# Peterson's®
# How to Get Money
# for College
# 2016

PETERSON'S®

**About Peterson's®**

Peterson's® is excited to be celebrating 50 years of trusted educational publishing. It's a milestone we're quite proud of, as we continue to provide the most accurate, dependable, high-quality education content in the field, providing you with everything you need to succeed. No matter where you are on your academic or professional path, you can rely on Peterson's publications and its online information at **www.petersons.com** for the most up-to-date education exploration data, expert test-prep tools, and the highest quality career success resources—everything you need to achieve your educational goals.

For more information, contact Peterson's, 3 Columbia Circle, Albany, NY 12203-5158; 800-338-3282 Ext. 54229; or visit us online at **www.petersons.com**.

Previous editions published as *How to Get Money for College* © 2009, 2010, 2011, 2012, 2013, 2014; *Peterson's College Money Handbook* © 1983, 1984, 1985, 1986, 1987, 1988, 1989, 1990, 1991, 1997, 1998, 1999, 2000, 2001, 2002, 2003, 2004, 2005, 2006, 2007, 2008; and as *Paying Less for College* © 1992, 1993, 1994, 1995, 1996

Peterson's makes reasonable efforts to obtain accurate, complete, and timely data from reliable sources. Nevertheless, Peterson's and the third-party data suppliers make no representation or warranty, either expressed or implied, as to the accuracy, timeliness, or completeness of the data or the results to be obtained from using the data, including, but not limited to, its quality, performance, merchantability, or fitness for a particular purpose, non-infringement or otherwise.

Neither Peterson's nor the third-party data suppliers warrant, guarantee, or make any representations that the results from using the data will be successful or will satisfy users' requirements. The entire risk to the results and performance is assumed by the user.

ISSN 1544-2330
ISBN: 978-0-7689-3964-4

Printed in the United States of America

10 9 8 7 6 5 4 3 2 1     17 16 15

Thirty-third Edition

By producing this book on recycled paper (10% post-consumer waste) 210 trees were saved.

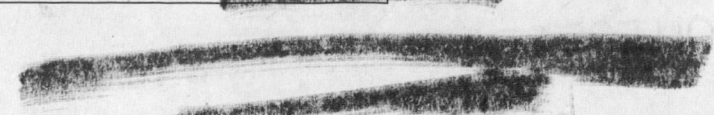

SUSTAINABLE FORESTRY INITIATIVE

Certified Sourcing
www.sfiprogram.org
SFI-00453

**Sustainability—Its Importance to Peterson's**

What does sustainability mean to Peterson's? As a leading publisher, we are aware that our business has a direct impact on vital resources—most importantly the raw material used to make our books. Peterson's is proud that its products are printed at SFI Chain-of-Custody certified facilities and that all of its books are printed on SFI certified paper with 10 percent post-consumer waste using vegetable-based ink.

Supporting the Sustainable Forestry Initiative® (SFI®) means that we only use vendors—from paper suppliers to printers—who have undergone rigorous certification audits by independent parties to demonstrate that they meet the standards.

Peterson's continuously strives to find new ways to incorporate responsible sourcing throughout all aspects of its business.

# Contents

# A Note from the Peterson's® Editors

The news media seem to constantly remind us that a college education is expensive. It certainly appears to be beyond the means of many Americans. The sticker price for four years at state-supported colleges can be more than $45,000, and private colleges and universities can cost more than $150,000. And these numbers continue to rise.

But there is good news. The system operates to provide the needed money so that most families and students are able to afford a college education while making only a reasonable financial sacrifice. However, because the college financial aid system is complex, finding the money is often easier said than done. That is why the process demands study, planning, calculation, flexibility, filling out forms, and meeting deadlines. Fortunately, for most people, it can produce positive results. There are many ways to manage college costs and many channels through which you can receive help. Be sure to take full advantage of the opportunities that have been opened up to students and their families by the many organizations, foundations, and businesses that have organized to help you with the burden of college expenses.

For nearly forty years, Peterson's has given students and parents the most comprehensive, up-to-date information on how to get their fair share of the financial aid pie. *Peterson's How to Get Money for College* is both a quick reference and a comprehensive resource that puts valuable information about college costs and financial aid opportunities at your fingertips.

- **The ABCs of Paying for College** provides insight into federal financial aid programs that are available, offers an overview of the financial aid landscape, walks you through the process of filing for aid, and provides proven tips on how to successfully navigate the financial aid process to obtain the federal, state, and institutional aid you deserve.

- The **Quick-Reference Chart** offers a snapshot comparison of the financial aid programs available at more than 2,300 four-year institutions across the country.

- The **Profiles of College Financial Aid Programs** provide unbiased financial aid data for each of the more than 2,300 four-year institutions listed.

- The **Appendix** lists the state scholarship and grant programs offered by all fifty states and the District of Columbia.

- The six **Indexes** included in the back of the book allow you to search for specific award programs based on a variety of criteria, including merit-based awards, athletic grants, ROTC programs, and much more.

Peterson's publishes a full line of books—financial aid, education exploration, test prep, and career preparation. Peterson's publications can be found at high school guidance offices, college libraries and career centers, and your local bookstore and library. Peterson's books are also available as eBooks and online at www.petersonsbooks.com.

We welcome any comments or suggestions you may have about this publication. Your feedback will help us make educational dreams possible for you—and others like you.

# The ABC's of Paying for College

# What You Need to Know About the FAFSA

The Free Application for Federal Student Aid or FAFSA (https://fafsa.ed.gov/FAFSA/app/fafsa) is a critical form that anyone seeking college financial aid must complete.

## WHY YOU MUST FILE THE FAFSA

The FAFSA is required in order for a student to be considered for any type of federal financial aid, including grants and loans. Even if you think your family makes too much for you to qualify for need-based aid, you should still complete the FAFSA. For one thing, many people are surprised to find that they may actually qualify for need-based aid—the eligibility for which is determined by a number of factors, in addition to household income.

Also, the FAFSA is required to apply for students loans (for which there is no need-based element such as income limits). If you don't initially think you want to apply for student loans but later change your mind, having a completed FAFSA already on file will help speed up the process.

In addition, most schools will require a student to have a completed FAFSA on file before the student can be considered for any school-based aid programs such as scholarships. A completed FAFSA is also required for federal work study jobs.

## IT'S EASIER TO FILE ONLINE

While you can opt to print and complete a paper version of the FAFSA, it is much quicker and easier to complete the online version. The system walks you through the process and can alert you to sections you can skip if they don't apply to you.

If you have completed a FAFSA in the past, some of your information will be automatically entered when you start to work on your newest one, giving you a head start. You will further save a lot of time by using the IRS data retrieval tool, which will be discussed later in this article.

Filing online means your form will be processed faster, and it also eliminates the worry that your paperwork will be lost or delayed in the mail.

For those who want or need to print and submit a paper version of the FAFSA, you can print a PDF version of the FAFSA online. Students and parents can request up to three copies of the paper FAFSA (in English or Spanish) by calling the Federal Student Aid Information Center toll-free at 800-4-FED-AID.

## THE NEW FEDERAL STUDENT AID ID

In order for a student to complete the online FAFSA, he or she must obtain a Federal Student Aid (FSA) ID. You can get this online at https://fsaid.ed.gov/npas/index.htm. Starting in May 2015, the FSA ID replaced the PIN system that was previously used. Parents of dependent students also need to obtain their own FSA ID in order to sign their child's FAFSA electronically online.

The FSA ID can be used to access several federal aid-related websites, including FAFSA.gov and StudentLoans.gov. It consists of a username and password and can be used to electronically sign Federal Student Aid documents, access your personal records, and make binding legal obligations. The FSA ID is beneficial in several ways:

- It removes your personal identifiable personally identifiable information (PII), such as your Social Security number, from your log-in credentials.
- It creates a more secure and efficient way to verify your information when you log in to access to your federal student aid information online.
- It gives you the ability to easily update your personal information.
- It allows you to easily retrieve your username and password by requesting a secure code be sent to your e-mail address or by answering challenge questions.

It's relatively simple to create an FSA ID and should only take a few minutes. In addition, you will have an opportunity to link your current Federal Student Aid PIN (if you already have one) to your FSA ID. The final step is to confirm your e-mail address. You will receive a secure code to the e-mail address you provided when you set up your FSA ID. Once you retrieve the code from your e-mail account and enter it—to confirm your e-mail address is valid—you will be able to use this e-mail address instead of your username to log in to any of the federal aid-related websites, making the log-in process even simpler for you and your parents.

When you initially create your FSA ID, your information will need to be verified with the Social Security Administration. This process can take anywhere from one to three days. For that reason, it's a good idea to take care of setting up your FSA ID as early as possible, so it will be all set when you are ready to begin completing your FAFSA.

IMPORTANT NOTE: Since your FSA ID provides access to your personal information and is used to sign online documents, it's imperative that you protect this ID. Don't share it with *anyone* or write it down in an insecure location—you could place yourself at great risk for identify theft.

If your FSA ID is lost or stolen, you must do one of the following:

- Contact Federal Student Aid's Customer Service center at 800-433-3243 (toll-free).
- Update your username and password by selecting "Edit My FSA ID".
- Disable your FSA ID so that no one can use it by selecting "Edit My FSA ID" and then selecting Disable My FSA ID.

## INFORMATION YOU WILL NEED

Completing your FAFSA (or updating one you have already started) will be much easier if you have some basic information and documentation handy when you prepare to complete the form. The first section of the FAFSA involves your basic personal information that you should know offhand, such as your name, address, and Social Security number. After that, you will need to provide details about your income, assets, and other financial issues. If you file taxes, much of this information will be taken from your tax return. If you haven't yet completed your taxes for that year, you can enter estimated figures and update the form with the final numbers later.

If you're a student who is married, you will also need to provide information about your spouse and their finances. If you're a dependent student, information about one or both or your parents and their finances will be required.

You will also need to provide information about the school(s) you attend or plan to attend. If you haven't made your final school choices yet, you can list the ones you know at this point and add others later.

## BE MINDFUL OF DEADLINES

The new FAFSA for the upcoming school year is available online starting on January 1. It is smart to complete your FAFSA as early as possible. If you file taxes, you will need information from your tax return (and from your parents, too, if you are a dependent student). However, you can complete your FAFSA before you file your tax return by entering estimated information and then returning to the online system and making any necessary updates once you have filed your taxes.

For federal aid, the final deadline to submit your FAFSA is June 30 at the end of the school year for which you are applying. So for the 2016–17 school year, the final deadline to submit your FAFSA would be June 30, 2017. However, you would normally want to apply for aid before the start of a semester—and ideally, as far in advance as possible. That's because schools frequently require all of your financial aid to be processed (or at least be in process) before your registration is considered official.

It can sometimes be tricky to keep track of other financial aid deadlines because the deadlines for different types of aid can vary by state and school. Be sure to check with your school—or the schools you are considering attending—to find out their financial aid deadlines so you can get all of your forms submitted in time.

Check the website for your state's department of education to find out the deadlines to submit the FAFSA and other forms in order to be considered for any state-funded financial aid that may be available to you.

## DEPENDENCY

One of the biggest misconceptions—or most misunderstood aspects of the FAFSA and financial aid—is that a student can simply declare himself or herself independent, and then their parents' information will not be considered. In the past, dependency wasn't viewed in such strict terms, and it was easier for a student who lived on their own to be considered independent.

It's important to keep in mind that dependency for financial aid purposes has nothing to do with tax status or whether a student's parents claimed the student as a dependent on their tax return. Dependency for taxes and financial aid are two completely different and separate things.

There are now strict criteria that determine a student's dependency status. To be considered independent, a student must meet one of the following conditions:

- Age 24 or older by December 31 of the school year for which the student is applying for aid
- Married
- Have children or other dependents for whom the student provides more than half of their support
- Currently serving in the military
- Having been homeless, in foster care, or a ward of the court

Even if one of these conditions applies, that doesn't necessarily grant the student automatic independent status. There may still be additional required documentation or other conditions that must be met.

## IRS DATA RETRIEVAL TOOL

A common complaint about the FAFSA is that it takes too long to complete. But a fairly recent change has made the form considerably less time-consuming for many people. The IRS Data Retrieval tool now allows the tax information of students or parents to be automatically imported into the FAFSA.

Once you reach the section of the online FAFSA that deals with financial information of the student (and parent, if applicable), you will see a button that says "Link to IRS" if that option is available to you. You will then follow the steps to log into the IRS system and have your information transferred to your FAFSA. In order to access the Data Retrieval Tool, the information you enter on the IRS login screen—including your name, address, and filing status—must exactly match the information on your most recent tax return.

Those who decide to skip this step for whatever reason should know that there's a good chance they will then be required to submit copies of their tax return and possibly even an IRS transcript in order to verify their tax information. (An IRS transcript is an official document that must be obtained from the IRS. That can be a time-consuming and inconvenient process, so you are usually better off just using the IRA data retrieval tool in the first place.)

There are certain situations in which the FAFSA will not allow you to use the Data Retrieval Tool. This tool is not an option for students or parents who are married and filed as Married Filing Separately, are married and filed as Head of Household, filed a Form 1040X amended tax return, or filed a Puerto Rican or foreign tax return. If you fall into one of these categories, you will need to enter your tax information manually.

Also, if you have just filed your tax return within a few weeks prior to completing the FAFSA, your current information may not be in the IRS system yet and may not be accessible by the Data Retrieval Tool.

## PARENTS' MARITAL STATUS

For dependent students, their parents' marital status can have a big impact on financial aid eligibility. If the parents are married, financial information for both parents must be reported. If the parents are separated but still living together, they are still listed as "married or remarried" on the FAFSA. Parents who are legally separated or living in separate households are classified as "divorced or separated."

If parents are divorced, the FAFSA must be completed by the parent with whom the student lived with most during the previous twelve-month period. If the student lived equally with both parents, the form would be completed by the parent who provided the most support.

## LISTING SCHOOL CHOICES

When completing the FAFSA, you must specify which colleges should receive the report generated by your FAFSA application. On the paper FAFSA, you can only list four colleges. On the online version, you can list ten. If you complete the paper version and want to have your information provided to more than four schools, you can go online to the FAFSA website after your form has been processed and add more schools to your list (up to a total of ten).

From a federal aid standpoint, it doesn't matter in what order you list the colleges. However, the FAFSA instructions note that for state aid purposes, you may want to list the colleges in order of preference. Keep in mind that each school on your list will see everything on your FAFSA—including the names of the other colleges you have listed. There have been reports that schools are using students' college listings to determine how likely a specific student is to attend their particular school (based on the theory that students tend to list colleges in the order of how much they want to attend each). The speculation is that a college may reserve its best financial aid offers for students who seem most interested in attending. While most schools won't confirm that practice, it is probably in your best interest to list your colleges in order of the ones you most want to attend.

# Falsifying Information on Your FAFSA Could Bring Big Problems

With the cost of college rising each year and college graduates saddled with more than $1 trillion in debt to pay for their postsecondary studies, more and more families are desperate to secure payment-free options for higher education. Nothing illuminates this fact better than the meteoric rise in applications for financial aid through the annually Free Application for Federal Student Aid (FAFSA). In the 2004–05 academic year, more than 11 million students sent in FAFSA applications. Less than seven years later, that number doubled to more than 22 million. With more and more students applying for federal financial aid, there is, unfortunately, an increased temptation to commit fraud. Parents try to do whatever they can to lower their Expected Family Contribution (EFC), and sometimes this can lead to falsifying information. This is a big no-no, but that doesn't stop people from trying.

A quick search on Google, and you can find parents and students asking boldly, "Do people lying on their FAFSA really get caught?" or "How do I hide the fact that I have money from FAFSA?" Cheating on the FAFSA seems as intuitive as forgetting to report that second job you have to the Internal Revenue Service.

A report released by the Government Accountability Office, the Congress-created financial watchdog, found that fifteen for-profit universities encouraged fraud and/or engaged in deceptive marketing practices. The report stated that one college admission worker encouraged an undercover applicant to not report $250,000 in savings on the student's FAFSA. Another college representative told an undercover applicant to falsify the number of dependents he had from 0 to 3.

It all seems so deceptively easy—giving thousands of dollars in savings to a student's uncle temporarily to hide that asset; writing down grandma's address to gain in-state tuition rates; forgetting to mention your true immigration status; or the extreme example of one Alaskan woman who used a false identity. In that situation, after claiming she suffered from years of child abuse, the woman used an obscure federal law to secure a new identity to hide from her accused abuser. (The abuser she named was never charged with a crime.) She received a new social security number and card. But instead of living a new life in anonymity, she used her *old* identity to apply for federal student loans—a lot of them. Arrested and convicted, the woman was sentenced to five years in prison and ordered to pay back nearly $1 million.

The prospect of going to jail for filling out false information on your FAFSA application may not have crossed your mind, but it is certainly a possibility. Falsifying information—knowingly or unknowingly—is a federal crime. It is punishable by up to $20,000 in fines and up to five years in prison. And though there are books offering tantalizing options to "game," the federal student aid system—do not be tempted.

You do not want to start your college career by committing a crime against the government. It's just not worth it. Your FAFSA is checked against your IRS documents by professionals who do not want to take the chance that they will use their precious scarce financial aid resources to support students who really do not need it. Students who falsify information to get financial aid leave deserving cash-strapped students out in the cold. Fortunately, though, fraud in the federal aid system is low—a recent government study found that about 5 percent of applications contain false information.

Even if you do not intend to defraud the government, inaccurate information on your FAFSA can get you into trouble. It is critical that you fill the application out as accurately as possible. It may look like an innocuous document, but it amounts to a partnership between you and the federal government, and it is essential that partnership is based upon trust.

Here are some tips to avoid making mistakes on your FAFSA that could cost you financial aid or even your freedom:

- Accurately report your assets, address, dependents, income, and so on. It just doesn't make sense to lie. All that information is easily verifiable. Income includes wages, tips, social security payments, child support payments, and other untaxed income. But retirement income such as those in a 401K or IRA does not have to be reported. Check with your tax advisor when filling out your FAFSA application.

- Fill out your FAFSA completely. Mistakes can cost you time as you might have to reapply, and that will literally cost you money.

- Avoid books, consultants, and websites that promise to lower your EFC by questionable means. Trying to "game," the federal aid system is just going to cause you headaches.

College is expensive, and families are smart to try to lower that expense as much as possible. But planning, saving, and focusing on academic pursuits to garner scholarships and grants is a much better way of acquiring money for college than trying to put one over on the federal government. Being honest is always the best policy—especially when applying for federal financial aid.

# Tips for Financing Your Child's College Education

## Don Betterton

Given the lifelong benefit of a college degree (college graduates are projected to earn in a lifetime $1 million more than those with only a high school diploma), higher education is a worthwhile investment. However, it is also an expensive one made even more difficult to manage by cost increases that have outpaced both inflation and gains in family income. The reality of higher education economics is that paying for a child's college education is an issue that shows no sign of getting easier.

Because of the high cost involved (even the most inexpensive four-year education at a public institution costs about $10,000 a year), good information about college budgets and strategies for reducing the "sticker price" is essential. You have made a good start by taking the time to read *Peterson's How to Get Money for College*. In the pages that follow, you will find valuable information about the four main sources of aid—federal, state, institutional, and private. Before you learn about the various programs, however, it will be helpful if you have an overview of how the college financial aid system operates and what long-range financing strategies are available.

## FINANCIAL AID

Financial aid refers to money that is awarded to a student, usually in a "package" that consists of gift aid (commonly called a scholarship or grant), a student loan, and/or a campus job.

## COLLEGE COSTS

The starting point for organizing a plan to pay for your child's college education is to make a good estimate of the yearly cost of attendance. You can use the **College Cost Worksheet** on the next page to do this.

To estimate your college costs for 2016–17, refer to the tuition and fees and room and board figures shown in the **College Cost Worksheet**. If your child will commute from your home, use $2,500 instead of the college's room and board charges and $900 for transportation. We have used $800 for books and $1,500 for personal expenses. Finally, estimate the cost of two round trips if your home is more than a few hundred miles from the college. Add the items to calculate the total budget. You should now have a reasonably good estimate of college costs for 2016–17. (To determine the costs for later years, adding 4 percent per year will probably give you a fairly accurate estimate.)

## DO YOU QUALIFY FOR NEED-BASED AID?

The next step is to evaluate whether or not you are likely to qualify for financial aid based on need. This step is critical, since more than 90 percent of the yearly total of $128 billion in student aid is awarded only after a determination is made that the family lacks sufficient financial resources to pay the full cost of college on its own. To judge your chance of receiving need-based aid, it is necessary to estimate an Expected Family Contribution (EFC) according to a government formula known as the Federal Methodology (FM). The official Federal Student Aid Website provides a FAFSA4caster tool (similar to an EFC calculator) that helps you get a head start on the financial aid process, including getting an early estimate of your eligibility for federal aid. The tool will also allow you to transfer the information provided into the actual Free Application for Federal Student Aid (FAFSA) form when you are ready to complete it. You can find the tool at http://www.fafsa4caster.ed.gov/F4CApp/index/index.jsf.

## APPLYING FOR NEED-BASED AID

Because the federal government provides about 67 percent of all aid awarded, the application, FAFSA, and need evaluation process is controlled by the U.S. Department of Education. In addition, nearly every state that offers student assistance uses the federal government's system to award its own aid. Furthermore, in addition to arranging for the payment of federal and state aid, many colleges use the FAFSA to award their own funds to eligible students. (Note: In addition to the FAFSA, many private colleges and universities also ask the family to complete the CSS/Financial Aid PROFILE® application.)

The FAFSA is your "passport" to receiving your share of the billions of dollars awarded annually in need-based aid. If you didn't read the first article in this section about the FAFSA, go back and take a look at it now. You will find the latest information on the FAFSA, including important details on the change from the PIN to the new FSA ID.

## AWARDING AID

The colleges you list on the FAFSA will receive your information in order to calculate a financial aid award in a package that typi-

## College Cost Worksheet

| | College 1 | College 2 | College 3 | Commuter College |
|---|---|---|---|---|
| Tuition and Fees | _____ | _____ | _____ | _____ |
| Room and Board | _____ | _____ | _____ | $2,500 |
| Books | $ 800 | $ 800 | $ 800 | $ 750 |
| Personal Expenses | $1,500 | $1,500 | $1,500 | $1,500 |
| Travel | _____ | _____ | _____ | $ 900 |
| Total Budget | _____ | _____ | _____ | _____ |

cally includes aid from at least one of the major sources—federal, state, college, or private. In addition, the award will probably consist of a combination of a scholarship, grant, loan, or campus job. These last two pieces—loan and job—are called self-help aid because they require effort on your child's part (that is, the aid must be either earned through work or paid back later). Scholarships or grants are outright gifts that have no such obligation.

It is important that you understand each part of the package. You'll want to know, for example, how much aid is a gift, the interest rate and repayment terms of the student loan, or how many hours per week the campus job requires. There should be an enclosure with the award letter that answers these questions. If not, make a list of your questions and call or visit the financial aid office.

Once you understand the terms of each item in the award letter, you should turn your attention to the "bottom line"—how much you will have to pay at each college where your child is accepted. In addition to understanding the aid award, this means having a good estimate of the college budget so you can

accurately calculate how much you and your child will have to contribute. (Often, an aid package does not cover the entire need.) Colleges differ in how much detail they include in their award notifications. Many colleges provide full information—types and amounts of aid, yearly costs, and the EFC for the parent and student shares. If these important items are missing or incomplete, you can do the work on your own. (See the **Comparing Financial Aid Awards and Family Contribution Worksheet** on the next page.) For example, if the award letter only shows the college's direct charges—tuition, room, and board— you need to estimate indirect costs such as books, personal expenses, and travel. Then subtract the total aid awarded from the yearly cost to get the EFC. A portion of that amount may be your child's contribution (35 percent of student assets and 50 percent of student earnings over $2,200) and the remainder is the parental share. If you can afford this amount at your child's first-choice college, the financial aid system has worked well for you, and your child's college enrollment plans can go forward.

## How Need Is Calculated and Aid Is Awarded

| | College 1 | College 2 |
|---|---|---|
| Total Cost of Attendance | $10,000 | $ 24,000 |
| − Expected Family Contribution | − 5,500 | − 5,500 |
| = Financial Need | $ 4,500 | $ 18,500 |
| − Grant Aid Awarded | − 675 | −14,575 |
| − Campus Job (Work-Study) Awarded | − 1,400 | − 1,300 |
| − Student Loan Awarded | − 2,425 | − 2,625 |
| = Unmet Need | 0 | 0 |

**Note:** Sometimes an institution is unable to meet all need. The amount of unmet need is called "the gap."

## Comparing Financial Aid Awards and Family Contribution Worksheet

| | College 1 | College 2 | College 3 |
|---|---|---|---|
| Cost of Attendance | _____ | _____ | _____ |
| Aid Awarded | _____ | _____ | _____ |
|    Grant/Scholarship | _____ | _____ | _____ |
|    Loan | _____ | _____ | _____ |
|    Job | _____ | _____ | _____ |
| Total Aid | _____ | _____ | _____ |
| Expected Family Contribution | _____ | _____ | _____ |
|    Student Contribution | _____ | _____ | _____ |
|    Parent Contribution | _____ | _____ | _____ |

But if you think your EFC is too high, you should contact the college's financial aid office and ask whether additional aid is available. Many private high-cost colleges are willing to work with families to help make attendance at their institutions possible. Most colleges also allow applicants to appeal their financial aid awards, the budget used for you, or any of the elements used to determine the family contribution, especially if there are extenuating circumstances or if the information has changed since the application was submitted. Some colleges may also reconsider an award based on a "competitive appeal," the submission of a more favorable award letter from another college.

If your appeal is unsuccessful and there is still a gap between the expected family contribution and what you feel you can pay from income and savings, you are left with two choices. One option is for your child to attend a college where paying your share of the bill will not be a problem. (This assumes that an affordable option was included on your child's original list of colleges, a wise admission application strategy.) The second is to look into alternate methods of financing. At this stage, parental loans and tuition payment plans are the best financing options. A parental loan can bring the yearly cost down to a manageable level by spreading payments over a number of years. This is the type of financing that families use when purchasing a home or automobile. A tuition payment plan is essentially a short-term loan and allows you to pay the costs over ten to twelve months. It is an option for families who have the resources available but need help with managing their cash flow.

## NON-NEED-BASED AID

Regardless of whether you might qualify for a need-based award, it is always worthwhile to look into merit, or non-need, scholarships from sources such as foundations, agencies, religious groups, and service organizations. For a family that isn't eligible for need-based aid, merit scholarships are the only form of gift aid available. If your child later qualifies for a need-based award, a merit scholarship can be quite helpful in providing additional resources if the aid does not fully cover the costs. Even if the college meets 100 percent of need, a merit scholarship reduces the self-help (loan and job) portion of an award.

In searching for merit-based scholarships, keep in mind that there are relatively few awards (compared to those that are need-based), and most of them are highly competitive. Use the following checklist in your search.

- Take advantage of any scholarships for which your child is automatically eligible based on parents' employer benefits, military service, association or church membership, other affiliations, or student or parent attributes (ethnic background, nationality, and so on). Company or union tuition remissions are the most common examples of these awards.

- Look for other awards for which your child might be eligible based on the previous characteristics and affiliations but where there is a selection process and an application is required. Free computerized searches are available on the Internet. (You should not pay a fee for a scholarship search.) Peterson's free scholarship search can be accessed by logging on to www.petersons.com/finaid. Scholarship directories, such as *Peterson's Scholarships, Grants & Prizes*, which details more than 4,000 scholarship programs, and *Peterson's Best Scholarships for Best Students* are useful resources and can be found in bookstores, high school guidance offices, or your local library. You can also find these books at www.petersonsbooks.com.

- See if your state has a merit scholarship program.

- Look into national scholarship competitions. High school guidance counselors usually know about these scholarships. Examples of these awards are the National Meritt Scholarship Program, the Coca-Cola Scholarship, Gates Millennium Scholars, Intel Science Talent Search, and the U.S. Senate Youth Program.

- ROTC (Reserve Officers' Training Corps) scholarships are offered by the Army, Navy, Air Force, and Marine Corps. A full ROTC scholarship covers tuition, fees, textbook costs, and, in some cases, a stipend. Acceptance of an ROTC scholarship entails a commitment to take military science courses and to serve for a specific number of years as an officer in the sponsoring branch of the service. Competition is heavy, and preference may be given to students in certain fields of study, such as engineering, languages, science, and health professions. Application procedures vary by service. Contact an armed services recruiter or high school guidance counselor for further information.

- Investigate community scholarships. High school guidance counselors usually have a list of these awards, and announcements are published in local newspapers. Most common are awards given by service organizations like the American Legion, Rotary International, and the local women's club.

- If your child is strong academically or is very talented in fields such as athletics or performing/creative arts, you may want to consider colleges that offer their own merit awards to gifted students they wish to enroll. Refer to the Non-Need Scholarships for Undergraduates index in the back part of this guide.

In addition to merit scholarships, there are loan and job opportunities for students who do not qualify for need-based aid. Some of the organizations that sponsor scholarships—for example, the Air Force Aid Society—also provide loans.

Work opportunities during the academic year are another type of assistance that is not restricted to aid recipients. Many colleges will, after assigning jobs to students on aid, open campus positions to all students looking for work. In addition, there are usually off-campus employment opportunities available to everyone.

## FINANCING YOUR CHILD'S COLLEGE EDUCATION

"Financing" means putting together resources to pay the balance due the college over and above payments from the primary sources of aid—grants, scholarships, student loans, and jobs. Financing strategies are important because the high cost of a college education today often requires a family, whether or not it receives aid, to think about stretching its college payment beyond the four-year period of enrollment. For high-cost colleges, it is not unreasonable to think about a 10-4-10 plan: ten years of saving; four years of paying college bills out of current income, savings, and borrowing; and ten years to repay a parental loan.

### Note

*A point of clarification about whether to put college savings in your name or your child's: If you are certain that your child will not be a candidate for need-based aid, there may be a tax advantage to accumulating money in his or her name. However, when it comes to maximizing aid eligibility, it is important to understand that student assets are assessed at a 20 percent rate and parental assets at about 5 percent. Therefore, if your college savings are in your child's name, it may be wise to reestablish title to these funds before applying for financial aid. You should contact your financial planner or accountant before making any modifications to your asset structure.*

### Savings

Although saving for college is always a good idea, many families are unclear about its advantages. Some families do not save because after normal living expenses have been covered, they do not have much money to set aside. An affordable but regular savings plan through a payroll deduction is usually the answer to the problem of spending your entire paycheck every month.

The second reason why saving for college is not a high priority is the belief that the financial aid system penalizes a family by lowering aid eligibility. The Federal Methodology of need determination is very kind to families that save. In fact, savings are ignored completely for most families that earn less than $50,000. Savings in the form of home equity, retirement plans, and most annuities are excluded from the calculation. And even when savings are counted, a maximum of 5 percent of the total is expected each year. In other words, if a family has $40,000 in savings after an asset protection allowance is considered, the contribution is no greater than $2,000. Given the impact of compound interest it is easy to see that a long-term savings plan can make paying for college much easier.

A sensible savings plan is important because of the financial advantage of saving compared to borrowing. The amount of money students borrow for college is now greater than the amount they receive in grants and scholarships. With

# What Is CSS/Financial Aid PROFILE

There are many complexities in the financial aid process: knowing which aid is merit-based and which aid is need-based; understanding the difference between grants, loans, and work-study; and determining whether funds are from federal, state, institutional, or private sources.

In addition, the aid application process itself can be confusing. It can involve more than the Free Application for Federal Student Aid (FAFSA) and the Federal Methodology (FM). Many colleges feel that the federal aid system (FAFSA and FM) does not collect or evaluate information thoroughly enough for them to award their own institutional funds. These colleges have made an arrangement with the College Scholarship Service, a branch of the College Board, to establish a separate application system.

The application is called the CSS/Financial Aid PROFILE®, and the need-analysis formula is referred to as the Institutional Methodology (IM). If you apply for financial aid at one of the colleges that uses the PROFILE, the admission material will state that the PROFILE is required in addition to the FAFSA. You should read the information carefully and file the PROFILE to meet the earliest college deadline. Before you can receive the PROFILE, however, you must register, either by phone or online at https://student.collegeboard.org/css-financial-aid-profile, providing enough basic information so the PROFILE package can be designed specifically for you. The FAFSA is free, but there is a charge for the PROFILE. As with the FAFSA, the PROFILE can be submitted via the Internet.

In addition to the requirement by certain colleges that you submit both the FAFSA and PROFILE (when used, the PROFILE is always in addition to the FAFSA; it does not replace it), you should understand that each system has its own method for analyzing a family's ability to pay for college. The main differences between PROFILE's Institutional Methodology and the FAFSA's Federal Methodology are:

- PROFILE includes equity in the family home as an asset; the FAFSA doesn't.

- PROFILE takes a broader look at assets not included on the FAFSA.

- PROFILE expects a minimum student contribution, usually in the form of summer earnings; the FAFSA has no such minimum.

- PROFILE may collect information on the noncustodial parent; the FAFSA does not.

- PROFILE allows for more professional judgment than the FAFSA. Medical expenses, private secondary school costs, and a variety of special circumstances are considered under PROFILE, subject to the discretion of the aid counselor on campus.

- PROFILE includes information on assets not reported on the FAFSA, including life insurance, annuities, retirement plans, etc.

To summarize: PROFILE's Institutional Methodology tends to be both more complete in its data collection and more rigorous in its analysis than the FAFSA's Federal Methodology. When IM results are compared to FM results for thousands of applicants, IM will usually come up with a somewhat higher expected parental contribution than FM.

# Creditworthiness

If you will be borrowing to pay for your child's college education, making sure you qualify for a loan is critical. For the most part, that means your credit record must be free of default or delinquency. You can check your credit history with one or more of the following three major credit bureaus and clean up any adverse information that appears. The numbers below will offer specific information on what you need to provide to obtain a report. All of the credit bureaus accept credit report requests over their Web sites. You will usually be asked to provide your full name, phone number, social security number, birth date, and addresses for the last five years. You are entitled to a free report from each bureau.

Equifax Credit Information
P.O. Box 740241
Atlanta, GA 30374
800-685-1111
http://www.equifax.com

Trans Union
800-888-4213
http://www.transunion.com

Experian
888-397-3742
http://www.experian.com

loans becoming so widespread, savings should be carefully considered as an alternative to borrowing. Your incentive for saving is that a dollar saved is a dollar not borrowed.

## Borrowing

Once you've calculated your "bottom-line" parental contribution and determined that the amount is not affordable out of your current income and assets, the most likely alternative is borrowing. Beginning July 1, 2010, as a result of the Health Care and Education Reconciliation Act, federal student loans are no longer made by private lenders under the Federal Family Education Loan (FFEL) Program. Instead, all new federal student loans come directly from the U.S. Department of Education under the Direct Loan Program, which offers subsidized and unsubsidized (Stafford) loans for students, PLUS loans for parents and graduate/professional students, and consolidation loans for both students and parents. For additional information, go online to https://studentloans.gov/myDirectLoan/index.action or call 800-4-FED-AID (toll-free).

For the Direct PLUS Loan, parents must complete a Direct PLUS Loan application and promissory note, contained in a single form that can be obtained from a school's financial aid office. The yearly limit on a PLUS Loan is equal to the student's cost of attendance minus any other financial aid the student receives. For example, if your cost of attendance is $6,000, and you receive $4,500 in other financial aid, your parents can borrow up to $1,500. Loans disbursed between July 1, 2014 and June 30, 2015 have a fixed interest rate of 7.21 percent. For Direct PLUS Loans first disbursed on or after July 1, 2015, and before July 1, 2016, the interest rate is 6.84%. These are fixed interest rates for the life of the loan. Interest is charged on a PLUS Loan from the date of the first disbursement until the loan is paid in full. A PLUS Loan made to the parent cannot be transferred to the student. The parent is responsible for repaying the PLUS Loan. For more details about PLUS Loans, visit www.direct.ed.gov/about.html.

## MAKE FINANCIAL AID WORK FOR YOU

If you are like millions of families that benefit from financial aid, it is likely that your child's college plans can go forward without undue worry about the costs involved. The key is to understand the financial aid system and to follow the best path for your family. The result of good information and good planning should be that you will receive your fair share of the billions of dollars available each year and that the cost of college will not prevent your child from attending.

*Don Betterton is a former Director of Undergraduate Financial Aid at Princeton University and a Certified College Planner (CCP).*

# Federal Financial Aid Programs

There are a number of sources of financial aid available to students: federal and state governments, private agencies, and the colleges themselves. In addition, there are three different forms of aid: grants, earnings, and loans.

The federal government is the single largest source of financial aid for students. In recent years, the U.S. Department of Education's student financial aid programs made more than $80 billion available in loans, grants, and other aid to 14 million students. At present, there are four federal grant programs—Federal Pell Grant, Federal Supplemental Educational Opportunity Grant (FSEOG), Teacher Education Assistance for College and Higher Education (TEACH) Grant, and Iraq and Afghanistan Service Grant. There are two federal loan programs: Federal Perkins Loan Program and the William D. Ford Federal Direct Loan Program. The federal government also has a job program, Federal Work-Study Program (FWS), which helps colleges provide employment for students. In addition to the student aid programs, there are also tuition tax credits and deductions. They are the American Opportunity Credit, the Lifetime Learning Credit, the Tuition and Fees Tax Deduction, and the Student Loan Interest Tax Deduction. Also, there is AmeriCorps. AmeriCorps will pay the interest that is accrued on qualified student loans for members who complete the service program.

The majority of federal higher education loans are made in the Direct Loan Program, which makes available two kinds of loans: loans to students and PLUS loans to parents or to graduate or professional students. These loans are either subsidized or unsubsidized. Subsidized loans are made on the basis of demonstrated student need, and the interest is paid by the government during the time the student is in school or deferment. For the unsubsidized (non-need-based) loans and PLUS loans, interest begins to accrue as funds are disbursed.

All new federal student loans come directly from the U.S. Department of Education under the Direct Loan Program. Students interested in receiving federal student aid should continue to complete a Free Application for Federal Student Aid (FAFSA) for each school year that they wish to be considered for aid. For more information about applying for federal student aid, call 800-4-FED-AID (800-433-3243)(toll-free) or visit www.fafsa.ed.gov.

## FEDERAL PELL GRANT

The Federal Pell Grant is the largest grant program; more than 9 million students receive Pell Grants annually. This grant is intended to be the starting point of assistance for lower-income families. Eligibility for a Pell Grant is based on the Expected Family Contribution. The amount you receive will depend on your EFC and the cost of education at the college you will attend. The highest award depends on how much funding the program receives from the government. For the 2015–16 award year (July 1, 2015 to June 30, 2016), the maximum award is $5,775. For the 2016–17 award year, this amount is expected to increase to $5,915. As of July 1, 2012, a student can not receive a Federal Pell Grant for more than 12 semesters or the equivalent. A student will receive notice when he/she is close to their limit.

## FEDERAL SUPPLEMENTAL EDUCATIONAL OPPORTUNITY GRANT (FSEOG)

As its name implies, Federal Supplemental Educational Opportunity Grants provide additional need-based federal grant money to supplement the Federal Pell Grant Program. Each participating college is given funds to award to especially needy students. The maximum award is $4,000 per year, but the amount you receive depends on the college's awarding policy, the availability of FSEOG funds, the total cost of education, and the amount of other aid awarded.

## FEDERAL WORK-STUDY PROGRAM (FWS)

This program provides jobs for students who demonstrate need. Salaries are paid by funds from the federal government as well as the college. Students work on an hourly basis on or off campus and must be paid at least the federal minimum wage. Students may earn only up to the amount awarded in the financial aid package.

## FEDERAL PERKINS LOAN PROGRAM

This is a low-interest (5%) loan for students with exceptional financial need. Perkins Loans are made through the college's financial aid office with the college as the lender. Undergraduate students can borrow a maximum of $5,500 per year, and there is a cumulative limit of $27,500. The annual limit for graduate and professional-degree-seeking students is $8,000 with a total cumulative limit (including the $27,500) of $60,000. Borrowers may take up to ten years to repay the loan, beginning nine months after they graduate, leave school, or drop below half-time status. No interest accrues while they are in school, and, under certain conditions (e.g., they teach in low-income areas, work in law enforcement, are full-time nurses or medical technicians, serve as Peace Corps or VISTA volunteers, etc.), some or all of the loan can be cancelled. In addition, payments can be deferred under certain conditions such as unemployment.

## FEDERAL DIRECT LOANS

A Direct Loan is borrowed directly from the U.S. Department of Education through the college's financial aid office.

The interest rate on Direct Subsidized and Unsubsidized Loans for undergraduates with a first disbursement date

# Federal Financial Aid Programs

| Name of Program | Type of Program | Maximum Award Per Year |
|---|---|---|
| Federal Pell Grant | need-based grant | $5,645 |
| Federal Supplemental Educational Opportunity Grant (FSEOG) | need-based grant | $4,000 |
| Teacher Education Assistance for College and Higher Education (TEACH) Grants | need/merit | up to $4,000 a year (based on strict criteria being met) |
| Iraq and Afghanistan Service Grant | need/merit | $5,645 (based on strict criteria being met) |
| Federal Work-Study Program (FWS) | need-based part-time job | no maximum |
| Federal Perkins Loan Program | need-based loan | $5,500 |
| Subsidized Federal Direct Loan | need-based grant student loan | $3,500 (first year) |
| Unsubsidized Federal Direct Loan | non-need based | $5,500 (first year, dependent student) |

between July 1, 2015, and June 30, 2016, is 4.29 percent. For those loans with a first disbursement date between July 1, 2014, and June 30, 2015, the interest rate was 4.66 percent.

The maximum amount dependent students may borrow in any one year is $5,500 for freshmen, $6,500 for sophomores, and $7,500 for juniors and seniors, with a maximum of $31,000 for the total undergraduate program (of which not more than $23,000 can be subsidized). The maximum amount independent students can borrow is $9,500 for freshmen (of which no more than $3,500 can be subsidized), $10,500 for sophomores (of which no more than $4,500 can be subsidized), and $12,500 for juniors and seniors (of which no more than $5,500 can be subsidized). Independent students can borrow up to $57,500 (of which no more than $23,000 can be subsidized) for the total undergraduate program. Borrowers may be charged a small origination fee, which is deducted from the loan proceeds. See the helpful, easy-to-read chart on the next page for maximum annual and total subsidized and unsubsidized loan limits.

To apply for a Federal Student Loan, you must first complete the FAFSA to determine eligibility for a subsidized loan and then complete a separate loan application that is submitted to the Department of Education. The Department of Education will send a master promissory for completion. The proceeds of the loan, less the origination fee, will be sent to the college to be either credited to your account or released to you directly. Direct loans are processed by the financial aid office as part of the overall financial aid package.

Once the repayment period starts, borrowers of both subsidized and unsubsidized Federal Direct Loans have to pay a combination of interest and principal monthly for up to a 25-year period. There are a number of repayment options as well as opportunities to consolidate federal loans. There are also provisions for extended repayments, deferments, and repayment forbearance, if needed. Note: If you receive a Direct Subsidized Loan that is first disbursed between July 1, 2012, and July 1, 2014, you will be responsible for paying any interest that accrues during your grace period (first six months after graduation). If you choose not to pay the interest that accrues during your grace period, the interest will be added to your principal balance.

## DIRECT PLUS LOANS

PLUS loans are for parents of dependent students to help families with the cost of education. There is no needs test to qualify. For Direct PLUS Loans first disbursed on or after July 1, 2014, and before July 1, 2015, the interest rate is 7.21 percent. For Direct PLUS Loans first disbursed on or after July 1, 2015, and before July 1, 2016, the interest rate is 6.84 percent. There is no yearly limit; you can borrow up to the cost of your child's education, less other financial aid received. Repayment begins sixty days after the funds are disbursed. The origination fee is approximately 4 percent and may be subtracted from the proceeds. Parent borrowers must generally have a good credit record to qualify.

## Maximum Annual and Total Subsidized and Unsubsidized Loan Limits as of July 1, 2014

| Year | Dependent Students (except students whose parents are unable to obtain PLUS Loans) | Independent Students (and dependent undergraduate students whose parents are unable to obtain PLUS Loans) |
|---|---|---|
| First-Year Undergraduate | $5,500—No more than $3,500 of this amount may be in subsidized loans. | $9,500—No more than $3,500 of this amount may be in subsidized loans. |
| Second-Year Undergraduate | $6,500—No more than $4,500 of this amount may be in subsidized loans. | $10,500—No more than $4,500 of this amount may be in subsidized loans. |
| Third-Year and Beyond Undergraduate | $7,500 per year—No more than $5,500 of this amount may be in subsidized loans. | $12,500 per year—No more than $5,500 of this amount may be in subsidized loans. |
| Graduate or Professional Degree Students | Not Applicable | $20,500 |
| **Maximum Total Debt from Subsidized and Unsubsidized Loans** | $31,000—No more than $23,000 of this amount may be in subsidized loans. | $57,500 for undergraduates—No more than $23,000 of this amount may be in subsidized loans.<br><br>$138,500 for graduate or professional students—No more than $65,500 of this amount may be in subsidized loans. The graduate debt limit includes all federal loans received for undergraduate study. |

*Source:* https://studentaid.ed.gov/sa/types/loans/subsidized-unsubsidized

## AMERICAN OPPORTUNITY CREDIT AND LIFETIME LEARNING CREDIT

Tuition tax credits allow families to reduce their tax bill by the out-of-pocket college tuition expense. Unlike a tax deduction, which is modified according to your tax bracket, a tax credit is a dollar-for-dollar reduction in taxes paid.

There are two programs: the American Opportunity Credit and the Lifetime Learning Credit. As is true of many federal programs, there are numerous rules and restrictions that apply. You should check with your tax preparer, financial adviser, or IRS Publication 970 for information about your own particular situation.

### American Opportunity Credit

The American Opportunity Credit (formerly the Hope Credit) can be claimed for expenses for the first four years of postsecondary education. This is a change from the previous Hope Credit. The American Opportunity Credit can be claimed now through tax-year 2017 for expenses for course-related books, supplies, and equipment. It is a tax credit of up to $2,500 of the cost of qualifying tuition and expenses, and up to 40 percent of the credit is refundable (up to $1,000).

Eligibility also differs from the former Hope Credit. A taxpayer who pays qualified tuition and related expenses and whose federal income tax return has a modified adjusted gross income of $80,000 or less ($160,000 or less for joint filers) is eligible for the credit. The credit is reduced ratably if a taxpayer's modified adjusted gross income exceeds those amounts. A taxpayer whose modified adjusted gross income is greater than $90,000 ($180,000 for joint filers) cannot benefit from this credit.

For more information about the American Opportunity Tax Credit, go online to http://www.irs.gov/uac/American-Opportunity-Tax-Credit:-Questions-and-Answers.

### Lifetime Learning Credit

The Lifetime Learning Credit is the counterpart of the American Opportunity Credit. The qualifying taxpayer can claim an annual tax credit of up to $2,000—20 percent of the first $10,000 of tuition. The credit is available for net tuition and fees, less grant aid. The total credit available is limited to $2,000 per year per taxpayer (or joint-filing couple). There is no limit on the number of years the lifetime learning credit can be claimed for each student. However, a taxpayer cannot claim both the American Opportunity Credit and Lifetime Learning Credit for the same student in one year. For more information, visit http://www.irs.gov/Individuals/LLC.

## TUITION AND FEES TAX DEDUCTION

The Tuition and Fees Tax Deduction could reduce taxable income by as much as $4,000. This deduction is taken as an adjustment to income, which means you can claim this deduction even if you do not itemize deductions on Schedule A of Form 1040. This deduction may benefit taxpayers who do not qualify for either the American Opportunity Credit or Lifetime Learning Credit.

Up to $4,000 may be deducted for tuition and fees required for enrollment or attendance at an eligible postsecondary institution. Personal living and family expenses, including room and board, insurance, medical, and transportation, are not deductible expenses.

The exact amount of the Tuition and Fees Tax Deduction depends on the amount of qualified tuition and related expenses paid for one's self, spouse, or dependents, and your Adjusted Gross Income. Consult the IRS or your tax preparer for more information.

## STUDENT LOAN INTEREST TAX DEDUCTION

If you made student loan interest payments, you may be able to reduce your taxable income by up to $2,500. You should check with your lender with regards to the amount of interest you paid if you did not receive an IRS Form 1098-E and your tax preparer or IRS Publication 970 for additional information, which can be found online at http://www.irs.gov/publications/p970/ch04.html.

## AMERICORPS

AmeriCorps is a national umbrella group of service programs for students. Participants work in a public or private nonprofit agency and provide service to the community in one of four priority areas: education, human services, the environment, and public safety. For all AmeriCorps programs, members receive a modest living allowance, and some programs provide housing. Individuals may not save much money during their year of service, but most find the living allowance to be adequate to cover their needs. AmeriCorps members who complete a term of service also receive an AmeriCorps Education Award. Many student-loan lenders will postpone the repayment of student loans during service in AmeriCorps, and AmeriCorps will pay the interest that is accrued on qualified student loans for members who complete the service program. Participants can work before, during, or after college and can use the funds to either pay current educational expenses or repay federal student loans. For more information, visit http://www.nationalservice.gov/programs/americorps.

# Inside the Federal Work-Study Program

If you're like millions of other families with college-age youth you may have had that moment. It's the stomach-churning wrinkle in time when you realize that the gap between the amount of money you've saved for your child's college education and the cost of that dream university seems as insurmountable as crossing the ocean on a surfboard. Even as you fill out the Free Application for Federal Student Aid (FAFSA) and your child gets the award letter from the college, the sticker shock can be depressing. But there is glimmer of hope, and it's called the Federal Work-Study Program (FWS).

The federally funded FWS, formerly known as the College Campus Work-Study Program, was a part of the anti-poverty legislation that swept the country in the 1960s. FWS partners with 3,400 institutions in the country to pay students to work on a college or university campus. Looking at the words "work study," may instill fear in some parent's hearts. They may think of nightmarish scenarios where their son or daughter spends so much time guarding the science building that they won't have time for their studies. This isn't necessarily true. There are several aspects to the federally supported work-study program that makes it an attractive option for students looking to lower their college bill.

## WORK-STUDY CAN BE A VALUABLE EXPERIENCE

The Federal Work-Study (FWS) Program is a federal student aid program that provides part-time employment while you are enrolled in school to help pay your education expenses. The Federal Work-Study Program emphasizes, whenever possible, employment in civic education and work that is related to your course of study.

If you work on campus, you'll most likely work for your school. If you work off campus, your employer might be a private nonprofit organization or a public agency, and the work performed must be in the public interest.

Colleges and universities like that the FWS is federally subsidized, so they will offer this option as part of a financial aid package first because it saves them money. So send your FASFA as early as possible, especially if you want to beat out the millions of students who seek work-study jobs! Also, don't forget to indicate on your FASFA that you are interested in a work-study job.

In addition, it may be best to choose work-study over outside employment. You may believe that work is work, but when it comes to work-study jobs that sentiment is not true. Work-study jobs are usually better for students because the payment you receive is NOT counted against you when applying for financial aid. This could make a huge difference in how much aid you receive from your chosen institution.

## WORK-STUDY JOBS—NOT ALWAYS "BORING"

Not all work-study jobs have to be through educational institutions. The program also funds jobs at a federal, state, or local public agency; a private nonprofit organization; or even a private for-profit organization. Check and see if your school has a partnership with an off-campus workplace. You might be able to find a work-study position in your field of study. This allows you to gain valuable experience and not just collect "man hours" while you pay down your college price tag.

Still, the type of job a student is privy to largely depends upon the intuition's work-study program. Some programs focus on interesting options such as janitorial services, cafeteria work, or even telemarketer. But with a little ingenuity, students can find a work-study assignment that fits their academic and financial need. For example, at Colorado College, a private school in Colorado Springs, work-study students can apply for jobs as diverse as stage manager for theater productions or work off campus at a nonprofit such as the Children's Literacy Center. To ensure you get a work-study position that fits your career goals, it's best to talk to officials at your institution early and often about available work-study options. For example, according to the U.S. Department of Education, a college must use 7 percent of its work-study funds to support students "working in community service jobs, including reading tutors for preschool age or elementary school children, mathematics tutors for students enrolled in elementary school through ninth grade, literacy tutors in a family literacy project performing family literacy activities, or emergency preparedness and response." When you talk to your institution's financial aid office you might mention your experience in any of these areas. This won't guarantee you a "better" work-study job, but it certainly can't hurt.

## TAKE ANOTHER LOOK AT WORK-STUDY

With flexible hours, guaranteed pay and the ability to help your institution and community, the work-study option is an attractive way for students to pay for their college education. Do not over look its benefits. Indicate work-study on your FAFSA application, and apply early. Who knows? You could end up as a tennis racquet stringer at Colorado College. For more information about FWS, go to http://www2.ed.gov/programs/fws/index.html.

# Analyzing Financial Aid Award Letters

## Richard Woodland

You have just received the financial aid award letters. Now what? This is the time to do a detailed analysis of each college's offer to help you pay for your child's education. Remember, accepting financial aid is a family matter. More often than not, parents need to borrow money to send their dependent children to college. You need to clearly understand the types of aid you and your child are being offered. How much is "free" money in the form of grants and/or scholarships that does not have to be repaid? If your financial aid award package includes loans, what are the terms and conditions for these loans? A good tool to have with you is the federal government's most recent issue of *Funding Your Education or 2015–16 Do You Need Money for College? Federal Student Aid at a Glance,* available from the school's financial aid office or at http://www.fsapubs.gov. This publication is very helpful in explaining the federal grant and loan programs that are usually a part of the aid package.

Let's take a minute to explain what is meant by "financial aid award package." A college will offer an aid applicant a combination of aid types, "packaged" in the form of grants and scholarships, loans, and a work-study job, based on the information provided on the FAFSA and/or another application. Many schools use a priority filing date, which guarantees that all applications received by this date will be considered for the full range of institutional aid programs available. Late applicants (by even one day!) often are only awarded the basic aid programs from state and federal sources. *It is important to apply on time.*

### EVALUATE EACH LETTER

As each award letter comes in, read it through carefully. The following are some critical points to consider:

- **Does the Cost of Attendance (COA) include all projected costs?** Each award letter should state the school's academic year COA. Tuition, fees, room, board, books, transportation, and personal expenses are what normally make up the COA. Does the award letter itemize all these components? Or does it omit some? This is crucial because this is what you will need to budget for. If you need additional information, be sure to contact the financial aid office. They will be glad to provide you with information or answer any questions you may have about their costs.

- **What is your Expected Family Contribution (EFC)?** Is the school's—not just the federal government's—EFC listed on the award letter? Some schools may require a higher EFC than you expected. Be aware that the EFC may increase or decrease each year depending on the information you provide on the renewal FAFSA or other financial aid application.

- **Is there unmet need?** Does the aid package cover the difference between the COA and the EFC? Not every school can cover your full need. If the aid package does not cover your full need, does the information with the award letter provide you with alternative loan options? If not, contact the financial aid office for more information.

- **Is the scholarship renewable for four years?** If your child is awarded a scholarship based on scholastic achievement or talent, you need to ask these questions: Is there a minimum grade point average he has to maintain? Can he switch majors but keep the scholarship? Does he need to participate in an "honors college" program to maintain the scholarship? If he needs to change to part-time status, will the award amount be prorated, or does he need to maintain full-time status? If it is an athletic or "special talent" scholarship, will he continue to receive the award if for some reason he cannot continue with the specific program? Renewal of scholarship funds is often the biggest misunderstanding between families and colleges. Be sure you clearly understand the terms and conditions of all grants and scholarships.

- **What will the college do to your child's award if she receives outside, noninstitutional scholarships?** Will the award be used to cover unmet need or reduce her student loans? Will the college reduce her institutional grants or scholarships? Or will they reduce her work-study award? (This is a good time to compare each school's policy on this matter.) Remember, your overall aid cannot total more than the COA, and many programs cannot exceed your financial need.

- **What are the interest rates of the loans that are offered?** Did another school offer you more than one loan and why? *Do not* sign the award letter until you understand your loan obligations. Again, *Funding Education Beyond High School: The Guide to Federal Student Aid* can be very helpful with this part of the analysis.

- **Is the school likely to cover the same expenses every year?** In particular, ask if grant or scholarship funds are normally reduced or increased after the freshman year, even if family income and EFC remain the same. Some colleges will *increase* the self-help (loan, job) percentage every year but not necessarily the free money.

- **If work-study was awarded, how many hours a week will your child be expected to work?** If you feel working that many hours will have a negative impact on your child's academic performance, you may want to request that the awarded job funds be changed to a loan. You must ask immediately because funds are limited. Many schools are flexible with these funds early in the process.

- **What happens if (or more likely, when) tuition increases?** Check with the financial aid office to find out what its policy is for renewing an aid package. If, for example, tuition increases by 5 percent each of the next three years and your EFC remains the same, what will happen to your scholarships, grants, and loans?

You can always appeal your award letter if you feel that your needs are not being met, if your family situation has changed, or if you have received a better award from a competitive school. You have the right to ask for a reconsideration of your award. (Do not use the word *negotiate*.) When asking for reconsideration, be sure to provide the aid officer with all relevant information.

## COMPARE LETTERS

After you have received and reviewed all the award letters from the schools your child is considering, the next step is to compare them and determine which schools are offering the best aid packages. Following are three sample award letters and a sample spreadsheet that shows you how to analyze and compare each school's awards.

(Note: These award letters are simply for discussion purposes. They should not be considered to be representative award letters with an EFC of $9,550.)

Once you have entered all the information into a spreadsheet of your own and come up with the balances, here are some things to consider for each school:

- **How much is the balance?** Ideally, your balance should be $0, but look to see which school has the lowest balance amount.

- **What part of the aid package comes in the form of grants and scholarships?** It is important to note this because these awards (gift aid) do not have to be paid back.

- **Look at the loans.** Usually, the best financial deal contains more money in scholarships and less in loan dollars. Based on expected freshman-year borrowing, determine the debt burden at each school once your child graduates. You have to multiply the amount of your loan by four or five years, depending on how long it will take for your child to graduate.

# UNIVERSITY A
## FINANCIAL AID AWARD LETTER
## 2015-2016

Date: 4/21/15
ID#: 0000000009

Dear Jane Smith,

We are pleased to inform you that you are eligible to receive the financial assistance indictate in the area labled "Your Financial Aid." We estimated your budget based on the following assumptions:

In-state resident and living on campus.

|  | FALL | SPRING | TOTAL |
| --- | --- | --- | --- |
| Tuition and Fees | $3,849 | $3,849 | $7,698 |
| Room & Board | 3,769 | 3,770 | 7,539 |
| Books | 420 | 420 | 840 |
| Transportation | 973 | 974 | 1,947 |
| Personal expenses | 369 | 369 | 738 |
| **Estimated Coast of Attendance** | **$9,380** | **$9,382** | **$18,762** |

**Your Financial Aid**

|  | FALL | SPRING | TOTAL |
| --- | --- | --- | --- |
| Federal Pell Grant | $1,950 | $1,950 | $3,900 |
| Federal Direct Subsidized Loan | $1,750 | $1,750 | $3,500 |
| State Grant | 432 | 432 | 864 |
| **Total Financial Aid** | **$4,132** | **$4,132** | **$8,264** |
| **Unmet Need** | **$5,248** | **$5,250** | **$10,498** |

What to Do Next:

- Verify that accurate assumptions have been used to determine your awards.
- Carefully review and follow the instructions on the Data Changes Form.
- To reduce or decline all or part of your loans, you must complete and return the Data Changes Form.
- We will assume you fully accept the awards above unless you submit changes to us immediately.
- Return corrections and required documents promptly.
- Retain this letter for your records.

# UNIVERSITY B
## FINANCIAL AID AWARD LETTER
### 2015-2016

Date: 4/21/15
ID#: 0000000009

Dear Jane Smith,

We are pleased to inform you that you are eligible to receive the financial assistance indictate in the area labled "Your Financial Aid." We estimated your budget based on the following assumptions:

Nonresident and living on campus.

| | FALL | SPRING | TOTAL |
|---|---|---|---|
| Tuition and Fees | $9,805 | $9,085 | $18,170 |
| Room & Board | 2,835 | 2,835 | 5,670 |
| Books | 410 | 410 | 820 |
| Transportation | 875 | 875 | 1,750 |
| Personal Expenses | 378 | 377 | 755 |
| **Estimated Coast of Attendance** | **$13,583** | **$13,582** | **$27,165** |

**Your Financial Aid**

| | FALL | SPRING | TOTAL |
|---|---|---|---|
| Federal Pell Grant | $1,950 | $1,950 | $3,900 |
| Federal SEOG Grant | 225 | 225 | 450 |
| Academic Excellence Scholarship | 500 | 500 | 1,000 |
| Federal Work-Study | 1,050 | 1,050 | 2,100 |
| Federal Perkins Loan Program | 1,250 | 1,250 | 2,500 |
| Subsidized Federal Stafford Student Loan | 1,750 | 1,750 | 3,500 |
| University Student Loan | 2,000 | 2,000 | 4,000 |
| **Total Financial Aid** | **$8,725** | **$8,725** | **$17,450** |
| **Unmet Need** | **$4,858** | **$4,857** | **$9,715** |

What to Do Next:
- Verify that accurate assumptions have been used to determine your awards.
- Carefully review and follow the instructions on the Data Changes Form.
- To reduce or decline all or part of your loans, you must complete and return the Data Changes Form.
- We will assume you fully accept the awards above unless you submit changes to us immediately.
- Return corrections and required documents promptly.
- Retain this letter for your records.

# UNIVERSITY C
## FINANCIAL AID AWARD LETTER
## 2015-2016

Date: 4/21/15
ID#: 0000000009

Dear Jane Smith,

We are pleased to inform you that you are eligible to receive the financial assistance indictate in the area labled "Your Financial Aid." We estimated your budget based on the following assumptions:

Living on campus.

|  | FALL | SPRING | TOTAL |
|---|---|---|---|
| Tuition and Fees | $14,955 | $14,955 | $29,910 |
| Room & Board | 4,194 | 4,193 | 8,387 |
| Books | 450 | 450 | 900 |
| Transportation | 350 | 350 | 700 |
| Personal Expenses | 1,295 | 1,293 | 2,588 |
| **Estimated Coast of Attendance** | **$21,244** | **$21,241** | **$42,485** |

**Your Financial Aid**

|  | FALL | SPRING | TOTAL |
|---|---|---|---|
| Institutional Grant | $10,805 | $10,805 | $21,610 |
| Federal Pell Grant | $1,950 | $1,950 | $3,900 |
| Federal SEOG Grant | 2,000 | 2,000 | 4,000 |
| Federal Work-Study Program | 1,713 | 1,712 | 3,425 |
| **Total Financial Aid** | **$16,468** | **$16,467** | **$32,935** |
| **Unmet Need** | **$4,776** | **$4,774** | **$9,550** |

What to Do Next:
- Verify that accurate assumptions have been used to determine your awards.
- Carefully review and follow the instructions on the Data Changes Form.
- To reduce or decline all or part of your loans, you must complete and return the Data Changes Form.
- We will assume you fully accept the awards above unless you submit changes to us immediately.
- Return corrections and required documents promptly.
- Retain this letter for your records.

# Comparison Grid

| | University A (State University) | University B (Nonresident State University) | University C (Private College) |
|---|---|---|---|
| **Cost of Attendance** | $18,762 | $27,165 | $42,485 |
| Tuition and Fees | 7,698 | 18,170 | 29,910 |
| Room & Board | 7,539 | 5,670 | 8,367 |
| Books | 840 | 820 | 900 |
| Transportation | 1,947 | 1,750 | 700 |
| Personal Expenses | 738 | 755 | 2,558 |
| | | | |
| **Grants and Scholarships** | 4,764 | 5,350 | 29,510 |
| **Loans** | 3,500 | 10,000 | 0 |
| **Work-Study** | 0 | 2,00 | 3,425 |
| **Expected Family Contribution** | 9,550 | 9,550 | 9,550 |
| | | | |
| **Balance** | $948 | $165 | $0 |

Some things to notice:

- At all schools, the federal Pell Grant remains the same.
- The loan amounts varied greatly among these schools.
- Even though University C (a private college) has the highest "sticker price," the net cost is less than the state schools.
- University B is a state university, but you are classified as an out-of-state resident (or nonresident). Many Students in this situation find that the higher out-of-state costs combined with lower grant aid make this a costly decision.
- All schools assume that you will be residing in on-campus housing. But if you choose to commute to University A, you would save a substatial amount because you would not have the $7,539 room and board cost.

And remember that the loan amounts will probably increase each year. You also should take into consideration that you will have to borrow even more as the COA increases each year. To determine the best loan deal, consider:

—What are the terms of the loans?

—What are interest rates?

—Do you pay the yearly interest rate during enrollment or is the interest subsidized or paid by the government?

—Is any money due during enrollment or is it deferred until after graduation? Figuring out how much you will owe at each school at graduation will give you a clear picture of what your financial situation will be after graduation.

However, unless cost is your only concern, you shouldn't simply choose the school offering the lowest loan amounts. Many other factors need to be considered, such as academic and social environment. And you should never reject a school based solely on insufficient financial aid. Consult with an aid administrator to discuss possible alternatives.

Finally, if the college that costs the most is still the one your child wants to attend, there are a number of ways to find money to cover the gap between the aid package and your actual cost, including paying more than the EFC figure, increasing student borrowing, working more hours, and taking out a PLUS loan.

*Richard Woodland is Vice President of Development for ProEd Solutions. He previously served as Director of Financial Aid at Rutgers University–Camden and as Director of Student Services and Financial Assistance at the Curtis Institute of Music.*

# Parents' and Students' Common Questions Answered

**Q** *Are a student's chances of being admitted to a college reduced if the student applies for financial aid?*

**A** Generally no. Nearly all colleges have a policy of "need-blind" admissions, which means that a student's financial need is not taken into account in the admission decision. There are a few selective colleges, however, that do consider ability to pay before deciding whether or not to admit a student. Some colleges will mention this in their literature; others may not. The best advice is to apply for financial aid if the student needs assistance to attend college.

**Q** *Are parents penalized for saving money for college?*

**A** No. As a matter of fact, families that have made a concerted effort to save money for college are in a much better position than those that have not. For example, a student from a family that has saved money may not have to borrow as much. Furthermore, the "taxing rate" on savings is quite low—only about 5 percent of the parents' assets are assessed and neither the home equity nor retirement savings are included. For example, a single 40-year-old parent who saved $40,000 for college expenses will have about $1,900 counted as part of the parental contribution. Two parents, if the older one is 40 years old (a parent's age factors into the formulation), would have about $300 counted. (Note: The "taxing rate" for student assets is much higher—20 percent—compared to 5 percent for parents.)

**Q** *How does the financial aid system work in cases of divorce or separation? How are stepparents treated?*

**A** In cases of divorce or separation, the financial aid application(s) should be completed by the parent with whom the student lived for the longest period of time in the past twelve months (custodial parent). If the custodial parent has remarried, the stepparent is considered a family member and must complete the application along with the biological parent. If your family has any special circumstances, you should discuss these directly with the financial aid office. (Note: Colleges that award their own aid may ask the noncustodial biological parent to complete a separate aid application and a contribution will be calculated.)

**Q** *When are students considered independent of parental support in applying for financial aid?*

**A** The student must be at least 24 years of age in order to be considered independent. If younger than 24, the student must be married, be a graduate or professional student, have legal dependents other than a spouse, be an orphan or ward of the court, or be a veteran of the armed forces or on active military duty. However, in very unusual situations, students who can clearly document estrangement from their parents can appeal to the financial aid office for additional consideration.

**Q** *What can a family do if a job loss occurs?*

**A** Financial aid eligibility is based on the previous year's income. So the family's 2015 income would be reported to determine eligibility for the 2016–17 academic year. In that way, the family's income can be verified with an income tax return. But the previous year's income may not accurately reflect the current financial situation, particularly if a parent lost a job or retired. In these instances, the projected income for the coming year can be used instead. Families should discuss the situation directly with the financial aid office and be prepared to provide appropriate documentation.

**Q** *When my daughter first went to college, we applied for financial aid and were denied because our Expected Family Contribution was too high. Now, my son is a high school senior, and we will soon have two in college. Will we get the same results?*

**A** The results will definitely be different. Both your son and your daughter should apply. As described earlier, need-based financial aid is based on your Expected Family Contribution, or EFC. When you have two children in college, this amount is divided in half for each child.

**Q** *I've heard about the "middle-income squeeze" in regard to financial aid. What is it?*

**A** The so-called "middle-income squeeze" is the idea that low-income families qualify for aid, high-income families have adequate resources to pay for education, and those in the middle are not eligible for aid but do not have the ability to pay full college costs. There is no provision in the Federal Methodology that treats middle-income students differently than others (such as an income cutoff for eligibility). The Expected Family Contribution rises proportionately as income and assets increase. If a middle-income family does not qualify for aid, it is because the need analysis formula yields a contribution that exceeds college costs. But keep in mind that if a $65,000-income family does not qualify for grant aid at a public university with a $16,000 cost, the same family will likely be eligible for aid at a private college with a cost of $25,000 or more. Also, there are loan programs available to parents and students that are not based on need. Middle-income families should realize, however, that many of the grant programs funded by federal and state governments are directed at lower-income families. It is therefore likely that a larger share of an aid package for a middle-income student will consist of loans rather than grants.

**Q** *Given our financial condition, my daughter will be receiving financial aid. We will help out as much as we can, and, in fact, we ourselves will be borrowing. But I am concerned that she will have to take on a lot of loans in order to go to the college of her choice. Does she have any options?*

**A** She does. If offered a loan, she can decline all or part of it. One option is for her to ask in the financial aid office to have some of the loan changed to a work-study job. If this is not possible, she can find her own part-time work. Often there is an employment office on campus that can help her locate a job. In most cases, the more she works, the less she has to borrow. It is important to remember that the education loans offered to students have very attractive terms and conditions, with flexible repayment options. Students should look upon these loans as a long-term investment that will reap significant rewards.

**Q** *What are some easy ways to improve my chances of receiving aid?*

**A** When filling out your scholarship or financial aid application, it's important to remember that the smallest mistake could hurt your chances for landing free money, or even worse, it could disqualify you completely from an awards contest. Grants and scholarships are highly competitive, so it's a good idea to make a list of what's needed and make sure you have everything before submitting your application. If you are submitting an essay, have another pair of eyes look at it for any spelling and grammar errors. Keep a file on everything you're applying for so that you don't miss any elements of an application. Make sure you're using reputable sites to conduct your free scholarship searches. If you have to pay to apply for an award or look for scholarships, chances are

you're being scammed. In a nutshell, the best advice is to follow all directions, and make sure that you meet all deadlines.

In addition, when filling out the FAFSA, it's important to pay close attention to the details, since any errors may delay the application process. These days, it's preferable to fill out the FAFSA online, since mailed forms can take weeks to process. If you're confused or concerned about something on the application, contact the Federal Student Aid Information Center at 1-800-4FED-AID; questions can also be asked through the FAFSA Web site. Your college's financial aid office should also be able to assist you. The FAFSA is available each year starting Jan. 1, and it's essential that you don't miss the deadline to apply. The sooner you apply, the sooner you'll know the kind of funding package you are likely to receive, and this will help you determine if you need to apply for any additional aid.

**Q** *Is it possible to change your financial aid package?*

**A** Yes. Most colleges have an appeal process. A request to change a need-based loan to a work-study job is usually approved if funds are available. A request to consider special financial circumstances may also be granted. At most colleges, a request for more grant money is rarely approved unless it is based on a change in the information reported. Applicants should speak with the financial aid office if they have concerns about their financial package. Some colleges may even respond to a competitive appeal, that is, a request to match another college's offer.

**Q** *The cost of attending college seems to be going up so much faster than the Consumer Price Index. Why is that, and how can I plan for my child's four years?*

**A** The cost of higher education cannot be compared to the Consumer Price Index (CPI). The CPI does not take into account most of the costs faced by colleges. For example, the dollars that universities spend on grants and scholarships have risen rapidly. Many universities have increased enrollment of students from less affluent families, further increasing the need for institutional financial aid. Colleges are expected to be on the cutting edge of technology, not only in research but also in the classroom and in the library. Many colleges have deferred needed maintenance and repairs that can now no longer be put off. In addition, there is market pressure to provide many expensive lifestyle amenities that were not expected ten years ago. In general, you can expect that college costs will rise at least 2 to 3 percent faster than inflation.

**Q** *I'm struggling with the idea that all students should apply to the college of their choice, regardless of cost, because financial aid will level the playing field. I feel I will be penalized because I have saved for college. My son has been required to save half of his allowance since age six* for his college education. Will that count against him when he applies for financial aid? It's difficult to explain to him that his college choices may be limited because of the responsible choices and sacrifices we have made as a family. What can we do to make the most of our situation?

A In general, it is always better to have planned ahead for college by saving. Families that have put away sufficient funds to pay for college will quickly realize that they have made the burden easier for themselves and their children. In today's college financing world, schools assume that paying for the cost of attendance is a ten-year commitment. So by saving when your child is young, you reap significant advantages from compound interest on the assets and reduce the need to borrow as much while in school. This should reduce the number of years after college that you will be burdened with loans. Families should spend the student's assets first, since the financial aid formulas count these more heavily than parental assets. Then, after the first year, you can explain to the college how you spent these assets, and why you might now need assistance. When looking at parental information, the income of the family is by far the most important component. Contrary to popular belief, parental assets play a minor role in the calculation of need. With this strategy, you have done the right thing, and in the long run, it should prove to be a wise financial plan.

Picking the right college also involves other factors. Students should select the colleges to which they are going to apply in two ways. First, and most important, is to look at colleges that meet your son's academic and lifestyle interests. Most experts will tell him to pick a few "reach" schools (i.e., schools where he is not sure he has the grades and scores required) and at least one or two academically "safe" schools. He should also select one or two financially "safe" schools that you are sure you can afford with either moderate or little financial aid. Most students do not get into all of their first-choice schools, and not everyone can afford the schools to which they are admitted. By working closely with the guidance office in high school and the admissions and financial aid offices at the college, you can maximize your options.

Q My son was awarded a $2,500 scholarship. This can be split and used for two years. When filling out the FAFSA, do we have to claim the full amount, or just the $1,250 he plans to use the first year?

A Congratulations to your son on the scholarship. Nowhere on the FAFSA should you report this scholarship. It is not considered income or an asset. However, once you choose a school to attend, you must notify the financial aid office for its advice on how to take the funds. But remember, do NOT report it on the FAFSA.

Q I will be receiving a scholarship from my local high school. How will this scholarship be treated in my financial aid award?

A Federal student aid regulations specify that all forms of aid must be included within the defined level of need. This means that additional aid, such as outside scholarships, must be combined with any need-based aid you receive; it may not be kept separate and used to reduce your family's contribution. If the college has not filled 100 percent of your need, it will usually allow outside scholarships to close the gap. Once your total need has been met, the college must reduce other aid and replace it with the outside award. Most colleges will allow you to use some, if not all, of an outside scholarship to replace self-help aid (loans and Federal Work-Study Program awards) rather than grant aid.

Q I know we're supposed to apply for financial aid as soon as possible after January 1. What if I don't have my W-2s yet and my tax return isn't done?

A The first financial aid application deadlines usually fall in early February. Most colleges use either March 1 or March 15 as their "priority filing date." Chances are you'll have your W-2 forms by then, but you won't have a completed tax return. If that is the case, complete the financial aid application using your best estimates. Then, when you receive the Student Aid Report (SAR), you can use your tax return to make corrections. Just be sure to check with each college for its deadline.

Q Is there enough aid available to make it worthwhile for me to consider colleges that are more expensive than I can afford?

A Definitely. More than $100 billion in aid is awarded to undergraduates every year. With more than half of all enrolled students qualifying for some type of assistance, this totals more than $5,500 per student. You should view financial aid as a large, national system of tuition discounts, some given according to a student's ability and talent, others based on what a student's family can afford to pay. If you qualify for need-based financial aid, you will essentially pay only your calculated family contribution, regardless of the cost of the college. You will not pay the "sticker price" (the cost of attendance listed in the college catalog) but a lower rate that is reduced by the amount of aid you receive. No college should be ruled out until after financial aid is considered. In addition, when deciding which college to attend, consider that the short-term cost of a college education is only one criterion. If the college meets your educational needs and you are convinced it can launch you on an exciting career, a significant up-front investment may turn out to be a bargain over the long run.

# Q If I don't qualify for need-based aid, what options are available?

A You should try to put together your own aid package to help reduce your parents' share. There are three sources to look into. First, search for merit scholarships. Second, seek employment, during both the summer and the academic year. The student employment office should be able to help you find a campus job. Third, look into borrowing. Even if you don't qualify for the need-based loan programs, the unsubsidized Federal Direct Loan is available to all students. The terms and conditions are the same as the subsidized loan programs except that interest accrues while you are in college.

After you have contributed what you can through scholarships, employment, and loans, your parents will be faced with their share of the college bill. Many colleges have monthly payment plans that allow families to spread their payments over the academic year. If these monthly payments turn out to be more than your parents can afford, they can take out a parent loan. By borrowing from the college itself, from a commercial agency or lender, or through PLUS, your parents can extend the payments over a ten-year period or longer. Borrowing reduces the monthly obligation to its lowest level, but the total amount paid will be the highest due to principal and interest payments. Before making a decision on where to borrow parental loan funds, be sure to first check with the financial aid office to determine what is the best source of alternative funds.

# How to Use This Guide

## QUICK-REFERENCE CHART

The amount of aid available at colleges can vary greatly. "College Costs At-a-Glance" lists the percent of freshmen who applied for and received need-based gift aid and the percent of those whose need was fully met. Also listed are the average freshman financial aid package, the average cost after aid, and the average indebtedness upon graduation.

## PROFILES OF COLLEGE FINANCIAL AID PROGRAMS

After the federal government, colleges provide the largest amount of financial aid to students. In addition, they control most of the money channeled to students from the federal government. The amount and makeup of your financial aid package will depend on the institution's particular circumstances and its decisions concerning your application. The main section of this book shows you the pattern and extent of each college's current awards. The profiles present detailed factual and statistical data for each school in a uniform format to enable easy, quick references and comparisons. Items that could not be collected in time for publication for specific institutions do not appear in those institutions' profiles. Colleges that supplied no data are listed by name and address only so that you do not overlook them in your search for colleges.

There is much anecdotal evidence that students and their families fail to apply for financial aid under the misconception that student aid goes only to poor families. Financial need in the context of college expenses is not the same as being needy in the broad social context. Middle-class families typically qualify for need-based financial aid; at expensive schools, even upper-middle income families can qualify for need-based financial aid. Peterson's encourages you to apply for financial aid whether or not you think that you will qualify.

To help you understand the definition and significance of each item, the following outline of the profile format explains what is covered in each section. The term college or colleges is frequently used throughout to refer to any institution of higher education, regardless of its official definition.

## The College

The name of the college is the official name as it appears on the institution's charter. The city and state listed are the official location of the school. The subhead line shows tuition and required fees, as they were charged to the majority of full-time undergraduate students in the 2014–15 academic year. Any exceptions to the 2014–15 academic year are so noted. For a public institution, the tuition and fees shown are for state residents, and this is noted. If a college's annual expenses are expressed as a comprehensive fee (including full-time tuition, mandatory fees, and college room and board), this is noted, as

are any unusual definitions, such as tuition only. The average undergraduate aid package is the average total package of grant, loan, and work-study aid that was awarded to meet the officially defined financial need of full-time undergraduates enrolled in fall 2014 (or fall 2013) who applied for financial aid, were determined to have need, and then actually received financial aid. This information appears in more detail in each profile.

## About the Institution

This paragraph gives the reader a brief introduction to a college. It contains the following elements:

### Institutional Control

Private institutions are designated as *independent* (nonprofit), *independent/religious* (sponsored by or affiliated with a religious group or having a nondenominational or interdenominational religious orientation), or *proprietary* (profit-making). Public institutions are designated by their primary source of support, such as *federal, state, commonwealth* (Puerto Rico), *territory* (U.S. territories), *county, district* (an administrative unit of public education, often having boundaries different from those of units of local government), *state-and locally-supported* ("locally" refers to county, district, or city), *state-supported* (funded by the state), or *state-related* (funded primarily by the state but administered autonomously).

### Type of Student Body

The categories are *men* (100 percent of student body), *coed primarily men, women* (100 percent of student body), *coed-primarily women,* and *coed*. A few schools are designated as *undergraduate: women only, graduate: coed* or *undergraduate: men only, graduate: coed*.

### Degrees Awarded

*Associate, bachelor's* (baccalaureate), *master's, doctoral* (doctorate), and *first professional* (in such fields as law and medicine). There are no institutions in this book that award the associate degree only. Many award the bachelor's as the highest degree.

### Number of Undergraduate Majors

This shows the number of academic fields in which the institution offers associate and/or bachelor's degrees. The purpose of this is to give you an indication of the range of subjects available.

### Enrollment

These figures are based on the actual number of full-time and part-time students enrolled in degree programs as of fall 2014 (or 2013 if the 2014 figure was not available). In most instances, they are designated as *total enrollment* (for the specific college or university) and *freshmen*. If the institution is a university and its total enrollment figure includes graduate students, a separate figure for *undergraduates* may be provided. If the profiled institution is a subunit of a university, the figures may be designated *total university enrollment* for the entire university and *total unit enrollment* for the specific subunit.

## Methodology Used for Determining Need

Private colleges usually have larger financial aid programs, but public colleges usually have lower sticker prices, especially for in-state or local students. At a public college, your financial need will be less, and you will receive a smaller financial aid package. This note on whether a college uses federal (FAFSA) or institutional methodology (usually CSS/Financial Aid PRO-FILE®) will let you know whether you will have to complete one or two kinds of financial aid application forms. Federal Methodology is the needs-analysis formula used by the U.S. Department of Education to determine the Expected Family Contribution (EFC), which, when subtracted from the cost of attendance at an institution, determines the financial need of a student. There is no relative advantage or disadvantage to using one methodology over the other.

## Undergraduate Expenses

If provided by the institution, the one-time application fee is listed. Costs are given for the 2015–16 academic year or for the 2014–15 academic year if 2015–16 figures were not yet available. (Peterson's collects information for freshmen specifically.) Annual expenses may be expressed as a comprehensive fee (including full-time tuition, mandatory fees, and college room and board) or may be given as separate figures for full-time tuition, fees, room and board, or room only. For public institutions where tuition differs according to state residence, separate figures are given for area or state residents and for nonresidents. Part-time tuition is expressed in terms of a per-unit rate (per credit, per semester hour, etc.), as specified by the institution.

The tuition structure at some institutions is complex. Freshmen and sophomores may be charged a different rate from that charged juniors and seniors, a professional or vocational division may have a different fee structure from the liberal arts division of the same institution, or part-time tuition may be prorated on a sliding scale according to the number of credit hours taken. Tuition and fees may vary according to academic program, campus/location, class time (day, evening, weekend), course/credit load, course level, degree level, reciprocity agreements, and student level. If tuition and fees differ for international students, the rate charged is listed.

Room and board charges are reported as a double occupancy and nineteen meals per week plan or the equivalent and may vary according to board plan selected, campus/location, gender, type of housing facility, or student level. If no college-owned or -operated housing facilities are offered, the phrase *college housing not available* will appear.

If a college offers a *guaranteed tuition* plan, it promises that the tuition rate of an entering student will not increase for the entire term of enrollment, from entrance to graduation. Other payment plans might include *tuition prepayment*, which allows an entering student to lock in the current tuition rate for the entire term of enrollment by paying the full amount in advance rather than year by year, and *installment* and *deferred payment* plans, which allow students to delay the payment of the full tuition.

Guaranteed tuition and tuition prepayment help you to plan the total cost of education and can save you from the financial distress sometimes caused by tuition hikes. Colleges that offer such plans may also help you to arrange financing, which in the long run can cost less than the total of four years of increasing tuition rates. Deferred payment or installment payments may better fit your personal financial situation, especially if you do not qualify for financial aid and, due to other financial commitments, find that obtaining the entire amount due is burdensome. Carefully investigate these plans, however, to see what premium you may pay at the end to allow you to defer immediate payment.

## Freshman Financial Aid

Usually, these are actual figures for the 2013–14 term, beginning in fall 2013; figures may also be estimated for the 2014–15 term. The particular term for which these data apply is indicated. The figures are for degree-seeking full-time freshman students. The first figure is the number of freshmen who applied for any kind of financial aid. The next figure is the percentage of those freshmen financial aid applicants who were determined to have financial need—that is, through the formal needs-assessment process, had a calculated expected family contribution that was less than the total college cost. The next figure is the percentage of this group of eligible freshmen who received any financial aid. The next figure is the percentage of this preceding group of eligible aid recipients whose need was fully met by financial aid. The *Average percent of need met* is the average percentage of financial need met for freshmen who received any need-based aid. The *Average financial aid package* is the average dollar amount awarded (need-based or non-need-based) to freshmen who applied for aid, were deemed eligible, and received any aid; awards used to reduce the expected family contribution are excluded from this average. The final line in most profiles is the percentage of freshmen who had no financial need but who received non-need-based aid other than athletic scholarships or special-group tuition benefits.

What do these data mean to you? If financial aid is important in your comparison of colleges, the relative percentage of students who received any aid, whose need was fully met, and the average percentage of need met have the most weight. These figures reflect the relative abundance of student aid available to the average eligible applicant. The average dollar amount of the aid package has real meaning, but only in relation to the college's expense; you will be especially interested in the difference between this figure and the costs figure, which is what the average student (in any given statistical group, there actually may be no average individual) will have to pay. Of course, if the financial aid package is largely loans rather than grants, you will have to pay this amount eventually. Relative differences in the figures of the number of students who apply for aid and who are deemed eligible can hinge on any number of factors: the relative sticker price of the college, the relative level of wealth of the students' families, the proportion of only children in college and students with siblings in college (families with two or more children in college are more likely to apply for aid and be considered eligible), or the relative sophistication in financial aid matters (or quality of college counseling they may have received) of the students and their families. While these may be interesting, they will not mean too much to most students and families. If you are among the unlucky (or, perhaps, lucky) families who do not qualify for need-based financial aid, the final sentence of this paragraph in the profile will be of interest because it reveals the relative policies that the college has in distributing merit-based aid to students who cannot demonstrate need.

## Undergraduate Financial Aid

This is the parallel paragraph to the Freshman Financial Aid paragraph. The same definitions apply, except that the group being considered is degree-seeking full-time undergraduate students (including freshmen).

There are cases of students who chose a particular college because they received a really generous financial aid package in their freshman year and then had to scramble to pay the tuition bill in their later years. If a financial aid package is a key factor in the decision to attend a particular college, you want to be certain that the package offered to all undergraduates is not too far from that offered to freshmen. The key figures are those for the percentage of students who received any aid, the percentage of financial aid recipients whose need was fully met, the average percentage of need met, and the dollar figure of the average financial aid package. Generally, colleges assume that after the freshman year, students develop study habits and time-management skills that will allow them to take on part-time and summer employment without hurting their academic performance. So, the proportion of self-help aid (work-study and student loans) in the financial aid package tends to increase after the freshman year. This pattern, which is true of most colleges, can be verified in the freshman-undergraduate figures in the paragraph on Gift Aid (Need-Based).

## Gift Aid (Need-Based)

*Total amount* is the total dollar figure in 2014–15 (estimated) or 2013–14 (actual) of need-based scholarships and grant (gift) aid awarded to degree-seeking full-time and part-time students that was used to meet financial need. The percentages of this aid from federal, state, institutional (college or university), and external (e.g., foundations, civic organizations, etc.) sources are shown. *Receiving aid* shows the percentages (and number, in parentheses) of freshmen and of all undergraduates who applied for aid, were considered eligible, and received any need-based gift aid. *Average award* is the average dollar amount of awards to freshmen and all undergraduates who applied for aid, were considered eligible, and received any need-based gift aid. *Scholarships, grants, and awards* cites major categories of need-based gift aid provided by the college; these include Federal Pell Grants, Federal Supplemental Educational Opportunity Grants (FSEOG), state scholarships, private scholarships, college/university gift aid from institutional funds,

United Negro College Fund aid, Federal Nursing Scholarships, and others.

Scholarships and grants are gifts awarded to students that do not need to be repaid. These are preferable to loans, which have to be repaid, or work-study wages, which may take time away from studies and personal pursuits. The total amount of need-based gift aid has to be placed into the context of the total number of undergraduate students (shown in the About the Institution paragraph) and the relative expense of the institution. Filing the FAFSA automatically puts you in line to receive any available federal grants for which you may qualify. However, if the college being considered has a higher than usual proportion of gift aid coming from state, institutional, or external sources, be sure to check with the financial aid office to find out what these sources may be and how to apply for them. For almost all colleges, the percentage of freshmen receiving need-based gift aid will be higher than the percentage of all undergraduates receiving need-based gift aid. However, if you are dependent on need-based gift aid and the particular college under consideration shows a sharper drop from the freshman to undergraduate years than other colleges of a similar type, you might want to think about how this change will affect your ability to pay for later years at this college.

## Gift Aid (Non-Need-Based)

*Total amount* is the total dollar figure in 2014–15 (estimated) or 2013–14 (actual) of non-need-based scholarships and grant (gift) aid awarded to degree-seeking full-time and part-time students. Non-need-based aid that was used to meet financial need is not included in this total. The percentages of this aid from federal, state, institutional (college or university), and external (e.g., National Merit Scholarships, civic, religious, fraternal organizations, etc.) sources are shown. *Receiving aid* shows the percentages (and number, in parentheses) of freshmen and of all undergraduates who were determined to have need and received non-need-based gift aid. *Average award* is the average dollar amount of awards to freshmen and all undergraduates determined to have no need but received non-need-based awards. *Scholarships, grants, and awards by category* cites the major categories in which non-need-based awards are available and the number of awards made in that category (in parentheses, the total dollar value of these awards). The categories listed are *Academic interests/achievement, Creative arts/performance, Special achievements/activities*, and *Special characteristics. Tuition waivers* indicate special categories of students (minority students, children of alumni, college employees or children of employees, adult students, and senior citizens) who may qualify for a full or partial waiver of tuition. *ROTC* indicates Army, Naval, and Air Force ROTC programs that are offered on campus; a program offered by arrangement on another campus is indicated by the word *cooperative.*

This section covers college-administered scholarships awarded to undergraduates on the basis of merit or personal attributes without regard to need. If you do not qualify for financial aid but nevertheless lack the resources to pay for college, non-need-based awards will be of special interest to you. Some personal characteristics are completely beyond an individual's control, and talents and achievements take a number of years to develop or attain. However, certain criteria for these awards, such as religious involvement, community service, and special academic interests can be attained in a relatively brief period of time. ROTC programs offer such benefits as tuition, the cost of textbooks, and living allowances. In return, you must fulfill a service obligation after graduating from college. Because they can be a significant help in paying for college, these programs have become quite competitive. Certain subject areas, such as nursing, health care, or the technical fields, are in stronger demand than others. Among the obligations to consider about ROTC are that you must spend a regular portion of your available time in military training programs and that ROTC entails a multiyear commitment after your graduation to serve as an officer in the armed services branch sponsoring the program.

## Loans

The figures here represent loans that are part of the financial aid award package. *Student loans* represents the total dollar amount of loans from all sources to full-time and part-time degree-seeking undergraduates or their parents. *Average need-based loan* represents the percentage of these loans that goes to meet financial need, and the percentage that goes to pay the non-need portion (the expected family contribution) are indicated. The percentage of a past graduating class who borrowed through any loan program (except parent loans) while enrolled at the college is shown, as is the average dollar figure per-borrower of cumulative undergraduate indebtedness (this does not include loans from other institutions). *Parent loans* shows the total amount borrowed through parent loan programs as well as the percentages that were applied to the need-based and non-needbased portions of financial need. *Programs* indicates the major loan programs available to undergraduates. These include Direct Student Loans (subsidized and unsubsidized and PLUS), Perkins Loans, Federal Nursing Loans, state loans, college/university loans, and other types.

Note: As a result of the Health Care and Education Reconciliation Act, as of July 1, 2010, federal student loans are no longer made by private lenders under the Federal Family Education Loan (FFEL) Program. Instead, all new federal student loans come directly from the U.S. Department of Education under the Direct Loan Program. Any FFEL loans noted in this section of an institution's profile are no longer available.

Loans are forms of aid that must be repaid with interest. Most people will borrow money to pay college costs. The loans available through financial aid programs are offered at very favorable interest rates. In comparing colleges, the dollar amount of total indebtedness is a factor to be considered. Typically, this amount would increase proportionate to the tuition. However, if it does not, this could mean that the college provides relatively generous grant or work-study aid rather than loans in its financial aid package.

## Work-Study

The total dollar amounts, number, and average dollar amount of *Federal work-study* (FWS) jobs appear first. The total dollar figure of *State or other work-study/employment*, if available, is shown, as is the percentage of those dollars that go to meet financial need. The number of part-time jobs available on campus to undergraduates, other than work-study, is shown last.

FWS is a federally funded program that enables students with demonstrated need to earn money by working on or off campus, usually in a nonprofit organization. FWS jobs are a special category of jobs that are open to students only through the financial aid office. Other kinds of part-time jobs are routinely available at most colleges and may vary widely. In comparing colleges, you may find characteristic differences in how the "self-help" amounts (loans and work-study) are apportioned.

## Athletic Awards

The total dollar amount of athletic scholarships given by the college to undergraduate students, including percentages that are need-based and non-need-based, is indicated.

## Applying for Financial Aid

*Required financial aid forms* include the FAFSA (Free Application for Federal Student Aid), the institution's own form, CSS/Financial Aid PROFILE, a state aid form, a noncustodial (divorced/separated) parent's statement, a business/farm supplement, and others. The college's financial aid application deadline is noted as the *Financial aid deadline* and is shown in one of three ways: as a specific date if it is an absolute deadline; noted as *continuous*, which means processing goes on without a deadline or until all available aid has been awarded; or as a date with the note *(priority)*, meaning that you are encouraged to apply before that date in order to have the best chance of obtaining aid. *Notification date* is listed as either a specific date or *continuous*. The date by which a reply to the college with the decision to accept or decline its financial aid package is listed as either a specific date or as a number of weeks from the date of notification.

Be prepared to check early with the colleges as to exactly which forms will be required. All colleges require the FAFSA for students applying for federal aid. In most cases, colleges have a limited amount of funds set aside to use as financial aid. It is possible that the first eligible students will get a larger share of what is available.

## Contact

The name, title, address, telephone and fax numbers, and e-mail address of the person to contact for further information (student financial aid contact) are given at the end of the profile. You should feel free to write or call for any materials you need or if you have questions.

## APPENDIX

This section lists more than 300 state-specific grants and loans. Award amounts, number of awards, eligibility requirements, application requirements, and deadlines are given for all programs.

## INDEXES

Six indexes in the back of the book allow you to search for particular award programs based on the following criteria:

### Non-Need Scholarships for Undergraduates

This index lists the colleges that report that they offer scholarships based on academic interests, abilities, achievements, or personal characteristics other than financial need. Specific categories appear in alphabetical order under the following broad groups:

- Academic Interests/Achievements
- Creative Arts/Performance
- Special Achievements/Activities
- Special Characteristics

See the index for specific categories in each group.

### Athletic Grants for Undergraduates

This index lists the colleges that report offering scholarships on the basis of athletic abilities.

### Co-op Programs

This index lists colleges that report offering cooperative education programs. These are formal arrangements with off-campus employers that are designed to allow students to combine study and work, often in a position related to the student's field of study. Salaries typically are set at regular marketplace levels, and academic credit is often given.

### ROTC Programs

This index lists colleges that offer Reserve Officers' Training Corps programs. The index is arranged by the branch of service that sponsors the program.

### Tuition Waivers

This index lists colleges that report offering full or partial tuition waivers for certain categories of students. A majority of colleges offer tuition waivers to employees or children of employees.

Because this benefit is so common and the affected employees usually are aware of it, no separate index of schools offering this option is provided. However, this information is included in the individual college profiles.

### Tuition Payment Alternatives

This index lists colleges that report offering tuition payment alternatives. These payment alternatives include deferred payment plans, guaranteed tuition plans, installment payment plans, and prepayment plans.

## DATA COLLECTION PROCEDURES

The data contained in the college chart, profiles, and indexes were collected in winter and spring 2015 through *Peterson's*

*Annual Survey of Undergraduate Financial Aid* and *Peterson's Annual Survey of Undergraduate Institutions.* Questionnaires were sent to the more than 4,600 institutions of higher education that are accredited in the United States and U.S. territories and offer full four- or five-year baccalaureate degrees via full-time on-campus programs of study. Officials at the colleges—usually financial aid or admission officers but sometimes registrars or institutional research staff members—completed and returned the forms. Peterson's has every reason to believe that the data presented in this book are accurate. However, students should always confirm costs and other facts with a specific school at the time of application, since colleges can and do change policies and fees whenever necessary.

The state aid data presented in *Peterson's How to Get Money for College* was submitted by state officials (usually the director of the state scholarship commission) to Peterson's in the spring of 2015. Because regulations for any government-sponsored program may be changed at any time, you should request written descriptive materials from the office administering a program in which you are interested.

## CRITERIA FOR INCLUSION IN THIS BOOK

To be included in this guide, an institution must have full accreditation or be a candidate for accreditation (preaccreditation) status by an institutional or specialized accrediting body recognized by the U.S. Department of Education or the Council for Higher Education Accreditation (CHEA). Institutional accrediting bodies, which review each institution as a whole, include the six regional associations of schools and colleges (Middle States, New England, North Central, Northwest, Southern, and Western), each of which is responsible for a specified portion of the United States and its territories. Other institutional accrediting bodies are national in scope and accredit specific kinds of institutions (e.g., Bible colleges, independent colleges, and rabbinical and Talmudic schools). Program registration by the New York State Board of Regents is considered to be the equivalent of institutional accreditation, since the board requires that all programs offered by an institution meet its standards before recognition is granted. There are recognized specialized or professional accrediting bodies in more than forty different fields, each of which is authorized to accredit institutions or specific programs in its particular field. For specialized institutions that offer programs in one field only, we designate this to be the equivalent of institutional accreditation. A full explanation of the accrediting process and complete information on recognized, institutional (regional and national) and specialized accrediting bodies can be found online at www.chea.org or at www.ed.gov/admins/finaid/accred/index.html.

# Quick-Reference Chart

# College Costs At-a-Glance

To help shed some light on the typical patterns of financial aid offered by colleges, we have prepared the following chart. This chart can help you to better understand financial aid practices in general, form realistic expectations about the amounts of aid that might be provided by specific colleges or universities, and prepare for meaningful discussions with the financial aid officers at colleges being considered. The data appearing in the chart have been supplied by the schools themselves and are also shown in the individual college profiles.

Tuition and fees are based on the total of full-time tuition and mandatory fees for the 2014–15 academic year or for the 2013–14 academic year if 2014–15 figures are not available. More information about these costs, as well as the costs of room and board and the year for which they are current, can be found in the individual college profiles. For institutions that have two or more tuition rates for different categories of students or types of programs, the lowest rate is used in figuring the cost.

The colleges are listed alphabetically by state. An "NR" in any individual column indicates that the applicable data element was "Not Reported."

The chart is divided into eight columns of information for each college:

### 1. Institutional Control
Whether the school is independent (ind.), including independent, independent–religious, and proprietary, or public (pub.), including federal, state, commonwealth, territory, county, district, city, state, local, and state-related.

### 2. Tuition and Fees
Based on the total of full-time tuition and mandatory fees. An asterisk indicates that the school includes room and board in their mandatory fees.

### 3. Room and Board
If a school has room and board costs that vary according to the type of accommodation and meal plan, either the lowest figures are represented or the figures are for the most common room arrangement and a full meal plan. If a school has only housing arrangements, a dagger appears to the right of the number. An "NA" will appear in this column if no college-owned or -operated housing facilities are offered.

### 4. Percent of Eligible Freshmen Receiving Need-Based Gift Awards
Calculated by dividing the number of freshman students determined to have need who received need-based gift aid by the number of full-time freshmen.

### 5. Percent of Freshmen Whose Need Was Fully Met
Calculated by dividing the number of freshman students whose financial need was fully met by the number of freshmen with need.

### 6. Average Financial Aid Package for Freshmen
The average dollar amount from all sources, including *gift aid* (scholarships and grants) and *self-help* (jobs and loans), awarded to freshmen receiving aid. Note that this aid package may exceed tuition and fees if the average aid package included coverage of room and board expenses.

### 7. Average Net Cost After Aid
Average aid package subtracted from published costs (tuition, fees, room, and board) to produce what the average student will have to pay.

### 8. Average Indebtedness Upon Graduation
Average per-student indebtedness of graduating seniors.

Because personal situations vary widely, it is very important to note that an individual's aid package can be quite different from the averages. Moreover, the data shown for each school can fluctuate widely from year to year, depending on the number of applicants, the amount of need to be met, and the financial resources and policies of the college. Peterson's intent in presenting this chart is to provide you with useful facts and figures that can serve as general guidelines in the pursuit of financial aid. We caution you to use the data only as a jumping-off point for further investigation and analysis, not as a means to rank or select colleges.

After you have narrowed down the choice of colleges based on academic and personal criteria, we recommend that you carefully study this chart. From it, you can develop a list of questions for financial aid officers at the colleges under serious consideration. Here are just a few questions you might want to ask: About the Institution

- What are the specific types and sources of aid provided to freshmen at this school?

- What factors does this college consider in determining whether a financial aid applicant is qualified for its need-based aid programs?

- How does the college determine the combination of types of aid that make up an individual's package?

- How are non-need-based awards treated: as a part of the aid package or as a part of the parental/family contribution?

- Does this school "guarantee" financial aid and, if so, how is its policy implemented? Guaranteed aid means that, by policy, 100 percent of need is met for all students judged to have need. Implementation determines *how* need is met and varies widely from school to school. For example, grade point average may determine the apportioning of scholarship, loan, and work-study aid. Rules for freshmen may be different from those for upperclass students.

- To what degree is the admission process "need-blind"? Need-blind means that admission decisions are made without regard to the student's need for financial aid.

- What are the norms and practices for upperclass students? Peterson's chart presents information on *freshmen* financial aid only; however, the financial aid office should be able and willing to provide you with comparable figures for upperclass students. A college might offer a wonderful package for the freshman year, then leave students mostly on their own to fund the remaining three years. Or the school may provide a higher proportion of scholarship money for freshmen, then rebalance its aid packages to contain more self-help aid (loans and work-study) in upperclass years.

There is an assumption that, all other factors being equal, students who have settled into the pattern of college time management can handle more work-study hours than freshmen. Grade point average, tuition increases, changes in parental financial circumstances, and other factors may also affect the redistribution.

*Michael Steidel is Director of Admission at Carnegie Mellon University.*

# College Costs At-a-Glance

| | Institutional Control ind.=independent; pub.=public | Tuition and Fees | Room and Board | Percent of Eligible Freshmen Receiving Need-Based Gift Awards | Percent of Freshmen Whose Need Was Fully Met | Average Financial Aid Package for Freshmen | Average Net Cost After Aid | Average Indebtedness Upon Graduation |
|---|---|---|---|---|---|---|---|---|
| **Alabama** | | | | | | | | |
| Alabama Agricultural and Mechanical University | pub. | $9090 | $5440 | 97% | 8% | $11,417 | $3113 | $38,819 |
| Alabama State University | pub. | $6936 | $5422 | 86% | 22% | $14,444 | — | $32,629 |
| Amridge University | ind. | $6900 | NA | 100% | 17% | $9078 | — | $10,500 |
| Athens State University | pub. | $6120 | NA | NR | NR | NR | NR | NR |
| Auburn University | pub. | $10,200 | $12,178 | 86% | 18% | $10,824 | $11,554 | $27,146 |
| Auburn University at Montgomery | pub. | $9080 | $5390 | 74% | 17% | $7506 | $6964 | NR |
| Birmingham-Southern College | ind. | $33,128 | $11,350 | 68% | 34% | $29,063 | $15,415 | $31,872 |
| Faulkner University | ind. | $18,750 | $6970 | 80% | 8% | $6300 | $19,420 | $29,000 |
| Heritage Christian University | ind. | $9792 | $3840 | 100% | 20% | $11,446 | $2186 | NR |
| Huntingdon College | ind. | $24,550 | $8550 | 100% | 14% | $18,215 | $14,885 | $28,322 |
| Jacksonville State University | pub. | $8790 | $6985 | 49% | NR | $9437 | $6338 | NR |
| Samford University | ind. | $28,370 | $10,234 | 99% | 23% | $17,470 | $21,134 | $26,543 |
| Spring Hill College | ind. | $32,468 | $11,696 | 99% | 16% | $28,172 | $15,992 | $31,855 |
| Troy University | pub. | $7564 | $6498 | 58% | NR | $3640 | $10,422 | NR |
| Tuskegee University | ind. | $19,120 | $9104 | 85% | 68% | $19,250 | $8974 | $26,500 |
| The University of Alabama | pub. | $9826 | $8866 | 79% | 25% | $13,271 | $5421 | $29,320 |
| The University of Alabama at Birmingham | pub. | $9280 | $5720† | 62% | 9% | $10,685 | $4315 | $30,642 |
| The University of Alabama in Huntsville | pub. | $9158 | $8433 | 89% | 28% | $12,556 | $5035 | $29,421 |
| University of Mobile | ind. | $19,700 | $9550 | 70% | 100% | $18,602 | $10,648 | $28,250 |
| University of Montevallo | pub. | $10,660 | $6400 | 90% | 13% | $10,495 | $6565 | $27,090 |
| University of North Alabama | pub. | $9073 | $6327 | 72% | 12% | $6666 | $8734 | $29,839 |
| University of South Alabama | pub. | $8610 | $7100 | 90% | 14% | $9665 | $6045 | NR |
| The University of West Alabama | pub. | $8018 | $6256 | 73% | NR | $10,159 | $4115 | $31,901 |
| **Alaska** | | | | | | | | |
| Alaska Pacific University | ind. | $19,680 | $7000 | 56% | NR | $12,560 | $14,120 | $8922 |
| University of Alaska Anchorage | pub. | $6074 | $11,179 | 89% | 31% | $8423 | $8830 | $26,569 |
| University of Alaska Fairbanks | pub. | $7370 | $8242 | 92% | 21% | $7630 | $7982 | $29,906 |
| **Arizona** | | | | | | | | |
| Arizona Christian University | ind. | $23,220 | $9890 | 99% | NR | $15,794 | $17,316 | $26,228 |
| Arizona State University at the Downtown Phoenix campus | pub. | $10,127 | $11,974 | 98% | 22% | $15,644 | $6457 | $22,498 |
| Arizona State University at the Polytechnic campus | pub. | $9811 | $10,720 | 98% | 24% | $13,628 | $6903 | $26,463 |
| Arizona State University at the Tempe campus | pub. | $10,127 | $10,010 | 99% | 24% | $15,063 | $5074 | $21,920 |
| Arizona State University at the West campus | pub. | $9811 | $9440 | 99% | 28% | $14,512 | $4739 | $18,585 |
| Embry-Riddle Aeronautical University–Prescott | ind. | $33,144 | $9900 | 100% | NR | $17,695 | $25,349 | NR |
| Northern Arizona University | pub. | $9990 | $9020 | 72% | 14% | $11,167 | $7843 | $23,602 |
| Prescott College | ind. | NR | NR | 100% | 3% | $21,076 | — | $24,651 |
| The University of Arizona | pub. | $10,581 | $9700 | 96% | 12% | $12,564 | $7717 | $22,761 |
| **Arkansas** | | | | | | | | |
| Arkansas State University | pub. | $7720 | $7750 | 98% | 40% | $10,000 | $5470 | $25,000 |
| Arkansas Tech University | pub. | $7248 | $6734 | 85% | 8% | $8756 | $5226 | $29,865 |
| Harding University | ind. | $17,040 | $6516 | 98% | 40% | $16,450 | $7106 | $24,120 |

NA = not applicable; NR = not reported; * = includes room and board; † = room only; — = not available.

# College Costs At-a-Glance

| | Institutional Control ind.=independent; pub.=public | Tuition and Fees | Room and Board | Percent of Eligible Freshmen Receiving Need-Based Gift Awards | Percent of Freshmen Whose Need Was Fully Met | Average Financial Aid Package for Freshmen | Average Net Cost After Aid | Average Indebtedness Upon Graduation |
|---|---|---|---|---|---|---|---|---|
| Henderson State University | pub. | $7561 | $6350 | 70% | 14% | $11,830 | $2081 | $23,641 |
| Hendrix College | ind. | $40,870 | $11,244 | 100% | 39% | $32,106 | $20,008 | $26,203 |
| John Brown University | ind. | $24,468 | $8664 | 93% | 14% | $19,242 | $13,890 | $24,525 |
| Lyon College | ind. | $25,280 | $8110 | 100% | 26% | $19,398 | $13,992 | $22,321 |
| Ouachita Baptist University | ind. | $23,320 | $6900 | 99% | 31% | $20,358 | $9862 | $24,252 |
| Philander Smith College | ind. | $12,414 | $9064 | 99% | 8% | $14,611 | $6867 | $35,968 |
| University of Arkansas | pub. | $8210 | $9454 | 85% | 17% | $8941 | $8723 | $24,120 |
| Williams Baptist College | ind. | $16,430 | $7000 | 74% | NR | $14,196 | $9234 | $20,077 |
| **California** | | | | | | | | |
| Academy of Art University | ind. | $25,350 | $14,160 | 75% | 1% | $9374 | $30,136 | $25,575 |
| Alliant International University–San Diego | ind. | $15,812 | $11,268 | 100% | NR | $15,785 | $11,295 | $15,000 |
| American Jewish University | ind. | $29,132 | $15,102 | 100% | NR | $29,132 | $15,102 | $30,000 |
| Azusa Pacific University | ind. | $33,096 | $5290† | 87% | 10% | $17,443 | $20,943 | $20,612 |
| Biola University | ind. | $34,498 | NR | 99% | 9% | $18,380 | $16,118 | $34,107 |
| California Baptist University | ind. | $29,422 | $9370 | 78% | 9% | $19,320 | $19,472 | $33,409 |
| California Christian College | ind. | $8540 | $4800 | 100% | NR | $13,745 | — | NR |
| California Institute of Integral Studies | ind. | $25,095 | NA | NR | NR | NR | NR | NR |
| California Institute of Technology | ind. | $43,362 | $12,918 | 100% | 100% | $41,990 | $14,290 | $12,104 |
| California Institute of the Arts | ind. | $43,976 | $6100† | 99% | 8% | $32,155 | $17,921 | $38,770 |
| California Lutheran University | ind. | $37,590 | $12,400 | 100% | 18% | $26,470 | $23,520 | $24,230 |
| California Polytechnic State University, San Luis Obispo | pub. | $8919 | $11,447 | 83% | 8% | $9935 | $10,431 | NR |
| California State Polytechnic University, Pomona | pub. | $6872 | $13,284 | 82% | 2% | $10,754 | $9402 | $22,245 |
| California State University, Bakersfield | pub. | $5473 | $10,926 | 100% | 10% | $4225 | $12,174 | $11,735 |
| California State University, Chico | pub. | $8532 | $11,626 | 76% | 15% | $17,380 | $2778 | NR |
| California State University, Dominguez Hills | pub. | $6134 | $10,956 | 88% | 2% | $5516 | $11,574 | $16,768 |
| California State University, East Bay | pub. | $6564 | $12,246 | 96% | 3% | $12,807 | $6003 | $18,684 |
| California State University, Fresno | pub. | $6298 | $10,604 | 89% | 17% | $11,760 | $5142 | $12,851 |
| California State University, Fullerton | pub. | $6316 | $13,510 | 82% | 56% | $13,210 | $6616 | $14,965 |
| California State University, Long Beach | pub. | $6420 | $11,688 | 83% | 75% | $12,567 | $5541 | $16,579 |
| California State University, Los Angeles | pub. | $6340 | $12,833 | 95% | 16% | $9426 | $9747 | $14,788 |
| California State University, Monterey Bay | pub. | $5963 | $10,112 | 81% | 16% | $11,169 | $4906 | $18,992 |
| California State University, Sacramento | pub. | $6602 | $6538† | 88% | 7% | $11,117 | $2023 | $4402 |
| California State University, San Bernardino | pub. | $6558 | $9933 | 97% | 26% | $8790 | $7701 | $20,077 |
| California State University, San Marcos | pub. | $7164 | NR | 82% | 1% | $5178 | $1986 | $22,024 |
| California State University, Stanislaus | pub. | $6491 | $11,900 | 73% | 9% | $7800 | $10,591 | NR |
| Chapman University | ind. | $47,260 | $13,830 | 92% | 12% | $33,988 | $27,102 | $27,979 |
| Claremont McKenna College | ind. | $47,395 | $14,820 | 97% | 100% | $41,556 | $20,659 | $23,232 |
| Concordia University | ind. | $31,690 | $9890 | 99% | 13% | $22,017 | $19,563 | $28,072 |
| Fresno Pacific University | ind. | $26,638 | $7360 | 79% | 23% | $21,091 | $12,907 | $21,992 |
| Harvey Mudd College | ind. | $48,594 | $15,833 | 98% | 100% | $42,282 | $22,145 | $24,503 |
| Hope International University | ind. | $28,550 | $9050 | 60% | 19% | $19,418 | $18,182 | $24,091 |
| Humboldt State University | pub. | $7190 | $12,114 | 87% | 10% | $13,365 | $5939 | $19,351 |

NA = not applicable; NR = not reported; * = includes room and board; † = room only; — = not available.

# College Costs At-a-Glance

| | Institutional Control ind.=independent; pub.=public | Tuition and Fees | Room and Board | Percent of Eligible Freshmen Receiving Need-Based Gift Awards | Percent of Freshmen Whose Need Was Fully Met | Average Financial Aid Package for Freshmen | Average Net Cost After Aid | Average Indebtedness Upon Graduation |
|---|---|---|---|---|---|---|---|---|
| John Paul the Great Catholic University | ind. | $24,900 | $8100† | 100% | NR | $16,196 | $16,804 | NR |
| Laguna College of Art & Design | ind. | $28,100 | $9100† | 85% | NR | $10,600 | $26,600 | $38,000 |
| La Sierra University | ind. | $30,470 | $7800 | 100% | 10% | $24,552 | $13,718 | $36,251 |
| Loyola Marymount University | ind. | $41,372 | $14,395 | 98% | 16% | $24,774 | $30,993 | $30,243 |
| Marymount California University | ind. | $31,657 | $12,998 | 98% | 4% | $24,842 | $19,813 | $9421 |
| The Master's College and Seminary | ind. | $29,860 | $9720 | 100% | 13% | $22,662 | $16,918 | $26,442 |
| Menlo College | ind. | $38,750 | $12,630 | 100% | 10% | $27,990 | $23,390 | $29,943 |
| Mills College | ind. | $42,918 | $12,914 | 99% | 18% | $42,452 | $13,380 | $31,273 |
| Mount Saint Mary's University | ind. | $35,944 | $11,117 | 100% | NR | $29,525 | $17,536 | NR |
| National University | ind. | NR | NA | 59% | 24% | $6207 | — | $12,076 |
| Notre Dame de Namur University | ind. | $31,822 | $12,494 | 100% | 8% | $27,813 | $16,503 | $31,348 |
| Occidental College | ind. | NR | NR | 92% | 100% | $42,608 | — | $29,962 |
| Otis College of Art and Design | ind. | $37,380 | $950 | 100% | 10% | $24,098 | $14,232 | $33,694 |
| Pepperdine University | ind. | $46,692 | $13,390 | 99% | 28% | $34,868 | $25,214 | $31,884 |
| Pitzer College | ind. | $46,992 | $14,758 | 100% | 100% | $44,719 | $17,031 | $19,422 |
| Point Loma Nazarene University | ind. | $31,406 | $9600 | 94% | 16% | $20,692 | $20,314 | $32,649 |
| Pomona College | ind. | $45,832 | $14,700 | 100% | 100% | $43,912 | $16,620 | $16,273 |
| Saint Mary's College of California | ind. | $41,380 | $14,140 | 100% | 8% | $31,995 | $23,525 | $32,803 |
| San Diego State University | pub. | $6866 | $14,745 | 69% | 4% | $10,300 | $11,311 | $18,400 |
| San Francisco Art Institute | ind. | $40,096 | $15,666 | 89% | 15% | $36,933 | $18,829 | $25,931 |
| San Francisco Conservatory of Music | ind. | $40,992 | $7000† | 100% | 16% | $31,825 | $16,167 | $24,500 |
| San Francisco State University | pub. | $6468 | NR | 96% | 31% | $11,564 | — | $22,741 |
| San Jose State University | pub. | $7323 | $11,810 | 74% | 26% | $14,881 | $4252 | $23,467 |
| Santa Clara University | ind. | $43,812 | $12,921 | 86% | 45% | $32,665 | $24,068 | $26,759 |
| Scripps College | ind. | $47,378 | $14,562 | 100% | 100% | $37,680 | $24,260 | $20,060 |
| Simpson University | ind. | $24,300 | $7900 | 100% | 14% | $20,111 | $12,089 | $28,161 |
| Soka University of America | ind. | $30,642 | $11,468 | 100% | 31% | $34,486 | $7624 | $19,563 |
| Sonoma State University | pub. | $7276 | $11,799 | 74% | 14% | $10,384 | $8691 | $20,744 |
| Southern California Institute of Architecture | ind. | $2450 | NA | 83% | NR | $20,942 | — | $39,287 |
| Stanford University | ind. | $45,729 | $14,107 | 99% | 95% | $44,790 | $15,046 | $19,230 |
| Thomas Aquinas College | ind. | $24,500 | $7950 | 93% | 100% | $21,178 | $11,272 | $16,263 |
| University of California, Berkeley | pub. | $12,972 | $15,438 | 99% | 74% | $26,871 | $1539 | $17,584 |
| University of California, Davis | pub. | $13,896 | $14,218 | 99% | 16% | $22,899 | $5215 | $19,705 |
| University of California, Irvine | pub. | $14,757 | $12,638 | 99% | 26% | $23,303 | $4092 | $20,319 |
| University of California, Los Angeles | pub. | $13,029 | $13,135 | 97% | 25% | $23,903 | $2261 | $20,759 |
| University of California, Merced | pub. | $14,813 | $14,718 | 99% | 35% | $26,712 | $2819 | $20,408 |
| University of California, Riverside | pub. | $13,307 | $15,000 | 99% | 29% | $24,523 | $3784 | $21,166 |
| University of California, San Diego | pub. | $13,456 | $12,254 | 98% | 33% | $23,076 | $2634 | $21,790 |
| University of California, Santa Barbara | pub. | $13,860 | $14,128 | 99% | 29% | $25,326 | $2662 | $21,045 |
| University of California, Santa Cruz | pub. | $13,398 | $14,730 | 98% | 18% | $24,303 | $3825 | $22,583 |
| University of La Verne | ind. | $38,560 | $12,510 | 98% | 9% | $30,662 | $20,408 | $28,215 |
| University of Redlands | ind. | $43,186 | $12,710 | NR | NR | NR | NR | NR |

NA = not applicable; NR = not reported; * = includes room and board; † = room only; — = not available.

# College Costs At-a-Glance

| | Institutional Control ind.=independent; pub.=public | Tuition and Fees | Room and Board | Percent of Eligible Freshmen Receiving Need-Based Gift Awards | Percent of Freshmen Whose Need Was Fully Met | Average Financial Aid Package for Freshmen | Average Net Cost After Aid | Average Indebtedness Upon Graduation |
|---|---|---|---|---|---|---|---|---|
| University of San Diego | ind. | $42,908 | $11,910 | 98% | 15% | $32,328 | $22,490 | $30,225 |
| University of San Francisco | ind. | $42,634 | $13,650 | 96% | 11% | $38,481 | $17,803 | $31,098 |
| University of Southern California | ind. | $48,280 | $13,334 | 87% | 98% | $45,044 | $16,570 | $28,541 |
| University of the Pacific | ind. | $41,342 | $12,582 | 98% | 17% | $29,594 | $24,330 | NR |
| Vanguard University of Southern California | ind. | $30,050 | $9420 | 64% | 16% | $12,944 | $26,526 | NR |
| Westmont College | ind. | $39,990 | $12,580 | 99% | 13% | $30,188 | $22,382 | $34,428 |
| Whittier College | ind. | $41,636 | $12,245 | 84% | 24% | $34,377 | $19,504 | $37,379 |
| William Jessup University | ind. | $26,480 | $10,278 | 100% | 16% | $21,347 | $15,411 | $23,636 |
| Woodbury University | ind. | NR | NR | 99% | 6% | $23,700 | — | $40,699 |
| **Colorado** | | | | | | | | |
| Adams State University | pub. | $7951 | $8400 | 97% | NR | $11,265 | $5086 | $30,211 |
| The Colorado College | ind. | $46,410 | $10,752 | 95% | 100% | $49,031 | $8131 | $19,756 |
| Colorado Mesa University | pub. | $7115 | $8706 | 83% | 18% | $7655 | $8166 | $26,740 |
| Colorado Mountain College | pub. | NR | NR | 47% | NR | NR | NR | NR |
| Colorado School of Mines | pub. | $16,918 | $10,484 | 55% | 25% | $10,354 | $17,048 | $23,667 |
| Colorado State University | pub. | $9897 | $10,488 | 79% | 27% | $10,158 | $10,227 | $23,721 |
| Colorado State University–Pueblo | pub. | $7834 | $9016 | 89% | 10% | $9344 | $7506 | $29,914 |
| Fort Lewis College | pub. | $7601 | $9130 | 89% | 16% | $14,093 | $2638 | $19,507 |
| Metropolitan State University of Denver | pub. | NR | NA | 73% | 1% | $6517 | — | $28,468 |
| Naropa University | ind. | $30,580 | $9604 | 100% | 10% | $23,370 | $16,814 | $23,755 |
| Nazarene Bible College | ind. | $11,400 | NA | 90% | 80% | $7940 | $3460 | $33,289 |
| Platt College | ind. | NR | NA | 67% | NR | $7500 | — | NR |
| Regis University | ind. | $33,710 | $9830 | 98% | 16% | $30,557 | $12,983 | $28,461 |
| University of Colorado Boulder | pub. | $10,789 | $12,810 | 78% | 43% | $15,782 | $7817 | $25,126 |
| University of Colorado Colorado Springs | pub. | $9143 | $9150 | 63% | 3% | $7865 | $10,428 | $19,780 |
| University of Colorado Denver | pub. | $9985 | $11,140 | 85% | 4% | $8565 | $12,560 | $21,502 |
| University of Denver | ind. | $42,090 | $11,109 | 99% | 37% | $34,610 | $18,589 | $29,050 |
| University of Northern Colorado | pub. | $7733 | $10,360 | 92% | 39% | $7114 | $10,979 | $25,446 |
| Western State Colorado University | pub. | $7874 | $9050 | 94% | 21% | $13,054 | $3870 | $21,251 |
| **Connecticut** | | | | | | | | |
| Albertus Magnus College | ind. | $28,930 | $12,960 | 94% | 6% | $20,894 | $20,996 | $33,975 |
| Central Connecticut State University | pub. | $8877 | $10,872 | 81% | 5% | $9602 | $10,147 | $24,000 |
| Connecticut College | ind. | $47,740 | $13,155 | 96% | 100% | $38,556 | $22,339 | $28,321 |
| Eastern Connecticut State University | pub. | $9560 | $11,650 | 81% | 10% | $9762 | $11,448 | $26,921 |
| Fairfield University | ind. | $44,875 | $13,520 | 86% | 17% | $30,240 | $28,155 | $27,918 |
| Post University | ind. | $27,350 | $10,500 | 99% | 13% | $18,898 | $18,952 | $15,995 |
| Quinnipiac University | ind. | $42,270 | $14,820 | 98% | 15% | $26,791 | $30,299 | $45,711 |
| Sacred Heart University | ind. | $35,750 | $13,514 | 79% | 15% | $19,402 | $29,862 | $45,746 |
| Southern Connecticut State University | pub. | $9157 | $11,289 | 75% | 21% | $13,690 | $6756 | $23,781 |
| Trinity College | ind. | $50,776 | $13,144 | 95% | 100% | $43,931 | $19,989 | $28,237 |
| University of Bridgeport | ind. | $29,920 | $12,710 | 86% | 5% | $26,551 | $16,079 | $21,200 |
| University of Connecticut | pub. | $2842 | $12,174 | 69% | 14% | $14,256 | $760 | $24,999 |

NA = not applicable; NR = not reported; * = includes room and board; † = room only; — = not available.

# College Costs At-a-Glance

| | Institutional Control ind.=independent; pub.=public | Tuition and Fees | Room and Board | Percent of Eligible Freshmen Receiving Need-Based Gift Awards | Percent of Freshmen Whose Need Was Fully Met | Average Financial Aid Package for Freshmen | Average Net Cost After Aid | Average Indebtedness Upon Graduation |
|---|---|---|---|---|---|---|---|---|
| University of Hartford | ind. | $36,460 | $11,638 | 98% | 13% | $24,135 | $23,963 | NR |
| University of New Haven | ind. | $34,630 | $14,410 | 100% | 13% | $23,035 | $26,005 | $43,472 |
| University of Saint Joseph | ind. | $36,140 | $14,850 | 99% | 12% | $28,540 | $22,450 | $37,557 |
| Wesleyan University | ind. | $48,974 | $13,504 | 94% | 100% | $45,001 | $17,477 | $22,959 |
| Western Connecticut State University | pub. | $9077 | $11,311 | NR | NR | NR | NR | NR |
| Yale University | ind. | $47,600 | $14,600 | 100% | 100% | $48,926 | $13,274 | $14,853 |
| **Delaware** | | | | | | | | |
| Delaware State University | pub. | $7336 | $10,708 | 67% | 8% | $11,620 | $6424 | $38,702 |
| University of Delaware | pub. | $12,342 | $11,558 | 97% | 51% | $15,989 | $7911 | $32,705 |
| **District of Columbia** | | | | | | | | |
| American University | ind. | $42,556 | $14,354 | 90% | 39% | $31,735 | $25,175 | NR |
| The Catholic University of America | ind. | $39,726 | $14,518 | 98% | 43% | $26,413 | $27,831 | NR |
| Gallaudet University | ind. | $15,604 | $12,630 | 99% | 12% | $19,948 | $8286 | $15,970 |
| Georgetown University | ind. | $46,744 | $14,024 | 91% | 100% | $38,969 | $21,799 | $22,464 |
| The George Washington University | ind. | $50,435 | $12,050 | 97% | 47% | $41,501 | $20,984 | $31,337 |
| Howard University | ind. | $23,970 | $13,646 | 62% | 12% | $17,752 | $19,864 | $32,071 |
| University of the District of Columbia | pub. | $5128 | $10,300 | 93% | 31% | $8000 | $7428 | NR |
| **Florida** | | | | | | | | |
| Adventist University of Health Sciences | ind. | $13,030 | $4000† | NR | NR | NR | NR | NR |
| Ave Maria University | ind. | $18,479 | $10,137 | 100% | 27% | $14,749 | $13,867 | NR |
| The Baptist College of Florida | ind. | $9700 | $4138 | 100% | 9% | $9262 | $4576 | $17,258 |
| Barry University | ind. | $28,160 | $10,400 | 87% | 4% | $23,297 | $15,263 | $38,342 |
| Beacon College | ind. | $34,680 | $10,249 | 42% | NR | $7000 | $37,929 | $27,000 |
| Bethune-Cookman University | ind | $14,410 | $8548 | 99% | 4% | $13,856 | $9102 | $23,525 |
| Carlos Albizu University, Miami Campus | ind | $12,384 | NA | 100% | NR | $7428 | $4956 | $16,500 |
| Eckerd College | ind. | $38,668 | $10,550 | 100% | 21% | $31,498 | $17,720 | $33,697 |
| Embry-Riddle Aeronautical University–Daytona | ind. | $33,218 | $10,382 | 99% | NR | $19,629 | $23,971 | NR |
| Everglades University | ind. | NR | NA | 100% | 80% | $9455 | — | $48,546 |
| Everglades University | ind. | NR | NA | 91% | 15% | $9002 | — | $60,735 |
| Everglades University | ind. | $16,000 | NA | 100% | NR | $14,579 | $1421 | $52,777 |
| Flagler College | ind. | $16,900 | $9350 | 100% | 14% | $11,788 | $14,462 | $27,853 |
| Florida Agricultural and Mechanical University | pub. | $5784 | $9576 | 99% | 17% | $13,299 | $2061 | $31,407 |
| Florida Atlantic University | pub. | $6039 | $11,924 | 82% | 9% | $9957 | $8006 | $21,448 |
| Florida Gulf Coast University | pub. | $6118 | $8359 | 66% | 6% | $8647 | $5830 | $22,718 |
| Florida Institute of Technology | ind. | $37,990 | $12,826 | 100% | 36% | $34,266 | $16,550 | $40,383 |
| Florida Southern College | ind. | $29,990 | $10,000 | 100% | 33% | $24,516 | $15,474 | $24,314 |
| Florida State University | pub. | $6507 | $10,208 | 73% | 8% | $8605 | $8110 | $24,347 |
| Hodges University | ind. | $13,220 | NA | 91% | 38% | $9110 | $4110 | $17,775 |
| Indian River State College | pub. | $2492 | $5700 | NR | NR | NR | NR | NR |
| Jacksonville University | ind. | $31,370 | $10,820 | 100% | 36% | $23,886 | $18,304 | NR |
| Keiser University | ind. | $17,596 | NA | 84% | NR | NR | NR | NR |

**NA** = not applicable; **NR** = not reported; * = includes room and board; † = room only; — = not available.

# College Costs At-a-Glance

| | Institutional Control ind.=independent; pub.=public | Tuition and Fees | Room and Board | Percent of Eligible Freshmen Receiving Need-Based Gift Awards | Percent of Freshmen Whose Need Was Fully Met | Average Financial Aid Package for Freshmen | Average Net Cost After Aid | Average Indebtedness Upon Graduation |
|---|---|---|---|---|---|---|---|---|
| Lynn University | ind. | $35,200 | $11,300 | 79% | 100% | $20,164 | $26,336 | $30,938 |
| New College of Florida | pub. | $7040 | $9009 | 95% | 42% | $14,178 | $1871 | $17,553 |
| Nova Southeastern University | ind. | $26,700 | $10,580 | 100% | 19% | $26,886 | $10,394 | $31,022 |
| Palm Beach Atlantic University | ind. | $26,274 | $8600 | 100% | 21% | $19,439 | $15,435 | $27,374 |
| Ringling College of Art and Design | ind. | $40,040 | $13,580 | 99% | 8% | $19,564 | $34,056 | $43,685 |
| Rollins College | ind. | $43,080 | $13,470 | 100% | 29% | $31,655 | $24,895 | $26,689 |
| Saint Leo University | ind. | $20,520 | $9870 | 100% | 12% | $18,548 | $11,842 | $27,436 |
| St. Thomas University | ind. | $27,150 | $5150 | 59% | 23% | NR | NR | NR |
| Stetson University | ind. | $41,590 | $6874† | 100% | 22% | $34,219 | $14,245 | $32,302 |
| Trinity College of Florida | ind. | $15,650 | $6450 | 100% | 7% | $15,210 | $6890 | $28,201 |
| University of Central Florida | pub. | $6368 | $9300 | 66% | 10% | $8213 | $7455 | $23,378 |
| University of Florida | pub. | $4477 | $9630 | 62% | 23% | $11,875 | $2232 | $20,642 |
| University of Miami | ind. | $44,350 | $12,684 | 98% | 28% | $35,536 | $21,498 | $26,793 |
| University of North Florida | pub. | $6385 | $9204 | 72% | 13% | $9199 | $6390 | $19,253 |
| University of South Florida | pub. | $6410 | $9400 | 97% | 8% | $10,581 | $5229 | $22,611 |
| The University of Tampa | ind. | $26,330 | $9624 | 100% | 10% | $16,395 | $19,559 | $33,673 |
| University of West Florida | pub. | $8400 | $9912 | 84% | 18% | $9078 | $9234 | NR |
| Webber International University | ind. | $23,816 | $8462 | 100% | 6% | $18,991 | $13,287 | $24,578 |
| **Georgia** | | | | | | | | |
| Agnes Scott College | ind. | $37,236 | $11,150 | 100% | 29% | $32,838 | $15,548 | $27,763 |
| Albany State University | pub. | $5192 | $7522 | 85% | 9% | $5077 | $7637 | $39,014 |
| Armstrong State University | pub. | $6214 | $10,266 | NR | NR | $8499 | $7981 | $6602 |
| Berry College | ind. | $30,530 | $10,660 | 100% | 28% | $26,564 | $14,626 | $23,997 |
| Brenau University | ind. | $25,478 | $11,998 | 100% | 23% | $23,643 | $13,833 | $33,376 |
| Clayton State University | pub. | $6194 | $9240 | 91% | 5% | $9067 | $6367 | $30,423 |
| Columbus State University | pub. | $6898 | $8880 | 69% | 15% | $9217 | $6561 | $30,142 |
| Covenant College | ind. | $30,160 | $8830 | 100% | 34% | $25,390 | $13,600 | $24,215 |
| Emmanuel College | ind. | $18,170 | $7200 | 100% | 25% | $13,884 | $11,486 | $29,202 |
| Emory University | ind. | $46,314 | $13,130 | 90% | 98% | $40,368 | $19,076 | $24,741 |
| Fort Valley State University | pub. | $6448 | $7920 | 16% | 28% | $1824 | $12,544 | NR |
| Georgia College & State University | pub. | $8960 | $9940 | 34% | NR | $9516 | $9384 | $21,919 |
| Georgia Institute of Technology | pub. | $11,394 | $12,840 | 96% | 33% | $12,900 | $11,334 | $24,891 |
| Georgia Regents University | pub. | NR | NR | NR | NR | NR | NR | $4846 |
| Georgia Southern University | pub. | $7190 | $9752 | 89% | 12% | $9390 | $7552 | $24,201 |
| Georgia Southwestern State University | pub. | $6070 | $8350 | 65% | 15% | $9950 | $4470 | $23,450 |
| Georgia State University | pub. | $10,240 | $13,342 | 75% | 10% | $12,138 | $11,444 | $27,295 |
| Kennesaw State University | pub. | $6932 | $7914 | 82% | 14% | $4422 | $10,424 | $24,740 |
| LaGrange College | ind. | $26,620 | $11,050 | 99% | 33% | $22,781 | $14,889 | $32,574 |
| Life University | ind. | $10,590 | $12,480 | 74% | NR | $9500 | $13,570 | $30,000 |
| Mercer University | ind. | $33,780 | $10,678 | 100% | 42% | $34,847 | $9611 | $30,018 |
| Morehouse College | ind. | $26,339 | $12,710 | 90% | 15% | $22,370 | $16,679 | $35,807 |
| Oglethorpe University | ind. | $32,500 | $11,700 | 100% | 12% | $30,335 | $13,865 | $24,058 |

NA = not applicable; NR = not reported; * = includes room and board; † = room only; — = not available.

# College Costs At-a-Glance

| | Institutional Control ind.=independent; pub.=public | Tuition and Fees | Room and Board | Percent of Eligible Freshmen Receiving Need-Based Gift Awards | Percent of Freshmen Whose Need Was Fully Met | Average Financial Aid Package for Freshmen | Average Net Cost After Aid | Average Indebtedness Upon Graduation |
|---|---|---|---|---|---|---|---|---|
| Piedmont College | ind. | $21,350 | $8786 | 100% | 20% | $19,080 | $11,056 | $23,481 |
| Reinhardt University | ind. | $20,266 | $7568 | 100% | 11% | $13,914 | $13,920 | $23,235 |
| Savannah College of Art and Design | ind. | $34,295 | $13,710 | 61% | 10% | $31,001 | $17,004 | $36,088 |
| Savannah State University | pub. | $6498 | $7330 | NR | NR | NR | NR | NR |
| Spelman College | ind. | $25,496 | $11,945 | 87% | 11% | $15,611 | $21,830 | $35,516 |
| Truett-McConnell College | ind. | $17,300 | $7120 | 100% | 13% | $14,546 | $9874 | $13,508 |
| University of Georgia | pub. | $10,836 | $9246 | 99% | 31% | $12,795 | $7287 | $21,638 |
| University of North Georgia | pub. | $6816 | $9162 | 62% | 62% | $9450 | $6528 | $12,892 |
| University of West Georgia | pub. | $6956 | $8532 | 67% | 53% | $7704 | $7784 | $27,494 |
| Valdosta State University | pub. | $6142 | $7864 | 90% | 22% | $16,069 | — | $27,308 |
| Wesleyan College | ind. | $19,900 | $8800 | 82% | 11% | $17,453 | $11,247 | $32,755 |
| **Hawaii** | | | | | | | | |
| Chaminade University of Honolulu | ind. | $20,940 | $11,640 | 97% | 24% | $19,211 | $13,369 | $26,323 |
| Hawai`i Pacific University | ind. | $22,360 | $13,610 | 57% | 19% | $22,419 | $13,551 | NR |
| University of Hawaii at Manoa | pub. | $10,584 | NR | 98% | 35% | $14,615 | — | $24,277 |
| University of Hawaii–West Oahu | pub. | $7380 | NA | 47% | NR | $6580 | $800 | NR |
| **Idaho** | | | | | | | | |
| Boise State University | pub. | $6640 | $6829 | 81% | 18% | $8975 | $4494 | $27,024 |
| The College of Idaho | ind. | $26,165 | $8990 | 100% | 19% | $26,628 | $8527 | $29,998 |
| Idaho State University | pub. | $6566 | $5963 | 78% | 6% | $9022 | $3507 | $26,445 |
| Lewis-Clark State College | pub. | $5900 | $6194 | 92% | 8% | $8168 | $3926 | $18,065 |
| Northwest Nazarene University | ind. | $27,950 | $6600 | 99% | 19% | $21,426 | $13,124 | $27,657 |
| University of Idaho | pub. | $6784 | $8022 | 74% | 42% | $13,573 | $1233 | $25,753 |
| **Illinois** | | | | | | | | |
| Augustana College | ind. | $38,466 | $9746 | 98% | 19% | $26,695 | $21,517 | $31,612 |
| Benedictine University | ind. | $28,240 | $8526 | 66% | NR | $20,846 | $15,920 | $26,750 |
| Blessing-Rieman College of Nursing | ind. | $21,810 | NR | NR | NR | NR | NR | $8475 |
| Bradley University | ind. | $30,844 | $9420 | 100% | 20% | $21,147 | $19,117 | $27,277 |
| Concordia University Chicago | ind. | $29,450 | $8992 | 99% | 15% | $21,417 | $17,025 | $32,408 |
| DePaul University | ind. | $35,071 | $12,552 | 86% | 13% | $23,440 | $24,183 | $27,498 |
| Dominican University | ind. | $30,670 | $9380 | 100% | 9% | $24,160 | $15,890 | $29,235 |
| Eastern Illinois University | pub. | $11,108 | $9358 | 78% | 8% | $12,129 | $8337 | $31,219 |
| Elmhurst College | ind. | $34,450 | $9666 | 100% | 35% | $24,842 | $19,274 | $28,068 |
| Governors State University | pub. | $9386 | $9000 | NR | NR | NR | NR | NR |
| Greenville College | ind. | $25,088 | $8288 | 100% | 12% | $19,564 | $13,812 | $28,452 |
| Illinois College | ind. | $29,210 | $9190 | 100% | 22% | $27,959 | $10,441 | $22,958 |
| Illinois Institute of Technology | ind. | $42,000 | NR | 100% | 22% | $37,589 | $4411 | $31,877 |
| Illinois State University | pub. | $13,296 | $9816 | 74% | 30% | $10,453 | $12,659 | $30,373 |
| Illinois Wesleyan University | ind. | $40,844 | $9446 | 100% | 44% | $30,984 | $19,306 | $32,101 |
| Knox College | ind. | $41,847 | $9012 | 98% | 28% | $36,017 | $14,842 | $29,085 |
| Lakeview College of Nursing | ind. | $15,040 | NA | NR | NR | NR | NR | $25,000 |

NA = not applicable; NR = not reported; * = includes room and board; † = room only; — = not available.

# College Costs At-a-Glance

| | Institutional Control ind.=independent; pub.=public | Tuition and Fees | Room and Board | Percent of Eligible Freshmen Receiving Need-Based Gift Awards | Percent of Freshmen Whose Need Was Fully Met | Average Financial Aid Package for Freshmen | Average Net Cost After Aid | Average Indebtedness Upon Graduation |
|---|---|---|---|---|---|---|---|---|
| Lewis University | ind. | $29,040 | $9930 | 100% | 21% | $22,768 | $16,202 | $33,748 |
| Lincoln Christian University | ind. | $16,050 | $7434 | 100% | 6% | $12,915 | $10,569 | $25,578 |
| Loyola University Chicago | ind. | $39,179 | $13,310 | 99% | 16% | $31,519 | $20,970 | $31,089 |
| MacMurray College | ind. | $23,600 | $8000 | 100% | 16% | $21,056 | $10,544 | $50,039 |
| McKendree University | ind. | $27,930 | $9020 | 100% | 24% | $24,083 | $12,867 | $21,731 |
| Millikin University | ind. | $29,620 | $9240 | 90% | 30% | $24,593 | $14,267 | $31,989 |
| Monmouth College | ind. | $34,200 | $8060 | 100% | 16% | $33,263 | $8997 | $31,154 |
| North Central College | ind. | $34,230 | $9795 | 100% | 24% | $26,156 | $17,869 | $32,086 |
| Northeastern Illinois University | pub. | $8612 | NA | 97% | 2% | $8375 | $237 | $13,366 |
| Northern Illinois University | pub. | $11,992 | $11,790 | 95% | 6% | $14,581 | $9201 | $33,234 |
| Northwestern University | ind. | $47,251 | $14,389 | 98% | 100% | $41,952 | $19,688 | $19,864 |
| Olivet Nazarene University | ind. | $32,790 | $7900 | 100% | 25% | $25,843 | $14,847 | $32,906 |
| Principia College | ind. | $27,440 | $10,810 | 100% | 42% | $29,677 | $8573 | $23,732 |
| Quincy University | ind. | $26,998 | $10,000 | 98% | 28% | $25,268 | $11,730 | $27,857 |
| Robert Morris University Illinois | ind. | $25,200 | $12,600 | 98% | 5% | $16,234 | $21,566 | $31,562 |
| Rockford University | ind. | $27,530 | $7710 | 99% | 15% | $19,248 | $15,992 | $39,619 |
| Roosevelt University | ind. | $27,300 | $12,532 | 86% | 22% | $24,450 | $15,382 | NR |
| Saint Anthony College of Nursing | ind. | $22,890 | NA | NR | NR | NR | NR | NR |
| Saint Francis Medical Center College of Nursing | ind. | $18,881 | $3400† | NR | NR | NR | NR | NR |
| Saint Xavier University | ind. | NR | NR | 86% | 10% | $26,245 | — | NR |
| School of the Art Institute of Chicago | ind. | $42,230 | $12,500 | 99% | 9% | $30,276 | $24,454 | $42,097 |
| Shimer College | ind. | $32,499 | $10,804 | 71% | 29% | $13,902 | $29,401 | $25,125 |
| Southern Illinois University Carbondale | pub. | $12,248 | $9694 | 71% | 8% | $16,057 | $5885 | $30,138 |
| Southern Illinois University Edwardsville | pub. | $9738 | $8781 | 83% | 24% | $11,911 | $6608 | $27,681 |
| Trinity Christian College | ind. | $25,290 | $9390 | 100% | 16% | $22,143 | $12,537 | $30,996 |
| University of Chicago | ind. | $48,253 | $14,205 | 99% | 100% | $43,402 | $19,056 | $23,223 |
| University of Illinois at Chicago | pub. | $13,634 | $10,871 | 86% | 7% | $14,240 | $10,265 | $23,158 |
| University of Illinois at Springfield | pub. | $11,413 | $11,550 | 98% | 23% | $16,291 | $6672 | $23,507 |
| University of St. Francis | ind. | $29,950 | NR | 69% | 72% | $25,881 | $4069 | $29,418 |
| VanderCook College of Music | ind. | $25,690 | $11,180 | 100% | NR | $16,596 | $20,274 | $38,861 |
| Western Illinois University | pub. | $11,282 | $9450 | 91% | 26% | $12,206 | $8526 | $28,785 |
| Wheaton College | ind. | $31,900 | $8820 | 99% | 37% | $24,629 | $16,091 | $25,939 |
| **Indiana** | | | | | | | | |
| Anderson University | ind. | $26,850 | $9250 | 99% | 39% | $25,945 | $10,155 | NR |
| Ball State University | pub. | $9384 | $9537 | 61% | 43% | $12,417 | $6504 | $27,627 |
| Butler University | ind. | $35,652 | $11,620 | 99% | 14% | $23,639 | $23,633 | $35,797 |
| Calumet College of Saint Joseph | ind. | $16,440 | NA | 71% | 12% | $11,856 | $4584 | $30,847 |
| DePauw University | ind. | $42,746 | $11,200 | 100% | 33% | $35,220 | $18,726 | $27,005 |
| Earlham College | ind. | $42,870 | $8600 | 96% | 15% | $40,538 | $10,932 | $27,421 |
| Franklin College | ind. | $29,025 | $8650 | 100% | 9% | $20,974 | $16,701 | $32,451 |
| Goshen College | ind. | $30,590 | $9985 | 100% | 24% | $25,615 | $14,960 | $26,586 |
| Hanover College | ind. | $34,514 | $10,452 | 100% | 29% | $27,663 | $17,303 | $31,004 |

NA = not applicable; NR = not reported; * = includes room and board; † = room only; — = not available.

# College Costs At-a-Glance

| | Institutional Control ind.=independent; pub.=public | Tuition and Fees | Room and Board | Percent of Eligible Freshmen Receiving Need-Based Gift Awards | Percent of Freshmen Whose Need Was Fully Met | Average Financial Aid Package for Freshmen | Average Net Cost After Aid | Average Indebtedness Upon Graduation |
|---|---|---|---|---|---|---|---|---|
| Huntington University | ind. | $24,771 | $8306 | 94% | 17% | $19,510 | $13,567 | $35,840 |
| Indiana State University | pub. | $8416 | $9182 | 71% | 10% | $10,101 | $7497 | $26,256 |
| Indiana Tech | ind. | $24,860 | $9521 | 87% | NR | $21,994 | $12,387 | $41,844 |
| Indiana University Bloomington | pub. | $10,388 | $9493 | 82% | 29% | $12,649 | $7232 | $27,300 |
| Indiana University East | pub. | $6787 | NA | 90% | 8% | $8669 | — | $29,952 |
| Indiana University Kokomo | pub. | $6811 | NA | 88% | 5% | $7707 | — | $26,651 |
| Indiana University Northwest | pub. | $6853 | NA | 83% | 4% | $7026 | — | $33,790 |
| Indiana University–Purdue University Fort Wayne | pub. | $7949 | $7632† | 62% | 3% | $8523 | $7058 | $29,452 |
| Indiana University–Purdue University Indianapolis | pub. | $8909 | $7981 | 86% | 9% | $10,041 | $6849 | $31,010 |
| Indiana University South Bend | pub. | $6905 | $7150† | 94% | 6% | $7901 | $6154 | $29,919 |
| Indiana University Southeast | pub. | $6827 | $6280† | 96% | 6% | $7510 | $5597 | $26,594 |
| Purdue University | pub. | $10,002 | $10,030 | 64% | 48% | $12,530 | $7502 | $28,343 |
| Purdue University Calumet | pub. | $6758 | $5485† | 64% | 4% | $4008 | $8235 | $28,600 |
| Rose-Hulman Institute of Technology | ind. | $41,283 | $12,057 | 88% | 20% | $29,661 | $23,679 | $35,420 |
| Saint Joseph's College | ind. | $27,485 | $8610 | 100% | 23% | $26,472 | $9623 | $30,899 |
| Saint Mary's College | ind. | $35,970 | $10,930 | 97% | 20% | $29,530 | $17,370 | $30,910 |
| Taylor University | ind. | $29,538 | $8283 | 100% | 25% | $20,074 | $17,747 | $25,125 |
| Trine University | ind. | $30,350 | $10,200 | 100% | 11% | $27,189 | $13,361 | $32,641 |
| University of Evansville | ind. | $31,776 | $10,880 | 100% | 25% | $27,491 | $15,165 | $29,441 |
| University of Indianapolis | ind. | $26,170 | $9324 | 63% | 14% | $19,556 | $15,938 | $35,689 |
| University of Notre Dame | ind. | $46,237 | $13,224 | 93% | 99% | $42,499 | $16,962 | $26,674 |
| University of Southern Indiana | pub. | $6957 | $7928 | 62% | 7% | $8781 | $6104 | $25,732 |
| Valparaiso University | ind. | $34,760 | $10,180 | 99% | 42% | $31,026 | $13,914 | $35,449 |
| Wabash College | ind. | $37,750 | $9130 | 100% | 63% | $32,745 | $14,135 | $30,734 |
| **Iowa** | | | | | | | | |
| Allen College | ind. | $19,295 | $7281 | 100% | NR | $26,429 | $147 | NR |
| Buena Vista University | ind. | $31,318 | $9046 | 100% | 67% | $28,498 | $11,866 | $34,173 |
| Central College | ind. | $33,345 | $9980 | 100% | 21% | $28,994 | $14,331 | $29,440 |
| Clarke University | ind. | $29,940 | $9000 | 100% | 22% | $25,714 | $13,226 | $37,200 |
| Coe College | ind. | $37,320 | $8230 | 100% | 20% | $33,073 | $12,477 | $31,992 |
| Cornell College | ind. | $37,725 | $8500 | 100% | 23% | $27,831 | $18,394 | $25,004 |
| Dordt College | ind. | NR | NR | 100% | 33% | $23,168 | — | $27,867 |
| Drake University | ind. | $32,246 | $9270 | 98% | 27% | $24,053 | $17,463 | $31,546 |
| Emmaus Bible College | ind. | $15,390 | $6560 | NR | NR | NR | NR | NR |
| Graceland University | ind. | $25,890 | $8100 | 100% | 12% | $24,215 | $9775 | $35,077 |
| Grand View University | ind. | $24,454 | $7866 | 91% | 31% | $21,654 | $10,666 | $38,160 |
| Grinnell College | ind. | $46,023 | $10,997 | 98% | 100% | $42,327 | $14,693 | $16,315 |
| Iowa State University of Science and Technology | pub. | $7736 | $8070 | 99% | 35% | $12,146 | $3660 | $28,880 |
| Iowa Wesleyan College | ind. | $27,286 | $9576 | 98% | 17% | $20,775 | $16,087 | $36,797 |
| Loras College | ind. | $29,729 | $8353 | 100% | 42% | $22,424 | $15,658 | $34,514 |
| Luther College | ind. | $39,190 | $7920 | 100% | 28% | $33,020 | $14,090 | $36,918 |
| Mercy College of Health Sciences | ind. | $15,642 | NA | NR | NR | NR | NR | NR |

NA = not applicable; NR = not reported; * = includes room and board; † = room only; — = not available.

# College Costs At-a-Glance

| | Institutional Control ind.=independent; pub.=public | Tuition and Fees | Room and Board | Percent of Eligible Freshmen Receiving Need-Based Gift Awards | Percent of Freshmen Whose Need Was Fully Met | Average Financial Aid Package for Freshmen | Average Net Cost After Aid | Average Indebtedness Upon Graduation |
|---|---|---|---|---|---|---|---|---|
| Morningside College | ind. | $27,180 | $8250 | 67% | 39% | $23,119 | $12,311 | $34,667 |
| Mount Mercy University | ind. | $28,226 | $8600 | 100% | 15% | $22,057 | $14,769 | $27,442 |
| St. Ambrose University | ind. | NR | NR | 100% | 24% | $21,117 | — | $34,937 |
| Simpson College | ind. | $32,550 | $7963 | 100% | 24% | $31,544 | $8969 | $35,205 |
| University of Dubuque | ind. | $26,950 | $8490 | 100% | 18% | $24,189 | $11,251 | $22,894 |
| The University of Iowa | pub. | $8104 | $9728 | 72% | 32% | $14,888 | $2944 | $28,716 |
| University of Northern Iowa | pub. | $7749 | $8046 | 56% | 26% | $7548 | $8247 | $23,163 |
| Upper Iowa University | ind. | $28,073 | $7910 | 98% | NR | $16,256 | $19,727 | $30,401 |
| Waldorf College | ind. | $20,884 | $6994 | 98% | 10% | $15,664 | $12,214 | $33,494 |
| Wartburg College | ind. | $37,190 | $9010 | 100% | 24% | $27,396 | $18,804 | $39,414 |
| **Kansas** | | | | | | | | |
| Barclay College | ind. | $14,990 | $8000 | 100% | 3% | $13,554 | $9436 | $7220 |
| Bethel College | ind. | $24,200 | $8240 | 88% | 27% | $24,117 | $8323 | $24,132 |
| Emporia State University | pub. | $5746 | $7582 | 94% | 16% | $8625 | $4703 | $30,488 |
| Fort Hays State University | pub. | NR | NR | 96% | 18% | $7207 | — | $25,172 |
| Friends University | ind. | $24,630 | $7320 | 90% | 29% | $18,027 | $13,923 | $15,289 |
| Kansas State University | pub. | $9034 | $8060 | 56% | 20% | $11,700 | $5394 | $26,779 |
| Kansas Wesleyan University | ind. | $26,600 | $8200 | 100% | 23% | $21,762 | $13,038 | $31,230 |
| Newman University | ind. | $24,730 | $7060 | 97% | 38% | $23,700 | $8090 | $23,843 |
| Pittsburg State University | pub. | $6230 | $6936 | 64% | 21% | $5866 | $7300 | $23,307 |
| Southwestern College | ind. | $25,946 | $7080 | 100% | 14% | $20,635 | $12,391 | $33,478 |
| Sterling College | ind. | $21,990 | $7931 | 94% | 24% | $19,893 | $10,028 | $28,221 |
| Tabor College | ind. | $23,900 | $8620 | 77% | 7% | $18,638 | $13,882 | $26,588 |
| The University of Kansas | pub. | $9706 | $7896 | 57% | 13% | $9160 | $8442 | $25,268 |
| Washburn University | pub. | $6038 | $6541 | 65% | 18% | $9767 | $2812 | $27,383 |
| Wichita State University | pub. | $7265 | $8373 | 73% | 75% | $5812 | $9826 | $23,534 |
| **Kentucky** | | | | | | | | |
| Alice Lloyd College | ind. | $11,460 | $5940 | 100% | 11% | $11,993 | $5407 | $9949 |
| Bellarmine University | ind. | $37,650 | $11,360 | 100% | 22% | $30,157 | $18,853 | $31,381 |
| Berea College | ind. | $870 | $6322 | 100% | NR | $31,547 | — | $6186 |
| Campbellsville University | ind. | $23,828 | $7770 | 100% | 17% | $20,205 | $11,393 | $22,261 |
| Centre College | ind. | $38,200 | $9620 | 99% | 35% | $29,897 | $17,923 | $25,994 |
| Clear Creek Baptist Bible College | ind. | NR | NR | 100% | NR | $6365 | — | NR |
| Eastern Kentucky University | pub. | $8150 | $4562† | 66% | 40% | $11,758 | $954 | $27,438 |
| Georgetown College | ind. | $32,960 | $8480 | 100% | 80% | $32,116 | $9324 | $19,076 |
| Kentucky Christian University | ind. | $17,810 | $7800 | 72% | 7% | $13,628 | $11,982 | $30,578 |
| Kentucky State University | pub. | $7404 | $6690 | 97% | 17% | $12,463 | $1631 | $34,110 |
| Kentucky Wesleyan College | ind. | $22,030 | $7800 | 100% | 21% | $16,118 | $13,712 | $24,150 |
| Lindsey Wilson College | ind. | $23,162 | $8900 | 100% | 19% | NR | NR | $26,249 |
| Morehead State University | pub. | $7866 | $7888 | 67% | 19% | $10,703 | $5051 | $28,147 |
| Murray State University | pub. | $7392 | $7912 | 92% | 23% | $11,221 | $4083 | $24,554 |
| Northern Kentucky University | pub. | $8856 | $8964 | 58% | 30% | $11,120 | $6700 | $27,594 |

NA = not applicable; NR = not reported; * = includes room and board; † = room only; — = not available.

# College Costs At-a-Glance

| | Institutional Control ind.=independent; pub.=public | Tuition and Fees | Room and Board | Percent of Eligible Freshmen Receiving Need-Based Gift Awards | Percent of Freshmen Whose Need Was Fully Met | Average Financial Aid Package for Freshmen | Average Net Cost After Aid | Average Indebtedness Upon Graduation |
|---|---|---|---|---|---|---|---|---|
| Thomas More College | ind. | $29,153 | $7770 | 100% | 28% | $19,660 | $17,263 | $31,014 |
| Transylvania University | ind. | $33,360 | $9300 | 100% | 29% | $27,367 | $15,293 | $28,079 |
| Union College | ind. | $24,075 | $7000 | 100% | 12% | $21,953 | $9122 | $32,691 |
| University of Louisville | pub. | $10,236 | $7710 | 98% | 28% | $12,078 | $5868 | $23,375 |
| University of Pikeville | ind. | $18,840 | $7210 | 100% | 36% | $20,993 | $5057 | $20,087 |
| University of the Cumberlands | ind. | $22,000 | $8500 | 100% | 22% | $21,032 | $9468 | $18,777 |
| Western Kentucky University | pub. | $9140 | $7171 | 64% | 29% | $13,575 | $2736 | $26,768 |
| **Louisiana** | | | | | | | | |
| Centenary College of Louisiana | ind. | $33,900 | $12,350 | 100% | 13% | $27,395 | $18,855 | $27,692 |
| Grambling State University | pub. | $6644 | $9372 | 86% | NR | $3850 | $12,166 | NR |
| Louisiana State University and Agricultural & Mechanical College | pub. | $8750 | $10,804 | 95% | 26% | $14,724 | $4830 | $22,294 |
| Louisiana Tech University | pub. | $8052 | $5520 | 97% | 27% | $9470 | $4102 | $16,855 |
| Loyola University New Orleans | ind. | $36,610 | $12,660 | 100% | 9% | $31,971 | $17,299 | $25,133 |
| Nicholls State University | pub. | $7304 | $8580 | 96% | 25% | $9919 | $5965 | $24,250 |
| Saint Joseph Seminary College | ind. | $16,240 | $13,830 | NR | NR | NR | NR | NR |
| Southeastern Louisiana University | pub. | $6547 | $7100 | 65% | 13% | $8358 | $5289 | NR |
| Tulane University | ind. | $48,306 | $12,556 | 97% | 69% | $32,424 | $28,438 | $31,653 |
| University of Louisiana at Lafayette | pub. | $6948 | $8566 | 98% | 15% | $9048 | $6466 | NR |
| University of New Orleans | pub. | $7482 | $9274 | 79% | 11% | $11,563 | $5193 | $18,850 |
| Xavier University of Louisiana | ind. | $21,552 | $8500 | 65% | NR | $21,750 | $8302 | $24,570 |
| **Maine** | | | | | | | | |
| Bates College | ind. | $60,720* | NR | 100% | 100% | $42,057 | $18,663 | $18,929 |
| Bowdoin College | ind. | $46,808 | $12,760 | 100% | 100% | $42,318 | $17,250 | $25,503 |
| Colby College | ind. | $47,350 | $12,150 | 100% | 100% | $46,029 | $13,471 | $21,958 |
| College of the Atlantic | ind. | $42,084 | $9432 | 100% | 92% | $39,777 | $11,739 | $23,926 |
| Husson University | ind. | $16,060 | $8922 | 98% | 8% | $14,536 | $10,446 | $32,343 |
| Maine Maritime Academy | pub. | $17,120 | $9830 | 78% | 8% | $7750 | $19,200 | $40,909 |
| Thomas College | ind. | NR | NR | 100% | 9% | $22,785 | — | $36,278 |
| Unity College | ind. | $25,820 | $9330 | 100% | 6% | $21,137 | $14,013 | NR |
| University of Maine | pub. | $10,606 | $9296 | 96% | 18% | $18,106 | $1796 | $33,875 |
| University of Maine at Augusta | pub. | $7448 | NA | 94% | 1% | $7976 | — | $30,827 |
| University of Maine at Farmington | pub. | $9217 | $8970 | 96% | 41% | $14,320 | $3867 | $31,792 |
| University of Maine at Fort Kent | pub. | $7575 | $7720 | 98% | 54% | $11,198 | $4097 | $24,028 |
| University of Maine at Machias | pub. | $7480 | $8178 | 97% | 69% | $13,737 | $1921 | $29,146 |
| University of Maine at Presque Isle | pub. | $7435 | $7656 | 100% | 63% | $11,418 | $3673 | $23,777 |
| University of Southern Maine | pub. | $8920 | $9150 | 93% | 41% | $12,911 | $5159 | NR |
| **Maryland** | | | | | | | | |
| Bowie State University | pub. | $7299 | $10,432 | 80% | 54% | $9321 | $8410 | $29,737 |
| Coppin State University | pub. | $4889 | $9236 | 98% | 11% | $9636 | $4489 | NR |
| Frostburg State University | pub. | $8488 | $8574 | 77% | 17% | $9315 | $7747 | $24,916 |

**NA = not applicable; NR = not reported; * = includes room and board; † = room only; — = not available.**

# College Costs At-a-Glance

| | Institutional Control ind.=independent; pub.=public | Tuition and Fees | Room and Board | Percent of Eligible Freshmen Receiving Need-Based Gift Awards | Percent of Freshmen Whose Need Was Fully Met | Average Financial Aid Package for Freshmen | Average Net Cost After Aid | Average Indebtedness Upon Graduation |
|---|---|---|---|---|---|---|---|---|
| Goucher College | ind. | $40,558 | $11,482 | 100% | 21% | $31,849 | $20,191 | $25,580 |
| Hood College | ind. | $35,150 | $11,840 | 100% | 16% | $28,497 | $18,493 | $31,229 |
| Johns Hopkins University | ind. | $49,210 | $14,540 | 93% | 98% | $38,105 | $25,645 | $23,627 |
| Loyola University Maryland | ind. | $44,255 | $12,790 | 92% | 90% | $28,420 | $28,625 | $34,190 |
| McDaniel College | ind. | $38,350 | $9100 | 100% | 27% | $35,043 | $12,407 | $31,568 |
| Mount St. Mary's University | ind. | $37,500 | $12,400 | 100% | 27% | $26,271 | $23,629 | $36,130 |
| Notre Dame of Maryland University | ind. | $33,670 | $10,930 | 100% | 25% | $28,928 | $15,672 | $32,346 |
| Peabody Conservatory of The Johns Hopkins University | ind. | $41,870 | $13,520 | 87% | 15% | $17,739 | $37,651 | $32,489 |
| St. John's College | ind. | $450 | $11,270 | 98% | 36% | $35,999 | — | $28,730 |
| St. Mary's College of Maryland | pub. | $13,824 | $11,930 | 90% | 12% | $15,694 | $10,060 | $24,621 |
| Salisbury University | pub. | $8560 | $10,620 | 90% | 15% | $8111 | $11,069 | $24,567 |
| Stevenson University | ind. | $28,980 | $12,490 | 100% | 10% | $20,739 | $20,731 | $32,503 |
| Towson University | pub. | $8650 | $11,260 | 56% | 14% | $9196 | $10,714 | $25,926 |
| University of Maryland, Baltimore County | pub. | $10,384 | $10,562 | 82% | 22% | $10,494 | $10,452 | $25,925 |
| University of Maryland, College Park | pub. | $9427 | $10,633 | 85% | 29% | $13,672 | $6388 | $25,131 |
| University of Maryland Eastern Shore | pub. | $9807 | $8994 | 86% | NR | $9968 | $8833 | $27,562 |
| University of Maryland University College | pub. | $6744 | NA | 80% | NR | $5271 | $1473 | NR |
| Washington College | ind. | $43,840 | $10,612 | 100% | 23% | $32,294 | $22,158 | $35,833 |
| **Massachusetts** | | | | | | | | |
| Amherst College | ind. | $48,526 | $12,680 | 100% | 100% | $49,469 | $11,737 | $14,490 |
| Anna Maria College | ind. | $34,060 | $12,730 | 99% | 3% | $25,752 | $21,038 | $51,934 |
| Assumption College | ind. | $36,160 | $10,962 | 100% | 20% | $25,788 | $21,334 | $34,417 |
| Babson College | ind. | $46,784 | $14,928 | 91% | 52% | $37,182 | $24,530 | $35,290 |
| Bay Path University | ind. | $30,859 | $12,240 | 100% | 8% | $28,106 | $14,993 | NR |
| Becker College | ind. | $32,870 | $12,000 | 76% | 12% | $24,330 | $20,540 | NR |
| Bentley University | ind. | $42,511 | $13,949 | 98% | 43% | $33,890 | $22,570 | $30,602 |
| Berklee College of Music | ind. | NR | NR | 77% | 9% | $8445 | — | $15,838 |
| Boston Architectural College | ind. | $19,706 | NR | 56% | NR | $5119 | $14,587 | NR |
| Boston College | ind. | $47,436 | $13,186 | 87% | 100% | $35,378 | $25,244 | $21,139 |
| Boston University | ind. | $46,664 | $14,030 | 98% | 37% | $39,436 | $21,258 | $39,166 |
| Brandeis University | ind. | $47,558 | $13,192 | 98% | 35% | $40,719 | $20,031 | $30,848 |
| Bridgewater State University | pub. | $8353 | $11,400 | 84% | 9% | $9054 | $10,699 | $32,040 |
| Clark University | ind. | $41,940 | $8200 | 99% | 65% | $34,602 | $15,538 | $24,990 |
| College of the Holy Cross | ind. | $47,176 | $12,748 | 84% | 100% | $36,532 | $23,392 | $28,354 |
| Curry College | ind. | $36,445 | $13,900 | 79% | 10% | $26,110 | $24,235 | $43,388 |
| Eastern Nazarene College | ind. | NR | NR | 100% | 30% | $31,739 | — | $25,251 |
| Elms College | ind. | $32,335 | $11,708 | 100% | 9% | $24,969 | $19,074 | $35,089 |
| Emerson College | ind. | $39,036 | $15,700 | 93% | 17% | $22,807 | $31,929 | $23,606 |
| Emmanuel College | ind. | $35,532 | $13,580 | 100% | 52% | $27,909 | $21,203 | $35,679 |
| Endicott College | ind. | $29,494 | $13,734 | 84% | 9% | $19,526 | $23,702 | $39,187 |
| Fisher College | ind. | $29,937 | $15,082 | 100% | NR | NR | NR | NR |
| Framingham State University | pub. | $8320 | $10,543 | 82% | 4% | $9149 | $9714 | $18,027 |

NA = not applicable; NR = not reported; * = includes room and board; † = room only; — = not available.

# College Costs At-a-Glance

| | Institutional Control ind.=independent; pub.=public | Tuition and Fees | Room and Board | Percent of Eligible Freshmen Receiving Need-Based Gift Awards | Percent of Freshmen Whose Need Was Fully Met | Average Financial Aid Package for Freshmen | Average Net Cost After Aid | Average Indebtedness Upon Graduation |
|---|---|---|---|---|---|---|---|---|
| Franklin W. Olin College of Engineering | ind. | $45,525 | $15,600 | 100% | 100% | $43,005 | $18,120 | $19,992 |
| Gordon College | ind. | $34,390 | $9930 | 100% | 17% | $23,043 | $21,277 | $38,456 |
| Hampshire College | ind. | $49,360 | $12,950 | 98% | 16% | $36,727 | $25,583 | $20,432 |
| Harvard University | ind. | $43,938 | $14,669 | 99% | 99% | $48,876 | $9731 | $15,117 |
| Lasell College | ind. | $31,000 | $12,750 | 100% | 23% | $24,587 | $19,163 | $37,302 |
| Lesley University | ind. | $25,550 | $14,830 | 100% | 18% | $15,925 | $24,455 | $23,000 |
| Massachusetts College of Art and Design | pub. | $11,225 | $13,000 | 85% | NR | $12,642 | $11,583 | $26,792 |
| Massachusetts College of Liberal Arts | pub. | $8975 | $9638 | 84% | 81% | $13,990 | $4623 | $28,817 |
| Massachusetts Institute of Technology | ind. | $45,016 | $13,224 | 97% | 100% | $39,495 | $18,745 | $19,064 |
| Massachusetts Maritime Academy | pub. | $7280 | $11,120 | NR | NR | NR | NR | $37,582 |
| MCPHS University | ind. | $30,530 | $15,240 | 65% | 6% | $16,330 | $29,440 | $14,618 |
| Merrimack College | ind. | $36,215 | $13,255 | 100% | 16% | $21,830 | $27,640 | NR |
| Montserrat College of Art | ind. | $28,700 | $9700 | NR | NR | NR | NR | NR |
| Mount Holyoke College | ind. | $43,886 | $12,860 | 100% | 100% | $36,827 | $19,919 | $23,914 |
| New England Conservatory of Music | ind. | $41,405 | $12,850 | 100% | 5% | $24,166 | $30,089 | $25,288 |
| Nichols College | ind. | $33,300 | $12,600 | 100% | 18% | $24,218 | $21,682 | $32,747 |
| Northeastern University | ind. | $43,440 | $14,570 | 98% | 100% | $34,399 | $23,611 | NR |
| Pine Manor College | ind. | $25,516 | $12,820 | 100% | 3% | $24,347 | $13,989 | $32,975 |
| School of the Museum of Fine Arts, Boston | ind. | $40,348 | $10,950† | 100% | 5% | $26,948 | $24,350 | $34,081 |
| Simmons College | ind. | $36,230 | $13,736 | 100% | 15% | $28,999 | $20,967 | NR |
| Smith College | ind. | $44,724 | $14,950 | 94% | 100% | $42,078 | $17,596 | $24,758 |
| Springfield College | ind. | $33,455 | $11,210 | 100% | 8% | $25,584 | $19,081 | $41,659 |
| Stonehill College | ind. | $37,426 | $14,290 | 99% | 57% | $31,183 | $20,533 | $31,622 |
| Suffolk University | ind. | $32,660 | $14,638 | 82% | 14% | $24,081 | $23,217 | $29,535 |
| Tufts University | ind. | $48,643 | $12,634 | 96% | 100% | $42,770 | $18,507 | $26,616 |
| University of Massachusetts Amherst | pub. | $1714 | $6137 | 92% | 13% | $14,887 | — | $30,453 |
| University of Massachusetts Boston | pub. | $11,966 | NA | 95% | 58% | $14,002 | — | $27,229 |
| University of Massachusetts Dartmouth | pub. | $11,681 | $11,435 | 93% | 39% | $16,523 | $6593 | $31,070 |
| University of Massachusetts Lowell | pub. | $12,447 | $11,278 | 93% | 48% | $14,771 | $8954 | $30,505 |
| Wellesley College | ind. | $45,078 | $13,960 | 96% | 100% | $40,932 | $18,106 | $12,956 |
| Wentworth Institute of Technology | ind. | $30,765 | $12,840 | NR | NR | NR | NR | NR |
| Western New England University | ind. | $33,466 | $12,688 | 100% | 11% | $25,375 | $20,779 | NR |
| Westfield State University | pub. | $8682 | $10,236 | 73% | 51% | $6673 | $12,245 | $26,326 |
| Wheaton College | ind. | $46,423 | $11,840 | 99% | 54% | $37,255 | $21,008 | $29,651 |
| Wheelock College | ind. | $32,830 | $13,600 | 100% | 15% | $25,443 | $20,987 | $46,690 |
| Williams College | ind. | $48,310 | $12,760 | 100% | 100% | $47,675 | $13,395 | $12,627 |
| Worcester Polytechnic Institute | ind. | $44,222 | $13,082 | 100% | 54% | $34,302 | $23,002 | NR |
| Worcester State University | pub. | $8557 | $11,255 | 89% | 34% | $11,209 | $8603 | $25,654 |
| **Michigan** | | | | | | | | |
| Adrian College | ind. | $32,660 | $9740 | 100% | 10% | $27,013 | $15,387 | $27,741 |
| Albion College | ind. | $37,300 | $10,550 | 100% | 25% | $30,767 | $17,083 | $37,151 |
| Alma College | ind. | $34,585 | $9490 | 100% | 19% | $25,384 | $18,691 | $32,389 |

NA = not applicable; NR = not reported; * = includes room and board; † = room only; — = not available.

# College Costs At-a-Glance

| | Institutional Control ind.=independent; pub.=public | Tuition and Fees | Room and Board | Percent of Eligible Freshmen Receiving Need-Based Gift Awards | Percent of Freshmen Whose Need Was Fully Met | Average Financial Aid Package for Freshmen | Average Net Cost After Aid | Average Indebtedness Upon Graduation |
|---|---|---|---|---|---|---|---|---|
| Andrews University | ind. | $26,262 | $8302 | 69% | 19% | $25,616 | $8948 | $36,536 |
| Aquinas College | ind. | $28,820 | $8558 | 100% | 40% | $21,912 | $15,466 | $22,396 |
| Calvin College | ind. | $29,635 | $9485 | 100% | 18% | $23,871 | $15,249 | $29,403 |
| Central Michigan University | pub. | $11,550 | $8780 | 85% | 52% | $13,814 | $6516 | $33,545 |
| Concordia University Ann Arbor | ind. | $25,990 | $8975 | 97% | 19% | $22,442 | $12,523 | $17,853 |
| Cornerstone University | ind. | $25,112 | $8226 | 100% | 12% | $20,881 | $12,457 | $27,919 |
| Eastern Michigan University | pub. | $9663 | $8940 | 71% | 5% | $10,241 | $8362 | $25,781 |
| Ferris State University | pub. | $11,190 | $9208 | 72% | 17% | $12,250 | $8148 | $35,720 |
| Grand Valley State University | pub. | $10,752 | $8200 | 88% | 14% | $10,569 | $8383 | $30,222 |
| Hillsdale College | ind. | $24,591 | $9760 | 68% | 38% | $13,134 | $21,217 | $25,502 |
| Hope College | ind. | $30,550 | $9390 | 87% | 20% | $25,203 | $14,737 | $31,717 |
| Kalamazoo College | ind. | $41,061 | $8679 | 98% | 59% | $36,012 | $13,728 | $28,405 |
| Lawrence Technological University | ind. | $30,200 | $8986 | 99% | 18% | $23,061 | $16,125 | $38,966 |
| Michigan State University | pub. | $13,200 | $9154 | 72% | 16% | $13,254 | $9100 | $26,122 |
| Michigan Technological University | pub. | $14,040 | $9516 | 82% | 20% | $14,870 | $8686 | $36,041 |
| Northern Michigan University | pub. | $9388 | $8954 | 59% | 14% | $9229 | $9113 | $29,618 |
| Oakland University | pub. | $10,613 | $8895 | 83% | 8% | $13,567 | $5941 | $26,724 |
| Olivet College | ind. | $23,801 | $3950† | 90% | 25% | $17,556 | $10,195 | $26,222 |
| Saginaw Valley State University | pub. | $8691 | $8400 | 77% | NR | NR | NR | NR |
| Spring Arbor University | ind. | $24,350 | $8460 | 100% | 20% | $22,184 | $10,626 | $36,866 |
| University of Michigan | pub. | $13,486 | $10,246 | 75% | 78% | $20,207 | $3525 | $26,510 |
| University of Michigan–Dearborn | pub. | $11,222 | NA | 73% | 11% | $9692 | $1530 | $22,168 |
| University of Michigan–Flint | pub. | $10,138 | $7911 | 77% | 3% | $10,759 | $7290 | $32,107 |
| Wayne State University | pub. | $12,349 | $9713 | 81% | 8% | $11,527 | $10,535 | $23,785 |
| Western Michigan University | pub. | $10,685 | $8943 | 69% | 25% | $15,300 | $4328 | $32,720 |
| **Minnesota** | | | | | | | | |
| Bemidji State University | pub. | $8134 | $7470 | 65% | 10% | $7631 | $7973 | NR |
| Bethany Lutheran College | ind. | $25,170 | $7710 | 100% | 29% | $19,511 | $13,369 | $33,384 |
| Bethel University | ind. | $32,990 | $9440 | 100% | 18% | $25,905 | $16,525 | $33,685 |
| Carleton College | ind. | $47,736 | $12,366 | 100% | 100% | $39,757 | $20,345 | $18,302 |
| College of Saint Benedict | ind. | $39,402 | $9956 | 99% | 49% | $33,343 | $16,015 | $39,437 |
| The College of St. Scholastica | ind. | $33,994 | $8932 | 80% | 26% | $26,367 | $16,559 | $42,792 |
| Concordia College | ind. | $35,464 | $7600 | 99% | 19% | $27,366 | $15,698 | NR |
| Concordia University, St. Paul | ind. | $20,750 | $8300 | 100% | 11% | $15,682 | $13,368 | $30,747 |
| Gustavus Adolphus College | ind. | $40,080 | $9250 | 98% | 24% | $34,947 | $14,383 | $36,636 |
| Hamline University | ind. | $36,270 | $9392 | 100% | 21% | $30,738 | $14,924 | $36,006 |
| Martin Luther College | ind. | $13,565 | $5355 | 98% | 11% | $11,264 | $7656 | $17,391 |
| McNally Smith College of Music | ind. | $25,210 | $5100 | 48% | NR | $9112 | $21,198 | $46,230 |
| Metropolitan State University | pub. | $6642 | NA | NR | NR | NR | NR | NR |
| Minneapolis College of Art and Design | ind. | $34,146 | $7030 | 100% | 16% | $24,714 | $16,462 | $33,400 |
| Minnesota State University Mankato | pub. | $8481 | $8042 | 68% | 20% | $9119 | $7404 | $31,568 |
| Minnesota State University Moorhead | pub. | $7829 | $7398 | 67% | NR | NR | NR | NR |

NA = not applicable; NR = not reported; * = includes room and board; † = room only; — = not available.

# College Costs At-a-Glance

| | Institutional Control ind.=independent; pub.=public | Tuition and Fees | Room and Board | Percent of Eligible Freshmen Receiving Need-Based Gift Awards | Percent of Freshmen Whose Need Was Fully Met | Average Financial Aid Package for Freshmen | Average Net Cost After Aid | Average Indebtedness Upon Graduation |
|---|---|---|---|---|---|---|---|---|
| St. Catherine University | ind. | $36,420 | $8894 | 86% | 24% | $35,807 | $9507 | $39,748 |
| St. Cloud State University | pub. | $7554 | $7560 | 74% | 12% | $9406 | $5708 | $31,953 |
| Saint John's University | ind. | $38,704 | $9280 | 99% | 43% | $32,415 | $15,569 | $38,089 |
| Saint Mary's University of Minnesota | ind. | $31,335 | $8240 | 100% | 28% | $26,200 | $13,375 | $33,216 |
| St. Olaf College | ind. | $42,940 | $9790 | 100% | 88% | $36,286 | $16,444 | $28,396 |
| University of Minnesota, Crookston | pub. | $11,468 | $7350 | 97% | 18% | $11,793 | $7025 | $23,621 |
| University of Minnesota, Duluth | pub. | $12,802 | $7004 | 89% | 17% | $10,790 | $9016 | $31,244 |
| University of Minnesota, Twin Cities Campus | pub. | $13,626 | $8920 | 87% | 29% | $12,815 | $9731 | $26,796 |
| University of St. Thomas | ind. | $36,682 | $5770† | 99% | 17% | $26,552 | $15,900 | $37,131 |
| Winona State University | pub. | $8750 | $7890 | 74% | 11% | $6733 | $9907 | $35,131 |
| **Mississippi** | | | | | | | | |
| Alcorn State University | pub. | $6192 | $8650 | 95% | 10% | $14,826 | $16 | $34,725 |
| Belhaven University | ind. | $21,626 | $8000 | 98% | 8% | $20,093 | $9533 | $26,800 |
| Blue Mountain College | ind. | $10,534 | $4800 | 55% | 36% | $12,451 | $2883 | $24,571 |
| Delta State University | pub. | $6562 | $7200 | 57% | NR | $4054 | $9708 | NR |
| Jackson State University | pub. | $6602 | NR | 84% | 1% | $13,005 | — | $31,576 |
| Millsaps College | ind. | $33,982 | $11,878 | 100% | 34% | $31,847 | $14,013 | $29,021 |
| Mississippi College | ind. | $15,458 | $8408 | 96% | 11% | $15,863 | $8003 | $29,189 |
| Mississippi State University | pub. | $7140 | $8954 | 92% | 29% | $15,020 | $1074 | $29,365 |
| Mississippi University for Women | pub. | $5640 | $6381 | 75% | 16% | $10,534 | $1487 | $21,095 |
| University of Mississippi | pub. | $7096 | $9908 | 91% | 15% | $10,956 | $6048 | $26,443 |
| University of Southern Mississippi | pub. | $7224 | $7640 | 67% | 29% | $12,046 | $2818 | $17,806 |
| **Missouri** | | | | | | | | |
| Calvary Bible College and Theological Seminary | ind. | $10,360 | $5440 | 63% | NR | $7058 | $8742 | $9993 |
| Central Methodist University | ind. | $22,360 | $7340 | 73% | 15% | $19,183 | $10,517 | $28,902 |
| City Vision University | ind. | $6000 | NR | 100% | 100% | $5081 | $919 | NR |
| Columbia College | ind. | $20,936 | $8240 | 67% | 16% | $16,190 | $12,986 | $14,591 |
| Conception Seminary College | ind. | $20,304 | $12,074 | 100% | 44% | $28,026 | $4352 | $27,243 |
| Culver-Stockton College | ind. | $24,900 | $7950 | 100% | 19% | $19,357 | $13,493 | $24,487 |
| Drury University | ind. | $23,885 | $7394 | 100% | 25% | $20,111 | $11,168 | $25,336 |
| Evangel University | ind. | $20,796 | $7200 | 99% | 10% | $16,288 | $11,708 | $30,179 |
| Fontbonne University | ind. | $23,790 | $8811 | 80% | 13% | $13,462 | $19,139 | $24,281 |
| Kansas City Art Institute | ind. | $35,270 | $10,240 | 100% | 12% | $22,375 | $23,135 | $25,000 |
| Lincoln University | pub. | $6838 | $5531 | 94% | 5% | $11,259 | $1110 | $30,225 |
| Lindenwood University | ind. | $15,580 | $7880 | 98% | 89% | $11,610 | $11,850 | NR |
| Logan University | ind. | $6880 | NA | NR | NR | NR | NR | NR |
| Maryville University of Saint Louis | ind. | $25,884 | $9972 | 99% | 15% | $23,942 | $11,914 | $31,696 |
| Missouri Baptist University | ind. | $22,760 | $9070 | 80% | 22% | $19,529 | $12,301 | $25,337 |
| Missouri Southern State University | pub. | $5762 | $6299 | 87% | 8% | $8162 | $3899 | $29,405 |
| Missouri State University | pub. | $7796 | $7678 | 90% | 18% | $9457 | $6017 | $24,655 |
| Missouri University of Science and Technology | pub. | $9537 | $9540 | 95% | 96% | $16,123 | $2954 | $27,591 |
| Missouri Valley College | ind. | $19,350 | $8100 | 100% | 40% | $13,450 | $14,000 | $25,200 |

NA = not applicable; NR = not reported; * = includes room and board; † = room only; — = not available.

# College Costs At-a-Glance

| | Institutional Control ind.=independent; pub.=public | Tuition and Fees | Room and Board | Percent of Eligible Freshmen Receiving Need-Based Gift Awards | Percent of Freshmen Whose Need Was Fully Met | Average Financial Aid Package for Freshmen | Average Net Cost After Aid | Average Indebtedness Upon Graduation |
|---|---|---|---|---|---|---|---|---|
| Missouri Western State University | pub. | $6498 | $7346 | 98% | 14% | $8558 | $5286 | $26,015 |
| Northwest Missouri State University | pub. | $8276 | $9192 | 87% | 70% | $11,121 | $6347 | $24,710 |
| Park University | ind. | $10,600 | $7980 | 74% | 22% | $11,544 | $7036 | $22,115 |
| Rockhurst University | ind. | $32,865 | $9080 | 68% | 30% | $25,848 | $16,097 | $24,852 |
| Saint Louis Christian College | ind. | $10,075 | $4600 | 89% | 11% | $7486 | $7189 | $32,975 |
| St. Louis College of Pharmacy | ind. | $28,264 | $9783 | 100% | 7% | $13,826 | $24,221 | $104,713 |
| Saint Louis University | ind. | $37,966 | $10,380 | 97% | 24% | $26,055 | $22,291 | $35,615 |
| Southeast Missouri State University | pub. | $6938 | $8432 | 95% | 13% | $8788 | $6582 | $26,508 |
| Southwest Baptist University | ind. | $20,840 | $6800 | 72% | 27% | $19,540 | $8100 | $26,615 |
| Stephens College | ind. | $28,510 | $9532 | 85% | 10% | $24,869 | $13,173 | $26,824 |
| Truman State University | pub. | $7374 | NR | 100% | 41% | $12,466 | — | $23,585 |
| University of Central Missouri | pub. | $7264 | $7828 | 61% | 13% | $8531 | $6561 | $27,424 |
| University of Missouri | pub. | $9433 | $9386 | 88% | 17% | $15,678 | $3141 | $25,321 |
| University of Missouri–Kansas City | pub. | $9475 | $9815 | 95% | 12% | $10,863 | $8427 | $29,464 |
| University of Missouri–St. Louis | pub. | $10,065 | $9052 | 97% | 22% | $12,727 | $6390 | $25,208 |
| Washington University in St. Louis | ind. | $48,093 | $15,280 | 96% | 100% | $38,410 | $24,963 | $23,858 |
| Webster University | ind. | $24,500 | $10,600 | 91% | 2% | $27,757 | $7343 | $30,413 |
| Westminster College | ind. | $22,560 | $9160 | 100% | 69% | $22,339 | $9381 | $29,004 |
| William Jewell College | ind. | $32,330 | $8880 | 100% | 25% | $24,492 | $16,718 | $29,885 |
| William Woods University | ind. | $22,160 | $8960 | 100% | 22% | $17,688 | $13,432 | $21,260 |
| **Montana** | | | | | | | | |
| Carroll College | ind. | $29,280 | $8950 | 100% | 26% | $20,401 | $17,829 | $26,996 |
| Montana State University | pub. | $5330 | NR | 78% | 7% | $11,948 | — | $27,200 |
| Montana State University Billings | pub. | $5780 | $6980 | 89% | 5% | $9210 | $3550 | $27,225 |
| Montana Tech of The University of Montana | pub. | $6752 | $8238 | 90% | 21% | $9858 | $5132 | $24,448 |
| Rocky Mountain College | ind. | $25,252 | $7944 | 100% | 27% | $21,481 | $11,715 | $29,206 |
| University of Great Falls | ind. | $21,556 | $6800 | 92% | 2% | $20,158 | $8198 | $23,340 |
| The University of Montana | pub. | $6330 | $8006 | 68% | 12% | $10,836 | $3500 | $27,203 |
| The University of Montana Western | pub. | $4797 | $6536 | NR | NR | NR | NR | NR |
| **Nebraska** | | | | | | | | |
| College of Saint Mary | ind. | $28,964 | $7400 | 100% | 25% | $21,308 | $15,056 | $29,538 |
| Concordia University, Nebraska | ind. | $27,110 | $7260 | 100% | 27% | $22,263 | $12,107 | $29,002 |
| Creighton University | ind. | $35,360 | $9996 | 100% | 27% | $27,779 | $17,577 | $33,428 |
| Doane College | ind. | $2720 | NR | 100% | 39% | $22,791 | — | $29,994 |
| Hastings College | ind. | $27,300 | $8080 | 100% | 31% | $20,242 | $15,138 | $27,784 |
| Nebraska Christian College | ind. | $13,200 | $7700 | NR | NR | NR | NR | NR |
| Nebraska Methodist College | ind. | $18,109 | $6460† | 91% | 3% | $9971 | $14,598 | $31,591 |
| Union College | ind. | $21,970 | $6730 | 100% | 25% | $17,604 | $11,096 | $29,020 |
| University of Nebraska at Kearney | pub. | $6584 | $8850 | 90% | 24% | $11,904 | $3530 | $23,229 |
| University of Nebraska at Omaha | pub. | $6750 | $8408 | 63% | 28% | $10,637 | $4521 | $26,866 |
| University of Nebraska–Lincoln | pub. | $8070 | $9961 | 84% | 21% | $13,753 | $4278 | $23,395 |
| Wayne State College | pub. | $5604 | $6420 | 78% | 47% | $8660 | $3364 | NR |

NA = not applicable; NR = not reported; * = includes room and board; † = room only; — = not available.

# College Costs At-a-Glance

| | Institutional Control ind.=independent; pub.=public | Tuition and Fees | Room and Board | Percent of Eligible Freshmen Receiving Need-Based Gift Awards | Percent of Freshmen Whose Need Was Fully Met | Average Financial Aid Package for Freshmen | Average Net Cost After Aid | Average Indebtedness Upon Graduation |
|---|---|---|---|---|---|---|---|---|
| **Nevada** | | | | | | | | |
| University of Nevada, Las Vegas | pub. | $6590 | $10,730 | 72% | 10% | $11,374 | $5946 | $18,542 |
| University of Nevada, Reno | pub. | $6872 | $10,868 | 71% | 12% | $8508 | $9232 | $22,500 |
| **New Hampshire** | | | | | | | | |
| Colby-Sawyer College | ind. | $38,610 | NR | NR | NR | NR | NR | NR |
| Dartmouth College | ind. | $48,108 | $13,839 | 98% | 100% | $49,359 | $12,588 | $17,171 |
| Franklin Pierce University | ind. | $31,782 | $12,060 | 100% | 24% | $23,238 | $20,604 | $38,546 |
| Keene State College | pub. | $12,938 | $9712† | 72% | 8% | $11,476 | $11,174 | $33,796 |
| New England College | ind. | $34,566 | $13,388 | 98% | 14% | $28,103 | $19,851 | $31,073 |
| Plymouth State University | pub. | $12,677 | $10,728 | 71% | 17% | $9906 | $13,499 | $32,327 |
| Saint Anselm College | ind. | NR | NR | 100% | 24% | $27,051 | — | $35,601 |
| University of New Hampshire | pub. | $16,552 | $10,360 | 76% | 18% | $23,716 | $3196 | $36,965 |
| University of New Hampshire at Manchester | pub. | $13,757 | NA | 46% | 11% | $10,821 | $2936 | $29,393 |
| **New Jersey** | | | | | | | | |
| Bloomfield College | ind. | $27,800 | $11,300 | 100% | 8% | $23,014 | $16,086 | $33,443 |
| Caldwell University | ind. | $30,050 | NR | 74% | 3% | $25,000 | $5050 | $22,250 |
| The College of New Jersey | pub. | $15,024 | $11,677 | 41% | 9% | $11,065 | $15,636 | $33,635 |
| College of Saint Elizabeth | ind. | $31,095 | $12,744 | 89% | 8% | $28,447 | $15,392 | NR |
| Drew University | ind. | $45,214 | $12,302 | 100% | 17% | $37,597 | $19,919 | $24,778 |
| Felician College | ind. | $30,605 | $11,650 | 77% | 11% | $31,735 | $10,520 | NR |
| Georgian Court University | ind. | $30,998 | $10,596 | 98% | 36% | $28,891 | $12,703 | $40,551 |
| Kean University | pub. | $11,243 | $12,200 | 76% | 6% | $10,305 | $13,138 | $32,886 |
| Monmouth University | ind. | $32,310 | $11,798 | 60% | 15% | $24,607 | $19,501 | $30,678 |
| Montclair State University | pub. | $11,540 | $14,010 | 65% | 1% | $8868 | $16,682 | $28,070 |
| New Jersey City University | pub. | $10,852 | $10,604 | 86% | 7% | $14,864 | $6592 | $20,763 |
| New Jersey Institute of Technology | pub. | $15,648 | $13,280 | 86% | 15% | $14,728 | $14,200 | NR |
| Princeton University | ind. | $43,450 | $14,160 | 100% | 100% | $45,467 | $12,143 | $6600 |
| Ramapo College of New Jersey | pub. | $8650 | $11,550 | 46% | 13% | $13,850 | $6350 | $29,972 |
| Rider University | ind. | $36,830 | $13,330 | 100% | 14% | $29,235 | $20,925 | $28,080 |
| Rowan University | pub. | $12,616 | $11,406 | 48% | 30% | $8681 | $15,341 | $31,759 |
| Rutgers, The State University of New Jersey, Camden | pub. | $13,683 | $11,438 | 76% | 4% | $14,858 | $10,263 | $28,651 |
| Rutgers, The State University of New Jersey, Newark | pub. | $13,297 | $12,509 | 85% | 2% | $14,912 | $10,894 | $26,993 |
| Rutgers, The State University of New Jersey, New Brunswick | pub. | $13,813 | $11,749 | 67% | 5% | $14,880 | $10,682 | $25,228 |
| Stockton University | pub. | $12,568 | $11,164 | 70% | 40% | $17,072 | $6660 | $33,543 |
| William Paterson University of New Jersey | pub. | $12,244 | $10,670 | 73% | 38% | $10,647 | $12,267 | $25,062 |
| **New Mexico** | | | | | | | | |
| Eastern New Mexico University | pub. | $4856 | $6452 | 98% | 100% | $10,864 | $444 | $4895 |
| New Mexico Highlands University | pub. | $4500 | $7404 | 89% | 6% | $1573 | $10,331 | $14,106 |
| New Mexico Institute of Mining and Technology | pub. | $6256 | $6740 | 62% | 20% | $9972 | $3024 | $20,944 |
| New Mexico State University | pub. | $5950 | $8100 | 99% | 12% | $8638 | $5412 | $18,628 |
| St. John's College | ind. | $48,994 | $10,890 | 80% | 95% | $36,485 | $23,399 | $25,570 |

**NA = not applicable; NR = not reported; \* = includes room and board; † = room only; — = not available.**

# College Costs At-a-Glance

| | Institutional Control ind.=independent; pub.=public | Tuition and Fees | Room and Board | Percent of Eligible Freshmen Receiving Need-Based Gift Awards | Percent of Freshmen Whose Need Was Fully Met | Average Financial Aid Package for Freshmen | Average Net Cost After Aid | Average Indebtedness Upon Graduation |
|---|---|---|---|---|---|---|---|---|
| Santa Fe University of Art and Design | ind. | NR | NR | 100% | 9% | $20,013 | — | NR |
| Western New Mexico University | pub. | NR | NR | 83% | 11% | $2759 | — | $29,758 |
| **New York** | | | | | | | | |
| Adelphi University | ind. | $32,340 | $13,620 | 71% | NR | $20,900 | $25,060 | $32,328 |
| Albany College of Pharmacy and Health Sciences | ind. | $30,131 | $10,240 | 100% | 15% | $16,398 | $23,973 | NR |
| Bard College | ind. | $48,240 | $13,772 | 97% | 32% | $44,925 | $17,087 | $26,599 |
| Barnard College | ind. | $46,040 | $14,660 | 97% | 97% | $45,066 | $15,634 | $17,660 |
| Baruch College of the City University of New York | pub. | $6861 | NR | 73% | 93% | $5767 | $1094 | $5511 |
| Binghamton University, State University of New York | pub. | $8620 | $13,028 | 81% | 12% | $11,236 | $10,412 | $25,727 |
| Brooklyn College of the City University of New York | pub. | $6283 | $8990† | 88% | 81% | $7500 | $7773 | $12,500 |
| Buffalo State College, State University of New York | pub. | $7347 | $11,964 | 85% | 12% | $13,420 | $5891 | $24,290 |
| Canisius College | ind. | $34,000 | $12,516 | 100% | 29% | $33,313 | $13,203 | $40,913 |
| Cazenovia College | ind. | $30,560 | $12,344 | 100% | 21% | $31,000 | $11,904 | $29,998 |
| City College of the City University of New York | pub. | $6330 | NR | 93% | 70% | $8757 | — | $16,942 |
| Clarkson University | ind. | $44,630 | $13,844 | 100% | 24% | $40,738 | $17,736 | $28,000 |
| Colgate University | ind. | $48,175 | $11,970 | 100% | 100% | $46,696 | $13,449 | $21,405 |
| The College at Brockport, State University of New York | pub. | $7562 | $11,440 | 78% | 14% | $11,511 | $7491 | $27,666 |
| College of Mount Saint Vincent | ind. | NR | NR | 93% | 15% | $22,853 | — | NR |
| The College of New Rochelle | ind. | $32,300 | $12,200 | 85% | 5% | $29,132 | $15,368 | $37,437 |
| The College of Saint Rose | ind. | $29,016 | $11,532 | 91% | 17% | $20,846 | $19,702 | $34,482 |
| College of Staten Island of the City University of New York | pub. | $479 | $12,364† | 97% | 2% | $9153 | $3690 | NR |
| Columbia University | ind. | $51,008 | $12,432 | 96% | 100% | $48,086 | $15,354 | NR |
| Columbia University, School of General Studies | ind. | $49,476 | $11,430 | NR | NR | NR | NR | NR |
| Cooper Union for the Advancement of Science and Art | ind. | $41,450 | $15,220 | 100% | 73% | $39,600 | $17,070 | $19,072 |
| Cornell University | ind. | $47,286 | $13,678 | 98% | 100% | $44,400 | $16,564 | $21,411 |
| The Culinary Institute of America | ind. | $28,240 | $9652 | 85% | 44% | $16,156 | $21,736 | $35,617 |
| Dominican College | ind. | $26,450 | $12,200 | 100% | 10% | $22,060 | $16,590 | $22,640 |
| Dowling College | ind. | $29,100 | $10,770 | 94% | 7% | $22,417 | $17,453 | $39,116 |
| D'Youville College | ind. | $23,462 | $10,800 | 100% | 18% | $18,098 | $16,164 | $33,169 |
| Elmira College | ind. | $39,950 | $12,000 | 100% | 20% | $30,477 | $21,473 | $26,471 |
| Farmingdale State College | pub. | $7483 | $12,190 | 89% | 9% | $8323 | $11,350 | NR |
| Fashion Institute of Technology | pub. | $5200 | $13,162 | 69% | 38% | $10,670 | $7692 | $27,303 |
| Five Towns College | ind. | $21,000 | NR | 53% | 11% | $15,647 | $5353 | $26,993 |
| Fordham University | ind. | $45,623 | $15,965 | 98% | 30% | $31,845 | $29,743 | $37,607 |
| Hamilton College | ind. | $47,820 | $12,150 | 100% | 100% | $43,909 | $16,061 | $18,941 |
| Hartwick College | ind. | $40,070 | $10,800 | 73% | 12% | $34,280 | $16,590 | $26,708 |
| Hilbert College | ind. | $20,350 | $9160 | 99% | 20% | $14,476 | $15,034 | $20,139 |
| Hobart and William Smith Colleges | ind. | $47,908 | $12,126 | 99% | 65% | $32,788 | $27,246 | $34,330 |
| Hofstra University | ind. | $38,900 | $13,510 | 96% | 25% | $28,000 | $24,410 | NR |
| Houghton College | ind. | $28,556 | $8252 | 96% | 11% | $22,544 | $14,264 | $26,550 |
| Iona College | ind. | $34,030 | $13,570 | 37% | 20% | $23,272 | $24,328 | $30,885 |
| Ithaca College | ind. | $39,532 | $14,332 | 95% | 56% | $33,873 | $19,991 | NR |

NA = not applicable; NR = not reported; * = includes room and board; † = room only; — = not available.

# College Costs At-a-Glance

| | Institutional Control ind.=independent; pub.=public | Tuition and Fees | Room and Board | Percent of Eligible Freshmen Receiving Need-Based Gift Awards | Percent of Freshmen Whose Need Was Fully Met | Average Financial Aid Package for Freshmen | Average Net Cost After Aid | Average Indebtedness Upon Graduation |
|---|---|---|---|---|---|---|---|---|
| John Jay College of Criminal Justice of the City University of New York | pub. | $6059 | NA | 53% | NR | $9445 | — | $11,246 |
| The Juilliard School | ind. | $38,490 | $14,290 | 95% | 40% | $33,854 | $18,926 | $26,712 |
| Keuka College | ind. | $28,235 | $10,800 | 92% | 7% | $22,663 | $16,372 | NR |
| The King's College | ind. | $33,270 | $0† | 100% | 10% | $22,202 | $11,068 | $28,117 |
| Lehman College of the City University of New York | pub. | $6429 | NR | 97% | NR | NR | NR | $8525 |
| Le Moyne College | ind. | $31,340 | $12,130 | 100% | 27% | $24,792 | $18,678 | $34,500 |
| LIM College | ind. | $24,225 | $19,850 | 77% | 2% | $10,585 | $33,490 | $35,743 |
| Long Island University–LIU Brooklyn | ind. | $34,852 | $12,330 | 97% | 6% | $22,787 | $24,395 | $41,554 |
| Long Island University–LIU Post | ind. | $34,852 | $12,808 | 73% | 16% | $20,952 | $26,708 | $35,474 |
| Manhattan College | ind. | $37,498 | $13,740 | 99% | 42% | $25,805 | $25,433 | $37,449 |
| Manhattan School of Music | ind. | $42,500 | $14,224 | 91% | NR | NR | NR | $3694 |
| Manhattanville College | ind. | $36,220 | $14,520 | 73% | 18% | $26,787 | $23,953 | $33,444 |
| Marist College | ind. | $32,500 | $13,600 | 74% | 22% | $19,490 | $26,610 | $34,801 |
| Marymount Manhattan College | ind. | $27,636 | $15,000 | 99% | 4% | $15,264 | $27,372 | $29,419 |
| Medgar Evers College of the City University of New York | pub. | $6332 | NA | 98% | NR | $7914 | — | NR |
| Mercy College | ind. | $17,766 | $12,690 | 91% | 3% | $15,144 | $15,312 | $17,399 |
| Molloy College | ind. | $26,850 | $13,590 | 97% | 8% | $18,217 | $22,223 | NR |
| Monroe College | ind. | $13,740 | $9200 | 99% | 64% | $14,334 | $8606 | $27,986 |
| Morrisville State College | pub. | $7642 | $12,858 | 90% | NR | $9746 | $10,754 | $29,023 |
| Mount Saint Mary College | ind. | $27,312 | $13,556 | 100% | 17% | $18,750 | $22,118 | $31,764 |
| Nazareth College of Rochester | ind. | $30,562 | $12,598 | 100% | 26% | $25,715 | $17,445 | $35,396 |
| The New School for Jazz and Contemporary Music | ind. | NR | NR | 62% | 25% | $18,152 | — | $28,966 |
| New York Institute of Technology | ind. | $32,180 | $12,830 | 90% | NR | $23,003 | $22,007 | NR |
| New York School of Interior Design | ind. | $30,790 | $15,610† | 82% | NR | $12,685 | $33,715 | $33,146 |
| New York University | ind. | $46,170 | $16,782 | 93% | 11% | $33,980 | $28,972 | $27,977 |
| Niagara University | ind. | $29,060 | $11,950 | 100% | 51% | $25,245 | $15,765 | $30,289 |
| Nyack College | ind. | $24,300 | $8950 | 100% | 5% | $20,158 | $13,092 | $37,577 |
| Pace University | ind. | $39,697 | $15,774 | 100% | 13% | $31,015 | $24,456 | $35,442 |
| Pratt Institute | ind. | $46,586 | $11,496 | 85% | NR | $22,466 | $35,616 | $34,877 |
| Purchase College, State University of New York | pub. | $7933 | $12,232 | 81% | 4% | $9476 | $10,689 | $26,348 |
| Queens College of the City University of New York | pub. | $6638 | $11,000† | 76% | 72% | $6800 | $10,838 | NR |
| Rensselaer Polytechnic Institute | ind. | $47,908 | $13,620 | 100% | 26% | $37,760 | $23,768 | $41,814 |
| Roberts Wesleyan College | ind. | $28,068 | $9840 | 100% | 17% | $25,944 | $11,964 | $35,461 |
| Rochester Institute of Technology | ind. | $36,038 | $11,568 | 95% | 81% | $24,500 | $23,106 | $26,000 |
| The Sage Colleges | ind. | $28,200 | $11,830 | 88% | NR | NR | NR | $26,534 |
| St. Bonaventure University | ind. | $30,475 | $11,100 | 100% | 20% | $26,138 | $15,437 | $35,627 |
| St. Francis College | ind. | $22,300 | $12,000† | 100% | 8% | $14,280 | $20,020 | $23,835 |
| St. John Fisher College | ind. | $29,550 | $11,158 | 100% | 37% | $22,096 | $18,612 | $32,982 |
| St. John's University | ind. | $38,680 | $16,390 | 86% | 12% | $28,262 | $26,808 | $32,950 |
| St. Joseph's College, Long Island Campus | ind. | $24,130 | NA | 79% | 34% | $15,995 | $8135 | $23,603 |
| St. Joseph's College, New York | ind. | $24,130 | NR | 100% | 21% | $17,588 | $6542 | $23,772 |

NA = not applicable; NR = not reported; * = includes room and board; † = room only; — = not available.

# College Costs At-a-Glance

| | Institutional Control ind.=independent; pub.=public | Tuition and Fees | Room and Board | Percent of Eligible Freshmen Receiving Need-Based Gift Awards | Percent of Freshmen Whose Need Was Fully Met | Average Financial Aid Package for Freshmen | Average Net Cost After Aid | Average Indebtedness Upon Graduation |
|---|---|---|---|---|---|---|---|---|
| St. Lawrence University | ind. | $47,686 | $12,286 | 99% | 22% | $39,913 | $20,059 | $26,792 |
| St. Thomas Aquinas College | ind. | $28,130 | $11,680 | 94% | 15% | $13,815 | $25,995 | $28,750 |
| Sarah Lawrence College | ind. | $50,736 | $14,504 | 73% | 40% | $28,307 | $36,933 | $18,483 |
| School of Visual Arts | ind. | NR | NR | 79% | 3% | $15,651 | — | $33,172 |
| Siena College | ind. | $33,415 | $13,595 | 100% | 24% | $27,232 | $19,778 | $32,678 |
| Skidmore College | ind. | $47,314 | $12,628 | 100% | 100% | $40,200 | $19,742 | $22,887 |
| State University of New York at Fredonia | pub. | $7740 | $12,100 | 77% | 15% | $11,456 | $8384 | $28,900 |
| State University of New York at New Paltz | pub. | $7418 | $10,896 | 59% | 5% | $11,227 | $7087 | $25,874 |
| State University of New York at Oswego | pub. | $7581 | $12,690 | 95% | 10% | $11,391 | $8880 | $28,362 |
| State University of New York at Plattsburgh | pub. | $7497 | $11,304 | 90% | 22% | $12,168 | $6633 | $28,125 |
| State University of New York College at Cortland | pub. | $7719 | $12,040 | 67% | 11% | $13,607 | $6152 | $27,472 |
| State University of New York College at Geneseo | pub. | $7774 | $11,518 | 77% | 60% | $10,911 | $8381 | $23,308 |
| State University of New York College at Old Westbury | pub. | $7323 | $10,390 | NR | NR | NR | NR | NR |
| State University of New York College at Potsdam | pub. | $7553 | $10,920 | 90% | 44% | $15,189 | $3284 | $21,531 |
| State University of New York College of Agriculture and Technology at Cobleskill | pub. | $7609 | $12,140 | 100% | 1% | $8606 | $11,143 | $24,952 |
| State University of New York College of Environmental Science and Forestry | pub. | $7398 | $15,120 | 89% | 45% | $14,600 | $7918 | $25,399 |
| State University of New York College of Technology at Canton | pub. | $7509 | $11,300 | 92% | 17% | $10,622 | $8187 | $30,905 |
| State University of New York College of Technology at Delhi | pub. | $7530 | $10,970 | 86% | NR | NR | NR | NR |
| State University of New York Maritime College | pub. | $7446 | $11,040 | 64% | 4% | $6226 | $12,260 | NR |
| State University of New York Polytechnic Institute | pub. | $7440 | $11,236 | 90% | 99% | $9845 | $8831 | NR |
| Stony Brook University, State University of New York | pub. | $8430 | $11,648 | 89% | 21% | $12,474 | $7604 | $24,884 |
| Syracuse University | ind. | $41,886 | $14,460 | 92% | 42% | $35,510 | $20,836 | $34,584 |
| Union College | ind. | $48,384 | $11,856 | 96% | 100% | $37,631 | $22,609 | $29,586 |
| University at Albany, State University of New York | pub. | $8527 | $11,986 | 88% | 8% | $10,235 | $10,278 | $24,779 |
| University at Buffalo, the State University of New York | pub. | $8871 | $12,400 | 98% | 54% | $9558 | $11,713 | NR |
| University of Rochester | ind. | $46,960 | $13,708 | 100% | 91% | $42,161 | $18,507 | $30,604 |
| Utica College | ind. | $33,736 | $11,934 | 100% | 10% | $30,140 | $15,530 | $42,083 |
| Vassar College | ind. | $49,570 | $11,570 | 99% | 100% | $48,398 | $12,742 | $17,476 |
| Villa Maria College | ind. | $19,170 | NA | 100% | 57% | $14,358 | $4812 | $22,658 |
| Wagner College | ind. | $40,750 | $12,450 | 100% | 25% | $30,510 | $22,690 | NR |
| Webb Institute | ind. | $46,000 | $14,050 | 100% | NR | $46,250 | $13,800 | $10,000 |
| Wells College | ind. | $37,500 | $13,000 | 90% | 10% | $33,910 | $16,590 | $36,498 |
| Yeshiva University | ind. | $38,730 | $11,250 | 94% | 35% | $33,744 | $16,236 | $22,769 |
| York College of the City University of New York | pub. | $6447 | NA | 94% | 100% | $8302 | — | $4745 |
| **North Carolina** | | | | | | | | |
| Appalachian State University | pub. | $6553 | $7675 | 72% | 22% | $8876 | $5352 | $21,693 |
| Belmont Abbey College | ind. | $18,500 | $10,094 | 100% | 16% | $12,619 | $15,975 | $27,341 |
| Brevard College | ind. | $26,170 | $9375 | 82% | 1% | $10,466 | $25,079 | $35,211 |
| Cabarrus College of Health Sciences | ind. | $11,970 | NA | 100% | NR | NR | NR | NR |
| Campbell University | ind. | $27,530 | $9860 | 71% | 14% | $29,353 | $8037 | $27,578 |

NA = not applicable; NR = not reported; * = includes room and board; † = room only; — = not available.

# College Costs At-a-Glance

| | Institutional Control ind.=independent; pub.=public | Tuition and Fees | Room and Board | Percent of Eligible Freshmen Receiving Need-Based Gift Awards | Percent of Freshmen Whose Need Was Fully Met | Average Financial Aid Package for Freshmen | Average Net Cost After Aid | Average Indebtedness Upon Graduation |
|---|---|---|---|---|---|---|---|---|
| Catawba College | ind. | $28,730 | $10,360 | 81% | 16% | $25,419 | $13,671 | $28,132 |
| Charlotte Christian College and Theological Seminary | ind. | NR | NA | 100% | 100% | $8726 | — | $39,607 |
| Chowan University | ind. | $23,400 | $8680 | 100% | NR | $21,444 | $10,636 | $33,992 |
| Davidson College | ind. | $45,377 | $12,769 | 100% | 100% | $38,584 | $19,562 | $21,365 |
| Duke University | ind. | $48,562 | $12,576 | 94% | 100% | $43,452 | $17,686 | $20,556 |
| East Carolina University | pub. | $6143 | $8833 | 74% | 8% | $9718 | $5258 | $29,699 |
| Elizabeth City State University | pub. | $4428 | $7213 | 90% | NR | NR | NR | NR |
| Elon University | ind. | $31,247 | $10,667 | 87% | 16% | $15,874 | $26,040 | $27,176 |
| Fayetteville State University | pub. | $2743 | $6445 | 99% | 12% | $11,759 | — | $24,029 |
| Gardner-Webb University | ind. | $26,885 | $8780 | 83% | 20% | $22,219 | $13,446 | $29,543 |
| Greensboro College | ind. | $26,900 | $10,100 | 92% | 85% | $43,191 | — | NR |
| Guilford College | ind. | $33,430 | $9370 | 91% | 5% | $27,854 | $14,946 | $25,360 |
| Johnson C. Smith University | ind. | $18,236 | $7100 | 96% | 5% | $16,748 | $8588 | $33,377 |
| Lees-McRae College | ind. | $24,854 | $9782 | 100% | 3% | $22,790 | $11,846 | NR |
| Lenoir-Rhyne University | ind. | $32,140 | $11,060 | 100% | 14% | $26,842 | $16,358 | $27,814 |
| Meredith College | ind. | $32,220 | $9516 | 100% | 18% | $24,989 | $16,747 | $34,535 |
| Methodist University | ind. | NR | NR | 98% | 9% | $22,085 | — | $35,525 |
| Mid-Atlantic Christian University | ind. | $13,440 | $8200 | 100% | 5% | $11,514 | $10,126 | $33,980 |
| Montreat College | ind. | $24,240 | $8266 | 100% | 54% | $22,228 | $10,278 | $19,899 |
| North Carolina Agricultural and Technical State University | pub. | $5535 | $6755 | 76% | 14% | $14,536 | — | $26,265 |
| North Carolina Central University | pub. | $5525 | $8165 | 84% | 6% | $11,804 | $1886 | $31,747 |
| North Carolina State University | pub. | $8296 | $10,030 | 96% | 26% | $13,773 | $4553 | $20,482 |
| Piedmont International University | ind. | $9580 | $6542 | 75% | 5% | $6206 | $9916 | $17,929 |
| Queens University of Charlotte | ind. | NR | NR | 100% | 17% | $24,788 | — | $28,359 |
| St. Andrews University | ind. | $23,682 | $9898 | 100% | 4% | $22,338 | $11,242 | $27,760 |
| Salem College | ind. | $25,356 | $11,764 | NR | NR | NR | NR | NR |
| University of Mount Olive | ind. | $17,800 | $7200 | 99% | 20% | $15,647 | $9353 | $28,241 |
| University of North Carolina at Asheville | pub. | $6392 | $8332 | 94% | 21% | $10,787 | $3937 | $21,105 |
| The University of North Carolina at Chapel Hill | pub. | $8336 | $10,592 | 93% | 78% | $17,797 | $1131 | $18,945 |
| The University of North Carolina at Charlotte | pub. | $6277 | $9270 | 88% | 15% | $10,645 | $4902 | $26,488 |
| The University of North Carolina at Greensboro | pub. | $6442 | $7688 | 91% | 22% | $9951 | $4179 | $23,265 |
| The University of North Carolina at Pembroke | pub. | $5287 | $8101 | 86% | 6% | $9233 | $4155 | $24,860 |
| University of North Carolina School of the Arts | pub. | $8363 | $8570 | 89% | 7% | $12,273 | $4660 | $22,697 |
| The University of North Carolina Wilmington | pub. | $6392 | $9124 | 89% | 11% | $9380 | $6136 | $6630 |
| Wake Forest University | ind. | $47,682 | $12,996 | 93% | 80% | $41,169 | $19,509 | $34,745 |
| Warren Wilson College | ind. | $32,560 | $9900 | 87% | 15% | $29,801 | $12,659 | $24,839 |
| Western Carolina University | pub. | $6531 | $8016 | 98% | 11% | $8709 | $5838 | $23,806 |
| William Peace University | ind. | $25,850 | $9900 | 88% | 16% | $24,109 | $11,641 | $32,000 |
| Wingate University | ind. | $28,110 | $10,600 | 100% | 25% | $21,332 | $17,378 | $29,939 |
| **North Dakota** | | | | | | | | |
| Dickinson State University | pub. | $6050 | $5850 | 86% | 43% | $15,301 | — | $24,244 |
| Mayville State University | pub. | $6489 | $5430 | 88% | 26% | $13,827 | — | $31,681 |

NA = not applicable; NR = not reported; * = includes room and board; † = room only; — = not available.

# College Costs At-a-Glance

| | Institutional Control ind.=independent; pub.=public | Tuition and Fees | Room and Board | Percent of Eligible Freshmen Receiving Need-Based Gift Awards | Percent of Freshmen Whose Need Was Fully Met | Average Financial Aid Package for Freshmen | Average Net Cost After Aid | Average Indebtedness Upon Graduation |
|---|---|---|---|---|---|---|---|---|
| Minot State University | pub. | $6086 | $5550 | 97% | 31% | $8582 | $3054 | $24,856 |
| University of Jamestown | ind. | $19,870 | $6860 | 100% | 27% | $14,330 | $12,400 | $26,530 |
| Valley City State University | pub. | $6674 | $5938 | 91% | 32% | $8641 | $3971 | $27,756 |
| **Ohio** | | | | | | | | |
| Antioch University Midwest | ind. | $19,407 | NA | NR | NR | NR | NR | NR |
| Ashland University | ind. | $19,852 | $9502 | 95% | NR | $17,592 | $11,762 | $36,779 |
| Baldwin Wallace University | ind. | $28,814 | $8048 | 100% | 31% | $24,907 | $11,955 | $32,526 |
| Bluffton University | ind. | $29,316 | $9832 | 100% | 42% | $28,765 | $10,383 | $35,883 |
| Bowling Green State University | pub. | $10,726 | $8244 | 91% | 14% | $14,042 | $4928 | $30,307 |
| Capital University | ind. | $31,990 | $9060 | 99% | 26% | $27,037 | $14,013 | $33,833 |
| Case Western Reserve University | ind. | $43,158 | $13,376 | 80% | 29% | $38,625 | $17,909 | $33,343 |
| Cedarville University | ind. | $27,206 | $6542 | 86% | 41% | $17,899 | $15,849 | $29,105 |
| Cincinnati Christian University | ind. | $16,216 | $7860 | 97% | 9% | $14,350 | $9726 | $32,675 |
| Cleveland Institute of Art | ind. | $38,320 | $11,455 | 100% | 8% | $25,723 | $24,052 | $30,681 |
| Cleveland Institute of Music | ind. | $45,627 | $13,357 | 100% | 35% | $29,346 | $29,638 | $27,157 |
| Cleveland State University | pub. | $9686 | $11,858 | 83% | 9% | $9168 | $12,376 | $24,856 |
| The College of Wooster | ind. | $43,350 | $10,250 | 99% | 56% | $38,821 | $14,779 | $24,506 |
| Columbus College of Art & Design | ind. | $29,892 | $7980 | 100% | 4% | $19,011 | $18,861 | $32,006 |
| Denison University | ind. | $47,290 | $11,570 | 100% | 36% | $41,384 | $17,476 | NR |
| Franciscan University of Steubenville | ind. | $24,780 | $8300 | 100% | 18% | $13,523 | $19,557 | $32,443 |
| Heidelberg University | ind. | $27,480 | $9226 | 100% | 15% | $23,863 | $12,843 | $36,962 |
| John Carroll University | ind. | $37,180 | $10,920 | 98% | 26% | $28,900 | $19,200 | $30,837 |
| Kent State University | pub. | $10,012 | $9908 | 52% | 13% | $9571 | $10,349 | $32,393 |
| Kent State University at Geauga | pub. | $5664 | NA | 71% | 5% | $6229 | — | NR |
| Kent State University at Stark | pub. | $5664 | NA | 73% | 5% | $5715 | — | NR |
| Kenyon College | ind. | $49,140 | $11,890 | 97% | 58% | $39,738 | $21,292 | $20,323 |
| Lake Erie College | ind. | $29,162 | $9178 | 99% | 11% | $24,876 | $13,464 | $34,114 |
| Malone University | ind. | $27,440 | $9266 | 100% | 19% | $23,406 | $13,300 | $30,679 |
| Marietta College | ind. | $33,140 | $10,395 | 95% | 20% | $29,061 | $14,474 | $39,708 |
| Mercy College of Ohio | ind. | NR | NR | 57% | 4% | $4707 | — | $28,842 |
| Miami University | pub. | $14,287 | $11,109 | 66% | 24% | $12,599 | $12,797 | $27,181 |
| Mount Carmel College of Nursing | ind. | $12,016 | $5000† | 55% | 31% | $6036 | $10,980 | $35,952 |
| Mount St. Joseph University | ind. | $26,850 | $8710 | 100% | 23% | $20,464 | $15,096 | NR |
| Muskingum University | ind. | NR | NR | 100% | 25% | $25,588 | — | $33,488 |
| Oberlin College | ind. | $50,564 | $13,630 | 99% | 100% | $37,344 | $26,850 | $25,018 |
| The Ohio State University | pub. | $10,037 | $9850 | 90% | 26% | $13,179 | $6708 | $26,830 |
| Ohio University | pub. | $10,602 | $10,478 | 91% | 28% | $8975 | $12,105 | $27,645 |
| Ohio University–Chillicothe | pub. | NR | NA | 86% | 8% | $6968 | — | $27,645 |
| Ohio University–Eastern | pub. | $4872 | NA | 87% | 17% | $5672 | — | $27,645 |
| Ohio University–Lancaster | pub. | NR | NA | 83% | 16% | $6320 | — | $27,645 |
| Ohio University–Southern Campus | pub. | NR | NA | 92% | 9% | $7448 | — | $27,645 |
| Ohio University–Zanesville | pub. | NR | NR | 90% | 13% | $6724 | — | $27,645 |

NA = not applicable; NR = not reported; * = includes room and board; † = room only; — = not available.

# College Costs At-a-Glance

| | Institutional Control ind.=independent; pub.=public | Tuition and Fees | Room and Board | Percent of Eligible Freshmen Receiving Need-Based Gift Awards | Percent of Freshmen Whose Need Was Fully Met | Average Financial Aid Package for Freshmen | Average Net Cost After Aid | Average Indebtedness Upon Graduation |
|---|---|---|---|---|---|---|---|---|
| Ohio Wesleyan University | ind. | $41,920 | $11,210 | 100% | 25% | $32,555 | $20,575 | $28,516 |
| Otterbein University | ind. | $31,624 | $9460 | 98% | 21% | $23,871 | $17,213 | $37,388 |
| Shawnee State University | pub. | $7364 | $9552 | NR | NR | NR | NR | NR |
| Tiffin University | ind. | $21,560 | $9870 | 100% | 11% | $18,639 | $12,791 | $32,679 |
| The University of Akron | pub. | $10,260 | $10,968 | 55% | 9% | $7825 | $13,403 | $23,124 |
| University of Cincinnati | pub. | $3318 | $10,750 | 41% | 7% | $8662 | $5406 | $28,228 |
| University of Dayton | ind. | $37,230 | $11,840 | 100% | 31% | $26,436 | $22,634 | $35,278 |
| The University of Findlay | ind. | $30,640 | $9350 | 100% | 18% | $20,543 | $19,447 | $34,434 |
| University of Mount Union | ind. | $27,990 | $9200 | 100% | 10% | $21,906 | $15,284 | $34,586 |
| University of Rio Grande | ind. | $21,930 | $9450 | 73% | 74% | $5555 | $25,825 | $28,617 |
| The University of Toledo | pub. | $9463 | $10,304 | 98% | 17% | $11,753 | $8014 | $27,928 |
| Ursuline College | ind. | $28,520 | $9490 | 100% | 19% | $24,288 | $13,722 | $29,542 |
| Wittenberg University | ind. | $38,090 | $10,028 | 100% | 23% | $33,733 | $14,385 | $30,748 |
| Wright State University | pub. | $8730 | $9108 | 88% | 19% | $10,735 | $7103 | $30,778 |
| Xavier University | ind. | $33,960 | $11,020 | 97% | 19% | $20,827 | $24,153 | $34,365 |
| Youngstown State University | pub. | $8317 | $8645 | 81% | 11% | $8226 | $8736 | $30,481 |
| **Oklahoma** | | | | | | | | |
| Cameron University | pub. | $5340 | $4664 | 81% | 15% | $8579 | $1425 | $20,512 |
| East Central University | pub. | $5599 | $5158 | 97% | NR | $9218 | $1539 | $21,806 |
| Hillsdale Free Will Baptist College | ind. | $11,980 | $6830 | 69% | NR | $10,000 | $8810 | $23,500 |
| Langston University | pub. | $4801 | $8720 | 94% | 25% | $14,598 | — | NR |
| Northeastern State University | pub. | $5284 | $6300 | 91% | 90% | $10,560 | $1024 | $24,431 |
| Northwestern Oklahoma State University | pub. | $5843 | $4230 | 86% | NR | NR | NR | $16,932 |
| Oklahoma Baptist University | ind. | $24,000 | $6780 | 82% | 26% | $19,822 | $10,958 | $26,557 |
| Oklahoma Christian University | ind. | $19,890 | $7030 | 65% | 46% | $21,135 | $5785 | $27,065 |
| Oklahoma City University | ind. | $30,726 | $9750 | 100% | 82% | $22,310 | $18,166 | $27,819 |
| Oklahoma State University | pub. | $7441 | $7390 | 78% | 17% | $13,284 | $1547 | $22,591 |
| Oklahoma Wesleyan University | ind. | $23,180 | $7488 | 100% | 13% | $15,264 | $15,404 | $28,072 |
| Oral Roberts University | ind. | $23,410 | $9765 | 98% | 35% | $24,133 | $9042 | $32,750 |
| Rogers State University | pub. | $5321 | $8830 | 82% | 7% | $9469 | $4682 | $13,403 |
| Southeastern Oklahoma State University | pub. | $5688 | $6143 | 73% | 9% | $10,410 | $1421 | $19,368 |
| Southwestern Oklahoma State University | pub. | NR | NR | 89% | 27% | $5631 | — | $16,262 |
| University of Central Oklahoma | pub. | $6686 | $9862 | 82% | 22% | $8588 | $7960 | $24,530 |
| University of Oklahoma | pub. | $7695 | $9126 | 55% | 82% | $11,633 | $5188 | $23,151 |
| University of Science and Arts of Oklahoma | pub. | $6270 | $5470 | 98% | 25% | $10,779 | $961 | $20,074 |
| The University of Tulsa | ind. | $39,036 | $10,680 | 30% | 56% | $28,252 | $21,464 | $29,161 |
| **Oregon** | | | | | | | | |
| Corban University | ind. | $28,640 | $8892 | 98% | 16% | $21,012 | $16,520 | $26,407 |
| George Fox University | ind. | $31,866 | $9864 | 84% | 44% | $27,919 | $13,811 | $25,143 |
| Lewis & Clark College | ind. | $43,382 | $11,000 | 99% | 21% | $36,083 | $18,299 | $27,421 |
| Linfield College | ind. | $37,346 | $10,330 | 84% | 32% | $32,134 | $15,542 | $28,697 |
| Marylhurst University | ind. | $20,345 | NA | NR | NR | NR | NR | $34,399 |

**NA = not applicable; NR = not reported; * = includes room and board; † = room only; — = not available.**

# College Costs At-a-Glance

| | Institutional Control ind.=independent; pub.=public | Tuition and Fees | Room and Board | Percent of Eligible Freshmen Receiving Need-Based Gift Awards | Percent of Freshmen Whose Need Was Fully Met | Average Financial Aid Package for Freshmen | Average Net Cost After Aid | Average Indebtedness Upon Graduation |
|---|---|---|---|---|---|---|---|---|
| Northwest Christian University | ind. | $26,180 | $8200 | 100% | 25% | $21,760 | $12,620 | $29,485 |
| Oregon Institute of Technology | pub. | NR | NR | 77% | 38% | $7246 | — | $29,685 |
| Oregon State University | pub. | $9122 | $11,151 | 82% | 9% | $11,695 | $8578 | $21,955 |
| Pacific University | ind. | $39,858 | $11,448 | 70% | 17% | $32,804 | $18,502 | $25,844 |
| Portland State University | pub. | $7794 | $11,349 | 79% | 8% | $10,078 | $9065 | $28,410 |
| Reed College | ind. | $47,760 | $12,200 | 98% | 99% | $47,253 | $12,707 | $19,151 |
| Southern Oregon University | pub. | $7720 | $11,397 | 84% | 9% | $8560 | $10,557 | $30,936 |
| University of Oregon | pub. | $9918 | $11,442 | 77% | 12% | $10,187 | $11,173 | $24,508 |
| University of Portland | ind. | $38,520 | $11,444 | 80% | 8% | $28,002 | $21,962 | $26,557 |
| Warner Pacific College | ind. | $20,300 | $8230 | 64% | 16% | $18,796 | $9734 | $31,338 |
| Western Oregon University | pub. | $8723 | $9416 | 87% | 10% | $9866 | $8273 | $28,331 |
| Willamette University | ind. | $44,076 | $10,820 | 97% | 34% | $34,279 | $20,617 | $26,936 |
| **Pennsylvania** | | | | | | | | |
| Albright College | ind. | $38,220 | $10,400 | 100% | 9% | $35,460 | $13,160 | $28,541 |
| Allegheny College | ind. | $42,470 | $10,740 | 100% | 43% | $35,861 | $17,349 | NR |
| Alvernia University | ind. | $31,100 | $10,820 | 100% | 8% | $21,851 | $20,069 | $39,560 |
| Arcadia University | ind. | $39,560 | $13,200 | 100% | 12% | $29,998 | $22,762 | NR |
| Bloomsburg University of Pennsylvania | pub. | $8914 | $8168 | 64% | 8% | $8183 | $8899 | $29,661 |
| Bryn Mawr College | ind. | $47,140 | $14,850 | 100% | 100% | $42,724 | $19,266 | $24,466 |
| Bucknell University | ind. | $50,152 | $12,216 | 94% | 90% | $31,500 | $30,868 | $22,500 |
| Cabrini College | ind. | $29,842 | $12,226 | 82% | 21% | $14,689 | $27,379 | $35,880 |
| Cairn University | ind. | $23,920 | $9350 | 100% | 13% | $20,728 | $12,542 | $33,016 |
| California University of Pennsylvania | pub. | $9556 | $10,086 | 86% | 9% | $10,041 | $9601 | $29,105 |
| Carnegie Mellon University | ind. | $49,022 | $12,400 | 95% | 30% | $34,870 | $26,552 | $31,905 |
| Cedar Crest College | ind. | $34,504 | $10,549 | 100% | 14% | $29,266 | $15,787 | $41,939 |
| Chatham University | ind. | $34,440 | $10,720 | 93% | 40% | $30,217 | $14,943 | $32,814 |
| Chestnut Hill College | ind. | $33,120 | $10,200 | 99% | 10% | $25,572 | $17,748 | $35,376 |
| Clarion University of Pennsylvania | pub. | $9788 | $8152 | 81% | 27% | $11,625 | $6315 | $21,507 |
| Delaware Valley University | ind. | NR | NR | 99% | 11% | $24,327 | — | $39,671 |
| DeSales University | ind. | $32,350 | $11,760 | 100% | 22% | $25,398 | $18,712 | $36,798 |
| Dickinson College | ind. | $47,692 | $11,972 | 97% | 68% | $38,630 | $21,034 | $25,392 |
| Drexel University | ind. | $47,051 | $14,367 | 100% | 22% | $33,002 | $28,416 | NR |
| Duquesne University | ind. | $32,636 | $11,084 | 100% | 28% | $24,850 | $18,870 | $34,522 |
| Eastern University | ind. | $30,590 | $10,188 | 74% | 28% | $22,088 | $18,690 | $34,662 |
| East Stroudsburg University of Pennsylvania | pub. | $9376 | $7980 | 68% | NR | $3834 | $13,522 | $27,730 |
| Elizabethtown College | ind. | $41,710 | $10,140 | 100% | 26% | $28,192 | $23,658 | $30,355 |
| Franklin & Marshall College | ind. | $48,514 | $12,285 | 98% | 100% | $45,769 | $15,030 | $27,474 |
| Gannon University | ind. | $28,368 | $11,240 | 98% | 20% | $24,282 | $15,326 | NR |
| Geneva College | ind. | $25,450 | $9630 | 100% | 17% | $20,783 | $14,297 | $32,673 |
| Gettysburg College | ind. | $47,480 | $11,340 | 97% | 90% | $36,825 | $21,995 | $27,714 |
| Grove City College | ind. | $15,550 | $8472 | 99% | 9% | $6958 | $17,064 | $31,634 |
| Gwynedd Mercy University | ind. | $31,360 | $11,010 | 100% | 12% | $23,366 | $19,004 | $37,860 |

NA = not applicable; NR = not reported; * = includes room and board; † = room only; — = not available.

# College Costs At-a-Glance

| | Institutional Control ind.=independent; pub.=public | Tuition and Fees | Room and Board | Percent of Eligible Freshmen Receiving Need-Based Gift Awards | Percent of Freshmen Whose Need Was Fully Met | Average Financial Aid Package for Freshmen | Average Net Cost After Aid | Average Indebtedness Upon Graduation |
|---|---|---|---|---|---|---|---|---|
| Haverford College | ind. | $49,098 | $14,888 | 95% | 100% | $43,864 | $20,122 | $15,540 |
| Holy Family University | ind. | $29,168 | $13,576 | 100% | 17% | $25,349 | $17,395 | $40,363 |
| Indiana University of Pennsylvania | pub. | $9470 | $11,346 | 67% | 7% | $10,111 | $10,705 | $33,807 |
| Juniata College | ind. | $40,600 | $11,140 | 100% | 25% | $31,877 | $19,863 | $33,421 |
| Keystone College | ind. | $21,900 | $9900 | 100% | 12% | $18,996 | $12,804 | NR |
| King's College | ind. | $31,816 | $11,686 | 98% | 16% | $23,188 | $20,314 | $29,432 |
| Kutztown University of Pennsylvania | pub. | $8833 | $8430 | 62% | 6% | $7602 | $9661 | $33,376 |
| Lafayette College | ind. | $45,635 | $13,520 | 97% | 91% | $42,316 | $16,839 | $27,497 |
| Lancaster Bible College | ind. | NR | NR | 98% | 7% | $12,854 | — | $20,959 |
| La Roche College | ind. | $25,500 | $10,324 | 95% | 38% | $28,966 | $6858 | $26,713 |
| La Salle University | ind. | $39,800 | $13,940 | 99% | 14% | $28,051 | $25,689 | $35,327 |
| Lebanon Valley College | ind. | $37,470 | $10,100 | 99% | 20% | $31,010 | $16,560 | $36,752 |
| Lehigh University | ind. | $44,890 | $11,880 | 97% | 40% | $36,551 | $20,219 | $31,877 |
| Lincoln University | pub. | $10,232 | $8686 | 100% | 100% | NR | NR | $12,082 |
| Lock Haven University of Pennsylvania | pub. | $9276 | $8752 | 80% | 42% | $11,178 | $6850 | $29,353 |
| Lycoming College | ind. | $35,900 | $10,884 | 100% | 23% | $33,897 | $12,887 | NR |
| Mansfield University of Pennsylvania | pub. | $9526 | $10,936 | 69% | 8% | $8535 | $11,927 | $33,799 |
| Marywood University | ind. | $32,692 | $13,900 | 85% | 21% | $25,721 | $20,871 | $41,559 |
| Mercyhurst University | ind. | $31,485 | $10,800 | 96% | 18% | $26,758 | $15,527 | $24,739 |
| Messiah College | ind. | $32,240 | $9630 | 99% | 21% | $23,466 | $18,404 | $34,301 |
| Millersville University of Pennsylvania | pub. | $10,268 | $11,380 | 76% | 9% | $8025 | $13,623 | $29,791 |
| Misericordia University | ind. | $29,010 | $12,050 | 99% | 25% | $20,101 | $20,959 | $35,140 |
| Moravian College | ind. | $37,572 | $11,082 | 100% | 12% | $29,241 | $19,413 | NR |
| Mount Aloysius College | ind. | NR | NR | 100% | NR | $15,525 | — | NR |
| Muhlenberg College | ind. | $44,145 | $10,450 | 99% | 86% | $31,900 | $22,695 | $29,702 |
| Peirce College | ind. | $13,800 | NA | 100% | NR | $14,150 | — | NR |
| Penn State Abington | pub. | $13,942 | NA | 84% | 3% | $11,384 | $2558 | $36,935 |
| Penn State Altoona | pub. | $14,588 | $10,520 | 62% | 7% | $10,875 | $14,233 | $36,935 |
| Penn State Beaver | pub. | $13,636 | $10,520 | 71% | 5% | $11,363 | $12,793 | $36,935 |
| Penn State Berks | pub. | $14,588 | $11,500 | 71% | 2% | $9863 | $16,225 | $36,935 |
| Penn State Brandywine | pub. | $13,942 | NA | 76% | 8% | $9841 | $4101 | $36,935 |
| Penn State Erie, The Behrend College | pub. | $14,588 | $10,520 | 67% | 3% | $10,811 | $14,297 | $36,935 |
| Penn State Greater Allegheny | pub. | $13,648 | $10,520 | 85% | 7% | $13,069 | $11,099 | $36,935 |
| Penn State Harrisburg | pub. | $14,588 | $11,980 | 63% | 7% | $10,644 | $15,924 | $36,935 |
| Penn State Hazleton | pub. | $13,882 | $10,520 | 74% | 3% | $10,929 | $13,473 | $36,935 |
| Penn State Lehigh Valley | pub. | $13,930 | NA | 77% | 3% | $9310 | $4620 | $36,935 |
| Penn State New Kensington | pub. | $13,588 | NR | 82% | 6% | $10,761 | $2827 | $36,935 |
| Penn State Schuylkill | pub. | $13,870 | $7886 | 84% | 8% | $13,076 | $8680 | $36,935 |
| Penn State University Park | pub. | $17,502 | $10,520 | 45% | 8% | $10,039 | $17,983 | $36,935 |
| Penn State Wilkes-Barre | pub. | $13,588 | NA | 77% | 8% | $9949 | $3639 | $36,935 |
| Penn State Worthington Scranton | pub. | $13,882 | NA | 87% | 6% | $9957 | $3925 | $36,935 |
| Penn State York | pub. | $13,930 | NA | 79% | 8% | $10,442 | $3488 | $36,935 |

NA = not applicable; NR = not reported; * = includes room and board; † = room only; — = not available.

# College Costs At-a-Glance

| | Institutional Control ind.=independent; pub.=public | Tuition and Fees | Room and Board | Percent of Eligible Freshmen Receiving Need-Based Gift Awards | Percent of Freshmen Whose Need Was Fully Met | Average Financial Aid Package for Freshmen | Average Net Cost After Aid | Average Indebtedness Upon Graduation |
|---|---|---|---|---|---|---|---|---|
| Pennsylvania College of Technology | pub. | $15,450 | $10,836 | 79% | NR | $11,579 | $14,707 | NR |
| Philadelphia University | ind. | $35,080 | $11,610 | 100% | 28% | $28,420 | $18,270 | $40,101 |
| Robert Morris University | ind. | $26,054 | $11,810 | 100% | 13% | $22,315 | $15,549 | $37,531 |
| Rosemont College | ind. | $31,580 | $12,880 | 99% | 14% | $35,709 | $8751 | $40,792 |
| Saint Francis University | ind. | $32,128 | $11,082 | 55% | 20% | $22,960 | $20,250 | $36,656 |
| Saint Joseph's University | ind. | $40,580 | $14,426 | 97% | 22% | $26,081 | $28,925 | NR |
| Saint Vincent College | ind. | $30,706 | $9538 | 64% | 24% | $28,780 | $11,464 | $29,464 |
| Seton Hill University | ind. | $32,037 | $10,739 | 100% | 22% | $25,414 | $17,362 | $36,295 |
| Shippensburg University of Pennsylvania | pub. | $9774 | $11,160 | 75% | 8% | $8221 | $12,713 | $29,988 |
| Slippery Rock University of Pennsylvania | pub. | $9309 | $9794 | 61% | 13% | $8314 | $10,789 | $30,458 |
| Susquehanna University | ind. | $40,350 | $10,800 | 100% | 24% | $30,922 | $20,228 | $29,734 |
| Swarthmore College | ind. | $46,060 | $13,550 | 100% | 100% | $43,934 | $15,676 | $21,866 |
| Temple University | pub. | $15,096 | $10,738 | 86% | 30% | $16,444 | $9390 | $35,760 |
| Thiel College | ind. | $27,828 | $10,900 | 100% | 9% | $23,644 | $15,084 | $37,932 |
| Thomas Jefferson University | ind. | NR | NR | NR | NR | NR | NR | $55,363 |
| University of Pennsylvania | ind. | $47,668 | $13,464 | 99% | 100% | $43,166 | $17,966 | $19,442 |
| University of Pittsburgh | pub. | $17,772 | $10,800 | 79% | 11% | $14,031 | $14,541 | $36,466 |
| University of Pittsburgh at Bradford | pub. | $13,322 | $8480 | 94% | 10% | $14,106 | $7696 | $37,157 |
| University of Pittsburgh at Greensburg | pub. | $13,372 | $9490 | 85% | 15% | $11,753 | $11,109 | $34,451 |
| University of Pittsburgh at Johnstown | pub. | $13,374 | $9080 | 83% | 15% | $11,154 | $11,300 | $34,162 |
| The University of Scranton | ind. | $39,956 | $13,566 | 98% | 12% | $24,093 | $29,429 | $38,640 |
| University of the Sciences | ind. | $36,096 | $14,108 | 85% | 43% | $20,894 | $29,310 | NR |
| University of Valley Forge | ind. | $20,364 | $8116 | 99% | 12% | $13,286 | $15,194 | $31,570 |
| Ursinus College | ind. | $46,080 | $11,500 | 100% | 24% | $36,276 | $21,304 | $35,360 |
| Villanova University | ind. | $45,966 | $12,278 | 94% | 19% | $35,413 | $22,831 | $35,122 |
| Washington & Jefferson College | ind. | $41,282 | $10,884 | 89% | 15% | $34,720 | $17,446 | NR |
| Waynesburg University | ind. | $21,290 | $8860 | 100% | 26% | $17,898 | $12,252 | $30,250 |
| West Chester University of Pennsylvania | pub. | $9054 | $8042 | 47% | 7% | $6983 | $10,113 | $30,881 |
| Westminster College | ind. | $33,410 | $10,160 | 100% | 15% | $26,945 | $16,625 | $35,333 |
| Widener University | ind. | $39,830 | $12,588 | 97% | 41% | $32,294 | $20,124 | NR |
| Wilkes University | ind. | $31,262 | $12,808 | 99% | 10% | $25,626 | $18,444 | $38,082 |
| Wilson College | ind. | $24,380 | $10,700 | 99% | 19% | $23,120 | $11,960 | $30,423 |
| York College of Pennsylvania | ind. | $18,240 | $10,160 | 61% | 27% | $14,074 | $14,326 | $35,669 |
| **Puerto Rico** | | | | | | | | |
| Inter American University of Puerto Rico, Bayamón Campus | ind. | $5860 | NR | 84% | 1% | $241 | $5619 | NR |
| Inter American University of Puerto Rico, Guayama Campus | ind. | $5534 | NA | 23% | 1% | $197 | $5337 | NR |
| Universidad Teolgica del Caribe | ind. | $4448 | $2400 | 100% | NR | NR | NR | NR |
| **Rhode Island** | | | | | | | | |
| Brown University | ind. | $47,434 | $11,994 | 96% | 100% | $43,239 | $16,189 | $24,300 |
| Bryant University | ind. | $39,808 | $14,553 | 71% | 50% | $20,968 | $33,393 | $39,283 |
| Providence College | ind. | $44,323 | $13,060 | 100% | 25% | $28,448 | $28,935 | $32,475 |
| Rhode Island College | pub. | $7602 | $10,094 | 88% | 14% | $9501 | $8195 | $25,567 |

NA = not applicable; NR = not reported; * = includes room and board; † = room only; — = not available.

# College Costs At-a-Glance

| | Institutional Control ind.=independent; pub.=public | Tuition and Fees | Room and Board | Percent of Eligible Freshmen Receiving Need-Based Gift Awards | Percent of Freshmen Whose Need Was Fully Met | Average Financial Aid Package for Freshmen | Average Net Cost After Aid | Average Indebtedness Upon Graduation |
|---|---|---|---|---|---|---|---|---|
| Rhode Island School of Design | ind. | $44,594 | $12,640 | 73% | 3% | $27,500 | $29,734 | $30,376 |
| Roger Williams University | ind. | $31,750 | $14,546 | 76% | 9% | $20,071 | $26,225 | $40,612 |
| Salve Regina University | ind. | $35,690 | $12,860 | 100% | 13% | $27,310 | $21,240 | $38,425 |
| University of Rhode Island | pub. | $12,506 | $7256 | 89% | 99% | $16,091 | $3671 | $30,731 |
| **South Carolina** | | | | | | | | |
| Anderson University | ind. | $23,750 | $8674 | 63% | 48% | $18,913 | $13,511 | $32,298 |
| Bob Jones University | ind. | $14,220 | $6090 | NR | NR | NR | NR | NR |
| The Citadel, The Military College of South Carolina | pub. | $12,568 | $6381 | 82% | 18% | $14,073 | $4876 | $29,701 |
| Clemson University | pub. | $13,808 | $8358 | 94% | 23% | $12,640 | $9526 | $30,213 |
| Coastal Carolina University | pub. | $10,140 | $8440 | 52% | 9% | $10,100 | $8480 | $35,207 |
| Coker College | ind. | $25,536 | $7830 | 95% | 28% | $22,483 | $10,883 | NR |
| College of Charleston | pub. | NR | NR | 74% | 23% | $13,290 | | $25,644 |
| Columbia International University | ind. | $20,430 | $7530 | 100% | 15% | $16,021 | $11,939 | $24,428 |
| Converse College | ind. | $16,500 | $9500 | 100% | 21% | $14,925 | $11,075 | $32,063 |
| Francis Marion University | pub. | $9738 | $7256 | 98% | 12% | $12,169 | $4825 | $28,979 |
| Furman University | ind. | $44,668 | $11,204 | 100% | 36% | $36,743 | $19,129 | $25,903 |
| Newberry College | ind. | $24,300 | $9300 | 100% | 16% | $22,604 | $10,996 | $31,951 |
| Presbyterian College | ind. | $34,828 | $9344 | 100% | 38% | $32,936 | $11,236 | $30,835 |
| University of South Carolina | pub. | $11,158 | $9248 | 41% | 23% | $9411 | $10,995 | $28,233 |
| University of South Carolina Aiken | pub. | $9602 | $7110 | 93% | 13% | $9999 | $6713 | $28,104 |
| University of South Carolina Upstate | pub. | $10,518 | $7682 | 72% | 13% | $9434 | $8766 | $22,660 |
| Winthrop University | pub. | $13,812 | $8182 | 99% | 18% | $13,733 | $8261 | $32,165 |
| Wofford College | ind. | $37,120 | $10,730 | 100% | 35% | $32,533 | $15,317 | $24,999 |
| **South Dakota** | | | | | | | | |
| Augustana College | ind. | $29,214 | $7028 | 100% | 32% | $25,651 | $10,591 | $35,385 |
| Dakota State University | pub. | $8286 | $5941 | 56% | 8% | $7250 | $6977 | $24,728 |
| Dakota Wesleyan University | ind. | $23,650 | $6800 | 100% | 24% | $22,250 | $8200 | $32,752 |
| Mount Marty College | ind. | $22,892 | $6978 | 99% | 49% | $27,730 | $2140 | $33,945 |
| Northern State University | pub. | $8043 | $6942 | 92% | 29% | $10,303 | $4682 | $27,487 |
| South Dakota School of Mines and Technology | pub. | $10,040 | $6370 | 74% | 46% | $13,500 | $2910 | $22,810 |
| South Dakota State University | pub. | $7713 | $6985 | 47% | 37% | $11,975 | $2723 | $23,183 |
| The University of South Dakota | pub. | $8022 | $7089 | 55% | 68% | $5867 | $9244 | $25,554 |
| **Tennessee** | | | | | | | | |
| American Baptist College of American Baptist Theological Seminary | ind. | $9622 | $5840 | 100% | 67% | $10,412 | $5050 | $9743 |
| Belmont University | ind. | $28,660 | $10,530 | 85% | 10% | $15,369 | $23,821 | $28,306 |
| Carson-Newman University | ind. | $25,360 | $8270 | 100% | 23% | $23,193 | $10,437 | $25,555 |
| Christian Brothers University | ind. | $30,106 | $7000 | 100% | 21% | $25,607 | $11,499 | $22,759 |
| Cumberland University | ind. | $21,210 | $7550 | 48% | 18% | $18,281 | $10,479 | $25,827 |
| Freed-Hardeman University | ind. | $20,468 | $7390 | 100% | 25% | $19,364 | $8494 | $31,185 |
| King University | ind. | $25,708 | $8180 | 97% | 19% | $22,492 | $11,396 | $21,091 |

**NA = not applicable; NR = not reported; \* = includes room and board; † = room only; — = not available.**

# College Costs At-a-Glance

| | Institutional Control ind.=independent; pub.=public | Tuition and Fees | Room and Board | Percent of Eligible Freshmen Receiving Need-Based Gift Awards | Percent of Freshmen Whose Need Was Fully Met | Average Financial Aid Package for Freshmen | Average Net Cost After Aid | Average Indebtedness Upon Graduation |
|---|---|---|---|---|---|---|---|---|
| Lee University | ind. | $15,000 | $7045 | 93% | 23% | $12,764 | $9281 | $32,163 |
| LeMoyne-Owen College | ind. | $10,900 | $5910 | 100% | 3% | $10,676 | $6134 | $27,441 |
| Lincoln Memorial University | ind. | $20,546 | $7300 | 95% | 16% | $18,281 | $9565 | $19,987 |
| Lipscomb University | ind. | $27,390 | $10,350 | 36% | 28% | $19,062 | $18,678 | $30,480 |
| Maryville College | ind. | $32,866 | $10,442 | 100% | 18% | $32,550 | $10,758 | NR |
| Middle Tennessee State University | pub. | $7876 | $8302 | 65% | 14% | $10,518 | $5660 | $24,834 |
| Milligan College | ind. | $29,830 | $6500 | 100% | 34% | $22,236 | $14,094 | $25,626 |
| Rhodes College | ind. | $43,224 | $10,746 | 100% | 56% | $34,061 | $19,909 | $27,077 |
| Sewanee: The University of the South | ind. | $38,700 | $11,050 | 99% | 36% | $31,889 | $17,861 | $21,277 |
| Tennessee State University | pub. | $6930 | $6240 | 84% | 9% | $11,434 | $1736 | $35,645 |
| Tennessee Technological University | pub. | $7498 | $8296 | 53% | 10% | $10,292 | $5502 | $18,467 |
| Tennessee Wesleyan College | ind. | $22,900 | $7310 | 100% | 18% | $18,112 | $12,098 | $21,280 |
| Trevecca Nazarene University | ind. | $23,126 | $8060 | NR | NR | NR | NR | $28,430 |
| Tusculum College | ind. | $22,670 | $8500 | 86% | 14% | $20,448 | $10,722 | $29,162 |
| Union University | ind. | $28,190 | $8430 | 77% | 15% | $23,634 | $12,986 | $29,187 |
| University of Memphis | pub. | $8973 | $8976 | 81% | 25% | $10,415 | $7534 | $25,244 |
| The University of Tennessee | pub. | $11,876 | $10,296 | 95% | 29% | $13,793 | $8379 | $23,870 |
| The University of Tennessee at Chattanooga | pub. | $8138 | $8110 | 96% | 18% | $10,611 | $5637 | $21,420 |
| The University of Tennessee at Martin | pub. | $8024 | $5786 | 68% | 24% | $13,637 | $173 | $28,701 |
| Vanderbilt University | ind. | $43,838 | $14,382 | 91% | 100% | $45,640 | $12,580 | $20,790 |
| **Texas** | | | | | | | | |
| Abilene Christian University | ind. | $29,450 | $9000 | 100% | 27% | $23,064 | $15,386 | $43,841 |
| Angelo State University | pub. | $7642 | $7602 | 80% | 20% | $12,240 | $3004 | $25,508 |
| Austin College | ind. | $34,840 | $11,503 | 100% | 29% | $33,055 | $13,288 | NR |
| Baylor University | ind. | $40,198 | $11,360 | 100% | 15% | $27,086 | $24,472 | NR |
| College of Biblical Studies–Houston | ind. | $7316 | NA | 89% | 100% | $5043 | $2273 | NR |
| Concordia University Texas | ind. | $28,160 | $9284 | 98% | 23% | $23,088 | $14,356 | $24,882 |
| The Criswell College | ind. | NR | NA | 94% | 71% | NR | NR | $4030 |
| Dallas Baptist University | ind. | $23,650 | $6930 | 60% | 45% | $14,753 | $15,827 | $28,279 |
| East Texas Baptist University | ind. | $23,280 | $8297 | 78% | 13% | $17,600 | $13,977 | $30,718 |
| Hardin-Simmons University | ind. | $24,500 | $7740 | 71% | 24% | $24,614 | $7626 | $34,380 |
| Houston Baptist University | ind. | $29,800 | $7715 | 100% | 20% | $26,077 | $11,438 | NR |
| Howard Payne University | ind. | $25,600 | $7489 | 85% | 24% | $19,529 | $13,560 | $33,329 |
| Huston-Tillotson University | ind. | $13,544 | $7568 | 91% | NR | $11,536 | $9576 | NR |
| Lamar University | pub. | $9251 | $8302 | 87% | NR | $6482 | $11,071 | NR |
| LeTourneau University | ind. | $26,910 | $9300 | 100% | 17% | $22,151 | $14,059 | $38,211 |
| Lubbock Christian University | ind. | $19,400 | $6908 | 99% | 9% | $14,917 | $11,391 | $27,949 |
| McMurry University | ind. | $24,844 | $7988 | 100% | 14% | $20,495 | $12,337 | $34,742 |
| Midland College | pub. | $2340 | NR | NR | NR | NR | NR | NR |
| Midwestern State University | pub. | $7753 | $6810 | 91% | 17% | $10,367 | $4196 | $25,550 |
| Our Lady of the Lake University of San Antonio | ind. | $24,596 | $7436 | 93% | 19% | $21,174 | $10,858 | $28,362 |
| Prairie View A&M University | pub. | $8098 | $7467 | 94% | 1% | $14,745 | $820 | $27,500 |

NA = not applicable; NR = not reported; * = includes room and board; † = room only; — = not available.

# College Costs At-a-Glance

| | Institutional Control ind.=independent; pub.=public | Tuition and Fees | Room and Board | Percent of Eligible Freshmen Receiving Need-Based Gift Awards | Percent of Freshmen Whose Need Was Fully Met | Average Financial Aid Package for Freshmen | Average Net Cost After Aid | Average Indebtedness Upon Graduation |
|---|---|---|---|---|---|---|---|---|
| Rice University | ind. | $40,566 | $13,400 | 98% | 100% | $38,034 | $15,932 | $22,241 |
| St. Edward's University | ind. | $38,720 | $11,664 | 92% | 10% | $32,068 | $18,316 | $34,444 |
| Sam Houston State University | pub. | $8932 | $8324 | 87% | 19% | $12,173 | $5083 | $31,433 |
| Schreiner University | ind. | $24,360 | $10,610 | 100% | 20% | $18,367 | $16,603 | $29,364 |
| Southern Methodist University | ind. | $48,190 | $15,575 | 69% | 41% | $38,600 | $25,165 | $34,671 |
| Southwestern Christian College | ind. | NR | NR | 39% | 49% | $14,370 | — | NR |
| Southwestern University | ind. | $37,560 | $12,108 | 100% | 26% | $32,220 | $17,448 | $30,935 |
| Stephen F. Austin State University | pub. | $8892 | $8868 | 73% | 14% | $11,783 | $5977 | $27,278 |
| Sul Ross State University | pub. | $6900 | $7416 | 100% | NR | NR | NR | NR |
| Tarleton State University | pub. | $8246 | $9042 | 94% | 6% | $9001 | $8287 | $26,267 |
| Texas A&M International University | pub. | $7558 | $8028 | 98% | 3% | $10,131 | $5455 | $17,394 |
| Texas A&M University | pub. | $9180 | $9522 | 96% | 48% | $16,417 | $2285 | $23,703 |
| Texas A&M University–Commerce | pub. | $7096 | $8106 | 94% | 12% | $12,948 | $2254 | NR |
| Texas A&M University–Corpus Christi | pub. | $7591 | $8583 | 83% | 19% | $9823 | $6351 | $26,445 |
| Texas Christian University | ind. | $38,600 | $11,380 | 93% | 26% | $24,644 | $25,336 | $39,584 |
| Texas Lutheran University | ind. | $26,800 | $9240 | 100% | 33% | $23,262 | $12,778 | $31,576 |
| Texas Southern University | pub. | $8126 | $9438 | 94% | 94% | $19,711 | — | $43,600 |
| Texas State University | pub. | $9516 | $7612 | 85% | 7% | $11,472 | $5656 | $26,031 |
| Texas Tech University | pub. | $9308 | $8405 | 88% | 17% | $14,231 | $3482 | $25,306 |
| Texas Wesleyan University | ind. | $23,144 | $8238 | 99% | 22% | $23,424 | $7958 | $37,014 |
| Texas Woman's University | pub. | $7995 | $6780 | 94% | 31% | $9976 | $4799 | NR |
| Trinity University | ind. | $36,214 | $11,936 | 100% | 88% | $36,648 | $11,502 | $35,318 |
| University of Dallas | ind. | $35,800 | $11,300 | 100% | 22% | $30,165 | $16,935 | $36,561 |
| University of Houston | pub. | $10,518 | $9278 | 92% | 19% | $13,138 | $6658 | $18,453 |
| University of Houston–Clear Lake | pub. | $6936 | $9682† | NR | NR | NR | NR | NR |
| University of Houston–Downtown | pub. | $6614 | NA | 95% | 99% | $8032 | — | $23,249 |
| University of Mary Hardin-Baylor | ind. | $24,460 | $7020 | 87% | 7% | $17,835 | $13,645 | $37,048 |
| University of North Texas | pub. | $9706 | $7760 | 75% | 20% | $13,107 | $4359 | NR |
| University of St. Thomas | ind. | $29,440 | $8250 | 97% | 15% | $23,529 | $14,161 | $36,497 |
| The University of Texas at Arlington | pub. | $8878 | $8156 | 100% | 22% | $12,229 | $4805 | $23,210 |
| The University of Texas at Austin | pub. | $9830 | $11,456 | 91% | 27% | $13,209 | $8077 | $27,207 |
| The University of Texas at Brownsville | pub. | NR | NR | 91% | NR | $10,261 | — | NR |
| The University of Texas at Dallas | pub. | $11,806 | $9542 | 91% | 34% | $15,278 | $6070 | $19,613 |
| The University of Texas at El Paso | pub. | $7255 | $9180 | 87% | 14% | $11,537 | $4898 | $24,000 |
| The University of Texas at San Antonio | pub. | $8737 | $7624 | 91% | 20% | $10,677 | $5684 | $27,337 |
| The University of Texas Health Science Center at Houston | pub. | $6507 | NA | NR | NR | NR | NR | NR |
| The University of Texas–Pan American | pub. | $5173 | $5952 | 98% | 3% | $9796 | $1329 | $14,900 |
| University of the Incarnate Word | ind. | $27,798 | $11,364 | 96% | 32% | $19,939 | $19,223 | $29,744 |
| Wayland Baptist University | ind. | $16,980 | $6690 | 99% | 13% | $13,775 | $9895 | $25,725 |
| West Texas A&M University | pub. | $6105 | $7196 | 81% | 4% | $8467 | $4834 | $20,682 |
| **Utah** | | | | | | | | |
| Brigham Young University | ind. | $5000 | $7330 | 56% | 2% | $6404 | $5926 | $14,021 |

NA = not applicable; NR = not reported; * = includes room and board; † = room only; — = not available.

# College Costs At-a-Glance

| | Institutional Control ind.=independent; pub.=public | Tuition and Fees | Room and Board | Percent of Eligible Freshmen Receiving Need-Based Gift Awards | Percent of Freshmen Whose Need Was Fully Met | Average Financial Aid Package for Freshmen | Average Net Cost After Aid | Average Indebtedness Upon Graduation |
|---|---|---|---|---|---|---|---|---|
| Dixie State University | pub. | $4454 | $5918 | 70% | 5% | $9169 | $1203 | $24,441 |
| Neumont University | ind. | $24,000 | $5400† | NR | NR | NR | NR | NR |
| Southern Utah University | pub. | $6138 | $3100† | 99% | 9% | $8630 | $608 | $14,978 |
| University of Utah | pub. | $7835 | $8528 | 88% | 14% | $18,997 | — | $20,019 |
| Utah State University | pub. | $6384 | $5680 | 67% | 8% | $8600 | $3464 | $21,200 |
| Utah Valley University | pub. | $5270 | NA | 70% | 12% | $7375 | — | $16,784 |
| Weber State University | pub. | $5184 | $8400 | 68% | 48% | $2865 | $10,719 | NR |
| Western Governors University | ind. | $6070 | NA | 100% | NR | $5115 | $955 | $19,880 |
| Westminster College | ind. | $30,364 | $8456 | 100% | 28% | $24,900 | $13,920 | $27,523 |
| **Vermont** | | | | | | | | |
| Bennington College | ind. | $46,658 | $13,652 | 100% | 3% | $45,704 | $14,606 | $26,073 |
| Castleton State College | pub. | $10,772 | $9414 | NR | NR | NR | NR | NR |
| Champlain College | ind. | $32,900 | $13,750 | 100% | 15% | $23,589 | $23,061 | $35,444 |
| Goddard College | ind. | $14,930 | $1488 | 100% | NR | $5258 | $11,160 | $22,888 |
| Marlboro College | ind. | NR | NR | 100% | NR | $31,838 | — | $29,478 |
| Middlebury College | ind. | $46,044 | $13,116 | 98% | 100% | $43,346 | $15,814 | $17,975 |
| Norwich University | ind. | $32,812 | $11,984 | 100% | 20% | $30,302 | $14,494 | $32,498 |
| Saint Michael's College | ind. | $40,750 | $10,975 | 100% | 33% | $30,604 | $21,121 | $36,967 |
| University of Vermont | pub. | $16,226 | $10,780 | 98% | 15% | $24,308 | $2698 | $27,276 |
| Vermont Technical College | pub. | $13,200 | $9414 | 78% | 4% | $9322 | $13,292 | $23,530 |
| **Virginia** | | | | | | | | |
| Averett University | ind. | $30,900 | $8700 | 100% | 13% | $23,107 | $16,493 | $31,876 |
| Bluefield College | ind. | $23,296 | $8527 | 100% | 13% | $18,720 | $13,103 | $24,344 |
| Bridgewater College | ind. | $31,480 | $11,520 | 100% | 28% | $27,710 | $15,290 | $33,326 |
| Christendom College | ind. | $790 | $8980 | 78% | 89% | $19,514 | — | $31,991 |
| Christopher Newport University | pub. | $11,646 | $10,314 | 73% | 14% | $8168 | $13,792 | $28,135 |
| The College of William and Mary | pub. | $17,656 | $10,344 | 81% | 27% | $17,011 | $10,989 | $25,733 |
| Emory & Henry College | ind. | $30,900 | $10,510 | 99% | 21% | $27,661 | $13,749 | $28,126 |
| George Mason University | pub. | $10,382 | $10,100 | 83% | 7% | $12,243 | $8239 | $27,206 |
| Hampden-Sydney College | ind. | $39,604 | $12,312 | 100% | 25% | $31,383 | $20,533 | $30,644 |
| Hampton University | ind. | $21,760 | $9692 | 82% | 46% | $5591 | $25,861 | $9231 |
| Hollins University | ind. | $35,635 | $12,300 | 100% | 20% | $36,269 | $11,666 | $37,332 |
| James Madison University | pub. | $9662 | $8828 | 56% | 88% | $8699 | $9791 | $23,732 |
| Jefferson College of Health Sciences | ind. | $23,380 | $7670 | 100% | NR | NR | NR | NR |
| Liberty University | ind. | $22,000 | $8786 | 100% | 12% | $14,073 | $16,713 | $20,451 |
| Longwood University | pub. | $11,910 | $10,272 | 80% | 29% | $13,904 | $8278 | $27,644 |
| Lynchburg College | ind. | $34,545 | $9330 | 100% | 17% | $29,114 | $14,761 | $33,592 |
| Mary Baldwin College | ind. | $29,595 | $8650 | 100% | 12% | $25,833 | $12,412 | $32,117 |
| Marymount University | ind. | $27,470 | $12,010 | 57% | 23% | $21,010 | $18,470 | $26,528 |
| Old Dominion University | pub. | $9250 | $10,233 | 84% | 15% | $10,504 | $8979 | $29,357 |
| Patrick Henry College | ind. | $27,098 | $10,728 | 100% | NR | $10,600 | $27,226 | $35,400 |
| Radford University | pub. | $9360 | $8406 | 63% | 26% | $8776 | $8990 | $26,333 |

NA = not applicable; NR = not reported; * = includes room and board; † = room only; — = not available.

# College Costs At-a-Glance

| | Institutional Control ind.=independent; pub.=public | Tuition and Fees | Room and Board | Percent of Eligible Freshmen Receiving Need-Based Gift Awards | Percent of Freshmen Whose Need Was Fully Met | Average Financial Aid Package for Freshmen | Average Net Cost After Aid | Average Indebtedness Upon Graduation |
|---|---|---|---|---|---|---|---|---|
| Randolph College | ind. | $34,110 | $11,650 | 100% | 33% | $28,259 | $17,501 | $33,854 |
| Randolph-Macon College | ind. | $36,340 | $10,750 | 100% | 29% | $28,144 | $18,946 | NR |
| Regent University | ind. | $17,150 | $8250 | 98% | 16% | $11,974 | $13,426 | $36,564 |
| Roanoke College | ind. | $39,666 | $12,370 | 100% | 22% | $31,100 | $20,936 | $34,320 |
| Shenandoah University | ind. | $30,760 | $9920 | 43% | 42% | $29,611 | $11,069 | $28,831 |
| University of Management and Technology | ind. | NR | NA | 100% | NR | NR | NR | NR |
| University of Mary Washington | pub. | $10,252 | $9430 | 70% | 15% | $8466 | $11,216 | $17,460 |
| University of Richmond | ind. | $46,680 | $10,790 | 98% | 89% | $44,626 | $12,844 | $22,550 |
| University of Virginia | pub. | $12,998 | $10,052 | 82% | 100% | $24,920 | — | $22,933 |
| The University of Virginia's College at Wise | pub. | $8868 | $10,340 | 94% | 43% | $14,275 | $4933 | $12,662 |
| Virginia Commonwealth University | pub. | $14,573 | $9318 | 85% | 7% | $11,283 | $12,608 | $32,411 |
| Virginia Military Institute | pub. | $15,518 | $8372 | 90% | 45% | $17,430 | $6460 | $26,720 |
| Virginia Polytechnic Institute and State University | pub. | NR | NR | 70% | 16% | $16,745 | — | $27,865 |
| Virginia State University | pub. | $8002 | $10,128 | 80% | 34% | $10,834 | $7296 | $28,250 |
| Virginia Union University | ind. | $14,930 | $8074 | 97% | 7% | $12,238 | $10,766 | $33,286 |
| Virginia Wesleyan College | ind. | $34,428 | $8680 | 100% | 18% | $23,272 | $19,836 | $31,891 |
| Washington and Lee University | ind. | $45,617 | $10,645 | 99% | 100% | $47,862 | $8400 | $23,224 |
| **Washington** | | | | | | | | |
| Bastyr University | ind. | $23,355 | $6975† | NR | NR | NR | NR | NR |
| Central Washington University | pub. | $8321 | $9316 | 86% | 55% | $11,941 | $5696 | $26,360 |
| Cornish College of the Arts | ind. | $35,800 | $9800 | 98% | 7% | $21,502 | $24,098 | $32,179 |
| Eastern Washington University | pub. | $7982 | $9628 | 79% | 9% | $10,838 | $6772 | $27,259 |
| The Evergreen State College | pub. | $8523 | $9492 | 70% | 7% | $9147 | $8868 | $21,054 |
| Gonzaga University | ind. | $37,990 | $10,835 | 100% | 28% | $24,846 | $23,979 | $29,513 |
| Northwest College of Art & Design | ind. | $19,050 | NA | 56% | NR | $7940 | $11,110 | $20,426 |
| Northwest University | ind. | $27,700 | $7790 | 97% | 17% | $17,773 | $17,717 | $27,479 |
| Pacific Lutheran University | ind. | $37,950 | $10,330 | 100% | 29% | $35,650 | $12,630 | $32,459 |
| Saint Martin's University | ind. | $31,688 | $9990 | 100% | 29% | $26,115 | $15,563 | $27,944 |
| Seattle Pacific University | ind. | $35,472 | $10,086 | 100% | 9% | $31,276 | $14,282 | $28,844 |
| Seattle University | ind. | $38,205 | $10,830 | 91% | 11% | $29,590 | $19,445 | $29,044 |
| University of Puget Sound | ind. | $43,428 | $11,180 | 98% | 19% | $28,459 | $26,149 | $27,776 |
| University of Washington | pub. | $12,394 | $10,833 | 80% | 39% | $17,500 | $5727 | $21,532 |
| University of Washington, Bothell | pub. | $12,517 | $10,833 | 92% | 13% | $17,000 | $6350 | $19,536 |
| University of Washington, Tacoma | pub. | $12,262 | $10,833 | 98% | 22% | $17,000 | $6095 | $23,396 |
| Walla Walla University | ind. | $25,866 | $6855 | 76% | 31% | $20,779 | $11,942 | $38,778 |
| Washington State University | pub. | $12,428 | $11,276 | 80% | 19% | $12,786 | $10,918 | $24,298 |
| Western Washington University | pub. | $8965 | $10,042 | 87% | 22% | $14,590 | $4417 | $21,520 |
| Whitman College | ind. | $44,800 | $11,228 | 100% | 45% | $34,801 | $21,227 | $19,147 |
| Whitworth University | ind. | $37,630 | $10,278 | 100% | 18% | $33,144 | $14,764 | $26,132 |
| **West Virginia** | | | | | | | | |
| Alderson Broaddus University | ind. | $22,740 | $7236 | 100% | 76% | $24,542 | $5434 | $26,765 |
| Bethany College | ind. | $25,736 | $9636 | NR | NR | NR | NR | NR |

**NA = not applicable; NR = not reported; * = includes room and board; † = room only; — = not available.**

# College Costs At-a-Glance

| | Institutional Control ind.=independent; pub.=public | Tuition and Fees | Room and Board | Percent of Eligible Freshmen Receiving Need-Based Gift Awards | Percent of Freshmen Whose Need Was Fully Met | Average Financial Aid Package for Freshmen | Average Net Cost After Aid | Average Indebtedness Upon Graduation |
|---|---|---|---|---|---|---|---|---|
| Bluefield State College | pub. | $5832 | NA | 89% | 16% | $3300 | $2532 | $27,000 |
| Concord University | pub. | $6580 | $7818 | 88% | 65% | $7675 | $6723 | $21,273 |
| Fairmont State University | pub. | $6306 | $7800 | 91% | 11% | $9056 | $5050 | $26,420 |
| Glenville State College | pub. | NR | NR | 90% | 12% | $13,468 | — | $27,932 |
| Marshall University | pub. | $6526 | $9546 | 80% | 30% | $11,015 | $5057 | $26,625 |
| Shepherd University | pub. | $6830 | $9682 | 66% | 35% | $11,773 | $4739 | $27,938 |
| University of Charleston | ind. | $24,200 | $9100 | 75% | 7% | $20,712 | $12,588 | NR |
| West Virginia University | pub. | $6960 | $9582 | 75% | 30% | $6860 | $9682 | $27,332 |
| West Virginia University Institute of Technology | pub. | $6048 | $8902 | 82% | 15% | $7437 | $7513 | $20,893 |
| West Virginia Wesleyan College | ind. | $28,792 | $4040 | 100% | 39% | $28,054 | $4778 | $31,044 |
| Wheeling Jesuit University | ind. | $28,030 | $5470 | 65% | 39% | $25,267 | $8233 | $29,131 |
| **Wisconsin** | | | | | | | | |
| Alverno College | ind. | $24,434 | $7500 | 100% | NR | $20,742 | $11,192 | $38,642 |
| Beloit College | ind. | $42,500 | $7470 | 100% | 36% | $34,275 | $15,695 | $28,768 |
| Cardinal Stritch University | ind. | $26,570 | $7470 | 99% | 17% | $23,924 | $10,116 | $29,473 |
| Carroll University | ind. | $28,550 | $8550 | 100% | 28% | $22,239 | $14,861 | $32,931 |
| Columbia College of Nursing | ind. | NR | NA | NR | NR | NR | NR | $28,203 |
| Concordia University Wisconsin | ind. | $26,160 | $9780 | 98% | 31% | $23,007 | $12,933 | $30,880 |
| Edgewood College | ind. | $25,590 | $8973 | 100% | 10% | $21,816 | $12,747 | $31,522 |
| Lawrence University | ind. | $42,657 | $8808 | 100% | 39% | $36,415 | $15,050 | $33,755 |
| Maranatha Baptist University | ind. | $13,510 | $6480 | 100% | 7% | $10,492 | $9498 | $14,851 |
| Marian University | ind. | $25,930 | $6490 | 100% | 15% | $18,678 | $13,742 | $31,000 |
| Marquette University | ind. | $37,170 | NR | 98% | 25% | $24,395 | $12,775 | $35,211 |
| Milwaukee School of Engineering | ind. | $36,540 | $8613 | 100% | 24% | $26,284 | $18,869 | $37,243 |
| Mount Mary University | ind. | $25,852 | $7738 | 99% | 11% | $24,121 | $9469 | $29,759 |
| Northland College | ind. | $31,480 | $7858 | 100% | 23% | $36,811 | $2527 | $30,637 |
| St. Norbert College | ind. | $33,023 | $8455 | 98% | 23% | $24,600 | $16,878 | $31,438 |
| University of Wisconsin–Eau Claire | pub. | $8744 | $6986 | 80% | 76% | $9260 | $6470 | $26,210 |
| University of Wisconsin–Green Bay | pub. | $7758 | $7224 | 75% | 23% | $9414 | $5568 | $27,239 |
| University of Wisconsin–La Crosse | pub. | $8795 | $5910 | 42% | 18% | $7060 | $7645 | $25,932 |
| University of Wisconsin–Madison | pub. | $10,410 | $8600 | 83% | 37% | $13,229 | $5781 | $26,579 |
| University of Wisconsin–Milwaukee | pub. | $9391 | $9126 | 60% | 28% | $7133 | $11,384 | $33,234 |
| University of Wisconsin–Oshkosh | pub. | $7437 | $7386 | 53% | 40% | $6414 | $8409 | $23,989 |
| University of Wisconsin–Parkside | pub. | $8334 | $6572 | 75% | NR | NR | NR | NR |
| University of Wisconsin–River Falls | pub. | $7751 | $6435 | 58% | 1% | $6524 | $7662 | $27,134 |
| University of Wisconsin–Stevens Point | pub. | $7669 | $6786 | 67% | 6% | $7209 | $7246 | $25,871 |
| University of Wisconsin–Stout | pub. | $9025 | $6434 | 52% | 14% | $10,101 | $5358 | $27,397 |
| University of Wisconsin–Superior | pub. | $7994 | $6320 | 56% | 13% | $10,574 | $3740 | $29,410 |
| University of Wisconsin–Whitewater | pub. | $7600 | $6144 | 58% | 41% | $7236 | $6508 | $27,623 |
| Wisconsin Lutheran College | ind. | $25,960 | $8900 | 100% | 17% | $22,097 | $12,763 | $26,896 |
| **Wyoming** | | | | | | | | |
| University of Wyoming | pub. | $4646 | $9755 | 61% | 25% | $9864 | $4537 | $23,708 |

NA = not applicable; NR = not reported; * = includes room and board; † = room only; — = not available.

# Profiles of College Financial Aid Programs

# ABILENE CHRISTIAN UNIVERSITY
## Abilene, TX

| Tuition & fees: $29,450 | Average undergraduate aid package: $20,931 |
|---|---|

**ABOUT THE INSTITUTION** Independent Church of Christ, coed. *Awards:* certificates, associate, bachelor's, master's, and doctoral degrees. 70 undergraduate majors. *Total enrollment:* 4,427. Undergraduates: 3,650. Freshmen: 974. Federal methodology is used as a basis for awarding need-based institutional aid.

**UNDERGRADUATE EXPENSES for 2015–2016** *Application fee:* $50. *Comprehensive fee:* $38,450 includes full-time tuition ($29,450) and room and board ($9000). *College room only:* $4180. Full-time tuition and fees vary according to course load. Room and board charges vary according to board plan and housing facility. *Part-time tuition:* $1090 per credit hour. Part-time tuition and fees vary according to course load. *Payment plan:* Tuition prepayment.

**FRESHMAN FINANCIAL AID (Fall 2014, est.)** 847 applied for aid; of those 83% were deemed to have need. 100% of freshmen with need received aid; of those 27% had need fully met. *Average percent of need met:* 73% (excluding resources awarded to replace EFC). *Average financial aid package:* $23,064 (excluding resources awarded to replace EFC). 29% of all full-time freshmen had no need and received non-need-based gift aid.

**UNDERGRADUATE FINANCIAL AID (Fall 2014, est.)** 2,696 applied for aid; of those 84% were deemed to have need. 100% of undergraduates with need received aid; of those 27% had need fully met. *Average percent of need met:* 69% (excluding resources awarded to replace EFC). *Average financial aid package:* $20,931 (excluding resources awarded to replace EFC). 33% of all full-time undergraduates had no need and received non-need-based gift aid.

**GIFT AID (NEED-BASED)** *Total amount:* $38,265,546 (11% federal, 8% state, 78% institutional, 3% external sources). *Receiving aid:* Freshmen: 72% (700); all full-time undergraduates: 66% (2,254). *Average award:* Freshmen: $20,695; Undergraduates: $18,066. *Scholarships, grants, and awards:* Federal Pell, FSEOG, state, private, college/university gift aid from institutional funds.

**GIFT AID (NON-NEED-BASED)** *Total amount:* $13,387,281 (1% federal, 97% institutional, 2% external sources). *Receiving aid:* Freshmen: 72% (700). Undergraduates: 64% (2,182). *Average award:* Freshmen: $11,758. Undergraduates: $10,590. *Scholarships, grants, and awards by category: Academic interests/ achievement:* agriculture, biological sciences, business, communication, education, engineering/technologies, English, foreign languages, general academic interests/ achievements, mathematics, physical sciences, religion/biblical studies, social sciences. *Creative arts/performance:* art/fine arts, debating, journalism/publications, music, theater/drama. *Special achievements/activities:* cheerleading/drum major, leadership. *Special characteristics:* children of faculty/staff, ethnic background, first-generation college students, local/state students, members of minority groups, out-of-state students, previous college experience, relatives of clergy, religious affiliation. *Tuition waivers:* Full or partial for employees or children of employees.

**LOANS** *Student loans:* $22,067,455 (31% need-based, 69% non-need-based). 67% of past graduating class borrowed through all loan programs. *Average indebtedness per student:* $43,841. *Average need-based loan:* Freshmen: $3577. Undergraduates: $4424. *Parent loans:* $4,185,920 (100% non-need-based). *Programs:* Federal Direct (Subsidized and Unsubsidized Stafford, PLUS), Perkins, state.

**WORK-STUDY** *Federal work-study:* Total amount: $635,679; jobs available. *State or other work-study/employment:* Total amount: $1,261,051 (2% need-based, 98% non-need-based). Part-time jobs available.

**ATHLETIC AWARDS** Total amount: $5,188,030 (50% need-based, 50% non-need-based).

**APPLYING FOR FINANCIAL AID** *Required financial aid form:* FAFSA. *Financial aid deadline (priority):* 3/1. *Notification date:* Continuous beginning 4/1. Students must reply within 3 weeks of notification.

**CONTACT** Ed Kerestly, Director of Student Financial Services, Abilene Christian University, ACU Box 29007, Abilene, TX 79699-9007, 325-674-2130 or toll-free 800-460-6228. *E-mail:* thedepot@acu.edu. *Website:* http://www.acu.edu/.

# ABRAHAM BALDWIN AGRICULTURAL COLLEGE
## Tifton, GA

| Tuition & fees: N/R | Average undergraduate aid package: N/A |
|---|---|

**ABOUT THE INSTITUTION** State-supported, coed. *Awards:* certificates, associate, and bachelor's degrees. 48 undergraduate majors. *Total enrollment:* 3,327. Undergraduates: 3,327. Freshmen: 1,117. Federal methodology is used as a basis for awarding need-based institutional aid.

**GIFT AID (NEED-BASED)** *Total amount:* $6,779,666 (100% federal). *Scholarships, grants, and awards:* Federal Pell, FSEOG, state, private, college/university gift aid from institutional funds.

**GIFT AID (NON-NEED-BASED)** *Total amount:* $5,780,109 (38% state, 62% institutional).

**LOANS** *Student loans:* $9,406,737 (46% need-based, 54% non-need-based). *Parent loans:* $363,900 (100% non-need-based). *Programs:* Federal Direct (Subsidized and Unsubsidized Stafford, PLUS), state.

**WORK-STUDY** *Federal work-study:* 133 jobs averaging $1539.

**ATHLETIC AWARDS** Total amount: $220,121 (100% non-need-based).

**APPLYING FOR FINANCIAL AID** *Required financial aid form:* FAFSA. *Financial aid deadline:* 7/1. *Notification date:* Continuous beginning 5/15.

**CONTACT** Michael Wright, Director of Student Financial Services, Abraham Baldwin Agricultural College, 2802 Moore Highway, ABAC 23, Tifton, GA 31793-2601, 229-391-4910 or toll-free 800-733-3653. *Fax:* 229-391-4871. *E-mail:* sfs@abac.edu. *Website:* http://www.abac.edu/.

# ACADEMY COLLEGE
## Bloomington, MN

**CONTACT** Kellye MacLeod, Director of Financial Aid, Academy College, 1101 East 78th Street, Bloomington, MN 55420, 952-851-0066 or toll-free 800-292-9149. *Fax:* 952-851-0094 *E-mail:* finaid@academycollege.edu. *Website:* http://www.academycollege.edu/.

# ACADEMY OF ART UNIVERSITY
## San Francisco, CA

| Tuition & fees: $25,350 | Average undergraduate aid package: $10,229 |
|---|---|

**ABOUT THE INSTITUTION** Proprietary, coed. *Awards:* certificates, associate, bachelor's, and master's degrees. 26 undergraduate majors. *Total enrollment:* 15,212. Undergraduates: 10,044. Freshmen: 1,159. Federal methodology is used as a basis for awarding need-based institutional aid.

**UNDERGRADUATE EXPENSES for 2015–2016** *Application fee:* $100. *Comprehensive fee:* $39,510 includes full-time tuition ($25,050), mandatory fees ($300), and room and board ($14,160). Full-time tuition and fees vary according to course load. Room and board charges vary according to board plan and housing facility. *Part-time tuition:* $835 per unit. Part-time tuition and fees vary according to course load.

**FRESHMAN FINANCIAL AID (Fall 2013)** 394 applied for aid; of those 88% were deemed to have need. 97% of freshmen with need received aid; of those 1% had need fully met. *Average percent of need met:* 30% (excluding resources awarded to replace EFC). *Average financial aid package:* $9374 (excluding resources awarded to replace EFC). 3% of all full-time freshmen had no need and received non-need-based gift aid.

**UNDERGRADUATE FINANCIAL AID (Fall 2013)** 2,924 applied for aid; of those 92% were deemed to have need. 97% of undergraduates with need received aid; of those 2% had need fully met. *Average percent of need met:* 33% (excluding resources awarded to replace EFC). *Average financial aid package:* $10,229 (excluding resources awarded to replace EFC). 1% of all full-time undergraduates had no need and received non-need-based gift aid.

**GIFT AID (NEED-BASED)** *Total amount:* $24,693,877 (59% federal, 13% state, 3% institutional, 25% external sources). *Receiving aid:* Freshmen: 38% (253); all full-time undergraduates: 34% (1,913). *Average award:* Freshmen: $8689; Undergrad-

uates: $9020. **Scholarships, grants, and awards:** Federal Pell, FSEOG, state, private, college/university gift aid from institutional funds.

**GIFT AID (NON-NEED-BASED) Total amount:** $4,885,662 (11% institutional, 89% external sources). **Receiving aid:** Freshmen: 3% (19). Undergraduates: 2% (132). **Average award:** Freshmen: $5626. Undergraduates: $6936.

**LOANS Student loans:** $51,382,319 (91% need-based, 9% non-need-based). 62% of past graduating class borrowed through all loan programs. **Average indebtedness per student:** $25,575. **Average need-based loan:** Freshmen: $3146. Undergraduates: $3970. **Parent loans:** $25,743,793 (66% need-based, 34% non-need-based). **Programs:** Federal Direct (Subsidized and Unsubsidized Stafford, PLUS), alternative loans.

**WORK-STUDY Federal work-study:** 117 jobs averaging $3604.

**ATHLETIC AWARDS** Total amount: $2,888,522 (43% need-based, 57% non-need-based).

**APPLYING FOR FINANCIAL AID Required financial aid forms:** FAFSA, institution's own form. **Financial aid deadline:** Continuous. **Notification date:** Continuous. Students must reply within 3 weeks of notification.

**CONTACT** Mr. Joe Vollaro, Executive Vice President of Financial Aid and Compliance, Academy of Art University, 79 New Montgomery Street, San Francisco, CA 94105-3410, 415-618-6528 or toll-free 800-544-ARTS. **Fax:** 415-618-6273. **E-mail:** jvollaro@academyart.edu.
**Website:** http://www.academyart.edu/.

---

# ADAMS STATE UNIVERSITY
### Alamosa, CO

| Tuition & fees (CO res): $7951 | Average undergraduate aid package: $12,058 |
|---|---|

**ABOUT THE INSTITUTION** State-supported, coed. **Awards:** associate, bachelor's, master's, and doctoral degrees. 78 undergraduate majors. **Total enrollment:** 3,152. Undergraduates: 2,138. Freshmen: 493. Federal methodology is used as a basis for awarding need-based institutional aid.

**UNDERGRADUATE EXPENSES for 2015–2016 Application fee:** $30. **Tuition, state resident:** full-time $5160; part-time $215 per credit hour. **Tuition, nonresident:** full-time $15,960; part-time $665 per credit hour. **Required fees:** full-time $2791; $114.78 per credit hour. Full-time tuition and fees vary according to course load. Part-time tuition and fees vary according to course load. **College room and board:** $8400; **Room only:** $4000. Room and board charges vary according to board plan and housing facility.

**FRESHMAN FINANCIAL AID (Fall 2013)** 505 applied for aid; of those 84% were deemed to have need. 99% of freshmen with need received aid; of those .5% had need fully met. **Average percent of need met:** 57% (excluding resources awarded to replace EFC). **Average financial aid package:** $11,265 (excluding resources awarded to replace EFC).

**UNDERGRADUATE FINANCIAL AID (Fall 2013)** 1,765 applied for aid; of those 86% were deemed to have need. 98% of undergraduates with need received aid; of those 1% had need fully met. **Average percent of need met:** 58% (excluding resources awarded to replace EFC). **Average financial aid package:** $12,058 (excluding resources awarded to replace EFC).

**GIFT AID (NEED-BASED) Total amount:** $10,018,907 (51% federal, 12% state, 32% institutional, 5% external sources). **Receiving aid:** Freshmen: 78% (408); all full-time undergraduates: 74% (1,407). **Average award:** Freshmen: $7164; Undergraduates: $7099. **Scholarships, grants, and awards:** Federal Pell, FSEOG, state, private, college/university gift aid from institutional funds.

**GIFT AID (NON-NEED-BASED) Tuition waivers:** Full or partial for employees or children of employees, senior citizens.

**LOANS Student loans:** $11,590,134 (40% need-based, 60% non-need-based). 72% of past graduating class borrowed through all loan programs. **Average indebtedness per student:** $30,211. **Average need-based loan:** Freshmen: $3120. Undergraduates: $3785. **Parent loans:** $1,693,256 (100% non-need-based). **Programs:** Federal Direct (Subsidized and Unsubsidized Stafford, PLUS), Perkins, alternative loans.

**WORK-STUDY Federal work-study:** 295 jobs averaging $952. **State or other work-study/employment:** Total amount: $380,733 (62% need-based, 38% non-need-based). 328 part-time jobs averaging $1155.

**ATHLETIC AWARDS** Total amount: $1,739,197 (100% need-based).

---

**APPLYING FOR FINANCIAL AID Required financial aid form:** FAFSA. **Financial aid deadline:** Continuous. **Notification date:** Continuous beginning 3/1.

**CONTACT** Philip Schroeder, Director of Financial Aid, Adams State University, 208 Edgemont Boulevard, Alamosa, CO 81101, 719-587-7306 or toll-free 800-824-6494. **Fax:** 719-587-7366. **E-mail:** financialaid@adams.edu.
**Website:** http://www.adams.edu/.

---

# ADELPHI UNIVERSITY
### Garden City, NY

| Tuition & fees: $32,340 | Average undergraduate aid package: $20,900 |
|---|---|

**ABOUT THE INSTITUTION** Independent, coed. **Awards:** certificates, associate, bachelor's, master's, and doctoral degrees. 47 undergraduate majors. **Total enrollment:** 7,610. Undergraduates: 5,071. Freshmen: 975. Federal methodology is used as a basis for awarding need-based institutional aid.

**UNDERGRADUATE EXPENSES for 2015–2016 Application fee:** $40. **Comprehensive fee:** $45,960 includes full-time tuition ($30,840), mandatory fees ($1500), and room and board ($13,620). **College room only:** $7110. Full-time tuition and fees vary according to course level, course load, location, program, and student level. Room and board charges vary according to board plan and housing facility. **Part-time tuition:** $945 per credit hour. Part-time tuition and fees vary according to course level, course load, location, program, and student level. **Payment plan:** Tuition prepayment.

**FRESHMAN FINANCIAL AID (Fall 2014, est.)** 842 applied for aid; of those 85% were deemed to have need. 97% of freshmen with need received aid. **Average percent of need met:** 21% (excluding resources awarded to replace EFC). **Average financial aid package:** $20,900 (excluding resources awarded to replace EFC). 20% of all full-time freshmen had no need and received non-need-based gift aid.

**UNDERGRADUATE FINANCIAL AID (Fall 2014, est.)** 3,696 applied for aid; of those 90% were deemed to have need. 91% of undergraduates with need received aid; of those .3% had need fully met. **Average percent of need met:** 19% (excluding resources awarded to replace EFC). **Average financial aid package:** $20,900 (excluding resources awarded to replace EFC). 21% of all full-time undergraduates had no need and received non-need-based gift aid.

**GIFT AID (NEED-BASED) Total amount:** $41,124,746 (16% federal, 12% state, 72% institutional). **Receiving aid:** Freshmen: 52% (496); all full-time undergraduates: 46% (2,090). **Average award:** Freshmen: $7172; Undergraduates: $7015. **Scholarships, grants, and awards:** Federal Pell, FSEOG, state, private, college/university gift aid from institutional funds, United Negro College Fund, endowed and restricted scholarships and grants.

**GIFT AID (NON-NEED-BASED) Total amount:** $15,859,075 (94% institutional, 6% external sources). **Receiving aid:** Freshmen: 63% (600). Undergraduates: 58% (2,644). **Average award:** Freshmen: $15,336. Undergraduates: $12,698. **Scholarships, grants, and awards by category:** Academic interests/achievement: 3,277 awards ($40,281,695 total): business, communication, computer science, foreign languages, general academic interests/achievements, mathematics, physical sciences. Creative arts/performance: 82 awards ($684,265 total): art/fine arts, cinema/film/broadcasting, dance, music, performing arts, theater/drama. Special achievements/activities: 1,685 awards ($1,441,125 total): community service, general special achievements/activities, leadership, memberships. Special characteristics: 370 awards ($3,114,081 total): adult students, children and siblings of alumni, children of faculty/staff, veterans. **Tuition waivers:** Full or partial for children of alumni, employees or children of employees, senior citizens. **ROTC:** Army cooperative, Air Force cooperative.

**LOANS Student loans:** $32,170,759 (40% need-based, 60% non-need-based). 75% of past graduating class borrowed through all loan programs. **Average indebtedness per student:** $32,328. **Average need-based loan:** Freshmen: $3981. Undergraduates: $4240. **Parent loans:** $9,606,411 (90% need-based, 10% non-need-based). **Programs:** Federal Direct (Subsidized and Unsubsidized Stafford, PLUS), Perkins, Federal Nursing.

**WORK-STUDY Federal work-study:** Total amount: $1,577,266; 407 jobs averaging $1508. **State or other work-study/employment:** Total amount: $2,226,704 (100% non-need-based). 1,160 part-time jobs averaging $1920.

**ATHLETIC AWARDS** Total amount: $3,364,355 (51% need-based, 49% non-need-based).

---

**APPLYING FOR FINANCIAL AID** *Required financial aid forms:* FAFSA, state aid form. *Financial aid deadline (priority):* 3/1. *Notification date:* Continuous beginning 3/1.

**CONTACT** Ms. Debra Evans, Senior Associate Director of Student Financial Services, Adelphi University, 1 South Avenue, PO Box 701, Garden City, NY 11530, 516-877-3394 or toll-free 800-ADELPHI. *Fax:* 516-877-3380. *E-mail:* evans@adelphi.edu.
*Website:* http://www.adelphi.edu/.

# ADRIAN COLLEGE
## Adrian, MI

| Tuition & fees: $32,660 | Average undergraduate aid package: $26,336 |
|---|---|

**ABOUT THE INSTITUTION** Independent United Methodist Church, coed. *Awards:* associate, bachelor's, and master's degrees. 72 undergraduate majors. *Total enrollment:* 1,656. Undergraduates: 1,647. Freshmen: 447. Both federal and institutional methodology are used as a basis for awarding need-based institutional aid.

**UNDERGRADUATE EXPENSES for 2015–2016** *Comprehensive fee:* $42,400 includes full-time tuition ($31,870), mandatory fees ($790), and room and board ($9740). *College room only:* $4680. Room and board charges vary according to board plan and housing facility. *Part-time tuition:* $890 per credit.

**FRESHMAN FINANCIAL AID (Fall 2013)** 386 applied for aid; of those 92% were deemed to have need. 100% of freshmen with need received aid; of those 10% had need fully met. *Average percent of need met:* 77% (excluding resources awarded to replace EFC). *Average financial aid package:* $27,013 (excluding resources awarded to replace EFC). 16% of all full-time freshmen had no need and received non-need-based gift aid.

**UNDERGRADUATE FINANCIAL AID (Fall 2013)** 1,408 applied for aid; of those 95% were deemed to have need. 100% of undergraduates with need received aid; of those 11% had need fully met. *Average percent of need met:* 76% (excluding resources awarded to replace EFC). *Average financial aid package:* $26,336 (excluding resources awarded to replace EFC). 13% of all full-time undergraduates had no need and received non-need-based gift aid.

**GIFT AID (NEED-BASED)** *Total amount:* $28,534,394 (10% federal, 5% state, 78% institutional, 7% external sources). *Receiving aid:* Freshmen: 84% (356); all full-time undergraduates: 86% (1,327). *Average award:* Freshmen: $22,843; Undergraduates: $21,336. *Scholarships, grants, and awards:* Federal Pell, FSEOG, state, private, college/university gift aid from institutional funds.

**GIFT AID (NON-NEED-BASED)** *Total amount:* $34,751,523 (99% institutional, 1% external sources). *Receiving aid:* Freshmen: 6% (25). Undergraduates: 6% (91). *Average award:* Freshmen: $15,800. Undergraduates: $14,942. *Scholarships, grants, and awards by category:* Academic interests/achievement: 1,528 awards ($10,418,451 total): business, general academic interests/achievements. *Creative arts/performance:* 200 awards ($504,317 total): art/fine arts, music, theater/drama. *Special achievements/activities:* 40 awards ($70,500 total): religious involvement. *Special characteristics:* 333 awards ($3,263,164 total): children and siblings of alumni, children of faculty/staff, children of union members/company employees, first-generation college students, general special characteristics, international students, religious affiliation, veterans, veterans' children. *Tuition waivers:* Full or partial for children of alumni, employees or children of employees. *ROTC:* Army cooperative.

**LOANS** *Student loans:* $13,737,575 (78% need-based, 22% non-need-based). 87% of past graduating class borrowed through all loan programs. *Average indebtedness per student:* $27,741. *Average need-based loan:* Freshmen: $3296. Undergraduates: $4368. *Parent loans:* $3,419,032 (46% need-based, 54% non-need-based). *Programs:* Federal Direct (Subsidized and Unsubsidized Stafford, PLUS), Perkins.

**WORK-STUDY** *Federal work-study:* 1,275 jobs averaging $1500. *State or other work-study/employment:* Total amount: $113,400 (100% non-need-based). 75 part-time jobs averaging $1500.

**APPLYING FOR FINANCIAL AID** *Required financial aid form:* FAFSA. *Financial aid deadline (priority):* 3/1. *Notification date:* Continuous beginning 3/15. Students must reply by 5/1 or within 2 weeks of notification.

**CONTACT** Mr. Matthew Rheinecker, Director of Financial Aid, Adrian College, 110 South Madison Street, Adrian, MI 49221-2575, 517-264-3109 or toll-free 800-877-2246. *Fax:* 517-264-3394. *E-mail:* mrheinecker@adrian.edu.
*Website:* http://www.adrian.edu/.

# ADVENTIST UNIVERSITY OF HEALTH SCIENCES
## Orlando, FL

| Tuition & fees: $13,030 | Average undergraduate aid package: N/A |
|---|---|

**ABOUT THE INSTITUTION** Independent, coed. *Awards:* associate, bachelor's, master's, and doctoral degrees. 8 undergraduate majors. *Total enrollment:* 2,090. Undergraduates: 1,950. Freshmen: 88. Federal methodology is used as a basis for awarding need-based institutional aid.

**UNDERGRADUATE EXPENSES for 2015–2016** *Application fee:* $20. *Tuition:* full-time $12,450; part-time $415 per credit hour. *Required fees:* full-time $580; $290 per term. Full-time tuition and fees vary according to course load, degree level, and program. Part-time tuition and fees vary according to course load, degree level, and program.

**GIFT AID (NEED-BASED)** *Total amount:* $2,646,248 (86% federal, 8% state, 5% institutional, 1% external sources). *Scholarships, grants, and awards:* Federal Pell, FSEOG, state, private, college/university gift aid from institutional funds.

**GIFT AID (NON-NEED-BASED)** *Total amount:* $2,072,309 (61% state, 4% institutional, 35% external sources). *Tuition waivers:* Full or partial for employees or children of employees.

**LOANS** *Student loans:* $12,324,691 (31% need-based, 69% non-need-based). *Parent loans:* $2,099,417 (100% non-need-based). *Programs:* Federal Direct (Subsidized and Unsubsidized Stafford, PLUS), private loans.

**APPLYING FOR FINANCIAL AID** *Required financial aid forms:* FAFSA, institution's own form. *Financial aid deadline:* 7/22 (priority: 4/10). *Notification date:* Continuous beginning 3/15. Students must reply within 2 weeks of notification.

**CONTACT** Rebecca Valencia, Director of Financial Aid, Adventist University of Health Sciences, 671 Winyah Drive, Orlando, FL 32803, 407-303-9203 or toll-free 800-500-7747. *Fax:* 407-303-7680. *E-mail:* rebecca.valencia@adu.edu.
*Website:* http://www.adu.edu/.

# AGNES SCOTT COLLEGE
## Decatur, GA

| Tuition & fees: $37,236 | Average undergraduate aid package: $33,244 |
|---|---|

**ABOUT THE INSTITUTION** Independent Presbyterian Church (U.S.A.), women only. *Awards:* bachelor's degrees. 36 undergraduate majors. *Total enrollment:* 873. Undergraduates: 873. Freshmen: 225. Both federal and institutional methodology are used as a basis for awarding need-based institutional aid.

**UNDERGRADUATE EXPENSES for 2015–2016** *Comprehensive fee:* $48,386 includes full-time tuition ($36,996), mandatory fees ($240), and room and board ($11,150). Room and board charges vary according to board plan and housing facility. Part-time tuition and fees vary according to course load.

**FRESHMAN FINANCIAL AID (Fall 2014, est.)** 203 applied for aid; of those 91% were deemed to have need. 100% of freshmen with need received aid; of those 29% had need fully met. *Average percent of need met:* 86% (excluding resources awarded to replace EFC). *Average financial aid package:* $32,838 (excluding resources awarded to replace EFC). 18% of all full-time freshmen had no need and received non-need-based gift aid.

**UNDERGRADUATE FINANCIAL AID (Fall 2014, est.)** 674 applied for aid; of those 92% were deemed to have need. 100% of undergraduates with need received aid; of those 20% had need fully met. *Average percent of need met:* 85% (excluding resources awarded to replace EFC). *Average financial aid package:* $33,244 (excluding resources awarded to replace EFC). 22% of all full-time undergraduates had no need and received non-need-based gift aid.

**GIFT AID (NEED-BASED)** *Total amount:* $16,925,586 (9% federal, 6% state, 83% institutional, 2% external sources). *Receiving aid:* Freshmen: 82% (185); all full-time undergraduates: 78% (621). *Average award:* Freshmen: $27,517; Undergraduates: $27,245. *Scholarships, grants, and awards:* Federal Pell, FSEOG, state, private, college/university gift aid from institutional funds.

**GIFT AID (NON-NEED-BASED)** *Total amount:* $4,619,926 (8% state, 89% institutional, 3% external sources). *Receiving aid:* Freshmen: 24% (53). Undergraduates: 16% (127). *Average award:* Freshmen: $23,440. Undergraduates: $22,131. *Scholarships, grants, and awards by category:* Academic interests/

*achievement:* general academic interests/achievements. *Creative arts/performance:* music. *Special achievements/activities:* community service, leadership. *Special characteristics:* adult students, children of educators, children of faculty/staff, international students, local/state students, religious affiliation, veterans, veterans' children. *Tuition waivers:* Full or partial for employees or children of employees. *ROTC:* Army cooperative, Air Force cooperative.

**LOANS** *Student loans:* $4,880,063 (50% need-based, 50% non-need-based). 71% of past graduating class borrowed through all loan programs. *Average indebtedness per student:* $27,763. *Average need-based loan:* Freshmen: $3373. Undergraduates: $4524. *Parent loans:* $1,620,470 (45% need-based, 55% non-need-based). *Programs:* Federal Direct (Subsidized and Unsubsidized Stafford, PLUS).

**WORK-STUDY** *Federal work-study:* Total amount: $595,069; jobs available. *State or other work-study/employment:* Total amount: $32,200 (100% non-need-based). Part-time jobs available.

**APPLYING FOR FINANCIAL AID** *Required financial aid forms:* FAFSA, federal income tax form(s). *Financial aid deadline:* 5/1 (priority: 2/15). *Notification date:* Continuous beginning 3/1. Students must reply within 2 weeks of notification.

**CONTACT** Patrick Bonones, Director of Financial Aid, Agnes Scott College, 141 East College Avenue, Decatur, GA 30030-3797, 404-471-6395 or toll-free 800-868-8602. *Fax:* 404-471-6159. *E-mail:* finaid@agnesscott.edu. *Website:* http://www.agnesscott.edu/.

# ALABAMA AGRICULTURAL AND MECHANICAL UNIVERSITY
## Huntsville, AL

| Tuition & fees (AL res): $9090 | Average undergraduate aid package: $10,708 |
|---|---|

**ABOUT THE INSTITUTION** State-supported, coed. 36 undergraduate majors. Federal methodology is used as a basis for awarding need-based institutional aid.

**UNDERGRADUATE EXPENSES for 2015–2016** *One-time required fee:* $100. *Tuition, state resident:* full-time $7500; part-time $250 per credit hour. *Tuition, nonresident:* full-time $15,000; part-time $500 per credit hour. *Required fees:* full-time $1590; $1590 per year. Full-time tuition and fees vary according to course load. Part-time tuition and fees vary according to course load. *College room and board:* $5440; *Room only:* $2400. Room and board charges vary according to board plan, housing facility, and location. *Payment plan:* Guaranteed tuition.

**FRESHMAN FINANCIAL AID (Fall 2013)** 1,184 applied for aid; of those 96% were deemed to have need. 98% of freshmen with need received aid; of those 8% had need fully met. *Average percent of need met:* 74% (excluding resources awarded to replace EFC). *Average financial aid package:* $11,417 (excluding resources awarded to replace EFC). 4% of all full-time freshmen had no need and received non-need-based gift aid.

**UNDERGRADUATE FINANCIAL AID (Fall 2013)** 3,784 applied for aid; of those 96% were deemed to have need. 98% of undergraduates with need received aid; of those 7% had need fully met. *Average percent of need met:* 72% (excluding resources awarded to replace EFC). *Average financial aid package:* $10,708 (excluding resources awarded to replace EFC). 3% of all full-time undergraduates had no need and received non-need-based gift aid.

**GIFT AID (NEED-BASED)** *Total amount:* $22,656,458 (66% federal, 31% institutional, 3% external sources). *Receiving aid:* Freshmen: 90% (1,075); all full-time undergraduates: 83% (3,244). *Average award:* Freshmen: $8415; Undergraduates: $7581. *Scholarships, grants, and awards:* Federal Pell, FSEOG, state, private, college/university gift aid from institutional funds.

**GIFT AID (NON-NEED-BASED)** *Total amount:* $930,584 (85% institutional, 15% external sources). *Receiving aid:* Freshmen: 3% (33). Undergraduates: 1% (53). *Average award:* Freshmen: $5035. Undergraduates: $6921. *Scholarships, grants, and awards by category:* Academic interests/achievement: agriculture, biological sciences, engineering/technologies, general academic interests/achievements, health fields, mathematics, military science, physical sciences, social sciences. *Creative arts/performance:* art/fine arts, music. *Tuition waivers:* Full or partial for employees or children of employees.

**LOANS** *Student loans:* $28,914,137 (95% need-based, 5% non-need-based). 77% of past graduating class borrowed through all loan programs. *Average indebtedness per student:* $38,819. *Average need-based loan:* Freshmen: $3563. Undergrad-

uates: $4023. *Parent loans:* $9,134,218 (83% need-based, 17% non-need-based). *Programs:* Federal Direct (Subsidized and Unsubsidized Stafford, PLUS), Perkins, Sallie Mae Smart Option Loans.

**WORK-STUDY** *Federal work-study:* jobs available.

**ATHLETIC AWARDS** Total amount: $3,195,098 (75% need-based, 25% non-need-based).

**APPLYING FOR FINANCIAL AID** *Required financial aid form:* FAFSA. *Financial aid deadline (priority):* 3/1. *Notification date:* Continuous beginning 2/15. Students must reply within 2 weeks of notification.

**CONTACT** Ms. Deborah Gordon, Financial Aid Officer, Alabama Agricultural and Mechanical University, PO Box 907, Huntsville, AL 35762, 256-372-4853 or toll-free 800-553-0816. *Fax:* 256-372-5407. *E-mail:* deborah.gordon@aamu.edu. *Website:* http://www.aamu.edu/.

# ALABAMA STATE UNIVERSITY
## Montgomery, AL

| Tuition & fees (AL res): $6936 | Average undergraduate aid package: $18,385 |
|---|---|

**ABOUT THE INSTITUTION** State-supported, coed. *Awards:* certificates, bachelor's, master's, and doctoral degrees. 34 undergraduate majors. *Total enrollment:* 5,510. Undergraduates: 4,803. Freshmen: 1,081. Federal methodology is used as a basis for awarding need-based institutional aid.

**UNDERGRADUATE EXPENSES for 2015–2016** *Application fee:* $25. *One-time required fee:* $150. *Tuition, state resident:* full-time $6936; part-time $289 per credit hour. *Tuition, nonresident:* full-time $13,872; part-time $578 per credit hour. *Required fees:* $446 per term. Full-time tuition and fees vary according to course load and degree level. Part-time tuition and fees vary according to course load and degree level. *College room and board:* $5422. Room and board charges vary according to board plan and housing facility.

**FRESHMAN FINANCIAL AID (Fall 2014, est.)** 872 applied for aid; of those 100% were deemed to have need. 94% of freshmen with need received aid; of those 22% had need fully met. *Average percent of need met:* 76% (excluding resources awarded to replace EFC). *Average financial aid package:* $14,444 (excluding resources awarded to replace EFC). 2% of all full-time freshmen had no need and received non-need-based gift aid.

**UNDERGRADUATE FINANCIAL AID (Fall 2014, est.)** 4,320 applied for aid; of those 97% were deemed to have need. 100% of undergraduates with need received aid; of those 41% had need fully met. *Average percent of need met:* 83% (excluding resources awarded to replace EFC). *Average financial aid package:* $18,385 (excluding resources awarded to replace EFC). 2% of all full-time undergraduates had no need and received non-need-based gift aid.

**GIFT AID (NEED-BASED)** *Total amount:* $18,532,937 (96% federal, 1% state, 3% institutional). *Receiving aid:* Freshmen: 66% (704); all full-time undergraduates: 82% (3,607). *Average award:* Freshmen: $5364; Undergraduates: $4642. *Scholarships, grants, and awards:* Federal Pell, FSEOG, state, private, college/university gift aid from institutional funds, United Negro College Fund.

**GIFT AID (NON-NEED-BASED)** *Total amount:* $14,558,743 (1% federal, 28% state, 59% institutional, 12% external sources). *Receiving aid:* Freshmen: 23% (247). Undergraduates: 45% (1,950). *Average award:* Freshmen: $9461. Undergraduates: $9669. *Scholarships, grants, and awards by category:* Academic interests/achievement: general academic interests/achievements. *Creative arts/performance:* general creative arts/performance, music, theater/drama. *Special achievements/activities:* leadership. *Special characteristics:* general special characteristics, members of minority groups. *Tuition waivers:* Full or partial for employees or children of employees. *ROTC:* Army cooperative, Air Force.

**LOANS** *Student loans:* $29,831,723 (45% need-based, 55% non-need-based). 90% of past graduating class borrowed through all loan programs. *Average indebtedness per student:* $32,629. *Average need-based loan:* Freshmen: $3215. Undergraduates: $3297. *Parent loans:* $6,474,842 (89% need-based, 11% non-need-based). *Programs:* Federal Direct (Subsidized and Unsubsidized Stafford, PLUS), Perkins.

**WORK-STUDY** *Federal work-study:* Total amount: $1,383,062; 651 jobs averaging $1800. *State or other work-study/employment:* Total amount: $838,066 (100% non-need-based). Part-time jobs available.

**ATHLETIC AWARDS** Total amount: $3,620,413 (86% need-based, 14% non-need-based).

**APPLYING FOR FINANCIAL AID** *Required financial aid form:* FAFSA. *Financial aid deadline (priority):* 4/1. *Notification date:* Continuous beginning 5/1.

**CONTACT** Mr. Marcus Byrd, Interim Director of Financial Aid, Alabama State University, PO Box 271, Montgomery, AL 36101-0271, 334-229-4323 or toll-free 800-253-5037. *Fax:* 334-299-4924. *E-mail:* mbyrd@alasu.edu.
*Website:* http://www.alasu.edu/.

---

# ALASKA BIBLE COLLEGE
## Glennallen, AK

**Tuition & fees: N/R**      **Average undergraduate aid package: N/A**

**ABOUT THE INSTITUTION** Independent nondenominational, coed. *Awards:* certificates, associate, and bachelor's degrees. 1 undergraduate major. *Total enrollment:* 31. Undergraduates: 31. Freshmen: 9. Institutional methodology is used as a basis for awarding need-based institutional aid.

**GIFT AID (NEED-BASED)** *Total amount:* $45,222 (100% federal). *Scholarships, grants, and awards:* Federal Pell, FSEOG, private, college/university gift aid from institutional funds.

**GIFT AID (NON-NEED-BASED)** *Total amount:* $20,222 (62% state, 38% external sources). *Scholarships, grants, and awards by category:* Academic interests/achievement: general academic interests/achievements, religion/biblical studies. Creative arts/performance: music. Special achievements/activities: religious involvement. Special characteristics: children of faculty/staff, married students, spouses of current students.

**LOANS** *Student loans:* $37,852 (100% need-based). *Programs:* Federal Direct (Subsidized and Unsubsidized Stafford), state.

**WORK-STUDY** *Federal work-study:* Total amount: $5000; jobs available. *State or other work-study/employment:* Part-time jobs available.

**APPLYING FOR FINANCIAL AID** *Required financial aid form:* FAFSA. *Financial aid deadline:* 7/1. *Notification date:* 8/1. Students must reply within 2 weeks of notification.

**CONTACT** Financial Aid Office, Alaska Bible College, 248 East Elmwood Avenue, Palmer, AK 99645, 907-745-3201 or toll-free 800-478-7884. *Fax:* 907-745-3210. *E-mail:* info@akbible.edu.
*Website:* http://www.akbible.edu/.

---

# ALASKA PACIFIC UNIVERSITY
## Anchorage, AK

**Tuition & fees: $19,680**      **Average undergraduate aid package: $9714**

**ABOUT THE INSTITUTION** Independent, coed. *Awards:* certificates, associate, bachelor's, master's, and doctoral degrees. 10 undergraduate majors. *Total enrollment:* 606. Undergraduates: 326. Freshmen: 19. Federal methodology is used as a basis for awarding need-based institutional aid.

**UNDERGRADUATE EXPENSES** for 2015–2016 *Application fee:* $25. *Comprehensive fee:* $26,680 includes full-time tuition ($19,500), mandatory fees ($180), and room and board ($7000). Full-time tuition and fees vary according to course load, degree level, program, and reciprocity agreements. Room and board charges vary according to board plan and housing facility. *Part-time tuition:* $812 per semester hour. Part-time tuition and fees vary according to course load, degree level, and program.

**FRESHMAN FINANCIAL AID (Fall 2014, est.)** 18 applied for aid; of those 89% were deemed to have need. 100% of freshmen with need received aid. *Average percent of need met:* 40% (excluding resources awarded to replace EFC). *Average financial aid package:* $12,560 (excluding resources awarded to replace EFC). 6% of all full-time freshmen had no need and received non-need-based gift aid.

**UNDERGRADUATE FINANCIAL AID (Fall 2014, est.)** 181 applied for aid; of those 88% were deemed to have need. 100% of undergraduates with need received aid. *Average percent of need met:* 30% (excluding resources awarded to replace EFC). *Average financial aid package:* $9714 (excluding resources awarded to

replace EFC). 8% of all full-time undergraduates had no need and received non-need-based gift aid.

**GIFT AID (NEED-BASED)** *Total amount:* $545,243 (74% federal, 8% state, 9% institutional, 9% external sources). *Receiving aid:* Freshmen: 50% (9); all full-time undergraduates: 42% (110). *Average award:* Freshmen: $3747; Undergraduates: $4406. *Scholarships, grants, and awards:* Federal Pell, FSEOG, state, private, college/university gift aid from institutional funds, Bureau of Indian Affairs Grants, Yellow Ribbon Grant Program, Native Alaskan Scholarships.

**GIFT AID (NON-NEED-BASED)** *Total amount:* $1,272,976 (4% state, 84% institutional, 12% external sources). *Receiving aid:* Freshmen: 89% (16). Undergraduates: 41% (108). *Average award:* Freshmen: $11,000. Undergraduates: $6627. *Scholarships, grants, and awards by category:* Academic interests/achievement: biological sciences, business, communication, education, English, general academic interests/achievements, health fields, humanities, mathematics, physical sciences, religion/biblical studies, social sciences. Creative arts/performance: art/fine arts, journalism/publications, music, theater/drama. Special achievements/activities: community service, general special achievements/activities, leadership, religious involvement. Special characteristics: adult students, children and siblings of alumni, children of faculty/staff, ethnic background, general special characteristics, international students, local/state students, members of minority groups, out-of-state students, previous college experience, religious affiliation. *Tuition waivers:* Full or partial for employees or children of employees. *ROTC:* Army cooperative, Air Force cooperative.

**LOANS** *Student loans:* $1,450,735 (45% need-based, 55% non-need-based). 63% of past graduating class borrowed through all loan programs. *Average indebtedness per student:* $8922. *Average need-based loan:* Freshmen: $3435. Undergraduates: $4347. *Parent loans:* $137,233 (100% non-need-based). *Programs:* Federal Direct (Subsidized and Unsubsidized Stafford, PLUS), state, alternative loans.

**WORK-STUDY** *Federal work-study:* Total amount: $17,154; 20 jobs averaging $748. *State or other work-study/employment:* Part-time jobs available.

**APPLYING FOR FINANCIAL AID** *Required financial aid form:* FAFSA. *Financial aid deadline (priority):* 6/30. *Notification date:* Continuous beginning 2/1. Students must reply by 2/1 or within 4 weeks of notification.

**CONTACT** Mr. Phong Moua, Director of Student Financial Services, Alaska Pacific University, 4101 University Drive, Carr-Gottstein Room 106, Anchorage, AK 99508-4672, 907-564-8342 or toll-free 800-252-7528. *Fax:* 907-564-8317. *E-mail:* pmoua@alaskapacific.edu.
*Website:* http://www.alaskapacific.edu/.

---

# ALBANY COLLEGE OF PHARMACY AND HEALTH SCIENCES
## Albany, NY

**Tuition & fees: $30,131**      **Average undergraduate aid package: $14,578**

**ABOUT THE INSTITUTION** Independent, coed. *Awards:* bachelor's, master's, and doctoral degrees. 6 undergraduate majors. *Total enrollment:* 1,559. Undergraduates: 1,078. Freshmen: 213. Both federal and institutional methodology are used as a basis for awarding need-based institutional aid.

**UNDERGRADUATE EXPENSES** for 2015–2016 *Application fee:* $75. *Comprehensive fee:* $40,371 includes full-time tuition ($29,400), mandatory fees ($731), and room and board ($10,240). *College room only:* $6600. Full-time tuition and fees vary according to degree level, program, and student level. Room and board charges vary according to board plan, housing facility, and location. *Part-time tuition:* $980 per credit hour. Part-time tuition and fees vary according to degree level, program, and student level.

**FRESHMAN FINANCIAL AID (Fall 2014, est.)** 203 applied for aid; of those 85% were deemed to have need. 99% of freshmen with need received aid; of those 15% had need fully met. *Average percent of need met:* 54% (excluding resources awarded to replace EFC). *Average financial aid package:* $16,398 (excluding resources awarded to replace EFC). 17% of all full-time freshmen had no need and received non-need-based gift aid.

**UNDERGRADUATE FINANCIAL AID (Fall 2014, est.)** 872 applied for aid; of those 89% were deemed to have need. 100% of undergraduates with need received aid; of those 9% had need fully met. *Average percent of need met:* 44% (excluding resources awarded to replace EFC). *Average financial aid package:* $14,578

---

(excluding resources awarded to replace EFC). 15% of all full-time undergraduates had no need and received non-need-based gift aid.

**GIFT AID (NEED-BASED) Total amount:** $8,701,672 (15% federal, 10% state, 71% institutional, 4% external sources). **Receiving aid:** Freshmen: 80% (171); all full-time undergraduates: 77% (731). **Average award:** Freshmen: $13,341; Undergraduates: $10,774. **Scholarships, grants, and awards:** Federal Pell, FSEOG, state, private, college/university gift aid from institutional funds.

**GIFT AID (NON-NEED-BASED) Total amount:** $1,798,731 (1% state, 92% institutional, 7% external sources). **Receiving aid:** Freshmen: 8% (17). Undergraduates: 5% (45). **Average award:** Freshmen: $10,011. Undergraduates: $9463. **Scholarships, grants, and awards by category:** Academic interests/achievement: biological sciences, general academic interests/achievements, health fields, physical sciences, premedicine. Special characteristics: children and siblings of alumni, children of faculty/staff, international students, siblings of current students. **Tuition waivers:** Full or partial for employees or children of employees.

**LOANS Student loans:** $16,665,652 (78% need-based, 22% non-need-based). **Average need-based loan:** Freshmen: $3300. Undergraduates: $4617. **Parent loans:** $3,566,724 (66% need-based, 34% non-need-based). **Programs:** Federal Direct (Subsidized and Unsubsidized Stafford, PLUS), Perkins, state, Health Professions Student Loans (HPSL).

**WORK-STUDY Federal work-study:** Total amount: $164,494; jobs available. **State or other work-study/employment:** Total amount: $13,680 (37% need-based, 63% non-need-based). Part-time jobs available.

**ATHLETIC AWARDS** Total amount: $1750 (100% non-need-based).

**APPLYING FOR FINANCIAL AID Required financial aid form:** FAFSA. **Financial aid deadline:** 5/1 (priority: 2/1). **Notification date:** 3/1. Students must reply within 2 weeks of notification.

**CONTACT** Kathleen Montague, Director of Financial Aid, Albany College of Pharmacy and Health Sciences, 106 New Scotland Avenue, Albany, NY 12208-3425, 518-694-7256 or toll-free 888-203-8010. Fax: 518-694-7322. E-mail: financial_aid@acphs.edu.
Website: http://www.acphs.edu/.

# ALBANY STATE UNIVERSITY
## Albany, GA

| Tuition & fees (GA res): $5192 | Average undergraduate aid package: $5164 |
| --- | --- |

**ABOUT THE INSTITUTION** State-supported, coed. **Awards:** certificates, bachelor's, and master's degrees. 34 undergraduate majors. **Total enrollment:** 3,910. Undergraduates: 3,316. Freshmen: 426. Federal methodology is used as a basis for awarding need-based institutional aid.

**UNDERGRADUATE EXPENSES for 2015–2016 Application fee:** $25. **Tuition, state resident:** full-time $3792; part-time $158 per credit hour. **Tuition, nonresident:** full-time $13,797; part-time $574.87 per credit hour. **Required fees:** full-time $1400. Full-time tuition and fees vary according to course load and degree level. Part-time tuition and fees vary according to course load and degree level. **College room and board:** $7522; **Room only:** $4674. Room and board charges vary according to board plan and housing facility.

**FRESHMAN FINANCIAL AID (Fall 2014, est.)** 422 applied for aid; of those 96% were deemed to have need. 99% of freshmen with need received aid; of those 9% had need fully met. **Average percent of need met:** 59% (excluding resources awarded to replace EFC). **Average financial aid package:** $5077 (excluding resources awarded to replace EFC).

**UNDERGRADUATE FINANCIAL AID (Fall 2014, est.)** 2,729 applied for aid; of those 96% were deemed to have need. 100% of undergraduates with need received aid; of those 9% had need fully met. **Average percent of need met:** 71% (excluding resources awarded to replace EFC). **Average financial aid package:** $5164 (excluding resources awarded to replace EFC). 1% of all full-time undergraduates had no need and received non-need-based gift aid.

**GIFT AID (NEED-BASED) Total amount:** $11,450,629 (100% federal). **Receiving aid:** Freshmen: 80% (341); all full-time undergraduates: 78% (2,165). **Average award:** Freshmen: $2608; Undergraduates: $2595. **Scholarships, grants, and awards:** Federal Pell, FSEOG, state, private, college/university gift aid from institutional funds, United Negro College Fund, Federal Nursing.

**GIFT AID (NON-NEED-BASED) Total amount:** $2,446,457 (90% state, 1% institutional, 9% external sources). **Receiving aid:** Freshmen: 48% (203). Undergraduates: 25% (693). **Average award:** Undergraduates: $1500. **Scholarships, grants,**

and awards by category: Academic interests/achievement: biological sciences, computer science, education, general academic interests/achievements, health fields, mathematics, social sciences. **Creative arts/performance:** music. **Special characteristics:** children and siblings of alumni, local/state students. **Tuition waivers:** Full or partial for employees or children of employees, senior citizens. **ROTC:** Army.

**LOANS Student loans:** $24,630,645 (48% need-based, 52% non-need-based). 93% of past graduating class borrowed through all loan programs. Average indebtedness per student: $39,014. **Average need-based loan:** Freshmen: $1765. Undergraduates: $2402. **Parent loans:** $2,800,393 (100% non-need-based). **Programs:** Federal Direct (Subsidized and Unsubsidized Stafford, PLUS), Perkins, state.

**WORK-STUDY Federal work-study:** Total amount: $409,650; jobs available. **State or other work-study/employment:** Part-time jobs available.

**ATHLETIC AWARDS** Total amount: $699,081 (100% non-need-based).

**APPLYING FOR FINANCIAL AID Required financial aid form:** FAFSA. **Financial aid deadline:** 6/30 (priority: 4/15). **Notification date:** Continuous.

**CONTACT** Mr. Thomas A. Harris, Director of Financial Aid, Albany State University, 504 College Drive, Albany, GA 31705-2717, 229-430-4650 or toll-free 800-822-7267. Fax: 229-430-3936.
Website: http://www.asurams.edu/.

# ALBERTUS MAGNUS COLLEGE
## New Haven, CT

| Tuition & fees: $28,930 | Average undergraduate aid package: $15,366 |
| --- | --- |

**ABOUT THE INSTITUTION** Independent Roman Catholic, coed. **Awards:** certificates, diplomas, associate, bachelor's, and master's degrees. 45 undergraduate majors. **Total enrollment:** 1,550. Undergraduates: 1,256. Freshmen: 159. Federal methodology is used as a basis for awarding need-based institutional aid.

**UNDERGRADUATE EXPENSES for 2015–2016 Application fee:** $35. **Comprehensive fee:** $41,890 includes full-time tuition ($28,440), mandatory fees ($490), and room and board ($12,960). Full-time tuition and fees vary according to program. Room and board charges vary according to board plan. **Part-time tuition:** $1185 per credit. Part-time tuition and fees vary according to program.

**FRESHMAN FINANCIAL AID (Fall 2014, est.)** 529 applied for aid; of those 97% were deemed to have need. 100% of freshmen with need received aid; of those 6% had need fully met. **Average percent of need met:** 52% (excluding resources awarded to replace EFC). **Average financial aid package:** $20,894 (excluding resources awarded to replace EFC). 1% of all full-time freshmen had no need and received non-need-based gift aid.

**UNDERGRADUATE FINANCIAL AID (Fall 2014, est.)** 1,119 applied for aid; of those 97% were deemed to have need. 99% of undergraduates with need received aid; of those 4% had need fully met. **Average percent of need met:** 44% (excluding resources awarded to replace EFC). **Average financial aid package:** $15,366 (excluding resources awarded to replace EFC). 1% of all full-time undergraduates had no need and received non-need-based gift aid.

**GIFT AID (NEED-BASED) Total amount:** $10,746,620 (26% federal, 15% state, 59% institutional). **Receiving aid:** Freshmen: 85% (484); all full-time undergraduates: 77% (961). **Average award:** Freshmen: $15,117; Undergraduates: $11,176. **Scholarships, grants, and awards:** Federal Pell, FSEOG, state, college/university gift aid from institutional funds.

**GIFT AID (NON-NEED-BASED) Total amount:** $1,520,795 (97% institutional, 3% external sources). **Receiving aid:** Freshmen: 25% (145). Undergraduates: 13% (169). **Average award:** Freshmen: $16,734. Undergraduates: $15,445. **Scholarships, grants, and awards by category:** Academic interests/achievement: biological sciences, business, communication, computer science, education, English, foreign languages, general academic interests/achievements, humanities, international studies, mathematics, physical sciences, premedicine, religion/biblical studies, social sciences. **Creative arts/performance:** art/fine arts, performing arts, theater/drama. **Special achievements/activities:** community service, leadership. **Special characteristics:** local/state students, religious affiliation, siblings of current students. **Tuition waivers:** Full or partial for employees or children of employees, senior citizens.

**LOANS Student loans:** $9,687,474 (43% need-based, 57% non-need-based). 87% of past graduating class borrowed through all loan programs. Average indebtedness per student: $33,975. **Average need-based loan:** Freshmen: $4136. Undergraduates: $4228. **Parent loans:** $741,450 (100% non-need-based). **Programs:** Federal Direct (Subsidized and Unsubsidized Stafford, PLUS), Perkins.

**WORK-STUDY** *Federal work-study:* Total amount: $159,136; 97 jobs averaging $1633.

**APPLYING FOR FINANCIAL AID** *Required financial aid form:* FAFSA. *Financial aid deadline (priority):* 3/15. *Notification date:* 4/15. Students must reply within 2 weeks of notification.

**CONTACT** Michelle Cochran, Director of Financial Aid, Albertus Magnus College, 700 Prospect Street, New Haven, CT 06511-1189, 203-773-8508 or toll-free 800-578-9160. *Fax:* 203-773-8972. *E-mail:* financial_aid@albertus.edu. *Website:* http://www.albertus.edu/.

# ALBION COLLEGE
## Albion, MI

| Tuition & fees: $37,300 | Average undergraduate aid package: $29,076 |
|---|---|

**ABOUT THE INSTITUTION** Independent Methodist, coed. *Awards:* bachelor's degrees. 63 undergraduate majors. *Total enrollment:* 1,268. Undergraduates: 1,268. Freshmen: 357. Federal methodology is used as a basis for awarding need-based institutional aid.

**UNDERGRADUATE EXPENSES for 2015–2016** *One-time required fee:* $185. *Comprehensive fee:* $47,850 includes full-time tuition ($36,872), mandatory fees ($428), and room and board ($10,550). *College room only:* $5160. Full-time tuition and fees vary according to course load. Room and board charges vary according to board plan and housing facility. *Part-time tuition:* $1560 per semester hour. Part-time tuition and fees vary according to course load.

**FRESHMAN FINANCIAL AID (Fall 2014, est.)** 320 applied for aid; of those 87% were deemed to have need. 100% of freshmen with need received aid; of those 25% had need fully met. *Average percent of need met:* 86% (excluding resources awarded to replace EFC). *Average financial aid package:* $30,767 (excluding resources awarded to replace EFC). 22% of all full-time freshmen had no need and received non-need-based gift aid.

**UNDERGRADUATE FINANCIAL AID (Fall 2014, est.)** 1,016 applied for aid; of those 89% were deemed to have need. 100% of undergraduates with need received aid; of those 21% had need fully met. *Average percent of need met:* 82% (excluding resources awarded to replace EFC). *Average financial aid package:* $29,076 (excluding resources awarded to replace EFC). 27% of all full-time undergraduates had no need and received non-need-based gift aid.

**GIFT AID (NEED-BASED)** *Total amount:* $22,277,896 (7% federal, 5% state, 86% institutional, 2% external sources). *Receiving aid:* Freshmen: 78% (278); all full-time undergraduates: 73% (907). *Average award:* Freshmen: $25,673; Undergraduates: $24,065. *Scholarships, grants, and awards:* Federal Pell, FSEOG, state, private, college/university gift aid from institutional funds.

**GIFT AID (NON-NEED-BASED)** *Total amount:* $5,829,816 (99% institutional, 1% external sources). *Receiving aid:* Freshmen: 77% (274). Undergraduates: 69% (860). *Average award:* Freshmen: $19,384. Undergraduates: $17,458. *Scholarships, grants, and awards by category: Academic interests/achievement:* 999 awards ($16,700,634 total): business, communication, general academic interests/achievements, mathematics. *Creative arts/performance:* 58 awards ($58,875 total): art/fine arts, music, performing arts, theater/drama. *Special characteristics:* 126 awards ($129,850 total): children and siblings of alumni, relatives of clergy. *Tuition waivers:* Full or partial for employees or children of employees.

**LOANS** *Student loans:* $9,475,702 (57% need-based, 43% non-need-based). 65% of past graduating class borrowed through all loan programs. *Average indebtedness per student:* $37,151. *Average need-based loan:* Freshmen: $5104. Undergraduates: $5301. *Parent loans:* $2,457,071 (100% non-need-based). *Programs:* Federal Direct (Subsidized and Unsubsidized Stafford, PLUS), Perkins.

**WORK-STUDY** *Federal work-study:* Total amount: $421,650; 312 jobs averaging $1317. *State or other work-study/employment:* Total amount: $88,545 (99% need-based, 1% non-need-based). 68 part-time jobs averaging $955.

**APPLYING FOR FINANCIAL AID** *Required financial aid form:* FAFSA. *Financial aid deadline (priority):* 2/1. *Notification date:* Continuous beginning 3/15.

**CONTACT** Ms. Ann Whitmer, Director of Student Financial Services, Albion College, Kellogg Center Box 4670, Albion, MI 49224-1831, 517-629-0440 or toll-free 800-858-6770. *Fax:* 517-629-0581. *E-mail:* financialaid@albion.edu. *Website:* http://www.albion.edu/.

# ALBRIGHT COLLEGE
## Reading, PA

| Tuition & fees: $38,220 | Average undergraduate aid package: $32,847 |
|---|---|

**ABOUT THE INSTITUTION** Independent United Methodist Church, coed. *Awards:* certificates, bachelor's, and master's degrees. 42 undergraduate majors. *Total enrollment:* 1,808. Undergraduates: 1,775. Freshmen: 540. Federal methodology is used as a basis for awarding need-based institutional aid.

**UNDERGRADUATE EXPENSES for 2015–2016** *Application fee:* $25. *Comprehensive fee:* $48,620 includes full-time tuition ($37,320), mandatory fees ($900), and room and board ($10,400). *College room only:* $5770. Full-time tuition and fees vary according to degree level. Room and board charges vary according to board plan and housing facility. *Part-time tuition:* $4665 per course. Part-time tuition and fees vary according to degree level.

**FRESHMAN FINANCIAL AID (Fall 2014, est.)** 509 applied for aid; of those 98% were deemed to have need. 100% of freshmen with need received aid; of those 9% had need fully met. *Average percent of need met:* 83% (excluding resources awarded to replace EFC). *Average financial aid package:* $35,460 (excluding resources awarded to replace EFC). 4% of all full-time freshmen had no need and received non-need-based gift aid.

**UNDERGRADUATE FINANCIAL AID (Fall 2014, est.)** 1,627 applied for aid; of those 97% were deemed to have need. 100% of undergraduates with need received aid; of those 10% had need fully met. *Average percent of need met:* 78% (excluding resources awarded to replace EFC). *Average financial aid package:* $32,847 (excluding resources awarded to replace EFC). 7% of all full-time undergraduates had no need and received non-need-based gift aid.

**GIFT AID (NEED-BASED)** *Total amount:* $42,372,984 (11% federal, 5% state, 80% institutional, 4% external sources). *Receiving aid:* Freshmen: 92% (496); all full-time undergraduates: 90% (1,567). *Average award:* Freshmen: $28,962; Undergraduates: $27,027. *Scholarships, grants, and awards:* Federal Pell, FSEOG, state, private, college/university gift aid from institutional funds, Academic Competitiveness Grants, National SMART Grants.

**GIFT AID (NON-NEED-BASED)** *Total amount:* $3,022,315 (85% institutional, 15% external sources). *Receiving aid:* Freshmen: 6% (34). Undergraduates: 6% (112). *Average award:* Freshmen: $14,354. Undergraduates: $14,176. *Scholarships, grants, and awards by category: Creative arts/performance:* art/fine arts, journalism/publications, music, theater/drama. *Special achievements/activities:* general special achievements/activities, memberships, religious involvement. *Special characteristics:* children and siblings of alumni, ethnic background, siblings of current students. *Tuition waivers:* Full or partial for employees or children of employees, adult students, senior citizens. *ROTC:* Army cooperative.

**LOANS** *Student loans:* $15,870,513 (80% need-based, 20% non-need-based). 88% of past graduating class borrowed through all loan programs. *Average indebtedness per student:* $28,541. *Average need-based loan:* Freshmen: $5437. Undergraduates: $5113. *Parent loans:* $4,533,555 (100% non-need-based). *Programs:* Federal Direct (Subsidized and Unsubsidized Stafford, PLUS), Perkins, private loans.

**WORK-STUDY** *Federal work-study:* Total amount: $1,881,590; jobs available. *State or other work-study/employment:* Total amount: $32,640 (37% need-based, 63% non-need-based). Part-time jobs available.

**APPLYING FOR FINANCIAL AID** *Financial aid deadline (priority):* 3/1. *Notification date:* 3/1. Students must reply by 3/1 or within 2 weeks of notification.

**CONTACT** Chris Hanlon, Director of Financial Aid, Albright College, PO Box 15234, Reading, PA 19612-5234, 610-921-7515 or toll-free 800-252-1856. *Fax:* 610-921-7729. *E-mail:* chanlon@alb.edu. *Website:* http://www.albright.edu/.

# ALCORN STATE UNIVERSITY
## Lorman, MS

| Tuition & fees (MS res): $6192 | Average undergraduate aid package: $15,322 |
|---|---|

**ABOUT THE INSTITUTION** State-supported, coed. *Awards:* certificates, associate, bachelor's, and master's degrees. 26 undergraduate majors. *Total enrollment:*

3,639. Undergraduates: 3,006. Freshmen: 517. Both federal and institutional methodology are used as a basis for awarding need-based institutional aid.

**UNDERGRADUATE EXPENSES** for 2015–2016 *Tuition, state resident:* full-time $6192. *Tuition, nonresident:* full-time $15,426. *College room and board:* $8650; *Room only:* $5902.

**FRESHMAN FINANCIAL AID (Fall 2014, est.)** 494 applied for aid; of those 100% were deemed to have need. 100% of freshmen with need received aid; of those 10% had need fully met. *Average percent of need met:* 52% (excluding resources awarded to replace EFC). *Average financial aid package:* $14,826 (excluding resources awarded to replace EFC). 27% of all full-time freshmen had no need and received non-need-based gift aid.

**UNDERGRADUATE FINANCIAL AID (Fall 2014, est.)** 1,650 applied for aid; of those 96% were deemed to have need. 100% of undergraduates with need received aid; of those 9% had need fully met. *Average percent of need met:* 48% (excluding resources awarded to replace EFC). *Average financial aid package:* $15,322 (excluding resources awarded to replace EFC). 19% of all full-time undergraduates had no need and received non-need-based gift aid.

**GIFT AID (NEED-BASED)** *Total amount:* $17,490,909 (70% federal, 2% state, 28% institutional). *Receiving aid:* Freshmen: 95% (470); all full-time undergraduates: 58% (1,487). *Average award:* Freshmen: $5516; Undergraduates: $5388. *Scholarships, grants, and awards:* Federal Pell, FSEOG, state, private, college/university gift aid from institutional funds.

**GIFT AID (NON-NEED-BASED)** *Receiving aid:* Freshmen: 33% (163). Undergraduates: 15% (384). *Average award:* Freshmen: $8456. Undergraduates: $7556. *Scholarships, grants, and awards by category: Academic interests/achievement:* 162 awards ($1,532,973 total): general academic interests/achievements. *Creative arts/performance:* 171 awards ($1,064,836 total): music. *Special achievements/activities:* 1 award ($15,776 total): leadership. *Special characteristics:* 55 awards ($208,400 total): children of faculty/staff. *Tuition waivers:* Full or partial for employees or children of employees. *ROTC:* Army.

**LOANS** *Student loans:* $28,763,198 (31% need-based, 69% non-need-based). 90% of past graduating class borrowed through all loan programs. *Average indebtedness per student:* $34,725. *Average need-based loan:* Freshmen: $3313. Undergraduates: $4168. *Parent loans:* $1,578,602 (100% non-need-based). *Programs:* Federal Direct (Subsidized and Unsubsidized Stafford, PLUS).

**WORK-STUDY** *Federal work-study:* Total amount: $317,818; 276 jobs averaging $1172. *State or other work-study/employment:* Total amount: $35,960 (100% need-based). Part-time jobs available.

**ATHLETIC AWARDS** Total amount: $2,385,498 (100% non-need-based).

**APPLYING FOR FINANCIAL AID** *Required financial aid forms:* FAFSA, institution's own form. *Financial aid deadline (priority):* 3/15. *Notification date:* Continuous beginning 4/1. Students must reply within 4 weeks of notification.

**CONTACT** Mrs. Juanita M. Russell, Director of Financial Aid, Alcorn State University, 1000 ASU Drive #28, Alcorn State, MS 39096-7500, 601-877-6190 or toll-free 800-222-6790. *Fax:* 601-877-6110. *E-mail:* juanita@alcorn.edu.
*Website:* http://www.alcorn.edu/.

# ALDERSON BROADDUS UNIVERSITY
## Philippi, WV

| Tuition & fees: $22,740 | Average undergraduate aid package: $25,574 |
| --- | --- |

**ABOUT THE INSTITUTION** Independent American Baptist Churches in the U.S.A., coed. *Awards:* certificates, associate, bachelor's, and master's degrees. 33 undergraduate majors. *Total enrollment:* 1,117. Undergraduates: 1,052. Freshmen: 438. Federal methodology is used as a basis for awarding need-based institutional aid.

**UNDERGRADUATE EXPENSES** for 2015–2016 *Comprehensive fee:* $29,976 includes full-time tuition ($22,530), mandatory fees ($210), and room and board ($7236). Room and board charges vary according to housing facility. *Part-time tuition:* $751 per credit. *Part-time fees:* $52.50 per term.

**FRESHMAN FINANCIAL AID (Fall 2013)** 438 applied for aid; of those 87% were deemed to have need. 100% of freshmen with need received aid; of those 76% had need fully met. *Average percent of need met:* 81% (excluding resources awarded to replace EFC). *Average financial aid package:* $24,542 (excluding resources awarded to replace EFC). 11% of all full-time freshmen had no need and received non-need-based gift aid.

**UNDERGRADUATE FINANCIAL AID (Fall 2013)** 976 applied for aid; of those 88% were deemed to have need. 100% of undergraduates with need received aid; of

those 71% had need fully met. *Average percent of need met:* 82% (excluding resources awarded to replace EFC). *Average financial aid package:* $25,574 (excluding resources awarded to replace EFC). 10% of all full-time undergraduates had no need and received non-need-based gift aid.

**GIFT AID (NEED-BASED)** *Total amount:* $12,528,939 (17% federal, 7% state, 74% institutional, 2% external sources). *Receiving aid:* Freshmen: 87% (381); all full-time undergraduates: 86% (850). *Average award:* Freshmen: $15,942; Undergraduates: $16,106. *Scholarships, grants, and awards:* Federal Pell, FSEOG, state, private, college/university gift aid from institutional funds, Federal Nursing, Scholarships for Disadvantaged Students (SDS), National Health Service Corps Scholarships.

**GIFT AID (NON-NEED-BASED)** *Total amount:* $1,689,279 (1% federal, 9% state, 86% institutional, 4% external sources). *Receiving aid:* Freshmen: 18% (81). Undergraduates: 9% (94). *Average award:* Freshmen: $10,581. Undergraduates: $10,285. *Scholarships, grants, and awards by category: Academic interests/achievement:* 696 awards ($5,802,069 total): biological sciences, business, communication, computer science, education, general academic interests/achievements, health fields, humanities, mathematics, physical sciences, premedicine, religion/biblical studies, social sciences. *Creative arts/performance:* 25 awards ($386,700 total): art/fine arts, creative writing, debating, journalism/publications, music, performing arts, theater/drama. *Special achievements/activities:* 634 awards ($1,193,018 total): general special achievements/activities, leadership. *Special characteristics:* 43 awards ($555,534 total): children of faculty/staff, ethnic background, general special characteristics, international students, religious affiliation. *Tuition waivers:* Full or partial for employees or children of employees.

**LOANS** *Student loans:* $6,456,265 (70% need-based, 30% non-need-based). 82% of past graduating class borrowed through all loan programs. *Average indebtedness per student:* $26,765. *Average need-based loan:* Freshmen: $3470. Undergraduates: $3719. *Parent loans:* $837,366 (28% need-based, 72% non-need-based). *Programs:* Federal Direct (Subsidized and Unsubsidized Stafford, PLUS), Perkins, Federal Nursing.

**WORK-STUDY** *Federal work-study:* 479 jobs averaging $1304. *State or other work-study/employment:* Total amount: $287,635 (22% need-based, 78% non-need-based). 116 part-time jobs averaging $2440.

**ATHLETIC AWARDS** Total amount: $1,663,462 (76% need-based, 24% non-need-based).

**APPLYING FOR FINANCIAL AID** *Required financial aid form:* FAFSA. *Financial aid deadline (priority):* 3/1. *Notification date:* Continuous beginning 3/1. Students must reply within 2 weeks of notification.

**CONTACT** Amy L. King, Director of Financial Aid, Alderson Broaddus University, College Hill Road, Philippi, WV 26416, 304-457-6354 or toll-free 800-263-1549. *Fax:* 304-457-6391.
*Website:* http://www.ab.edu/.

# ALFRED UNIVERSITY
## Alfred, NY

**ABOUT THE INSTITUTION** Independent, coed. 41 undergraduate majors.

**GIFT AID (NEED-BASED)** *Scholarships, grants, and awards:* Federal Pell, FSEOG, state, private, college/university gift aid from institutional funds.

**GIFT AID (NON-NEED-BASED)** *Scholarships, grants, and awards by category: Academic interests/achievement:* biological sciences, business, communication, education, engineering/technologies, English, foreign languages, general academic interests/achievements, humanities, international studies, mathematics, military science, physical sciences, premedicine, social sciences. *Creative arts/performance:* art/fine arts, creative writing, general creative arts/performance, performing arts. *Special achievements/activities:* leadership. *Special characteristics:* children of educators, children of faculty/staff, international students.

**LOANS** *Programs:* Federal Direct (Subsidized and Unsubsidized Stafford, PLUS), Perkins, college/university, alternative loans.

**WORK-STUDY** *Federal work-study:* jobs available.

**APPLYING FOR FINANCIAL AID** *Required financial aid forms:* FAFSA, institution's own form, state aid form, noncustodial (divorced/separated) parent's statement, business/farm supplement.

**CONTACT** Mr. Earl Pierce Jr., Director of Student Financial Aid, Alfred University, Alumni Hall, One Saxon Drive, Alfred, NY 14802-1205, 607-871-2159 or toll-free 800-541-9229. *Fax:* 607-871-2252. *E-mail:* pierce@alfred.edu.
*Website:* http://www.alfred.edu/.

## ALICE LLOYD COLLEGE
### Pippa Passes, KY

| Tuition & fees: $11,460 | Average undergraduate aid package: $13,001 |
|---|---|

**ABOUT THE INSTITUTION** Independent, coed. *Awards:* bachelor's degrees. 16 undergraduate majors. *Total enrollment:* 619. Undergraduates: 619. Freshmen: 184. Federal methodology is used as a basis for awarding need-based institutional aid.

**UNDERGRADUATE EXPENSES for 2015–2016** *Comprehensive fee:* $17,400 includes full-time tuition ($9600), mandatory fees ($1860), and room and board ($5940). *College room only:* $2850. *Part-time tuition:* $212 per credit hour. Part-time tuition and fees vary according to course load.

**FRESHMAN FINANCIAL AID (Fall 2014, est.)** 193 applied for aid; of those 95% were deemed to have need. 100% of freshmen with need received aid; of those 11% had need fully met. *Average percent of need met:* 67% (excluding resources awarded to replace EFC). *Average financial aid package:* $11,993 (excluding resources awarded to replace EFC). 5% of all full-time freshmen had no need and received non-need-based gift aid.

**UNDERGRADUATE FINANCIAL AID (Fall 2014, est.)** 596 applied for aid; of those 94% were deemed to have need. 100% of undergraduates with need received aid; of those 14% had need fully met. *Average percent of need met:* 72% (excluding resources awarded to replace EFC). *Average financial aid package:* $13,001 (excluding resources awarded to replace EFC). 6% of all full-time undergraduates had no need and received non-need-based gift aid.

**GIFT AID (NEED-BASED)** *Total amount:* $5,211,134 (31% federal, 42% state, 27% institutional). *Receiving aid:* Freshmen: 95% (183); all full-time undergraduates: 93% (555). *Average award:* Freshmen: $8645; Undergraduates: $9389. *Scholarships, grants, and awards:* Federal Pell, FSEOG, state, private, college/university gift aid from institutional funds.

**GIFT AID (NON-NEED-BASED)** *Total amount:* $294,628 (70% state, 10% institutional, 20% external sources). *Receiving aid:* Freshmen: 9% (17). Undergraduates: 11% (63). *Average award:* Freshmen: $7027. Undergraduates: $6562. *Scholarships, grants, and awards by category:* Special achievements/activities: general special achievements/activities. *Special characteristics:* members of minority groups. *Tuition waivers:* Full or partial for employees or children of employees.

**LOANS** *Student loans:* $1,816,095 (80% need-based, 20% non-need-based). 52% of past graduating class borrowed through all loan programs. *Average indebtedness per student:* $9949. *Average need-based loan:* Freshmen: $1889. Undergraduates: $2166. *Parent loans:* $7500 (100% non-need-based). *Programs:* Federal Direct (Subsidized and Unsubsidized Stafford, PLUS), college/university, Bagby Loans .

**WORK-STUDY** *Federal work-study:* Total amount: $947,157; 456 jobs averaging $2320. *State or other work-study/employment:* Total amount: $322,820 (13% need-based, 87% non-need-based). 137 part-time jobs averaging $2320.

**ATHLETIC AWARDS** Total amount: $293,116 (100% non-need-based).

**APPLYING FOR FINANCIAL AID** *Required financial aid form:* FAFSA. *Financial aid deadline (priority):* 2/15. *Notification date:* Continuous beginning 5/1.

**CONTACT** Ms. Jacqueline Stewart, Director of Financial Aid, Alice Lloyd College, 100 Purpose Road, Pippa Passes, KY 41844, 606-368-6058 or toll-free 888-280-4252. *E-mail:* jacquelinestewart@alc.edu. *Website:* http://www.alc.edu/.

## ALLEGHENY COLLEGE
### Meadville, PA

| Tuition & fees: $42,470 | Average undergraduate aid package: $33,833 |
|---|---|

**ABOUT THE INSTITUTION** Independent, coed. *Awards:* bachelor's degrees. 47 undergraduate majors. *Total enrollment:* 2,023. Undergraduates: 2,023. Freshmen: 476. Federal methodology is used as a basis for awarding need-based institutional aid.

**UNDERGRADUATE EXPENSES for 2015–2016** *Comprehensive fee:* $53,210 includes full-time tuition ($41,970), mandatory fees ($500), and room and board ($10,740). *College room only:* $5650. Room and board charges vary according to board plan and housing facility. *Part-time tuition:* $1749 per credit

hour. *Part-time fees:* $250 per term. Part-time tuition and fees vary according to course load.

**FRESHMAN FINANCIAL AID (Fall 2014, est.)** 424 applied for aid; of those 90% were deemed to have need. 100% of freshmen with need received aid; of those 43% had need fully met. *Average percent of need met:* 92% (excluding resources awarded to replace EFC). *Average financial aid package:* $35,861 (excluding resources awarded to replace EFC). 19% of all full-time freshmen had no need and received non-need-based gift aid.

**UNDERGRADUATE FINANCIAL AID (Fall 2014, est.)** 1,624 applied for aid; of those 89% were deemed to have need. 100% of undergraduates with need received aid; of those 34% had need fully met. *Average percent of need met:* 90% (excluding resources awarded to replace EFC). *Average financial aid package:* $33,833 (excluding resources awarded to replace EFC). 24% of all full-time undergraduates had no need and received non-need-based gift aid.

**GIFT AID (NEED-BASED)** *Total amount:* $37,074,873 (7% federal, 4% state, 86% institutional, 3% external sources). *Receiving aid:* Freshmen: 80% (380); all full-time undergraduates: 74% (1,445). *Average award:* Freshmen: $29,162; Undergraduates: $26,535. *Scholarships, grants, and awards:* Federal Pell, FSEOG, state, private, college/university gift aid from institutional funds, Veterans Education Benefits (GI Bill), Yellow Ribbon Grant Program.

**GIFT AID (NON-NEED-BASED)** *Total amount:* $9,489,812 (95% institutional, 5% external sources). *Receiving aid:* Freshmen: 20% (95). Undergraduates: 13% (255). *Average award:* Freshmen: $17,266. Undergraduates: $16,174. *Scholarships, grants, and awards by category:* Academic interests/achievement: 1,648 awards ($25,887,020 total): general academic interests/achievements. *Special characteristics:* 119 awards ($3,017,542 total): adult students, children of educators, children of faculty/staff, international students. *Tuition waivers:* Full or partial for employees or children of employees.

**LOANS** *Student loans:* $12,543,118 (47% need-based, 53% non-need-based). *Average need-based loan:* Freshmen: $4350. Undergraduates: $5216. *Parent loans:* $4,078,598 (100% non-need-based). *Programs:* Federal Direct (Subsidized and Unsubsidized Stafford, PLUS), Perkins, private loans.

**WORK-STUDY** *Federal work-study:* Total amount: $2,243,869; 1,139 jobs averaging $1970. *State or other work-study/employment:* Total amount: $583,795 (100% non-need-based). 113 part-time jobs averaging $5166.

**APPLYING FOR FINANCIAL AID** *Required financial aid form:* FAFSA. *Financial aid deadline (priority):* 2/15. *Notification date:* Continuous beginning 3/1. Students must reply by 5/1 or within 4 weeks of notification.

**CONTACT** Mr. Jonathan Boleratz, Director of Financial Aid, Allegheny College, 520 North Main Street, Meadville, PA 16335, 800-835-7780 or toll-free 800-521-5293. *Fax:* 814-332-2349. *E-mail:* fao@allegheny.edu. *Website:* http://www.allegheny.edu/.

## ALLEGHENY WESLEYAN COLLEGE
### Salem, OH

| Tuition & fees: N/R | Average undergraduate aid package: N/A |
|---|---|

**ABOUT THE INSTITUTION** Independent Wesleyan, coed. 2 undergraduate majors. Both federal and institutional methodology are used as a basis for awarding need-based institutional aid.

**GIFT AID (NEED-BASED)** *Total amount:* $38,037 (53% federal, 47% institutional). *Scholarships, grants, and awards:* Federal Pell, FSEOG, private, college/university gift aid from institutional funds.

**GIFT AID (NON-NEED-BASED)** *Total amount:* $15,742 (87% institutional, 13% external sources). *Scholarships, grants, and awards by category:* Creative arts/performance: 5 awards ($12,000 total): music.

**LOANS** *Student loans:* $96,778 (100% need-based). *Programs:* Federal Direct (Subsidized and Unsubsidized Stafford, PLUS).

**WORK-STUDY** *State or other work-study/employment:* Total amount: $59,779 (91% need-based, 9% non-need-based). 30 part-time jobs averaging $1992.

**APPLYING FOR FINANCIAL AID** *Required financial aid forms:* FAFSA, institution's own form. *Financial aid deadline (priority):* 7/31. *Notification date:* 8/15. Students must reply within 3 weeks of notification.

**CONTACT** Esther Phelps, Financial Aid Director, Allegheny Wesleyan College, 2161 Woodsdale Road, Salem, OH 44460, 330-337-6403 Ext. 111 or toll-free 800-292-3153. *Fax:* 424-228-3006. *E-mail:* ephelps@awc.edu. *Website:* http://www.awc.edu/.

## ALLEN COLLEGE
### Waterloo, IA

| Tuition & fees: $19,295 | Average undergraduate aid package: $12,215 |
| --- | --- |

**ABOUT THE INSTITUTION** Independent, coed, primarily women. **Awards:** certificates, associate, bachelor's, master's, and doctoral degrees (liberal arts and general education courses offered at either University of North Iowa or Wartburg College). 5 undergraduate majors. **Total enrollment:** 580. Undergraduates: 397. Freshmen: 1. Federal methodology is used as a basis for awarding need-based institutional aid.

**UNDERGRADUATE EXPENSES for 2015–2016 Application fee:** $50. **Comprehensive fee:** $26,576 includes full-time tuition ($17,262), mandatory fees ($2033), and room and board ($7281). **College room only:** $3641. Full-time tuition and fees vary according to course load and program. **Part-time tuition:** $557 per credit hour. **Part-time fees:** $75 per credit. Part-time tuition and fees vary according to course load and program.

**FRESHMAN FINANCIAL AID (Fall 2013)** 1 applied for aid; of those 100% were deemed to have need. 100% of freshmen with need received aid. **Average percent of need met:** 69% (excluding resources awarded to replace EFC). **Average financial aid package:** $26,429 (excluding resources awarded to replace EFC).

**UNDERGRADUATE FINANCIAL AID (Fall 2013)** 294 applied for aid; of those 90% were deemed to have need. 100% of undergraduates with need received aid; of those 7% had need fully met. **Average percent of need met:** 51% (excluding resources awarded to replace EFC). **Average financial aid package:** $12,215 (excluding resources awarded to replace EFC). 5% of all full-time undergraduates had no need and received non-need-based gift aid.

**GIFT AID (NEED-BASED) Total amount:** $1,848,842 (25% federal, 40% state, 23% institutional, 12% external sources). **Receiving aid:** Freshmen: 100% (1); all full-time undergraduates: 80% (237). **Average award:** Freshmen: $23,929; Undergraduates: $6977. **Scholarships, grants, and awards:** Federal Pell, FSEOG, state, private, college/university gift aid from institutional funds, Federal Nursing, Scholarships for Disadvantaged Students (SDS).

**GIFT AID (NON-NEED-BASED) Total amount:** $37,090 (89% institutional, 11% external sources). **Average award:** Undergraduates: $2071. **Scholarships, grants, and awards by category:** Academic interests/achievement: health fields. Special achievements/activities: community service, general special achievements/activities, leadership. Special characteristics: children of faculty/staff, general special characteristics, local/state students, members of minority groups, out-of-state students. **Tuition waivers:** Full or partial for employees or children of employees. **ROTC:** Army cooperative.

**LOANS Student loans:** $2,936,779 (87% need-based, 13% non-need-based). **Average need-based loan:** Freshmen: $2500. Undergraduates: $5119. **Parent loans:** $967,952 (51% need-based, 49% non-need-based). **Programs:** Federal Direct (Subsidized and Unsubsidized Stafford, PLUS), Perkins, Federal Nursing, state, college/university.

**WORK-STUDY Federal work-study:** 9 jobs averaging $2177.

**APPLYING FOR FINANCIAL AID Required financial aid forms:** FAFSA, institution's own form. **Financial aid deadline:** Continuous. **Notification date:** Continuous beginning 4/1. Students must reply within 2 weeks of notification.

**CONTACT** Kathie S. Aswegan, Financial Aid Coordinator, Allen College, Barrett Forum, 1825 Logan Avenue, Waterloo, IA 50703-1990, 319-226-2003. *Fax:* 319-226-2051. *E-mail:* kathie.aswegan@allencollege.edu.
*Website:* http://www.allencollege.edu/.

## ALLEN UNIVERSITY
### Columbia, SC

**CONTACT** Ms. Donna Foster, Director of Financial Aid, Allen University, 1530 Harden Street, Columbia, SC 29204-1085, 803-376-5736 or toll-free 877-625-5368. *E-mail:* donnaf@allenuniversity.edu.
*Website:* http://www.allenuniversity.edu/.

## ALLIANT INTERNATIONAL UNIVERSITY–SAN DIEGO
### San Diego, CA

| Tuition & fees: $15,812 | Average undergraduate aid package: $17,285 |
| --- | --- |

**ABOUT THE INSTITUTION** Independent, coed. **Awards:** certificates, bachelor's, master's, and doctoral degrees. 4 undergraduate majors. **Total enrollment:** 3,523. Undergraduates: 237. Federal methodology is used as a basis for awarding need-based institutional aid.

**UNDERGRADUATE EXPENSES for 2015–2016 Application fee:** $65. **Comprehensive fee:** $27,080 includes full-time tuition ($15,336), mandatory fees ($476), and room and board ($11,268). **College room only:** $7560. **Part-time tuition:** $639 per credit. **Part-time fees:** $130 per term.

**FRESHMAN FINANCIAL AID (Fall 2014, est.)** 4 applied for aid; of those 100% were deemed to have need. 100% of freshmen with need received aid. **Average percent of need met:** 67% (excluding resources awarded to replace EFC). **Average financial aid package:** $15,785 (excluding resources awarded to replace EFC).

**UNDERGRADUATE FINANCIAL AID (Fall 2014, est.)** 146 applied for aid; of those 99% were deemed to have need. 100% of undergraduates with need received aid; of those 2% had need fully met. **Average percent of need met:** 67% (excluding resources awarded to replace EFC). **Average financial aid package:** $17,285 (excluding resources awarded to replace EFC). 13% of all full-time undergraduates had no need and received non-need-based gift aid.

**GIFT AID (NEED-BASED) Total amount:** $893,342 (79% federal, 21% state). **Receiving aid:** Freshmen: 80% (4); all full-time undergraduates: 59% (108). **Average award:** Freshmen: $11,725; Undergraduates: $13,925. **Scholarships, grants, and awards:** Federal Pell, FSEOG, state, private, college/university gift aid from institutional funds.

**GIFT AID (NON-NEED-BASED) Total amount:** $666,860 (100% institutional). **Receiving aid:** Freshmen: 60% (3). Undergraduates: 61% (112). **Average award:** Undergraduates: $4000. **Scholarships, grants, and awards by category:** Academic interests/achievement: business, communication, computer science, education, English, foreign languages, general academic interests/achievements, humanities, international studies, social sciences. Special achievements/activities: community service, general special achievements/activities, leadership. Special characteristics: children and siblings of alumni, children of current students, children of faculty/staff, international students, local/state students, siblings of current students, spouses of current students, veterans.

**LOANS Student loans:** $766,203 (49% need-based, 51% non-need-based). 74% of past graduating class borrowed through all loan programs. **Average indebtedness per student:** $15,000. **Average need-based loan:** Freshmen: $3500. Undergraduates: $5500. **Parent loans:** $65,801 (100% non-need-based). **Programs:** Federal Direct (Subsidized and Unsubsidized Stafford, PLUS), Perkins, alternative loans.

**WORK-STUDY Federal work-study:** Total amount: $77,603; 37 jobs averaging $2500. **State or other work-study/employment:** Part-time jobs available.

**APPLYING FOR FINANCIAL AID Required financial aid form:** FAFSA. **Financial aid deadline (priority):** 3/2. **Notification date:** Continuous beginning 3/15. Students must reply within 3 weeks of notification.

**CONTACT** Deborah Spindler, Director of Financial Aid, Alliant International University–San Diego, 10455 Pomerado Road, San Diego, CA 92131-1799, 858-635-4559 Ext. 4700 or toll-free 866-825-5426. *Fax:* 858-635-4848. *E-mail:* dspindler@alliant.edu.
*Website:* http://www.alliant.edu/.

## ALLIED AMERICAN UNIVERSITY
### Laguna Hills, CA

**CONTACT** Financial Aid Office, Allied American University, 22952 Alcade Drive, Laguna Hills, CA 92653, 888-384-0849.
*Website:* http://allied.edu/.

# ALLIED HEALTH INSTITUTE
## Plantation, FL

**CONTACT** Financial Aid Office, Allied Health Institute, 51 North State Road 7, Plantation, FL 33317, 866-251-4134.
*Website:* http://www.alliedhealthinstitute.edu/.

# ALMA COLLEGE
## Alma, MI

| Tuition & fees: $34,585 | Average undergraduate aid package: $23,452 |
|---|---|

**ABOUT THE INSTITUTION** Independent Presbyterian, coed. *Awards:* bachelor's degrees. 63 undergraduate majors. *Total enrollment:* 1,396. Undergraduates: 1,396. Freshmen: 356. Federal methodology is used as a basis for awarding need-based institutional aid.

**UNDERGRADUATE EXPENSES for 2015–2016** *Application fee:* $25. *Comprehensive fee:* $44,075 includes full-time tuition ($34,190), mandatory fees ($395), and room and board ($9490). *College room only:* $4745. Full-time tuition and fees vary according to student level. Room and board charges vary according to board plan. *Part-time tuition:* $1100 per credit hour. Part-time tuition and fees vary according to course load and student level.

**FRESHMAN FINANCIAL AID (Fall 2014, est.)** 351 applied for aid; of those 90% were deemed to have need. 100% of freshmen with need received aid; of those 19% had need fully met. *Average percent of need met:* 72% (excluding resources awarded to replace EFC). *Average financial aid package:* $25,384 (excluding resources awarded to replace EFC). 11% of all full-time freshmen had no need and received non-need-based gift aid.

**UNDERGRADUATE FINANCIAL AID (Fall 2014, est.)** 1,248 applied for aid; of those 90% were deemed to have need. 100% of undergraduates with need received aid; of those 17% had need fully met. *Average percent of need met:* 68% (excluding resources awarded to replace EFC). *Average financial aid package:* $23,452 (excluding resources awarded to replace EFC). 17% of all full-time undergraduates had no need and received non-need-based gift aid.

**GIFT AID (NEED-BASED)** *Total amount:* $24,536,871 (8% federal, 6% state, 85% institutional, 1% external sources). *Receiving aid:* Freshmen: 89% (317); all full-time undergraduates: 83% (1,118). *Average award:* Freshmen: $24,110; Undergraduates: $22,473. *Scholarships, grants, and awards:* Federal Pell, FSEOG, state, private, college/university gift aid from institutional funds.

**GIFT AID (NON-NEED-BASED)** *Total amount:* $4,865,645 (98% institutional, 2% external sources). *Receiving aid:* Freshmen: 13% (46). Undergraduates: 10% (133). *Average award:* Freshmen: $20,217. Undergraduates: $17,604. *Scholarships, grants, and awards by category: Academic interests/achievement:* 1,278 awards ($15,907,839 total): general academic interests/achievements. *Creative arts/performance:* 297 awards ($733,971 total): art/fine arts, dance, music, performing arts, theater/drama. *Special achievements/activities:* 12 awards ($11,875 total): religious involvement. *Special characteristics:* 185 awards ($170,100 total): children and siblings of alumni, siblings of current students. *Tuition waivers:* Full or partial for employees or children of employees. *ROTC:* Army cooperative.

**LOANS** *Student loans:* $11,419,608 (56% need-based, 44% non-need-based). 79% of past graduating class borrowed through all loan programs. *Average indebtedness per student:* $32,389. *Average need-based loan:* Freshmen: $3848. Undergraduates: $4959. *Parent loans:* $4,985,358 (19% need-based, 81% non-need-based). *Programs:* Federal Direct (Subsidized and Unsubsidized Stafford, PLUS), Perkins, college/university, alternative loans.

**WORK-STUDY** *Federal work-study:* Total amount: $404,087; 372 jobs averaging $1086.

**APPLYING FOR FINANCIAL AID** *Required financial aid form:* FAFSA. *Financial aid deadline (priority):* 3/1. *Notification date:* Continuous beginning 3/1. Students must reply within 3 weeks of notification.

**CONTACT** Mrs. Michelle L. McNier, Director of Financial Aid, Alma College, 614 West Superior Street, Alma, MI 48801-1599, 989-463-7347 or toll-free 800-321-ALMA. *Fax:* 989-463-7993. *E-mail:* mcnierml@alma.edu.
*Website:* http://www.alma.edu/.

# ALVERNIA UNIVERSITY
## Reading, PA

| Tuition & fees: $31,100 | Average undergraduate aid package: $19,151 |
|---|---|

**ABOUT THE INSTITUTION** Independent Roman Catholic, coed. *Awards:* associate, bachelor's, master's, and doctoral degrees. 39 undergraduate majors. *Total enrollment:* 2,917. Undergraduates: 2,442. Freshmen: 376. Federal methodology is used as a basis for awarding need-based institutional aid.

**UNDERGRADUATE EXPENSES for 2015–2016** *Application fee:* $25. *Comprehensive fee:* $41,920 includes full-time tuition ($30,500), mandatory fees ($600), and room and board ($10,820). *College room only:* $5380. Full-time tuition and fees vary according to class time and reciprocity agreements. Room and board charges vary according to board plan and housing facility. *Part-time tuition:* $810 per credit. Part-time tuition and fees vary according to class time and course load.

**FRESHMAN FINANCIAL AID (Fall 2014, est.)** 369 applied for aid; of those 93% were deemed to have need. 100% of freshmen with need received aid; of those 8% had need fully met. *Average percent of need met:* 65% (excluding resources awarded to replace EFC). *Average financial aid package:* $21,851 (excluding resources awarded to replace EFC). 7% of all full-time freshmen had no need and received non-need-based gift aid.

**UNDERGRADUATE FINANCIAL AID (Fall 2014, est.)** 1,512 applied for aid; of those 92% were deemed to have need. 99% of undergraduates with need received aid; of those 9% had need fully met. *Average percent of need met:* 62% (excluding resources awarded to replace EFC). *Average financial aid package:* $19,151 (excluding resources awarded to replace EFC). 9% of all full-time undergraduates had no need and received non-need-based gift aid.

**GIFT AID (NEED-BASED)** *Total amount:* $22,709,318 (18% federal, 13% state, 63% institutional, 6% external sources). *Receiving aid:* Freshmen: 91% (344); all full-time undergraduates: 75% (1,349). *Average award:* Freshmen: $17,592; Undergraduates: $14,682. *Scholarships, grants, and awards:* Federal Pell, FSEOG, state, private, college/university gift aid from institutional funds.

**GIFT AID (NON-NEED-BASED)** *Total amount:* $2,931,675 (1% state, 71% institutional, 28% external sources). *Receiving aid:* Freshmen: 6% (21). Undergraduates: 5% (82). *Average award:* Freshmen: $15,356. Undergraduates: $10,078. *Scholarships, grants, and awards by category: Academic interests/achievement:* general academic interests/achievements. *Special achievements/activities:* community service, leadership, memberships, religious involvement. *Special characteristics:* children and siblings of alumni, children of faculty/staff, general special characteristics, local/state students, siblings of current students. *Tuition waivers:* Full or partial for employees or children of employees, senior citizens. *ROTC:* Army cooperative.

**LOANS** *Student loans:* $20,591,622 (77% need-based, 23% non-need-based). 84% of past graduating class borrowed through all loan programs. *Average indebtedness per student:* $39,560. *Average need-based loan:* Freshmen: $3338. Undergraduates: $4232. *Parent loans:* $5,775,821 (54% need-based, 46% non-need-based). *Programs:* Federal Direct (Subsidized and Unsubsidized Stafford, PLUS), Perkins.

**WORK-STUDY** *Federal work-study:* Total amount: $1,353,175; jobs available. *State or other work-study/employment:* Part-time jobs available

**APPLYING FOR FINANCIAL AID** *Required financial aid forms:* FAFSA, state aid form. *Financial aid deadline (priority):* 5/1. *Notification date:* Continuous beginning 2/10. Students must reply by 5/1 or within 2 weeks of notification.

**CONTACT** Ms. Christine Saadi, Director of Student Financial Planning, Alvernia University, 400 Saint Bernardine Street, Reading, PA 19607-1799, 610-796-8213 or toll-free 888-ALVERNIA (in-state). *Fax:* 610-796-8336. *E-mail:* christine.saadi@alvernia.edu.
*Website:* http://www.alvernia.edu/.

# ALVERNO COLLEGE
## Milwaukee, WI

| Tuition & fees: $24,434 | Average undergraduate aid package: $18,262 |
|---|---|

**ABOUT THE INSTITUTION** Independent Roman Catholic, undergraduate: women only; graduate: coed. *Awards:* certificates, associate, bachelor's, and master's degrees (also offers weekend program with significant enrollment not reflected in profile). 41 undergraduate majors. *Total enrollment:* 2,389. Undergraduates: 1,723. Freshmen: 198. Federal methodology is used as a basis for awarding need-based institutional aid.

**UNDERGRADUATE EXPENSES for 2015–2016** *Comprehensive fee:* $31,934 includes full-time tuition ($23,784), mandatory fees ($650), and room and board ($7500). Full-time tuition and fees vary according to program. Room and board charges vary according to board plan and housing facility. *Part-time tuition:* $991 per credit hour. Part-time tuition and fees vary according to program.

**FRESHMAN FINANCIAL AID (Fall 2014, est.)** 185 applied for aid; of those 98% were deemed to have need. 100% of freshmen with need received aid. *Average financial aid package:* $20,742 (excluding resources awarded to replace EFC). 6% of all full-time freshmen had no need and received non-need-based gift aid.

**UNDERGRADUATE FINANCIAL AID (Fall 2014, est.)** 1,206 applied for aid; of those 95% were deemed to have need. 100% of undergraduates with need received aid. *Average financial aid package:* $18,262 (excluding resources awarded to replace EFC). 8% of all full-time undergraduates had no need and received non-need-based gift aid.

**GIFT AID (NEED-BASED)** *Total amount:* $18,000,780 (25% federal, 14% state, 59% institutional, 2% external sources). *Receiving aid:* Freshmen: 94% (181); all full-time undergraduates: 89% (1,130). *Average award:* Freshmen: $17,736; Undergraduates: $14,160. *Scholarships, grants, and awards:* Federal Pell, FSEOG, state, private, college/university gift aid from institutional funds.

**GIFT AID (NON-NEED-BASED)** *Total amount:* $1,011,119 (96% institutional, 4% external sources). *Receiving aid:* Freshmen: 90% (174). Undergraduates: 78% (996). *Average award:* Freshmen: $10,571. Undergraduates: $8617. *Scholarships, grants, and awards by category:* Academic interests/achievement: 2,263 awards ($8,587,438 total): general academic interests/achievements. *Creative arts/performance:* 22 awards ($34,957 total): art/fine arts, music. *Special achievements/activities:* 4 awards ($94,040 total): community service. *Special characteristics:* 27 awards ($218,532 total): children of faculty/staff, international students. *Tuition waivers:* Full or partial for employees or children of employees. *ROTC:* Army cooperative, Air Force cooperative.

**LOANS** *Student loans:* $13,088,651 (89% need-based, 11% non-need-based). 93% of past graduating class borrowed through all loan programs. *Average indebtedness per student:* $38,642. *Average need-based loan:* Freshmen: $3006. Undergraduates: $3836. *Parent loans:* $583,290 (67% need-based, 33% non-need-based). *Programs:* Federal Direct (Subsidized and Unsubsidized Stafford, PLUS), Perkins, state.

**WORK-STUDY** *Federal work-study:* Total amount: $322,120; 111 jobs averaging $1497. *State or other work-study/employment:* Total amount: $688,714 (100% non-need-based). Part-time jobs available.

**APPLYING FOR FINANCIAL AID** *Required financial aid forms:* FAFSA, institution's own form. *Financial aid deadline (priority):* 3/15. *Notification date:* Continuous beginning 3/15. Students must reply within 2 weeks of notification.

**CONTACT** Ms. Amy Christen, Director of Financial Aid, Alverno College, 3400 South 43rd Street, PO Box 343922, Milwaukee, WI 53234-3922, 414-382-6040 or toll-free 800-933-3401. *Fax:* 414-382-6354. *E-mail:* amy.christen@alverno.edu. *Website:* http://www.alverno.edu/.

---

# AMERICAN ACADEMY OF ART
## Chicago, IL

**CONTACT** Ms. Ione Fitzgerald, Director of Financial Aid, American Academy of Art, 332 South Michigan Avenue, Suite 300, Chicago, IL 60604, 312-461-0600 or toll-free 888-461-0600. *Fax:* 312-294-9570. *Website:* http://www.aaart.edu/.

---

# AMERICAN BAPTIST COLLEGE OF AMERICAN BAPTIST THEOLOGICAL SEMINARY
## Nashville, TN

| Tuition & fees: $9622 | Average undergraduate aid package: $10,412 |
|---|---|

**ABOUT THE INSTITUTION** Independent Baptist, coed. *Awards:* diplomas, associate, and bachelor's degrees. 4 undergraduate majors. *Total enrollment:* 157. Undergraduates: 157. Freshmen: 14. Federal methodology is used as a basis for awarding need-based institutional aid.

**UNDERGRADUATE EXPENSES for 2015–2016** *Application fee:* $30. *Comprehensive fee:* $15,462 includes full-time tuition ($8688), mandatory fees ($934), and room and board ($5840). *College room only:* $3840. Room and board charges vary according to housing facility. *Part-time tuition:* $362 per credit.

**FRESHMAN FINANCIAL AID (Fall 2014, est.)** 15 applied for aid; of those 100% were deemed to have need. 100% of freshmen with need received aid; of those 67% had need fully met. *Average percent of need met:* 40% (excluding resources awarded to replace EFC). *Average financial aid package:* $10,412 (excluding resources awarded to replace EFC).

**UNDERGRADUATE FINANCIAL AID (Fall 2014, est.)** 128 applied for aid; of those 100% were deemed to have need. 100% of undergraduates with need received aid. *Average percent of need met:* 40% (excluding resources awarded to replace EFC). *Average financial aid package:* $10,412 (excluding resources awarded to replace EFC).

**GIFT AID (NEED-BASED)** *Total amount:* $794,827 (71% federal, 10% state, 18% institutional, 1% external sources). *Receiving aid:* Freshmen: 100% (15); all full-time undergraduates: 62% (80). *Average award:* Freshmen: $8263; Undergraduates: $8263. *Scholarships, grants, and awards:* Federal Pell, FSEOG, state, college/university gift aid from institutional funds.

**LOANS** *Student loans:* $1,157,334 (100% need-based). 83% of past graduating class borrowed through all loan programs. *Average indebtedness per student:* $9743. *Average need-based loan:* Freshmen: $3823. Undergraduates: $3823. *Parent loans:* $22,940 (100% need-based). *Programs:* Federal Direct (Subsidized and Unsubsidized Stafford, PLUS).

**WORK-STUDY** *Federal work-study:* Total amount: $7452; 5 jobs averaging $7452.

**APPLYING FOR FINANCIAL AID** *Required financial aid form:* FAFSA. *Financial aid deadline:* 7/23 (priority: 1/1). *Notification date:* Continuous beginning 7/30. Students must reply by 8/1 or within 2 weeks of notification.

**CONTACT** Miss Sharonda Campbell, Financial Aid Administrator, American Baptist College of American Baptist Theological Seminary, 1800 Baptist World Center Drive, Nashville, TN 37207, 615-687-6903. *Fax:* 615-226-7855. *E-mail:* scampbell@abcnash.edu. *Website:* http://www.abcnash.edu/.

---

# AMERICAN BUSINESS & TECHNOLOGY UNIVERSITY
## Saint Joseph, MO

**CONTACT** Financial Aid Office, American Business & Technology University, 2300 Frederick Avenue, Saint Joseph, MO 64506, 800-908-9329. *Website:* http://www.abtu.edu/.

---

# AMERICAN COLLEGE FOR MEDICAL CAREERS
## Orlando, FL

**CONTACT** Financial Aid Office, American College for Medical Careers, 5959 Lake Ellenor Drive, Orlando, FL 32809, 407-738-4488 or toll-free 888-599-7887. *Website:* http://www.acmc.edu/.

# AMERICAN INDIAN COLLEGE OF THE ASSEMBLIES OF GOD, INC.
### Phoenix, AZ

**CONTACT** Nadine Waldrop, Director of Student Financial Aid, American Indian College of the Assemblies of God, Inc., 10020 North Fifteenth Avenue, Phoenix, AZ 85021-2199, 602-944-3335 Ext. 223. *Fax:* 602-944-1952. *E-mail:* nwaldrop@aicag.edu. *Website:* http://www.aicag.edu/.

# AMERICAN INTERCONTINENTAL UNIVERSITY ATLANTA
### Atlanta, GA

**CONTACT** Financial Aid Office, American InterContinental University Atlanta, 6600 Peachtree-Dunwoody Road, 500 Embassy Row, Atlanta, GA 30328, 404-965-6500 or toll-free 800-353-1744. *Website:* http://www.aiuniv.edu/.

# AMERICAN INTERCONTINENTAL UNIVERSITY HOUSTON
### Houston, TX

**CONTACT** Financial Aid Office, American InterContinental University Houston, 9999 Richmond Avenue, Houston, TX 77042, 832-242-5788 or toll-free 888-607-9888. *Website:* http://www.aiuniv.edu/.

# AMERICAN INTERCONTINENTAL UNIVERSITY ONLINE
### Schaumburg, IL

**CONTACT** Financial Aid Office, American InterContinental University Online, 231 N. Martingale Road, 6th Floor, Schaumburg, IL 60173, 847-851-5000 or toll-free 877-701-3800. *Website:* http://www.aiuniv.edu/.

# AMERICAN INTERNATIONAL COLLEGE
### Springfield, MA

**ABOUT THE INSTITUTION** Independent, coed. *Awards:* certificates, associate, bachelor's, master's, and doctoral degrees. 32 undergraduate majors. *Total enrollment:* 3,629. Undergraduates: 1,473. Freshmen: 309.

**GIFT AID (NEED-BASED)** *Scholarships, grants, and awards:* Federal Pell, FSEOG, state, private, college/university gift aid from institutional funds.

**GIFT AID (NON-NEED-BASED)** *Scholarships, grants, and awards by category:* Academic interests/achievement: general academic interests/achievements. *Special characteristics:* children and siblings of alumni, children of faculty/staff, children of public servants.

**LOANS** *Programs:* Federal Direct (Subsidized and Unsubsidized Stafford, PLUS), Perkins.

**WORK-STUDY** *Federal work-study:* 466 jobs averaging $640. *State or other work-study/employment:* Total amount: $273,909 (100% non-need-based). 161 part-time jobs averaging $1190.

**APPLYING FOR FINANCIAL AID** *Required financial aid form:* FAFSA.

**CONTACT** Ms. Sage Stachowiak, Director of Financial Aid, American International College, 1000 State Street, Springfield, MA 01109-3189, 413-205-3521 or toll-free 800-242-3142. *Fax:* 413-205-3912. *E-mail:* sage.stachowiak@aic.edu. *Website:* http://www.aic.edu/.

# AMERICAN JEWISH UNIVERSITY
### Bel Air, CA

| Tuition & fees: $29,132 | Average undergraduate aid package: $29,132 |
|---|---|

**ABOUT THE INSTITUTION** Independent Jewish, coed. *Awards:* bachelor's and master's degrees. 10 undergraduate majors. *Total enrollment:* 229. Undergraduates: 112. Freshmen: 7. Both federal and institutional methodology are used as a basis for awarding need-based institutional aid.

**UNDERGRADUATE EXPENSES for 2015–2016** *Application fee:* $35. *Comprehensive fee:* $44,234 includes full-time tuition ($27,312), mandatory fees ($1820), and room and board ($15,102). *College room only:* $7098. Full-time tuition and fees vary according to course load and degree level. Room and board charges vary according to board plan and housing facility. *Part-time tuition:* $1138 per unit. Part-time tuition and fees vary according to course load and degree level.

**FRESHMAN FINANCIAL AID (Fall 2014, est.)** 8 applied for aid; of those 100% were deemed to have need. 100% of freshmen with need received aid. *Average percent of need met:* 100% (excluding resources awarded to replace EFC). *Average financial aid package:* $29,132 (excluding resources awarded to replace EFC). 8% of all full-time freshmen had no need and received non-need-based gift aid.

**UNDERGRADUATE FINANCIAL AID (Fall 2014, est.)** 58 applied for aid; of those 100% were deemed to have need. 100% of undergraduates with need received aid. *Average percent of need met:* 95% (excluding resources awarded to replace EFC). *Average financial aid package:* $29,132 (excluding resources awarded to replace EFC). 11% of all full-time undergraduates had no need and received non-need-based gift aid.

**GIFT AID (NEED-BASED)** *Total amount:* $656,612 (33% federal, 21% state, 46% institutional). *Receiving aid:* Freshmen: 62% (8); all full-time undergraduates: 63% (58). *Average award:* Freshmen: $8961; Undergraduates: $8229. *Scholarships, grants, and awards:* Federal Pell, FSEOG, state, private, college/university gift aid from institutional funds.

**GIFT AID (NON-NEED-BASED)** *Total amount:* $484,600 (100% institutional). *Receiving aid:* Freshmen: 62% (8). Undergraduates: 27% (25). *Average award:* Freshmen: $3000. Undergraduates: $3000. *Scholarships, grants, and awards by category:* Academic interests/achievement: business, general academic interests/achievements, premedicine. *Special achievements/activities:* leadership. *Tuition waivers:* Full or partial for employees or children of employees.

**LOANS** *Student loans:* $430,250 (42% need-based, 58% non-need-based). 90% of past graduating class borrowed through all loan programs. *Average indebtedness per student:* $30,000. *Average need-based loan:* Freshmen: $3500. Undergraduates: $5500. *Parent loans:* $176,113 (100% non-need-based). *Programs:* Federal Direct (Subsidized and Unsubsidized Stafford, PLUS), alternative loans.

**WORK-STUDY** *Federal work-study:* Total amount: $27,520, 33 jobs averaging $834.

**APPLYING FOR FINANCIAL AID** *Required financial aid forms:* FAFSA, institution's own form, federal income tax form(s). *Financial aid deadline (priority):* 3/2. *Notification date:* Continuous beginning 3/15. Students must reply within 3 weeks of notification.

**CONTACT** Larisa Zadoyen, Director of Financial Aid, American Jewish University, 15600 Mulholland Drive, Bel Air, CA 90077-1599, 310-476-9777 Ext. 252 or toll-free 888-853-6763. *Fax:* 310-476-4613. *E-mail:* lzadoyen@aju.edu. *Website:* http://www.aju.edu/.

# AMERICAN MUSICAL AND DRAMATIC ACADEMY, LOS ANGELES

## Los Angeles, CA

**CONTACT** Financial Aid Office, American Musical and Dramatic Academy, Los Angeles, 6305 Yucca Street, Los Angeles, CA 90028, 323-469-3300 or toll-free 888-474-9444.
*Website:* http://www.amda.edu/.

# AMERICAN NATIONAL UNIVERSITY

## Salem, VA

**CONTACT** Financial Aid Office, American National University, 1813 East Main Street, Salem, VA 24153, 540-986-1800 or toll-free 888-9-JOBREADY.
*Website:* http://www.national-college.edu/.

# AMERICAN SENTINEL UNIVERSITY

## Aurora, CO

**CONTACT** Financial Aid Office, American Sentinel University, 2260 South Xanadu Way, Suite 310, Aurora, CO 80014 or toll-free 800-729-2427.
*Website:* http://www.americansentinel.edu/.

# AMERICAN UNIVERSITY

## Washington, DC

| Tuition & fees: $42,556 | Average undergraduate aid package: $29,054 |
|---|---|

**ABOUT THE INSTITUTION** Independent Methodist, coed. *Awards:* certificates, associate, bachelor's, master's, and doctoral degrees. 69 undergraduate majors. *Total enrollment:* 13,061. Undergraduates: 7,706. Freshmen: 1,787. Institutional methodology is used as a basis for awarding need-based institutional aid.

**UNDERGRADUATE EXPENSES for 2015–2016 Application fee:** $70. *Comprehensive fee:* $56,910 includes full-time tuition ($42,556) and room and board ($14,354). *College room only:* $9704. Full-time tuition and fees vary according to course load and location. Room and board charges vary according to board plan, housing facility, and location. *Part-time tuition:* $1417 per credit hour. Part-time tuition and fees vary according to course load and location. *Payment plan:* Tuition prepayment.

**FRESHMAN FINANCIAL AID (Fall 2014, est.)** 1,423 applied for aid; of those 76% were deemed to have need. 99% of freshmen with need received aid; of those 39% had need fully met. *Average percent of need met:* 86% (excluding resources awarded to replace EFC). *Average financial aid package:* $31,735 (excluding resources awarded to replace EFC). 16% of all full-time freshmen had no need and received non-need-based gift aid.

**UNDERGRADUATE FINANCIAL AID (Fall 2014, est.)** 4,459 applied for aid; of those 85% were deemed to have need. 99% of undergraduates with need received aid; of those 19% had need fully met. *Average percent of need met:* 71% (excluding resources awarded to replace EFC). *Average financial aid package:* $29,054 (excluding resources awarded to replace EFC). 12% of all full-time undergraduates had no need and received non-need-based gift aid.

**GIFT AID (NEED-BASED) Receiving aid:** Freshmen: 54% (963); all full-time undergraduates: 45% (3,104). *Average award:* Freshmen: $24,437; Undergraduates: $22,757. *Scholarships, grants, and awards:* Federal Pell, FSEOG, private, college/university gift aid from institutional funds.

**GIFT AID (NON-NEED-BASED) Receiving aid:** Freshmen: 22% (389). Undergraduates: 18% (1,255). *Average award:* Freshmen: $12,218. Undergraduates: $13,989. *Scholarships, grants, and awards by category:* Academic interests/achievement: general academic interests/achievements. Creative arts/performance: general creative arts/performance. Special achievements/activities: general special achievements/activities, leadership, memberships. Special characteristics: adult students, children and siblings of alumni, children of faculty/staff, ethnic background, first-generation college students, local/state students, members of minority groups, previous college experience, relatives of clergy, spouses of current students, veterans, veterans' children. *Tuition waivers:* Full or partial for employees or children of employees. *ROTC:* Army cooperative, Air Force cooperative.

**LOANS Average need-based loan:** Freshmen: $3422. Undergraduates: $4380. *Programs:* Federal Direct (Subsidized and Unsubsidized Stafford, PLUS), Perkins, college/university.

**WORK-STUDY** Federal work-study jobs available.

**APPLYING FOR FINANCIAL AID Required financial aid forms:** FAFSA, CSS Financial Aid PROFILE. *Financial aid deadline:* 2/15. *Notification date:* 4/1. Students must reply within 4 weeks of notification.

**CONTACT** Brian Lee Sang, Assistant Vice Provost, Financial Aid, American University, 4400 Massachusetts Avenue, NW, Washington, DC 20016-8001, 202-885-6500. *Fax:* 202-885-1025. *E-mail:* facounselor@american.edu.
*Website:* http://www.american.edu/.

# AMERICAN UNIVERSITY OF HEALTH SCIENCES

## Signal Hill, CA

**CONTACT** Financial Aid Office, American University of Health Sciences, 1600 East Hill Street, Building #1, Signal Hill, CA 90755, 562-988-2278.
*Website:* http://www.auhs.edu/.

# AMERICAN UNIVERSITY OF PUERTO RICO

## Bayamón, PR

**CONTACT** Mr. Yahaira Melendez, Financial Aid Director, American University of Puerto Rico, PO Box 2037, Bayamón, PR 00960-2037, 787-620-2040 Ext. 2031. *Fax:* 787-785-7377. *E-mail:* melendezy@aupr.edu.
*Website:* http://www.aupr.edu/.

# AMHERST COLLEGE

## Amherst, MA

| Tuition & fees: $48,526 | Average undergraduate aid package: $48,535 |
|---|---|

**ABOUT THE INSTITUTION** Independent, coed. *Awards:* bachelor's degrees. 38 undergraduate majors. *Total enrollment:* 1,792. Undergraduates: 1,792. Freshmen: 469. Institutional methodology is used as a basis for awarding need-based institutional aid.

**UNDERGRADUATE EXPENSES for 2015–2016 Application fee:** $60. *Comprehensive fee:* $61,206 includes full-time tuition ($47,720), mandatory fees ($806), and room and board ($12,680). *College room only:* $6870.

**FRESHMAN FINANCIAL AID (Fall 2014, est.)** 345 applied for aid; of those 84% were deemed to have need. 100% of freshmen with need received aid; of those 100% had need fully met. *Average percent of need met:* 100% (excluding resources awarded to replace EFC). *Average financial aid package:* $49,469 (excluding resources awarded to replace EFC).

**UNDERGRADUATE FINANCIAL AID (Fall 2014, est.)** 1,245 applied for aid; of those 89% were deemed to have need. 100% of undergraduates with need received aid; of those 100% had need fully met. *Average percent of need met:* 100% (excluding resources awarded to replace EFC). *Average financial aid package:* $48,535 (excluding resources awarded to replace EFC).

**GIFT AID (NEED-BASED) Total amount:** $52,086,621 (5% federal, 94% institutional, 1% external sources). *Receiving aid:* Freshmen: 62% (290); all full-time undergraduates: 58% (1,100). *Average award:* Freshmen: $48,105; Undergraduates: $47,243. *Scholarships, grants, and awards:* Federal Pell, FSEOG, state, private, college/university gift aid from institutional funds.

**GIFT AID (NON-NEED-BASED)** *Total amount:* $874,700 (100% external sources). *Receiving aid:* Undergraduates: 1. **ROTC:** Army cooperative, Air Force cooperative.

**LOANS** *Student loans:* $2,452,458 (30% need-based, 70% non-need-based). 31% of past graduating class borrowed through all loan programs. *Average indebtedness per student:* $14,490. *Average need-based loan:* Freshmen: $357. Undergraduates: $330. *Parent loans:* $2,139,738 (100% non-need-based). *Programs:* Federal Direct (Subsidized and Unsubsidized Stafford, PLUS), Perkins, college/university.

**WORK-STUDY** *Federal work-study:* Total amount: $1,087,152; 694 jobs averaging $1602. *State or other work-study/employment:* Total amount: $370,235 (100% need-based). 227 part-time jobs averaging $1658.

**APPLYING FOR FINANCIAL AID** *Required financial aid forms:* FAFSA, CSS Financial Aid PROFILE, noncustodial (divorced/separated) parent's statement, business/farm supplement, federal income tax form(s), W-2 forms. *Financial aid deadline (priority):* 2/15. *Notification date:* 4/1. Students must reply by 5/1.

**CONTACT** Gail W. Holt, Dean of Financial Aid, Amherst College, B-5 Converse Hall, PO Box 5000, Amherst, MA 01002-5000, 413-542-2296. *Fax:* 413-542-2628. *E-mail:* finaid@amherst.edu.

*Website:* http://www.amherst.edu/.

---

# AMRIDGE UNIVERSITY
## Montgomery, AL

| Tuition & fees: $6900 | Average undergraduate aid package: $8735 |
|---|---|

**ABOUT THE INSTITUTION** Independent Church of Christ, coed. *Awards:* associate, bachelor's, master's, and doctoral degrees. 4 undergraduate majors. *Total enrollment:* 618. Undergraduates: 278. Freshmen: 10. Federal methodology is used as a basis for awarding need-based institutional aid.

**UNDERGRADUATE EXPENSES** for 2015–2016 *Application fee:* $50. *Tuition:* full-time $6000; part-time $400 per semester hour. *Required fees:* full-time $900; $450 per term. Full-time tuition and fees vary according to course load and student level. Part-time tuition and fees vary according to course load and student level. *Payment plan:* Guaranteed tuition.

**FRESHMAN FINANCIAL AID (Fall 2013)** 6 applied for aid; of those 100% were deemed to have need. 100% of freshmen with need received aid; of those 17% had need fully met. *Average percent of need met:* 41% (excluding resources awarded to replace EFC). *Average financial aid package:* $9078 (excluding resources awarded to replace EFC).

**UNDERGRADUATE FINANCIAL AID (Fall 2013)** 322 applied for aid; of those 83% were deemed to have need. 100% of undergraduates with need received aid; of those 38% had need fully met. *Average percent of need met:* 52% (excluding resources awarded to replace EFC). *Average financial aid package:* $8735 (excluding resources awarded to replace EFC).

**GIFT AID (NEED-BASED)** *Total amount:* $1,990,429 (88% federal, 1% state, 11% institutional). *Receiving aid:* Freshmen: 100% (6); all full-time undergraduates: 83% (266). *Average award:* Freshmen: $4612; Undergraduates: $3065. *Scholarships, grants, and awards:* Federal Pell, FSEOG, state, private, college/university gift aid from institutional funds.

**GIFT AID (NON-NEED-BASED)** *Receiving aid:* Freshmen: 100% (6). Undergraduates: 73% (235). *Average award:* Freshmen: $3248. Undergraduates: $2980. *Scholarships, grants, and awards by category:* Special achievements/activities: religious involvement. *Special characteristics:* children of educators, children of faculty/staff, veterans. *Tuition waivers:* Full or partial for employees or children of employees.

**LOANS** *Student loans:* $2,098,371 (42% need-based, 58% non-need-based). 63% of past graduating class borrowed through all loan programs. *Average indebtedness per student:* $10,500. *Programs:* Federal Direct (Subsidized and Unsubsidized Stafford, PLUS).

**WORK-STUDY** Federal work-study jobs available.

**APPLYING FOR FINANCIAL AID** *Required financial aid forms:* FAFSA, institution's own form, state aid form. *Financial aid deadline:* Continuous. *Notification date:* 7/30. Students must reply within 2 weeks of notification.

**CONTACT** Starr Fain, Director of Financial Aid, Amridge University, 1200 Taylor Road, Montgomery, AL 36117, 334-387-3877 Ext. 7523 or toll-free 888-790-8080. *Fax:* 334-387-3878. *E-mail:* starrfain@amridgeuniversity.edu.

*Website:* http://www.amridgeuniversity.edu/.

---

# ANDERSON UNIVERSITY
## Anderson, IN

| Tuition & fees: $26,850 | Average undergraduate aid package: $23,905 |
|---|---|

**ABOUT THE INSTITUTION** Independent Church of God, coed. *Awards:* associate, bachelor's, master's, and doctoral degrees. 64 undergraduate majors. *Total enrollment:* 2,399. Undergraduates: 1,976. Freshmen: 441. Federal methodology is used as a basis for awarding need-based institutional aid.

**UNDERGRADUATE EXPENSES** for 2015–2016 *Application fee:* $25. *Comprehensive fee:* $36,100 includes full-time tuition ($26,770), mandatory fees ($80), and room and board ($9250). *College room only:* $5920. Room and board charges vary according to board plan and housing facility. *Part-time tuition:* $1116 per semester hour. Part-time tuition and fees vary according to course load.

**FRESHMAN FINANCIAL AID (Fall 2014, est.)** 422 applied for aid; of those 90% were deemed to have need. 100% of freshmen with need received aid; of those 39% had need fully met. *Average percent of need met:* 97% (excluding resources awarded to replace EFC). *Average financial aid package:* $25,945 (excluding resources awarded to replace EFC). 13% of all full-time freshmen had no need and received non-need-based gift aid.

**UNDERGRADUATE FINANCIAL AID (Fall 2014, est.)** 1,549 applied for aid; of those 91% were deemed to have need. 100% of undergraduates with need received aid; of those 43% had need fully met. *Average percent of need met:* 88% (excluding resources awarded to replace EFC). *Average financial aid package:* $23,905 (excluding resources awarded to replace EFC). 18% of all full-time undergraduates had no need and received non-need-based gift aid.

**GIFT AID (NEED-BASED)** *Total amount:* $21,428,557 (14% federal, 12% state, 70% institutional, 4% external sources). *Receiving aid:* Freshmen: 85% (373); all full-time undergraduates: 82% (1,374). *Average award:* Freshmen: $17,248; Undergraduates: $15,932. *Scholarships, grants, and awards:* Federal Pell, FSEOG, state, private, college/university gift aid from institutional funds.

**GIFT AID (NON-NEED-BASED)** *Total amount:* $4,796,480 (90% institutional, 10% external sources). *Receiving aid:* Freshmen: 4% (17). Undergraduates: 4% (67). *Average award:* Freshmen: $14,030. Undergraduates: $14,313. *Scholarships, grants, and awards by category:* Academic interests/achievement: general academic interests/achievements. *Creative arts/performance:* art/fine arts, music. *Special achievements/activities:* leadership. *Special characteristics:* adult students, children of faculty/staff, international students, relatives of clergy. *Tuition waivers:* Full or partial for employees or children of employees.

**LOANS** *Student loans:* $16,549,856 (67% need-based, 33% non-need-based). *Average need-based loan:* Freshmen: $9742. Undergraduates: $10,011. *Programs:* Federal Direct (Subsidized and Unsubsidized Stafford, PLUS), Perkins.

**WORK-STUDY** *Federal work-study:* Total amount: $138,731; jobs available. *State or other work-study/employment:* Total amount: $317,184 (30% need-based, 70% non-need-based). Part-time jobs available.

**APPLYING FOR FINANCIAL AID** *Required financial aid form:* FAFSA. *Financial aid deadline (priority):* 3/1. *Notification date:* Continuous beginning 3/1.

**CONTACT** Mr. Kenneth Nieman, Director of Financial Aid, Anderson University, 1100 East Fifth Street, Anderson, IN 46012-3495, 765-641-4180 or toll-free 800-428-6414. *Fax:* 765-641-3831. *E-mail:* kfnieman@anderson.edu.

*Website:* http://www.anderson.edu/.

# ANDERSON UNIVERSITY
## Anderson, SC

| Tuition & fees: $23,750 | Average undergraduate aid package: $18,123 |
|---|---|

**ABOUT THE INSTITUTION** Independent Baptist, coed. *Awards:* bachelor's, master's, and doctoral degrees. 30 undergraduate majors. *Total enrollment:* 2,922. Undergraduates: 2,630. Freshmen: 538. Federal methodology is used as a basis for awarding need-based institutional aid.

**UNDERGRADUATE EXPENSES for 2015–2016** *Application fee:* $25. *Comprehensive fee:* $32,424 includes full-time tuition ($21,660), mandatory fees ($2090), and room and board ($8674). *College room only:* $4490. Full-time tuition and fees vary according to course load and program. Room and board charges vary according to board plan and housing facility. Part-time tuition and fees vary according to program.

**FRESHMAN FINANCIAL AID (Fall 2014, est.)** 626 applied for aid; of those 86% were deemed to have need. 100% of freshmen with need received aid; of those 48% had need fully met. *Average percent of need met:* 71% (excluding resources awarded to replace EFC). *Average financial aid package:* $18,913 (excluding resources awarded to replace EFC). 13% of all full-time freshmen had no need and received non-need-based gift aid.

**UNDERGRADUATE FINANCIAL AID (Fall 2014, est.)** 2,110 applied for aid; of those 88% were deemed to have need. 100% of undergraduates with need received aid; of those 40% had need fully met. *Average percent of need met:* 67% (excluding resources awarded to replace EFC). *Average financial aid package:* $18,123 (excluding resources awarded to replace EFC). 11% of all full-time undergraduates had no need and received non-need-based gift aid.

**GIFT AID (NEED-BASED)** *Total amount:* $34,263,126 (15% federal, 28% state, 56% institutional, 1% external sources). *Receiving aid:* Freshmen: 52% (339); all full-time undergraduates: 58% (1,326). *Average award:* Freshmen: $16,312; Undergraduates: $15,082. *Scholarships, grants, and awards:* Federal Pell, FSEOG, state, private, college/university gift aid from institutional funds.

**GIFT AID (NON-NEED-BASED)** *Total amount:* $21,068,379 (21% federal, 24% state, 54% institutional, 1% external sources). *Receiving aid:* Freshmen: 82% (539). Undergraduates: 81% (1,847). *Average award:* Freshmen: $9434. Undergraduates: $9734. *Scholarships, grants, and awards by category:* Academic interests/achievement: 1,890 awards ($12,075,591 total): business, education, general academic interests/achievements, religion/biblical studies. Creative arts/performance: 270 awards ($408,897 total): art/fine arts, music, performing arts, theater/drama. Special achievements/activities: 199 awards ($336,900 total): cheerleading/drum major, leadership, memberships. Special characteristics: 1,520 awards ($3,297,677 total): children of faculty/staff, ethnic background, general special characteristics, international students, members of minority groups, out-of-state students, religious affiliation, veterans, veterans' children. *Tuition waivers:* Full or partial for employees or children of employees. *ROTC:* Army cooperative, Air Force cooperative.

**LOANS** *Student loans:* $18,804,674 (72% need-based, 28% non-need-based). 100% of past graduating class borrowed through all loan programs. *Average indebtedness per student:* $32,298. *Average need-based loan:* Freshmen: $3648. Undergraduates: $4608. *Parent loans:* $2,464,215 (41% need-based, 59% non-need-based). *Programs:* Federal Direct (Subsidized and Unsubsidized Stafford, PLUS), Perkins, state, private loans.

**WORK-STUDY** *Federal work-study:* Total amount: $229,442; 182 jobs averaging $885. *State or other work-study/employment:* 245 part-time jobs averaging $1046.

**ATHLETIC AWARDS** Total amount: $1,681,242 (54% need-based, 46% non-need-based).

**APPLYING FOR FINANCIAL AID** *Required financial aid form:* FAFSA. *Financial aid deadline:* 7/30 (priority: 3/1). *Notification date:* Continuous beginning 3/15. Students must reply within 2 weeks of notification.

**CONTACT** Allison Sullivan, Director of Financial Aid Planning, Anderson University, 316 Boulevard, Anderson, SC 29621-4035, 864-231-2181 or toll-free 800-542-3594. *Fax:* 864-231-2008. *E-mail:* myohe@andersonuniversity.edu. *Website:* http://www.andersonuniversity.edu/.

# ANDREWS UNIVERSITY
## Berrien Springs, MI

| Tuition & fees: $26,262 | Average undergraduate aid package: $27,265 |
|---|---|

**ABOUT THE INSTITUTION** Independent Seventh-day Adventist, coed. *Awards:* certificates, associate, bachelor's, master's, and doctoral degrees. 64 undergraduate majors. *Total enrollment:* 3,418. Undergraduates: 1,805. Freshmen: 273. Federal methodology is used as a basis for awarding need-based institutional aid.

**UNDERGRADUATE EXPENSES for 2015–2016** *Application fee:* $30. *Comprehensive fee:* $34,564 includes full-time tuition ($25,416), mandatory fees ($846), and room and board ($8302). *College room only:* $4302. Full-time tuition and fees vary according to course load. Room and board charges vary according to board plan. *Part-time tuition:* $1059 per semester hour. Part-time tuition and fees vary according to course load.

**FRESHMAN FINANCIAL AID (Fall 2014, est.)** 188 applied for aid; of those 91% were deemed to have need. 100% of freshmen with need received aid; of those 19% had need fully met. *Average percent of need met:* 82% (excluding resources awarded to replace EFC). *Average financial aid package:* $25,616 (excluding resources awarded to replace EFC). 34% of all full-time freshmen had no need and received non-need-based gift aid.

**UNDERGRADUATE FINANCIAL AID (Fall 2014, est.)** 1,007 applied for aid; of those 93% were deemed to have need. 100% of undergraduates with need received aid; of those 14% had need fully met. *Average percent of need met:* 83% (excluding resources awarded to replace EFC). *Average financial aid package:* $27,265 (excluding resources awarded to replace EFC). 37% of all full-time undergraduates had no need and received non-need-based gift aid.

**GIFT AID (NEED-BASED)** *Total amount:* $21,407,419 (12% federal, 1% state, 70% institutional, 17% external sources). *Receiving aid:* Freshmen: 46% (119); all full-time undergraduates: 46% (710). *Average award:* Freshmen: $6721; Undergraduates: $7285. *Scholarships, grants, and awards:* Federal Pell, FSEOG, state, private, college/university gift aid from institutional funds.

**GIFT AID (NON-NEED-BASED)** *Receiving aid:* Freshmen: 66% (172). Undergraduates: 60% (931). *Average award:* Freshmen: $10,855. Undergraduates: $9580. *Scholarships, grants, and awards by category:* Academic interests/achievement: 1,456 awards ($8,981,420 total): general academic interests/achievements. Creative arts/performance: 43 awards ($43,100 total): music. Special achievements/activities: 227 awards ($310,705 total): leadership, religious involvement. Special characteristics: 107 awards ($1,173,076 total): children of faculty/staff, general special characteristics, international students. *Tuition waivers:* Full or partial for employees or children of employees, senior citizens.

**LOANS** *Student loans:* $18,179,763 (33% need-based, 67% non-need-based). 62% of past graduating class borrowed through all loan programs. *Average indebtedness per student:* $36,536. *Average need-based loan:* Freshmen: $3212. Undergraduates: $4807. *Parent loans:* $3,824,208 (100% non-need-based). *Programs:* Federal Direct (Subsidized and Unsubsidized Stafford, PLUS), Perkins.

**WORK-STUDY** *Federal work-study:* Total amount: $651,908; 695 jobs averaging $938. *State or other work-study/employment:* Part-time jobs available.

**APPLYING FOR FINANCIAL AID** *Required financial aid forms:* FAFSA, institution's own form. *Financial aid deadline:* Continuous. *Notification date:* Continuous.

**CONTACT** Cynthia Gammon, Assistant Director of Student Financial Services, Andrews University, Student Financial Services Administration Building, Berrien Springs, MI 49104, 800-253-2874. *Fax:* 269-471-3228. *E-mail:* sfs@andrews.edu. *Website:* http://www.andrews.edu/.

# ANGELES COLLEGE
## Los Angeles, CA

**CONTACT** Financial Aid Office, Angeles College, 3440 Wilshire Boulevard, Suite 310, Los Angeles, CA 90010, 213-487-2211. *Website:* http://www.angelescollege.org/.

# ANGELO STATE UNIVERSITY
## San Angelo, TX

| Tuition & fees (TX res): $7642 | Average undergraduate aid package: $11,311 |
|---|---|

**ABOUT THE INSTITUTION** State-supported, coed. *Awards:* bachelor's, master's, and doctoral degrees. 36 undergraduate majors. *Total enrollment:* 6,494. Undergraduates: 5,425. Freshmen: 1,316. Federal methodology is used as a basis for awarding need-based institutional aid.

**UNDERGRADUATE EXPENSES** for 2015–2016 *Application fee:* $35. *Tuition, state resident:* full-time $4700; part-time $157 per credit hour. *Tuition, nonresident:* full-time $15,560; part-time $519 per credit hour. *Required fees:* full-time $2942. *College room and board:* $7602.

**FRESHMAN FINANCIAL AID (Fall 2013)** 1,094 applied for aid; of those 76% were deemed to have need. 100% of freshmen with need received aid; of those 20% had need fully met. *Average percent of need met:* 91% (excluding resources awarded to replace EFC). *Average financial aid package:* $12,240 (excluding resources awarded to replace EFC). 19% of all full-time freshmen had no need and received non-need-based gift aid.

**UNDERGRADUATE FINANCIAL AID (Fall 2013)** 3,793 applied for aid; of those 82% were deemed to have need. 99% of undergraduates with need received aid; of those 14% had need fully met. *Average percent of need met:* 82% (excluding resources awarded to replace EFC). *Average financial aid package:* $11,311 (excluding resources awarded to replace EFC). 16% of all full-time undergraduates had no need and received non-need-based gift aid.

**GIFT AID (NEED-BASED)** *Total amount:* $24,726,347 (56% federal, 44% state). *Receiving aid:* Freshmen: 55% (663); all full-time undergraduates: 56% (2,642). *Average award:* Freshmen: $3819; Undergraduates: $3315. *Scholarships, grants, and awards:* Federal Pell, FSEOG, state, private, college/university gift aid from institutional funds, Federal Nursing, Carr Academic Scholarships.

**GIFT AID (NON-NEED-BASED)** *Total amount:* $14,293,305 (5% state, 88% institutional, 7% external sources). *Receiving aid:* Freshmen: 46% (556). Undergraduates: 23% (1,064). *Average award:* Freshmen: $2980. Undergraduates: $2958. *Scholarships, grants, and awards by category:* Academic interests/achievement: agriculture, biological sciences, business, communication, computer science, education, English, foreign languages, general academic interests/achievements, humanities, international studies, mathematics, military science, physical sciences, pre-medicine, social sciences. Creative arts/performance: art/fine arts, dance, journalism/publications, music, performing arts, theater/drama. Special achievements/activities: cheerleading/drum major, general special achievements/activities, hobbies/interests, leadership, memberships, rodeo. Special characteristics: first-generation college students, local/state students. *ROTC:* Air Force.

**LOANS** *Student loans:* $58,526,499 (31% need-based, 69% non-need-based). 67% of past graduating class borrowed through all loan programs. *Average indebtedness per student:* $25,508. *Average need-based loan:* Freshmen: $3298. Undergraduates: $3919. *Parent loans:* $23,626,439 (100% non-need-based). *Programs:* Federal Direct (Subsidized and Unsubsidized Stafford, PLUS), Perkins, Federal Nursing, state, college/university, alternative loans.

**WORK-STUDY** *Federal work-study:* jobs available. *State or other work-study/employment:* Total amount: $328,556 (100% need-based). Part-time jobs available.

**ATHLETIC AWARDS** Total amount: $1,676,928 (100% non-need-based).

**APPLYING FOR FINANCIAL AID** *Required financial aid form:* FAFSA. *Financial aid deadline:* Continuous. *Notification date:* Continuous beginning 4/1. Students must reply within 4 weeks of notification.

**CONTACT** Mr. William R. Bloom, Director of Financial Aid, Angelo State University, ASU Station #11015, San Angelo, TX 76909-1015, 325-942-2246 or toll-free 800-946-8627. *Fax:* 325-942-2082. *E-mail:* william.bloom@angelo.edu. *Website:* http://www.angelo.edu/.

# ANNA MARIA COLLEGE
## Paxton, MA

| Tuition & fees: $34,060 | Average undergraduate aid package: $26,543 |
|---|---|

**ABOUT THE INSTITUTION** Independent Roman Catholic, coed. *Awards:* certificates, bachelor's, master's, and doctoral degrees. 58 undergraduate majors. *Total enrollment:* 1,455. Undergraduates: 1,116. Freshmen: 169. Federal methodology is used as a basis for awarding need-based institutional aid.

**UNDERGRADUATE EXPENSES** for 2015–2016 *Application fee:* $40. *Comprehensive fee:* $46,790 includes full-time tuition ($31,920), mandatory fees ($2140), and room and board ($12,730). *Part-time tuition:* $1185 per course.

**FRESHMAN FINANCIAL AID (Fall 2014, est.)** 162 applied for aid; of those 90% were deemed to have need. 99% of freshmen with need received aid; of those 3% had need fully met. *Average percent of need met:* 21% (excluding resources awarded to replace EFC). *Average financial aid package:* $25,752 (excluding resources awarded to replace EFC). 13% of all full-time freshmen had no need and received non-need-based gift aid.

**UNDERGRADUATE FINANCIAL AID (Fall 2014, est.)** 721 applied for aid; of those 93% were deemed to have need. 100% of undergraduates with need received aid; of those 3% had need fully met. *Average percent of need met:* 23% (excluding resources awarded to replace EFC). *Average financial aid package:* $26,543 (excluding resources awarded to replace EFC). 5% of all full-time undergraduates had no need and received non-need-based gift aid.

**GIFT AID (NEED-BASED)** *Total amount:* $6,082,228 (25% federal, 6% state, 69% institutional). *Receiving aid:* Freshmen: 85% (144); all full-time undergraduates: 84% (648). *Average award:* Freshmen: $8828; Undergraduates: $8998. *Scholarships, grants, and awards:* Federal Pell, FSEOG, state, private, college/university gift aid from institutional funds.

**GIFT AID (NON-NEED-BASED)** *Total amount:* $7,210,884 (96% institutional, 4% external sources). *Receiving aid:* Freshmen: 85% (144). Undergraduates: 85% (657). *Average award:* Freshmen: $10,840. Undergraduates: $9947. *Scholarships, grants, and awards by category:* Academic interests/achievement: general academic interests/achievements. Creative arts/performance: music. Special achievements/activities: religious involvement. Special characteristics: children of faculty/staff, general special characteristics, local/state students, previous college experience. *ROTC:* Air Force cooperative.

**LOANS** *Student loans:* $9,124,561 (33% need-based, 67% non-need-based). 95% of past graduating class borrowed through all loan programs. *Average indebtedness per student:* $51,934. *Average need-based loan:* Freshmen: $3133. Undergraduates: $4381. *Parent loans:* $2,922,929 (100% non-need-based). *Programs:* Federal Direct (Subsidized and Unsubsidized Stafford, PLUS), Perkins, state.

**WORK-STUDY** *Federal work-study:* Total amount: $1,023,678; jobs available. *State or other work-study/employment:* Part-time jobs available.

**APPLYING FOR FINANCIAL AID** *Required financial aid form:* FAFSA. *Financial aid deadline (priority):* 3/1. *Notification date:* Continuous beginning 3/15. Students must reply within 4 weeks of notification.

**CONTACT** Sandra J. Pereira, Director of Financial Aid, Anna Maria College, 50 Sunset Lane, Paxton, MA 01612-1198, 508-849-3363. *Fax:* 508-849-3229. *E-mail:* spereira@annamaria.edu. *Website:* http://www.annamaria.edu/.

# ANTIOCH UNIVERSITY MIDWEST
## Yellow Springs, OH

| Tuition & fees: $19,407 | Average undergraduate aid package: N/A |
|---|---|

**ABOUT THE INSTITUTION** Independent, coed. *Awards:* certificates, bachelor's, and master's degrees. 11 undergraduate majors. *Total enrollment:* 256. Undergraduates: 81. Federal methodology is used as a basis for awarding need-based institutional aid.

**UNDERGRADUATE EXPENSES** for 2015–2016 *Application fee:* $45. *Tuition:* full-time $18,972; part-time $527 per credit.

**GIFT AID (NEED-BASED)** *Total amount:* $468,082 (77% federal, 23% state). *Scholarships, grants, and awards:* Federal Pell, FSEOG, state.

**GIFT AID (NON-NEED-BASED)** *Scholarships, grants, and awards by category:* *Academic interests/achievement:* education, health fields.
**LOANS** *Programs:* Federal Direct (Subsidized and Unsubsidized Stafford, PLUS), Perkins.
**WORK-STUDY** *Federal work-study:* Total amount: $245,743; jobs available.
**APPLYING FOR FINANCIAL AID** *Required financial aid forms:* FAFSA, institution's own form. *Financial aid deadline:* Continuous. *Notification date:* Continuous beginning 4/1.
**CONTACT** Tricia Webb, Assistant Director of Financial Aid , Antioch University Midwest, 900 Dayton Street, Yellow Springs, OH 45387, 937-769-1883. *Fax:* 937-769-1804. *E-mail:* twebb@antioch.edu.
*Website:* http://midwest.antioch.edu/.

# ANTIOCH UNIVERSITY SANTA BARBARA
## Santa Barbara, CA

**CONTACT** Cecilia Schneider, Financial Aid Director, Antioch University Santa Barbara, 801 Garden Street, Santa Barbara, CA 93101-1580, 805-962-8179 Ext. 108 or toll-free 866-526-8462. *Fax:* 805-962-4786.
*Website:* http://www.antiochsb.edu/.

# ANTIOCH UNIVERSITY SEATTLE
## Seattle, WA

**CONTACT** Katy Stahl, Director of Financial Aid, Antioch University Seattle, 2326 Sixth Avenue, Seattle, WA 98121-1814, 206-268-4004 or toll-free 888-268-4477. *Fax:* 206-268-4242. *E-mail:* kstahl@antiochseattle.edu.
*Website:* http://www.antiochsea.edu/.

# APEX SCHOOL OF THEOLOGY
## Durham, NC

**CONTACT** Financial Aid Office, Apex School of Theology, 2945 South Miami Boulevard, Suite 114, Durham, NC 27703, 919-572-1625.
*Website:* http://www.apexsot.edu/.

# APPALACHIAN BIBLE COLLEGE
## Bradley, WV

**CONTACT** Deana Steinke, Director of Financial Aid, Appalachian Bible College, 161 College Drive, Mount Hope, WV 25880, 304-877-6428 Ext. 3247 or toll-free 800-678-9ABC. *Fax:* 304-877-5082. *E-mail:* deana.steinke@abc.edu.
*Website:* http://www.abc.edu/.

# APPALACHIAN STATE UNIVERSITY
## Boone, NC

| Tuition & fees (NC res): $6553 | Average undergraduate aid package: $9551 |
|---|---|

**ABOUT THE INSTITUTION** State-supported, coed. *Awards:* certificates, bachelor's, master's, and doctoral degrees. 78 undergraduate majors. *Total enrollment:* 18,026. Undergraduates: 16,255. Freshmen: 3,033. Federal methodology is used as a basis for awarding need-based institutional aid.
**UNDERGRADUATE EXPENSES** for 2015–2016 *Application fee:* $55. *Tuition, state resident:* full-time $3772; part-time $127.50 per credit hour. *Tuition, nonresident:* full-time $16,939; part-time $572.50 per credit hour. *Required fees:* full-time $2781; $17 per credit hour. Part-time tuition and fees vary

according to course load. *College room and board:* $7675; *Room only:* $4125. Room and board charges vary according to board plan and housing facility.
**FRESHMAN FINANCIAL AID (Fall 2014, est.)** 1,602 applied for aid; of those 98% were deemed to have need. 93% of freshmen with need received aid; of those 22% had need fully met. *Average percent of need met:* 63% (excluding resources awarded to replace EFC). *Average financial aid package:* $8876 (excluding resources awarded to replace EFC). 3% of all full-time freshmen had no need and received non-need-based gift aid.
**UNDERGRADUATE FINANCIAL AID (Fall 2014, est.)** 7,948 applied for aid; of those 97% were deemed to have need. 96% of undergraduates with need received aid; of those 26% had need fully met. *Average percent of need met:* 67% (excluding resources awarded to replace EFC). *Average financial aid package:* $9551 (excluding resources awarded to replace EFC). 3% of all full-time undergraduates had no need and received non-need-based gift aid.
**GIFT AID (NEED-BASED)** *Total amount:* $44,128,089 (42% federal, 28% state, 25% institutional, 5% external sources). *Receiving aid:* Freshmen: 35% (1,055); all full-time undergraduates: 36% (5,437). *Average award:* Freshmen: $8203; Undergraduates: $8057. *Scholarships, grants, and awards:* Federal Pell, FSEOG, state, private, college/university gift aid from institutional funds.
**GIFT AID (NON-NEED-BASED)** *Total amount:* $2,825,271 (10% state, 47% institutional, 43% external sources). *Receiving aid:* Freshmen: 19% (564). Undergraduates: 18% (2,711). *Average award:* Freshmen: $3788. Undergraduates: $2768. *Scholarships, grants, and awards by category:* *Academic interests/achievement:* general academic interests/achievements. *Creative arts/performance:* general creative arts/performance. *Special achievements/activities:* general special achievements/activities. *Special characteristics:* general special characteristics. *Tuition waivers:* Full or partial for employees or children of employees. *ROTC:* Army.
**LOANS** *Student loans:* $52,802,052 (76% need-based, 24% non-need-based). 57% of past graduating class borrowed through all loan programs. *Average indebtedness per student:* $21,693. *Average need-based loan:* Freshmen: $3322. Undergraduates: $4318. *Parent loans:* $27,290,029 (64% need-based, 36% non-need-based). *Programs:* Federal Direct (Subsidized and Unsubsidized Stafford, PLUS), Perkins.
**WORK-STUDY** *Federal work-study:* Total amount: $522,000; 309 jobs averaging $1669.
**ATHLETIC AWARDS** Total amount: $4,571,936 (44% need-based, 56% non-need-based).
**APPLYING FOR FINANCIAL AID** *Required financial aid form:* FAFSA. *Financial aid deadline:* Continuous. *Notification date:* Continuous beginning 4/1. Students must reply within 3 weeks of notification.
**CONTACT** Lori Townsend, Interim Director of Student Financial Aid, Appalachian State University, John E. Thomas Hall, ASU Box 32059, Boone, NC 28608-2059, 828-262-2190. *Fax:* 828-262-2585. *E-mail:* financialaid@appstate.edu.
*Website:* http://www.appstate.edu/.

# AQUINAS COLLEGE
## Grand Rapids, MI

| Tuition & fees: $28,820 | Average undergraduate aid package: $20,213 |
|---|---|

**ABOUT THE INSTITUTION** Independent Roman Catholic, coed. *Awards:* associate, bachelor's, and master's degrees. 51 undergraduate majors. *Total enrollment:* 1,933. Undergraduates: 1,789. Freshmen: 354. Federal methodology is used as a basis for awarding need-based institutional aid.
**UNDERGRADUATE EXPENSES** for 2015–2016 *Comprehensive fee:* $37,378 includes full-time tuition ($28,426), mandatory fees ($394), and room and board ($8558). *College room only:* $4014. Full-time tuition and fees vary according to course load. Room and board charges vary according to board plan and housing facility. *Part-time tuition:* $498 per credit hour. Part-time tuition and fees vary according to course load.
**FRESHMAN FINANCIAL AID (Fall 2014, est.)** 333 applied for aid; of those 90% were deemed to have need. 100% of freshmen with need received aid; of those 40% had need fully met. *Average percent of need met:* 78% (excluding resources awarded to replace EFC). *Average financial aid package:* $21,912 (excluding resources awarded to replace EFC). 16% of all full-time freshmen had no need and received non-need-based gift aid.
**UNDERGRADUATE FINANCIAL AID (Fall 2014, est.)** 1,308 applied for aid; of those 91% were deemed to have need. 100% of undergraduates with need received aid; of those 40% had need fully met. *Average percent of need met:* 78%

(excluding resources awarded to replace EFC). *Average financial aid package:* $20,213 (excluding resources awarded to replace EFC). 20% of all full-time undergraduates had no need and received non-need-based gift aid.

**GIFT AID (NEED-BASED)** *Total amount:* $24,793,299 (10% federal, 6% state, 84% institutional). *Receiving aid:* Freshmen: 84% (299); all full-time undergraduates: 80% (1,190). *Average award:* Freshmen: $19,501; Undergraduates: $17,381. *Scholarships, grants, and awards:* Federal Pell, FSEOG, state, private, college/university gift aid from institutional funds.

**GIFT AID (NON-NEED-BASED)** *Total amount:* $5,193,994 (100% institutional). *Receiving aid:* Freshmen: 16% (55). Undergraduates: 20% (305). *Average award:* Freshmen: $14,054. Undergraduates: $12,706. *Scholarships, grants, and awards by category:* Academic interests/achievement: general academic interests/achievements. *Special characteristics:* children and siblings of alumni, children of faculty/staff. *Tuition waivers:* Full or partial for children of alumni, employees or children of employees. *ROTC:* Army cooperative.

**LOANS** *Student loans:* $7,411,325 (50% need-based, 50% non-need-based). 76% of past graduating class borrowed through all loan programs. *Average indebtedness per student:* $22,396. *Average need-based loan:* Freshmen: $2411. Undergraduates: $2832. *Parent loans:* $1,441,453 (92% need-based, 8% non-need-based). *Programs:* Federal Direct (Subsidized and Unsubsidized Stafford, PLUS), Perkins.

**WORK-STUDY** *Federal work-study:* Total amount: $134,000; jobs available. *State or other work-study/employment:* Part-time jobs available.

**ATHLETIC AWARDS** Total amount: $954,210 (100% need-based).

**APPLYING FOR FINANCIAL AID** *Required financial aid form:* FAFSA. *Financial aid deadline:* 8/15 (priority: 3/1). *Notification date:* Continuous. Students must reply within 2 weeks of notification.

**CONTACT** David J. Steffee, Director of Financial Aid, Aquinas College, 1607 Robinson Road, Grand Rapids, MI 49506-1799, 616-459-8281 Ext. 5127 or toll-free 800-678-9593. *Fax:* 616-732-4547. *E-mail:* steffdav@aquinas.edu. *Website:* http://www.aquinas.edu/.

# AQUINAS COLLEGE
## Nashville, TN

**CONTACT** Mrs. Kylie Pruitt, Director of Financial Aid, Aquinas College, 4210 Harding Road, Nashville, TN 37205-2005, 615-297-7545 Ext. 431 or toll-free 800-649-9956. *Fax:* 615-279-3891. *E-mail:* pruittk@aquinascollege.edu. *Website:* http://www.aquinascollege.edu/.

# ARCADIA UNIVERSITY
## Glenside, PA

| Tuition & fees: $39,560 | Average undergraduate aid package: $28,791 |
|---|---|

**ABOUT THE INSTITUTION** Independent Presbyterian Church (U.S.A.), coed. *Awards:* certificates, bachelor's, master's, and doctoral degrees. 66 undergraduate majors. *Total enrollment:* 3,939. Undergraduates: 2,594. Freshmen: 673. Federal methodology is used as a basis for awarding need-based institutional aid.

**UNDERGRADUATE EXPENSES for 2015–2016** *Application fee:* $30. *Comprehensive fee:* $52,760 includes full-time tuition ($38,900), mandatory fees ($660), and room and board ($13,200). *College room only:* $9000. Full-time tuition and fees vary according to course load, degree level, and program. Room and board charges vary according to board plan. *Part-time tuition:* $640 per credit.

**FRESHMAN FINANCIAL AID (Fall 2014, est.)** 656 applied for aid; of those 88% were deemed to have need. 100% of freshmen with need received aid; of those 12% had need fully met. *Average percent of need met:* 74% (excluding resources awarded to replace EFC). *Average financial aid package:* $29,998 (excluding resources awarded to replace EFC). 18% of all full-time freshmen had no need and received non-need-based gift aid.

**UNDERGRADUATE FINANCIAL AID (Fall 2014, est.)** 2,140 applied for aid; of those 87% were deemed to have need. 100% of undergraduates with need received aid; of those 14% had need fully met. *Average percent of need met:* 74% (excluding resources awarded to replace EFC). *Average financial aid package:*

$28,791 (excluding resources awarded to replace EFC). 19% of all full-time undergraduates had no need and received non-need-based gift aid.

**GIFT AID (NEED-BASED)** *Total amount:* $47,870,888 (8% federal, 5% state, 85% institutional, 2% external sources). *Receiving aid:* Freshmen: 85% (572); all full-time undergraduates: 75% (1,839). *Average award:* Freshmen: $26,376; Undergraduates: $24,478. *Scholarships, grants, and awards:* Federal Pell, FSEOG, state, private, college/university gift aid from institutional funds, Academic Competitiveness Grants, National SMART Grants, TEACH Grants.

**GIFT AID (NON-NEED-BASED)** *Total amount:* $7,933,224 (100% institutional). *Receiving aid:* Freshmen: 9% (61). Undergraduates: 8% (190). *Average award:* Freshmen: $15,994. Undergraduates: $16,975. *Scholarships, grants, and awards by category:* Academic interests/achievement: 2,413 awards ($35,232,622 total): general academic interests/achievements. Creative arts/performance: applied art and design, art/fine arts, theater/drama. *Special achievements/activities:* community service, general special achievements/activities, leadership, memberships. *Special characteristics:* 39 awards ($87,500 total): children and siblings of alumni, relatives of clergy, religious affiliation.

**LOANS** *Student loans:* $48,388,861 (84% need-based, 16% non-need-based). 88% of past graduating class borrowed through all loan programs. *Average need-based loan:* Freshmen: $3214. Undergraduates: $4061. *Parent loans:* $5,243,675 (88% need-based, 12% non-need-based). *Programs:* Federal Direct (Subsidized and Unsubsidized Stafford, PLUS), Perkins.

**WORK-STUDY** *Federal work-study:* Total amount: $2,569,223; 1,548 jobs averaging $1660. *State or other work-study/employment:* Total amount: $358,005 (100% non-need-based). 213 part-time jobs averaging $1681.

**APPLYING FOR FINANCIAL AID** *Required financial aid forms:* FAFSA, institution's own form. *Financial aid deadline (priority):* 3/1. *Notification date:* Continuous beginning 3/1. Students must reply by 5/1.

**CONTACT** Alison Venditti, Assistant Director of Financial Aid, Arcadia University, 450 South Easton Road, Glenside, PA 19038, 215-572-2837 or toll-free 877-ARCADIA. *Fax:* 215-572-4049. *E-mail:* venditta@arcadia.edu. *Website:* http://www.arcadia.edu/.

# ARGOSY UNIVERSITY, ATLANTA
## Atlanta, GA

**CONTACT** Financial Aid Office, Argosy University, Atlanta, 980 Hammond Drive, Suite 100, Atlanta, GA 30328, 770-671-1200 or toll-free 888-671-4777. *Website:* http://www.argosy.edu/locations/atlanta/.

# ARGOSY UNIVERSITY, CHICAGO
## Chicago, IL

**CONTACT** Financial Aid Office, Argosy University, Chicago, 225 North Michigan Avenue, Suite 1300, Chicago, IL 60601, 312-777-7600 or toll-free 800-626-4123. *Website:* http://www.argosy.edu/chicago-illinois/default.aspx.

# ARGOSY UNIVERSITY, DALLAS
## Farmers Branch, TX

**CONTACT** Financial Aid Office, Argosy University, Dallas, 5001 Lyndon B. Johnson Freeway, Heritage Square, Farmers Branch, TX 75244, 214-890-9900 or toll-free 866-954-9900. *Website:* http://www.argosy.edu/dallas-texas/default.aspx.

# ARGOSY UNIVERSITY, DENVER
## Denver, CO

**CONTACT** Financial Aid Office, Argosy University, Denver, 7600 East Eastman Avenue, Denver, CO 80231, 303-923-4110 or toll-free 866-431-5981. *Website:* http://www.argosy.edu/locations/denver/.

## ARGOSY UNIVERSITY, HAWAII
### Honolulu, HI

CONTACT Financial Aid Office, Argosy University, Hawaii, 1001 Bishop Street, Suite 400, Honolulu, HI 96813, 808-536-5555 or toll-free 888-323-2777.
*Website:* http://www.argosy.edu/locations/hawaii/.

## ARGOSY UNIVERSITY, INLAND EMPIRE
### Ontario, CA

CONTACT Financial Aid Office, Argosy University, Inland Empire, 3401 Centre Lake Drive, Suite 200, Ontario, CA 91761, 909-472-0800 or toll-free 866-217-9075.
*Website:* http://www.argosy.edu/locations/inland-empire/.

## ARGOSY UNIVERSITY, NASHVILLE
### Nashville, TN

CONTACT Financial Aid Office, Argosy University, Nashville, 100 Centerview Drive, Suite 225, Nashville, TN 37214, 615-525-2800 or toll-free 866-833-6598.
*Website:* http://www.argosy.edu/locations/nashville/.

## ARGOSY UNIVERSITY, ORANGE COUNTY
### Orange, CA

CONTACT Financial Aid Office, Argosy University, Orange County, 601 South Lewis Street, Orange, CA 92868, 714-620-3700 or toll-free 800-716-9598.
*Website:* http://www.argosy.edu/locations/los-angeles-orange-county/.

## ARGOSY UNIVERSITY, PHOENIX
### Phoenix, AZ

CONTACT Financial Aid Office, Argosy University, Phoenix, 2233 West Dunlap Avenue, Phoenix, AZ 85021, 602-216-2600 or toll-free 866-216-2777.
*Website:* http://www.argosy.edu/phoenix-arizona/default.aspx.

## ARGOSY UNIVERSITY, SALT LAKE CITY
### Draper, UT

CONTACT Financial Aid Office, Argosy University, Salt Lake City, 121 Election Road, Suite 300, Draper, UT 84020, 801-601-5000 or toll-free 888-639-4756.
*Website:* http://www.argosy.edu/locations/salt-lake-city/.

## ARGOSY UNIVERSITY, SAN DIEGO
### San Diego, CA

CONTACT Financial Aid Office, Argosy University, San Diego, 1615 Murray Canyon Road, Suite 100, San Diego, CA 92108, 619-321-3000 or toll-free 866-505-0333.
*Website:* http://www.argosy.edu/locations/san-diego/.

## ARGOSY UNIVERSITY, SAN FRANCISCO BAY AREA
### Alameda, CA

CONTACT Financial Aid Office, Argosy University, San Francisco Bay Area, 1005 Atlantic Avenue, Alameda, CA 94501, 510-217-4700 or toll-free 866-215-2777.
*Website:* http://www.argosy.edu/locations/san-francisco/.

## ARGOSY UNIVERSITY, SARASOTA
### Sarasota, FL

CONTACT Financial Aid Office, Argosy University, Sarasota, 5250 17th Street, Sarasota, FL 34235, 941-379-0404 or toll-free 800-331-5995.
*Website:* http://www.argosy.edu/locations/sarasota/.

## ARGOSY UNIVERSITY, SCHAUMBURG
### Schaumburg, IL

CONTACT Financial Aid Office, Argosy University, Schaumburg, 999 North Plaza Drive, Suite 111, Schaumburg, IL 60173-5403, 847-969-4900 or toll-free 866-290-2777.
*Website:* http://www.argosy.edu/locations/chicago-schaumburg/.

## ARGOSY UNIVERSITY, SEATTLE
### Seattle, WA

CONTACT Financial Aid Office, Argosy University, Seattle, 2601-A Elliott Avenue, Seattle, WA 98121, 206-283-4500 or toll-free 866-283-2777.
*Website:* http://www.argosy.edu/locations/seattle/.

## ARGOSY UNIVERSITY, TAMPA
### Tampa, FL

CONTACT Financial Aid Office, Argosy University, Tampa, 1403 North Howard Avenue, Tampa, FL 33607, 813-393-5290 or toll-free 800-850-6488.
*Website:* http://www.argosy.edu/locations/tampa/.

## ARGOSY UNIVERSITY, TWIN CITIES
### Eagan, MN

CONTACT Financial Aid Office, Argosy University, Twin Cities, 1515 Central Parkway, Eagan, MN 55121, 651-846-2882 or toll-free 888-844-2004.
*Website:* http://www.argosy.edu/locations/twin-cities/.

## ARGOSY UNIVERSITY, WASHINGTON DC
### Arlington, VA

CONTACT Financial Aid Office, Argosy University, Washington DC, 1550 Wilson Boulevard, Suite 600, Arlington, VA 22209, 703-526-5800 or toll-free 866-703-2777.
*Website:* http://www.argosy.edu/locations/washington-dc/.

# ARIZONA CHRISTIAN UNIVERSITY
### Phoenix, AZ

| Tuition & fees: $23,220 | Average undergraduate aid package: $15,811 |
|---|---|

**ABOUT THE INSTITUTION** Independent Conservative Baptist, coed. **Awards:** associate and bachelor's degrees. 21 undergraduate majors. **Total enrollment:** 737. Undergraduates: 737. Freshmen: 154. Federal methodology is used as a basis for awarding need-based institutional aid.

**UNDERGRADUATE EXPENSES for 2015–2016 Comprehensive fee:** $33,110 includes full-time tuition ($22,230), mandatory fees ($990), and room and board ($9890). Full-time tuition and fees vary according to class time, course load, and program. Room and board charges vary according to board plan. **Part-time tuition:** $930 per credit hour. **Part-time fees:** $495 per term. Part-time tuition and fees vary according to class time, course load, and program.

**FRESHMAN FINANCIAL AID (Fall 2014, est.)** 147 applied for aid; of those 85% were deemed to have need. 100% of freshmen with need received aid. **Average financial aid package:** $15,794 (excluding resources awarded to replace EFC). 14% of all full-time freshmen had no need and received non-need-based gift aid.

**UNDERGRADUATE FINANCIAL AID (Fall 2014, est.)** 503 applied for aid; of those 89% were deemed to have need. 100% of undergraduates with need received aid. **Average financial aid package:** $15,811 (excluding resources awarded to replace EFC). 9% of all full-time undergraduates had no need and received non-need-based gift aid.

**GIFT AID (NEED-BASED) Total amount:** $4,547,124 (24% federal, 74% institutional, 2% external sources). **Receiving aid:** Freshmen: 81% (124); all full-time undergraduates: 77% (444). **Average award:** Freshmen: $13,769; Undergraduates: $13,195. **Scholarships, grants, and awards:** Federal Pell, FSEOG, state, private, college/university gift aid from institutional funds.

**GIFT AID (NON-NEED-BASED) Total amount:** $926,379 (1% federal, 94% institutional, 5% external sources). **Average award:** Freshmen: $6228. Undergraduates: $5414. **Scholarships, grants, and awards by category:** Academic interests/achievement: general academic interests/achievements. Creative arts/performance: music. Special achievements/activities: community service, general special achievements/activities, leadership. **Tuition waivers:** Full or partial for employees or children of employees. **ROTC:** Air Force cooperative.

**LOANS Student loans:** $2,555,525 (92% need-based, 8% non-need-based). 72% of past graduating class borrowed through all loan programs. **Average indebtedness per student:** $26,228. **Average need-based loan:** Freshmen: $3024. Undergraduates: $3705. **Parent loans:** $1,569,995 (38% need-based, 62% non-need-based). **Programs:** Federal Direct (Subsidized and Unsubsidized Stafford, PLUS).

**WORK-STUDY** Federal work-study jobs available.

**ATHLETIC AWARDS** Total amount: $1,602,911 (91% need-based, 9% non-need-based).

**APPLYING FOR FINANCIAL AID Required financial aid forms:** FAFSA, institution's own form. **Financial aid deadline:** 6/5. **Notification date:** Continuous beginning 4/15. Students must reply by 6/1 or within 2 weeks of notification.

**CONTACT** Mr. Steven Young, Director of Financial Aid, Arizona Christian University, 2625 East Cactus Road, Phoenix, AZ 85032-7042, 602-386-4115 or toll-free 800-247-2697. Fax: 602-404-2159. E-mail: steven.young@arizonachristian.edu. Website: http://arizonachristian.edu/.

# ARIZONA COLLEGE–MESA
### Mesa, AZ

**CONTACT** Financial Aid Office, Arizona College–Mesa, 163 N Dobson Road, Mesa, AZ 85201. Website: http://www.arizonacollege.edu/.

# ARIZONA STATE UNIVERSITY AT THE DOWNTOWN PHOENIX CAMPUS
### Phoenix, AZ

| Tuition & fees (AZ res): $10,127 | Average undergraduate aid package: $13,166 |
|---|---|

**ABOUT THE INSTITUTION** State-supported, coed. **Awards:** certificates, bachelor's, master's, and doctoral degrees. 26 undergraduate majors. **Total enrollment:** 11,217. Undergraduates: 9,150. Federal methodology is used as a basis for awarding need-based institutional aid.

**UNDERGRADUATE EXPENSES for 2015–2016 Application fee:** $50. **Tuition, state resident:** full-time $9454; part-time $677 per credit hour. **Tuition, nonresident:** full-time $23,830; part-time $993 per credit hour. **Required fees:** full-time $673. Full-time tuition and fees vary according to program. Part-time tuition and fees vary according to program. **College room and board:** $11,974; **Room only:** $8334. Room and board charges vary according to board plan and housing facility.

**FRESHMAN FINANCIAL AID (Fall 2013)** 980 applied for aid; of those 82% were deemed to have need. 100% of freshmen with need received aid; of those 22% had need fully met. **Average percent of need met:** 68% (excluding resources awarded to replace EFC). **Average financial aid package:** $15,644 (excluding resources awarded to replace EFC). 20% of all full-time freshmen had no need and received non-need-based gift aid.

**UNDERGRADUATE FINANCIAL AID (Fall 2013)** 6,131 applied for aid; of those 87% were deemed to have need. 100% of undergraduates with need received aid; of those 17% had need fully met. **Average percent of need met:** 58% (excluding resources awarded to replace EFC). **Average financial aid package:** $13,166 (excluding resources awarded to replace EFC). 12% of all full-time undergraduates had no need and received non-need-based gift aid.

**GIFT AID (NEED-BASED) Total amount:** $44,288,573 (38% federal, 53% institutional, 9% external sources). **Receiving aid:** Freshmen: 74% (787); all full-time undergraduates: 61% (1,847). **Average award:** Freshmen: $11,700; Undergraduates: $8705. **Scholarships, grants, and awards:** Federal Pell, FSEOG, state, private, college/university gift aid from institutional funds, United Negro College Fund.

**GIFT AID (NON-NEED-BASED) Total amount:** $10,833,032 (7% federal, 71% institutional, 22% external sources). **Receiving aid:** Freshmen: 8% (82). Undergraduates: 4% (324). **Average award:** Freshmen: $7998. Undergraduates: $7349. **Scholarships, grants, and awards by category:** Academic interests/achievement: general academic interests/achievements. Special achievements/activities: leadership. Special characteristics: children of faculty/staff, international students, local/state students, out-of-state students. **Tuition waivers:** Full or partial for employees or children of employees. **ROTC:** Army cooperative, Naval cooperative, Air Force cooperative.

**LOANS Student loans:** $42,075,084 (79% need-based, 21% non-need-based). 65% of past graduating class borrowed through all loan programs. **Average indebtedness per student:** $22,498. **Average need-based loan:** Freshmen: $3007. Undergraduates: $4191. **Parent loans:** $14,529,178 (40% need-based, 60% non-need-based). **Programs:** Federal Direct (Subsidized and Unsubsidized Stafford, PLUS), Perkins, Federal Nursing, state, private loans from endowment funds.

**WORK-STUDY Federal work-study:** 343 jobs averaging $2669. **State or other work-study/employment:** Total amount: $4,025,910 (37% need-based, 63% non-need-based). 1,083 part-time jobs averaging $3714.

**ATHLETIC AWARDS** Total amount: $1,065,743 (45% need-based, 55% non-need-based).

**APPLYING FOR FINANCIAL AID Required financial aid form:** FAFSA. **Financial aid deadline (priority):** 3/1. **Notification date:** Continuous beginning 3/1.

**CONTACT** Student Financial Assistance Office, Arizona State University at the Downtown Phoenix campus, PO Box 870412, Tempe, AZ 85287-0412, 855-278-5080. Fax: 480-965-9484. Website: https://campus.asu.edu/downtown/.

# ARIZONA STATE UNIVERSITY AT THE POLYTECHNIC CAMPUS
## Mesa, AZ

| Tuition & fees (AZ res): $9811 | Average undergraduate aid package: $13,733 |
|---|---|

**ABOUT THE INSTITUTION** State-supported, coed. **Awards:** certificates, bachelor's, master's, and doctoral degrees. 33 undergraduate majors. **Total enrollment:** 4,094. Undergraduates: 3,750. Federal methodology is used as a basis for awarding need-based institutional aid.

**UNDERGRADUATE EXPENSES for 2015–2016 Application fee:** $50. **Tuition, state resident:** full-time $9138; part-time $677 per credit hour. **Tuition, nonresident:** full-time $22,639; part-time $993 per credit hour. **Required fees:** full-time $673. Full-time tuition and fees vary according to program. Part-time tuition and fees vary according to program. **College room and board:** $10,720; **Room only:** $7080. Room and board charges vary according to board plan and housing facility.

**FRESHMAN FINANCIAL AID (Fall 2013)** 322 applied for aid; of those 75% were deemed to have need. 100% of freshmen with need received aid; of those 24% had need fully met. **Average percent of need met:** 67% (excluding resources awarded to replace EFC). **Average financial aid package:** $13,628 (excluding resources awarded to replace EFC). 24% of all full-time freshmen had no need and received non-need-based gift aid.

**UNDERGRADUATE FINANCIAL AID (Fall 2013)** 2,123 applied for aid; of those 88% were deemed to have need. 100% of undergraduates with need received aid; of those 20% had need fully met. **Average percent of need met:** 57% (excluding resources awarded to replace EFC). **Average financial aid package:** $13,733 (excluding resources awarded to replace EFC). 9% of all full-time undergraduates had no need and received non-need-based gift aid.

**GIFT AID (NEED-BASED) Total amount:** $15,199,319 (48% federal, 42% institutional, 10% external sources). **Receiving aid:** Freshmen: 60% (236); all full-time undergraduates: 60% (1,671). **Average award:** Freshmen: $10,382; Undergraduates: $8454. **Scholarships, grants, and awards:** Federal Pell, FSEOG, state, private, college/university gift aid from institutional funds, United Negro College Fund.

**GIFT AID (NON-NEED-BASED) Total amount:** $7,107,237 (15% federal, 27% institutional, 58% external sources). **Receiving aid:** Freshmen: 7% (29). Undergraduates: 4% (112). **Average award:** Freshmen: $5976. Undergraduates: $6263. **Scholarships, grants, and awards by category:** Academic interests/achievement: general academic interests/achievements. Special achievements/activities: leadership. Special characteristics: children of faculty/staff, international students, local/state students, out-of-state students. **Tuition waivers:** Full or partial for employees or children of employees. **ROTC:** Army cooperative, Naval cooperative, Air Force cooperative.

**LOANS Student loans:** $16,171,449 (79% need-based, 21% non-need-based). 63% of past graduating class borrowed through all loan programs. **Average indebtedness per student:** $26,463. **Average need-based loan:** Freshmen: $2932. Undergraduates: $4338. **Parent loans:** $4,733,483 (44% need-based, 56% non-need-based). **Programs:** Federal Direct (Subsidized and Unsubsidized Stafford, PLUS), Perkins, state, private loans from endowment funds.

**WORK-STUDY Federal work-study:** 110 jobs averaging $2916. **State or other work-study/employment:** Total amount: $2,479,788 (36% need-based, 64% non-need-based). 584 part-time jobs averaging $4246.

**ATHLETIC AWARDS** Total amount: $59,903 (54% need-based, 46% non-need-based).

**APPLYING FOR FINANCIAL AID Required financial aid form:** FAFSA. **Financial aid deadline (priority):** 3/1. **Notification date:** Continuous beginning 3/1.

**CONTACT** Student Financial Assistance Office, Arizona State University at the Polytechnic campus, PO Box 870412, Tempe, AZ 85287-0412, 855-278-5080. *Fax:* 480-965-9484.
*Website:* https://campus.asu.edu/polytechnic.

# ARIZONA STATE UNIVERSITY AT THE TEMPE CAMPUS
## Tempe, AZ

| Tuition & fees (AZ res): $10,127 | Average undergraduate aid package: $13,362 |
|---|---|

**ABOUT THE INSTITUTION** State-supported, coed. **Awards:** certificates, bachelor's, master's, and doctoral degrees (profile includes data for the West, Polytechnic and Downtown Phoenix campuses). 93 undergraduate majors. **Total enrollment:** 50,358. Undergraduates: 39,968. Freshmen: 7,647. Federal methodology is used as a basis for awarding need-based institutional aid.

**UNDERGRADUATE EXPENSES for 2015–2016 Application fee:** $50. **Tuition, state resident:** full-time $9454; part-time $677 per credit hour. **Tuition, nonresident:** full-time $23,830; part-time $993 per credit hour. **Required fees:** full-time $673. Full-time tuition and fees vary according to program. Part-time tuition and fees vary according to program. **College room and board:** $10,010; **Room only:** $6370. Room and board charges vary according to board plan and housing facility.

**FRESHMAN FINANCIAL AID (Fall 2013)** 5,588 applied for aid; of those 74% were deemed to have need. 100% of freshmen with need received aid; of those 24% had need fully met. **Average percent of need met:** 71% (excluding resources awarded to replace EFC). **Average financial aid package:** $15,063 (excluding resources awarded to replace EFC). 29% of all full-time freshmen had no need and received non-need-based gift aid.

**UNDERGRADUATE FINANCIAL AID (Fall 2013)** 24,421 applied for aid; of those 83% were deemed to have need. 100% of undergraduates with need received aid; of those 19% had need fully met. **Average percent of need met:** 61% (excluding resources awarded to replace EFC). **Average financial aid package:** $13,362 (excluding resources awarded to replace EFC). 19% of all full-time undergraduates had no need and received non-need-based gift aid.

**GIFT AID (NEED-BASED) Total amount:** $174,410,356 (35% federal, 1% state, 57% institutional, 7% external sources). **Receiving aid:** Freshmen: 58% (4,116); all full-time undergraduates: 54% (18,706). **Average award:** Freshmen: $11,359; Undergraduates: $9007. **Scholarships, grants, and awards:** Federal Pell, FSEOG, state, private, college/university gift aid from institutional funds, United Negro College Fund.

**GIFT AID (NON-NEED-BASED) Total amount:** $90,959,664 (3% federal, 64% institutional, 33% external sources). **Receiving aid:** Freshmen: 9% (627). Undergraduates: 5% (1,751). **Average award:** Freshmen: $8006. Undergraduates: $7688. **Scholarships, grants, and awards by category:** Academic interests/achievement: general academic interests/achievements. Creative arts/performance: art/fine arts, dance, music, theater/drama. Special achievements/activities: leadership. Special characteristics: children of faculty/staff, international students, local/state students, out-of-state students. **Tuition waivers:** Full or partial for employees or children of employees. **ROTC:** Army, Naval, Air Force.

**LOANS Student loans:** $142,374,571 (75% need-based, 25% non-need-based). 54% of past graduating class borrowed through all loan programs. **Average indebtedness per student:** $21,920. **Average need-based loan:** Freshmen: $3008. Undergraduates: $4150. **Parent loans:** $54,862,226 (38% need-based, 62% non-need-based). **Programs:** Federal Direct (Subsidized and Unsubsidized Stafford, PLUS), Perkins, state, private loans from endowment funds.

**WORK-STUDY Federal work-study:** 1,077 jobs averaging $2406. **State or other work-study/employment:** Total amount: $18,454,718 (33% need-based, 67% non-need-based). 5,551 part-time jobs averaging $3324.

**ATHLETIC AWARDS** Total amount: $7,115,161 (43% need-based, 57% non-need-based).

**APPLYING FOR FINANCIAL AID Required financial aid form:** FAFSA. **Financial aid deadline (priority):** 3/1. **Notification date:** Continuous beginning 3/1.

**CONTACT** Student Financial Assistance Office, Arizona State University at the Tempe campus, PO Box 870412, Tempe, AZ 85287-0412, 855-278-5080. *Fax:* 480-965-9484.
*Website:* http://www.asu.edu/.

# ARIZONA STATE UNIVERSITY AT THE WEST CAMPUS
### Glendale, AZ

| Tuition & fees (AZ res): $9811 | Average undergraduate aid package: $11,817 |
| --- | --- |

**ABOUT THE INSTITUTION** State-supported, coed. *Awards:* certificates, bachelor's, master's, and doctoral degrees. 28 undergraduate majors. *Total enrollment:* 3,693. Undergraduates: 3,296. Federal methodology is used as a basis for awarding need-based institutional aid.

**UNDERGRADUATE EXPENSES for 2015–2016** *Application fee:* $50. *Tuition, state resident:* full-time $9138; part-time $677 per credit hour. *Tuition, nonresident:* full-time $22,639; part-time $993 per credit hour. *Required fees:* full-time $673. Full-time tuition and fees vary according to program. Part-time tuition and fees vary according to program. *College room and board:* $9440; *Room only:* $5800. Room and board charges vary according to board plan and housing facility.

**FRESHMAN FINANCIAL AID (Fall 2013)** 246 applied for aid; of those 84% were deemed to have need. 100% of freshmen with need received aid; of those 28% had need fully met. *Average percent of need met:* 74% (excluding resources awarded to replace EFC). *Average financial aid package:* $14,512 (excluding resources awarded to replace EFC). 17% of all full-time freshmen had no need and received non-need-based gift aid.

**UNDERGRADUATE FINANCIAL AID (Fall 2013)** 2,288 applied for aid; of those 92% were deemed to have need. 100% of undergraduates with need received aid; of those 14% had need fully met. *Average percent of need met:* 59% (excluding resources awarded to replace EFC). *Average financial aid package:* $11,817 (excluding resources awarded to replace EFC). 6% of all full-time undergraduates had no need and received non-need-based gift aid.

**GIFT AID (NEED-BASED)** *Total amount:* $16,627,801 (50% federal, 1% state, 42% institutional, 7% external sources). *Receiving aid:* Freshmen: 76% (203); all full-time undergraduates: 71% (1,900). *Average award:* Freshmen: $11,153; Undergraduates: $8077. *Scholarships, grants, and awards:* Federal Pell, FSEOG, state, private, college/university gift aid from institutional funds, United Negro College Fund.

**GIFT AID (NON-NEED-BASED)** *Total amount:* $2,261,358 (15% federal, 65% institutional, 20% external sources). *Receiving aid:* Freshmen: 10% (27). Undergraduates: 4% (103). *Average award:* Freshmen: $6091. Undergraduates: $6575. *Scholarships, grants, and awards by category:* Academic interests/achievement: general academic interests/achievements. *Special achievements/activities:* leadership. *Special characteristics:* children of faculty/staff, international students, local/state students, out-of-state students. *Tuition waivers:* Full or partial for employees or children of employees. *ROTC:* Army cooperative, Naval cooperative, Air Force cooperative.

**LOANS** *Student loans:* $15,999,686 (83% need-based, 17% non-need-based). 65% of past graduating class borrowed through all loan programs. *Average indebtedness per student:* $18,585. *Average need-based loan:* Freshmen: $3135. Undergraduates: $4328. *Parent loans:* $2,220,125 (43% need-based, 57% non-need-based). *Programs:* Federal Direct (Subsidized and Unsubsidized Stafford, PLUS), Perkins, state, private loans from endowment funds.

**WORK-STUDY** *Federal work-study:* 120 jobs averaging $2509. *State or other work-study/employment:* Total amount: $1,452,680 (39% need-based, 61% non-need-based). 435 part-time jobs averaging $3339.

**APPLYING FOR FINANCIAL AID** *Required financial aid form:* FAFSA. *Financial aid deadline (priority):* 3/1. *Notification date:* Continuous beginning 3/1.

**CONTACT** Student Financial Assistance Office, Arizona State University at the West campus, PO Box 870412, Tempe, AZ 85287-0412, 855-278-5080. *Fax:* 480-965-9484. *Website:* https://campus.asu.edu/west.

# ARKANSAS BAPTIST COLLEGE
### Little Rock, AR

**CONTACT** Office of Financial Aid, Arkansas Baptist College, 1600 Bishop Street, Little Rock, AR 72202-6067, 501-374-7856. *Website:* http://www.arkansasbaptist.edu/.

# ARKANSAS STATE UNIVERSITY
### Jonesboro, AR

| Tuition & fees (AR res): $7720 | Average undergraduate aid package: $10,500 |
| --- | --- |

**ABOUT THE INSTITUTION** State-supported, coed. *Awards:* certificates, associate, bachelor's, master's, and doctoral degrees. 73 undergraduate majors. *Total enrollment:* 13,144. Undergraduates: 9,857. Freshmen: 1,698. Both federal and institutional methodology are used as a basis for awarding need-based institutional aid.

**UNDERGRADUATE EXPENSES for 2015–2016** *Application fee:* $15. *Tuition, state resident:* full-time $5760; part-time $192 per credit hour. *Tuition, nonresident:* full-time $11,520; part-time $384 per credit hour. *Required fees:* full-time $1960; $63 per credit hour or $35 per term. Full-time tuition and fees vary according to course load, location, and program. Part-time tuition and fees vary according to course load, location, and program. *College room and board:* $7750. Room and board charges vary according to board plan, housing facility, and student level.

**FRESHMAN FINANCIAL AID (Fall 2014, est.)** 1,479 applied for aid; of those 99% were deemed to have need. 97% of freshmen with need received aid; of those 40% had need fully met. *Average percent of need met:* 62% (excluding resources awarded to replace EFC). *Average financial aid package:* $10,000 (excluding resources awarded to replace EFC). 13% of all full-time freshmen had no need and received non-need-based gift aid.

**UNDERGRADUATE FINANCIAL AID (Fall 2014, est.)** 6,567 applied for aid; of those 99% were deemed to have need. 97% of undergraduates with need received aid; of those 55% had need fully met. *Average percent of need met:* 51% (excluding resources awarded to replace EFC). *Average financial aid package:* $10,500 (excluding resources awarded to replace EFC). 10% of all full-time undergraduates had no need and received non-need-based gift aid.

**GIFT AID (NEED-BASED)** *Total amount:* $60,300,000 (43% federal, 23% state, 31% institutional, 3% external sources). *Receiving aid:* Freshmen: 83% (1,403); all full-time undergraduates: 81% (6,021). *Average award:* Freshmen: $10,000; Undergraduates: $10,000. *Scholarships, grants, and awards:* Federal Pell, FSEOG, state, private, college/university gift aid from institutional funds.

**GIFT AID (NON-NEED-BASED)** *Receiving aid:* Freshmen: 39% (653). Undergraduates: 46% (3,401). *Average award:* Freshmen: $5000. Undergraduates: $5575. *Scholarships, grants, and awards by category:* Academic interests/achievement: 2,520 awards ($14,183,623 total): agriculture, area/ethnic studies, biological sciences, business, communication, computer science, education, engineering/technologies, English, general academic interests/achievements, health fields, humanities, library science, mathematics, military science, physical sciences, premedicine, social sciences. Creative arts/performance: 310 awards ($757,350 total): art/fine arts, cinema/film/broadcasting, debating, journalism/publications, music, performing arts, theater/drama. *Special achievements/activities:* 66 awards ($56,755 total): cheerleading/drum major, community service, general special achievements/activities, leadership. *Special characteristics:* 152 awards ($491,780 total): adult students, children and siblings of alumni, children of faculty/staff, ethnic background, first-generation college students, general special characteristics, handicapped students, local/state students, members of minority groups, out-of-state students, veterans, veterans' children. *Tuition waivers:* Full or partial for employees or children of employees, senior citizens. *ROTC:* Army.

**LOANS** *Student loans:* $59,000,000 (95% need-based, 5% non-need-based). 67% of past graduating class borrowed through all loan programs. *Average indebtedness per student:* $25,000. *Average need-based loan:* Freshmen: $6100. Undergraduates: $8100. *Programs:* Federal Direct (Subsidized and Unsubsidized Stafford, PLUS), Perkins.

**WORK-STUDY** *Federal work-study:* Total amount: $575,000; 180 jobs averaging $3400. *State or other work-study/employment:* Total amount: $2,500,000 (100% non-need-based). 350 part-time jobs averaging $3800.

**ATHLETIC AWARDS** Total amount: $4,400,000 (77% need-based, 23% non-need-based).

**APPLYING FOR FINANCIAL AID** *Required financial aid forms:* FAFSA, institution's own form. *Financial aid deadline:* 7/1 (priority: 2/15). *Notification date:* Continuous beginning 6/1. Students must reply within 2 weeks of notification.

**CONTACT** Mr. Terry Finney, Director of Financial Aid, Arkansas State University, PO Box 1620, State University, AR 72467, 870-972-2310 or toll-free 800-382-3030. *Fax:* 870-972-2794. *E-mail:* finaid@astate.edu. *Website:* http://www.astate.edu/.

## ARKANSAS TECH UNIVERSITY
### Russellville, AR

| Tuition & fees (AR res): $7248 | Average undergraduate aid package: $8760 |
| --- | --- |

**ABOUT THE INSTITUTION** State-supported, coed. *Awards:* certificates, associate, bachelor's, and master's degrees. 72 undergraduate majors. *Total enrollment:* 12,002. Undergraduates: 11,099. Freshmen: 1,946. Federal methodology is used as a basis for awarding need-based institutional aid.

**UNDERGRADUATE EXPENSES for 2015–2016** *Tuition, state resident:* full-time $6270; part-time $209 per credit hour. *Tuition, nonresident:* full-time $12,540; part-time $418 per credit hour. *Required fees:* full-time $978; $22 per credit hour or $159 per term. Full-time tuition and fees vary according to course load and location. Part-time tuition and fees vary according to course load and location. *College room and board:* $6734; *Room only:* $3972. Room and board charges vary according to board plan, housing facility, and location.

**FRESHMAN FINANCIAL AID (Fall 2013)** 1,632 applied for aid; of those 72% were deemed to have need. 98% of freshmen with need received aid; of those 8% had need fully met. *Average percent of need met:* 62% (excluding resources awarded to replace EFC). *Average financial aid package:* $8756 (excluding resources awarded to replace EFC). 18% of all full-time freshmen had no need and received non-need-based gift aid.

**UNDERGRADUATE FINANCIAL AID (Fall 2013)** 6,331 applied for aid; of those 76% were deemed to have need. 98% of undergraduates with need received aid; of those 9% had need fully met. *Average percent of need met:* 62% (excluding resources awarded to replace EFC). *Average financial aid package:* $8760 (excluding resources awarded to replace EFC). 12% of all full-time undergraduates had no need and received non-need-based gift aid.

**GIFT AID (NEED-BASED)** *Total amount:* $21,569,039 (97% federal, 3% state). *Receiving aid:* Freshmen: 58% (979); all full-time undergraduates: 56% (3,922). *Average award:* Freshmen: $4480; Undergraduates: $4411. *Scholarships, grants, and awards:* Federal Pell, FSEOG, state, private.

**GIFT AID (NON-NEED-BASED)** *Total amount:* $25,093,826 (46% state, 42% institutional, 12% external sources). *Receiving aid:* Freshmen: 45% (759). Undergraduates: 31% (2,162). *Average award:* Freshmen: $6368. Undergraduates: $6450. *Scholarships, grants, and awards by category: Academic interests/achievement:* biological sciences, business, computer science, education, engineering/technologies, general academic interests/achievements, health fields, humanities, military science, physical sciences, social sciences. *Creative arts/performance:* cinema/film/broadcasting, creative writing, journalism/publications, theater/drama. *Special achievements/activities:* general special achievements/activities, hobbies/interests, junior miss, leadership, memberships. *Special characteristics:* children of faculty/staff, general special characteristics, international students, out-of-state students, public servants. *Tuition waivers:* Full or partial for employees or children of employees, senior citizens. *ROTC:* Army cooperative.

**LOANS** *Student loans:* $38,777,783 (43% need-based, 57% non-need-based). 62% of past graduating class borrowed through all loan programs. *Average indebtedness per student:* $29,865. *Average need-based loan:* Freshmen: $2960. Undergraduates: $3694. *Parent loans:* $775,806 (100% non-need-based). *Programs:* Federal Direct (Subsidized and Unsubsidized Stafford, PLUS), Perkins.

**WORK-STUDY** *Federal work-study:* jobs available. *State or other work-study/employment:* Total amount: $340,202 (21% need-based, 79% non-need-based). Part-time jobs available.

**ATHLETIC AWARDS** Total amount: $1,287,730 (100% non-need-based).

**APPLYING FOR FINANCIAL AID** *Required financial aid forms:* FAFSA, institution's own form. *Financial aid deadline (priority):* 4/15. *Notification date:* Continuous beginning 5/1. Students must reply within 2 weeks of notification.

**CONTACT** Financial Aid Office, Arkansas Tech University, 1605 Coliseum Drive, Suite 117, Russellville, AR 72801, 479-968-0399 or toll-free 800-582-6953. *Fax:* 479-964-0857. *E-mail:* fa.help@atu.edu. *Website:* http://www.atu.edu/.

## ARLINGTON BAPTIST COLLEGE
### Arlington, TX

**CONTACT** Mr. David B. Clogston Jr., Business Manager, Arlington Baptist College, 3001 West Division Street, Arlington, TX 76012-3425, 817-461-8741 Ext. 110. *Fax:* 817-274-1138. *Website:* http://www.arlingtonbaptistcollege.edu/.

## ARMSTRONG STATE UNIVERSITY
### Savannah, GA

| Tuition & fees (GA res): $6214 | Average undergraduate aid package: $8499 |
| --- | --- |

**ABOUT THE INSTITUTION** State-supported, coed. *Awards:* certificates, associate, bachelor's, master's, and doctoral degrees. 34 undergraduate majors. *Total enrollment:* 7,094. Undergraduates: 6,346. Freshmen: 812. Federal methodology is used as a basis for awarding need-based institutional aid.

**UNDERGRADUATE EXPENSES for 2015–2016** *Tuition, state resident:* full-time $4740; part-time $158 per credit hour. *Tuition, nonresident:* full-time $17,246; part-time $574.87 per credit hour. *Required fees:* full-time $1474; $612 per term. Full-time tuition and fees vary according to course load, location, and program. Part-time tuition and fees vary according to course load, location, and program. *College room and board:* $10,266; *Room only:* $6288. Room and board charges vary according to board plan and housing facility.

**FRESHMAN FINANCIAL AID (Fall 2014, est.)** 806 applied for aid. *Average percent of need met:* 86% (excluding resources awarded to replace EFC). *Average financial aid package:* $8499 (excluding resources awarded to replace EFC). 5% of all full-time freshmen had no need and received non-need-based gift aid.

**UNDERGRADUATE FINANCIAL AID (Fall 2014, est.)** 3,069 applied for aid. *Average percent of need met:* 86% (excluding resources awarded to replace EFC). *Average financial aid package:* $8499 (excluding resources awarded to replace EFC). 2% of all full-time undergraduates had no need and received non-need-based gift aid.

**GIFT AID (NEED-BASED)** *Total amount:* $12,193,567 (97% federal, 2% state, 1% institutional). *Average award:* Freshmen: $1500; Undergraduates: $1500. *Scholarships, grants, and awards:* Federal Pell, FSEOG, state, private, college/university gift aid from institutional funds, Federal Nursing.

**GIFT AID (NON-NEED-BASED)** *Total amount:* $3,270,679 (89% state, 2% institutional, 9% external sources). *Average award:* Freshmen: $1500. Undergraduates: $1500. *Scholarships, grants, and awards by category: Academic interests/achievement:* biological sciences, computer science, education, engineering/technologies, English, foreign languages, general academic interests/achievements, health fields, humanities, international studies, mathematics, military science, physical sciences. *Creative arts/performance:* art/fine arts, general creative arts/performance, music. *Special achievements/activities:* community service. *Special characteristics:* ethnic background, international students, religious affiliation. *Tuition waivers:* Full or partial for employees or children of employees, senior citizens. *ROTC:* Army, Naval cooperative.

**LOANS** *Student loans:* $35,474,678 (39% need-based, 61% non-need-based). 53% of past graduating class borrowed through all loan programs. *Average indebtedness per student:* $6602. *Average need-based loan:* Freshmen: $4750. Undergraduates: $4750. *Parent loans:* $2,460,903 (100% non-need-based). *Programs:* Federal Direct (Subsidized and Unsubsidized Stafford, PLUS), state, college/university, alternative loans.

**WORK-STUDY** *Federal work-study:* Total amount: $10,741; 63 jobs averaging $2000. *State or other work-study/employment:* Part-time jobs available.

**ATHLETIC AWARDS** Total amount: $768,074 (100% non-need-based).

**APPLYING FOR FINANCIAL AID** *Required financial aid forms:* FAFSA, general scholarship application form. *Financial aid deadline (priority):* 3/15. *Notification date:* Continuous beginning 2/1. Students must reply by 4/15 or within 6 weeks of notification.

**CONTACT** Director of Financial Aid, Armstrong State University, 11935 Abercorn Street, Victor Hall, 2nd floor, Savannah, GA 31419-1997, 912-344-3266 or toll-free 800-633-2349. *Fax:* 912-344-3448. *E-mail:* fin.aid@armstrong.edu. *Website:* http://www.armstrong.edu/.

# ART ACADEMY OF CINCINNATI
## Cincinnati, OH

**CONTACT** Ms. Karen Geiger, Director of Financial Aid, Art Academy of Cincinnati, 1212 Jackson Street, Cincinnati, OH 45202, 513-562-8773 or toll-free 800-323-5692. *Fax:* 513-562-8778. *E-mail:* financialaid@artacademy.edu. *Website:* http://www.artacademy.edu/.

# ART CENTER COLLEGE OF DESIGN
## Pasadena, CA

**CONTACT** Clema McKenzie, Director of Financial Aid, Art Center College of Design, 1700 Lida Street, Pasadena, CA 91103-1999, 626-396-2215. *Fax:* 626-683-8684. *Website:* http://www.artcenter.edu/.

# THE ART INSTITUTE OF AUSTIN, A BRANCH OF THE ART INSTITUTE OF HOUSTON
## Austin, TX

**CONTACT** Financial Aid Office, The Art Institute of Austin, a branch of The Art Institute of Houston, 101 W. Louis Henna Boulevard, Suite 100, Austin, TX 78728, 512-691-1707 or toll-free 866-583-7952. *Website:* http://www.artinstitutes.edu/austin.

# THE ART INSTITUTE OF CALIFORNIA–HOLLYWOOD, A CAMPUS OF ARGOSY UNIVERSITY
## North Hollywood, CA

Financial Aid Office, The Art Institute of California–Hollywood, a campus of Argosy University, 5250 Lankershim Boulevard, North Hollywood, CA 91601, 818-299-5100 or toll-free 877-468-6232.

# THE ART INSTITUTE OF CALIFORNIA–INLAND EMPIRE, A CAMPUS OF ARGOSY UNIVERSITY
## San Bernardino, CA

**CONTACT** Financial Aid Office, The Art Institute of California–Inland Empire, a campus of Argosy University, 674 East Brier Drive, San Bernardino, CA 92408, 909-915-2100 or toll-free 800-353-0812. *Website:* http://www.artinstitutes.edu/inlandempire/.

# THE ART INSTITUTE OF CALIFORNIA–LOS ANGELES, A CAMPUS OF ARGOSY UNIVERSITY
## Santa Monica, CA

**CONTACT** Financial Aid Office, The Art Institute of California–Los Angeles, a campus of Argosy University, 2900 31st Street, Santa Monica, CA 90405-3035, 310-752-4700 or toll-free 888-646-4610. *Website:* http://www.artinstitutes.edu/losangeles/.

# THE ART INSTITUTE OF CALIFORNIA–ORANGE COUNTY, A CAMPUS OF ARGOSY UNIVERSITY
## Santa Ana, CA

**CONTACT** Financial Aid Office, The Art Institute of California–Orange County, a campus of Argosy University, 3601 West Sunflower Avenue, Santa Ana, CA 92704, 714-830-0200 or toll-free 888-549-3055. *Website:* http://www.artinstitutes.edu/orangecounty/.

# THE ART INSTITUTE OF CALIFORNIA–SACRAMENTO, A CAMPUS OF ARGOSY UNIVERSITY
## Sacramento, CA

**CONTACT** Financial Aid Office, The Art Institute of California–Sacramento, a campus of Argosy University, 2850 Gateway Oaks Drive, Suite 100, Sacramento, CA 95833, 916-830-6320 or toll-free 800-477-1957. *Website:* http://www.artinstitutes.edu/sacramento/.

# THE ART INSTITUTE OF CALIFORNIA–SAN DIEGO, A CAMPUS OF ARGOSY UNIVERSITY
## San Diego, CA

Financial Aid Office, The Art Institute of California–San Diego, a campus of Argosy University, 10025 Mesa Rim Road, San Diego, CA 92121, 619-546-0602 or toll-free 866-275-2422.

# THE ART INSTITUTE OF CALIFORNIA–SAN FRANCISCO, A CAMPUS OF ARGOSY UNIVERSITY
## San Francisco, CA

Financial Aid Office, The Art Institute of California–San Francisco, a campus of Argosy University, 1170 Market Street, San Francisco, CA 94102-4908, 415-865-0198 or toll-free 888-493-3261. *Fax:* 415-863-5831.

## THE ART INSTITUTE OF CHARLESTON, A BRANCH OF THE ART INSTITUTE OF ATLANTA
### Charleston, SC

CONTACT Financial Aid Office, The Art Institute of Charleston, a branch of The Art Institute of Atlanta, 24 North Market Street, Charleston, SC 29401, 843-727-3500 or toll-free 866-211-0107.
Website: http://www.artinstitutes.edu/charleston/.

## THE ART INSTITUTE OF CHARLOTTE, A CAMPUS OF SOUTH UNIVERSITY
### Charlotte, NC

CONTACT Financial Aid Office, The Art Institute of Charlotte, a campus of South University, Three LakePointe Plaza, 2110 Water Ridge Parkway, Charlotte, NC 28217, 704-357-8020 or toll-free 800-872-4417.
Website: http://www.artinstitutes.edu/charlotte/.

## THE ART INSTITUTE OF COLORADO
### Denver, CO

CONTACT Financial Aid Office, The Art Institute of Colorado, 1200 Lincoln Street, Denver, CO 80203, 303-837-0825 or toll-free 800-275-2420.
Website: http://www.artinstitutes.edu/denver/.

## THE ART INSTITUTE OF DALLAS, A CAMPUS OF SOUTH UNIVERSITY
### Dallas, TX

CONTACT Financial Aid Office, The Art Institute of Dallas, a campus of South University, 8080 Park Lane, Suite 100, Dallas, TX 75231-5993, 214-692-8080 or toll-free 800-275-4243.
Website: http://www.artinstitutes.edu/dallas/.

## THE ART INSTITUTE OF FORT LAUDERDALE
### Fort Lauderdale, FL

Financial Aid Office, The Art Institute of Fort Lauderdale, 1799 Southeast 17th Street Causeway, Fort Lauderdale, FL 33316-3000, 954-527-1799 or toll-free 800-275-7603.

## THE ART INSTITUTE OF HOUSTON
### Houston, TX

Financial Aid Office, The Art Institute of Houston, 4140 Southwest Freeway, Houston, TX 77027, 713-623-2040 or toll-free 800-275-4244.

## THE ART INSTITUTE OF INDIANAPOLIS
### Indianapolis, IN

CONTACT Financial Aid Office, The Art Institute of Indianapolis, 3500 Depauw Boulevard, Suite 1010, Indianapolis, IN 46268, 317-613-4800 or toll-free 866-441-9031.
Website: http://www.artinstitutes.edu/indianapolis/.

## THE ART INSTITUTE OF LAS VEGAS
### Henderson, NV

CONTACT Financial Aid Office, The Art Institute of Las Vegas, 2350 Corporate Circle Drive, Henderson, NV 89074, 702-369-9944 or toll-free 800-833-2678.
Website: http://www.artinstitutes.edu/lasvegas/.

## THE ART INSTITUTE OF MICHIGAN
### Novi, MI

CONTACT Financial Aid Office, The Art Institute of Michigan, 28125 Cabot Drive, Suite 120, Novi, MI 48377, 248-675-3800 or toll-free 800-479-0087.
Website: http://www.artinstitutes.edu/detroit/.

## THE ART INSTITUTE OF PHILADELPHIA
### Philadelphia, PA

Financial Aid Office, The Art Institute of Philadelphia, 1622 Chestnut Street, Philadelphia, PA 19103, 215-567-7080 or toll-free 800-275-2474.

## THE ART INSTITUTE OF PHOENIX
### Phoenix, AZ

CONTACT Financial Aid Office, The Art Institute of Phoenix, 2233 West Dunlap Avenue, Phoenix, AZ 85021-2859, 602-331-7500 or toll-free 800-474-2479.
Website: http://www.artinstitutes.edu/phoenix/.

## THE ART INSTITUTE OF PITTSBURGH
### Pittsburgh, PA

Financial Aid Office, The Art Institute of Pittsburgh, 420 Boulevard of the Allies, Pittsburgh, PA 15219, 412-263-6600 or toll-free 800-275-2470.

## THE ART INSTITUTE OF PORTLAND
### Portland, OR

CONTACT Financial Aid Office, The Art Institute of Portland, 1122 NW Davis Street, Portland, OR 97209, 503-228-6528 or toll-free 888-228-6528.
Website: http://www.artinstitutes.edu/portland/.

# THE ART INSTITUTE OF RALEIGH-DURHAM, A CAMPUS OF SOUTH UNIVERSITY
### Durham, NC

CONTACT Financial Aid Office, The Art Institute of Raleigh-Durham, a campus of South University, 410 Blackwell Street, Suite 200, Durham, NC 27701, 919-317-3050 or toll-free 888-245-9593.
Website: http://www.artinstitutes.edu/raleigh-durham.

# THE ART INSTITUTE OF ST. LOUIS
### St. Charles, MO

CONTACT Financial Aid Office, The Art Institute of St. Louis, 1520 South Fifth Street, St. Charles, MO 63303, 636-688-3010.
Website: http://www.artinstitutes.edu/st-louis/.

# THE ART INSTITUTE OF SAN ANTONIO, A BRANCH OF THE ART INSTITUTE OF HOUSTON
### San Antonio, TX

CONTACT Financial Aid Office, The Art Institute of San Antonio, a branch of The Art Institute of Houston, 1000 IH-10 West, Suite 200, San Antonio, TX 78230, 210-338-7320 or toll-free 888-222-0040.
Website: http://www.artinstitutes.edu/san-antonio/.

# THE ART INSTITUTE OF SEATTLE
### Seattle, WA

Financial Aid Office, The Art Institute of Seattle, 2323 Elliott Avenue, Seattle, WA 98121-1642, 206-448-6600 or toll-free 800-275-2471.

# THE ART INSTITUTE OF TAMPA, A BRANCH OF MIAMI INTERNATIONAL UNIVERSITY OF ART & DESIGN
### Tampa, FL

CONTACT Financial Aid Office, The Art Institute of Tampa, a branch of Miami International University of Art & Design, Parkside at Tampa Bay Park, 4401 North Himes Avenue, Suite 150, Tampa, FL 33614, 813-873-2112 or toll-free 866-703-3277.
Website: http://www.artinstitutes.edu/tampa/.

# THE ART INSTITUTE OF TENNESSEE-NASHVILLE, A BRANCH OF THE ART INSTITUTE OF ATLANTA
### Nashville, TN

CONTACT Financial Aid Office, The Art Institute of Tennessee-Nashville, a branch of The Art Institute of Atlanta, 100 Centerview Drive, Suite 250, Nashville, TN 37214, 615-874-1067 or toll-free 866-747-5770.
Website: http://www.artinstitutes.edu/nashville/.

# THE ART INSTITUTE OF TUCSON
### Tucson, AZ

CONTACT Financial Aid Office, The Art Institute of Tucson, 5099 East Grant Road, Suite 100, Tucson, AZ 85712, 520-318-2700 or toll-free 866-690-8850.
Website: http://www.artinstitutes.edu/tucson/.

# THE ART INSTITUTE OF VIRGINIA BEACH, A BRANCH OF THE ART INSTITUTE OF ATLANTA
### Virginia Beach, VA

CONTACT Financial Aid Office, The Art Institute of Virginia Beach, a branch of The Art Institute of Atlanta, Two Columbus Center, 4500 Main Street, Suite 100, Virginia Beach, VA 23462, 757-493-6700 or toll-free 877-437-4428.
Website: http://www.artinstitutes.edu/virginia-beach/.

# THE ART INSTITUTE OF WASHINGTON, A BRANCH OF THE ART INSTITUTE OF ATLANTA
### Arlington, VA

Financial Aid Office, The Art Institute of Washington, a branch of The Art Institute of Atlanta, 1820 North Fort Myer Drive, Arlington, VA 22209, 703-247-6849 or toll-free 877-303-3771. Fax: 703-247-6829.

# THE ART INSTITUTES INTERNATIONAL MINNESOTA
### Minneapolis, MN

Financial Aid Office, The Art Institutes International Minnesota, 15 South 9th Street, Minneapolis, MN 55402, 612-332-3361 or toll-free 800-777-3643.

# ASBURY UNIVERSITY
### Wilmore, KY

ABOUT THE INSTITUTION Independent nondenominational, coed. *Awards:* associate, bachelor's, and master's degrees. 45 undergraduate majors. *Total enrollment:* 1,854. Undergraduates: 1,622. Freshmen: 303.

GIFT AID (NEED-BASED) *Scholarships, grants, and awards:* Federal Pell, FSEOG, state, private, college/university gift aid from institutional funds.

GIFT AID (NON-NEED-BASED) *Scholarships, grants, and awards by category: Academic interests/achievement:* business, general academic interests/achievements. *Creative arts/performance:* art/fine arts, music, theater/drama. *Special achievements/activities:* leadership. *Special characteristics:* children and siblings of alumni, children of faculty/staff, ethnic background, international students, out-of-state students, relatives of clergy, siblings of current students.

LOANS *Programs:* Federal Direct (Subsidized and Unsubsidized Stafford, PLUS), Perkins, college/university, private loans.

WORK-STUDY *Federal work-study:* 593 jobs averaging $1622.

CONTACT Mr. Ronald Anderson, Director of Financial Aid, Asbury University, One Macklem Drive, Wilmore, KY 40390, 859-858-3511 Ext. 2195 or toll-free 800-888-1818. Fax: 859-858-9149. E-mail: ron.anderson@asbury.edu.
Website: http://www.asbury.edu/.

# ASHFORD UNIVERSITY
## Clinton, IA

**CONTACT** Lisa Kramer, Director of Financial Aid, Ashford University, 400 North Bluff Boulevard, PO Box 2967, Clinton, IA 52733-2967, 563-242-4023 Ext. 1243 or toll-free 866-711-1700. *Fax:* 563-242-8684.
*Website:* http://www.ashford.edu/.

# ASHLAND UNIVERSITY
## Ashland, OH

| Tuition & fees: $19,852 | Average undergraduate aid package: $17,689 |
| --- | --- |

**ABOUT THE INSTITUTION** Independent Brethren Church, coed. *Awards:* certificates, diplomas, associate, bachelor's, master's, and doctoral degrees. 83 undergraduate majors. *Total enrollment:* 5,979. Undergraduates: 3,198. Freshmen: 623. Federal methodology is used as a basis for awarding need-based institutional aid.
**UNDERGRADUATE EXPENSES for 2015–2016** *Tuition:* full-time . Full-time tuition and fees vary according to location and program. Part-time tuition and fees vary according to course load, location, and program. Room and board charges vary according to board plan, housing facility, and location.
**FRESHMAN FINANCIAL AID (Fall 2014, est.)** 568 applied for aid; of those 83% were deemed to have need. 100% of freshmen with need received aid. *Average financial aid package:* $17,592 (excluding resources awarded to replace EFC). 15% of all full-time freshmen had no need and received non-need-based gift aid.
**UNDERGRADUATE FINANCIAL AID (Fall 2014, est.)** 2,191 applied for aid; of those 88% were deemed to have need. 100% of undergraduates with need received aid. *Average financial aid package:* $17,689 (excluding resources awarded to replace EFC). 10% of all full-time undergraduates had no need and received non-need-based gift aid.
**GIFT AID (NEED-BASED) Total amount:** $16,455,107 (24% federal, 9% state, 65% institutional, 2% external sources). *Receiving aid:* Freshmen: 75% (450); all full-time undergraduates: 69% (1,755). *Average award:* Freshmen: $11,415; Undergraduates: $10,445. *Scholarships, grants, and awards:* Federal Pell, FSEOG, state, private, college/university gift aid from institutional funds.
**GIFT AID (NON-NEED-BASED) Total amount:** $2,080,903 (1% federal, 97% institutional, 2% external sources). *Average award:* Freshmen: $6915. Undergraduates: $5248. *Scholarships, grants, and awards by category: Academic interests/achievement:* general academic interests/achievements, mathematics, physical sciences, social sciences. *Creative arts/performance:* 101 awards ($202,880 total): art/fine arts, music, theater/drama. *Special achievements/activities:* 19 awards ($10,750 total): cheerleading/drum major, leadership, religious involvement. *Special characteristics:* 236 awards ($2,074,563 total): children and siblings of alumni, children of faculty/staff, ethnic background, international students, members of minority groups, out-of-state students, relatives of clergy, religious affiliation, siblings of current students, veterans. *Tuition waivers:* Full or partial for children of alumni, employees or children of employees, senior citizens. *ROTC:* Army cooperative, Air Force cooperative.
**LOANS Student loans:** $14,808,540 (84% need-based, 16% non-need-based). 89% of past graduating class borrowed through all loan programs. *Average indebtedness per student:* $36,779. *Average need-based loan:* Freshmen: $4119. Undergraduates: $4836. *Parent loans:* $4,584,956 (89% need-based, 11% non-need-based). *Programs:* Federal Direct (Subsidized and Unsubsidized Stafford, PLUS), Perkins, college/university.
**WORK-STUDY** *Federal work-study:* Total amount: $3,660,357; 1,380 jobs averaging $2589. *State or other work-study/employment:* Total amount: $835,670 (100% non-need-based). Part-time jobs available.
**ATHLETIC AWARDS** Total amount: $2,482,156 (65% need-based, 35% non-need-based).
**APPLYING FOR FINANCIAL AID** *Required financial aid form:* FAFSA. *Financial aid deadline (priority):* 3/15. *Notification date:* Continuous beginning 3/1.
**CONTACT** Mr. Stephen C. Howell, Director of Financial Aid, Ashland University, 401 College Avenue, Ashland, OH 44805-3702, 419-289-5944 or toll-free 800-882-1548. *Fax:* 419-289-5976. *E-mail:* showell@ashland.edu.
*Website:* http://www.ashland.edu/.

# ASHWORTH COLLEGE
## Norcross, GA

**CONTACT** Financial Aid Office, Ashworth College, 6625 The Corners Parkway, Suite 500, Norcross, GA 30092, 770-729-8400 or toll-free 800-957-5412.
*Website:* http://www.ashworthcollege.edu/.

# ASPEN UNIVERSITY
## Denver, CO

**CONTACT** Jennifer Quinn, Director of Financial Aid, Aspen University, 720 South Colorado Bouleavrd #1150N, Denver, CO 80246, 800-441-4746. *Fax:* 303-336-1144.
*E-mail:* jquinn@aspen.edu.
*Website:* http://www.aspen.edu/.

# ASSUMPTION COLLEGE
## Worcester, MA

| Tuition & fees: $36,160 | Average undergraduate aid package: $26,459 |
| --- | --- |

**ABOUT THE INSTITUTION** Independent Roman Catholic, coed. *Awards:* certificates, bachelor's, and master's degrees. 35 undergraduate majors. *Total enrollment:* 2,502. Undergraduates: 2,008. Freshmen: 571. Federal methodology is used as a basis for awarding need-based institutional aid.
**UNDERGRADUATE EXPENSES for 2015–2016** *Application fee:* $50. *Comprehensive fee:* $47,122 includes full-time tuition ($35,510), mandatory fees ($650), and room and board ($10,962). *College room only:* $6914. Full-time tuition and fees vary according to course load and reciprocity agreements. Room and board charges vary according to housing facility. *Part-time tuition:* $1183.67 per credit hour. Part-time tuition and fees vary according to course load. *Payment plan:* Guaranteed tuition.
**FRESHMAN FINANCIAL AID (Fall 2014, est.)** 522 applied for aid; of those 87% were deemed to have need. 100% of freshmen with need received aid; of those 20% had need fully met. *Average percent of need met:* 72% (excluding resources awarded to replace EFC). *Average financial aid package:* $25,788 (excluding resources awarded to replace EFC). 18% of all full-time freshmen had no need and received non-need-based gift aid.
**UNDERGRADUATE FINANCIAL AID (Fall 2014, est.)** 1,718 applied for aid; of those 90% were deemed to have need. 100% of undergraduates with need received aid; of those 19% had need fully met. *Average percent of need met:* 74% (excluding resources awarded to replace EFC). *Average financial aid package:* $26,459 (excluding resources awarded to replace EFC). 18% of all full-time undergraduates had no need and received non-need-based gift aid.
**GIFT AID (NEED-BASED) Total amount:** $30,369,564 (7% federal, 3% state, 89% institutional, 1% external sources). *Receiving aid:* Freshmen: 80% (454); all full-time undergraduates: 77% (1,543). *Average award:* Freshmen: $21,215; Undergraduates: $21,039. *Scholarships, grants, and awards:* Federal Pell, FSEOG, state, private, college/university gift aid from institutional funds, Academic Competitiveness Grants, National SMART Grants.
**GIFT AID (NON-NEED-BASED) Total amount:** $5,728,564 (98% institutional, 2% external sources). *Receiving aid:* Freshmen: 13% (73). Undergraduates: 10% (203). *Average award:* Freshmen: $14,741. Undergraduates: $13,158. *Scholarships, grants, and awards by category: Academic interests/achievement:* 1,474 awards ($19,218,250 total): general academic interests/achievements. *Special characteristics:* members of minority groups. *Tuition waivers:* Full or partial for employees or children of employees. *ROTC:* Army cooperative, Air Force cooperative.
**LOANS Student loans:** $16,730,848 (67% need-based, 33% non-need-based). 81% of past graduating class borrowed through all loan programs. *Average indebtedness per student:* $34,417. *Average need-based loan:* Freshmen: $3778. Undergraduates: $4937. *Parent loans:* $6,834,793 (39% need-based, 61% non-need-based). *Programs:* Federal Direct (Subsidized and Unsubsidized Stafford, PLUS), Perkins, state, college/university.
**WORK-STUDY** *Federal work-study:* Total amount: $541,927; 393 jobs averaging $1398.

**ATHLETIC AWARDS** Total amount: $2,363,937 (52% need-based, 48% non-need-based).
**APPLYING FOR FINANCIAL AID** *Required financial aid form:* FAFSA. *Financial aid deadline:* 2/15. *Notification date:* Continuous beginning 2/16. Students must reply by 5/1.
**CONTACT** William C. Smith, Director of Financial Aid, Assumption College, 500 Salisbury Street, Worcester, MA 01609-1296, 508-767-7157 or toll-free 866-477-7776. *Fax:* 508-767-7376. *E-mail:* fa@assumption.edu.
*Website:* http://www.assumption.edu/.

# ATENAS COLLEGE
## Manati, PR

**CONTACT** Financial Aid Office, Atenas College, Paseo de La Atenas #101 Altos, Manati, PR 00674, 787-884-3838.
*Website:* http://www.atenascollege.edu/.

# ATHENS STATE UNIVERSITY
## Athens, AL

| Tuition & fees (AL res): $6120 | Average undergraduate aid package: $9334 |
| --- | --- |

**ABOUT THE INSTITUTION** State-supported, coed. *Awards:* certificates and bachelor's degrees. 35 undergraduate majors. *Total enrollment:* 3,128. Undergraduates: 3,129. Federal methodology is used as a basis for awarding need-based institutional aid.
**UNDERGRADUATE EXPENSES for 2015–2016** *Application fee:* $30. *Tuition, state resident:* full-time $5370. *Tuition, nonresident:* full-time $10,740. *Required fees:* full-time $750.
**UNDERGRADUATE FINANCIAL AID (Fall 2013)** 1,053 applied for aid; of those 88% were deemed to have need. 99% of undergraduates with need received aid; of those 3% had need fully met. *Average percent of need met:* 3% (excluding resources awarded to replace EFC). *Average financial aid package:* $9334 (excluding resources awarded to replace EFC).
**GIFT AID (NEED-BASED)** *Total amount:* $5,179,349 (99% federal, 1% external sources). *Receiving aid:* All full-time undergraduates: 47% (639). *Average award:* Undergraduates: $4081. *Scholarships, grants, and awards:* Federal Pell, FSEOG, state, private, college/university gift aid from institutional funds.
**GIFT AID (NON-NEED-BASED)** *Total amount:* $102,311 (100% federal). *Receiving aid:* Undergraduates: 2% (29). *Tuition waivers:* Full or partial for employees or children of employees, senior citizens.
**LOANS** *Student loans:* $13,513,203 (45% need-based, 55% non-need-based). *Average need-based loan:* Undergraduates: $3177. *Programs:* Federal Direct (Subsidized and Unsubsidized Stafford, PLUS), college/university.
**WORK-STUDY** *Federal work-study:* jobs available.
**APPLYING FOR FINANCIAL AID** *Required financial aid form:* FAFSA. *Financial aid deadline:* Continuous. *Notification date:* Continuous beginning 5/1. Students must reply within 2 weeks of notification.
**CONTACT** Mary Chambliss, Financial Aid Director, Athens State University, 300 North Beaty Street, Athens, AL 35611, 256-233-8161 or toll-free 800-522-0272. *Fax:* 256-233-8161. *E-mail:* finaid@athens.edu.
*Website:* http://www.athens.edu/.

# ATLANTIC UNIVERSITY COLLEGE
## Guaynabo, PR

**CONTACT** Mrs. Velma Aponte, Financial Aid Coordinator, Atlantic University College, Calle Colton #9, Guaynabo, PR 00970, 787-720-1092. *E-mail:* atlaneco@coqui.net.
*Website:* http://www.atlanticu.edu/.

# AUBURN UNIVERSITY
## Auburn University, AL

| Tuition & fees (AL res): $10,200 | Average undergraduate aid package: $10,804 |
| --- | --- |

**ABOUT THE INSTITUTION** State-supported, coed. *Awards:* certificates, bachelor's, master's, and doctoral degrees. 145 undergraduate majors. *Total enrollment:* 25,912. Undergraduates: 20,629. Freshmen: 4,592. Federal methodology is used as a basis for awarding need-based institutional aid.
**UNDERGRADUATE EXPENSES for 2015–2016** *Application fee:* $50. *Tuition, state resident:* full-time $8592; part-time $358 per semester hour. *Tuition, nonresident:* full-time $25,776; part-time $1074 per semester hour. *Required fees:* full-time $1608; $804 per term. Full-time tuition and fees vary according to program and reciprocity agreements. Part-time tuition and fees vary according to course load, program, and reciprocity agreements. *College room and board:* $12,178; *Room only:* $6892. Room and board charges vary according to board plan and housing facility.
**FRESHMAN FINANCIAL AID (Fall 2013)** 2,237 applied for aid; of those 62% were deemed to have need. 100% of freshmen with need received aid; of those 18% had need fully met. *Average percent of need met:* 51% (excluding resources awarded to replace EFC). *Average financial aid package:* $10,824 (excluding resources awarded to replace EFC). 32% of all full-time freshmen had no need and received non-need-based gift aid.
**UNDERGRADUATE FINANCIAL AID (Fall 2013)** 11,762 applied for aid; of those 58% were deemed to have need. 100% of undergraduates with need received aid; of those 14% had need fully met. *Average percent of need met:* 45% (excluding resources awarded to replace EFC). *Average financial aid package:* $10,804 (excluding resources awarded to replace EFC). 16% of all full-time undergraduates had no need and received non-need-based gift aid.
**GIFT AID (NEED-BASED)** *Total amount:* $37,095,782 (37% federal, 4% state, 49% institutional, 10% external sources). *Receiving aid:* Freshmen: 32% (1,203); all full-time undergraduates: 28% (5,027). *Average award:* Freshmen: $7277; Undergraduates: $7109. *Scholarships, grants, and awards:* Federal Pell, FSEOG, state, private, college/university gift aid from institutional funds.
**GIFT AID (NON-NEED-BASED)** *Total amount:* $46,413,222 (9% state, 76% institutional, 15% external sources). *Receiving aid:* Freshmen: 5% (184). Undergraduates: 3% (599). *Average award:* Freshmen: $5661. Undergraduates: $5265. *Scholarships, grants, and awards by category:* Academic interests/achievement: agriculture, architecture, biological sciences, business, communication, computer science, education, engineering/technologies, English, foreign languages, general academic interests/achievements, health fields, home economics, humanities, mathematics, physical sciences, premedicine, social sciences. *Creative arts/performance:* applied art and design, art/fine arts, cinema/film/broadcasting, creative writing, journalism/publications, music, performing arts, theater/drama. *Special achievements/activities:* cheerleading/drum major, leadership, memberships. *Special characteristics:* children and siblings of alumni, children of faculty/staff, children of union members/company employees, ethnic background, local/state students, married students, out-of-state students. *Tuition waivers:* Full or partial for employees or children of employees. *ROTC:* Army, Naval, Air Force.
**LOANS** *Student loans:* $64,059,638 (72% need-based, 28% non-need-based). 41% of past graduating class borrowed through all loan programs. *Average indebtedness per student:* $27,146. *Average need-based loan:* Freshmen: $3791. Undergraduates: $4553. *Parent loans:* $29,616,613 (51% need-based, 49% non-need-based). *Programs:* Federal Direct (Subsidized and Unsubsidized Stafford, PLUS), Perkins, Federal Nursing, college/university.
**WORK-STUDY** *Federal work-study:* 211 jobs averaging $3902.
**ATHLETIC AWARDS** Total amount: $11,568,733 (5% need-based, 95% non-need-based).
**APPLYING FOR FINANCIAL AID** *Required financial aid form:* FAFSA. *Financial aid deadline (priority):* 3/1. *Notification date:* Continuous beginning 10/2. Students must reply by 5/1.
**CONTACT** Mr. Mike Reynolds, Director of Student Financial Services, Auburn University, 203 Mary Martin Hall, Auburn University, AL 36849, 334-844-4634 or toll-free 800-AUBURN9. *Fax:* 334-844-6085. *E-mail:* finaid7@auburn.edu.
*Website:* http://www.auburn.edu/.

# AUBURN UNIVERSITY AT MONTGOMERY
## Montgomery, AL

| Tuition & fees (AL res): $9080 | Average undergraduate aid package: $7236 |
|---|---|

**ABOUT THE INSTITUTION** State-supported, coed. **Awards:** certificates, bachelor's, master's, and doctoral degrees. 32 undergraduate majors. **Total enrollment:** 5,057. Undergraduates: 4,377. Freshmen: 613. Federal methodology is used as a basis for awarding need-based institutional aid.

**UNDERGRADUATE EXPENSES for 2015–2016 Tuition, state resident:** full-time $8430; part-time $281 per credit hour. **Tuition, nonresident:** full-time $18,990; part-time $633 per credit hour. **Required fees:** full-time $650. Full-time tuition and fees vary according to course load and degree level. Part-time tuition and fees vary according to course load and degree level. **College room and board:** $5390; **Room only:** $4190. Room and board charges vary according to housing facility.

**FRESHMAN FINANCIAL AID (Fall 2014, est.)** 536 applied for aid; of those 100% were deemed to have need. 98% of freshmen with need received aid; of those 17% had need fully met. **Average financial aid package:** $7506 (excluding resources awarded to replace EFC). 5% of all full-time freshmen had no need and received non-need-based gift aid.

**UNDERGRADUATE FINANCIAL AID (Fall 2014, est.)** 2,310 applied for aid; of those 96% were deemed to have need. 98% of undergraduates with need received aid; of those 18% had need fully met. **Average financial aid package:** $7236 (excluding resources awarded to replace EFC). 2% of all full-time undergraduates had no need and received non-need-based gift aid.

**GIFT AID (NEED-BASED) Total amount:** $9,052,442 (100% federal). **Receiving aid:** Freshmen: 72% (386); all full-time undergraduates: 49% (1,512). **Average award:** Freshmen: $5139; Undergraduates: $4730. **Scholarships, grants, and awards:** Federal Pell, FSEOG, state, college/university gift aid from institutional funds.

**GIFT AID (NON-NEED-BASED) Total amount:** $3,707,815 (91% institutional, 9% external sources). **Receiving aid:** Freshmen: 25% (133). Undergraduates: 15% (463). **Average award:** Freshmen: $3778. Undergraduates: $3966. **Scholarships, grants, and awards by category:** Academic interests/achievement: general academic interests/achievements. **Tuition waivers:** Full or partial for employees or children of employees, senior citizens. **ROTC:** Army, Air Force cooperative.

**LOANS Student loans:** $19,286,084 (49% need-based, 51% non-need-based). **Average need-based loan:** Freshmen: $3589. Undergraduates: $4071. **Parent loans:** $1,008,191 (100% non-need-based). **Programs:** Federal Direct (Subsidized and Unsubsidized Stafford, PLUS), Perkins.

**WORK-STUDY Federal work-study:** Total amount: $186,834; jobs available.

**APPLYING FOR FINANCIAL AID Required financial aid form:** FAFSA. **Financial aid deadline (priority):** 3/1. **Notification date:** Continuous beginning 4/15.

**CONTACT** Mr. Anthony Richey, Senior Director of Financial Aid, Auburn University at Montgomery, PO Box 244023, Montgomery, AL 36124-4023, 334-244-3571 or toll-free 800-227-2649. Fax: 334-244-3913. E-mail: aumfinancialaidoffice@aum.edu. Website: http://www.aum.edu/.

# AUGSBURG COLLEGE
## Minneapolis, MN

**ABOUT THE INSTITUTION** Independent Lutheran, coed. **Awards:** certificates, bachelor's, master's, and doctoral degrees. 72 undergraduate majors. **Total enrollment:** 3,580. Undergraduates: 2,620. Freshmen: 393.

**GIFT AID (NEED-BASED) Scholarships, grants, and awards:** Federal Pell, FSEOG, state, private, college/university gift aid from institutional funds, Federal Nursing.

**GIFT AID (NON-NEED-BASED) Scholarships, grants, and awards by category:** Academic interests/achievement: biological sciences, business, communication, computer science, education, English, foreign languages, general academic interests/achievements, health fields, international studies, mathematics, physical sciences, religion/biblical studies, social sciences. Creative arts/performance: art/fine arts, music, performing arts, theater/drama. Special achievements/activities: community

service, general special achievements/activities, junior miss, leadership, religious involvement. Special characteristics: children and siblings of alumni, international students, members of minority groups, relatives of clergy, siblings of current students.

**LOANS Programs:** Federal Direct (Subsidized and Unsubsidized Stafford, PLUS), Perkins, Federal Nursing, state.

**APPLYING FOR FINANCIAL AID Required financial aid form:** FAFSA.

**CONTACT** Mr. Paul L. Terrio, Director of Student Financial Services, Augsburg College, 2211 Riverside Avenue, Minneapolis, MN 55454-1351, 612-330-1049 or toll-free 800-788-5678. Fax: 612-330-1308. E-mail: terriop@augsburg.edu. Website: http://www.augsburg.edu/.

# AUGUSTANA COLLEGE
## Rock Island, IL

| Tuition & fees: $38,466 | Average undergraduate aid package: $25,989 |
|---|---|

**ABOUT THE INSTITUTION** Independent Evangelical Lutheran Church in America, coed. **Awards:** bachelor's degrees. 61 undergraduate majors. **Total enrollment:** 2,500. Undergraduates: 2,500. Freshmen: 726. Federal methodology is used as a basis for awarding need-based institutional aid.

**UNDERGRADUATE EXPENSES for 2015–2016 Comprehensive fee:** $48,212 includes full-time tuition ($38,466) and room and board ($9746). Room and board charges vary according to board plan and housing facility. **Part-time tuition:** $1650 per credit. Part-time tuition and fees vary according to course load. **Payment plan:** Tuition prepayment.

**FRESHMAN FINANCIAL AID (Fall 2013)** 582 applied for aid; of those 85% were deemed to have need. 100% of freshmen with need received aid; of those 19% had need fully met. **Average percent of need met:** 84% (excluding resources awarded to replace EFC). **Average financial aid package:** $26,695 (excluding resources awarded to replace EFC). 21% of all full-time freshmen had no need and received non-need-based gift aid.

**UNDERGRADUATE FINANCIAL AID (Fall 2013)** 2,283 applied for aid; of those 85% were deemed to have need. 100% of undergraduates with need received aid; of those 19% had need fully met. **Average percent of need met:** 84% (excluding resources awarded to replace EFC). **Average financial aid package:** $25,989 (excluding resources awarded to replace EFC). 21% of all full-time undergraduates had no need and received non-need-based gift aid.

**GIFT AID (NEED-BASED) Total amount:** $38,952,287 (7% federal, 8% state, 84% institutional, 1% external sources). **Receiving aid:** Freshmen: 77% (482); all full-time undergraduates: 76% (1,895). **Average award:** Freshmen: $21,667; Undergraduates: $20,527. **Scholarships, grants, and awards:** Federal Pell, FSEOG, state, private, college/university gift aid from institutional funds.

**GIFT AID (NON-NEED-BASED) Total amount:** $11,281,451 (99% institutional, 1% external sources). **Receiving aid:** Freshmen: 12% (75). Undergraduates: 11% (269). **Average award:** Freshmen: $18,188. Undergraduates: $16,568. **Scholarships, grants, and awards by category:** Academic interests/achievement: 2,622 awards ($30,350,080 total): area/ethnic studies, biological sciences, business, communication, computer science, education, English, foreign languages, general academic interests/achievements, humanities, mathematics, physical sciences, religion/biblical studies, social sciences. Creative arts/performance: 525 awards ($966,675 total): art/fine arts, creative writing, debating, music, theater/drama. Special achievements/activities: 43 awards ($42,420 total): leadership. Special characteristics: 563 awards ($4,037,994 total): children and siblings of alumni, children of faculty/staff, ethnic background, international students, members of minority groups, religious affiliation, siblings of current students. **Tuition waivers:** Full or partial for employees or children of employees.

**LOANS Student loans:** $16,167,408 (72% need-based, 28% non-need-based). 77% of past graduating class borrowed through all loan programs. Average indebtedness per student: $31,612. **Average need-based loan:** Freshmen: $3766. Undergraduates: $4649. **Parent loans:** $4,907,547 (37% need-based, 63% non-need-based). **Programs:** Federal Direct (Subsidized and Unsubsidized Stafford, PLUS), Perkins.

**WORK-STUDY Federal work-study:** 1,344 jobs averaging $2331.

**APPLYING FOR FINANCIAL AID Required financial aid forms:** FAFSA, institution's own form. **Financial aid deadline (priority):** 2/1. **Notification date:** Continuous beginning 3/1. Students must reply by 5/1.

CONTACT Ms. Sue Standley, Director of Financial Aid, Augustana College, 639 38th Street, Rock Island, IL 61201-2296, 309-794-7207 Ext. 7447 or toll-free 800-798-8100. *Fax:* 309-794-7174. *E-mail:* suestandley@augustana.edu. *Website:* http://www.augustana.edu/.

## AUGUSTANA COLLEGE
### Sioux Falls, SD

| Tuition & fees: $29,214 | Average undergraduate aid package: $23,975 |
| --- | --- |

**ABOUT THE INSTITUTION** Independent Evangelical Lutheran Church in America, coed. *Awards:* bachelor's and master's degrees. 64 undergraduate majors. *Total enrollment:* 1,823. Undergraduates: 1,671. Freshmen: 396. Federal methodology is used as a basis for awarding need-based institutional aid.

**UNDERGRADUATE EXPENSES for 2015–2016** *Comprehensive fee:* $36,242 includes full-time tuition ($28,764), mandatory fees ($450), and room and board ($7028). *College room only:* $3360. Full-time tuition and fees vary according to course load and degree level. Room and board charges vary according to board plan and housing facility. *Part-time tuition:* $450 per credit hour. Part-time tuition and fees vary according to course load and degree level.

**FRESHMAN FINANCIAL AID (Fall 2014, est.)** 329 applied for aid; of those 81% were deemed to have need. 100% of freshmen with need received aid; of those 32% had need fully met. *Average percent of need met:* 99% (excluding resources awarded to replace EFC). *Average financial aid package:* $25,651 (excluding resources awarded to replace EFC). 33% of all full-time freshmen had no need and received non-need-based gift aid.

**UNDERGRADUATE FINANCIAL AID (Fall 2014, est.)** 1,177 applied for aid; of those 84% were deemed to have need. 100% of undergraduates with need received aid; of those 27% had need fully met. *Average percent of need met:* 91% (excluding resources awarded to replace EFC). *Average financial aid package:* $23,975 (excluding resources awarded to replace EFC). 37% of all full-time undergraduates had no need and received non-need-based gift aid.

**GIFT AID (NEED-BASED)** *Total amount:* $15,780,186 (12% federal, 83% institutional, 5% external sources). *Receiving aid:* Freshmen: 67% (265); all full-time undergraduates: 62% (984). *Average award:* Freshmen: $22,028; Undergraduates: $19,796. *Scholarships, grants, and awards:* Federal Pell, FSEOG, state, private, college/university gift aid from institutional funds, need-linked special talent scholarships, minority scholarships.

**GIFT AID (NON-NEED-BASED)** *Total amount:* $9,672,470 (1% federal, 5% state, 91% institutional, 3% external sources). *Receiving aid:* Freshmen: 66% (260), Undergraduates: 61% (965). *Average award:* Freshmen: $15,959. Undergraduates: $14,322. *Scholarships, grants, and awards by category: Academic interests/achievement:* biological sciences, business, communication, computer science, education, English, foreign languages, general academic interests/achievements, health fields, humanities, international studies, mathematics, physical sciences, premedicine, religion/biblical studies, social sciences. *Creative arts/performance:* art/fine arts, creative writing, dance, journalism/publications, music, performing arts, theater/drama. *Special achievements/activities:* cheerleading/drum major, community service, general special achievements/activities, leadership, religious involvement. *Special characteristics:* adult students, children and siblings of alumni, children of current students, children of faculty/staff, ethnic background, international students, local/state students, members of minority groups, religious affiliation, siblings of current students, spouses of current students, veterans. *Tuition waivers:* Full or partial for employees or children of employees. *ROTC:* Army cooperative, Air Force cooperative.

**LOANS** *Student loans:* $9,379,356 (57% need-based, 43% non-need-based). 74% of past graduating class borrowed through all loan programs. *Average indebtedness per student:* $35,385. *Average need-based loan:* Freshmen: $4596. Undergraduates: $5037. *Parent loans:* $937,843 (19% need-based, 81% non-need-based). *Programs:* Federal Direct (Subsidized and Unsubsidized Stafford, PLUS), Perkins, Federal Nursing, college/university, private loans, Minnesota SELF Loans.

**WORK-STUDY** *Federal work-study:* Total amount: $621,009; 357 jobs averaging $1806. *State or other work-study/employment:* Total amount: $100,242 (2% need-based, 98% non-need-based). 120 part-time jobs averaging $950.

**ATHLETIC AWARDS** Total amount: $3,384,475 (37% need-based, 63% non-need-based).

**APPLYING FOR FINANCIAL AID** *Required financial aid form:* FAFSA. *Financial aid deadline (priority):* 3/1. *Notification date:* Continuous beginning 4/1. Students must reply by 5/1 or within 3 weeks of notification.
CONTACT Ms. Brenda L. Murtha, Director of Financial Aid, Augustana College, 2001 South Summit Avenue, Sioux Falls, SD 57197, 605-274-5216 or toll-free 800-727-2844. *Fax:* 605-274-5295. *E-mail:* brenda.murtha@augie.edu. *Website:* http://www.augie.edu/.

## AULTMAN COLLEGE OF NURSING AND HEALTH SCIENCES
### Canton, OH

CONTACT Financial Aid Office, Aultman College of Nursing and Health Sciences, 2600 6th Street, SW, Canton, OH 44710-1797, 330-438-6347. *Website:* http://www.aultmancollege.edu/.

## AURORA UNIVERSITY
### Aurora, IL

**ABOUT THE INSTITUTION** Independent, coed. *Awards:* certificates, bachelor's, master's, and doctoral degrees. 34 undergraduate majors. *Total enrollment:* 4,946. Undergraduates: 3,246. Freshmen: 647.

**GIFT AID (NEED-BASED)** *Scholarships, grants, and awards:* Federal Pell, FSEOG, state, private, college/university gift aid from institutional funds.

**GIFT AID (NON-NEED-BASED)** *Scholarships, grants, and awards by category: Academic interests/achievement:* business, education, general academic interests/achievements. *Creative arts/performance:* art/fine arts, music, theater/drama. *Special achievements/activities:* leadership. *Special characteristics:* children and siblings of alumni, children of current students, children of faculty/staff, out of state students, parents of current students, religious affiliation, siblings of current students, spouses of current students, veterans, veterans' children.

**LOANS** *Programs:* Federal Direct (Subsidized and Unsubsidized Stafford, PLUS), Perkins, private loans.

**WORK-STUDY** *Federal work-study:* 1,456 jobs averaging $1609. *State or other work-study/employment:* Total amount: $443,190 (100% non-need-based). 32 part-time jobs averaging $7648.

**APPLYING FOR FINANCIAL AID** *Required financial aid form:* FAFSA.

CONTACT Mrs. Heather McKane, Dean of Student Financial Services, Aurora University, 347 South Gladstone Avenue, Aurora, IL 60506-4892, 630-844-6190 or toll-free 800-742-5281. *Fax:* 630-844-6191. *E-mail:* finaid@aurora.edu. *Website:* http://www.aurora.edu/.

## AUSTIN COLLEGE
### Sherman, TX

| Tuition & fees: $34,840 | Average undergraduate aid package: $30,701 |
| --- | --- |

**ABOUT THE INSTITUTION** Independent Presbyterian, coed. *Awards:* bachelor's and master's degrees. 50 undergraduate majors. *Total enrollment:* 1,301. Undergraduates: 1,278. Freshmen: 357. Federal methodology is used as a basis for awarding need-based institutional aid.

**UNDERGRADUATE EXPENSES for 2015–2016** *One-time required fee:* $25. *Comprehensive fee:* $46,343 includes full-time tuition ($34,655), mandatory fees ($185), and room and board ($11,503). *College room only:* $5360. Full-time tuition and fees vary according to student level. Room and board charges vary according to board plan. *Part-time tuition:* $5025 per course.

**FRESHMAN FINANCIAL AID (Fall 2014, est.)** 292 applied for aid; of those 83% were deemed to have need. 100% of freshmen with need received aid; of those 29% had need fully met. *Average percent of need met:* 85% (excluding resources awarded to replace EFC). *Average financial aid package:* $33,055 (excluding resources awarded to replace EFC). 14% of all full-time freshmen had no need and received non-need-based gift aid.

**UNDERGRADUATE FINANCIAL AID (Fall 2014, est.)** 986 applied for aid; of those 85% were deemed to have need. 100% of undergraduates with need received aid; of those 27% had need fully met. *Average percent of need met:* 80% (excluding resources awarded to replace EFC). *Average financial aid package:* $30,701 (excluding resources awarded to replace EFC). 12% of all full-time undergraduates had no need and received non-need-based gift aid.

**GIFT AID (NEED-BASED)** *Total amount:* $23,293,352 (8% federal, 6% state, 84% institutional, 2% external sources). *Receiving aid:* Freshmen: 68% (241); all full-time undergraduates: 65% (829). *Average award:* Freshmen: $28,026; Undergraduates: $25,926. *Scholarships, grants, and awards:* Federal Pell, FSEOG, state, private, college/university gift aid from institutional funds.

**GIFT AID (NON-NEED-BASED)** *Total amount:* $6,036,179 (99% institutional, 1% external sources). *Receiving aid:* Freshmen: 19% (67). Undergraduates: 11% (138). *Average award:* Freshmen: $21,951. Undergraduates: $19,297. *Scholarships, grants, and awards by category: Academic interests/achievement:* biological sciences, business, communication, education, engineering/technologies, English, foreign languages, general academic interests/achievements, health fields, humanities, international studies, physical sciences, premedicine, religion/biblical studies, social sciences. *Creative arts/performance:* art/fine arts, music, theater/drama. *Special achievements/activities:* community service, general special achievements/activities, leadership, religious involvement. *Special characteristics:* children of faculty/staff, first-generation college students, general special characteristics, international students, local/state students, out-of-state students, previous college experience, relatives of clergy, religious affiliation, veterans. *Tuition waivers:* Full or partial for employees or children of employees.

**LOANS** *Student loans:* $6,634,442 (55% need-based, 45% non-need-based). *Average need-based loan:* Freshmen: $4964. Undergraduates: $5133. *Parent loans:* $4,609,113 (24% need-based, 76% non-need-based). *Programs:* Federal Direct (Subsidized and Unsubsidized Stafford, PLUS), Perkins, state, private loans.

**WORK-STUDY** *Federal work-study:* Total amount: $625,845; jobs available. *State or other work-study/employment:* Total amount: $124,575 (28% need-based, 72% non-need-based). Part-time jobs available.

**APPLYING FOR FINANCIAL AID** *Required financial aid form:* FAFSA. *Financial aid deadline (priority):* 4/1. *Notification date:* Continuous beginning 2/15. Students must reply by 5/1.

**CONTACT** Mrs. Laurie Coulter, Assistant Vice President for Institutional Enrollment/Executive Director of Financial Aid, Austin College, 900 North Grand Avenue, Sherman, TX 75090, 903-813-2900 or toll-free 800-596-4276 (in-state), 800-526.4276 (out-of-state). *Fax:* 903-813-3198. *E-mail:* finaid@austincollege.edu. *Website:* http://www.austincollege.edu/.

# AUSTIN GRADUATE SCHOOL OF THEOLOGY
## Austin, TX

**CONTACT** David Arthur, Director of Financial Aid, Austin Graduate School of Theology, 7640 Guadalupe Street, Austin, TX 78752, 512-476-2772 Ext. 105 or toll-free 866-AUS-GRAD. *Fax:* 512-476-3919. *E-mail:* darthur@austingrad.edu. *Website:* http://www.austingrad.edu/.

# AUSTIN PEAY STATE UNIVERSITY
## Clarksville, TN

| Tuition & fees: N/R | Average undergraduate aid package: $9972 |
|---|---|

**ABOUT THE INSTITUTION** State-supported, coed. *Awards:* certificates, associate, bachelor's, and master's degrees. 31 undergraduate majors. *Total enrollment:* 10,111. Undergraduates: 9,246. Freshmen: 1,494. Federal methodology is used as a basis for awarding need-based institutional aid.

**UNDERGRADUATE EXPENSES for 2015–2016** *Application fee:* $15. *Tuition, state resident:* part-time $246 per credit hour. *Tuition, nonresident:* part-time $850 per credit hour. Full-time tuition and fees vary according to location and program. Part-time tuition and fees vary according to location and program. Room and board charges vary according to board plan and housing facility.

**FRESHMAN FINANCIAL AID (Fall 2013)** 1,205 applied for aid; of those 84% were deemed to have need. 99% of freshmen with need received aid. *Average financial aid package:* $10,976 (excluding resources awarded to replace EFC). 13% of all full-time freshmen had no need and received non-need-based gift aid.

**UNDERGRADUATE FINANCIAL AID (Fall 2013)** 6,311 applied for aid; of those 88% were deemed to have need. 99% of undergraduates with need received aid. *Average financial aid package:* $9972 (excluding resources awarded to replace EFC). 8% of all full-time undergraduates had no need and received non-need-based gift aid.

**GIFT AID (NEED-BASED)** *Total amount:* $26,587,412 (85% federal, 15% state). *Receiving aid:* Freshmen: 66% (812); all full-time undergraduates: 70% (4,788). *Average award:* Freshmen: $7045; Undergraduates: $7376. *Scholarships, grants, and awards:* Federal Pell, FSEOG, state, private, college/university gift aid from institutional funds.

**GIFT AID (NON-NEED-BASED)** *Total amount:* $22,769,828 (44% state, 11% institutional, 45% external sources). *Receiving aid:* Freshmen: 66% (822). Undergraduates: 44% (2,992). *Average award:* Freshmen: $4834. Undergraduates: $4313. *Scholarships, grants, and awards by category: Academic interests/achievement:* 522 awards ($1,542,365 total): agriculture, biological sciences, business, communication, computer science, education, English, foreign languages, general academic interests/achievements, health fields, humanities, international studies, mathematics, military science, physical sciences, social sciences. *Creative arts/performance:* 410 awards ($383,351 total): art/fine arts, creative writing, debating, journalism/publications, music, performing arts, theater/drama. *Special achievements/activities:* 245 awards ($239,144 total): general special achievements/activities, leadership, memberships. *Special characteristics:* 77 awards ($98,402 total): children of educators, children of faculty/staff, ethnic background, general special characteristics, members of minority groups, veterans. *Tuition waivers:* Full or partial for employees or children of employees, senior citizens. *ROTC:* Army, Air Force cooperative.

**LOANS** *Student loans:* $40,122,136 (46% need-based, 54% non-need-based). 60% of past graduating class borrowed through all loan programs. *Average indebtedness per student:* $28,820. *Average need-based loan:* Freshmen: $3104. Undergraduates: $3895. *Parent loans:* $3,042,360 (100% non-need-based). *Programs:* Federal Direct (Subsidized and Unsubsidized Stafford, PLUS), Perkins.

**WORK-STUDY** *Federal work-study:* 127 jobs averaging $2199. *State or other work-study/employment:* Total amount: $637,784 (100% non-need-based). 422 part-time jobs averaging $1511.

**ATHLETIC AWARDS** *Total amount:* $3,025,759 (100% non-need-based).

**APPLYING FOR FINANCIAL AID** *Required financial aid form:* FAFSA. *Financial aid deadline:* Continuous. *Notification date:* Continuous beginning 4/7.

**CONTACT** Ms. Donna Price, Director of Student Financial Aid, Austin Peay State University, PO Box 4546, Clarksville, TN 37044, 931-221-7907 or toll-free 800-844-2778. *Fax:* 931-221-6329. *E-mail:* priced@apsu.edu. *Website:* http://www.apsu.edu/.

# AVE MARIA UNIVERSITY
## Ave Maria, FL

| Tuition & fees: $18,479 | Average undergraduate aid package: $15,647 |
|---|---|

**ABOUT THE INSTITUTION** Independent Roman Catholic, coed. *Awards:* bachelor's, master's, and doctoral degrees. 30 undergraduate majors. *Total enrollment:* 1,081. Undergraduates: 1,027. Freshmen: 304. Federal methodology is used as a basis for awarding need-based institutional aid.

**UNDERGRADUATE EXPENSES for 2015–2016** *Comprehensive fee:* $28,616 includes full-time tuition ($17,712), mandatory fees ($767), and room and board ($10,137).

**FRESHMAN FINANCIAL AID (Fall 2014, est.)** 257 applied for aid; of those 81% were deemed to have need. 100% of freshmen with need received aid; of those 27% had need fully met. *Average percent of need met:* 72% (excluding resources awarded to replace EFC). *Average financial aid package:* $14,749 (excluding resources awarded to replace EFC). 25% of all full-time freshmen had no need and received non-need-based gift aid.

**UNDERGRADUATE FINANCIAL AID (Fall 2014, est.)** 798 applied for aid; of those 85% were deemed to have need. 100% of undergraduates with need received aid; of those 23% had need fully met. *Average percent of need met:* 72% (excluding resources awarded to replace EFC). *Average financial aid package:*

$15,647 (excluding resources awarded to replace EFC). 27% of all full-time undergraduates had no need and received non-need-based gift aid.

**GIFT AID (NEED-BASED)** *Total amount:* $6,310,381 (22% federal, 18% state, 58% institutional, 2% external sources). *Receiving aid:* Freshmen: 66% (208); all full-time undergraduates: 65% (678). *Average award:* Freshmen: $11,749; Undergraduates: $12,226. *Scholarships, grants, and awards:* Federal Pell, FSEOG, state, private, college/university gift aid from institutional funds.

**GIFT AID (NON-NEED-BASED)** *Total amount:* $2,780,027 (12% state, 84% institutional, 4% external sources). *Receiving aid:* Freshmen: 14% (43). Undergraduates: 11% (111). *Average award:* Freshmen: $7971. Undergraduates: $7477. *Scholarships, grants, and awards by category:* Creative arts/performance: 28 awards ($52,875 total): music. *Special achievements/activities:* 141 awards ($301,850 total): leadership. *Special characteristics:* 348 awards ($789,957 total): children of faculty/staff, religious affiliation, siblings of current students. *Tuition waivers:* Full or partial for employees or children of employees.

**LOANS** *Student loans:* $4,174,774 (66% need-based, 34% non-need-based). *Average need-based loan:* Freshmen: $2950. Undergraduates: $3851. *Parent loans:* $1,301,228 (35% need-based, 65% non-need-based). *Programs:* Federal Direct (Subsidized and Unsubsidized Stafford, PLUS), college/university.

**WORK-STUDY** *Federal work-study:* Total amount: $142,223; 97 jobs averaging $1466. *State or other work-study/employment:* Total amount: $1500 (100% need-based). 1 part-time job averaging $1500.

**ATHLETIC AWARDS** Total amount: $2,869,198 (64% need-based, 36% non-need-based).

**APPLYING FOR FINANCIAL AID** *Required financial aid forms:* FAFSA, state aid form. *Financial aid deadline (priority):* 4/1. *Notification date:* Continuous beginning 2/15.

**CONTACT** Anne Hart, Financial Aid Director, Ave Maria University, 5050 Ave Maria Boulevard, Ave Maria, FL 34142, 239-280-1669 or toll-free 877-283-8648. *Fax:* 239-280-2566. *E-mail:* amufinancialaid@avemaria.edu.
*Website:* http://www.avemaria.edu/.

# AVERETT UNIVERSITY
## Danville, VA

| Tuition & fees: $30,900 | Average undergraduate aid package: $23,741 |
| --- | --- |

**ABOUT THE INSTITUTION** Independent Baptist General Association of Virginia, coed. *Awards:* associate, bachelor's, and master's degrees. 56 undergraduate majors. *Total enrollment:* 877. Undergraduates: 858. Freshmen: 202. Federal methodology is used as a basis for awarding need-based institutional aid.

**UNDERGRADUATE EXPENSES for 2015–2016** *Comprehensive fee:* $39,600 includes full-time tuition ($30,900) and room and board ($8700). *College room only:* $5870. Full-time tuition and fees vary according to class time, course load, location, and program. Room and board charges vary according to board plan and housing facility. *Part-time tuition:* $960 per credit. Part-time tuition and fees vary according to class time, course load, location, and program.

**FRESHMAN FINANCIAL AID (Fall 2014, est.)** 190 applied for aid; of those 94% were deemed to have need. 100% of freshmen with need received aid; of those 13% had need fully met. *Average percent of need met:* 69% (excluding resources awarded to replace EFC). *Average financial aid package:* $23,107 (excluding resources awarded to replace EFC). 13% of all full-time freshmen had no need and received non-need-based gift aid.

**UNDERGRADUATE FINANCIAL AID (Fall 2014, est.)** 743 applied for aid; of those 95% were deemed to have need. 100% of undergraduates with need received aid; of those 11% had need fully met. *Average percent of need met:* 74% (excluding resources awarded to replace EFC). *Average financial aid package:* $23,741 (excluding resources awarded to replace EFC). 13% of all full-time undergraduates had no need and received non-need-based gift aid.

**GIFT AID (NEED-BASED)** *Total amount:* $13,981,394 (15% federal, 12% state, 64% institutional, 9% external sources). *Receiving aid:* Freshmen: 87% (179); all full-time undergraduates: 87% (703). *Average award:* Freshmen: $19,730; Undergraduates: $19,619. *Scholarships, grants, and awards:* Federal Pell, FSEOG, state, private, college/university gift aid from institutional funds.

**GIFT AID (NON-NEED-BASED)** *Total amount:* $1,896,088 (11% state, 81% institutional, 8% external sources). *Receiving aid:* Freshmen: 9% (18). Undergraduates: 7% (57). *Average award:* Freshmen: $13,144. Undergraduates: $12,178.

*Scholarships, grants, and awards by category:* Academic interests/achievement: 308 awards ($576,460 total): biological sciences, business, education, engineering/technologies, English, foreign languages, general academic interests/achievements, health fields, home economics, humanities, mathematics, physical sciences, premedicine, religion/biblical studies. *Creative arts/performance:* 11 awards ($14,174 total): art/fine arts, journalism/publications, music, theater/drama. *Special achievements/activities:* 94 awards ($139,658 total): general special achievements/activities, leadership, memberships, religious involvement. *Special characteristics:* 226 awards ($300,697 total): adult students, children and siblings of alumni, children of union members/company employees, first-generation college students, general special characteristics, international students, local/state students, out-of-state students, relatives of clergy, religious affiliation. *Tuition waivers:* Full or partial for employees or children of employees, senior citizens.

**LOANS** *Student loans:* $6,299,119 (84% need-based, 16% non-need-based). 73% of past graduating class borrowed through all loan programs. *Average indebtedness per student:* $31,876. *Average need-based loan:* Freshmen: $3926. Undergraduates: $4739. *Parent loans:* $2,615,203 (46% need-based, 54% non-need-based). *Programs:* Federal Direct (Subsidized and Unsubsidized Stafford, PLUS), Perkins, state, alternative loans.

**WORK-STUDY** *Federal work-study:* Total amount: $11,700; 127 jobs averaging $926.

**APPLYING FOR FINANCIAL AID** *Required financial aid forms:* FAFSA, state aid form. *Financial aid deadline (priority):* 4/1. *Notification date:* Continuous. Students must reply within 2 weeks of notification.

**CONTACT** Carl Bradsher, Dean of Financial Assistance, Averett University, 420 West Main Street, Danville, VA 24541-3692, 434-791-5646 or toll-free 800-AVERETT. *Fax:* 434-791-5647. *E-mail:* carl.bradsher@averett.edu.
*Website:* http://www.averett.edu/.

# AVILA UNIVERSITY
## Kansas City, MO

**CONTACT** Nancy Merz, Director of Financial Aid, Avila University, 11901 Wornall Road, Kansas City, MO 64145, 816-501-3782 or toll-free 800-GO-AVILA. *Fax:* 816-501-2462. *E-mail:* nancy.merz@avila.edu.
*Website:* http://www.avila.edu/.

# AZUSA PACIFIC UNIVERSITY
## Azusa, CA

| Tuition & fees: $33,096 | Average undergraduate aid package: $18,522 |
| --- | --- |

**ABOUT THE INSTITUTION** Independent nondenominational, coed. *Awards:* certificates, bachelor's, master's, and doctoral degrees. 36 undergraduate majors. *Total enrollment:* 10,325. Undergraduates: 6,160. Freshmen: 1,046. Federal methodology is used as a basis for awarding need-based institutional aid.

**UNDERGRADUATE EXPENSES for 2015–2016** *Application fee:* $45. *Tuition:* full-time $32,516. Room and board charges vary according to board plan and housing facility.

**FRESHMAN FINANCIAL AID (Fall 2013)** 1,158 applied for aid; of those 82% were deemed to have need. 100% of freshmen with need received aid; of those 10% had need fully met. *Average percent of need met:* 31% (excluding resources awarded to replace EFC). *Average financial aid package:* $17,443 (excluding resources awarded to replace EFC). 16% of all full-time freshmen had no need and received non-need-based gift aid.

**UNDERGRADUATE FINANCIAL AID (Fall 2013)** 5,292 applied for aid; of those 80% were deemed to have need. 100% of undergraduates with need received aid; of those 9% had need fully met. *Average percent of need met:* 35% (excluding resources awarded to replace EFC). *Average financial aid package:* $18,522 (excluding resources awarded to replace EFC). 16% of all full-time undergraduates had no need and received non-need-based gift aid.

**GIFT AID (NEED-BASED)** *Total amount:* $64,004,505 (13% federal, 15% state, 71% institutional, 1% external sources). *Receiving aid:* Freshmen: 67% (815); all full-time undergraduates: 65% (3,699). *Average award:* Freshmen: $8787; Undergrad-

uates: $10,107. **Scholarships, grants, and awards:** Federal Pell, FSEOG, state, private, college/university gift aid from institutional funds, Federal Nursing.
**GIFT AID (NON-NEED-BASED) Total amount:** $8,717,054 (96% institutional, 4% external sources). **Receiving aid:** Freshmen: 62% (755). Undergraduates: 57% (3,226). **Average award:** Freshmen: $7949. Undergraduates: $7704. **Scholarships, grants, and awards by category:** *Academic interests/achievement:* general academic interests/achievements. *Creative arts/performance:* general creative arts/performance. *Special achievements/activities:* leadership. *Special characteristics:* members of minority groups, religious affiliation. *ROTC:* Army, Air Force cooperative.
**LOANS Student loans:** $27,561,742 (87% need-based, 13% non-need-based). 74% of past graduating class borrowed through all loan programs. *Average indebtedness per student:* $20,612. **Average need-based loan:** Freshmen: $3686. Undergraduates: $4303. **Parent loans:** $12,506,827 (61% need-based, 39% non-need-based). **Programs:** Federal Direct (Subsidized and Unsubsidized Stafford, PLUS), Perkins, Federal Nursing.
**WORK-STUDY Federal work-study:** jobs available.
**ATHLETIC AWARDS** Total amount: $3,140,708 (74% need-based, 26% non-need-based).
**APPLYING FOR FINANCIAL AID Required financial aid forms:** FAFSA, institution's own form. **Notification date:** Continuous.
**CONTACT** Todd Ross, Interim Director of Student Financial Services, Azusa Pacific University, 901 East Alosta Avenue, PO Box 7000, Azusa, CA 91702-7000, 626-812-3009 or toll-free 800-TALK-APU. *E-mail:* tross@apu.edu. *Website:* http://www.apu.edu/.

# BABSON COLLEGE
## Wellesley, MA

| Tuition & fees: $46,784 | Average undergraduate aid package: $38,749 |
| --- | --- |

**ABOUT THE INSTITUTION** Independent, coed. **Awards:** certificates, bachelor's, and master's degrees. 24 undergraduate majors. **Total enrollment:** 3,049. Undergraduates: 2,107. Freshmen: 506. Both federal and institutional methodology are used as a basis for awarding need-based institutional aid.
**UNDERGRADUATE EXPENSES** for 2015–2016 *Application fee:* $75. **Comprehensive fee:** $61,712 includes full-time tuition ($46,784) and room and board ($14,928). **College room only:** $9634. Room and board charges vary according to board plan and housing facility.
**FRESHMAN FINANCIAL AID (Fall 2014, est.)** 276 applied for aid; of those 82% were deemed to have need. 100% of freshmen with need received aid; of those 52% had need fully met. **Average percent of need met:** 98% (excluding resources awarded to replace EFC). **Average financial aid package:** $37,182 (excluding resources awarded to replace EFC). 5% of all full-time freshmen had no need and received non-need-based gift aid.
**UNDERGRADUATE FINANCIAL AID (Fall 2014, est.)** 1,013 applied for aid; of those 89% were deemed to have need. 100% of undergraduates with need received aid; of those 50% had need fully met. **Average percent of need met:** 96% (excluding resources awarded to replace EFC). **Average financial aid package:** $38,749 (excluding resources awarded to replace EFC). 7% of all full-time undergraduates had no need and received non-need-based gift aid.
**GIFT AID (NEED-BASED) Total amount:** $29,925,000 (6% federal, 1% state, 93% institutional). **Receiving aid:** Freshmen: 41% (205); all full-time undergraduates: 40% (847). **Average award:** Freshmen: $33,705; Undergraduates: $35,332. **Scholarships, grants, and awards:** Federal Pell, FSEOG, state, college/university gift aid from institutional funds.
**GIFT AID (NON-NEED-BASED) Total amount:** $3,289,000 (84% institutional, 16% external sources). **Receiving aid:** Freshmen: 6% (32). Undergraduates: 7% (137). **Average award:** Freshmen: $24,649. Undergraduates: $19,462. **Scholarships, grants, and awards by category:** *Academic interests/achievement:* general academic interests/achievements. *Special achievements/activities:* leadership. *Special characteristics:* veterans. *Tuition waivers:* Full or partial for employees or children of employees. *ROTC:* Army cooperative, Naval cooperative, Air Force cooperative.
**LOANS Student loans:** $7,535,000 (48% need-based, 52% non-need-based). 43% of past graduating class borrowed through all loan programs. *Average indebtedness per student:* $35,290. **Average need-based loan:** Freshmen: $3441. Undergrad-

uates: $4532. **Parent loans:** $2,826,000 (100% non-need-based). **Programs:** Federal Direct (Subsidized and Unsubsidized Stafford, PLUS), Perkins, state.
**WORK-STUDY Federal work-study:** Total amount: $1,375,000; jobs available. **State or other work-study/employment:** Total amount: $67,000 (100% need-based). Part-time jobs available.
**APPLYING FOR FINANCIAL AID Required financial aid forms:** FAFSA, CSS Financial Aid PROFILE, noncustodial (divorced/separated) parent's statement, federal income tax form(s), W-2 forms, verification worksheet. **Financial aid deadline:** 2/15. **Notification date:** 4/1. Students must reply by 5/1.
**CONTACT** Ms. Melissa Shaak, Director of Student Financial Services, Babson College, Hollister Hall, Third Floor, Babson Park, MA 02457-0310, 781-239-4219 or toll-free 800-488-3696. *Fax:* 781-239-5510. *E-mail:* shaak@babson.edu. *Website:* http://www.babson.edu/.

# BACONE COLLEGE
## Muskogee, OK

**CONTACT** Mrs. Kathye Watson, Office of Financial Aid, Bacone College, 2299 Old Bacone Road, Muskogee, OK 74403-1597, 918-781-7294 or toll-free 888-682-5514 Ext. 7340. *Fax:* 918-781-7416. *E-mail:* financialaid@bacone.edu. *Website:* http://www.bacone.edu/.

# BAIS BINYOMIN ACADEMY
## Stamford, CT

**CONTACT** Financial Aid Office, Bais Binyomin Academy, 132 Prospect Street, Stamford, CT 06901-1202, 203-325-4351.

# BAIS HAMEDRASH AND MESIVTA OF BALTIMORE
## Baltimore, MD

**CONTACT** Financial Aid Office, Bais HaMedrash and Mesivta of Baltimore, 6823 Old Pimlico Road, Baltimore, MD 21209, 410-486-0006.

# BAKER COLLEGE
## Flint, MI

**CONTACT** Financial Aid Office, Baker College, Baker College System Headquarters, 1050 West Bristol Road, Flint, MI 48507-5508, 810-766-4280 or toll-free 800-964-4299.
*Website:* http://www.baker.edu/.

# BAKER UNIVERSITY
## Baldwin City, KS

**CONTACT** Mrs. Jeanne Mott, Financial Aid Director, Baker University, Box 65, Baldwin City, KS 66006-0065, 785-594-4595 or toll-free 800-873-4282. *Fax:* 785-594-8358.
*Website:* http://www.bakeru.edu/.

# BALDWIN WALLACE UNIVERSITY
## Berea, OH

| Tuition & fees: $28,814 | Average undergraduate aid package: $21,666 |
|---|---|

**ABOUT THE INSTITUTION** Independent Methodist, coed. *Awards:* certificates, bachelor's, and master's degrees. 76 undergraduate majors. *Total enrollment:* 3,979. Undergraduates: 3,362. Freshmen: 717. Federal methodology is used as a basis for awarding need-based institutional aid.

**UNDERGRADUATE EXPENSES for 2015–2016** *Application fee:* $25. *Comprehensive fee:* $36,862 includes full-time tuition ($28,814) and room and board ($8048). *College room only:* $4648. Full-time tuition and fees vary according to class time, course level, course load, degree level, program, and reciprocity agreements. Room and board charges vary according to housing facility. *Part-time tuition:* $895 per semester hour. Part-time tuition and fees vary according to class time, course level, course load, degree level, program, and reciprocity agreements.

**FRESHMAN FINANCIAL AID (Fall 2014, est.)** 678 applied for aid; of those 87% were deemed to have need. 100% of freshmen with need received aid; of those 31% had need fully met. *Average percent of need met:* 88% (excluding resources awarded to replace EFC). *Average financial aid package:* $24,907 (excluding resources awarded to replace EFC). 16% of all full-time freshmen had no need and received non-need-based gift aid.

**UNDERGRADUATE FINANCIAL AID (Fall 2014, est.)** 2,585 applied for aid; of those 91% were deemed to have need. 100% of undergraduates with need received aid; of those 36% had need fully met. *Average percent of need met:* 87% (excluding resources awarded to replace EFC). *Average financial aid package:* $21,666 (excluding resources awarded to replace EFC). 16% of all full-time undergraduates had no need and received non-need-based gift aid.

**GIFT AID (NEED-BASED)** *Total amount:* $38,481,671 (12% federal, 5% state, 81% institutional, 2% external sources). *Receiving aid:* Freshmen: 82% (589); all full-time undergraduates: 80% (2,354). *Average award:* Freshmen: $20,203; Undergraduates: $16,201. *Scholarships, grants, and awards:* Federal Pell, FSEOG, state, private, college/university gift aid from institutional funds.

**GIFT AID (NON-NEED-BASED)** *Total amount:* $7,120,370 (1% state, 98% institutional, 1% external sources). *Receiving aid:* Freshmen: 12% (86). Undergraduates: 14% (422). *Average award:* Freshmen: $13,440. Undergraduates: $12,080. *Scholarships, grants, and awards by category:* Academic interests/achievement: 2,260 awards ($19,914,000 total): general academic interests/achievement. Creative arts/performance: 197 awards ($730,000 total): music. Special achievements/activities: leadership. Special characteristics: 1,306 awards ($3,731,000 total): children and siblings of alumni, members of minority groups, religious affiliation, siblings of current students. *Tuition waivers:* Full or partial for children of alumni, employees or children of employees. *ROTC:* Army cooperative, Air Force cooperative.

**LOANS** *Student loans:* $18,418,862 (53% need-based, 47% non-need-based). 80% of past graduating class borrowed through all loan programs. *Average indebtedness per student:* $32,526. *Average need-based loan:* Freshmen: $3004. Undergraduates: $4034. *Parent loans:* $10,146,203 (87% need-based, 13% non-need-based). *Programs:* Federal Direct (Subsidized and Unsubsidized Stafford, PLUS), Perkins.

**WORK-STUDY** *Federal work-study:* Total amount: $466,000; 1,017 jobs averaging $1273. *State or other work-study/employment:* Total amount: $901,000 (100% non-need-based). 378 part-time jobs averaging $1273.

**APPLYING FOR FINANCIAL AID** *Required financial aid form:* FAFSA. *Financial aid deadline (priority):* 8/15. *Notification date:* Continuous beginning 2/15.

**CONTACT** Dr. George L. Rolleston, Director of Financial Aid, Baldwin Wallace University, 275 Eastland Road, Berea, OH 44017-2088, 440-826-2108 or toll-free 877-BW-APPLY. *Fax:* 440-826-8048. *E-mail:* grollest@bw.edu. *Website:* http://www.bw.edu/.

# BALL STATE UNIVERSITY
## Muncie, IN

| Tuition & fees (IN res): $9384 | Average undergraduate aid package: $11,822 |
|---|---|

**ABOUT THE INSTITUTION** State-supported, coed. *Awards:* certificates, associate, bachelor's, master's, and doctoral degrees. 85 undergraduate majors. *Total enrollment:* 20,655. Undergraduates: 16,415. Freshmen: 3,597. Federal methodology is used as a basis for awarding need-based institutional aid.

**UNDERGRADUATE EXPENSES for 2015–2016** *Application fee:* $55. *Tuition, state resident:* full-time $8722; part-time $327 per credit. *Tuition, non-resident:* full-time $23,948; part-time $989 per credit. *Required fees:* full-time $662. Full-time tuition and fees vary according to course load, program, and reciprocity agreements. Part-time tuition and fees vary according to course load and reciprocity agreements. *College room and board:* $9537; *Room only:* $4343. Room and board charges vary according to board plan and housing facility.

**FRESHMAN FINANCIAL AID (Fall 2014, est.)** 3,419 applied for aid; of those 76% were deemed to have need. 100% of freshmen with need received aid; of those 43% had need fully met. *Average percent of need met:* 69% (excluding resources awarded to replace EFC). *Average financial aid package:* $12,417 (excluding resources awarded to replace EFC). 13% of all full-time freshmen had no need and received non-need-based gift aid.

**UNDERGRADUATE FINANCIAL AID (Fall 2014, est.)** 12,480 applied for aid; of those 81% were deemed to have need. 100% of undergraduates with need received aid; of those 38% had need fully met. *Average percent of need met:* 68% (excluding resources awarded to replace EFC). *Average financial aid package:* $11,822 (excluding resources awarded to replace EFC). 12% of all full-time undergraduates had no need and received non-need-based gift aid.

**GIFT AID (NEED-BASED)** *Total amount:* $35,228,960 (69% federal, 19% state, 12% institutional). *Receiving aid:* Freshmen: 44% (1,595); all full-time undergraduates: 40% (5,976). *Average award:* Freshmen: $5399; Undergraduates: $5756. *Scholarships, grants, and awards:* Federal Pell, FSEOG, state, private, college/university gift aid from institutional funds.

**GIFT AID (NON-NEED-BASED)** *Total amount:* $55,376,056 (2% federal, 32% state, 53% institutional, 13% external sources). *Receiving aid:* Freshmen: 50% (1,804). Undergraduates: 34% (5,077). *Average award:* Freshmen: $6823. Undergraduates: $7174. *Scholarships, grants, and awards by category:* Academic interests/achievement: architecture, biological sciences, business, communication, education, engineering/technologies, English, foreign languages, general academic interests/achievements, health fields, humanities, international studies, mathematics, military science, physical sciences, social sciences. Creative arts/performance: cinema/film/broadcasting, dance, debating, general creative arts/performance, journalism/publications, music, performing arts, theater/drama. Special achievements/activities: community service, general special achievements/activities, leadership. Special characteristics: adult students, children of faculty/staff, ethnic background, general special characteristics, international students, local/state students, members of minority groups, out-of-state students, veterans, veterans' children. *Tuition waivers:* Full or partial for employees or children of employees, senior citizens. *ROTC:* Army.

**LOANS** *Student loans:* $101,706,377 (41% need-based, 59% non-need-based). 72% of past graduating class borrowed through all loan programs. *Average indebtedness per student:* $27,627. *Average need-based loan:* Freshmen: $3493. Undergraduates: $4408. *Parent loans:* $27,569,209 (100% non-need-based). *Programs:* Federal Direct (Subsidized and Unsubsidized Stafford, PLUS), Perkins.

**WORK-STUDY** *Federal work-study:* Total amount: $2,820,371; jobs available. *State or other work-study/employment:* Total amount: $9,336,146 (100% non-need-based). Part-time jobs available.

**ATHLETIC AWARDS** Total amount: $6,479,091 (100% non-need-based).

**APPLYING FOR FINANCIAL AID** *Required financial aid form:* FAFSA. *Financial aid deadline (priority):* 3/10. *Notification date:* Continuous beginning 4/1.

**CONTACT** Dr. John McPherson, Director of Scholarships and Financial Aid, Ball State University, Lucina Hall, Room 245, Muncie, IN 47306-1099, 800-227-4017 or toll-free 800-482-4BSU. *Fax:* 765-285-4247. *E-mail:* finaid@bsu.edu. *Website:* http://www.bsu.edu/.

# BAPTIST BIBLE COLLEGE
### Springfield, MO

**CONTACT** Bob Kotulski, Director of Financial Aid, Baptist Bible College, 628 East Kearney, Springfield, MO 65803-3498, 417-268-6036 or toll-free 800-228-5754. *Fax:* 417-268-6694.
*Website:* https://gobbc.edu/.

# THE BAPTIST COLLEGE OF FLORIDA
### Graceville, FL

| Tuition & fees: $9700 | Average undergraduate aid package: $8628 |
|---|---|

**ABOUT THE INSTITUTION** Independent Southern Baptist, coed. *Awards:* certificates, associate, bachelor's, and master's degrees. 9 undergraduate majors. *Total enrollment:* 486. Undergraduates: 462. Freshmen: 35. Federal methodology is used as a basis for awarding need-based institutional aid.

**UNDERGRADUATE EXPENSES for 2015–2016** *Application fee:* $25. *Comprehensive fee:* $13,838 includes full-time tuition ($9300), mandatory fees ($400), and room and board ($4138). Full-time tuition and fees vary according to location and program. Room and board charges vary according to board plan and housing facility. *Part-time tuition:* $310 per credit hour. Part-time tuition and fees vary according to location and program.

**FRESHMAN FINANCIAL AID (Fall 2014, est.)** 55 applied for aid; of those 73% were deemed to have need. 58% of freshmen with need received aid; of those 9% had need fully met. *Average percent of need met:* 40% (excluding resources awarded to replace EFC). *Average financial aid package:* $9262 (excluding resources awarded to replace EFC). 3% of all full-time freshmen had no need and received non-need-based gift aid.

**UNDERGRADUATE FINANCIAL AID (Fall 2014, est.)** 399 applied for aid; of those 85% were deemed to have need. 78% of undergraduates with need received aid; of those 7% had need fully met. *Average percent of need met:* 42% (excluding resources awarded to replace EFC). *Average financial aid package:* $8628 (excluding resources awarded to replace EFC). 4% of all full-time undergraduates had no need and received non-need-based gift aid.

**GIFT AID (NEED-BASED)** *Total amount:* $1,853,677 (60% federal, 21% state, 16% institutional, 3% external sources). *Receiving aid:* Freshmen: 14% (23); all full-time undergraduates: 36% (264). *Average award:* Freshmen: $7743; Undergraduates: $6071. *Scholarships, grants, and awards:* Federal Pell, FSEOG, state, private, college/university gift aid from institutional funds.

**GIFT AID (NON-NEED-BASED)** *Total amount:* $148,456 (53% state, 35% institutional, 12% external sources). *Receiving aid:* Freshmen: 1% (1). Undergraduates: 2% (12). *Average award:* Freshmen: $1160. Undergraduates: $1399. *Scholarships, grants, and awards by category:* Academic interests/achievement: 212 awards ($248,882 total): education, religion/biblical studies. *Creative arts/performance:* music. *Special characteristics:* 159 awards ($162,590 total): children with a deceased or disabled parent, religious affiliation, spouses of current students. *Tuition waivers:* Full or partial for employees or children of employees.

**LOANS** *Student loans:* $1,567,684 (83% need-based, 17% non-need-based). 62% of past graduating class borrowed through all loan programs. *Average indebtedness per student:* $17,258. *Average need-based loan:* Freshmen: $3176. Undergraduates: $3810. *Parent loans:* $35,650 (35% need-based, 65% non-need-based). *Programs:* Federal Direct (Subsidized and Unsubsidized Stafford, PLUS).

**WORK-STUDY** *Federal work-study:* Total amount: $52,159; 23 jobs averaging $2268.

**APPLYING FOR FINANCIAL AID** *Required financial aid forms:* FAFSA, institution's own form, state aid form, business/farm supplement, student authorization form. *Financial aid deadline:* 4/15 (priority: 4/1). *Notification date:* Continuous beginning 6/15. Students must reply within 4 weeks of notification.

**CONTACT** Stephanie E. Powell, Director of Financial Aid, The Baptist College of Florida, 5400 College Drive, Graceville, FL 32440-3306, 850-263-3261 Ext. 461 or toll-free 800-328-2660 Ext. 460. *Fax:* 850-263-2141. *E-mail:* finaid@baptistcollege.edu.
*Website:* http://www.baptistcollege.edu/.

# BAPTIST COLLEGE OF HEALTH SCIENCES
### Memphis, TN

**CONTACT** Leanne Smith, Financial Aid Officer, Baptist College of Health Sciences, 1003 Monroe Avenue, Memphis, TN 38104, 901-227-6805 or toll-free 866-575-2247. *Fax:* 901-227-4311. *E-mail:* leanne.smith@bchs.edu.
*Website:* http://www.bchs.edu/.

# BAPTIST HEALTH SYSTEM SCHOOL OF HEALTH PROFESSIONS
### San Antonio, TX

**CONTACT** Financial Aid Office, Baptist Health System School of Health Professions, 8400 Datapoint Drive, San Antonio, TX 78229, 210-297-9636.
*Website:* http://www.bshp.edu/.

# BAPTIST MISSIONARY ASSOCIATION THEOLOGICAL SEMINARY
### Jacksonville, TX

**ABOUT THE INSTITUTION** Independent Baptist, coed, primarily men. 1 undergraduate major.

**GIFT AID (NEED-BASED)** *Scholarships, grants, and awards:* Federal Pell, private.

**LOANS** *Programs:* Federal Direct (Subsidized and Unsubsidized Stafford).

**APPLYING FOR FINANCIAL AID** *Required financial aid forms:* FAFSA, institution's own form.

**CONTACT** Dr. Philip Attebery, Dean/Registrar, Baptist Missionary Association Theological Seminary, 1530 East Pine Street, PO Box 670, Jacksonville, TX 75766-5407, 903-586-2501 or toll-free 800-259-5673. *Fax:* 903-586-0378. *E-mail:* bmatsem@bmats.edu.
*Website:* http://www.bmats.edu/.

# BAPTIST UNIVERSITY OF THE AMERICAS
### San Antonio, TX

| Tuition & fees: $5760 | Average undergraduate aid package: N/A |
|---|---|

**ABOUT THE INSTITUTION** Independent Baptist, coed. *Awards:* certificates, diplomas, associate, and bachelor's degrees (associate degree in Cross-Cultural Studies). 7 undergraduate majors. *Total enrollment:* 168. Undergraduates: 168. Freshmen: 22.

**UNDERGRADUATE EXPENSES for 2015–2016** *Tuition:* full-time $5040; part-time $210 per credit. Room and board charges vary according to housing facility.

**GIFT AID (NEED-BASED)** *Scholarships, grants, and awards:* Federal Pell, FSEOG, private, college/university gift aid from institutional funds.

**GIFT AID (NON-NEED-BASED)** *Tuition waivers:* Full or partial for employees or children of employees.

**LOANS** *Programs:* Federal Direct (Subsidized and Unsubsidized Stafford).

**APPLYING FOR FINANCIAL AID** *Required financial aid forms:* FAFSA, institution's own form. *Financial aid deadline:* Continuous. *Notification date:* Continuous.

**CONTACT** Mrs. Araceli G. Acosta, Financial Aid Director, Baptist University of the Americas, 8019 South Pan Am Expressway, San Antonio, TX 78224, 210-924-4338 Ext. 214 or toll-free 800-721-1396. *Fax:* 210-924-2701. *E-mail:* araceli.acosta@bua.edu.
*Website:* http://www.bua.edu/.

# BARCLAY COLLEGE
## Haviland, KS

| Tuition & fees: $14,990 | Average undergraduate aid package: $18,656 |
|---|---|

**ABOUT THE INSTITUTION** Independent Society of Friends, coed. *Awards:* certificates, associate, bachelor's, and master's degrees. 9 undergraduate majors. *Total enrollment:* 251. Undergraduates: 229. Freshmen: 52. Federal methodology is used as a basis for awarding need-based institutional aid.

**UNDERGRADUATE EXPENSES for 2015–2016** *Application fee:* $15. *Comprehensive fee:* $22,990 includes full-time tuition ($11,000), mandatory fees ($3990), and room and board ($8000). Room and board charges vary according to board plan and housing facility. *Part-time tuition:* $295 per credit hour. *Part-time fees:* $295 per credit hour. Part-time tuition and fees vary according to course load.

**FRESHMAN FINANCIAL AID (Fall 2013)** 30 applied for aid; of those 100% were deemed to have need. 100% of freshmen with need received aid; of those 3% had need fully met. *Average percent of need met:* 75% (excluding resources awarded to replace EFC). *Average financial aid package:* $13,554 (excluding resources awarded to replace EFC). 11% of all full-time freshmen had no need and received non-need-based gift aid.

**UNDERGRADUATE FINANCIAL AID (Fall 2013)** 186 applied for aid; of those 100% were deemed to have need. 100% of undergraduates with need received aid; of those 12% had need fully met. *Average percent of need met:* 72% (excluding resources awarded to replace EFC). *Average financial aid package:* $18,656 (excluding resources awarded to replace EFC). 6% of all full-time undergraduates had no need and received non-need-based gift aid.

**GIFT AID (NEED-BASED)** *Total amount:* $1,356,228 (36% federal, 63% institutional, 1% external sources). *Receiving aid:* Freshmen: 81% (30); all full-time undergraduates: 84% (186). *Average award:* Freshmen: $8231; Undergraduates: $13,830. *Scholarships, grants, and awards:* Federal Pell, FSEOG, state, private, college/university gift aid from institutional funds.

**GIFT AID (NON-NEED-BASED)** *Total amount:* $406,154 (93% institutional, 7% external sources). *Receiving aid:* Freshmen: 81% (30). Undergraduates: 84% (186). *Average award:* Freshmen: $11,000. Undergraduates: $11,000. *Scholarships, grants, and awards by category:* Academic interests/achievement: general academic interests/achievements. Creative arts/performance: art/fine arts, music. Special achievements/activities: general special achievements/activities, leadership. Special characteristics: children and siblings of alumni, children of current students, children of faculty/staff, international students, local/state students, married students, parents of current students, relatives of clergy, religious affiliation, siblings of current students, spouses of current students. *Tuition waivers:* Full or partial for employees or children of employees.

**LOANS** *Student loans:* $834,947 (77% need-based, 23% non-need-based). 72% of past graduating class borrowed through all loan programs. *Average indebtedness per student:* $7220. *Average need-based loan:* Freshmen: $2498. Undergraduates: $3736. *Parent loans:* $3800 (100% need-based).

**WORK-STUDY** *Federal work-study:* jobs available. *State or other work-study/employment:* Total amount: $50,631 (100% need-based). Part-time jobs available.

**APPLYING FOR FINANCIAL AID** *Required financial aid form:* FAFSA. *Financial aid deadline (priority):* 3/15. *Notification date:* Continuous. Students must reply by 8/1 or within 4 weeks of notification.

**CONTACT** Ryan Haase, Financial Aid Coordinator, Barclay College, 607 North Kingman, Haviland, KS 67059, 800-862-0226. *Fax:* 620-862-5403. *E-mail:* financialaid@barclaycollege.edu. *Website:* http://www.barclaycollege.edu/.

# BARD COLLEGE
## Annandale-on-Hudson, NY

| Tuition & fees: $48,240 | Average undergraduate aid package: $40,938 |
|---|---|

**ABOUT THE INSTITUTION** Independent, coed. *Awards:* bachelor's, master's, and doctoral degrees. 59 undergraduate majors. *Total enrollment:* 2,306. Under-

graduates: 2,059. Freshmen: 560. Both federal and institutional methodology are used as a basis for awarding need-based institutional aid.

**UNDERGRADUATE EXPENSES for 2015–2016** *Application fee:* $50. *One-time required fee:* $1614. *Comprehensive fee:* $62,012 includes full-time tuition ($47,560), mandatory fees ($680), and room and board ($13,772). Full-time tuition and fees vary according to degree level and location. Room and board charges vary according to location. *Part-time tuition:* $1486 per credit hour. Part-time tuition and fees vary according to degree level and location. *Payment plan:* Tuition prepayment.

**FRESHMAN FINANCIAL AID (Fall 2014, est.)** 406 applied for aid; of those 97% were deemed to have need. 100% of freshmen with need received aid; of those 32% had need fully met. *Average percent of need met:* 92% (excluding resources awarded to replace EFC). *Average financial aid package:* $44,925 (excluding resources awarded to replace EFC). 1% of all full-time freshmen had no need and received non-need-based gift aid.

**UNDERGRADUATE FINANCIAL AID (Fall 2014, est.)** 1,418 applied for aid; of those 97% were deemed to have need. 100% of undergraduates with need received aid; of those 28% had need fully met. *Average percent of need met:* 81% (excluding resources awarded to replace EFC). *Average financial aid package:* $40,938 (excluding resources awarded to replace EFC). 2% of all full-time undergraduates had no need and received non-need-based gift aid.

**GIFT AID (NEED-BASED)** *Total amount:* $47,646,151 (5% federal, 2% state, 91% institutional, 2% external sources). *Receiving aid:* Freshmen: 68% (381); all full-time undergraduates: 67% (1,317). *Average award:* Freshmen: $40,614; Undergraduates: $36,796. *Scholarships, grants, and awards:* Federal Pell, FSEOG, state, private, college/university gift aid from institutional funds.

**GIFT AID (NON-NEED-BASED)** *Total amount:* $814,488 (2% federal, 87% institutional, 11% external sources). *Average award:* Freshmen: $20,071. Undergraduates: $20,154. *Scholarships, grants, and awards by category:* Special achievements/activities: 1 award ($5000 total): leadership. Special characteristics: 7 awards ($246,516 total): children of educators, children of faculty/staff. *Tuition waivers:* Full or partial for employees or children of employees.

**LOANS** *Student loans:* $7,750,446 (96% need-based, 4% non-need-based). 52% of past graduating class borrowed through all loan programs. *Average indebtedness per student:* $26,599. *Average need-based loan:* Freshmen: $5402. Undergraduates: $6100. *Parent loans:* $4,221,476 (89% need-based, 11% non-need-based). *Programs:* Federal Direct (Subsidized and Unsubsidized Stafford, PLUS), Perkins, college/university loans from institutional funds (international students only).

**WORK-STUDY** *Federal work-study:* Total amount: $1,255,225; 818 jobs averaging $1500. *State or other work-study/employment:* Part-time jobs available.

**APPLYING FOR FINANCIAL AID** *Required financial aid forms:* FAFSA, CSS Financial Aid PROFILE, state aid form, noncustodial (divorced/separated) parent's statement. *Financial aid deadline:* 2/15. *Notification date:* 4/1. Students must reply by 5/1 or within 2 weeks of notification.

**CONTACT** Denise Ann Ackerman, Director of Financial Aid, Bard College, Annandale Road, Annandale-on-Hudson, NY 12504, 845-758-7525. *Fax:* 845-758-7336. *E-mail:* finaid@bard.edu. *Website:* http://www.bard.edu/.

# BARD COLLEGE AT SIMON'S ROCK
## Great Barrington, MA

**CONTACT** Ms. Ann Murtagh Gitto, Director of Financial Aid, Bard College at Simon's Rock, 84 Alford Road, Great Barrington, MA 01230-9702, 413-528-7297 or toll-free 800-235-7186. *Fax:* 413-528-7339. *E-mail:* agitto@simons-rock.edu. *Website:* http://www.simons-rock.edu/.

# BARNARD COLLEGE
## New York, NY

| Tuition & fees: $46,040 | Average undergraduate aid package: $44,040 |
|---|---|

**ABOUT THE INSTITUTION** Independent, women only. *Awards:* bachelor's degrees. 51 undergraduate majors. *Total enrollment:* 2,577. Undergraduates: 2,577.

Freshmen: 619. Both federal and institutional methodology are used as a basis for awarding need-based institutional aid.

**UNDERGRADUATE EXPENSES for 2015–2016** *Application fee:* $65. *Comprehensive fee:* $60,700 includes full-time tuition ($44,300), mandatory fees ($1740), and room and board ($14,660). Room and board charges vary according to board plan and housing facility. *Part-time fees:* $1480 per credit hour. *Payment plan:* Tuition prepayment.

**FRESHMAN FINANCIAL AID (Fall 2014, est.)** 359 applied for aid; of those 80% were deemed to have need. 100% of freshmen with need received aid; of those 97% had need fully met. *Average percent of need met:* 100% (excluding resources awarded to replace EFC). *Average financial aid package:* $45,066 (excluding resources awarded to replace EFC).

**UNDERGRADUATE FINANCIAL AID (Fall 2014, est.)** 1,186 applied for aid; of those 87% were deemed to have need. 100% of undergraduates with need received aid; of those 98% had need fully met. *Average percent of need met:* 100% (excluding resources awarded to replace EFC). *Average financial aid package:* $44,040 (excluding resources awarded to replace EFC).

**GIFT AID (NEED-BASED)** *Total amount:* $39,215,099 (6% federal, 3% state, 88% institutional, 3% external sources). *Receiving aid:* Freshmen: 45% (278); all full-time undergraduates: 40% (1,008). *Average award:* Freshmen: $41,753; Undergraduates: $38,842. *Scholarships, grants, and awards:* Federal Pell, FSEOG, state, private, college/university gift aid from institutional funds.

**GIFT AID (NON-NEED-BASED)** *Total amount:* $950,988 (6% state, 94% external sources). *Tuition waivers:* Full or partial for employees or children of employees. *ROTC:* Army cooperative, Naval cooperative, Air Force cooperative.

**LOANS** *Student loans:* $5,879,441 (66% need-based, 34% non-need-based). 49% of past graduating class borrowed through all loan programs. *Average indebtedness per student:* $17,660. *Average need-based loan:* Freshmen: $3395. Undergraduates: $4477. *Parent loans:* $4,696,508 (100% non-need-based). *Programs:* Federal Direct (Subsidized and Unsubsidized Stafford, PLUS), Perkins, state, college/university.

**WORK-STUDY** *Federal work-study:* Total amount: $577,730; 273 jobs averaging $2116. *State or other work-study/employment:* Total amount: $1,357,176 (86% need-based, 14% non-need-based). 554 part-time jobs averaging $2096.

**APPLYING FOR FINANCIAL AID** *Required financial aid forms:* FAFSA, CSS Financial Aid PROFILE, state aid form, noncustodial (divorced/separated) parent's statement, federal income tax form(s). *Financial aid deadline:* 2/15. *Notification date:* 3/31. Students must reply by 5/1.

**CONTACT** Nanette DiLauro, Director of Financial Aid, Barnard College, 3009 Broadway, New York, NY 10027-6598, 212-854-2154. *Fax:* 212-854-2902. *E-mail:* finaid@barnard.edu.
*Website:* http://www.barnard.edu/.

# BARRY UNIVERSITY
## Miami Shores, FL

| Tuition & fees: $28,160 | Average undergraduate aid package: $20,058 |
| --- | --- |

**ABOUT THE INSTITUTION** Independent Roman Catholic, coed. *Awards:* certificates, bachelor's, master's, and doctoral degrees. 58 undergraduate majors. *Total enrollment:* 8,518. Undergraduates: 3,996. Freshmen: 460. Federal methodology is used as a basis for awarding need-based institutional aid.

**UNDERGRADUATE EXPENSES for 2015–2016** *Application fee:* $30. *Comprehensive fee:* $38,560 includes full-time tuition ($28,160) and room and board ($10,400). Room and board charges vary according to board plan. *Part-time tuition:* $845 per credit. Part-time tuition and fees vary according to course load.

**FRESHMAN FINANCIAL AID (Fall 2014, est.)** 404 applied for aid; of those 97% were deemed to have need. 99% of freshmen with need received aid; of those 4% had need fully met. *Average percent of need met:* 57% (excluding resources awarded to replace EFC). *Average financial aid package:* $23,297 (excluding resources awarded to replace EFC). 9% of all full-time freshmen had no need and received non-need-based gift aid.

**UNDERGRADUATE FINANCIAL AID (Fall 2014, est.)** 2,782 applied for aid; of those 97% were deemed to have need. 99% of undergraduates with need received aid; of those 4% had need fully met. *Average percent of need met:* 49% (excluding resources awarded to replace EFC). *Average financial aid package:* $20,058 (excluding resources awarded to replace EFC). 8% of all full-time undergraduates had no need and received non-need-based gift aid.

**GIFT AID (NEED-BASED)** *Total amount:* $16,845,253 (55% federal, 8% state, 37% institutional). *Receiving aid:* Freshmen: 73% (337); all full-time undergraduates: 63% (2,118). *Average award:* Freshmen: $10,936; Undergraduates: $7690. *Scholarships, grants, and awards:* Federal Pell, FSEOG, state, private, college/university gift aid from institutional funds, Federal Nursing.

**GIFT AID (NON-NEED-BASED)** *Total amount:* $26,795,159 (20% state, 79% institutional, 1% external sources). *Receiving aid:* Freshmen: 76% (349). Undergraduates: 74% (2,500). *Average award:* Freshmen: $9808. Undergraduates: $8662. *ROTC:* Army cooperative, Air Force cooperative.

**LOANS** *Student loans:* $27,064,399 (43% need-based, 57% non-need-based). 71% of past graduating class borrowed through all loan programs. *Average indebtedness per student:* $38,342. *Average need-based loan:* Freshmen: $3233. Undergraduates: $4671. *Parent loans:* $3,414,079 (100% non-need-based). *Programs:* Perkins, Federal Nursing, college/university, alternative loans.

**WORK-STUDY** *Federal work-study:* Total amount: $589,217; jobs available. *State or other work-study/employment:* Total amount: $429,360 (100% non-need-based). Part-time jobs available.

**ATHLETIC AWARDS** Total amount: $3,120,780 (100% non-need-based).

**APPLYING FOR FINANCIAL AID** *Required financial aid form:* FAFSA. *Financial aid deadline:* Continuous. *Notification date:* Continuous beginning 1/25.

**CONTACT** Mr. Dart Humeston, Assistant Dean of Enrollment Services/Director of Financial Aid, Barry University, 11300 Northeast Second Avenue, Miami Shores, FL 33161-6695, 305-899-3673 or toll-free 800-695-2279. *E-mail:* finaid@mail.barry.edu. *Website:* http://www.barry.edu/.

# BARTON COLLEGE
## Wilson, NC

**ABOUT THE INSTITUTION** Independent Christian Church (Disciples of Christ), coed. *Awards:* bachelor's and master's degrees. 32 undergraduate majors. *Total enrollment:* 1,065. Undergraduates: 1,057. Freshmen: 217.

**GIFT AID (NEED-BASED)** *Scholarships, grants, and awards:* Federal Pell, FSEOG, state, private, college/university gift aid from institutional funds.

**GIFT AID (NON-NEED-BASED)** *Scholarships, grants, and awards by category:* Academic interests/achievement: biological sciences, business, communication, computer science, education, English, general academic interests/achievements, health fields, humanities, international studies, mathematics, physical sciences, religion/biblical studies, social sciences. Creative arts/performance: art/fine arts, music, theater/drama. Special achievements/activities: general special achievements/activities, leadership, religious involvement. Special characteristics: adult students, children and siblings of alumni, children of faculty/staff, international students, local/state students, relatives of clergy, religious affiliation, siblings of current students, veterans.

**LOANS** *Programs:* Federal Direct (Subsidized and Unsubsidized Stafford, PLUS), Perkins, alternative loans.

**WORK-STUDY** *Federal work-study:* jobs available. *State or other work-study/employment:* Part-time jobs available.

**APPLYING FOR FINANCIAL AID** *Required financial aid form:* FAFSA.

**CONTACT** Mrs. Bridget Ellis, Director of Financial Aid, Barton College, Box 5000, Wilson, NC 27893, 252-399-6371 or toll-free 800-345-4973. *Fax:* 252-399-6572. *E-mail:* aid@barton.edu.
*Website:* http://www.barton.edu/.

# BARUCH COLLEGE OF THE CITY UNIVERSITY OF NEW YORK
## New York, NY

| Tuition & fees (NY res): $6861 | Average undergraduate aid package: $4882 |
| --- | --- |

**ABOUT THE INSTITUTION** State and locally supported, coed. *Awards:* certificates, bachelor's, and master's degrees. 25 undergraduate majors. *Total enrollment:* 18,090. Undergraduates: 14,857. Freshmen: 1,282. Federal methodology is used as a basis for awarding need-based institutional aid.

**UNDERGRADUATE EXPENSES for 2015–2016 Application fee:** $65. **Tuition, state resident:** full-time $6330; part-time $275 per credit. **Tuition, nonresident:** full-time $16,800; part-time $560 per credit. **Required fees:** full-time $531. Full-time tuition and fees vary according to course load. Part-time tuition and fees vary according to course load. Room and board charges vary according to housing facility.

**FRESHMAN FINANCIAL AID (Fall 2014, est.)** 982 applied for aid; of those 79% were deemed to have need. 96% of freshmen with need received aid; of those 93% had need fully met. **Average percent of need met:** 70% (excluding resources awarded to replace EFC). **Average financial aid package:** $5767 (excluding resources awarded to replace EFC). 28% of all full-time freshmen had no need and received non-need-based gift aid.

**UNDERGRADUATE FINANCIAL AID (Fall 2014, est.)** 7,011 applied for aid; of those 93% were deemed to have need. 95% of undergraduates with need received aid; of those 16% had need fully met. **Average percent of need met:** 18% (excluding resources awarded to replace EFC). **Average financial aid package:** $4882 (excluding resources awarded to replace EFC). 9% of all full-time undergraduates had no need and received non-need-based gift aid.

**GIFT AID (NEED-BASED) Total amount:** $64,272,740 (50% federal, 45% state, 4% institutional, 1% external sources). **Receiving aid:** Freshmen: 44% (543); all full-time undergraduates: 46% (4,443). **Average award:** Freshmen: $5186; Undergraduates: $4898. **Scholarships, grants, and awards:** Federal Pell, FSEOG, state, college/university gift aid from institutional funds.

**GIFT AID (NON-NEED-BASED) Receiving aid:** Freshmen: 52% (645). Undergraduates: 8% (791). **Average award:** Freshmen: $4006. Undergraduates: $4264. **Scholarships, grants, and awards by category:** Academic interests/achievement: general academic interests/achievements. **Tuition waivers:** Full or partial for employees or children of employees, senior citizens. **ROTC:** Army cooperative.

**LOANS Student loans:** $22,766,421 (30% need-based, 70% non-need-based). 21% of past graduating class borrowed through all loan programs. **Average indebtedness per student:** $5511. **Average need-based loan:** Freshmen: $3043. Undergraduates: $4195. **Parent loans:** $544,324 (100% non-need-based). **Programs:** Federal Direct (Subsidized and Unsubsidized Stafford, PLUS), Perkins.

**WORK-STUDY Federal work-study:** Total amount: $3,144,124; 1,898 jobs averaging $1432. **State or other work-study/employment:** Total amount: $69,059 (100% need-based). 40 part-time jobs averaging $1726.

**APPLYING FOR FINANCIAL AID Required financial aid forms:** FAFSA, state aid form. **Financial aid deadline (priority):** 4/15. **Notification date:** Continuous beginning 4/21. Students must reply by 6/1 or within 2 weeks of notification.

**CONTACT** Ms. Elizabeth Riquez, Financial Aid Services , Baruch College of the City University of New York, One Bernard Baruch Way , Box H-880, New York, NY 10010-5585, 646-312-1399. *Fax:* 646-312-1361. *E-mail:* elizabeth.riquez@baruch.cuny.edu. *Website:* http://www.baruch.cuny.edu/.

# BASTYR UNIVERSITY
## Kenmore, WA

| Tuition & fees: $23,355 | Average undergraduate aid package: $18,159 |
| --- | --- |

**ABOUT THE INSTITUTION** Independent, coed. **Awards:** certificates, bachelor's, master's, and doctoral degrees. 7 undergraduate majors. **Total enrollment:** 1,195. Undergraduates: 267. Federal methodology is used as a basis for awarding need-based institutional aid.

**UNDERGRADUATE EXPENSES for 2015–2016 Application fee:** $60. **Tuition:** full-time $23,355; part-time $613 per credit. Full-time tuition and fees vary according to course load and program. Part-time tuition and fees vary according to course load and program. Room and board charges vary according to housing facility.

**UNDERGRADUATE FINANCIAL AID (Fall 2013)** 186 applied for aid; of those 94% were deemed to have need. 100% of undergraduates with need received aid. **Average percent of need met:** 45% (excluding resources awarded to replace EFC). **Average financial aid package:** $18,159 (excluding resources awarded to replace EFC).

**GIFT AID (NEED-BASED) Total amount:** $1,152,319 (39% federal, 33% state, 23% institutional, 5% external sources). **Receiving aid:** All full-time undergraduates: 71% (160). **Average award:** Undergraduates: $10,230. **Scholarships, grants, and**

**awards:** Federal Pell, FSEOG, state, private, college/university gift aid from institutional funds.

**GIFT AID (NON-NEED-BASED) Receiving aid:** Undergraduates: 1% (3). **Scholarships, grants, and awards by category:** Academic interests/achievement: health fields. **Tuition waivers:** Full or partial for employees or children of employees.

**LOANS Student loans:** $2,660,573 (100% need-based). **Average need-based loan:** Undergraduates: $11,000. **Parent loans:** $334,689 (100% need-based). **Programs:** Federal Direct (Subsidized and Unsubsidized Stafford, PLUS), Perkins.

**WORK-STUDY Federal work-study:** jobs available. **State or other work-study/employment:** Total amount: $22,992 (100% need-based). Part-time jobs available.

**APPLYING FOR FINANCIAL AID Required financial aid forms:** FAFSA, institution's own form. **Financial aid deadline (priority):** 4/15. **Notification date:** Continuous beginning 3/1. Students must reply within 2 weeks of notification.

**CONTACT** Danette Carter, Director of Financial Aid, Bastyr University, 14500 Juanita Drive NE, Kenmore, WA 98028-4966, 425-602-3083. *Fax:* 425-602-3094. *E-mail:* finaid@bastyr.edu.

*Website:* http://www.bastyr.edu/.

# BATES COLLEGE
## Lewiston, ME

| Comprehensive fee: $60,720 | Average undergraduate aid package: $42,718 |
| --- | --- |

**ABOUT THE INSTITUTION** Independent, coed. **Awards:** bachelor's degrees. 37 undergraduate majors. **Total enrollment:** 1,773. Undergraduates: 1,773. Freshmen: 491. Institutional methodology is used as a basis for awarding need-based institutional aid.

**UNDERGRADUATE EXPENSES for 2015–2016 Application fee:** $60. **Comprehensive fee:** $60,720. **Payment plan:** Tuition prepayment.

**FRESHMAN FINANCIAL AID (Fall 2014, est.)** 244 applied for aid; of those 86% were deemed to have need. 100% of freshmen with need received aid; of those 100% had need fully met. **Average percent of need met:** 100% (excluding resources awarded to replace EFC). **Average financial aid package:** $42,057 (excluding resources awarded to replace EFC).

**UNDERGRADUATE FINANCIAL AID (Fall 2014, est.)** 876 applied for aid; of those 89% were deemed to have need. 100% of undergraduates with need received aid; of those 100% had need fully met. **Average percent of need met:** 100% (excluding resources awarded to replace EFC). **Average financial aid package:** $42,718 (excluding resources awarded to replace EFC).

**GIFT AID (NEED-BASED) Total amount:** $30,397,271 (4% federal, 95% institutional, 1% external sources). **Receiving aid:** Freshmen: 43% (210); all full-time undergraduates: 44% (781). **Average award:** Freshmen: $38,752; Undergraduates: $38,921. **Scholarships, grants, and awards:** Federal Pell, FSEOG, state, private, college/university gift aid from institutional funds.

**GIFT AID (NON-NEED-BASED) Total amount:** $50,950 (100% external sources). **Tuition waivers:** Full or partial for employees or children of employees.

**LOANS Student loans:** $3,179,729 (51% need-based, 49% non-need-based). 40% of past graduating class borrowed through all loan programs. **Average indebtedness per student:** $18,929. **Average need-based loan:** Freshmen: $2284. Undergraduates: $3169. **Parent loans:** $1,412,431 (100% non-need-based). **Programs:** Federal Direct (Subsidized and Unsubsidized Stafford, PLUS), Perkins, state.

**WORK-STUDY Federal work-study:** Total amount: $825,141; 465 jobs averaging $1774. **State or other work-study/employment:** Total amount: $505,350 (100% need-based). 289 part-time jobs averaging $1749.

**APPLYING FOR FINANCIAL AID Required financial aid forms:** FAFSA, CSS Financial Aid PROFILE, noncustodial (divorced/separated) parent's statement. **Financial aid deadline:** 2/15. **Notification date:** 4/1. Students must reply by 5/1.

**CONTACT** Ms. Wendy G. Glass, Director of Student Financial Services, Bates College, 44 Mountain Avenue, Lewiston, ME 04240, 207-786-6096 or toll-free 855-228-3755. *Fax:* 207-786-8350. *E-mail:* wglass@bates.edu. *Website:* http://www.bates.edu/.

# BAYAMÓN CENTRAL UNIVERSITY
## Bayamón, PR

**CONTACT** Financial Aid Director, Bayamón Central University, PO Box 1725, Bayamón, PR 00960-1725, 787-786-3030 Ext. 2115. *Fax:* 787-785-4365. *Website:* http://www.ucb.edu.pr/.

# BAYLOR UNIVERSITY
## Waco, TX

| Tuition & fees: $40,198 | Average undergraduate aid package: $26,017 |
|---|---|

**ABOUT THE INSTITUTION** Independent Baptist, coed. *Awards:* certificates, bachelor's, master's, and doctoral degrees. 123 undergraduate majors. *Total enrollment:* 16,263. Undergraduates: 13,859. Freshmen: 3,625. Federal methodology is used as a basis for awarding need-based institutional aid.

**UNDERGRADUATE EXPENSES for 2015–2016** *Application fee:* $50. *Comprehensive fee:* $51,558 includes full-time tuition ($36,360), mandatory fees ($3838), and room and board ($11,360). *College room only:* $6160. Room and board charges vary according to board plan and housing facility. *Part-time tuition:* $1515 per semester hour. *Part-time fees:* $160 per semester hour.

**FRESHMAN FINANCIAL AID (Fall 2014, est.)** 2,815 applied for aid; of those 78% were deemed to have need. 100% of freshmen with need received aid; of those 15% had need fully met. *Average percent of need met:* 67% (excluding resources awarded to replace EFC). *Average financial aid package:* $27,086 (excluding resources awarded to replace EFC). 36% of all full-time freshmen had no need and received non-need-based gift aid.

**UNDERGRADUATE FINANCIAL AID (Fall 2014, est.)** 9,114 applied for aid; of those 84% were deemed to have need. 100% of undergraduates with need received aid; of those 16% had need fully met. *Average percent of need met:* 65% (excluding resources awarded to replace EFC). *Average financial aid package:* $26,017 (excluding resources awarded to replace EFC). 34% of all full-time undergraduates had no need and received non-need-based gift aid.

**GIFT AID (NEED-BASED)** *Total amount:* $145,700,421 (8% federal, 7% state, 82% institutional, 3% external sources). *Receiving aid:* Freshmen: 61% (2,196); all full-time undergraduates: 55% (7,423). *Average award:* Freshmen: $21,411; Undergraduates: $20,015. *Scholarships, grants, and awards:* Federal Pell, FSEOG, state, college/university gift aid from institutional funds.

**GIFT AID (NON-NEED-BASED)** *Total amount:* $66,551,935 (98% institutional, 2% external sources). *Receiving aid:* Freshmen: 60% (2,168). Undergraduates: 52% (7,077). *Average award:* Freshmen: $14,179. Undergraduates: $13,131. *Scholarships, grants, and awards by category: Academic interests/achievement:* 12,730 awards ($128,685,983 total): business, communication, computer science, education, engineering/technologies, English, foreign languages, general academic interests/achievements, health fields, home economics, humanities, international studies, mathematics, military science, physical sciences, premedicine, religion/biblical studies, social sciences. *Creative arts/performance:* 524 awards ($2,707,606 total): art/fine arts, cinema/film/broadcasting, debating, journalism/publications, music, theater/drama. *Special achievements/activities:* community service, leadership, religious involvement. *Special characteristics:* 207 awards ($5,263,651 total): children of faculty/staff, veterans, veterans' children. *Tuition waivers:* Full or partial for employees or children of employees. *ROTC:* Army, Air Force.

**LOANS** *Student loans:* $89,361,598 (67% need-based, 33% non-need-based). *Average need-based loan:* Freshmen: $2890. Undergraduates: $3782. *Parent loans:* $28,785,166 (46% need-based, 54% non-need-based). *Programs:* Federal Direct (Subsidized and Unsubsidized Stafford, PLUS), Perkins, Federal Nursing, state, private loans.

**WORK-STUDY** *Federal work-study:* Total amount: $15,449,044; 5,367 jobs averaging $2879. *State or other work-study/employment:* Part-time jobs available.

**ATHLETIC AWARDS** Total amount: $11,545,243 (40% need-based, 60% non-need-based).

**APPLYING FOR FINANCIAL AID** *Required financial aid forms:* FAFSA, state residency affirmation (TX residents only). *Financial aid deadline (priority):* 3/1. *Notification date:* Continuous beginning 3/1. Students must reply by 5/1 or within 2 weeks of notification.

**CONTACT** Office of Admission Services, Baylor University, PO Box 97056, Waco, TX 76798-7056, 254-710-3435 or toll-free 800-BAYLORU. *Fax:* 254-710-3436. *E-mail:* admissions@baylor.edu. *Website:* http://www.baylor.edu/.

# BAY PATH UNIVERSITY
## Longmeadow, MA

| Tuition & fees: $30,859 | Average undergraduate aid package: $24,708 |
|---|---|

**ABOUT THE INSTITUTION** Independent, undergraduate: women only; graduate: coed. *Awards:* certificates, associate, bachelor's, and master's degrees. 27 undergraduate majors. *Total enrollment:* 2,593. Undergraduates: 1,590. Freshmen: 129. Federal methodology is used as a basis for awarding need-based institutional aid.

**UNDERGRADUATE EXPENSES for 2015–2016** *Application fee:* $25. *Comprehensive fee:* $43,099 includes full-time tuition ($30,859) and room and board ($12,240). Room and board charges vary according to board plan. *Part-time tuition:* $490 per credit hour. Part-time tuition and fees vary according to course load.

**FRESHMAN FINANCIAL AID (Fall 2014, est.)** 116 applied for aid; of those 95% were deemed to have need. 100% of freshmen with need received aid; of those 8% had need fully met. *Average percent of need met:* 77% (excluding resources awarded to replace EFC). *Average financial aid package:* $28,106 (excluding resources awarded to replace EFC). 12% of all full-time freshmen had no need and received non-need-based gift aid.

**UNDERGRADUATE FINANCIAL AID (Fall 2014, est.)** 585 applied for aid; of those 96% were deemed to have need. 100% of undergraduates with need received aid; of those 8% had need fully met. *Average percent of need met:* 73% (excluding resources awarded to replace EFC). *Average financial aid package:* $24,708 (excluding resources awarded to replace EFC). 9% of all full-time undergraduates had no need and received non-need-based gift aid.

**GIFT AID (NEED-BASED)** *Total amount:* $11,026,592 (14% federal, 3% state, 81% institutional, 2% external sources). *Receiving aid:* Freshmen: 87% (110); all full-time undergraduates: 91% (559). *Average award:* Freshmen: $22,400; Undergraduates: $19,475. *Scholarships, grants, and awards:* Federal Pell, FSEOG, state, private, college/university gift aid from institutional funds.

**GIFT AID (NON-NEED-BASED)** *Total amount:* $1,005,399 (99% institutional, 1% external sources). *Receiving aid:* Freshmen: 5% (6). Undergraduates: 5% (33). *Average award:* Freshmen: $15,251. Undergraduates: $14,177. *Scholarships, grants, and awards by category: Academic interests/achievement:* general academic interests/achievements. *Special characteristics:* adult students, children of faculty/staff, children with a deceased or disabled parent, general special characteristics, international students, siblings of current students. *Tuition waivers:* Full or partial for children of alumni, employees or children of employees. *ROTC:* Army cooperative, Air Force cooperative.

**LOANS** *Student loans:* $5,094,243 (54% need-based, 46% non-need-based). 91% of past graduating class borrowed through all loan programs. *Average need-based loan:* Freshmen: $5048. Undergraduates: $5193. *Parent loans:* $1,076,329 (52% need-based, 48% non-need-based). *Programs:* Federal Direct (Subsidized and Unsubsidized Stafford, PLUS), Perkins.

**WORK-STUDY** *Federal work-study:* Total amount: $288,475; jobs available. *State or other work-study/employment:* Total amount: $139,435 (100% non-need-based). Part-time jobs available.

**APPLYING FOR FINANCIAL AID** *Required financial aid form:* FAFSA. *Financial aid deadline (priority):* 3/1. *Notification date:* Continuous beginning 3/1. Students must reply within 2 weeks of notification.

**CONTACT** Stephanie King, Director of Student Financial Services, Bay Path University, 588 Longmeadow Street, Longmeadow, MA 01106-2292, 413-565-1345 or toll-free 800-782-7284 Ext. 1331. *Fax:* 413-565-1101. *E-mail:* pbrand@baypath.edu. *Website:* http://www.baypath.edu/.

# BEACON COLLEGE
## Leesburg, FL

| Tuition & fees: $34,680 | Average undergraduate aid package: $3000 |
|---|---|

**ABOUT THE INSTITUTION** Independent, coed. *Awards:* associate and bachelor's degrees. 7 undergraduate majors. *Total enrollment:* 223. Undergraduates: 223. Freshmen: 52. Both federal and institutional methodology are used as a basis for awarding need-based institutional aid.

**UNDERGRADUATE EXPENSES for 2015–2016** *Application fee:* $50. *One-time required fee:* $300. *Comprehensive fee:* $44,929 includes full-time tuition ($33,480), mandatory fees ($1200), and room and board ($10,249). *College room only:* $6514. Room and board charges vary according to housing facility. *Part-time tuition:* $940 per credit. *Part-time fees:* $600 per term. Part-time tuition and fees vary according to course load.

**FRESHMAN FINANCIAL AID (Fall 2014, est.)** 36 applied for aid; of those 33% were deemed to have need. 100% of freshmen with need received aid. *Average percent of need met:* 75% (excluding resources awarded to replace EFC). *Average financial aid package:* $7000 (excluding resources awarded to replace EFC). 19% of all full-time freshmen had no need and received non-need-based gift aid.

**UNDERGRADUATE FINANCIAL AID (Fall 2014, est.)** 131 applied for aid; of those 44% were deemed to have need. 100% of undergraduates with need received aid. *Average percent of need met:* 80% (excluding resources awarded to replace EFC). *Average financial aid package:* $3000 (excluding resources awarded to replace EFC). 8% of all full-time undergraduates had no need and received non-need-based gift aid.

**GIFT AID (NEED-BASED)** *Total amount:* $1,108,367 (26% federal, 1% state, 70% institutional, 3% external sources). *Receiving aid:* Freshmen: 10% (5); all full-time undergraduates: 6% (14). *Average award:* Freshmen: $3500; Undergraduates: $1500. *Scholarships, grants, and awards:* Federal Pell, FSEOG, state, private, college/university gift aid from institutional funds.

**GIFT AID (NON-NEED-BASED)** *Total amount:* $254,810 (54% state, 46% institutional). *Receiving aid:* Freshmen: 23% (12). Undergraduates: 26% (57). *Average award:* Freshmen: $7000. Undergraduates: $6000. *Tuition waivers:* Full or partial for employees or children of employees.

**LOANS** *Student loans:* $649,250 (48% need-based, 52% non-need-based). 60% of past graduating class borrowed through all loan programs. *Average indebtedness per student:* $27,000. *Average need-based loan:* Freshmen: $4500. Undergraduates: $5500. *Parent loans:* $1,332,579 (100% non-need-based). *Programs:* Federal Direct (Subsidized and Unsubsidized Stafford, PLUS).

**WORK-STUDY** *Federal work-study:* Total amount: $15,144; jobs available. *State or other work-study/employment:* Total amount: $2687 (100% need-based). Part-time jobs available.

**APPLYING FOR FINANCIAL AID** *Required financial aid forms:* FAFSA, state aid form. *Financial aid deadline (priority):* 4/1. *Notification date:* 5/1. Students must reply within 2 weeks of notification.

**CONTACT** Mrs. Shawna L. Wells-Booth, Director of Financial Aid, Beacon College, 105 East Main Street, Leesburg, FL 34788, 352-638-9733. *Fax:* 800-360-1974. *E-mail:* financialaid@beaconcollege.edu. *Website:* http://www.beaconcollege.edu/.

# BECKER COLLEGE
## Worcester, MA

| Tuition & fees: $32,870 | Average undergraduate aid package: $21,776 |
|---|---|

**ABOUT THE INSTITUTION** Independent, coed. *Awards:* certificates, associate, and bachelor's degrees (also includes Leicester, MA small town campus). 26 undergraduate majors. *Total enrollment:* 2,021. Undergraduates: 2,021. Freshmen: 407. Federal methodology is used as a basis for awarding need-based institutional aid.

**UNDERGRADUATE EXPENSES for 2015–2016** *Comprehensive fee:* $44,870 includes full-time tuition ($31,320), mandatory fees ($1550), and room and board ($12,000). *College room only:* $5850. Full-time tuition and fees vary according to class time, course load, program, and student level. Room and board charges vary according to board plan and housing facility. *Part-time tuition:* $1305

per credit. Part-time tuition and fees vary according to class time, course load, program, and student level. *Payment plan:* Guaranteed tuition.

**FRESHMAN FINANCIAL AID (Fall 2014, est.)** 345 applied for aid; of those 92% were deemed to have need. 100% of freshmen with need received aid; of those 12% had need fully met. *Average percent of need met:* 68% (excluding resources awarded to replace EFC). *Average financial aid package:* $24,330 (excluding resources awarded to replace EFC). 13% of all full-time freshmen had no need and received non-need-based gift aid.

**UNDERGRADUATE FINANCIAL AID (Fall 2014, est.)** 1,330 applied for aid; of those 93% were deemed to have need. 100% of undergraduates with need received aid; of those 10% had need fully met. *Average percent of need met:* 64% (excluding resources awarded to replace EFC). *Average financial aid package:* $21,776 (excluding resources awarded to replace EFC). 14% of all full-time undergraduates had no need and received non-need-based gift aid.

**GIFT AID (NEED-BASED)** *Total amount:* $22,774,959 (16% federal, 4% state, 79% institutional, 1% external sources). *Receiving aid:* Freshmen: 65% (239); all full-time undergraduates: 59% (860). *Average award:* Freshmen: $11,636; Undergraduates: $8675. *Scholarships, grants, and awards:* Federal Pell, FSEOG, state, private, college/university gift aid from institutional funds.

**GIFT AID (NON-NEED-BASED)** *Total amount:* $2,837,209 (98% institutional, 2% external sources). *Receiving aid:* Freshmen: 82% (300). Undergraduates: 79% (1,161). *Average award:* Freshmen: $17,499. Undergraduates: $17,224. *Scholarships, grants, and awards by category:* Academic interests/achievement: general academic interests/achievements. Special achievements/activities: leadership. Special characteristics: 63 awards ($724,149 total): children of faculty/staff, siblings of current students. *Tuition waivers:* Full or partial for employees or children of employees, senior citizens. *ROTC:* Army cooperative, Air Force cooperative.

**LOANS** *Student loans:* $21,056,513 (79% need-based, 21% non-need-based). *Average need-based loan:* Freshmen: $3450. Undergraduates: $4292. *Parent loans:* $5,748,435 (61% need-based, 39% non-need-based). *Programs:* Federal Direct (Subsidized and Unsubsidized Stafford, PLUS), state, alternative loans.

**WORK-STUDY** *Federal work-study:* Total amount: $381,190; 255 jobs averaging $1227.

**APPLYING FOR FINANCIAL AID** *Required financial aid form:* FAFSA. *Financial aid deadline (priority):* 3/15. *Notification date:* Continuous beginning 3/15. Students must reply within 2 weeks of notification.

**CONTACT** Mr. Heather Ruland, Director of Financial Aid, Becker College, 61 Sever Street, Worcester, MA 01615-0071, 508-373-9430 or toll-free 877-5BECKER. *Fax:* 508-890-1511. *E-mail:* financialaid@becker.edu. *Website:* http://www.becker.edu/.

# BE'ER YAAKOV TALMUDIC SEMINARY
## Spring Valley, NY

**CONTACT** Financial Aid Office, Be'er Yaakov Talmudic Seminary, 12 Jefferson Avenue, Spring Valley, NY 10977, 845-406-9699.

# BEIS MEDRASH HEICHAL DOVID
## Far Rockaway, NY

**CONTACT** Financial Aid Office, Beis Medrash Heichal Dovid, 257 Beach 17th Street, Far Rockaway, NY 11691, 718-868-2300.

# BELHAVEN UNIVERSITY
## Jackson, MS

| Tuition & fees: $21,626 | Average undergraduate aid package: $17,067 |
|---|---|

**ABOUT THE INSTITUTION** Independent Presbyterian, coed. *Awards:* certificates, associate, bachelor's, and master's degrees. 36 undergraduate majors. *Total enrollment:* 4,120. Undergraduates: 2,567. Freshmen: 343. Federal methodology is used as a basis for awarding need-based institutional aid.

**UNDERGRADUATE EXPENSES for 2015–2016** *Application fee:* $25. *Comprehensive fee:* $29,626 includes full-time tuition ($21,626) and room and board ($8000). Room and board charges vary according to housing facility. *Part-time tuition:* $425 per hour. Part-time tuition and fees vary according to course load.
**FRESHMAN FINANCIAL AID (Fall 2014, est.)** 242 applied for aid; of those 93% were deemed to have need. 100% of freshmen with need received aid; of those 8% had need fully met. *Average percent of need met:* 66% (excluding resources awarded to replace EFC). *Average financial aid package:* $20,093 (excluding resources awarded to replace EFC). 11% of all full-time freshmen had no need and received non-need-based gift aid.
**UNDERGRADUATE FINANCIAL AID (Fall 2014, est.)** 1,051 applied for aid; of those 94% were deemed to have need. 100% of undergraduates with need received aid; of those 7% had need fully met. *Average percent of need met:* 57% (excluding resources awarded to replace EFC). *Average financial aid package:* $17,067 (excluding resources awarded to replace EFC). 20% of all full-time undergraduates had no need and received non-need-based gift aid.
**GIFT AID (NEED-BASED)** *Total amount:* $10,340,557 (29% federal, 2% state, 69% institutional). *Receiving aid:* Freshmen: 77% (220); all full-time undergraduates: 73% (928). *Average award:* Freshmen: $14,878; Undergraduates: $12,178. *Scholarships, grants, and awards:* Federal Pell, FSEOG, state, private, college/university gift aid from institutional funds.
**GIFT AID (NON-NEED-BASED)** *Total amount:* $828,333 (13% state, 60% institutional, 27% external sources). *Receiving aid:* Freshmen: 77% (220). Undergraduates: 64% (816). *Average award:* Freshmen: $17,100. Undergraduates: $13,190. *Scholarships, grants, and awards by category: Academic interests/ achievement:* biological sciences, business, communication, education, English, foreign languages, general academic interests/achievements, humanities, international studies, mathematics, premedicine, religion/biblical studies, social sciences. *Creative arts/performance:* applied art and design, art/fine arts, creative writing, dance, journalism/publications, music, performing arts, theater/drama. *Special achievements/activities:* cheerleading/drum major, general special achievements/activities, junior miss, leadership. *Special characteristics:* children of faculty/staff, general special characteristics, international students, local/state students. *Tuition waivers:* Full or partial for employees or children of employees. *ROTC:* Army cooperative, Air Force cooperative.
**LOANS** *Student loans:* $7,450,384 (47% need-based, 53% non-need-based). 61% of past graduating class borrowed through all loan programs. *Average indebtedness per student:* $26,800. *Average need-based loan:* Freshmen: $3264. Undergraduates: $4203. *Parent loans:* $1,179,448 (92% need-based, 8% non-need-based). *Programs:* Federal Direct (Subsidized and Unsubsidized Stafford, PLUS), Perkins, state.
**WORK-STUDY** *Federal work-study:* Total amount: $346,039; jobs available. *State or other work-study/employment:* Total amount: $360,481 (94% need-based, 6% non-need-based). Part-time jobs available.
**ATHLETIC AWARDS** Total amount: $2,038,933 (100% non-need-based).
**APPLYING FOR FINANCIAL AID** *Required financial aid form:* FAFSA. *Financial aid deadline (priority):* 5/1. *Notification date:* Continuous.
**CONTACT** Mrs. Debbi Braswell, Director of Financial Aid, Belhaven University, 1500 Peachtree Street, Box 159, Jackson, MS 39202-1789, 601-968-5933 or toll-free 800-960-5940. *E-mail:* dbraswell@belhaven.edu.
*Website:* http://www.belhaven.edu/.

# BELLARMINE UNIVERSITY
## Louisville, KY

| Tuition & fees: $37,650 | Average undergraduate aid package: $28,838 |
| --- | --- |

**ABOUT THE INSTITUTION** Independent Roman Catholic, coed. *Awards:* certificates, bachelor's, master's, and doctoral degrees. 40 undergraduate majors. *Total enrollment:* 3,609. Undergraduates: 2,585. Freshmen: 666. Both federal and institutional methodology are used as a basis for awarding need-based institutional aid.
**UNDERGRADUATE EXPENSES for 2015–2016** *Application fee:* $25. *One-time required fee:* $400. *Comprehensive fee:* $49,010 includes full-time tuition ($36,210), mandatory fees ($1440), and room and board ($11,360). *College room only:* $7130. Room and board charges vary according to board plan and housing facility. *Part-time tuition:* $850 per credit hour.
**FRESHMAN FINANCIAL AID (Fall 2014, est.)** 643 applied for aid; of those 87% were deemed to have need. 100% of freshmen with need received aid; of those 22%

had need fully met. *Average percent of need met:* 76% (excluding resources awarded to replace EFC). *Average financial aid package:* $30,157 (excluding resources awarded to replace EFC). 16% of all full-time freshmen had no need and received non-need-based gift aid.
**UNDERGRADUATE FINANCIAL AID (Fall 2014, est.)** 2,053 applied for aid; of those 89% were deemed to have need. 97% of undergraduates with need received aid; of those 21% had need fully met. *Average percent of need met:* 75% (excluding resources awarded to replace EFC). *Average financial aid package:* $28,838 (excluding resources awarded to replace EFC). 21% of all full-time undergraduates had no need and received non-need-based gift aid.
**GIFT AID (NEED-BASED)** *Total amount:* $41,534,821 (8% federal, 12% state, 79% institutional, 1% external sources). *Receiving aid:* Freshmen: 84% (558); all full-time undergraduates: 75% (1,773). *Average award:* Freshmen: $22,660; Undergraduates: $21,414. *Scholarships, grants, and awards:* Federal Pell, FSEOG, state, private, college/university gift aid from institutional funds.
**GIFT AID (NON-NEED-BASED)** *Total amount:* $12,432,611 (6% state, 92% institutional, 2% external sources). *Receiving aid:* Freshmen: 27% (180). Undergraduates: 24% (568). *Average award:* Freshmen: $21,276. Undergraduates: $19,958. *Scholarships, grants, and awards by category: Academic interests/ achievement:* biological sciences, business, education, general academic interests/ achievements, health fields, physical sciences. *Creative arts/performance:* art/fine arts, music. *Special achievements/activities:* cheerleading/drum major, community service, general special achievements/activities, leadership, religious involvement. *Special characteristics:* adult students, children and siblings of alumni, children of faculty/staff, ethnic background, international students, local/state students, members of minority groups, out-of-state students, previous college experience, religious affiliation. *Tuition waivers:* Full or partial for employees or children of employees, senior citizens. *ROTC:* Army cooperative, Air Force cooperative.
**LOANS** *Student loans:* $14,358,109 (77% need-based, 23% non-need-based). 71% of past graduating class borrowed through all loan programs. *Average indebtedness per student:* $31,381. *Average need-based loan:* Freshmen: $3530. Undergraduates: $4237. *Parent loans:* $2,875,366 (55% need-based, 45% non-need-based). *Programs:* Federal Direct (Subsidized and Unsubsidized Stafford, PLUS).
**WORK-STUDY** *Federal work-study:* Total amount: $477,835; 259 jobs averaging $1844. *State or other work-study/employment:* Total amount: $168,650 (72% need-based, 28% non-need-based). Part-time jobs available.
**ATHLETIC AWARDS** Total amount: $2,627,401 (47% need-based, 53% non-need-based).
**APPLYING FOR FINANCIAL AID** *Required financial aid form:* FAFSA. *Financial aid deadline (priority):* 3/1. *Notification date:* Continuous beginning 3/15. Students must reply by 5/1.
**CONTACT** Ms. Heather Boutell, Director of Financial Aid, Bellarmine University, 2001 Newburg Road, Louisville, KY 40205-0671, 502-452-8124 or toll-free 800-274-4723 Ext. 8131. *Fax:* 502-452-8002. *E-mail:* hboutell@bellarmine.edu.
*Website:* http://www.bellarmine.edu/.

# BELLEVUE UNIVERSITY
## Bellevue, NE

**ABOUT THE INSTITUTION** Independent, coed. 27 undergraduate majors.
**GIFT AID (NEED-BASED)** *Scholarships, grants, and awards:* Federal Pell, FSEOG, state.
**GIFT AID (NON-NEED-BASED)** *Scholarships, grants, and awards by category: Academic interests/achievement:* business, general academic interests/achievements, humanities, mathematics, social sciences.
**APPLYING FOR FINANCIAL AID** *Required financial aid forms:* FAFSA, institution's own form.
**CONTACT** Ms. Janet Yale, Director of Financial Aid, Bellevue University, 1000 Galvin Road South, Bellevue, NE 68005, 402-293-2000 or toll-free 800-756-7920. *Fax:* 402-557-5425.
*Website:* http://www.bellevue.edu/.

# BELLIN COLLEGE
## Green Bay, WI

**CONTACT** Mrs. Lena C. Goodman, Director of Financial Aid, Bellin College, 3201 Eaton Road, Green Bay, WI 54311, 920-433-6638 or toll-free 800-236-8707. *Fax:* 920-433-1922. *E-mail:* lena.goodman@bellincollege.edu. *Website:* http://www.bellincollege.edu/.

# BELMONT ABBEY COLLEGE
## Belmont, NC

| Tuition & fees: $18,500 | Average undergraduate aid package: $12,140 |
| --- | --- |

**ABOUT THE INSTITUTION** Independent Roman Catholic, coed. *Awards:* bachelor's degrees. 15 undergraduate majors. *Total enrollment:* 1,560. Undergraduates: 1,560. Freshmen: 293. Federal methodology is used as a basis for awarding need-based institutional aid.

**UNDERGRADUATE EXPENSES for 2015–2016 Application fee:** $35. *One-time required fee:* $400. *Comprehensive fee:* $28,594 includes full-time tuition ($18,500) and room and board ($10,094). *College room only:* $5828. Full-time tuition and fees vary according to course load and reciprocity agreements. Room and board charges vary according to board plan and housing facility. *Part-time tuition:* $617 per credit hour. Part-time tuition and fees vary according to course load and reciprocity agreements.

**FRESHMAN FINANCIAL AID (Fall 2014, est.)** 250 applied for aid; of those 79% were deemed to have need. 99% of freshmen with need received aid; of those 16% had need fully met. *Average percent of need met:* 55% (excluding resources awarded to replace EFC). *Average financial aid package:* $12,619 (excluding resources awarded to replace EFC). 31% of all full-time freshmen had no need and received non-need-based gift aid.

**UNDERGRADUATE FINANCIAL AID (Fall 2014, est.)** 1,222 applied for aid; of those 89% were deemed to have need. 100% of undergraduates with need received aid; of those 10% had need fully met. *Average percent of need met:* 51% (excluding resources awarded to replace EFC). *Average financial aid package:* $12,140 (excluding resources awarded to replace EFC). 19% of all full-time undergraduates had no need and received non-need-based gift aid.

**GIFT AID (NEED-BASED) Total amount:** $7,655,228 (40% federal, 23% state, 36% institutional, 1% external sources). *Receiving aid:* Freshmen: 67% (196); all full-time undergraduates: 72% (1,039). *Average award:* Freshmen: $8916; Undergraduates: $7815. *Scholarships, grants, and awards:* Federal Pell, FSEOG, state, private, college/university gift aid from institutional funds.

**GIFT AID (NON-NEED-BASED) Total amount:** $1,744,282 (97% institutional, 3% external sources). *Receiving aid:* Freshmen: 8% (22). Undergraduates: 3% (50). *Average award:* Freshmen: $4283. Undergraduates: $5645. *Scholarships, grants, and awards by category:* Academic interests/achievement: 638 awards ($5,400,799 total): general academic interests/achievements. *Creative arts/performance:* theater/drama. *Special characteristics:* 33 awards ($267,728 total): children of faculty/staff. *Tuition waivers:* Full or partial for employees or children of employees. *ROTC:* Army cooperative, Air Force cooperative.

**LOANS Student loans:** $11,348,360 (83% need-based, 17% non-need-based). 69% of past graduating class borrowed through all loan programs. *Average indebtedness per student:* $27,341. *Average need-based loan:* Freshmen: $3555. Undergraduates: $4538. *Parent loans:* $7,383,683 (33% need-based, 67% non-need-based). *Programs:* Federal Direct (Subsidized and Unsubsidized Stafford, PLUS).

**WORK-STUDY Federal work-study:** Total amount: $144,000; jobs available.

**ATHLETIC AWARDS** Total amount: $1,166,420 (49% need-based, 51% non-need-based).

**APPLYING FOR FINANCIAL AID Required financial aid form:** FAFSA. *Financial aid deadline (priority):* 4/1. *Notification date:* Continuous beginning 3/15. Students must reply within 2 weeks of notification.

**CONTACT** Ms. Julie Hodge, Associate Director of Financial Aid, Belmont Abbey College, 100 Belmont Mt. Holly Road, Belmont, NC 28012-1802, 704-461-6720 or toll-free 888-BAC-0110. *Fax:* 704-461-6882. *E-mail:* juliehodge@bac.edu. *Website:* http://www.belmontabbeycollege.edu/.

# BELMONT UNIVERSITY
## Nashville, TN

| Tuition & fees: $28,660 | Average undergraduate aid package: $14,105 |
| --- | --- |

**ABOUT THE INSTITUTION** Independent Christian, coed. *Awards:* certificates, bachelor's, master's, and doctoral degrees. 94 undergraduate majors. *Total enrollment:* 7,244. Undergraduates: 5,837. Freshmen: 1,392. Federal methodology is used as a basis for awarding need-based institutional aid.

**UNDERGRADUATE EXPENSES for 2015–2016 Application fee:** $50. *Comprehensive fee:* $39,190 includes full-time tuition ($27,320), mandatory fees ($1340), and room and board ($10,530). *College room only:* $5850. Full-time tuition and fees vary according to course load. Room and board charges vary according to board plan and housing facility. *Part-time tuition:* $1040 per credit hour. Part-time tuition and fees vary according to course load.

**FRESHMAN FINANCIAL AID (Fall 2013)** 990 applied for aid; of those 69% were deemed to have need. 100% of freshmen with need received aid; of those 10% had need fully met. *Average percent of need met:* 54% (excluding resources awarded to replace EFC). *Average financial aid package:* $15,369 (excluding resources awarded to replace EFC). 24% of all full-time freshmen had no need and received non-need-based gift aid.

**UNDERGRADUATE FINANCIAL AID (Fall 2013)** 3,585 applied for aid; of those 78% were deemed to have need. 100% of undergraduates with need received aid; of those 8% had need fully met. *Average percent of need met:* 49% (excluding resources awarded to replace EFC). *Average financial aid package:* $14,105 (excluding resources awarded to replace EFC). 19% of all full-time undergraduates had no need and received non-need-based gift aid.

**GIFT AID (NEED-BASED) Total amount:** $28,003,818 (16% federal, 14% state, 70% institutional). *Receiving aid:* Freshmen: 47% (583); all full-time undergraduates: 44% (2,250). *Average award:* Freshmen: $14,018; Undergraduates: $12,096. *Scholarships, grants, and awards:* Federal Pell, FSEOG, state, private, college/university gift aid from institutional funds.

**GIFT AID (NON-NEED-BASED) Total amount:** $7,265,269 (18% state, 82% institutional). *Receiving aid:* Freshmen: 6% (69). Undergraduates: 4% (221). *Average award:* Freshmen: $7287. Undergraduates: $7438. *Scholarships, grants, and awards by category:* Academic interests/achievement: biological sciences, business, general academic interests/achievements, health fields, religion/biblical studies, social sciences. *Creative arts/performance:* applied art and design, art/fine arts, music, performing arts. *Special achievements/activities:* cheerleading/drum major, general special achievements/activities, leadership, religious involvement. *Special characteristics:* children and siblings of alumni, children of faculty/staff, members of minority groups, siblings of current students, veterans, veterans' children. *Tuition waivers:* Full or partial for employees or children of employees, senior citizens. *ROTC:* Army cooperative, Naval cooperative, Air Force cooperative.

**LOANS Student loans:** $9,756,198 (100% need-based). 56% of past graduating class borrowed through all loan programs. *Average indebtedness per student:* $28,306. *Average need-based loan:* Freshmen: $3574. Undergraduates: $4420. *Parent loans:* $22,409,146 (85% need-based, 15% non-need-based). *Programs:* Federal Direct (Subsidized and Unsubsidized Stafford, PLUS), Perkins.

**WORK-STUDY Federal work-study:** jobs available.

**ATHLETIC AWARDS** Total amount: $3,973,147 (33% need-based, 67% non-need-based).

**APPLYING FOR FINANCIAL AID Required financial aid form:** FAFSA. *Financial aid deadline (priority):* 3/1. *Notification date:* Continuous beginning 3/15. Students must reply by 5/1 or within 2 weeks of notification.

**CONTACT** Mrs. Pat Smedley, Director of Student Financial Services, Belmont University, 1900 Belmont Boulevard, Nashville, TN 37212-3757, 615-460-6403. *E-mail:* pat.smedley@belmont.edu. *Website:* http://www.belmont.edu/.

# BELOIT COLLEGE
## Beloit, WI

| Tuition & fees: $42,500 | Average undergraduate aid package: $33,965 |
|---|---|

**ABOUT THE INSTITUTION** Independent, coed. *Awards:* bachelor's degrees. 50 undergraduate majors. *Total enrollment:* 1,303. Undergraduates: 1,303. Freshmen: 299. Both federal and institutional methodology are used as a basis for awarding need-based institutional aid.

**UNDERGRADUATE EXPENSES for 2015–2016** *Comprehensive fee:* $49,970 includes full-time tuition ($42,220), mandatory fees ($280), and room and board ($7470). *College room only:* $4320. Room and board charges vary according to board plan. *Part-time tuition:* $1320 per credit hour.

**FRESHMAN FINANCIAL AID (Fall 2014, est.)** 240 applied for aid; of those 83% were deemed to have need. 100% of freshmen with need received aid; of those 36% had need fully met. *Average percent of need met:* 93% (excluding resources awarded to replace EFC). *Average financial aid package:* $34,275 (excluding resources awarded to replace EFC). 32% of all full-time freshmen had no need and received non-need-based gift aid.

**UNDERGRADUATE FINANCIAL AID (Fall 2014, est.)** 950 applied for aid; of those 88% were deemed to have need. 100% of undergraduates with need received aid; of those 31% had need fully met. *Average percent of need met:* 92% (excluding resources awarded to replace EFC). *Average financial aid package:* $33,965 (excluding resources awarded to replace EFC). 28% of all full-time undergraduates had no need and received non-need-based gift aid.

**GIFT AID (NEED-BASED)** *Total amount:* $21,397,959 (7% federal, 2% state, 90% institutional, 1% external sources). *Receiving aid:* Freshmen: 67% (200); all full-time undergraduates: 68% (833). *Average award:* Freshmen: $26,034; Undergraduates: $25,688. *Scholarships, grants, and awards:* Federal Pell, FSEOG, state, private, college/university gift aid from institutional funds.

**GIFT AID (NON-NEED-BASED)** *Total amount:* $7,514,187 (99% institutional, 1% external sources). *Receiving aid:* Freshmen: 36% (109). Undergraduates: 35% (431). *Average award:* Freshmen: $18,171. Undergraduates: $17,256. *Scholarships, grants, and awards by category:* Academic interests/achievement: general academic interests/achievements. Creative arts/performance: music. Special achievements/activities: community service, general special achievements/activities, leadership. Special characteristics: siblings of current students, veterans. *Tuition waivers:* Full or partial for employees or children of employees.

**LOANS** *Student loans:* $7,385,840 (66% need-based, 34% non-need-based). 65% of past graduating class borrowed through all loan programs. *Average indebtedness per student:* $28,768. *Average need-based loan:* Freshmen: $3690. Undergraduates: $4933. *Parent loans:* $1,683,713 (33% need-based, 67% non-need-based). *Programs:* Federal Direct (Subsidized and Unsubsidized Stafford, PLUS), Perkins, college/university.

**WORK-STUDY** *Federal work-study:* Total amount: $879,296; 465 jobs averaging $1891. *State or other work-study/employment:* Total amount: $442,073 (54% need-based, 46% non-need-based). 373 part-time jobs averaging $1176.

**APPLYING FOR FINANCIAL AID** *Required financial aid form:* FAFSA. *Financial aid deadline:* 3/1. *Notification date:* Continuous beginning 3/1. Students must reply by 5/1.

**CONTACT** Mr. Jon Urish, Director of Student Financial Services, Beloit College, 700 College Street, Beloit, WI 53511-5596, 608-363-2663 or toll-free 800-9-BELOIT. *Fax:* 608-363-2075. *E-mail:* urishj@beloit.edu. *Website:* http://www.beloit.edu/.

# BEMIDJI STATE UNIVERSITY
## Bemidji, MN

| Tuition & fees (MN res): $8134 | Average undergraduate aid package: $8764 |
|---|---|

**ABOUT THE INSTITUTION** State-supported, coed. *Awards:* certificates, associate, bachelor's, and master's degrees. 70 undergraduate majors. *Total enrollment:* 4,906. Undergraduates: 4,697. Freshmen: 802. Federal methodology is used as a basis for awarding need-based institutional aid.

**UNDERGRADUATE EXPENSES for 2015–2016** *Application fee:* $20. *Tuition, state resident:* full-time $7146; part-time $249.85 per credit. *Tuition,*

*nonresident:* full-time $7146; part-time $249.85 per credit. *Required fees:* full-time $988; $22 per credit. Full-time tuition and fees vary according to course load, location, program, and reciprocity agreements. Part-time tuition and fees vary according to course load, location, program, and reciprocity agreements. *College room and board:* $7470. Room and board charges vary according to board plan and housing facility.

**FRESHMAN FINANCIAL AID (Fall 2013)** 469 applied for aid; of those 72% were deemed to have need. 99% of freshmen with need received aid; of those 10% had need fully met. *Average percent of need met:* 56% (excluding resources awarded to replace EFC). *Average financial aid package:* $7631 (excluding resources awarded to replace EFC). 23% of all full-time freshmen had no need and received non-need-based gift aid.

**UNDERGRADUATE FINANCIAL AID (Fall 2013)** 2,890 applied for aid; of those 79% were deemed to have need. 99% of undergraduates with need received aid; of those 14% had need fully met. *Average percent of need met:* 61% (excluding resources awarded to replace EFC). *Average financial aid package:* $8764 (excluding resources awarded to replace EFC). 16% of all full-time undergraduates had no need and received non-need-based gift aid.

**GIFT AID (NEED-BASED)** *Total amount:* $10,853,039 (67% federal, 32% state, 1% external sources). *Receiving aid:* Freshmen: 40% (219); all full-time undergraduates: 46% (1,597). *Average award:* Freshmen: $5299; Undergraduates: $5339. *Scholarships, grants, and awards:* Federal Pell, FSEOG, state, private, college/university gift aid from institutional funds.

**GIFT AID (NON-NEED-BASED)** *Total amount:* $5,742,356 (12% federal, 11% state, 59% institutional, 18% external sources). *Receiving aid:* Freshmen: 46% (247). Undergraduates: 47% (1,652). *Average award:* Freshmen: $9262. Undergraduates: $10,309. *Scholarships, grants, and awards by category:* Academic interests/achievement: 844 awards ($902,893 total): biological sciences, business, communication, computer science, education, engineering/technologies, English, foreign languages, general academic interests/achievements, health fields, humanities, international studies, mathematics, physical sciences, premedicine, social sciences. Creative arts/performance: 76 awards ($146,886 total): applied art and design, art/fine arts, cinema/film/broadcasting, creative writing, general creative arts/performance, journalism/publications, music, performing arts. Special achievements/activities: 20 awards ($37,500 total): general special achievements/activities, leadership. Special characteristics: 247 awards ($506,034 total): children and siblings of alumni, children of faculty/staff, handicapped students, international students, members of minority groups, out-of-state students, previous college experience. *Tuition waivers:* Full or partial for employees or children of employees, senior citizens.

**LOANS** *Student loans:* $25,234,934 (40% need-based, 60% non-need-based). *Average need-based loan:* Freshmen: $3398. Undergraduates: $4104. *Parent loans:* $635,604 (100% non-need-based). *Programs:* Federal Direct (Subsidized and Unsubsidized Stafford, PLUS), Perkins, state, alternative loans.

**WORK-STUDY** *Federal work-study:* 285 jobs averaging $1693. *State or other work-study/employment:* Total amount: $326,311 (100% need-based). 176 part-time jobs averaging $1863.

**ATHLETIC AWARDS** Total amount: $1,302,154 (100% non-need-based).

**APPLYING FOR FINANCIAL AID** *Required financial aid forms:* FAFSA, institution's own form. *Financial aid deadline (priority):* 3/31. *Notification date:* Continuous beginning 6/15.

**CONTACT** Financial Aid Office, Bemidji State University, 1500 Birchmont Drive NE #14, Bemidji, MN 56601-2699, 218-755-2034 or toll-free 800-475-2001. *Fax:* 218-755-4361. *E-mail:* financialaid@bemidjistate.edu. *Website:* http://www.bemidjistate.edu/.

# BENEDICT COLLEGE
## Columbia, SC

**ABOUT THE INSTITUTION** Independent Baptist, coed. 32 undergraduate majors.

**GIFT AID (NEED-BASED)** *Scholarships, grants, and awards:* Federal Pell, FSEOG, state, private, TEACH Grants.

**GIFT AID (NON-NEED-BASED)** *Scholarships, grants, and awards by category:* Academic interests/achievement: general academic interests/achievements. Creative arts/performance: general creative arts/performance, music.

**LOANS** *Programs:* Federal Direct (Subsidized and Unsubsidized Stafford, PLUS), Perkins, state, college/university.

**WORK-STUDY** Federal work-study jobs available.

**APPLYING FOR FINANCIAL AID** *Required financial aid form:* FAFSA.

**CONTACT** Mrs. Bichevia Green, Associate Director of Financial Aid, Benedict College, 1600 Harden Street, Columbia, SC 29204, 803-705-4418 or toll-free 800-868-6598. *Fax:* 803-705-6629. *E-mail:* greenb@benedict.edu. *Website:* http://www.benedict.edu/.

# BENEDICTINE COLLEGE
### Atchison, KS

**ABOUT THE INSTITUTION** Independent Roman Catholic, coed. *Awards:* bachelor's and master's degrees. 46 undergraduate majors. *Total enrollment:* 2,138. Undergraduates: 2,100. Freshmen: 488.

**GIFT AID (NEED-BASED)** *Scholarships, grants, and awards:* Federal Pell, FSEOG, state, private, college/university gift aid from institutional funds.

**GIFT AID (NON-NEED-BASED)** *Scholarships, grants, and awards by category: Academic interests/achievement:* general academic interests/achievements. *Creative arts/performance:* music, theater/drama. *Special achievements/activities:* general special achievements/activities. *Special characteristics:* children of educators, ethnic background, general special characteristics, international students, local/state students, members of minority groups, out-of-state students, religious affiliation, veterans' children.

**LOANS** *Programs:* Perkins, alternative loans.

**WORK-STUDY** *Federal work-study:* 335 jobs averaging $606. *State or other work-study/employment:* Part-time jobs available.

**APPLYING FOR FINANCIAL AID** *Required financial aid form:* FAFSA.

**CONTACT** Mr. Tony Tanking, Director of Financial Aid, Benedictine College, 1020 North Second Street, Atchison, KS 66002-1499, 913-360-7484 or toll-free 800-467-5340. *Fax:* 913-367-5462. *E-mail:* ttanking@benedictine.edu. *Website:* http://www.benedictine.edu/.

# BENEDICTINE UNIVERSITY
### Lisle, IL

| Tuition & fees: $28,240 | Average undergraduate aid package: $19,374 |
| --- | --- |

**ABOUT THE INSTITUTION** Independent Roman Catholic, coed. *Awards:* certificates, associate, bachelor's, master's, and doctoral degrees. 51 undergraduate majors. *Total enrollment:* 6,307. Undergraduates: 3,818. Freshmen: 672. Federal methodology is used as a basis for awarding need-based institutional aid.

**UNDERGRADUATE EXPENSES for 2015–2016** *Application fee:* $40. *Comprehensive fee:* $36,766 includes full-time tuition ($27,140), mandatory fees ($1100), and room and board ($8526). *College room only:* $5846. Full-time tuition and fees vary according to course load, degree level, and location. Room and board charges vary according to board plan, housing facility, and location. *Part-time tuition:* $905 per hour. *Part-time fees:* $55 per credit hour. Part-time tuition and fees vary according to course load, degree level, and location.

**FRESHMAN FINANCIAL AID (Fall 2014, est.)** 602 applied for aid; of those 91% were deemed to have need. 100% of freshmen with need received aid. *Average financial aid package:* $20,846 (excluding resources awarded to replace EFC). 13% of all full-time freshmen had no need and received non-need-based gift aid.

**UNDERGRADUATE FINANCIAL AID (Fall 2014, est.)** 2,530 applied for aid; of those 94% were deemed to have need. 99% of undergraduates with need received aid. *Average financial aid package:* $19,374 (excluding resources awarded to replace EFC). 15% of all full-time undergraduates had no need and received non-need-based gift aid.

**GIFT AID (NEED-BASED)** *Total amount:* $12,428,049 (54% federal, 40% state, 6% institutional). *Receiving aid:* Freshmen: 54% (358); all full-time undergraduates: 52% (1,594). *Average award:* Freshmen: $7202; Undergraduates: $7365. *Scholarships, grants, and awards:* Federal Pell, FSEOG, state, college/university gift aid from institutional funds.

**GIFT AID (NON-NEED-BASED)** *Total amount:* $27,552,856 (99% institutional, 1% external sources). *Receiving aid:* Freshmen: 81% (540). Undergraduates: 66% (2,025). *Average award:* Freshmen: $9611. Undergraduates: $9353. *Scholarships, grants, and awards by category: Academic interests/achievement:* general academic interests/achievements. *Creative arts/performance:* music. *Special achievements/activities:* community service, general special achievements/activities,

leadership, memberships. *Special characteristics:* children and siblings of alumni, children of faculty/staff, general special characteristics, international students, local/state students, out-of-state students, relatives of clergy, siblings of current students, veterans, veterans' children. *Tuition waivers:* Full or partial for employees or children of employees. **ROTC:** Army cooperative.

**LOANS** *Student loans:* $18,900,056 (45% need-based, 55% non-need-based). 76% of past graduating class borrowed through all loan programs. *Average indebtedness per student:* $26,750. *Average need-based loan:* Freshmen: $3405. Undergraduates: $4296. *Parent loans:* $4,011,829 (100% non-need-based). *Programs:* Federal Direct (Subsidized and Unsubsidized Stafford, PLUS), Perkins.

**WORK-STUDY** *Federal work-study:* Total amount: $282,346; jobs available. *State or other work-study/employment:* Part-time jobs available.

**APPLYING FOR FINANCIAL AID** *Required financial aid form:* FAFSA. *Financial aid deadline:* Continuous. *Notification date:* Continuous beginning 2/1. Students must reply within 2 weeks of notification.

**CONTACT** Diane Battistella, Senior Associate Dean of Financial Aid, Benedictine University, 5700 College Road, Lisle, IL 60532, 630-829-6415 or toll-free 888-829-6363 (out-of-state). *Fax:* 630-829-6101. *E-mail:* dbattistella@ben.edu. *Website:* http://www.ben.edu/.

# BENNETT COLLEGE
### Greensboro, NC

**CONTACT** Ms. Keisha Ragsdale, Director of Financial Aid, Bennett College, 900 East Washington Street, Greensboro, NC 27401, 336-370-8678 or toll-free 800-413-5323. *Fax:* 336-517-2204. *E-mail:* kragsdale@bennett.edu. *Website:* http://www.bennett.edu/.

# BENNINGTON COLLEGE
### Bennington, VT

| Tuition & fees: $46,658 | Average undergraduate aid package: $42,405 |
| --- | --- |

**ABOUT THE INSTITUTION** Independent, coed. *Awards:* certificates, bachelor's, and master's degrees. 87 undergraduate majors. *Total enrollment:* 755. Undergraduates: 660. Freshmen: 192. Both federal and institutional methodology are used as a basis for awarding need-based institutional aid.

**UNDERGRADUATE EXPENSES for 2015–2016** *Application fee:* $60. *Comprehensive fee:* $60,310 includes full-time tuition ($46,048), mandatory fees ($610), and room and board ($13,652). *College room only:* $7328. Room and board charges vary according to board plan. *Part-time tuition:* $1535 per credit hour.

**FRESHMAN FINANCIAL AID (Fall 2014, est.)** 155 applied for aid; of those 100% were deemed to have need. 100% of freshmen with need received aid; of those 3% had need fully met. *Average percent of need met:* 77% (excluding resources awarded to replace EFC). *Average financial aid package:* $45,704 (excluding resources awarded to replace EFC). 17% of all full-time freshmen had no need and received non-need-based gift aid.

**UNDERGRADUATE FINANCIAL AID (Fall 2014, est.)** 448 applied for aid; of those 100% were deemed to have need. 100% of undergraduates with need received aid; of those 10% had need fully met. *Average percent of need met:* 58% (excluding resources awarded to replace EFC). *Average financial aid package:* $42,405 (excluding resources awarded to replace EFC). 23% of all full-time undergraduates had no need and received non-need-based gift aid.

**GIFT AID (NEED-BASED)** *Total amount:* $12,909,562 (6% federal, 92% institutional, 2% external sources). *Receiving aid:* Freshmen: 81% (155); all full-time undergraduates: 71% (448). *Average award:* Freshmen: $25,079; Undergraduates: $24,475. *Scholarships, grants, and awards:* Federal Pell, FSEOG, state, private, college/university gift aid from institutional funds.

**GIFT AID (NON-NEED-BASED)** *Total amount:* $5,844,450 (95% institutional, 5% external sources). *Receiving aid:* Freshmen: 79% (152). Undergraduates: 65% (408). *Average award:* Freshmen: $14,283. Undergraduates: $13,181. *Scholarships, grants, and awards by category: Academic interests/achievement:* general academic interests/achievements. *Special characteristics:* children of educators, children of faculty/staff, veterans, veterans' children. *Tuition waivers:* Full or partial for employees or children of employees.

**LOANS** *Student loans:* $2,847,405 (81% need-based, 19% non-need-based). 59% of past graduating class borrowed through all loan programs. *Average indebtedness per student:* $26,073. *Average need-based loan:* Freshmen: $3116. Undergraduates: $3891. *Parent loans:* $1,270,692 (42% need-based, 58% non-need-based). *Programs:* Federal Direct (Subsidized and Unsubsidized Stafford, PLUS).

**WORK-STUDY** *Federal work-study:* Total amount: $636,327; jobs available. *State or other work-study/employment:* Total amount: $172,500 (100% non-need-based). Part-time jobs available.

**APPLYING FOR FINANCIAL AID** *Required financial aid forms:* FAFSA, institution's own form, CSS Financial Aid PROFILE, noncustodial (divorced/separated) parent's statement, federal income tax form(s), W-2 forms. *Financial aid deadline:* 2/15 (priority: 1/15). *Notification date:* 4/1. Students must reply by 5/1 or within 2 weeks of notification.

**CONTACT** Heather Clifford, Director of Financial Aid, Bennington College, One College Drive, Bennington, VT 05201, 802-440-4325 or toll-free 800-833-6845. *Fax:* 802-440-4880. *E-mail:* finaid@bennington.edu. *Website:* http://www.bennington.edu/.

# BENTLEY UNIVERSITY
## Waltham, MA

| Tuition & fees: $42,511 | Average undergraduate aid package: $33,956 |
| --- | --- |

**ABOUT THE INSTITUTION** Independent, coed. *Awards:* certificates, bachelor's, master's, and doctoral degrees. 22 undergraduate majors. *Total enrollment:* 5,568. Undergraduates: 4,264. Freshmen: 978. Both federal and institutional methodology are used as a basis for awarding need-based institutional aid.

**UNDERGRADUATE EXPENSES** for 2015–2016 *Application fee:* $50. *Comprehensive fee:* $56,460 includes full-time tuition ($40,990), mandatory fees ($1521), and room and board ($13,949). *College room only:* $8449. Room and board charges vary according to board plan and housing facility. *Part-time tuition:* $2080 per course. *Part-time fees:* $26 per year. Part-time tuition and fees vary according to class time and course load.

**FRESHMAN FINANCIAL AID (Fall 2013)** 679 applied for aid; of those 67% were deemed to have need. 100% of freshmen with need received aid; of those 43% had need fully met. *Average percent of need met:* 95% (excluding resources awarded to replace EFC). *Average financial aid package:* $33,890 (excluding resources awarded to replace EFC). 21% of all full-time freshmen had no need and received non-need-based gift aid.

**UNDERGRADUATE FINANCIAL AID (Fall 2013)** 2,486 applied for aid; of those 74% were deemed to have need. 100% of undergraduates with need received aid; of those 39% had need fully met. *Average percent of need met:* 94% (excluding resources awarded to replace EFC). *Average financial aid package:* $33,956 (excluding resources awarded to replace EFC). 20% of all full-time undergraduates had no need and received non-need-based gift aid.

**GIFT AID (NEED-BASED)** *Total amount:* $48,697,416 (7% federal, 2% state, 91% institutional). *Receiving aid:* Freshmen: 45% (443); all full-time undergraduates: 44% (1,793). *Average award:* Freshmen: $30,000; Undergraduates: $29,025. *Scholarships, grants, and awards:* Federal Pell, FSEOG, state, private, college/university gift aid from institutional funds.

**GIFT AID (NON-NEED-BASED)** *Total amount:* $16,322,747 (91% institutional, 9% external sources). *Receiving aid:* Freshmen: 9% (90). Undergraduates: 6% (235). *Average award:* Freshmen: $16,917. Undergraduates: $16,761. *Scholarships, grants, and awards by category: Academic interests/achievement:* 1,447 awards ($25,256,938 total): general academic interests/achievements. *Special achievements/activities:* 15 awards ($113,750 total): community service. *Special characteristics:* 40 awards ($498,200 total): international students, members of minority groups. *Tuition waivers:* Full or partial for employees or children of employees. *ROTC:* Army cooperative, Air Force cooperative.

**LOANS** *Student loans:* $22,275,862 (48% need-based, 52% non-need-based). 57% of past graduating class borrowed through all loan programs. *Average indebtedness per student:* $30,602. *Average need-based loan:* Freshmen: $4038. Undergraduates: $5370. *Parent loans:* $8,256,008 (100% non-need-based). *Programs:* Federal Direct (Subsidized and Unsubsidized Stafford, PLUS), Perkins, state.

**WORK-STUDY** *Federal work-study:* 839 jobs averaging $1637. *State or other work-study/employment:* Total amount: $534,400 (100% non-need-based). 733 part-time jobs averaging $956.

**ATHLETIC AWARDS** Total amount: $2,413,542 (28% need-based, 72% non-need-based).

**APPLYING FOR FINANCIAL AID** *Required financial aid forms:* FAFSA, CSS Financial Aid PROFILE, noncustodial (divorced/separated) parent's statement, business/farm supplement, federal income tax form(s). *Financial aid deadline:* 2/1. *Notification date:* 3/31.

**CONTACT** Donna Kendall, Executive Director of Enrollment Management and Financial Assistance, Bentley University, 175 Forest Street, Waltham, MA 02452-4705, 781-891-3441 or toll-free 800-523-2354. *Fax:* 781-891-2448. *E-mail:* finaid@bentley.edu. *Website:* http://www.bentley.edu/.

# BEREA COLLEGE
## Berea, KY

| Tuition & fees: $870 | Average undergraduate aid package: $30,448 |
| --- | --- |

**ABOUT THE INSTITUTION** Independent, coed. *Awards:* bachelor's degrees. 38 undergraduate majors. *Total enrollment:* 1,621. Undergraduates: 1,621. Freshmen: 416. Federal methodology is used as a basis for awarding need-based institutional aid.

**UNDERGRADUATE EXPENSES** for 2015–2016 Room and board charges vary according to board plan. Financial aid is provided to all students for tuition costs.

**FRESHMAN FINANCIAL AID (Fall 2014, est.)** 416 applied for aid; of those 100% were deemed to have need. 100% of freshmen with need received aid. *Average percent of need met:* 94% (excluding resources awarded to replace EFC). *Average financial aid package:* $31,547 (excluding resources awarded to replace EFC).

**UNDERGRADUATE FINANCIAL AID (Fall 2014, est.)** 1,577 applied for aid; of those 100% were deemed to have need. 100% of undergraduates with need received aid. *Average percent of need met:* 91% (excluding resources awarded to replace EFC). *Average financial aid package:* $30,448 (excluding resources awarded to replace EFC).

**GIFT AID (NEED-BASED)** *Total amount:* $45,062,968 (15% federal, 7% state, 77% institutional, 1% external sources). *Receiving aid:* Freshmen: 100% (416); all full-time undergraduates: 100% (1,577). *Average award:* Freshmen: $29,921; Undergraduates: $28,182. *Scholarships, grants, and awards:* Federal Pell, FSEOG, state, private, college/university gift aid from institutional funds.

**LOANS** *Student loans:* $805,748 (36% need-based, 64% non-need-based). 64% of past graduating class borrowed through all loan programs. *Average indebtedness per student:* $6186. *Average need-based loan:* Freshmen: $40. Undergraduates: $181. *Parent loans:* $4500 (100% non-need-based). *Programs:* Federal Direct (Subsidized and Unsubsidized Stafford, PLUS), Perkins, college/university.

**WORK-STUDY** *Federal work-study:* Total amount: $2,813,839; jobs available. *State or other work-study/employment:* Total amount: $521,015 (100% need-based). Part-time jobs available.

**APPLYING FOR FINANCIAL AID** *Required financial aid form:* FAFSA. *Financial aid deadline:* 3/1 (priority: 1/31). *Notification date:* Continuous beginning 3/1. Students must reply by 5/1.

**CONTACT** Nancy Melton, Director of Student Financial Aid Services, Berea College, CPO 2172, Berea, KY 40404, 859-985-3313 or toll-free 800-326-5948. *Fax:* 859-985-3914. *E-mail:* meltonn@berea.edu. *Website:* http://www.berea.edu/.

# BERGIN UNIVERSITY OF CANINE STUDIES
## Rohnert Park, CA

**CONTACT** Financial Aid Office, Bergin University of Canine Studies, 5860 Labath Avenue, Rohnert Park, CA 94928, 707-545-3647. *Website:* http://www.berginu.edu/.

# BERKELEY COLLEGE
## Woodland Park, NJ

**CONTACT** Office of Financial Aid, Berkeley College, 44 Rifle Camp Road, Woodland Park, NJ 07424-3353, 800-446-5400. *E-mail:* financialaid@berkeleycollege.edu. *Website:* http://www.berkeleycollege.edu/.

# BERKELEY COLLEGE–NEW YORK CITY CAMPUS
## New York, NY

| Tuition & fees: $24,300 | Average undergraduate aid package: N/A |
|---|---|

**ABOUT THE INSTITUTION** Proprietary, coed. *Awards:* certificates, associate, and bachelor's degrees. 12 undergraduate majors. *Total enrollment:* 4,029. Undergraduates: 4,029. Freshmen: 570.

**UNDERGRADUATE EXPENSES for 2015–2016 Application fee:** $50. *Tuition:* full-time $23,100; part-time $525 per quarter hour. *Required fees:* full-time $1200; $275 per term. Full-time tuition and fees vary according to course load. Part-time tuition and fees vary according to course load. *Payment plan:* Guaranteed tuition.

**GIFT AID (NEED-BASED)** *Scholarships, grants, and awards:* Federal Pell, FSEOG, state, private.

**GIFT AID (NON-NEED-BASED)** *Tuition waivers:* Full or partial for employees or children of employees.

**LOANS** *Programs:* Federal Direct (Subsidized and Unsubsidized Stafford), alternative loans.

**APPLYING FOR FINANCIAL AID** *Required financial aid form:* state income tax form(s). *Notification date:* Continuous.

**CONTACT** Office of Financial Aid, Berkeley College–New York City Campus, 3 East 43rd Street, New York, NY 10017, 800-446-5400. *E-mail:* financialaid@berkeleycollege.edu. *Website:* http://www.berkeleycollege.edu/.

# BERKLEE COLLEGE OF MUSIC
## Boston, MA

| Tuition & fees: N/R | Average undergraduate aid package: $8365 |
|---|---|

**ABOUT THE INSTITUTION** Independent, coed. 13 undergraduate majors. Both federal and institutional methodology are used as a basis for awarding need-based institutional aid.

**FRESHMAN FINANCIAL AID (Fall 2014, est.)** 451 applied for aid; of those 85% were deemed to have need. 91% of freshmen with need received aid; of those 9% had need fully met. *Average percent of need met:* 33% (excluding resources awarded to replace EFC). *Average financial aid package:* $8445 (excluding resources awarded to replace EFC). 6% of all full-time freshmen had no need and received non-need-based gift aid.

**UNDERGRADUATE FINANCIAL AID (Fall 2014, est.)** 1,723 applied for aid; of those 96% were deemed to have need. 95% of undergraduates with need received aid; of those 2% had need fully met. *Average percent of need met:* 54% (excluding resources awarded to replace EFC). *Average financial aid package:* $8365 (excluding resources awarded to replace EFC). 1% of all full-time undergraduates had no need and received non-need-based gift aid.

**GIFT AID (NEED-BASED)** *Total amount:* $34,978,447 (7% federal, 1% state, 88% institutional, 4% external sources). *Receiving aid:* Freshmen: 35% (270); all full-time undergraduates: 34% (1,200). *Average award:* Freshmen: $21,292; Undergraduates: $17,636. *Scholarships, grants, and awards:* Federal Pell, FSEOG, state, private, college/university gift aid from institutional funds.

**GIFT AID (NON-NEED-BASED)** *Total amount:* $979,416 (98% institutional, 2% external sources). *Average award:* Freshmen: $13,739. Undergraduates: $13,419. *Scholarships, grants, and awards by category:* Academic interests/achievement: education, engineering/technologies, general academic interests/achieve-ments. *Creative arts/performance:* music. *Special characteristics:* children and siblings of alumni, children of faculty/staff.

**LOANS** *Student loans:* $22,759,070 (96% need-based, 4% non-need-based). 37% of past graduating class borrowed through all loan programs. *Average indebtedness per student:* $15,838. *Average need-based loan:* Freshmen: $4162. Undergraduates: $4982. *Parent loans:* $14,975,269 (91% need-based, 9% non-need-based). *Programs:* Federal Direct (Subsidized and Unsubsidized Stafford, PLUS), Perkins, state, private loans.

**WORK-STUDY** *Federal work-study:* Total amount: $627,800; jobs available. *State or other work-study/employment:* Total amount: $118,700 (100% need-based). Part-time jobs available.

**APPLYING FOR FINANCIAL AID** *Required financial aid forms:* FAFSA, CSS Financial Aid PROFILE, noncustodial (divorced/separated) parent's statement. *Financial aid deadline (priority):* 3/1. *Notification date:* Continuous beginning 12/31.

**CONTACT** Office of Financial Aid, Berklee College of Music, 921 Boylston Street, Boston, MA 02215-3693, 617-747-2274 or toll-free 800-BERKLEE. *Fax:* 617-747-2073. *E-mail:* financialaid@berklee.edu. *Website:* http://www.berklee.edu/.

# BERRY COLLEGE
## Mount Berry, GA

| Tuition & fees: $30,530 | Average undergraduate aid package: $25,079 |
|---|---|

**ABOUT THE INSTITUTION** Independent interdenominational, coed. *Awards:* bachelor's and master's degrees. 43 undergraduate majors. *Total enrollment:* 2,177. Undergraduates: 2,085. Freshmen: 568. Federal methodology is used as a basis for awarding need-based institutional aid.

**UNDERGRADUATE EXPENSES for 2015–2016 Comprehensive fee:** $41,190 includes full-time tuition ($30,330), mandatory fees ($200), and room and board ($10,660). *College room only:* $6020. Room and board charges vary according to board plan and housing facility. *Part-time tuition:* $1011 per credit hour.

**FRESHMAN FINANCIAL AID (Fall 2014, est.)** 516 applied for aid; of those 79% were deemed to have need. 100% of freshmen with need received aid; of those 28% had need fully met. *Average percent of need met:* 85% (excluding resources awarded to replace EFC). *Average financial aid package:* $26,564 (excluding resources awarded to replace EFC). 28% of all full-time freshmen had no need and received non-need-based gift aid.

**UNDERGRADUATE FINANCIAL AID (Fall 2014, est.)** 1,802 applied for aid; of those 83% were deemed to have need. 100% of undergraduates with need received aid; of those 29% had need fully met. *Average percent of need met:* 82% (excluding resources awarded to replace EFC). *Average financial aid package:* $25,079 (excluding resources awarded to replace EFC). 27% of all full-time undergraduates had no need and received non-need-based gift aid.

**GIFT AID (NEED-BASED)** *Total amount:* $30,336,772 (8% federal, 10% state, 80% institutional, 2% external sources). *Receiving aid:* Freshmen: 72% (409); all full-time undergraduates: 72% (1,486). *Average award:* Freshmen: $22,519; Undergraduates: $20,510. *Scholarships, grants, and awards:* Federal Pell, FSEOG, state, private, college/university gift aid from institutional funds.

**GIFT AID (NON-NEED-BASED)** *Total amount:* $10,382,016 (19% state, 77% institutional, 4% external sources). *Receiving aid:* Freshmen: 17% (97). Undergraduates: 16% (326). *Average award:* Freshmen: $12,241. Undergraduates: $11,976. *Scholarships, grants, and awards by category:* Academic interests/achievement: agriculture, business, communication, education, English, general academic interests/achievements, humanities, religion/biblical studies. *Creative arts/performance:* art/fine arts, debating, journalism/publications, music, theater/drama. *Special achievements/activities:* community service, leadership, religious involvement. *Special characteristics:* adult students, children of faculty/staff, ethnic background, first-generation college students, international students, local/state students, members of minority groups, out-of-state students, veterans, veterans' children. *Tuition waivers:* Full or partial for employees or children of employees, senior citizens.

**LOANS** *Student loans:* $13,416,369 (62% need-based, 38% non-need-based). 65% of past graduating class borrowed through all loan programs. *Average indebtedness per student:* $23,997. *Average need-based loan:* Freshmen: $4550. Undergraduates: $5083. *Parent loans:* $3,390,513 (25% need-based, 75% non-need-based).

**Programs:** Federal Direct (Subsidized and Unsubsidized Stafford, PLUS), Perkins, state, college/university.
**WORK-STUDY Federal work-study:** Total amount: $493,724; 398 jobs averaging $2101. **State or other work-study/employment:** Total amount: $443,700 (66% need-based, 34% non-need-based). 144 part-time jobs averaging $4390.
**APPLYING FOR FINANCIAL AID Required financial aid forms:** FAFSA, state aid form. **Financial aid deadline (priority):** 3/1. **Notification date:** Continuous beginning 2/15. Students must reply by 3/1.
**CONTACT** Mrs. Donna Childres, Director of Financial Aid, Berry College, 2277 Martha Berry Highway, NW, Mount Berry, GA 30149-5007, 706-236-1714 or toll-free 800-237-7942. **Fax:** 706-290-2160. **E-mail:** financialaid@berry.edu.
**Website:** http://www.berry.edu/.

# BETHANY COLLEGE
## Lindsborg, KS

**CONTACT** Ms. Amber Maneth, Office of Financial Aid, Bethany College, 335 East Swensson, Lindsborg, KS 67456-1897, 785-227-3311 Ext. 8248 or toll-free 800-826-2281. **Fax:** 785-227-2004. **E-mail:** manetha@bethanylb.edu.
**Website:** http://www.bethanylb.edu/.

# BETHANY COLLEGE
## Bethany, WV

| Tuition & fees: $25,736 | Average undergraduate aid package: N/A |
|---|---|

**ABOUT THE INSTITUTION** Independent Christian Church (Disciples of Christ), coed. **Awards:** bachelor's and master's degrees. 59 undergraduate majors. **Total enrollment:** 935. Undergraduates: 905. Freshmen: 246. Both federal and institutional methodology are used as a basis for awarding need-based institutional aid.
**UNDERGRADUATE EXPENSES for 2015–2016 Comprehensive fee:** $35,372 includes full-time tuition ($24,836), mandatory fees ($900), and room and board ($9636). **College room only:** $5000. Full-time tuition and fees vary according to course load. Room and board charges vary according to board plan and housing facility. **Part-time tuition:** $675 per credit hour. **Part-time fees:** $112.50 per credit hour. Part-time tuition and fees vary according to course load.
**GIFT AID (NEED-BASED) Total amount:** $7,109,424 (28% federal, 2% state, 70% institutional). **Scholarships, grants, and awards:** Federal Pell, FSEOG, state, private, college/university gift aid from institutional funds.
**GIFT AID (NON-NEED-BASED) Total amount:** $5,247,486 (3% state, 95% institutional, 2% external sources). **Scholarships, grants, and awards by category:** Academic interests/achievement: general academic interests/achievements. Creative arts/performance: music. Special achievements/activities: community service, hobbies/interests, leadership, religious involvement. Special characteristics: children and siblings of alumni, children of faculty/staff, international students, local/ state students, out-of-state students, relatives of clergy, religious affiliation. **Tuition waivers:** Full or partial for employees or children of employees.
**LOANS Student loans:** $5,989,962 (43% need-based, 57% non-need-based). **Parent loans:** $1,216,706 (100% non-need-based). **Programs:** Federal Direct (Subsidized and Unsubsidized Stafford, PLUS), Perkins, alternative loans.
**WORK-STUDY Federal work-study:** Total amount: $581,806; jobs available. **State or other work-study/employment:** Total amount: $234,512 (100% non-need-based). Part-time jobs available.
**APPLYING FOR FINANCIAL AID Required financial aid form:** FAFSA. **Financial aid deadline:** Continuous. **Notification date:** Continuous beginning 2/15. Students must reply within 2 weeks of notification.
**CONTACT** Jason McClain, Director of Financial Aid, Bethany College, Center for Enrollment and Financial Aid #4, 31 East Campus Drive, Bethany, WV 26032, 304-829-7611 or toll-free 800-922-7611. **Fax:** 304-829-7142. **E-mail:** enrollment@bethanywv.edu.
**Website:** http://www.bethanywv.edu/.

# BETHANY LUTHERAN COLLEGE
## Mankato, MN

| Tuition & fees: $25,170 | Average undergraduate aid package: $19,087 |
|---|---|

**ABOUT THE INSTITUTION** Independent Lutheran, coed. **Awards:** bachelor's degrees. 25 undergraduate majors. **Total enrollment:** 533. Undergraduates: 533. Freshmen: 142. Federal methodology is used as a basis for awarding need-based institutional aid.
**UNDERGRADUATE EXPENSES for 2015–2016 One-time required fee:** $130. **Comprehensive fee:** $32,880 includes full-time tuition ($24,720), mandatory fees ($450), and room and board ($7710). Room and board charges vary according to board plan, housing facility, and student level. **Part-time tuition:** $1050 per credit hour. **Part-time fees:** $225. Part-time tuition and fees vary according to course load.
**FRESHMAN FINANCIAL AID (Fall 2013)** 141 applied for aid; of those 91% were deemed to have need. 100% of freshmen with need received aid; of those 29% had need fully met. **Average percent of need met:** 86% (excluding resources awarded to replace EFC). **Average financial aid package:** $19,511 (excluding resources awarded to replace EFC). 8% of all full-time freshmen had no need and received non-need-based gift aid.
**UNDERGRADUATE FINANCIAL AID (Fall 2013)** 518 applied for aid; of those 94% were deemed to have need. 100% of undergraduates with need received aid; of those 19% had need fully met. **Average percent of need met:** 81% (excluding resources awarded to replace EFC). **Average financial aid package:** $19,087 (excluding resources awarded to replace EFC). 8% of all full-time undergraduates had no need and received non-need-based gift aid.
**GIFT AID (NEED-BASED) Total amount:** $6,361,037 (15% federal, 14% state, 69% institutional, 2% external sources). **Receiving aid:** Freshmen: 88% (129); all full-time undergraduates: 88% (489). **Average award:** Freshmen: $15,134; Undergraduates: $14,155. **Scholarships, grants, and awards:** Federal Pell, FSEOG, state, private, college/university gift aid from institutional funds.
**GIFT AID (NON-NEED-BASED) Total amount:** $558,937 (89% institutional, 11% external sources). **Receiving aid:** Freshmen: 10% (15). Undergraduates: 7% (40). **Average award:** Freshmen: $5936. Undergraduates: $5862. **Scholarships, grants, and awards by category:** Creative arts/performance: 62 awards ($112,000 total): art/fine arts, debating, journalism/publications, music, theater/drama. Special characteristics: 16 awards ($327,616 total): children of faculty/staff. **Tuition waivers:** Full or partial for employees or children of employees, senior citizens. **ROTC:** Army cooperative.
**LOANS Student loans:** $3,746,631 (73% need-based, 27% non-need-based). 85% of past graduating class borrowed through all loan programs. **Average indebtedness per student:** $33,384. **Average need-based loan:** Freshmen: $4411. Undergraduates: $5039. **Parent loans:** $330,464 (21% need-based, 79% non-need-based). **Programs:** Federal Direct (Subsidized and Unsubsidized Stafford, PLUS), Perkins, state, alternative loans.
**WORK-STUDY Federal work-study:** 27 jobs averaging $1620. **State or other work-study/employment:** Total amount: $214,775 (63% need-based, 37% non-need-based). 273 part-time jobs averaging $787.
**APPLYING FOR FINANCIAL AID Required financial aid forms:** FAFSA, institution's own form, business/farm supplement. **Financial aid deadline (priority):** 4/15. **Notification date:** Continuous beginning 3/1. Students must reply within 4 weeks of notification.
**CONTACT** Financial Aid Office, Bethany Lutheran College, 700 Luther Drive, Mankato, MN 56001-6163, 507-344-7328 or toll-free 800-944-3066. **Fax:** 507-344-7376. **E-mail:** finaid@blc.edu.
**Website:** http://www.blc.edu/.

# BETHEL COLLEGE
## Mishawaka, IN

**ABOUT THE INSTITUTION** Independent Missionary Church, coed. **Awards:** associate, bachelor's, and master's degrees. 51 undergraduate majors. **Total enrollment:** 1,792. Undergraduates: 1,600. Freshmen: 224.
**GIFT AID (NEED-BASED) Scholarships, grants, and awards:** Federal Pell, FSEOG, state, private, college/university gift aid from institutional funds, Federal Nursing.

**GIFT AID (NON-NEED-BASED)** *Scholarships, grants, and awards by category:* *Academic interests/achievement:* biological sciences, business, communication, education, engineering/technologies, English, general academic interests/achievements, health fields, mathematics, physical sciences, premedicine, religion/biblical studies, social sciences. *Creative arts/performance:* art/fine arts, music, theater/drama. *Special achievements/activities:* cheerleading/drum major, general special achievements/activities, leadership, religious involvement. *Special characteristics:* children and siblings of alumni, children of faculty/staff, international students, members of minority groups, relatives of clergy, religious affiliation, siblings of current students, spouses of current students.

**LOANS** *Programs:* Federal Direct (Subsidized and Unsubsidized Stafford, PLUS), Perkins, Federal Nursing.

**WORK-STUDY** Federal work-study jobs available.

**APPLYING FOR FINANCIAL AID** *Required financial aid forms:* FAFSA, institution's own form.

**CONTACT** Ms. Andrea Helmuth, Assistant Vice President for Admission and Financial Aid, Bethel College, 1001 Bethel Circle, Mishawaka, IN 46545-5591, 574-807-7600 or toll-free 800-422-4101. *Fax:* 574-807-7122. *E-mail:* andrea.helmuth@bethelcollege.edu.

*Website:* http://www.bethelcollege.edu/.

# BETHEL COLLEGE
## North Newton, KS

| Tuition & fees: $24,200 | Average undergraduate aid package: $23,801 |
|---|---|

**ABOUT THE INSTITUTION** Independent Mennonite Church USA, coed. *Awards:* certificates and bachelor's degrees. 17 undergraduate majors. *Total enrollment:* 483. Undergraduates: 483. Freshmen: 110. Federal methodology is used as a basis for awarding need-based institutional aid.

**UNDERGRADUATE EXPENSES** for 2015–2016 *Application fee:* $20. *One-time required fee:* $200. *Comprehensive fee:* $32,440 includes full-time tuition ($24,200) and room and board ($8240). *College room only:* $4420. Room and board charges vary according to board plan, housing facility, and student level. *Part-time tuition:* $865 per credit hour. Part-time tuition and fees vary according to course load.

**FRESHMAN FINANCIAL AID (Fall 2013)** 115 applied for aid; of those 98% were deemed to have need. 100% of freshmen with need received aid; of those 27% had need fully met. *Average percent of need met:* 87% (excluding resources awarded to replace EFC). *Average financial aid package:* $24,117 (excluding resources awarded to replace EFC). 7% of all full-time freshmen had no need and received non-need-based gift aid.

**UNDERGRADUATE FINANCIAL AID (Fall 2013)** 443 applied for aid; of those 93% were deemed to have need. 100% of undergraduates with need received aid; of those 32% had need fully met. *Average percent of need met:* 89% (excluding resources awarded to replace EFC). *Average financial aid package:* $23,801 (excluding resources awarded to replace EFC). 14% of all full-time undergraduates had no need and received non-need-based gift aid.

**GIFT AID (NEED-BASED)** *Total amount:* $1,485,701 (66% federal, 29% state, 5% institutional). *Receiving aid:* Freshmen: 82% (99); all full-time undergraduates: 72% (351). *Average award:* Freshmen: $4910; Undergraduates: $4859. *Scholarships, grants, and awards:* Federal Pell, FSEOG, state, college/university gift aid from institutional funds.

**GIFT AID (NON-NEED-BASED)** *Total amount:* $4,676,042 (93% institutional, 7% external sources). *Receiving aid:* Freshmen: 93% (113). Undergraduates: 85% (413). *Average award:* Freshmen: $9631. Undergraduates: $9154. *Scholarships, grants, and awards by category:* *Academic interests/achievement:* biological sciences, communication, general academic interests/achievements, social sciences. *Creative arts/performance:* art/fine arts, debating, music, theater/drama. *Special achievements/activities:* cheerleading/drum major. *Special characteristics:* children and siblings of alumni, children of current students, children of faculty/staff, ethnic background, general special characteristics, international students, local/state students, previous college experience, relatives of clergy, religious affiliation, siblings of current students, spouses of current students. *Tuition waivers:* Full or partial for employees or children of employees, senior citizens.

**LOANS** *Student loans:* $3,040,533 (100% need-based). 82% of past graduating class borrowed through all loan programs. *Average indebtedness per student:*

$24,132. *Average need-based loan:* Freshmen: $5933. Undergraduates: $7969. *Parent loans:* $569,883 (100% non-need-based). *Programs:* Federal Direct (Subsidized and Unsubsidized Stafford, PLUS), Perkins.

**WORK-STUDY** *Federal work-study:* 154 jobs averaging $1239. *State or other work-study/employment:* 195 part-time jobs averaging $1331.

**ATHLETIC AWARDS** Total amount: $1,179,148 (100% non-need-based).

**APPLYING FOR FINANCIAL AID** *Required financial aid form:* FAFSA. *Financial aid deadline (priority):* 4/1. *Notification date:* Continuous beginning 2/1. Students must reply by 5/1 or within 2 weeks of notification.

**CONTACT** Mr. Tony Graber, Director of Financial Aid, Bethel College, 300 East 27th Street, North Newton, KS 67117, 316-284-5232 or toll-free 800-522-1887 Ext. 230. *Fax:* 316-284-5845. *E-mail:* tgraber@bethelks.edu.

*Website:* http://www.bethelks.edu/.

# BETHEL COLLEGE
## Hampton, VA

**CONTACT** Financial Aid Office, Bethel College, 1705 Todds Lane, Hampton, VA 23666, 757-826-1426.

*Website:* http://bethel-college.com/.

# BETHEL UNIVERSITY
## St. Paul, MN

| Tuition & fees: $32,990 | Average undergraduate aid package: $24,292 |
|---|---|

**ABOUT THE INSTITUTION** Independent Baptist General Conference, coed. *Awards:* certificates, associate, bachelor's, master's, and doctoral degrees. 52 undergraduate majors. *Total enrollment:* 4,884. Undergraduates: 3,051. Freshmen: 604. Federal methodology is used as a basis for awarding need-based institutional aid.

**UNDERGRADUATE EXPENSES** for 2015–2016 *Comprehensive fee:* $42,430 includes full-time tuition ($32,840), mandatory fees ($150), and room and board ($9440). *College room only:* $5400. Room and board charges vary according to board plan. *Part-time tuition:* $1370 per credit. Part-time tuition and fees vary according to course load. *Payment plan:* Tuition prepayment.

**FRESHMAN FINANCIAL AID (Fall 2014, est.)** 556 applied for aid; of those 82% were deemed to have need. 100% of freshmen with need received aid; of those 18% had need fully met. *Average percent of need met:* 80% (excluding resources awarded to replace EFC). *Average financial aid package:* $25,905 (excluding resources awarded to replace EFC). 24% of all full-time freshmen had no need and received non-need-based gift aid.

**UNDERGRADUATE FINANCIAL AID (Fall 2014, est.)** 2,150 applied for aid; of those 84% were deemed to have need. 100% of undergraduates with need received aid; of those 17% had need fully met. *Average percent of need met:* 78% (excluding resources awarded to replace EFC). *Average financial aid package:* $24,292 (excluding resources awarded to replace EFC). 25% of all full-time undergraduates had no need and received non-need-based gift aid.

**GIFT AID (NEED-BASED)** *Total amount:* $31,377,580 (10% federal, 10% state, 78% institutional, 2% external sources). *Receiving aid:* Freshmen: 76% (456); all full-time undergraduates: 74% (1,791). *Average award:* Freshmen: $19,827; Undergraduates: $18,217. *Scholarships, grants, and awards:* Federal Pell, FSEOG, state, private, college/university gift aid from institutional funds.

**GIFT AID (NON-NEED-BASED)** *Total amount:* $7,355,885 (1% federal, 96% institutional, 3% external sources). *Receiving aid:* Freshmen: 10% (58). Undergraduates: 8% (203). *Average award:* Freshmen: $10,702. Undergraduates: $10,497. *Scholarships, grants, and awards by category:* *Academic interests/achievement:* general academic interests/achievements. *Creative arts/performance:* art/fine arts, debating, music, theater/drama. *Special achievements/activities:* community service, junior miss, leadership, religious involvement. *Special characteristics:* children and siblings of alumni, children of faculty/staff, ethnic background, international students, members of minority groups, out-of-state students, relatives of clergy, religious affiliation. *Tuition waivers:* Full or partial for employees or children of employees. *ROTC:* Army cooperative, Air Force cooperative.

**LOANS** *Student loans:* $18,715,365 (67% need-based, 33% non-need-based). 80% of past graduating class borrowed through all loan programs. *Average indebtedness*

*per student:* $33,685. **Average need-based loan:** Freshmen: $4040. Undergraduates: $4368. **Parent loans:** $4,364,751 (40% need-based, 60% non-need-based). **Programs:** Federal Direct (Subsidized and Unsubsidized Stafford, PLUS), Perkins, state, alternative loans.
**WORK-STUDY** *Federal work-study:* Total amount: $600,000; 350 jobs averaging $2500. **State or other work-study/employment:** Total amount: $2,366,894 (67% need-based, 33% non-need-based). 1,500 part-time jobs averaging $2500.
**APPLYING FOR FINANCIAL AID** *Required financial aid form:* FAFSA. *Financial aid deadline (priority):* 4/15. *Notification date:* Continuous beginning 3/1.
**CONTACT** Mr. Jeffrey D. Olson, Director of Financial Aid, Bethel University, 3900 Bethel Drive, St. Paul, MN 55112-6999, 651-638-6241 or toll-free 800-255-8706 Ext. 6242. *Fax:* 651-635-1491. *E-mail:* finaid@bethel.edu.
*Website:* http://www.bethel.edu/.

# BETHEL UNIVERSITY
## McKenzie, TN

**CONTACT** Laura Bateman, Office of Financial Aid, Bethel University, 325 Cherry Avenue, McKenzie, TN 38201, 901-352-4007. *Fax:* 901-352-4069.
*Website:* http://www.bethelu.edu/.

# BETHESDA UNIVERSITY
## Anaheim, CA

**CONTACT** Ms. Grace Choi, Financial Aid Administrator, Bethesda University, 730 North Euclid Street, Anaheim, CA 92801, 714-683-1413. *Fax:* 714-517-1948. *E-mail:* financialaid@bcu.edu.
*Website:* http://www.buc.edu/.

# BETH HAMEDRASH SHAAREI YOSHER INSTITUTE
## Brooklyn, NY

**CONTACT** Financial Aid Office, Beth HaMedrash Shaarei Yosher Institute, 4102-10 16th Avenue, Brooklyn, NY 11204, 718-854-2290.

# BETH HATALMUD RABBINICAL COLLEGE
## Brooklyn, NY

**CONTACT** Financial Aid Office, Beth Hatalmud Rabbinical College, 2127 82nd Street, Brooklyn, NY 11204, 718-259-2525.

# BETH MEDRASH GOVOHA
## Lakewood, NJ

**CONTACT** Financial Aid Office, Beth Medrash Govoha, 617 Sixth Street, Lakewood, NJ 08701-2797, 732-367-1060.

# BETHUNE-COOKMAN UNIVERSITY
## Daytona Beach, FL

| Tuition & fees: $14,410 | Average undergraduate aid package: $13,672 |
|---|---|

**ABOUT THE INSTITUTION** Independent Methodist, coed. **Awards:** bachelor's and master's degrees. 38 undergraduate majors. **Total enrollment:** 4,045. Undergraduates: 3,900. Freshmen: 965. Federal methodology is used as a basis for awarding need-based institutional aid.
**UNDERGRADUATE EXPENSES for 2015-2016** *Application fee:* $25. **Comprehensive fee:** $22,958 includes full-time tuition ($13,440), mandatory fees ($970), and room and board ($8548). **College room only:** $6710. Full-time tuition and fees vary according to course load and degree level. Room and board charges vary according to housing facility. **Part-time tuition:** $50 per credit hour. Part-time tuition and fees vary according to course load and degree level.
**FRESHMAN FINANCIAL AID (Fall 2014, est.)** 927 applied for aid; of those 97% were deemed to have need. 100% of freshmen with need received aid; of those 4% had need fully met. **Average percent of need met:** 52% (excluding resources awarded to replace EFC). **Average financial aid package:** $13,856 (excluding resources awarded to replace EFC). 1% of all full-time freshmen had no need and received non-need-based gift aid.
**UNDERGRADUATE FINANCIAL AID (Fall 2014, est.)** 3,243 applied for aid; of those 97% were deemed to have need. 100% of undergraduates with need received aid; of those 5% had need fully met. **Average percent of need met:** 50% (excluding resources awarded to replace EFC). **Average financial aid package:** $13,672 (excluding resources awarded to replace EFC). 1% of all full-time undergraduates had no need and received non-need-based gift aid.
**GIFT AID (NEED-BASED)** *Total amount:* $30,818,176 (51% federal, 26% state, 21% institutional, 2% external sources). **Receiving aid:** Freshmen: 96% (892); all full-time undergraduates: 94% (3,056). **Average award:** Freshmen: $10,571; Undergraduates: $10,070. **Scholarships, grants, and awards:** Federal Pell, FSEOG, state, private, college/university gift aid from institutional funds, United Negro College Fund.
**GIFT AID (NON-NEED-BASED)** *Total amount:* $1,011,332 (29% state, 65% institutional, 6% external sources). **Receiving aid:** Freshmen: 3% (32). Undergraduates: 3% (82). **Average award:** Freshmen: $7480. Undergraduates: $8387. **Scholarships, grants, and awards by category:** Academic interests/achievement: 277 awards ($2,023,411 total): general academic interests/achievements. **Tuition waivers:** Full or partial for employees or children of employees. **ROTC:** Army cooperative, Air Force cooperative.
**LOANS** *Student loans:* $29,569,821 (95% need-based, 5% non-need-based). 95% of past graduating class borrowed through all loan programs. *Average indebtedness per student:* $23,525. **Average need-based loan:** Freshmen: $3633. Undergraduates: $4072. **Parent loans:** $6,975,388 (82% need-based, 18% non-need-based). **Programs:** Federal Direct (Subsidized and Unsubsidized Stafford, PLUS), alternative loans.
**WORK-STUDY** *Federal work-study:* Total amount: $513,160; 200 jobs averaging $2500. **State or other work-study/employment:** 100 part-time jobs averaging $2000.
**ATHLETIC AWARDS** Total amount: $3,408,041 (89% need-based, 11% non-need-based).
**APPLYING FOR FINANCIAL AID** *Required financial aid form:* FAFSA. *Financial aid deadline (priority):* 4/1. *Notification date:* Continuous beginning 4/1. Students must reply within 3 weeks of notification.
**CONTACT** Mr. Calvin Davis, Director of Financial Aid, Bethune-Cookman University, 640 Dr. Mary McLeod Bethune Boulevard, Daytona Beach, FL 32114-3099, 386-481-2781 or toll-free 800-448-0228. *Fax:* 386-481-2621. *E-mail:* davisca@cookman.edu.
*Website:* http://www.cookman.edu/.

# BEULAH HEIGHTS UNIVERSITY
## Atlanta, GA

**CONTACT** Ms. Patricia Banks, Director of Financial Aid, Beulah Heights University, 892 Berne Street, SE, Atlanta, GA 30316, 404-627-2681 or toll-free 888-777-BHBC. *Fax:* 404-627-0702. *E-mail:* pat.banks@beulah.org.
*Website:* http://www.beulah.org/.

# BINGHAMTON UNIVERSITY, STATE UNIVERSITY OF NEW YORK
## Vestal, NY

| Tuition & fees (NY res): $8620 | Average undergraduate aid package: $12,449 |
|---|---|

**ABOUT THE INSTITUTION** State-supported, coed. *Awards:* certificates, bachelor's, master's, and doctoral degrees. 76 undergraduate majors. *Total enrollment:* 16,695. Undergraduates: 13,412. Freshmen: 2,602. Federal methodology is used as a basis for awarding need-based institutional aid.

**UNDERGRADUATE EXPENSES for 2015–2016 Application fee:** $50. *Tuition, state resident:* full-time $6170; part-time $257 per credit hour. *Tuition, nonresident:* full-time $17,810; part-time $742 per credit hour. *Required fees:* full-time $2450; $100.60 per credit hour or $24.50 per term. Full-time tuition and fees vary according to program. Part-time tuition and fees vary according to course load and program. *College room and board:* $13,028. Room and board charges vary according to board plan and housing facility.

**FRESHMAN FINANCIAL AID (Fall 2014, est.)** 2,053 applied for aid; of those 60% were deemed to have need. 100% of freshmen with need received aid; of those 12% had need fully met. *Average percent of need met:* 63% (excluding resources awarded to replace EFC). *Average financial aid package:* $11,236 (excluding resources awarded to replace EFC). 2% of all full-time freshmen had no need and received non-need-based gift aid.

**UNDERGRADUATE FINANCIAL AID (Fall 2014, est.)** 8,776 applied for aid; of those 72% were deemed to have need. 100% of undergraduates with need received aid; of those 15% had need fully met. *Average percent of need met:* 72% (excluding resources awarded to replace EFC). *Average financial aid package:* $12,449 (excluding resources awarded to replace EFC). 3% of all full-time undergraduates had no need and received non-need-based gift aid.

**GIFT AID (NEED-BASED) Total amount:** $42,506,423 (44% federal, 48% state, 6% institutional, 2% external sources) *Receiving aid:* Freshmen: 40% (1,004); all full-time undergraduates: 41% (5,285). *Average award:* Freshmen: $8453; Undergraduates: $8065. *Scholarships, grants, and awards:* Federal Pell, FSEOG, state, private, college/university gift aid from institutional funds.

**GIFT AID (NON-NEED-BASED) Total amount:** $3,188,004 (49% state, 28% institutional, 23% external sources). *Receiving aid:* Freshmen: 6% (150). Undergraduates: 3% (381). *Average award:* Freshmen: $6905. Undergraduates: $7237. *Scholarships, grants, and awards by category: Academic interests/achievement:* 373 awards ($1,333,035 total): area/ethnic studies, biological sciences, business, computer science, education, engineering/technologies, English, foreign languages, general academic interests/achievements, health fields, humanities, international studies, mathematics, physical sciences, premedicine, social sciences. *Creative arts/performance:* 14 awards ($15,000 total): art/fine arts, cinema/film/broadcasting, creative writing, dance, general creative arts/performance, journalism/publications, music, performing arts, theater/drama. *Special achievements/activities:* 66 awards ($116,290 total): community service, general special achievements/activities, leadership. *Special characteristics:* 82 awards ($279,750 total): adult students, children and siblings of alumni, children of faculty/staff, ethnic background, first-generation college students, handicapped students, international students, local/state students, married students, members of minority groups, out-of-state students, veterans, veterans' children. *ROTC:* Army cooperative, Air Force cooperative.

**LOANS Student loans:** $75,178,548 (74% need-based, 26% non-need-based). 53% of past graduating class borrowed through all loan programs. *Average indebtedness per student:* $25,727. *Average need-based loan:* Freshmen: $3769. Undergraduates: $4971. *Parent loans:* $14,833,732 (72% need-based, 28% non-need-based). *Programs:* Federal Direct (Subsidized and Unsubsidized Stafford, PLUS), Perkins, Federal Nursing, college/university.

**WORK-STUDY Federal work-study:** Total amount: $500,000; 302 jobs averaging $1450.

**ATHLETIC AWARDS** Total amount: $4,470,735 (100% non-need-based).

**APPLYING FOR FINANCIAL AID Required financial aid forms:** FAFSA, state aid form. *Financial aid deadline (priority):* 2/1. *Notification date:* Continuous beginning 3/4. Students must reply within 2 weeks of notification.

**CONTACT** Mr. Dennis Chavez, Director of Student Financial Aid and Student Records, Binghamton University, State University of New York, PO Box 6000, Binghamton, NY 13902-6000, 607-777-2428. *Fax:* 607-777-6897. *E-mail:* finaid@binghamton.edu.
*Website:* http://www.binghamton.edu/.

# BIOLA UNIVERSITY
## La Mirada, CA

| Tuition & fees: $34,498 | Average undergraduate aid package: $18,515 |
|---|---|

**ABOUT THE INSTITUTION** Independent interdenominational, coed. *Awards:* certificates, bachelor's, master's, and doctoral degrees. 98 undergraduate majors. *Total enrollment:* 6,358. Undergraduates: 4,373. Freshmen: 944. Both federal and institutional methodology are used as a basis for awarding need-based institutional aid.

**UNDERGRADUATE EXPENSES for 2015–2016 Application fee:** $55. *Tuition:* full-time $34,498; part-time $1438 per unit. Room and board charges vary according to board plan, housing facility, and location.

**FRESHMAN FINANCIAL AID (Fall 2013)** 769 applied for aid; of those 80% were deemed to have need. 99% of freshmen with need received aid; of those 9% had need fully met. *Average percent of need met:* 51% (excluding resources awarded to replace EFC). *Average financial aid package:* $18,380 (excluding resources awarded to replace EFC). 25% of all full-time freshmen had no need and received non-need-based gift aid.

**UNDERGRADUATE FINANCIAL AID (Fall 2013)** 3,246 applied for aid; of those 88% were deemed to have need. 99% of undergraduates with need received aid; of those 6% had need fully met. *Average percent of need met:* 49% (excluding resources awarded to replace EFC). *Average financial aid package:* $18,515 (excluding resources awarded to replace EFC). 22% of all full-time undergraduates had no need and received non-need-based gift aid.

**GIFT AID (NEED-BASED) Total amount:** $37,070,635 (16% federal, 19% state, 65% institutional). *Receiving aid:* Freshmen: 68% (604); all full-time undergraduates: 67% (2,763). *Average award:* Freshmen: $14,007; Undergraduates: $13,164. *Scholarships, grants, and awards:* Federal Pell, FSEOG, state, private, college/university gift aid from institutional funds.

**GIFT AID (NON-NEED-BASED) Total amount:** $6,925,348 (100% institutional). *Receiving aid:* Freshmen: 4% (37). Undergraduates: 2% (98). *Average award:* Freshmen: $8289. Undergraduates: $7028. *Scholarships, grants, and awards by category: Academic interests/achievement:* 2,202 awards: biological sciences, communication, general academic interests/achievements. *Creative arts/performance:* 257 awards: cinema/film/broadcasting, journalism/publications, music, theater/drama. *Special achievements/activities:* 76 awards: community service, leadership. *Special characteristics:* 318 awards: children of faculty/staff, ethnic background, international students, members of minority groups, relatives of clergy. *ROTC:* Army cooperative, Air Force cooperative.

**LOANS Student loans:** $26,594,757 (79% need-based, 21% non-need-based). 68% of past graduating class borrowed through all loan programs. *Average indebtedness per student:* $34,107. *Average need-based loan:* Freshmen: $3131. Undergraduates: $3751. *Parent loans:* $12,393,606 (56% need-based, 44% non-need-based). *Programs:* Federal Direct (Subsidized and Unsubsidized Stafford, PLUS), Perkins, Federal Nursing, college/university, alternative loans.

**WORK-STUDY Federal work-study:** 324 jobs averaging $1475.

**ATHLETIC AWARDS** Total amount: $2,003,309 (62% need-based, 38% non-need-based).

**APPLYING FOR FINANCIAL AID Required financial aid forms:** FAFSA, state aid form. *Financial aid deadline (priority):* 3/1. *Notification date:* Continuous beginning 3/1.

**CONTACT** Office of Financial Aid, Biola University, 13800 Biola Avenue, La Mirada, CA 90639-0001, 562-903-4742 or toll-free 800-652-4652. *Fax:* 562-906-4541. *E-mail:* finaid@biola.edu.
*Website:* http://www.biola.edu/.

# BIRMINGHAM-SOUTHERN COLLEGE
## Birmingham, AL

| Tuition & fees: $33,128 | Average undergraduate aid package: $30,038 |
|---|---|

**ABOUT THE INSTITUTION** Independent Methodist, coed. *Awards:* bachelor's degrees. 42 undergraduate majors. *Total enrollment:* 1,231. Undergraduates: 1,231. Freshmen: 327. Federal methodology is used as a basis for awarding need-based institutional aid.

**UNDERGRADUATE EXPENSES for 2015–2016** *Application fee:* $40. *One-time required fee:* $200. *Comprehensive fee:* $44,478 includes full-time tuition ($31,954), mandatory fees ($1174), and room and board ($11,350). *College room only:* $6600. Full-time tuition and fees vary according to program and reciprocity agreements. Room and board charges vary according to board plan and housing facility. Part-time tuition and fees vary according to course load, program, and reciprocity agreements.

**FRESHMAN FINANCIAL AID (Fall 2014, est.)** 272 applied for aid; of those 76% were deemed to have need. 100% of freshmen with need received aid; of those 34% had need fully met. *Average percent of need met:* 75% (excluding resources awarded to replace EFC). *Average financial aid package:* $29,063 (excluding resources awarded to replace EFC). 41% of all full-time freshmen had no need and received non-need-based gift aid.

**UNDERGRADUATE FINANCIAL AID (Fall 2014, est.)** 812 applied for aid; of those 79% were deemed to have need. 100% of undergraduates with need received aid; of those 31% had need fully met. *Average percent of need met:* 82% (excluding resources awarded to replace EFC). *Average financial aid package:* $30,038 (excluding resources awarded to replace EFC). 43% of all full-time undergraduates had no need and received non-need-based gift aid.

**GIFT AID (NEED-BASED)** *Total amount:* $5,200,120 (22% federal, 1% state, 77% institutional). *Receiving aid:* Freshmen: 40% (140); all full-time undergraduates: 42% (492). *Average award:* Freshmen: $6901; Undergraduates: $10,098. *Scholarships, grants, and awards:* Federal Pell, FSEOG, state, private, college/university gift aid from institutional funds.

**GIFT AID (NON-NEED-BASED)** *Total amount:* $21,160,294 (1% state, 98% institutional, 1% external sources). *Receiving aid:* Freshmen: 59% (207). Undergraduates: 53% (629). *Average award:* Freshmen: $21,525. Undergraduates: $18,073. *Scholarships, grants, and awards by category: Academic interests/achievement:* area/ethnic studies, biological sciences, business, communication, computer science, education, engineering/technologies, English, foreign languages, general academic interests/achievements, health fields, humanities, international studies, mathematics, physical sciences, premedicine, religion/biblical studies, social sciences. *Creative arts/performance:* art/fine arts, dance, music, performing arts, theater/drama. *Special achievements/activities:* junior miss, leadership, memberships, religious involvement. *Special characteristics:* adult students, children and siblings of alumni, children of faculty/staff, ethnic background, first-generation college students, general special characteristics, international students, local/state students, previous college experience, relatives of clergy, religious affiliation, veterans, veterans' children. *Tuition waivers:* Full or partial for employees or children of employees. *ROTC:* Army cooperative, Air Force cooperative.

**LOANS** *Student loans:* $6,595,109 (37% need-based, 63% non-need-based). 50% of past graduating class borrowed through all loan programs. *Average indebtedness per student:* $31,872. *Average need-based loan:* Freshmen: $4155. Undergraduates: $5015. *Parent loans:* $1,861,782 (100% non-need-based). *Programs:* Federal Direct (Subsidized and Unsubsidized Stafford, PLUS), Perkins, college/university.

**WORK-STUDY** *Federal work-study:* Total amount: $237,333; 169 jobs averaging $1250. *State or other work-study/employment:* Total amount: $163,426 (25% need-based, 75% non-need-based). 65 part-time jobs averaging $1250.

**APPLYING FOR FINANCIAL AID** *Required financial aid forms:* FAFSA, state aid form. *Financial aid deadline (priority):* 3/1. *Notification date:* 3/1. Students must reply by 5/1.

**CONTACT** Financial Aid Office, Birmingham-Southern College, 900 Arkadelphia Road, Birmingham, AL 35254, 205-226-4688 or toll-free 800-523-5793. *Fax:* 205-226-3082. *E-mail:* finaid@bsc.edu.
*Website:* http://www.bsc.edu/.

# BIRTHINGWAY COLLEGE OF MIDWIFERY
## Portland, OR

**CONTACT** Financial Aid Office, Birthingway College of Midwifery, 12113 SE Foster Road, Portland, OR 97299, 503-760-3131.
*Website:* http://www.birthingway.edu/.

# BLACKBURN COLLEGE
## Carlinville, IL

**CONTACT** Mrs. Jane Kelsey, Financial Aid Administrator, Blackburn College, 700 College Avenue, Carlinville, IL 62626-1498, 217-854-3231 Ext. 4227 or toll-free 800-233-3550. *Fax:* 217-854-3731.
*Website:* http://www.blackburn.edu/.

# BLACK HILLS STATE UNIVERSITY
## Spearfish, SD

**CONTACT** Ms. Deb Henriksen, Director of Financial Aid, Black Hills State University, 1200 University Street, Spearfish, SD 57799-9670, 605-642-6581 or toll-free 800-255-2478. *Fax:* 605-642-6913. *E-mail:* deb.henriksen@bhsu.edu.
*Website:* http://www.bhsu.edu/.

# BLESSING-RIEMAN COLLEGE OF NURSING
## Quincy, IL

| Tuition & fees: $21,810 | Average undergraduate aid package: $12,429 |
| --- | --- |

**ABOUT THE INSTITUTION** Independent, coed, primarily women. *Awards:* bachelor's and master's degrees. 1 undergraduate major. *Total enrollment:* 253. Undergraduates: 234. Federal methodology is used as a basis for awarding need-based institutional aid.

**UNDERGRADUATE EXPENSES for 2015–2016** *Tuition:* full-time $21,810; part-time $727 per credit hour. Full-time tuition and fees vary according to course load, degree level, and student level. Part-time tuition and fees vary according to course load, degree level, and student level. Room and board charges vary according to student level.

**UNDERGRADUATE FINANCIAL AID (Fall 2014, est.)** 177 applied for aid; of those 100% were deemed to have need. 100% of undergraduates with need received aid; of those 100% had need fully met. *Average percent of need met:* 100% (excluding resources awarded to replace EFC). *Average financial aid package:* $12,429 (excluding resources awarded to replace EFC).

**GIFT AID (NEED-BASED)** *Total amount:* $1,228,049 (20% federal, 13% state, 57% institutional, 10% external sources). *Receiving aid:* All full-time undergraduates: 100% (177). *Average award:* Undergraduates: $4294. *Scholarships, grants, and awards:* Federal Pell, state, private, college/university gift aid from institutional funds.

**GIFT AID (NON-NEED-BASED)** *Receiving aid:* Undergraduates: 83% (147). *Scholarships, grants, and awards by category: Academic interests/achievement:* general academic interests/achievements.

**LOANS** *Student loans:* $1,017,533 (100% non-need-based). 72% of past graduating class borrowed through all loan programs. *Average indebtedness per student:* $8475. *Parent loans:* $40,545 (100% non-need-based). *Programs:* Federal Direct (Subsidized and Unsubsidized Stafford, PLUS), Federal Nursing, college/university.

**APPLYING FOR FINANCIAL AID** *Required financial aid form:* FAFSA. *Financial aid deadline:* Continuous. *Notification date:* Continuous beginning 4/1.

**CONTACT** Mr. Kevin Turnbull, Financial Aid Coordinator, Blessing-Rieman College of Nursing, Broadway at 11th Street, PO Box 7005, Quincy, IL 62301, 217-223-8400 Ext. 6993 or toll-free 800-877-9140 Ext. 6964. *Fax:* 217-223-1781. *E-mail:* kturnbull@brcn.edu@brcn.edu.
*Website:* http://www.brcn.edu/.

# BLOOMFIELD COLLEGE
Bloomfield, NJ

| Tuition & fees: $27,800 | Average undergraduate aid package: $20,634 |
|---|---|

**ABOUT THE INSTITUTION** Independent Presbyterian Church (U.S.A.), coed. *Awards:* certificates, bachelor's, and master's degrees. 21 undergraduate majors. *Total enrollment:* 2,012. Undergraduates: 2,007. Freshmen: 447. Federal methodology is used as a basis for awarding need-based institutional aid.

**UNDERGRADUATE EXPENSES for 2015–2016** *Application fee:* $40. *Comprehensive fee:* $39,100 includes full-time tuition ($27,800) and room and board ($11,300). *College room only:* $5650. Full-time tuition and fees vary according to degree level. Room and board charges vary according to housing facility. *Part-time tuition:* $3475 per course. Part-time tuition and fees vary according to course load and degree level.

**FRESHMAN FINANCIAL AID (Fall 2014, est.)** 431 applied for aid; of those 97% were deemed to have need. 100% of freshmen with need received aid; of those 8% had need fully met. *Average percent of need met:* 25% (excluding resources awarded to replace EFC). *Average financial aid package:* $23,014 (excluding resources awarded to replace EFC). 3% of all full-time freshmen had no need and received non-need-based gift aid.

**UNDERGRADUATE FINANCIAL AID (Fall 2014, est.)** 1,658 applied for aid; of those 93% were deemed to have need. 100% of undergraduates with need received aid; of those 9% had need fully met. *Average percent of need met:* 25% (excluding resources awarded to replace EFC). *Average financial aid package:* $20,634 (excluding resources awarded to replace EFC). 6% of all full-time undergraduates had no need and received non-need-based gift aid.

**GIFT AID (NEED-BASED)** *Total amount:* $27,936,745 (23% federal, 39% state, 38% institutional). *Receiving aid:* Freshmen: 96% (415); all full-time undergraduates: 91% (1,522). *Average award:* Freshmen: $19,745; Undergraduates: $17,229. *Scholarships, grants, and awards:* Federal Pell, FSEOG, state, private, college/university gift aid from institutional funds.

**GIFT AID (NON-NEED-BASED)** *Total amount:* $3,926,577 (96% institutional, 4% external sources). *Receiving aid:* Freshmen: 31% (133). Undergraduates: 34% (566). *Average award:* Freshmen: $22,063. Undergraduates: $18,601. *Scholarships, grants, and awards by category:* Academic interests/achievement: 502 awards ($2,931,872 total): biological sciences, business, computer science, education, English, general academic interests/achievements, health fields, humanities, mathematics, physical sciences, religion/biblical studies, social sciences. *Creative arts/performance:* 1 award ($6320 total): applied art and design, art/fine arts; cinema/film/broadcasting, general creative arts/performance, performing arts, theater/drama. *Special achievements/activities:* 347 awards ($2,659,324 total): community service, general special achievements/activities, leadership. *Special characteristics:* 43 awards ($107,181 total): adult students, children and siblings of alumni, children of current students, general special characteristics, international students, out-of-state students, siblings of current students, spouses of current students. *Tuition waivers:* Full or partial for employees or children of employees, senior citizens. *ROTC:* Army cooperative.

**LOANS** *Student loans:* $12,625,722 (49% need-based, 51% non-need-based). 92% of past graduating class borrowed through all loan programs. *Average indebtedness per student:* $33,443. *Average need-based loan:* Freshmen: $3297. Undergraduates: $4056. *Parent loans:* $2,039,883 (100% non-need-based). *Programs:* Federal Direct (Subsidized and Unsubsidized Stafford, PLUS).

**WORK-STUDY** *Federal work-study:* Total amount: $807,774; 365 jobs averaging $2193. *State or other work-study/employment:* Part-time jobs available.

**ATHLETIC AWARDS** Total amount: $1,559,854 (100% non-need-based).

**APPLYING FOR FINANCIAL AID** *Required financial aid form:* FAFSA. *Financial aid deadline:* 6/1 (priority: 3/15). *Notification date:* Continuous beginning 3/15. Students must reply within 2 weeks of notification.

**CONTACT** Ms. Breanne Simkin, Director of Financial Aid, Bloomfield College, 467 Franklin Street, Bloomfield, NJ 07003-9981, 973-748-9000 Ext. 1213 or toll-free 800-848-4555 Ext. 230. *Fax:* 973-748-9735. *E-mail:* breanne_simkin@bloomfield.edu. *Website:* http://www.bloomfield.edu/.

# BLOOMSBURG UNIVERSITY OF PENNSYLVANIA
Bloomsburg, PA

| Tuition & fees (PA res): $8914 | Average undergraduate aid package: $8750 |
|---|---|

**ABOUT THE INSTITUTION** State-supported, coed. *Awards:* certificates, bachelor's, master's, and doctoral degrees. 41 undergraduate majors. *Total enrollment:* 9,998. Undergraduates: 9,319. Freshmen: 2,171. Federal methodology is used as a basis for awarding need-based institutional aid.

**UNDERGRADUATE EXPENSES for 2015–2016** *Application fee:* $35. *Tuition, state resident:* full-time $6820; part-time $284 per credit. *Tuition, non-resident:* full-time $17,050; part-time $710 per credit. *Required fees:* full-time $2094; $76.75 per credit or $75 per term. Full-time tuition and fees vary according to course load and location. Part-time tuition and fees vary according to course load and location. *College room and board:* $8168; *Room only:* $5154. Room and board charges vary according to board plan and housing facility.

**FRESHMAN FINANCIAL AID (Fall 2014, est.)** 2,031 applied for aid; of those 74% were deemed to have need. 98% of freshmen with need received aid; of those 8% had need fully met. *Average percent of need met:* 51% (excluding resources awarded to replace EFC). *Average financial aid package:* $8183 (excluding resources awarded to replace EFC). 3% of all full-time freshmen had no need and received non-need-based gift aid.

**UNDERGRADUATE FINANCIAL AID (Fall 2014, est.)** 7,617 applied for aid; of those 73% were deemed to have need. 99% of undergraduates with need received aid; of those 11% had need fully met. *Average percent of need met:* 57% (excluding resources awarded to replace EFC). *Average financial aid package:* $8750 (excluding resources awarded to replace EFC). 2% of all full-time undergraduates had no need and received non-need-based gift aid.

**GIFT AID (NEED-BASED)** *Total amount:* $22,050,538 (60% federal, 38% state, 2% institutional). *Receiving aid:* Freshmen: 44% (943); all full-time undergraduates: 41% (3,485). *Average award:* Freshmen: $6342; Undergraduates: $5835. *Scholarships, grants, and awards:* Federal Pell, FSEOG, state, private, college/university gift aid from institutional funds.

**GIFT AID (NON-NEED-BASED)** *Total amount:* $3,217,891 (11% state, 37% institutional, 52% external sources). *Receiving aid:* Freshmen: 16% (341). Undergraduates: 10% (869). *Average award:* Freshmen: $2099. Undergraduates: $1810. *Scholarships, grants, and awards by category:* Academic interests/achievement: 596 awards ($1,032,954 total): biological sciences, business, communication, computer science, education, English, foreign languages, general academic interests/achievements, health fields, humanities, international studies, mathematics, physical sciences, religion/biblical studies, social sciences. *Special characteristics:* 285 awards ($1,023,307 total): children of faculty/staff, international students. *Tuition waivers:* Full or partial for employees or children of employees, senior citizens. *ROTC:* Army, Air Force cooperative.

**LOANS** *Student loans:* $61,630,928 (37% need-based, 63% non-need-based). 75% of past graduating class borrowed through all loan programs. *Average indebtedness per student:* $29,661. *Average need-based loan:* Freshmen: $3333. Undergraduates: $4158. *Parent loans:* $12,086,602 (100% non-need-based). *Programs:* Federal Direct (Subsidized and Unsubsidized Stafford, PLUS), Perkins, state, alternative loans.

**WORK-STUDY** *Federal work-study:* Total amount: $3,260,749; 1,042 jobs averaging $3088. *State or other work-study/employment:* Total amount: $4,862,261 (100% non-need-based). 1,371 part-time jobs averaging $3434.

**ATHLETIC AWARDS** Total amount: $382,181 (100% non-need-based).

**APPLYING FOR FINANCIAL AID** *Required financial aid form:* FAFSA. *Financial aid deadline (priority):* 3/15. *Notification date:* Continuous beginning 4/1.

**CONTACT** Mr. John J. Bieryla, Director of Financial Aid, Bloomsburg University of Pennsylvania, 119 Warren Student Services Center, 400 East 2nd Street, Bloomsburg, PA 17815-1301, 570-389-4279. *Fax:* 570-389-4795. *E-mail:* stfinaid@bloomu.edu. *Website:* http://www.bloomu.edu/.

# BLUEFIELD COLLEGE
## Bluefield, VA

| Tuition & fees: $23,296 | Average undergraduate aid package: $15,576 |
|---|---|

**ABOUT THE INSTITUTION** Independent Southern Baptist, coed. *Awards:* bachelor's and master's degrees. 41 undergraduate majors. *Total enrollment:* 942. Undergraduates: 926. Freshmen: 160. Federal methodology is used as a basis for awarding need-based institutional aid.

**UNDERGRADUATE EXPENSES** for 2015–2016 *Comprehensive fee:* $31,823 includes full-time tuition ($23,296) and room and board ($8527). *College room only:* $3672. Full-time tuition and fees vary according to course load and program. Room and board charges vary according to housing facility. *Part-time tuition:* $953 per credit. Part-time tuition and fees vary according to course load and program.

**FRESHMAN FINANCIAL AID (Fall 2014, est.)** 156 applied for aid; of those 94% were deemed to have need. 100% of freshmen with need received aid; of those 13% had need fully met. *Average percent of need met:* 62% (excluding resources awarded to replace EFC). *Average financial aid package:* $18,720 (excluding resources awarded to replace EFC). 8% of all full-time freshmen had no need and received non-need-based gift aid.

**UNDERGRADUATE FINANCIAL AID (Fall 2014, est.)** 671 applied for aid; of those 96% were deemed to have need. 100% of undergraduates with need received aid; of those 9% had need fully met. *Average percent of need met:* 54% (excluding resources awarded to replace EFC). *Average financial aid package:* $15,576 (excluding resources awarded to replace EFC). 9% of all full-time undergraduates had no need and received non-need-based gift aid.

**GIFT AID (NEED-BASED)** *Total amount:* $6,160,536 (30% federal, 21% state, 40% institutional, 9% external sources). *Receiving aid:* Freshmen: 93% (147); all full-time undergraduates: 88% (638). *Average award:* Freshmen: $15,598; Undergraduates: $11,647. *Scholarships, grants, and awards:* Federal Pell, FSEOG, state, private, college/university gift aid from institutional funds.

**GIFT AID (NON-NEED-BASED)** *Total amount:* $794,380 (23% state, 68% institutional, 9% external sources). *Receiving aid:* Freshmen: 9% (15). Undergraduates: 7% (48). *Average award:* Freshmen: $7458. Undergraduates: $6975. *Scholarships, grants, and awards by category:* Academic interests/achievement: general academic interests/achievements. Creative arts/performance: 51 awards ($142,600 total): art/fine arts, music, performing arts, theater/drama. Special achievements/activities: 2 awards ($8000 total): cheerleading/drum major. Special characteristics: 110 awards ($289,464 total): adult students, children of faculty/staff, first-generation college students, general special characteristics, local/state students, out-of-state students, religious affiliation, veterans, veterans' children. *Tuition waivers:* Full or partial for employees or children of employees, senior citizens.

**LOANS** *Student loans:* $5,814,081 (90% need-based, 10% non-need-based). 86% of past graduating class borrowed through all loan programs. *Average indebtedness per student:* $24,344. *Average need-based loan:* Freshmen: $3460. Undergraduates: $4376. *Parent loans:* $695,687 (58% need-based, 42% non-need-based). *Programs:* Federal Direct (Subsidized and Unsubsidized Stafford, PLUS), alternative loans.

**WORK-STUDY** *Federal work-study:* Total amount: $61,900; 73 jobs averaging $856. *State or other work-study/employment:* Total amount: $7000 (54% need-based, 46% non-need-based). 16 part-time jobs averaging $469.

**ATHLETIC AWARDS** Total amount: $1,945,871 (75% need-based, 25% non-need-based).

**APPLYING FOR FINANCIAL AID** *Required financial aid forms:* FAFSA, state aid form. *Financial aid deadline (priority):* 6/1. *Notification date:* Continuous. Students must reply by 8/24.

**CONTACT** Ms. Carly Jean Kestner, Director of Financial Aid, Bluefield College, 3000 College Drive, Bluefield, VA 24605, 276-326-4215 or toll-free 800-872-0175. *Fax:* 276-326-4356. *E-mail:* ckestner@bluefield.edu. *Website:* http://www.bluefield.edu/.

# BLUEFIELD STATE COLLEGE
## Bluefield, WV

| Tuition & fees (WV res): $5832 | Average undergraduate aid package: $3600 |
|---|---|

**ABOUT THE INSTITUTION** State-supported, coed. *Awards:* associate and bachelor's degrees. 18 undergraduate majors. *Total enrollment:* 1,563. Undergraduates: 1,563. Freshmen: 242. Federal methodology is used as a basis for awarding need-based institutional aid.

**UNDERGRADUATE EXPENSES** for 2015–2016 *Tuition, state resident:* full-time $5832; part-time $243 per credit hour. *Tuition, nonresident:* full-time $11,064; part-time $460 per credit hour.

**FRESHMAN FINANCIAL AID (Fall 2014, est.)** 290 applied for aid; of those 81% were deemed to have need. 95% of freshmen with need received aid; of those 16% had need fully met. *Average percent of need met:* 65% (excluding resources awarded to replace EFC). *Average financial aid package:* $3300 (excluding resources awarded to replace EFC). 1% of all full-time freshmen had no need and received non-need-based gift aid.

**UNDERGRADUATE FINANCIAL AID (Fall 2014, est.)** 1,300 applied for aid; of those 92% were deemed to have need. 95% of undergraduates with need received aid; of those 13% had need fully met. *Average percent of need met:* 68% (excluding resources awarded to replace EFC). *Average financial aid package:* $3600 (excluding resources awarded to replace EFC). 1% of all full-time undergraduates had no need and received non-need-based gift aid.

**GIFT AID (NEED-BASED)** *Total amount:* $5,835,207 (76% federal, 24% state). *Receiving aid:* Freshmen: 67% (200); all full-time undergraduates: 62% (1,000). *Average award:* Freshmen: $3800; Undergraduates: $3800. *Scholarships, grants, and awards:* Federal Pell, FSEOG, state.

**GIFT AID (NON-NEED-BASED)** *Total amount:* $1,261,113 (42% state, 22% institutional, 36% external sources). *Receiving aid:* Freshmen: 23% (70). Undergraduates: 11% (180). *Average award:* Freshmen: $900. Undergraduates: $900. *Scholarships, grants, and awards by category:* Academic interests/achievement: engineering/technologies, general academic interests/achievements. Special achievements/activities: cheerleading/drum major, general special achievements/activities, junior miss, leadership. Special characteristics: general special characteristics. *Tuition waivers:* Full or partial for adult students, senior citizens.

**LOANS** *Student loans:* $7,999,172 (45% need-based, 55% non-need-based). 72% of past graduating class borrowed through all loan programs. *Average indebtedness per student:* $27,000. *Average need-based loan:* Freshmen: $3400. Undergraduates: $4300. *Parent loans:* $80,000 (100% non-need-based). *Programs:* Federal Direct (Subsidized and Unsubsidized Stafford, PLUS).

**WORK-STUDY** *Federal work-study:* Total amount: $130,000; 51 jobs averaging $2600. *State or other work-study/employment:* Total amount: $312,000 (100% non-need-based). Part-time jobs available.

**ATHLETIC AWARDS** Total amount: $375,000 (100% non-need-based).

**APPLYING FOR FINANCIAL AID** *Required financial aid forms:* FAFSA, institution's own form. *Financial aid deadline (priority):* 3/1. *Notification date:* 6/1.

**CONTACT** Mr. Tom Ilse, Director of Financial Aid, Bluefield State College, 219 Rock Street, Bluefield, WV 24701-2198, 304-327-4020 or toll-free 800-344-8892 Ext. 4065 (in-state), 800-654-7798 Ext. 4065 (out-of-state). *Fax:* 304-325-7747. *E-mail:* tilse@bluefieldstate.edu. *Website:* http://www.bluefieldstate.edu/.

# BLUE MOUNTAIN COLLEGE
## Blue Mountain, MS

| Tuition & fees: $10,534 | Average undergraduate aid package: $10,156 |
|---|---|

**ABOUT THE INSTITUTION** Independent Southern Baptist, coed. *Awards:* bachelor's and master's degrees. 23 undergraduate majors. *Total enrollment:* 544. Undergraduates: 520. Freshmen: 76. Federal methodology is used as a basis for awarding need-based institutional aid.

**UNDERGRADUATE EXPENSES** for 2015–2016 *Application fee:* $10. *Comprehensive fee:* $15,334 includes full-time tuition ($9240), mandatory fees ($1294), and room and board ($4800). Full-time tuition and fees vary according to course load, degree level, and program. Room and board charges vary according to gender, housing facility, and location. *Part-time tuition:* $308 per hour. *Part-time fees:* $509 per term. Part-time tuition and fees vary according to course load, degree level, and program.

**FRESHMAN FINANCIAL AID (Fall 2014, est.)** 109 applied for aid; of those 100% were deemed to have need. 100% of freshmen with need received aid; of those 36% had need fully met. *Average percent of need met:* 67% (excluding resources awarded to replace EFC). *Average financial aid package:* $12,451 (excluding resources awarded to replace EFC). 26% of all full-time freshmen had no need and received non-need-based gift aid.

**UNDERGRADUATE FINANCIAL AID (Fall 2014, est.)** 451 applied for aid; of those 83% were deemed to have need. 100% of undergraduates with need received aid; of those 87% had need fully met. *Average percent of need met:* 59% (excluding resources awarded to replace EFC). *Average financial aid package:* $10,156 (excluding resources awarded to replace EFC). 83% of all full-time undergraduates had no need and received non-need-based gift aid.

**GIFT AID (NEED-BASED)** *Total amount:* $2,287,972 (47% federal, 10% state, 43% institutional). *Receiving aid:* Freshmen: 55% (60); all full-time undergraduates: 56% (259). *Average award:* Freshmen: $4923; Undergraduates: $3700. *Scholarships, grants, and awards:* Federal Pell, FSEOG, state, private, college/university gift aid from institutional funds.

**GIFT AID (NON-NEED-BASED)** *Total amount:* $1,853,506 (52% federal, 38% institutional, 10% external sources). *Receiving aid:* Freshmen: 2% (2). Undergraduates: 33% (152). *Average award:* Freshmen: $4973. Undergraduates: $2616. *Scholarships, grants, and awards by category:* Academic interests/achievement: biological sciences, business, education, English, general academic interests/achievements, health fields, humanities, library science, mathematics, physical sciences, premedicine, religion/biblical studies, social sciences. *Creative arts/performance:* art/fine arts, music, theater/drama. *Special achievements/activities:* general special achievements/activities, leadership, memberships, religious involvement. *Special characteristics:* children and siblings of alumni, children of current students, children of faculty/staff, married students, parents of current students, religious affiliation, siblings of current students, spouses of current students, twins. *Tuition waivers:* Full or partial for employees or children of employees.

**LOANS** *Student loans:* $1,988,309 (55% need-based, 45% non-need-based). 71% of past graduating class borrowed through all loan programs. *Average indebtedness per student:* $24,571. *Average need-based loan:* Freshmen: $3190. Undergraduates: $5005. *Parent loans:* $124,445 (100% non-need-based). *Programs:* Federal Direct (Subsidized and Unsubsidized Stafford, PLUS), Perkins.

**WORK-STUDY** *Federal work-study:* Total amount: $49,152; 49 jobs averaging $812. *State or other work-study/employment:* Total amount: $55,000 (100% non-need-based). 52 part-time jobs averaging $834.

**ATHLETIC AWARDS** Total amount: $859,529 (100% non-need-based).

**APPLYING FOR FINANCIAL AID** *Required financial aid forms:* FAFSA, state aid form. *Financial aid deadline (priority):* 3/1. *Notification date:* Continuous beginning 4/1. Students must reply within 2 weeks of notification.

**CONTACT** Mrs. Michelle L. Hall, Director of Financial Aid, Blue Mountain College, PO Box 160, Blue Mountain, MS 38610-0160, 662-685-4771 Ext. 141 or toll-free 800-235-0136. *Fax:* 662-685-4776. *E-mail:* financialaid@bmc.edu. *Website:* http://www.bmc.edu/.

# BLUFFTON UNIVERSITY
## Bluffton, OH

| Tuition & fees: $29,316 | Average undergraduate aid package: $27,372 |
| --- | --- |

**ABOUT THE INSTITUTION** Independent Mennonite, coed. *Awards:* certificates, bachelor's, and master's degrees. 39 undergraduate majors. *Total enrollment:* 1,094. Undergraduates: 997. Freshmen: 218. Both federal and institutional methodology are used as a basis for awarding need-based institutional aid.

**UNDERGRADUATE EXPENSES** for 2015–2016 *Application fee:* $20. *Comprehensive fee:* $39,148 includes full-time tuition ($28,866), mandatory fees ($450), and room and board ($9832). Full-time tuition and fees vary according to course load and reciprocity agreements. Room and board charges vary according to board plan and housing facility. *Part-time tuition:* $1203 per credit hour. *Part-time fees:* $113 per term. Part-time tuition and fees vary according to course load.

**FRESHMAN FINANCIAL AID (Fall 2014, est.)** 212 applied for aid; of those 97% were deemed to have need. 100% of freshmen with need received aid; of those 42% had need fully met. *Average percent of need met:* 92% (excluding resources awarded to replace EFC). *Average financial aid package:* $28,765 (excluding resources awarded to replace EFC). 6% of all full-time freshmen had no need and received non-need-based gift aid.

**UNDERGRADUATE FINANCIAL AID (Fall 2014, est.)** 703 applied for aid; of those 95% were deemed to have need. 100% of undergraduates with need received aid; of those 48% had need fully met. *Average percent of need met:* 91% (excluding resources awarded to replace EFC). *Average financial aid package:* $27,372 (excluding resources awarded to replace EFC). 9% of all full-time undergraduates had no need and received non-need-based gift aid.

**GIFT AID (NEED-BASED)** *Total amount:* $12,619,549 (14% federal, 5% state, 76% institutional, 5% external sources). *Receiving aid:* Freshmen: 94% (205); all full-time undergraduates: 85% (669). *Average award:* Freshmen: $22,697; Undergraduates: $20,652. *Scholarships, grants, and awards:* Federal Pell, FSEOG, state, private, college/university gift aid from institutional funds.

**GIFT AID (NON-NEED-BASED)** *Total amount:* $2,227,115 (93% institutional, 7% external sources). *Receiving aid:* Freshmen: 7% (16). Undergraduates: 8% (62). *Average award:* Freshmen: $12,912. Undergraduates: $14,013. *Scholarships, grants, and awards by category:* Academic interests/achievement: 629 awards ($6,969,901 total): biological sciences, general academic interests/achievements, mathematics, physical sciences, premedicine. *Creative arts/performance:* 70 awards ($157,000 total): art/fine arts, music, performing arts. *Special achievements/activities:* 3 awards ($9000 total): leadership. *Special characteristics:* 386 awards ($1,137,559 total): children and siblings of alumni, children of faculty/staff, international students, members of minority groups, out-of-state students, religious affiliation. *Tuition waivers:* Full or partial for employees or children of employees.

**LOANS** *Student loans:* $7,572,306 (94% need-based, 6% non-need-based). 82% of past graduating class borrowed through all loan programs. *Average indebtedness per student:* $35,883. *Average need-based loan:* Freshmen: $4397. Undergraduates: $4910. *Parent loans:* $1,845,922 (71% need-based, 29% non-need-based). *Programs:* Federal Direct (Subsidized and Unsubsidized Stafford, PLUS), Perkins, alternative loans.

**WORK-STUDY** *Federal work-study:* Total amount: $1,236,790; 537 jobs averaging $2290. *State or other work-study/employment:* Total amount: $491,925 (64% need-based, 36% non-need-based). 200 part-time jobs averaging $2423.

**APPLYING FOR FINANCIAL AID** *Required financial aid form:* FAFSA. *Financial aid deadline:* 10/1 (priority: 5/1). *Notification date:* Continuous beginning 3/1. Students must reply within 3 weeks of notification.

**CONTACT** Chris Fowler, Director of Financial Aid, Bluffton University, 1 University Drive, Bluffton, OH 45817-2104, 419-358-3266 or toll-free 800-488-3257. *Fax:* 419-358-3073. *E-mail:* fowlerc@bluffton.edu. *Website:* http://www.bluffton.edu/.

# BOB JONES UNIVERSITY
## Greenville, SC

| Tuition & fees: $14,220 | Average undergraduate aid package: N/A |
| --- | --- |

**ABOUT THE INSTITUTION** Independent Christian, coed. *Awards:* certificates, associate, bachelor's, master's, and doctoral degrees. 48 undergraduate majors. *Total enrollment:* 3,108. Undergraduates: 2,721. Freshmen: 610. Federal methodology is used as a basis for awarding need-based institutional aid.

**UNDERGRADUATE EXPENSES** for 2015–2016 *Comprehensive fee:* $20,310 includes full-time tuition ($13,570), mandatory fees ($650), and room and board ($6090). Full-time tuition and fees vary according to course load and program. *Part-time tuition:* $680 per credit hour. Part-time tuition and fees vary according to course load and program.

**UNDERGRADUATE FINANCIAL AID (Fall 2013)** 1,502 applied for aid; of those 100% were deemed to have need. 100% of undergraduates with need received aid; of those 36% had need fully met. *Average percent of need met:* 24% (excluding resources awarded to replace EFC).

**GIFT AID (NEED-BASED)** *Total amount:* $13,400,000 (37% federal, 11% state, 45% institutional, 7% external sources). *Receiving aid:* All full-time undergraduates: 100% (1,502). *Scholarships, grants, and awards:* Federal Pell, FSEOG, state, private, college/university gift aid from institutional funds.

**GIFT AID (NON-NEED-BASED)** *Total amount:* $2,200,000 (100% state). *Receiving aid:* Undergraduates: 39% (590). *Tuition waivers:* Full or partial for employees or children of employees, senior citizens.

**LOANS** *Student loans:* $6,500,000 (100% need-based). *Parent loans:* $850,000 (100% non-need-based). *Programs:* Federal Direct (Subsidized and Unsubsidized Stafford, PLUS), college/university.

**WORK-STUDY** *Federal work-study:* jobs available. *State or other work-study/employment:* Part-time jobs available.

**APPLYING FOR FINANCIAL AID** *Required financial aid form:* FAFSA. *Financial aid deadline:* Continuous. *Notification date:* Continuous.

**CONTACT** Office of Financial Aid, Bob Jones University, 1700 Wade Hampton Boulevard, Greenville, SC 29614, 864-242-5100 Ext. 3040 or toll-free 800-252-6363. *E-mail:* finaid@bju.edu. *Website:* http://www.bju.edu/.

# BOISE BIBLE COLLEGE
## Boise, ID

**CONTACT** Beth Turner, Financial Aid Counselor, Boise Bible College, 8695 West Marigold Street, Boise, ID 83714-1220, 208-376-7731 Ext. 12 or toll-free 800-893-7755. *Fax:* 208-376-7743. *E-mail:* betht@boisebible.edu. *Website:* http://www.boisebible.edu/.

# BOISE STATE UNIVERSITY
## Boise, ID

| Tuition & fees (ID res): $6640 | Average undergraduate aid package: $8912 |
|---|---|

**ABOUT THE INSTITUTION** State-supported, coed. *Awards:* certificates, associate, bachelor's, master's, and doctoral degrees. 89 undergraduate majors. *Total enrollment:* 21,981. Undergraduates: 19,026. Freshmen: 2,194. Federal methodology is used as a basis for awarding need-based institutional aid.

**UNDERGRADUATE EXPENSES** for 2015–2016 *Application fee:* $60. *One-time required fee:* $175. *Tuition, state resident:* full-time $4620; part-time $169.25 per credit hour. *Tuition, nonresident:* full-time $17,472; part-time $369.25 per credit hour. *Required fees:* full-time $2020; $94.75 per credit hour. Full-time tuition and fees vary according to course load and reciprocity agreements. Part-time tuition and fees vary according to course load. *College room and board:* $6829; *Room only:* $3609. Room and board charges vary according to board plan and housing facility.

**FRESHMAN FINANCIAL AID (Fall 2013)** 1,316 applied for aid; of those 97% were deemed to have need. 99% of freshmen with need received aid; of those 18% had need fully met. *Average percent of need met:* 61% (excluding resources awarded to replace EFC). *Average financial aid package:* $8975 (excluding resources awarded to replace EFC). 6% of all full-time freshmen had no need and received non-need-based gift aid.

**UNDERGRADUATE FINANCIAL AID (Fall 2013)** 8,020 applied for aid; of those 97% were deemed to have need. 97% of undergraduates with need received aid; of those 9% had need fully met. *Average percent of need met:* 57% (excluding resources awarded to replace EFC). *Average financial aid package:* $8912 (excluding resources awarded to replace EFC). 5% of all full-time undergraduates had no need and received non-need-based gift aid.

**GIFT AID (NEED-BASED)** *Total amount:* $35,074,402 (77% federal, 4% state, 12% institutional, 7% external sources). *Receiving aid:* Freshmen: 46% (1,011); all full-time undergraduates: 48% (5,938). *Average award:* Freshmen: $4697; Undergraduates: $4827. *Scholarships, grants, and awards:* Federal Pell, FSEOG, state, private, college/university gift aid from institutional funds, Federal Nursing, Leveraging Educational Assistance Program (LEAP).

**GIFT AID (NON-NEED-BASED)** *Total amount:* $1,762,232 (4% federal, 14% state, 52% institutional, 30% external sources). *Receiving aid:* Freshmen: 5% (105). Undergraduates: 2% (214). *Average award:* Freshmen: $1926. Undergraduates: $1246. *Scholarships, grants, and awards by category:* Academic interests/achievement: biological sciences, business, communication, computer science, education, engineering/technologies, English, foreign languages, general academic interests/achievements, health fields, humanities, international studies, mathematics, military science, physical sciences, premedicine, social sciences. *Creative arts/performance:* art/fine arts, dance, debating, general creative arts/performance, journalism/publications, music, performing arts, theater/drama. *Special achievements/activities:* cheerleading/drum major, community service, leadership, rodeo. *Special characteristics:* ethnic background, first-generation college students, general special characteristics, handicapped students, international students, local/state students, members of minority groups, out-of-state students, previous college experience, spouses of current students, veterans, veterans' children. *Tuition waivers:* Full or partial for employees or children of employees, senior citizens. *ROTC:* Army.

**LOANS** *Student loans:* $73,271,207 (82% need-based, 18% non-need-based). 76% of past graduating class borrowed through all loan programs. *Average indebtedness per student:* $27,024. *Average need-based loan:* Freshmen: $3267. Undergraduates: $4289. *Parent loans:* $4,694,618 (35% need-based, 65% non-need-based). *Programs:* Federal Direct (Subsidized and Unsubsidized Stafford, PLUS), Perkins, Federal Nursing, college/university, Alaska loans.

**WORK-STUDY** *Federal work-study:* 245 jobs averaging $2098. *State or other work-study/employment:* Total amount: $1,276,394 (100% need-based). 203 part-time jobs averaging $3653.

**ATHLETIC AWARDS** Total amount: $6,252,376 (85% need-based, 15% non-need-based).

**APPLYING FOR FINANCIAL AID** *Required financial aid form:* FAFSA. *Financial aid deadline:* 6/30 (priority: 2/15). *Notification date:* Continuous beginning 3/15. Students must reply by 4/12 or within 4 weeks of notification.

**CONTACT** Office of Financial Aid and Scholarships, Boise State University, Administration Building, Room 113, Boise, ID 83725-1315, 800-824-7017. *Fax:* 208-426-1305. *E-mail:* faquest@boisestate.edu. *Website:* http://www.boisestate.edu/.

# BON SECOURS MEMORIAL COLLEGE OF NURSING
## Richmond, VA

**CONTACT** Financial Aid Office, Bon Secours Memorial College of Nursing, 8550 Magellan Parkway, Suite 1100, Richmond, VA 23227-1149, 804-627-5300 or toll-free 866-238-7414. *Website:* http://www.bsmcon.edu/.

# BORICUA COLLEGE
## New York, NY

**CONTACT** Ms. Rosalia Cruz, Financial Aid Administrator, Boricua College, 3755 Broadway, New York, NY 10032-1560, 212-694-1000 Ext. 611. *Fax:* 212-694-1015. *E-mail:* rcruz@boricuacollege.edu. *Website:* http://www.boricuacollege.edu/.

# BOSTON ARCHITECTURAL COLLEGE
## Boston, MA

| Tuition & fees: $19,706 | Average undergraduate aid package: $9818 |
|---|---|

**ABOUT THE INSTITUTION** Independent, coed. *Awards:* certificates, bachelor's, and master's degrees. 4 undergraduate majors. *Total enrollment:* 878. Undergraduates: 472. Freshmen: 24. Federal methodology is used as a basis for awarding need-based institutional aid.

**UNDERGRADUATE EXPENSES** for 2015–2016 *Tuition:* full-time $19,056; part-time $1588 per credit hour. *Required fees:* full-time $650; $175. Full-time tuition and fees vary according to course load, degree level, and program. Part-time tuition and fees vary according to course load, degree level, and program.

**FRESHMAN FINANCIAL AID (Fall 2014, est.)** 10 applied for aid; of those 90% were deemed to have need. 100% of freshmen with need received aid. *Average percent of need met:* 18% (excluding resources awarded to replace EFC). *Average financial aid package:* $5119 (excluding resources awarded to replace EFC).

**UNDERGRADUATE FINANCIAL AID (Fall 2014, est.)** 62 applied for aid; of those 92% were deemed to have need. 96% of undergraduates with need received aid. *Average percent of need met:* 28% (excluding resources awarded to replace EFC). *Average financial aid package:* $9818 (excluding resources awarded to replace EFC). 22% of all full-time undergraduates had no need and received non-need-based gift aid.
**GIFT AID (NEED-BASED)** *Total amount:* $1,103,730 (49% federal, 4% state, 33% institutional, 14% external sources). *Receiving aid:* Freshmen: 42% (5); all full-time undergraduates: 46% (40). *Average award:* Freshmen: $3930; Undergraduates: $6641. *Scholarships, grants, and awards:* Federal Pell, FSEOG, state, private, college/university gift aid from institutional funds.
**GIFT AID (NON-NEED-BASED)** *Total amount:* $124,270 (72% institutional, 28% external sources). *Average award:* Undergraduates: $2844. *Scholarships, grants, and awards by category: Academic interests/achievement:* 67 awards ($241,864 total): architecture, general academic interests/achievements. *Special achievements/activities:* 5 awards ($30,000 total): leadership. *Tuition waivers:* Full or partial for employees or children of employees.
**LOANS** *Student loans:* $2,839,273 (88% need-based, 12% non-need-based). *Average need-based loan:* Freshmen: $2936. Undergraduates: $5072. *Parent loans:* $949,950 (83% need-based, 17% non-need-based). *Programs:* Federal Direct (Subsidized and Unsubsidized Stafford, PLUS), private loans.
**WORK-STUDY** *Federal work-study:* Total amount: $72,101; 30 jobs averaging $3281.
**APPLYING FOR FINANCIAL AID** *Required financial aid form:* FAFSA. *Financial aid deadline (priority):* 4/15. *Notification date:* Continuous beginning 5/1. Students must reply within 2 weeks of notification.
**CONTACT** Ms. Janice Wilkos-Greenberg, Director of Financial Aid , Boston Architectural College, 320 Newbury Street, Boston, MA 02115, 617-585-0183. *Fax:* 617-585-0131. *E-mail:* janice.greenberg@the-bac.edu.
*Website:* http://www.the-bac.edu/.

# BOSTON BAPTIST COLLEGE
## Boston, MA

**CONTACT** Financial Aid Office, Boston Baptist College, 950 Metropolitan Avenue, Boston, MA 02136, 617-364-3510 or toll-free 888-235-2014.
*Website:* http://www.boston.edu/.

# BOSTON COLLEGE
## Chestnut Hill, MA

| Tuition & fees: $47,436 | Average undergraduate aid package: $36,793 |
|---|---|

**ABOUT THE INSTITUTION** Independent Roman Catholic (Jesuit), coed. *Awards:* certificates, bachelor's, master's, and doctoral degrees (also offers continuing education program with significant enrollment not reflected in profile). 47 undergraduate majors. *Total enrollment:* 13,575. Undergraduates: 9,154. Freshmen: 2,344. Institutional methodology is used as a basis for awarding need-based institutional aid.
**UNDERGRADUATE EXPENSES for 2015–2016** *Application fee:* $70. *One-time required fee:* $474. *Comprehensive fee:* $60,622 includes full-time tuition ($46,670), mandatory fees ($766), and room and board ($13,186). *College room only:* $8180. Room and board charges vary according to housing facility.
**FRESHMAN FINANCIAL AID (Fall 2013)** 1,095 applied for aid; of those 85% were deemed to have need. 100% of freshmen with need received aid; of those 100% had need fully met. *Average percent of need met:* 100% (excluding resources awarded to replace EFC). *Average financial aid package:* $35,378 (excluding resources awarded to replace EFC). 2% of all full-time freshmen had no need and received non-need-based gift aid.
**UNDERGRADUATE FINANCIAL AID (Fall 2013)** 4,346 applied for aid; of those 89% were deemed to have need. 100% of undergraduates with need received aid; of those 100% had need fully met. *Average percent of need met:* 100% (excluding resources awarded to replace EFC). *Average financial aid package:* $36,793 (excluding resources awarded to replace EFC). 2% of all full-time undergraduates had no need and received non-need-based gift aid.

**GIFT AID (NEED-BASED)** *Total amount:* $109,406,338 (6% federal, 1% state, 90% institutional, 3% external sources). *Receiving aid:* Freshmen: 37% (810); all full-time undergraduates: 37% (3,384). *Average award:* Freshmen: $32,146; Undergraduates: $32,330. *Scholarships, grants, and awards:* Federal Pell, FSEOG, state, private, college/university gift aid from institutional funds.
**GIFT AID (NON-NEED-BASED)** *Total amount:* $6,707,400 (25% federal, 53% institutional, 22% external sources). *Receiving aid:* Freshmen: 1% (17). Undergraduates: 1% (59). *Average award:* Freshmen: $19,222. Undergraduates: $18,337. *Scholarships, grants, and awards by category: Academic interests/ achievement:* 99 awards ($2,617,790 total): general academic interests/achievements, military science. *Tuition waivers:* Full or partial for employees or children of employees. *ROTC:* Army cooperative, Naval cooperative, Air Force cooperative.
**LOANS** *Student loans:* $21,417,219 (84% need-based, 16% non-need-based). 51% of past graduating class borrowed through all loan programs. *Average indebtedness per student:* $21,139. *Average need-based loan:* Freshmen: $4112. Undergraduates: $5182. *Parent loans:* $31,475,846 (100% non-need-based). *Programs:* Perkins, Federal Nursing, state.
**WORK-STUDY** *Federal work-study:* jobs available.
**ATHLETIC AWARDS** Total amount: $16,610,246 (13% need-based, 87% non-need-based).
**APPLYING FOR FINANCIAL AID** *Required financial aid forms:* FAFSA, CSS Financial Aid PROFILE, business/farm supplement, federal income tax form(s), W-2 forms. *Financial aid deadline (priority):* 2/1. *Notification date:* 4/1. Students must reply by 5/1.
**CONTACT** Office of Student Services, Boston College, Lyons Hall, 140 Commonwealth Avenue, Chestnut Hill, MA 02467, 617-552-3300 or toll-free 800-360-2522. *Fax:* 617-552-4889. *E-mail:* studentservices@bc.edu.
*Website:* http://www.bc.edu/.

# THE BOSTON CONSERVATORY
## Boston, MA

**CONTACT** Jessica Raine, Financial Aid Assistant, The Boston Conservatory, 8 The Fenway, Boston, MA 02215, 617-912-9147. *Fax:* 617-536-1496. *E-mail:* jraine@ bostonconservatory.edu.
*Website:* http://www.bostonconservatory.edu/.

# BOSTON UNIVERSITY
## Boston, MA

| Tuition & fees: $46,664 | Average undergraduate aid package: $35,766 |
|---|---|

**ABOUT THE INSTITUTION** Independent, coed. *Awards:* certificates, bachelor's, master's, and doctoral degrees. 103 undergraduate majors. *Total enrollment:* 32,112. Undergraduates: 18,017. Freshmen: 3,915. Institutional methodology is used as a basis for awarding need-based institutional aid.
**UNDERGRADUATE EXPENSES for 2015–2016** *Application fee:* $80. *Comprehensive fee:* $60,694 includes full-time tuition ($45,686), mandatory fees ($978), and room and board ($14,030). *College room only:* $9200. Full-time tuition and fees vary according to class time. Room and board charges vary according to board plan, housing facility, and location. *Part-time tuition:* $1428 per credit hour. *Part-time fees:* $60 per term. Part-time tuition and fees vary according to class time and course load. *Payment plan:* Tuition prepayment.
**FRESHMAN FINANCIAL AID (Fall 2014, est.)** 1,946 applied for aid; of those 78% were deemed to have need. 100% of freshmen with need received aid; of those 37% had need fully met. *Average percent of need met:* 91% (excluding resources awarded to replace EFC). *Average financial aid package:* $39,436 (excluding resources awarded to replace EFC). 7% of all full-time freshmen had no need and received non-need-based gift aid.
**UNDERGRADUATE FINANCIAL AID (Fall 2014, est.)** 7,037 applied for aid; of those 89% were deemed to have need. 100% of undergraduates with need received aid; of those 29% had need fully met. *Average percent of need met:* 86% (excluding resources awarded to replace EFC). *Average financial aid package:*

$35,766 (excluding resources awarded to replace EFC). 8% of all full-time undergraduates had no need and received non-need-based gift aid.

**GIFT AID (NEED-BASED)** *Total amount:* $181,889,232 (7% federal, 1% state, 90% institutional, 2% external sources). *Receiving aid:* Freshmen: 38% (1,480); all full-time undergraduates: 38% (6,156). *Average award:* Freshmen: $34,004; Undergraduates: $29,854. *Scholarships, grants, and awards:* Federal Pell, FSEOG, state, private, college/university gift aid from institutional funds.

**GIFT AID (NON-NEED-BASED)** *Total amount:* $35,405,659 (2% federal, 70% institutional, 28% external sources). *Receiving aid:* Freshmen: 3% (129). Undergraduates: 2% (342). *Average award:* Freshmen: $17,409. Undergraduates: $17,594. *Scholarships, grants, and awards by category: Academic interests/ achievement:* 1,583 awards ($25,152,687 total): engineering/technologies, general academic interests/achievements, military science. *Creative arts/performance:* 216 awards ($2,176,386 total): art/fine arts, music, theater/drama. *Special achievements/activities:* 47 awards ($2,044,301 total): general special achievements/activities, memberships. *Special characteristics:* 338 awards ($7,152,464 total): children and siblings of alumni, children of faculty/staff, general special characteristics, local/state students, members of minority groups, relatives of clergy, religious affiliation, veterans, veterans' children. *Tuition waivers:* Full or partial for employees or children of employees. *ROTC:* Army, Naval, Air Force.

**LOANS** *Student loans:* $75,066,543 (54% need-based, 46% non-need-based). 57% of past graduating class borrowed through all loan programs. *Average indebtedness per student:* $39,166. *Average need-based loan:* Freshmen: $5409. Undergraduates: $5526. *Parent loans:* $35,307,059 (25% need-based, 75% non-need-based). *Programs:* Federal Direct (Subsidized and Unsubsidized Stafford, PLUS), Perkins, state, alternative loans.

**WORK-STUDY** *Federal work-study:* Total amount: $6,050,124; 3,129 jobs averaging $1934. *State or other work-study/employment:* Part-time jobs available.

**ATHLETIC AWARDS** Total amount: $14,197,978 (9% need-based, 91% non-need-based).

**APPLYING FOR FINANCIAL AID** *Required financial aid forms:* FAFSA, CSS Financial Aid PROFILE, noncustodial (divorced/separated) parent's statement. *Financial aid deadline:* 2/15. *Notification date:* Continuous beginning 3/15. Students must reply by 5/1 or within 2 weeks of notification.

**CONTACT** Julie Wickstrom, Director of Financial Assistance, Boston University, 881 Commonwealth Avenue, Boston, MA 02215, 617-353-4176. *Fax:* 617-353-8200. *E-mail:* finaid@bu.edu.
*Website:* http://www.bu.edu/.

# BOWDOIN COLLEGE
## Brunswick, ME

| Tuition & fees: $46,808 | Average undergraduate aid package: $40,549 |
|---|---|

**ABOUT THE INSTITUTION** Independent, coed. *Awards:* bachelor's degrees. 42 undergraduate majors. *Total enrollment:* 1,805. Undergraduates: 1,805. Freshmen: 501. Institutional methodology is used as a basis for awarding need-based institutional aid.

**UNDERGRADUATE EXPENSES** for 2015–2016 *Application fee:* $60. *Comprehensive fee:* $59,568 includes full-time tuition ($46,354), mandatory fees ($454), and room and board ($12,760). *College room only:* $5964. Room and board charges vary according to board plan.

**FRESHMAN FINANCIAL AID (Fall 2014, est.)** 285 applied for aid; of those 78% were deemed to have need. 100% of freshmen with need received aid; of those 100% had need fully met. *Average percent of need met:* 100% (excluding resources awarded to replace EFC). *Average financial aid package:* $42,318 (excluding resources awarded to replace EFC). 3% of all full-time freshmen had no need and received non-need-based gift aid.

**UNDERGRADUATE FINANCIAL AID (Fall 2014, est.)** 930 applied for aid; of those 86% were deemed to have need. 100% of undergraduates with need received aid; of those 100% had need fully met. *Average percent of need met:* 100% (excluding resources awarded to replace EFC). *Average financial aid package:* $40,549 (excluding resources awarded to replace EFC). 3% of all full-time undergraduates had no need and received non-need-based gift aid.

**GIFT AID (NEED-BASED)** *Total amount:* $31,998,936 (5% federal, 92% institutional, 3% external sources). *Receiving aid:* Freshmen: 44% (222); all full-time undergraduates: 45% (800). *Average award:* Freshmen: $40,680; Undergraduates:

$38,978. *Scholarships, grants, and awards:* Federal Pell, FSEOG, state, private, college/university gift aid from institutional funds.

**GIFT AID (NON-NEED-BASED)** *Total amount:* $652,550 (9% institutional, 91% external sources). *Average award:* Freshmen: $1000. Undergraduates: $1000. *Scholarships, grants, and awards by category: Academic interests/ achievement:* 54 awards ($54,000 total): general academic interests/achievements. *Special achievements/activities:* leadership. *Special characteristics:* children of faculty/ staff. *Tuition waivers:* Full or partial for employees or children of employees.

**LOANS** *Student loans:* 32% of past graduating class borrowed through all loan programs. *Average indebtedness per student:* $25,503. *Programs:* Federal Direct (Subsidized and Unsubsidized Stafford), Perkins, state.

**WORK-STUDY** *Federal work-study:* Total amount: $832,651; 481 jobs averaging $1731. *State or other work-study/employment:* Total amount: $424,569 (100% need-based). 240 part-time jobs averaging $1769.

**APPLYING FOR FINANCIAL AID** *Required financial aid forms:* FAFSA, CSS Financial Aid PROFILE, noncustodial (divorced/separated) parent's statement, business/farm supplement. *Financial aid deadline:* 2/15. *Notification date:* 4/5. Students must reply by 5/1 or within 1 week of notification.

**CONTACT** Mr. Michael D. Bartini, Director of Student Aid, Bowdoin College, 5300 College Station, Brunswick, ME 04011-8444, 207-725-3146. *Fax:* 207-725-3864. *E-mail:* mbartini@bowdoin.edu.
*Website:* http://www.bowdoin.edu/.

# BOWIE STATE UNIVERSITY
## Bowie, MD

| Tuition & fees (MD res): $7299 | Average undergraduate aid package: $8993 |
|---|---|

**ABOUT THE INSTITUTION** State-supported, coed. *Awards:* certificates, bachelor's, master's, and doctoral degrees. 29 undergraduate majors. *Total enrollment:* 5,561. Undergraduates: 4,358. Freshmen: 629. Federal methodology is used as a basis for awarding need-based institutional aid.

**UNDERGRADUATE EXPENSES** for 2015–2016 *Application fee:* $40. *Tuition, state resident:* full-time $4969; part-time $219 per credit hour. *Tuition, nonresident:* full-time $15,545; part-time $653 per credit hour. *Required fees:* full-time $2330; $91.16 per credit hour. Part-time tuition and fees vary according to course load. *College room and board:* $10,432; *Room only:* $6702. Room and board charges vary according to board plan and housing facility.

**FRESHMAN FINANCIAL AID (Fall 2013)** 436 applied for aid; of those 100% were deemed to have need. 100% of freshmen with need received aid; of those 54% had need fully met. *Average percent of need met:* 47% (excluding resources awarded to replace EFC). *Average financial aid package:* $9321 (excluding resources awarded to replace EFC). 4% of all full-time freshmen had no need and received non-need-based gift aid.

**UNDERGRADUATE FINANCIAL AID (Fall 2013)** 2,580 applied for aid; of those 100% were deemed to have need. 100% of undergraduates with need received aid; of those 40% had need fully met. *Average percent of need met:* 45% (excluding resources awarded to replace EFC). *Average financial aid package:* $8993 (excluding resources awarded to replace EFC). 2% of all full-time undergraduates had no need and received non-need-based gift aid.

**GIFT AID (NEED-BASED)** *Total amount:* $19,259,957 (48% federal, 25% state, 26% institutional, 1% external sources). *Receiving aid:* Freshmen: 61% (349); all full-time undergraduates: 68% (2,109). *Average award:* Freshmen: $8006; Undergraduates: $6825. *Scholarships, grants, and awards:* Federal Pell, FSEOG, state, private, college/university gift aid from institutional funds, United Negro College Fund, Federal Nursing.

**GIFT AID (NON-NEED-BASED)** *Total amount:* $490,247 (2% federal, 14% state, 80% institutional, 4% external sources). *Receiving aid:* Freshmen: 66% (379). Undergraduates: 68% (2,108). *Scholarships, grants, and awards by category: Academic interests/achievement:* biological sciences, business, communication, computer science, engineering/technologies, mathematics, military science. *Creative arts/ performance:* applied art and design, art/fine arts, general creative arts/performance, music. *Special achievements/activities:* 244 awards ($2,008,925 total): general special achievements/activities. *Special characteristics:* 460 awards ($575,440 total): first-generation college students, general special characteristics. *Tuition waivers:* Full or partial for employees or children of employees, senior citizens. *ROTC:* Army.

**LOANS** *Student loans:* $22,329,031 (84% need-based, 16% non-need-based). 83% of past graduating class borrowed through all loan programs. *Average indebtedness per student:* $29,737. *Average need-based loan:* Freshmen: $3317. Undergraduates: $4098. *Parent loans:* $2,993,289 (40% need-based, 60% non-need-based). *Programs:* Federal Direct (Subsidized and Unsubsidized Stafford, PLUS), Perkins, Federal Nursing, state, college/university.
**WORK-STUDY** *Federal work-study:* 76 jobs averaging $2567.
**ATHLETIC AWARDS** Total amount: $775,338 (59% need-based, 41% non-need-based).
**APPLYING FOR FINANCIAL AID** *Required financial aid forms:* FAFSA, institution's own form. *Financial aid deadline (priority):* 3/1. *Notification date:* Continuous beginning 4/1. Students must reply within 2 weeks of notification.
**CONTACT** Clayton Steen, Acting Director of Financial Aid, Bowie State University, 14000 Jericho Park Road, Bowie, MD 20715, 301-860-3543 or toll-free 877-772-6943. *Fax:* 301-860-3549. *E-mail:* dstanley@bowiestate.edu.
*Website:* http://www.bowiestate.edu/.

# BOWLING GREEN STATE UNIVERSITY
## Bowling Green, OH

| Tuition & fees (OH res): $10,726 | Average undergraduate aid package: $13,927 |
| --- | --- |

**ABOUT THE INSTITUTION** State-supported, coed. *Awards:* certificates, bachelor's, master's, and doctoral degrees. 216 undergraduate majors. *Total enrollment:* 16,554. Undergraduates: 14,099. Freshmen: 3,030. Federal methodology is used as a basis for awarding need-based institutional aid.
**UNDERGRADUATE EXPENSES for 2015–2016** *Application fee:* $45. *Tuition, state resident:* full-time $9096; part-time $379 per credit hour. *Tuition, nonresident:* full-time $16,404; part-time $684 per credit hour. *Required fees:* full-time $1630; $67.25 per credit hour. Full-time tuition and fees vary according to course load and location. Part-time tuition and fees vary according to course load and location. *College room and board:* $8244. Room and board charges vary according to board plan and housing facility.
**FRESHMAN FINANCIAL AID (Fall 2014, est.)** 2,669 applied for aid; of those 79% were deemed to have need. 100% of freshmen with need received aid; of those 14% had need fully met. *Average percent of need met:* 75% (excluding resources awarded to replace EFC). *Average financial aid package:* $14,042 (excluding resources awarded to replace EFC). 21% of all full-time freshmen had no need and received non-need-based gift aid.
**UNDERGRADUATE FINANCIAL AID (Fall 2014, est.)** 10,391 applied for aid; of those 82% were deemed to have need. 100% of undergraduates with need received aid; of those 12% had need fully met. *Average percent of need met:* 74% (excluding resources awarded to replace EFC). *Average financial aid package:* $13,927 (excluding resources awarded to replace EFC). 19% of all full-time undergraduates had no need and received non-need-based gift aid.
**GIFT AID (NEED-BASED)** *Total amount:* $46,290,068 (43% federal, 7% state, 44% institutional, 6% external sources). *Receiving aid:* Freshmen: 63% (1,912); all full-time undergraduates: 55% (7,064). *Average award:* Freshmen: $6756; Undergraduates: $6448. *Scholarships, grants, and awards:* Federal Pell, FSEOG, state, private, college/university gift aid from institutional funds.
**GIFT AID (NON-NEED-BASED)** *Total amount:* $16,419,384 (3% state, 79% institutional, 18% external sources). *Receiving aid:* Freshmen: 7% (218). Undergraduates: 5% (638). *Average award:* Freshmen: $4815. Undergraduates: $4676. *Scholarships, grants, and awards by category:* Academic interests/achievement: biological sciences, business, communication, computer science, education, engineering/technologies, English, foreign languages, general academic interests/achievements, health fields, home economics, humanities, international studies, mathematics, military science, physical sciences, social sciences. *Creative arts/performance:* art/fine arts, cinema/film/broadcasting, creative writing, dance, debating, journalism/publications, music, performing arts, theater/drama. *Special achievements/activities:* general special achievements/activities, leadership. *Special characteristics:* children and siblings of alumni, children of faculty/staff, general special characteristics, international students, members of minority groups. *Tuition waivers:* Full or partial for employees or children of employees, senior citizens. *ROTC:* Army, Air Force.
**LOANS** *Student loans:* $76,530,974 (74% need-based, 26% non-need-based). 76% of past graduating class borrowed through all loan programs. *Average indebtedness per student:* $30,307. *Average need-based loan:* Freshmen: $6684. Undergrad-

uates: $7441. *Parent loans:* $31,511,212 (43% need-based, 57% non-need-based). *Programs:* Federal Direct (Subsidized and Unsubsidized Stafford, PLUS), Perkins, Federal Nursing, state, college/university, alternative loans.
**WORK-STUDY** *Federal work-study:* Total amount: $550,041; 447 jobs averaging $1264.
**ATHLETIC AWARDS** Total amount: $5,726,851 (40% need-based, 60% non-need-based).
**APPLYING FOR FINANCIAL AID** *Required financial aid form:* FAFSA. *Financial aid deadline:* Continuous. *Notification date:* Continuous beginning 4/15. Students must reply within 3 weeks of notification.
**CONTACT** Eric Bucks, Associate Director of Student Financial Aid, Bowling Green State University, 231 Administration Building, Bowling Green, OH 43403, 419-372-2651. *Fax:* 419-372-0404.
*Website:* http://www.bgsu.edu/.

# BRADLEY UNIVERSITY
## Peoria, IL

| Tuition & fees: $30,844 | Average undergraduate aid package: $20,117 |
| --- | --- |

**ABOUT THE INSTITUTION** Independent, coed. *Awards:* certificates, bachelor's, master's, and doctoral degrees. 104 undergraduate majors. *Total enrollment:* 5,300. Undergraduates: 4,589. Freshmen: 948. Federal methodology is used as a basis for awarding need-based institutional aid.
**UNDERGRADUATE EXPENSES for 2015–2016** *Application fee:* $35. *One-time required fee:* $200. *Comprehensive fee:* $40,264 includes full-time tuition ($30,500), mandatory fees ($344), and room and board ($9420). *College room only:* $5460. Full-time tuition and fees vary according to course load and program. Room and board charges vary according to board plan. *Part-time tuition:* $940 per credit hour. *Part-time fees:* $810 per credit hour. Part-time tuition and fees vary according to course load and program.
**FRESHMAN FINANCIAL AID (Fall 2014, est.)** 837 applied for aid; of those 77% were deemed to have need. 100% of freshmen with need received aid; of those 20% had need fully met. *Average percent of need met:* 72% (excluding resources awarded to replace EFC). *Average financial aid package:* $21,147 (excluding resources awarded to replace EFC). 12% of all full-time freshmen had no need and received non-need-based gift aid.
**UNDERGRADUATE FINANCIAL AID (Fall 2014, est.)** 4,087 applied for aid; of those 85% were deemed to have need. 99% of undergraduates with need received aid; of those 15% had need fully met. *Average percent of need met:* 67% (excluding resources awarded to replace EFC). *Average financial aid package:* $20,117 (excluding resources awarded to replace EFC). 17% of all full-time undergraduates had no need and received non-need-based gift aid.
**GIFT AID (NEED-BASED)** *Total amount:* $51,455,772 (9% federal, 10% state, 78% institutional, 3% external sources). *Receiving aid:* Freshmen: 68% (644); all full-time undergraduates: 61% (2,824). *Average award:* Freshmen: $15,901; Undergraduates: $15,016. *Scholarships, grants, and awards:* Federal Pell, FSEOG, state, private, college/university gift aid from institutional funds.
**GIFT AID (NON-NEED-BASED)** *Total amount:* $7,309,417 (95% institutional, 5% external sources). *Receiving aid:* Freshmen: 11% (100). Undergraduates: 7% (320). *Average award:* Freshmen: $9871. Undergraduates: $10,012. *Scholarships, grants, and awards by category:* Academic interests/achievement: general academic interests/achievements. *Creative arts/performance:* art/fine arts, music, theater/drama. *Special achievements/activities:* community service, leadership. *Special characteristics:* children and siblings of alumni, children of faculty/staff. *Tuition waivers:* Full or partial for employees or children of employees, senior citizens. *ROTC:* Army.
**LOANS** *Student loans:* $30,256,855 (63% need-based, 37% non-need-based). 75% of past graduating class borrowed through all loan programs. *Average indebtedness per student:* $27,277. *Average need-based loan:* Freshmen: $4704. Undergraduates: $6379. *Parent loans:* $80,476,386 (7% need-based, 93% non-need-based). *Programs:* Federal Direct (Subsidized and Unsubsidized Stafford, PLUS), Perkins, Federal Nursing.
**WORK-STUDY** *Federal work-study:* Total amount: $452,913; 280 jobs averaging $2000.
**ATHLETIC AWARDS** Total amount: $3,833,244 (45% need-based, 55% non-need-based).

**APPLYING FOR FINANCIAL AID** *Required financial aid form:* FAFSA. *Financial aid deadline (priority):* 3/1. *Notification date:* Continuous beginning 3/1.

**CONTACT** Mr. David L. Pardieck, Director of Financial Assistance, Bradley University, 1501 West Bradley Avenue, Peoria, IL 61625-0002, 309-677-3089 or toll-free 800-447-6460. *E-mail:* dlp@bradley.edu. *Website:* http://www.bradley.edu/.

# BRANDEIS UNIVERSITY
## Waltham, MA

| Tuition & fees: $47,558 | Average undergraduate aid package: $37,276 |
|---|---|

**ABOUT THE INSTITUTION** Independent, coed. *Awards:* bachelor's, master's, and doctoral degrees. 43 undergraduate majors. *Total enrollment:* 5,945. Undergraduates: 3,729. Freshmen: 859. Institutional methodology is used as a basis for awarding need-based institutional aid.

**UNDERGRADUATE EXPENSES** for 2015–2016 *Application fee:* $75. *One-time required fee:* $275. *Comprehensive fee:* $60,750 includes full-time tuition ($46,022), mandatory fees ($1536), and room and board ($13,192). *College room only:* $7492. Full-time tuition and fees vary according to student level. Room and board charges vary according to board plan and housing facility. *Part-time tuition:* $5753 per course. *Part-time fees:* $768 per term. Part-time tuition and fees vary according to course load. *Payment plan:* Tuition prepayment.

**FRESHMAN FINANCIAL AID (Fall 2013)** 545 applied for aid; of those 82% were deemed to have need. 99% of freshmen with need received aid; of those 35% had need fully met. *Average percent of need met:* 96% (excluding resources awarded to replace EFC). *Average financial aid package:* $40,719 (excluding resources awarded to replace EFC). 6% of all full-time freshmen had no need and received non-need-based gift aid.

**UNDERGRADUATE FINANCIAL AID (Fall 2013)** 2,174 applied for aid; of those 88% were deemed to have need. 99% of undergraduates with need received aid; of those 23% had need fully met. *Average percent of need met:* 91% (excluding resources awarded to replace EFC). *Average financial aid package:* $37,276 (excluding resources awarded to replace EFC). 5% of all full-time undergraduates had no need and received non-need-based gift aid.

**GIFT AID (NEED-BASED)** *Total amount:* $60,074,973 (7% federal, 1% state, 89% institutional, 3% external sources). *Receiving aid:* Freshmen: 52% (431); all full-time undergraduates: 51% (1,821). *Average award:* Freshmen: $37,733; Undergraduates: $32,276. *Scholarships, grants, and awards:* Federal Pell, FSEOG, state, private, college/university gift aid from institutional funds.

**GIFT AID (NON-NEED-BASED)** *Total amount:* $5,311,882 (1% federal, 66% institutional, 33% external sources). *Receiving aid:* Freshmen: 5% (43). Undergraduates: 3% (116). *Average award:* Freshmen: $14,049. Undergraduates: $17,895. *Tuition waivers:* Full or partial for employees or children of employees. *ROTC:* Army cooperative, Air Force cooperative.

**LOANS** *Student loans:* $16,409,476 (68% need-based, 32% non-need-based). 60% of past graduating class borrowed through all loan programs. *Average indebtedness per student:* $30,848. *Average need-based loan:* Freshmen: $3530. Undergraduates: $5007. *Parent loans:* $5,350,259 (13% need-based, 87% non-need-based). *Programs:* Federal Direct (Subsidized and Unsubsidized Stafford, PLUS), Perkins, state, college/university.

**WORK-STUDY** *Federal work-study:* jobs available. *State or other work-study/employment:* Total amount: $785,750 (27% need-based, 73% non-need-based). Part-time jobs available.

**APPLYING FOR FINANCIAL AID** *Required financial aid forms:* FAFSA, CSS Financial Aid PROFILE, state aid form, noncustodial (divorced/separated) parent's statement. *Financial aid deadline (priority):* 2/1. *Notification date:* 4/1. Students must reply by 5/1.

**CONTACT** Nicole Bonanni, Assistant Director for Student Services, Brandeis University, Usdan Student Center, 415 South Street, Waltham, MA 02454-9110, 781-736-3700 or toll-free 800-622-0622 (out-of-state). *Fax:* 781-736-3719. *E-mail:* sfs@brandeis.edu. *Website:* http://www.brandeis.edu/.

# BRANDMAN UNIVERSITY
## Irvine, CA

**CONTACT** Financial Aid Office, Brandman University, 16355 Laguna Canyon Road, Irvine, CA 92618, 949-753-4774 or toll-free 800-746-0082. *Website:* http://www.brandman.edu/irvine/.

# BRENAU UNIVERSITY
## Gainesville, GA

| Tuition & fees: $25,478 | Average undergraduate aid package: $16,472 |
|---|---|

**ABOUT THE INSTITUTION** Independent, women only. *Awards:* associate, bachelor's, and master's degrees (also offers coed evening and weekend programs with significant enrollment not reflected in profile). 31 undergraduate majors. *Total enrollment:* 2,789. Undergraduates: 1,596. Freshmen: 231. Federal methodology is used as a basis for awarding need-based institutional aid.

**UNDERGRADUATE EXPENSES** for 2015–2016 *Application fee:* $35. *Comprehensive fee:* $37,476 includes full-time tuition ($25,478) and room and board ($11,998). Full-time tuition and fees vary according to course load, location, and program. *Part-time tuition:* $849 per credit. Part-time tuition and fees vary according to course load, location, and program.

**FRESHMAN FINANCIAL AID (Fall 2014, est.)** 216 applied for aid; of those 96% were deemed to have need. 100% of freshmen with need received aid; of those 23% had need fully met. *Average percent of need met:* 75% (excluding resources awarded to replace EFC). *Average financial aid package:* $23,643 (excluding resources awarded to replace EFC). 8% of all full-time freshmen had no need and received non-need-based gift aid.

**UNDERGRADUATE FINANCIAL AID (Fall 2014, est.)** 901 applied for aid; of those 94% were deemed to have need. 98% of undergraduates with need received aid; of those 24% had need fully met. *Average percent of need met:* 66% (excluding resources awarded to replace EFC). *Average financial aid package:* $16,472 (excluding resources awarded to replace EFC). 9% of all full-time undergraduates had no need and received non-need-based gift aid.

**GIFT AID (NEED-BASED)** *Total amount:* $12,828,034 (26% federal, 13% state, 60% institutional, 1% external sources). *Receiving aid:* Freshmen: 89% (205); all full-time undergraduates: 83% (831). *Average award:* Freshmen: $16,782; Undergraduates: $13,249. *Scholarships, grants, and awards:* Federal Pell, FSEOG, private, college/university gift aid from institutional funds.

**GIFT AID (NON-NEED-BASED)** *Total amount:* $608,591 (39% state, 59% institutional, 2% external sources). *Receiving aid:* Freshmen: 5% (11). Undergraduates: 5% (53). *Average award:* Freshmen: $16,701. Undergraduates: $13,303. *Scholarships, grants, and awards by category:* Academic interests/achievement: biological sciences, business, communication, education, English, general academic interests/achievements, health fields, humanities. *Creative arts/performance:* applied art and design, art/fine arts, cinema/film/broadcasting, creative writing, dance, journalism/publications, music, performing arts, theater/drama. *Special achievements/activities:* cheerleading/drum major, community service, general special achievements/activities, leadership. *Special characteristics:* children of faculty/staff, first-generation college students, general special characteristics, international students. *Tuition waivers:* Full or partial for employees or children of employees.

**LOANS** *Student loans:* $11,378,679 (86% need-based, 14% non-need-based). 75% of past graduating class borrowed through all loan programs. *Average indebtedness per student:* $33,376. *Average need-based loan:* Freshmen: $8108. Undergraduates: $9332. *Parent loans:* $494,736 (19% need-based, 81% non-need-based). *Programs:* Federal Direct (Subsidized and Unsubsidized Stafford, PLUS), Perkins, Federal Nursing, state.

**WORK-STUDY** *Federal work-study:* Total amount: $255,577; jobs available.

**ATHLETIC AWARDS** Total amount: $1,753,036 (77% need-based, 23% non-need-based).

**APPLYING FOR FINANCIAL AID** *Required financial aid forms:* FAFSA, state aid form. *Financial aid deadline (priority):* 4/1. *Notification date:* Continuous beginning 3/1.

**CONTACT** Mrs. Pam Barrett, Associate Vice President and Director of Financial Aid, Brenau University, 500 Washington Street, SE, Gainesville, GA 30501-3697, 770-534-6176 or toll-free 800-252-5119. *Fax:* 770-538-4306. *E-mail:* pbarrett@brenau.edu. *Website:* http://www.brenau.edu/.

# BRESCIA UNIVERSITY
## Owensboro, KY

**CONTACT** Mr. Britton Hibbitt, Administrative Assistant to Financial Aid, Brescia University, 717 Frederica Street, Owensboro, KY 42301-3023, 270-686-4253 or toll-free 877-273-7242. *Fax:* 270-686-4253. *E-mail:* financial.aid@brescia.edu. *Website:* http://www.brescia.edu/.

# BREVARD COLLEGE
## Brevard, NC

| Tuition & fees: $26,170 | Average undergraduate aid package: $10,851 |
|---|---|

**ABOUT THE INSTITUTION** Independent United Methodist, coed. *Awards:* bachelor's degrees. 21 undergraduate majors. *Total enrollment:* 705. Undergraduates: 705. Freshmen: 218. Both federal and institutional methodology are used as a basis for awarding need-based institutional aid.

**UNDERGRADUATE EXPENSES for 2015–2016** *Comprehensive fee:* $35,545 includes full-time tuition ($25,950), mandatory fees ($220), and room and board ($9375). Full-time tuition and fees vary according to course load. Room and board charges vary according to board plan and housing facility. *Part-time tuition:* $510 per credit hour. Part-time tuition and fees vary according to course load.

**FRESHMAN FINANCIAL AID (Fall 2014, est.)** 189 applied for aid; of those 90% were deemed to have need. 100% of freshmen with need received aid; of those 1% had need fully met. *Average percent of need met:* 66% (excluding resources awarded to replace EFC). *Average financial aid package:* $10,466 (excluding resources awarded to replace EFC). 15% of all full-time freshmen had no need and received non-need-based gift aid.

**UNDERGRADUATE FINANCIAL AID (Fall 2014, est.)** 578 applied for aid; of those 90% were deemed to have need. 100% of undergraduates with need received aid; of those 16% had need fully met. *Average percent of need met:* 59% (excluding resources awarded to replace EFC). *Average financial aid package:* $10,851 (excluding resources awarded to replace EFC). 16% of all full-time undergraduates had no need and received non-need-based gift aid.

**GIFT AID (NEED-BASED)** *Total amount:* $7,070,140 (18% federal, 16% state, 60% institutional, 6% external sources). *Receiving aid:* Freshmen: 64% (140); all full-time undergraduates: 60% (417). *Average award:* Freshmen: $8472; Undergraduates: $8154. *Scholarships, grants, and awards:* Federal Pell, FSEOG, state, private, college/university gift aid from institutional funds.

**GIFT AID (NON-NEED-BASED)** *Total amount:* $1,311,471 (93% institutional, 7% external sources). *Receiving aid:* Freshmen: 78% (171). Undergraduates: 45% (316). *Average award:* Freshmen: $8318. Undergraduates: $8703. *Scholarships, grants, and awards by category:* Academic interests/achievement: general academic interests/achievements. Creative arts/performance: art/fine arts, music, theater/drama. Special achievements/activities: cheerleading/drum major, community service, general special achievements/activities, leadership. Special characteristics: children of faculty/staff, international students, local/state students, previous college experience, veterans' children. *Tuition waivers:* Full or partial for employees or children of employees, senior citizens.

**LOANS** *Student loans:* $3,673,055 (76% need-based, 24% non-need-based). 76% of past graduating class borrowed through all loan programs. *Average indebtedness per student:* $35,211. *Average need-based loan:* Freshmen: $3137. Undergraduates: $3748. *Parent loans:* $1,317,755 (39% need-based, 61% non-need-based). *Programs:* Federal Direct (Subsidized and Unsubsidized Stafford, PLUS), Perkins.

**WORK-STUDY** *Federal work-study:* Total amount: $38,580; jobs available. *State or other work-study/employment:* Total amount: $105,919 (65% need-based, 35% non-need-based). Part-time jobs available.

**ATHLETIC AWARDS** Total amount: $1,823,972 (77% need-based, 23% non-need-based).

**APPLYING FOR FINANCIAL AID** *Required financial aid form:* FAFSA. *Financial aid deadline (priority):* 2/1. *Notification date:* Continuous beginning 2/1. Students must reply by 5/1 or within 4 weeks of notification.

**CONTACT** Ms. Caron Surrett, Director of Financial Aid, Brevard College, 1 Brevard College Drive, Brevard, NC 28712, 828-884-8261 or toll-free 800-527-9090. *Fax:* 828-884-3790. *E-mail:* finaid@brevard.edu. *Website:* http://www.brevard.edu/.

# BREWTON-PARKER COLLEGE
## Mt. Vernon, GA

**CONTACT** Mrs. Shannon Mullins, Executive Director of Financial Aid, Brewton-Parker College, PO Box 197, Mt. Vernon, GA 30445-0197, 800-342-1087 Ext. 213 or toll-free 800-342-1087. *Fax:* 912-583-3598. *E-mail:* smullins@bpc.edu. *Website:* http://www.bpc.edu/.

# BRIARCLIFFE COLLEGE
## Bethpage, NY

**CONTACT** Johanna Kelly, Financial Aid Director, Briarcliffe College, 1055 Stewart Avenue, Bethpage, NY 11714, 516-918-3600 or toll-free 888-349-4999 (in-state), 888-348-4999 (out-of-state). *Website:* http://www.briarcliffe.edu/.

# BRIAR CLIFF UNIVERSITY
## Sioux City, IA

**ABOUT THE INSTITUTION** Independent Roman Catholic, coed. *Awards:* certificates, associate, bachelor's, and master's degrees. 29 undergraduate majors. *Total enrollment:* 1,174. Undergraduates: 1,042. Freshmen: 180.

**GIFT AID (NEED-BASED)** *Scholarships, grants, and awards:* Federal Pell, FSEOG, state, private, college/university gift aid from institutional funds.

**GIFT AID (NON-NEED-BASED)** *Scholarships, grants, and awards by category:* Academic interests/achievement: biological sciences, business, communication, computer science, education, English, foreign languages, general academic interests/achievements, health fields, humanities, mathematics, physical sciences, religion/biblical studies, social sciences. Creative arts/performance: art/fine arts, music, theater/drama. Special achievements/activities: leadership, religious involvement. Special characteristics: children and siblings of alumni, first-generation college students, international students, members of minority groups.

**LOANS** *Programs:* Federal Direct (Subsidized and Unsubsidized Stafford, PLUS), Perkins, alternative loans, partnership loans, Minnesota SELF Loans.

**APPLYING FOR FINANCIAL AID** *Required financial aid forms:* FAFSA, federal income tax form(s).

**CONTACT** Brian K. Eben, Office of Student Financial Aid, Briar Cliff University, 3303 Rebecca Street, PO Box 2100, Sioux City, IA 51104-2100, 712-279-5239 or toll free 800-662-3303. *Fax:* 712-279-1632. *Website:* http://www.briarcliff.edu/.

# BRIDGEWATER COLLEGE
## Bridgewater, VA

| Tuition & fees: $31,480 | Average undergraduate aid package: $26,549 |
|---|---|

**ABOUT THE INSTITUTION** Independent Church of the Brethren, coed. *Awards:* bachelor's degrees. 29 undergraduate majors. *Total enrollment:* 1,785. Undergraduates: 1,785. Freshmen: 488. Federal methodology is used as a basis for awarding need-based institutional aid.

**UNDERGRADUATE EXPENSES for 2015–2016** *Comprehensive fee:* $43,000 includes full-time tuition ($30,800), mandatory fees ($680), and room and board ($11,520). Room and board charges vary according to housing facility. *Part-time tuition:* $1070 per credit hour.

**FRESHMAN FINANCIAL AID (Fall 2014, est.)** 464 applied for aid; of those 89% were deemed to have need. 100% of freshmen with need received aid; of those 28% had need fully met. *Average percent of need met:* 88% (excluding resources awarded to replace EFC). *Average financial aid package:* $27,710 (excluding resources awarded to replace EFC). 15% of all full-time freshmen had no need and received non-need-based gift aid.

**UNDERGRADUATE FINANCIAL AID (Fall 2014, est.)** 1,553 applied for aid; of those 91% were deemed to have need. 100% of undergraduates with need received

aid; of those 30% had need fully met. *Average percent of need met:* 86% (excluding resources awarded to replace EFC). *Average financial aid package:* $26,549 (excluding resources awarded to replace EFC). 19% of all full-time undergraduates had no need and received non-need-based gift aid.
**GIFT AID (NEED-BASED)** *Total amount:* $26,384,311 (8% federal, 12% state, 79% institutional, 1% external sources). *Receiving aid:* Freshmen: 85% (415); all full-time undergraduates: 81% (1,417). *Average award:* Freshmen: $24,595; Undergraduates: $22,846. *Scholarships, grants, and awards:* Federal Pell, FSEOG, state, private, college/university gift aid from institutional funds.
**GIFT AID (NON-NEED-BASED)** *Total amount:* $12,285,974 (7% state, 91% institutional, 2% external sources). *Receiving aid:* Freshmen: 85% (415). Undergraduates: 81% (1,417). *Average award:* Freshmen: $18,243. Undergraduates: $16,753. *Scholarships, grants, and awards by category: Academic interests/ achievement:* 1,553 awards ($25,482,195 total): general academic interests/achievements. *Creative arts/performance:* 60 awards ($101,230 total): music. *Special characteristics:* 656 awards ($2,715,060 total): children of educators, children of faculty/staff, international students, members of minority groups, out-of-state students, previous college experience, religious affiliation. *Tuition waivers:* Full or partial for employees or children of employees, senior citizens.
**LOANS** *Student loans:* $11,693,679 (60% need-based, 40% non-need-based). 79% of past graduating class borrowed through all loan programs. *Average indebtedness per student:* $33,326. *Average need-based loan:* Freshmen: $4364. Undergraduates: $5004. *Parent loans:* $4,151,922 (11% need-based, 89% non-need-based). *Programs:* Federal Direct (Subsidized and Unsubsidized Stafford, PLUS), Perkins.
**WORK-STUDY** *Federal work-study:* Total amount: $363,466; 324 jobs averaging $1226. *State or other work-study/employment:* Total amount: $143,390 (100% non-need-based). 168 part-time jobs averaging $853.
**APPLYING FOR FINANCIAL AID** *Required financial aid forms:* FAFSA, state aid form. *Financial aid deadline (priority):* 3/1. *Notification date:* Continuous beginning 3/15. Students must reply by 5/1 or within 2 weeks of notification.
**CONTACT** Mr. Scott Morrison, Director of Financial Aid, Bridgewater College, 402 East College Street, Bridgewater, VA 22812-1599, 540-828-5377 or toll-free 800-759-8328. *Fax:* 540-828-5671. *E-mail:* smorriso@bridgewater.edu. *Website:* http://www.bridgewater.edu/.

# BRIDGEWATER STATE UNIVERSITY
## Bridgewater, MA

| Tuition & fees (MA res): $8353 | Average undergraduate aid package: $8085 |
| --- | --- |

**ABOUT THE INSTITUTION** State-supported, coed. *Awards:* certificates, bachelor's, and master's degrees. 80 undergraduate majors. *Total enrollment:* 11,187. Undergraduates: 9,628. Freshmen: 1,540. Federal methodology is used as a basis for awarding need-based institutional aid.
**UNDERGRADUATE EXPENSES for 2015–2016** *Application fee:* $40. *Tuition, state resident:* full-time $910; part-time $38 per credit hour. *Tuition, nonresident:* full-time $7050; part-time $294 per credit hour. *Required fees:* full-time $7443; $304.71 per credit hour. Full-time tuition and fees vary according to course load. *College room and board:* $11,400; *Room only:* $7500. Room and board charges vary according to board plan and housing facility.
**FRESHMAN FINANCIAL AID (Fall 2013)** 1,369 applied for aid; of those 78% were deemed to have need. 98% of freshmen with need received aid; of those 9% had need fully met. *Average percent of need met:* 66% (excluding resources awarded to replace EFC). *Average financial aid package:* $9054 (excluding resources awarded to replace EFC). 1% of all full-time freshmen had no need and received non-need-based gift aid.
**UNDERGRADUATE FINANCIAL AID (Fall 2013)** 7,197 applied for aid; of those 80% were deemed to have need. 98% of undergraduates with need received aid; of those 12% had need fully met. *Average percent of need met:* 42% (excluding resources awarded to replace EFC). *Average financial aid package:* $8085 (excluding resources awarded to replace EFC). 1% of all full-time undergraduates had no need and received non-need-based gift aid.
**GIFT AID (NEED-BASED)** *Total amount:* $20,742,333 (64% federal, 18% state, 18% institutional). *Receiving aid:* Freshmen: 59% (884); all full-time undergraduates: 53% (4,204). *Average award:* Freshmen: $3080; Undergraduates: $4732. *Scholarships, grants, and awards:* Federal Pell, FSEOG, state, private, college/university gift aid from institutional funds.

**GIFT AID (NON-NEED-BASED)** *Total amount:* $4,338,427 (3% federal, 28% state, 15% institutional, 54% external sources). *Receiving aid:* Freshmen: 17% (251). Undergraduates: 13% (1,031). *Average award:* Freshmen: $3821. Undergraduates: $5680. *Scholarships, grants, and awards by category: Academic interests/ achievement:* general academic interests/achievements. *Special characteristics:* local/ state students, members of minority groups. *Tuition waivers:* Full or partial for employees or children of employees, senior citizens. *ROTC:* Army cooperative, Air Force cooperative.
**LOANS** *Student loans:* $49,076,833 (47% need-based, 53% non-need-based). 66% of past graduating class borrowed through all loan programs. *Average indebtedness per student:* $32,040. *Average need-based loan:* Freshmen: $2246. Undergraduates: $4452. *Parent loans:* $7,203,092 (100% non-need-based). *Programs:* Federal Direct (Subsidized and Unsubsidized Stafford, PLUS), Perkins, state, private loans.
**WORK-STUDY** *Federal work-study:* 459 jobs averaging $1800.
**APPLYING FOR FINANCIAL AID** *Required financial aid form:* FAFSA. *Financial aid deadline (priority):* 3/1. *Notification date:* Continuous beginning 3/30.
**CONTACT** Office of Financial Aid, Bridgewater State University, Tillinghast Hall, Room 100, 45 School Street, Bridgewater, MA 02325-0001, 508-531-1341. *Fax:* 508-531-1728. *E-mail:* finaid@bridgew.edu. *Website:* http://www.bridgew.edu/.

# BRIGHAM YOUNG UNIVERSITY
## Provo, UT

| Tuition & fees: $5000 | Average undergraduate aid package: $7258 |
| --- | --- |

**ABOUT THE INSTITUTION** Independent The Church of Jesus Christ of Latter-day Saints, coed. *Awards:* certificates, bachelor's, master's, and doctoral degrees. 102 undergraduate majors. *Total enrollment:* 30,484. Undergraduates: 27,163. Freshmen: 4,060. Both federal and institutional methodology are used as a basis for awarding need-based institutional aid.
**UNDERGRADUATE EXPENSES for 2015–2016** *Application fee:* $35. *Comprehensive fee:* $12,330 includes full-time tuition ($5000) and room and board ($7330). Room and board charges vary according to board plan, housing facility, and location. *Part-time tuition:* $257 per credit hour. Part-time tuition and fees vary according to course load. Latter Day Saints full-time student $5,000 per year, non-LDS full-time student $10,000.
**FRESHMAN FINANCIAL AID (Fall 2013)** 2,258 applied for aid; of those 63% were deemed to have need. 89% of freshmen with need received aid; of those 2% had need fully met. *Average percent of need met:* 27% (excluding resources awarded to replace EFC). *Average financial aid package:* $6404 (excluding resources awarded to replace EFC). 34% of all full-time freshmen had no need and received non-need-based gift aid.
**UNDERGRADUATE FINANCIAL AID (Fall 2013)** 14,722 applied for aid; of those 85% were deemed to have need. 94% of undergraduates with need received aid; of those 45% had need fully met. *Average percent of need met:* 34% (excluding resources awarded to replace EFC). *Average financial aid package:* $7258 (excluding resources awarded to replace EFC). 23% of all full-time undergraduates had no need and received non-need-based gift aid.
**GIFT AID (NEED-BASED)** *Total amount:* $51,345,496 (86% federal, 14% institutional). *Receiving aid:* Freshmen: 16% (718); all full-time undergraduates: 39% (9,776). *Average award:* Freshmen: $4428; Undergraduates: $4897. *Scholarships, grants, and awards:* Federal Pell, private, college/university gift aid from institutional funds.
**GIFT AID (NON-NEED-BASED)** *Total amount:* $49,976,864 (85% institutional, 15% external sources). *Receiving aid:* Freshmen: 20% (893). Undergraduates: 26% (6,401). *Average award:* Freshmen: $3624. Undergraduates: $3944. *Scholarships, grants, and awards by category: Academic interests/achievement:* general academic interests/achievements. *Creative arts/performance:* art/fine arts, music, theater/drama. *Special achievements/activities:* leadership, religious involvement. *Special characteristics:* local/state students, members of minority groups, religious affiliation. *Tuition waivers:* Full or partial for employees or children of employees. *ROTC:* Army, Air Force.
**LOANS** *Student loans:* $32,374,618 (56% need-based, 44% non-need-based). 26% of past graduating class borrowed through all loan programs. *Average indebtedness per student:* $14,021. *Average need-based loan:* Freshmen: $3107. Undergrad-

uates: $4215. **Parent loans:** $1,107,620 (100% non-need-based). **Programs:** Federal Direct (Subsidized and Unsubsidized Stafford, PLUS).
**WORK-STUDY** *State or other work-study/employment:* Part-time jobs available.
**ATHLETIC AWARDS** Total amount: $4,630,910 (100% non-need-based).
**APPLYING FOR FINANCIAL AID** *Required financial aid form:* FAFSA. *Financial aid deadline (priority):* 4/15. *Notification date:* Continuous beginning 4/1.
**CONTACT** Stephen E. Hill, Director of Financial Aid, Brigham Young University, C-144 ASB, Provo, UT 84602, 801-422-4104. *Fax:* 801-422-0234. *Website:* http://www.byu.edu/.

# BRIGHAM YOUNG UNIVERSITY–HAWAII
## Laie, HI

**CONTACT** Mr. Wes Duke, Director of Financial Aid, Brigham Young University–Hawaii, BYUH #1980, 55-220 Kulanui Street, Laie, HI 96762, 808-293-3530. *Fax:* 808-293-3349. *E-mail:* duekw@byuh.edu. *Website:* http://www.byuh.edu/.

# BRIGHAM YOUNG UNIVERSITY–IDAHO
## Rexburg, ID

**CONTACT** Financial Aid Office, Brigham Young University–Idaho, Rexburg, ID 83460, 208-496-2011. *Website:* http://www.byui.edu/.

# BRISTOL UNIVERSITY
## Anaheim, CA

**CONTACT** Financial Aid Office, Bristol University, 2390 Orangewood Avenue, Suite 485, Anaheim, CA 92806, 714-542-8086. *Website:* http://bristoluniversity.edu/.

# BROADVIEW ENTERTAINMENT ARTS UNIVERSITY
## Salt Lake City, UT

**CONTACT** Office of Financial Aid, Broadview Entertainment Arts University, 240 East Morris Avenue, Salt Lake City, UT 84115, 801-300-4300 or toll-free 877-801-8889. *Fax:* 801-300-4301. *Website:* http://www.broadviewuniversity.edu/.

# BROADVIEW UNIVERSITY–BOISE
## Meridian, ID

**CONTACT** Office of Financial Aid, Broadview University–Boise, 2750 East Gala Court, Meridian, ID 83642, 208-577-2900 or toll-free 877-572-5757. *Fax:* 208-577-2901. *Website:* http://www.broadviewuniversity.edu/.

# BROADVIEW UNIVERSITY–LAYTON
## Layton, UT

**CONTACT** Office of Financial Aid, Broadview University–Layton, 869 West Hill Field Road, Layton, UT 84041, 801-660-6000 or toll-free 866-253-7744. *Fax:* 801-669-6001. *Website:* http://www.broadviewuniversity.edu/.

# BROADVIEW UNIVERSITY–OREM
## Orem, UT

**CONTACT** Office of Financial Aid, Broadview University–Orem, 898 North 1200 West, Orem, UT 84057, 801-822-5800 or toll-free 877-822-5838. *Fax:* 801-822-5801. *Website:* http://www.broadviewuniversity.edu/.

# BROADVIEW UNIVERSITY–WEST JORDAN
## West Jordan, UT

**CONTACT** Office of Financial Aid, Broadview University–West Jordan, 1902 West 7800 South, West Jordan, UT 84088, 801-304-4224 or toll-free 866-304-4224. *Fax:* 801-304-4229. *Website:* http://www.broadviewuniversity.edu/.

# BROOKLINE COLLEGE
## Phoenix, AZ

**CONTACT** Financial Aid Office, Brookline College, 2445 West Dunlap Avenue, Suite 100, Phoenix, AZ 85021, 602-242-6265 or toll-free 800-793-2428. *Website:* http://brooklinecollege.edu/.

# BROOKLINE COLLEGE
## Tempe, AZ

**CONTACT** Financial Aid Office, Brookline College, 1140-1150 South Priest Drive, Tempe, AZ 85281, 480-545-8755 or toll-free 888-886-2428. *Website:* http://brooklinecollege.edu/.

# BROOKLINE COLLEGE
## Tucson, AZ

**CONTACT** Financial Aid Office, Brookline College, 5441 East 22nd Street, Suite 125, Tucson, AZ 85711, 520-748-9799 or toll-free 888-292-2428. *Website:* http://brooklinecollege.edu/.

# BROOKLINE COLLEGE
## Albuquerque, NM

**CONTACT** Financial Aid Office, Brookline College, 4201 Central Avenue NW, Suite J, Albuquerque, NM 87105-1649, 505-880-2877 or toll-free 888-660-2428. *Website:* http://brooklinecollege.edu/.

# BROOKLYN COLLEGE OF THE CITY UNIVERSITY OF NEW YORK
### Brooklyn, NY

| Tuition & fees (NY res): $6283 | Average undergraduate aid package: $7500 |
| --- | --- |

**ABOUT THE INSTITUTION** State and locally supported, coed. 76 undergraduate majors. Federal methodology is used as a basis for awarding need-based institutional aid.

**UNDERGRADUATE EXPENSES for 2015–2016 Tuition, state resident:** full-time $6030; part-time $260 per credit. **Tuition, nonresident:** full-time $12,840; part-time $535 per credit. **Required fees:** full-time $253. **Room only:** $8990.

**FRESHMAN FINANCIAL AID (Fall 2013)** 1,013 applied for aid; of those 83% were deemed to have need. 94% of freshmen with need received aid; of those 81% had need fully met. **Average percent of need met:** 94% (excluding resources awarded to replace EFC). **Average financial aid package:** $7500 (excluding resources awarded to replace EFC). 22% of all full-time freshmen had no need and received non-need-based gift aid.

**UNDERGRADUATE FINANCIAL AID (Fall 2013)** 8,998 applied for aid; of those 87% were deemed to have need. 89% of undergraduates with need received aid; of those 76% had need fully met. **Average percent of need met:** 95% (excluding resources awarded to replace EFC). **Average financial aid package:** $7500 (excluding resources awarded to replace EFC). 11% of all full-time undergraduates had no need and received non-need-based gift aid.

**GIFT AID (NEED-BASED) Total amount:** $52,556,630 (57% federal, 43% state). **Receiving aid:** Freshmen: 61% (690); all full-time undergraduates: 74% (6,831). **Average award:** Freshmen: $3300; Undergraduates: $3300. **Scholarships, grants, and awards:** Federal Pell, FSEOG, state, private, college/university gift aid from institutional funds.

**GIFT AID (NON-NEED-BASED) Total amount:** $1,252,748 (4% federal, 3% state, 88% institutional, 5% external sources). **Receiving aid:** Freshmen: 25% (288). Undergraduates: 22% (2,005). **Average award:** Freshmen: $3500. Undergraduates: $3500. **Scholarships, grants, and awards by category:** Academic interests/achievement: 209 awards ($630,000 total): general academic interests/achievements. Creative arts/performance: 16 awards ($32,000 total): general creative arts/performance.

**LOANS Student loans:** $31,315,475 (98% need-based, 2% non-need-based). 48% of past graduating class borrowed through all loan programs. **Average indebtedness per student:** $12,500. **Average need-based loan:** Freshmen: $3200. Undergraduates: $3200. **Parent loans:** $404,049 (100% need-based). **Programs:** Federal Direct (Subsidized and Unsubsidized Stafford, PLUS), Perkins.

**WORK-STUDY Federal work-study:** 1,350 jobs averaging $1400. **State or other work-study/employment:** Total amount: $123,915 (100% need-based). Part-time jobs available.

**APPLYING FOR FINANCIAL AID Required financial aid forms:** FAFSA, state aid form. **Financial aid deadline:** 5/1. **Notification date:** Continuous beginning 5/15.

**CONTACT** Mr. Ahad Farhang, Director of Financial Aid, Brooklyn College of the City University of New York, 2900 Bedford Avenue, Brooklyn, NY 11210-2889, 718-951-5669. Fax: 718-951-4778. E-mail: afarhang@brooklyn.cuny.edu. Website: http://www.brooklyn.cuny.edu/.

# BROOKS INSTITUTE
### Ventura, CA

| Tuition & fees: N/R | Average undergraduate aid package: N/A |
| --- | --- |

**ABOUT THE INSTITUTION** Proprietary, coed. 4 undergraduate majors. Federal methodology is used as a basis for awarding need-based institutional aid.

**GIFT AID (NEED-BASED) Scholarships, grants, and awards:** Federal Pell, FSEOG, state, private, college/university gift aid from institutional funds, Veterans Education Benefits (GI Bill), Yellow Ribbon Grant Program.

**GIFT AID (NON-NEED-BASED) Scholarships, grants, and awards by category:** Creative arts/performance: applied art and design, art/fine arts, cinema/film/broadcasting, journalism/publications. Special achievements/activities: general special achievements/activities.

**LOANS Programs:** Federal Direct (Subsidized and Unsubsidized Stafford, PLUS), alternative loans.

**APPLYING FOR FINANCIAL AID Required financial aid forms:** FAFSA, institution's own form. **Financial aid deadline:** Continuous. **Notification date:** Continuous. Students must reply within 4 weeks of notification.

**CONTACT** Stacey Eymann, Student Finance Manager, Brooks Institute, 5301 North Ventura Avenue, Ventura, CA 93001, 888-304-3456 Ext. 58065 or toll-free 888-276-4999. Fax: 805-679-6920. E-mail: seymann@brooks.edu. Website: http://www.brooks.edu/.

# BROWN MACKIE COLLEGE–BIRMINGHAM
### Birmingham, AL

**CONTACT** Financial Aid Office, Brown Mackie College–Birmingham, 105 Vulcan Road, Suite 100, Birmingham, AL 35209, 205-909-1500 or toll-free 888-299-4699. Website: http://www.brownmackie.edu/birmingham.

# BROWN MACKIE COLLEGE–DALLAS/FT. WORTH
### Bedford, TX

**CONTACT** Financial Aid Office, Brown Mackie College–Dallas/Ft. Worth, 2200 Hwy 121, Suite 270, Bedford, TX 76021, 817-799-0500. Website: http://www.brownmackie.edu/dallas/.

# BROWN MACKIE COLLEGE–SAN ANTONIO
### San Antonio, TX

**CONTACT** Financial Aid Office, Brown Mackie College–San Antonio, 4715 Fredericksburg Road, Suite 100, San Antonio, TX 78229, 210-428-2210 or toll-free 877-460-1714. Website: http://www.brownmackie.edu/san-antonio.

# BROWN UNIVERSITY
### Providence, RI

| Tuition & fees: $47,434 | Average undergraduate aid package: $42,468 |
| --- | --- |

**ABOUT THE INSTITUTION** Independent, coed. **Awards:** bachelor's, master's, and doctoral degrees. 76 undergraduate majors. **Total enrollment:** 9,181. Undergraduates: 6,548. Freshmen: 1,559. Both federal and institutional methodology are used as a basis for awarding need-based institutional aid.

**UNDERGRADUATE EXPENSES for 2015–2016 Application fee:** $75. **Comprehensive fee:** $59,428 includes full-time tuition ($46,408), mandatory fees ($1026), and room and board ($11,994). **College room only:** $7416. Room and board charges vary according to board plan.

**FRESHMAN FINANCIAL AID (Fall 2014, est.)** 873 applied for aid; of those 87% were deemed to have need. 100% of freshmen with need received aid; of those 100% had need fully met. **Average percent of need met:** 100% (excluding resources awarded to replace EFC). **Average financial aid package:** $43,239 (excluding resources awarded to replace EFC). 1% of all full-time freshmen had no need and received non-need-based gift aid.

**UNDERGRADUATE FINANCIAL AID (Fall 2014, est.)** 3,088 applied for aid; of those 91% were deemed to have need. 100% of undergraduates with need received aid; of those 99% had need fully met. **Average percent of need met:** 100% (excluding resources awarded to replace EFC). **Average financial aid package:** $42,468 (excluding resources awarded to replace EFC). 1% of all full-time undergraduates had no need and received non-need-based gift aid.

**GIFT AID (NEED-BASED)** *Total amount:* $111,303,115 (5% federal, 90% institutional, 5% external sources). *Receiving aid:* Freshmen: 47% (727); all full-time undergraduates: 45% (2,791). *Average award:* Freshmen: $41,098; Undergraduates: $40,917. *Scholarships, grants, and awards:* Federal Pell, FSEOG, state, private, college/university gift aid from institutional funds.

**GIFT AID (NON-NEED-BASED)** *Total amount:* $4,153,253 (1% institutional, 99% external sources). *Average award:* Freshmen: $10,000. Undergraduates: $9452. *Scholarships, grants, and awards by category: Special characteristics:* 21 awards ($178,003 total): veterans, veterans' children. *Tuition waivers:* Full or partial for employees or children of employees. *ROTC:* Army cooperative.

**LOANS** *Student loans:* $10,986,717 (74% need-based, 26% non-need-based). 35% of past graduating class borrowed through all loan programs. *Average indebtedness per student:* $24,300. *Average need-based loan:* Freshmen: $5065. Undergraduates: $5628. *Parent loans:* $8,101,535 (1% need-based, 99% non-need-based). *Programs:* Federal Direct (Subsidized and Unsubsidized Stafford, PLUS), Perkins, college/university.

**WORK-STUDY** *Federal work-study:* Total amount: $3,800,252; 1,537 jobs averaging $2472. *State or other work-study/employment:* Total amount: $927,421 (100% need-based). 369 part-time jobs averaging $2513.

**APPLYING FOR FINANCIAL AID** *Required financial aid forms:* FAFSA, CSS Financial Aid PROFILE, noncustodial (divorced/separated) parent's statement. *Financial aid deadline:* 2/1. *Notification date:* 4/1. Students must reply by 5/1.

**CONTACT** Office of Financial Aid, Brown University, PO Box 1827, Providence, RI 02912, 401-863-2721. *Fax:* 401-863-7575. *E-mail:* financial_aid@brown.edu. *Website:* http://www.brown.edu/.

# BRYAN COLLEGE
## Dayton, TN

**CONTACT** Rick Taphorn, Director of Financial Aid, Bryan College, PO Box 7000, Dayton, TN 37321-7000, 423-775-7339 or toll-free 800-277-9522. *Fax:* 423-775-7300. *E-mail:* finaid@bryan.edu. *Website:* http://www.bryan.edu/.

# BRYAN COLLEGE OF HEALTH SCIENCES
## Lincoln, NE

**CONTACT** Financial Aid Office, Bryan College of Health Sciences, 5035 Everett Street, Lincoln, NE 68506-1398, 402-481-3801. *Website:* http://www.bryanhealth.com/CollegeofHealthSciences.

# BRYANT & STRATTON COLLEGE–AKRON CAMPUS
## Akron, OH

**CONTACT** Financial Aid Office, Bryant & Stratton College–Akron Campus, 190 Montrose West Avenue, Akron, OH 44321, 330-598-2500. *Website:* http://www.bryantstratton.edu/.

# BRYANT & STRATTON COLLEGE–CLEVELAND CAMPUS
## Cleveland, OH

**CONTACT** Bill Davenport, Financial Aid Supervisor, Bryant & Stratton College–Cleveland Campus, 1700 East 13th Street, Cleveland, OH 44114-3203, 216-771-1700. *Fax:* 216-771-7787. *Website:* http://www.bryantstratton.edu/.

# BRYANT & STRATTON COLLEGE–HAMPTON CAMPUS
## Hampton, VA

**CONTACT** Financial Aid Office, Bryant & Stratton College–Hampton Campus, 4410 East Claiborne Square, Suite 233, Hampton, VA 23666, 757-896-6001. *Website:* http://www.bryantstratton.edu/.

# BRYANT & STRATTON COLLEGE–WAUWATOSA CAMPUS
## Wauwatosa, WI

**CONTACT** Financial Aid Office, Bryant & Stratton College–Wauwatosa Campus, 10950 W. Potter Road, Wauwatosa, WI 53226, 414-302-7000. *Website:* http://www.bryantstratton.edu/.

# BRYANT UNIVERSITY
## Smithfield, RI

| Tuition & fees: $39,808 | Average undergraduate aid package: $21,753 |
|---|---|

**ABOUT THE INSTITUTION** Independent, coed. *Awards:* bachelor's and master's degrees. 46 undergraduate majors. *Total enrollment:* 3,462. Undergraduates: 3,320. Freshmen: 826. Federal methodology is used as a basis for awarding need-based institutional aid.

**UNDERGRADUATE EXPENSES for 2015–2016** *Application fee:* $50. *Comprehensive fee:* $54,361 includes full-time tuition ($39,421), mandatory fees ($387), and room and board ($14,553). *College room only:* $8542. Room and board charges vary according to board plan and housing facility. *Part-time tuition:* $977.16 per credit hour. Part-time tuition and fees vary according to course load.

**FRESHMAN FINANCIAL AID (Fall 2014, est.)** 700 applied for aid; of those 83% were deemed to have need. 99% of freshmen with need received aid; of those 50% had need fully met. *Average percent of need met:* 51% (excluding resources awarded to replace EFC). *Average financial aid package:* $20,968 (excluding resources awarded to replace EFC). 25% of all full-time freshmen had no need and received non-need-based gift aid.

**UNDERGRADUATE FINANCIAL AID (Fall 2014, est.)** 2,310 applied for aid; of those 88% were deemed to have need. 100% of undergraduates with need received aid; of those 50% had need fully met. *Average percent of need met:* 52% (excluding resources awarded to replace EFC). *Average financial aid package:* $21,753 (excluding resources awarded to replace EFC). 21% of all full-time undergraduates had no need and received non-need-based gift aid.

**GIFT AID (NEED-BASED)** *Total amount:* $26,345,218 (8% federal, 1% state, 88% institutional, 3% external sources). *Receiving aid:* Freshmen: 44% (409); all full-time undergraduates: 48% (1,559). *Average award:* Freshmen: $9008; Undergraduates: $10,320. *Scholarships, grants, and awards:* Federal Pell, FSEOG, state, private, college/university gift aid from institutional funds.

**GIFT AID (NON-NEED-BASED)** *Total amount:* $17,406,206 (96% institutional, 4% external sources). *Receiving aid:* Freshmen: 47% (432). Undergraduates: 41% (1,341). *Average award:* Freshmen: $13,820. Undergraduates: $13,406. *Scholarships, grants, and awards by category: Academic interests/achievement:* general academic interests/achievements. *Special characteristics:* international students, members of minority groups, siblings of current students. *Tuition waivers:* Full or partial for employees or children of employees. *ROTC:* Army cooperative.

**LOANS** *Student loans:* $27,493,852 (38% need-based, 62% non-need-based). 78% of past graduating class borrowed through all loan programs. *Average indebtedness per student:* $39,283. *Average need-based loan:* Freshmen: $3978. Undergraduates: $5115. *Parent loans:* $9,061,113 (32% need-based, 68% non-need-based). *Programs:* Federal Direct (Subsidized and Unsubsidized Stafford, PLUS), Perkins, private loans.

**WORK-STUDY** *Federal work-study:* Total amount: $295,455; jobs available. *State or other work-study/employment:* Total amount: $1,510,811 (30% need-based, 70% non-need-based). Part-time jobs available.

**ATHLETIC AWARDS** Total amount: $6,402,195 (42% need-based, 58% non-need-based).

**APPLYING FOR FINANCIAL AID** *Required financial aid form:* FAFSA. *Financial aid deadline (priority):* 2/15. *Notification date:* 3/24. Students must reply by 5/1.

**CONTACT** Mr. John B. Canning, Director of Financial Aid, Bryant University, 1150 Douglas Pike, Smithfield, RI 02917-1284, 401-232-6020 or toll-free 800-622-7001. *Fax:* 401-232-6293. *E-mail:* jcanning@bryant.edu. *Website:* http://www.bryant.edu/.

---

# BRYAN UNIVERSITY
## Springfield, MO

**CONTACT** Financial Aid Office, Bryan University, 4255 Nature Center Way, Springfield, MO 65804, 417-862-5700 or toll-free 855-566-0650. *Website:* http://www.bryanu.edu/campus-locations/springfield-missouri/.

---

# BRYN ATHYN COLLEGE OF THE NEW CHURCH
## Bryn Athyn, PA

**CONTACT** Wendy Cooper, Associate Director of Financial Aid, Bryn Athyn College of the New Church, Box 717, Bryn Athyn, PA 19009, 267-502-2630 or toll-free 800-767-9552. *Fax:* 267-502-4866. *E-mail:* financialaid@brynathyn.edu. *Website:* http://www.brynathyn.edu/.

---

# BRYN MAWR COLLEGE
## Bryn Mawr, PA

| Tuition & fees: $47,140 | Average undergraduate aid package: $42,369 |
|---|---|

**ABOUT THE INSTITUTION** Independent, undergraduate: women only; graduate: coed. *Awards:* certificates, bachelor's, master's, and doctoral degrees. 33 undergraduate majors. *Total enrollment:* 1,709. Undergraduates: 1,308. Freshmen: 351. Institutional methodology is used as a basis for awarding need-based institutional aid.

**UNDERGRADUATE EXPENSES for 2015–2016** *Application fee:* $50. *Comprehensive fee:* $61,990 includes full-time tuition ($46,030), mandatory fees ($1110), and room and board ($14,850). *College room only:* $8470. *Part-time tuition:* $5755 per course.

**FRESHMAN FINANCIAL AID (Fall 2014, est.)** 225 applied for aid; of those 78% were deemed to have need. 100% of freshmen with need received aid; of those 100% had need fully met. *Average percent of need met:* 100% (excluding resources awarded to replace EFC). *Average financial aid package:* $42,724 (excluding resources awarded to replace EFC). 9% of all full-time freshmen had no need and received non-need-based gift aid.

**UNDERGRADUATE FINANCIAL AID (Fall 2014, est.)** 778 applied for aid; of those 87% were deemed to have need. 98% of undergraduates with need received aid; of those 100% had need fully met. *Average percent of need met:* 100% (excluding resources awarded to replace EFC). *Average financial aid package:* $42,369 (excluding resources awarded to replace EFC). 5% of all full-time undergraduates had no need and received non-need-based gift aid.

**GIFT AID (NEED-BASED)** *Total amount:* $26,883,803 (4% federal, 1% state, 93% institutional, 2% external sources). *Receiving aid:* Freshmen: 50% (176); all full-time undergraduates: 52% (664). *Average award:* Freshmen: $36,525; Undergraduates: $36,402. *Scholarships, grants, and awards:* Federal Pell, FSEOG, state, college/university gift aid from institutional funds.

**GIFT AID (NON-NEED-BASED)** *Total amount:* $1,260,018 (97% institutional, 3% external sources). *Receiving aid:* Freshmen: 4% (13). Undergraduates: 2% (30). *Average award:* Freshmen: $10,750. Undergraduates: $10,833. *Scholarships, grants, and awards by category:* Academic interests/achievement: general academic interests/achievements. Special achievements/activities: leadership. *ROTC:* Air Force cooperative.

**LOANS** *Student loans:* $4,088,147 (63% need-based, 37% non-need-based). 64% of past graduating class borrowed through all loan programs. *Average indebtedness per student:* $24,466. *Average need-based loan:* Freshmen: $4671. Undergraduates: $4821. *Parent loans:* $1,077,558 (100% non-need-based). *Programs:* Federal Direct (Subsidized and Unsubsidized Stafford, PLUS), Perkins.

**WORK-STUDY** *Federal work-study:* Total amount: $838,172; jobs available. *State or other work-study/employment:* Total amount: $395,797 (100% need-based). Part-time jobs available.

**APPLYING FOR FINANCIAL AID** *Required financial aid forms:* FAFSA, CSS Financial Aid PROFILE. *Financial aid deadline:* 3/1. *Notification date:* Continuous beginning 3/23. Students must reply by 5/1.

**CONTACT** Ethel M. Desmarais, Director of Student Financial Services, Bryn Mawr College, 101 North Merion Avenue, Bryn Mawr, PA 19010-2899, 610-526-7922 or toll-free 800-BMC-1885. *Fax:* 610-526-5249. *E-mail:* edesmara@brynmawr.edu. *Website:* http://www.brynmawr.edu/.

---

# BUCKNELL UNIVERSITY
## Lewisburg, PA

| Tuition & fees: $50,152 | Average undergraduate aid package: $30,000 |
|---|---|

**ABOUT THE INSTITUTION** Independent, coed. *Awards:* bachelor's and master's degrees. 68 undergraduate majors. *Total enrollment:* 3,624. Undergraduates: 3,565. Freshmen: 939. Both federal and institutional methodology are used as a basis for awarding need-based institutional aid.

**UNDERGRADUATE EXPENSES for 2015–2016** *Application fee:* $40. *Comprehensive fee:* $62,368 includes full-time tuition ($49,878), mandatory fees ($274), and room and board ($12,216). *College room only:* $7450. Room and board charges vary according to board plan and housing facility. *Part-time tuition:* $1369 per credit hour. *Payment plan:* Tuition prepayment.

**FRESHMAN FINANCIAL AID (Fall 2014, est.)** 530 applied for aid; of those 72% were deemed to have need. 100% of freshmen with need received aid; of those 90% had need fully met. *Average percent of need met:* 91% (excluding resources awarded to replace EFC). *Average financial aid package:* $31,500 (excluding resources awarded to replace EFC). 12% of all full-time freshmen had no need and received non-need-based gift aid.

**UNDERGRADUATE FINANCIAL AID (Fall 2014, est.)** 1,797 applied for aid; of those 83% were deemed to have need. 100% of undergraduates with need received aid; of those 90% had need fully met. *Average percent of need met:* 91% (excluding resources awarded to replace EFC). *Average financial aid package:* $30,000 (excluding resources awarded to replace EFC). 9% of all full-time undergraduates had no need and received non-need-based gift aid.

**GIFT AID (NEED-BASED)** *Total amount:* $49,647,251 (4% federal, 2% state, 91% institutional, 3% external sources). *Receiving aid:* Freshmen: 38% (360); all full-time undergraduates: 40% (1,404). *Average award:* Freshmen: $26,700; Undergraduates: $24,000. *Scholarships, grants, and awards:* Federal Pell, FSEOG, state, private, college/university gift aid from institutional funds.

**GIFT AID (NON-NEED-BASED)** *Total amount:* $3,797,700 (100% institutional). *Receiving aid:* Freshmen: 11% (104). Undergraduates: 8% (284). *Average award:* Freshmen: $11,668. Undergraduates: $13,808. *Scholarships, grants, and awards by category:* Academic interests/achievement: 200 awards ($2,578,000 total): business, engineering/technologies, general academic interests/achievements, mathematics, physical sciences. Creative arts/performance: 128 awards ($734,759 total): art/fine arts, creative writing, dance, music, performing arts, theater/drama. Special achievements/activities: 120 awards ($5,748,419 total): general special achievements/activities, leadership. *Tuition waivers:* Full or partial for employees or children of employees. *ROTC:* Army.

**LOANS** *Student loans:* $12,224,718 (100% need-based). 55% of past graduating class borrowed through all loan programs. *Average indebtedness per student:* $22,500. *Average need-based loan:* Freshmen: $3500. Undergraduates: $5500. *Parent loans:* $6,432,075 (100% non-need-based). *Programs:* Federal Direct (Subsidized and Unsubsidized Stafford, PLUS), Perkins.

**WORK-STUDY** *Federal work-study:* Total amount: $350,000; 600 jobs averaging $1500. *State or other work-study/employment:* Total amount: $30,000 (100% need-based). 50 part-time jobs averaging $1500.

**ATHLETIC AWARDS** Total amount: $6,255,368 (48% need-based, 52% non-need-based).

**APPLYING FOR FINANCIAL AID** *Required financial aid forms:* FAFSA, CSS Financial Aid PROFILE, noncustodial (divorced/separated) parent's statement. *Financial aid deadline:* 1/15. *Notification date:* 4/1. Students must reply by 5/1.
**CONTACT** Andrea Leithner Stauffer, Director of Financial Aid, Bucknell University, 1 Dent Drive, Lewisburg, PA 17837, 570-577-1331. *Fax:* 570-577-1481. *E-mail:* finaid@bucknell.edu.
*Website:* http://www.bucknell.edu/.

# BUENA VISTA UNIVERSITY
## Storm Lake, IA

| Tuition & fees: $31,318 | Average undergraduate aid package: $27,355 |
|---|---|

**ABOUT THE INSTITUTION** Independent Presbyterian Church (U.S.A.), coed. *Awards:* bachelor's and master's degrees. 59 undergraduate majors. *Total enrollment:* 914. Undergraduates: 861. Freshmen: 201. Federal methodology is used as a basis for awarding need-based institutional aid.
**UNDERGRADUATE EXPENSES for 2015–2016** *Comprehensive fee:* $40,364 includes full-time tuition ($31,318) and room and board ($9046). Full-time tuition and fees vary according to location. Room and board charges vary according to board plan. Part-time tuition and fees vary according to location.
**FRESHMAN FINANCIAL AID (Fall 2014, est.)** 180 applied for aid; of those 91% were deemed to have need. 100% of freshmen with need received aid; of those 67% had need fully met. *Average percent of need met:* 91% (excluding resources awarded to replace EFC). *Average financial aid package:* $28,498 (excluding resources awarded to replace EFC). 8% of all full-time freshmen had no need and received non-need-based gift aid.
**UNDERGRADUATE FINANCIAL AID (Fall 2014, est.)** 750 applied for aid; of those 92% were deemed to have need. 100% of undergraduates with need received aid; of those 32% had need fully met. *Average percent of need met:* 89% (excluding resources awarded to replace EFC). *Average financial aid package:* $27,355 (excluding resources awarded to replace EFC). 7% of all full-time undergraduates had no need and received non-need-based gift aid.
**GIFT AID (NEED-BASED)** *Total amount:* $18,351,390 (10% federal, 10% state, 80% institutional). *Receiving aid:* Freshmen: 81% (163); all full-time undergraduates: 83% (691). *Average award:* Freshmen: $22,426; Undergraduates: $21,480. *Scholarships, grants, and awards:* Federal Pell, FSEOG, state, private, college/university gift aid from institutional funds.
**GIFT AID (NON-NEED-BASED)** *Total amount:* $12,439,179 (1% state, 97% institutional, 2% external sources). *Receiving aid:* Freshmen: 69% (138). Undergraduates: 70% (580). *Average award:* Freshmen: $19,601. Undergraduates: $17,766. *Scholarships, grants, and awards by category:* Academic interests/achievement: biological sciences, business, computer science, education, general academic interests/achievements, humanities, international studies, mathematics. *Creative arts/performance:* art/fine arts, music, theater/drama. *Special achievements/activities:* general special achievements/activities, leadership. *Special characteristics:* children of faculty/staff, ethnic background, international students, out-of-state students, religious affiliation, siblings of current students. *Tuition waivers:* Full or partial for employees or children of employees. *ROTC:* Army.
**LOANS** *Student loans:* $6,900,935 (45% need-based, 55% non-need-based). 80% of past graduating class borrowed through all loan programs. *Average indebtedness per student:* $34,173. *Average need-based loan:* Freshmen: $5149. Undergraduates: $5700. *Parent loans:* $1,142,724 (100% non-need-based). *Programs:* Federal Direct (Subsidized and Unsubsidized Stafford, PLUS), Perkins, college/university.
**WORK-STUDY** *Federal work-study:* Total amount: $421,900; jobs available. *State or other work-study/employment:* Total amount: $204,446 (100% non-need-based). Part-time jobs available.
**APPLYING FOR FINANCIAL AID** *Required financial aid form:* FAFSA. *Financial aid deadline (priority):* 6/1. *Notification date:* Continuous beginning 2/1.
**CONTACT** Mrs. Leanne Valentine, Director of Financial Assistance, Buena Vista University, 610 West Fourth Street, Storm Lake, IA 50588, 712-749-2164 or toll-free 800-383-9600. *Fax:* 712-749-1451. *E-mail:* valentinel@bvu.edu.
*Website:* http://www.bvu.edu/.

# BUFFALO STATE COLLEGE, STATE UNIVERSITY OF NEW YORK
## Buffalo, NY

| Tuition & fees (NY res): $7347 | Average undergraduate aid package: $12,749 |
|---|---|

**ABOUT THE INSTITUTION** State-supported, coed. *Awards:* certificates, bachelor's, and master's degrees. 79 undergraduate majors. *Total enrollment:* 11,083. Undergraduates: 9,475. Freshmen: 1,869. Federal methodology is used as a basis for awarding need-based institutional aid.
**UNDERGRADUATE EXPENSES for 2015–2016** *Application fee:* $50. *Tuition, state resident:* full-time $6170; part-time $257 per credit hour. *Tuition, nonresident:* full-time $15,820; part-time $659 per credit hour. *Required fees:* full-time $1177. Part-time tuition and fees vary according to course load. *College room and board:* $11,964; *Room only:* $7060. Room and board charges vary according to board plan, housing facility, and student level.
**FRESHMAN FINANCIAL AID (Fall 2014, est.)** 1,760 applied for aid; of those 96% were deemed to have need. 99% of freshmen with need received aid; of those 12% had need fully met. *Average percent of need met:* 14% (excluding resources awarded to replace EFC). *Average financial aid package:* $13,420 (excluding resources awarded to replace EFC). 9% of all full-time freshmen had no need and received non-need-based gift aid.
**UNDERGRADUATE FINANCIAL AID (Fall 2014, est.)** 7,355 applied for aid; of those 99% were deemed to have need. 98% of undergraduates with need received aid; of those 18% had need fully met. *Average percent of need met:* 23% (excluding resources awarded to replace EFC). *Average financial aid package:* $12,749 (excluding resources awarded to replace EFC). 7% of all full-time undergraduates had no need and received non-need-based gift aid.
**GIFT AID (NEED-BASED)** *Total amount:* $39,598,689 (53% federal, 47% state). *Receiving aid:* Freshmen: 76% (1,419); all full-time undergraduates: 68% (5,651). *Average award:* Freshmen: $7578; Undergraduates: $6850. *Scholarships, grants, and awards:* Federal Pell, FSEOG, state, private.
**GIFT AID (NON-NEED-BASED)** *Total amount:* $2,809,191 (13% federal, 1% state, 40% institutional, 46% external sources). *Receiving aid:* Freshmen: 16% (300). Undergraduates: 12% (976). *Average award:* Freshmen: $1894. Undergraduates: $1959. *Scholarships, grants, and awards by category:* Academic interests/achievement: 496 awards: biological sciences, business, communication, computer science, education, engineering/technologies, foreign languages, general academic interests/achievements, health fields, home economics, mathematics, physical sciences, social sciences. *Creative arts/performance:* 124 awards: applied art and design, art/fine arts, general creative arts/performance, music, performing arts, theater/drama. *Special achievements/activities:* general special achievements/activities. *Special characteristics:* 24 awards: general special characteristics, international students. *Tuition waivers:* Full or partial for employees or children of employees. *ROTC:* Army cooperative.
**LOANS** *Student loans:* $36,232,779 (57% need-based, 43% non-need-based). 73% of past graduating class borrowed through all loan programs. *Average indebtedness per student:* $24,290. *Average need-based loan:* Freshmen: $3582. Undergraduates: $4180. *Parent loans:* $9,617,695 (47% need-based, 53% non-need-based). *Programs:* Federal Direct (Subsidized and Unsubsidized Stafford, PLUS), Perkins.
**WORK-STUDY** *Federal work-study:* Total amount: $941,230; 372 jobs averaging $2593. *State or other work-study/employment:* 400 part-time jobs averaging $3317.
**APPLYING FOR FINANCIAL AID** *Required financial aid form:* FAFSA. *Financial aid deadline (priority):* 3/1. *Notification date:* Continuous beginning 5/1.
**CONTACT** Connie F. Cooke, Director of Financial Aid, Buffalo State College, State University of New York, 1300 Elmwood Avenue, Buffalo, NY 14222-1095, 716-878-4902. *Fax:* 716-878-4903. *E-mail:* finaid@buffalostate.edu.
*Website:* http://www.buffalostate.edu/.

# BURLINGTON COLLEGE
## Burlington, VT
**ABOUT THE INSTITUTION** Independent, coed. 18 undergraduate majors.

**GIFT AID (NEED-BASED)** *Scholarships, grants, and awards:* Federal Pell, FSEOG, state, private, college/university gift aid from institutional funds.

**GIFT AID (NON-NEED-BASED)** *Scholarships, grants, and awards by category:* *Academic interests/achievement:* general academic interests/achievements. *Special achievements/activities:* community service, general special achievements/activities, leadership.

**LOANS** *Programs:* Federal Direct (Subsidized and Unsubsidized Stafford, PLUS), Perkins.

**WORK-STUDY** *Federal work-study:* jobs available. *State or other work-study/employment:* Total amount: $4000 (100% non-need-based). Part-time jobs available.

**APPLYING FOR FINANCIAL AID** *Required financial aid form:* FAFSA.

**CONTACT** Ms. Lindy Walsh, Director of Financial Aid, Burlington College, 351 North Avenue, Burlington, VT 05401, 802-862-9616 or toll-free 800-862-9616. *Fax:* 802-846-3072. *E-mail:* lwalsh@burlington.edu. *Website:* http://www.burlington.edu/.

# BUTLER UNIVERSITY
## Indianapolis, IN

| Tuition & fees: $35,652 | Average undergraduate aid package: $23,034 |
| --- | --- |

**ABOUT THE INSTITUTION** Independent, coed. *Awards:* associate, bachelor's, master's, and doctoral degrees. 64 undergraduate majors. *Total enrollment:* 4,848. Undergraduates: 4,062. Freshmen: 971. Federal methodology is used as a basis for awarding need-based institutional aid.

**UNDERGRADUATE EXPENSES** for 2015–2016 *Application fee:* $35. *Comprehensive fee:* $47,272 includes full-time tuition ($34,750), mandatory fees ($902), and room and board ($11,620). *College room only:* $5460. Full-time tuition and fees vary according to course load, degree level, and program. Room and board charges vary according to housing facility. *Part-time tuition:* $1450 per credit hour. Part-time tuition and fees vary according to course load, degree level, and program.

**FRESHMAN FINANCIAL AID (Fall 2014, est.)** 920 applied for aid; of those 65% were deemed to have need. 100% of freshmen with need received aid; of those 14% had need fully met. *Average percent of need met:* 68% (excluding resources awarded to replace EFC). *Average financial aid package:* $23,639 (excluding resources awarded to replace EFC). 32% of all full-time freshmen had no need and received non-need-based gift aid.

**UNDERGRADUATE FINANCIAL AID (Fall 2014, est.)** 3,853 applied for aid; of those 69% were deemed to have need. 100% of undergraduates with need received aid; of those 13% had need fully met. *Average percent of need met:* 68% (excluding resources awarded to replace EFC). *Average financial aid package:* $23,034 (excluding resources awarded to replace EFC). 27% of all full-time undergraduates had no need and received non-need-based gift aid.

**GIFT AID (NEED-BASED)** *Total amount:* $47,391,916 (6% federal, 7% state, 80% institutional, 7% external sources). *Receiving aid:* Freshmen: 62% (596); all full-time undergraduates: 62% (2,600). *Average award:* Freshmen: $19,143; Undergraduates: $18,704. *Scholarships, grants, and awards:* Federal Pell, FSEOG, state, private, college/university gift aid from institutional funds.

**GIFT AID (NON-NEED-BASED)** *Total amount:* $16,083,295 (87% institutional, 13% external sources). *Receiving aid:* Freshmen: 10% (95). Undergraduates: 9% (363). *Average award:* Freshmen: $13,157. Undergraduates: $11,979. *Scholarships, grants, and awards by category:* *Academic interests/achievement:* biological sciences, business, communication, computer science, education, engineering/technologies, English, foreign languages, general academic interests/achievements, health fields, humanities, international studies, mathematics, physical sciences, premedicine, religion/biblical studies, social sciences. *Creative arts/performance:* applied art and design, art/fine arts, cinema/film/broadcasting, dance, journalism/publications, music, performing arts, theater/drama. *Special characteristics:* veterans, veterans' children. *Tuition waivers:* Full or partial for employees or children of employees. **ROTC:** Army, Air Force cooperative.

**LOANS** *Student loans:* $29,473,174 (71% need-based, 29% non-need-based). 68% of past graduating class borrowed through all loan programs. *Average indebtedness per student:* $35,797. *Average need-based loan:* Freshmen: $4141. Undergraduates: $5192. *Parent loans:* $9,325,431 (38% need-based, 62% non-need-based). *Programs:* Federal Direct (Subsidized and Unsubsidized Stafford, PLUS), Perkins.

**WORK-STUDY** *Federal work-study:* Total amount: $355,777; 193 jobs averaging $962.

**ATHLETIC AWARDS** Total amount: $4,173,729 (31% need-based, 69% non-need-based).

**APPLYING FOR FINANCIAL AID** *Required financial aid form:* FAFSA. *Financial aid deadline (priority):* 3/1. *Notification date:* 3/15. Students must reply within 3 weeks of notification.

**CONTACT** Mrs. Leslie Middleton, Associate Director of Financial Aid, Butler University, 4600 Sunset Avenue, Indianapolis, IN 46208-3485, 317-940-8200 or toll-free 888-940-8100. *Fax:* 317-940-8250. *E-mail:* lmmiddle@butler.edu. *Website:* http://www.butler.edu/.

# CABARRUS COLLEGE OF HEALTH SCIENCES
## Concord, NC

| Tuition & fees: $11,970 | Average undergraduate aid package: N/A |
| --- | --- |

**ABOUT THE INSTITUTION** Independent, coed, primarily women. *Awards:* certificates, diplomas, associate, bachelor's, and master's degrees. 10 undergraduate majors. *Total enrollment:* 448. Undergraduates: 438. Freshmen: 31. Federal methodology is used as a basis for awarding need-based institutional aid.

**UNDERGRADUATE EXPENSES** for 2015–2016 *Application fee:* $50. *Tuition:* full-time $11,650. Full-time tuition and fees vary according to course load. Part-time tuition and fees vary according to course load.

**FRESHMAN FINANCIAL AID (Fall 2013)** 23 applied for aid; of those 91% were deemed to have need. 100% of freshmen with need received aid.

**GIFT AID (NEED-BASED)** *Total amount:* $1,611,707 (42% federal, 44% state, 12% institutional, 2% external sources). *Receiving aid:* Freshmen: 84% (21). *Scholarships, grants, and awards:* Federal Pell, FSEOG, state, college/university gift aid from institutional funds.

**GIFT AID (NON-NEED-BASED)** *Scholarships, grants, and awards by category:* *Special characteristics:* first-generation college students.

**LOANS** *Student loans:* $3,342,903 (42% need-based, 58% non-need-based). *Parent loans:* $18,300 (100% non-need-based). *Programs:* Federal Direct (Subsidized and Unsubsidized Stafford, PLUS), state.

**WORK-STUDY** *Federal work-study:* 12 jobs averaging $1062. *State or other work-study/employment:* Total amount: $37,750 (100% non-need-based). Part-time jobs available.

**APPLYING FOR FINANCIAL AID** *Required financial aid form:* FAFSA. *Financial aid deadline (priority):* 4/15. *Notification date:* Continuous beginning 7/1. Students must reply within 2 weeks of notification.

**CONTACT** Valerie Richard, Director of Financial Aid, Cabarrus College of Health Sciences, 401 Medical Park Drive, Concord, NC 28025, 704-403-3507. *Fax:* 704-403-2077. *E-mail:* valerie.richard@carolinashealthcare.org. *Website:* http://www.cabarruscollege.edu/.

# CABRINI COLLEGE
## Radnor, PA

| Tuition & fees: $29,842 | Average undergraduate aid package: $16,687 |
| --- | --- |

**ABOUT THE INSTITUTION** Independent Roman Catholic, coed. *Awards:* bachelor's and master's degrees. 36 undergraduate majors. *Total enrollment:* 2,203. Undergraduates: 1,406. Freshmen: 393. Federal methodology is used as a basis for awarding need-based institutional aid.

**UNDERGRADUATE EXPENSES** for 2015–2016 *Application fee:* $35. *Comprehensive fee:* $42,068 includes full-time tuition ($28,932), mandatory fees ($910), and room and board ($12,226). Room and board charges vary according to board plan and housing facility. *Part-time tuition:* $525 per credit hour. Part-time tuition and fees vary according to course load.

**FRESHMAN FINANCIAL AID (Fall 2013)** 298 applied for aid; of those 88% were deemed to have need. 100% of freshmen with need received aid; of those 21% had need fully met. *Average percent of need met:* 56% (excluding resources awarded to replace EFC). *Average financial aid package:* $14,689 (excluding resources

awarded to replace EFC). 14% of all full-time freshmen had no need and received non-need-based gift aid.

**UNDERGRADUATE FINANCIAL AID (Fall 2013)** 1,212 applied for aid; of those 80% were deemed to have need. 100% of undergraduates with need received aid; of those 27% had need fully met. *Average percent of need met:* 53% (excluding resources awarded to replace EFC). *Average financial aid package:* $16,687 (excluding resources awarded to replace EFC). 22% of all full-time undergraduates had no need and received non-need-based gift aid.

**GIFT AID (NEED-BASED)** *Total amount:* $18,273,053 (12% federal, 7% state, 80% institutional, 1% external sources). *Receiving aid:* Freshmen: 70% (213); all full-time undergraduates: 61% (750). *Average award:* Freshmen: $8168; Undergraduates: $8079. *Scholarships, grants, and awards:* Federal Pell, FSEOG, state, private, college/university gift aid from institutional funds.

**GIFT AID (NON-NEED-BASED)** *Total amount:* $2,670,270 (100% institutional). *Receiving aid:* Freshmen: 83% (251). Undergraduates: 78% (956). *Average award:* Freshmen: $10,941. Undergraduates: $11,677. *Scholarships, grants, and awards by category: Academic interests/achievement:* general academic interests/achievements. *Special characteristics:* children and siblings of alumni, out-of-state students, religious affiliation, siblings of current students. *Tuition waivers:* Full or partial for children of alumni, employees or children of employees, senior citizens. *ROTC:* Army cooperative, Air Force cooperative.

**LOANS** *Student loans:* $10,148,764 (96% need-based, 4% non-need-based). 100% of past graduating class borrowed through all loan programs. *Average indebtedness per student:* $35,880. *Average need-based loan:* Freshmen: $2889. Undergraduates: $3777. *Parent loans:* $3,125,443 (88% need-based, 12% non-need-based). *Programs:* Federal Direct (Subsidized and Unsubsidized Stafford, PLUS), Perkins.

**WORK-STUDY** *Federal work-study:* 272 jobs averaging $1429.

**APPLYING FOR FINANCIAL AID** *Required financial aid form:* FAFSA. *Financial aid deadline (priority):* 2/15. *Notification date:* Continuous beginning 3/1. Students must reply by 5/1.

**CONTACT** Ms. Elizabeth Gingerich, Director of Financial Aid, Cabrini College, 610 King of Prussia Road, Grace Hall, First Floor, Radnor, PA 19087-3698, 610-902-8424 or toll-free 800-848-1003. *Fax:* 610-902-8426. *E-mail:* egs34@cabrini.edu. *Website:* http://www.cabrini.edu/.

# CAIRN UNIVERSITY
### Langhorne, PA

| Tuition & fees: $23,920 | Average undergraduate aid package: $18,367 |
|---|---|

**ABOUT THE INSTITUTION** Independent nondenominational, coed. *Awards:* certificates, bachelor's, and master's degrees. 18 undergraduate majors. *Total enrollment:* 1,062. Undergraduates: 817. Freshmen: 159. Federal methodology is used as a basis for awarding need-based institutional aid.

**UNDERGRADUATE EXPENSES** for 2015–2016 *Application fee:* $25. *Comprehensive fee:* $33,270 includes full-time tuition ($23,710), mandatory fees ($210), and room and board ($9350). *College room only:* $4895. Full-time tuition and fees vary according to course load. Room and board charges vary according to board plan and location. *Part-time tuition:* $703 per credit. Part-time tuition and fees vary according to course load.

**FRESHMAN FINANCIAL AID (Fall 2014, est.)** 141 applied for aid; of those 89% were deemed to have need. 100% of freshmen with need received aid; of those 13% had need fully met. *Average percent of need met:* 76% (excluding resources awarded to replace EFC). *Average financial aid package:* $20,728 (excluding resources awarded to replace EFC). 20% of all full-time freshmen had no need and received non-need-based gift aid.

**UNDERGRADUATE FINANCIAL AID (Fall 2014, est.)** 681 applied for aid; of those 93% were deemed to have need. 100% of undergraduates with need received aid; of those 14% had need fully met. *Average percent of need met:* 73% (excluding resources awarded to replace EFC). *Average financial aid package:* $18,367 (excluding resources awarded to replace EFC). 15% of all full-time undergraduates had no need and received non-need-based gift aid.

**GIFT AID (NEED-BASED)** *Total amount:* $8,368,557 (18% federal, 7% state, 74% institutional, 1% external sources). *Receiving aid:* Freshmen: 79% (126); all full-time undergraduates: 79% (611). *Average award:* Freshmen: $16,454; Undergraduates: $13,987. *Scholarships, grants, and awards:* Federal Pell, FSEOG, state, private, college/university gift aid from institutional funds.

**GIFT AID (NON-NEED-BASED)** *Total amount:* $1,438,436 (97% institutional, 3% external sources). *Receiving aid:* Freshmen: 9% (14). Undergraduates: 8% (61). *Average award:* Freshmen: $11,200. Undergraduates: $10,065. *Scholarships, grants, and awards by category: Academic interests/achievement:* general academic interests/achievements. *Creative arts/performance:* music. *Special achievements/activities:* general special achievements/activities. *Special characteristics:* children of faculty/staff, relatives of clergy. *Tuition waivers:* Full or partial for employees or children of employees. *ROTC:* Air Force cooperative.

**LOANS** *Student loans:* $5,639,700 (78% need-based, 22% non-need-based). 76% of past graduating class borrowed through all loan programs. *Average indebtedness per student:* $33,016. *Average need-based loan:* Freshmen: $3707. Undergraduates: $4735. *Parent loans:* $829,459 (54% need-based, 46% non-need-based). *Programs:* Federal Direct (Subsidized and Unsubsidized Stafford, PLUS).

**WORK-STUDY** *Federal work-study:* Total amount: $255,410; jobs available.

**APPLYING FOR FINANCIAL AID** *Required financial aid form:* FAFSA. *Financial aid deadline:* Continuous. *Notification date:* Continuous beginning 2/15. Students must reply within 2 weeks of notification.

**CONTACT** Mr. Stephen Cassel, Director of Financial Aid, Cairn University, 200 Manor Avenue, Langhorne, PA 19047-2990, 215-702-4243 or toll-free 800-366-0049. *Fax:* 215-702-4248. *E-mail:* scassel@cairn.edu. *Website:* http://cairn.edu/.

# CALDWELL UNIVERSITY
### Caldwell, NJ

| Tuition & fees: $30,050 | Average undergraduate aid package: $22,000 |
|---|---|

**ABOUT THE INSTITUTION** Independent Roman Catholic, coed. *Awards:* certificates, bachelor's, master's, and doctoral degrees. 28 undergraduate majors. *Total enrollment:* 2,103. Undergraduates: 1,595. Freshmen: 371. Both federal and institutional methodology are used as a basis for awarding need-based institutional aid.

**UNDERGRADUATE EXPENSES** for 2015–2016 *Application fee:* $40. *Tuition:* full-time $28,900; part-time $802 per credit hour. *Required fees:* full-time $1150; $200 per term. Full-time tuition and fees vary according to course load and location. Part-time tuition and fees vary according to course load and location. Room and board charges vary according to housing facility.

**FRESHMAN FINANCIAL AID (Fall 2014, est.)** 343 applied for aid; of those 100% were deemed to have need. 99% of freshmen with need received aid; of those 3% had need fully met. *Average percent of need met:* 76% (excluding resources awarded to replace EFC). *Average financial aid package:* $25,000 (excluding resources awarded to replace EFC). 5% of all full-time freshmen had no need and received non-need-based gift aid.

**UNDERGRADUATE FINANCIAL AID (Fall 2014, est.)** 1,236 applied for aid; of those 86% were deemed to have need. 100% of undergraduates with need received aid; of those 2% had need fully met. *Average percent of need met:* 73% (excluding resources awarded to replace EFC). *Average financial aid package:* $22,000 (excluding resources awarded to replace EFC). 4% of all full-time undergraduates had no need and received non-need-based gift aid.

**GIFT AID (NEED-BASED)** *Total amount:* $13,690,788 (22% federal, 37% state, 41% institutional). *Receiving aid:* Freshmen: 68% (251); all full-time undergraduates: 66% (875). *Average award:* Freshmen: $18,655; Undergraduates: $15,485. *Scholarships, grants, and awards:* Federal Pell, FSEOG, state, private, college/university gift aid from institutional funds.

**GIFT AID (NON-NEED-BASED)** *Total amount:* $10,519,733 (1% state, 97% institutional, 2% external sources). *Receiving aid:* Freshmen: 54% (201). Undergraduates: 45% (592). *Average award:* Freshmen: $17,292. Undergraduates: $16,246. *Scholarships, grants, and awards by category: Academic interests/achievement:* 699 awards ($9,649,274 total): biological sciences, general academic interests/achievements, health fields. *Creative arts/performance:* 54 awards ($83,913 total): art/fine arts, music. *Special achievements/activities:* 169 awards ($399,091 total): community service, general special achievements/activities, religious involvement. *Special characteristics:* 104 awards ($235,294 total): children of current students, children of faculty/staff, general special characteristics, local/state students, parents of current students, public servants, relatives of clergy, religious affiliation, siblings of current students, spouses of current students, twins, veterans. *Tuition* *waivers:* Full or partial for children of alumni, employees or children of employees, adult students, senior citizens. **ROTC:** Army cooperative.

**LOANS** *Student loans:* $8,955,909 (39% need-based, 61% non-need-based). 85% of past graduating class borrowed through all loan programs. *Average indebtedness per student:* $22,250. *Average need-based loan:* Freshmen: $3438. Undergraduates: $4297. *Parent loans:* $3,470,185 (100% non-need-based). *Programs:* Federal Direct (Subsidized and Unsubsidized Stafford, PLUS), state, private loans.

**WORK-STUDY** *Federal work-study:* Total amount: $115,000; 92 jobs averaging $1200. *State or other work-study/employment:* Total amount: $713,733 (100% non-need-based). 263 part-time jobs averaging $2714.

**ATHLETIC AWARDS** Total amount: $1,234,738 (12% need-based, 88% non-need-based).

**APPLYING FOR FINANCIAL AID** *Required financial aid forms:* FAFSA, state aid form. *Financial aid deadline:* Continuous. *Notification date:* Continuous beginning 2/15.

**CONTACT** Ms. Eileen Felske, Director of Financial Aid, Caldwell University, 120 Bloomfield Avenue, Caldwell, NJ 07006, 973-618-3221. *Fax:* 973-618-3650. *E-mail:* financialaid@caldwell.edu. *Website:* http://www.caldwell.edu/.

# CALIFORNIA BAPTIST UNIVERSITY
## Riverside, CA

| Tuition & fees: $29,422 | Average undergraduate aid package: $16,344 |
|---|---|

**ABOUT THE INSTITUTION** Independent Southern Baptist, coed. *Awards:* certificates, bachelor's, and master's degrees. 67 undergraduate majors. *Total enrollment:* 7,957. Undergraduates: 6,435. Freshmen: 1,099. Federal methodology is used as a basis for awarding need-based institutional aid.

**UNDERGRADUATE EXPENSES** for 2015–2016 *Application fee:* $45. *One-time required fee:* $310. *Comprehensive fee:* $38,792 includes full-time tuition ($27,612), mandatory fees ($1810), and room and board ($9370). *College room only:* $4940. Full-time tuition and fees vary according to course load and location. Room and board charges vary according to board plan and housing facility. *Part-time tuition:* $1062 per unit. *Part-time fees:* $175 per term. Part-time tuition and fees vary according to course load and location.

**FRESHMAN FINANCIAL AID (Fall 2014, est.)** 975 applied for aid; of those 89% were deemed to have need. 92% of freshmen with need received aid; of those 9% had need fully met. *Average percent of need met:* 56% (excluding resources awarded to replace EFC). *Average financial aid package:* $19,320 (excluding resources awarded to replace EFC). 8% of all full-time freshmen had no need and received non-need-based gift aid.

**UNDERGRADUATE FINANCIAL AID (Fall 2014, est.)** 5,075 applied for aid; of those 93% were deemed to have need. 99% of undergraduates with need received aid; of those 7% had need fully met. *Average percent of need met:* 51% (excluding resources awarded to replace EFC). *Average financial aid package:* $16,344 (excluding resources awarded to replace EFC). 5% of all full-time undergraduates had no need and received non-need-based gift aid.

**GIFT AID (NEED-BASED)** *Total amount:* $58,676,968 (22% federal, 24% state, 53% institutional, 1% external sources). *Receiving aid:* Freshmen: 59% (623); all full-time undergraduates: 58% (3,209). *Average award:* Freshmen: $15,232; Undergraduates: $12,329. *Scholarships, grants, and awards:* Federal Pell, FSEOG, state, private, college/university gift aid from institutional funds, Federal Nursing.

**GIFT AID (NON-NEED-BASED)** *Total amount:* $1,918,063 (98% institutional, 2% external sources). *Receiving aid:* Freshmen: 54% (578). Undergraduates: 44% (2,461). *Average award:* Freshmen: $7397. Undergraduates: $6959. *Scholarships, grants, and awards by category: Academic interests/achievement:* architecture, engineering/technologies, general academic interests/achievements, health fields, religion/biblical studies. *Creative arts/performance:* applied art and design, art/fine arts, cinema/film/broadcasting, debating, journalism/publications, music, theater/drama. *Special achievements/activities:* cheerleading/drum major. *Special characteristics:* adult students, children of faculty/staff, international students, relatives of clergy, religious affiliation, siblings of current students, veterans, veterans' children. *Tuition waivers:* Full or partial for employees or children of employees. *ROTC:* Army, Air Force cooperative.

**LOANS** *Student loans:* $50,643,600 (94% need-based, 6% non-need-based). 80% of past graduating class borrowed through all loan programs. *Average indebtedness per student:* $33,409. *Average need-based loan:* Freshmen: $3455. Undergraduates: $4495. *Parent loans:* $13,694,504 (92% need-based, 8% non-need-based). *Programs:* Federal Direct (Subsidized and Unsubsidized Stafford, PLUS), Perkins, alternative loans.

**WORK-STUDY** *Federal work-study:* Total amount: $250,000; 294 jobs averaging $949.

**ATHLETIC AWARDS** Total amount: $4,831,852 (93% need-based, 7% non-need-based).

**APPLYING FOR FINANCIAL AID** *Required financial aid forms:* FAFSA, state aid form. *Financial aid deadline:* Continuous. *Notification date:* Continuous beginning 3/2. Students must reply by 6/1.

**CONTACT** Ms. Rebecca Sanchez, Financial Aid Director, California Baptist University, 8432 Magnolia Avenue, Riverside, CA 92504-3297, 951-343-4236 or toll-free 877-228-8866. *Fax:* 951-343-4518. *E-mail:* finaid@calbaptist.edu. *Website:* http://www.calbaptist.edu/.

# CALIFORNIA CHRISTIAN COLLEGE
## Fresno, CA

| Tuition & fees: $8540 | Average undergraduate aid package: $13,547 |
|---|---|

**ABOUT THE INSTITUTION** Independent Free Will Baptist, coed. *Awards:* associate and bachelor's degrees. 1 undergraduate major. *Total enrollment:* 20. Undergraduates: 20. Federal methodology is used as a basis for awarding need-based institutional aid.

**UNDERGRADUATE EXPENSES** for 2015–2016 *Application fee:* $40. *Comprehensive fee:* $13,340 includes full-time tuition ($7920), mandatory fees ($620), and room and board ($4800). *Part-time tuition:* $330 per unit.

**FRESHMAN FINANCIAL AID (Fall 2013)** 1 applied for aid; of those 100% were deemed to have need. 100% of freshmen with need received aid. *Average percent of need met:* 56% (excluding resources awarded to replace EFC). *Average financial aid package:* $13,745 (excluding resources awarded to replace EFC).

**UNDERGRADUATE FINANCIAL AID (Fall 2013)** 14 applied for aid; of those 93% were deemed to have need. 100% of undergraduates with need received aid. *Average percent of need met:* 70% (excluding resources awarded to replace EFC). *Average financial aid package:* $13,547 (excluding resources awarded to replace EFC).

**GIFT AID (NEED-BASED)** *Total amount:* $76,882 (98% federal, 2% external sources). *Receiving aid:* Freshmen: 50% (1); all full-time undergraduates: 68% (13). *Average award:* Freshmen: $6045; Undergraduates: $4965. *Scholarships, grants, and awards:* Federal Pell, FSEOG, state, private, college/university gift aid from institutional funds.

**LOANS** *Student loans:* $110,450 (100% need-based). *Average need-based loan:* Freshmen: $3500. Undergraduates: $4063. *Programs:* Federal Direct (Subsidized and Unsubsidized Stafford, PLUS).

**WORK-STUDY** *Federal work-study:* 5 jobs averaging $1824.

**APPLYING FOR FINANCIAL AID** *Required financial aid forms:* FAFSA, institution's own form, Cal Grant forms, GPA verification form (CA residents only). *Financial aid deadline (priority):* 3/2. *Notification date:* 8/15.

**CONTACT** Mindy Scroggins, Financial Aid Coordinator, California Christian College, 4881 East University Avenue, Fresno, CA 93703, 559-251-4215 Ext. 5580. *Fax:* 559-251-4231. *E-mail:* financialaid@calchristiancollege.edu. *Website:* http://www.calchristiancollege.edu/.

# CALIFORNIA COAST UNIVERSITY
## Santa Ana, CA

**CONTACT** Financial Aid Office, California Coast University, 925 North Spurgeon Street, Santa Ana, CA 92701, 714-547-9625 or toll-free 888-CCU-UNIV. *Website:* http://www.calcoast.edu/.

# CALIFORNIA COLLEGE OF THE ARTS
## San Francisco, CA

| Tuition & fees: N/R | Average undergraduate aid package: $27,460 |
| --- | --- |

**ABOUT THE INSTITUTION** Independent, coed. *Awards:* bachelor's and master's degrees. 22 undergraduate majors. *Total enrollment:* 1,998. Undergraduates: 1,572. Freshmen: 273. Federal methodology is used as a basis for awarding need-based institutional aid.

**UNDERGRADUATE EXPENSES for 2015–2016** *Tuition:* part-time $1733 per credit. Full-time tuition and fees vary according to degree level. Part-time tuition and fees vary according to degree level. Room and board charges vary according to housing facility.

**FRESHMAN FINANCIAL AID (Fall 2014, est.)** 158 applied for aid; of those 92% were deemed to have need. 100% of freshmen with need received aid; of those 5% had need fully met. *Average percent of need met:* 63% (excluding resources awarded to replace EFC). *Average financial aid package:* $29,493 (excluding resources awarded to replace EFC). 32% of all full-time freshmen had no need and received non-need-based gift aid.

**UNDERGRADUATE FINANCIAL AID (Fall 2014, est.)** 918 applied for aid; of those 95% were deemed to have need. 100% of undergraduates with need received aid; of those 4% had need fully met. *Average percent of need met:* 59% (excluding resources awarded to replace EFC). *Average financial aid package:* $27,460 (excluding resources awarded to replace EFC). 19% of all full-time undergraduates had no need and received non-need-based gift aid.

**GIFT AID (NEED-BASED)** *Total amount:* $19,589,457 (13% federal, 9% state, 73% institutional, 5% external sources). *Receiving aid:* Freshmen: 54% (146); all full-time undergraduates: 59% (869). *Average award:* Freshmen: $25,417; Undergraduates: $22,574. *Scholarships, grants, and awards:* Federal Pell, FSEOG, state, private, college/university gift aid from institutional funds.

**GIFT AID (NON-NEED-BASED)** *Total amount:* $2,657,698 (99% institutional, 1% external sources). *Receiving aid:* Freshmen: 47% (129). Undergraduates: 37% (534). *Average award:* Freshmen: $10,859. Undergraduates: $9292. *Scholarships, grants, and awards by category:* Academic interests/achievement: general academic interests/achievements. *Tuition waivers:* Full or partial for employees or children of employees.

**LOANS** *Student loans:* $4,636,258 (87% need-based, 13% non-need-based). 61% of past graduating class borrowed through all loan programs. *Average indebtedness per student:* $34,237. *Average need-based loan:* Freshmen: $3540. Undergraduates: $4848. *Parent loans:* $3,321,486 (71% need-based, 29% non-need-based). *Programs:* Federal Direct (Subsidized and Unsubsidized Stafford, PLUS), Perkins, private loans.

**WORK-STUDY** *Federal work-study:* Total amount: $345,521; 798 jobs averaging $2922. *State or other work-study/employment:* Total amount: $864,779 (100% non-need-based). 74 part-time jobs averaging $3672.

**APPLYING FOR FINANCIAL AID** *Required financial aid form:* FAFSA. *Financial aid deadline (priority):* 3/1. *Notification date:* Continuous beginning 4/1. Students must reply by 5/1 or within 3 weeks of notification.

**CONTACT** Dr. Scott C. Cline, Director of Financial Aid, California College of the Arts, 1111 Eighth Street, San Francisco, CA 94107, 415-703-9528 or toll-free 800-447-1ART. *Fax:* 415-551-9261. *E-mail:* finaid@cca.edu. *Website:* http://www.cca.edu/.

# CALIFORNIA COLLEGE SAN DIEGO
## National City, CA

**CONTACT** Financial Aid Office, California College San Diego, 22 West 35th Street, National City, CA 91950, 619-680-4421 or toll-free 800-622-3188. *Website:* http://www.cc-sd.edu/.

# CALIFORNIA COLLEGE SAN DIEGO
## San Diego, CA

**CONTACT** Raul Rivera, Senior Financial Aid Officer, California College San Diego, 6602 Convoy Court, #100, San Diego, CA 92111, 619-680-4430 Ext. 1507 or toll-free 800-622-3188. *Fax:* 619-695-5793. *E-mail:* raul.rivera@cc-sd.edu. *Website:* http://www.cc-sd.edu/.

# CALIFORNIA COLLEGE SAN DIEGO
## San Marcos, CA

**CONTACT** Financial Aid Office, California College San Diego, 277 Rancheros Drive, Suite 200, San Marcos, CA 92069, 760- 621-4333 or toll-free 800-622-3188. *Website:* http://www.cc-sd.edu/.

# CALIFORNIA INSTITUTE OF INTEGRAL STUDIES
## San Francisco, CA

| Tuition & fees: $25,095 | Average undergraduate aid package: $10,954 |
| --- | --- |

**ABOUT THE INSTITUTION** Independent, coed. *Awards:* certificates, bachelor's, master's, and doctoral degrees. 1 undergraduate major. *Total enrollment:* 1,256. Undergraduates: 104. Entering class: 55. Federal methodology is used as a basis for awarding need-based institutional aid.

**UNDERGRADUATE EXPENSES for 2015–2016** *Application fee:* $65. *Tuition:* full-time $24,840; part-time $690 per credit. *Required fees:* full-time $255; $255 per year or $85 per term.

**UNDERGRADUATE FINANCIAL AID (Fall 2013)** 62 applied for aid; of those 97% were deemed to have need. 100% of undergraduates with need received aid. *Average percent of need met:* 32% (excluding resources awarded to replace EFC). *Average financial aid package:* $10,954 (excluding resources awarded to replace EFC).

**GIFT AID (NEED-BASED)** *Total amount:* $351,077 (47% federal, 6% state, 33% institutional, 14% external sources). *Receiving aid:* All full-time undergraduates: 88% (60). *Average award:* Undergraduates: $5819. *Scholarships, grants, and awards:* Federal Pell, FSEOG, state, private, college/university gift aid from institutional funds, Yellow Ribbon Grant Program.

**GIFT AID (NON-NEED-BASED)** *Scholarships, grants, and awards by category:* Special characteristics: 1 award ($1000 total): International students.

**LOANS** *Student loans:* $614,997 (100% need-based). *Average need-based loan:* Undergraduates: $6009. *Programs:* Federal Direct (Subsidized and Unsubsidized Stafford, PLUS), private loans.

**WORK-STUDY** *Federal work-study:* 6 jobs averaging $3275.

**APPLYING FOR FINANCIAL AID** *Notification date:* Continuous.

**CONTACT** Financial Aid Office, California Institute of Integral Studies, 1453 Mission Street, San Francisco, CA 94103, 415-575-6122. *Fax:* 415-575-1268. *E-mail:* finaid@ciis.edu. *Website:* http://www.ciis.edu/.

# CALIFORNIA INSTITUTE OF TECHNOLOGY
## Pasadena, CA

| Tuition & fees: $43,362 | Average undergraduate aid package: $41,669 |
| --- | --- |

**ABOUT THE INSTITUTION** Independent, coed. *Awards:* certificates, bachelor's, master's, and doctoral degrees. 25 undergraduate majors. *Total* *enrollment:* 2,209. Undergraduates: 983. Freshmen: 226. Both federal and institutional methodology are used as a basis for awarding need-based institutional aid.

**UNDERGRADUATE EXPENSES for 2015–2016** *Application fee:* $75. *One-time required fee:* $500. *Comprehensive fee:* $56,280 includes full-time tuition ($41,790), mandatory fees ($1572), and room and board ($12,918). *College room only:* $7281. Room and board charges vary according to housing facility. *Part-time tuition:* $387 per credit.

**FRESHMAN FINANCIAL AID (Fall 2014, est.)** 167 applied for aid; of those 75% were deemed to have need. 100% of freshmen with need received aid; of those 100% had need fully met. *Average percent of need met:* 100% (excluding resources awarded to replace EFC). *Average financial aid package:* $41,990 (excluding resources awarded to replace EFC).

**UNDERGRADUATE FINANCIAL AID (Fall 2014, est.)** 596 applied for aid; of those 83% were deemed to have need. 100% of undergraduates with need received aid; of those 100% had need fully met. *Average percent of need met:* 100% (excluding resources awarded to replace EFC). *Average financial aid package:* $41,669 (excluding resources awarded to replace EFC).

**GIFT AID (NEED-BASED)** *Total amount:* $17,891,295 (5% federal, 1% state, 93% institutional, 1% external sources). *Receiving aid:* Freshmen: 55% (125); all full-time undergraduates: 50% (495). *Average award:* Freshmen: $40,060; Undergraduates: $37,557. *Scholarships, grants, and awards:* Federal Pell, FSEOG, state, private, college/university gift aid from institutional funds.

**GIFT AID (NON-NEED-BASED)** *Total amount:* $339,153 (100% external sources). *Receiving aid:* Undergraduates: 1% (7). *Tuition waivers:* Full or partial for employees or children of employees. *ROTC:* Army cooperative, Air Force cooperative.

**LOANS** *Student loans:* $1,464,028 (80% need-based, 20% non-need-based). 32% of past graduating class borrowed through all loan programs. *Average indebtedness per student:* $12,104. *Average need-based loan:* Freshmen: $2989. Undergraduates: $4624. *Parent loans:* $356,082 (5% need-based, 95% non-need-based). *Programs:* Federal Direct (Subsidized and Unsubsidized Stafford, PLUS), Perkins, college/university.

**WORK-STUDY** *Federal work-study:* Total amount: $887,566; 278 jobs averaging $3193. *State or other work-study/employment:* Total amount: $80,866 (100% need-based). 31 part-time jobs averaging $2609.

**APPLYING FOR FINANCIAL AID** *Required financial aid forms:* FAFSA, institution's own form, CSS Financial Aid PROFILE, state aid form, noncustodial (divorced/separated) parent's statement, business/farm supplement. *Financial aid deadline (priority):* 2/1. *Notification date:* Continuous beginning 3/30. Students must reply by 5/1 or within 2 weeks of notification.

**CONTACT** Don Crewell, Director of Financial Aid, California Institute of Technology, 1200 East California Boulevard, MC 20-90, Pasadena, CA 91125-3405, 626-395-6280. *Fax:* 626-564-8136. *E-mail:* dcrewell@caltech.edu. *Website:* http://www.caltech.edu/.

# CALIFORNIA INSTITUTE OF THE ARTS
## Valencia, CA

| Tuition & fees: $43,976 | Average undergraduate aid package: $32,090 |
| --- | --- |

**ABOUT THE INSTITUTION** Independent, coed. *Awards:* certificates, bachelor's, master's, and doctoral degrees. 10 undergraduate majors. *Total enrollment:* 1,454. Undergraduates: 895. Freshmen: 151. Federal methodology is used as a basis for awarding need-based institutional aid.

**UNDERGRADUATE EXPENSES for 2015–2016** *Application fee:* $70. *Tuition:* full-time $43,400.

**FRESHMAN FINANCIAL AID (Fall 2014, est.)** 121 applied for aid; of those 91% were deemed to have need. 100% of freshmen with need received aid; of those 8% had need fully met. *Average percent of need met:* 75% (excluding resources awarded to replace EFC). *Average financial aid package:* $32,155 (excluding resources awarded to replace EFC). 6% of all full-time freshmen had no need and received non-need-based gift aid.

**UNDERGRADUATE FINANCIAL AID (Fall 2014, est.)** 788 applied for aid; of those 87% were deemed to have need. 100% of undergraduates with need received aid; of those 4% had need fully met. *Average percent of need met:* 75% (excluding resources awarded to replace EFC). *Average financial aid package:* $32,090

(excluding resources awarded to replace EFC). 5% of all full-time undergraduates had no need and received non-need-based gift aid.

**GIFT AID (NEED-BASED)** *Total amount:* $7,657,432 (24% federal, 14% state, 60% institutional, 2% external sources). *Receiving aid:* Freshmen: 63% (109); all full-time undergraduates: 67% (667). *Average award:* Freshmen: $16,660; Undergraduates: $16,210. *Scholarships, grants, and awards:* Federal Pell, FSEOG, state, private, college/university gift aid from institutional funds.

**GIFT AID (NON-NEED-BASED)** *Total amount:* $754,644 (100% institutional). *Average award:* Freshmen: $5548. Undergraduates: $8570. *Scholarships, grants, and awards by category:* Creative arts/performance: 77 awards ($546,710 total): applied art and design, art/fine arts, cinema/film/broadcasting, creative writing, dance, music, performing arts, theater/drama.

**LOANS** *Student loans:* $7,663,547 (94% need-based, 6% non-need-based). 76% of past graduating class borrowed through all loan programs. *Average indebtedness per student:* $38,770. *Average need-based loan:* Freshmen: $8235. Undergraduates: $10,422. *Parent loans:* $2,572,030 (75% need-based, 25% non-need-based). *Programs:* Federal Direct (Subsidized and Unsubsidized Stafford, PLUS), Perkins, college/university, private loans.

**WORK-STUDY** *Federal work-study:* Total amount: $420,235; 357 jobs averaging $1500. *State or other work-study/employment:* Total amount: $9875 (100% need-based). 12 part-time jobs averaging $1500.

**APPLYING FOR FINANCIAL AID** *Required financial aid forms:* FAFSA, CSS Financial Aid PROFILE. *Financial aid deadline (priority):* 2/15. *Notification date:* Continuous beginning 4/1. Students must reply by 5/1 or within 3 weeks of notification.

**CONTACT** Dr. Robin Bailey-Chen, Director of Financial Aid, California Institute of the Arts, 24700 McBean Parkway, Valencia, CA 91355-2340, 661-253-7869 or toll-free 800-545-2787. *Fax:* 661-287-3816. *E-mail:* bheuer@calarts.edu. *Website:* http://www.calarts.edu/.

# CALIFORNIA INTERCONTINENTAL UNIVERSITY
## Diamond Bar, CA

**CONTACT** Financial Aid Office, California Intercontinental University, 1470 Valley Vista Drive, Suite 150, Diamond Bar, CA 91765, 909-396-6090 or toll-free 866-687-2258. *Website:* http://caluniversity.edu/.

# CALIFORNIA LUTHERAN UNIVERSITY
## Thousand Oaks, CA

| Tuition & fees: $37,590 | Average undergraduate aid package: $25,730 |
| --- | --- |

**ABOUT THE INSTITUTION** Independent Lutheran, coed. *Awards:* certificates, bachelor's, master's, and doctoral degrees. 52 undergraduate majors. *Total enrollment:* 4,160. Undergraduates: 2,808. Freshmen: 556. Both federal and institutional methodology are used as a basis for awarding need-based institutional aid.

**UNDERGRADUATE EXPENSES for 2015–2016** *Application fee:* $25. *Comprehensive fee:* $49,990 includes full-time tuition ($37,140), mandatory fees ($450), and room and board ($12,400). *College room only:* $6730. Room and board charges vary according to board plan and housing facility. *Part-time tuition:* $1180 per credit hour.

**FRESHMAN FINANCIAL AID (Fall 2014, est.)** 555 applied for aid; of those 80% were deemed to have need. 100% of freshmen with need received aid; of those 18% had need fully met. *Average percent of need met:* 69% (excluding resources awarded to replace EFC). *Average financial aid package:* $26,470 (excluding resources awarded to replace EFC). 16% of all full-time freshmen had no need and received non-need-based gift aid.

**UNDERGRADUATE FINANCIAL AID (Fall 2014, est.)** 2,502 applied for aid; of those 72% were deemed to have need. 95% of undergraduates with need received aid; of those 13% had need fully met. *Average percent of need met:* 64% (excluding resources awarded to replace EFC). *Average financial aid package:* $25,730 (excluding resources awarded to replace EFC). 27% of all full-time undergraduates had no need and received non-need-based gift aid.

**GIFT AID (NEED-BASED)** *Total amount:* $37,781,124 (9% federal, 13% state, 77% institutional, 1% external sources). *Receiving aid:* Freshmen: 79% (442); all full-time undergraduates: 64% (1,704). *Average award:* Freshmen: $23,870; Undergraduates: $22,100. *Scholarships, grants, and awards:* Federal Pell, FSEOG, state, private, college/university gift aid from institutional funds.

**GIFT AID (NON-NEED-BASED)** *Total amount:* $11,111,186 (99% institutional, 1% external sources). *Receiving aid:* Freshmen: 69% (385). Undergraduates: 60% (1,578). *Average award:* Freshmen: $16,820. Undergraduates: $15,150. *Scholarships, grants, and awards by category: Academic interests/achievement:* biological sciences, business, communication, computer science, education, English, foreign languages, general academic interests/achievements, humanities, international studies, mathematics, physical sciences, religion/biblical studies, social sciences. *Creative arts/performance:* art/fine arts, creative writing, journalism/publications, music, performing arts, theater/drama. *Special achievements/activities:* community service, general special achievements/activities, leadership, religious involvement. *Special characteristics:* adult students, children and siblings of alumni, children of faculty/staff, international students, relatives of clergy, religious affiliation, veterans, veterans' children. *ROTC:* Army cooperative, Air Force cooperative.

**LOANS** *Student loans:* $13,913,572 (90% need-based, 10% non-need-based). 74% of past graduating class borrowed through all loan programs. *Average indebtedness per student:* $24,230. *Average need-based loan:* Freshmen: $3480. Undergraduates: $4720. *Parent loans:* $9,586,342 (89% need-based, 11% non-need-based). *Programs:* Federal Direct (Subsidized and Unsubsidized Stafford, PLUS), Perkins.

**WORK-STUDY** *Federal work-study:* Total amount: $500,000; 360 jobs averaging $2500.

**APPLYING FOR FINANCIAL AID** *Required financial aid forms:* FAFSA, Cal Grant forms, GPA verification form (CA residents only). *Financial aid deadline (priority):* 3/1. *Notification date:* Continuous beginning 3/15. Students must reply by 5/1 or within 2 weeks of notification.

**CONTACT** Jerry McKeen, Director of Financial Aid, California Lutheran University, 60 West Olsen Road, Thousand Oaks, CA 91360-2787, 805-493-3115 or toll-free 877-258-3678. *Fax:* 805-493-3114. *E-mail:* jmckeen@callutheran.edu. *Website:* http://www.callutheran.edu/.

# CALIFORNIA MARITIME ACADEMY
### Vallejo, CA

**ABOUT THE INSTITUTION** State-supported, coed. 4 undergraduate majors.

**GIFT AID (NEED-BASED)** *Scholarships, grants, and awards:* Federal Pell, FSEOG, state, private, college/university gift aid from institutional funds.

**GIFT AID (NON-NEED-BASED)** *Scholarships, grants, and awards by category: Academic interests/achievement:* general academic interests/achievements.

**LOANS** *Programs:* Federal Direct (Subsidized and Unsubsidized Stafford, PLUS), Perkins.

**WORK-STUDY** *Federal work-study:* 76 jobs averaging $1452.

**APPLYING FOR FINANCIAL AID** *Required financial aid forms:* FAFSA, state aid form.

**CONTACT** Nicole Hill, Director of Financial Aid, California Maritime Academy, 200 Maritime Academy Drive, Vallejo, CA 94590-0644, 707-654-1275 or toll-free 800-561-1945. *Fax:* 707-654-1007. *E-mail:* finaid@csum.edu. *Website:* http://www.csum.edu/.

# CALIFORNIA MIRAMAR UNIVERSITY
### San Diego, CA

**CONTACT** Financial Aid Office, California Miramar University, 9750 Miramar Road, Suite 180, San Diego, CA 92126, 858-653-3000 or toll-free 877-570-5678. *Website:* http://www.calmu.edu/.

# CALIFORNIA NATIONAL UNIVERSITY FOR ADVANCED STUDIES
### Northridge, CA

**CONTACT** Office of Academic Affairs, California National University for Advanced Studies, 16909 Parthenia Street, North Hills, CA 91343, 800-782-2422. *Website:* http://www.cnuas.edu/.

# CALIFORNIA POLYTECHNIC STATE UNIVERSITY, SAN LUIS OBISPO
### San Luis Obispo, CA

| Tuition & fees (CA res): $8919 | Average undergraduate aid package: $10,279 |
| --- | --- |

**ABOUT THE INSTITUTION** State-supported, coed. *Awards:* bachelor's and master's degrees. 64 undergraduate majors. *Total enrollment:* 20,186. Undergraduates: 19,246. Freshmen: 4,662. Federal methodology is used as a basis for awarding need-based institutional aid.

**UNDERGRADUATE EXPENSES** for 2015–2016 *Application fee:* $55. *Tuition, state resident:* full-time $5472; part-time $3174 per year. *Tuition, nonresident:* full-time $16,632; part-time $7638 per year. *Required fees:* full-time $3447; $3003 per year. Full-time tuition and fees vary according to course load, degree level, and program. Part-time tuition and fees vary according to course load, degree level, and program. *College room and board:* $11,447; *Room only:* $6754. Room and board charges vary according to housing facility.

**FRESHMAN FINANCIAL AID (Fall 2013)** 3,900 applied for aid; of those 55% were deemed to have need. 89% of freshmen with need received aid; of those 8% had need fully met. *Average percent of need met:* 59% (excluding resources awarded to replace EFC). *Average financial aid package:* $9935 (excluding resources awarded to replace EFC). 11% of all full-time freshmen had no need and received non-need-based gift aid.

**UNDERGRADUATE FINANCIAL AID (Fall 2013)** 11,184 applied for aid; of those 69% were deemed to have need. 91% of undergraduates with need received aid; of those 8% had need fully met. *Average percent of need met:* 59% (excluding resources awarded to replace EFC). *Average financial aid package:* $10,279 (excluding resources awarded to replace EFC). 9% of all full-time undergraduates had no need and received non-need-based gift aid.

**GIFT AID (NEED-BASED)** *Total amount:* $48,592,337 (34% federal, 30% state, 28% institutional, 8% external sources). *Receiving aid:* Freshmen: 33% (1,590); all full-time undergraduates: 31% (5,522). *Average award:* Freshmen: $3225; Undergraduates: $3488. *Scholarships, grants, and awards:* Federal Pell, FSEOG, state, private, college/university gift aid from institutional funds, TEACH Grants.

**GIFT AID (NON-NEED-BASED)** *Total amount:* $6,422,904 (54% institutional, 46% external sources). *Receiving aid:* Freshmen: 1% (56). Undergraduates: 1% (115). *Average award:* Freshmen: $1955. Undergraduates: $1978. *Scholarships, grants, and awards by category: Academic interests/achievement:* agriculture, architecture, biological sciences, business, communication, computer science, education, engineering/technologies, English, foreign languages, general academic interests/achievements, health fields, home economics, humanities, international studies, library science, mathematics, military science, physical sciences, social sciences. *Creative arts/performance:* applied art and design, art/fine arts, cinema/film/broadcasting, creative writing, dance, debating, general creative arts/performance, journalism/publications, music, performing arts, theater/drama. *Special achievements/activities:* community service, leadership, rodeo. *Special characteristics:* children and siblings of alumni, general special characteristics, local/state students. *Tuition waivers:* Full or partial for employees or children of employees. *ROTC:* Army.

**LOANS** *Student loans:* $45,406,240 (67% need-based, 33% non-need-based). *Average need-based loan:* Freshmen: $3251. Undergraduates: $3977. *Parent loans:* $28,454,190 (26% need-based, 74% non-need-based). *Programs:* Federal Direct (Subsidized and Unsubsidized Stafford, PLUS), Perkins, college/university, alternative loans.

**WORK-STUDY** *Federal work-study:* jobs available.

**ATHLETIC AWARDS** Total amount: $4,023,543 (34% need-based, 66% non-need-based).

**APPLYING FOR FINANCIAL AID** *Required financial aid form:* FAFSA. *Financial aid deadline (priority):* 3/2. *Notification date:* Continuous beginning 4/1.
**CONTACT** Lois Kelly, Director of Financial Aid, California Polytechnic State University, San Luis Obispo, Administration Building, Room 212, San Luis Obispo, CA 93407, 805-756-2927. *Fax:* 805-756-7243. *E-mail:* financialaid@calpoly.edu. *Website:* http://www.calpoly.edu/.

# CALIFORNIA STATE POLYTECHNIC UNIVERSITY, POMONA
## Pomona, CA

| Tuition & fees (CA res): $6872 | Average undergraduate aid package: $10,915 |
|---|---|

**ABOUT THE INSTITUTION** State-supported, coed. *Awards:* bachelor's, master's, and doctoral degrees. 52 undergraduate majors. *Total enrollment:* 23,966. Undergraduates: 22,395. Freshmen: 3,658. Federal methodology is used as a basis for awarding need-based institutional aid.
**UNDERGRADUATE EXPENSES for 2015–2016** *Application fee:* $55. *Tuition, state resident:* full-time $5472. *Tuition, nonresident:* full-time $16,632. *Required fees:* full-time $1400; $248 per credit. Full-time tuition and fees vary according to course load, degree level, and program. Part-time tuition and fees vary according to course load, degree level, and program. *College room and board:* $13,284; *Room only:* $8112. Room and board charges vary according to board plan and housing facility.
**FRESHMAN FINANCIAL AID (Fall 2014, est.)** 3,050 applied for aid; of those 80% were deemed to have need. 96% of freshmen with need received aid; of those 2% had need fully met. *Average percent of need met:* 60% (excluding resources awarded to replace EFC). *Average financial aid package:* $10,754 (excluding resources awarded to replace EFC).
**UNDERGRADUATE FINANCIAL AID (Fall 2014, est.)** 15,319 applied for aid; of those 87% were deemed to have need. 96% of undergraduates with need received aid; of those 4% had need fully met. *Average percent of need met:* 55% (excluding resources awarded to replace EFC). *Average financial aid package:* $10,915 (excluding resources awarded to replace EFC). 1% of all full-time undergraduates had no need and received non-need-based gift aid.
**GIFT AID (NEED-BASED)** *Total amount:* $139,541,523 (46% federal, 24% state, 30% institutional). *Receiving aid:* Freshmen: 54% (1,908); all full-time undergraduates: 54% (10,518). *Average award:* Freshmen: $9910; Undergraduates: $9708. *Scholarships, grants, and awards:* Federal Pell, FSEOG, state, private, college/university gift aid from institutional funds.
**GIFT AID (NON-NEED-BASED)** *Total amount:* $4,674,844 (50% state, 5% institutional, 45% external sources). *Receiving aid:* Freshmen: 18% (656). Undergraduates: 17% (3,342). *Average award:* Undergraduates: $1159. *Scholarships, grants, and awards by category:* Academic interests/achievement: agriculture, architecture, biological sciences, business, computer science, education, engineering/technologies, general academic interests/achievements, humanities, mathematics, physical sciences, social sciences. *Special achievements/activities:* hobbies/interests, leadership. *Special characteristics:* children and siblings of alumni, children of current students, members of minority groups. *Tuition waivers:* Full or partial for employees or children of employees. *ROTC:* Army.
**LOANS** *Student loans:* $67,873,761 (52% need-based, 48% non-need-based). 50% of past graduating class borrowed through all loan programs. *Average indebtedness per student:* $22,245. *Average need-based loan:* Freshmen: $3548. Undergraduates: $4486. *Parent loans:* $3,719,362 (100% non-need-based). *Programs:* Perkins, college/university, alternative loans.
**WORK-STUDY** *Federal work-study:* Total amount: $619,803; 239 jobs averaging $2585.
**ATHLETIC AWARDS** Total amount: $684,033 (100% non-need-based).
**APPLYING FOR FINANCIAL AID** *Required financial aid form:* FAFSA. *Financial aid deadline:* Continuous. *Notification date:* Continuous beginning 4/1. Students must reply within 6 weeks of notification.
**CONTACT** Diana Minor, Director of Financial Aid and Scholarships, California State Polytechnic University, Pomona, 3801 West Temple Avenue, Pomona, CA 91768-2557, 909-869-3704. *Fax:* 909-869-4757. *E-mail:* dyminor@cpp.edu. *Website:* http://www.cpp.edu/.

# CALIFORNIA STATE UNIVERSITY, BAKERSFIELD
## Bakersfield, CA

| Tuition & fees (CA res): $5473 | Average undergraduate aid package: $4245 |
|---|---|

**ABOUT THE INSTITUTION** State-supported, coed. *Awards:* bachelor's and master's degrees. 30 undergraduate majors. *Total enrollment:* 8,720. Undergraduates: 7,544. Freshmen: 1,425. Federal methodology is used as a basis for awarding need-based institutional aid.
**UNDERGRADUATE EXPENSES for 2015–2016** *Application fee:* $55. *Tuition, state resident:* full-time $5473. *Tuition, nonresident:* full-time $16,632; part-time $248 per credit hour. *College room and board:* $10,926; *Room only:* $6369.
**FRESHMAN FINANCIAL AID (Fall 2014, est.)** 1,087 applied for aid; of those 81% were deemed to have need. 94% of freshmen with need received aid; of those 10% had need fully met. *Average percent of need met:* 72% (excluding resources awarded to replace EFC). *Average financial aid package:* $4225 (excluding resources awarded to replace EFC).
**UNDERGRADUATE FINANCIAL AID (Fall 2014, est.)** 4,969 applied for aid; of those 81% were deemed to have need. 100% of undergraduates with need received aid; of those 8% had need fully met. *Average percent of need met:* 72% (excluding resources awarded to replace EFC). *Average financial aid package:* $4245 (excluding resources awarded to replace EFC).
**GIFT AID (NEED-BASED)** *Total amount:* $50,440,977 (43% federal, 54% state, 2% institutional, 1% external sources). *Receiving aid:* Freshmen: 65% (831); all full-time undergraduates: 69% (4,004). *Average award:* Freshmen: $3742; Undergraduates: $3513. *Scholarships, grants, and awards:* Federal Pell, FSEOG, state, private, college/university gift aid from institutional funds, Federal Nursing.
**GIFT AID (NON-NEED-BASED)** *Total amount:* $500 (100% state). *Receiving aid:* Freshmen: 7% (87). Undergraduates: 5% (314). *Scholarships, grants, and awards by category:* Academic interests/achievement: agriculture, architecture, biological sciences, business, communication, education, foreign languages, general academic interests/achievements, health fields, humanities, mathematics, physical sciences, premedicine, religion/biblical studies, social sciences. *Creative arts/performance:* art/fine arts, dance, music, theater/drama. *Special achievements/activities:* community service, general special achievements/activities, leadership. *Special characteristics:* children of faculty/staff, children of union members/company employees, ethnic background, first-generation college students, local/state students, veterans.
**LOANS** *Student loans:* $19,969,898 (100% need-based). 90% of past graduating class borrowed through all loan programs. *Average indebtedness per student:* $11,735. *Average need-based loan:* Freshmen: $1140. Undergraduates: $1450. *Parent loans:* $274,150 (100% need-based). *Programs:* Federal Direct (Subsidized and Unsubsidized Stafford, PLUS), Perkins, Federal Nursing, college/university.
**WORK-STUDY** *Federal work-study:* Total amount: $232,036; jobs available.
**ATHLETIC AWARDS** Total amount: $1,833,418 (100% need-based).
**APPLYING FOR FINANCIAL AID** *Required financial aid forms:* FAFSA, state aid form. *Financial aid deadline (priority):* 3/2. *Notification date:* Continuous beginning 4/15. Students must reply within 3 weeks of notification.
**CONTACT** Dr. Ron Radney, Director of Financial Aid and Scholarships, California State University, Bakersfield, 9001 Stockdale Highway, Bakersfield, CA 93311-1022, 661-654-3271 or toll-free 800-788-2782. *Fax:* 661-654-6800. *E-mail:* rradney@csub.edu. *Website:* http://www.csub.edu/.

# CALIFORNIA STATE UNIVERSITY CHANNEL ISLANDS
## Camarillo, CA

**CONTACT** Financial Aid Office, California State University Channel Islands, One University Drive, Camarillo, CA 93012, 805-437-8400. *Website:* http://www.csuci.edu/.

# CALIFORNIA STATE UNIVERSITY, CHICO
## Chico, CA

| Tuition & fees (CA res): $8532 | Average undergraduate aid package: $16,090 |
|---|---|

**ABOUT THE INSTITUTION** State-supported, coed. *Awards:* certificates, bachelor's, and master's degrees. 53 undergraduate majors. *Total enrollment:* 17,462. Undergraduates: 16,255. Freshmen: 2,945. Federal methodology is used as a basis for awarding need-based institutional aid.

**UNDERGRADUATE EXPENSES for 2015–2016** *Application fee:* $55. *Tuition, state resident:* full-time $7002. *Tuition, nonresident:* full-time $18,162. *Required fees:* full-time $1530. Full-time tuition and fees vary according to degree level. Part-time tuition and fees vary according to course load and degree level. *College room and board:* $11,626. Room and board charges vary according to board plan and housing facility.

**FRESHMAN FINANCIAL AID (Fall 2013)** 1,947 applied for aid; of those 76% were deemed to have need. 98% of freshmen with need received aid; of those 15% had need fully met. *Average percent of need met:* 66% (excluding resources awarded to replace EFC). *Average financial aid package:* $17,380 (excluding resources awarded to replace EFC). 1% of all full-time freshmen had no need and received non-need-based gift aid.

**UNDERGRADUATE FINANCIAL AID (Fall 2013)** 10,838 applied for aid; of those 84% were deemed to have need. 97% of undergraduates with need received aid; of those 16% had need fully met. *Average percent of need met:* 63% (excluding resources awarded to replace EFC). *Average financial aid package:* $16,090 (excluding resources awarded to replace EFC). 1% of all full-time undergraduates had no need and received non-need-based gift aid.

**GIFT AID (NEED-BASED)** *Total amount:* $68,400,161 (46% federal, 54% state). *Receiving aid:* Freshmen: 48% (1,111); all full-time undergraduates: 50% (7,061). *Average award:* Freshmen: $10,538; Undergraduates: $9865. *Scholarships, grants, and awards:* Federal Pell, FSEOG, state, private, college/university gift aid from institutional funds, United Negro College Fund.

**GIFT AID (NON-NEED-BASED)** *Total amount:* $2,735,700 (38% institutional, 62% external sources). *Receiving aid:* Freshmen: 14% (335). Undergraduates: 8% (1,188). *Average award:* Freshmen: $1625. Undergraduates: $1868. *Scholarships, grants, and awards by category: Academic interests/achievement:* agriculture, area/ethnic studies, biological sciences, business, communication, computer science, education, engineering/technologies, English, foreign languages, general academic interests/achievements, health fields, humanities, international studies, mathematics, physical sciences, social sciences. *Creative arts/performance:* applied art and design, art/fine arts, cinema/film/broadcasting, creative writing, dance, debating, general creative arts/performance, journalism/publications, music, performing arts, theater/drama. *Special achievements/activities:* community service, general special achievements/activities, hobbies/interests, leadership, memberships. *Special characteristics:* adult students, children of faculty/staff, ethnic background, first-generation college students, handicapped students, international students, local/state students, married students, members of minority groups, out-of-state students. *Tuition waivers:* Full or partial for employees or children of employees, senior citizens.

**LOANS** *Student loans:* $46,966,952 (57% need-based, 43% non-need-based). *Average need-based loan:* Freshmen: $3448. Undergraduates: $4598. *Programs:* Federal Direct (Subsidized and Unsubsidized Stafford, PLUS), Perkins, college/university.

**WORK-STUDY** *Federal work-study:* jobs available.

**ATHLETIC AWARDS** Total amount: $630,006 (100% non-need-based).

**APPLYING FOR FINANCIAL AID** *Required financial aid forms:* FAFSA, institution's own form. *Financial aid deadline:* Continuous. *Notification date:* Continuous beginning 3/2.

**CONTACT** Dan Reed, Director of Financial Aid and Scholarships, California State University, Chico, 400 West First Street, Student Services Center, Room 250, Chico, CA 95929-0705, 530-898-6451 or toll-free 800-542-4426 (out-of-state). *Fax:* 530-898-6883. *E-mail:* finaid@csuchico.edu.
*Website:* http://www.csuchico.edu/.

# CALIFORNIA STATE UNIVERSITY, DOMINGUEZ HILLS
## Carson, CA

| Tuition & fees (CA res): $6134 | Average undergraduate aid package: $6278 |
|---|---|

**ABOUT THE INSTITUTION** State-supported, coed. *Awards:* certificates, bachelor's, and master's degrees. 68 undergraduate majors. *Total enrollment:* 14,687. Undergraduates: 12,617. Freshmen: 1,342. Federal methodology is used as a basis for awarding need-based institutional aid.

**UNDERGRADUATE EXPENSES for 2015–2016** *Application fee:* $55. *Tuition, state resident:* full-time $5472. *Tuition, nonresident:* full-time $16,632; part-time $372 per credit. *Required fees:* full-time $662. *College room and board:* $10,956. Room and board charges vary according to housing facility.

**FRESHMAN FINANCIAL AID (Fall 2014, est.)** 1,248 applied for aid; of those 92% were deemed to have need. 99% of freshmen with need received aid; of those 2% had need fully met. *Average percent of need met:* 36% (excluding resources awarded to replace EFC). *Average financial aid package:* $5516 (excluding resources awarded to replace EFC). 5% of all full-time freshmen had no need and received non-need-based gift aid.

**UNDERGRADUATE FINANCIAL AID (Fall 2014, est.)** 6,931 applied for aid; of those 96% were deemed to have need. 98% of undergraduates with need received aid; of those 2% had need fully met. *Average percent of need met:* 35% (excluding resources awarded to replace EFC). *Average financial aid package:* $6278 (excluding resources awarded to replace EFC). 2% of all full-time undergraduates had no need and received non-need-based gift aid.

**GIFT AID (NEED-BASED)** *Total amount:* $40,347,887 (45% federal, 53% state, 1% institutional, 1% external sources). *Receiving aid:* Freshmen: 78% (1,001); all full-time undergraduates: 65% (5,678). *Average award:* Freshmen: $5320; Undergraduates: $5134. *Scholarships, grants, and awards:* Federal Pell, FSEOG, state, private, college/university gift aid from institutional funds.

**GIFT AID (NON-NEED-BASED)** *Total amount:* $63,899 (49% institutional, 51% external sources). *Receiving aid:* Freshmen: 17% (212). Undergraduates: 20% (1,760). *Average award:* Freshmen: $3792. Undergraduates: $4025. *Tuition waivers:* Full or partial for employees or children of employees, senior citizens. **ROTC:** Army, Air Force cooperative.

**LOANS** *Student loans:* $16,311,226 (93% need-based, 7% non-need-based). 60% of past graduating class borrowed through all loan programs. *Average indebtedness per student:* $16,768. *Average need-based loan:* Freshmen: $1551. Undergraduates: $2211. *Parent loans:* $412,046 (51% need-based, 49% non-need-based). *Programs:* Federal Direct (Subsidized and Unsubsidized Stafford, PLUS), Perkins, college/university.

**WORK-STUDY** *Federal work-study:* Total amount: $366,018; 233 jobs averaging $1571.

**ATHLETIC AWARDS** Total amount: $244,586 (90% need-based, 10% non-need-based).

**APPLYING FOR FINANCIAL AID** *Required financial aid form:* FAFSA. *Financial aid deadline:* 5/15 (priority: 3/2). *Notification date:* Continuous beginning 3/15. Students must reply within 2 weeks of notification.

**CONTACT** Mrs. Delores S. Lee, Director of Financial Aid, California State University, Dominguez Hills, 1000 East Victoria Street, Carson, CA 90747-0001, 310-243-3189. *Fax:* 310-516-4498. *E-mail:* dslee@csudh.edu.
*Website:* http://www.csudh.edu/.

# CALIFORNIA STATE UNIVERSITY, EAST BAY
## Hayward, CA

| Tuition & fees (CA res): $6564 | Average undergraduate aid package: $11,016 |
|---|---|

**ABOUT THE INSTITUTION** State-supported, coed. *Awards:* certificates, bachelor's, master's, and doctoral degrees. 90 undergraduate majors. *Total enrollment:* 14,526. Undergraduates: 12,060. Freshmen: 1,511. Federal methodology is used as a basis for awarding need-based institutional aid.

**UNDERGRADUATE EXPENSES** for 2015–2016 *Application fee:* $55. *Tuition, state resident:* full-time $6564; part-time $1058 per term. *Tuition, nonresident:* full-time $15,492; part-time $2546 per term. *Required fees:* $364 per term. Full-time tuition and fees vary according to course load and reciprocity agreements. Part-time tuition and fees vary according to course load and reciprocity agreements. *College room and board:* $12,246. Room and board charges vary according to board plan.

**FRESHMAN FINANCIAL AID (Fall 2014, est.)** 619 applied for aid; of those 93% were deemed to have need. 98% of freshmen with need received aid; of those 3% had need fully met. *Average percent of need met:* 64% (excluding resources awarded to replace EFC). *Average financial aid package:* $12,807 (excluding resources awarded to replace EFC).

**UNDERGRADUATE FINANCIAL AID (Fall 2014, est.)** 7,378 applied for aid; of those 97% were deemed to have need. 98% of undergraduates with need received aid; of those 3% had need fully met. *Average percent of need met:* 59% (excluding resources awarded to replace EFC). *Average financial aid package:* $11,016 (excluding resources awarded to replace EFC).

**GIFT AID (NEED-BASED) Total amount:** $63,711,590 (42% federal, 28% state, 29% institutional, 1% external sources). *Receiving aid:* Freshmen: 37% (549); all full-time undergraduates: 58% (6,816). *Average award:* Freshmen: $10,329; Undergraduates: $8564. *Scholarships, grants, and awards:* Federal Pell, FSEOG, state, private, college/university gift aid from institutional funds.

**GIFT AID (NON-NEED-BASED) Scholarships, grants, and awards by category:** *Academic interests/achievement:* general academic interests/achievements. *Creative arts/performance:* music. *Tuition waivers:* Full or partial for employees or children of employees, senior citizens.

**LOANS Student loans:** $33,398,657 (86% need-based, 14% non-need-based). 47% of past graduating class borrowed through all loan programs. *Average indebtedness per student:* $18,684. *Average need-based loan:* Freshmen: $5450. Undergraduates: $6751. *Parent loans:* $4,525,320 (35% need-based, 65% non-need-based). *Programs:* Federal Direct (Subsidized and Unsubsidized Stafford, PLUS), Perkins, college/university.

**WORK-STUDY Federal work-study:** Total amount: $709,179; jobs available.

**ATHLETIC AWARDS** Total amount: $831,031 (100% need-based).

**APPLYING FOR FINANCIAL AID** *Required financial aid form:* FAFSA. *Financial aid deadline (priority):* 3/2. *Notification date:* Continuous beginning 3/31. Students must reply within 4 weeks of notification.

**CONTACT** Office of Financial Aid, California State University, East Bay, 25800 Carlos Bee Boulevard, Hayward, CA 94542-3028, 510-885-2784. *Fax:* 510-885-2161. *E-mail:* finaid@csueastbay.edu. *Website:* http://www.csueastbay.edu/.

# CALIFORNIA STATE UNIVERSITY, FRESNO

## Fresno, CA

| Tuition & fees (CA res): $6298 | Average undergraduate aid package: $12,478 |
| --- | --- |

**ABOUT THE INSTITUTION** State-supported, coed. *Awards:* certificates, bachelor's, master's, and doctoral degrees. 87 undergraduate majors. *Total enrollment:* 23,179. Undergraduates: 20,510. Freshmen: 3,422. Federal methodology is used as a basis for awarding need-based institutional aid.

**UNDERGRADUATE EXPENSES** for 2015–2016 *Application fee:* $55. *Tuition, state resident:* full-time $6298. *Tuition, nonresident:* full-time $17,446; part-time $372 per credit hour. *College room and board:* $10,604. Room and board charges vary according to board plan.

**FRESHMAN FINANCIAL AID (Fall 2014, est.)** 2,967 applied for aid; of those 89% were deemed to have need. 99% of freshmen with need received aid; of those 17% had need fully met. *Average percent of need met:* 73% (excluding resources awarded to replace EFC). *Average financial aid package:* $11,760 (excluding resources awarded to replace EFC). 6% of all full-time freshmen had no need and received non-need-based gift aid.

**UNDERGRADUATE FINANCIAL AID (Fall 2014, est.)** 14,478 applied for aid; of those 93% were deemed to have need. 98% of undergraduates with need received aid; of those 18% had need fully met. *Average percent of need met:* 73% (excluding resources awarded to replace EFC). *Average financial aid package:*

$12,478 (excluding resources awarded to replace EFC). 4% of all full-time undergraduates had no need and received non-need-based gift aid.

**GIFT AID (NEED-BASED) Total amount:** $128,224,491 (45% federal, 55% state). *Receiving aid:* Freshmen: 69% (2,340); all full-time undergraduates: 65% (11,594). *Average award:* Freshmen: $10,630; Undergraduates: $10,319. *Scholarships, grants, and awards:* Federal Pell, FSEOG, state, private, college/university gift aid from institutional funds.

**GIFT AID (NON-NEED-BASED) Total amount:** $7,759,049 (21% state, 44% institutional, 35% external sources). *Receiving aid:* Freshmen: 29% (970). Undergraduates: 22% (3,852). *Average award:* Freshmen: $1603. Undergraduates: $1269. *Scholarships, grants, and awards by category:* *Academic interests/achievement:* 1,016 awards ($2,762,983 total): agriculture, area/ethnic studies, biological sciences, business, communication, education, engineering/technologies, English, foreign languages, general academic interests/achievements, health fields, humanities, mathematics, physical sciences, social sciences. *Creative arts/performance:* 179 awards ($230,169 total): art/fine arts, journalism/publications, music, theater/drama. *Special achievements/activities:* 21 awards ($28,750 total): community service, leadership. *Special characteristics:* 3 awards ($3898 total): handicapped students, local/state students. *ROTC:* Army, Air Force.

**LOANS Student loans:** $42,358,211 (57% need-based, 43% non-need-based). 78% of past graduating class borrowed through all loan programs. *Average indebtedness per student:* $12,851. *Average need-based loan:* Freshmen: $2982. Undergraduates: $3999. *Parent loans:* $1,317,009 (100% non-need-based). *Programs:* Federal Direct (Subsidized and Unsubsidized Stafford, PLUS), Perkins, Federal Nursing, college/university, alternative loans.

**WORK-STUDY Federal work-study:** Total amount: $974,513; 224 jobs averaging $4261.

**ATHLETIC AWARDS** Total amount: $4,701,757 (100% non-need-based).

**APPLYING FOR FINANCIAL AID** *Required financial aid form:* FAFSA. *Financial aid deadline (priority):* 3/2. *Notification date:* Continuous beginning 4/1. Students must reply within 3 weeks of notification.

**CONTACT** Denise Tardell, Assistant Director of Financial Aid, California State University, Fresno, 5150 North Maple Avenue, JA64, Fresno, CA 93740, 559-278-2182. *Fax:* 559-278-4833. *E-mail:* dtardell@csufresno.edu. *Website:* http://www.csufresno.edu/.

# CALIFORNIA STATE UNIVERSITY, FULLERTON

## Fullerton, CA

| Tuition & fees (CA res): $6316 | Average undergraduate aid package: $13,546 |
| --- | --- |

**ABOUT THE INSTITUTION** State-supported, coed. *Awards:* certificates, bachelor's, master's, and doctoral degrees. 66 undergraduate majors. *Total enrollment:* 38,128. Undergraduates: 32,726. Freshmen: 4,357. Federal methodology is used as a basis for awarding need-based institutional aid.

**UNDERGRADUATE EXPENSES** for 2015–2016 *Application fee:* $55. *Tuition, state resident:* full-time $5472; part-time $4016 per year. *Tuition, nonresident:* full-time $16,632; part-time $6249 per year. *Required fees:* full-time $844; $844 per year. Full-time tuition and fees vary according to course load. Part-time tuition and fees vary according to course load. *College room and board:* $13,510. Room and board charges vary according to board plan and housing facility.

**FRESHMAN FINANCIAL AID (Fall 2013)** 3,835 applied for aid; of those 95% were deemed to have need. 83% of freshmen with need received aid; of those 56% had need fully met. *Average percent of need met:* 56% (excluding resources awarded to replace EFC). *Average financial aid package:* $13,210 (excluding resources awarded to replace EFC). 9% of all full-time freshmen had no need and received non-need-based gift aid.

**UNDERGRADUATE FINANCIAL AID (Fall 2013)** 24,175 applied for aid; of those 81% were deemed to have need. 87% of undergraduates with need received aid; of those 56% had need fully met. *Average percent of need met:* 56% (excluding resources awarded to replace EFC). *Average financial aid package:* $13,546 (excluding resources awarded to replace EFC). 5% of all full-time undergraduates had no need and received non-need-based gift aid.

**GIFT AID (NEED-BASED) Total amount:** $162,149,888 (40% federal, 26% state, 33% institutional, 1% external sources). *Receiving aid:* Freshmen: 55% (2,476); all full-time undergraduates: 51% (17,036). *Average award:* Freshmen: $8994;

Undergraduates: $10,010. *Scholarships, grants, and awards:* Federal Pell, FSEOG, state, private, college/university gift aid from institutional funds, Federal Nursing.
**GIFT AID (NON-NEED-BASED) Total amount:** $561,794 (100% external sources). *Receiving aid:* Freshmen: 9% (423). Undergraduates: 5% (1,528). *Average award:* Freshmen: $7802. Undergraduates: $7989. *Scholarships, grants, and awards by category: Academic interests/achievement:* 2,544 awards ($3,807,905 total): area/ethnic studies, biological sciences, business, communication, computer science, education, engineering/technologies, English, foreign languages, general academic interests/achievements, health fields, humanities, mathematics, military science, physical sciences, religion/biblical studies, social sciences. *Creative arts/performance:* 300 awards ($193,669 total): art/fine arts, cinema/film/broadcasting, dance, journalism/publications, music, performing arts, theater/drama. *Special achievements/activities:* 273 awards ($284,172 total): general special achievements/activities, leadership. *Special characteristics:* 158 awards ($671,972 total): general special characteristics. *Tuition waivers:* Full or partial for employees or children of employees, senior citizens. *ROTC:* Army.
**LOANS Student loans:** $75,196,083 (53% need-based, 47% non-need-based). 42% of past graduating class borrowed through all loan programs. *Average indebtedness per student:* $14,965. *Average need-based loan:* Freshmen: $3498. Undergraduates: $5765. *Parent loans:* $3,472,984 (100% non-need-based). *Programs:* Federal Direct (Subsidized and Unsubsidized Stafford, PLUS), Perkins, college/university, private loans.
**WORK-STUDY Federal work-study:** 227 jobs averaging $3805.
**ATHLETIC AWARDS** Total amount: $2,327,543 (84% need-based, 16% non-need-based).
**APPLYING FOR FINANCIAL AID** *Required financial aid form:* FAFSA. *Financial aid deadline (priority):* 3/2. *Notification date:* Continuous beginning 4/22. Students must reply within 4 weeks of notification.
**CONTACT** Ms. Cecilia Schouwe, Director of Financial Aid, California State University, Fullerton, 800 North State College Boulevard, Fullerton, CA 92831-3599, 657-278-3128. *Fax:* 657-278-7090. *E-mail:* cschouwe@fullerton.edu. *Website:* http://www.fullerton.edu/.

# CALIFORNIA STATE UNIVERSITY, LONG BEACH
## Long Beach, CA

| Tuition & fees (CA res): $6420 | Average undergraduate aid package: $13,662 |
|---|---|

**ABOUT THE INSTITUTION** State-supported, coed. *Awards:* certificates, bachelor's, master's, and doctoral degrees. 148 undergraduate majors. *Total enrollment:* 36,809. Undergraduates: 31,523. Freshmen: 4,335. Federal methodology is used as a basis for awarding need-based institutional aid.
**UNDERGRADUATE EXPENSES for 2015–2016 Application fee:** $55. *Tuition, state resident:* full-time $5440. *Tuition, nonresident:* full-time $14,368; part-time $372 per unit. *Required fees:* full-time $980. Full-time tuition and fees vary according to degree level and program. Part-time tuition and fees vary according to course load, degree level, and program. *College room and board:* $11,688. Room and board charges vary according to board plan.
**FRESHMAN FINANCIAL AID (Fall 2014, est.)** 3,811 applied for aid; of those 81% were deemed to have need. 97% of freshmen with need received aid; of those 75% had need fully met. *Average percent of need met:* 80% (excluding resources awarded to replace EFC). *Average financial aid package:* $12,567 (excluding resources awarded to replace EFC). 11% of all full-time freshmen had no need and received non-need-based gift aid.
**UNDERGRADUATE FINANCIAL AID (Fall 2014, est.)** 22,097 applied for aid; of those 91% were deemed to have need. 94% of undergraduates with need received aid; of those 48% had need fully met. *Average percent of need met:* 83% (excluding resources awarded to replace EFC). *Average financial aid package:* $13,662 (excluding resources awarded to replace EFC). 8% of all full-time undergraduates had no need and received non-need-based gift aid.
**GIFT AID (NEED-BASED) Total amount:** $180,084,306 (42% federal, 54% state, 3% institutional, 1% external sources). *Receiving aid:* Freshmen: 57% (2,476); all full-time undergraduates: 61% (15,981). *Average award:* Freshmen: $7786;

Undergraduates: $6538. *Scholarships, grants, and awards:* Federal Pell, FSEOG, state, private, college/university gift aid from institutional funds.
**GIFT AID (NON-NEED-BASED) Total amount:** $27,596 (100% federal). *Receiving aid:* Freshmen: 17% (753). Undergraduates: 19% (4,839). *Average award:* Freshmen: $1847. Undergraduates: $2356. *Tuition waivers:* Full or partial for employees or children of employees, senior citizens. *ROTC:* Army.
**LOANS Student loans:** $122,451,359 (57% need-based, 43% non-need-based). 43% of past graduating class borrowed through all loan programs. *Average indebtedness per student:* $16,579. *Average need-based loan:* Freshmen: $3021. Undergraduates: $3811. *Parent loans:* $3,152,717 (100% non-need-based). *Programs:* Federal Direct (Subsidized and Unsubsidized Stafford, PLUS), Perkins.
**WORK-STUDY Federal work-study:** Total amount: $3,037,439; jobs available.
**ATHLETIC AWARDS** Total amount: $2,248,705 (100% non-need-based).
**APPLYING FOR FINANCIAL AID** *Required financial aid form:* FAFSA. *Financial aid deadline (priority):* 3/2. *Notification date:* 4/1. Students must reply within 4 weeks of notification.
**CONTACT** Nicolas Valdivia, Office of Financial Aid, California State University, Long Beach, 1250 Bellflower Boulevard, Long Beach, CA 90840, 562-985-8403. *Website:* http://www.csulb.edu/.

# CALIFORNIA STATE UNIVERSITY, LOS ANGELES
## Los Angeles, CA

| Tuition & fees (CA res): $6340 | Average undergraduate aid package: $11,764 |
|---|---|

**ABOUT THE INSTITUTION** State-supported, coed. *Awards:* certificates, bachelor's, master's, and doctoral degrees. 62 undergraduate majors. *Total enrollment:* 24,488. Undergraduates: 20,668. Freshmen: 3,230. Federal methodology is used as a basis for awarding need-based institutional aid.
**UNDERGRADUATE EXPENSES for 2015–2016 Application fee:** $55. *Tuition, state resident:* full-time $5472. *Tuition, nonresident:* full-time $14,400. *Required fees:* full-time $868. Full-time tuition and fees vary according to course level and course load. Part-time tuition and fees vary according to course level and course load. *College room and board:* $12,833. Room and board charges vary according to board plan and housing facility.
**FRESHMAN FINANCIAL AID (Fall 2014, est.)** 2,504 applied for aid; of those 97% were deemed to have need. 100% of freshmen with need received aid; of those 16% had need fully met. *Average percent of need met:* 60% (excluding resources awarded to replace EFC). *Average financial aid package:* $9426 (excluding resources awarded to replace EFC). 1% of all full-time freshmen had no need and received non-need-based gift aid.
**UNDERGRADUATE FINANCIAL AID (Fall 2014, est.)** 15,370 applied for aid; of those 97% were deemed to have need. 100% of undergraduates with need received aid; of those 15% had need fully met. *Average percent of need met:* 68% (excluding resources awarded to replace EFC). *Average financial aid package:* $11,764 (excluding resources awarded to replace EFC). 1% of all full-time undergraduates had no need and received non-need-based gift aid.
**GIFT AID (NEED-BASED) Total amount:** $153,802,204 (46% federal, 52% state, 2% institutional). *Receiving aid:* Freshmen: 73% (2,308); all full-time undergraduates: 81% (14,326). *Average award:* Freshmen: $9006; Undergraduates: $9668. *Scholarships, grants, and awards:* Federal Pell, FSEOG, state, private, college/university gift aid from institutional funds.
**GIFT AID (NON-NEED-BASED) Total amount:** $515,441 (25% state, 75% institutional). *Average award:* Freshmen: $2437. Undergraduates: $2888. *Scholarships, grants, and awards by category: Academic interests/achievement:* biological sciences, business, communication, computer science, education, engineering/technologies, English, foreign languages, general academic interests/achievements, health fields, mathematics, physical sciences, social sciences. *Creative arts/performance:* art/fine arts, general creative arts/performance, journalism/publications, music, theater/drama. *Special achievements/activities:* community service, general special achievements/activities. *Special characteristics:* general special characteristics. *Tuition waivers:* Full or partial for employees or children of employees. *ROTC:* Army cooperative, Air Force cooperative.
**LOANS Student loans:** $54,010,451 (96% need-based, 4% non-need-based). 54% of past graduating class borrowed through all loan programs. *Average indebtedness*

*per student:* $14,788. *Average need-based loan:* Freshmen: $3087. Undergraduates: $4214. *Parent loans:* $980,404 (65% need-based, 35% non-need-based). *Programs:* Federal Direct (Subsidized and Unsubsidized Stafford, PLUS), Perkins, Federal Nursing.

**WORK-STUDY** *Federal work-study:* Total amount: $923,060; jobs available.

**ATHLETIC AWARDS** Total amount: $509,606 (82% need-based, 18% non-need-based).

**APPLYING FOR FINANCIAL AID** *Required financial aid form:* FAFSA. *Financial aid deadline (priority):* 3/3. *Notification date:* Continuous beginning 4/1.

**CONTACT** Tamie L. Nguyen, Director of Financial Aid, California State University, Los Angeles, 5151 State University Drive, Los Angeles, CA 90032, 323-343-6260. *Fax:* 323-343-3166. *E-mail:* tnguyen10@cslanet.calstatela.edu. *Website:* http://www.calstatela.edu/.

# CALIFORNIA STATE UNIVERSITY, MONTEREY BAY
## Seaside, CA

| Tuition & fees (CA res): $5963 | Average undergraduate aid package: $11,055 |
| --- | --- |

**ABOUT THE INSTITUTION** State-supported, coed. *Awards:* bachelor's and master's degrees. 23 undergraduate majors. *Total enrollment:* 6,631. Undergraduates: 6,234. Freshmen: 1,305. Federal methodology is used as a basis for awarding need-based institutional aid.

**UNDERGRADUATE EXPENSES for 2015–2016** *Application fee:* $55. *Tuition, state resident:* full-time $0. *Tuition, nonresident:* full-time $11,160; part-time $372 per credit hour. *Required fees:* full-time $5963; $1832 per term. Full-time tuition and fees vary according to course load and degree level. Part-time tuition and fees vary according to course load and degree level. *College room and board:* $10,112. Room and board charges vary according to board plan and housing facility.

**FRESHMAN FINANCIAL AID (Fall 2014, est.)** 1,194 applied for aid; of those 79% were deemed to have need. 95% of freshmen with need received aid; of those 16% had need fully met. *Average percent of need met:* 65% (excluding resources awarded to replace EFC). *Average financial aid package:* $11,169 (excluding resources awarded to replace EFC). 2% of all full-time freshmen had no need and received non-need-based gift aid.

**UNDERGRADUATE FINANCIAL AID (Fall 2014, est.)** 4,520 applied for aid; of those 86% were deemed to have need. 94% of undergraduates with need received aid; of those 15% had need fully met. *Average percent of need met:* 73% (excluding resources awarded to replace EFC). *Average financial aid package:* $11,055 (excluding resources awarded to replace EFC). 1% of all full-time undergraduates had no need and received non-need-based gift aid.

**GIFT AID (NEED-BASED)** Total amount: $30,679,986 (45% federal, 28% state, 27% institutional). *Receiving aid:* Freshmen: 56% (724); all full-time undergraduates: 53% (3,056). *Average award:* Freshmen: $10,431; Undergraduates: $9595. *Scholarships, grants, and awards:* Federal Pell, FSEOG, state, private, college/university gift aid from institutional funds.

**GIFT AID (NON-NEED-BASED)** Total amount: $669,379 (6% federal, 37% institutional, 57% external sources). *Receiving aid:* Freshmen: 11% (136). Undergraduates: 6% (327). *Average award:* Freshmen: $3945. Undergraduates: $2980. *Scholarships, grants, and awards by category:* Academic interests/achievement: business, general academic interests/achievements. *Special achievements/activities:* leadership. *Special characteristics:* children and siblings of alumni, general special characteristics, local/state students. *Tuition waivers:* Full or partial for employees or children of employees, senior citizens.

**LOANS** *Student loans:* $15,843,196 (65% need-based, 35% non-need-based). 73% of past graduating class borrowed through all loan programs. *Average indebtedness per student:* $18,992. *Average need-based loan:* Freshmen: $3374. Undergraduates: $4342. *Parent loans:* $2,332,134 (100% non-need-based). *Programs:* Federal Direct (Subsidized and Unsubsidized Stafford, PLUS), Perkins, private loans.

**WORK-STUDY** *Federal work-study:* Total amount: $107,300; jobs available. *State or other work-study/employment:* Part-time jobs available.

**ATHLETIC AWARDS** Total amount: $479,404 (100% non-need-based).

**APPLYING FOR FINANCIAL AID** *Required financial aid forms:* FAFSA, state aid form. *Financial aid deadline:* 6/1 (priority: 3/2). *Notification date:* Continuous beginning 4/1.

**CONTACT** Office of Financial Aid, California State University, Monterey Bay, 100 Campus Center, Building 47, Seaside, CA 93955-8001, 831-582-5100. *Fax:* 831-582-3782. *Website:* http://www.csumb.edu/.

# CALIFORNIA STATE UNIVERSITY, NORTHRIDGE
## Northridge, CA

**ABOUT THE INSTITUTION** State-supported, coed. *Awards:* bachelor's and master's degrees. 59 undergraduate majors. *Total enrollment:* 40,131. Undergraduates: 35,206. Freshmen: 5,526.

**GIFT AID (NEED-BASED)** *Scholarships, grants, and awards:* Federal Pell, FSEOG, state, private, college/university gift aid from institutional funds.

**GIFT AID (NON-NEED-BASED)** *Scholarships, grants, and awards by category:* Academic interests/achievement: business, communication, computer science, education, engineering/technologies, English, general academic interests/achievements, mathematics, social sciences. *Creative arts/performance:* journalism/publications, music. *Special achievements/activities:* leadership.

**LOANS** *Programs:* Perkins.

**APPLYING FOR FINANCIAL AID** *Required financial aid form:* FAFSA.

**CONTACT** Lili Vidal, Director of Financial Aid and Scholarships, California State University, Northridge, 18111 Nordhoff Street, Northridge, CA 91330-8307, 818-677-4085. *Fax:* 818-677-6787. *E-mail:* financial.aid@csun.edu. *Website:* http://www.csun.edu/.

# CALIFORNIA STATE UNIVERSITY, SACRAMENTO
## Sacramento, CA

| Tuition & fees (CA res): $6602 | Average undergraduate aid package: $10,808 |
| --- | --- |

**ABOUT THE INSTITUTION** State-supported, coed. *Awards:* bachelor's, master's, and doctoral degrees. 55 undergraduate majors. *Total enrollment:* 29,349. Undergraduates: 26,648. Freshmen: 3,695. Federal methodology is used as a basis for awarding need-based institutional aid.

**UNDERGRADUATE EXPENSES for 2015–2016** *Application fee:* $55. *Tuition, state resident:* full-time $5472. *Tuition, nonresident:* full-time $16,632; part-time $372 per credit hour. *Required fees:* full-time $1130. *Room only:* $6538. Room and board charges vary according to board plan and housing facility.

**FRESHMAN FINANCIAL AID (Fall 2013)** 2,916 applied for aid; of those 86% were deemed to have need. 94% of freshmen with need received aid; of those 7% had need fully met. *Average percent of need met:* 63% (excluding resources awarded to replace EFC). *Average financial aid package:* $11,117 (excluding resources awarded to replace EFC). 1% of all full-time freshmen had no need and received non-need-based gift aid.

**UNDERGRADUATE FINANCIAL AID (Fall 2013)** 17,289 applied for aid; of those 91% were deemed to have need. 94% of undergraduates with need received aid; of those 6% had need fully met. *Average percent of need met:* 60% (excluding resources awarded to replace EFC). *Average financial aid package:* $10,808 (excluding resources awarded to replace EFC). 1% of all full-time undergraduates had no need and received non-need-based gift aid.

**GIFT AID (NEED-BASED)** Total amount: $146,156,201 (43% federal, 28% state, 29% institutional). *Receiving aid:* Freshmen: 64% (2,061); all full-time undergraduates: 61% (12,788). *Average award:* Freshmen: $10,678; Undergraduates: $9625. *Scholarships, grants, and awards:* Federal Pell, FSEOG, state, private, college/university gift aid from institutional funds, Federal Nursing.

**GIFT AID (NON-NEED-BASED)** Total amount: $4,326,828 (2% federal, 1% state, 27% institutional, 70% external sources). *Receiving aid:* Freshmen: 9% (304). Undergraduates: 5% (1,072). *Average award:* Freshmen: $1038. Undergraduates: $1047. *ROTC:* Army cooperative, Air Force.

**LOANS** *Student loans:* $92,900,562 (46% need-based, 54% non-need-based). 38% of past graduating class borrowed through all loan programs. *Average indebtedness per student:* $4402. *Average need-based loan:* Freshmen: $3322. Undergraduates: $4350. *Parent loans:* $9,245,505 (100% non-need-based). *Programs:* Federal Direct (Subsidized and Unsubsidized Stafford, PLUS), Perkins, Federal Nursing, college/university.
**WORK-STUDY** *Federal work-study:* jobs available. *State or other work-study/employment:* Part-time jobs available.
**ATHLETIC AWARDS** Total amount: $4,165,568 (100% need-based).
**APPLYING FOR FINANCIAL AID** *Required financial aid form:* FAFSA. *Financial aid deadline:* Continuous. *Notification date:* Continuous beginning 4/23.
**CONTACT** Anita Kermes, Director of Financial Aid, California State University, Sacramento, 6000 J Street, Sacramento, CA 95819-6044, 916-278-6554. *Fax:* 916-278-6082.
*Website:* http://www.csus.edu/.

# CALIFORNIA STATE UNIVERSITY, SAN BERNARDINO
## San Bernardino, CA

| Tuition & fees (CA res): $6558 | Average undergraduate aid package: $8781 |
|---|---|

**ABOUT THE INSTITUTION** State-supported, coed. *Awards:* certificates, bachelor's, master's, and doctoral degrees. 42 undergraduate majors. *Total enrollment:* 18,952. Undergraduates: 16,676. Freshmen: 2,724. Federal methodology is used as a basis for awarding need-based institutional aid.
**UNDERGRADUATE EXPENSES** for 2015–2016 *Application fee:* $55. *Tuition, state resident:* full-time $5472; part-time $3174 per year. *Tuition, nonresident:* full-time $16,632; part-time $248 per unit. *Required fees:* full-time $1086; $1086 per year. Part-time tuition and fees vary according to course load. *College room and board:* $9933. Room and board charges vary according to board plan and housing facility.
**FRESHMAN FINANCIAL AID (Fall 2014, est.)** 2,443 applied for aid; of those 91% were deemed to have need. 97% of freshmen with need received aid; of those 26% had need fully met. *Average percent of need met:* 76% (excluding resources awarded to replace EFC). *Average financial aid package:* $8790 (excluding resources awarded to replace EFC). 1% of all full-time freshmen had no need and received non-need-based gift aid.
**UNDERGRADUATE FINANCIAL AID (Fall 2014, est.)** 13,020 applied for aid; of those 94% were deemed to have need. 97% of undergraduates with need received aid; of those 22% had need fully met. *Average percent of need met:* 74% (excluding resources awarded to replace EFC). *Average financial aid package:* $8781 (excluding resources awarded to replace EFC). 1% of all full-time undergraduates had no need and received non-need-based gift aid.
**GIFT AID (NEED-BASED)** *Total amount:* $109,636,690 (46% federal, 52% state, 1% institutional, 1% external sources). *Receiving aid:* Freshmen: 80% (2,089); all full-time undergraduates: 78% (11,541). *Average award:* Freshmen: $8909; Undergraduates: $8834. *Scholarships, grants, and awards:* Federal Pell, FSEOG, state, private, college/university gift aid from institutional funds.
**GIFT AID (NON-NEED-BASED)** *Total amount:* $872,355 (76% institutional, 24% external sources). *Receiving aid:* Freshmen: 20% (518). Undergraduates: 11% (1,599). *Average award:* Freshmen: $1963. Undergraduates: $3849. *Scholarships, grants, and awards by category:* Academic interests/achievement: 655 awards ($1,403,819 total): biological sciences, business, computer science, education, foreign languages, general academic interests/achievements, health fields, international studies, mathematics, physical sciences, social sciences. *Creative arts/performance:* 18 awards ($29,155 total): art/fine arts, general creative arts/performance, journalism/publications, music, theater/drama. *Special achievements/activities:* community service, general special achievements/activities, hobbies/interests, memberships. *Special characteristics:* 13 awards ($47,670 total): children of public servants, children with a deceased or disabled parent, first-generation college students, handicapped students, veterans, veterans' children. *Tuition waivers:* Full or partial for employees or children of employees, senior citizens. *ROTC:* Army, Air Force.
**LOANS** *Student loans:* $41,674,191 (67% need-based, 33% non-need-based). 66% of past graduating class borrowed through all loan programs. *Average indebtedness*

*per student:* $19,575. *Average need-based loan:* Freshmen: $3187. Undergraduates: $4091. *Parent loans:* $2,746,083 (9% need-based, 91% non-need-based). *Programs:* Federal Direct (Subsidized and Unsubsidized Stafford, PLUS), Perkins.
**WORK-STUDY** *Federal work-study:* Total amount: $1,412,120; 306 jobs averaging $3966.
**ATHLETIC AWARDS** Total amount: $576,162 (68% need-based, 32% non-need-based).
**APPLYING FOR FINANCIAL AID** *Required financial aid forms:* FAFSA, state aid form. *Financial aid deadline (priority):* 3/2. *Notification date:* Continuous beginning 4/1.
**CONTACT** Ms. Roseanna Ruiz, Director of Financial Aid, California State University, San Bernardino, 5500 University Parkway, San Bernardino, CA 92407-2397, 909-537-5227. *Fax:* 909-537-4024.
*Website:* http://www.csusb.edu/.

# CALIFORNIA STATE UNIVERSITY, SAN MARCOS
## San Marcos, CA

| Tuition & fees (CA res): $7164 | Average undergraduate aid package: $5259 |
|---|---|

**ABOUT THE INSTITUTION** State-supported, coed. *Awards:* bachelor's, master's, and doctoral degrees. 38 undergraduate majors. *Total enrollment:* 12,150. Undergraduates: 11,555. Freshmen: 2,167. Federal methodology is used as a basis for awarding need-based institutional aid.
**UNDERGRADUATE EXPENSES** for 2015–2016 *Application fee:* $55. *Tuition, state resident:* full-time $0. *Tuition, nonresident:* full-time $16,092; part-time $372 per unit. *Required fees:* full-time $7164; $2433 per term. Part-time tuition and fees vary according to course load. Room and board charges vary according to housing facility.
**FRESHMAN FINANCIAL AID (Fall 2013)** 1,774 applied for aid; of those 80% were deemed to have need. 99% of freshmen with need received aid; of those 1% had need fully met. *Average percent of need met:* 63% (excluding resources awarded to replace EFC). *Average financial aid package:* $5178 (excluding resources awarded to replace EFC).
**UNDERGRADUATE FINANCIAL AID (Fall 2013)** 6,777 applied for aid; of those 86% were deemed to have need. 98% of undergraduates with need received aid; of those 2% had need fully met. *Average percent of need met:* 64% (excluding resources awarded to replace EFC). *Average financial aid package:* $5259 (excluding resources awarded to replace EFC). 1% of all full-time undergraduates had no need and received non-need-based gift aid.
**GIFT AID (NEED-BASED)** *Total amount:* $25,301,624 (44% federal, 26% state, 27% institutional, 3% external sources). *Receiving aid:* Freshmen: 63% (1,152); all full-time undergraduates: 66% (4,726). *Average award:* Freshmen: $5038; Undergraduates: $4789. *Scholarships, grants, and awards:* Federal Pell, FSEOG, state, private, college/university gift aid from institutional funds.
**GIFT AID (NON-NEED-BASED)** *Total amount:* $132,387 (7% institutional, 93% external sources). *Average award:* Undergraduates: $2133. *Scholarships, grants, and awards by category:* Academic interests/achievement: general academic interests/achievements, mathematics. *Special achievements/activities:* leadership. *Special characteristics:* local/state students. *Tuition waivers:* Full or partial for employees or children of employees, senior citizens. *ROTC:* Army cooperative, Naval cooperative, Air Force cooperative.
**LOANS** *Student loans:* $14,027,389 (83% need-based, 17% non-need-based). 50% of past graduating class borrowed through all loan programs. *Average indebtedness per student:* $22,024. *Average need-based loan:* Freshmen: $1113. Undergraduates: $1394. *Parent loans:* $396,072 (20% need-based, 80% non-need-based). *Programs:* Federal Direct (Subsidized and Unsubsidized Stafford, PLUS), Perkins, college/university.
**WORK-STUDY** *Federal work-study:* jobs available. *State or other work-study/employment:* Total amount: $14,185,971 (83% need-based, 17% non-need-based). Part-time jobs available.
**ATHLETIC AWARDS** Total amount: $262,859 (90% need-based, 10% non-need-based).
**APPLYING FOR FINANCIAL AID** *Required financial aid form:* FAFSA. *Financial aid deadline (priority):* 3/4. *Notification date:* 2/25.

**CONTACT** Financial Aid and Scholarships Office, California State University, San Marcos, 333 South Twin Oaks Valley Road, San Marcos, CA 92096-0001, 760-750-4850. *Fax:* 760-750-3047. *E-mail:* finaid@csusm.edu.
*Website:* http://www.csusm.edu/.

# CALIFORNIA STATE UNIVERSITY, STANISLAUS
## Turlock, CA

| Tuition & fees (CA res): $6491 | Average undergraduate aid package: $8006 |
| --- | --- |

**ABOUT THE INSTITUTION** State-supported, coed. *Awards:* certificates, bachelor's, master's, and doctoral degrees. 50 undergraduate majors. *Total enrollment:* 9,045. Undergraduates: 7,847. Freshmen: 1,232. Federal methodology is used as a basis for awarding need-based institutional aid.

**UNDERGRADUATE EXPENSES for 2015–2016 Application fee:** $55. *Tuition, state resident:* full-time $5472. *Tuition, nonresident:* full-time $16,632. *Required fees:* full-time $1019; $1019 per term. Full-time tuition and fees vary according to course load, degree level, and reciprocity agreements. Part-time tuition and fees vary according to course load, degree level, and reciprocity agreements. *College room and board:* $11,900. Room and board charges vary according to board plan and housing facility.

**FRESHMAN FINANCIAL AID (Fall 2014, est.)** 1,119 applied for aid; of those 91% were deemed to have need. 100% of freshmen with need received aid; of those 9% had need fully met. *Average percent of need met:* 51% (excluding resources awarded to replace EFC). *Average financial aid package:* $7800 (excluding resources awarded to replace EFC). 3% of all full-time freshmen had no need and received non-need-based gift aid.

**UNDERGRADUATE FINANCIAL AID (Fall 2014, est.)** 5,918 applied for aid; of those 93% were deemed to have need. 100% of undergraduates with need received aid; of those 11% had need fully met. *Average percent of need met:* 49% (excluding resources awarded to replace EFC). *Average financial aid package:* $8006 (excluding resources awarded to replace EFC). 1% of all full-time undergraduates had no need and received non-need-based gift aid.

**GIFT AID (NEED-BASED) Total amount:** $52,725,863 (41% federal, 31% state, 27% institutional, 1% external sources). *Receiving aid:* Freshmen: 62% (745); all full-time undergraduates: 40% (2,710). *Average award:* Freshmen: $5171; Undergraduates: $4641. *Scholarships, grants, and awards:* Federal Pell, FSEOG, state, private, college/university gift aid from institutional funds.

**GIFT AID (NON-NEED-BASED) Total amount:** $496,485 (1% federal, 41% state, 27% institutional, 31% external sources). *Receiving aid:* Freshmen: 2% (29). Undergraduates: 1% (87). *Average award:* Freshmen: $1600. Undergraduates: $1745. *Scholarships, grants, and awards by category: Academic interests/achievement:* agriculture, area/ethnic studies, biological sciences, business, communication, computer science, education, English, foreign languages, general academic interests/achievements, health fields, humanities, international studies, mathematics, physical sciences, premedicine, social sciences. *Creative arts/performance:* art/fine arts, music. *Special achievements/activities:* community service, general special achievements/activities, leadership, memberships. *Special characteristics:* children of faculty/staff, first-generation college students, general special characteristics, local/state students. *Tuition waivers:* Full or partial for employees or children of employees.

**LOANS Student loans:** $35,563,148 (90% need-based, 10% non-need-based). *Average need-based loan:* Freshmen: $3152. Undergraduates: $3956. *Parent loans:* $11,720,805 (73% need-based, 27% non-need-based). *Programs:* Federal Direct (Subsidized and Unsubsidized Stafford, PLUS), Perkins, private loans.

**WORK-STUDY Federal work-study:** Total amount: $528,083; jobs available. *State or other work-study/employment:* Part-time jobs available.

**ATHLETIC AWARDS** Total amount: $678,775 (48% need-based, 52% non-need-based).

**APPLYING FOR FINANCIAL AID Required financial aid forms:** FAFSA, state aid form. *Financial aid deadline (priority):* 3/2. *Notification date:* Continuous beginning 3/15. Students must reply within 3 weeks of notification.

**CONTACT** Ms. Lisa Fields, Research Analyst, California State University, Stanislaus, One University Circle, Turlock, CA 95382, 209-667-3281 or toll-free 800-300-7420. *Fax:* 209-664-7069. *E-mail:* lfields@csustan.edu.
*Website:* http://www.csustan.edu/.

# CALIFORNIA UNIVERSITY OF MANAGEMENT AND SCIENCES
## Anaheim, CA

**CONTACT** Financial Aid Office, California University of Management and Sciences, 721 North Euclid Street, Anaheim, CA 92801, 714-533-3946.
*Website:* http://www.calums.edu/.

# CALIFORNIA UNIVERSITY OF PENNSYLVANIA
## California, PA

| Tuition & fees (PA res): $9556 | Average undergraduate aid package: $9446 |
| --- | --- |

**ABOUT THE INSTITUTION** State-supported, coed. *Awards:* certificates, associate, bachelor's, and master's degrees. 52 undergraduate majors. *Total enrollment:* 7,978. Undergraduates: 6,076. Freshmen: 1,023. Federal methodology is used as a basis for awarding need-based institutional aid.

**UNDERGRADUATE EXPENSES for 2015–2016 Application fee:** $25. *Tuition, state resident:* full-time $6820; part-time $284 per credit hour. *Tuition, nonresident:* full-time $10,230; part-time $426 per credit hour. *Required fees:* full-time $2736. Full-time tuition and fees vary according to course load, location, and student level. Part-time tuition and fees vary according to course load, location, and student level. *College room and board:* $10,086; *Room only:* $6592. Room and board charges vary according to board plan and housing facility.

**FRESHMAN FINANCIAL AID (Fall 2013)** 1,125 applied for aid; of those 83% were deemed to have need. 100% of freshmen with need received aid; of those 9% had need fully met. *Average percent of need met:* 64% (excluding resources awarded to replace EFC). *Average financial aid package:* $10,041 (excluding resources awarded to replace EFC). 2% of all full-time freshmen had no need and received non-need-based gift aid.

**UNDERGRADUATE FINANCIAL AID (Fall 2013)** 5,185 applied for aid; of those 84% were deemed to have need. 100% of undergraduates with need received aid; of those 7% had need fully met. *Average percent of need met:* 62% (excluding resources awarded to replace EFC). *Average financial aid package:* $9446 (excluding resources awarded to replace EFC). 2% of all full-time undergraduates had no need and received non-need-based gift aid.

**GIFT AID (NEED-BASED) Total amount:** $24,936,554 (52% federal, 35% state, 10% institutional, 3% external sources). *Receiving aid:* Freshmen: 69% (806); all full-time undergraduates: 57% (3,233). *Average award:* Freshmen: $6381; Undergraduates: $5688. *Scholarships, grants, and awards:* Federal Pell, FSEOG, state, private, college/university gift aid from institutional funds.

**GIFT AID (NON-NEED-BASED) Total amount:** $3,487,730 (6% federal, 2% state, 56% institutional, 36% external sources). *Receiving aid:* Freshmen: 26% (304). Undergraduates: 15% (862). *Average award:* Freshmen: $3543. Undergraduates: $3097. *Scholarships, grants, and awards by category: Academic interests/achievement:* general academic interests/achievements. *Creative arts/performance:* general creative arts/performance. *Special achievements/activities:* general special achievements/activities. *Special characteristics:* ethnic background, international students, members of minority groups, veterans. *Tuition waivers:* Full or partial for employees or children of employees. *ROTC:* Army.

**LOANS Student loans:** $49,633,317 (41% need-based, 59% non-need-based). 80% of past graduating class borrowed through all loan programs. *Average indebtedness per student:* $29,105. *Average need-based loan:* Freshmen: $2995. Undergraduates: $3870. *Parent loans:* $8,836,918 (100% non-need-based). *Programs:* Federal Direct (Subsidized and Unsubsidized Stafford, PLUS), Perkins, college/university.

**WORK-STUDY Federal work-study:** jobs available. *State or other work-study/employment:* Total amount: $1,729,545 (31% need-based, 69% non-need-based). Part-time jobs available.

**ATHLETIC AWARDS** Total amount: $2,398,513 (100% non-need-based).

**APPLYING FOR FINANCIAL AID Required financial aid form:** FAFSA. *Financial aid deadline:* Continuous. *Notification date:* Continuous beginning 4/1.

CONTACT Jill Fernandes, Director of Financial Aid, California University of Pennsylvania, 250 University Avenue, California, PA 15419-1394, 724-938-4415 or toll-free 888-412-0479.
*Website:* http://www.calu.edu/.

## CALUMET COLLEGE OF SAINT JOSEPH
### Whiting, IN

| Tuition & fees: $16,440 | Average undergraduate aid package: $12,417 |
|---|---|

**ABOUT THE INSTITUTION** Independent Roman Catholic, coed. *Awards:* certificates, associate, bachelor's, and master's degrees. 21 undergraduate majors. *Total enrollment:* 1,072. Undergraduates: 907. Freshmen: 126. Both federal and institutional methodology are used as a basis for awarding need-based institutional aid.

**UNDERGRADUATE EXPENSES for 2015–2016 Tuition:** full-time $16,170; part-time $510 per credit hour. *Required fees:* full-time $270; $135 per term. Full-time tuition and fees vary according to course load and program. Part-time tuition and fees vary according to course load and program. *Payment plan:* Guaranteed tuition.

**FRESHMAN FINANCIAL AID (Fall 2013)** 136 applied for aid; of those 92% were deemed to have need. 96% of freshmen with need received aid; of those 12% had need fully met. *Average percent of need met:* 60% (excluding resources awarded to replace EFC). *Average financial aid package:* $11,856 (excluding resources awarded to replace EFC). 1% of all full-time freshmen had no need and received non-need-based gift aid.

**UNDERGRADUATE FINANCIAL AID (Fall 2013)** 557 applied for aid; of those 91% were deemed to have need. 99% of undergraduates with need received aid; of those 12% had need fully met. *Average percent of need met:* 60% (excluding resources awarded to replace EFC). *Average financial aid package:* $12,417 (excluding resources awarded to replace EFC). 3% of all full-time undergraduates had no need and received non-need-based gift aid.

**GIFT AID (NEED-BASED) Total amount:** $3,267,011 (53% federal, 27% state, 19% institutional, 1% external sources). *Receiving aid:* Freshmen: 57% (85); all full-time undergraduates: 60% (364). *Average award:* Freshmen: $7573; Undergraduates: $7738. *Scholarships, grants, and awards:* Federal Pell, FSEOG, state, private, college/university gift aid from institutional funds, United Negro College Fund.

**GIFT AID (NON-NEED-BASED) Total amount:** $1,041,751 (48% institutional, 52% external sources). *Receiving aid:* Freshmen: 58% (87). Undergraduates: 50% (305). *Average award:* Freshmen: $4228. Undergraduates: $2959. *Scholarships, grants, and awards by category: Academic interests/achievement:* 52 awards ($128,489 total): general academic interests/achievements. *Creative arts/performance:* art/fine arts, creative writing, general creative arts/performance, theater/drama. *Special achievements/activities:* 33 awards ($46,625 total): leadership. *Special characteristics:* 55 awards ($169,101 total): children and siblings of alumni, children of faculty/staff, general special characteristics, previous college experience, religious affiliation. *Tuition waivers:* Full or partial for children of alumni, employees or children of employees, senior citizens.

**LOANS Student loans:** $3,849,983 (47% need-based, 53% non-need-based). 77% of past graduating class borrowed through all loan programs. *Average indebtedness per student:* $30,847. *Average need-based loan:* Freshmen: $3818. Undergraduates: $2984. *Parent loans:* $114,741 (100% non-need-based). *Programs:* Federal Direct (Subsidized and Unsubsidized Stafford, PLUS).

**WORK-STUDY Federal work-study:** 23 jobs averaging $1816. *State or other work-study/employment:* Total amount: $1284 (100% need-based). 1 part-time job averaging $1284.

**ATHLETIC AWARDS** Total amount: $1,438,357 (100% non-need-based).

**APPLYING FOR FINANCIAL AID Required financial aid form:** FAFSA. *Financial aid deadline (priority):* 3/10. *Notification date:* Continuous beginning 4/1.

CONTACT Gina Pirtle, Director of Financial Aid and Business Office Operations, Calumet College of Saint Joseph, 2400 New York Avenue, Whiting, IN 46394, 219-473-4379 or toll-free 877-700-9100. E-mail: gpirtle@ccsj.edu.
*Website:* http://www.ccsj.edu/.

## CALVARY BIBLE COLLEGE AND THEOLOGICAL SEMINARY
### Kansas City, MO

| Tuition & fees: $10,360 | Average undergraduate aid package: $7780 |
|---|---|

**ABOUT THE INSTITUTION** Independent nondenominational, coed. *Awards:* certificates, associate, bachelor's, and master's degrees. 34 undergraduate majors. *Total enrollment:* 314. Undergraduates: 250. Freshmen: 38. Both federal and institutional methodology are used as a basis for awarding need-based institutional aid.

**UNDERGRADUATE EXPENSES for 2015–2016 One-time required fee:** $100. *Comprehensive fee:* $15,800 includes full-time tuition ($9520), mandatory fees ($840), and room and board ($5440). Full-time tuition and fees vary according to course load. Room and board charges vary according to housing facility. *Part-time tuition:* $340 per credit hour. *Part-time fees:* $30 per credit hour; $60 per term. Part-time tuition and fees vary according to course load.

**FRESHMAN FINANCIAL AID (Fall 2013)** 27 applied for aid; of those 100% were deemed to have need. 100% of freshmen with need received aid. *Average financial aid package:* $7058 (excluding resources awarded to replace EFC).

**UNDERGRADUATE FINANCIAL AID (Fall 2013)** 129 applied for aid; of those 95% were deemed to have need. 100% of undergraduates with need received aid. *Average financial aid package:* $7780 (excluding resources awarded to replace EFC).

**GIFT AID (NEED-BASED) Total amount:** $899,108 (56% federal, 38% institutional, 6% external sources). *Receiving aid:* Freshmen: 47% (17); all full-time undergraduates: 42% (72). *Average award:* Freshmen: $3351; Undergraduates: $4429. *Scholarships, grants, and awards:* Federal Pell, FSEOG, private, college/university gift aid from institutional funds.

**GIFT AID (NON-NEED-BASED) Receiving aid:** Freshmen: 50% (18). Undergraduates: 38% (66). *Scholarships, grants, and awards by category: Academic interests/achievement:* general academic interests/achievements. *Creative arts/performance:* general creative arts/performance. *Special achievements/activities:* general special achievements/activities, religious involvement. *Special characteristics:* children and siblings of alumni, children of educators, children of faculty/staff, relatives of clergy, religious affiliation, siblings of current students, spouses of current students. *Tuition waivers:* Full or partial for employees or children of employees. *ROTC:* Army cooperative.

**LOANS Student loans:** $853,672 (100% need-based). 42% of past graduating class borrowed through all loan programs. *Average indebtedness per student:* $9993. *Average need-based loan:* Freshmen: $3488. Undergraduates: $4245. *Parent loans:* $19,870 (100% need-based). *Programs:* Federal Direct (Subsidized and Unsubsidized Stafford, PLUS).

**APPLYING FOR FINANCIAL AID Required financial aid forms:** FAFSA, institution's own form. *Financial aid deadline:* 4/1 (priority: 3/1). *Notification date:* Continuous beginning 5/1.

CONTACT Mr. Robert Crank, Director of Financial Aid, Calvary Bible College and Theological Seminary, 15800 Calvary Road, Kansas City, MO 64147-1341, 816-322-0110 Ext. 1323 or toll-free 800-326-3960. Fax: 816-331-4474. E-mail: finaid@calvary.edu.
*Website:* http://www.calvary.edu/.

## CALVIN COLLEGE
### Grand Rapids, MI

| Tuition & fees: $29,635 | Average undergraduate aid package: $21,920 |
|---|---|

**ABOUT THE INSTITUTION** Independent Christian Reformed, coed. *Awards:* bachelor's and master's degrees. 102 undergraduate majors. *Total enrollment:* 3,993. Undergraduates: 3,894. Freshmen: 951. Both federal and institutional methodology are used as a basis for awarding need-based institutional aid.

**UNDERGRADUATE EXPENSES for 2015–2016 Application fee:** $35. *Comprehensive fee:* $39,120 includes full-time tuition ($29,400), mandatory fees ($235), and room and board ($9485). Full-time tuition and fees vary according to degree level and program. Room and board charges vary according to board plan and housing facility. **Part-time tuition:** $700 per credit hour. Part-time tuition and fees vary according to course load and degree level. **Payment plan:** Tuition prepayment.

**FRESHMAN FINANCIAL AID (Fall 2014, est.)** 856 applied for aid; of those 73% were deemed to have need. 100% of freshmen with need received aid; of those 18% had need fully met. **Average percent of need met:** 78% (excluding resources awarded to replace EFC). **Average financial aid package:** $23,871 (excluding resources awarded to replace EFC). 32% of all full-time freshmen had no need and received non-need-based gift aid.

**UNDERGRADUATE FINANCIAL AID (Fall 2014, est.)** 3,063 applied for aid; of those 76% were deemed to have need. 100% of undergraduates with need received aid; of those 15% had need fully met. **Average percent of need met:** 72% (excluding resources awarded to replace EFC). **Average financial aid package:** $21,920 (excluding resources awarded to replace EFC). 33% of all full-time undergraduates had no need and received non-need-based gift aid.

**GIFT AID (NEED-BASED) Total amount:** $35,852,437 (12% federal, 5% state, 81% institutional, 2% external sources). **Receiving aid:** Freshmen: 66% (625); all full-time undergraduates: 61% (2,301). **Average award:** Freshmen: $17,278; Undergraduates: $15,097. **Scholarships, grants, and awards:** Federal Pell, FSEOG, state, private, college/university gift aid from institutional funds.

**GIFT AID (NON-NEED-BASED) Total amount:** $14,008,551 (96% institutional, 4% external sources). **Receiving aid:** Freshmen: 8% (77). Undergraduates: 5% (200). **Average award:** Freshmen: $8423. Undergraduates: $7640. **Scholarships, grants, and awards by category:** Academic interests/achievement: $19,600,000 total: architecture, area/ethnic studies, biological sciences, business, communication, computer science, education, engineering/technologies, English, foreign languages, general academic interests/achievements, health fields, humanities, international studies, mathematics, physical sciences, premedicine, religion/biblical studies, social sciences. Creative arts/performance: $167,000 total: applied art and design, art/fine arts, cinema/film/broadcasting, creative writing, journalism/publications, music, performing arts, theater/drama. Special achievements/activities: $664,200 total: community service, leadership, religious involvement. Special characteristics: $11,864,500 total: adult students, children and siblings of alumni, children of faculty/staff, children of union members/company employees, children of workers in trades, children with a deceased or disabled parent, ethnic background, first-generation college students, handicapped students, international students, local/state students, members of minority groups, out-of-state students, religious affiliation, twins, veterans, veterans' children. **Tuition waivers:** Full or partial for employees or children of employees. **ROTC:** Army cooperative.

**LOANS Student loans:** $25,148,101 (74% need-based, 26% non-need-based). 67% of past graduating class borrowed through all loan programs. Average indebtedness per student: $29,403. **Average need-based loan:** Freshmen: $4932. Undergraduates: $6919. **Parent loans:** $3,529,523 (50% need-based, 50% non-need-based). **Programs:** Federal Direct (Subsidized and Unsubsidized Stafford, PLUS), Perkins, state, college/university, alternative loans.

**WORK-STUDY Federal work-study:** Total amount: $1,781,918; 1,306 jobs averaging $1344. **State or other work-study/employment:** Total amount: $1,333,831 (100% non-need-based). 1,073 part-time jobs averaging $1220.

**APPLYING FOR FINANCIAL AID Required financial aid form:** FAFSA. **Financial aid deadline (priority):** 2/15. **Notification date:** Continuous beginning 3/15.

**CONTACT** Mr. Craig Heerema, Financial Aid Administrator, Calvin College, Spoelhof Center 263, Grand Rapids, MI 49546, 616-526-6134 or toll-free 800-688-0122. Fax: 616-526-6883. E-mail: cheerema@calvin.edu. Website: http://www.calvin.edu/.

---

# CAMBRIDGE COLLEGE
## Cambridge, MA

**CONTACT** Dr. Frank Lauder, Director of Financial Aid, Cambridge College, 1000 Massachusetts Avenue, Cambridge, MA 02138, 617-868-1000 Ext. 1440 or toll-free 800-877-4723. Fax: 617-349-3561. E-mail: francis.lauder@cambridgecollege.edu. Website: http://www.cambridgecollege.edu/.

---

# CAMERON UNIVERSITY
## Lawton, OK

| Tuition & fees (OK res): $5340 | Average undergraduate aid package: $10,109 |
|---|---|

**ABOUT THE INSTITUTION** State-supported, coed. **Awards:** certificates, associate, bachelor's, and master's degrees. 39 undergraduate majors. **Total enrollment:** 5,538. Undergraduates: 5,056. Freshmen: 826. Federal methodology is used as a basis for awarding need-based institutional aid.

**UNDERGRADUATE EXPENSES for 2015–2016 Application fee:** $15. **Tuition, state resident:** full-time $3720; part-time $124 per credit hour. **Tuition, nonresident:** full-time $11,760; part-time $392 per credit hour. **Required fees:** full-time $1620; $54 per credit hour. Full-time tuition and fees vary according to course level, course load, and program. Part-time tuition and fees vary according to course level, course load, and program. **College room and board:** $4664; **Room only:** $1792. Room and board charges vary according to board plan and housing facility.

**FRESHMAN FINANCIAL AID (Fall 2013)** 726 applied for aid; of those 85% were deemed to have need. 97% of freshmen with need received aid; of those 15% had need fully met. **Average percent of need met:** 52% (excluding resources awarded to replace EFC). **Average financial aid package:** $8579 (excluding resources awarded to replace EFC). 5% of all full-time freshmen had no need and received non-need-based gift aid.

**UNDERGRADUATE FINANCIAL AID (Fall 2013)** 2,872 applied for aid; of those 89% were deemed to have need. 96% of undergraduates with need received aid; of those 10% had need fully met. **Average percent of need met:** 52% (excluding resources awarded to replace EFC). **Average financial aid package:** $10,109 (excluding resources awarded to replace EFC). 3% of all full-time undergraduates had no need and received non-need-based gift aid.

**GIFT AID (NEED-BASED) Total amount:** $16,218,538 (81% federal, 15% state, 3% institutional, 1% external sources). **Receiving aid:** Freshmen: 59% (487); all full-time undergraduates: 58% (2,063). **Average award:** Freshmen: $6121; Undergraduates: $5895. **Scholarships, grants, and awards:** Federal Pell, FSEOG, state, private, college/university gift aid from institutional funds.

**GIFT AID (NON-NEED-BASED) Total amount:** $956,368 (14% state, 39% institutional, 47% external sources). **Receiving aid:** Freshmen: 25% (204). Undergraduates: 15% (521). **Average award:** Freshmen: $1326. Undergraduates: $1742. **Scholarships, grants, and awards by category:** Academic interests/achievement: agriculture, biological sciences, business, communication, computer science, education, engineering/technologies, English, foreign languages, general academic interests/achievements, health fields, mathematics, military science, physical sciences, social sciences. Creative arts/performance: art/fine arts, cinema/film/broadcasting, creative writing, debating, journalism/publications, music, performing arts, theater/drama. Special achievements/activities: cheerleading/drum major, general special achievements/activities, leadership. Special characteristics: children of faculty/staff, international students, members of minority groups, out-of-state students, veterans, veterans' children. **Tuition waivers:** Full or partial for employees or children of employees, senior citizens. **ROTC:** Army.

**LOANS Student loans:** $16,749,960 (47% need-based, 53% non-need-based). 44% of past graduating class borrowed through all loan programs. Average indebtedness per student: $20,512. **Average need-based loan:** Freshmen: $3038. Undergraduates: $3831. **Parent loans:** $72,941 (100% non-need-based). **Programs:** Federal Direct (Subsidized and Unsubsidized Stafford, PLUS).

**WORK-STUDY Federal work-study:** 64 jobs averaging $2386. **State or other work-study/employment:** Total amount: $1,083,780 (100% non-need-based). 330 part-time jobs averaging $3186.

**ATHLETIC AWARDS** Total amount: $728,361 (100% non-need-based).

**APPLYING FOR FINANCIAL AID Required financial aid form:** FAFSA. **Financial aid deadline:** Continuous. **Notification date:** Continuous beginning 4/1. Students must reply by 8/1 or within 2 weeks of notification.

**CONTACT** Mr. Donald Hall, Director of Financial Aid, Cameron University, 2800 West Gore Boulevard, Lawton, OK 73505-6377, 580-581-2293 or toll-free 888-454-7600. Fax: 580-581-2556. E-mail: dhall@cameron.edu. Website: http://www.cameron.edu/.

# CAMPBELLSVILLE UNIVERSITY
## Campbellsville, KY

| Tuition & fees: $23,828 | Average undergraduate aid package: $18,861 |
|---|---|

**ABOUT THE INSTITUTION** Independent Kentucky Baptist Convention, coed. *Awards:* certificates, associate, bachelor's, and master's degrees. 56 undergraduate majors. *Total enrollment:* 3,484. Undergraduates: 3,062. Freshmen: 523. Federal methodology is used as a basis for awarding need-based institutional aid.

**UNDERGRADUATE EXPENSES for 2015–2016** *Application fee:* $20. *Comprehensive fee:* $31,598 includes full-time tuition ($23,328), mandatory fees ($500), and room and board ($7770). Full-time tuition and fees vary according to location. Room and board charges vary according to housing facility. *Part-time tuition:* $972 per credit hour. Part-time tuition and fees vary according to location.

**FRESHMAN FINANCIAL AID (Fall 2013)** 450 applied for aid; of those 94% were deemed to have need. 98% of freshmen with need received aid; of those 17% had need fully met. *Average percent of need met:* 81% (excluding resources awarded to replace EFC). *Average financial aid package:* $20,205 (excluding resources awarded to replace EFC). 7% of all full-time freshmen had no need and received non-need-based gift aid.

**UNDERGRADUATE FINANCIAL AID (Fall 2013)** 1,597 applied for aid; of those 95% were deemed to have need. 99% of undergraduates with need received aid; of those 18% had need fully met. *Average percent of need met:* 79% (excluding resources awarded to replace EFC). *Average financial aid package:* $18,861 (excluding resources awarded to replace EFC). 7% of all full-time undergraduates had no need and received non-need-based gift aid.

**GIFT AID (NEED-BASED)** *Total amount:* $23,537,217 (20% federal, 22% state, 53% institutional, 5% external sources). *Receiving aid:* Freshmen: 86% (415); all full-time undergraduates: 88% (1,480). *Average award:* Freshmen: $17,813; Undergraduates: $16,117. *Scholarships, grants, and awards:* Federal Pell, FSEOG, state, college/university gift aid from institutional funds.

**GIFT AID (NON-NEED-BASED)** *Total amount:* $2,424,763 (1% federal, 15% state, 66% institutional, 18% external sources). *Receiving aid:* Freshmen: 10% (48). Undergraduates: 10% (174). *Average award:* Freshmen: $10,128. Undergraduates: $10,046. *Scholarships, grants, and awards by category:* Academic interests/achievement: 1,125 awards ($9,357,816 total): biological sciences, business, communication, computer science, education, English, general academic interests/achievements, health fields, humanities, mathematics, physical sciences, premedicine, religion/biblical studies, social sciences. *Creative arts/performance:* 170 awards ($421,245 total): art/fine arts, journalism/publications, music, theater/drama. *Special achievements/activities:* 40 awards ($72,250 total): cheerleading/drum major, junior miss, leadership, religious involvement. *Special characteristics:* 158 awards ($790,473 total): adult students, children of educators, children of faculty/staff, international students, relatives of clergy, religious affiliation, veterans. *Tuition waivers:* Full or partial for employees or children of employees, adult students, senior citizens. *ROTC:* Army cooperative.

**LOANS** *Student loans:* $9,921,288 (78% need-based, 22% non-need-based). 55% of past graduating class borrowed through all loan programs. *Average indebtedness per student:* $22,261. *Average need-based loan:* Freshmen: $2805. Undergraduates: $3580. *Parent loans:* $1,260,010 (38% need-based, 62% non-need-based). *Programs:* Federal Direct (Subsidized and Unsubsidized Stafford, PLUS), Perkins, college/university.

**WORK-STUDY** *Federal work-study:* 275 jobs averaging $1400. *State or other work-study/employment:* Total amount: $43,850 (53% need-based, 47% non-need-based). 30 part-time jobs averaging $1200.

**ATHLETIC AWARDS** Total amount: $3,276,204 (56% need-based, 44% non-need-based).

**APPLYING FOR FINANCIAL AID** *Required financial aid form:* FAFSA. *Financial aid deadline (priority):* 1/15. *Notification date:* Continuous beginning 3/15. Students must reply within 3 weeks of notification.

**CONTACT** Chris Mapes, Director of Financial Aid, Campbellsville University, 1 University Drive, Campbellsville, KY 42718, 270-789-5013 or toll-free 800-264-6014. *Fax:* 270-789-5079. *E-mail:* finaid@campbellsville.edu. *Website:* http://www.campbellsville.edu/.

# CAMPBELL UNIVERSITY
## Buies Creek, NC

| Tuition & fees: $27,530 | Average undergraduate aid package: $21,799 |
|---|---|

**ABOUT THE INSTITUTION** Independent North Carolina Baptist State Convention, coed. 85 undergraduate majors. Federal methodology is used as a basis for awarding need-based institutional aid.

**UNDERGRADUATE EXPENSES for 2015–2016** *Comprehensive fee:* $37,390 includes full-time tuition ($26,550), mandatory fees ($980), and room and board ($9860). *College room only:* $4700. Full-time tuition and fees vary according to course load, location, and program. Room and board charges vary according to board plan and housing facility. *Part-time tuition:* $550 per credit hour. Part-time tuition and fees vary according to course load, location, and program.

**FRESHMAN FINANCIAL AID (Fall 2014, est.)** 808 applied for aid; of those 93% were deemed to have need. 100% of freshmen with need received aid; of those 14% had need fully met. *Average percent of need met:* 82% (excluding resources awarded to replace EFC). *Average financial aid package:* $29,353 (excluding resources awarded to replace EFC). 14% of all full-time freshmen had no need and received non-need-based gift aid.

**UNDERGRADUATE FINANCIAL AID (Fall 2014, est.)** 2,928 applied for aid; of those 94% were deemed to have need. 100% of undergraduates with need received aid; of those 14% had need fully met. *Average percent of need met:* 82% (excluding resources awarded to replace EFC). *Average financial aid package:* $21,799 (excluding resources awarded to replace EFC). 15% of all full-time undergraduates had no need and received non-need-based gift aid.

**GIFT AID (NEED-BASED)** *Total amount:* $54,794,736 (14% federal, 14% state, 69% institutional, 3% external sources). *Receiving aid:* Freshmen: 61% (531); all full-time undergraduates: 61% (2,031). *Average award:* Freshmen: $4594; Undergraduates: $6890. *Scholarships, grants, and awards:* Federal Pell, FSEOG, state, private, college/university gift aid from institutional funds.

**GIFT AID (NON-NEED-BASED)** *Total amount:* $6,679,657 (93% institutional, 7% external sources). *Receiving aid:* Freshmen: 84% (733). Undergraduates: 79% (2,662). *Average award:* Freshmen: $13,326. Undergraduates: $13,061. *Scholarships, grants, and awards by category:* Academic interests/achievement: 2,491 awards ($25,330,883 total): general academic interests/achievements. *Creative arts/performance:* 44 awards ($36,250 total): art/fine arts, creative writing, journalism/publications, music, theater/drama. *Special achievements/activities:* 36 awards ($113,700 total): cheerleading/drum major, religious involvement. *Special characteristics:* 94 awards ($1,711,616 total): children of faculty/staff. *Tuition waivers:* Full or partial for employees or children of employees.

**LOANS** *Student loans:* $30,951,797 (94% need-based, 6% non-need-based). 71% of past graduating class borrowed through all loan programs. *Average indebtedness per student:* $27,578. *Average need-based loan:* Freshmen: $2935. Undergraduates: $3689. *Parent loans:* $40,798,543 (91% need-based, 9% non-need-based). *Programs:* Federal Direct (Subsidized and Unsubsidized Stafford, PLUS), Perkins, state.

**WORK-STUDY** *Federal work-study:* Total amount: $665,700; 557 jobs averaging $1420. *State or other work-study/employment:* 673 part-time jobs averaging $771.

**ATHLETIC AWARDS** Total amount: $5,430,778 (53% need-based, 47% non-need-based).

**APPLYING FOR FINANCIAL AID** *Required financial aid form:* FAFSA. *Financial aid deadline (priority):* 2/15. *Notification date:* Continuous. Students must reply within 2 weeks of notification.

**CONTACT** Financial Aid Office, Campbell University, PO Box 36, Buies Creek, NC 27506, 910-893-1310 or toll-free 800-334-4111. *Fax:* 910-814-5788. *Website:* http://www.campbell.edu/.

## CANISIUS COLLEGE
### Buffalo, NY

| Tuition & fees: $34,000 | Average undergraduate aid package: $29,284 |
|---|---|

**ABOUT THE INSTITUTION** Independent Roman Catholic (Jesuit), coed. **Awards:** certificates, associate, bachelor's, and master's degrees. 112 undergraduate majors. **Total enrollment:** 4,181. Undergraduates: 2,868. Freshmen: 613. Federal methodology is used as a basis for awarding need-based institutional aid.

**UNDERGRADUATE EXPENSES for 2015–2016 Application fee:** $40. **Comprehensive fee:** $46,516 includes full-time tuition ($32,630), mandatory fees ($1370), and room and board ($12,516). **College room only:** $7354. Room and board charges vary according to board plan and housing facility. **Part-time tuition:** $932 per credit hour.

**FRESHMAN FINANCIAL AID (Fall 2014, est.)** 565 applied for aid; of those 90% were deemed to have need. 100% of freshmen with need received aid; of those 29% had need fully met. **Average percent of need met:** 86% (excluding resources awarded to replace EFC). **Average financial aid package:** $33,313 (excluding resources awarded to replace EFC). 15% of all full-time freshmen had no need and received non-need-based gift aid.

**UNDERGRADUATE FINANCIAL AID (Fall 2014, est.)** 2,281 applied for aid; of those 91% were deemed to have need. 100% of undergraduates with need received aid; of those 22% had need fully met. **Average percent of need met:** 80% (excluding resources awarded to replace EFC). **Average financial aid package:** $29,284 (excluding resources awarded to replace EFC). 20% of all full-time undergraduates had no need and received non-need-based gift aid.

**GIFT AID (NEED-BASED) Total amount:** $44,850,015 (11% federal, 8% state, 81% institutional). **Receiving aid:** Freshmen: 83% (508); all full-time undergraduates: 76% (2,063). **Average award:** Freshmen: $26,616; Undergraduates: $22,616. **Scholarships, grants, and awards:** Federal Pell, FSEOG, state, private, college/university gift aid from institutional funds.

**GIFT AID (NON-NEED-BASED) Total amount:** $4,185,195 (1% federal, 98% institutional, 1% external sources). **Receiving aid:** Freshmen: 21% (126). Undergraduates: 16% (445). **Average award:** Freshmen: $16,528. Undergraduates: $15,623. **Scholarships, grants, and awards by category:** Academic interests/achievement: 2,048 awards ($26,220,955 total): general academic interests/achievements. Creative arts/performance: 76 awards ($145,000 total): art/fine arts, dance, music. Special achievements/activities: 1 award ($2295 total): religious involvement. Special characteristics: 439 awards ($3,697,826 total): children and siblings of alumni, children of educators, children of faculty/staff, international students, religious affiliation. **Tuition waivers:** Full or partial for employees or children of employees. **ROTC:** Army.

**LOANS Student loans:** $17,604,596 (72% need-based, 28% non-need-based). 70% of past graduating class borrowed through all loan programs. **Average indebtedness per student:** $40,913. **Average need-based loan:** Freshmen: $3788. Undergraduates: $4515. **Parent loans:** $6,995,333 (33% need-based, 67% non-need-based). **Programs:** Federal Direct (Subsidized and Unsubsidized Stafford, PLUS), Perkins.

**WORK-STUDY Federal work-study:** Total amount: $741,477; 429 jobs averaging $1728. **State or other work-study/employment:** Total amount: $39,925 (86% need-based, 14% non-need-based). Part-time jobs available.

**ATHLETIC AWARDS** Total amount: $1,882,577 (55% need-based, 45% non-need-based).

**APPLYING FOR FINANCIAL AID Required financial aid forms:** FAFSA, state aid form. **Financial aid deadline (priority):** 2/15. **Notification date:** Continuous beginning 3/15. Students must reply by 5/1.

**CONTACT** Ms. Mary Koehneke, Interim Director of Student Financial Aid, Canisius College, 2001 Main Street, Buffalo, NY 14208-1098, 716-888-2300 or toll-free 800-843-1517. Fax: 716-888-2377. E-mail: mkoehnek@canisius.edu. Website: http://www.canisius.edu/.

## CAPELLA UNIVERSITY
### Minneapolis, MN

**CONTACT** University Services, Capella University, 222 South Ninth Street, Minneapolis, MN 55402, 888-227-3552 or toll-free 866-283-7921. Website: http://www.capella.edu/.

## CAPITAL UNIVERSITY
### Columbus, OH

| Tuition & fees: $31,990 | Average undergraduate aid package: $25,472 |
|---|---|

**ABOUT THE INSTITUTION** Independent Evangelical Lutheran Church in America, coed. **Awards:** certificates, bachelor's, master's, and doctoral degrees. 60 undergraduate majors. **Total enrollment:** 3,494. Undergraduates: 2,742. Freshmen: 710. Federal methodology is used as a basis for awarding need-based institutional aid.

**UNDERGRADUATE EXPENSES for 2015–2016 Application fee:** $25. **Comprehensive fee:** $41,050 includes full-time tuition ($31,990) and room and board ($9060). Full-time tuition and fees vary according to course load. Room and board charges vary according to board plan and housing facility. **Part-time tuition:** $1066 per credit hour. Part-time tuition and fees vary according to course load.

**FRESHMAN FINANCIAL AID (Fall 2013)** 650 applied for aid; of those 91% were deemed to have need. 100% of freshmen with need received aid; of those 26% had need fully met. **Average percent of need met:** 81% (excluding resources awarded to replace EFC). **Average financial aid package:** $27,037 (excluding resources awarded to replace EFC). 14% of all full-time freshmen had no need and received non-need-based gift aid.

**UNDERGRADUATE FINANCIAL AID (Fall 2013)** 2,153 applied for aid; of those 92% were deemed to have need. 100% of undergraduates with need received aid; of those 24% had need fully met. **Average percent of need met:** 78% (excluding resources awarded to replace EFC). **Average financial aid package:** $25,472 (excluding resources awarded to replace EFC). 16% of all full-time undergraduates had no need and received non-need-based gift aid.

**GIFT AID (NEED-BASED) Total amount:** $45,243,042 (9% federal, 3% state, 88% institutional). **Receiving aid:** Freshmen: 85% (586); all full-time undergraduates: 78% (1,879). **Average award:** Freshmen: $21,675; Undergraduates: $19,945. **Scholarships, grants, and awards:** Federal Pell, FSEOG, state, private, college/university gift aid from institutional funds.

**GIFT AID (NON-NEED-BASED) Total amount:** $1,474,196 (3% institutional, 97% external sources). **Receiving aid:** Freshmen: 85% (585). Undergraduates: 76% (1,830). **Average award:** Freshmen: $19,309. Undergraduates: $17,689. **Scholarships, grants, and awards by category:** Academic interests/achievement: general academic interests/achievements. Creative arts/performance: music, performing arts. Special achievements/activities: hobbies/interests, leadership, religious involvement. Special characteristics: children and siblings of alumni, children of faculty/staff, ethnic background, international students, members of minority groups, out-of-state students, relatives of clergy, religious affiliation, siblings of current students. **Tuition waivers:** Full or partial for employees or children of employees, senior citizens. **ROTC:** Army, Air Force cooperative.

**LOANS Student loans:** $19,993,788 (41% need-based, 59% non-need-based). 83% of past graduating class borrowed through all loan programs. **Average indebtedness per student:** $33,833. **Average need-based loan:** Freshmen: $4146. Undergraduates: $4814. **Parent loans:** $6,720,409 (100% non-need-based). **Programs:** Federal Direct (Subsidized and Unsubsidized Stafford, PLUS), Perkins, Federal Nursing, college/university.

**WORK-STUDY Federal work-study:** jobs available. **State or other work-study/employment:** Part-time jobs available.

**APPLYING FOR FINANCIAL AID Required financial aid form:** FAFSA. **Financial aid deadline (priority):** 3/1. **Notification date:** Continuous beginning 3/15. Students must reply by 5/1.

**CONTACT** Ms. Susan Kannenwischer, Office of Financial Aid, Capital University, 1 College and Main Street, Columbus, OH 43209-2394, 614-236-6511 or toll-free 866-544-6175. Fax: 614-236-6926. E-mail: finaid@capital.edu. Website: http://www.capital.edu/.

## CAPITOL TECHNOLOGY UNIVERSITY
### Laurel, MD

**CONTACT** Suzanne Thompson, Director of Financial Aid, Capitol Technology University, 11301 Springfield Road, Laurel, MD 20708-9759, 301-369-2800 Ext. 3037 or toll-free 800-950-1992. Fax: 301-369-2328. E-mail: sthompson@capitol-college.edu. Website: http://www.captechu.edu/.

# CARDINAL STRITCH UNIVERSITY
## Milwaukee, WI

| Tuition & fees: $26,570 | Average undergraduate aid package: $13,949 |
| --- | --- |

**ABOUT THE INSTITUTION** Independent Roman Catholic, coed. *Awards:* certificates, associate, bachelor's, master's, and doctoral degrees. 38 undergraduate majors. *Total enrollment:* 3,811. Undergraduates: 2,308. Freshmen: 188. Federal methodology is used as a basis for awarding need-based institutional aid.

**UNDERGRADUATE EXPENSES** for 2015–2016 *Comprehensive fee:* $34,040 includes full-time tuition ($25,920), mandatory fees ($650), and room and board ($7470). Full-time tuition and fees vary according to degree level and program. Room and board charges vary according to board plan and housing facility. *Part-time tuition:* $810 per credit. *Part-time fees:* $325 per term. Part-time tuition and fees vary according to course load, degree level, and program.

**FRESHMAN FINANCIAL AID (Fall 2014, est.)** 157 applied for aid; of those 91% were deemed to have need. 100% of freshmen with need received aid; of those 17% had need fully met. *Average percent of need met:* 78% (excluding resources awarded to replace EFC). *Average financial aid package:* $23,924 (excluding resources awarded to replace EFC). 23% of all full-time freshmen had no need and received non-need-based gift aid.

**UNDERGRADUATE FINANCIAL AID (Fall 2014, est.)** 1,519 applied for aid; of those 85% were deemed to have need. 98% of undergraduates with need received aid; of those 9% had need fully met. *Average percent of need met:* 52% (excluding resources awarded to replace EFC). *Average financial aid package:* $13,949 (excluding resources awarded to replace EFC). 10% of all full-time undergraduates had no need and received non-need-based gift aid.

**GIFT AID (NEED-BASED)** *Total amount:* $12,857,329 (28% federal, 9% state, 61% institutional, 2% external sources). *Receiving aid:* Freshmen: 75% (141); all full-time undergraduates: 60% (1,058). *Average award:* Freshmen: $19,924; Undergraduates: $11,704. *Scholarships, grants, and awards:* Federal Pell, FSEOG, state, private, college/university gift aid from institutional funds.

**GIFT AID (NON-NEED-BASED)** *Total amount:* $2,944,211 (8% federal, 90% institutional, 2% external sources). *Receiving aid:* Freshmen: 8% (15). Undergraduates: 4% (66). *Average award:* Freshmen: $17,366. Undergraduates: $13,307. *Scholarships, grants, and awards by category:* Academic interests/achievement: general academic interests/achievements. Creative arts/performance: art/fine arts, music, theater/drama. Special characteristics: children and siblings of alumni, children of current students, children of faculty/staff, international students, religious affiliation, siblings of current students, spouses of current students. *Tuition waivers:* Full or partial for employees or children of employees.

**LOANS** *Student loans:* $11,947,611 (87% need-based, 13% non-need-based). 83% of past graduating class borrowed through all loan programs. *Average indebtedness per student:* $29,473. *Average need-based loan:* Freshmen: $3227. Undergraduates: $3974. *Parent loans:* $564,156 (51% need-based, 49% non-need-based). *Programs:* Federal Direct (Subsidized and Unsubsidized Stafford, PLUS), Perkins, state.

**WORK-STUDY** *Federal work-study:* Total amount: $840,470; jobs available. *State or other work-study/employment:* Total amount: $489,738 (75% need-based, 25% non-need-based). Part-time jobs available.

**ATHLETIC AWARDS** Total amount: $1,099,768 (56% need-based, 44% non-need-based).

**APPLYING FOR FINANCIAL AID** *Required financial aid forms:* FAFSA, institution's own form. *Financial aid deadline:* Continuous. *Notification date:* Continuous beginning 3/1. Students must reply within 2 weeks of notification.

**CONTACT** Financial Aid Office, Cardinal Stritch University, 6801 North Yates Road, Milwaukee, WI 53217-3985, 414-410-4048 or toll-free 800-347-8822 Ext. 4040. *Website:* http://www.stritch.edu/.

# CAREER POINT COLLEGE
## San Antonio, TX

**CONTACT** Financial Aid Office, Career Point College, 4522 Fredericksburg Road, San Antonio, TX 78201, 210-732-3000. *Website:* http://www.careerpointcollege.edu/.

# CAREERS UNLIMITED
## Orem, UT

**CONTACT** Financial Aid Office, Careers Unlimited, 1176 South 1480 West, Orem, UT 84058, 801-426-8234. *Website:* http://www.ucdh.edu/.

# CARIBBEAN UNIVERSITY
## Bayamón, PR

**CONTACT** Financial Aid Office, Caribbean University, Box 493, Bayamón, PR 00960-0493, 787-780-0070. *Website:* http://www.caribbean.edu/.

# CARLETON COLLEGE
## Northfield, MN

| Tuition & fees: $47,736 | Average undergraduate aid package: $38,623 |
| --- | --- |

**ABOUT THE INSTITUTION** Independent, coed. *Awards:* bachelor's degrees. 39 undergraduate majors. *Total enrollment:* 2,057. Undergraduates: 2,057. Freshmen: 521. Both federal and institutional methodology are used as a basis for awarding need-based institutional aid.

**UNDERGRADUATE EXPENSES** for 2015–2016 *Application fee:* $30. *Comprehensive fee:* $60,102 includes full-time tuition ($47,460), mandatory fees ($276), and room and board ($12,366). *College room only:* $6468. Room and board charges vary according to board plan.

**FRESHMAN FINANCIAL AID (Fall 2013)** 393 applied for aid; of those 71% were deemed to have need. 100% of freshmen with need received aid; of those 100% had need fully met. *Average percent of need met:* 100% (excluding resources awarded to replace EFC). *Average financial aid package:* $39,757 (excluding resources awarded to replace EFC). 6% of all full-time freshmen had no need and received non-need-based gift aid.

**UNDERGRADUATE FINANCIAL AID (Fall 2013)** 1,763 applied for aid; of those 64% were deemed to have need. 100% of undergraduates with need received aid; of those 100% had need fully met. *Average percent of need met:* 100% (excluding resources awarded to replace EFC). *Average financial aid package:* $38,623 (excluding resources awarded to replace EFC). 7% of all full-time undergraduates had no need and received non-need-based gift aid.

**GIFT AID (NEED-BASED)** *Total amount:* $36,830,646 (4% federal, 1% state, 91% institutional, 4% external sources). *Receiving aid:* Freshmen: 53% (278); all full-time undergraduates: 55% (1,129). *Average award:* Freshmen: $36,030; Undergraduates: $34,050. *Scholarships, grants, and awards:* Federal Pell, FSEOG, state, private, college/university gift aid from institutional funds.

**GIFT AID (NON-NEED-BASED)** *Total amount:* $1,256,597 (30% institutional, 70% external sources). *Receiving aid:* Freshmen: 7% (37). Undergraduates: 9% (179). *Average award:* Freshmen: $4773. Undergraduates: $3095. *Scholarships, grants, and awards by category:* Academic interests/achievement: 238 awards ($377,242 total): general academic interests/achievements. Creative arts/performance: 1 award ($1100 total): music. *Tuition waivers:* Full or partial for employees or children of employees.

**LOANS** *Student loans:* $5,444,926 (95% need-based, 5% non-need-based). 39% of past graduating class borrowed through all loan programs. *Average indebtedness per student:* $18,302. *Average need-based loan:* Freshmen: $4243. Undergraduates: $5281. *Parent loans:* $1,347,143 (86% need-based, 14% non-need-based). *Programs:* Federal Direct (Subsidized and Unsubsidized Stafford, PLUS), Perkins, state, college/university.

**WORK-STUDY** *Federal work-study:* 350 jobs averaging $2510. *State or other work-study/employment:* Total amount: $3,411,006 (57% need-based, 43% non-need-based). 1,342 part-time jobs averaging $2539.

**APPLYING FOR FINANCIAL AID** *Required financial aid forms:* FAFSA, CSS Financial Aid PROFILE, noncustodial (divorced/separated) parent's statement. *Financial aid deadline:* 2/15. *Notification date:* 3/31. Students must reply by 5/1 or within 2 weeks of notification.

CONTACT Mr. Rodney M. Oto, Director of Student Financial Services, Carleton College, One North College Street, Northfield, MN 55057-4001, 507-222-4138 or toll-free 800-995-2275. *Fax:* 507-222-4269.
*Website:* http://www.carleton.edu/.

# CARLOS ALBIZU UNIVERSITY
## San Juan, PR

**ABOUT THE INSTITUTION** Independent, coed. *Awards:* bachelor's, master's, and doctoral degrees. 3 undergraduate majors. *Total enrollment:* 919. Undergraduates: 142.

**GIFT AID (NEED-BASED)** *Scholarships, grants, and awards:* Federal Pell, FSEOG, state, college/university gift aid from institutional funds.

**GIFT AID (NON-NEED-BASED)** *Scholarships, grants, and awards by category:* Academic interests/achievement: social sciences.

**LOANS** *Programs:* Federal Direct (Subsidized and Unsubsidized Stafford, PLUS).

**WORK-STUDY** *Federal work-study:* 2 jobs averaging $1094.

CONTACT Mrs. Doris J. Quero, Director, Carlos Albizu University, PO Box 9023711, San Juan, PR 00901, 787-725-6500 Ext. 1529. *Fax:* 787-721-4008. *E-mail:* dquero@albizu.edu.
*Website:* http://www.albizu.edu/.

# CARLOS ALBIZU UNIVERSITY, MIAMI CAMPUS
## Miami, FL

| Tuition & fees: $12,384 | Average undergraduate aid package: $7428 |
| --- | --- |

**ABOUT THE INSTITUTION** Independent, coed. *Awards:* certificates, diplomas, bachelor's, master's, and doctoral degrees. 5 undergraduate majors. *Total enrollment:* 1,000. Undergraduates: 305. Freshmen: 12. Federal methodology is used as a basis for awarding need-based institutional aid.

**UNDERGRADUATE EXPENSES for 2015–2016** *Application fee:* $25. *Tuition:* full-time $11,628; part-time $323 per credit. *Required fees:* full-time $756; $252 per term. Full-time tuition and fees vary according to course load, degree level, and program. Part-time tuition and fees vary according to course load, degree level, and program.

**FRESHMAN FINANCIAL AID (Fall 2014, est.)** 10 applied for aid; of those 60% were deemed to have need. 100% of freshmen with need received aid. *Average percent of need met:* 65% (excluding resources awarded to replace EFC). *Average financial aid package:* $7428 (excluding resources awarded to replace EFC).

**UNDERGRADUATE FINANCIAL AID (Fall 2014, est.)** 170 applied for aid; of those 86% were deemed to have need. 100% of undergraduates with need received aid. *Average percent of need met:* 50% (excluding resources awarded to replace EFC). *Average financial aid package:* $7428 (excluding resources awarded to replace EFC).

**GIFT AID (NEED-BASED)** *Total amount:* $1,120,253 (79% federal, 21% state). *Receiving aid:* Freshmen: 50% (6); all full-time undergraduates: 72% (138). *Average award:* Freshmen: $4850; Undergraduates: $4850. *Scholarships, grants, and awards:* Federal Pell, FSEOG, state, college/university gift aid from institutional funds.

**GIFT AID (NON-NEED-BASED)** *Scholarships, grants, and awards by category:* Special characteristics: children of faculty/staff. *Tuition waivers:* Full or partial for employees or children of employees.

**LOANS** *Student loans:* $1,948,700 (62% need-based, 38% non-need-based). 23% of past graduating class borrowed through all loan programs. *Average indebtedness per student:* $16,500. *Average need-based loan:* Freshmen: $4826. Undergraduates: $4826. *Parent loans:* $30,946 (100% need-based). *Programs:* Federal Direct (Subsidized and Unsubsidized Stafford, PLUS), college/university.

**WORK-STUDY** *Federal work-study:* Total amount: $77,702; jobs available.

**APPLYING FOR FINANCIAL AID** *Required financial aid forms:* FAFSA, institution's own form. *Financial aid deadline (priority):* 6/1. *Notification date:* Continuous.

CONTACT Suset Menendez, Financial Aid Officer, Carlos Albizu University, Miami Campus, 2173 Northwest 99th Avenue, Miami, FL 33172, 305-593-1223 Ext. 3269 or toll-free 888-GO-TO-CAU (in-state), 800-GO-TO-CAU (out-of-state). *Fax:* 305-593-8902. *E-mail:* smenendez@albizu.edu.
*Website:* http://www.albizu.edu/.

# CARLOW UNIVERSITY
## Pittsburgh, PA

CONTACT Ms. Natalie Wilson, Director of Financial Aid, Carlow University, 3333 Fifth Avenue, Pittsburgh, PA 15213-3165, 412-578-6171 or toll-free 800-333-CARLOW.
*Website:* http://www.carlow.edu/.

# CARNEGIE MELLON UNIVERSITY
## Pittsburgh, PA

| Tuition & fees: $49,022 | Average undergraduate aid package: $36,001 |
| --- | --- |

**ABOUT THE INSTITUTION** Independent, coed. *Awards:* certificates, bachelor's, master's, and doctoral degrees. 71 undergraduate majors. *Total enrollment:* 12,991. Undergraduates: 6,306. Freshmen: 1,442. Both federal and institutional methodology are used as a basis for awarding need-based institutional aid.

**UNDERGRADUATE EXPENSES for 2015–2016** *Application fee:* $70. *One-time required fee:* $236. *Comprehensive fee:* $61,422 includes full-time tuition ($48,030), mandatory fees ($992), and room and board ($12,400). *College room only:* $7280. Full-time tuition and fees vary according to student level. Room and board charges vary according to board plan and housing facility. Part-time tuition and fees vary according to student level.

**FRESHMAN FINANCIAL AID (Fall 2014, est.)** 940 applied for aid; of those 73% were deemed to have need. 99% of freshmen with need received aid; of those 30% had need fully met. *Average percent of need met:* 83% (excluding resources awarded to replace EFC). *Average financial aid package:* $34,870 (excluding resources awarded to replace EFC). 4% of all full-time freshmen had no need and received non-need-based gift aid.

**UNDERGRADUATE FINANCIAL AID (Fall 2014, est.)** 3,287 applied for aid; of those 85% were deemed to have need. 98% of undergraduates with need received aid; of those 25% had need fully met. *Average percent of need met:* 83% (excluding resources awarded to replace EFC). *Average financial aid package:* $36,001 (excluding resources awarded to replace EFC). 4% of all full-time undergraduates had no need and received non-need-based gift aid.

**GIFT AID (NEED-BASED)** *Total amount:* $78,153,672 (6% federal, 1% state, 91% institutional, 2% external sources). *Receiving aid:* Freshmen: 44% (650); all full-time undergraduates: 44% (2,656). *Average award:* Freshmen: $30,552; Undergraduates: $30,068. *Scholarships, grants, and awards:* Federal Pell, FSEOG, state, private, college/university gift aid from institutional funds.

**GIFT AID (NON-NEED-BASED)** *Total amount:* $5,037,702 (70% institutional, 30% external sources). *Receiving aid:* Freshmen: 9% (126). Undergraduates: 4% (269). *Average award:* Freshmen: $11,804. Undergraduates: $10,867. *Scholarships, grants, and awards by category:* Academic interests/achievement: general academic interests/achievements. Creative arts/performance: art/fine arts, music. Special achievements/activities: leadership. Special characteristics: local/state students, members of minority groups, out-of-state students. *ROTC:* Army, Naval, Air Force.

**LOANS** *Student loans:* $23,728,886 (67% need-based, 33% non-need-based). 45% of past graduating class borrowed through all loan programs. *Average indebtedness per student:* $31,905. *Average need-based loan:* Freshmen: $4749. Undergraduates: $5445. *Parent loans:* $6,637,064 (27% need-based, 73% non-need-based). *Programs:* Federal Direct (Subsidized and Unsubsidized Stafford, PLUS), Perkins.

**WORK-STUDY** *Federal work-study:* Total amount: $5,220,403; jobs available. *State or other work-study/employment:* Part-time jobs available.

**APPLYING FOR FINANCIAL AID** *Required financial aid forms:* FAFSA, institution's own form, CSS Financial Aid PROFILE, noncustodial (divorced/separated) parent's statement, federal income tax form(s). *Financial aid deadline (priority):* 2/15. *Notification date:* 3/15.

**CONTACT** Office of Enrollment Services, Carnegie Mellon University, 5000 Forbes Avenue, Pittsburgh, PA 15213-3890, 412-268-8186. *Fax:* 412-268-8084. *E-mail:* thehub@andrew.cmu.edu.
*Website:* http://www.cmu.edu/.

# CAROLINA CHRISTIAN COLLEGE
## Winston-Salem, NC

**ABOUT THE INSTITUTION** Independent nondenominational, coed. *Awards:* associate, bachelor's, and master's degrees. 1 undergraduate major. *Total enrollment:* 44. Undergraduates: 36. Freshmen: 2.

**GIFT AID (NEED-BASED)** *Scholarships, grants, and awards:* Federal Pell, FSEOG.

**LOANS** *Programs:* Federal Direct (Subsidized and Unsubsidized Stafford, PLUS).

**APPLYING FOR FINANCIAL AID** *Required financial aid form:* FAFSA.

**CONTACT** LaTanya V. Lucas, Academic Dean, Carolina Christian College, 4209 Indiana Avenue, Winston Salem, NC 27105, 336-744-0900 Ext. 106. *E-mail:* latanya@carolina.edu.
*Website:* http://www.carolina.edu/.

# CAROLINA COLLEGE OF BIBLICAL STUDIES
## Fayetteville, NC

**CONTACT** Financial Aid Office, Carolina College of Biblical Studies, 817 South McPherson Church Road, Fayetteville, NC 28303, 910-323-5614.
*Website:* http://carolinabiblecollege.org/.

# CARROLL COLLEGE
## Helena, MT

| Tuition & fees: $29,280 | Average undergraduate aid package: $20,324 |
| --- | --- |

**ABOUT THE INSTITUTION** Independent Roman Catholic, coed. *Awards:* associate and bachelor's degrees. 50 undergraduate majors. *Total enrollment:* 1,430. Undergraduates: 1,430. Freshmen: 354. Federal methodology is used as a basis for awarding need-based institutional aid.

**UNDERGRADUATE EXPENSES** for 2015–2016 *Application fee:* $35. *Comprehensive fee:* $38,230 includes full-time tuition ($28,670), mandatory fees ($610), and room and board ($8950). *College room only:* $4552. Full-time tuition and fees vary according to course load. Room and board charges vary according to board plan and housing facility. *Part-time tuition:* $1194 per credit hour. Part-time tuition and fees vary according to course load.

**FRESHMAN FINANCIAL AID (Fall 2013)** 271 applied for aid; of those 80% were deemed to have need. 100% of freshmen with need received aid; of those 26% had need fully met. *Average percent of need met:* 77% (excluding resources awarded to replace EFC). *Average financial aid package:* $20,401 (excluding resources awarded to replace EFC). 30% of all full-time freshmen had no need and received non-need-based gift aid.

**UNDERGRADUATE FINANCIAL AID (Fall 2013)** 1,009 applied for aid; of those 85% were deemed to have need. 100% of undergraduates with need received aid; of those 17% had need fully met. *Average percent of need met:* 71% (excluding resources awarded to replace EFC). *Average financial aid package:* $20,324 (excluding resources awarded to replace EFC). 34% of all full-time undergraduates had no need and received non-need-based gift aid.

**GIFT AID (NEED-BASED)** *Total amount:* $12,376,895 (14% federal, 79% institutional, 7% external sources). *Receiving aid:* Freshmen: 69% (218); all full-time undergraduates: 63% (845). *Average award:* Freshmen: $16,384; Undergraduates: $15,278. *Scholarships, grants, and awards:* Federal Pell, FSEOG, state, private, college/university gift aid from institutional funds.

**GIFT AID (NON-NEED-BASED)** *Total amount:* $6,810,595 (14% federal, 79% institutional, 7% external sources). *Receiving aid:* Freshmen: 18% (56). Undergrad-

uates: 11% (142). *Average award:* Freshmen: $12,981. Undergraduates: $11,323. *Scholarships, grants, and awards by category:* Academic interests/achievement: general academic interests/achievements. Creative arts/performance: 40 awards ($50,750 total): art/fine arts, creative writing, debating, music, performing arts, theater/drama. Special achievements/activities: 76 awards ($157,958 total): cheerleading/drum major, general special achievements/activities, leadership, religious involvement. Special characteristics: 93 awards ($1,183,264 total): children of faculty/staff, children of union members/company employees, international students, religious affiliation, siblings of current students, spouses of current students, veterans. *Tuition waivers:* Full or partial for employees or children of employees, senior citizens. *ROTC:* Army.

**LOANS** *Student loans:* $7,329,683 (53% need-based, 47% non-need-based). 66% of past graduating class borrowed through all loan programs. *Average indebtedness per student:* $26,996. *Average need-based loan:* Freshmen: $3237. Undergraduates: $4298. *Parent loans:* $3,079,404 (45% need-based, 55% non-need-based). *Programs:* Federal Direct (Subsidized and Unsubsidized Stafford, PLUS), Perkins, private loans.

**WORK-STUDY** *Federal work-study:* 235 jobs averaging $2180. *State or other work-study/employment:* Part-time jobs available.

**ATHLETIC AWARDS** Total amount: $2,048,500 (46% need-based, 54% non-need-based).

**APPLYING FOR FINANCIAL AID** *Required financial aid form:* FAFSA. *Financial aid deadline (priority):* 3/1. *Notification date:* Continuous. Students must reply within 2 weeks of notification.

**CONTACT** Ms. Janet Riis, Director of Financial Aid, Carroll College, 1601 North Benton Avenue, Helena, MT 59625-0002, 406-447-5423 or toll-free 800-992-3648. *Fax:* 406-447-4533. *E-mail:* jriis@carroll.edu.
*Website:* http://www.carroll.edu/.

# CARROLL UNIVERSITY
## Waukesha, WI

| Tuition & fees: $28,550 | Average undergraduate aid package: $21,258 |
| --- | --- |

**ABOUT THE INSTITUTION** Independent Presbyterian, coed. 77 undergraduate majors. Federal methodology is used as a basis for awarding need-based institutional aid.

**UNDERGRADUATE EXPENSES** for 2015–2016 *One-time required fee:* $270. *Comprehensive fee:* $37,100 includes full-time tuition ($27,850), mandatory fees ($700), and room and board ($8550). *College room only:* $4672. Full-time tuition and fees vary according to program. Room and board charges vary according to board plan and housing facility. *Part-time tuition:* $355 per credit hour. Part-time tuition and fees vary according to course load and program.

**FRESHMAN FINANCIAL AID (Fall 2014, est.)** 702 applied for aid; of those 90% were deemed to have need. 100% of freshmen with need received aid; of those 28% had need fully met. *Average percent of need met:* 87% (excluding resources awarded to replace EFC). *Average financial aid package:* $22,239 (excluding resources awarded to replace EFC). 16% of all full-time freshmen had no need and received non-need-based gift aid.

**UNDERGRADUATE FINANCIAL AID (Fall 2014, est.)** 2,495 applied for aid; of those 88% were deemed to have need. 100% of undergraduates with need received aid; of those 27% had need fully met. *Average percent of need met:* 85% (excluding resources awarded to replace EFC). *Average financial aid package:* $21,258 (excluding resources awarded to replace EFC). 18% of all full-time undergraduates had no need and received non-need-based gift aid.

**GIFT AID (NEED-BASED)** *Total amount:* $39,032,587 (8% federal, 6% state, 85% institutional, 1% external sources). *Receiving aid:* Freshmen: 85% (630); all full-time undergraduates: 82% (2,207). *Average award:* Freshmen: $17,807; Undergraduates: $16,463. *Scholarships, grants, and awards:* Federal Pell, FSEOG, state, private, college/university gift aid from institutional funds.

**GIFT AID (NON-NEED-BASED)** *Total amount:* $2,932,630 (1% federal, 14% state, 65% institutional, 20% external sources). *Receiving aid:* Freshmen: 16% (120). Undergraduates: 13% (339). *Average award:* Freshmen: $14,566. Undergraduates: $12,798. *Scholarships, grants, and awards by category:* Academic interests/achievement: 2,349 awards ($27,178,262 total): biological sciences, business, computer science, education, general academic interests/achievements, health fields, humanities, international studies, mathematics, physical sciences, premedicine, social sciences. *Creative arts/performance:* 74 awards ($114,000 total): art/fine arts, journalism/publications, music, performing arts, theater/drama. *Special achievements/activities:* 456 awards ($257,951 total): general special achievements/activities, junior miss, leadership, memberships, religious involvement. *Special characteristics:* 717 awards ($1,256,992 total): adult students, children and siblings of alumni, children of current students, children of faculty/staff, general special characteristics, international students, siblings of current students, spouses of current students. *Tuition waivers:* Full or partial for employees or children of employees.

**LOANS** *Student loans:* $21,197,714 (39% need-based, 61% non-need-based). 80% of past graduating class borrowed through all loan programs. *Average indebtedness per student:* $32,931. *Average need-based loan:* Freshmen: $3700. Undergraduates: $4584. *Parent loans:* $3,945,960 (75% need-based, 25% non-need-based). *Programs:* Federal Direct (Subsidized and Unsubsidized Stafford, PLUS), Perkins, state, college/university.

**WORK-STUDY** *Federal work-study:* Total amount: $814,212; 347 jobs averaging $2346. *State or other work-study/employment:* Total amount: $3,553,125 (100% non-need-based). 1,520 part-time jobs averaging $2368.

**APPLYING FOR FINANCIAL AID** *Required financial aid form:* FAFSA. *Financial aid deadline:* Continuous. *Notification date:* Continuous beginning 2/15. Students must reply by 5/1 or within 2 weeks of notification.

**CONTACT** Dawn Scott, Director of Financial Aid, Carroll University, 100 North East Avenue, Waukesha, WI 53186-5593, 262-524-7297 or toll-free 800-CARROLL. *Fax:* 262-951-3037. *E-mail:* dscott@carrollu.edu.
*Website:* http://www.carrollu.edu/.

# CARSON-NEWMAN UNIVERSITY
### Jefferson City, TN

| Tuition & fees: $25,360 | Average undergraduate aid package: $21,549 |
| --- | --- |

**ABOUT THE INSTITUTION** Independent Southern Baptist, coed. *Awards:* certificates, associate, bachelor's, master's, and doctoral degrees. 63 undergraduate majors. *Total enrollment:* 2,362. Undergraduates: 1,757. Freshmen: 491. Federal methodology is used as a basis for awarding need-based institutional aid.

**UNDERGRADUATE EXPENSES** for 2015–2016 *Comprehensive fee:* $33,630 includes full-time tuition ($24,200), mandatory fees ($1160), and room and board ($8270). *College room only:* $3930. Full-time tuition and fees vary according to class time and course load. Room and board charges vary according to board plan, gender, and housing facility. *Part-time tuition:* $1010 per credit hour.

**FRESHMAN FINANCIAL AID (Fall 2013)** 422 applied for aid; of those 100% were deemed to have need. 100% of freshmen with need received aid; of those 23% had need fully met. *Average percent of need met:* 84% (excluding resources awarded to replace EFC). *Average financial aid package:* $23,193 (excluding resources awarded to replace EFC). 12% of all full-time freshmen had no need and received non-need-based gift aid.

**UNDERGRADUATE FINANCIAL AID (Fall 2013)** 1,320 applied for aid; of those 100% were deemed to have need. 100% of undergraduates with need received aid; of those 22% had need fully met. *Average percent of need met:* 82% (excluding resources awarded to replace EFC). *Average financial aid package:* $21,549 (excluding resources awarded to replace EFC). 10% of all full-time undergraduates had no need and received non-need-based gift aid.

**GIFT AID (NEED-BASED)** *Total amount:* $21,638,957 (15% federal, 20% state, 63% institutional, 2% external sources). *Receiving aid:* Freshmen: 88% (420); all full-time undergraduates: 83% (1,304). *Average award:* Freshmen: $18,118; Undergraduates: $16,082. *Scholarships, grants, and awards:* Federal Pell, FSEOG, state, private, college/university gift aid from institutional funds.

**GIFT AID (NON-NEED-BASED)** *Total amount:* $2,633,526 (1% federal, 19% state, 73% institutional, 7% external sources). *Receiving aid:* Freshmen: 12% (56). Undergraduates: 15% (231). *Average award:* Freshmen: $9787. Undergraduates: $9326. *Scholarships, grants, and awards by category:* Academic interests/achievement: biological sciences, business, education, general academic interests/achievements, home economics, mathematics, military science, religion/biblical studies. *Creative arts/performance:* art/fine arts, debating, journalism/publications, music. *Special achievements/activities:* leadership, memberships. *Special characteristics:* children and siblings of alumni, members of minority groups, relatives of clergy, siblings of current students. *Tuition waivers:* Full or partial for employees or children of employees, senior citizens. *ROTC:* Army.

**LOANS** *Student loans:* $8,873,617 (95% need-based, 5% non-need-based). 70% of past graduating class borrowed through all loan programs. *Average indebtedness per student:* $25,555. *Average need-based loan:* Freshmen: $3071. Undergraduates: $3840. *Parent loans:* $1,455,225 (90% need-based, 10% non-need-based). *Programs:* Perkins, state, college/university, alternative loans.

**WORK-STUDY** *Federal work-study:* jobs available. *State or other work-study/employment:* Total amount: $113,365 (98% need-based, 2% non-need-based). Part-time jobs available.

**ATHLETIC AWARDS** Total amount: $2,756,522 (74% need-based, 26% non-need-based).

**APPLYING FOR FINANCIAL AID** *Required financial aid forms:* FAFSA, institution's own form. *Financial aid deadline (priority):* 2/1. *Notification date:* Continuous. Students must reply within 2 weeks of notification.

**CONTACT** Danette Seale, Director of Financial Aid, Carson-Newman University, 1646 Russell Avenue, Jefferson City, TN 37760, 865-471-3247 or toll-free 800-678-9061. *Fax:* 865-471-3502. *E-mail:* dseale@cn.edu.
*Website:* http://www.cn.edu/.

# CARTHAGE COLLEGE
### Kenosha, WI

**CONTACT** Vatistas Vatistas, Director of Financial Aid, Carthage College, 2001 Alford Park Drive, Kenosha, WI 53140, 262-551-6001 or toll-free 800-351-4058. *Fax:* 262-551-5762. *E-mail:* vvatistas@carthage.edu.
*Website:* http://www.carthage.edu/.

# CASE WESTERN RESERVE UNIVERSITY
### Cleveland, OH

| Tuition & fees: $43,158 | Average undergraduate aid package: $37,356 |
| --- | --- |

**ABOUT THE INSTITUTION** Independent, coed. *Awards:* certificates, bachelor's, master's, and doctoral degrees. 68 undergraduate majors. *Total enrollment:* 10,771. Undergraduates: 4,911. Freshmen: 1,282. Federal methodology is used as a basis for awarding need-based institutional aid.

**UNDERGRADUATE EXPENSES** for 2015–2016 *One-time required fee:* $495. *Comprehensive fee:* $56,534 includes full-time tuition ($42,766), mandatory fees ($392), and room and board ($13,376). *College room only:* $7730. Room and board charges vary according to board plan, housing facility, and student level. *Part-time tuition:* $1792 per credit hour. Part-time tuition and fees vary according to course load.

**FRESHMAN FINANCIAL AID (Fall 2014, est.)** 911 applied for aid; of those 80% were deemed to have need. 100% of freshmen with need received aid; of those 29% had need fully met. *Average percent of need met:* 87% (excluding resources awarded to replace EFC). *Average financial aid package:* $38,625 (excluding resources awarded to replace EFC). 29% of all full-time freshmen had no need and received non-need-based gift aid.

**UNDERGRADUATE FINANCIAL AID (Fall 2014, est.)** 3,141 applied for aid; of those 86% were deemed to have need. 100% of undergraduates with need received aid; of those 23% had need fully met. *Average percent of need met:* 84% (excluding resources awarded to replace EFC). *Average financial aid package:* $37,356 (excluding resources awarded to replace EFC). 28% of all full-time undergraduates had no need and received non-need-based gift aid.

**GIFT AID (NEED-BASED)** *Total amount:* $74,186,923 (7% federal, 1% state, 88% institutional, 4% external sources). *Receiving aid:* Freshmen: 45% (581); all full-time undergraduates: 48% (2,285). *Average award:* Freshmen: $29,986; Undergraduates: $26,983. *Scholarships, grants, and awards:* Federal Pell, FSEOG, state, private, college/university gift aid from institutional funds.

**GIFT AID (NON-NEED-BASED)** *Total amount:* $35,749,847 (95% institutional, 5% external sources). *Receiving aid:* Freshmen: 10% (131). Undergraduates: 7% (338). *Average award:* Freshmen: $22,009. Undergraduates: $22,087. *Scholarships, grants, and awards by category:* Academic interests/achievement: 3,282 awards ($68,372,156 total): biological sciences, business, communication, computer

science, engineering/technologies, English, foreign languages, general academic interests/achievements, health fields, humanities, international studies, mathematics, physical sciences, premedicine, religion/biblical studies, social sciences. *Creative arts/ performance:* 49 awards ($1,370,557 total): art/fine arts, creative writing, dance, general creative arts/performance, music, performing arts, theater/drama. *Special achievements/activities:* 62 awards ($226,000 total): leadership. *Special characteristics:* 166 awards ($6,251,693 total): children of faculty/staff. *Tuition waivers:* Full or partial for employees or children of employees. *ROTC:* Army, Air Force cooperative.
**LOANS** *Student loans:* $21,613,528 (80% need-based, 20% non-need-based). 60% of past graduating class borrowed through all loan programs. *Average indebtedness per student:* $33,343. *Average need-based loan:* Freshmen: $3930. Undergraduates: $5107. *Parent loans:* $14,780,833 (69% need-based, 31% non-need-based). *Programs:* Federal Direct (Subsidized and Unsubsidized Stafford, PLUS), Perkins, Federal Nursing, college/university, alternative loans.
**WORK-STUDY** *Federal work-study:* Total amount: $4,080,390; 1,877 jobs averaging $2153.
**APPLYING FOR FINANCIAL AID** *Required financial aid forms:* FAFSA, institution's own form, CSS Financial Aid PROFILE. *Financial aid deadline (priority):* 2/15. *Notification date:* Continuous beginning 3/15. Students must reply by 5/1 or within 2 weeks of notification.
**CONTACT** Mrs. Venus M. Puliafico, Director of University Financial Aid, Case Western Reserve University, 2049 Martin Luther King Jr. Drive, Cleveland, OH 44106-7049, 216-368-4530. *Fax:* 216-368-5054. *E-mail:* vxp4@case.edu.
*Website:* http://www.case.edu/.

# CASTLETON STATE COLLEGE
## Castleton, VT

| Tuition & fees (VT res): $10,772 | Average undergraduate aid package: N/A |
|---|---|

**ABOUT THE INSTITUTION** State-supported, coed. *Awards:* certificates, associate, bachelor's, and master's degrees. 67 undergraduate majors. *Total enrollment:* 2,184. Undergraduates: 1,985. Freshmen: 369. Federal methodology is used as a basis for awarding need-based institutional aid.
**UNDERGRADUATE EXPENSES for 2015–2016** *Application fee:* $40. *One-time required fee:* $200. *Tuition, state resident:* full-time $9768; part-time $407 per credit. *Tuition, nonresident:* full-time $24,432; part-time $1018 per credit. *Required fees:* full-time $1004; $42 per credit or $502 per term. Full-time tuition and fees vary according to course load and program. Part-time tuition and fees vary according to course load and program. *College room and board:* $9414; *Room only:* $5606. Room and board charges vary according to board plan.
**GIFT AID (NEED-BASED)** *Total amount:* $7,852,681 (45% federal, 14% state, 30% institutional, 11% external sources). *Scholarships, grants, and awards:* Federal Pell, FSEOG, state, private, college/university gift aid from institutional funds.
**GIFT AID (NON-NEED-BASED)** *Scholarships, grants, and awards by category:* Academic interests/achievement: biological sciences, business, communication, education, English, foreign languages, general academic interests/achievements, health fields, humanities, mathematics. *Creative arts/performance:* applied art and design, art/fine arts, cinema/film/broadcasting, general creative arts/performance, music, performing arts, theater/drama. *Special achievements/activities:* community service, general special achievements/activities. *Special characteristics:* children and siblings of alumni, children of faculty/staff, general special characteristics, international students, veterans. *Tuition waivers:* Full or partial for employees or children of employees, senior citizens. *ROTC:* Army.
**LOANS** *Student loans:* $16,293,298 (100% need-based). *Parent loans:* $3,709,401 (100% need-based). *Programs:* Federal Direct (Subsidized and Unsubsidized Stafford, PLUS), Perkins.
**WORK-STUDY** *Federal work-study:* 325 jobs averaging $1249.
**APPLYING FOR FINANCIAL AID** *Required financial aid forms:* FAFSA, state aid form. *Financial aid deadline (priority):* 4/1. *Notification date:* Continuous beginning 2/15. Students must reply by 5/1 or within 2 weeks of notification.
**CONTACT** Kathleen O'Meara, Director of Financial Aid, Castleton State College, Castleton, VT 05735, 802-468-1292 or toll-free 800-639-8521. *Fax:* 802-468-5237. *E-mail:* kathy.omeara@castleton.edu.
*Website:* http://www.castleton.edu/.

# CATAWBA COLLEGE
## Salisbury, NC

| Tuition & fees: $28,730 | Average undergraduate aid package: $21,440 |
|---|---|

**ABOUT THE INSTITUTION** Independent United Church of Christ, coed. *Awards:* bachelor's and master's degrees. 46 undergraduate majors. *Total enrollment:* 1,316. Undergraduates: 1,309. Freshmen: 345. Federal methodology is used as a basis for awarding need-based institutional aid.
**UNDERGRADUATE EXPENSES for 2015–2016** *Comprehensive fee:* $39,090 includes full-time tuition ($28,730) and room and board ($10,360). Full-time tuition and fees vary according to class time, course load, and degree level. *Part-time tuition:* $750 per credit hour. Part-time tuition and fees vary according to class time, course load, and degree level.
**FRESHMAN FINANCIAL AID (Fall 2013)** 314 applied for aid; of those 93% were deemed to have need. 100% of freshmen with need received aid; of those 16% had need fully met. *Average percent of need met:* 78% (excluding resources awarded to replace EFC). *Average financial aid package:* $25,419 (excluding resources awarded to replace EFC). 13% of all full-time freshmen had no need and received non-need-based gift aid.
**UNDERGRADUATE FINANCIAL AID (Fall 2013)** 1,086 applied for aid; of those 93% were deemed to have need. 100% of undergraduates with need received aid; of those 17% had need fully met. *Average percent of need met:* 74% (excluding resources awarded to replace EFC). *Average financial aid package:* $21,440 (excluding resources awarded to replace EFC). 13% of all full-time undergraduates had no need and received non-need-based gift aid.
**GIFT AID (NEED-BASED)** *Total amount:* $6,706,845 (39% federal, 43% state, 11% institutional, 7% external sources). *Receiving aid:* Freshmen: 70% (235); all full-time undergraduates: 70% (836). *Average award:* Freshmen: $7725; Undergraduates: $7175. *Scholarships, grants, and awards:* Federal Pell, FSEOG, state, private, college/university gift aid from institutional funds.
**GIFT AID (NON-NEED-BASED)** *Total amount:* $10,123,912 (100% institutional). *Receiving aid:* Freshmen: 86% (290). Undergraduates: 71% (842). *Average award:* Freshmen: $14,011. Undergraduates: $11,081. *Scholarships, grants, and awards by category:* Academic interests/achievement: education, general academic interests/achievements. *Creative arts/performance:* music, theater/drama. *Special achievements/activities:* general special achievements/activities, leadership. *Special characteristics:* local/state students. *Tuition waivers:* Full or partial for employees or children of employees. *ROTC:* Army cooperative, Air Force cooperative.
**LOANS** *Student loans:* $7,959,531 (52% need-based, 48% non-need-based). 72% of past graduating class borrowed through all loan programs. *Average indebtedness per student:* $28,132. *Average need-based loan:* Freshmen: $4445. Undergraduates: $4679. *Parent loans:* $1,626,397 (100% non-need-based). *Programs:* Federal Direct (Subsidized and Unsubsidized Stafford, PLUS), Perkins, state, college/university, alternative loans.
**WORK-STUDY** *Federal work-study:* jobs available. *State or other work-study/employment:* Total amount: $226,812 (100% need-based). Part-time jobs available.
**ATHLETIC AWARDS** Total amount: $3,151,274 (100% non-need-based).
**APPLYING FOR FINANCIAL AID** *Required financial aid form:* FAFSA. *Financial aid deadline (priority):* 3/15. *Notification date:* Continuous beginning 2/15. Students must reply within 2 weeks of notification.
**CONTACT** Dawn Snook, Director of Financial Aid, Catawba College, 2300 West Innes Street, Salisbury, NC 28144-2488, 704-637-4416 or toll-free 800-CATAWBA. *Fax:* 704-637-4252. *E-mail:* dasnook@catawba.edu.
*Website:* http://www.catawba.edu/.

# THE CATHOLIC UNIVERSITY OF AMERICA
## Washington, DC

| Tuition & fees: $39,726 | Average undergraduate aid package: $25,560 |
|---|---|

**ABOUT THE INSTITUTION** Independent Roman Catholic Church, coed. *Awards:* certificates, bachelor's, master's, and doctoral degrees. 60 undergraduate majors. **Total enrollment:** 6,699. Undergraduates: 3,572. Freshmen: 832. Federal methodology is used as a basis for awarding need-based institutional aid.

**UNDERGRADUATE EXPENSES for 2015–2016 Application fee:** $55. **One-time required fee:** $425. **Comprehensive fee:** $54,244 includes full-time tuition ($39,200), mandatory fees ($526), and room and board ($14,518). Full-time tuition and fees vary according to program. Room and board charges vary according to board plan and housing facility. **Part-time tuition:** $1550 per credit hour. **Part-time fees:** $302.50 per year. Part-time tuition and fees vary according to course load and program.

**FRESHMAN FINANCIAL AID (Fall 2014, est.)** 675 applied for aid; of those 80% were deemed to have need. 100% of freshmen with need received aid; of those 43% had need fully met. **Average percent of need met:** 78% (excluding resources awarded to replace EFC). **Average financial aid package:** $26,413 (excluding resources awarded to replace EFC). 30% of all full-time freshmen had no need and received non-need-based gift aid.

**UNDERGRADUATE FINANCIAL AID (Fall 2014, est.)** 2,300 applied for aid; of those 85% were deemed to have need. 100% of undergraduates with need received aid; of those 43% had need fully met. **Average percent of need met:** 79% (excluding resources awarded to replace EFC). **Average financial aid package:** $25,560 (excluding resources awarded to replace EFC). 31% of all full-time undergraduates had no need and received non-need-based gift aid.

**GIFT AID (NEED-BASED) Total amount:** $41,366,000 (6% federal, 93% institutional, 1% external sources). **Receiving aid:** Freshmen: 64% (531); all full-time undergraduates: 57% (1,906). **Average award:** Freshmen: $22,213; Undergraduates: $21,601. **Scholarships, grants, and awards:** Federal Pell, FSEOG, state, private, college/university gift aid from institutional funds.

**GIFT AID (NON-NEED-BASED) Total amount:** $16,047,472 (99% institutional, 1% external sources). **Average award:** Freshmen: $16,379. Undergraduates: $15,620. **Scholarships, grants, and awards by category:** Academic interests/achievement: general academic interests/achievements. Creative arts/performance: music, theater/drama. Special characteristics: children and siblings of alumni, children of faculty/staff, religious affiliation, siblings of current students, twins, veterans, veterans' children. **Tuition waivers:** Full or partial for children of alumni, employees or children of employees. ROTC: Army, Naval cooperative, Air Force cooperative.

**LOANS Student loans:** $21,298,285 (86% need-based, 14% non-need-based). **Average need-based loan:** Freshmen: $4412. Undergraduates: $4937. **Parent loans:** $10,515,562 (91% need-based, 9% non-need-based). **Programs:** Federal Direct (Subsidized and Unsubsidized Stafford, PLUS), Perkins, Federal Nursing, private loans.

**WORK-STUDY Federal work-study:** Total amount: $614,214; 318 jobs averaging $1932.

**APPLYING FOR FINANCIAL AID Required financial aid forms:** FAFSA, CSS Financial Aid PROFILE, alumni and parish scholarship application form. **Financial aid deadline:** 4/10 (priority: 2/15). **Notification date:** Continuous beginning 3/10. Students must reply by 5/1 or within 2 weeks of notification.

**CONTACT** Mr. Joseph Dobrota, Director of Financial Aid, The Catholic University of America, 620 Michigan Avenue, NE, Washington, DC 20064, 202-319-5307 or toll-free 800-673-2772. Fax: 202-319-5573. E-mail: dobrota@cua.edu.

Website: http://www.cua.edu/.

# CAZENOVIA COLLEGE
## Cazenovia, NY

| Tuition & fees: $30,560 | Average undergraduate aid package: $29,600 |
| --- | --- |

**ABOUT THE INSTITUTION** Independent, coed. **Awards:** certificates, associate, and bachelor's degrees. 24 undergraduate majors. **Total enrollment:** 1,091. Undergraduates: 1,091. Freshmen: 265. Federal methodology is used as a basis for awarding need-based institutional aid.

**UNDERGRADUATE EXPENSES for 2015–2016 Application fee:** $30. **Comprehensive fee:** $42,904 includes full-time tuition ($30,028), mandatory fees ($532), and room and board ($12,344). **College room only:** $6920. Full-time tuition and fees vary according to class time, course load, and program. Room and board charges vary according to board plan and housing facility. **Part-time tuition:** $640 per credit hour. Part-time tuition and fees vary according to class time and course load.

**FRESHMAN FINANCIAL AID (Fall 2014, est.)** 254 applied for aid; of those 96% were deemed to have need. 100% of freshmen with need received aid; of those 21% had need fully met. **Average percent of need met:** 83% (excluding resources

awarded to replace EFC). **Average financial aid package:** $31,000 (excluding resources awarded to replace EFC). 8% of all full-time freshmen had no need and received non-need-based gift aid.

**UNDERGRADUATE FINANCIAL AID (Fall 2014, est.)** 923 applied for aid; of those 95% were deemed to have need. 100% of undergraduates with need received aid; of those 10% had need fully met. **Average percent of need met:** 80% (excluding resources awarded to replace EFC). **Average financial aid package:** $29,600 (excluding resources awarded to replace EFC). 9% of all full-time undergraduates had no need and received non-need-based gift aid.

**GIFT AID (NEED-BASED) Total amount:** $21,747,909 (11% federal, 9% state, 79% institutional, 1% external sources). **Receiving aid:** Freshmen: 92% (243); all full-time undergraduates: 87% (836). **Average award:** Freshmen: $13,700; Undergraduates: $16,011. **Scholarships, grants, and awards:** Federal Pell, FSEOG, state, private, college/university gift aid from institutional funds.

**GIFT AID (NON-NEED-BASED) Total amount:** $2,282,843 (2% state, 98% institutional). **Receiving aid:** Freshmen: 8% (22). Undergraduates: 10% (101). **Average award:** Freshmen: $18,500. Undergraduates: $14,600. **Scholarships, grants, and awards by category:** Academic interests/achievement: general academic interests/achievements. **Tuition waivers:** Full or partial for employees or children of employees. ROTC: Army cooperative, Air Force cooperative.

**LOANS Student loans:** $8,631,306 (55% need-based, 45% non-need-based). 83% of past graduating class borrowed through all loan programs. **Average indebtedness per student:** $29,998. **Average need-based loan:** Freshmen: $3450. Undergraduates: $4300. **Parent loans:** $2,787,860 (46% need-based, 54% non-need-based). **Programs:** Federal Direct (Subsidized and Unsubsidized Stafford, PLUS).

**WORK-STUDY Federal work-study:** Total amount: $296,250; jobs available.

**APPLYING FOR FINANCIAL AID Required financial aid forms:** FAFSA, state aid form. **Financial aid deadline (priority):** 3/1. **Notification date:** Continuous. Students must reply by 5/1 or within 2 weeks of notification.

**CONTACT** Christine L. Mandel, Director of Financial Aid, Cazenovia College, 3 Sullivan Street, Cazenovia, NY 13035, 315-655-7887 or toll-free 800-654-3210. Fax: 315-655-7219. E-mail: finaid@cazenovia.edu.

Website: http://www.cazenovia.edu/.

# CEDAR CREST COLLEGE
## Allentown, PA

| Tuition & fees: $34,504 | Average undergraduate aid package: $26,519 |
| --- | --- |

**ABOUT THE INSTITUTION** Independent United Church of Christ, coed, primarily women. **Awards:** certificates, bachelor's, and master's degrees. 41 undergraduate majors. **Total enrollment:** 1,531. Undergraduates: 1,344. Freshmen: 170. Federal methodology is used as a basis for awarding need-based institutional aid.

**UNDERGRADUATE EXPENSES for 2015–2016 Comprehensive fee:** $45,053 includes full-time tuition ($33,904), mandatory fees ($600), and room and board ($10,549). **College room only:** $5160. Full-time tuition and fees vary according to class time, course load, and program. Room and board charges vary according to board plan and housing facility. **Part-time tuition:** $1130 per credit. **Part-time fees:** $150 per term. Part-time tuition and fees vary according to class time, course load, and program.

**FRESHMAN FINANCIAL AID (Fall 2014, est.)** 165 applied for aid; of those 97% were deemed to have need. 100% of freshmen with need received aid; of those 14% had need fully met. **Average percent of need met:** 80% (excluding resources awarded to replace EFC). **Average financial aid package:** $29,266 (excluding resources awarded to replace EFC). 5% of all full-time freshmen had no need and received non-need-based gift aid.

**UNDERGRADUATE FINANCIAL AID (Fall 2014, est.)** 518 applied for aid; of those 95% were deemed to have need. 100% of undergraduates with need received aid; of those 13% had need fully met. **Average percent of need met:** 75% (excluding resources awarded to replace EFC). **Average financial aid package:** $26,519 (excluding resources awarded to replace EFC). 7% of all full-time undergraduates had no need and received non-need-based gift aid.

**GIFT AID (NEED-BASED) Total amount:** $11,165,169 (12% federal, 8% state, 77% institutional, 3% external sources). **Receiving aid:** Freshmen: 94% (160); all full-time undergraduates: 92% (493). **Average award:** Freshmen: $25,884; Undergraduates: $22,296. **Scholarships, grants, and awards:** Federal Pell, FSEOG, state, private, college/university gift aid from institutional funds, Federal Nursing.

**GIFT AID (NON-NEED-BASED)** *Total amount:* $794,979 (1% state, 98% institutional, 1% external sources). *Receiving aid:* Freshmen: 11% (18). Undergraduates: 8% (45). *Average award:* Freshmen: $18,625. Undergraduates: $13,523. *Scholarships, grants, and awards by category: Academic interests/achievement:* business, communication, English, general academic interests/achievements. *Creative arts/performance:* art/fine arts, dance, performing arts, theater/drama. *Special achievements/activities:* community service, general special achievements/activities, junior miss, leadership, memberships, religious involvement. *Special characteristics:* adult students, children and siblings of alumni, general special characteristics, previous college experience, relatives of clergy, siblings of current students. *Tuition waivers:* Full or partial for children of alumni, employees or children of employees. *ROTC:* Army cooperative.

**LOANS** *Student loans:* $5,729,448 (80% need-based, 20% non-need-based). 92% of past graduating class borrowed through all loan programs. *Average indebtedness per student:* $41,939. *Average need-based loan:* Freshmen: $3537. Undergraduates: $4531. *Parent loans:* $1,393,325 (52% need-based, 48% non-need-based). *Programs:* Federal Direct (Subsidized and Unsubsidized Stafford, PLUS), Perkins, Federal Nursing.

**WORK-STUDY** *Federal work-study:* Total amount: $114,779; jobs available. *State or other work-study/employment:* Total amount: $19,720 (71% need-based, 29% non-need-based). Part-time jobs available.

**APPLYING FOR FINANCIAL AID** *Required financial aid form:* FAFSA. *Financial aid deadline (priority):* 5/1. *Notification date:* Continuous beginning 9/15.

**CONTACT** Ms. Valerie D. Kreiser, Director of Student Financial Services, Cedar Crest College, Room 212 Blaney Hall, 100 College Drive, Allentown, PA 18104-6196, 610-606-4666 Ext. 3314 or toll-free 800-360-1222. *Fax:* 610-606-4653. *E-mail:* financialservices@cedarcrest.edu. *Website:* http://www.cedarcrest.edu/.

# CEDARVILLE UNIVERSITY
### Cedarville, OH

| Tuition & fees: $27,206 | Average undergraduate aid package: $17,006 |
|---|---|

**ABOUT THE INSTITUTION** Independent Baptist, coed. *Awards:* certificates, bachelor's, master's, and doctoral degrees. 71 undergraduate majors. *Total enrollment:* 3,585. Undergraduates: 3,303. Freshmen: 787. Federal methodology is used as a basis for awarding need-based institutional aid.

**UNDERGRADUATE EXPENSES** for 2015–2016 *Application fee:* $30. *Comprehensive fee:* $33,748 includes full-time tuition ($27,006), mandatory fees ($200), and room and board ($6542). *College room only:* $3708. Room and board charges vary according to board plan and housing facility. *Part-time tuition:* $1022 per credit hour. *Part-time fees:* $50 per term. Part-time tuition and fees vary according to course load.

**FRESHMAN FINANCIAL AID (Fall 2014, est.)** 693 applied for aid; of those 82% were deemed to have need. 100% of freshmen with need received aid; of those 41% had need fully met. *Average percent of need met:* 28% (excluding resources awarded to replace EFC). *Average financial aid package:* $17,899 (excluding resources awarded to replace EFC). 25% of all full-time freshmen had no need and received non-need-based gift aid.

**UNDERGRADUATE FINANCIAL AID (Fall 2014, est.)** 2,388 applied for aid; of those 87% were deemed to have need. 100% of undergraduates with need received aid; of those 41% had need fully met. *Average percent of need met:* 33% (excluding resources awarded to replace EFC). *Average financial aid package:* $17,006 (excluding resources awarded to replace EFC). 25% of all full-time undergraduates had no need and received non-need-based gift aid.

**GIFT AID (NEED-BASED)** *Total amount:* $9,470,807 (29% federal, 4% state, 66% institutional, 1% external sources). *Receiving aid:* Freshmen: 62% (489); all full-time undergraduates: 59% (1,787). *Average award:* Freshmen: $4197; Undergraduates: $4289. *Scholarships, grants, and awards:* Federal Pell, FSEOG, state, private, college/university gift aid from institutional funds, Federal Nursing.

**GIFT AID (NON-NEED-BASED)** *Total amount:* $27,936,072 (85% institutional, 15% external sources). *Receiving aid:* Freshmen: 68% (537). Undergraduates: 61% (1,834). *Average award:* Freshmen: $17,825. Undergraduates: $15,983. *Scholarships, grants, and awards by category: Academic interests/achievement:*

2,015 awards ($15,620,812 total): general academic interests/achievements. *Creative arts/performance:* 32 awards ($27,850 total): debating, music. *Special achievements/activities:* 17 awards ($334,305 total): leadership. *Special characteristics:* 212 awards ($3,327,172 total): children of faculty/staff, ethnic background, general special characteristics, religious affiliation, veterans. *Tuition waivers:* Full or partial for employees or children of employees, adult students, senior citizens. *ROTC:* Army cooperative, Air Force cooperative.

**LOANS** *Student loans:* $18,159,888 (39% need-based, 61% non-need-based). 67% of past graduating class borrowed through all loan programs. *Average indebtedness per student:* $29,105. *Average need-based loan:* Freshmen: $4573. Undergraduates: $5660. *Parent loans:* $14,803,781 (100% non-need-based). *Programs:* Federal Direct (Subsidized and Unsubsidized Stafford, PLUS), Perkins, Federal Nursing, college/university.

**WORK-STUDY** *Federal work-study:* Total amount: $223,740; 396 jobs averaging $1103. *State or other work-study/employment:* Total amount: $1,747,046 (100% non-need-based). 1,597 part-time jobs averaging $1094.

**ATHLETIC AWARDS** Total amount: $1,231,846 (100% non-need-based).

**APPLYING FOR FINANCIAL AID** *Required financial aid form:* FAFSA. *Financial aid deadline (priority):* 3/1. *Notification date:* Continuous beginning 3/1. Students must reply within 4 weeks of notification.

**CONTACT** Mr. Russell Kim Jenerette, Executive Director of Financial Aid, Cedarville University, 251 North Main Street, Cedarville, OH 45314-0601, 937-766-7866 Ext. 3640 or toll-free 800-233-2784. *E-mail:* kimjenerette@cedarville.edu. *Website:* http://www.cedarville.edu/.

# CENTENARY COLLEGE
### Hackettstown, NJ

**CONTACT** Michelle Burwell, Associate Director of Financial Aid, Centenary College, 400 Jefferson Street, Hackettstown, NJ 07840-2100, 908-852-1400 Ext. 2240 or toll-free 800-236-8679. *Fax:* 908-813-2632. *E-mail:* burwellm@centenarycollege.edu. *Website:* http://www.centenarycollege.edu/.

# CENTENARY COLLEGE OF LOUISIANA
### Shreveport, LA

| Tuition & fees: $33,900 | Average undergraduate aid package: $25,657 |
|---|---|

**ABOUT THE INSTITUTION** Independent United Methodist, coed. *Awards:* bachelor's and master's degrees. 23 undergraduate majors. *Total enrollment:* 619. Undergraduates: 553. Freshmen: 141. Federal methodology is used as a basis for awarding need-based institutional aid.

**UNDERGRADUATE EXPENSES** for 2015–2016 *One-time required fee:* $250. *Comprehensive fee:* $46,250 includes full-time tuition ($33,900) and room and board ($12,350). Full-time tuition and fees vary according to course load, degree level, and student level. Room and board charges vary according to board plan, housing facility, and student level. Part-time tuition and fees vary according to course load, degree level, and student level.

**FRESHMAN FINANCIAL AID (Fall 2014, est.)** 132 applied for aid; of those 95% were deemed to have need. 98% of freshmen with need received aid; of those 13% had need fully met. *Average percent of need met:* 69% (excluding resources awarded to replace EFC). *Average financial aid package:* $27,395 (excluding resources awarded to replace EFC). 10% of all full-time freshmen had no need and received non-need-based gift aid.

**UNDERGRADUATE FINANCIAL AID (Fall 2014, est.)** 479 applied for aid; of those 89% were deemed to have need. 100% of undergraduates with need received aid; of those 19% had need fully met. *Average percent of need met:* 75% (excluding resources awarded to replace EFC). *Average financial aid package:* $25,657 (excluding resources awarded to replace EFC). 23% of all full-time undergraduates had no need and received non-need-based gift aid.

**GIFT AID (NEED-BASED)** *Total amount:* $9,324,676 (10% federal, 12% state, 77% institutional, 1% external sources). *Receiving aid:* Freshmen: 88% (123); all full-

time undergraduates: 78% (424). *Average award:* Freshmen: $23,565; Undergraduates: $21,909. *Scholarships, grants, and awards:* Federal Pell, FSEOG, state, private, college/university gift aid from institutional funds.

**GIFT AID (NON-NEED-BASED)** *Total amount:* $2,843,037 (10% state, 89% institutional, 1% external sources). *Receiving aid:* Freshmen: 11% (15). Undergraduates: 12% (63). *Average award:* Freshmen: $16,308. Undergraduates: $15,863. *Scholarships, grants, and awards by category: Academic interests/achievement:* $5,664,521 total: biological sciences, business, communication, education, engineering/technologies, English, foreign languages, general academic interests/achievements, health fields, humanities, mathematics, physical sciences, premedicine, religion/biblical studies, social sciences. *Creative arts/performance:* $330,300 total: art/fine arts, dance, general creative arts/performance, music, performing arts, theater/drama. *Special achievements/activities:* $812,985 total: community service, general special achievements/activities, hobbies/interests, religious involvement. *Special characteristics:* $892,245 total: children and siblings of alumni, children of educators, children of faculty/staff, ethnic background, first-generation college students, general special characteristics, international students, local/state students, members of minority groups, out-of-state students, relatives of clergy, religious affiliation, siblings of current students. *Tuition waivers:* Full or partial for employees or children of employees.

**LOANS** *Student loans:* $2,496,658 (48% need-based, 52% non-need-based). 54% of past graduating class borrowed through all loan programs. *Average indebtedness per student:* $27,692. *Average need-based loan:* Freshmen: $3351. Undergraduates: $4398. *Parent loans:* $880,285 (95% need-based, 5% non-need-based). *Programs:* Federal Direct (Subsidized and Unsubsidized Stafford, PLUS), Perkins.

**WORK-STUDY** *Federal work-study:* Total amount: $401,828; 184 jobs averaging $2184. *State or other work-study/employment:* Total amount: $54,700 (100% non-need-based). 42 part-time jobs averaging $1396.

**APPLYING FOR FINANCIAL AID** *Required financial aid form:* FAFSA. *Financial aid deadline (priority):* 2/15. *Notification date:* Continuous beginning 3/15. Students must reply by 5/1.

**CONTACT** Mrs. Lynette Viskozki, Director of Financial Aid, Centenary College of Louisiana, PO Box 41188, Shreveport, LA 71134-1188, 318-869-5137 or toll-free 800-234-4448. *Fax:* 318-841-7266. *E-mail:* lviskozk@centenary.edu. *Website:* http://www.centenary.edu/.

---

# CENTRAL BAPTIST COLLEGE
## Conway, AR

**CONTACT** Christi Bell, Financial Aid Director, Central Baptist College, 1501 College Avenue, Conway, AR 72032-6470, 800-205-6872 Ext. 185 or toll-free 800-205-6872. *Fax:* 501-329-2941. *E-mail:* financialaid@cbc.edu. *Website:* http://www.cbc.edu/.

---

# CENTRAL CHRISTIAN COLLEGE OF KANSAS
## McPherson, KS

**CONTACT** Mike Reimer, Financial Aid Director, Central Christian College of Kansas, 1200 South Main, PO Box 1403, McPherson, KS 67460, 620-241-0723 Ext. 333 or toll-free 800-835-0078. *Fax:* 620-241-6032. *E-mail:* miker@centralchristian.edu. *Website:* http://www.centralchristian.edu/.

---

# CENTRAL CHRISTIAN COLLEGE OF THE BIBLE
## Moberly, MO

| Tuition & fees: N/R | Average undergraduate aid package: N/A |
|---|---|

**ABOUT THE INSTITUTION** Independent Christian Churches and Churches of Christ, coed. 2 undergraduate majors. Institutional methodology is used as a basis for awarding need-based institutional aid.

**FRESHMAN FINANCIAL AID (Fall 2013)** 33 applied for aid.

**UNDERGRADUATE FINANCIAL AID (Fall 2013)** 286 applied for aid.

**GIFT AID (NEED-BASED)** *Total amount:* $926,873 (100% federal). *Scholarships, grants, and awards:* Federal Pell, FSEOG, private, college/university gift aid from institutional funds.

**GIFT AID (NON-NEED-BASED)** *Total amount:* $2,268,581 (94% institutional, 6% external sources). *Scholarships, grants, and awards by category: Academic interests/achievement:* religion/biblical studies.

**LOANS** *Student loans:* $1,070,260 (56% need-based, 44% non-need-based). *Parent loans:* $28,840 (100% non-need-based). *Programs:* Federal Direct (Subsidized and Unsubsidized Stafford, PLUS), alternative loans.

**WORK-STUDY** *Federal work-study:* jobs available.

**APPLYING FOR FINANCIAL AID** *Financial aid deadline:* Continuous. *Notification date:* Continuous beginning 3/1. Students must reply by 6/15 or within 4 weeks of notification.

**CONTACT** Rhonda J. Dunham, Financial Aid Director, Central Christian College of the Bible, 911 East Urbandale Drive, Moberly, MO 65270-1997, 660-263-3900 Ext. 121 or toll-free 888-263-3900. *Fax:* 660-263-3936. *E-mail:* rdunham@cccb.edu. *Website:* http://www.cccb.edu/.

---

# CENTRAL COLLEGE
## Pella, IA

| Tuition & fees: $33,345 | Average undergraduate aid package: $24,872 |
|---|---|

**ABOUT THE INSTITUTION** Independent Reformed Church in America, coed. *Awards:* bachelor's degrees. 37 undergraduate majors. *Total enrollment:* 1,411. Undergraduates: 1,411. Freshmen: 429. Federal methodology is used as a basis for awarding need-based institutional aid.

**UNDERGRADUATE EXPENSES for 2015–2016** *Application fee:* $25. *Comprehensive fee:* $43,325 includes full-time tuition ($33,345) and room and board ($9980). *College room only:* $4892. Room and board charges vary according to board plan. *Part-time tuition:* $1389 per credit hour. Part-time tuition and fees vary according to course load.

**FRESHMAN FINANCIAL AID (Fall 2014, est.)** 411 applied for aid; of those 89% were deemed to have need. 100% of freshmen with need received aid; of those 21% had need fully met. *Average percent of need met:* 84% (excluding resources awarded to replace EFC). *Average financial aid package:* $28,994 (excluding resources awarded to replace EFC). 15% of all full-time freshmen had no need and received non-need-based gift aid.

**UNDERGRADUATE FINANCIAL AID (Fall 2014, est.)** 1,164 applied for aid; of those 91% were deemed to have need. 100% of undergraduates with need received aid; of those 19% had need fully met. *Average percent of need met:* 80% (excluding resources awarded to replace EFC). *Average financial aid package:* $24,872 (excluding resources awarded to replace EFC). 19% of all full-time undergraduates had no need and received non-need-based gift aid.

**GIFT AID (NEED-BASED)** *Total amount:* $23,525,893 (7% federal, 10% state, 81% institutional, 2% external sources). *Receiving aid:* Freshmen: 85% (366); all full-time undergraduates: 81% (1,056). *Average award:* Freshmen: $25,114; Undergraduates: $22,088. *Scholarships, grants, and awards:* Federal Pell, FSEOG, state, private, college/university gift aid from institutional funds.

**GIFT AID (NON-NEED-BASED)** *Total amount:* $5,380,182 (7% federal, 91% institutional, 2% external sources). *Receiving aid:* Freshmen: 16% (69). Undergraduates: 8% (103). *Average award:* Freshmen: $18,855. Undergraduates: $16,292. *Scholarships, grants, and awards by category: Academic interests/achievement:* biological sciences, business, communication, computer science, education, foreign languages, general academic interests/achievements, health fields, humanities, international studies, mathematics, physical sciences, premedicine, religion/biblical studies, social sciences. *Creative arts/performance:* art/fine arts, creative writing, music, theater/drama. *Special achievements/activities:* community service, religious involvement. *Special characteristics:* children and siblings of alumni, children of current students, children of faculty/staff, general special characteristics, handicapped students, international students, local/state students, members of minority groups, out-of-state students, previous college experience, religious affiliation, siblings of current students, twins, veterans, veterans' children. *Tuition waivers:* Full or partial for employees or children of employees.

**LOANS** *Student loans:* $9,122,720 (73% need-based, 27% non-need-based). 82% of past graduating class borrowed through all loan programs. *Average indebtedness per student:* $29,440. *Average need-based loan:* Freshmen: $3115. Undergrad-

uates: $3045. *Parent loans:* $2,688,751 (34% need-based, 66% non-need-based). *Programs:* Federal Direct (Subsidized and Unsubsidized Stafford, PLUS), Perkins, college/university, alternative loans.

**WORK-STUDY** *Federal work-study:* Total amount: $838,188; jobs available. *State or other work-study/employment:* Total amount: $689,075 (100% non-need-based). Part-time jobs available.

**APPLYING FOR FINANCIAL AID** *Required financial aid form:* FAFSA. *Financial aid deadline (priority):* 3/1. *Notification date:* Continuous beginning 3/1. Students must reply by 5/1 or within 2 weeks of notification.

**CONTACT** Wayne Dille, Director of Financial Aid, Central College, 812 University Street, Campus Box 5800, Pella, IA 50219-1999, 641-628-5336 or toll-free 877-462-3687. *Fax:* 641-628-7199. *E-mail:* dillew@central.edu. *Website:* http://www.central.edu/.

# CENTRAL CONNECTICUT STATE UNIVERSITY
### New Britain, CT

| Tuition & fees (CT res): $8877 | Average undergraduate aid package: $8672 |
|---|---|

**ABOUT THE INSTITUTION** State-supported, coed. *Awards:* certificates, bachelor's, master's, and doctoral degrees. 53 undergraduate majors. *Total enrollment:* 12,037. Undergraduates: 9,911. Freshmen: 1,369. Federal methodology is used as a basis for awarding need-based institutional aid.

**UNDERGRADUATE EXPENSES for 2015–2016** *Application fee:* $50. *Tuition, state resident:* full-time $4600; part-time $193 per credit hour. *Tuition, nonresident:* full-time $14,886; part-time $197 per credit hour. *Required fees:* full-time $4277; $232 per credit hour. Full-time tuition and fees vary according to course level, course load, and program. Part-time tuition and fees vary according to course level, course load, and program. *College room and board:* $10,872; *Room only:* $6322. Room and board charges vary according to board plan.

**FRESHMAN FINANCIAL AID (Fall 2014, est.)** 1,215 applied for aid; of those 79% were deemed to have need. 94% of freshmen with need received aid; of those 5% had need fully met. *Average percent of need met:* 61% (excluding resources awarded to replace EFC). *Average financial aid package:* $9602 (excluding resources awarded to replace EFC). 4% of all full-time freshmen had no need and received non-need-based gift aid.

**UNDERGRADUATE FINANCIAL AID (Fall 2014, est.)** 7,030 applied for aid; of those 86% were deemed to have need. 86% of undergraduates with need received aid; of those 6% had need fully met. *Average percent of need met:* 61% (excluding resources awarded to replace EFC). *Average financial aid package:* $8672 (excluding resources awarded to replace EFC). 3% of all full-time undergraduates had no need and received non-need-based gift aid.

**GIFT AID (NEED-BASED)** *Total amount:* $24,381,846 (57% federal, 18% state, 25% institutional). *Receiving aid:* Freshmen: 54% (727); all full-time undergraduates: 49% (3,743). *Average award:* Freshmen: $5547; Undergraduates: $5880. *Scholarships, grants, and awards:* Federal Pell, FSEOG, state, college/university gift aid from institutional funds.

**GIFT AID (NON-NEED-BASED)** *Total amount:* $3,592,872 (2% state, 67% institutional, 31% external sources). *Receiving aid:* Freshmen: 14% (192). Undergraduates: 12% (938). *Average award:* Freshmen: $2966. Undergraduates: $4008. *Scholarships, grants, and awards by category:* Academic interests/achievement: general academic interests/achievements. *Special characteristics:* members of minority groups. *Tuition waivers:* Full or partial for employees or children of employees, senior citizens. *ROTC:* Army cooperative, Air Force cooperative.

**LOANS** *Student loans:* $54,083,686 (38% need-based, 62% non-need-based). 53% of past graduating class borrowed through all loan programs. *Average indebtedness per student:* $24,000. *Average need-based loan:* Freshmen: $3183. Undergraduates: $4272. *Parent loans:* $6,238,028 (100% non-need-based). *Programs:* Federal Direct (Subsidized and Unsubsidized Stafford, PLUS), Perkins.

**WORK-STUDY** *Federal work-study:* Total amount: $395,626; 286 jobs averaging $1426. *State or other work-study/employment:* Total amount: $2,304,374 (100% non-need-based). Part-time jobs available.

**ATHLETIC AWARDS** Total amount: $3,448,142 (100% non-need-based).

**APPLYING FOR FINANCIAL AID** *Required financial aid form:* FAFSA. *Financial aid deadline:* 9/15 (priority: 3/1). *Notification date:* Continuous beginning 3/30. Students must reply within 2 weeks of notification.

**CONTACT** Mr. Dennis Williams, Associate Director of Financial Aid, Central Connecticut State University, Davidson Hall, Room 221, New Britain, CT 06050-4010, 860-832-2200 or toll-free 860-832-2278 (in-state), 860-733-2278 (out-of-state). *Fax:* 860-832-3330. *E-mail:* finaid@ccsu.edu. *Website:* http://www.ccsu.edu/.

# CENTRAL METHODIST UNIVERSITY
### Fayette, MO

| Tuition & fees: $22,360 | Average undergraduate aid package: $24,015 |
|---|---|

**ABOUT THE INSTITUTION** Independent Methodist, coed. *Awards:* associate, bachelor's, and master's degrees. 45 undergraduate majors. *Total enrollment:* 1,185. Undergraduates: 1,185. Freshmen: 331. Federal methodology is used as a basis for awarding need-based institutional aid.

**UNDERGRADUATE EXPENSES for 2015–2016** *One-time required fee:* $100. *Comprehensive fee:* $29,700 includes full-time tuition ($21,630), mandatory fees ($730), and room and board ($7340). Full-time tuition and fees vary according to program and reciprocity agreements. Room and board charges vary according to board plan and housing facility. *Part-time tuition:* $210 per credit hour. *Part-time fees:* $30. Part-time tuition and fees vary according to course load and program.

**FRESHMAN FINANCIAL AID (Fall 2014, est.)** 322 applied for aid; of those 91% were deemed to have need. 100% of freshmen with need received aid; of those 15% had need fully met. *Average percent of need met:* 25% (excluding resources awarded to replace EFC). *Average financial aid package:* $19,183 (excluding resources awarded to replace EFC). 10% of all full-time freshmen had no need and received non-need-based gift aid.

**UNDERGRADUATE FINANCIAL AID (Fall 2014, est.)** 1,041 applied for aid; of those 91% were deemed to have need. 100% of undergraduates with need received aid; of those 18% had need fully met. *Average percent of need met:* 74% (excluding resources awarded to replace EFC). *Average financial aid package:* $24,015 (excluding resources awarded to replace EFC). 13% of all full-time undergraduates had no need and received non-need-based gift aid.

**GIFT AID (NEED-BASED)** *Total amount:* $2,940,199 (75% federal, 25% state). *Receiving aid:* Freshmen: 64% (212); all full-time undergraduates: 55% (629). *Average award:* Freshmen: $4916; Undergraduates: $4784. *Scholarships, grants, and awards:* Federal Pell, FSEOG, state, private, college/university gift aid from institutional funds.

**GIFT AID (NON-NEED-BASED)** *Total amount:* $9,078,458 (95% institutional, 5% external sources). *Receiving aid:* Freshmen: 88% (291). Undergraduates: 83% (947). *Average award:* Freshmen: $8305. Undergraduates: $9233. *Scholarships, grants, and awards by category:* Academic interests/achievement: biological sciences, business, communication, computer science, education, English, foreign languages, general academic interests/achievements, health fields, humanities, mathematics, physical sciences, premedicine, religion/biblical studies, social sciences. *Creative arts/performance:* music, theater/drama. *Special achievements/activities:* cheerleading/drum major, leadership, religious involvement. *Special characteristics:* children and siblings of alumni, children of faculty/staff, general special characteristics, international students, relatives of clergy, religious affiliation, siblings of current students, spouses of current students. *Tuition waivers:* Full or partial for children of alumni, employees or children of employees. *ROTC:* Army cooperative, Air Force cooperative.

**LOANS** *Student loans:* $7,223,219 (44% need-based, 56% non-need-based). 79% of past graduating class borrowed through all loan programs. *Average indebtedness per student:* $28,902. *Average need-based loan:* Freshmen: $3512. Undergraduates: $4146. *Parent loans:* $1,536,681 (100% non-need-based). *Programs:* Federal Direct (Subsidized and Unsubsidized Stafford, PLUS), Perkins.

**WORK-STUDY** *Federal work-study:* Total amount: $172,417; jobs available. *State or other work-study/employment:* Total amount: $92,611 (100% non-need-based). Part-time jobs available.

**ATHLETIC AWARDS** Total amount: $4,793,683 (100% non-need-based).

**APPLYING FOR FINANCIAL AID** *Required financial aid form:* FAFSA. *Financial aid deadline:* Continuous. *Notification date:* Continuous beginning 1/1. Students must reply by 8/5.

**CONTACT** Mrs. Kristen M. Gibbs, Director of Financial Assistance, Central Methodist University, 411 Central Methodist Square, Fayette, MO 65248-1198, 660-248-6244 or toll-free 888-CMU-1854 (in-state), 877-CMU-1854 (out-of-state). *Fax:* 660-248-6288. *E-mail:* kgibbs@centralmethodist.edu. *Website:* http://www.centralmethodist.edu/.

# CENTRAL MICHIGAN UNIVERSITY
## Mount Pleasant, MI

| Tuition & fees (MI res): $11,550 | Average undergraduate aid package: $12,940 |
|---|---|

**ABOUT THE INSTITUTION** State-supported, coed. *Awards:* certificates, bachelor's, master's, and doctoral degrees. 130 undergraduate majors. *Total enrollment:* 27,002. Undergraduates: 20,794. Freshmen: 3,811. Federal methodology is used as a basis for awarding need-based institutional aid.

**UNDERGRADUATE EXPENSES for 2015–2016** *Application fee:* $35. *Tuition, state resident:* full-time $11,550; part-time $385 per credit hour. *Tuition, nonresident:* full-time $23,670; part-time $789 per credit hour. Full-time tuition and fees vary according to location. Part-time tuition and fees vary according to location. *College room and board:* $8780; *Room only:* $4390. Room and board charges vary according to board plan and housing facility.

**FRESHMAN FINANCIAL AID (Fall 2013)** 2,666 applied for aid; of those 76% were deemed to have need. 96% of freshmen with need received aid; of those 52% had need fully met. *Average percent of need met:* 83% (excluding resources awarded to replace EFC). *Average financial aid package:* $13,814 (excluding resources awarded to replace EFC). 14% of all full-time freshmen had no need and received non-need-based gift aid.

**UNDERGRADUATE FINANCIAL AID (Fall 2013)** 14,115 applied for aid; of those 80% were deemed to have need. 98% of undergraduates with need received aid; of those 49% had need fully met. *Average percent of need met:* 79% (excluding resources awarded to replace EFC). *Average financial aid package:* $12,940 (excluding resources awarded to replace EFC). 9% of all full-time undergraduates had no need and received non-need-based gift aid.

**GIFT AID (NEED-BASED)** *Total amount:* $48,330,123 (54% federal, 3% state, 40% institutional, 3% external sources). *Receiving aid:* Freshmen: 56% (1,661); all full-time undergraduates: 48% (8,395). *Average award:* Freshmen: $8069; Undergraduates: $5961. *Scholarships, grants, and awards:* Federal Pell, FSEOG, state, private, college/university gift aid from institutional funds.

**GIFT AID (NON-NEED-BASED)** *Total amount:* $8,036,764 (1% state, 88% institutional, 11% external sources). *Receiving aid:* Freshmen: 4% (110). Undergraduates: 2% (387). *Average award:* Freshmen: $4161. Undergraduates: $3838. *Scholarships, grants, and awards by category: Academic interests/achievement:* 4,184 awards ($13,045,195 total): biological sciences, business, communication, computer science, education, engineering/technologies, English, foreign languages, general academic interests/achievements, health fields, home economics, humanities, international studies, mathematics, military science, physical sciences, premedicine, religion/biblical studies, social sciences. *Creative arts/performance:* 155 awards ($295,343 total): applied art and design, art/fine arts, cinema/film/broadcasting, creative writing, dance, general creative arts/performance, journalism/publications, music, performing arts, theater/drama. *Special achievements/activities:* 726 awards ($6,187,062 total): general special achievements/activities, leadership. *Special characteristics:* 205 awards ($1,213,999 total): children and siblings of alumni, children of faculty/staff, ethnic background, international students, local/state students, out-of-state students. *Tuition waivers:* Full or partial for children of alumni, employees or children of employees, senior citizens. *ROTC:* Army, Air Force cooperative.

**LOANS** *Student loans:* $98,470,118 (72% need-based, 28% non-need-based). 74% of past graduating class borrowed through all loan programs. *Average indebtedness per student:* $33,545. *Average need-based loan:* Freshmen: $6190. Undergraduates: $7296. *Parent loans:* $31,738,191 (31% need-based, 69% non-need-based). *Programs:* Federal Direct (Subsidized and Unsubsidized Stafford, PLUS), Perkins, college/university.

**WORK-STUDY** *Federal work-study:* 861 jobs averaging $1471. *State or other work-study/employment:* Total amount: $10,427,160 (31% need-based, 69% non-need-based). 4,468 part-time jobs averaging $2334.

**ATHLETIC AWARDS** Total amount: $4,762,179 (36% need-based, 64% non-need-based).

**APPLYING FOR FINANCIAL AID** *Required financial aid form:* FAFSA. *Financial aid deadline (priority):* 3/1. *Notification date:* Continuous beginning 3/25. Students must reply by 4/1.

**CONTACT** Mr. Kirk M. Yats, Director of Scholarships and Financial Aid, Central Michigan University, Mount Pleasant, MI 48859, 989-774-3674 or toll-free 888-292-5366. *Fax:* 989-774-3634. *E-mail:* cmuosfa@cmich.edu. *Website:* http://www.cmich.edu/.

# CENTRAL PENN COLLEGE
## Summerdale, PA

**CONTACT** Kathy Shepard, Financial Aid Director, Central Penn College, College Hill and Valley Roads, Summerdale, PA 17093, 717-728-2261 or toll-free 800-759-2727. *Fax:* 717-728-2350. *E-mail:* financial-aid@centralpenn.edu. *Website:* http://www.centralpenn.edu/.

# CENTRAL STATE UNIVERSITY
## Wilberforce, OH

**ABOUT THE INSTITUTION** State-supported, coed. *Awards:* bachelor's degrees. 35 undergraduate majors. *Total enrollment:* 1,751. Undergraduates: 1,733. Freshmen: 402.

**GIFT AID (NEED-BASED)** *Scholarships, grants, and awards:* Federal Pell, FSEOG, state, private, college/university gift aid from institutional funds.

**GIFT AID (NON-NEED-BASED)** *Scholarships, grants, and awards by category: Academic interests/achievement:* business, computer science, education, engineering/technologies, general academic interests/achievements, physical sciences. *Creative arts/performance:* music. *Special characteristics:* children of faculty/staff, veterans, veterans' children.

**APPLYING FOR FINANCIAL AID** *Required financial aid form:* FAFSA.

**CONTACT** Sonia Slomba, Director of Student Financial Aid, Central State University, PO Box 1004, Wilberforce, OH 45384, 937-376-6579 or toll-free 800-388-CSU1 (in-state), 800-388-2781 (out-of-state). *Fax:* 937-376-6519. *E-mail:* sslomba@ centralstate.edu. *Website:* http://www.centralstate.edu/.

# CENTRAL WASHINGTON UNIVERSITY
## Ellensburg, WA

| Tuition & fees (WA res): $8321 | Average undergraduate aid package: $11,495 |
|---|---|

**ABOUT THE INSTITUTION** State-supported, coed. *Awards:* certificates, bachelor's, and master's degrees. 138 undergraduate majors. *Total enrollment:* 11,794. Undergraduates: 10,964. Freshmen: 1,362. Federal methodology is used as a basis for awarding need-based institutional aid.

**UNDERGRADUATE EXPENSES for 2015–2016** *Application fee:* $50. *Tuition, state resident:* full-time $7245; part-time $265 per credit hour. *Tuition, nonresident:* full-time $20,304; part-time $680 per credit hour. *Required fees:* full-time $1076; $15.50 per credit or $303 per term. Full-time tuition and fees vary according to course load, degree level, location, and reciprocity agreements. Part-time tuition and fees vary according to course load, degree level, location, and reciprocity agreements. *College room and board:* $9316. Room and board charges vary according to board plan and housing facility.

**FRESHMAN FINANCIAL AID (Fall 2013)** 1,340 applied for aid; of those 73% were deemed to have need. 99% of freshmen with need received aid; of those 55% had need fully met. *Average percent of need met:* 88% (excluding resources awarded to replace EFC). *Average financial aid package:* $11,941 (excluding resources awarded to replace EFC).

**UNDERGRADUATE FINANCIAL AID (Fall 2013)** 8,776 applied for aid; of those 79% were deemed to have need. 91% of undergraduates with need received aid; of those 50% had need fully met. *Average percent of need met:* 83% (excluding resources awarded to replace EFC). *Average financial aid package:* $11,495 (excluding resources awarded to replace EFC). 1% of all full-time undergraduates had no need and received non-need-based gift aid.

**GIFT AID (NEED-BASED)** *Total amount:* $41,801,040 (41% federal, 44% state, 9% institutional, 6% external sources). *Receiving aid:* Freshmen: 57% (836); all full-time undergraduates: 55% (5,196). *Average award:* Freshmen: $9213; Undergraduates: $8407. *Scholarships, grants, and awards:* Federal Pell, FSEOG, state, private, college/university gift aid from institutional funds.

**GIFT AID (NON-NEED-BASED)** *Total amount:* $464,608 (5% state, 5% institutional, 90% external sources). *Receiving aid:* Freshmen: 43% (635). Undergraduates: 22% (2,017). *Average award:* Undergraduates: $1448. *Scholarships, grants, and awards by category:* Academic interests/achievement: general academic interests/achievements. *Creative arts/performance:* art/fine arts, general creative arts/performance, music, theater/drama. *Special achievements/activities:* leadership. *Special characteristics:* children and siblings of alumni, children of faculty/staff, children of public servants, local/state students, members of minority groups, out-of-state students, public servants, veterans, veterans' children. *Tuition waivers:* Full or partial for employees or children of employees, senior citizens. *ROTC:* Army, Air Force.

**LOANS** *Student loans:* $47,049,866 (86% need-based, 14% non-need-based). 69% of past graduating class borrowed through all loan programs. *Average indebtedness per student:* $26,360. *Average need-based loan:* Freshmen: $3820. Undergraduates: $4382. *Parent loans:* $18,792,394 (66% need-based, 34% non-need-based). *Programs:* Federal Direct (Subsidized and Unsubsidized Stafford, PLUS), Perkins, college/university.

**WORK-STUDY** *Federal work-study:* jobs available. *State or other work-study/employment:* Total amount: $286,248 (100% need-based). Part-time jobs available.

**ATHLETIC AWARDS** Total amount: $1,354,299 (70% need-based, 30% non-need-based).

**APPLYING FOR FINANCIAL AID** *Required financial aid form:* FAFSA. *Financial aid deadline (priority):* 3/1. *Notification date:* Continuous beginning 5/15. Students must reply within 4 weeks of notification.

**CONTACT** Mr. Adrian Naranjo, Director of Student Financial Services, Central Washington University, 400 East University Way, Ellensburg, WA 98926-7495, 509-963-2091. *Fax:* 509-963-1788. *E-mail:* finaid@cwu.edu.
*Website:* http://www.cwu.edu/.

# CENTRAL YESHIVA TOMCHEI TMIMIM-LUBAVITCH
## Brooklyn, NY

**CONTACT** Rabbi Moshe M. Gluckowsky, Director of Financial Aid , Central Yeshiva Tomchei Tmimim Lubavitch, 841-853 Ocean Parkway, Brooklyn, NY 11230, 718-859-2277.

# CENTRE COLLEGE
## Danville, KY

| Tuition & fees: $38,200 | Average undergraduate aid package: $28,761 |
| --- | --- |

**ABOUT THE INSTITUTION** Independent Presbyterian Church (U.S.A.), coed. *Awards:* bachelor's degrees. 28 undergraduate majors. *Total enrollment:* 1,387. Undergraduates: 1,387. Freshmen: 386. Both federal and institutional methodology are used as a basis for awarding need-based institutional aid.

**UNDERGRADUATE EXPENSES** for 2015–2016 *Comprehensive fee:* $47,820 Includes full-time tuition ($38,200) and room and board ($9620). *College room only:* $4810. *Part-time tuition:* $1375 per credit hour.

**FRESHMAN FINANCIAL AID (Fall 2014, est.)** 313 applied for aid; of those 76% were deemed to have need. 100% of freshmen with need received aid; of those 35% had need fully met. *Average percent of need met:* 86% (excluding resources awarded to replace EFC). *Average financial aid package:* $29,897 (excluding resources awarded to replace EFC). 35% of all full-time freshmen had no need and received non-need-based gift aid.

**UNDERGRADUATE FINANCIAL AID (Fall 2014, est.)** 979 applied for aid; of those 82% were deemed to have need. 100% of undergraduates with need received aid; of those 28% had need fully met. *Average percent of need met:* 84% (excluding resources awarded to replace EFC). *Average financial aid package:* $28,761 (excluding resources awarded to replace EFC). 38% of all full-time undergraduates had no need and received non-need-based gift aid.

**GIFT AID (NEED-BASED)** *Total amount:* $20,255,629 (5% federal, 11% state, 82% institutional, 2% external sources). *Receiving aid:* Freshmen: 61% (237); all full-time undergraduates: 58% (796). *Average award:* Freshmen: $27,338; Undergraduates: $25,491. *Scholarships, grants, and awards:* Federal Pell, FSEOG, state, private, college/university gift aid from institutional funds.

**GIFT AID (NON-NEED-BASED)** *Total amount:* $9,946,133 (6% state, 92% institutional, 2% external sources). *Average award:* Freshmen: $18,619. Undergraduates: $18,766. *Scholarships, grants, and awards by category:* Academic interests/achievement: foreign languages, general academic interests/achievements. *Creative arts/performance:* music, theater/drama. *Special achievements/activities:* community service. *Special characteristics:* children and siblings of alumni, children of faculty/staff, ethnic background, first-generation college students. *Tuition waivers:* Full or partial for employees or children of employees. *ROTC:* Army cooperative, Air Force cooperative.

**LOANS** *Student loans:* $5,014,087 (57% need-based, 43% non-need-based). 54% of past graduating class borrowed through all loan programs. *Average indebtedness per student:* $25,994. *Average need-based loan:* Freshmen: $3282. Undergraduates: $4485. *Parent loans:* $1,905,821 (100% non-need-based). *Programs:* Federal Direct (Subsidized and Unsubsidized Stafford, PLUS), Perkins, college/university.

**WORK-STUDY** *Federal work-study:* Total amount: $592,944; jobs available. *State or other work-study/employment:* Part-time jobs available.

**APPLYING FOR FINANCIAL AID** *Required financial aid forms:* FAFSA, institution's own form. *Financial aid deadline:* 1/31. *Notification date:* 3/19. Students must reply by 5/1.

**CONTACT** Mr. Kevin Lamb, Director of Financial Aid/Associate Dean of Admission and Financial Aid, Centre College, 600 West Walnut Street, Danville, KY 40422-1394, 859-238-5365 or toll-free 800-423-6236. *Fax:* 859-238-8719. *E-mail:* finaid@centre.edu.
*Website:* http://www.centre.edu/.

# CENTRO DE ESTUDIOS MULTIDISCIPLINARIOS
## Bayamn, PR

**CONTACT** Financial Aid Office, Centro de Estudios Multidisciplinarios, 25 Degetau Street, Bayamn, PR 00961, 787-780-8900.
*Website:* http://www.cempr.edu/.

# CENTRO DE ESTUDIOS MULTIDISCIPLINARIOS
## Humacao, PR

**CONTACT** Financial Aid Office, Centro de Estudios Multidisciplinarios, 6 Dr. Vidal Street, Humacao, PR 00791, 809-852-5530.
*Website:* http://www.cempr.edu/.

# CHADRON STATE COLLEGE
## Chadron, NE

**CONTACT** Ms. Sherry Douglas, Director of Financial Aid, Chadron State College, 1000 Main Street, Chadron, NE 69337, 308-432-6230 or toll-free 800-242-3766. *Fax:* 308-432-6229. *E-mail:* finaid@csc.edu.
*Website:* http://www.csc.edu/.

## CHAMBERLAIN COLLEGE OF NURSING
### Phoenix, AZ

**CONTACT** Financial Aid Office, Chamberlain College of Nursing, 2149 West Dunlap Avenue, Phoenix, AZ 85021, 602-331-2720 or toll-free 888-556-8CCN.
*Website:* http://www.chamberlain.edu/.

## CHAMBERLAIN COLLEGE OF NURSING
### Jacksonville, FL

**CONTACT** Financial Aid Office, Chamberlain College of Nursing, 5200 Belfort Road, Jacksonville, FL 32256-6040, 904-251-8100 or toll-free 888-556-8CCN.
*Website:* http://www.chamberlain.edu/.

## CHAMBERLAIN COLLEGE OF NURSING
### Miramar, FL

**CONTACT** Financial Aid Office, Chamberlain College of Nursing, 2300 SW 145th Avenue, Miramar, FL 33027, 954-885-3510.
*Website:* http://www.chamberlain.edu/.

## CHAMBERLAIN COLLEGE OF NURSING
### Atlanta, GA

**CONTACT** Financial Aid Office, Chamberlain College of Nursing, 5775 Peachtree-Dunwoody Road, NE, Suite A100, Atlanta, GA 30342, 404-250-8500.
*Website:* http://www.chamberlain.edu/.

## CHAMBERLAIN COLLEGE OF NURSING
### Addison, IL

**CONTACT** Financial Aid Office, Chamberlain College of Nursing, 1221 N. Swift Road, Addison, IL 60101-6106, 630-953-3680 or toll-free 888-556-8CCN.
*Website:* http://www.chamberlain.edu/.

## CHAMBERLAIN COLLEGE OF NURSING
### Chicago, IL

**CONTACT** Financial Aid Office, Chamberlain College of Nursing, 3300 N. Campbell Avenue, Chicago, IL 60618, 773-961-3000 or toll-free 888-556-8CCN.
*Website:* http://www.chamberlain.edu/.

## CHAMBERLAIN COLLEGE OF NURSING
### Tinley Park, IL

**CONTACT** Financial Aid Office, Chamberlain College of Nursing, 18624 West Creek Drive, Tinley Park, IL 60477, 708-560-2000.
*Website:* http://www.chamberlain.edu/.

## CHAMBERLAIN COLLEGE OF NURSING
### Indianapolis, IN

**CONTACT** Financial Aid Office, Chamberlain College of Nursing, 9100 Keystone Crossing, Suite 600, Indianapolis, IN 46240, 317-816-7335.
*Website:* http://www.chamberlain.edu/.

## CHAMBERLAIN COLLEGE OF NURSING
### Troy, MI

**CONTACT** Financial Aid Office, Chamberlain College of Nursing, 200 Kirts Boulevard, Troy, MI 48084, 248-817-4140.
*Website:* http://www.chamberlain.edu/.

## CHAMBERLAIN COLLEGE OF NURSING
### St. Louis, MO

**CONTACT** Financial Aid Counselor, Chamberlain College of Nursing, 11830 Westline Industrial Drive, Suite 106, St. Louis, MO 63146, 314-991-6200 or toll-free 888-556-8CCN.
*Website:* http://www.chamberlain.edu/.

## CHAMBERLAIN COLLEGE OF NURSING
### Las Vegas, NV

**CONTACT** Financial Aid Office, Chamberlain College of Nursing, 9901 Covington Cross Drive, Las Vegas, NV 89144, 702-786-1660.
*Website:* http://www.chamberlain.edu/.

## CHAMBERLAIN COLLEGE OF NURSING
### North Brunswick, NJ

**CONTACT** Financial Aid Office, Chamberlain College of Nursing, 630 U.S. Highway One, North Brunswick, NJ 08902, 732-875-1300.
*Website:* http://www.chamberlain.edu/.

# CHAMBERLAIN COLLEGE OF NURSING
### Cleveland, OH

**CONTACT** Financial Aid Office, Chamberlain College of Nursing, 6700 Euclid Avenue, Suite 201, Cleveland, OH 44103, 216-361-6005. *Website:* http://www.chamberlain.edu/.

# CHAMBERLAIN COLLEGE OF NURSING
### Columbus, OH

**CONTACT** Financial Aid Office, Chamberlain College of Nursing, 1350 Alum Creek Drive, Columbus, OH 43209, 614-252-8890 or toll-free 888-556-8CCN. *Website:* http://www.chamberlain.edu/.

# CHAMBERLAIN COLLEGE OF NURSING
### Houston, TX

**CONTACT** Financial Aid Office, Chamberlain College of Nursing, 11025 Equity Drive, Houston, TX 77041, 713-277-9800. *Website:* http://www.chamberlain.edu/.

# CHAMBERLAIN COLLEGE OF NURSING
### Pearland, TX

**CONTACT** Financial Aid Office, Chamberlain College of Nursing, 12000 Shadow Creek Parkway, Pearland, TX 77584, 832-664-7000. *Website:* http://www.chamberlain.edu/.

# CHAMBERLAIN COLLEGE OF NURSING
### Arlington, VA

**CONTACT** Financial Aid Office, Chamberlain College of Nursing, 2450 Crystal Drive, Arlington, VA 22202, 703-416-7300 or toll-free 888-556-8CCN. *Website:* http://www.chamberlain.edu/.

# CHAMINADE UNIVERSITY OF HONOLULU
### Honolulu, HI

| Tuition & fees: $20,940 | Average undergraduate aid package: $18,271 |
|---|---|

**ABOUT THE INSTITUTION** Independent Roman Catholic, coed. *Awards:* certificates, associate, bachelor's, and master's degrees. 27 undergraduate majors. *Total enrollment:* 1,976. Undergraduates: 1,306. Freshmen: 239. Federal methodology is used as a basis for awarding need-based institutional aid.

**UNDERGRADUATE EXPENSES for 2015-2016** *Application fee:* $50. *Comprehensive fee:* $32,580 includes full-time tuition ($20,810), mandatory fees ($130), and room and board ($11,640). Full-time tuition and fees vary according to course load and program. Room and board charges vary according to board plan and housing facility. *Part-time tuition:* $694 per credit. Part-time tuition and fees vary according to course load and program.

**FRESHMAN FINANCIAL AID (Fall 2013)** 231 applied for aid; of those 85% were deemed to have need. 100% of freshmen with need received aid; of those 24% had need fully met. *Average percent of need met:* 78% (excluding resources awarded to replace EFC). *Average financial aid package:* $19,211 (excluding resources awarded to replace EFC). 10% of all full-time freshmen had no need and received non-need-based gift aid.

**UNDERGRADUATE FINANCIAL AID (Fall 2013)** 971 applied for aid; of those 91% were deemed to have need. 100% of undergraduates with need received aid; of those 16% had need fully met. *Average percent of need met:* 71% (excluding resources awarded to replace EFC). *Average financial aid package:* $18,271 (excluding resources awarded to replace EFC). 19% of all full-time undergraduates had no need and received non-need-based gift aid.

**GIFT AID (NEED-BASED)** *Receiving aid:* Freshmen: 74% (192); all full-time undergraduates: 65% (794). *Average award:* Freshmen: $4644; Undergraduates: $4802. *Scholarships, grants, and awards:* Federal Pell, FSEOG, private, college/university gift aid from institutional funds, Academic Competitiveness Grants, National SMART Grants, TEACH Grants, LEAP grants.

**GIFT AID (NON-NEED-BASED)** *Receiving aid:* Freshmen: 76% (196). Undergraduates: 69% (841). *Average award:* Freshmen: $6851. Undergraduates: $6631. *Scholarships, grants, and awards by category: Academic interests/achievement:* 1,154 awards ($7,837,557 total): general academic interests/achievements. *Special achievements/activities:* 103 awards ($1,191,770 total): community service, memberships, religious involvement. *Special characteristics:* 146 awards ($1,547,780 total): children of faculty/staff, ethnic background, religious affiliation, siblings of current students. *ROTC:* Army cooperative, Air Force cooperative.

**LOANS** *Student loans:* 64% of past graduating class borrowed through all loan programs. *Average indebtedness per student:* $26,323. *Average need-based loan:* Freshmen: $3234. Undergraduates: $4217. *Programs:* Federal Direct (Subsidized and Unsubsidized Stafford, PLUS), alternative loans.

**WORK-STUDY** *Federal work-study:* 813 jobs averaging $2615.

**APPLYING FOR FINANCIAL AID** *Required financial aid form:* FAFSA. *Financial aid deadline:* Continuous. *Notification date:* Continuous.

**CONTACT** Amy Takiguchi, Director of Financial Aid, Chaminade University of Honolulu, 3140 Waialae Avenue, Honolulu, HI 96816-1578, 808-735-4780 or toll-free 800-735-3733. *Fax:* 808-739-8362. *E-mail:* finaid@chaminade.edu. *Website:* http://www.chaminade.edu/.

# CHAMPLAIN COLLEGE
### Burlington, VT

| Tuition & fees: $32,900 | Average undergraduate aid package: $21,773 |
|---|---|

**ABOUT THE INSTITUTION** Independent, coed. *Awards:* certificates, associate, bachelor's, and master's degrees. 47 undergraduate majors. *Total enrollment:* 3,585. Undergraduates: 3,124. Freshmen: 637. Federal methodology is used as a basis for awarding need-based institutional aid.

**UNDERGRADUATE EXPENSES for 2015-2016** *Comprehensive fee:* $46,650 includes full-time tuition ($32,800), mandatory fees ($100), and room and board ($13,750). *Part-time tuition:* $1367 per credit hour. *Payment plan:* Tuition prepayment.

**FRESHMAN FINANCIAL AID (Fall 2014, est.)** 551 applied for aid; of those 85% were deemed to have need. 100% of freshmen with need received aid; of those 15% had need fully met. *Average percent of need met:* 69% (excluding resources awarded to replace EFC). *Average financial aid package:* $23,589 (excluding resources awarded to replace EFC). 21% of all full-time freshmen had no need and received non-need-based gift aid.

**UNDERGRADUATE FINANCIAL AID (Fall 2014, est.)** 1,852 applied for aid; of those 87% were deemed to have need. 100% of undergraduates with need received aid; of those 13% had need fully met. *Average percent of need met:* 66% (excluding resources awarded to replace EFC). *Average financial aid package:* $21,773 (excluding resources awarded to replace EFC). 20% of all full-time undergraduates had no need and received non-need-based gift aid.

**GIFT AID (NEED-BASED)** *Total amount:* $26,111,452 (16% federal, 5% state, 77% institutional, 2% external sources). *Receiving aid:* Freshmen: 73% (465); all full-time undergraduates: 69% (1,593). *Average award:* Freshmen: $17,089; Undergrad-

uates: $15,566. **Scholarships, grants, and awards:** Federal Pell, FSEOG, state, private, college/university gift aid from institutional funds.
**GIFT AID (NON-NEED-BASED) Total amount:** $4,577,015 (15% federal, 85% institutional). **Receiving aid:** Freshmen: 8% (48). Undergraduates: 6% (133). **Average award:** Freshmen: $8182. Undergraduates: $8144. **Scholarships, grants, and awards by category:** Academic interests/achievement: business, communication, computer science, education, engineering/technologies, general academic interests/achievement, health fields, social sciences. Special achievements/activities: leadership. Special characteristics: first-generation college students, general special characteristics, international students, members of minority groups. **Tuition waivers:** Full or partial for employees or children of employees. **ROTC:** Army cooperative.
**LOANS Student loans:** $15,582,854 (85% need-based, 15% non-need-based). 73% of past graduating class borrowed through all loan programs. Average indebtedness per student: $35,444. **Average need-based loan:** Freshmen: $4189. Undergraduates: $4650. **Parent loans:** $11,948,636 (57% need-based, 43% non-need-based). **Programs:** Federal Direct (Subsidized and Unsubsidized Stafford, PLUS), Perkins, state.
**WORK-STUDY Federal work-study:** Total amount: $2,896,473; jobs available.
**APPLYING FOR FINANCIAL AID Required financial aid form:** FAFSA. **Financial aid deadline:** 2/15. **Notification date:** 3/30. Students must reply by 5/1 or within 2 weeks of notification.
**CONTACT** Kristi Jovell, Director of Financial Aid, Champlain College, 163 South Willard Street, Burlington, VT 05401, 802-860-2777 or toll-free 800-570-5858. Fax: 802-860-2775. E-mail: kjovell@champlain.edu.
Website: http://www.champlain.edu/.

# CHAPMAN UNIVERSITY
## Orange, CA

| Tuition & fees: $47,260 | Average undergraduate aid package: $32,247 |
|---|---|

**ABOUT THE INSTITUTION** Independent Christian Church (Disciples of Christ), coed. **Awards:** bachelor's, master's, and doctoral degrees. 49 undergraduate majors. **Total enrollment:** 8,132. Undergraduates: 5,281. Freshmen: 1,422. Both federal and institutional methodology are used as a basis for awarding need-based institutional aid.
**UNDERGRADUATE EXPENSES for 2015–2016 Application fee:** $65. **Comprehensive fee:** $61,090 includes full-time tuition ($46,500), mandatory fees ($760), and room and board ($13,830). **College room only:** $9444. Room and board charges vary according to board plan and housing facility. **Part-time tuition:** $1445 per credit. **Payment plan:** Tuition prepayment.
**FRESHMAN FINANCIAL AID (Fall 2014, est.)** 1,080 applied for aid; of those 80% were deemed to have need. 100% of freshmen with need received aid; of those 12% had need fully met. **Average percent of need met:** 77% (excluding resources awarded to replace EFC). **Average financial aid package:** $33,988 (excluding resources awarded to replace EFC). 24% of all full-time freshmen had no need and received non-need-based gift aid.
**UNDERGRADUATE FINANCIAL AID (Fall 2014, est.)** 4,038 applied for aid; of those 87% were deemed to have need. 99% of undergraduates with need received aid; of those 12% had need fully met. **Average percent of need met:** 72% (excluding resources awarded to replace EFC). **Average financial aid package:** $32,247 (excluding resources awarded to replace EFC). 23% of all full-time undergraduates had no need and received non-need-based gift aid.
**GIFT AID (NEED-BASED) Total amount:** $88,556,626 (7% federal, 7% state, 85% institutional, 1% external sources). **Receiving aid:** Freshmen: 57% (803); all full-time undergraduates: 53% (3,161). **Average award:** Freshmen: $16,732; Undergraduates: $15,855. **Scholarships, grants, and awards:** Federal Pell, FSEOG, state, private, college/university gift aid from institutional funds.
**GIFT AID (NON-NEED-BASED) Total amount:** $23,082,895 (98% institutional, 2% external sources). **Receiving aid:** Freshmen: 47% (662). Undergraduates: 39% (2,340). **Average award:** Freshmen: $15,999. Undergraduates: $16,618. **Scholarships, grants, and awards by category:** Academic interests/achievement: 3,452 awards ($57,025,654 total): biological sciences, general academic interests/achievements, physical sciences. Creative arts/performance: 380 awards ($1,304,534 total): art/fine arts, cinema/film/broadcasting, creative writing, dance, music, performing arts, theater/drama. Special characteristics: 61 awards ($60,428 total):

children and siblings of alumni. **Tuition waivers:** Full or partial for employees or children of employees. **ROTC:** Army cooperative, Air Force cooperative.
**LOANS Student loans:** $35,971,139 (87% need-based, 13% non-need-based). 62% of past graduating class borrowed through all loan programs. Average indebtedness per student: $27,979. **Average need-based loan:** Freshmen: $3785. Undergraduates: $4825. **Parent loans:** $6,931,314 (37% need-based, 63% non-need-based). **Programs:** Federal Direct (Subsidized and Unsubsidized Stafford), Perkins.
**WORK-STUDY Federal work-study:** Total amount: $9,003,458; 3,018 jobs averaging $2942.
**APPLYING FOR FINANCIAL AID Required financial aid forms:** FAFSA, state aid form. **Financial aid deadline (priority):** 3/2. **Notification date:** Continuous beginning 3/15. Students must reply within 3 weeks of notification.
**CONTACT** Mr. Jim Whitaker, Associate Vice Chancellor, Enrollment Management/Chief Financial Aid Officer, Chapman University, One University Drive, Orange, CA 92866, 714-532-6050 or toll-free 888-CUAPPLY. Fax: 714-997-6743. E-mail: whitaker@chapman.edu.
Website: http://www.chapman.edu/.

# CHARLES DREW UNIVERSITY OF MEDICINE AND SCIENCE
## Los Angeles, CA

**CONTACT** Financial Aid Office, Charles Drew University of Medicine and Science, 1731 East 120th Street, Los Angeles, CA 90059, 323-563-4824. Fax: 323-569-0597.
Website: http://www.cdrewu.edu/.

# CHARLESTON SOUTHERN UNIVERSITY
## Charleston, SC

**CONTACT** Mr. Jim Rhoden, Director of Admissions, Charleston Southern University, PO Box 118087, 9200 University Boulevard, Charleston, SC 29423-8087, 843-863-7050 or toll-free 800-947-7474. Fax: 843-863-7070.
Website: http://www.charlestonsouthern.edu/.

# CHARLOTTE CHRISTIAN COLLEGE AND THEOLOGICAL SEMINARY
## Charlotte, NC

| Tuition & fees: N/R | Average undergraduate aid package: $8416 |
|---|---|

**ABOUT THE INSTITUTION** Independent Christian, coed. 2 undergraduate majors. Federal methodology is used as a basis for awarding need-based institutional aid.
**FRESHMAN FINANCIAL AID (Fall 2014, est.)** 2 applied for aid; of those 100% were deemed to have need. 100% of freshmen with need received aid; of those 100% had need fully met. **Average percent of need met:** 100% (excluding resources awarded to replace EFC). **Average financial aid package:** $8726 (excluding resources awarded to replace EFC).
**UNDERGRADUATE FINANCIAL AID (Fall 2014, est.)** 49 applied for aid; of those 100% were deemed to have need. 100% of undergraduates with need received aid; of those 100% had need fully met. **Average percent of need met:** 100% (excluding resources awarded to replace EFC). **Average financial aid package:** $8416 (excluding resources awarded to replace EFC).
**GIFT AID (NEED-BASED) Total amount:** $873,761 (97% federal, 3% institutional). **Receiving aid:** Freshmen: 100% (2); all full-time undergraduates: 84% (43). **Average award:** Freshmen: $8227; Undergraduates: $5396. **Scholarships, grants, and awards:** Federal Pell, FSEOG, private, college/university gift aid from institutional funds, Veterans Education Benefits (GI Bill).
**GIFT AID (NON-NEED-BASED) Total amount:** $24,304 (100% institutional). **Scholarships, grants, and awards by category:** Academic interests/

*achievement:* education, foreign languages, general academic interests/achievements, religion/biblical studies. *Special achievements/activities:* memberships, religious involvement. *Special characteristics:* religious affiliation.

**LOANS Student loans:** $849,457 (100% need-based). 25% of past graduating class borrowed through all loan programs. *Average indebtedness per student:* $39,607. **Average need-based loan:** Freshmen: $3500. Undergraduates: $3536. **Programs:** Federal Direct (Subsidized and Unsubsidized Stafford, PLUS).

**WORK-STUDY Federal work-study:** Total amount: $9514; 4 jobs averaging $1758.

**APPLYING FOR FINANCIAL AID Required financial aid form:** FAFSA. *Financial aid deadline:* Continuous. *Notification date:* 3/15. Students must reply within 2 weeks of notification.

**CONTACT** Mr. Kenneth Neal Roach, Financial Aid Officer, Charlotte Christian College and Theological Seminary, 3117 Whiting Avenue, PO Box 790106, Charlotte, NC 28206-7901, 704-334-6882 Ext. 114. *Fax:* 704-334-6885. *E-mail:* kroach@charlottechristian.edu.

*Website:* http://www.charlottechristian.edu/.

# CHARTER OAK STATE COLLEGE
## New Britain, CT

**CONTACT** Velma Walters, Director, Financial Aid, Charter Oak State College, 55 Paul J. Manafort Drive, New Britain, CT 06053-2142, 860-832-3872. *Fax:* 860-832-3999. *E-mail:* sfa@charteroak.edu.
*Website:* http://www.charteroak.edu/.

# CHATHAM UNIVERSITY
## Pittsburgh, PA

| Tuition & fees: $34,440 | Average undergraduate aid package: $23,512 |
|---|---|

**ABOUT THE INSTITUTION** Independent, coed, primarily women. *Awards:* certificates, bachelor's, master's, and doctoral degrees. 43 undergraduate majors. *Total enrollment:* 2,134. Undergraduates: 932. Freshmen: 104. Both federal and institutional methodology are used as a basis for awarding need-based institutional aid.

**UNDERGRADUATE EXPENSES for 2015–2016 Application fee:** $35. **Comprehensive fee:** $45,160 includes full-time tuition ($33,200), mandatory fees ($1240), and room and board ($10,720). **College room only:** $5470. Room and board charges vary according to board plan and housing facility. **Part-time tuition:** $805 per credit. Part-time tuition and fees vary according to course load.

**FRESHMAN FINANCIAL AID (Fall 2014, est.)** 97 applied for aid; of those 89% were deemed to have need. 87% of freshmen with need received aid; of those 40% had need fully met. *Average percent of need met:* 80% (excluding resources awarded to replace EFC). *Average financial aid package:* $30,217 (excluding resources awarded to replace EFC). 12% of all full-time freshmen had no need and received non-need-based gift aid.

**UNDERGRADUATE FINANCIAL AID (Fall 2014, est.)** 476 applied for aid; of those 95% were deemed to have need. 100% of undergraduates with need received aid; of those 9% had need fully met. *Average percent of need met:* 82% (excluding resources awarded to replace EFC). *Average financial aid package:* $23,512 (excluding resources awarded to replace EFC). 5% of all full-time undergraduates had no need and received non-need-based gift aid.

**GIFT AID (NEED-BASED) Total amount:** $9,097,455 (12% federal, 8% state, 79% institutional, 1% external sources). *Receiving aid:* Freshmen: 69% (70); all full-time undergraduates: 64% (359). *Average award:* Freshmen: $8628; Undergraduates: $8351. *Scholarships, grants, and awards:* Federal Pell, FSEOG, state, private, college/university gift aid from institutional funds.

**GIFT AID (NON-NEED-BASED) Total amount:** $1,068,200 (1% federal, 95% institutional, 4% external sources). *Receiving aid:* Freshmen: 74% (75). Undergraduates: 62% (350). *Average award:* Freshmen: $17,750. Undergraduates: $16,007. *Scholarships, grants, and awards by category:* Academic interests/achievement: 488 awards ($6,725,178 total): general academic interests/achievements. *Creative arts/performance:* 13 awards ($23,000 total): applied art and design, art/fine arts, music. *Special achievements/activities:* 289 awards ($721,500 total): leadership.

---

*Special characteristics:* 19 awards ($2000 total): children and siblings of alumni, siblings of current students. *Tuition waivers:* Full or partial for employees or children of employees. *ROTC:* Army cooperative, Naval cooperative, Air Force cooperative.

**LOANS Student loans:** $3,177,792 (52% need-based, 48% non-need-based). 74% of past graduating class borrowed through all loan programs. *Average indebtedness per student:* $32,814. **Average need-based loan:** Freshmen: $3185. Undergraduates: $4591. **Parent loans:** $1,208,672 (87% need-based, 13% non-need-based). *Programs:* Federal Direct (Subsidized and Unsubsidized Stafford, PLUS), Perkins.

**WORK-STUDY Federal work-study:** Total amount: $375,380; 179 jobs averaging $2200. *State or other work-study/employment:* Total amount: $75,000 (100% non-need-based). Part-time jobs available.

**APPLYING FOR FINANCIAL AID Required financial aid form:** FAFSA. *Financial aid deadline:* Continuous. *Notification date:* Continuous beginning 3/1. Students must reply within 3 weeks of notification.

**CONTACT** Dr. Jennifer Burns, Director of Financial Aid, Chatham University, Woodland Road, Pittsburgh, PA 15232-2826, 412-365-1849 or toll-free 800-837-1290. *Fax:* 412-365-1643. *E-mail:* jburns@chatham.edu.

*Website:* http://www.chatham.edu/.

# CHESTNUT HILL COLLEGE
## Philadelphia, PA

| Tuition & fees: $33,120 | Average undergraduate aid package: $21,138 |
|---|---|

**ABOUT THE INSTITUTION** Independent Roman Catholic, coed. *Awards:* certificates, associate, bachelor's, master's, and doctoral degrees (profile includes figures from both traditional and accelerated (part-time) programs). 42 undergraduate majors. *Total enrollment:* 2,063. Undergraduates: 1,491. Freshmen: 186. Federal methodology is used as a basis for awarding need-based institutional aid.

**UNDERGRADUATE EXPENSES for 2015–2016 Application fee:** $35. **One-time required fee:** $425. **Comprehensive fee:** $43,320 includes full-time tuition ($32,930), mandatory fees ($190), and room and board ($10,200). Room and board charges vary according to board plan and housing facility. **Part-time tuition:** $705 per credit.

**FRESHMAN FINANCIAL AID (Fall 2014, est.)** 167 applied for aid; of those 86% were deemed to have need. 100% of freshmen with need received aid; of those 10% had need fully met. *Average percent of need met:* 71% (excluding resources awarded to replace EFC). *Average financial aid package:* $25,572 (excluding resources awarded to replace EFC). 4% of all full-time freshmen had no need and received non-need-based gift aid.

**UNDERGRADUATE FINANCIAL AID (Fall 2014, est.)** 1,082 applied for aid; of those 94% were deemed to have need. 100% of undergraduates with need received aid; of those 7% had need fully met. *Average percent of need met:* 62% (excluding resources awarded to replace EFC). *Average financial aid package:* $21,138 (excluding resources awarded to replace EFC). 2% of all full-time undergraduates had no need and received non-need-based gift aid.

**GIFT AID (NEED-BASED) Total amount:** $24,608,678 (13% federal, 7% state, 75% institutional, 5% external sources). *Receiving aid:* Freshmen: 71% (142); all full-time undergraduates: 85% (1,006). *Average award:* Freshmen: $21,715; Undergraduates: $16,914. *Scholarships, grants, and awards:* Federal Pell, FSEOG, state, private, college/university gift aid from institutional funds.

**GIFT AID (NON-NEED-BASED) Total amount:** $2,201,574 (1% state, 66% institutional, 33% external sources). *Receiving aid:* Freshmen: 5% (10). Undergraduates: 4% (50). *Average award:* Undergraduates: $9108. *Scholarships, grants, and awards by category:* Academic interests/achievement: general academic interests/achievements. *Tuition waivers:* Full or partial for employees or children of employees, senior citizens.

**LOANS Student loans:** $12,863,996 (84% need-based, 16% non-need-based). 90% of past graduating class borrowed through all loan programs. *Average indebtedness per student:* $35,376. **Parent loans:** $2,089,895 (48% need-based, 52% non-need-based). *Programs:* Federal Direct (Subsidized and Unsubsidized Stafford, PLUS), Perkins.

**WORK-STUDY Federal work-study:** Total amount: $185,922; 462 jobs averaging $1182.

**ATHLETIC AWARDS** Total amount: $1,236,031 (53% need-based, 47% non-need-based).

**APPLYING FOR FINANCIAL AID** *Required financial aid form:* FAFSA. *Financial aid deadline:* Continuous. *Notification date:* Continuous beginning 2/26.
**CONTACT** Ms. Sarah Fevig, Director of Financial Aid, Chestnut Hill College, 9601 Germantown Avenue, Philadelphia, PA 19118-2693, 215-248-7017 or toll-free 800-248-0052. *Fax:* 215-248-7217. *E-mail:* fevigs@chc.edu. *Website:* http://www.chc.edu/.

# CHEYNEY UNIVERSITY OF PENNSYLVANIA
## Cheyney, PA

**CONTACT** Mr. James Brown, Director of Financial Aid, Cheyney University of Pennsylvania, 1837 University Circle, Cheyney, PA 19319, 610-399-2302 or toll-free 800-CHEYNEY. *Fax:* 610-399-2411. *E-mail:* jbrown@cheyney.edu. *Website:* http://www.cheyney.edu/.

# CHICAGO STATE UNIVERSITY
## Chicago, IL

**ABOUT THE INSTITUTION** State-supported, coed. *Awards:* certificates, bachelor's, master's, and doctoral degrees. 34 undergraduate majors. *Total enrollment:* 5,211. Undergraduates: 3,912. Freshmen: 260.
**GIFT AID (NEED-BASED)** *Scholarships, grants, and awards:* Federal Pell, FSEOG, state, private, college/university gift aid from institutional funds, Federal Nursing.
**GIFT AID (NON-NEED-BASED)** *Scholarships, grants, and awards by category: Academic interests/achievement:* general academic interests/achievements, physical sciences. *Creative arts/performance:* art/fine arts, journalism/publications, music. *Special achievements/activities:* leadership.
**LOANS** *Programs:* Federal Direct (Subsidized and Unsubsidized Stafford, PLUS), Perkins, Federal Nursing.
**WORK-STUDY** *Federal work-study:* jobs available. *State or other work-study/employment:* Part-time jobs available.
**APPLYING FOR FINANCIAL AID** *Required financial aid form:* FAFSA.
**CONTACT** Ms. Cathy Davis, Director of Student Financial Aid, Chicago State University, 9501 South Martin Luther King Drive, Chicago, IL 60628, 773-995-2304. *E-mail:* cdavis58@csu.edu. *Website:* http://www.csu.edu/.

# CHOWAN UNIVERSITY
## Murfreesboro, NC

| Tuition & fees: $23,400 | Average undergraduate aid package: $28,876 |
|---|---|

**ABOUT THE INSTITUTION** Independent Baptist, coed. *Awards:* associate, bachelor's, and master's degrees. 50 undergraduate majors. *Total enrollment:* 1,484. Undergraduates: 1,478. Freshmen: 531. Federal methodology is used as a basis for awarding need-based institutional aid.
**UNDERGRADUATE EXPENSES** for 2015–2016 *Application fee:* $20. *Comprehensive fee:* $32,080 includes full-time tuition ($23,400) and room and board ($8680). Full-time tuition and fees vary according to class time, course load, and program. Room and board charges vary according to board plan and housing facility. *Part-time tuition:* $385 per credit. Part-time tuition and fees vary according to class time and program.
**FRESHMAN FINANCIAL AID (Fall 2014, est.)** 526 applied for aid; of those 98% were deemed to have need. 100% of freshmen with need received aid. *Average percent of need met:* 63% (excluding resources awarded to replace EFC). *Average financial aid package:* $21,444 (excluding resources awarded to replace EFC). 3% of all full-time freshmen had no need and received non-need-based gift aid.
**UNDERGRADUATE FINANCIAL AID (Fall 2014, est.)** 1,422 applied for aid; of those 98% were deemed to have need. 100% of undergraduates with need received

aid; of those 2% had need fully met. *Average percent of need met:* 72% (excluding resources awarded to replace EFC). *Average financial aid package:* $28,876 (excluding resources awarded to replace EFC). 2% of all full-time undergraduates had no need and received non-need-based gift aid.
**GIFT AID (NEED-BASED)** *Total amount:* $21,192,632 (26% federal, 13% state, 59% institutional, 2% external sources). *Receiving aid:* Freshmen: 97% (517); all full-time undergraduates: 95% (1,390). *Average award:* Freshmen: $16,641; Undergraduates: $16,904. *Scholarships, grants, and awards:* Federal Pell, FSEOG, state, private, college/university gift aid from institutional funds.
**GIFT AID (NON-NEED-BASED)** *Total amount:* $138,778 (9% federal, 91% state). *Receiving aid:* Freshmen: 1% (7). Undergraduates: 1% (16). *Average award:* Freshmen: $7084. Undergraduates: $5998. *Scholarships, grants, and awards by category: Academic interests/achievement:* 1,390 awards ($6,228,493 total): general academic interests/achievements. *Creative arts/performance:* 23 awards ($68,650 total): music. *Special achievements/activities:* 558 awards ($1,482,291 total): leadership. *Special characteristics:* 21 awards ($173,288 total): children of educators, children of faculty/staff, children of public servants, children of union members/company employees, first-generation college students, general special characteristics, handicapped students, international students, local/state students, out-of-state students, public servants, relatives of clergy, religious affiliation, veterans, veterans' children. *Tuition waivers:* Full or partial for employees or children of employees, senior citizens.
**LOANS** *Student loans:* $12,199,867 (43% need-based, 57% non-need-based). 96% of past graduating class borrowed through all loan programs. *Average indebtedness per student:* $33,992. *Average need-based loan:* Freshmen: $3605. Undergraduates: $3979. *Parent loans:* $3,350,766 (100% non-need-based). *Programs:* Federal Direct (Subsidized and Unsubsidized Stafford, PLUS), Perkins, state, alternative loans.
**WORK-STUDY** *Federal work-study:* Total amount: $539,231; 360 jobs averaging $1443. *State or other work-study/employment:* Total amount: $2000 (100% non-need-based). 162 part-time jobs averaging $1381.
**ATHLETIC AWARDS** Total amount: $1,992,564 (100% need-based).
**APPLYING FOR FINANCIAL AID** *Required financial aid form:* FAFSA. *Financial aid deadline (priority):* 5/1. *Notification date:* Continuous beginning 4/1. Students must reply within 2 weeks of notification.
**CONTACT** Mrs. Sharon W. Rose, Director of Financial Aid, Chowan University, One University Place, Murfreesboro, NC 27855, 252-398-1229 or toll-free 888-4-CHOWAN. *Fax:* 252-398-6513. *E-mail:* roses1@chowan.edu. *Website:* http://www.chowan.edu/.

# CHRISTENDOM COLLEGE
## Front Royal, VA

| Tuition & fees: $790 | Average undergraduate aid package: $19,350 |
|---|---|

**ABOUT THE INSTITUTION** Independent Roman Catholic, coed. *Awards:* associate, bachelor's, and master's degrees. 8 undergraduate majors. *Total enrollment:* 541. Undergraduates: 433. Freshmen: 122. Institutional methodology is used as a basis for awarding need-based institutional aid.
**UNDERGRADUATE EXPENSES** for 2015–2016 *Application fee:* $25.
**FRESHMAN FINANCIAL AID (Fall 2014, est.)** 99 applied for aid; of those 86% were deemed to have need. 100% of freshmen with need received aid; of those 89% had need fully met. *Average percent of need met:* 85% (excluding resources awarded to replace EFC). *Average financial aid package:* $19,514 (excluding resources awarded to replace EFC). 19% of all full-time freshmen had no need and received non-need-based gift aid.
**UNDERGRADUATE FINANCIAL AID (Fall 2014, est.)** 274 applied for aid; of those 94% were deemed to have need. 100% of undergraduates with need received aid; of those 94% had need fully met. *Average percent of need met:* 85% (excluding resources awarded to replace EFC). *Average financial aid package:* $19,350 (excluding resources awarded to replace EFC). 19% of all full-time undergraduates had no need and received non-need-based gift aid.
**GIFT AID (NEED-BASED)** *Total amount:* $2,562,953 (100% institutional). *Receiving aid:* Freshmen: 54% (66); all full-time undergraduates: 56% (243). *Average award:* Freshmen: $6590; Undergraduates: $8260. *Scholarships, grants, and awards:* private, college/university gift aid from institutional funds.
**GIFT AID (NON-NEED-BASED)** *Total amount:* $681,540 (100% institutional). *Receiving aid:* Freshmen: 30% (36). Undergraduates: 24% (102). *Average award:* Freshmen: $9715. Undergraduates: $8785. *Scholarships, grants, and awards by*

*category:* Academic interests/achievement: 188 awards ($1,302,350 total): general academic interests/achievements. **Tuition waivers:** Full or partial for employees or children of employees.
**LOANS Student loans:** $2,590,764 (69% need-based, 31% non-need-based). 66% of past graduating class borrowed through all loan programs. *Average indebtedness per student:* $31,991. **Average need-based loan:** Freshmen: $7515. Undergraduates: $7115. *Programs:* college/university.
**WORK-STUDY** *State or other work-study/employment:* Total amount: $287,100 (100% non-need-based). 145 part-time jobs averaging $2100.
**APPLYING FOR FINANCIAL AID** *Required financial aid form:* institution's own form. **Financial aid deadline (priority):** 4/1. **Notification date:** Continuous beginning 3/1. Students must reply within 4 weeks of notification.
**CONTACT** Ms. Alisa Polk, Financial Aid Officer, Christendom College, 134 Christendom Drive, Front Royal, VA 22630-5103, 800-877-5456 Ext. 1214 or toll-free 800-877-5456. *Fax:* 540-631-0297. *E-mail:* apolk@christendom.edu. *Website:* http://www.christendom.edu/.

# CHRISTIAN BROTHERS UNIVERSITY
## Memphis, TN

| Tuition & fees: $30,106 | Average undergraduate aid package: $23,390 |
|---|---|

**ABOUT THE INSTITUTION** Independent Roman Catholic, coed. *Awards:* certificates, associate, bachelor's, and master's degrees. 38 undergraduate majors. *Total enrollment:* 1,670. Undergraduates: 1,299. Freshmen: 354. Federal methodology is used as a basis for awarding need-based institutional aid.
**UNDERGRADUATE EXPENSES for 2015–2016** *Application fee:* $25. **Comprehensive fee:** $37,106 includes full-time tuition ($29,316), mandatory fees ($790), and room and board ($7000). Full-time tuition and fees vary according to class time and program. Room and board charges vary according to board plan and housing facility. **Part-time tuition:** $1050.63 per credit. **Part-time fees:** $225 per term. Part-time tuition and fees vary according to class time and program.
**FRESHMAN FINANCIAL AID (Fall 2013)** 263 applied for aid; of those 80% were deemed to have need. 100% of freshmen with need received aid; of those 21% had need fully met. *Average percent of need met:* 81% (excluding resources awarded to replace EFC). *Average financial aid package:* $25,607 (excluding resources awarded to replace EFC). 20% of all full-time freshmen had no need and received non-need-based gift aid.
**UNDERGRADUATE FINANCIAL AID (Fall 2013)** 1,013 applied for aid; of those 80% were deemed to have need. 100% of undergraduates with need received aid; of those 19% had need fully met. *Average percent of need met:* 76% (excluding resources awarded to replace EFC). *Average financial aid package:* $23,390 (excluding resources awarded to replace EFC). 20% of all full-time undergraduates had no need and received non-need-based gift aid.
**GIFT AID (NEED-BASED)** *Total amount:* $14,109,530 (17% federal, 15% state, 68% institutional). *Receiving aid:* Freshmen: 79% (209); all full-time undergraduates: 77% (788). *Average award:* Freshmen: $19,955; Undergraduates: $17,557. *Scholarships, grants, and awards:* Federal Pell, FSEOG, state, private, college/university gift aid from institutional funds.
**GIFT AID (NON-NEED-BASED)** *Total amount:* $4,018,279 (14% state, 83% institutional, 3% external sources). *Receiving aid:* Freshmen: 14% (36). Undergraduates: 12% (118). *Average award:* Freshmen: $13,639. Undergraduates: $13,031. *Scholarships, grants, and awards by category:* Academic interests/achievement: 1,139 awards ($10,285,186 total): engineering/technologies, general academic interests/achievements, health fields. Creative arts/performance: 6 awards ($52,315 total): art/fine arts, performing arts. Special achievements/activities: 43 awards ($87,000 total): general special achievements/activities, leadership, memberships. Special characteristics: 272 awards ($317,506 total): adult students, children and siblings of alumni, ethnic background, general special characteristics, local/state students, out-of-state students, veterans, veterans' children. **Tuition waivers:** Full or partial for employees or children of employees. **ROTC:** Army cooperative, Naval cooperative, Air Force cooperative.
**LOANS Student loans:** $6,121,116 (82% need-based, 18% non-need-based). 70% of past graduating class borrowed through all loan programs. *Average indebtedness per student:* $22,759. *Average need-based loan:* Freshmen: $3586. Undergraduates: $4431. *Parent loans:* $702,767 (50% need-based, 50% non-need-based). **Pro-**

**grams:** Federal Direct (Subsidized and Unsubsidized Stafford, PLUS), Perkins, college/university, alternative loans.
**WORK-STUDY** *Federal work-study:* 224 jobs averaging $980. **State or other work-study/employment:** Total amount: $110,560 (34% need-based, 66% non-need-based). 116 part-time jobs averaging $1140.
**ATHLETIC AWARDS** Total amount: $1,572,548 (37% need-based, 63% non-need-based).
**APPLYING FOR FINANCIAL AID** *Required financial aid form:* FAFSA. **Financial aid deadline (priority):** 2/15. **Notification date:** Continuous beginning 2/28. Students must reply by 5/1 or within 2 weeks of notification.
**CONTACT** Mr. John H. Lewis, IV, Director of Financial Aid, Christian Brothers University, 650 East Parkway South, Memphis, TN 38104, 901-321-3305 or toll-free 877-321-4CBU. *Fax:* 901-321-3327. *E-mail:* john.lewis@cbu.edu. *Website:* http://www.cbu.edu/.

# CHRISTIAN LIFE COLLEGE
## Mount Prospect, IL

**ABOUT THE INSTITUTION** Independent Christian, coed. *Awards:* diplomas, associate, and bachelor's degrees. 1 undergraduate major. *Total enrollment:* 40. Undergraduates: 40. Freshmen: 6.
**GIFT AID (NEED-BASED)** *Scholarships, grants, and awards:* Federal Pell, FSEOG.
**GIFT AID (NON-NEED-BASED)** *Scholarships, grants, and awards by category:* Special characteristics: children of faculty/staff, general special characteristics, relatives of clergy, religious affiliation.
**LOANS** *Programs:* Federal Direct (Subsidized and Unsubsidized Stafford, PLUS).
**APPLYING FOR FINANCIAL AID** *Required financial aid form:* FAFSA.
**CONTACT** Christina Bell, Office of Financial Aid, Christian Life College, 400 East Gregory Street, Mt. Prospect, IL 60056, 847-259-1840. *Fax:* 847-259-3888. *Website:* http://www.christianlifecollege.edu/.

# CHRISTOPHER NEWPORT UNIVERSITY
## Newport News, VA

| Tuition & fees (VA res): $11,646 | Average undergraduate aid package: $8511 |
|---|---|

**ABOUT THE INSTITUTION** State-supported, coed. *Awards:* bachelor's and master's degrees. 39 undergraduate majors. *Total enrollment:* 5,221. Undergraduates: 5,096. Freshmen: 1,228. Federal methodology is used as a basis for awarding need-based institutional aid.
**UNDERGRADUATE EXPENSES for 2015–2016** *Application fee:* $50. *Tuition, state resident:* full-time $6928; part-time $288 per credit hour. *Tuition, nonresident:* full-time $16,860; part-time $702 per credit hour. *Required fees:* full-time $4718; $196 per credit hour. Full-time tuition and fees vary according to course load. Part-time tuition and fees vary according to course load. *College room and board:* $10,314; *Room only:* $6564. Room and board charges vary according to board plan and housing facility.
**FRESHMAN FINANCIAL AID (Fall 2014, est.)** 975 applied for aid; of those 59% were deemed to have need. 94% of freshmen with need received aid; of those 14% had need fully met. *Average percent of need met:* 61% (excluding resources awarded to replace EFC). *Average financial aid package:* $8168 (excluding resources awarded to replace EFC). 14% of all full-time freshmen had no need and received non-need-based gift aid.
**UNDERGRADUATE FINANCIAL AID (Fall 2014, est.)** 3,251 applied for aid; of those 69% were deemed to have need. 96% of undergraduates with need received aid; of those 16% had need fully met. *Average percent of need met:* 63% (excluding resources awarded to replace EFC). *Average financial aid package:* $8511 (excluding resources awarded to replace EFC). 12% of all full-time undergraduates had no need and received non-need-based gift aid.
**GIFT AID (NEED-BASED)** *Total amount:* $9,008,863 (36% federal, 51% state, 13% institutional). *Receiving aid:* Freshmen: 32% (392); all full-time undergraduates: 30% (1,518). *Average award:* Freshmen: $5742; Undergraduates: $5599. **Scholar-**

ships, grants, and awards: Federal Pell, FSEOG, state, private, college/university gift aid from institutional funds.

**GIFT AID (NON-NEED-BASED)** *Total amount:* $3,397,670 (2% state, 65% institutional, 33% external sources). *Receiving aid:* Freshmen: 21% (252). Undergraduates: 13% (662). *Average award:* Freshmen: $2016. Undergraduates: $2093. *Scholarships, grants, and awards by category: Academic interests/achievement:* 75 awards ($182,750 total): biological sciences, business, communication, computer science, education, engineering/technologies, English, foreign languages, general academic interests/achievements, humanities, mathematics, physical sciences, premedicine, social sciences. *Creative arts/performance:* 70 awards ($86,300 total): art/fine arts, music, performing arts, theater/drama. *Special achievements/activities:* 928 awards ($1,767,000 total): community service, general special achievements/activities, leadership. *Special characteristics:* 10 awards ($32,429 total): children and siblings of alumni, first-generation college students, general special characteristics, local/state students. *Tuition waivers:* Full or partial for employees or children of employees, senior citizens. *ROTC:* Army.

**LOANS** *Student loans:* $24,394,184 (32% need-based, 68% non-need-based). 54% of past graduating class borrowed through all loan programs. *Average indebtedness per student:* $28,135. *Average need-based loan:* Freshmen: $3256. Undergraduates: $4205. *Parent loans:* $7,097,412 (100% non-need-based). *Programs:* Federal Direct (Subsidized and Unsubsidized Stafford, PLUS).

**WORK-STUDY** *Federal work-study:* Total amount: $60,381; 90 jobs averaging $699. *State or other work-study/employment:* Total amount: $2,898,162 (100% non-need-based). 1,397 part-time jobs averaging $2133.

**APPLYING FOR FINANCIAL AID** *Required financial aid form:* FAFSA. *Financial aid deadline (priority):* 3/1. *Notification date:* Continuous beginning 3/1. Students must reply by 5/1.

**CONTACT** Christina Russell, Director of Financial Aid, Christopher Newport University, 1 Avenue of the Arts, Newport News, VA 23606, 757-594-7170 or toll-free 800-333-4268. *Fax:* 757-594-7113. *E-mail:* christina.russell@cnu.edu. *Website:* http://www.cnu.edu/.

# CINCINNATI CHRISTIAN UNIVERSITY
## Cincinnati, OH

| Tuition & fees: $16,216 | Average undergraduate aid package: $12,550 |
| --- | --- |

**ABOUT THE INSTITUTION** Independent Church of Christ, coed. *Awards:* associate, bachelor's, and master's degrees. 11 undergraduate majors. *Total enrollment:* 838. Undergraduates: 620. Freshmen: 100. Federal methodology is used as a basis for awarding need-based institutional aid.

**UNDERGRADUATE EXPENSES** for 2015–2016 *Application fee:* $40. *Comprehensive fee:* $24,076 includes full-time tuition ($15,966), mandatory fees ($250), and room and board ($7860). *College room only:* $3760. Full-time tuition and fees vary according to course load and student level. Room and board charges vary according to board plan, housing facility, and student level. *Part-time tuition:* $570 per semester hour. Part-time tuition and fees vary according to course load and student level.

**FRESHMAN FINANCIAL AID (Fall 2013)** 101 applied for aid; of those 87% were deemed to have need. 100% of freshmen with need received aid; of those 9% had need fully met. *Average percent of need met:* 65% (excluding resources awarded to replace EFC). *Average financial aid package:* $14,350 (excluding resources awarded to replace EFC). 11% of all full-time freshmen had no need and received non-need-based gift aid.

**UNDERGRADUATE FINANCIAL AID (Fall 2013)** 518 applied for aid; of those 93% were deemed to have need. 100% of undergraduates with need received aid; of those 7% had need fully met. *Average percent of need met:* 55% (excluding resources awarded to replace EFC). *Average financial aid package:* $12,550 (excluding resources awarded to replace EFC). 11% of all full-time undergraduates had no need and received non-need-based gift aid.

**GIFT AID (NEED-BASED)** *Total amount:* $3,793,446 (36% federal, 7% state, 51% institutional, 6% external sources). *Receiving aid:* Freshmen: 78% (85); all full-time undergraduates: 79% (447). *Average award:* Freshmen: $10,818; Undergraduates: $8988. *Scholarships, grants, and awards:* Federal Pell, FSEOG, state, private, college/university gift aid from institutional funds.

**GIFT AID (NON-NEED-BASED)** *Total amount:* $560,107 (80% institutional, 20% external sources). *Receiving aid:* Freshmen: 6% (7). Undergraduates: 5% (27).

*Average award:* Freshmen: $6022. Undergraduates: $6376. *Scholarships, grants, and awards by category: Academic interests/achievement:* education, general academic interests/achievements, religion/biblical studies. *Creative arts/performance:* music. *Special achievements/activities:* general special achievements/activities, leadership, religious involvement. *Special characteristics:* children of faculty/staff, international students, married students, members of minority groups, parents of current students, siblings of current students, spouses of current students. *Tuition waivers:* Full or partial for employees or children of employees.

**LOANS** *Student loans:* $4,584,484 (86% need-based, 14% non-need-based). 86% of past graduating class borrowed through all loan programs. *Average indebtedness per student:* $32,675. *Average need-based loan:* Freshmen: $3032. Undergraduates: $3873. *Parent loans:* $736,663 (57% need-based, 43% non-need-based). *Programs:* Federal Direct (Subsidized and Unsubsidized Stafford, PLUS), college/university, private loans.

**WORK-STUDY** *Federal work-study:* 228 jobs averaging $1375.

**ATHLETIC AWARDS** Total amount: $635,860 (72% need-based, 28% non-need-based).

**APPLYING FOR FINANCIAL AID** *Required financial aid form:* FAFSA. *Financial aid deadline (priority):* 3/1. *Notification date:* Continuous beginning 4/1. Students must reply by 8/1.

**CONTACT** Marcella Farmer, Associate Director of Financial Aid, Cincinnati Christian University, 2700 Glenway Avenue, Cincinnati, OH 45204-1799, 513-244-8130 or toll-free 800-949-4228 (in-state), 800-949-4CCU (out-of-state). *Fax:* 513-244-8453. *E-mail:* financialaid@ccuniversity.edu. *Website:* http://www.ccuniversity.edu/.

# CINCINNATI COLLEGE OF MORTUARY SCIENCE
## Cincinnati, OH

**CONTACT** Ms. Pat Leon, Financial Aid Officer , Cincinnati College of Mortuary Science, 645 West North Bend Road, Cincinnati, OH 45224-1428, 513-761-2020 or toll-free 888-377-8433. *Website:* http://www.ccms.edu/.

# THE CITADEL, THE MILITARY COLLEGE OF SOUTH CAROLINA
## Charleston, SC

| Tuition & fees (SC res): $12,568 | Average undergraduate aid package: $14,819 |
| --- | --- |

**ABOUT THE INSTITUTION** State-supported, coed, primarily men. *Awards:* certificates, bachelor's, and master's degrees. 19 undergraduate majors. *Total enrollment:* 3,592. Undergraduates: 2,763. Freshmen: 618. Federal methodology is used as a basis for awarding need-based institutional aid.

**UNDERGRADUATE EXPENSES** for 2015–2016 *Application fee:* $40. *Tuition, state resident:* full-time $11,098; part-time $432 per credit. *Tuition, nonresident:* full-time $30,706; part-time $792 per credit. *Required fees:* full-time $1470. *College room and board:* $6381.

**FRESHMAN FINANCIAL AID (Fall 2014, est.)** 543 applied for aid; of those 76% were deemed to have need. 96% of freshmen with need received aid; of those 18% had need fully met. *Average percent of need met:* 50% (excluding resources awarded to replace EFC). *Average financial aid package:* $14,073 (excluding resources awarded to replace EFC). 20% of all full-time freshmen had no need and received non-need-based gift aid.

**UNDERGRADUATE FINANCIAL AID (Fall 2014, est.)** 1,890 applied for aid; of those 77% were deemed to have need. 96% of undergraduates with need received aid; of those 24% had need fully met. *Average percent of need met:* 58% (excluding resources awarded to replace EFC). *Average financial aid package:* $14,819 (excluding resources awarded to replace EFC). 20% of all full-time undergraduates had no need and received non-need-based gift aid.

**GIFT AID (NEED-BASED)** *Total amount:* $13,819,435 (24% federal, 16% state, 26% institutional, 34% external sources). *Receiving aid:* Freshmen: 53% (328); all full-time undergraduates: 45% (1,131). *Average award:* Freshmen: $13,941; Under-

graduates: $14,451. *Scholarships, grants, and awards:* Federal Pell, FSEOG, state, private, college/university gift aid from institutional funds.
**GIFT AID (NON-NEED-BASED)** *Total amount:* $7,712,939 (20% state, 31% institutional, 49% external sources). *Receiving aid:* Freshmen: 9% (58). Undergraduates: 9% (223). *Average award:* Freshmen: $10,096. Undergraduates: $15,380. *Scholarships, grants, and awards by category:* Academic interests/achievement: biological sciences, business, engineering/technologies, general academic interests/achievements, humanities, military science, religion/biblical studies. *Creative arts/performance:* journalism/publications, music. *Special achievements/activities:* community service, leadership, religious involvement. *Special characteristics:* children and siblings of alumni, children with a deceased or disabled parent, local/state students, out-of-state students. *Tuition waivers:* Full or partial for employees or children of employees, senior citizens. *ROTC:* Army, Naval, Air Force.
**LOANS** *Student loans:* $8,564,743 (85% need-based, 15% non-need-based). 65% of past graduating class borrowed through all loan programs. *Average indebtedness per student:* $29,701. *Average need-based loan:* Freshmen: $3649. Undergraduates: $4404. *Parent loans:* $12,291,939 (83% need-based, 17% non-need-based). *Programs:* Federal Direct (Subsidized and Unsubsidized Stafford, PLUS), Perkins, state.
**WORK-STUDY** *Federal work-study:* Total amount: $159,162; 82 jobs averaging $2500. *State or other work-study/employment:* Total amount: $5000 (100% non-need-based). Part-time jobs available.
**ATHLETIC AWARDS** Total amount: $5,242,923 (50% need-based, 50% non-need-based).
**APPLYING FOR FINANCIAL AID** *Required financial aid form:* FAFSA. *Financial aid deadline (priority):* 3/1. *Notification date:* 4/1. Students must reply within 2 weeks of notification.
**CONTACT** Lt. Col. Hank M. Fuller, Director of Financial Aid and Scholarships, The Citadel, The Military College of South Carolina, 171 Moultrie Street, Charleston, SC 29409, 843-953-5187 or toll-free 800-868-1842. *Fax:* 843-953-6759. *E-mail:* hank.fuller@citadel.edu.
*Website:* http://www.citadel.edu/.

# CITY COLLEGE
## Hollywood, FL

**CONTACT** Financial Aid Office, City College, 6565 Taft Street, Hollywood, FL 33024, 954-744-1777 or toll-free 866-314-5681.
*Website:* http://www.citycollege.edu/.

# CITY COLLEGE OF THE CITY UNIVERSITY OF NEW YORK
## New York, NY

| Tuition & fees (NY res): $6330 | Average undergraduate aid package: $8878 |
|---|---|

**ABOUT THE INSTITUTION** State and locally supported, coed. *Awards:* certificates, bachelor's, master's, and doctoral degrees. 68 undergraduate majors. *Total enrollment:* 15,620. Undergraduates: 16,463. Freshmen: 1,444. Federal methodology is used as a basis for awarding need-based institutional aid.
**UNDERGRADUATE EXPENSES** for 2015–2016 *Application fee:* $65. *Tuition, state resident:* full-time $6330. *Tuition, nonresident:* full-time $16,800. Full-time tuition and fees vary according to course load and program. Part-time tuition and fees vary according to course load and program. Room and board charges vary according to housing facility.
**FRESHMAN FINANCIAL AID (Fall 2014, est.)** 1,279 applied for aid; of those 90% were deemed to have need. 97% of freshmen with need received aid; of those 70% had need fully met. *Average percent of need met:* 84% (excluding resources awarded to replace EFC). *Average financial aid package:* $8757 (excluding resources awarded to replace EFC). 7% of all full-time freshmen had no need and received non-need-based gift aid.
**UNDERGRADUATE FINANCIAL AID (Fall 2014, est.)** 8,866 applied for aid; of those 95% were deemed to have need. 99% of undergraduates with need received aid; of those 82% had need fully met. *Average percent of need met:* 82% (excluding

resources awarded to replace EFC). *Average financial aid package:* $8878 (excluding resources awarded to replace EFC). 6% of all full-time undergraduates had no need and received non-need-based gift aid.
**GIFT AID (NEED-BASED)** *Total amount:* $81,854,696 (52% federal, 43% state, 4% institutional, 1% external sources). *Receiving aid:* Freshmen: 73% (1,044); all full-time undergraduates: 79% (8,238). *Average award:* Freshmen: $7989; Undergraduates: $7910. *Scholarships, grants, and awards:* Federal Pell, FSEOG, state, private, college/university gift aid from institutional funds.
**GIFT AID (NON-NEED-BASED)** *Total amount:* $4,040,920 (8% state, 73% institutional, 19% external sources). *Receiving aid:* Freshmen: 42% (605). Undergraduates: 9% (977). *Average award:* Freshmen: $3106. Undergraduates: $4120. *Scholarships, grants, and awards by category:* Academic interests/achievement: architecture, area/ethnic studies, biological sciences, communication, computer science, education, engineering/technologies, English, foreign languages, general academic interests/achievements, humanities, international studies, mathematics, premedicine, social sciences. *Creative arts/performance:* applied art and design, art/fine arts, cinema/film/broadcasting, creative writing, general creative arts/performance, music, performing arts. *Special achievements/activities:* community service, general special achievements/activities, leadership. *Special characteristics:* children and siblings of alumni, local/state students. *Tuition waivers:* Full or partial for senior citizens. *ROTC:* Army.
**LOANS** *Student loans:* $26,359,620 (92% need-based, 8% non-need-based). 22% of past graduating class borrowed through all loan programs. *Average indebtedness per student:* $16,942. *Average need-based loan:* Freshmen: $2121. Undergraduates: $4024. *Parent loans:* $1,073,696 (100% non-need-based). *Programs:* Federal Direct (Subsidized and Unsubsidized Stafford, PLUS), Perkins.
**WORK-STUDY** *Federal work-study:* Total amount: $5,207,374; jobs available. *State or other work-study/employment:* Part-time jobs available.
**APPLYING FOR FINANCIAL AID** *Required financial aid forms:* FAFSA, state aid form. *Financial aid deadline (priority):* 3/15. *Notification date:* Continuous beginning 4/1.
**CONTACT** Thelma Mason, Director of Financial Aid, City College of the City University of New York, 160 Convent Avenue, Wille Administration Building, Room 104, New York, NY 10031, 212-650-5816. *Fax:* 212-650-5829. *E-mail:* tmason@ccny.cuny.edu.
*Website:* http://www.ccny.cuny.edu/.

# CITY VISION UNIVERSITY
## Kansas City, MO

| Tuition & fees: $6000 | Average undergraduate aid package: $3653 |
|---|---|

**ABOUT THE INSTITUTION** Independent Christian, coed. *Awards:* certificates, bachelor's, and master's degrees. 3 undergraduate majors. *Total enrollment:* 80. Undergraduates: 72. Entering class: 5. Both federal and institutional methodology are used as a basis for awarding need-based institutional aid.
**UNDERGRADUATE EXPENSES** for 2015–2016 *Application fee:* $25. *One-time required fee:* $25. *Tuition:* full-time $6000; part-time $3000 per year. Full-time tuition and fees vary according to course load and degree level. Part-time tuition and fees vary according to course load and degree level.
**UNDERGRADUATE FINANCIAL AID (Fall 2013)** 67 applied for aid; of those 100% were deemed to have need. 100% of undergraduates with need received aid; of those 76% had need fully met. *Average percent of need met:* 100% (excluding resources awarded to replace EFC). *Average financial aid package:* $3653 (excluding resources awarded to replace EFC). 33% of all full-time undergraduates had no need and received non-need-based gift aid.
**GIFT AID (NEED-BASED)** *Total amount:* $83,240 (100% federal). *Receiving aid:* Entering class: 50% (1); all full-time undergraduates: 37% (29). *Average award:* Freshmen: $5081; Undergraduates: $1468. *Scholarships, grants, and awards:* Federal Pell, college/university gift aid from institutional funds.
**GIFT AID (NON-NEED-BASED)** *Total amount:* $55,600 (100% institutional). *Receiving aid:* Undergraduates: 55% (43). *Average award:* Undergraduates: $1041. *Scholarships, grants, and awards by category:* Special achievements/activities: 43 awards ($55,600 total): memberships. *Special characteristics:* veterans. *Tuition waivers:* Full or partial for employees or children of employees.

**LOANS** *Student loans:* $105,905 (100% need-based). *Average need-based loan:* Freshmen: $9409. Undergraduates: $4814. *Programs:* Federal Direct (Subsidized and Unsubsidized Stafford), private loans.

**APPLYING FOR FINANCIAL AID** *Required financial aid forms:* FAFSA, institution's own form. *Financial aid deadline:* Continuous. *Notification date:* Continuous.

**CONTACT** Mrs. Ann Marie Cameron-Thompson, Director of Financial Aid, City Vision University, 48 Pleasant Street, Dorchester, MA 02125, 617-282-9798 Ext. 108. *Fax:* 816-256-8471. *E-mail:* financialaid@cityvision.edu .
*Website:* http://www.cityvision.edu/.

---

# CLAFLIN UNIVERSITY
## Orangeburg, SC

**CONTACT** Ms. Yolanda Frazier, Interim Director of Financial Aid, Claflin University, Tingly Hall, Suite 12, 400 Magnolia Street, Orangeburg, SC 29115, 803-535-5720 or toll-free 800-922-1276. *Fax:* 803-535-5383. *E-mail:* yfrazier@claflin.edu.
*Website:* http://www.claflin.edu/.

---

# CLAREMONT MCKENNA COLLEGE
## Claremont, CA

| Tuition & fees: $47,395 | Average undergraduate aid package: $42,538 |
| --- | --- |

**ABOUT THE INSTITUTION** Independent, coed. *Awards:* bachelor's and master's degrees. 33 undergraduate majors. *Total enrollment:* 1,324. Undergraduates: 1,301. Freshmen: 327. Both federal and institutional methodology are used as a basis for awarding need-based institutional aid.

**UNDERGRADUATE EXPENSES for 2015–2016** *Application fee:* $60. *Comprehensive fee:* $62,215 includes full-time tuition ($47,150), mandatory fees ($245), and room and board ($14,820). *College room only:* $7900. Room and board charges vary according to board plan and housing facility. *Part-time tuition:* $7858.33 per course. Part-time tuition and fees vary according to course load.

**FRESHMAN FINANCIAL AID (Fall 2014, est.)** 176 applied for aid; of those 72% were deemed to have need. 100% of freshmen with need received aid; of those 100% had need fully met. *Average percent of need met:* 100% (excluding resources awarded to replace EFC). *Average financial aid package:* $41,556 (excluding resources awarded to replace EFC). 5% of all full-time freshmen had no need and received non-need-based gift aid.

**UNDERGRADUATE FINANCIAL AID (Fall 2014, est.)** 673 applied for aid; of those 75% were deemed to have need. 100% of undergraduates with need received aid; of those 91% had need fully met. *Average percent of need met:* 100% (excluding resources awarded to replace EFC). *Average financial aid package:* $42,538 (excluding resources awarded to replace EFC). 6% of all full-time undergraduates had no need and received non-need-based gift aid.

**GIFT AID (NEED-BASED)** *Total amount:* $19,992,686 (4% federal, 5% state, 88% institutional, 3% external sources). *Receiving aid:* Freshmen: 38% (123); all full-time undergraduates: 38% (494). *Average award:* Freshmen: $38,850; Undergraduates: $40,438. *Scholarships, grants, and awards:* Federal Pell, FSEOG, state, private, college/university gift aid from institutional funds.

**GIFT AID (NON-NEED-BASED)** *Total amount:* $1,993,290 (63% institutional, 37% external sources). *Receiving aid:* Freshmen: 23% (74). Undergraduates: 17% (224). *Average award:* Freshmen: $9829. Undergraduates: $15,732. *Scholarships, grants, and awards by category:* Academic interests/achievement: general academic interests/achievements, military science. *Special achievements/activities:* leadership. *Special characteristics:* veterans, veterans' children. *Tuition waivers:* Full or partial for employees or children of employees. *ROTC:* Army, Air Force cooperative.

**LOANS** *Student loans:* $1,922,843 (28% need-based, 72% non-need-based). 31% of past graduating class borrowed through all loan programs. *Average indebtedness per student:* $23,232. *Average need-based loan:* Freshmen: $3681. Undergraduates: $3970. *Parent loans:* $1,204,006 (100% non-need-based). *Programs:* Federal Direct (Subsidized and Unsubsidized Stafford, PLUS), Perkins, college/university, alternative loans.

**WORK-STUDY** *Federal work-study:* Total amount: $776,464; 373 jobs averaging $2082. *State or other work-study/employment:* Total amount: $136,100 (93% need-based, 7% non-need-based). 65 part-time jobs averaging $2094.

**APPLYING FOR FINANCIAL AID** *Required financial aid forms:* FAFSA, CSS Financial Aid PROFILE, state aid form, noncustodial (divorced/separated) parent's statement, business/farm supplement. *Financial aid deadline:* 2/1 (priority: 1/1). *Notification date:* 4/1. Students must reply by 5/1.

**CONTACT** Ms. Georgette R. DeVeres, Associate Vice President and Dean of Admission and Financial Aid, Claremont McKenna College, Kravis Center, Lower Court, 888 Columbia Avenue, Claremont, CA 91711, 909-621-8356. *Fax:* 909-607-0661. *E-mail:* georgette.deveres@claremontmckenna.edu.
*Website:* http://www.claremontmckenna.edu/.

---

# CLARION UNIVERSITY OF PENNSYLVANIA
## Clarion, PA

| Tuition & fees (PA res): $9788 | Average undergraduate aid package: $12,863 |
| --- | --- |

**ABOUT THE INSTITUTION** State-supported, coed. *Awards:* certificates, associate, bachelor's, master's, and doctoral degrees. 54 undergraduate majors. *Total enrollment:* 5,712. Undergraduates: 4,911. Freshmen: 989. Federal methodology is used as a basis for awarding need-based institutional aid.

**UNDERGRADUATE EXPENSES for 2015–2016** *One-time required fee:* $50. *Tuition, state resident:* full-time $6820; part-time $284 per credit. *Tuition, nonresident:* full-time $10,230; part-time $426 per credit. *Required fees:* full-time $2968; $174.25 per credit hour. Full-time tuition and fees vary according to course load, degree level, and location. Part-time tuition and fees vary according to course load, degree level, and location. *College room and board:* $8152; *Room only:* $5138. Room and board charges vary according to board plan, housing facility, and location.

**FRESHMAN FINANCIAL AID (Fall 2013)** 969 applied for aid; of those 87% were deemed to have need. 98% of freshmen with need received aid; of those 27% had need fully met. *Average percent of need met:* 62% (excluding resources awarded to replace EFC). *Average financial aid package:* $11,625 (excluding resources awarded to replace EFC). 4% of all full-time freshmen had no need and received non-need-based gift aid.

**UNDERGRADUATE FINANCIAL AID (Fall 2013)** 3,857 applied for aid; of those 88% were deemed to have need. 98% of undergraduates with need received aid; of those 21% had need fully met. *Average percent of need met:* 69% (excluding resources awarded to replace EFC). *Average financial aid package:* $12,863 (excluding resources awarded to replace EFC). 3% of all full-time undergraduates had no need and received non-need-based gift aid.

**GIFT AID (NEED-BASED)** *Total amount:* $17,292,963 (52% federal, 36% state, 5% institutional, 7% external sources). *Receiving aid:* Freshmen: 67% (665); all full-time undergraduates: 58% (2,530). *Average award:* Freshmen: $6188; Undergraduates: $5899. *Scholarships, grants, and awards:* Federal Pell, FSEOG, state, private, college/university gift aid from institutional funds, United Negro College Fund.

**GIFT AID (NON-NEED-BASED)** *Total amount:* $410,570 (1% federal, 12% state, 63% institutional, 24% external sources). *Receiving aid:* Freshmen: 31% (312). Undergraduates: 19% (832). *Average award:* Freshmen: $1801. Undergraduates: $1854. *Scholarships, grants, and awards by category:* Academic interests/achievement: biological sciences, business, communication, computer science, education, English, foreign languages, general academic interests/achievements, health fields, humanities, international studies, library science, mathematics, military science, physical sciences, premedicine, social sciences. *Creative arts/performance:* art/fine arts, general creative arts/performance, music, theater/drama. *Special achievements/activities:* leadership, memberships. *Special characteristics:* children and siblings of alumni, children of faculty/staff, children of union members/company employees, first-generation college students, local/state students, members of minority groups, previous college experience, spouses of current students. *Tuition waivers:* Full or partial for employees or children of employees, senior citizens. *ROTC:* Army cooperative.

**LOANS** *Student loans:* $37,628,230 (93% need-based, 7% non-need-based). 78% of past graduating class borrowed through all loan programs. *Average indebtedness per student:* $21,507. *Average need-based loan:* Freshmen: $3276. Undergraduates: $4105. *Parent loans:* $6,103,754 (86% need-based, 14% non-need-based).

---

**Programs:** Federal Direct (Subsidized and Unsubsidized Stafford, PLUS), Perkins, private loans.
**WORK-STUDY** *Federal work-study:* jobs available. *State or other work-study/employment:* Total amount: $589,356 (100% non-need-based). Part-time jobs available.
**ATHLETIC AWARDS** Total amount: $670,463 (74% need-based, 26% non-need-based).
**APPLYING FOR FINANCIAL AID** *Required financial aid forms:* FAFSA, state aid form. *Financial aid deadline (priority):* 5/1. *Notification date:* Continuous beginning 3/30.
**CONTACT** Ms. Ragan Griffin, Student Financial Services, Clarion University of Pennsylvania, B-16 Carrier Hall, Clarion, PA 16214, 814-393-2315 or toll-free 800-672-7171. *Fax:* 814-393-2520. *E-mail:* stfinservice@clarion.edu.
*Website:* http://www.clarion.edu/.

# CLARK ATLANTA UNIVERSITY
## Atlanta, GA

**CONTACT** Office of Financial Aid, Clark Atlanta University, 223 James P. Brawley Drive, Atlanta, GA 30314, 404-880-8992 or toll-free 800-688-3228. *Fax:* 404-880-8070. *E-mail:* studentfinancialaid@cau.edu.
*Website:* http://www.cau.edu/.

# CLARKE UNIVERSITY
## Dubuque, IA

| Tuition & fees: $29,940 | Average undergraduate aid package: $23,657 |
| --- | --- |

**ABOUT THE INSTITUTION** Independent Roman Catholic, coed. *Awards:* associate, bachelor's, master's, and doctoral degrees. 29 undergraduate majors. *Total enrollment:* 1,200. Undergraduates: 949. Freshmen: 183. Federal methodology is used as a basis for awarding need-based institutional aid.
**UNDERGRADUATE EXPENSES for 2015–2016** *Application fee:* $25. *Comprehensive fee:* $38,940 includes full-time tuition ($29,000), mandatory fees ($940), and room and board ($9000). *College room only:* $4300. Room and board charges vary according to housing facility. *Part-time tuition:* $690 per credit.
**FRESHMAN FINANCIAL AID (Fall 2014, est.)** 177 applied for aid; of those 92% were deemed to have need. 100% of freshmen with need received aid; of those 22% had need fully met. *Average percent of need met:* 76% (excluding resources awarded to replace EFC). *Average financial aid package:* $25,714 (excluding resources awarded to replace EFC). 12% of all full-time freshmen had no need and received non-need-based gift aid.
**UNDERGRADUATE FINANCIAL AID (Fall 2014, est.)** 752 applied for aid; of those 93% were deemed to have need. 100% of undergraduates with need received aid; of those 21% had need fully met. *Average percent of need met:* 71% (excluding resources awarded to replace EFC). *Average financial aid package:* $23,657 (excluding resources awarded to replace EFC). 12% of all full-time undergraduates had no need and received non-need-based gift aid.
**GIFT AID (NEED-BASED)** *Total amount:* $10,055,583 (14% federal, 14% state, 70% institutional, 2% external sources). *Receiving aid:* Freshmen: 88% (162); all full-time undergraduates: 86% (693). *Average award:* Freshmen: $21,459; Undergraduates: $18,750. *Scholarships, grants, and awards:* Federal Pell, FSEOG, state, private, college/university gift aid from institutional funds.
**GIFT AID (NON-NEED-BASED)** *Total amount:* $884,783 (99% institutional, 1% external sources). *Receiving aid:* Freshmen: 87% (160). Undergraduates: 81% (659). *Average award:* Freshmen: $18,844. Undergraduates: $18,107. *Scholarships, grants, and awards by category:* Academic interests/achievement: general academic interests/achievements. Creative arts/performance: art/fine arts, music, theater/drama. Special achievements/activities: leadership. Special characteristics: children and siblings of alumni, children of faculty/staff, relatives of clergy. *Tuition waivers:* Full or partial for children of alumni, employees or children of employees, adult students, senior citizens. *ROTC:* Army cooperative.
**LOANS** *Student loans:* $8,690,729 (36% need-based, 64% non-need-based). 90% of past graduating class borrowed through all loan programs. *Average indebtedness*

---

*per student:* $37,200. *Average need-based loan:* Freshmen: $3491. Undergraduates: $4582. *Parent loans:* $1,218,764 (92% need-based, 8% non-need-based). *Programs:* Federal Direct (Subsidized and Unsubsidized Stafford, PLUS), Perkins, Federal Nursing, college/university, private loans.
**WORK-STUDY** *Federal work-study:* Total amount: $650,928; 343 jobs averaging $1840.
**ATHLETIC AWARDS** Total amount: $1,712,565 (100% non-need-based).
**APPLYING FOR FINANCIAL AID** *Financial aid deadline (priority):* 4/15. *Notification date:* Continuous beginning 3/1. Students must reply within 2 weeks of notification.
**CONTACT** Amy Norton, Director of Financial Aid, Clarke University, 1550 Clarke Drive, Dubuque, IA 52001-3198, 563-588-6327 or toll-free 800-383-2345. *Fax:* 563-584-8605. *E-mail:* amy.norton@clarke.edu.
*Website:* http://www.clarke.edu/.

# CLARKSON COLLEGE
## Omaha, NE

**CONTACT** Pam Shelton, Director of Financial Aid, Clarkson College, 101 South 42nd Street, Omaha, NE 68131-2739, 402-552-2749 or toll-free 800-647-5500. *Fax:* 402-552-6165. *E-mail:* shelton@clarksoncollege.edu.
*Website:* http://www.clarksoncollege.edu/.

# CLARKSON UNIVERSITY
## Potsdam, NY

| Tuition & fees: $44,630 | Average undergraduate aid package: $40,409 |
| --- | --- |

**ABOUT THE INSTITUTION** Independent, coed. *Awards:* certificates, bachelor's, master's, and doctoral degrees. 35 undergraduate majors. *Total enrollment:* 3,873. Undergraduates: 3,247. Freshmen: 767. Federal methodology is used as a basis for awarding need-based institutional aid.
**UNDERGRADUATE EXPENSES for 2015–2016** *Application fee:* $50. *Comprehensive fee:* $58,474 includes full-time tuition ($43,690), mandatory fees ($940), and room and board ($13,844). *College room only:* $7334. Full-time tuition and fees vary according to course load. Room and board charges vary according to board plan and housing facility. *Part-time tuition:* $1457 per credit hour. Part-time tuition and fees vary according to course load.
**FRESHMAN FINANCIAL AID (Fall 2014, est.)** 690 applied for aid; of those 91% were deemed to have need. 100% of freshmen with need received aid; of those 24% had need fully met. *Average percent of need met:* 90% (excluding resources awarded to replace EFC). *Average financial aid package:* $40,738 (excluding resources awarded to replace EFC). 17% of all full-time freshmen had no need and received non-need-based gift aid.
**UNDERGRADUATE FINANCIAL AID (Fall 2014, est.)** 2,815 applied for aid; of those 94% were deemed to have need. 100% of undergraduates with need received aid; of those 19% had need fully met. *Average percent of need met:* 90% (excluding resources awarded to replace EFC). *Average financial aid package:* $40,409 (excluding resources awarded to replace EFC). 15% of all full-time undergraduates had no need and received non-need-based gift aid.
**GIFT AID (NEED-BASED)** *Total amount:* $76,121,784 (8% federal, 4% state, 87% institutional, 1% external sources). *Receiving aid:* Freshmen: 81% (622); all full-time undergraduates: 84% (2,613). *Average award:* Freshmen: $29,947; Undergraduates: $29,179. *Scholarships, grants, and awards:* Federal Pell, FSEOG, state, private, college/university gift aid from institutional funds, Higher Education Opportunity Program (HEOP).
**GIFT AID (NON-NEED-BASED)** *Total amount:* $13,264,114 (11% federal, 1% state, 86% institutional, 2% external sources). *Receiving aid:* Freshmen: 14% (109). Undergraduates: 11% (328). *Average award:* Freshmen: $21,360. Undergraduates: $19,191. *Scholarships, grants, and awards by category:* Academic interests/achievement: 3,221 awards ($40,675,895 total): biological sciences, business, communication, computer science, engineering/technologies, general academic interests/achievements, humanities, mathematics, military science, physical sciences, social sciences. Special achievements/activities: 652 awards ($3,491,865 total): general special achievements/activities, leadership. Special characteristics: 952 awards ($3,059,800

total): children and siblings of alumni, children of faculty/staff, general special characteristics, international students, local/state students, members of minority groups, veterans. **Tuition waivers:** Full or partial for employees or children of employees. **ROTC:** Army, Air Force.

**LOANS Student loans:** $26,965,916 (75% need-based, 25% non-need-based). 85% of past graduating class borrowed through all loan programs. **Average indebtedness per student:** $28,000. **Average need-based loan:** Freshmen: $4548. Undergraduates: $5533. **Parent loans:** $7,221,351 (51% need-based, 49% non-need-based). **Programs:** Federal Direct (Subsidized and Unsubsidized Stafford, PLUS), Perkins, college/university, alternative loans.

**WORK-STUDY Federal work-study:** Total amount: $500,829; 1,760 jobs averaging $1600. **State or other work-study/employment:** Total amount: $504,714 (60% need-based, 40% non-need-based). 74 part-time jobs averaging $9230. **ATHLETIC AWARDS** Total amount: $1,835,651 (7% need-based, 93% non-need-based).

**APPLYING FOR FINANCIAL AID Required financial aid forms:** FAFSA, state aid form. **Financial aid deadline:** 3/1 (priority: 2/15). **Notification date:** Continuous beginning 3/17. Students must reply by 5/1 or within 2 weeks of notification.

**CONTACT** Mrs. Pamela A. Nichols, Director of Financial Aid, Clarkson University, 8 Clarkson Avenue, Box 5615, Potsdam, NY 13699, 315-268-6413 or toll-free 800-527-6577. *Fax:* 315-268-3899. *E-mail:* pnichols@clarkson.edu. *Website:* http://www.clarkson.edu/.

# CLARK UNIVERSITY
## Worcester, MA

| Tuition & fees: $41,940 | Average undergraduate aid package: $33,231 |
|---|---|

**ABOUT THE INSTITUTION** Independent, coed. **Awards:** certificates, bachelor's, master's, and doctoral degrees. 48 undergraduate majors. **Total enrollment:** 3,423. Undergraduates: 2,301. Freshmen: 548. Institutional methodology is used as a basis for awarding need-based institutional aid.

**UNDERGRADUATE EXPENSES for 2015–2016 Application fee:** $55. **Comprehensive fee:** $50,140 includes full-time tuition ($41,590), mandatory fees ($350), and room and board ($8200). **College room only:** $4700. Room and board charges vary according to board plan and housing facility. **Part-time tuition:** $1300 per credit. **Payment plan:** Tuition prepayment.

**FRESHMAN FINANCIAL AID (Fall 2014, est.)** 399 applied for aid; of those 80% were deemed to have need. 99% of freshmen with need received aid; of those 65% had need fully met. **Average percent of need met:** 95% (excluding resources awarded to replace EFC). **Average financial aid package:** $34,602 (excluding resources awarded to replace EFC). 31% of all full-time freshmen had no need and received non-need-based gift aid.

**UNDERGRADUATE FINANCIAL AID (Fall 2014, est.)** 1,647 applied for aid; of those 80% were deemed to have need. 99% of undergraduates with need received aid; of those 69% had need fully met. **Average percent of need met:** 95% (excluding resources awarded to replace EFC). **Average financial aid package:** $33,231 (excluding resources awarded to replace EFC). 31% of all full-time undergraduates had no need and received non-need-based gift aid.

**GIFT AID (NEED-BASED) Total amount:** $30,728,564 (9% federal, 2% state, 89% institutional). **Receiving aid:** Freshmen: 57% (313); all full-time undergraduates: 59% (1,294). **Average award:** Freshmen: $26,602; Undergraduates: $25,826. **Scholarships, grants, and awards:** Federal Pell, FSEOG, state, college/university gift aid from institutional funds.

**GIFT AID (NON-NEED-BASED) Total amount:** $12,535,041 (100% institutional). **Receiving aid:** Freshmen: 25% (139). Undergraduates: 23% (512). **Average award:** Freshmen: $17,042. Undergraduates: $16,362. **Scholarships, grants, and awards by category:** *Academic interests/achievement:* general academic interests/achievements. *Special achievements/activities:* community service, general special achievements/activities. **Tuition waivers:** Full or partial for employees or children of employees. **ROTC:** Army cooperative, Naval cooperative, Air Force cooperative.

**LOANS Student loans:** $10,825,871 (62% need-based, 38% non-need-based). 91% of past graduating class borrowed through all loan programs. **Average indebtedness per student:** $24,990. **Average need-based loan:** Freshmen: $4780. Undergraduates: $4089. **Parent loans:** $3,112,698 (10% need-based, 90% non-need-based).

**Programs:** Federal Direct (Subsidized and Unsubsidized Stafford, PLUS), Perkins, state.

**WORK-STUDY Federal work-study:** Total amount: $1,443,147; 1,000 jobs averaging $2000.

**APPLYING FOR FINANCIAL AID Required financial aid forms:** FAFSA, CSS Financial Aid PROFILE, noncustodial (divorced/separated) parent's statement. **Financial aid deadline:** 2/1. **Notification date:** 3/31. Students must reply by 5/1.

**CONTACT** Ms. Mary Ellen Severance, Director of Financial Assistance, Clark University, 950 Main Street, Worcester, MA 01610-1477, 508-793-7478 or toll-free 800-GO-CLARK. *Fax:* 508-793-8802. *E-mail:* finaid@clarku.edu. *Website:* http://www.clarku.edu/.

# CLAYTON STATE UNIVERSITY
## Morrow, GA

| Tuition & fees (GA res): $6194 | Average undergraduate aid package: $9007 |
|---|---|

**ABOUT THE INSTITUTION** State-supported, coed. **Awards:** certificates, associate, bachelor's, and master's degrees. 34 undergraduate majors. **Total enrollment:** 7,022. Undergraduates: 6,632. Freshmen: 532. Federal methodology is used as a basis for awarding need-based institutional aid.

**UNDERGRADUATE EXPENSES for 2015–2016 Application fee:** $40. **Tuition, state resident:** full-time $4740. **Tuition, nonresident:** full-time $17,246. **Required fees:** full-time $1454. Full-time tuition and fees vary according to course load. Part-time tuition and fees vary according to course load. **College room and board:** $9240. Room and board charges vary according to board plan and housing facility.

**FRESHMAN FINANCIAL AID (Fall 2014, est.)** 412 applied for aid; of those 91% were deemed to have need. 100% of freshmen with need received aid; of those 5% had need fully met. **Average percent of need met:** 52% (excluding resources awarded to replace EFC). **Average financial aid package:** $9067 (excluding resources awarded to replace EFC). 1% of all full-time freshmen had no need and received non-need-based gift aid.

**UNDERGRADUATE FINANCIAL AID (Fall 2014, est.)** 3,344 applied for aid; of those 94% were deemed to have need. 100% of undergraduates with need received aid; of those 3% had need fully met. **Average percent of need met:** 46% (excluding resources awarded to replace EFC). **Average financial aid package:** $9007 (excluding resources awarded to replace EFC). 1% of all full-time undergraduates had no need and received non-need-based gift aid.

**GIFT AID (NEED-BASED) Total amount:** $22,112,725 (84% federal, 14% state, 1% institutional, 1% external sources). **Receiving aid:** Freshmen: 79% (343); all full-time undergraduates: 76% (2,722). **Average award:** Freshmen: $6535; Undergraduates: $5947. **Scholarships, grants, and awards:** Federal Pell, FSEOG, state, private, college/university gift aid from institutional funds, Federal Nursing.

**GIFT AID (NON-NEED-BASED) Total amount:** $594,944 (84% state, 12% institutional, 4% external sources). **Receiving aid:** Freshmen: 9% (37). Undergraduates: 3% (119). **Average award:** Freshmen: $2041. Undergraduates: $2321. **Tuition waivers:** Full or partial for employees or children of employees, senior citizens. **ROTC:** Army, Naval cooperative, Air Force cooperative.

**LOANS Student loans:** $44,692,051 (94% need-based, 6% non-need-based). 84% of past graduating class borrowed through all loan programs. **Average indebtedness per student:** $30,423. **Average need-based loan:** Freshmen: $3402. Undergraduates: $4179. **Parent loans:** $1,481,816 (66% need-based, 34% non-need-based). **Programs:** Federal Direct (Subsidized and Unsubsidized Stafford, PLUS), state.

**WORK-STUDY Federal work-study:** Total amount: $263,084; 62 jobs averaging $4733.

**ATHLETIC AWARDS** Total amount: $87,165 (86% need-based, 14% non-need-based).

**APPLYING FOR FINANCIAL AID Required financial aid form:** FAFSA. **Financial aid deadline (priority):** 7/15. **Notification date:** Continuous beginning 4/15.

**CONTACT** Patricia Barton, Director of Financial Aid, Clayton State University, 2000 Clayton State Boulevard, Morrow, GA 30260, 678-466-4181. *Fax:* 678-466-4189. *E-mail:* financialaid@mail.clayton.edu. *Website:* http://www.clayton.edu/.

# CLEAR CREEK BAPTIST BIBLE COLLEGE

## Pineville, KY

| Tuition & fees: N/R | Average undergraduate aid package: $8103 |
|---|---|

**ABOUT THE INSTITUTION** Independent Southern Baptist, coed, primarily men. 2 undergraduate majors. Institutional methodology is used as a basis for awarding need-based institutional aid.

**FRESHMAN FINANCIAL AID (Fall 2014, est.)** 10 applied for aid; of those 100% were deemed to have need. 100% of freshmen with need received aid. *Average percent of need met:* 50% (excluding resources awarded to replace EFC). *Average financial aid package:* $6365 (excluding resources awarded to replace EFC). 9% of all full-time freshmen had no need and received non-need-based gift aid.

**UNDERGRADUATE FINANCIAL AID (Fall 2014, est.)** 97 applied for aid; of those 100% were deemed to have need. 100% of undergraduates with need received aid. *Average percent of need met:* 50% (excluding resources awarded to replace EFC). *Average financial aid package:* $8103 (excluding resources awarded to replace EFC). 5% of all full-time undergraduates had no need and received non-need-based gift aid.

**GIFT AID (NEED-BASED)** *Total amount:* $713,680 (62% federal, 29% institutional, 9% external sources). *Receiving aid:* Freshmen: 91% (10); all full-time undergraduates: 98% (97). *Average award:* Freshmen: $6365; Undergraduates: $8103. *Scholarships, grants, and awards:* Federal Pell, FSEOG, state, private, college/university gift aid from institutional funds.

**GIFT AID (NON-NEED-BASED)** *Total amount:* $69,090 (44% federal, 56% institutional). *Receiving aid:* Freshmen: 18% (2). Undergraduates: 49% (49). *Average award:* Freshmen: $800. Undergraduates: $2967. *Scholarships, grants, and awards by category:* Academic interests/achievement: 3 awards ($540 total): general academic interests/achievements. Creative arts/performance: music. Special characteristics: 2 awards ($1138 total): handicapped students, international students.

**LOANS** *Student loans:* $55,804 (100% need-based).

**WORK-STUDY** *Federal work-study:* Total amount: $38,081; 52 jobs averaging $692.

**APPLYING FOR FINANCIAL AID** *Required financial aid forms:* FAFSA, institution's own form. *Financial aid deadline:* Continuous. *Notification date:* Continuous beginning 6/1.

**CONTACT** Mr. Sam Risner, Director of Financial Aid, Clear Creek Baptist Bible College, 300 Clear Creek Road, Pineville, KY 40977-9754, 606-337-3196 Ext. 142. *Fax:* 606-337-1631. *E-mail:* srisner@ccbbc.edu.
*Website:* http://www.ccbbc.edu/.

# CLEARY UNIVERSITY

## Ann Arbor, MI

**ABOUT THE INSTITUTION** Independent, coed. 9 undergraduate majors.

**GIFT AID (NEED-BASED)** *Scholarships, grants, and awards:* Federal Pell, FSEOG, state, private, college/university gift aid from institutional funds.

**GIFT AID (NON-NEED-BASED)** *Scholarships, grants, and awards by category:* Academic interests/achievement: business, computer science, general academic interests/achievements. Special characteristics: children and siblings of alumni, children of faculty/staff, veterans.

**LOANS** *Programs:* Federal Direct (Subsidized and Unsubsidized Stafford, PLUS).

**WORK-STUDY** *Federal work-study:* 16 jobs averaging $1970. *State or other work-study/employment:* 27 part-time jobs averaging $1382.

**APPLYING FOR FINANCIAL AID** *Required financial aid form:* FAFSA.

**CONTACT** Vesta Smith-Campbell, Director of Financial Aid, Cleary University, 3750 Cleary Drive, Howell, MI 48843, 517-338-3042 or toll-free 800-686-1883. *Fax:* 517-552-8022. *E-mail:* vscampbell@cleary.edu.
*Website:* http://www.cleary.edu/.

# CLEMSON UNIVERSITY

## Clemson, SC

| Tuition & fees (SC res): $13,808 | Average undergraduate aid package: $10,812 |
|---|---|

**ABOUT THE INSTITUTION** State-supported, coed. *Awards:* certificates, bachelor's, master's, and doctoral degrees. 71 undergraduate majors. *Total enrollment:* 21,303. Undergraduates: 16,931. Freshmen: 3,289. Federal methodology is used as a basis for awarding need-based institutional aid.

**UNDERGRADUATE EXPENSES for 2015–2016** *Application fee:* $100. *Tuition, state resident:* full-time $13,808; part-time $562 per credit hour. *Tuition, nonresident:* full-time $31,824; part-time $1345 per credit hour. Full-time tuition and fees vary according to course load, location, and program. Part-time tuition and fees vary according to program. *College room and board:* $8358. Room and board charges vary according to board plan, housing facility, and location.

**FRESHMAN FINANCIAL AID (Fall 2014, est.)** 2,785 applied for aid; of those 63% were deemed to have need. 99% of freshmen with need received aid; of those 23% had need fully met. *Average percent of need met:* 58% (excluding resources awarded to replace EFC). *Average financial aid package:* $12,640 (excluding resources awarded to replace EFC). 27% of all full-time freshmen had no need and received non-need-based gift aid.

**UNDERGRADUATE FINANCIAL AID (Fall 2014, est.)** 10,892 applied for aid; of those 73% were deemed to have need. 96% of undergraduates with need received aid; of those 18% had need fully met. *Average percent of need met:* 52% (excluding resources awarded to replace EFC). *Average financial aid package:* $10,812 (excluding resources awarded to replace EFC). 24% of all full-time undergraduates had no need and received non-need-based gift aid.

**GIFT AID (NEED-BASED)** *Total amount:* $58,313,659 (23% federal, 43% state, 28% institutional, 6% external sources). *Receiving aid:* Freshmen: 46% (1,617); all full-time undergraduates: 37% (6,367). *Average award:* Freshmen: $10,670; Undergraduates: $8590. *Scholarships, grants, and awards:* Federal Pell, FSEOG, state, private, college/university gift aid from institutional funds, Federal Nursing.

**GIFT AID (NON-NEED-BASED)** *Total amount:* $50,824,605 (51% state, 44% institutional, 5% external sources). *Receiving aid:* Freshmen: 32% (1,108). Undergraduates: 23% (3,994). *Average award:* Freshmen: $7643. Undergraduates: $5280. *Scholarships, grants, and awards by category:* Academic interests/achievement: agriculture, architecture, biological sciences, business, communication, computer science, education, engineering/technologies, English, foreign languages, general academic interests/achievements, health fields, humanities, international studies, mathematics, military science, physical sciences, premedicine, social sciences. Creative arts/performance: applied art and design, art/fine arts, performing arts, theater/drama. Special achievements/activities: community service, general special achievements/activities, leadership. Special characteristics: children of faculty/staff, ethnic background, local/state students, members of minority groups, veterans. *Tuition waivers:* Full or partial for senior citizens. *ROTC:* Army, Air Force.

**LOANS** *Student loans:* $71,506,819 (78% need-based, 22% non-need-based). 49% of past graduating class borrowed through all loan programs. *Average indebtedness per student:* $30,213. *Average need-based loan:* Freshmen: $3551. Undergraduates: $4413. *Parent loans:* $23,350,985 (78% need-based, 22% non-need-based). *Programs:* Federal Direct (Subsidized and Unsubsidized Stafford, PLUS), Perkins, state, college/university.

**WORK-STUDY** *Federal work-study:* Total amount: $2,171,694; 939 jobs averaging $2362. *State or other work-study/employment:* Part-time jobs available.

**ATHLETIC AWARDS** Total amount: $6,579,719 (47% need-based, 53% non-need-based).

**APPLYING FOR FINANCIAL AID** *Required financial aid form:* FAFSA. *Financial aid deadline (priority):* 3/1. *Notification date:* Continuous beginning 4/1. Students must reply within 3 weeks of notification.

**CONTACT** Mr. Chuck Knepfle, Director of Financial Aid, Clemson University, G-01 Sikes Hall, Box 345123, Clemson, SC 29634-5123, 864-656-2280. *Fax:* 864-656-1831. *E-mail:* finaid@clemson.edu.
*Website:* http://www.clemson.edu/.

# CLEVELAND INSTITUTE OF ART
## Cleveland, OH

| Tuition & fees: $38,320 | Average undergraduate aid package: $26,939 |
| --- | --- |

**ABOUT THE INSTITUTION** Independent, coed. **Awards:** bachelor's degrees. 15 undergraduate majors. **Total enrollment:** 559. Undergraduates: 559. Freshmen: 139. Federal methodology is used as a basis for awarding need-based institutional aid.

**UNDERGRADUATE EXPENSES for 2015–2016 Application fee:** $30. **Comprehensive fee:** $49,775 includes full-time tuition ($35,980), mandatory fees ($2340), and room and board ($11,455). **College room only:** $7325. Full-time tuition and fees vary according to program, reciprocity agreements, and student level. Room and board charges vary according to board plan and housing facility. **Part-time tuition:** $1499 per credit. Part-time tuition and fees vary according to course load, program, reciprocity agreements, and student level.

**FRESHMAN FINANCIAL AID (Fall 2014, est.)** 123 applied for aid; of those 96% were deemed to have need. 100% of freshmen with need received aid; of those 8% had need fully met. **Average percent of need met:** 58% (excluding resources awarded to replace EFC). **Average financial aid package:** $25,723 (excluding resources awarded to replace EFC). 15% of all full-time freshmen had no need and received non-need-based gift aid.

**UNDERGRADUATE FINANCIAL AID (Fall 2014, est.)** 463 applied for aid; of those 97% were deemed to have need. 100% of undergraduates with need received aid; of those 8% had need fully met. **Average percent of need met:** 62% (excluding resources awarded to replace EFC). **Average financial aid package:** $26,939 (excluding resources awarded to replace EFC). 16% of all full-time undergraduates had no need and received non-need-based gift aid.

**GIFT AID (NEED-BASED) Total amount:** $9,613,074 (11% federal, 4% state, 83% institutional, 2% external sources). **Receiving aid:** Freshmen: 79% (118); all full-time undergraduates: 82% (447). **Average award:** Freshmen: $21,075; Undergraduates: $21,514. **Scholarships, grants, and awards:** Federal Pell, FSEOG, state, private, college/university gift aid from institutional funds.

**GIFT AID (NON-NEED-BASED) Total amount:** $1,259,831 (100% institutional). **Receiving aid:** Freshmen: 5% (8). Undergraduates: 5% (28). **Average award:** Freshmen: $12,652. Undergraduates: $2988. **Scholarships, grants, and awards by category:** Creative arts/performance: applied art and design, art/fine arts. **Special characteristics:** children of faculty/staff, veterans. **Tuition waivers:** Full or partial for employees or children of employees.

**LOANS Student loans:** $4,884,459 (87% need-based, 13% non-need-based). 87% of past graduating class borrowed through all loan programs. **Average indebtedness per student:** $30,681. **Average need-based loan:** Freshmen: $4015. Undergraduates: $4643. **Parent loans:** $2,104,340 (79% need-based, 21% non-need-based). **Programs:** Federal Direct (Subsidized and Unsubsidized Stafford, PLUS), Perkins.

**WORK-STUDY Federal work-study:** Total amount: $484,602; 150 jobs averaging $1082.

**APPLYING FOR FINANCIAL AID Required financial aid form:** FAFSA. **Financial aid deadline (priority):** 3/15. **Notification date:** Continuous beginning 3/1. Students must reply by 5/1 or within 3 weeks of notification.

**CONTACT** Mr. Martin Joseph Carney Jr., Director of Financial Aid, Cleveland Institute of Art, 11141 East Boulevard, Cleveland, OH 44106-1700, 216-421-7425 or toll-free 800-223-4700. Fax: 216-754-3634. E-mail: financialaid@cia.edu. Website: http://www.cia.edu/.

# CLEVELAND INSTITUTE OF MUSIC
## Cleveland, OH

| Tuition & fees: $45,627 | Average undergraduate aid package: $29,573 |
| --- | --- |

**ABOUT THE INSTITUTION** Independent, coed. 3 undergraduate majors. Both federal and institutional methodology are used as a basis for awarding need-based institutional aid.

**UNDERGRADUATE EXPENSES for 2015–2016 Comprehensive fee:** $58,984 includes full-time tuition ($44,200), mandatory fees ($1427), and room and board ($13,357). Room and board charges vary according to board plan. **Part-time tuition:** $1842 per credit hour. **Part-time fees:** $1427 per year.

**FRESHMAN FINANCIAL AID (Fall 2014, est.)** 45 applied for aid; of those 82% were deemed to have need. 100% of freshmen with need received aid; of those 35% had need fully met. **Average percent of need met:** 78% (excluding resources awarded to replace EFC). **Average financial aid package:** $29,346 (excluding resources awarded to replace EFC). 31% of all full-time freshmen had no need and received non-need-based gift aid.

**UNDERGRADUATE FINANCIAL AID (Fall 2014, est.)** 161 applied for aid; of those 87% were deemed to have need. 100% of undergraduates with need received aid; of those 24% had need fully met. **Average percent of need met:** 73% (excluding resources awarded to replace EFC). **Average financial aid package:** $29,573 (excluding resources awarded to replace EFC). 38% of all full-time undergraduates had no need and received non-need-based gift aid.

**GIFT AID (NEED-BASED) Total amount:** $3,711,144 (4% federal, 93% institutional, 3% external sources). **Receiving aid:** Freshmen: 69% (37); all full-time undergraduates: 62% (140). **Average award:** Freshmen: $26,807; Undergraduates: $25,684. **Scholarships, grants, and awards:** Federal Pell, FSEOG, state, private, college/university gift aid from institutional funds.

**GIFT AID (NON-NEED-BASED) Total amount:** $2,371,562 (95% institutional, 5% external sources). **Receiving aid:** Freshmen: 24% (13). Undergraduates: 14% (31). **Average award:** Freshmen: $18,411. Undergraduates: $21,916. **Scholarships, grants, and awards by category:** Creative arts/performance: music. **Special characteristics:** children of faculty/staff. **Tuition waivers:** Full or partial for employees or children of employees.

**LOANS Student loans:** $997,969 (71% need-based, 29% non-need-based). 59% of past graduating class borrowed through all loan programs. **Average indebtedness per student:** $27,157. **Average need-based loan:** Freshmen: $3664. Undergraduates: $5002. **Parent loans:** $718,277 (42% need-based, 58% non-need-based). **Programs:** Federal Direct (Subsidized and Unsubsidized Stafford, PLUS), Perkins, college/university, private loans.

**WORK-STUDY Federal work-study:** Total amount: $64,350; jobs available. **State or other work-study/employment:** Total amount: $20,621 (26% need-based, 74% non-need-based). Part-time jobs available.

**APPLYING FOR FINANCIAL AID Required financial aid forms:** FAFSA, CSS Financial Aid PROFILE. **Financial aid deadline (priority):** 2/15. **Notification date:** 4/1. Students must reply by 5/1.

**CONTACT** Ms. Kristie Gripp, Director of Financial Aid, Cleveland Institute of Music, 11021 East Boulevard, Cleveland, OH 44106-1776, 216-795-3192. Fax: 216-707-4519. E-mail: kristine.gripp@cim.edu. Website: http://www.cim.edu/.

# CLEVELAND STATE UNIVERSITY
## Cleveland, OH

| Tuition & fees (OH res): $9686 | Average undergraduate aid package: $8935 |
| --- | --- |

**ABOUT THE INSTITUTION** State-supported, coed. **Awards:** certificates, bachelor's, master's, and doctoral degrees. 77 undergraduate majors. **Total enrollment:** 17,301. Undergraduates: 12,194. Freshmen: 1,591. Federal methodology is used as a basis for awarding need-based institutional aid.

**UNDERGRADUATE EXPENSES for 2015–2016 Application fee:** $30. **Tuition, state resident:** full-time $9636; part-time $401.50 per credit hour. **Tuition, nonresident:** full-time $12,878; part-time $536.60 per credit hour. **Required fees:** full-time $50; $25 per term. Full-time tuition and fees vary according to course load, degree level, and program. Part-time tuition and fees vary according to course load, degree level, and program. **College room and board:** $11,858; **Room only:** $8108. Room and board charges vary according to board plan and housing facility.

**FRESHMAN FINANCIAL AID (Fall 2014, est.)** 1,310 applied for aid; of those 87% were deemed to have need. 98% of freshmen with need received aid; of those 9% had need fully met. **Average percent of need met:** 48% (excluding resources awarded to replace EFC). **Average financial aid package:** $9168 (excluding resources awarded to replace EFC). 8% of all full-time freshmen had no need and received non-need-based gift aid.

**UNDERGRADUATE FINANCIAL AID (Fall 2014, est.)** 7,299 applied for aid; of those 90% were deemed to have need. 97% of undergraduates with need received aid; of those 7% had need fully met. **Average percent of need met:** 45% (excluding resources awarded to replace EFC). **Average financial aid package:** $8935

(excluding resources awarded to replace EFC). 5% of all full-time undergraduates had no need and received non-need-based gift aid.

**GIFT AID (NEED-BASED) Total amount:** $34,986,274 (65% federal, 13% state, 13% institutional, 9% external sources). **Receiving aid:** Freshmen: 60% (923); all full-time undergraduates: 58% (5,009). **Average award:** Freshmen: $6904; Undergraduates: $6397. **Scholarships, grants, and awards:** Federal Pell, FSEOG, state, private, college/university gift aid from institutional funds.

**GIFT AID (NON-NEED-BASED) Total amount:** $3,346,770 (2% federal, 4% state, 69% institutional, 25% external sources). **Receiving aid:** Freshmen: 4% (56). Undergraduates: 2% (189). **Average award:** Freshmen: $4430. Undergraduates: $4839. **Scholarships, grants, and awards by category:** Academic interests/achievement: biological sciences, business, communication, computer science, education, engineering/technologies, English, general academic interests/achievements, health fields, humanities, mathematics, physical sciences, premedicine, social sciences. Creative arts/performance: art/fine arts, creative writing, dance, journalism/publications, music, performing arts, theater/drama. Special achievements/activities: cheerleading/drum major. Special characteristics: children of faculty/staff, general special characteristics, out-of-state students. **Tuition waivers:** Full or partial for employees or children of employees, senior citizens. **ROTC:** Army cooperative, Air Force cooperative.

**LOANS Student loans:** $61,272,392 (87% need-based, 13% non-need-based). 57% of past graduating class borrowed through all loan programs. **Average indebtedness per student:** $24,856. **Average need-based loan:** Freshmen: $3957. Undergraduates: $4443. **Parent loans:** $3,163,182 (49% need-based, 51% non-need-based). **Programs:** Federal Direct (Subsidized and Unsubsidized Stafford, PLUS), Perkins, state, alternative loans.

**WORK-STUDY Federal work-study:** Total amount: $1,583,712; 414 jobs averaging $3560. **State or other work-study/employment:** Part-time jobs available.

**ATHLETIC AWARDS** Total amount: $2,626,103 (37% need-based, 63% non-need-based).

**APPLYING FOR FINANCIAL AID Required financial aid forms:** FAFSA, federal income tax form(s). **Financial aid deadline (priority):** 2/15. **Notification date:** Continuous beginning 3/15. Students must reply within 4 weeks of notification.

**CONTACT** Financial Aid Office, Cleveland State University, 1621 Euclid Avenue, Cleveland, OH 44115, 216-687-5594 or toll-free 888-CSU-OHIO. E-mail: campus411@csuohio.edu.
Website: http://www.csuohio.edu/.

# COASTAL CAROLINA UNIVERSITY
## Conway, SC

**Tuition & fees (SC res): $10,140** | **Average undergraduate aid package: $9855**

**ABOUT THE INSTITUTION** State-supported, coed. **Awards:** certificates, bachelor's, master's, and doctoral degrees. 41 undergraduate majors. **Total enrollment:** 9,976. Undergraduates: 9,364. Freshmen: 2,375. Federal methodology is used as a basis for awarding need-based institutional aid.

**UNDERGRADUATE EXPENSES for 2015–2016 Application fee:** $45. **Tuition, state resident:** full-time $9960; part-time $425 per credit hour. **Tuition, nonresident:** full-time $23,300; part-time $975 per credit hour. **Required fees:** full-time $180. Full-time tuition and fees vary according to course load and degree level. Part-time tuition and fees vary according to course load and degree level. **College room and board:** $8440; **Room only:** $5440. Room and board charges vary according to board plan and housing facility.

**FRESHMAN FINANCIAL AID (Fall 2013)** 1,904 applied for aid; of those 82% were deemed to have need. 99% of freshmen with need received aid; of those 9% had need fully met. **Average percent of need met:** 50% (excluding resources awarded to replace EFC). **Average financial aid package:** $10,100 (excluding resources awarded to replace EFC). 18% of all full-time freshmen had no need and received non-need-based gift aid.

**UNDERGRADUATE FINANCIAL AID (Fall 2013)** 6,839 applied for aid; of those 85% were deemed to have need. 99% of undergraduates with need received aid; of those 9% had need fully met. **Average percent of need met:** 48% (excluding resources awarded to replace EFC). **Average financial aid package:** $9855 (excluding resources awarded to replace EFC). 16% of all full-time undergraduates had no need and received non-need-based gift aid.

**GIFT AID (NEED-BASED) Total amount:** $15,952,963 (92% federal, 8% state). **Receiving aid:** Freshmen: 38% (802); all full-time undergraduates: 40% (3,205). **Average award:** Freshmen: $5069; Undergraduates: $4798. **Scholarships, grants, and awards:** Federal Pell, FSEOG, state, private, college/university gift aid from institutional funds.

**GIFT AID (NON-NEED-BASED) Total amount:** $13,575,246 (66% state, 21% institutional, 13% external sources). **Receiving aid:** Freshmen: 34% (705). Undergraduates: 21% (1,708). **Average award:** Freshmen: $11,822. Undergraduates: $12,574. **Scholarships, grants, and awards by category:** Academic interests/achievement: 2,557 awards ($7,442,857 total): biological sciences, business, communication, computer science, education, English, foreign languages, general academic interests/achievements, humanities, international studies, mathematics, physical sciences, social sciences. Creative arts/performance: 55 awards ($60,988 total): art/fine arts, music, performing arts, theater/drama. Special achievements/activities: 31 awards ($32,500 total): cheerleading/drum major. Special characteristics: 1,812 awards ($5,400,108 total): general special characteristics, international students, local/state students, out-of-state students, veterans' children. **Tuition waivers:** Full or partial for employees or children of employees, senior citizens. **ROTC:** Army.

**LOANS Student loans:** $60,824,916 (33% need-based, 67% non-need-based). 78% of past graduating class borrowed through all loan programs. **Average indebtedness per student:** $35,207. **Average need-based loan:** Freshmen: $8904. Undergraduates: $8846. **Parent loans:** $17,375,624 (100% non-need-based). **Programs:** Federal Direct (Subsidized and Unsubsidized Stafford, PLUS), Perkins, state.

**WORK-STUDY Federal work-study:** 122 jobs averaging $2446. **State or other work-study/employment:** Total amount: $2,853,067 (11% need-based, 89% non-need-based). 1,035 part-time jobs averaging $2459.

**ATHLETIC AWARDS** Total amount: $4,168,775 (100% non-need-based).

**APPLYING FOR FINANCIAL AID Required financial aid form:** FAFSA. **Financial aid deadline (priority):** 3/1. **Notification date:** Continuous beginning 3/1. Students must reply by 5/15.

**CONTACT** Ms. Wendy H. Watts, Director of Financial Aid and Scholarships, Coastal Carolina University, PO Box 261954, Conway, SC 29528-6054, 843-349-2190 or toll-free 800-277-7000. Fax: 843-349-2347. E-mail: wwatts@coastal.edu.
Website: http://www.coastal.edu/.

# COE COLLEGE
## Cedar Rapids, IA

**Tuition & fees: $37,320** | **Average undergraduate aid package: $30,351**

**ABOUT THE INSTITUTION** Independent Presbyterian Church, coed. **Awards:** bachelor's degrees. 65 undergraduate majors. **Total enrollment:** 1,436. Undergraduates: 1,435. Freshmen: 376. Federal methodology is used as a basis for awarding need-based institutional aid.

**UNDERGRADUATE EXPENSES for 2015–2016 Application fee:** $30. **Comprehensive fee:** $45,550 includes full-time tuition ($36,990), mandatory fees ($330), and room and board ($8230). **College room only:** $3730. Room and board charges vary according to board plan and housing facility. **Part-time tuition:** $4155 per course. Part-time tuition and fees vary according to course load.

**FRESHMAN FINANCIAL AID (Fall 2014, est.)** 357 applied for aid; of those 92% were deemed to have need. 100% of freshmen with need received aid; of those 20% had need fully met. **Average percent of need met:** 87% (excluding resources awarded to replace EFC). **Average financial aid package:** $33,073 (excluding resources awarded to replace EFC). 13% of all full-time freshmen had no need and received non-need-based gift aid.

**UNDERGRADUATE FINANCIAL AID (Fall 2014, est.)** 1,210 applied for aid; of those 93% were deemed to have need. 100% of undergraduates with need received aid; of those 20% had need fully met. **Average percent of need met:** 83% (excluding resources awarded to replace EFC). **Average financial aid package:** $30,351 (excluding resources awarded to replace EFC). 15% of all full-time undergraduates had no need and received non-need-based gift aid.

**GIFT AID (NEED-BASED) Total amount:** $27,448,231 (7% federal, 6% state, 84% institutional, 3% external sources). **Receiving aid:** Freshmen: 87% (327); all full-time undergraduates: 84% (1,124). **Average award:** Freshmen: $28,086; Undergraduates: $25,079. **Scholarships, grants, and awards:** Federal Pell, FSEOG, state, private, college/university gift aid from institutional funds, Federal Nursing, ROTC Scholarships.

**GIFT AID (NON-NEED-BASED)** *Total amount:* $5,721,800 (2% federal, 92% institutional, 6% external sources). *Receiving aid:* Freshmen: 14% (51). Undergraduates: 13% (169). *Average award:* Freshmen: $21,781. Undergraduates: $20,313. *Scholarships, grants, and awards by category: Academic interests/ achievement:* 1,789 awards ($19,740,105 total): biological sciences, business, English, foreign languages, general academic interests/achievements, mathematics, physical sciences, premedicine. *Creative arts/performance:* 51 awards ($379,180 total): art/fine arts, creative writing, music, performing arts, theater/drama. *Special achievements/ activities:* 7 awards ($6000 total): community service. *Special characteristics:* 376 awards ($2,288,967 total): adult students, children and siblings of alumni, children of educators, children of faculty/staff, ethnic background, general special characteristics, international students, members of minority groups, religious affiliation, siblings of current students, veterans, veterans' children. *Tuition waivers:* Full or partial for employees or children of employees, adult students, senior citizens. *ROTC:* Army, Air Force cooperative.

**LOANS** *Student loans:* $9,593,997 (76% need-based, 24% non-need-based). 77% of past graduating class borrowed through all loan programs. *Average indebtedness per student:* $31,992. *Average need-based loan:* Freshmen: $4979. Undergraduates: $5491. *Parent loans:* $2,490,465 (37% need-based, 63% non-need-based). *Programs:* Federal Direct (Subsidized and Unsubsidized Stafford, PLUS), Perkins, college/university.

**WORK-STUDY** *Federal work-study:* Total amount: $834,887; 651 jobs averaging $1668. *State or other work-study/employment:* Total amount: $327,700 (15% need-based, 85% non-need-based). 224 part-time jobs averaging $1449.

**APPLYING FOR FINANCIAL AID** *Required financial aid form:* FAFSA. *Financial aid deadline (priority):* 3/1. *Notification date:* Continuous beginning 3/15. Students must reply by 5/1 or within 2 weeks of notification.

**CONTACT** Ms. Barbara Hoffman, Director of Financial Aid, Coe College, 1220 First Avenue, NE, Cedar Rapids, IA 52402-5070, 319-399-8540 or toll-free 877-225-5263. *Fax:* 319-399-8886.
*Website:* http://www.coe.edu/.

# COGSWELL POLYTECHNICAL COLLEGE
## Sunnyvale, CA

**CONTACT** Lisa Mandy, Director of Financial Aid, Cogswell Polytechnical College, 1175 Bordeaux Drive, Sunnyvale, CA 94089, 408-498-5107 or toll-free 800-264-7955. *Fax:* 408-747-0765. *E-mail:* lmandy@cogswell.edu.
*Website:* http://www.cogswell.edu/.

# COKER COLLEGE
## Hartsville, SC

| Tuition & fees: $25,536 | Average undergraduate aid package: $19,754 |
|---|---|

**ABOUT THE INSTITUTION** Independent, coed. *Awards:* bachelor's and master's degrees (also offers evening program with significant enrollment not reflected in profile). 41 undergraduate majors. *Total enrollment:* 1,219. Undergraduates: 1,165. Freshmen: 239. Both federal and institutional methodology are used as a basis for awarding need-based institutional aid.

**UNDERGRADUATE EXPENSES** for 2015–2016 *Application fee:* $25. *Comprehensive fee:* $33,366 includes full-time tuition ($25,536) and room and board ($7830). Full-time tuition and fees vary according to course load, degree level, location, and program. Room and board charges vary according to board plan and housing facility. *Part-time tuition:* $1064 per credit hour. Part-time tuition and fees vary according to course load, degree level, location, and program.

**FRESHMAN FINANCIAL AID (Fall 2014, est.)** 209 applied for aid; of those 90% were deemed to have need. 100% of freshmen with need received aid; of those 28% had need fully met. *Average percent of need met:* 45% (excluding resources awarded to replace EFC). *Average financial aid package:* $22,483 (excluding resources awarded to replace EFC). 7% of all full-time freshmen had no need and received non-need-based gift aid.

**UNDERGRADUATE FINANCIAL AID (Fall 2014, est.)** 910 applied for aid; of those 93% were deemed to have need. 100% of undergraduates with need received

aid; of those 18% had need fully met. *Average percent of need met:* 47% (excluding resources awarded to replace EFC). *Average financial aid package:* $19,754 (excluding resources awarded to replace EFC). 4% of all full-time undergraduates had no need and received non-need-based gift aid.

**GIFT AID (NEED-BASED)** *Receiving aid:* Freshmen: 79% (180); all full-time undergraduates: 70% (817). *Average award:* Freshmen: $9385; Undergraduates: $7807. *Scholarships, grants, and awards:* Federal Pell, FSEOG, state, private, college/university gift aid from institutional funds.

**GIFT AID (NON-NEED-BASED)** *Receiving aid:* Freshmen: 76% (173). Undergraduates: 53% (617). *Average award:* Freshmen: $9603. Undergraduates: $7996. *Scholarships, grants, and awards by category: Academic interests/ achievement:* biological sciences, general academic interests/achievements. *Creative arts/performance:* art/fine arts, creative writing, dance, general creative arts/performance, music, theater/drama. *Special achievements/activities:* cheerleading/drum major, leadership. *Special characteristics:* children and siblings of alumni, children of faculty/staff, international students, local/state students, out-of-state students, previous college experience, veterans. *Tuition waivers:* Full or partial for employees or children of employees.

**LOANS** *Student loans:* 81% of past graduating class borrowed through all loan programs. *Average need-based loan:* Freshmen: $3249. Undergraduates: $4487. *Programs:* Federal Direct (Subsidized and Unsubsidized Stafford, PLUS), Perkins, state, private loans.

**WORK-STUDY** Federal work-study jobs available. *State or other work-study/ employment:* Part-time jobs available.

**APPLYING FOR FINANCIAL AID** *Required financial aid form:* FAFSA. *Financial aid deadline:* 6/1 (priority: 4/1). *Notification date:* Continuous beginning 3/1. Students must reply by 5/1 or within 3 weeks of notification.

**CONTACT** Mrs. Betty Williams, Director of Financial Aid, Coker College, 300 East College Avenue, Hartsville, SC 29550, 843-383-8055 or toll-free 800-950-1908. *Fax:* 843-383-8056. *E-mail:* bwilliams@coker.edu.
*Website:* http://www.coker.edu/.

# THE COLBURN SCHOOL CONSERVATORY OF MUSIC
## Los Angeles, CA

**CONTACT** Ms. Kathleen Tesar, Associate Dean, The Colburn School Conservatory of Music, 200 South Grand Avenue, Los Angeles, CA 90012, 213-621-4534. *Fax:* 213-625-0371. *E-mail:* admissions@colburnschool.edu.
*Website:* http://www.colburnschool.edu/.

# COLBY COLLEGE
## Waterville, ME

| Tuition & fees: $47,350 | Average undergraduate aid package: $42,858 |
|---|---|

**ABOUT THE INSTITUTION** Independent, coed. *Awards:* bachelor's degrees. 47 undergraduate majors. *Total enrollment:* 1,847. Undergraduates: 1,847. Freshmen: 480. Both federal and institutional methodology are used as a basis for awarding need-based institutional aid.

**UNDERGRADUATE EXPENSES** for 2015–2016 *Comprehensive fee:* $59,500 includes full-time tuition ($45,360), mandatory fees ($1990), and room and board ($12,150). Room and board charges vary according to housing facility. *Part-time fees:* $1740 per credit hour. Part-time tuition and fees vary according to course load.

**FRESHMAN FINANCIAL AID (Fall 2014, est.)** 239 applied for aid; of those 72% were deemed to have need. 100% of freshmen with need received aid; of those 100% had need fully met. *Average percent of need met:* 100% (excluding resources awarded to replace EFC). *Average financial aid package:* $46,029 (excluding resources awarded to replace EFC). 1% of all full-time freshmen had no need and received non-need-based gift aid.

**UNDERGRADUATE FINANCIAL AID (Fall 2014, est.)** 915 applied for aid; of those 78% were deemed to have need. 100% of undergraduates with need received aid; of those 100% had need fully met. *Average percent of need met:* 100%

(excluding resources awarded to replace EFC). *Average financial aid package:* $42,858 (excluding resources awarded to replace EFC). 1% of all full-time undergraduates had no need and received non-need-based gift aid.

**GIFT AID (NEED-BASED)** *Total amount:* $29,156,133 (5% federal, 94% institutional, 1% external sources). *Receiving aid:* Freshmen: 36% (171); all full-time undergraduates: 38% (710). *Average award:* Freshmen: $44,014; Undergraduates: $41,033. *Scholarships, grants, and awards:* Federal Pell, FSEOG, state, private, college/university gift aid from institutional funds, Academic Competitiveness Grants, National SMART Grants, Colby National Merit Scholarships.

**GIFT AID (NON-NEED-BASED)** *Total amount:* $484,523 (39% federal, 46% institutional, 15% external sources). *Receiving aid:* Freshmen: 1% (4). Undergraduates: 1% (16). *Average award:* Freshmen: $500. Undergraduates: $500. *Scholarships, grants, and awards by category:* Academic interests/achievement: 26 awards ($9300 total): general academic interests/achievements. *Special characteristics:* 13 awards ($211,275 total): general special characteristics. *Tuition waivers:* Full or partial for employees or children of employees. *ROTC:* Army cooperative.

**LOANS** *Student loans:* $2,226,190 (10% need-based, 90% non-need-based). 33% of past graduating class borrowed through all loan programs. *Average indebtedness per student:* $21,958. *Average need-based loan:* Freshmen: $4150. Undergraduates: $3942. *Parent loans:* $1,882,142 (100% non-need-based). *Programs:* Federal Direct (Subsidized and Unsubsidized Stafford, PLUS), Perkins, state, college/university, alternative loans.

**WORK-STUDY** *Federal work-study:* Total amount: $631,125; 370 jobs averaging $1706. *State or other work-study/employment:* Total amount: $258,875 (100% need-based). 146 part-time jobs averaging $1733.

**APPLYING FOR FINANCIAL AID** *Required financial aid forms:* FAFSA, CSS Financial Aid PROFILE, federal income tax form(s). *Financial aid deadline:* 2/1. *Notification date:* 4/1. Students must reply by 5/1.

**CONTACT** David Jones, Director of Operations and New Student Aid, Colby College, 4850 Mayflower Hill, Waterville, ME 04901-8848, 800-723-3032. *Fax:* 207-859-4828. *E-mail:* finaid@colby.edu.
*Website:* http://www.colby.edu/.

# COLBY-SAWYER COLLEGE
## New London, NH

| Tuition & fees: $38,610 | Average undergraduate aid package: N/A |
| --- | --- |

**ABOUT THE INSTITUTION** Independent, coed. *Awards:* certificates, associate, and bachelor's degrees. 27 undergraduate majors. *Total enrollment:* 1,369. Undergraduates: 1,369. Freshmen: 331. Federal methodology is used as a basis for awarding need-based institutional aid.

**UNDERGRADUATE EXPENSES for 2015–2016** *Application fee:* $45. *Tuition:* full-time $38,610; part-time $1287 per credit. Part-time tuition and fees vary according to course load. Room and board charges vary according to housing facility.

**GIFT AID (NEED-BASED)** *Total amount:* $11,179,261 (23% federal, 1% state, 76% institutional). *Scholarships, grants, and awards:* Federal Pell, FSEOG, state, private, college/university gift aid from institutional funds.

**GIFT AID (NON-NEED-BASED)** *Total amount:* $25,445,714 (100% institutional). *Scholarships, grants, and awards by category:* Academic interests/achievement: general academic interests/achievements. *Creative arts/performance:* applied art and design, art/fine arts, creative writing. *Special achievements/activities:* community service, leadership. *Special characteristics:* children of faculty/staff. *Tuition waivers:* Full or partial for employees or children of employees. *ROTC:* Army cooperative.

**LOANS** *Student loans:* $9,456,147 (41% need-based, 59% non-need-based). *Parent loans:* $2,511,754 (100% non-need-based). *Programs:* Federal Direct (Subsidized and Unsubsidized Stafford, PLUS), Perkins.

**WORK-STUDY** *Federal work-study:* Total amount: $3,897,767; jobs available.

**APPLYING FOR FINANCIAL AID** *Required financial aid form:* FAFSA. *Financial aid deadline:* 3/1 (priority: 2/15). *Notification date:* Continuous beginning 2/1. Students must reply by 5/1.

**CONTACT** Ms. Beth Renzulli, Director of Financial Aid, Colby-Sawyer College, 541 Main Street, New London, NH 03257-7835, 603-526-3717 or toll-free 800-272-1015. *Fax:* 603-526-3737. *E-mail:* cscfinaid@colby-sawyer.edu.
*Website:* http://www.colby-sawyer.edu/.

# COLEGIO UNIVERSITARIO DE SAN JUAN
## San Juan, PR

**ABOUT THE INSTITUTION** City-supported, coed. 12 undergraduate majors.

**GIFT AID (NEED-BASED)** *Scholarships, grants, and awards:* Federal Pell, FSEOG, state, private, college/university gift aid from institutional funds.

**GIFT AID (NON-NEED-BASED)** *Scholarships, grants, and awards by category:* Academic interests/achievement: agriculture, architecture, area/ethnic studies, biological sciences, business, communication, computer science, engineering/technologies, English, foreign languages, general academic interests/achievements, health fields, humanities, mathematics, physical sciences, premedicine, social sciences. *Creative arts/performance:* applied art and design, art/fine arts, creative writing, general creative arts/performance, journalism/publications, music, performing arts, theater/drama. *Special characteristics:* ethnic background, first-generation college students, handicapped students, local/state students, members of minority groups, veterans.

**LOANS** *Programs:* private loans.

**WORK-STUDY** Federal work-study jobs available. *State or other work-study/employment:* Part-time jobs available.

**APPLYING FOR FINANCIAL AID** *Required financial aid forms:* FAFSA, California Dream Application.

**CONTACT** Ken Lira, Director of Financial Aid, Colegio Universitario de San Juan, 43-500 Monterey Avenue, Palm Desert, AB 92260, 760-776-7428. *Fax:* 760-776-7338. *E-mail:* klira@collegeofthedesert.edu.
*Website:* http://www.cunisanjuan.edu/.

# COLEMAN UNIVERSITY
## San Diego, CA

**CONTACT** Financial Aid Office, Coleman University, 8888 Balboa Avenue, San Diego, CA 92123, 858-499-0202 or toll-free 800-430-2030. *Fax:* 858-499-0233. *E-mail:* faoffice@coleman.edu.
*Website:* http://www.coleman.edu/.

# COLGATE UNIVERSITY
## Hamilton, NY

| Tuition & fees: $48,175 | Average undergraduate aid package: $45,594 |
| --- | --- |

**ABOUT THE INSTITUTION** Independent, coed. *Awards:* bachelor's and master's degrees. 51 undergraduate majors. *Total enrollment:* 2,898. Undergraduates: 2,890. Freshmen: 759. Institutional methodology is used as a basis for awarding need-based institutional aid.

**UNDERGRADUATE EXPENSES for 2015–2016** *Application fee:* $60. *One-time required fee:* $50. *Comprehensive fee:* $60,145 includes full-time tuition ($47,855), mandatory fees ($320), and room and board ($11,970). *College room only:* $5775. Full-time tuition and fees vary according to course load. Room and board charges vary according to board plan and housing facility. *Part-time tuition:* $5981.88 per course. Part-time tuition and fees vary according to course load. *Payment plan:* Tuition prepayment.

**FRESHMAN FINANCIAL AID (Fall 2014, est.)** 307 applied for aid; of those 86% were deemed to have need. 100% of freshmen with need received aid; of those 100% had need fully met. *Average percent of need met:* 100% (excluding resources awarded to replace EFC). *Average financial aid package:* $46,696 (excluding resources awarded to replace EFC).

**UNDERGRADUATE FINANCIAL AID (Fall 2014, est.)** 1,086 applied for aid; of those 92% were deemed to have need. 100% of undergraduates with need received aid; of those 100% had need fully met. *Average percent of need met:* 100% (excluding resources awarded to replace EFC). *Average financial aid package:* $45,594 (excluding resources awarded to replace EFC).

**GIFT AID (NEED-BASED)** *Total amount:* $42,782,068 (4% federal, 2% state, 92% institutional, 2% external sources). *Receiving aid:* Freshmen: 34% (264); all full-time undergraduates: 34% (991). *Average award:* Freshmen: $43,023; Undergrad-

uates: $41,428. **Scholarships, grants, and awards:** Federal Pell, FSEOG, state, college/university gift aid from institutional funds.

**GIFT AID (NON-NEED-BASED) Total amount:** $1,108,166 (18% institutional, 82% external sources). **Scholarships, grants, and awards by category:** Special characteristics: 15 awards ($203,901 total): veterans, veterans' children. **Tuition waivers:** Full or partial for employees or children of employees. **ROTC:** Army cooperative.

**LOANS Student loans:** $5,229,023 (44% need-based, 56% non-need-based). 31% of past graduating class borrowed through all loan programs. Average indebtedness per student: $21,405. **Average need-based loan:** Freshmen: $1414. Undergraduates: $3612. **Parent loans:** $4,331,743 (100% non-need-based). **Programs:** Federal Direct (Subsidized and Unsubsidized Stafford, PLUS), Perkins.

**WORK-STUDY Federal work-study:** Total amount: $1,305,690; 583 jobs averaging $2241. **State or other work-study/employment:** Total amount: $582,397 (97% need-based, 3% non-need-based). 277 part-time jobs averaging $2039.

**ATHLETIC AWARDS** Total amount: $9,316,084 (100% non-need-based).

**APPLYING FOR FINANCIAL AID Required financial aid forms:** CSS Financial Aid PROFILE, noncustodial (divorced/separated) parent's statement. **Financial aid deadline:** 1/15. **Notification date:** 4/1. Students must reply by 5/1 or within 2 weeks of notification.

**CONTACT** Office of Financial Aid, Colgate University, 13 Oak Drive, Hamilton, NY 13346, 315-228-7431. Fax: 315-228-7050. E-mail: finaid@colgate.edu. Website: http://www.colgate.edu/.

---

# COLLEGEAMERICA–CHEYENNE
## Cheyenne, WY

**CONTACT** Financial Aid Office, CollegeAmerica–Cheyenne, 6101 Yellowstone Road, Cheyenne, WY 82009, 800-622-2894. Website: http://www.collegeamerica.edu/.

---

# THE COLLEGE AT BROCKPORT, STATE UNIVERSITY OF NEW YORK
## Brockport, NY

| Tuition & fees (NY res): $7562 | Average undergraduate aid package: $10,374 |
|---|---|

**ABOUT THE INSTITUTION** State-supported, coed. **Awards:** certificates, bachelor's, and master's degrees. 43 undergraduate majors. **Total enrollment:** 8,106. Undergraduates: 7,040. Freshmen: 1,090. Federal methodology is used as a basis for awarding need-based institutional aid.

**UNDERGRADUATE EXPENSES for 2015–2016 Application fee:** $50. **Tuition, state resident:** full-time $6170; part-time $257 per credit. **Tuition, non-resident:** full-time $15,820; part-time $659 per credit. **Required fees:** full-time $1392. Part-time tuition and fees vary according to course load. **College room and board:** $11,440; **Room only:** $7130. Room and board charges vary according to board plan and housing facility.

**FRESHMAN FINANCIAL AID (Fall 2014, est.)** 922 applied for aid; of those 78% were deemed to have need. 97% of freshmen with need received aid; of those 14% had need fully met. **Average percent of need met:** 75% (excluding resources awarded to replace EFC). **Average financial aid package:** $11,511 (excluding resources awarded to replace EFC). 8% of all full-time freshmen had no need and received non-need-based gift aid.

**UNDERGRADUATE FINANCIAL AID (Fall 2014, est.)** 4,584 applied for aid; of those 80% were deemed to have need. 98% of undergraduates with need received aid; of those 16% had need fully met. **Average percent of need met:** 75% (excluding resources awarded to replace EFC). **Average financial aid package:** $10,374 (excluding resources awarded to replace EFC). 3% of all full-time undergraduates had no need and received non-need-based gift aid.

**GIFT AID (NEED-BASED) Total amount:** $22,030,833 (55% federal, 44% state, 1% external sources). **Receiving aid:** Freshmen: 55% (549); all full-time undergraduates: 56% (2,944). **Average award:** Freshmen: $6922; Undergraduates: $6361. **Scholarships, grants, and awards:** Federal Pell, FSEOG, state, private, college/university gift aid from institutional funds.

**GIFT AID (NON-NEED-BASED) Total amount:** $5,214,889 (12% federal, 7% state, 61% institutional, 20% external sources). **Receiving aid:** Freshmen: 26% (255). Undergraduates: 15% (771). **Average award:** Freshmen: $4238. Undergraduates: $4627. **Scholarships, grants, and awards by category:** Academic interests/achievement: 713 awards ($2,411,884 total): biological sciences, business, communication, computer science, education, English, foreign languages, general academic interests/achievements, health fields, humanities, international studies, mathematics, military science, physical sciences, premedicine, social sciences. Creative arts/performance: 51 awards ($44,800 total): art/fine arts, cinema/film/broadcasting, creative writing, dance, general creative arts/performance, journalism/publications, music, theater/drama. Special achievements/activities: 38 awards ($33,500 total): community service, general special achievements/activities, hobbies/interests, leadership, religious involvement. Special characteristics: 45 awards ($61,965 total): children and siblings of alumni, ethnic background, first-generation college students, general special characteristics, international students, married students, members of minority groups, previous college experience, religious affiliation, veterans. **Tuition waivers:** Full or partial for employees or children of employees, senior citizens. **ROTC:** Army, Naval cooperative, Air Force cooperative.

**LOANS Student loans:** $39,490,815 (45% need-based, 55% non-need-based). 82% of past graduating class borrowed through all loan programs. Average indebtedness per student: $27,666. **Average need-based loan:** Freshmen: $4772. Undergraduates: $4760. **Parent loans:** $4,642,983 (100% non-need-based). **Programs:** Federal Direct (Subsidized and Unsubsidized Stafford, PLUS), Perkins, Federal Nursing, alternative loans.

**WORK-STUDY Federal work-study:** Total amount: $1,140,397; 572 jobs averaging $2033. **State or other work-study/employment:** Total amount: $2,423,773 (100% non-need-based). 1,683 part-time jobs averaging $1440.

**APPLYING FOR FINANCIAL AID Required financial aid forms:** FAFSA, state aid form. **Financial aid deadline (priority):** 3/15. **Notification date:** Continuous beginning 3/15. Students must reply by 5/1.

**CONTACT** Mr. J. Scott Atkinson, Director of Enrollment Services, The College at Brockport, State University of New York, 350 New Campus Drive, Brockport, NY 14420-2937, 585-395-2501. Fax: 585-395-5445. E-mail: satkinso@brockport.edu. Website: http://www.brockport.edu/.

---

# COLLEGE FOR CREATIVE STUDIES
## Detroit, MI

**CONTACT** Office of Financial Aid, College for Creative Studies, 201 East Kirby, Detroit, MI 48202-4034, 313-664-7495 or toll-free 800-952-ARTS. Fax: 313-872-1521. E-mail: finaid@collegeforcreativestudies.edu. Website: http://www.collegeforcreativestudies.edu/.

---

# COLLEGE OF BIBLICAL STUDIES–HOUSTON
## Houston, TX

| Tuition & fees: $7316 | Average undergraduate aid package: N/A |
|---|---|

**ABOUT THE INSTITUTION** Independent nondenominational, coed. **Awards:** certificates, associate, and bachelor's degrees. 7 undergraduate majors. **Total enrollment:** 496. Undergraduates: 496. Freshmen: 42. Federal methodology is used as a basis for awarding need-based institutional aid.

**UNDERGRADUATE EXPENSES for 2015–2016 Application fee:** $40. **Tuition:** full-time $6946; part-time $274 per credit hour. **Required fees:** full-time $370; $185 per term. Full-time tuition and fees vary according to program. Part-time tuition and fees vary according to program.

**FRESHMAN FINANCIAL AID (Fall 2014, est.)** 9 applied for aid; of those 100% were deemed to have need. 100% of freshmen with need received aid; of those 100% had need fully met. **Average financial aid package:** $5043 (excluding resources awarded to replace EFC).

**GIFT AID (NEED-BASED) Total amount:** $1,782,889 (61% federal, 36% institutional, 3% external sources). **Receiving aid:** Freshmen: 80% (8). **Average award:** Freshmen: $1019. **Scholarships, grants, and awards:** college/university gift aid from institutional funds.

**GIFT AID (NON-NEED-BASED)** *Tuition waivers:* Full or partial for employees or children of employees.
**LOANS** *Student loans:* $1,929,860 (100% need-based). *Programs:* Federal Direct (Subsidized and Unsubsidized Stafford).
**APPLYING FOR FINANCIAL AID** *Required financial aid form:* FAFSA. *Financial aid deadline:* 8/5. *Notification date:* Continuous.
**CONTACT** Roshanna Hardison, Director of Student Financial Services, College of Biblical Studies–Houston, 7000 Regency Square Boulevard, Houston, TX 77036, 832-252-0728 or toll-free 844-227-9673. *E-mail:* roshanna.hardison@cbshouston.edu. *Website:* http://www.cbshouston.edu/.

# COLLEGE OF BUSINESS AND TECHNOLOGY–MIAMI GARDENS
## Miami Gardens, FL

**CONTACT** Financial Aid Office, College of Business and Technology–Miami Gardens, 5190 NW 167 Street, Miami Gardens, FL 33014-6338. *Website:* http://www.cbt.edu/.

# COLLEGE OF CHARLESTON
## Charleston, SC

| Tuition & fees: N/R | Average undergraduate aid package: $13,248 |
|---|---|

**ABOUT THE INSTITUTION** State-supported, coed. *Awards:* certificates, bachelor's, and master's degrees (also offers graduate degree programs through University of Charleston, South Carolina), 57 undergraduate majors. *Total enrollment:* 11,456. Undergraduates: 10,440. Freshmen: 2,166. Federal methodology is used as a basis for awarding need-based institutional aid.
**FRESHMAN FINANCIAL AID (Fall 2014, est.)** 1,567 applied for aid; of those 68% were deemed to have need. 96% of freshmen with need received aid; of those 23% had need fully met. *Average percent of need met:* 58% (excluding resources awarded to replace EFC). *Average financial aid package:* $13,290 (excluding resources awarded to replace EFC). 25% of all full-time freshmen had no need and received non-need-based gift aid.
**UNDERGRADUATE FINANCIAL AID (Fall 2014, est.)** 5,948 applied for aid; of those 77% were deemed to have need. 96% of undergraduates with need received aid; of those 19% had need fully met. *Average percent of need met:* 57% (excluding resources awarded to replace EFC). *Average financial aid package:* $13,248 (excluding resources awarded to replace EFC). 19% of all full-time undergraduates had no need and received non-need-based gift aid.
**GIFT AID (NEED-BASED)** *Total amount:* $27,109,046 (39% federal, 32% state, 24% institutional, 5% external sources). *Receiving aid:* Freshmen: 35% (755); all full-time undergraduates: 33% (3,113). *Average award:* Freshmen: $3317; Undergraduates: $3176. *Scholarships, grants, and awards:* Federal Pell, FSEOG, state, private, college/university gift aid from institutional funds.
**GIFT AID (NON-NEED-BASED)** *Total amount:* $19,699,667 (54% state, 40% institutional, 6% external sources). *Receiving aid:* Freshmen: 37% (798). Undergraduates: 22% (2,070). *Average award:* Freshmen: $10,240. Undergraduates: $11,255. *Scholarships, grants, and awards by category:* Academic interests/achievement: biological sciences, business, communication, computer science, education, engineering/technologies, English, foreign languages, general academic interests/achievements, health fields, humanities, mathematics, physical sciences, premedicine, social sciences. *Creative arts/performance:* art/fine arts, music, performing arts, theater/drama. *Special characteristics:* general special characteristics. *ROTC:* Air Force cooperative.
**LOANS** *Student loans:* $36,806,421 (65% need-based, 35% non-need-based). 52% of past graduating class borrowed through all loan programs. *Average indebtedness per student:* $25,644. *Average need-based loan:* Freshmen: $2968. Undergraduates: $3597. *Parent loans:* $27,151,430 (56% need-based, 44% non-need-based). *Programs:* Federal Direct (Subsidized and Unsubsidized Stafford, PLUS), Perkins.
**WORK-STUDY** *Federal work-study:* Total amount: $318,685; jobs available. *State or other work-study/employment:* Part-time jobs available.

**ATHLETIC AWARDS** Total amount: $4,245,718 (25% need-based, 75% non-need-based).
**APPLYING FOR FINANCIAL AID** *Required financial aid form:* FAFSA. *Financial aid deadline (priority):* 3/1. *Notification date:* Continuous beginning 4/10. Students must reply within 8 weeks of notification.
**CONTACT** Mr. Don Griggs, Director of Financial Aid, College of Charleston, 66 George Street, Charleston, SC 29424, 843-953-5540. *Fax:* 843-953-7192. *Website:* http://www.cofc.edu/.

# COLLEGE OF COASTAL GEORGIA
## Brunswick, GA

**CONTACT** Financial Aid Office, College of Coastal Georgia, One College Drive, Brunswick, GA 31520, 912-264-7235 or toll-free 800-675-7235. *Website:* http://www.ccga.edu/.

# THE COLLEGE OF IDAHO
## Caldwell, ID

| Tuition & fees: $26,165 | Average undergraduate aid package: $25,976 |
|---|---|

**ABOUT THE INSTITUTION** Independent, coed. *Awards:* bachelor's and master's degrees. 36 undergraduate majors. *Total enrollment:* 1,144. Undergraduates: 1,120. Freshmen: 336. Federal methodology is used as a basis for awarding need-based institutional aid.
**UNDERGRADUATE EXPENSES** for 2015–2016 *Comprehensive fee:* $35,155 includes full-time tuition ($25,410), mandatory fees ($755), and room and board ($8990). *Part-time tuition:* $1009 per credit.
**FRESHMAN FINANCIAL AID (Fall 2014, est.)** 252 applied for aid; of those 100% were deemed to have need. 100% of freshmen with need received aid; of those 19% had need fully met. *Average percent of need met:* 91% (excluding resources awarded to replace EFC). *Average financial aid package:* $26,628 (excluding resources awarded to replace EFC). 20% of all full-time freshmen had no need and received non-need-based gift aid.
**UNDERGRADUATE FINANCIAL AID (Fall 2014, est.)** 884 applied for aid; of those 89% were deemed to have need. 100% of undergraduates with need received aid; of those 17% had need fully met. *Average percent of need met:* 93% (excluding resources awarded to replace EFC). *Average financial aid package:* $25,976 (excluding resources awarded to replace EFC). 29% of all full-time undergraduates had no need and received non-need-based gift aid.
**GIFT AID (NEED-BASED)** *Total amount:* $4,743,535 (50% federal, 3% state, 12% institutional, 35% external sources). *Receiving aid:* Freshmen: 76% (252); all full-time undergraduates: 61% (657). *Average award:* Freshmen: $8497; Undergraduates: $7833. *Scholarships, grants, and awards:* Federal Pell, FSEOG, state, private, college/university gift aid from institutional funds.
**GIFT AID (NON-NEED-BASED)** *Total amount:* $13,616,400 (100% institutional). *Receiving aid:* Freshmen: 76% (252). Undergraduates: 72% (781). *Average award:* Freshmen: $16,313. Undergraduates: $14,708. *Scholarships, grants, and awards by category:* Academic interests/achievement: 1,226 awards ($2,617,974 total): biological sciences, business, education, English, foreign languages, general academic interests/achievements, humanities, mathematics, physical sciences, premedicine, religion/biblical studies, social sciences. *Creative arts/performance:* 198 awards ($203,389 total): art/fine arts, debating, music, performing arts, theater/drama. *Special achievements/activities:* 2 awards ($2600 total): leadership. *Special characteristics:* 103 awards ($62,636 total): children and siblings of alumni, children of educators, children of faculty/staff, first-generation college students, international students, local/state students, married students, members of minority groups, out-of-state students, siblings of current students, veterans' children. *ROTC:* Army cooperative.
**LOANS** *Student loans:* $6,702,608 (91% need-based, 9% non-need-based). 75% of past graduating class borrowed through all loan programs. *Average indebtedness per student:* $29,998. *Average need-based loan:* Freshmen: $3841. Undergraduates: $4763. *Parent loans:* $965,131 (100% need-based). *Programs:* Federal Direct (Subsidized and Unsubsidized Stafford, PLUS), Perkins, private loans.

**WORK-STUDY** *Federal work-study:* Total amount: $162,064; 215 jobs averaging $1000. *State or other work-study/employment:* Total amount: $40,000 (47% need-based, 53% non-need-based). 57 part-time jobs averaging $1000.

**ATHLETIC AWARDS** Total amount: $1,673,327 (88% need-based, 12% non-need-based).

**APPLYING FOR FINANCIAL AID** *Required financial aid forms:* FAFSA, institution's own form. *Financial aid deadline (priority):* 2/15. *Notification date:* Continuous. Students must reply within 3 weeks of notification.

**CONTACT** Jennifer Worden, Director of Financial Aid Services, The College of Idaho, 2112 Cleveland Boulevard, Caldwell, ID 83605, 208-459-5307 or toll-free 800-244-3246. *Fax:* 208-459-5844. *E-mail:* jworden@collegeofidaho.edu. *Website:* http://www.collegeofidaho.edu/.

# COLLEGE OF MOUNT SAINT VINCENT
## Riverdale, NY

| Tuition & fees: N/R | Average undergraduate aid package: $19,829 |
|---|---|

**ABOUT THE INSTITUTION** Independent, coed. *Awards:* certificates, associate, bachelor's, and master's degrees. 25 undergraduate majors. *Total enrollment:* 1,918. Undergraduates: 1,649. Freshmen: 386. Federal methodology is used as a basis for awarding need-based institutional aid.

**FRESHMAN FINANCIAL AID (Fall 2013)** 380 applied for aid; of those 91% were deemed to have need. 100% of freshmen with need received aid; of those 15% had need fully met. *Average percent of need met:* 71% (excluding resources awarded to replace EFC). *Average financial aid package:* $22,853 (excluding resources awarded to replace EFC). 7% of all full-time freshmen had no need and received non-need-based gift aid.

**UNDERGRADUATE FINANCIAL AID (Fall 2013)** 1,362 applied for aid; of those 92% were deemed to have need. 100% of undergraduates with need received aid; of those 14% had need fully met. *Average percent of need met:* 68% (excluding resources awarded to replace EFC). *Average financial aid package:* $19,829 (excluding resources awarded to replace EFC). 8% of all full-time undergraduates had no need and received non-need-based gift aid.

**GIFT AID (NEED-BASED)** *Receiving aid:* Freshmen: 84% (323); all full-time undergraduates: 82% (1,175). *Average award:* Freshmen: $8620; Undergraduates: $10,243. *Scholarships, grants, and awards:* Federal Pell, FSEOG, state, private, college/university gift aid from institutional funds.

**GIFT AID (NON-NEED-BASED)** *Receiving aid:* Freshmen: 83% (321). Undergraduates: 75% (1,078). *Average award:* Freshmen: $15,746. Undergraduates: $12,904. *Scholarships, grants, and awards by category:* Academic interests/achievement: general academic interests/achievements. Special achievements/activities: leadership. Special characteristics: children and siblings of alumni, children of faculty/staff, siblings of current students. ROTC: Air Force cooperative.

**LOANS** *Average need-based loan:* Freshmen: $2525. Undergraduates: $4333. *Programs:* Federal Direct (Subsidized and Unsubsidized Stafford, PLUS), Perkins.

**WORK-STUDY** Federal work-study jobs available.

**APPLYING FOR FINANCIAL AID** *Required financial aid forms:* FAFSA, state aid form. *Financial aid deadline:* Continuous. *Notification date:* Continuous beginning 3/15. Students must reply by 5/1 or within 2 weeks of notification.

**CONTACT** Mr. Emmett Cooper, Director of Financial Aid, College of Mount Saint Vincent, 6301 Riverdale Avenue, Riverdale, NY 10471, 718-405-3309 or toll-free 800-665-CMSV. *Fax:* 718-405-3490. *E-mail:* emmett.cooper@mountsaintvincent.edu. *Website:* http://www.mountsaintvincent.edu/.

# THE COLLEGE OF NEW JERSEY
## Ewing, NJ

| Tuition & fees (NJ res): $15,024 | Average undergraduate aid package: $11,106 |
|---|---|

**ABOUT THE INSTITUTION** State-supported, coed. *Awards:* certificates, bachelor's, and master's degrees. 48 undergraduate majors. *Total enrollment:* 7,409.

Undergraduates: 6,743. Freshmen: 1,417. Federal methodology is used as a basis for awarding need-based institutional aid.

**UNDERGRADUATE EXPENSES** for 2015–2016 *Application fee:* $75. *Tuition, state resident:* full-time $10,562; part-time $374.29 per credit hour. *Tuition, nonresident:* full-time $21,175; part-time $749.49 per credit hour. *Required fees:* full-time $4462; $177.76 per credit hour. Part-time tuition and fees vary according to course load. *College room and board:* $11,677; *Room only:* $8411. Room and board charges vary according to board plan.

**FRESHMAN FINANCIAL AID (Fall 2014, est.)** 1,229 applied for aid; of those 64% were deemed to have need. 91% of freshmen with need received aid; of those 9% had need fully met. *Average percent of need met:* 42% (excluding resources awarded to replace EFC). *Average financial aid package:* $11,065 (excluding resources awarded to replace EFC). 11% of all full-time freshmen had no need and received non-need-based gift aid.

**UNDERGRADUATE FINANCIAL AID (Fall 2014, est.)** 4,664 applied for aid; of those 72% were deemed to have need. 94% of undergraduates with need received aid; of those 12% had need fully met. *Average percent of need met:* 46% (excluding resources awarded to replace EFC). *Average financial aid package:* $11,106 (excluding resources awarded to replace EFC). 8% of all full-time undergraduates had no need and received non-need-based gift aid.

**GIFT AID (NEED-BASED)** *Total amount:* $21,815,004 (25% federal, 32% state, 35% institutional, 8% external sources). *Receiving aid:* Freshmen: 21% (293); all full-time undergraduates: 21% (1,303). *Average award:* Freshmen: $14,316; Undergraduates: $12,074. *Scholarships, grants, and awards:* Federal Pell, FSEOG, state, private, college/university gift aid from institutional funds, Federal Nursing.

**GIFT AID (NON-NEED-BASED)** *Total amount:* $5,598,477 (85% institutional, 15% external sources). *Receiving aid:* Freshmen: 16% (222). Undergraduates: 14% (859). *Average award:* Freshmen: $4550. Undergraduates: $5330. *Scholarships, grants, and awards by category:* Academic interests/achievement: general academic interests/achievements. Creative arts/performance: art/fine arts, music. Special characteristics: children with a deceased or disabled parent, members of minority groups. Tuition waivers: Full or partial for employees or children of employees, senior citizens. ROTC: Army cooperative, Air Force cooperative.

**LOANS** *Student loans:* $35,656,599 (78% need-based, 22% non-need-based). 60% of past graduating class borrowed through all loan programs. *Average indebtedness per student:* $33,635. *Average need-based loan:* Freshmen: $3632. Undergraduates: $4695. *Parent loans:* $5,400,399 (78% need-based, 22% non-need-based). *Programs:* Federal Direct (Subsidized and Unsubsidized Stafford, PLUS), Perkins, Federal Nursing.

**WORK-STUDY** *Federal work-study:* Total amount: $172,560; jobs available.

**APPLYING FOR FINANCIAL AID** *Required financial aid form:* FAFSA. *Financial aid deadline (priority):* 3/1. *Notification date:* Continuous beginning 6/1. Students must reply within 2 weeks of notification.

**CONTACT** Mr. Wilbert Casaine, Director of Financial Aid, The College of New Jersey, PO Box 7718, Ewing, NJ 08628, 609-771-2602. *Fax:* 609-637-5154. *E-mail:* casainew@tcnj.edu. *Website:* http://www.tcnj.edu/.

# THE COLLEGE OF NEW ROCHELLE
## New Rochelle, NY

| Tuition & fees: $32,300 | Average undergraduate aid package: $22,358 |
|---|---|

**ABOUT THE INSTITUTION** Independent, coed, primarily women. *Awards:* certificates, bachelor's, and master's degrees (also offers a non-traditional adult program with significant enrollment not reflected in profile). 35 undergraduate majors. *Total enrollment:* 1,478. Undergraduates: 820. Freshmen: 92. Federal methodology is used as a basis for awarding need-based institutional aid.

**UNDERGRADUATE EXPENSES** for 2015–2016 *Application fee:* $35. *Comprehensive fee:* $44,500 includes full-time tuition ($31,200), mandatory fees ($1100), and room and board ($12,200). Full-time tuition and fees vary according to course load, location, and program. Room and board charges vary according to housing facility. *Part-time tuition:* $896 per credit. *Part-time fees:* $400 per term. Part-time tuition and fees vary according to course load, location, and program.

**FRESHMAN FINANCIAL AID (Fall 2013)** 78 applied for aid; of those 96% were deemed to have need. 100% of freshmen with need received aid; of those 5% had need fully met. *Average percent of need met:* 73% (excluding resources awarded to replace EFC). *Average financial aid package:* $29,132 (excluding resources awarded to replace EFC). 4% of all full-time freshmen had no need and received non-need-based gift aid.

**UNDERGRADUATE FINANCIAL AID (Fall 2013)** 532 applied for aid; of those 96% were deemed to have need. 100% of undergraduates with need received aid; of those 5% had need fully met. *Average percent of need met:* 59% (excluding resources awarded to replace EFC). *Average financial aid package:* $22,358 (excluding resources awarded to replace EFC). 4% of all full-time undergraduates had no need and received non-need-based gift aid.

**GIFT AID (NEED-BASED)** *Total amount:* $9,462,330 (19% federal, 10% state, 70% institutional, 1% external sources). *Receiving aid:* Freshmen: 82% (64); all full-time undergraduates: 83% (443). *Average award:* Freshmen: $12,056; Undergraduates: $9146. *Scholarships, grants, and awards:* Federal Pell, FSEOG, state, private, college/university gift aid from institutional funds.

**GIFT AID (NON-NEED-BASED)** *Total amount:* $337,040 (96% institutional, 4% external sources). *Receiving aid:* Freshmen: 96% (75). Undergraduates: 86% (460). *Average award:* Freshmen: $19,000. Undergraduates: $13,843. *Scholarships, grants, and awards by category:* Academic interests/achievement: 240 awards ($2,875,000 total): area/ethnic studies, biological sciences, business, communication, education, English, foreign languages, general academic interests/achievements, health fields, humanities, mathematics, physical sciences, premedicine, religion/biblical studies, social sciences. *Creative arts/performance:* 39 awards ($275,000 total): applied art and design, art/fine arts, cinema/film/broadcasting, creative writing, debating, journalism/publications, music, theater/drama. *Special achievements/activities:* 68 awards ($71,000 total): community service, general special achievements/activities, hobbies/interests, leadership, memberships, religious involvement. *Special characteristics:* 47 awards ($235,750 total): children and siblings of alumni, children of faculty/staff, children of union members/company employees, children of workers in trades, general special characteristics, out-of-state students, parents of current students, previous college experience, siblings of current students, spouses of current students, spouses of deceased or disabled public servants, veterans, veterans' children. *Tuition waivers:* Full or partial for employees or children of employees.

**LOANS** *Student loans:* $28,449,592 (91% need-based, 9% non-need-based). 89% of past graduating class borrowed through all loan programs. *Average indebtedness per student:* $37,437. *Average need-based loan:* Freshmen: $4902. Undergraduates: $5522. *Parent loans:* $665,334 (96% need-based, 4% non-need-based). *Programs:* Federal Direct (Subsidized and Unsubsidized Stafford, PLUS), Perkins, Federal Nursing.

**WORK-STUDY** *Federal work-study:* 365 jobs averaging $2500. *State or other work-study/employment:* Part-time jobs available.

**APPLYING FOR FINANCIAL AID** *Required financial aid forms:* FAFSA, institution's own form. *Financial aid deadline:* Continuous. *Notification date:* Continuous beginning 1/1. Students must reply within 2 weeks of notification.

**CONTACT** Anne Pelak, Director of Financial Aid, The College of New Rochelle, 29 Castle Place, New Rochelle, NY 10805-2339, 914-654-5225 or toll-free 800-933-5923. *Fax:* 914-654-5420. *E-mail:* apelak@cnr.edu.
*Website:* http://www.cnr.edu/.

---

# COLLEGE OF SAINT BENEDICT
### Saint Joseph, MN

| Tuition & fees: $39,402 | Average undergraduate aid package: $31,995 |
| --- | --- |

**ABOUT THE INSTITUTION** Independent Roman Catholic, women only. *Awards:* bachelor's degrees (coordinate with Saint John's University for men). 50 undergraduate majors. *Total enrollment:* 2,020. Undergraduates: 2,020. Freshmen: 542. Federal methodology is used as a basis for awarding need-based institutional aid.

**UNDERGRADUATE EXPENSES for 2015–2016** *Comprehensive fee:* $49,358 includes full-time tuition ($38,428), mandatory fees ($974), and room and board ($9956). *College room only:* $4782. Room and board charges vary according to board plan and housing facility. *Part-time tuition:* $1601 per credit hour. Part-time tuition and fees vary according to course load.

**FRESHMAN FINANCIAL AID (Fall 2014, est.)** 473 applied for aid; of those 86% were deemed to have need. 100% of freshmen with need received aid; of those 49% had need fully met. *Average percent of need met:* 92% (excluding resources awarded to replace EFC). *Average financial aid package:* $33,343 (excluding

---

resources awarded to replace EFC. 22% of all full-time freshmen had no need and received non-need-based gift aid.

**UNDERGRADUATE FINANCIAL AID (Fall 2014, est.)** 1,608 applied for aid; of those 87% were deemed to have need. 100% of undergraduates with need received aid; of those 42% had need fully met. *Average percent of need met:* 89% (excluding resources awarded to replace EFC). *Average financial aid package:* $31,995 (excluding resources awarded to replace EFC). 24% of all full-time undergraduates had no need and received non-need-based gift aid.

**GIFT AID (NEED-BASED)** *Total amount:* $35,801,959 (7% federal, 7% state, 83% institutional, 3% external sources). *Receiving aid:* Freshmen: 74% (401); all full-time undergraduates: 69% (1,365). *Average award:* Freshmen: $27,478; Undergraduates: $25,770. *Scholarships, grants, and awards:* Federal Pell, FSEOG, state, private, college/university gift aid from institutional funds.

**GIFT AID (NON-NEED-BASED)** *Total amount:* $10,211,986 (93% institutional, 7% external sources). *Receiving aid:* Freshmen: 72% (390). Undergraduates: 67% (1,339). *Average award:* Freshmen: $17,962. Undergraduates: $15,708. *Scholarships, grants, and awards by category:* Academic interests/achievement: 1,821 awards ($25,952,698 total): computer science, engineering/technologies, general academic interests/achievements, mathematics, military science, physical sciences. *Creative arts/performance:* 201 awards ($480,878 total): art/fine arts, music, theater/drama. *Special characteristics:* 483 awards ($2,535,180 total): children and siblings of alumni, international students, out-of-state students. *Tuition waivers:* Full or partial for employees or children of employees. *ROTC:* Army cooperative.

**LOANS** *Student loans:* $15,838,046 (89% need-based, 11% non-need-based). 75% of past graduating class borrowed through all loan programs. *Average indebtedness per student:* $39,437. *Average need-based loan:* Freshmen: $3530. Undergraduates: $4287. *Parent loans:* $1,355,348 (81% need-based, 19% non-need-based). *Programs:* Federal Direct (Subsidized and Unsubsidized Stafford, PLUS), Perkins, state, private loans.

**WORK-STUDY** *Federal work-study:* Total amount: $1,136,204; 423 jobs averaging $2691. *State or other work-study/employment:* Total amount: $2,769,581 (75% need-based, 25% non-need-based). 1,102 part-time jobs averaging $2689.

**APPLYING FOR FINANCIAL AID** *Required financial aid forms:* FAFSA, institution's own form. *Financial aid deadline (priority):* 3/15. *Notification date:* Continuous beginning 3/15. Students must reply by 5/1.

**CONTACT** Mr. Stuart Perry, Executive Director of Financial Aid, College of Saint Benedict, 37 South College Avenue, Saint Joseph, MN 56374-2099, 320-363-5388 or toll-free 800-544-1489. *Fax:* 320-363-6090. *E-mail:* sperry@csbsju.edu.
*Website:* http://www.csbsju.edu/.

---

# COLLEGE OF SAINT ELIZABETH
### Morristown, NJ

| Tuition & fees: $31,095 | Average undergraduate aid package: $23,749 |
| --- | --- |

**ABOUT THE INSTITUTION** Independent Roman Catholic, coed, primarily women. *Awards:* certificates, bachelor's, master's, and doctoral degrees (also offers coed adult undergraduate degree program and coed graduate programs). 29 undergraduate majors. *Total enrollment:* 1,411. Undergraduates: 895. Freshmen: 141. Both federal and institutional methodology are used as a basis for awarding need-based institutional aid.

**UNDERGRADUATE EXPENSES for 2015–2016** *Application fee:* $35. *Comprehensive fee:* $43,839 includes full-time tuition ($29,148), mandatory fees ($1947), and room and board ($12,744). Room and board charges vary according to board plan. *Part-time tuition:* $911 per credit hour. Part-time tuition and fees vary according to course load and location.

**FRESHMAN FINANCIAL AID (Fall 2013)** 124 applied for aid; of those 93% were deemed to have need. 100% of freshmen with need received aid; of those 8% had need fully met. *Average percent of need met:* 87% (excluding resources awarded to replace EFC). *Average financial aid package:* $28,447 (excluding resources awarded to replace EFC). 1% of all full-time freshmen had no need and received non-need-based gift aid.

**UNDERGRADUATE FINANCIAL AID (Fall 2013)** 541 applied for aid; of those 91% were deemed to have need. 100% of undergraduates with need received aid; of those 10% had need fully met. *Average percent of need met:* 98% (excluding resources awarded to replace EFC). *Average financial aid package:* $23,749

(excluding resources awarded to replace EFC). 1% of all full-time undergraduates had no need and received non-need-based gift aid.

**GIFT AID (NEED-BASED) Total amount:** $5,952,414 (29% federal, 51% state, 20% institutional). **Receiving aid:** Freshmen: 82% (102); all full-time undergraduates: 71% (396). **Average award:** Freshmen: $16,003; Undergraduates: $14,708. **Scholarships, grants, and awards:** Federal Pell, FSEOG, state, private, college/university gift aid from institutional funds.

**GIFT AID (NON-NEED-BASED) Total amount:** $6,338,177 (100% institutional). **Receiving aid:** Freshmen: 93% (115). Undergraduates: 78% (431). **Average award:** Freshmen: $29,070. Undergraduates: $29,070. **Scholarships, grants, and awards by category:** Academic interests/achievement: general academic interests/achievements. Special achievements/activities: community service, leadership. Special characteristics: adult students, children and siblings of alumni. **Tuition waivers:** Full or partial for children of alumni, employees or children of employees, senior citizens. **LOANS Student loans:** $5,195,201 (44% need-based, 56% non-need-based). **Programs:** Perkins. **WORK-STUDY Federal work-study:** jobs available.

**APPLYING FOR FINANCIAL AID Required financial aid form:** FAFSA. **Financial aid deadline:** Continuous. **Notification date:** Continuous beginning 11/15. Students must reply by 5/1 or within 2 weeks of notification.

**CONTACT** Mr. James Kulhaway, Assistant Director of Financial Aid, College of Saint Elizabeth, 2 Convent Road, Morristown, NJ 07960-6989, 973-290-4432 or toll-free 800-210-7900. E-mail: jkulhaway@cse.edu.

Website: http://www.cse.edu/.

# COLLEGE OF ST. JOSEPH
## Rutland, VT

**CONTACT** Julie Rosmus, Director of Financial Aid, College of St. Joseph, 71 Clement Road, Rutland, VT 05701-3899, 802-773-5900 Ext. 3274 or toll-free 877-270-9998. Fax: 802-776-5275. E-mail: jrosmus@csj.edu.

Website: http://www.csj.edu/.

# COLLEGE OF SAINT MARY
## Omaha, NE

| Tuition & fees: $28,964 | Average undergraduate aid package: $20,059 |
|---|---|

**ABOUT THE INSTITUTION** Independent Roman Catholic, women only. **Awards:** certificates, associate, bachelor's, master's, and doctoral degrees. 30 undergraduate majors. **Total enrollment:** 1,018. Undergraduates: 770. Freshmen: 71. Federal methodology is used as a basis for awarding need-based institutional aid.

**UNDERGRADUATE EXPENSES for 2015–2016 Application fee:** $30. **Comprehensive fee:** $36,364 includes full-time tuition ($28,964) and room and board ($7400). Full-time tuition and fees vary according to program. Part-time tuition and fees vary according to course load and program.

**FRESHMAN FINANCIAL AID (Fall 2014, est.)** 64 applied for aid; of those 92% were deemed to have need. 100% of freshmen with need received aid; of those 25% had need fully met. **Average percent of need met:** 78% (excluding resources awarded to replace EFC). **Average financial aid package:** $21,308 (excluding resources awarded to replace EFC). 6% of all full-time freshmen had no need and received non-need-based gift aid.

**UNDERGRADUATE FINANCIAL AID (Fall 2014, est.)** 588 applied for aid; of those 93% were deemed to have need. 100% of undergraduates with need received aid; of those 14% had need fully met. **Average percent of need met:** 69% (excluding resources awarded to replace EFC). **Average financial aid package:** $20,059 (excluding resources awarded to replace EFC). 6% of all full-time undergraduates had no need and received non-need-based gift aid.

**GIFT AID (NEED-BASED) Total amount:** $6,874,489 (21% federal, 3% state, 72% institutional, 4% external sources). **Receiving aid:** Freshmen: 92% (59); all full-time undergraduates: 91% (533). **Average award:** Freshmen: $17,146; Undergraduates: $13,519. **Scholarships, grants, and awards:** Federal Pell, FSEOG, state, private, college/university gift aid from institutional funds, Federal Nursing.

**GIFT AID (NON-NEED-BASED) Total amount:** $660,675 (1% federal, 84% institutional, 15% external sources). **Receiving aid:** Freshmen: 19% (12). Undergrad-

uates: 9% (53). **Average award:** Freshmen: $15,500. Undergraduates: $10,375. **Scholarships, grants, and awards by category:** Academic interests/achievement: 618 awards ($3,814,300 total): biological sciences, education, general academic interests/achievements, mathematics. Creative arts/performance: 7 awards ($10,250 total): art/fine arts, debating, music. Special achievements/activities: 136 awards ($149,375 total): community service, general special achievements/activities, leadership, religious involvement. Special characteristics: 71 awards ($128,638 total): children of faculty/staff, first-generation college students, general special characteristics, international students. **Tuition waivers:** Full or partial for employees or children of employees, senior citizens. **ROTC:** Army cooperative, Air Force cooperative.

**LOANS Student loans:** $6,099,612 (83% need-based, 17% non-need-based). 68% of past graduating class borrowed through all loan programs. Average indebtedness per student: $29,538. Average need-based loan: Freshmen: $3685. Undergraduates: $5896. **Parent loans:** $840,814 (45% need-based, 55% non-need-based). **Programs:** Federal Direct (Subsidized and Unsubsidized Stafford, PLUS), Perkins, Federal Nursing.

**WORK-STUDY Federal work-study:** Total amount: $446,877; 161 jobs averaging $2846. **State or other work-study/employment:** Total amount: $40,400 (65% need-based, 35% non-need-based). 14 part-time jobs averaging $4279.

**ATHLETIC AWARDS** Total amount: $789,150 (67% need-based, 33% non-need-based).

**APPLYING FOR FINANCIAL AID Required financial aid form:** FAFSA. **Financial aid deadline (priority):** 3/15. **Notification date:** Continuous beginning 3/15. Students must reply within 2 weeks of notification.

**CONTACT** Beth Sisk, Director of Financial Aid and the Express Center, College of Saint Mary, 7000 Mercy Road, Omaha, NE 68106, 402-399-2362 or toll-free 800-926-5534. Fax: 402-399-2480. E-mail: finaid@csm.edu.

Website: http://www.csm.edu/.

# THE COLLEGE OF SAINT ROSE
## Albany, NY

| Tuition & fees: $29,016 | Average undergraduate aid package: $18,419 |
|---|---|

**ABOUT THE INSTITUTION** Independent, coed. **Awards:** certificates, bachelor's, and master's degrees. 50 undergraduate majors. **Total enrollment:** 4,509. Undergraduates: 2,773. Freshmen: 534. Federal methodology is used as a basis for awarding need-based institutional aid.

**UNDERGRADUATE EXPENSES for 2015–2016 Application fee:** $40. **Comprehensive fee:** $40,548 includes full-time tuition ($28,036), mandatory fees ($980), and room and board ($11,532). **College room only:** $5800. Full-time tuition and fees vary according to class time and course load. Room and board charges vary according to board plan and housing facility. **Part-time tuition:** $932 per credit hour. **Part-time fees:** $31 per credit hour; $85 per semester hour. Part-time tuition and fees vary according to class time and course load.

**FRESHMAN FINANCIAL AID (Fall 2014, est.)** 598 applied for aid; of those 91% were deemed to have need. 99% of freshmen with need received aid; of those 17% had need fully met. **Average percent of need met:** 78% (excluding resources awarded to replace EFC). **Average financial aid package:** $20,846 (excluding resources awarded to replace EFC). 10% of all full-time freshmen had no need and received non-need-based gift aid.

**UNDERGRADUATE FINANCIAL AID (Fall 2014, est.)** 2,443 applied for aid; of those 92% were deemed to have need. 99% of undergraduates with need received aid; of those 16% had need fully met. **Average percent of need met:** 75% (excluding resources awarded to replace EFC). **Average financial aid package:** $18,419 (excluding resources awarded to replace EFC). 10% of all full-time undergraduates had no need and received non-need-based gift aid.

**GIFT AID (NEED-BASED) Total amount:** $21,103,150 (22% federal, 16% state, 59% institutional, 3% external sources). **Receiving aid:** Freshmen: 79% (489); all full-time undergraduates: 76% (2,013). **Average award:** Freshmen: $12,162; Undergraduates: $9611. **Scholarships, grants, and awards:** Federal Pell, FSEOG, state, private, college/university gift aid from institutional funds.

**GIFT AID (NON-NEED-BASED) Total amount:** $17,895,775 (96% institutional, 4% external sources). **Receiving aid:** Freshmen: 74% (461). Undergraduates: 64% (1,692). **Average award:** Freshmen: $12,934. Undergraduates: $11,508. **Scholarships, grants, and awards by category:** Academic interests/achievement: business, communication, education, engineering/technologies, English, foreign languages, general academic interests/achievements, humanities, mathematics, premedicine, social sciences. *Creative arts/performance:* art/fine arts, music. *Special achievements/activities:* community service. *Special characteristics:* adult students, children and siblings of alumni, children of faculty/staff, children of union members/company employees, ethnic background, general special characteristics, members of minority groups, out-of-state students, siblings of current students, twins. *Tuition waivers:* Full or partial for employees or children of employees. *ROTC:* Army cooperative, Naval cooperative, Air Force cooperative.

**LOANS** *Student loans:* $15,111,617 (56% need-based, 44% non-need-based). 87% of past graduating class borrowed through all loan programs. *Average indebtedness per student:* $34,482. *Average need-based loan:* Freshmen: $3418. Undergraduates: $4400. *Parent loans:* $6,857,521 (77% need-based, 23% non-need-based). *Programs:* Federal Direct (Subsidized and Unsubsidized Stafford, PLUS), Perkins.

**WORK-STUDY** *Federal work-study:* Total amount: $411,582; jobs available. *State or other work-study/employment:* Total amount: $17,950 (100% non-need-based). Part-time jobs available.

**ATHLETIC AWARDS** Total amount: $2,577,820 (35% need-based, 65% non-need-based).

**APPLYING FOR FINANCIAL AID** *Required financial aid form:* FAFSA. *Financial aid deadline:* 4/1 (priority: 2/1). *Notification date:* 2/20. Students must reply by 5/1 or within 2 weeks of notification.

**CONTACT** Steven Dwire, Assistant Vice President of Financial Aid and Enrollment Management, The College of Saint Rose, 432 Western Avenue, Albertus Hall, Room 206, Albany, NY 12203-1419, 518-458-4915 or toll-free 800-637-8556. *Fax:* 518-454-2802. *E-mail:* finaid@strose.edu.
*Website:* http://www.strose.edu/.

# THE COLLEGE OF ST. SCHOLASTICA
### Duluth, MN

| Tuition & fees: $33,994 | Average undergraduate aid package: $21,774 |
|---|---|

**ABOUT THE INSTITUTION** Independent Roman Catholic Church, coed. *Awards:* certificates, bachelor's, master's, and doctoral degrees. 38 undergraduate majors. *Total enrollment:* 4,237. Undergraduates: 2,859. Freshmen: 461. Federal methodology is used as a basis for awarding need-based institutional aid.

**UNDERGRADUATE EXPENSES** for 2015–2016 *Comprehensive fee:* $42,926 includes full-time tuition ($33,784), mandatory fees ($210), and room and board ($8932). *College room only:* $4928. Full-time tuition and fees vary according to class time and program. Room and board charges vary according to board plan and housing facility. *Part-time tuition:* $1056 per credit. Part-time tuition and fees vary according to class time, course load, and program.

**FRESHMAN FINANCIAL AID (Fall 2014, est.)** 416 applied for aid; of those 88% were deemed to have need. 100% of freshmen with need received aid; of those 26% had need fully met. *Average percent of need met:* 76% (excluding resources awarded to replace EFC). *Average financial aid package:* $26,367 (excluding resources awarded to replace EFC). 10% of all full-time freshmen had no need and received non-need-based gift aid.

**UNDERGRADUATE FINANCIAL AID (Fall 2014, est.)** 1,993 applied for aid; of those 91% were deemed to have need. 99% of undergraduates with need received aid; of those 20% had need fully met. *Average percent of need met:* 70% (excluding resources awarded to replace EFC). *Average financial aid package:* $21,774 (excluding resources awarded to replace EFC). 6% of all full-time undergraduates had no need and received non-need-based gift aid.

**GIFT AID (NEED-BASED)** *Total amount:* $10,798,151 (36% federal, 31% state, 33% institutional). *Receiving aid:* Freshmen: 64% (295); all full-time undergraduates: 62% (1,441). *Average award:* Freshmen: $7517; Undergraduates: $7093. *Scholarships, grants, and awards:* Federal Pell, FSEOG, state, private, college/university gift aid from institutional funds.

**GIFT AID (NON-NEED-BASED)** *Total amount:* $29,015,343 (1% federal, 1% state, 95% institutional, 3% external sources). *Receiving aid:* Freshmen: 80% (368). Undergraduates: 65% (1,492). *Average award:* Freshmen: $16,402. Undergraduates: $14,630. *Scholarships, grants, and awards by category: Academic interests/achievement:* general academic interests/achievements. *Creative arts/performance:* music. *Special characteristics:* children and siblings of alumni, children of faculty/staff, ethnic background, handicapped students, international students, local/state students, members of minority groups, previous college experience, religious affiliation, siblings

of current students, spouses of current students. *Tuition waivers:* Full or partial for employees or children of employees, senior citizens. *ROTC:* Air Force cooperative.

**LOANS** *Student loans:* $21,625,346 (33% need-based, 67% non-need-based). 77% of past graduating class borrowed through all loan programs. *Average indebtedness per student:* $42,792. *Average need-based loan:* Freshmen: $3628. Undergraduates: $4693. *Parent loans:* $1,927,193 (100% non-need-based). *Programs:* Federal Direct (Subsidized and Unsubsidized Stafford, PLUS), Perkins, Federal Nursing, state.

**WORK-STUDY** *Federal work-study:* Total amount: $347,078; jobs available. *State or other work-study/employment:* Total amount: $1,957,680 (16% need-based, 84% non-need-based). Part-time jobs available.

**APPLYING FOR FINANCIAL AID** *Required financial aid form:* FAFSA. *Financial aid deadline (priority):* 3/1. *Notification date:* Continuous beginning 3/1. Students must reply within 2 weeks of notification.

**CONTACT** Mr. Jon P. Erickson, Director of Financial Aid, The College of St. Scholastica, 1200 Kenwood Avenue, Duluth, MN 55811-4199, 218-723-6725 or toll-free 800-249-6412. *Fax:* 218-733-2229. *E-mail:* jerickso@css.edu.
*Website:* http://www.css.edu/.

# COLLEGE OF STATEN ISLAND OF THE CITY UNIVERSITY OF NEW YORK
### Staten Island, NY

| Tuition & fees (area res): $479 | Average undergraduate aid package: $8200 |
|---|---|

**ABOUT THE INSTITUTION** State and locally supported, coed. *Awards:* certificates, associate, bachelor's, master's, and doctoral degrees. 45 undergraduate majors. *Total enrollment:* 14,344. Undergraduates: 13,343. Freshmen: 2,492. Federal methodology is used as a basis for awarding need-based institutional aid.

**UNDERGRADUATE EXPENSES** for 2015–2016 *Tuition, area resident:* full-time . *Tuition, state resident:* full-time $6030; part-time $260 per credit hour. *Tuition, nonresident:* full-time $16,050; part-time $535 per credit hour. *Required fees:* full-time $479; $141.10 per term. *Room only:* $12,364. Room and board charges vary according to board plan and housing facility.

**FRESHMAN FINANCIAL AID (Fall 2013)** 2,277 applied for aid; of those 81% were deemed to have need. 95% of freshmen with need received aid; of those 2% had need fully met. *Average percent of need met:* 63% (excluding resources awarded to replace EFC). *Average financial aid package:* $9153 (excluding resources awarded to replace EFC). 6% of all full-time freshmen had no need and received non-need-based gift aid.

**UNDERGRADUATE FINANCIAL AID (Fall 2013)** 7,738 applied for aid; of those 86% were deemed to have need. 96% of undergraduates with need received aid; of those 2% had need fully met. *Average percent of need met:* 60% (excluding resources awarded to replace EFC). *Average financial aid package:* $8200 (excluding resources awarded to replace EFC). 4% of all full-time undergraduates had no need and received non-need-based gift aid.

**GIFT AID (NEED-BASED)** *Total amount:* $45,651,643 (59% federal, 33% state, 8% external sources). *Receiving aid:* Freshmen: 64% (1,693); all full-time undergraduates: 62% (6,090). *Average award:* Freshmen: $7320; Undergraduates: $6577. *Scholarships, grants, and awards:* Federal Pell, FSEOG, state, private, college/university gift aid from institutional funds, United Negro College Fund, Federal Nursing.

**GIFT AID (NON-NEED-BASED)** *Total amount:* $1,842,220 (20% federal, 25% state, 55% external sources). *Receiving aid:* Freshmen: 58% (1,521). Undergraduates: 54% (5,275). *Average award:* Freshmen: $1745. Undergraduates: $2697. *Scholarships, grants, and awards by category: Academic interests/achievement:* architecture, area/ethnic studies, biological sciences, business, communication, computer science, education, engineering/technologies, English, foreign languages, general academic interests/achievements, health fields, home economics, humanities, international studies, library science, mathematics, physical sciences, premedicine, social sciences. *Creative arts/performance:* applied art and design, art/fine arts, cinema/film/broadcasting, creative writing, dance, debating, general creative arts/performance, journalism/publications, music, performing arts, theater/drama. *Special achievements/activities:* community service, general special achievements/activities, hobbies/interests, leadership. *Special characteristics:* adult students, children and siblings of alumni, children of current students, children of educators, children of faculty/staff, children of public servants, children of union members/company employees, children of workers in trades, children with a deceased or disabled parent, ethnic background, first-generation college students, general special characteristics, handicapped students, international students, local/state students, married students, members of minority groups, out-of-state students, parents of current students, previous college experience, public servants, siblings of current students, spouses of current students, spouses of deceased or disabled public servants, veterans, veterans' children. *Tuition waivers:* Full or partial for employees or children of employees, senior citizens.

**LOANS** *Student loans:* $12,501,182 (100% need-based). *Average need-based loan:* Freshmen: $4769. Undergraduates: $4980. *Programs:* Federal Direct (Subsidized and Unsubsidized Stafford, PLUS), Perkins.

**WORK-STUDY** *Federal work-study:* jobs available. *State or other work-study/employment:* Total amount: $6150 (100% non-need-based). Part-time jobs available.

**APPLYING FOR FINANCIAL AID** *Required financial aid forms:* FAFSA, state aid form. *Financial aid deadline (priority):* 3/30. *Notification date:* Continuous beginning 6/1.

**CONTACT** Mr. Philippe Marius, Director of Financial Aid, College of Staten Island of the City University of New York, 2800 Victory Boulevard, 2A-401A, Staten Island, NY 10314-6600, 718-982-2030. *Fax:* 718-982-2037. *E-mail:* financialaid@csi.cuny.edu. *Website:* http://www.csi.cuny.edu/.

# COLLEGE OF THE ATLANTIC
## Bar Harbor, ME

| Tuition & fees: $42,084 | Average undergraduate aid package: $37,812 |
| --- | --- |

**ABOUT THE INSTITUTION** Independent, coed. *Awards:* bachelor's and master's degrees. 42 undergraduate majors. *Total enrollment:* 386. Undergraduates: 378. Freshmen: 79. Both federal and institutional methodology are used as a basis for awarding need-based institutional aid.

**UNDERGRADUATE EXPENSES for 2015–2016** *Application fee:* $50. *Comprehensive fee:* $51,516 includes full-time tuition ($41,535), mandatory fees ($549), and room and board ($9432). *College room only:* $6000. Full-time tuition and fees vary according to course load and degree level. Room and board charges vary according to board plan. *Part-time tuition:* $4615 per credit. *Part-time fees:* $183 per term. Part-time tuition and fees vary according to course load and degree level.

**FRESHMAN FINANCIAL AID (Fall 2014, est.)** 76 applied for aid; of those 93% were deemed to have need. 100% of freshmen with need received aid; of those 92% had need fully met. *Average percent of need met:* 96% (excluding resources awarded to replace EFC). *Average financial aid package:* $39,777 (excluding resources awarded to replace EFC). 8% of all full-time freshmen had no need and received non-need-based gift aid.

**UNDERGRADUATE FINANCIAL AID (Fall 2014, est.)** 322 applied for aid; of those 95% were deemed to have need. 100% of undergraduates with need received aid; of those 90% had need fully met. *Average percent of need met:* 92% (excluding resources awarded to replace EFC). *Average financial aid package:* $37,812 (excluding resources awarded to replace EFC). 9% of all full-time undergraduates had no need and received non-need-based gift aid.

**GIFT AID (NEED-BASED)** *Total amount:* $9,693,415 (6% federal, 1% state, 92% institutional, 1% external sources). *Receiving aid:* Freshmen: 90% (71); all full-time undergraduates: 85% (304). *Average award:* Freshmen: $33,765; Undergraduates: $31,578. *Scholarships, grants, and awards:* Federal Pell, FSEOG, state, private, college/university gift aid from institutional funds.

**GIFT AID (NON-NEED-BASED)** *Total amount:* $354,933 (98% institutional, 2% external sources). *Receiving aid:* Undergraduates: 1% (3). *Average award:* Freshmen: $11,433. Undergraduates: $9693. *Scholarships, grants, and awards by category:* Academic interests/achievement: 38 awards ($346,833 total): general academic interests/achievements. *Tuition waivers:* Full or partial for employees or children of employees.

**LOANS** *Student loans:* $1,611,160 (61% need-based, 39% non-need-based). 67% of past graduating class borrowed through all loan programs. *Average indebtedness per student:* $23,926. *Average need-based loan:* Freshmen: $3879. Undergraduates: $4722. *Parent loans:* $219,365 (100% non-need-based). *Programs:* Federal Direct (Subsidized and Unsubsidized Stafford, PLUS), Perkins.

**WORK-STUDY** *Federal work-study:* Total amount: $848,404; 245 jobs averaging $2795. *State or other work-study/employment:* Total amount: $230,731 (71% need-based, 29% non-need-based). 80 part-time jobs averaging $2884.

**APPLYING FOR FINANCIAL AID** *Required financial aid forms:* FAFSA, institution's own form, noncustodial (divorced/separated) parent's statement. *Financial aid deadline (priority):* 2/15. *Notification date:* 4/1. Students must reply by 5/1 or within 2 weeks of notification.

**CONTACT** Bruce Hazam, Director of Financial Aid, College of the Atlantic, 105 Eden Street, Bar Harbor, ME 04609-1198, 207-801-5645 or toll-free 800-528-0025. *Fax:* 207-288-4126. *E-mail:* bhazam@coa.edu. *Website:* http://www.coa.edu/.

# COLLEGE OF THE HOLY CROSS
## Worcester, MA

| Tuition & fees: $47,176 | Average undergraduate aid package: $35,279 |
| --- | --- |

**ABOUT THE INSTITUTION** Independent Roman Catholic (Jesuit), coed. *Awards:* bachelor's degrees. 34 undergraduate majors. *Total enrollment:* 2,937. Undergraduates: 2,937. Freshmen: 773. Both federal and institutional methodology are used as a basis for awarding need-based institutional aid.

**UNDERGRADUATE EXPENSES for 2015–2016** *Application fee:* $60. *Comprehensive fee:* $59,924 includes full-time tuition ($46,550), mandatory fees ($626), and room and board ($12,748). *College room only:* $6878. Room and board charges vary according to housing facility.

**FRESHMAN FINANCIAL AID (Fall 2014, est.)** 565 applied for aid; of those 76% were deemed to have need. 100% of freshmen with need received aid; of those 100% had need fully met. *Average percent of need met:* 100% (excluding resources awarded to replace EFC). *Average financial aid package:* $36,532 (excluding resources awarded to replace EFC). 1% of all full-time freshmen had no need and received non-need-based gift aid.

**UNDERGRADUATE FINANCIAL AID (Fall 2014, est.)** 1,909 applied for aid; of those 84% were deemed to have need. 100% of undergraduates with need received aid; of those 100% had need fully met. *Average percent of need met:* 100% (excluding resources awarded to replace EFC). *Average financial aid package:* $35,279 (excluding resources awarded to replace EFC). 2% of all full-time undergraduates had no need and received non-need-based gift aid.

**GIFT AID (NEED-BASED)** *Total amount:* $42,973,866 (6% federal, 2% state, 92% institutional). *Receiving aid:* Freshmen: 46% (357); all full-time undergraduates: 46% (1,326). *Average award:* Freshmen: $33,991; Undergraduates: $32,207. *Scholarships, grants, and awards:* Federal Pell, FSEOG, state, private, college/university gift aid from institutional funds.

**GIFT AID (NON-NEED-BASED)** *Total amount:* $4,877,118 (62% institutional, 38% external sources). *Receiving aid:* Freshmen: 2% (14). Undergraduates: 1% (42). *Average award:* Freshmen: $45,080. Undergraduates: $33,308. *Scholarships, grants, and awards by category:* Academic interests/achievement: 66 awards ($2,301,230 total): general academic interests/achievements, humanities, military science. Creative arts/performance: 4 awards ($180,320 total): music. Special characteristics: 37 awards ($1,667,960 total): children of faculty/staff. *Tuition waivers:* Full or partial for employees or children of employees. *ROTC:* Army cooperative, Naval, Air Force cooperative.

**LOANS** *Student loans:* $13,077,222 (82% need-based, 18% non-need-based). 59% of past graduating class borrowed through all loan programs. *Average indebtedness per student:* $28,354. *Average need-based loan:* Freshmen: $4952. Undergraduates: $5441. *Parent loans:* $7,841,167 (100% non-need-based). *Programs:* Federal Direct (Subsidized and Unsubsidized Stafford, PLUS), Perkins.

**WORK-STUDY** *Federal work-study:* Total amount: $1,795,222; 1,106 jobs averaging $1620.

**ATHLETIC AWARDS** Total amount: $8,863,837 (65% need-based, 35% non-need-based).

**APPLYING FOR FINANCIAL AID** *Required financial aid forms:* FAFSA, CSS Financial Aid PROFILE, noncustodial (divorced/separated) parent's statement, business/farm supplement, federal income tax form(s). *Financial aid deadline:* 2/1. *Notification date:* 4/1. Students must reply by 5/1.

**CONTACT** Ms. Lynne Myers, Director of Financial Aid, College of the Holy Cross, One College Street, Worcester, MA 01610-2395, 508-793-2265 or toll-free 800-442-2421. *Fax:* 508-793-2527. *Website:* http://www.holycross.edu/.

## COLLEGE OF THE OZARKS
### Point Lookout, MO

| Tuition & fees: N/R | Average undergraduate aid package: $20,097 |
|---|---|

**ABOUT THE INSTITUTION** Independent Presbyterian, coed. **Awards:** bachelor's degrees. 67 undergraduate majors. **Total enrollment:** 1,433. Undergraduates: 1,433. Freshmen: 255. Federal methodology is used as a basis for awarding need-based institutional aid.

**UNDERGRADUATE EXPENSES for 2015–2016 Tuition:** part-time $310 per credit hour. Part-time tuition and fees vary according to course load.

**FRESHMAN FINANCIAL AID (Fall 2014, est.)** 247 applied for aid; of those 96% were deemed to have need. 100% of freshmen with need received aid; of those 18% had need fully met. **Average percent of need met:** 84% (excluding resources awarded to replace EFC). **Average financial aid package:** $19,855 (excluding resources awarded to replace EFC). 21% of all full-time freshmen had no need and received non-need-based gift aid.

**UNDERGRADUATE FINANCIAL AID (Fall 2014, est.)** 1,256 applied for aid; of those 97% were deemed to have need. 100% of undergraduates with need received aid; of those 31% had need fully met. **Average percent of need met:** 87% (excluding resources awarded to replace EFC). **Average financial aid package:** $20,097 (excluding resources awarded to replace EFC). 7% of all full-time undergraduates had no need and received non-need-based gift aid.

**GIFT AID (NEED-BASED) Total amount:** $22,023,787 (16% federal, 5% state, 78% institutional, 1% external sources). **Receiving aid:** Freshmen: 78% (237); all full-time undergraduates: 92% (1,215). **Average award:** Freshmen: $16,202; Undergraduates: $16,877. **Scholarships, grants, and awards:** Federal Pell, FSEOG, state, private, college/university gift aid from institutional funds.

**GIFT AID (NON-NEED-BASED) Total amount:** $2,416,299 (1% federal, 1% state, 96% institutional, 2% external sources). **Receiving aid:** Freshmen: 5% (16). Undergraduates: 11% (150). **Average award:** Freshmen: $13,546. Undergraduates: $13,560. **ROTC:** Army.

**LOANS Student loans:** 8% of past graduating class borrowed through all loan programs. **Average indebtedness per student:** $6282.

**WORK-STUDY Federal work-study:** Total amount: $3,253,530; 220 jobs averaging $3935. **State or other work-study/employment:** Total amount: $2,427,222 (39% need-based, 61% non-need-based). 85 part-time jobs averaging $3935.

**ATHLETIC AWARDS** Total amount: $296,130 (50% need-based, 50% non-need-based).

**APPLYING FOR FINANCIAL AID Required financial aid form:** FAFSA. **Financial aid deadline (priority):** 2/15. **Notification date:** 8/1.

**CONTACT** Office of Financial Aid, College of the Ozarks, PO Box 17, Point Lookout, MO 65726, 417-690-3290 or toll-free 800-222-0525. *Fax:* 417-690-3286. *Website:* http://www.cofo.edu/.

## THE COLLEGE OF WILLIAM AND MARY
### Williamsburg, VA

| Tuition & fees (VA res): $17,656 | Average undergraduate aid package: $18,442 |
|---|---|

**ABOUT THE INSTITUTION** State-supported, coed. **Awards:** certificates, bachelor's, master's, and doctoral degrees. 41 undergraduate majors. **Total enrollment:** 8,437. Undergraduates: 6,299. Freshmen: 1,511. Federal methodology is used as a basis for awarding need-based institutional aid.

**UNDERGRADUATE EXPENSES for 2015–2016 Application fee:** $70. **Tuition, state resident:** full-time $12,428; part-time $350 per credit hour. **Tuition, nonresident:** full-time $34,132; part-time $1080 per credit hour. **Required fees:** full-time $5228. Full-time tuition and fees vary according to program. **College room and board:** $10,344; **Room only:** $6398. Room and board charges vary according to board plan and housing facility. **Payment plan:** Guaranteed tuition.

**FRESHMAN FINANCIAL AID (Fall 2013)** 990 applied for aid; of those 53% were deemed to have need. 94% of freshmen with need received aid; of those 27% had need fully met. **Average percent of need met:** 74% (excluding resources awarded to replace EFC). **Average financial aid package:** $17,011 (excluding resources awarded to replace EFC). 2% of all full-time freshmen had no need and received non-need-based gift aid.

**UNDERGRADUATE FINANCIAL AID (Fall 2013)** 3,098 applied for aid; of those 69% were deemed to have need. 97% of undergraduates with need received aid; of those 26% had need fully met. **Average percent of need met:** 76% (excluding resources awarded to replace EFC). **Average financial aid package:** $18,442 (excluding resources awarded to replace EFC). 5% of all full-time undergraduates had no need and received non-need-based gift aid.

**GIFT AID (NEED-BASED) Total amount:** $26,421,616 (13% federal, 12% state, 70% institutional, 5% external sources). **Receiving aid:** Freshmen: 27% (404); all full-time undergraduates: 28% (1,703). **Average award:** Freshmen: $13,609; Undergraduates: $13,914. **Scholarships, grants, and awards:** Federal Pell, FSEOG, state, private, college/university gift aid from institutional funds.

**GIFT AID (NON-NEED-BASED) Total amount:** $3,575,025 (5% federal, 67% institutional, 28% external sources). **Receiving aid:** Freshmen: 16% (236). Undergraduates: 12% (731). **Average award:** Freshmen: $11,088. Undergraduates: $6673. **Scholarships, grants, and awards by category:** Academic interests/achievement: 19 awards ($457,213 total): general academic interests/achievements. Creative arts/performance: 77 awards ($51,924 total): music, theater/drama. Special characteristics: 169 awards ($2,350,667 total): general special characteristics. **Tuition waivers:** Full or partial for employees or children of employees, senior citizens. **ROTC:** Army.

**LOANS Student loans:** $15,538,870 (72% need-based, 28% non-need-based). 38% of past graduating class borrowed through all loan programs. **Average indebtedness per student:** $25,733. **Average need-based loan:** Freshmen: $3384. Undergraduates: $4463. **Parent loans:** $6,136,884 (71% need-based, 29% non-need-based). **Programs:** Federal Direct (Subsidized and Unsubsidized Stafford, PLUS), Perkins.

**WORK-STUDY Federal work-study:** 120 jobs averaging $1108.

**ATHLETIC AWARDS** Total amount: $7,122,337 (17% need-based, 83% non-need-based).

**APPLYING FOR FINANCIAL AID Required financial aid forms:** FAFSA, CSS Financial Aid PROFILE. **Financial aid deadline (priority):** 3/15. **Notification date:** Continuous beginning 3/15. Students must reply by 5/1 or within 2 weeks of notification.

**CONTACT** Mr. Edward P. Irish, Director of Financial Aid, The College of William and Mary, PO Box 8795, Williamsburg, VA 23187, 757-221-2425. *Fax:* 757-221-2515. *E-mail:* epiris@wm.edu. *Website:* http://www.wm.edu/.

## THE COLLEGE OF WOOSTER
### Wooster, OH

| Tuition & fees: $43,350 | Average undergraduate aid package: $39,304 |
|---|---|

**ABOUT THE INSTITUTION** Independent Presbyterian Church (U.S.A.), coed. **Awards:** bachelor's degrees. 46 undergraduate majors. **Total enrollment:** 2,066. Undergraduates: 2,066. Freshmen: 547. Both federal and institutional methodology are used as a basis for awarding need-based institutional aid.

**UNDERGRADUATE EXPENSES for 2015–2016 Application fee:** $45. **Comprehensive fee:** $53,600 includes full-time tuition ($42,920), mandatory fees ($430), and room and board ($10,250). **College room only:** $4950. Full-time tuition and fees vary according to course load. Room and board charges vary according to board plan and housing facility. **Part-time tuition:** $1335 per credit. Part-time tuition and fees vary according to course load.

**FRESHMAN FINANCIAL AID (Fall 2014, est.)** 413 applied for aid; of those 85% were deemed to have need. 100% of freshmen with need received aid; of those 56% had need fully met. **Average percent of need met:** 95% (excluding resources awarded to replace EFC). **Average financial aid package:** $38,821 (excluding resources awarded to replace EFC). 35% of all full-time freshmen had no need and received non-need-based gift aid.

**UNDERGRADUATE FINANCIAL AID (Fall 2014, est.)** 1,333 applied for aid; of those 90% were deemed to have need. 100% of undergraduates with need received aid; of those 53% had need fully met. **Average percent of need met:** 94% (excluding resources awarded to replace EFC). **Average financial aid package:** $39,304 (excluding resources awarded to replace EFC). 38% of all full-time undergraduates had no need and received non-need-based gift aid.

**GIFT AID (NEED-BASED)** *Total amount:* $35,024,384 (6% federal, 1% state, 91% institutional, 2% external sources). *Receiving aid:* Freshmen: 63% (345); all full-time undergraduates: 59% (1,181). *Average award:* Freshmen: $30,163; Undergraduates: $29,304. *Scholarships, grants, and awards:* Federal Pell, FSEOG, state, private, college/university gift aid from institutional funds.

**GIFT AID (NON-NEED-BASED)** *Total amount:* $15,529,695 (98% institutional, 2% external sources). *Receiving aid:* Freshmen: 10% (52). Undergraduates: 6% (127). *Average award:* Freshmen: $21,747. Undergraduates: $19,329. *Scholarships, grants, and awards by category:* Academic interests/achievement: 1,565 awards ($25,743,806 total): general academic interests/achievements. *Creative arts/ performance:* 141 awards ($571,710 total): dance, music, theater/drama. *Special achievements/activities:* 211 awards ($1,446,250 total): community service, religious involvement. *Special characteristics:* 311 awards ($8,563,258 total): children of educators, children of faculty/staff, international students, members of minority groups. *Tuition waivers:* Full or partial for employees or children of employees.

**LOANS** *Student loans:* $9,728,675 (71% need-based, 29% non-need-based). 56% of past graduating class borrowed through all loan programs. *Average indebtedness per student:* $24,506. *Average need-based loan:* Freshmen: $5810. Undergraduates: $6872. *Parent loans:* $3,867,339 (23% need-based, 77% non-need-based). *Programs:* Federal Direct (Subsidized and Unsubsidized Stafford, PLUS), Perkins.

**WORK-STUDY** *Federal work-study:* Total amount: $1,833,876; 932 jobs averaging $1968. *State or other work-study/employment:* Total amount: $319,500 (100% non-need-based). 116 part-time jobs averaging $2754.

**APPLYING FOR FINANCIAL AID** *Required financial aid forms:* FAFSA, institution's own form. *Financial aid deadline (priority):* 2/15. *Notification date:* Continuous beginning 2/15. Students must reply by 5/1.

**CONTACT** Mr. Joseph Winge, Director of Financial Aid, The College of Wooster, Pearl House, 804 Beall Avenue, Wooster, OH 44691, 800-877-3688 or toll-free 800-877-9905. *Fax:* 330-263-2634. *E-mail:* financialaid@wooster.edu. *Website:* http://www.wooster.edu/.

# COLORADO CHRISTIAN UNIVERSITY
## Lakewood, CO

**CONTACT** Mr. Steve Woodburn, Director of Financial Aid, Colorado Christian University, 180 South Garrison Street, Lakewood, CO 80226-7499, 303-963-3230 or toll-free 800-44-FAITH. *Fax:* 303-963-3231. *E-mail:* sfs@ccu.edu. *Website:* http://www.ccu.edu/.

# THE COLORADO COLLEGE
## Colorado Springs, CO

| Tuition & fees: $46,410 | Average undergraduate aid package: $45,111 |
| --- | --- |

**ABOUT THE INSTITUTION** Independent, coed. *Awards:* bachelor's and master's degrees (master's degree in education only). 49 undergraduate majors. *Total enrollment:* 2,067. Undergraduates: 2,050. Freshmen: 549. Both federal and institutional methodology are used as a basis for awarding need-based institutional aid.

**UNDERGRADUATE EXPENSES for 2015–2016** *Application fee:* $60. *One-time required fee:* $150. *Comprehensive fee:* $57,162 includes full-time tuition ($46,000), mandatory fees ($410), and room and board ($10,752). *College room only:* $6176. Room and board charges vary according to board plan and housing facility. *Part-time tuition:* $7667 per course. Part-time tuition and fees vary according to course load.

**FRESHMAN FINANCIAL AID (Fall 2014, est.)** 280 applied for aid; of those 72% were deemed to have need. 100% of freshmen with need received aid; of those 100% had need fully met. *Average percent of need met:* 100% (excluding resources awarded to replace EFC). *Average financial aid package:* $49,031 (excluding resources awarded to replace EFC). 3% of all full-time freshmen had no need and received non-need-based gift aid.

**UNDERGRADUATE FINANCIAL AID (Fall 2014, est.)** 1,022 applied for aid; of those 73% were deemed to have need. 100% of undergraduates with need received aid; of those 100% had need fully met. *Average percent of need met:* 100% (excluding resources awarded to replace EFC). *Average financial aid package:* $45,111 (excluding resources awarded to replace EFC). 7% of all full-time undergraduates had no need and received non-need-based gift aid.

**GIFT AID (NEED-BASED)** *Total amount:* $27,368,720 (4% federal, 95% institutional, 1% external sources). *Receiving aid:* Freshmen: 35% (192); all full-time undergraduates: 35% (719). *Average award:* Freshmen: $43,884; Undergraduates: $38,556. *Scholarships, grants, and awards:* Federal Pell, FSEOG, state, private, college/university gift aid from institutional funds.

**GIFT AID (NON-NEED-BASED)** *Total amount:* $3,676,596 (1% state, 56% institutional, 43% external sources). *Receiving aid:* Freshmen: 13% (74). Undergraduates: 8% (155). *Average award:* Freshmen: $9792. Undergraduates: $11,490. *Scholarships, grants, and awards by category:* Academic interests/ achievement: 157 awards ($1,884,028 total): biological sciences, general academic interests/achievements, mathematics, physical sciences. *Special characteristics:* 17 awards ($607,938 total): children of faculty/staff, international students. *Tuition waivers:* Full or partial for employees or children of employees. *ROTC:* Army cooperative.

**LOANS** *Student loans:* $4,895,336 (43% need-based, 57% non-need-based). 34% of past graduating class borrowed through all loan programs. *Average indebtedness per student:* $19,756. *Average need-based loan:* Freshmen: $3102. Undergraduates: $4589. *Parent loans:* $1,618,535 (100% non-need-based). *Programs:* Federal Direct (Subsidized and Unsubsidized Stafford, PLUS), Perkins.

**WORK-STUDY** *Federal work-study:* Total amount: $702,505; 206 jobs averaging $1828. *State or other work-study/employment:* Total amount: $292,131 (100% need-based). 130 part-time jobs averaging $1875.

**ATHLETIC AWARDS** Total amount: $1,746,288 (13% need-based, 87% non-need-based).

**APPLYING FOR FINANCIAL AID** *Required financial aid forms:* FAFSA, CSS Financial Aid PROFILE, noncustodial (divorced/separated) parent's statement, federal income tax form(s), W-2 forms. *Financial aid deadline:* 2/15. *Notification date:* 3/20. Students must reply by 5/1.

**CONTACT** Mr. James M. Swanson, Director of Financial Aid, The Colorado College, 14 East Cache La Poudre Street, Colorado Springs, CO 80903-3294, 719-389-6651 or toll-free 800-542-7214. *Fax:* 719-389-6173. *E-mail:* financialaid@coloradocollege.edu. *Website:* http://www.coloradocollege.edu/.

# COLORADO HEIGHTS UNIVERSITY
## Denver, CO

**ABOUT THE INSTITUTION** Independent, coed. *Awards:* certificates, bachelor's, and master's degrees. 2 undergraduate majors. *Total enrollment:* 375. Undergraduates: 343. Freshmen: 35.

**GIFT AID (NEED-BASED)** *Scholarships, grants, and awards:* Federal Pell, FSEOG, college/university gift aid from institutional funds.

**LOANS** *Programs:* Federal Direct (Subsidized and Unsubsidized Stafford, PLUS).

**APPLYING FOR FINANCIAL AID** *Required financial aid forms:* FAFSA, institution's own form.

**CONTACT** Amber Bartlett, Financial Aid Advisor, Colorado Heights University, 3001 South Federal Boulevard, Room 2013, Denver, CO 80236, 303-937-4200. *Fax:* 303-937-4224. *Website:* http://www.chu.edu/.

# COLORADO MESA UNIVERSITY
## Grand Junction, CO

| Tuition & fees (CO res): $7115 | Average undergraduate aid package: $8317 |
| --- | --- |

**ABOUT THE INSTITUTION** State-supported, coed. *Awards:* certificates, associate, bachelor's, master's, and doctoral degrees. 55 undergraduate majors. *Total enrollment:* 9,116. Undergraduates: 9,003. Freshmen: 1,872. Federal methodology is used as a basis for awarding need-based institutional aid.

**UNDERGRADUATE EXPENSES for 2015–2016** *Application fee:* $30. *Tuition, state resident:* full-time $6357; part-time $227 per credit hour. *Tuition, nonresident:* full-time $16,961; part-time $606 per credit hour. *Required fees:* full-time $758; $27.10 per credit hour. Full-time tuition and fees vary according to course load. Part-time tuition and fees vary according to course load. *College room* and board: $8706; Room only: $4616. Room and board charges vary according to board plan and housing facility.

FRESHMAN FINANCIAL AID (Fall 2013) 1,888 applied for aid; of those 77% were deemed to have need. 97% of freshmen with need received aid; of those 18% had need fully met. Average percent of need met: 60% (excluding resources awarded to replace EFC). Average financial aid package: $7655 (excluding resources awarded to replace EFC). 8% of all full-time freshmen had no need and received non-need-based gift aid.

UNDERGRADUATE FINANCIAL AID (Fall 2013) 6,044 applied for aid; of those 82% were deemed to have need. 98% of undergraduates with need received aid; of those 15% had need fully met. Average percent of need met: 59% (excluding resources awarded to replace EFC). Average financial aid package: $8317 (excluding resources awarded to replace EFC). 5% of all full-time undergraduates had no need and received non-need-based gift aid.

GIFT AID (NEED-BASED) Total amount: $25,518,477 (63% federal, 15% state, 13% institutional, 9% external sources). Receiving aid: Freshmen: 57% (1,176); all full-time undergraduates: 56% (4,061). Average award: Freshmen: $5815; Undergraduates: $5853. Scholarships, grants, and awards: Federal Pell, FSEOG, state, private, college/university gift aid from institutional funds.

GIFT AID (NON-NEED-BASED) Total amount: $3,734,873 (22% federal, 61% institutional, 17% external sources). Receiving aid: Freshmen: 6% (123). Undergraduates: 4% (282). Average award: Freshmen: $3029. Undergraduates: $2939. Scholarships, grants, and awards by category: Academic interests/achievement: biological sciences, business, communication, computer science, education, engineering/technologies, English, foreign languages, general academic interests/achievements, health fields, humanities, mathematics, physical sciences, social sciences. Creative arts/performance: art/fine arts, creative writing, dance, journalism/publications, music, performing arts, theater/drama. Special achievements/activities: general special achievements/activities, hobbies/interests, leadership. Special characteristics: adult students, first-generation college students, international students, local/state students, members of minority groups, out-of-state students. Tuition waivers: Full or partial for employees or children of employees.

LOANS Student loans: $42,157,813 (85% need-based, 15% non-need-based). 66% of past graduating class borrowed through all loan programs. Average indebtedness per student: $26,740. Average need-based loan: Freshmen: $3063. Undergraduates: $3676. Parent loans: $14,118,079 (60% need-based, 40% non-need-based). Programs: Federal Direct (Subsidized and Unsubsidized Stafford, PLUS), Perkins.

WORK-STUDY Federal work-study: jobs available. State or other work-study/employment: Total amount: $4,191,891 (24% need-based, 76% non-need-based). Part-time jobs available.

ATHLETIC AWARDS Total amount: $1,507,755 (57% need-based, 43% non-need-based).

APPLYING FOR FINANCIAL AID Required financial aid form: FAFSA. Financial aid deadline: Continuous. Notification date: Continuous beginning 3/1. Students must reply within 2 weeks of notification.

CONTACT Mr. Curt Martin, Director of Financial Aid, Colorado Mesa University, 1100 North Avenue, Grand Junction, CO 81501-3122, 970-248-1065 or toll-free 800-982-MESA. Fax: 970-248-1191. E-mail: cumartin@coloradomesa.edu. Website: http://www.coloradomesa.edu/.

---

# COLORADO MOUNTAIN COLLEGE
## Glenwood Springs, CO

| Tuition & fees: N/R | Average undergraduate aid package: N/A |
|---|---|

ABOUT THE INSTITUTION District-supported, coed. 26 undergraduate majors. Federal methodology is used as a basis for awarding need-based institutional aid.

FRESHMAN FINANCIAL AID (Fall 2013) 10% of all full-time freshmen had no need and received non-need-based gift aid.

UNDERGRADUATE FINANCIAL AID (Fall 2013) 11% of all full-time undergraduates had no need and received non-need-based gift aid.

GIFT AID (NEED-BASED) Total amount: $4,223,780 (84% federal, 16% state). Receiving aid: Freshmen: 38% (153); all full-time undergraduates: 39% (670). Scholarships, grants, and awards: Federal Pell, FSEOG, state, private, college/university gift aid from institutional funds.

GIFT AID (NON-NEED-BASED) Total amount: $983,086 (68% institutional, 32% external sources). Receiving aid: Freshmen: 15% (59). Undergraduates: 17%

---

(295). Average award: Freshmen: $831. Undergraduates: $1143. Scholarships, grants, and awards by category: Special characteristics: local/state students.

LOANS Student loans: $5,042,069 (55% need-based, 45% non-need-based). Parent loans: $526,939 (100% non-need-based). Programs: Federal Direct (Subsidized and Unsubsidized Stafford, PLUS), Perkins, Federal Nursing, state.

WORK-STUDY Federal work-study: jobs available. State or other work-study/employment: Total amount: $262,784 (27% need-based, 73% non-need-based). Part-time jobs available.

APPLYING FOR FINANCIAL AID Required financial aid form: FAFSA. Financial aid deadline (priority): 3/31. Notification date: Continuous.

CONTACT Mr. Thomas S. Valles, Director of Financial Aid, Colorado Mountain College, 802 Grand Avenue, Glenwood Springs, CO 81601, 970-947-8338 or toll-free 800-621-8559. E-mail: tvalles@coloradomtn.edu. Website: http://www.coloradomtn.edu/.

---

# COLORADO MOUNTAIN COLLEGE
## Leadville, CO

CONTACT Financial Aid Office, Colorado Mountain College, 901 South Highway 24, Leadville, CO 80461, 719-486-2015 or toll-free 800-621-8559. Website: http://www.coloradomtn.edu/.

---

# COLORADO MOUNTAIN COLLEGE
## Steamboat Springs, CO

| Tuition & fees: N/R | Average undergraduate aid package: N/A |
|---|---|

ABOUT THE INSTITUTION District-supported, coed. 27 undergraduate majors. Federal methodology is used as a basis for awarding need-based institutional aid.

GIFT AID (NEED-BASED) Scholarships, grants, and awards: Federal Pell, FSEOG, state, college/university gift aid from institutional funds.

LOANS Programs: Federal Direct (Subsidized and Unsubsidized Stafford, PLUS).

WORK-STUDY Federal work-study jobs available. State or other work-study/employment: Part-time jobs available.

APPLYING FOR FINANCIAL AID Required financial aid form: FAFSA. Financial aid deadline (priority): 3/31. Notification date: Continuous beginning 5/15.

CONTACT Mr. Thomas S. Valles, Director of Financial Aid, Colorado Mountain College, 802 Grand Avenue, Glenwood Springs, CO 81601, 800-621-8559 Ext. 8338 or toll-free 800-621-8559. Fax: 970-947-8318. E-mail: finaid@coloradomtn.edu. Website: http://www.coloradomtn.edu/.

---

# COLORADO SCHOOL OF MINES
## Golden, CO

| Tuition & fees (CO res): $16,918 | Average undergraduate aid package: $12,191 |
|---|---|

ABOUT THE INSTITUTION State-supported, coed. Awards: certificates, bachelor's, master's, and doctoral degrees. 17 undergraduate majors. Total enrollment: 5,795. Undergraduates: 4,456. Freshmen: 1,000. Federal methodology is used as a basis for awarding need-based institutional aid.

UNDERGRADUATE EXPENSES for 2015–2016 Application fee: $45. Tuition, state resident: full-time $14,790; part-time $493 per credit hour. Tuition, nonresident: full-time $31,470; part-time $1049 per credit hour. Required fees: full-time $2128. Full-time tuition and fees vary according to course load. College room and board: $10,484. Room and board charges vary according to board plan and housing facility.

FRESHMAN FINANCIAL AID (Fall 2013) 779 applied for aid; of those 65% were deemed to have need. 100% of freshmen with need received aid; of those 25% had need fully met. Average percent of need met: 46% (excluding resources awarded to replace EFC). Average financial aid package: $10,354 (excluding resources

awarded to replace EFC). 31% of all full-time freshmen had no need and received non-need-based gift aid.

**UNDERGRADUATE FINANCIAL AID (Fall 2013)** 2,788 applied for aid; of those 75% were deemed to have need. 100% of undergraduates with need received aid; of those 20% had need fully met. *Average percent of need met:* 55% (excluding resources awarded to replace EFC). *Average financial aid package:* $12,191 (excluding resources awarded to replace EFC). 25% of all full-time undergraduates had no need and received non-need-based gift aid.

**GIFT AID (NEED-BASED)** *Total amount:* $15,744,698 (22% federal, 5% state, 57% institutional, 16% external sources). *Receiving aid:* Freshmen: 29% (278); all full-time undergraduates: 27% (1,106). *Average award:* Freshmen: $4220; Undergraduates: $4835. *Scholarships, grants, and awards:* Federal Pell, FSEOG, state, private, college/university gift aid from institutional funds.

**GIFT AID (NON-NEED-BASED)** *Total amount:* $8,872,440 (88% institutional, 12% external sources). *Receiving aid:* Freshmen: 42% (400). Undergraduates: 33% (1,319). *Average award:* Freshmen: $7983. Undergraduates: $7666. *Scholarships, grants, and awards by category: Academic interests/achievement:* business, computer science, engineering/technologies, general academic interests/achievements, mathematics, military science, physical sciences. *Tuition waivers:* Full or partial for employees or children of employees. *ROTC:* Army, Air Force.

**LOANS** *Student loans:* $27,050,622 (50% need-based, 50% non-need-based). 66% of past graduating class borrowed through all loan programs. *Average indebtedness per student:* $23,667. *Average need-based loan:* Freshmen: $3642. Undergraduates: $4764. *Parent loans:* $11,970,799 (62% need-based, 38% non-need-based). *Programs:* Federal Direct (Subsidized and Unsubsidized Stafford, PLUS), Perkins, college/university.

**WORK-STUDY** *Federal work-study:* 303 jobs averaging $1572. *State or other work-study/employment:* Total amount: $3,376,354 (59% need-based, 41% non-need-based). 1,530 part-time jobs averaging $2242.

**ATHLETIC AWARDS** Total amount: $2,061,379 (50% need-based, 50% non-need-based).

**APPLYING FOR FINANCIAL AID** *Required financial aid form:* FAFSA. *Financial aid deadline (priority):* 3/1. *Notification date:* Continuous beginning 3/1.

**CONTACT** Jill Robertson, Director of Financial Aid, Colorado School of Mines, 1600 Maple Street, Golden, CO 80401-1887, 303-273-3301 or toll-free 800-446-9488 Ext. 3220. Fax: 303-384-2252. *E-mail:* finaid@mines.edu.
*Website:* http://www.mines.edu/.

# COLORADO STATE UNIVERSITY
### Fort Collins, CO

| Tuition & fees (CO res): $9897 | Average undergraduate aid package: $10,498 |
| --- | --- |

**ABOUT THE INSTITUTION** State-supported, coed. *Awards:* certificates, bachelor's, master's, and doctoral degrees. 119 undergraduate majors. *Total enrollment:* 31,449. Undergraduates: 23,858. Freshmen: 4,353. Federal methodology is used as a basis for awarding need-based institutional aid.

**UNDERGRADUATE EXPENSES for 2015–2016** *Application fee:* $50. *Tuition, state resident:* full-time $7868; part-time $357.30 per credit hour. *Tuition, nonresident:* full-time $24,048; part-time $1202 per credit hour. *Required fees:* full-time $2029; $45.87 per credit hour or $229.35 per term. Full-time tuition and fees vary according to course level, course load, program, and student level. Part-time tuition and fees vary according to course level, course load, program, and student level. *College room and board:* $10,488; *Room only:* $5104. Room and board charges vary according to board plan, housing facility, and location.

**FRESHMAN FINANCIAL AID (Fall 2013)** 3,545 applied for aid; of those 63% were deemed to have need. 91% of freshmen with need received aid; of those 27% had need fully met. *Average percent of need met:* 74% (excluding resources awarded to replace EFC). *Average financial aid package:* $10,158 (excluding resources awarded to replace EFC). 14% of all full-time freshmen had no need and received non-need-based gift aid.

**UNDERGRADUATE FINANCIAL AID (Fall 2013)** 15,008 applied for aid; of those 73% were deemed to have need. 91% of undergraduates with need received aid; of those 26% had need fully met. *Average percent of need met:* 73% (excluding resources awarded to replace EFC). *Average financial aid package:* $10,498 (excluding resources awarded to replace EFC). 11% of all full-time undergraduates had no need and received non-need-based gift aid.

**GIFT AID (NEED-BASED)** *Total amount:* $66,352,478 (36% federal, 8% state, 48% institutional, 8% external sources). *Receiving aid:* Freshmen: 37% (1,625); all full-time undergraduates: 34% (7,108). *Average award:* Freshmen: $7653; Undergraduates: $6749. *Scholarships, grants, and awards:* Federal Pell, FSEOG, state, private, college/university gift aid from institutional funds.

**GIFT AID (NON-NEED-BASED)** *Total amount:* $14,740,163 (2% federal, 2% state, 76% institutional, 20% external sources). *Receiving aid:* Freshmen: 16. Undergraduates: 85. *Average award:* Freshmen: $3996. Undergraduates: $4214. *Scholarships, grants, and awards by category: Academic interests/achievement:* general academic interests/achievements. *Creative arts/performance:* art/fine arts, creative writing, dance, music, theater/drama. *Special achievements/activities:* general special achievements/activities. *Special characteristics:* children of faculty/staff, first-generation college students, international students. *Tuition waivers:* Full or partial for employees or children of employees. *ROTC:* Army, Air Force.

**LOANS** *Student loans:* $84,921,035 (69% need-based, 31% non-need-based). 56% of past graduating class borrowed through all loan programs. *Average indebtedness per student:* $23,721. *Average need-based loan:* Freshmen: $5145. Undergraduates: $6675. *Parent loans:* $41,017,046 (29% need-based, 71% non-need-based). *Programs:* Federal Direct (Subsidized and Unsubsidized Stafford, PLUS), Perkins, alternative loans.

**WORK-STUDY** *Federal work-study:* jobs available. *State or other work-study/employment:* Total amount: $1,742,905 (79% need-based, 21% non-need-based). Part-time jobs available.

**ATHLETIC AWARDS** Total amount: $7,376,527 (34% need-based, 66% non-need-based).

**APPLYING FOR FINANCIAL AID** *Required financial aid form:* FAFSA. *Financial aid deadline (priority):* 3/1. *Notification date:* Continuous beginning 3/1.

**CONTACT** Student Financial Services Office, Colorado State University, Room 103, Centennial Hall, Fort Collins, CO 80523-8024, 970-491-6321. *E-mail:* sfs@colostate.edu.
*Website:* http://www.colostate.edu/.

# COLORADO STATE UNIVERSITY– GLOBAL CAMPUS
### Greenwood Village, CO

**CONTACT** Financial Aid Office, Colorado State University–Global Campus, 8000 E. Maplewood Avenue, Greenwood Village, CO 80111, 720-279-0159 or toll-free 800-920-6723.
*Website:* http://csuglobal.edu/.

# COLORADO STATE UNIVERSITY– PUEBLO
### Pueblo, CO

| Tuition & fees (CO res): $7834 | Average undergraduate aid package: $9669 |
| --- | --- |

**ABOUT THE INSTITUTION** State-supported, coed. *Awards:* bachelor's and master's degrees. 27 undergraduate majors. *Total enrollment:* 7,256. Undergraduates: 5,192. Freshmen: 910. Federal methodology is used as a basis for awarding need-based institutional aid.

**UNDERGRADUATE EXPENSES for 2015–2016** *Application fee:* $25. *Tuition, state resident:* full-time $5824; part-time $216 per credit hour. *Tuition, nonresident:* full-time $16,765; part-time $650 per credit hour. *Required fees:* full-time $2010; $67 per credit hour. Full-time tuition and fees vary according to course load and reciprocity agreements. Part-time tuition and fees vary according to course load and reciprocity agreements. *College room and board:* $9016; *Room only:* $5410. Room and board charges vary according to board plan.

**FRESHMAN FINANCIAL AID (Fall 2014, est.)** 615 applied for aid; of those 80% were deemed to have need. 100% of freshmen with need received aid; of those 10% had need fully met. *Average percent of need met:* 60% (excluding resources awarded to replace EFC). *Average financial aid package:* $9344 (excluding

resources awarded to replace EFC). 11% of all full-time freshmen had no need and received non-need-based gift aid.

**UNDERGRADUATE FINANCIAL AID (Fall 2014, est.)** 2,358 applied for aid; of those 85% were deemed to have need. 99% of undergraduates with need received aid; of those 8% had need fully met. *Average percent of need met:* 58% (excluding resources awarded to replace EFC). *Average financial aid package:* $9669 (excluding resources awarded to replace EFC). 9% of all full-time undergraduates had no need and received non-need-based gift aid.

**GIFT AID (NEED-BASED) Total amount:** $15,349,956 (58% federal, 20% state, 18% institutional, 4% external sources). *Receiving aid:* Freshmen: 70% (432); all full-time undergraduates: 63% (1,702). *Average award:* Freshmen: $7461; Undergraduates: $7064. *Scholarships, grants, and awards:* Federal Pell, FSEOG, state, private, college/university gift aid from institutional funds, Federal Nursing, TEACH Grants.

**GIFT AID (NON-NEED-BASED) Total amount:** $1,464,021 (2% state, 84% institutional, 14% external sources). *Receiving aid:* Freshmen: 5% (33). Undergraduates: 3% (84). *Average award:* Freshmen: $3224. Undergraduates: $3557. *Scholarships, grants, and awards by category:* Academic interests/achievement: biological sciences, business, communication, computer science, education, engineering/technologies, English, foreign languages, general academic interests/achievements, health fields, mathematics, physical sciences, premedicine, social sciences. *Creative arts/performance:* applied art and design, art/fine arts, cinema/film/broadcasting, journalism/publications, music. *Special achievements/activities:* community service, general special achievements/activities, leadership. *Special characteristics:* adult students, children and siblings of alumni, children of current students, children of faculty/staff, ethnic background, first-generation college students, general special characteristics, handicapped students, international students, local/state students, married students, members of minority groups, out-of-state students. *Tuition waivers:* Full or partial for employees or children of employees, senior citizens. *ROTC:* Army.

**LOANS Student loans:** $19,289,291 (80% need-based, 20% non-need-based). 74% of past graduating class borrowed through all loan programs. *Average indebtedness per student:* $29,914. *Average need-based loan:* Freshmen: $3066. Undergraduates: $3730. *Parent loans:* $2,575,500 (41% need-based, 59% non-need-based). *Programs:* Federal Direct (Subsidized and Unsubsidized Stafford, PLUS), Perkins, Federal Nursing.

**WORK-STUDY Federal work-study:** Total amount: $315,596; jobs available. *State or other work-study/employment:* Total amount: $1,059,493 (63% need-based, 37% non-need-based). Part-time jobs available.

**ATHLETIC AWARDS** Total amount: $1,992,303 (58% need-based, 42% non-need-based).

**APPLYING FOR FINANCIAL AID Required financial aid forms:** FAFSA, institution's own form. *Financial aid deadline (priority):* 3/1. *Notification date:* Continuous beginning 3/10. Students must reply within 3 weeks of notification.

**CONTACT** Sean McGivney, Director of Financial Aid, Colorado State University–Pueblo, 2200 Bonforte Boulevard, Pueblo, CO 81001-4901, 719-549-2913. *Fax:* 719-549-2088. *E-mail:* sean.mcgivney@csupueblo.edu. *Website:* http://www.csupueblo.edu/.

# COLORADO TECHNICAL UNIVERSITY COLORADO SPRINGS
## Colorado Springs, CO

**CONTACT** Jacqueline Harris, Senior Director of Student Finance Services, Colorado Technical University Colorado Springs, 4435 North Chestnut Street, Colorado Springs, CO 80907-3896, 719-598-0200 or toll-free 866-942-6555. *Fax:* 719-598-3740. *Website:* http://www.coloradotech.edu/.

# COLORADO TECHNICAL UNIVERSITY DENVER SOUTH
## Aurora, CO

**CONTACT** Ms. Natalie Dietsch, Financial Aid Manager, Colorado Technical University Denver South, 5775 Denver Tech Center Boulevard, Suite 100, Greenwood Village, CO 80111, 303-694-6600 or toll-free 888-309-6555. *Fax:* 303-694-6673. *Website:* http://www.coloradotech.edu/.

# COLUMBIA CENTRO UNIVERSITARIO
## Caguas, PR

**CONTACT** Financial Aid Officer, Columbia Centro Universitario, Carr 183, Km 1.7, PO Box 8517, Caguas, PR 00726, 787-743-4041 Ext. 244. *Fax:* 787-744-7031. *Website:* http://www.columbiaco.edu/.

# COLUMBIA CENTRO UNIVERSITARIO
## Yauco, PR

**CONTACT** Financial Aid Office, Columbia Centro Universitario, Calle Betances #3, Box 3062, Yauco, PR 00698, 787-856-0945. *Website:* http://www.columbiaco.edu/.

# COLUMBIA COLLEGE
## Columbia, MO

| Tuition & fees: $20,936 | Average undergraduate aid package: $14,981 |
| --- | --- |

**ABOUT THE INSTITUTION** Independent Christian Church (Disciples of Christ), coed. *Awards:* associate, bachelor's, and master's degrees (offers continuing education program with significant enrollment not reflected in profile). 41 undergraduate majors. *Total enrollment:* 1,199. Undergraduates: 966. Freshmen: 133. Federal methodology is used as a basis for awarding need-based institutional aid.

**UNDERGRADUATE EXPENSES** for 2015–2016 *Application fee:* $35. *Comprehensive fee:* $29,176 includes full-time tuition ($20,936) and room and board ($8240). *College room only:* $5462. Full-time tuition and fees vary according to class time, course load, degree level, program, and reciprocity agreements. Room and board charges vary according to board plan and housing facility. *Part-time tuition:* $450 per credit hour. Part-time tuition and fees vary according to class time, course load, degree level, location, and reciprocity agreements. *Payment plan:* Guaranteed tuition.

**FRESHMAN FINANCIAL AID (Fall 2013)** 108 applied for aid; of those 95% were deemed to have need. 98% of freshmen with need received aid; of those 16% had need fully met. *Average percent of need met:* 62% (excluding resources awarded to replace EFC). *Average financial aid package:* $16,190 (excluding resources awarded to replace EFC). 9% of all full-time freshmen had no need and received non-need-based gift aid.

**UNDERGRADUATE FINANCIAL AID (Fall 2013)** 574 applied for aid; of those 92% were deemed to have need. 98% of undergraduates with need received aid; of those 12% had need fully met. *Average percent of need met:* 56% (excluding resources awarded to replace EFC). *Average financial aid package:* $14,981 (excluding resources awarded to replace EFC). 10% of all full-time undergraduates had no need and received non-need-based gift aid.

**GIFT AID (NEED-BASED) Total amount:** $2,165,157 (64% federal, 27% state, 9% institutional). *Receiving aid:* Freshmen: 53% (68); all full-time undergraduates: 48% (374). *Average award:* Freshmen: $5342; Undergraduates: $5063. *Scholarships, grants, and awards:* Federal Pell, FSEOG, state, private.

**GIFT AID (NON-NEED-BASED) Total amount:** $4,264,225 (1% state, 96% institutional, 3% external sources). *Receiving aid:* Freshmen: 72% (93). Undergraduates: 52% (404). *Average award:* Freshmen: $9385. Undergraduates: $9926. *Scholarships, grants, and awards by category:* Academic interests/

*achievement:* 408 awards ($2,024,166 total): biological sciences, business, communication, computer science, education, English, general academic interests/achievements, humanities, mathematics, physical sciences, religion/biblical studies, social sciences. *Creative arts/performance:* 23 awards ($20,675 total): art/fine arts, creative writing, music. *Special achievements/activities:* 186 awards ($997,968 total): community service, general special achievements/activities, leadership, religious involvement. *Special characteristics:* 296 awards ($522,541 total): adult students, children and siblings of alumni, children of current students, children of educators, children of faculty/staff, children of union members/company employees, ethnic background, first-generation college students, general special characteristics, international students, local/state students, members of minority groups, parents of current students, previous college experience, religious affiliation, siblings of current students, spouses of current students, veterans, veterans' children. *Tuition waivers:* Full or partial for children of alumni, employees or children of employees, senior citizens. *ROTC:* Army cooperative, Naval cooperative, Air Force cooperative.

**LOANS** *Student loans:* $3,940,013 (41% need-based, 59% non-need-based). 55% of past graduating class borrowed through all loan programs. *Average indebtedness per student:* $14,591. *Average need-based loan:* Freshmen: $2553. Undergraduates: $3691. *Parent loans:* $433,494 (100% non-need-based). *Programs:* Federal Direct (Subsidized and Unsubsidized Stafford, PLUS).

**WORK-STUDY** *Federal work-study:* 200 jobs averaging $2528. *State or other work-study/employment:* Total amount: $333,355 (100% need-based). 224 part-time jobs averaging $1666.

**ATHLETIC AWARDS** Total amount: $1,771,231 (100% non-need-based).

**APPLYING FOR FINANCIAL AID** *Required financial aid form:* FAFSA. *Financial aid deadline (priority):* 3/1. *Notification date:* Continuous beginning 3/1.

**CONTACT** Sharon Abernathy, Director of Financial Aid, Columbia College, 1001 Rogers Street, Columbia, MO 65216-0002, 573-875-7360 or toll-free 800-231-2391. *Fax:* 573-875-7452. *E-mail:* saabernathy@ccis.edu. *Website:* http://www.ccis.edu/.

# COLUMBIA COLLEGE
## Columbia, SC

**CONTACT** Anita Kaminer Elliott, Director of Financial Aid, Columbia College, 1301 Columbia College Drive, Columbia, SC 29203-5998, 803-786-3612 or toll-free 800-277-1301. *Fax:* 803-786-3560. *Website:* http://www.columbiasc.edu/.

# COLUMBIA COLLEGE CHICAGO
## Chicago, IL

**CONTACT** Ms. Jennifer Waters, Executive Director of Student Financial Services, Columbia College Chicago, 600 South Michigan Avenue, Chicago, IL 60605-1996, 312-369-7831. *Fax:* 312-986-7008. *E-mail:* jwaters@colum.edu. *Website:* http://www.colum.edu/.

# COLUMBIA COLLEGE HOLLYWOOD
## Tarzana, CA

**CONTACT** Mr. Jan Hastings, Financial Aid Administrator, Columbia College Hollywood, 18618 Oxnard Street, Tarzana, CA 91356, 818-401-1030 or toll-free 800-785-0585. *Fax:* 818-345-8660. *E-mail:* finaid@columbiacollege.edu. *Website:* http://www.columbiacollege.edu/.

# COLUMBIA COLLEGE OF NURSING
## Glendale, WI

| Tuition & fees: N/R | Average undergraduate aid package: $15,155 |
|---|---|

**ABOUT THE INSTITUTION** Independent, coed, primarily women. 1 undergraduate major. Both federal and institutional methodology are used as a basis for awarding need-based institutional aid.

**UNDERGRADUATE FINANCIAL AID (Fall 2014, est.)** 156 applied for aid; of those 78% were deemed to have need. 100% of undergraduates with need received aid; of those 7% had need fully met. *Average percent of need met:* 48% (excluding resources awarded to replace EFC). *Average financial aid package:* $15,155 (excluding resources awarded to replace EFC). 11% of all full-time undergraduates had no need and received non-need-based gift aid.

**GIFT AID (NEED-BASED)** *Total amount:* $779,755 (24% federal, 19% state, 42% institutional, 15% external sources). *Receiving aid:* All full-time undergraduates: 49% (81). *Average award:* Undergraduates: $8865. *Scholarships, grants, and awards:* Federal Pell, FSEOG, state, private, college/university gift aid from institutional funds.

**GIFT AID (NON-NEED-BASED)** *Total amount:* $95,864 (100% institutional). *Receiving aid:* Undergraduates: 69% (116). *Average award:* Undergraduates: $5000. *Scholarships, grants, and awards by category: Academic interests/achievement:* 153 awards ($592,938 total): general academic interests/achievements.

**LOANS** *Student loans:* $1,333,704 (78% need-based, 22% non-need-based). 96% of past graduating class borrowed through all loan programs. *Average indebtedness per student:* $28,203. *Average need-based loan:* Undergraduates: $4939. *Parent loans:* $88,309 (58% need-based, 42% non-need-based). *Programs:* Federal Direct (Subsidized and Unsubsidized Stafford, PLUS).

**APPLYING FOR FINANCIAL AID** *Notification date:* Continuous.

**CONTACT** Wendy Hilvo, Financial Aid Director, Columbia College of Nursing, 4425 North Port Washington Road, Suite 302, Glendale, WI 53212, 414-326-2337. *Fax:* 414-326-2362. *E-mail:* financialaid@ccon.edu. *Website:* http://www.ccon.edu/.

# COLUMBIA INTERNATIONAL UNIVERSITY
## Columbia, SC

| Tuition & fees: $20,430 | Average undergraduate aid package: $15,803 |
|---|---|

**ABOUT THE INSTITUTION** Independent nondenominational, coed. *Awards:* certificates, associate, bachelor's, master's, and doctoral degrees. 18 undergraduate majors. *Total enrollment:* 1,104. Undergraduates: 560. Freshmen: 101. Federal methodology is used as a basis for awarding need-based institutional aid.

**UNDERGRADUATE EXPENSES for 2015–2016** *Comprehensive fee:* $27,960 includes full-time tuition ($19,890), mandatory fees ($540), and room and board ($7530). Full-time tuition and fees vary according to course load, program, and reciprocity agreements. Room and board charges vary according to board plan and housing facility. *Part-time tuition:* $795 per credit hour. *Part-time fees:* $10 per credit hour; $120 per term. Part-time tuition and fees vary according to course load, program, and reciprocity agreements.

**FRESHMAN FINANCIAL AID (Fall 2013)** 94 applied for aid; of those 89% were deemed to have need. 100% of freshmen with need received aid; of those 15% had need fully met. *Average percent of need met:* 63% (excluding resources awarded to replace EFC). *Average financial aid package:* $16,021 (excluding resources awarded to replace EFC). 11% of all full-time freshmen had no need and received non-need-based gift aid.

**UNDERGRADUATE FINANCIAL AID (Fall 2013)** 434 applied for aid; of those 90% were deemed to have need. 100% of undergraduates with need received aid; of those 17% had need fully met. *Average percent of need met:* 61% (excluding resources awarded to replace EFC). *Average financial aid package:* $15,803 (excluding resources awarded to replace EFC). 20% of all full-time undergraduates had no need and received non-need-based gift aid.

**GIFT AID (NEED-BASED)** *Total amount:* $4,644,677 (23% federal, 24% state, 49% institutional, 4% external sources). *Receiving aid:* Freshmen: 87% (84); all full-time undergraduates: 78% (390). *Average award:* Freshmen: $13,556; Undergrad-

uates: $12,843. *Scholarships, grants, and awards:* Federal Pell, FSEOG, state, private, college/university gift aid from institutional funds.
**GIFT AID (NON-NEED-BASED)** *Total amount:* $892,343 (31% state, 65% institutional, 4% external sources). *Receiving aid:* Freshmen: 11% (11). Undergraduates: 10% (50). *Average award:* Freshmen: $7353. Undergraduates: $5082. *Scholarships, grants, and awards by category: Academic interests/achievement:* general academic interests/achievements. *Special achievements/activities:* general special achievements/activities, leadership, religious involvement. *Special characteristics:* 220 awards ($355,922 total): children and siblings of alumni, children of faculty/staff, ethnic background, international students, local/state students, members of minority groups, spouses of current students, veterans, veterans' children. *Tuition waivers:* Full or partial for employees or children of employees.
**LOANS** *Student loans:* $2,514,888 (80% need-based, 20% non-need-based). 55% of past graduating class borrowed through all loan programs. *Average indebtedness per student:* $24,428. *Average need-based loan:* Freshmen: $3196. Undergraduates: $3676. *Parent loans:* $1,524,216 (46% need-based, 54% non-need-based). *Programs:* Federal Direct (Subsidized and Unsubsidized Stafford, PLUS).
**WORK-STUDY** *Federal work-study:* 106 jobs averaging $1424. *State or other work-study/employment:* 248 part-time jobs averaging $1899.
**ATHLETIC AWARDS** Total amount: $145,400 (89% need-based, 11% non-need-based).
**APPLYING FOR FINANCIAL AID** *Required financial aid forms:* FAFSA, institution's own form, state aid form. *Financial aid deadline (priority):* 4/15. *Notification date:* Continuous beginning 3/1. Students must reply within 2 weeks of notification.
**CONTACT** Mrs. Patty Jean Hix, Financial Aid Director, Columbia International University, 7435 Monticello Road, Columbia, SC 29203, 800-777-2227 Ext. 5037 or toll-free 800-777-2227 Ext. 5024. *Fax:* 803-223-2505. *E-mail:* phix@ciu.edu. *Website:* http://www.ciu.edu/.

# COLUMBIA UNIVERSITY
## New York, NY

| Tuition & fees: $51,008 | Average undergraduate aid package: $46,516 |
|---|---|

**ABOUT THE INSTITUTION** Independent, coed. *Awards:* bachelor's, master's, and doctoral degrees. 78 undergraduate majors. *Total enrollment:* 6,170. Undergraduates: 6,170. Freshmen: 1,424. Both federal and institutional methodology are used as a basis for awarding need-based institutional aid.
**UNDERGRADUATE EXPENSES for 2015–2016** *Application fee:* $80. *Comprehensive fee:* $63,440 includes full-time tuition ($48,646), mandatory fees ($2362), and room and board ($12,432).
**FRESHMAN FINANCIAL AID (Fall 2014, est.)** 856 applied for aid; of those 87% were deemed to have need. 100% of freshmen with need received aid; of those 100% had need fully met. *Average percent of need met:* 100% (excluding resources awarded to replace EFC). *Average financial aid package:* $48,086 (excluding resources awarded to replace EFC).
**UNDERGRADUATE FINANCIAL AID (Fall 2014, est.)** 3,352 applied for aid; of those 91% were deemed to have need. 100% of undergraduates with need received aid; of those 100% had need fully met. *Average percent of need met:* 100% (excluding resources awarded to replace EFC). *Average financial aid package:* $46,516 (excluding resources awarded to replace EFC).
**GIFT AID (NEED-BASED)** *Total amount:* $134,426,622 (5% federal, 1% state, 92% institutional, 2% external sources). *Receiving aid:* Freshmen: 50% (717); all full-time undergraduates: 48% (2,939). *Average award:* Freshmen: $47,895; Undergraduates: $44,887. *Scholarships, grants, and awards:* Federal Pell, FSEOG, state, private, college/university gift aid from institutional funds.
**GIFT AID (NON-NEED-BASED)** *Total amount:* $604,543 (13% federal, 1% state, 86% external sources). *Receiving aid:* Freshmen: 5. Undergraduates: 17. *Tuition waivers:* Full or partial for employees or children of employees. *ROTC:* Army cooperative, Naval, Air Force cooperative.
**LOANS** *Student loans:* $5,663,815 (53% need-based, 47% non-need-based). *Average need-based loan:* Freshmen: $2277. Undergraduates: $3919. *Parent loans:* $5,510,281 (15% need-based, 85% non-need-based). *Programs:* Federal Direct (Subsidized and Unsubsidized Stafford, PLUS), Perkins, alternative loans.

**WORK-STUDY** *Federal work-study:* Total amount: $5,139,177; jobs available. *State or other work-study/employment:* Total amount: $1,861,636 (83% need-based, 17% non-need-based). Part-time jobs available.
**APPLYING FOR FINANCIAL AID** *Required financial aid forms:* FAFSA, CSS Financial Aid PROFILE, noncustodial (divorced/separated) parent's statement, federal income tax form(s). *Financial aid deadline:* 3/1. *Notification date:* 3/31. Students must reply by 5/1.
**CONTACT** Kathryn Tuman, Executive Director of Financial Aid, Columbia University, 100 Hamilton Hall, MC 2802, 1130 Amsterdam Avenue, New York, NY 10027, 212-854-3711. *Fax:* 212-854-5353. *E-mail:* kat56@columbia.edu. *Website:* http://www.columbia.edu/.

# COLUMBIA UNIVERSITY, SCHOOL OF GENERAL STUDIES
## New York, NY

| Tuition & fees: $49,476 | Average undergraduate aid package: N/A |
|---|---|

**ABOUT THE INSTITUTION** Independent, coed. *Awards:* certificates and bachelor's degrees. 79 undergraduate majors. *Total enrollment:* 1,898. Undergraduates: 1,898. Freshmen: 121. Both federal and institutional methodology are used as a basis for awarding need-based institutional aid.
**UNDERGRADUATE EXPENSES for 2015–2016** *Application fee:* $80. *Comprehensive fee:* $60,906 includes full-time tuition ($47,100), mandatory fees ($2376), and room and board ($11,430). *College room only:* $7020. Full-time tuition and fees vary according to course load and program. Room and board charges vary according to board plan and housing facility. *Part-time tuition:* $1570 per credit hour. Part-time tuition and fees vary according to course load and program. *Payment plan:* Tuition prepayment.
**GIFT AID (NEED-BASED)** *Total amount:* $19,070,106 (22% federal, 3% state, 73% institutional, 2% external sources). *Scholarships, grants, and awards:* Federal Pell, FSEOG, state, private, college/university gift aid from institutional funds.
**GIFT AID (NON-NEED-BASED)** *Total amount:* $4,022,533 (94% institutional, 6% external sources). *Scholarships, grants, and awards by category: Academic interests/achievement:* general academic interests/achievements. *Tuition waivers:* Full or partial for employees or children of employees. *ROTC:* Army cooperative, Naval, Air Force cooperative.
**LOANS** *Student loans:* $18,849,243 (93% need-based, 7% non-need-based). *Parent loans:* $1,643,815 (63% need-based, 37% non-need-based). *Programs:* Federal Direct (Subsidized and Unsubsidized Stafford, PLUS), Perkins, college/university.
**WORK-STUDY** *Federal work-study:* jobs available.
**APPLYING FOR FINANCIAL AID** *Required financial aid forms:* FAFSA, institution's own form. *Financial aid deadline:* 6/1. *Notification date:* Continuous.
**CONTACT** Mr. William Skip Bailey, Director of Educational Financing, Columbia University, School of General Studies, 408 Lewisohn Hall, 2970 Broadway, New York, NY 10027, 212-854-5410 or toll-free 800-895-1169. *Fax:* 212-854-6316. *E-mail:* gs_financial_aid@columbia.edu. *Website:* http://www.gs.columbia.edu/.

# COLUMBUS COLLEGE OF ART & DESIGN
## Columbus, OH

| Tuition & fees: $29,892 | Average undergraduate aid package: $19,911 |
|---|---|

**ABOUT THE INSTITUTION** Independent, coed. *Awards:* bachelor's and master's degrees. 7 undergraduate majors. *Total enrollment:* 1,347. Undergraduates: 1,314. Freshmen: 247. Federal methodology is used as a basis for awarding need-based institutional aid.
**UNDERGRADUATE EXPENSES for 2015–2016** *Application fee:* $40. *Comprehensive fee:* $37,872 includes full-time tuition ($28,872), mandatory fees

($1020), and room and board ($7980). Full-time tuition and fees vary according to course load. Room and board charges vary according to board plan, housing facility, location, and student level. *Part-time tuition:* $1203 per credit hour. Part-time tuition and fees vary according to course load.

**FRESHMAN FINANCIAL AID (Fall 2014, est.)** 240 applied for aid; of those 92% were deemed to have need. 97% of freshmen with need received aid; of those 4% had need fully met. *Average percent of need met:* 48% (excluding resources awarded to replace EFC). *Average financial aid package:* $19,011 (excluding resources awarded to replace EFC). 19% of all full-time freshmen had no need and received non-need-based gift aid.

**UNDERGRADUATE FINANCIAL AID (Fall 2014, est.)** 1,014 applied for aid; of those 93% were deemed to have need. 98% of undergraduates with need received aid; of those 7% had need fully met. *Average percent of need met:* 52% (excluding resources awarded to replace EFC). *Average financial aid package:* $19,911 (excluding resources awarded to replace EFC). 18% of all full-time undergraduates had no need and received non-need-based gift aid.

**GIFT AID (NEED-BASED)** *Total amount:* $13,132,162 (17% federal, 5% state, 77% institutional, 1% external sources). *Receiving aid:* Freshmen: 78% (215); all full-time undergraduates: 79% (916). *Average award:* Freshmen: $14,796; Undergraduates: $13,775. *Scholarships, grants, and awards:* Federal Pell, FSEOG, state, private, college/university gift aid from institutional funds.

**GIFT AID (NON-NEED-BASED)** *Total amount:* $2,416,065 (99% institutional, 1% external sources). *Receiving aid:* Freshmen: 2% (5). Undergraduates: 3% (31). *Average award:* Freshmen: $10,423. Undergraduates: $10,430. *Scholarships, grants, and awards by category:* Creative arts/performance: 1,107 awards ($12,488,561 total): art/fine arts. *Special characteristics:* 10 awards ($201,855 total): children of educators, children of faculty/staff, local/state students. *Tuition waivers:* Full or partial for employees or children of employees.

**LOANS** *Student loans:* $9,276,761 (89% need-based, 11% non-need-based). 83% of past graduating class borrowed through all loan programs. *Average indebtedness per student:* $32,006. *Average need-based loan:* Freshmen: $5287. Undergraduates: $6777. *Parent loans:* $6,063,272 (64% need-based, 36% non-need-based). *Programs:* Federal Direct (Subsidized and Unsubsidized Stafford, PLUS), Perkins, state.

**WORK-STUDY** *Federal work-study:* Total amount: $506,306; 156 jobs averaging $3550. *State or other work-study/employment:* 283 part-time jobs averaging $3550.

**APPLYING FOR FINANCIAL AID** *Required financial aid forms:* FAFSA, institution's own form, federal income tax form(s), verification worksheet. *Financial aid deadline (priority):* 3/1. *Notification date:* 3/15. Students must reply within 2 weeks of notification.

**CONTACT** Mrs. Anna Marie Schofield, Director of Financial Aid, Columbus College of Art & Design, 60 Cleveland Avenue, Columbus, OH 43215-1758, 614-224-9101 Ext. 3274 or toll-free 877-997-2223. *Fax:* 614-222-4034. *E-mail:* aschofield@ccad.edu. *Website:* http://www.ccad.edu/.

# COLUMBUS STATE UNIVERSITY
## Columbus, GA

| Tuition & fees (GA res): $6898 | Average undergraduate aid package: $9057 |
| --- | --- |

**ABOUT THE INSTITUTION** State-supported, coed. *Awards:* certificates, associate, bachelor's, master's, and doctoral degrees. 40 undergraduate majors. *Total enrollment:* 8,164. Undergraduates: 7,021. Freshmen: 1,044. Federal methodology is used as a basis for awarding need-based institutional aid.

**UNDERGRADUATE EXPENSES for 2015–2016** *Application fee:* $40. *Tuition, state resident:* full-time $5098; part-time $109.03 per credit hour. *Tuition, nonresident:* full-time $17,994; part-time $600.80 per credit hour. *Required fees:* full-time $1800; $767.50 per term. Full-time tuition and fees vary according to course load, degree level, and program. Part-time tuition and fees vary according to course load, degree level, and program. *College room and board:* $8880; *Room only:* $4080. Room and board charges vary according to board plan and housing facility.

**FRESHMAN FINANCIAL AID (Fall 2014, est.)** 765 applied for aid; of those 83% were deemed to have need. 98% of freshmen with need received aid; of those 15% had need fully met. *Average percent of need met:* 67% (excluding resources awarded to replace EFC). *Average financial aid package:* $9217 (excluding resources

awarded to replace EFC). 5% of all full-time freshmen had no need and received non-need-based gift aid.

**UNDERGRADUATE FINANCIAL AID (Fall 2014, est.)** 4,175 applied for aid; of those 85% were deemed to have need. 98% of undergraduates with need received aid; of those 14% had need fully met. *Average percent of need met:* 68% (excluding resources awarded to replace EFC). *Average financial aid package:* $9057 (excluding resources awarded to replace EFC). 5% of all full-time undergraduates had no need and received non-need-based gift aid.

**GIFT AID (NEED-BASED)** *Total amount:* $15,387,775 (100% federal). *Receiving aid:* Freshmen: 52% (428); all full-time undergraduates: 53% (2,528). *Average award:* Freshmen: $4834; Undergraduates: $4833. *Scholarships, grants, and awards:* Federal Pell, FSEOG, state, private, college/university gift aid from institutional funds.

**GIFT AID (NON-NEED-BASED)** *Total amount:* $9,208,461 (85% state, 8% institutional, 7% external sources). *Receiving aid:* Freshmen: 49% (402). Undergraduates: 29% (1,365). *Average award:* Freshmen: $2438. Undergraduates: $1874. *Scholarships, grants, and awards by category:* Academic interests/achievement: biological sciences, business, communication, computer science, education, English, general academic interests/achievements, health fields, humanities, international studies, mathematics, military science, physical sciences. *Creative arts/performance:* art/fine arts, dance, music, performing arts, theater/drama. *Special achievements/activities:* cheerleading/drum major, community service, general special achievements/activities, leadership. *ROTC:* Army.

**LOANS** *Student loans:* $33,311,515 (45% need-based, 55% non-need-based). 70% of past graduating class borrowed through all loan programs. *Average indebtedness per student:* $30,142. *Average need-based loan:* Freshmen: $3368. Undergraduates: $4249. *Parent loans:* $1,934,416 (100% non-need-based). *Programs:* Federal Direct (Subsidized and Unsubsidized Stafford, PLUS), Perkins, Federal Nursing, state, college/university.

**WORK-STUDY** *Federal work-study:* Total amount: $506,170; jobs available.

**ATHLETIC AWARDS** Total amount: $1,106,431 (100% non-need-based).

**APPLYING FOR FINANCIAL AID** *Required financial aid form:* FAFSA. *Financial aid deadline (priority):* 5/1. *Notification date:* Continuous beginning 5/1.

**CONTACT** Ms. Patricia Garrett, Associate Director of Financial Aid, Columbus State University, 4225 University Avenue, Columbus, GA 31907-5645, 706-507-8800 or toll-free 866-264-2035. *Fax:* 706-568-2230. *E-mail:* garrett_patricia2@columbusstate.edu. *Website:* http://www.columbusstate.edu/.

# COMPASS COLLEGE OF CINEMATIC ARTS
## Grand Rapids, MI

**CONTACT** Financial Aid Office, Compass College of Cinematic Arts, 41 Sheldon Boulevard SE, Grand Rapids, MI 49503, 616-988-1000. *Website:* http://www.compass.edu/.

# CONCEPTION SEMINARY COLLEGE
## Conception, MO

| Tuition & fees: $20,304 | Average undergraduate aid package: $25,889 |
| --- | --- |

**ABOUT THE INSTITUTION** Independent Roman Catholic, men only. *Awards:* certificates and bachelor's degrees. 3 undergraduate majors. *Total enrollment:* 86. Undergraduates: 86. Freshmen: 16. Federal methodology is used as a basis for awarding need-based institutional aid.

**UNDERGRADUATE EXPENSES for 2015–2016** *Comprehensive fee:* $32,378 includes full-time tuition ($20,104), mandatory fees ($200), and room and board ($12,074). *College room only:* $5050. *Part-time tuition:* $200 per credit hour.

**FRESHMAN FINANCIAL AID (Fall 2014, est.)** 9 applied for aid; of those 100% were deemed to have need. 100% of freshmen with need received aid; of those 44% had need fully met. *Average percent of need met:* 90% (excluding resources awarded to replace EFC). *Average financial aid package:* $28,026 (excluding

resources awarded to replace EFC). 45% of all full-time freshmen had no need and received non-need-based gift aid.

**UNDERGRADUATE FINANCIAL AID (Fall 2014, est.)** 36 applied for aid; of those 86% were deemed to have need. 100% of undergraduates with need received aid; of those 68% had need fully met. *Average percent of need met:* 90% (excluding resources awarded to replace EFC). *Average financial aid package:* $25,889 (excluding resources awarded to replace EFC). 24% of all full-time undergraduates had no need and received non-need-based gift aid.

**GIFT AID (NEED-BASED)** *Total amount:* $558,023 (31% federal, 19% institutional, 50% external sources). *Receiving aid:* Freshmen: 45% (9); all full-time undergraduates: 36% (31). *Average award:* Freshmen: $5924; Undergraduates: $4580. *Scholarships, grants, and awards:* Federal Pell, FSEOG, private, college/university gift aid from institutional funds.

**GIFT AID (NON-NEED-BASED)** *Total amount:* $1,719,645 (4% institutional, 96% external sources). *Receiving aid:* Freshmen: 45% (9). Undergraduates: 36% (31). *Average award:* Freshmen: $1417. Undergraduates: $2222. *Scholarships, grants, and awards by category:* Academic interests/achievement: general academic interests/achievements. *Special characteristics:* religious affiliation. *Tuition waivers:* Full or partial for employees or children of employees.

**LOANS** *Student loans:* $211,237 (52% need-based, 48% non-need-based). 43% of past graduating class borrowed through all loan programs. *Average indebtedness per student:* $27,243. *Average need-based loan:* Freshmen: $3500. Undergraduates: $3341. *Parent loans:* $13,000 (100% non-need-based). *Programs:* Federal Direct (Subsidized and Unsubsidized Stafford, PLUS).

**WORK-STUDY** *Federal work-study:* Total amount: $21,175; jobs available. *State or other work-study/employment:* Part-time jobs available.

**APPLYING FOR FINANCIAL AID** *Required financial aid form:* FAFSA. *Financial aid deadline:* Continuous. *Notification date:* Continuous beginning 6/1. Students must reply within 4 weeks of notification.

**CONTACT** Br. Justin Hernandez, PhD, Financial Aid Director, Conception Seminary College, PO Box 502, Conception, MO 64433-0502, 660-944-2851. *Fax:* 660-944-2829. *E-mail:* justin@conception.edu. *Website:* http://www.conception.edu/.

## CONCORDIA COLLEGE
### Moorhead, MN

| Tuition & fees: $35,464 | Average undergraduate aid package: $27,360 |
|---|---|

**ABOUT THE INSTITUTION** Independent Evangelical Lutheran Church in America, coed. *Awards:* bachelor's and master's degrees. 58 undergraduate majors. *Total enrollment:* 2,398. Undergraduates: 2,381. Freshmen: 540. Federal methodology is used as a basis for awarding need-based institutional aid.

**UNDERGRADUATE EXPENSES for 2015–2016** *Application fee:* $20. *Comprehensive fee:* $43,064 includes full-time tuition ($35,250), mandatory fees ($214), and room and board ($7600). *College room only:* $3260. Full-time tuition and fees vary according to course load and degree level. Room and board charges vary according to board plan and housing facility. *Part-time tuition:* $1380 per credit hour. Part-time tuition and fees vary according to course load and degree level.

**FRESHMAN FINANCIAL AID (Fall 2013)** 624 applied for aid; of those 86% were deemed to have need. 100% of freshmen with need received aid; of those 19% had need fully met. *Average percent of need met:* 92% (excluding resources awarded to replace EFC). *Average financial aid package:* $27,366 (excluding resources awarded to replace EFC). 21% of all full-time freshmen had no need and received non-need-based gift aid.

**UNDERGRADUATE FINANCIAL AID (Fall 2013)** 2,069 applied for aid; of those 88% were deemed to have need. 100% of undergraduates with need received aid; of those 16% had need fully met. *Average percent of need met:* 90% (excluding resources awarded to replace EFC). *Average financial aid package:* $27,360 (excluding resources awarded to replace EFC). 24% of all full-time undergraduates had no need and received non-need-based gift aid.

**GIFT AID (NEED-BASED)** *Total amount:* $33,797,909 (9% federal, 9% state, 79% institutional, 3% external sources). *Receiving aid:* Freshmen: 78% (531); all full-time undergraduates: 72% (1,782). *Average award:* Freshmen: $20,726; Undergraduates: $18,955. *Scholarships, grants, and awards:* Federal Pell, FSEOG, state, private, college/university gift aid from institutional funds.

**GIFT AID (NON-NEED-BASED)** *Total amount:* $9,686,997 (3% federal, 93% institutional, 4% external sources). *Receiving aid:* Freshmen: 11% (76). Undergraduates: 9% (220). *Average award:* Freshmen: $14,465. Undergraduates: $12,974. *Scholarships, grants, and awards by category:* Academic interests/achievement: general academic interests/achievements. *Creative arts/performance:* art/fine arts, debating, music, theater/drama. *Special characteristics:* international students. *Tuition waivers:* Full or partial for employees or children of employees. *ROTC:* Army cooperative, Air Force cooperative.

**LOANS** *Student loans:* $19,503,765 (64% need-based, 36% non-need-based). *Average need-based loan:* Freshmen: $6883. Undergraduates: $8730. *Parent loans:* $2,084,430 (27% need-based, 73% non-need-based). *Programs:* Federal Direct (Subsidized and Unsubsidized Stafford, PLUS), Perkins, state, college/university, private loans.

**WORK-STUDY** *Federal work-study:* jobs available. *State or other work-study/employment:* Total amount: $1,884,317 (20% need-based, 80% non-need-based). Part-time jobs available.

**APPLYING FOR FINANCIAL AID** *Required financial aid form:* FAFSA. *Financial aid deadline:* Continuous. *Notification date:* Continuous beginning 3/15. Students must reply within 6 weeks of notification.

**CONTACT** Mr. Eric Addington, Director of Financial Aid, Concordia College, 901 South 8th Street, Moorhead, MN 56562, 218-299-3010 or toll-free 800-699-9897. *Fax:* 218-299-3025. *E-mail:* eaddingt@cord.edu. *Website:* http://www.concordiacollege.edu/.

## CONCORDIA COLLEGE ALABAMA
### Selma, AL

**CONTACT** Mrs. T. H. Bridges, Financial Aid Office, Concordia College Alabama, 1804 Green Street, Selma, AL 36701, 334-874-5700. *Fax:* 334-874-3728. *E-mail:* tbridges@concordiaselma.edu. *Website:* http://www.ccal.edu/.

## CONCORDIA COLLEGE–NEW YORK
### Bronxville, NY

**CONTACT** Janice Spikereit, Director of Financial Aid, Concordia College–New York, 171 White Plains Road, Bronxville, NY 10708, 914-337-9300 Ext. 2146 or toll-free 800-YES-COLLEGE. *Fax:* 914-395-4500. *E-mail:* financialaid@concordia-ny.edu. *Website:* http://www.concordia-ny.edu/.

## CONCORDIA UNIVERSITY
### Irvine, CA

| Tuition & fees: $31,690 | Average undergraduate aid package: $18,883 |
|---|---|

**ABOUT THE INSTITUTION** Independent Lutheran Church–Missouri Synod, coed. *Awards:* associate, bachelor's, master's, and doctoral degrees (associate's degree for international students only). 28 undergraduate majors. *Total enrollment:* 4,311. Undergraduates: 1,918. Freshmen: 352. Federal methodology is used as a basis for awarding need-based institutional aid.

**UNDERGRADUATE EXPENSES for 2015–2016** *Application fee:* $50. *Comprehensive fee:* $41,580 includes full-time tuition ($31,040), mandatory fees ($650), and room and board ($9890). *College room only:* $5700. Full-time tuition and fees vary according to course load. Room and board charges vary according to board plan and housing facility. *Part-time tuition:* $925 per unit. *Part-time fees:* $325 per term. Part-time tuition and fees vary according to course load.

**FRESHMAN FINANCIAL AID (Fall 2014, est.)** 313 applied for aid; of those 82% were deemed to have need. 100% of freshmen with need received aid; of those 13% had need fully met. *Average percent of need met:* 67% (excluding resources awarded to replace EFC). *Average financial aid package:* $22,017 (excluding resources awarded to replace EFC). 19% of all full-time freshmen had no need and received non-need-based gift aid.

**UNDERGRADUATE FINANCIAL AID (Fall 2014, est.)** 1,418 applied for aid; of those 85% were deemed to have need. 99% of undergraduates with need received aid; of those 13% had need fully met. *Average percent of need met:* 60% (excluding resources awarded to replace EFC). *Average financial aid package:* $18,883 (excluding resources awarded to replace EFC). 16% of all full-time undergraduates had no need and received non-need-based gift aid.

**GIFT AID (NEED-BASED) *Total amount:*** $15,105,499 (16% federal, 20% state, 64% institutional). *Receiving aid:* Freshmen: 72% (254); all full-time undergraduates: 62% (1,090). *Average award:* Freshmen: $18,281; Undergraduates: $15,811. *Scholarships, grants, and awards:* Federal Pell, FSEOG, state, private, college/university gift aid from institutional funds.

**GIFT AID (NON-NEED-BASED) *Total amount:*** $3,374,747 (100% institutional). *Receiving aid:* Freshmen: 8% (27). Undergraduates: 6% (108). *Average award:* Freshmen: $10,083. Undergraduates: $8409. *Scholarships, grants, and awards by category:* Academic interests/achievement: 1,262 awards ($7,424,324 total): general academic interests/achievements. Creative arts/performance: 220 awards ($969,889 total): debating, music, theater/drama. Special characteristics: 299 awards ($1,211,120 total): children of faculty/staff, first-generation college students, religious affiliation. *Tuition waivers:* Full or partial for employees or children of employees.

**LOANS *Student loans:*** $12,964,927 (35% need-based, 65% non-need-based). 74% of past graduating class borrowed through all loan programs. *Average indebtedness per student:* $28,072. *Average need-based loan:* Freshmen: $3307. Undergraduates: $4445. *Parent loans:* $4,606,709 (100% non-need-based). *Programs:* Federal Direct (Subsidized and Unsubsidized Stafford, PLUS), private loans.

**WORK-STUDY *Federal work-study:*** Total amount: $131,250; 60 jobs averaging $2145. *State or other work-study/employment:* Part-time jobs available.

**ATHLETIC AWARDS** Total amount: $3,800,754 (65% need-based, 35% non-need-based).

**APPLYING FOR FINANCIAL AID *Required financial aid forms:*** FAFSA, state aid form, department scholarship application form. *Financial aid deadline:* 3/2. *Notification date:* Continuous beginning 3/15. Students must reply within 4 weeks of notification.

**CONTACT** Lori McDonald, Director of Financial Aid, Concordia University, 1530 Concordia West, Irvine, CA 92612-3299, 949-214-3074 or toll-free 800-229-1200. *Fax:* 949-214-3500. *E-mail:* lori.mcdonald@cui.edu.
*Website:* http://www.cui.edu/.

# CONCORDIA UNIVERSITY
## Portland, OR

**ABOUT THE INSTITUTION** Independent Lutheran Church–Missouri Synod, coed. 33 undergraduate majors.

**GIFT AID (NEED-BASED) *Scholarships, grants, and awards:*** Federal Pell, FSEOG, state, college/university gift aid from institutional funds.

**GIFT AID (NON-NEED-BASED) *Scholarships, grants, and awards by category:*** Academic interests/achievement: general academic interests/achievements, religion/biblical studies. Creative arts/performance: music. Special achievements/activities: leadership, religious involvement. Special characteristics: children of faculty/staff, relatives of clergy, religious affiliation.

**LOANS *Programs:*** Federal Direct (Subsidized and Unsubsidized Stafford, PLUS), Perkins, state, alternative loans.

**APPLYING FOR FINANCIAL AID *Required financial aid form:*** FAFSA.

**CONTACT** Mr. Robert Clarke, Director of Financial Aid, Concordia University, 2811 Northeast Holman Street, Portland, OR 97211-6099, 503-493-6555 or toll-free 800-321-9371. *Fax:* 503-280-8661. *E-mail:* jcullen@cu-portland.edu.
*Website:* http://www.cu-portland.edu/.

# CONCORDIA UNIVERSITY ANN ARBOR
## Ann Arbor, MI

| Tuition & fees: $25,990 | Average undergraduate aid package: $22,210 |
|---|---|

**ABOUT THE INSTITUTION** Independent Lutheran Church–Missouri Synod, coed. 35 undergraduate majors. Federal methodology is used as a basis for awarding need-based institutional aid.

**UNDERGRADUATE EXPENSES for 2015–2016 *Comprehensive fee:*** $34,965 includes full-time tuition ($25,930), mandatory fees ($60), and room and board ($8975). Full-time tuition and fees vary according to location and program. Room and board charges vary according to housing facility. *Part-time tuition:* $1080 per credit. *Part-time fees:* $30 per term. Part-time tuition and fees vary according to course load, location, and program.

**FRESHMAN FINANCIAL AID (Fall 2014, est.)** 167 applied for aid; of those 93% were deemed to have need. 100% of freshmen with need received aid; of those 19% had need fully met. *Average percent of need met:* 70% (excluding resources awarded to replace EFC). *Average financial aid package:* $22,442 (excluding resources awarded to replace EFC). 2% of all full-time freshmen had no need and received non-need-based gift aid.

**UNDERGRADUATE FINANCIAL AID (Fall 2014, est.)** 562 applied for aid; of those 93% were deemed to have need. 100% of undergraduates with need received aid; of those 20% had need fully met. *Average percent of need met:* 72% (excluding resources awarded to replace EFC). *Average financial aid package:* $22,210 (excluding resources awarded to replace EFC). 5% of all full-time undergraduates had no need and received non-need-based gift aid.

**GIFT AID (NEED-BASED) *Total amount:*** $6,507,458 (15% federal, 7% state, 73% institutional, 5% external sources). *Receiving aid:* Freshmen: 89% (152); all full-time undergraduates: 86% (510). *Average award:* Freshmen: $16,876; Undergraduates: $15,415. *Scholarships, grants, and awards:* Federal Pell, FSEOG, state, private, college/university gift aid from institutional funds.

**GIFT AID (NON-NEED-BASED) *Total amount:*** $1,234,963 (100% institutional). *Receiving aid:* Freshmen: 16% (27). Undergraduates: 15% (91). *Average award:* Freshmen: $13,982. Undergraduates: $12,145. *Scholarships, grants, and awards by category:* Academic interests/achievement: $1,768,958 total: business, education, general academic interests/achievements, religion/biblical studies. Creative arts/performance: $285,965 total: art/fine arts, music, performing arts, theater/drama. Special characteristics: $795,860 total: children and siblings of alumni, children of faculty/staff, ethnic background, general special characteristics, out-of-state students, religious affiliation, siblings of current students. *Tuition waivers:* Full or partial for employees or children of employees.

**LOANS *Student loans:*** $4,216,289 (65% need-based, 35% non-need-based). 82% of past graduating class borrowed through all loan programs. *Average indebtedness per student:* $17,853. *Average need-based loan:* Freshmen: $4899. Undergraduates: $6030. *Parent loans:* $1,322,603 (100% non-need-based). *Programs:* Federal Direct (Subsidized and Unsubsidized Stafford, PLUS), Perkins.

**WORK-STUDY *Federal work-study:*** Total amount: $405,698; 115 jobs averaging $569. *State or other work-study/employment:* Part-time jobs available.

**ATHLETIC AWARDS** Total amount: $1,783,079 (86% need-based, 14% non-need-based).

**APPLYING FOR FINANCIAL AID *Required financial aid form:*** FAFSA. *Financial aid deadline (priority):* 3/15. *Notification date:* Continuous beginning 2/1. Students must reply by 5/1 or within 3 weeks of notification.

**CONTACT** Mr. Steven P. Taylor, Financial Aid Office, Concordia University Ann Arbor, 4090 Geddes Road, Ann Arbor, MI 48105-2797, 734-995-7408 or toll-free 877-995-7520 (in-state), 877-955-7520 (out-of-state). *Fax:* 734-995-4610. *E-mail:* steve.taylor@cuaa.edu.
*Website:* http://www.cuaa.edu/.

# CONCORDIA UNIVERSITY CHICAGO
## River Forest, IL

| Tuition & fees: $29,450 | Average undergraduate aid package: $19,289 |
| --- | --- |

**ABOUT THE INSTITUTION** Independent Lutheran Church–Missouri Synod, coed. *Awards:* certificates, bachelor's, master's, and doctoral degrees. 61 undergraduate majors. *Total enrollment:* 5,038. Undergraduates: 1,538. Freshmen: 300. Federal methodology is used as a basis for awarding need-based institutional aid.

**UNDERGRADUATE EXPENSES for 2015–2016** *Comprehensive fee:* $38,442 includes full-time tuition ($28,660), mandatory fees ($790), and room and board ($8992). *College room only:* $4374. Full-time tuition and fees vary according to course load, degree level, program, and reciprocity agreements. Room and board charges vary according to board plan and housing facility. *Part-time tuition:* $895 per credit hour. Part-time tuition and fees vary according to course load, degree level, program, and reciprocity agreements.

**FRESHMAN FINANCIAL AID (Fall 2013)** 370 applied for aid; of those 92% were deemed to have need. 100% of freshmen with need received aid; of those 15% had need fully met. *Average percent of need met:* 74% (excluding resources awarded to replace EFC). *Average financial aid package:* $21,417 (excluding resources awarded to replace EFC). 9% of all full-time freshmen had no need and received non-need-based gift aid.

**UNDERGRADUATE FINANCIAL AID (Fall 2013)** 1,402 applied for aid; of those 91% were deemed to have need. 99% of undergraduates with need received aid; of those 17% had need fully met. *Average percent of need met:* 74% (excluding resources awarded to replace EFC). *Average financial aid package:* $19,289 (excluding resources awarded to replace EFC). 11% of all full-time undergraduates had no need and received non-need-based gift aid.

**GIFT AID (NEED-BASED)** *Total amount:* $18,352,585 (16% federal, 13% state, 71% institutional). *Receiving aid:* Freshmen: 90% (338); all full-time undergraduates: 83% (1,225). *Average award:* Freshmen: $17,867; Undergraduates: $14,880. *Scholarships, grants, and awards:* Federal Pell, FSEOG, state, private, college/university gift aid from institutional funds.

**GIFT AID (NON-NEED-BASED)** *Total amount:* $3,637,271 (76% institutional, 24% external sources). *Receiving aid:* Freshmen: 11% (41). Undergraduates: 11% (169). *Average award:* Freshmen: $11,789. Undergraduates: $11,656. *Scholarships, grants, and awards by category: Academic interests/achievement:* biological sciences, business, communication, computer science, education, English, foreign languages, general academic interests/achievements, mathematics, religion/biblical studies. *Creative arts/performance:* music. *Special characteristics:* children and siblings of alumni, children of faculty/staff, international students, religious affiliation. *Tuition waivers:* Full or partial for children of alumni, employees or children of employees, senior citizens.

**LOANS** *Student loans:* $10,079,317 (43% need-based, 57% non-need-based). 80% of past graduating class borrowed through all loan programs. *Average indebtedness per student:* $32,408. *Average need-based loan:* Freshmen: $3156. Undergraduates: $4222. *Parent loans:* $1,754,213 (100% non-need-based). *Programs:* Federal Direct (Subsidized and Unsubsidized Stafford, PLUS), Perkins.

**WORK-STUDY** *Federal work-study:* jobs available. *State or other work-study/employment:* Total amount: $711,478 (100% need-based). Part-time jobs available.

**APPLYING FOR FINANCIAL AID** *Required financial aid form:* FAFSA. *Financial aid deadline:* 6/1 (priority: 2/1). *Notification date:* Continuous beginning 1/24.

**CONTACT** Aida Asencio-Pinto, Director of Financial Aid, Concordia University Chicago, 7400 Augusta Street, River Forest, IL 60305-1499, 708-209-3113 or toll-free 800-285-2668. *Fax:* 708-488-4102. *E-mail:* aida.asenciopinto@cuchicago.edu. *Website:* http://www.cuchicago.edu/.

# CONCORDIA UNIVERSITY, NEBRASKA
## Seward, NE

| Tuition & fees: $27,110 | Average undergraduate aid package: $20,709 |
| --- | --- |

**ABOUT THE INSTITUTION** Independent Lutheran Church–Missouri Synod, coed. *Awards:* certificates, bachelor's, and master's degrees. 85 undergraduate majors. *Total enrollment:* 2,332. Undergraduates: 1,607. Freshmen: 326. Federal methodology is used as a basis for awarding need-based institutional aid.

**UNDERGRADUATE EXPENSES for 2015–2016** *Comprehensive fee:* $34,370 includes full-time tuition ($26,810), mandatory fees ($300), and room and board ($7260). *College room only:* $2980. Room and board charges vary according to board plan and housing facility. *Part-time tuition:* $825 per credit hour.

**FRESHMAN FINANCIAL AID (Fall 2014, est.)** 293 applied for aid; of those 87% were deemed to have need. 100% of freshmen with need received aid; of those 27% had need fully met. *Average percent of need met:* 82% (excluding resources awarded to replace EFC). *Average financial aid package:* $22,263 (excluding resources awarded to replace EFC). 10% of all full-time freshmen had no need and received non-need-based gift aid.

**UNDERGRADUATE FINANCIAL AID (Fall 2014, est.)** 996 applied for aid; of those 87% were deemed to have need. 100% of undergraduates with need received aid; of those 24% had need fully met. *Average percent of need met:* 78% (excluding resources awarded to replace EFC). *Average financial aid package:* $20,709 (excluding resources awarded to replace EFC). 11% of all full-time undergraduates had no need and received non-need-based gift aid.

**GIFT AID (NEED-BASED)** *Total amount:* $12,309,391 (13% federal, 1% state, 74% institutional, 12% external sources). *Receiving aid:* Freshmen: 78% (255); all full-time undergraduates: 73% (870). *Average award:* Freshmen: $17,844; Undergraduates: $16,212. *Scholarships, grants, and awards:* Federal Pell, FSEOG, state, private, college/university gift aid from institutional funds.

**GIFT AID (NON-NEED-BASED)** *Total amount:* $4,069,947 (100% institutional). *Receiving aid:* Freshmen: 17% (54). Undergraduates: 12% (148). *Average award:* Freshmen: $14,777. Undergraduates: $11,475. *Scholarships, grants, and awards by category: Academic interests/achievement:* biological sciences, business, communication, computer science, education, English, general academic interests/achievements, health fields, humanities, mathematics, physical sciences, premedicine, religion/biblical studies, social sciences. *Creative arts/performance:* applied art and design, art/fine arts, dance, debating, music, theater/drama. *Special achievements/activities:* cheerleading/drum major. *Special characteristics:* children and siblings of alumni, children of educators, children of faculty/staff, international students, local/state students, members of minority groups, religious affiliation, veterans, veterans' children. *Tuition waivers:* Full or partial for employees or children of employees. *ROTC:* Army cooperative, Air Force cooperative.

**LOANS** *Student loans:* $5,797,995 (46% need-based, 54% non-need-based). 73% of past graduating class borrowed through all loan programs. *Average indebtedness per student:* $29,002. *Average need-based loan:* Freshmen: $3584. Undergraduates: $4515. *Parent loans:* $1,415,137 (100% non-need-based). *Programs:* Federal Direct (Subsidized and Unsubsidized Stafford, PLUS), Perkins.

**WORK-STUDY** *Federal work-study:* Total amount: $101,788; 80 jobs averaging $1400.

**ATHLETIC AWARDS** Total amount: $3,130,680 (70% need-based, 30% non-need-based).

**APPLYING FOR FINANCIAL AID** *Required financial aid form:* FAFSA. *Financial aid deadline (priority):* 3/1. *Notification date:* Continuous beginning 3/1. Students must reply within 4 weeks of notification.

**CONTACT** Mr. Aaron W. Roberts, Director of Undergraduate Recruitment, Concordia University, Nebraska, 800 North Columbia Avenue, Seward, NE 68434-1556, 800-535-5494. *Fax:* 402-643-4073. *E-mail:* admiss@cune.edu. *Website:* http://www.cune.edu/.

# CONCORDIA UNIVERSITY, ST. PAUL
## St. Paul, MN

| Tuition & fees: $20,750 | Average undergraduate aid package: $13,706 |
| --- | --- |

**ABOUT THE INSTITUTION** Independent Lutheran Church–Missouri Synod, coed. *Awards:* certificates, associate, bachelor's, master's, and doctoral degrees. 58 undergraduate majors. *Total enrollment:* 4,057. Undergraduates: 2,420. Freshmen: 242. Federal methodology is used as a basis for awarding need-based institutional aid.

**UNDERGRADUATE EXPENSES for 2015–2016** *Application fee:* $30. *Comprehensive fee:* $29,050 includes full-time tuition ($20,750) and room and board ($8300). Full-time tuition and fees vary according to degree level and program. Room and board charges vary according to board plan and housing facility. *Part-time* *tuition:* $650 per credit. Part-time tuition and fees vary according to course load, degree level, and program.

**FRESHMAN FINANCIAL AID (Fall 2014, est.)** 219 applied for aid; of those 88% were deemed to have need. 99% of freshmen with need received aid; of those 11% had need fully met. *Average percent of need met:* 66% (excluding resources awarded to replace EFC). *Average financial aid package:* $15,682 (excluding resources awarded to replace EFC). 10% of all full-time freshmen had no need and received non-need-based gift aid.

**UNDERGRADUATE FINANCIAL AID (Fall 2014, est.)** 1,123 applied for aid; of those 89% were deemed to have need. 99% of undergraduates with need received aid; of those 10% had need fully met. *Average percent of need met:* 58% (excluding resources awarded to replace EFC). *Average financial aid package:* $13,706 (excluding resources awarded to replace EFC). 9% of all full-time undergraduates had no need and received non-need-based gift aid.

**GIFT AID (NEED-BASED)** *Total amount:* $9,850,224 (39% federal, 24% state, 35% institutional, 2% external sources). *Receiving aid:* Freshmen: 79% (191); all full-time undergraduates: 73% (945). *Average award:* Freshmen: $11,602; Undergraduates: $9632. *Scholarships, grants, and awards:* Federal Pell, FSEOG, state, private, college/university gift aid from institutional funds.

**GIFT AID (NON-NEED-BASED)** *Total amount:* $910,450 (1% federal, 1% state, 98% institutional). *Receiving aid:* Freshmen: 7% (18). Undergraduates: 4% (57). *Average award:* Freshmen: $4266. Undergraduates: $4316. *Scholarships, grants, and awards by category: Academic interests/achievement:* 734 awards ($1,979,157 total): general academic interests/achievements, mathematics, religion/biblical studies. *Creative arts/performance:* 83 awards ($72,250 total): music, theater/drama. *Special characteristics:* 127 awards ($202,471 total): children of faculty/staff, religious affiliation, veterans, veterans' children. *Tuition waivers:* Full or partial for employees or children of employees. *ROTC:* Army cooperative, Air Force cooperative.

**LOANS** *Student loans:* $14,168,838 (39% need-based, 61% non-need-based). 82% of past graduating class borrowed through all loan programs. *Average indebtedness per student:* $30,747. *Average need-based loan:* Freshmen: $3417. Undergraduates: $4447. *Parent loans:* $916,891 (100% non-need-based). *Programs:* Federal Direct (Subsidized and Unsubsidized Stafford, PLUS), Perkins, state, private loans.

**WORK-STUDY** *Federal work-study:* Total amount: $232,980; 99 jobs averaging $2351. *State or other work-study/employment:* Total amount: $478,592 (100% need-based). 219 part-time jobs averaging $2377.

**ATHLETIC AWARDS** Total amount: $1,742,298 (76% need-based, 24% non-need-based).

**APPLYING FOR FINANCIAL AID** *Required financial aid forms:* FAFSA, institution's own form. *Financial aid deadline (priority):* 5/1. *Notification date:* Continuous beginning 5/10.

**CONTACT** Ms. Jeanie Peck, Financial Aid Director, Concordia University, St. Paul, 1282 Concordia Avenue, St. Paul, MN 55104-5494, 651-603-6300 or toll-free 800-333-4705. *Fax:* 651-603-6298. *E-mail:* finaid@csp.edu. *Website:* http://www.csp.edu/.

# CONCORDIA UNIVERSITY TEXAS
### Austin, TX

| Tuition & fees: $28,160 | Average undergraduate aid package: $20,814 |
| --- | --- |

**ABOUT THE INSTITUTION** Independent Lutheran Church–Missouri Synod, coed. *Awards:* associate, bachelor's, and master's degrees. 24 undergraduate majors. *Total enrollment:* 2,504. Undergraduates: 1,567. Freshmen: 242. Federal methodology is used as a basis for awarding need-based institutional aid.

**UNDERGRADUATE EXPENSES for 2015–2016** *Application fee:* $25. *Comprehensive fee:* $37,444 includes full-time tuition ($27,600), mandatory fees ($560), and room and board ($9284). *College room only:* $4954. Full-time tuition and fees vary according to course load, degree level, and program. Room and board charges vary according to board plan. *Part-time tuition:* $905 per credit hour. Part-time tuition and fees vary according to course load, degree level, and program.

**FRESHMAN FINANCIAL AID (Fall 2014, est.)** 189 applied for aid; of those 83% were deemed to have need. 99% of freshmen with need received aid; of those 23% had need fully met. *Average percent of need met:* 80% (excluding resources awarded to replace EFC). *Average financial aid package:* $23,088 (excluding resources awarded to replace EFC). 21% of all full-time freshmen had no need and received non-need-based gift aid.

**UNDERGRADUATE FINANCIAL AID (Fall 2014, est.)** 872 applied for aid; of those 88% were deemed to have need. 99% of undergraduates with need received aid; of those 16% had need fully met. *Average percent of need met:* 74% (excluding resources awarded to replace EFC). *Average financial aid package:* $20,814 (excluding resources awarded to replace EFC). 17% of all full-time undergraduates had no need and received non-need-based gift aid.

**GIFT AID (NEED-BASED)** *Total amount:* $12,910,773 (23% federal, 14% state, 63% institutional). *Receiving aid:* Freshmen: 74% (153); all full-time undergraduates: 71% (732). *Average award:* Freshmen: $17,802; Undergraduates: $15,528. *Scholarships, grants, and awards:* Federal Pell, FSEOG, state, private, college/university gift aid from institutional funds.

**GIFT AID (NON-NEED-BASED)** *Total amount:* $2,814,044 (100% institutional). *Receiving aid:* Freshmen: 15% (32). Undergraduates: 10% (102). *Average award:* Freshmen: $13,083. Undergraduates: $12,008. *Scholarships, grants, and awards by category: Academic interests/achievement:* biological sciences, business, communication, computer science, education, English, foreign languages, general academic interests/achievements, health fields, international studies, mathematics, physical sciences, religion/biblical studies, social sciences. *Creative arts/performance:* music. *Special achievements/activities:* junior miss, leadership, religious involvement. *Special characteristics:* adult students, children and siblings of alumni, children of faculty/staff, religious affiliation, veterans, veterans' children. *Tuition waivers:* Full or partial for employees or children of employees. *ROTC:* Army cooperative, Air Force cooperative.

**LOANS** *Student loans:* $9,317,795 (49% need-based, 51% non-need-based). 75% of past graduating class borrowed through all loan programs. *Average indebtedness per student:* $24,882. *Average need-based loan:* Freshmen: $5076. Undergraduates: $5486. *Parent loans:* $2,145,811 (100% non-need-based). *Programs:* Federal Direct (Subsidized and Unsubsidized Stafford, PLUS), state.

**WORK-STUDY** *Federal work-study:* Total amount: $451,600; jobs available. *State or other work-study/employment:* Total amount: $23,250 (100% need-based). Part-time jobs available.

**APPLYING FOR FINANCIAL AID** *Required financial aid forms:* FAFSA, state aid form. *Financial aid deadline:* Continuous. *Notification date:* Continuous beginning 2/15. Students must reply within 2 weeks of notification.

**CONTACT** Mr. Russell Jeffrey, Director of Student Financial Services, Concordia University Texas, 11400 Concordia University Drive, Austin, TX 78726, 512-313-4672 or toll-free 800-865-4282. *Fax:* 512-313-1670. *E-mail:* russell.jeffrey@concordia.edu. *Website:* http://www.concordia.edu/.

# CONCORDIA UNIVERSITY WISCONSIN
### Mequon, WI

| Tuition & fees: $26,160 | Average undergraduate aid package: $19,601 |
| --- | --- |

**ABOUT THE INSTITUTION** Independent Lutheran Church–Missouri Synod, coed. *Awards:* certificates, associate, bachelor's, master's, and doctoral degrees. 73 undergraduate majors. *Total enrollment:* 8,161. Undergraduates: 4,377. Freshmen: 640. Federal methodology is used as a basis for awarding need-based institutional aid.

**UNDERGRADUATE EXPENSES for 2015–2016** *Application fee:* $35. *Comprehensive fee:* $35,940 includes full-time tuition ($25,930), mandatory fees ($230), and room and board ($9780). Full-time tuition and fees vary according to program. Room and board charges vary according to board plan. Part-time tuition and fees vary according to program.

**FRESHMAN FINANCIAL AID (Fall 2014, est.)** 607 applied for aid; of those 87% were deemed to have need. 100% of freshmen with need received aid; of those 31% had need fully met. *Average percent of need met:* 79% (excluding resources awarded to replace EFC). *Average financial aid package:* $23,007 (excluding resources awarded to replace EFC). 16% of all full-time freshmen had no need and received non-need-based gift aid.

**UNDERGRADUATE FINANCIAL AID (Fall 2014, est.)** 2,645 applied for aid; of those 89% were deemed to have need. 100% of undergraduates with need received aid; of those 22% had need fully met. *Average percent of need met:* 68% (excluding resources awarded to replace EFC). *Average financial aid package:* $19,601 (excluding resources awarded to replace EFC). 13% of all full-time undergraduates had no need and received non-need-based gift aid.

**GIFT AID (NEED-BASED)** *Total amount:* $30,111,252 (19% federal, 8% state, 69% institutional, 4% external sources). *Receiving aid:* Freshmen: 83% (522); all full-time undergraduates: 75% (2,187). *Average award:* Freshmen: $14,926; Undergraduates: $12,887. *Scholarships, grants, and awards:* Federal Pell, FSEOG, state, private, college/university gift aid from institutional funds.

**GIFT AID (NON-NEED-BASED)** *Total amount:* $6,921,169 (100% institutional). *Receiving aid:* Freshmen: 22% (138). Undergraduates: 14% (409). *Average award:* Freshmen: $11,662. Undergraduates: $10,326. *Scholarships, grants, and awards by category:* Academic interests/achievement: 225 awards ($2,468,594 total): religion/biblical studies. Creative arts/performance: 118 awards ($200,568 total): music. Special characteristics: 419 awards ($807,053 total): out-of-state students.

**LOANS** *Student loans:* $26,586,473 (58% need-based, 42% non-need-based). 82% of past graduating class borrowed through all loan programs. *Average indebtedness per student:* $30,880. *Average need-based loan:* Freshmen: $6479. Undergraduates: $6659. *Parent loans:* $4,238,721 (100% non-need-based). *Programs:* Federal Direct (Subsidized and Unsubsidized Stafford, PLUS), state.

**WORK-STUDY** *Federal work-study:* Total amount: $350,000; 195 jobs averaging $1358.

**APPLYING FOR FINANCIAL AID** *Required financial aid form:* FAFSA. *Financial aid deadline (priority):* 3/15. *Notification date:* Continuous beginning 1/21. Students must reply within 3 weeks of notification.

**CONTACT** Mr. Steven P. Taylor, Director of Financial Aid, Concordia University Wisconsin, 12800 North Lake Shore Drive, Mequon, WI 53097-2402, 262-243-4392 or toll-free 888-628-9472. *Fax:* 262-243-2992. *E-mail:* steve.taylor@cuw.edu. *Website:* http://www.cuw.edu/.

# CONCORD UNIVERSITY
## Athens, WV

| Tuition & fees (WV res): $6580 | Average undergraduate aid package: $8896 |
|---|---|

**ABOUT THE INSTITUTION** State-supported, coed. *Awards:* associate, bachelor's, and master's degrees. 38 undergraduate majors. *Total enrollment:* 2,563. Undergraduates: 2,259. Freshmen: 427. Federal methodology is used as a basis for awarding need-based institutional aid.

**UNDERGRADUATE EXPENSES** for 2015–2016 *Tuition, state resident:* full-time $6422; part-time $268 per credit hour. *Tuition, nonresident:* full-time $14,118; part-time $588 per credit hour. *Required fees:* full-time $158. Full-time tuition and fees vary according to course load and program. Part-time tuition and fees vary according to course load and program. *College room and board:* $7818; *Room only:* $3982.

**FRESHMAN FINANCIAL AID (Fall 2014, est.)** 387 applied for aid; of those 81% were deemed to have need. 90% of freshmen with need received aid; of those 65% had need fully met. *Average percent of need met:* 91% (excluding resources awarded to replace EFC). *Average financial aid package:* $7675 (excluding resources awarded to replace EFC). 14% of all full-time freshmen had no need and received non-need-based gift aid.

**UNDERGRADUATE FINANCIAL AID (Fall 2014, est.)** 1,804 applied for aid; of those 85% were deemed to have need. 92% of undergraduates with need received aid; of those 52% had need fully met. *Average percent of need met:* 88% (excluding resources awarded to replace EFC). *Average financial aid package:* $8896 (excluding resources awarded to replace EFC). 10% of all full-time undergraduates had no need and received non-need-based gift aid.

**GIFT AID (NEED-BASED)** *Total amount:* $7,102,055 (75% federal, 23% state, 2% external sources). *Receiving aid:* Freshmen: 59% (248); all full-time undergraduates: 59% (1,203). *Average award:* Freshmen: $5375; Undergraduates: $6194. *Scholarships, grants, and awards:* Federal Pell, FSEOG, state, private, college/university gift aid from institutional funds.

**GIFT AID (NON-NEED-BASED)** *Total amount:* $4,511,708 (37% state, 37% institutional, 26% external sources). *Receiving aid:* Freshmen: 46% (192). Undergraduates: 34% (688). *Average award:* Freshmen: $3470. Undergraduates: $3201. *Scholarships, grants, and awards by category:* Academic interests/achievement: 927 awards ($938,310 total): business, communication, education, English, general academic interests/achievements, mathematics, physical sciences, pre-medicine, social sciences. Creative arts/performance: 86 awards ($166,042 total): art/fine arts, journalism/publications, music, theater/drama. Special achievements/activ-

ities: 71 awards ($19,502 total): community service, general special achievements/activities, leadership. *Special characteristics:* 37 awards ($193,001 total): children of faculty/staff, veterans, veterans' children. *Tuition waivers:* Full or partial for employees or children of employees.

**LOANS** *Student loans:* $10,646,943 (43% need-based, 57% non-need-based). 94% of past graduating class borrowed through all loan programs. *Average indebtedness per student:* $21,273. *Average need-based loan:* Freshmen: $3096. Undergraduates: $3715. *Parent loans:* $585,156 (100% non-need-based). *Programs:* Federal Direct (Subsidized and Unsubsidized Stafford, PLUS), Perkins.

**WORK-STUDY** *Federal work-study:* Total amount: $315,557; 238 jobs averaging $1352.

**ATHLETIC AWARDS** Total amount: $1,396,448 (100% non-need-based).

**APPLYING FOR FINANCIAL AID** *Required financial aid forms:* FAFSA, institution's own form, state aid form, verification worksheet. *Financial aid deadline:* 4/15. *Notification date:* Continuous beginning 5/15. Students must reply within 3 weeks of notification.

**CONTACT** Debra Turner, Director of Financial Aid, Concord University, PO Box 1000, Athens, WV 24712-1000, 304-384-6069 or toll-free 888-384-5249. *Fax:* 304-384-3084. *E-mail:* turner@concord.edu. *Website:* http://www.concord.edu/.

# CONNECTICUT COLLEGE
## New London, CT

| Tuition & fees: $47,740 | Average undergraduate aid package: $39,458 |
|---|---|

**ABOUT THE INSTITUTION** Independent, coed. *Awards:* bachelor's and master's degrees. 47 undergraduate majors. *Total enrollment:* 1,900. Undergraduates: 1,893. Freshmen: 498. Both federal and institutional methodology are used as a basis for awarding need-based institutional aid.

**UNDERGRADUATE EXPENSES** for 2015–2016 *Application fee:* $60. *Comprehensive fee:* $60,895 includes full-time tuition ($47,420), mandatory fees ($320), and room and board ($13,155). *College room only:* $7590. Room and board charges vary according to board plan. *Part-time tuition:* $1412 per credit hour.

**FRESHMAN FINANCIAL AID (Fall 2014, est.)** 297 applied for aid; of those 86% were deemed to have need. 100% of freshmen with need received aid; of those 100% had need fully met. *Average percent of need met:* 100% (excluding resources awarded to replace EFC). *Average financial aid package:* $38,556 (excluding resources awarded to replace EFC).

**UNDERGRADUATE FINANCIAL AID (Fall 2014, est.)** 1,077 applied for aid; of those 90% were deemed to have need. 100% of undergraduates with need received aid; of those 100% had need fully met. *Average percent of need met:* 100% (excluding resources awarded to replace EFC). *Average financial aid package:* $39,458 (excluding resources awarded to replace EFC).

**GIFT AID (NEED-BASED)** *Total amount:* $33,800,735 (4% federal, 1% state, 91% institutional, 4% external sources). *Receiving aid:* Freshmen: 49% (245); all full-time undergraduates: 49% (918). *Average award:* Freshmen: $35,877; Undergraduates: $35,885. *Scholarships, grants, and awards:* Federal Pell, FSEOG, state, college/university gift aid from institutional funds.

**GIFT AID (NON-NEED-BASED)** *Tuition waivers:* Full or partial for employees or children of employees, senior citizens.

**LOANS** *Student loans:* $8,129,916 (47% need-based, 53% non-need-based). 42% of past graduating class borrowed through all loan programs. *Average indebtedness per student:* $28,321. *Average need-based loan:* Freshmen: $3527. Undergraduates: $4621. *Parent loans:* $2,941,079 (100% non-need-based). *Programs:* Federal Direct (Subsidized and Unsubsidized Stafford, PLUS), Perkins.

**WORK-STUDY** *Federal work-study:* Total amount: $1,436,097; jobs available.

**APPLYING FOR FINANCIAL AID** *Required financial aid forms:* FAFSA, CSS Financial Aid PROFILE, noncustodial (divorced/separated) parent's statement. *Financial aid deadline (priority):* 2/1. *Notification date:* 4/1. Students must reply by 5/1.

**CONTACT** Mr. Sean Martin, Director of Financial Aid Services, Connecticut College, 270 Mohegan Avenue, New London, CT 06320-4196, 860-439-2058. *Fax:* 860-439-5357. *E-mail:* finaid@conncoll.edu. *Website:* http://www.connecticutcollege.edu/.

# CONSERVATORIO DE MUSICA DE PUERTO RICO
### San Juan, PR

**CONTACT** Mr. Michael Rajaballey, Director of Financial Aid, Conservatorio de Musica de Puerto Rico, 951 Ave. Ponce de Leon, Miramar, San Juan, PR 00907, 787-751-0160 Ext. 231. *Fax:* 787-763-3886. *E-mail:* mrajaballey@cmpr.gobierno.pr. *Website:* http://www.cmpr.edu/.

# CONVERSE COLLEGE
### Spartanburg, SC

| Tuition & fees: $16,500 | Average undergraduate aid package: $14,940 |
|---|---|

**ABOUT THE INSTITUTION** Independent, undergraduate: women only; graduate: coed. *Awards:* certificates, bachelor's, and master's degrees. 47 undergraduate majors. *Total enrollment:* 1,335. Undergraduates: 748. Freshmen: 232. Federal methodology is used as a basis for awarding need-based institutional aid.

**UNDERGRADUATE EXPENSES for 2015–2016** *Comprehensive fee:* $26,000 includes full-time tuition ($15,500), mandatory fees ($1000), and room and board ($9500). Full-time tuition and fees vary according to course load and program. Room and board charges vary according to board plan. Part-time tuition and fees vary according to course load and program.

**FRESHMAN FINANCIAL AID (Fall 2014, est.)** 225 applied for aid; of those 85% were deemed to have need. 100% of freshmen with need received aid; of those 21% had need fully met. *Average percent of need met:* 70% (excluding resources awarded to replace EFC). *Average financial aid package:* $14,925 (excluding resources awarded to replace EFC). 16% of all full-time freshmen had no need and received non-need-based gift aid.

**UNDERGRADUATE FINANCIAL AID (Fall 2014, est.)** 662 applied for aid; of those 87% were deemed to have need. 100% of undergraduates with need received aid; of those 19% had need fully met. *Average percent of need met:* 69% (excluding resources awarded to replace EFC). *Average financial aid package:* $14,940 (excluding resources awarded to replace EFC). 17% of all full-time undergraduates had no need and received non-need-based gift aid.

**GIFT AID (NEED-BASED)** *Total amount:* $6,107,667 (27% federal, 41% state, 29% institutional, 3% external sources). *Receiving aid:* Freshmen: 82% (192); all full-time undergraduates: 79% (563). *Average award:* Freshmen: $11,262; Undergraduates: $10,903. *Scholarships, grants, and awards:* Federal Pell, FSEOG, state, private, college/university gift aid from institutional funds.

**GIFT AID (NON-NEED-BASED)** *Total amount:* $1,517,328 (1% federal, 42% state, 54% institutional, 3% external sources). *Receiving aid:* Freshmen: 12% (29). Undergraduates: 10% (72). *Average award:* Freshmen: $3789. Undergraduates: $6061. *Scholarships, grants, and awards by category:* Academic interests/achievement: 525 awards ($2,179,094 total): general academic interests/achievements. Creative arts/performance: 160 awards ($286,090 total): applied art and design, general creative arts/performance, music, theater/drama. *Special characteristics:* 4 awards ($25,740 total): children and siblings of alumni, children of faculty/staff. *Tuition waivers:* Full or partial for employees or children of employees. *ROTC:* Army cooperative.

**LOANS** *Student loans:* $5,466,405 (77% need-based, 23% non-need-based). 81% of past graduating class borrowed through all loan programs. *Average indebtedness per student:* $32,063. *Average need-based loan:* Freshmen: $4460. Undergraduates: $5075. *Parent loans:* $830,536 (40% need-based, 60% non-need-based). *Programs:* Federal Direct (Subsidized and Unsubsidized Stafford, PLUS), Perkins, state.

**WORK-STUDY** *Federal work-study:* Total amount: $111,127; 83 jobs averaging $1608. *State or other work-study/employment:* 86 part-time jobs averaging $1343.

**ATHLETIC AWARDS** Total amount: $572,995 (50% need-based, 50% non-need-based).

**APPLYING FOR FINANCIAL AID** *Required financial aid form:* FAFSA. *Financial aid deadline (priority):* 5/1. *Notification date:* Continuous beginning 3/1. Students must reply by 5/1 or within 2 weeks of notification.

**CONTACT** Mrs. Nancy T. Garmroth, Director of Financial Planning, Converse College, 580 East Main Street, Spartanburg, SC 29302-0006, 864-596-9019 or toll-free 800-766-1125. *Fax:* 864-596-9749. *E-mail:* nancy.garmroth@converse.edu. *Website:* http://www.converse.edu/.

# COOPER UNION FOR THE ADVANCEMENT OF SCIENCE AND ART
### New York, NY

| Tuition & fees: $41,450 | Average undergraduate aid package: $39,600 |
|---|---|

**ABOUT THE INSTITUTION** Independent, coed. *Awards:* certificates, bachelor's, and master's degrees (also offers master's program primarily made up of currently-enrolled students). 8 undergraduate majors. *Total enrollment:* 949. Undergraduates: 876. Freshmen: 220. Both federal and institutional methodology are used as a basis for awarding need-based institutional aid.

**UNDERGRADUATE EXPENSES for 2015–2016** *Comprehensive fee:* $56,670 includes full-time tuition ($39,600), mandatory fees ($1850), and room and board ($15,220). *College room only:* $11,220. Room and board charges vary according to housing facility.

**FRESHMAN FINANCIAL AID (Fall 2013)** 114 applied for aid; of those 43% were deemed to have need. 100% of freshmen with need received aid; of those 73% had need fully met. *Average percent of need met:* 91% (excluding resources awarded to replace EFC). *Average financial aid package:* $39,600 (excluding resources awarded to replace EFC). 72% of all full-time freshmen had no need and received non-need-based gift aid.

**UNDERGRADUATE FINANCIAL AID (Fall 2013)** 409 applied for aid; of those 67% were deemed to have need. 100% of undergraduates with need received aid; of those 48% had need fully met. *Average percent of need met:* 91% (excluding resources awarded to replace EFC). *Average financial aid package:* $39,600 (excluding resources awarded to replace EFC). 68% of all full-time undergraduates had no need and received non-need-based gift aid.

**GIFT AID (NEED-BASED)** *Total amount:* $2,902,139 (28% federal, 11% state, 18% institutional, 43% external sources). *Receiving aid:* Freshmen: 28% (49); all full-time undergraduates: 32% (272). *Average award:* Freshmen: $45,405; Undergraduates: $45,915. *Scholarships, grants, and awards:* Federal Pell, FSEOG, state, private, college/university gift aid from institutional funds.

**GIFT AID (NON-NEED-BASED)** *Total amount:* $32,292,046 (100% institutional). *Receiving aid:* Freshmen: 28% (49). Undergraduates: 32% (272). *Average award:* Freshmen: $39,600. Undergraduates: $39,600. *Scholarships, grants, and awards by category:* Academic interests/achievement: 579 awards ($20,145,100 total): architecture, engineering/technologies. Creative arts/performance: 276 awards ($9,920,000 total): art/fine arts. *ROTC:* Army cooperative.

**LOANS** *Student loans:* $921,528 (88% need-based, 12% non-need-based). 26% of past graduating class borrowed through all loan programs. *Average indebtedness per student:* $19,072. *Average need-based loan:* Freshmen: $3329. Undergraduates: $3723. *Parent loans:* $153,150 (40% need-based, 60% non-need-based). *Programs:* Federal Direct (Subsidized and Unsubsidized Stafford, PLUS), Perkins, college/university.

**WORK-STUDY** *Federal work-study:* 47 jobs averaging $846. *State or other work-study/employment:* Total amount: $472,670 (22% need-based, 78% non-need-based). 355 part-time jobs averaging $1034.

**APPLYING FOR FINANCIAL AID** *Required financial aid forms:* FAFSA, CSS Financial Aid PROFILE. *Financial aid deadline:* 5/1 (priority: 3/15). *Notification date:* 6/1. Students must reply by 6/30 or within 2 weeks of notification.

**CONTACT** Ms. Mary Ruokonen, Director of Financial Aid, Cooper Union for the Advancement of Science and Art, 30 Cooper Square, New York, NY 10003-7120, 212-353-4130. *Fax:* 212-353-4343. *E-mail:* ruokon@cooper.edu. *Website:* http://www.cooper.edu/.

# COPPIN STATE UNIVERSITY
## Baltimore, MD

| Tuition & fees (MD res): $4889 | Average undergraduate aid package: $11,871 |
| --- | --- |

**ABOUT THE INSTITUTION** State-supported, coed. 20 undergraduate majors. Federal methodology is used as a basis for awarding need-based institutional aid.

**UNDERGRADUATE EXPENSES for 2015–2016 Tuition, state resident:** full-time $4089; part-time $175 per credit hour. **Tuition, nonresident:** full-time $9350; part-time $521 per credit hour. **Required fees:** full-time $800. **College room and board:** $9236; **Room only:** $5534.

**FRESHMAN FINANCIAL AID (Fall 2013)** 311 applied for aid; of those 99% were deemed to have need. 100% of freshmen with need received aid; of those 11% had need fully met. **Average percent of need met:** 53% (excluding resources awarded to replace EFC). **Average financial aid package:** $9636 (excluding resources awarded to replace EFC). 2% of all full-time freshmen had no need and received non-need-based gift aid.

**UNDERGRADUATE FINANCIAL AID (Fall 2013)** 1,889 applied for aid; of those 99% were deemed to have need. 100% of undergraduates with need received aid; of those 9% had need fully met. **Average percent of need met:** 70% (excluding resources awarded to replace EFC). **Average financial aid package:** $11,871 (excluding resources awarded to replace EFC). 1% of all full-time undergraduates had no need and received non-need-based gift aid.

**GIFT AID (NEED-BASED) Total amount:** $12,723,145 (70% federal, 16% state, 14% institutional). **Receiving aid:** Freshmen: 91% (302); all full-time undergraduates: 90% (1,842). **Average award:** Freshmen: $7446; Undergraduates: $7744. **Scholarships, grants, and awards:** Federal Pell, FSEOG, state, private, college/university gift aid from institutional funds, Federal Nursing.

**GIFT AID (NON-NEED-BASED) Total amount:** $513,170 (20% federal, 22% state, 54% institutional, 4% external sources). **Receiving aid:** Freshmen: 55% (181). Undergraduates: 50% (1,034). **Average award:** Freshmen: $2768. Undergraduates: $2999. **Scholarships, grants, and awards by category:** Academic interests/achievement: general academic interests/achievements.

**LOANS Student loans:** $12,616,708 (85% need-based, 15% non-need-based). **Average need-based loan:** Freshmen: $3483. Undergraduates: $4242. **Parent loans:** $621,673 (67% need-based, 33% non-need-based). **Programs:** Federal Direct (Subsidized and Unsubsidized Stafford, PLUS), Perkins, alternative loans.

**WORK-STUDY Federal work-study:** jobs available.

**ATHLETIC AWARDS** Total amount: $1,087,572 (75% need-based, 25% non-need-based).

**APPLYING FOR FINANCIAL AID Required financial aid form:** FAFSA. **Financial aid deadline (priority):** 3/1. **Notification date:** 4/15. Students must reply within 4 weeks of notification.

**CONTACT** Ms. Thelma Ross, Director of Financial Aid, Coppin State University, 2500 West North Avenue, Baltimore, MD 21216-3698, 410-951-3633 or toll-free 800-635-3674. *Fax:* 410-951-3637. *E-mail:* thross@coppin.edu. *Website:* http://www.coppin.edu/.

# CORBAN UNIVERSITY
## Salem, OR

| Tuition & fees: $28,640 | Average undergraduate aid package: $20,591 |
| --- | --- |

**ABOUT THE INSTITUTION** Independent Christian, coed. **Awards:** certificates, associate, bachelor's, master's, and doctoral degrees. 48 undergraduate majors. **Total enrollment:** 1,212. Undergraduates: 1,024. Freshmen: 220. Federal methodology is used as a basis for awarding need-based institutional aid.

**UNDERGRADUATE EXPENSES for 2015–2016 Application fee:** $40. **One-time required fee:** $100. **Comprehensive fee:** $37,532 includes full-time tuition ($27,980), mandatory fees ($660), and room and board ($8892). **College room only:** $5152. Full-time tuition and fees vary according to course level, degree level, program, reciprocity agreements, and student level. Room and board charges vary according to board plan. **Part-time tuition:** $1166 per credit hour. Part-time tuition and fees vary according to course level, course load, degree level, program, reciprocity agreements, and student level.

**FRESHMAN FINANCIAL AID (Fall 2014, est.)** 188 applied for aid; of those 92% were deemed to have need. 100% of freshmen with need received aid; of those 16% had need fully met. **Average percent of need met:** 67% (excluding resources awarded to replace EFC). **Average financial aid package:** $21,012 (excluding resources awarded to replace EFC). 10% of all full-time freshmen had no need and received non-need-based gift aid.

**UNDERGRADUATE FINANCIAL AID (Fall 2014, est.)** 733 applied for aid; of those 93% were deemed to have need. 100% of undergraduates with need received aid; of those 16% had need fully met. **Average percent of need met:** 67% (excluding resources awarded to replace EFC). **Average financial aid package:** $20,591 (excluding resources awarded to replace EFC). 12% of all full-time undergraduates had no need and received non-need-based gift aid.

**GIFT AID (NEED-BASED) Total amount:** $8,810,324 (20% federal, 3% state, 67% institutional, 10% external sources). **Receiving aid:** Freshmen: 77% (169); all full-time undergraduates: 79% (673). **Average award:** Freshmen: $18,547; Undergraduates: $17,422. **Scholarships, grants, and awards:** Federal Pell, FSEOG, state, private, college/university gift aid from institutional funds.

**GIFT AID (NON-NEED-BASED) Total amount:** $1,233,790 (3% federal, 82% institutional, 15% external sources). **Receiving aid:** Freshmen: 10% (22). Undergraduates: 9% (79). **Average award:** Freshmen: $8470. Undergraduates: $8605. **Scholarships, grants, and awards by category:** Academic interests/achievement: 541 awards ($3,648,445 total): general academic interests/achievements. Creative arts/performance: 68 awards ($164,144 total): music, performing arts. Special achievements/activities: 437 awards ($461,144 total): general special achievements/activities, hobbies/interests, leadership, memberships, religious involvement. Special characteristics: 305 awards ($1,101,740 total): children and siblings of alumni, children of faculty/staff, international students, relatives of clergy, siblings of current students, veterans, veterans' children. **Tuition waivers:** Full or partial for employees or children of employees, senior citizens. **ROTC:** Army cooperative.

**LOANS Student loans:** $5,715,832 (79% need-based, 21% non-need-based). 80% of past graduating class borrowed through all loan programs. **Average indebtedness per student:** $26,407. **Average need-based loan:** Freshmen: $3821. Undergraduates: $4532. **Parent loans:** $1,410,629 (59% need-based, 41% non-need-based). **Programs:** Federal Direct (Subsidized and Unsubsidized Stafford, PLUS), Perkins, state.

**WORK-STUDY** Federal work-study jobs available.

**ATHLETIC AWARDS** Total amount: $3,322,809 (69% need-based, 31% non-need-based).

**APPLYING FOR FINANCIAL AID Required financial aid form:** FAFSA. **Financial aid deadline (priority):** 2/15. **Notification date:** Continuous beginning 3/1.

**CONTACT** Ellen Zarfas, Director of Financial Aid, Corban University, 5000 Deer Park Drive, SE, Salem, OR 97317, 503-375-7006 or toll-free 800-845-3005. *Fax:* 503-585-4316. *E-mail:* financialaid@corban.edu. *Website:* http://www.corban.edu/.

# CORNELL COLLEGE
## Mount Vernon, IA

| Tuition & fees: $37,725 | Average undergraduate aid package: $32,245 |
| --- | --- |

**ABOUT THE INSTITUTION** Independent Methodist, coed. **Awards:** bachelor's degrees. 47 undergraduate majors. **Total enrollment:** 1,075. Undergraduates: 1,077. Freshmen: 262. Federal methodology is used as a basis for awarding need-based institutional aid.

**UNDERGRADUATE EXPENSES for 2015–2016 Application fee:** $30. **Comprehensive fee:** $46,225 includes full-time tuition ($37,500), mandatory fees ($225), and room and board ($8500). **College room only:** $3800. Room and board charges vary according to board plan and housing facility. **Part-time tuition:** $1520 per credit. Part-time tuition and fees vary according to course load.

**FRESHMAN FINANCIAL AID (Fall 2014, est.)** 235 applied for aid; of those 83% were deemed to have need. 100% of freshmen with need received aid; of those 23% had need fully met. **Average percent of need met:** 79% (excluding resources awarded to replace EFC). **Average financial aid package:** $27,831 (excluding resources awarded to replace EFC). 25% of all full-time freshmen had no need and received non-need-based gift aid.

UNDERGRADUATE FINANCIAL AID (Fall 2014, est.) 895 applied for aid; of those 91% were deemed to have need. 100% of undergraduates with need received aid; of those 14% had need fully met. **Average percent of need met:** 80% (excluding resources awarded to replace EFC). **Average financial aid package:** $32,245 (excluding resources awarded to replace EFC). 22% of all full-time undergraduates had no need and received non-need-based gift aid.

**GIFT AID (NEED-BASED)** *Total amount:* $21,086,484 (9% federal, 2% state, 87% institutional, 2% external sources). *Receiving aid:* Freshmen: 74% (195); all full-time undergraduates: 76% (809). *Average award:* Freshmen: $24,662; Undergraduates: $23,447. *Scholarships, grants, and awards:* Federal Pell, FSEOG, state, private, college/university gift aid from institutional funds, TEACH Grants.

**GIFT AID (NON-NEED-BASED)** *Total amount:* $4,824,587 (99% institutional, 1% external sources). *Receiving aid:* Freshmen: 74% (194). Undergraduates: 70% (752). *Average award:* Freshmen: $20,576. Undergraduates: $18,292. *Scholarships, grants, and awards by category:* Academic interests/achievement: 772 awards ($11,411,611 total): general academic interests/achievements. Creative arts/performance: 123 awards ($737,700 total): art/fine arts, music, performing arts, theater/drama. Special achievements/activities: 12 awards ($177,275 total). Special characteristics: 159 awards ($2,890,619 total): children and siblings of alumni, children of faculty/staff. *Tuition waivers:* Full or partial for employees or children of employees.

**LOANS** *Student loans:* $6,426,434 (82% need-based, 18% non-need-based). 79% of past graduating class borrowed through all loan programs. *Average indebtedness per student:* $25,004. *Average need-based loan:* Freshmen: $3461. Undergraduates: $4805. *Parent loans:* $2,287,625 (100% non-need-based). *Programs:* Federal Direct (Subsidized and Unsubsidized Stafford, PLUS), Perkins, college/university, United Methodist Student Loans.

**WORK-STUDY** *Federal work-study:* Total amount: $751,128; 493 jobs averaging $1521. *State or other work-study/employment:* Total amount: $99,324 (100% non-need-based). 87 part-time jobs averaging $1141.

**APPLYING FOR FINANCIAL AID** *Required financial aid form:* FAFSA. *Financial aid deadline:* 3/1. *Notification date:* Continuous beginning 3/1. Students must reply by 5/1 or within 2 weeks of notification.

**CONTACT** Ms. Shannon Amundson, Director of Financial Assistance, Cornell College, Peter Paul Luce Admission Center, 600 First Street West, Mount Vernon, IA 52314-1098, 319-895-4216 or toll-free 800-747-1112. *Fax:* 319-895-4106. *E-mail:* samundson@cornellcollege.edu.
*Website:* http://www.cornellcollege.edu/.

# CORNELL UNIVERSITY
## Ithaca, NY

| Tuition & fees: $47,286 | Average undergraduate aid package: $43,416 |
| --- | --- |

**ABOUT THE INSTITUTION** Independent, coed. *Awards:* bachelor's, master's, and doctoral degrees. 123 undergraduate majors. *Total enrollment:* 21,850. Undergraduates: 14,453. Freshmen: 3,225. Institutional methodology is used as a basis for awarding need-based institutional aid.

**UNDERGRADUATE EXPENSES** for 2015–2016 *Application fee:* $75. *Comprehensive fee:* $60,964 includes full-time tuition ($47,050), mandatory fees ($236), and room and board ($13,678). *College room only:* $8112. Full-time tuition and fees vary according to degree level. Room and board charges vary according to board plan and housing facility.

**FRESHMAN FINANCIAL AID (Fall 2014, est.)** 1,791 applied for aid; of those 84% were deemed to have need. 100% of freshmen with need received aid; of those 100% had need fully met. *Average percent of need met:* 100% (excluding resources awarded to replace EFC). *Average financial aid package:* $44,400 (excluding resources awarded to replace EFC).

**UNDERGRADUATE FINANCIAL AID (Fall 2014, est.)** 7,671 applied for aid; of those 89% were deemed to have need. 100% of undergraduates with need received aid; of those 100% had need fully met. *Average percent of need met:* 100% (excluding resources awarded to replace EFC). *Average financial aid package:* $43,416 (excluding resources awarded to replace EFC).

**GIFT AID (NEED-BASED)** *Total amount:* $251,512,483 (6% federal, 2% state, 89% institutional, 3% external sources). *Receiving aid:* Freshmen: 46% (1,470); all full-time undergraduates: 46% (6,669). *Average award:* Freshmen: $38,758; Undergraduates: $37,559. *Scholarships, grants, and awards:* Federal Pell, FSEOG, state, private, college/university gift aid from institutional funds.

**GIFT AID (NON-NEED-BASED)** *Tuition waivers:* Full or partial for employees or children of employees. *ROTC:* Army, Naval, Air Force.

**LOANS** *Student loans:* $28,014,541 (100% need-based). 45% of past graduating class borrowed through all loan programs. *Average indebtedness per student:* $21,411. *Average need-based loan:* Freshmen: $4577. Undergraduates: $4802. *Parent loans:* $9,523,950 (100% need-based). *Programs:* Federal Direct (Subsidized and Unsubsidized Stafford, PLUS), Perkins, college/university.

**WORK-STUDY** *Federal work-study:* Total amount: $10,445,875; 4,950 jobs averaging $2110. *State or other work-study/employment:* Total amount: $2,200,192 (100% need-based). 1,100 part-time jobs averaging $2000.

**APPLYING FOR FINANCIAL AID** *Required financial aid forms:* FAFSA, CSS Financial Aid PROFILE, noncustodial (divorced/separated) parent's statement. *Financial aid deadline:* 2/15. *Notification date:* 4/1. Students must reply by 5/1.

**CONTACT** Ms. Susan Hitchcock, Director of Financial Aid and Student Employment, Cornell University, 203 Day Hall, Ithaca, NY 14853-2488, 607-255-5145.
*Website:* http://www.cornell.edu/.

# CORNERSTONE UNIVERSITY
## Grand Rapids, MI

| Tuition & fees: $25,112 | Average undergraduate aid package: $19,871 |
| --- | --- |

**ABOUT THE INSTITUTION** Independent nondenominational, coed. *Awards:* diplomas, associate, bachelor's, and master's degrees. 49 undergraduate majors. *Total enrollment:* 2,770. Undergraduates: 2,153. Freshmen: 323. Federal methodology is used as a basis for awarding need-based institutional aid.

**UNDERGRADUATE EXPENSES** for 2015–2016 *Application fee:* $25. *Comprehensive fee:* $33,338 includes full-time tuition ($24,542), mandatory fees ($570), and room and board ($8226). Full-time tuition and fees vary according to course load and reciprocity agreements. Room and board charges vary according to board plan and housing facility. *Part-time tuition:* $941 per credit hour. *Part-time fees:* $185 per term. Part-time tuition and fees vary according to course load.

**FRESHMAN FINANCIAL AID (Fall 2014, est.)** 275 applied for aid; of those 92% were deemed to have need. 100% of freshmen with need received aid; of those 12% had need fully met. *Average percent of need met:* 71% (excluding resources awarded to replace EFC). *Average financial aid package:* $20,881 (excluding resources awarded to replace EFC). 15% of all full-time freshmen had no need and received non-need-based gift aid.

**UNDERGRADUATE FINANCIAL AID (Fall 2014, est.)** 1,056 applied for aid; of those 91% were deemed to have need. 100% of undergraduates with need received aid; of those 14% had need fully met. *Average percent of need met:* 68% (excluding resources awarded to replace EFC). *Average financial aid package:* $19,871 (excluding resources awarded to replace EFC). 17% of all full-time undergraduates had no need and received non-need-based gift aid.

**GIFT AID (NEED-BASED)** *Total amount:* $13,729,652 (16% federal, 8% state, 74% institutional, 2% external sources). *Receiving aid:* Freshmen: 85% (253); all full-time undergraduates: 82% (956). *Average award:* Freshmen: $17,642; Undergraduates: $15,814. *Scholarships, grants, and awards:* Federal Pell, FSEOG, state, private, college/university gift aid from institutional funds.

**GIFT AID (NON-NEED-BASED)** *Total amount:* $2,127,993 (99% institutional, 1% external sources). *Receiving aid:* Freshmen: 8% (24). Undergraduates: 7% (84). *Average award:* Freshmen: $10,614. Undergraduates: $9356. *Scholarships, grants, and awards by category:* Academic interests/achievement: business, communication, education, English, foreign languages, general academic interests/achievements, humanities, mathematics, physical sciences, religion/biblical studies, social sciences. Creative arts/performance: journalism/publications, music. Special characteristics: children of faculty/staff, ethnic background, international students, members of minority groups, relatives of clergy. *Tuition waivers:* Full or partial for employees or children of employees. *ROTC:* Army cooperative.

**LOANS** *Student loans:* $6,993,773 (48% need-based, 52% non-need-based). 80% of past graduating class borrowed through all loan programs. *Average indebtedness per student:* $27,919. *Average need-based loan:* Freshmen: $3496. Undergraduates: $4232. *Parent loans:* $1,233,534 (100% non-need-based). *Programs:* Federal Direct (Subsidized and Unsubsidized Stafford, PLUS), Perkins.

**WORK-STUDY** *Federal work-study:* Total amount: $192,965; 241 jobs averaging $1426.

**ATHLETIC AWARDS** Total amount: $1,498,554 (64% need-based, 36% non-need-based).

APPLYING FOR FINANCIAL AID *Required financial aid form:* FAFSA. *Financial aid deadline:* Continuous. *Notification date:* Continuous beginning 3/1. Students must reply within 4 weeks of notification.

CONTACT Mrs. Carol S. Carpenter, Director of Student Financial Services, Cornerstone University, 1001 East Beltline Avenue, NE, Grand Rapids, MI 49525-5897, 616-222-1424 or toll-free 800-787-9778. *Fax:* 616-222-1400. *E-mail:* carol.carpenter@cornerstone.edu. *Website:* http://www.cornerstone.edu/.

# CORNISH COLLEGE OF THE ARTS
## Seattle, WA

| Tuition & fees: $35,800 | Average undergraduate aid package: $22,119 |
| --- | --- |

**ABOUT THE INSTITUTION** Independent, coed. *Awards:* certificates and bachelor's degrees. 16 undergraduate majors. *Total enrollment:* 767. Undergraduates: 765. Freshmen: 161. Federal methodology is used as a basis for awarding need-based institutional aid.

**UNDERGRADUATE EXPENSES for 2015–2016 *Application fee:* $40. *Comprehensive fee:* $45,600 includes full-time tuition ($35,400), mandatory fees ($400), and room and board ($9800). *College room only:* $6900. Full-time tuition and fees vary according to program. Room and board charges vary according to board plan. *Part-time tuition:* $1475 per credit hour. Part-time tuition and fees vary according to program.

**FRESHMAN FINANCIAL AID (Fall 2014, est.)** 123 applied for aid; of those 94% were deemed to have need. 100% of freshmen with need received aid; of those 7% had need fully met. *Average percent of need met:* 54% (excluding resources awarded to replace EFC). *Average financial aid package:* $21,502 (excluding resources awarded to replace EFC). 19% of all full-time freshmen had no need and received non-need-based gift aid.

**UNDERGRADUATE FINANCIAL AID (Fall 2014, est.)** 629 applied for aid; of those 90% were deemed to have need. 100% of undergraduates with need received aid; of those 5% had need fully met. *Average percent of need met:* 56% (excluding resources awarded to replace EFC). *Average financial aid package:* $22,119 (excluding resources awarded to replace EFC). 20% of all full-time undergraduates had no need and received non-need-based gift aid.

**GIFT AID (NEED-BASED)** *Total amount:* $9,351,238 (16% federal, 12% state, 68% institutional, 4% external sources). *Receiving aid:* Freshmen: 80% (114); all full-time undergraduates: 80% (561). *Average award:* Freshmen: $17,190; Undergraduates: $15,977. *Scholarships, grants, and awards:* Federal Pell, FSEOG, state, private, college/university gift aid from institutional funds.

**GIFT AID (NON-NEED-BASED)** *Total amount:* $1,319,175 (87% institutional, 13% external sources). *Receiving aid:* Freshmen: 3% (5). Undergraduates: 3% (22). *Average award:* Freshmen: $7566. Undergraduates: $7282. *Scholarships, grants, and awards by category:* Academic interests/achievement: general academic interests/achievements. Creative arts/performance: art/fine arts, dance, music, theater/drama. *Tuition waivers:* Full or partial for employees or children of employees.

**LOANS** *Student loans:* $6,125,030 (86% need-based, 14% non-need-based). 82% of past graduating class borrowed through all loan programs. *Average indebtedness per student:* $32,179. *Average need-based loan:* Freshmen: $3171. Undergraduates: $4538. *Parent loans:* $3,850,050 (61% need-based, 39% non-need-based). *Programs:* Federal Direct (Subsidized and Unsubsidized Stafford, PLUS), Perkins.

**WORK-STUDY** *Federal work-study:* Total amount: $516,955; 262 jobs averaging $2000. *State or other work-study/employment:* Total amount: $658,564 (96% need-based, 4% non-need-based). 241 part-time jobs averaging $2000.

**APPLYING FOR FINANCIAL AID** *Required financial aid form:* FAFSA. *Financial aid deadline (priority):* 2/15. *Notification date:* 3/1. Students must reply by 5/1 or within 2 weeks of notification.

**CONTACT** Sharron Starling, Office of Admissions, Cornish College of the Arts, 1000 Lenora Street, Seattle, WA 98121, 206-726-5017 or toll-free 800-726-ARTS. *Fax:* 206-720-1011. *E-mail:* admissions@cornish.edu. *Website:* http://www.cornish.edu/.

# COVENANT COLLEGE
## Lookout Mountain, GA

| Tuition & fees: $30,160 | Average undergraduate aid package: $24,435 |
| --- | --- |

**ABOUT THE INSTITUTION** Independent Presbyterian Church in America, coed. *Awards:* bachelor's and master's degrees (master's degree in education only). 27 undergraduate majors. *Total enrollment:* 1,173. Undergraduates: 1,105. Freshmen: 265. Federal methodology is used as a basis for awarding need-based institutional aid.

**UNDERGRADUATE EXPENSES for 2015–2016 *Application fee:* $35. *Comprehensive fee:* $38,990 includes full-time tuition ($29,300), mandatory fees ($860), and room and board ($8830). Full-time tuition and fees vary according to course load. Room and board charges vary according to board plan and housing facility. *Part-time tuition:* $1245 per credit hour. Part-time tuition and fees vary according to course load.

**FRESHMAN FINANCIAL AID (Fall 2013)** 251 applied for aid; of those 80% were deemed to have need. 100% of freshmen with need received aid; of those 34% had need fully met. *Average percent of need met:* 84% (excluding resources awarded to replace EFC). *Average financial aid package:* $25,390 (excluding resources awarded to replace EFC). 26% of all full-time freshmen had no need and received non-need-based gift aid.

**UNDERGRADUATE FINANCIAL AID (Fall 2013)** 752 applied for aid; of those 86% were deemed to have need. 100% of undergraduates with need received aid; of those 31% had need fully met. *Average percent of need met:* 82% (excluding resources awarded to replace EFC). *Average financial aid package:* $24,435 (excluding resources awarded to replace EFC). 30% of all full-time undergraduates had no need and received non-need-based gift aid.

**GIFT AID (NEED-BASED)** *Total amount:* $12,834,664 (11% federal, 4% state, 82% institutional, 3% external sources). *Receiving aid:* Freshmen: 67% (199); all full-time undergraduates: 62% (636). *Average award:* Freshmen: $18,816; Undergraduates: $17,752. *Scholarships, grants, and awards:* Federal Pell, FSEOG, state, private, college/university gift aid from institutional funds.

**GIFT AID (NON-NEED-BASED)** *Total amount:* $3,942,187 (4% state, 91% institutional, 5% external sources). *Receiving aid:* Freshmen: 12% (36). Undergraduates: 9% (97). *Average award:* Freshmen: $12,206. Undergraduates: $11,585. *Scholarships, grants, and awards by category:* Academic interests/achievement: general academic interests/achievements. Creative arts/performance: music. Special achievements/activities: leadership. Special characteristics: children of faculty/staff, international students, members of minority groups, religious affiliation. *Tuition waivers:* Full or partial for employees or children of employees, senior citizens. ROTC: Army cooperative.

**LOANS** *Student loans:* $4,534,735 (92% need-based, 8% non-need-based). 69% of past graduating class borrowed through all loan programs. *Average indebtedness per student:* $24,215. *Average need-based loan:* Freshmen: $6847. Undergraduates: $6847. *Parent loans:* $990,214 (88% need-based, 12% non-need-based). *Programs:* Perkins, state, college/university.

**WORK-STUDY** *Federal work-study:* jobs available. *State or other work-study/employment:* Total amount: $980,728 (87% need-based, 13% non-need-based). Part-time jobs available.

**APPLYING FOR FINANCIAL AID** *Required financial aid forms:* FAFSA, state aid form. *Financial aid deadline:* Continuous. *Notification date:* Continuous beginning 2/1. Students must reply within 3 weeks of notification.

**CONTACT** Mrs. Margaret Stewart, Assistant Director of Financial Aid, Covenant College, 14049 Scenic Highway, Lookout Mountain, GA 30750, 706-419-1152 or toll-free 888-451-2683. *Fax:* 706-820-2820. *E-mail:* margaret.stewart@covenant.edu. *Website:* http://www.covenant.edu/.

# COX COLLEGE
## Springfield, MO

| Tuition & fees: N/R | Average undergraduate aid package: N/A |
| --- | --- |

**ABOUT THE INSTITUTION** Independent, coed, primarily women. 1 undergraduate major. Federal methodology is used as a basis for awarding need-based institutional aid.

**GIFT AID (NEED-BASED) Total amount:** $2,163,723 (71% federal, 14% state, 13% institutional, 2% external sources). **Scholarships, grants, and awards:** Federal Pell, FSEOG, state, private, college/university gift aid from institutional funds, United Negro College Fund, Federal Nursing.
**LOANS Student loans:** $5,460,484 (100% need-based). **Parent loans:** $143,975 (100% need-based). **Programs:** Federal Direct (Subsidized and Unsubsidized Stafford, PLUS).
**WORK-STUDY Federal work-study:** 8 jobs averaging $3465. **State or other work-study/employment:** Part-time jobs available.
**APPLYING FOR FINANCIAL AID Required financial aid forms:** FAFSA, institution's own form. **Financial aid deadline (priority):** 4/1. **Notification date:** Continuous beginning 5/20.
**CONTACT** Victoria L. Jacobson, Financial Aid Counselor, Cox College, 1423 North Jefferson Avenue, Springfield, MO 65802, 417-269-3458 or toll-free 866-898-5355 (in-state). Fax: 417-269-3586. E-mail: victoria.jacobson@coxcollege.edu. Website: http://www.coxcollege.edu/.

---

# CREATIVE CENTER
## Omaha, NE

**CONTACT** Financial Aid Office, Creative Center, 10850 Emmet Street, Omaha, NE 68164, 402-898-1000 or toll-free 888-898-1789. Website: http://www.creativecenter.edu/.

---

# CREIGHTON UNIVERSITY
## Omaha, NE

| Tuition & fees: $35,360 | Average undergraduate aid package: $28,375 |
|---|---|

**ABOUT THE INSTITUTION** Independent Roman Catholic (Jesuit), coed. **Awards:** certificates, associate, bachelor's, master's, and doctoral degrees. 79 undergraduate majors. **Total enrollment:** 8,236. Undergraduates: 4,065. Freshmen: 1,025. Federal methodology is used as a basis for awarding need-based institutional aid.
**UNDERGRADUATE EXPENSES for 2015–2016 Application fee:** $40. **Comprehensive fee:** $45,356 includes full-time tuition ($33,796), mandatory fees ($1564), and room and board ($9996). Full-time tuition and fees vary according to course load and program. Room and board charges vary according to board plan and housing facility. **Part-time tuition:** $1058 per credit hour. Part-time tuition and fees vary according to course load and program.
**FRESHMAN FINANCIAL AID (Fall 2014, est.)** 833 applied for aid; of those 74% were deemed to have need. 100% of freshmen with need received aid; of those 27% had need fully met. **Average percent of need met:** 85% (excluding resources awarded to replace EFC). **Average financial aid package:** $27,779 (excluding resources awarded to replace EFC). 36% of all full-time freshmen had no need and received non-need-based gift aid.
**UNDERGRADUATE FINANCIAL AID (Fall 2014, est.)** 2,487 applied for aid; of those 82% were deemed to have need. 100% of undergraduates with need received aid; of those 36% had need fully met. **Average percent of need met:** 87% (excluding resources awarded to replace EFC). **Average financial aid package:** $28,375 (excluding resources awarded to replace EFC). 36% of all full-time undergraduates had no need and received non-need-based gift aid.
**GIFT AID (NEED-BASED) Total amount:** $41,960,177 (7% federal, 1% state, 89% institutional, 3% external sources). **Receiving aid:** Freshmen: 60% (616); all full-time undergraduates: 53% (2,031). **Average award:** Freshmen: $22,750; Undergraduates: $22,665. **Scholarships, grants, and awards:** Federal Pell, FSEOG, state, private, college/university gift aid from institutional funds.
**GIFT AID (NON-NEED-BASED) Total amount:** $18,988,733 (98% institutional, 2% external sources). **Receiving aid:** Freshmen: 57% (580). Undergraduates: 49% (1,865). **Average award:** Freshmen: $14,873. Undergraduates: $14,200. **Scholarships, grants, and awards by category:** Academic interests/achievement: 2,750 awards ($33,000,000 total): business, education, general academic interests/achievements, military science. Creative arts/performance: 20 awards ($77,300 total): art/fine arts, dance, music, performing arts, theater/drama. Special achievements/activities: 270 awards ($520,000 total): community service, leadership. Special characteristics: 50 awards ($1,250,000 total): first-generation college students, members of minority groups. **Tuition waivers:** Full or partial for employees or children of employees, adult students, senior citizens. **ROTC:** Army, Air Force cooperative.
**LOANS Student loans:** $23,484,169 (82% need-based, 18% non-need-based). 64% of past graduating class borrowed through all loan programs. Average indebtedness per student: $33,428. **Average need-based loan:** Freshmen: $4981. Undergraduates: $6061. **Parent loans:** $4,889,715 (100% non-need-based). **Programs:** Federal Direct (Subsidized and Unsubsidized Stafford, PLUS), Perkins, Federal Nursing.
**WORK-STUDY Federal work-study:** Total amount: $1,635,238; 735 jobs averaging $2074.
**ATHLETIC AWARDS** Total amount: $4,255,791 (36% need-based, 64% non-need-based).
**APPLYING FOR FINANCIAL AID Required financial aid forms:** FAFSA, institution's own form. **Financial aid deadline (priority):** 3/1. **Notification date:** Continuous beginning 3/15. Students must reply within 4 weeks of notification.
**CONTACT** Ms. Paula S. Kohles, Director of Financial Aid, Creighton University, 2500 California Plaza, Omaha, NE 68178, 402-280-2731 or toll-free 800-282-5835. Fax: 402-280-2895. E-mail: paulakohles@creighton.edu. Website: http://www.creighton.edu/.

---

# THE CRISWELL COLLEGE
## Dallas, TX

| Tuition & fees: N/R | Average undergraduate aid package: $9115 |
|---|---|

**ABOUT THE INSTITUTION** Independent Southern Baptist Convention, coed. 2 undergraduate majors. Institutional methodology is used as a basis for awarding need-based institutional aid.
**FRESHMAN FINANCIAL AID (Fall 2014, est.)** 77 applied for aid; of those 100% were deemed to have need. 100% of freshmen with need received aid; of those 71% had need fully met. **Average percent of need met:** 87% (excluding resources awarded to replace EFC). 14% of all full-time freshmen had no need and received non-need-based gift aid.
**UNDERGRADUATE FINANCIAL AID (Fall 2014, est.)** 150 applied for aid; of those 100% were deemed to have need. 100% of undergraduates with need received aid; of those 100% had need fully met. **Average percent of need met:** 65% (excluding resources awarded to replace EFC). **Average financial aid package:** $9115 (excluding resources awarded to replace EFC). 13% of all full-time undergraduates had no need and received non-need-based gift aid.
**GIFT AID (NEED-BASED) Total amount:** $540,921 (87% federal, 13% institutional). **Receiving aid:** Freshmen: 83% (72); all full-time undergraduates: 89% (150). **Average award:** Freshmen: $1685; Undergraduates: $5460. **Scholarships, grants, and awards:** Federal Pell, private, college/university gift aid from institutional funds.
**GIFT AID (NON-NEED-BASED) Total amount:** $168,226 (100% institutional). **Receiving aid:** Freshmen: 53% (46). Undergraduates: 70% (118). **Average award:** Freshmen: $470. Undergraduates: $980. **Scholarships, grants, and awards by category:** Academic interests/achievement: 153 awards ($301,345 total): general academic interests/achievements, religion/biblical studies. Special achievements/activities: 38 awards ($32,839 total): religious involvement. Special characteristics: 31 awards ($83,474 total): children and siblings of alumni, children of faculty/staff, international students, local/state students, out-of-state students, religious affiliation, veterans.
**LOANS Student loans:** $1,178,764 (33% need-based, 67% non-need-based). 68% of past graduating class borrowed through all loan programs. Average indebtedness per student: $4030. **Average need-based loan:** Freshmen: $1920. Undergraduates: $5100. **Parent loans:** $21,529 (100% non-need-based). **Programs:** Federal Direct (Subsidized and Unsubsidized Stafford, PLUS), college/university.
**APPLYING FOR FINANCIAL AID Required financial aid forms:** FAFSA, institution's own form, CSS Financial Aid PROFILE. **Financial aid deadline (priority):** 4/15. **Notification date:** Continuous beginning 7/15. Students must reply within 6 weeks of notification.
**CONTACT** TaLisa Pollard, Financial Aid Director, The Criswell College, 4010 Gaston Avenue, Dallas, TX 75246, 800-899-0012. Fax: 214-818-1393. E-mail: tpollard@criswell.edu. Website: http://www.criswell.edu/.

# CROSSROADS BIBLE COLLEGE
## Indianapolis, IN

| Tuition & fees: N/R | Average undergraduate aid package: N/A |
|---|---|

**ABOUT THE INSTITUTION** Independent Baptist, coed. 8 undergraduate majors. Institutional methodology is used as a basis for awarding need-based institutional aid.

**GIFT AID (NEED-BASED)** *Total amount:* $1,021,464 (61% federal, 31% state, 8% institutional). *Scholarships, grants, and awards:* Federal Pell, FSEOG, state, college/university gift aid from institutional funds.

**GIFT AID (NON-NEED-BASED)** *Scholarships, grants, and awards by category: Academic interests/achievement:* religion/biblical studies. *Special achievements/activities:* religious involvement. *Special characteristics:* children of faculty/staff, married students, siblings of current students, spouses of current students.

**LOANS** *Student loans:* $1,577,971 (100% need-based). *Programs:* Federal Direct (Subsidized and Unsubsidized Stafford, PLUS).

**WORK-STUDY** *Federal work-study:* jobs available.

**APPLYING FOR FINANCIAL AID** *Required financial aid forms:* FAFSA, institution's own form. *Financial aid deadline:* 6/30 (priority: 5/31). *Notification date:* 7/31. Students must reply within 2 weeks of notification.

**CONTACT** Mrs. Phyllis Dodson, Senior Director of Financial Aid, Crossroads Bible College, 601 North Shortridge Road, Indianapolis, IN 46219, 317-789-8250 or toll-free 800-822-3119. *Fax:* 317-789-8253. *E-mail:* pdodson@crossroads.edu. *Website:* http://www.crossroads.edu/.

# CROSSROADS COLLEGE
## Rochester, MN

**CONTACT** Polly Kellogg Bradley, Director of Financial Aid, Crossroads College, 920 Mayowood Road SW, Rochester, MN 55902, 507-288-4563 or toll-free 800-456-7651. *Fax:* 507-288-9046. *E-mail:* financialaid@crossroadscollege.edu. *Website:* http://www.crossroadscollege.edu/.

# CROWN COLLEGE
## St. Bonifacius, MN

**CONTACT** Mrs. Shannon Schaaf, Director of Financial Aid, Crown College, 8700 College View Drive, St. Bonifacius, MN 55375-9001, 952-446-4175 or toll-free 800-68-CROWN. *Fax:* 952-446-4178. *E-mail:* finaid@crown.edu. *Website:* http://www.crown.edu/.

# THE CULINARY INSTITUTE OF AMERICA
## Hyde Park, NY

| Tuition & fees: $28,240 | Average undergraduate aid package: $14,037 |
|---|---|

**ABOUT THE INSTITUTION** Independent, coed. *Awards:* certificates, associate, and bachelor's degrees. 4 undergraduate majors. *Total enrollment:* 2,778. Undergraduates: 2,778. Freshmen: 511. Federal methodology is used as a basis for awarding need-based institutional aid.

**UNDERGRADUATE EXPENSES** for 2015–2016 *Application fee:* $50. *Comprehensive fee:* $37,892 includes full-time tuition ($26,950), mandatory fees ($1290), and room and board ($9652). *College room only:* $6880. Full-time tuition and fees vary according to degree level. Room and board charges vary according to board plan and housing facility.

**FRESHMAN FINANCIAL AID (Fall 2014, est.)** 453 applied for aid; of those 91% were deemed to have need. 100% of freshmen with need received aid; of those 44% had need fully met. *Average percent of need met:* 80% (excluding resources awarded to replace EFC). *Average financial aid package:* $16,156 (excluding resources awarded to replace EFC). 15% of all full-time freshmen had no need and received non-need-based gift aid.

**UNDERGRADUATE FINANCIAL AID (Fall 2014, est.)** 1,999 applied for aid; of those 91% were deemed to have need. 99% of undergraduates with need received aid; of those 32% had need fully met. *Average percent of need met:* 70% (excluding resources awarded to replace EFC). *Average financial aid package:* $14,037 (excluding resources awarded to replace EFC). 17% of all full-time undergraduates had no need and received non-need-based gift aid.

**GIFT AID (NEED-BASED)** *Total amount:* $17,209,094 (19% federal, 4% state, 74% institutional, 3% external sources). *Receiving aid:* Freshmen: 68% (349); all full-time undergraduates: 53% (1,505). *Average award:* Freshmen: $12,102; Undergraduates: $9569. *Scholarships, grants, and awards:* Federal Pell, FSEOG, state, private, college/university gift aid from institutional funds.

**GIFT AID (NON-NEED-BASED)** *Total amount:* $1,814,095 (3% federal, 1% state, 88% institutional, 8% external sources). *Receiving aid:* Freshmen: 73% (373). Undergraduates: 49% (1,388). *Average award:* Freshmen: $5648. Undergraduates: $3783. *Scholarships, grants, and awards by category: Academic interests/achievement:* 1,578 awards ($4,781,013 total): general academic interests/achievements. *Creative arts/performance:* 103 awards ($559,705 total): general creative arts/performance. *Special achievements/activities:* 54 awards ($109,000 total): general special achievements/activities. *Special characteristics:* 613 awards ($1,244,845 total): general special characteristics, veterans, veterans' children.

**LOANS** *Student loans:* $18,047,254 (85% need-based, 15% non-need-based). 92% of past graduating class borrowed through all loan programs. *Average indebtedness per student:* $35,617. *Average need-based loan:* Freshmen: $3116. Undergraduates: $4017. *Parent loans:* $6,245,923 (100% non-need-based). *Programs:* Federal Direct (Subsidized and Unsubsidized Stafford, PLUS), Perkins, alternative loans.

**WORK-STUDY** *Federal work-study:* Total amount: $1,948,720; 808 jobs averaging $2227. *State or other work-study/employment:* Total amount: $439,094 (72% need-based, 28% non-need-based). Part-time jobs available.

**APPLYING FOR FINANCIAL AID** *Required financial aid form:* FAFSA. *Financial aid deadline (priority):* 4/15. *Notification date:* Continuous beginning 3/5. Students must reply within 2 weeks of notification.

**CONTACT** Kathleen Gailor, Director of Financial Aid, The Culinary Institute of America, 1946 Campus Drive, Hyde Park, NY 12538-1499, 845-451-1500 or toll-free 800-CULINARY. *Fax:* 845-905-4030. *E-mail:* finaid@culinary.edu. *Website:* http://www.ciachef.edu/.

# CULINARY INSTITUTE OF VIRGINIA
## Norfolk, VA

**CONTACT** Ms. Lynn Robinson, Director of Financial Aid, Culinary Institute of Virginia, 8 Abbott Park Place, Providence, RI 02903, 401-598-4648 or toll-free 866-619-CHEF. *Fax:* 401-598-1040. *E-mail:* fp@jwu.edu. *Website:* http://www.chefva.com/.

# CULVER-STOCKTON COLLEGE
## Canton, MO

| Tuition & fees: $24,900 | Average undergraduate aid package: $20,407 |
|---|---|

**ABOUT THE INSTITUTION** Independent Christian Church (Disciples of Christ), coed. *Awards:* bachelor's and master's degrees. 35 undergraduate majors. *Total enrollment:* 971. Undergraduates: 957. Freshmen: 290. Federal methodology is used as a basis for awarding need-based institutional aid.

**UNDERGRADUATE EXPENSES** for 2015–2016 *One-time required fee:* $200. *Comprehensive fee:* $32,850 includes full-time tuition ($24,500), mandatory fees ($400), and room and board ($7950). *College room only:* $3560. Room and board charges vary according to board plan and housing facility. *Part-time tuition:* $570 per credit hour. *Part-time fees:* $16.67 per credit hour.

**FRESHMAN FINANCIAL AID (Fall 2014, est.)** 255 applied for aid; of those 93% were deemed to have need. 100% of freshmen with need received aid; of those 19% had need fully met. *Average percent of need met:* 73% (excluding resources awarded to replace EFC). *Average financial aid package:* $19,357 (excluding

resources awarded to replace EFC). 14% of all full-time freshmen had no need and received non-need-based gift aid.

**UNDERGRADUATE FINANCIAL AID (Fall 2014, est.)** 769 applied for aid; of those 94% were deemed to have need. 100% of undergraduates with need received aid; of those 17% had need fully met. *Average percent of need met:* 74% (excluding resources awarded to replace EFC). *Average financial aid package:* $20,407 (excluding resources awarded to replace EFC). 13% of all full-time undergraduates had no need and received non-need-based gift aid.

**GIFT AID (NEED-BASED)** *Total amount:* $9,342,793 (22% federal, 6% state, 70% institutional, 2% external sources). *Receiving aid:* Freshmen: 82% (237); all full-time undergraduates: 85% (722). *Average award:* Freshmen: $16,460; Undergraduates: $16,673. *Scholarships, grants, and awards:* Federal Pell, FSEOG, state, private, college/university gift aid from institutional funds.

**GIFT AID (NON-NEED-BASED)** *Total amount:* $1,386,186 (2% state, 89% institutional, 9% external sources). *Receiving aid:* Freshmen: 12% (34). Undergraduates: 11% (90). *Average award:* Freshmen: $6433. Undergraduates: $8765. *Scholarships, grants, and awards by category: Academic interests/achievement:* 835 awards ($5,517,648 total): general academic interests/achievements. *Creative arts/performance:* 113 awards ($454,000 total): art/fine arts, debating, music, theater/drama. *Special achievements/activities:* 101 awards ($270,500 total): cheerleading/drum major, general special achievements/activities, leadership. *Special characteristics:* 104 awards ($511,280 total): children and siblings of alumni, children of faculty/staff, international students, local/state students, religious affiliation, veterans, veterans' children. *Tuition waivers:* Full or partial for employees or children of employees, senior citizens.

**LOANS** *Student loans:* $6,947,044 (78% need-based, 22% non-need-based). 85% of past graduating class borrowed through all loan programs. *Average indebtedness per student:* $24,487. *Average need-based loan:* Freshmen: $3409. Undergraduates: $4173. *Parent loans:* $1,379,853 (40% need-based, 60% non-need-based). *Programs:* Federal Direct (Subsidized and Unsubsidized Stafford, PLUS), Perkins, Federal Nursing, state, college/university.

**WORK-STUDY** *Federal work-study:* Total amount: $74,126; 115 jobs averaging $655. *State or other work-study/employment:* Total amount: $357,140 (54% need-based, 46% non-need-based). 341 part-time jobs averaging $1047.

**ATHLETIC AWARDS** Total amount: $3,692,101 (76% need-based, 24% non-need-based).

**APPLYING FOR FINANCIAL AID** *Required financial aid form:* FAFSA. *Financial aid deadline:* 6/1 (priority: 3/1). *Notification date:* Continuous. Students must reply within 2 weeks of notification.

**CONTACT** Ms. Tina M. Wiseman, Director of Financial Aid, Culver-Stockton College, One College Hill, Canton, MO 63435, 573-288-6307 or toll-free 800-537-1883. *Fax:* 573-288-6308. *E-mail:* twiseman@culver.edu. *Website:* http://www.culver.edu/.

# CUMBERLAND UNIVERSITY
## Lebanon, TN

| Tuition & fees: $21,210 | Average undergraduate aid package: $16,665 |
| --- | --- |

**ABOUT THE INSTITUTION** Independent, coed. *Awards:* associate, bachelor's, and master's degrees. 37 undergraduate majors. *Total enrollment:* 1,481. Undergraduates: 1,254. Freshmen: 178. Both federal and institutional methodology are used as a basis for awarding need-based institutional aid.

**UNDERGRADUATE EXPENSES for 2015–2016** *Application fee:* $25. *One-time required fee:* $100. *Comprehensive fee:* $28,760 includes full-time tuition ($20,160), mandatory fees ($1050), and room and board ($7550). Full-time tuition and fees vary according to degree level. Room and board charges vary according to housing facility. *Part-time tuition:* $840 per credit hour. Part-time tuition and fees vary according to course load and degree level.

**FRESHMAN FINANCIAL AID (Fall 2013)** 203 applied for aid; of those 91% were deemed to have need. 100% of freshmen with need received aid; of those 18% had need fully met. *Average percent of need met:* 61% (excluding resources awarded to replace EFC). *Average financial aid package:* $18,281 (excluding resources awarded to replace EFC). 3% of all full-time freshmen had no need and received non-need-based gift aid.

**UNDERGRADUATE FINANCIAL AID (Fall 2013)** 983 applied for aid; of those 93% were deemed to have need. 100% of undergraduates with need received aid; of those 15% had need fully met. *Average percent of need met:* 69% (excluding

resources awarded to replace EFC). *Average financial aid package:* $16,665 (excluding resources awarded to replace EFC). 6% of all full-time undergraduates had no need and received non-need-based gift aid.

**GIFT AID (NEED-BASED)** *Total amount:* $2,656,268 (82% federal, 18% state). *Receiving aid:* Freshmen: 42% (89); all full-time undergraduates: 41% (430). *Average award:* Freshmen: $5829; Undergraduates: $5590. *Scholarships, grants, and awards:* Federal Pell, FSEOG, state, private, college/university gift aid from institutional funds.

**GIFT AID (NON-NEED-BASED)** *Total amount:* $6,659,515 (26% state, 67% institutional, 7% external sources). *Receiving aid:* Freshmen: 77% (164). Undergraduates: 69% (731). *Average award:* Freshmen: $3833. Undergraduates: $4096. *Scholarships, grants, and awards by category: Academic interests/achievement:* general academic interests/achievements. *Creative arts/performance:* art/fine arts, music, performing arts, theater/drama. *Special achievements/activities:* leadership. *Special characteristics:* children of faculty/staff. *Tuition waivers:* Full or partial for employees or children of employees. *ROTC:* Army.

**LOANS** *Student loans:* $8,857,406 (33% need-based, 67% non-need-based). 63% of past graduating class borrowed through all loan programs. *Average indebtedness per student:* $25,827. *Average need-based loan:* Freshmen: $3004. Undergraduates: $4065. *Parent loans:* $542,488 (100% non-need-based). *Programs:* Perkins, alternative loans.

**WORK-STUDY** *Federal work-study:* 120 jobs averaging $750. *State or other work-study/employment:* Total amount: $15,707 (100% non-need-based). 15 part-time jobs averaging $750.

**ATHLETIC AWARDS** Total amount: $55,101,426 (100% non-need-based).

**APPLYING FOR FINANCIAL AID** *Required financial aid form:* FAFSA. *Financial aid deadline (priority):* 2/15. *Notification date:* Continuous beginning 3/1. Students must reply within 2 weeks of notification.

**CONTACT** Ms. Beatrice LaChance, Executive Director of Enrollment Services, Cumberland University, 1 Cumberland Square, Lebanon, TN 37087-3554, 615-444-2562 Ext. 1244 or toll-free 800-467-0562. *Fax:* 615-443-8424. *E-mail:* lvaughan@cumberland.edu. *Website:* http://www.cumberland.edu/.

# CURRY COLLEGE
## Milton, MA

| Tuition & fees: $36,445 | Average undergraduate aid package: $24,327 |
| --- | --- |

**ABOUT THE INSTITUTION** Independent, coed. *Awards:* bachelor's and master's degrees. 20 undergraduate majors. *Total enrollment:* 3,141. Undergraduates: 2,900. Freshmen: 649. Federal methodology is used as a basis for awarding need-based institutional aid.

**UNDERGRADUATE EXPENSES for 2015–2016** *Application fee:* $50. *One-time required fee:* $320. *Comprehensive fee:* $50,345 includes full-time tuition ($34,730), mandatory fees ($1715), and room and board ($13,900). *College room only:* $7800. Full-time tuition and fees vary according to class time, course load, location, and program. Room and board charges vary according to board plan and housing facility. *Part-time tuition:* $1158 per credit. Part-time tuition and fees vary according to class time, course load, location, and program.

**FRESHMAN FINANCIAL AID (Fall 2014, est.)** 525 applied for aid; of those 100% were deemed to have need. 100% of freshmen with need received aid; of those 10% had need fully met. *Average percent of need met:* 69% (excluding resources awarded to replace EFC). *Average financial aid package:* $26,110 (excluding resources awarded to replace EFC). 19% of all full-time freshmen had no need and received non-need-based gift aid.

**UNDERGRADUATE FINANCIAL AID (Fall 2014, est.)** 1,591 applied for aid; of those 100% were deemed to have need. 100% of undergraduates with need received aid; of those 8% had need fully met. *Average percent of need met:* 69% (excluding resources awarded to replace EFC). *Average financial aid package:* $24,327 (excluding resources awarded to replace EFC). 17% of all full-time undergraduates had no need and received non-need-based gift aid.

**GIFT AID (NEED-BASED)** *Total amount:* $29,802,636 (11% federal, 3% state, 85% institutional, 1% external sources). *Receiving aid:* Freshmen: 64% (413); all full-time undergraduates: 64% (1,346). *Average award:* Freshmen: $10,918; Undergraduates: $12,318. *Scholarships, grants, and awards:* Federal Pell, FSEOG, state, private, college/university gift aid from institutional funds, TEACH Grants.

**GIFT AID (NON-NEED-BASED)** *Total amount:* $4,530,910 (8% federal, 90% institutional, 2% external sources). *Receiving aid:* Freshmen: 6% (42). Undergraduates: 4% (90). *Average award:* Freshmen: $12,244. Undergraduates: $9572. *Scholarships, grants, and awards by category: Academic interests/achievement:* 1,657 awards ($13,526,750 total): general academic interests/achievements. *Special characteristics:* 42 awards ($968,680 total): children and siblings of alumni, children of current students, children of faculty/staff, siblings of current students, spouses of current students. *Tuition waivers:* Full or partial for children of alumni, employees or children of employees. *ROTC:* Army cooperative, Air Force cooperative.

**LOANS** *Student loans:* $20,503,223 (35% need-based, 65% non-need-based). 81% of past graduating class borrowed through all loan programs. *Average indebtedness per student:* $43,388. *Average need-based loan:* Freshmen: $3663. Undergraduates: $4474. *Parent loans:* $9,803,799 (100% non-need-based). *Programs:* Federal Direct (Subsidized and Unsubsidized Stafford, PLUS), Perkins, state.

**WORK-STUDY** *Federal work-study:* Total amount: $1,805,600; 910 jobs averaging $1971.

**APPLYING FOR FINANCIAL AID** *Required financial aid form:* FAFSA. *Financial aid deadline (priority):* 3/1. *Notification date:* Continuous beginning 3/1.

**CONTACT** Linda Brennan, Director of Financial Aid, Curry College, 1071 Blue Hill Avenue, Milton, MA 02186-2395, 617-333-2354 or toll-free 800-669-0686. *Fax:* 617-333-2915. *E-mail:* fin-aid@curry.edu. *Website:* http://www.curry.edu/.

# CURTIS INSTITUTE OF MUSIC
## Philadelphia, PA

**CONTACT** Veronica McAuley, Director of Student Financial Assistance, Curtis Institute of Music, 1726 Locust Street, Philadelphia, PA 19103-6107, 215-717-3188. *E-mail:* veronica.mcauley@curtis.edu. *Website:* http://www.curtis.edu/.

# DADE MEDICAL COLLEGE
## Hollywood, FL

**CONTACT** Financial Aid Office, Dade Medical College, 6837 Taft Street, Hollywood, FL 33024, 954-843-7930 or toll-free 855-DMC-4488. *Website:* http://www.dademedical.edu/.

# DADE MEDICAL COLLEGE
## Homestead, FL

**CONTACT** Financial Aid Office, Dade Medical College, 381 N. Krome Ave, Homestead, FL 33030, 786-454-9070. *Website:* http://www.dademedical.edu/.

# DADE MEDICAL COLLEGE
## Jacksonville, FL

**CONTACT** Financial Aid Office, Dade Medical College, 9550 Regency Square Boulevard, Suite 1200, Jacksonville, FL 32225, 904-345-5678 or toll-free 855-DMC-4488. *Website:* http://www.dademedical.edu/.

# DADE MEDICAL COLLEGE
## Miami, FL

**CONTACT** Financial Aid Office, Dade Medical College, 3721-1 NW 7th Street, Miami, FL 33126, 786-363-4924. *Website:* http://www.dademedical.edu/.

# DADE MEDICAL COLLEGE
## Miami Lakes, FL

**CONTACT** Financial Aid Office, Dade Medical College, 5875 NW 163rd Street, Suite 101, Miami Lakes, FL 33014, 786-363-3340. *Website:* http://www.dademedical.edu/.

# DADE MEDICAL COLLEGE
## West Palm Beach, FL

**CONTACT** Financial Aid Office, Dade Medical College, 2601 South Military Trail, West Palm Beach, FL 33415, 561-345-7240. *Website:* http://www.dademedical.edu/.

# DAEMEN COLLEGE
## Amherst, NY

**ABOUT THE INSTITUTION** Independent, coed. *Awards:* certificates, bachelor's, master's, and doctoral degrees. 35 undergraduate majors. *Total enrollment:* 2,800. Undergraduates: 2,044. Freshmen: 420.

**GIFT AID (NEED-BASED)** *Scholarships, grants, and awards:* Federal Pell, FSEOG, state, private, college/university gift aid from institutional funds.

**GIFT AID (NON-NEED-BASED)** *Scholarships, grants, and awards by category: Academic interests/achievement:* general academic interests/achievements, health fields. *Creative arts/performance:* art/fine arts. *Special achievements/activities:* leadership. *Special characteristics:* children of faculty/staff, international students, siblings of current students, veterans, veterans' children.

**LOANS** *Programs:* Federal Direct (Subsidized and Unsubsidized Stafford, PLUS), Perkins, alternative loans.

**WORK-STUDY** *Federal work-study:* 755 jobs averaging $2161. *State or other work-study/employment:* Total amount: $291,598 (32% need-based, 68% non-need-based). 58 part-time jobs averaging $5028.

**APPLYING FOR FINANCIAL AID** *Required financial aid forms:* FAFSA, state aid form.

**CONTACT** Mr. Jeffrey Pagano, Director of Financial Aid, Daemen College, 4380 Main Street, Amherst, NY 14226-3592, 716-839-8254 or toll-free 800-462-7652. *Fax:* 716-839-8378. *E-mail:* jpagano@daemen.edu. *Website:* http://www.daemen.edu/.

# DAKOTA STATE UNIVERSITY
## Madison, SD

| Tuition & fees (SD res): $8286 | Average undergraduate aid package: $7997 |
| --- | --- |

**ABOUT THE INSTITUTION** State-supported, coed. *Awards:* certificates, associate, bachelor's, master's, and doctoral degrees. 29 undergraduate majors. *Total enrollment:* 3,047. Undergraduates: 2,736. Freshmen: 291. Federal methodology is used as a basis for awarding need-based institutional aid.

**UNDERGRADUATE EXPENSES** for 2015–2016 *Application fee:* $20. *Tuition, state resident:* full-time $3993; part-time $133 per credit hour. *Tuition, nonresident:* full-time $5993; part-time $200 per credit hour. *Required fees:* full-time $4293. Full-time tuition and fees vary according to location and reciprocity agree-

ments. Part-time tuition and fees vary according to location and reciprocity agreements. **College room and board:** $5941; **Room only:** $3231. Room and board charges vary according to board plan and housing facility.
**FRESHMAN FINANCIAL AID (Fall 2013)** 256 applied for aid; of those 78% were deemed to have need. 100% of freshmen with need received aid; of those 8% had need fully met. **Average percent of need met:** 75% (excluding resources awarded to replace EFC). **Average financial aid package:** $7250 (excluding resources awarded to replace EFC). 13% of all full-time freshmen had no need and received non-need-based gift aid.
**UNDERGRADUATE FINANCIAL AID (Fall 2013)** 995 applied for aid; of those 81% were deemed to have need. 100% of undergraduates with need received aid; of those 9% had need fully met. **Average percent of need met:** 73% (excluding resources awarded to replace EFC). **Average financial aid package:** $7997 (excluding resources awarded to replace EFC). 8% of all full-time undergraduates had no need and received non-need-based gift aid.
**GIFT AID (NEED-BASED) Total amount:** $3,733,661 (78% federal, 4% state, 10% institutional, 8% external sources). **Receiving aid:** Freshmen: 39% (111); all full-time undergraduates: 39% (459). **Average award:** Freshmen: $4091; Undergraduates: $4424. **Scholarships, grants, and awards:** Federal Pell, FSEOG, state, private, college/university gift aid from institutional funds, Agency Assistance (Veterans Benefits/Department of Labor).
**GIFT AID (NON-NEED-BASED) Total amount:** $370,826 (13% federal, 15% state, 40% institutional, 32% external sources). **Receiving aid:** Freshmen: 48% (138). Undergraduates: 30% (357). **Average award:** Freshmen: $4059. Undergraduates: $3980. **Scholarships, grants, and awards by category:** Academic interests/achievement: 355 awards ($454,725 total): business, communication, computer science, education, English, general academic interests/achievements, mathematics. Creative arts/performance: 6 awards ($1350 total): music. **Tuition waivers:** Full or partial for employees or children of employees, senior citizens. **ROTC:** Air Force cooperative.
**LOANS Student loans:** $9,677,827 (71% need-based, 29% non-need-based). 79% of past graduating class borrowed through all loan programs. Average indebtedness per student: $24,728. **Average need-based loan:** Freshmen: $3502. Undergraduates: $4203. **Parent loans:** $913,644 (71% need-based, 29% non-need-based). **Programs:** Federal Direct (Subsidized and Unsubsidized Stafford, PLUS), Perkins, alternative loans.
**WORK-STUDY Federal work-study:** 151 jobs averaging $1676. **State or other work-study/employment:** Total amount: $112,800 (100% non-need-based). 20 part-time jobs averaging $5640.
**ATHLETIC AWARDS** Total amount: $279,766 (71% need-based, 29% non-need-based).
**APPLYING FOR FINANCIAL AID Required financial aid forms:** FAFSA, institutional scholarship application form. **Financial aid deadline (priority):** 3/1. **Notification date:** Continuous beginning 4/1. Students must reply within 2 weeks of notification.
**CONTACT** Denise Grayson, Financial Aid Director, Dakota State University, 103 Heston Hall, 820 North Washington Avenue, Madison, SD 57042-1799, 605-256-5158 or toll-free 888-DSU-9988. Fax: 605-256-5020. E-mail: fa@dsu.edu.
Website: http://www.dsu.edu/.

# DAKOTA WESLEYAN UNIVERSITY
## Mitchell, SD

| Tuition & fees: $23,650 | Average undergraduate aid package: $21,800 |
|---|---|

**ABOUT THE INSTITUTION** Independent United Methodist, coed. 46 undergraduate majors. Federal methodology is used as a basis for awarding need-based institutional aid.
**UNDERGRADUATE EXPENSES for 2015–2016 Comprehensive fee:** $30,450 includes full-time tuition ($23,550), mandatory fees ($100), and room and board ($6800). Room and board charges vary according to board plan and housing facility.
**FRESHMAN FINANCIAL AID (Fall 2014, est.)** 126 applied for aid; of those 89% were deemed to have need. 100% of freshmen with need received aid; of those 24% had need fully met. **Average percent of need met:** 91% (excluding resources awarded to replace EFC). **Average financial aid package:** $22,250 (excluding resources awarded to replace EFC). 20% of all full-time freshmen had no need and received non-need-based gift aid.

**UNDERGRADUATE FINANCIAL AID (Fall 2014, est.)** 591 applied for aid; of those 91% were deemed to have need. 100% of undergraduates with need received aid; of those 20% had need fully met. **Average percent of need met:** 82% (excluding resources awarded to replace EFC). **Average financial aid package:** $21,800 (excluding resources awarded to replace EFC). 17% of all full-time undergraduates had no need and received non-need-based gift aid.
**GIFT AID (NEED-BASED) Total amount:** $6,698,586 (18% federal, 2% state, 77% institutional, 3% external sources). **Receiving aid:** Freshmen: 80% (112); all full-time undergraduates: 78% (528). **Average award:** Freshmen: $15,500; Undergraduates: $14,042. **Scholarships, grants, and awards:** Federal Pell, FSEOG, state, college/university gift aid from institutional funds.
**GIFT AID (NON-NEED-BASED) Total amount:** $1,602,340 (4% state, 91% institutional, 5% external sources). **Receiving aid:** Freshmen: 16% (23). Undergraduates: 12% (84). **Average award:** Freshmen: $10,870. Undergraduates: $10,384. **Scholarships, grants, and awards by category:** Academic interests/achievement: 31 awards ($67,240 total): biological sciences, business, education, general academic interests/achievements, health fields, mathematics, premedicine. Creative arts/performance: 46 awards ($85,400 total): art/fine arts, music, theater/drama. Special achievements/activities: 7 awards ($14,250 total): cheerleading/drum major, general special achievements/activities. Special characteristics: 77 awards ($192,816 total): children of faculty/staff, religious affiliation. **Tuition waivers:** Full or partial for senior citizens.
**LOANS Student loans:** $5,968,865 (72% need-based, 28% non-need-based). 93% of past graduating class borrowed through all loan programs. Average indebtedness per student: $32,752. **Average need-based loan:** Freshmen: $3530. Undergraduates: $4863. **Parent loans:** $593,889 (52% need-based, 48% non-need-based). **Programs:** Federal Direct (Subsidized and Unsubsidized Stafford, PLUS), Perkins, private loans, United Methodist Student Loans (for members of Methodist Church).
**WORK-STUDY Federal work-study:** Total amount: $104,099; 109 jobs averaging $1550.
**ATHLETIC AWARDS** Total amount: $1,394,221 (59% need-based, 41% non-need-based).
**APPLYING FOR FINANCIAL AID Financial aid deadline (priority):** 4/1. **Notification date:** Continuous beginning 3/1. Students must reply within 2 weeks of notification.
**CONTACT** Kristy O'Kief, Director of Financial Aid, Dakota Wesleyan University, 1200 West University Avenue, Mitchell, SD 57301, 605-995-2656 or toll-free 800-333-8506. Fax: 605-995-2638. E-mail: krokief@dwu.edu.
Website: http://www.dwu.edu/.

# DALLAS BAPTIST UNIVERSITY
## Dallas, TX

| Tuition & fees: $23,650 | Average undergraduate aid package: $15,583 |
|---|---|

**ABOUT THE INSTITUTION** Independent Baptist General Convention of Texas, coed. **Awards:** certificates, associate, bachelor's, master's, and doctoral degrees. 50 undergraduate majors. **Total enrollment:** 5,445. Undergraduates: 3,457. Freshmen: 494. Federal methodology is used as a basis for awarding need-based institutional aid.
**UNDERGRADUATE EXPENSES for 2015–2016 Application fee:** $25. **Comprehensive fee:** $30,580 includes full-time tuition ($23,250), mandatory fees ($400), and room and board ($6930). **College room only:** $3313. Room and board charges vary according to board plan and housing facility. **Part-time tuition:** $775 per credit hour. **Part-time fees:** $200 per term.
**FRESHMAN FINANCIAL AID (Fall 2014, est.)** 449 applied for aid; of those 78% were deemed to have need. 99% of freshmen with need received aid; of those 45% had need fully met. **Average percent of need met:** 59% (excluding resources awarded to replace EFC). **Average financial aid package:** $14,753 (excluding resources awarded to replace EFC). 20% of all full-time freshmen had no need and received non-need-based gift aid.
**UNDERGRADUATE FINANCIAL AID (Fall 2014, est.)** 1,965 applied for aid; of those 80% were deemed to have need. 97% of undergraduates with need received aid; of those 36% had need fully met. **Average percent of need met:** 59% (excluding resources awarded to replace EFC). **Average financial aid package:** $15,583 (excluding resources awarded to replace EFC). 18% of all full-time undergraduates had no need and received non-need-based gift aid.

**GIFT AID (NEED-BASED)** *Total amount:* $6,856,692 (56% federal, 44% state). *Receiving aid:* Freshmen: 42% (208); all full-time undergraduates: 40% (967). *Average award:* Freshmen: $3766; Undergraduates: $3987. *Scholarships, grants, and awards:* Federal Pell, FSEOG, state, private, college/university gift aid from institutional funds.

**GIFT AID (NON-NEED-BASED)** *Total amount:* $16,290,660 (88% institutional, 12% external sources). *Receiving aid:* Freshmen: 65% (318). Undergraduates: 56% (1,334). *Average award:* Freshmen: $8013. Undergraduates: $8219. *Scholarships, grants, and awards by category:* Academic interests/achievement: 946 awards ($2,595,460 total): biological sciences, business, communication, computer science, education, English, general academic interests/achievements, humanities, mathematics, physical sciences, premedicine, religion/biblical studies, social sciences. Creative arts/performance: 92 awards ($332,496 total): art/fine arts, music. Special achievements/activities: 1,688 awards ($7,053,277 total): community service, general special achievements/activities, leadership, memberships, religious involvement. Special characteristics: 328 awards ($1,287,518 total): children of faculty/staff, general special characteristics, relatives of clergy, religious affiliation, veterans, veterans' children. *Tuition waivers:* Full or partial for employees or children of employees. *ROTC:* Army cooperative, Air Force cooperative.

**LOANS** *Student loans:* $15,502,205 (36% need-based, 64% non-need-based). 80% of past graduating class borrowed through all loan programs. *Average indebtedness per student:* $28,279. *Average need-based loan:* Freshmen: $3370. Undergraduates: $4146. *Parent loans:* $5,492,346 (100% non-need-based). *Programs:* Federal Direct (Subsidized and Unsubsidized Stafford, PLUS), state.

**WORK-STUDY** *Federal work-study:* Total amount: $408,474; 168 jobs averaging $2279. *State or other work-study/employment:* Total amount: $31,020 (100% need-based). 25 part-time jobs averaging $1324.

**ATHLETIC AWARDS** Total amount: $1,956,530 (100% non-need-based).

**APPLYING FOR FINANCIAL AID** *Required financial aid forms:* FAFSA, institution's own form. *Financial aid deadline:* Continuous. *Notification date:* Continuous beginning 2/1.

**CONTACT** Mr. Lee Ferguson, Director of Financial Aid, Dallas Baptist University, 3000 Mountain Creek Parkway, Dallas, TX 75211-9299, 214-333-5363 or toll-free 800-460-1328. *Fax:* 214-333-5586. *E-mail:* lee@dbu.edu. *Website:* http://www.dbu.edu/.

# DALLAS CHRISTIAN COLLEGE
## Dallas, TX

**CONTACT** Robin L. Walker, Director of Student Financial Aid, Dallas Christian College, 2700 Christian Parkway, Dallas, TX 75234-7299, 972-241-3371 Ext. 105 or toll-free 800-688-1029. *Fax:* 972-241-8021. *E-mail:* finaid@dallas.edu. *Website:* http://www.dallas.edu/.

# DALTON STATE COLLEGE
## Dalton, GA

**CONTACT** Holly Woods, Assistant Director of Financial Aid, Dalton State College, 650 College Drive, Dalton, GA 30720, 706-272-4545 or toll-free 800-829-4436. *Fax:* 706-272-2458. *E-mail:* finaid@daltonstate.edu. *Website:* http://www.daltonstate.edu/.

# DANIEL WEBSTER COLLEGE
## Nashua, NH

**CONTACT** Darla Ammidown, Director of Financial Aid , Daniel Webster College, 20 University Drive, Nashua, NH 03063-1300, 603-577-6533 or toll-free 800-325-6876. *Fax:* 603-577-6593. *E-mail:* dammidown@dwc.edu. *Website:* http://www.dwc.edu/.

# DARTMOUTH COLLEGE
## Hanover, NH

| Tuition & fees: $48,108 | Average undergraduate aid package: $45,359 |
| --- | --- |

**ABOUT THE INSTITUTION** Independent, coed. *Awards:* bachelor's, master's, and doctoral degrees. 60 undergraduate majors. *Total enrollment:* 6,298. Undergraduates: 4,289. Freshmen: 1,152. Both federal and institutional methodology are used as a basis for awarding need-based institutional aid.

**UNDERGRADUATE EXPENSES** for 2015–2016 *Application fee:* $80. *One-time required fee:* $170. *Comprehensive fee:* $61,947 includes full-time tuition ($46,764), mandatory fees ($1344), and room and board ($13,839). *College room only:* $8286. Room and board charges vary according to board plan. *Payment plan:* Tuition prepayment.

**FRESHMAN FINANCIAL AID (Fall 2014, est.)** 646 applied for aid; of those 86% were deemed to have need. 100% of freshmen with need received aid; of those 100% had need fully met. *Average percent of need met:* 100% (excluding resources awarded to replace EFC). *Average financial aid package:* $49,359 (excluding resources awarded to replace EFC).

**UNDERGRADUATE FINANCIAL AID (Fall 2014, est.)** 2,379 applied for aid; of those 89% were deemed to have need. 100% of undergraduates with need received aid; of those 100% had need fully met. *Average percent of need met:* 100% (excluding resources awarded to replace EFC). *Average financial aid package:* $45,359 (excluding resources awarded to replace EFC).

**GIFT AID (NEED-BASED)** *Total amount:* $86,014,506 (5% federal, 92% institutional, 3% external sources). *Receiving aid:* Freshmen: 47% (543); all full-time undergraduates: 49% (2,033). *Average award:* Freshmen: $44,847; Undergraduates: $42,299. *Scholarships, grants, and awards:* Federal Pell, FSEOG, state, private, college/university gift aid from institutional funds.

**GIFT AID (NON-NEED-BASED)** *Total amount:* $1,023,591 (13% federal, 87% external sources). *ROTC:* Army cooperative.

**LOANS** *Student loans:* $10,078,093 (66% need-based, 34% non-need-based). 46% of past graduating class borrowed through all loan programs. *Average indebtedness per student:* $17,171. *Average need-based loan:* Freshmen: $4258. Undergraduates: $3951. *Parent loans:* $3,956,350 (100% non-need-based). *Programs:* Federal Direct (Subsidized and Unsubsidized Stafford, PLUS), Perkins, state, college/university.

**WORK-STUDY** *Federal work-study:* Total amount: $2,664,004; 1,247 jobs averaging $2136. *State or other work-study/employment:* Total amount: $1,261,548 (100% need-based). 579 part-time jobs averaging $2178.

**APPLYING FOR FINANCIAL AID** *Required financial aid forms:* FAFSA, CSS Financial Aid PROFILE, noncustodial (divorced/separated) parent's statement, business/farm supplement, federal income tax form(s), W-2 forms. *Financial aid deadline:* 2/1. *Notification date:* 4/2. Students must reply by 5/1.

**CONTACT** Ms. Virginia S. Hazen, Director of Financial Aid, Dartmouth College, 6024 McNutt Hall, Hanover, NH 03755, 603-646-2451. *Fax:* 603-646-1414. *E-mail:* virginia.s.hazen@dartmouth.edu. *Website:* http://www.dartmouth.edu/.

# DAVENPORT UNIVERSITY
## Grand Rapids, MI

**ABOUT THE INSTITUTION** Independent, coed. *Awards:* certificates, diplomas, associate, bachelor's, and master's degrees. 20 undergraduate majors. *Total enrollment:* 10,221. Undergraduates: 7,876. Freshmen: 653.

**GIFT AID (NEED-BASED)** *Scholarships, grants, and awards:* Federal Pell, FSEOG, state, private, college/university gift aid from institutional funds.

**GIFT AID (NON-NEED-BASED)** *Scholarships, grants, and awards by category:* Academic interests/achievement: general academic interests/achievements. Special achievements/activities: memberships.

**LOANS** *Programs:* private loans.

**APPLYING FOR FINANCIAL AID** *Required financial aid form:* FAFSA.

**CONTACT** David DeBoer, Executive Director of Financial Aid, Davenport University, 6191 Kraft Avenue SE, Grand Rapids, MI 49512, 616-732-1132 or toll-free 800-925-3884 (in-state), 866-925-3884 (out-of-state). *Fax:* 616-732-1167. *E-mail:* david.debore@davenport.edu. *Website:* http://www.davenport.edu/.

# DAVIDSON COLLEGE
## Davidson, NC

| Tuition & fees: $45,377 | Average undergraduate aid package: $37,228 |
| --- | --- |

**ABOUT THE INSTITUTION** Independent Presbyterian, coed. **Awards:** bachelor's degrees. 27 undergraduate majors. **Total enrollment:** 1,770. Undergraduates: 1,770. Freshmen: 502. Both federal and institutional methodology are used as a basis for awarding need-based institutional aid.

**UNDERGRADUATE EXPENSES** for 2015–2016 **Application fee:** $50. **Comprehensive fee:** $58,146 includes full-time tuition ($44,928), mandatory fees ($449), and room and board ($12,769). **College room only:** $6499. Room and board charges vary according to board plan.

**FRESHMAN FINANCIAL AID (Fall 2013)** 296 applied for aid; of those 80% were deemed to have need. 100% of freshmen with need received aid; of those 100% had need fully met. **Average percent of need met:** 100% (excluding resources awarded to replace EFC). **Average financial aid package:** $38,584 (excluding resources awarded to replace EFC). 6% of all full-time freshmen had no need and received non-need-based gift aid.

**UNDERGRADUATE FINANCIAL AID (Fall 2013)** 949 applied for aid; of those 91% were deemed to have need. 100% of undergraduates with need received aid; of those 100% had need fully met. **Average percent of need met:** 100% (excluding resources awarded to replace EFC). **Average financial aid package:** $37,228 (excluding resources awarded to replace EFC). 7% of all full-time undergraduates had no need and received non-need-based gift aid.

**GIFT AID (NEED-BASED) Total amount:** $30,532,195 (4% federal, 2% state, 92% institutional, 2% external sources). **Receiving aid:** Freshmen: 49% (236); all full-time undergraduates: 48% (852). **Average award:** Freshmen: $37,259; Undergraduates: $35,836. **Scholarships, grants, and awards:** Federal Pell, FSEOG, state, private, college/university gift aid from institutional funds, need-linked special talent scholarships.

**GIFT AID (NON-NEED-BASED) Total amount:** $4,113,325 (11% federal, 63% institutional, 26% external sources). **Receiving aid:** Freshmen: 9% (42). Undergraduates: 10% (170). **Average award:** Freshmen: $26,540. Undergraduates: $21,269. **Scholarships, grants, and awards by category:** Academic interests/achievement: 145 awards ($1,601,961 total): biological sciences, business, education, foreign languages, general academic interests/achievements, health fields, international studies, mathematics, physical sciences, premedicine, religion/biblical studies, social sciences. Creative arts/performance: 32 awards ($163,020 total): art/fine arts, creative writing, music, performing arts, theater/drama. Special achievements/activities: 83 awards ($2,214,347 total): community service, general special achievements/activities, leadership, religious involvement. Special characteristics: 63 awards ($449,902 total): first-generation college students, general special characteristics, local/state students, out-of-state students, relatives of clergy, religious affiliation. **Tuition waivers:** Full or partial for employees or children of employees. **ROTC:** Army, Air Force cooperative.

**LOANS Student loans:** $2,861,819 (29% need-based, 71% non-need-based). 31% of past graduating class borrowed through all loan programs. Average indebtedness per student: $21,365. **Average need-based loan:** Freshmen: $2594. Undergraduates: $3405. **Parent loans:** $2,347,569 (100% non-need-based). **Programs:** Federal Direct (Subsidized and Unsubsidized Stafford, PLUS), alternative loans.

**WORK-STUDY Federal work-study:** 334 jobs averaging $1517. **State or other work-study/employment:** Total amount: $210,373 (100% need-based). 129 part-time jobs averaging $1631.

**ATHLETIC AWARDS Total amount:** $2,922,686 (100% non-need-based).

**APPLYING FOR FINANCIAL AID Required financial aid forms:** FAFSA, CSS Financial Aid PROFILE, noncustodial (divorced/separated) parent's statement, business/farm supplement, federal income tax form(s), W-2 forms. **Financial aid deadline:** 2/15. **Notification date:** 4/1. Students must reply by 5/1.

**CONTACT** Mr. David R. Gelinas, Director of Financial Aid, Davidson College, 413 North Main Street, PO Box 7157, Davidson, NC 28035-7157, 704-894-2232 or toll-free 800-768-0380. Fax: 704-894-2845. E-mail: dagelinas@davidson.edu. Website: http://www.davidson.edu/.

# DAVIS & ELKINS COLLEGE
## Elkins, WV

**CONTACT** Susan M. George, Director of Financial Planning, Davis & Elkins College, 100 Campus Drive, Elkins, WV 26241-3996, 304-637-1373 or toll-free 800-624-3157. Fax: 304-637-1986. E-mail: ssw@davisandelkins.edu. Website: http://www.dewv.edu/.

# DAVIS COLLEGE
## Johnson City, NY

**CONTACT** Stephanie D. Baker, Financial Aid Director, Davis College, 400 Riverside Drive, Johnson City, NY 13790, 607-729-1581 Ext. 401 or toll-free 877-949-3248. Fax: 607-770-6886. E-mail: financialaid@davisny.edu. Website: http://www.davisny.edu/.

# DAYMAR INSTITUTE
## Clarksville, TN

**CONTACT** Financial Aid Office, Daymar Institute, 2691 Trenton Road, Clarksville, TN 37040, 931-552-7600. Website: http://www.daymarinstitute.edu/.

# DAYMAR INSTITUTE
## Murfreesboro, TN

**CONTACT** Financial Aid Office, Daymar Institute, 415 Golden Bear Court, Murfreesboro, TN 37128, 615-217-9347. Website: http://www.daymarinstitute.edu/.

# DEFIANCE COLLEGE
## Defiance, OH

**ABOUT THE INSTITUTION** Independent United Church of Christ, coed. **Awards:** associate, bachelor's, and master's degrees. 33 undergraduate majors. **Total enrollment:** 920. Undergraduates: 824. Freshmen: 233.

**GIFT AID (NEED-BASED) Scholarships, grants, and awards:** Federal Pell, FSEOG, state, private, college/university gift aid from institutional funds.

**GIFT AID (NON-NEED-BASED) Scholarships, grants, and awards by category:** Academic interests/achievement: biological sciences, business, communication, education, English, general academic interests/achievements, health fields, humanities, international studies, mathematics, physical sciences, premedicine, religion/biblical studies, social sciences. Creative arts/performance: applied art and design, music. Special achievements/activities: community service, general special achievements/activities, leadership, religious involvement. Special characteristics: children and siblings of alumni, children of faculty/staff, international students, members of minority groups, out-of-state students, religious affiliation, veterans, veterans' children.

**LOANS Programs:** Federal Direct (Subsidized and Unsubsidized Stafford, PLUS), Perkins, alternative loans.

**WORK-STUDY Federal work-study:** 419 jobs averaging $2441. **State or other work-study/employment:** Total amount: $142,650 (100% non-need-based). 62 part-time jobs averaging $2301.

**APPLYING FOR FINANCIAL AID Required financial aid form:** FAFSA.

**CONTACT** Amy Francis, Director of Financial Aid, Defiance College, 701 North Clinton Street, Defiance, OH 43512-1610, 419-783-2376 or toll-free 800-520-4632. Fax: 419-783-2579. E-mail: afrancis@defiance.edu. Website: http://www.defiance.edu/.

# DELAWARE STATE UNIVERSITY
## Dover, DE

| Tuition & fees (DE res): $7336 | Average undergraduate aid package: $11,479 |
|---|---|

**ABOUT THE INSTITUTION** State-supported, coed. **Awards:** bachelor's, master's, and doctoral degrees. 137 undergraduate majors. **Total enrollment:** 4,397. Undergraduates: 4,012. Freshmen: 894. Federal methodology is used as a basis for awarding need-based institutional aid.

**UNDERGRADUATE EXPENSES for 2015–2016 Application fee:** $35. **Tuition, state resident:** full-time $7336; part-time $272 per credit hour. **Tuition, nonresident:** full-time $15,692; part-time $620 per credit hour. **Required fees:** $300 per term. Full-time tuition and fees vary according to course load. Part-time tuition and fees vary according to course load. **College room and board:** $10,708; **Room only:** $6976. Room and board charges vary according to board plan and housing facility.

**FRESHMAN FINANCIAL AID (Fall 2013)** 882 applied for aid; of those 88% were deemed to have need. 99% of freshmen with need received aid; of those 8% had need fully met. **Average percent of need met:** 72% (excluding resources awarded to replace EFC). **Average financial aid package:** $11,620 (excluding resources awarded to replace EFC). 2% of all full-time freshmen had no need and received non-need-based gift aid.

**UNDERGRADUATE FINANCIAL AID (Fall 2013)** 3,277 applied for aid; of those 90% were deemed to have need. 98% of undergraduates with need received aid; of those 82% had need fully met. **Average percent of need met:** 71% (excluding resources awarded to replace EFC). **Average financial aid package:** $11,479 (excluding resources awarded to replace EFC). 1% of all full-time undergraduates had no need and received non-need-based gift aid.

**GIFT AID (NEED-BASED) Total amount:** $22,213,774 (40% federal, 23% state, 36% institutional, 1% external sources). **Receiving aid:** Freshmen: 57% (514); all full-time undergraduates: 58% (2,088). **Average award:** Freshmen: $5191; Undergraduates: $5011. **Scholarships, grants, and awards:** Federal Pell, FSEOG, state, college/university gift aid from institutional funds, Federal Nursing.

**GIFT AID (NON-NEED-BASED) Receiving aid:** Freshmen: 44% (396). Undergraduates: 29% (1,041). **Average award:** Freshmen: $15,213. Undergraduates: $15,445. **Scholarships, grants, and awards by category:** Academic interests/achievement: general academic interests/achievements. Creative arts/performance: music. Special achievements/activities: general special achievements/activities. Special characteristics: out-of-state students. **Tuition waivers:** Full or partial for employees or children of employees, senior citizens. **ROTC:** Army, Air Force cooperative.

**LOANS Student loans:** $19,640,873 (100% need-based). 89% of past graduating class borrowed through all loan programs. **Average indebtedness per student:** $38,702. **Average need-based loan:** Freshmen: $3270. Undergraduates: $5423. **Parent loans:** $9,894,414 (100% need-based). **Programs:** Federal Direct (Subsidized and Unsubsidized Stafford, PLUS), Perkins, Federal Nursing.

**WORK-STUDY Federal work-study:** jobs available. **State or other work-study/employment:** Part-time jobs available.

**ATHLETIC AWARDS Total amount:** $4,195,091 (100% non-need-based).

**APPLYING FOR FINANCIAL AID Required financial aid form:** FAFSA. **Financial aid deadline (priority):** 3/15. **Notification date:** Continuous beginning 3/1. Students must reply by 7/10.

**CONTACT** Stephen J. Ampersand, Assistant Vice President for Financial Aid Services, Delaware State University, 1200 North DuPont Highway, Dover, DE 19901-2277, 302-857-6250 or toll-free 800-845-2544. *E-mail:* sampersand@desu.edu. *Website:* http://www.desu.edu/.

# DELAWARE VALLEY UNIVERSITY
## Doylestown, PA

| Tuition & fees: N/R | Average undergraduate aid package: $22,896 |
|---|---|

**ABOUT THE INSTITUTION** Independent, coed. 29 undergraduate majors. Federal methodology is used as a basis for awarding need-based institutional aid.

**FRESHMAN FINANCIAL AID (Fall 2014, est.)** 461 applied for aid; of those 89% were deemed to have need. 100% of freshmen with need received aid; of those 11% had need fully met. **Average percent of need met:** 70% (excluding resources awarded to replace EFC). **Average financial aid package:** $24,327 (excluding resources awarded to replace EFC). 15% of all full-time freshmen had no need and received non-need-based gift aid.

**UNDERGRADUATE FINANCIAL AID (Fall 2014, est.)** 1,476 applied for aid; of those 91% were deemed to have need. 100% of undergraduates with need received aid; of those 12% had need fully met. **Average percent of need met:** 68% (excluding resources awarded to replace EFC). **Average financial aid package:** $22,896 (excluding resources awarded to replace EFC). 18% of all full-time undergraduates had no need and received non-need-based gift aid.

**GIFT AID (NEED-BASED) Total amount:** $25,311,496 (9% federal, 6% state, 83% institutional, 2% external sources). **Receiving aid:** Freshmen: 84% (409); all full-time undergraduates: 79% (1,335). **Average award:** Freshmen: $20,538; Undergraduates: $18,901. **Scholarships, grants, and awards:** Federal Pell, FSEOG, state, private, college/university gift aid from institutional funds.

**GIFT AID (NON-NEED-BASED) Total amount:** $5,252,843 (98% institutional, 2% external sources). **Receiving aid:** Freshmen: 8% (38). Undergraduates: 7% (124). **Average award:** Freshmen: $14,957. Undergraduates: $14,380. **Scholarships, grants, and awards by category:** Academic interests/achievement: general academic interests/achievements. Creative arts/performance: general creative arts/performance. Special characteristics: children and siblings of alumni.

**LOANS Student loans:** $14,998,064 (74% need-based, 26% non-need-based). 83% of past graduating class borrowed through all loan programs. **Average indebtedness per student:** $39,671. **Average need-based loan:** Freshmen: $3874. Undergraduates: $4610. **Parent loans:** $6,493,831 (54% need-based, 46% non-need-based). **Programs:** Federal Direct (Subsidized and Unsubsidized Stafford, PLUS), Perkins, alternative loans.

**WORK-STUDY Federal work-study:** Total amount: $210,116; 131 jobs averaging $1262. **State or other work-study/employment:** Part-time jobs available.

**APPLYING FOR FINANCIAL AID Required financial aid forms:** FAFSA, state aid form. **Financial aid deadline:** 4/1. **Notification date:** Continuous beginning 2/15. Students must reply by 5/1 or within 2 weeks of notification.

**CONTACT** Ms. Joan Hock, Director of Student Financial Aid, Delaware Valley University, 700 East Butler Avenue, Doylestown, PA 18901-2697, 215-489-2975 or toll-free 800-2DELVAL. *E-mail:* finaid@delval.edu. *Website:* http://www.delval.edu/.

# DELTA STATE UNIVERSITY
## Cleveland, MS

| Tuition & fees (MS res): $6562 | Average undergraduate aid package: $4288 |
|---|---|

**ABOUT THE INSTITUTION** State-supported, coed. **Awards:** certificates, bachelor's, master's, and doctoral degrees. 38 undergraduate majors. **Total enrollment:** 3,614. Undergraduates: 2,778. Freshmen: 419. Federal methodology is used as a basis for awarding need-based institutional aid.

**UNDERGRADUATE EXPENSES for 2015–2016 Application fee:** $25. **Tuition, state resident:** full-time $6012; part-time $251 per hour. **Tuition, nonresident:** full-time $6012; part-time $251 per hour. **Required fees:** full-time $550; $376 per year. Part-time tuition and fees vary according to course load. **College room and board:** $7200; **Room only:** $7200. Room and board charges vary according to housing facility.

**FRESHMAN FINANCIAL AID (Fall 2014, est.) Average financial aid package:** $4054 (excluding resources awarded to replace EFC).

**UNDERGRADUATE FINANCIAL AID (Fall 2014, est.) Average financial aid package:** $4288 (excluding resources awarded to replace EFC).

**GIFT AID (NEED-BASED) Total amount:** $5,388,598 (97% federal, 3% state). **Receiving aid:** Freshmen: 51% (208); all full-time undergraduates: 51% (1,166). **Average award:** Freshmen: $2590; Undergraduates: $2552. **Scholarships, grants, and awards:** Federal Pell, FSEOG, state, private, college/university gift aid from institutional funds.

**GIFT AID (NON-NEED-BASED) Total amount:** $2,687,416 (30% state, 25% institutional, 45% external sources). **Receiving aid:** Freshmen: 70% (287). Undergraduates: 54% (1,257). **Scholarships, grants, and awards by category:** Academic interests/achievement: biological sciences, business, computer science, education, English, foreign languages, general academic interests/achievements, health fields, humanities, mathematics, physical sciences, premedicine, social sciences. *Creative arts/performance:* art/fine arts, creative writing, journalism/publications, music, performing arts. *Special achievements/activities:* cheerleading/drum major, general special achievements/activities, leadership, memberships. *Special characteristics:* children and siblings of alumni, children of faculty/staff, general special characteristics, out-of-state students. *Tuition waivers:* Full or partial for children of alumni, employees or children of employees, senior citizens. *ROTC:* Army.

**LOANS** *Student loans:* $11,457,361 (46% need-based, 54% non-need-based). *Parent loans:* $769,274 (100% non-need-based). *Programs:* Federal Direct (Subsidized and Unsubsidized Stafford, PLUS), Perkins.

**WORK-STUDY** *Federal work-study:* Total amount: $364,094; 219 jobs averaging $635. *State or other work-study/employment:* Total amount: $311,024 (100% non-need-based). 126 part-time jobs averaging $4348.

**ATHLETIC AWARDS** Total amount: $1,204,200 (100% non-need-based).

**APPLYING FOR FINANCIAL AID** *Required financial aid forms:* FAFSA, institution's own form. *Financial aid deadline (priority):* 3/1. *Notification date:* Continuous beginning 5/1.

**CONTACT** Ms. Christie Rocconi, Director of Student Financial Assistance, Delta State University, Kent Wyatt Hall 144, Highway 8 West, Cleveland, MS 38733-0001, 662-846-4670 or toll-free 800-468-6378. *Fax:* 662-846-4683. *E-mail:* finaid@deltastate.edu. *Website:* http://www.deltastate.edu/.

# DENISON UNIVERSITY
## Granville, OH

| Tuition & fees: $47,290 | Average undergraduate aid package: $40,637 |
|---|---|

**ABOUT THE INSTITUTION** Independent, coed. *Awards:* bachelor's degrees. 38 undergraduate majors. *Total enrollment:* 2,280. Undergraduates: 2,280. Freshmen: 611. Federal methodology is used as a basis for awarding need-based institutional aid.

**UNDERGRADUATE EXPENSES for 2015–2016** *Comprehensive fee:* $58,860 includes full-time tuition ($46,250), mandatory fees ($1040), and room and board ($11,570). *College room only:* $6370. Room and board charges vary according to board plan and housing facility. Part-time tuition and fees vary according to course load.

**FRESHMAN FINANCIAL AID (Fall 2014, est.)** 418 applied for aid; of those 85% were deemed to have need. 100% of freshmen with need received aid; of those 36% had need fully met. *Average percent of need met:* 97% (excluding resources awarded to replace EFC). *Average financial aid package:* $41,384 (excluding resources awarded to replace EFC). 40% of all full-time freshmen had no need and received non-need-based gift aid.

**UNDERGRADUATE FINANCIAL AID (Fall 2014, est.)** 1,384 applied for aid; of those 87% were deemed to have need. 100% of undergraduates with need received aid; of those 36% had need fully met. *Average percent of need met:* 96% (excluding resources awarded to replace EFC). *Average financial aid package:* $40,637 (excluding resources awarded to replace EFC). 44% of all full-time undergraduates had no need and received non-need-based gift aid.

**GIFT AID (NEED-BASED)** *Total amount:* $21,418,758 (10% federal, 1% state, 89% institutional). *Receiving aid:* Freshmen: 58% (357); all full-time undergraduates: 53% (1,202). *Average award:* Freshmen: $36,053; Undergraduates: $34,254. *Scholarships, grants, and awards:* Federal Pell, FSEOG, state, private, college/university gift aid from institutional funds.

**GIFT AID (NON-NEED-BASED)** *Total amount:* $39,154,640 (98% institutional, 2% external sources). *Receiving aid:* Freshmen: 55% (336). Undergraduates: 49% (1,115). *Average award:* Freshmen: $22,114. Undergraduates: $18,537. *Scholarships, grants, and awards by category:* Academic interests/achievement: biological sciences, English, foreign languages, mathematics, physical sciences. *Special characteristics:* children of faculty/staff, veterans. *Tuition waivers:* Full or partial for employees or children of employees. *ROTC:* Army cooperative.

**LOANS** *Student loans:* $9,126,806 (100% need-based). *Average need-based loan:* Freshmen: $4320. Undergraduates: $5127. *Parent loans:* $3,495,728 (100% non-need-based). *Programs:* Federal Direct (Subsidized and Unsubsidized Stafford, PLUS), Perkins, college/university.

**WORK-STUDY** *Federal work-study:* Total amount: $1,197,219; jobs available. *State or other work-study/employment:* Part-time jobs available.

**APPLYING FOR FINANCIAL AID** *Required financial aid form:* FAFSA. *Financial aid deadline (priority):* 3/15. *Notification date:* Continuous beginning 3/28. Students must reply within 2 weeks of notification.

**CONTACT** Ms. Nancy Hoover, Director of Financial Aid, Denison University, PO Box M, Granville, OH 43023-0613, 740-587-6279 or toll-free 800-DENISON. *Fax:* 740-587-5706. *E-mail:* hoover@denison.edu. *Website:* http://www.denison.edu/.

# DENVER SCHOOL OF NURSING
## Denver, CO

**CONTACT** Financial Aid Office, Denver School of Nursing, 1401 19th Street, Denver, CO 80202, 303-292-0015 or toll-free 888-479-5550. *Website:* http://www.denverschoolofnursing.edu/.

# DEPAUL UNIVERSITY
## Chicago, IL

| Tuition & fees: $35,071 | Average undergraduate aid package: $21,294 |
|---|---|

**ABOUT THE INSTITUTION** Independent Roman Catholic, coed. *Awards:* certificates, bachelor's, master's, and doctoral degrees. 107 undergraduate majors. *Total enrollment:* 23,799. Undergraduates: 16,153. Freshmen: 2,544. Federal methodology is used as a basis for awarding need-based institutional aid.

**UNDERGRADUATE EXPENSES for 2015–2016** *Application fee:* $25. *Comprehensive fee:* $47,623 includes full-time tuition ($34,390), mandatory fees ($681), and room and board ($12,552). *College room only:* $9027. Full-time tuition and fees vary according to course load and program. Room and board charges vary according to board plan, housing facility, and location. *Part-time tuition:* $570 per credit hour. Part-time tuition and fees vary according to course load and program.

**FRESHMAN FINANCIAL AID (Fall 2013)** 2,110 applied for aid; of those 85% were deemed to have need. 99% of freshmen with need received aid; of those 13% had need fully met. *Average percent of need met:* 66% (excluding resources awarded to replace EFC). *Average financial aid package:* $23,440 (excluding resources awarded to replace EFC). 21% of all full-time freshmen had no need and received non-need-based gift aid.

**UNDERGRADUATE FINANCIAL AID (Fall 2013)** 10,613 applied for aid; of those 90% were deemed to have need. 99% of undergraduates with need received aid; of those 12% had need fully met. *Average percent of need met:* 61% (excluding resources awarded to replace EFC). *Average financial aid package:* $21,294 (excluding resources awarded to replace EFC). 14% of all full-time undergraduates had no need and received non-need-based gift aid.

**GIFT AID (NEED-BASED)** *Total amount:* $110,900,000 (27% federal, 18% state, 55% institutional). *Receiving aid:* Freshmen: 63% (1,527); all full-time undergraduates: 60% (8,111). *Average award:* Freshmen: $11,204; Undergraduates: $12,719. *Scholarships, grants, and awards:* Federal Pell, FSEOG, state, private, college/university gift aid from institutional funds, TEACH Grants, Veteran Awards.

**GIFT AID (NON-NEED-BASED)** *Total amount:* $78,000,000 (97% institutional, 3% external sources). *Receiving aid:* Freshmen: 67% (1,634). Undergraduates: 41% (5,610). *Average award:* Freshmen: $10,941. Undergraduates: $10,011. *Scholarships, grants, and awards by category:* Academic interests/achievement: general academic interests/achievements. Creative arts/performance: art/fine arts, music, performing arts, theater/drama. *Special achievements/activities:* community service, leadership. *Special characteristics:* children of faculty/staff, local/state students, veterans, veterans' children. *Tuition waivers:* Full or partial for employees or children of employees. *ROTC:* Army.

**LOANS** *Student loans:* $70,900,000 (54% need-based, 46% non-need-based). 60% of past graduating class borrowed through all loan programs. *Average indebtedness per student:* $27,498. *Average need-based loan:* Freshmen: $3422. Undergraduates: $4558. *Parent loans:* $53,700,000 (100% non-need-based). *Programs:* Federal Direct (Subsidized and Unsubsidized Stafford, PLUS), Perkins, private loans.

**WORK-STUDY** *Federal work-study:* 471 jobs averaging $3132. *State or other work-study/employment:* Total amount: $6,900,000 (59% need-based, 41% non-need-based). 2,568 part-time jobs averaging $3101.

**ATHLETIC AWARDS** Total amount: $5,400,000 (100% non-need-based).

APPLYING FOR FINANCIAL AID *Required financial aid form:* FAFSA. *Financial aid deadline (priority):* 2/15. *Notification date:* Continuous beginning 3/15. Students must reply by 5/1 or within 4 weeks of notification.
CONTACT DePaul Central, Office of Financial Aid, DePaul University, 1 East Jackson Boulevard, Chicago, IL 60604-2287, 312-362-8610 or toll-free 800-4DE-PAUL (out-of-state). *Fax:* 312-362-5748.
*Website:* http://www.depaul.edu/.

# DEPAUW UNIVERSITY
## Greencastle, IN

| Tuition & fees: $42,746 | Average undergraduate aid package: $35,694 |
|---|---|

ABOUT THE INSTITUTION Independent United Methodist Church, coed. *Awards:* bachelor's degrees. 45 undergraduate majors. *Total enrollment:* 2,216. Undergraduates: 2,216. Freshmen: 514. Both federal and institutional methodology are used as a basis for awarding need-based institutional aid.
UNDERGRADUATE EXPENSES for 2015–2016 *Application fee:* $40. *Comprehensive fee:* $53,946 includes full-time tuition ($42,050), mandatory fees ($696), and room and board ($11,200). Room and board charges vary according to board plan. *Part-time tuition:* $1314.06 per credit hour.
FRESHMAN FINANCIAL AID (Fall 2014, est.) 419 applied for aid; of those 79% were deemed to have need. 100% of freshmen with need received aid; of those 33% had need fully met. *Average percent of need met:* 89% (excluding resources awarded to replace EFC). *Average financial aid package:* $35,220 (excluding resources awarded to replace EFC). 34% of all full-time freshmen had no need and received non-need-based gift aid.
UNDERGRADUATE FINANCIAL AID (Fall 2014, est.) 1,389 applied for aid; of those 86% were deemed to have need. 100% of undergraduates with need received aid; of those 27% had need fully met. *Average percent of need met:* 89% (excluding resources awarded to replace EFC). *Average financial aid package:* $35,694 (excluding resources awarded to replace EFC). 42% of all full-time undergraduates had no need and received non-need-based gift aid.
GIFT AID (NEED-BASED) *Total amount:* $35,884,646 (5% federal, 3% state, 86% institutional, 6% external sources). *Receiving aid:* Freshmen: 65% (332); all full-time undergraduates: 55% (1,198). *Average award:* Freshmen: $31,067; Undergraduates: $30,895. *Scholarships, grants, and awards:* Federal Pell, FSEOG, state, private, college/university gift aid from institutional funds.
GIFT AID (NON-NEED-BASED) *Total amount:* $18,568,562 (92% institutional, 8% external sources). *Receiving aid:* Freshmen: 16% (80). Undergraduates: 11% (233). *Average award:* Freshmen: $16,702. Undergraduates: $16,764. *Scholarships, grants, and awards by category:* Academic interests/achievement: general academic interests/achievements. *Special achievements/activities:* community service. *Special characteristics:* children and siblings of alumni. *Tuition waivers:* Full or partial for employees or children of employees. *ROTC:* Army cooperative, Air Force cooperative.
LOANS *Student loans:* $11,185,553 (61% need-based, 39% non-need-based). 51% of past graduating class borrowed through all loan programs. *Average indebtedness per student:* $27,005. *Average need-based loan:* Freshmen: $4173. Undergraduates: $4752. *Parent loans:* $4,060,359 (27% need-based, 73% non-need-based). *Programs:* Federal Direct (Subsidized and Unsubsidized Stafford, PLUS), Perkins, college/university.
WORK-STUDY *Federal work-study:* Total amount: $947,283; jobs available. *State or other work-study/employment:* Total amount: $948,498 (34% need-based, 66% non-need-based). Part-time jobs available.
APPLYING FOR FINANCIAL AID *Required financial aid forms:* FAFSA, CSS Financial Aid PROFILE. *Financial aid deadline:* 2/1 (priority: 1/15). *Notification date:* 3/15. Students must reply by 5/1.
CONTACT Craig Slaughter, Director of Financial Aid, DePauw University, 200 East Seminary, Greencastle, IN 46135-0037, 765-658-4030 or toll-free 800-447-2495. *Fax:* 765-658-4137. *E-mail:* financialaid@depauw.edu.
*Website:* http://www.depauw.edu/.

# DESALES UNIVERSITY
## Center Valley, PA

| Tuition & fees: $32,350 | Average undergraduate aid package: $23,059 |
|---|---|

ABOUT THE INSTITUTION Independent Roman Catholic, coed. *Awards:* certificates, bachelor's, master's, and doctoral degrees. 43 undergraduate majors. *Total enrollment:* 3,198. Undergraduates: 2,381. Freshmen: 408. Federal methodology is used as a basis for awarding need-based institutional aid.
UNDERGRADUATE EXPENSES for 2015–2016 *Application fee:* $30. *Comprehensive fee:* $44,110 includes full-time tuition ($31,000), mandatory fees ($1350), and room and board ($11,760). Full-time tuition and fees vary according to class time and course load. Room and board charges vary according to board plan and housing facility. *Part-time tuition:* $1290 per credit hour. *Part-time fees:* $446 per credit hour. Part-time tuition and fees vary according to class time and course load.
FRESHMAN FINANCIAL AID (Fall 2014, est.) 386 applied for aid; of those 90% were deemed to have need. 100% of freshmen with need received aid; of those 22% had need fully met. *Average percent of need met:* 71% (excluding resources awarded to replace EFC). *Average financial aid package:* $25,398 (excluding resources awarded to replace EFC). 14% of all full-time freshmen had no need and received non-need-based gift aid.
UNDERGRADUATE FINANCIAL AID (Fall 2014, est.) 1,570 applied for aid; of those 92% were deemed to have need. 99% of undergraduates with need received aid; of those 19% had need fully met. *Average percent of need met:* 67% (excluding resources awarded to replace EFC). *Average financial aid package:* $23,059 (excluding resources awarded to replace EFC). 14% of all full-time undergraduates had no need and received non-need-based gift aid.
GIFT AID (NEED-BASED) *Total amount:* $24,196,994 (13% federal, 8% state, 78% institutional, 1% external sources). *Receiving aid:* Freshmen: 86% (349); all full-time undergraduates: 76% (1,358). *Average award:* Freshmen: $20,398; Undergraduates: $17,738. *Scholarships, grants, and awards:* Federal Pell, FSEOG, state, private, college/university gift aid from institutional funds.
GIFT AID (NON-NEED-BASED) *Total amount:* $3,894,914 (3% federal, 92% institutional, 5% external sources). *Receiving aid:* Freshmen: 81% (330). Undergraduates: 63% (1,127). *Average award:* Freshmen: $13,014. Undergraduates: $11,076. *Scholarships, grants, and awards by category:* Academic interests/achievement: 1,558 awards ($7,833,499 total): biological sciences, business, communication, computer science, education, English, foreign languages, general academic interests/achievements, health fields, humanities, mathematics, physical sciences, premedicine, religion/biblical studies, social sciences. Creative arts/performance: 209 awards ($375,568 total): cinema/film/broadcasting, dance, performing arts, theater/drama. *Special achievements/activities:* community service. *Tuition waivers:* Full or partial for employees or children of employees, adult students, senior citizens. *ROTC:* Army cooperative.
LOANS *Student loans:* $18,931,433 (74% need-based, 26% non-need-based). 82% of past graduating class borrowed through all loan programs. *Average indebtedness per student:* $36,798. *Average need-based loan:* Freshmen: $3541. Undergraduates: $4655. *Parent loans:* $3,969,349 (45% need-based, 55% non-need-based). *Programs:* Federal Direct (Subsidized and Unsubsidized Stafford, PLUS), Perkins, Federal Nursing.
WORK-STUDY *Federal work-study:* Total amount: $880,503; 521 jobs averaging $1951. *State or other work-study/employment:* Total amount: $497,337 (13% need-based, 87% non-need-based). 293 part-time jobs averaging $1948.
APPLYING FOR FINANCIAL AID *Required financial aid forms:* FAFSA, state aid form, PHEAA form (PA residents only). *Financial aid deadline:* 5/1 (priority: 2/15). *Notification date:* Continuous beginning 2/15. Students must reply by 5/1 or within 2 weeks of notification.
CONTACT Mrs. Joyce Farmer, Director of Financial Aid, DeSales University, 2755 Station Avenue, Center Valley, PA 18034-9568, 610-282-1100 Ext. 1208 or toll-free 877-4-333725 (in-state), 877-4-33725 (out-of-state). *Fax:* 610-282-0131. *E-mail:* joyce.farmer@desales.edu.
*Website:* http://www.desales.edu/.

# DESIGN INSTITUTE OF SAN DIEGO
## San Diego, CA

**CONTACT** Financial Aid Office, Design Institute of San Diego, 8555 Commerce Avenue, San Diego, CA 92121, 858-566-1200 or toll-free 800-619-4337. *Website:* http://www.disd.edu/.

# DEVRY COLLEGE OF NEW YORK
## New York, NY

**CONTACT** Elvira Senese, Dean of Student Finance, DeVry College of New York, 30-20 Thomson Avenue, Long Island City, NY 11101, 718-472-2728 or toll-free 866-338-7941. *Fax:* 718-269-4284. *Website:* http://www.devry.edu/.

# DEVRY UNIVERSITY
## Mesa, AZ

**CONTACT** Financial Aid Office, DeVry University, 1201 South Alma School Road, Suite 5450, Mesa, AZ 85210-2011, 480-827-1511 or toll-free 866-338-7941. *Website:* http://www.devry.edu/.

# DEVRY UNIVERSITY
## Phoenix, AZ

**CONTACT** Student Finance Office, DeVry University, 2149 West Dunlap Avenue, Phoenix, AZ 85021-2995, 602-749-4545 or toll-free 866-338-7941. *Website:* http://www.devry.edu/.

# DEVRY UNIVERSITY
## Alhambra, CA

**CONTACT** Financial Aid Office, DeVry University, 1000 S. Freemont Avenue, Building A-11, Alhambra, CA 91803, 626-293-4300 or toll-free 866-338-7941. *Website:* http://www.devry.edu/.

# DEVRY UNIVERSITY
## Anaheim, CA

**CONTACT** Financial Aid Office, DeVry University, 1900 South State College Boulevard, Suite 150, Anaheim, CA 92806-6136, 714-935-3200 or toll-free 866-338-7941. *Website:* http://www.devry.edu/.

# DEVRY UNIVERSITY
## Bakersfield, CA

**CONTACT** Financial Aid Office, DeVry University, 3000 Ming Avenue, Bakersfield, CA 93304-4136, 661-833-7120 or toll-free 866-338-7941. *Website:* http://www.devry.edu/.

# DEVRY UNIVERSITY
## Fremont, CA

**CONTACT** Kim Kane, Director of Student Finance, DeVry University, 6600 Dumbarton Circle, Fremont, CA 94555, 510-574-1100 or toll-free 866-338-7941. *Fax:* 510-742-0868. *Website:* http://www.devry.edu/.

# DEVRY UNIVERSITY
## Long Beach, CA

**CONTACT** Kathy Odom, Director of Financial Aid, DeVry University, 3880 Kilroy Airport Way, Long Beach, CA 90806, 562-427-0861 or toll-free 866-338-7941. *Fax:* 562-989-1578. *Website:* http://www.devry.edu/.

# DEVRY UNIVERSITY
## Oakland, CA

**CONTACT** Financial Aid Office, DeVry University, 505 14th Street, Suite 100, Oakland, CA 94612, 866-473-3879 or toll-free 866-338-7941. *Website:* http://www.devry.edu/.

# DEVRY UNIVERSITY
## Oxnard, CA

**CONTACT** Financial Aid Office, DeVry University, 300 E. Esplanade Drive, Suite 100, Oxnard, CA 93036, 805-604-3350 or toll-free 866-338-7941. *Website:* http://www.devry.edu/.

# DEVRY UNIVERSITY
## Palmdale, CA

**CONTACT** Ann Logan, Dean of Student Finance, DeVry University, 22801 Roscoe Boulevard, West Hills, CA 91304, 818-932-3001 or toll-free 866-338-7941. *Fax:* 818-932-3131. *Website:* http://www.devry.edu/.

# DEVRY UNIVERSITY
## Pomona, CA

**CONTACT** Student Finance Office, DeVry University, 901 Corporate Center Drive, Pomona, CA 91768-2642, 909-622-8866 or toll-free 866-338-7941. *Website:* http://www.devry.edu/.

# DEVRY UNIVERSITY
## San Diego, CA

**CONTACT** Financial Aid Office, DeVry University, 2655 Camino Del Rio North, Suite 350, San Diego, CA 92108-1633, 619-683-2446 or toll-free 866-338-7941. *Website:* http://www.devry.edu/.

## DEVRY UNIVERSITY
### Sherman Oaks, CA

**CONTACT** Financial Aid Office, DeVry University, 15301 Ventura Boulevard, D-100, Sherman Oaks, CA 91403, 888-610-0800 or toll-free 866-338-7941.
*Website:* http://www.devry.edu/.

## DEVRY UNIVERSITY
### Colorado Springs, CO

**CONTACT** Carol Oppman, Director of Financial Aid, DeVry University, 225 South Union Boulevard, Colorado Springs, CO 80910, 719-632-3000 or toll-free 866-338-7941. *Fax:* 719-632-1909.
*Website:* http://www.devry.edu/.

## DEVRY UNIVERSITY
### Westminster, CO

**CONTACT** Office of Financial Aid, DeVry University, 1870 West 122nd Avenue, Westminster, CO 80234-2010, 303-280-7400 or toll-free 866-338-7941.
*Website:* http://www.devry.edu/.

## DEVRY UNIVERSITY
### Jacksonville, FL

**CONTACT** Financial Aid Office, DeVry University, 5200 Belfort Road, Suite 175, Jacksonville, FL 32256-6040.
*Website:* http://www.devry.edu/.

## DEVRY UNIVERSITY
### Miramar, FL

**CONTACT** Office of Financial Aid, DeVry University, 2300 Southwest 145th Avenue, Miramar, FL 33027, 954-499-9700 or toll-free 866-338-7941.
*Website:* http://www.devry.edu/.

## DEVRY UNIVERSITY
### Orlando, FL

**CONTACT** Estrella Velazquez-Domenech, Director of Student Finance, DeVry University, 4000 Millenia Boulevard, Orlando, FL 32839, 407-345-2816 or toll-free 866-338-7941. *Fax:* 407-355-4855.
*Website:* http://www.devry.edu/.

## DEVRY UNIVERSITY
### Alpharetta, GA

**CONTACT** David Pickett, Assistant Director of Financial Aid, DeVry University, 2555 Northwinds Parkway, Alpharetta, GA 30004, 770-521-4900 or toll-free 866-338-7941. *Fax:* 770-664-8024.
*Website:* http://www.devry.edu/.

## DEVRY UNIVERSITY
### Decatur, GA

**CONTACT** Student Finance Office, DeVry University, 1 West Court Square, Suite 100, Decatur, GA 30030-2556, 404-270-2702 or toll-free 866-338-7941.
*Website:* http://www.devry.edu/.

## DEVRY UNIVERSITY
### Duluth, GA

**CONTACT** Financial Aid Office, DeVry University, 3505 Koger Boulevard, Suite 170, Duluth, GA 30096-7671, 678-380-9780 or toll-free 866-338-7941.
*Website:* http://www.devry.edu/.

## DEVRY UNIVERSITY
### Addison, IL

**CONTACT** Sejal Amin, Director of Student Finance, DeVry University, 1221 North Swift Road, Addison, IL 60101-6106, 630-953-1300 or toll-free 866-338-7941.
*Website:* http://www.devry.edu/.

## DEVRY UNIVERSITY
### Chicago, IL

**CONTACT** Milena Dobrina, Director of Financial Aid, DeVry University, 3300 North Campbell Avenue, Chicago, IL 60618-5994, 773-929-8500 or toll-free 866-338-7941. *Fax:* 773-348-1780.
*Website:* http://www.devry.edu/.

## DEVRY UNIVERSITY
### Downers Grove, IL

**CONTACT** Financial Aid Office, DeVry University, 3005 Highland Parkway, Suite 100, Downers Grove, IL 60515, 630-515-3000 or toll-free 866-338-7941.
*Website:* http://www.devry.edu/.

## DEVRY UNIVERSITY
### Elgin, IL

**CONTACT** Financial Aid Office, DeVry University, Randall Point, 2250 Point Boulevard, Suite 250, Elgin, IL 60123, 847-649-3980 or toll-free 866-338-7941.
*Website:* http://www.devry.edu/.

## DEVRY UNIVERSITY
### Gurnee, IL

**CONTACT** Financial Aid Office, DeVry University, 1075 Tri-State Parkway, Suite 800, Gurnee, IL 60031-9126, 847-855-2649 or toll-free 866-338-7941.
*Website:* http://www.devry.edu/.

## DEVRY UNIVERSITY
### Naperville, IL

**CONTACT** Financial Aid Office, DeVry University, 2056 Westings Avenue, Suite 40, Naperville, IL 60563-2361, 630-428-9086 or toll-free 866-338-7941.
*Website:* http://www.devry.edu/.

## DEVRY UNIVERSITY
### Tinley Park, IL

**CONTACT** Director of Student Finance, DeVry University, 18624 West Creek Drive, Tinley Park, IL 60477, 708-342-3300 or toll-free 866-338-7941. *Fax:* 708-342-3120.
*Website:* http://www.devry.edu/.

## DEVRY UNIVERSITY
### Merrillville, IN

**CONTACT** Financial Aid Office, DeVry University, 100 East 80th Place, Suite 222 Mall, Merrillville, IN 46410-5673, 219-736-7440 or toll-free 866-338-7941.
*Website:* http://www.devry.edu/.

## DEVRY UNIVERSITY
### Louisville, KY

**CONTACT** Financial Aid Office, DeVry University, 10172 Linn Station Road, Suite 300, Louisville, KY 40223 or toll-free 866-338-7941.
*Website:* http://www.devry.edu/.

## DEVRY UNIVERSITY
### Bethesda, MD

**CONTACT** Financial Aid Office, DeVry University, 4550 Montgomery Avenue, Suite 100 North, Bethesda, MD 20814-3304, 301-652-8477 or toll-free 866-338-7941.
*Website:* http://www.devry.edu/.

## DEVRY UNIVERSITY
### Kansas City, MO

**CONTACT** Maureen Kelly, Senior Associate Director of Financial Aid, DeVry University, 11224 Holmes Street, Kansas City, MO 64131-3698, 816-941-0430 or toll-free 866-338-7941.
*Website:* http://www.devry.edu/.

## DEVRY UNIVERSITY
### Kansas City, MO

**CONTACT** Financial Aid Office, DeVry University, City Center Square, 1100 Main Street, Suite 118, Kansas City, MO 64105-2112, 816-221-1300 or toll-free 866-338-7941.
*Website:* http://www.devry.edu/.

## DEVRY UNIVERSITY
### Henderson, NV

**CONTACT** Financial Aid Office, DeVry University, 2490 Paseo Verde Parkway, Suite 150, Henderson, NV 89074-7120, 702-933-9700 or toll-free 866-338-7941.
*Website:* http://www.devry.edu/.

## DEVRY UNIVERSITY
### North Brunswick, NJ

**CONTACT** Student Finance Office, DeVry University, 630 U.S. Highway 1, North Brunswick, NJ 08902, 732-729-3777 or toll-free 866-338-7941.
*Website:* http://www.devry.edu/.

## DEVRY UNIVERSITY
### Paramus, NJ

**CONTACT** Financial Aid Office, DeVry University, 35 Plaza, 81 East State Route 4, Suite 102, Paramus, NJ 07652, 201-556-2840 or toll-free 866-338-7941.
*Website:* http://www.devry.edu/.

## DEVRY UNIVERSITY
### Charlotte, NC

**CONTACT** Financial Aid Office, DeVry University, 2015 Ayrsley Town Boulevard, Suite 109, Charlotte, NC 28273-4068, 704-362-2345 or toll-free 866-338-7941.
*Website:* http://www.devry.edu/.

## DEVRY UNIVERSITY
### Columbus, OH

**CONTACT** Student Finance Office, DeVry University, 1350 Alum Creek Drive, Columbus, OH 43209-2705, 614-253-7291 or toll-free 866-338-7941. *Fax:* 614-252-4108.
*Website:* http://www.devry.edu/.

## DEVRY UNIVERSITY
### Seven Hills, OH

**CONTACT** Financial Aid Office, DeVry University, 4141 Rockside Road, Seven Hills, OH 44131, 216-328-8754 or toll-free 866-338-7941.
*Website:* http://www.devry.edu/.

## DEVRY UNIVERSITY
### Oklahoma City, OK

**CONTACT** Financial Aid Office, DeVry University, Lakepointe Towers, 4013 Northwest Expressway Street, Suite 100, Oklahoma City, OK 73116, 405-767-9516 or toll-free 866-338-7941.
*Website:* http://www.devry.edu/.

## DEVRY UNIVERSITY
### Fort Washington, PA

**CONTACT** Financial Aid Office, DeVry University, 1140 Virginia Drive, Fort Washington, PA 19034, 215-591-5700 or toll-free 866-338-7941.
*Website:* http://www.devry.edu/.

## DEVRY UNIVERSITY
### King of Prussia, PA

**CONTACT** Financial Aid Office, DeVry University, 150 Allendale Road, Suite 3250, King of Prussia, PA 19406-2926, 610-205-3130 or toll-free 866-338-7941.
*Website:* http://www.devry.edu/.

## DEVRY UNIVERSITY
### Philadelphia, PA

**CONTACT** Financial Aid Office, DeVry University, Philadelphia Downtown Center, 1800 JFK Boulevard, Suite 200, Philadelphia, PA 19103-7421 or toll-free 866-338-7941.
*Website:* http://www.devry.edu/.

## DEVRY UNIVERSITY
### Nashville, TN

**CONTACT** Financial Aid Office, DeVry University, 3343 Perimeter Hill Drive, Suite 200, Nashville, TN 37211-4147, 615-445-3456 or toll free 866-338-7941.
*Website:* http://www.devry.edu/.

## DEVRY UNIVERSITY
### Irving, TX

**CONTACT** Student Finance Office, DeVry University, 4800 Regent Boulevard, Irving, TX 75063-2440, 972-929-9310 or toll-free 866-338-7941.
*Website:* http://www.devry.edu/.

## DEVRY UNIVERSITY
### San Antonio, TX

**CONTACT** Financial Aid Office, DeVry University, 618 NW Loop, Suite 202, San Antonio, TX 78216, 210-524-5400.
*Website:* http://www.devry.edu/.

## DEVRY UNIVERSITY
### Sandy, UT

**CONTACT** Financial Aid Office, DeVry University, 9350 South 150 E, Suite 420, Sandy, UT 84070, 801-565-5110 or toll-free 866-338-7941.
*Website:* http://www.devry.edu/.

## DEVRY UNIVERSITY
### Arlington, VA

**CONTACT** Roberta McDevitt, Director of Student Finance, DeVry University, 2341 Jefferson Davis Highway, Arlington, VA 22202, 866-338-7932 or toll-free 866-338-7941. *Fax:* 703-414-4040.
*Website:* http://www.devry.edu/.

## DEVRY UNIVERSITY
### Chesapeake, VA

**CONTACT** Financial Aid Office, DeVry University, 1317 Executive Boulevard, Suite 100, Chesapeake, VA 23320-3671, 757-382-5680 or toll-free 866-338-7941.
*Website:* http://www.devry.edu/.

## DEVRY UNIVERSITY
### Manassas, VA

**CONTACT** Financial Aid Office, DeVry University, 10432 Balls Ford Road, Suite 130, Manassas, VA 20109-3173, 703-396-6611 or toll-free 866-338-7941.
*Website:* http://www.devry.edu/.

## DEVRY UNIVERSITY ONLINE
### Addison, IL

**CONTACT** Financial Aid Office, DeVry University Online, 1221 North Swift Road, Addison, IL 60101-6106 or toll-free 866-338-7941.
*Website:* http://www.devry.edu/.

## DEWEY UNIVERSITY–CAROLINA
### Carolina, PR

**CONTACT** Financial Aid Office, Dewey University–Carolina, Carr. #3, Km. 11, Parque Industrial de Carolina, Lote 7, Carolina, PR 00986, 787-769-1515.
*Website:* http://www.dewey.edu/.

## DEWEY UNIVERSITY–HATO REY
### Hato Rey, PR

**CONTACT** Financial Aid Office, Dewey University–Hato Rey, 427 Avenida Barbosa, Hato Rey, PR 00910-9538, 787-753-0039.
*Website:* http://www.dewey.edu/.

## DEWEY UNIVERSITY–JUANA DIAZ
### Juana Diaz, PR

**CONTACT** Financial Aid Office, Dewey University–Juana Diaz, Carr. 149, Km. 55.9, Parque Industrial Lomas, Juana Diaz, PR 00910, 787-260-1023 Ext.0.
*Website:* http://www.dewey.edu/.

# DEWEY UNIVERSITY–MANATI
## Manati, PR

**CONTACT** Financial Aid Office, Dewey University–Manati, Road 604, Km. 49.1 Barrio Tierras Nuevas, Salientes, Manati, PR 00674, 787-854-3800 or toll-free 866-773-3939.
*Website:* http://www.dewey.edu/.

# DICKINSON COLLEGE
## Carlisle, PA

| Tuition & fees: $47,692 | Average undergraduate aid package: $38,290 |
| --- | --- |

**ABOUT THE INSTITUTION** Independent, coed. *Awards:* bachelor's degrees. 43 undergraduate majors. *Total enrollment:* 2,364. Undergraduates: 2,364. Freshmen: 618. Both federal and institutional methodology are used as a basis for awarding need-based institutional aid.

**UNDERGRADUATE EXPENSES** for 2015–2016 *Application fee:* $65. *One-time required fee:* $25. *Comprehensive fee:* $59,664 includes full-time tuition ($47,242), mandatory fees ($450), and room and board ($11,972). *College room only:* $6174. Room and board charges vary according to board plan and housing facility. *Part-time tuition:* $5910 per course. *Part-time fees:* $56 per course.

**FRESHMAN FINANCIAL AID (Fall 2014, est.)** 422 applied for aid; of those 84% were deemed to have need. 99% of freshmen with need received aid; of those 68% had need fully met. *Average percent of need met:* 99% (excluding resources awarded to replace EFC). *Average financial aid package:* $38,630 (excluding resources awarded to replace EFC). 15% of all full-time freshmen had no need and received non-need-based gift aid.

**UNDERGRADUATE FINANCIAL AID (Fall 2014, est.)** 1,420 applied for aid; of those 90% were deemed to have need. 99% of undergraduates with need received aid; of those 58% had need fully met. *Average percent of need met:* 96% (excluding resources awarded to replace EFC). *Average financial aid package:* $38,290 (excluding resources awarded to replace EFC). 15% of all full-time undergraduates had no need and received non-need-based gift aid.

**GIFT AID (NEED-BASED)** *Total amount:* $40,299,784 (4% federal, 1% state, 93% institutional, 2% external sources). *Receiving aid:* Freshmen: 55% (341); all full-time undergraduates: 53% (1,228). *Average award:* Freshmen: $33,363; Undergraduates: $32,786. *Scholarships, grants, and awards:* Federal Pell, FSEOG, state, private, college/university gift aid from institutional funds.

**GIFT AID (NON-NEED-BASED)** *Total amount:* $6,176,211 (27% federal, 63% institutional, 10% external sources). *Receiving aid:* Freshmen: 6% (37). Undergraduates: 4% (102). *Average award:* Freshmen: $9044. Undergraduates: $10,151. *Scholarships, grants, and awards by category: Academic interests/achievement:* 813 awards ($12,278,732 total): general academic interests/achievements, military science. *Special characteristics:* 45 awards ($1,200,065 total): children and siblings of alumni, children of faculty/staff, veterans, veterans' children. *Tuition waivers:* Full or partial for employees or children of employees, senior citizens. *ROTC:* Army.

**LOANS** *Student loans:* $8,943,232 (71% need-based, 29% non-need-based). 57% of past graduating class borrowed through all loan programs. *Average indebtedness per student:* $25,392. *Average need-based loan:* Freshmen: $4479. Undergraduates: $5001. *Parent loans:* $3,946,757 (25% need-based, 75% non-need-based). *Programs:* Federal Direct (Subsidized and Unsubsidized Stafford, PLUS), Perkins, college/university.

**WORK-STUDY** *Federal work-study:* Total amount: $2,153,204; 931 jobs averaging $2313. *State or other work-study/employment:* Total amount: $599,942 (72% need-based, 28% non-need-based). 152 part-time jobs averaging $3947.

**APPLYING FOR FINANCIAL AID** *Required financial aid forms:* FAFSA, CSS Financial Aid PROFILE, state aid form, noncustodial (divorced/separated) parent's statement. *Financial aid deadline:* 2/1 (priority: 11/15). *Notification date:* 3/20. Students must reply by 5/1 or within 2 weeks of notification.

**CONTACT** Rick A. Heckman, Director of Financial Aid, Dickinson College, PO Box 1773, Carlisle, PA 17013-2896, 717-245-1308 or toll-free 800-644-1773. *Fax:* 717-245-1972. *E-mail:* finaid@dickinson.edu.
*Website:* http://www.dickinson.edu/.

# DICKINSON STATE UNIVERSITY
## Dickinson, ND

| Tuition & fees (ND res): $6050 | Average undergraduate aid package: $13,818 |
| --- | --- |

**ABOUT THE INSTITUTION** State-supported, coed. *Awards:* certificates, associate, and bachelor's degrees. 43 undergraduate majors. *Total enrollment:* 1,479. Undergraduates: 1,475. Freshmen: 193. Federal methodology is used as a basis for awarding need-based institutional aid.

**UNDERGRADUATE EXPENSES** for 2015–2016 *Application fee:* $35. *Tuition, state resident:* full-time $4891; part-time $203.78 per credit. *Tuition, nonresident:* full-time $7337; part-time $305.66 per credit. *Required fees:* full-time $1159; $48.31 per credit or $48.31 per credit. Full-time tuition and fees vary according to course load, location, program, and reciprocity agreements. Part-time tuition and fees vary according to course load, location, program, and reciprocity agreements. *College room and board:* $5850; *Room only:* $2400. Room and board charges vary according to board plan.

**FRESHMAN FINANCIAL AID (Fall 2014, est.)** 162 applied for aid; of those 64% were deemed to have need. 97% of freshmen with need received aid; of those 43% had need fully met. *Average percent of need met:* 67% (excluding resources awarded to replace EFC). *Average financial aid package:* $15,301 (excluding resources awarded to replace EFC). 22% of all full-time freshmen had no need and received non-need-based gift aid.

**UNDERGRADUATE FINANCIAL AID (Fall 2014, est.)** 729 applied for aid; of those 72% were deemed to have need. 97% of undergraduates with need received aid; of those 39% had need fully met. *Average percent of need met:* 46% (excluding resources awarded to replace EFC). *Average financial aid package:* $13,818 (excluding resources awarded to replace EFC). 23% of all full-time undergraduates had no need and received non-need-based gift aid.

**GIFT AID (NEED-BASED)** *Total amount:* $2,341,171 (67% federal, 15% state, 9% institutional, 9% external sources). *Receiving aid:* Freshmen: 48% (87); all full-time undergraduates: 45% (437). *Average award:* Freshmen: $5329; Undergraduates: $4832. *Scholarships, grants, and awards:* Federal Pell, FSEOG, state, private.

**GIFT AID (NON-NEED-BASED)** *Total amount:* $291,373 (3% federal, 23% state, 43% institutional, 31% external sources). *Receiving aid:* Freshmen: 27% (49). Undergraduates: 12% (115). *Average award:* Freshmen: $1320. Undergraduates: $1532. *Scholarships, grants, and awards by category: Academic interests/achievement:* agriculture, biological sciences, business, communication, computer science, education, English, foreign languages, general academic interests/achievements, health fields, humanities, mathematics, physical sciences, premedicine, social sciences. *Creative arts/performance:* art/fine arts, creative writing, journalism/publications, music, theater/drama. *Special achievements/activities:* cheerleading/drum major, leadership, rodeo. *Special characteristics:* children of faculty/staff, children with a deceased or disabled parent, ethnic background, general special characteristics, international students, members of minority groups, veterans, veterans' children. *Tuition waivers:* Full or partial for minority students, children of alumni, employees or children of employees, senior citizens.

**LOANS** *Student loans:* $4,623,636 (58% need-based, 42% non-need-based). 68% of past graduating class borrowed through all loan programs. *Average indebtedness per student:* $24,244. *Average need-based loan:* Freshmen: $5778. Undergraduates: $6220. *Parent loans:* $119,276 (5% need-based, 95% non-need-based). *Programs:* Federal Direct (Subsidized and Unsubsidized Stafford, PLUS), Perkins, Federal Nursing, private loans, Alaska Loans.

**WORK-STUDY** *Federal work-study:* Total amount: $187,639; 68 jobs averaging $2992. *State or other work-study/employment:* Part-time jobs available.

**ATHLETIC AWARDS** Total amount: $308,548 (68% need-based, 32% non-need-based).

**APPLYING FOR FINANCIAL AID** *Required financial aid form:* FAFSA. *Financial aid deadline (priority):* 4/15. *Notification date:* Continuous beginning 6/15. Students must reply within 4 weeks of notification.

**CONTACT** Ms. Sandy Klein, Director of Financial Aid, Dickinson State University, 291 Campus Drive, Dickinson, ND 58601-4896, 701-483-2566 or toll-free 800-279-4295. *Fax:* 701-483-2720. *E-mail:* sandy.klein@dickinsonstate.edu.
*Website:* http://www.dickinsonstate.edu/.

# DIGIPEN INSTITUTE OF TECHNOLOGY
## Redmond, WA

**CONTACT** Mrs. Kimberly King, Director of Financial Aid, DigiPen Institute of Technology, 9931 Willows Road, Redmond, WA 98052, 425-895-4446 or toll-free 866-478-5236. *Fax:* 425-558-0378. *E-mail:* kimking@digipen.edu. *Website:* http://www.digipen.edu/.

# DILLARD UNIVERSITY
## New Orleans, LA

**ABOUT THE INSTITUTION** Independent interdenominational, coed. *Awards:* bachelor's degrees. 23 undergraduate majors. *Total enrollment:* 1,183. Undergraduates: 1,183. Freshmen: 229.

**GIFT AID (NEED-BASED)** *Scholarships, grants, and awards:* Federal Pell, FSEOG, state, private, college/university gift aid from institutional funds, United Negro College Fund, Federal Nursing.

**GIFT AID (NON-NEED-BASED)** *Scholarships, grants, and awards by category: Academic interests/achievement:* general academic interests/achievements. *Creative arts/performance:* art/fine arts, music, theater/drama. *Special characteristics:* children of faculty/staff, relatives of clergy, religious affiliation.

**LOANS** *Programs:* Federal Direct (Subsidized and Unsubsidized Stafford, PLUS), Perkins, Federal Nursing, alternative loans.

**WORK-STUDY** *Federal work-study:* 204 jobs averaging $1632.

**APPLYING FOR FINANCIAL AID** *Required financial aid forms:* FAFSA, institution's own form.

**CONTACT** Mr. Theodis Wright, Director of Financial Aid and Scholarships, Dillard University, 2601 Gentilly Boulevard, New Orleans, LA 70122-3097, 504-816-4677 or toll free 800-216-8094. *Fax:* 504-816-5456. *E-mail:* twright@dillard.edu. *Website:* http://www.dillard.edu/.

# DIXIE STATE UNIVERSITY
## St. George, UT

| Tuition & fees (UT res): $4454 | Average undergraduate aid package: $9835 |
| --- | --- |

**ABOUT THE INSTITUTION** State-supported, coed. *Awards:* certificates, diplomas, associate, and bachelor's degrees. 60 undergraduate majors. *Total enrollment:* 8,570. Undergraduates: 8,570. Freshmen: 1,925. Federal methodology is used as a basis for awarding need-based institutional aid.

**UNDERGRADUATE EXPENSES for 2015–2016** *Application fee:* $35. *Tuition, state resident:* full-time $3792; part-time $158 per credit hour. *Tuition, nonresident:* full-time $12,120; part-time $505 per credit hour. *Required fees:* full-time $662; $158 per credit hour. Full-time tuition and fees vary according to course load. Part-time tuition and fees vary according to course load. *College room and board:* $5918; *Room only:* $3260. Room and board charges vary according to board plan, housing facility, and location.

**FRESHMAN FINANCIAL AID (Fall 2013)** 1,212 applied for aid; of those 95% were deemed to have need. 88% of freshmen with need received aid; of those 5% had need fully met. *Average percent of need met:* 53% (excluding resources awarded to replace EFC). *Average financial aid package:* $9169 (excluding resources awarded to replace EFC). 1% of all full-time freshmen had no need and received non-need-based gift aid.

**UNDERGRADUATE FINANCIAL AID (Fall 2013)** 3,962 applied for aid; of those 98% were deemed to have need. 91% of undergraduates with need received aid; of those 3% had need fully met. *Average percent of need met:* 57% (excluding resources awarded to replace EFC). *Average financial aid package:* $9835 (excluding resources awarded to replace EFC). 1% of all full-time undergraduates had no need and received non-need-based gift aid.

**GIFT AID (NEED-BASED)** *Total amount:* $24,447,909 (81% federal, 14% state, 3% institutional, 2% external sources). *Receiving aid:* Freshmen: 43% (704); all full-time undergraduates: 52% (2,739). *Average award:* Freshmen: $4810; Undergraduates: $4892. *Scholarships, grants, and awards:* Federal Pell, FSEOG, state, private, college/university gift aid from institutional funds.

**GIFT AID (NON-NEED-BASED)** *Total amount:* $390,046 (81% state, 8% institutional, 11% external sources). *Receiving aid:* Freshmen: 34% (553). Undergraduates: 26% (1,345). *Average award:* Freshmen: $6867. Undergraduates: $13,294. *Scholarships, grants, and awards by category: Academic interests/achievement:* 1,566 awards ($6,235,614 total): general academic interests/achievements. *Tuition waivers:* Full or partial for employees or children of employees, senior citizens. *ROTC:* Army.

**LOANS** *Student loans:* $43,819,584 (100% need-based). 57% of past graduating class borrowed through all loan programs. *Average indebtedness per student:* $24,441. *Average need-based loan:* Freshmen: $3407. Undergraduates: $4248. *Parent loans:* $7,631,538 (86% need-based, 14% non-need-based). *Programs:* Federal Direct (Subsidized and Unsubsidized Stafford, PLUS), Perkins.

**WORK-STUDY** *Federal work-study:* 116 jobs averaging $3558. *State or other work-study/employment:* Total amount: $193,303 (100% need-based). 51 part-time jobs averaging $3790.

**ATHLETIC AWARDS** Total amount: $1,069,520 (95% need-based, 5% non-need-based).

**APPLYING FOR FINANCIAL AID** *Required financial aid forms:* FAFSA, institution's own form. *Financial aid deadline:* 6/30 (priority: 5/1). *Notification date:* Continuous beginning 3/1. Students must reply within 2 weeks of notification.

**CONTACT** J. D. Robertson, Director of Financial Aid, Dixie State University, 225 South 700 East, St. George, UT 84770, 435-652-7575. *Fax:* 435-656-4087. *E-mail:* finaid@dixie.edu. *Website:* http://www.dixie.edu/.

# DOANE COLLEGE
## Crete, NE

| Tuition & fees: $2720 | Average undergraduate aid package: $21,187 |
| --- | --- |

**ABOUT THE INSTITUTION** Independent United Church of Christ, coed. *Awards:* certificates, bachelor's, and master's degrees (non-traditional undergraduate programs and graduate programs offered at Lincoln campus). 42 undergraduate majors. *Total enrollment:* 1,067. Undergraduates: 1,067. Freshmen: 268. Both federal and institutional methodology are used as a basis for awarding need-based institutional aid.

**UNDERGRADUATE EXPENSES for 2015–2016** *Tuition:* full-time $2720. Full-time tuition and fees vary according to location. Part-time tuition and fees vary according to course load and location. Room and board charges vary according to board plan, housing facility, and location.

**FRESHMAN FINANCIAL AID (Fall 2014, est.)** 254 applied for aid; of those 89% were deemed to have need. 100% of freshmen with need received aid; of those 39% had need fully met. *Average percent of need met:* 95% (excluding resources awarded to replace EFC). *Average financial aid package:* $22,791 (excluding resources awarded to replace EFC). 4% of all full-time freshmen had no need and received non-need-based gift aid.

**UNDERGRADUATE FINANCIAL AID (Fall 2014, est.)** 912 applied for aid; of those 88% were deemed to have need. 100% of undergraduates with need received aid; of those 31% had need fully met. *Average percent of need met:* 87% (excluding resources awarded to replace EFC). *Average financial aid package:* $21,187 (excluding resources awarded to replace EFC). 8% of all full-time undergraduates had no need and received non-need-based gift aid.

**GIFT AID (NEED-BASED)** *Total amount:* $10,885,708 (16% federal, 4% state, 76% institutional, 4% external sources). *Receiving aid:* Freshmen: 85% (227); all full-time undergraduates: 76% (806). *Average award:* Freshmen: $19,533; Undergraduates: $17,439. *Scholarships, grants, and awards:* Federal Pell, FSEOG, state, private, college/university gift aid from institutional funds.

**GIFT AID (NON-NEED-BASED)** *Total amount:* $2,793,531 (8% federal, 91% institutional, 1% external sources). *Receiving aid:* Freshmen: 47% (126). Undergraduates: 38% (398). *Average award:* Freshmen: $7414. Undergraduates: $13,431. *Scholarships, grants, and awards by category: Academic interests/achievement:* general academic interests/achievements. *Creative arts/performance:* art/fine arts, debating, music, performing arts, theater/drama. *Special characteristics:* children and siblings of alumni, children of faculty/staff, religious affiliation, siblings of current students. *Tuition waivers:* Full or partial for employees or children of employees, senior citizens. *ROTC:* Army cooperative, Air Force cooperative.

**LOANS Student loans:** $6,293,064 (46% need-based, 54% non-need-based). 76% of past graduating class borrowed through all loan programs. *Average indebtedness per student:* $29,994. *Average need-based loan:* Freshmen: $3708. Undergraduates: $4653. *Parent loans:* $2,939,895 (100% non-need-based). *Programs:* Federal Direct (Subsidized and Unsubsidized Stafford, PLUS), Perkins.

**WORK-STUDY Federal work-study:** Total amount: $441,713; jobs available. *State or other work-study/employment:* Total amount: $433,959 (100% non-need-based). Part-time jobs available.

**ATHLETIC AWARDS** Total amount: $3,867,834 (75% need-based, 25% non-need-based).

**APPLYING FOR FINANCIAL AID Required financial aid form:** FAFSA. *Financial aid deadline:* Continuous. *Notification date:* Continuous beginning 3/15. Students must reply within 4 weeks of notification.

**CONTACT** Peggy Tvrdy, Director of Financial Aid, Doane College, 1014 Boswell Avenue, Crete, NE 68333-2430, 402-826-8260 or toll-free 800-333-6263. *Fax:* 402-826-8600. *E-mail:* peggy.tvrdy@doane.edu. *Website:* http://www.doane.edu/.

# DOMINICAN COLLEGE
## Orangeburg, NY

| Tuition & fees: $26,450 | Average undergraduate aid package: $19,805 |
|---|---|

**ABOUT THE INSTITUTION** Independent, coed. *Awards:* certificates, associate, bachelor's, master's, and doctoral degrees. 35 undergraduate majors. *Total enrollment:* 1,971. Undergraduates: 1,483. Freshmen: 290. Federal methodology is used as a basis for awarding need-based institutional aid.

**UNDERGRADUATE EXPENSES for 2015–2016 Application fee:** $35. *Comprehensive fee:* $38,650 includes full-time tuition ($25,680), mandatory fees ($770), and room and board ($12,200). Full-time tuition and fees vary according to degree level. Room and board charges vary according to board plan and housing facility. *Part-time tuition:* $776 per credit hour. *Part-time fees:* $180 per term. Part-time tuition and fees vary according to degree level and program.

**FRESHMAN FINANCIAL AID (Fall 2014, est.)** 286 applied for aid; of those 88% were deemed to have need. 100% of freshmen with need received aid; of those 10% had need fully met. *Average percent of need met:* 68% (excluding resources awarded to replace EFC). *Average financial aid package:* $22,060 (excluding resources awarded to replace EFC). 11% of all full-time freshmen had no need and received non-need-based gift aid.

**UNDERGRADUATE FINANCIAL AID (Fall 2014, est.)** 1,074 applied for aid; of those 91% were deemed to have need. 99% of undergraduates with need received aid; of those 12% had need fully met. *Average percent of need met:* 64% (excluding resources awarded to replace EFC). *Average financial aid package:* $19,805 (excluding resources awarded to replace EFC). 8% of all full-time undergraduates had no need and received non-need-based gift aid.

**GIFT AID (NEED-BASED) Total amount:** $14,185,395 (19% federal, 12% state, 67% institutional, 2% external sources). *Receiving aid:* Freshmen: 88% (253); all full-time undergraduates: 90% (968). *Average award:* Freshmen: $8558; Undergraduates: $15,410. *Scholarships, grants, and awards:* Federal Pell, FSEOG, state, private, college/university gift aid from institutional funds.

**GIFT AID (NON-NEED-BASED) Total amount:** $1,060,701 (3% state, 92% institutional, 5% external sources). *Receiving aid:* Freshmen: 6% (18). Undergraduates: 7% (75). *Average award:* Freshmen: $10,465. Undergraduates: $9170. *Scholarships, grants, and awards by category:* Academic interests/achievement: education, general academic interests/achievements, health fields. *Special characteristics:* children of faculty/staff, general special characteristics, relatives of clergy. *Tuition waivers:* Full or partial for employees or children of employees, senior citizens.

**LOANS Student loans:** $8,728,244 (83% need-based, 17% non-need-based). 94% of past graduating class borrowed through all loan programs. *Average indebtedness per student:* $22,640. *Average need-based loan:* Freshmen: $3447. Undergraduates: $4803. *Parent loans:* $4,380,761 (61% need-based, 39% non-need-based). *Programs:* Federal Direct (Subsidized and Unsubsidized Stafford, PLUS), Perkins, Federal Nursing.

**WORK-STUDY Federal work-study:** Total amount: $300,885; 343 jobs averaging $1500. *State or other work-study/employment:* Total amount: $265,993 (62% need-based, 38% non-need-based). Part-time jobs available.

**ATHLETIC AWARDS** Total amount: $1,537,510 (78% need-based, 22% non-need-based).

**APPLYING FOR FINANCIAL AID Required financial aid forms:** FAFSA, state aid form. *Financial aid deadline (priority):* 2/15. *Notification date:* Continuous beginning 2/15. Students must reply within 4 weeks of notification.

**CONTACT** Ms. Stacy Salinas, Director of Financial Aid, Dominican College, 470 Western Highway, Orangeburg, NY 10962-1210, 845-848-7818 or toll-free 866-432-4636. *Fax:* 845-359-4317. *E-mail:* stacy.salinas@dc.edu. *Website:* http://www.dc.edu/.

# DOMINICAN UNIVERSITY
## River Forest, IL

| Tuition & fees: $30,670 | Average undergraduate aid package: $22,638 |
|---|---|

**ABOUT THE INSTITUTION** Independent Roman Catholic, coed. *Awards:* certificates, bachelor's, master's, and doctoral degrees. 64 undergraduate majors. *Total enrollment:* 3,498. Undergraduates: 2,180. Freshmen: 473. Federal methodology is used as a basis for awarding need-based institutional aid.

**UNDERGRADUATE EXPENSES for 2015–2016 Application fee:** $25. *One-time required fee:* $150. *Comprehensive fee:* $40,050 includes full-time tuition ($30,300), mandatory fees ($370), and room and board ($9380). Full-time tuition and fees vary according to course load, program, and reciprocity agreements. Room and board charges vary according to board plan and housing facility. *Part-time tuition:* $1010 per credit hour. *Part-time fees:* $90 per term. Part-time tuition and fees vary according to course load, program, and reciprocity agreements.

**FRESHMAN FINANCIAL AID (Fall 2014, est.)** 454 applied for aid; of those 94% were deemed to have need. 100% of freshmen with need received aid; of those 9% had need fully met. *Average percent of need met:* 76% (excluding resources awarded to replace EFC). *Average financial aid package:* $24,160 (excluding resources awarded to replace EFC). 9% of all full-time freshmen had no need and received non-need-based gift aid.

**UNDERGRADUATE FINANCIAL AID (Fall 2014, est.)** 1,552 applied for aid; of those 94% were deemed to have need. 100% of undergraduates with need received aid; of those 11% had need fully met. *Average percent of need met:* 71% (excluding resources awarded to replace EFC). *Average financial aid package:* $22,638 (excluding resources awarded to replace EFC). 8% of all full-time undergraduates had no need and received non-need-based gift aid.

**GIFT AID (NEED-BASED) Total amount:** $24,140,530 (22% federal, 21% state, 55% institutional, 2% external sources). *Receiving aid:* Freshmen: 90% (426); all full-time undergraduates: 87% (1,411). *Average award:* Freshmen: $20,517; Undergraduates: $19,096. *Scholarships, grants, and awards:* Federal Pell, FSEOG, state, private, college/university gift aid from institutional funds.

**GIFT AID (NON-NEED-BASED) Total amount:** $1,423,335 (90% institutional, 10% external sources). *Receiving aid:* Freshmen: 7% (34). Undergraduates: 7% (114). *Average award:* Freshmen: $6993. Undergraduates: $7108. *Scholarships, grants, and awards by category:* Academic interests/achievement: general academic interests/achievements. *Creative arts/performance:* applied art and design, art/fine arts. *Special characteristics:* children and siblings of alumni, children of faculty/staff, siblings of current students. *Tuition waivers:* Full or partial for employees or children of employees.

**LOANS Student loans:** $13,414,450 (85% need-based, 15% non-need-based). 85% of past graduating class borrowed through all loan programs. *Average indebtedness per student:* $29,235. *Average need-based loan:* Freshmen: $3342. Undergraduates: $4276. *Parent loans:* $2,256,600 (43% need-based, 57% non-need-based). *Programs:* Federal Direct (Subsidized and Unsubsidized Stafford, PLUS).

**WORK-STUDY Federal work-study:** Total amount: $588,735; jobs available. *State or other work-study/employment:* Total amount: $314,050 (43% need-based, 57% non-need-based). Part-time jobs available.

**APPLYING FOR FINANCIAL AID Required financial aid form:** FAFSA. *Financial aid deadline (priority):* 2/15. *Notification date:* Continuous beginning 2/15. Students must reply within 2 weeks of notification.

**CONTACT** Victoria Lamick, Director of Financial Aid, Dominican University, 7900 West Division Street, River Forest, IL 60305-1099, 708-524-6950 or toll-free 800-828-8475. *Fax:* 708-366-6478. *E-mail:* vlamick@dom.edu. *Website:* http://www.dom.edu/.

# DOMINICAN UNIVERSITY OF CALIFORNIA
## San Rafael, CA

**ABOUT THE INSTITUTION** Independent Roman Catholic Church, coed. *Awards:* bachelor's and master's degrees. 24 undergraduate majors. *Total enrollment:* 2,001. Undergraduates: 1,478. Freshmen: 262.

**GIFT AID (NEED-BASED)** *Scholarships, grants, and awards:* Federal Pell, FSEOG, state, private, college/university gift aid from institutional funds, Scholarships for Disadvantaged Students (SDS).

**GIFT AID (NON-NEED-BASED)** *Scholarships, grants, and awards by category:* Academic interests/achievement: general academic interests/achievements. Creative arts/performance: music. Special achievements/activities: community service, leadership. Special characteristics: adult students, children and siblings of alumni, children of faculty/staff, international students, members of minority groups, veterans, veterans' children.

**LOANS** *Programs:* Federal Direct (Subsidized and Unsubsidized Stafford, PLUS), Perkins, private loans.

**APPLYING FOR FINANCIAL AID** *Required financial aid forms:* FAFSA, institution's own form.

**CONTACT** Ms. Shanon Little, Director of Financial Aid, Dominican University of California, 50 Acacia Avenue, San Rafael, CA 94901-2298, 415-257-1302 or toll-free 888-323-6763. *Fax:* 415-485-3294. *E-mail:* shanon.little@dominican.edu. *Website:* http://www.dominican.edu/.

# DORDT COLLEGE
## Sioux Center, IA

| Tuition & fees: N/R | Average undergraduate aid package: $21,965 |
| --- | --- |

**ABOUT THE INSTITUTION** Independent Christian Reformed, coed. *Awards:* associate, bachelor's, and master's degrees. 86 undergraduate majors. *Total enrollment:* 1,405. Undergraduates: 1,376. Freshmen: 380. Federal methodology is used as a basis for awarding need-based institutional aid.

**FRESHMAN FINANCIAL AID (Fall 2014, est.)** 303 applied for aid; of those 85% were deemed to have need. 100% of freshmen with need received aid; of those 33% had need fully met. *Average percent of need met:* 77% (excluding resources awarded to replace EFC). *Average financial aid package:* $23,168 (excluding resources awarded to replace EFC). 20% of all full-time freshmen had no need and received non-need-based gift aid.

**UNDERGRADUATE FINANCIAL AID (Fall 2014, est.)** 1,079 applied for aid; of those 86% were deemed to have need. 100% of undergraduates with need received aid; of those 32% had need fully met. *Average percent of need met:* 76% (excluding resources awarded to replace EFC). *Average financial aid package:* $21,965 (excluding resources awarded to replace EFC). 22% of all full-time undergraduates had no need and received non-need-based gift aid.

**GIFT AID (NEED-BASED)** *Total amount:* $15,672,272 (10% federal, 8% state, 73% institutional, 9% external sources). *Receiving aid:* Freshmen: 72% (258); all full-time undergraduates: 70% (924). *Average award:* Freshmen: $16,465; Undergraduates: $14,967. *Scholarships, grants, and awards:* Federal Pell, FSEOG, state, private, college/university gift aid from institutional funds.

**GIFT AID (NON-NEED-BASED)** *Total amount:* $2,764,612 (92% institutional, 8% external sources). *Receiving aid:* Freshmen: 12% (44). Undergraduates: 11% (149). *Average award:* Freshmen: $19,579. Undergraduates: $18,363. *Scholarships, grants, and awards by category:* Academic interests/achievement: agriculture, biological sciences, business, communication, computer science, education, engineering/technologies, English, foreign languages, general academic interests/achievements, humanities, mathematics, physical sciences, premedicine, religion/biblical studies, social sciences. Creative arts/performance: debating, journalism/publications,

music, theater/drama. Special achievements/activities: community service, general special achievements/activities, leadership. Special characteristics: children and siblings of alumni, children of faculty/staff, general special characteristics, handicapped students, international students, local/state students, members of minority groups, out-of-state students, religious affiliation.

**LOANS** *Student loans:* $9,790,478 (89% need-based, 11% non-need-based). 82% of past graduating class borrowed through all loan programs. *Average indebtedness per student:* $27,867. *Average need-based loan:* Freshmen: $5229. Undergraduates: $5367. *Parent loans:* $5,989,421 (84% need-based, 16% non-need-based). *Programs:* Federal Direct (Subsidized and Unsubsidized Stafford, PLUS), Perkins, state, college/university, alternative loans.

**WORK-STUDY** *Federal work-study:* Total amount: $722,855; 400 jobs averaging $1600. *State or other work-study/employment:* Total amount: $1,219,380 (75% need-based, 25% non-need-based). 500 part-time jobs averaging $1600.

**ATHLETIC AWARDS** Total amount: $2,488,490 (79% need-based, 21% non-need-based).

**APPLYING FOR FINANCIAL AID** *Required financial aid forms:* FAFSA, institution's own form. *Financial aid deadline (priority):* 4/1. *Notification date:* Continuous beginning 3/1. Students must reply within 3 weeks of notification.

**CONTACT** Mr. Michael Epema, Director of Financial Aid, Dordt College, 498 4th Avenue NE, Sioux Center, IA 51250-1697, 712-722-6087 or toll-free 800-343-6738. *Fax:* 712-722-6035. *E-mail:* michael.epema@dordt.edu. *Website:* http://www.dordt.edu/.

# DOWLING COLLEGE
## Oakdale, NY

| Tuition & fees: $29,100 | Average undergraduate aid package: $19,348 |
| --- | --- |

**ABOUT THE INSTITUTION** Independent, coed. *Awards:* certificates, bachelor's, master's, and doctoral degrees. 50 undergraduate majors. *Total enrollment:* 2,453. Undergraduates: 1,783. Freshmen: 188. Federal methodology is used as a basis for awarding need-based institutional aid.

**UNDERGRADUATE EXPENSES for 2015–2016** *Application fee:* $35. *Comprehensive fee:* $39,870 includes full-time tuition ($27,300), mandatory fees ($1800), and room and board ($10,770).

**FRESHMAN FINANCIAL AID (Fall 2013)** 188 applied for aid; of those 97% were deemed to have need. 98% of freshmen with need received aid; of those 7% had need fully met. *Average percent of need met:* 68% (excluding resources awarded to replace EFC). *Average financial aid package:* $22,417 (excluding resources awarded to replace EFC). 37% of all full-time freshmen had no need and received non-need-based gift aid.

**UNDERGRADUATE FINANCIAL AID (Fall 2013)** 1,065 applied for aid; of those 99% were deemed to have need. 99% of undergraduates with need received aid; of those 6% had need fully met. *Average percent of need met:* 58% (excluding resources awarded to replace EFC). *Average financial aid package:* $19,348 (excluding resources awarded to replace EFC). 38% of all full-time undergraduates had no need and received non-need-based gift aid.

**GIFT AID (NEED-BASED)** *Total amount:* $10,039,960 (27% federal, 20% state, 52% institutional, 1% external sources). *Receiving aid:* Freshmen: 72% (169); all full-time undergraduates: 66% (947). *Average award:* Freshmen: $12,681; Undergraduates: $10,084. *Scholarships, grants, and awards:* Federal Pell, FSEOG, state, private, college/university gift aid from institutional funds.

**GIFT AID (NON-NEED-BASED)** *Total amount:* $5,910,173 (11% federal, 2% state, 87% institutional). *Receiving aid:* Freshmen: 44% (104). Undergraduates: 44% (639). *Average award:* Freshmen: $6908. Undergraduates: $6906. *Scholarships, grants, and awards by category:* Academic interests/achievement: 33 awards ($716,989 total): business, education, general academic interests/achievements, mathematics, social sciences. Special achievements/activities: general special achievements/activities. Special characteristics: adult students, children and siblings of alumni, children of educators, children of faculty/staff, children of public servants, children of union members/company employees, children of workers in trades, ethnic background, first-generation college students, general special characteristics, local/state students, members of minority groups, previous college experience, public servants, siblings of current students, twins, veterans. *Tuition waivers:* Full or partial for employees or children of employees. *ROTC:* Army cooperative, Air Force cooperative.

**LOANS** *Student loans:* $10,118,082 (40% need-based, 60% non-need-based). 85% of past graduating class borrowed through all loan programs. *Average indebtedness per student:* $39,116. *Average need-based loan:* Freshmen: $3335. Undergraduates: $4484. *Parent loans:* $3,908,629 (100% need-based). *Programs:* Federal Direct (Subsidized and Unsubsidized Stafford, PLUS), Perkins, state, private loans.

**WORK-STUDY** *Federal work-study:* 660 jobs averaging $3023. *State or other work-study/employment:* 34 part-time jobs averaging $1846.

**ATHLETIC AWARDS** Total amount: $2,245,904 (100% non-need-based).

**APPLYING FOR FINANCIAL AID** *Required financial aid forms:* FAFSA, state aid form. *Financial aid deadline (priority):* 2/15. *Notification date:* Continuous beginning 3/15.

**CONTACT** Ms. Carla Guevara, Director of Financial Aid, Dowling College, 150 Idle Hour Boulevard, Oakdale, NY 11769-1999, 631-244-3220 or toll-free 800-DOWLING. *E-mail:* guevarac@dowling.edu.
*Website:* http://www.dowling.edu/.

---

# DRAKE UNIVERSITY
## Des Moines, IA

| Tuition & fees: $32,246 | Average undergraduate aid package: $25,015 |
|---|---|

**ABOUT THE INSTITUTION** Independent, coed. *Awards:* certificates, bachelor's, master's, and doctoral degrees. 66 undergraduate majors. *Total enrollment:* 5,062. Undergraduates: 3,364. Freshmen: 870. Federal methodology is used as a basis for awarding need-based institutional aid.

**UNDERGRADUATE EXPENSES for 2015–2016** *Application fee:* $25. *Comprehensive fee:* $41,516 includes full-time tuition ($32,100), mandatory fees ($146), and room and board ($9270). *College room only:* $4950. Full-time tuition and fees vary according to course load, degree level, program, and student level. Room and board charges vary according to board plan. *Part-time tuition:* $635 per credit hour. Part-time tuition and fees vary according to class time, degree level, and program.

**FRESHMAN FINANCIAL AID (Fall 2014, est.)** 748 applied for aid; of those 76% were deemed to have need. 100% of freshmen with need received aid; of those 27% had need fully met. *Average percent of need met:* 76% (excluding resources awarded to replace EFC). *Average financial aid package:* $24,053 (excluding resources awarded to replace EFC). 29% of all full-time freshmen had no need and received non-need-based gift aid.

**UNDERGRADUATE FINANCIAL AID (Fall 2014, est.)** 2,301 applied for aid; of those 82% were deemed to have need. 100% of undergraduates with need received aid; of those 25% had need fully met. *Average percent of need met:* 79% (excluding resources awarded to replace EFC). *Average financial aid package:* $25,015 (excluding resources awarded to replace EFC). 34% of all full-time undergraduates had no need and received non-need-based gift aid.

**GIFT AID (NEED-BASED)** *Total amount:* $30,986,497 (9% federal, 5% state, 83% institutional, 3% external sources). *Receiving aid:* Freshmen: 64% (558); all full-time undergraduates: 58% (1,842). *Average award:* Freshmen: $18,126; Undergraduates: $16,669. *Scholarships, grants, and awards:* Federal Pell, FSEOG, state, private, college/university gift aid from institutional funds.

**GIFT AID (NON-NEED-BASED)** *Total amount:* $17,561,016 (3% federal, 94% institutional, 3% external sources). *Receiving aid:* Freshmen: 14% (118). Undergraduates: 10% (317). *Average award:* Freshmen: $14,213. Undergraduates: $12,889. *Scholarships, grants, and awards by category: Academic interests/achievement:* 2,584 awards ($29,707,797 total): general academic interests/achievements. *Creative arts/performance:* 299 awards ($1,620,655 total): art/fine arts, music, theater/drama. *Special characteristics:* 230 awards ($339,455 total): children and siblings of alumni, international students. *Tuition waivers:* Full or partial for children of alumni, employees or children of employees, senior citizens. *ROTC:* Army cooperative, Air Force cooperative.

**LOANS** *Student loans:* $30,598,800 (48% need-based, 52% non-need-based). 63% of past graduating class borrowed through all loan programs. *Average indebtedness per student:* $31,546. *Average need-based loan:* Freshmen: $3102. Undergraduates: $6152. *Parent loans:* $43,056,033 (19% need-based, 81% non-need-based). *Programs:* Federal Direct (Subsidized and Unsubsidized Stafford, PLUS), Perkins, college/university, Health Professions Student Loans (HPSL).

**WORK-STUDY** *Federal work-study:* Total amount: $2,927,381; 1,529 jobs averaging $1915.

---

**ATHLETIC AWARDS** Total amount: $3,896,856 (26% need-based, 74% non-need-based).

**APPLYING FOR FINANCIAL AID** *Required financial aid form:* FAFSA. *Financial aid deadline:* Continuous. *Notification date:* Continuous beginning 3/1. Students must reply by 5/1 or within 3 weeks of notification.

**CONTACT** Office of Student Financial Planning, Drake University, 2507 University Avenue, Des Moines, IA 50311-4516, 800-443-7253 Ext. 2905 or toll-free 800-44-DRAKE Ext. 3181. *Fax:* 515-271-4042. *E-mail:* financialaid@drake.edu. *Website:* http://www.drake.edu/.

---

# DREW UNIVERSITY
## Madison, NJ

| Tuition & fees: $45,214 | Average undergraduate aid package: $35,607 |
|---|---|

**ABOUT THE INSTITUTION** Independent United Methodist Church, coed. *Awards:* certificates, bachelor's, master's, and doctoral degrees. 29 undergraduate majors. *Total enrollment:* 2,113. Undergraduates: 1,417. Freshmen: 302. Federal methodology is used as a basis for awarding need-based institutional aid.

**UNDERGRADUATE EXPENSES for 2015–2016** *Application fee:* $60. *Comprehensive fee:* $57,516 includes full-time tuition ($44,232), mandatory fees ($982), and room and board ($12,302). *College room only:* $7914. Room and board charges vary according to board plan and housing facility. *Part-time tuition:* $1843 per credit hour. Part-time tuition and fees vary according to course load. *Payment plan:* Tuition prepayment.

**FRESHMAN FINANCIAL AID (Fall 2013)** 343 applied for aid; of those 90% were deemed to have need. 100% of freshmen with need received aid; of those 17% had need fully met. *Average percent of need met:* 81% (excluding resources awarded to replace EFC). *Average financial aid package:* $37,597 (excluding resources awarded to replace EFC). 19% of all full-time freshmen had no need and received non-need-based gift aid.

**UNDERGRADUATE FINANCIAL AID (Fall 2013)** 1,110 applied for aid; of those 92% were deemed to have need. 100% of undergraduates with need received aid; of those 14% had need fully met. *Average percent of need met:* 77% (excluding resources awarded to replace EFC). *Average financial aid package:* $35,607 (excluding resources awarded to replace EFC). 23% of all full-time undergraduates had no need and received non-need-based gift aid.

**GIFT AID (NEED-BASED)** *Total amount:* $31,021,453 (8% federal, 10% state, 81% institutional, 1% external sources). *Receiving aid:* Freshmen: 77% (309); all full-time undergraduates: 71% (1,014). *Average award:* Freshmen: $32,927; Undergraduates: $35,607. *Scholarships, grants, and awards:* Federal Pell, FSEOG, state, private, college/university gift aid from institutional funds.

**GIFT AID (NON-NEED-BASED)** *Total amount:* $5,692,684 (99% institutional, 1% external sources). *Receiving aid:* Freshmen: 7% (27). Undergraduates: 5% (71). *Average award:* Freshmen: $18,346. Undergraduates: $14,991. *Scholarships, grants, and awards by category: Academic interests/achievement:* area/ethnic studies, biological sciences, computer science, English, foreign languages, general academic interests/achievements, humanities, mathematics, physical sciences, religion/biblical studies, social sciences. *Creative arts/performance:* art/fine arts, creative writing, general creative arts/performance, music, theater/drama. *Special characteristics:* members of minority groups. *Tuition waivers:* Full or partial for employees or children of employees.

**LOANS** *Student loans:* $6,137,135 (56% need-based, 44% non-need-based). 74% of past graduating class borrowed through all loan programs. *Average indebtedness per student:* $24,778. *Average need-based loan:* Freshmen: $3298. Undergraduates: $4495. *Parent loans:* $6,940,096 (55% need-based, 45% non-need-based). *Programs:* Federal Direct (Subsidized and Unsubsidized Stafford, PLUS), Perkins, state.

**WORK-STUDY** *Federal work-study:* jobs available. *State or other work-study/employment:* Total amount: $3,055,392 (98% need-based, 2% non-need-based). Part-time jobs available.

**APPLYING FOR FINANCIAL AID** *Required financial aid form:* FAFSA. *Financial aid deadline:* 2/15. *Notification date:* 3/30. Students must reply by 5/1.

**CONTACT** Renee Volak, Director of Financial Assistance, Drew University, 36 Madison Avenue, Madison, NJ 07940-1493, 973-408-3112. *Fax:* 973-408-3188. *E-mail:* finaid@drew.edu. *Website:* http://www.drew.edu/.

# DREXEL UNIVERSITY
## Philadelphia, PA

| Tuition & fees: $47,051 | Average undergraduate aid package: $25,190 |
|---|---|

**ABOUT THE INSTITUTION** Independent, coed. *Awards:* certificates, associate, bachelor's, master's, and doctoral degrees. 80 undergraduate majors. *Total enrollment:* 26,359. Undergraduates: 16,896. Freshmen: 2,928. Federal methodology is used as a basis for awarding need-based institutional aid.

**UNDERGRADUATE EXPENSES for 2015–2016 Application fee:** $50. *Comprehensive fee:* $61,418 includes full-time tuition ($44,646), mandatory fees ($2405), and room and board ($14,367). Full-time tuition and fees vary according to course load, location, program, and student level. Room and board charges vary according to board plan and housing facility. *Part-time tuition:* $1004 per credit hour. Part-time tuition and fees vary according to course load and program.

**FRESHMAN FINANCIAL AID (Fall 2014, est.)** 2,394 applied for aid; of those 85% were deemed to have need. 100% of freshmen with need received aid; of those 22% had need fully met. *Average percent of need met:* 62% (excluding resources awarded to replace EFC). *Average financial aid package:* $33,002 (excluding resources awarded to replace EFC). 12% of all full-time freshmen had no need and received non-need-based gift aid.

**UNDERGRADUATE FINANCIAL AID (Fall 2014, est.)** 9,326 applied for aid; of those 88% were deemed to have need. 99% of undergraduates with need received aid; of those 20% had need fully met. *Average percent of need met:* 56% (excluding resources awarded to replace EFC). *Average financial aid package:* $25,190 (excluding resources awarded to replace EFC). 7% of all full-time undergraduates had no need and received non-need-based gift aid.

**GIFT AID (NEED-BASED) Total amount:** $164,761,356 (11% federal, 3% state, 82% institutional, 4% external sources). *Receiving aid:* Freshmen: 69% (2,023); all full-time undergraduates: 54% (7,696). *Average award:* Freshmen: $28,234; Undergraduates: $21,813. *Scholarships, grants, and awards:* Federal Pell, FSEOG, state, private, college/university gift aid from institutional funds, United Negro College Fund.

**GIFT AID (NON-NEED-BASED) Total amount:** $78,390,842 (97% institutional, 3% external sources). *Receiving aid:* Freshmen: 7% (214). Undergraduates: 2% (284). *Average award:* Freshmen: $18,723. Undergraduates: $16,410. *Scholarships, grants, and awards by category:* Academic interests/achievement: general academic interests/achievements. *Creative arts/performance:* dance, music, performing arts, theater/drama. *Special achievements/activities:* cheerleading/drum major. *Special characteristics:* children and siblings of alumni, siblings of current students, twins. *Tuition waivers:* Full or partial for children of alumni, employees or children of employees. *ROTC:* Army, Naval cooperative, Air Force cooperative.

**LOANS Student loans:** $108,944,527 (75% need-based, 25% non-need-based). *Average need-based loan:* Freshmen: $3554. Undergraduates: $4400. *Parent loans:* $41,909,990 (100% non-need-based). *Programs:* Federal Direct (Subsidized and Unsubsidized Stafford, PLUS), Perkins, Federal Nursing, college/university.

**WORK-STUDY Federal work-study:** Total amount: $1,852,358; jobs available.

**ATHLETIC AWARDS** Total amount: $8,038,911 (31% need-based, 69% non-need-based).

**APPLYING FOR FINANCIAL AID Required financial aid form:** FAFSA. *Financial aid deadline:* 3/1. *Notification date:* Continuous beginning 3/15.

**CONTACT** Helen Gourousis, Director of Financial Aid, Drexel University, 3141 Chestnut Street, Philadelphia, PA 19104-2875, 215-895-5928 or toll-free 800-2-DREXEL. *Fax:* 215-895-6903. *E-mail:* gouroush@drexel.edu. *Website:* http://www.drexel.edu/.

# DRURY UNIVERSITY
## Springfield, MO

| Tuition & fees: $23,885 | Average undergraduate aid package: $19,321 |
|---|---|

**ABOUT THE INSTITUTION** Independent, coed. *Awards:* bachelor's and master's degrees (also offers evening program with significant enrollment not reflected in profile). 44 undergraduate majors. *Total enrollment:* 1,751. Undergraduates: 1,454. Freshmen: 310. Federal methodology is used as a basis for awarding need-based institutional aid.

**UNDERGRADUATE EXPENSES for 2015–2016 Application fee:** $50. *One-time required fee:* $150. *Comprehensive fee:* $31,279 includes full-time tuition ($22,750), mandatory fees ($1135), and room and board ($7394). Full-time tuition and fees vary according to class time. Room and board charges vary according to board plan and housing facility. Part-time tuition and fees vary according to class time. *Payment plan:* Tuition prepayment.

**FRESHMAN FINANCIAL AID (Fall 2014, est.)** 252 applied for aid; of those 81% were deemed to have need. 100% of freshmen with need received aid; of those 25% had need fully met. *Average percent of need met:* 76% (excluding resources awarded to replace EFC). *Average financial aid package:* $20,111 (excluding resources awarded to replace EFC). 36% of all full-time freshmen had no need and received non-need-based gift aid.

**UNDERGRADUATE FINANCIAL AID (Fall 2014, est.)** 1,007 applied for aid; of those 87% were deemed to have need. 100% of undergraduates with need received aid; of those 20% had need fully met. *Average percent of need met:* 73% (excluding resources awarded to replace EFC). *Average financial aid package:* $19,321 (excluding resources awarded to replace EFC). 31% of all full-time undergraduates had no need and received non-need-based gift aid.

**GIFT AID (NEED-BASED) Total amount:** $12,182,098 (18% federal, 6% state, 70% institutional, 6% external sources). *Receiving aid:* Freshmen: 65% (203); all full-time undergraduates: 61% (868). *Average award:* Freshmen: $15,621; Undergraduates: $14,987. *Scholarships, grants, and awards:* Federal Pell, FSEOG, state, private, college/university gift aid from institutional funds.

**GIFT AID (NON-NEED-BASED) Total amount:** $4,926,935 (3% state, 93% institutional, 4% external sources). *Receiving aid:* Freshmen: 13% (40). Undergraduates: 8% (117). *Average award:* Freshmen: $8404. Undergraduates: $8263. *Scholarships, grants, and awards by category:* Academic interests/achievement: 1,298 awards ($7,339,738 total): architecture, biological sciences, business, communication, computer science, education, English, foreign languages, general academic interests/achievements, health fields, humanities, mathematics, physical sciences, premedicine, social sciences. *Creative arts/performance:* 190 awards ($480,040 total): art/fine arts, creative writing, debating, music, theater/drama. *Special achievements/activities:* 23 awards ($23,750 total): cheerleading/drum major, leadership, religious involvement. *Special characteristics:* 124 awards ($1,271,109 total): children and siblings of alumni, children of faculty/staff, ethnic background, international students, members of minority groups, relatives of clergy, religious affiliation, veterans. *Tuition waivers:* Full or partial for minority students, children of alumni, employees or children of employees. *ROTC:* Army cooperative.

**LOANS Student loans:** $9,432,776 (62% need-based, 38% non-need-based). 59% of past graduating class borrowed through all loan programs. *Average indebtedness per student:* $25,336. *Average need-based loan:* Freshmen: $5345. Undergraduates: $5073. *Parent loans:* $1,929,736 (33% need-based, 67% non-need-based). *Programs:* Federal Direct (Subsidized and Unsubsidized Stafford, PLUS), Perkins.

**WORK-STUDY Federal work-study:** Total amount: $278,486; 177 jobs averaging $2338. *State or other work-study/employment:* Part-time jobs available.

**ATHLETIC AWARDS** Total amount: $3,014,864 (32% need-based, 68% non-need-based).

**APPLYING FOR FINANCIAL AID Required financial aid forms:** FAFSA, institution's own form. *Financial aid deadline (priority):* 1/10. *Notification date:* Continuous beginning 3/1. Students must reply by 5/1 or within 2 weeks of notification.

**CONTACT** Ms. Becky Ahrens, Interim Director of Financial Aid, Drury University, 900 North Benton Avenue, Springfield, MO 65802-3791, 417-873-7312 or toll-free 800-922-2274. *Fax:* 417-873-6906. *E-mail:* baherns@drury.edu. *Website:* http://www.drury.edu/.

# DUKE UNIVERSITY
## Durham, NC

| Tuition & fees: $48,562 | Average undergraduate aid package: $44,635 |
|---|---|

**ABOUT THE INSTITUTION** Independent United Methodist Church, coed. 45 undergraduate majors. Both federal and institutional methodology are used as a basis for awarding need-based institutional aid.

**UNDERGRADUATE EXPENSES** for 2015–2016 *Comprehensive fee:* $61,138 includes full-time tuition ($47,488), mandatory fees ($1074), and room and board ($12,576). *College room only:* $6526.

**FRESHMAN FINANCIAL AID (Fall 2014, est.)** 876 applied for aid; of those 83% were deemed to have need. 100% of freshmen with need received aid; of those 100% had need fully met. *Average percent of need met:* 100% (excluding resources awarded to replace EFC). *Average financial aid package:* $43,452 (excluding resources awarded to replace EFC). 13% of all full-time freshmen had no need and received non-need-based gift aid.

**UNDERGRADUATE FINANCIAL AID (Fall 2014, est.)** 3,331 applied for aid; of those 88% were deemed to have need. 100% of undergraduates with need received aid; of those 100% had need fully met. *Average percent of need met:* 100% (excluding resources awarded to replace EFC). *Average financial aid package:* $44,635 (excluding resources awarded to replace EFC). 12% of all full-time undergraduates had no need and received non-need-based gift aid.

**GIFT AID (NEED-BASED)** *Total amount:* $112,443,140 (4% federal, 91% institutional, 5% external sources). *Receiving aid:* Freshmen: 40% (680); all full-time undergraduates: 41% (2,763). *Average award:* Freshmen: $40,841; Undergraduates: $41,910. *Scholarships, grants, and awards:* Federal Pell, FSEOG, state, private, college/university gift aid from institutional funds.

**GIFT AID (NON-NEED-BASED)** *Total amount:* $16,089,702 (67% institutional, 33% external sources). *Receiving aid:* Freshmen: 6% (96). Undergraduates: 4% (280). *Average award:* Freshmen: $13,689. Undergraduates: $20,714. *Scholarships, grants, and awards by category: Academic interests/achievement:* 121 awards ($7,231,475 total): general academic interests/achievements, mathematics. *Creative arts/performance:* creative writing. *Special achievements/activities:* 80 awards ($4,811,171 total): general special achievements/activities, leadership. *Special characteristics:* 58 awards ($3,623,707 total): children and siblings of alumni, ethnic background, international students, local/state students.

**LOANS** *Student loans:* $17,245,736 (80% need-based, 20% non-need-based). 36% of past graduating class borrowed through all loan programs. *Average indebtedness per student:* $20,556. *Average need-based loan:* Freshmen: $3914. Undergraduates: $4061. *Parent loans:* $6,477,790 (76% need-based, 24% non-need-based). *Programs:* Federal Direct (Subsidized and Unsubsidized Stafford, PLUS), Perkins, college/university, alternative loans.

**WORK-STUDY** *Federal work-study:* Total amount: $3,938,963; 1,952 jobs averaging $2018. *State or other work-study/employment:* Total amount: $1,988,750 (57% need-based, 43% non-need-based). 908 part-time jobs averaging $1524.

**ATHLETIC AWARDS** Total amount: $16,870,989 (25% need-based, 75% non-need-based).

**APPLYING FOR FINANCIAL AID** *Required financial aid forms:* FAFSA, CSS Financial Aid PROFILE, noncustodial (divorced/separated) parent's statement, business/farm supplement, federal income tax form(s), W-2 forms. *Financial aid deadline:* 3/15. *Notification date:* 4/1. Students must reply by 5/1.

**CONTACT** Alison Rabil, Director of Financial Aid, Duke University, 2127 Campus Drive Addition, Box 90397, Durham, NC 27708-0397, 919-684-6225. *Fax:* 919-660-9811. *E-mail:* finaid@duke.edu.
*Website:* http://www.duke.edu/.

# DUNLAP-STONE UNIVERSITY
## Phoenix, AZ

| Tuition & fees: N/R | Average undergraduate aid package: N/A |
|---|---|

**ABOUT THE INSTITUTION** Proprietary, coed. *Awards:* certificates, associate, and bachelor's degrees. 1 undergraduate major. *Total enrollment:* 500. Undergraduates: 500. Institutional methodology is used as a basis for awarding need-based institutional aid.

**APPLYING FOR FINANCIAL AID** *Notification date:* Continuous.

**CONTACT** Office of the Bursar, Dunlap-Stone University, 19820 North 7th Street, Suite #100, Phoenix, AZ 85024, 800-474-8013. *E-mail:* info@expandglobal.com. *Website:* http://www.dunlap-stone.edu/.

# DUQUESNE UNIVERSITY
## Pittsburgh, PA

| Tuition & fees: $32,636 | Average undergraduate aid package: $22,848 |
|---|---|

**ABOUT THE INSTITUTION** Independent Roman Catholic, coed. *Awards:* certificates, bachelor's, master's, and doctoral degrees. 71 undergraduate majors. *Total enrollment:* 9,648. Undergraduates: 5,995. Freshmen: 1,343. Federal methodology is used as a basis for awarding need-based institutional aid.

**UNDERGRADUATE EXPENSES** for 2015–2016 *Application fee:* $50. *Comprehensive fee:* $43,720 includes full-time tuition ($30,070), mandatory fees ($2566), and room and board ($11,084). *College room only:* $6044. Full-time tuition and fees vary according to course load and program. Room and board charges vary according to board plan and housing facility. *Part-time tuition:* $981 per credit. *Part-time fees:* $100 per credit. Part-time tuition and fees vary according to course load and program.

**FRESHMAN FINANCIAL AID (Fall 2013)** 1,394 applied for aid; of those 81% were deemed to have need. 100% of freshmen with need received aid; of those 28% had need fully met. *Average percent of need met:* 84% (excluding resources awarded to replace EFC). *Average financial aid package:* $24,850 (excluding resources awarded to replace EFC). 26% of all full-time freshmen had no need and received non-need-based gift aid.

**UNDERGRADUATE FINANCIAL AID (Fall 2013)** 4,749 applied for aid; of those 84% were deemed to have need. 100% of undergraduates with need received aid; of those 23% had need fully met. *Average percent of need met:* 79% (excluding resources awarded to replace EFC). *Average financial aid package:* $22,848 (excluding resources awarded to replace EFC). 27% of all full-time undergraduates had no need and received non-need-based gift aid.

**GIFT AID (NEED-BASED)** *Total amount:* $63,197,585 (9% federal, 9% state, 78% institutional, 4% external sources). *Receiving aid:* Freshmen: 73% (1,124); all full-time undergraduates: 69% (3,948). *Average award:* Freshmen: $17,409; Undergraduates: $18,059. *Scholarships, grants, and awards:* Federal Pell, FSEOG, state, private, college/university gift aid from institutional funds, United Negro College Fund.

**GIFT AID (NON-NEED-BASED)** *Total amount:* $17,561,168 (1% state, 95% institutional, 4% external sources). *Receiving aid:* Freshmen: 73% (1,124). Undergraduates: 66% (3,759). *Average award:* Freshmen: $12,103. Undergraduates: $10,804. *Scholarships, grants, and awards by category: Academic interests/achievement:* 5,051 awards ($48,779,781 total): education, general academic interests/achievements. *Creative arts/performance:* 274 awards ($1,917,120 total): dance, music. *Special characteristics:* 1,241 awards ($11,820,902 total): children and siblings of alumni, children of faculty/staff, ethnic background, general special characteristics, international students, members of minority groups, relatives of clergy, religious affiliation, veterans, veterans' children. *Tuition waivers:* Full or partial for employees or children of employees, senior citizens. *ROTC:* Army, Naval cooperative, Air Force cooperative.

**LOANS** *Student loans:* $51,662,989 (88% need-based, 12% non-need-based). 75% of past graduating class borrowed through all loan programs. *Average indebtedness per student:* $34,522. *Average need-based loan:* Freshmen: $4114. Undergraduates: $4675. *Parent loans:* $19,366,230 (92% need-based, 8% non-need-based). *Programs:* Federal Direct (Subsidized and Unsubsidized Stafford, PLUS), Perkins, Federal Nursing, private loans.

**WORK-STUDY** *Federal work-study:* 3,160 jobs averaging $2482.

**ATHLETIC AWARDS** Total amount: $6,400,746 (50% need-based, 50% non-need-based).

**APPLYING FOR FINANCIAL AID** *Required financial aid form:* FAFSA. *Financial aid deadline:* 5/1. *Notification date:* Continuous beginning 3/1. Students must reply by 5/1 or within 3 weeks of notification.

**CONTACT** Mr. Richard C. Esposito, Director of Financial Aid, Duquesne University, 600 Forbes Avenue, Pittsburgh, PA 15282-0299, 412-396-6607 or toll-free 800-456-0590. *Fax:* 412-396-5284. *E-mail:* esposito@duq.edu.
*Website:* http://www.duq.edu/.

# D'YOUVILLE COLLEGE
## Buffalo, NY

| Tuition & fees: $23,462 | Average undergraduate aid package: $17,951 |
|---|---|

**ABOUT THE INSTITUTION** Independent, coed. **Awards:** certificates, bachelor's, master's, and doctoral degrees. 24 undergraduate majors. **Total enrollment:** 3,150. Undergraduates: 2,023. Freshmen: 251. Federal methodology is used as a basis for awarding need-based institutional aid.

**UNDERGRADUATE EXPENSES for 2015–2016 Comprehensive fee:** $34,262 includes full-time tuition ($23,092), mandatory fees ($370), and room and board ($10,800). Full-time tuition and fees vary according to course load, degree level, and program. Room and board charges vary according to board plan and housing facility. **Part-time tuition:** $720 per credit hour. **Part-time fees:** $3 per credit; $55 per term. Part-time tuition and fees vary according to course load, degree level, and program. **Payment plan:** Guaranteed tuition.

**FRESHMAN FINANCIAL AID (Fall 2014, est.)** 199 applied for aid; of those 91% were deemed to have need. 100% of freshmen with need received aid; of those 18% had need fully met. **Average percent of need met:** 71% (excluding resources awarded to replace EFC). **Average financial aid package:** $18,098 (excluding resources awarded to replace EFC). 10% of all full-time freshmen had no need and received non-need-based gift aid.

**UNDERGRADUATE FINANCIAL AID (Fall 2014, est.)** 758 applied for aid; of those 89% were deemed to have need. 99% of undergraduates with need received aid; of those 26% had need fully met. **Average percent of need met:** 70% (excluding resources awarded to replace EFC). **Average financial aid package:** $17,951 (excluding resources awarded to replace EFC). 11% of all full-time undergraduates had no need and received non-need-based gift aid.

**GIFT AID (NEED-BASED) Total amount:** $10,292,407 (17% federal, 15% state, 66% institutional, 2% external sources). **Receiving aid:** Freshmen: 74% (181); all full-time undergraduates: 82% (670). **Average award:** Freshmen: $14,587; Undergraduates: $14,161. **Scholarships, grants, and awards:** Federal Pell, FSEOG, state, private, college/university gift aid from institutional funds.

**GIFT AID (NON-NEED-BASED) Total amount:** $1,471,379 (2% state, 95% institutional, 3% external sources). **Receiving aid:** Freshmen: 8% (19). Undergraduates: 11% (87). **Average award:** Freshmen: $10,056. Undergraduates: $9848. **Scholarships, grants, and awards by category:** Academic interests/ achievement: biological sciences, business, education, English, general academic interests/achievements, health fields, humanities, international studies, mathematics, premedicine, social sciences. **Special characteristics:** children and siblings of alumni, children of faculty/staff, veterans. **Tuition waivers:** Full or partial for children of alumni, employees or children of employees, senior citizens. **ROTC:** Army cooperative.

**LOANS Student loans:** $7,724,354 (68% need-based, 32% non-need-based). 93% of past graduating class borrowed through all loan programs. **Average indebtedness per student:** $33,169. **Average need-based loan:** Freshmen: $3729. Undergraduates: $4370. **Parent loans:** $1,228,788 (54% need-based, 46% non-need-based). **Programs:** Federal Direct (Subsidized and Unsubsidized Stafford, PLUS), Perkins, Federal Nursing.

**WORK-STUDY Federal work-study:** Total amount: $213,337; 250 jobs averaging $1500. **State or other work-study/employment:** Total amount: $12,110 (8% need-based, 92% non-need-based). 400 part-time jobs averaging $1000.

**APPLYING FOR FINANCIAL AID Required financial aid forms:** FAFSA, state aid form. **Financial aid deadline (priority):** 2/15. **Notification date:** Continuous beginning 3/15. Students must reply within 2 weeks of notification.

**CONTACT** Mr. Matthew R. Metz, Director of Financial Aid, D'Youville College, 320 Porter Avenue, Buffalo, NY 14201-1084, 716-829-7500 or toll-free 800-777-3921. Fax: 716-829-7779. E-mail: metzm@dyc.edu. Website: http://www.dyc.edu/.

# EAGLE GATE COLLEGE
## Layton, UT

**CONTACT** Financial Aid Office, Eagle Gate College, 915 North 400 West, Layton, UT 84041 or toll-free 866-29-EAGLE. Website: http://eaglegatecollege.edu/.

# EAGLE GATE COLLEGE
## Murray, UT

**CONTACT** Financial Aid Office, Eagle Gate College, 5588 South Green Street, Murray, UT 84123, 801-268-9271 or toll-free 866-29-EAGLE. Website: http://eaglegatecollege.edu/.

# EARLHAM COLLEGE
## Richmond, IN

| Tuition & fees: $42,870 | Average undergraduate aid package: $38,857 |
|---|---|

**ABOUT THE INSTITUTION** Independent Society of Friends, coed. **Awards:** bachelor's and master's degrees. 36 undergraduate majors. **Total enrollment:** 1,074. Undergraduates: 993. Freshmen: 270. Federal methodology is used as a basis for awarding need-based institutional aid.

**UNDERGRADUATE EXPENSES for 2015–2016 Comprehensive fee:** $51,470 includes full-time tuition ($42,000), mandatory fees ($870), and room and board ($8600). **College room only:** $4400. Room and board charges vary according to board plan. **Part-time tuition:** $1400 per credit. **Payment plan:** Tuition prepayment.

**FRESHMAN FINANCIAL AID (Fall 2013)** 193 applied for aid; of those 95% were deemed to have need. 100% of freshmen with need received aid; of those 15% had need fully met. **Average percent of need met:** 90% (excluding resources awarded to replace EFC). **Average financial aid package:** $40,538 (excluding resources awarded to replace EFC). 9% of all full-time freshmen had no need and received non-need-based gift aid.

**UNDERGRADUATE FINANCIAL AID (Fall 2013)** 697 applied for aid; of those 96% were deemed to have need. 100% of undergraduates with need received aid; of those 23% had need fully met. **Average percent of need met:** 88% (excluding resources awarded to replace EFC). **Average financial aid package:** $38,857 (excluding resources awarded to replace EFC). 11% of all full-time undergraduates had no need and received non-need-based gift aid.

**GIFT AID (NEED-BASED) Total amount:** $21,737,865 (7% federal, 2% state, 90% institutional, 1% external sources). **Receiving aid:** Freshmen: 71% (177); all full-time undergraduates: 64% (635). **Average award:** Freshmen: $32,972; Undergraduates: $30,350. **Scholarships, grants, and awards:** Federal Pell, FSEOG, state, private, college/university gift aid from institutional funds.

**GIFT AID (NON-NEED-BASED) Total amount:** $1,477,917 (94% institutional, 6% external sources). **Receiving aid:** Freshmen: 22% (55). Undergraduates: 27% (267). **Average award:** Freshmen: $14,039. Undergraduates: $12,143. **Scholarships, grants, and awards by category:** Academic interests/achievement: general academic interests/achievements. **Special achievements/activities:** religious involvement. **Special characteristics:** ethnic background. **Tuition waivers:** Full or partial for employees or children of employees.

**LOANS Student loans:** $4,687,673 (96% need-based, 4% non-need-based). 57% of past graduating class borrowed through all loan programs. **Average indebtedness per student:** $27,421. **Average need-based loan:** Freshmen: $4380. Undergraduates: $5147. **Parent loans:** $815,851 (25% need-based, 75% non-need-based). **Programs:** Federal Direct (Subsidized and Unsubsidized Stafford, PLUS), Perkins, college/university.

**WORK-STUDY Federal work-study:** 676 jobs averaging $2086. **State or other work-study/employment:** Total amount: $30,324 (100% need-based). 37 part-time jobs averaging $600.

**APPLYING FOR FINANCIAL AID Required financial aid form:** FAFSA. **Financial aid deadline:** 3/1. **Notification date:** Continuous beginning 3/1. Students must reply by 5/1 or within 3 weeks of notification.

**CONTACT** Kathy Gottschalk, Director of Financial Aid, Earlham College, National Road West, Richmond, IN 47374-4095, 765-983-1217 or toll-free 800-327-5426. Fax: 765-983-1299. E-mail: gottska@earlham.edu. Website: http://www.earlham.edu/.

# EAST CAROLINA UNIVERSITY
## Greenville, NC

| Tuition & fees (NC res): $6143 | Average undergraduate aid package: $10,661 |
|---|---|

**ABOUT THE INSTITUTION** State-supported, coed. *Awards:* certificates, bachelor's, master's, and doctoral degrees. 83 undergraduate majors. *Total enrollment:* 27,511. Undergraduates: 22,252. Freshmen: 4,226. Federal methodology is used as a basis for awarding need-based institutional aid.
**UNDERGRADUATE EXPENSES for 2015–2016** *Application fee:* $70. *Tuition, state resident:* full-time $3959; part-time $165 per credit hour. *Tuition, nonresident:* full-time $19,156; part-time $798 per credit hour. *Required fees:* full-time $2184. Full-time tuition and fees vary according to location. Part-time tuition and fees vary according to course load and location. *College room and board:* $8833; *Room only:* $4910. Room and board charges vary according to board plan and housing facility.
**FRESHMAN FINANCIAL AID (Fall 2014, est.)** 3,492 applied for aid; of those 76% were deemed to have need. 97% of freshmen with need received aid; of those 8% had need fully met. *Average percent of need met:* 60% (excluding resources awarded to replace EFC). *Average financial aid package:* $9718 (excluding resources awarded to replace EFC). 2% of all full-time freshmen had no need and received non-need-based gift aid.
**UNDERGRADUATE FINANCIAL AID (Fall 2014, est.)** 14,301 applied for aid; of those 83% were deemed to have need. 97% of undergraduates with need received aid; of those 9% had need fully met. *Average percent of need met:* 64% (excluding resources awarded to replace EFC). *Average financial aid package:* $10,661 (excluding resources awarded to replace EFC). 1% of all full-time undergraduates had no need and received non-need-based gift aid.
**GIFT AID (NEED-BASED)** *Total amount:* $80,101,130 (44% federal, 22% state, 31% institutional, 3% external sources). *Receiving aid:* Freshmen: 45% (1,891); all full-time undergraduates: 46% (8,717). *Average award:* Freshmen: $7730; Undergraduates: $7771. *Scholarships, grants, and awards:* Federal Pell, FSEOG, state, private, college/university gift aid from institutional funds, Federal Nursing.
**GIFT AID (NON-NEED-BASED)** *Total amount:* $568,919 (15% state, 46% institutional, 39% external sources). *Receiving aid:* Freshmen: 14% (602). Undergraduates: 9% (1,790). *Average award:* Freshmen: $4161. Undergraduates: $3756. *Scholarships, grants, and awards by category: Academic interests/achievement:* biological sciences, business, communication, computer science, education, engineering/technologies, English, foreign languages, general academic interests/achievements, health fields, home economics, humanities, international studies, library science, mathematics, military science, physical sciences, social sciences. *Creative arts/performance:* applied art and design, art/fine arts, dance, music, performing arts. *Special characteristics:* adult students, children and siblings of alumni, children of faculty/staff, ethnic background, general special characteristics, handicapped students. *Tuition waivers:* Full or partial for employees or children of employees, senior citizens. *ROTC:* Army, Air Force.
**LOANS** *Student loans:* $106,408,647 (97% need-based, 3% non-need-based). 67% of past graduating class borrowed through all loan programs. *Average indebtedness per student:* $29,699. *Average need-based loan:* Freshmen: $5972. Undergraduates: $7066. *Parent loans:* $17,627,090 (100% need-based). *Programs:* Federal Direct (Subsidized and Unsubsidized Stafford, PLUS), Perkins, Federal Nursing, state.
**WORK-STUDY** *Federal work-study:* Total amount: $1,271,666; 406 jobs averaging $2741. *State or other work-study/employment:* 1,992 part-time jobs averaging $2026.
**ATHLETIC AWARDS** Total amount: $6,098,084 (93% need-based, 7% non-need-based).
**APPLYING FOR FINANCIAL AID** *Required financial aid forms:* FAFSA, general scholarship application form. *Financial aid deadline (priority):* 3/1. *Notification date:* 4/1. Students must reply within 3 weeks of notification.
**CONTACT** Ms. Julie Poorman, Director of Financial Aid, East Carolina University, East 5th Street, Greenville, NC 27858-4353, 252-328-6610. Fax: 252-328-4347. E-mail: poormanj@ecu.edu. *Website:* http://www.ecu.edu/.

# EAST CENTRAL UNIVERSITY
## Ada, OK

| Tuition & fees (OK res): $5599 | Average undergraduate aid package: $10,502 |
|---|---|

**ABOUT THE INSTITUTION** State-supported, coed. *Awards:* certificates, bachelor's, and master's degrees. 70 undergraduate majors. *Total enrollment:* 4,428. Undergraduates: 3,637. Freshmen: 605. Federal methodology is used as a basis for awarding need-based institutional aid.
**UNDERGRADUATE EXPENSES for 2015–2016** *Application fee:* $20. *Tuition, state resident:* full-time $4236; part-time $141.20 per semester hour. *Tuition, nonresident:* full-time $12,149; part-time $404.96 per semester hour. *Required fees:* full-time $1363; $41.80 per semester hour or $54.50 per term. *College room and board:* $5158; *Room only:* $2100. Room and board charges vary according to board plan and housing facility. *Payment plan:* Guaranteed tuition.
**FRESHMAN FINANCIAL AID (Fall 2013)** 472 applied for aid; of those 82% were deemed to have need. 100% of freshmen with need received aid. *Average financial aid package:* $9218 (excluding resources awarded to replace EFC). 22% of all full-time freshmen had no need and received non-need-based gift aid.
**UNDERGRADUATE FINANCIAL AID (Fall 2013)** 2,323 applied for aid; of those 87% were deemed to have need. 100% of undergraduates with need received aid. *Average financial aid package:* $10,502 (excluding resources awarded to replace EFC). 19% of all full-time undergraduates had no need and received non-need-based gift aid.
**GIFT AID (NEED-BASED)** *Total amount:* $10,907,832 (74% federal, 26% state). *Receiving aid:* Freshmen: 63% (375); all full-time undergraduates: 62% (1,904). *Average award:* Freshmen: $7410; Undergraduates: $7123. *Scholarships, grants, and awards:* Federal Pell, FSEOG, state, private, college/university gift aid from institutional funds.
**GIFT AID (NON-NEED-BASED)** *Total amount:* $3,504,756 (4% state, 27% institutional, 69% external sources). *Receiving aid:* Freshmen: 16% (93). Undergraduates: 15% (448). *Average award:* Freshmen: $1718. Undergraduates: $1641. *Scholarships, grants, and awards by category: Academic interests/achievement:* 688 awards ($1,227,876 total): communication, general academic interests/achievements. *Creative arts/performance:* 242 awards ($419,783 total): music, performing arts, theater/drama. *Special achievements/activities:* 29 awards ($15,986 total): cheerleading/drum major. *Special characteristics:* 859 awards ($4,244,549 total): children of faculty/staff, general special characteristics, international students, members of minority groups, out-of-state students, veterans, veterans' children. *Tuition waivers:* Full or partial for employees or children of employees, senior citizens.
**LOANS** *Student loans:* $15,978,496 (100% need-based). 64% of past graduating class borrowed through all loan programs. *Average indebtedness per student:* $21,806. *Average need-based loan:* Freshmen: $4803. Undergraduates: $6376. *Parent loans:* $107,935 (100% need-based). *Programs:* Federal Direct (Subsidized and Unsubsidized Stafford, PLUS).
**WORK-STUDY** *Federal work-study:* 515 jobs averaging $643. *State or other work-study/employment:* Part-time jobs available.
**ATHLETIC AWARDS** Total amount: $1,111,308 (100% non-need-based).
**APPLYING FOR FINANCIAL AID** *Required financial aid form:* FAFSA. *Financial aid deadline (priority):* 3/1. *Notification date:* Continuous beginning 4/15. Students must reply within 2 weeks of notification.
**CONTACT** Becky Isaacs, Director of Financial Aid, East Central University, 1100 East 14th, Ada, OK 74820-6999, 580-332-8000 Ext. 242. Fax: 580-436-5612. E-mail: bisaacs@ecok.edu. *Website:* http://www.ecok.edu/.

# EASTERN CONNECTICUT STATE UNIVERSITY
## Willimantic, CT

| Tuition & fees (CT res): $9560 | Average undergraduate aid package: $8659 |
|---|---|

**ABOUT THE INSTITUTION** State-supported, coed. *Awards:* associate, bachelor's, and master's degrees. 29 undergraduate majors. *Total enrollment:* 5,287.

Undergraduates: 5,139. Freshmen: 883. Federal methodology is used as a basis for awarding need-based institutional aid.

**UNDERGRADUATE EXPENSES for 2015–2016** *Application fee:* $50. *Tuition, state resident:* full-time $4600; part-time $433 per credit hour. *Tuition, nonresident:* full-time $14,886; part-time $437 per credit hour. *Required fees:* full-time $4960. Part-time tuition and fees vary according to course load. *College room and board:* $11,650; *Room only:* $6682. Room and board charges vary according to board plan and housing facility.

**FRESHMAN FINANCIAL AID (Fall 2013)** 861 applied for aid; of those 76% were deemed to have need. 96% of freshmen with need received aid; of those 10% had need fully met. *Average percent of need met:* 62% (excluding resources awarded to replace EFC). *Average financial aid package:* $9762 (excluding resources awarded to replace EFC). 3% of all full-time freshmen had no need and received non-need-based gift aid.

**UNDERGRADUATE FINANCIAL AID (Fall 2013)** 3,574 applied for aid; of those 81% were deemed to have need. 96% of undergraduates with need received aid; of those 9% had need fully met. *Average percent of need met:* 56% (excluding resources awarded to replace EFC). *Average financial aid package:* $8659 (excluding resources awarded to replace EFC). 3% of all full-time undergraduates had no need and received non-need-based gift aid.

**GIFT AID (NEED-BASED)** *Total amount:* $13,004,729 (47% federal, 11% state, 39% institutional, 3% external sources). *Receiving aid:* Freshmen: 53% (510); all full-time undergraduates: 47% (2,059). *Average award:* Freshmen: $7858; Undergraduates: $6010. *Scholarships, grants, and awards:* Federal Pell, FSEOG, state, private, college/university gift aid from institutional funds.

**GIFT AID (NON-NEED-BASED)** *Total amount:* $998,371 (5% state, 77% institutional, 18% external sources). *Receiving aid:* Freshmen: 8% (81). Undergraduates: 5% (212). *Average award:* Freshmen: $4279. Undergraduates: $2927. *Scholarships, grants, and awards by category:* Academic interests/achievement: general academic interests/achievements. *Tuition waivers:* Full or partial for employees or children of employees. *ROTC:* Army cooperative, Air Force cooperative.

**LOANS** *Student loans:* $27,641,035 (72% need-based, 28% non-need-based). 72% of past graduating class borrowed through all loan programs. *Average indebtedness per student:* $26,921. *Average need-based loan:* Freshmen: $3500. Undergraduates: $4403. *Parent loans:* $4,548,339 (37% need-based, 63% non-need-based). *Programs:* Federal Direct (Subsidized and Unsubsidized Stafford, PLUS), Perkins, alternative loans.

**WORK-STUDY** *Federal work-study:* jobs available. *State or other work-study/employment:* Part-time jobs available.

**APPLYING FOR FINANCIAL AID** *Required financial aid form:* FAFSA. *Financial aid deadline:* Continuous. *Notification date:* Continuous. Students must reply within 2 weeks of notification.

**CONTACT** Edwin Harris, Director of Enrollment Management and Financial Aid, Eastern Connecticut State University, 83 Windham Street, Gelsi-Young Hall, Room 320, Willimantic, CT 06226-2295, 860-465-5775. *E-mail:* harrised@easternct.edu. *Website:* http://www.easternct.edu/.

# EASTERN ILLINOIS UNIVERSITY
## Charleston, IL

| Tuition & fees (IL res): $11,108 | Average undergraduate aid package: $11,392 |
|---|---|

**ABOUT THE INSTITUTION** State-supported, coed. *Awards:* certificates, bachelor's, and master's degrees. 47 undergraduate majors. *Total enrollment:* 8,913. Undergraduates: 7,640. Freshmen: 1,126. Federal methodology is used as a basis for awarding need-based institutional aid.

**UNDERGRADUATE EXPENSES for 2015–2016** *Application fee:* $30. *Tuition, state resident:* full-time $8490; part-time $283 per credit hour. *Tuition, nonresident:* full-time $25,470; part-time $849 per credit hour. *Required fees:* full-time $2618; $96 per credit hour. Full-time tuition and fees vary according to course load and student level. Part-time tuition and fees vary according to course load and student level. *College room and board:* $9358. Room and board charges vary according to board plan and housing facility. *Payment plan:* Guaranteed tuition.

**FRESHMAN FINANCIAL AID (Fall 2014, est.)** 1,024 applied for aid; of those 79% were deemed to have need. 100% of freshmen with need received aid; of those 8% had need fully met. *Average percent of need met:* 64% (excluding resources

awarded to replace EFC). *Average financial aid package:* $12,129 (excluding resources awarded to replace EFC). 14% of all full-time freshmen had no need and received non-need-based gift aid.

**UNDERGRADUATE FINANCIAL AID (Fall 2014, est.)** 6,483 applied for aid; of those 71% were deemed to have need. 100% of undergraduates with need received aid; of those 9% had need fully met. *Average percent of need met:* 64% (excluding resources awarded to replace EFC). *Average financial aid package:* $11,392 (excluding resources awarded to replace EFC). 11% of all full-time undergraduates had no need and received non-need-based gift aid.

**GIFT AID (NEED-BASED)** *Total amount:* $30,711,332 (45% federal, 32% state, 18% institutional, 5% external sources). *Receiving aid:* Freshmen: 59% (628); all full-time undergraduates: 51% (3,414). *Average award:* Freshmen: $3431; Undergraduates: $3447. *Scholarships, grants, and awards:* Federal Pell, FSEOG, state, private, college/university gift aid from institutional funds.

**GIFT AID (NON-NEED-BASED)** *Total amount:* $3,048,868 (4% federal, 17% state, 58% institutional, 21% external sources). *Receiving aid:* Freshmen: 44% (466). Undergraduates: 30% (1,976). *Average award:* Freshmen: $3286. Undergraduates: $3537. *Scholarships, grants, and awards by category:* Academic interests/achievement: 2,195 awards ($3,960,336 total): biological sciences, business, communication, computer science, education, engineering/technologies, English, foreign languages, general academic interests/achievements, health fields, home economics, humanities, international studies, mathematics, physical sciences, premedicine, social sciences. Creative arts/performance: 479 awards ($595,172 total): applied art and design, art/fine arts, cinema/film/broadcasting, creative writing, debating, general creative arts/performance, journalism/publications, music, performing arts, theater/drama. Special achievements/activities: 652 awards ($3,424,137 total): general special achievements/activities, leadership. *Tuition waivers:* Full or partial for employees or children of employees, senior citizens. *ROTC:* Army.

**LOANS** *Student loans:* $39,603,825 (86% need-based, 14% non-need-based). 82% of past graduating class borrowed through all loan programs. *Average indebtedness per student:* $31,219. *Average need-based loan:* Freshmen: $3134. Undergraduates: $4201. *Parent loans:* $8,330,482 (77% need-based, 23% non-need-based). *Programs:* Federal Direct (Subsidized and Unsubsidized Stafford, PLUS), Perkins, college/university.

**WORK-STUDY** *Federal work-study:* Total amount: $373,910; 208 jobs averaging $980. *State or other work-study/employment:* 2,342 part-time jobs averaging $1489.

**ATHLETIC AWARDS** Total amount: $3,245,966 (51% need-based, 49% non-need-based).

**APPLYING FOR FINANCIAL AID** *Required financial aid form:* FAFSA. *Financial aid deadline (priority):* 3/1. *Notification date:* Continuous beginning 3/1. Students must reply within 2 weeks of notification.

**CONTACT** Carol Waldmann, Interim Director of Financial Aid, Eastern Illinois University, 600 Lincoln Avenue, Charleston, IL 61920, 217-581-3713 or toll-free 077-581-2348. *Fax:* 217-581-6422. *E-mail:* finald@eiu.edu. *Website:* http://www.eiu.edu/.

# EASTERN KENTUCKY UNIVERSITY
## Richmond, KY

| Tuition & fees (KY res): $8150 | Average undergraduate aid package: $10,970 |
|---|---|

**ABOUT THE INSTITUTION** State-supported, coed. *Awards:* certificates, associate, bachelor's, master's, and doctoral degrees. 101 undergraduate majors. *Total enrollment:* 16,305. Undergraduates: 13,949. Freshmen: 2,608. Federal methodology is used as a basis for awarding need-based institutional aid.

**UNDERGRADUATE EXPENSES for 2015–2016** *Application fee:* $35. *Tuition, state resident:* full-time $8150; part-time $340 per credit hour. *Tuition, nonresident:* full-time $17,640; part-time $735 per credit hour. Full-time tuition and fees vary according to degree level and location. Part-time tuition and fees vary according to course load. *Room only:* $4562. Room and board charges vary according to board plan and housing facility.

**FRESHMAN FINANCIAL AID (Fall 2014, est.)** 2,350 applied for aid; of those 84% were deemed to have need. 100% of freshmen with need received aid; of those 40% had need fully met. *Average percent of need met:* 85% (excluding resources awarded to replace EFC). *Average financial aid package:* $11,758 (excluding

resources awarded to replace EFC). 9% of all full-time freshmen had no need and received non-need-based gift aid.

**UNDERGRADUATE FINANCIAL AID (Fall 2014, est.)** 9,375 applied for aid; of those 87% were deemed to have need. 98% of undergraduates with need received aid; of those 40% had need fully met. *Average percent of need met:* 84% (excluding resources awarded to replace EFC). *Average financial aid package:* $10,970 (excluding resources awarded to replace EFC). 11% of all full-time undergraduates had no need and received non-need-based gift aid.

**GIFT AID (NEED-BASED)** *Total amount:* $50,389,365 (54% federal, 26% state, 18% institutional, 2% external sources). *Receiving aid:* Freshmen: 52% (1,313); all full-time undergraduates: 48% (5,395). *Average award:* Freshmen: $6260; Undergraduates: $5765. *Scholarships, grants, and awards:* Federal Pell, FSEOG, state, private, college/university gift aid from institutional funds.

**GIFT AID (NON-NEED-BASED)** *Total amount:* $8,404,868 (1% federal, 33% state, 62% institutional, 4% external sources). *Receiving aid:* Freshmen: 71% (1,801). Undergraduates: 43% (4,859). *Average award:* Freshmen: $5346. Undergraduates: $5455. *Scholarships, grants, and awards by category:* Academic interests/achievement: 3,004 awards ($13,442,212 total): general academic interests/achievements. *Creative arts/performance:* 136 awards ($380,147 total): music. *Special achievements/activities:* 35 awards ($24,500 total): cheerleading/drum major. *Special characteristics:* 360 awards ($1,568,742 total): children and siblings of alumni, children of faculty/staff, members of minority groups. *Tuition waivers:* Full or partial for employees or children of employees, senior citizens. *ROTC:* Army, Air Force cooperative.

**LOANS** *Student loans:* $65,838,764 (89% need-based, 11% non-need-based). 71% of past graduating class borrowed through all loan programs. *Average indebtedness per student:* $27,438. *Average need-based loan:* Freshmen: $2905. Undergraduates: $3876. *Parent loans:* $30,915,476 (74% need-based, 26% non-need-based). *Programs:* Federal Direct (Subsidized and Unsubsidized Stafford, PLUS), Perkins, college/university.

**WORK-STUDY** *Federal work-study:* Total amount: $4,804,798; 1,200 jobs averaging $2400. *State or other work-study/employment:* Total amount: $3,122,472 (100% non-need-based). 1,200 part-time jobs averaging $2400.

**ATHLETIC AWARDS** Total amount: $4,190,367 (39% need-based, 61% non-need-based).

**APPLYING FOR FINANCIAL AID** *Required financial aid form:* FAFSA. *Financial aid deadline (priority):* 2/1. *Notification date:* Continuous beginning 4/1.

**CONTACT** Office of Financial Aid, Eastern Kentucky University, 521 Lancaster Avenue, Whitlock Building, CPO Box 59, Richmond, KY 40475-3102, 859-622-2361 or toll-free 800-465-9191. *Fax:* 859-622-2019. *E-mail:* finaid@eku.edu. *Website:* http://www.eku.edu/.

# EASTERN MENNONITE UNIVERSITY
## Harrisonburg, VA

**CONTACT** Ms. Renee Leap, Assistant Director of Financial Assistance, Eastern Mennonite University, 1200 Park Road, Harrisonburg, VA 22802-2462, 540-432-4138 or toll-free 800-368-2665. *Fax:* 540-432-4081. *E-mail:* leapr@emu.edu. *Website:* http://www.emu.edu/.

# EASTERN MICHIGAN UNIVERSITY
## Ypsilanti, MI

| Tuition & fees (MI res): $9663 | Average undergraduate aid package: $9291 |
| --- | --- |

**ABOUT THE INSTITUTION** State-supported, coed. *Awards:* certificates, bachelor's, master's, and doctoral degrees. 131 undergraduate majors. *Total enrollment:* 22,261. Undergraduates: 18,208. Freshmen: 2,630. Federal methodology is used as a basis for awarding need-based institutional aid.

**UNDERGRADUATE EXPENSES for 2015–2016** *Application fee:* $35. *One-time required fee:* $310. *Tuition, state resident:* full-time $8244; part-time $274.80 per credit hour. *Tuition, nonresident:* full-time $24,286; part-time $809.55 per credit hour. *Required fees:* full-time $1419; $43.85 per credit hour or $51.60 per term. Full-time tuition and fees vary according to course level and reciprocity agreements. Part-time tuition and fees vary according to course level and reciprocity agreements. *College room and board:* $8940; *Room only:* $4676. Room and board charges vary according to board plan, housing facility, and location.

**FRESHMAN FINANCIAL AID (Fall 2013)** 2,633 applied for aid; of those 80% were deemed to have need. 99% of freshmen with need received aid; of those 5% had need fully met. *Average percent of need met:* 45% (excluding resources awarded to replace EFC). *Average financial aid package:* $10,241 (excluding resources awarded to replace EFC). 23% of all full-time freshmen had no need and received non-need-based gift aid.

**UNDERGRADUATE FINANCIAL AID (Fall 2013)** 11,263 applied for aid; of those 85% were deemed to have need. 99% of undergraduates with need received aid; of those 3% had need fully met. *Average percent of need met:* 48% (excluding resources awarded to replace EFC). *Average financial aid package:* $9291 (excluding resources awarded to replace EFC). 14% of all full-time undergraduates had no need and received non-need-based gift aid.

**GIFT AID (NEED-BASED)** *Total amount:* $37,038,917 (95% federal, 2% state, 3% institutional). *Receiving aid:* Freshmen: 52% (1,491); all full-time undergraduates: 52% (7,062). *Average award:* Freshmen: $5967; Undergraduates: $4845. *Scholarships, grants, and awards:* Federal Pell, FSEOG, state, private, college/university gift aid from institutional funds.

**GIFT AID (NON-NEED-BASED)** *Total amount:* $26,232,147 (94% institutional, 6% external sources). *Receiving aid:* Freshmen: 58% (1,660). Undergraduates: 31% (4,223). *Average award:* Freshmen: $4386. Undergraduates: $4785. *Scholarships, grants, and awards by category:* Academic interests/achievement: 5,902 awards ($17,298,661 total): agriculture, architecture, biological sciences, business, communication, computer science, education, engineering/technologies, English, foreign languages, general academic interests/achievements, health fields, home economics, humanities, mathematics, physical sciences, religion/biblical studies, social sciences. *Creative arts/performance:* 116 awards ($200,325 total): applied art and design, art/fine arts, cinema/film/broadcasting, creative writing, dance, debating, general creative arts/performance, music, performing arts, theater/drama. *Special achievements/activities:* 172 awards ($200,325 total): general special achievements/activities, leadership, memberships, religious involvement. *Special characteristics:* 413 awards ($5,373,322 total): children and siblings of alumni, ethnic background, international students, members of minority groups, out-of-state students, previous college experience, religious affiliation. *Tuition waivers:* Full or partial for employees or children of employees. *ROTC:* Army, Naval cooperative, Air Force cooperative.

**LOANS** *Student loans:* $102,897,131 (41% need-based, 59% non-need-based). 69% of past graduating class borrowed through all loan programs. *Average indebtedness per student:* $25,781. *Average need-based loan:* Freshmen: $3208. Undergraduates: $4112. *Parent loans:* $13,097,733 (100% non-need-based). *Programs:* Federal Direct (Subsidized and Unsubsidized Stafford, PLUS), Perkins, private loans.

**WORK-STUDY** *Federal work-study:* 675 jobs averaging $1612. *State or other work-study/employment:* Part-time jobs available.

**ATHLETIC AWARDS** Total amount: $5,027,630 (100% non-need-based).

**APPLYING FOR FINANCIAL AID** *Required financial aid form:* FAFSA. *Financial aid deadline:* Continuous. *Notification date:* Continuous beginning 3/1.

**CONTACT** Donna Holubik, Director of Financial Aid, Eastern Michigan University, 403 Pierce Hall, Ypsilanti, MI 48197, 734-487-1048 or toll-free 800-GO TO EMU. *Fax:* 734-487-0174. *E-mail:* dholubik@emich.edu. *Website:* http://www.emich.edu/.

# EASTERN NAZARENE COLLEGE
## Quincy, MA

| Tuition & fees: N/R | Average undergraduate aid package: $29,431 |
| --- | --- |

**ABOUT THE INSTITUTION** Independent Church of the Nazarene, coed. 106 undergraduate majors. Federal methodology is used as a basis for awarding need-based institutional aid.

**FRESHMAN FINANCIAL AID (Fall 2014, est.)** 162 applied for aid; of those 90% were deemed to have need. 97% of freshmen with need received aid; of those 30% had need fully met. *Average percent of need met:* 81% (excluding resources awarded to replace EFC). *Average financial aid package:* $31,739 (excluding resources awarded to replace EFC). 10% of all full-time freshmen had no need and received non-need-based gift aid.

**UNDERGRADUATE FINANCIAL AID (Fall 2014, est.)** 761 applied for aid; of those 52% were deemed to have need. 98% of undergraduates with need received aid; of those 33% had need fully met. *Average percent of need met:* 80% (excluding resources awarded to replace EFC). *Average financial aid package:* $29,431 (excluding resources awarded to replace EFC). 8% of all full-time undergraduates had no need and received non-need-based gift aid.
**GIFT AID (NEED-BASED)** *Total amount:* $10,194,178 (14% federal, 2% state, 83% institutional, 1% external sources). *Receiving aid:* Freshmen: 84% (142); all full-time undergraduates: 44% (384). *Average award:* Freshmen: $22,442; Undergraduates: $17,673. *Scholarships, grants, and awards:* Federal Pell, FSEOG, state, private, college/university gift aid from institutional funds, United Negro College Fund.
**GIFT AID (NON-NEED-BASED)** *Total amount:* $1,355,380 (96% institutional, 4% external sources). *Receiving aid:* Freshmen: 6% (10). Undergraduates: 4% (33). *Average award:* Freshmen: $9100. Undergraduates: $13,644. *Scholarships, grants, and awards by category:* Academic interests/achievement: general academic interests/achievements. Special achievements/activities: hobbies/interests, leadership, religious involvement. Special characteristics: children and siblings of alumni, children of faculty/staff, international students, religious affiliation, veterans.
**LOANS** *Student loans:* $6,170,836 (55% need-based, 45% non-need-based). 77% of past graduating class borrowed through all loan programs. *Average indebtedness per student:* $25,251. *Average need-based loan:* Freshmen: $6200. Undergraduates: $8837. *Parent loans:* $1,421,914 (64% need-based, 36% non-need-based). *Programs:* Federal Direct (Subsidized and Unsubsidized Stafford, PLUS), Perkins, state, alternative loans.
**WORK-STUDY** *Federal work-study:* Total amount: $81,000; 40 jobs averaging $2500. *State or other work-study/employment:* Part-time jobs available.
**APPLYING FOR FINANCIAL AID** *Required financial aid form:* FAFSA. *Financial aid deadline (priority):* 3/1. *Notification date:* Continuous beginning 1/15. Students must reply within 2 weeks of notification.
**CONTACT** Lisa Seals, Interim Director of Financial Aid, Eastern Nazarene College, 23 East Elm Avenue, Quincy, MA 02170, 617-745-3869 or toll-free 800-88-ENC88. *Fax:* 617-745-3992. *E-mail:* lisa.seals@enc .edu.
*Website:* http://www.enc.edu/.

# EASTERN NEW MEXICO UNIVERSITY
## Portales, NM

| Tuition & fees (NM res): $4856 | Average undergraduate aid package: $10,675 |
| --- | --- |

**ABOUT THE INSTITUTION** State-supported, coed. *Awards:* certificates, associate, bachelor's, and master's degrees. 52 undergraduate majors. *Total enrollment:* 5,887. Undergraduates: 4,600. Freshmen: 639. Federal methodology is used as a basis for awarding need-based institutional aid.
**UNDERGRADUATE EXPENSES for 2015–2016** *Tuition, state resident:* full-time $3064; part-time $127.70 per credit hour. *Tuition, nonresident:* full-time $8838; part-time $368.32 per credit hour. *Required fees:* full-time $1792; $74.70 per credit hour. Full-time tuition and fees vary according to course load and reciprocity agreements. Part-time tuition and fees vary according to course load. *College room and board:* $6452; *Room only:* $3108. Room and board charges vary according to board plan and housing facility.
**FRESHMAN FINANCIAL AID (Fall 2014, est.)** 414 applied for aid; of those 100% were deemed to have need. 100% of freshmen with need received aid; of those 100% had need fully met. *Average percent of need met:* 39% (excluding resources awarded to replace EFC). *Average financial aid package:* $10,864 (excluding resources awarded to replace EFC). 3% of all full-time freshmen had no need and received non-need-based gift aid.
**UNDERGRADUATE FINANCIAL AID (Fall 2014, est.)** 1,617 applied for aid; of those 100% were deemed to have need. 100% of undergraduates with need received aid; of those 100% had need fully met. *Average percent of need met:* 40% (excluding resources awarded to replace EFC). *Average financial aid package:* $10,675 (excluding resources awarded to replace EFC). 2% of all full-time undergraduates had no need and received non-need-based gift aid.
**GIFT AID (NEED-BASED)** *Total amount:* $13,020,652 (68% federal, 32% state). *Receiving aid:* Freshmen: 65% (406); all full-time undergraduates: 58% (1,584). *Average award:* Freshmen: $4460; Undergraduates: $4301. *Scholarships, grants, and awards:* Federal Pell, FSEOG, state, private, college/university gift aid from institutional funds.

**GIFT AID (NON-NEED-BASED)** *Total amount:* $2,730,865 (71% institutional, 29% external sources). *Receiving aid:* Freshmen: 56% (352). Undergraduates: 36% (991). *Average award:* Freshmen: $3593. Undergraduates: $4803. *Scholarships, grants, and awards by category:* Academic interests/achievement: agriculture, biological sciences, business, communication, computer science, education, engineering/technologies, English, foreign languages, general academic interests/achievements, health fields, home economics, humanities, mathematics, military science, physical sciences, premedicine, religion/biblical studies, social sciences. *Creative arts/performance:* applied art and design, art/fine arts, cinema/film/broadcasting, creative writing, dance, debating, general creative arts/performance, journalism/publications, music, performing arts, theater/drama. *Special achievements/activities:* community service, general special achievements/activities, hobbies/interests, leadership, memberships, rodeo. *Special characteristics:* children and siblings of alumni, ethnic background, first-generation college students, general special characteristics, international students, members of minority groups, out-of-state students, veterans. *Tuition waivers:* Full or partial for employees or children of employees, senior citizens.
**LOANS** *Student loans:* $11,727,817 (45% need-based, 55% non-need-based). 2% of past graduating class borrowed through all loan programs. *Average indebtedness per student:* $4895. *Average need-based loan:* Freshmen: $3150. Undergraduates: $3904. *Parent loans:* $167,286 (100% non-need-based). *Programs:* Federal Direct (Subsidized and Unsubsidized Stafford, PLUS), Perkins, state, college/university.
**WORK-STUDY** *Federal work-study:* Total amount: $1,260,744; jobs available. *State or other work-study/employment:* Total amount: $261,587 (100% need-based). Part-time jobs available.
**ATHLETIC AWARDS** Total amount: $1,188,920 (100% non-need-based).
**APPLYING FOR FINANCIAL AID** *Required financial aid form:* FAFSA. *Financial aid deadline:* Continuous. *Notification date:* Continuous beginning 3/1.
**CONTACT** Mr. Brent Small, Director of Financial Aid, Eastern New Mexico University, Station 20, 1500 South Avenue K, Portales, NM 88130, 575-562-2194 or toll-free 800-367-3668. *Fax:* 575-562-2198. *E-mail:* brent.small@enmu.edu. *Website:* http://www.enmu.edu/.

# EASTERN OREGON UNIVERSITY
## La Grande, OR

**CONTACT** Financial Aid Office, Eastern Oregon University, One University Boulevard, Inlow Hall, Room 201, La Grande, OR 97850-2899, 541-962-3550 or toll-free 800-452-8639. *Fax:* 541-962-3661. *E-mail:* fao@eou.edu. *Website:* http://www.eou.edu/.

# EASTERN UNIVERSITY
## St. Davids, PA

| Tuition & fees: $30,590 | Average undergraduate aid package: $18,517 |
| --- | --- |

**ABOUT THE INSTITUTION** Independent Christian, coed. *Awards:* certificates, diplomas, associate, bachelor's, master's, and doctoral degrees. 38 undergraduate majors. *Total enrollment:* 3,762. Undergraduates: 2,402. Freshmen: 446. Federal methodology is used as a basis for awarding need-based institutional aid.
**UNDERGRADUATE EXPENSES for 2015–2016** *Application fee:* $35. *One-time required fee:* $50. *Comprehensive fee:* $40,778 includes full-time tuition ($30,250), mandatory fees ($340), and room and board ($10,188). *College room only:* $5432. Full-time tuition and fees vary according to course load, degree level, and program. Room and board charges vary according to housing facility and location. *Part-time tuition:* $660 per credit. Part-time tuition and fees vary according to course load, degree level, and program.
**FRESHMAN FINANCIAL AID (Fall 2013)** 285 applied for aid; of those 88% were deemed to have need. 100% of freshmen with need received aid; of those 28% had need fully met. *Average percent of need met:* 74% (excluding resources awarded to replace EFC). *Average financial aid package:* $22,088 (excluding resources awarded to replace EFC). 8% of all full-time freshmen had no need and received non-need-based gift aid.
**UNDERGRADUATE FINANCIAL AID (Fall 2013)** 1,974 applied for aid; of those 93% were deemed to have need. 99% of undergraduates with need received aid;

of those 17%. had need fully met. *Average percent of need met:* 62% (excluding resources awarded to replace EFC). *Average financial aid package:* $18,517 (excluding resources awarded to replace EFC). 6% of all full-time undergraduates had no need and received non-need-based gift aid.

**GIFT AID (NEED-BASED)** *Total amount:* $10,139,510 (46% federal, 24% state, 30% institutional). *Receiving aid:* Freshmen: 45% (186); all full-time undergraduates: 75% (1,485). *Average award:* Freshmen: $6585; Undergraduates: $6527. *Scholarships, grants, and awards:* Federal Pell, FSEOG, state, private, college/university gift aid from institutional funds.

**GIFT AID (NON-NEED-BASED)** *Total amount:* $18,035,252 (1% state, 95% institutional, 4% external sources). *Receiving aid:* Freshmen: 60% (245). Undergraduates: 76% (1,519). *Average award:* Freshmen: $13,109. Undergraduates: $10,267. *Scholarships, grants, and awards by category: Academic interests/achievement:* business, general academic interests/achievements, religion/biblical studies. *Creative arts/performance:* dance, music. *Special achievements/activities:* community service, leadership, memberships. *Special characteristics:* children and siblings of alumni, children of faculty/staff, international students, relatives of clergy. *Tuition waivers:* Full or partial for children of alumni, employees or children of employees. *ROTC:* Army cooperative, Air Force cooperative.

**LOANS** *Student loans:* $19,318,501 (40% need-based, 60% non-need-based). 80% of past graduating class borrowed through all loan programs. *Average indebtedness per student:* $34,662. *Average need-based loan:* Freshmen: $3797. Undergraduates: $4281. *Parent loans:* $2,792,091 (100% non-need-based). *Programs:* Federal Direct (Subsidized and Unsubsidized Stafford, PLUS), Perkins.

**WORK-STUDY** *Federal work-study:* 418 jobs averaging $1200. *State or other work-study/employment:* Part-time jobs available.

**APPLYING FOR FINANCIAL AID** *Required financial aid forms:* FAFSA, monthly income form. *Financial aid deadline:* Continuous. *Notification date:* Continuous beginning 4/1.

**CONTACT** Office of Student Financial Aid, Eastern University, 1300 Eagle Road, St. Davids, PA 19087-3696, 610-225-5102 or toll-free 800-452-0996. *Fax:* 610-225-5651. *E-mail:* finaid@eastern.edu.
*Website:* http://www.eastern.edu/.

uates: $8319. *Scholarships, grants, and awards:* Federal Pell, FSEOG, state, private, college/university gift aid from institutional funds.

**GIFT AID (NON-NEED-BASED)** *Total amount:* $3,911,224 (2% institutional, 98% external sources). *Receiving aid:* Freshmen: 39% (570). Undergraduates: 15% (1,523). *Average award:* Freshmen: $3598. Undergraduates: $3958. *Scholarships, grants, and awards by category: Academic interests/achievement:* 1,162 awards ($1,655,000 total): area/ethnic studies, biological sciences, business, communication, computer science, education, engineering/technologies, English, foreign languages, general academic interests/achievements, health fields, humanities, international studies, mathematics, military science, physical sciences, premedicine, social sciences. *Creative arts/performance:* 85 awards ($106,250 total): art/fine arts, cinema/film/broadcasting, creative writing, journalism/publications, music, theater/drama. *Special characteristics:* 700 awards ($1,053,000 total): adult students, children and siblings of alumni, children of union members/company employees, ethnic background, first-generation college students, handicapped students, local/state students, married students, spouses of deceased or disabled public servants, veterans, veterans' children. *Tuition waivers:* Full or partial for employees or children of employees. *ROTC:* Army.

**LOANS** *Student loans:* $46,760,041 (87% need-based, 13% non-need-based). 57% of past graduating class borrowed through all loan programs. *Average indebtedness per student:* $27,259. *Average need-based loan:* Freshmen: $3169. Undergraduates: $4160. *Parent loans:* $9,827,599 (69% need-based, 31% non-need-based). *Programs:* Federal Direct (Subsidized and Unsubsidized Stafford, PLUS), Perkins.

**WORK-STUDY** *Federal work-study:* 185 jobs averaging $2484. *State or other work-study/employment:* Total amount: $448,824 (100% need-based). 182 part-time jobs averaging $2573.

**ATHLETIC AWARDS** Total amount: $2,465,663 (27% need-based, 73% non-need-based).

**APPLYING FOR FINANCIAL AID** *Required financial aid form:* FAFSA. *Financial aid deadline (priority):* 2/15. *Notification date:* Continuous beginning 4/15. Students must reply within 4 weeks of notification.

**CONTACT** Mr. Bruce DeFrates, Director of Financial Aid and Scholarships, Eastern Washington University, 102 Sutton Hall, Cheney, WA 99004-2447, 509-359-6329. *Fax:* 509-359-4330. *E-mail:* bdefrates@ewu.edu.
*Website:* http://www.ewu.edu/.

# EASTERN WASHINGTON UNIVERSITY
## Cheney, WA

| Tuition & fees (WA res): $7982 | Average undergraduate aid package: $10,884 |
| --- | --- |

**ABOUT THE INSTITUTION** State-supported, coed. *Awards:* certificates, bachelor's, master's, and doctoral degrees. 93 undergraduate majors. *Total enrollment:* 12,791. Undergraduates: 11,678. Freshmen: 1,486. Federal methodology is used as a basis for awarding need-based institutional aid.

**UNDERGRADUATE EXPENSES** for 2015–2016 *Tuition, state resident:* full-time $7372; part-time $245.73 per credit hour. *Tuition, nonresident:* full-time $20,503; part-time $683.42 per credit hour. *Required fees:* full-time $610. Full-time tuition and fees vary according to course level, course load, degree level, program, reciprocity agreements, and student level. Part-time tuition and fees vary according to course level, course load, degree level, program, reciprocity agreements, and student level. *College room and board:* $9628; *Room only:* $5278. Room and board charges vary according to board plan and housing facility.

**FRESHMAN FINANCIAL AID (Fall 2013)** 1,305 applied for aid; of those 79% were deemed to have need. 97% of freshmen with need received aid; of those 9% had need fully met. *Average percent of need met:* 53% (excluding resources awarded to replace EFC). *Average financial aid package:* $10,838 (excluding resources awarded to replace EFC). 9% of all full-time freshmen had no need and received non-need-based gift aid.

**UNDERGRADUATE FINANCIAL AID (Fall 2013)** 7,800 applied for aid; of those 85% were deemed to have need. 97% of undergraduates with need received aid; of those 8% had need fully met. *Average percent of need met:* 55% (excluding resources awarded to replace EFC). *Average financial aid package:* $10,884 (excluding resources awarded to replace EFC). 5% of all full-time undergraduates had no need and received non-need-based gift aid.

**GIFT AID (NEED-BASED)** *Total amount:* $44,333,587 (44% federal, 43% state, 8% institutional, 5% external sources). *Receiving aid:* Freshmen: 54% (790); all full-time undergraduates: 52% (5,073). *Average award:* Freshmen: $8576; Undergrad-

# EAST STROUDSBURG UNIVERSITY OF PENNSYLVANIA
## East Stroudsburg, PA

| Tuition & fees (PA res): $9376 | Average undergraduate aid package: $3992 |
| --- | --- |

**ABOUT THE INSTITUTION** State-supported, coed. *Awards:* associate, bachelor's, and master's degrees. 49 undergraduate majors. *Total enrollment:* 6,778. Undergraduates: 6,186. Freshmen: 1,212. Federal methodology is used as a basis for awarding need-based institutional aid.

**UNDERGRADUATE EXPENSES** for 2015–2016 *Application fee:* $25. *Tuition, state resident:* full-time $6820; part-time $284 per credit. *Tuition, nonresident:* full-time $17,050; part-time $710 per credit. *Required fees:* full-time $2556; $102.77 per credit. Full-time tuition and fees vary according to course load, location, and program. Part-time tuition and fees vary according to location and program. *College room and board:* $7980; *Room only:* $5372. Room and board charges vary according to board plan and housing facility.

**FRESHMAN FINANCIAL AID (Fall 2013)** 1,072 applied for aid; of those 82% were deemed to have need. 94% of freshmen with need received aid; of those .2% had need fully met. *Average percent of need met:* 37% (excluding resources awarded to replace EFC). *Average financial aid package:* $3834 (excluding resources awarded to replace EFC).

**UNDERGRADUATE FINANCIAL AID (Fall 2013)** 4,718 applied for aid; of those 84% were deemed to have need. 95% of undergraduates with need received aid; of those .3% had need fully met. *Average percent of need met:* 37% (excluding resources awarded to replace EFC). *Average financial aid package:* $3992 (excluding resources awarded to replace EFC).

**GIFT AID (NEED-BASED)** *Total amount:* $14,673,828 (60% federal, 33% state, 3% institutional, 4% external sources). *Receiving aid:* Freshmen: 49% (566); all full-time undergraduates: 44% (2,442). *Average award:* Freshmen: $2928; Undergraduates: $2952. *Scholarships, grants, and awards:* Federal Pell, FSEOG, state, private, college/university gift aid from institutional funds.

**GIFT AID (NON-NEED-BASED)** *Scholarships, grants, and awards by category:* *Academic interests/achievement:* biological sciences, business, communication, computer science, education, English, foreign languages, general academic interests/achievements, health fields, mathematics, physical sciences, social sciences. *Creative arts/performance:* applied art and design, art/fine arts, music, theater/drama. *Special achievements/activities:* general special achievements/activities, leadership. *Special characteristics:* adult students, children and siblings of alumni, handicapped students, international students, local/state students, members of minority groups. *Tuition waivers:* Full or partial for employees or children of employees, senior citizens. **ROTC:** Army, Air Force.

**LOANS** *Student loans:* $28,345,683 (51% need-based, 49% non-need-based). 69% of past graduating class borrowed through all loan programs. *Average indebtedness per student:* $27,730. *Average need-based loan:* Freshmen: $810. Undergraduates: $1034. *Parent loans:* $17,645,460 (100% need-based). *Programs:* Federal Direct (Subsidized and Unsubsidized Stafford, PLUS), Perkins.

**WORK-STUDY** *Federal work-study:* jobs available. *State or other work-study/employment:* Total amount: $777,202 (79% need-based, 21% non-need-based). Part-time jobs available.

**ATHLETIC AWARDS** Total amount: $955,135 (100% need-based).

**APPLYING FOR FINANCIAL AID** *Required financial aid form:* FAFSA. *Financial aid deadline:* 3/1. *Notification date:* 4/1. Students must reply by 5/1.

**CONTACT** Kizzy Morris, Registrar/Director of Enrollment Services, East Stroudsburg University of Pennsylvania, 200 Prospect Street, East Stroudsburg, PA 18301-2999, 570-422-2820 or toll-free 877-230-5547. *Fax:* 570-422-2849. *Website:* http://www.esu.edu/.

# EAST TENNESSEE STATE UNIVERSITY
## Johnson City, TN

**ABOUT THE INSTITUTION** State-supported, coed. *Awards:* certificates, bachelor's, master's, and doctoral degrees. 49 undergraduate majors. *Total enrollment:* 14,434. Undergraduates: 11,550. Freshmen: 2,055.

**GIFT AID (NEED-BASED)** *Scholarships, grants, and awards:* Federal Pell, FSEOG, state, private, college/university gift aid from institutional funds, Federal Nursing.

**GIFT AID (NON-NEED-BASED)** *Scholarships, grants, and awards by category:* *Academic interests/achievement:* biological sciences, business, computer science, education, engineering/technologies, English, general academic interests/achievements, health fields, mathematics, military science, social sciences. *Creative arts/performance:* art/fine arts, journalism/publications, music, theater/drama. *Special achievements/activities:* leadership, memberships. *Special characteristics:* children of union members/company employees, members of minority groups.

**LOANS** *Programs:* Federal Direct (Subsidized and Unsubsidized Stafford, PLUS), Perkins, Federal Nursing, state, college/university.

**APPLYING FOR FINANCIAL AID** *Required financial aid form:* FAFSA.

**CONTACT** Financial Aid Counselor, East Tennessee State University, PO Box 70722, 105 Burgin Dossett, Johnson City, TN 37614-1710, 423-439-4300 or toll-free 800-462-3878. *Fax:* 423-439-5855. *E-mail:* finaid@etsu.edu. *Website:* http://www.etsu.edu/.

# EAST TEXAS BAPTIST UNIVERSITY
## Marshall, TX

| Tuition & fees: $23,280 | Average undergraduate aid package: $16,873 |
|---|---|

**ABOUT THE INSTITUTION** Independent Baptist, coed. *Awards:* certificates, bachelor's, and master's degrees. 41 undergraduate majors. *Total enrollment:* 1,299. Undergraduates: 1,231. Freshmen: 363. Federal methodology is used as a basis for awarding need-based institutional aid.

**UNDERGRADUATE EXPENSES** for 2015–2016 *Application fee:* $25. *Comprehensive fee:* $31,577 includes full-time tuition ($22,350), mandatory fees ($930), and room and board ($8297). *College room only:* $4400. Room and board charges vary according to board plan and housing facility. *Part-time tuition:* $745 per credit hour. *Part-time fees:* $39 per credit hour.

**FRESHMAN FINANCIAL AID (Fall 2013)** 328 applied for aid; of those 91% were deemed to have need. 100% of freshmen with need received aid; of those 13% had need fully met. *Average percent of need met:* 33% (excluding resources awarded to replace EFC). *Average financial aid package:* $17,600 (excluding resources awarded to replace EFC). 13% of all full-time freshmen had no need and received non-need-based gift aid.

**UNDERGRADUATE FINANCIAL AID (Fall 2013)** 1,016 applied for aid; of those 91% were deemed to have need. 100% of undergraduates with need received aid; of those 12% had need fully met. *Average percent of need met:* 34% (excluding resources awarded to replace EFC). *Average financial aid package:* $16,873 (excluding resources awarded to replace EFC). 13% of all full-time undergraduates had no need and received non-need-based gift aid.

**GIFT AID (NEED-BASED)** *Total amount:* $3,931,346 (60% federal, 40% state). *Receiving aid:* Freshmen: 69% (233); all full-time undergraduates: 66% (705). *Average award:* Freshmen: $6374; Undergraduates: $5989. *Scholarships, grants, and awards:* Federal Pell, FSEOG, state, private, college/university gift aid from institutional funds.

**GIFT AID (NON-NEED-BASED)** *Total amount:* $9,520,241 (95% institutional, 5% external sources). *Receiving aid:* Freshmen: 86% (293). Undergraduates: 84% (891). *Average award:* Freshmen: $9631. Undergraduates: $8974. *Scholarships, grants, and awards by category:* *Academic interests/achievement:* 869 awards ($4,592,168 total): biological sciences, business, communication, education, English, general academic interests/achievements, health fields, humanities, mathematics, physical sciences, religion/biblical studies, social sciences. *Creative arts/performance:* 99 awards ($240,528 total): music, theater/drama. *Special achievements/activities:* 650 awards ($1,569,122 total): general special achievements/activities, leadership, religious involvement. *Special characteristics:* 113 awards ($511,241 total): children and siblings of alumni, children of faculty/staff, general special characteristics, international students, religious affiliation. *Tuition waivers:* Full or partial for employees or children of employees.

**LOANS** *Student loans:* $7,363,389 (43% need-based, 57% non-need-based). 88% of past graduating class borrowed through all loan programs. *Average indebtedness per student:* $30,718. *Average need-based loan:* Freshmen: $3385. Undergraduates: $4129. *Parent loans:* $1,271,782 (100% non-need-based). *Programs:* Federal Direct (Subsidized and Unsubsidized Stafford, PLUS), Perkins, state.

**WORK-STUDY** *Federal work-study:* 143 jobs averaging $1409. *State or other work-study/employment:* Total amount: $254,564 (6% need-based, 94% non-need-based). 186 part-time jobs averaging $1364.

**APPLYING FOR FINANCIAL AID** *Required financial aid forms:* FAFSA, institution's own form. *Financial aid deadline (priority):* 6/1. *Notification date:* Continuous beginning 1/1.

**CONTACT** Tommy Young, Director of Financial Aid, East Texas Baptist University, One Tiger Drive, Marshall, TX 75670-1498, 903-923-2137 or toll-free 800-804-ETBU. *Fax:* 903-934-8120. *E-mail:* tyoung@etbu.edu. *Website:* http://www.etbu.edu/.

# EAST-WEST UNIVERSITY
## Chicago, IL

**ABOUT THE INSTITUTION** Independent, coed. 7 undergraduate majors.

**GIFT AID (NEED-BASED)** *Scholarships, grants, and awards:* Federal Pell, FSEOG, state, college/university gift aid from institutional funds.

**GIFT AID (NON-NEED-BASED)** *Scholarships, grants, and awards by category:* *Academic interests/achievement:* general academic interests/achievements.

**LOANS** *Programs:* Federal Direct (Subsidized and Unsubsidized Stafford, PLUS).

**APPLYING FOR FINANCIAL AID** *Required financial aid form:* FAFSA.

**CONTACT** Cesar Campos, Director of Financial Aid, East-West University, 816 South Michigan Avenue, Chicago, IL 60605-2103, 312-939-0111 Ext. 1806. *Fax:* 312-939-0083. *E-mail:* cesar@eastwest.edu. *Website:* http://www.eastwest.edu/.

# ECCLESIA COLLEGE
## Springdale, AR

**CONTACT** Financial Aid Office, Ecclesia College, 9653 Nations Drive, Springdale, AR 72762, 479-248-7236.
*Website:* http://www.ecollege.edu/.

# ECKERD COLLEGE
## St. Petersburg, FL

| Tuition & fees: $38,668 | Average undergraduate aid package: $31,297 |
| --- | --- |

**ABOUT THE INSTITUTION** Independent Presbyterian, coed. *Awards:* bachelor's degrees. 38 undergraduate majors. *Total enrollment:* 1,802. Undergraduates: 1,802. Freshmen: 512. Federal methodology is used as a basis for awarding need-based institutional aid.

**UNDERGRADUATE EXPENSES for 2015–2016** *Application fee:* $40. *Comprehensive fee:* $49,218 includes full-time tuition ($38,342), mandatory fees ($326), and room and board ($10,550). *College room only:* $5310. Room and board charges vary according to board plan and housing facility. *Part-time tuition:* $4514 per course.

**FRESHMAN FINANCIAL AID (Fall 2014, est.)** 448 applied for aid; of those 82% were deemed to have need. 100% of freshmen with need received aid; of those 21% had need fully met. *Average percent of need met:* 88% (excluding resources awarded to replace EFC). *Average financial aid package:* $31,498 (excluding resources awarded to replace EFC). 39% of all full-time freshmen had no need and received non-need-based gift aid.

**UNDERGRADUATE FINANCIAL AID (Fall 2014, est.)** 1,234 applied for aid; of those 86% were deemed to have need. 100% of undergraduates with need received aid; of those 22% had need fully met. *Average percent of need met:* 87% (excluding resources awarded to replace EFC). *Average financial aid package:* $31,297 (excluding resources awarded to replace EFC). 51% of all full-time undergraduates had no need and received non-need-based gift aid.

**GIFT AID (NEED-BASED)** *Total amount:* $22,375,002 (7% federal, 5% state, 86% institutional, 2% external sources). *Receiving aid:* Freshmen: 82% (368); all full-time undergraduates: 86% (1,058). *Average award:* Freshmen: $22,273; Undergraduates: $21,747. *Scholarships, grants, and awards:* Federal Pell, FSEOG, state, college/university gift aid from institutional funds.

**GIFT AID (NON-NEED-BASED)** *Total amount:* $11,393,382 (4% state, 93% institutional, 3% external sources). *Average award:* Freshmen: $16,280. Undergraduates: $14,326. *Scholarships, grants, and awards by category:* Academic interests/achievement: general academic interests/achievements. *Creative arts/performance:* art/fine arts, creative writing, music, theater/drama. *Special characteristics:* children of faculty/staff, international students, local/state students, religious affiliation. *Tuition waivers:* Full or partial for employees or children of employees. *ROTC:* Army cooperative, Air Force cooperative.

**LOANS** *Student loans:* $11,020,650 (64% need-based, 36% non-need-based). 59% of past graduating class borrowed through all loan programs. *Average indebtedness per student:* $33,697. *Average need-based loan:* Freshmen: $3328. Undergraduates: $3836. *Parent loans:* $4,834,974 (36% need-based, 64% non-need-based). *Programs:* Federal Direct (Subsidized and Unsubsidized Stafford, PLUS), Perkins, college/university.

**WORK-STUDY** *Federal work-study:* Total amount: $1,435,880; jobs available. *State or other work-study/employment:* Total amount: $26,000 (100% non-need-based). Part-time jobs available.

**ATHLETIC AWARDS** Total amount: $1,852,594 (43% need-based, 57% non-need-based).

**APPLYING FOR FINANCIAL AID** *Required financial aid form:* FAFSA. *Financial aid deadline (priority):* 3/1. *Notification date:* Continuous beginning 2/20. Students must reply by 5/1.

**CONTACT** Dr. Pat Garrett Watkins, Director of Financial Aid, Eckerd College, 4200 54th Avenue, South, St. Petersburg, FL 33711, 727-864-8334 or toll-free 800-456-9009. *Fax:* 727-866-2304. *E-mail:* watkinpe@eckerd.edu.
*Website:* http://www.eckerd.edu/.

# ECPI UNIVERSITY
## Virginia Beach, VA

| Tuition & fees: N/R | Average undergraduate aid package: N/A |
| --- | --- |

**ABOUT THE INSTITUTION** Proprietary, coed. 28 undergraduate majors. Federal methodology is used as a basis for awarding need-based institutional aid.

**FRESHMAN FINANCIAL AID (Fall 2013)** 797 applied for aid.

**UNDERGRADUATE FINANCIAL AID (Fall 2013)** 11,856 applied for aid.

**GIFT AID (NEED-BASED)** *Total amount:* $56,907,077 (92% federal, 8% institutional). *Scholarships, grants, and awards:* Federal Pell, FSEOG, state, private, college/university gift aid from institutional funds.

**GIFT AID (NON-NEED-BASED)** *Total amount:* $2,561,362 (13% state, 78% institutional, 9% external sources). *Scholarships, grants, and awards by category:* Academic interests/achievement: business, computer science, engineering/technologies, health fields. *Special achievements/activities:* community service, general special achievements/activities. *Special characteristics:* adult students, children and siblings of alumni, children of current students, children of faculty/staff, general special characteristics, parents of current students, veterans, veterans' children.

**LOANS** *Student loans:* $110,239,629 (42% need-based, 58% non-need-based). *Parent loans:* $3,392,018 (100% non-need-based). *Programs:* Federal Direct (Subsidized and Unsubsidized Stafford, PLUS), Perkins, college/university, private loans.

**WORK-STUDY** *Federal work-study:* jobs available. *State or other work-study/employment:* Part-time jobs available.

**APPLYING FOR FINANCIAL AID** *Required financial aid forms:* FAFSA, institution's own form. *Financial aid deadline:* Continuous. *Notification date:* Continuous beginning 3/1. Students must reply within 12 weeks of notification.

**CONTACT** Mrs. Kathi Turner, Director of Financial Aid, ECPI University, 5555 Greenwich Road, Suite 300, Virginia Beach, VA 23462, 757-490-9090 or toll-free 866-499-0336. *Fax:* 757-671-8661. *E-mail:* kturner@ecpi.edu.
*Website:* http://www.ecpi.edu/.

# EDGEWOOD COLLEGE
## Madison, WI

| Tuition & fees: $25,590 | Average undergraduate aid package: $20,413 |
| --- | --- |

**ABOUT THE INSTITUTION** Independent Roman Catholic, coed. *Awards:* certificates, bachelor's, master's, and doctoral degrees. 52 undergraduate majors. *Total enrollment:* 2,980. Undergraduates: 1,935. Freshmen: 290. Federal methodology is used as a basis for awarding need-based institutional aid.

**UNDERGRADUATE EXPENSES for 2015–2016** *Application fee:* $30. *Comprehensive fee:* $34,563 includes full-time tuition ($25,590) and room and board ($8973). Full-time tuition and fees vary according to degree level. Room and board charges vary according to housing facility. *Part-time tuition:* $805 per credit. Part-time tuition and fees vary according to course load and degree level.

**FRESHMAN FINANCIAL AID (Fall 2013)** 265 applied for aid; of those 92% were deemed to have need. 100% of freshmen with need received aid; of those 10% had need fully met. *Average percent of need met:* 79% (excluding resources awarded to replace EFC). *Average financial aid package:* $21,816 (excluding resources awarded to replace EFC). 14% of all full-time freshmen had no need and received non-need-based gift aid.

**UNDERGRADUATE FINANCIAL AID (Fall 2013)** 1,277 applied for aid; of those 91% were deemed to have need. 100% of undergraduates with need received aid; of those 11% had need fully met. *Average percent of need met:* 75% (excluding resources awarded to replace EFC). *Average financial aid package:* $20,413 (excluding resources awarded to replace EFC). 18% of all full-time undergraduates had no need and received non-need-based gift aid.

**GIFT AID (NEED-BASED)** *Total amount:* $19,352,152 (17% federal, 11% state, 64% institutional, 8% external sources). *Receiving aid:* Freshmen: 83% (242); all full-time undergraduates: 75% (1,136). *Average award:* Freshmen: $16,849; Undergraduates: $14,030. *Scholarships, grants, and awards:* Federal Pell, FSEOG, state, private, college/university gift aid from institutional funds.

**GIFT AID (NON-NEED-BASED)** *Total amount:* $2,908,033 (8% federal, 58% institutional, 34% external sources). *Receiving aid:* Freshmen: 6% (18). Undergraduates: 4% (68). *Average award:* Freshmen: $6060. Undergraduates: $5020. *Scholarships, grants, and awards by category:* Academic interests/achievement:

1,359 awards ($6,062,552 total): area/ethnic studies, foreign languages, general academic interests/achievements. *Creative arts/performance:* 141 awards ($196,750 total): art/fine arts, creative writing, music, performing arts, theater/drama. *Special achievements/activities:* 54 awards ($304,195 total): community service. *Special characteristics:* 72 awards ($759,489 total): children of faculty/staff. *Tuition waivers:* Full or partial for employees or children of employees. *ROTC:* Army cooperative, Naval cooperative, Air Force cooperative.

**LOANS** *Student loans:* $14,270,290 (75% need-based, 25% non-need-based). 77% of past graduating class borrowed through all loan programs. *Average indebtedness per student:* $31,522. *Average need-based loan:* Freshmen: $3846. Undergraduates: $5408. *Parent loans:* $1,914,835 (42% need-based, 58% non-need-based). *Programs:* Federal Direct (Subsidized and Unsubsidized Stafford, PLUS), Perkins, state.

**WORK-STUDY** *Federal work-study:* 390 jobs averaging $2051. *State or other work-study/employment:* Total amount: $2,139,310 (51% need-based, 49% non-need-based). 807 part-time jobs averaging $1943.

**APPLYING FOR FINANCIAL AID** *Required financial aid form:* FAFSA. *Financial aid deadline (priority):* 3/1. *Notification date:* Continuous beginning 3/15. Students must reply by 5/1.

**CONTACT** Ms. Kari J. Gribble, Director of Financial Aid and Edgewood Central, Edgewood College, 1000 Edgewood College Drive, Madison, WI 53711-1997, 608-663-4300 or toll-free 800-444-4861 Ext. 2294. *E-mail:* ecentral@edgewood.edu. *Website:* http://www.edgewood.edu/.

# EDINBORO UNIVERSITY OF PENNSYLVANIA
## Edinboro, PA

**ABOUT THE INSTITUTION** State-supported, coed. *Awards:* certificates, associate, bachelor's, master's, and doctoral degrees. 39 undergraduate majors. *Total enrollment:* 6,837. Undergraduates: 5,585. Freshmen: 1,239.

**GIFT AID (NEED-BASED)** *Scholarships, grants, and awards:* Federal Pell, FSEOG, state, private, college/university gift aid from institutional funds.

**GIFT AID (NON-NEED-BASED)** *Scholarships, grants, and awards by category:* Academic interests/achievement: biological sciences, business, communication, computer science, education, engineering/technologies, English, foreign languages, general academic interests/achievements, health fields, humanities, mathematics, military science, physical sciences, premedicine, religion/biblical studies, social sciences. *Creative arts/performance:* applied art and design, art/fine arts, cinema/film/broadcasting, creative writing, journalism/publications, music, theater/drama. *Special achievements/activities:* community service, general special achievements/activities, leadership, memberships. *Special characteristics:* adult students, children and siblings of alumni, children of faculty/staff, children of union members/company employees, children with a deceased or disabled parent, first-generation college students, general special characteristics, handicapped students, international students, local/state students, members of minority groups, out-of-state students, religious affiliation, veterans, veterans' children.

**LOANS** *Programs:* Federal Direct (Subsidized and Unsubsidized Stafford, PLUS), Perkins, Federal Nursing.

**APPLYING FOR FINANCIAL AID** *Required financial aid forms:* FAFSA, state aid form.

**CONTACT** Ms. Alyssa Dobson, Director of Financial Aid, Edinboro University of Pennsylvania, Hamilton Hall, Edinboro, PA 16444, 814-732-3500 or toll-free 888-846-2676. *Fax:* 814-732-2129. *E-mail:* finaid@edinboro.edu. *Website:* http://www.edinboro.edu/.

# EDP UNIVERSITY OF PUERTO RICO
## Hato Rey, PR

**CONTACT** Yaitzaenid Gonzalez, Financial Aid Administrator, EDP University of Puerto Rico, PO Box 192303, San Juan, PR 00919-2303, 787-765-3560 Ext. 253. *Fax:* 787-777-0025. *E-mail:* ygonzalez@edpcollege.edu. *Website:* http://www.edpuniversity.edu/.

# EDP UNIVERSITY OF PUERTO RICO–SAN SEBASTIAN
## San Sebastian, PR

**ABOUT THE INSTITUTION** Proprietary, coed. *Awards:* associate, bachelor's, and master's degrees. 11 undergraduate majors. *Total enrollment:* 1,204. Undergraduates: 1,168. Freshmen: 292.

**GIFT AID (NEED-BASED)** *Scholarships, grants, and awards:* Federal Pell, FSEOG, state.

**GIFT AID (NON-NEED-BASED)** *Scholarships, grants, and awards by category:* Special characteristics: veterans, veterans' children.

**LOANS** *Programs:* Federal Direct (Subsidized and Unsubsidized Stafford, PLUS).

**APPLYING FOR FINANCIAL AID** *Required financial aid form:* FAFSA.

**CONTACT** Mrs. Yaitzaenid Gonzalez, Financial Aid Administrator, EDP University of Puerto Rico–San Sebastian, PO Box 192303, San Juan , PR 00919, 787-765-3560 Ext. 253. *Fax:* 787-777-0025. *E-mail:* ygonzalez@edpcollege.edu. *Website:* http://www.edpuniversity.edu/.

# EDWARD WATERS COLLEGE
## Jacksonville, FL

**CONTACT** Gabriel Mbomeh, Director of Financial Aid, Edward Waters College, 1658 Kings Road, Jacksonville, FL 32209-6199, 904-366-2528 or toll-free 888-898-3191. *Website:* http://www.ewc.edu/.

# ELIZABETH CITY STATE UNIVERSITY
## Elizabeth City, NC

| Tuition & fees (NC res): $4428 | Average undergraduate aid package: N/A |
|---|---|

**ABOUT THE INSTITUTION** State-supported, coed. *Awards:* bachelor's and master's degrees. 35 undergraduate majors. *Total enrollment:* 2,421. Undergraduates: 2,336. Freshmen: 323. Federal methodology is used as a basis for awarding need-based institutional aid.

**UNDERGRADUATE EXPENSES for 2015–2016** *Application fee:* $30. *Tuition, state resident:* full-time $2776; part-time $347 per credit hour. *Tuition, nonresident:* full-time $13,639; part-time $1704.11 per credit hour. *Required fees:* full-time $1652. *College room and board:* $7213. Room and board charges vary according to housing facility.

**FRESHMAN FINANCIAL AID (Fall 2013)** 315 applied for aid; of those 100% were deemed to have need. 100% of freshmen with need received aid. *Average percent of need met:* 75% (excluding resources awarded to replace EFC).

**UNDERGRADUATE FINANCIAL AID (Fall 2013)** 2,248 applied for aid; of those 100% were deemed to have need. 100% of undergraduates with need received aid.

**GIFT AID (NEED-BASED)** *Total amount:* $13,795,863 (59% federal, 31% state, 10% institutional). *Receiving aid:* Freshmen: 89% (285); all full-time undergraduates: 87% (2,038). *Average award:* Freshmen: $8452. *Scholarships, grants, and awards:* Federal Pell, FSEOG, state, private, college/university gift aid from institutional funds, United Negro College Fund.

**GIFT AID (NON-NEED-BASED)** *Total amount:* $399,926 (100% institutional). *Receiving aid:* Freshmen: 11% (34). *Scholarships, grants, and awards by category:* Academic interests/achievement: computer science, education, general academic interests/achievements, mathematics, military science. *Creative arts/performance:* music, performing arts. *Special characteristics:* ethnic background, handicapped students, international students, members of minority groups, veterans, veterans' children. *ROTC:* Army.

**LOANS** *Student loans:* $11,525,839 (55% need-based, 45% non-need-based). *Average need-based loan:* Freshmen: $5160. *Parent loans:* $909,940 (100% need-based). *Programs:* Federal Direct (Subsidized and Unsubsidized Stafford, PLUS), Perkins.

**WORK-STUDY** *Federal work-study:* jobs available.

**ATHLETIC AWARDS** Total amount: $509,411 (100% need-based).

**APPLYING FOR FINANCIAL AID** *Required financial aid forms:* FAFSA, noncustodial (divorced/separated) parent's statement. *Financial aid deadline:* 6/1 (priority: 3/15). *Notification date:* Continuous beginning 6/1. Students must reply by 6/30.

**CONTACT** LaTonya M. Gregory, Assistant Director of Financial Aid, Elizabeth City State University, 1704 Weeksville Road, Campus Box 914, Elizabeth City, NC 27909-7806, 252-335-3285 or toll-free 800-347-3278. *Fax:* 252-335-3716.
*Website:* http://www.ecsu.edu/.

# ELIZABETHTOWN COLLEGE
### Elizabethtown, PA

| Tuition & fees: $41,710 | Average undergraduate aid package: $27,722 |
|---|---|

**ABOUT THE INSTITUTION** Independent Church of the Brethren, coed. *Awards:* bachelor's and master's degrees. 43 undergraduate majors. *Total enrollment:* 1,822. Undergraduates: 1,788. Freshmen: 447. Both federal and institutional methodology are used as a basis for awarding need-based institutional aid.

**UNDERGRADUATE EXPENSES for 2015–2016** *Application fee:* $30. *Comprehensive fee:* $51,850 includes full-time tuition ($41,710) and room and board ($10,140). *College room only:* $5020. Full-time tuition and fees vary according to course load. Room and board charges vary according to board plan and housing facility. Part-time tuition and fees vary according to course load.

**FRESHMAN FINANCIAL AID (Fall 2014, est.)** 401 applied for aid; of those 88% were deemed to have need. 100% of freshmen with need received aid; of those 26% had need fully met. *Average percent of need met:* 81% (excluding resources awarded to replace EFC). *Average financial aid package:* $28,192 (excluding resources awarded to replace EFC). 24% of all full-time freshmen had no need and received non-need-based gift aid.

**UNDERGRADUATE FINANCIAL AID (Fall 2014, est.)** 1,433 applied for aid; of those 91% were deemed to have need. 100% of undergraduates with need received aid; of those 19% had need fully met. *Average percent of need met:* 79% (excluding resources awarded to replace EFC). *Average financial aid package:* $27,722 (excluding resources awarded to replace EFC). 23% of all full-time undergraduates had no need and received non-need-based gift aid.

**GIFT AID (NEED-BASED)** *Total amount:* $30,123,796 (6% federal, 5% state, 82% institutional, 7% external sources). *Receiving aid:* Freshmen: 79% (351); all full-time undergraduates: 75% (1,303). *Average award:* Freshmen: $24,506; Undergraduates: $23,087. *Scholarships, grants, and awards:* Federal Pell, FSEOG, state, private, college/university gift aid from institutional funds.

**GIFT AID (NON-NEED-BASED)** *Total amount:* $10,613,707 (84% institutional, 16% external sources). *Receiving aid:* Freshmen: 18% (79). Undergraduates: 11% (197). *Average award:* Freshmen: $20,043. Undergraduates: $18,489. *Scholarships, grants, and awards by category:* Academic interests/achievement: biological sciences, business, communication, computer science, education, engineering/technologies, English, foreign languages, general academic interests/achievements, health fields, humanities, international studies, mathematics, physical sciences, premedicine, religion/biblical studies, social sciences. *Creative arts/performance:* art/fine arts, music, performing arts, theater/drama. *Special achievements/activities:* religious involvement. *Special characteristics:* children of faculty/staff, international students, local/state students, members of minority groups, religious affiliation, siblings of current students. *Tuition waivers:* Full or partial for employees or children of employees.

**LOANS** *Student loans:* $13,537,906 (64% need-based, 36% non-need-based). 75% of past graduating class borrowed through all loan programs. *Average indebtedness per student:* $30,355. *Average need-based loan:* Freshmen: $3941. Undergraduates: $4680. *Parent loans:* $6,229,975 (36% need-based, 64% non-need-based). *Programs:* Federal Direct (Subsidized and Unsubsidized Stafford, PLUS), Perkins.

**WORK-STUDY** *Federal work-study:* Total amount: $1,014,235; 780 jobs averaging $1319.

**APPLYING FOR FINANCIAL AID** *Required financial aid forms:* FAFSA, state aid form, federal income tax form(s), W-2 forms. *Financial aid deadline (priority):* 3/15. *Notification date:* Continuous beginning 3/1. Students must reply by 5/1 or within 2 weeks of notification.

**CONTACT** Ms. Elizabeth K. McCloud, Director of Financial Aid, Elizabethtown College, 1 Alpha Drive, Elizabethtown, PA 17022, 717-361-1404. *Fax:* 717-361-1514. *E-mail:* mcclouek@etown.edu.
*Website:* http://www.etown.edu/.

# ELLIS UNIVERSITY
### Oakbrook Terrace, IL

**CONTACT** Financial Aid Office, Ellis University, 2 Mid America Plaza, Suite 824AB, Oakbrook Terrace, IL 60181 or toll-free 877-355-4762.
*Website:* http://www.ellis.edu/.

# ELMHURST COLLEGE
### Elmhurst, IL

| Tuition & fees: $34,450 | Average undergraduate aid package: $27,279 |
|---|---|

**ABOUT THE INSTITUTION** Independent United Church of Christ, coed. *Awards:* bachelor's and master's degrees. 70 undergraduate majors. *Total enrollment:* 3,257. Undergraduates: 2,853. Freshmen: 510. Federal methodology is used as a basis for awarding need-based institutional aid.

**UNDERGRADUATE EXPENSES for 2015–2016** *Comprehensive fee:* $44,116 includes full-time tuition ($34,200), mandatory fees ($250), and room and board ($9666). *College room only:* $5856. Room and board charges vary according to board plan and housing facility. Part-time tuition and fees vary according to course load.

**FRESHMAN FINANCIAL AID (Fall 2014, est.)** 465 applied for aid; of those 86% were deemed to have need. 100% of freshmen with need received aid; of those 35% had need fully met. *Average percent of need met:* 82% (excluding resources awarded to replace EFC). *Average financial aid package:* $24,842 (excluding resources awarded to replace EFC). 13% of all full-time freshmen had no need and received non-need-based gift aid.

**UNDERGRADUATE FINANCIAL AID (Fall 2014, est.)** 2,323 applied for aid; of those 81% were deemed to have need. 100% of undergraduates with need received aid; of those 35% had need fully met. *Average percent of need met:* 76% (excluding resources awarded to replace EFC). *Average financial aid package:* $27,279 (excluding resources awarded to replace EFC). 17% of all full-time undergraduates had no need and received non-need-based gift aid.

**GIFT AID (NEED-BASED)** *Total amount:* $41,374,630 (10% federal, 9% state, 80% institutional, 1% external sources). *Receiving aid:* Freshmen: 78% (398); all full-time undergraduates: 72% (1,889). *Average award:* Freshmen: $22,363; Undergraduates: $22,002. *Scholarships, grants, and awards:* Federal Pell, FSEOG, state, private, college/university gift aid from institutional funds.

**GIFT AID (NON-NEED-BASED)** *Total amount:* $11,180,448 (98% institutional, 2% external sources). *Receiving aid:* Freshmen: 27% (138). Undergraduates: 25% (658). *Average award:* Freshmen: $18,144. Undergraduates: $13,248. *Scholarships, grants, and awards by category:* Academic interests/achievement: 1,354 awards ($18,348,787 total): biological sciences, business, communication, computer science, education, English, foreign languages, general academic interests/achievements, health fields, humanities, international studies, mathematics, physical sciences, premedicine, religion/biblical studies, social sciences. *Creative arts/performance:* 120 awards ($1,129,271 total): art/fine arts, music, theater/drama. *Special characteristics:* 718 awards ($3,590,728 total): children and siblings of alumni, children of current students, children with a deceased or disabled parent, ethnic background, members of minority groups, religious affiliation, siblings of current students, spouses of current students, veterans, veterans' children. *Tuition waivers:* Full or partial for employees or children of employees, senior citizens. *ROTC:* Army cooperative, Air Force cooperative.

**LOANS** *Student loans:* $17,041,252 (38% need-based, 62% non-need-based). 89% of past graduating class borrowed through all loan programs. *Average indebtedness per student:* $28,068. *Average need-based loan:* Freshmen: $3636. Undergraduates: $4634. *Parent loans:* $4,673,921 (73% need-based, 27% non-need-based). *Programs:* Federal Direct (Subsidized and Unsubsidized Stafford, PLUS), Perkins, alternative loans.

**WORK-STUDY** *Federal work-study:* Total amount: $330,974; 372 jobs averaging $1236. *State or other work-study/employment:* Total amount: $382,534 (100% non-need-based). 238 part-time jobs averaging $1607.

**APPLYING FOR FINANCIAL AID** *Required financial aid form:* FAFSA. *Financial aid deadline (priority):* 2/14. *Notification date:* Continuous beginning 3/1. Students must reply within 3 weeks of notification.

**CONTACT** Ruth A. Pusich, Director of Student Financial Services, Elmhurst College, Goebel Hall 106A, 190 Prospect Avenue, Elmhurst, IL 60126-3296, 630-617-3080 or toll-free 800-697-1871. *Fax:* 630-617-3487. *E-mail:* ruthp@elmhurst.edu.
*Website:* http://www.elmhurst.edu/.

# ELMIRA COLLEGE
## Elmira, NY

| Tuition & fees: $39,950 | Average undergraduate aid package: $30,559 |
|---|---|

**ABOUT THE INSTITUTION** Independent, coed. *Awards:* certificates, associate, bachelor's, and master's degrees. 49 undergraduate majors. *Total enrollment:* 1,482. Undergraduates: 1,365. Freshmen: 331. Federal methodology is used as a basis for awarding need-based institutional aid.

**UNDERGRADUATE EXPENSES for 2015–2016** *Application fee:* $50. *Comprehensive fee:* $51,950 includes full-time tuition ($38,300), mandatory fees ($1650), and room and board ($12,000). *College room only:* $6400. Room and board charges vary according to board plan and housing facility. *Part-time fees:* $55 per year. Part-time tuition and fees vary according to course load and degree level. *Payment plan:* Tuition prepayment.

**FRESHMAN FINANCIAL AID (Fall 2014, est.)** 299 applied for aid; of those 91% were deemed to have need. 100% of freshmen with need received aid; of those 20% had need fully met. *Average percent of need met:* 78% (excluding resources awarded to replace EFC). *Average financial aid package:* $30,477 (excluding resources awarded to replace EFC). 17% of all full-time freshmen had no need and received non-need-based gift aid.

**UNDERGRADUATE FINANCIAL AID (Fall 2014, est.)** 1,032 applied for aid; of those 94% were deemed to have need. 100% of undergraduates with need received aid; of those 21% had need fully met. *Average percent of need met:* 79% (excluding resources awarded to replace EFC). *Average financial aid package:* $30,559 (excluding resources awarded to replace EFC). 17% of all full-time undergraduates had no need and received non-need-based gift aid.

**GIFT AID (NEED-BASED)** *Total amount:* $25,049,934 (6% federal, 4% state, 87% institutional, 3% external sources). *Receiving aid:* Freshmen: 83% (272); all full-time undergraduates: 82% (964). *Average award:* Freshmen: $27,500; Undergraduates: $26,624. *Scholarships, grants, and awards:* Federal Pell, FSEOG, state, private, college/university gift aid from institutional funds.

**GIFT AID (NON-NEED-BASED)** *Total amount:* $6,557,443 (1% state, 90% institutional, 9% external sources). *Receiving aid:* Freshmen: 15% (50). Undergraduates: 13% (156). *Average award:* Freshmen: $23,750. Undergraduates: $23,065. *Scholarships, grants, and awards by category:* Academic interests/achievement: 856 awards ($20,675,065 total): general academic interests/achievements. *Special achievements/activities:* 64 awards ($735,450 total): leadership. *Special characteristics:* 474 awards ($2,706,753 total): children of faculty/staff, international students, local/state students, out-of-state students, previous college experience, siblings of current students, veterans. *Tuition waivers:* Full or partial for employees or children of employees, adult students. *ROTC:* Army, Air Force cooperative.

**LOANS** *Student loans:* $9,342,705 (70% need-based, 30% non-need-based). 82% of past graduating class borrowed through all loan programs. *Average indebtedness per student:* $26,471. *Average need-based loan:* Freshmen: $3721. Undergraduates: $4635. *Parent loans:* $3,957,215 (44% need-based, 56% non-need-based). *Programs:* Federal Direct (Subsidized and Unsubsidized Stafford, PLUS), Perkins.

**WORK-STUDY** *Federal work-study:* Total amount: $214,393; 191 jobs averaging $1600. *State or other work-study/employment:* Total amount: $266,670 (28% need-based, 72% non-need-based). 340 part-time jobs averaging $1300.

**APPLYING FOR FINANCIAL AID** *Required financial aid forms:* FAFSA, state aid form. *Financial aid deadline (priority):* 2/1. *Notification date:* Continuous beginning 2/15. Students must reply by 5/1 or within 3 weeks of notification.

**CONTACT** Kathleen L. Cohen, Dean of Financial Aid, Elmira College, One Park Place, Elmira, NY 14901-2099, 607-735-1728 or toll-free 800-935-6472. *Fax:* 607-735-1718. *E-mail:* kcohen@elmira.edu.
*Website:* http://www.elmira.edu/.

# ELMS COLLEGE
## Chicopee, MA

| Tuition & fees: $32,335 | Average undergraduate aid package: $22,246 |
|---|---|

**ABOUT THE INSTITUTION** Independent Roman Catholic, coed. *Awards:* certificates, associate, bachelor's, master's, and doctoral degrees. 33 undergraduate majors. *Total enrollment:* 1,717. Undergraduates: 1,396. Freshmen: 187. Federal methodology is used as a basis for awarding need-based institutional aid.

**UNDERGRADUATE EXPENSES for 2015–2016** *Application fee:* $30. *Comprehensive fee:* $44,043 includes full-time tuition ($30,768), mandatory fees ($1567), and room and board ($11,708). Room and board charges vary according to board plan. Part-time tuition and fees vary according to location and program.

**FRESHMAN FINANCIAL AID (Fall 2014, est.)** 181 applied for aid; of those 97% were deemed to have need. 100% of freshmen with need received aid; of those 9% had need fully met. *Average percent of need met:* 70% (excluding resources awarded to replace EFC). *Average financial aid package:* $24,969 (excluding resources awarded to replace EFC). 6% of all full-time freshmen had no need and received non-need-based gift aid.

**UNDERGRADUATE FINANCIAL AID (Fall 2014, est.)** 953 applied for aid; of those 95% were deemed to have need. 100% of undergraduates with need received aid; of those 8% had need fully met. *Average percent of need met:* 63% (excluding resources awarded to replace EFC). *Average financial aid package:* $22,246 (excluding resources awarded to replace EFC). 9% of all full-time undergraduates had no need and received non-need-based gift aid.

**GIFT AID (NEED-BASED)** *Total amount:* $16,029,918 (16% federal, 4% state, 76% institutional, 4% external sources). *Receiving aid:* Freshmen: 94% (175); all full-time undergraduates: 85% (874). *Average award:* Freshmen: $21,857; Undergraduates: $18,179. *Scholarships, grants, and awards:* Federal Pell, FSEOG, state, private, college/university gift aid from institutional funds.

**GIFT AID (NON-NEED-BASED)** *Total amount:* $1,704,206 (91% institutional, 9% external sources). *Receiving aid:* Freshmen: 7% (14). Undergraduates: 5% (48). *Average award:* Freshmen: $15,520. Undergraduates: $14,164. *Scholarships, grants, and awards by category:* Academic interests/achievement: 828 awards ($9,242,508 total): general academic interests/achievements. *Special characteristics:* 42 awards ($327,166 total): children of faculty/staff, general special characteristics, religious affiliation, siblings of current students. *Tuition waivers:* Full or partial for employees or children of employees, senior citizens. *ROTC:* Army cooperative, Air Force cooperative.

**LOANS** *Student loans:* $11,997,975 (86% need-based, 14% non-need-based). 88% of past graduating class borrowed through all loan programs. *Average indebtedness per student:* $35,089. *Average need-based loan:* Freshmen: $3435. Undergraduates: $4714. *Parent loans:* $2,196,643 (56% need-based, 44% non-need-based). *Programs:* Federal Direct (Subsidized and Unsubsidized Stafford, PLUS), Perkins.

**WORK-STUDY** *Federal work-study:* Total amount: $110,892; 114 jobs averaging $1164.

**APPLYING FOR FINANCIAL AID** *Required financial aid form:* FAFSA. *Financial aid deadline (priority):* 3/1. *Notification date:* Continuous beginning 3/15. Students must reply within 2 weeks of notification.

**CONTACT** Financial Aid Office, Elms College, 291 Springfield Street, Chicopee, MA 01013, 413-265-2249 or toll-free 800-255-ELMS. *E-mail:* finaid@elms.edu.
*Website:* http://www.elms.edu/.

# ELON UNIVERSITY
### Elon, NC

**Tuition & fees: $31,247** | **Average undergraduate aid package: $17,306**

**ABOUT THE INSTITUTION** Independent United Church of Christ, coed. *Awards:* bachelor's, master's, and doctoral degrees. 73 undergraduate majors. *Total enrollment:* 6,483. Undergraduates: 5,782. Freshmen: 1,497. Institutional methodology is used as a basis for awarding need-based institutional aid.

**UNDERGRADUATE EXPENSES for 2015–2016** *Application fee:* $50. *Comprehensive fee:* $41,914 includes full-time tuition ($30,848), mandatory fees ($399), and room and board ($10,667). *College room only:* $5231. Room and board charges vary according to board plan and housing facility. *Part-time tuition:* $983 per semester hour. Part-time tuition and fees vary according to course load.

**FRESHMAN FINANCIAL AID (Fall 2014, est.)** 860 applied for aid; of those 59% were deemed to have need. 99% of freshmen with need received aid; of those 16% had need fully met. *Average percent of need met:* 57% (excluding resources awarded to replace EFC). *Average financial aid package:* $15,874 (excluding resources awarded to replace EFC). 19% of all full-time freshmen had no need and received non-need-based gift aid.

**UNDERGRADUATE FINANCIAL AID (Fall 2014, est.)** 2,647 applied for aid; of those 72% were deemed to have need. 100% of undergraduates with need received aid; of those 18% had need fully met. *Average percent of need met:* 60% (excluding resources awarded to replace EFC). *Average financial aid package:* $17,306 (excluding resources awarded to replace EFC). 20% of all full-time undergraduates had no need and received non-need-based gift aid.

**GIFT AID (NEED-BASED)** *Total amount:* $19,374,077 (12% federal, 7% state, 79% institutional, 2% external sources). *Receiving aid:* Freshmen: 30% (440); all full-time undergraduates: 30% (1,703). *Average award:* Freshmen: $12,474; Undergraduates: $13,722. *Scholarships, grants, and awards:* Federal Pell, FSEOG, state, private, college/university gift aid from institutional funds.

**GIFT AID (NON-NEED-BASED)** *Total amount:* $8,337,585 (1% state, 96% institutional, 3% external sources). *Receiving aid:* Freshmen: 15% (218). Undergraduates: 15% (819). *Average award:* Freshmen: $6303. Undergraduates: $6603. *Scholarships, grants, and awards by category:* Academic interests/achievement: 2,303 awards ($10,330,767 total): biological sciences, business, communication, computer science, education, engineering/technologies, general academic interests/achievements, mathematics, military science, physical sciences, premedicine, religion/biblical studies, social sciences. *Creative arts/performance:* 118 awards ($324,142 total): art/fine arts, journalism/publications, music, performing arts, theater/drama. *Special achievements/activities:* 164 awards ($348,966 total): community service, general special achievements/activities, leadership, religious involvement. *Special characteristics:* 170 awards ($2,426,438 total): adult students, children of faculty/staff, ethnic background, first-generation college students, international students, members of minority groups, relatives of clergy, veterans. *Tuition waivers:* Full or partial for employees or children of employees. *ROTC:* Army, Air Force cooperative.

**LOANS** *Student loans:* $17,547,011 (65% need-based, 35% non-need-based). 43% of past graduating class borrowed through all loan programs. *Average indebtedness per student:* $27,176. *Average need-based loan:* Freshmen: $3394. Undergraduates: $4514. *Parent loans:* $11,158,060 (56% need-based, 44% non-need-based). *Programs:* Federal Direct (Subsidized and Unsubsidized Stafford, PLUS), Perkins, state, college/university, alternative loans.

**WORK-STUDY** *Federal work-study:* Total amount: $3,203,779; 1,418 jobs averaging $2309.

**ATHLETIC AWARDS** Total amount: $8,179,276 (36% need-based, 64% non-need-based).

**APPLYING FOR FINANCIAL AID** *Required financial aid forms:* FAFSA, institution's own form, CSS Financial Aid PROFILE. *Financial aid deadline (priority):* 2/15. *Notification date:* 3/30.

**CONTACT** Dr. Patrick Murphy, Director of Financial Planning, Elon University, 2725 Campus Box, Elon, NC 27244, 336-278-7640 or toll-free 800-334-8448. *Fax:* 336-278-7639. *E-mail:* finaid@elon.edu.
*Website:* http://www.elon.edu/.

# EMBRY-RIDDLE AERONAUTICAL UNIVERSITY–DAYTONA
### Daytona Beach, FL

**Tuition & fees: $33,218** | **Average undergraduate aid package: $15,986**

**ABOUT THE INSTITUTION** Independent, coed. *Awards:* associate, bachelor's, master's, and doctoral degrees. 23 undergraduate majors. *Total enrollment:* 5,538. Undergraduates: 4,967. Freshmen: 1,217. Federal methodology is used as a basis for awarding need-based institutional aid.

**UNDERGRADUATE EXPENSES for 2015–2016** *Application fee:* $50. *Comprehensive fee:* $43,600 includes full-time tuition ($31,944), mandatory fees ($1274), and room and board ($10,382). *College room only:* $6160. Room and board charges vary according to board plan, housing facility, and location. *Part-time tuition:* $1331 per credit hour.

**FRESHMAN FINANCIAL AID (Fall 2014, est.)** 1,103 applied for aid; of those 87% were deemed to have need. 100% of freshmen with need received aid. *Average financial aid package:* $19,629 (excluding resources awarded to replace EFC).

**UNDERGRADUATE FINANCIAL AID (Fall 2014, est.)** 3,866 applied for aid; of those 82% were deemed to have need. 100% of undergraduates with need received aid. *Average financial aid package:* $15,986 (excluding resources awarded to replace EFC).

**GIFT AID (NEED-BASED)** *Total amount:* $52,243,345 (14% federal, 7% state, 62% institutional, 17% external sources). *Receiving aid:* Freshmen: 78% (946); all full-time undergraduates: 64% (2,994). *Average award:* Freshmen: $17,305; Undergraduates: $13,233. *Scholarships, grants, and awards:* Federal Pell, FSEOG, state, private, college/university gift aid from institutional funds.

**GIFT AID (NON-NEED-BASED)** *Scholarships, grants, and awards by category:* Special achievements/activities: leadership. *Tuition waivers:* Full or partial for employees or children of employees. *ROTC:* Army, Naval, Air Force.

**LOANS** *Student loans:* $33,928,040 (100% need-based). *Average need-based loan:* Freshmen: $3990. Undergraduates: $4849. *Parent loans:* $27,370,697 (100% need-based). *Programs:* Federal Direct (Subsidized and Unsubsidized Stafford, PLUS), Perkins.

**WORK-STUDY** *Federal work-study:* Total amount: $315,759; 163 jobs averaging $1756. *State or other work-study/employment:* Total amount: $5,204,091 (100% need-based). 1,658 part-time jobs averaging $3304.

**ATHLETIC AWARDS** Total amount: $3,027,136 (100% need-based).

**APPLYING FOR FINANCIAL AID** *Required financial aid form:* FAFSA. *Financial aid deadline (priority):* 3/1. *Notification date:* Continuous beginning 3/1. Students must reply within 4 weeks of notification.

**CONTACT** Barbara Dryden, Director of Financial Aid, Embry-Riddle Aeronautical University–Daytona, 600 South Clyde Morris Boulevard, Daytona Beach, FL 32114-3900, 800-943-6279 or toll-free 800-862-2416. *Fax:* 386-226-6307. *E-mail:* dbfinaid@erau.edu.
*Website:* http://www.embryriddle.edu/.

# EMBRY-RIDDLE AERONAUTICAL UNIVERSITY–PRESCOTT
### Prescott, AZ

**Tuition & fees: $33,144** | **Average undergraduate aid package: $16,608**

**ABOUT THE INSTITUTION** Independent, coed. *Awards:* bachelor's and master's degrees. 18 undergraduate majors. *Total enrollment:* 2,035. Undergraduates: 1,984. Freshmen: 505. Federal methodology is used as a basis for awarding need-based institutional aid.

**UNDERGRADUATE EXPENSES for 2015–2016** *Application fee:* $50. *Comprehensive fee:* $43,044 includes full-time tuition ($31,944), mandatory fees ($1200), and room and board ($9900). *College room only:* $5600. Room and board charges vary according to board plan, housing facility, and location. *Part-time tuition:* $1331 per credit hour.

**FRESHMAN FINANCIAL AID (Fall 2014, est.)** 467 applied for aid; of those 87% were deemed to have need. 99% of freshmen with need received aid. *Average financial aid package:* $17,695 (excluding resources awarded to replace EFC).
**UNDERGRADUATE FINANCIAL AID (Fall 2014, est.)** 1,613 applied for aid; of those 80% were deemed to have need. 100% of undergraduates with need received aid. *Average financial aid package:* $16,608 (excluding resources awarded to replace EFC).
**GIFT AID (NEED-BASED)** *Total amount:* $23,147,904 (10% federal, 74% institutional, 16% external sources). *Receiving aid:* Freshmen: 80% (402); all full-time undergraduates: 65% (1,222). *Average award:* Freshmen: $15,896; Undergraduates: $14,191. *Scholarships, grants, and awards:* Federal Pell, FSEOG, state, private, college/university gift aid from institutional funds.
**GIFT AID (NON-NEED-BASED)** *Tuition waivers:* Full or partial for employees or children of employees. *ROTC:* Army, Air Force.
**LOANS** *Student loans:* $13,006,044 (100% need-based). *Average need-based loan:* Freshmen: $3606. Undergraduates: $4232. *Parent loans:* $8,983,586 (100% need-based). *Programs:* Federal Direct (Subsidized and Unsubsidized Stafford, PLUS), Perkins, college/university.
**WORK-STUDY** *Federal work-study:* Total amount: $76,016; 28 jobs averaging $1147. *State or other work-study/employment:* Total amount: $1,212,958 (100% need-based). 537 part-time jobs averaging $2311.
**ATHLETIC AWARDS** Total amount: $1,314,989 (100% need-based).
**APPLYING FOR FINANCIAL AID** *Required financial aid form:* FAFSA. *Financial aid deadline (priority):* 3/1. *Notification date:* Continuous beginning 3/1. Students must reply within 4 weeks of notification.
**CONTACT** Ms. Debra Hintz, Director of Financial Aid, Prescott Campus, Embry-Riddle Aeronautical University–Prescott, 3700 Willow Creek Road, Prescott, AZ 86301-3720, 800-888-3728. *Fax:* 928-777-3893. *E-mail:* prfinaid@erau.edu. *Website:* http://www.embryriddle.edu/.

# EMBRY-RIDDLE AERONAUTICAL UNIVERSITY–WORLDWIDE

## Daytona Beach, FL

**ABOUT THE INSTITUTION** Independent, coed. *Awards:* certificates, associate, bachelor's, master's, and doctoral degrees (programs offered at 100 military bases worldwide). 8 undergraduate majors. *Total enrollment:* 15,173. Undergraduates: 10,561.
**GIFT AID (NEED-BASED)** *Scholarships, grants, and awards:* Federal Pell, state, private, college/university gift aid from institutional funds.
**GIFT AID (NON-NEED-BASED)** *Scholarships, grants, and awards by category:* Academic interests/achievement: general academic interests/achievements. Special achievements/activities: leadership.
**LOANS** *Programs:* Federal Direct (Subsidized and Unsubsidized Stafford, PLUS).
**APPLYING FOR FINANCIAL AID** *Required financial aid form:* FAFSA.
**CONTACT** Ms. Joan D. Bowen, Director of Financial Aid - Worldwide, Embry-Riddle Aeronautical University–Worldwide, 600 South Clyde Morris Boulevard, Daytona Beach, FL 32114-3900, 866-567-7202 or toll-free 800-522-6787. *Fax:* 386-226-6915. *E-mail:* wwfinaid@erau.edu.
*Website:* http://www.embryriddle.edu/.

# EMERSON COLLEGE

## Boston, MA

| Tuition & fees: $39,036 | Average undergraduate aid package: $20,840 |
| --- | --- |

**ABOUT THE INSTITUTION** Independent, coed. *Awards:* certificates, bachelor's, master's, and doctoral degrees. 28 undergraduate majors. *Total enrollment:* 4,533. Undergraduates: 3,765. Freshmen: 857. Institutional methodology is used as a basis for awarding need-based institutional aid.
**UNDERGRADUATE EXPENSES for 2015–2016** *Application fee:* $65. *Comprehensive fee:* $54,736 includes full-time tuition ($38,304), mandatory fees ($732), and room and board ($15,700). Full-time tuition and fees vary according to student

level. Room and board charges vary according to board plan. *Part-time tuition:* $1197 per credit. Part-time tuition and fees vary according to student level.
**FRESHMAN FINANCIAL AID (Fall 2014, est.)** 656 applied for aid; of those 70% were deemed to have need. 98% of freshmen with need received aid; of those 17% had need fully met. *Average percent of need met:* 68% (excluding resources awarded to replace EFC). *Average financial aid package:* $22,807 (excluding resources awarded to replace EFC). 10% of all full-time freshmen had no need and received non-need-based gift aid.
**UNDERGRADUATE FINANCIAL AID (Fall 2014, est.)** 2,552 applied for aid; of those 78% were deemed to have need. 99% of undergraduates with need received aid; of those 14% had need fully met. *Average percent of need met:* 59% (excluding resources awarded to replace EFC). *Average financial aid package:* $20,840 (excluding resources awarded to replace EFC). 9% of all full-time undergraduates had no need and received non-need-based gift aid.
**GIFT AID (NEED-BASED)** *Total amount:* $29,795,019 (10% federal, 1% state, 88% institutional, 1% external sources). *Receiving aid:* Freshmen: 49% (418); all full-time undergraduates: 46% (1,730). *Average award:* Freshmen: $19,175; Undergraduates: $17,140. *Scholarships, grants, and awards:* Federal Pell, FSEOG, state, private, college/university gift aid from institutional funds.
**GIFT AID (NON-NEED-BASED)** *Total amount:* $6,502,673 (94% institutional, 6% external sources). *Receiving aid:* Freshmen: 12% (102). Undergraduates: 8% (294). *Average award:* Freshmen: $16,191. Undergraduates: $14,675. *Scholarships, grants, and awards by category:* Academic interests/achievement: 691 awards ($10,219,682 total): general academic interests/achievements. Creative arts/performance: 17 awards ($238,000 total): performing arts. *Tuition waivers:* Full or partial for employees or children of employees.
**LOANS** *Student loans:* $26,969,161 (75% need-based, 25% non-need-based). 62% of past graduating class borrowed through all loan programs. *Average indebtedness per student:* $23,606. *Average need-based loan:* Freshmen: $3966. Undergraduates: $4857. *Parent loans:* $10,996,414 (36% need-based, 64% non-need-based). *Programs:* Federal Direct (Subsidized and Unsubsidized Stafford, PLUS), Perkins, state.
**WORK-STUDY** *Federal work-study:* Total amount: $540,382; 402 jobs averaging $1409. *State or other work-study/employment:* Total amount: $925,044 (42% need-based, 58% non-need-based). 75 part-time jobs averaging $13,065.
**APPLYING FOR FINANCIAL AID** *Required financial aid forms:* FAFSA, CSS Financial Aid PROFILE, noncustodial (divorced/separated) parent's statement, business/farm supplement. *Financial aid deadline (priority):* 3/2. *Notification date:* 4/1. Students must reply by 5/1 or within 3 weeks of notification.
**CONTACT** James Olick, Director of Financial Aid, Emerson College, 120 Boylston Street, Boston, MA 02116-4624, 617-824-8655. *Fax:* 617-824-8619. *E-mail:* finaid@emerson.edu.
*Website:* http://www.emerson.edu/.

# EMMANUEL COLLEGE

## Franklin Springs, GA

| Tuition & fees: $18,170 | Average undergraduate aid package: $15,519 |
| --- | --- |

**ABOUT THE INSTITUTION** Independent Pentecostal Holiness Church, coed. *Awards:* associate and bachelor's degrees. 24 undergraduate majors. *Total enrollment:* 816. Undergraduates: 816. Freshmen: 193. Federal methodology is used as a basis for awarding need-based institutional aid.
**UNDERGRADUATE EXPENSES for 2015–2016** *Application fee:* $25. *Comprehensive fee:* $25,370 includes full-time tuition ($18,000), mandatory fees ($170), and room and board ($7200). Room and board charges vary according to housing facility. *Part-time tuition:* $750 per credit hour.
**FRESHMAN FINANCIAL AID (Fall 2014, est.)** 174 applied for aid; of those 90% were deemed to have need. 100% of freshmen with need received aid; of those 25% had need fully met. *Average percent of need met:* 65% (excluding resources awarded to replace EFC). *Average financial aid package:* $13,884 (excluding resources awarded to replace EFC). 16% of all full-time freshmen had no need and received non-need-based gift aid.
**UNDERGRADUATE FINANCIAL AID (Fall 2014, est.)** 605 applied for aid; of those 90% were deemed to have need. 100% of undergraduates with need received aid; of those 18% had need fully met. *Average percent of need met:* 68% (excluding resources awarded to replace EFC). *Average financial aid package:*

$15,519 (excluding resources awarded to replace EFC). 18% of all full-time undergraduates had no need and received non-need-based gift aid.

**GIFT AID (NEED-BASED)** *Total amount:* $5,292,607 (30% federal, 16% state, 50% institutional, 4% external sources). *Receiving aid:* Freshmen: 83% (156); all full-time undergraduates: 81% (544). *Average award:* Freshmen: $11,283; Undergraduates: $11,770. *Scholarships, grants, and awards:* Federal Pell, FSEOG, state, college/university gift aid from institutional funds.

**GIFT AID (NON-NEED-BASED)** *Total amount:* $2,223,489 (16% state, 32% institutional, 52% external sources). *Receiving aid:* Freshmen: 16% (30). Undergraduates: 10% (69). *Average award:* Freshmen: $5664. Undergraduates: $4930. *Scholarships, grants, and awards by category: Academic interests/achievement:* 501 awards ($2,113,680 total): business, communication, education, English, general academic interests/achievements, health fields, religion/biblical studies. *Creative arts/performance:* 23 awards ($36,031 total): applied art and design, art/fine arts, creative writing, dance, general creative arts/performance, journalism/publications, music, performing arts, theater/drama. *Special achievements/activities:* 20 awards ($77,820 total): cheerleading/drum major, general special achievements/activities, hobbies/interests, leadership, memberships, religious involvement. *Special characteristics:* 769 awards ($954,270 total): adult students, children of current students, children of educators, children of faculty/staff, first-generation college students, general special characteristics, international students, local/state students, married students, parents of current students, relatives of clergy, religious affiliation, siblings of current students, spouses of current students, twins. *Tuition waivers:* Full or partial for employees or children of employees, senior citizens.

**LOANS** *Student loans:* $3,788,677 (82% need-based, 18% non-need-based). 70% of past graduating class borrowed through all loan programs. *Average indebtedness per student:* $29,202. *Average need-based loan:* Freshmen: $2822. Undergraduates: $3762. *Parent loans:* $1,245,563 (44% need-based, 56% non-need-based). *Programs:* Federal Direct (Subsidized and Unsubsidized Stafford, PLUS), state.

**WORK-STUDY** *Federal work-study:* Total amount: $493,284; 120 jobs averaging $883. *State or other work-study/employment:* 132 part-time jobs averaging $939.

**ATHLETIC AWARDS** Total amount: $1,992,591 (61% need-based, 39% non-need-based).

**APPLYING FOR FINANCIAL AID** *Required financial aid forms:* FAFSA, institution's own form, state aid form. *Financial aid deadline:* 6/15 (priority: 5/1). *Notification date:* Continuous beginning 3/1. Students must reply within 2 weeks of notification.

**CONTACT** Mrs. Niki Stinson, Director of Financial Aid, Emmanuel College, PO Box 129, Franklin Springs, GA 30639-0129, 706-245-2871 or toll-free 800-860-8800. *Fax:* 706-245-2846. *E-mail:* nstinson@ec.edu. *Website:* http://www.ec.edu/.

# EMMANUEL COLLEGE
## Boston, MA

| Tuition & fees: $35,532 | Average undergraduate aid package: $27,346 |
| --- | --- |

**ABOUT THE INSTITUTION** Independent Roman Catholic, coed. *Awards:* certificates, bachelor's, and master's degrees. 44 undergraduate majors. *Total enrollment:* 2,311. Undergraduates: 2,082. Freshmen: 524. Federal methodology is used as a basis for awarding need-based institutional aid.

**UNDERGRADUATE EXPENSES** for 2015–2016 *Application fee:* $60. *One-time required fee:* $280. *Comprehensive fee:* $49,112 includes full-time tuition ($35,312), mandatory fees ($220), and room and board ($13,580). Room and board charges vary according to housing facility. *Part-time tuition:* $1104 per credit hour.

**FRESHMAN FINANCIAL AID (Fall 2014, est.)** 485 applied for aid; of those 91% were deemed to have need. 100% of freshmen with need received aid; of those 52% had need fully met. *Average percent of need met:* 76% (excluding resources awarded to replace EFC). *Average financial aid package:* $27,909 (excluding resources awarded to replace EFC). 14% of all full-time freshmen had no need and received non-need-based gift aid.

**UNDERGRADUATE FINANCIAL AID (Fall 2014, est.)** 1,604 applied for aid; of those 92% were deemed to have need. 100% of undergraduates with need received aid; of those 55% had need fully met. *Average percent of need met:* 75% (excluding resources awarded to replace EFC). *Average financial aid package:* $27,346 (excluding resources awarded to replace EFC). 17% of all full-time undergraduates had no need and received non-need-based gift aid.

**GIFT AID (NEED-BASED)** *Total amount:* $30,277,272 (9% federal, 2% state, 86% institutional, 3% external sources). *Receiving aid:* Freshmen: 84% (442); all full-time undergraduates: 81% (1,474). *Average award:* Freshmen: $21,343; Undergraduates: $19,872. *Scholarships, grants, and awards:* Federal Pell, FSEOG, state, private, college/university gift aid from institutional funds.

**GIFT AID (NON-NEED-BASED)** *Total amount:* $3,382,862 (1% federal, 97% institutional, 2% external sources). *Receiving aid:* Freshmen: 84% (441). Undergraduates: 79% (1,443). *Average award:* Freshmen: $13,902. Undergraduates: $12,505. *Scholarships, grants, and awards by category: Academic interests/achievement:* general academic interests/achievements. *Creative arts/performance:* general creative arts/performance. *Special achievements/activities:* community service, general special achievements/activities, leadership. *Special characteristics:* children and siblings of alumni, children of educators, children of faculty/staff, children of union members/company employees, ethnic background, general special characteristics, handicapped students, international students, local/state students, religious affiliation, siblings of current students, veterans, veterans' children. *Tuition waivers:* Full or partial for children of alumni, employees or children of employees. *ROTC:* Army cooperative, Air Force cooperative.

**LOANS** *Student loans:* $14,432,206 (94% need-based, 6% non-need-based). 78% of past graduating class borrowed through all loan programs. *Average indebtedness per student:* $35,679. *Average need-based loan:* Freshmen: $3731. Undergraduates: $4869. *Parent loans:* $9,295,423 (100% non-need-based). *Programs:* Federal Direct (Subsidized and Unsubsidized Stafford, PLUS), Perkins, state.

**WORK-STUDY** *Federal work-study:* Total amount: $145,813; 453 jobs averaging $1993. *State or other work-study/employment:* Total amount: $1,107,905 (100% non-need-based). Part-time jobs available.

**APPLYING FOR FINANCIAL AID** *Required financial aid form:* FAFSA. *Financial aid deadline (priority):* 2/15. *Notification date:* Continuous beginning 3/1.

**CONTACT** Jennifer Porter, Associate Vice President for Student Financial Services, Emmanuel College, 400 The Fenway, Boston, MA 02115, 617-735-9938. *Fax:* 617-735-9939. *E-mail:* financialservices@emmanuel.edu. *Website:* http://www.emmanuel.edu/.

# EMMAUS BIBLE COLLEGE
## Dubuque, IA

| Tuition & fees: $15,390 | Average undergraduate aid package: N/A |
| --- | --- |

**ABOUT THE INSTITUTION** Independent nondenominational, coed. *Awards:* certificates, associate, and bachelor's degrees. 12 undergraduate majors. *Total enrollment:* 207. Undergraduates: 207. Federal methodology is used as a basis for awarding need-based institutional aid.

**UNDERGRADUATE EXPENSES** for 2015–2016 *Application fee:* $25. *Comprehensive fee:* $21,950 includes full-time tuition ($14,600), mandatory fees ($790), and room and board ($6560). *Part-time tuition:* $642 per credit.

**GIFT AID (NEED-BASED)** *Scholarships, grants, and awards:* Federal Pell, FSEOG, state, private, college/university gift aid from institutional funds.

**GIFT AID (NON-NEED-BASED)** *Scholarships, grants, and awards by category: Academic interests/achievement:* general academic interests/achievements. *Special achievements/activities:* leadership, religious involvement. *Special characteristics:* children and siblings of alumni, children of faculty/staff, ethnic background, international students, relatives of clergy.

**LOANS** *Programs:* Federal Direct (Subsidized and Unsubsidized Stafford).

**APPLYING FOR FINANCIAL AID** *Financial aid deadline:* Continuous. *Notification date:* Continuous.

**CONTACT** Steve Seeman, Financial Aid Director, Emmaus Bible College, 2570 Asbury Road, Dubuque, IA 52001-3097, 800-397-2425 Ext. 1309 or toll-free 800-397-2425. *Fax:* 563-588-1216. *E-mail:* financialaid@emmaus.edu. *Website:* http://www.emmaus.edu/.

# EMORY & HENRY COLLEGE
## Emory, VA

| Tuition & fees: $30,900 | Average undergraduate aid package: $27,315 |
|---|---|

**ABOUT THE INSTITUTION** Independent United Methodist, coed. **Awards:** bachelor's and master's degrees. 66 undergraduate majors. **Total enrollment:** 1,038. Undergraduates: 1,012. Freshmen: 253. Federal methodology is used as a basis for awarding need-based institutional aid.

**UNDERGRADUATE EXPENSES for 2015–2016 Comprehensive fee:** $41,410 includes full-time tuition ($30,700), mandatory fees ($200), and room and board ($10,510). **College room only:** $5220. Full-time tuition and fees vary according to course load, degree level, and location. Room and board charges vary according to board plan, housing facility, and location. Part-time tuition and fees vary according to course load, degree level, and location.

**FRESHMAN FINANCIAL AID (Fall 2014, est.)** 271 applied for aid; of those 88% were deemed to have need. 100% of freshmen with need received aid; of those 21% had need fully met. **Average percent of need met:** 94% (excluding resources awarded to replace EFC). **Average financial aid package:** $27,661 (excluding resources awarded to replace EFC). 15% of all full-time freshmen had no need and received non-need-based gift aid.

**UNDERGRADUATE FINANCIAL AID (Fall 2014, est.)** 884 applied for aid; of those 90% were deemed to have need. 100% of undergraduates with need received aid; of those 23% had need fully met. **Average percent of need met:** 82% (excluding resources awarded to replace EFC). **Average financial aid package:** $27,315 (excluding resources awarded to replace EFC). 18% of all full-time undergraduates had no need and received non-need-based gift aid.

**GIFT AID (NEED-BASED) Total amount:** $17,406,401 (10% federal, 8% state, 80% institutional, 2% external sources). **Receiving aid:** Freshmen: 83% (237); all full-time undergraduates: 80% (794). **Average award:** Freshmen: $24,615; Undergraduates: $23,496. **Scholarships, grants, and awards:** Federal Pell, FSEOG, state, private, college/university gift aid from institutional funds.

**GIFT AID (NON-NEED-BASED) Total amount:** $3,881,330 (10% state, 85% institutional, 5% external sources). **Receiving aid:** Freshmen: 1% (2). Undergraduates: 1% (5). **Average award:** Freshmen: $15,767. Undergraduates: $15,530. **Scholarships, grants, and awards by category:** Academic interests/achievement: general academic interests/achievements, premedicine, religion/biblical studies. Creative arts/performance: art/fine arts, music, theater/drama. Special characteristics: children of educators, children of faculty/staff, out-of-state students. **Tuition waivers:** Full or partial for employees or children of employees.

**LOANS Student loans:** $5,358,303 (83% need-based, 17% non-need-based). 65% of past graduating class borrowed through all loan programs. Average indebtedness per student: $28,126. **Average need-based loan:** Freshmen: $3696. Undergraduates: $4559. **Parent loans:** $3,580,876 (37% need-based, 63% non-need-based). **Programs:** Federal Direct (Subsidized and Unsubsidized Stafford, PLUS), Perkins.

**WORK-STUDY Federal work-study:** Total amount: $298,864; 177 jobs averaging $1720.

**APPLYING FOR FINANCIAL AID Required financial aid forms:** FAFSA, state aid form. **Financial aid deadline (priority):** 3/1. **Notification date:** Continuous beginning 2/15. Students must reply within 2 weeks of notification.

**CONTACT** Ms. Scarlett C. Blevins, Director of Financial Aid, Emory & Henry College, PO Box 947, Emory, VA 24327-0010, 276-944-6115 or toll-free 800-848-5493. Fax: 276-944-6884. E-mail: scblevins@ehc.edu.
Website: http://www.ehc.edu/.

# EMORY UNIVERSITY
## Atlanta, GA

| Tuition & fees: $46,314 | Average undergraduate aid package: $40,309 |
|---|---|

**ABOUT THE INSTITUTION** Independent Methodist, coed. **Awards:** certificates, associate, bachelor's, master's, and doctoral degrees (enrollment figures include Emory University, Oxford College; application data for main campus only). 65 undergraduate majors. **Total enrollment:** 14,769. Undergraduates: 7,829. Freshmen: 1,824. Both federal and institutional methodology are used as a basis for awarding need-based institutional aid.

**UNDERGRADUATE EXPENSES for 2015–2016 Application fee:** $75. **Comprehensive fee:** $59,444 includes full-time tuition ($45,700), mandatory fees ($614), and room and board ($13,130). **College room only:** $7720. Full-time tuition and fees vary according to degree level and location. Room and board charges vary according to board plan, housing facility, location, and student level. **Part-time tuition:** $1904 per credit hour.

**FRESHMAN FINANCIAL AID (Fall 2014, est.)** 642 applied for aid; of those 81% were deemed to have need. 100% of freshmen with need received aid; of those 98% had need fully met. **Average percent of need met:** 97% (excluding resources awarded to replace EFC). **Average financial aid package:** $40,368 (excluding resources awarded to replace EFC). 4% of all full-time freshmen had no need and received non-need-based gift aid.

**UNDERGRADUATE FINANCIAL AID (Fall 2014, est.)** 2,813 applied for aid; of those 89% were deemed to have need. 100% of undergraduates with need received aid; of those 93% had need fully met. **Average percent of need met:** 97% (excluding resources awarded to replace EFC). **Average financial aid package:** $40,309 (excluding resources awarded to replace EFC). 5% of all full-time undergraduates had no need and received non-need-based gift aid.

**GIFT AID (NEED-BASED) Total amount:** $87,818,884 (7% federal, 2% state, 90% institutional, 1% external sources). **Receiving aid:** Freshmen: 35% (473); all full-time undergraduates: 40% (2,255). **Average award:** Freshmen: $38,283; Undergraduates: $37,657. **Scholarships, grants, and awards:** Federal Pell, FSEOG, private, college/university gift aid from institutional funds.

**GIFT AID (NON-NEED-BASED) Total amount:** $10,404,590 (18% state, 72% institutional, 10% external sources). **Receiving aid:** Freshmen: 12% (168). Undergraduates: 13% (716). **Average award:** Freshmen: $22,432. Undergraduates: $22,538. **Scholarships, grants, and awards by category:** Academic interests/achievement: business, general academic interests/achievements, humanities, physical sciences. Creative arts/performance: art/fine arts, cinema/film/broadcasting, debating, music, theater/drama. Special achievements/activities: leadership. Special characteristics: children of faculty/staff, local/state students, religious affiliation, veterans, veterans' children. **Tuition waivers:** Full or partial for employees or children of employees. **ROTC:** Army cooperative, Naval cooperative, Air Force cooperative.

**LOANS Student loans:** $15,785,838 (56% need-based, 44% non-need-based). 48% of past graduating class borrowed through all loan programs. Average indebtedness per student: $24,741. **Average need-based loan:** Freshmen: $3793. Undergraduates: $4620. **Parent loans:** $5,467,226 (3% need-based, 97% non-need-based). **Programs:** Federal Direct (Subsidized and Unsubsidized Stafford, PLUS), Perkins, Federal Nursing, state, college/university, alternative loans.

**WORK-STUDY Federal work-study:** Total amount: $5,101,718; jobs available. **State or other work-study/employment:** Total amount: $498,960 (39% need-based, 61% non-need-based). Part-time jobs available.

**APPLYING FOR FINANCIAL AID Required financial aid forms:** FAFSA, CSS Financial Aid PROFILE, noncustodial (divorced/separated) parent's statement. **Financial aid deadline:** 3/1 (priority: 2/15). **Notification date:** 4/1. Students must reply by 5/1.

**CONTACT** Mr. John Leach, Director of Financial Aid, Emory University, Boisfeuillet Jones Center, Suite 300, 200 Dowman Drive, Atlanta, GA 30322-1960, 404-727-6039 or toll-free 800-727-6036. Fax: 404-727-6709. E-mail: john.blanchard.leach@emory.edu.
Website: http://www.emory.edu/.

# EMPORIA STATE UNIVERSITY
## Emporia, KS

| Tuition & fees (KS res): $5746 | Average undergraduate aid package: $8805 |
|---|---|

**ABOUT THE INSTITUTION** State-supported, coed. **Awards:** certificates, bachelor's, master's, and doctoral degrees. 34 undergraduate majors. **Total enrollment:** 6,114. Undergraduates: 3,924. Freshmen: 755. Federal methodology is used as a basis for awarding need-based institutional aid.

**UNDERGRADUATE EXPENSES for 2015–2016 Application fee:** $30. **Tuition, state resident:** full-time $4500; part-time $150 per credit hour. **Tuition, nonresident:** full-time $16,650; part-time $555 per credit hour. **Required fees:** full-time $1246; $75 per credit hour. Full-time tuition and fees vary according to course load, degree level, and location. Part-time tuition and fees vary according to course load, degree level, and location. *College room and board:* $7582; *Room only:* $4182. Room and board charges vary according to board plan, housing facility, and location.

**FRESHMAN FINANCIAL AID (Fall 2014, est.)** 662 applied for aid; of those 80% were deemed to have need. 100% of freshmen with need received aid; of those 16% had need fully met. *Average percent of need met:* 64% (excluding resources awarded to replace EFC). *Average financial aid package:* $8625 (excluding resources awarded to replace EFC). 20% of all full-time freshmen had no need and received non-need-based gift aid.

**UNDERGRADUATE FINANCIAL AID (Fall 2014, est.)** 2,740 applied for aid; of those 83% were deemed to have need. 99% of undergraduates with need received aid; of those 14% had need fully met. *Average percent of need met:* 62% (excluding resources awarded to replace EFC). *Average financial aid package:* $8805 (excluding resources awarded to replace EFC). 15% of all full-time undergraduates had no need and received non-need-based gift aid.

**GIFT AID (NEED-BASED) Total amount:** $10,988,188 (62% federal, 6% state, 20% institutional, 12% external sources). *Receiving aid:* Freshmen: 68% (498); all full-time undergraduates: 58% (1,996). *Average award:* Freshmen: $5937; Undergraduates: $5833. *Scholarships, grants, and awards:* Federal Pell, FSEOG, state, private, college/university gift aid from institutional funds, Jones Foundation Grants.

**GIFT AID (NON-NEED-BASED) Total amount:** $2,954,275 (1% federal, 44% institutional, 55% external sources). *Receiving aid:* Freshmen: 4% (31). Undergraduates: 3% (98). *Average award:* Freshmen: $1947. Undergraduates: $2315. *Scholarships, grants, and awards by category:* Academic interests/achievement: 1,470 awards ($2,841,447 total): biological sciences, business, communication, computer science, education, engineering/technologies, English, foreign languages, general academic interests/achievements, health fields, humanities, mathematics, physical sciences, premedicine, social sciences. *Creative arts/performance:* 148 awards ($187,527 total): art/fine arts, creative writing, debating, music, theater/drama. *Special achievements/activities:* 53 awards ($35,393 total): general special achievements/activities, leadership, memberships. *Special characteristics:* 126 awards ($241,388 total): children and siblings of alumni, children of faculty/staff, children of union members/company employees, first-generation college students, general special characteristics, handicapped students, international students, members of minority groups, religious affiliation, veterans, veterans' children. *Tuition waivers:* Full or partial for employees or children of employees, senior citizens.

**LOANS Student loans:** $16,903,841 (74% need-based, 26% non-need-based). 69% of past graduating class borrowed through all loan programs. *Average indebtedness per student:* $30,488. *Average need-based loan:* Freshmen: $5106. Undergraduates: $6240. *Parent loans:* $6,553,111 (24% need-based, 76% non-need-based). *Programs:* Federal Direct (Subsidized and Unsubsidized Stafford, PLUS), Perkins, alternative loans, Alaska Loans.

**WORK-STUDY Federal work-study:** Total amount: $431,040; 224 jobs averaging $1904. *State or other work-study/employment:* Total amount: $29,137 (70% need-based, 30% non-need-based). 13 part-time jobs averaging $2241.

**ATHLETIC AWARDS** Total amount: $1,406,202 (57% need-based, 43% non-need-based).

**APPLYING FOR FINANCIAL AID Required financial aid forms:** FAFSA, state aid form. *Financial aid deadline (priority):* 3/15. *Notification date:* Continuous. Students must reply within 2 weeks of notification.

**CONTACT** Elaine Henrie, Director of Financial Aid, Emporia State University, 1 Kellogg Circle, Emporia, KS 66801-5087, 620-341-5457 or toll-free 877-GOTOESU (in-state), 877-468-6378 (out-of-state). *Fax:* 620-341-6088. *E-mail:* ehenrie@emporia.edu. *Website:* http://www.emporia.edu/.

---

## ENDICOTT COLLEGE
### Beverly, MA

| Tuition & fees: $29,494 | Average undergraduate aid package: $20,277 |
|---|---|

**ABOUT THE INSTITUTION** Independent, coed. *Awards:* certificates, associate, bachelor's, master's, and doctoral degrees. 39 undergraduate majors. *Total enrollment:* 4,655. Undergraduates: 2,963. Freshmen: 763. Federal methodology is used as a basis for awarding need-based institutional aid.

**UNDERGRADUATE EXPENSES for 2015–2016 Application fee:** $50. *Comprehensive fee:* $43,228 includes full-time tuition ($28,994), mandatory fees ($500),

and room and board ($13,734). *College room only:* $9468. Full-time tuition and fees vary according to location. Room and board charges vary according to board plan and housing facility. *Part-time tuition:* $890 per credit hour. Part-time tuition and fees vary according to location. *Payment plan:* Tuition prepayment.

**FRESHMAN FINANCIAL AID (Fall 2014, est.)** 704 applied for aid; of those 77% were deemed to have need. 100% of freshmen with need received aid; of those 9% had need fully met. *Average percent of need met:* 63% (excluding resources awarded to replace EFC). *Average financial aid package:* $19,526 (excluding resources awarded to replace EFC). 18% of all full-time freshmen had no need and received non-need-based gift aid.

**UNDERGRADUATE FINANCIAL AID (Fall 2014, est.)** 2,302 applied for aid; of those 74% were deemed to have need. 99% of undergraduates with need received aid; of those 10% had need fully met. *Average percent of need met:* 65% (excluding resources awarded to replace EFC). *Average financial aid package:* $20,277 (excluding resources awarded to replace EFC). 18% of all full-time undergraduates had no need and received non-need-based gift aid.

**GIFT AID (NEED-BASED) Total amount:** $23,297,771 (9% federal, 2% state, 89% institutional). *Receiving aid:* Freshmen: 60% (451); all full-time undergraduates: 56% (1,421). *Average award:* Freshmen: $10,207; Undergraduates: $10,925. *Scholarships, grants, and awards:* Federal Pell, FSEOG, state, private, college/university gift aid from institutional funds.

**GIFT AID (NON-NEED-BASED) Total amount:** $4,646,398 (90% institutional, 10% external sources). *Receiving aid:* Freshmen: 52% (393). Undergraduates: 43% (1,101). *Average award:* Freshmen: $8501. Undergraduates: $8248. *Scholarships, grants, and awards by category:* Academic interests/achievement: 1,311 awards ($10,539,922 total): business, education, general academic interests/achievements, health fields. *Creative arts/performance:* 2 awards ($3500 total): art/fine arts, music, performing arts. *Special achievements/activities:* 9 awards ($14,500 total): community service, general special achievements/activities, leadership, religious involvement. *Special characteristics:* 104 awards ($442,744 total): children and siblings of alumni, children of educators, general special characteristics, international students, local/state students, religious affiliation. *Tuition waivers:* Full or partial for employees or children of employees. *ROTC:* Army cooperative.

**LOANS Student loans:** $20,845,952 (33% need-based, 67% non-need-based). 74% of past graduating class borrowed through all loan programs. *Average indebtedness per student:* $39,187. *Average need-based loan:* Freshmen: $3798. Undergraduates: $4573. *Parent loans:* $5,881,131 (100% non-need-based). *Programs:* Federal Direct (Subsidized and Unsubsidized Stafford, PLUS), Perkins.

**WORK-STUDY Federal work-study:** Total amount: $1,229,896; 625 jobs averaging $2000.

**APPLYING FOR FINANCIAL AID Required financial aid forms:** FAFSA, institution's own form. *Financial aid deadline (priority):* 3/15. *Notification date:* Continuous beginning 3/1. Students must reply within 2 weeks of notification.

**CONTACT** Ms. Marcia Toomey, Director of Financial Aid, Endicott College, 376 Hale Street, Beverly, MA 01915-2096, 978-232-2060 or toll-free 800-325-1114. *Fax:* 978-232-2085. *E-mail:* mtoomey@endicott.edu. *Website:* http://www.endicott.edu/.

---

## EPIC BIBLE COLLEGE
### Sacramento, CA

**CONTACT** Financial Aid Office, Epic Bible College, 5225 Hillsdale Boulevard, Sacramento, CA 95842, 916-348-4689. *Website:* http://epic.edu/.

---

## ERSKINE COLLEGE
### Due West, SC

**CONTACT** Mrs. Becky Pressley, Director of Financial Aid, Erskine College, PO Box 337, Due West, SC 29639, 864-379-8832 or toll-free 800-241-8721. *Fax:* 864-379-2172. *E-mail:* pressley@erskine.edu. *Website:* http://www.erskine.edu/.

# ESCUELA DE ARTES PLASTICAS DE PUERTO RICO

## San Juan, PR

**CONTACT** Mr. Alfred Diaz Melendez, Financial Aid Administrator, Escuela de Artes Plasticas de Puerto Rico, PO Box 9021112, San Juan, PR 00902-1112, 787-725-8120 Ext. 317. *Fax:* 787-725-3798. *E-mail:* adiaz@eap.edu. *Website:* http://www.eap.edu/.

# EUGENE LANG COLLEGE THE NEW SCHOOL FOR LIBERAL ARTS

## New York, NY

**ABOUT THE INSTITUTION** Independent, coed. *Awards:* bachelor's degrees. 16 undergraduate majors. *Total enrollment:* 1,487. Undergraduates: 1,487. Freshmen: 291.

**GIFT AID (NEED-BASED)** *Scholarships, grants, and awards:* Federal Pell, FSEOG, state, private, college/university gift aid from institutional funds.

**GIFT AID (NON-NEED-BASED)** *Scholarships, grants, and awards by category: Academic interests/achievement:* general academic interests/achievements. *Special achievements/activities:* general special achievements/activities, leadership. *Special characteristics:* local/state students, members of minority groups.

**LOANS** *Programs:* Federal Direct (Subsidized and Unsubsidized Stafford, PLUS), Perkins.

**APPLYING FOR FINANCIAL AID** *Required financial aid forms:* FAFSA, state aid form.

**CONTACT** Office of Student Financial Services, Eugene Lang College The New School for Liberal Arts, 72 Fifth Avenue, New York, NY 10011, 212-229-8930 or toll-free 800-292-3040. *E-mail:* sfs@newschool.edu. *Website:* http://www.newschool.edu/lang.

# EUREKA COLLEGE

## Eureka, IL

| Tuition & fees: N/R | Average undergraduate aid package: $15,558 |
|---|---|

**ABOUT THE INSTITUTION** Independent Christian Church (Disciples of Christ), coed. *Awards:* bachelor's degrees. 26 undergraduate majors. *Total enrollment:* 664. Undergraduates: 664. Freshmen: 168. Both federal and institutional methodology are used as a basis for awarding need-based institutional aid.

**UNDERGRADUATE EXPENSES for 2015–2016** *Tuition:* part-time $550 per semester hour. Full-time tuition and fees vary according to course load and program. Part-time tuition and fees vary according to course load and program. Room and board charges vary according to board plan and housing facility.

**FRESHMAN FINANCIAL AID (Fall 2014, est.)** 162 applied for aid; of those 86% were deemed to have need. 100% of freshmen with need received aid; of those 10% had need fully met. *Average percent of need met:* 80% (excluding resources awarded to replace EFC). *Average financial aid package:* $18,218 (excluding resources awarded to replace EFC). 17% of all full-time freshmen had no need and received non-need-based gift aid.

**UNDERGRADUATE FINANCIAL AID (Fall 2014, est.)** 564 applied for aid; of those 89% were deemed to have need. 100% of undergraduates with need received aid; of those 19% had need fully met. *Average percent of need met:* 72% (excluding resources awarded to replace EFC). *Average financial aid package:* $15,558 (excluding resources awarded to replace EFC). 21% of all full-time undergraduates had no need and received non-need-based gift aid.

**GIFT AID (NEED-BASED)** *Total amount:* $5,562,597 (22% federal, 23% state, 55% institutional). *Receiving aid:* Freshmen: 83% (140); all full-time undergraduates: 79% (504). *Average award:* Freshmen: $14,332; Undergraduates: $11,278. *Scholarships, grants, and awards:* Federal Pell, FSEOG, state, private, college/university gift aid from institutional funds.

**GIFT AID (NON-NEED-BASED)** *Total amount:* $905,855 (100% institutional). *Average award:* Freshmen: $8792. Undergraduates: $6773. *Scholarships, grants,*

*and awards by category: Academic interests/achievement:* 662 awards ($2,912,751 total): general academic interests/achievements. *Creative arts/performance:* 183 awards ($146,250 total): art/fine arts, music, performing arts, theater/drama. *Special achievements/activities:* 296 awards ($559,418 total): community service, leadership, religious involvement. *Special characteristics:* 108 awards ($299,089 total): children and siblings of alumni, children of faculty/staff, relatives of clergy, religious affiliation, siblings of current students. *Tuition waivers:* Full or partial for employees or children of employees, senior citizens.

**LOANS** *Student loans:* $4,731,713 (91% need-based, 9% non-need-based). 87% of past graduating class borrowed through all loan programs. *Average indebtedness per student:* $30,194. *Average need-based loan:* Freshmen: $3328. Undergraduates: $4396. *Parent loans:* $572,372 (89% need-based, 11% non-need-based). *Programs:* Federal Direct (Subsidized and Unsubsidized Stafford, PLUS), Perkins, alternative loans.

**WORK-STUDY** *Federal work-study:* Total amount: $73,907; 103 jobs averaging $823. *State or other work-study/employment:* Total amount: $246,353 (100% non-need-based). 98 part-time jobs averaging $1066.

**APPLYING FOR FINANCIAL AID** *Required financial aid form:* FAFSA. *Financial aid deadline (priority):* 2/1. *Notification date:* Continuous beginning 2/15. Students must reply within 2 weeks of notification.

**CONTACT** Ms. Erin Bline, Director of Financial Aid, Eureka College, 300 East College Avenue, Eureka, IL 61530, 309-467-6311 or toll-free 888-4-EUREKA. *Fax:* 309-467-6897. *E-mail:* eraid@eureka.edu. *Website:* http://www.eureka.edu/.

# EVANGEL UNIVERSITY

## Springfield, MO

| Tuition & fees: $20,796 | Average undergraduate aid package: $16,429 |
|---|---|

**ABOUT THE INSTITUTION** Independent Assemblies of God, coed. *Awards:* associate, bachelor's, master's, and doctoral degrees. 48 undergraduate majors. *Total enrollment:* 2,000. Undergraduates: 1,788. Freshmen: 329. Federal methodology is used as a basis for awarding need-based institutional aid.

**UNDERGRADUATE EXPENSES for 2015–2016** *Application fee:* $25. *Comprehensive fee:* $27,996 includes full-time tuition ($19,676), mandatory fees ($1120), and room and board ($7200). *College room only:* $3720. Full-time tuition and fees vary according to course load. Room and board charges vary according to board plan. *Part-time tuition:* $820 per credit hour. Part-time tuition and fees vary according to course load.

**FRESHMAN FINANCIAL AID (Fall 2013)** 393 applied for aid; of those 87% were deemed to have need. 100% of freshmen with need received aid; of those 10% had need fully met. *Average percent of need met:* 66% (excluding resources awarded to replace EFC). *Average financial aid package:* $16,288 (excluding resources awarded to replace EFC). 9% of all full-time freshmen had no need and received non-need-based gift aid.

**UNDERGRADUATE FINANCIAL AID (Fall 2013)** 1,804 applied for aid; of those 88% were deemed to have need. 100% of undergraduates with need received aid; of those 9% had need fully met. *Average percent of need met:* 64% (excluding resources awarded to replace EFC). *Average financial aid package:* $16,429 (excluding resources awarded to replace EFC). 8% of all full-time undergraduates had no need and received non-need-based gift aid.

**GIFT AID (NEED-BASED)** *Total amount:* $14,583,006 (30% federal, 1% state, 53% institutional, 16% external sources). *Receiving aid:* Freshmen: 74% (341); all full-time undergraduates: 83% (1,563). *Average award:* Freshmen: $12,104; Undergraduates: $11,073. *Scholarships, grants, and awards:* Federal Pell, FSEOG, state, private, college/university gift aid from institutional funds.

**GIFT AID (NON-NEED-BASED)** *Total amount:* $1,585,241 (1% federal, 74% institutional, 25% external sources). *Receiving aid:* Freshmen: 7% (30). Undergraduates: 6% (111). *Average award:* Freshmen: $5867. Undergraduates: $4879. *Scholarships, grants, and awards by category: Academic interests/achievement:* 1,107 awards ($4,221,980 total): biological sciences, business, communication, computer science, education, engineering/technologies, English, foreign languages, general academic interests/achievements, health fields, humanities, international studies, mathematics, physical sciences, premedicine, religion/biblical studies, social sciences. *Creative arts/performance:* 215 awards ($230,115 total): art/fine arts, debating, music, theater/drama. *Special achievements/activities:* 237 awards ($185,479 total): cheerleading/drum major, general special achievements/activities, leadership, religious involvement. *Special characteristics:* 336 awards ($2,169,656 total): adult students, children and siblings of alumni, children of educators, children of faculty/staff, general special characteristics, out-of-state students, relatives of clergy, religious affiliation. *Tuition waivers:* Full or partial for employees or children of employees. *ROTC:* Army cooperative.

**LOANS** *Student loans:* $16,894,869 (79% need-based, 21% non-need-based). 79% of past graduating class borrowed through all loan programs. *Average indebtedness per student:* $30,179. *Average need-based loan:* Freshmen: $3585. Undergraduates: $4781. *Parent loans:* $2,842,799 (53% need-based, 47% non-need-based). *Programs:* Federal Direct (Subsidized and Unsubsidized Stafford, PLUS), Perkins, college/university.

**WORK-STUDY** *Federal work-study:* 1,273 jobs averaging $1652. *State or other work-study/employment:* Total amount: $38,950 (63% need-based, 37% non-need-based). Part-time jobs available.

**ATHLETIC AWARDS** Total amount: $2,212,495 (73% need-based, 27% non-need-based).

**APPLYING FOR FINANCIAL AID** *Required financial aid form:* FAFSA. *Financial aid deadline:* 7/1 (priority: 3/1). *Notification date:* Continuous beginning 3/1. Students must reply within 4 weeks of notification.

**CONTACT** Mrs. Valerie Sharp, Director of Student Financial Services, Evangel University, 1111 North Glenstone Avenue, Springfield, MO 65802-2191, 417-865-2811 Ext. 7302 or toll-free 800-382-6435. *Fax:* 417-575-5478. *E-mail:* sharpv@evangel.edu. *Website:* http://www.evangel.edu/.

## EVEREST UNIVERSITY
### Jacksonville, FL

**CONTACT** Financial Aid Office, Everest University, 8226 Phillips Highway, Jacksonville, FL 32256, 904-731-4949 or toll-free 888-741-4270. *Website:* http://www.everest.edu/.

## EVEREST UNIVERSITY
### Lakeland, FL

**CONTACT** Brian Jones, Senior Finance Officer, Everest University, Office of Financial Aid, 995 East Memorial Boulevard, Lakeland, FL 33801, 863-686-1444 Ext. 118 or toll-free 888-741-4270. *Fax:* 863-682-1077. *Website:* http://www.everest.edu/.

## EVEREST UNIVERSITY
### Largo, FL

**CONTACT** Mr. Will Scott, Director of Student Finance, Everest University, 1199 East Bay Drive, Largo, FL 33770, 727-725-2688 Ext. 166 or toll-free 888-741-4270. *Fax:* 727-373-4408. *E-mail:* wscott@cci.edu. *Website:* http://www.everest.edu/.

## EVEREST UNIVERSITY
### Melbourne, FL

**CONTACT** Ida C. Liska, Director of Student Finance, Everest University, 2401 North Harbor City Boulevard, Melbourne, FL 32935-6657, 321-253-2929 Ext. 142. *E-mail:* iliska@cci.edu. *Website:* http://www.everest.edu/.

## EVEREST UNIVERSITY
### Orlando, FL

**CONTACT** Ms. Linda Kaisrlik, Director of Student Finance, Everest University, 5421 Diplomat Circle, Orlando, FL 32810-5674, 407-628-5870 Ext. 118 or toll-free 800-628-5870. *Website:* http://www.everest.edu/.

## EVEREST UNIVERSITY
### Orlando, FL

**CONTACT** Sherri Williams, Director of Financial Aid, Everest University, 2411 Sand Lake Road, Orlando, FL 32809, 407-851-2525 or toll-free 888-741-4270 (in-state), 888-471-4270 (out-of-state). *Website:* http://www.everest.edu/.

## EVEREST UNIVERSITY
### Pompano Beach, FL

**CONTACT** Sharon Scheible, Director of Student Financial Aid, Everest University, 1040 Bayview Drive, Fort Lauderdale, FL 33304-2522, 954-568-1600 Ext. 52. *Fax:* 954-564-5283. *E-mail:* scheible@cci.edu. *Website:* http://www.everest.edu/.

## EVEREST UNIVERSITY
### Tampa, FL

**CONTACT** Mr. Rod Kirkwood, Financial Aid Director, Everest University, 3319 West Hillsborough Avenue, Tampa, FL 33614, 813-879-6000 Ext. 145. *Fax:* 813-871-2483. *E-mail:* rkirkwoo@cci.edu. *Website:* http://www.everest.edu/.

## EVEREST UNIVERSITY
### Tampa, FL

**CONTACT** Ms. Ginger Waymire, Director of Financial Aid, Everest University, 3924 Coconut Palm Drive, Tampa, FL 33619, 813-621-0041 Ext. 118 or toll-free 888-741-4270. *Fax:* 813-621-6283. *E-mail:* gwaymire@cci.edu. *Website:* http://www.everest.edu/.

## EVERGLADES UNIVERSITY
### Altamonte Springs, FL

| Tuition & fees: N/R | Average undergraduate aid package: $10,350 |
|---|---|

**ABOUT THE INSTITUTION** Independent, coed. 6 undergraduate majors. Federal methodology is used as a basis for awarding need-based institutional aid.

**FRESHMAN FINANCIAL AID (Fall 2014, est.)** 5 applied for aid; of those 100% were deemed to have need. 100% of freshmen with need received aid; of those 80% had need fully met. *Average percent of need met:* 53% (excluding resources awarded to replace EFC). *Average financial aid package:* $9455 (excluding resources awarded to replace EFC).

**UNDERGRADUATE FINANCIAL AID (Fall 2014, est.)** 144 applied for aid; of those 94% were deemed to have need. 100% of undergraduates with need received aid; of those 81% had need fully met. *Average percent of need met:* 72% (excluding resources awarded to replace EFC). *Average financial aid package:* $10,350 (excluding resources awarded to replace EFC).

**GIFT AID (NEED-BASED)** *Total amount:* $658,674 (87% federal, 3% state, 10% institutional). *Receiving aid:* Freshmen: 62% (5); all full-time undergraduates: 89% (128). *Average award:* Freshmen: $5230; Undergraduates: $8991. *Scholarships, grants, and awards:* Federal Pell, FSEOG, state, private, college/university gift aid from institutional funds.

**GIFT AID (NON-NEED-BASED)** *Total amount:* $261,909 (100% state). *Receiving aid:* Freshmen: 50% (4). Undergraduates: 75% (108). *Scholarships, grants, and awards by category:* Special characteristics: 1 award ($763 total): general special characteristics, local/state students, veterans.

**LOANS** *Student loans:* $1,309,945 (43% need-based, 57% non-need-based). 100% of past graduating class borrowed through all loan programs. *Average indebtedness per student:* $48,546. *Average need-based loan:* Freshmen: $3031. Undergraduates: $5164. *Parent loans:* $31,731 (100% need-based). *Programs:* Federal Direct (Subsidized and Unsubsidized Stafford, PLUS), Perkins.

**WORK-STUDY** Federal work-study jobs available.

**APPLYING FOR FINANCIAL AID** *Required financial aid forms:* FAFSA, institution's own form. *Financial aid deadline:* Continuous. *Notification date:* Continuous beginning 1/1. Students must reply within 2 weeks of notification.

**CONTACT** Miss Seeta Singh Moonilall, Regional Director of Financial Aid, Everglades University, 5002 T-Rex Avenue, Suite 100, Boca Raton, FL 33431, 561-912-1211 or toll-free 866-289-1078. *Fax:* 561-912-1191. *E-mail:* smoonilall@evergladesuniversity.edu.
*Website:* http://www.evergladesuniversity.edu/.

# EVERGLADES UNIVERSITY
## Boca Raton, FL

| Tuition & fees: N/R | Average undergraduate aid package: $8245 |
| --- | --- |

**ABOUT THE INSTITUTION** Independent, coed. 6 undergraduate majors. Federal methodology is used as a basis for awarding need-based institutional aid.

**FRESHMAN FINANCIAL AID (Fall 2014, est.)** 42 applied for aid; of those 81% were deemed to have need. 100% of freshmen with need received aid; of those 15% had need fully met. *Average percent of need met:* 38% (excluding resources awarded to replace EFC). *Average financial aid package:* $9002 (excluding resources awarded to replace EFC). 19% of all full-time freshmen had no need and received non-need-based gift aid.

**UNDERGRADUATE FINANCIAL AID (Fall 2014, est.)** 965 applied for aid; of those 98% were deemed to have need. 100% of undergraduates with need received aid; of those 25% had need fully met. *Average percent of need met:* 67% (excluding resources awarded to replace EFC). *Average financial aid package:* $8245 (excluding resources awarded to replace EFC). 2% of all full-time undergraduates had no need and received non-need-based gift aid.

**GIFT AID (NEED-BASED)** *Total amount:* $3,691,880 (82% federal, 1% state, 17% institutional). *Receiving aid:* Freshmen: 74% (31); all full-time undergraduates: 75% (722). *Average award:* Freshmen: $8970; Undergraduates: $9586. *Scholarships, grants, and awards:* Federal Pell, FSEOG, state, private, college/university gift aid from institutional funds.

**GIFT AID (NON-NEED-BASED)** *Total amount:* $853,543 (75% state, 25% institutional). *Receiving aid:* Freshmen: 29% (12). Undergraduates: 33% (322). *Average award:* Freshmen: $125. Undergraduates: $2125. *Scholarships, grants, and awards by category:* Special characteristics: 143 awards ($216,844 total): general special characteristics, local/state students, veterans.

**LOANS** *Student loans:* $8,783,904 (37% need-based, 63% non-need-based). 96% of past graduating class borrowed through all loan programs. *Average indebtedness per student:* $60,735. *Average need-based loan:* Freshmen: $4007. Undergraduates: $4863. *Parent loans:* $235,611 (100% need-based). *Programs:* Federal Direct (Subsidized and Unsubsidized Stafford, PLUS), Perkins.

**WORK-STUDY** Federal work-study jobs available.

**APPLYING FOR FINANCIAL AID** *Required financial aid forms:* FAFSA, institution's own form. *Financial aid deadline:* Continuous. *Notification date:* Continuous beginning 1/1. Students must reply within 2 weeks of notification.

**CONTACT** Miss Seeta Singh Moonilall, Regional Director of Financial Aid, Everglades University, 5002 T-Rex Avenue, Suite 100, Boca Raton, FL 33431, 561-912-1211 or toll-free 888-772-6077. *Fax:* 561-912-1191. *E-mail:* smoonilall@evergladesuniversity.edu.
*Website:* http://www.evergladesuniversity.edu/.

# EVERGLADES UNIVERSITY
## Sarasota, FL

| Tuition & fees: $16,000 | Average undergraduate aid package: $8455 |
| --- | --- |

**ABOUT THE INSTITUTION** Independent, coed. *Awards:* bachelor's and master's degrees. 7 undergraduate majors. *Total enrollment:* 1,451. Undergraduates: 1,313. Freshmen: 53. Federal methodology is used as a basis for awarding need-based institutional aid.

**UNDERGRADUATE EXPENSES for 2015–2016** *Application fee:* $50. *One-time required fee:* $195. *Tuition:* full-time $14,400.

**FRESHMAN FINANCIAL AID (Fall 2014, est.)** 3 applied for aid; of those 100% were deemed to have need. 100% of freshmen with need received aid. *Average percent of need met:* 91% (excluding resources awarded to replace EFC). *Average financial aid package:* $14,579 (excluding resources awarded to replace EFC).

**UNDERGRADUATE FINANCIAL AID (Fall 2014, est.)** 190 applied for aid; of those 94% were deemed to have need. 100% of undergraduates with need received aid; of those 25% had need fully met. *Average percent of need met:* 59% (excluding resources awarded to replace EFC). *Average financial aid package:* $8455 (excluding resources awarded to replace EFC).

**GIFT AID (NEED-BASED)** *Total amount:* $910,075 (76% federal, 2% state, 22% institutional). *Receiving aid:* Freshmen: 100% (3); all full-time undergraduates: 92% (174). *Average award:* Freshmen: $6963; Undergraduates: $5230. *Scholarships, grants, and awards:* Federal Pell, FSEOG, state, private, college/university gift aid from institutional funds.

**GIFT AID (NON-NEED-BASED)** *Total amount:* $309,025 (97% state, 3% institutional). *Receiving aid:* Freshmen: 67% (2). Undergraduates: 73% (138). *Scholarships, grants, and awards by category:* Special characteristics: 12 awards ($10,268 total): general special characteristics, local/state students, veterans.

**LOANS** *Student loans:* $1,595,958 (39% need-based, 61% non-need-based). 89% of past graduating class borrowed through all loan programs. *Average indebtedness per student:* $52,777. *Average need-based loan:* Freshmen: $6115. Undergraduates: $4782. *Parent loans:* $9574 (100% need-based). *Programs:* Federal Direct (Subsidized and Unsubsidized Stafford, PLUS), Perkins.

**WORK-STUDY** Federal work-study jobs available.

**APPLYING FOR FINANCIAL AID** *Required financial aid forms:* FAFSA, institution's own form. *Financial aid deadline:* Continuous. *Notification date:* Continuous beginning 1/1. Students must reply within 2 weeks of notification.

**CONTACT** Miss Seeta Singh Moonilall, Regional Director of Financial Aid, Everglades University, 5002 T-Rex Avenue, Suite 100, Boca Raton, FL 33431, 561-912-1211 or toll-free 888-854-8308. *Fax:* 561-912-1191. *E-mail:* smoonilall@evergladesuniversity.edu.
*Website:* http://www.evergladesuniversity.edu/.

# THE EVERGREEN STATE COLLEGE
## Olympia, WA

| Tuition & fees (WA res): $8523 | Average undergraduate aid package: $10,111 |
| --- | --- |

**ABOUT THE INSTITUTION** State-supported, coed. *Awards:* bachelor's and master's degrees. 45 undergraduate majors. *Total enrollment:* 4,219. Undergraduates: 3,878. Freshmen: 543. Federal methodology is used as a basis for awarding need-based institutional aid.

**UNDERGRADUATE EXPENSES for 2015–2016** *Application fee:* $50. *Tuition, state resident:* full-time $7845; part-time $261.50 per credit hour. *Tuition, nonresident:* full-time $20,901; part-time $696.70 per credit hour. *Required fees:* full-time $678; $9.25 per credit hour or $5 per term. Full-time tuition and fees vary according to course load, location, and program. Part-time tuition and fees vary according to course load, location, and program. *College room and board:* $9492; *Room only:* $6270. Room and board charges vary according to board plan, housing facility, location, and student level.

**FRESHMAN FINANCIAL AID (Fall 2013)** 396 applied for aid; of those 78% were deemed to have need. 94% of freshmen with need received aid; of those 7% had need fully met. *Average percent of need met:* 66% (excluding resources awarded to replace EFC). **Average financial aid package:** $9147 (excluding resources awarded to replace EFC). 1% of all full-time freshmen had no need and received non-need-based gift aid.

**UNDERGRADUATE FINANCIAL AID (Fall 2013)** 2,903 applied for aid; of those 91% were deemed to have need. 95% of undergraduates with need received aid; of those 8% had need fully met. **Average percent of need met:** 70% (excluding resources awarded to replace EFC). **Average financial aid package:** $10,111 (excluding resources awarded to replace EFC). 1% of all full-time undergraduates had no need and received non-need-based gift aid.

**GIFT AID (NEED-BASED) Total amount:** $20,129,694 (42% federal, 48% state, 9% institutional, 1% external sources). **Receiving aid:** Freshmen: 41% (202); all full-time undergraduates: 55% (2,072). **Average award:** Freshmen: $9021; Undergraduates: $10,258. **Scholarships, grants, and awards:** Federal Pell, FSEOG, state, private, college/university gift aid from institutional funds.

**GIFT AID (NON-NEED-BASED) Total amount:** $135,581 (14% state, 48% institutional, 38% external sources). **Receiving aid:** Freshmen: 2% (9). Undergraduates: 1% (28). **Average award:** Freshmen: $6971. Undergraduates: $4679. **Scholarships, grants, and awards by category:** Academic interests/achievement: general academic interests/achievements. Creative arts/performance: general creative arts/performance. Special achievements/activities: general special achievements/activities. Special characteristics: adult students, ethnic background, first-generation college students, general special characteristics, local/state students, out-of-state students, veterans, veterans' children. **Tuition waivers:** Full or partial for employees or children of employees, senior citizens.

**LOANS Student loans:** $15,845,095 (93% need-based, 7% non-need-based). 51% of past graduating class borrowed through all loan programs. **Average indebtedness per student:** $21,054. **Average need-based loan:** Freshmen: $3604. Undergraduates: $4233. **Parent loans:** $3,840,058 (78% need-based, 22% non-need-based). **Programs:** Federal Direct (Subsidized and Unsubsidized Stafford, PLUS), Perkins, college/university.

**WORK-STUDY Federal work-study:** jobs available. **State or other work-study/employment:** Total amount: $744,530 (100% need-based). Part-time jobs available.

**ATHLETIC AWARDS** Total amount: $226,917 (82% need-based, 18% non-need-based).

**APPLYING FOR FINANCIAL AID Required financial aid form:** FAFSA. **Financial aid deadline (priority):** 3/1. **Notification date:** Continuous beginning 4/1. Students must reply within 6 weeks of notification.

**CONTACT** Financial Aid Office, The Evergreen State College, 2700 Evergreen Parkway NW, Olympia, WA 98505, 360-867-6205. Fax: 360-866-6576. E-mail: finaid@evergreen.edu.
Website: http://www.evergreen.edu/.

---

# EXCELSIOR COLLEGE
## Albany, NY

| Tuition & fees: N/R | Average undergraduate aid package: N/A |
|---|---|

**ABOUT THE INSTITUTION** Independent, coed. **Awards:** certificates, associate, bachelor's, and master's degrees (offers only external degree programs). 32 undergraduate majors. **Total enrollment:** 38,825. Undergraduates: 35,901. Federal methodology is used as a basis for awarding need-based institutional aid.

**UNDERGRADUATE EXPENSES for 2015-2016 Application fee:** $100. **Tuition:** part-time $465 per credit hour. Part-time tuition and fees vary according to reciprocity agreements.

**GIFT AID (NEED-BASED) Total amount:** $8,342,630 (78% federal, 8% state, 5% institutional, 9% external sources). **Scholarships, grants, and awards:** Federal Pell, FSEOG, state, private, college/university gift aid from institutional funds, Federal Nursing, Veterans Education Benefits (GI Bill).

**GIFT AID (NON-NEED-BASED) Tuition waivers:** Full or partial for employees or children of employees.

**LOANS Student loans:** $17,473,467 (100% need-based). **Parent loans:** $25,194 (100% non-need-based). **Programs:** Federal Direct (Subsidized and Unsubsidized Stafford, PLUS), Federal Nursing.

**APPLYING FOR FINANCIAL AID Financial aid deadline:** Continuous. **Notification date:** Continuous.

**CONTACT** Christina Roarke, Director of Financial Aid, Excelsior College, 7 Columbia Circle, Albany, NY 12203-5159, 518-464-8500 or toll-free 888-647-2388. Fax: 518-464-8777.
Website: http://www.excelsior.edu/.

---

# EX'PRESSION COLLEGE FOR DIGITAL ARTS
## Emeryville, CA

**CONTACT** Financial Aid Office, Ex'pression College for Digital Arts, 6601 Shellmound Street, Emeryville, CA 94608, 510-654-2934 or toll-free 877-833-8800.
Website: http://www.expression.edu/.

---

# FAIRFIELD UNIVERSITY
## Fairfield, CT

| Tuition & fees: $44,875 | Average undergraduate aid package: $30,054 |
|---|---|

**ABOUT THE INSTITUTION** Independent Roman Catholic (Jesuit), coed. **Awards:** certificates, bachelor's, master's, and doctoral degrees. 37 undergraduate majors. **Total enrollment:** 5,123. Undergraduates: 3,982. Freshmen: 1,056. Both federal and institutional methodology are used as a basis for awarding need-based institutional aid.

**UNDERGRADUATE EXPENSES for 2015-2016 Application fee:** $60. **One-time required fee:** $230. **Comprehensive fee:** $58,395 includes full-time tuition ($44,250), mandatory fees ($625), and room and board ($13,520). **College room only:** $8280. Full-time tuition and fees vary according to class time, course level, course load, degree level, and program. Room and board charges vary according to board plan and housing facility. **Part-time tuition:** $725 per credit hour. **Part-time fees:** $60 per term. Part-time tuition and fees vary according to class time, course level, course load, degree level, and program.

**FRESHMAN FINANCIAL AID (Fall 2014, est.)** 779 applied for aid; of those 68% were deemed to have need. 100% of freshmen with need received aid; of those 17% had need fully met. **Average percent of need met:** 87% (excluding resources awarded to replace EFC). **Average financial aid package:** $30,240 (excluding resources awarded to replace EFC). 39% of all full-time freshmen had no need and received non-need-based gift aid.

**UNDERGRADUATE FINANCIAL AID (Fall 2014, est.)** 2,467 applied for aid; of those 73% were deemed to have need. 100% of undergraduates with need received aid; of those 16% had need fully met. **Average percent of need met:** 87% (excluding resources awarded to replace EFC). **Average financial aid package:** $30,054 (excluding resources awarded to replace EFC). 33% of all full-time undergraduates had no need and received non-need-based gift aid.

**GIFT AID (NEED-BASED) Total amount:** $43,208,744 (5% federal, 3% state, 92% institutional). **Receiving aid:** Freshmen: 43% (457); all full-time undergraduates: 43% (1,586). **Average award:** Freshmen: $14,847; Undergraduates: $15,682. **Scholarships, grants, and awards:** Federal Pell, FSEOG, state, private, college/university gift aid from institutional funds, Federal Nursing.

**GIFT AID (NON-NEED-BASED) Total amount:** $15,428,265 (95% institutional, 5% external sources). **Receiving aid:** Freshmen: 45% (471). Undergraduates: 39% (1,433). **Average award:** Freshmen: $16,684. Undergraduates: $15,452. **Scholarships, grants, and awards by category:** Academic interests/achievement: 1,224 awards ($14,508,834 total): general academic interests/achievements. Creative arts/performance: 28 awards ($20,114 total): general creative arts/performance. Special achievements/activities: 8 awards ($39,103 total): general special achievements/activities. Special characteristics: 194 awards ($3,131,617 total): children and siblings of alumni, children of faculty/staff, children with a deceased or disabled parent, ethnic background, first-generation college students, general special characteristics, veterans, veterans' children. **Tuition waivers:** Full or partial for employees or children of employees. **ROTC:** Army cooperative, Air Force cooperative.

**LOANS Student loans:** $14,462,876 (55% need-based, 45% non-need-based). 65% of past graduating class borrowed through all loan programs. **Average indebtedness per student:** $27,918. **Average need-based loan:** Freshmen: $3938. Undergraduates: $4938. **Parent loans:** $7,724,518 (100% non-need-based). **Programs:** Federal

Direct (Subsidized and Unsubsidized Stafford, PLUS), Perkins, Federal Nursing, alternative loans.

**WORK-STUDY** *Federal work-study:* Total amount: $280,490; 277 jobs averaging $1012.

**ATHLETIC AWARDS** Total amount: $5,911,096 (100% non-need-based).

**APPLYING FOR FINANCIAL AID** *Required financial aid forms:* FAFSA, CSS Financial Aid PROFILE, noncustodial (divorced/separated) parent's statement, business/farm supplement. *Financial aid deadline:* 2/15. *Notification date:* 4/1. Students must reply by 5/1.

**CONTACT** Diana Draper, Director of Financial Aid, Fairfield University, 1073 North Benson Road, Fairfield, CT 06824, 203-254-4125. *Fax:* 203-254-4008. *E-mail:* finaid@fairfield.edu.

*Website:* http://www.fairfield.edu/.

# FAIRLEIGH DICKINSON UNIVERSITY, COLLEGE AT FLORHAM
## Madison, NJ

**CONTACT** Financial Aid Office, Fairleigh Dickinson University, College at Florham, 285 Madison Avenue, Madison, NJ 07940-1099, 973-443-8700 or toll-free 800-338-8803.

*Website:* http://www.fdu.edu/.

# FAIRLEIGH DICKINSON UNIVERSITY, METROPOLITAN CAMPUS
## Teaneck, NJ

**CONTACT** Financial Aid Office, Fairleigh Dickinson University, Metropolitan Campus, 100 River Road, Teaneck, NJ 07666-1914, 201-692-2363 or toll-free 800-338-8803.

*Website:* http://www.fdu.edu/.

# FAIRMONT STATE UNIVERSITY
## Fairmont, WV

| Tuition & fees (WV res): $6306 | Average undergraduate aid package: $8643 |
| --- | --- |

**ABOUT THE INSTITUTION** State-supported, coed. *Awards:* associate, bachelor's, and master's degrees. 42 undergraduate majors. *Total enrollment:* 4,035. Undergraduates: 3,785. Freshmen: 689. Federal methodology is used as a basis for awarding need-based institutional aid.

**UNDERGRADUATE EXPENSES for 2015–2016** *Tuition, state resident:* full-time $6306; part-time $255 per credit hour. *Tuition, nonresident:* full-time $13,306; part-time $546 per credit hour. Full-time tuition and fees vary according to location. Part-time tuition and fees vary according to course load and location. *College room and board:* $7800; *Room only:* $4026. Room and board charges vary according to board plan and housing facility.

**FRESHMAN FINANCIAL AID (Fall 2013)** 710 applied for aid; of those 76% were deemed to have need. 98% of freshmen with need received aid; of those 11% had need fully met. *Average percent of need met:* 72% (excluding resources awarded to replace EFC). *Average financial aid package:* $9056 (excluding resources awarded to replace EFC). 12% of all full-time freshmen had no need and received non-need-based gift aid.

**UNDERGRADUATE FINANCIAL AID (Fall 2013)** 3,092 applied for aid; of those 83% were deemed to have need. 98% of undergraduates with need received aid; of those 6% had need fully met. *Average percent of need met:* 65% (excluding resources awarded to replace EFC). *Average financial aid package:* $8643 (excluding resources awarded to replace EFC). 8% of all full-time undergraduates had no need and received non-need-based gift aid.

**GIFT AID (NEED-BASED)** Total amount: $14,337,593 (55% federal, 40% state, 5% institutional). *Receiving aid:* Freshmen: 65% (479); all full-time undergraduates: 64% (2,199). *Average award:* Freshmen: $6836; Undergraduates: $5940. *Scholar-

ships, grants, and awards:* Federal Pell, FSEOG, state, private, college/university gift aid from institutional funds.

**GIFT AID (NON-NEED-BASED)** *Total amount:* $743,639 (4% state, 34% institutional, 62% external sources). *Receiving aid:* Freshmen: 33% (244). Undergraduates: 19% (636). *Average award:* Freshmen: $5376. Undergraduates: $5299. *Scholarships, grants, and awards by category:* Academic interests/achievement: 515 awards ($2,048,226 total): architecture, biological sciences, business, computer science, education, engineering/technologies, English, general academic interests/achievements, health fields, humanities, international studies, mathematics, physical sciences, social sciences. *Creative arts/performance:* 660 awards ($2,714,901 total): art/fine arts, creative writing, debating, general creative arts/performance, journalism/publications, music, theater/drama. *Special achievements/activities:* 100 awards ($90,075 total): cheerleading/drum major, general special achievements/activities, leadership. *Special characteristics:* 26 awards ($35,500 total): adult students, children and siblings of alumni, children of faculty/staff, ethnic background, first-generation college students, general special characteristics, handicapped students, international students, local/state students, members of minority groups, out-of-state students, previous college experience, veterans, veterans' children. *Tuition waivers:* Full or partial for employees or children of employees. *ROTC:* Army, Air Force cooperative.

**LOANS** *Student loans:* $18,102,377 (40% need-based, 60% non-need-based). 68% of past graduating class borrowed through all loan programs. *Average indebtedness per student:* $26,420. *Average need-based loan:* Freshmen: $2982. Undergraduates: $3791. *Parent loans:* $601,160 (100% non-need-based). *Programs:* Federal Direct (Subsidized and Unsubsidized Stafford, PLUS), Perkins.

**WORK-STUDY** *Federal work-study:* 143 jobs averaging $1344. *State or other work-study/employment:* Total amount: $672,744 (100% non-need-based). 660 part-time jobs averaging $2100.

**ATHLETIC AWARDS** Total amount: $1,182,197 (70% need-based, 30% non-need-based).

**APPLYING FOR FINANCIAL AID** *Required financial aid form:* FAFSA. *Financial aid deadline (priority):* 3/1. *Notification date:* Continuous beginning 4/1. Students must reply within 2 weeks of notification.

**CONTACT** Patricia Wiemer, Director of Financial Aid and Scholarships, Fairmont State University, 1201 Locust Avenue, Fairmont, WV 26554, 304-367-4892 or toll-free 800-641-5678. *Fax:* 304-367-4789. *E-mail:* patricia.weimer@fairmontstate.edu.

*Website:* http://www.fairmontstate.edu/.

# FAITH BAPTIST BIBLE COLLEGE AND THEOLOGICAL SEMINARY
## Ankeny, IA

**CONTACT** Mr. Breck Appell, Director of Financial Assistance, Faith Baptist Bible College and Theological Seminary, 1900 Northwest 4th Street, Ankeny, IA 50021-2152, 515-964-0601 or toll-free 888-FAITH 4U. *Fax:* 515-964-1638.

*Website:* http://www.faith.edu/.

# FAITH THEOLOGICAL SEMINARY
## Baltimore, MD

**CONTACT** Financial Aid Office, Faith Theological Seminary, 529 Walker Avenue, Baltimore, MD 21212, 410-323-6211.

*Website:* http://www.faiththeological.org/.

# FAMILY OF FAITH COLLEGE
## Shawnee, OK

**CONTACT** Financial Aid Office, Family of Faith College, 30 Kinville, Shawnee, OK 74802, 405-273-5331.

*Website:* http://www.familyoffaithcollege.edu/.

# FARMINGDALE STATE COLLEGE
## Farmingdale, NY

| Tuition & fees (NY res): $7483 | Average undergraduate aid package: $7717 |
|---|---|

**ABOUT THE INSTITUTION** State-supported, coed. *Awards:* certificates, associate, and bachelor's degrees. 27 undergraduate majors. *Total enrollment:* 8,394. Undergraduates: 8,394. Freshmen: 1,068. Federal methodology is used as a basis for awarding need-based institutional aid.

**UNDERGRADUATE EXPENSES** for 2015–2016 *Application fee:* $50. *Tuition, state resident:* full-time $6170; part-time $257 per credit. *Tuition, nonresident:* full-time $15,820; part-time $659 per credit. *Required fees:* full-time $1313; $53.15 per credit or $10 per term. Full-time tuition and fees vary according to program. Part-time tuition and fees vary according to course load and program. *College room and board:* $12,190; *Room only:* $7440. Room and board charges vary according to board plan and housing facility.

**FRESHMAN FINANCIAL AID (Fall 2013)** 892 applied for aid; of those 72% were deemed to have need. 91% of freshmen with need received aid; of those 9% had need fully met. *Average percent of need met:* 62% (excluding resources awarded to replace EFC). *Average financial aid package:* $8323 (excluding resources awarded to replace EFC). 1% of all full-time freshmen had no need and received non-need-based gift aid.

**UNDERGRADUATE FINANCIAL AID (Fall 2013)** 4,167 applied for aid; of those 77% were deemed to have need. 94% of undergraduates with need received aid; of those 8% had need fully met. *Average percent of need met:* 57% (excluding resources awarded to replace EFC). *Average financial aid package:* $7717 (excluding resources awarded to replace EFC). 1% of all full-time undergraduates had no need and received non-need-based gift aid.

**GIFT AID (NEED-BASED)** *Total amount:* $16,470,295 (56% federal, 44% state). *Receiving aid:* Freshmen: 47% (516); all full-time undergraduates: 43% (2,567). *Average award:* Freshmen: $6942; Undergraduates: $6038. *Scholarships, grants, and awards:* Federal Pell, FSEOG, state, private, college/university gift aid from institutional funds.

**GIFT AID (NON-NEED-BASED)** *Total amount:* $1,114,891 (37% state, 21% institutional, 42% external sources). *Receiving aid:* Freshmen: 5% (51). Undergraduates: 4% (252). *Average award:* Freshmen: $965. Undergraduates: $1624. *ROTC:* Army cooperative, Naval cooperative, Air Force cooperative.

**LOANS** *Student loans:* $17,455,601 (42% need-based, 58% non-need-based). *Average need-based loan:* Freshmen: $4029. Undergraduates: $4282. *Parent loans:* $1,135,879 (100% non-need-based). *Programs:* Federal Direct (Subsidized and Unsubsidized Stafford, PLUS), Perkins, alternative loans.

**WORK-STUDY** *Federal work-study:* jobs available. *State or other work-study/employment:* Total amount: $322,784 (100% non-need-based). Part-time jobs available.

**APPLYING FOR FINANCIAL AID** *Required financial aid form:* FAFSA. *Financial aid deadline (priority):* 4/1. *Notification date:* Continuous beginning 3/1.

**CONTACT** Office of Financial Aid, Farmingdale State College, 2350 Broadhollow Road, Laffin Hall, Room 324, Farmingdale, NY 11735, 631-420-2578. *Fax:* 631-420-3662. *E-mail:* faoffice@farmingdale.edu. *Website:* http://www.farmingdale.edu/.

# FASHION INSTITUTE OF TECHNOLOGY
## New York, NY

| Tuition & fees (NY res): $5200 | Average undergraduate aid package: $11,882 |
|---|---|

**ABOUT THE INSTITUTION** State and locally supported, coed, primarily women. *Awards:* certificates, associate, bachelor's, and master's degrees. 23 undergraduate majors. *Total enrollment:* 9,764. Undergraduates: 9,567. Freshmen: 1,322. Federal methodology is used as a basis for awarding need-based institutional aid.

**UNDERGRADUATE EXPENSES** for 2015–2016 *Application fee:* $50. *Tuition, state resident:* full-time $4500; part-time $257 per credit hour. *Tuition, nonresident:* full-time $13,500; part-time $742 per credit hour. *Required fees:* full-time $700. Full-time tuition and fees vary according to degree level. Part-time tuition and fees vary according to degree level. *College room and board:* $13,162. Room and board charges vary according to board plan and housing facility.

**FRESHMAN FINANCIAL AID (Fall 2013)** 969 applied for aid; of those 71% were deemed to have need. 100% of freshmen with need received aid; of those 38% had need fully met. *Average percent of need met:* 77% (excluding resources awarded to replace EFC). *Average financial aid package:* $10,670 (excluding resources awarded to replace EFC). 3% of all full-time freshmen had no need and received non-need-based gift aid.

**UNDERGRADUATE FINANCIAL AID (Fall 2013)** 4,713 applied for aid; of those 80% were deemed to have need. 100% of undergraduates with need received aid; of those 35% had need fully met. *Average percent of need met:* 72% (excluding resources awarded to replace EFC). *Average financial aid package:* $11,882 (excluding resources awarded to replace EFC). 1% of all full-time undergraduates had no need and received non-need-based gift aid.

**GIFT AID (NEED-BASED)** *Total amount:* $16,990,117 (64% federal, 29% state, 7% institutional). *Receiving aid:* Freshmen: 37% (475); all full-time undergraduates: 38% (2,735). *Average award:* Freshmen: $6112; Undergraduates: $5751. *Scholarships, grants, and awards:* Federal Pell, FSEOG, state, private, college/university gift aid from institutional funds.

**GIFT AID (NON-NEED-BASED)** *Total amount:* $78,000 (100% institutional). *Receiving aid:* Freshmen: 1% (16). Undergraduates: 1% (64). *Average award:* Freshmen: $477. Undergraduates: $477. *Scholarships, grants, and awards by category:* Creative arts/performance: applied art and design. *Tuition waivers:* Full or partial for employees or children of employees, senior citizens.

**LOANS** *Student loans:* $36,085,822 (36% need-based, 64% non-need-based). 57% of past graduating class borrowed through all loan programs. *Average indebtedness per student:* $27,303. *Average need-based loan:* Freshmen: $2627. Undergraduates: $3500. *Parent loans:* $8,694,021 (100% non-need-based). *Programs:* Federal Direct (Subsidized and Unsubsidized Stafford, PLUS), Perkins, alternative loans.

**WORK-STUDY** *Federal work-study:* jobs available.

**APPLYING FOR FINANCIAL AID** *Required financial aid forms:* FAFSA, state aid form. *Financial aid deadline (priority):* 2/15. *Notification date:* Continuous beginning 4/1. Students must reply within 2 weeks of notification.

**CONTACT** Financial Aid Office, Fashion Institute of Technology, Seventh Avenue at 27th Street, New York, NY 10001-5992, 212-217-3560. *Website:* http://www.fitnyc.edu/.

# FAULKNER UNIVERSITY
## Montgomery, AL

| Tuition & fees: $18,750 | Average undergraduate aid package: $5950 |
|---|---|

**ABOUT THE INSTITUTION** Independent Church of Christ, coed. *Awards:* associate, bachelor's, master's, and doctoral degrees. 14 undergraduate majors. *Total enrollment:* 3,335. Undergraduates: 2,668. Freshmen: 407. Federal methodology is used as a basis for awarding need-based institutional aid.

**UNDERGRADUATE EXPENSES** for 2015–2016 *Application fee:* $25. *One-time required fee:* $575. *Comprehensive fee:* $25,720 includes full-time tuition ($17,020), mandatory fees ($1730), and room and board ($6970). *College room only:* $3330. Full-time tuition and fees vary according to class time, location, and program. Room and board charges vary according to board plan and housing facility. *Part-time tuition:* $500 per semester hour. *Part-time fees:* $288 per term. Part-time tuition and fees vary according to class time, location, and program.

**FRESHMAN FINANCIAL AID (Fall 2013)** 240 applied for aid; of those 79% were deemed to have need. 100% of freshmen with need received aid; of those 8% had need fully met. *Average percent of need met:* 57% (excluding resources awarded to replace EFC). *Average financial aid package:* $6300 (excluding resources awarded to replace EFC). 7% of all full-time freshmen had no need and received non-need-based gift aid.

**UNDERGRADUATE FINANCIAL AID (Fall 2013)** 1,521 applied for aid; of those 79% were deemed to have need. 100% of undergraduates with need received aid; of those 3% had need fully met. *Average percent of need met:* 59% (excluding resources awarded to replace EFC). *Average financial aid package:* $5950 (excluding resources awarded to replace EFC). 4% of all full-time undergraduates had no need and received non-need-based gift aid.

**GIFT AID (NEED-BASED)** *Total amount:* $7,340,467 (100% federal). *Receiving aid:* Freshmen: 53% (151); all full-time undergraduates: 50% (900).

*Average award:* Freshmen: $3600; Undergraduates: $5700. ***Scholarships, grants, and awards:*** Federal Pell, FSEOG, state, private, college/university gift aid from institutional funds.

**GIFT AID (NON-NEED-BASED)** *Total amount:* $5,568,451 (7% state, 89% institutional, 4% external sources). *Receiving aid:* Freshmen: 60% (171). Undergraduates: 56% (1,008). *Average award:* Undergraduates: $2200. ***Scholarships, grants, and awards by category:*** *Academic interests/achievement:* general academic interests/achievements, religion/biblical studies. *Creative arts/performance:* journalism/publications, music, theater/drama. *Special achievements/activities:* cheerleading/drum major, leadership, religious involvement. *Special characteristics:* adult students, children and siblings of alumni, children of faculty/staff, local/state students, out-of-state students, relatives of clergy, religious affiliation, siblings of current students. *Tuition waivers:* Full or partial for employees or children of employees, adult students. *ROTC:* Army cooperative, Air Force cooperative.

**LOANS** *Student loans:* $32,802,838 (27% need-based, 73% non-need-based). 89% of past graduating class borrowed through all loan programs. *Average indebtedness per student:* $29,000. *Average need-based loan:* Freshmen: $3400. Undergraduates: $5300. *Parent loans:* $1,620,469 (100% non-need-based). *Programs:* Federal Direct (Subsidized and Unsubsidized Stafford, PLUS), Perkins.

**WORK-STUDY** *Federal work-study:* jobs available. *State or other work-study/employment:* Total amount: $3800 (100% non-need-based). Part-time jobs available.

**ATHLETIC AWARDS** Total amount: $3,331,156 (100% non-need-based).

**APPLYING FOR FINANCIAL AID** *Required financial aid forms:* FAFSA, institution's own form, state aid form. *Financial aid deadline:* 8/1 (priority: 3/15). *Notification date:* 5/1. Students must reply within 3 weeks of notification.

**CONTACT** Mr. William G. Jackson II, Director of Financial Aid, Faulkner University, 5345 Atlanta Highway, Montgomery, AL 36109-3398, 334-386-7195 or toll-free 800-879-9816. *Fax:* 334-386-7201. *E-mail:* faid@faulkner.edu. *Website:* http://www.faulkner.edu/.

# FAYETTEVILLE STATE UNIVERSITY
## Fayetteville, NC

| Tuition & fees (NC res): $2743 | Average undergraduate aid package: $10,666 |
|---|---|

**ABOUT THE INSTITUTION** State-supported, coed. *Awards:* bachelor's, master's, and doctoral degrees. 41 undergraduate majors. *Total enrollment:* 5,899. Undergraduates: 5,247. Freshmen: 476. Federal methodology is used as a basis for awarding need-based institutional aid.

**UNDERGRADUATE EXPENSES for 2015–2016** *Application fee:* $40. *Tuition, state resident:* full-time $2743. *Tuition, nonresident:* full-time $14,351. Full-time tuition and fees vary according to course level, course load, degree level, location, and program. Part-time tuition and fees vary according to course level, course load, degree level, location, and program. *College room and board:* $6445; *Room only:* $3529. Room and board charges vary according to board plan and housing facility.

**FRESHMAN FINANCIAL AID (Fall 2014, est.)** 686 applied for aid; of those 96% were deemed to have need. 99% of freshmen with need received aid; of those 12% had need fully met. *Average percent of need met:* 78% (excluding resources awarded to replace EFC). *Average financial aid package:* $11,759 (excluding resources awarded to replace EFC).

**UNDERGRADUATE FINANCIAL AID (Fall 2014, est.)** 3,740 applied for aid; of those 95% were deemed to have need. 98% of undergraduates with need received aid; of those 12% had need fully met. *Average percent of need met:* 73% (excluding resources awarded to replace EFC). *Average financial aid package:* $10,666 (excluding resources awarded to replace EFC).

**GIFT AID (NEED-BASED)** *Total amount:* $26,548,591 (63% federal, 19% state, 15% institutional, 3% external sources). *Receiving aid:* Freshmen: 90% (643); all full-time undergraduates: 85% (3,378). *Average award:* Freshmen: $8675; Undergraduates: $6987. *Scholarships, grants, and awards:* Federal Pell, FSEOG, state, private, college/university gift aid from institutional funds, United Negro College Fund, Federal Nursing.

**GIFT AID (NON-NEED-BASED)** *Total amount:* $15,128 (100% external sources). *Receiving aid:* Freshmen: 4% (28). Undergraduates: 2% (63). ***Scholarships, grants, and awards by category:*** *Academic interests/achievement:* general academic interests/achievements. *Creative arts/performance:* music. *Special*

*characteristics:* local/state students. *Tuition waivers:* Full or partial for employees or children of employees, senior citizens. *ROTC:* Army cooperative, Air Force.

**LOANS** *Student loans:* $31,408,529 (96% need-based, 4% non-need-based). 90% of past graduating class borrowed through all loan programs. *Average indebtedness per student:* $24,029. *Average need-based loan:* Freshmen: $3420. Undergraduates: $4325. *Parent loans:* $641,421 (69% need-based, 31% non-need-based). *Programs:* Federal Direct (Subsidized and Unsubsidized Stafford, PLUS), Perkins.

**WORK-STUDY** *Federal work-study:* Total amount: $423,363; jobs available. *State or other work-study/employment:* Part-time jobs available.

**ATHLETIC AWARDS** Total amount: $645,251 (100% non-need-based).

**APPLYING FOR FINANCIAL AID** *Required financial aid forms:* FAFSA, federal income tax form(s), W-2 forms. *Financial aid deadline:* 3/1. *Notification date:* Continuous beginning 4/1.

**CONTACT** Mr. Keith Townsend, Administrative Assistant, Fayetteville State University, 1200 Murchison Road, Fayetteville, NC 28301-4298, 910-672-1327 or toll-free 800-222-2594. *Fax:* 910-672-1423. *E-mail:* ktownse7@uncfsu.edu. *Website:* http://www.uncfsu.edu/.

# FELICIAN COLLEGE
## Lodi, NJ

| Tuition & fees: $30,605 | Average undergraduate aid package: $26,716 |
|---|---|

**ABOUT THE INSTITUTION** Independent Roman Catholic, coed. *Awards:* certificates, associate, bachelor's, master's, and doctoral degrees. 31 undergraduate majors. *Total enrollment:* 1,933. Undergraduates: 1,621. Freshmen: 153. Federal methodology is used as a basis for awarding need-based institutional aid.

**UNDERGRADUATE EXPENSES for 2015–2016** *Application fee:* $30. *Comprehensive fee:* $42,255 includes full-time tuition ($28,950), mandatory fees ($1655), and room and board ($11,650). Full-time tuition and fees vary according to program. Room and board charges vary according to housing facility. *Part-time tuition:* $955 per credit hour. Part-time tuition and fees vary according to course load and program.

**FRESHMAN FINANCIAL AID (Fall 2014, est.)** 264 applied for aid; of those 96% were deemed to have need. 100% of freshmen with need received aid; of those 11% had need fully met. *Average percent of need met:* 77% (excluding resources awarded to replace EFC). *Average financial aid package:* $31,735 (excluding resources awarded to replace EFC). 6% of all full-time freshmen had no need and received non-need-based gift aid.

**UNDERGRADUATE FINANCIAL AID (Fall 2014, est.)** 1,267 applied for aid; of those 96% were deemed to have need. 99% of undergraduates with need received aid; of those 10% had need fully met. *Average percent of need met:* 70% (excluding resources awarded to replace EFC). *Average financial aid package:* $26,716 (excluding resources awarded to replace EFC). 7% of all full-time undergraduates had no need and received non-need-based gift aid.

**GIFT AID (NEED-BASED)** *Total amount:* $11,222,211 (35% federal, 56% state, 9% institutional). *Receiving aid:* Freshmen: 72% (195); all full-time undergraduates: 63% (875). *Average award:* Freshmen: $13,699; Undergraduates: $12,562. *Scholarships, grants, and awards:* Federal Pell, FSEOG, state, private, college/university gift aid from institutional funds.

**GIFT AID (NON-NEED-BASED)** *Total amount:* $13,661,782 (5% federal, 94% institutional, 1% external sources). *Receiving aid:* Freshmen: 94% (254). Undergraduates: 70% (969). *Average award:* Freshmen: $16,477. Undergraduates: $13,837. ***Scholarships, grants, and awards by category:*** *Academic interests/achievement:* 1,057 awards ($14,739,204 total): business, education, English, general academic interests/achievements, health fields, religion/biblical studies. *Special characteristics:* 26 awards ($262,923 total): children of faculty/staff, siblings of current students. *Tuition waivers:* Full or partial for employees or children of employees.

**LOANS** *Student loans:* $10,545,620 (43% need-based, 57% non-need-based). *Average need-based loan:* Freshmen: $3305. Undergraduates: $4324. *Parent loans:* $2,184,209 (100% non-need-based). *Programs:* Federal Direct (Subsidized and Unsubsidized Stafford, PLUS), state.

**WORK-STUDY** Federal work-study jobs available. *State or other work-study/employment:* Part-time jobs available.

**ATHLETIC AWARDS** Total amount: $2,018,399 (100% non-need-based).

APPLYING FOR FINANCIAL AID *Required financial aid form:* FAFSA. *Financial aid deadline:* Continuous. *Notification date:* Continuous beginning 4/1.
CONTACT Ms. Cynthia Montalvo, Financial Aid Director, Felician College, 262 South Main Street, Lodi, NJ 07644, 201-559-6040. *Fax:* 201-559-6025. *E-mail:* montalvoc@felician.edu.
*Website:* http://www.felician.edu/.

# FERRIS STATE UNIVERSITY
## Big Rapids, MI

| Tuition & fees (MI res): $11,190 | Average undergraduate aid package: $10,950 |
|---|---|

**ABOUT THE INSTITUTION** State-supported, coed. *Awards:* certificates, associate, bachelor's, master's, and doctoral degrees. 111 undergraduate majors. *Total enrollment:* 14,600. Undergraduates: 13,357. Freshmen: 1,926. Federal methodology is used as a basis for awarding need-based institutional aid.

**UNDERGRADUATE EXPENSES for 2015–2016** *Application fee:* $30. *One-time required fee:* $162. *Tuition, state resident:* full-time $11,190; part-time $373 per credit hour. *Tuition, nonresident:* full-time $16,800; part-time $560 per credit hour. Full-time tuition and fees vary according to location, program, and student level. Part-time tuition and fees vary according to location and student level. *College room and board:* $9208. Room and board charges vary according to board plan and housing facility.

**FRESHMAN FINANCIAL AID (Fall 2014, est.)** 1,747 applied for aid; of those 84% were deemed to have need. 99% of freshmen with need received aid; of those 17% had need fully met. *Average percent of need met:* 70% (excluding resources awarded to replace EFC). *Average financial aid package:* $12,250 (excluding resources awarded to replace EFC). 14% of all full-time freshmen had no need and received non-need-based gift aid.

**UNDERGRADUATE FINANCIAL AID (Fall 2014, est.)** 8,749 applied for aid; of those 81% were deemed to have need. 99% of undergraduates with need received aid; of those 14% had need fully met. *Average percent of need met:* 64% (excluding resources awarded to replace EFC). *Average financial aid package:* $10,950 (excluding resources awarded to replace EFC). 12% of all full-time undergraduates had no need and received non-need-based gift aid.

**GIFT AID (NEED-BASED)** *Total amount:* $30,383,950 (83% federal, 2% state, 15% institutional). *Receiving aid:* Freshmen: 55% (1,044); all full-time undergraduates: 53% (5,085). *Average award:* Freshmen: $4860; Undergraduates: $5030. *Scholarships, grants, and awards:* Federal Pell, FSEOG, state, private, college/university gift aid from institutional funds.

**GIFT AID (NON-NEED-BASED)** *Total amount:* $30,931,020 (1% federal, 31% state, 52% institutional, 16% external sources). *Receiving aid:* Freshmen: 63% (1,189). Undergraduates: 41% (3,953). *Average award:* Freshmen: $4940. Undergraduates: $4270. *Scholarships, grants, and awards by category:* Academic interests/achievement: 3,682 awards ($10,222,066 total): agriculture, architecture, biological sciences, business, communication, computer science, education, engineering/technologies, general academic interests/achievements, health fields, mathematics. Creative arts/performance: 622 awards ($1,915,409 total): applied art and design, art/fine arts, debating, general creative arts/performance, journalism/publications, music, theater/drama. Special achievements/activities: 94 awards ($31,223 total): general special achievements/activities, memberships. Special characteristics: 150 awards ($152,900 total): adult students, children and siblings of alumni, ethnic background, general special characteristics, international students, local/state students, members of minority groups, previous college experience, veterans. *Tuition waivers:* Full or partial for employees or children of employees. *ROTC:* Army cooperative.

**LOANS** *Student loans:* $74,008,522 (42% need-based, 58% non-need-based). 83% of past graduating class borrowed through all loan programs. *Average indebtedness per student:* $35,720. *Average need-based loan:* Freshmen: $3640. Undergraduates: $4450. *Parent loans:* $9,265,550 (100% non-need-based). *Programs:* Federal Direct (Subsidized and Unsubsidized Stafford, PLUS), Perkins, Federal Nursing, college/university, alternative loans.

**WORK-STUDY** *Federal work-study:* Total amount: $1,013,120; 448 jobs averaging $2250. *State or other work-study/employment:* Total amount: $1,498,490 (100% non-need-based). 245 part-time jobs averaging $1780.

**ATHLETIC AWARDS** Total amount: $2,027,300 (100% non-need-based).

APPLYING FOR FINANCIAL AID *Required financial aid form:* FAFSA. *Financial aid deadline (priority):* 2/15. *Notification date:* Continuous beginning 3/15. Students must reply within 3 weeks of notification.
CONTACT Nancy Wencl, Assistant Director of Financial Aid, Ferris State University, 1201 South State Street, Big Rapids, MI 49307-2020, 231-591-2100 or toll-free 800-433-7747. *Fax:* 231-591-2950. *E-mail:* wencln@ferris.edu.
*Website:* http://www.ferris.edu/.

# FERRUM COLLEGE
## Ferrum, VA

**ABOUT THE INSTITUTION** Independent United Methodist, coed. *Awards:* bachelor's degrees. 31 undergraduate majors. *Total enrollment:* 1,451. Undergraduates: 1,451. Freshmen: 499.

**GIFT AID (NEED-BASED)** *Scholarships, grants, and awards:* Federal Pell, FSEOG, state, private, college/university gift aid from institutional funds.

**GIFT AID (NON-NEED-BASED)** *Scholarships, grants, and awards by category:* Academic interests/achievement: general academic interests/achievements. Special achievements/activities: general special achievements/activities, leadership, religious involvement. Special characteristics: children of faculty/staff, international students, local/state students, relatives of clergy, religious affiliation.

**LOANS** *Programs:* Federal Direct (Subsidized and Unsubsidized Stafford, PLUS), Perkins.

**APPLYING FOR FINANCIAL AID** *Required financial aid forms:* FAFSA, state aid form.

CONTACT Heather Hollandsworth, Director of Financial Aid, Ferrum College, PO Box 1000, Ferrum, VA 24088, 540-365-4282 or toll-free 800-868-9797. *Fax:* 540-365-4266. *E-mail:* hhollandsworth@ferrum.edu.
*Website:* http://www.ferrum.edu/.

# FINLANDIA UNIVERSITY
## Hancock, MI

CONTACT Sandra Turnquist, Director of Financial Aid, Finlandia University, 601 Quincy Street, Hancock, MI 49930, 906-487-7240 or toll-free 877-202-5491. *Fax:* 906-487-7383. *E-mail:* sandra.turnquist@finlandia.edu.
*Website:* http://www.finlandia.edu/.

# FISHER COLLEGE
## Boston, MA

| Tuition & fees: $29,937 | Average undergraduate aid package: N/A |
|---|---|

**ABOUT THE INSTITUTION** Independent, coed. *Awards:* certificates, associate, bachelor's, and master's degrees. 23 undergraduate majors. *Total enrollment:* 1,875. Undergraduates: 1,875. Freshmen: 429. Federal methodology is used as a basis for awarding need-based institutional aid.

**UNDERGRADUATE EXPENSES for 2015–2016** *Comprehensive fee:* $45,019 includes full-time tuition ($28,942), mandatory fees ($995), and room and board ($15,082). Room and board charges vary according to housing facility. Part-time tuition and fees vary according to course load.

**FRESHMAN FINANCIAL AID (Fall 2013)** 251 applied for aid; of those 100% were deemed to have need. 100% of freshmen with need received aid.

**UNDERGRADUATE FINANCIAL AID (Fall 2013)** 1,084 applied for aid; of those 92% were deemed to have need. 100% of undergraduates with need received aid.

**GIFT AID (NEED-BASED)** *Total amount:* $11,702,241 (59% federal, 3% state, 38% institutional). *Receiving aid:* Freshmen: 86% (251); all full-time undergraduates: 86% (1,002). *Scholarships, grants, and awards:* Federal Pell, FSEOG, state, private, college/university gift aid from institutional funds.

**GIFT AID (NON-NEED-BASED)** *Total amount:* $5,960,635 (31% federal, 69% institutional). *Scholarships, grants, and awards by category:* Academic interests/achievement: general academic interests/achievements. *ROTC:* Army cooperative.

LOANS *Student loans:* $6,622,350 (72% need-based, 28% non-need-based). 60% of past graduating class borrowed through all loan programs. *Programs:* Federal Direct (Subsidized and Unsubsidized Stafford, PLUS), Perkins.
**WORK-STUDY** *Federal work-study:* jobs available.
**APPLYING FOR FINANCIAL AID** *Required financial aid form:* FAFSA. *Financial aid deadline:* Continuous. *Notification date:* Continuous beginning 3/1.
**CONTACT** Pamela Walker, Director of Financial Aid, Fisher College, 1 Arlington Street, Third Floor, Boston, MA 02116, 617-236-5470. *E-mail:* pwalker@fisher.edu. *Website:* http://www.fisher.edu/.

## FISK UNIVERSITY
### Nashville, TN

**CONTACT** Mary Chambliss, Director of Financial Aid, Fisk University, 1000 17th Avenue North, Nashville, TN 37208-3051, 615-329-8735 or toll-free 888-702-0022. *E-mail:* mchambliss@fisk.edu. *Website:* http://www.fisk.edu/.

## FITCHBURG STATE UNIVERSITY
### Fitchburg, MA

**ABOUT THE INSTITUTION** State-supported, coed. *Awards:* certificates, bachelor's, and master's degrees. 61 undergraduate majors. *Total enrollment:* 6,818. Undergraduates: 4,212. Freshmen: 727.
**GIFT AID (NEED-BASED)** *Scholarships, grants, and awards:* Federal Pell, FSEOG, state, private, college/university gift aid from institutional funds.
**GIFT AID (NON-NEED-BASED)** *Scholarships, grants, and awards by category:* Academic interests/achievement, biological sciences, business, communication, computer science, education, engineering/technologies, English, foreign languages, general academic interests/achievements, health fields, mathematics, social sciences. *Special achievements/activities:* general special achievements/activities, leadership. *Special characteristics:* adult students, children and siblings of alumni, ethnic background, local/state students, members of minority groups, out-of-state students, previous college experience, veterans.
**LOANS** *Programs:* Federal Direct (Subsidized and Unsubsidized Stafford, PLUS), Perkins, Federal Nursing, state.
**WORK-STUDY** *Federal work-study:* 192 jobs averaging $1760.
**APPLYING FOR FINANCIAL AID** *Required financial aid form:* FAFSA.
**CONTACT** Office of Financial Aid, Fitchburg State University, 160 Pearl Street, Fitchburg, MA 01420, 978-665-3156 or toll-free 800-705-9692. *Fax:* 978-665-3559. *E-mail:* finaid@fitchburgstate.edu. *Website:* http://www.fitchburgstate.edu/.

## FIVE TOWNS COLLEGE
### Dix Hills, NY

| Tuition & fees: $21,000 | Average undergraduate aid package: $14,472 |
|---|---|

**ABOUT THE INSTITUTION** Independent, coed. *Awards:* associate, bachelor's, master's, and doctoral degrees. 19 undergraduate majors. *Total enrollment:* 686. Undergraduates: 649. Freshmen: 118. Federal methodology is used as a basis for awarding need-based institutional aid.
**UNDERGRADUATE EXPENSES** for 2015–2016 *Application fee:* $35. *Tuition:* full-time $21,000; part-time $875 per credit. Full-time tuition and fees vary according to course level, course load, degree level, program, and student level. Part-time tuition and fees vary according to course level, course load, degree level, program, and student level.
**FRESHMAN FINANCIAL AID (Fall 2014, est.)** 109 applied for aid; of those 94% were deemed to have need. 100% of freshmen with need received aid; of those 11% had need fully met. *Average percent of need met:* 55% (excluding resources awarded to replace EFC). *Average financial aid package:* $15,647 (excluding

resources awarded to replace EFC). 10% of all full-time freshmen had no need and received non-need-based gift aid.
**UNDERGRADUATE FINANCIAL AID (Fall 2014, est.)** 550 applied for aid; of those 96% were deemed to have need. 100% of undergraduates with need received aid; of those 7% had need fully met. *Average percent of need met:* 51% (excluding resources awarded to replace EFC). *Average financial aid package:* $14,472 (excluding resources awarded to replace EFC). 6% of all full-time undergraduates had no need and received non-need-based gift aid.
**GIFT AID (NEED-BASED)** *Total amount:* $2,572,450 (60% federal, 40% state). *Receiving aid:* Freshmen: 47% (55); all full-time undergraduates: 53% (306). *Average award:* Freshmen: $2939; Undergraduates: $3102. *Scholarships, grants, and awards:* Federal Pell, FSEOG, state, private, college/university gift aid from institutional funds.
**GIFT AID (NON-NEED-BASED)** *Total amount:* $3,419,126 (3% state, 89% institutional, 8% external sources). *Receiving aid:* Freshmen: 85% (100). Undergraduates: 84% (484). *Average award:* Freshmen: $3904. Undergraduates: $4015. *Scholarships, grants, and awards by category:* Academic interests/achievement: 340 awards ($1,193,503 total): business, education, general academic interests/achievements. Creative arts/performance: 452 awards ($1,679,411 total): cinema/film/broadcasting, music, theater/drama. *Tuition waivers:* Full or partial for employees or children of employees.
**LOANS** *Student loans:* $3,219,518 (55% need-based, 45% non-need-based). 96% of past graduating class borrowed through all loan programs. *Average indebtedness per student:* $26,993. *Average need-based loan:* Freshmen: $3369. Undergraduates: $4371. *Parent loans:* $1,760,267 (100% non-need-based). *Programs:* Federal Direct (Subsidized and Unsubsidized Stafford, PLUS).
**WORK-STUDY** *Federal work-study:* Total amount: $51,908; 113 jobs averaging $1276. *State or other work-study/employment:* Total amount: $928,862 (100% non-need-based). Part-time jobs available.
**APPLYING FOR FINANCIAL AID** *Required financial aid forms:* FAFSA, state aid form. *Financial aid deadline (priority):* 4/30. *Notification date:* Continuous beginning 3/1. Students must reply within 4 weeks of notification.
**CONTACT** Mr. Jason LaBonte, Financial Aid Director, Five Towns College, 305 North Service Road, Dix Hills, NY 11746-5871, 631-656-2113. *Fax:* 631-656-2191. *E-mail:* jason.labonte@ftc.edu. *Website:* http://www.ftc.edu/.

## FLAGLER COLLEGE
### St. Augustine, FL

| Tuition & fees: $16,900 | Average undergraduate aid package: $12,194 |
|---|---|

**ABOUT THE INSTITUTION** Independent, coed. *Awards:* bachelor's degrees. 34 undergraduate majors. *Total enrollment:* 2,774. Undergraduates: 2,774. Freshmen: 673. Federal methodology is used as a basis for awarding need-based institutional aid.
**UNDERGRADUATE EXPENSES** for 2015–2016 *Application fee:* $50. *Comprehensive fee:* $26,250 includes full-time tuition ($16,800), mandatory fees ($100), and room and board ($9350). *College room only:* $4450. Full-time tuition and fees vary according to location. Room and board charges vary according to board plan and housing facility. *Part-time tuition:* $560 per credit hour. Part-time tuition and fees vary according to location.
**FRESHMAN FINANCIAL AID (Fall 2014, est.)** 553 applied for aid; of those 76% were deemed to have need. 99% of freshmen with need received aid; of those 14% had need fully met. *Average percent of need met:* 57% (excluding resources awarded to replace EFC). *Average financial aid package:* $11,788 (excluding resources awarded to replace EFC). 16% of all full-time freshmen had no need and received non-need-based gift aid.
**UNDERGRADUATE FINANCIAL AID (Fall 2014, est.)** 2,149 applied for aid; of those 79% were deemed to have need. 99% of undergraduates with need received aid; of those 13% had need fully met. *Average percent of need met:* 59% (excluding resources awarded to replace EFC). *Average financial aid package:* $12,194 (excluding resources awarded to replace EFC). 9% of all full-time undergraduates had no need and received non-need-based gift aid.
**GIFT AID (NEED-BASED)** *Total amount:* $12,756,073 (29% federal, 33% state, 36% institutional, 2% external sources). *Receiving aid:* Freshmen: 62% (415); all full-time undergraduates: 61% (1,627). *Average award:* Freshmen: $8811; Undergrad-

uates: $8563. *Scholarships, grants, and awards:* Federal Pell, FSEOG, state, private, college/university gift aid from institutional funds.

**GIFT AID (NON-NEED-BASED)** *Total amount:* $2,422,163 (70% state, 27% institutional, 3% external sources). *Receiving aid:* Freshmen: 4% (29). Undergraduates: 4% (107). *Average award:* Freshmen: $1838. Undergraduates: $2498. *Scholarships, grants, and awards by category: Academic interests/achievement:* business, communication, education, English, foreign languages, general academic interests/achievements, humanities, religion/biblical studies, social sciences. *Creative arts/performance:* applied art and design, art/fine arts, cinema/film/broadcasting, performing arts, theater/drama. *Special achievements/activities:* general special achievements/activities, leadership, memberships, religious involvement. *Special characteristics:* children of educators, children of faculty/staff, ethnic background, first-generation college students, general special characteristics, local/state students, members of minority groups, out-of-state students. *Tuition waivers:* Full or partial for employees or children of employees.

**LOANS** *Student loans:* $17,076,706 (66% need-based, 34% non-need-based). 51% of past graduating class borrowed through all loan programs. *Average indebtedness per student:* $27,853. *Average need-based loan:* Freshmen: $3203. Undergraduates: $4108. *Parent loans:* $2,724,793 (40% need-based, 60% non-need-based). *Programs:* Federal Direct (Subsidized and Unsubsidized Stafford, PLUS), Perkins.

**WORK-STUDY** *Federal work-study:* Total amount: $250,570; jobs available. *State or other work-study/employment:* Total amount: $66,480 (1% need-based, 99% non-need-based). Part-time jobs available.

**ATHLETIC AWARDS** Total amount: $1,440,750 (54% need-based, 46% non-need-based).

**APPLYING FOR FINANCIAL AID** *Required financial aid forms:* FAFSA, institution's own form. *Financial aid deadline (priority):* 4/1. *Notification date:* Continuous beginning 3/1. Students must reply within 2 weeks of notification.

**CONTACT** Office of Financial Aid, Flagler College, PO Box 1027, St. Augustine, FL 32085-1027, 904-819-6225 or toll-free 800-304-4208. *Fax:* 904-819-6453. *E-mail:* financialaid@flagler.edu.
*Website:* http://www.flagler.edu/.

# FLORIDA AGRICULTURAL AND MECHANICAL UNIVERSITY
## Tallahassee, FL

| Tuition & fees (FL res): $5784 | Average undergraduate aid package: $13,259 |
| --- | --- |

**ABOUT THE INSTITUTION** State-supported, coed. *Awards:* certificates, associate, bachelor's, master's, and doctoral degrees. 55 undergraduate majors. *Total enrollment:* 10,241. Undergraduates: 8,495. Freshmen: 1,400. Federal methodology is used as a basis for awarding need-based institutional aid.

**UNDERGRADUATE EXPENSES** for 2015–2016 *Application fee:* $30. *One-time required fee:* $35. *Tuition, state resident:* full-time $5644; part-time $188.16 per credit. *Tuition, nonresident:* full-time $17,586; part-time $586.16 per credit. *Required fees:* full-time $140. *College room and board:* $9576; *Room only:* $5558. Room and board charges vary according to board plan and housing facility. *Payment plan:* Tuition prepayment.

**FRESHMAN FINANCIAL AID (Fall 2014, est.)** 1,204 applied for aid; of those 86% were deemed to have need. 100% of freshmen with need received aid; of those 17% had need fully met. *Average percent of need met:* 73% (excluding resources awarded to replace EFC). *Average financial aid package:* $13,299 (excluding resources awarded to replace EFC). 1% of all full-time freshmen had no need and received non-need-based gift aid.

**UNDERGRADUATE FINANCIAL AID (Fall 2014, est.)** 7,768 applied for aid; of those 86% were deemed to have need. 100% of undergraduates with need received aid; of those 15% had need fully met. *Average percent of need met:* 72% (excluding resources awarded to replace EFC). *Average financial aid package:* $13,259 (excluding resources awarded to replace EFC). 1% of all full-time undergraduates had no need and received non-need-based gift aid.

**GIFT AID (NEED-BASED)** *Total amount:* $35,827,187 (72% federal, 9% state, 19% institutional). *Receiving aid:* Freshmen: 80% (1,017); all full-time undergraduates: 69% (5,584). *Average award:* Freshmen: $5967; Undergraduates: $6724. *Scholarships, grants, and awards:* Federal Pell, FSEOG, state, private, college/university gift aid from institutional funds, United Negro College Fund.

**GIFT AID (NON-NEED-BASED)** *Total amount:* $11,664,349 (38% state, 13% institutional, 49% external sources). *Receiving aid:* Freshmen: 41% (524). Undergraduates: 30% (2,432). *Average award:* Freshmen: $6061. Undergraduates: $10,922. *Scholarships, grants, and awards by category: Academic interests/achievement:* agriculture, architecture, area/ethnic studies, biological sciences, business, communication, computer science, education, engineering/technologies, English, foreign languages, general academic interests/achievements, health fields, humanities, mathematics, military science, physical sciences, premedicine, social sciences. *Creative arts/performance:* applied art and design, art/fine arts, cinema/film/broadcasting, creative writing, dance, journalism/publications, music, performing arts, theater/drama. *Special achievements/activities:* cheerleading/drum major, community service, general special achievements/activities, leadership. *Special characteristics:* 417 awards ($1,975,329 total): ethnic background, first-generation college students, general special characteristics, local/state students, out-of-state students. *Tuition waivers:* Full or partial for employees or children of employees, senior citizens. *ROTC:* Army, Naval, Air Force cooperative.

**LOANS** *Student loans:* $46,802,639 (49% need-based, 51% non-need-based). 87% of past graduating class borrowed through all loan programs. *Average indebtedness per student:* $31,407. *Average need-based loan:* Freshmen: $3443. Undergraduates: $4274. *Parent loans:* $8,433,721 (100% non-need-based). *Programs:* Federal Direct (Subsidized and Unsubsidized Stafford, PLUS), Perkins, private loans.

**WORK-STUDY** *Federal work-study:* Total amount: $591,382; 270 jobs averaging $2153.

**ATHLETIC AWARDS** Total amount: $2,329,040 (100% non-need-based).

**APPLYING FOR FINANCIAL AID** *Required financial aid form:* FAFSA. *Financial aid deadline (priority):* 3/1. *Notification date:* Continuous beginning 4/15.

**CONTACT** Ms. Lisa A. Stewart, Director of Financial Aid, Florida Agricultural and Mechanical University, 101 Foote-Hilyer Administration Center, Tallahassee, FL 32307, 850-599-3730 or toll-free 866-642-1198.
*Website:* http://www.famu.edu/.

# FLORIDA ATLANTIC UNIVERSITY
## Boca Raton, FL

| Tuition & fees (FL res): $6039 | Average undergraduate aid package: $10,199 |
| --- | --- |

**ABOUT THE INSTITUTION** State-supported, coed. *Awards:* certificates, associate, bachelor's, master's, and doctoral degrees. 63 undergraduate majors. *Total enrollment:* 30,364. Undergraduates: 25,209. Freshmen: 3,072. Federal methodology is used as a basis for awarding need-based institutional aid.

**UNDERGRADUATE EXPENSES** for 2015–2016 *Application fee:* $30. *Tuition, state resident:* full-time $6039; part-time $105.07 per credit hour. *Tuition, nonresident:* full-time $21,595; part-time $598.93 per credit hour. Full-time tuition and fees vary according to course load. Part-time tuition and fees vary according to course load. *College room and board:* $11,924. Room and board charges vary according to board plan and housing facility. *Payment plan:* Tuition prepayment.

**FRESHMAN FINANCIAL AID (Fall 2014, est.)** 2,411 applied for aid; of those 74% were deemed to have need. 98% of freshmen with need received aid; of those 9% had need fully met. *Average percent of need met:* 60% (excluding resources awarded to replace EFC). *Average financial aid package:* $9957 (excluding resources awarded to replace EFC). 4% of all full-time freshmen had no need and received non-need-based gift aid.

**UNDERGRADUATE FINANCIAL AID (Fall 2014, est.)** 11,846 applied for aid; of those 81% were deemed to have need. 97% of undergraduates with need received aid; of those 11% had need fully met. *Average percent of need met:* 63% (excluding resources awarded to replace EFC). *Average financial aid package:* $10,199 (excluding resources awarded to replace EFC). 1% of all full-time undergraduates had no need and received non-need-based gift aid.

**GIFT AID (NEED-BASED)** *Total amount:* $61,679,142 (69% federal, 15% state, 12% institutional, 4% external sources). *Receiving aid:* Freshmen: 50% (1,454); all full-time undergraduates: 52% (7,943). *Average award:* Freshmen: $6134; Undergraduates: $5800. *Scholarships, grants, and awards:* Federal Pell, FSEOG, state, private, college/university gift aid from institutional funds, Federal Nursing.

**GIFT AID (NON-NEED-BASED)** *Total amount:* $6,201,485 (61% state, 16% institutional, 23% external sources). *Receiving aid:* Freshmen: 2% (68). Undergraduates: 2% (348). *Average award:* Freshmen: $2533. Undergraduates: $2495. *Schol-*

arships, grants, and awards by category: *Academic interests/achievement:* business, engineering/technologies, general academic interests/achievements, physical sciences, social sciences. *Creative arts/performance:* music, performing arts. **Tuition waivers:** Full or partial for employees or children of employees, senior citizens. **ROTC:** Army, Air Force cooperative.

**LOANS** *Student loans:* $85,325,974 (75% need-based, 25% non-need-based). 50% of past graduating class borrowed through all loan programs. *Average indebtedness per student:* $21,448. **Average need-based loan:** Freshmen: $5395. Undergraduates: $6533. **Parent loans:** $4,755,883 (46% need-based, 54% non-need-based). **Programs:** Federal Direct (Subsidized and Unsubsidized Stafford, PLUS), Perkins, college/university.

**WORK-STUDY** *Federal work-study:* Total amount: $753,861; 228 jobs averaging $2920. **State or other work-study/employment:** Total amount: $16,000 (100% need-based). 5 part-time jobs averaging $2385.

**ATHLETIC AWARDS** Total amount: $3,506,726 (39% need-based, 61% non-need-based).

**APPLYING FOR FINANCIAL AID** *Required financial aid form:* FAFSA. *Financial aid deadline:* 6/30 (priority: 3/1). **Notification date:** Continuous beginning 3/15. Students must reply by 8/23.

**CONTACT** Tracy Boulukos, Director of Student Financial Aid, Florida Atlantic University, 777 Glades Road, Boca Raton, FL 33431-0991, 561-297-3528. *E-mail:* tbouluko@fau.edu.
*Website:* http://www.fau.edu/.

# FLORIDA COLLEGE
## Temple Terrace, FL

**ABOUT THE INSTITUTION** Independent, coed. *Awards:* associate and bachelor's degrees. 10 undergraduate majors. *Total enrollment:* 555. Undergraduates: 555. Freshmen: 199.

**GIFT AID (NEED-BASED)** *Scholarships, grants, and awards:* Federal Pell, FSEOG, state, private, college/university gift aid from institutional funds.

**GIFT AID (NON-NEED-BASED)** *Scholarships, grants, and awards by category:* Academic interests/achievement: business, education, general academic interests/achievements, religion/biblical studies. *Creative arts/performance:* music. *Special achievements/activities:* general special achievements/activities. *Special characteristics:* children of faculty/staff.

**LOANS** *Programs:* Federal Direct (Subsidized and Unsubsidized Stafford, PLUS), Perkins.

**APPLYING FOR FINANCIAL AID** *Required financial aid form:* FAFSA.

**CONTACT** Stephen Blaylock, Director of Financial Aid, Florida College, 119 North Glen Arven Avenue, Temple Terrace, FL 33617, 813-988-5131 Ext. 130. *Fax:* 813-899-6772. *E-mail:* blaylocks@floridacollege.edu.
*Website:* http://www.floridacollege.edu/.

# FLORIDA GULF COAST UNIVERSITY
## Fort Myers, FL

| Tuition & fees (FL res): $6118 | Average undergraduate aid package: $9386 |
|---|---|

**ABOUT THE INSTITUTION** State-supported, coed. *Awards:* certificates, associate, bachelor's, master's, and doctoral degrees. 42 undergraduate majors. *Total enrollment:* 14,492. Undergraduates: 13,300. Freshmen: 2,782. Federal methodology is used as a basis for awarding need-based institutional aid.

**UNDERGRADUATE EXPENSES** for 2015–2016 *Application fee:* $30. *Tuition, state resident:* full-time $4191. *Tuition, nonresident:* full-time $22,381. *Required fees:* full-time $1927. Full-time tuition and fees vary according to course load. Part-time tuition and fees vary according to course load. **College room and board:** $8359; *Room only:* $4820. Room and board charges vary according to board plan and housing facility.

**FRESHMAN FINANCIAL AID (Fall 2013)** 2,684 applied for aid; of those 54% were deemed to have need. 100% of freshmen with need received aid; of those 6% had need fully met. *Average percent of need met:* 52% (excluding resources awarded to replace EFC). *Average financial aid package:* $8647 (excluding resources

awarded to replace EFC). 3% of all full-time freshmen had no need and received non-need-based gift aid.

**UNDERGRADUATE FINANCIAL AID (Fall 2013)** 8,044 applied for aid; of those 68% were deemed to have need. 100% of undergraduates with need received aid; of those 6% had need fully met. *Average percent of need met:* 59% (excluding resources awarded to replace EFC). *Average financial aid package:* $9386 (excluding resources awarded to replace EFC). 3% of all full-time undergraduates had no need and received non-need-based gift aid.

**GIFT AID (NEED-BASED)** *Total amount:* $30,235,837 (59% federal, 21% state, 16% institutional, 4% external sources). *Receiving aid:* Freshmen: 35% (968); all full-time undergraduates: 35% (3,738). *Average award:* Freshmen: $5017; Undergraduates: $5250. *Scholarships, grants, and awards:* Federal Pell, FSEOG, state, private, college/university gift aid from institutional funds.

**GIFT AID (NON-NEED-BASED)** *Total amount:* $5,337,251 (1% federal, 62% state, 23% institutional, 14% external sources). *Receiving aid:* Freshmen: 31% (841). Undergraduates: 19% (2,015). *Average award:* Freshmen: $2979. Undergraduates: $3562. *Scholarships, grants, and awards by category:* Academic interests/achievement: biological sciences, business, education, engineering/technologies, general academic interests/achievements, health fields, humanities, mathematics, physical sciences, religion/biblical studies, social sciences. *Creative arts/performance:* art/fine arts, music. *Special achievements/activities:* community service, leadership. *Special characteristics:* adult students, ethnic background, handicapped students, international students, local/state students, members of minority groups, out-of-state students.

**LOANS** *Student loans:* $41,528,909 (82% need-based, 18% non-need-based). 46% of past graduating class borrowed through all loan programs. *Average indebtedness per student:* $22,718. *Average need-based loan:* Freshmen: $6313. Undergraduates: $6982. *Programs:* Federal Direct (Subsidized and Unsubsidized Stafford, PLUS).

**WORK-STUDY** *Federal work-study:* jobs available. *State or other work-study/employment:* Total amount: $19,389,530 (100% need-based). Part-time jobs available.

**ATHLETIC AWARDS** Total amount: $754,683 (100% non-need-based).

**APPLYING FOR FINANCIAL AID** *Required financial aid forms:* FAFSA, institution's own form, state aid form. *Financial aid deadline:* 6/30 (priority: 3/1). *Notification date:* Continuous.

**CONTACT** Jorge Lopez-Rosado, Director of Student Financial Services, Florida Gulf Coast University, 10501 FGCU Boulevard South, Fort Myers, FL 33965, 239-590-1210 or toll-free 888-889-1095. *Fax:* 239-590-7923. *E-mail:* faso@fgcu.edu.
*Website:* http://www.fgcu.edu/.

# FLORIDA INSTITUTE OF TECHNOLOGY
## Melbourne, FL

| Tuition & fees: $37,990 | Average undergraduate aid package: $34,092 |
|---|---|

**ABOUT THE INSTITUTION** Independent, coed. *Awards:* certificates, bachelor's, master's, and doctoral degrees. 63 undergraduate majors. *Total enrollment:* 6,393. Undergraduates: 3,656. Freshmen: 791. Federal methodology is used as a basis for awarding need-based institutional aid.

**UNDERGRADUATE EXPENSES** for 2015–2016 *Comprehensive fee:* $50,816 includes full-time tuition ($37,240), mandatory fees ($750), and room and board ($12,826). *College room only:* $7510. Full-time tuition and fees vary according to course load and program. Room and board charges vary according to board plan and housing facility. *Part-time tuition:* $1075 per credit hour.

**FRESHMAN FINANCIAL AID (Fall 2014, est.)** 477 applied for aid; of those 88% were deemed to have need. 100% of freshmen with need received aid; of those 36% had need fully met. *Average percent of need met:* 83% (excluding resources awarded to replace EFC). *Average financial aid package:* $34,266 (excluding resources awarded to replace EFC). 36% of all full-time freshmen had no need and received non-need-based gift aid.

**UNDERGRADUATE FINANCIAL AID (Fall 2014, est.)** 1,852 applied for aid; of those 90% were deemed to have need. 100% of undergraduates with need received aid; of those 33% had need fully met. *Average percent of need met:* 82% (excluding resources awarded to replace EFC). *Average financial aid package:*

$34,092 (excluding resources awarded to replace EFC). 28% of all full-time undergraduates had no need and received non-need-based gift aid.

**GIFT AID (NEED-BASED) Total amount:** $37,126,776 (17% federal, 10% state, 72% institutional, 1% external sources). **Receiving aid:** Freshmen: 54% (418); all full-time undergraduates: 52% (1,667). **Average award:** Freshmen: $25,376; Undergraduates: $23,464. **Scholarships, grants, and awards:** Federal Pell, FSEOG, state, private, college/university gift aid from institutional funds.

**GIFT AID (NON-NEED-BASED) Total amount:** $17,169,620 (8% federal, 3% state, 88% institutional, 1% external sources). **Receiving aid:** Freshmen: 54% (415). Undergraduates: 50% (1,624). **Average award:** Freshmen: $15,422. Undergraduates: $14,171. **Scholarships, grants, and awards by category:** *Academic interests/achievement:* 1,926 awards ($27,050,833 total): business, engineering/technologies, general academic interests/achievements, military science. *Creative arts/performance:* 29 awards ($32,500 total): music. *Special achievements/activities:* 101 awards ($1,281,000 total): hobbies/interests, leadership, memberships. *Special characteristics:* 1,728 awards ($6,867,281 total): children and siblings of alumni, children of faculty/staff, general special characteristics, international students, previous college experience, siblings of current students. *Tuition waivers:* Full or partial for employees or children of employees, senior citizens. ROTC: Army.

**LOANS Student loans:** $13,340,032 (93% need-based, 7% non-need-based). 60% of past graduating class borrowed through all loan programs. *Average indebtedness per student:* $40,383. **Average need-based loan:** Freshmen: $4406. Undergraduates: $5235. **Parent loans:** $9,817,249 (95% need-based, 5% non-need-based). **Programs:** Federal Direct (Subsidized and Unsubsidized Stafford, PLUS), Perkins, state, college/university.

**WORK-STUDY Federal work-study:** Total amount: $1,404,489; 711 jobs averaging $1975. **State or other work-study/employment:** Total amount: $30,922 (100% need-based). 10 part-time jobs averaging $3092.

**ATHLETIC AWARDS** Total amount: $6,014,842 (52% need-based, 48% non-need-based).

**APPLYING FOR FINANCIAL AID Required financial aid forms:** FAFSA, state aid form. **Financial aid deadline (priority):** 3/1. **Notification date:** Continuous beginning 2/15. Students must reply by 5/1 or within 4 weeks of notification.

**CONTACT** Mr. John W. Duncan, Office of Financial Aid, Florida Institute of Technology, 150 West University Boulevard, Melbourne, FL 32901-6975, 321-674-8063 or toll-free 800-888-4348. Fax: 321-724-2778. E-mail: finaid@fit.edu.
Website: http://www.fit.edu/.

# FLORIDA INTERNATIONAL UNIVERSITY
## Miami, FL

**ABOUT THE INSTITUTION** State-supported, coed. **Awards:** certificates, bachelor's, master's, and doctoral degrees. 64 undergraduate majors. **Total enrollment:** 49,703. Undergraduates: 40,974. Freshmen: 4,144.

**GIFT AID (NEED-BASED) Scholarships, grants, and awards:** Federal Pell, FSEOG, state, private, college/university gift aid from institutional funds.

**GIFT AID (NON-NEED-BASED) Scholarships, grants, and awards by category:** *Academic interests/achievement:* architecture, biological sciences, business, communication, computer science, education, engineering/technologies, English, foreign languages, general academic interests/achievements, health fields, humanities, mathematics, physical sciences, social sciences. *Creative arts/performance:* art/fine arts, dance, journalism/publications, music, performing arts, theater/drama. *Special characteristics:* first-generation college students, veterans, veterans' children.

**LOANS Programs:** Federal Direct (Subsidized and Unsubsidized Stafford, PLUS), Perkins, college/university.

**APPLYING FOR FINANCIAL AID Required financial aid form:** FAFSA.

**CONTACT** Francisco Valines, Director of Financial Aid, Florida International University, 11200 SW 8th Street, PC 125, Miami, FL 33199, 305-348-7272. Fax: 305-348-2346. E-mail: francisco.valines@fiu.edu.
Website: http://www.fiu.edu/.

# FLORIDA MEMORIAL UNIVERSITY
## Miami-Dade, FL

**CONTACT** Brian Phillip, Director of Financial Aid, Florida Memorial University, 15800 Northwest 42nd Avenue, Miami, FL 33054, 305-626-3745 or toll-free 800-822-1362. Fax: 305-626-3106.
Website: http://www.fmuniv.edu/.

# FLORIDA NATIONAL UNIVERSITY
## Hialeah, FL

| Tuition & fees: N/R | Average undergraduate aid package: N/A |
|---|---|

**ABOUT THE INSTITUTION** Proprietary, coed. **Awards:** certificates, diplomas, associate, bachelor's, and master's degrees. 36 undergraduate majors. **Total enrollment:** 2,401. Undergraduates: 2,376. Freshmen: 472. Federal methodology is used as a basis for awarding need-based institutional aid.

**UNDERGRADUATE EXPENSES for 2015–2016 Tuition:** part-time $525 per credit. **Payment plans:** Guaranteed tuition, tuition prepayment.

**FRESHMAN FINANCIAL AID (Fall 2013)** 275 applied for aid; of those 97% were deemed to have need. 96% of freshmen with need received aid.

**UNDERGRADUATE FINANCIAL AID (Fall 2013)** 1,885 applied for aid; of those 99% were deemed to have need. 100% of undergraduates with need received aid.

**GIFT AID (NEED-BASED) Total amount:** $10,464,474 (96% federal, 4% state). **Receiving aid:** Freshmen: 90% (255); all full-time undergraduates: 93% (1,845). **Average award:** Freshmen: $5069; Undergraduates: $5069. **Scholarships, grants, and awards:** Federal Pell, FSEOG, state, private, college/university gift aid from institutional funds.

**GIFT AID (NON-NEED-BASED) Tuition waivers:** Full or partial for employees or children of employees.

**LOANS Student loans:** $17,534,617 (100% need-based). 91% of past graduating class borrowed through all loan programs. *Average indebtedness per student:* $10,000. **Parent loans:** $471,383 (100% need-based). **Programs:** Federal Direct (Subsidized and Unsubsidized Stafford, PLUS), Perkins.

**WORK-STUDY Federal work-study:** 14 jobs averaging $8320. **State or other work-study/employment:** Part-time jobs available.

**APPLYING FOR FINANCIAL AID Required financial aid form:** FAFSA. **Financial aid deadline:** Continuous. **Notification date:** Continuous.

**CONTACT** Mr. Omar Sanchez, Director of Financial Aid, Florida National University, 4425 West Jose Regueiro (20th) Avenue, Hialeah, FL 33012, 305-821-3333 Ext. 1003. Fax: 305-362-0595. E-mail: omarsnc@fnu.edu.
Website: http://www.fnu.edu/.

# FLORIDA SOUTHERN COLLEGE
## Lakeland, FL

| Tuition & fees: $29,990 | Average undergraduate aid package: $24,441 |
|---|---|

**ABOUT THE INSTITUTION** Independent United Methodist Church, coed. **Awards:** bachelor's, master's, and doctoral degrees. 56 undergraduate majors. **Total enrollment:** 2,439. Undergraduates: 2,172. Freshmen: 581. Federal methodology is used as a basis for awarding need-based institutional aid.

**UNDERGRADUATE EXPENSES for 2015–2016 Application fee:** $30. **Comprehensive fee:** $39,990 includes full-time tuition ($29,340), mandatory fees ($650), and room and board ($10,000). **College room only:** $5740. Room and board charges vary according to board plan and housing facility. **Part-time tuition:** $840 per credit hour. Part-time tuition and fees vary according to class time and course load.

**FRESHMAN FINANCIAL AID (Fall 2014, est.)** 531 applied for aid; of those 81% were deemed to have need. 100% of freshmen with need received aid; of those 33% had need fully met. *Average percent of need met:* 75% (excluding resources awarded to replace EFC). **Average financial aid package:** $24,516 (excluding resources awarded to replace EFC). 25% of all full-time freshmen had no need and received non-need-based gift aid.

**UNDERGRADUATE FINANCIAL AID (Fall 2014, est.)** 1,745 applied for aid; of those 85% were deemed to have need. 100% of undergraduates with need received aid; of those 28% had need fully met. **Average percent of need met:** 74% (excluding resources awarded to replace EFC). **Average financial aid package:** $24,441 (excluding resources awarded to replace EFC). 29% of all full-time undergraduates had no need and received non-need-based gift aid.
**GIFT AID (NEED-BASED) Total amount:** $30,203,343 (10% federal, 15% state, 67% institutional, 8% external sources). **Receiving aid:** Freshmen: 74% (429); all full-time undergraduates: 69% (1,462). **Average award:** Freshmen: $19,461; Undergraduates: $17,949. **Scholarships, grants, and awards:** Federal Pell, FSEOG, state, private, college/university gift aid from institutional funds, Federal Nursing.
**GIFT AID (NON-NEED-BASED) Total amount:** $8,815,327 (15% state, 78% institutional, 7% external sources). **Receiving aid:** Freshmen: 45% (257). Undergraduates: 47% (998). **Average award:** Freshmen: $16,908. Undergraduates: $16,411. **Scholarships, grants, and awards by category:** Academic interests/achievement: agriculture, biological sciences, business, communication, education, general academic interests/achievements, health fields, physical sciences, religion/biblical studies, social sciences. Creative arts/performance: art/fine arts, music, theater/drama. Special achievements/activities: community service, general special achievements/activities, leadership. Special characteristics: children and siblings of alumni, children of faculty/staff, general special characteristics, local/state students, out-of-state students, relatives of clergy, religious affiliation, siblings of current students. **Tuition waivers:** Full or partial for children of alumni, employees or children of employees. **ROTC:** Army, Air Force cooperative.
**LOANS Student loans:** $15,171,535 (88% need-based, 12% non-need-based). 71% of past graduating class borrowed through all loan programs. Average indebtedness per student: $24,314. **Average need-based loan:** Freshmen: $4547. Undergraduates: $5787. **Parent loans:** $5,080,165 (87% need-based, 13% non-need-based). **Programs:** Federal Direct (Subsidized and Unsubsidized Stafford, PLUS), Perkins.
**WORK-STUDY Federal work-study:** Total amount: $255,146; 140 jobs averaging $1822. **State or other work-study/employment:** Total amount: $615,868 (70% need-based, 30% non-need-based). 223 part-time jobs averaging $1921.
**ATHLETIC AWARDS** Total amount: $3,319,824 (54% need-based, 46% non-need-based).
**APPLYING FOR FINANCIAL AID Required financial aid forms:** FAFSA, institution's own form. **Financial aid deadline:** 7/1 (priority: 3/1). **Notification date:** Continuous beginning 3/1. Students must reply within 3 weeks of notification.
**CONTACT** Mr. William L. Healy, Director of Financial Aid, Florida Southern College, 111 Lake Hollingsworth Drive, Lakeland, FL 33801-5698, 863-680-4140 or toll-free 800-274-4131. Fax: 863-680-4567. E-mail: whealy@flsouthern.edu.
Website: http://www.flsouthern.edu/.

# FLORIDA STATE UNIVERSITY
## Tallahassee, FL

| Tuition & fees (FL res): $6507 | Average undergraduate aid package: $8370 |
|---|---|

**ABOUT THE INSTITUTION** State-supported, coed. **Awards:** certificates, associate, bachelor's, master's, and doctoral degrees. 49 undergraduate majors. **Total enrollment:** 41,226. Undergraduates: 32,948. Freshmen: 5,994. Federal methodology is used as a basis for awarding need-based institutional aid.
**UNDERGRADUATE EXPENSES for 2015–2016 Application fee:** $30. **Tuition, state resident:** full-time $4640; part-time $105.07 per credit hour. **Tuition, nonresident:** full-time $19,806; part-time $610.62 per credit hour. **Required fees:** full-time $1867; $110.48 per credit hour or $20 per term. Full-time tuition and fees vary according to course load, degree level, and location. Part-time tuition and fees vary according to course load, degree level, and location. **College room and board:** $10,208; **Room only:** $6160. Room and board charges vary according to board plan and housing facility. **Payment plan:** Tuition prepayment.
**FRESHMAN FINANCIAL AID (Fall 2014, est.)** 4,989 applied for aid; of those 61% were deemed to have need. 97% of freshmen with need received aid; of those 8% had need fully met. **Average percent of need met:** 34% (excluding resources awarded to replace EFC). **Average financial aid package:** $8605 (excluding resources awarded to replace EFC). 8% of all full-time freshmen had no need and received non-need-based gift aid.
**UNDERGRADUATE FINANCIAL AID (Fall 2014, est.)** 22,688 applied for aid; of those 67% were deemed to have need. 98% of undergraduates with need received

aid; of those 6% had need fully met. **Average percent of need met:** 33% (excluding resources awarded to replace EFC). **Average financial aid package:** $8370 (excluding resources awarded to replace EFC). 6% of all full-time undergraduates had no need and received non-need-based gift aid.
**GIFT AID (NEED-BASED) Total amount:** $95,293,118 (42% federal, 33% state, 21% institutional, 4% external sources). **Receiving aid:** Freshmen: 36% (2,130); all full-time undergraduates: 35% (10,109). **Average award:** Freshmen: $4641; Undergraduates: $4940. **Scholarships, grants, and awards:** Federal Pell, FSEOG, state, private, college/university gift aid from institutional funds, Academic Competitiveness Grants, National SMART Grants.
**GIFT AID (NON-NEED-BASED) Total amount:** $18,444,793 (73% state, 19% institutional, 8% external sources). **Receiving aid:** Freshmen: 38% (2,269). Undergraduates: 34% (9,827). **Average award:** Freshmen: $2461. Undergraduates: $2282. **Scholarships, grants, and awards by category:** Academic interests/achievement: general academic interests/achievements. Creative arts/performance: cinema/film/broadcasting, dance, music, theater/drama. Special characteristics: local/state students. **Tuition waivers:** Full or partial for employees or children of employees, senior citizens. **ROTC:** Army, Naval cooperative, Air Force.
**LOANS Student loans:** $87,172,439 (72% need-based, 28% non-need-based). 54% of past graduating class borrowed through all loan programs. Average indebtedness per student: $24,347. **Average need-based loan:** Freshmen: $3340. Undergraduates: $4118. **Parent loans:** $10,267,252 (36% need-based, 64% non-need-based). **Programs:** Federal Direct (Subsidized and Unsubsidized Stafford, PLUS), Perkins, college/university.
**WORK-STUDY Federal work-study:** Total amount: $1,737,453; 716 jobs averaging $2400. **State or other work-study/employment:** Total amount: $53,064 (100% need based). 39 part-time jobs averaging $2400.
**ATHLETIC AWARDS** Total amount: $616,042 (78% need-based, 22% non-need-based).
**APPLYING FOR FINANCIAL AID Required financial aid form:** FAFSA. **Financial aid deadline:** Continuous. **Notification date:** Continuous beginning 3/1.
**CONTACT** Darryl Marshall, Director of Financial Aid, Florida State University, University Center A4400, Tallahassee, FL 32306-2430, 850-644-5716. Fax: 850-644-6404. E-mail: ofacs@admin.fsu.edu.
Website: http://www.fsu.edu/.

# FONTBONNE UNIVERSITY
## St. Louis, MO

| Tuition & fees: $23,790 | Average undergraduate aid package: $14,870 |
|---|---|

**ABOUT THE INSTITUTION** Independent Roman Catholic, coed. **Awards:** certificates, bachelor's, and master's degrees. 38 undergraduate majors. **Total enrollment:** 1,819. Undergraduates: 1,213. Freshmen: 113. Both federal and institutional methodology are used as a basis for awarding need-based institutional aid.
**UNDERGRADUATE EXPENSES for 2015–2016 Application fee:** $25. **Comprehensive fee:** $32,601 includes full-time tuition ($23,430), mandatory fees ($360), and room and board ($8811). Full-time tuition and fees vary according to course load and program. Room and board charges vary according to board plan and housing facility. **Part-time tuition:** $626 per credit. **Part-time fees:** $18 per credit. Part-time tuition and fees vary according to course load and program.
**FRESHMAN FINANCIAL AID (Fall 2014, est.)** 100 applied for aid; of those 82% were deemed to have need. 100% of freshmen with need received aid; of those 13% had need fully met. **Average percent of need met:** 97% (excluding resources awarded to replace EFC). **Average financial aid package:** $13,462 (excluding resources awarded to replace EFC). 7% of all full-time freshmen had no need and received non-need-based gift aid.
**UNDERGRADUATE FINANCIAL AID (Fall 2014, est.)** 612 applied for aid; of those 89% were deemed to have need. 100% of undergraduates with need received aid; of those 2% had need fully met. **Average percent of need met:** 97% (excluding resources awarded to replace EFC). **Average financial aid package:** $14,870 (excluding resources awarded to replace EFC). 1% of all full-time undergraduates had no need and received non-need-based gift aid.
**GIFT AID (NEED-BASED) Total amount:** $3,666,937 (47% federal, 11% state, 42% institutional). **Receiving aid:** Freshmen: 59% (66); all full-time undergraduates: 53% (468). **Average award:** Freshmen: $6017; Undergraduates: $5358. **Scholar-

ships, grants, and awards: Federal Pell, FSEOG, state, private, college/university gift aid from institutional funds.

**GIFT AID (NON-NEED-BASED)** *Total amount:* $6,771,613 (1% federal, 96% institutional, 3% external sources). *Receiving aid:* Freshmen: 73% (81). Undergraduates: 60% (531). *Average award:* Freshmen: $9437. Undergraduates: $9437. *Scholarships, grants, and awards by category: Academic interests/achievement:* 27 awards ($19,500 total): computer science, English, general academic interests/achievements. *Creative arts/performance:* 30 awards ($21,750 total): art/fine arts, creative writing, theater/drama. *Special achievements/activities:* community service, general special achievements/activities, leadership. *Special characteristics:* 224 awards ($186,000 total): religious affiliation, siblings of current students. *Tuition waivers:* Full or partial for employees or children of employees. *ROTC:* Army cooperative, Air Force cooperative.

**LOANS** *Student loans:* $7,585,493 (42% need-based, 58% non-need-based). 77% of past graduating class borrowed through all loan programs. *Average indebtedness per student:* $24,281. *Average need-based loan:* Freshmen: $4416. Undergraduates: $4548. *Parent loans:* $1,061,926 (100% non-need-based). *Programs:* Perkins, CitiAssist loans.

**WORK-STUDY** *Federal work-study:* Total amount: $88,049; 92 jobs averaging $967. *State or other work-study/employment:* Total amount: $74,317 (100% non-need-based). 89 part-time jobs averaging $835.

**APPLYING FOR FINANCIAL AID** *Required financial aid forms:* FAFSA, institution's own form. *Financial aid deadline (priority):* 4/30. *Notification date:* Continuous. Students must reply within 3 weeks of notification.

**CONTACT** Financial Aid Office, Fontbonne University, 6800 Wydown Boulevard, St. Louis, MO 63105-3098, 314-889-1414 or toll-free 800-205-5862. *Fax:* 314-889-1457. *E-mail:* fbufinaid@fontbonne.edu.
*Website:* http://www.fontbonne.edu/.

# FORDHAM UNIVERSITY
## New York, NY

| Tuition & fees: $45,623 | Average undergraduate aid package: $30,051 |
|---|---|

**ABOUT THE INSTITUTION** Independent Roman Catholic (Jesuit), coed. *Awards:* certificates, bachelor's, master's, and doctoral degrees (branch locations at Rose Hill and Lincoln Center). 76 undergraduate majors. *Total enrollment:* 15,231. Undergraduates: 8,633. Freshmen: 2,258. Both federal and institutional methodology are used as a basis for awarding need-based institutional aid.

**UNDERGRADUATE EXPENSES for 2015–2016** *Application fee:* $70. *Comprehensive fee:* $61,588 includes full-time tuition ($44,450), mandatory fees ($1173), and room and board ($15,965). Room and board charges vary according to board plan, housing facility, and location. *Part-time tuition:* $1482 per credit hour. Part-time tuition and fees vary according to class time and course load.

**FRESHMAN FINANCIAL AID (Fall 2013)** 1,730 applied for aid; of those 76% were deemed to have need. 100% of freshmen with need received aid; of those 30% had need fully met. *Average percent of need met:* 80% (excluding resources awarded to replace EFC). *Average financial aid package:* $31,845 (excluding resources awarded to replace EFC). 21% of all full-time freshmen had no need and received non-need-based gift aid.

**UNDERGRADUATE FINANCIAL AID (Fall 2013)** 6,422 applied for aid; of those 77% were deemed to have need. 100% of undergraduates with need received aid; of those 26% had need fully met. *Average percent of need met:* 75% (excluding resources awarded to replace EFC). *Average financial aid package:* $30,051 (excluding resources awarded to replace EFC). 18% of all full-time undergraduates had no need and received non-need-based gift aid.

**GIFT AID (NEED-BASED)** *Total amount:* $99,037,009 (8% federal, 6% state, 81% institutional, 5% external sources). *Receiving aid:* Freshmen: 66% (1,284); all full-time undergraduates: 61% (4,712). *Average award:* Freshmen: $24,608; Undergraduates: $22,251. *Scholarships, grants, and awards:* Federal Pell, FSEOG, state, private, college/university gift aid from institutional funds.

**GIFT AID (NON-NEED-BASED)** *Total amount:* $26,060,499 (2% state, 87% institutional, 11% external sources). *Receiving aid:* Freshmen: 14% (264). Undergraduates: 11% (840). *Average award:* Freshmen: $13,822. Undergraduates: $13,165. *Scholarships, grants, and awards by category: Academic interests/achievement:* biological sciences, business, communication, foreign languages, general academic interests/achievements. *Creative arts/performance:* dance, music. *Special*

achievements/activities: general special achievements/activities. *Special characteristics:* adult students, children and siblings of alumni, children of faculty/staff, children with a deceased or disabled parent, handicapped students. *Tuition waivers:* Full or partial for employees or children of employees. *ROTC:* Army, Naval cooperative, Air Force cooperative.

**LOANS** *Student loans:* $44,099,472 (69% need-based, 31% non-need-based). 62% of past graduating class borrowed through all loan programs. *Average indebtedness per student:* $37,607. *Average need-based loan:* Freshmen: $5311. Undergraduates: $6507. *Parent loans:* $22,839,475 (47% need-based, 53% non-need-based). *Programs:* Federal Direct (Subsidized and Unsubsidized Stafford, PLUS), Perkins.

**WORK-STUDY** *Federal work-study:* jobs available. *State or other work-study/employment:* Part-time jobs available.

**ATHLETIC AWARDS** Total amount: $11,289,849 (65% need-based, 35% non-need-based).

**APPLYING FOR FINANCIAL AID** *Required financial aid forms:* FAFSA, CSS Financial Aid PROFILE, state aid form, noncustodial (divorced/separated) parent's statement, business/farm supplement. *Financial aid deadline:* 2/1. *Notification date:* Continuous beginning 3/31. Students must reply by 5/1 or within 2 weeks of notification.

**CONTACT** Angela Van Dekker, Assistant Vice President of Student Financial Services, Fordham University, 441 East Fordham Road, Thebaud Hall, Room 208, New York, NY 10458, 718-817-3804 or toll-free 800-FORDHAM. *Fax:* 718-817-3817. *E-mail:* avandekker@fordham.edu.
*Website:* http://www.fordham.edu/.

# FORT HAYS STATE UNIVERSITY
## Hays, KS

| Tuition & fees: N/R | Average undergraduate aid package: $7199 |
|---|---|

**ABOUT THE INSTITUTION** State-supported, coed. *Awards:* certificates, associate, bachelor's, and master's degrees. 66 undergraduate majors. *Total enrollment:* 13,825. Undergraduates: 11,643. Freshmen: 1,025. Federal methodology is used as a basis for awarding need-based institutional aid.

**FRESHMAN FINANCIAL AID (Fall 2013)** 695 applied for aid; of those 77% were deemed to have need. 98% of freshmen with need received aid; of those 18% had need fully met. *Average percent of need met:* 56% (excluding resources awarded to replace EFC). *Average financial aid package:* $7207 (excluding resources awarded to replace EFC). 24% of all full-time freshmen had no need and received non-need-based gift aid.

**UNDERGRADUATE FINANCIAL AID (Fall 2013)** 3,826 applied for aid; of those 84% were deemed to have need. 97% of undergraduates with need received aid; of those 10% had need fully met. *Average percent of need met:* 52% (excluding resources awarded to replace EFC). *Average financial aid package:* $7199 (excluding resources awarded to replace EFC). 10% of all full-time undergraduates had no need and received non-need-based gift aid.

**GIFT AID (NEED-BASED)** *Total amount:* $15,799,752 (78% federal, 5% state, 7% institutional, 10% external sources). *Receiving aid:* Freshmen: 54% (504); all full-time undergraduates: 54% (2,529). *Average award:* Freshmen: $5074; Undergraduates: $4810. *Scholarships, grants, and awards:* Federal Pell, FSEOG, state, private, college/university gift aid from institutional funds.

**GIFT AID (NON-NEED-BASED)** *Total amount:* $2,875,917 (1% state, 26% institutional, 73% external sources). *Receiving aid:* Freshmen: 6% (56). Undergraduates: 2% (111). *Average award:* Freshmen: $1406. Undergraduates: $1427. *Scholarships, grants, and awards by category: Academic interests/achievement:* agriculture, area/ethnic studies, biological sciences, business, communication, computer science, education, engineering/technologies, English, foreign languages, general academic interests/achievements, health fields, home economics, humanities, international studies, mathematics, military science, physical sciences, premedicine, religion/biblical studies, social sciences. *Creative arts/performance:* applied art and design, art/fine arts, cinema/film/broadcasting, creative writing, dance, debating, general creative arts/performance, journalism/publications, music, performing arts, theater/drama. *Special achievements/activities:* cheerleading/drum major, leadership, rodeo. *Special characteristics:* adult students, children and siblings of alumni, children of faculty/staff, general special characteristics, international students, spouses of current students, veterans, veterans' children.

**LOANS** *Student loans:* $32,661,058 (81% need-based, 19% non-need-based). 71% of past graduating class borrowed through all loan programs. *Average indebtedness*

per student: $25,172. **Average need-based loan:** Freshmen: $2953. Undergraduates: $3753. **Parent loans:** $2,669,537 (27% need-based, 73% non-need-based). **Programs:** Federal Direct (Subsidized and Unsubsidized Stafford, PLUS), Perkins, college/university.

**WORK-STUDY** *Federal work-study:* jobs available. **State or other work-study/employment:** Total amount: $141,610 (51% need-based, 49% non-need-based). Part-time jobs available.

**ATHLETIC AWARDS** Total amount: $1,765,601 (51% need-based, 49% non-need-based).

**APPLYING FOR FINANCIAL AID** *Required financial aid forms:* FAFSA, institution's own form, state aid form. **Financial aid deadline (priority):** 3/1. **Notification date:** Continuous beginning 3/15. Students must reply within 2 weeks of notification.

**CONTACT** Craig Karlin, Director of Financial Assistance, Fort Hays State University, Custer Hall, Room 306, 600 Park Street, Hays, KS 67601, 785-628-4408 or toll-free 800-628-FHSU. *Fax:* 785-628-4014. *E-mail:* finaid@fhsu.edu. *Website:* http://www.fhsu.edu/.

# FORTIS COLLEGE
## Cutler Bay, FL

**CONTACT** Financial Aid Office, Fortis College, 19600 South Dixie Highway, Suite B, Cutler Bay, FL 33157, 786-345-5300 or toll-free 855-4-FORTIS. *Website:* http://www.fortis.edu/.

# FORT LEWIS COLLEGE
## Durango, CO

| Tuition & fees (CO res): $7601 | Average undergraduate aid package: $13,918 |
|---|---|

**ABOUT THE INSTITUTION** State-supported, coed. *Awards:* certificates, bachelor's, and master's degrees. 55 undergraduate majors. **Total enrollment:** 3,776. Undergraduates: 3,751. Freshmen: 779. Federal methodology is used as a basis for awarding need-based institutional aid.

**UNDERGRADUATE EXPENSES for 2015–2016** *Application fee:* $40. **Tuition, state resident:** full-time $5856; part-time $244 per credit hour. **Tuition, nonresident:** full-time $16,072; part-time $670 per credit hour. **Required fees:** full-time $1745. Full-time tuition and fees vary according to course load and reciprocity agreements. Part-time tuition and fees vary according to course load and reciprocity agreements. **College room and board:** $9130; **Room only:** $4530. Room and board charges vary according to board plan and housing facility.

**FRESHMAN FINANCIAL AID (Fall 2013)** 710 applied for aid; of those 80% were deemed to have need. 99% of freshmen with need received aid; of those 16% had need fully met. **Average percent of need met:** 92% (excluding resources awarded to replace EFC). **Average financial aid package:** $14,093 (excluding resources awarded to replace EFC). 6% of all full-time freshmen had no need and received non-need-based gift aid.

**UNDERGRADUATE FINANCIAL AID (Fall 2013)** 2,779 applied for aid; of those 84% were deemed to have need. 100% of undergraduates with need received aid; of those 17% had need fully met. **Average percent of need met:** 92% (excluding resources awarded to replace EFC). **Average financial aid package:** $13,918 (excluding resources awarded to replace EFC). 8% of all full-time undergraduates had no need and received non-need-based gift aid.

**GIFT AID (NEED-BASED)** *Total amount:* $12,324,093 (45% federal, 7% state, 31% institutional, 17% external sources). **Receiving aid:** Freshmen: 60% (507); all full-time undergraduates: 60% (2,014). **Average award:** Freshmen: $4813; Undergraduates: $4808. **Scholarships, grants, and awards:** Federal Pell, FSEOG, state, private, college/university gift aid from institutional funds.

**GIFT AID (NON-NEED-BASED)** *Total amount:* $2,792,260 (1% state, 79% institutional, 20% external sources). **Receiving aid:** Freshmen: 5% (40). Undergraduates: 3% (105). **Average award:** Freshmen: $5578. Undergraduates: $3748. **Scholarships, grants, and awards by category:** Academic interests/achievement: area/ethnic studies, biological sciences, business, communication, education, English, general academic interests/achievements, humanities, mathematics, physical sciences, social sciences. Creative arts/performance: art/fine arts, music, performing arts,

theater/drama. Special achievements/activities: general special achievements/activities, leadership. Special characteristics: adult students, children and siblings of alumni, children of faculty/staff, ethnic background, first-generation college students, general special characteristics, handicapped students, international students, local/state students, out-of-state students, veterans' children. **Tuition waivers:** Full or partial for minority students, employees or children of employees.

**LOANS** *Student loans:* $18,933,517 (55% need-based, 45% non-need-based). 62% of past graduating class borrowed through all loan programs. *Average indebtedness per student:* $19,507. **Average need-based loan:** Freshmen: $3843. Undergraduates: $3748. **Parent loans:** $18,494,475 (13% need-based, 87% non-need-based). **Programs:** Federal Direct (Subsidized and Unsubsidized Stafford, PLUS), Perkins.

**WORK-STUDY** *Federal work-study:* jobs available. **State or other work-study/employment:** Total amount: $393,849 (87% need-based, 13% non-need-based). Part-time jobs available.

**ATHLETIC AWARDS** Total amount: $2,032,849 (44% need-based, 56% non-need-based).

**APPLYING FOR FINANCIAL AID** *Required financial aid form:* FAFSA. **Financial aid deadline (priority):** 2/15. **Notification date:** Continuous beginning 3/1.

**CONTACT** Ms. Tracey Piccoli, Director of Financial Aid, Fort Lewis College, 1000 Rim Drive, 101 Miller Student Services Building, Durango, CO 81301, 800-352-7512 or toll-free 877-FLC-COLO. *Fax:* 970-247-7108. *E-mail:* finaid_off@fortlewis.edu. *Website:* http://www.fortlewis.edu/.

# FORT VALLEY STATE UNIVERSITY
## Fort Valley, GA

| Tuition & fees (GA res): $6448 | Average undergraduate aid package: $2124 |
|---|---|

**ABOUT THE INSTITUTION** State-supported, coed. *Awards:* certificates, bachelor's, and master's degrees. 35 undergraduate majors. **Total enrollment:** 2,594. Undergraduates: 2,229. Freshmen: 224. Federal methodology is used as a basis for awarding need-based institutional aid.

**UNDERGRADUATE EXPENSES for 2015–2016** *Application fee:* $20. **Tuition, state resident:** full-time $4740; part-time $158 per credit hour. **Tuition, nonresident:** full-time $17,246; part-time $574.87 per credit hour. **Required fees:** full-time $1708. Full-time tuition and fees vary according to course load, degree level, and student level. Part-time tuition and fees vary according to course load, degree level, and student level. **College room and board:** $7920. Room and board charges vary according to board plan, housing facility, and student level.

**FRESHMAN FINANCIAL AID (Fall 2014, est.)** 217 applied for aid; of those 100% were deemed to have need. 100% of freshmen with need received aid; of those 28% had need fully met. **Average percent of need met:** 28% (excluding resources awarded to replace EFC). **Average financial aid package:** $1824 (excluding resources awarded to replace EFC).

**UNDERGRADUATE FINANCIAL AID (Fall 2014, est.)** 1,855 applied for aid; of those 100% were deemed to have need. 100% of undergraduates with need received aid; of those 60% had need fully met. **Average percent of need met:** 60% (excluding resources awarded to replace EFC). **Average financial aid package:** $2124 (excluding resources awarded to replace EFC).

**GIFT AID (NEED-BASED)** *Total amount:* $9,159,929 (83% federal, 13% state, 3% institutional, 1% external sources). **Receiving aid:** Freshmen: 16% (34); all full-time undergraduates: 30% (584). **Average award:** Freshmen: $2055; Undergraduates: $2196. **Scholarships, grants, and awards:** Federal Pell, FSEOG, state, private, college/university gift aid from institutional funds.

**GIFT AID (NON-NEED-BASED)** *Scholarships, grants, and awards by category:* Academic interests/achievement: agriculture, business, general academic interests/achievements, home economics, military science, premedicine, social sciences. Creative arts/performance: journalism/publications, music. Special achievements/activities: general special achievements/activities. Special characteristics: handicapped students, international students, out-of-state students. **Tuition waivers:** Full or partial for senior citizens. **ROTC:** Army.

**LOANS** *Student loans:* $24,044,982 (64% need-based, 36% non-need-based). *Average need-based loan:* Freshmen: $1899. Undergraduates: $2207. **Parent loans:** $9,703,626 (50% need-based, 50% non-need-based). **Programs:** Federal Direct (Subsidized and Unsubsidized Stafford, PLUS), Perkins.

**WORK-STUDY** *Federal work-study:* Total amount: $308,094; jobs available.

**ATHLETIC AWARDS** Total amount: $309,457 (100% need-based).
**APPLYING FOR FINANCIAL AID** *Required financial aid form:* FAFSA. *Financial aid deadline (priority):* 3/1. *Notification date:* Continuous beginning 4/15.
**CONTACT** Mr. James Stotts, Office of Financial Aid, Fort Valley State University, 1005 State University Drive, Fort Valley, GA 31030, 478-825-6182 or toll-free 877-462-3878. *Fax:* 478-825-6976.
*Website:* http://www.fvsu.edu/.

# FRAMINGHAM STATE UNIVERSITY
## Framingham, MA

| Tuition & fees (MA res): $8320 | Average undergraduate aid package: $8631 |
|---|---|

**ABOUT THE INSTITUTION** State-supported, coed. *Awards:* certificates, bachelor's, and master's degrees. 28 undergraduate majors. *Total enrollment:* 6,499. Undergraduates: 4,609. Freshmen: 808. Federal methodology is used as a basis for awarding need-based institutional aid.
**UNDERGRADUATE EXPENSES** for 2015–2016 *Application fee:* $45. *Tuition, state resident:* full-time $970; part-time $162 per course. *Tuition, nonresident:* full-time $7050; part-time $1175 per course. *Required fees:* full-time $7350; $1290 per course. Full-time tuition and fees vary according to class time and degree level. Part-time tuition and fees vary according to class time, course load, and degree level. *College room and board:* $10,543; *Room only:* $7114. Room and board charges vary according to board plan and housing facility. *Payment plan:* Tuition prepayment.
**FRESHMAN FINANCIAL AID (Fall 2013)** 713 applied for aid; of those 80% were deemed to have need. 100% of freshmen with need received aid; of those 4% had need fully met. *Average percent of need met:* 59% (excluding resources awarded to replace EFC). *Average financial aid package:* $9149 (excluding resources awarded to replace EFC). 5% of all full-time freshmen had no need and received non-need-based gift aid.
**UNDERGRADUATE FINANCIAL AID (Fall 2013)** 3,072 applied for aid; of those 81% were deemed to have need. 100% of undergraduates with need received aid; of those 2% had need fully met. *Average percent of need met:* 58% (excluding resources awarded to replace EFC). *Average financial aid package:* $8631 (excluding resources awarded to replace EFC). 3% of all full-time undergraduates had no need and received non-need-based gift aid.
**GIFT AID (NEED-BASED)** *Total amount:* $10,762,979 (51% federal, 27% state, 19% institutional, 3% external sources). *Receiving aid:* Freshmen: 58% (471); all full-time undergraduates: 51% (1,942). *Average award:* Freshmen: $5650; Undergraduates: $5373. *Scholarships, grants, and awards:* Federal Pell, FSEOG, state, private, college/university gift aid from institutional funds.
**GIFT AID (NON-NEED-BASED)** *Total amount:* $659,843 (33% state, 57% institutional, 10% external sources). *Receiving aid:* Freshmen: 1% (7). Undergraduates: 1% (27). *Average award:* Freshmen: $1847. Undergraduates: $2189. *Scholarships, grants, and awards by category:* Academic interests/achievement: biological sciences, education, engineering/technologies, English, general academic interests/achievements, home economics, mathematics, physical sciences. *Special characteristics:* children of faculty/staff, children of public servants, children of union members/company employees, veterans. *Tuition waivers:* Full or partial for employees or children of employees, senior citizens.
**LOANS** *Student loans:* $15,674,626 (95% need-based, 5% non-need-based). 81% of past graduating class borrowed through all loan programs. *Average indebtedness per student:* $18,027. *Average need-based loan:* Freshmen: $4029. Undergraduates: $4308. *Parent loans:* $3,634,427 (8% need-based, 92% non-need-based). *Programs:* Federal Direct (Subsidized and Unsubsidized Stafford, PLUS), Perkins, state.
**WORK-STUDY** *Federal work-study:* jobs available. *State or other work-study/employment:* Total amount: $42,747 (100% need-based). Part-time jobs available.
**APPLYING FOR FINANCIAL AID** *Required financial aid form:* FAFSA. *Financial aid deadline (priority):* 3/1. *Notification date:* Continuous beginning 3/15. Students must reply by 5/1 or within 2 weeks of notification.
**CONTACT** Office of Financial Aid, Framingham State University, 100 State Street, PO Box 9101, Framingham, MA 01701-9101, 508-626-4534. *Fax:* 508-626-4598.
*Website:* http://www.framingham.edu/.

# FRANCISCAN UNIVERSITY OF STEUBENVILLE
## Steubenville, OH

| Tuition & fees: $24,780 | Average undergraduate aid package: $13,829 |
|---|---|

**ABOUT THE INSTITUTION** Independent Roman Catholic, coed. *Awards:* associate, bachelor's, and master's degrees. 31 undergraduate majors. *Total enrollment:* 2,714. Undergraduates: 2,135. Freshmen: 464. Federal methodology is used as a basis for awarding need-based institutional aid.
**UNDERGRADUATE EXPENSES** for 2015–2016 *Application fee:* $20. *Comprehensive fee:* $33,080 includes full-time tuition ($24,320), mandatory fees ($460), and room and board ($8300). *College room only:* $4800. Room and board charges vary according to board plan. *Part-time tuition:* $805 per credit hour. Part-time tuition and fees vary according to class time and course load.
**FRESHMAN FINANCIAL AID (Fall 2014, est.)** 384 applied for aid; of those 80% were deemed to have need. 100% of freshmen with need received aid; of those 18% had need fully met. *Average percent of need met:* 59% (excluding resources awarded to replace EFC). *Average financial aid package:* $13,523 (excluding resources awarded to replace EFC). 31% of all full-time freshmen had no need and received non-need-based gift aid.
**UNDERGRADUATE FINANCIAL AID (Fall 2014, est.)** 1,546 applied for aid; of those 80% were deemed to have need. 100% of undergraduates with need received aid; of those 16% had need fully met. *Average percent of need met:* 57% (excluding resources awarded to replace EFC). *Average financial aid package:* $13,829 (excluding resources awarded to replace EFC). 25% of all full-time undergraduates had no need and received non-need-based gift aid.
**GIFT AID (NEED-BASED)** *Total amount:* $11,178,135 (18% federal, 2% state, 68% institutional, 12% external sources). *Receiving aid:* Freshmen: 66% (306); all full-time undergraduates: 61% (1,216). *Average award:* Freshmen: $10,607; Undergraduates: $9988. *Scholarships, grants, and awards:* Federal Pell, FSEOG, state, private, college/university gift aid from institutional funds.
**GIFT AID (NON-NEED-BASED)** *Total amount:* $3,597,492 (87% institutional, 13% external sources). *Receiving aid:* Freshmen: 8% (39). Undergraduates: 6% (111). *Average award:* Freshmen: $6168. Undergraduates: $5438. *Scholarships, grants, and awards by category:* Academic interests/achievement: general academic interests/achievements. *Special achievements/activities:* religious involvement. *Special characteristics:* children of faculty/staff, international students, local/state students, religious affiliation, siblings of current students. *Tuition waivers:* Full or partial for employees or children of employees. *ROTC:* Army, Air Force cooperative.
**LOANS** *Student loans:* $15,227,150 (64% need-based, 36% non-need-based). 76% of past graduating class borrowed through all loan programs. *Average indebtedness per student:* $32,443. *Average need-based loan:* Freshmen: $3379. Undergraduates: $4356. *Parent loans:* $3,655,269 (48% need-based, 52% non-need-based). *Programs:* Federal Direct (Subsidized and Unsubsidized Stafford, PLUS), Perkins, Federal Nursing.
**WORK-STUDY** *Federal work-study:* Total amount: $164,398; jobs available. *State or other work-study/employment:* Total amount: $1,324,987 (80% need-based, 20% non-need-based). Part-time jobs available.
**APPLYING FOR FINANCIAL AID** *Required financial aid form:* FAFSA. *Financial aid deadline (priority):* 4/1. *Notification date:* Continuous beginning 2/15. Students must reply within 3 weeks of notification.
**CONTACT** John Herrmann, Director of Student Financial Services, Franciscan University of Steubenville, 1235 University Boulevard, Steubenville, OH 43952-1763, 740-284-5215 or toll-free 800-783-6220. *Fax:* 740-284-5469. *E-mail:* jherrmann@franciscan.edu.
*Website:* http://www.franciscan.edu/.

# FRANCIS MARION UNIVERSITY
## Florence, SC

| Tuition & fees (SC res): $9738 | Average undergraduate aid package: $11,317 |
|---|---|

**ABOUT THE INSTITUTION** State-supported, coed. *Awards:* certificates, bachelor's, and master's degrees. 33 undergraduate majors. *Total enrollment:* 3,944.

Undergraduates: 3,605. Freshmen: 757. Federal methodology is used as a basis for awarding need-based institutional aid.

**UNDERGRADUATE EXPENSES for 2015–2016** *Application fee:* $35. *Tuition, state resident:* full-time $9266; part-time $463.30 per credit hour. *Tuition, nonresident:* full-time $18,532; part-time $926.60 per credit hour. *Required fees:* full-time $472; $14 per credit hour or $57 per term. Full-time tuition and fees vary according to degree level and program. Part-time tuition and fees vary according to course load, degree level, and program. *College room and board:* $7256; *Room only:* $4088. Room and board charges vary according to board plan and housing facility.

**FRESHMAN FINANCIAL AID (Fall 2014, est.)** 693 applied for aid; of those 92% were deemed to have need. 100% of freshmen with need received aid; of those 12% had need fully met. *Average percent of need met:* 66% (excluding resources awarded to replace EFC). *Average financial aid package:* $12,169 (excluding resources awarded to replace EFC). 3% of all full-time freshmen had no need and received non-need-based gift aid.

**UNDERGRADUATE FINANCIAL AID (Fall 2014, est.)** 2,720 applied for aid; of those 92% were deemed to have need. 100% of undergraduates with need received aid; of those 11% had need fully met. *Average percent of need met:* 61% (excluding resources awarded to replace EFC). *Average financial aid package:* $11,317 (excluding resources awarded to replace EFC). 2% of all full-time undergraduates had no need and received non-need-based gift aid.

**GIFT AID (NEED-BASED)** *Total amount:* $16,229,607 (56% federal, 38% state, 4% institutional, 2% external sources). *Receiving aid:* Freshmen: 83% (625); all full-time undergraduates: 76% (2,360). *Average award:* Freshmen: $8637; Undergraduates: $7156. *Scholarships, grants, and awards:* Federal Pell, FSEOG, state, private, college/university gift aid from institutional funds.

**GIFT AID (NON-NEED-BASED)** *Total amount:* $1,204,922 (82% state, 15% institutional, 3% external sources). *Receiving aid:* Freshmen: 5% (40). Undergraduates: 3% (106). *Average award:* Freshmen: $2750. Undergraduates: $2650. *Scholarships, grants, and awards by category:* Academic interests/achievement: biological sciences, business, computer science, education, English, general academic interests/achievements, health fields, humanities, mathematics, premedicine, social sciences. Creative arts/performance: art/fine arts, music, theater/drama. Special achievements/activities: cheerleading/drum major. Special characteristics: adult students, children and siblings of alumni, children of faculty/staff, children of union members/company employees, handicapped students, international students, out-of-state students, spouses of deceased or disabled public servants, veterans, veterans' children. *Tuition waivers:* Full or partial for employees or children of employees, senior citizens. *ROTC:* Army.

**LOANS** *Student loans:* $18,133,554 (88% need-based, 12% non-need-based). 61% of past graduating class borrowed through all loan programs. *Average indebtedness per student:* $28,979. *Average need-based loan:* Freshmen: $2279. Undergraduates: $3344. *Parent loans:* $2,052,280 (54% need-based, 46% non-need-based). *Programs:* Federal Direct (Subsidized and Unsubsidized Stafford, PLUS), state, college/university.

**WORK-STUDY** *Federal work-study:* Total amount: $321,515; jobs available. *State or other work-study/employment:* Total amount: $157,625 (100% non-need-based). Part-time jobs available.

**ATHLETIC AWARDS** Total amount: $786,163 (45% need-based, 55% non-need-based).

**APPLYING FOR FINANCIAL AID** *Required financial aid forms:* FAFSA, institution's own form. *Financial aid deadline (priority):* 3/1. *Notification date:* Continuous beginning 1/30.

**CONTACT** Miss Kim Ellisor, Director of Financial Assistance, Francis Marion University, PO Box 100547, Florence, SC 29502-0547, 843-661-1190 or toll-free 800-368-7551.
*Website:* http://www.fmarion.edu/.

# FRANKLIN & MARSHALL COLLEGE
## Lancaster, PA

| Tuition & fees: $48,514 | Average undergraduate aid package: $43,852 |
| --- | --- |

**ABOUT THE INSTITUTION** Independent, coed. *Awards:* bachelor's degrees. 40 undergraduate majors. *Total enrollment:* 2,209. Undergraduates: 2,209. Freshmen:

592. Both federal and institutional methodology are used as a basis for awarding need-based institutional aid.

**UNDERGRADUATE EXPENSES for 2015–2016** *Application fee:* $60. *One-time required fee:* $200. *Comprehensive fee:* $60,799 includes full-time tuition ($48,414), mandatory fees ($100), and room and board ($12,285). *College room only:* $7330. Room and board charges vary according to board plan and housing facility. *Part-time tuition:* $6052 per course. Part-time tuition and fees vary according to course load.

**FRESHMAN FINANCIAL AID (Fall 2014, est.)** 397 applied for aid; of those 85% were deemed to have need. 100% of freshmen with need received aid; of those 100% had need fully met. *Average percent of need met:* 100% (excluding resources awarded to replace EFC). *Average financial aid package:* $45,769 (excluding resources awarded to replace EFC). 1% of all full-time freshmen had no need and received non-need-based gift aid.

**UNDERGRADUATE FINANCIAL AID (Fall 2014, est.)** 1,371 applied for aid; of those 87% were deemed to have need. 100% of undergraduates with need received aid; of those 100% had need fully met. *Average percent of need met:* 100% (excluding resources awarded to replace EFC). *Average financial aid package:* $43,852 (excluding resources awarded to replace EFC). 1% of all full-time undergraduates had no need and received non-need-based gift aid.

**GIFT AID (NEED-BASED)** *Total amount:* $45,696,993 (4% federal, 1% state, 93% institutional, 2% external sources). *Receiving aid:* Freshmen: 56% (330); all full-time undergraduates: 50% (1,155). *Average award:* Freshmen: $41,770; Undergraduates: $39,564. *Scholarships, grants, and awards:* Federal Pell, FSEOG, state, private, college/university gift aid from institutional funds.

**GIFT AID (NON-NEED-BASED)** *Total amount:* $1,844,550 (1% federal, 42% institutional, 57% external sources). *Receiving aid:* Freshmen: 14% (82). Undergraduates: 14% (320). *Average award:* Freshmen: $2375. Undergraduates: $12,636. *Scholarships, grants, and awards by category:* Creative arts/performance: music. *Tuition waivers:* Full or partial for employees or children of employees. *ROTC:* Army cooperative.

**LOANS** *Student loans:* $9,189,336 (56% need-based, 44% non-need-based). 50% of past graduating class borrowed through all loan programs. *Average indebtedness per student:* $27,474. *Average need-based loan:* Freshmen: $3282. Undergraduates: $4253. *Parent loans:* $3,802,293 (3% need-based, 97% non-need-based). *Programs:* Federal Direct (Subsidized and Unsubsidized Stafford, PLUS), Perkins, college/university.

**WORK-STUDY** *Federal work-study:* Total amount: $1,592,769; jobs available. *State or other work-study/employment:* Total amount: $328,288 (100% need-based). Part-time jobs available.

**APPLYING FOR FINANCIAL AID** *Required financial aid forms:* FAFSA, CSS Financial Aid PROFILE, state aid form, noncustodial (divorced/separated) parent's statement, federal income tax form(s). *Financial aid deadline:* 2/15. *Notification date:* 4/1.

**CONTACT** Mr. Clarke Paine, Director of Financial Aid, Franklin & Marshall College, PO Box 3003, Lancaster, PA 17604-3003, 717-291-3991 or toll-free 877-678-9111. *Fax:* 717-291-4462. *E-mail:* clarke.paine@fandm.edu.
*Website:* http://www.fandm.edu/.

# FRANKLIN COLLEGE
## Franklin, IN

| Tuition & fees: $29,025 | Average undergraduate aid package: $21,465 |
| --- | --- |

**ABOUT THE INSTITUTION** Independent American Baptist Churches in the U.S.A., coed. *Awards:* bachelor's and master's degrees. 31 undergraduate majors. *Total enrollment:* 1,075. Undergraduates: 1,075. Freshmen: 328. Federal methodology is used as a basis for awarding need-based institutional aid.

**UNDERGRADUATE EXPENSES for 2015–2016** *Comprehensive fee:* $37,675 includes full-time tuition ($28,840), mandatory fees ($185), and room and board ($8650). *College room only:* $5150. Room and board charges vary according to board plan.

**FRESHMAN FINANCIAL AID (Fall 2013)** 262 applied for aid; of those 90% were deemed to have need. 100% of freshmen with need received aid; of those 9% had need fully met. *Average percent of need met:* 67% (excluding resources awarded to replace EFC). *Average financial aid package:* $20,974 (excluding resources

awarded to replace EFC). 13% of all full-time freshmen had no need and received non-need-based gift aid.

**UNDERGRADUATE FINANCIAL AID (Fall 2013)** 883 applied for aid; of those 90% were deemed to have need. 100% of undergraduates with need received aid; of those 9% had need fully met. *Average percent of need met:* 71% (excluding resources awarded to replace EFC). *Average financial aid package:* $21,465 (excluding resources awarded to replace EFC). 15% of all full-time undergraduates had no need and received non-need-based gift aid.

**GIFT AID (NEED-BASED)** *Total amount:* $13,287,913 (12% federal, 16% state, 68% institutional, 4% external sources). *Receiving aid:* Freshmen: 87% (236); all full-time undergraduates: 84% (793). *Average award:* Freshmen: $17,240; Undergraduates: $17,058. *Scholarships, grants, and awards:* Federal Pell, FSEOG, state, private, college/university gift aid from institutional funds.

**GIFT AID (NON-NEED-BASED)** *Total amount:* $2,442,370 (1% state, 89% institutional, 10% external sources). *Receiving aid:* Freshmen: 78% (212). Undergraduates: 75% (710). *Average award:* Freshmen: $12,880. Undergraduates: $12,648. *Scholarships, grants, and awards by category:* Academic interests/achievement: general academic interests/achievements. Creative arts/performance: art/fine arts, journalism/publications, music, performing arts, theater/drama. Special characteristics: children and siblings of alumni, children of faculty/staff, ethnic background, members of minority groups, out-of-state students, religious affiliation, siblings of current students. *Tuition waivers:* Full or partial for employees or children of employees, senior citizens. *ROTC:* Army cooperative.

**LOANS** *Student loans:* $7,994,385 (75% need-based, 25% non-need-based). 80% of past graduating class borrowed through all loan programs. *Average indebtedness per student:* $32,451. *Average need-based loan:* Freshmen: $3916. Undergraduates: $4660. *Parent loans:* $2,312,483 (53% need-based, 47% non-need-based). *Programs:* Federal Direct (Subsidized and Unsubsidized Stafford, PLUS), Perkins, college/university.

**WORK-STUDY** *Federal work-study:* jobs available. *State or other work-study/employment:* Total amount: $6400 (40% need-based, 60% non-need-based). Part-time jobs available.

**APPLYING FOR FINANCIAL AID** *Required financial aid forms:* FAFSA, institution's own form. *Financial aid deadline (priority):* 3/10. *Notification date:* Continuous beginning 3/1. Students must reply by 5/1 or within 4 weeks of notification.

**CONTACT** Elizabeth Sappenfield, Director of Financial Aid, Franklin College, 101 Branigin Boulevard, Franklin, IN 46131-2598, 317-738-8075 or toll-free 800-852-0232. *Fax:* 317-738-8072. *E-mail:* finaid@franklincollege.edu. *Website:* http://www.franklincollege.edu/.

# FRANKLIN PIERCE UNIVERSITY
## Rindge, NH

| Tuition & fees: $31,782 | Average undergraduate aid package: $23,887 |
|---|---|

**ABOUT THE INSTITUTION** Independent, coed. *Awards:* certificates, associate, bachelor's, master's, and doctoral degrees (profile does not reflect significant enrollment at 6 continuing education sites; master's degree is only offered at these sites). 45 undergraduate majors. *Total enrollment:* 2,204. Undergraduates: 1,671. Freshmen: 450. Federal methodology is used as a basis for awarding need-based institutional aid.

**UNDERGRADUATE EXPENSES for 2015–2016** *Application fee:* $40. *Comprehensive fee:* $43,842 includes full-time tuition ($29,682), mandatory fees ($2100), and room and board ($12,060). *College room only:* $7040. Full-time tuition and fees vary according to course load, degree level, location, and program. Room and board charges vary according to board plan, housing facility, and student level. *Part-time tuition:* $990 per credit hour. Part-time tuition and fees vary according to course load, degree level, location, and program.

**FRESHMAN FINANCIAL AID (Fall 2013)** 422 applied for aid; of those 92% were deemed to have need. 100% of freshmen with need received aid; of those 24% had need fully met. *Average percent of need met:* 73% (excluding resources awarded to replace EFC). *Average financial aid package:* $23,238 (excluding resources awarded to replace EFC). 15% of all full-time freshmen had no need and received non-need-based gift aid.

**UNDERGRADUATE FINANCIAL AID (Fall 2013)** 1,235 applied for aid; of those 92% were deemed to have need. 100% of undergraduates with need received aid; of those 20% had need fully met. *Average percent of need met:* 73%

(excluding resources awarded to replace EFC). *Average financial aid package:* $23,887 (excluding resources awarded to replace EFC). 15% of all full-time undergraduates had no need and received non-need-based gift aid.

**GIFT AID (NEED-BASED)** *Total amount:* $19,908,161 (10% federal, 1% state, 88% institutional, 1% external sources). *Receiving aid:* Freshmen: 84% (386); all full-time undergraduates: 82% (1,122). *Average award:* Freshmen: $19,718; Undergraduates: $19,445. *Scholarships, grants, and awards:* Federal Pell, FSEOG, state, private, college/university gift aid from institutional funds.

**GIFT AID (NON-NEED-BASED)** *Total amount:* $3,632,335 (100% institutional). *Receiving aid:* Freshmen: 16% (75). Undergraduates: 12% (160). *Average award:* Freshmen: $13,424. Undergraduates: $13,304. *Scholarships, grants, and awards by category:* Academic interests/achievement: communication, general academic interests/achievements. Creative arts/performance: performing arts, theater/drama. Special achievements/activities: general special achievements/activities, leadership. Special characteristics: adult students, children and siblings of alumni, children of current students, children of educators, children of faculty/staff, general special characteristics, international students, local/state students, married students, parents of current students, siblings of current students, spouses of current students. *Tuition waivers:* Full or partial for employees or children of employees, senior citizens. *ROTC:* Army cooperative, Air Force cooperative.

**LOANS** *Student loans:* $11,976,877 (70% need-based, 30% non-need-based). 86% of past graduating class borrowed through all loan programs. *Average indebtedness per student:* $38,546. *Average need-based loan:* Freshmen: $4164. Undergraduates: $4974. *Parent loans:* $6,336,285 (46% need-based, 54% non-need-based). *Programs:* Federal Direct (Subsidized and Unsubsidized Stafford, PLUS), Perkins.

**WORK-STUDY** *Federal work-study:* jobs available. *State or other work-study/employment:* Part-time jobs available.

**ATHLETIC AWARDS** Total amount: $1,773,954 (42% need-based, 58% non-need-based).

**APPLYING FOR FINANCIAL AID** *Required financial aid form:* FAFSA. *Financial aid deadline (priority):* 3/1. *Notification date:* Continuous beginning 3/1.

**CONTACT** Kenneth Ferreira, Executive Director of Student Financial Services, Franklin Pierce University, 40 University Drive, Rindge, NH 03461-0060, 603-899-4180 or toll-free 800-437-0048. *Fax:* 603-899-4372. *E-mail:* ferreirak@franklinpierce.edu. *Website:* http://www.franklinpierce.edu/.

# FRANKLIN UNIVERSITY
## Columbus, OH

**CONTACT** Ms. Marlowe Collier, Financial Aid Assistant, Franklin University, 201 South Grant Avenue, Columbus, OH 43215-5399, 614-797-4700 or toll-free 877-341-6300. *Fax:* 614-220-8931. *E-mail:* finaid@franklin.edu. *Website:* http://www.franklin.edu/.

# FRANKLIN W. OLIN COLLEGE OF ENGINEERING
## Needham, MA

| Tuition & fees: $45,525 | Average undergraduate aid package: $41,000 |
|---|---|

**ABOUT THE INSTITUTION** Independent, coed. *Awards:* bachelor's degrees. 3 undergraduate majors. *Total enrollment:* 370. Undergraduates: 370. Freshmen: 79. Federal methodology is used as a basis for awarding need-based institutional aid.

**UNDERGRADUATE EXPENSES for 2015–2016** *Application fee:* $80. *One-time required fee:* $2656. *Comprehensive fee:* $61,125 includes full-time tuition ($45,000), mandatory fees ($525), and room and board ($15,600). *College room only:* $9300.

**FRESHMAN FINANCIAL AID (Fall 2014, est.)** 57 applied for aid; of those 72% were deemed to have need. 100% of freshmen with need received aid; of those 100% had need fully met. *Average percent of need met:* 100% (excluding resources awarded to replace EFC). *Average financial aid package:* $43,005 (excluding resources awarded to replace EFC). 48% of all full-time freshmen had no need and received non-need-based gift aid.

**UNDERGRADUATE FINANCIAL AID (Fall 2014, est.)** 192 applied for aid; of those 87% were deemed to have need. 100% of undergraduates with need received aid; of those 93% had need fully met. **Average percent of need met:** 99% (excluding resources awarded to replace EFC). **Average financial aid package:** $41,000 (excluding resources awarded to replace EFC). 51% of all full-time undergraduates had no need and received non-need-based gift aid.

**GIFT AID (NEED-BASED) Total amount:** $6,135,851 (3% federal, 96% institutional, 1% external sources). **Receiving aid:** Freshmen: 52% (41); all full-time undergraduates: 49% (167). **Average award:** Freshmen: $38,050; Undergraduates: $36,611. **Scholarships, grants, and awards:** Federal Pell, FSEOG, private, college/university gift aid from institutional funds.

**GIFT AID (NON-NEED-BASED) Total amount:** $4,172,382 (98% institutional, 2% external sources). **Receiving aid:** Freshmen: 52% (41). Undergraduates: 49% (167). **Average award:** Freshmen: $21,882. Undergraduates: $21,749. **Scholarships, grants, and awards by category:** Academic interests/achievement: general academic interests/achievements.

**LOANS Student loans:** $757,713 (43% need-based, 57% non-need-based). 44% of past graduating class borrowed through all loan programs. **Average indebtedness per student:** $19,992. **Average need-based loan:** Freshmen: $3133. Undergraduates: $3417. **Parent loans:** $174,418 (100% non-need-based). **Programs:** Federal Direct (Subsidized and Unsubsidized Stafford, PLUS).

**APPLYING FOR FINANCIAL AID Required financial aid form:** FAFSA. **Financial aid deadline:** 2/15. **Notification date:** Continuous beginning 3/21. Students must reply by 5/1 or within 2 weeks of notification.

**CONTACT** Ms. Jean Ricker, Director of Financial Aid, Franklin W. Olin College of Engineering, 1000 Olin Way, Needham, MA 02492-1200, 781-292-2343. *E-mail:* jean.ricker@olin.edu.
*Website:* http://www.olin.edu/.

# FREED-HARDEMAN UNIVERSITY
## Henderson, TN

| Tuition & fees: $20,468 | Average undergraduate aid package: $17,710 |
| --- | --- |

**ABOUT THE INSTITUTION** Independent Church of Christ, coed. **Awards:** certificates, associate, bachelor's, master's, and doctoral degrees. 40 undergraduate majors. **Total enrollment:** 1,811. Undergraduates: 1,386. Freshmen: 356. Federal methodology is used as a basis for awarding need-based institutional aid.

**UNDERGRADUATE EXPENSES for 2015–2016 Comprehensive fee:** $27,858 includes full-time tuition ($20,468) and room and board ($7390). **College room only:** $3980. Room and board charges vary according to board plan and housing facility. **Part-time tuition:** $650 per credit hour.

**FRESHMAN FINANCIAL AID (Fall 2014, est.)** 329 applied for aid; of those 80% were deemed to have need. 100% of freshmen with need received aid; of those 25% had need fully met. **Average percent of need met:** 76% (excluding resources awarded to replace EFC). **Average financial aid package:** $19,364 (excluding resources awarded to replace EFC). 21% of all full-time freshmen had no need and received non-need-based gift aid.

**UNDERGRADUATE FINANCIAL AID (Fall 2014, est.)** 1,188 applied for aid; of those 84% were deemed to have need. 100% of undergraduates with need received aid; of those 21% had need fully met. **Average percent of need met:** 68% (excluding resources awarded to replace EFC). **Average financial aid package:** $17,710 (excluding resources awarded to replace EFC). 18% of all full-time undergraduates had no need and received non-need-based gift aid.

**GIFT AID (NEED-BASED) Total amount:** $11,630,342 (16% federal, 13% state, 65% institutional, 6% external sources). **Receiving aid:** Freshmen: 77% (262); all full-time undergraduates: 77% (975). **Average award:** Freshmen: $13,503; Undergraduates: $11,999. **Scholarships, grants, and awards:** Federal Pell, FSEOG, state, private, college/university gift aid from institutional funds, Academic Competitiveness Grants, TEACH Grants.

**GIFT AID (NON-NEED-BASED) Total amount:** $4,026,784 (18% state, 74% institutional, 8% external sources). **Receiving aid:** Freshmen: 18% (62). Undergraduates: 15% (186). **Average award:** Freshmen: $11,105. Undergraduates: $10,285. **Tuition waivers:** Full or partial for employees or children of employees.

**LOANS Student loans:** $5,269,257 (77% need-based, 23% non-need-based). 75% of past graduating class borrowed through all loan programs. **Average indebtedness per student:** $31,185. **Average need-based loan:** Freshmen: $3023. Undergrad-

uates: $3839. **Parent loans:** $3,098,387 (54% need-based, 46% non-need-based). **Programs:** Federal Direct (Subsidized and Unsubsidized Stafford, PLUS), Perkins, alternative loans.

**WORK-STUDY Federal work-study:** Total amount: $1,248,957; jobs available. **State or other work-study/employment:** Part-time jobs available.

**ATHLETIC AWARDS** Total amount: $1,735,922 (42% need-based, 58% non-need-based).

**APPLYING FOR FINANCIAL AID Required financial aid forms:** FAFSA, institution's own form. **Financial aid deadline:** Continuous. **Notification date:** Continuous beginning 3/1.

**CONTACT** Mrs. Summer Judd, Director of Financial Aid, Freed-Hardeman University, 158 East Main Street, Henderson, TN 38340-2399, 731-989-6662 or toll-free 800-FHU-FHU-1. *Fax:* 731-989-6775. *E-mail:* sjudd@fhu.edu.
*Website:* http://www.fhu.edu/.

# FRESNO PACIFIC UNIVERSITY
## Fresno, CA

| Tuition & fees: $26,638 | Average undergraduate aid package: $15,829 |
| --- | --- |

**ABOUT THE INSTITUTION** Independent Mennonite Brethren Church, coed. **Awards:** certificates, associate, bachelor's, and master's degrees. 23 undergraduate majors. **Total enrollment:** 3,483. Undergraduates: 2,412. Freshmen: 223. Federal methodology is used as a basis for awarding need-based institutional aid.

**UNDERGRADUATE EXPENSES for 2015–2016 Application fee:** $40. **Comprehensive fee:** $33,998 includes full-time tuition ($26,250), mandatory fees ($388), and room and board ($7360). **College room only:** $2700. Full-time tuition and fees vary according to course level, degree level, and program. Room and board charges vary according to board plan and housing facility. **Part-time tuition:** $938 per unit. **Part-time fees:** $194 per term. Part-time tuition and fees vary according to course level, degree level, and program.

**FRESHMAN FINANCIAL AID (Fall 2014, est.)** 179 applied for aid; of those 95% were deemed to have need. 100% of freshmen with need received aid; of those 23% had need fully met. **Average percent of need met:** 75% (excluding resources awarded to replace EFC). **Average financial aid package:** $21,091 (excluding resources awarded to replace EFC). 10% of all full-time freshmen had no need and received non-need-based gift aid.

**UNDERGRADUATE FINANCIAL AID (Fall 2014, est.)** 2,014 applied for aid; of those 93% were deemed to have need. 99% of undergraduates with need received aid; of those 7% had need fully met. **Average percent of need met:** 69% (excluding resources awarded to replace EFC). **Average financial aid package:** $15,829 (excluding resources awarded to replace EFC). 9% of all full-time undergraduates had no need and received non-need-based gift aid.

**GIFT AID (NEED-BASED) Total amount:** $12,759,075 (44% federal, 45% state, 11% institutional). **Receiving aid:** Freshmen: 71% (134); all full-time undergraduates: 70% (1,556). **Average award:** Freshmen: $11,981; Undergraduates: $8308. **Scholarships, grants, and awards:** Federal Pell, FSEOG, state, private, college/university gift aid from institutional funds.

**GIFT AID (NON-NEED-BASED) Total amount:** $9,201,668 (98% institutional, 2% external sources). **Receiving aid:** Undergraduates: 52% (1,165). **Average award:** Freshmen: $10,118. Undergraduates: $9555. **Scholarships, grants, and awards by category:** Academic interests/achievement: business, general academic interests/achievements, humanities, social sciences. Creative arts/performance: music, performing arts, theater/drama. Special characteristics: children of faculty/staff, members of minority groups, relatives of clergy, religious affiliation, spouses of current students. **Tuition waivers:** Full or partial for employees or children of employees.

**LOANS Student loans:** $13,725,005 (100% need-based). 75% of past graduating class borrowed through all loan programs. **Average indebtedness per student:** $21,992. **Average need-based loan:** Freshmen: $5563. Undergraduates: $5246. **Parent loans:** $1,124,386 (100% need-based). **Programs:** Federal Direct (Subsidized and Unsubsidized Stafford, PLUS), Perkins.

**WORK-STUDY Federal work-study:** Total amount: $92,259; jobs available. **State or other work-study/employment:** Total amount: $1,883,884 (100% need-based). Part-time jobs available.

**ATHLETIC AWARDS** Total amount: $2,467,553 (100% non-need-based).

**APPLYING FOR FINANCIAL AID Required financial aid forms:** FAFSA, institution's own form. **Financial aid deadline (priority):** 3/2. **Notification**

**date:** Continuous beginning 3/2. Students must reply by 7/30 or within 3 weeks of notification.

**CONTACT** April Powell, Director of Financial Aid, Fresno Pacific University, 1717 South Chestnut Avenue, #2004, Fresno, CA 93702, 559-453-2041 or toll-free 800-660-6089. *Fax:* 559-453-5595. *E-mail:* sfs@fresno.edu.
*Website:* http://www.fresno.edu/.

# FRIENDS UNIVERSITY
## Wichita, KS

| Tuition & fees: $24,630 | Average undergraduate aid package: $14,589 |
|---|---|

**ABOUT THE INSTITUTION** Independent Christian non-denominational, coed. **Awards:** associate, bachelor's, and master's degrees. 48 undergraduate majors. **Total enrollment:** 1,882. Undergraduates: 1,344. Freshmen: 182. Federal methodology is used as a basis for awarding need-based institutional aid.

**UNDERGRADUATE EXPENSES for 2015–2016 Application fee:** $35. **Comprehensive fee:** $31,950 includes full-time tuition ($24,450), mandatory fees ($180), and room and board ($7320). **College room only:** $3550. Full-time tuition and fees vary according to class time, course load, degree level, and location. Room and board charges vary according to board plan and housing facility. **Part-time tuition:** $855 per credit hour. Part-time tuition and fees vary according to class time, course load, degree level, and location.

**FRESHMAN FINANCIAL AID (Fall 2014, est.)** 162 applied for aid; of those 91% were deemed to have need. 100% of freshmen with need received aid; of those 29% had need fully met. **Average percent of need met:** 92% (excluding resources awarded to replace EFC). **Average financial aid package:** $18,027 (excluding resources awarded to replace EFC). 8% of all full-time freshmen had no need and received non-need-based gift aid.

**UNDERGRADUATE FINANCIAL AID (Fall 2014, est.)** 994 applied for aid; of those 93% were deemed to have need. 100% of undergraduates with need received aid; of those 16% had need fully met. **Average percent of need met:** 80% (excluding resources awarded to replace EFC). **Average financial aid package:** $14,589 (excluding resources awarded to replace EFC). 6% of all full-time undergraduates had no need and received non-need-based gift aid.

**GIFT AID (NEED-BASED) Total amount:** $10,817,643 (43% federal, 9% state, 45% institutional, 3% external sources). **Receiving aid:** Freshmen: 71% (132); all full-time undergraduates: 76% (867). **Average award:** Freshmen: $7805; Undergraduates: $8269. **Scholarships, grants, and awards:** Federal Pell, FSEOG, state, private, college/university gift aid from institutional funds.

**GIFT AID (NON-NEED-BASED) Total amount:** $414,581 (4% state, 88% institutional, 8% external sources). **Receiving aid:** Freshmen: 79% (147). Undergraduates: 78% (892). **Average award:** Freshmen: $2537. Undergraduates: $7232. **Scholarships, grants, and awards by category:** Academic interests/achievement: 769 awards ($4,881,750 total): biological sciences, general academic interests/achievements, health fields, religion/biblical studies. **Creative arts/performance:** 272 awards ($816,892 total): applied art and design, art/fine arts, dance, music, performing arts, theater/drama. **Special achievements/activities:** 95 awards ($134,700 total): cheerleading/drum major, leadership, religious involvement. **Special characteristics:** 217 awards ($445,690 total): children and siblings of alumni, international students, out-of-state students, relatives of clergy. **Tuition waivers:** Full or partial for employees or children of employees, senior citizens.

**LOANS Student loans:** $20,043,234 (27% need-based, 73% non-need-based). 75% of past graduating class borrowed through all loan programs. *Average indebtedness per student:* $15,289. *Average need-based loan:* Freshmen: $2788. Undergraduates: $4236. **Parent loans:** $879,627 (95% need-based, 5% non-need-based). **Programs:** Federal Direct (Subsidized and Unsubsidized Stafford, PLUS), Perkins.

**WORK-STUDY Federal work-study:** Total amount: $262,645; 206 jobs averaging $1275. **State or other work-study/employment:** 223 part-time jobs averaging $1762.

**ATHLETIC AWARDS** Total amount: $1,741,272 (95% need-based, 5% non-need-based).

**APPLYING FOR FINANCIAL AID Required financial aid form:** FAFSA. **Financial aid deadline (priority):** 3/15. **Notification date:** Continuous beginning 3/1. Students must reply within 3 weeks of notification.

**CONTACT** Tony Lubbers, Director of Financial Aid, Friends University, 2100 University Street, Wichita, KS 67213, 316-295-5599 or toll-free 800-794-6945. *Fax:* 316-295-5703. *E-mail:* lubberst@friends.edu.
*Website:* http://www.friends.edu/.

# FROSTBURG STATE UNIVERSITY
## Frostburg, MD

| Tuition & fees (MD res): $8488 | Average undergraduate aid package: $9335 |
|---|---|

**ABOUT THE INSTITUTION** State-supported, coed. **Awards:** certificates, bachelor's, master's, and doctoral degrees. 47 undergraduate majors. **Total enrollment:** 5,645. Undergraduates: 4,915. Freshmen: 958. Federal methodology is used as a basis for awarding need-based institutional aid.

**UNDERGRADUATE EXPENSES for 2015–2016 Application fee:** $30. **Tuition, state resident:** full-time $6214; part-time $257 per credit. **Tuition, non-resident:** full-time $18,314; part-time $514 per credit. **Required fees:** full-time $2274; $106 per credit or $25 per term. Full-time tuition and fees vary according to location. Part-time tuition and fees vary according to course load and location. **College room and board:** $8574; **Room only:** $4110. Room and board charges vary according to board plan and housing facility.

**FRESHMAN FINANCIAL AID (Fall 2014, est.)** 854 applied for aid; of those 74% were deemed to have need. 100% of freshmen with need received aid; of those 17% had need fully met. **Average percent of need met:** 60% (excluding resources awarded to replace EFC). **Average financial aid package:** $9315 (excluding resources awarded to replace EFC). 17% of all full-time freshmen had no need and received non-need-based gift aid.

**UNDERGRADUATE FINANCIAL AID (Fall 2014, est.)** 3,698 applied for aid; of those 83% were deemed to have need. 92% of undergraduates with need received aid; of those 15% had need fully met. **Average percent of need met:** 61% (excluding resources awarded to replace EFC). **Average financial aid package:** $9335 (excluding resources awarded to replace EFC). 18% of all full-time undergraduates had no need and received non-need-based gift aid.

**GIFT AID (NEED-BASED) Total amount:** $15,708,811 (51% federal, 24% state, 20% institutional, 5% external sources). **Receiving aid:** Freshmen: 50% (488); all full-time undergraduates: 48% (2,124). **Average award:** Freshmen: $7515; Undergraduates: $6870. **Scholarships, grants, and awards:** Federal Pell, FSEOG, state, private, college/university gift aid from institutional funds.

**GIFT AID (NON-NEED-BASED) Total amount:** $3,906,973 (1% federal, 14% state, 57% institutional, 28% external sources). **Receiving aid:** Freshmen: 17% (170). Undergraduates: 18% (803). **Average award:** Freshmen: $2465. Undergraduates: $3108. **Scholarships, grants, and awards by category:** Academic interests/achievement: biological sciences, business, communication, computer science, education, engineering/technologies, English, foreign languages, general academic interests/achievements, health fields, humanities, international studies, mathematics, physical sciences, premedicine, social sciences. **Creative arts/performance:** art/fine arts, creative writing, journalism/publications, music, performing arts, theater/drama. **Special achievements/activities:** community service, leadership. **Special characteristics:** adult students, children of union members/company employees, international students, local/state students, out-of-state students, veterans, veterans' children. **Tuition waivers:** Full or partial for employees or children of employees, senior citizens.

**LOANS Student loans:** $22,798,251 (39% need-based, 61% non-need-based). 66% of past graduating class borrowed through all loan programs. *Average indebtedness per student:* $24,916. *Average need-based loan:* Freshmen: $3217. Undergraduates: $3865. **Parent loans:** $4,229,057 (100% non-need-based). **Programs:** Federal Direct (Subsidized and Unsubsidized Stafford, PLUS), Perkins.

**WORK-STUDY Federal work-study:** Total amount: $103,592; 156 jobs averaging $664. **State or other work-study/employment:** Part-time jobs available.

**APPLYING FOR FINANCIAL AID Required financial aid form:** FAFSA. **Financial aid deadline (priority):** 3/1. **Notification date:** Continuous beginning 3/15. Students must reply within 3 weeks of notification.

**CONTACT** Mrs. Angela Hovatter, Director of Financial Aid, Frostburg State University, 114 Pullen Hall, Frostburg, MD 21532-1099, 301-687-4301. *Fax:* 301-687-7074. *E-mail:* ahovatter@frostburg.edu.
*Website:* http://www.frostburg.edu/.

# FULL SAIL UNIVERSITY
## Winter Park, FL

**CONTACT** Financial Aid Office, Full Sail University, 3300 University Boulevard, Winter Park, FL 32792, 800-575-1142 or toll-free 800-226-7625. *Website:* http://www.fullsail.edu/.

# FURMAN UNIVERSITY
## Greenville, SC

| Tuition & fees: $44,668 | Average undergraduate aid package: $35,321 |
|---|---|

**ABOUT THE INSTITUTION** Independent, coed. *Awards:* certificates, bachelor's, and master's degrees. 50 undergraduate majors. *Total enrollment:* 2,973. Undergraduates: 2,810. Freshmen: 725. Both federal and institutional methodology are used as a basis for awarding need-based institutional aid.

**UNDERGRADUATE EXPENSES for 2015–2016 *Application fee:*** $50. *Comprehensive fee:* $55,872 includes full-time tuition ($44,288), mandatory fees ($380), and room and board ($11,204). *College room only:* $6022. Room and board charges vary according to board plan and housing facility. *Part-time tuition:* $1384 per credit. Part-time tuition and fees vary according to course load.

**FRESHMAN FINANCIAL AID (Fall 2014, est.)** 504 applied for aid; of those 76% were deemed to have need. 100% of freshmen with need received aid; of those 36% had need fully met. *Average percent of need met:* 80% (excluding resources awarded to replace EFC). *Average financial aid package:* $36,743 (excluding resources awarded to replace EFC). 37% of all full-time freshmen had no need and received non-need-based gift aid.

**UNDERGRADUATE FINANCIAL AID (Fall 2014, est.)** 1,398 applied for aid; of those 83% were deemed to have need. 100% of undergraduates with need received aid; of those 33% had need fully met. *Average percent of need met:* 77% (excluding resources awarded to replace EFC). *Average financial aid package:* $35,321 (excluding resources awarded to replace EFC). 41% of all full-time undergraduates had no need and received non-need-based gift aid.

**GIFT AID (NEED-BASED)** *Total amount:* $30,955,133 (6% federal, 4% state, 85% institutional, 5% external sources). *Receiving aid:* Freshmen: 53% (382); all full-time undergraduates: 43% (1,154). *Average award:* Freshmen: $33,708; Undergraduates: $31,665. *Scholarships, grants, and awards:* Federal Pell, FSEOG, state, private, college/university gift aid from institutional funds.

**GIFT AID (NON-NEED-BASED)** *Total amount:* $23,071,029 (15% state, 82% institutional, 3% external sources). *Receiving aid:* Freshmen: 53% (382). Undergraduates: 43% (1,153). *Average award:* Freshmen: $18,441. Undergraduates: $17,166. *Scholarships, grants, and awards by category:* Academic interests/achievement: area/ethnic studies, biological sciences, business, communication, computer science, education, engineering/technologies, English, foreign languages, general academic interests/achievements, health fields, humanities, international studies, mathematics, military science, physical sciences, premedicine, religion/biblical studies, social sciences. *Creative arts/performance:* art/fine arts, creative writing, music, theater/drama. *Special achievements/activities:* community service, leadership, religious involvement. *Special characteristics:* children of faculty/staff, ethnic background, international students, local/state students, relatives of clergy, religious affiliation, veterans. *Tuition waivers:* Full or partial for employees or children of employees. *ROTC:* Army.

**LOANS** *Student loans:* $8,592,405 (84% need-based, 16% non-need-based). 42% of past graduating class borrowed through all loan programs. *Average indebtedness per student:* $25,903. *Average need-based loan:* Freshmen: $4442. Undergraduates: $5130. *Parent loans:* $4,098,388 (85% need-based, 15% non-need-based). *Programs:* Federal Direct (Subsidized and Unsubsidized Stafford, PLUS), Perkins, state, alternative loans.

**WORK-STUDY** *Federal work-study:* Total amount: $817,249; 583 jobs averaging $1552.

**ATHLETIC AWARDS** Total amount: $10,412,325 (39% need-based, 61% non-need-based).

**APPLYING FOR FINANCIAL AID** *Required financial aid forms:* FAFSA, CSS Financial Aid PROFILE, state aid form. *Financial aid deadline:* 1/15. *Notification date:* 4/1. Students must reply by 5/1 or within 2 weeks of notification.

**CONTACT** Mr. Forrest Stuart, Associate Vice President of Financial Aid, Furman University, 3300 Poinsett Highway, Greenville, SC 29613, 864-294-2204. *Fax:* 864-294-3127. *E-mail:* forrest.stuart@furman.edu. *Website:* http://www.furman.edu/.

# GALEN COLLEGE OF NURSING
## Cincinnati, OH

**CONTACT** Financial Aid Office, Galen College of Nursing, 100 East Business Way, Suite 200, Cincinnati, OH 45241, 513-475-3636. *Website:* http://www.galencollege.edu/.

# GALLAUDET UNIVERSITY
## Washington, DC

| Tuition & fees: $15,604 | Average undergraduate aid package: $19,027 |
|---|---|

**ABOUT THE INSTITUTION** Independent, coed. *Awards:* certificates, bachelor's, master's, and doctoral degrees (Undergraduate programs are open primarily to the students with hearing-impairments). 21 undergraduate majors. *Total enrollment:* 1,488. Undergraduates: 1,031. Freshmen: 182. Federal methodology is used as a basis for awarding need-based institutional aid.

**UNDERGRADUATE EXPENSES for 2015–2016 *Application fee:*** $50. *Comprehensive fee:* $28,234 includes full-time tuition ($15,078), mandatory fees ($526), and room and board ($12,630). *College room only:* $7080. Full-time tuition and fees vary according to course load. Room and board charges vary according to board plan. *Part-time tuition:* $628.25 per credit. Part-time tuition and fees vary according to course load.

**FRESHMAN FINANCIAL AID (Fall 2013)** 164 applied for aid; of those 92% were deemed to have need. 100% of freshmen with need received aid; of those 12% had need fully met. *Average percent of need met:* 73% (excluding resources awarded to replace EFC). *Average financial aid package:* $19,948 (excluding resources awarded to replace EFC). 3% of all full-time freshmen had no need and received non-need-based gift aid.

**UNDERGRADUATE FINANCIAL AID (Fall 2013)** 948 applied for aid; of those 100% were deemed to have need. 92% of undergraduates with need received aid; of those 11% had need fully met. *Average percent of need met:* 71% (excluding resources awarded to replace EFC). *Average financial aid package:* $19,027 (excluding resources awarded to replace EFC). 3% of all full-time undergraduates had no need and received non-need-based gift aid.

**GIFT AID (NEED-BASED)** *Total amount:* $35,647,902 (63% federal, 23% state, 13% institutional, 1% external sources). *Receiving aid:* Freshmen: 75% (150); all full-time undergraduates: 86% (867). *Average award:* Freshmen: $18,659; Undergraduates: $17,213. *Scholarships, grants, and awards:* Federal Pell, FSEOG, state, private, college/university gift aid from institutional funds.

**GIFT AID (NON-NEED-BASED)** *Total amount:* $876,371 (70% state, 29% institutional, 1% external sources). *Receiving aid:* Freshmen: 14% (27). Undergraduates: 15% (155). *Average award:* Freshmen: $9600. Undergraduates: $7837. *Scholarships, grants, and awards by category:* Academic interests/achievement: general academic interests/achievements. *Special achievements/activities:* leadership. *Special characteristics:* members of minority groups. *Tuition waivers:* Full or partial for employees or children of employees.

**LOANS** *Student loans:* $3,178,382 (95% need-based, 5% non-need-based). 62% of past graduating class borrowed through all loan programs. *Average indebtedness per student:* $15,970. *Average need-based loan:* Freshmen: $3093. Undergraduates: $4010. *Parent loans:* $483,088 (67% need-based, 33% non-need-based). *Programs:* Federal Direct (Subsidized and Unsubsidized Stafford, PLUS), Perkins.

**WORK-STUDY** *Federal work-study:* jobs available.

**APPLYING FOR FINANCIAL AID** *Required financial aid forms:* FAFSA, institution's own form. *Financial aid deadline:* Continuous. *Notification date:* Continuous beginning 3/1.

CONTACT Shondra Dickson, Director of Financial Aid, Gallaudet University, Chapel Hall, Room G-02, 800 Florida Avenue, NE, Washington, DC 20002, 202-651-5290 or toll-free 800-995-0550. *Fax:* 202-651-5740. *E-mail:* financial.aid@gallaudet.edu. *Website:* http://www.gallaudet.edu/.

# GANNON UNIVERSITY
## Erie, PA

| Tuition & fees: $28,368 | Average undergraduate aid package: $23,719 |
|---|---|

**ABOUT THE INSTITUTION** Independent Roman Catholic, coed. *Awards:* certificates, associate, bachelor's, master's, and doctoral degrees. 61 undergraduate majors. *Total enrollment:* 4,410. Undergraduates: 3,205. Freshmen: 595. Federal methodology is used as a basis for awarding need-based institutional aid.

**UNDERGRADUATE EXPENSES** for 2015–2016 *Application fee:* $25. *Comprehensive fee:* $39,608 includes full-time tuition ($27,760), mandatory fees ($608), and room and board ($11,240). *College room only:* $5890. Full-time tuition and fees vary according to class time, course load, degree level, and program. Room and board charges vary according to board plan and housing facility. *Part-time tuition:* $670 per credit hour. *Part-time fees:* $18 per credit hour. Part-time tuition and fees vary according to class time, course load, degree level, and program.

**FRESHMAN FINANCIAL AID (Fall 2014, est.)** 540 applied for aid; of those 92% were deemed to have need. 100% of freshmen with need received aid; of those 20% had need fully met. *Average percent of need met:* 79% (excluding resources awarded to replace EFC). *Average financial aid package:* $24,282 (excluding resources awarded to replace EFC). 13% of all full-time freshmen had no need and received non-need-based gift aid.

**UNDERGRADUATE FINANCIAL AID (Fall 2014, est.)** 2,232 applied for aid; of those 91% were deemed to have need. 100% of undergraduates with need received aid; of those 21% had need fully met. *Average percent of need met:* 76% (excluding resources awarded to replace EFC). *Average financial aid package:* $23,719 (excluding resources awarded to replace EFC). 15% of all full-time undergraduates had no need and received non-need-based gift aid.

**GIFT AID (NEED-BASED)** *Total amount:* $37,706,493 (10% federal, 9% state, 76% institutional, 5% external sources). *Receiving aid:* Freshmen: 82% (485); all full-time undergraduates: 78% (2,026). *Average award:* Freshmen: $20,887; Undergraduates: $19,545. *Scholarships, grants, and awards:* Federal Pell, FSEOG, state, private, college/university gift aid from institutional funds, Federal Nursing.

**GIFT AID (NON-NEED-BASED)** *Total amount:* $9,059,513 (67% institutional, 33% external sources). *Receiving aid:* Freshmen: 13% (80). Undergraduates: 11% (290). *Average award:* Freshmen: $12,710. Undergraduates: $12,212. *Scholarships, grants, and awards by category:* Academic interests/achievement: 836 awards ($10,978,998 total): biological sciences, business, education, engineering/technologies, English, foreign languages, general academic interests/achievements, humanities, international studies, mathematics, premedicine, religion/biblical studies, social sciences. *Creative arts/performance:* 74 awards ($119,500 total): music, performing arts, theater/drama. *Special achievements/activities:* 81 awards ($129,400 total): community service, leadership. *Special characteristics:* 990 awards ($2,301,982 total): adult students, ethnic background, international students, members of minority groups, religious affiliation, veterans. *Tuition waivers:* Full or partial for employees or children of employees, senior citizens. *ROTC:* Army.

**LOANS** *Student loans:* $18,480,235 (67% need-based, 33% non-need-based). 76% of past graduating class borrowed through all loan programs. *Average need-based loan:* Freshmen: $3370. Undergraduates: $4293. *Parent loans:* $4,717,210 (82% need-based, 18% non-need-based). *Programs:* Federal Direct (Subsidized and Unsubsidized Stafford, PLUS), Perkins, Federal Nursing.

**WORK-STUDY** *Federal work-study:* Total amount: $800,197; 507 jobs averaging $2300. *State or other work-study/employment:* Total amount: $278,945 (100% non-need-based). 169 part-time jobs averaging $2300.

**ATHLETIC AWARDS** Total amount: $3,971,310 (68% need-based, 32% non-need-based).

**APPLYING FOR FINANCIAL AID** *Required financial aid form:* FAFSA. *Financial aid deadline (priority):* 3/15. *Notification date:* Continuous beginning 11/1.

**CONTACT** Ms. Sharon Krahe, Director of Financial Aid, Gannon University, 109 University Square, Erie, PA 16541, 814-871-7670 or toll-free 800-GANNONU. *Fax:* 814-871-5826. *E-mail:* krahe001@gannon.edu. *Website:* http://www.gannon.edu/.

# GARDNER-WEBB UNIVERSITY
## Boiling Springs, NC

| Tuition & fees: $26,885 | Average undergraduate aid package: $21,535 |
|---|---|

**ABOUT THE INSTITUTION** Independent Baptist, coed. *Awards:* certificates, associate, bachelor's, master's, and doctoral degrees. 66 undergraduate majors. *Total enrollment:* 4,636. Undergraduates: 2,572. Freshmen: 434. Federal methodology is used as a basis for awarding need-based institutional aid.

**UNDERGRADUATE EXPENSES** for 2015–2016 *Application fee:* $40. *Comprehensive fee:* $35,665 includes full-time tuition ($26,690), mandatory fees ($195), and room and board ($8780). *College room only:* $4490. Full-time tuition and fees vary according to degree level. Room and board charges vary according to board plan and housing facility. *Part-time tuition:* $426 per credit hour. Part-time tuition and fees vary according to course load.

**FRESHMAN FINANCIAL AID (Fall 2014, est.)** 455 applied for aid; of those 90% were deemed to have need. 100% of freshmen with need received aid; of those 20% had need fully met. *Average percent of need met:* 71% (excluding resources awarded to replace EFC). *Average financial aid package:* $22,219 (excluding resources awarded to replace EFC). 16% of all full-time freshmen had no need and received non-need-based gift aid.

**UNDERGRADUATE FINANCIAL AID (Fall 2014, est.)** 1,409 applied for aid; of those 90% were deemed to have need. 100% of undergraduates with need received aid; of those 20% had need fully met. *Average percent of need met:* 69% (excluding resources awarded to replace EFC). *Average financial aid package:* $21,535 (excluding resources awarded to replace EFC). 17% of all full-time undergraduates had no need and received non-need-based gift aid.

**GIFT AID (NEED-BASED)** *Total amount:* $18,769,171 (15% federal, 18% state, 65% institutional, 2% external sources). *Receiving aid:* Freshmen: 69% (339); all full-time undergraduates: 61% (974). *Average award:* Freshmen: $7366; Undergraduates: $7102. *Scholarships, grants, and awards:* Federal Pell, FSEOG, state, private, college/university gift aid from institutional funds.

**GIFT AID (NON-NEED-BASED)** *Total amount:* $2,851,949 (99% institutional, 1% external sources). *Receiving aid:* Freshmen: 81% (397). Undergraduates: 72% (1,144). *Average award:* Freshmen: $9816. Undergraduates: $10,506. *Scholarships, grants, and awards by category:* Academic interests/achievement: biological sciences, business, communication, computer science, education, English, foreign languages, general academic interests/achievements, health fields, humanities, mathematics, physical sciences, premedicine, religion/biblical studies, social sciences. *Creative arts/performance:* art/fine arts, music, theater/drama. *Special achievements/activities:* cheerleading/drum major, religious involvement. *Special characteristics:* children of faculty/staff, handicapped students, local/state students, members of minority groups, out-of-state students, previous college experience, relatives of clergy. *Tuition waivers:* Full or partial for employees or children of employees. *ROTC:* Army, Air Force cooperative.

**LOANS** *Student loans:* $9,955,984 (95% need-based, 5% non-need-based). 77% of past graduating class borrowed through all loan programs. *Average indebtedness per student:* $29,543. *Average need-based loan:* Freshmen: $3670. Undergraduates: $4612. *Parent loans:* $3,959,436 (96% need-based, 4% non-need-based). *Programs:* Federal Direct (Subsidized and Unsubsidized Stafford, PLUS), Perkins, state, alternative loans.

**WORK-STUDY** *Federal work-study:* Total amount: $358,368; 261 jobs averaging $1386. *State or other work-study/employment:* Total amount: $50,971 (89% need-based, 11% non-need-based). 38 part-time jobs averaging $1377.

**ATHLETIC AWARDS** Total amount: $6,278,574 (64% need-based, 36% non-need-based).

**APPLYING FOR FINANCIAL AID** *Required financial aid forms:* FAFSA, state aid form. *Financial aid deadline (priority):* 3/15. *Notification date:* 3/1. Students must reply within 2 weeks of notification.

**CONTACT** Summer Nance, Assistant Vice President of Financial Planning, Gardner-Webb University, PO Box 955, Boiling Springs, NC 28017, 704-406-4243 or toll-free 800-253-6472. *Fax:* 704-406-4102. *Website:* http://www.gardner-webb.edu/.

# GENEVA COLLEGE
## Beaver Falls, PA

| Tuition & fees: $25,450 | Average undergraduate aid package: $20,159 |
| --- | --- |

**ABOUT THE INSTITUTION** Independent Reformed Presbyterian Church of North America, coed. **Awards:** associate, bachelor's, and master's degrees (also offers non-traditional programs in Philadelphia and western Pennsylvania with significant enrollment not reflected in profile). 35 undergraduate majors. **Total enrollment:** 1,568. Undergraduates: 1,267. Freshmen: 311. Federal methodology is used as a basis for awarding need-based institutional aid.

**UNDERGRADUATE EXPENSES for 2015–2016 Application fee:** $40. **Comprehensive fee:** $35,080 includes full-time tuition ($25,450) and room and board ($9630). Full-time tuition and fees vary according to course load. Room and board charges vary according to board plan. **Part-time tuition:** $860 per credit. Part-time tuition and fees vary according to course load.

**FRESHMAN FINANCIAL AID (Fall 2014, est.)** 301 applied for aid; of those 89% were deemed to have need. 99% of freshmen with need received aid; of those 17% had need fully met. **Average percent of need met:** 77% (excluding resources awarded to replace EFC). **Average financial aid package:** $20,783 (excluding resources awarded to replace EFC). 14% of all full-time freshmen had no need and received non-need-based gift aid.

**UNDERGRADUATE FINANCIAL AID (Fall 2014, est.)** 1,123 applied for aid; of those 91% were deemed to have need. 100% of undergraduates with need received aid; of those 19% had need fully met. **Average percent of need met:** 77% (excluding resources awarded to replace EFC). **Average financial aid package:** $20,159 (excluding resources awarded to replace EFC). 15% of all full-time undergraduates had no need and received non-need-based gift aid.

**GIFT AID (NEED-BASED) Total amount:** $15,837,385 (14% federal, 11% state, 71% institutional, 4% external sources). **Receiving aid:** Freshmen: 84% (266); all full-time undergraduates: 82% (1,013). **Average award:** Freshmen: $16,853; Undergraduates: $15,958. **Scholarships, grants, and awards:** Federal Pell, FSEOG, state, private, college/university gift aid from institutional funds.

**GIFT AID (NON-NEED-BASED) Total amount:** $2,609,041 (1% federal, 1% state, 85% institutional, 13% external sources). **Receiving aid:** Freshmen: 9% (30). Undergraduates: 10% (118). **Average award:** Freshmen: $10,802. Undergraduates: $9952. **Scholarships, grants, and awards by category:** Academic interests/achievement: engineering/technologies, general academic interests/achievements, religion/biblical studies. Creative arts/performance: music. Special characteristics: children of faculty/staff, religious affiliation. **Tuition waivers:** Full or partial for employees or children of employees. **ROTC:** Army cooperative.

**LOANS Student loans:** $8,689,090 (69% need-based, 31% non-need-based). 80% of past graduating class borrowed through all loan programs. **Average indebtedness per student:** $32,673. **Average need-based loan:** Freshmen: $3473. Undergraduates: $4108. **Parent loans:** $1,943,544 (39% need-based, 61% non-need-based). **Programs:** Federal Direct (Subsidized and Unsubsidized Stafford, PLUS), Perkins.

**WORK-STUDY Federal work-study:** Total amount: $200,000; 250 jobs averaging $2000.

**APPLYING FOR FINANCIAL AID Required financial aid form:** FAFSA. **Financial aid deadline (priority):** 3/15. **Notification date:** Continuous beginning 3/1. Students must reply within 4 weeks of notification.

**CONTACT** Mr. Steven Bell, Director of Financial Aid, Geneva College, 3200 College Avenue, Beaver Falls, PA 15010-3599, 724-847-6530 or toll-free 800-847-8255. *Fax:* 724-847-6776. *E-mail:* financialaid@geneva.edu.

*Website:* http://www.geneva.edu/.

# GEORGE FOX UNIVERSITY
## Newberg, OR

| Tuition & fees: $31,866 | Average undergraduate aid package: $27,296 |
| --- | --- |

**ABOUT THE INSTITUTION** Independent Friends, coed. **Awards:** certificates, bachelor's, master's, and doctoral degrees. 46 undergraduate majors. **Total enrollment:** 3,712. Undergraduates: 2,383. Freshmen: 772. Federal methodology is used as a basis for awarding need-based institutional aid.

**UNDERGRADUATE EXPENSES for 2015–2016 Application fee:** $40. **Comprehensive fee:** $41,730 includes full-time tuition ($31,510), mandatory fees ($356), and room and board ($9864). **College room only:** $5754. Room and board charges vary according to board plan. **Part-time tuition:** $954 per credit hour. Part-time tuition and fees vary according to course load.

**FRESHMAN FINANCIAL AID (Fall 2014, est.)** 541 applied for aid; of those 88% were deemed to have need. 100% of freshmen with need received aid; of those 44% had need fully met. **Average percent of need met:** 87% (excluding resources awarded to replace EFC). **Average financial aid package:** $27,919 (excluding resources awarded to replace EFC). 11% of all full-time freshmen had no need and received non-need-based gift aid.

**UNDERGRADUATE FINANCIAL AID (Fall 2014, est.)** 1,889 applied for aid; of those 91% were deemed to have need. 100% of undergraduates with need received aid; of those 37% had need fully met. **Average percent of need met:** 85% (excluding resources awarded to replace EFC). **Average financial aid package:** $27,296 (excluding resources awarded to replace EFC). 7% of all full-time undergraduates had no need and received non-need-based gift aid.

**GIFT AID (NEED-BASED) Total amount:** $32,660,714 (11% federal, 2% state, 83% institutional, 4% external sources). **Receiving aid:** Freshmen: 62% (398); all full-time undergraduates: 64% (1,446). **Average award:** Freshmen: $7896; Undergraduates: $8443. **Scholarships, grants, and awards:** Federal Pell, FSEOG, state, private, college/university gift aid from institutional funds, Academic Competitiveness Grants, National SMART Grants, TEACH Grants.

**GIFT AID (NON-NEED-BASED) Total amount:** $2,629,772 (95% institutional, 5% external sources). **Receiving aid:** Freshmen: 74% (473). Undergraduates: 67% (1,518). **Average award:** Freshmen: $11,561. Undergraduates: $10,470. **Scholarships, grants, and awards by category:** Academic interests/achievement: biological sciences, business, communication, computer science, education, engineering/technologies, English, foreign languages, general academic interests/achievements, health fields, home economics, humanities, international studies, mathematics, physical sciences, religion/biblical studies, social sciences. Creative arts/performance: art/fine arts, cinema/film/broadcasting, debating, music, theater/drama. Special achievements/activities: leadership, religious involvement. Special characteristics: children and siblings of alumni, children of faculty/staff, ethnic background, international students, members of minority groups, out-of-state students, relatives of clergy, religious affiliation. **Tuition waivers:** Full or partial for employees or children of employees, senior citizens. **ROTC:** Air Force cooperative.

**LOANS Student loans:** $12,402,132 (84% need-based, 16% non-need-based). 75% of past graduating class borrowed through all loan programs. **Average indebtedness per student:** $25,143. **Average need-based loan:** Freshmen: $2872. Undergraduates: $3577. **Parent loans:** $1,372,458 (53% need-based, 47% non-need-based). **Programs:** Federal Direct (Subsidized and Unsubsidized Stafford, PLUS), Perkins, alternative loans.

**WORK-STUDY Federal work-study:** Total amount: $2,720,555; jobs available. **State or other work-study/employment:** Total amount: $237,837 (100% non-need-based). Part-time jobs available.

**APPLYING FOR FINANCIAL AID Required financial aid forms:** FAFSA, state aid form. **Financial aid deadline (priority):** 2/1. **Notification date:** Continuous beginning 3/1. Students must reply within 6 weeks of notification.

**CONTACT** James Oshiro, Director of Financial Aid, George Fox University, 414 North Meridian Street, Newberg, OR 97132-2697, 503-554-2290 or toll-free 800-765-4369. *Fax:* 503-554-3880. *E-mail:* sfs@georgefox.edu.

*Website:* http://www.georgefox.edu/.

# GEORGE MASON UNIVERSITY
## Fairfax, VA

| Tuition & fees (VA res): $10,382 | Average undergraduate aid package: $11,955 |
| --- | --- |

**ABOUT THE INSTITUTION** State-supported, coed. **Awards:** certificates, bachelor's, master's, and doctoral degrees. 67 undergraduate majors. **Total enrollment:** 33,723. Undergraduates: 22,343. Freshmen: 3,078. Federal methodology is used as a basis for awarding need-based institutional aid.

**UNDERGRADUATE EXPENSES for 2015–2016 Tuition, state resident:** full-time $7562; part-time $315 per credit hour. **Tuition, nonresident:** full-time $27,140; part-time $1131 per credit hour. **Required fees:** full-time $2820; $118 per credit hour. Full-time tuition and fees vary according to course load. Part-time tuition

and fees vary according to course load. **College room and board:** $10,100; **Room only:** $6000. Room and board charges vary according to board plan and housing facility.
**FRESHMAN FINANCIAL AID (Fall 2013)** 2,445 applied for aid; of those 69% were deemed to have need. 97% of freshmen with need received aid; of those 7% had need fully met. **Average percent of need met:** 61% (excluding resources awarded to replace EFC). **Average financial aid package:** $12,243 (excluding resources awarded to replace EFC). 4% of all full-time freshmen had no need and received non-need-based gift aid.
**UNDERGRADUATE FINANCIAL AID (Fall 2013)** 11,714 applied for aid; of those 79% were deemed to have need. 96% of undergraduates with need received aid; of those 5% had need fully met. **Average percent of need met:** 56% (excluding resources awarded to replace EFC). **Average financial aid package:** $11,955 (excluding resources awarded to replace EFC). 3% of all full-time undergraduates had no need and received non-need-based gift aid.
**GIFT AID (NEED-BASED) Total amount:** $45,538,601 (51% federal, 37% state, 12% institutional). **Receiving aid:** Freshmen: 45% (1,358); all full-time undergraduates: 42% (7,205). **Average award:** Freshmen: $6483; Undergraduates: $5889. **Scholarships, grants, and awards:** Federal Pell, FSEOG, state, private, college/university gift aid from institutional funds.
**GIFT AID (NON-NEED-BASED) Total amount:** $9,286,092 (71% institutional, 29% external sources). **Receiving aid:** Freshmen: 17% (523). Undergraduates: 8% (1,388). **Average award:** Freshmen: $5525. Undergraduates: $6936. **Scholarships, grants, and awards by category:** Academic interests/achievement: 1,364 awards ($6,526,385 total): general academic interests/achievements. Creative arts/performance: general creative arts/performance. Special characteristics: general special characteristics. **Tuition waivers:** Full or partial for employees or children of employees, senior citizens. **ROTC:** Army, Air Force cooperative.
**LOANS Student loans:** $87,030,071 (76% need-based, 24% non-need-based). 60% of past graduating class borrowed through all loan programs. Average indebtedness per student: $27,206. **Average need-based loan:** Freshmen: $3523. Undergraduates: $4591. **Parent loans:** $20,214,855 (48% need-based, 52% non-need-based). **Programs:** Federal Direct (Subsidized and Unsubsidized Stafford, PLUS), Perkins, Federal Nursing.
**WORK-STUDY Federal work-study:** 331 jobs averaging $2234.
**ATHLETIC AWARDS Total amount:** $5,055,392 (100% non-need-based).
**APPLYING FOR FINANCIAL AID Required financial aid form:** FAFSA. **Financial aid deadline (priority):** 3/1. **Notification date:** Continuous beginning 4/1. Students must reply within 3 weeks of notification.
**CONTACT** Heidi Granger, Office of Student Financial Aid, George Mason University, Mail Stop 3B5, Fairfax, VA 22030-4444, 703-993-2353 or toll-free 888-627-6612. Fax: 703-993-2350. E-mail: finaid@gmu.edu.
Website: http://www.gmu.edu/.

# GEORGETOWN COLLEGE
## Georgetown, KY

| Tuition & fees: $32,960 | Average undergraduate aid package: $32,160 |
|---|---|

**ABOUT THE INSTITUTION** Independent Baptist Church, coed. **Awards:** certificates, bachelor's, and master's degrees. 33 undergraduate majors. **Total enrollment:** 1,262. Undergraduates: 979. Freshmen: 273. Federal methodology is used as a basis for awarding need-based institutional aid.
**UNDERGRADUATE EXPENSES for 2015–2016 Comprehensive fee:** $41,440 includes full-time tuition ($32,960) and room and board ($8480). **College room only:** $4090. Full-time tuition and fees vary according to course load and degree level. Room and board charges vary according to board plan and housing facility. **Part-time tuition:** $1020 per credit hour. Part-time tuition and fees vary according to degree level.
**FRESHMAN FINANCIAL AID (Fall 2013)** 232 applied for aid; of those 92% were deemed to have need. 100% of freshmen with need received aid; of those 80% had need fully met. **Average percent of need met:** 78% (excluding resources awarded to replace EFC). **Average financial aid package:** $32,116 (excluding resources awarded to replace EFC). 13% of all full-time freshmen had no need and received non-need-based gift aid.
**UNDERGRADUATE FINANCIAL AID (Fall 2013)** 936 applied for aid; of those 89% were deemed to have need. 100% of undergraduates with need received aid; of those 55% had need fully met. **Average percent of need met:** 76% (excluding

resources awarded to replace EFC). **Average financial aid package:** $32,160 (excluding resources awarded to replace EFC). 19% of all full-time undergraduates had no need and received non-need-based gift aid.
**GIFT AID (NEED-BASED) Total amount:** $17,871,148 (10% federal, 10% state, 75% institutional, 5% external sources). **Receiving aid:** Freshmen: 88% (213); all full-time undergraduates: 83% (833). **Average award:** Freshmen: $17,700; Undergraduates: $17,764. **Scholarships, grants, and awards:** Federal Pell, FSEOG, state, private, college/university gift aid from institutional funds.
**GIFT AID (NON-NEED-BASED) Total amount:** $742,403 (5% federal, 11% state, 73% institutional, 11% external sources). **Receiving aid:** Freshmen: 13% (32). Undergraduates: 15% (151). **Average award:** Freshmen: $14,493. Undergraduates: $15,594. **Scholarships, grants, and awards by category:** Academic interests/achievement: communication, general academic interests/achievements, international studies. Creative arts/performance: art/fine arts, music, performing arts, theater/drama. Special achievements/activities: junior miss, leadership, religious involvement. Special characteristics: children and siblings of alumni, children of faculty/staff, local/state students, members of minority groups, out-of-state students, relatives of clergy, religious affiliation, veterans, veterans' children. **Tuition waivers:** Full or partial for employees or children of employees. **ROTC:** Army cooperative, Air Force cooperative.
**LOANS Student loans:** $9,061,298 (93% need-based, 7% non-need-based). 73% of past graduating class borrowed through all loan programs. Average indebtedness per student: $19,076. **Average need-based loan:** Freshmen: $3886. Undergraduates: $4775. **Parent loans:** $1,671,781 (97% need-based, 3% non-need-based). **Programs:** Federal Direct (Subsidized and Unsubsidized Stafford, PLUS), Perkins, college/university.
**WORK-STUDY Federal work-study:** 575 jobs averaging $966.
**ATHLETIC AWARDS Total amount:** $2,168,166 (92% need-based, 8% non-need-based).
**APPLYING FOR FINANCIAL AID Required financial aid forms:** FAFSA, institution's own form. **Financial aid deadline (priority):** 2/1. **Notification date:** Continuous beginning 3/1. Students must reply by 5/1 or within 3 weeks of notification.
**CONTACT** Tiffany Hornberger, Director of Student Financial Planning, Georgetown College, 400 East College Street, Georgetown, KY 40324-1696, 502-863-8027 or toll-free 800-788-9985. Fax: 502-868-7733. E-mail: financialaid@georgetowncollege.edu. Website: http://www.georgetowncollege.edu/.

# GEORGETOWN UNIVERSITY
## Washington, DC

| Tuition & fees: $46,744 | Average undergraduate aid package: $39,693 |
|---|---|

**ABOUT THE INSTITUTION** Independent Roman Catholic (Jesuit), coed. **Awards:** certificates, bachelor's, master's, and doctoral degrees. 48 undergraduate majors. **Total enrollment:** 17,858. Undergraduates: 7,595. Freshmen: 1,578. Both federal and institutional methodology are used as a basis for awarding need-based institutional aid.
**UNDERGRADUATE EXPENSES for 2015–2016 Application fee:** $75. **Comprehensive fee:** $60,768 includes full-time tuition ($46,200), mandatory fees ($544), and room and board ($14,024). **College room only:** $9548. Full-time tuition and fees vary according to course load and program. Room and board charges vary according to board plan and housing facility. **Part-time tuition:** $1925 per credit hour. Part-time tuition and fees vary according to course load and program.
**FRESHMAN FINANCIAL AID (Fall 2014, est.)** 1,029 applied for aid; of those 61% were deemed to have need. 100% of freshmen with need received aid; of those 100% had need fully met. **Average percent of need met:** 100% (excluding resources awarded to replace EFC). **Average financial aid package:** $38,969 (excluding resources awarded to replace EFC).
**UNDERGRADUATE FINANCIAL AID (Fall 2014, est.)** 4,017 applied for aid; of those 69% were deemed to have need. 100% of undergraduates with need received aid; of those 100% had need fully met. **Average percent of need met:** 100% (excluding resources awarded to replace EFC). **Average financial aid package:** $39,693 (excluding resources awarded to replace EFC).
**GIFT AID (NEED-BASED) Total amount:** $99,241,000 (5% federal, 90% institutional, 5% external sources). **Receiving aid:** Freshmen: 36% (567); all full-time undergraduates: 35% (2,516). **Average award:** Freshmen: $37,376; Undergraduates:

$36,878. **Scholarships, grants, and awards:** Federal Pell, FSEOG, state, private, college/university gift aid from institutional funds.
**GIFT AID (NON-NEED-BASED) Total amount:** $1,552,000 (92% federal, 8% institutional). **Receiving aid:** Freshmen: 16% (250). Undergraduates: 11% (800). **Scholarships, grants, and awards by category:** Special characteristics: 150 awards ($4,028,151 total): children of faculty/staff. **ROTC:** Army, Naval cooperative, Air Force cooperative.
**LOANS Student loans:** $17,210,000 (46% need-based, 54% non-need-based). 39% of past graduating class borrowed through all loan programs. *Average indebtedness per student:* $22,464. **Average need-based loan:** Freshmen: $2755. Undergraduates: $4318. **Parent loans:** $10,700,000 (100% non-need-based). **Programs:** Federal Direct (Subsidized and Unsubsidized Stafford, PLUS), Perkins, Federal Nursing, alternative loans.
**WORK-STUDY Federal work-study:** Total amount: $6,600,000; 2,614 jobs averaging $2933.
**ATHLETIC AWARDS** Total amount: $7,785,000 (25% need-based, 75% non-need-based).
**APPLYING FOR FINANCIAL AID Required financial aid forms:** FAFSA, CSS Financial Aid PROFILE, federal income tax form(s). **Financial aid deadline:** 2/1. **Notification date:** 4/1. Students must reply by 5/1 or within 2 weeks of notification.
**CONTACT** Ms. Patricia A. McWade, Dean of Student Financial Services, Georgetown University, 37th and O Street, NW, Box 1252, Washington, DC 20057, 202-687-4547. *Fax:* 202-687-6542. *E-mail:* mcwadep@georgetown.edu. *Website:* http://www.georgetown.edu/.

# THE GEORGE WASHINGTON UNIVERSITY
### Washington, DC

| Tuition & fees: $50,435 | Average undergraduate aid package: $42,335 |
| --- | --- |

**ABOUT THE INSTITUTION** Independent, coed. **Awards:** certificates, associate, bachelor's, master's, and doctoral degrees. 81 undergraduate majors. **Total enrollment:** 25,613. Undergraduates: 10,740. Freshmen: 2,416. Federal methodology is used as a basis for awarding need-based institutional aid.
**UNDERGRADUATE EXPENSES for 2015–2016 Application fee:** $75. **Comprehensive fee:** $62,484 Includes full-time tuition ($50,367), mandatory fees ($68), and room and board ($12,050). Full-time tuition and fees vary according to student level. Room and board charges vary according to housing facility. **Part-time tuition:** $1430 per credit hour. **Part-time fees:** $2.25 per credit hour. Part-time tuition and fees vary according to course load. **Payment plan:** Guaranteed tuition.
**FRESHMAN FINANCIAL AID (Fall 2013)** 1,554 applied for aid; of those 74% were deemed to have need. 98% of freshmen with need received aid; of those 47% had need fully met. **Average percent of need met:** 89% (excluding resources awarded to replace EFC). **Average financial aid package:** $41,501 (excluding resources awarded to replace EFC). 20% of all full-time freshmen had no need and received non-need-based gift aid.
**UNDERGRADUATE FINANCIAL AID (Fall 2013)** 5,371 applied for aid; of those 84% were deemed to have need. 98% of undergraduates with need received aid; of those 55% had need fully met. **Average percent of need met:** 89% (excluding resources awarded to replace EFC). **Average financial aid package:** $42,335 (excluding resources awarded to replace EFC). 20% of all full-time undergraduates had no need and received non-need-based gift aid.
**GIFT AID (NEED-BASED) Total amount:** $142,369,336 (6% federal, 94% institutional). **Receiving aid:** Freshmen: 47% (1,107); all full-time undergraduates: 45% (4,291). **Average award:** Freshmen: $29,833; Undergraduates: $29,879. **Scholarships, grants, and awards:** Federal Pell, FSEOG, state, college/university gift aid from institutional funds.
**GIFT AID (NON-NEED-BASED) Total amount:** $26,183,727 (100% institutional). **Receiving aid:** Freshmen: 12% (290). Undergraduates: 13% (1,205). **Average award:** Freshmen: $18,307. Undergraduates: $18,780. **Scholarships, grants, and awards by category:** Academic interests/achievement: general academic interests/achievements. Creative arts/performance: general creative arts/performance. **Tuition waivers:** Full or partial for employees or children of employees. **ROTC:** Army cooperative, Naval, Air Force cooperative.

**LOANS Student loans:** $36,936,539 (74% need-based, 26% non-need-based). 49% of past graduating class borrowed through all loan programs. *Average indebtedness per student:* $31,337. **Average need-based loan:** Freshmen: $4986. Undergraduates: $5758. **Parent loans:** $20,790,300 (20% need-based, 80% non-need-based). **Programs:** Perkins.
**WORK-STUDY Federal work-study:** jobs available.
**ATHLETIC AWARDS** Total amount: $8,514,832 (20% need-based, 80% non-need-based).
**APPLYING FOR FINANCIAL AID Required financial aid forms:** FAFSA, CSS Financial Aid PROFILE. **Financial aid deadline:** 2/1. **Notification date:** Continuous beginning 3/24. Students must reply by 5/1.
**CONTACT** Dan Small, Associate Vice President for Financial Assistance, The George Washington University, 2121 I Street, NW, Rice Hall, Suite 301, Washington, DC 21044, 202-994-6620. *Fax:* 202-994-0906. *E-mail:* finaid@gwu.edu. *Website:* http://www.gwu.edu/.

# GEORGIA CHRISTIAN UNIVERSITY
### Atlanta, GA

**CONTACT** Financial Aid Office, Georgia Christian University, 6789 Peachtree Industrial Boulevard, Atlanta, GA 30360, 770-279-0507. *Website:* http://www.gcuniv.edu/.

# GEORGIA COLLEGE & STATE UNIVERSITY
### Milledgeville, GA

| Tuition & fees (GA res): $8960 | Average undergraduate aid package: $9534 |
| --- | --- |

**ABOUT THE INSTITUTION** State-supported, coed. **Awards:** certificates, bachelor's, master's, and doctoral degrees. 37 undergraduate majors. **Total enrollment:** 6,772. Undergraduates: 5,927. Freshmen: 1,465. Federal methodology is used as a basis for awarding need-based institutional aid.
**UNDERGRADUATE EXPENSES for 2015–2016 Application fee:** $40. **Tuition, state resident:** full-time $6970. **Tuition, nonresident:** full-time $25,318. **Required fees:** full-time $1990. Full-time tuition and fees vary according to course load, location, and program. Part-time tuition and fees vary according to course load, location, and program. **College room and board:** $9940; **Room only:** $5860. Room and board charges vary according to board plan and housing facility.
**FRESHMAN FINANCIAL AID (Fall 2013)** 1,261 applied for aid; of those 61% were deemed to have need. 99% of freshmen with need received aid. **Average percent of need met:** 25% (excluding resources awarded to replace EFC). **Average financial aid package:** $9516 (excluding resources awarded to replace EFC). 2% of all full-time freshmen had no need and received non-need-based gift aid.
**UNDERGRADUATE FINANCIAL AID (Fall 2013)** 4,258 applied for aid; of those 69% were deemed to have need. 98% of undergraduates with need received aid. **Average percent of need met:** 30% (excluding resources awarded to replace EFC). **Average financial aid package:** $9534 (excluding resources awarded to replace EFC). 2% of all full-time undergraduates had no need and received non-need-based gift aid.
**GIFT AID (NEED-BASED) Total amount:** $5,633,652 (97% federal, 3% institutional). **Receiving aid:** Freshmen: 19% (263); all full-time undergraduates: 22% (1,170). **Average award:** Freshmen: $4299; Undergraduates: $4346. **Scholarships, grants, and awards:** Federal Pell, FSEOG, state, college/university gift aid from institutional funds.
**GIFT AID (NON-NEED-BASED) Total amount:** $22,930,011 (94% state, 3% institutional, 3% external sources). **Receiving aid:** Freshmen: 52% (725). Undergraduates: 43% (2,243). **Average award:** Freshmen: $1771. Undergraduates: $1613. **Scholarships, grants, and awards by category:** Academic interests/achievement: biological sciences, business, computer science, education, humanities, international studies, physical sciences, social sciences. Creative arts/performance: art/fine arts, journalism/publications, music. Special achievements/activities: general special achievements/activities. Special characteristics: adult students, children of faculty/staff, general special characteristics, local/state students, out-of-state students,

public servants. **Tuition waivers:** Full or partial for employees or children of employees, senior citizens. **ROTC:** Army cooperative.
**LOANS Student loans:** $29,592,251 (31% need-based, 69% non-need-based). 51% of past graduating class borrowed through all loan programs. *Average indebtedness per student:* $21,919. **Average need-based loan:** Freshmen: $3435. Undergraduates: $4248. **Parent loans:** $3,706,523 (100% non-need-based). **Programs:** Federal Direct (Subsidized and Unsubsidized Stafford, PLUS), Perkins.
**WORK-STUDY Federal work-study:** jobs available.
**ATHLETIC AWARDS** Total amount: $555,117 (100% non-need-based).
**APPLYING FOR FINANCIAL AID Required financial aid form:** FAFSA. *Financial aid deadline (priority):* 3/1. *Notification date:* Continuous beginning 3/1. Students must reply within 2 weeks of notification.
**CONTACT** Ms. Cathy Crawley, Director of Financial Aid, Georgia College & State University, Campus Box 30, Milledgeville, GA 31061, 478-445-5149 or toll-free 800-342-0471. *Fax:* 478-445-0729. *E-mail:* cathy.crawley@gcsu.edu. *Website:* http://www.gcsu.edu/.

# GEORGIA GWINNETT COLLEGE
## Lawrenceville, GA

**CONTACT** Financial Aid Office, Georgia Gwinnett College, 1000 University Center Lane, Lawrenceville, GA 30043, 678-407-5000 or toll-free 877-704-4422. *Website:* http://www.ggc.edu/.

# GEORGIA INSTITUTE OF TECHNOLOGY
## Atlanta, GA

| Tuition & fees (GA res): $11,394 | Average undergraduate aid package: $11,566 |
|---|---|

**ABOUT THE INSTITUTION** State-supported, coed. **Awards:** bachelor's, master's, and doctoral degrees. 34 undergraduate majors. **Total enrollment:** 23,109. Undergraduates: 14,682. Freshmen: 2,809. Federal methodology is used as a basis for awarding need-based institutional aid.
**UNDERGRADUATE EXPENSES for 2015–2016 Application fee:** $75. **Tuition, state resident:** full-time $9002; part-time $2675 per term. **Tuition, nonresident:** full-time $28,306; part-time $8399 per term. **Required fees:** full-time $2392; $1196 per term or $1196 per term. Part-time tuition and fees vary according to course load. **College room and board:** $12,840; **Room only:** $8488. Room and board charges vary according to board plan and housing facility.
**FRESHMAN FINANCIAL AID (Fall 2013)** 2,204 applied for aid; of those 52% were deemed to have need. 97% of freshmen with need received aid; of those 33% had need fully met. **Average percent of need met:** 60% (excluding resources awarded to replace EFC). **Average financial aid package:** $12,900 (excluding resources awarded to replace EFC). 10% of all full-time freshmen had no need and received non-need-based gift aid.
**UNDERGRADUATE FINANCIAL AID (Fall 2013)** 9,371 applied for aid; of those 64% were deemed to have need. 96% of undergraduates with need received aid; of those 24% had need fully met. **Average percent of need met:** 50% (excluding resources awarded to replace EFC). **Average financial aid package:** $11,566 (excluding resources awarded to replace EFC). 7% of all full-time undergraduates had no need and received non-need-based gift aid.
**GIFT AID (NEED-BASED) Total amount:** $47,216,496 (24% federal, 44% state, 27% institutional, 5% external sources). **Receiving aid:** Freshmen: 40% (1,071); all full-time undergraduates: 39% (5,162). **Average award:** Freshmen: $11,168; Undergraduates: $9522. **Scholarships, grants, and awards:** Federal Pell, FSEOG, state, private, college/university gift aid from institutional funds, United Negro College Fund.
**GIFT AID (NON-NEED-BASED) Total amount:** $24,637,088 (79% state, 16% institutional, 5% external sources). **Receiving aid:** Freshmen: 32% (853). Undergraduates: 26% (3,468). **Average award:** Freshmen: $4393. Undergraduates: $4367. **Scholarships, grants, and awards by category:** Academic interests/achievement: 2,657 awards ($13,694,265 total): architecture, biological sciences, computer science, engineering/technologies, general academic interests/achievements, physical sciences. Special achievements/activities: 518 awards ($691,425 total): cheerleading/drum major, general special achievements/activities, leadership. Special charac-

teristics: 6,108 awards ($44,131,035 total): children with a deceased or disabled parent, local/state students, members of minority groups, out-of-state students, veterans, veterans' children. **Tuition waivers:** Full or partial for employees or children of employees, senior citizens. **ROTC:** Army, Naval, Air Force.
**LOANS Student loans:** $44,904,886 (83% need-based, 17% non-need-based). 43% of past graduating class borrowed through all loan programs. *Average indebtedness per student:* $24,891. **Average need-based loan:** Freshmen: $5545. Undergraduates: $6446. **Parent loans:** $23,671,995 (76% need-based, 24% non-need-based). **Programs:** Federal Direct (Subsidized and Unsubsidized Stafford, PLUS), Perkins, state, college/university.
**WORK-STUDY Federal work-study:** 386 jobs averaging $2191.
**ATHLETIC AWARDS** Total amount: $5,764,586 (45% need-based, 55% non-need-based).
**APPLYING FOR FINANCIAL AID Required financial aid forms:** FAFSA, institution's own form, CSS Financial Aid PROFILE. *Financial aid deadline:* 2/15. *Notification date:* 4/15. Students must reply by 5/1.
**CONTACT** Ms. Marie Mons, Director of Student Financial Planning and Services, Georgia Institute of Technology, 225 North Avenue, NW, Atlanta, GA 30332-0460, 404-894-4160. *Fax:* 404-894-7412. *E-mail:* marie.mons@finaid.gatech.edu. *Website:* http://www.gatech.edu/.

# GEORGIAN COURT UNIVERSITY
## Lakewood, NJ

| Tuition & fees: $30,998 | Average undergraduate aid package: $26,664 |
|---|---|

**ABOUT THE INSTITUTION** Independent Roman Catholic, coed. **Awards:** certificates, bachelor's, and master's degrees. 28 undergraduate majors. **Total enrollment:** 2,308. Undergraduates: 1,621. Freshmen: 230. Federal methodology is used as a basis for awarding need-based institutional aid.
**UNDERGRADUATE EXPENSES for 2015–2016 Application fee:** $40. **Comprehensive fee:** $41,594 includes full-time tuition ($29,566), mandatory fees ($1432), and room and board ($10,596). **Part-time tuition:** $676 per credit hour. **Part-time fees:** $358 per term. Part-time tuition and fees vary according to location.
**FRESHMAN FINANCIAL AID (Fall 2014, est.)** 221 applied for aid; of those 91% were deemed to have need. 100% of freshmen with need received aid; of those 36% had need fully met. **Average percent of need met:** 89% (excluding resources awarded to replace EFC). **Average financial aid package:** $28,891 (excluding resources awarded to replace EFC). 11% of all full-time freshmen had no need and received non-need-based gift aid.
**UNDERGRADUATE FINANCIAL AID (Fall 2014, est.)** 1,162 applied for aid; of those 93% were deemed to have need. 100% of undergraduates with need received aid; of those 31% had need fully met. **Average percent of need met:** 84% (excluding resources awarded to replace EFC). **Average financial aid package:** $26,664 (excluding resources awarded to replace EFC). 11% of all full-time undergraduates had no need and received non-need-based gift aid.
**GIFT AID (NEED-BASED) Total amount:** $19,492,668 (16% federal, 22% state, 62% institutional). **Receiving aid:** Freshmen: 86% (196); all full-time undergraduates: 79% (1,024). **Average award:** Freshmen: $21,704; Undergraduates: $17,870. **Scholarships, grants, and awards:** Federal Pell, FSEOG, state, private, college/university gift aid from institutional funds.
**GIFT AID (NON-NEED-BASED) Total amount:** $2,393,020 (1% federal, 99% institutional). **Receiving aid:** Freshmen: 9% (21). Undergraduates: 6% (75). **Average award:** Freshmen: $14,642. Undergraduates: $13,076. **Scholarships, grants, and awards by category:** Academic interests/achievement: biological sciences, business, education, English, general academic interests/achievements, health fields, mathematics, physical sciences. Creative arts/performance: art/fine arts, dance. Special achievements/activities: general special achievements/activities. Special characteristics: children of faculty/staff, local/state students, religious affiliation, veterans. **Tuition waivers:** Full or partial for employees or children of employees.
**LOANS Student loans:** $10,786,222 (73% need-based, 27% non-need-based). 90% of past graduating class borrowed through all loan programs. *Average indebtedness per student:* $40,551. **Average need-based loan:** Freshmen: $4771. Undergraduates: $6829. **Parent loans:** $1,486,268 (46% need-based, 54% non-need-based). **Programs:** Federal Direct (Subsidized and Unsubsidized Stafford, PLUS), state.

**WORK-STUDY** *Federal work-study:* Total amount: $192,442; jobs available. *State or other work-study/employment:* Total amount: $19,642 (8% need-based, 92% non-need-based). Part-time jobs available.

**ATHLETIC AWARDS** Total amount: $1,449,974 (59% need-based, 41% non-need-based).

**APPLYING FOR FINANCIAL AID** *Required financial aid form:* FAFSA. *Financial aid deadline:* 7/1 (priority: 4/15). *Notification date:* Continuous beginning 2/1. Students must reply within 2 weeks of notification.

**CONTACT** Office of Financial Aid, Georgian Court University, 900 Lakewood Avenue, Lakewood, NJ 08701-2697, 732-987-2254 or toll-free 800-458-8422. *Fax:* 732-987-2023. *E-mail:* financialaid@georgian.edu.

*Website:* http://www.georgian.edu/.

# GEORGIA REGENTS UNIVERSITY
## Augusta, GA

| Tuition & fees: N/R | Average undergraduate aid package: $2189 |
|---|---|

**ABOUT THE INSTITUTION** State-supported, coed. *Awards:* certificates, associate, bachelor's, master's, and doctoral degrees. 40 undergraduate majors. *Total enrollment:* 7,977. Undergraduates: 5,224. Freshmen: 745. Federal methodology is used as a basis for awarding need-based institutional aid.

**UNDERGRADUATE FINANCIAL AID (Fall 2014, est.)** 3,060 applied for aid; of those 78% were deemed to have need. 98% of undergraduates with need received aid; of those 9% had need fully met. *Average financial aid package:* $2189 (excluding resources awarded to replace EFC). 1% of all full-time undergraduates had no need and received non-need-based gift aid.

**GIFT AID (NEED-BASED)** *Total amount:* $10,390,806 (93% federal, 7% external sources). *Receiving aid:* All full-time undergraduates: 42% (1,697). *Average award:* Undergraduates: $2268. *Scholarships, grants, and awards:* Federal Pell, FSEOG, state, private, college/university gift aid from institutional funds, Federal Nursing.

**GIFT AID (NON-NEED-BASED)** *Total amount:* $7,348,909 (50% state, 40% institutional, 10% external sources). *Receiving aid:* Undergraduates: 5% (209). *Average award:* Undergraduates: $1809. *Scholarships, grants, and awards by category:* Academic interests/achievement: business, computer science, education, general academic interests/achievements, health fields, mathematics. *Creative arts/performance:* art/fine arts, music. *Special characteristics:* religious affiliation. *ROTC:* Army.

**LOANS** *Student loans:* $24,037,148 (44% need-based, 56% non-need-based). 19% of past graduating class borrowed through all loan programs. *Average indebtedness per student:* $4846. *Average need-based loan:* Undergraduates: $2039. *Parent loans:* $880,520 (100% need-based). *Programs:* Federal Direct (Subsidized and Unsubsidized Stafford, PLUS), Perkins, Federal Nursing, state, college/university.

**WORK-STUDY** *Federal work-study:* Total amount: $308,307; Jobs available.

**ATHLETIC AWARDS** Total amount: $746,760 (100% non-need-based).

**APPLYING FOR FINANCIAL AID** *Required financial aid form:* FAFSA. *Financial aid deadline:* 3/1. *Notification date:* Continuous beginning 3/1.

**CONTACT** Paula Stribling, Interim Director of Financial Aid, Georgia Regents University, 1120 Fifteenth Street, Fanning Hall, Augusta, GA 30912-7320, 706-729-2316 or toll-free 800-519-3388. *Fax:* 706-737-1777. *E-mail:* pstribling@gru.edu. *Website:* http://www.gru.edu/.

# GEORGIA SOUTHERN UNIVERSITY
## Statesboro, GA

| Tuition & fees (GA res): $7190 | Average undergraduate aid package: $9309 |
|---|---|

**ABOUT THE INSTITUTION** State-supported, coed. *Awards:* certificates, bachelor's, master's, and doctoral degrees. 80 undergraduate majors. *Total enrollment:* 20,517. Undergraduates: 18,004. Freshmen: 3,498. Federal methodology is used as a basis for awarding need-based institutional aid.

**UNDERGRADUATE EXPENSES** for 2015–2016 *Application fee:* $30. *Tuition, state resident:* full-time $5098; part-time $170 per credit hour. *Tuition, nonresident:* full-time $17,994; part-time $600 per credit hour. *Required fees:* full-time $2092; $1046 per term. Full-time tuition and fees vary according to course load, degree level, location, and program. Part-time tuition and fees vary according to course load, degree level, location, and program. *College room and board:* $9752; *Room only:* $6052. Room and board charges vary according to board plan and housing facility.

**FRESHMAN FINANCIAL AID (Fall 2013)** 3,366 applied for aid; of those 73% were deemed to have need. 98% of freshmen with need received aid; of those 12% had need fully met. *Average percent of need met:* 54% (excluding resources awarded to replace EFC). *Average financial aid package:* $9390 (excluding resources awarded to replace EFC). 2% of all full-time freshmen had no need and received non-need-based gift aid.

**UNDERGRADUATE FINANCIAL AID (Fall 2013)** 14,243 applied for aid; of those 77% were deemed to have need. 98% of undergraduates with need received aid; of those 8% had need fully met. *Average percent of need met:* 49% (excluding resources awarded to replace EFC). *Average financial aid package:* $9309 (excluding resources awarded to replace EFC). 1% of all full-time undergraduates had no need and received non-need-based gift aid.

**GIFT AID (NEED-BASED)** *Total amount:* $56,296,714 (56% federal, 41% state, 1% institutional, 2% external sources). *Receiving aid:* Freshmen: 60% (2,134); all full-time undergraduates: 57% (8,914). *Average award:* Freshmen: $6927; Undergraduates: $6347. *Scholarships, grants, and awards:* Federal Pell, FSEOG, state, private, college/university gift aid from institutional funds, Hope Scholarships, TEACH Grants.

**GIFT AID (NON-NEED-BASED)** *Total amount:* $11,246,837 (93% state, 4% institutional, 3% external sources). *Receiving aid:* Freshmen: 1% (39). Undergraduates: 1% (100). *Average award:* Freshmen: $1624. Undergraduates: $1775. *Scholarships, grants, and awards by category:* Academic interests/achievement: 616 awards ($945,125 total): biological sciences, business, communication, computer science, education, engineering/technologies, English, foreign languages, general academic interests/achievements, health fields, humanities, international studies, mathematics, military science, social sciences. *Creative arts/performance:* 65 awards ($65,430 total): art/fine arts, cinema/film/broadcasting, general creative arts/performance, music, theater/drama. *Special achievements/activities:* 155 awards ($201,200 total): cheerleading/drum major, community service, junior miss, leadership, memberships, religious involvement. *Special characteristics:* 31 awards ($81,950 total): adult students, children and siblings of alumni, children of public servants, first-generation college students, general special characteristics, handicapped students, married students, members of minority groups, religious affiliation. *Tuition waivers:* Full or partial for employees or children of employees, senior citizens. *ROTC:* Army.

**LOANS** *Student loans:* $83,252,007 (84% need-based, 16% non-need-based). 72% of past graduating class borrowed through all loan programs. *Average indebtedness per student:* $24,201. *Average need-based loan:* Freshmen: $4156. Undergraduates: $4765. *Parent loans:* $10,700,416 (75% need-based, 25% non-need-based). *Programs:* Federal Direct (Subsidized and Unsubsidized Stafford, PLUS), Perkins, state, alternative loans.

**WORK-STUDY** *Federal work-study:* 261 jobs averaging $1768.

**ATHLETIC AWARDS** Total amount: $3,969,388 (66% need-based, 34% non-need-based).

**APPLYING FOR FINANCIAL AID** *Required financial aid form:* FAFSA. *Financial aid deadline (priority):* 4/20. *Notification date:* Continuous beginning 4/20.

**CONTACT** Mrs. Elise Boyett, Associate Director of Financial Aid, Georgia Southern University, PO Box 8065, Statesboro, GA 30460-8065, 912-478-5413. *Fax:* 912-478-0573. *E-mail:* eboyett@georgiasouthern.edu. *Website:* http://www.georgiasouthern.edu/.

# GEORGIA SOUTHWESTERN STATE UNIVERSITY
### Americus, GA

| Tuition & fees (GA res): $6070 | Average undergraduate aid package: $9373 |
|---|---|

**ABOUT THE INSTITUTION** State-supported, coed. **Awards:** certificates, bachelor's, and master's degrees. 23 undergraduate majors. **Total enrollment:** 2,666. Undergraduates: 2,527. Freshmen: 392. Federal methodology is used as a basis for awarding need-based institutional aid.

**UNDERGRADUATE EXPENSES for 2015–2016 Application fee:** $25. **Tuition, state resident:** full-time $4740; part-time $158 per credit hour. **Tuition, nonresident:** full-time $17,246; part-time $574.87 per credit hour. **Required fees:** full-time $1330; $665 per term. Full-time tuition and fees vary according to course load and location. Part-time tuition and fees vary according to course load and location. **College room and board:** $8350; **Room only:** $4830. Room and board charges vary according to board plan and housing facility.

**FRESHMAN FINANCIAL AID (Fall 2014, est.)** 357 applied for aid; of those 79% were deemed to have need. 100% of freshmen with need received aid; of those 15% had need fully met. **Average percent of need met:** 64% (excluding resources awarded to replace EFC). **Average financial aid package:** $9950 (excluding resources awarded to replace EFC). 9% of all full-time freshmen had no need and received non-need-based gift aid.

**UNDERGRADUATE FINANCIAL AID (Fall 2014, est.)** 1,551 applied for aid; of those 85% were deemed to have need. 99% of undergraduates with need received aid; of those 10% had need fully met. **Average percent of need met:** 58% (excluding resources awarded to replace EFC). **Average financial aid package:** $9373 (excluding resources awarded to replace EFC). 6% of all full-time undergraduates had no need and received non-need-based gift aid.

**GIFT AID (NEED-BASED) Total amount:** $5,383,116 (100% federal). **Receiving aid:** Freshmen: 47% (183); all full-time undergraduates: 52% (904). **Average award:** Freshmen: $4839; Undergraduates: $4751. **Scholarships, grants, and awards:** Federal Pell, FSEOG, state, private, college/university gift aid from institutional funds.

**GIFT AID (NON-NEED-BASED) Total amount:** $3,420,348 (78% state, 18% institutional, 4% external sources). **Receiving aid:** Freshmen: 58% (223). Undergraduates: 35% (619). **Average award:** Freshmen: $1183. Undergraduates: $1444. **Scholarships, grants, and awards by category:** Academic interests/achievement: 144 awards ($264,526 total): general academic interests/achievements. Creative arts/performance: 49 awards ($38,433 total): art/fine arts, music, theater/drama. Special achievements/activities: leadership. Special characteristics: children and siblings of alumni, general special characteristics, local/state students.

**LOANS Student loans:** $14,506,329 (43% need-based, 57% non-need-based). 75% of past graduating class borrowed through all loan programs. **Average indebtedness per student:** $23,450. **Average need-based loan:** Freshmen: $3358. Undergraduates: $4205. **Parent loans:** $307,050 (100% non-need-based). **Programs:** Federal Direct (Subsidized and Unsubsidized Stafford, PLUS), Perkins, state.

**WORK-STUDY Federal work-study:** Total amount: $106,810; 52 jobs averaging $2054.

**ATHLETIC AWARDS** Total amount: $501,932 (100% non-need-based).

**APPLYING FOR FINANCIAL AID Required financial aid form:** FAFSA. **Financial aid deadline:** 6/15 (priority: 4/15). **Notification date:** Continuous beginning 5/1. Students must reply within 8 weeks of notification.

**CONTACT** Angela Bryant, Director of Financial Aid, Georgia Southwestern State University, 800 Georgia Southwestern State University Drive, Americus, GA 31709-4693, 229-928-1378 or toll-free 800-338-0082. *Fax:* 229-931-2061. *E-mail:* finaid@gsw.edu.
*Website:* http://www.gsw.edu/.

# GEORGIA STATE UNIVERSITY
### Atlanta, GA

| Tuition & fees (GA res): $10,240 | Average undergraduate aid package: $10,659 |
|---|---|

**ABOUT THE INSTITUTION** State-supported, coed. **Awards:** certificates, bachelor's, master's, and doctoral degrees. 49 undergraduate majors. **Total enrollment:** 32,542. Undergraduates: 25,315. Freshmen: 3,696. Federal methodology is used as a basis for awarding need-based institutional aid.

**UNDERGRADUATE EXPENSES for 2015–2016 Application fee:** $60. **Tuition, state resident:** full-time $8112; part-time $270.40 per credit hour. **Tuition, nonresident:** full-time $26,322; part-time $867 per credit hour. **Required fees:** full-time $2128; $1064 per term. Part-time tuition and fees vary according to course load. **College room and board:** $13,342; **Room only:** $9616. Room and board charges vary according to housing facility.

**FRESHMAN FINANCIAL AID (Fall 2013)** 3,246 applied for aid; of those 84% were deemed to have need. 98% of freshmen with need received aid; of those 10% had need fully met. **Average percent of need met:** 63% (excluding resources awarded to replace EFC). **Average financial aid package:** $12,138 (excluding resources awarded to replace EFC).

**UNDERGRADUATE FINANCIAL AID (Fall 2013)** 16,435 applied for aid; of those 88% were deemed to have need. 98% of undergraduates with need received aid; of those 7% had need fully met. **Average percent of need met:** 58% (excluding resources awarded to replace EFC). **Average financial aid package:** $10,659 (excluding resources awarded to replace EFC).

**GIFT AID (NEED-BASED) Total amount:** $61,519,974 (96% federal, 4% institutional). **Receiving aid:** Freshmen: 59% (2,003); all full-time undergraduates: 58% (10,624). **Average award:** Freshmen: $5058; Undergraduates: $4855. **Scholarships, grants, and awards:** Federal Pell, FSEOG, state, private, college/university gift aid from institutional funds, United Negro College Fund.

**GIFT AID (NON-NEED-BASED) Total amount:** $65,858,833 (93% state, 7% institutional). **Receiving aid:** Freshmen: 73% (2,456). Undergraduates: 73% (13,341). **Tuition waivers:** Full or partial for employees or children of employees, senior citizens. **ROTC:** Army, Naval cooperative, Air Force cooperative.

**LOANS Student loans:** $120,504,221 (46% need-based, 54% non-need-based). 73% of past graduating class borrowed through all loan programs. **Average indebtedness per student:** $27,295. **Parent loans:** $11,774,724 (100% non-need-based). **Programs:** Federal Direct (Subsidized and Unsubsidized Stafford, PLUS), Perkins, Federal Nursing, state.

**WORK-STUDY Federal work-study:** jobs available. **State or other work-study/employment:** Part-time jobs available.

**ATHLETIC AWARDS** Total amount: $225,900 (100% non-need-based).

**APPLYING FOR FINANCIAL AID Required financial aid form:** FAFSA. **Financial aid deadline:** 4/1. **Notification date:** Continuous beginning 3/1. Students must reply by 4/1 or within 3 weeks of notification.

**CONTACT** Louis Scott, Director of Student Financial Aid, Georgia State University, PO Box 4040, Atlanta, GA 30302, 404-413-2600. *Fax:* 404-413-2102. *E-mail:* onestopshop@gsu.edu.
*Website:* http://www.gsu.edu/.

# GETTYSBURG COLLEGE
### Gettysburg, PA

| Tuition & fees: $47,480 | Average undergraduate aid package: $37,087 |
|---|---|

**ABOUT THE INSTITUTION** Independent Evangelical Lutheran Church in America, coed. **Awards:** bachelor's degrees. 82 undergraduate majors. **Total enrollment:** 2,451. Undergraduates: 2,451. Freshmen: 720. Both federal and institutional methodology are used as a basis for awarding need-based institutional aid.

**UNDERGRADUATE EXPENSES for 2015–2016 Application fee:** $60. **Comprehensive fee:** $58,820 includes full-time tuition ($47,480) and room and board ($11,340). Room and board charges vary according to board plan and housing facility.

**FRESHMAN FINANCIAL AID (Fall 2014, est.)** 530 applied for aid; of those 82% were deemed to have need. 99% of freshmen with need received aid; of those 90% had need fully met. **Average percent of need met:** 90% (excluding resources awarded to replace EFC). **Average financial aid package:** $36,825 (excluding resources

awarded to replace EFC). 17% of all full-time freshmen had no need and received non-need-based gift aid.

**UNDERGRADUATE FINANCIAL AID (Fall 2014, est.)** 1,721 applied for aid; of those 86% were deemed to have need. 97% of undergraduates with need received aid; of those 90% had need fully met. *Average percent of need met:* 90% (excluding resources awarded to replace EFC). *Average financial aid package:* $37,087 (excluding resources awarded to replace EFC). 17% of all full-time undergraduates had no need and received non-need-based gift aid.

**GIFT AID (NEED-BASED)** *Total amount:* $48,541,620 (4% federal, 1% state, 93% institutional, 2% external sources). *Receiving aid:* Freshmen: 58% (421); all full-time undergraduates: 59% (1,423). *Average award:* Freshmen: $33,185; Undergraduates: $32,458. *Scholarships, grants, and awards:* Federal Pell, FSEOG, state, private, college/university gift aid from institutional funds.

**GIFT AID (NON-NEED-BASED)** *Total amount:* $6,653,159 (10% federal, 84% institutional, 6% external sources). *Receiving aid:* Freshmen: 30% (213). Undergraduates: 30% (739). *Average award:* Freshmen: $11,832. Undergraduates: $12,401. *Scholarships, grants, and awards by category:* Academic interests/achievement: 1,082 awards ($14,064,000 total): general academic interests/achievements. Creative arts/performance: 19 awards ($190,000 total): music. **Tuition waivers:** Full or partial for employees or children of employees. **ROTC:** Army cooperative.

**LOANS** *Student loans:* $10,581,743 (49% need-based, 51% non-need-based). 57% of past graduating class borrowed through all loan programs. *Average indebtedness per student:* $27,714. *Average need-based loan:* Freshmen: $3997. Undergraduates: $5019. *Parent loans:* $5,926,320 (100% need-based). *Programs:* Federal Direct (Subsidized and Unsubsidized Stafford, PLUS), Perkins, college/university.

**WORK-STUDY** *Federal work-study:* Total amount: $264,038; 300 jobs averaging $880. *State or other work-study/employment:* Total amount: $1,151,267 (100% non-need-based). 935 part-time jobs averaging $1231.

**APPLYING FOR FINANCIAL AID** *Required financial aid forms:* FAFSA, CSS Financial Aid PROFILE, federal income tax form(s), verification worksheet. *Financial aid deadline:* 2/1. *Notification date:* 3/27. Students must reply by 5/1.

**CONTACT** Christina Gormley, Director of Financial Aid, Gettysburg College, 300 North Washington Street, Gettysburg, PA 17325, 717-337-6620 or toll-free 800-431-0803. *Fax:* 717-337-8555. *E-mail:* finaid@gettysburg.edu. *Website:* http://www.gettysburg.edu/.

# GLENVILLE STATE COLLEGE
## Glenville, WV

| Tuition & fees: N/R | Average undergraduate aid package: $13,554 |
| --- | --- |

**ABOUT THE INSTITUTION** State-supported, coed. *Awards:* associate and bachelor's degrees. 32 undergraduate majors. *Total enrollment:* 1,850. Undergraduates: 1,850. Freshmen: 314. Federal methodology is used as a basis for awarding need-based institutional aid.

**FRESHMAN FINANCIAL AID (Fall 2014, est.)** 257 applied for aid; of those 88% were deemed to have need. 100% of freshmen with need received aid; of those 12% had need fully met. *Average percent of need met:* 73% (excluding resources awarded to replace EFC). *Average financial aid package:* $13,468 (excluding resources awarded to replace EFC). 5% of all full-time freshmen had no need and received non-need-based gift aid.

**UNDERGRADUATE FINANCIAL AID (Fall 2014, est.)** 948 applied for aid; of those 89% were deemed to have need. 99% of undergraduates with need received aid; of those 18% had need fully met. *Average percent of need met:* 74% (excluding resources awarded to replace EFC). *Average financial aid package:* $13,554 (excluding resources awarded to replace EFC). 5% of all full-time undergraduates had no need and received non-need-based gift aid.

**GIFT AID (NEED-BASED)** *Total amount:* $4,257,803 (71% federal, 28% state, 1% institutional). *Receiving aid:* Freshmen: 77% (203); all full-time undergraduates: 69% (720). *Average award:* Freshmen: $6281; Undergraduates: $6193. *Scholarships, grants, and awards:* Federal Pell, FSEOG, state, private, college/university gift aid from institutional funds.

**GIFT AID (NON-NEED-BASED)** *Total amount:* $1,475,963 (47% state, 32% institutional, 21% external sources). *Receiving aid:* Freshmen: 58% (154). Undergraduates: 49% (510). *Average award:* Freshmen: $2409. Undergraduates: $1967. *Scholarships, grants, and awards by category:* Academic interests/

achievement: 221 awards ($289,744 total): biological sciences, business, education, English, general academic interests/achievements, mathematics, social sciences. Creative arts/performance: 39 awards ($45,426 total): journalism/publications, music. Special achievements/activities: 3 awards ($4000 total): cheerleading/drum major. Special characteristics: 184 awards ($636,553 total): children of faculty/staff, first-generation college students, out-of-state students, veterans, veterans' children. **ROTC:** Army.

**LOANS** *Student loans:* $4,929,457 (46% need-based, 54% non-need-based). 76% of past graduating class borrowed through all loan programs. *Average indebtedness per student:* $27,932. *Average need-based loan:* Freshmen: $3174. Undergraduates: $3753. *Parent loans:* $461,588 (100% non-need-based). *Programs:* Federal Direct (Subsidized and Unsubsidized Stafford, PLUS), private loans.

**WORK-STUDY** *Federal work-study:* Total amount: $137,056; 134 jobs averaging $994. *State or other work-study/employment:* Total amount: $386,707 (100% non-need-based). 245 part-time jobs averaging $1772.

**ATHLETIC AWARDS** Total amount: $1,323,067 (100% non-need-based).

**APPLYING FOR FINANCIAL AID** *Required financial aid form:* FAFSA. *Financial aid deadline (priority):* 2/1. *Notification date:* Continuous beginning 3/1. Students must reply within 3 weeks of notification.

**CONTACT** Ms. Karen Lay, Director of Financial Aid, Glenville State College, 200 High Street, Glenville, WV 26351-1200, 304-462-4103 Ext. 5 or toll-free 800-924-2010. *Fax:* 304-462-4407. *E-mail:* karen.lay@glenville.edu. *Website:* http://www.glenville.edu/.

# GLOBE INSTITUTE OF TECHNOLOGY
## New York, NY

**CONTACT** Office of Admissions, Globe Institute of Technology, 291 Broadway, 2nd Floor, New York, NY 10007, 212-349-4330 or toll-free 888-51-GLOBE (in-state), 800-51-GLOBE (out-of-state). *Fax:* 212-227-5920. *E-mail:* admission@globe.edu. *Website:* http://www.globe.edu/.

# GLOBE UNIVERSITY–APPLETON
## Grand Chute, WI

**CONTACT** Office of Financial Aid, Globe University–Appleton, 5045 West Grande Market Drive, Grand Chute, MN 54913, 920-384-1100. *Fax:* 920-364-1101. *Website:* http://www.globeuniversity.edu/.

# GLOBE UNIVERSITY–EAU CLAIRE
## Eau Claire, WI

**CONTACT** Office of Financial Aid, Globe University–Eau Claire, 4955 Bullis Farm Road, Eau Claire, WI 54701-5168, 715-855-6600 or toll-free 877-303-6060 (in-state), 377-303-6060 (out-of-state). *Fax:* 715-855-6601. *Website:* http://www.globeuniversity.edu/.

# GLOBE UNIVERSITY–GREEN BAY
## Bellevue, WI

**CONTACT** Office of Financial Aid, Globe University–Green Bay, 2620 Development Drive, Bellevue, WI 54311, 920-264-1600. *Fax:* 920-264-1601. *Website:* http://www.globeuniversity.edu/.

# GLOBE UNIVERSITY–LA CROSSE
## Onalaska, WI

**CONTACT** Office of Financial Aid, Globe University–La Crosse, 2651 Midwest Drive, Onalaska, WI 54650, 608-779-2600. *Fax:* 608-779-2601. *Website:* http://www.globeuniversity.edu/.

# GLOBE UNIVERSITY–MADISON EAST
## Madison, WI

**CONTACT** Office of Financial Aid, Globe University–Madison East, 4901 Eastpark Boulevard, Madison, WI 53718, 608-216-9400. *Fax:* 608-216-9401. *Website:* http://www.globeuniversity.edu/.

# GLOBE UNIVERSITY–MADISON WEST
## Middleton, WI

**CONTACT** Office of Financial Aid, Globe University–Madison West, 1345 Deming Way, Middleton, WI 53562, 608-830-6900. *Fax:* 608-830-6901. *Website:* http://www.globeuniversity.edu/.

# GLOBE UNIVERSITY–MINNEAPOLIS
## Minneapolis, MN

**CONTACT** Office of Financial Aid, Globe University–Minneapolis, 80 South 8th Street, Suite 51, Minneapolis, MN 55402, 612-455-3000. *Fax:* 612-455-3001. *Website:* http://www.globeuniversity.edu/.

# GLOBE UNIVERSITY–MOORHEAD
## Moorhead, MN

**CONTACT** Office of Financial Aid, Globe University–Moorhead, 2777 34th Street South, Moorhead , MN 56560, 218-422-1000. *Fax:* 218-422-1001. *Website:* http://www.globeuniversity.edu/.

# GLOBE UNIVERSITY–SIOUX FALLS
## Sioux Falls, SD

**CONTACT** Office of Financial Aid, Globe University–Sioux Falls, 5101 South Broadband Lane, Sioux Falls, SD 57108-2208, 605-977-0705 or toll-free 866-437-0705. *Fax:* 605-977-0784. *Website:* http://www.globeuniversity.edu/.

# GLOBE UNIVERSITY–WAUSAU
## Rothschild, WI

**CONTACT** Office of Financial Aid, Globe University–Wausau, 1480 Country Road XX, Rothschild, WI 54474, 715-301-1300. *Fax:* 715-301-1301. *Website:* http://www.globeuniversity.edu/.

# GLOBE UNIVERSITY–WOODBURY
## Woodbury, MN

**CONTACT** Office of Financial Aid, Globe University–Woodbury, 8089 Globe Drive, Woodbury, MN 55125, 651-730-5100 or toll-free 800-231-0660. *Fax:* 651-730-5151. *Website:* http://www.globeuniversity.edu/.

# GODDARD COLLEGE
## Plainfield, VT

| Tuition & fees: $14,930 | Average undergraduate aid package: $8467 |
| --- | --- |

**ABOUT THE INSTITUTION** Independent, coed. *Awards:* bachelor's and master's degrees. 51 undergraduate majors. *Total enrollment:* 538. Undergraduates: 191. Freshmen: 5. Federal methodology is used as a basis for awarding need-based institutional aid.

**UNDERGRADUATE EXPENSES for 2015–2016** *Application fee:* $40. *Comprehensive fee:* $16,418 includes full-time tuition ($14,738), mandatory fees ($192), and room and board ($1488). Full-time tuition and fees vary according to course load, location, program, and reciprocity agreements. Room and board charges vary according to location. Part-time tuition and fees vary according to program.

**FRESHMAN FINANCIAL AID (Fall 2013)** 2 applied for aid; of those 50% were deemed to have need. 100% of freshmen with need received aid. *Average percent of need met:* 9% (excluding resources awarded to replace EFC). *Average financial aid package:* $5258 (excluding resources awarded to replace EFC).

**UNDERGRADUATE FINANCIAL AID (Fall 2013)** 237 applied for aid; of those 100% were deemed to have need. 98% of undergraduates with need received aid; of those 1% had need fully met. *Average percent of need met:* 36% (excluding resources awarded to replace EFC). *Average financial aid package:* $8467 (excluding resources awarded to replace EFC). 3% of all full-time undergraduates had no need and received non-need-based gift aid.

**GIFT AID (NEED-BASED)** *Total amount:* $788,099 (80% federal, 8% state, 10% institutional, 2% external sources). *Receiving aid:* Freshmen: 33% (1); all full-time undergraduates: 60% (165). *Average award:* Freshmen: $3508; Undergraduates: $4755. *Scholarships, grants, and awards:* Federal Pell, FSEOG, state, private, college/university gift aid from institutional funds.

**GIFT AID (NON-NEED-BASED)** *Total amount:* $20,794 (100% institutional). *Receiving aid:* Undergraduates: 12% (34). *Average award:* Undergraduates: $666. *Scholarships, grants, and awards by category:* Creative arts/performance: creative writing. *Tuition waivers:* Full or partial for employees or children of employees.

**LOANS** *Student loans:* $1,805,132 (96% need-based, 4% non-need-based). 77% of past graduating class borrowed through all loan programs. *Average indebtedness per student:* $22,888. *Average need-based loan:* Freshmen: $1750. Undergraduates: $4555. *Parent loans:* $42,277 (83% need-based, 17% non-need-based). *Programs:* Federal Direct (Subsidized and Unsubsidized Stafford, PLUS), Perkins.

**APPLYING FOR FINANCIAL AID** *Required financial aid form:* FAFSA. *Financial aid deadline:* Continuous. *Notification date:* Continuous. Students must reply within 2 weeks of notification.

**CONTACT** Shannon Trainor, Assistant Director of Financial Aid, Goddard College, 123 Pitkin Road, Plainfield, VT 05667, 802-454-8311 Ext. 303 or toll-free 800-906-8312. *Fax:* 802-322-1000. *E-mail:* shannon.trainor@goddard.edu. *Website:* http://www.goddard.edu/.

# GOD'S BIBLE SCHOOL AND COLLEGE
## Cincinnati, OH

**CONTACT** Mrs. Lori Waggoner, Financial Aid Director, God's Bible School and College, 1810 Young Street, Cincinnati, OH 45202-6899, 513-721-7944 Ext. 205 or toll-free 800-486-4637. *Fax:* 513-721-1357. *E-mail:* lwaggoner@gbs.edu. *Website:* http://www.gbs.edu/.

# GOLDEN GATE UNIVERSITY
## San Francisco, CA

| Tuition & fees: N/R | Average undergraduate aid package: $10,350 |
| --- | --- |

**ABOUT THE INSTITUTION** Independent, coed. 8 undergraduate majors. Federal methodology is used as a basis for awarding need-based institutional aid.

**UNDERGRADUATE FINANCIAL AID (Fall 2013)** 299 applied for aid; of those 80% were deemed to have need. 100% of undergraduates with need received aid; of those 21% had need fully met. **Average percent of need met:** 20% (excluding resources awarded to replace EFC). **Average financial aid package:** $10,350 (excluding resources awarded to replace EFC). 12% of all full-time undergraduates had no need and received non-need-based gift aid.

**GIFT AID (NEED-BASED)** **Total amount:** $148,521 (45% federal, 38% institutional, 17% external sources). **Receiving aid:** All full-time undergraduates: 52% (205). **Average award:** Undergraduates: $3750. **Scholarships, grants, and awards:** Federal Pell, FSEOG, state, private, college/university gift aid from institutional funds.

**GIFT AID (NON-NEED-BASED)** **Total amount:** $842,702 (100% institutional). **Receiving aid:** Undergraduates: 41% (162). **Average award:** Undergraduates: $3750. **Scholarships, grants, and awards by category:** Academic interests/achievement: business, computer science, general academic interests/achievements, international studies. Special achievements/activities: community service, leadership. Special characteristics: adult students, children and siblings of alumni, children of faculty/staff, first-generation college students, general special characteristics, international students, members of minority groups, previous college experience, veterans.

**LOANS** **Student loans:** $4,883,731 (72% need-based, 28% non-need-based). **Average need-based loan:** Undergraduates: $5500. **Parent loans:** $25,000 (100% need-based). **Programs:** Federal Direct (Subsidized and Unsubsidized Stafford, PLUS), Perkins.

**WORK-STUDY** **Federal work-study:** 18 jobs averaging $5000.

**APPLYING FOR FINANCIAL AID** **Required financial aid forms:** FAFSA, institution's own form. **Financial aid deadline:** Continuous. **Notification date:** Continuous beginning 4/1. Students must reply within 3 weeks of notification.

**CONTACT** Kathleen Kelly, Interim Director of Financial Services, Golden Gate University, 536 Mission Street, San Francisco, CA 94105-2968, 415-442-7297 or toll-free 800-448-3381. Fax: 415-442-7819. E-mail: kkelly@ggu.edu. Website: http://www.ggu.edu/.

# GOLDEY-BEACOM COLLEGE
## Wilmington, DE

**CONTACT** Jane H. Lysle, Dean of Enrollment Management, Goldey-Beacom College, 4701 Limestone Road, Wilmington, DE 19808-1999, 302-225-6274 or toll-free 800-833-4877. Fax: 302-998-8631. E-mail: lyslej@gbc.edu. Website: http://www.gbc.edu/.

# GOLDFARB SCHOOL OF NURSING AT BARNES-JEWISH COLLEGE
## St. Louis, MO

| Tuition & fees: N/R | Average undergraduate aid package: N/A |
| --- | --- |

**ABOUT THE INSTITUTION** Independent, coed, primarily women. **Awards:** certificates, bachelor's, master's, and doctoral degrees. 1 undergraduate major. **Total enrollment:** 752. Undergraduates: 630. Federal methodology is used as a basis for awarding need-based institutional aid.

**UNDERGRADUATE EXPENSES** for 2015–2016 **Application fee:** $50. **Tuition:** part-time $698 per credit hour. Full-time tuition and fees vary according to course load and degree level. Part-time tuition and fees vary according to course load and degree level.

**GIFT AID (NEED-BASED)** **Total amount:** $1,245,000 (72% federal, 21% state, 7% external sources). **Scholarships, grants, and awards:** Federal Pell, FSEOG, state, private, college/university gift aid from institutional funds.

**GIFT AID (NON-NEED-BASED)** **Total amount:** $429,000 (100% institutional). **Scholarships, grants, and awards by category:** Academic interests/achievement: general academic interests/achievements.

**LOANS** **Student loans:** $9,829,089 (36% need-based, 64% non-need-based). **Parent loans:** $721,584 (100% non-need-based). **Programs:** Federal Direct (Subsidized and Unsubsidized Stafford, PLUS).

**WORK-STUDY** **Federal work-study:** 19 jobs averaging $1289.

**APPLYING FOR FINANCIAL AID** **Required financial aid forms:** FAFSA, institution's own form. **Financial aid deadline (priority):** 4/1. **Notification date:** Continuous beginning 4/1. Students must reply within 2 weeks of notification.

**CONTACT** Jason Crowe, Director of Financial Aid, Goldfarb School of Nursing at Barnes-Jewish College, 4483 Duncan, St. Louis, MO 63110-1091, 314-454-7770 or toll-free 800-832-9009. E-mail: jcrowe@bjc.org. Website: http://www.barnesjewishcollege.edu/.

# GONZAGA UNIVERSITY
## Spokane, WA

| Tuition & fees: $37,990 | Average undergraduate aid package: $25,554 |
| --- | --- |

**ABOUT THE INSTITUTION** Independent Roman Catholic, coed. **Awards:** bachelor's, master's, and doctoral degrees. 57 undergraduate majors. **Total enrollment:** 7,352. Undergraduates: 4,837. Freshmen: 1,048. Federal methodology is used as a basis for awarding need-based institutional aid.

**UNDERGRADUATE EXPENSES** for 2015–2016 **Application fee:** $50. **Comprehensive fee:** $48,825 includes full-time tuition ($37,480), mandatory fees ($510), and room and board ($10,835). **College room only:** $5565. Full-time tuition and fees vary according to course load, location, program, reciprocity agreements, and student level. Room and board charges vary according to board plan, housing facility, and location. **Part-time tuition:** $1055 per credit. **Part-time fees:** $200 per term. Part-time tuition and fees vary according to course load, location, program, reciprocity agreements, and student level.

**FRESHMAN FINANCIAL AID (Fall 2013)** 1,055 applied for aid; of those 74% were deemed to have need. 100% of freshmen with need received aid; of those 28% had need fully met. **Average percent of need met:** 81% (excluding resources awarded to replace EFC). **Average financial aid package:** $24,846 (excluding resources awarded to replace EFC). 34% of all full-time freshmen had no need and received non-need-based gift aid.

**UNDERGRADUATE FINANCIAL AID (Fall 2013)** 3,443 applied for aid; of those 80% were deemed to have need. 100% of undergraduates with need received aid; of those 27% had need fully met. **Average percent of need met:** 80% (excluding resources awarded to replace EFC). **Average financial aid package:** $25,554 (excluding resources awarded to replace EFC). 38% of all full-time undergraduates had no need and received non-need-based gift aid.

**GIFT AID (NEED-BASED)** **Total amount:** $39,908,375 (10% federal, 8% state, 78% institutional, 4% external sources). **Receiving aid:** Freshmen: 63% (785); all full-time undergraduates: 57% (2,754). **Average award:** Freshmen: $19,339; Undergraduates: $19,305. **Scholarships, grants, and awards:** Federal Pell, FSEOG, state, private, college/university gift aid from institutional funds, Federal Nursing.

**GIFT AID (NON-NEED-BASED)** **Total amount:** $38,298,364 (99% institutional, 1% external sources). **Receiving aid:** Freshmen: 14% (171). Undergraduates: 11% (536). **Average award:** Freshmen: $11,885. Undergraduates: $12,083. **Scholarships, grants, and awards by category:** Academic interests/achievement: 141 awards ($409,031 total): business, engineering/technologies, military science. Creative arts/performance: 110 awards ($182,280 total): debating, music. Special achievements/activities: 168 awards ($576,336 total): leadership, memberships. Special characteristics: 393 awards ($3,194,227 total): children and siblings of alumni, children of faculty/staff, international students, members of minority groups, siblings of current students. **Tuition waivers:** Full or partial for employees or children of employees. **ROTC:** Army.

**LOANS** **Student loans:** $32,699,793 (70% need-based, 30% non-need-based). 60% of past graduating class borrowed through all loan programs. **Average indebtedness per student:** $29,513. **Average need-based loan:** Freshmen: $4795. Undergrad-

uates: $5595. **Parent loans:** $8,094,721 (81% need-based, 19% non-need-based).
**Programs:** Federal Direct (Subsidized and Unsubsidized Stafford, PLUS), Perkins, Federal Nursing, state, college/university.

**WORK-STUDY** *Federal work-study:* 461 jobs averaging $2612. **State or other work-study/employment:** Total amount: $638,224 (100% need-based). 429 part-time jobs averaging $4086.

**ATHLETIC AWARDS** Total amount: $4,120,564 (26% need-based, 74% non-need-based).

**APPLYING FOR FINANCIAL AID** *Required financial aid form:* FAFSA. **Financial aid deadline (priority):** 2/1. **Notification date:** Continuous beginning 3/1. Students must reply by 5/1 or within 3 weeks of notification.

**CONTACT** James White, Dean of Student Financial Services, Gonzaga University, 502 East Boone Avenue, Spokane, WA 99258-0072, 509-313-6568 or toll-free 800-322-2584 Ext. 6572. *Fax:* 509-313-5816. *E-mail:* whitej@gonzaga.edu. *Website:* http://www.gonzaga.edu/.

# GORDON COLLEGE
## Wenham, MA

| Tuition & fees: $34,390 | Average undergraduate aid package: $22,562 |
|---|---|

**ABOUT THE INSTITUTION** Independent nondenominational, coed. **Awards:** bachelor's and master's degrees. 36 undergraduate majors. **Total enrollment:** 2,079. Undergraduates: 1,736. Freshmen: 402. Federal methodology is used as a basis for awarding need-based institutional aid.

**UNDERGRADUATE EXPENSES** for 2015–2016 *Application fee:* $50. **Comprehensive fee:** $44,320 includes full-time tuition ($32,930), mandatory fees ($1460), and room and board ($9930). **College room only:** $6560. Full-time tuition and fees vary according to course load and program. Room and board charges vary according to board plan and housing facility. **Part-time tuition:** $1165 per credit. Part-time tuition and fees vary according to course load and program.

**FRESHMAN FINANCIAL AID (Fall 2014, est.)** 353 applied for aid; of those 83% were deemed to have need. 100% of freshmen with need received aid; of those 17% had need fully met. **Average percent of need met:** 69% (excluding resources awarded to replace EFC). **Average financial aid package:** $23,043 (excluding resources awarded to replace EFC). 26% of all full-time freshmen had no need and received non-need-based gift aid.

**UNDERGRADUATE FINANCIAL AID (Fall 2014, est.)** 1,305 applied for aid; of those 87% were deemed to have need. 100% of undergraduates with need received aid; of those 16% had need fully met. **Average percent of need met:** 68% (excluding resources awarded to replace EFC). **Average financial aid package:** $22,562 (excluding resources awarded to replace EFC). 28% of all full-time undergraduates had no need and received non-need-based gift aid.

**GIFT AID (NEED-BASED) Total amount:** $20,803,254 (9% federal, 1% state, 78% institutional, 12% external sources). **Receiving aid:** Freshmen: 72% (294); all full-time undergraduates: 70% (1,132). **Average award:** Freshmen: $19,433; Undergraduates: $17,663. **Scholarships, grants, and awards:** Federal Pell, FSEOG, state, private, college/university gift aid from institutional funds.

**GIFT AID (NON-NEED-BASED) Total amount:** $8,108,083 (85% institutional, 15% external sources). **Receiving aid:** Freshmen: 10% (40). Undergraduates: 8% (126). **Average award:** Freshmen: $13,045. Undergraduates: $13,460. **Scholarships, grants, and awards by category:** Academic interests/achievement: 1,389 awards ($14,712,496 total): general academic interests/achievements. Creative arts/performance: 112 awards ($315,694 total): art/fine arts, music, theater/drama. Special achievements/activities: 149 awards ($1,590,971 total): leadership. Special characteristics: 400 awards ($3,323,395 total): children and siblings of alumni, children of faculty/staff, international students, relatives of clergy, veterans, veterans' children. **Tuition waivers:** Full or partial for employees or children of employees. **ROTC:** Army cooperative.

**LOANS Student loans:** $13,894,042 (70% need-based, 30% non-need-based). 84% of past graduating class borrowed through all loan programs. *Average indebtedness per student:* $38,456. **Average need-based loan:** Freshmen: $3634. Undergraduates: $4826. **Parent loans:** $4,008,928 (54% need-based, 46% non-need-based). **Programs:** Federal Direct (Subsidized and Unsubsidized Stafford, PLUS), Perkins, state.

**WORK-STUDY** *Federal work-study:* Total amount: $240,542; 488 jobs averaging $504.

**APPLYING FOR FINANCIAL AID** *Required financial aid form:* FAFSA. **Financial aid deadline (priority):** 3/1. **Notification date:** Continuous beginning 2/15. Students must reply by 5/1 or within 2 weeks of notification.

**CONTACT** Daniel O'Connell, Senior Director of Student Financial Services, Gordon College, 255 Grapevine Road, Wenham, MA 01984-1899, 978-867-4246 or toll-free 866-464-6736. *Fax:* 978-867-4657. *E-mail:* daniel.oconnell@gordon.edu. *Website:* http://www.gordon.edu/.

# GOSHEN COLLEGE
## Goshen, IN

| Tuition & fees: $30,590 | Average undergraduate aid package: $24,844 |
|---|---|

**ABOUT THE INSTITUTION** Independent Mennonite, coed. **Awards:** bachelor's and master's degrees. 38 undergraduate majors. **Total enrollment:** 842. Undergraduates: 774. Freshmen: 159. Federal methodology is used as a basis for awarding need-based institutional aid.

**UNDERGRADUATE EXPENSES** for 2015–2016 *Application fee:* $25. **Comprehensive fee:** $40,575 includes full-time tuition ($30,590) and room and board ($9985). **College room only:** $5350. Full-time tuition and fees vary according to degree level and program. Room and board charges vary according to board plan and housing facility. **Part-time tuition:** $1250 per credit hour. Part-time tuition and fees vary according to course load, degree level, and program.

**FRESHMAN FINANCIAL AID (Fall 2014, est.)** 138 applied for aid; of those 89% were deemed to have need. 100% of freshmen with need received aid; of those 24% had need fully met. **Average percent of need met:** 82% (excluding resources awarded to replace EFC). **Average financial aid package:** $25,615 (excluding resources awarded to replace EFC). 22% of all full-time freshmen had no need and received non-need-based gift aid.

**UNDERGRADUATE FINANCIAL AID (Fall 2014, est.)** 541 applied for aid; of those 91% were deemed to have need. 100% of undergraduates with need received aid; of those 20% had need fully met. **Average percent of need met:** 82% (excluding resources awarded to replace EFC). **Average financial aid package:** $24,844 (excluding resources awarded to replace EFC). 26% of all full-time undergraduates had no need and received non-need-based gift aid.

**GIFT AID (NEED-BASED) Total amount:** $8,688,397 (16% federal, 11% state, 57% institutional, 16% external sources). **Receiving aid:** Freshmen: 77% (123); all full-time undergraduates: 71% (481). **Average award:** Freshmen: $22,070; Undergraduates: $20,195. **Scholarships, grants, and awards:** Federal Pell, FSEOG, state, private, college/university gift aid from institutional funds.

**GIFT AID (NON-NEED-BASED) Total amount:** $3,279,326 (1% state, 79% institutional, 20% external sources). **Receiving aid:** Freshmen: 15% (24). Undergraduates: 11% (78). **Average award:** Freshmen: $15,804. Undergraduates: $13,569. **Scholarships, grants, and awards by category:** Academic interests/achievement: business, communication, education, general academic interests/achievements. Creative arts/performance: music, theater/drama. Special achievements/activities: community service, junior miss. Special characteristics: children of educators, children of faculty/staff, ethnic background, international students, members of minority groups. **Tuition waivers:** Full or partial for employees or children of employees.

**LOANS Student loans:** $4,436,022 (76% need-based, 24% non-need-based). 73% of past graduating class borrowed through all loan programs. *Average indebtedness per student:* $26,586. **Average need-based loan:** Freshmen: $3941. Undergraduates: $5498. **Parent loans:** $391,330 (52% need-based, 48% non-need-based). **Programs:** Federal Direct (Subsidized and Unsubsidized Stafford, PLUS), Perkins, Federal Nursing.

**WORK-STUDY** *Federal work-study:* Total amount: $321,766; 282 jobs averaging $1090. **State or other work-study/employment:** Total amount: $85,800 (100% non-need-based). 49 part-time jobs averaging $1678.

**ATHLETIC AWARDS** Total amount: $1,383,934 (64% need-based, 36% non-need-based).

**APPLYING FOR FINANCIAL AID** *Required financial aid form:* FAFSA. **Financial aid deadline (priority):** 3/1. **Notification date:** Continuous beginning 2/1. Students must reply by 5/1 or within 2 weeks of notification.

**CONTACT** Mr. Joel D. Short, Director of Student Financial Aid, Goshen College, 1700 South Main Street, Goshen, IN 46526-4794, 574-535-7525 or toll-free 800-348-7422. *Fax:* 574-535-7654. *E-mail:* joelds@goshen.edu.
*Website:* http://www.goshen.edu/.

# GOUCHER COLLEGE
## Baltimore, MD

| Tuition & fees: $40,558 | Average undergraduate aid package: $31,019 |
|---|---|

**ABOUT THE INSTITUTION** Independent, coed. *Awards:* certificates, bachelor's, and master's degrees. 33 undergraduate majors. *Total enrollment:* 2,114. Undergraduates: 1,471. Freshmen: 403. Both federal and institutional methodology are used as a basis for awarding need-based institutional aid.
**UNDERGRADUATE EXPENSES for 2015–2016** *Application fee:* $55. *Comprehensive fee:* $52,040 includes full-time tuition ($39,808), mandatory fees ($750), and room and board ($11,482). *College room only:* $6798. Room and board charges vary according to board plan and housing facility. *Part-time tuition:* $1327 per credit hour. *Payment plan:* Tuition prepayment.
**FRESHMAN FINANCIAL AID (Fall 2014, est.)** 342 applied for aid; of those 84% were deemed to have need. 100% of freshmen with need received aid; of those 21% had need fully met. *Average percent of need met:* 79% (excluding resources awarded to replace EFC). *Average financial aid package:* $31,849 (excluding resources awarded to replace EFC). 26% of all full-time freshmen had no need and received non-need-based gift aid.
**UNDERGRADUATE FINANCIAL AID (Fall 2014, est.)** 1,040 applied for aid; of those 89% were deemed to have need. 100% of undergraduates with need received aid; of those 20% had need fully met. *Average percent of need met:* 61% (excluding resources awarded to replace EFC). *Average financial aid package:* $31,019 (excluding resources awarded to replace EFC). 24% of all full-time undergraduates had no need and received non-need-based gift aid.
**GIFT AID (NEED-BASED)** *Total amount:* $25,406,193 (8% federal, 3% state, 86% institutional, 3% external sources). *Receiving aid:* Freshmen: 71% (286); all full-time undergraduates: 65% (916). *Average award:* Freshmen: $28,191; Undergraduates: $26,977. *Scholarships, grants, and awards:* Federal Pell, FSEOG, state, private, college/university gift aid from institutional funds.
**GIFT AID (NON-NEED-BASED)** *Total amount:* $6,937,473 (91% institutional, 9% external sources). *Receiving aid:* Freshmen: 11% (45). Undergraduates: 8% (108). *Average award:* Freshmen: $16,099. Undergraduates: $15,740. *Scholarships, grants, and awards by category: Creative arts/performance:* 14 awards ($135,000 total): art/fine arts, dance, music, performing arts, theater/drama. *Tuition waivers:* Full or partial for employees or children of employees. *ROTC:* Army cooperative, Air Force cooperative.
**LOANS** *Student loans:* $8,672,075 (71% need-based, 29% non-need-based). 57% of past graduating class borrowed through all loan programs. *Average indebtedness per student:* $25,580. *Average need-based loan:* Freshmen: $3485. Undergraduates: $4609. *Parent loans:* $2,700,799 (42% need-based, 58% non-need-based). *Programs:* Federal Direct (Subsidized and Unsubsidized Stafford, PLUS), Perkins, college/university.
**WORK-STUDY** *Federal work-study:* Total amount: $485,785; 418 jobs averaging $1095. *State or other work-study/employment:* Part-time jobs available.
**APPLYING FOR FINANCIAL AID** *Required financial aid forms:* FAFSA, CSS Financial Aid PROFILE, noncustodial (divorced/separated) parent's statement. *Financial aid deadline (priority):* 2/1. *Notification date:* 4/1. Students must reply by 5/1 or within 2 weeks of notification.
**CONTACT** Stephanie Bender, Director of Student Financial Aid, Goucher College, 1021 Dulaney Valley Road, Baltimore, MD 21204-2794, 410-337-6141 or toll-free 800-468-2437. *Fax:* 410-337-6504.
*Website:* http://www.goucher.edu/.

# GOVERNORS STATE UNIVERSITY
## University Park, IL

| Tuition & fees (IL res): $9386 | Average undergraduate aid package: N/A |
|---|---|

**ABOUT THE INSTITUTION** State-supported, coed. *Awards:* certificates, bachelor's, master's, and doctoral degrees. 30 undergraduate majors. *Total enrollment:* 5,776. Undergraduates: 3,585. Freshmen: 160. Federal methodology is used as a basis for awarding need-based institutional aid.
**UNDERGRADUATE EXPENSES for 2015–2016** *Application fee:* $25. *Tuition, state resident:* full-time $7650; part-time $255 per credit hour. *Tuition, nonresident:* full-time $15,300; part-time $510 per credit hour. *Required fees:* full-time $1736; $49 per credit hour or $133 per term. Full-time tuition and fees vary according to course load, degree level, reciprocity agreements, and student level. Part-time tuition and fees vary according to course load, degree level, reciprocity agreements, and student level. *College room and board:* $9000; *Room only:* $5238. Room and board charges vary according to housing facility. *Payment plan:* Guaranteed tuition.
**GIFT AID (NEED-BASED)** *Total amount:* $9,983,819 (74% federal, 26% state). *Scholarships, grants, and awards:* Federal Pell, FSEOG, state, college/university gift aid from institutional funds.
**GIFT AID (NON-NEED-BASED)** *Total amount:* $1,969,702 (26% federal, 50% state, 17% institutional, 7% external sources). *Scholarships, grants, and awards by category: Academic interests/achievement:* biological sciences, business, communication, education, English, general academic interests/achievements, health fields, mathematics, physical sciences, social sciences. *Creative arts/performance:* general creative arts/performance. *Special achievements/activities:* general special achievements/activities. *Special characteristics:* children of educators, children of public servants, members of minority groups, veterans. *Tuition waivers:* Full or partial for employees or children of employees, senior citizens.
**LOANS** *Student loans:* $15,954,899 (57% need-based, 43% non-need-based). *Parent loans:* $60,006 (100% non-need-based). *Programs:* Federal Direct (Subsidized and Unsubsidized Stafford, PLUS), Perkins.
**WORK-STUDY** *Federal work-study:* jobs available. *State or other work-study/employment:* Part-time jobs available.
**APPLYING FOR FINANCIAL AID** *Required financial aid form:* FAFSA. *Financial aid deadline (priority):* 3/15. *Notification date:* Continuous.
**CONTACT** John Perry, Director of Financial Aid, Governors State University, 1 University Parkway, University Park, IL 60484, 708-534-4483 or toll-free 800-478-8478. *Fax:* 708-534-1172. *E-mail:* jperry@govst.edu.
*Website:* http://www.govst.edu/.

# GRACE BIBLE COLLEGE
## Grand Rapids, MI

**CONTACT** Mr. Kurt Postma, Director of Financial Aid, Grace Bible College, 1011 Aldon Street, SW, Grand Rapids, MI 49509-1921, 616-538-2330 or toll-free 800-968-1887. *Fax:* 616-538-0599. *E-mail:* kpostma@gbcol.edu.
*Website:* http://www.gbcol.edu/.

# GRACE COLLEGE
## Winona Lake, IN

**CONTACT** Charlette Sauders, Director of Financial Aid, Grace College, 200 Seminary Drive, Winona Lake, IN 46590-1294, 574-372-5100 Ext. 6161 or toll-free 800-54-GRACE. *Fax:* 574-372-5144. *E-mail:* charlette.sauders@grace.edu.
*Website:* http://www.grace.edu/.

# GRACE COLLEGE OF DIVINITY
## Fayetteville, NC

**CONTACT** Financial Aid Office, Grace College of Divinity, 5117 Cliffdale Road, Fayetteville, NC 28314, 910-221-2224.
*Website:* http://www.gcdivinity.org/.

# GRACELAND UNIVERSITY
## Lamoni, IA

| Tuition & fees: $25,890 | Average undergraduate aid package: $22,106 |
|---|---|

**ABOUT THE INSTITUTION** Independent Community of Christ, coed. *Awards:* certificates, bachelor's, master's, and doctoral degrees. 47 undergraduate majors. *Total enrollment:* 2,407. Undergraduates: 1,594. Freshmen: 282. Federal methodology is used as a basis for awarding need-based institutional aid.
**UNDERGRADUATE EXPENSES for 2015–2016** *Comprehensive fee:* $33,990 includes full-time tuition ($25,420), mandatory fees ($470), and room and board ($8100). Full-time tuition and fees vary according to course load. Room and board charges vary according to board plan, housing facility, and location. *Part-time tuition:* $775 per credit. Part-time tuition and fees vary according to course load.
**FRESHMAN FINANCIAL AID (Fall 2014, est.)** 270 applied for aid; of those 94% were deemed to have need. 99% of freshmen with need received aid; of those 12% had need fully met. *Average percent of need met:* 76% (excluding resources awarded to replace EFC). *Average financial aid package:* $24,215 (excluding resources awarded to replace EFC). 6% of all full-time freshmen had no need and received non-need-based gift aid.
**UNDERGRADUATE FINANCIAL AID (Fall 2014, est.)** 1,150 applied for aid; of those 93% were deemed to have need. 96% of undergraduates with need received aid; of those 17% had need fully met. *Average percent of need met:* 75% (excluding resources awarded to replace EFC). *Average financial aid package:* $22,106 (excluding resources awarded to replace EFC). 13% of all full-time undergraduates had no need and received non-need-based gift aid.
**GIFT AID (NEED-BASED)** *Total amount:* $14,395,951 (24% federal, 6% state, 68% institutional, 2% external sources). *Receiving aid:* Freshmen: 87% (253); all full-time undergraduates: 76% (1,009). *Average award:* Freshmen: $19,336; Undergraduates: $17,148. *Scholarships, grants, and awards:* Federal Pell, FSEOG, state, private, college/university gift aid from institutional funds.
**GIFT AID (NON-NEED-BASED)** *Total amount:* $2,203,562 (2% federal, 93% institutional, 5% external sources). *Receiving aid:* Freshmen: 22% (65). Undergraduates: 23% (303). *Average award:* Freshmen: $14,114. Undergraduates: $12,039. *Scholarships, grants, and awards by category: Academic interests/achievement:* 566 awards ($3,276,196 total): computer science, engineering/technologies, English, general academic interests/achievements, physical sciences. *Creative arts/performance:* 157 awards ($346,873 total): applied art and design, creative writing, dance, music, theater/drama. *Special achievements/activities:* 202 awards ($290,328 total): cheerleading/drum major, general special achievements/activities, leadership, religious involvement. *Special characteristics:* 1,144 awards ($7,450,565 total): children and siblings of alumni, children of faculty/staff, first-generation college students, general special characteristics, international students, local/state students, members of minority groups, religious affiliation. *Tuition waivers:* Full or partial for employees or children of employees, senior citizens.
**LOANS** *Student loans:* $9,750,324 (84% need-based, 16% non-need-based). 78% of past graduating class borrowed through all loan programs. *Average indebtedness per student:* $35,077. *Average need-based loan:* Freshmen: $4366. Undergraduates: $5108. *Parent loans:* $1,298,555 (38% need-based, 62% non-need-based). *Programs:* Federal Direct (Subsidized and Unsubsidized Stafford, PLUS), Perkins, state, college/university.
**WORK-STUDY** *Federal work-study:* Total amount: $321,238; 163 jobs averaging $1522. *State or other work-study/employment:* Total amount: $1,020,893 (46% need-based, 54% non-need-based). 652 part-time jobs averaging $1558.
**ATHLETIC AWARDS** Total amount: $3,591,094 (76% need-based, 24% non-need-based).
**APPLYING FOR FINANCIAL AID** *Required financial aid form:* FAFSA. *Financial aid deadline:* Continuous. *Notification date:* Continuous beginning 2/1. Students must reply within 2 weeks of notification.

**CONTACT** Talia Brown, Director of Financial Aid, Graceland University, 1 University Place, Lamoni, IA 50140, 641-784-5117 or toll-free 866-GRACELAND. *Fax:* 641-784-5242. *E-mail:* talia.brown@graceland.edu.
*Website:* http://www.graceland.edu/.

# GRACE MISSION UNIVERSITY
## Fullerton, CA

**CONTACT** Financial Aid Office, Grace Mission University, 1645 West Valencia Drive, Fullerton, CA 92833, 714-525-0088.
*Website:* http://www.gm.edu/.

# GRACE UNIVERSITY
## Omaha, NE

**CONTACT** Marcy Pierce, Director of Financial Aid, Grace University, 1311 South Ninth Street, Omaha, NE 68108-3629, 402-449-2810 or toll-free 800-383-1422. *Fax:* 402-449-2921. *E-mail:* gufinaid@graceu.edu.
*Website:* http://www.graceuniversity.edu/.

# GRAMBLING STATE UNIVERSITY
## Grambling, LA

| Tuition & fees (LA res): $6644 | Average undergraduate aid package: $3935 |
|---|---|

**ABOUT THE INSTITUTION** State-supported, coed. *Awards:* certificates, bachelor's, master's, and doctoral degrees. 28 undergraduate majors. *Total enrollment:* 4,504. Undergraduates: 3,524. Freshmen: 406. Federal methodology is used as a basis for awarding need-based institutional aid.
**UNDERGRADUATE EXPENSES for 2015–2016** *Application fee:* $20. *Tuition, state resident:* full-time $4895; part-time $204 per credit hour. *Tuition, nonresident:* full-time $14,114; part-time $204 per credit hour. *Required fees:* full-time $1749; $204 per credit hour. Full-time tuition and fees vary according to course load, degree level, and student level. Part-time tuition and fees vary according to course load, degree level, and student level. *College room and board:* $9372; *Room only:* $5948. Room and board charges vary according to housing facility.
**FRESHMAN FINANCIAL AID (Fall 2014, est.)** 396 applied for aid; of those 100% were deemed to have need. 99% of freshmen with need received aid. *Average financial aid package:* $3850 (excluding resources awarded to replace EFC). 23% of all full-time freshmen had no need and received non-need-based gift aid.
**UNDERGRADUATE FINANCIAL AID (Fall 2014, est.)** 3,076 applied for aid; of those 100% were deemed to have need. 99% of undergraduates with need received aid. *Average financial aid package:* $3935 (excluding resources awarded to replace EFC). 14% of all full-time undergraduates had no need and received non-need-based gift aid.
**GIFT AID (NEED-BASED)** *Total amount:* $15,072,653 (95% federal, 5% state). *Receiving aid:* Freshmen: 83% (336); all full-time undergraduates: 81% (2,659). *Average award:* Freshmen: $3888; Undergraduates: $3852. *Scholarships, grants, and awards:* Federal Pell, FSEOG, state.
**GIFT AID (NON-NEED-BASED)** *Total amount:* $1,955,131 (5% federal, 41% state, 49% institutional, 5% external sources). *Receiving aid:* Freshmen: 96% (391). Undergraduates: 19% (613). *Average award:* Freshmen: $4488. Undergraduates: $3386. *Scholarships, grants, and awards by category: Academic interests/achievement:* biological sciences, business, communication, computer science, education, engineering/technologies, English, foreign languages, general academic interests/achievements, health fields, home economics, humanities, mathematics, military science, physical sciences, premedicine, social sciences. *Creative arts/performance:* dance, general creative arts/performance, music, performing arts, theater/drama. *Special achievements/activities:* cheerleading/drum major, junior miss, leadership. *Special characteristics:* children and siblings of alumni, children of faculty/staff, children of public servants, ethnic background, international students, local/state students, members of minority groups, out-of-state students, public servants, veterans, veterans'

children. **Tuition waivers:** Full or partial for children of alumni, employees or children of employees, senior citizens. **ROTC:** Army, Air Force cooperative.

**LOANS Student loans:** $42,023,312 (27% need-based, 73% non-need-based). **Average need-based loan:** Freshmen: $3464. Undergraduates: $4064. **Parent loans:** $4,425,492 (100% non-need-based). **Programs:** Federal Direct (Subsidized and Unsubsidized Stafford, PLUS), alternative loans.

**WORK-STUDY Federal work-study:** Total amount: $338,575; jobs available. **State or other work-study/employment:** Part-time jobs available.

**ATHLETIC AWARDS** Total amount: $1,786,192 (100% non-need-based).

**APPLYING FOR FINANCIAL AID Required financial aid form:** FAFSA. **Financial aid deadline:** 6/1 (priority: 4/1). **Notification date:** Continuous beginning 3/1. Students must reply within 2 weeks of notification.

**CONTACT** Mr. Gavin Hamms, Director of Student Financial Aid and Scholarships, Grambling State University, PO Box 629, Grambling, LA 71245, 318-274-6328 or toll-free 800-569-4714. *Fax:* 318-274-3358.

*Website:* http://www.gram.edu/.

# GRAND CANYON UNIVERSITY
## Phoenix, AZ

**CONTACT** Director of Financial Aid, Grand Canyon University, 3300 West Camelback Road, PO Box 11097, Phoenix, AZ 85017-3030, 800-800-9776 Ext. 2885 or toll-free 800-800-9776. *Fax:* 602-589-2044.

*Website:* http://www.gcu.edu/.

# GRAND VALLEY STATE UNIVERSITY
## Allendale, MI

| Tuition & fees (MI res): $10,752 | Average undergraduate aid package: $9357 |
| --- | --- |

**ABOUT THE INSTITUTION** State-supported, coed. **Awards:** certificates, bachelor's, master's, and doctoral degrees. 105 undergraduate majors. **Total enrollment:** 25,094. Undergraduates: 21,636. Freshmen: 4,199. Federal methodology is used as a basis for awarding need-based institutional aid.

**UNDERGRADUATE EXPENSES for 2015–2016 Application fee:** $30. **Tuition, state resident:** full-time $10,752; part-time $448 per credit hour. **Tuition, nonresident:** full-time $15,408; part-time $642 per credit hour. Full-time tuition and fees vary according to course load, program, and student level. Part-time tuition and fees vary according to course load, program, and student level. **College room and board:** $8200. Room and board charges vary according to board plan and housing facility.

**FRESHMAN FINANCIAL AID (Fall 2014, est.)** 3,707 applied for aid; of those 70% were deemed to have need. 99% of freshmen with need received aid; of those 14% had need fully met. **Average percent of need met:** 70% (excluding resources awarded to replace EFC). **Average financial aid package:** $10,569 (excluding resources awarded to replace EFC). 16% of all full-time freshmen had no need and received non-need-based gift aid.

**UNDERGRADUATE FINANCIAL AID (Fall 2014, est.)** 15,525 applied for aid; of those 75% were deemed to have need. 99% of undergraduates with need received aid; of those 16% had need fully met. **Average percent of need met:** 66% (excluding resources awarded to replace EFC). **Average financial aid package:** $9357 (excluding resources awarded to replace EFC). 15% of all full-time undergraduates had no need and received non-need-based gift aid.

**GIFT AID (NEED-BASED) Total amount:** $61,305,873 (50% federal, 4% state, 42% institutional, 4% external sources). **Receiving aid:** Freshmen: 54% (2,267); all full-time undergraduates: 50% (9,541). **Average award:** Freshmen: $7616; Undergraduates: $6277. **Scholarships, grants, and awards:** Federal Pell, FSEOG, state, private, college/university gift aid from institutional funds.

**GIFT AID (NON-NEED-BASED) Total amount:** $9,497,259 (1% federal, 87% institutional, 12% external sources). **Receiving aid:** Freshmen: 3% (117). Undergraduates: 2% (349). **Average award:** Freshmen: $2777. Undergraduates: $2676. **Scholarships, grants, and awards by category:** Academic interests/achievement: business, communication, computer science, education, engineering/technologies, English, foreign languages, general academic interests/achievements, health fields, humanities, international studies, mathematics, physical sciences, premedicine, social

sciences. *Creative arts/performance:* applied art and design, art/fine arts, cinema/film/broadcasting, dance, journalism/publications, music, theater/drama. *Special characteristics:* adult students, children and siblings of alumni, children of faculty/staff, children of union members/company employees, children of workers in trades, general special characteristics, handicapped students, international students, local/state students, out-of-state students, public servants, spouses of deceased or disabled public servants, veterans, veterans' children. **Tuition waivers:** Full or partial for employees or children of employees.

**LOANS Student loans:** $117,737,643 (41% need-based, 59% non-need-based). 73% of past graduating class borrowed through all loan programs. *Average indebtedness per student:* $30,222. **Average need-based loan:** Freshmen: $3667. Undergraduates: $4340. **Parent loans:** $65,390,031 (100% non-need-based). **Programs:** Federal Direct (Subsidized and Unsubsidized Stafford, PLUS), Perkins, Federal Nursing.

**WORK-STUDY Federal work-study:** Total amount: $3,645,931; 1,487 jobs averaging $2452. **State or other work-study/employment:** Part-time jobs available.

**ATHLETIC AWARDS** Total amount: $3,239,458 (38% need-based, 62% non-need-based).

**APPLYING FOR FINANCIAL AID Required financial aid form:** FAFSA. **Financial aid deadline (priority):** 3/1. **Notification date:** 3/10. Students must reply by 5/1 or within 4 weeks of notification.

**CONTACT** Michelle Rhodes, Office of Financial Aid, Grand Valley State University, 100 Student Services Building, Allendale, MI 49401, 616-331-3234 or toll-free 800-748-0246. *Fax:* 616-331-3180. *E-mail:* rhodesmi@gvsu.edu.

*Website:* http://www.gvsu.edu/.

# GRAND VIEW UNIVERSITY
## Des Moines, IA

| Tuition & fees: $24,454 | Average undergraduate aid package: $17,223 |
| --- | --- |

**ABOUT THE INSTITUTION** Independent Evangelical Lutheran Church in America, coed. **Awards:** certificates, bachelor's, and master's degrees. 40 undergraduate majors. **Total enrollment:** 2,064. Undergraduates: 2,005. Freshmen: 279. Federal methodology is used as a basis for awarding need-based institutional aid.

**UNDERGRADUATE EXPENSES for 2015–2016 Comprehensive fee:** $32,320 includes full-time tuition ($23,864), mandatory fees ($590), and room and board ($7866). Full-time tuition and fees vary according to class time and course load. Room and board charges vary according to board plan and housing facility. **Part-time tuition:** $593 per credit hour. Part-time tuition and fees vary according to class time and course load.

**FRESHMAN FINANCIAL AID (Fall 2014, est.)** 260 applied for aid; of those 89% were deemed to have need. 100% of freshmen with need received aid; of those 31% had need fully met. **Average percent of need met:** 85% (excluding resources awarded to replace EFC). **Average financial aid package:** $21,654 (excluding resources awarded to replace EFC). 16% of all full-time freshmen had no need and received non-need-based gift aid.

**UNDERGRADUATE FINANCIAL AID (Fall 2014, est.)** 1,522 applied for aid; of those 89% were deemed to have need. 100% of undergraduates with need received aid; of those 21% had need fully met. **Average percent of need met:** 74% (excluding resources awarded to replace EFC). **Average financial aid package:** $17,223 (excluding resources awarded to replace EFC). 16% of all full-time undergraduates had no need and received non-need-based gift aid.

**GIFT AID (NEED-BASED) Total amount:** $16,705,813 (21% federal, 25% state, 52% institutional, 2% external sources). **Receiving aid:** Freshmen: 76% (211); all full-time undergraduates: 75% (1,258). **Average award:** Freshmen: $19,446; Undergraduates: $15,092. **Scholarships, grants, and awards:** Federal Pell, FSEOG, state, private, college/university gift aid from institutional funds.

**GIFT AID (NON-NEED-BASED) Total amount:** $2,053,654 (2% state, 88% institutional, 10% external sources). **Receiving aid:** Freshmen: 13% (36). Undergraduates: 9% (143). **Average award:** Freshmen: $10,220. Undergraduates: $8180. **Scholarships, grants, and awards by category:** Academic interests/achievement: 1,639 awards ($9,120,995 total): biological sciences, business, communication, education, English, general academic interests/achievements, health fields, mathematics, physical sciences, religion/biblical studies, social sciences. *Creative arts/performance:* 128 awards ($20,869 total): applied art and design, art/fine arts, dance, music, theater/drama. *Special achievements/activities:* 47 awards ($62,750 total): cheerleading/drum major, community service, junior miss, memberships, religious involvement. *Special characteristics:* 143 awards ($734,250 total): adult students, children and siblings of alumni, children of educators, children of faculty/staff, ethnic background, religious affiliation, veterans. *Tuition waivers:* Full or partial for children of alumni, employees or children of employees, senior citizens. *ROTC:* Army cooperative, Air Force cooperative.

**LOANS** *Student loans:* $15,757,804 (70% need-based, 30% non-need-based). 89% of past graduating class borrowed through all loan programs. *Average indebtedness per student:* $38,160. *Average need-based loan:* Freshmen: $3932. Undergraduates: $4470. *Parent loans:* $2,100,857 (11% need-based, 89% non-need-based). *Programs:* Federal Direct (Subsidized and Unsubsidized Stafford, PLUS), Perkins, college/university, private loans.

**WORK-STUDY** *Federal work-study:* Total amount: $482,605; 330 jobs averaging $1386. *State or other work-study/employment:* Part-time jobs available.

**ATHLETIC AWARDS** Total amount: $3,886,127 (71% need-based, 29% non-need-based).

**APPLYING FOR FINANCIAL AID** *Financial aid deadline (priority):* 3/1. *Notification date:* Continuous beginning 3/10. Students must reply by 5/1 or within 3 weeks of notification.

**CONTACT** Michele Dunne, Director of Financial Aid, Grand View University, 1200 Grandview Avenue, Des Moines, IA 50316-1599, 515-263-2820 or toll-free 800-444-6083. *Fax:* 515-263-6191. *E-mail:* mdunne@grandview.edu. *Website:* http://www.grandview.edu/.

# GRANTHAM UNIVERSITY
## Lenexa, KS

**CONTACT** Financial Aid Office, Grantham University, 16025 West 113th Street, Lenexa, KS 66219 or toll-free 800-955-2527. *Website:* http://www.grantham.edu/.

# GREAT LAKES CHRISTIAN COLLEGE
## Lansing, MI

**CONTACT** Financial Aid Officer, Great Lakes Christian College, 6211 West Willow Highway, Lansing, MI 48917-1299, 517-321-0242 or toll-free 800-YES-GLCC. *Website:* http://www.glcc.edu/.

# GREEN MOUNTAIN COLLEGE
## Poultney, VT

**CONTACT** Wendy J. Ellis, Director of Student Financial Services, Green Mountain College, One Brennan Circle, Poultney, VT 05764-1199, 800-776-6675 Ext. 8209 or toll-free 800-776-6675. *Fax:* 802-287-8096. *E-mail:* ellisw@greenmtn.edu. *Website:* http://www.greenmtn.edu/.

# GREENSBORO COLLEGE
## Greensboro, NC

| Tuition & fees: $26,900 | Average undergraduate aid package: $39,948 |
| --- | --- |

**ABOUT THE INSTITUTION** Independent United Methodist, coed. *Awards:* certificates, bachelor's, and master's degrees. 53 undergraduate majors. *Total enrollment:* 1,264. Undergraduates: 1,117. Freshmen: 192. Federal methodology is used as a basis for awarding need-based institutional aid.

**UNDERGRADUATE EXPENSES** for 2015–2016 *Application fee:* $35. *Comprehensive fee:* $37,000 includes full-time tuition ($26,300), mandatory fees ($600), and room and board ($10,100). *College room only:* $5000. Full-time tuition and fees vary according to course load and program. Room and board charges vary according to housing facility. *Part-time tuition:* $725 per credit hour. Part-time tuition and fees vary according to program.

**FRESHMAN FINANCIAL AID (Fall 2014, est.)** 177 applied for aid; of those 94% were deemed to have need. 100% of freshmen with need received aid; of those 85% had need fully met. *Average percent of need met:* 94% (excluding resources awarded to replace EFC). *Average financial aid package:* $43,191 (excluding resources awarded to replace EFC). 5% of all full-time freshmen had no need and received non-need-based gift aid.

**UNDERGRADUATE FINANCIAL AID (Fall 2014, est.)** 646 applied for aid; of those 95% were deemed to have need. 100% of undergraduates with need received aid; of those 81% had need fully met. *Average percent of need met:* 93% (excluding resources awarded to replace EFC). *Average financial aid package:* $39,948 (excluding resources awarded to replace EFC). 5% of all full-time undergraduates had no need and received non-need-based gift aid.

**GIFT AID (NEED-BASED)** *Total amount:* $10,422,540 (18% federal, 14% state, 65% institutional, 3% external sources). *Receiving aid:* Freshmen: 84% (153); all full-time undergraduates: 80% (558). *Average award:* Freshmen: $20,138; Undergraduates: $17,348. *Scholarships, grants, and awards:* Federal Pell, FSEOG, state, private, college/university gift aid from institutional funds.

**GIFT AID (NON-NEED-BASED)** *Receiving aid:* Freshmen: 77% (141). Undergraduates: 66% (459). *Average award:* Freshmen: $23,540. Undergraduates: $21,562. *Scholarships, grants, and awards by category:* Academic interests/achievement: general academic interests/achievements. Creative arts/performance: art/fine arts, music, theater/drama. Special achievements/activities: community service, leadership, religious involvement. *Special characteristics:* adult students, children and siblings of alumni, children of faculty/staff, international students, relatives of clergy, religious affiliation, siblings of current students, veterans. *Tuition waivers:* Full or partial for employees or children of employees, adult students, senior citizens. *ROTC:* Army cooperative, Air Force cooperative.

**LOANS** *Student loans:* $6,523,153 (100% need-based). 93% of past graduating class borrowed through all loan programs. *Average need-based loan:* Freshmen: $8146. Undergraduates: $9399. *Parent loans:* $3,106,521 (31% need-based, 69% non-need-based). *Programs:* Federal Direct (Subsidized and Unsubsidized Stafford, PLUS), Perkins, college/university.

**WORK-STUDY** *Federal work-study:* Total amount: $146,300; 131 jobs averaging $717.

**APPLYING FOR FINANCIAL AID** *Required financial aid forms:* FAFSA, institution's own form, state aid form. *Financial aid deadline (priority):* 4/15. *Notification date:* Continuous. Students must reply within 2 weeks of notification.

**CONTACT** Lindsay Latham, Director of Financial Aid, Greensboro College, 815 West Market Street, Greensboro, NC 27401-1875, 336-272-7102 Ext. 217 or toll-free 800-346-8226. *Fax:* 336-230-9622. *E-mail:* dvanarsdale@greensborocollege.edu. *Website:* http://www.greensboro.edu/.

# GREENVILLE COLLEGE
## Greenville, IL

| Tuition & fees: $25,088 | Average undergraduate aid package: $19,031 |
| --- | --- |

**ABOUT THE INSTITUTION** Independent Free Methodist, coed. *Awards:* bachelor's and master's degrees. 54 undergraduate majors. *Total enrollment:* 1,307. Undergraduates: 1,103. Freshmen: 269. Federal methodology is used as a basis for awarding need-based institutional aid.

**UNDERGRADUATE EXPENSES** for 2015–2016 *Application fee:* $30. *Comprehensive fee:* $33,376 includes full-time tuition ($24,864), mandatory fees ($224), and room and board ($8288). *College room only:* $4012. Full-time tuition and fees vary according to degree level. Room and board charges vary according to housing facility. *Part-time tuition:* $526 per credit. Part-time tuition and fees vary according to course load and degree level.

**FRESHMAN FINANCIAL AID (Fall 2014, est.)** 236 applied for aid; of those 92% were deemed to have need. 100% of freshmen with need received aid; of those 12% had need fully met. *Average percent of need met:* 77% (excluding resources awarded to replace EFC). *Average financial aid package:* $19,564 (excluding resources awarded to replace EFC). 13% of all full-time freshmen had no need and received non-need-based gift aid.

**UNDERGRADUATE FINANCIAL AID (Fall 2014, est.)** 847 applied for aid; of those 92% were deemed to have need. 100% of undergraduates with need received aid; of those 14% had need fully met. *Average percent of need met:* 74% (excluding resources awarded to replace EFC). *Average financial aid package:*

$19,031 (excluding resources awarded to replace EFC). 13% of all full-time undergraduates had no need and received non-need-based gift aid.

**GIFT AID (NEED-BASED) Total amount:** $13,239,897 (15% federal, 10% state, 72% institutional, 3% external sources). **Receiving aid:** Freshmen: 86% (215); all full-time undergraduates: 83% (759). **Average award:** Freshmen: $16,621; Undergraduates: $15,526. **Scholarships, grants, and awards:** Federal Pell, FSEOG, state, private, college/university gift aid from institutional funds.

**GIFT AID (NON-NEED-BASED) Total amount:** $1,457,763 (1% federal, 98% institutional, 1% external sources). **Receiving aid:** Freshmen: 9% (22). Undergraduates: 8% (75). **Average award:** Freshmen: $8477. Undergraduates: $9208. **Scholarships, grants, and awards by category:** Academic interests/achievement: biological sciences, engineering/technologies, mathematics, physical sciences. Creative arts/performance: applied art and design, art/fine arts, music, performing arts. Special achievements/activities: leadership, memberships, religious involvement. Special characteristics: children and siblings of alumni, children of faculty/staff, international students, local/state students, out-of-state students, relatives of clergy, religious affiliation, siblings of current students. **Tuition waivers:** Full or partial for employees or children of employees, senior citizens.

**LOANS Student loans:** $7,283,851 (80% need-based, 20% non-need-based). 78% of past graduating class borrowed through all loan programs. **Average indebtedness per student:** $28,452. **Average need-based loan:** Freshmen: $3487. Undergraduates: $4353. **Parent loans:** $2,232,281 (31% need-based, 69% non-need-based). **Programs:** Federal Direct (Subsidized and Unsubsidized Stafford, PLUS), Perkins, college/university.

**WORK-STUDY Federal work-study:** Total amount: $193,576; jobs available. **State or other work-study/employment:** Part-time jobs available.

**APPLYING FOR FINANCIAL AID Required financial aid form:** FAFSA. **Financial aid deadline (priority):** 2/1. **Notification date:** Continuous beginning 3/1. Students must reply within 3 weeks of notification.

**CONTACT** Marilae Latham, Director of Financial Aid, Greenville College, 315 East College Avenue, Greenville, IL 62246-0159, 618-664-7110 or toll-free 800-345-4440. Fax: 618-664-7198. E-mail: marilae.latham@greenville.edu. Website: http://www.greenville.edu/.

# GRINNELL COLLEGE
## Grinnell, IA

| Tuition & fees: $46,023 | Average undergraduate aid package: $43,287 |
| --- | --- |

**ABOUT THE INSTITUTION** Independent, coed. **Awards:** bachelor's degrees. 27 undergraduate majors. **Total enrollment:** 1,734. Undergraduates: 1,734. Freshmen: 435. Both federal and institutional methodology are used as a basis for awarding need-based institutional aid.

**UNDERGRADUATE EXPENSES for 2015–2016 Comprehensive fee:** $57,020 includes full-time tuition ($45,620), mandatory fees ($403), and room and board ($10,997). **College room only:** $5152. Room and board charges vary according to board plan and housing facility. **Part-time tuition:** $1413 per credit hour.

**FRESHMAN FINANCIAL AID (Fall 2014, est.)** 366 applied for aid; of those 84% were deemed to have need. 100% of freshmen with need received aid; of those 100% had need fully met. **Average percent of need met:** 100% (excluding resources awarded to replace EFC). **Average financial aid package:** $42,327 (excluding resources awarded to replace EFC). 15% of all full-time freshmen had no need and received non-need-based gift aid.

**UNDERGRADUATE FINANCIAL AID (Fall 2014, est.)** 1,263 applied for aid; of those 93% were deemed to have need. 100% of undergraduates with need received aid; of those 100% had need fully met. **Average percent of need met:** 100% (excluding resources awarded to replace EFC). **Average financial aid package:** $43,287 (excluding resources awarded to replace EFC). 15% of all full-time undergraduates had no need and received non-need-based gift aid.

**GIFT AID (NEED-BASED) Total amount:** $43,056,570 (4% federal, 1% state, 94% institutional, 1% external sources). **Receiving aid:** Freshmen: 69% (301); all full-time undergraduates: 70% (1,158). **Average award:** Freshmen: $35,514; Undergraduates: $37,153. **Scholarships, grants, and awards:** Federal Pell, FSEOG, state, private, college/university gift aid from institutional funds.

**GIFT AID (NON-NEED-BASED) Total amount:** $5,870,168 (87% institutional, 13% external sources). **Receiving aid:** Freshmen: 10% (42). Undergraduates: 7%

(122). **Average award:** Freshmen: $18,473. Undergraduates: $16,968. **Scholarships, grants, and awards by category:** Academic interests/achievement: general academic interests/achievements. **Tuition waivers:** Full or partial for employees or children of employees.

**LOANS Student loans:** $3,785,559 (86% need-based, 14% non-need-based). 56% of past graduating class borrowed through all loan programs. **Average indebtedness per student:** $16,315. **Average need-based loan:** Freshmen: $3703. Undergraduates: $3894. **Programs:** Federal Direct (Subsidized and Unsubsidized Stafford, PLUS), Perkins, state.

**WORK-STUDY Federal work-study:** Total amount: $1,427,214; 711 jobs averaging $1863. **State or other work-study/employment:** Total amount: $1,060,560 (38% need-based, 62% non-need-based). 390 part-time jobs averaging $2141.

**APPLYING FOR FINANCIAL AID Required financial aid forms:** FAFSA, CSS Financial Aid PROFILE, noncustodial (divorced/separated) parent's statement. **Financial aid deadline:** 2/1. **Notification date:** 4/1. Students must reply by 5/1.

**CONTACT** Mr. Brad Lindberg, Director of Student Financial Aid, Grinnell College, 1103 Park Street, Grinnell, IA 50112-1690, 641-269-3250 or toll-free 800-247-0113. Fax: 641-269-4937. E-mail: lindbergb@grinnell.edu. Website: http://www.grinnell.edu/.

# GROVE CITY COLLEGE
## Grove City, PA

| Tuition & fees: $15,550 | Average undergraduate aid package: $6777 |
| --- | --- |

**ABOUT THE INSTITUTION** Independent Presbyterian, coed. **Awards:** bachelor's degrees. 38 undergraduate majors. **Total enrollment:** 2,509. Undergraduates: 2,509. Freshmen: 637. Institutional methodology is used as a basis for awarding need-based institutional aid.

**UNDERGRADUATE EXPENSES for 2015–2016 Application fee:** $50. **Comprehensive fee:** $24,022 includes full-time tuition ($15,550) and room and board ($8472). Room and board charges vary according to housing facility. **Part-time tuition:** $486 per credit hour.

**FRESHMAN FINANCIAL AID (Fall 2014, est.)** 405 applied for aid; of those 75% were deemed to have need. 99% of freshmen with need received aid; of those 9% had need fully met. **Average percent of need met:** 51% (excluding resources awarded to replace EFC). **Average financial aid package:** $6958 (excluding resources awarded to replace EFC). 6% of all full-time freshmen had no need and received non-need-based gift aid.

**UNDERGRADUATE FINANCIAL AID (Fall 2014, est.)** 1,304 applied for aid; of those 82% were deemed to have need. 99% of undergraduates with need received aid; of those 9% had need fully met. **Average percent of need met:** 49% (excluding resources awarded to replace EFC). **Average financial aid package:** $6777 (excluding resources awarded to replace EFC). 16% of all full-time undergraduates had no need and received non-need-based gift aid.

**GIFT AID (NEED-BASED) Total amount:** $7,129,363 (15% state, 76% institutional, 9% external sources). **Receiving aid:** Freshmen: 47% (299); all full-time undergraduates: 42% (1,047). **Average award:** Freshmen: $6958; Undergraduates: $6777. **Scholarships, grants, and awards:** state, private, college/university gift aid from institutional funds.

**GIFT AID (NON-NEED-BASED) Total amount:** $1,771,424 (2% state, 50% institutional, 48% external sources). **Receiving aid:** Freshmen: 4% (26). Undergraduates: 4% (89). **Average award:** Freshmen: $4370. Undergraduates: $1926. **Scholarships, grants, and awards by category:** Academic interests/achievement: 643 awards ($958,622 total): biological sciences, business, communication, education, engineering/technologies, English, foreign languages, general academic interests/achievements, mathematics, physical sciences, religion/biblical studies, social sciences. Creative arts/performance: 11 awards ($11,900 total): creative writing, music. Special achievements/activities: 27 awards ($86,500 total): general special achievements/activities, leadership, memberships, religious involvement. Special characteristics: 27 awards ($191,700 total): ethnic background, first-generation college students, general special characteristics, handicapped students, members of minority groups. **Tuition waivers:** Full or partial for employees or children of employees.

**LOANS Student loans:** $13,267,487 (37% need-based, 63% non-need-based). 56% of past graduating class borrowed through all loan programs. **Average indebtedness per student:** $31,634. **Programs:** state, private loans.

**APPLYING FOR FINANCIAL AID** *Required financial aid form:* institution's own form. *Financial aid deadline:* 4/15. *Notification date:* Continuous beginning 3/18. Students must reply by 5/1.

**CONTACT** Mr. Thomas G. Ball, Director of Financial Aid, Grove City College, 100 Campus Drive, Grove City, PA 16127-2104, 724-458-3300. *Fax:* 724-450-4040. *E-mail:* financialaid@gcc.edu.
*Website:* http://www.gcc.edu/.

# GUILFORD COLLEGE
## Greensboro, NC

| Tuition & fees: $33,430 | Average undergraduate aid package: $21,140 |
|---|---|

**ABOUT THE INSTITUTION** Independent Society of Friends, coed. *Awards:* certificates and bachelor's degrees. 36 undergraduate majors. *Total enrollment:* 2,137. Undergraduates: 2,137. Freshmen: 351. Federal methodology is used as a basis for awarding need-based institutional aid.

**UNDERGRADUATE EXPENSES** for 2015–2016 *Comprehensive fee:* $42,800 includes full-time tuition ($33,050), mandatory fees ($380), and room and board ($9370). Room and board charges vary according to board plan and housing facility. *Part-time tuition:* $1012 per credit hour. Part-time tuition and fees vary according to course load.

**FRESHMAN FINANCIAL AID (Fall 2014, est.)** 306 applied for aid; of those 81% were deemed to have need. 100% of freshmen with need received aid; of those 5% had need fully met. *Average percent of need met:* 83% (excluding resources awarded to replace EFC). *Average financial aid package:* $27,854 (excluding resources awarded to replace EFC). 16% of all full-time freshmen had no need and received non-need-based gift aid.

**UNDERGRADUATE FINANCIAL AID (Fall 2014, est.)** 1,645 applied for aid; of those 95% were deemed to have need. 100% of undergraduates with need received aid; of those 5% had need fully met. *Average percent of need met:* 84% (excluding resources awarded to replace EFC). *Average financial aid package:* $21,140 (excluding resources awarded to replace EFC). 9% of all full-time undergraduates had no need and received non-need-based gift aid.

**GIFT AID (NEED-BASED)** *Total amount:* $24,956,436 (16% federal, 9% state, 72% institutional, 3% external sources). *Receiving aid:* Freshmen: 65% (227); all full-time undergraduates: 86% (1,443). *Average award:* Freshmen: $26,997; Undergraduates: $19,797. *Scholarships, grants, and awards:* Federal Pell, FSEOG, state, private, college/university gift aid from institutional funds.

**GIFT AID (NON-NEED-BASED)** *Total amount:* $3,172,530 (93% institutional, 7% external sources). *Receiving aid:* Freshmen: 68% (240). Undergraduates: 53% (880). *Average award:* Freshmen: $14,758. Undergraduates: $11,897. *Scholarships, grants, and awards by category:* Academic interests/achievement: biological sciences, general academic interests/achievements. Creative arts/performance: music, theater/drama. Special achievements/activities: religious involvement. Special characteristics: children of faculty/staff, first-generation college students, local/state students. *Tuition waivers:* Full or partial for employees or children of employees.

**LOANS** *Student loans:* $11,312,717 (89% need-based, 11% non-need-based). 79% of past graduating class borrowed through all loan programs. *Average indebtedness per student:* $25,360. *Average need-based loan:* Freshmen: $6872. Undergraduates: $9501. *Parent loans:* $2,126,878 (100% need-based). *Programs:* Perkins, college/university.

**WORK-STUDY** *Federal work-study:* Total amount: $237,590; jobs available. *State or other work-study/employment:* Total amount: $237,346 (100% need-based). Part-time jobs available.

**APPLYING FOR FINANCIAL AID** *Required financial aid forms:* FAFSA, noncustodial (divorced/separated) parent's statement, business/farm supplement. *Financial aid deadline (priority):* 3/1. *Notification date:* Continuous. Students must reply within 2 weeks of notification.

**CONTACT** Mr. Paul J. Coscia, Director of Student Financial Services, Guilford College, 5800 West Friendly Avenue, Greensboro, NC 27410, 336-316-2395 or toll-free 800-992-7759. *Fax:* 336-316-2942. *E-mail:* pcoscia@guilford.edu.
*Website:* http://www.guilford.edu/.

# GUSTAVUS ADOLPHUS COLLEGE
## St. Peter, MN

| Tuition & fees: $40,080 | Average undergraduate aid package: $33,495 |
|---|---|

**ABOUT THE INSTITUTION** Independent Evangelical Lutheran Church in America, coed. *Awards:* bachelor's degrees. 67 undergraduate majors. *Total enrollment:* 2,456. Undergraduates: 2,456. Freshmen: 599. Both federal and institutional methodology are used as a basis for awarding need-based institutional aid.

**UNDERGRADUATE EXPENSES** for 2015–2016 *One-time required fee:* $460. *Comprehensive fee:* $49,330 includes full-time tuition ($39,550), mandatory fees ($530), and room and board ($9250). *College room only:* $5950. Room and board charges vary according to board plan and housing facility. *Part-time tuition:* $5400 per course. *Payment plan:* Tuition prepayment.

**FRESHMAN FINANCIAL AID (Fall 2013)** 546 applied for aid; of those 87% were deemed to have need. 100% of freshmen with need received aid; of those 24% had need fully met. *Average percent of need met:* 92% (excluding resources awarded to replace EFC). *Average financial aid package:* $34,947 (excluding resources awarded to replace EFC). 24% of all full-time freshmen had no need and received non-need-based gift aid.

**UNDERGRADUATE FINANCIAL AID (Fall 2013)** 1,971 applied for aid; of those 90% were deemed to have need. 100% of undergraduates with need received aid; of those 24% had need fully met. *Average percent of need met:* 89% (excluding resources awarded to replace EFC). *Average financial aid package:* $33,495 (excluding resources awarded to replace EFC). 28% of all full-time undergraduates had no need and received non-need-based gift aid.

**GIFT AID (NEED-BASED)** *Total amount:* $46,905,416 (6% federal, 7% state, 84% institutional, 3% external sources). *Receiving aid:* Freshmen: 74% (466); all full-time undergraduates: 71% (1,743). *Average award:* Freshmen: $28,463; Undergraduates: $26,393. *Scholarships, grants, and awards:* Federal Pell, FSEOG, state, private, college/university gift aid from institutional funds.

**GIFT AID (NON-NEED-BASED)** *Total amount:* $9,358,274 (95% institutional, 5% external sources). *Receiving aid:* Freshmen: 7% (47). Undergraduates: 7% (163). *Average award:* Freshmen: $18,784. Undergraduates: $16,668. *Scholarships, grants, and awards by category:* Academic interests/achievement: general academic interests/achievements. Creative arts/performance: art/fine arts, dance, debating, music, theater/drama. Special achievements/activities: junior miss. Special characteristics: children and siblings of alumni, ethnic background, first-generation college students, international students, members of minority groups, out-of-state students, siblings of current students. *Tuition waivers:* Full or partial for employees or children of employees. *ROTC:* Army cooperative.

**LOANS** *Student loans:* $16,731,115 (38% need-based, 62% non-need-based). 76% of past graduating class borrowed through all loan programs. *Average indebtedness per student:* $36,636. *Average need-based loan:* Freshmen: $3807. Undergraduates: $4060. *Programs:* Federal Direct (Subsidized and Unsubsidized Stafford, PLUS), Perkins, state.

**WORK-STUDY** *Federal work-study:* jobs available. *State or other work-study/employment:* Total amount: $1,026,576 (69% need-based, 31% non-need-based). Part-time jobs available.

**APPLYING FOR FINANCIAL AID** *Required financial aid form:* FAFSA. *Financial aid deadline:* 4/15 (priority: 3/15). *Notification date:* Continuous beginning 3/15. Students must reply by 5/1 or within 2 weeks of notification.

**CONTACT** Mr. Doug Minter, Dean of Financial Aid, Gustavus Adolphus College, 800 West College Avenue, St. Peter, MN 56082-1498, 507-933-7527 or toll-free 800-GUSTAVU(S). *Fax:* 507-933-7727. *E-mail:* finaid@gustavus.edu.
*Website:* http://www.gustavus.edu/.

# GUTENBERG COLLEGE
## Eugene, OR

**CONTACT** Financial Aid Office, Gutenberg College, 1883 University Street, Eugene, OR 97403, 541-683-5141.
*Website:* http://www.gutenberg.edu/.

# GWYNEDD MERCY UNIVERSITY
## Gwynedd Valley, PA

| Tuition & fees: $31,360 | Average undergraduate aid package: $21,574 |
|---|---|

**ABOUT THE INSTITUTION** Independent Roman Catholic, coed. **Awards:** certificates, associate, bachelor's, master's, and doctoral degrees. 32 undergraduate majors. **Total enrollment:** 2,477. Undergraduates: 1,983. Freshmen: 206. Federal methodology is used as a basis for awarding need-based institutional aid.

**UNDERGRADUATE EXPENSES for 2015–2016 Application fee:** $25. **Comprehensive fee:** $42,370 includes full-time tuition ($30,760), mandatory fees ($600), and room and board ($11,010). **College room only:** $5360. Full-time tuition and fees vary according to program. Room and board charges vary according to board plan and housing facility. **Part-time tuition:** $675 per contact hour. Part-time tuition and fees vary according to program.

**FRESHMAN FINANCIAL AID (Fall 2014, est.)** 196 applied for aid; of those 91% were deemed to have need. 100% of freshmen with need received aid; of those 12% had need fully met. **Average percent of need met:** 70% (excluding resources awarded to replace EFC). **Average financial aid package:** $23,366 (excluding resources awarded to replace EFC). 11% of all full-time freshmen had no need and received non-need-based gift aid.

**UNDERGRADUATE FINANCIAL AID (Fall 2014, est.)** 1,269 applied for aid; of those 86% were deemed to have need. 99% of undergraduates with need received aid; of those 14% had need fully met. **Average percent of need met:** 68% (excluding resources awarded to replace FFC). **Average financial aid package:** $21,574 (excluding resources awarded to replace EFC). 11% of all full-time undergraduates had no need and received non-need-based gift aid.

**GIFT AID (NEED-BASED) Total amount:** $20,800,964 (16% federal, 10% state, 66% institutional, 8% external sources). **Receiving aid:** Freshmen: 89% (178); all full-time undergraduates: 72% (1,083). **Average award:** Freshmen: $19,791; Undergraduates: $17,863. **Scholarships, grants, and awards:** Federal Pell, FSEOG, state, private, college/university gift aid from institutional funds.

**GIFT AID (NON-NEED-BASED) Total amount:** $3,015,337 (4% federal, 1% state, 82% institutional, 13% external sources). **Receiving aid:** Freshmen: 10% (19). Undergraduates: 8% (124). **Average award:** Freshmen: $12,630. Undergraduates: $11,140. **Scholarships, grants, and awards by category:** Academic interests/achievement: general academic interests/achievements. Special achievements/activities: general special achievements/activities. Special characteristics: children and siblings of alumni, children of faculty/staff, siblings of current students, veterans, veterans' children. **Tuition waivers:** Full or partial for employees or children of employees.

**LOANS Student loans:** $14,687,672 (75% need-based, 25% non-need-based). 83% of past graduating class borrowed through all loan programs. Average indebtedness per student: $37,860. **Average need-based loan:** Freshmen: $3450. Undergraduates: $4209. **Parent loans:** $2,481,735 (45% need-based, 55% non-need-based). **Programs:** Federal Direct (Subsidized and Unsubsidized Stafford, PLUS), Perkins, Federal Nursing, alternative loans.

**WORK-STUDY Federal work-study:** Total amount: $331,826, jobs available. **State or other work-study/employment:** Part-time jobs available.

**APPLYING FOR FINANCIAL AID Required financial aid forms:** FAFSA, institution's own form. **Financial aid deadline:** 5/1 (priority: 3/15). **Notification date:** Continuous beginning 2/15. Students must reply by 5/1 or within 2 weeks of notification.

**CONTACT** Mrs. Elizabeth R. Howard, Director of Student Financial Aid, Gwynedd Mercy University, PO Box 901, Gwynedd Valley, PA 19437-0901, 215-646-7300 Ext. 483 or toll-free 800-DIAL-GMC. Fax: 215-641-5556. E-mail: howard.e@gmercyu.edu. Website: http://www.gmercyu.edu/.

# HALLMARK UNIVERSITY
## San Antonio, TX

**CONTACT** Financial Aid Office, Hallmark University, 10401 IH 10 West, San Antonio, TX 78230, 210-690-9000 or toll-free 800-880-6600. Website: http://www.hallmarkuniversity.edu/.

# HAMILTON COLLEGE
## Clinton, NY

| Tuition & fees: $47,820 | Average undergraduate aid package: $43,256 |
|---|---|

**ABOUT THE INSTITUTION** Independent, coed. **Awards:** bachelor's degrees. 43 undergraduate majors. **Total enrollment:** 1,900. Undergraduates: 1,900. Freshmen: 469. Both federal and institutional methodology are used as a basis for awarding need-based institutional aid.

**UNDERGRADUATE EXPENSES for 2015–2016 Application fee:** $70. **Comprehensive fee:** $59,970 includes full-time tuition ($47,350), mandatory fees ($470), and room and board ($12,150). **College room only:** $6640. Room and board charges vary according to board plan. **Part-time tuition:** $5918.75 per course.

**FRESHMAN FINANCIAL AID (Fall 2014, est.)** 250 applied for aid; of those 96% were deemed to have need. 100% of freshmen with need received aid; of those 100% had need fully met. **Average percent of need met:** 100% (excluding resources awarded to replace EFC). **Average financial aid package:** $43,909 (excluding resources awarded to replace EFC).

**UNDERGRADUATE FINANCIAL AID (Fall 2014, est.)** 920 applied for aid; of those 96% were deemed to have need. 100% of undergraduates with need received aid; of those 100% had need fully met. **Average percent of need met:** 100% (excluding resources awarded to replace EFC). **Average financial aid package:** $43,256 (excluding resources awarded to replace EFC).

**GIFT AID (NEED-BASED) Total amount:** $35,398,221 (4% federal, 2% state, 92% institutional, 2% external sources). **Receiving aid:** Freshmen: 51% (239); all full-time undergraduates: 47% (880). **Average award:** Freshmen: $40,165; Undergraduates: $38,762. **Scholarships, grants, and awards:** Federal Pell, FSEOG, state, private, college/university gift aid from institutional funds.

**GIFT AID (NON-NEED-BASED) Total amount:** $851,776 (2% federal, 4% state, 23% institutional, 71% external sources). **Tuition waivers:** Full or partial for employees or children of employees. **ROTC:** Army cooperative, Air Force cooperative.

**LOANS Student loans:** $2,988,784 (100% need-based). 44% of past graduating class borrowed through all loan programs. Average indebtedness per student: $18,941. **Average need-based loan:** Freshmen: $3286. Undergraduates: $4268. **Programs:** Federal Direct (Subsidized and Unsubsidized Stafford, PLUS), Perkins, college/university.

**WORK-STUDY Federal work-study:** Total amount: $1,048,840; 576 jobs averaging $1821. **State or other work-study/employment:** Total amount: $94,100 (100% need-based). 49 part-time jobs averaging $1920.

**APPLYING FOR FINANCIAL AID Required financial aid forms:** FAFSA, institution's own form, CSS Financial Aid PROFILE, state aid form, noncustodial (divorced/separated) parent's statement, business/farm supplement. **Financial aid deadline:** 2/15. **Notification date:** 4/1. Students must reply by 5/1.

**CONTACT** Office of Financial Aid, Hamilton College, 198 College Hill Road, Clinton, NY 13323, 315-859-4434 or toll-free 800-843-2655. Fax: 315-859-4962. E-mail: finaid@hamilton.edu. Website: http://www.hamilton.edu/.

# HAMILTON TECHNICAL COLLEGE
## Davenport, IA

**CONTACT** Ms. Lisa Boyd, Executive Vice President/Director of Financial Aid, Hamilton Technical College, 1011 East 53rd Street, Davenport, IA 52807-2653, 563-386-3570 Ext. 33 or toll-free 866-966-4825. Fax: 563-386-6756. Website: http://www.hamiltontechcollege.edu/.

# HAMLINE UNIVERSITY
## St. Paul, MN

| Tuition & fees: $36,270 | Average undergraduate aid package: $28,520 |
| --- | --- |

**ABOUT THE INSTITUTION** Independent United Methodist Church, coed. **Awards:** certificates, bachelor's, master's, and doctoral degrees. 52 undergraduate majors. **Total enrollment:** 4,469. Undergraduates: 2,242. Freshmen: 521. Federal methodology is used as a basis for awarding need-based institutional aid.

**UNDERGRADUATE EXPENSES for 2015–2016 Comprehensive fee:** $45,662 includes full-time tuition ($35,710), mandatory fees ($560), and room and board ($9392). **College room only:** $4794. Room and board charges vary according to board plan and housing facility. **Part-time tuition:** $1116 per credit. **Part-time fees:** $486 per year. Part-time tuition and fees vary according to course load.

**FRESHMAN FINANCIAL AID (Fall 2014, est.)** 484 applied for aid; of those 90% were deemed to have need. 100% of freshmen with need received aid; of those 21% had need fully met. **Average percent of need met:** 85% (excluding resources awarded to replace EFC). **Average financial aid package:** $30,738 (excluding resources awarded to replace EFC). 14% of all full-time freshmen had no need and received non-need-based gift aid.

**UNDERGRADUATE FINANCIAL AID (Fall 2014, est.)** 1,909 applied for aid; of those 92% were deemed to have need. 100% of undergraduates with need received aid; of those 17% had need fully met. **Average percent of need met:** 79% (excluding resources awarded to replace EFC). **Average financial aid package:** $28,520 (excluding resources awarded to replace EFC). 15% of all full-time undergraduates had no need and received non-need-based gift aid.

**GIFT AID (NEED-BASED) Total amount:** $38,041,184 (11% federal, 10% state, 78% institutional, 1% external sources). **Receiving aid:** Freshmen: 84% (437); all full-time undergraduates: 83% (1,758). **Average award:** Freshmen: $24,164; Undergraduates: $21,916. **Scholarships, grants, and awards:** Federal Pell, FSEOG, state, private, college/university gift aid from institutional funds, Academic Competitiveness Grants, National SMART Grants, TEACH Grants, United Methodist Scholarships.

**GIFT AID (NON-NEED-BASED) Total amount:** $6,636,244 (1% federal, 97% institutional, 2% external sources). **Receiving aid:** Freshmen: 12% (64). Undergraduates: 9% (193). **Average award:** Freshmen: $15,889. Undergraduates: $15,238. **Scholarships, grants, and awards by category:** Academic interests/achievement: 1,811 awards ($24,836,056 total): biological sciences, business, communication, education, English, foreign languages, general academic interests/achievements, health fields, humanities, international studies, mathematics, physical sciences, premedicine, religion/biblical studies, social sciences. Creative arts/performance: 165 awards ($529,601 total): applied art and design, art/fine arts, creative writing, general creative arts/performance, journalism/publications, music, performing arts, theater/drama. Special achievements/activities: 265 awards ($669,306 total): community service, general special achievements/activities, leadership, memberships. Special characteristics: 436 awards ($1,673,731 total): children and siblings of alumni, ethnic background, general special characteristics, handicapped students, international students, local/state students, members of minority groups, out-of-state students, previous college experience, relatives of clergy, religious affiliation, veterans. **Tuition waivers:** Full or partial for employees or children of employees. **ROTC:** Army cooperative, Air Force cooperative.

**LOANS Student loans:** $15,343,923 (76% need-based, 24% non-need-based). 82% of past graduating class borrowed through all loan programs. **Average indebtedness per student:** $36,006. **Average need-based loan:** Freshmen: $4013. Undergraduates: $4955. **Parent loans:** $4,792,479 (37% need-based, 63% non-need-based). **Programs:** Federal Direct (Subsidized and Unsubsidized Stafford, PLUS), Perkins, state, alternative loans, United Methodist Student Loans.

**WORK-STUDY Federal work-study:** Total amount: $1,172,395; 489 jobs averaging $2398. **State or other work-study/employment:** Total amount: $2,414,420 (55% need-based, 45% non-need-based). 884 part-time jobs averaging $2731.

**APPLYING FOR FINANCIAL AID Required financial aid form:** FAFSA. **Financial aid deadline (priority):** 3/15. **Notification date:** Continuous beginning 3/15. Students must reply by 5/1 or within 2 weeks of notification.

**CONTACT** Ms. Lynette Wahl, Office of Financial Aid, Hamline University, 1536 Hewitt Avenue, MS C1915, St. Paul, MN 55104, 651-523-3000 or toll-free 800-753-9753. Fax: 651-523-2585. E-mail: finaid@hamline.edu. Website: http://www.hamline.edu/.

# HAMPDEN-SYDNEY COLLEGE
## Hampden-Sydney, VA

| Tuition & fees: $39,604 | Average undergraduate aid package: $31,035 |
| --- | --- |

**ABOUT THE INSTITUTION** Independent Presbyterian Church (U.S.A.), men only. **Awards:** bachelor's degrees. 25 undergraduate majors. **Total enrollment:** 1,105. Undergraduates: 1,105. Freshmen: 322. Both federal and institutional methodology are used as a basis for awarding need-based institutional aid.

**UNDERGRADUATE EXPENSES for 2015–2016 Application fee:** $30. **Comprehensive fee:** $51,916 includes full-time tuition ($38,018), mandatory fees ($1586), and room and board ($12,312). **College room only:** $5156. Room and board charges vary according to board plan and housing facility. **Part-time tuition:** $1200 per credit hour.

**FRESHMAN FINANCIAL AID (Fall 2014, est.)** 259 applied for aid; of those 85% were deemed to have need. 100% of freshmen with need received aid; of those 25% had need fully met. **Average percent of need met:** 80% (excluding resources awarded to replace EFC). **Average financial aid package:** $31,383 (excluding resources awarded to replace EFC). 31% of all full-time freshmen had no need and received non-need-based gift aid.

**UNDERGRADUATE FINANCIAL AID (Fall 2014, est.)** 809 applied for aid; of those 88% were deemed to have need. 100% of undergraduates with need received aid; of those 21% had need fully met. **Average percent of need met:** 79% (excluding resources awarded to replace EFC). **Average financial aid package:** $31,035 (excluding resources awarded to replace EFC). 34% of all full-time undergraduates had no need and received non-need-based gift aid.

**GIFT AID (NEED-BASED) Total amount:** $18,870,319 (6% federal, 8% state, 85% institutional, 1% external sources). **Receiving aid:** Freshmen: 68% (220); all full-time undergraduates: 64% (711). **Average award:** Freshmen: $27,644; Undergraduates: $26,540. **Scholarships, grants, and awards:** Federal Pell, FSEOG, state, private, college/university gift aid from institutional funds.

**GIFT AID (NON-NEED-BASED) Total amount:** $6,700,986 (14% state, 83% institutional, 3% external sources). **Receiving aid:** Freshmen: 12% (38). Undergraduates: 9% (98). **Average award:** Freshmen: $15,151. Undergraduates: $13,692. **Scholarships, grants, and awards by category:** Academic interests/achievement: biological sciences, education, general academic interests/achievements, health fields, international studies, premedicine. Creative arts/performance: music. Special achievements/activities: general special achievements/activities, leadership. Special characteristics: children of educators, children of faculty/staff, ethnic background, international students, members of minority groups, out-of-state students, veterans, veterans' children. **Tuition waivers:** Full or partial for employees or children of employees. **ROTC:** Army cooperative.

**LOANS Student loans:** $6,543,338 (66% need-based, 34% non-need-based). 59% of past graduating class borrowed through all loan programs. **Average indebtedness per student:** $30,644. **Average need-based loan:** Freshmen: $3848. Undergraduates: $4889. **Parent loans:** $3,631,174 (34% need-based, 66% non-need-based). **Programs:** Federal Direct (Subsidized and Unsubsidized Stafford, PLUS), Perkins, college/university.

**WORK-STUDY Federal work-study:** Total amount: $335,309; 205 jobs averaging $1385.

**APPLYING FOR FINANCIAL AID Required financial aid forms:** FAFSA, state aid form. **Financial aid deadline (priority):** 3/1. **Notification date:** 3/15. Students must reply by 5/1.

**CONTACT** Ms. Zita Marie Barree, Director of Financial Aid, Hampden-Sydney College, PO Box 726, Hampden-Sydney, VA 23943-0726, 434-223-6119 or toll-free 800-755-0733. Fax: 434-223-6075. E-mail: hsfinaid@hsc.edu. Website: http://www.hsc.edu/.

# HAMPSHIRE COLLEGE
## Amherst, MA

| Tuition & fees: $49,360 | Average undergraduate aid package: $35,078 |
| --- | --- |

**ABOUT THE INSTITUTION** Independent, coed. **Awards:** bachelor's degrees. 57 undergraduate majors. **Total enrollment:** 1,376. Undergraduates: 1,376. Freshmen:

324. Institutional methodology is used as a basis for awarding need-based institutional aid.

**UNDERGRADUATE EXPENSES for 2015–2016** *Application fee:* $60. *Comprehensive fee:* $62,310 includes full-time tuition ($47,620), mandatory fees ($1740), and room and board ($12,950). *College room only:* $8110. Room and board charges vary according to board plan.

**FRESHMAN FINANCIAL AID (Fall 2014, est.)** 267 applied for aid; of those 83% were deemed to have need. 100% of freshmen with need received aid; of those 16% had need fully met. *Average percent of need met:* 86% (excluding resources awarded to replace EFC). *Average financial aid package:* $36,727 (excluding resources awarded to replace EFC). 25% of all full-time freshmen had no need and received non-need-based gift aid.

**UNDERGRADUATE FINANCIAL AID (Fall 2014, est.)** 941 applied for aid; of those 86% were deemed to have need. 100% of undergraduates with need received aid; of those 16% had need fully met. *Average percent of need met:* 86% (excluding resources awarded to replace EFC). *Average financial aid package:* $35,078 (excluding resources awarded to replace EFC). 27% of all full-time undergraduates had no need and received non-need-based gift aid.

**GIFT AID (NEED-BASED)** *Total amount:* $23,577,896 (8% federal, 1% state, 89% institutional, 2% external sources). *Receiving aid:* Freshmen: 66% (215); all full-time undergraduates: 58% (786). *Average award:* Freshmen: $32,985; Undergraduates: $30,256. *Scholarships, grants, and awards:* Federal Pell, FSEOG, state, private, college/university gift aid from institutional funds.

**GIFT AID (NON-NEED-BASED)** *Total amount:* $6,131,720 (1% federal, 90% institutional, 9% external sources). *Receiving aid:* Freshmen: 10% (31). Undergraduates: 8% (113). *Average award:* Freshmen: $12,719. Undergraduates: $13,583. *Scholarships, grants, and awards by category:* Academic interests/achievement: biological sciences, English, general academic interests/achievements, humanities, international studies, mathematics, physical sciences, social sciences. Creative arts/performance: creative writing. Special achievements/activities: community service, leadership. Special characteristics: children of faculty/staff. *Tuition waivers:* Full or partial for employees or children of employees. *ROTC:* Army cooperative.

**LOANS** *Student loans:* $7,073,113 (73% need-based, 27% non-need based). 65% of past graduating class borrowed through all loan programs. *Average indebtedness per student:* $20,432. *Average need-based loan:* Freshmen: $3144. Undergraduates: $4246. *Parent loans:* $2,843,248 (28% need-based, 72% non-need-based). *Programs:* Federal Direct (Subsidized and Unsubsidized Stafford, PLUS), Perkins.

**WORK-STUDY** *Federal work-study:* Total amount: $1,025,543; 763 jobs averaging $2600. *State or other work-study/employment:* Total amount: $392,178 (14% need-based, 86% non-need-based). Part-time jobs available.

**APPLYING FOR FINANCIAL AID** *Required financial aid forms:* FAFSA, CSS Financial Aid PROFILE, noncustodial (divorced/separated) parent's statement. *Financial aid deadline (priority):* 2/1. *Notification date:* 4/1. Students must reply by 5/1 or within 2 weeks of notification.

**CONTACT** Ms. Jennifer Garratt Lawton, Director of Financial Aid, Hampshire College, 893 West Street, Amherst, MA 01002, 413-559-5484 or toll-free 877-937-4267. *Fax:* 413-559-5585. *E-mail:* financialaid@hampshire.edu.
*Website:* http://www.hampshire.edu/.

# HAMPTON UNIVERSITY
## Hampton, VA

| Tuition & fees: $21,760 | Average undergraduate aid package: $5789 |
| --- | --- |

**ABOUT THE INSTITUTION** Independent, coed. *Awards:* certificates, associate, bachelor's, master's, and doctoral degrees. 77 undergraduate majors. *Total enrollment:* 4,397. Undergraduates: 3,504. Freshmen: 882. Federal methodology is used as a basis for awarding need-based institutional aid.

**UNDERGRADUATE EXPENSES for 2015–2016** *Application fee:* $35. *Comprehensive fee:* $31,452 includes full-time tuition ($19,548), mandatory fees ($2212), and room and board ($9692). *College room only:* $5040. Full-time tuition and fees vary according to course load, degree level, location, program, and reciprocity agreements. Room and board charges vary according to board plan, housing facility, and location. *Part-time tuition:* $496 per credit hour. Part-time tuition and fees vary according to class time, course load, location, and reciprocity agreements.

**FRESHMAN FINANCIAL AID (Fall 2014, est.)** 651 applied for aid; of those 85% were deemed to have need. 96% of freshmen with need received aid; of those 46% had

need fully met. *Average percent of need met:* 46% (excluding resources awarded to replace EFC). *Average financial aid package:* $5591 (excluding resources awarded to replace EFC). 4% of all full-time freshmen had no need and received non-need-based gift aid.

**UNDERGRADUATE FINANCIAL AID (Fall 2014, est.)** 2,046 applied for aid; of those 85% were deemed to have need. 95% of undergraduates with need received aid; of those 33% had need fully met. *Average percent of need met:* 52% (excluding resources awarded to replace EFC). *Average financial aid package:* $5789 (excluding resources awarded to replace EFC). 1% of all full-time undergraduates had no need and received non-need-based gift aid.

**GIFT AID (NEED-BASED)** *Total amount:* $7,235,121 (86% federal, 9% state, 2% institutional, 3% external sources). *Receiving aid:* Freshmen: 56% (434); all full-time undergraduates: 21% (617). *Average award:* Freshmen: $5137; Undergraduates: $5003. *Scholarships, grants, and awards:* Federal Pell, FSEOG, state, private, college/university gift aid from institutional funds, Federal Nursing.

**GIFT AID (NON-NEED-BASED)** *Total amount:* $17,674,079 (8% state, 70% institutional, 22% external sources). *Receiving aid:* Freshmen: 42% (329). Undergraduates: 14% (411). *Average award:* Freshmen: $12,217. Undergraduates: $12,424. *Scholarships, grants, and awards by category:* Academic interests/achievement: 150 awards ($1,973,890 total): architecture, biological sciences, business, communication, computer science, education, engineering/technologies, general academic interests/achievements, health fields, physical sciences. Creative arts/performance: 9 awards ($52,000 total): music. Special achievements/activities: 18 awards ($45,000 total): leadership. Special characteristics: 659 awards ($2,151,711 total): adult students, children of faculty/staff, international students, members of minority groups, veterans, veterans' children. *Tuition waivers:* Full or partial for employees or children of employees. *ROTC:* Army, Naval.

**LOANS** *Student loans:* $20,553,615 (92% need-based, 8% non-need-based). 72% of past graduating class borrowed through all loan programs. *Average indebtedness per student:* $9231. *Average need-based loan:* Freshmen: $5254. Undergraduates: $5502. *Parent loans:* $24,288,384 (87% need-based, 13% non-need-based). *Programs:* Federal Direct (Subsidized and Unsubsidized Stafford, PLUS), Perkins, Federal Nursing, college/university, private loans.

**WORK-STUDY** *Federal work-study:* Total amount: $123,989; 172 jobs averaging $655. *State or other work-study/employment:* Total amount: $217,045 (86% need-based, 14% non-need-based). 138 part-time jobs averaging $967.

**ATHLETIC AWARDS** Total amount: $5,013,876 (100% non-need-based).

**APPLYING FOR FINANCIAL AID** *Required financial aid forms:* FAFSA, state aid form (VA residents only). *Financial aid deadline:* 4/15 (priority: 2/15). *Notification date:* Continuous beginning 4/15. Students must reply within 2 weeks of notification.

**CONTACT** Martin Miles, Director of Financial Aid, Hampton University, Whipple Barn, 2nd Floor, Hampton, VA 23668, 757-727-5332 or toll-free 800-624-3328. *Fax:* 757-728-6567. *E-mail:* martin.miles@hamptonu.edu.
*Website:* http://www.hamptonu.edu/.

# HANNIBAL-LAGRANGE UNIVERSITY
## Hannibal, MO

**CONTACT** Brice Baumgardner, Director of Financial Aid, Hannibal-LaGrange University, 2800 Palmyra Road, Hannibal, MO 63401-1940, 573-629-3279 Ext. 3279 or toll-free 800-HLG-1119. *Fax:* 573-248-0954. *E-mail:* bbaumgardner@hlg.edu. *Website:* http://www.hlg.edu/.

# HANOVER COLLEGE
## Hanover, IN

| Tuition & fees: $34,514 | Average undergraduate aid package: $27,889 |
| --- | --- |

**ABOUT THE INSTITUTION** Independent Presbyterian, coed. *Awards:* bachelor's degrees. 31 undergraduate majors. *Total enrollment:* 1,145. Undergraduates: 1,145. Freshmen: 293. Federal methodology is used as a basis for awarding need-based institutional aid.

**UNDERGRADUATE EXPENSES** for 2015–2016 *Application fee:* $40. *One-time required fee:* $250. *Comprehensive fee:* $44,966 includes full-time tuition ($33,744), mandatory fees ($770), and room and board ($10,452). *College room only:* $5200. Full-time tuition and fees vary according to reciprocity agreements. Room and board charges vary according to housing facility. *Part-time tuition:* $3750 per unit. Part-time tuition and fees vary according to course load and reciprocity agreements.

**FRESHMAN FINANCIAL AID (Fall 2013)** 257 applied for aid; of those 86% were deemed to have need. 100% of freshmen with need received aid; of those 29% had need fully met. *Average percent of need met:* 81% (excluding resources awarded to replace EFC). *Average financial aid package:* $27,663 (excluding resources awarded to replace EFC). 22% of all full-time freshmen had no need and received non-need-based gift aid.

**UNDERGRADUATE FINANCIAL AID (Fall 2013)** 964 applied for aid; of those 90% were deemed to have need. 100% of undergraduates with need received aid; of those 25% had need fully met. *Average percent of need met:* 82% (excluding resources awarded to replace EFC). *Average financial aid package:* $27,889 (excluding resources awarded to replace EFC). 22% of all full-time undergraduates had no need and received non-need-based gift aid.

**GIFT AID (NEED-BASED)** *Total amount:* $19,821,539 (8% federal, 9% state, 79% institutional, 4% external sources). *Receiving aid:* Freshmen: 75% (221); all full-time undergraduates: 76% (865). *Average award:* Freshmen: $24,350; Undergraduates: $23,577. *Scholarships, grants, and awards:* Federal Pell, FSEOG, state, private, college/university gift aid from institutional funds.

**GIFT AID (NON-NEED-BASED)** *Total amount:* $5,721,762 (1% state, 96% institutional, 3% external sources). *Receiving aid:* Freshmen: 17% (49). Undergraduates: 13% (147). *Average award:* Freshmen: $20,693. Undergraduates: $18,221. *Scholarships, grants, and awards by category:* Academic interests/achievement: general academic interests/achievements. Creative arts/performance: art/fine arts, music, theater/drama. Special characteristics: children and siblings of alumni, children of faculty/staff, international students, members of minority groups, out-of-state students, religious affiliation, siblings of current students. *Tuition waivers:* Full or partial for employees or children of employees, senior citizens.

**LOANS** *Student loans:* $7,765,810 (64% need-based, 36% non-need-based). 70% of past graduating class borrowed through all loan programs. *Average indebtedness per student:* $31,004. *Average need-based loan:* Freshmen: $3339. Undergraduates: $4292. *Parent loans:* $3,369,053 (34% need-based, 66% non-need-based). *Programs:* Federal Direct (Subsidized and Unsubsidized Stafford, PLUS), college/university.

**WORK-STUDY** *Federal work-study:* 528 jobs averaging $1311.

**APPLYING FOR FINANCIAL AID** *Required financial aid form:* FAFSA. *Financial aid deadline (priority):* 3/1. *Notification date:* Continuous beginning 3/1. Students must reply by 5/1.

**CONTACT** Mr. Richard A. Nash, Director of Financial Aid, Hanover College, PO Box 108, Hanover, IN 47243-0108, 800-213-2178 Ext. 7029 or toll-free 800-213-2178. *Fax:* 812-866-7284. *E-mail:* finaid@hanover.edu. *Website:* http://www.hanover.edu/.

---

# HARDING UNIVERSITY
## Searcy, AR

| Tuition & fees: $17,040 | Average undergraduate aid package: $15,108 |
|---|---|

**ABOUT THE INSTITUTION** Independent Church of Christ, coed. *Awards:* certificates, bachelor's, master's, and doctoral degrees. 85 undergraduate majors. *Total enrollment:* 6,238. Undergraduates: 4,428. Freshmen: 1,041. Federal methodology is used as a basis for awarding need-based institutional aid.

**UNDERGRADUATE EXPENSES** for 2015–2016 *Application fee:* $50. *Comprehensive fee:* $23,556 includes full-time tuition ($16,560), mandatory fees ($480), and room and board ($6516). *College room only:* $3290. Full-time tuition and fees vary according to course load. Room and board charges vary according to board plan and housing facility. *Part-time tuition:* $552 per credit hour. *Part-time fees:* $25 per credit hour. Part-time tuition and fees vary according to course load. *Payment plan:* Tuition prepayment.

**FRESHMAN FINANCIAL AID (Fall 2013)** 895 applied for aid; of those 73% were deemed to have need. 99% of freshmen with need received aid; of those 40% had need fully met. *Average percent of need met:* 83% (excluding resources awarded to

replace EFC). *Average financial aid package:* $16,450 (excluding resources awarded to replace EFC). 22% of all full-time freshmen had no need and received non-need-based gift aid.

**UNDERGRADUATE FINANCIAL AID (Fall 2013)** 3,185 applied for aid; of those 80% were deemed to have need. 99% of undergraduates with need received aid; of those 34% had need fully met. *Average percent of need met:* 72% (excluding resources awarded to replace EFC). *Average financial aid package:* $15,108 (excluding resources awarded to replace EFC). 12% of all full-time undergraduates had no need and received non-need-based gift aid.

**GIFT AID (NEED-BASED)** *Total amount:* $19,824,177 (27% federal, 9% state, 61% institutional, 3% external sources). *Receiving aid:* Freshmen: 61% (638); all full-time undergraduates: 52% (2,321). *Average award:* Freshmen: $9749; Undergraduates: $8837. *Scholarships, grants, and awards:* Federal Pell, FSEOG, state, private, college/university gift aid from institutional funds.

**GIFT AID (NON-NEED-BASED)** *Total amount:* $12,265,683 (10% state, 87% institutional, 3% external sources). *Receiving aid:* Freshmen: 12% (128). Undergraduates: 9% (420). *Average award:* Freshmen: $6269. Undergraduates: $6157. *Scholarships, grants, and awards by category:* Academic interests/achievement: 2,358 awards ($13,511,556 total): communication, computer science, engineering/technologies, English, general academic interests/achievements, health fields, religion/biblical studies. Creative arts/performance: 218 awards ($219,782 total): art/fine arts, cinema/film/broadcasting, debating, general creative arts/performance, journalism/publications, music. Special achievements/activities: 97 awards ($75,572 total): cheerleading/drum major, general special achievements/activities, leadership, religious involvement. Special characteristics: 559 awards ($3,457,617 total): children of faculty/staff, children with a deceased or disabled parent, general special characteristics, international students, relatives of clergy, siblings of current students. *Tuition waivers:* Full or partial for employees or children of employees, senior citizens.

**LOANS** *Student loans:* $21,392,206 (81% need-based, 19% non-need-based). 63% of past graduating class borrowed through all loan programs. *Average indebtedness per student:* $24,120. *Average need-based loan:* Freshmen: $6409. Undergraduates: $6547. *Parent loans:* $5,633,943 (71% need-based, 29% non-need-based). *Programs:* Federal Direct (Subsidized and Unsubsidized Stafford, PLUS), Perkins, Federal Nursing, state, college/university.

**WORK-STUDY** *Federal work-study:* 522 jobs averaging $780. *State or other work-study/employment:* Total amount: $2,162,837 (60% need-based, 40% non-need-based). 1,581 part-time jobs averaging $1666.

**ATHLETIC AWARDS** Total amount: $2,354,207 (40% need-based, 60% non-need-based).

**APPLYING FOR FINANCIAL AID** *Required financial aid form:* FAFSA. *Financial aid deadline (priority):* 4/15. *Notification date:* Continuous. Students must reply within 2 weeks of notification.

**CONTACT** Dr. Jonathan C. Roberts, Director of Student Financial Services, Harding University, PO Box 12282, Searcy, AR 72149-2282, 501-279-4257 or toll-free 800-477-4407. *Fax:* 501-279-4129. *E-mail:* jroberts@harding.edu. *Website:* http://www.harding.edu/.

---

# HARDIN-SIMMONS UNIVERSITY
## Abilene, TX

| Tuition & fees: $24,500 | Average undergraduate aid package: $19,036 |
|---|---|

**ABOUT THE INSTITUTION** Independent Baptist, coed. *Awards:* certificates, bachelor's, master's, and doctoral degrees. 66 undergraduate majors. *Total enrollment:* 2,084. Undergraduates: 1,640. Freshmen: 339. Federal methodology is used as a basis for awarding need-based institutional aid.

**UNDERGRADUATE EXPENSES** for 2015–2016 *Comprehensive fee:* $32,240 includes full-time tuition ($24,500) and room and board ($7740). *College room only:* $3600. Full-time tuition and fees vary according to program. Room and board charges vary according to board plan and housing facility. *Part-time tuition:* $750 per credit hour. *Part-time fees:* $525 per term. Part-time tuition and fees vary according to course load and program. *Payment plan:* Guaranteed tuition.

**FRESHMAN FINANCIAL AID (Fall 2014, est.)** 336 applied for aid; of those 76% were deemed to have need. 100% of freshmen with need received aid; of those 24% had need fully met. *Average percent of need met:* 66% (excluding resources awarded to replace EFC). *Average financial aid package:* $24,614 (excluding resources awarded to replace EFC). 64% of all full-time freshmen had no need and received non-need-based gift aid.

**UNDERGRADUATE FINANCIAL AID (Fall 2014, est.)** 1,413 applied for aid; of those 73% were deemed to have need. 100% of undergraduates with need received aid; of those 17% had need fully met. *Average percent of need met:* 67% (excluding resources awarded to replace EFC). *Average financial aid package:* $19,036 (excluding resources awarded to replace EFC). 55% of all full-time undergraduates had no need and received non-need-based gift aid.

**GIFT AID (NEED-BASED)** *Total amount:* $5,392,100 (48% federal, 36% state, 16% institutional). *Receiving aid:* Freshmen: 53% (180); all full-time undergraduates: 51% (742). *Average award:* Freshmen: $6117; Undergraduates: $5708. *Scholarships, grants, and awards:* Federal Pell, FSEOG, state, private, college/university gift aid from institutional funds.

**GIFT AID (NON-NEED-BASED)** *Total amount:* $12,616,504 (96% institutional, 4% external sources). *Receiving aid:* Freshmen: 73% (248). Undergraduates: 64% (936). *Average award:* Freshmen: $10,614. Undergraduates: $9015. *Scholarships, grants, and awards by category: Academic interests/achievement:* biological sciences, business, communication, computer science, education, English, foreign languages, general academic interests/achievements, health fields, humanities, mathematics, physical sciences, premedicine, religion/biblical studies, social sciences. *Creative arts/performance:* applied art and design, art/fine arts, creative writing, journalism/publications, music, performing arts, theater/drama. *Special achievements/activities:* general special achievements/activities. *Special characteristics:* children and siblings of alumni, children of educators, children of faculty/staff, ethnic background, general special characteristics, handicapped students, out-of-state students, public servants, relatives of clergy, religious affiliation, siblings of current students, veterans, veterans' children. *Tuition waivers:* Full or partial for employees or children of employees.

**LOANS** *Student loans:* $15,527,412 (22% need-based, 78% non-need-based). 75% of past graduating class borrowed through all loan programs. *Average indebtedness per student:* $34,380. *Average need-based loan:* Freshmen: $2975. Undergraduates: $4055. *Parent loans:* $3,398,422 (100% non-need-based). *Programs:* Federal Direct (Subsidized and Unsubsidized Stafford, PLUS), Perkins, Federal Nursing, state, college/university.

**WORK-STUDY** *Federal work-study:* Total amount: $152,214; jobs available. *State or other work-study/employment:* Total amount: $18,048 (100% need-based). Part-time jobs available.

**APPLYING FOR FINANCIAL AID** *Required financial aid form:* FAFSA. *Financial aid deadline (priority):* 3/1. *Notification date:* Continuous beginning 2/1. Students must reply within 2 weeks of notification.

**CONTACT** Mrs. Bridget Moore, Director of Financial Aid and Scholarships, Hardin-Simmons University, Box 16050, Abilene, TX 79698, 325-670-1482 or toll-free 877-464-7889. *Fax:* 325-670-5822. *E-mail:* bnmoore@hsutx.edu.
*Website:* http://www.hsutx.edu/.

# HARRISBURG UNIVERSITY OF SCIENCE AND TECHNOLOGY
## Harrisburg, PA

**CONTACT** Mr. Vince P. Frank, Director of Financial Aid Services, Harrisburg University of Science and Technology, 326 Market Street, Harrisburg, PA 17101-2208, 717-901-5115 or toll-free 866-HBG-UNIV. *Fax:* 717-901-3115. *E-mail:* vfrank@harrisburgu.edu.
*Website:* http://www.HarrisburgU.edu/.

# HARRISON COLLEGE
## Indianapolis, IN

**CONTACT** Financial Aid Office, Harrison College, 550 East Washington Street, Indianapolis, IN 46204, 317-264-5656 or toll-free 888-544-4422.
*Website:* http://www.harrison.edu/.

# HARRISON COLLEGE
## Grove City, OH

**CONTACT** Financial Aid Office, Harrison College, 3880 Jackpot Road, Grove City, OH 43123, 614-539-8800 or toll-free 888-544-4422.
*Website:* http://www.harrison.edu/.

# HARRIS-STOWE STATE UNIVERSITY
## St. Louis, MO

**CONTACT** Regina Blackshear, Director of Financial Aid, Harris-Stowe State University, 3026 Laclede Avenue, St. Louis, MO 63103-2136, 314-340-3502. *Fax:* 314-340-3503.
*Website:* http://www.hssu.edu/.

# HARTWICK COLLEGE
## Oneonta, NY

| Tuition & fees: $40,070 | Average undergraduate aid package: $32,197 |
| --- | --- |

**ABOUT THE INSTITUTION** Independent, coed. *Awards:* bachelor's degrees. 33 undergraduate majors. *Total enrollment:* 1,540. Undergraduates: 1,540. Freshmen: 419. Federal methodology is used as a basis for awarding need-based institutional aid.

**UNDERGRADUATE EXPENSES for 2015–2016** *One-time required fee:* $400. *Comprehensive fee:* $50,870 includes full-time tuition ($39,260), mandatory fees ($810), and room and board ($10,800). *College room only:* $5120. Full-time tuition and fees vary according to course load. Room and board charges vary according to board plan and housing facility. *Part-time tuition:* $1260 per credit hour. Part-time tuition and fees vary according to course load.

**FRESHMAN FINANCIAL AID (Fall 2014, est.)** 395 applied for aid; of those 93% were deemed to have need. 100% of freshmen with need received aid; of those 12% had need fully met. *Average percent of need met:* 80% (excluding resources awarded to replace EFC). *Average financial aid package:* $34,280 (excluding resources awarded to replace EFC). 12% of all full-time freshmen had no need and received non-need-based gift aid.

**UNDERGRADUATE FINANCIAL AID (Fall 2014, est.)** 1,331 applied for aid; of those 93% were deemed to have need. 100% of undergraduates with need received aid; of those 13% had need fully met. *Average percent of need met:* 79% (excluding resources awarded to replace EFC). *Average financial aid package:* $32,197 (excluding resources awarded to replace EFC). 17% of all full-time undergraduates had no need and received non-need-based gift aid.

**GIFT AID (NEED-BASED)** *Total amount:* $30,333,336 (8% federal, 6% state, 83% institutional, 3% external sources). *Receiving aid:* Freshmen: 63% (266); all full-time undergraduates: 82% (1,237). *Average award:* Freshmen: $28,153; Undergraduates: $26,491. *Scholarships, grants, and awards:* Federal Pell, FSEOG, state, private, college/university gift aid from institutional funds.

**GIFT AID (NON-NEED-BASED)** *Total amount:* $5,948,937 (96% institutional, 4% external sources). *Receiving aid:* Freshmen: 6% (26). Undergraduates: 7% (98). *Average award:* Freshmen: $20,788. Undergraduates: $19,257. *Scholarships, grants, and awards by category: Academic interests/achievement:* general academic interests/achievements. *Creative arts/performance:* 6 awards ($11,400 total): art/fine arts, music. *Special achievements/activities:* 811 awards ($1,780,993 total): general special achievements/activities. *Special characteristics:* 196 awards ($1,869,932 total): children and siblings of alumni, children of faculty/staff, international students, siblings of current students, veterans. *Tuition waivers:* Full or partial for employees or children of employees.

**LOANS** *Student loans:* $13,793,494 (79% need-based, 21% non-need-based). 78% of past graduating class borrowed through all loan programs. *Average indebtedness per student:* $26,708. *Average need-based loan:* Freshmen: $4992. Undergraduates: $4273. *Parent loans:* $17,254,967 (28% need-based, 72% non-need-based). *Programs:* Federal Direct (Subsidized and Unsubsidized Stafford, PLUS), Perkins, Federal Nursing, college/university, alternative loans.

**WORK-STUDY** *Federal work-study:* Total amount: $1,941,951; 938 jobs averaging $1795.

**ATHLETIC AWARDS** Total amount: $793,906 (14% need-based, 86% non-need-based).

**APPLYING FOR FINANCIAL AID** *Required financial aid form:* FAFSA. *Financial aid deadline:* Continuous. *Notification date:* Continuous beginning 2/6. Students must reply by 5/1 or within 2 weeks of notification.

**CONTACT** Mrs. Melissa Allen, Director of Financial Aid, Hartwick College, One Hartwick Drive, Oneonta, NY 13820, 607-431-4130 or toll-free 888-HARTWICK. *Fax:* 607-431-4006. *E-mail:* allenm@hartwick.edu. *Website:* http://www.hartwick.edu/.

# HARVARD UNIVERSITY
## Cambridge, MA

| Tuition & fees: $43,938 | Average undergraduate aid package: $47,475 |
|---|---|

**ABOUT THE INSTITUTION** Independent, coed. *Awards:* bachelor's, master's, and doctoral degrees. 47 undergraduate majors. *Total enrollment:* 10,803. Undergraduates: 6,694. Freshmen: 1,650. Institutional methodology is used as a basis for awarding need-based institutional aid.

**UNDERGRADUATE EXPENSES** for 2015–2016 *Application fee:* $75. *Comprehensive fee:* $58,607 includes full-time tuition ($40,418), mandatory fees ($3520), and room and board ($14,669). *College room only:* $9009. *Payment plan:* Tuition prepayment.

**FRESHMAN FINANCIAL AID (Fall 2013)** 1,087 applied for aid; of those 86% were deemed to have need. 100% of freshmen with need received aid; of those 99% had need fully met. *Average percent of need met:* 100% (excluding resources awarded to replace EFC). *Average financial aid package:* $48,876 (excluding resources awarded to replace EFC).

**UNDERGRADUATE FINANCIAL AID (Fall 2013)** 4,291 applied for aid; of those 93% were deemed to have need. 100% of undergraduates with need received aid; of those 99% had need fully met. *Average percent of need met:* 100% (excluding resources awarded to replace EFC). *Average financial aid package:* $47,475 (excluding resources awarded to replace EFC). 1% of all full-time undergraduates had no need and received non-need-based gift aid.

**GIFT AID (NEED-BASED)** *Total amount:* $176,440,505 (5% federal, 92% institutional, 3% external sources). *Receiving aid:* Freshmen: 56% (930); all full-time undergraduates: 58% (3,960). *Average award:* Freshmen: $47,053; Undergraduates: $44,430. *Scholarships, grants, and awards:* Federal Pell, FSEOG, state, private, college/university gift aid from institutional funds.

**GIFT AID (NON-NEED-BASED)** *Total amount:* $5,138,238 (13% federal, 4% institutional, 83% external sources). *Average award:* Undergraduates: $20,827. *ROTC:* Army cooperative, Naval, Air Force cooperative.

**LOANS** *Student loans:* $5,937,181 (70% need-based, 30% non-need-based). 26% of past graduating class borrowed through all loan programs. *Average indebtedness per student:* $15,117. *Average need-based loan:* Freshmen: $3569. Undergraduates: $4462. *Parent loans:* $5,702,271 (100% non-need-based). *Programs:* Federal Direct (Subsidized and Unsubsidized Stafford, PLUS), Perkins, state, college/university.

**WORK-STUDY** *Federal work-study:* 1,024 jobs averaging $2781. *State or other work-study/employment:* Total amount: $6,075,680 (87% need-based, 13% non-need-based). 2,128 part-time jobs averaging $2855.

**APPLYING FOR FINANCIAL AID** *Required financial aid forms:* FAFSA, CSS Financial Aid PROFILE, noncustodial (divorced/separated) parent's statement, business/farm supplement, federal income tax form(s). *Financial aid deadline (priority):* 2/1. *Notification date:* 4/1. Students must reply by 5/1 or within 2 weeks of notification.

**CONTACT** Financial Aid Office, Harvard University, 86 Brattle Street, Cambridge, MA 02138, 617-495-1581. *Fax:* 617-496-0256. *Website:* http://www.harvard.edu/.

# HARVEY MUDD COLLEGE
## Claremont, CA

| Tuition & fees: $48,594 | Average undergraduate aid package: $38,557 |
|---|---|

**ABOUT THE INSTITUTION** Independent, coed. *Awards:* bachelor's degrees. 7 undergraduate majors. *Total enrollment:* 804. Undergraduates: 804. Freshmen: 194. Both federal and institutional methodology are used as a basis for awarding need-based institutional aid.

**UNDERGRADUATE EXPENSES** for 2015–2016 *Application fee:* $70. *One-time required fee:* $100. *Comprehensive fee:* $64,427 includes full-time tuition ($48,315), mandatory fees ($279), and room and board ($15,833). *College room only:* $8494. Room and board charges vary according to board plan. *Part-time tuition:* $1509.84 per unit. Part-time tuition and fees vary according to course load.

**FRESHMAN FINANCIAL AID (Fall 2013)** 155 applied for aid; of those 74% were deemed to have need. 100% of freshmen with need received aid; of those 100% had need fully met. *Average percent of need met:* 100% (excluding resources awarded to replace EFC). *Average financial aid package:* $42,282 (excluding resources awarded to replace EFC). 20% of all full-time freshmen had no need and received non-need-based gift aid.

**UNDERGRADUATE FINANCIAL AID (Fall 2013)** 495 applied for aid; of those 85% were deemed to have need. 100% of undergraduates with need received aid; of those 100% had need fully met. *Average percent of need met:* 100% (excluding resources awarded to replace EFC). *Average financial aid package:* $38,557 (excluding resources awarded to replace EFC). 22% of all full-time undergraduates had no need and received non-need-based gift aid.

**GIFT AID (NEED-BASED)** *Total amount:* $14,290,472 (4% federal, 4% state, 89% institutional, 3% external sources). *Receiving aid:* Freshmen: 52% (112); all full-time undergraduates: 50% (410). *Average award:* Freshmen: $40,188; Undergraduates: $35,558. *Scholarships, grants, and awards:* Federal Pell, FSEOG, state, private, college/university gift aid from institutional funds.

**GIFT AID (NON-NEED-BASED)** *Total amount:* $2,252,754 (83% institutional, 17% external sources). *Receiving aid:* Freshmen: 11% (24). Undergraduates: 6% (50). *Average award:* Freshmen: $9410. Undergraduates: $10,546. *Scholarships, grants, and awards by category:* Academic interests/achievement: 322 awards ($3,408,646 total): general academic interests/achievements. *Special characteristics:* 2 awards ($50,000 total): international students. *Tuition waivers:* Full or partial for employees or children of employees. *ROTC:* Army cooperative, Air Force.

**LOANS** *Student loans:* $2,612,899 (89% need-based, 11% non-need-based). 51% of past graduating class borrowed through all loan programs. *Average indebtedness per student:* $24,503. *Average need-based loan:* Freshmen: $4187. Undergraduates: $5039. *Parent loans:* $1,749,276 (78% need-based, 22% non-need-based). *Programs:* Federal Direct (Subsidized and Unsubsidized Stafford, PLUS), Perkins, college/university, alternative loans.

**WORK-STUDY** *Federal work-study:* 157 jobs averaging $574. *State or other work-study/employment:* Total amount: $161,971 (74% need-based, 26% non-need-based). 28 part-time jobs averaging $5785.

**APPLYING FOR FINANCIAL AID** *Required financial aid forms:* FAFSA, CSS Financial Aid PROFILE, state aid form, noncustodial (divorced/separated) parent's statement, business/farm supplement. *Financial aid deadline:* 2/1. *Notification date:* 4/1. Students must reply by 5/1.

**CONTACT** Mrs. Gilma Lopez, Director of Financial Aid, Harvey Mudd College, 301 Platt Boulevard, Claremont, CA 91711-5994, 909-621-8055. *Fax:* 909-607-7046. *E-mail:* financial_aid@hmc.edu. *Website:* http://www.hmc.edu/.

# HASKELL INDIAN NATIONS UNIVERSITY
## Lawrence, KS

**CONTACT** Reta Brewer, Director of Financial Aid, Haskell Indian Nations University, 155 Indian Avenue, Box 5027, Lawrence, KS 66046-4800, 785-749-8468. *Fax:* 785-832-6617. *Website:* http://www.haskell.edu/.

# HASTINGS COLLEGE
### Hastings, NE

| Tuition & fees: $27,300 | Average undergraduate aid package: $21,151 |
| --- | --- |

**ABOUT THE INSTITUTION** Independent Presbyterian, coed. *Awards:* bachelor's and master's degrees. 83 undergraduate majors. *Total enrollment:* 1,212. Undergraduates: 1,183. Freshmen: 345. Federal methodology is used as a basis for awarding need-based institutional aid.

**UNDERGRADUATE EXPENSES** for 2015–2016 *Comprehensive fee:* $35,380 includes full-time tuition ($26,110), mandatory fees ($1190), and room and board ($8080). Room and board charges vary according to board plan and housing facility. *Part-time tuition:* $1070 per credit hour. *Part-time fees:* $316 per term. Part-time tuition and fees vary according to course load.

**FRESHMAN FINANCIAL AID (Fall 2014, est.)** 310 applied for aid; of those 86% were deemed to have need. 100% of freshmen with need received aid; of those 31% had need fully met. *Average percent of need met:* 81% (excluding resources awarded to replace EFC). *Average financial aid package:* $20,242 (excluding resources awarded to replace EFC). 21% of all full-time freshmen had no need and received non-need-based gift aid.

**UNDERGRADUATE FINANCIAL AID (Fall 2014, est.)** 932 applied for aid; of those 90% were deemed to have need. 100% of undergraduates with need received aid; of those 27% had need fully met. *Average percent of need met:* 79% (excluding resources awarded to replace EFC). *Average financial aid package:* $21,151 (excluding resources awarded to replace EFC). 24% of all full-time undergraduates had no need and received non-need-based gift aid.

**GIFT AID (NEED-BASED)** *Total amount:* $12,850,443 (11% federal, 2% state, 82% institutional, 5% external sources). *Receiving aid:* Freshmen: 78% (268); all full-time undergraduates: 75% (838). *Average award:* Freshmen: $17,705; Undergraduates: $17,634. *Scholarships, grants, and awards:* Federal Pell, FSEOG, state, private, college/university gift aid from institutional funds.

**GIFT AID (NON-NEED-BASED)** *Total amount:* $5,093,779 (90% institutional, 10% external sources). *Receiving aid:* Freshmen: 23% (78). Undergraduates: 17% (191). *Average award:* Freshmen: $15,664. Undergraduates: $13,915. *Scholarships, grants, and awards by category: Academic interests/achievement:* communication, general academic interests/achievements, religion/biblical studies. *Creative arts/performance:* art/fine arts, cinema/film/broadcasting, dance, debating, journalism/publications, music, performing arts, theater/drama. *Special achievements/activities:* cheerleading/drum major, memberships, rodeo. *Special characteristics:* adult students, children and siblings of alumni, children of educators, children of faculty/staff, international students, previous college experience, religious affiliation, siblings of current students, spouses of current students. *Tuition waivers:* Full or partial for employees or children of employees, adult students.

**LOANS** *Student loans:* $5,633,704 (70% need-based, 30% non-need-based). 71% of past graduating class borrowed through all loan programs. *Average indebtedness per student:* $27,784. *Average need-based loan:* Freshmen: $3709. Undergraduates: $4583. *Parent loans:* $1,812,062 (40% need-based, 60% non-need-based). *Programs:* Federal Direct (Subsidized and Unsubsidized Stafford, PLUS), Perkins, college/university.

**WORK-STUDY** *Federal work-study:* Total amount: $104,430; 70 jobs averaging $1663. *State or other work-study/employment:* Total amount: $167,660 (52% need-based, 48% non-need-based). Part-time jobs available.

**ATHLETIC AWARDS** Total amount: $3,071,033 (67% need-based, 33% non-need-based).

**APPLYING FOR FINANCIAL AID** *Required financial aid forms:* FAFSA, institution's own form. *Financial aid deadline:* 9/1 (priority: 5/1). *Notification date:* Continuous beginning 2/15. Students must reply within 2 weeks of notification.

**CONTACT** Ms. Terri Lynn Graham, Director of Student Financial Aid, Hastings College, 710 North Turner Avenue, Hastings, NE 68901, 402-461-7431 or toll-free 800-532-7642. *Fax:* 402-461-7714. *E-mail:* tgraham@hastings.edu. *Website:* http://www.hastings.edu/.

# HAVERFORD COLLEGE
### Haverford, PA

| Tuition & fees: $49,098 | Average undergraduate aid package: $42,851 |
| --- | --- |

**ABOUT THE INSTITUTION** Independent, coed. *Awards:* bachelor's degrees. 38 undergraduate majors. *Total enrollment:* 1,194. Undergraduates: 1,194. Freshmen: 338. Institutional methodology is used as a basis for awarding need-based institutional aid.

**UNDERGRADUATE EXPENSES** for 2015–2016 *Application fee:* $60. *One-time required fee:* $230. *Comprehensive fee:* $63,986 includes full-time tuition ($48,656), mandatory fees ($442), and room and board ($14,888). *College room only:* $8494. *Payment plan:* Tuition prepayment.

**FRESHMAN FINANCIAL AID (Fall 2014, est.)** 218 applied for aid; of those 81% were deemed to have need. 100% of freshmen with need received aid; of those 100% had need fully met. *Average percent of need met:* 100% (excluding resources awarded to replace EFC). *Average financial aid package:* $43,864 (excluding resources awarded to replace EFC).

**UNDERGRADUATE FINANCIAL AID (Fall 2014, est.)** 670 applied for aid; of those 89% were deemed to have need. 100% of undergraduates with need received aid; of those 100% had need fully met. *Average percent of need met:* 100% (excluding resources awarded to replace EFC). *Average financial aid package:* $42,851 (excluding resources awarded to replace EFC).

**GIFT AID (NEED-BASED)** *Total amount:* $24,783,683 (3% federal, 1% state, 93% institutional, 3% external sources). *Receiving aid:* Freshmen: 50% (168); all full-time undergraduates: 49% (575). *Average award:* Freshmen: $40,607; Undergraduates: $42,621. *Scholarships, grants, and awards:* Federal Pell, FSEOG, state, college/university gift aid from institutional funds.

**GIFT AID (NON-NEED-BASED)** *Tuition waivers:* Full or partial for employees or children of employees.

**LOANS** *Student loans:* $1,118,444 (51% need-based, 49% non-need-based). 26% of past graduating class borrowed through all loan programs. *Average indebtedness per student:* $15,540. *Average need-based loan:* Freshmen: $780. Undergraduates: $844. *Parent loans:* $1,504,745 (100% non-need-based). *Programs:* Federal Direct (Subsidized and Unsubsidized Stafford, PLUS), Perkins.

**WORK-STUDY** *Federal work-study:* Total amount: $102,305; jobs available. *State or other work-study/employment:* Total amount: $893,233 (44% need-based, 56% non-need-based). Part-time jobs available.

**APPLYING FOR FINANCIAL AID** *Required financial aid forms:* FAFSA, CSS Financial Aid PROFILE, noncustodial (divorced/separated) parent's statement, business/farm supplement. *Financial aid deadline (priority):* 2/1. *Notification date:* 4/1. Students must reply by 5/1.

**CONTACT** Mr. David J. Hoy, Director of Financial Aid, Haverford College, 370 Lancaster Avenue, Haverford, PA 19041-1392, 610-896-1350. *Fax:* 610-896-1338. *E-mail:* finaid@haverford.edu. *Website:* http://www.haverford.edu/.

# HAWAII PACIFIC UNIVERSITY
### Honolulu, HI

| Tuition & fees: $22,360 | Average undergraduate aid package: $20,234 |
| --- | --- |

**ABOUT THE INSTITUTION** Independent, coed. *Awards:* certificates, associate, bachelor's, and master's degrees. 63 undergraduate majors. *Total enrollment:* 5,827. Undergraduates: 4,835. Freshmen: 590. Federal methodology is used as a basis for awarding need-based institutional aid.

**UNDERGRADUATE EXPENSES** for 2015–2016 *Application fee:* $50. *Comprehensive fee:* $35,970 includes full-time tuition ($22,160), mandatory fees ($200), and room and board ($13,610). Full-time tuition and fees vary according to course level, course load, degree level, location, program, and student level. Room and board charges vary according to housing facility. *Part-time tuition:* $740 per credit. *Part-time fees:* $25 per term. Part-time tuition and fees vary according to course level, course load, degree level, location, program, and student level.

**FRESHMAN FINANCIAL AID (Fall 2013)** 462 applied for aid; of those 72% were deemed to have need. 100% of freshmen with need received aid; of those 19% had need fully met. *Average percent of need met:* 81% (excluding resources awarded to replace EFC). *Average financial aid package:* $22,419 (excluding resources awarded to replace EFC). 8% of all full-time freshmen had no need and received non-need-based gift aid.

**UNDERGRADUATE FINANCIAL AID (Fall 2013)** 2,262 applied for aid; of those 64% were deemed to have need. 99% of undergraduates with need received aid; of those 16% had need fully met. *Average percent of need met:* 70% (excluding resources awarded to replace EFC). *Average financial aid package:* $20,234 (excluding resources awarded to replace EFC). 4% of all full-time undergraduates had no need and received non-need-based gift aid.

**GIFT AID (NEED-BASED)** *Total amount:* $5,327,141 (100% federal). *Receiving aid:* Freshmen: 39% (188); all full-time undergraduates: 32% (840). *Average award:* Freshmen: $1163; Undergraduates: $1766. *Scholarships, grants, and awards:* Federal Pell, FSEOG, private, college/university gift aid from institutional funds, Federal Nursing.

**GIFT AID (NON-NEED-BASED)** *Total amount:* $906,990 (11% institutional, 89% external sources). *Receiving aid:* Freshmen: 5% (26). Undergraduates: 6% (159). *Average award:* Freshmen: $4164. Undergraduates: $889. *Scholarships, grants, and awards by category: Academic interests/achievement:* biological sciences, business, communication, general academic interests/achievements, health fields, social sciences. *Creative arts/performance:* dance, debating, journalism/publications, music. *Special achievements/activities:* cheerleading/drum major, community service, hobbies/interests, leadership, memberships, religious involvement. *Special characteristics:* ethnic background, international students, local/state students, out-of-state students, previous college experience, relatives of clergy, religious affiliation. *Tuition waivers:* Full or partial for employees or children of employees. *ROTC:* Army cooperative, Air Force cooperative.

**LOANS** *Student loans:* $14,377,914 (49% need-based, 51% non-need-based). *Average need-based loan:* Freshmen: $4495. Undergraduates: $6080. *Parent loans:* $8,723,085 (100% non-need-based). *Programs:* Federal Direct (Subsidized and Unsubsidized Stafford, PLUS), Perkins, Federal Nursing.

**WORK-STUDY** *Federal work-study:* 242 jobs averaging $3000.

**ATHLETIC AWARDS** Total amount: $2,237,566 (100% non-need-based).

**APPLYING FOR FINANCIAL AID** *Required financial aid form:* FAFSA. *Financial aid deadline (priority):* 3/1. *Notification date:* Continuous beginning 3/15. Students must reply within 3 weeks of notification.

**CONTACT** Adam Hatch, Director of Financial Aid, Hawaii Pacific University, 1164 Bishop Street, Suite 201, Honolulu, HI 96813-2785, 808-544-0253 or toll-free 866-225-5478. *Fax:* 808-544-0884. *E-mail:* financialaid@hpu.edu.
*Website:* http://www.hpu.edu/.

had need fully met. *Average percent of need met:* 78% (excluding resources awarded to replace EFC). *Average financial aid package:* $23,863 (excluding resources awarded to replace EFC). 9% of all full-time freshmen had no need and received non-need-based gift aid.

**UNDERGRADUATE FINANCIAL AID (Fall 2014, est.)** 1,005 applied for aid; of those 93% were deemed to have need. 100% of undergraduates with need received aid; of those 16% had need fully met. *Average percent of need met:* 79% (excluding resources awarded to replace EFC). *Average financial aid package:* $23,339 (excluding resources awarded to replace EFC). 9% of all full-time undergraduates had no need and received non-need-based gift aid.

**GIFT AID (NEED-BASED)** *Total amount:* $16,109,631 (14% federal, 5% state, 79% institutional, 2% external sources). *Receiving aid:* Freshmen: 88% (319); all full-time undergraduates: 88% (932). *Average award:* Freshmen: $18,385; Undergraduates: $17,190. *Scholarships, grants, and awards:* Federal Pell, FSEOG, state, private, college/university gift aid from institutional funds.

**GIFT AID (NON-NEED-BASED)** *Total amount:* $1,434,746 (96% institutional, 4% external sources). *Receiving aid:* Freshmen: 81% (293). Undergraduates: 64% (678). *Average award:* Freshmen: $13,521. Undergraduates: $11,945. *Scholarships, grants, and awards by category: Academic interests/achievement:* 707 awards ($7,989,100 total): general academic interests/achievements. *Creative arts/performance:* 60 awards ($113,250 total): music, performing arts. *Special characteristics:* 210 awards ($990,144 total): children of faculty/staff, international students, out-of-state students, relatives of clergy, religious affiliation. *Tuition waivers:* Full or partial for employees or children of employees. *ROTC:* Army cooperative, Air Force cooperative.

**LOANS** *Student loans:* $8,747,457 (96% need-based, 4% non-need-based). 94% of past graduating class borrowed through all loan programs. *Average indebtedness per student:* $36,962. *Average need-based loan:* Freshmen: $4019. Undergraduates: $5010. *Parent loans:* $2,683,042 (94% need-based, 6% non-need-based). *Programs:* Federal Direct (Subsidized and Unsubsidized Stafford, PLUS), Perkins.

**WORK-STUDY** *Federal work-study:* Total amount: $1,280,365; 659 jobs averaging $2000. *State or other work-study/employment:* Total amount: $60,837 (58% need-based, 42% non-need-based). 61 part-time jobs averaging $1000.

**APPLYING FOR FINANCIAL AID** *Required financial aid form:* FAFSA. *Financial aid deadline:* Continuous. *Notification date:* Continuous beginning 3/1. Students must reply by 5/1.

**CONTACT** Ms. Juli L. Weininger, Director of Financial Aid, Heidelberg University, 310 East Market Street, Tiffin, OH 44883-2462, 419-448-2293 or toll-free 800-434-3352. *Fax:* 419-448-2296.
*Website:* http://www.heidelberg.edu/.

---

# HEBREW THEOLOGICAL COLLEGE
## Skokie, IL

**CONTACT** Ms. Rhoda Morris, Financial Aid Administrator , Hebrew Theological College, 7135 Carpenter Road, Skokie, IL 60077-3263, 847-982-2500. *Fax:* 847-674-6381.
*Website:* http://www.htc.edu/.

---

# HELLENIC COLLEGE
## Brookline, MA

**CONTACT** Gregory Floor, Director of Admissions/Financial Aid, Hellenic College, 50 Goddard Avenue, Brookline, MA 02146-7496, 617-731-3500 Ext. 1285 or toll-free 866-424-2338. *Fax:* 617-850-1465. *E-mail:* gfloor@hchc.edu.
*Website:* http://www.hchc.edu/.

---

# HEIDELBERG UNIVERSITY
## Tiffin, OH

| Tuition & fees: $27,480 | Average undergraduate aid package: $23,339 |
| --- | --- |

**ABOUT THE INSTITUTION** Independent United Church of Christ, coed. *Awards:* bachelor's and master's degrees. 46 undergraduate majors. *Total enrollment:* 1,337. Undergraduates: 1,106. Freshmen: 364. Federal methodology is used as a basis for awarding need-based institutional aid.

**UNDERGRADUATE EXPENSES** for 2015–2016 *Comprehensive fee:* $36,706 includes full-time tuition ($26,900), mandatory fees ($580), and room and board ($9226). Full-time tuition and fees vary according to course load and degree level. Room and board charges vary according to housing facility. *Part-time fees:* $695 per credit. Part-time tuition and fees vary according to course load and degree level.

**FRESHMAN FINANCIAL AID (Fall 2014, est.)** 342 applied for aid; of those 93% were deemed to have need. 100% of freshmen with need received aid; of those 15%

---

# HENDERSON STATE UNIVERSITY
## Arkadelphia, AR

| Tuition & fees (AR res): $7561 | Average undergraduate aid package: $11,778 |
| --- | --- |

**ABOUT THE INSTITUTION** State-supported, coed. *Awards:* certificates, bachelor's, and master's degrees. 38 undergraduate majors. *Total enrollment:* 3,583. Undergraduates: 3,199. Freshmen: 704. Federal methodology is used as a basis for awarding need-based institutional aid.

**UNDERGRADUATE EXPENSES** for 2015–2016 *Tuition, state resident:* full-time $5970; part-time $191 per credit hour. *Tuition, nonresident:* full-time $12,330; part-time $395 per credit hour. *Required fees:* full-time $1591. Full-time tuition and fees vary according to course load and location. Part-time tuition and fees vary according to course load and location. *College room and board:* $6350. Room and board charges vary according to board plan and housing facility.

**FRESHMAN FINANCIAL AID (Fall 2014, est.)** 754 applied for aid; of those 88% were deemed to have need. 98% of freshmen with need received aid; of those 14% had need fully met. *Average percent of need met:* 57% (excluding resources awarded to replace EFC). *Average financial aid package:* $11,830 (excluding resources awarded to replace EFC). 8% of all full-time freshmen had no need and received non-need-based gift aid.

**UNDERGRADUATE FINANCIAL AID (Fall 2014, est.)** 2,703 applied for aid; of those 90% were deemed to have need. 99% of undergraduates with need received aid; of those 11% had need fully met. *Average percent of need met:* 57% (excluding resources awarded to replace EFC). *Average financial aid package:* $11,778 (excluding resources awarded to replace EFC). 5% of all full-time undergraduates had no need and received non-need-based gift aid.

**GIFT AID (NEED-BASED)** *Total amount:* $8,397,888 (97% federal, 3% state). *Receiving aid:* Freshmen: 59% (453); all full-time undergraduates: 57% (1,678). *Average award:* Freshmen: $4545; Undergraduates: $4572. *Scholarships, grants, and awards:* Federal Pell, FSEOG, state, private.

**GIFT AID (NON-NEED-BASED)** *Total amount:* $12,226,726 (5% federal, 36% state, 49% institutional, 10% external sources). *Receiving aid:* Freshmen: 55% (424). Undergraduates: 43% (1,261). *Average award:* Freshmen: $6079. Undergraduates: $5730. *Scholarships, grants, and awards by category: Academic interests/achievement:* biological sciences, education, general academic interests/achievements, international studies, mathematics. *Creative arts/performance:* art/fine arts, cinema/film/broadcasting, dance, debating, journalism/publications, music, performing arts, theater/drama. *Special achievements/activities:* cheerleading/drum major, general special achievements/activities, leadership. *Special characteristics:* children and siblings of alumni, children of faculty/staff, international students, out-of-state students. *Tuition waivers:* Full or partial for children of alumni, employees or children of employees, senior citizens. *ROTC:* Army cooperative.

**LOANS** *Student loans:* $17,324,511 (38% need-based, 62% non-need-based). 66% of past graduating class borrowed through all loan programs. *Average indebtedness per student:* $23,641. *Average need-based loan:* Freshmen: $2839. Undergraduates: $3714. *Parent loans:* $634,767 (100% non-need-based). *Programs:* Federal Direct (Subsidized and Unsubsidized Stafford, PLUS), Perkins.

**WORK-STUDY** *Federal work-study:* Total amount: $261,169; jobs available. *State or other work-study/employment:* Total amount: $279,376 (100% non-need-based). Part-time jobs available.

**ATHLETIC AWARDS** Total amount: $1,750,222 (100% non-need-based).

**APPLYING FOR FINANCIAL AID** *Required financial aid form:* FAFSA. *Financial aid deadline (priority):* 6/1. *Notification date:* Continuous beginning 4/15.

**CONTACT** Ms. Vicki Taylor, Director of Financial Aid, Henderson State University, 1100 Henderson Street, HSU Box 7812, Arkadelphia, AR 71999-0001, 870-230-5138 or toll-free 800-228-7333. *Fax:* 870-230-5481. *E-mail:* taylorv@hsu.edu. *Website:* http://www.hsu.edu/.

# HENDRIX COLLEGE
## Conway, AR

| Tuition & fees: $40,870 | Average undergraduate aid package: $30,702 |
| --- | --- |

**ABOUT THE INSTITUTION** Independent United Methodist, coed. *Awards:* bachelor's and master's degrees. 31 undergraduate majors. *Total enrollment:* 1,358. Undergraduates: 1,348. Freshmen: 314. Federal methodology is used as a basis for awarding need-based institutional aid.

**UNDERGRADUATE EXPENSES for 2015–2016** *Application fee:* $40. *Comprehensive fee:* $52,114 includes full-time tuition ($40,520), mandatory fees ($350), and room and board ($11,244). *College room only:* $5790. Full-time tuition and fees vary according to course load and student level. Room and board charges vary according to board plan and housing facility. *Part-time tuition:* $4874 per course. Part-time tuition and fees vary according to course load and student level.

**FRESHMAN FINANCIAL AID (Fall 2014, est.)** 291 applied for aid; of those 73% were deemed to have need. 100% of freshmen with need received aid; of those 39% had need fully met. *Average percent of need met:* 84% (excluding resources awarded to replace EFC). *Average financial aid package:* $32,106 (excluding resources awarded to replace EFC). 33% of all full-time freshmen had no need and received non-need-based gift aid.

**UNDERGRADUATE FINANCIAL AID (Fall 2014, est.)** 1,036 applied for aid; of those 78% were deemed to have need. 100% of undergraduates with need received aid; of those 37% had need fully met. *Average percent of need met:* 81% (excluding resources awarded to replace EFC). *Average financial aid package:* $30,702 (excluding resources awarded to replace EFC). 38% of all full-time undergraduates had no need and received non-need-based gift aid.

**GIFT AID (NEED-BASED)** *Total amount:* $20,731,416 (7% federal, 5% state, 87% institutional, 1% external sources). *Receiving aid:* Freshmen: 67% (211); all full-time undergraduates: 61% (811). *Average award:* Freshmen: $28,606; Undergraduates: $26,759. *Scholarships, grants, and awards:* Federal Pell, FSEOG, state, private, college/university gift aid from institutional funds.

**GIFT AID (NON-NEED-BASED)** *Total amount:* $16,445,762 (12% state, 87% institutional, 1% external sources). *Receiving aid:* Freshmen: 23% (71). Undergraduates: 19% (251). *Average award:* Freshmen: $26,138. Undergraduates: $25,014. *Scholarships, grants, and awards by category: Academic interests/achievement:* $20,024,041 total: general academic interests/achievements. *Creative arts/performance:* $209,500 total: art/fine arts, dance, music, theater/drama. *Special achievements/activities:* $4,971,375 total: community service, general special achievements/activities, leadership, religious involvement. *Special characteristics:* $1,875,768 total: children of educators, children of faculty/staff, international students, previous college experience, relatives of clergy. *Tuition waivers:* Full or partial for employees or children of employees. *ROTC:* Army cooperative.

**LOANS** *Student loans:* $4,938,889 (61% need-based, 39% non-need-based). 44% of past graduating class borrowed through all loan programs. *Average indebtedness per student:* $26,203. *Average need-based loan:* Freshmen: $3498. Undergraduates: $4175. *Parent loans:* $2,198,645 (38% need-based, 62% non-need-based). *Programs:* Federal Direct (Subsidized and Unsubsidized Stafford, PLUS), Perkins, United Methodist Student Loans.

**WORK-STUDY** *Federal work-study:* Total amount: $975,193; 524 jobs averaging $1884. *State or other work-study/employment:* Total amount: $347,097 (11% need-based, 89% non-need-based). 264 part-time jobs averaging $1537.

**APPLYING FOR FINANCIAL AID** *Required financial aid forms:* FAFSA, state aid form. *Financial aid deadline (priority):* 3/1. *Notification date:* Continuous beginning 3/1. Students must reply by 5/1.

**CONTACT** Ms. Kristina Burford, Associate Vice President for Enrollment/Director of Financial Aid, Hendrix College, 1600 Washington Avenue, Conway, AR 72032, 501-450-1368 or toll-free 800-277-9017. *Fax:* 501-450-3871. *E-mail:* burford@hendrix.edu. *Website:* http://www.hendrix.edu/.

# HENLEY-PUTNAM UNIVERSITY
## San Jose, CA

**CONTACT** Financial Aid Office, Henley-Putnam University, 2107 N. First Street, Suite 210, San Jose, CA 95131, 408-453-9900 or toll-free 88-852-8746 (in-state), 888-852-8746 (out-of-state). *Website:* http://www.henley-putnam.edu/.

# HERITAGE BIBLE COLLEGE
## Dunn, NC

**ABOUT THE INSTITUTION** Independent Pentecostal Free Will Baptist, coed. *Awards:* associate and bachelor's degrees. 2 undergraduate majors. *Total enrollment:* 69. Undergraduates: 69. Freshmen: 10.

**GIFT AID (NEED-BASED)** *Scholarships, grants, and awards:* Federal Pell, FSEOG, private, college/university gift aid from institutional funds.

**GIFT AID (NON-NEED-BASED)** *Scholarships, grants, and awards by category: Academic interests/achievement:* religion/biblical studies.

**WORK-STUDY** *Federal work-study:* 5 jobs averaging $5268.

**APPLYING FOR FINANCIAL AID** *Required financial aid forms:* FAFSA, institution's own form, verification documents.

**CONTACT** Mrs. Iris Prince, Director of Financial Aid, Heritage Bible College, PO Box 1628, Dunn, NC 28335, 800-297-6351 Ext. 226 or toll-free 800-297-6351. *Fax:* 910-892-1809. *E-mail:* iprince@heritagebiblecollege.edu. *Website:* http://www.heritagebiblecollege.edu/.

# HERITAGE CHRISTIAN UNIVERSITY
## Florence, AL

| Tuition & fees: $9792 | Average undergraduate aid package: $9951 |
|---|---|

**ABOUT THE INSTITUTION** Independent Church of Christ, coed, primarily men. 1 undergraduate major. Federal methodology is used as a basis for awarding need-based institutional aid.

**UNDERGRADUATE EXPENSES for 2015–2016** *One-time required fee:* $300. *Comprehensive fee:* $13,632 includes full-time tuition ($8952), mandatory fees ($840), and room and board ($3840). *College room only:* $3000. Full-time tuition and fees vary according to course load. Room and board charges vary according to housing facility. *Part-time tuition:* $373 per credit hour. *Part-time fees:* $35 per credit hour. Part-time tuition and fees vary according to course load.

**FRESHMAN FINANCIAL AID (Fall 2013)** 5 applied for aid; of those 100% were deemed to have need. 100% of freshmen with need received aid; of those 20% had need fully met. *Average percent of need met:* 93% (excluding resources awarded to replace EFC). *Average financial aid package:* $11,446 (excluding resources awarded to replace EFC).

**UNDERGRADUATE FINANCIAL AID (Fall 2013)** 37 applied for aid; of those 100% were deemed to have need. 100% of undergraduates with need received aid; of those 38% had need fully met. *Average percent of need met:* 93% (excluding resources awarded to replace EFC). *Average financial aid package:* $9951 (excluding resources awarded to replace EFC).

**GIFT AID (NEED-BASED)** *Total amount:* $433,572 (36% federal, 63% institutional, 1% external sources). *Receiving aid:* Freshmen: 100% (5); all full-time undergraduates: 100% (37). *Average award:* Freshmen: $11,446; Undergraduates: $9951. *Scholarships, grants, and awards:* Federal Pell, FSEOG, college/university gift aid from institutional funds, donor-funded scholarships.

**GIFT AID (NON-NEED-BASED)** *Receiving aid:* Undergraduates: 14% (5). *Scholarships, grants, and awards by category: Academic interests/achievement:* 14 awards ($33,861 total): religion/biblical studies. *Special achievements/activities:* religious involvement. *Special characteristics:* 5 awards ($18,309 total): children of educators, children of faculty/staff, married students, relatives of clergy, spouses of current students. *Tuition waivers:* Full or partial for employees or children of employees.

**LOANS** *Student loans:* $139,052 (100% need-based). *Average need-based loan:* Undergraduates: $3345. *Programs:* Federal Direct (Subsidized and Unsubsidized Stafford, PLUS), college/university.

**WORK-STUDY** *Federal work-study:* 1 job averaging $1275.

**APPLYING FOR FINANCIAL AID** *Required financial aid forms:* FAFSA, institutional scholarship application form. *Financial aid deadline (priority):* 6/1. *Notification date:* Continuous beginning 7/15. Students must reply within 2 weeks of notification.

**CONTACT** Mechelle R. Thompson, Associate Director of Financial Aid, Heritage Christian University, PO Box HCU, Florence, AL 35630, 800-367-3565 Ext. 303 or toll-free 800-367-3565. *Fax:* 256-716-8021. *E-mail:* mthompson@hcu.edu. *Website:* http://www.hcu.edu/.

# HERITAGE UNIVERSITY
## Toppenish, WA

**CONTACT** Mr. Norberto Espindola, Director of Enrollment Management Services, Heritage University, 3240 Fort Road, Toppenish, WA 98948-9599, 509-865-8500 or toll-free 888-272-6190. *Fax:* 509-865-8659. *E-mail:* financial_aid@heritage.edu. *Website:* http://www.heritage.edu/.

# HERZING UNIVERSITY
## Birmingham, AL

**CONTACT** Financial Aid Office, Herzing University, 280 West Valley Avenue, Birmingham, AL 35209, 205-916-2800 or toll-free 800-596-0724. *Website:* http://www.herzing.edu/birmingham/.

# HERZING UNIVERSITY
## Winter Park, FL

**CONTACT** Financial Aid Office, Herzing University, 1595 South Semoran Boulevard, Winter Park, FL 32792, 407-478-0500 or toll-free 800-596-0724. *Website:* http://www.herzing.edu/.

# HERZING UNIVERSITY
## Atlanta, GA

**CONTACT** Financial Aid Office, Herzing University, 3393 Peachtree Road, Suite 1003, Atlanta, GA 30326, 404-816-4533 or toll-free 800-596-0724. *Website:* http://www.herzing.edu/atlanta/.

# HERZING UNIVERSITY
## Kenner, LA

**CONTACT** Financial Aid Office, Herzing University, 2500 Williams Boulevard, Kenner, LA 70062, 504-733-0074 or toll-free 800-596-0724. *Website:* http://www.herzing.edu/.

# HERZING UNIVERSITY
## Brookfield, WI

**CONTACT** Financial Aid Office, Herzing University, 555 South Executive Drive, Brookfield, WI 53005, 262-649-1710 or toll-free 800-596-0724. *Website:* http://www.herzing.edu/brookfield.

# HERZING UNIVERSITY
## Kenosha, WI

**CONTACT** Financial Aid Office, Herzing University, 4006 Washington Road, Kenosha, WI 53144, 262-671-0675 or toll-free 800-596-0724. *Website:* http://www.herzing.edu/kenosha.

# HERZING UNIVERSITY
## Madison, WI

**CONTACT** Financial Aid Office, Herzing University, 5218 East Terrace Drive, Madison, WI 53718, 608-249-6611 or toll-free 800-596-0724. *Website:* http://www.herzing.edu/madison/.

# HERZING UNIVERSITY ONLINE
## Milwaukee, WI

**CONTACT** Financial Aid Office, Herzing University Online, 525 North 6th Street, Milwaukee, WI 53203, 866-508-0748. *Website:* http://www.herzingonline.edu/.

# HICKEY COLLEGE
## St. Louis, MO

**CONTACT** Financial Aid Office, Hickey College, 940 West Port Plaza, Suite 101, St. Louis, MO 63146, 314-434-2212 or toll-free 800-777-1544. *Website:* http://www.hickeycollege.edu/.

# HIGH POINT UNIVERSITY
## High Point, NC

**ABOUT THE INSTITUTION** Independent United Methodist, coed. *Awards:* certificates, bachelor's, master's, and doctoral degrees. 44 undergraduate majors. *Total enrollment:* 4,399. Undergraduates: 4,208. Freshmen: 1,386.

**GIFT AID (NEED-BASED) Scholarships, grants, and awards:** Federal Pell, FSEOG, state, private, college/university gift aid from institutional funds.

**GIFT AID (NON-NEED-BASED) Scholarships, grants, and awards by category:** *Academic interests/achievement:* biological sciences, business, education, English, foreign languages, general academic interests/achievements, humanities, international studies, mathematics, physical sciences, premedicine, religion/biblical studies. *Creative arts/performance:* art/fine arts, music. *Special achievements/activities:* general special achievements/activities. *Special characteristics:* relatives of clergy.

**LOANS Programs:** Federal Direct (Subsidized and Unsubsidized Stafford, PLUS), Perkins.

**APPLYING FOR FINANCIAL AID** *Required financial aid forms:* FAFSA, state aid form.

**CONTACT** Mr. Ron Elmore, Director of Student Financial Planning, High Point University, Box 3232, University Station, 833 Montlieu Avenue, High Point, NC 27262, 336-841-9128 or toll-free 800-345-6993. *Fax:* 336-884-0221. *E-mail:* relmore@highpoint.edu.
*Website:* http://www.highpoint.edu/.

# HILBERT COLLEGE
## Hamburg, NY

| Tuition & fees: $20,350 | Average undergraduate aid package: $14,073 |
|---|---|

**ABOUT THE INSTITUTION** Independent, coed. *Awards:* associate, bachelor's, and master's degrees. 18 undergraduate majors. *Total enrollment:* 1,012. Undergraduates: 960. Freshmen: 168. Federal methodology is used as a basis for awarding need-based institutional aid.

**UNDERGRADUATE EXPENSES for 2015–2016 Application fee:** $25. **Comprehensive fee:** $29,510 includes full-time tuition ($20,050), mandatory fees ($300), and room and board ($9160). **College room only:** $4730. Room and board charges vary according to board plan and housing facility. **Part-time tuition:** $505 per credit. **Part-time fees:** $300 per term.

**FRESHMAN FINANCIAL AID (Fall 2014, est.)** 162 applied for aid; of those 94% were deemed to have need. 100% of freshmen with need received aid; of those 20% had need fully met. *Average percent of need met:* 73% (excluding resources awarded to replace EFC). *Average financial aid package:* $14,476 (excluding resources awarded to replace EFC). 6% of all full-time freshmen had no need and received non-need-based gift aid.

**UNDERGRADUATE FINANCIAL AID (Fall 2014, est.)** 761 applied for aid; of those 90% were deemed to have need. 100% of undergraduates with need received aid; of those 18% had need fully met. *Average percent of need met:* 71% (excluding resources awarded to replace EFC). *Average financial aid package:* $14,073 (excluding resources awarded to replace EFC). 10% of all full-time undergraduates had no need and received non-need-based gift aid.

**GIFT AID (NEED-BASED) Total amount:** $6,775,721 (28% federal, 18% state, 46% institutional, 8% external sources). *Receiving aid:* Freshmen: 93% (151); all full-time undergraduates: 88% (680). *Average award:* Freshmen: $10,833; Undergraduates: $9696. *Scholarships, grants, and awards:* Federal Pell, FSEOG, state, private, college/university gift aid from institutional funds.

**GIFT AID (NON-NEED-BASED) Total amount:** $548,394 (3% state, 72% institutional, 25% external sources). *Receiving aid:* Freshmen: 6% (9). Undergraduates: 4% (31). *Average award:* Freshmen: $3950. Undergraduates: $4284. *Scholarships, grants, and awards by category:* *Academic interests/achievement:* general academic interests/achievements. *Special achievements/activities:* leadership. *Special characteristics:* children and siblings of alumni, members of minority groups, siblings of current students. *Tuition waivers:* Full or partial for minority students, children of alumni, employees or children of employees, adult students, senior citizens. *ROTC:* Army cooperative.

**LOANS Student loans:** $6,695,704 (75% need-based, 25% non-need-based). 84% of past graduating class borrowed through all loan programs. *Average indebtedness*

per student: $20,139. *Average need-based loan:* Freshmen: $4097. Undergraduates: $4925. *Parent loans:* $1,200,805 (41% need-based, 59% non-need-based).
**Programs:** Federal Direct (Subsidized and Unsubsidized Stafford, PLUS), Perkins.

**WORK-STUDY Federal work-study:** Total amount: $90,772; 49 jobs averaging $1852.

**APPLYING FOR FINANCIAL AID** *Required financial aid forms:* FAFSA, state aid form. *Financial aid deadline (priority):* 4/1. *Notification date:* Continuous beginning 3/1. Students must reply within 2 weeks of notification.

**CONTACT** Beverly Chudy-Szczur, Director of Financial Aid, Hilbert College, 5200 South Park Avenue, Hamburg, NY 14075-1597, 716-649-7900 Ext. 207 or toll-free 800-649-8003. *Fax:* 716-649-1152. *E-mail:* bchudy@hilbert.edu.
*Website:* http://www.hilbert.edu/.

# HILLSDALE COLLEGE
## Hillsdale, MI

| Tuition & fees: $24,591 | Average undergraduate aid package: $16,245 |
|---|---|

**ABOUT THE INSTITUTION** Independent, coed. *Awards:* bachelor's, master's, and doctoral degrees. 35 undergraduate majors. *Total enrollment:* 1,504. Undergraduates: 1,472. Freshmen: 360. Both federal and institutional methodology are used as a basis for awarding need-based institutional aid.

**UNDERGRADUATE EXPENSES for 2015–2016 Application fee:** $35. **One-time required fee:** $300. **Comprehensive fee:** $34,351 includes full-time tuition ($23,840), mandatory fees ($751), and room and board ($9760). **College room only:** $4800. Full-time tuition and fees vary according to degree level. Room and board charges vary according to board plan. **Part-time tuition:** $950 per credit. **Part-time fees:** $85 per credit; $751 per year. Part-time tuition and fees vary according to degree level. **Payment plan:** Tuition prepayment.

**FRESHMAN FINANCIAL AID (Fall 2014, est.)** 245 applied for aid; of those 76% were deemed to have need. 96% of freshmen with need received aid; of those 38% had need fully met. *Average percent of need met:* 60% (excluding resources awarded to replace EFC). *Average financial aid package:* $13,134 (excluding resources awarded to replace EFC). 47% of all full-time freshmen had no need and received non-need-based gift aid.

**UNDERGRADUATE FINANCIAL AID (Fall 2014, est.)** 811 applied for aid; of those 96% were deemed to have need. 92% of undergraduates with need received aid; of those 43% had need fully met. *Average percent of need met:* 65% (excluding resources awarded to replace EFC). *Average financial aid package:* $16,245 (excluding resources awarded to replace EFC). 43% of all full-time undergraduates had no need and received non-need-based gift aid.

**GIFT AID (NEED-BASED) Total amount:** $4,211,572 (100% institutional). *Receiving aid:* Freshmen: 32% (122); all full-time undergraduates: 33% (474). *Average award:* Freshmen: $7554; Undergraduates: $7905. *Scholarships, grants, and awards:* private, college/university gift aid from institutional funds.

**GIFT AID (NON-NEED-BASED) Total amount:** $16,093,896 (89% institutional, 11% external sources). *Receiving aid:* Freshmen: 38% (144). Undergraduates: 41% (595). *Average award:* Freshmen: $4887. Undergraduates: $5531. *Scholarships, grants, and awards by category:* *Academic interests/achievement:* 987 awards ($5,586,185 total): biological sciences, business, education, English, foreign languages, general academic interests/achievements, health fields, humanities, international studies, mathematics, physical sciences, premedicine, religion/biblical studies, social sciences. *Creative arts/performance:* 93 awards ($412,000 total): art/fine arts, debating, journalism/publications, music, theater/drama. *Special achievements/activities:* 131 awards ($1,448,872 total): community service, general special achievements/activities, leadership. *Special characteristics:* 59 awards ($910,724 total): children of faculty/staff, international students. *Tuition waivers:* Full or partial for children of alumni, employees or children of employees.

**LOANS Student loans:** $5,826,466 (53% need-based, 47% non-need-based). 56% of past graduating class borrowed through all loan programs. *Average indebtedness per student:* $25,502. *Average need-based loan:* Freshmen: $6130. Undergraduates: $6189. *Programs:* college/university, alternative loans.

**ATHLETIC AWARDS** Total amount: $2,946,134 (100% non-need-based).

**APPLYING FOR FINANCIAL AID** *Required financial aid form:* institution's own form. *Financial aid deadline (priority):* 4/1. *Notification date:* Continuous beginning 12/1. Students must reply within 4 weeks of notification.

CONTACT Mr. Rich Moeggengberg, Director of Student Financial Aid, Hillsdale College, 33 East College Street, Hillsdale, MI 49242-1298, 517-607-2350. *Fax:* 517-607-2298. *E-mail:* rmoeggenberg@hillsdale.edu. *Website:* http://www.hillsdale.edu/.

# HILLSDALE FREE WILL BAPTIST COLLEGE
## Moore, OK

| Tuition & fees: $11,980 | Average undergraduate aid package: $10,500 |
| --- | --- |

**ABOUT THE INSTITUTION** Independent Free Will Baptist, coed. *Awards:* associate, bachelor's, and master's degrees. 24 undergraduate majors. *Total enrollment:* 233. Undergraduates: 225. Freshmen: 41. Both federal and institutional methodology are used as a basis for awarding need-based institutional aid.

**UNDERGRADUATE EXPENSES for 2015-2016** *Application fee:* $20. *Comprehensive fee:* $18,810 includes full-time tuition ($9300), mandatory fees ($2680), and room and board ($6830). *College room only:* $2660. Full-time tuition and fees vary according to course load. Room and board charges vary according to board plan and housing facility. *Part-time tuition:* $387.50 per credit hour. *Part-time fees:* $37 per credit hour; $245 per term. Part-time tuition and fees vary according to course load.

**FRESHMAN FINANCIAL AID (Fall 2013)** 50 applied for aid; of those 84% were deemed to have need. 100% of freshmen with need received aid. *Average percent of need met:* 55% (excluding resources awarded to replace EFC). *Average financial aid package:* $10,000 (excluding resources awarded to replace EFC). 19% of all full-time freshmen had no need and received non-need-based gift aid.

**UNDERGRADUATE FINANCIAL AID (Fall 2013)** 165 applied for aid; of those 88% were deemed to have need. 100% of undergraduates with need received aid. *Average percent of need met:* 55% (excluding resources awarded to replace EFC). *Average financial aid package:* $10,500 (excluding resources awarded to replace EFC). 21% of all full-time undergraduates had no need and received non-need-based gift aid.

**GIFT AID (NEED-BASED)** *Total amount:* $819,746 (62% federal, 36% state, 2% institutional). *Receiving aid:* Freshmen: 56% (29); all full-time undergraduates: 61% (113). *Average award:* Freshmen: $6700; Undergraduates: $6900. *Scholarships, grants, and awards:* Federal Pell, FSEOG, state, private, college/university gift aid from institutional funds, Bureau of Indian Affairs Grants.

**GIFT AID (NON-NEED-BASED)** *Total amount:* $513,767 (85% institutional, 15% external sources). *Receiving aid:* Freshmen: 69% (36). Undergraduates: 70% (128). *Average award:* Freshmen: $2900. Undergraduates: $2600. *Scholarships, grants, and awards by category:* Academic interests/achievement: 128 awards ($319,550 total): business, education, English, general academic interests/achievements, health fields, religion/biblical studies. *Creative arts/performance:* 15 awards ($13,200 total): music, theater/drama. *Special achievements/activities:* 10 awards ($21,300 total): religious involvement. *Special characteristics:* 65 awards ($166,500 total): children and siblings of alumni, children of faculty/staff, general special characteristics, relatives of clergy, religious affiliation, veterans, veterans' children. *Tuition waivers:* Full or partial for children of alumni, employees or children of employees, senior citizens.

**LOANS** *Student loans:* $1,029,874 (43% need-based, 57% non-need-based). 76% of past graduating class borrowed through all loan programs. *Average indebtedness per student:* $23,500. *Average need-based loan:* Freshmen: $3500. Undergraduates: $4150. *Parent loans:* $90,959 (100% non-need-based). *Programs:* Federal Direct (Subsidized and Unsubsidized Stafford, PLUS).

**WORK-STUDY** *Federal work-study:* 19 jobs averaging $2500.

**APPLYING FOR FINANCIAL AID** *Required financial aid forms:* FAFSA, institution's own form. *Financial aid deadline (priority):* 6/30. *Notification date:* Continuous beginning 4/1. Students must reply within 4 weeks of notification.

CONTACT Denise Conklin, Director of Financial Aid, Hillsdale Free Will Baptist College, PO Box 7208, Moore, OK 73153-1208, 405-912-9012. *Fax:* 405-912-9050. *E-mail:* dconklin@hc.edu. *Website:* http://www.hc.edu/.

# HIRAM COLLEGE
## Hiram, OH

CONTACT Ann Marie Gruber, Associate Director of Financial Aid, Hiram College, Box 67, Hiram, OH 44234-0067, 330-569-5107 or toll-free 800-362-5280. *Fax:* 330-569-5499. *Website:* http://www.hiram.edu/.

# HOBART AND WILLIAM SMITH COLLEGES
## Geneva, NY

| Tuition & fees: $47,908 | Average undergraduate aid package: $33,069 |
| --- | --- |

**ABOUT THE INSTITUTION** Independent, coed. *Awards:* certificates, bachelor's, and master's degrees. 47 undergraduate majors. *Total enrollment:* 2,425. Undergraduates: 2,421. Freshmen: 643. Both federal and institutional methodology are used as a basis for awarding need-based institutional aid.

**UNDERGRADUATE EXPENSES for 2015-2016** *Application fee:* $45. *Comprehensive fee:* $60,034 includes full-time tuition ($46,852), mandatory fees ($1056), and room and board ($12,126). Room and board charges vary according to board plan. *Payment plan:* Tuition prepayment.

**FRESHMAN FINANCIAL AID (Fall 2014, est.)** 438 applied for aid; of those 81% were deemed to have need. 100% of freshmen with need received aid; of those 65% had need fully met. *Average percent of need met:* 80% (excluding resources awarded to replace EFC). *Average financial aid package:* $32,788 (excluding resources awarded to replace EFC). 35% of all full-time freshmen had no need and received non-need-based gift aid.

**UNDERGRADUATE FINANCIAL AID (Fall 2014, est.)** 1,589 applied for aid; of those 85% were deemed to have need. 100% of undergraduates with need received aid; of those 60% had need fully met. *Average percent of need met:* 78% (excluding resources awarded to replace EFC). *Average financial aid package:* $33,069 (excluding resources awarded to replace EFC). 32% of all full-time undergraduates had no need and received non-need-based gift aid.

**GIFT AID (NEED-BASED)** *Total amount:* $38,731,449 (6% federal, 3% state, 86% institutional, 5% external sources). *Receiving aid:* Freshmen: 63% (350); all full-time undergraduates: 65% (1,334). *Average award:* Freshmen: $29,828; Undergraduates: $29,012. *Scholarships, grants, and awards:* Federal Pell, FSEOG, state, private, college/university gift aid from institutional funds.

**GIFT AID (NON-NEED-BASED)** *Total amount:* $13,095,195 (89% institutional, 11% external sources). *Receiving aid:* Freshmen: 16% (87). Undergraduates: 12% (236). *Average award:* Freshmen: $13,586. Undergraduates: $15,377. *Scholarships, grants, and awards by category:* Academic interests/achievement: 169 awards ($3,481,713 total): general academic interests/achievements, premedicine. *Creative arts/performance:* 28 awards ($224,600 total): art/fine arts, creative writing, dance, music, performing arts. *Special achievements/activities:* 57 awards ($839,490 total): community service, leadership. *Special characteristics:* 66 awards ($320,619 total): children and siblings of alumni, relatives of clergy, veterans' children. *Tuition waivers:* Full or partial for employees or children of employees. *ROTC:* Army cooperative, Air Force cooperative.

**LOANS** *Student loans:* $12,197,500 (63% need-based, 37% non-need-based). 57% of past graduating class borrowed through all loan programs. *Average indebtedness per student:* $34,330. *Average need-based loan:* Freshmen: $3290. Undergraduates: $4145. *Parent loans:* $6,170,710 (39% need-based, 61% non-need-based). *Programs:* Federal Direct (Subsidized and Unsubsidized Stafford, PLUS), Perkins, college/university.

**WORK-STUDY** *Federal work-study:* Total amount: $1,174,706; 887 jobs averaging $1814. *State or other work-study/employment:* Total amount: $1,270,058 (13% need-based, 87% non-need-based). 518 part-time jobs averaging $1830.

**APPLYING FOR FINANCIAL AID** *Required financial aid forms:* FAFSA, CSS Financial Aid PROFILE, state aid form, noncustodial (divorced/separated) parent's statement, federal income tax form(s). *Financial aid deadline:* 2/15. *Notification date:* 4/1. Students must reply by 5/1.

**CONTACT** Beth Nepa, Director of Financial Aid, Hobart and William Smith Colleges, Demarest Hall, 300 Pulteney Street, Geneva, NY 14456-3397, 315-781-3315 or toll-free 800-852-2256. *Fax:* 315-781-4048. *E-mail:* nepa@hws.edu. *Website:* http://www.hws.edu/.

# HOBE SOUND BIBLE COLLEGE
## Hobe Sound, FL

**CONTACT** Director of Financial Aid, Hobe Sound Bible College, PO Box 1065, Hobe Sound, FL 33475-1065, 561-546-5534. *Fax:* 561-545-1422. *Website:* http://www.hsbc.edu/.

# HODGES UNIVERSITY
## Naples, FL

| Tuition & fees: $13,220 | Average undergraduate aid package: $10,050 |
|---|---|

**ABOUT THE INSTITUTION** Independent, coed. *Awards:* certificates, associate, bachelor's, and master's degrees. 8 undergraduate majors. *Total enrollment:* 1,882. Undergraduates: 1,678. Freshmen: 134. Federal methodology is used as a basis for awarding need-based institutional aid.

**UNDERGRADUATE EXPENSES for 2015–2016 Application fee:** $20. *Tuition:* full-time $12,720; part-time $530 per credit hour.

**FRESHMAN FINANCIAL AID (Fall 2014, est.)** 102 applied for aid; of those 92% were deemed to have need. 100% of freshmen with need received aid; of those 38% had need fully met. *Average percent of need met:* 71% (excluding resources awarded to replace EFC). *Average financial aid package:* $9110 (excluding resources awarded to replace EFC). 4% of all full-time freshmen had no need and received non-need-based gift aid.

**UNDERGRADUATE FINANCIAL AID (Fall 2014, est.)** 1,104 applied for aid; of those 98% were deemed to have need. 100% of undergraduates with need received aid; of those 18% had need fully met. *Average percent of need met:* 80% (excluding resources awarded to replace EFC). *Average financial aid package:* $10,050 (excluding resources awarded to replace EFC). 3% of all full-time undergraduates had no need and received non-need-based gift aid.

**GIFT AID (NEED-BASED) Total amount:** $9,193,844 (98% federal, 2% state). *Receiving aid:* Freshmen: 80% (86); all full-time undergraduates: 92% (1,051). *Average award:* Freshmen: $3010; Undergraduates: $2900. *Scholarships, grants, and awards:* Federal Pell, FSEOG, state, private, college/university gift aid from institutional funds.

**GIFT AID (NON-NEED-BASED) Total amount:** $3,387,542 (86% state, 12% institutional, 2% external sources). *Receiving aid:* Freshmen: 56% (61). Undergraduates: 69% (782). *Average award:* Freshmen: $300. Undergraduates: $300. *Scholarships, grants, and awards by category:* Special achievements/activities: general special achievements/activities. *Special characteristics:* children of current students, first-generation college students, general special characteristics, spouses of current students, veterans, veterans' children. *Tuition waivers:* Full or partial for employees or children of employees.

**LOANS Student loans:** $16,600,000 (45% need-based, 55% non-need-based). 79% of past graduating class borrowed through all loan programs. *Average indebtedness per student:* $17,775. *Average need-based loan:* Freshmen: $2900. Undergraduates: $2975. *Parent loans:* $50,000 (100% need-based). *Programs:* Federal Direct (Subsidized and Unsubsidized Stafford, PLUS).

**WORK-STUDY Federal work-study:** Total amount: $168,168; 45 jobs averaging $3733.

**APPLYING FOR FINANCIAL AID Required financial aid form:** FAFSA. *Financial aid deadline:* Continuous. *Notification date:* Continuous.

**CONTACT** Mr. Joe Gilchrist, Vice President of Student Financial Services, Hodges University, 2655 Northbrooke Drive, Naples, FL 34119, 239-598-6116 or toll-free 800-466-8017. *Fax:* 239-598-6257. *E-mail:* jgilchrist@hodges.edu. *Website:* http://www.hodges.edu/.

# HOFSTRA UNIVERSITY
## Hempstead, NY

| Tuition & fees: $38,900 | Average undergraduate aid package: $26,000 |
|---|---|

**ABOUT THE INSTITUTION** Independent, coed. *Awards:* certificates, bachelor's, master's, and doctoral degrees. 129 undergraduate majors. *Total enrollment:* 10,953. Undergraduates: 6,904. Freshmen: 1,714. Federal methodology is used as a basis for awarding need-based institutional aid.

**UNDERGRADUATE EXPENSES for 2015–2016 Application fee:** $70. *Comprehensive fee:* $52,410 includes full-time tuition ($37,850), mandatory fees ($1050), and room and board ($13,510). *College room only:* $9050. Full-time tuition and fees vary according to course load. Room and board charges vary according to board plan and housing facility. *Part-time tuition:* $1275 per credit hour. *Part-time fees:* $155 per term. Part-time tuition and fees vary according to course load. *Payment plan:* Guaranteed tuition.

**FRESHMAN FINANCIAL AID (Fall 2014, est.)** 1,479 applied for aid; of those 84% were deemed to have need. 100% of freshmen with need received aid; of those 25% had need fully met. *Average percent of need met:* 67% (excluding resources awarded to replace EFC). *Average financial aid package:* $28,000 (excluding resources awarded to replace EFC). 21% of all full-time freshmen had no need and received non-need-based gift aid.

**UNDERGRADUATE FINANCIAL AID (Fall 2014, est.)** 5,206 applied for aid; of those 84% were deemed to have need. 100% of undergraduates with need received aid; of those 22% had need fully met. *Average percent of need met:* 62% (excluding resources awarded to replace EFC). *Average financial aid package:* $26,000 (excluding resources awarded to replace EFC). 20% of all full-time undergraduates had no need and received non-need-based gift aid.

**GIFT AID (NEED-BASED) Total amount:** $69,740,000 (12% federal, 7% state, 80% institutional, 1% external sources). *Receiving aid:* Freshmen: 70% (1,199); all full-time undergraduates: 64% (4,131). *Average award:* Freshmen: $20,000; Undergraduates: $17,000. *Scholarships, grants, and awards:* Federal Pell, FSEOG, state, private, college/university gift aid from institutional funds, United Negro College Fund.

**GIFT AID (NON-NEED-BASED) Total amount:** $27,040,000 (2% federal, 1% state, 95% institutional, 2% external sources). *Receiving aid:* Freshmen: 14% (240). Undergraduates: 10% (661). *Average award:* Freshmen: $18,000. Undergraduates: $15,000. *Scholarships, grants, and awards by category:* Academic interests/achievement: 5,962 awards ($69,708,467 total): communication, engineering/technologies, general academic interests/achievements. *Creative arts/performance:* 229 awards ($710,059 total): applied art and design, art/fine arts, cinema/film/broadcasting, dance, journalism/publications, music, performing arts, theater/drama. *Special achievements/activities:* 263 awards ($6,189,515 total): cheerleading/drum major, general special achievements/activities, leadership. *Special characteristics:* 404 awards ($9,171,688 total): children and siblings of alumni, children of faculty/staff, children of union members/company employees, general special characteristics, handicapped students, local/state students, members of minority groups, public servants, veterans, veterans' children. *Tuition waivers:* Full or partial for employees or children of employees, senior citizens. *ROTC:* Army.

**LOANS Student loans:** $51,300,000 (67% need-based, 33% non-need-based). 67% of past graduating class borrowed through all loan programs. *Average need-based loan:* Freshmen: $3000. Undergraduates: $5000. *Parent loans:* $35,710,000 (58% need-based, 42% non-need-based). *Programs:* Federal Direct (Subsidized and Unsubsidized Stafford, PLUS), Perkins, state, college/university.

**WORK-STUDY Federal work-study:** Total amount: $5,160,000; 1,771 jobs averaging $2913. *State or other work-study/employment:* Total amount: $4,470,000 (24% need-based, 76% non-need-based). 1,461 part-time jobs averaging $3061.

**ATHLETIC AWARDS** Total amount: $6,170,000 (48% need-based, 52% non-need-based).

**APPLYING FOR FINANCIAL AID Required financial aid forms:** FAFSA, state aid form. *Financial aid deadline (priority):* 2/15. *Notification date:* Continuous beginning 3/1. Students must reply by 5/1 or within 2 weeks of notification.

**CONTACT** Sandra Mervius, Director of Financial Aid, Hofstra University, 126 Hofstra University, Hempstead, NY 11549, 516-463-4335 or toll-free 800-HOFSTRA. *Fax:* 516-463-4936. *E-mail:* sandra.a.filbry@hofstra.edu. *Website:* http://www.hofstra.edu/.

# HOLLINS UNIVERSITY
## Roanoke, VA

| Tuition & fees: $35,635 | Average undergraduate aid package: $33,342 |
|---|---|

**ABOUT THE INSTITUTION** Independent, undergraduate: women only; graduate: coed. *Awards:* certificates, bachelor's, and master's degrees. 27 undergraduate majors. *Total enrollment:* 769. Undergraduates: 596. Freshmen: 165. Federal methodology is used as a basis for awarding need-based institutional aid.

**UNDERGRADUATE EXPENSES** for 2015–2016 *Comprehensive fee:* $47,935 includes full-time tuition ($35,000), mandatory fees ($635), and room and board ($12,300). *Part-time tuition:* $1094 per credit hour. *Part-time fees:* $322.50 per year. *Payment plan:* Tuition prepayment.

**FRESHMAN FINANCIAL AID (Fall 2014, est.)** 153 applied for aid; of those 96% were deemed to have need. 100% of freshmen with need received aid; of those 20% had need fully met. *Average percent of need met:* 86% (excluding resources awarded to replace EFC). *Average financial aid package:* $36,269 (excluding resources awarded to replace EFC). 11% of all full-time freshmen had no need and received non-need-based gift aid.

**UNDERGRADUATE FINANCIAL AID (Fall 2014, est.)** 500 applied for aid; of those 92% were deemed to have need. 100% of undergraduates with need received aid; of those 20% had need fully met. *Average percent of need met:* 83% (excluding resources awarded to replace EFC). *Average financial aid package:* $33,342 (excluding resources awarded to replace EFC). 19% of all full-time undergraduates had no need and received non-need-based gift aid.

**GIFT AID (NEED-BASED)** *Total amount:* $12,533,291 (10% federal, 6% state, 82% institutional, 2% external sources). *Receiving aid:* Freshmen: 89% (147); all full-time undergraduates: 80% (462). *Average award:* Freshmen: $32,095; Undergraduates: $28,320. *Scholarships, grants, and awards:* Federal Pell, FSEOG, state, private, college/university gift aid from institutional funds.

**GIFT AID (NON-NEED-BASED)** *Total amount:* $3,102,452 (6% state, 93% institutional, 1% external sources). *Receiving aid:* Freshmen: 89% (147). Undergraduates: 80% (462). *Average award:* Freshmen: $25,837. Undergraduates: $23,067. *Scholarships, grants, and awards by category: Academic interests/ achievement:* general academic interests/achievements. *Creative arts/performance:* art/fine arts, cinema/film/broadcasting, creative writing, dance, music, theater/drama. *Special achievements/activities:* community service, general special achievements/ activities, hobbies/interests, leadership. *Special characteristics:* adult students, children and siblings of alumni, children of faculty/staff, international students, local/state students, out-of-state students, previous college experience, veterans. *Tuition waivers:* Full or partial for employees or children of employees.

**LOANS** *Student loans:* $3,517,090 (88% need-based, 12% non-need-based). 77% of past graduating class borrowed through all loan programs. *Average indebtedness per student:* $37,332. *Average need-based loan:* Freshmen: $4555. Undergraduates: $5164. *Parent loans:* $947,451 (42% need-based, 58% non-need-based). *Programs:* Federal Direct (Subsidized and Unsubsidized Stafford, PLUS), Perkins, college/ university.

**WORK-STUDY** *Federal work-study:* Total amount: $169,750; jobs available. *State or other work-study/employment:* Total amount: $351,264 (46% need-based, 54% non-need-based). Part-time jobs available.

**APPLYING FOR FINANCIAL AID** *Required financial aid forms:* FAFSA, state aid form. *Financial aid deadline (priority):* 2/15. *Notification date:* Continuous beginning 3/1. Students must reply by 5/1.

**CONTACT** Mrs. MaryJean Sullivan, Director of Scholarships and Financial Assistance, Hollins University, PO Box 9718, Roanoke, VA 24020-1718, 540-362-6332 or toll-free 800-456-9595. *Fax:* 540-362-6093. *E-mail:* sfa@hollins.edu. *Website:* http://www.hollins.edu/.

# HOLY FAMILY UNIVERSITY
## Philadelphia, PA

| Tuition & fees: $29,168 | Average undergraduate aid package: $20,394 |
|---|---|

**ABOUT THE INSTITUTION** Independent Roman Catholic, coed. *Awards:* certificates, associate, bachelor's, master's, and doctoral degrees. 43 undergraduate majors. *Total enrollment:* 2,623. Undergraduates: 1,985. Freshmen: 252. Federal methodology is used as a basis for awarding need-based institutional aid.

**UNDERGRADUATE EXPENSES** for 2015–2016 *Application fee:* $25. *Comprehensive fee:* $42,744 includes full-time tuition ($28,198), mandatory fees ($970), and room and board ($13,576). *College room only:* $7140. Full-time tuition and fees vary according to class time, course level, course load, degree level, program, reciprocity agreements, and student level. Room and board charges vary according to board plan and housing facility. *Part-time tuition:* $603 per credit hour. *Part-time fees:* $108 per term. Part-time tuition and fees vary according to class time, course level, course load, degree level, program, reciprocity agreements, and student level.

**FRESHMAN FINANCIAL AID (Fall 2014, est.)** 245 applied for aid; of those 94% were deemed to have need. 100% of freshmen with need received aid; of those 17% had need fully met. *Average percent of need met:* 82% (excluding resources awarded to replace EFC). *Average financial aid package:* $25,349 (excluding resources awarded to replace EFC). 8% of all full-time freshmen had no need and received non-need-based gift aid.

**UNDERGRADUATE FINANCIAL AID (Fall 2014, est.)** 1,256 applied for aid; of those 93% were deemed to have need. 99% of undergraduates with need received aid; of those 17% had need fully met. *Average percent of need met:* 71% (excluding resources awarded to replace EFC). *Average financial aid package:* $20,394 (excluding resources awarded to replace EFC). 10% of all full-time undergraduates had no need and received non-need-based gift aid.

**GIFT AID (NEED-BASED)** *Total amount:* $18,259,249 (16% federal, 13% state, 70% institutional, 1% external sources). *Receiving aid:* Freshmen: 92% (230); all full-time undergraduates: 85% (1,138). *Average award:* Freshmen: $20,112; Undergraduates: $15,358. *Scholarships, grants, and awards:* Federal Pell, FSEOG, state, private, college/university gift aid from institutional funds.

**GIFT AID (NON-NEED-BASED)** *Total amount:* $1,435,278 (99% institutional, 1% external sources). *Receiving aid:* Freshmen: 92% (230). Undergraduates: 81% (1,082). *Average award:* Freshmen: $15,022. Undergraduates: $11,018. *Scholarships, grants, and awards by category: Academic interests/achievement:* 1,240 awards ($16,063,697 total): general academic interests/achievements. *Tuition waivers:* Full or partial for employees or children of employees, senior citizens. *ROTC:* Army cooperative.

**LOANS** *Student loans:* $11,374,580 (94% need-based, 6% non-need-based). 83% of past graduating class borrowed through all loan programs. *Average indebtedness per student:* $40,363. *Average need-based loan:* Freshmen: $3746. Undergraduates: $4505. *Parent loans:* $1,803,620 (93% need-based, 7% non-need-based). *Programs:* Federal Direct (Subsidized and Unsubsidized Stafford, PLUS), Perkins, Federal Nursing.

**WORK-STUDY** *Federal work-study:* Total amount: $385,126; 332 jobs averaging $1156.

**ATHLETIC AWARDS** Total amount: $1,605,651 (82% need-based, 18% non-need-based).

**APPLYING FOR FINANCIAL AID** *Required financial aid form:* FAFSA. *Financial aid deadline (priority):* 3/1. *Notification date:* Continuous beginning 3/15.

**CONTACT** Financial Aid Office, Holy Family University, 9801 Frankford Avenue, Philadelphia, PA 19114-2094, 215-637-7700 Ext. 3233. *Fax:* 215-599-1694. *E-mail:* finaid@holyfamily.edu. *Website:* http://www.holyfamily.edu/.

# HOLY CROSS COLLEGE
## Notre Dame, IN

**CONTACT** Robert Benjamin, Director of Financial Aid, Holy Cross College, PO Box 308, Notre Dame, IN 46556, 574-239-8362. *E-mail:* rbenjamin@hcc-nd.edu. *Website:* http://www.hcc-nd.edu/.

# HOLY NAMES UNIVERSITY
## Oakland, CA

**CONTACT** Christina Miller, Director of Financial Aid, Holy Names University, 3500 Mountain Boulevard, Oakland, CA 94619-1699, 510-436-1327 or toll-free 800-430-1321. *Fax:* 510-436-1199. *E-mail:* miller@hnu.edu. *Website:* http://www.hnu.edu/.

# HOOD COLLEGE
## Frederick, MD

| Tuition & fees: $35,150 | Average undergraduate aid package: $26,070 |
|---|---|

**ABOUT THE INSTITUTION** Independent, coed. *Awards:* certificates, bachelor's, and master's degrees (also offers adult program with significant enrollment not reflected in profile). 37 undergraduate majors. *Total enrollment:* 2,365. Undergraduates: 1,359. Freshmen: 289. Federal methodology is used as a basis for awarding need-based institutional aid.

**UNDERGRADUATE EXPENSES for 2015–2016** *Application fee:* $35. *Comprehensive fee:* $46,990 includes full-time tuition ($34,630), mandatory fees ($520), and room and board ($11,840). *College room only:* $6200. Room and board charges vary according to board plan and housing facility. *Part-time tuition:* $1005 per credit. *Part-time fees:* $260 per term.

**FRESHMAN FINANCIAL AID (Fall 2014, est.)** 268 applied for aid; of those 91% were deemed to have need. 100% of freshmen with need received aid; of those 16% had need fully met. *Average percent of need met:* 77% (excluding resources awarded to replace EFC). *Average financial aid package:* $28,497 (excluding resources awarded to replace EFC). 13% of all full-time freshmen had no need and received non-need-based gift aid.

**UNDERGRADUATE FINANCIAL AID (Fall 2014, est.)** 1,122 applied for aid; of those 93% were deemed to have need. 100% of undergraduates with need received aid; of those 17% had need fully met. *Average percent of need met:* 73% (excluding resources awarded to replace EFC). *Average financial aid package:* $26,070 (excluding resources awarded to replace EFC). 14% of all full-time undergraduates had no need and received non-need-based gift aid.

**GIFT AID (NEED-BASED)** *Total amount:* $22,386,124 (90% federal, 8% state, 80% institutional, 2% external sources). *Receiving aid:* Freshmen: 85% (244); all full-time undergraduates: 83% (1,037). *Average award:* Freshmen: $24,814; Undergraduates: $21,937. *Scholarships, grants, and awards:* Federal Pell, FSEOG, state, private, college/university gift aid from institutional funds.

**GIFT AID (NON-NEED-BASED)** *Total amount:* $3,997,432 (90% institutional, 10% external sources). *Receiving aid:* Freshmen: 9% (27). Undergraduates: 10% (120). *Average award:* Freshmen: $15,776. Undergraduates: $15,678. *Scholarships, grants, and awards by category:* Academic interests/achievement: general academic interests/achievements. Creative arts/performance: music. Special achievements/activities: leadership. Special characteristics: children and siblings of alumni, children of faculty/staff, international students, local/state students, religious affiliation, siblings of current students. *Tuition waivers:* Full or partial for employees or children of employees, senior citizens. *ROTC:* Army.

**LOANS** *Student loans:* $8,916,392 (78% need-based, 22% non-need-based). 82% of past graduating class borrowed through all loan programs. *Average indebtedness per student:* $31,229. *Average need-based loan:* Freshmen: $3899. Undergraduates: $4405. *Parent loans:* $3,258,745 (35% need-based, 65% non-need-based). *Programs:* Federal Direct (Subsidized and Unsubsidized Stafford, PLUS), Perkins.

**WORK-STUDY** *Federal work-study:* Total amount: $521,503; 367 jobs averaging $2000. *State or other work-study/employment:* Total amount: $142,000 (7% need-based, 93% non-need-based). 75 part-time jobs averaging $2000.

**APPLYING FOR FINANCIAL AID** *Required financial aid form:* FAFSA. *Financial aid deadline:* Continuous. *Notification date:* Continuous beginning 3/1. Students must reply by 5/1 or within 4 weeks of notification.

**CONTACT** Ms. Brenda DiSorbo, Director of Financial Aid, Hood College, 401 Rosemont Avenue, Frederick, MD 21701-8575, 301-696-3411 or toll-free 800-922-1599. *Fax:* 301-696-3812. *E-mail:* disorbo@hood.edu. *Website:* http://www.hood.edu/.

# HOPE COLLEGE
## Holland, MI

| Tuition & fees: $30,550 | Average undergraduate aid package: $23,850 |
|---|---|

**ABOUT THE INSTITUTION** Independent Reformed Church in America, coed. *Awards:* bachelor's degrees. 63 undergraduate majors. *Total enrollment:* 3,455. Undergraduates: 3,455. Freshmen: 830. Federal methodology is used as a basis for awarding need-based institutional aid.

**UNDERGRADUATE EXPENSES for 2015–2016** *Application fee:* $35. *Comprehensive fee:* $39,940 includes full-time tuition ($30,370), mandatory fees ($180), and room and board ($9390). *College room only:* $4310. Room and board charges vary according to board plan. Part-time tuition and fees vary according to course load and program.

**FRESHMAN FINANCIAL AID (Fall 2014, est.)** 702 applied for aid; of those 77% were deemed to have need. 100% of freshmen with need received aid; of those 20% had need fully met. *Average percent of need met:* 80% (excluding resources awarded to replace EFC). *Average financial aid package:* $25,203 (excluding resources awarded to replace EFC). 26% of all full-time freshmen had no need and received non-need-based gift aid.

**UNDERGRADUATE FINANCIAL AID (Fall 2014, est.)** 2,353 applied for aid; of those 82% were deemed to have need. 99% of undergraduates with need received aid; of those 22% had need fully met. *Average percent of need met:* 79% (excluding resources awarded to replace EFC). *Average financial aid package:* $23,850 (excluding resources awarded to replace EFC). 26% of all full-time undergraduates had no need and received non-need-based gift aid.

**GIFT AID (NEED-BASED)** *Total amount:* $29,092,412 (11% federal, 6% state, 83% institutional). *Receiving aid:* Freshmen: 58% (468); all full-time undergraduates: 51% (1,666). *Average award:* Freshmen: $20,315; Undergraduates: $18,044. *Scholarships, grants, and awards:* Federal Pell, FSEOG, state, private, college/university gift aid from institutional funds.

**GIFT AID (NON-NEED-BASED)** *Total amount:* $10,452,870 (4% federal, 86% institutional, 10% external sources). *Receiving aid:* Freshmen: 52% (422). Undergraduates: 43% (1,390). *Average award:* Freshmen: $8227. Undergraduates: $8286. *Scholarships, grants, and awards by category:* Academic interests/achievement: 2,151 awards ($14,211,981 total): general academic interests/achievements. Creative arts/performance: 142 awards ($348,250 total): art/fine arts, creative writing, dance, music, theater/drama. Special characteristics: 165 awards ($1,588,407 total): ethnic background. *Tuition waivers:* Full or partial for employees or children of employees. *ROTC:* Army cooperative.

**LOANS** *Student loans:* $16,152,071 (47% need-based, 53% non-need-based). 63% of past graduating class borrowed through all loan programs. *Average indebtedness per student:* $31,717. *Average need-based loan:* Freshmen: $4071. Undergraduates: $5114. *Parent loans:* $4,578,270 (100% non-need-based). *Programs:* Federal Direct (Subsidized and Unsubsidized Stafford, PLUS), Perkins.

**WORK-STUDY** *Federal work-study:* Total amount: $294,469; 179 jobs averaging $1534. *State or other work-study/employment:* Total amount: $2,200,000 (59% need-based, 41% non-need-based). 577 part-time jobs averaging $909.

**APPLYING FOR FINANCIAL AID** *Required financial aid forms:* FAFSA, institution's own form. *Financial aid deadline (priority):* 3/1. *Notification date:* Continuous beginning 3/15. Students must reply within 2 weeks of notification.

**CONTACT** Ms. Jill Nutt, Director of Financial Aid, Hope College, 141 East 12th Street, Holland, MI 49422-9000, 616-395-7765 or toll-free 800-968-7850. *Fax:* 616-395-7160. *E-mail:* nutt@hope.edu. *Website:* http://www.hope.edu/.

# HOPE INTERNATIONAL UNIVERSITY
## Fullerton, CA

| Tuition & fees: $28,550 | Average undergraduate aid package: $15,340 |
|---|---|

**ABOUT THE INSTITUTION** Independent Christian Churches and Churches of Christ, coed. *Awards:* certificates, associate, bachelor's, and master's degrees. 17 undergraduate majors. *Total enrollment:* 1,276. Undergraduates: 819. Freshmen: 94. Federal methodology is used as a basis for awarding need-based institutional aid.

**UNDERGRADUATE EXPENSES for 2015–2016** *Application fee:* $40. *Comprehensive fee:* $37,600 includes full-time tuition ($27,900), mandatory fees ($650), and room and board ($9050). *College room only:* $4800. Full-time tuition and fees vary according to course level, course load, degree level, location, program, and reciprocity agreements. Room and board charges vary according to board plan. *Part-time tuition:* $1230 per unit. Part-time tuition and fees vary according to course level, course load, degree level, location, program, and reciprocity agreements.

**FRESHMAN FINANCIAL AID (Fall 2013)** 67 applied for aid; of those 93% were deemed to have need. 100% of freshmen with need received aid; of those 19% had need fully met. *Average percent of need met:* 62% (excluding resources awarded to replace EFC). *Average financial aid package:* $19,418 (excluding resources awarded to replace EFC). 18% of all full-time freshmen had no need and received non-need-based gift aid.

**UNDERGRADUATE FINANCIAL AID (Fall 2013)** 619 applied for aid; of those 95% were deemed to have need. 100% of undergraduates with need received aid; of those 8% had need fully met. *Average percent of need met:* 52% (excluding resources awarded to replace EFC). *Average financial aid package:* $15,340 (excluding resources awarded to replace EFC). 2% of all full-time undergraduates had no need and received non-need-based gift aid.

**GIFT AID (NEED-BASED)** *Total amount:* $3,845,838 (48% federal, 37% state, 15% institutional). *Receiving aid:* Freshmen: 54% (37); all full-time undergraduates: 57% (387). *Average award:* Freshmen: $10,010; Undergraduates: $8366. *Scholarships, grants, and awards:* Federal Pell, FSEOG, state, private, college/university gift aid from institutional funds.

**GIFT AID (NON-NEED-BASED)** *Total amount:* $2,397,673 (91% institutional, 9% external sources). *Receiving aid:* Freshmen: 82% (56). Undergraduates: 58% (390). *Average award:* Freshmen: $14,282. Undergraduates: $10,875. *Scholarships, grants, and awards by category:* Academic interests/achievement: 170 awards ($1,545,738 total): general academic interests/achievements. *Special achievements/activities:* 50 awards ($446,750 total): leadership. *Special characteristics:* 19 awards ($149,437 total): children of faculty/staff, veterans. *Tuition waivers:* Full or partial for employees or children of employees. *ROTC:* Army cooperative.

**LOANS** *Student loans:* $5,974,666 (48% need-based, 52% non-need-based). 83% of past graduating class borrowed through all loan programs. *Average indebtedness per student:* $24,091. *Average need-based loan:* Freshmen: $3500. Undergraduates: $4256. *Parent loans:* $1,175,660 (92% need-based, 8% non-need-based). *Programs:* Federal Direct (Subsidized and Unsubsidized Stafford, PLUS).

**WORK-STUDY** *Federal work-study:* 53 jobs averaging $2000. *State or other work-study/employment:* Total amount: $389,681 (100% non-need-based). 87 part-time jobs averaging $2000.

**ATHLETIC AWARDS** Total amount: $1,930,686 (100% non-need-based).

**APPLYING FOR FINANCIAL AID** *Required financial aid forms:* FAFSA, institution's own form. *Financial aid deadline (priority):* 3/2. *Notification date:* Continuous beginning 3/1. Students must reply within 2 weeks of notification.

**CONTACT** Ms. Shannon O'Shields, Director of Student Financial Services, Hope International University, 2500 East Nutwood Avenue, Fullerton, CA 92831, 714-879-3901 Ext. 2207 or toll-free 866-722-HOPE. *Fax:* 714-681-7421. *E-mail:* soshields@hiu.edu.
*Website:* http://www.hiu.edu/.

# HORIZON UNIVERSITY
## San Diego, CA

**CONTACT** Financial Aid Office, Horizon University, 5331 Mt. Alifan Drive, San Diego, CA 92111, 858-695-8587 or toll-free 800-553-HORIZON.
*Website:* http://www.horizonuniversity.edu/.

# HOUGHTON COLLEGE
## Houghton, NY

| Tuition & fees: $28,556 | Average undergraduate aid package: $19,967 |
|---|---|

**ABOUT THE INSTITUTION** Independent Wesleyan, coed. *Awards:* associate, bachelor's, and master's degrees. 66 undergraduate majors. *Total enrollment:* 1,078. Undergraduates: 1,048. Freshmen: 237. Federal methodology is used as a basis for awarding need-based institutional aid.

**UNDERGRADUATE EXPENSES** for 2015–2016 *Application fee:* $40. *Comprehensive fee:* $36,808 includes full-time tuition ($28,406), mandatory fees ($150), and room and board ($8252). *College room only:* $4426. Full-time tuition and fees vary according to location. Room and board charges vary according to board plan and housing facility. *Part-time tuition:* $1194 per credit hour. Part-time tuition and fees vary according to location.

**FRESHMAN FINANCIAL AID (Fall 2014, est.)** 210 applied for aid; of those 91% were deemed to have need. 100% of freshmen with need received aid; of those 11%

had need fully met. *Average percent of need met:* 56% (excluding resources awarded to replace EFC). *Average financial aid package:* $22,544 (excluding resources awarded to replace EFC). 5% of all full-time freshmen had no need and received non-need-based gift aid.

**UNDERGRADUATE FINANCIAL AID (Fall 2014, est.)** 855 applied for aid; of those 94% were deemed to have need. 100% of undergraduates with need received aid; of those 10% had need fully met. *Average percent of need met:* 52% (excluding resources awarded to replace EFC). *Average financial aid package:* $19,967 (excluding resources awarded to replace EFC). 4% of all full-time undergraduates had no need and received non-need-based gift aid.

**GIFT AID (NEED-BASED)** *Total amount:* $7,987,796 (23% federal, 14% state, 63% institutional). *Receiving aid:* Freshmen: 78% (185); all full-time undergraduates: 75% (745). *Average award:* Freshmen: $13,685; Undergraduates: $11,583. *Scholarships, grants, and awards:* Federal Pell, FSEOG, state, private, college/university gift aid from institutional funds.

**GIFT AID (NON-NEED-BASED)** *Total amount:* $7,674,611 (92% institutional, 8% external sources). *Receiving aid:* Freshmen: 63% (150). Undergraduates: 58% (578). *Average award:* Freshmen: $7962. Undergraduates: $9046. *Scholarships, grants, and awards by category:* Academic interests/achievement: 574 awards ($4,811,723 total): English, general academic interests/achievements, physical sciences, religion/biblical studies. *Creative arts/performance:* 106 awards ($310,690 total): art/fine arts, music, performing arts. *Special achievements/activities:* 71 awards ($370,462 total): community service, general special achievements/activities, hobbies/interests, leadership, memberships, religious involvement. *Special characteristics:* 475 awards ($3,036,323 total): adult students, children and siblings of alumni, children of faculty/staff, general special characteristics, handicapped students, international students, local/state students, relatives of clergy, religious affiliation, siblings of current students, veterans. *Tuition waivers:* Full or partial for employees or children of employees. *ROTC:* Army cooperative.

**LOANS** *Student loans:* $6,848,664 (49% need-based, 51% non-need-based). 70% of past graduating class borrowed through all loan programs. *Average indebtedness per student:* $26,550. *Average need-based loan:* Freshmen: $4024. Undergraduates: $4558. *Parent loans:* $1,552,492 (100% non-need-based). *Programs:* Federal Direct (Subsidized and Unsubsidized Stafford, PLUS), Perkins, state, alternative loans.

**WORK-STUDY** *Federal work-study:* Total amount: $1,045,587; 543 jobs averaging $1972. *State or other work-study/employment:* Total amount: $75,600 (100% non-need-based). 25 part-time jobs averaging $2100.

**APPLYING FOR FINANCIAL AID** *Required financial aid forms:* FAFSA, state aid form. *Financial aid deadline (priority):* 3/1. *Notification date:* Continuous beginning 3/1. Students must reply by 5/1 or within 4 weeks of notification.

**CONTACT** Mrs. Marianne Loper, Director of Financial Aid, Houghton College, One Willard Avenue, Houghton, NY 14744, 585-567-9328 or toll-free 800-777-2556. *Fax:* 585-567-9610. *E-mail:* marianne.loper@houghton.edu.
*Website:* http://www.houghton.edu/.

# HOUSTON BAPTIST UNIVERSITY
## Houston, TX

| Tuition & fees: $29,800 | Average undergraduate aid package: $25,617 |
|---|---|

**ABOUT THE INSTITUTION** Independent Baptist, coed. *Awards:* bachelor's and master's degrees. 59 undergraduate majors. *Total enrollment:* 3,128. Undergraduates: 2,288. Freshmen: 615. Federal methodology is used as a basis for awarding need-based institutional aid.

**UNDERGRADUATE EXPENSES** for 2015–2016 *Comprehensive fee:* $37,515 includes full-time tuition ($27,950), mandatory fees ($1850), and room and board ($7715). *College room only:* $4500. Room and board charges vary according to board plan and housing facility. Part-time tuition and fees vary according to course load.

**FRESHMAN FINANCIAL AID (Fall 2014, est.)** 523 applied for aid; of those 91% were deemed to have need. 100% of freshmen with need received aid; of those 20% had need fully met. *Average percent of need met:* 73% (excluding resources awarded to replace EFC). *Average financial aid package:* $26,077 (excluding resources awarded to replace EFC). 22% of all full-time freshmen had no need and received non-need-based gift aid.

**UNDERGRADUATE FINANCIAL AID (Fall 2014, est.)** 1,656 applied for aid; of those 94% were deemed to have need. 100% of undergraduates with need received aid; of those 18% had need fully met. *Average percent of need met:* 70%

(excluding resources awarded to replace EFC). **Average financial aid package:** $25,617 (excluding resources awarded to replace EFC). 23% of all full-time undergraduates had no need and received non-need-based gift aid.

**GIFT AID (NEED-BASED) Total amount:** $24,246,117 (20% federal, 8% state, 70% institutional, 2% external sources). **Receiving aid:** Freshmen: 78% (477); all full-time undergraduates: 72% (1,539). **Average award:** Freshmen: $18,327; Undergraduates: $17,558. **Scholarships, grants, and awards:** Federal Pell, FSEOG, state, private, college/university gift aid from institutional funds.

**GIFT AID (NON-NEED-BASED) Total amount:** $7,126,319 (98% institutional, 2% external sources). **Receiving aid:** Freshmen: 78% (477). Undergraduates: 69% (1,472). **Average award:** Freshmen: $14,181. Undergraduates: $13,153. **Scholarships, grants, and awards by category:** Academic interests/achievement: 2,838 awards ($21,436,270 total): general academic interests/achievements, health fields, religion/biblical studies. Creative arts/performance: 48 awards ($165,900 total): art/fine arts, music. Special achievements/activities: 152 awards ($204,301 total): cheerleading/drum major, community service, leadership, religious involvement. Special characteristics: 61 awards ($351,351 total): children of faculty/staff, relatives of clergy. **Tuition waivers:** Full or partial for employees or children of employees. **ROTC:** Army cooperative, Naval cooperative, Air Force cooperative.

**LOANS Student loans:** $17,643,577 (77% need-based, 23% non-need-based). **Average need-based loan:** Freshmen: $5147. Undergraduates: $5233. **Parent loans:** $5,017,520 (7% need-based, 93% non-need-based). **Programs:** Federal Direct (Subsidized and Unsubsidized Stafford, PLUS).

**WORK-STUDY Federal work-study:** Total amount: $2,013,834; 1,064 jobs averaging $1893. **State or other work-study/employment:** Part-time jobs available.

**ATHLETIC AWARDS** Total amount: $7,198,899 (47% need-based, 53% non-need-based).

**APPLYING FOR FINANCIAL AID Required financial aid form:** FAFSA. **Financial aid deadline:** 4/15 (priority: 3/1). **Notification date:** Continuous beginning 3/10.

**CONTACT** Veronica Jene Gabbard, Senior Director of Financial Aid and Scholarships, Houston Baptist University, 7502 Fondren Road, Houston, TX 77074-3298, 281-649-3747 or toll-free 800-696-3210. *Fax:* 281-649-3298. *E-mail:* financialaid@hbu.edu. *Website:* http://www.hbu.edu/.

# HOWARD PAYNE UNIVERSITY
## Brownwood, TX

| Tuition & fees: $25,600 | Average undergraduate aid package: $18,654 |
|---|---|

**ABOUT THE INSTITUTION** Independent Baptist General Convention of Texas, coed. **Awards:** certificates, bachelor's, and master's degrees. 69 undergraduate majors. **Total enrollment:** 1,137. Undergraduates: 1,073. Freshmen: 302. Federal methodology is used as a basis for awarding need-based institutional aid.

**UNDERGRADUATE EXPENSES for 2015–2016 Comprehensive fee:** $33,089 includes full-time tuition ($23,600), mandatory fees ($2000), and room and board ($7489). Full-time tuition and fees vary according to course load, location, and program. Room and board charges vary according to board plan and housing facility. **Part-time tuition:** $760 per credit. Part-time tuition and fees vary according to location and program.

**FRESHMAN FINANCIAL AID (Fall 2014, est.)** 288 applied for aid; of those 94% were deemed to have need. 100% of freshmen with need received aid; of those 24% had need fully met. **Average percent of need met:** 78% (excluding resources awarded to replace EFC). **Average financial aid package:** $19,529 (excluding resources awarded to replace EFC). 9% of all full-time freshmen had no need and received non-need-based gift aid.

**UNDERGRADUATE FINANCIAL AID (Fall 2014, est.)** 848 applied for aid; of those 93% were deemed to have need. 100% of undergraduates with need received aid; of those 26% had need fully met. **Average percent of need met:** 76% (excluding resources awarded to replace EFC). **Average financial aid package:** $18,654 (excluding resources awarded to replace EFC). 15% of all full-time undergraduates had no need and received non-need-based gift aid.

**GIFT AID (NEED-BASED) Total amount:** $10,568,760 (19% federal, 12% state, 66% institutional, 3% external sources). **Receiving aid:** Freshmen: 76% (228); all full-time undergraduates: 70% (658). **Average award:** Freshmen: $17,215; Undergrad-

uates: $15,809. **Scholarships, grants, and awards:** Federal Pell, FSEOG, state, private, college/university gift aid from institutional funds.

**GIFT AID (NON-NEED-BASED) Total amount:** $3,918,291 (97% institutional, 3% external sources). **Receiving aid:** Freshmen: 17% (52). Undergraduates: 16% (151). **Average award:** Freshmen: $13,488. Undergraduates: $12,021. **Scholarships, grants, and awards by category:** Academic interests/achievement: biological sciences, business, communication, education, English, general academic interests/achievements, mathematics, physical sciences, premedicine, religion/biblical studies, social sciences. Creative arts/performance: art/fine arts, music, theater/drama. Special achievements/activities: community service, leadership, religious involvement. Special characteristics: children and siblings of alumni, children of faculty/staff, local/state students, relatives of clergy, religious affiliation, siblings of current students. **Tuition waivers:** Full or partial for employees or children of employees.

**LOANS Student loans:** $6,733,091 (60% need-based, 40% non-need-based). 67% of past graduating class borrowed through all loan programs. **Average indebtedness per student:** $33,329. **Average need-based loan:** Freshmen: $3412. Undergraduates: $4031. **Parent loans:** $1,220,217 (35% need-based, 65% non-need-based). **Programs:** Federal Direct (Subsidized and Unsubsidized Stafford, PLUS), Perkins, state.

**WORK-STUDY Federal work-study:** Total amount: $98,842; jobs available. **State or other work-study/employment:** Total amount: $6779 (100% need-based). Part-time jobs available.

**APPLYING FOR FINANCIAL AID Required financial aid forms:** FAFSA, institution's own form, Core Residency Form. **Financial aid deadline (priority):** 3/15. **Notification date:** Continuous beginning 2/1. Students must reply within 2 weeks of notification.

**CONTACT** Mrs. Glenda Huff, Director of Financial Aid, Howard Payne University, 1000 Fisk Avenue, Brownwood, TX 76801, 325-649-8014 or toll-free 800-880-4478. *Fax:* 325-649-8973. *E-mail:* ghuff@hputx.edu. *Website:* http://www.hputx.edu/.

# HOWARD UNIVERSITY
## Washington, DC

| Tuition & fees: $23,970 | Average undergraduate aid package: $14,864 |
|---|---|

**ABOUT THE INSTITUTION** Independent, coed. **Awards:** certificates, bachelor's, master's, and doctoral degrees. 65 undergraduate majors. **Total enrollment:** 10,265. Undergraduates: 7,013. Freshmen: 1,479. Federal methodology is used as a basis for awarding need-based institutional aid.

**UNDERGRADUATE EXPENSES for 2015–2016 Application fee:** $45. **Comprehensive fee:** $37,616 includes full-time tuition ($22,737), mandatory fees ($1233), and room and board ($13,646). **College room only:** $9506. Full-time tuition and fees vary according to course load. Room and board charges vary according to board plan and housing facility. **Part-time tuition:** $980 per credit hour. **Part-time fees:** $1233 per term. Part-time tuition and fees vary according to course load.

**FRESHMAN FINANCIAL AID (Fall 2014, est.)** 1,286 applied for aid; of those 93% were deemed to have need. 98% of freshmen with need received aid; of those 12% had need fully met. **Average percent of need met:** 13% (excluding resources awarded to replace EFC). **Average financial aid package:** $17,752 (excluding resources awarded to replace EFC). 11% of all full-time freshmen had no need and received non-need-based gift aid.

**UNDERGRADUATE FINANCIAL AID (Fall 2014, est.)** 5,636 applied for aid; of those 94% were deemed to have need. 98% of undergraduates with need received aid; of those 9% had need fully met. **Average percent of need met:** 10% (excluding resources awarded to replace EFC). **Average financial aid package:** $14,864 (excluding resources awarded to replace EFC). 7% of all full-time undergraduates had no need and received non-need-based gift aid.

**GIFT AID (NEED-BASED) Receiving aid:** Freshmen: 50% (721); all full-time undergraduates: 53% (3,344). **Average award:** Freshmen: $5729; Undergraduates: $7291. **Scholarships, grants, and awards:** Federal Pell, FSEOG, state, private, college/university gift aid from institutional funds, Federal Nursing.

**GIFT AID (NON-NEED-BASED) Receiving aid:** Freshmen: 47% (667). Undergraduates: 39% (2,441). **Average award:** Freshmen: $27,266. Undergraduates: $24,835. **Scholarships, grants, and awards by category:** Academic interests/achievement: architecture, biological sciences, business, communication, computer science, education, engineering/technologies, English, foreign languages, health fields, humanities, international studies, mathematics, military science, physical sciences, pre-medicine, religion/biblical studies, social sciences. *Creative arts/performance:* applied art and design, art/fine arts, cinema/film/broadcasting, dance, journalism/publications, music, performing arts, theater/drama. *Special achievements/activities:* cheerleading/drum major, general special achievements/activities, leadership, memberships, religious involvement. *Special characteristics:* adult students, ethnic background, first-generation college students, handicapped students, international students, local/state students, married students, members of minority groups, previous college experience, religious affiliation. *Tuition waivers:* Full or partial for employees or children of employees. *ROTC:* Army, Air Force.

**LOANS** *Student loans:* $43,167,279 (100% non-need-based). 82% of past graduating class borrowed through all loan programs. *Average indebtedness per student:* $32,071. *Average need-based loan:* Freshmen: $3524. Undergraduates: $4440. *Parent loans:* $38,493,813 (100% non-need-based). *Programs:* Federal Direct (Subsidized and Unsubsidized Stafford, PLUS), Perkins, Federal Nursing, district, college/university.

**WORK-STUDY** *Federal work-study:* Total amount: $2,168,180; 467 jobs averaging $4214. *State or other work-study/employment:* Total amount: $1,358,139 (100% non-need-based). 233 part-time jobs averaging $4896.

**ATHLETIC AWARDS** Total amount: $3,762,305 (100% non-need-based).

**APPLYING FOR FINANCIAL AID** *Required financial aid form:* FAFSA. *Financial aid deadline:* 5/1 (priority: 2/1). *Notification date:* Continuous beginning 2/16. Students must reply by 2/16 or within 3 weeks of notification.

**CONTACT** Derek Kindle, Director of Financial Aid , Howard University, 2400 Sixth Street, NW, Washington, DC 20059, 202-806-2741 or toll-free 800-822-6363. *Fax:* 202-806-2818. *E-mail:* dkindle@howard.edu.
*Website:* http://www.howard.edu/.

# HULT INTERNATIONAL BUSINESS SCHOOL
## Cambridge, MA

**CONTACT** Financial Aid Office, Hult International Business School, One Education Street, Cambridge, MA 02141, 617-746-1990.
*Website:* http://www.hult.edu/.

# HUMBOLDT STATE UNIVERSITY
## Arcata, CA

| Tuition & fees (CA res): $7190 | Average undergraduate aid package: $13,368 |
|---|---|

**ABOUT THE INSTITUTION** State-supported, coed. *Awards:* certificates, bachelor's, and master's degrees. 67 undergraduate majors. *Total enrollment:* 8,485. Undergraduates: 7,962. Freshmen: 1,386. Federal methodology is used as a basis for awarding need-based institutional aid.

**UNDERGRADUATE EXPENSES** for 2015–2016 *Application fee:* $55. *Tuition, state resident:* full-time $7190; part-time $372 per credit. *Tuition, non-resident:* full-time $18,350; part-time $372 per credit. *Required fees:* $1266 per term. Full-time tuition and fees vary according to degree level. Part-time tuition and fees vary according to course load and degree level. *College room and board:* $12,114; *Room only:* $7434. Room and board charges vary according to board plan and housing facility.

**FRESHMAN FINANCIAL AID (Fall 2013)** 1,233 applied for aid; of those 83% were deemed to have need. 95% of freshmen with need received aid; of those 10% had need fully met. *Average percent of need met:* 70% (excluding resources awarded to replace EFC). *Average financial aid package:* $13,365 (excluding resources awarded to replace EFC). 2% of all full-time freshmen had no need and received non-need-based gift aid.

**UNDERGRADUATE FINANCIAL AID (Fall 2013)** 6,231 applied for aid; of those 89% were deemed to have need. 97% of undergraduates with need received aid; of those 8% had need fully met. *Average percent of need met:* 70% (excluding resources awarded to replace EFC). *Average financial aid package:* $13,368 (excluding resources awarded to replace EFC). 2% of all full-time undergraduates had no need and received non-need-based gift aid.

**GIFT AID (NEED-BASED)** *Total amount:* $44,824,462 (43% federal, 25% state, 28% institutional, 4% external sources). *Receiving aid:* Freshmen: 63% (850); all full-time undergraduates: 64% (4,619). *Average award:* Freshmen: $8853; Undergraduates: $7992. *Scholarships, grants, and awards:* Federal Pell, FSEOG, state, private, college/university gift aid from institutional funds.

**GIFT AID (NON-NEED-BASED)** *Total amount:* $331,180 (23% institutional, 77% external sources). *Receiving aid:* Freshmen: 1% (7). Undergraduates: 1% (57). *Average award:* Freshmen: $208. Undergraduates: $357. *Scholarships, grants, and awards by category:* Academic interests/achievement: general academic interests/achievements. *Tuition waivers:* Full or partial for employees or children of employees.

**LOANS** *Student loans:* $32,310,930 (85% need-based, 15% non-need-based). 74% of past graduating class borrowed through all loan programs. *Average indebtedness per student:* $19,351. *Average need-based loan:* Freshmen: $5790. Undergraduates: $6978. *Parent loans:* $3,789,305 (28% need-based, 72% non-need-based). *Programs:* Federal Direct (Subsidized and Unsubsidized Stafford, PLUS), Perkins, college/university.

**WORK-STUDY** *Federal work-study:* jobs available.

**ATHLETIC AWARDS** Total amount: $864,376 (59% need-based, 41% non-need-based).

**APPLYING FOR FINANCIAL AID** *Required financial aid form:* FAFSA. *Financial aid deadline (priority):* 3/2. *Notification date:* Continuous beginning 4/1. Students must reply within 4 weeks of notification.

**CONTACT** Peggy Metzger, Director of Financial Aid, Humboldt State University, 1 Harpst Street, Arcata, CA 95521-8299, 707-826-4321 or toll-free 866-850-9556. *E-mail:* pmetzger@humboldt.edu.
*Website:* http://www.humboldt.edu/.

# HUMPHREYS COLLEGE
## Stockton, CA

**CONTACT** Rita Franco, Director of Financial Aid, Humphreys College, 6650 Inglewood Avenue, Stockton, CA 95207-3896, 209-478-0800. *Fax:* 209-235-2983.
*Website:* http://www.humphreys.edu/.

# HUNTER COLLEGE OF THE CITY UNIVERSITY OF NEW YORK
## New York, NY

**ABOUT THE INSTITUTION** State and locally supported, coed. *Awards:* certificates, bachelor's, master's, and doctoral degrees. 63 undergraduate majors. *Total enrollment:* 23,112. Undergraduates: 16,879. Freshmen: 2,080.

**GIFT AID (NEED-BASED)** *Scholarships, grants, and awards:* Federal Pell, FSEOG, state, private, college/university gift aid from institutional funds.

**GIFT AID (NON-NEED-BASED)** *Scholarships, grants, and awards by category:* Academic interests/achievement: general academic interests/achievements.

**LOANS** *Programs:* Federal Direct (Subsidized and Unsubsidized Stafford, PLUS), Perkins.

**WORK-STUDY** *Federal work-study:* jobs available. *State or other work-study/employment:* Part-time jobs available.

**APPLYING FOR FINANCIAL AID** *Required financial aid forms:* FAFSA, state aid form.

**CONTACT** Aristalia Cortorreal Diaz, Director of Financial Aid, Hunter College of the City University of New York, 695 Park Avenue, New York, NY 10065-5085, 212-772-4400. *Fax:* 212-650-3666. *E-mail:* aristalia@hunter.cuny.edu.
*Website:* http://www.hunter.cuny.edu/.

# HUNTINGDON COLLEGE
## Montgomery, AL

| Tuition & fees: $24,550 | Average undergraduate aid package: $17,249 |
| --- | --- |

**ABOUT THE INSTITUTION** Independent United Methodist, coed. *Awards:* bachelor's degrees. 36 undergraduate majors. *Total enrollment:* 1,160. Undergraduates: 1,160. Freshmen: 227. Both federal and institutional methodology are used as a basis for awarding need-based institutional aid.

**UNDERGRADUATE EXPENSES for 2015–2016** *Comprehensive fee:* $33,100 includes full-time tuition ($23,500), mandatory fees ($1050), and room and board ($8550). Full-time tuition and fees vary according to course load, program, and student level. Room and board charges vary according to housing facility. *Part-time tuition:* $980 per credit hour. Part-time tuition and fees vary according to course load and program. *Payment plan:* Guaranteed tuition.

**FRESHMAN FINANCIAL AID (Fall 2014, est.)** 206 applied for aid; of those 82% were deemed to have need. 100% of freshmen with need received aid; of those 14% had need fully met. *Average percent of need met:* 66% (excluding resources awarded to replace EFC). *Average financial aid package:* $18,215 (excluding resources awarded to replace EFC). 25% of all full-time freshmen had no need and received non-need-based gift aid.

**UNDERGRADUATE FINANCIAL AID (Fall 2014, est.)** 766 applied for aid; of those 89% were deemed to have need. 100% of undergraduates with need received aid; of those 16% had need fully met. *Average percent of need met:* 68% (excluding resources awarded to replace EFC). *Average financial aid package:* $17,249 (excluding resources awarded to replace EFC). 24% of all full-time undergraduates had no need and received non-need-based gift aid.

**GIFT AID (NEED-BASED)** *Total amount:* $9,430,856 (25% federal, 2% state, 67% institutional, 6% external sources). *Receiving aid:* Freshmen: 74% (169); all full-time undergraduates: 73% (673). *Average award:* Freshmen: $15,159; Undergraduates: $13,291. *Scholarships, grants, and awards:* Federal Pell, FSEOG, state, private, college/university gift aid from institutional funds.

**GIFT AID (NON-NEED-BASED)** *Total amount:* $3,259,392 (2% state, 78% institutional, 20% external sources). *Receiving aid:* Freshmen: 8% (19). Undergraduates: 8% (70). *Average award:* Freshmen: $11,613. Undergraduates: $10,489. *Scholarships, grants, and awards by category: Academic interests/achievement:* 130 awards ($1,234,700 total): biological sciences, computer science, general academic interests/achievements, mathematics. *Creative arts/performance:* 123 awards ($868,090 total): dance, music, performing arts. *Special achievements/activities:* 17 awards ($175,305 total): cheerleading/drum major, community service, junior miss. *Special characteristics:* 348 awards ($3,205,010 total): children and siblings of alumni, children of faculty/staff, children of workers in trades, international students, local/state students, religious affiliation, spouses of current students, veterans, veterans' children. *Tuition waivers:* Full or partial for children of alumni, employees or children of employees. *ROTC:* Army cooperative, Air Force cooperative.

**LOANS** *Student loans:* $6,949,259 (79% need-based, 21% non-need-based). 80% of past graduating class borrowed through all loan programs. *Average indebtedness per student:* $28,322. *Average need-based loan:* Freshmen: $3606. Undergraduates: $4401. *Parent loans:* $1,660,271 (43% need-based, 57% non-need-based). *Programs:* Federal Direct (Subsidized and Unsubsidized Stafford, PLUS), Perkins.

**WORK-STUDY** *Federal work-study:* Total amount: $101,400; 147 jobs averaging $974.

**APPLYING FOR FINANCIAL AID** *Required financial aid form:* FAFSA. *Financial aid deadline (priority):* 3/1. *Notification date:* Continuous beginning 3/1. Students must reply by 5/1 or within 2 weeks of notification.

**CONTACT** Ms. Brittany Nicole Davis, Associate Director of Financial Aid, Huntingdon College, 1500 East Fairview Avenue, Montgomery, AL 36106-2148, 334-833-4428 or toll-free 800-763-0313. Fax: 334-833-4235. E-mail: finaid@huntingdon.edu.
*Website:* http://www.huntingdon.edu/.

# HUNTINGTON UNIVERSITY
## Huntington, IN

| Tuition & fees: $24,771 | Average undergraduate aid package: $17,228 |
| --- | --- |

**ABOUT THE INSTITUTION** Independent Church of the United Brethren in Christ, coed. *Awards:* associate, bachelor's, and master's degrees. 77 undergraduate majors. *Total enrollment:* 1,134. Undergraduates: 1,053. Freshmen: 226. Both federal and institutional methodology are used as a basis for awarding need-based institutional aid.

**UNDERGRADUATE EXPENSES for 2015–2016** *Application fee:* $20. *Comprehensive fee:* $33,077 includes full-time tuition ($23,976), mandatory fees ($795), and room and board ($8306). Full-time tuition and fees vary according to course load, degree level, and program. Room and board charges vary according to board plan. Part-time tuition and fees vary according to course load, degree level, and program.

**FRESHMAN FINANCIAL AID (Fall 2014, est.)** 211 applied for aid; of those 90% were deemed to have need. 98% of freshmen with need received aid; of those 17% had need fully met. *Average percent of need met:* 73% (excluding resources awarded to replace EFC). *Average financial aid package:* $19,510 (excluding resources awarded to replace EFC). 15% of all full-time freshmen had no need and received non-need-based gift aid.

**UNDERGRADUATE FINANCIAL AID (Fall 2014, est.)** 793 applied for aid; of those 98% were deemed to have need. 97% of undergraduates with need received aid; of those 5% had need fully met. *Average percent of need met:* 71% (excluding resources awarded to replace EFC). *Average financial aid package:* $17,228 (excluding resources awarded to replace EFC). 16% of all full-time undergraduates had no need and received non-need-based gift aid.

**GIFT AID (NEED-BASED)** *Total amount:* $11,514,737 (15% federal, 12% state, 70% institutional, 3% external sources). *Receiving aid:* Freshmen: 77% (174); all full-time undergraduates: 84% (752). *Average award:* Freshmen: $16,985; Undergraduates: $14,901. *Scholarships, grants, and awards:* Federal Pell, FSEOG, state, private, college/university gift aid from institutional funds.

**GIFT AID (NON-NEED-BASED)** *Total amount:* $3,435,166 (98% institutional, 2% external sources). *Receiving aid:* Freshmen: 20% (45). Undergraduates: 21% (187). *Average award:* Freshmen: $11,715. Undergraduates: $11,525. *Scholarships, grants, and awards by category: Academic interests/achievement:* biological sciences, business, communication, computer science, education, English, general academic interests/achievements, health fields, mathematics. *Creative arts/performance:* applied art and design, art/fine arts, cinema/film/broadcasting, creative writing, journalism/publications, music, theater/drama. *Special achievements/activities:* cheerleading/drum major, religious involvement. *Special characteristics:* children of faculty/staff, ethnic background, international students, local/state students, previous college experience, relatives of clergy, religious affiliation, veterans, veterans' children. *Tuition waivers:* Full or partial for minority students, children of alumni, employees or children of employees.

**LOANS** *Student loans:* $9,506,854 (84% need-based, 16% non-need-based). 66% of past graduating class borrowed through all loan programs. *Average indebtedness per student:* $35,840. *Average need-based loan:* Freshmen: $3810. Undergraduates: $4750. *Parent loans:* $1,548,332 (100% need-based). *Programs:* Federal Direct (Subsidized and Unsubsidized Stafford, PLUS), Perkins.

**WORK-STUDY** *Federal work-study:* Total amount: $119,261; jobs available.

**ATHLETIC AWARDS** Total amount: $1,270,556 (91% need-based, 9% non-need-based).

**APPLYING FOR FINANCIAL AID** *Required financial aid form:* FAFSA. *Financial aid deadline (priority):* 3/10. *Notification date:* Continuous beginning 2/15. Students must reply by 5/1 or within 2 weeks of notification.

**CONTACT** Mr. Jerry W. Davis, Director of Financial Aid, Huntington University, 2303 College Avenue, Huntington, IN 46750, 260-359-4014 or toll-free 800-642-6493. Fax: 260-358-3699. E-mail: finaid@huntington.edu.
*Website:* http://www.huntington.edu/.

# HUNTSVILLE BIBLE COLLEGE
## Huntsville, AL

**CONTACT** Financial Aid Office, Huntsville Bible College, 904 Oakwood Avenue, Huntsville, AL 35811-1632, 256-539-0834.
*Website:* http://www.hbc1.edu/.

# HUSSON UNIVERSITY
## Bangor, ME

| Tuition & fees: $16,060 | Average undergraduate aid package: $13,469 |
| --- | --- |

**ABOUT THE INSTITUTION** Independent, coed. *Awards:* certificates, associate, bachelor's, master's, and doctoral degrees. 42 undergraduate majors. *Total enrollment:* 3,414. Undergraduates: 2,704. Freshmen: 517. Federal methodology is used as a basis for awarding need-based institutional aid.

**UNDERGRADUATE EXPENSES for 2015–2016** *Application fee:* $40. *One-time required fee:* $100. *Comprehensive fee:* $24,982 includes full-time tuition ($15,660), mandatory fees ($400), and room and board ($8922). Full-time tuition and fees vary according to class time and location. Room and board charges vary according to board plan and housing facility. *Part-time tuition:* $522 per credit. Part-time tuition and fees vary according to class time, course load, and location. *Payment plan:* Tuition prepayment.

**FRESHMAN FINANCIAL AID (Fall 2013)** 376 applied for aid; of those 91% were deemed to have need. 98% of freshmen with need received aid; of those 8% had need fully met. *Average percent of need met:* 71% (excluding resources awarded to replace EFC). *Average financial aid package:* $14,536 (excluding resources awarded to replace EFC). 6% of all full-time freshmen had no need and received non-need-based gift aid.

**UNDERGRADUATE FINANCIAL AID (Fall 2013)** 1,537 applied for aid; of those 90% were deemed to have need. 98% of undergraduates with need received aid; of those 6% had need fully met. *Average percent of need met:* 66% (excluding resources awarded to replace EFC). *Average financial aid package:* $13,469 (excluding resources awarded to replace EFC). 8% of all full-time undergraduates had no need and received non-need-based gift aid.

**GIFT AID (NEED-BASED)** *Total amount:* $13,883,103 (43% federal, 5% state, 45% institutional, 7% external sources). *Receiving aid:* Freshmen: 61% (328); all full-time undergraduates: 64% (1,294). *Average award:* Freshmen: $10,799; Undergraduates: $9215. *Scholarships, grants, and awards:* Federal Pell, FSEOG, state, private, college/university gift aid from institutional funds.

**GIFT AID (NON-NEED-BASED)** *Total amount:* $837,231 (79% institutional, 21% external sources). *Receiving aid:* Freshmen: 1% (7). Undergraduates: 1% (30). *Average award:* Freshmen: $3275. Undergraduates: $2749. *Scholarships, grants, and awards by category:* Academic interests/achievement: biological sciences, business, computer science, education, English, general academic interests/achievements, health fields, social sciences. Special achievements/activities: general special achievements/activities, leadership. Special characteristics: children of union members/company employees. Tuition waivers: Full or partial for employees or children of employees, senior citizens. ROTC: Army, Naval cooperative.

**LOANS** *Student loans:* $15,425,334 (78% need-based, 22% non-need-based). 89% of past graduating class borrowed through all loan programs. *Average indebtedness per student:* $32,343. *Average need-based loan:* Freshmen: $3222. Undergraduates: $4069. *Parent loans:* $1,914,257 (43% need-based, 57% non-need-based). *Programs:* Federal Direct (Subsidized and Unsubsidized Stafford, PLUS), Perkins, state, alternative loans.

**WORK-STUDY** *Federal work-study:* jobs available.

**APPLYING FOR FINANCIAL AID** *Required financial aid form:* FAFSA. *Financial aid deadline:* 4/15. *Notification date:* Continuous beginning 3/15. Students must reply by 5/1 or within 2 weeks of notification.

**CONTACT** Nicole Vachon, Director of Financial Aid, Husson University, 1 College Circle, Bangor, ME 04401, 207-973-1091 or toll-free 800-4-HUSSON. *Fax:* 207-941-7932. *E-mail:* vachonni@husson.edu. *Website:* http://www.husson.edu/.

# HUSTON-TILLOTSON UNIVERSITY
## Austin, TX

| Tuition & fees: $13,544 | Average undergraduate aid package: $13,980 |
| --- | --- |

**ABOUT THE INSTITUTION** Independent interdenominational, coed. *Awards:* certificates, bachelor's, and master's degrees. 22 undergraduate majors. *Total enrollment:* 1,031. Undergraduates: 975. Freshmen: 206. Federal methodology is used as a basis for awarding need-based institutional aid.

**UNDERGRADUATE EXPENSES for 2015–2016** *Application fee:* $25. *Comprehensive fee:* $21,112 includes full-time tuition ($11,460), mandatory fees ($2084), and room and board ($7568). *College room only:* $3642. Full-time tuition and fees vary according to course load. Room and board charges vary according to housing facility. *Part-time tuition:* $383 per credit hour. *Part-time fees:* $457 per term. Part-time tuition and fees vary according to course load.

**FRESHMAN FINANCIAL AID (Fall 2013)** *Average financial aid package:* $11,536 (excluding resources awarded to replace EFC).

**UNDERGRADUATE FINANCIAL AID (Fall 2013)** *Average financial aid package:* $13,980 (excluding resources awarded to replace EFC).

**GIFT AID (NEED-BASED)** *Total amount:* $5,991,544 (48% federal, 24% state, 25% institutional, 3% external sources). *Receiving aid:* Freshmen: 97% (196); all full-time undergraduates: 76% (704). *Average award:* Freshmen: $8783; Undergraduates: $7860. *Scholarships, grants, and awards:* Federal Pell, FSEOG, state, private, college/university gift aid from institutional funds.

**GIFT AID (NON-NEED-BASED)** *Total amount:* $182,214 (37% federal, 63% state). *Receiving aid:* Undergraduates: 5% (44). *Scholarships, grants, and awards by category:* Academic interests/achievement: general academic interests/achievements. Creative arts/performance: music. Special characteristics: general special characteristics. Tuition waivers: Full or partial for employees or children of employees. ROTC: Army cooperative, Naval cooperative, Air Force cooperative.

**LOANS** *Student loans:* $6,388,668 (44% need-based, 56% non-need-based). *Average need-based loan:* Freshmen: $3059. Undergraduates: $3747. *Parent loans:* $725,243 (100% non-need-based). *Programs:* Federal Direct (Subsidized and Unsubsidized Stafford, PLUS), state, alternative loans.

**WORK-STUDY** *Federal work-study:* jobs available. *State or other work-study/employment:* Total amount: $8775 (100% need-based). Part-time jobs available.

**ATHLETIC AWARDS** Total amount: $379,277 (100% need-based).

**APPLYING FOR FINANCIAL AID** *Required financial aid form:* FAFSA. *Financial aid deadline (priority):* 3/15. *Notification date:* Continuous. Students must reply within 2 weeks of notification.

**CONTACT** Director of Financial Aid, Huston-Tillotson University, 900 Chicon Street, Austin, TX 78702, 512-505-3031. *Fax:* 512-505-3192. *Website:* http://www.htu.edu/.

# IDAHO STATE UNIVERSITY
## Pocatello, ID

| Tuition & fees (ID res): $6566 | Average undergraduate aid package: $9452 |
| --- | --- |

**ABOUT THE INSTITUTION** State-supported, coed. *Awards:* certificates, associate, bachelor's, master's, and doctoral degrees. 94 undergraduate majors. *Total enrollment:* 13,804. Undergraduates: 11,792. Freshmen: 1,739. Federal methodology is used as a basis for awarding need-based institutional aid.

**UNDERGRADUATE EXPENSES for 2015–2016** *Application fee:* $50. *Tuition, state resident:* full-time $4910; part-time $328 per credit hour. *Tuition, nonresident:* full-time $17,020; part-time $535 per credit hour. *Required fees:* full-time $1656. Full-time tuition and fees vary according to course load, program, and reciprocity agreements. Part-time tuition and fees vary according to course load. *College room and board:* $5963; *Room only:* $2550. Room and board charges vary according to board plan, housing facility, and location.

**FRESHMAN FINANCIAL AID (Fall 2013)** 956 applied for aid; of those 84% were deemed to have need. 99% of freshmen with need received aid; of those 6% had need fully met. *Average percent of need met:* 47% (excluding resources awarded to replace EFC). *Average financial aid package:* $9022 (excluding resources awarded to replace EFC). 5% of all full-time freshmen had no need and received non-need-based gift aid.

**UNDERGRADUATE FINANCIAL AID (Fall 2013)** 6,353 applied for aid; of those 79% were deemed to have need. 99% of undergraduates with need received aid; of those 3% had need fully met. *Average percent of need met:* 45% (excluding resources awarded to replace EFC). *Average financial aid package:* $9452 (excluding resources awarded to replace EFC). 5% of all full-time undergraduates had no need and received non-need-based gift aid.

**GIFT AID (NEED-BASED)** *Total amount:* $23,933,513 (85% federal, 2% state, 10% institutional, 3% external sources). *Receiving aid:* Freshmen: 49% (620); all full-time undergraduates: 48% (3,931). *Average award:* Freshmen: $4560; Undergraduates: $4595. *Scholarships, grants, and awards:* Federal Pell, FSEOG, state, private, college/university gift aid from institutional funds, Federal Nursing.

**GIFT AID (NON-NEED-BASED)** *Total amount:* $2,018,746 (9% state, 68% institutional, 23% external sources). *Receiving aid:* Freshmen: 40% (503). Undergraduates: 18% (1,473). *Average award:* Freshmen: $3091. Undergraduates: $2303. *Scholarships, grants, and awards by category:* Academic interests/achievement: architecture, biological sciences, business, communication, computer science, education, engineering/technologies, English, foreign languages, general academic interests/achievements, health fields, humanities, international studies, mathematics, military science, physical sciences, premedicine, social sciences. *Creative arts/performance:* art/fine arts, dance, debating, journalism/publications, music, performing arts, theater/drama. *Special achievements/activities:* cheerleading/drum major, general special achievements/activities. *Special characteristics:* children of faculty/staff, children with a deceased or disabled parent, ethnic background, first-generation college students, general special characteristics, handicapped students, international students, local/state students, members of minority groups, out-of-state students. *Tuition waivers:* Full or partial for employees or children of employees, senior citizens. **ROTC:** Army.

**LOANS** *Student loans:* $61,158,477 (97% need-based, 3% non-need-based). 67% of past graduating class borrowed through all loan programs. *Average indebtedness per student:* $26,445. *Average need-based loan:* Freshmen: $3091. Undergraduates: $3920. *Parent loans:* $831,585 (85% need-based, 15% non-need-based). *Programs:* Federal Direct (Subsidized and Unsubsidized Stafford, PLUS), Perkins, Federal Nursing.

**WORK-STUDY** *Federal work-study:* Total amount: $592,647; jobs available. *State or other work-study/employment:* Total amount: $347,338 (100% need-based). Part-time jobs available.

**ATHLETIC AWARDS** Total amount: $2,164,575 (32% need-based, 68% non-need-based).

**APPLYING FOR FINANCIAL AID** *Required financial aid form:* FAFSA. *Financial aid deadline (priority):* 3/1. *Notification date:* Continuous beginning 4/1.

**CONTACT** Mr. James R. Martin, Director of Financial Aid, Idaho State University, 921 South 8th Avenue, Museum Building 337, Stop 8077, Pocatello, ID 83209-8077, 208-282-2756. *Fax:* 208-282-4755. *E-mail:* finaidem@isu.edu.
*Website:* http://www.isu.edu/.

## ILLINOIS COLLEGE
### Jacksonville, IL

| Tuition & fees: $29,210 | Average undergraduate aid package: $26,431 |
| --- | --- |

**ABOUT THE INSTITUTION** Independent interdenominational, coed. *Awards:* bachelor's and master's degrees. 44 undergraduate majors. *Total enrollment:* 965. Undergraduates: 957. Freshmen: 253. Federal methodology is used as a basis for awarding need-based institutional aid.

**UNDERGRADUATE EXPENSES for 2015–2016** *Comprehensive fee:* $38,400 includes full-time tuition ($28,660), mandatory fees ($550), and room and board ($9190). *College room only:* $4890. Room and board charges vary according to board plan and housing facility. *Part-time tuition:* $890 per credit hour. *Part-time fees:* $137.50 per term.

**FRESHMAN FINANCIAL AID (Fall 2014, est.)** 225 applied for aid; of those 93% were deemed to have need. 100% of freshmen with need received aid; of those 22% had need fully met. *Average percent of need met:* 87% (excluding resources awarded to replace EFC). *Average financial aid package:* $27,959 (excluding resources awarded to replace EFC). 13% of all full-time freshmen had no need and received non-need-based gift aid.

**UNDERGRADUATE FINANCIAL AID (Fall 2014, est.)** 853 applied for aid; of those 92% were deemed to have need. 100% of undergraduates with need received aid; of those 22% had need fully met. *Average percent of need met:* 86% (excluding resources awarded to replace EFC). *Average financial aid package:* $26,431 (excluding resources awarded to replace EFC). 16% of all full-time undergraduates had no need and received non-need-based gift aid.

**GIFT AID (NEED-BASED)** *Total amount:* $16,463,073 (11% federal, 10% state, 77% institutional, 2% external sources). *Receiving aid:* Freshmen: 87% (209); all full-time undergraduates: 84% (789). *Average award:* Freshmen: $22,939; Undergraduates: $20,864. *Scholarships, grants, and awards:* Federal Pell, FSEOG, state, private, college/university gift aid from institutional funds.

**GIFT AID (NON-NEED-BASED)** *Total amount:* $3,227,452 (97% institutional, 3% external sources). *Receiving aid:* Freshmen: 13% (31). Undergraduates: 12% (110). *Average award:* Freshmen: $16,548. Undergraduates: $15,492. *Scholarships, grants, and awards by category:* Academic interests/achievement: general academic interests/achievements. *Creative arts/performance:* art/fine arts, music, theater/drama. *Special characteristics:* children of faculty/staff, international students, previous college experience. *Tuition waivers:* Full or partial for employees or children of employees.

**LOANS** *Student loans:* $7,145,763 (71% need-based, 29% non-need-based). 76% of past graduating class borrowed through all loan programs. *Average indebtedness per student:* $22,958. *Average need-based loan:* Freshmen: $4500. Undergraduates: $5192. *Parent loans:* $1,315,268 (28% need-based, 72% non-need-based). *Programs:* Federal Direct (Subsidized and Unsubsidized Stafford, PLUS), Perkins.

**WORK-STUDY** *Federal work-study:* Total amount: $882,088; 559 jobs averaging $1960. *State or other work-study/employment:* Part-time jobs available.

**APPLYING FOR FINANCIAL AID** *Required financial aid form:* FAFSA. *Financial aid deadline (priority):* 1/31. *Notification date:* Continuous beginning 3/1. Students must reply within 2 weeks of notification.

**CONTACT** Kate Taylor, Director of Financial Aid, Illinois College, 1101 West College Avenue, Jacksonville, IL 62650-2299, 217-245-3035 or toll-free 866-464-5265. *Fax:* 217-245-3274. *E-mail:* kataylor@mail.ic.edu.
*Website:* http://www.ic.edu/.

## THE ILLINOIS INSTITUTE OF ART–CHICAGO
### Chicago, IL

Financial Aid Office, The Illinois Institute of Art–Chicago, 350 North Orleans Street, Suite 136, Chicago, IL 60654-1593, 800-351-3450.

## THE ILLINOIS INSTITUTE OF ART–SCHAUMBURG
### Schaumburg, IL

**CONTACT** Financial Aid Office, The Illinois Institute of Art–Schaumburg, 1000 North Plaza Drive, Suite 100, Schaumburg, IL 60173, 847-619-3450 or toll-free 800-314-3450.
*Website:* http://www.artinstitutes.edu/schaumburg/.

## ILLINOIS INSTITUTE OF TECHNOLOGY
### Chicago, IL

| Tuition & fees: $42,000 | Average undergraduate aid package: $35,527 |
| --- | --- |

**ABOUT THE INSTITUTION** Independent, coed. *Awards:* certificates, bachelor's, master's, and doctoral degrees. 38 undergraduate majors. *Total enrollment:* 7,898. Undergraduates: 3,099. Freshmen: 440. Federal methodology is used as a basis for awarding need-based institutional aid.

**UNDERGRADUATE EXPENSES for 2015–2016** *Tuition:* full-time $42,000; part-time $1313 per credit hour. Full-time tuition and fees vary according to student level. Part-time tuition and fees vary according to course load and student level. Room and board charges vary according to board plan and housing facility.

**FRESHMAN FINANCIAL AID (Fall 2014, est.)** 309 applied for aid; of those 92% were deemed to have need. 100% of freshmen with need received aid; of those 22%

had need fully met. **Average percent of need met:** 83% (excluding resources awarded to replace EFC). **Average financial aid package:** $37,589 (excluding resources awarded to replace EFC). 35% of all full-time freshmen had no need and received non-need-based gift aid.

**UNDERGRADUATE FINANCIAL AID (Fall 2014, est.)** 1,672 applied for aid; of those 96% were deemed to have need. 100% of undergraduates with need received aid; of those 13% had need fully met. **Average percent of need met:** 75% (excluding resources awarded to replace EFC). **Average financial aid package:** $35,527 (excluding resources awarded to replace EFC). 36% of all full-time undergraduates had no need and received non-need-based gift aid.

**GIFT AID (NEED-BASED) Total amount:** $47,755,150 (11% federal, 7% state, 81% institutional, 1% external sources). **Receiving aid:** Freshmen: 64% (282); all full-time undergraduates: 54% (1,586). **Average award:** Freshmen: $32,136; Undergraduates: $29,733. **Scholarships, grants, and awards:** Federal Pell, FSEOG, state, private, college/university gift aid from institutional funds.

**GIFT AID (NON-NEED-BASED) Total amount:** $26,294,953 (2% federal, 97% institutional, 1% external sources). **Receiving aid:** Freshmen: 12% (54). Undergraduates: 6% (161). **Average award:** Freshmen: $24,656. Undergraduates: $22,595. **Scholarships, grants, and awards by category:** Academic interests/achievement: architecture, business, engineering/technologies, general academic interests/achievements. Creative arts/performance: applied art and design. Special achievements/activities: community service, general special achievements/activities, hobbies/interests, leadership, memberships. Special characteristics: children and siblings of alumni, children of faculty/staff, children of public servants, general special characteristics, international students, local/state students, previous college experience, veterans, veterans' children. **Tuition waivers:** Full or partial for employees or children of employees. **ROTC:** Army, Naval, Air Force.

**LOANS Student loans:** $12,001,539 (85% need-based, 15% non-need-based). 60% of past graduating class borrowed through all loan programs. **Average indebtedness per student:** $31,877. **Average need-based loan:** Freshmen: $3657. Undergraduates: $5001. **Parent loans:** $5,283,105 (49% need-based, 51% non-need-based). **Programs:** Perkins.

**WORK-STUDY Federal work-study:** Total amount: $1,777,769; jobs available. **State or other work-study/employment:** Part-time jobs available.

**APPLYING FOR FINANCIAL AID Required financial aid form:** FAFSA. **Financial aid deadline (priority):** 2/1. **Notification date:** Continuous beginning 3/1.

**CONTACT** Abby McGrath, Director of Financial Aid, Illinois Institute of Technology, 3300 South Federal Street, Chicago, IL 60616, 312-567-5730 or toll-free 800-448-2329. Fax: 312-567-3982. E-mail: finaid@iit.edu.
Website: http://www.iit.edu/.

# ILLINOIS STATE UNIVERSITY
### Normal, IL

| Tuition & fees (IL res): $13,296 | Average undergraduate aid package: $10,482 |
|---|---|

**ABOUT THE INSTITUTION** State-supported, coed. **Awards:** certificates, bachelor's, master's, and doctoral degrees. 70 undergraduate majors. **Total enrollment:** 20,615. Undergraduates: 18,155. Freshmen: 3,589. Federal methodology is used as a basis for awarding need-based institutional aid.

**UNDERGRADUATE EXPENSES for 2015–2016 Application fee:** $40. **Tuition, state resident:** full-time $10,470; part-time $349 per credit hour. **Tuition, nonresident:** full-time $18,060; part-time $602 per credit hour. **Required fees:** full-time $2826; $78.66 per credit hour. Full-time tuition and fees vary according to course load and degree level. Part-time tuition and fees vary according to course load and degree level. **College room and board:** $9816; **Room only:** $5282. Room and board charges vary according to board plan, housing facility, and location. **Payment plan:** Guaranteed tuition.

**FRESHMAN FINANCIAL AID (Fall 2014, est.)** 3,157 applied for aid; of those 77% were deemed to have need. 93% of freshmen with need received aid; of those 30% had need fully met. **Average percent of need met:** 72% (excluding resources awarded to replace EFC). **Average financial aid package:** $10,453 (excluding resources awarded to replace EFC). 8% of all full-time freshmen had no need and received non-need-based gift aid.

**UNDERGRADUATE FINANCIAL AID (Fall 2014, est.)** 13,132 applied for aid; of those 84% were deemed to have need. 92% of undergraduates with need received

aid; of those 31% had need fully met. **Average percent of need met:** 72% (excluding resources awarded to replace EFC). **Average financial aid package:** $10,482 (excluding resources awarded to replace EFC). 5% of all full-time undergraduates had no need and received non-need-based gift aid.

**GIFT AID (NEED-BASED) Total amount:** $63,434,071 (37% federal, 34% state, 27% institutional, 2% external sources). **Receiving aid:** Freshmen: 47% (1,671); all full-time undergraduates: 39% (6,691). **Average award:** Freshmen: $9873; Undergraduates: $9785. **Scholarships, grants, and awards:** Federal Pell, FSEOG, state, private, college/university gift aid from institutional funds, Federal Nursing.

**GIFT AID (NON-NEED-BASED) Total amount:** $7,956,029 (4% federal, 53% state, 33% institutional, 10% external sources). **Receiving aid:** Freshmen: 27% (960). Undergraduates: 17% (2,957). **Average award:** Freshmen: $2769. Undergraduates: $2706. **Scholarships, grants, and awards by category:** Academic interests/achievement: 1,262 awards ($3,001,702 total): agriculture, biological sciences, business, communication, computer science, education, engineering/technologies, English, foreign languages, general academic interests/achievements, health fields, home economics, humanities, international studies, library science, mathematics, military science, physical sciences, premedicine, social sciences. Creative arts/performance: 150 awards ($424,287 total): applied art and design, art/fine arts, cinema/film/broadcasting, creative writing, debating, general creative arts/performance, music, performing arts, theater/drama. Special achievements/activities: 1 award ($1000 total): community service, leadership. Special characteristics: 368 awards ($1,509,449 total): children of faculty/staff, children of union members/company employees, children with a deceased or disabled parent, first-generation college students, general special characteristics, members of minority groups, previous college experience. **Tuition waivers:** Full or partial for minority students, employees or children of employees, senior citizens. **ROTC:** Army.

**LOANS Student loans:** $96,730,236 (73% need-based, 27% non-need-based). 65% of past graduating class borrowed through all loan programs. **Average indebtedness per student:** $30,373. **Average need-based loan:** Freshmen: $3545. Undergraduates: $4517. **Parent loans:** $34,075,124 (38% need-based, 62% non-need-based). **Programs:** Federal Direct (Subsidized and Unsubsidized Stafford, PLUS), Perkins, Federal Nursing.

**WORK-STUDY Federal work-study:** Total amount: $1,624,291; 307 jobs averaging $2034. **State or other work-study/employment:** Total amount: $78,993 (57% need-based, 43% non-need-based). 51 part-time jobs averaging $2462.

**ATHLETIC AWARDS** Total amount: $2,891,266 (36% need-based, 64% non-need-based).

**APPLYING FOR FINANCIAL AID Required financial aid form:** FAFSA. **Financial aid deadline (priority):** 3/1. **Notification date:** Continuous beginning 4/1.

**CONTACT** Mr. David Krueger, Associate Director of Financial Aid, Illinois State University, Campus Box 2320, Normal, IL 61790-2320, 309-438-2231 or toll-free 800-366-2478. Fax: 309-438-3755. E-mail: financialaid@illinoisitate.edu.
Website: http://www.illinoisstate.edu/.

# ILLINOIS WESLEYAN UNIVERSITY
### Bloomington, IL

| Tuition & fees: $40,844 | Average undergraduate aid package: $29,999 |
|---|---|

**ABOUT THE INSTITUTION** Independent, coed. **Awards:** bachelor's degrees. 48 undergraduate majors. **Total enrollment:** 1,893. Undergraduates: 1,893. Freshmen: 455. Both federal and institutional methodology are used as a basis for awarding need-based institutional aid.

**UNDERGRADUATE EXPENSES for 2015–2016 Comprehensive fee:** $50,290 includes full-time tuition ($40,664), mandatory fees ($180), and room and board ($9446). **College room only:** $5926. Room and board charges vary according to housing facility. **Part-time tuition:** $1271 per unit. **Part-time fees:** $4892 per unit.

**FRESHMAN FINANCIAL AID (Fall 2014, est.)** 373 applied for aid; of those 77% were deemed to have need. 100% of freshmen with need received aid; of those 44% had need fully met. **Average percent of need met:** 88% (excluding resources awarded to replace EFC). **Average financial aid package:** $30,984 (excluding resources awarded to replace EFC). 37% of all full-time freshmen had no need and received non-need-based gift aid.

**UNDERGRADUATE FINANCIAL AID (Fall 2014, est.)** 1,457 applied for aid; of those 82% were deemed to have need. 100% of undergraduates with need received

aid; of those 38% had need fully met. *Average percent of need met:* 85% (excluding resources awarded to replace EFC). *Average financial aid package:* $29,999 (excluding resources awarded to replace EFC). 34% of all full-time undergraduates had no need and received non-need-based gift aid.

**GIFT AID (NEED-BASED)** *Total amount:* $27,638,756 (7% federal, 7% state, 85% institutional, 1% external sources). *Receiving aid:* Freshmen: 63% (287); all full-time undergraduates: 64% (1,193). *Average award:* Freshmen: $25,346; Undergraduates: $23,480. *Scholarships, grants, and awards:* Federal Pell, FSEOG, state, private, college/university gift aid from institutional funds.

**GIFT AID (NON-NEED-BASED)** *Total amount:* $10,768,187 (100% institutional). *Receiving aid:* Freshmen: 9% (39). Undergraduates: 5% (103). *Average award:* Freshmen: $16,566. Undergraduates: $15,760. *Scholarships, grants, and awards by category:* Academic interests/achievement: general academic interests/achievements. Creative arts/performance: art/fine arts, general creative arts/performance, music, theater/drama. Special characteristics: children of faculty/staff, general special characteristics, international students. *Tuition waivers:* Full or partial for employees or children of employees. *ROTC:* Army cooperative.

**LOANS** *Student loans:* $10,816,379 (49% need-based, 51% non-need-based). 69% of past graduating class borrowed through all loan programs. *Average indebtedness per student:* $32,101. *Average need-based loan:* Freshmen: $4264. Undergraduates: $5594. *Parent loans:* $4,520,537 (100% non-need-based). *Programs:* Federal Direct (Subsidized and Unsubsidized Stafford, PLUS), Perkins, Federal Nursing, college/university.

**WORK-STUDY** *Federal work-study:* Total amount: $331,989; jobs available. *State or other work-study/employment:* Total amount: $1,919,850 (83% need-based, 17% non-need-based). Part-time jobs available.

**APPLYING FOR FINANCIAL AID** *Required financial aid forms:* FAFSA, institution's own form. *Financial aid deadline (priority):* 3/1. *Notification date:* Continuous beginning 3/1. Students must reply by 5/1.

**CONTACT** Mr. Scott Seibring, Director of Financial Aid, Illinois Wesleyan University, 1312 North Park Street, PO Box 2900, Bloomington, IL 61702-2900, 309-556-3393 or toll-free 800-332-2498. *Fax:* 309-556-3833. *E-mail:* seibring@iwu.edu. *Website:* http://www.iwu.edu/.

# IMMACULATA UNIVERSITY
## Immaculata, PA

**CONTACT** Mr. Peter Lysionek, Director of Student Financial Aid, Immaculata University, 1145 King Road, Box 500, Immaculata, PA 19345, 610-647-4400 Ext. 3026 or toll-free 877-428-6329. *Fax:* 610-640-0836. *E-mail:* plysionek@immaculata.edu. *Website:* http://www.immaculata.edu/.

# INDEPENDENCE UNIVERSITY
## Salt Lake City, UT

**CONTACT** Financial Aid Director, Independence University, 2423 Hoover Avenue, National City, CA 91950-6605, 619-477-4800 or toll-free 800-972-5149. *Fax:* 619-477-5202. *Website:* http://www.independence.edu/.

# INDIANA STATE UNIVERSITY
## Terre Haute, IN

| Tuition & fees (IN res): $8416 | Average undergraduate aid package: $9995 |
| --- | --- |

**ABOUT THE INSTITUTION** State-supported, coed. *Awards:* certificates, associate, bachelor's, master's, and doctoral degrees. 70 undergraduate majors. *Total enrollment:* 13,183. Undergraduates: 10,881. Freshmen: 2,739. Federal methodology is used as a basis for awarding need-based institutional aid.

**UNDERGRADUATE EXPENSES** for 2015–2016 *Application fee:* $25. *Tuition, state resident:* full-time $8216; part-time $298 per credit hour. *Tuition, nonresident:* full-time $18,146; part-time $643 per credit hour. *Required fees:*

full-time $200; $100 per term. Full-time tuition and fees vary according to reciprocity agreements. Part-time tuition and fees vary according to course load and reciprocity agreements. *College room and board:* $9182. Room and board charges vary according to board plan and housing facility.

**FRESHMAN FINANCIAL AID (Fall 2013)** 2,497 applied for aid; of those 87% were deemed to have need. 98% of freshmen with need received aid; of those 10% had need fully met. *Average percent of need met:* 79% (excluding resources awarded to replace EFC). *Average financial aid package:* $10,101 (excluding resources awarded to replace EFC). 9% of all full-time freshmen had no need and received non-need-based gift aid.

**UNDERGRADUATE FINANCIAL AID (Fall 2013)** 7,883 applied for aid; of those 86% were deemed to have need. 97% of undergraduates with need received aid; of those 11% had need fully met. *Average percent of need met:* 80% (excluding resources awarded to replace EFC). *Average financial aid package:* $9995 (excluding resources awarded to replace EFC). 11% of all full-time undergraduates had no need and received non-need-based gift aid.

**GIFT AID (NEED-BASED)** *Total amount:* $25,546,315 (76% federal, 16% state, 7% institutional, 1% external sources). *Receiving aid:* Freshmen: 57% (1,505); all full-time undergraduates: 48% (4,365). *Average award:* Freshmen: $5638; Undergraduates: $5625. *Scholarships, grants, and awards:* Federal Pell, FSEOG, state, private, college/university gift aid from institutional funds.

**GIFT AID (NON-NEED-BASED)** *Total amount:* $25,131,474 (54% state, 37% institutional, 9% external sources). *Receiving aid:* Freshmen: 63% (1,676). Undergraduates: 44% (3,974). *Average award:* Freshmen: $3052. Undergraduates: $3462. *Scholarships, grants, and awards by category:* Academic interests/achievement: area/ethnic studies, biological sciences, business, communication, computer science, education, engineering/technologies, English, foreign languages, general academic interests/achievements, health fields, humanities, mathematics, physical sciences, premedicine, social sciences. Creative arts/performance: applied art and design, art/fine arts, music, performing arts, theater/drama. Special characteristics: children and siblings of alumni, children of faculty/staff, members of minority groups, previous college experience, veterans. *Tuition waivers:* Full or partial for employees or children of employees, senior citizens. *ROTC:* Army, Air Force.

**LOANS** *Student loans:* $48,189,923 (45% need-based, 55% non-need-based). 72% of past graduating class borrowed through all loan programs. *Average indebtedness per student:* $26,256. *Average need-based loan:* Freshmen: $3227. Undergraduates: $3971. *Parent loans:* $9,640,483 (100% non-need-based). *Programs:* Federal Direct (Subsidized and Unsubsidized Stafford, PLUS), Perkins.

**WORK-STUDY** *Federal work-study:* jobs available. *State or other work-study/employment:* Part-time jobs available.

**ATHLETIC AWARDS** Total amount: $4,027,871 (100% non-need-based).

**APPLYING FOR FINANCIAL AID** *Required financial aid form:* FAFSA. *Financial aid deadline:* 7/1 (priority: 3/1). *Notification date:* Continuous beginning 3/15.

**CONTACT** Crystal Baker, Director of Student Financial Aid, Indiana State University, 150 Tirey Hall, Terre Haute, IN 47809-1401, 812-237-2215 or toll-free 800-468-6478. *Fax:* 812-237-4330. *E-mail:* isu-finaid@indstate.edu. *Website:* http://www.indstate.edu/.

# INDIANA TECH
## Fort Wayne, IN

| Tuition & fees: $24,860 | Average undergraduate aid package: $18,712 |
| --- | --- |

**ABOUT THE INSTITUTION** Independent, coed. *Awards:* associate, bachelor's, master's, and doctoral degrees. 31 undergraduate majors. *Total enrollment:* 6,355. Undergraduates: 5,738. Freshmen: 875. Federal methodology is used as a basis for awarding need-based institutional aid.

**UNDERGRADUATE EXPENSES** for 2015–2016 *Application fee:* $50. *Comprehensive fee:* $34,381 includes full-time tuition ($24,450), mandatory fees ($410), and room and board ($9521). Full-time tuition and fees vary according to class time, course load, and program. Room and board charges vary according to board plan and housing facility. *Part-time tuition:* $480 per credit hour. Part-time tuition and fees vary according to class time, course load, and program.

**FRESHMAN FINANCIAL AID (Fall 2014, est.)** 679 applied for aid; of those 95% were deemed to have need. 100% of freshmen with need received aid. *Average percent of need met:* 30% (excluding resources awarded to replace EFC).

*Average financial aid package:* $21,994 (excluding resources awarded to replace EFC). 4% of all full-time freshmen had no need and received non-need-based gift aid.
**UNDERGRADUATE FINANCIAL AID (Fall 2014, est.)** 3,776 applied for aid; of those 96% were deemed to have need. 99% of undergraduates with need received aid. *Average percent of need met:* 39% (excluding resources awarded to replace EFC). *Average financial aid package:* $18,712 (excluding resources awarded to replace EFC). 1% of all full-time undergraduates had no need and received non-need-based gift aid.
**GIFT AID (NEED-BASED)** *Total amount:* $38,593,730 (50% federal, 28% state, 21% institutional, 1% external sources). *Receiving aid:* Freshmen: 81% (563); all full-time undergraduates: 78% (3,122). *Average award:* Freshmen: $7811; Undergraduates: $8419. *Scholarships, grants, and awards:* Federal Pell, FSEOG, state, private, college/university gift aid from institutional funds.
**GIFT AID (NON-NEED-BASED)** *Receiving aid:* Freshmen: 53% (370). Undergraduates: 23% (914). *Average award:* Freshmen: $9553. Undergraduates: $8490. *Scholarships, grants, and awards by category: Academic interests/achievement:* 913 awards: computer science, engineering/technologies, general academic interests/achievement. *Special characteristics:* 132 awards ($870,522 total): children of current students, children of faculty/staff, married students, siblings of current students, spouses of current students. *Tuition waivers:* Full or partial for employees or children of employees. *ROTC:* Army cooperative.
**LOANS** *Student loans:* $43,315,044 (42% need-based, 58% non-need-based). 74% of past graduating class borrowed through all loan programs. *Average indebtedness per student:* $41,844. *Average need-based loan:* Freshmen: $3224. Undergraduates: $3813. *Parent loans:* $2,276,374 (100% non-need-based). *Programs:* Federal Direct (Subsidized and Unsubsidized Stafford, PLUS), Perkins.
**WORK-STUDY** *Federal work-study:* Total amount: $185,669; 124 jobs averaging $1497. *State or other work-study/employment:* Part-time jobs available.
**ATHLETIC AWARDS** Total amount: $5,392,675 (100% non-need-based).
**APPLYING FOR FINANCIAL AID** *Required financial aid form:* FAFSA. *Financial aid deadline (priority):* 3/1. *Notification date:* Continuous beginning 2/20. Students must reply within 2 weeks of notification.
**CONTACT** Mrs. Lisa Claudette Green, Systems Analyst, Indiana Tech, 1600 East Washington Boulevard, Fort Wayne, IN 46803-1297, 800-937-2448 Ext. 2334 or toll-free 800-937-2448. *Fax:* 219-422-1578. *E-mail:* financialaid@indianatech.edu.
*Website:* http://www.indianatech.edu/.

# INDIANA UNIVERSITY BLOOMINGTON
### Bloomington, IN

| Tuition & fees (IN res): $10,388 | Average undergraduate aid package: $11,998 |
|---|---|

**ABOUT THE INSTITUTION** State-supported, coed. *Awards:* certificates, associate, bachelor's, master's, and doctoral degrees. 104 undergraduate majors. *Total enrollment:* 46,416. Undergraduates: 36,419. Freshmen: 6,985. Federal methodology is used as a basis for awarding need-based institutional aid.
**UNDERGRADUATE EXPENSES** for 2015–2016 *Application fee:* $60. *Tuition, state resident:* full-time $9087; part-time $283.92 per credit hour. *Tuition, nonresident:* full-time $31,940; part-time $998.13 per credit hour. *Required fees:* full-time $1301. Full-time tuition and fees vary according to location and program. Part-time tuition and fees vary according to course load, location, and program. *College room and board:* $9493. Room and board charges vary according to board plan and housing facility.
**FRESHMAN FINANCIAL AID (Fall 2013)** 5,364 applied for aid; of those 64% were deemed to have need. 94% of freshmen with need received aid; of those 29% had need fully met. *Average percent of need met:* 66% (excluding resources awarded to replace EFC). *Average financial aid package:* $12,649 (excluding resources awarded to replace EFC). 19% of all full-time freshmen had no need and received non-need-based gift aid.
**UNDERGRADUATE FINANCIAL AID (Fall 2013)** 18,540 applied for aid; of those 73% were deemed to have need. 96% of undergraduates with need received aid; of those 19% had need fully met. *Average percent of need met:* 64% (excluding resources awarded to replace EFC). *Average financial aid package:* $11,998 (excluding resources awarded to replace EFC). 27% of all full-time undergraduates had no need and received non-need-based gift aid.

**GIFT AID (NEED-BASED)** *Total amount:* $107,150,361 (26% federal, 27% state, 42% institutional, 5% external sources). *Receiving aid:* Freshmen: 35% (2,658); all full-time undergraduates: 35% (10,838). *Average award:* Freshmen: $11,965; Undergraduates: $10,137. *Scholarships, grants, and awards:* Federal Pell, FSEOG, state, private, college/university gift aid from institutional funds.
**GIFT AID (NON-NEED-BASED)** *Total amount:* $61,343,264 (2% federal, 2% state, 84% institutional, 12% external sources). *Receiving aid:* Freshmen: 8% (591). Undergraduates: 5% (1,684). *Average award:* Freshmen: $8061. Undergraduates: $5446. *Tuition waivers:* Full or partial for employees or children of employees. *ROTC:* Army, Air Force.
**LOANS** *Student loans:* $102,356,149 (61% need-based, 39% non-need-based). 51% of past graduating class borrowed through all loan programs. *Average indebtedness per student:* $27,300. *Average need-based loan:* Freshmen: $3203. Undergraduates: $4356. *Parent loans:* $37,784,304 (37% need-based, 63% non-need-based). *Programs:* Federal Direct (Subsidized and Unsubsidized Stafford, PLUS), Perkins, Federal Nursing, college/university.
**WORK-STUDY** *Federal work-study:* jobs available. *State or other work-study/employment:* Total amount: $31,445 (81% need-based, 19% non-need-based). Part-time jobs available.
**ATHLETIC AWARDS** Total amount: $11,315,609 (32% need-based, 68% non-need-based).
**APPLYING FOR FINANCIAL AID** *Required financial aid form:* FAFSA. *Financial aid deadline (priority):* 3/10. *Notification date:* Continuous beginning 4/1.
**CONTACT** Jackie Kennedy-Fletcher , Director of Student Financial Assistance, Indiana University Bloomington, 408 North Union Street, Bloomington, IN 47405, 812-855-6500. *Fax:* 812-855-7615. *E-mail:* rsvposfa@indiana.edu.
*Website:* http://www.iub.edu/.

# INDIANA UNIVERSITY EAST
### Richmond, IN

| Tuition & fees (IN res): $6787 | Average undergraduate aid package: $8834 |
|---|---|

**ABOUT THE INSTITUTION** State-supported, coed. *Awards:* certificates, bachelor's, and master's degrees. 23 undergraduate majors. *Total enrollment:* 4,573. Undergraduates: 4,430. Freshmen: 397. Federal methodology is used as a basis for awarding need-based institutional aid.
**UNDERGRADUATE EXPENSES** for 2015–2016 *Application fee:* $35. *Tuition, state resident:* full-time $6196; part-time $206.53 per credit hour. *Tuition, nonresident:* full-time $17,490; part-time $583 per credit hour. *Required fees:* full-time $591. Full-time tuition and fees vary according to course load, location, program, and reciprocity agreements. Part-time tuition and fees vary according to course load, location, program, and reciprocity agreements.
**FRESHMAN FINANCIAL AID (Fall 2013)** 375 applied for aid; of those 84% were deemed to have need. 97% of freshmen with need received aid; of those 8% had need fully met. *Average percent of need met:* 68% (excluding resources awarded to replace EFC). *Average financial aid package:* $8669 (excluding resources awarded to replace EFC). 9% of all full-time freshmen had no need and received non-need-based gift aid.
**UNDERGRADUATE FINANCIAL AID (Fall 2013)** 1,791 applied for aid; of those 90% were deemed to have need. 95% of undergraduates with need received aid; of those 6% had need fully met. *Average percent of need met:* 63% (excluding resources awarded to replace EFC). *Average financial aid package:* $8834 (excluding resources awarded to replace EFC). 5% of all full-time undergraduates had no need and received non-need-based gift aid.
**GIFT AID (NEED-BASED)** *Total amount:* $10,287,138 (60% federal, 29% state, 8% institutional, 3% external sources). *Receiving aid:* Freshmen: 71% (275); all full-time undergraduates: 69% (1,324). *Average award:* Freshmen: $7823; Undergraduates: $6834. *Scholarships, grants, and awards:* Federal Pell, FSEOG, state, private, college/university gift aid from institutional funds.
**GIFT AID (NON-NEED-BASED)** *Total amount:* $574,820 (7% federal, 12% state, 48% institutional, 33% external sources). *Receiving aid:* Freshmen: 4% (15). Undergraduates: 3% (55). *Average award:* Freshmen: $2401. Undergraduates: $2148. *Tuition waivers:* Full or partial for employees or children of employees.
**LOANS** *Student loans:* $12,874,731 (82% need-based, 18% non-need-based). 78% of past graduating class borrowed through all loan programs. *Average indebtedness*

per student: $29,952. *Average need-based loan:* Freshmen: $2782. Undergraduates: $3776. *Parent loans:* $87,658 (28% need-based, 72% non-need-based). *Programs:* Federal Direct (Subsidized and Unsubsidized Stafford, PLUS), Perkins, college/university.

**WORK-STUDY** *Federal work-study:* jobs available.

**ATHLETIC AWARDS** Total amount: $199,710 (70% need-based, 30% non-need-based).

**APPLYING FOR FINANCIAL AID** *Required financial aid forms:* FAFSA, institution's own form. *Financial aid deadline (priority):* 3/10. *Notification date:* Continuous beginning 5/1. Students must reply within 2 weeks of notification.

**CONTACT** Sarah Soper, Director of Financial Aid and Scholarships, Indiana University East, Whitewater Hall 112, 2325 Chester Boulevard, Richmond, IN 47374-1289, 765-973-8206 or toll-free 800-959-EAST. *Fax:* 765-973-8288. *E-mail:* eaosfa@iue.edu.

*Website:* http://www.iue.edu/.

---

# INDIANA UNIVERSITY KOKOMO
## Kokomo, IN

| Tuition & fees (IN res): $6811 | Average undergraduate aid package: $8311 |
|---|---|

**ABOUT THE INSTITUTION** State-supported, coed. *Awards:* certificates, associate, bachelor's, and master's degrees. 29 undergraduate majors. *Total enrollment:* 4,180. Undergraduates: 4,004. Freshmen: 523. Federal methodology is used as a basis for awarding need-based institutional aid.

**UNDERGRADUATE EXPENSES for 2015–2016** *Application fee:* $35. *Tuition, state resident:* full-time $6220; part-time $207.32 per credit hour. *Tuition, nonresident:* full-time $17,490; part-time $583 per credit hour. *Required fees:* full-time $591. Full-time tuition and fees vary according to course load, location, and program. Part-time tuition and fees vary according to course load, location, and program.

**FRESHMAN FINANCIAL AID (Fall 2013)** 438 applied for aid; of those 76% were deemed to have need. 95% of freshmen with need received aid; of those 5% had need fully met. *Average percent of need met:* 62% (excluding resources awarded to replace EFC). *Average financial aid package:* $7707 (excluding resources awarded to replace EFC). 5% of all full-time freshmen had no need and received non-need-based gift aid.

**UNDERGRADUATE FINANCIAL AID (Fall 2013)** 1,807 applied for aid; of those 83% were deemed to have need. 96% of undergraduates with need received aid; of those 3% had need fully met. *Average percent of need met:* 62% (excluding resources awarded to replace EFC). *Average financial aid package:* $8311 (excluding resources awarded to replace EFC). 5% of all full-time undergraduates had no need and received non-need-based gift aid.

**GIFT AID (NEED-BASED)** *Total amount:* $9,319,782 (59% federal, 34% state, 4% institutional, 3% external sources). *Receiving aid:* Freshmen: 60% (275); all full-time undergraduates: 60% (1,208). *Average award:* Freshmen: $6966; Undergraduates: $6627. *Scholarships, grants, and awards:* Federal Pell, FSEOG, state, private, college/university gift aid from institutional funds.

**GIFT AID (NON-NEED-BASED)** *Total amount:* $640,065 (18% federal, 25% state, 24% institutional, 33% external sources). *Receiving aid:* Freshmen: 2% (11). Undergraduates: 2% (37). *Average award:* Freshmen: $2031. Undergraduates: $1194. *Tuition waivers:* Full or partial for employees or children of employees. **ROTC:** Army.

**LOANS** *Student loans:* $10,641,694 (78% need-based, 22% non-need-based). 74% of past graduating class borrowed through all loan programs. *Average indebtedness per student:* $26,651. *Average need-based loan:* Freshmen: $2826. Undergraduates: $3689. *Parent loans:* $86,490 (26% need-based, 74% non-need-based). *Programs:* Federal Direct (Subsidized and Unsubsidized Stafford, PLUS), Perkins, Federal Nursing, college/university.

**WORK-STUDY** *Federal work-study:* jobs available. *State or other work-study/employment:* Total amount: $1175 (100% need-based). Part-time jobs available.

**ATHLETIC AWARDS** Total amount: $34,000 (84% need-based, 16% non-need-based).

**APPLYING FOR FINANCIAL AID** *Required financial aid form:* FAFSA. *Financial aid deadline:* 6/30 (priority: 3/10). *Notification date:* Continuous beginning 3/25. Students must reply by 6/1.

---

**CONTACT** John Delaney, Assistant Director of Financial Aid, Indiana University Kokomo, Kelley Student Center, Room 230, 2300 South Washington Street, Kokomo, IN 46904-9003, 765-455-9216 or toll-free 888-875-4485. *Fax:* 765-455-9537. *E-mail:* finaidko@iuk.edu.

*Website:* http://www.iuk.edu/.

---

# INDIANA UNIVERSITY NORTHWEST
## Gary, IN

| Tuition & fees (IN res): $6853 | Average undergraduate aid package: $8186 |
|---|---|

**ABOUT THE INSTITUTION** State-supported, coed. *Awards:* certificates, associate, bachelor's, and master's degrees. 41 undergraduate majors. *Total enrollment:* 6,052. Undergraduates: 5,661. Freshmen: 711. Federal methodology is used as a basis for awarding need-based institutional aid.

**UNDERGRADUATE EXPENSES for 2015–2016** *Application fee:* $35. *Tuition, state resident:* full-time $6262; part-time $208.75 per credit hour. *Tuition, nonresident:* full-time $17,490; part-time $583 per credit hour. *Required fees:* full-time $591. Full-time tuition and fees vary according to course load, location, and program. Part-time tuition and fees vary according to course load, location, and program.

**FRESHMAN FINANCIAL AID (Fall 2013)** 619 applied for aid; of those 74% were deemed to have need. 93% of freshmen with need received aid; of those 4% had need fully met. *Average percent of need met:* 62% (excluding resources awarded to replace EFC). *Average financial aid package:* $7026 (excluding resources awarded to replace EFC). 7% of all full-time freshmen had no need and received non-need-based gift aid.

**UNDERGRADUATE FINANCIAL AID (Fall 2013)** 2,795 applied for aid; of those 83% were deemed to have need. 95% of undergraduates with need received aid; of those 3% had need fully met. *Average percent of need met:* 62% (excluding resources awarded to replace EFC). *Average financial aid package:* $8186 (excluding resources awarded to replace EFC). 6% of all full-time undergraduates had no need and received non-need-based gift aid.

**GIFT AID (NEED-BASED)** *Total amount:* $14,389,120 (63% federal, 29% state, 6% institutional, 2% external sources). *Receiving aid:* Freshmen: 50% (351); all full-time undergraduates: 58% (1,834). *Average award:* Freshmen: $6600; Undergraduates: $6589. *Scholarships, grants, and awards:* Federal Pell, FSEOG, state, private, college/university gift aid from institutional funds, United Negro College Fund, Federal Nursing, .

**GIFT AID (NON-NEED-BASED)** *Total amount:* $1,040,055 (9% federal, 10% state, 72% institutional, 9% external sources). *Receiving aid:* Freshmen: 1% (10). Undergraduates: 1% (30). *Average award:* Freshmen: $3768. Undergraduates: $3485. *Tuition waivers:* Full or partial for employees or children of employees. **ROTC:** Army.

**LOANS** *Student loans:* $18,073,788 (78% need-based, 22% non-need-based). 78% of past graduating class borrowed through all loan programs. *Average indebtedness per student:* $33,790. *Average need-based loan:* Freshmen: $2898. Undergraduates: $3618. *Parent loans:* $227,737 (22% need-based, 78% non-need-based). *Programs:* Federal Direct (Subsidized and Unsubsidized Stafford, PLUS), Perkins, college/university.

**WORK-STUDY** *Federal work-study:* jobs available.

**ATHLETIC AWARDS** Total amount: $46,700 (56% need-based, 44% non-need-based).

**APPLYING FOR FINANCIAL AID** *Required financial aid form:* FAFSA. *Financial aid deadline (priority):* 3/10. *Notification date:* Continuous beginning 4/15. Students must reply by 6/30.

**CONTACT** Harold Burtley, Director of Scholarships and Financial Aid, Indiana University Northwest, 3400 Broadway, Hawthorn Hall, Room 111, Gary, IN 46408, 219-980-6778 or toll-free 800-968-7486. *Fax:* 219-981-5622. *E-mail:* finaidnw@iun.edu.

*Website:* http://www.iun.edu/.

---

# INDIANA UNIVERSITY OF PENNSYLVANIA
## Indiana, PA

| Tuition & fees (PA res): $9470 | Average undergraduate aid package: $9270 |
| --- | --- |

**ABOUT THE INSTITUTION** State-supported, coed. **Awards:** certificates, associate, bachelor's, master's, and doctoral degrees. 62 undergraduate majors. **Total enrollment:** 14,369. Undergraduates: 12,130. Freshmen: 2,733. Federal methodology is used as a basis for awarding need-based institutional aid.

**UNDERGRADUATE EXPENSES for 2015–2016 Application fee:** $50. **Tuition, state resident:** full-time $6820; part-time $284 per credit hour. **Tuition, nonresident:** full-time $17,050; part-time $710 per credit hour. **Required fees:** full-time $2650; $63.20 per credit hour or $229.50 per credit hour. Full-time tuition and fees vary according to course load and reciprocity agreements. Part-time tuition and fees vary according to course load and reciprocity agreements. **College room and board:** $11,346; **Room only:** $8290. Room and board charges vary according to board plan, housing facility, and location.

**FRESHMAN FINANCIAL AID (Fall 2013)** 2,485 applied for aid; of those 81% were deemed to have need. 98% of freshmen with need received aid; of those 7% had need fully met. **Average percent of need met:** 59% (excluding resources awarded to replace EFC). **Average financial aid package:** $10,111 (excluding resources awarded to replace EFC). 3% of all full-time freshmen had no need and received non-need-based gift aid.

**UNDERGRADUATE FINANCIAL AID (Fall 2013)** 9,954 applied for aid; of those 83% were deemed to have need. 98% of undergraduates with need received aid; of those 7% had need fully met. **Average percent of need met:** 56% (excluding resources awarded to replace EFC). **Average financial aid package:** $9270 (excluding resources awarded to replace EFC). 2% of all full-time undergraduates had no need and received non-need-based gift aid.

**GIFT AID (NEED-BASED) Total amount:** $32,107,410 (62% federal, 38% state). **Receiving aid:** Freshmen: 50% (1,314); all full-time undergraduates: 45% (5,326). **Average award:** Freshmen: $6529; Undergraduates: $5913. **Scholarships, grants, and awards:** Federal Pell, FSEOG, state, private, college/university gift aid from institutional funds, United Negro College Fund.

**GIFT AID (NON-NEED-BASED) Total amount:** $5,112,481 (14% state, 26% institutional, 60% external sources). **Receiving aid:** Freshmen: 24% (640). Undergraduates: 14% (1,620). **Average award:** Freshmen: $1831. Undergraduates: $1787. **Scholarships, grants, and awards by category:** Academic interests/achievement: 1,462 awards ($3,311,134 total): area/ethnic studies, biological sciences, business, communication, computer science, education, engineering/technologies, English, foreign languages, general academic interests/achievements, health fields, home economics, humanities, international studies, mathematics, military science, physical sciences, premedicine, religion/biblical studies, social sciences. Creative arts/performance: applied art and design, art/fine arts, dance, general creative arts/performance, journalism/publications, music, performing arts, theater/drama. Special achievements/activities: community service, general special achievements/activities, hobbies/interests, leadership. Special characteristics: adult students, children of faculty/staff, ethnic background, international students. **Tuition waivers:** Full or partial for employees or children of employees, senior citizens. **ROTC:** Army.

**LOANS Student loans:** $82,097,308 (39% need-based, 61% non-need-based). 82% of past graduating class borrowed through all loan programs. **Average indebtedness per student:** $33,807. **Average need-based loan:** Freshmen: $3623. Undergraduates: $4233. **Parent loans:** $17,602,354 (100% non-need-based). **Programs:** Federal Direct (Subsidized and Unsubsidized Stafford, PLUS), Perkins, private loans.

**WORK-STUDY Federal work-study:** 930 jobs averaging $1988. **State or other work-study/employment:** Total amount: $1,032,742 (100% non-need-based). 1,663 part-time jobs averaging $2519.

**ATHLETIC AWARDS Total amount:** $1,385,952 (100% non-need-based).

**APPLYING FOR FINANCIAL AID Required financial aid form:** FAFSA. **Financial aid deadline (priority):** 4/15. **Notification date:** Continuous beginning 3/14.

**CONTACT** Mrs. Stacy Hopkins, Director of Financial Aid, Indiana University of Pennsylvania, 213 Clark Hall, Indiana, PA 15705, 724-357-2218 or toll-free 800-442-6830. Fax: 724-357-2094. E-mail: stacy.hopkins@iup.edu.
Website: http://www.iup.edu/.

# INDIANA UNIVERSITY–PURDUE UNIVERSITY FORT WAYNE
## Fort Wayne, IN

| Tuition & fees (IN res): $7949 | Average undergraduate aid package: $9525 |
| --- | --- |

**ABOUT THE INSTITUTION** State-supported, coed. **Awards:** certificates, associate, bachelor's, and master's degrees. 103 undergraduate majors. **Total enrollment:** 13,214. Undergraduates: 12,674. Freshmen: 1,559. Federal methodology is used as a basis for awarding need-based institutional aid.

**UNDERGRADUATE EXPENSES for 2015–2016 Application fee:** $50. **Tuition, state resident:** full-time $6938; part-time $231.25 per credit hour. **Tuition, nonresident:** full-time $18,081; part-time $602.70 per credit hour. **Required fees:** full-time $1011; $33.70 per credit hour. Full-time tuition and fees vary according to course load. Part-time tuition and fees vary according to course load. **Room only:** $7632. Room and board charges vary according to housing facility.

**FRESHMAN FINANCIAL AID (Fall 2014, est.)** 1,441 applied for aid; of those 81% were deemed to have need. 94% of freshmen with need received aid; of those 3% had need fully met. **Average percent of need met:** 48% (excluding resources awarded to replace EFC). **Average financial aid package:** $8523 (excluding resources awarded to replace EFC). 1% of all full-time freshmen had no need and received non-need-based gift aid.

**UNDERGRADUATE FINANCIAL AID (Fall 2014, est.)** 6,395 applied for aid; of those 86% were deemed to have need. 96% of undergraduates with need received aid; of those 2% had need fully met. **Average percent of need met:** 47% (excluding resources awarded to replace EFC). **Average financial aid package:** $9525 (excluding resources awarded to replace EFC). 1% of all full-time undergraduates had no need and received non-need-based gift aid.

**GIFT AID (NEED-BASED) Total amount:** $32,000,000 (52% federal, 39% state, 6% institutional, 3% external sources). **Receiving aid:** Freshmen: 43% (677); all full-time undergraduates: 50% (3,641). **Average award:** Freshmen: $4943; Undergraduates: $5437. **Scholarships, grants, and awards:** Federal Pell, FSEOG, state, private, college/university gift aid from institutional funds.

**GIFT AID (NON-NEED-BASED) Receiving aid:** Freshmen: 31% (490). Undergraduates: 19% (1,396). **Average award:** Freshmen: $5738. Undergraduates: $3660. **Scholarships, grants, and awards by category:** Academic interests/achievement: biological sciences, engineering/technologies, general academic interests/achievements, premedicine. Creative arts/performance: art/fine arts, music, theater/drama. Special achievements/activities: leadership. Special characteristics: children and siblings of alumni, general special characteristics, local/state students. **Tuition waivers:** Full or partial for employees or children of employees, senior citizens. **ROTC:** Army.

**LOANS Student loans:** $45,750,000 (98% need-based, 2% non-need-based). 12% of past graduating class borrowed through all loan programs. **Average indebtedness per student:** $29,452. **Average need-based loan:** Freshmen: $3059. Undergraduates: $3870. **Parent loans:** $2,015,000 (99% need-based, 1% non-need-based). **Programs:** Federal Direct (Subsidized and Unsubsidized Stafford, PLUS), Perkins.

**WORK-STUDY Federal work-study:** Total amount: $400,000; 200 jobs averaging $3000.

**ATHLETIC AWARDS Total amount:** $2,100,000 (40% need-based, 60% non-need-based).

**APPLYING FOR FINANCIAL AID Required financial aid forms:** FAFSA, general scholarship application form. **Financial aid deadline (priority):** 3/10. **Notification date:** Continuous beginning 4/1.

**CONTACT** Mr. David Peterson, Director of Financial Aid, Indiana University–Purdue University Fort Wayne, 2101 East Coliseum Boulevard, Fort Wayne, IN 46805-1499, 260-481-6240 or toll-free 800-324-4739. E-mail: finaid@ipfw.edu.
Website: http://www.ipfw.edu/.

# INDIANA UNIVERSITY–PURDUE UNIVERSITY INDIANAPOLIS
## Indianapolis, IN

**Tuition & fees (IN res):** $8909 | **Average undergraduate aid package:** $9862

**ABOUT THE INSTITUTION** State-supported, coed. **Awards:** certificates, associate, bachelor's, master's, and doctoral degrees. 88 undergraduate majors. **Total enrollment:** 30,690. Undergraduates: 22,525. Freshmen: 3,779. Federal methodology is used as a basis for awarding need-based institutional aid.

**UNDERGRADUATE EXPENSES for 2015–2016 Application fee:** $55. **Tuition, state resident:** full-time $7878; part-time $262.61 per credit hour. **Tuition, nonresident:** full-time $29,058; part-time $968.59 per credit hour. **Required fees:** full-time $1031. Full-time tuition and fees vary according to course load, location, and program. Part-time tuition and fees vary according to course load, location, and program. **College room and board:** $7981. Room and board charges vary according to board plan and housing facility.

**FRESHMAN FINANCIAL AID (Fall 2013)** 3,173 applied for aid; of those 79% were deemed to have need. 96% of freshmen with need received aid; of those 9% had need fully met. **Average percent of need met:** 63% (excluding resources awarded to replace EFC). **Average financial aid package:** $10,041 (excluding resources awarded to replace EFC). 9% of all full-time freshmen had no need and received non-need-based gift aid.

**UNDERGRADUATE FINANCIAL AID (Fall 2013)** 13,984 applied for aid; of those 84% were deemed to have need. 96% of undergraduates with need received aid; of those 6% had need fully met. **Average percent of need met:** 61% (excluding resources awarded to replace EFC). **Average financial aid package:** $9862 (excluding resources awarded to replace EFC). 8% of all full-time undergraduates had no need and received non-need-based gift aid.

**GIFT AID (NEED-BASED) Total amount:** $78,563,709 (48% federal, 34% state, 15% institutional, 3% external sources). **Receiving aid:** Freshmen: 59% (2,077); all full-time undergraduates: 56% (9,324). **Average award:** Freshmen: $8561; Undergraduates: $7816. **Scholarships, grants, and awards:** Federal Pell, FSEOG, state, private, college/university gift aid from institutional funds.

**GIFT AID (NON-NEED-BASED) Total amount:** $20,890,119 (5% federal, 6% state, 37% institutional, 52% external sources). **Receiving aid:** Freshmen: 5% (172). Undergraduates: 3% (520). **Average award:** Freshmen: $6434. Undergraduates: $4658. **Tuition waivers:** Full or partial for employees or children of employees. **ROTC:** Army, Air Force cooperative.

**LOANS Student loans:** $92,160,962 (78% need-based, 22% non-need-based). 73% of past graduating class borrowed through all loan programs. **Average indebtedness per student:** $31,010. **Average need-based loan:** Freshmen: $3443. Undergraduates: $4196. **Parent loans:** $7,103,062 (34% need-based, 66% non-need-based). **Programs:** Federal Direct (Subsidized and Unsubsidized Stafford, PLUS), Perkins, Federal Nursing, college/university.

**WORK-STUDY Federal work-study:** jobs available. **State or other work-study/employment:** Total amount: $44,794 (78% need-based, 22% non-need-based). Part-time jobs available.

**ATHLETIC AWARDS** Total amount: $2,122,137 (42% need-based, 58% non-need-based).

**APPLYING FOR FINANCIAL AID Required financial aid form:** FAFSA. **Financial aid deadline (priority):** 3/10. **Notification date:** Continuous beginning 4/1.

**CONTACT** Marvin Smith, Director of Student Financial Services, Indiana University–Purdue University Indianapolis, 420 University Boulevard, CE 250, Indianapolis, IN 46202-5145, 317-274-4162. Fax: 317-274-3664. E-mail: finaid@iupui.edu. Website: http://www.iupui.edu/.

# INDIANA UNIVERSITY SOUTH BEND
## South Bend, IN

**Tuition & fees (IN res):** $6905 | **Average undergraduate aid package:** $8661

**ABOUT THE INSTITUTION** State-supported, coed. **Awards:** certificates, diplomas, associate, bachelor's, and master's degrees. 58 undergraduate majors. **Total enrollment:** 7,859. Undergraduates: 7,293. Freshmen: 938. Federal methodology is used as a basis for awarding need-based institutional aid.

**UNDERGRADUATE EXPENSES for 2015–2016 Application fee:** $35. **Tuition, state resident:** full-time $6314; part-time $210.47 per credit hour. **Tuition, nonresident:** full-time $17,490; part-time $583 per credit hour. **Required fees:** full-time $591. Full-time tuition and fees vary according to course load, location, and program. Part-time tuition and fees vary according to course load, location, and program. **Room only:** $7150. Room and board charges vary according to housing facility.

**FRESHMAN FINANCIAL AID (Fall 2013)** 769 applied for aid; of those 83% were deemed to have need. 94% of freshmen with need received aid; of those 6% had need fully met. **Average percent of need met:** 62% (excluding resources awarded to replace EFC). **Average financial aid package:** $7901 (excluding resources awarded to replace EFC). 7% of all full-time freshmen had no need and received non-need-based gift aid.

**UNDERGRADUATE FINANCIAL AID (Fall 2013)** 3,501 applied for aid; of those 88% were deemed to have need. 95% of undergraduates with need received aid; of those 4% had need fully met. **Average percent of need met:** 61% (excluding resources awarded to replace EFC). **Average financial aid package:** $8661 (excluding resources awarded to replace EFC). 4% of all full-time undergraduates had no need and received non-need-based gift aid.

**GIFT AID (NEED-BASED) Total amount:** $19,203,733 (58% federal, 32% state, 7% institutional, 3% external sources). **Receiving aid:** Freshmen: 67% (563); all full-time undergraduates: 65% (2,565). **Average award:** Freshmen: $6541; Undergraduates: $6688. **Scholarships, grants, and awards:** Federal Pell, FSEOG, state, private, college/university gift aid from institutional funds.

**GIFT AID (NON-NEED-BASED) Total amount:** $1,455,642 (9% federal, 8% state, 26% institutional, 57% external sources). **Receiving aid:** Freshmen: 3% (27). Undergraduates: 2% (73). **Average award:** Freshmen: $1316. Undergraduates: $1709. **Tuition waivers:** Full or partial for employees or children of employees. **ROTC:** Army cooperative, Naval cooperative, Air Force cooperative.

**LOANS Student loans:** $21,259,583 (83% need-based, 17% non-need-based). 75% of past graduating class borrowed through all loan programs. **Average indebtedness per student:** $29,919. **Average need-based loan:** Freshmen: $2844. Undergraduates: $3833. **Parent loans:** $497,746 (32% need-based, 68% non-need-based). **Programs:** Federal Direct (Subsidized and Unsubsidized Stafford, PLUS), Perkins, state.

**WORK-STUDY Federal work-study:** jobs available. **State or other work-study/employment:** Total amount: $3661 (100% need-based). Part-time jobs available.

**ATHLETIC AWARDS** Total amount: $295,950 (63% need-based, 37% non-need-based).

**APPLYING FOR FINANCIAL AID Required financial aid forms:** FAFSA, institution's own form. **Financial aid deadline (priority):** 3/10. **Notification date:** Continuous beginning 5/1.

**CONTACT** Cathy Buckman, Interim Director of Financial Aid, Indiana University South Bend, 1700 Mishawaka Avenue, PO Box 7111, Building 157, South Bend, IN 46634-7111, 574-520-4357 or toll-free 877-GO-2-IUSB. Fax: 574-520-5561. E-mail: sbfinaid@iusb.edu. Website: http://www.iusb.edu/.

# INDIANA UNIVERSITY SOUTHEAST
## New Albany, IN

**Tuition & fees (IN res):** $6827 | **Average undergraduate aid package:** $7667

**ABOUT THE INSTITUTION** State-supported, coed. **Awards:** certificates, associate, bachelor's, and master's degrees. 36 undergraduate majors. **Total enrollment:**

6,442. Undergraduates: 5,989. Freshmen: 923. Federal methodology is used as a basis for awarding need-based institutional aid.

**UNDERGRADUATE EXPENSES for 2015–2016** *Application fee:* $35. *Tuition, state resident:* full-time $6236; part-time $207.88 per credit hour. *Tuition, nonresident:* full-time $17,490; part-time $583 per credit hour. *Required fees:* full-time $591. Full-time tuition and fees vary according to course load, location, program, and reciprocity agreements. Part-time tuition and fees vary according to course load, location, program, and reciprocity agreements. *Room only:* $6280. Room and board charges vary according to board plan and housing facility.

**FRESHMAN FINANCIAL AID (Fall 2013)** 826 applied for aid; of those 79% were deemed to have need. 97% of freshmen with need received aid; of those 6% had need fully met. *Average percent of need met:* 60% (excluding resources awarded to replace EFC). *Average financial aid package:* $7510 (excluding resources awarded to replace EFC). 18% of all full-time freshmen had no need and received non-need-based gift aid.

**UNDERGRADUATE FINANCIAL AID (Fall 2013)** 3,081 applied for aid; of those 82% were deemed to have need. 96% of undergraduates with need received aid; of those 5% had need fully met. *Average percent of need met:* 58% (excluding resources awarded to replace EFC). *Average financial aid package:* $7667 (excluding resources awarded to replace EFC). 9% of all full-time undergraduates had no need and received non-need-based gift aid.

**GIFT AID (NEED-BASED)** *Total amount:* $14,461,238 (62% federal, 27% state, 6% institutional, 5% external sources). *Receiving aid:* Freshmen: 67% (606); all full-time undergraduates: 57% (2,065). *Average award:* Freshmen: $5967; Undergraduates: $5876. *Scholarships, grants, and awards:* Federal Pell, FSEOG, state, private, college/university gift aid from institutional funds.

**GIFT AID (NON-NEED-BASED)** *Total amount:* $1,486,779 (16% federal, 18% state, 32% institutional, 34% external sources). *Receiving aid:* Freshmen: 4% (32). Undergraduates: 2% (84). *Average award:* Freshmen: $561. Undergraduates: $1056. *Tuition waivers:* Full or partial for employees or children of employees. *ROTC:* Army cooperative, Air Force cooperative.

**LOANS** *Student loans:* $18,486,066 (77% need-based, 23% non-need-based). 67% of past graduating class borrowed through all loan programs. *Average indebtedness per student:* $26,594. *Average need-based loan:* Freshmen: $2935. Undergraduates: $3708. *Parent loans:* $520,120 (32% need-based, 68% non-need-based). *Programs:* Federal Direct (Subsidized and Unsubsidized Stafford, PLUS), Perkins, college/university.

**WORK-STUDY** *Federal work-study:* jobs available. *State or other work-study/employment:* Total amount: $17,981 (91% need-based, 9% non-need-based). Part-time jobs available.

**ATHLETIC AWARDS** Total amount: $107,301 (66% need-based, 34% non-need-based).

**APPLYING FOR FINANCIAL AID** *Required financial aid form:* FAFSA. *Financial aid deadline (priority):* 3/10. *Notification date:* Continuous beginning 5/1.

**CONTACT** Traci Armes, Director of Financial Aid, Indiana University Southeast, University Center, South Room 105, New Albany, IN 47150, 812-941-2246 or toll-free 800-852-8835. *Fax:* 812-941-2546. *E-mail:* financialaid@ius.edu.
*Website:* http://www.ius.edu/.

# INDIANA WESLEYAN UNIVERSITY
## Marion, IN

**ABOUT THE INSTITUTION** Independent Wesleyan, coed. *Awards:* certificates, associate, bachelor's, master's, and doctoral degrees (also offers adult program with significant enrollment not reflected in profile). 86 undergraduate majors. *Total enrollment:* 3,018. Undergraduates: 2,933. Freshmen: 718.

**GIFT AID (NEED-BASED)** *Scholarships, grants, and awards:* Federal Pell, FSEOG, state, private, college/university gift aid from institutional funds.

**GIFT AID (NON-NEED-BASED)** *Scholarships, grants, and awards by category: Academic interests/achievement:* biological sciences, business, communication, computer science, education, English, foreign languages, general academic interests/achievements, health fields, international studies, mathematics, physical sciences, premedicine, religion/biblical studies, social sciences. *Creative arts/performance:* art/fine arts, music, theater/drama. *Special achievements/activities:* cheerleading/drum major, community service, hobbies/interests, religious involvement. *Special characteristics:* children and siblings of alumni, children of faculty/staff, relatives of clergy, religious affiliation, siblings of current students, veterans.

**LOANS** *Programs:* Federal Direct (Subsidized and Unsubsidized Stafford, PLUS), Perkins, college/university.

**APPLYING FOR FINANCIAL AID** *Required financial aid form:* FAFSA.

**CONTACT** Daniel Solms, Financial Aid Office, Indiana Wesleyan University, 4201 South Washington Street, Marion, IN 46953-4999, 765-677-2116 or toll-free 866-468-6498. *Fax:* 765-677-2809. *E-mail:* finaid@indwes.edu.
*Website:* http://www.indwes.edu/.

# INDIAN RIVER STATE COLLEGE
## Fort Pierce, FL

| Tuition & fees (FL res): $2492 | Average undergraduate aid package: N/A |
| --- | --- |

**ABOUT THE INSTITUTION** State-supported, coed. *Awards:* certificates, diplomas, associate, and bachelor's degrees. 92 undergraduate majors. *Total enrollment:* 17,665. Undergraduates: 17,665. Freshmen: 1,877.

**UNDERGRADUATE EXPENSES for 2015–2016** *Tuition, state resident:* full-time $2492; part-time $103.83 per credit hour. *Tuition, nonresident:* full-time $9372; part-time $390.49 per credit hour. Full-time tuition and fees vary according to course load and degree level. Part-time tuition and fees vary according to course load and degree level. *College room and board:* $5700; *Room only:* $3150.

**GIFT AID (NEED-BASED)** *Scholarships, grants, and awards:* Federal Pell, FSEOG, state, private, college/university gift aid from institutional funds.

**LOANS** *Programs:* Federal Direct (Subsidized and Unsubsidized Stafford, PLUS).

**WORK-STUDY** Federal work-study jobs available.

**APPLYING FOR FINANCIAL AID** *Required financial aid forms:* FAFSA, institution's own form. *Financial aid deadline (priority):* 7/16. *Notification date:* Continuous.

**CONTACT** Mary Lewis, Director of Financial Aid, Indian River State College, W Building, Main Campus, Fort Pierce, FL 34981, 772-462-7450 or toll-free 866-792-4772. *E-mail:* financialaid-info@irsc.edu.
*Website:* http://www.irsc.edu/.

# INSTE BIBLE COLLEGE
## Ankeny, IA

**CONTACT** Financial Aid Office, INSTE Bible College, 2302 SW 3rd Street, Ankeny, IA 50023, 515-289-9200.
*Website:* http://www.inste.edu/.

# INSTITUTE OF AMERICAN INDIAN ARTS
## Santa Fe, NM

**CONTACT** Lala M. Gallegos, Director of Financial Aid, Institute of American Indian Arts, 83 Avan Nu Po Road, Santa Fe, NM 87508, 505-424-5724. *Fax:* 505-424-0909. *E-mail:* lgallegos@iaia.edu.
*Website:* http://www.iaia.edu/.

# INTER AMERICAN UNIVERSITY OF PUERTO RICO, AGUADILLA CAMPUS
## Aguadilla, PR

**CONTACT** Mr. Juan Gonzalez, Director of Financial Aid , Inter American University of Puerto Rico, Aguadilla Campus, PO Box 20000, Aguadilla, PR 00605, 787-891-0925 Ext. 2108. *Fax:* 787-882-3020.
*Website:* http://www.aguadilla.inter.edu/.

# INTER AMERICAN UNIVERSITY OF PUERTO RICO, ARECIBO CAMPUS
## Arecibo, PR

**CONTACT** Ramón O. de Jesús, Financial Aid Director, Inter American University of Puerto Rico, Arecibo Campus, PO Box 4050, Arecibo, PR 00614-4050, 787-878-5475 Ext. 2275. *Fax:* 787-880-1624.
*Website:* http://www.arecibo.inter.edu/.

# INTER AMERICAN UNIVERSITY OF PUERTO RICO, BARRANQUITAS CAMPUS
## Barranquitas, PR

**CONTACT** Mr. Eduardo Fontanez Colon, Financial Aid Officer, Inter American University of Puerto Rico, Barranquitas Campus, Box 517, Barranquitas, PR 00794, 787-857-3600 Ext. 2049. *Fax:* 787-857-2244.
*Website:* http://www.br.inter.edu/.

# INTER AMERICAN UNIVERSITY OF PUERTO RICO, BAYAMÓN CAMPUS
## Bayamón, PR

| Tuition & fees: $5860 | Average undergraduate aid package: $1458 |
| --- | --- |

**ABOUT THE INSTITUTION** Independent, coed. *Awards:* certificates, associate, bachelor's, and master's degrees. 36 undergraduate majors. *Total enrollment:* 4,825. Undergraduates: 4,717. Freshmen: 1,080. Federal methodology is used as a basis for awarding need-based institutional aid.
**UNDERGRADUATE EXPENSES for 2015–2016** *Tuition:* full-time $5340; part-time $260 per semester hour. Full-time tuition and fees vary according to class time, course load, and program. Part-time tuition and fees vary according to class time, course load, and program.
**FRESHMAN FINANCIAL AID (Fall 2014, est.)** 1,193 applied for aid; of those 99% were deemed to have need. 47% of freshmen with need received aid; of those 1% had need fully met. *Average percent of need met:* 2% (excluding resources awarded to replace EFC). *Average financial aid package:* $241 (excluding resources awarded to replace EFC).
**UNDERGRADUATE FINANCIAL AID (Fall 2014, est.)** 2,760 applied for aid; of those 99% were deemed to have need. 69% of undergraduates with need received aid; of those 1% had need fully met. *Average percent of need met:* 11% (excluding resources awarded to replace EFC). *Average financial aid package:* $1458 (excluding resources awarded to replace EFC).
**GIFT AID (NEED-BASED)** *Total amount:* $1,890,170 (16% federal, 51% state, 33% institutional). *Receiving aid:* Freshmen: 39% (469); all full-time undergraduates: 53% (1,519). *Average award:* Freshmen: $174; Undergraduates: $482. *Scholarships, grants, and awards:* Federal Pell, state, college/university gift aid from institutional funds.
**GIFT AID (NON-NEED-BASED)** *ROTC:* Army cooperative.
**LOANS** *Student loans:* $3,316,293 (100% need-based). *Average need-based loan:* Freshmen: $184. Undergraduates: $2375. *Parent loans:* $174,530 (100% need-based). *Programs:* Perkins.
**WORK-STUDY** *Federal work-study:* Total amount: $378,306; jobs available.
**ATHLETIC AWARDS** Total amount: $71,335 (100% need-based).
**APPLYING FOR FINANCIAL AID** *Required financial aid form:* FAFSA. *Notification date:* Continuous.
**CONTACT** Mrs. Sonya Matos, Interim Director of Student Services, Inter American University of Puerto Rico, Bayamón Campus, 500 Dr. John Will Harris Road, Bayamon, PR 00957, 787-279-1912 Ext. 2017. *E-mail:* smatos@bayamon.inter.edu.
*Website:* http://bayamon.inter.edu/.

# INTER AMERICAN UNIVERSITY OF PUERTO RICO, FAJARDO CAMPUS
## Fajardo, PR

**CONTACT** Financial Aid Director, Inter American University of Puerto Rico, Fajardo Campus, Call Box 700003, Fajardo, PR 00738-7003, 787-863-2390 Ext. 2208.
*Website:* http://www.fajardo.inter.edu/.

# INTER AMERICAN UNIVERSITY OF PUERTO RICO, GUAYAMA CAMPUS
## Guayama, PR

| Tuition & fees: $5534 | Average undergraduate aid package: $1904 |
| --- | --- |

**ABOUT THE INSTITUTION** Independent, coed. *Awards:* certificates, associate, bachelor's, and master's degrees. 16 undergraduate majors. *Total enrollment:* 2,151. Undergraduates: 2,069. Freshmen: 350. Institutional methodology is used as a basis for awarding need-based institutional aid.
**UNDERGRADUATE EXPENSES for 2015–2016** *Tuition:* full-time $4272.
**FRESHMAN FINANCIAL AID (Fall 2014, est.)** 186 applied for aid; of those 96% were deemed to have need. 44% of freshmen with need received aid; of those 1% had need fully met. *Average percent of need met:* 1% (excluding resources awarded to replace EFC). *Average financial aid package:* $197 (excluding resources awarded to replace EFC).
**UNDERGRADUATE FINANCIAL AID (Fall 2014, est.)** 1,246 applied for aid; of those 97% were deemed to have need. 54% of undergraduates with need received aid; of those .2% had need fully met. *Average percent of need met:* 31% (excluding resources awarded to replace EFC). *Average financial aid package:* $1904 (excluding resources awarded to replace EFC).
**GIFT AID (NEED-BASED)** *Total amount:* $4,949,673 (95% federal, 2% state, 3% institutional). *Receiving aid:* Freshmen: 6% (18); all full-time undergraduates: 11% (197). *Average award:* Freshmen: $43; Undergraduates: $697. *Scholarships, grants, and awards:* Federal Pell, FSEOG, state, college/university gift aid from institutional funds.
**GIFT AID (NON-NEED-BASED)** *Tuition waivers:* Full or partial for employees or children of employees. *ROTC:* Army cooperative.
**LOANS** *Student loans:* $1,537,860 (100% need-based). *Average need-based loan:* Freshmen: $202. Undergraduates: $1818. *Programs:* Federal Direct (Subsidized and Unsubsidized Stafford, PLUS).
**WORK-STUDY** *Federal work-study:* Total amount: $98,296; jobs available.
**ATHLETIC AWARDS** Total amount: $12,200 (100% need-based).
**APPLYING FOR FINANCIAL AID** *Required financial aid form:* FAFSA. *Financial aid deadline:* Continuous. *Notification date:* Continuous beginning 7/1. Students must reply within 5 weeks of notification.
**CONTACT** Mr. Jose A. Vechini, Director of Financial Aid, Inter American University of Puerto Rico, Guayama Campus, Call Box 10004, Guayama, PR 00785, 787-864-2222 Ext. 2206. *Fax:* 787-864-8232. *E-mail:* jose.vechini@guayama.inter.edu.
*Website:* http://www.guayama.inter.edu/.

# INTER AMERICAN UNIVERSITY OF PUERTO RICO, METROPOLITAN CAMPUS
## San Juan, PR

**CONTACT** Mrs. Luz M. Medina, Acting Director of Financial Aid, Inter American University of Puerto Rico, Metropolitan Campus, PO Box 191293, San Juan, PR 00919-1293, 787-758-2891. *Fax:* 787-250-0782.
*Website:* http://metro.inter.edu/.

# INTER AMERICAN UNIVERSITY OF PUERTO RICO, PONCE CAMPUS

### Mercedita, PR

**ABOUT THE INSTITUTION** Independent, coed. *Awards:* certificates, associate, bachelor's, and master's degrees. 46 undergraduate majors. *Total enrollment:* 5,734. Undergraduates: 5,361. Freshmen: 980.

**GIFT AID (NEED-BASED)** *Scholarships, grants, and awards:* Federal Pell, FSEOG, state, college/university gift aid from institutional funds, Federal Nursing.

**LOANS** *Programs:* Federal Direct (Subsidized and Unsubsidized Stafford, PLUS), Perkins.

**APPLYING FOR FINANCIAL AID** *Required financial aid form:* FAFSA.

**CONTACT** Debra Martinez, Financial Aid Officer, Inter American University of Puerto Rico, Ponce Campus, 104 Turpeaux Industrial Park, Mercedita, PR 00715-2201, 787-284-1912 Ext. 2161. *Fax:* 787-841-0103. *E-mail:* dmartinez@ponce.inter.edu. *Website:* http://www.ponce.inter.edu/.

# INTER AMERICAN UNIVERSITY OF PUERTO RICO, SAN GERMÁN CAMPUS

### San Germán, PR

**CONTACT** Ms. Maria I. Lugo, Financial Aid Director, Inter American University of Puerto Rico, San Germán Campus, PO Box 5100, San German, PR 00683-5008, 787-264-1912 Ext. 7252 or toll-free 800-981-8075 (in-state). *Fax:* 787-892-6350. *Website:* http://www.sg.inter.edu/.

# INTERIOR DESIGNERS INSTITUTE

### Newport Beach, CA

**CONTACT** Office of Financial Aid, Interior Designers Institute, 1061 Camelback Road, Newport Beach, CA 92660, 949-675-4451. *Website:* http://www.idi.edu/.

# INTERNATIONAL BAPTIST COLLEGE AND SEMINARY

### Chandler, AZ

**CONTACT** Financial Aid Office, International Baptist College and Seminary, 2211 West Germann Road, Chandler, AZ 85286, 480-838-7070 Ext. 268 or toll-free 800-422-4858. *Fax:* 480-838-5432. *E-mail:* financialaid@ibconline.edu. *Website:* http://www.ibcs.edu/.

# INTERNATIONAL BUSINESS COLLEGE

### Fort Wayne, IN

**CONTACT** Financial Aid Office, International Business College, 5699 Coventry Lane, Fort Wayne, IN 46804, 219-459-4500 or toll-free 800-589-6363. *Website:* http://www.ibcfortwayne.edu/.

# IONA COLLEGE

### New Rochelle, NY

| Tuition & fees: $34,030 | Average undergraduate aid package: $21,845 |
| --- | --- |

**ABOUT THE INSTITUTION** Independent Roman Catholic Church, coed. *Awards:* certificates, bachelor's, and master's degrees. 50 undergraduate majors.

*Total enrollment:* 3,909. Undergraduates: 3,301. Freshmen: 802. Federal methodology is used as a basis for awarding need-based institutional aid.

**UNDERGRADUATE EXPENSES for 2015–2016** *Application fee:* $50. *Comprehensive fee:* $47,600 includes full-time tuition ($31,880), mandatory fees ($2150), and room and board ($13,570). Room and board charges vary according to housing facility. *Part-time tuition:* $1060 per credit. *Part-time fees:* $540 per term. Part-time tuition and fees vary according to course load.

**FRESHMAN FINANCIAL AID (Fall 2014, est.)** 797 applied for aid; of those 83% were deemed to have need. 100% of freshmen with need received aid; of those 20% had need fully met. *Average percent of need met:* 14% (excluding resources awarded to replace EFC). *Average financial aid package:* $23,272 (excluding resources awarded to replace EFC). 17% of all full-time freshmen had no need and received non-need-based gift aid.

**UNDERGRADUATE FINANCIAL AID (Fall 2014, est.)** 2,920 applied for aid; of those 83% were deemed to have need. 99% of undergraduates with need received aid; of those 20% had need fully met. *Average percent of need met:* 20% (excluding resources awarded to replace EFC). *Average financial aid package:* $21,845 (excluding resources awarded to replace EFC). 16% of all full-time undergraduates had no need and received non-need-based gift aid.

**GIFT AID (NEED-BASED)** *Total amount:* $39,385,321 (10% federal, 8% state, 80% institutional, 2% external sources). *Receiving aid:* Freshmen: 31% (249); all full-time undergraduates: 39% (1,180). *Average award:* Freshmen: $4982; Undergraduates: $5654. *Scholarships, grants, and awards:* Federal Pell, FSEOG, state, private, college/university gift aid from institutional funds.

**GIFT AID (NON-NEED-BASED)** *Total amount:* $8,604,311 (3% state, 94% institutional, 3% external sources). *Receiving aid:* Freshmen: 83% (665). Undergraduates: 79% (2,356). *Average award:* Freshmen: $15,453. Undergraduates: $15,493. *Scholarships, grants, and awards by category:* Academic interests/achievement: 2,144 awards ($17,822,386 total): general academic interests/achievements. Creative arts/performance: 26 awards ($97,500 total): music. Special achievements/activities: 12 awards ($81,420 total): community service. Special characteristics: 318 awards ($732,823 total): children and siblings of alumni, religious affiliation, siblings of current students, veterans, veterans' children. *Tuition waivers:* Full or partial for children of alumni, employees or children of employees. *ROTC:* Army cooperative, Air Force cooperative.

**LOANS** *Student loans:* $17,023,391 (71% need-based, 29% non-need-based). 76% of past graduating class borrowed through all loan programs. *Average indebtedness per student:* $30,885. *Average need-based loan:* Freshmen: $2865. Undergraduates: $4030. *Parent loans:* $10,821,681 (53% need-based, 47% non-need-based). *Programs:* Federal Direct (Subsidized and Unsubsidized Stafford, PLUS), Perkins.

**WORK-STUDY** *Federal work-study:* Total amount: $505,751; 359 jobs averaging $1333. *State or other work-study/employment:* Part-time jobs available.

**ATHLETIC AWARDS** Total amount: $3,958,318 (58% need-based, 42% non-need-based).

**APPLYING FOR FINANCIAL AID** *Required financial aid forms:* FAFSA, state aid form. *Financial aid deadline:* 4/15. *Notification date:* Continuous beginning 3/1. Students must reply by 5/1 or within 2 weeks of notification.

**CONTACT** Mary Grant, Director of Financial Aid, Iona College, 715 North Avenue, New Rochelle, NY 10801-1890, 914-633-2676 or toll-free 800-231-IONA. *Fax:* 914-633-2486. *E-mail:* mgrant@iona.edu. *Website:* http://www.iona.edu/.

# IOWA STATE UNIVERSITY OF SCIENCE AND TECHNOLOGY

### Ames, IA

| Tuition & fees (IA res): $7736 | Average undergraduate aid package: $11,793 |
| --- | --- |

**ABOUT THE INSTITUTION** State-supported, coed. *Awards:* certificates, bachelor's, master's, and doctoral degrees. 116 undergraduate majors. *Total enrollment:* 34,435. Undergraduates: 28,893. Freshmen: 6,041. Federal methodology is used as a basis for awarding need-based institutional aid.

**UNDERGRADUATE EXPENSES for 2015–2016** *Application fee:* $40. *Tuition, state resident:* full-time $6648; part-time $277 per semester hour. *Tuition, nonresident:* full-time $19,768; part-time $824 per semester hour. *Required fees:* full-time $1088. Full-time tuition and fees vary according to class time, degree level, and program. Part-time tuition and fees vary according to class time, course load, degree level, and program. *College room and board:* $8070; *Room only:* $4279. Room and board charges vary according to board plan and housing facility.

**FRESHMAN FINANCIAL AID (Fall 2013)** 5,052 applied for aid; of those 62% were deemed to have need. 99% of freshmen with need received aid; of those 35% had need fully met. *Average percent of need met:* 83% (excluding resources awarded to replace EFC). *Average financial aid package:* $12,146 (excluding resources awarded to replace EFC). 36% of all full-time freshmen had no need and received non-need-based gift aid.

**UNDERGRADUATE FINANCIAL AID (Fall 2013)** 19,967 applied for aid; of those 68% were deemed to have need. 99% of undergraduates with need received aid; of those 34% had need fully met. *Average percent of need met:* 80% (excluding resources awarded to replace EFC). *Average financial aid package:* $11,793 (excluding resources awarded to replace EFC). 31% of all full-time undergraduates had no need and received non-need-based gift aid.

**GIFT AID (NEED-BASED)** *Total amount:* $90,072,882 (31% federal, 2% state, 62% institutional, 5% external sources). *Receiving aid:* Freshmen: 51% (3,084); all full-time undergraduates: 52% (13,387). *Average award:* Freshmen: $8189; Undergraduates: $6814. *Scholarships, grants, and awards:* Federal Pell, FSEOG, state, college/university gift aid from institutional funds.

**GIFT AID (NON-NEED-BASED)** *Total amount:* $36,332,757 (6% federal, 1% state, 71% institutional, 22% external sources). *Receiving aid:* Freshmen: 24% (1,473). Undergraduates: 24% (6,164). *Average award:* Freshmen: $3805. Undergraduates: $2916. *Scholarships, grants, and awards by category:* Academic interests/achievement: agriculture, architecture, area/ethnic studies, biological sciences, business, communication, computer science, education, engineering/technologies, English, foreign languages, general academic interests/achievements, health fields, home economics, humanities, international studies, library science, mathematics, military science, physical sciences, premedicine, social sciences. *Creative arts/performance:* applied art and design, art/fine arts, journalism/publications, music, theater/drama. *Special achievements/activities:* community service, general special achievements/activities, leadership. *Special characteristics:* adult students, children and siblings of alumni, ethnic background, first-generation college students, general special characteristics, international students, local/state students, members of minority groups, out-of-state students. *ROTC:* Army, Naval, Air Force.

**LOANS** *Student loans:* $118,771,116 (61% need-based, 39% non-need-based). 62% of past graduating class borrowed through all loan programs. *Average indebtedness per student:* $28,880. *Average need-based loan:* Freshmen: $3460. Undergraduates: $4420. *Parent loans:* $30,566,690 (23% need-based, 77% non-need-based). *Programs:* Federal Direct (Subsidized and Unsubsidized Stafford, PLUS), Perkins, college/university, private loans.

**WORK-STUDY** *Federal work-study:* jobs available. *State or other work-study/employment:* Total amount: $1,420,734 (100% need-based). Part-time jobs available.

**ATHLETIC AWARDS** Total amount: $6,749,529 (43% need-based, 57% non-need-based).

**APPLYING FOR FINANCIAL AID** *Required financial aid form:* FAFSA. *Financial aid deadline (priority):* 3/1. *Notification date:* Continuous beginning 4/1. Students must reply by 5/1.

**CONTACT** Ms. Roberta Johnson, Director of Financial Aid, Iowa State University of Science and Technology, 0210 Beardshear Hall, Ames, IA 50011, 515-294-2223 or toll-free 800-262-3810. *Fax:* 515-294-3622. *E-mail:* rljohns@iastate.edu. *Website:* http://www.iastate.edu/.

# IOWA WESLEYAN COLLEGE
## Mount Pleasant, IA

| Tuition & fees: $27,286 | Average undergraduate aid package: $19,292 |
| --- | --- |

**ABOUT THE INSTITUTION** Independent United Methodist, coed. *Awards:* bachelor's degrees. 27 undergraduate majors. *Total enrollment:* 473. Undergraduates: 473. Freshmen: 75. Federal methodology is used as a basis for awarding need-based institutional aid.

**UNDERGRADUATE EXPENSES** for 2015–2016 *Application fee:* $20. *Comprehensive fee:* $36,862 includes full-time tuition ($26,806), mandatory fees ($480), and room and board ($9576). *College room only:* $3644. Room and board charges vary according to housing facility. *Part-time tuition:* $675 per credit hour. *Part-*

time fees: $20 per credit hour. Part-time tuition and fees vary according to class time, course load, and location.

**FRESHMAN FINANCIAL AID (Fall 2013)** 102 applied for aid; of those 90% were deemed to have need. 100% of freshmen with need received aid; of those 17% had need fully met. *Average percent of need met:* 71% (excluding resources awarded to replace EFC). *Average financial aid package:* $20,775 (excluding resources awarded to replace EFC). 11% of all full-time freshmen had no need and received non-need-based gift aid.

**UNDERGRADUATE FINANCIAL AID (Fall 2013)** 423 applied for aid; of those 94% were deemed to have need. 100% of undergraduates with need received aid; of those 15% had need fully met. *Average percent of need met:* 68% (excluding resources awarded to replace EFC). *Average financial aid package:* $19,292 (excluding resources awarded to replace EFC). 13% of all full-time undergraduates had no need and received non-need-based gift aid.

**GIFT AID (NEED-BASED)** *Total amount:* $6,773,459 (19% federal, 14% state, 65% institutional, 2% external sources). *Receiving aid:* Freshmen: 87% (90); all full-time undergraduates: 84% (394). *Average award:* Freshmen: $17,460; Undergraduates: $15,275. *Scholarships, grants, and awards:* Federal Pell, FSEOG, state, private, college/university gift aid from institutional funds.

**GIFT AID (NON-NEED-BASED)** *Total amount:* $49,053 (100% federal). *Average award:* Freshmen: $15,181. Undergraduates: $11,362. *Scholarships, grants, and awards by category:* Academic interests/achievement: $3,235,539 total: business, education, English, general academic interests/achievements, health fields, social sciences. *Creative arts/performance:* $97,489 total: art/fine arts, music. *Special characteristics:* $842,019 total: children and siblings of alumni, children of faculty/staff, international students, out-of-state students, siblings of current students. *Tuition waivers:* Full or partial for employees or children of employees.

**LOANS** *Student loans:* $4,805,314 (47% need-based, 53% non-need-based). 91% of past graduating class borrowed through all loan programs. *Average indebtedness per student:* $36,797. *Average need-based loan:* Freshmen: $3315. Undergraduates: $4016. *Parent loans:* $511,514 (100% need-based). *Programs:* Federal Direct (Subsidized and Unsubsidized Stafford, PLUS), Perkins, alternative loans.

**WORK-STUDY** *Federal work-study:* 115 jobs averaging $2000.

**APPLYING FOR FINANCIAL AID** *Required financial aid form:* FAFSA. *Financial aid deadline (priority):* 4/1. *Notification date:* Continuous beginning 3/15.

**CONTACT** Renae Armentrout, Director of Financial Aid, Iowa Wesleyan College, 601 North Main Street, Mount Pleasant, IA 52641-1398, 319-385-6242 or toll-free 800-582-2383. *Fax:* 319-385-6203. *E-mail:* rarmentrout@iwc.edu. *Website:* http://www.iwc.edu/.

# ITHACA COLLEGE
## Ithaca, NY

| Tuition & fees: $39,532 | Average undergraduate aid package: $33,300 |
| --- | --- |

**ABOUT THE INSTITUTION** Independent, coed. *Awards:* certificates, bachelor's, master's, and doctoral degrees. 102 undergraduate majors. *Total enrollment:* 6,587. Undergraduates: 6,124. Freshmen: 1,560. Institutional methodology is used as a basis for awarding need-based institutional aid.

**UNDERGRADUATE EXPENSES** for 2015–2016 *Application fee:* $60. *Comprehensive fee:* $53,864 includes full-time tuition ($39,532) and room and board ($14,332). *College room only:* $7752. Room and board charges vary according to board plan and housing facility. *Part-time tuition:* $1318 per credit hour.

**FRESHMAN FINANCIAL AID (Fall 2014, est.)** 1,332 applied for aid; of those 82% were deemed to have need. 100% of freshmen with need received aid; of those 56% had need fully met. *Average percent of need met:* 90% (excluding resources awarded to replace EFC). *Average financial aid package:* $33,873 (excluding resources awarded to replace EFC). 24% of all full-time freshmen had no need and received non-need-based gift aid.

**UNDERGRADUATE FINANCIAL AID (Fall 2014, est.)** 4,674 applied for aid; of those 87% were deemed to have need. 100% of undergraduates with need received aid; of those 45% had need fully met. *Average percent of need met:* 86% (excluding resources awarded to replace EFC). *Average financial aid package:* $33,300 (excluding resources awarded to replace EFC). 22% of all full-time undergraduates had no need and received non-need-based gift aid.

**GIFT AID (NEED-BASED)** *Total amount:* $93,430,565 (6% federal, 4% state, 88% institutional, 2% external sources). *Receiving aid:* Freshmen: 67% (1,040); all full-time undergraduates: 66% (3,933). *Average award:* Freshmen: $24,749; Undergraduates: $23,640. *Scholarships, grants, and awards:* Federal Pell, FSEOG, state, private, college/university gift aid from institutional funds.

**GIFT AID (NON-NEED-BASED)** *Total amount:* $23,750,546 (4% federal, 91% institutional, 5% external sources). *Receiving aid:* Freshmen: 22% (349). Undergraduates: 15% (918). *Average award:* Freshmen: $13,103. Undergraduates: $13,029. *Scholarships, grants, and awards by category: Academic interests/ achievement:* 4,081 awards ($50,930,643 total): communication, general academic interests/achievements. *Creative arts/performance:* 149 awards ($497,044 total): cinema/film/broadcasting, dance, journalism/publications, music, performing arts, theater/drama. *Special achievements/activities:* 239 awards ($1,316,000 total): leadership. *Special characteristics:* 704 awards ($3,700,385 total): children and siblings of alumni, children of faculty/staff, general special characteristics, members of minority groups, siblings of current students. *Tuition waivers:* Full or partial for children of alumni, employees or children of employees. *ROTC:* Army cooperative, Air Force cooperative.

**LOANS** *Student loans:* $31,471,293 (76% need-based, 24% non-need-based). *Average need-based loan:* Freshmen: $5306. Undergraduates: $6434. *Parent loans:* $30,836,381 (38% need-based, 62% non-need-based). *Programs:* Federal Direct (Subsidized and Unsubsidized Stafford, PLUS), Perkins, alternative loans.

**WORK-STUDY** *Federal work-study:* Total amount: $1,500,000; 3,035 jobs averaging $2344. *State or other work-study/employment:* Total amount: $9,456,882 (65% need-based, 35% non-need-based). 1,624 part-time jobs averaging $2402.

**APPLYING FOR FINANCIAL AID** *Required financial aid forms:* FAFSA, CSS Financial Aid PROFILE. *Financial aid deadline (priority):* 2/1. *Notification date:* Continuous beginning 2/15. Students must reply by 5/1.

**CONTACT** Ms. Lisa Hoskey, Director of Student Financial Services, Ithaca College, 953 Danby Road, Ithaca, NY 14850-7002, 800-429-4275 or toll-free 800-429-4274. *Fax:* 607-274-1895. *E-mail:* finaid@ithaca.edu. *Website:* http://www.ithaca.edu/.

# ITT TECHNICAL INSTITUTE
## Tempe, AZ

**CONTACT** Financial Aid Office, ITT Technical Institute, 5005 S. Wendler Drive, Tempe, AZ 85282, 602-437-7500 or toll-free 800-879-4881. *Website:* http://www.itt-tech.edu/.

# ITT TECHNICAL INSTITUTE
## Clovis, CA

**CONTACT** Financial Aid Office, ITT Technical Institute, 362 N. Clovis Avenue, Clovis, CA 93612, 559-325-5400 or toll-free 800-564-9771. *Website:* http://www.itt-tech.edu/.

# ITT TECHNICAL INSTITUTE
## Concord, CA

**CONTACT** Financial Aid Office, ITT Technical Institute, 1140 Galaxy Way, Suite 400, Concord, CA 94520, 925-674-8200 or toll-free 800-211-7062. *Website:* http://www.itt-tech.edu/.

# ITT TECHNICAL INSTITUTE
## Corona, CA

**CONTACT** Financial Aid Office, ITT Technical Institute, 4160 Temescal Canyon Road, Suite 100, Corona, CA 92883, 951-277-5400 or toll-free 877-764-9661. *Website:* http://www.itt-tech.edu/.

# ITT TECHNICAL INSTITUTE
## Deerfield Beach, FL

**CONTACT** Financial Aid Office, ITT Technical Institute, 700 W. Hillsboro Boulevard, Suite 100, Building 1, Deerfield Beach, FL 33441, 954-360-4701 or toll-free 877-243-8548. *Website:* http://www.itt-tech.edu/.

# ITT TECHNICAL INSTITUTE
## West Palm Beach, FL

**CONTACT** Financial Aid Office, ITT Technical Institute, 1756 N. Congress Avenue, West Palm Beach, FL 33409, 561-233-4900 or toll-free 877-236-8164. *Website:* http://www.itt-tech.edu/.

# ITT TECHNICAL INSTITUTE
## Douglasville, GA

**CONTACT** Financial Aid Office, ITT Technical Institute, 5905 Stewart Parkway, Douglasville, GA 30135, 678-715-2100 or toll-free 877-215-1173. *Website:* http://www.itt-tech.edu/.

# ITT TECHNICAL INSTITUTE
## Springfield, IL

**CONTACT** Financial Aid Office, ITT Technical Institute, 2501 Wabash Avenue, Springfield, IL 62704, 217-547-5700 or toll-free 877-263-2374. *Website:* http://www.itt-tech.edu/.

# ITT TECHNICAL INSTITUTE
## Indianapolis, IN

**CONTACT** Financial Aid Office, ITT Technical Institute, 2525 N. Shadeland Avenue, Suite 103, Indianapolis, IN 46219, 317-351-3800 or toll-free 877-264-1057. *Website:* http://www.itt-tech.edu/.

# ITT TECHNICAL INSTITUTE
## Indianapolis, IN

**CONTACT** Financial Aid Office, ITT Technical Institute, 9511 Angola Court, Indianapolis, IN 46268-1119, 317-875-8640 or toll-free 800-937-4488. *Website:* http://www.itt-tech.edu/.

# ITT TECHNICAL INSTITUTE
## South Bend, IN

**CONTACT** Financial Aid Office, ITT Technical Institute, 17390 Dugdale Drive, Suite 100, South Bend, IN 46635, 574-247-8300 or toll-free 877-474-1926. *Website:* http://www.itt-tech.edu/.

## ITT TECHNICAL INSTITUTE
### Overland Park, KS

**CONTACT** Financial Aid Office, ITT Technical Institute, 7600 West 119th Street, Suite 100, Overland Park, KS 66213, 913-253-1300 or toll-free 877-327-9026. *Website:* http://www.itt-tech.edu/.

## ITT TECHNICAL INSTITUTE
### Wichita, KS

**CONTACT** Financial Aid Office, ITT Technical Institute, 8111 E. 32nd Street North, Suite 103, Wichita, KS 67226, 316-609-4100 or toll-free 877-207-1047. *Website:* http://www.itt-tech.edu/.

## ITT TECHNICAL INSTITUTE
### Lexington, KY

**CONTACT** Financial Aid Office, ITT Technical Institute, 2473 Fortune Drive, Suite 180, Lexington, KY 40509, 859-246-3300 or toll-free 800-519-8151. *Website:* http://www.itt-tech.edu/.

## ITT TECHNICAL INSTITUTE
### Hanover, MD

**CONTACT** Financial Aid Office, ITT Technical Institute, 7030 Dorsey Road, Suite 100, Hanover, MD 21076, 410-694-4700 or toll-free 877-243-6993. *Website:* http://www.itt-tech.edu/.

## ITT TECHNICAL INSTITUTE
### Madison, MS

**CONTACT** Financial Aid Office, ITT Technical Institute, 382 Galleria Parkway, Suite 100, Madison, MS 39110, 601-607-4500 or toll-free 800-209-2521. *Website:* http://www.itt-tech.edu/.

## ITT TECHNICAL INSTITUTE
### Springfield, MO

**CONTACT** Financial Aid Office, ITT Technical Institute, 3216 South National Avenue, Springfield, MO 65807, 417-877-4800 or toll-free 877-219-4387. *Website:* http://www.itt-tech.edu/.

## ITT TECHNICAL INSTITUTE
### Charlotte, NC

**CONTACT** Financial Aid Office, ITT Technical Institute, 10926 David Taylor Drive, Suite 100, Charlotte, NC 28262, 704-548-2300 or toll-free 877-243-7685. *Website:* http://www.itt-tech.edu/.

## ITT TECHNICAL INSTITUTE
### Durham, NC

**CONTACT** Financial Aid Office, ITT Technical Institute, 3518 Westgate Drive, Suite 150, Durham, NC 27707, 919-401-1400 or toll-free 877-452-8662. *Website:* http://www.itt-tech.edu/.

## ITT TECHNICAL INSTITUTE
### Oklahoma City, OK

**CONTACT** Financial Aid Office, ITT Technical Institute, 50 Penn Place Office Tower, 1900 Northwest Expressway, Suite 305R, Oklahoma City, OK 73118, 405-810-4100 or toll-free 800-518-1612. *Website:* http://www.itt-tech.edu/.

## ITT TECHNICAL INSTITUTE
### Salem, OR

**CONTACT** Financial Aid Office, ITT Technical Institute, 4825 Commercial Street SE, Suite 100, Salem, OR 97302-2177, 503-576-2300 or toll-free 877-273-7397. *Website:* http://www.itt-tech.edu/.

## JACKSON STATE UNIVERSITY
### Jackson, MS

| Tuition & fees (MS res): $6602 | Average undergraduate aid package: $10,504 |
|---|---|

**ABOUT THE INSTITUTION** State-supported, coed. *Awards:* certificates, bachelor's, master's, and doctoral degrees. 42 undergraduate majors. *Total enrollment:* 9,508. Undergraduates: 7,199. Freshmen: 1,196. Federal methodology is used as a basis for awarding need-based institutional aid.

**UNDERGRADUATE EXPENSES for 2015–2016** *Tuition, state resident:* full-time $6602. *Tuition, nonresident:* full-time $16,174. Room and board charges vary according to housing facility.

**FRESHMAN FINANCIAL AID (Fall 2013)** 1,043 applied for aid; of those 92% were deemed to have need. 99% of freshmen with need received aid; of those 1% had need fully met. *Average percent of need met:* 36% (excluding resources awarded to replace EFC). *Average financial aid package:* $13,005 (excluding resources awarded to replace EFC). 3% of all full-time freshmen had no need and received non-need-based gift aid.

**UNDERGRADUATE FINANCIAL AID (Fall 2013)** 5,606 applied for aid; of those 93% were deemed to have need. 99% of undergraduates with need received aid; of those 1% had need fully met. *Average percent of need met:* 37% (excluding resources awarded to replace EFC). *Average financial aid package:* $10,504 (excluding resources awarded to replace EFC). 3% of all full-time undergraduates had no need and received non-need-based gift aid.

**GIFT AID (NEED-BASED)** *Total amount:* $23,614,582 (100% federal). *Receiving aid:* Freshmen: 77% (804); all full-time undergraduates: 75% (4,206). *Average award:* Freshmen: $5256; Undergraduates: $4724. *Scholarships, grants, and awards:* Federal Pell, FSEOG, state, private, college/university gift aid from institutional funds.

**GIFT AID (NON-NEED-BASED)** *Total amount:* $23,774,454 (14% state, 80% institutional, 6% external sources). *Receiving aid:* Freshmen: 58% (608). Undergraduates: 37% (2,080). *Average award:* Freshmen: $9117. Undergraduates: $7004. *Scholarships, grants, and awards by category:* Academic interests/achievement: 2,261 awards ($18,420,413 total): general academic interests/achievements. Creative arts/performance: 221 awards ($732,314 total): music. Special achievements/activities: 98 awards ($103,277 total): leadership. Special characteristics: 65 awards ($198,127 total): children and siblings of alumni, children of faculty/staff. *Tuition waivers:* Full or partial for children of alumni, employees or children of employees. *ROTC:* Army, Air Force.

**LOANS** *Student loans:* $76,703,610 (27% need-based, 73% non-need-based). 89% of past graduating class borrowed through all loan programs. *Average indebtedness per student:* $31,576. *Average need-based loan:* Freshmen: $3355. Undergraduates: $4032. *Parent loans:* $4,690,856 (100% non-need-based). *Programs:* Federal Direct (Subsidized and Unsubsidized Stafford, PLUS), Perkins.

**WORK-STUDY** *Federal work-study:* 1,080 jobs averaging $2368.

**ATHLETIC AWARDS** Total amount: $2,559,951 (100% non-need-based).

**APPLYING FOR FINANCIAL AID** *Required financial aid forms:* FAFSA, institution's own form, state aid form. *Financial aid deadline (priority):* 4/15. *Notification date:* Continuous beginning 5/1.

**CONTACT** Mrs. Betty Moncure, Director, Jackson State University, 1400 J.R. Lynch Street, PO Box 17065, Jackson, MS 39217, 601-979-2227 or toll-free 800-848-6817. *Fax:* 601-979-2237. *E-mail:* betty.j.moncure@jsums.edu. *Website:* http://www.jsums.edu/.

# JACKSONVILLE STATE UNIVERSITY
## Jacksonville, AL

| Tuition & fees (AL res): $8790 | Average undergraduate aid package: $9254 |
| --- | --- |

**ABOUT THE INSTITUTION** State-supported, coed. *Awards:* certificates, bachelor's, master's, and doctoral degrees. 60 undergraduate majors. *Total enrollment:* 8,659. Undergraduates: 7,647. Freshmen: 1,185. Federal methodology is used as a basis for awarding need-based institutional aid.

**UNDERGRADUATE EXPENSES for 2015–2016** *Application fee:* $35. *Tuition, state resident:* full-time $8490; part-time $283 per credit hour. *Tuition, nonresident:* full-time $16,980; part-time $566 per credit hour. *Required fees:* full-time $300; $150 per term. *College room and board:* $6985. Room and board charges vary according to board plan and housing facility.

**FRESHMAN FINANCIAL AID (Fall 2013)** 1,066 applied for aid; of those 99% were deemed to have need. 100% of freshmen with need received aid. *Average financial aid package:* $9437 (excluding resources awarded to replace EFC).

**UNDERGRADUATE FINANCIAL AID (Fall 2013)** 5,040 applied for aid; of those 99% were deemed to have need. 100% of undergraduates with need received aid. *Average financial aid package:* $9254 (excluding resources awarded to replace EFC).

**GIFT AID (NEED-BASED)** *Total amount:* $29,581,817 (49% federal, 1% state, 47% institutional, 3% external sources). *Receiving aid:* Freshmen: 45% (519); all full-time undergraduates: 49% (2,806). *Average award:* Undergraduates: $4464. *Scholarships, grants, and awards:* Federal Pell, FSEOG, state, private, college/university gift aid from institutional funds.

**GIFT AID (NON-NEED-BASED)** *Receiving aid:* Freshmen: 61% (701). Undergraduates: 39% (2,274). *Scholarships, grants, and awards by category:* Academic interests/achievement: biological sciences, business, communication, computer science, education, English, general academic interests/achievements, health fields, home economics, humanities, mathematics, military science, physical sciences, social sciences. *Creative arts/performance:* art/fine arts, journalism/publications, music, theater/drama. *Special achievements/activities:* general special achievements/activities, leadership. *Special characteristics:* children and siblings of alumni, local/state students. *Tuition waivers:* Full or partial for employees or children of employees. *ROTC:* Army.

**LOANS** *Student loans:* $42,586,829 (39% need-based, 61% non-need-based). *Average need-based loan:* Freshmen: $1000. Undergraduates: $984. *Parent loans:* $2,286,237 (100% non-need-based). *Programs:* Federal Direct (Subsidized and Unsubsidized Stafford, PLUS), state, college/university.

**WORK-STUDY** *Federal work-study:* jobs available. *State or other work-study/employment:* Total amount: $1,869,900 (100% non-need-based). Part-time jobs available.

**ATHLETIC AWARDS** Total amount: $4,531,801 (100% non-need-based).

**APPLYING FOR FINANCIAL AID** *Required financial aid forms:* FAFSA, institution's own form. *Financial aid deadline (priority):* 3/15. *Notification date:* Continuous beginning 4/16. Students must reply within 2 weeks of notification.

**CONTACT** Ms. Vickie Adams, Director of Financial Aid, Jacksonville State University, 700 Pelham Road North, Jacksonville, AL 36265-9982, 256-782-5006 Ext. 8399 or toll-free 800-231-5291. *Fax:* 256-782-5476. *E-mail:* finaid@jsu.edu. *Website:* http://www.jsu.edu/.

# JACKSONVILLE UNIVERSITY
## Jacksonville, FL

| Tuition & fees: $31,370 | Average undergraduate aid package: $23,040 |
| --- | --- |

**ABOUT THE INSTITUTION** Independent, coed. *Awards:* certificates, bachelor's, master's, and doctoral degrees. 71 undergraduate majors. *Total enrollment:* 4,085. Undergraduates: 3,223. Freshmen: 394. Federal methodology is used as a basis for awarding need-based institutional aid.

**UNDERGRADUATE EXPENSES for 2015–2016** *Application fee:* $30. *Comprehensive fee:* $42,190 includes full-time tuition ($31,370) and room and board ($10,820). *College room only:* $6480. Full-time tuition and fees vary according to course load, degree level, and program. Room and board charges vary according to board plan and housing facility. *Part-time tuition:* $1042 per credit hour. *Part-time fees:* $523 per credit hour. Part-time tuition and fees vary according to course load, degree level, and program.

**FRESHMAN FINANCIAL AID (Fall 2014, est.)** 385 applied for aid; of those 86% were deemed to have need. 100% of freshmen with need received aid; of those 36% had need fully met. *Average percent of need met:* 86% (excluding resources awarded to replace EFC). *Average financial aid package:* $23,886 (excluding resources awarded to replace EFC). 10% of all full-time freshmen had no need and received non-need-based gift aid.

**UNDERGRADUATE FINANCIAL AID (Fall 2014, est.)** 2,058 applied for aid; of those 73% were deemed to have need. 100% of undergraduates with need received aid; of those 36% had need fully met. *Average percent of need met:* 73% (excluding resources awarded to replace EFC). *Average financial aid package:* $23,040 (excluding resources awarded to replace EFC). 21% of all full-time undergraduates had no need and received non-need-based gift aid.

**GIFT AID (NEED-BASED)** *Total amount:* $23,783,944 (17% federal, 16% state, 67% institutional). *Receiving aid:* Freshmen: 84% (330); all full-time undergraduates: 71% (1,497). *Average award:* Freshmen: $18,493; Undergraduates: $16,847. *Scholarships, grants, and awards:* Federal Pell, FSEOG, state, private, college/university gift aid from institutional funds.

**GIFT AID (NON-NEED-BASED)** *Total amount:* $5,772,060 (17% state, 83% institutional). *Receiving aid:* Freshmen: 14% (55). Undergraduates: 27% (563). *Average award:* Freshmen: $14,721. Undergraduates: $10,435. *Scholarships, grants, and awards by category:* Academic interests/achievement: general academic interests/achievements. *Creative arts/performance:* art/fine arts, general creative arts/performance, music, theater/drama. *Special achievements/activities:* general special achievements/activities, leadership. *Special characteristics:* children of educators, children of faculty/staff, international students. *Tuition waivers:* Full or partial for employees or children of employees. *ROTC:* Army, Naval.

**LOANS** *Student loans:* $17,682,407 (85% need-based, 15% non-need-based). *Average need-based loan:* Freshmen: $2330. Undergraduates: $3545. *Parent loans:* $1,594,482 (84% need-based, 16% non-need-based). *Programs:* Federal Direct (Subsidized and Unsubsidized Stafford, PLUS), Perkins.

**WORK-STUDY** *Federal work-study:* Total amount: $57,539; 119 jobs averaging $484. *State or other work-study/employment:* Total amount: $141,797 (68% need-based, 32% non-need-based). 155 part-time jobs averaging $645.

**ATHLETIC AWARDS** Total amount: $4,674,431 (68% need-based, 32% non-need-based).

**APPLYING FOR FINANCIAL AID** *Required financial aid forms:* FAFSA, institution's own form, proof of medical insurance coverage and waiver form. *Financial aid deadline (priority):* 3/31. *Notification date:* Continuous beginning 2/20.

**CONTACT** Karen Laverdiere, Director of Financial Aid, Jacksonville University, 2800 University Boulevard North, Jacksonville, FL 32211, 904-256-7243 or toll-free 800-225-2027. *Fax:* 904-256-7148. *E-mail:* kfisher2@ju.edu. *Website:* http://www.ju.edu/.

# JAMES MADISON UNIVERSITY
## Harrisonburg, VA

| Tuition & fees (VA res): $9662 | Average undergraduate aid package: $10,025 |
| --- | --- |

**ABOUT THE INSTITUTION** State-supported, coed. **Awards:** bachelor's, master's, and doctoral degrees (also offers specialist in education degree). 46 undergraduate majors. **Total enrollment:** 20,853. Undergraduates: 19,142. Freshmen: 4,364. Federal methodology is used as a basis for awarding need-based institutional aid.

**UNDERGRADUATE EXPENSES for 2015–2016 Application fee:** $60. **Tuition, state resident:** full-time $5406; part-time $179 per credit hour. **Tuition, nonresident:** full-time $20,266; part-time $656 per credit hour. **Required fees:** full-time $4256. **College room and board:** $8828; **Room only:** $4564.

**FRESHMAN FINANCIAL AID (Fall 2014, est.)** 3,084 applied for aid; of those 64% were deemed to have need. 89% of freshmen with need received aid; of those 88% had need fully met. **Average percent of need met:** 39% (excluding resources awarded to replace EFC). **Average financial aid package:** $8699 (excluding resources awarded to replace EFC). 1% of all full-time freshmen had no need and received non-need-based gift aid.

**UNDERGRADUATE FINANCIAL AID (Fall 2014, est.)** 10,592 applied for aid; of those 69% were deemed to have need. 92% of undergraduates with need received aid; of those 75% had need fully met. **Average percent of need met:** 43% (excluding resources awarded to replace EFC). **Average financial aid package:** $10,025 (excluding resources awarded to replace EFC). 1% of all full-time undergraduates had no need and received non-need-based gift aid.

**GIFT AID (NEED-BASED) Total amount:** $29,540,783 (39% federal, 25% state, 25% institutional, 11% external sources). **Receiving aid:** Freshmen: 23% (984); all full-time undergraduates: 18% (3,239). **Average award:** Freshmen: $7611; Undergraduates: $7613. **Scholarships, grants, and awards:** Federal Pell, FSEOG, state, private, college/university gift aid from institutional funds.

**GIFT AID (NON-NEED-BASED) Total amount:** $5,464,329 (3% state, 91% institutional, 6% external sources). **Receiving aid:** Freshmen: 6% (251). Undergraduates: 8% (1,353). **Average award:** Freshmen: $3347. Undergraduates: $3172. **Scholarships, grants, and awards by category:** Academic interests/achievement: architecture, biological sciences, business, computer science, education, engineering/technologies, English, general academic interests/achievements, health fields, humanities, international studies, mathematics, military science, physical sciences, premedicine, religion/biblical studies, social sciences. Creative arts/performance: art/fine arts, cinema/film/broadcasting, dance, journalism/publications, music, theater/drama. Special achievements/activities: cheerleading/drum major, general special achievements/activities, leadership. Special characteristics: children and siblings of alumni, children of faculty/staff, handicapped students, International students, local/state students, members of minority groups, out-of-state students, siblings of current students. **ROTC:** Army, Air Force cooperative.

**LOANS Student loans:** $61,563,060 (36% need-based, 64% non-need-based). 52% of past graduating class borrowed through all loan programs. Average indebtedness per student: $23,732. **Average need-based loan:** Freshmen: $3618. Undergraduates: $4670. **Parent loans:** $34,588,436 (100% non-need-based). **Programs:** Federal Direct (Subsidized and Unsubsidized Stafford, PLUS), Perkins.

**WORK-STUDY Federal work-study:** Total amount: $478,800; jobs available. **State or other work-study/employment:** Total amount: $6,278,720 (100% non-need-based). Part-time jobs available.

**ATHLETIC AWARDS Total amount:** $6,520,552 (100% non-need-based).

**APPLYING FOR FINANCIAL AID Required financial aid form:** FAFSA. **Financial aid deadline (priority):** 3/1. **Notification date:** Continuous beginning 4/1. Students must reply within 4 weeks of notification.

**CONTACT** Lisa L. Tumer, Director of Financial Aid and Scholarships, James Madison University, 800 South Main Street, MSC 3519, Harrisonburg, VA 22807, 540-568-7820. Fax: 540-568-7994. E-mail: fin_aid@jmu.edu.
Website: http://www.jmu.edu/.

# JARVIS CHRISTIAN COLLEGE
## Hawkins, TX

**CONTACT** Alice Copeland, Director of Financial Aid, Jarvis Christian College, PO Box 1470, Hawkins, TX 75765, 903-730-4890 Ext. 2402. Fax: 903-730-4891. E-mail: alice.copeland@jarvis.edu.
Website: http://www.jarvis.edu/.

# JEFFERSON COLLEGE OF HEALTH SCIENCES
## Roanoke, VA

| Tuition & fees: $23,380 | Average undergraduate aid package: N/A |
| --- | --- |

**ABOUT THE INSTITUTION** Independent, coed. **Awards:** certificates, associate, bachelor's, and master's degrees. 11 undergraduate majors. **Total enrollment:** 1,131. Undergraduates: 876. Freshmen: 76. Federal methodology is used as a basis for awarding need-based institutional aid.

**UNDERGRADUATE EXPENSES for 2015–2016 Application fee:** $35. **Comprehensive fee:** $31,050 includes full-time tuition ($23,080), mandatory fees ($300), and room and board ($7670). Full-time tuition and fees vary according to course load. **Part-time tuition:** $670 per credit hour. Part-time tuition and fees vary according to course load.

**FRESHMAN FINANCIAL AID (Fall 2013)** 66 applied for aid; of those 100% were deemed to have need. 100% of freshmen with need received aid.

**UNDERGRADUATE FINANCIAL AID (Fall 2013)** 686 applied for aid; of those 100% were deemed to have need. 100% of undergraduates with need received aid.

**GIFT AID (NEED-BASED) Total amount:** $6,096,217 (23% federal, 27% state, 44% institutional, 6% external sources). **Receiving aid:** Freshmen: 100% (66); all full-time undergraduates: 100% (684). **Scholarships, grants, and awards:** Federal Pell, FSEOG, state, private, college/university gift aid from institutional funds.

**GIFT AID (NON-NEED-BASED) Total amount:** $329,083 (55% federal, 26% state, 19% institutional). **Receiving aid:** Freshmen: 35% (23). Undergraduates: 25% (174). **Scholarships, grants, and awards by category:** Academic interests/achievement: biological sciences, health fields. Special characteristics: local/state students. **Tuition waivers:** Full or partial for employees or children of employees.

**LOANS Student loans:** $7,428,591 (35% need-based, 65% non-need-based). **Parent loans:** $1,176,231 (100% non-need-based). **Programs:** Federal Direct (Subsidized and Unsubsidized Stafford, PLUS), alternative loans.

**WORK-STUDY Federal work-study:** jobs available. **State or other work-study/employment:** Total amount: $16,793 (100% non-need-based). Part-time jobs available.

**APPLYING FOR FINANCIAL AID Required financial aid forms:** FAFSA, state aid form. **Financial aid deadline (priority):** 5/1. **Notification date:** Continuous beginning 5/1.

**CONTACT** Debra A. Johnson, Director of Financial Aid, Jefferson College of Health Sciences, 101 Elm Avenue SE, Roanoke, VA 24013-2222, 540-985-8492 or toll-free 888-985-8483. Fax: 540-224-6916. E-mail: djjohnson@jchs.edu.
Website: http://www.jchs.edu/.

# THE JEWISH THEOLOGICAL SEMINARY
## New York, NY

**CONTACT** Linda Levine, Registrar/Director of Financial Aid, The Jewish Theological Seminary, 3080 Broadway, New York, NY 10027-4649, 212-678-8007. Fax: 212-678-8947. E-mail: financialaid@jtsa.edu.
Website: http://www.jtsa.edu/.

# JOHN BROWN UNIVERSITY
## Siloam Springs, AR

| Tuition & fees: $24,468 | Average undergraduate aid package: $18,043 |
| --- | --- |

**ABOUT THE INSTITUTION** Independent interdenominational, coed. *Awards:* associate, bachelor's, and master's degrees. 87 undergraduate majors. *Total enrollment:* 2,400. Undergraduates: 1,781. Freshmen: 300. Federal methodology is used as a basis for awarding need-based institutional aid.

**UNDERGRADUATE EXPENSES for 2015–2016** *Application fee:* $25. *Comprehensive fee:* $33,132 includes full-time tuition ($23,398), mandatory fees ($1070), and room and board ($8664). Full-time tuition and fees vary according to course load. Room and board charges vary according to board plan and housing facility. *Part-time tuition:* $752 per credit hour. Part-time tuition and fees vary according to course load.

**FRESHMAN FINANCIAL AID (Fall 2013)** 265 applied for aid; of those 84% were deemed to have need. 100% of freshmen with need received aid; of those 14% had need fully met. *Average percent of need met:* 77% (excluding resources awarded to replace EFC). *Average financial aid package:* $19,242 (excluding resources awarded to replace EFC). 25% of all full-time freshmen had no need and received non-need-based gift aid.

**UNDERGRADUATE FINANCIAL AID (Fall 2013)** 1,042 applied for aid; of those 87% were deemed to have need. 100% of undergraduates with need received aid; of those 12% had need fully met. *Average percent of need met:* 71% (excluding resources awarded to replace EFC). *Average financial aid package:* $18,043 (excluding resources awarded to replace EFC). 29% of all full-time undergraduates had no need and received non-need-based gift aid.

**GIFT AID (NEED-BASED)** *Total amount:* $11,445,754 (19% federal, 9% state, 70% institutional, 2% external sources). *Receiving aid:* Freshmen: 68% (207); all full-time undergraduates: 65% (844). *Average award:* Freshmen: $16,076; Undergraduates: $14,447. *Scholarships, grants, and awards:* Federal Pell, FSEOG, state, private, college/university gift aid from institutional funds.

**GIFT AID (NON-NEED-BASED)** *Total amount:* $6,833,939 (5% state, 64% institutional, 31% external sources). *Receiving aid:* Freshmen: 68% (207). Undergraduates: 56% (728). *Average award:* Freshmen: $16,202. Undergraduates: $14,329. *Scholarships, grants, and awards by category: Academic interests/achievement:* general academic interests/achievements. *Creative arts/performance:* art/fine arts, journalism/publications, music, theater/drama. *Tuition waivers:* Full or partial for employees or children of employees. *ROTC:* Army cooperative, Air Force cooperative.

**LOANS** *Student loans:* $5,457,819 (69% need-based, 31% non-need-based). 61% of past graduating class borrowed through all loan programs. *Average indebtedness per student:* $24,525. *Average need-based loan:* Freshmen: $2580. Undergraduates: $3217. *Parent loans:* $1,598,007 (16% need-based, 84% non-need-based). *Programs:* Federal Direct (Subsidized and Unsubsidized Stafford, PLUS), Perkins, college/university.

**WORK-STUDY** *Federal work-study:* jobs available. *State or other work-study/employment:* Total amount: $280,654 (98% need-based, 2% non-need-based). Part-time jobs available.

**ATHLETIC AWARDS** Total amount: $1,928,552 (58% need-based, 42% non-need-based).

**APPLYING FOR FINANCIAL AID** *Required financial aid forms:* FAFSA, state aid form. *Financial aid deadline (priority):* 3/1. *Notification date:* Continuous beginning 3/1. Students must reply by 5/1 or within 2 weeks of notification.

**CONTACT** Mr. Kim Eldridge, Director of Student Financial Aid, John Brown University, 2000 West University Street, Siloam Springs, AR 72761-2121, 479-524-7424 or toll-free 877-JBU-INFO. *Fax:* 479-524-7405. *E-mail:* keldridg@jbu.edu. *Website:* http://www.jbu.edu/.

# JOHN CARROLL UNIVERSITY
## University Heights, OH

| Tuition & fees: $37,180 | Average undergraduate aid package: $28,538 |
| --- | --- |

**ABOUT THE INSTITUTION** Independent Roman Catholic (Jesuit), coed. *Awards:* certificates, bachelor's, and master's degrees. 53 undergraduate majors. *Total enrollment:* 3,700. Undergraduates: 3,125. Freshmen: 799. Federal methodology is used as a basis for awarding need-based institutional aid.

**UNDERGRADUATE EXPENSES for 2015–2016** *One-time required fee:* $325. *Comprehensive fee:* $48,100 includes full-time tuition ($35,930), mandatory fees ($1250), and room and board ($10,920). Room and board charges vary according to board plan and housing facility. *Part-time tuition:* $1095 per credit hour. Part-time tuition and fees vary according to course load.

**FRESHMAN FINANCIAL AID (Fall 2014, est.)** 720 applied for aid; of those 87% were deemed to have need. 94% of freshmen with need received aid; of those 26% had need fully met. *Average percent of need met:* 83% (excluding resources awarded to replace EFC). *Average financial aid package:* $28,900 (excluding resources awarded to replace EFC). 26% of all full-time freshmen had no need and received non-need-based gift aid.

**UNDERGRADUATE FINANCIAL AID (Fall 2014, est.)** 2,595 applied for aid; of those 85% were deemed to have need. 100% of undergraduates with need received aid; of those 16% had need fully met. *Average percent of need met:* 79% (excluding resources awarded to replace EFC). *Average financial aid package:* $28,538 (excluding resources awarded to replace EFC). 17% of all full-time undergraduates had no need and received non-need-based gift aid.

**GIFT AID (NEED-BASED)** *Total amount:* $47,823,304 (8% federal, 2% state, 89% institutional, 1% external sources). *Receiving aid:* Freshmen: 72% (577); all full-time undergraduates: 72% (2,170). *Average award:* Freshmen: $23,823; Undergraduates: $23,250. *Scholarships, grants, and awards:* Federal Pell, FSEOG, state, private, college/university gift aid from institutional funds.

**GIFT AID (NON-NEED-BASED)** *Total amount:* $15,972,882 (99% institutional, 1% external sources). *Receiving aid:* Freshmen: 73% (582). Undergraduates: 72% (2,178). *Average award:* Freshmen: $18,393. Undergraduates: $16,297. *Scholarships, grants, and awards by category: Academic interests/achievement:* biological sciences, business, communication, computer science, education, English, foreign languages, health fields, mathematics, military science, physical sciences, pre-medicine, religion/biblical studies, social sciences. *Special achievements/activities:* community service, leadership. *Special characteristics:* children of educators, children of faculty/staff, local/state students, veterans, veterans' children. *Tuition waivers:* Full or partial for employees or children of employees, senior citizens. *ROTC:* Army.

**LOANS** *Student loans:* $18,763,316 (64% need-based, 36% non-need-based). 82% of past graduating class borrowed through all loan programs. *Average indebtedness per student:* $30,837. *Average need-based loan:* Freshmen: $2971. Undergraduates: $4049. *Parent loans:* $5,841,832 (41% need-based, 59% non-need-based). *Programs:* Federal Direct (Subsidized and Unsubsidized Stafford, PLUS), Perkins.

**WORK-STUDY** *Federal work-study:* Total amount: $745,793; jobs available. *State or other work-study/employment:* Part-time jobs available.

**APPLYING FOR FINANCIAL AID** *Required financial aid form:* FAFSA. *Financial aid deadline:* 3/15 (priority: 2/15). *Notification date:* Continuous beginning 2/15. Students must reply by 5/1 or within 4 weeks of notification.

**CONTACT** Ms. Claudia A. Wenzel, Director of Financial Aid, John Carroll University, 20700 North Park Boulevard, University Heights, OH 44118-4581, 216-397-4248 or toll-free 888-335-6800. *Fax:* 216-397-3098. *E-mail:* jcuofa@jcu.edu. *Website:* http://www.jcu.edu/.

# JOHN F. KENNEDY UNIVERSITY
## Pleasant Hill, CA

**CONTACT** Mindy Bergeron, Director of Financial Aid, John F. Kennedy University, 100 Ellinwood Way, Pleasant Hill, CA 94523, 925-969-3385 or toll-free 800-696-JFKU. *Fax:* 925-969-3390. *E-mail:* bergeron@jfku.edu. *Website:* http://www.jfku.edu/.

# JOHN JAY COLLEGE OF CRIMINAL JUSTICE OF THE CITY UNIVERSITY OF NEW YORK
### New York, NY

| Tuition & fees (NY res): $6059 | Average undergraduate aid package: $9445 |
|---|---|

**ABOUT THE INSTITUTION** State and locally supported, coed. **Awards:** certificates, bachelor's, and master's degrees. 17 undergraduate majors. **Total enrollment:** 15,008. Undergraduates: 13,215. Freshmen: 1,861. Federal methodology is used as a basis for awarding need-based institutional aid.
**UNDERGRADUATE EXPENSES for 2015–2016 Application fee:** $65. **Tuition, state resident:** full-time $5730. **Tuition, nonresident:** full-time $15,300; part-time $485 per credit. **Required fees:** full-time $329.
**FRESHMAN FINANCIAL AID (Fall 2013)** 2,998 applied for aid; of those 92% were deemed to have need. 92% of freshmen with need received aid. **Average percent of need met:** 85% (excluding resources awarded to replace EFC). **Average financial aid package:** $9445 (excluding resources awarded to replace EFC).
**UNDERGRADUATE FINANCIAL AID (Fall 2013)** 9,641 applied for aid; of those 92% were deemed to have need. 92% of undergraduates with need received aid. **Average percent of need met:** 85% (excluding resources awarded to replace EFC). **Average financial aid package:** $9445 (excluding resources awarded to replace EFC).
**GIFT AID (NEED-BASED) Total amount:** $57,915,447 (60% federal, 39% state, 1% institutional). **Receiving aid:** Freshmen: 10% (1,337); all full-time undergraduates: 61% (7,517). **Average award:** Freshmen: $2954; Undergraduates: $2954. **Scholarships, grants, and awards:** Federal Pell, FSEOG, state, college/university gift aid from institutional funds.
**GIFT AID (NON-NEED-BASED) Receiving aid:** Freshmen: 1% (207). Undergraduates: 2% (218). **Scholarships, grants, and awards by category:** Academic interests/achievement: general academic interests/achievements.
**LOANS Student loans:** $22,133,588 (33% need-based, 67% non-need-based). 20% of past graduating class borrowed through all loan programs. **Average indebtedness per student:** $11,246. **Average need-based loan:** Freshmen: $4245. Undergraduates: $4245. **Parent loans:** $736,703 (100% non-need-based). **Programs:** Federal Direct (Subsidized and Unsubsidized Stafford, PLUS), Perkins.
**WORK-STUDY Federal work-study:** jobs available. **State or other work-study/employment:** Part-time jobs available.
**APPLYING FOR FINANCIAL AID Required financial aid forms:** FAFSA, state aid form. **Financial aid deadline:** Continuous. **Notification date:** 4/1. Students must reply within 2 weeks of notification.
**CONTACT** Sylvia Lopez-Crespo, Director of Financial Aid, John Jay College of Criminal Justice of the City University of New York, 445 West 59th Street, New York, NY 10019-1093, 212-237-8897 or toll-free 877-JOHNJAY. Fax: 212-237-8936. E-mail: slopez@jjay.cuny.edu. Website: http://www.jjay.cuny.edu/.

# JOHN PAUL THE GREAT CATHOLIC UNIVERSITY
### Escondido, CA

| Tuition & fees: $24,900 | Average undergraduate aid package: $16,928 |
|---|---|

**ABOUT THE INSTITUTION** Independent religious, coed. **Awards:** certificates, bachelor's, and master's degrees. 2 undergraduate majors. **Total enrollment:** 286. Undergraduates: 196. Freshmen: 59. Both federal and institutional methodology are used as a basis for awarding need-based institutional aid.
**UNDERGRADUATE EXPENSES for 2015–2016 Application fee:** $20. **Tuition:** full-time $24,000; part-time $667 per credit. **Payment plan:** Guaranteed tuition.
**FRESHMAN FINANCIAL AID (Fall 2013)** 45 applied for aid; of those 100% were deemed to have need. 100% of freshmen with need received aid. **Average percent**

of need met: 53% (excluding resources awarded to replace EFC). **Average financial aid package:** $16,196 (excluding resources awarded to replace EFC).
**UNDERGRADUATE FINANCIAL AID (Fall 2013)** 104 applied for aid; of those 100% were deemed to have need. 100% of undergraduates with need received aid. **Average percent of need met:** 53% (excluding resources awarded to replace EFC). **Average financial aid package:** $16,928 (excluding resources awarded to replace EFC).
**GIFT AID (NEED-BASED) Total amount:** $1,313,788 (14% federal, 83% institutional, 3% external sources). **Receiving aid:** Freshmen: 96% (45); all full-time undergraduates: 81% (104). **Average award:** Freshmen: $11,410; Undergraduates: $11,816. **Scholarships, grants, and awards:** Federal Pell, private, college/university gift aid from institutional funds.
**GIFT AID (NON-NEED-BASED) Total amount:** $266,865 (99% institutional, 1% external sources). **Scholarships, grants, and awards by category:** Academic interests/achievement: general academic interests/achievements. Creative arts/performance: general creative arts/performance. Special achievements/activities: community service, leadership, religious involvement.
**LOANS Student loans:** $902,857 (83% need-based, 17% non-need-based). **Average need-based loan:** Freshmen: $3451. Undergraduates: $3921. **Parent loans:** $247,965 (71% need-based, 29% non-need-based). **Programs:** Federal Direct (Subsidized and Unsubsidized Stafford, PLUS), private loans.
**APPLYING FOR FINANCIAL AID Required financial aid forms:** FAFSA, institution's own form. **Financial aid deadline:** 4/15. **Notification date:** Continuous beginning 10/1. Students must reply by 5/1 or within 2 weeks of notification.
**CONTACT** Lisa Williams, Director of Financial Aid, John Paul the Great Catholic University, 155 West Grand Avenue, San Diego, CA 92025, 858-653-6740 Ext. 1303. Fax: 858-653-3791. E-mail: lwilliams@jpcatholic.com. Website: http://www.jpcatholic.com/.

# JOHNS HOPKINS UNIVERSITY
### Baltimore, MD

| Tuition & fees: $49,210 | Average undergraduate aid package: $37,462 |
|---|---|

**ABOUT THE INSTITUTION** Independent, coed. **Awards:** certificates, diplomas, bachelor's, master's, and doctoral degrees. 66 undergraduate majors. **Total enrollment:** 7,306. Undergraduates: 5,365. Freshmen: 1,414. Institutional methodology is used as a basis for awarding need-based institutional aid.
**UNDERGRADUATE EXPENSES for 2015–2016 Application fee:** $70. **Comprehensive fee:** $63,750 includes full-time tuition ($48,710), mandatory fees ($500), and room and board ($14,540). **College room only:** $8400. Room and board charges vary according to board plan and housing facility. **Part-time tuition:** $1624 per credit hour.
**FRESHMAN FINANCIAL AID (Fall 2014, est.)** 914 applied for aid; of those 78% were deemed to have need. 100% of freshmen with need received aid; of those 98% had need fully met. **Average percent of need met:** 98% (excluding resources awarded to replace EFC). **Average financial aid package:** $38,105 (excluding resources awarded to replace EFC). 1% of all full-time freshmen had no need and received non-need-based gift aid.
**UNDERGRADUATE FINANCIAL AID (Fall 2014, est.)** 2,966 applied for aid; of those 83% were deemed to have need. 100% of undergraduates with need received aid; of those 99% had need fully met. **Average percent of need met:** 99% (excluding resources awarded to replace EFC). **Average financial aid package:** $37,462 (excluding resources awarded to replace EFC). 2% of all full-time undergraduates had no need and received non-need-based gift aid.
**GIFT AID (NEED-BASED) Total amount:** $79,710,817 (5% federal, 92% institutional, 3% external sources). **Receiving aid:** Freshmen: 47% (666); all full-time undergraduates: 43% (2,289). **Average award:** Freshmen: $35,792; Undergraduates: $34,462. **Scholarships, grants, and awards:** Federal Pell, FSEOG, state, private, college/university gift aid from institutional funds.
**GIFT AID (NON-NEED-BASED) Total amount:** $4,645,439 (20% federal, 1% state, 56% institutional, 23% external sources). **Receiving aid:** Freshmen: 16% (227). Undergraduates: 10% (546). **Average award:** Freshmen: $30,263. Undergraduates: $30,165. **Scholarships, grants, and awards by category:** Academic interests/achievement: 82 awards ($2,510,860 total): engineering/technologies, general academic interests/achievements. Special characteristics: 102 awards ($3,281,224 total):

children of faculty/staff, local/state students. *Tuition waivers:* Full or partial for employees or children of employees. *ROTC:* Army, Air Force cooperative.

**LOANS** *Student loans:* $13,512,326 (58% need-based, 42% non-need-based). 48% of past graduating class borrowed through all loan programs. *Average indebtedness per student:* $23,627. *Average need-based loan:* Freshmen: $3301. Undergraduates: $4380. *Parent loans:* $8,258,803 (5% need-based, 95% non-need-based). *Programs:* Federal Direct (Subsidized and Unsubsidized Stafford, PLUS), Perkins, college/university.

**WORK-STUDY** *Federal work-study:* Total amount: $4,399,815; 1,839 jobs averaging $2392. *State or other work-study/employment:* Total amount: $303,548 (100% need-based). Part-time jobs available.

**ATHLETIC AWARDS** Total amount: $1,338,879 (18% need-based, 82% non-need-based).

**APPLYING FOR FINANCIAL AID** *Required financial aid forms:* FAFSA, CSS Financial Aid PROFILE, noncustodial (divorced/separated) parent's statement, federal income tax form(s). *Financial aid deadline:* 3/1. *Notification date:* 4/1. Students must reply by 5/1 or within 2 weeks of notification.

**CONTACT** Mr. Tom McDermott, Director of Student Financial Services, Johns Hopkins University, 146 Garland Hall, Baltimore, MD 21218, 410-516-8028. *Fax:* 410-516-6015. *E-mail:* tmcderm1@jhu.edu.
*Website:* http://www.jhu.edu/.

# JOHNSON & WALES UNIVERSITY
## Denver, CO

**CONTACT** Ms. Lynn Robinson, Executive Director of Student Financial Services, Johnson & Wales University, 8 Abbott Park Place, Providence, RI 02903, 401-598-4648 or toll-free 877-598-3368. *Fax:* 401-598-1040. *E-mail:* fp@jwu.edu.
*Website:* http://www.jwu.edu/denver/.

# JOHNSON & WALES UNIVERSITY
## North Miami, FL

**CONTACT** Ms. Lynn Robinson, Executive Director of Student Financial Services, Johnson & Wales University, 8 Abbott Park Place, Providence, RI 02903, 401-598-4648 or toll-free 866-598-3567. *Fax:* 401-598-1040. *E-mail:* fp@jwu.edu.
*Website:* http://www.jwu.edu/northmiami/.

# JOHNSON & WALES UNIVERSITY
## Charlotte, NC

**CONTACT** Ms. Lynn Robinson, Executive Director of Student Financial Services, Johnson & Wales University, 8 Abbott Park Place, Providence, RI 02903, 401-598-1648 or toll-free 866-598-2427. *Fax:* 401-598-4751. *E-mail:* fp@jwu.edu.
*Website:* http://www.jwu.edu/charlotte/.

# JOHNSON & WALES UNIVERSITY
## Providence, RI

**CONTACT** Ms. Lynn Robinson, Executive Director of Student Financial Services, Johnson & Wales University, 8 Abbott Park Place, Providence, RI 02903, 401-598-4648 or toll-free 800-342-5598. *Fax:* 401-598-1040. *E-mail:* fp@jwu.edu.
*Website:* http://www.jwu.edu/providence/.

# JOHNSON C. SMITH UNIVERSITY
## Charlotte, NC

| Tuition & fees: $18,236 | Average undergraduate aid package: $15,885 |
| --- | --- |

**ABOUT THE INSTITUTION** Independent, coed. *Awards:* bachelor's and master's degrees. 25 undergraduate majors. *Total enrollment:* 1,402. Undergraduates: 1,375. Freshmen: 268. Federal methodology is used as a basis for awarding need-based institutional aid.

**UNDERGRADUATE EXPENSES** for 2015–2016 *Application fee:* $25. *Comprehensive fee:* $25,336 includes full-time tuition ($18,236) and room and board ($7100). *College room only:* $4086. Full-time tuition and fees vary according to course load. Room and board charges vary according to board plan and housing facility. *Part-time tuition:* $418 per credit hour. Part-time tuition and fees vary according to course load.

**FRESHMAN FINANCIAL AID (Fall 2014, est.)** 252 applied for aid; of those 97% were deemed to have need. 100% of freshmen with need received aid; of those 5% had need fully met. *Average percent of need met:* 58% (excluding resources awarded to replace EFC). *Average financial aid package:* $16,748 (excluding resources awarded to replace EFC). 4% of all full-time freshmen had no need and received non-need-based gift aid.

**UNDERGRADUATE FINANCIAL AID (Fall 2014, est.)** 1,199 applied for aid; of those 97% were deemed to have need. 100% of undergraduates with need received aid; of those 8% had need fully met. *Average percent of need met:* 57% (excluding resources awarded to replace EFC). *Average financial aid package:* $15,885 (excluding resources awarded to replace EFC). 9% of all full-time undergraduates had no need and received non-need-based gift aid.

**GIFT AID (NEED-BASED)** *Total amount:* $11,887,570 (43% federal, 18% state, 36% institutional, 3% external sources). *Receiving aid:* Freshmen: 88% (233); all full-time undergraduates: 84% (1,111). *Average award:* Freshmen: $13,158; Undergraduates: $11,579. *Scholarships, grants, and awards:* Federal Pell, FSEOG, state, private, college/university gift aid from institutional funds, United Negro College Fund.

**GIFT AID (NON-NEED-BASED)** *Total amount:* $2,546,668 (3% state, 95% institutional, 2% external sources). *Receiving aid:* Freshmen: 4% (11). Undergraduates: 6% (77). *Average award:* Freshmen: $12,500. Undergraduates: $19,057. *Scholarships, grants, and awards by category: Academic interests/achievement:* biological sciences, computer science, engineering/technologies, foreign languages, general academic interests/achievements. *Creative arts/performance:* music. *Special achievements/activities:* general special achievements/activities. *Special characteristics:* children of faculty/staff, ethnic background, general special characteristics, international students, out-of-state students, siblings of current students. *Tuition waivers:* Full or partial for children of alumni, employees or children of employees. *ROTC:* Army, Air Force cooperative.

**LOANS** *Student loans:* $10,540,762 (94% need-based, 6% non-need-based). 78% of past graduating class borrowed through all loan programs. *Average indebtedness per student:* $33,377. *Average need-based loan:* Freshmen: $4014. Undergraduates: $4400. *Parent loans:* $2,981,920 (71% need-based, 29% non-need-based). *Programs:* Perkins, alternative loans.

**WORK-STUDY** *Federal work-study:* Total amount: $485,000; 217 jobs averaging $2008. *State or other work-study/employment:* Total amount: $380,566 (62% need-based, 38% non-need-based). Part-time jobs available.

**ATHLETIC AWARDS** Total amount: $1,792,245 (69% need-based, 31% non-need-based).

**APPLYING FOR FINANCIAL AID** *Required financial aid form:* FAFSA. *Financial aid deadline (priority):* 3/1. *Notification date:* Continuous beginning 3/1. Students must reply within 2 weeks of notification.

**CONTACT** Office of Financial Aid, Johnson C. Smith University, 100 Beatties Ford Road, Charlotte, NC 28216, 704-378-1498 or toll-free 800-782-7303. *Fax:* 704-378-1292.
*Website:* http://www.jcsu.edu/.

# JOHNSON STATE COLLEGE
## Johnson, VT

**ABOUT THE INSTITUTION** State-supported, coed. *Awards:* certificates, associate, bachelor's, and master's degrees. 58 undergraduate majors. *Total enrollment:* 1,662. Undergraduates: 1,458. Freshmen: 222.

**GIFT AID (NEED-BASED)** *Scholarships, grants, and awards:* Federal Pell, FSEOG, state, private, college/university gift aid from institutional funds.
**GIFT AID (NON-NEED-BASED)** *Scholarships, grants, and awards by category:* Academic interests/achievement: business, education, general academic interests/achievements, mathematics. *Creative arts/performance:* art/fine arts, dance, music, performing arts, theater/drama. *Special achievements/activities:* community service, general special achievements/activities, leadership, memberships. *Special characteristics:* general special characteristics, international students, local/state students, members of minority groups.
**LOANS** *Programs:* Federal Direct (Subsidized and Unsubsidized Stafford, PLUS), Perkins.
**WORK-STUDY** *Federal work-study:* jobs available.
**APPLYING FOR FINANCIAL AID** *Required financial aid form:* FAFSA.
**CONTACT** Ms. Kimberly Goodell, Financial Aid Officer, Johnson State College, 337 College Hill, Johnson, VT 05656-9405, 802-635-2356 or toll-free 800-635-2356. *Fax:* 802-635-1463. *E-mail:* goodellk@badger.jsc.vsc.edu.
*Website:* http://www.jsc.edu/.

## JOHNSON UNIVERSITY
### Knoxville, TN

**CONTACT** Mr. Lawrence Rector, CPA, Financial Aid Director, Johnson University, 7900 Johnson Drive, Knoxville, TN 37998, 865-251-2303 Ext. 2316 or toll-free 800-827-2122. *Fax:* 865-251-2337. *E-mail:* lrector@jbc.edu.
*Website:* http://www.johnsonu.edu/.

## JOHNSON UNIVERSITY FLORIDA
### Kissimmee, FL

**CONTACT** Ms. Sandra Peppard, Director of Student Financial Aid, Johnson University Florida, 1011 Bill Beck Boulevard, Kissimmee, FL 34744-5301, 407-847-8966 Ext. 365 or toll-free 888-GO-TO-FCC. *Fax:* 407-847-3925. *E-mail:* sandi.peppard@fcc.edu.
*Website:* http://www.johnsonu.edu/.

## JONES COLLEGE
### Jacksonville, FL

**CONTACT** Mrs. Becky Davis, Director of Financial Assistance, Jones College, 5353 Arlington Expressway, Jacksonville, FL 32211-5540, 904-743-1122 or toll-free 800-631-4056. *Fax:* 904-743-4446.
*Website:* http://www.jones.edu/.

## JOSE MARIA VARGAS UNIVERSITY
### Pembroke Pines, FL

**CONTACT** Financial Aid Office, Jose Maria Vargas University, 10131 Pines Boulevard, Pembroke Pines, FL 33026, 954-322-4446.
*Website:* http://www.jmvu.edu/.

## JUDSON COLLEGE
### Marion, AL

**ABOUT THE INSTITUTION** Independent Baptist, coed, primarily women. *Awards:* associate and bachelor's degrees. 22 undergraduate majors. *Total enrollment:* 376. Undergraduates: 376. Freshmen: 83.
**GIFT AID (NEED-BASED)** *Scholarships, grants, and awards:* Federal Pell, FSEOG, state, private, college/university gift aid from institutional funds, Academic Competitiveness Grants, National SMART Grants, TEACH Grants.

**GIFT AID (NON-NEED-BASED)** *Scholarships, grants, and awards by category:* Academic interests/achievement: biological sciences, general academic interests/achievements, premedicine. *Creative arts/performance:* art/fine arts, music. *Special achievements/activities:* general special achievements/activities. *Special characteristics:* children of educators, children of faculty/staff, relatives of clergy, religious affiliation.
**LOANS** *Programs:* Perkins, college/university.
**APPLYING FOR FINANCIAL AID** *Required financial aid forms:* FAFSA, institution's own form, state aid form.
**CONTACT** Mrs. Ashley D. Clemons, Director of Financial Aid, Judson College, 302 Bibb Street, Marion, AL 36756, 334-683-5170 or toll-free 800-447-9472. *Fax:* 334-683-5282. *E-mail:* aclemons@judson.edu.
*Website:* http://www.judson.edu/.

## JUDSON UNIVERSITY
### Elgin, IL

**ABOUT THE INSTITUTION** Independent Baptist, coed. *Awards:* certificates, diplomas, bachelor's, master's, and doctoral degrees. 45 undergraduate majors. *Total enrollment:* 1,288. Undergraduates: 1,154. Freshmen: 201.
**GIFT AID (NEED-BASED)** *Scholarships, grants, and awards:* Federal Pell, FSEOG, state, private, college/university gift aid from institutional funds.
**GIFT AID (NON-NEED-BASED)** *Scholarships, grants, and awards by category:* Academic interests/achievement: general academic interests/achievements. *Creative arts/performance:* art/fine arts, music, theater/drama. *Special achievements/activities:* leadership.
**LOANS** *Programs:* Federal Direct (Subsidized and Unsubsidized Stafford, PLUS), Perkins.
**WORK-STUDY** *Federal work-study:* 100 jobs averaging $1075. *State or other work-study/employment:* Total amount: $314,361 (100% non-need-based). Part-time jobs available.
**APPLYING FOR FINANCIAL AID** *Required financial aid form:* FAFSA.
**CONTACT** Roberto Santizo, Director of Financial Aid, Judson University, 1151 North State Street, Elgin, IL 60123-1498, 847-628-2532 or toll-free 800-879-5376. *Fax:* 847-628-2533. *E-mail:* rsantizo@judsonu.edu.
*Website:* http://www.judsonu.edu/.

## THE JUILLIARD SCHOOL
### New York, NY

| Tuition & fees: $38,490 | Average undergraduate aid package: $34,916 |
|---|---|

**ABOUT THE INSTITUTION** Independent, coed. *Awards:* certificates, diplomas, bachelor's, master's, and doctoral degrees. 4 undergraduate majors. *Total enrollment:* 927. Undergraduates: 570. Freshmen: 129. Federal methodology is used as a basis for awarding need-based institutional aid.
**UNDERGRADUATE EXPENSES** for 2015–2016 *Application fee:* $110. *One-time required fee:* $250. *Comprehensive fee:* $52,780 includes full-time tuition ($38,190), mandatory fees ($300), and room and board ($14,290).
**FRESHMAN FINANCIAL AID (Fall 2014, est.)** 125 applied for aid; of those 78% were deemed to have need. 100% of freshmen with need received aid; of those 40% had need fully met. *Average percent of need met:* 79% (excluding resources awarded to replace EFC). *Average financial aid package:* $33,854 (excluding resources awarded to replace EFC). 11% of all full-time freshmen had no need and received non-need-based gift aid.
**UNDERGRADUATE FINANCIAL AID (Fall 2014, est.)** 459 applied for aid; of those 85% were deemed to have need. 100% of undergraduates with need received aid; of those 31% had need fully met. *Average percent of need met:* 79% (excluding resources awarded to replace EFC). *Average financial aid package:* $34,916 (excluding resources awarded to replace EFC). 9% of all full-time undergraduates had no need and received non-need-based gift aid.
**GIFT AID (NEED-BASED)** *Total amount:* $10,831,101 (5% federal, 1% state, 91% institutional, 3% external sources). *Receiving aid:* Freshmen: 71% (92); all full-time undergraduates: 75% (381). *Average award:* Freshmen: $43,966; Undergrad-

uates: $28,381. **Scholarships, grants, and awards:** Federal Pell, FSEOG, state, private, college/university gift aid from institutional funds.

**GIFT AID (NON-NEED-BASED) Total amount:** $1,136,210 (93% institutional, 7% external sources). **Average award:** Freshmen: $24,712. Undergraduates: $21,983. **Scholarships, grants, and awards by category:** Creative arts/performance: dance, music, performing arts, theater/drama. **Tuition waivers:** Full or partial for employees or children of employees.

**LOANS Student loans:** $1,623,714 (93% need-based, 7% non-need-based). 53% of past graduating class borrowed through all loan programs. Average indebtedness per student: $26,712. **Average need-based loan:** Freshmen: $3488. Undergraduates: $5001. **Parent loans:** $628,994 (97% need-based, 3% non-need-based). **Programs:** Federal Direct (Subsidized and Unsubsidized Stafford, PLUS), Perkins.

**WORK-STUDY Federal work-study:** Total amount: $373,416; 211 jobs averaging $2010. **State or other work-study/employment:** Total amount: $505,858 (74% need-based, 26% non-need-based). 231 part-time jobs averaging $1936.

**APPLYING FOR FINANCIAL AID Required financial aid forms:** FAFSA, institution's own form. **Financial aid deadline:** 3/1. **Notification date:** 4/1. Students must reply by 5/1.

**CONTACT** Tina Gonzalez, Director of Financial Aid, The Juilliard School, 60 Lincoln Center Plaza, New York, NY 10023, 212-799-5000 Ext. 211. Fax: 646-505-4161. E-mail: financialaid@juilliard.edu.
Website: http://www.juilliard.edu/.

# JUNIATA COLLEGE
### Huntingdon, PA

| Tuition & fees: $40,600 | Average undergraduate aid package: $30,563 |
|---|---|

**ABOUT THE INSTITUTION** Independent Church of the Brethren, coed. **Awards:** bachelor's and master's degrees. 60 undergraduate majors. **Total enrollment:** 1,632. Undergraduates: 1,615. Freshmen: 423. Federal methodology is used as a basis for awarding need-based institutional aid.

**UNDERGRADUATE EXPENSES for 2015–2016 Comprehensive fee:** $51,740 includes full-time tuition ($39,840), mandatory fees ($760), and room and board ($11,140). **College room only:** $5930. Full-time tuition and fees vary according to course load and program. Room and board charges vary according to board plan. **Part-time tuition:** $1610 per credit.

**FRESHMAN FINANCIAL AID (Fall 2014, est.)** 351 applied for aid; of those 87% were deemed to have need. 100% of freshmen with need received aid; of those 25% had need fully met. **Average percent of need met:** 86% (excluding resources awarded to replace EFC). **Average financial aid package:** $31,877 (excluding resources awarded to replace EFC). 27% of all full-time freshmen had no need and received non-need-based gift aid.

**UNDERGRADUATE FINANCIAL AID (Fall 2014, est.)** 1,222 applied for aid; of those 88% were deemed to have need. 99% of undergraduates with need received aid; of those 22% had need fully met. **Average percent of need met:** 81% (excluding resources awarded to replace EFC). **Average financial aid package:** $30,563 (excluding resources awarded to replace EFC). 29% of all full-time undergraduates had no need and received non-need-based gift aid.

**GIFT AID (NEED-BASED) Total amount:** $26,572,662 (7% federal, 5% state, 87% institutional, 1% external sources). **Receiving aid:** Freshmen: 72% (304); all full-time undergraduates: 69% (1,063). **Average award:** Freshmen: $26,934; Undergraduates: $24,997. **Scholarships, grants, and awards:** Federal Pell, FSEOG, state, private, college/university gift aid from institutional funds.

**GIFT AID (NON-NEED-BASED) Total amount:** $9,241,094 (99% institutional, 1% external sources). **Receiving aid:** Freshmen: 14% (58). Undergraduates: 10% (161). **Average award:** Freshmen: $19,204. Undergraduates: $18,054. **Scholarships, grants, and awards by category:** Academic interests/achievement: biological sciences, business, communication, computer science, education, foreign languages, general academic interests/achievements, health fields, humanities, international studies, mathematics, physical sciences, premedicine, social sciences. Creative arts/performance: art/fine arts, music, performing arts, theater/drama. Special achievements/activities: community service, general special achievements/activities, leadership. Special characteristics: children of faculty/staff, ethnic background, international students, local/state students. **Tuition waivers:** Full or partial for employees or children of employees, senior citizens.

**LOANS Student loans:** $9,569,508 (65% need-based, 35% non-need-based). 72% of past graduating class borrowed through all loan programs. Average indebtedness per student: $33,421. **Average need-based loan:** Freshmen: $4558. Undergraduates: $5171. **Parent loans:** $2,724,203 (41% need-based, 59% non-need-based). **Programs:** Federal Direct (Subsidized and Unsubsidized Stafford, PLUS), Perkins, college/university.

**WORK-STUDY Federal work-study:** Total amount: $1,108,164; jobs available. **State or other work-study/employment:** Total amount: $1,244,999 (9% need-based, 91% non-need-based). Part-time jobs available.

**APPLYING FOR FINANCIAL AID Required financial aid form:** FAFSA. **Financial aid deadline (priority):** 2/15. **Notification date:** Continuous beginning 3/1. Students must reply by 5/1 or within 2 weeks of notification.

**CONTACT** Shane Himes, Director of Student Financial Planning, Juniata College, 1700 Moore Street, Huntingdon, PA 16652-2119, 814-641-3140 or toll-free 877-JUNIATA. Fax: 814-641-5311. E-mail: himess@juniata.edu.
Website: http://www.juniata.edu/.

# KALAMAZOO COLLEGE
### Kalamazoo, MI

| Tuition & fees: $41,061 | Average undergraduate aid package: $34,463 |
|---|---|

**ABOUT THE INSTITUTION** Independent American Baptist Churches in the U.S.A., coed. **Awards:** bachelor's degrees. 28 undergraduate majors. **Total enrollment:** 1,461. Undergraduates: 1,461. Freshmen: 357. Both federal and institutional methodology are used as a basis for awarding need-based institutional aid.

**UNDERGRADUATE EXPENSES for 2015–2016 Comprehensive fee:** $49,740 includes full-time tuition ($40,728), mandatory fees ($333), and room and board ($8679). **College room only:** $4233. Room and board charges vary according to board plan and housing facility.

**FRESHMAN FINANCIAL AID (Fall 2014, est.)** 314 applied for aid; of those 84% were deemed to have need. 100% of freshmen with need received aid; of those 59% had need fully met. **Average percent of need met:** 95% (excluding resources awarded to replace EFC). **Average financial aid package:** $36,012 (excluding resources awarded to replace EFC). 25% of all full-time freshmen had no need and received non-need-based gift aid.

**UNDERGRADUATE FINANCIAL AID (Fall 2014, est.)** 1,074 applied for aid; of those 89% were deemed to have need. 100% of undergraduates with need received aid; of those 46% had need fully met. **Average percent of need met:** 91% (excluding resources awarded to replace EFC). **Average financial aid package:** $34,463 (excluding resources awarded to replace EFC). 30% of all full-time undergraduates had no need and received non-need-based gift aid.

**GIFT AID (NEED-BASED) Total amount:** $25,447,190 (7% federal, 3% state, 89% institutional, 1% external sources). **Receiving aid:** Freshmen: 73% (259); all full-time undergraduates: 66% (939). **Average award:** Freshmen: $28,977; Undergraduates: $26,990. **Scholarships, grants, and awards:** Federal Pell, FSEOG, state, private, college/university gift aid from institutional funds.

**GIFT AID (NON-NEED-BASED) Total amount:** $9,668,375 (83% institutional, 17% external sources). **Receiving aid:** Freshmen: 17% (62). Undergraduates: 13% (181). **Average award:** Freshmen: $18,028. Undergraduates: $16,358. **Scholarships, grants, and awards by category:** Academic interests/achievement: general academic interests/achievements. Creative arts/performance: art/fine arts, music, performing arts. Special achievements/activities: leadership. Special characteristics: children and siblings of alumni. **Tuition waivers:** Full or partial for employees or children of employees. **ROTC:** Army cooperative.

**LOANS Student loans:** $8,068,128 (66% need-based, 34% non-need-based). 58% of past graduating class borrowed through all loan programs. Average indebtedness per student: $28,405. **Average need-based loan:** Freshmen: $4881. Undergraduates: $5747. **Parent loans:** $2,160,105 (100% non-need-based). **Programs:** Federal Direct (Subsidized and Unsubsidized Stafford, PLUS), Perkins.

**WORK-STUDY Federal work-study:** Total amount: $1,206,238; 491 jobs averaging $2440. **State or other work-study/employment:** Total amount: $174,573 (100% need-based). Part-time jobs available.

**APPLYING FOR FINANCIAL AID Required financial aid forms:** FAFSA, institution's own form. **Financial aid deadline (priority):** 2/15. **Notification date:** Continuous beginning 3/23. Students must reply by 5/1.

**CONTACT** Marian Stowers, Director of Financial Aid, Kalamazoo College, 1200 Academy Street, Kalamazoo, MI 49006-3295, 269-337-7192 or toll-free 800-253-3602. *Fax:* 269-337-7390.
*Website:* http://www.kzoo.edu/.

# KANSAS CITY ART INSTITUTE
## Kansas City, MO

| Tuition & fees: $35,270 | Average undergraduate aid package: $23,526 |
|---|---|

**ABOUT THE INSTITUTION** Independent, coed. *Awards:* certificates and bachelor's degrees. 13 undergraduate majors. *Total enrollment:* 655. Undergraduates: 655. Freshmen: 134. Federal methodology is used as a basis for awarding need-based institutional aid.
**UNDERGRADUATE EXPENSES for 2015–2016** *Application fee:* $45. *Comprehensive fee:* $45,510 includes full-time tuition ($35,120), mandatory fees ($150), and room and board ($10,240). Full-time tuition and fees vary according to program. Room and board charges vary according to board plan. *Part-time tuition:* $1465 per credit hour. Part-time tuition and fees vary according to program.
**FRESHMAN FINANCIAL AID (Fall 2014, est.)** 159 applied for aid; of those 91% were deemed to have need. 97% of freshmen with need received aid; of those 12% had need fully met. *Average percent of need met:* 54% (excluding resources awarded to replace EFC). *Average financial aid package:* $22,375 (excluding resources awarded to replace EFC). 13% of all full-time freshmen had no need and received non-need-based gift aid.
**UNDERGRADUATE FINANCIAL AID (Fall 2014, est.)** 637 applied for aid; of those 92% were deemed to have need. 98% of undergraduates with need received aid; of those 13% had need fully met. *Average percent of need met:* 59% (excluding resources awarded to replace EFC). *Average financial aid package:* $23,526 (excluding resources awarded to replace EFC). 17% of all full-time undergraduates had no need and received non-need-based gift aid.
**GIFT AID (NEED-BASED)** *Total amount:* $11,119,181 (14% federal, 2% state, 78% institutional, 6% external sources). *Receiving aid:* Freshmen: 88% (140); all full-time undergraduates: 89% (570). *Average award:* Freshmen: $19,453; Undergraduates: $19,266. *Scholarships, grants, and awards:* Federal Pell, FSEOG, state, private, college/university gift aid from institutional funds.
**GIFT AID (NON-NEED-BASED)** *Total amount:* $2,142,136 (94% institutional, 6% external sources). *Receiving aid:* Freshmen: 8% (13). Undergraduates: 8% (50). *Average award:* Freshmen: $17,928. Undergraduates: $15,298. *Scholarships, grants, and awards by category:* Creative arts/performance: art/fine arts. *Tuition waivers:* Full or partial for employees or children of employees.
**LOANS** *Student loans:* $5,121,773 (79% need-based, 21% non-need-based). 85% of past graduating class borrowed through all loan programs. *Average indebtedness per student:* $25,000. *Average need-based loan:* Freshmen: $3731. Undergraduates: $4740. *Parent loans:* $1,296,853 (65% need-based, 35% non-need-based). *Programs:* Federal Direct (Subsidized and Unsubsidized Stafford, PLUS), Perkins, alternative loans.
**WORK-STUDY** *Federal work-study:* Total amount: $114,940; 119 jobs averaging $1026. *State or other work-study/employment:* Total amount: $211,250 (57% need-based, 43% non-need-based). 219 part-time jobs averaging $1200.
**APPLYING FOR FINANCIAL AID** *Required financial aid form:* FAFSA. *Financial aid deadline (priority):* 3/15. *Notification date:* Continuous beginning 3/15. Students must reply within 2 weeks of notification.
**CONTACT** Mrs. Darchelle Renee Webster, Financial Aid Director, Kansas City Art Institute, 4415 Warwick Boulevard, Kansas City, MO 64111-1874, 816-802-3337 or toll-free 800-522-5224. *Fax:* 816-802-3453. *E-mail:* financialaid@kcai.edu. *Website:* http://www.kcai.edu/.

# KANSAS STATE UNIVERSITY
## Manhattan, KS

| Tuition & fees (KS res): $9034 | Average undergraduate aid package: $11,773 |
|---|---|

**ABOUT THE INSTITUTION** State-supported, coed. *Awards:* certificates, associate, bachelor's, master's, and doctoral degrees. 87 undergraduate majors. *Total enrollment:* 24,766. Undergraduates: 20,327. Freshmen: 3,757. Federal methodology is used as a basis for awarding need-based institutional aid.
**UNDERGRADUATE EXPENSES for 2015–2016** *Application fee:* $30. *Tuition, state resident:* full-time $8223. *Tuition, nonresident:* full-time $21,813. *Required fees:* full-time $811. Full-time tuition and fees vary according to course load, degree level, location, program, and reciprocity agreements. Part-time tuition and fees vary according to course load, degree level, location, program, and reciprocity agreements. *College room and board:* $8060. Room and board charges vary according to board plan, housing facility, and location.
**FRESHMAN FINANCIAL AID (Fall 2013)** 2,906 applied for aid; of those 70% were deemed to have need. 98% of freshmen with need received aid; of those 20% had need fully met. *Average percent of need met:* 78% (excluding resources awarded to replace EFC). *Average financial aid package:* $11,700 (excluding resources awarded to replace EFC). 16% of all full-time freshmen had no need and received non-need-based gift aid.
**UNDERGRADUATE FINANCIAL AID (Fall 2013)** 12,227 applied for aid; of those 77% were deemed to have need. 97% of undergraduates with need received aid; of those 17% had need fully met. *Average percent of need met:* 77% (excluding resources awarded to replace EFC). *Average financial aid package:* $11,773 (excluding resources awarded to replace EFC). 7% of all full-time undergraduates had no need and received non-need-based gift aid.
**GIFT AID (NEED-BASED)** *Total amount:* $47,047,831 (42% federal, 6% state, 44% institutional, 8% external sources). *Receiving aid:* Freshmen: 30% (1,113); all full-time undergraduates: 30% (5,324). *Average award:* Freshmen: $4363; Undergraduates: $4298. *Scholarships, grants, and awards:* Federal Pell, FSEOG, state, private, college/university gift aid from institutional funds.
**GIFT AID (NON-NEED-BASED)** *Total amount:* $7,535,816 (1% federal, 80% institutional, 19% external sources). *Receiving aid:* Freshmen: 39% (1,447). Undergraduates: 25% (4,485). *Average award:* Freshmen: $4594. Undergraduates: $3736. *Tuition waivers:* Full or partial for employees or children of employees. *ROTC:* Army, Air Force.
**LOANS** *Student loans:* $75,306,700 (72% need-based, 28% non-need-based). 63% of past graduating class borrowed through all loan programs. *Average indebtedness per student:* $26,779. *Average need-based loan:* Freshmen: $3521. Undergraduates: $4247. *Parent loans:* $26,336,207 (28% need-based, 72% non-need-based). *Programs:* Federal Direct (Subsidized and Unsubsidized Stafford, PLUS), Perkins, college/university.
**WORK-STUDY** *Federal work-study:* jobs available. *State or other work-study/employment:* Total amount: $8,178,420 (83% need-based, 17% non-need-based). Part-time jobs available.
**ATHLETIC AWARDS** Total amount: $5,459,186 (89% need-based, 11% non-need-based).
**APPLYING FOR FINANCIAL AID** *Required financial aid form:* FAFSA. *Financial aid deadline (priority):* 3/1. *Notification date:* Continuous beginning 4/1. Students must reply within 2 weeks of notification.
**CONTACT** Mr. Larry Moeder, Director of Admissions and Student Financial Assistance, Kansas State University, 104 Fairchild Hall, Manhattan, KS 66506, 785-532-6420 or toll-free 800-432-8270. *E-mail:* larrym@ksu.edu. *Website:* http://www.k-state.edu/.

# KANSAS WESLEYAN UNIVERSITY
## Salina, KS

| Tuition & fees: $26,600 | Average undergraduate aid package: $20,771 |
|---|---|

**ABOUT THE INSTITUTION** Independent United Methodist, coed. *Awards:* associate, bachelor's, and master's degrees. 63 undergraduate majors. *Total* *enrollment:* 710. Undergraduates: 667. Freshmen: 144. Federal methodology is used as a basis for awarding need-based institutional aid.

**UNDERGRADUATE EXPENSES for 2015–2016** *Application fee:* $20. *One-time required fee:* $200. *Comprehensive fee:* $34,800 includes full-time tuition ($26,600) and room and board ($8200). *College room only:* $2800. Room and board charges vary according to housing facility. *Part-time tuition:* $2400 per term. Part-time tuition and fees vary according to course load.

**FRESHMAN FINANCIAL AID (Fall 2014, est.)** 141 applied for aid; of those 90% were deemed to have need. 100% of freshmen with need received aid; of those 23% had need fully met. *Average percent of need met:* 74% (excluding resources awarded to replace EFC). *Average financial aid package:* $21,762 (excluding resources awarded to replace EFC). 9% of all full-time freshmen had no need and received non-need-based gift aid.

**UNDERGRADUATE FINANCIAL AID (Fall 2014, est.)** 619 applied for aid; of those 89% were deemed to have need. 100% of undergraduates with need received aid; of those 19% had need fully met. *Average percent of need met:* 75% (excluding resources awarded to replace EFC). *Average financial aid package:* $20,771 (excluding resources awarded to replace EFC). 8% of all full-time undergraduates had no need and received non-need-based gift aid.

**GIFT AID (NEED-BASED)** *Total amount:* $2,713,981 (49% federal, 22% state, 19% institutional, 10% external sources). *Receiving aid:* Freshmen: 89% (127); all full-time undergraduates: 86% (539). *Average award:* Freshmen: $9003; Undergraduates: $8229. *Scholarships, grants, and awards:* Federal Pell, FSEOG, state, private, college/university gift aid from institutional funds.

**GIFT AID (NON-NEED-BASED)** *Total amount:* $5,889,260 (99% institutional, 1% external sources). *Receiving aid:* Freshmen: 78% (111). Undergraduates: 76% (474). *Average award:* Freshmen: $11,808. Undergraduates: $10,006. *Scholarships, grants, and awards by category:* Academic interests/achievement: 532 awards ($4,849,686 total): biological sciences, business, communication, computer science, education, English, foreign languages, general academic interests/achievements, mathematics, physical sciences, premedicine, religion/biblical studies, social sciences. Creative arts/performance: 60 awards ($141,581 total): dance, music, theater/drama. Special achievements/activities: 7 awards ($15,025 total): cheerleading/drum major, junior miss. Special characteristics: 152 awards ($520,873 total): children and siblings of alumni, children of faculty/staff, siblings of current students. *Tuition waivers:* Full or partial for children of alumni, employees or children of employees, senior citizens.

**LOANS** *Student loans:* $4,990,668 (49% need-based, 51% non-need-based). 87% of past graduating class borrowed through all loan programs. *Average indebtedness per student:* $31,230. *Average need-based loan:* Freshmen: $3842. Undergraduates: $4674. *Parent loans:* $1,479,332 (100% non-need-based). *Programs:* Federal Direct (Subsidized and Unsubsidized Stafford, PLUS), Perkins.

**WORK-STUDY** *Federal work-study:* Total amount: $144,983; 86 jobs averaging $1686. *State or other work-study/employment:* Total amount: $16,384 (100% non-need-based). 9 part-time jobs averaging $1820.

**ATHLETIC AWARDS** Total amount: $445,966 (100% non-need-based).

**APPLYING FOR FINANCIAL AID** *Required financial aid form:* FAFSA. *Financial aid deadline (priority):* 3/15. *Notification date:* Continuous beginning 2/15.

**CONTACT** Mrs. Lois Elizabeth Madsen, Director of Student Financial Planning, Kansas Wesleyan University, 100 East Claflin, Hall of the Pioneers, Room 285, Salina, KS 67401-6196, 785-827-5541 Ext. 1132 or toll-free 800-874-1154 Ext. 1285. *Fax:* 785-827-0927. *E-mail:* lois.madsen@kwu.edu. *Website:* http://www.kwu.edu/.

# KAPLAN UNIVERSITY, AUGUSTA
## Augusta, ME

**CONTACT** Financial Aid Office, Kaplan University, Augusta, 14 Marketplace Drive, Augusta, ME 04330, 207-213-2500 or toll-free 888-561-4343. *Website:* http://www.kaplanuniversity.edu/.

# KAPLAN UNIVERSITY, DAVENPORT CAMPUS
## Davenport, IA

**CONTACT** Financial Aid Office, Kaplan University, Davenport Campus, 1801 East Kimberly Road, Suite 1, Davenport, IA 52807-2095, 563-355-3500 or toll-free 866-527-5268 (in-state), 800-527-5268 (out-of-state). *Website:* http://www.kaplanuniversity.edu/.

# KAPLAN UNIVERSITY, MASON CITY CAMPUS
## Mason City, IA

**CONTACT** Financial Aid Office, Kaplan University, Mason City Campus, 2570 4th Street, SW, Mason City, IA 50401, 641-423-2530 or toll-free 866-527-5268 (in-state), 800-527-5268 (out-of-state). *Website:* http://www.kaplanuniversity.edu/.

# KEAN UNIVERSITY
## Union, NJ

| Tuition & fees (NJ res): $11,243 | Average undergraduate aid package: $10,300 |
|---|---|

**ABOUT THE INSTITUTION** State-supported, coed. *Awards:* certificates, bachelor's, master's, and doctoral degrees. 47 undergraduate majors. *Total enrollment:* 14,359. Undergraduates: 11,987. Freshmen: 1,502. Federal methodology is used as a basis for awarding need-based institutional aid.

**UNDERGRADUATE EXPENSES for 2015–2016** *Application fee:* $75. *Tuition, state resident:* full-time $7345; part-time $286 per credit. *Tuition, non-resident:* full-time $13,754; part-time $485 per credit. *Required fees:* full-time $3898; $143 per credit. Part-time tuition and fees vary according to course load. *College room and board:* $12,200; *Room only:* $9378. Room and board charges vary according to board plan, housing facility, and student level.

**FRESHMAN FINANCIAL AID (Fall 2014, est.)** 1,334 applied for aid; of those 86% were deemed to have need. 90% of freshmen with need received aid; of those 6% had need fully met. *Average percent of need met:* 76% (excluding resources awarded to replace EFC). *Average financial aid package:* $10,305 (excluding resources awarded to replace EFC). 2% of all full-time freshmen had no need and received non-need-based gift aid.

**UNDERGRADUATE FINANCIAL AID (Fall 2014, est.)** 7,780 applied for aid; of those 86% were deemed to have need. 96% of undergraduates with need received aid; of those 13% had need fully met. *Average percent of need met:* 81% (excluding resources awarded to replace EFC). *Average financial aid package:* $10,300 (excluding resources awarded to replace EFC). 1% of all full-time undergraduates had no need and received non-need-based gift aid.

**GIFT AID (NEED-BASED)** *Total amount:* $40,818,328 (60% federal, 35% state, 4% institutional, 1% external sources). *Receiving aid:* Freshmen: 53% (781); all full-time undergraduates: 51% (4,689). *Average award:* Freshmen: $8479; Undergraduates: $7935. *Scholarships, grants, and awards:* Federal Pell, FSEOG, state, private, college/university gift aid from institutional funds.

**GIFT AID (NON-NEED-BASED)** *Total amount:* $32,650 (100% state). *Receiving aid:* Freshmen: 10% (146). Undergraduates: 7% (638). *Average award:* Freshmen: $4463. Undergraduates: $4222. *Scholarships, grants, and awards by category:* Academic interests/achievement: area/ethnic studies, biological sciences, business, communication, computer science, education, engineering/technologies, English, foreign languages, general academic interests/achievements, health fields, humanities, international studies, mathematics, physical sciences, premedicine, social sciences. Creative arts/performance: applied art and design, art/fine arts, cinema/film/broadcasting, dance, general creative arts/performance, music, performing arts, theater/drama. Special achievements/activities: general special achievements/activities. Special characteristics: general special characteristics. *Tuition waivers:* Full or partial for employees or children of employees, senior citizens. *ROTC:* Army cooperative, Air Force cooperative.

**LOANS** *Student loans:* $67,071,678 (41% need-based, 59% non-need-based). 73% of past graduating class borrowed through all loan programs. *Average indebtedness per student:* $32,886. *Average need-based loan:* Freshmen: $3478. Undergraduates: $4369. *Parent loans:* $6,972,794 (100% non-need-based). *Programs:* Federal Direct (Subsidized and Unsubsidized Stafford, PLUS), Perkins.

**WORK-STUDY** *Federal work-study:* Total amount: $527,972; jobs available.

**APPLYING FOR FINANCIAL AID** *Required financial aid form:* FAFSA. *Financial aid deadline (priority):* 4/17. *Notification date:* Continuous beginning 3/1. Students must reply by 5/1.

**CONTACT** Ms. Sherrell Watson-Hall, Director of Financial Aid, Kean University, 1000 Morris Avenue, Union, NJ 07083, 908-737-3220. *Fax:* 908-737-3200. *E-mail:* finaid@kean.edu.

*Website:* http://www.kean.edu/.

# KEENE STATE COLLEGE
### Keene, NH

| Tuition & fees (NH res): $12,938 | Average undergraduate aid package: $10,785 |
|---|---|

**ABOUT THE INSTITUTION** State-supported, coed. *Awards:* certificates, bachelor's, and master's degrees. 69 undergraduate majors. *Total enrollment:* 4,957. Undergraduates: 4,841. Freshmen: 1,267. Federal methodology is used as a basis for awarding need-based institutional aid.

**UNDERGRADUATE EXPENSES** for 2015–2016 *Application fee:* $50. *Tuition, state resident:* full-time $10,410; part-time $440 per credit hour. *Tuition, nonresident:* full-time $18,880; part-time $790 per credit hour. *Required fees:* full-time $2528; $101 per credit hour. Part-time tuition and fees vary according to course load. *Room only:* $9712. Room and board charges vary according to board plan and housing facility.

**FRESHMAN FINANCIAL AID (Fall 2013)** 1,148 applied for aid; of those 78% were deemed to have need. 98% of freshmen with need received aid; of those 8% had need fully met. *Average percent of need met:* 61% (excluding resources awarded to replace EFC). *Average financial aid package:* $11,476 (excluding resources awarded to replace EFC). 15% of all full-time freshmen had no need and received non-need-based gift aid.

**UNDERGRADUATE FINANCIAL AID (Fall 2013)** 3,807 applied for aid; of those 79% were deemed to have need. 99% of undergraduates with need received aid; of those 11% had need fully met. *Average percent of need met:* 61% (excluding resources awarded to replace EFC). *Average financial aid package:* $10,785 (excluding resources awarded to replace EFC). 10% of all full-time undergraduates had no need and received non-need-based gift aid.

**GIFT AID (NEED-BASED)** *Total amount:* $13,206,508 (39% federal, 2% state, 50% institutional, 9% external sources). *Receiving aid:* Freshmen: 50% (633); all full-time undergraduates: 43% (1,953). *Average award:* Freshmen: $6890; Undergraduates: $6459. *Scholarships, grants, and awards:* Federal Pell, FSEOG, state, private, college/university gift aid from institutional funds.

**GIFT AID (NON-NEED-BASED)** *Total amount:* $5,688,001 (88% institutional, 12% external sources). *Receiving aid:* Freshmen: 39% (488). Undergraduates: 25% (1,150). *Average award:* Freshmen: $3545. Undergraduates: $3224. *Scholarships, grants, and awards by category:* Academic interests/achievement: 1,373 awards ($3,752,851 total): general academic interests/achievements. Creative arts/performance: 18 awards ($54,000 total): applied art and design, art/fine arts, cinema/film/broadcasting, dance, general creative arts/performance, music, theater/drama. Special achievements/activities: 62 awards ($113,000 total): general special achievements/activities, leadership. Special characteristics: children and siblings of alumni. *Tuition waivers:* Full or partial for employees or children of employees, senior citizens. *ROTC:* Army cooperative, Air Force cooperative.

**LOANS** *Student loans:* $36,764,343 (32% need-based, 68% non-need-based). 85% of past graduating class borrowed through all loan programs. *Average indebtedness per student:* $33,796. *Average need-based loan:* Freshmen: $3535. Undergraduates: $4295. *Parent loans:* $10,202,651 (100% non-need-based). *Programs:* Federal Direct (Subsidized and Unsubsidized Stafford, PLUS), Perkins, college/university.

**WORK-STUDY** *Federal work-study:* 1,324 jobs averaging $2299. *State or other work-study/employment:* Total amount: $1,048,532 (100% non-need-based). 721 part-time jobs averaging $1454.

**APPLYING FOR FINANCIAL AID** *Required financial aid form:* FAFSA. *Financial aid deadline:* 3/1. *Notification date:* Continuous. Students must reply within 4 weeks of notification.

**CONTACT** Ms. Patricia Blodgett, Director of Financial Aid, Keene State College, 229 Main Street, Keene, NH 03435-2606, 603-358-2280 or toll-free 800-KSC-1909. *Fax:* 603-358-2794. *E-mail:* pblodget@keene.edu.

*Website:* http://www.keene.edu/.

# KEHILATH YAKOV RABBINICAL SEMINARY
### Ossining, NY

**CONTACT** Financial Aid Office, Kehilath Yakov Rabbinical Seminary, 206 Wilson Street, Brooklyn, NY 11211-7207, 718-963-1212.

*Website:* http://kehilathyakov.com/.

# KEISER UNIVERSITY
### Fort Lauderdale, FL

| Tuition & fees: $17,596 | Average undergraduate aid package: N/A |
|---|---|

**ABOUT THE INSTITUTION** Independent, coed. *Awards:* certificates, associate, bachelor's, master's, and doctoral degrees (profile includes data from campuses located in Daytona Beach, Fort Lauderdale, Fort Myers, Jacksonville, Lakeland, Melbourne, Miami, Orlando, Pembroke Pines, Port St. Lucie, Sarasota, Tallahassee, Tampa, and West Palm Beach; not all programs offered at all locations, but many classes offered 100% online). 57 undergraduate majors. *Total enrollment:* 17,129. Undergraduates: 16,039. Freshmen: 2,289. Federal methodology is used as a basis for awarding need-based institutional aid.

**UNDERGRADUATE EXPENSES** for 2015–2016 *Application fee:* $50. *Tuition:* full-time $16,056; part-time $669 per credit hour. Full-time tuition and fees vary according to course load and program. Part-time tuition and fees vary according to course load and program.

**FRESHMAN FINANCIAL AID (Fall 2013)** 1,697 applied for aid; of those 100% were deemed to have need. 100% of freshmen with need received aid.

**UNDERGRADUATE FINANCIAL AID (Fall 2013)** 11,067 applied for aid; of those 100% were deemed to have need. 100% of undergraduates with need received aid.

**GIFT AID (NEED-BASED)** *Total amount:* $118,663,261 (54% federal, 8% state, 30% institutional). *Receiving aid:* Freshmen: 71% (1,126); all full-time undergraduates: 59% (9,530). *Scholarships, grants, and awards:* Federal Pell, FSEOG, state, private, college/university gift aid from institutional funds.

**LOANS** *Student loans:* $186,888,372 (100% need-based). *Parent loans:* $5,621,584 (100% need-based). *Programs:* Federal Direct (Subsidized and Unsubsidized Stafford, PLUS), Perkins.

**WORK-STUDY** *Federal work-study:* jobs available.

**APPLYING FOR FINANCIAL AID** *Required financial aid form:* FAFSA. *Financial aid deadline:* Continuous. *Notification date:* Continuous. Students must reply within 2 weeks of notification.

**CONTACT** Fred Pfeffer, Associate Vice Chancellor for Student Financial Services, Keiser University, 1500 NW 49 Street, Fort Lauderdale, FL 33309, 954-776-4456 or toll-free 888-534-7379. *Fax:* 954-749-4456. *E-mail:* fredp@keiseruniversity.edu.

*Website:* http://www.keiseruniversity.edu/.

# KENDALL COLLEGE
### Chicago, IL

**CONTACT** Chris Miller, Director of Financial Aid, Kendall College, 900 N. North Branch Street, Chicago, IL 60642, 312-752-2428 or toll-free 888-90-KENDALL. *Fax:* 312-752-2267.

*Website:* http://www.kendall.edu/.

# KENNESAW STATE UNIVERSITY
## Kennesaw, GA

| Tuition & fees (GA res): $6932 | Average undergraduate aid package: $4322 |
| --- | --- |

**ABOUT THE INSTITUTION** State-supported, coed. *Awards:* certificates, bachelor's, master's, and doctoral degrees. 52 undergraduate majors. *Total enrollment:* 25,714. Undergraduates: 23,592. Freshmen: 3,674. Federal methodology is used as a basis for awarding need-based institutional aid.

**UNDERGRADUATE EXPENSES for 2015–2016** *Application fee:* $40. *Tuition, state resident:* full-time $5098; part-time $170 per credit hour. *Tuition, nonresident:* full-time $17,994; part-time $600 per credit hour. *Required fees:* full-time $1834; $917 per term. Part-time tuition and fees vary according to course load. *College room and board:* $7914. Room and board charges vary according to board plan, housing facility, and student level.

**FRESHMAN FINANCIAL AID (Fall 2014, est.)** 3,330 applied for aid; of those 75% were deemed to have need. 96% of freshmen with need received aid; of those 14% had need fully met. *Average percent of need met:* 84% (excluding resources awarded to replace EFC). *Average financial aid package:* $4422 (excluding resources awarded to replace EFC). 1% of all full-time freshmen had no need and received non-need-based gift aid.

**UNDERGRADUATE FINANCIAL AID (Fall 2014, est.)** 14,813 applied for aid; of those 82% were deemed to have need. 96% of undergraduates with need received aid; of those 18% had need fully met. *Average percent of need met:* 67% (excluding resources awarded to replace EFC). *Average financial aid package:* $4322 (excluding resources awarded to replace EFC). 1% of all full-time undergraduates had no need and received non-need-based gift aid.

**GIFT AID (NEED-BASED)** *Total amount:* $39,946,406 (97% federal, 2% state, 1% institutional). *Receiving aid:* Freshmen: 53% (1,948); all full-time undergraduates: 58% (10,365). *Average award:* Freshmen: $2833; Undergraduates: $3407. *Scholarships, grants, and awards:* Federal Pell, FSEOG, state, private, college/university gift aid from institutional funds.

**GIFT AID (NON-NEED-BASED)** *Total amount:* $34,124,096 (97% state, 3% institutional). *Receiving aid:* Freshmen: 48% (1,751). Undergraduates: 29% (5,221). *Average award:* Freshmen: $935. Undergraduates: $1218. *Scholarships, grants, and awards by category:* Academic interests/achievement: biological sciences, business, communication, computer science, education, English, foreign languages, general academic interests/achievements, health fields, humanities, international studies, mathematics, physical sciences, premedicine, social sciences. *Creative arts/performance:* art/fine arts, dance, music, performing arts, theater/drama. *Special achievements/activities:* community service, leadership, memberships. *Special characteristics:* children and siblings of alumni, children of union members/company employees, children of workers in trades, ethnic background, general special characteristics, handicapped students, international students, local/state students, members of minority groups, religious affiliation, veterans' children. *Tuition waivers:* Full or partial for employees or children of employees, senior citizens. *ROTC:* Army cooperative, Air Force cooperative.

**LOANS** *Student loans:* $91,988,749 (48% need-based, 52% non-need-based). 63% of past graduating class borrowed through all loan programs. *Average indebtedness per student:* $24,740. *Average need-based loan:* Freshmen: $1295. Undergraduates: $1789. *Parent loans:* $7,480,819 (100% non-need-based). *Programs:* Federal Direct (Subsidized and Unsubsidized Stafford, PLUS), Perkins.

**WORK-STUDY** *Federal work-study:* Total amount: $456,381; 162 jobs averaging $2817.

**ATHLETIC AWARDS** Total amount: $1,759,900 (100% non-need-based).

**APPLYING FOR FINANCIAL AID** *Required financial aid form:* FAFSA. *Financial aid deadline (priority):* 4/1. *Notification date:* Continuous beginning 4/1.

**CONTACT** Mr. Ron H. Day, Director of Student Financial Aid, Kennesaw State University, 585 Cobb Avenue, NW, Mail Drop #0119, Kennesaw, GA 30144-5591, 770-423-6074. *Fax:* 470-578-9096. *E-mail:* finaid@kennesaw.edu. *Website:* http://www.kennesaw.edu/.

# KENT STATE UNIVERSITY
## Kent, OH

| Tuition & fees (OH res): $10,012 | Average undergraduate aid package: $8888 |
| --- | --- |

**ABOUT THE INSTITUTION** State-supported, coed. *Awards:* certificates, bachelor's, master's, and doctoral degrees. 92 undergraduate majors. *Total enrollment:* 29,477. Undergraduates: 23,328. Freshmen: 4,272. Federal methodology is used as a basis for awarding need-based institutional aid.

**UNDERGRADUATE EXPENSES for 2015–2016** *Application fee:* $45. *One-time required fee:* $150. *Tuition, state resident:* full-time $10,012; part-time $456 per credit hour. *Tuition, nonresident:* full-time $17,972; part-time $818 per credit hour. Full-time tuition and fees vary according to course load. Part-time tuition and fees vary according to course load. *College room and board:* $9908; *Room only:* $6108. Room and board charges vary according to board plan and housing facility.

**FRESHMAN FINANCIAL AID (Fall 2014, est.)** 3,755 applied for aid; of those 81% were deemed to have need. 99% of freshmen with need received aid; of those 13% had need fully met. *Average percent of need met:* 55% (excluding resources awarded to replace EFC). *Average financial aid package:* $9571 (excluding resources awarded to replace EFC). 19% of all full-time freshmen had no need and received non-need-based gift aid.

**UNDERGRADUATE FINANCIAL AID (Fall 2014, est.)** 14,951 applied for aid; of those 85% were deemed to have need. 98% of undergraduates with need received aid; of those 8% had need fully met. *Average percent of need met:* 46% (excluding resources awarded to replace EFC). *Average financial aid package:* $8888 (excluding resources awarded to replace EFC). 15% of all full-time undergraduates had no need and received non-need-based gift aid.

**GIFT AID (NEED-BASED)** *Total amount:* $66,341,579 (47% federal, 7% state, 40% institutional, 6% external sources). *Receiving aid:* Freshmen: 37% (1,578); all full-time undergraduates: 36% (6,969). *Average award:* Freshmen: $5292; Undergraduates: $5190. *Scholarships, grants, and awards:* Federal Pell, FSEOG, state, private, college/university gift aid from institutional funds.

**GIFT AID (NON-NEED-BASED)** *Total amount:* $16,470,875 (12% federal, 9% state, 72% institutional, 7% external sources). *Receiving aid:* Freshmen: 55% (2,315). Undergraduates: 33% (6,424). *Average award:* Freshmen: $5274. Undergraduates: $4660. *Scholarships, grants, and awards by category:* Academic interests/achievement: architecture, area/ethnic studies, biological sciences, business, communication, computer science, education, engineering/technologies, English, foreign languages, general academic interests/achievements, health fields, humanities, international studies, library science, mathematics, military science, physical sciences, premedicine, religion/biblical studies, social sciences. *Creative arts/performance:* applied art and design, art/fine arts, cinema/film/broadcasting, creative writing, dance, general creative arts/performance, journalism/publications, music, performing arts, theater/drama. *Special achievements/activities:* community service, general special achievements/activities, leadership. *Special characteristics:* adult students, children and siblings of alumni, children of faculty/staff, children of union members/company employees, ethnic background, first-generation college students, handicapped students, international students, local/state students, members of minority groups, out-of-state students, previous college experience, veterans, veterans' children. *Tuition waivers:* Full or partial for employees or children of employees, senior citizens. *ROTC:* Army, Air Force.

**LOANS** *Student loans:* $118,979,090 (43% need-based, 57% non-need-based). 75% of past graduating class borrowed through all loan programs. *Average indebtedness per student:* $32,393. *Average need-based loan:* Freshmen: $4099. Undergraduates: $4564. *Parent loans:* $30,720,786 (57% need-based, 43% non-need-based). *Programs:* Federal Direct (Subsidized and Unsubsidized Stafford, PLUS), Perkins, Federal Nursing, state, college/university, alternative loans.

**WORK-STUDY** *Federal work-study:* Total amount: $2,147,973; 709 jobs averaging $2745.

**ATHLETIC AWARDS** Total amount: $5,893,067 (57% need-based, 43% non-need-based).

**APPLYING FOR FINANCIAL AID** *Required financial aid form:* FAFSA. *Financial aid deadline (priority):* 3/1. *Notification date:* 3/15. Students must reply within 2 weeks of notification.

**CONTACT** Mark A. Evans, Director of Student Financial Aid, Kent State University, 103 Schwartz Center, Kent, OH 44242-0001, 330-672-2972 or toll-free 800-988-KENT. *Fax:* 330-672-4014. *E-mail:* mevans@kent.edu. *Website:* http://www.kent.edu/.

# KENT STATE UNIVERSITY AT GEAUGA
## Burton, OH

| Tuition & fees (OH res): $5664 | Average undergraduate aid package: $6607 |
|---|---|

**ABOUT THE INSTITUTION** State-supported, coed. **Awards:** associate, bachelor's, and master's degrees. 10 undergraduate majors. **Total enrollment:** 2,725. Undergraduates: 2,725. Freshmen: 340. Federal methodology is used as a basis for awarding need-based institutional aid.

**UNDERGRADUATE EXPENSES for 2015–2016 Application fee:** $40. **One-time required fee:** $150. **Tuition, state resident:** full-time $5664; part-time $258 per credit hour. **Tuition, nonresident:** full-time $13,624; part-time $620 per credit hour. Full-time tuition and fees vary according to course level and course load. Part-time tuition and fees vary according to course level and course load.

**FRESHMAN FINANCIAL AID (Fall 2014, est.)** 236 applied for aid; of those 85% were deemed to have need. 95% of freshmen with need received aid; of those 5% had need fully met. **Average percent of need met:** 45% (excluding resources awarded to replace EFC). **Average financial aid package:** $6229 (excluding resources awarded to replace EFC). 2% of all full-time freshmen had no need and received non-need-based gift aid.

**UNDERGRADUATE FINANCIAL AID (Fall 2014, est.)** 650 applied for aid; of those 88% were deemed to have need. 96% of undergraduates with need received aid; of those 5% had need fully met. **Average percent of need met:** 41% (excluding resources awarded to replace EFC). **Average financial aid package:** $6607 (excluding resources awarded to replace EFC). 1% of all full-time undergraduates had no need and received non-need-based gift aid.

**GIFT AID (NEED-BASED) Total amount:** $2,834,786 (97% federal, 2% institutional, 1% external sources). **Receiving aid:** Freshmen: 48% (134); all full-time undergraduates: 48% (385). **Average award:** Freshmen: $4657; Undergraduates: $4522. **Scholarships, grants, and awards:** Federal Pell, FSEOG, state, private, college/university gift aid from institutional funds.

**GIFT AID (NON-NEED-BASED) Total amount:** $84,767 (43% federal, 35% state, 15% institutional, 7% external sources). **Receiving aid:** Freshmen: 8% (21). Undergraduates: 7% (56). **Average award:** Freshmen: $917. Undergraduates: $953. **Scholarships, grants, and awards by category:** Academic interests/achievement: business, education, general academic interests/achievements, health fields, humanities. Special characteristics: children of faculty/staff, out-of-state students. Tuition waivers: Full or partial for employees or children of employees, senior citizens. ROTC: Army cooperative, Air Force cooperative.

**LOANS Student loans:** $6,904,950 (46% need-based, 54% non-need-based). **Average need-based loan:** Freshmen: $3442. Undergraduates: $3817. **Parent loans:** $298,284 (59% need-based, 41% non-need-based). **Programs:** Federal Direct (Subsidized and Unsubsidized Stafford, PLUS), Perkins, Federal Nursing, state, college/university, alternative loans.

**WORK-STUDY Federal work-study:** Total amount: $54,981; jobs available.

**APPLYING FOR FINANCIAL AID Required financial aid form:** FAFSA. **Financial aid deadline (priority):** 3/1. **Notification date:** 3/15. Students must reply within 2 weeks of notification.

**CONTACT** Donna Holcomb, Financial Aid Advisor, Kent State University at Geauga, 14111 Claridon-Troy Road, Burton, OH 44021, 440-834-3737. *Fax:* 440-834-8846. *E-mail:* dholcomb@kent.edu.
*Website:* http://www.geauga.kent.edu/.

# KENT STATE UNIVERSITY AT STARK
## Canton, OH

| Tuition & fees (OH res): $5664 | Average undergraduate aid package: $6718 |
|---|---|

**ABOUT THE INSTITUTION** State-supported, coed. **Awards:** associate, bachelor's, and master's degrees. 18 undergraduate majors. **Total enrollment:** 4,678. Undergraduates: 4,639. Freshmen: 631. Federal methodology is used as a basis for awarding need-based institutional aid.

**UNDERGRADUATE EXPENSES for 2015–2016 Application fee:** $40. **One-time required fee:** $150. **Tuition, state resident:** full-time $5664; part-time $258 per credit hour. **Tuition, nonresident:** full-time $13,624; part-time $620 per credit hour. Full-time tuition and fees vary according to course level and course load. Part-time tuition and fees vary according to course level and course load.

**FRESHMAN FINANCIAL AID (Fall 2014, est.)** 479 applied for aid; of those 86% were deemed to have need. 97% of freshmen with need received aid; of those 5% had need fully met. **Average percent of need met:** 45% (excluding resources awarded to replace EFC). **Average financial aid package:** $5715 (excluding resources awarded to replace EFC). 9% of all full-time freshmen had no need and received non-need-based gift aid.

**UNDERGRADUATE FINANCIAL AID (Fall 2014, est.)** 2,002 applied for aid; of those 90% were deemed to have need. 98% of undergraduates with need received aid; of those 5% had need fully met. **Average percent of need met:** 43% (excluding resources awarded to replace EFC). **Average financial aid package:** $6718 (excluding resources awarded to replace EFC). 4% of all full-time undergraduates had no need and received non-need-based gift aid.

**GIFT AID (NEED-BASED) Total amount:** $8,961,291 (90% federal, 8% institutional, 2% external sources). **Receiving aid:** Freshmen: 53% (292); all full-time undergraduates: 61% (1,415). **Average award:** Freshmen: $4389; Undergraduates: $4193. **Scholarships, grants, and awards:** Federal Pell, FSEOG, state, private, college/university gift aid from institutional funds.

**GIFT AID (NON-NEED-BASED) Total amount:** $488,074 (28% federal, 21% state, 41% institutional, 10% external sources). **Receiving aid:** Freshmen: 26% (140). Undergraduates: 13% (293). **Average award:** Freshmen: $1809. Undergraduates: $1994. **Scholarships, grants, and awards by category:** Academic interests/achievement: business, communication, education, foreign languages, general academic interests/achievements, health fields, social sciences. Creative arts/performance: journalism/publications, music, performing arts, theater/drama. Special achievements/activities: community service. Special characteristics: adult students, children and siblings of alumni, children of faculty/staff, first-generation college students, general special characteristics, members of minority groups, out-of-state students, public servants, veterans. Tuition waivers: Full or partial for employees or children of employees, senior citizens. ROTC: Army cooperative, Air Force cooperative.

**LOANS Student loans:** $17,085,721 (49% need-based, 51% non-need-based). **Average need-based loan:** Freshmen: $3332. Undergraduates: $3958. **Parent loans:** $418,884 (55% need-based, 45% non-need-based). **Programs:** Federal Direct (Subsidized and Unsubsidized Stafford, PLUS), Perkins, Federal Nursing, state, college/university, alternative loans.

**WORK-STUDY Federal work-study:** Total amount: $101,850; jobs available.

**APPLYING FOR FINANCIAL AID Required financial aid form:** FAFSA. **Financial aid deadline (priority):** 3/1. **Notification date:** 3/15. Students must reply within 2 weeks of notification.

**CONTACT** Amber Wallace, Assistant Director for Financial Aid, Kent State University at Stark, 134 Main Hall, North Canton, OH 44720, 330-244-3257. *Fax:* 330-499-0301. *E-mail:* gpukys@kent.edu.
*Website:* http://www.stark.kent.edu/.

# KENTUCKY CHRISTIAN UNIVERSITY
## Grayson, KY

| Tuition & fees: $17,810 | Average undergraduate aid package: $14,428 |
|---|---|

**ABOUT THE INSTITUTION** Independent Christian Churches and Churches of Christ, coed. **Awards:** bachelor's and master's degrees. 20 undergraduate majors. **Total enrollment:** 637. Undergraduates: 602. Freshmen: 171. Federal methodology is used as a basis for awarding need-based institutional aid.

**UNDERGRADUATE EXPENSES for 2015–2016 Application fee:** $30. **Comprehensive fee:** $25,610 includes full-time tuition ($17,400), mandatory fees ($410), and room and board ($7800). Full-time tuition and fees vary according to course load. Room and board charges vary according to housing facility. **Part-time tuition:** $580 per credit. Part-time tuition and fees vary according to class time, course load, and program.

**FRESHMAN FINANCIAL AID (Fall 2013)** 125 applied for aid; of those 95% were deemed to have need. 100% of freshmen with need received aid; of those 7% had need fully met. **Average percent of need met:** 58% (excluding resources awarded to replace EFC). **Average financial aid package:** $13,628 (excluding resources

awarded to replace EFC). 8% of all full-time freshmen had no need and received non-need-based gift aid.

**UNDERGRADUATE FINANCIAL AID (Fall 2013)** 485 applied for aid; of those 93% were deemed to have need. 100% of undergraduates with need received aid; of those 9% had need fully met. *Average percent of need met:* 62% (excluding resources awarded to replace EFC). *Average financial aid package:* $14,428 (excluding resources awarded to replace EFC). 10% of all full-time undergraduates had no need and received non-need-based gift aid.

**GIFT AID (NEED-BASED)** *Total amount:* $1,795,279 (67% federal, 33% state). *Receiving aid:* Freshmen: 67% (86); all full-time undergraduates: 64% (325). *Average award:* Freshmen: $5282; Undergraduates: $5354. *Scholarships, grants, and awards:* Federal Pell, FSEOG, state, private, college/university gift aid from institutional funds.

**GIFT AID (NON-NEED-BASED)** *Total amount:* $3,284,836 (8% state, 81% institutional, 11% external sources). *Receiving aid:* Freshmen: 92% (119). Undergraduates: 89% (453). *Average award:* Freshmen: $7966. Undergraduates: $7313. *Scholarships, grants, and awards by category: Academic interests/achievement:* 331 awards ($945,672 total): business, education, general academic interests/achievements, health fields, humanities, international studies, premedicine, religion/biblical studies. *Creative arts/performance:* 43 awards ($111,166 total): debating, music, performing arts, theater/drama. *Special achievements/activities:* 310 awards ($1,139,255 total): cheerleading/drum major, community service, general special achievements/activities, leadership, religious involvement. *Special characteristics:* 220 awards ($480,514 total): children and siblings of alumni, children of faculty/staff, ethnic background, general special characteristics, international students, local/state students, members of minority groups, previous college experience, religious affiliation, spouses of current students. *Tuition waivers:* Full or partial for employees or children of employees.

**LOANS** *Student loans:* $3,420,794 (45% need-based, 55% non-need-based). 61% of past graduating class borrowed through all loan programs. *Average indebtedness per student:* $30,578. *Average need-based loan:* Freshmen: $3218. Undergraduates: $3986. *Parent loans:* $460,891 (100% non-need-based). *Programs:* Federal Direct (Subsidized and Unsubsidized Stafford, PLUS), Perkins.

**WORK-STUDY** *Federal work-study:* 234 jobs averaging $1261. *State or other work-study/employment:* Total amount: $65,786 (100% non-need-based). 44 part-time jobs averaging $1495.

**ATHLETIC AWARDS** Total amount: $521,431 (100% non-need-based).

**APPLYING FOR FINANCIAL AID** *Required financial aid form:* FAFSA. *Financial aid deadline (priority):* 3/1. *Notification date:* Continuous beginning 3/15. Students must reply within 2 weeks of notification.

**CONTACT** Mrs. Jennie M. Bender, Director of Financial Aid, Kentucky Christian University, 100 Academic Parkway, Grayson, KY 41143-2205, 606-474-3226 or toll-free 800-522-3181. *Fax:* 606-474-3268. *E-mail:* jbender@kcu.edu. *Website:* http://www.kcu.edu/.

# KENTUCKY MOUNTAIN BIBLE COLLEGE
## Vancleve, KY

**CONTACT** Mrs. Rosita Marshall, Director of Financial Aid, Kentucky Mountain Bible College, PO Box 10, Vancleve, KY 41385-0010, 800-879-KMBC Ext. 175 or toll-free 800-879-KMBC. *Fax:* 800-659-4324. *E-mail:* finaid@kmbc.edu. *Website:* http://www.kmbc.edu/.

# KENTUCKY STATE UNIVERSITY
## Frankfort, KY

| Tuition & fees (KY res): $7404 | Average undergraduate aid package: $12,182 |
|---|---|

**ABOUT THE INSTITUTION** State-related, coed. *Awards:* associate, bachelor's, master's, and doctoral degrees. 26 undergraduate majors. *Total enrollment:* 1,895. Undergraduates: 1,754. Freshmen: 289. Federal methodology is used as a basis for awarding need-based institutional aid.

**UNDERGRADUATE EXPENSES** for 2015–2016 *Tuition, state resident:* full-time $7014; part-time $292.25 per credit hour. *Tuition, nonresident:* full-time

$16,824; part-time $701 per credit hour. *Required fees:* full-time $390; $13 per credit hour. Full-time tuition and fees vary according to course load and degree level. Part-time tuition and fees vary according to course load and degree level. *College room and board:* $6690; *Room only:* $3340. Room and board charges vary according to board plan and housing facility.

**FRESHMAN FINANCIAL AID (Fall 2014, est.)** 274 applied for aid; of those 95% were deemed to have need. 98% of freshmen with need received aid; of those 17% had need fully met. *Average percent of need met:* 59% (excluding resources awarded to replace EFC). *Average financial aid package:* $12,463 (excluding resources awarded to replace EFC). 4% of all full-time freshmen had no need and received non-need-based gift aid.

**UNDERGRADUATE FINANCIAL AID (Fall 2014, est.)** 1,300 applied for aid; of those 95% were deemed to have need. 99% of undergraduates with need received aid; of those 12% had need fully met. *Average percent of need met:* 59% (excluding resources awarded to replace EFC). *Average financial aid package:* $12,182 (excluding resources awarded to replace EFC). 3% of all full-time undergraduates had no need and received non-need-based gift aid.

**GIFT AID (NEED-BASED)** *Total amount:* $9,972,449 (57% federal, 8% state, 34% institutional, 1% external sources). *Receiving aid:* Freshmen: 87% (246); all full-time undergraduates: 83% (1,149). *Average award:* Freshmen: $8919; Undergraduates: $8090. *Scholarships, grants, and awards:* Federal Pell, FSEOG, state, college/university gift aid from institutional funds.

**GIFT AID (NON-NEED-BASED)** *Total amount:* $742,631 (2% federal, 14% state, 82% institutional, 2% external sources). *Receiving aid:* Freshmen: 6% (16). Undergraduates: 4% (52). *Average award:* Freshmen: $9724. Undergraduates: $9663. *Scholarships, grants, and awards by category: Academic interests/achievement:* 315 awards ($851,458 total): computer science, general academic interests/achievements. *Creative arts/performance:* 44 awards ($119,167 total): art/fine arts, music, performing arts. *Special achievements/activities:* 62 awards ($344,280 total): cheerleading/drum major. *Special characteristics:* 82 awards ($354,808 total): adult students, children of faculty/staff, children with a deceased or disabled parent, ethnic background, local/state students, previous college experience, public servants, veterans. *Tuition waivers:* Full or partial for employees or children of employees, senior citizens. *ROTC:* Army cooperative, Air Force cooperative.

**LOANS** *Student loans:* $10,362,122 (92% need-based, 8% non-need-based). 54% of past graduating class borrowed through all loan programs. *Average indebtedness per student:* $34,110. *Average need-based loan:* Freshmen: $3386. Undergraduates: $4132. *Parent loans:* $1,601,959 (72% need-based, 28% non-need-based). *Programs:* Federal Direct (Subsidized and Unsubsidized Stafford, PLUS), alternative loans.

**WORK-STUDY** *Federal work-study:* Total amount: $527,188; 115 jobs averaging $4584. *State or other work-study/employment:* Total amount: $153,010 (54% need-based, 46% non-need-based). 96 part-time jobs averaging $1594.

**ATHLETIC AWARDS** Total amount: $1,038,798 (87% need-based, 13% non-need-based).

**APPLYING FOR FINANCIAL AID** *Required financial aid form:* FAFSA. *Financial aid deadline (priority):* 4/15. *Notification date:* Continuous beginning 3/15. Students must reply within 4 weeks of notification.

**CONTACT** Ms. Victoria Owens, Director of Financial Aid, Kentucky State University, 400 East Main Street, Frankfort, KY 40601, 502-597-6033 or toll-free 877-367-5978. *Fax:* 502-597-5950. *E-mail:* victoria.owens@kysu.edu. *Website:* http://www.kysu.edu/.

# KENTUCKY WESLEYAN COLLEGE
## Owensboro, KY

| Tuition & fees: $22,030 | Average undergraduate aid package: $16,223 |
|---|---|

**ABOUT THE INSTITUTION** Independent Methodist, coed. *Awards:* bachelor's degrees. 39 undergraduate majors. *Total enrollment:* 709. Undergraduates: 709. Freshmen: 239. Federal methodology is used as a basis for awarding need-based institutional aid.

**UNDERGRADUATE EXPENSES** for 2015–2016 *Comprehensive fee:* $29,830 includes full-time tuition ($21,400), mandatory fees ($630), and room and board ($7800). Full-time tuition and fees vary according to course load. Room and board charges vary according to board plan and housing facility. *Part-time tuition:* $610 per credit. Part-time tuition and fees vary according to course load.

**FRESHMAN FINANCIAL AID (Fall 2013)** 161 applied for aid; of those 89% were deemed to have need. 98% of freshmen with need received aid; of those 21% had need fully met. *Average percent of need met:* 68% (excluding resources awarded to replace EFC). *Average financial aid package:* $16,118 (excluding resources awarded to replace EFC). 13% of all full-time freshmen had no need and received non-need-based gift aid.

**UNDERGRADUATE FINANCIAL AID (Fall 2013)** 657 applied for aid; of those 92% were deemed to have need. 99% of undergraduates with need received aid; of those 20% had need fully met. *Average percent of need met:* 72% (excluding resources awarded to replace EFC). *Average financial aid package:* $16,223 (excluding resources awarded to replace EFC). 12% of all full-time undergraduates had no need and received non-need-based gift aid.

**GIFT AID (NEED-BASED)** *Total amount:* $7,743,809 (20% federal, 20% state, 52% institutional, 8% external sources). *Receiving aid:* Freshmen: 84% (141); all full-time undergraduates: 85% (590). *Average award:* Freshmen: $13,646; Undergraduates: $13,036. *Scholarships, grants, and awards:* Federal Pell, FSEOG, state, private, college/university gift aid from institutional funds.

**GIFT AID (NON-NEED-BASED)** *Total amount:* $1,403,180 (9% state, 77% institutional, 14% external sources). *Receiving aid:* Freshmen: 13% (21). Undergraduates: 10% (67). *Average award:* Freshmen: $12,589. Undergraduates: $9746. *Scholarships, grants, and awards by category: Academic interests/ achievement:* general academic interests/achievements. *Creative arts/performance:* art/fine arts, creative writing, general creative arts/performance, music, performing arts. *Special achievements/activities:* general special achievements/activities, junior miss, leadership. *Special characteristics:* children and siblings of alumni, children of faculty/staff, general special characteristics, local/state students, out-of-state students, relatives of clergy, religious affiliation, veterans. *Tuition waivers:* Full or partial for children of alumni, employees or children of employees, senior citizens. *ROTC:* Army cooperative.

**LOANS** *Student loans:* $3,798,534 (76% need-based, 24% non-need-based). 83% of past graduating class borrowed through all loan programs. *Average indebtedness per student:* $24,150. *Average need-based loan:* Freshmen: $3157. Undergraduates: $3914. *Parent loans:* $489,464 (42% need-based, 58% non-need-based). *Programs:* Federal Direct (Subsidized and Unsubsidized Stafford, PLUS), Perkins.

**WORK-STUDY** *Federal work-study:* jobs available. *State or other work-study/employment:* Part-time jobs available.

**APPLYING FOR FINANCIAL AID** *Required financial aid form:* FAFSA. *Financial aid deadline:* 3/15. *Notification date:* Continuous. Students must reply within 2 weeks of notification.

**CONTACT** Mrs. Samantha Hays, Director of Financial Aid, Kentucky Wesleyan College, 3000 Frederica Street, Owensboro, KY 42301, 270-852-3130 or toll-free 800-999-0592 (in-state), 800-990-0592 (out-of-state). *Fax:* 270-852-3133. *E-mail:* shays@kwc.edu. *Website:* http://www.kwc.edu/.

# KENYON COLLEGE
## Gambier, OH

| Tuition & fees: $49,140 | Average undergraduate aid package: $40,946 |
| --- | --- |

**ABOUT THE INSTITUTION** Independent, coed. *Awards:* bachelor's degrees. 35 undergraduate majors. *Total enrollment:* 1,662. Undergraduates: 1,662. Freshmen: 448. Both federal and institutional methodology are used as a basis for awarding need-based institutional aid.

**UNDERGRADUATE EXPENSES** for 2015–2016 *Comprehensive fee:* $61,030 includes full-time tuition ($47,220), mandatory fees ($1920), and room and board ($11,890). *College room only:* $5170. Full-time tuition and fees vary according to reciprocity agreements. Room and board charges vary according to housing facility and student level. Part-time tuition and fees vary according to reciprocity agreements.

**FRESHMAN FINANCIAL AID (Fall 2014, est.)** 270 applied for aid; of those 81% were deemed to have need. 100% of freshmen with need received aid; of those 58% had need fully met. *Average percent of need met:* 95% (excluding resources awarded to replace EFC). *Average financial aid package:* $39,738 (excluding resources awarded to replace EFC). 6% of all full-time freshmen had no need and received non-need-based gift aid.

**UNDERGRADUATE FINANCIAL AID (Fall 2014, est.)** 853 applied for aid; of those 85% were deemed to have need. 100% of undergraduates with need received aid; of those 61% had need fully met. *Average percent of need met:* 95% (excluding resources awarded to replace EFC). *Average financial aid package:* $40,946 (excluding resources awarded to replace EFC). 11% of all full-time undergraduates had no need and received non-need-based gift aid.

**GIFT AID (NEED-BASED)** *Total amount:* $26,741,420 (4% federal, 93% institutional, 3% external sources). *Receiving aid:* Freshmen: 47% (212); all full-time undergraduates: 39% (703). *Average award:* Freshmen: $37,450; Undergraduates: $38,039. *Scholarships, grants, and awards:* Federal Pell, FSEOG, state, private, college/university gift aid from institutional funds.

**GIFT AID (NON-NEED-BASED)** *Total amount:* $4,679,069 (70% institutional, 30% external sources). *Receiving aid:* Freshmen: 9% (41). Undergraduates: 6% (110). *Average award:* Freshmen: $12,884. Undergraduates: $13,311. *Scholarships, grants, and awards by category: Academic interests/achievement:* 244 awards ($3,364,000 total): general academic interests/achievements. *Creative arts/performance:* 21 awards ($279,000 total): art/fine arts, creative writing, music. *Special characteristics:* 53 awards ($1,036,660 total): ethnic background, first-generation college students. *Tuition waivers:* Full or partial for employees or children of employees.

**LOANS** *Student loans:* $5,049,444 (57% need-based, 43% non-need-based). 46% of past graduating class borrowed through all loan programs. *Average indebtedness per student:* $20,323. *Average need-based loan:* Freshmen: $2712. Undergraduates: $3900. *Parent loans:* $1,784,844 (7% need-based, 93% non-need-based). *Programs:* Federal Direct (Subsidized and Unsubsidized Stafford, PLUS), Perkins, college/university.

**WORK-STUDY** *Federal work-study:* Total amount: $344,233; 277 jobs averaging $1691. *State or other work-study/employment:* Total amount: $574,552 (63% need-based, 37% non-need-based). 139 part-time jobs averaging $1710.

**APPLYING FOR FINANCIAL AID** *Required financial aid forms:* FAFSA, CSS Financial Aid PROFILE, noncustodial (divorced/separated) parent's statement, federal income tax form(s). *Financial aid deadline (priority):* 2/15. *Notification date:* 4/1. Students must reply by 5/1.

**CONTACT** Mr. Craig Daugherty, Director of Financial Aid, Kenyon College, Edelstein House, Gambier, OH 43022-9623, 740-427-5430 or toll-free 800-848-2468. *Fax:* 740-427-5240. *E-mail:* daugherty@kenyon.edu. *Website:* http://www.kenyon.edu/.

# KETTERING COLLEGE
## Kettering, OH

**CONTACT** Financial Aid Office, Kettering College, 3737 Southern Boulevard, Kettering, OH 45429-1299, 937-395-8601 or toll-free 800-433-5262. *Website:* http://www.kc.edu/.

# KETTERING UNIVERSITY
## Flint, MI

**ABOUT THE INSTITUTION** Independent, coed. *Awards:* bachelor's and master's degrees. 15 undergraduate majors. *Total enrollment:* 2,089. Undergraduates: 1,741. Freshmen: 364.

**GIFT AID (NEED-BASED)** *Scholarships, grants, and awards:* Federal Pell, FSEOG, state, private, college/university gift aid from institutional funds, United Negro College Fund.

**GIFT AID (NON-NEED-BASED)** *Scholarships, grants, and awards by category: Academic interests/achievement:* business, computer science, engineering/technologies, general academic interests/achievements, mathematics, physical sciences. *Special achievements/activities:* general special achievements/activities, leadership, memberships. *Special characteristics:* children of faculty/staff, siblings of current students.

**LOANS** *Programs:* Federal Direct (Subsidized and Unsubsidized Stafford, PLUS).

**WORK-STUDY** *Federal work-study:* jobs available.

**APPLYING FOR FINANCIAL AID** *Required financial aid form:* FAFSA.

**CONTACT** Diane Bice, Director of Financial Aid, Kettering University, 1700 University Avenue, Flint, MI 48504, 800-955-4464 Ext. 7859 or toll-free 800-955-4464 Ext. 7865 (in-state), 800-955-4464 (out-of-state). *Fax:* 810-762-9807. *E-mail:* finaid@ kettering.edu.
*Website:* http://www.kettering.edu/.

# KEUKA COLLEGE
### Keuka Park, NY

| Tuition & fees: $28,235 | Average undergraduate aid package: $18,697 |
|---|---|

**ABOUT THE INSTITUTION** Independent American Baptist Churches in the U.S.A., coed. *Awards:* bachelor's and master's degrees. 34 undergraduate majors. *Total enrollment:* 1,999. Undergraduates: 1,803. Freshmen: 220. Federal methodology is used as a basis for awarding need-based institutional aid.

**UNDERGRADUATE EXPENSES for 2015–2016** *Application fee:* $30. *Comprehensive fee:* $39,035 includes full-time tuition ($27,260), mandatory fees ($975), and room and board ($10,800). *College room only:* $5130. Full-time tuition and fees vary according to degree level and program. Room and board charges vary according to board plan and housing facility. *Part-time tuition:* $910 per credit hour. Part-time tuition and fees vary according to program.

**FRESHMAN FINANCIAL AID (Fall 2013)** 222 applied for aid; of those 96% were deemed to have need. 100% of freshmen with need received aid; of those 7% had need fully met. *Average percent of need met:* 70% (excluding resources awarded to replace EFC). *Average financial aid package:* $22,663 (excluding resources awarded to replace EFC). 3% of all full-time freshmen had no need and received non-need-based gift aid.

**UNDERGRADUATE FINANCIAL AID (Fall 2013)** 1,248 applied for aid; of those 95% were deemed to have need. 100% of undergraduates with need received aid; of those 10% had need fully met. *Average percent of need met:* 65% (excluding resources awarded to replace EFC). *Average financial aid package:* $18,697 (excluding resources awarded to replace EFC). 2% of all full-time undergraduates had no need and received non-need-based gift aid.

**GIFT AID (NEED-BASED)** *Total amount:* $14,216,921 (18% federal, 12% state, 68% institutional, 2% external sources). *Receiving aid:* Freshmen: 88% (197); all full-time undergraduates: 73% (970). *Average award:* Freshmen: $9996; Undergraduates: $8059. *Scholarships, grants, and awards:* Federal Pell, FSEOG, state, college/university gift aid from institutional funds.

**GIFT AID (NON-NEED-BASED)** *Total amount:* $1,515,411 (17% federal, 10% state, 63% institutional, 10% external sources). *Receiving aid:* Freshmen: 81% (182). Undergraduates: 55% (737). *Average award:* Freshmen: $9911. Undergraduates: $12,952. *Scholarships, grants, and awards by category:* Academic interests/achievement: general academic interests/achievements, international studies. *Special achievements/activities:* community service, general special achievements/activities, leadership. *Special characteristics:* children and siblings of alumni, children of faculty/staff, international students, siblings of current students. *Tuition waivers:* Full or partial for employees or children of employees.

**LOANS** *Student loans:* $13,120,826 (88% need-based, 12% non-need-based). *Average need-based loan:* Freshmen: $3584. Undergraduates: $4332. *Programs:* Perkins.

**WORK-STUDY** *Federal work-study:* jobs available. *State or other work-study/employment:* Total amount: $138,926 (23% need-based, 77% non-need-based). Part-time jobs available.

**APPLYING FOR FINANCIAL AID** *Required financial aid form:* FAFSA. *Financial aid deadline:* Continuous. *Notification date:* Continuous beginning 3/1. Students must reply by 5/1 or within 2 weeks of notification.

**CONTACT** Jennifer Bates, Director of Financial Aid, Keuka College, 141 Central Avenue, Keuka Park, NY 14478-0098, 315-279-5232 or toll-free 800-33-KEUKA. *Fax:* 315-536-5327. *E-mail:* jbates@keuka.edu.
*Website:* http://www.keuka.edu/.

# KEYSTONE COLLEGE
### La Plume, PA

| Tuition & fees: $21,900 | Average undergraduate aid package: $17,679 |
|---|---|

**ABOUT THE INSTITUTION** Independent, coed. *Awards:* certificates, associate, bachelor's, and master's degrees. 42 undergraduate majors. *Total enrollment:* 1,484. Undergraduates: 1,461. Freshmen: 314. Federal methodology is used as a basis for awarding need-based institutional aid.

**UNDERGRADUATE EXPENSES for 2015–2016** *Application fee:* $30. *One-time required fee:* $500. *Comprehensive fee:* $31,800 includes full-time tuition ($21,000), mandatory fees ($900), and room and board ($9900). *College room only:* $4950. Room and board charges vary according to board plan and housing facility. *Part-time tuition:* $425 per credit. *Part-time fees:* $275 per term. Part-time tuition and fees vary according to course load.

**FRESHMAN FINANCIAL AID (Fall 2014, est.)** 290 applied for aid; of those 91% were deemed to have need. 100% of freshmen with need received aid; of those 12% had need fully met. *Average percent of need met:* 70% (excluding resources awarded to replace EFC). *Average financial aid package:* $18,996 (excluding resources awarded to replace EFC). 1% of all full-time freshmen had no need and received non-need-based gift aid.

**UNDERGRADUATE FINANCIAL AID (Fall 2014, est.)** 1,182 applied for aid; of those 93% were deemed to have need. 99% of undergraduates with need received aid; of those 11% had need fully met. *Average percent of need met:* 66% (excluding resources awarded to replace EFC). *Average financial aid package:* $17,679 (excluding resources awarded to replace EFC). 1% of all full-time undergraduates had no need and received non-need-based gift aid.

**GIFT AID (NEED-BASED)** *Total amount:* $5,920,993 (56% federal, 35% state, 7% institutional, 2% external sources). *Receiving aid:* Freshmen: 85% (264); all full-time undergraduates: 90% (1,087). *Average award:* Freshmen: $15,708; Undergraduates: $13,989. *Scholarships, grants, and awards:* Federal Pell, FSEOG, state, private, college/university gift aid from institutional funds.

**GIFT AID (NON-NEED-BASED)** *Total amount:* $107,897 (26% federal, 41% state, 19% institutional, 14% external sources). *Receiving aid:* Freshmen: 5% (15). Undergraduates: 6% (72). *Average award:* Freshmen: $1051. Undergraduates: $1467. *Scholarships, grants, and awards by category:* Academic interests/achievement: agriculture, computer science, health fields. *Special characteristics:* children and siblings of alumni, international students, siblings of current students. *Tuition waivers:* Full or partial for employees or children of employees, senior citizens. *ROTC:* Army cooperative, Air Force cooperative.

**LOANS** *Student loans:* $10,509,319 (81% need-based, 19% non-need-based). *Average need-based loan:* Freshmen: $3036. Undergraduates: $3671. *Parent loans:* $2,738,179 (46% need-based, 54% non-need-based). *Programs:* Federal Direct (Subsidized and Unsubsidized Stafford, PLUS), Perkins, alternative loans.

**WORK-STUDY** *Federal work-study:* Total amount: $512,502; jobs available. *State or other work-study/employment:* Total amount: $256,396 (28% need-based, 72% non-need-based). Part-time jobs available.

**APPLYING FOR FINANCIAL AID** *Required financial aid forms:* FAFSA, state aid form. *Financial aid deadline:* 5/1 (priority: 4/1). *Notification date:* Continuous beginning 3/1. Students must reply within 3 weeks of notification.

**CONTACT** Director of Financial Assistance and Planning, Keystone College, One College Green, La Plume, PA 18440, 570-945-8134 or toll-free 877-4-COLLEGE. *Fax:* 570-945-8134. *E-mail:* financialaid@keystone.edu.
*Website:* http://www.keystone.edu/.

# THE KING'S COLLEGE
### New York, NY

| Tuition & fees: $33,270 | Average undergraduate aid package: $23,549 |
|---|---|

**ABOUT THE INSTITUTION** Independent nondenominational, coed. *Awards:* bachelor's degrees. 2 undergraduate majors. *Total enrollment:* 487. Undergraduates: 487. Freshmen: 144. Federal methodology is used as a basis for awarding need-based institutional aid.

**UNDERGRADUATE EXPENSES for 2015–2016** *Application fee:* $30. *Tuition:* full-time $32,870; part-time $1370 per credit. *Required fees:* full-time

$400; $200 per term. Full-time tuition and fees vary according to course load. Part-time tuition and fees vary according to course load. Room and board charges vary according to location.

**FRESHMAN FINANCIAL AID (Fall 2013)** 108 applied for aid; of those 92% were deemed to have need. 100% of freshmen with need received aid; of those 10% had need fully met. *Average percent of need met:* 67% (excluding resources awarded to replace EFC). *Average financial aid package:* $22,202 (excluding resources awarded to replace EFC). 19% of all full-time freshmen had no need and received non-need-based gift aid.

**UNDERGRADUATE FINANCIAL AID (Fall 2013)** 393 applied for aid; of those 93% were deemed to have need. 100% of undergraduates with need received aid; of those 17% had need fully met. *Average percent of need met:* 71% (excluding resources awarded to replace EFC). *Average financial aid package:* $23,549 (excluding resources awarded to replace EFC). 25% of all full-time undergraduates had no need and received non-need-based gift aid.

**GIFT AID (NEED-BASED)** *Total amount:* $7,580,378 (8% federal, 1% state, 89% institutional, 2% external sources). *Receiving aid:* Freshmen: 79% (99); all full-time undergraduates: 74% (365). *Average award:* Freshmen: $20,079; Undergraduates: $20,667. *Scholarships, grants, and awards:* Federal Pell, FSEOG, state, private, college/university gift aid from institutional funds.

**GIFT AID (NON-NEED-BASED)** *Total amount:* $2,005,094 (99% institutional, 1% external sources). *Receiving aid:* Freshmen: 9% (11). Undergraduates: 62% (305). *Average award:* Freshmen: $14,527. Undergraduates: $15,994. *Scholarships, grants, and awards by category:* Academic interests/achievement: 129 awards ($1,992,869 total): general academic interests/achievements. *Tuition waivers:* Full or partial for employees or children of employees. *ROTC:* Army cooperative.

**LOANS** *Student loans:* $2,854,028 (95% need-based, 5% non-need-based). 75% of past graduating class borrowed through all loan programs. *Average indebtedness per student:* $28,117. *Average need-based loan:* Freshmen: $3234. Undergraduates: $7276. *Parent loans:* $674,173 (92% need-based, 8% non-need-based). *Programs:* Federal Direct (Subsidized and Unsubsidized Stafford, PLUS), private loans.

**APPLYING FOR FINANCIAL AID** *Required financial aid form:* FAFSA. *Financial aid deadline (priority):* 3/15. *Notification date:* Continuous beginning 2/1.

**CONTACT** Anna Peters, Director of Financial Aid, The King's College, 56 Broadway, New York, NY 10004, 212-659-7281 or toll-free 888-969-7200 Ext. 3610. *Fax:* 212-659-3613. *E-mail:* apeters@tkc.edu.
*Website:* http://www.tkc.edu/.

# KING'S COLLEGE
## Wilkes-Barre, PA

| Tuition & fees: $31,816 | Average undergraduate aid package: $22,682 |
| --- | --- |

**ABOUT THE INSTITUTION** Independent Roman Catholic, coed. *Awards:* certificates, associate, bachelor's, and master's degrees. 40 undergraduate majors. *Total enrollment:* 2,308. Undergraduates: 2,002. Freshmen: 487. Federal methodology is used as a basis for awarding need-based institutional aid.

**UNDERGRADUATE EXPENSES for 2015–2016** *Application fee:* $30. *Comprehensive fee:* $43,502 includes full-time tuition ($31,416), mandatory fees ($400), and room and board ($11,686). *College room only:* $5708. Room and board charges vary according to board plan. *Part-time tuition:* $530 per credit hour.

**FRESHMAN FINANCIAL AID (Fall 2014, est.)** 470 applied for aid; of those 90% were deemed to have need. 100% of freshmen with need received aid; of those 16% had need fully met. *Average percent of need met:* 70% (excluding resources awarded to replace EFC). *Average financial aid package:* $23,188 (excluding resources awarded to replace EFC). 13% of all full-time freshmen had no need and received non-need-based gift aid.

**UNDERGRADUATE FINANCIAL AID (Fall 2014, est.)** 1,651 applied for aid; of those 90% were deemed to have need. 100% of undergraduates with need received aid; of those 16% had need fully met. *Average percent of need met:* 70% (excluding resources awarded to replace EFC). *Average financial aid package:* $22,682 (excluding resources awarded to replace EFC). 16% of all full-time undergraduates had no need and received non-need-based gift aid.

**GIFT AID (NEED-BASED)** *Total amount:* $25,367,157 (11% federal, 10% state, 78% institutional, 1% external sources). *Receiving aid:* Freshmen: 85% (413); all full-

time undergraduates: 80% (1,448). *Average award:* Freshmen: $18,434; Undergraduates: $17,071. *Scholarships, grants, and awards:* Federal Pell, FSEOG, state, private, college/university gift aid from institutional funds.

**GIFT AID (NON-NEED-BASED)** *Total amount:* $5,356,010 (8% federal, 89% institutional, 3% external sources). *Receiving aid:* Freshmen: 10% (48). Undergraduates: 7% (134). *Average award:* Freshmen: $15,428. Undergraduates: $13,452. *Scholarships, grants, and awards by category:* Academic interests/achievement: 1,487 awards ($16,271,821 total): biological sciences, business, communication, computer science, education, engineering/technologies, English, foreign languages, general academic interests/achievements, health fields, humanities, mathematics, physical sciences, premedicine, religion/biblical studies, social sciences. *Special achievements/activities:* 1,363 awards ($3,699,322 total): community service, general special achievements/activities, leadership. *Special characteristics:* 382 awards ($2,798,078 total): children and siblings of alumni, children of educators, children of faculty/staff, international students, relatives of clergy, siblings of current students, veterans. *Tuition waivers:* Full or partial for employees or children of employees, senior citizens. *ROTC:* Army, Air Force cooperative.

**LOANS** *Student loans:* $14,880,427 (70% need-based, 30% non-need-based). 86% of past graduating class borrowed through all loan programs. *Average indebtedness per student:* $29,432. *Average need-based loan:* Freshmen: $3442. Undergraduates: $4348. *Parent loans:* $4,656,070 (79% need-based, 21% non-need-based). *Programs:* Federal Direct (Subsidized and Unsubsidized Stafford, PLUS), Perkins, private loans.

**WORK-STUDY** *Federal work-study:* Total amount: $360,000; 357 jobs averaging $1008. *State or other work-study/employment:* Total amount: $275,000 (25% need-based, 75% non-need-based). 163 part-time jobs averaging $1687.

**APPLYING FOR FINANCIAL AID** *Required financial aid forms:* FAFSA, institution's own form. *Financial aid deadline (priority):* 2/15. *Notification date:* Continuous beginning 3/1. Students must reply by 5/1 or within 2 weeks of notification.

**CONTACT** Ms. Donna Cerza, Director of Financial Aid, King's College, 133 North River Street, Wilkes-Barre, PA 18711-0801, 570-208-5868 or toll-free 888-KINGSPA. *Fax:* 570-208-6015. *E-mail:* finaid@kings.edu.
*Website:* http://www.kings.edu/.

# KING'S UNIVERSITY
## Southlake, TX

**CONTACT** Mr. Norman V. Stoppenbrink Jr., Financial Aid Officer, King's University, 14800 Sherman Way, Los Angeles, CA 91405, 818-779-8040 Ext. 8278 or toll-free 888-779-8040. *Fax:* 818-779-8251. *E-mail:* financialaid@kingsuniversity.edu.
*Website:* http://www.tku.edu/.

# KING UNIVERSITY
## Bristol, TN

| Tuition & fees: $25,708 | Average undergraduate aid package: $14,128 |
| --- | --- |

**ABOUT THE INSTITUTION** Independent Presbyterian Church (U.S.A.), coed. *Awards:* certificates, associate, bachelor's, master's, and doctoral degrees. 55 undergraduate majors. *Total enrollment:* 2,898. Undergraduates: 2,431. Freshmen: 185. Federal methodology is used as a basis for awarding need-based institutional aid.

**UNDERGRADUATE EXPENSES for 2015–2016** *One-time required fee:* $125. *Comprehensive fee:* $33,888 includes full-time tuition ($24,316), mandatory fees ($1392), and room and board ($8180). *College room only:* $4108. Full-time tuition and fees vary according to course load, degree level, and program. Room and board charges vary according to board plan and housing facility. *Part-time tuition:* $600 per credit hour. *Part-time fees:* $100 per credit hour. Part-time tuition and fees vary according to course load, degree level, and program.

**FRESHMAN FINANCIAL AID (Fall 2014, est.)** 160 applied for aid; of those 90% were deemed to have need. 100% of freshmen with need received aid; of those 19% had need fully met. *Average percent of need met:* 80% (excluding resources awarded to replace EFC). *Average financial aid package:* $22,492 (excluding resources awarded to replace EFC). 15% of all full-time freshmen had no need and received non-need-based gift aid.

**UNDERGRADUATE FINANCIAL AID (Fall 2014, est.)** 1,915 applied for aid; of those 92% were deemed to have need. 99% of undergraduates with need received aid; of those 14% had need fully met. *Average percent of need met:* 65% (excluding resources awarded to replace EFC). *Average financial aid package:* $14,128 (excluding resources awarded to replace EFC). 6% of all full-time undergraduates had no need and received non-need-based gift aid.

**GIFT AID (NEED-BASED)** *Total amount:* $15,521,124 (33% federal, 11% state, 51% institutional, 5% external sources). *Receiving aid:* Freshmen: 78% (140); all full-time undergraduates: 70% (1,396). *Average award:* Freshmen: $19,018; Undergraduates: $11,789. *Scholarships, grants, and awards:* Federal Pell, FSEOG, state, private, college/university gift aid from institutional funds.

**GIFT AID (NON-NEED-BASED)** *Total amount:* $2,320,774 (1% federal, 13% state, 62% institutional, 24% external sources). *Receiving aid:* Freshmen: 13% (23). Undergraduates: 7% (134). *Average award:* Freshmen: $10,740. Undergraduates: $9648. *Scholarships, grants, and awards by category: Academic interests/achievement:* 740 awards ($6,322,312 total): general academic interests/achievements. *Creative arts/performance:* 85 awards ($338,250 total): art/fine arts, music, performing arts, theater/drama. *Special achievements/activities:* 94 awards ($114,500 total): general special achievements/activities. *Special characteristics:* children of faculty/staff, out-of-state students, veterans, veterans' children. *Tuition waivers:* Full or partial for employees or children of employees, senior citizens.

**LOANS** *Student loans:* $21,053,265 (83% need-based, 17% non-need-based). 86% of past graduating class borrowed through all loan programs. *Average indebtedness per student:* $21,091. *Average need-based loan:* Freshmen: $3966. Undergraduates: $4789. *Parent loans:* $687,878 (36% need-based, 64% non-need-based). *Programs:* Federal Direct (Subsidized and Unsubsidized Stafford, PLUS), Perkins, state, college/university.

**WORK-STUDY** *Federal work-study:* Total amount: $330,056; 83 jobs averaging $1610. *State or other work-study/employment:* 131 part-time jobs averaging $1401.

**ATHLETIC AWARDS** Total amount: $2,823,733 (60% need-based, 40% non-need-based).

**APPLYING FOR FINANCIAL AID** *Required financial aid form:* FAFSA. *Financial aid deadline (priority):* 3/1. *Notification date:* Continuous beginning 3/1. Students must reply within 2 weeks of notification.

**CONTACT** Richard J. Brand, Director of Financial Aid, King University, 1350 King College Road, Bristol, TN 37620-2699, 423-652-4728 or toll-free 800-362-0014. *Fax:* 423-652-6039. *E-mail:* rjbrand@king.edu.
*Website:* http://www.king.edu/.

# KNOX COLLEGE
## Galesburg, IL

| Tuition & fees: $41,847 | Average undergraduate aid package: $32,942 |
| --- | --- |

**ABOUT THE INSTITUTION** Independent, coed. *Awards:* bachelor's degrees. 42 undergraduate majors. *Total enrollment:* 1,399. Undergraduates: 1,399. Freshmen: 362. Both federal and institutional methodology are used as a basis for awarding need-based institutional aid.

**UNDERGRADUATE EXPENSES for 2015–2016** *Application fee:* $40. *Comprehensive fee:* $50,859 includes full-time tuition ($41,094), mandatory fees ($753), and room and board ($9012). *College room only:* $4512. Full-time tuition and fees vary according to course load. Room and board charges vary according to housing facility. *Part-time tuition:* $4566 per credit. Part-time tuition and fees vary according to course load.

**FRESHMAN FINANCIAL AID (Fall 2013)** 334 applied for aid; of those 91% were deemed to have need. 100% of freshmen with need received aid; of those 28% had need fully met. *Average percent of need met:* 91% (excluding resources awarded to replace EFC). *Average financial aid package:* $36,017 (excluding resources awarded to replace EFC). 15% of all full-time freshmen had no need and received non-need-based gift aid.

**UNDERGRADUATE FINANCIAL AID (Fall 2013)** 1,176 applied for aid; of those 93% were deemed to have need. 100% of undergraduates with need received aid; of those 24% had need fully met. *Average percent of need met:* 87% (excluding resources awarded to replace EFC). *Average financial aid package:* $32,942 (excluding resources awarded to replace EFC). 19% of all full-time undergraduates had no need and received non-need-based gift aid.

**GIFT AID (NEED-BASED)** *Total amount:* $30,407,957 (8% federal, 5% state, 86% institutional, 1% external sources). *Receiving aid:* Freshmen: 83% (299); all full-time undergraduates: 79% (1,075). *Average award:* Freshmen: $30,014; Undergraduates: $27,887. *Scholarships, grants, and awards:* Federal Pell, FSEOG, state, private, college/university gift aid from institutional funds.

**GIFT AID (NON-NEED-BASED)** *Total amount:* $4,140,426 (98% institutional, 2% external sources). *Receiving aid:* Freshmen: 17% (62). Undergraduates: 11% (156). *Average award:* Freshmen: $19,183. Undergraduates: $15,785. *Scholarships, grants, and awards by category: Academic interests/achievement:* general academic interests/achievements, mathematics. *Creative arts/performance:* art/fine arts, creative writing, dance, music, theater/drama. *Special achievements/activities:* community service. *Special characteristics:* children of faculty/staff, veterans. *Tuition waivers:* Full or partial for employees or children of employees.

**LOANS** *Student loans:* $8,573,520 (61% need-based, 39% non-need-based). 68% of past graduating class borrowed through all loan programs. *Average indebtedness per student:* $29,085. *Average need-based loan:* Freshmen: $4997. Undergraduates: $5168. *Parent loans:* $1,682,538 (100% non-need-based). *Programs:* Federal Direct (Subsidized and Unsubsidized Stafford, PLUS), Perkins, college/university, private loans.

**WORK-STUDY** *Federal work-study:* jobs available. *State or other work-study/employment:* Total amount: $297,675 (100% need-based). Part-time jobs available.

**APPLYING FOR FINANCIAL AID** *Required financial aid forms:* FAFSA, institution's own form. *Financial aid deadline (priority):* 2/1. *Notification date:* Continuous beginning 3/1. Students must reply by 5/1 or within 2 weeks of notification.

**CONTACT** Ms. Ann M. Brill, Director of Financial Aid, Knox College, 2 East South Street, Galesburg, IL 61401, 309-341-7149 or toll-free 800-678-KNOX. *Fax:* 309-341-7453. *E-mail:* abrill@knox.edu.
*Website:* http://www.knox.edu/.

# KUTZTOWN UNIVERSITY OF PENNSYLVANIA
## Kutztown, PA

| Tuition & fees (PA res): $8833 | Average undergraduate aid package: $8197 |
| --- | --- |

**ABOUT THE INSTITUTION** State-supported, coed. *Awards:* certificates, bachelor's, and master's degrees. 43 undergraduate majors. *Total enrollment:* 9,218. Undergraduates: 8,570. Freshmen: 1,782. Federal methodology is used as a basis for awarding need-based institutional aid.

**UNDERGRADUATE EXPENSES for 2015–2016** *Application fee:* $35. *One-time required fee:* $238. *Tuition, state resident:* full-time $6820; part-time $284 per credit hour. *Tuition, nonresident:* full-time $17,050; part-time $710 per credit hour. *Required fees:* full-time $2013; $81.36 per credit hour. Full-time tuition and fees vary according to course load. Part-time tuition and fees vary according to course load. *College room and board:* $8430; *Room only:* $5552. Room and board charges vary according to board plan and housing facility.

**FRESHMAN FINANCIAL AID (Fall 2013)** 1,675 applied for aid; of those 80% were deemed to have need. 96% of freshmen with need received aid; of those 6% had need fully met. *Average percent of need met:* 46% (excluding resources awarded to replace EFC). *Average financial aid package:* $7602 (excluding resources awarded to replace EFC). 1% of all full-time freshmen had no need and received non-need-based gift aid.

**UNDERGRADUATE FINANCIAL AID (Fall 2013)** 6,869 applied for aid; of those 82% were deemed to have need. 97% of undergraduates with need received aid; of those 7% had need fully met. *Average percent of need met:* 50% (excluding resources awarded to replace EFC). *Average financial aid package:* $8197 (excluding resources awarded to replace EFC). 1% of all full-time undergraduates had no need and received non-need-based gift aid.

**GIFT AID (NEED-BASED)** *Total amount:* $21,817,398 (53% federal, 40% state, 2% institutional, 5% external sources). *Receiving aid:* Freshmen: 44% (792); all full-time undergraduates: 42% (3,383). *Average award:* Freshmen: $5907; Undergraduates: $5730. *Scholarships, grants, and awards:* Federal Pell, FSEOG, state, private, college/university gift aid from institutional funds.

**GIFT AID (NON-NEED-BASED)** *Total amount:* $512,908 (20% state, 25% institutional, 55% external sources). *Receiving aid:* Freshmen: 5% (90). Undergraduates: 5% (427). *Average award:* Freshmen: $1440. Undergraduates: $1240. *Scholarships, grants, and awards by category:* Academic interests/achievement: 375 awards ($1,339,807 total): biological sciences, business, communication, computer science, education, English, foreign languages, general academic interests/achievements, humanities, international studies, library science, mathematics, physical sciences. *Creative arts/performance:* 37 awards ($31,889 total): applied art and design, art/fine arts, dance, music. *Special achievements/activities:* 269 awards ($545,677 total): community service, general special achievements/activities, leadership, religious involvement. *Special characteristics:* 134 awards ($906,979 total): children of faculty/staff, children of union members/company employees, first-generation college students, handicapped students, local/state students. *Tuition waivers:* Full or partial for employees or children of employees, senior citizens. *ROTC:* Army cooperative.

**LOANS** *Student loans:* $60,485,242 (82% need-based, 18% non-need-based). 81% of past graduating class borrowed through all loan programs. *Average indebtedness per student:* $33,376. *Average need-based loan:* Freshmen: $3417. Undergraduates: $4175. *Parent loans:* $11,209,314 (81% need-based, 19% non-need-based). *Programs:* Federal Direct (Subsidized and Unsubsidized Stafford, PLUS), Perkins.

**WORK-STUDY** *Federal work-study:* 411 jobs averaging $708.

**ATHLETIC AWARDS** Total amount: $603,889 (73% need-based, 27% non-need-based).

**APPLYING FOR FINANCIAL AID** *Required financial aid form:* FAFSA. *Financial aid deadline (priority):* 3/1. *Notification date:* Continuous beginning 3/30. Students must reply by 5/1 or within 4 weeks of notification.

**CONTACT** Mr. Bernard McCree, Director of Financial Aid, Kutztown University of Pennsylvania, 209 Stratton Administration Center, Kutztown, PA 19530-0730, 610-683-4032 or toll-free 877-628-1915. *Fax:* 610-683-1380. *E-mail:* mccree@kutztown.edu.

*Website:* http://www.kutztown.edu/.

# KUYPER COLLEGE
## Grand Rapids, MI

**ABOUT THE INSTITUTION** Independent Christian, coed. *Awards:* certificates, associate, and bachelor's degrees. 26 undergraduate majors. *Total enrollment:* 274. Undergraduates: 272. Freshmen: 54.

**GIFT AID (NEED-BASED)** *Scholarships, grants, and awards:* Federal Pell, FSEOG, state, private, college/university gift aid from institutional funds.

**GIFT AID (NON-NEED-BASED)** *Scholarships, grants, and awards by category:* Academic interests/achievement: general academic interests/achievements. Creative arts/performance: music. Special achievements/activities: leadership, religious involvement. Special characteristics: children and siblings of alumni, children of faculty/staff, international students, members of minority groups, siblings of current students.

**LOANS** *Programs:* Federal Direct (Subsidized and Unsubsidized Stafford, PLUS), alternative loans.

**WORK-STUDY** *Federal work-study:* 12 jobs averaging $2487. *State or other work-study/employment:* Total amount: $325,704 (100% non-need-based). 110 part-time jobs averaging $2636.

**APPLYING FOR FINANCIAL AID** *Required financial aid form:* FAFSA.

**CONTACT** Ms. Agnes Russell, Director of Financial Aid, Kuyper College, 3333 East Beltline NE, Grand Rapids, MI 49525-9749, 616-222-3000 Ext. 656. *Fax:* 616-222-3045. *E-mail:* arussell@kuyper.edu.

*Website:* http://www.kuyper.edu/.

# LAFAYETTE COLLEGE
## Easton, PA

| Tuition & fees: $45,635 | Average undergraduate aid package: $41,206 |
| --- | --- |

**ABOUT THE INSTITUTION** Independent Presbyterian Church (U.S.A.), coed. *Awards:* bachelor's degrees. 35 undergraduate majors. *Total enrollment:* 2,503.

Undergraduates: 2,503. Freshmen: 648. Institutional methodology is used as a basis for awarding need-based institutional aid.

**UNDERGRADUATE EXPENSES for 2015–2016** *One-time required fee:* $750. *Comprehensive fee:* $59,155 includes full-time tuition ($45,230), mandatory fees ($405), and room and board ($13,520). *College room only:* $8360. Full-time tuition and fees vary according to course load. Room and board charges vary according to board plan, housing facility, and student level. *Part-time tuition:* $5655 per course. Part-time tuition and fees vary according to course load.

**FRESHMAN FINANCIAL AID (Fall 2014, est.)** 375 applied for aid; of those 54% were deemed to have need. 100% of freshmen with need received aid; of those 91% had need fully met. *Average percent of need met:* 99% (excluding resources awarded to replace EFC). *Average financial aid package:* $42,316 (excluding resources awarded to replace EFC). 6% of all full-time freshmen had no need and received non-need-based gift aid.

**UNDERGRADUATE FINANCIAL AID (Fall 2014, est.)** 1,344 applied for aid; of those 67% were deemed to have need. 100% of undergraduates with need received aid; of those 87% had need fully met. *Average percent of need met:* 98% (excluding resources awarded to replace EFC). *Average financial aid package:* $41,206 (excluding resources awarded to replace EFC). 9% of all full-time undergraduates had no need and received non-need-based gift aid.

**GIFT AID (NEED-BASED)** *Total amount:* $30,956,580 (4% federal, 1% state, 94% institutional, 1% external sources). *Receiving aid:* Freshmen: 30% (194); all full-time undergraduates: 36% (870). *Average award:* Freshmen: $36,661; Undergraduates: $35,412. *Scholarships, grants, and awards:* Federal Pell, FSEOG, state, private, college/university gift aid from institutional funds.

**GIFT AID (NON-NEED-BASED)** *Total amount:* $6,589,070 (83% institutional, 17% external sources). *Receiving aid:* Freshmen: 9% (59). Undergraduates: 7% (175). *Average award:* Freshmen: $25,737. Undergraduates: $23,469. *Scholarships, grants, and awards by category:* Academic interests/achievement: general academic interests/achievements. Creative arts/performance: applied art and design, art/fine arts, cinema/film/broadcasting, creative writing, dance, general creative arts/performance, music, performing arts, theater/drama. *Tuition waivers:* Full or partial for employees or children of employees. *ROTC:* Army cooperative.

**LOANS** *Student loans:* $8,809,465 (50% need-based, 50% non-need-based). 51% of past graduating class borrowed through all loan programs. *Average indebtedness per student:* $27,497. *Average need-based loan:* Freshmen: $4205. Undergraduates: $4707. *Parent loans:* $2,727,703 (100% non-need-based). *Programs:* Federal Direct (Subsidized and Unsubsidized Stafford, PLUS), Perkins, college/university.

**WORK-STUDY** *Federal work-study:* Total amount: $606,579; 440 jobs averaging $1379. *State or other work-study/employment:* Total amount: $1,191,335 (46% need-based, 54% non-need-based). Part-time jobs available.

**ATHLETIC AWARDS** Total amount: $3,466,107 (100% non-need-based).

**APPLYING FOR FINANCIAL AID** *Required financial aid forms:* FAFSA, CSS Financial Aid PROFILE, noncustodial (divorced/separated) parent's statement, federal income tax form(s). *Financial aid deadline:* 3/1 (priority: 1/15). *Notification date:* 4/1. Students must reply by 5/1.

**CONTACT** Ms. Ashley Bianchi, Director of Financial Aid, Lafayette College, 730 High Street, 107 Markle Hall, Easton, PA 18042-1777, 610-330-5055. *Fax:* 610-330-5758. *E-mail:* bianchia@lafayette.edu.

*Website:* http://www.lafayette.edu/.

# LAGRANGE COLLEGE
## LaGrange, GA

| Tuition & fees: $26,620 | Average undergraduate aid package: $22,667 |
| --- | --- |

**ABOUT THE INSTITUTION** Independent United Methodist, coed. *Awards:* certificates, bachelor's, and master's degrees. 30 undergraduate majors. *Total enrollment:* 964. Undergraduates: 880. Freshmen: 238. Federal methodology is used as a basis for awarding need-based institutional aid.

**UNDERGRADUATE EXPENSES for 2015–2016** *One-time required fee:* $150. *Comprehensive fee:* $37,670 includes full-time tuition ($26,290), mandatory fees ($330), and room and board ($11,050). *College room only:* $6310. Full-time tuition and fees vary according to class time, course load, and program. Room and board charges vary according to board plan and housing facility. *Part-time tuition:* $1080 per semester hour. Part-time tuition and fees vary according to class time, course load, and program.

**FRESHMAN FINANCIAL AID (Fall 2013)** 225 applied for aid; of those 95% were deemed to have need. 100% of freshmen with need received aid; of those 33% had need fully met. *Average percent of need met:* 75% (excluding resources awarded to replace EFC). *Average financial aid package:* $22,781 (excluding resources awarded to replace EFC). 5% of all full-time freshmen had no need and received non-need-based gift aid.

**UNDERGRADUATE FINANCIAL AID (Fall 2013)** 765 applied for aid; of those 90% were deemed to have need. 100% of undergraduates with need received aid; of those 23% had need fully met. *Average percent of need met:* 86% (excluding resources awarded to replace EFC). *Average financial aid package:* $22,667 (excluding resources awarded to replace EFC). 9% of all full-time undergraduates had no need and received non-need-based gift aid.

**GIFT AID (NEED-BASED)** *Total amount:* $9,911,994 (17% federal, 13% state, 63% institutional, 7% external sources). *Receiving aid:* Freshmen: 91% (211); all full-time undergraduates: 81% (650). *Average award:* Freshmen: $15,282; Undergraduates: $14,244. *Scholarships, grants, and awards:* Federal Pell, FSEOG, private, college/university gift aid from institutional funds.

**GIFT AID (NON-NEED-BASED)** *Total amount:* $3,400,637 (12% state, 73% institutional, 15% external sources). *Receiving aid:* Freshmen: 5% (12). Undergraduates: 9% (71). *Average award:* Freshmen: $10,067. Undergraduates: $11,088. *Scholarships, grants, and awards by category:* Academic interests/achievement: education, general academic interests/achievements, health fields. Creative arts/performance: art/fine arts, music, theater/drama. Special achievements/activities: leadership. Special characteristics: children of faculty/staff, ethnic background, first-generation college students, relatives of clergy, religious affiliation. Tuition waivers: Full or partial for employees or children of employees, senior citizens.

**LOANS** *Student loans:* $6,731,388 (90% need-based, 10% non-need-based). 78% of past graduating class borrowed through all loan programs. *Average indebtedness per student:* $32,574. *Average need-based loan:* Freshmen: $3274. Undergraduates: $4145. *Parent loans:* $1,023,632 (34% need-based, 66% non-need-based). *Programs:* Federal Direct (Subsidized and Unsubsidized Stafford, PLUS), state.

**WORK-STUDY** *Federal work-study:* jobs available. *State or other work-study/employment:* Total amount: $395,541 (75% need-based, 25% non-need-based). Part-time jobs available.

**APPLYING FOR FINANCIAL AID** *Required financial aid forms:* FAFSA, state aid form. *Financial aid deadline (priority):* 3/1. *Notification date:* Continuous beginning 3/15. Students must reply within 4 weeks of notification.

**CONTACT** Michelle Reeves, Assistant Director, LaGrange College, 601 Broad Street, LaGrange, GA 30240-2999, 888-253-9918 or toll-free 800-593-2885. *Fax:* 706-880-8348. *E-mail:* mreeves@lagrange.edu.
*Website:* http://www.lagrange.edu/.

# LAGUNA COLLEGE OF ART & DESIGN
## Laguna Beach, CA

| Tuition & fees: $28,100 | Average undergraduate aid package: $16,101 |
| --- | --- |

**ABOUT THE INSTITUTION** Independent, coed. *Awards:* certificates, bachelor's, and master's degrees. 14 undergraduate majors. *Total enrollment:* 544. Undergraduates: 510. Freshmen: 68. Federal methodology is used as a basis for awarding need-based institutional aid.

**UNDERGRADUATE EXPENSES** for 2015–2016 *Application fee:* $45. *Tuition:* full-time $28,100; part-time $1170 per credit. Full-time tuition and fees vary according to degree level. Part-time tuition and fees vary according to course load and degree level.

**FRESHMAN FINANCIAL AID (Fall 2014, est.)** 68 applied for aid; of those 96% were deemed to have need. 100% of freshmen with need received aid. *Average percent of need met:* 71% (excluding resources awarded to replace EFC). *Average financial aid package:* $10,600 (excluding resources awarded to replace EFC). 3% of all full-time freshmen had no need and received non-need-based gift aid.

**UNDERGRADUATE FINANCIAL AID (Fall 2014, est.)** 434 applied for aid; of those 91% were deemed to have need. 100% of undergraduates with need received aid; of those 1% had need fully met. *Average percent of need met:* 72% (excluding resources awarded to replace EFC). *Average financial aid package:* $16,101 (excluding resources awarded to replace EFC). 2% of all full-time undergraduates had no need and received non-need-based gift aid.

**GIFT AID (NEED-BASED)** *Total amount:* $1,907,767 (53% federal, 38% state, 6% institutional, 3% external sources). *Receiving aid:* Freshmen: 77% (55); all full-time undergraduates: 83% (379). *Average award:* Freshmen: $6000; Undergraduates: $5500. *Scholarships, grants, and awards:* Federal Pell, FSEOG, state, private, college/university gift aid from institutional funds.

**GIFT AID (NON-NEED-BASED)** *Total amount:* $2,659,984 (100% institutional). *Receiving aid:* Freshmen: 92% (65). Undergraduates: 86% (395). *Average award:* Freshmen: $4500. Undergraduates: $4500. *Scholarships, grants, and awards by category:* Academic interests/achievement: general academic interests/achievements. Creative arts/performance: applied art and design, art/fine arts.

**LOANS** *Student loans:* $3,526,424 (39% need-based, 61% non-need-based). 90% of past graduating class borrowed through all loan programs. *Average indebtedness per student:* $38,000. *Average need-based loan:* Freshmen: $4000. Undergraduates: $5500. *Parent loans:* $2,868,465 (100% need-based). *Programs:* Federal Direct (Subsidized and Unsubsidized Stafford, PLUS).

**WORK-STUDY** *Federal work-study:* Total amount: $48,000; 20 jobs averaging $2400.

**APPLYING FOR FINANCIAL AID** *Required financial aid form:* FAFSA. *Financial aid deadline:* Continuous. *Notification date:* Continuous beginning 2/1.

**CONTACT** Christopher Brown, Director of Admissions and Financial Aid, Laguna College of Art & Design, 2825 Laguna Canyon Road, Laguna Beach, CA 92651-1136, 949-376-6000 or toll-free 800-255-0762. *Fax:* 949-715-4084. *E-mail:* cbrown@lcad.edu.
*Website:* http://www.lcad.edu/.

# LAKE ERIE COLLEGE
## Painesville, OH

| Tuition & fees: $29,162 | Average undergraduate aid package: $22,717 |
| --- | --- |

**ABOUT THE INSTITUTION** Independent, coed. *Awards:* certificates, bachelor's, and master's degrees. 34 undergraduate majors. *Total enrollment:* 1,114. Undergraduates: 903. Freshmen: 186. Federal methodology is used as a basis for awarding need-based institutional aid.

**UNDERGRADUATE EXPENSES** for 2015–2016 *Application fee:* $30. *One-time required fee:* $350. *Comprehensive fee:* $38,340 includes full-time tuition ($27,770), mandatory fees ($1392), and room and board ($9178). *College room only:* $4464. Full-time tuition and fees vary according to course load, degree level, and program. Room and board charges vary according to board plan. *Part-time tuition:* $736 per credit hour. *Part-time fees:* $51 per credit hour. Part-time tuition and fees vary according to course load, degree level, and program.

**FRESHMAN FINANCIAL AID (Fall 2014, est.)** 179 applied for aid; of those 93% were deemed to have need. 100% of freshmen with need received aid; of those 11% had need fully met. *Average percent of need met:* 74% (excluding resources awarded to replace EFC). *Average financial aid package:* $24,876 (excluding resources awarded to replace EFC). 10% of all full-time freshmen had no need and received non-need-based gift aid.

**UNDERGRADUATE FINANCIAL AID (Fall 2014, est.)** 650 applied for aid; of those 95% were deemed to have need. 100% of undergraduates with need received aid; of those 17% had need fully met. *Average percent of need met:* 72% (excluding resources awarded to replace EFC). *Average financial aid package:* $22,717 (excluding resources awarded to replace EFC). 13% of all full-time undergraduates had no need and received non-need-based gift aid.

**GIFT AID (NEED-BASED)** *Total amount:* $9,199,151 (15% federal, 4% state, 81% institutional). *Receiving aid:* Freshmen: 89% (165); all full-time undergraduates: 82% (614). *Average award:* Freshmen: $21,306; Undergraduates: $18,788. *Scholarships, grants, and awards:* Federal Pell, FSEOG, state, private, college/university gift aid from institutional funds.

**GIFT AID (NON-NEED-BASED)** *Total amount:* $1,561,985 (96% institutional, 4% external sources). *Receiving aid:* Freshmen: 8% (15). Undergraduates: 11% (80). *Average award:* Freshmen: $11,849. Undergraduates: $12,738. *Scholarships, grants, and awards by category:* Academic interests/achievement: biological sciences, business, communication, education, English, foreign languages, general academic interests/achievements, humanities, international studies, mathematics, physical sciences, social sciences. Creative arts/performance: art/fine arts, dance, general creative arts/performance, music, performing arts, theater/drama. Special achievements/

*activities:* community service, general special achievements/activities, hobbies/interests. *Special characteristics:* children of faculty/staff, twins, veterans, veterans' children. *Tuition waivers:* Full or partial for employees or children of employees, senior citizens. **LOANS** *Student loans:* $5,681,648 (76% need-based, 24% non-need-based). 83% of past graduating class borrowed through all loan programs. *Average indebtedness per student:* $34,114. *Average need-based loan:* Freshmen: $3454. Undergraduates: $4352. *Parent loans:* $1,255,130 (45% need-based, 55% non-need-based). *Programs:* Federal Direct (Subsidized and Unsubsidized Stafford, PLUS), Perkins. **WORK-STUDY** *Federal work-study:* Total amount: $108,361; jobs available. **ATHLETIC AWARDS** Total amount: $3,606,414 (63% need-based, 37% non-need-based).

**APPLYING FOR FINANCIAL AID** *Required financial aid form:* FAFSA. *Financial aid deadline:* Continuous. *Notification date:* Continuous beginning 2/15. Students must reply by 5/1 or within 4 weeks of notification.

**CONTACT** Patricia Pangonis, Director of Financial Aid, Lake Erie College, 391 West Washington Street, Painesville, OH 44077-3389, 440-375-7102 or toll-free 800-916-0904. *Fax:* 440-375-7103. *E-mail:* finaid@lec.edu.
*Website:* http://www.lec.edu/.

# LAKE FOREST COLLEGE
## Lake Forest, IL

**ABOUT THE INSTITUTION** Independent, coed. *Awards:* certificates, bachelor's, and master's degrees. 31 undergraduate majors. *Total enrollment:* 1,626. Undergraduates: 1,607. Freshmen: 410.

**GIFT AID (NEED-BASED)** *Scholarships, grants, and awards:* Federal Pell, FSEOG, state, private, college/university gift aid from institutional funds.

**GIFT AID (NON-NEED-BASED)** *Scholarships, grants, and awards by category: Academic interests/achievement:* biological sciences, computer science, English, foreign languages, general academic interests/achievements, mathematics, physical sciences, social sciences. *Creative arts/performance:* art/fine arts, creative writing, music, theater/drama. *Special achievements/activities:* leadership. *Special characteristics:* children and siblings of alumni, local/state students, previous college experience.

**LOANS** *Programs:* Federal Direct (Subsidized and Unsubsidized Stafford, PLUS), Perkins, private loans.

**WORK-STUDY** Federal work-study jobs available. *State or other work-study/employment:* Part-time jobs available.

**APPLYING FOR FINANCIAL AID** *Required financial aid forms:* FAFSA, institution's own form.

**CONTACT** Mr. Jerry Cebrzynski, Director of Financial Aid, Lake Forest College, 555 North Sheridan Road, Lake Forest, IL 60045-2399, 847-735-5104 or toll-free 800-828-4751. *Fax:* 847-735-6271. *E-mail:* cebrzynski@lakeforest.edu.
*Website:* http://www.lakeforest.edu/.

# LAKELAND COLLEGE
## Sheboygan, WI

**CONTACT** Ms. Patty Taylor, Director of Financial Aid, Lakeland College, PO Box 359, Sheboygan, WI 53082-0359, 920-565-1214 or toll-free 800-569-2166. *Fax:* 920-565-1470.
*Website:* http://www.lakeland.edu/.

# LAKE SUPERIOR STATE UNIVERSITY
## Sault Sainte Marie, MI

**ABOUT THE INSTITUTION** State-supported, coed. *Awards:* certificates, associate, bachelor's, and master's degrees. 70 undergraduate majors. *Total enrollment:* 2,438. Undergraduates: 2,432. Freshmen: 409.

**GIFT AID (NEED-BASED)** *Scholarships, grants, and awards:* Federal Pell, FSEOG, state, private, college/university gift aid from institutional funds, Federal Nursing, Academic Competitiveness Grants, National SMART Grants.

**GIFT AID (NON-NEED-BASED)** *Scholarships, grants, and awards by category: Academic interests/achievement:* general academic interests/achievements. **LOANS** *Programs:* Federal Direct (Subsidized and Unsubsidized Stafford, PLUS), Perkins, Federal Nursing, alternative loans. **APPLYING FOR FINANCIAL AID** *Required financial aid form:* FAFSA.

**CONTACT** Deborah Faust, Director of Financial Aid, Lake Superior State University, 650 West Easterday Avenue, Sault Sainte Marie, MI 49783, 906-635-2678 or toll-free 888-800-LSSU Ext. 2231. *Fax:* 906-635-6669. *E-mail:* finaid@lssu.edu.
*Website:* http://www.lssu.edu/.

# LAKEVIEW COLLEGE OF NURSING
## Danville, IL

| Tuition & fees: $15,040 | Average undergraduate aid package: $20,500 |
|---|---|

**ABOUT THE INSTITUTION** Independent, coed, primarily women. *Awards:* bachelor's degrees. 1 undergraduate major. *Total enrollment:* 322. Undergraduates: 322. Federal methodology is used as a basis for awarding need-based institutional aid. **UNDERGRADUATE EXPENSES for 2015–2016** *Application fee:* $100. *Tuition:* full-time $13,120; part-time $410 per credit hour. *Required fees:* full-time $1920; $60 per credit hour. Full-time tuition and fees vary according to course load and location. Part-time tuition and fees vary according to course load and location. **UNDERGRADUATE FINANCIAL AID (Fall 2014, est.)** 392 applied for aid; of those 92% were deemed to have need. 99% of undergraduates with need received aid; of those 86% had need fully met. *Average percent of need met:* 82% (excluding resources awarded to replace EFC). *Average financial aid package:* $20,500 (excluding resources awarded to replace EFC).

**GIFT AID (NEED-BASED)** *Total amount:* $990,434 (59% federal, 41% state). *Receiving aid:* All full-time undergraduates: 82% (357). *Average award:* Undergraduates: $2500. *Scholarships, grants, and awards:* Federal Pell, state, private, college/university gift aid from institutional funds.

**GIFT AID (NON-NEED-BASED)** *Total amount:* $200,000 (55% institutional, 45% external sources). *Receiving aid:* Undergraduates: 34% (148). *Scholarships, grants, and awards by category: Academic interests/achievement:* health fields. *Tuition waivers:* Full or partial for employees or children of employees. *ROTC:* Army cooperative.

**LOANS** *Student loans:* $2,600,000 (92% need-based, 8% non-need-based). 92% of past graduating class borrowed through all loan programs. *Average indebtedness per student:* $25,000. *Average need-based loan:* Undergraduates: $5500. *Parent loans:* $215,000 (100% non-need-based). *Programs:* Federal Direct (Subsidized and Unsubsidized Stafford, PLUS).

**APPLYING FOR FINANCIAL AID** *Financial aid deadline:* Continuous. *Notification date:* Continuous beginning 4/1. Students must reply within 4 weeks of notification.

**CONTACT** Ms. Janet Ingargiola, Director of Financial Aid, Lakeview College of Nursing, 903 North Logan Avenue, Danville, IL 61832, 217-709-0930. *Fax:* 217-709-0956. *E-mail:* jingarg@lakeviewcol.edu.
*Website:* http://www.lakeviewcol.edu/.

# LAMAR UNIVERSITY
## Beaumont, TX

| Tuition & fees (TX res): $9251 | Average undergraduate aid package: $6718 |
|---|---|

**ABOUT THE INSTITUTION** State-supported, coed. *Awards:* certificates, bachelor's, master's, and doctoral degrees. 55 undergraduate majors. *Total enrollment:* 14,895. Undergraduates: 9,279. Freshmen: 1,290. Federal methodology is used as a basis for awarding need-based institutional aid. **UNDERGRADUATE EXPENSES for 2015–2016** *One-time required fee:* $10. *Tuition, state resident:* full-time $6450; part-time $218 per credit hour. *Tuition, nonresident:* full-time $17,400; part-time $580 per credit hour. *Required fees:* full-time $2801; $382 per credit hour or $784 per credit hour. Full-time tuition and fees vary according to course load, location, and program. Part-time tuition and fees vary according to course load, location, and program. **College room and board:** $8302; **Room only:** $5252. Room and board charges vary according to board plan. **Payment plan:** Guaranteed tuition.

**FRESHMAN FINANCIAL AID (Fall 2013)** 1,157 applied for aid; of those 77% were deemed to have need. 98% of freshmen with need received aid. **Average percent of need met:** 33% (excluding resources awarded to replace EFC). **Average financial aid package:** $6482 (excluding resources awarded to replace EFC). 12% of all full-time freshmen had no need and received non-need-based gift aid.

**UNDERGRADUATE FINANCIAL AID (Fall 2013)** 5,535 applied for aid; of those 84% were deemed to have need. 98% of undergraduates with need received aid. **Average percent of need met:** 39% (excluding resources awarded to replace EFC). **Average financial aid package:** $6718 (excluding resources awarded to replace EFC). 18% of all full-time undergraduates had no need and received non-need-based gift aid.

**GIFT AID (NEED-BASED) Total amount:** $27,428,872 (61% federal, 36% state, 3% institutional). **Receiving aid:** Freshmen: 54% (758); all full-time undergraduates: 53% (3,807). **Average award:** Freshmen: $4610; Undergraduates: $4902. **Scholarships, grants, and awards:** Federal Pell, FSEOG, state, private, college/university gift aid from institutional funds, United Negro College Fund.

**GIFT AID (NON-NEED-BASED) Total amount:** $4,810,653 (2% state, 69% institutional, 29% external sources). **Receiving aid:** Freshmen: 24% (337). Undergraduates: 16% (1,160). **Average award:** Freshmen: $2325. Undergraduates: $2613. **Scholarships, grants, and awards by category:** Academic interests/achievement: general academic interests/achievements. Creative arts/performance: general creative arts/performance. Special achievements/activities: general special achievements/activities. **Tuition waivers:** Full or partial for employees or children of employees, senior citizens. **ROTC:** Air Force cooperative.

**LOANS Student loans:** $40,053,814 (43% need-based, 57% non-need-based). 17% of past graduating class borrowed through all loan programs. **Average need-based loan:** Freshmen: $3877. Undergraduates: $3914. **Parent loans:** $2,068,413 (100% non-need-based). **Programs:** Federal Direct (Subsidized and Unsubsidized Stafford, PLUS), Perkins, Federal Nursing, state.

**WORK-STUDY Federal work-study:** 206 jobs averaging $2345. **State or other work-study/employment:** Total amount: $114,672 (100% need-based). 51 part-time jobs averaging $2248.

**ATHLETIC AWARDS** Total amount: $3,926,965 (100% non-need-based).

**APPLYING FOR FINANCIAL AID Required financial aid forms:** FAFSA, institution's own form. **Financial aid deadline (priority):** 3/31. **Notification date:** Continuous beginning 5/15. Students must reply within 2 weeks of notification.

**CONTACT** Student Financial Assistance Office, Lamar University, PO Box 10042, Beaumont, TX 77710, 409-880-8450. Fax: 409-880-8934. E-mail: financialaid@lamar.edu.
Website: http://www.lamar.edu/.

# LANCASTER BIBLE COLLEGE
## Lancaster, PA

| Tuition & fees: N/R | Average undergraduate aid package: $12,476 |
|---|---|

**ABOUT THE INSTITUTION** Independent nondenominational, coed. 17 undergraduate majors. Federal methodology is used as a basis for awarding need-based institutional aid.

**FRESHMAN FINANCIAL AID (Fall 2014, est.)** 162 applied for aid; of those 88% were deemed to have need. 100% of freshmen with need received aid; of those 7% had need fully met. **Average percent of need met:** 60% (excluding resources awarded to replace EFC). **Average financial aid package:** $12,854 (excluding resources awarded to replace EFC). 14% of all full-time freshmen had no need and received non-need-based gift aid.

**UNDERGRADUATE FINANCIAL AID (Fall 2014, est.)** 707 applied for aid; of those 90% were deemed to have need. 100% of undergraduates with need received aid; of those 8% had need fully met. **Average percent of need met:** 60% (excluding resources awarded to replace EFC). **Average financial aid package:** $12,476 (excluding resources awarded to replace EFC). 17% of all full-time undergraduates had no need and received non-need-based gift aid.

**GIFT AID (NEED-BASED) Total amount:** $6,189,673 (31% federal, 14% state, 51% institutional, 4% external sources). **Receiving aid:** Freshmen: 84% (139); all full-time undergraduates: 78% (600). **Average award:** Freshmen: $10,264; Undergrad-

uates: $9519. **Scholarships, grants, and awards:** Federal Pell, FSEOG, state, private, college/university gift aid from institutional funds, Office of Vocational Rehabilitation Awards, Blindness and Visual Services Awards.

**GIFT AID (NON-NEED-BASED) Total amount:** $825,711 (96% institutional, 4% external sources). **Receiving aid:** Freshmen: 82% (136). Undergraduates: 67% (516). **Average award:** Freshmen: $4410. Undergraduates: $5358. **Scholarships, grants, and awards by category:** Academic interests/achievement: 419 awards ($1,284,425 total): general academic interests/achievements. Creative arts/performance: 68 awards ($144,170 total): general creative arts/performance, music. Special achievements/activities: 63 awards ($82,750 total): general special achievements/activities, leadership, religious involvement. Special characteristics: 325 awards ($937,256 total): adult students, children and siblings of alumni, children of current students, children of faculty/staff, international students, married students, previous college experience, relatives of clergy, religious affiliation, siblings of current students, spouses of current students, veterans.

**LOANS Student loans:** $5,527,164 (78% need-based, 22% non-need-based). 20% of past graduating class borrowed through all loan programs. **Average indebtedness per student:** $20,959. **Average need-based loan:** Freshmen: $3218. Undergraduates: $4071. **Parent loans:** $637,334 (54% need-based, 46% non-need-based). **Programs:** Federal Direct (Subsidized and Unsubsidized Stafford, PLUS), Perkins, state, alternative loans.

**WORK-STUDY Federal work-study:** Total amount: $137,196; 91 jobs averaging $1500.

**APPLYING FOR FINANCIAL AID Required financial aid forms:** FAFSA, state aid form. **Financial aid deadline (priority):** 5/1. **Notification date:** Continuous beginning 3/1. Students must reply within 3 weeks of notification.

**CONTACT** Karen Fox, Director of Financial Aid, Lancaster Bible College, 901 Eden Road, Lancaster, PA 17601, 717-560-8254 Ext. 5352 or toll-free 800-544-7335. Fax: 717-560-8216. E-mail: kfox@lbc.edu.
Website: http://www.lbc.edu/.

# LANDER UNIVERSITY
## Greenwood, SC

**CONTACT** Director of Financial Aid, Lander University, 320 Stanley Avenue, Greenwood, SC 29649, 864-388-8340 or toll-free 888-452-6337. Fax: 864-388-8811. E-mail: fhardin@lander.edu.
Website: http://www.lander.edu/.

# LANE COLLEGE
## Jackson, TN

**CONTACT** Mr. Tony Calhoun, Director of Financial Aid, Lane College, 545 Lane Avenue, Jackson, TN 38301, 731-426-7558 or toll-free 800-960-7533. Fax: 731-426-7652. E-mail: tcalhoun@lanecollege.edu.
Website: http://www.lanecollege.edu/.

# LANGSTON UNIVERSITY
## Langston, OK

| Tuition & fees (OK res): $4801 | Average undergraduate aid package: $14,990 |
|---|---|

**ABOUT THE INSTITUTION** State-supported, coed. **Awards:** associate, bachelor's, master's, and doctoral degrees. 37 undergraduate majors. **Total enrollment:** 2,576. Undergraduates: 2,272. Freshmen: 629. Federal methodology is used as a basis for awarding need-based institutional aid.

**UNDERGRADUATE EXPENSES for 2015–2016 Application fee:** $35. **Tuition, state resident:** full-time $3305; part-time $110.16 per credit hour. **Tuition, nonresident:** full-time $10,291; part-time $343.04 per credit hour. **Required fees:** full-time $1496; $110.16 per credit hour or $83 per credit hour. Full-time tuition and fees vary according to degree level and program. Part-time tuition and fees vary according to degree level and program. **College room and board:** $8720;

**Room only:** $5850. Room and board charges vary according to board plan and housing facility. **Payment plans:** Guaranteed tuition, tuition prepayment.

**FRESHMAN FINANCIAL AID (Fall 2014, est.)** 573 applied for aid; of those 96% were deemed to have need. 95% of freshmen with need received aid; of those 25% had need fully met. **Average percent of need met:** 74% (excluding resources awarded to replace EFC). **Average financial aid package:** $14,598 (excluding resources awarded to replace EFC). 6% of all full-time freshmen had no need and received non-need-based gift aid.

**UNDERGRADUATE FINANCIAL AID (Fall 2014, est.)** 2,048 applied for aid; of those 94% were deemed to have need. 94% of undergraduates with need received aid; of those 32% had need fully met. **Average percent of need met:** 79% (excluding resources awarded to replace EFC). **Average financial aid package:** $14,990 (excluding resources awarded to replace EFC). 8% of all full-time undergraduates had no need and received non-need-based gift aid.

**GIFT AID (NEED-BASED) Total amount:** $7,530,041 (93% federal, 4% state, 1% institutional, 2% external sources). **Receiving aid:** Freshmen: 84% (486); all full-time undergraduates: 77% (1,607). **Average award:** Freshmen: $5248; Undergraduates: $5163. **Scholarships, grants, and awards:** Federal Pell, FSEOG, state.

**GIFT AID (NON-NEED-BASED) Total amount:** $3,075,001 (84% state, 16% external sources). **Receiving aid:** Freshmen: 22% (125). Undergraduates: 24% (504). **Average award:** Freshmen: $6919. Undergraduates: $6872. **Scholarships, grants, and awards by category:** Academic interests/achievement: agriculture, business, education, engineering/technologies, general academic interests/achievements, health fields. Creative arts/performance: music. Special achievements/activities: cheerleading/drum major, leadership. Special characteristics: ethnic background. **Tuition waivers:** Full or partial for children of alumni, employees or children of employees. **ROTC:** Army cooperative.

**LOANS Student loans:** $247,315 (100% need-based). 96% of past graduating class borrowed through all loan programs. **Parent loans:** $1,601,503 (100% need-based). **Programs:** Federal Direct (Subsidized and Unsubsidized Stafford, PLUS).

**WORK-STUDY Federal work-study:** Total amount: $354,630; 237 jobs averaging $1349. **State or other work-study/employment:** Part-time jobs available.

**ATHLETIC AWARDS** Total amount: $1,095,920 (100% need-based).

**APPLYING FOR FINANCIAL AID Required financial aid forms:** FAFSA, institution's own form. **Financial aid deadline (priority):** 3/15. **Notification date:** 6/30.

**CONTACT** Sheila Mcgill, Director of Financial Aid, Langston University, Success Center, Langston, OK 73050, 405-466-3287. **Fax:** 405-466-2986. **E-mail:** smcgill@langston.edu.

**Website:** http://www.langston.edu/.

## LA ROCHE COLLEGE
### Pittsburgh, PA

| Tuition & fees: $25,500 | Average undergraduate aid package: $26,801 |
|---|---|

**ABOUT THE INSTITUTION** Independent Roman Catholic Church, coed. **Awards:** certificates, associate, bachelor's, and master's degrees. 35 undergraduate majors. **Total enrollment:** 1,412. Undergraduates: 1,305. Freshmen: 223. Federal methodology is used as a basis for awarding need-based institutional aid.

**UNDERGRADUATE EXPENSES for 2015–2016 Application fee:** $50. **Comprehensive fee:** $35,824 includes full-time tuition ($24,750), mandatory fees ($750), and room and board ($10,324). **College room only:** $6534. Room and board charges vary according to board plan and housing facility. **Part-time tuition:** $630 per credit hour.

**FRESHMAN FINANCIAL AID (Fall 2014, est.)** 148 applied for aid; of those 97% were deemed to have need. 100% of freshmen with need received aid; of those 38% had need fully met. **Average percent of need met:** 89% (excluding resources awarded to replace EFC). **Average financial aid package:** $28,966 (excluding resources awarded to replace EFC). 2% of all full-time freshmen had no need and received non-need-based gift aid.

**UNDERGRADUATE FINANCIAL AID (Fall 2014, est.)** 812 applied for aid; of those 94% were deemed to have need. 100% of undergraduates with need received aid; of those 35% had need fully met. **Average percent of need met:** 95% (excluding resources awarded to replace EFC). **Average financial aid package:** $26,801 (excluding resources awarded to replace EFC). 4% of all full-time undergraduates had no need and received non-need-based gift aid.

**GIFT AID (NEED-BASED) Total amount:** $4,843,360 (39% federal, 34% state, 27% institutional). **Receiving aid:** Freshmen: 61% (136); all full-time undergraduates: 55% (590). **Average award:** Freshmen: $9053; Undergraduates: $8077. **Scholarships, grants, and awards:** Federal Pell, FSEOG, state, private, college/university gift aid from institutional funds.

**GIFT AID (NON-NEED-BASED) Total amount:** $9,675,963 (95% institutional, 5% external sources). **Receiving aid:** Freshmen: 62% (139). Undergraduates: 71% (761). **Average award:** Freshmen: $15,680. Undergraduates: $15,680. **Scholarships, grants, and awards by category:** Academic interests/achievement: 941 awards ($8,258,630 total): general academic interests/achievements. **Tuition waivers:** Full or partial for employees or children of employees, senior citizens. **ROTC:** Army cooperative, Air Force cooperative.

**LOANS Student loans:** $8,857,364 (35% need-based, 65% non-need-based). 75% of past graduating class borrowed through all loan programs. **Average indebtedness per student:** $26,713. **Average need-based loan:** Freshmen: $4001. Undergraduates: $4855. **Parent loans:** $1,700,497 (100% non-need-based). **Programs:** Federal Direct (Subsidized and Unsubsidized Stafford, PLUS), Perkins, state.

**WORK-STUDY Federal work-study:** Total amount: $244,000; 159 jobs averaging $1530.

**APPLYING FOR FINANCIAL AID Required financial aid form:** FAFSA. **Financial aid deadline (priority):** 5/1. **Notification date:** Continuous beginning 3/1. Students must reply within 2 weeks of notification.

**CONTACT** Mrs. Sharon E. Platt, Director of Financial Aid, La Roche College, 9000 Babcock Boulevard, Pittsburgh, PA 15237-5898, 412-536-1125 or toll-free 800-838-4LRC. **Fax:** 412-536-1072. **E-mail:** sharon.platt@laroche.edu. **Website:** http://www.laroche.edu/.

## LA SALLE UNIVERSITY
### Philadelphia, PA

| Tuition & fees: $39,800 | Average undergraduate aid package: $27,790 |
|---|---|

**ABOUT THE INSTITUTION** Independent Roman Catholic, coed. **Awards:** certificates, associate, bachelor's, master's, and doctoral degrees. 62 undergraduate majors. **Total enrollment:** 6,255. Undergraduates: 4,322. Freshmen: 919. Federal methodology is used as a basis for awarding need-based institutional aid.

**UNDERGRADUATE EXPENSES for 2015–2016 Application fee:** $35. **One-time required fee:** $150. **Comprehensive fee:** $53,740 includes full-time tuition ($39,200), mandatory fees ($600), and room and board ($13,940). **College room only:** $6960. Full-time tuition and fees vary according to course load and program. Room and board charges vary according to board plan and housing facility. **Part-time tuition:** $540 per credit hour. **Part-time fees:** $150 per term. Part-time tuition and fees vary according to course load and program.

**FRESHMAN FINANCIAL AID (Fall 2013)** 857 applied for aid; of those 93% were deemed to have need. 100% of freshmen with need received aid; of those 14% had need fully met. **Average percent of need met:** 75% (excluding resources awarded to replace EFC). **Average financial aid package:** $28,051 (excluding resources awarded to replace EFC). 13% of all full-time freshmen had no need and received non-need-based gift aid.

**UNDERGRADUATE FINANCIAL AID (Fall 2013)** 3,083 applied for aid; of those 93% were deemed to have need. 100% of undergraduates with need received aid; of those 14% had need fully met. **Average percent of need met:** 76% (excluding resources awarded to replace EFC). **Average financial aid package:** $27,790 (excluding resources awarded to replace EFC). 16% of all full-time undergraduates had no need and received non-need-based gift aid.

**GIFT AID (NEED-BASED) Total amount:** $65,521,880 (12% federal, 7% state, 79% institutional, 2% external sources). **Receiving aid:** Freshmen: 85% (794); all full-time undergraduates: 80% (2,828). **Average award:** Freshmen: $23,623; Undergraduates: $22,651. **Scholarships, grants, and awards:** Federal Pell, FSEOG, state, private, college/university gift aid from institutional funds.

**GIFT AID (NON-NEED-BASED) Total amount:** $11,326,271 (97% institutional, 3% external sources). **Receiving aid:** Freshmen: 8% (74). Undergraduates: 7% (238). **Average award:** Freshmen: $17,891. Undergraduates: $16,336. **Scholarships, grants, and awards by category:** Academic interests/achievement: 3,306 awards ($47,035,684 total): general academic interests/achievements. Special achievements/activities: 16 awards ($160,000 total): community service. Special characteristics: 89 awards ($2,766,801 total): children of faculty/staff, relatives of clergy, veterans. **Tuition waivers:** Full or partial for employees or children of employees. **ROTC:** Army cooperative, Air Force cooperative.

**LOANS** *Student loans:* $36,836,259 (71% need-based, 29% non-need-based). 79% of past graduating class borrowed through all loan programs. *Average indebtedness per student:* $35,327. *Average need-based loan:* Freshmen: $3723. Undergraduates: $4795. *Parent loans:* $9,399,003 (48% need-based, 52% non-need-based). *Programs:* Federal Direct (Subsidized and Unsubsidized Stafford, PLUS), Perkins.

**WORK-STUDY** *Federal work-study:* 386 jobs averaging $1292.

**ATHLETIC AWARDS** Total amount: $5,264,739 (47% need-based, 53% non-need-based).

**APPLYING FOR FINANCIAL AID** *Required financial aid form:* FAFSA. *Financial aid deadline (priority):* 2/15. *Notification date:* Continuous beginning 3/15. Students must reply by 5/1 or within 2 weeks of notification.

**CONTACT** Joseph Alaimo, Financial Aid Director, La Salle University, 1900 West Olney Avenue, Philadelphia, PA 19141-1199, 215-951-1070 or toll-free 800-328-1910. *Fax:* 215-951-5098.

*Website:* http://www.lasalle.edu/.

# LASELL COLLEGE
## Newton, MA

| Tuition & fees: $31,000 | Average undergraduate aid package: $24,392 |
|---|---|

**ABOUT THE INSTITUTION** Independent, coed. *Awards:* bachelor's and master's degrees. 46 undergraduate majors. *Total enrollment:* 2,127. Undergraduates: 1,737. Freshmen: 501. Federal methodology is used as a basis for awarding need-based institutional aid.

**UNDERGRADUATE EXPENSES for 2015–2016** *Application fee:* $40. *Comprehensive fee:* $43,750 includes full-time tuition ($29,800), mandatory fees ($1200), and room and board ($12,750). Room and board charges vary according to board plan and housing facility. *Part-time tuition:* $980 per credit hour. *Part-time fees:* $310 per term. Part-time tuition and fees vary according to course load.

**FRESHMAN FINANCIAL AID (Fall 2014, est.)** 450 applied for aid; of those 89% were deemed to have need. 100% of freshmen with need received aid; of those 23% had need fully met. *Average percent of need met:* 73% (excluding resources awarded to replace EFC). *Average financial aid package:* $24,587 (excluding resources awarded to replace EFC). 16% of all full-time freshmen had no need and received non-need-based gift aid.

**UNDERGRADUATE FINANCIAL AID (Fall 2014, est.)** 1,510 applied for aid; of those 93% were deemed to have need. 100% of undergraduates with need received aid; of those 16% had need fully met. *Average percent of need met:* 72% (excluding resources awarded to replace EFC). *Average financial aid package:* $24,392 (excluding resources awarded to replace EFC). 14% of all full-time undergraduates had no need and received non-need-based gift aid.

**GIFT AID (NEED-BASED)** *Total amount:* $26,757,974 (10% federal, 2% state, 84% institutional, 4% external sources). *Receiving aid:* Freshmen: 80% (399); all full-time undergraduates: 82% (1,399). *Average award:* Freshmen: $21,142; Undergraduates: $19,754. *Scholarships, grants, and awards:* Federal Pell, FSEOG, state, private, college/university gift aid from institutional funds.

**GIFT AID (NON-NEED-BASED)** *Total amount:* $5,428,799 (67% institutional, 33% external sources). *Receiving aid:* Freshmen: 14% (68). Undergraduates: 9% (152). *Average award:* Freshmen: $13,945. Undergraduates: $12,241. *Scholarships, grants, and awards by category:* Academic interests/achievement: general academic interests/achievements. Special achievements/activities: community service, general special achievements/activities, leadership. Special characteristics: children and siblings of alumni, children of faculty/staff, siblings of current students, veterans, veterans' children. *Tuition waivers:* Full or partial for children of alumni, employees or children of employees.

**LOANS** *Student loans:* $14,252,285 (70% need-based, 30% non-need-based). 88% of past graduating class borrowed through all loan programs. *Average indebtedness per student:* $37,302. *Average need-based loan:* Freshmen: $3189. Undergraduates: $4281. *Parent loans:* $6,717,709 (44% need-based, 56% non-need-based). *Programs:* Federal Direct (Subsidized and Unsubsidized Stafford, PLUS), Perkins.

**WORK-STUDY** *Federal work-study:* Total amount: $1,204,444; 901 jobs averaging $1800.

**APPLYING FOR FINANCIAL AID** *Required financial aid form:* FAFSA. *Financial aid deadline (priority):* 2/15. *Notification date:* Continuous beginning 2/15. Students must reply by 5/1 or within 2 weeks of notification.

**CONTACT** Michele R. Kosboth, Director of Student Financial Planning, Lasell College, 1844 Commonwealth Avenue, Newton, MA 02466-2709, 617-243-2227 or toll-free 888-LASELL-4. *Fax:* 617-243-2326. *E-mail:* finaid@lasell.edu. *Website:* http://www.lasell.edu/.

# LA SIERRA UNIVERSITY
## Riverside, CA

| Tuition & fees: $30,470 | Average undergraduate aid package: $22,616 |
|---|---|

**ABOUT THE INSTITUTION** Independent Seventh-day Adventist, coed. *Awards:* certificates, bachelor's, master's, and doctoral degrees. 37 undergraduate majors. *Total enrollment:* 2,510. Undergraduates: 2,119. Freshmen: 467. Federal methodology is used as a basis for awarding need-based institutional aid.

**UNDERGRADUATE EXPENSES for 2015–2016** *Comprehensive fee:* $38,270 includes full-time tuition ($29,340), mandatory fees ($1130), and room and board ($7800). Full-time tuition and fees vary according to course load, degree level, and location. Room and board charges vary according to board plan and housing facility. *Part-time tuition:* $815 per quarter hour. Part-time tuition and fees vary according to course load, degree level, and location.

**FRESHMAN FINANCIAL AID (Fall 2014, est.)** 413 applied for aid; of those 93% were deemed to have need. 100% of freshmen with need received aid; of those 10% had need fully met. *Average percent of need met:* 73% (excluding resources awarded to replace EFC). *Average financial aid package:* $24,552 (excluding resources awarded to replace EFC). 17% of all full-time freshmen had no need and received non-need-based gift aid.

**UNDERGRADUATE FINANCIAL AID (Fall 2014, est.)** 1,617 applied for aid; of those 94% were deemed to have need. 100% of undergraduates with need received aid; of those 7% had need fully met. *Average percent of need met:* 69% (excluding resources awarded to replace EFC). *Average financial aid package:* $22,616 (excluding resources awarded to replace EFC). 17% of all full-time undergraduates had no need and received non-need-based gift aid.

**GIFT AID (NEED-BASED)** *Total amount:* $22,188,039 (25% federal, 27% state, 46% institutional, 2% external sources). *Receiving aid:* Freshmen: 83% (381); all full-time undergraduates: 80% (1,518). *Average award:* Freshmen: $23,398; Undergraduates: $20,429. *Scholarships, grants, and awards:* Federal Pell, FSEOG, state, private, college/university gift aid from institutional funds.

**GIFT AID (NON-NEED-BASED)** *Total amount:* $2,927,247 (98% institutional, 2% external sources). *Receiving aid:* Freshmen: 7% (32). Undergraduates: 4% (84). *Average award:* Freshmen: $11,333. Undergraduates: $8262. *Scholarships, grants, and awards by category:* Academic interests/achievement: biological sciences, business, education, English, foreign languages, general academic interests/achievements, religion/biblical studies. Creative arts/performance: applied art and design, art/fine arts, music, theater/drama. Special achievements/activities: leadership. Special characteristics: adult students, children of faculty/staff, public servants, relatives of clergy, religious affiliation, siblings of current students. *Tuition waivers:* Full or partial for employees or children of employees.

**LOANS** *Student loans:* $12,979,703 (97% need-based, 3% non-need-based). 71% of past graduating class borrowed through all loan programs. *Average indebtedness per student:* $36,251. *Average need-based loan:* Freshmen: $3493. Undergraduates: $5264. *Parent loans:* $4,307,747 (93% need-based, 7% non-need-based). *Programs:* Federal Direct (Subsidized and Unsubsidized Stafford, PLUS), Perkins, state.

**WORK-STUDY** *Federal work-study:* Total amount: $1,538,472; jobs available.

**ATHLETIC AWARDS** Total amount: $154,449 (95% need-based, 5% non-need-based).

**APPLYING FOR FINANCIAL AID** *Required financial aid forms:* FAFSA, state aid form. *Financial aid deadline:* 8/15 (priority: 3/2). *Notification date:* Continuous beginning 4/15. Students must reply by 8/5 or within 2 weeks of notification.

**CONTACT** Mrs. Elina Bascomb, Director of Financial Aid, La Sierra University, 4500 Riverwalk Parkway, Riverside, CA 92515, 951-785-2359 or toll-free 800-874-5587. *Fax:* 951-785-2942. *E-mail:* sfs@lasierra.edu. *Website:* http://www.lasierra.edu/.

# LAUREL UNIVERSITY
## High Point, NC

**CONTACT** Mrs. Shirley P. Carter, Director of Financial Aid, Laurel University, 1215 Eastchester Drive, High Point, NC 27265, 336-887-3000. *Fax:* 336-889-2261. *E-mail:* scarter@laureluniversity.edu.
*Website:* http://www.laureluniversity.edu/.

# LAWRENCE TECHNOLOGICAL UNIVERSITY
## Southfield, MI

| Tuition & fees: $30,200 | Average undergraduate aid package: $23,443 |
|---|---|

**ABOUT THE INSTITUTION** Independent, coed. *Awards:* certificates, associate, bachelor's, master's, and doctoral degrees. 50 undergraduate majors. *Total enrollment:* 4,015. Undergraduates: 2,798. Freshmen: 337. Federal methodology is used as a basis for awarding need-based institutional aid.

**UNDERGRADUATE EXPENSES for 2015–2016** *Application fee:* $30. *Comprehensive fee:* $39,186 includes full-time tuition ($29,580), mandatory fees ($620), and room and board ($8986). *College room only:* $5095. Full-time tuition and fees vary according to course level, degree level, location, program, and student level. Room and board charges vary according to board plan and housing facility. *Part-time tuition:* $986 per credit hour. *Part-time fees:* $310 per term. Part-time tuition and fees vary according to course level, degree level, location, program, and student level.

**FRESHMAN FINANCIAL AID (Fall 2013)** 311 applied for aid; of those 79% were deemed to have need. 99% of freshmen with need received aid; of those 18% had need fully met. *Average percent of need met:* 71% (excluding resources awarded to replace EFC). *Average financial aid package:* $23,061 (excluding resources awarded to replace EFC). 17% of all full-time freshmen had no need and received non-need-based gift aid.

**UNDERGRADUATE FINANCIAL AID (Fall 2013)** 1,230 applied for aid; of those 74% were deemed to have need. 99% of undergraduates with need received aid; of those 14% had need fully met. *Average percent of need met:* 68% (excluding resources awarded to replace EFC). *Average financial aid package:* $23,443 (excluding resources awarded to replace EFC). 18% of all full-time undergraduates had no need and received non-need-based gift aid.

**GIFT AID (NEED-BASED)** *Total amount:* $13,710,963 (17% federal, 9% state, 72% institutional, 2% external sources). *Receiving aid:* Freshmen: 68% (240); all full-time undergraduates: 59% (884). *Average award:* Freshmen: $15,881; Undergraduates: $14,033. *Scholarships, grants, and awards:* Federal Pell, FSEOG, state, private, college/university gift aid from institutional funds, Michigan National Guard and ROTC Scholarships.

**GIFT AID (NON-NEED-BASED)** *Total amount:* $3,479,759 (99% institutional, 1% external sources). *Receiving aid:* Freshmen: 62% (220). Undergraduates: 48% (716). *Average award:* Freshmen: $13,358. Undergraduates: $12,603. *Scholarships, grants, and awards by category:* Academic interests/achievement: 2,427 awards ($13,935,731 total): architecture, business, computer science, education, engineering/technologies, general academic interests/achievements, humanities, international studies, mathematics, military science, physical sciences. *Special achievements/activities:* 30 awards ($13,513 total): cheerleading/drum major, junior miss. *Special characteristics:* 63 awards ($1,003,562 total): children of faculty/staff, members of minority groups. *Tuition waivers:* Full or partial for employees or children of employees. *ROTC:* Air Force cooperative.

**LOANS** *Student loans:* $7,341,304 (97% need-based, 3% non-need-based). 69% of past graduating class borrowed through all loan programs. *Average indebtedness per student:* $38,966. *Average need-based loan:* Freshmen: $6112. Undergraduates: $7382. *Parent loans:* $6,020,201 (95% need-based, 5% non-need-based). *Programs:* Federal Direct (Subsidized and Unsubsidized Stafford, PLUS), Perkins, state, college/university, alternative loans.

**WORK-STUDY** *Federal work-study:* 80 jobs averaging $2259. *State or other work-study/employment:* Part-time jobs available.

**ATHLETIC AWARDS** Total amount: $1,644,233 (100% non-need-based).

**APPLYING FOR FINANCIAL AID** *Required financial aid form:* FAFSA. *Financial aid deadline (priority):* 4/1. *Notification date:* Continuous beginning 4/1. Students must reply within 2 weeks of notification.
**CONTACT** Mrs. Dee King, Interim Director of Financial Aid, Lawrence Technological University, 21000 West Ten Mile Road, Southfield, MI 48075-1058, 248-204-2127 or toll-free 800-225-5588. *Fax:* 248-204-2228. *E-mail:* dking@ltu.edu.
*Website:* http://www.ltu.edu/.

# LAWRENCE UNIVERSITY
## Appleton, WI

| Tuition & fees: $42,657 | Average undergraduate aid package: $35,069 |
|---|---|

**ABOUT THE INSTITUTION** Independent, coed. *Awards:* bachelor's degrees. 59 undergraduate majors. *Total enrollment:* 1,519. Undergraduates: 1,519. Freshmen: 385. Institutional methodology is used as a basis for awarding need-based institutional aid.

**UNDERGRADUATE EXPENSES for 2015–2016** *Application fee:* $40. *Comprehensive fee:* $51,465 includes full-time tuition ($42,357), mandatory fees ($300), and room and board ($8808). *College room only:* $4152.

**FRESHMAN FINANCIAL AID (Fall 2014, est.)** 306 applied for aid; of those 84% were deemed to have need. 100% of freshmen with need received aid; of those 39% had need fully met. *Average percent of need met:* 93% (excluding resources awarded to replace EFC). *Average financial aid package:* $36,415 (excluding resources awarded to replace EFC). 28% of all full-time freshmen had no need and received non-need-based gift aid.

**UNDERGRADUATE FINANCIAL AID (Fall 2014, est.)** 1,079 applied for aid; of those 88% were deemed to have need. 100% of undergraduates with need received aid; of those 33% had need fully met. *Average percent of need met:* 90% (excluding resources awarded to replace EFC). *Average financial aid package:* $35,069 (excluding resources awarded to replace EFC). 31% of all full-time undergraduates had no need and received non-need-based gift aid.

**GIFT AID (NEED-BASED)** *Total amount:* $27,033,969 (6% federal, 3% state, 88% institutional, 3% external sources). *Receiving aid:* Freshmen: 68% (257); all full-time undergraduates: 66% (952). *Average award:* Freshmen: $31,098; Undergraduates: $29,111. *Scholarships, grants, and awards:* Federal Pell, FSEOG, state, private, college/university gift aid from institutional funds.

**GIFT AID (NON-NEED-BASED)** *Total amount:* $8,358,508 (98% institutional, 2% external sources). *Receiving aid:* Freshmen: 2% (6). Undergraduates: 2% (34). *Average award:* Freshmen: $21,598. Undergraduates: $18,007. *Scholarships, grants, and awards by category:* Academic interests/achievement: 747 awards ($11,028,500 total): general academic interests/achievements. *Creative arts/performance:* 134 awards ($1,481,000 total): music. *Special achievements/activities:* 517 awards ($1,396,600 total): community service, general special achievements/activities. *Special characteristics:* 359 awards ($6,218,431 total): children and siblings of alumni, children of faculty/staff, ethnic background, international students, siblings of current students, veterans, veterans' children. *Tuition waivers:* Full or partial for employees or children of employees.

**LOANS** *Student loans:* $7,523,280 (53% need-based, 47% non-need-based). 67% of past graduating class borrowed through all loan programs. *Average indebtedness per student:* $33,755. *Average need-based loan:* Freshmen: $4648. Undergraduates: $5474. *Parent loans:* $1,948,815 (100% non-need-based). *Programs:* Federal Direct (Subsidized and Unsubsidized Stafford, PLUS), Perkins, private loans.

**WORK-STUDY** *Federal work-study:* Total amount: $1,421,933; 631 jobs averaging $2105. *State or other work-study/employment:* Total amount: $814,301 (100% non-need-based). 431 part-time jobs averaging $1937.

**APPLYING FOR FINANCIAL AID** *Required financial aid forms:* FAFSA, CSS Financial Aid PROFILE, noncustodial (divorced/separated) parent's statement, federal income tax form(s). *Financial aid deadline (priority):* 3/1. *Notification date:* Continuous beginning 3/1. Students must reply by 5/1.
**CONTACT** Mrs. Sara Beth Holman, Director of Financial Aid, Lawrence University, 711 East Boldt Way SPC 32, Appleton, WI 54911, 920-832-6583 or toll-free 800-227-0982. *Fax:* 920-832-6582. *E-mail:* sara.b.holman@lawrence.edu.
*Website:* http://www.lawrence.edu/.

# LEBANON VALLEY COLLEGE
### Annville, PA

| Tuition & fees: $37,470 | Average undergraduate aid package: $28,025 |
|---|---|

**ABOUT THE INSTITUTION** Independent United Methodist, coed. **Awards:** certificates, bachelor's, master's, and doctoral degrees. 37 undergraduate majors. **Total enrollment:** 1,901. Undergraduates: 1,683. Freshmen: 413. Federal methodology is used as a basis for awarding need-based institutional aid.

**UNDERGRADUATE EXPENSES for 2015–2016 Comprehensive fee:** $47,570 includes full-time tuition ($36,470), mandatory fees ($1000), and room and board ($10,100). **College room only:** $4880. Room and board charges vary according to board plan and housing facility. **Part-time tuition:** $595 per credit. Part-time tuition and fees vary according to class time and degree level.

**FRESHMAN FINANCIAL AID (Fall 2014, est.)** 400 applied for aid; of those 91% were deemed to have need. 100% of freshmen with need received aid; of those 20% had need fully met. **Average percent of need met:** 80% (excluding resources awarded to replace EFC). **Average financial aid package:** $31,010 (excluding resources awarded to replace EFC). 14% of all full-time freshmen had no need and received non-need-based gift aid.

**UNDERGRADUATE FINANCIAL AID (Fall 2014, est.)** 1,439 applied for aid; of those 93% were deemed to have need. 100% of undergraduates with need received aid; of those 28% had need fully met. **Average percent of need met:** 75% (excluding resources awarded to replace EFC). **Average financial aid package:** $28,025 (excluding resources awarded to replace EFC). 15% of all full-time undergraduates had no need and received non-need-based gift aid.

**GIFT AID (NEED-BASED) Total amount:** $27,504,280 (7% federal, 8% state, 85% institutional). **Receiving aid:** Freshmen: 87% (359); all full-time undergraduates: 84% (1,319). **Average award:** Freshmen: $24,817; Undergraduates: $23,715. **Scholarships, grants, and awards:** Federal Pell, FSEOG, state, private, college/university gift aid from institutional funds, TEACH Grants.

**GIFT AID (NON-NEED-BASED) Total amount:** $5,440,644 (1% federal, 1% state, 80% institutional, 18% external sources). **Receiving aid:** Freshmen: 7% (30). Undergraduates: 7% (116). **Average award:** Freshmen: $14,855. Undergraduates: $15,249. **Scholarships, grants, and awards by category:** Academic interests/achievement: 1,311 awards ($20,187,873 total): biological sciences, English, general academic interests/achievements, mathematics, physical sciences, religion/biblical studies, social sciences. Creative arts/performance: 48 awards ($93,084 total): music. Special achievements/activities: 67 awards ($34,780 total): general special achievements/activities. Special characteristics: 270 awards ($2,279,203 total): children and siblings of alumni, children of faculty/staff, ethnic background, international students, members of minority groups, veterans. **Tuition waivers:** Full or partial for employees or children of employees, senior citizens.

**LOANS Student loans:** $14,183,241 (37% need-based, 63% non-need-based). 80% of past graduating class borrowed through all loan programs. **Average indebtedness per student:** $36,752. **Average need-based loan:** Freshmen: $3974. Undergraduates: $4467. **Parent loans:** $6,880,478 (100% non-need-based). **Programs:** Federal Direct (Subsidized and Unsubsidized Stafford, PLUS), Perkins.

**WORK-STUDY Federal work-study:** Total amount: $1,544,864; 1,045 jobs averaging $1447.

**APPLYING FOR FINANCIAL AID Required financial aid form:** FAFSA. **Financial aid deadline (priority):** 3/1. **Notification date:** Continuous beginning 3/1. Students must reply by 5/1 or within 2 weeks of notification.

**CONTACT** Mrs. Kendra M. Feigert, Director of Financial Aid, Lebanon Valley College, 101 North College Avenue, Annville, PA 17003, 866-582-4236 or toll-free 866-LVC-4ADM. Fax: 717-867-6027. E-mail: feigert@lvc.edu. Website: http://www.lvc.edu/.

# LEES-MCRAE COLLEGE
### Banner Elk, NC

| Tuition & fees: $24,854 | Average undergraduate aid package: $22,736 |
|---|---|

**ABOUT THE INSTITUTION** Independent Presbyterian Church (U.S.A.), coed. **Awards:** bachelor's degrees. 24 undergraduate majors. **Total enrollment:** 940. Undergraduates: 940. Freshmen: 216. Both federal and institutional methodology are used as a basis for awarding need-based institutional aid.

**UNDERGRADUATE EXPENSES for 2015–2016 Application fee:** $35. **Comprehensive fee:** $34,636 includes full-time tuition ($24,154), mandatory fees ($700), and room and board ($9782). **College room only:** $4896. Full-time tuition and fees vary according to course load, location, and reciprocity agreements. Room and board charges vary according to housing facility. Part-time tuition and fees vary according to course load, location, and reciprocity agreements.

**FRESHMAN FINANCIAL AID (Fall 2014, est.)** 204 applied for aid; of those 92% were deemed to have need. 100% of freshmen with need received aid; of those 3% had need fully met. **Average percent of need met:** 70% (excluding resources awarded to replace EFC). **Average financial aid package:** $22,790 (excluding resources awarded to replace EFC). 8% of all full-time freshmen had no need and received non-need-based gift aid.

**UNDERGRADUATE FINANCIAL AID (Fall 2014, est.)** 781 applied for aid; of those 96% were deemed to have need. 100% of undergraduates with need received aid; of those 1% had need fully met. **Average percent of need met:** 71% (excluding resources awarded to replace EFC). **Average financial aid package:** $22,736 (excluding resources awarded to replace EFC). 13% of all full-time undergraduates had no need and received non-need-based gift aid.

**GIFT AID (NEED-BASED) Total amount:** $14,415,141 (14% federal, 11% state, 74% institutional, 1% external sources). **Receiving aid:** Freshmen: 87% (187). **Average award:** Freshmen: $9840; Undergraduates: $7487. **Scholarships, grants, and awards:** Federal Pell, FSEOG, state, private, college/university gift aid from institutional funds.

**GIFT AID (NON-NEED-BASED) Receiving aid:** Freshmen: 87% (187). Undergraduates: 80% (746). **Average award:** Freshmen: $9028. Undergraduates: $17,170. **Scholarships, grants, and awards by category:** Academic interests/achievement: biological sciences, education, general academic interests/achievements, mathematics. Creative arts/performance: dance, journalism/publications, performing arts, theater/drama. Special achievements/activities: cheerleading/drum major, general special achievements/activities. Special characteristics: children of educators, children of faculty/staff, children with a deceased or disabled parent, international students, local/state students, previous college experience, relatives of clergy, religious affiliation, veterans. **Tuition waivers:** Full or partial for employees or children of employees.

**LOANS Student loans:** $5,766,880 (100% need-based). **Average need-based loan:** Freshmen: $3500. Undergraduates: $5000. **Parent loans:** $1,576,260 (100% need-based). **Programs:** Federal Direct (Subsidized and Unsubsidized Stafford, PLUS), Perkins, state.

**WORK-STUDY Federal work-study:** Total amount: $182,740; jobs available. **State or other work-study/employment:** Total amount: $8800 (100% need-based). Part-time jobs available.

**ATHLETIC AWARDS** Total amount: $1,657,925 (100% need-based).

**APPLYING FOR FINANCIAL AID Required financial aid forms:** FAFSA, state aid form. **Financial aid deadline (priority):** 4/15. **Notification date:** Continuous beginning 3/1. Students must reply within 2 weeks of notification.

**CONTACT** Cathy Shell, Director of Financial Aid, Lees-McRae College, PO Box 128, Banner Elk, NC 28604-0128, 828-898-8740 or toll-free 800-280-4562. Fax: 828-898-8746. E-mail: shell@lmc.edu. Website: http://www.lmc.edu/.

# LEE UNIVERSITY
### Cleveland, TN

| Tuition & fees: $15,000 | Average undergraduate aid package: $11,183 |
|---|---|

**ABOUT THE INSTITUTION** Independent Church of God, coed. **Awards:** certificates, bachelor's, and master's degrees. 68 undergraduate majors. **Total enrollment:** 5,098. Undergraduates: 4,575. Freshmen: 757. Federal methodology is used as a basis for awarding need-based institutional aid.

**UNDERGRADUATE EXPENSES for 2015–2016 Comprehensive fee:** $22,045 includes full-time tuition ($14,400), mandatory fees ($600), and room and board ($7045). **College room only:** $3595. Full-time tuition and fees vary according to course load, location, and program. Room and board charges vary according to board plan and housing facility. **Part-time tuition:** $600 per credit hour. **Part-time fees:** $60 per term. Part-time tuition and fees vary according to course load, location, and program.

**FRESHMAN FINANCIAL AID (Fall 2014, est.)** 659 applied for aid; of those 79% were deemed to have need. 100% of freshmen with need received aid; of those 23% had need fully met. *Average percent of need met:* 61% (excluding resources awarded to replace EFC). *Average financial aid package:* $12,764 (excluding resources awarded to replace EFC). 19% of all full-time freshmen had no need and received non-need-based gift aid.

**UNDERGRADUATE FINANCIAL AID (Fall 2014, est.)** 3,193 applied for aid; of those 85% were deemed to have need. 99% of undergraduates with need received aid; of those 12% had need fully met. *Average percent of need met:* 47% (excluding resources awarded to replace EFC). *Average financial aid package:* $11,183 (excluding resources awarded to replace EFC). 14% of all full-time undergraduates had no need and received non-need-based gift aid.

**GIFT AID (NEED-BASED)** *Total amount:* $19,231,569 (39% federal, 20% state, 38% institutional, 3% external sources). *Receiving aid:* Freshmen: 65% (486); all full-time undergraduates: 64% (2,402). *Average award:* Freshmen: $10,616; Undergraduates: $8449. *Scholarships, grants, and awards:* Federal Pell, FSEOG, state, private, college/university gift aid from institutional funds.

**GIFT AID (NON-NEED-BASED)** *Total amount:* $5,872,930 (1% federal, 24% state, 71% institutional, 4% external sources). *Receiving aid:* Freshmen: 11% (79). Undergraduates: 6% (221). *Average award:* Freshmen: $8465. Undergraduates: $6898. *Scholarships, grants, and awards by category: Academic interests/achievement:* biological sciences, business, communication, education, general academic interests/achievements, religion/biblical studies. *Creative arts/performance:* music, theater/drama. *Special achievements/activities:* cheerleading/drum major, leadership, religious involvement. *Special characteristics:* children of faculty/staff, local/state students, siblings of current students, spouses of current students. *Tuition waivers:* Full or partial for employees or children of employees, senior citizens.

**LOANS** *Student loans:* $24,374,623 (80% need-based, 20% non-need-based). 62% of past graduating class borrowed through all loan programs. *Average indebtedness per student:* $32,163. *Average need-based loan:* Freshmen: $3528. Undergraduates: $4247. *Parent loans:* $3,671,903 (51% need-based, 49% non-need-based). *Programs:* Federal Direct (Subsidized and Unsubsidized Stafford, PLUS), Perkins, college/university.

**WORK-STUDY** *Federal work-study:* Total amount: $428,372; 251 jobs averaging $1632. *State or other work-study/employment:* Total amount: $4400 (100% non-need-based). 577 part-time jobs averaging $1358.

**ATHLETIC AWARDS** Total amount: $1,916,990 (40% need-based, 60% non-need-based).

**APPLYING FOR FINANCIAL AID** *Required financial aid form:* FAFSA. *Financial aid deadline (priority):* 3/15. *Notification date:* Continuous beginning 2/1.

**CONTACT** Mrs. Marian Dill, Director of Student Financial Aid, Lee University, 1120 North Ocoee Street, Cleveland, TN 37311, 423-614-8300 or toll-free 800-533-9930. *Fax:* 423-614-8308. *E-mail:* finaid@leeuniversity.edu. *Website:* http://www.leeuniversity.edu/.

# LEHIGH UNIVERSITY
## Bethlehem, PA

| Tuition & fees: $44,890 | Average undergraduate aid package: $38,996 |
|---|---|

**ABOUT THE INSTITUTION** Independent, coed. *Awards:* certificates, bachelor's, master's, and doctoral degrees. 69 undergraduate majors. *Total enrollment:* 7,119. Undergraduates: 5,062. Freshmen: 1,299. Both federal and institutional methodology are used as a basis for awarding need-based institutional aid.

**UNDERGRADUATE EXPENSES for 2015–2016** *Application fee:* $70. *Comprehensive fee:* $56,770 includes full-time tuition ($44,520), mandatory fees ($370), and room and board ($11,880). *College room only:* $6820. Room and board charges vary according to board plan and housing facility. *Part-time tuition:* $1860 per credit hour. *Payment plan:* Tuition prepayment.

**FRESHMAN FINANCIAL AID (Fall 2014, est.)** 820 applied for aid; of those 63% were deemed to have need. 100% of freshmen with need received aid; of those 40% had need fully met. *Average percent of need met:* 93% (excluding resources awarded to replace EFC). *Average financial aid package:* $36,551 (excluding resources awarded to replace EFC). 5% of all full-time freshmen had no need and received non-need-based gift aid.

**UNDERGRADUATE FINANCIAL AID (Fall 2014, est.)** 2,738 applied for aid; of those 74% were deemed to have need. 100% of undergraduates with need received aid; of those 62% had need fully met. *Average percent of need met:* 96% (excluding resources awarded to replace EFC). *Average financial aid package:* $38,996 (excluding resources awarded to replace EFC). 6% of all full-time undergraduates had no need and received non-need-based gift aid.

**GIFT AID (NEED-BASED)** *Total amount:* $63,588,774 (6% federal, 2% state, 92% institutional). *Receiving aid:* Freshmen: 39% (502); all full-time undergraduates: 40% (1,986). *Average award:* Freshmen: $31,819; Undergraduates: $32,995. *Scholarships, grants, and awards:* Federal Pell, FSEOG, state, private, college/university gift aid from institutional funds, United Negro College Fund.

**GIFT AID (NON-NEED-BASED)** *Total amount:* $7,297,625 (53% institutional, 47% external sources). *Receiving aid:* Freshmen: 5% (60). Undergraduates: 6% (293). *Average award:* Freshmen: $15,235. Undergraduates: $12,424. *Scholarships, grants, and awards by category: Academic interests/achievement:* 281 awards ($3,132,641 total): business, communication, engineering/technologies, general academic interests/achievements, international studies, military science. *Creative arts/performance:* 82 awards ($137,390 total): general creative arts/performance, journalism/publications, music, performing arts, theater/drama. *Special achievements/activities:* 11 awards ($16,000 total): general special achievements/activities. *Special characteristics:* 89 awards ($3,770,810 total): children of faculty/staff, members of minority groups. *Tuition waivers:* Full or partial for employees or children of employees. *ROTC:* Army.

**LOANS** *Student loans:* $25,182,812 (40% need-based, 60% non-need-based). 52% of past graduating class borrowed through all loan programs. *Average indebtedness per student:* $31,877. *Average need-based loan:* Freshmen: $4047. Undergraduates: $4714. *Parent loans:* $6,493,956 (100% non-need-based). *Programs:* Federal Direct (Subsidized and Unsubsidized Stafford, PLUS), Perkins, college/university.

**WORK-STUDY** *Federal work-study:* Total amount: $2,656,138; 1,285 jobs averaging $1664. *State or other work-study/employment:* Total amount: $805,856 (7% need-based, 93% non-need-based). 29 part-time jobs averaging $1891.

**ATHLETIC AWARDS** Total amount: $8,094,502 (5% need-based, 95% non-need-based).

**APPLYING FOR FINANCIAL AID** *Required financial aid forms:* FAFSA, CSS Financial Aid PROFILE, noncustodial (divorced/separated) parent's statement, business/farm supplement. *Financial aid deadline:* 2/15. *Notification date:* 3/30. Students must reply by 5/1 or within 3 weeks of notification.

**CONTACT** Jennifer Mertz, Director of Financial Aid, Lehigh University, 27 Memorial Drive West, Bethlehem, PA 18015-3094, 610-758-3181. *Fax:* 610-758-6211. *E-mail:* jlm207@lehigh.edu. *Website:* http://www.lehigh.edu/.

# LEHMAN COLLEGE OF THE CITY UNIVERSITY OF NEW YORK
## Bronx, NY

| Tuition & fees (NY res): $6429 | Average undergraduate aid package: N/A |
|---|---|

**ABOUT THE INSTITUTION** State and locally supported, coed. *Awards:* certificates, bachelor's, and master's degrees. 52 undergraduate majors. *Total enrollment:* 12,220. Undergraduates: 10,021. Freshmen: 588. Federal methodology is used as a basis for awarding need-based institutional aid.

**UNDERGRADUATE EXPENSES for 2015–2016** *Application fee:* $65. *Tuition, state resident:* full-time $6030; part-time $260 per credit hour. *Tuition, nonresident:* full-time $12,840; part-time $535 per credit hour. *Required fees:* full-time $399; $117.10 per term. Full-time tuition and fees vary according to course load. Part-time tuition and fees vary according to course load. Room and board charges vary according to housing facility.

**FRESHMAN FINANCIAL AID (Fall 2013)** 436 applied for aid; of those 100% were deemed to have need. 94% of freshmen with need received aid.

**UNDERGRADUATE FINANCIAL AID (Fall 2013)** 4,454 applied for aid; of those 97% were deemed to have need. 100% of undergraduates with need received aid.

**GIFT AID (NEED-BASED)** *Total amount:* $72,109,842 (98% federal, 2% state). *Receiving aid:* Freshmen: 74% (395); all full-time undergraduates: 75% (4,017). *Average award:* Freshmen: $1947; Undergraduates: $2130. *Scholarships, grants,*

and awards: Federal Pell, FSEOG, state, college/university gift aid from institutional funds.
**GIFT AID (NON-NEED-BASED)** *Total amount:* $20,922,097 (100% federal). *Receiving aid:* Freshmen: 5% (29). Undergraduates: 13% (685). **ROTC:** Army cooperative.
**LOANS** *Student loans:* $42,619,473 (51% need-based, 49% non-need-based). 25% of past graduating class borrowed through all loan programs. *Average indebtedness per student:* $8525. *Average need-based loan:* Freshmen: $1017. Undergraduates: $1160. *Parent loans:* $21,014 (100% non-need-based). *Programs:* Federal Direct (Subsidized and Unsubsidized Stafford, PLUS), Perkins.
**WORK-STUDY** *Federal work-study:* jobs available. *State or other work-study/employment:* Part-time jobs available.
**APPLYING FOR FINANCIAL AID** *Required financial aid forms:* FAFSA, state aid form. *Financial aid deadline:* Continuous. *Notification date:* Continuous beginning 3/1.
**CONTACT** David Martinez, Director of Financial Aid, Lehman College of the City University of New York, 250 Bedford Park Boulevard West, Bronx, NY 10468-1589, 718-960-8545 or toll-free 877-LEHMAN1. *Fax:* 718-960-8328. *E-mail:* idmlc@cunyvm.cuny.edu.
*Website:* http://www.lehman.cuny.edu/.

# LE MOYNE COLLEGE
## Syracuse, NY

| Tuition & fees: $31,340 | Average undergraduate aid package: $23,164 |
| --- | --- |

**ABOUT THE INSTITUTION** Independent Roman Catholic (Jesuit), coed. *Awards:* certificates, bachelor's, and master's degrees. 54 undergraduate majors. *Total enrollment:* 3,381. Undergraduates: 2,849. Freshmen: 678. Both federal and institutional methodology are used as a basis for awarding need-based institutional aid.
**UNDERGRADUATE EXPENSES for 2015–2016** *Application fee:* $35. *Comprehensive fee:* $43,470 includes full-time tuition ($30,350), mandatory fees ($990), and room and board ($12,130). *College room only:* $7650. Room and board charges vary according to board plan and housing facility. *Part-time tuition:* $637 per credit hour. Part-time tuition and fees vary according to class time and course load.
**FRESHMAN FINANCIAL AID (Fall 2013)** 592 applied for aid; of those 90% were deemed to have need. 100% of freshmen with need received aid; of those 27% had need fully met. *Average percent of need met:* 80% (excluding resources awarded to replace EFC). *Average financial aid package:* $24,792 (excluding resources awarded to replace EFC). 10% of all full-time freshmen had no need and received non-need-based gift aid.
**UNDERGRADUATE FINANCIAL AID (Fall 2013)** 2,166 applied for aid; of those 92% were deemed to have need. 100% of undergraduates with need received aid; of those 22% had need fully met. *Average percent of need met:* 75% (excluding resources awarded to replace EFC). *Average financial aid package:* $23,164 (excluding resources awarded to replace EFC). 7% of all full-time undergraduates had no need and received non-need-based gift aid.
**GIFT AID (NEED-BASED)** *Total amount:* $37,049,212 (10% federal, 9% state, 78% institutional, 3% external sources). *Receiving aid:* Freshmen: 86% (533); all full-time undergraduates: 83% (1,982). *Average award:* Freshmen: $20,669; Undergraduates: $18,568. *Scholarships, grants, and awards:* Federal Pell, FSEOG, state, private, college/university gift aid from institutional funds.
**GIFT AID (NON-NEED-BASED)** *Total amount:* $4,701,939 (90% institutional, 10% external sources). *Receiving aid:* Freshmen: 15% (96). Undergraduates: 11% (254). *Average award:* Freshmen: $7356. Undergraduates: $6733. *Scholarships, grants, and awards by category:* Academic interests/achievement: 592 awards ($10,416,150 total): general academic interests/achievements. Creative arts/performance: 25 awards ($7103 total): music. Special achievements/activities: 612 awards ($6,758,881 total): leadership. Special characteristics: 172 awards ($827,120 total): children and siblings of alumni, members of minority groups. *Tuition waivers:* Full or partial for employees or children of employees. **ROTC:** Army cooperative, Air Force cooperative.
**LOANS** *Student loans:* $19,619,091 (95% need-based, 5% non-need-based). 88% of past graduating class borrowed through all loan programs. *Average indebtedness per student:* $34,500. *Average need-based loan:* Freshmen: $3649. Undergrad-

uates: $4586. *Parent loans:* $5,750,940 (96% need-based, 4% non-need-based). *Programs:* Federal Direct (Subsidized and Unsubsidized Stafford, PLUS), Perkins.
**WORK-STUDY** *Federal work-study:* 428 jobs averaging $862. *State or other work-study/employment:* 472 part-time jobs averaging $1556.
**ATHLETIC AWARDS** *Total amount:* $1,528,064 (61% need-based, 39% non-need-based).
**APPLYING FOR FINANCIAL AID** *Required financial aid forms:* FAFSA, state aid form. *Financial aid deadline (priority):* 2/15. *Notification date:* 3/15. Students must reply by 5/1 or within 2 weeks of notification.
**CONTACT** Mrs. Sharon J. Halpin, Director of Financial Aid, Le Moyne College, 1419 Salt Springs Road, Syracuse, NY 13214-1301, 315-445-4400 or toll-free 800-333-4733. *Fax:* 315-445-4182. *E-mail:* halpins@lemoyne.edu.
*Website:* http://www.lemoyne.edu/.

# LEMOYNE-OWEN COLLEGE
## Memphis, TN

| Tuition & fees: $10,900 | Average undergraduate aid package: $10,423 |
| --- | --- |

**ABOUT THE INSTITUTION** Independent United Church of Christ, coed. *Awards:* certificates and bachelor's degrees. 22 undergraduate majors. *Total enrollment:* 1,023. Undergraduates: 1,023. Freshmen: 161. Federal methodology is used as a basis for awarding need-based institutional aid.
**UNDERGRADUATE EXPENSES for 2015–2016** *Application fee:* $25. *Comprehensive fee:* $16,810 includes full-time tuition ($10,680), mandatory fees ($220), and room and board ($5910). *College room only:* $3600. Room and board charges vary according to housing facility. *Part-time tuition:* $436 per credit hour.
**FRESHMAN FINANCIAL AID (Fall 2013)** 140 applied for aid; of those 99% were deemed to have need. 99% of freshmen with need received aid; of those 3% had need fully met. *Average percent of need met:* 49% (excluding resources awarded to replace EFC). *Average financial aid package:* $10,676 (excluding resources awarded to replace EFC). 3% of all full-time freshmen had no need and received non-need-based gift aid.
**UNDERGRADUATE FINANCIAL AID (Fall 2013)** 773 applied for aid; of those 99% were deemed to have need. 98% of undergraduates with need received aid; of those 2% had need fully met. *Average percent of need met:* 47% (excluding resources awarded to replace EFC). *Average financial aid package:* $10,423 (excluding resources awarded to replace EFC). 1% of all full-time undergraduates had no need and received non-need-based gift aid.
**GIFT AID (NEED-BASED)** *Total amount:* $5,914,410 (67% federal, 22% state, 6% institutional, 5% external sources). *Receiving aid:* Freshmen: 93% (136); all full-time undergraduates: 89% (700). *Average award:* Freshmen: $7800; Undergraduates: $7384. *Scholarships, grants, and awards:* Federal Pell, FSEOG, state, private, college/university gift aid from institutional funds, United Negro College Fund.
**GIFT AID (NON-NEED-BASED)** *Total amount:* $173,766 (2% federal, 6% state, 69% institutional, 23% external sources). *Receiving aid:* Freshmen: 1% (1). Undergraduates: 1% (10). *Average award:* Freshmen: $3819. Undergraduates: $11,002. *Scholarships, grants, and awards by category:* Academic interests/achievement: 52 awards: general academic interests/achievements. Creative arts/performance: 23 awards: journalism/publications, music. Special characteristics: 13 awards: children of faculty/staff. *Tuition waivers:* Full or partial for employees or children of employees. **ROTC:** Army cooperative, Air Force cooperative.
**LOANS** *Student loans:* $6,491,394 (97% need-based, 3% non-need-based). 96% of past graduating class borrowed through all loan programs. *Average indebtedness per student:* $27,441. *Average need-based loan:* Freshmen: $3084. Undergraduates: $3603. *Parent loans:* $211,135 (83% need-based, 17% non-need-based). *Programs:* Federal Direct (Subsidized and Unsubsidized Stafford, PLUS).
**WORK-STUDY** *Federal work-study:* 145 jobs averaging $1670.
**ATHLETIC AWARDS** *Total amount:* $311,873 (82% need-based, 18% non-need-based).
**APPLYING FOR FINANCIAL AID** *Required financial aid forms:* FAFSA, institution's own form. *Financial aid deadline (priority):* 4/1. *Notification date:* Continuous beginning 5/1. Students must reply within 2 weeks of notification.
**CONTACT** Office of Student Financial Services, LeMoyne-Owen College, 807 Walker Avenue, Memphis, TN 38126-6595, 901-435-1552 or toll-free 800-737-7778. *Fax:* 901-435-1574.
*Website:* http://www.loc.edu/.

# LENOIR-RHYNE UNIVERSITY
## Hickory, NC

| Tuition & fees: $32,140 | Average undergraduate aid package: $25,242 |
| --- | --- |

**ABOUT THE INSTITUTION** Independent Lutheran, coed. *Awards:* bachelor's and master's degrees. 49 undergraduate majors. *Total enrollment:* 2,143. Undergraduates: 1,524. Freshmen: 347. Federal methodology is used as a basis for awarding need-based institutional aid.

**UNDERGRADUATE EXPENSES for 2015–2016** *Application fee:* $35. *Comprehensive fee:* $43,200 includes full-time tuition ($32,140) and room and board ($11,060). *Part-time tuition:* $520 per credit. Part-time tuition and fees vary according to class time.

**FRESHMAN FINANCIAL AID (Fall 2013)** 278 applied for aid; of those 91% were deemed to have need. 100% of freshmen with need received aid; of those 14% had need fully met. *Average percent of need met:* 78% (excluding resources awarded to replace EFC). *Average financial aid package:* $26,842 (excluding resources awarded to replace EFC). 14% of all full-time freshmen had no need and received non-need-based gift aid.

**UNDERGRADUATE FINANCIAL AID (Fall 2013)** 1,031 applied for aid; of those 94% were deemed to have need. 100% of undergraduates with need received aid; of those 16% had need fully met. *Average percent of need met:* 74% (excluding resources awarded to replace EFC). *Average financial aid package:* $25,242 (excluding resources awarded to replace EFC). 11% of all full-time undergraduates had no need and received non-need-based gift aid.

**GIFT AID (NEED-BASED)** *Total amount:* $20,663,689 (13% federal, 18% state, 66% institutional, 3% external sources). *Receiving aid:* Freshmen: 84% (251); all full-time undergraduates: 88% (959). *Average award:* Freshmen: $22,779; Undergraduates: $20,624. *Scholarships, grants, and awards:* Federal Pell, FSEOG, state, private, college/university gift aid from institutional funds.

**GIFT AID (NON-NEED-BASED)** *Total amount:* $2,453,277 (2% state, 92% institutional, 6% external sources). *Receiving aid:* Freshmen: 8% (25). Undergraduates: 10% (110). *Average award:* Freshmen: $12,475. Undergraduates: $12,205. *Scholarships, grants, and awards by category:* Academic interests/achievement: general academic interests/achievements. Creative arts/performance: music. Special achievements/activities: cheerleading/drum major, leadership. Special characteristics: children and siblings of alumni, children of faculty/staff, ethnic background, local/state students, members of minority groups, relatives of clergy, religious affiliation, siblings of current students. *Tuition waivers:* Full or partial for employees or children of employees, senior citizens. *ROTC:* Army cooperative, Air Force cooperative.

**LOANS** *Student loans:* $8,798,186 (85% need-based, 15% non-need-based). 82% of past graduating class borrowed through all loan programs. *Average indebtedness per student:* $27,814. *Average need-based loan:* Freshmen: $3373. Undergraduates: $4316. *Parent loans:* $3,604,363 (58% need-based, 42% non-need-based). *Programs:* Federal Direct (Subsidized and Unsubsidized Stafford, PLUS), Perkins, state.

**WORK-STUDY** *Federal work-study:* jobs available. *State or other work-study/employment:* Part-time jobs available.

**ATHLETIC AWARDS** Total amount: $3,623,128 (68% need-based, 32% non-need-based).

**APPLYING FOR FINANCIAL AID** *Required financial aid form:* FAFSA. *Financial aid deadline (priority):* 3/1. *Notification date:* Continuous beginning 3/1. Students must reply by 8/31.

**CONTACT** Nick Jenkins, Financial Aid Counselor, Lenoir-Rhyne University, PO Box 7227, Hickory, NC 28603, 828-328-7301 or toll-free 800-277-5721. *Fax:* 828-328-7039. *E-mail:* finaid@lr.edu.
*Website:* http://www.lr.edu/.

# LESLEY UNIVERSITY
## Cambridge, MA

| Tuition & fees: $25,550 | Average undergraduate aid package: $14,007 |
| --- | --- |

**ABOUT THE INSTITUTION** Independent, coed, primarily women. *Awards:* certificates, associate, bachelor's, master's, and doctoral degrees. 22 undergraduate majors. *Total enrollment:* 4,422. Undergraduates: 1,492. Freshmen: 306. Both federal and institutional methodology are used as a basis for awarding need-based institutional aid.

**UNDERGRADUATE EXPENSES for 2015–2016** *Comprehensive fee:* $40,380 includes full-time tuition ($24,720), mandatory fees ($830), and room and board ($14,830). *College room only:* $9060. Full-time tuition and fees vary according to class time, course level, course load, degree level, location, program, reciprocity agreements, and student level. Room and board charges vary according to housing facility. *Part-time tuition:* $1030 per credit hour.

**FRESHMAN FINANCIAL AID (Fall 2014, est.)** 274 applied for aid; of those 83% were deemed to have need. 100% of freshmen with need received aid; of those 18% had need fully met. *Average percent of need met:* 75% (excluding resources awarded to replace EFC). *Average financial aid package:* $15,925 (excluding resources awarded to replace EFC). 24% of all full-time freshmen had no need and received non-need-based gift aid.

**UNDERGRADUATE FINANCIAL AID (Fall 2014, est.)** 1,036 applied for aid; of those 86% were deemed to have need. 100% of undergraduates with need received aid; of those 17% had need fully met. *Average percent of need met:* 70% (excluding resources awarded to replace EFC). *Average financial aid package:* $14,007 (excluding resources awarded to replace EFC). 29% of all full-time undergraduates had no need and received non-need-based gift aid.

**GIFT AID (NEED-BASED)** *Total amount:* $8,725,946 (17% federal, 2% state, 68% institutional, 13% external sources). *Receiving aid:* Freshmen: 74% (227); all full-time undergraduates: 66% (860). *Average award:* Freshmen: $10,531; Undergraduates: $9020. *Scholarships, grants, and awards:* Federal Pell, FSEOG, state, private, college/university gift aid from institutional funds.

**GIFT AID (NON-NEED-BASED)** *Total amount:* $2,103,178 (100% institutional). *Receiving aid:* Freshmen: 4% (12). Undergraduates: 1% (7). *Average award:* Freshmen: $7555. Undergraduates: $5775. *Scholarships, grants, and awards by category:* Special achievements/activities: general special achievements/activities. Special characteristics: ethnic background. *Tuition waivers:* Full or partial for employees or children of employees.

**LOANS** *Student loans:* $10,758,447 (65% need-based, 35% non-need-based). 75% of past graduating class borrowed through all loan programs. *Average indebtedness per student:* $23,000. *Average need-based loan:* Freshmen: $3868. Undergraduates: $4679. *Parent loans:* $4,039,414 (100% non-need-based). *Programs:* Federal Direct (Subsidized and Unsubsidized Stafford, PLUS), Perkins.

**WORK-STUDY** *Federal work-study:* Total amount: $500,000; jobs available. *State or other work-study/employment:* Part-time jobs available.

**APPLYING FOR FINANCIAL AID** *Required financial aid form:* FAFSA. *Financial aid deadline (priority):* 2/15. *Notification date:* Continuous beginning 2/1.

**CONTACT** Scott A. Jewell, Director of Student Financial Services, Lesley University, 29 Everett Street, Cambridge, MA 02138-2790, 617-349-8714 or toll-free 800-999-1959 Ext. 8800. *Fax:* 617-349-8667. *E-mail:* sjewell@lesley.edu.
*Website:* http://www.lesley.edu/.

# LETOURNEAU UNIVERSITY
## Longview, TX

| Tuition & fees: $26,910 | Average undergraduate aid package: $19,491 |
| --- | --- |

**ABOUT THE INSTITUTION** Independent nondenominational, coed. *Awards:* associate, bachelor's, and master's degrees. 75 undergraduate majors. *Total enrollment:* 2,667. Undergraduates: 2,250. Freshmen: 367. Both federal and institutional methodology are used as a basis for awarding need-based institutional aid.

**UNDERGRADUATE EXPENSES for 2015–2016** *Comprehensive fee:* $36,210 includes full-time tuition ($26,390), mandatory fees ($520), and room and board ($9300). Full-time tuition and fees vary according to course level, course load, location, and program. Room and board charges vary according to board plan. **Part-time tuition:** $1053 per credit hour. Part-time tuition and fees vary according to course level, course load, location, and program.

**FRESHMAN FINANCIAL AID (Fall 2014, est.)** 307 applied for aid; of those 86% were deemed to have need. 100% of freshmen with need received aid; of those 17% had need fully met. **Average percent of need met:** 74% (excluding resources awarded to replace EFC). **Average financial aid package:** $22,151 (excluding resources awarded to replace EFC). 18% of all full-time freshmen had no need and received non-need-based gift aid.

**UNDERGRADUATE FINANCIAL AID (Fall 2014, est.)** 1,243 applied for aid; of those 92% were deemed to have need. 99% of undergraduates with need received aid; of those 11% had need fully met. **Average percent of need met:** 61% (excluding resources awarded to replace EFC). **Average financial aid package:** $19,491 (excluding resources awarded to replace EFC). 13% of all full-time undergraduates had no need and received non-need-based gift aid.

**GIFT AID (NEED-BASED) Total amount:** $17,825,672 (20% federal, 11% state, 65% institutional, 4% external sources). **Receiving aid:** Freshmen: 81% (264); all full-time undergraduates: 85% (1,111). **Average award:** Freshmen: $17,277; Undergraduates: $15,122. **Scholarships, grants, and awards:** Federal Pell, FSEOG, state, private, college/university gift aid from institutional funds, United Negro College Fund.

**GIFT AID (NON-NEED-BASED) Total amount:** $2,260,910 (3% federal, 94% institutional, 3% external sources). **Receiving aid:** Freshmen: 10% (34). Undergraduates: 6% (78). **Average award:** Freshmen: $12,512. Undergraduates: $8037. **Tuition waivers:** Full or partial for employees or children of employees.

**LOANS Student loans:** $16,782,902 (84% need-based, 16% non-need-based). 76% of past graduating class borrowed through all loan programs. **Average indebtedness per student:** $38,211. **Average need-based loan:** Freshmen: $4446. Undergraduates: $5016. **Parent loans:** $3,007,231 (32% need-based, 68% non-need-based). **Programs:** Federal Direct (Subsidized and Unsubsidized Stafford, PLUS), Perkins, state.

**WORK-STUDY Federal work-study:** Total amount: $559,998; jobs available. **State or other work-study/employment:** Total amount: $20,533 (100% need-based). Part-time jobs available.

**APPLYING FOR FINANCIAL AID Required financial aid form:** FAFSA. **Financial aid deadline:** Continuous. **Notification date:** Continuous beginning 3/1. Students must reply within 2 weeks of notification.

**CONTACT** Financial Aid Office, LeTourneau University, PO Box 7001, Longview, TX 75607, 903-233-4312 or toll-free 800-759-8811. *Fax:* 903-233-4302. *E-mail:* financialaid@letu.edu.
*Website:* http://www.letu.edu/.

# LEWIS & CLARK COLLEGE
## Portland, OR

| Tuition & fees: $43,382 | Average undergraduate aid package: $36,865 |
| --- | --- |

**ABOUT THE INSTITUTION** Independent, coed. **Awards:** certificates, bachelor's, master's, and doctoral degrees. 31 undergraduate majors. **Total enrollment:** 3,504. Undergraduates: 2,179. Freshmen: 564. Both federal and institutional methodology are used as a basis for awarding need-based institutional aid.

**UNDERGRADUATE EXPENSES for 2015–2016 Comprehensive fee:** $54,382 includes full-time tuition ($43,022), mandatory fees ($360), and room and board ($11,000). **College room only:** $5894. Room and board charges vary according to board plan and housing facility. **Part-time tuition:** $2151 per credit hour.

**FRESHMAN FINANCIAL AID (Fall 2014, est.)** 470 applied for aid; of those 77% were deemed to have need. 100% of freshmen with need received aid; of those 21% had need fully met. **Average percent of need met:** 88% (excluding resources awarded to replace EFC). **Average financial aid package:** $36,083 (excluding resources awarded to replace EFC). 16% of all full-time freshmen had no need and received non-need-based gift aid.

**UNDERGRADUATE FINANCIAL AID (Fall 2014, est.)** 1,478 applied for aid; of those 82% were deemed to have need. 100% of undergraduates with need received aid; of those 20% had need fully met. **Average percent of need met:** 88% (excluding resources awarded to replace EFC). **Average financial aid package:** $36,865 (excluding resources awarded to replace EFC). 26% of all full-time undergraduates had no need and received non-need-based gift aid.

**GIFT AID (NEED-BASED) Total amount:** $40,351,601 (6% federal, 90% institutional, 4% external sources). **Receiving aid:** Freshmen: 64% (360); all full-time undergraduates: 59% (1,205). **Average award:** Freshmen: $28,655; Undergraduates: $29,334. **Scholarships, grants, and awards:** Federal Pell, FSEOG, state, private, college/university gift aid from institutional funds.

**GIFT AID (NON-NEED-BASED) Total amount:** $3,356,795 (96% institutional, 4% external sources). **Receiving aid:** Freshmen: 7% (39). Undergraduates: 5% (108). **Average award:** Freshmen: $13,839. Undergraduates: $13,832. **Scholarships, grants, and awards by category:** Academic interests/achievement: general academic interests/achievements. Creative arts/performance: debating, music. Special achievements/activities: community service, leadership. Special characteristics: children of faculty/staff. **Tuition waivers:** Full or partial for employees or children of employees. **ROTC:** Army cooperative.

**LOANS Student loans:** $10,126,235 (75% need-based, 25% non-need-based). 56% of past graduating class borrowed through all loan programs. **Average indebtedness per student:** $27,421. **Average need-based loan:** Freshmen: $4338. Undergraduates: $5047. **Parent loans:** $3,132,301 (69% need-based, 31% non-need-based). **Programs:** Federal Direct (Subsidized and Unsubsidized Stafford, PLUS), Perkins.

**WORK-STUDY Federal work-study:** Total amount: $2,362,348; 308 jobs averaging $2465. **State or other work-study/employment:** Total amount: $778,491 (83% need-based, 17% non-need-based). 14 part-time jobs averaging $2107.

**APPLYING FOR FINANCIAL AID Required financial aid forms:** FAFSA, CSS Financial Aid PROFILE. **Financial aid deadline (priority):** 2/15. **Notification date:** Continuous beginning 3/15. Students must reply by 7/1.

**CONTACT** Anastacia Dillon, Director of Financial Aid, Lewis & Clark College, Templeton Campus Center, MSC 56, Portland, OR 97219-7899, 503-768-7090 or toll-free 800-444-4111. *Fax:* 503-768-7074. *E-mail:* fao@lclark.edu.
*Website:* http://www.lclark.edu/.

# LEWIS-CLARK STATE COLLEGE
## Lewiston, ID

| Tuition & fees (ID res): $5900 | Average undergraduate aid package: $8602 |
| --- | --- |

**ABOUT THE INSTITUTION** State-supported, coed. **Awards:** certificates, associate, and bachelor's degrees. 50 undergraduate majors. **Total enrollment:** 4,304. Undergraduates: 4,304. Freshmen: 515. Federal methodology is used as a basis for awarding need-based institutional aid.

**UNDERGRADUATE EXPENSES for 2015–2016 Tuition, state resident:** full-time $5900; part-time $302 per credit hour. **Tuition, nonresident:** full-time $16,418; part-time $302 per credit hour. Full-time tuition and fees vary according to course load and reciprocity agreements. **College room and board:** $6194; **Room only:** $3200. Room and board charges vary according to board plan and housing facility.

**FRESHMAN FINANCIAL AID (Fall 2013)** 412 applied for aid; of those 83% were deemed to have need. 100% of freshmen with need received aid; of those 8% had need fully met. **Average percent of need met:** 58% (excluding resources awarded to replace EFC). **Average financial aid package:** $8168 (excluding resources awarded to replace EFC). 12% of all full-time freshmen had no need and received non-need-based gift aid.

**UNDERGRADUATE FINANCIAL AID (Fall 2013)** 2,070 applied for aid; of those 62% were deemed to have need. 97% of undergraduates with need received aid; of those 20% had need fully met. **Average percent of need met:** 72% (excluding resources awarded to replace EFC). **Average financial aid package:** $8602 (excluding resources awarded to replace EFC). 8% of all full-time undergraduates had no need and received non-need-based gift aid.

**GIFT AID (NEED-BASED) Total amount:** $8,072,339 (84% federal, 1% state, 5% institutional, 10% external sources). **Receiving aid:** Freshmen: 70% (312); all full-time undergraduates: 47% (1,120). **Average award:** Freshmen: $6245; Undergraduates: $5713. **Scholarships, grants, and awards:** Federal Pell, FSEOG, state, private, college/university gift aid from institutional funds.

**GIFT AID (NON-NEED-BASED) Total amount:** $1,445,499 (4% federal, 46% state, 50% institutional). **Receiving aid:** Freshmen: 50% (225). Undergraduates: 22% (523). **Average award:** Freshmen: $2539. Undergraduates: $2921. **Scholarships, grants, and awards by category:** Academic interests/achievement: 370 awards ($469,244 total): biological sciences, business, communication, education, engineering/technologies, English, general academic interests/achievements, health fields, humanities, mathematics, physical sciences, social sciences. *Creative arts/performance:* 13 awards ($18,743 total): art/fine arts, creative writing, debating, music, theater/drama. *Special achievements/activities:* 291 awards ($1,710,314 total): community service, general special achievements/activities, junior miss, leadership, rodeo. *Special characteristics:* 440 awards ($1,592,907 total): children and siblings of alumni, ethnic background, first-generation college students, general special characteristics, members of minority groups, out-of-state students, previous college experience. *Tuition waivers:* Full or partial for employees or children of employees, senior citizens. *ROTC:* Army cooperative, Naval cooperative, Air Force cooperative.

**LOANS** *Student loans:* $14,700,392 (47% need-based, 53% non-need-based). 68% of past graduating class borrowed through all loan programs. *Average indebtedness per student:* $18,065. *Average need-based loan:* Freshmen: $2079. Undergraduates: $3938. *Parent loans:* $387,091 (100% non-need-based). *Programs:* Federal Direct (Subsidized and Unsubsidized Stafford, PLUS), Perkins, Federal Nursing.

**WORK-STUDY** *Federal work-study:* 80 jobs averaging $1305. *State or other work-study/employment:* Total amount: $100,228 (77% need-based, 23% non-need-based). 79 part-time jobs averaging $1290.

**ATHLETIC AWARDS** Total amount: $1,850,270 (100% non-need-based).

**APPLYING FOR FINANCIAL AID** *Required financial aid form:* FAFSA. *Financial aid deadline (priority):* 3/1. *Notification date:* Continuous beginning 4/15. Students must reply within 2 weeks of notification.

**CONTACT** Ms. Laura Hughes, Director of Financial Aid, Lewis-Clark State College, 500 8th Avenue, Lewiston, ID 83501-2698, 208-792-2224 or toll-free 800-933-5272. *Fax:* 208-792-2063. *E-mail:* lhughes@lcsc.edu. *Website:* http://www.lcsc.edu/.

# LEWIS UNIVERSITY
## Romeoville, IL

| Tuition & fees: $29,040 | Average undergraduate aid package: $20,334 |
| --- | --- |

**ABOUT THE INSTITUTION** Independent Roman Catholic Church, coed. *Awards:* certificates, associate, bachelor's, master's, and doctoral degrees. 83 undergraduate majors. *Total enrollment:* 6,689. Undergraduates: 4,752. Freshmen: 744. Federal methodology is used as a basis for awarding need-based institutional aid.

**UNDERGRADUATE EXPENSES** for 2015–2016 *Application fee:* $40. *Comprehensive fee:* $38,970 includes full-time tuition ($28,940), mandatory fees ($100), and room and board ($9930). *College room only:* $6310. Full-time tuition and fees vary according to course load, location, and program. Room and board charges vary according to board plan and housing facility. *Part-time tuition:* $852 per credit. *Part-time fees:* $50 per term. Part-time tuition and fees vary according to course load, location, and program.

**FRESHMAN FINANCIAL AID (Fall 2014, est.)** 704 applied for aid; of those 88% were deemed to have need. 100% of freshmen with need received aid; of those 21% had need fully met. *Average percent of need met:* 81% (excluding resources awarded to replace EFC). *Average financial aid package:* $22,768 (excluding resources awarded to replace EFC). 15% of all full-time freshmen had no need and received non-need-based gift aid.

**UNDERGRADUATE FINANCIAL AID (Fall 2014, est.)** 3,273 applied for aid; of those 89% were deemed to have need. 100% of undergraduates with need received aid; of those 22% had need fully met. *Average percent of need met:* 75% (excluding resources awarded to replace EFC). *Average financial aid package:* $20,334 (excluding resources awarded to replace EFC). 17% of all full-time undergraduates had no need and received non-need-based gift aid.

**GIFT AID (NEED-BASED)** *Total amount:* $37,771,957 (19% federal, 15% state, 65% institutional, 1% external sources). *Receiving aid:* Freshmen: 83% (617); all full-time undergraduates: 73% (2,768). *Average award:* Freshmen: $16,766; Undergraduates: $14,019. *Scholarships, grants, and awards:* Federal Pell, FSEOG, state, private, college/university gift aid from institutional funds, Federal Nursing.

**GIFT AID (NON-NEED-BASED)** *Total amount:* $9,010,993 (10% federal, 1% state, 87% institutional, 2% external sources). *Receiving aid:* Freshmen: 11% (80). Undergraduates: 9% (348). *Average award:* Freshmen: $11,910. Undergraduates: $9998. *Scholarships, grants, and awards by category: Academic interests/achievement:* general academic interests/achievements. *Creative arts/performance:* art/fine arts, music, theater/drama. *Special achievements/activities:* cheerleading/drum major, community service, general special achievements/activities, leadership, memberships, religious involvement. *Special characteristics:* children and siblings of alumni,

children of faculty/staff, religious affiliation, veterans, veterans' children. *Tuition waivers:* Full or partial for children of alumni, employees or children of employees, adult students. *ROTC:* Army cooperative, Air Force cooperative.

**LOANS** *Student loans:* $32,638,039 (71% need-based, 29% non-need-based). 81% of past graduating class borrowed through all loan programs. *Average indebtedness per student:* $33,748. *Average need-based loan:* Freshmen: $3390. Undergraduates: $4421. *Parent loans:* $7,821,546 (38% need-based, 62% non-need-based). *Programs:* Federal Direct (Subsidized and Unsubsidized Stafford, PLUS), Perkins.

**WORK-STUDY** *Federal work-study:* Total amount: $7,121,067; 2,169 jobs averaging $3283. *State or other work-study/employment:* Total amount: $1,133,839 (27% need-based, 73% non-need-based). 267 part-time jobs averaging $4247.

**ATHLETIC AWARDS** Total amount: $3,350,468 (42% need-based, 58% non-need-based).

**APPLYING FOR FINANCIAL AID** *Required financial aid form:* FAFSA. *Financial aid deadline:* 5/1 (priority: 2/15). *Notification date:* Continuous beginning 2/1. Students must reply by 5/1 or within 2 weeks of notification.

**CONTACT** Ms. Janeen Decharinte, Director of Financial Aid Services, Lewis University, One University Parkway, Romeoville, IL 60446, 815-836-5263 or toll-free 800-897-9000. *Fax:* 815-836-5135. *E-mail:* decharja@lewisu.edu. *Website:* http://www.lewisu.edu/.

# LIBERTY UNIVERSITY
## Lynchburg, VA

| Tuition & fees: $22,000 | Average undergraduate aid package: $13,999 |
| --- | --- |

**ABOUT THE INSTITUTION** Independent nondenominational, coed. *Awards:* certificates, associate, bachelor's, master's, and doctoral degrees (also offers external degree program with significant enrollment not reflected in profile). 77 undergraduate majors. *Total enrollment:* 13,847. Undergraduates: 12,645. Freshmen: 2,719. Federal methodology is used as a basis for awarding need-based institutional aid.

**UNDERGRADUATE EXPENSES** for 2015–2016 *Application fee:* $40. *Comprehensive fee:* $30,786 includes full-time tuition ($21,300), mandatory fees ($700), and room and board ($8786). *College room only:* $5486. Full-time tuition and fees vary according to course load. Room and board charges vary according to housing facility. *Part-time tuition:* $730 per credit hour. Part-time tuition and fees vary according to course load.

**FRESHMAN FINANCIAL AID (Fall 2014, est.)** 2,534 applied for aid; of those 80% were deemed to have need. 100% of freshmen with need received aid; of those 12% had need fully met. *Average percent of need met:* 58% (excluding resources awarded to replace EFC). *Average financial aid package:* $14,073 (excluding resources awarded to replace EFC). 7% of all full-time freshmen had no need and received non-need-based gift aid.

**UNDERGRADUATE FINANCIAL AID (Fall 2014, est.)** 11,102 applied for aid; of those 80% were deemed to have need. 100% of undergraduates with need received aid; of those 11% had need fully met. *Average percent of need met:* 59% (excluding resources awarded to replace EFC). *Average financial aid package:* $13,999 (excluding resources awarded to replace EFC). 7% of all full-time undergraduates had no need and received non-need-based gift aid.

**GIFT AID (NEED-BASED)** *Total amount:* $88,725,405 (19% federal, 8% state, 70% institutional, 3% external sources). *Receiving aid:* Freshmen: 75% (2,021); all full-time undergraduates: 72% (8,795). *Average award:* Freshmen: $10,959; Undergraduates: $10,006. *Scholarships, grants, and awards:* Federal Pell, FSEOG, state, private, college/university gift aid from institutional funds.

**GIFT AID (NON-NEED-BASED)** *Total amount:* $28,873,938 (10% state, 87% institutional, 3% external sources). *Receiving aid:* Freshmen: 14% (371). Undergraduates: 13% (1,632). *Average award:* Freshmen: $6630. Undergraduates: $8404. *Scholarships, grants, and awards by category: Academic interests/achievement:* biological sciences, business, communication, computer science, education, engineering/technologies, English, general academic interests/achievements, mathematics, premedicine, religion/biblical studies. *Creative arts/performance:* cinema/film/broadcasting, debating, journalism/publications, music, performing arts. *Special achievements/activities:* cheerleading/drum major, leadership. *Special characteristics:* children of faculty/staff, international students, local/state students, religious affiliation, veterans. *Tuition waivers:* Full or partial for employees or children of employees. *ROTC:* Army, Air Force cooperative.

**LOANS** *Student loans:* $65,432,778 (81% need-based, 19% non-need-based). 64% of past graduating class borrowed through all loan programs. *Average indebtedness per student:* $20,451. *Average need-based loan:* Freshmen: $3337. Undergraduates: $4174. *Parent loans:* $21,154,050 (77% need-based, 23% non-need-based). *Programs:* Federal Direct (Subsidized and Unsubsidized Stafford, PLUS), state, college/university, Canadian federal and provincial loans.
**WORK-STUDY** *Federal work-study:* Total amount: $1,615,337; jobs available. *State or other work-study/employment:* Part-time jobs available.
**ATHLETIC AWARDS** Total amount: $5,638,041 (61% need-based, 39% non-need-based).
**APPLYING FOR FINANCIAL AID** *Required financial aid forms:* FAFSA, state aid form. *Financial aid deadline:* 3/1. *Notification date:* Continuous beginning 3/15. Students must reply within 3 weeks of notification.
**CONTACT** Robert Ritz, Vice President of Financial Aid, Liberty University, 1971 University Boulevard, Lynchburg, VA 24515, 434-582-2270 or toll-free 800-543-5317. *Fax:* 434-582-2053. *E-mail:* financialaid@liberty.edu.
*Website:* http://www.liberty.edu/.

# LIFE PACIFIC COLLEGE
## San Dimas, CA

**ABOUT THE INSTITUTION** Independent International Church of the Foursquare Gospel, coed. 3 undergraduate majors.
**GIFT AID (NEED-BASED)** *Scholarships, grants, and awards:* Federal Pell, FSEOG, state, private, college/university gift aid from institutional funds.
**GIFT AID (NON-NEED-BASED)** *Scholarships, grants, and awards by category:* Academic interests/achievement: general academic interests/achievements. *Special characteristics:* children of faculty/staff, relatives of clergy.
**LOANS** *Programs:* Federal Direct (Subsidized and Unsubsidized Stafford, PLUS).
**WORK-STUDY** Federal work-study jobs available.
**APPLYING FOR FINANCIAL AID** *Required financial aid forms:* FAFSA, state aid form.
**CONTACT** Mrs. Luci Perez, Director of Financial Aid, Life Pacific College, 1100 Covina Boulevard, San Dimas, CA 91773-3298, 909-599-5433 Ext. 322 or toll-free 877-886-5433 Ext. 314. *Fax:* 909-706-3031. *E-mail:* lperez@lifepacific.edu.
*Website:* http://www.lifepacific.edu/.

# LIFE UNIVERSITY
## Marietta, GA

| Tuition & fees: $10,590 | Average undergraduate aid package: $10,600 |
| --- | --- |

**ABOUT THE INSTITUTION** Independent, coed. *Awards:* certificates, associate, bachelor's, master's, and doctoral degrees. 11 undergraduate majors. *Total enrollment:* 2,754. Undergraduates: 774. Freshmen: 98. Federal methodology is used as a basis for awarding need-based institutional aid.
**UNDERGRADUATE EXPENSES for 2015–2016** *Application fee:* $50. *Comprehensive fee:* $23,070 includes full-time tuition ($9540), mandatory fees ($1050), and room and board ($12,480). Full-time tuition and fees vary according to course load, degree level, and student level. *Part-time tuition:* $210 per credit hour. *Part-time fees:* $350 per term. Part-time tuition and fees vary according to degree level and student level.
**FRESHMAN FINANCIAL AID (Fall 2013)** 64 applied for aid; of those 84% were deemed to have need. 100% of freshmen with need received aid. *Average percent of need met:* 28% (excluding resources awarded to replace EFC). *Average financial aid package:* $9500 (excluding resources awarded to replace EFC).
**UNDERGRADUATE FINANCIAL AID (Fall 2013)** 468 applied for aid; of those 94% were deemed to have need. 96% of undergraduates with need received aid. *Average percent of need met:* 32% (excluding resources awarded to replace EFC). *Average financial aid package:* $10,600 (excluding resources awarded to replace EFC).
**GIFT AID (NEED-BASED)** *Total amount:* $2,349,000 (100% federal). *Receiving aid:* Freshmen: 58% (40); all full-time undergraduates: 54% (290). *Average award:* Freshmen: $5100; Undergraduates: $5300. *Scholarships, grants, and awards:* Federal Pell, FSEOG.

**GIFT AID (NON-NEED-BASED)** *Total amount:* $429,000 (81% state, 16% institutional, 3% external sources). *Receiving aid:* Freshmen: 67% (46). Undergraduates: 55% (296). *Scholarships, grants, and awards by category:* Academic interests/achievement: 58 awards ($265,000 total): general academic interests/achievements. *Special achievements/activities:* 125 awards ($700,000 total): general special achievements/activities, leadership. *Special characteristics:* 23 awards ($100,000 total): children and siblings of alumni, general special characteristics, international students, local/state students, members of minority groups. *Tuition waivers:* Full or partial for employees or children of employees.
**LOANS** *Student loans:* $3,739,000 (40% need-based, 60% non-need-based). 76% of past graduating class borrowed through all loan programs. *Average indebtedness per student:* $30,000. *Average need-based loan:* Freshmen: $3500. Undergraduates: $4900. *Parent loans:* $342,000 (100% need-based). *Programs:* Federal Direct (Subsidized and Unsubsidized Stafford, PLUS), Perkins, state, college/university, alternative loans.
**WORK-STUDY** *Federal work-study:* 111 jobs averaging $2000. *State or other work-study/employment:* Part-time jobs available.
**ATHLETIC AWARDS** Total amount: $240,000 (100% non-need-based).
**APPLYING FOR FINANCIAL AID** *Required financial aid form:* FAFSA. *Financial aid deadline (priority):* 3/1. *Notification date:* Continuous beginning 4/1.
**CONTACT** Melissa Waters, Director of Financial Aid, Life University, 1269 Barclay Circle, Marietta, GA 30060, 770-426-2901 or toll-free 800-543-3202. *Fax:* 770-426-2926. *E-mail:* finaid@life.edu.
*Website:* http://www.life.edu/.

# LIM COLLEGE
## New York, NY

| Tuition & fees: $24,225 | Average undergraduate aid package: $9693 |
| --- | --- |

**ABOUT THE INSTITUTION** Proprietary, coed, primarily women. *Awards:* certificates, associate, bachelor's, and master's degrees. 5 undergraduate majors. *Total enrollment:* 1,737. Undergraduates: 1,552. Freshmen: 285. Both federal and institutional methodology are used as a basis for awarding need-based institutional aid.
**UNDERGRADUATE EXPENSES for 2015–2016** *Application fee:* $40. *Comprehensive fee:* $44,075 includes full-time tuition ($23,650), mandatory fees ($575), and room and board ($19,850). *College room only:* $15,850. *Part-time tuition:* $785 per credit.
**FRESHMAN FINANCIAL AID (Fall 2014, est.)** 271 applied for aid; of those 77% were deemed to have need. 98% of freshmen with need received aid; of those 2% had need fully met. *Average percent of need met:* 33% (excluding resources awarded to replace EFC). *Average financial aid package:* $10,585 (excluding resources awarded to replace EFC). 14% of all full-time freshmen had no need and received non-need-based gift aid.
**UNDERGRADUATE FINANCIAL AID (Fall 2014, est.)** 1,369 applied for aid; of those 69% were deemed to have need. 98% of undergraduates with need received aid; of those 2% had need fully met. *Average percent of need met:* 39% (excluding resources awarded to replace EFC). *Average financial aid package:* $9693 (excluding resources awarded to replace EFC). 12% of all full-time undergraduates had no need and received non-need-based gift aid.
**GIFT AID (NEED-BASED)** *Total amount:* $5,760,811 (38% federal, 8% state, 53% institutional, 1% external sources). *Receiving aid:* Freshmen: 56% (159); all full-time undergraduates: 49% (704). *Average award:* Freshmen: $9297; Undergraduates: $7396. *Scholarships, grants, and awards:* Federal Pell, FSEOG, state, private, college/university gift aid from institutional funds.
**GIFT AID (NON-NEED-BASED)** *Total amount:* $1,031,133 (16% federal, 1% state, 78% institutional, 5% external sources). *Receiving aid:* Freshmen: 43% (123). Undergraduates: 31% (447). *Average award:* Freshmen: $4881. Undergraduates: $4135. *Scholarships, grants, and awards by category:* Academic interests/achievement: general academic interests/achievements. *Special achievements/activities:* leadership, memberships. *Special characteristics:* children of faculty/staff, local/state students, siblings of current students.
**LOANS** *Student loans:* $10,282,442 (34% need-based, 66% non-need-based). 73% of past graduating class borrowed through all loan programs. *Average indebtedness per student:* $35,743. *Average need-based loan:* Freshmen: $3173. Undergrad-

uates: $4015. **Parent loans:** $8,560,213 (100% non-need-based). **Programs:** Federal Direct (Subsidized and Unsubsidized Stafford, PLUS).
**WORK-STUDY** Federal work-study jobs available.
**APPLYING FOR FINANCIAL AID Required financial aid forms:** FAFSA, state aid form. **Financial aid deadline:** 11/15 (priority: 3/1). **Notification date:** Continuous beginning 2/25. Students must reply by 7/31 or within 2 weeks of notification.
**CONTACT** Dean of Student Financial Services, LIM College, 12 East 53rd Street, New York, NY 10022-5268, 212-752-1530 Ext. 389 or toll-free 800-677-1323. **Fax:** 212-750-3473. **E-mail:** sfs@limcollege.edu.
**Website:** http://www.limcollege.edu/.

# LIMESTONE COLLEGE
## Gaffney, SC

**ABOUT THE INSTITUTION** Independent, coed. **Awards:** associate, bachelor's, and master's degrees. 61 undergraduate majors. **Total enrollment:** 1,263. Undergraduates: 1,188. Freshmen: 512.
**GIFT AID (NEED-BASED) Scholarships, grants, and awards:** Federal Pell, FSEOG, state, private, college/university gift aid from institutional funds.
**GIFT AID (NON-NEED-BASED) Scholarships, grants, and awards by category:** Academic interests/achievement: biological sciences, business, communication, computer science, education, English, general academic interests/achievements, health fields, humanities, mathematics, physical sciences, premedicine, religion/biblical studies, social sciences. Creative arts/performance: art/fine arts, music, performing arts, theater/drama. Special achievements/activities: cheerleading/drum major, general special achievements/activities, leadership, religious involvement. Special characteristics: children of faculty/staff, local/state students, out-of-state students, previous college experience, siblings of current students.
**LOANS Programs:** Federal Direct (Subsidized and Unsubsidized Stafford, PLUS), Perkins.
**WORK-STUDY Federal work-study:** 112 jobs averaging $1360. **State or other work-study/employment:** Total amount: $110,500 (50% need-based, 50% non-need-based). 121 part-time jobs averaging $768.
**APPLYING FOR FINANCIAL AID Required financial aid form:** FAFSA.
**CONTACT** Mr. Bobby Greer, Director of Financial Aid, Limestone College, 1115 College Drive, Gaffney, SC 29340-3799, 864-488-4567 or toll-free 800-795-7151. **Fax:** 864-487-8706. **E-mail:** bgreer@limestone.edu.
**Website:** http://www.limestone.edu/.

# LINCOLN CHRISTIAN UNIVERSITY
## Lincoln, IL

| Tuition & fees: $16,050 | Average undergraduate aid package: $10,673 |
|---|---|

**ABOUT THE INSTITUTION** Independent Christian Churches and Churches of Christ, coed. **Awards:** certificates, associate, bachelor's, master's, and doctoral degrees. 14 undergraduate majors. **Total enrollment:** 932. Undergraduates: 557. Freshmen: 64. Federal methodology is used as a basis for awarding need-based institutional aid.
**UNDERGRADUATE EXPENSES** for 2015–2016 **Application fee:** $25. **Comprehensive fee:** $23,484 includes full-time tuition ($15,810), mandatory fees ($240), and room and board ($7434). **College room only:** $5434. Full-time tuition and fees vary according to location and program. **Part-time tuition:** $527 per credit hour. Part-time tuition and fees vary according to location and program.
**FRESHMAN FINANCIAL AID (Fall 2013)** 77 applied for aid; of those 94% were deemed to have need. 100% of freshmen with need received aid; of those 6% had need fully met. **Average percent of need met:** 65% (excluding resources awarded to replace EFC). **Average financial aid package:** $12,915 (excluding resources awarded to replace EFC). 13% of all full-time freshmen had no need and received non-need-based gift aid.
**UNDERGRADUATE FINANCIAL AID (Fall 2013)** 598 applied for aid; of those 94% were deemed to have need. 100% of undergraduates with need received aid; of those 7% had need fully met. **Average percent of need met:** 60% (excluding resources awarded to replace EFC). **Average financial aid package:** $10,673

(excluding resources awarded to replace EFC). 9% of all full-time undergraduates had no need and received non-need-based gift aid.
**GIFT AID (NEED-BASED) Total amount:** $3,727,050 (36% federal, 19% state, 37% institutional, 8% external sources). **Receiving aid:** Freshmen: 91% (72); all full-time undergraduates: 85% (535). **Average award:** Freshmen: $9384; Undergraduates: $7085. **Scholarships, grants, and awards:** Federal Pell, FSEOG, state, private, college/university gift aid from institutional funds.
**GIFT AID (NON-NEED-BASED) Total amount:** $365,378 (84% institutional, 16% external sources). **Receiving aid:** Freshmen: 1% (1). Undergraduates: 3% (17). **Average award:** Freshmen: $4338. Undergraduates: $4461. **Scholarships, grants, and awards by category:** Academic interests/achievement: 160 awards ($496,800 total): general academic interests/achievements. Special characteristics: 19 awards ($167,250 total): children of faculty/staff, international students. **Tuition waivers:** Full or partial for employees or children of employees, senior citizens.
**LOANS Student loans:** $3,935,161 (78% need-based, 22% non-need-based). 77% of past graduating class borrowed through all loan programs. Average indebtedness per student: $25,578. **Average need-based loan:** Freshmen: $3911. Undergraduates: $3887. **Parent loans:** $372,235 (45% need-based, 55% non-need-based). **Programs:** Federal Direct (Subsidized and Unsubsidized Stafford, PLUS), Perkins, alternative loans.
**WORK-STUDY Federal work-study:** 65 jobs averaging $1590. **State or other work-study/employment:** Total amount: $196,501 (100% non-need-based). 125 part-time jobs averaging $1572.
**APPLYING FOR FINANCIAL AID Required financial aid form:** FAFSA. **Financial aid deadline (priority):** 3/1. **Notification date:** Continuous beginning 3/1. Students must reply within 4 weeks of notification.
**CONTACT** Nancy Siddens, Director of Financial Aid, Lincoln Christian University, 100 Campus View Drive, Lincoln, IL 62656, 217-732-3168 Ext. 2250 or toll-free 888-522-5228. **Fax:** 217-732-4199. **E-mail:** finaid@lincolnchristian.edu.
**Website:** http://www.lincolnchristian.edu/.

# LINCOLN COLLEGE–NORMAL
## Normal, IL

**CONTACT** Financial Aid Office, Lincoln College–Normal, 715 West Raab Road, Normal, IL 61761, 309-452-0500 or toll-free 800-569-0558.
**Website:** http://www.lincolncollege.edu/normal/.

# LINCOLN COLLEGE OF NEW ENGLAND
## Southington, CT

**CONTACT** Financial Aid Office, Lincoln College of New England, 2279 Mount Vernon Road, Southington, CT 06489-1057, 860-628-4751 or toll-free 800-825-0087.
**Website:** http://www.lincolncollegene.edu/.

# LINCOLN CULINARY INSTITUTE
## West Palm Beach, FL

**CONTACT** Financial Aid Office, Lincoln Culinary Institute, 2410 Metrocentre Boulevard, West Palm Beach, FL 33407, 561-842-8324.
**Website:** http://www.lincolnedu.com/campus/west-palm-beach-culinary-fl.

# LINCOLN MEMORIAL UNIVERSITY
## Harrogate, TN

| Tuition & fees: $20,546 | Average undergraduate aid package: $17,135 |
| --- | --- |

**ABOUT THE INSTITUTION** Independent, coed. *Awards:* certificates, associate, bachelor's, master's, and doctoral degrees. 43 undergraduate majors. *Total enrollment:* 3,735. Undergraduates: 1,699. Freshmen: 260. Federal methodology is used as a basis for awarding need-based institutional aid.

**UNDERGRADUATE EXPENSES for 2015–2016** *Application fee:* $25. *Comprehensive fee:* $27,846 includes full-time tuition ($20,016), mandatory fees ($530), and room and board ($7300). Room and board charges vary according to board plan and housing facility. *Part-time tuition:* $834 per credit hour. Part-time tuition and fees vary according to course load.

**FRESHMAN FINANCIAL AID (Fall 2013)** 168 applied for aid; of those 93% were deemed to have need. 99% of freshmen with need received aid; of those 16% had need fully met. *Average percent of need met:* 76% (excluding resources awarded to replace EFC). *Average financial aid package:* $18,281 (excluding resources awarded to replace EFC). 13% of all full-time freshmen had no need and received non-need-based gift aid.

**UNDERGRADUATE FINANCIAL AID (Fall 2013)** 1,182 applied for aid; of those 92% were deemed to have need. 99% of undergraduates with need received aid; of those 19% had need fully met. *Average percent of need met:* 77% (excluding resources awarded to replace EFC). *Average financial aid package:* $17,135 (excluding resources awarded to replace EFC). 12% of all full-time undergraduates had no need and received non-need-based gift aid.

**GIFT AID (NEED-BASED)** *Total amount:* $16,887,263 (45% federal, 37% state, 11% institutional, 7% external sources). *Receiving aid:* Freshmen: 81% (147); all full-time undergraduates: 79% (999). *Average award:* Freshmen: $7753; Undergraduates: $8992. *Scholarships, grants, and awards:* Federal Pell, FSEOG, state, private, college/university gift aid from institutional funds.

**GIFT AID (NON-NEED-BASED)** *Total amount:* $5,090,847 (9% state, 83% institutional, 8% external sources). *Receiving aid:* Freshmen: 19% (35). Undergraduates: 20% (257). *Average award:* Freshmen: $8794. Undergraduates: $9718. *Scholarships, grants, and awards by category: Academic interests/achievement:* general academic interests/achievements. *Creative arts/performance:* music. *Special achievements/activities:* cheerleading/drum major. *Special characteristics:* children and siblings of alumni, children of faculty/staff, local/state students, members of minority groups. *Tuition waivers:* Full or partial for children of alumni, employees or children of employees, senior citizens.

**LOANS** *Student loans:* $16,276,336 (85% need-based, 15% non-need-based). 57% of past graduating class borrowed through all loan programs. *Average indebtedness per student:* $19,987. *Average need-based loan:* Freshmen: $3316. Undergraduates: $4105. *Parent loans:* $690,680 (54% need-based, 46% non-need-based). *Programs:* Federal Direct (Subsidized and Unsubsidized Stafford, PLUS), Perkins, Federal Nursing.

**WORK-STUDY** *Federal work-study:* jobs available. *State or other work-study/employment:* Total amount: $151,050 (73% need-based, 27% non-need-based). Part-time jobs available.

**ATHLETIC AWARDS** Total amount: $2,419,852 (56% need-based, 44% non-need-based).

**APPLYING FOR FINANCIAL AID** *Required financial aid form:* FAFSA. *Financial aid deadline (priority):* 2/15. *Notification date:* 3/15.

**CONTACT** Bryan Erslan, Director of Financial Aid, Lincoln Memorial University, 6965 Cumberland Gap Parkway, Harrogate, TN 37752-1901, 423-869-6465 or toll-free 800-325-0900. *Fax:* 423-869-6347. *E-mail:* bryan.erslan@lmunet.edu.
*Website:* http://www.lmunet.edu/.

# LINCOLN UNIVERSITY
## Oakland, CA

**CONTACT** Financial Aid Office, Lincoln University, 401 15th Street, Oakland, CA 94612, 510-628-8010 or toll-free 888-810-9998.
*Website:* http://www.lincolnuca.edu/.

# LINCOLN UNIVERSITY
## Jefferson City, MO

| Tuition & fees (MO res): $6838 | Average undergraduate aid package: $10,788 |
| --- | --- |

**ABOUT THE INSTITUTION** State-supported, coed. *Awards:* certificates, associate, bachelor's, and master's degrees. 46 undergraduate majors. *Total enrollment:* 3,117. Undergraduates: 2,977. Freshmen: 534. Federal methodology is used as a basis for awarding need-based institutional aid.

**UNDERGRADUATE EXPENSES for 2015–2016** *Tuition, state resident:* full-time $6150; part-time $205 per credit hour. *Tuition, nonresident:* full-time $12,540; part-time $418 per credit hour. *Required fees:* full-time $688; $16.75 per credit hour or $92.70 per term. Full-time tuition and fees vary according to location and reciprocity agreements. Part-time tuition and fees vary according to location and reciprocity agreements. *College room and board:* $5531; *Room only:* $2786. Room and board charges vary according to board plan and housing facility.

**FRESHMAN FINANCIAL AID (Fall 2014, est.)** 496 applied for aid; of those 92% were deemed to have need. 100% of freshmen with need received aid; of those 5% had need fully met. *Average percent of need met:* 59% (excluding resources awarded to replace EFC). *Average financial aid package:* $11,259 (excluding resources awarded to replace EFC).

**UNDERGRADUATE FINANCIAL AID (Fall 2014, est.)** 1,837 applied for aid; of those 90% were deemed to have need. 100% of undergraduates with need received aid; of those 4% had need fully met. *Average percent of need met:* 62% (excluding resources awarded to replace EFC). *Average financial aid package:* $10,788 (excluding resources awarded to replace EFC). 1% of all full-time undergraduates had no need and received non-need-based gift aid.

**GIFT AID (NEED-BASED)** *Total amount:* $9,745,480 (77% federal, 9% state, 9% institutional, 5% external sources). *Receiving aid:* Freshmen: 82% (428); all full-time undergraduates: 75% (1,484). *Average award:* Freshmen: $6283; Undergraduates: $5762. *Scholarships, grants, and awards:* Federal Pell, FSEOG, state, private, college/university gift aid from institutional funds.

**GIFT AID (NON-NEED-BASED)** *Total amount:* $664,796 (10% federal, 2% state, 17% institutional, 71% external sources). *Receiving aid:* Freshmen: 1% (5). Undergraduates: 1% (28). *Average award:* Undergraduates: $4333. *Scholarships, grants, and awards by category: Academic interests/achievement:* 161 awards ($771,534 total): agriculture, general academic interests/achievements, military science. *Creative arts/performance:* 98 awards ($163,378 total): art/fine arts, journalism/publications, music, performing arts, theater/drama. *Special achievements/activities:* 20 awards ($12,170 total): cheerleading/drum major. *Special characteristics:* 333 awards ($1,579,118 total): adult students, children of faculty/staff, international students, out-of-state students. *Tuition waivers:* Full or partial for employees or children of employees, senior citizens. *ROTC:* Army, Naval cooperative, Air Force cooperative.

**LOANS** *Student loans:* $15,419,458 (40% need-based, 60% non-need-based). 73% of past graduating class borrowed through all loan programs. *Average indebtedness per student:* $30,225. *Average need-based loan:* Freshmen: $3456. Undergraduates: $4058. *Parent loans:* $1,303,692 (100% non-need-based). *Programs:* Federal Direct (Subsidized and Unsubsidized Stafford, PLUS), private loans.

**WORK-STUDY** *Federal work-study:* Total amount: $200,333; 169 jobs averaging $1214. *State or other work-study/employment:* Total amount: $382,812 (100% non-need-based). 156 part-time jobs averaging $3956.

**ATHLETIC AWARDS** Total amount: $1,043,422 (100% need-based).

**APPLYING FOR FINANCIAL AID** *Required financial aid forms:* FAFSA, institution's own form. *Financial aid deadline (priority):* 3/1. *Notification date:* Continuous beginning 3/15. Students must reply within 2 weeks of notification.

**CONTACT** Mr. Alfred Robinson, Director of Financial Aid, Lincoln University, 820 Chestnut Street, Jefferson City, MO 65102-0029, 573-681-6156. *Fax:* 573-681-5871. *E-mail:* robinsona@lincolnu.edu.
*Website:* http://www.lincolnu.edu/.

# LINCOLN UNIVERSITY
## Lincoln University, PA

**Tuition & fees (PA res): $10,232**     **Average undergraduate aid package: N/A**

**ABOUT THE INSTITUTION** State-related, coed. *Awards:* bachelor's and master's degrees. 46 undergraduate majors. *Total enrollment:* 1,819. Undergraduates: 1,589. Freshmen: 318. Federal methodology is used as a basis for awarding need-based institutional aid.

**UNDERGRADUATE EXPENSES for 2015–2016** *Application fee:* $20. *One-time required fee:* $202. *Tuition, state resident:* full-time $7160; part-time $301 per credit. *Tuition, nonresident:* full-time $11,836; part-time $497 per credit. *Required fees:* full-time $3072; $127 per year or $154 per year. Full-time tuition and fees vary according to degree level, program, and student level. Part-time tuition and fees vary according to course load, degree level, program, and student level. *College room and board:* $8686; *Room only:* $4634. Room and board charges vary according to board plan and housing facility. *Payment plan:* Guaranteed tuition.

**FRESHMAN FINANCIAL AID (Fall 2013)** 330 applied for aid; of those 100% were deemed to have need. 98% of freshmen with need received aid; of those 100% had need fully met. *Average percent of need met:* 98% (excluding resources awarded to replace EFC).

**UNDERGRADUATE FINANCIAL AID (Fall 2013)** 1,465 applied for aid; of those 100% were deemed to have need. 99% of undergraduates with need received aid; of those 100% had need fully met. *Average percent of need met:* 99% (excluding resources awarded to replace EFC).

**GIFT AID (NEED-BASED)** *Total amount:* $5,700,972 (43% federal, 11% state, 36% institutional, 10% external sources). *Receiving aid:* Freshmen: 97% (324); all full-time undergraduates: 96% (1,436). *Average award:* Freshmen: $1548; Undergraduates: $1675. *Scholarships, grants, and awards:* Federal Pell, FSEOG, state, private, college/university gift aid from institutional funds, United Negro College Fund.

**GIFT AID (NON-NEED-BASED)** *Scholarships, grants, and awards by category:* Academic interests/achievement: biological sciences, business, communication, computer science, education, English, general academic interests/achievements, humanities, mathematics, physical sciences, social sciences. *Creative arts/performance:* music. *Special achievements/activities:* general special achievements/activities. *Special characteristics:* children and siblings of alumni, children of faculty/staff, international students. *Tuition waivers:* Full or partial for children of alumni, employees or children of employees. *ROTC:* Army cooperative, Air Force cooperative.

**LOANS** *Student loans:* $2,711,000 (100% need-based). 91% of past graduating class borrowed through all loan programs. *Average indebtedness per student:* $12,082. *Average need-based loan:* Freshmen: $1695. Undergraduates: $2120. *Parent loans:* $2,100,978 (100% non-need-based). *Programs:* Federal Direct (Subsidized and Unsubsidized Stafford, PLUS), Perkins.

**WORK-STUDY** *Federal work-study:* jobs available.

**ATHLETIC AWARDS** Total amount: $294,746 (100% need-based).

**APPLYING FOR FINANCIAL AID** *Required financial aid form:* FAFSA. *Financial aid deadline:* 5/1 (priority: 4/1). *Notification date:* Continuous. Students must reply within 2 weeks of notification.

**CONTACT** Ms. Kim Anderson, Director of Financial Aid, Lincoln University, PO Box 179, Lincoln University, PA 19352, 484-365-7583 or toll-free 800-790-0191. *Fax:* 484-365-8198. *E-mail:* kanderson@lincoln.edu. *Website:* http://www.lincoln.edu/.

# LINDENWOOD UNIVERSITY
## St. Charles, MO

**Tuition & fees: $15,580**     **Average undergraduate aid package: $10,874**

**ABOUT THE INSTITUTION** Independent Presbyterian, coed. *Awards:* certificates, bachelor's, master's, and doctoral degrees. 106 undergraduate majors. *Total enrollment:* 12,151. Undergraduates: 8,541. Freshmen: 1,201. Both federal and institutional methodology are used as a basis for awarding need-based institutional aid.

**UNDERGRADUATE EXPENSES for 2015–2016** *Application fee:* $30. *Comprehensive fee:* $23,460 includes full-time tuition ($15,230), mandatory fees ($350), and room and board ($7880). *College room only:* $4290. *Part-time tuition:* $440 per credit hour. Part-time tuition and fees vary according to course load.

**FRESHMAN FINANCIAL AID (Fall 2014, est.)** 814 applied for aid; of those 80% were deemed to have need. 100% of freshmen with need received aid; of those 89% had need fully met. *Average percent of need met:* 94% (excluding resources awarded to replace EFC). *Average financial aid package:* $11,610 (excluding resources awarded to replace EFC). 39% of all full-time freshmen had no need and received non-need-based gift aid.

**UNDERGRADUATE FINANCIAL AID (Fall 2014, est.)** 5,089 applied for aid; of those 85% were deemed to have need. 100% of undergraduates with need received aid; of those 71% had need fully met. *Average percent of need met:* 90% (excluding resources awarded to replace EFC). *Average financial aid package:* $10,874 (excluding resources awarded to replace EFC). 49% of all full-time undergraduates had no need and received non-need-based gift aid.

**GIFT AID (NEED-BASED)** *Total amount:* $34,803,000 (34% federal, 11% state, 55% institutional). *Receiving aid:* Freshmen: 53% (637); all full-time undergraduates: 47% (3,494). *Average award:* Freshmen: $6634; Undergraduates: $6427. *Scholarships, grants, and awards:* Federal Pell, FSEOG, state, private, college/university gift aid from institutional funds.

**GIFT AID (NON-NEED-BASED)** *Total amount:* $13,312,700 (2% state, 98% institutional). *Receiving aid:* Freshmen: 34% (410). Undergraduates: 30% (2,228). *Average award:* Freshmen: $3929. Undergraduates: $4785. *Scholarships, grants, and awards by category:* Academic interests/achievement: biological sciences, business, communication, computer science, education, engineering/technologies, English, foreign languages, general academic interests/achievements, health fields, humanities, international studies, library science, mathematics, military science, physical sciences, premedicine, religion/biblical studies, social sciences. *Creative arts/performance:* applied art and design, art/fine arts, cinema/film/broadcasting, dance, debating, general creative arts/performance, music, performing arts, theater/drama. *Special achievements/activities:* cheerleading/drum major, community service, general special achievements/activities, junior miss, leadership. *Special characteristics:* children and siblings of alumni, children of faculty/staff, public servants, veterans, veterans' children. *Tuition waivers:* Full or partial for employees or children of employees, senior citizens. *ROTC:* Army, Air Force cooperative.

**LOANS** *Student loans:* $44,300,000 (46% need-based, 54% non-need-based). *Average need-based loan:* Freshmen: $3040. Undergraduates: $4382. *Parent loans:* $4,500,000 (100% non-need-based). *Programs:* Federal Direct (Subsidized and Unsubsidized Stafford, PLUS).

**WORK-STUDY** *Federal work-study:* Total amount: $400,000; 237 jobs averaging $2209. *State or other work-study/employment:* Total amount: $7,800,000 (60% need-based, 40% non-need-based). 733 part-time jobs averaging $2222.

**ATHLETIC AWARDS** Total amount: $4,200,000 (100% non-need-based).

**APPLYING FOR FINANCIAL AID** *Required financial aid form:* FAFSA. *Financial aid deadline (priority):* 4/1. *Notification date:* Continuous. Students must reply within 2 weeks of notification.

**CONTACT** Lori Bode, Director of Financial Aid, Lindenwood University, 209 South Kingshighway, St. Charles, MO 63301-1695, 636-949-4925. *Fax:* 636-949-4924. *E-mail:* lbode@lindenwood.edu. *Website:* http://www.lindenwood.edu/.

# LINDSEY WILSON COLLEGE
## Columbia, KY

**Tuition & fees: $23,162**     **Average undergraduate aid package: N/A**

**ABOUT THE INSTITUTION** Independent United Methodist, coed. *Awards:* associate, bachelor's, master's, and doctoral degrees. 34 undergraduate majors. *Total enrollment:* 2,641. Undergraduates: 2,205. Freshmen: 526. Federal methodology is used as a basis for awarding need-based institutional aid.

**UNDERGRADUATE EXPENSES for 2015–2016** *Comprehensive fee:* $32,062 includes full-time tuition ($22,920), mandatory fees ($242), and room and board ($8900). *College room only:* $3225. Full-time tuition and fees vary according to class time, degree level, and location. *Part-time tuition:* $955 per credit hour. *Part-time fees:* $48 per term. Part-time tuition and fees vary according to class time, degree level, and location.

**FRESHMAN FINANCIAL AID (Fall 2014, est.)** 512 applied for aid; of those 96% were deemed to have need. 100% of freshmen with need received aid; of those 19% had need fully met.

**UNDERGRADUATE FINANCIAL AID (Fall 2014, est.)** 2,121 applied for aid; of those 95% were deemed to have need. 100% of undergraduates with need received aid; of those 23% had need fully met.
**GIFT AID (NEED-BASED) Total amount:** $31,482,926 (18% federal, 20% state, 59% institutional, 3% external sources). **Receiving aid:** Freshmen: 96% (490); all full-time undergraduates: 92% (1,957). **Average award:** Freshmen: $19,278; Undergraduates: $17,472. **Scholarships, grants, and awards:** Federal Pell, FSEOG, state, private, college/university gift aid from institutional funds.
**GIFT AID (NON-NEED-BASED) Scholarships, grants, and awards by category:** Academic interests/achievement: biological sciences, business, education, English, general academic interests/achievements, mathematics, premedicine, religion/biblical studies. Creative arts/performance: applied art and design, music. Special achievements/activities: cheerleading/drum major, general special achievements/activities, junior miss, leadership, religious involvement. Special characteristics: children and siblings of alumni, children of faculty/staff, relatives of clergy, religious affiliation. **Tuition waivers:** Full or partial for employees or children of employees, senior citizens.
**LOANS Student loans:** $12,524,142 (100% need-based). 78% of past graduating class borrowed through all loan programs. Average indebtedness per student: $26,249. **Average need-based loan:** Freshmen: $8040. Undergraduates: $4522. **Parent loans:** $895,251 (100% need-based). **Programs:** Federal Direct (Subsidized and Unsubsidized Stafford, PLUS), Perkins, college/university.
**WORK-STUDY Federal work-study:** Total amount: $571,233; 282 jobs averaging $2145. **State or other work-study/employment:** Total amount: $31,186 (100% need-based). 23 part-time jobs averaging $2375.
**ATHLETIC AWARDS** Total amount: $2,604,929 (100% need-based).
**APPLYING FOR FINANCIAL AID Required financial aid form:** FAFSA. **Financial aid deadline (priority):** 4/1. **Notification date:** Continuous beginning 4/15. Students must reply within 2 weeks of notification.
**CONTACT** Ms. Marilyn D. Radford, Director of Student Financial Services, Lindsey Wilson College, 210 Lindsey Wilson Street, Columbia, KY 42728, 270-384-8022 or toll-free 800-264-0138. Fax: 270-384-8591. E-mail: radfordm@lindsey.edu. Website: http://www.lindsey.edu/.

---

# LINFIELD COLLEGE
## McMinnville, OR

| Tuition & fees: $37,346 | Average undergraduate aid package: $30,438 |
|---|---|

**ABOUT THE INSTITUTION** Independent American Baptist Churches in the USA, coed. **Awards:** bachelor's degrees (Linfield College includes the Linfield College McMinnville Campus in McMinnville, Oregon; the Linfield-Good Samaritan School of Nursing in Portland, Oregon(Portland Campus) and the Linfield College Adult Degree Program online). 49 undergraduate majors. **Total enrollment:** 1,683. Undergraduates: 1,683. Freshmen: 463. Federal methodology is used as a basis for awarding need-based institutional aid.
**UNDERGRADUATE EXPENSES for 2015–2016 Comprehensive fee:** $47,676 includes full-time tuition ($37,000), mandatory fees ($346), and room and board ($10,330). **College room only:** $5610. Full-time tuition and fees vary according to course load and location. Room and board charges vary according to board plan, housing facility, and location. **Part-time tuition:** $1152 per semester hour. **Part-time fees:** $202 per term. Part-time tuition and fees vary according to course load and location.
**FRESHMAN FINANCIAL AID (Fall 2014, est.)** 421 applied for aid; of those 86% were deemed to have need. 100% of freshmen with need received aid; of those 32% had need fully met. **Average percent of need met:** 85% (excluding resources awarded to replace EFC). **Average financial aid package:** $32,134 (excluding resources awarded to replace EFC). 12% of all full-time freshmen had no need and received non-need-based gift aid.
**UNDERGRADUATE FINANCIAL AID (Fall 2014, est.)** 1,375 applied for aid; of those 88% were deemed to have need. 100% of undergraduates with need received aid; of those 28% had need fully met. **Average percent of need met:** 81% (excluding resources awarded to replace EFC). **Average financial aid package:** $30,438 (excluding resources awarded to replace EFC). 22% of all full-time undergraduates had no need and received non-need-based gift aid.
**GIFT AID (NEED-BASED) Total amount:** $25,246,442 (10% federal, 2% state, 84% institutional, 4% external sources). **Receiving aid:** Freshmen: 67% (306); all full-time undergraduates: 61% (989). **Average award:** Freshmen: $26,477; Undergrad-

---

uates: $24,216. **Scholarships, grants, and awards:** Federal Pell, FSEOG, state, private, college/university gift aid from institutional funds.
**GIFT AID (NON-NEED-BASED) Total amount:** $7,486,480 (1% federal, 96% institutional, 3% external sources). **Receiving aid:** Freshmen: 68% (311). Undergraduates: 65% (1,057). **Average award:** Freshmen: $15,900. Undergraduates: $16,160. **Scholarships, grants, and awards by category:** Academic interests/achievement: 1,343 awards ($17,344,169 total): biological sciences, business, communication, computer science, education, English, foreign languages, general academic interests/achievements, health fields, humanities, international studies, mathematics, physical sciences, religion/biblical studies, social sciences. Creative arts/performance: 56 awards ($135,550 total): debating, music, theater/drama. Special achievements/activities: 110 awards ($217,050 total): community service, leadership. Special characteristics: 620 awards ($6,333,881 total): children of faculty/staff, international students, members of minority groups, previous college experience. **Tuition waivers:** Full or partial for employees or children of employees, senior citizens. **ROTC:** Air Force cooperative.
**LOANS Student loans:** $11,382,383 (65% need-based, 35% non-need-based). 70% of past graduating class borrowed through all loan programs. Average indebtedness per student: $28,697. **Average need-based loan:** Freshmen: $3358. Undergraduates: $4496. **Parent loans:** $3,779,360 (36% need-based, 64% non-need-based). **Programs:** Federal Direct (Subsidized and Unsubsidized Stafford, PLUS), Perkins, private loans.
**WORK-STUDY Federal work-study:** Total amount: $2,220,042; 522 jobs averaging $2516. **State or other work-study/employment:** Total amount: $1,737,365 (3% need-based, 97% non-need-based). 445 part-time jobs averaging $2332.
**APPLYING FOR FINANCIAL AID Required financial aid form:** FAFSA. **Financial aid deadline (priority):** 2/1. **Notification date:** 4/1. Students must reply by 5/1 or within 2 weeks of notification.
**CONTACT** Ms. Keri Burke, Director of Financial Aid, Linfield College, 900 Southeast Baker Street, A484, McMinnville, OR 97128-6894, 503-883-2269 or toll-free 800-640-2287. Fax: 503-883-2486. E-mail: finaid@linfield.edu. Website: http://www.linfield.edu/.

---

# LIPSCOMB UNIVERSITY
## Nashville, TN

| Tuition & fees: $27,390 | Average undergraduate aid package: $21,630 |
|---|---|

**ABOUT THE INSTITUTION** Independent Church of Christ, coed. **Awards:** certificates, associate, bachelor's, master's, and doctoral degrees. 95 undergraduate majors. **Total enrollment:** 4,489. Undergraduates: 2,883. Freshmen: 630. Federal methodology is used as a basis for awarding need-based institutional aid.
**UNDERGRADUATE EXPENSES for 2015–2016 Application fee:** $50. **Comprehensive fee:** $37,740 includes full-time tuition ($25,290), mandatory fees ($2100), and room and board ($10,350). **College room only:** $5730. Full-time tuition and fees vary according to course load. Room and board charges vary according to board plan and housing facility. **Part-time tuition:** $1055 per credit hour. Part-time tuition and fees vary according to course load.
**FRESHMAN FINANCIAL AID (Fall 2014, est.)** 622 applied for aid; of those 68% were deemed to have need. 100% of freshmen with need received aid; of those 28% had need fully met. **Average percent of need met:** 57% (excluding resources awarded to replace EFC). **Average financial aid package:** $19,062 (excluding resources awarded to replace EFC). 32% of all full-time freshmen had no need and received non-need-based gift aid.
**UNDERGRADUATE FINANCIAL AID (Fall 2014, est.)** 2,499 applied for aid; of those 67% were deemed to have need. 100% of undergraduates with need received aid; of those 28% had need fully met. **Average percent of need met:** 56% (excluding resources awarded to replace EFC). **Average financial aid package:** $21,630 (excluding resources awarded to replace EFC). 29% of all full-time undergraduates had no need and received non-need-based gift aid.
**GIFT AID (NEED-BASED) Total amount:** $24,307,257 (13% federal, 18% state, 62% institutional, 7% external sources). **Receiving aid:** Freshmen: 24% (150); all full-time undergraduates: 22% (560). **Average award:** Freshmen: $3497; Undergraduates: $3799. **Scholarships, grants, and awards:** Federal Pell, FSEOG, state, private, college/university gift aid from institutional funds.
**GIFT AID (NON-NEED-BASED) Total amount:** $9,022,453 (14% state, 81% institutional, 5% external sources). **Receiving aid:** Freshmen: 66% (415). Undergrad-

uates: 57% (1,464). *Average award:* Freshmen: $12,191. Undergraduates: $13,435. *Scholarships, grants, and awards by category: Academic interests/ achievement:* 803 awards ($11,447,424 total): biological sciences, business, communication, education, engineering/technologies, English, general academic interests/ achievements, home economics, mathematics, premedicine, religion/biblical studies. *Creative arts/performance:* 89 awards ($520,800 total): art/fine arts, journalism/publications, music, theater/drama. *Special achievements/activities:* 70 awards ($319,592 total): cheerleading/drum major, community service, general special achievements/ activities, leadership, religious involvement. *Special characteristics:* 229 awards ($2,225,767 total): adult students, children of educators, children of faculty/staff, children with a deceased or disabled parent, international students, local/state students, members of minority groups, relatives of clergy, religious affiliation. *Tuition waivers:* Full or partial for employees or children of employees, adult students. *ROTC:* Army cooperative, Air Force cooperative.

**LOANS** *Student loans:* $12,325,851 (88% need-based, 12% non-need-based). 61% of past graduating class borrowed through all loan programs. *Average indebtedness per student:* $30,480. *Average need-based loan:* Freshmen: $3547. Undergraduates: $5097. *Parent loans:* $5,043,278 (91% need-based, 9% non-need-based). *Programs:* Federal Direct (Subsidized and Unsubsidized Stafford, PLUS), Perkins.

**WORK-STUDY** *Federal work-study:* Total amount: $324,691; 133 jobs averaging $2441.

**ATHLETIC AWARDS** Total amount: $4,200,277 (67% need-based, 33% non-need-based).

**APPLYING FOR FINANCIAL AID** *Required financial aid form:* FAFSA. *Financial aid deadline (priority):* 1/31. *Notification date:* Continuous beginning 3/1.

**CONTACT** Ms. Tiffany Summers, Director of Financial Aid, Lipscomb University, One University Park Drive, Nashville, TN 37204-3951, 615-966-1791 or toll-free 877-582-4766. *Fax:* 615-966-7640. *E-mail:* tiffany.summers@lipscomb.edu. *Website:* http://www.lipscomb.edu/.

# LIVINGSTONE COLLEGE
## Salisbury, NC

**CONTACT** Mrs. Terry Jefferies, Financial Aid Director, Livingstone College, 701 West Monroe Street, Price Building, Salisbury, NC 28144-5298, 704-216-6069 or toll-free 800-835-3435. *Fax:* 704-216-6319. *E-mail:* tjefferies@livingstone.edu. *Website:* http://www.livingstone.edu/.

# LOCK HAVEN UNIVERSITY OF PENNSYLVANIA
## Lock Haven, PA

| Tuition & fees (PA res): $9276 | Average undergraduate aid package: $8511 |
|---|---|

**ABOUT THE INSTITUTION** State-supported, coed. *Awards:* associate, bachelor's, and master's degrees. 47 undergraduate majors. *Total enrollment:* 4,917. Undergraduates: 4,521. Freshmen: 935. Federal methodology is used as a basis for awarding need-based institutional aid.

**UNDERGRADUATE EXPENSES** for 2015–2016 *Application fee:* $25. *One-time required fee:* $30. *Tuition, state resident:* full-time $6820; part-time $284 per credit hour. *Tuition, nonresident:* full-time $15,050; part-time $284 per credit hour. *Required fees:* full-time $2456; $137.40 per credit hour or $40 per term. Full-time tuition and fees vary according to course load and location. Part-time tuition and fees vary according to course load and location. *College room and board:* $8752; *Room only:* $5600. Room and board charges vary according to board plan and housing facility.

**FRESHMAN FINANCIAL AID (Fall 2014, est.)** 857 applied for aid; of those 84% were deemed to have need. 98% of freshmen with need received aid; of those 42% had need fully met. *Average percent of need met:* 87% (excluding resources awarded to replace EFC). *Average financial aid package:* $11,178 (excluding resources awarded to replace EFC). 1% of all full-time freshmen had no need and received non-need-based gift aid.

**UNDERGRADUATE FINANCIAL AID (Fall 2014, est.)** 2,910 applied for aid; of those 90% were deemed to have need. 95% of undergraduates with need received aid; of those 43% had need fully met. *Average percent of need met:* 85% (excluding resources awarded to replace EFC). *Average financial aid package:* $8511 (excluding resources awarded to replace EFC). 1% of all full-time undergraduates had no need and received non-need-based gift aid.

**GIFT AID (NEED-BASED)** *Total amount:* $15,615,514 (55% federal, 40% state, 5% institutional). *Receiving aid:* Freshmen: 61% (557); all full-time undergraduates: 55% (2,290). *Average award:* Freshmen: $7696; Undergraduates: $5445. *Scholarships, grants, and awards:* Federal Pell, FSEOG, state, private, college/university gift aid from institutional funds.

**GIFT AID (NON-NEED-BASED)** *Total amount:* $1,559,803 (4% federal, 31% institutional, 65% external sources). *Receiving aid:* Freshmen: 16% (147). Undergraduates: 8% (319). *Average award:* Freshmen: $2062. Undergraduates: $2437. *Scholarships, grants, and awards by category: Academic interests/ achievement:* 536 awards ($603,407 total): biological sciences, business, communication, computer science, education, English, foreign languages, general academic interests/achievements, health fields, international studies, library science, mathematics, physical sciences, premedicine, social sciences. *Creative arts/performance:* 6 awards ($14,200 total): art/fine arts, journalism/publications, music, performing arts. *Special achievements/activities:* 58 awards ($62,225 total): community service, general special achievements/activities, leadership, memberships. *Special characteristics:* 55 awards ($59,275 total): adult students, ethnic background, handicapped students, international students, local/state students, married students, members of minority groups, previous college experience. *Tuition waivers:* Full or partial for minority students, employees or children of employees, senior citizens. *ROTC:* Army.

**LOANS** *Student loans:* $45,614,118 (30% need-based, 70% non-need-based). 82% of past graduating class borrowed through all loan programs. *Average indebtedness per student:* $29,353. *Average need-based loan:* Freshmen: $3260. Undergraduates: $4278. *Parent loans:* $5,834,091 (100% non-need-based). *Programs:* Federal Direct (Subsidized and Unsubsidized Stafford, PLUS), Perkins, college/university, alternative loans.

**WORK-STUDY** *Federal work-study:* Total amount: $284,607; 302 jobs averaging $557. *State or other work-study/employment:* Total amount: $302,400 (100% non-need-based). 431 part-time jobs averaging $1452.

**ATHLETIC AWARDS** Total amount: $648,578 (100% non-need-based).

**APPLYING FOR FINANCIAL AID** *Required financial aid forms:* FAFSA, state aid form. *Financial aid deadline (priority):* 3/15. *Notification date:* Continuous beginning 3/20. Students must reply within 2 weeks of notification.

**CONTACT** Robert Fryer, Director of Financial Aid, Lock Haven University of Pennsylvania, 401 North Fairview Street, 223 Ulmer Hall, Lock Haven, PA 17745-2390, 570-484-2452 or toll-free 800-332-8900 (in-state), 800-233-8978 (out-of-state). *Fax:* 570-484-2918. *E-mail:* rcf138@lhup.edu. *Website:* http://www.lhup.edu/.

# LOGAN UNIVERSITY
## Chesterfield, MO

| Tuition & fees: $6880 | Average undergraduate aid package: $7604 |
|---|---|

**ABOUT THE INSTITUTION** Independent, coed. *Awards:* bachelor's, master's, and doctoral degrees. 2 undergraduate majors. *Total enrollment:* 899. Undergraduates: 48. Federal methodology is used as a basis for awarding need-based institutional aid.

**UNDERGRADUATE EXPENSES** for 2015–2016 *Application fee:* $50. *Tuition:* full-time $6600; part-time $275 per credit hour. *Required fees:* full-time $280; $140 per term. Full-time tuition and fees vary according to course load and degree level. Part-time tuition and fees vary according to course load and degree level.

**UNDERGRADUATE FINANCIAL AID (Fall 2014, est.)** 31 applied for aid; of those 97% were deemed to have need. 100% of undergraduates with need received aid; of those 7% had need fully met. *Average percent of need met:* 46% (excluding resources awarded to replace EFC). *Average financial aid package:* $7604 (excluding resources awarded to replace EFC).

**GIFT AID (NEED-BASED)** *Total amount:* $70,970 (100% federal). *Receiving aid:* All full-time undergraduates: 52% (16). *Average award:* Undergraduates: $3684. *Scholarships, grants, and awards:* Federal Pell, FSEOG, state, private.

**GIFT AID (NON-NEED-BASED)** *Total amount:* $5620 (100% external sources). *Tuition waivers:* Full or partial for employees or children of employees.
**LOANS** *Student loans:* $217,916 (78% need-based, 22% non-need-based). *Average need-based loan:* Undergraduates: $4658. *Parent loans:* $9027 (40% need-based, 60% non-need-based). *Programs:* Federal Direct (Subsidized and Unsubsidized Stafford, PLUS), Perkins.
**WORK-STUDY** *Federal work-study:* Total amount: $17,325; 3 jobs averaging $1459.
**APPLYING FOR FINANCIAL AID** *Notification date:* Continuous. Students must reply within 2 weeks of notification.
**CONTACT** Kerry R. Hallahan, Director of Financial Aid, Logan University, 1851 Schoettler Road, Chesterfield, MO 63017, 636-230-1741 or toll-free 800-533-9210. *E-mail:* kerry.hallahan@logan.edu.
*Website:* http://www.logan.edu/.

# LOMA LINDA UNIVERSITY
## Loma Linda, CA

**CONTACT** Verdell Schaefer, Director of Financial Aid, Loma Linda University, 11139 Anderson Street, Loma Linda, CA 92350, 909-558-4509 or toll-free 800-422-4558. *Fax:* 909-558-4879. *E-mail:* finaid@univ.llu.edu.
*Website:* http://www.llu.edu/.

# LONG ISLAND UNIVERSITY–LIU BROOKLYN
## Brooklyn, NY

| Tuition & fees: $34,852 | Average undergraduate aid package: $19,220 |
|---|---|

**ABOUT THE INSTITUTION** Independent, coed. *Awards:* certificates, associate, bachelor's, master's, and doctoral degrees. 53 undergraduate majors. *Total enrollment:* 8,354. Undergraduates: 4,871. Freshmen: 842. Federal methodology is used as a basis for awarding need-based institutional aid.
**UNDERGRADUATE EXPENSES for 2015–2016** *Application fee:* $50. *Comprehensive fee:* $47,182 includes full-time tuition ($33,018), mandatory fees ($1834), and room and board ($12,330). Full-time tuition and fees vary according to program. Room and board charges vary according to board plan and housing facility. *Part-time tuition:* $1030 per credit. *Part-time fees:* $434 per term. Part-time tuition and fees vary according to program.
**FRESHMAN FINANCIAL AID (Fall 2013)** 827 applied for aid; of those 97% were deemed to have need. 97% of freshmen with need received aid; of those 6% had need fully met. *Average percent of need met:* 60% (excluding resources awarded to replace EFC). *Average financial aid package:* $22,787 (excluding resources awarded to replace EFC). 3% of all full-time freshmen had no need and received non-need-based gift aid.
**UNDERGRADUATE FINANCIAL AID (Fall 2013)** 4,014 applied for aid; of those 96% were deemed to have need. 97% of undergraduates with need received aid; of those 6% had need fully met. *Average percent of need met:* 51% (excluding resources awarded to replace EFC). *Average financial aid package:* $19,220 (excluding resources awarded to replace EFC). 4% of all full-time undergraduates had no need and received non-need-based gift aid.
**GIFT AID (NEED-BASED)** *Total amount:* $38,909,542 (46% federal, 21% state, 33% institutional). *Receiving aid:* Freshmen: 88% (757); all full-time undergraduates: 80% (3,344). *Average award:* Freshmen: $14,814; Undergraduates: $10,773. *Scholarships, grants, and awards:* Federal Pell, FSEOG, state, private, college/university gift aid from institutional funds, United Negro College Fund, Scholarships for Disadvantaged Students (SDS).
**GIFT AID (NON-NEED-BASED)** *Total amount:* $21,463,275 (98% institutional, 2% external sources). *Receiving aid:* Freshmen: 79% (686). Undergraduates: 83% (3,471). *Average award:* Freshmen: $9106. Undergraduates: $7738. *Scholarships, grants, and awards by category: Academic interests/achievement:* communication, education, general academic interests/achievements, health fields, international studies. *Creative arts/performance:* art/fine arts, cinema/film/broadcasting, creative writing, dance, journalism/publications, music; performing arts, theater/drama. *Special achievements/activities:* cheerleading/drum major, general

special achievements/activities, leadership. *Special characteristics:* children and siblings of alumni, children of educators, children of faculty/staff, ethnic background, first-generation college students, general special characteristics, handicapped students, international students, siblings of current students, veterans, veterans' children. *Tuition waivers:* Full or partial for employees or children of employees.
**LOANS** *Student loans:* $39,855,127 (35% need-based, 65% non-need-based). 81% of past graduating class borrowed through all loan programs. *Average indebtedness per student:* $41,554. *Average need-based loan:* Freshmen: $3673. Undergraduates: $4442. *Parent loans:* $15,906,749 (100% non-need-based). *Programs:* Federal Direct (Subsidized and Unsubsidized Stafford, PLUS), Perkins, Health Professions Student Loans (HPSL).
**WORK-STUDY** *Federal work-study:* 329 jobs averaging $3724.
**ATHLETIC AWARDS** *Total amount:* $6,483,968 (100% non-need-based).
**APPLYING FOR FINANCIAL AID** *Required financial aid forms:* FAFSA, state aid form. *Financial aid deadline:* Continuous. *Notification date:* Continuous beginning 2/15. Students must reply by 5/1 or within 2 weeks of notification.
**CONTACT** Ms. Margaret Nelson, Executive Director of Enrollment Services, Long Island University–LIU Brooklyn, 1 University Plaza, Brooklyn, NY 11201-8423, 718-488-1037 or toll-free 800-LIU-PLAN. *Fax:* 718-488-3343. *E-mail:* bklnenrollmentservices@liu.edu.
*Website:* http://www.liu.edu/.

# LONG ISLAND UNIVERSITY–LIU POST
## Brookville, NY

| Tuition & fees: $34,852 | Average undergraduate aid package: $19,276 |
|---|---|

**ABOUT THE INSTITUTION** Independent, coed. *Awards:* certificates, associate, bachelor's, master's, and doctoral degrees. 74 undergraduate majors. *Total enrollment:* 9,486. Undergraduates: 7,117. Freshmen: 563. Federal methodology is used as a basis for awarding need-based institutional aid.
**UNDERGRADUATE EXPENSES for 2015–2016** *Application fee:* $50. *Comprehensive fee:* $47,660 includes full-time tuition ($33,018), mandatory fees ($1834), and room and board ($12,808). Full-time tuition and fees vary according to program. Room and board charges vary according to board plan and housing facility. *Part-time tuition:* $1030 per credit. *Part-time fees:* $434 per term. Part-time tuition and fees vary according to program.
**FRESHMAN FINANCIAL AID (Fall 2013)** 539 applied for aid; of those 86% were deemed to have need. 100% of freshmen with need received aid; of those 16% had need fully met. *Average percent of need met:* 61% (excluding resources awarded to replace EFC). *Average financial aid package:* $20,952 (excluding resources awarded to replace EFC). 16% of all full-time freshmen had no need and received non-need-based gift aid.
**UNDERGRADUATE FINANCIAL AID (Fall 2013)** 3,058 applied for aid; of those 85% were deemed to have need. 98% of undergraduates with need received aid; of those 18% had need fully met. *Average percent of need met:* 58% (excluding resources awarded to replace EFC). *Average financial aid package:* $19,276 (excluding resources awarded to replace EFC). 14% of all full-time undergraduates had no need and received non-need-based gift aid.
**GIFT AID (NEED-BASED)** *Total amount:* $16,746,188 (42% federal, 26% state, 32% institutional). *Receiving aid:* Freshmen: 54% (339); all full-time undergraduates: 51% (1,838). *Average award:* Freshmen: $9021; Undergraduates: $8330. *Scholarships, grants, and awards:* Federal Pell, FSEOG, state, private, college/university gift aid from institutional funds, Scholarships for Disadvantaged Students (SDS).
**GIFT AID (NON-NEED-BASED)** *Total amount:* $27,856,757 (99% institutional, 1% external sources). *Receiving aid:* Freshmen: 47% (298). Undergraduates: 44% (1,601). *Average award:* Freshmen: $11,171. Undergraduates: $12,302. *Scholarships, grants, and awards by category: Academic interests/achievement:* biological sciences, business, computer science, education, English, general academic interests/achievements, health fields, international studies, library science, mathematics, premedicine, social sciences. *Creative arts/performance:* art/fine arts, cinema/film/broadcasting, dance, journalism/publications, music, performing arts, theater/drama. *Special achievements/activities:* leadership. *Special characteristics:* adult students, children and siblings of alumni, children of educators, children of faculty/staff, ethnic background, first-generation college students, handicapped students, international students, siblings of current students, veterans, veterans' children. *Tuition waivers:* Full or partial for employees or children of employees.

**LOANS** *Student loans:* $23,901,349 (35% need-based, 65% non-need-based). 64% of past graduating class borrowed through all loan programs. *Average indebtedness per student:* $35,474. *Average need-based loan:* Freshmen: $3771. Undergraduates: $4592. *Parent loans:* $15,561,596 (100% non-need-based). *Programs:* Federal Direct (Subsidized and Unsubsidized Stafford, PLUS), Perkins.
**WORK-STUDY** *Federal work-study:* 539 jobs averaging $1357.
**ATHLETIC AWARDS** Total amount: $5,165,906 (100% non-need-based).
**APPLYING FOR FINANCIAL AID** *Required financial aid forms:* FAFSA, state aid form. *Financial aid deadline:* Continuous. *Notification date:* Continuous beginning 2/15. Students must reply by 5/1 or within 2 weeks of notification.
**CONTACT** Ms. Joanne Graziano, Executive Director, Enrollment Services, Long Island University–LIU Post, 720 Northern Boulevard, Brookville, NY 11548-1300, 516-299-2553 or toll-free 800-LIU-PLAN. *Fax:* 516-299-3833. *E-mail:* post-enrollmentservices@liu.edu.
*Website:* http://www.liu.edu/.

## LONGWOOD UNIVERSITY
### Farmville, VA

| Tuition & fees (VA res): $11,910 | Average undergraduate aid package: $13,743 |
|---|---|

**ABOUT THE INSTITUTION** State-supported, coed. *Awards:* certificates, bachelor's, and master's degrees. 25 undergraduate majors. *Total enrollment:* 5,096. Undergraduates: 4,574. Freshmen: 1,097. Federal methodology is used as a basis for awarding need-based institutional aid.
**UNDERGRADUATE EXPENSES for 2015–2016** *Application fee:* $50. *Tuition, state resident:* full-time $7170; part-time $239 per credit. *Tuition, non-resident:* full-time $21,330; part-time $688 per credit. *Required fees:* full-time $4740; $158 per credit hour. Full-time tuition and fees vary according to course load. Part-time tuition and fees vary according to course load. *College room and board:* $10,272; *Room only:* $6394. Room and board charges vary according to board plan, housing facility, and location.
**FRESHMAN FINANCIAL AID (Fall 2013)** 894 applied for aid; of those 73% were deemed to have need. 93% of freshmen with need received aid; of those 29% had need fully met. *Average percent of need met:* 80% (excluding resources awarded to replace EFC). *Average financial aid package:* $13,904 (excluding resources awarded to replace EFC). 4% of all full-time freshmen had no need and received non-need-based gift aid.
**UNDERGRADUATE FINANCIAL AID (Fall 2013)** 3,046 applied for aid; of those 76% were deemed to have need. 96% of undergraduates with need received aid; of those 30% had need fully met. *Average percent of need met:* 82% (excluding resources awarded to replace EFC). *Average financial aid package:* $13,743 (excluding resources awarded to replace EFC). 5% of all full-time undergraduates had no need and received non-need-based gift aid.
**GIFT AID (NEED-BASED)** *Total amount:* $12,680,232 (37% federal, 35% state, 22% institutional, 6% external sources). *Receiving aid:* Freshmen: 45% (488); all full-time undergraduates: 40% (1,658). *Average award:* Freshmen: $7545; Undergraduates: $7375. *Scholarships, grants, and awards:* Federal Pell, FSEOG, state, private, college/university gift aid from institutional funds.
**GIFT AID (NON-NEED-BASED)** *Total amount:* $1,528,221 (4% state, 70% institutional, 26% external sources). *Receiving aid:* Freshmen: 2% (25). Undergraduates: 2% (87). *Average award:* Freshmen: $4683. Undergraduates: $4270. *Scholarships, grants, and awards by category:* Academic interests/achievement: biological sciences, business, computer science, education, English, general academic interests/achievements, humanities, international studies, mathematics, military science, social sciences. Creative arts/performance: art/fine arts, music, theater/drama. Special achievements/activities: community service, leadership, memberships. Special characteristics: children and siblings of alumni, general special characteristics, local/state students. *Tuition waivers:* Full or partial for employees or children of employees, senior citizens. *ROTC:* Army.
**LOANS** *Student loans:* $20,022,401 (68% need-based, 32% non-need-based). 65% of past graduating class borrowed through all loan programs. *Average indebtedness per student:* $27,644. *Average need-based loan:* Freshmen: $3763. Undergraduates: $4369. *Parent loans:* $12,532,556 (32% need-based, 68% non-need-based). *Programs:* Federal Direct (Subsidized and Unsubsidized Stafford, PLUS), Perkins, private loans.

**WORK-STUDY** *Federal work-study:* jobs available. *State or other work-study/employment:* Part-time jobs available.
**ATHLETIC AWARDS** Total amount: $2,259,965 (33% need-based, 67% non-need-based).
**APPLYING FOR FINANCIAL AID** *Required financial aid form:* FAFSA. *Financial aid deadline (priority):* 3/1. *Notification date:* Continuous beginning 4/1. Students must reply within 4 weeks of notification.
**CONTACT** Ms. Caroline Gibbs, Financial Aid Counselor, Longwood University, 201 High Street, Farmville, VA 23909, 434-395-2949 or toll-free 800-281-4677. *Fax:* 434-395-2829. *E-mail:* gibbsca@longwood.edu.
*Website:* http://www.longwood.edu/.

## LORAS COLLEGE
### Dubuque, IA

| Tuition & fees: $29,729 | Average undergraduate aid package: $20,971 |
|---|---|

**ABOUT THE INSTITUTION** Independent Roman Catholic, coed. *Awards:* associate, bachelor's, and master's degrees. 38 undergraduate majors. *Total enrollment:* 1,569. Undergraduates: 1,490. Freshmen: 374. Federal methodology is used as a basis for awarding need-based institutional aid.
**UNDERGRADUATE EXPENSES for 2015–2016** *Application fee:* $25. *Comprehensive fee:* $38,082 includes full-time tuition ($28,340), mandatory fees ($1389), and room and board ($8353). *College room only:* $3953. Full-time tuition and fees vary according to course load and degree level. Room and board charges vary according to board plan and housing facility. *Part-time tuition:* $590 per credit. *Part-time fees:* $25 per credit.
**FRESHMAN FINANCIAL AID (Fall 2014, est.)** 336 applied for aid; of those 87% were deemed to have need. 100% of freshmen with need received aid; of those 42% had need fully met. *Average percent of need met:* 90% (excluding resources awarded to replace EFC). *Average financial aid package:* $22,424 (excluding resources awarded to replace EFC). 21% of all full-time freshmen had no need and received non-need-based gift aid.
**UNDERGRADUATE FINANCIAL AID (Fall 2014, est.)** 1,251 applied for aid; of those 87% were deemed to have need. 100% of undergraduates with need received aid; of those 78% had need fully met. *Average percent of need met:* 84% (excluding resources awarded to replace EFC). *Average financial aid package:* $20,971 (excluding resources awarded to replace EFC). 27% of all full-time undergraduates had no need and received non-need-based gift aid.
**GIFT AID (NEED-BASED)** *Total amount:* $20,262,571 (8% federal, 5% state, 87% institutional). *Receiving aid:* Freshmen: 78% (291); all full-time undergraduates: 73% (1,051). *Average award:* Freshmen: $17,975; Undergraduates: $17,647. *Scholarships, grants, and awards:* Federal Pell, FSEOG, state, private, college/university gift aid from institutional funds.
**GIFT AID (NON-NEED-BASED)** *Total amount:* $5,651,451 (1% federal, 1% state, 93% institutional, 5% external sources). *Receiving aid:* Freshmen: 78% (291). Undergraduates: 76% (1,094). *Average award:* Freshmen: $17,896. Undergraduates: $15,082. *Scholarships, grants, and awards by category:* Academic interests/achievement: 1,376 awards ($18,309,978 total): engineering/technologies, general academic interests/achievements, physical sciences. Creative arts/performance: 93 awards ($112,650 total): music. *Tuition waivers:* Full or partial for employees or children of employees. *ROTC:* Army cooperative.
**LOANS** *Student loans:* $8,724,362 (43% need-based, 57% non-need-based). 73% of past graduating class borrowed through all loan programs. *Average indebtedness per student:* $34,514. *Average need-based loan:* Freshmen: $3585. Undergraduates: $4580. *Parent loans:* $1,850,137 (100% non-need-based). *Programs:* Federal Direct (Subsidized and Unsubsidized Stafford, PLUS), Perkins, college/university.
**WORK-STUDY** *Federal work-study:* Total amount: $200,000; 600 jobs averaging $1932. *State or other work-study/employment:* Total amount: $250,000 (100% non-need-based). 177 part-time jobs averaging $1951.
**APPLYING FOR FINANCIAL AID** *Required financial aid form:* FAFSA. *Financial aid deadline (priority):* 4/15. *Notification date:* Continuous beginning 3/1. Students must reply within 3 weeks of notification.

**CONTACT** Ms. Julie A. Dunn, Director of Financial Planning, Loras College, 1450 Alta Vista Street, Dubuque, IA 52001-4327, 563-588-7136 or toll-free 800-245-6727. *Fax:* 563-588-7119. *E-mail:* julie.dunn@loras.edu. *Website:* http://www.loras.edu/.

# LOS ANGELES FILM SCHOOL
## Hollywood, CA

**CONTACT** Financial Aid Office, Los Angeles Film School, 6363 Sunset Boulevard, Hollywood, CA 90028, 323-860-0789 or toll-free 877-952-3456. *Website:* http://www.lafilm.edu/.

# LOUISIANA COLLEGE
## Pineville, LA

**ABOUT THE INSTITUTION** Independent Southern Baptist, coed. *Awards:* associate, bachelor's, and master's degrees. 55 undergraduate majors. *Total enrollment:* 1,256. Undergraduates: 985. Freshmen: 236.

**GIFT AID (NEED-BASED)** *Scholarships, grants, and awards:* Federal Pell, FSEOG, state, private, college/university gift aid from institutional funds.

**GIFT AID (NON-NEED-BASED)** *Scholarships, grants, and awards by category:* Academic interests/achievement: business, general academic interests/achievements, health fields, religion/biblical studies. *Creative arts/performance:* music, performing arts, theater/drama. *Special achievements/activities:* leadership. *Special characteristics:* children of faculty/staff.

**LOANS** *Programs:* Federal Direct (Subsidized and Unsubsidized Stafford, PLUS).

**APPLYING FOR FINANCIAL AID** *Required financial aid forms:* FAFSA, institution's own form.

**CONTACT** David Barnard, Director of Financial Aid, Louisiana College, 1140 College Drive, Pineville, LA 71359-0001, 318-487-7387 or toll-free 800-487-1906. *Fax:* 318-487-7449. *E-mail:* gossett@lacollege.edu. *Website:* http://www.lacollege.edu/.

# LOUISIANA STATE UNIVERSITY AND AGRICULTURAL & MECHANICAL COLLEGE
## Baton Rouge, LA

| Tuition & fees (LA res): $8750 | Average undergraduate aid package: $14,798 |
| --- | --- |

**ABOUT THE INSTITUTION** State-supported, coed. *Awards:* certificates, bachelor's, master's, and doctoral degrees. 66 undergraduate majors. *Total enrollment:* 37,314. Undergraduates: 25,572. Freshmen: 5,655. Federal methodology is used as a basis for awarding need-based institutional aid.

**UNDERGRADUATE EXPENSES** for 2015–2016 *Application fee:* $40. *Tuition, state resident:* full-time $6678. *Tuition, nonresident:* full-time $24,395. *Required fees:* full-time $2072. Part-time tuition and fees vary according to course load. *College room and board:* $10,804; *Room only:* $6900. Room and board charges vary according to board plan and housing facility.

**FRESHMAN FINANCIAL AID (Fall 2013)** 3,873 applied for aid; of those 70% were deemed to have need. 100% of freshmen with need received aid; of those 26% had need fully met. *Average percent of need met:* 72% (excluding resources awarded to replace EFC). *Average financial aid package:* $14,724 (excluding resources awarded to replace EFC). 16% of all full-time freshmen had no need and received non-need-based gift aid.

**UNDERGRADUATE FINANCIAL AID (Fall 2013)** 12,945 applied for aid; of those 76% were deemed to have need. 100% of undergraduates with need received aid; of those 22% had need fully met. *Average percent of need met:* 68% (excluding resources awarded to replace EFC). *Average financial aid package:* $14,798 (excluding resources awarded to replace EFC). 14% of all full-time undergraduates had no need and received non-need-based gift aid.

**GIFT AID (NEED-BASED)** *Total amount:* $83,426,238 (27% federal, 40% state, 31% institutional, 2% external sources). *Receiving aid:* Freshmen: 47% (2,605); all full-time undergraduates: 38% (8,587). *Average award:* Freshmen: $10,405; Undergraduates: $10,097. *Scholarships, grants, and awards:* Federal Pell, FSEOG, state, private, college/university gift aid from institutional funds.

**GIFT AID (NON-NEED-BASED)** *Total amount:* $70,800,090 (2% federal, 68% state, 24% institutional, 6% external sources). *Receiving aid:* Freshmen: 2% (99). Undergraduates: 1% (253). *Average award:* Freshmen: $3188. Undergraduates: $5098. *Scholarships, grants, and awards by category:* Academic interests/achievement: 1,038 awards ($1,204,558 total): agriculture, architecture, biological sciences, business, communication, computer science, education, engineering/technologies, English, foreign languages, general academic interests/achievements, home economics, humanities, mathematics, military science, physical sciences, premedicine. *Creative arts/performance:* 138 awards ($380,689 total): applied art and design, journalism/publications, music, performing arts, theater/drama. *Special characteristics:* 143 awards ($1,541,253 total): children with a deceased or disabled parent, general special characteristics. *Tuition waivers:* Full or partial for employees or children of employees. *ROTC:* Army, Naval cooperative, Air Force.

**LOANS** *Student loans:* $66,406,217 (71% need-based, 29% non-need-based). 39% of past graduating class borrowed through all loan programs. *Average indebtedness per student:* $22,294. *Average need-based loan:* Freshmen: $5216. Undergraduates: $6354. *Parent loans:* $28,764,079 (45% need-based, 55% non-need-based). *Programs:* Federal Direct (Subsidized and Unsubsidized Stafford, PLUS), Perkins, college/university.

**WORK-STUDY** *Federal work-study:* 770 jobs averaging $2200. *State or other work-study/employment:* Total amount: $14,861,440 (30% need-based, 70% non-need-based). 4,700 part-time jobs averaging $2400.

**ATHLETIC AWARDS** Total amount: $10,883,134 (41% need-based, 59% non-need-based).

**APPLYING FOR FINANCIAL AID** *Required financial aid forms:* FAFSA, institution's own form. *Financial aid deadline (priority):* 4/1. *Notification date:* Continuous beginning 12/15. Students must reply by 5/1.

**CONTACT** Ms. Amy Marix , Associate Director of Undergraduate Admissions and Student Aid, Louisiana State University and Agricultural & Mechanical College, 1146 Pleasant Hall, Baton Rouge, LA 70803-3103, 225-578-3113. *Fax:* 225-578-6300. *E-mail:* financialaid@lsu.edu. *Website:* http://www.lsu.edu/.

# LOUISIANA STATE UNIVERSITY AT ALEXANDRIA
## Alexandria, LA

**CONTACT** Financial Aid Office, Louisiana State University at Alexandria, 8100 Highway 71 South, Alexandria, LA 71302-9121, 318-445-3672 or toll-free 888-473-6417. *Website:* http://www.lsua.edu/.

# LOUISIANA STATE UNIVERSITY HEALTH SCIENCES CENTER
## New Orleans, LA

**CONTACT** Mr. Patrick Gorman, Director of Financial Aid, Louisiana State University Health Sciences Center, 433 Bolivar Street, New Orleans, LA 70112, 504-568-4821. *Fax:* 504-599-1390. *Website:* http://www.lsuhsc.edu/.

# LOUISIANA STATE UNIVERSITY IN SHREVEPORT
## Shreveport, LA

**CONTACT** Office of Student Financial Aid, Louisiana State University in Shreveport, One University Place, Shreveport, LA 71115-2399, 318-797-5363 or toll-free 800-229-5957. *Fax:* 318-797-5366.
*Website:* http://www.lsus.edu/.

# LOUISIANA TECH UNIVERSITY
## Ruston, LA

| Tuition & fees (LA res): $8052 | Average undergraduate aid package: $9757 |
| --- | --- |

**ABOUT THE INSTITUTION** State-supported, coed. *Awards:* certificates, associate, bachelor's, master's, and doctoral degrees. 79 undergraduate majors. *Total enrollment:* 11,225. Undergraduates: 9,532. Freshmen: 1,857. Federal methodology is used as a basis for awarding need-based institutional aid.
**UNDERGRADUATE EXPENSES for 2015–2016 Application fee:** $20. *Tuition, state resident:* full-time $6233; part-time $336 per credit hour. *Tuition, nonresident:* full-time $20,816; part-time $943 per credit hour. *Required fees:* full-time $1819. Full-time tuition and fees vary according to course load, location, and program. Part-time tuition and fees vary according to course load, location, and program. *College room and board:* $5520. Room and board charges vary according to board plan and housing facility.
**FRESHMAN FINANCIAL AID (Fall 2013)** 615 applied for aid; of those 66% were deemed to have need. 98% of freshmen with need received aid; of those 27% had need fully met. *Average percent of need met:* 63% (excluding resources awarded to replace EFC). *Average financial aid package:* $9470 (excluding resources awarded to replace EFC). 24% of all full-time freshmen had no need and received non-need-based gift aid.
**UNDERGRADUATE FINANCIAL AID (Fall 2013)** 3,715 applied for aid; of those 69% were deemed to have need. 96% of undergraduates with need received aid; of those 22% had need fully met. *Average percent of need met:* 62% (excluding resources awarded to replace EFC). *Average financial aid package:* $9757 (excluding resources awarded to replace EFC). 18% of all full-time undergraduates had no need and received non-need-based gift aid.
**GIFT AID (NEED-BASED) Total amount:** $22,399,970 (36% federal, 43% state, 18% institutional, 3% external sources). *Receiving aid:* Freshmen: 26% (386); all full-time undergraduates: 35% (2,300). *Average award:* Freshmen: $8402; Undergraduates: $8375. *Scholarships, grants, and awards:* Federal Pell, FSEOG, state, private, college/university gift aid from institutional funds.
**GIFT AID (NON-NEED-BASED) Total amount:** $14,549,196 (57% state, 37% institutional, 6% external sources). *Receiving aid:* Freshmen: 7% (100). Undergraduates: 7% (485). *Average award:* Freshmen: $1882. Undergraduates: $3011. *Scholarships, grants, and awards by category: Academic interests/achievement:* agriculture, architecture, biological sciences, business, computer science, education, engineering/technologies, English, foreign languages, general academic interests/achievements, health fields, home economics, international studies, mathematics, military science, physical sciences, social sciences. *Creative arts/performance:* applied art and design, art/fine arts, creative writing, debating, general creative arts/performance, journalism/publications, music, performing arts, theater/drama. *Special achievements/activities:* cheerleading/drum major, junior miss. *Special characteristics:* children and siblings of alumni, children of faculty/staff, children of public servants, handicapped students, international students, members of minority groups, out-of-state students, spouses of deceased or disabled public servants, veterans, veterans' children. *Tuition waivers:* Full or partial for children of alumni, employees or children of employees, senior citizens. *ROTC:* Army cooperative, Air Force.
**LOANS Student loans:** $18,617,311 (70% need-based, 30% non-need-based). 51% of past graduating class borrowed through all loan programs. *Average indebtedness per student:* $16,855. *Average need-based loan:* Freshmen: $2670. Undergraduates: $3348. *Parent loans:* $4,249,239 (32% need-based, 68% non-need-based). *Programs:* Federal Direct (Subsidized and Unsubsidized Stafford, PLUS), Perkins.
**WORK-STUDY Federal work-study:** 280 jobs averaging $2067. *State or other work-study/employment:* 1,008 part-time jobs averaging $2356.

**ATHLETIC AWARDS Total amount:** $3,776,690 (48% need-based, 52% non-need-based).
**APPLYING FOR FINANCIAL AID Required financial aid forms:** FAFSA, institution's own form. *Financial aid deadline (priority):* 4/15. *Notification date:* Continuous beginning 4/1. Students must reply within 3 weeks of notification.
**CONTACT** Office of Financial Aid, Louisiana Tech University, PO Box 7925, Ruston, LA 71272, 318-257-2641 or toll-free 800-528-3241. *Fax:* 318-257-2628. *E-mail:* techaid@latech.edu.
*Website:* http://www.latech.edu/.

# LOURDES UNIVERSITY
## Sylvania, OH

**ABOUT THE INSTITUTION** Independent Roman Catholic, coed. *Awards:* certificates, associate, bachelor's, and master's degrees. 26 undergraduate majors. *Total enrollment:* 1,780. Undergraduates: 1,482. Freshmen: 162.
**GIFT AID (NEED-BASED) Scholarships, grants, and awards:** Federal Pell, FSEOG, state, private, college/university gift aid from institutional funds.
**GIFT AID (NON-NEED-BASED) Scholarships, grants, and awards by category: Academic interests/achievement:** general academic interests/achievements. *Creative arts/performance:* art/fine arts, dance, theater/drama. *Special achievements/activities:* cheerleading/drum major, general special achievements/activities, leadership. *Special characteristics:* adult students, ethnic background, local/state students, members of minority groups, out-of-state students, previous college experience, religious affiliation.
**LOANS Programs:** Federal Direct (Subsidized and Unsubsidized Stafford, PLUS), Perkins, state, college/university, alternative loans.
**WORK-STUDY Federal work-study:** 68 jobs averaging $1872. *State or other work-study/employment:* Total amount: $192,000 (100% need-based). 128 part-time jobs averaging $1500.
**APPLYING FOR FINANCIAL AID Required financial aid form:** FAFSA.
**CONTACT** Deb LaJeunesse, Director of Financial Aid, Lourdes University, 6832 Convent Boulevard, Sylvania, OH 43560-2898, 419-824-3732 or toll-free 800-878-3210. *Fax:* 419-517-8866. *E-mail:* finaid@lourdes.edu.
*Website:* http://www.lourdes.edu/.

# LOYOLA MARYMOUNT UNIVERSITY
## Los Angeles, CA

| Tuition & fees: $41,372 | Average undergraduate aid package: $26,949 |
| --- | --- |

**ABOUT THE INSTITUTION** Independent Roman Catholic, coed. *Awards:* certificates, bachelor's, master's, and doctoral degrees. 55 undergraduate majors. *Total enrollment:* 9,515. Undergraduates: 6,184. Freshmen: 1,348. Both federal and institutional methodology are used as a basis for awarding need-based institutional aid.
**UNDERGRADUATE EXPENSES for 2015–2016 Application fee:** $60. *One-time required fee:* $225. *Comprehensive fee:* $55,767 includes full-time tuition ($40,680), mandatory fees ($692), and room and board ($14,395). *College room only:* $9995. Full-time tuition and fees vary according to reciprocity agreements. Room and board charges vary according to board plan and housing facility. *Part-time tuition:* $1697 per credit hour. Part-time tuition and fees vary according to course load.
**FRESHMAN FINANCIAL AID (Fall 2013)** 1,088 applied for aid; of those 73% were deemed to have need. 100% of freshmen with need received aid; of those 16% had need fully met. *Average percent of need met:* 63% (excluding resources awarded to replace EFC). *Average financial aid package:* $24,774 (excluding resources awarded to replace EFC). 34% of all full-time freshmen had no need and received non-need-based gift aid.
**UNDERGRADUATE FINANCIAL AID (Fall 2013)** 4,510 applied for aid; of those 77% were deemed to have need. 99% of undergraduates with need received aid; of those 19% had need fully met. *Average percent of need met:* 65% (excluding resources awarded to replace EFC). *Average financial aid package:* $26,949 (excluding resources awarded to replace EFC). 22% of all full-time undergraduates had no need and received non-need-based gift aid.

**GIFT AID (NEED-BASED)** *Total amount:* $63,216,417 (10% federal, 13% state, 76% institutional, 1% external sources). *Receiving aid:* Freshmen: 58% (778); all full-time undergraduates: 55% (3,241). *Average award:* Freshmen: $18,325; Undergraduates: $19,402. *Scholarships, grants, and awards:* Federal Pell, FSEOG, state, private, college/university gift aid from institutional funds.

**GIFT AID (NON-NEED-BASED)** *Total amount:* $17,347,018 (90% institutional, 10% external sources). *Receiving aid:* Freshmen: 7% (93). Undergraduates: 7% (435). *Average award:* Freshmen: $7888. Undergraduates: $9432. *Scholarships, grants, and awards by category: Academic interests/achievement:* 2,879 awards ($30,077,517 total): biological sciences, business, communication, education, engineering/technologies, English, foreign languages, general academic interests/achievements, humanities, international studies, mathematics, physical sciences, religion/biblical studies, social sciences. *Creative arts/performance:* 51 awards ($290,424 total): applied art and design, art/fine arts, cinema/film/broadcasting, creative writing, general creative arts/performance, journalism/publications, music, performing arts, theater/drama. *Special achievements/activities:* 156 awards ($1,734,380 total): community service, general special achievements/activities, leadership, memberships, religious involvement. *Special characteristics:* 303 awards ($6,069,547 total): adult students, children and siblings of alumni, children of faculty/staff, ethnic background, first-generation college students, general special characteristics, handicapped students, international students, local/state students, members of minority groups, out-of-state students, previous college experience, religious affiliation, veterans. *Tuition waivers:* Full or partial for employees or children of employees. *ROTC:* Army cooperative, Naval cooperative, Air Force.

**LOANS** *Student loans:* $27,565,826 (76% need-based, 24% non-need-based). 59% of past graduating class borrowed through all loan programs. *Average indebtedness per student:* $30,243. *Average need-based loan:* Freshmen: $4729. Undergraduates: $5704. *Parent loans:* $24,978,186 (48% need-based, 52% non-need-based). *Programs:* Federal Direct (Subsidized and Unsubsidized Stafford, PLUS), Perkins, college/university.

**WORK-STUDY** *Federal work-study:* 1,525 jobs averaging $1876. *State or other work-study/employment:* Total amount: $4,195,766 (30% need-based, 70% non-need-based). 2,127 part-time jobs averaging $1972.

**ATHLETIC AWARDS** Total amount: $7,598,109 (47% need-based, 53% non-need-based).

**APPLYING FOR FINANCIAL AID** *Required financial aid form:* FAFSA. *Financial aid deadline:* 7/30 (priority: 2/1). *Notification date:* Continuous beginning 3/15. Students must reply by 5/1 or within 4 weeks of notification.

**CONTACT** Mrs. Catherine Graham, Director of Financial Aid, Loyola Marymount University, One LMU Drive, Suite 200, Los Angeles, CA 90045-8350, 310-338-2753 or toll-free 800-LMU-INFO. *Fax:* 310-338-2793. *E-mail:* finaid@lmu.edu. *Website:* http://www.lmu.edu/.

# LOYOLA UNIVERSITY CHICAGO
## Chicago, IL

| Tuition & fees: $39,179 | Average undergraduate aid package: $30,916 |
| --- | --- |

**ABOUT THE INSTITUTION** Independent Roman Catholic (Jesuit), coed. *Awards:* certificates, bachelor's, master's, and doctoral degrees (also offers adult part-time program with significant enrollment not reflected in profile). 74 undergraduate majors. *Total enrollment:* 15,902. Undergraduates: 10,322. Freshmen: 2,292. Federal methodology is used as a basis for awarding need-based institutional aid.

**UNDERGRADUATE EXPENSES** for 2015–2016 *Comprehensive fee:* $52,489 includes full-time tuition ($37,883), mandatory fees ($1296), and room and board ($13,310). *College room only:* $8380. Full-time tuition and fees vary according to location, program, and student level. Room and board charges vary according to board plan, housing facility, and location. *Part-time tuition:* $722 per credit. Part-time tuition and fees vary according to course load.

**FRESHMAN FINANCIAL AID (Fall 2014, est.)** 1,943 applied for aid; of those 82% were deemed to have need. 100% of freshmen with need received aid; of those 16% had need fully met. *Average percent of need met:* 79% (excluding resources awarded to replace EFC). *Average financial aid package:* $31,519 (excluding resources awarded to replace EFC). 26% of all full-time freshmen had no need and received non-need-based gift aid.

**UNDERGRADUATE FINANCIAL AID (Fall 2014, est.)** 7,284 applied for aid; of those 87% were deemed to have need. 99% of undergraduates with need received aid; of those 13% had need fully met. *Average percent of need met:* 78% (excluding resources awarded to replace EFC). *Average financial aid package:* $30,916 (excluding resources awarded to replace EFC). 23% of all full-time undergraduates had no need and received non-need-based gift aid.

**GIFT AID (NEED-BASED)** *Total amount:* $114,241,731 (13% federal, 8% state, 77% institutional, 2% external sources). *Receiving aid:* Freshmen: 69% (1,570); all full-time undergraduates: 66% (6,046). *Average award:* Freshmen: $19,927; Undergraduates: $18,875. *Scholarships, grants, and awards:* Federal Pell, FSEOG, state, private, college/university gift aid from institutional funds.

**GIFT AID (NON-NEED-BASED)** *Total amount:* $32,945,829 (4% federal, 93% institutional, 3% external sources). *Receiving aid:* Freshmen: 8% (193). Undergraduates: 6% (566). *Average award:* Freshmen: $15,284. Undergraduates: $13,220. *Scholarships, grants, and awards by category: Academic interests/achievement:* 6,422 awards ($83,766,354 total): general academic interests/achievements. *Creative arts/performance:* 43 awards ($122,200 total): art/fine arts, debating, journalism/publications, music, theater/drama. *Special achievements/activities:* 332 awards ($2,058,974 total): community service, general special achievements/activities, leadership, memberships. *Special characteristics:* 1,284 awards ($3,333,350 total): adult students, general special characteristics, religious affiliation. *Tuition waivers:* Full or partial for employees or children of employees, senior citizens. *ROTC:* Army, Naval cooperative, Air Force cooperative.

**LOANS** *Student loans:* $63,011,945 (77% need-based, 23% non-need-based). 72% of past graduating class borrowed through all loan programs. *Average indebtedness per student:* $31,089. *Average need-based loan:* Freshmen: $3779. Undergraduates: $4763. *Parent loans:* $39,517,242 (53% need-based, 47% non-need-based). *Programs:* Federal Direct (Subsidized and Unsubsidized Stafford, PLUS), Perkins, Federal Nursing.

**WORK-STUDY** *Federal work-study:* Total amount: $10,619,503; 4,649 jobs averaging $2196.

**ATHLETIC AWARDS** Total amount: $4,614,423 (47% need-based, 53% non-need-based).

**APPLYING FOR FINANCIAL AID** *Required financial aid form:* FAFSA. *Financial aid deadline:* Continuous. *Notification date:* Continuous beginning 2/15. Students must reply within 3 weeks of notification.

**CONTACT** Mrs. Nancy Merz, Director of Financial Aid, Loyola University Chicago, 6525 North Sheridan Road, Chicago, IL 60660, 773-508-7704 or toll-free 800-262-2373. *Fax:* 773-508-3397. *E-mail:* nmerz@luc.edu. *Website:* http://www.luc.edu/.

# LOYOLA UNIVERSITY MARYLAND
## Baltimore, MD

| Tuition & fees: $44,255 | Average undergraduate aid package: $28,440 |
| --- | --- |

**ABOUT THE INSTITUTION** Independent Roman Catholic (Jesuit), coed. *Awards:* certificates, bachelor's, master's, and doctoral degrees. 35 undergraduate majors. *Total enrollment:* 5,977. Undergraduates: 4,004. Freshmen: 1,096. Both federal and institutional methodology are used as a basis for awarding need-based institutional aid.

**UNDERGRADUATE EXPENSES** for 2015–2016 *Application fee:* $50. *Comprehensive fee:* $57,045 includes full-time tuition ($42,690), mandatory fees ($1565), and room and board ($12,790). Full-time tuition and fees vary according to course load. Room and board charges vary according to housing facility. *Part-time tuition:* $692 per credit. Part-time tuition and fees vary according to course load.

**FRESHMAN FINANCIAL AID (Fall 2013)** 843 applied for aid; of those 80% were deemed to have need. 100% of freshmen with need received aid; of those 90% had need fully met. *Average percent of need met:* 94% (excluding resources awarded to replace EFC). *Average financial aid package:* $28,420 (excluding resources awarded to replace EFC). 18% of all full-time freshmen had no need and received non-need-based gift aid.

**UNDERGRADUATE FINANCIAL AID (Fall 2013)** 2,705 applied for aid; of those 87% were deemed to have need. 100% of undergraduates with need received aid; of those 89% had need fully met. *Average percent of need met:* 91% (excluding resources awarded to replace EFC). *Average financial aid package:* $28,440 (excluding resources awarded to replace EFC). 12% of all full-time undergraduates had no need and received non-need-based gift aid.

**GIFT AID (NEED-BASED)** *Total amount:* $53,489,200 (6% federal, 1% state, 91% institutional, 2% external sources). *Receiving aid:* Freshmen: 56% (617); all full-time undergraduates: 52% (2,073). *Average award:* Freshmen: $23,190; Undergrad-

uates: $22,565. **Scholarships, grants, and awards:** Federal Pell, FSEOG, state, private, college/university gift aid from institutional funds.

**GIFT AID (NON-NEED-BASED) Total amount:** $9,040,555 (12% federal, 80% institutional, 8% external sources). **Receiving aid:** Freshmen: 29% (318). Undergraduates: 19% (770). **Average award:** Freshmen: $14,240. Undergraduates: $14,675. **Scholarships, grants, and awards by category:** Academic interests/achievement: general academic interests/achievements. **Tuition waivers:** Full or partial for employees or children of employees. **ROTC:** Army, Air Force cooperative.

**LOANS Student loans:** $20,902,306 (42% need-based, 58% non-need-based). 63% of past graduating class borrowed through all loan programs. Average indebtedness per student: $34,190. **Average need-based loan:** Freshmen: $3680. Undergraduates: $4250. **Parent loans:** $17,825,827 (100% non-need-based). **Programs:** Federal Direct (Subsidized and Unsubsidized Stafford, PLUS), Perkins, college/university.

**WORK-STUDY Federal work-study:** jobs available. **State or other work-study/employment:** Total amount: $1,011,724 (73% need-based, 27% non-need-based). Part-time jobs available.

**ATHLETIC AWARDS** Total amount: $5,306,983 (33% need-based, 67% non-need-based).

**APPLYING FOR FINANCIAL AID Required financial aid forms:** FAFSA, CSS Financial Aid PROFILE, noncustodial (divorced/separated) parent's statement. **Financial aid deadline:** 2/15. **Notification date:** 4/1. Students must reply by 5/1.

**CONTACT** Office of Financial Aid, Loyola University Maryland, Knott Humanities Center 211A, Baltimore, MD 21210, 410-617-2576 or toll-free 800-221-9107. Fax: 410-617-5149. E-mail: financialaid@loyola.edu.

Website: http://www.loyola.edu/.

# LOYOLA UNIVERSITY NEW ORLEANS
## New Orleans, LA

| Tuition & fees: $36,610 | Average undergraduate aid package: $29,614 |
|---|---|

**ABOUT THE INSTITUTION** Independent Roman Catholic (Jesuit), coed. **Awards:** certificates, bachelor's, master's, and doctoral degrees. 47 undergraduate majors. **Total enrollment:** 4,686. Undergraduates: 2,946. Freshmen: 624. Federal methodology is used as a basis for awarding need-based institutional aid.

**UNDERGRADUATE EXPENSES for 2015–2016 Application fee:** $20. **Comprehensive fee:** $49,270 includes full-time tuition ($35,504), mandatory fees ($1106), and room and board ($12,660). **College room only:** $7430. Room and board charges vary according to board plan and housing facility. **Part-time tuition:** $1012 per credit. **Part-time fees:** $294 per term.

**FRESHMAN FINANCIAL AID (Fall 2014, est.)** 534 applied for aid; of those 85% were deemed to have need. 100% of freshmen with need received aid; of those 9% had need fully met. **Average percent of need met:** 77% (excluding resources awarded to replace EFC). **Average financial aid package:** $31,971 (excluding resources awarded to replace EFC). 22% of all full-time freshmen had no need and received non-need-based gift aid.

**UNDERGRADUATE FINANCIAL AID (Fall 2014, est.)** 1,940 applied for aid; of those 88% were deemed to have need. 100% of undergraduates with need received aid; of those 11% had need fully met. **Average percent of need met:** 72% (excluding resources awarded to replace EFC). **Average financial aid package:** $29,614 (excluding resources awarded to replace EFC). 27% of all full-time undergraduates had no need and received non-need-based gift aid.

**GIFT AID (NEED-BASED) Total amount:** $43,015,293 (10% federal, 7% state, 80% institutional, 3% external sources). **Receiving aid:** Freshmen: 73% (453); all full-time undergraduates: 68% (1,689). **Average award:** Freshmen: $27,332; Undergraduates: $25,182. **Scholarships, grants, and awards:** Federal Pell, FSEOG, state, private, college/university gift aid from institutional funds, United Negro College Fund.

**GIFT AID (NON-NEED-BASED) Total amount:** $13,581,716 (6% state, 89% institutional, 5% external sources). **Receiving aid:** Freshmen: 6% (34). Undergraduates: 7% (164). **Average award:** Freshmen: $13,122. Undergraduates: $14,876. **Scholarships, grants, and awards by category:** Academic interests/achievement: general academic interests/achievements. Creative arts/performance: art/fine arts, general creative arts/performance. Special achievements/activities: leadership. Special characteristics: children and siblings of alumni, children of faculty/staff.

**Tuition waivers:** Full or partial for employees or children of employees, senior citizens. **ROTC:** Army cooperative, Naval cooperative, Air Force cooperative.

**LOANS Student loans:** $15,410,257 (78% need-based, 22% non-need-based). 64% of past graduating class borrowed through all loan programs. Average indebtedness per student: $25,133. **Average need-based loan:** Freshmen: $4321. Undergraduates: $4879. **Parent loans:** $5,468,928 (47% need-based, 53% non-need-based). **Programs:** Federal Direct (Subsidized and Unsubsidized Stafford, PLUS), Perkins.

**WORK-STUDY Federal work-study:** Total amount: $824,216; jobs available.

**ATHLETIC AWARDS** Total amount: $1,314,543 (62% need-based, 38% non-need-based).

**APPLYING FOR FINANCIAL AID Required financial aid form:** FAFSA. **Financial aid deadline (priority):** 3/1. **Notification date:** Continuous beginning 3/1. Students must reply by 5/1 or within 2 weeks of notification.

**CONTACT** Ms. Carrie E. Glass, Director of Scholarships and Financial Aid, Loyola University New Orleans, 6363 St. Charles Avenue, New Orleans, LA 70118-6195, 504-865-3231 or toll-free 800-4-LOYOLA. Fax: 504-865-3233. E-mail: finaid@loyno.edu.

Website: http://www.loyno.edu/.

# LUBBOCK CHRISTIAN UNIVERSITY
## Lubbock, TX

| Tuition & fees: $19,400 | Average undergraduate aid package: $15,287 |
|---|---|

**ABOUT THE INSTITUTION** Independent Church of Christ, coed. **Awards:** bachelor's and master's degrees. 61 undergraduate majors. **Total enrollment:** 1,902. Undergraduates: 1,439. Freshmen: 264. Federal methodology is used as a basis for awarding need-based institutional aid.

**UNDERGRADUATE EXPENSES for 2015–2016 Application fee:** $25. **Comprehensive fee:** $26,308 includes full-time tuition ($19,400) and room and board ($6908). Full-time tuition and fees vary according to degree level and program. Room and board charges vary according to board plan and housing facility. **Part-time tuition:** $621 per credit hour. **Part-time fees:** $60 per term. Part-time tuition and fees vary according to course load, degree level, and program.

**FRESHMAN FINANCIAL AID (Fall 2014, est.)** 176 applied for aid; of those 81% were deemed to have need. 100% of freshmen with need received aid; of those 9% had need fully met. **Average percent of need met:** 69% (excluding resources awarded to replace EFC). **Average financial aid package:** $14,917 (excluding resources awarded to replace EFC). 15% of all full-time freshmen had no need and received non-need-based gift aid.

**UNDERGRADUATE FINANCIAL AID (Fall 2014, est.)** 872 applied for aid; of those 85% were deemed to have need. 100% of undergraduates with need received aid; of those 11% had need fully met. **Average percent of need met:** 69% (excluding resources awarded to replace EFC). **Average financial aid package:** $15,287 (excluding resources awarded to replace EFC). 15% of all full-time undergraduates had no need and received non-need-based gift aid.

**GIFT AID (NEED-BASED) Total amount:** $7,024,313 (32% federal, 25% state, 33% institutional, 10% external sources). **Receiving aid:** Freshmen: 53% (141); all full-time undergraduates: 58% (714). **Average award:** Freshmen: $10,330; Undergraduates: $10,534. **Scholarships, grants, and awards:** Federal Pell, FSEOG, state, college/university gift aid from institutional funds.

**GIFT AID (NON-NEED-BASED) Total amount:** $1,440,443 (78% institutional, 22% external sources). **Receiving aid:** Freshmen: 5% (13). Undergraduates: 6% (71). **Average award:** Freshmen: $4640. Undergraduates: $5278. **Scholarships, grants, and awards by category:** Academic interests/achievement: 771 awards ($3,291,080 total): agriculture, business, communication, computer science, education, English, foreign languages, general academic interests/achievements, humanities, physical sciences, religion/biblical studies, social sciences. Creative arts/performance: 106 awards ($128,325 total): art/fine arts, journalism/publications, music, performing arts, theater/drama. Special achievements/activities: 30 awards ($22,172 total): cheerleading/drum major, leadership. Special characteristics: 33 awards ($445,602 total): children of faculty/staff, general special characteristics. **Tuition waivers:** Full or partial for employees or children of employees. **ROTC:** Army cooperative, Air Force cooperative.

**LOANS Student loans:** $10,826,283 (74% need-based, 26% non-need-based). 78% of past graduating class borrowed through all loan programs. Average indebtedness per student: $27,949. **Average need-based loan:** Freshmen: $4260. Undergraduates: $4740. **Parent loans:** $2,854,264 (36% need-based, 64% non-need-based). **Programs:** Federal Direct (Subsidized and Unsubsidized Stafford, PLUS), Perkins, state.

**WORK-STUDY** *Federal work-study:* Total amount: $820,631; 567 jobs averaging $1686. *State or other work-study/employment:* Total amount: $21,246 (61% need-based, 39% non-need-based). 70 part-time jobs averaging $304.

**ATHLETIC AWARDS** Total amount: $1,898,969 (47% need-based, 53% non-need-based).

**APPLYING FOR FINANCIAL AID** *Required financial aid forms:* FAFSA, institution's own form. *Financial aid deadline (priority):* 6/1. *Notification date:* Continuous beginning 3/1.

**CONTACT** Mrs. Amy Hardesty, Director of Financial Aid, Lubbock Christian University, 5601 19th Street, Lubbock, TX 79407, 806-720-7176 or toll-free 800-933-7601. *Fax:* 806-720-7185. *E-mail:* amy.hardesty@lcu.edu. *Website:* http://www.lcu.edu/.

# LUTHER COLLEGE
## Decorah, IA

| Tuition & fees: $39,190 | Average undergraduate aid package: $30,365 |
| --- | --- |

**ABOUT THE INSTITUTION** Independent Evangelical Lutheran Church in America, coed. **Awards:** bachelor's degrees. 40 undergraduate majors. **Total enrollment:** 2,385. Undergraduates: 2,385. Freshmen: 559. Federal methodology is used as a basis for awarding need-based institutional aid.

**UNDERGRADUATE EXPENSES** for 2015–2016 **Comprehensive fee:** $47,110 includes full-time tuition ($38,940), mandatory fees ($250), and room and board ($7920). **College room only:** $3570. Full-time tuition and fees vary according to course load. Room and board charges vary according to board plan and housing facility. **Part-time tuition:** $1392 per credit hour. Part-time tuition and fees vary according to course load.

**FRESHMAN FINANCIAL AID (Fall 2014, est.)** 493 applied for aid; of those 86% were deemed to have need. 100% of freshmen with need received aid; of those 28% had need fully met. *Average percent of need met:* 89% (excluding resources awarded to replace EFC). *Average financial aid package:* $33,020 (excluding resources awarded to replace EFC). 12% of all full-time freshmen had no need and received non-need-based gift aid.

**UNDERGRADUATE FINANCIAL AID (Fall 2014, est.)** 1,882 applied for aid; of those 85% were deemed to have need. 100% of undergraduates with need received aid; of those 27% had need fully met. *Average percent of need met:* 86% (excluding resources awarded to replace EFC). *Average financial aid package:* $30,365 (excluding resources awarded to replace EFC). 11% of all full-time undergraduates had no need and received non-need-based gift aid.

**GIFT AID (NEED-BASED)** *Total amount:* $37,619,603 (7% federal, 4% state, 86% institutional, 3% external sources). *Receiving aid:* Freshmen: 76% (423); all full-time undergraduates: 69% (1,590). *Average award:* Freshmen: $24,622; Undergraduates: $22,197. *Scholarships, grants, and awards:* Federal Pell, FSEOG, state, private, college/university gift aid from institutional funds.

**GIFT AID (NON-NEED-BASED)** *Total amount:* $15,294,360 (1% federal, 81% institutional, 18% external sources). *Receiving aid:* Freshmen: 10% (55). Undergraduates: 8% (187). *Average award:* Freshmen: $18,110. Undergraduates: $16,062. *Scholarships, grants, and awards by category:* Academic interests/achievement: 1,306 awards ($19,302,898 total): general academic interests/achievements. Creative arts/performance: 519 awards ($1,693,829 total): music. Special characteristics: 468 awards ($807,196 total): children and siblings of alumni, members of minority groups, religious affiliation. *Tuition waivers:* Full or partial for employees or children of employees.

**LOANS** *Student loans:* $11,683,989 (77% need-based, 23% non-need-based). 74% of past graduating class borrowed through all loan programs. *Average indebtedness per student:* $36,918. *Average need-based loan:* Freshmen: $5001. Undergraduates: $5017. *Parent loans:* $5,788,804 (33% need-based, 67% non-need-based). *Programs:* Federal Direct (Subsidized and Unsubsidized Stafford, PLUS), Perkins, college/university.

**WORK-STUDY** *Federal work-study:* Total amount: $2,074,993; 1,014 jobs averaging $2046. *State or other work-study/employment:* Total amount: $2,100,005 (13% need-based, 87% non-need-based). 1,071 part-time jobs averaging $1960.

**APPLYING FOR FINANCIAL AID** *Required financial aid forms:* FAFSA, institution's own form. *Financial aid deadline (priority):* 3/1. *Notification date:* Continuous beginning 3/15. Students must reply by 5/1.

**CONTACT** Ms. Janice Cordell, Director of Financial Aid, Luther College, 700 College Drive, Decorah, IA 52101-1045, 563-387-1018 or toll-free 800-458-8437. *Fax:* 563-387-2241. *E-mail:* cordellj@luther.edu. *Website:* http://www.luther.edu/.

# LUTHER RICE COLLEGE & SEMINARY
## Lithonia, GA

**CONTACT** Gary W. Cook, Director of Financial Aid, Luther Rice College & Seminary, 3038 Evans Mill Road, Lithonia, GA 30038-2418, 770-484-1204 Ext. 241 or toll-free 800-442-1577. *Fax:* 678-990-5388. *E-mail:* gcook@lru.edu. *Website:* http://www.lutherrice.edu/.

# LYCOMING COLLEGE
## Williamsport, PA

| Tuition & fees: $35,900 | Average undergraduate aid package: $30,635 |
| --- | --- |

**ABOUT THE INSTITUTION** Independent United Methodist, coed. **Awards:** bachelor's degrees. 40 undergraduate majors. **Total enrollment:** 1,357. Undergraduates: 1,357. Freshmen: 394. Federal methodology is used as a basis for awarding need-based institutional aid.

**UNDERGRADUATE EXPENSES** for 2015–2016 **Application fee:** $35. **One-time required fee:** $225. **Comprehensive fee:** $46,784 includes full-time tuition ($35,200), mandatory fees ($700), and room and board ($10,884). Room and board charges vary according to board plan and housing facility. **Part-time tuition:** $1100 per credit hour. Part-time tuition and fees vary according to course load.

**FRESHMAN FINANCIAL AID (Fall 2014, est.)** 366 applied for aid; of those 92% were deemed to have need. 100% of freshmen with need received aid; of those 23% had need fully met. *Average percent of need met:* 86% (excluding resources awarded to replace EFC). *Average financial aid package:* $33,897 (excluding resources awarded to replace EFC). 14% of all full-time freshmen had no need and received non-need-based gift aid.

**UNDERGRADUATE FINANCIAL AID (Fall 2014, est.)** 1,172 applied for aid; of those 92% were deemed to have need. 100% of undergraduates with need received aid; of those 30% had need fully met. *Average percent of need met:* 81% (excluding resources awarded to replace EFC). *Average financial aid package:* $30,635 (excluding resources awarded to replace EFC). 12% of all full-time undergraduates had no need and received non-need-based gift aid.

**GIFT AID (NEED-BASED)** *Total amount:* $28,216,706 (8% federal, 6% state, 84% institutional, 2% external sources). *Receiving aid:* Freshmen: 86% (337); all full-time undergraduates: 82% (1,082). *Average award:* Freshmen: $28,802; Undergraduates: $25,355. *Scholarships, grants, and awards:* Federal Pell, FSEOG, state, private, college/university gift aid from institutional funds.

**GIFT AID (NON-NEED-BASED)** *Total amount:* $4,198,745 (94% institutional, 6% external sources). *Receiving aid:* Freshmen: 15% (59). Undergraduates: 12% (157). *Average award:* Freshmen: $21,404. Undergraduates: $18,162. *Scholarships, grants, and awards by category:* Academic interests/achievement: biological sciences, business, communication, computer science, education, English, foreign languages, general academic interests/achievements, health fields, humanities, international studies, mathematics, physical sciences, premedicine, religion/biblical studies, social sciences. Creative arts/performance: applied art and design, art/fine arts, creative writing, music, theater/drama. Special achievements/activities: community service, general special achievements/activities, leadership. Special characteristics: children of educators, children of faculty/staff, local/state students, relatives of clergy. *Tuition waivers:* Full or partial for employees or children of employees. **ROTC:** Army cooperative.

**LOANS** *Student loans:* $10,051,431 (71% need-based, 29% non-need-based). 86% of past graduating class borrowed through all loan programs. *Average need-based loan:* Freshmen: $3565. Undergraduates: $4715. *Parent loans:* $3,584,710 (38% need-based, 62% non-need-based). *Programs:* Federal Direct (Subsidized and Unsubsidized Stafford, PLUS), Perkins, college/university.

**WORK-STUDY** *Federal work-study:* Total amount: $175,889; jobs available.
**APPLYING FOR FINANCIAL AID** *Required financial aid forms:* FAFSA, institution's own form, state aid form. *Financial aid deadline (priority):* 5/1. *Notification date:* Continuous beginning 3/1. Students must reply by 5/1.
**CONTACT** Mr. James S. Lakis, Director of Financial Aid, Lycoming College, 700 College Place, Williamsport, PA 17701-5192, 570-321-4040 or toll-free 800-345-3920 Ext. 4026. *Fax:* 570-321-4993. *E-mail:* lakis@lycoming.edu. *Website:* http://www.lycoming.edu/.

# LYME ACADEMY COLLEGE OF FINE ARTS
## Old Lyme, CT

**CONTACT** Mr. Stephen Podeszwa, Director of Financial Aid, Lyme Academy College of Fine Arts, 84 Lyme Street, Old Lyme, CT 06371, 860-434-3571 Ext. 114. *Fax:* 860-434-8725. *E-mail:* spodeszwa@lymeacademy.edu. *Website:* http://www.lymeacademy.edu/.

# LYNCHBURG COLLEGE
## Lynchburg, VA

| Tuition & fees: $34,545 | Average undergraduate aid package: $25,845 |
|---|---|

**ABOUT THE INSTITUTION** Independent Christian Church (Disciples of Christ), coed. *Awards:* certificates, bachelor's, master's, and doctoral degrees. 36 undergraduate majors. *Total enrollment:* 2,736. Undergraduates: 2,161. Freshmen: 512. Federal methodology is used as a basis for awarding need-based institutional aid.
**UNDERGRADUATE EXPENSES for 2015–2016** *Application fee:* $30. *Comprehensive fee:* $43,875 includes full-time tuition ($33,600), mandatory fees ($945), and room and board ($9330). *College room only:* $4720. Room and board charges vary according to board plan and housing facility. *Part-time tuition:* $460 per credit hour. *Part-time fees:* $5.10 per credit hour. Part-time tuition and fees vary according to course load. *Payment plan:* Tuition prepayment.
**FRESHMAN FINANCIAL AID (Fall 2014, est.)** 477 applied for aid; of those 91% were deemed to have need. 100% of freshmen with need received aid; of those 17% had need fully met. *Average percent of need met:* 84% (excluding resources awarded to replace EFC). *Average financial aid package:* $29,114 (excluding resources awarded to replace EFC). 14% of all full-time freshmen had no need and received non-need-based gift aid.
**UNDERGRADUATE FINANCIAL AID (Fall 2014, est.)** 1,642 applied for aid; of those 92% were deemed to have need. 100% of undergraduates with need received aid; of those 15% had need fully met. *Average percent of need met:* 78% (excluding resources awarded to replace EFC). *Average financial aid package:* $25,845 (excluding resources awarded to replace EFC). 19% of all full-time undergraduates had no need and received non-need-based gift aid.
**GIFT AID (NEED-BASED)** *Total amount:* $32,293,534 (10% federal, 9% state, 78% institutional, 3% external sources). *Receiving aid:* Freshmen: 85% (435); all full-time undergraduates: 75% (1,494). *Average award:* Freshmen: $25,261; Undergraduates: $22,164. *Scholarships, grants, and awards:* Federal Pell, FSEOG, state, private, college/university gift aid from institutional funds.
**GIFT AID (NON-NEED-BASED)** *Total amount:* $7,649,119 (1% federal, 13% state, 80% institutional, 6% external sources). *Receiving aid:* Freshmen: 11% (57). Undergraduates: 9% (172). *Average award:* Freshmen: $15,209. Undergraduates: $13,152. *Scholarships, grants, and awards by category:* Academic interests/achievement: 1,833 awards ($19,273,460 total): general academic interests/achievements. Creative arts/performance: 114 awards ($261,908 total): art/fine arts, music, theater/drama. *Tuition waivers:* Full or partial for employees or children of employees, adult students, senior citizens.
**LOANS** *Student loans:* $14,220,631 (66% need-based, 34% non-need-based). 83% of past graduating class borrowed through all loan programs. *Average indebtedness per student:* $33,592. *Average need-based loan:* Freshmen: $3521. Undergraduates: $3566. *Parent loans:* $3,793,146 (54% need-based, 46% non-need-based). *Programs:* Federal Direct (Subsidized and Unsubsidized Stafford, PLUS), Perkins.

**WORK-STUDY** *Federal work-study:* Total amount: $233,325; 445 jobs averaging $1550. *State or other work-study/employment:* Total amount: $451,623 (29% need-based, 71% non-need-based). 309 part-time jobs averaging $1534.
**APPLYING FOR FINANCIAL AID** *Required financial aid forms:* FAFSA, state aid form. *Financial aid deadline (priority):* 3/5. *Notification date:* Continuous beginning 3/5. Students must reply by 5/1 or within 2 weeks of notification.
**CONTACT** Ms. Chrystal Jefferson, Interim Director of Financial Aid, Lynchburg College, 1501 Lakeside Drive, Lynchburg, VA 24501, 434-544-8228 or toll-free 800-426-8101. *Fax:* 434-544-8653. *Website:* http://www.lynchburg.edu/.

# LYNDON STATE COLLEGE
## Lyndonville, VT

**CONTACT** Student Services Consultant, Lyndon State College, 1001 College Road, Lyndonville, VT 05851, 802-626-6396 or toll-free 800-225-1998. *Fax:* 802-626-9770. *E-mail:* financialaid@lyndonstate.edu. *Website:* http://www.lyndonstate.edu/.

# LYNN UNIVERSITY
## Boca Raton, FL

| Tuition & fees: $35,200 | Average undergraduate aid package: $20,349 |
|---|---|

**ABOUT THE INSTITUTION** Independent, coed. *Awards:* certificates, bachelor's, master's, and doctoral degrees. 25 undergraduate majors. *Total enrollment:* 2,613. Undergraduates: 1,976. Freshmen: 540. Federal methodology is used as a basis for awarding need-based institutional aid.
**UNDERGRADUATE EXPENSES for 2015–2016** *Application fee:* $45. *Comprehensive fee:* $46,500 includes full-time tuition ($33,450), mandatory fees ($1750), and room and board ($11,300). Full-time tuition and fees vary according to program. Room and board charges vary according to board plan and housing facility. *Part-time tuition:* $970 per credit. Part-time tuition and fees vary according to course load and program.
**FRESHMAN FINANCIAL AID (Fall 2014, est.)** 464 applied for aid; of those 53% were deemed to have need. 100% of freshmen with need received aid; of those 100% had need fully met. *Average percent of need met:* 53% (excluding resources awarded to replace EFC). *Average financial aid package:* $20,164 (excluding resources awarded to replace EFC). 35% of all full-time freshmen had no need and received non-need-based gift aid.
**UNDERGRADUATE FINANCIAL AID (Fall 2014, est.)** 1,402 applied for aid; of those 56% were deemed to have need. 99% of undergraduates with need received aid; of those 100% had need fully met. *Average percent of need met:* 53% (excluding resources awarded to replace EFC). *Average financial aid package:* $20,349 (excluding resources awarded to replace EFC). 22% of all full-time undergraduates had no need and received non-need-based gift aid.
**GIFT AID (NEED-BASED)** *Total amount:* $9,551,213 (20% federal, 13% state, 65% institutional, 2% external sources). *Receiving aid:* Freshmen: 36% (193); all full-time undergraduates: 34% (620). *Average award:* Freshmen: $10,007; Undergraduates: $9574. *Scholarships, grants, and awards:* Federal Pell, FSEOG, state, private, college/university gift aid from institutional funds.
**GIFT AID (NON-NEED-BASED)** *Total amount:* $4,435,930 (8% state, 90% institutional, 2% external sources). *Receiving aid:* Freshmen: 42% (225). Undergraduates: 38% (683). *Average award:* Freshmen: $9975. Undergraduates: $11,455. *Scholarships, grants, and awards by category:* Academic interests/achievement: biological sciences, business, communication, general academic interests/achievements, international studies. Creative arts/performance: music. Special achievements/activities: leadership. Special characteristics: children and siblings of alumni, children of educators, children of faculty/staff, out-of-state students, siblings of current students, veterans. *Tuition waivers:* Full or partial for employees or children of employees. *ROTC:* Air Force cooperative.
**LOANS** *Student loans:* $5,850,748 (86% need-based, 14% non-need-based). 38% of past graduating class borrowed through all loan programs. *Average indebtedness per student:* $30,938. *Average need-based loan:* Freshmen: $3840. Undergrad-

uates: $4559. **Parent loans:** $6,371,036 (89% need-based, 11% non-need-based). **Programs:** Federal Direct (Subsidized and Unsubsidized Stafford, PLUS), Perkins, state, college/university.

**WORK-STUDY** Federal work-study: Total amount: $207,167; jobs available. **State or other work-study/employment:** Total amount: $238,200 (64% need-based, 36% non-need-based). Part-time jobs available.

**ATHLETIC AWARDS** Total amount: $3,231,553 (57% need-based, 43% non-need-based).

**APPLYING FOR FINANCIAL AID** Required financial aid form: FAFSA. **Financial aid deadline (priority):** 3/1. **Notification date:** Continuous beginning 2/1. Students must reply within 2 weeks of notification.

**CONTACT** Mrs. Chan Park, Director of Student Financial Assistance , Lynn University, 3601 North Military Trail, Boca Raton, FL 33431-5598, 561-237-7186 or toll-free 800-888-5966. Fax: 561-237-7189. E-mail: cpark@lynn.edu.

Website: http://www.lynn.edu/.

---

# LYON COLLEGE
## Batesville, AR

| Tuition & fees: $25,280 | Average undergraduate aid package: $20,898 |
|---|---|

**ABOUT THE INSTITUTION** Independent Presbyterian, coed. **Awards:** bachelor's degrees. 14 undergraduate majors. **Total enrollment:** 711. Undergraduates: 711. Freshmen: 254. Federal methodology is used as a basis for awarding need-based institutional aid.

**UNDERGRADUATE EXPENSES for 2015–2016 Application fee:** $25. **Comprehensive fee:** $33,390 includes full-time tuition ($25,040), mandatory fees ($240), and room and board ($8110). Full-time tuition and fees vary according to course load. Room and board charges vary according to board plan and housing facility. **Part-time tuition:** $835 per credit hour.

**FRESHMAN FINANCIAL AID (Fall 2014, est.)** 232 applied for aid; of those 88% were deemed to have need. 100% of freshmen with need received aid; of those 26% had need fully met. **Average percent of need met:** 79% (excluding resources awarded to replace EFC). **Average financial aid package:** $19,398 (excluding resources awarded to replace EFC). 8% of all full-time freshmen had no need and received non-need-based gift aid.

**UNDERGRADUATE FINANCIAL AID (Fall 2014, est.)** 578 applied for aid; of those 90% were deemed to have need. 100% of undergraduates with need received aid; of those 25% had need fully met. **Average percent of need met:** 82% (excluding resources awarded to replace EFC). **Average financial aid package:** $20,898 (excluding resources awarded to replace EFC). 13% of all full-time undergraduates had no need and received non-need-based gift aid.

**GIFT AID (NEED-BASED) Total amount:** $6,719,863 (20% federal, 13% state, 62% institutional, 5% external sources). **Receiving aid:** Freshmen: 84% (204); all full-time undergraduates: 78% (519). **Average award:** Freshmen: $16,487; Undergraduates: $17,538. **Scholarships, grants, and awards:** Federal Pell, FSEOG, state, private, college/university gift aid from institutional funds.

**GIFT AID (NON-NEED-BASED) Total amount:** $2,218,388 (28% state, 65% institutional, 7% external sources). **Receiving aid:** Freshmen: 20% (49). Undergraduates: 17% (114). **Average award:** Freshmen: $13,437. Undergraduates: $13,869. **Scholarships, grants, and awards by category:** Academic interests/achievement: 315 awards ($4,026,111 total): business, general academic interests/achievements. Creative arts/performance: 23 awards ($189,245 total): art/fine arts, music, theater/drama. Special achievements/activities: 5 awards ($66,459 total): cheerleading/drum major, general special achievements/activities. Special characteristics: 13 awards ($161,314 total): children of faculty/staff, ethnic background, first-generation college students, local/state students, members of minority groups, religious affiliation. **Tuition waivers:** Full or partial for employees or children of employees.

**LOANS Student loans:** $3,399,536 (74% need-based, 26% non-need-based). 78% of past graduating class borrowed through all loan programs. Average indebtedness per student: $22,321. **Average need-based loan:** Freshmen: $3632. Undergraduates: $4220. **Parent loans:** $602,135 (41% need-based, 59% non-need-based). **Programs:** Federal Direct (Subsidized and Unsubsidized Stafford, PLUS), Perkins.

**WORK-STUDY** Federal work-study: Total amount: $112,347; 143 jobs averaging $737. **State or other work-study/employment:** 3 part-time jobs averaging $833.

**ATHLETIC AWARDS** Total amount: $3,790,907 (66% need-based, 34% non-need-based).

---

**APPLYING FOR FINANCIAL AID** Required financial aid form: FAFSA. **Financial aid deadline (priority):** 3/15. **Notification date:** Continuous beginning 9/1. Students must reply by 8/15.

**CONTACT** Mr. Tommy Tucker, Director of Student Assistance, Lyon College, 2300 Highland Road, Batesville, AR 72501, 870-307-7257 or toll-free 800-423-2542. Fax: 870-307-7542. E-mail: financialaid@lyon.edu.

Website: http://www.lyon.edu/.

---

# MACALESTER COLLEGE
## St. Paul, MN

| Tuition & fees: N/R | Average undergraduate aid package: $40,694 |
|---|---|

**ABOUT THE INSTITUTION** Independent Presbyterian, coed. **Awards:** bachelor's degrees. 37 undergraduate majors. **Total enrollment:** 2,039. Undergraduates: 2,039. Freshmen: 555. Both federal and institutional methodology are used as a basis for awarding need-based institutional aid.

**UNDERGRADUATE EXPENSES for 2015–2016 Application fee:** $40. **Tuition:** part-time $1521 per credit hour. Full-time tuition and fees vary according to course load. Part-time tuition and fees vary according to course load. Room and board charges vary according to board plan and housing facility.

**FRESHMAN FINANCIAL AID (Fall 2014, est.)** 438 applied for aid; of those 90% were deemed to have need. 100% of freshmen with need received aid; of those 100% had need fully met. **Average percent of need met:** 100% (excluding resources awarded to replace EFC). **Average financial aid package:** $40,994 (excluding resources awarded to replace EFC). 11% of all full-time freshmen had no need and received non-need-based gift aid.

**UNDERGRADUATE FINANCIAL AID (Fall 2014, est.)** 1,548 applied for aid; of those 91% were deemed to have need. 100% of undergraduates with need received aid; of those 100% had need fully met. **Average percent of need met:** 100% (excluding resources awarded to replace EFC). **Average financial aid package:** $40,694 (excluding resources awarded to replace EFC). 9% of all full-time undergraduates had no need and received non-need-based gift aid.

**GIFT AID (NEED-BASED) Total amount:** $48,877,866 (4% federal, 1% state, 93% institutional, 2% external sources). **Receiving aid:** Freshmen: 73% (393); all full-time undergraduates: 69% (1,401). **Average award:** Freshmen: $35,594; Undergraduates: $34,527. **Scholarships, grants, and awards:** Federal Pell, FSEOG, state, private, college/university gift aid from institutional funds.

**GIFT AID (NON-NEED-BASED) Total amount:** $2,528,487 (85% institutional, 15% external sources). **Receiving aid:** Freshmen: 4% (24). Undergraduates: 4% (77). **Average award:** Freshmen: $12,617. Undergraduates: $11,856. **Scholarships, grants, and awards by category:** Academic interests/achievement: general academic interests/achievements. Special characteristics: ethnic background. **Tuition waivers:** Full or partial for employees or children of employees. **ROTC:** Army cooperative, Naval cooperative, Air Force cooperative.

**LOANS Student loans:** $7,930,387 (93% need-based, 7% non-need-based). 68% of past graduating class borrowed through all loan programs. Average indebtedness per student: $24,156. **Average need-based loan:** Freshmen: $4001. Undergraduates: $4662. **Parent loans:** $1,689,350 (100% non-need-based). **Programs:** Federal Direct (Subsidized and Unsubsidized Stafford, PLUS), Perkins, state.

**WORK-STUDY** Federal work-study: Total amount: $500,972; jobs available. **State or other work-study/employment:** Total amount: $2,532,175 (95% need-based, 5% non-need-based). Part-time jobs available.

**APPLYING FOR FINANCIAL AID** Required financial aid forms: FAFSA, CSS Financial Aid PROFILE, noncustodial (divorced/separated) parent's statement, federal income tax form(s). **Financial aid deadline:** 3/1 (priority: 2/8). **Notification date:** 4/1. Students must reply by 5/1.

**CONTACT** Financial Aid Office, Macalester College, 1600 Grand Avenue, St. Paul, MN 55105, 651-696-6214 or toll-free 800-231-7974. Fax: 651-696-6866. E-mail: finaid@macalester.edu.

Website: http://www.macalester.edu/.

# MACHZIKEI HADATH RABBINICAL COLLEGE
## Brooklyn, NY

**CONTACT** Rabbi Baruch Rozmarin, Director of Financial Aid, Machzikei Hadath Rabbinical College, 5407 16th Avenue, Brooklyn, NY 11204-1805, 718-854-8777.

# MACMURRAY COLLEGE
## Jacksonville, IL

| Tuition & fees: $23,600 | Average undergraduate aid package: $20,581 |
|---|---|

**ABOUT THE INSTITUTION** Independent United Methodist, coed. 30 undergraduate majors. Federal methodology is used as a basis for awarding need-based institutional aid.

**UNDERGRADUATE EXPENSES for 2015–2016** *Comprehensive fee:* $31,600 includes full-time tuition ($22,900), mandatory fees ($700), and room and board ($8000). Full-time tuition and fees vary according to course load, location, and student level. Room and board charges vary according to housing facility. *Part-time tuition:* $732 per credit hour. *Part-time fees:* $30 per credit hour; $5 per term. Part-time tuition and fees vary according to course load, location, and student level.

**FRESHMAN FINANCIAL AID (Fall 2014, est.)** 112 applied for aid; of those 91% were deemed to have need. 100% of freshmen with need received aid; of those 16% had need fully met. *Average percent of need met:* 81% (excluding resources awarded to replace EFC). *Average financial aid package:* $21,056 (excluding resources awarded to replace EFC). 11% of all full-time freshmen had no need and received non-need-based gift aid.

**UNDERGRADUATE FINANCIAL AID (Fall 2014, est.)** 506 applied for aid; of those 92% were deemed to have need. 100% of undergraduates with need received aid; of those 14% had need fully met. *Average percent of need met:* 77% (excluding resources awarded to replace EFC). *Average financial aid package:* $20,581 (excluding resources awarded to replace EFC). 10% of all full-time undergraduates had no need and received non-need-based gift aid.

**GIFT AID (NEED-BASED) Total amount:** $6,744,472 (24% federal, 18% state, 57% institutional, 1% external sources). *Receiving aid:* Freshmen: 89% (102); all full-time undergraduates: 89% (468). *Average award:* Freshmen: $15,128; Undergraduates: $14,644. *Scholarships, grants, and awards:* Federal Pell, FSEOG, state, private, college/university gift aid from institutional funds.

**GIFT AID (NON-NEED-BASED) Total amount:** $687,892 (2% federal, 1% state, 94% institutional, 3% external sources). *Receiving aid:* Freshmen: 9% (10). Undergraduates: 7% (38). *Average award:* Freshmen: $8912. Undergraduates: $10,013. *Scholarships, grants, and awards by category: Academic interests/achievement:* 454 awards ($3,429,564 total): general academic interests/achievements. *Special achievements/activities:* 38 awards ($81,684 total): leadership, memberships, religious involvement. *Special characteristics:* 108 awards ($105,033 total): children and siblings of alumni, children of faculty/staff, first-generation college students, general special characteristics, out-of-state students, siblings of current students, veterans, veterans' children. *Tuition waivers:* Full or partial for children of alumni, employees or children of employees, senior citizens.

**LOANS Student loans:** $5,148,223 (81% need-based, 19% non-need-based). 86% of past graduating class borrowed through all loan programs. *Average indebtedness per student:* $50,039. *Average need-based loan:* Freshmen: $5713. Undergraduates: $5625. *Parent loans:* $1,025,000 (35% need-based, 65% non-need-based). *Programs:* Federal Direct (Subsidized and Unsubsidized Stafford, PLUS), Perkins, college/university.

**WORK-STUDY Federal work-study:** Total amount: $445,287; 321 jobs averaging $1567.

**APPLYING FOR FINANCIAL AID Required financial aid form:** FAFSA. *Financial aid deadline (priority):* 2/1. *Notification date:* Continuous beginning 3/1. Students must reply within 2 weeks of notification.

**CONTACT** Mrs. Laci N. Engelbrecht, Director of Financial Aid, MacMurray College, 447 East College Avenue, Jacksonville, IL 62650, 217-479-7041 or toll-free 800-252-7485. *Fax:* 217-291-0702. *E-mail:* financialaid@mac.edu. *Website:* http://www.mac.edu/.

# MADONNA UNIVERSITY
## Livonia, MI

**CONTACT** Cathy Durham, Financial Aid Secretary, Madonna University, 36600 Schoolcraft Road, Livonia, MI 48150-1173, 734-432-5663 or toll-free 800-852-4951. *Fax:* 734-432-5344. *E-mail:* finaid@madonna.edu. *Website:* http://www.madonna.edu/.

# MAHARISHI UNIVERSITY OF MANAGEMENT
## Fairfield, IA

**CONTACT** Mr. Bill Christensen, Director of Financial Aid, Maharishi University of Management, 1000 North 4th Street, DB 1127, Fairfield, IA 52557-1127, 641-472-1156 or toll-free 800-369-6480. *Fax:* 641-472-1133. *E-mail:* bchrist@mum.edu. *Website:* http://www.mum.edu/.

# MAINE COLLEGE OF ART
## Portland, ME

**CONTACT** Adrienne J. Amari, Director of Financial Aid, Maine College of Art, 522 Congress Street, Portland, ME 04101-3987, 207-775-3052 Ext. 5073 or toll-free 800-699-1509. *Fax:* 207-772-5069. *E-mail:* aamari@meca.edu. *Website:* http://www.meca.edu/.

# MAINE MARITIME ACADEMY
## Castine, ME

| Tuition & fees (area res): $17,120 | Average undergraduate aid package: $9245 |
|---|---|

**ABOUT THE INSTITUTION** State-supported, coed, primarily men. *Awards:* associate, bachelor's, and master's degrees. 11 undergraduate majors. *Total enrollment:* 1,066. Undergraduates: 1,037. Freshmen: 234. Federal methodology is used as a basis for awarding need-based institutional aid.

**UNDERGRADUATE EXPENSES for 2015–2016** *Tuition, area resident:* full-time $14,160. *Tuition, state resident:* full-time $9440. *Tuition, nonresident:* full-time $21,080. *Required fees:* full-time $2960. *College room and board:* $9830; *Room only:* $3880.

**FRESHMAN FINANCIAL AID (Fall 2013)** 200 applied for aid; of those 86% were deemed to have need. 99% of freshmen with need received aid; of those 8% had need fully met. *Average percent of need met:* 36% (excluding resources awarded to replace EFC). *Average financial aid package:* $7750 (excluding resources awarded to replace EFC). 5% of all full-time freshmen had no need and received non-need-based gift aid.

**UNDERGRADUATE FINANCIAL AID (Fall 2013)** 866 applied for aid; of those 87% were deemed to have need. 99% of undergraduates with need received aid; of those 9% had need fully met. *Average percent of need met:* 43% (excluding resources awarded to replace EFC). *Average financial aid package:* $9245 (excluding resources awarded to replace EFC). 5% of all full-time undergraduates had no need and received non-need-based gift aid.

**GIFT AID (NEED-BASED) Total amount:** $3,299,409 (41% federal, 6% state, 30% institutional, 23% external sources). *Receiving aid:* Freshmen: 65% (134); all full-time undergraduates: 61% (543). *Average award:* Freshmen: $5703; Undergraduates: $6318. *Scholarships, grants, and awards:* Federal Pell, FSEOG, state, private, college/university gift aid from institutional funds.

**GIFT AID (NON-NEED-BASED) Total amount:** $481,486 (10% state, 47% institutional, 43% external sources). *Receiving aid:* Freshmen: 3% (6). Undergraduates: 3% (29). *Average award:* Freshmen: $3867. Undergraduates: $4369. *Scholarships, grants, and awards by category: Academic interests/achievement:* 131 awards ($639,488 total): biological sciences, business, engineering/technologies, general academic interests/achievements. *Special characteristics:* 13 awards ($114,684 total): children of faculty/staff. *Tuition waivers:* Full or partial for employees or children of employees. *ROTC:* Army cooperative, Naval.

**LOANS** *Student loans:* $10,662,107 (71% need-based, 29% non-need-based). 88% of past graduating class borrowed through all loan programs. *Average indebtedness per student:* $40,909. *Average need-based loan:* Freshmen: $3639. Undergraduates: $4924. *Parent loans:* $3,003,261 (48% need-based, 52% non-need-based). *Programs:* Federal Direct (Subsidized and Unsubsidized Stafford, PLUS), Perkins, college/university, alternative loans.

**WORK-STUDY** *Federal work-study:* 153 jobs averaging $619.

**APPLYING FOR FINANCIAL AID** *Required financial aid form:* FAFSA. *Financial aid deadline (priority):* 4/1. *Notification date:* Continuous beginning 4/1. Students must reply within 4 weeks of notification.

**CONTACT** Mrs. Kathy S. Heath, Director of Financial Aid, Maine Maritime Academy, Pleasant Street, Castine, ME 04420, 207-326-2205 or toll-free 800-464-6565 (in-state), 800-227-8465 (out-of-state). *Fax:* 207-326-2515. *E-mail:* bbayle@mma.edu. *Website:* http://www.mainemaritime.edu/.

# MALONE UNIVERSITY
## Canton, OH

| Tuition & fees: $27,440 | Average undergraduate aid package: $21,583 |
| --- | --- |

**ABOUT THE INSTITUTION** Independent Evangelical Friends Church–Eastern Region, coed. *Awards:* certificates, bachelor's, and master's degrees. 42 undergraduate majors. *Total enrollment:* 1,980. Undergraduates: 1,565. Freshmen: 314. Federal methodology is used as a basis for awarding need-based institutional aid.

**UNDERGRADUATE EXPENSES** for 2015–2016 *Application fee:* $20. *Comprehensive fee:* $36,706 includes full-time tuition ($26,456), mandatory fees ($984), and room and board ($9266). *College room only:* $4640. Room and board charges vary according to board plan. *Part-time tuition:* $470 per credit. *Part-time fees:* $246 per term. Part-time tuition and fees vary according to course load.

**FRESHMAN FINANCIAL AID (Fall 2014, est.)** 289 applied for aid; of those 91% were deemed to have need. 100% of freshmen with need received aid; of those 19% had need fully met. *Average percent of need met:* 81% (excluding resources awarded to replace EFC). *Average financial aid package:* $23,406 (excluding resources awarded to replace EFC). 15% of all full-time freshmen had no need and received non-need-based gift aid.

**UNDERGRADUATE FINANCIAL AID (Fall 2014, est.)** 1,143 applied for aid; of those 93% were deemed to have need. 100% of undergraduates with need received aid; of those 19% had need fully met. *Average percent of need met:* 77% (excluding resources awarded to replace EFC). *Average financial aid package:* $21,583 (excluding resources awarded to replace EFC). 12% of all full-time undergraduates had no need and received non-need-based gift aid.

**GIFT AID (NEED-BASED)** *Total amount:* $16,103,938 (17% federal, 5% state, 74% institutional, 4% external sources). *Receiving aid:* Freshmen: 84% (262); all full-time undergraduates: 79% (1,049). *Average award:* Freshmen: $18,891; Undergraduates: $17,427. *Scholarships, grants, and awards:* Federal Pell, FSEOG, state, private, college/university gift aid from institutional funds.

**GIFT AID (NON-NEED-BASED)** *Total amount:* $2,169,939 (1% federal, 91% institutional, 8% external sources). *Receiving aid:* Freshmen: 11% (35). Undergraduates: 10% (134). *Average award:* Freshmen: $11,510. Undergraduates: $10,051. *Scholarships, grants, and awards by category: Academic interests/achievement:* 1,086 awards ($9,193,507 total): biological sciences, business, communication, education, general academic interests/achievements, health fields, mathematics, premedicine, religion/biblical studies, social sciences. *Creative arts/performance:* 61 awards ($121,780 total): creative writing, debating, journalism/publications, music, theater/drama. *Special achievements/activities:* 170 awards ($327,100 total): cheerleading/drum major, general special achievements/activities, leadership, religious involvement. *Special characteristics:* 108 awards ($1,048,148 total): children and siblings of alumni, handicapped students, international students, local/state students, members of minority groups, relatives of clergy, religious affiliation, veterans. *Tuition waivers:* Full or partial for employees or children of employees, senior citizens. *ROTC:* Army cooperative, Air Force cooperative.

**LOANS** *Student loans:* $9,617,425 (77% need-based, 23% non-need-based). 83% of past graduating class borrowed through all loan programs. *Average indebtedness per student:* $30,679. *Average need-based loan:* Freshmen: $4632. Undergraduates: $4837. *Parent loans:* $1,970,633 (37% need-based, 63% non-need-based).

*Programs:* Federal Direct (Subsidized and Unsubsidized Stafford, PLUS), Perkins, state, college/university, alternative loans.

**WORK-STUDY** *Federal work-study:* Total amount: $461,094; 314 jobs averaging $1950.

**ATHLETIC AWARDS** Total amount: $3,526,767 (58% need-based, 42% non-need-based).

**APPLYING FOR FINANCIAL AID** *Required financial aid form:* FAFSA. *Financial aid deadline:* 7/31 (priority: 3/1). *Notification date:* Continuous beginning 3/1. Students must reply within 2 weeks of notification.

**CONTACT** Mrs. Pamela Pustay, Director of Financial Aid, Malone University, 2600 Cleveland Avenue NW, Canton, OH 44709, 330-471-8161 or toll-free 800-521-1146. *Fax:* 330-471-8652. *E-mail:* ppustay@malone.edu. *Website:* http://www.malone.edu/.

# MANCHESTER UNIVERSITY
## North Manchester, IN

| Tuition & fees: N/R | Average undergraduate aid package: $25,265 |
| --- | --- |

**ABOUT THE INSTITUTION** Independent Church of the Brethren, coed. *Awards:* associate, bachelor's, master's, and doctoral degrees. 85 undergraduate majors. *Total enrollment:* 1,479. Undergraduates: 1,257. Freshmen: 441. Federal methodology is used as a basis for awarding need-based institutional aid.

**UNDERGRADUATE EXPENSES** for 2015–2016 *Application fee:* $25. *One-time required fee:* $250. *Tuition:* part-time $700 per credit hour. *Required fees:* $30 per credit hour. Part-time tuition and fees vary according to course load. Room and board charges vary according to board plan and housing facility.

**FRESHMAN FINANCIAL AID (Fall 2014, est.)** 418 applied for aid; of those 94% were deemed to have need. 100% of freshmen with need received aid; of those 24% had need fully met. *Average percent of need met:* 70% (excluding resources awarded to replace EFC). *Average financial aid package:* $26,997 (excluding resources awarded to replace EFC). 8% of all full-time freshmen had no need and received non-need-based gift aid.

**UNDERGRADUATE FINANCIAL AID (Fall 2014, est.)** 1,160 applied for aid; of those 94% were deemed to have need. 100% of undergraduates with need received aid; of those 23% had need fully met. *Average percent of need met:* 67% (excluding resources awarded to replace EFC). *Average financial aid package:* $25,265 (excluding resources awarded to replace EFC). 8% of all full-time undergraduates had no need and received non-need-based gift aid.

**GIFT AID (NEED-BASED)** *Total amount:* $23,917,268 (8% federal, 12% state, 78% institutional, 2% external sources). *Receiving aid:* Freshmen: 89% (393); all full-time undergraduates: 89% (1,085). *Average award:* Freshmen: $22,312; Undergraduates: $20,939. *Scholarships, grants, and awards:* Federal Pell, FSEOG, state, private, college/university gift aid from institutional funds.

**GIFT AID (NON-NEED-BASED)** *Total amount:* $1,819,165 (94% institutional, 6% external sources). *Receiving aid:* Freshmen: 10% (45). Undergraduates: 10% (120). *Average award:* Freshmen: $17,082. Undergraduates: $16,865. *Scholarships, grants, and awards by category: Academic interests/achievement:* general academic interests/achievements. *Creative arts/performance:* music. *Special achievements/activities:* leadership. *Special characteristics:* children and siblings of alumni, children of faculty/staff, international students, members of minority groups, out-of-state students, parents of current students, religious affiliation, siblings of current students, spouses of current students. *Tuition waivers:* Full or partial for employees or children of employees.

**LOANS** *Student loans:* $9,535,869 (59% need-based, 41% non-need-based). 82% of past graduating class borrowed through all loan programs. *Average indebtedness per student:* $30,141. *Average need-based loan:* Freshmen: $3317. Undergraduates: $4315. *Parent loans:* $3,176,203 (5% need-based, 95% non-need-based). *Programs:* Federal Direct (Subsidized and Unsubsidized Stafford, PLUS), Perkins.

**WORK-STUDY** *Federal work-study:* Total amount: $1,157,451; jobs available. *State or other work-study/employment:* Part-time jobs available.

**APPLYING FOR FINANCIAL AID** *Required financial aid form:* FAFSA. *Financial aid deadline (priority):* 3/1. *Notification date:* Continuous beginning 3/15. Students must reply by 5/1 or within 3 weeks of notification.

CONTACT Mrs. Sherri Shockey, Director of Student Financial Services, Manchester University, 604 East College Avenue, North Manchester, IN 46962-1225, 260-982-5066 or toll-free 800-852-3648. *Fax:* 260-982-5043. *E-mail:* slshockey@manchester.edu.
*Website:* http://www.manchester.edu/.

# MANHATTAN CHRISTIAN COLLEGE
## Manhattan, KS

CONTACT Mrs. Margaret Carlisle, Director of Financial Aid, Manhattan Christian College, 1415 Anderson Avenue, Manhattan, KS 66502-4081, 785-539-3571 or toll-free 877-246-4622. *E-mail:* carlisle@mccks.edu.
*Website:* http://www.mccks.edu/.

# MANHATTAN COLLEGE
## Riverdale, NY

| Tuition & fees: $37,498 | Average undergraduate aid package: $23,513 |
|---|---|

ABOUT THE INSTITUTION Independent Roman Catholic Church, coed. *Awards:* certificates, bachelor's, and master's degrees. 44 undergraduate majors. *Total enrollment:* 3,970. Undergraduates: 3,471. Freshmen: 747. Federal methodology is used as a basis for awarding need-based institutional aid.
UNDERGRADUATE EXPENSES for 2015–2016 *Application fee:* $60. *Comprehensive fee:* $51,238 includes full-time tuition ($34,300), mandatory fees ($3198), and room and board ($13,740). Full-time tuition and fees vary according to course load, program, and student level. Room and board charges vary according to board plan. *Part-time tuition:* $875 per credit. Part-time tuition and fees vary according to course load.
FRESHMAN FINANCIAL AID (Fall 2014, est.) 668 applied for aid; of those 88% were deemed to have need. 99% of freshmen with need received aid; of those 42% had need fully met. *Average percent of need met:* 69% (excluding resources awarded to replace EFC). *Average financial aid package:* $25,805 (excluding resources awarded to replace EFC). 21% of all full-time freshmen had no need and received non-need-based gift aid.
UNDERGRADUATE FINANCIAL AID (Fall 2014, est.) 2,725 applied for aid; of those 88% were deemed to have need. 99% of undergraduates with need received aid; of those 14% had need fully met. *Average percent of need met:* 67% (excluding resources awarded to replace EFC). *Average financial aid package:* $23,513 (excluding resources awarded to replace EFC). 24% of all full-time undergraduates had no need and received non-need-based gift aid.
GIFT AID (NEED-BASED) *Total amount:* $43,702,360 (11% federal, 8% state, 80% institutional, 1% external sources). *Receiving aid:* Freshmen: 78% (581); all full-time undergraduates: 67% (2,355). *Average award:* Freshmen: $20,100; Undergraduates: $19,090. *Scholarships, grants, and awards:* Federal Pell, FSEOG, state, private, college/university gift aid from institutional funds.
GIFT AID (NON-NEED-BASED) *Total amount:* $6,085,298 (1% state, 98% institutional, 1% external sources). *Receiving aid:* Freshmen: 11% (80). Undergraduates: 9% (315). *Average award:* Freshmen: $8305. Undergraduates: $6827. *Scholarships, grants, and awards by category:* Academic interests/achievement: biological sciences, business, computer science, foreign languages, general academic interests/achievements, mathematics, military science. Creative arts/performance: music. Special achievements/activities: community service, leadership. Special characteristics: children of faculty/staff. *Tuition waivers:* Full or partial for employees or children of employees. ROTC: Army cooperative, Air Force.
LOANS *Student loans:* $21,149,210 (91% need-based, 9% non-need-based). 75% of past graduating class borrowed through all loan programs. *Average indebtedness per student:* $37,449. *Average need-based loan:* Freshmen: $3431. Undergraduates: $4504. *Parent loans:* $10,754,226 (90% need-based, 10% non-need-based). *Programs:* Federal Direct (Subsidized and Unsubsidized Stafford, PLUS), Perkins.
WORK-STUDY *Federal work-study:* Total amount: $1,743,907; jobs available. *State or other work-study/employment:* Part-time jobs available.
ATHLETIC AWARDS Total amount: $4,982,937 (53% need-based, 47% non-need-based).

APPLYING FOR FINANCIAL AID *Required financial aid forms:* FAFSA, institution's own form, state aid form. *Financial aid deadline (priority):* 3/1. *Notification date:* 4/1. Students must reply by 5/1.
CONTACT Mr. Edward Keough, Director of Student Financial Services, Manhattan College, 4513 Manhattan College Parkway, Riverdale, NY 10471, 718-862-7100 or toll-free 800-622-9235. *Fax:* 718-862-8027. *E-mail:* finaid@manhattan.edu.
*Website:* http://www.manhattan.edu/.

# MANHATTAN SCHOOL OF MUSIC
## New York, NY

| Tuition & fees: $42,500 | Average undergraduate aid package: N/A |
|---|---|

ABOUT THE INSTITUTION Independent, coed. *Awards:* certificates, diplomas, bachelor's, master's, and doctoral degrees. 7 undergraduate majors. *Total enrollment:* 957. Undergraduates: 389. Freshmen: 113. Both federal and institutional methodology are used as a basis for awarding need-based institutional aid.
UNDERGRADUATE EXPENSES for 2015–2016 *Application fee:* $125. *Comprehensive fee:* $56,724 includes full-time tuition ($42,000), mandatory fees ($500), and room and board ($14,224). *College room only:* $9725. Room and board charges vary according to board plan and housing facility. *Part-time tuition:* $1750 per credit. Part-time tuition and fees vary according to course load.
FRESHMAN FINANCIAL AID (Fall 2014, est.) 78 applied for aid; of those 74% were deemed to have need. 100% of freshmen with need received aid.
UNDERGRADUATE FINANCIAL AID (Fall 2014, est.) 80 applied for aid; of those 84% were deemed to have need. 100% of undergraduates with need received aid.
GIFT AID (NEED-BASED) *Total amount:* $10,499,664 (4% federal, 96% institutional). *Receiving aid:* Freshmen: 47% (53); all full-time undergraduates: 21% (58). *Scholarships, grants, and awards:* Federal Pell, FSEOG, state, private, college/university gift aid from institutional funds.
GIFT AID (NON-NEED-BASED) *Total amount:* $963,845 (93% institutional, 7% external sources). *Receiving aid:* Undergraduates: 3% (9). *Scholarships, grants, and awards by category:* Creative arts/performance: music. *Tuition waivers:* Full or partial for employees or children of employees.
LOANS *Student loans:* $853,029 (67% need-based, 33% non-need-based). 28% of past graduating class borrowed through all loan programs. *Average indebtedness per student:* $3694. *Parent loans:* $1,555,649 (100% non-need-based). *Programs:* Federal Direct (Subsidized and Unsubsidized Stafford, PLUS), Perkins.
WORK-STUDY *Federal work-study:* Total amount: $51,708; jobs available.
APPLYING FOR FINANCIAL AID *Required financial aid forms:* FAFSA, CSS Financial Aid PROFILE. *Financial aid deadline:* 3/1. *Notification date:* 4/1. Students must reply by 5/1.
CONTACT Ms. Amy Anderson, Assistant Dean for Enrollment Management, Manhattan School of Music, 120 Claremont Avenue, New York, NY 10027-4698, 212-749-2802 Ext. 4501. *Fax:* 212-749-3025. *E-mail:* aanderson@msmnyc.edu.
*Website:* http://www.msmnyc.edu/.

# MANHATTANVILLE COLLEGE
## Purchase, NY

| Tuition & fees: $36,220 | Average undergraduate aid package: $29,347 |
|---|---|

ABOUT THE INSTITUTION Independent, coed. *Awards:* certificates, bachelor's, master's, and doctoral degrees. 41 undergraduate majors. *Total enrollment:* 2,865. Undergraduates: 1,798. Freshmen: 459. Federal methodology is used as a basis for awarding need-based institutional aid.
UNDERGRADUATE EXPENSES for 2015–2016 *Application fee:* $50. *Comprehensive fee:* $50,740 includes full-time tuition ($34,870), mandatory fees ($1350), and room and board ($14,520). *College room only:* $8680. Full-time tuition and fees vary according to course load. Room and board charges vary according to board plan. *Part-time tuition:* $810 per credit. *Part-time fees:* $60 per term. Part-time tuition and fees vary according to course load and program.

**FRESHMAN FINANCIAL AID (Fall 2014, est.)** 421 applied for aid; of those 86% were deemed to have need. 95% of freshmen with need received aid; of those 18% had need fully met. *Average percent of need met:* 71% (excluding resources awarded to replace EFC). *Average financial aid package:* $26,787 (excluding resources awarded to replace EFC). 20% of all full-time freshmen had no need and received non-need-based gift aid.

**UNDERGRADUATE FINANCIAL AID (Fall 2014, est.)** 1,424 applied for aid; of those 85% were deemed to have need. 99% of undergraduates with need received aid; of those 16% had need fully met. *Average percent of need met:* 75% (excluding resources awarded to replace EFC). *Average financial aid package:* $29,347 (excluding resources awarded to replace EFC). 21% of all full-time undergraduates had no need and received non-need-based gift aid.

**GIFT AID (NEED-BASED)** *Total amount:* $33,304,488 (8% federal, 6% state, 86% institutional). *Receiving aid:* Freshmen: 54% (250); all full-time undergraduates: 55% (934). *Average award:* Freshmen: $6572; Undergraduates: $7686. *Scholarships, grants, and awards:* Federal Pell, FSEOG, state, college/university gift aid from institutional funds.

**GIFT AID (NON-NEED-BASED)** *Total amount:* $8,595,581 (97% institutional, 3% external sources). *Receiving aid:* Freshmen: 75% (344). Undergraduates: 71% (1,195). *Average award:* Freshmen: $16,992. Undergraduates: $16,638. *Scholarships, grants, and awards by category:* Academic interests/achievement: general academic interests/achievements, mathematics. Creative arts/performance: dance, performing arts. Special achievements/activities: community service, leadership. Special characteristics: general special characteristics, previous college experience. *Tuition waivers:* Full or partial for employees or children of employees.

**LOANS** *Student loans:* $5,570,326 (64% need-based, 36% non-need-based). 72% of past graduating class borrowed through all loan programs. *Average indebtedness per student:* $33,444. *Average need-based loan:* Freshmen: $2435. Undergraduates: $4553. *Parent loans:* $4,196,531 (100% non-need-based). *Programs:* Federal Direct (Subsidized and Unsubsidized Stafford, PLUS), Perkins.

**WORK-STUDY** *Federal work-study:* Total amount: $686,026; jobs available. *State or other work-study/employment:* Total amount: $653,510 (100% non-need-based). Part-time jobs available.

**APPLYING FOR FINANCIAL AID** *Required financial aid forms:* FAFSA, state aid form. *Financial aid deadline (priority):* 3/1. *Notification date:* Continuous beginning 3/1. Students must reply by 5/1 or within 2 weeks of notification.

**CONTACT** Mr. Robert Gilmore, Director of Financial Aid, Manhattanville College, 2900 Purchase Street, Purchase, NY 10577-2132, 914-323-5357 or toll-free 800-328-4553. *Fax:* 914-323-5382. *E-mail:* robert.gilmore@mville.edu.
*Website:* http://www.mville.edu/.

# MANNES COLLEGE THE NEW SCHOOL FOR MUSIC
## New York, NY

**ABOUT THE INSTITUTION** Independent, coed. *Awards:* certificates, diplomas, bachelor's, and master's degrees. 7 undergraduate majors. *Total enrollment:* 354. Undergraduates: 158. Freshmen: 34.

**GIFT AID (NEED-BASED)** *Scholarships, grants, and awards:* Federal Pell, FSEOG, state, college/university gift aid from institutional funds.

**GIFT AID (NON-NEED-BASED)** *Scholarships, grants, and awards by category:* Academic interests/achievement: general academic interests/achievements. Creative arts/performance: music, performing arts. Special achievements/activities: leadership. Special characteristics: international students, local/state students, members of minority groups.

**LOANS** *Programs:* Federal Direct (Subsidized and Unsubsidized Stafford, PLUS), Perkins.

**APPLYING FOR FINANCIAL AID** *Required financial aid forms:* FAFSA, state aid form.

**CONTACT** Office of Student Financial Services, Mannes College The New School for Music, 72 Fifth Avenue, New York, NY 10024-4402, 212-229-8930 or toll-free 800-292-3040. *Fax:* 212-229-5919. *E-mail:* sfs@newschool.edu.
*Website:* http://www.mannes.edu/.

# MANSFIELD UNIVERSITY OF PENNSYLVANIA
## Mansfield, PA

| Tuition & fees (PA res): $9526 | Average undergraduate aid package: $9650 |
| --- | --- |

**ABOUT THE INSTITUTION** State-supported, coed. *Awards:* associate, bachelor's, and master's degrees. 65 undergraduate majors. *Total enrollment:* 2,752. Undergraduates: 2,587. Freshmen: 550. Federal methodology is used as a basis for awarding need-based institutional aid.

**UNDERGRADUATE EXPENSES for 2015–2016** *Application fee:* $25. *Tuition, state resident:* full-time $6820; part-time $284 per credit hour. *Tuition, nonresident:* full-time $17,050; part-time $710 per credit hour. *Required fees:* full-time $2706. Part-time tuition and fees vary according to course load. *College room and board:* $10,936; *Room only:* $7600. Room and board charges vary according to board plan and housing facility.

**FRESHMAN FINANCIAL AID (Fall 2013)** 661 applied for aid; of those 88% were deemed to have need. 100% of freshmen with need received aid; of those 8% had need fully met. *Average percent of need met:* 99% (excluding resources awarded to replace EFC). *Average financial aid package:* $8535 (excluding resources awarded to replace EFC). 4% of all full-time freshmen had no need and received non-need-based gift aid.

**UNDERGRADUATE FINANCIAL AID (Fall 2013)** 2,330 applied for aid; of those 88% were deemed to have need. 100% of undergraduates with need received aid; of those 10% had need fully met. *Average percent of need met:* 74% (excluding resources awarded to replace EFC). *Average financial aid package:* $9650 (excluding resources awarded to replace EFC). 1% of all full-time undergraduates had no need and received non-need-based gift aid.

**GIFT AID (NEED-BASED)** *Total amount:* $8,763,825 (61% federal, 33% state, 6% institutional). *Receiving aid:* Freshmen: 59% (402); all full-time undergraduates: 57% (1,447). *Average award:* Freshmen: $2904; Undergraduates: $2981. *Scholarships, grants, and awards:* Federal Pell, FSEOG, state, private, college/university gift aid from institutional funds.

**GIFT AID (NON-NEED-BASED)** *Total amount:* $1,285,141 (2% federal, 1% state, 58% institutional, 39% external sources). *Receiving aid:* Freshmen: 55% (376). Undergraduates: 53% (1,349). *Average award:* Freshmen: $1783. Undergraduates: $1404. *Scholarships, grants, and awards by category:* Academic interests/achievement: biological sciences, communication, education, general academic interests/achievements, health fields, mathematics, physical sciences. Creative arts/performance: art/fine arts, journalism/publications, music. Special achievements/activities: leadership. Special characteristics: children and siblings of alumni, local/state students, members of minority groups, religious affiliation. *Tuition waivers:* Full or partial for employees or children of employees, senior citizens. *ROTC:* Army cooperative.

**LOANS** *Student loans:* $20,397,335 (40% need-based, 60% non-need-based). 86% of past graduating class borrowed through all loan programs. *Average indebtedness per student:* $33,799. *Average need-based loan:* Freshmen: $1795. Undergraduates: $2708. *Parent loans:* $4,111,481 (100% non-need-based). *Programs:* Federal Direct (Subsidized and Unsubsidized Stafford, PLUS), Perkins.

**WORK-STUDY** *Federal work-study:* jobs available. *State or other work-study/employment:* Total amount: $1,041,938 (100% non-need-based). Part-time jobs available.

**ATHLETIC AWARDS** Total amount: $606,941 (100% non-need-based).

**APPLYING FOR FINANCIAL AID** *Required financial aid forms:* FAFSA, state aid form. *Financial aid deadline:* 6/30 (priority: 2/15). *Notification date:* Continuous beginning 2/17. Students must reply within 4 weeks of notification.

**CONTACT** Mr. Charles M. Scheetz, Director of Financial Aid, Mansfield University of Pennsylvania, 224 South Hall, 71 South Academy Street, Mansfield, PA 16933, 570-662-4129 or toll-free 800-577-6826. *Fax:* 570-662-4136.
*Website:* http://www.mansfield.edu/.

# MAPLE SPRINGS BAPTIST BIBLE COLLEGE AND SEMINARY
## Capitol Heights, MD

**CONTACT** Ms. Fannie G. Thompson, Director of Business Affairs, Maple Springs Baptist Bible College and Seminary, 4130 Belt Road, Capitol Heights, MD 20743, 301-736-3631. *Fax:* 301-735-6507.
*Website:* http://www.msbbcs.edu/.

# MARANATHA BAPTIST UNIVERSITY
## Watertown, WI

| Tuition & fees: $13,510 | Average undergraduate aid package: $10,382 |
| --- | --- |

**ABOUT THE INSTITUTION** Independent Baptist, coed. **Awards:** certificates, associate, bachelor's, and master's degrees. 31 undergraduate majors. **Total enrollment:** 1,042. Undergraduates: 942. Freshmen: 193. Federal methodology is used as a basis for awarding need-based institutional aid.

**UNDERGRADUATE EXPENSES for 2015–2016 Application fee:** $50. **Comprehensive fee:** $19,990 includes full-time tuition ($12,370), mandatory fees ($1140), and room and board ($6480). Full-time tuition and fees vary according to location and program. **Part-time tuition:** $515 per credit hour. **Part-time fees:** $48 per credit hour. Part-time tuition and fees vary according to course load.

**FRESHMAN FINANCIAL AID (Fall 2014, est.)** 123 applied for aid; of those 88% were deemed to have need. 100% of freshmen with need received aid; of those 7% had need fully met. **Average percent of need met:** 55% (excluding resources awarded to replace EFC). **Average financial aid package:** $10,492 (excluding resources awarded to replace EFC). 12% of all full-time freshmen had no need and received non-need-based gift aid.

**UNDERGRADUATE FINANCIAL AID (Fall 2014, est.)** 512 applied for aid; of those 91% were deemed to have need. 100% of undergraduates with need received aid; of those 10% had need fully met. **Average percent of need met:** 54% (excluding resources awarded to replace EFC). **Average financial aid package:** $10,382 (excluding resources awarded to replace EFC). 9% of all full-time undergraduates had no need and received non-need-based gift aid.

**GIFT AID (NEED-BASED) Total amount:** $3,212,337 (39% federal, 8% state, 37% institutional, 16% external sources). **Receiving aid:** Freshmen: 84% (108); all full-time undergraduates: 80% (434). **Average award:** Freshmen: $7320; Undergraduates: $6865. **Scholarships, grants, and awards:** Federal Pell, FSEOG, state, private, college/university gift aid from institutional funds.

**GIFT AID (NON-NEED-BASED) Total amount:** $371,921 (57% institutional, 43% external sources). **Receiving aid:** Freshmen: 1% (1). Undergraduates: 3% (15). **Average award:** Freshmen: $3248. Undergraduates: $3408. **Scholarships, grants, and awards by category:** Academic interests/achievement: business, general academic interests/achievements, religion/biblical studies. Creative arts/performance: music. Special characteristics: children and siblings of alumni, children of educators, children of faculty/staff, relatives of clergy, spouses of current students. **Tuition waivers:** Full or partial for employees or children of employees. **ROTC:** Army, Air Force cooperative.

**LOANS Student loans:** $4,387,192 (82% need-based, 18% non-need-based). 67% of past graduating class borrowed through all loan programs. *Average indebtedness per student:* $14,851. **Average need-based loan:** Freshmen: $3231. Undergraduates: $4195. **Parent loans:** $112,190 (39% need-based, 61% non-need-based). **Programs:** Federal Direct (Subsidized and Unsubsidized Stafford, PLUS), state, alternative loans.

**WORK-STUDY State or other work-study/employment:** Part-time jobs available.

**APPLYING FOR FINANCIAL AID Required financial aid form:** FAFSA. *Financial aid deadline (priority):* 3/1. *Notification date:* Continuous. Students must reply within 2 weeks of notification.

**CONTACT** Mr. Bruce Roth, Associate Director of Financial Aid, Maranatha Baptist University, 745 West Main Street, Watertown, WI 53094, 920-206-2318 or toll-free 800-622-2947. *Fax:* 920-261-9109. *E-mail:* financialaid@mbu.edu.
*Website:* http://www.mbu.edu/.

# MARIA COLLEGE
## Albany, NY

**CONTACT** Financial Aid Office, Maria College, 700 New Scotland Avenue, Albany, NY 12208-1798, 518-438-3111.
*Website:* http://www.mariacollege.edu/.

# MARIAN UNIVERSITY
## Indianapolis, IN

**CONTACT** Mr. John E. Shelton, Dean of Financial Aid, Marian University, 3200 Cold Spring Road, Indianapolis, IN 46222-1997, 317-955-6040 or toll-free 800-772-7264 (in-state). *Fax:* 317-955-6424. *E-mail:* jshelton@marian.edu.
*Website:* http://www.marian.edu/.

# MARIAN UNIVERSITY
## Fond du Lac, WI

| Tuition & fees: $25,930 | Average undergraduate aid package: $17,414 |
| --- | --- |

**ABOUT THE INSTITUTION** Independent Roman Catholic, coed. **Awards:** certificates, bachelor's, master's, and doctoral degrees. 47 undergraduate majors. **Total enrollment:** 2,130. Undergraduates: 1,628. Freshmen: 250. Both federal and institutional methodology are used as a basis for awarding need-based institutional aid.

**UNDERGRADUATE EXPENSES for 2015–2016 Application fee:** $20. **One-time required fee:** $100. **Comprehensive fee:** $32,420 includes full-time tuition ($25,510), mandatory fees ($420), and room and board ($6490). **College room only:** $3900. Full-time tuition and fees vary according to course load and program. Room and board charges vary according to board plan. Part-time tuition and fees vary according to course load and program.

**FRESHMAN FINANCIAL AID (Fall 2013)** 248 applied for aid; of those 92% were deemed to have need. 100% of freshmen with need received aid; of those 15% had need fully met. **Average percent of need met:** 72% (excluding resources awarded to replace EFC). **Average financial aid package:** $18,678 (excluding resources awarded to replace EFC). 8% of all full-time freshmen had no need and received non-need-based gift aid.

**UNDERGRADUATE FINANCIAL AID (Fall 2013)** 1,310 applied for aid; of those 92% were deemed to have need. 100% of undergraduates with need received aid; of those 13% had need fully met. **Average percent of need met:** 69% (excluding resources awarded to replace EFC). **Average financial aid package:** $17,414 (excluding resources awarded to replace EFC). 6% of all full-time undergraduates had no need and received non-need-based gift aid.

**GIFT AID (NEED-BASED) Total amount:** $16,694,009 (17% federal, 12% state, 63% institutional, 8% external sources). **Receiving aid:** Freshmen: 92% (227); all full-time undergraduates: 89% (1,186). **Average award:** Freshmen: $15,108; Undergraduates: $13,801. **Scholarships, grants, and awards:** Federal Pell, FSEOG, state, private, college/university gift aid from institutional funds, endowed and restricted scholarships and grants.

**GIFT AID (NON-NEED-BASED) Total amount:** $1,169,437 (1% state, 91% institutional, 8% external sources). **Receiving aid:** Freshmen: 13% (33). Undergraduates: 7% (98). **Average award:** Freshmen: $10,315. Undergraduates: $9124. **Scholarships, grants, and awards by category:** Academic interests/achievement: general academic interests/achievements. Creative arts/performance: music. Special characteristics: children of faculty/staff, children of union members/company employees, children with a deceased or disabled parent, local/state students, out-of-state students, siblings of current students, veterans. **Tuition waivers:** Full or partial for employees or children of employees, senior citizens. **ROTC:** Army.

**LOANS Student loans:** $10,464,924 (81% need-based, 19% non-need-based). 92% of past graduating class borrowed through all loan programs. *Average indebtedness per student:* $31,000. **Average need-based loan:** Freshmen: $3269. Undergraduates: $4374. **Parent loans:** $1,980,373 (43% need-based, 57% non-need-based). **Programs:** Federal Direct (Subsidized and Unsubsidized Stafford, PLUS), Perkins, Federal Nursing.

**WORK-STUDY** *Federal work-study:* jobs available. *State or other work-study/employment:* Total amount: $576,399 (100% non-need-based). 395 part-time jobs averaging $1447.

**APPLYING FOR FINANCIAL AID** *Required financial aid forms:* FAFSA, institution's own form. *Financial aid deadline (priority):* 3/1. *Notification date:* Continuous beginning 3/1. Students must reply within 4 weeks of notification.

**CONTACT** Ms. Pam Warren, Director of Financial Aid, Marian University, 45 South National Avenue, Fond du Lac, WI 54935-4699, 920-923-7614 or toll-free 800-2-MARIAN. *Fax:* 920-923-8767. *E-mail:* pwarren@marianuniversity.edu. *Website:* http://www.marianuniversity.edu/.

# MARIETTA COLLEGE
## Marietta, OH

| Tuition & fees: $33,140 | Average undergraduate aid package: $28,122 |
|---|---|

**ABOUT THE INSTITUTION** Independent, coed. *Awards:* certificates, associate, bachelor's, and master's degrees. 44 undergraduate majors. *Total enrollment:* 1,500. Undergraduates: 1,371. Freshmen: 357. Federal methodology is used as a basis for awarding need-based institutional aid.

**UNDERGRADUATE EXPENSES for 2015–2016** *Application fee:* $25. *Comprehensive fee:* $43,535 includes full-time tuition ($32,215), mandatory fees ($925), and room and board ($10,395). *College room only:* $5995. *Part-time tuition:* $1050 per credit.

**FRESHMAN FINANCIAL AID (Fall 2014, est.)** 320 applied for aid; of those 90% were deemed to have need. 100% of freshmen with need received aid; of those 20% had need fully met. *Average percent of need met:* 73% (excluding resources awarded to replace EFC). *Average financial aid package:* $29,061 (excluding resources awarded to replace EFC). 10% of all full-time freshmen had no need and received non-need-based gift aid.

**UNDERGRADUATE FINANCIAL AID (Fall 2014, est.)** 1,061 applied for aid; of those 89% were deemed to have need. 100% of undergraduates with need received aid; of those 23% had need fully met. *Average percent of need met:* 76% (excluding resources awarded to replace EFC). *Average financial aid package:* $28,122 (excluding resources awarded to replace EFC). 11% of all full-time undergraduates had no need and received non-need-based gift aid.

**GIFT AID (NEED-BASED)** *Total amount:* $12,502,612 (16% federal, 4% state, 80% institutional). *Receiving aid:* Freshmen: 77% (274); all full-time undergraduates: 70% (887). *Average award:* Freshmen: $18,919; Undergraduates: $18,902. *Scholarships, grants, and awards:* Federal Pell, FSEOG, state, private, college/university gift aid from institutional funds.

**GIFT AID (NON-NEED-BASED)** *Total amount:* $10,391,180 (1% state, 90% institutional, 9% external sources). *Receiving aid:* Freshmen: 74% (263). Undergraduates: 58% (735). *Average award:* Freshmen: $11,665. Undergraduates: $13,762. *Scholarships, grants, and awards by category:* Academic interests/achievement: 508 awards ($7,098,828 total): general academic interests/achievements, physical sciences. *Creative arts/performance:* 57 awards ($165,375 total): art/fine arts, music, performing arts, theater/drama. *Special characteristics:* 146 awards ($713,239 total): children and siblings of alumni, ethnic background, members of minority groups. *Tuition waivers:* Full or partial for employees or children of employees.

**LOANS** *Student loans:* $11,634,157 (32% need-based, 68% non-need-based). 73% of past graduating class borrowed through all loan programs. *Average indebtedness per student:* $39,708. *Average need-based loan:* Freshmen: $3504. Undergraduates: $4458. *Parent loans:* $2,768,519 (100% non-need-based). *Programs:* Federal Direct (Subsidized and Unsubsidized Stafford, PLUS), Perkins.

**WORK-STUDY** *Federal work-study:* Total amount: $1,575,257; 765 jobs averaging $1810.

**APPLYING FOR FINANCIAL AID** *Required financial aid form:* FAFSA. *Financial aid deadline (priority):* 2/15. *Notification date:* 3/1. Students must reply by 5/1 or within 2 weeks of notification.

**CONTACT** Mrs. Emily Schuck, Director of Financial Aid, Marietta College, 215 Fifth Street, Marietta, OH 45750-4000, 740-376-4712 or toll-free 800-331-7896. *Fax:* 740-376-4990. *E-mail:* finaid@marietta.edu. *Website:* http://www.marietta.edu/.

# MARIST COLLEGE
## Poughkeepsie, NY

| Tuition & fees: $32,500 | Average undergraduate aid package: $18,969 |
|---|---|

**ABOUT THE INSTITUTION** Independent, coed. *Awards:* certificates, bachelor's, and master's degrees. 43 undergraduate majors. *Total enrollment:* 6,356. Undergraduates: 5,516. Freshmen: 1,127. Federal methodology is used as a basis for awarding need-based institutional aid.

**UNDERGRADUATE EXPENSES for 2015–2016** *Application fee:* $50. *One-time required fee:* $90. *Comprehensive fee:* $46,100 includes full-time tuition ($32,000), mandatory fees ($500), and room and board ($13,600). *College room only:* $8700. Full-time tuition and fees vary according to course load and location. Room and board charges vary according to board plan, housing facility, and location. *Part-time tuition:* $634 per credit hour. *Part-time fees:* $40 per term. Part-time tuition and fees vary according to course load.

**FRESHMAN FINANCIAL AID (Fall 2014, est.)** 914 applied for aid; of those 74% were deemed to have need. 100% of freshmen with need received aid; of those 22% had need fully met. *Average percent of need met:* 69% (excluding resources awarded to replace EFC). *Average financial aid package:* $19,490 (excluding resources awarded to replace EFC). 26% of all full-time freshmen had no need and received non-need-based gift aid.

**UNDERGRADUATE FINANCIAL AID (Fall 2014, est.)** 3,482 applied for aid; of those 80% were deemed to have need. 100% of undergraduates with need received aid; of those 16% had need fully met. *Average percent of need met:* 64% (excluding resources awarded to replace EFC). *Average financial aid package:* $18,969 (excluding resources awarded to replace EFC). 26% of all full-time undergraduates had no need and received non-need-based gift aid.

**GIFT AID (NEED-BASED)** *Total amount:* $34,564,185 (9% federal, 6% state, 83% institutional, 2% external sources). *Receiving aid:* Freshmen: 44% (500); all full-time undergraduates: 42% (2,030). *Average award:* Freshmen: $17,152; Undergraduates: $15,447. *Scholarships, grants, and awards:* Federal Pell, FSEOG, state, private, college/university gift aid from institutional funds.

**GIFT AID (NON-NEED-BASED)** *Total amount:* $10,916,394 (1% federal, 2% state, 94% institutional, 3% external sources). *Receiving aid:* Freshmen: 58% (652). Undergraduates: 48% (2,336). *Average award:* Freshmen: $7802. Undergraduates: $7619. *Scholarships, grants, and awards by category:* Academic interests/achievement: 3,100 awards ($24,494,040 total): general academic interests/achievements. *Creative arts/performance:* 98 awards ($188,500 total): debating, music, theater/drama. *Special characteristics:* local/state students. *Tuition waivers:* Full or partial for employees or children of employees, adult students. *ROTC:* Army.

**LOANS** *Student loans:* $29,842,438 (76% need-based, 24% non-need-based). 68% of past graduating class borrowed through all loan programs. *Average indebtedness per student:* $34,801. *Average need-based loan:* Freshmen: $3717. Undergraduates: $4953. *Parent loans:* $10,593,771 (73% need-based, 27% non-need-based). *Programs:* Federal Direct (Subsidized and Unsubsidized Stafford, PLUS), Perkins, alternative loans.

**WORK-STUDY** *Federal work-study:* Total amount: $3,445,351; 1,390 jobs averaging $2479. *State or other work-study/employment:* Total amount: $1,034,270 (100% non-need-based). 583 part-time jobs averaging $1781.

**ATHLETIC AWARDS** Total amount: $4,330,179 (50% need-based, 50% non-need-based).

**APPLYING FOR FINANCIAL AID** *Required financial aid forms:* FAFSA, institution's own form. *Financial aid deadline:* 5/1 (priority: 2/15). *Notification date:* Continuous beginning 4/1. Students must reply by 5/1 or within 2 weeks of notification.

**CONTACT** Joseph R. Weglarz, Executive Director of Student Financial Services, Marist College, 3399 North Road, Poughkeepsie, NY 12601, 845-575-3230 or toll-free 800-436-5483. *Fax:* 845-575-3099. *E-mail:* joseph.weglarz@marist.edu. *Website:* http://www.marist.edu/.

# MARLBORO COLLEGE
## Marlboro, VT

| Tuition & fees: N/R | Average undergraduate aid package: $30,541 |
| --- | --- |

**ABOUT THE INSTITUTION** Independent, coed. 75 undergraduate majors. Federal methodology is used as a basis for awarding need-based institutional aid.
**FRESHMAN FINANCIAL AID (Fall 2014, est.)** 40 applied for aid; of those 92% were deemed to have need. 100% of freshmen with need received aid. *Average percent of need met:* 76% (excluding resources awarded to replace EFC). *Average financial aid package:* $31,838 (excluding resources awarded to replace EFC). 21% of all full-time freshmen had no need and received non-need-based gift aid.
**UNDERGRADUATE FINANCIAL AID (Fall 2014, est.)** 168 applied for aid; of those 93% were deemed to have need. 100% of undergraduates with need received aid. *Average percent of need met:* 80% (excluding resources awarded to replace EFC). *Average financial aid package:* $30,541 (excluding resources awarded to replace EFC). 15% of all full-time undergraduates had no need and received non-need-based gift aid.
**GIFT AID (NEED-BASED)** *Total amount:* $4,122,947 (10% federal, 2% state, 86% institutional, 2% external sources). *Receiving aid:* Freshmen: 79% (37); all full-time undergraduates: 78% (154). *Average award:* Freshmen: $24,755; Undergraduates: $23,237. *Scholarships, grants, and awards:* Federal Pell, FSEOG, state, private, college/university gift aid from institutional funds.
**GIFT AID (NON-NEED-BASED)** *Average award:* Freshmen: $15,345. Undergraduates: $12,867. *Scholarships, grants, and awards by category: Academic interests/achievement:* general academic interests/achievements. *Creative arts/performance:* art/fine arts, general creative arts/performance. *Special achievements/activities:* leadership.
**LOANS** *Student loans:* $1,900,561 (65% need-based, 35% non-need-based). 76% of past graduating class borrowed through all loan programs. *Average indebtedness per student:* $29,478. *Average need-based loan:* Freshmen: $3425. Undergraduates: $4457. *Parent loans:* $233,536 (100% need-based). *Programs:* Federal Direct (Subsidized and Unsubsidized Stafford, PLUS).
**WORK-STUDY** *Federal work-study:* Total amount: $294,535; jobs available. *State or other work-study/employment:* Part-time jobs available.
**APPLYING FOR FINANCIAL AID** *Required financial aid form:* FAFSA. *Financial aid deadline:* 3/1. *Notification date:* Continuous beginning 3/1. Students must reply by 5/1 or within 2 weeks of notification.
**CONTACT** Financial Aid Office, Marlboro College, PO Box A, 2582 South Road, Marlboro, VT 05344-0300, 802-258-9237 or toll-free 800-343-0049. *Fax:* 802-258-9300. *E-mail:* finaid@marlboro.edu.
*Website:* http://www.marlboro.edu/.

# MARQUETTE UNIVERSITY
## Milwaukee, WI

| Tuition & fees: $37,170 | Average undergraduate aid package: $24,753 |
| --- | --- |

**ABOUT THE INSTITUTION** Independent Roman Catholic (Jesuit), coed. *Awards:* certificates, bachelor's, master's, and doctoral degrees. 67 undergraduate majors. *Total enrollment:* 11,745. Undergraduates: 8,410. Freshmen: 1,992. Federal methodology is used as a basis for awarding need-based institutional aid.
**UNDERGRADUATE EXPENSES for 2015-2016** *Tuition:* full-time $36,720; part-time $995 per credit. Full-time tuition and fees vary according to course load and program. Part-time tuition and fees vary according to program. Room and board charges vary according to housing facility.
**FRESHMAN FINANCIAL AID (Fall 2014, est.)** 1,623 applied for aid; of those 73% were deemed to have need. 100% of freshmen with need received aid; of those 25% had need fully met. *Average percent of need met:* 76% (excluding resources awarded to replace EFC). *Average financial aid package:* $24,395 (excluding resources awarded to replace EFC). 38% of all full-time freshmen had no need and received non-need-based gift aid.
**UNDERGRADUATE FINANCIAL AID (Fall 2014, est.)** 5,847 applied for aid; of those 78% were deemed to have need. 100% of undergraduates with need received aid; of those 24% had need fully met. *Average percent of need met:* 77%

(excluding resources awarded to replace EFC). *Average financial aid package:* $24,753 (excluding resources awarded to replace EFC). 40% of all full-time undergraduates had no need and received non-need-based gift aid.
**GIFT AID (NEED-BASED)** *Total amount:* $78,497,773 (9% federal, 4% state, 81% institutional, 6% external sources). *Receiving aid:* Freshmen: 59% (1,169); all full-time undergraduates: 56% (4,496). *Average award:* Freshmen: $18,840; Undergraduates: $17,782. *Scholarships, grants, and awards:* Federal Pell, FSEOG, state, private, college/university gift aid from institutional funds, Veterans Benefits.
**GIFT AID (NON-NEED-BASED)** *Total amount:* $39,755,144 (90% institutional, 10% external sources). *Receiving aid:* Freshmen: 7% (146). Undergraduates: 7% (526). *Average award:* Freshmen: $11,095. Undergraduates: $10,294. *Scholarships, grants, and awards by category: Academic interests/achievement:* 7,040 awards ($67,688,229 total): biological sciences, business, communication, education, engineering/technologies, English, foreign languages, general academic interests/achievements, health fields, mathematics, physical sciences. *Creative arts/performance:* 9 awards ($7500 total): theater/drama. *Special characteristics:* 170 awards ($5,804,160 total): children of faculty/staff. *Tuition waivers:* Full or partial for employees or children of employees, senior citizens. *ROTC:* Army, Naval, Air Force.
**LOANS** *Student loans:* $49,800,318 (62% need-based, 38% non-need-based). 63% of past graduating class borrowed through all loan programs. *Average indebtedness per student:* $35,211. *Average need-based loan:* Freshmen: $4172. Undergraduates: $6665. *Parent loans:* $19,506,904 (35% need-based, 65% non-need-based). *Programs:* Federal Direct (Subsidized and Unsubsidized Stafford, PLUS), Perkins, Federal Nursing, state, college/university, private loans.
**WORK-STUDY** *Federal work-study:* Total amount: $3,854,506; jobs available. *State or other work-study/employment:* Part-time jobs available.
**ATHLETIC AWARDS** Total amount: $5,210,586 (33% need-based, 67% non-need-based).
**APPLYING FOR FINANCIAL AID** *Required financial aid form:* FAFSA. *Financial aid deadline:* Continuous. *Notification date:* Continuous beginning 3/5. Students must reply by 5/1 or within 3 weeks of notification.
**CONTACT** Susan Teerink, Director of Financial Aid, Marquette University, PO Box 1881, Milwaukee, WI 53201-1881, 414-288-4000 or toll-free 800-222-6544. *Fax:* 414-288-1718. *E-mail:* financialaid@marquette.edu.
*Website:* http://www.marquette.edu/.

# MARSHALL UNIVERSITY
## Huntington, WV

| Tuition & fees (WV res): $6526 | Average undergraduate aid package: $10,192 |
| --- | --- |

**ABOUT THE INSTITUTION** State-supported, coed. *Awards:* certificates, associate, bachelor's, master's, and doctoral degrees. 54 undergraduate majors. *Total enrollment:* 13,381. Undergraduates: 9,536. Freshmen: 1,848. Federal methodology is used as a basis for awarding need-based institutional aid.
**UNDERGRADUATE EXPENSES for 2015-2016** *Application fee:* $30. *Tuition, state resident:* full-time $5450; part-time $227.25 per credit hour. *Tuition, nonresident:* full-time $13,950; part-time $581.50 per credit hour. *Required fees:* full-time $1076; $45 per credit hour. Full-time tuition and fees vary according to degree level, location, program, and reciprocity agreements. Part-time tuition and fees vary according to course load, degree level, location, program, and reciprocity agreements. *College room and board:* $9546; *Room only:* $5908. Room and board charges vary according to board plan and housing facility.
**FRESHMAN FINANCIAL AID (Fall 2014, est.)** 1,781 applied for aid; of those 78% were deemed to have need. 99% of freshmen with need received aid; of those 30% had need fully met. *Average percent of need met:* 51% (excluding resources awarded to replace EFC). *Average financial aid package:* $11,015 (excluding resources awarded to replace EFC). 14% of all full-time freshmen had no need and received non-need-based gift aid.
**UNDERGRADUATE FINANCIAL AID (Fall 2014, est.)** 7,168 applied for aid; of those 80% were deemed to have need. 98% of undergraduates with need received aid; of those 28% had need fully met. *Average percent of need met:* 50% (excluding resources awarded to replace EFC). *Average financial aid package:* $10,192 (excluding resources awarded to replace EFC). 10% of all full-time undergraduates had no need and received non-need-based gift aid.
**GIFT AID (NEED-BASED)** *Total amount:* $27,800,562 (68% federal, 29% state, 3% institutional). *Receiving aid:* Freshmen: 60% (1,091); all full-time undergraduates:

55% (4,398). **Average award:** Freshmen: $6520; Undergraduates: $5984. **Scholarships, grants, and awards:** Federal Pell, FSEOG, state, private, college/university gift aid from institutional funds, Federal Nursing.

**GIFT AID (NON-NEED-BASED) Total amount:** $15,746,485 (56% state, 25% institutional, 19% external sources). **Receiving aid:** Freshmen: 44% (802). Undergraduates: 29% (2,309). **Average award:** Freshmen: $1438. Undergraduates: $1659. **Scholarships, grants, and awards by category:** Academic interests/achievement: general academic interests/achievements. Creative arts/performance: art/fine arts, general creative arts/performance. **Special characteristics:** children and siblings of alumni, children of faculty/staff, local/state students, members of minority groups. **Tuition waivers:** Full or partial for employees or children of employees, senior citizens. **ROTC:** Army.

**LOANS Student loans:** $41,138,484 (93% need-based, 7% non-need-based). 67% of past graduating class borrowed through all loan programs. **Average indebtedness per student:** $26,625. **Average need-based loan:** Freshmen: $5762. Undergraduates: $7078. **Parent loans:** $4,427,053 (100% non-need-based). **Programs:** Federal Direct (Subsidized and Unsubsidized Stafford, PLUS), Perkins, Federal Nursing.

**WORK-STUDY Federal work-study:** Total amount: $648,016; jobs available. **State or other work-study/employment:** Part-time jobs available.

**ATHLETIC AWARDS Total amount:** $5,195,929 (100% non-need-based).

**APPLYING FOR FINANCIAL AID Required financial aid forms:** FAFSA, state aid form. **Financial aid deadline (priority):** 3/1. **Notification date:** 5/1.

**CONTACT** Ms. Kathy Bialk, Director of Student Financial Aid, Marshall University, One John Marshall Drive, Huntington, WV 25755, 304-696-2280 or toll-free 800-642-3499. Fax: 304-696-3242. E-mail: bialkk@marshall.edu.
Website: http://www.marshall.edu/.

---

# MARS HILL UNIVERSITY
## Mars Hill, NC

**CONTACT** Amanda Randolph, Director of Financial Aid, Mars Hill University, PO Box 370, Mars Hill, NC 28754, 828-689-1123 or toll-free 866-648-4968. Fax: 828-689-1300. E-mail: arandolph@mhc.edu.
Website: http://www.mhu.edu/.

---

# MARTIN LUTHER COLLEGE
## New Ulm, MN

| Tuition & fees: $13,565 | Average undergraduate aid package: $10,830 |
|---|---|

**ABOUT THE INSTITUTION** Independent Wisconsin Evangelical Lutheran Synod, coed. **Awards:** certificates, diplomas, bachelor's, and master's degrees. 6 undergraduate majors. **Total enrollment:** 857. Undergraduates: 783. Freshmen: 189. Federal methodology is used as a basis for awarding need-based institutional aid.

**UNDERGRADUATE EXPENSES for 2015–2016 Comprehensive fee:** $18,920 includes full-time tuition ($13,565) and room and board ($5355).

**FRESHMAN FINANCIAL AID (Fall 2013)** 137 applied for aid; of those 83% were deemed to have need. 100% of freshmen with need received aid; of those 11% had need fully met. **Average percent of need met:** 73% (excluding resources awarded to replace EFC). **Average financial aid package:** $11,264 (excluding resources awarded to replace EFC). 18% of all full-time freshmen had no need and received non-need-based gift aid.

**UNDERGRADUATE FINANCIAL AID (Fall 2013)** 553 applied for aid; of those 86% were deemed to have need. 100% of undergraduates with need received aid; of those 18% had need fully met. **Average percent of need met:** 75% (excluding resources awarded to replace EFC). **Average financial aid package:** $10,830 (excluding resources awarded to replace EFC). 17% of all full-time undergraduates had no need and received non-need-based gift aid.

**GIFT AID (NEED-BASED) Total amount:** $3,243,892 (27% federal, 7% state, 52% institutional, 14% external sources). **Receiving aid:** Freshmen: 74% (112); all full-time undergraduates: 76% (467). **Average award:** Freshmen: $7650; Undergraduates: $6725. **Scholarships, grants, and awards:** Federal Pell, FSEOG, state, private, college/university gift aid from institutional funds.

**GIFT AID (NON-NEED-BASED) Total amount:** $505,959 (57% institutional, 43% external sources). **Receiving aid:** Freshmen: 3% (5). Undergraduates: 4% (26).

**Average award:** Freshmen: $2558. Undergraduates: $2521. **Scholarships, grants, and awards by category:** Academic interests/achievement: general academic interests/achievements. Creative arts/performance: music.

**LOANS Student loans:** $3,855,507 (69% need-based, 31% non-need-based). 90% of past graduating class borrowed through all loan programs. **Average indebtedness per student:** $17,391. **Average need-based loan:** Freshmen: $4051. Undergraduates: $4508. **Parent loans:** $100,426 (26% need-based, 74% non-need-based). **Programs:** Federal Direct (Subsidized and Unsubsidized Stafford, PLUS), Perkins, state, college/university, alternative loans.

**WORK-STUDY Federal work-study:** jobs available. **State or other work-study/employment:** Total amount: $16,379 (69% need-based, 31% non-need-based). Part-time jobs available.

**APPLYING FOR FINANCIAL AID Required financial aid forms:** FAFSA, institution's own form. **Financial aid deadline:** 4/15. **Notification date:** Continuous beginning 3/15. Students must reply by 9/1.

**CONTACT** Mr. Mark Bauer, Director of Financial Aid, Martin Luther College, 1995 Luther Court, New Ulm, MN 56073, 507-354-8221 or toll-free 877-MLC-1995. Fax: 507-354-8225. E-mail: bauermd@mlc-wels.edu.
Website: http://www.mlc-wels.edu/.

---

# MARTIN METHODIST COLLEGE
## Pulaski, TN

**CONTACT** Ms. Anita Beecham, Financial Aid Assistant, Martin Methodist College, 433 West Madison Street, Pulaski, TN 38478-2716, 931-363-9808 or toll-free 800-467-1273. Fax: 931-363-9818. E-mail: abeecham@martinmethodist.edu.
Website: http://www.martinmethodist.edu/.

---

# MARTIN UNIVERSITY
## Indianapolis, IN

**CONTACT** Berdia Marshall, Director of Financial Aid, Martin University, 2171 Avondale Place, Indianapolis, IN 46218-3867, 317-543-3670. Fax: 317-543-4790. E-mail: bmarshall@martin.edu.
Website: http://www.martin.edu/.

---

# MARY BALDWIN COLLEGE
## Staunton, VA

| Tuition & fees: $29,595 | Average undergraduate aid package: $22,492 |
|---|---|

**ABOUT THE INSTITUTION** Independent, coed, primarily women. **Awards:** certificates, bachelor's, master's, and doctoral degrees. 34 undergraduate majors. **Total enrollment:** 1,754. Undergraduates: 1,423. Freshmen: 257. Federal methodology is used as a basis for awarding need-based institutional aid.

**UNDERGRADUATE EXPENSES for 2015–2016 Comprehensive fee:** $38,245 includes full-time tuition ($29,210), mandatory fees ($385), and room and board ($8650). **College room only:** $5521. Full-time tuition and fees vary according to degree level. Room and board charges vary according to housing facility. **Part-time tuition:** $219 per credit hour. Part-time tuition and fees vary according to degree level.

**FRESHMAN FINANCIAL AID (Fall 2014, est.)** 251 applied for aid; of those 95% were deemed to have need. 100% of freshmen with need received aid; of those 12% had need fully met. **Average percent of need met:** 74% (excluding resources awarded to replace EFC). **Average financial aid package:** $25,833 (excluding resources awarded to replace EFC). 8% of all full-time freshmen had no need and received non-need-based gift aid.

**UNDERGRADUATE FINANCIAL AID (Fall 2014, est.)** 837 applied for aid; of those 95% were deemed to have need. 100% of undergraduates with need received aid; of those 11% had need fully met. **Average percent of need met:** 71% (excluding resources awarded to replace EFC). **Average financial aid package:** $22,492 (excluding resources awarded to replace EFC). 10% of all full-time undergraduates had no need and received non-need-based gift aid.

**GIFT AID (NEED-BASED)** *Total amount:* $15,613,847 (21% federal, 9% state, 65% institutional, 5% external sources). *Receiving aid:* Freshmen: 91% (239); all full-time undergraduates: 87% (784). *Average award:* Freshmen: $22,352; Undergraduates: $18,604. *Scholarships, grants, and awards:* Federal Pell, FSEOG, state, private, college/university gift aid from institutional funds.

**GIFT AID (NON-NEED-BASED)** *Total amount:* $1,970,142 (1% federal, 8% state, 74% institutional, 17% external sources). *Receiving aid:* Freshmen: 9% (23). Undergraduates: 8% (71). *Average award:* Freshmen: $16,060. Undergraduates: $14,978. *Scholarships, grants, and awards by category: Academic interests/achievement:* 771 awards ($8,452,729 total): general academic interests/achievements. *Special achievements/activities:* leadership. *Special characteristics:* children of educators, children of faculty/staff. *Tuition waivers:* Full or partial for employees or children of employees. *ROTC:* Army, Naval cooperative, Air Force cooperative.

**LOANS** *Student loans:* $9,317,038 (86% need-based, 14% non-need-based). 83% of past graduating class borrowed through all loan programs. *Average indebtedness per student:* $32,117. *Average need-based loan:* Freshmen: $3802. Undergraduates: $4246. *Parent loans:* $1,500,840 (42% need-based, 58% non-need-based). *Programs:* Federal Direct (Subsidized and Unsubsidized Stafford, PLUS), Perkins, alternative loans.

**WORK-STUDY** *Federal work-study:* Total amount: $313,278; 253 jobs averaging $1267. *State or other work-study/employment:* Total amount: $168,133 (47% need-based, 53% non-need-based). 114 part-time jobs averaging $1529.

**APPLYING FOR FINANCIAL AID** *Required financial aid forms:* FAFSA, state aid form (VA residents only). *Financial aid deadline:* Continuous. *Notification date:* Continuous beginning 3/15. Students must reply within 3 weeks of notification.

**CONTACT** Mrs. Robin Dietrich, Director of Financial Aid, Mary Baldwin College, PO Box 1500, Staunton, VA 24402, 540-887-7025 or toll-free 800-468-2262. *Fax:* 540-887-7229. *E-mail:* rdietric@mbc.edu.
*Website:* http://www.mbc.edu/.

# MARYGROVE COLLEGE
## Detroit, MI

**CONTACT** Mr. Donald Hurt, Director of Financial Aid, Marygrove College, 8425 West McNichols Road, Detroit, MI 48221-2599, 313-862-8000 Ext. 436 or toll-free 866-313-1297.
*Website:* http://www.marygrove.edu/.

# MARYLAND INSTITUTE COLLEGE OF ART
## Baltimore, MD

**CONTACT** Ms. Diane Prengaman, Associate Vice President for Financial Aid, Maryland Institute College of Art, 1300 Mount Royal Avenue, Baltimore, MD 21217, 410-225-2285. *Fax:* 410-225-2337. *E-mail:* dprengam@mica.edu.
*Website:* http://www.mica.edu/.

# MARYLHURST UNIVERSITY
## Marylhurst, OR

| Tuition & fees: $20,345 | Average undergraduate aid package: $15,600 |
|---|---|

**ABOUT THE INSTITUTION** Independent Roman Catholic, coed. *Awards:* certificates, bachelor's, and master's degrees. 20 undergraduate majors. *Total enrollment:* 1,273. Undergraduates: 696. Federal methodology is used as a basis for awarding need-based institutional aid.

**UNDERGRADUATE EXPENSES** for 2015–2016 *Application fee:* $50. *Tuition:* full-time $20,295; part-time $451 per quarter hour.

**UNDERGRADUATE FINANCIAL AID (Fall 2014, est.)** 101 applied for aid; of those 97% were deemed to have need. 100% of undergraduates with need received

aid; of those 5% had need fully met. *Average percent of need met:* 52% (excluding resources awarded to replace EFC). *Average financial aid package:* $15,600 (excluding resources awarded to replace EFC). 6% of all full-time undergraduates had no need and received non-need-based gift aid.

**GIFT AID (NEED-BASED)** *Total amount:* $2,701,540 (46% federal, 6% state, 42% institutional, 6% external sources). *Receiving aid:* All full-time undergraduates: 56% (95). *Average award:* Undergraduates: $9442. *Scholarships, grants, and awards:* Federal Pell, FSEOG, state, private, college/university gift aid from institutional funds, United Negro College Fund.

**GIFT AID (NON-NEED-BASED)** *Total amount:* $149,004 (99% institutional, 1% external sources). *Receiving aid:* Undergraduates: 1% (2). *Average award:* Undergraduates: $7114.

**LOANS** *Student loans:* $4,738,554 (90% need-based, 10% non-need-based). 100% of past graduating class borrowed through all loan programs. *Average indebtedness per student:* $34,399. *Average need-based loan:* Undergraduates: $4803. *Parent loans:* $48,155 (44% need-based, 56% non-need-based). *Programs:* Federal Direct (Subsidized and Unsubsidized Stafford, PLUS), Perkins.

**WORK-STUDY** *Federal work-study:* Total amount: $707,876; 168 jobs averaging $4835.

**APPLYING FOR FINANCIAL AID** *Required financial aid forms:* FAFSA, institution's own form. *Financial aid deadline:* Continuous. *Notification date:* Continuous beginning 4/1. Students must reply within 8 weeks of notification.

**CONTACT** Tracy Reisinger, Office of Financial Aid, Marylhurst University, 17600 Pacific Highway, PO Box 261, Marylhurst, OR 97036, 503-699-6253 or toll-free 800-634-9982. *Fax:* 503-635-6585. *E-mail:* treisinger@marylhurst.edu.
*Website:* http://www.marylhurst.edu/.

# MARYMOUNT CALIFORNIA UNIVERSITY
## Rancho Palos Verdes, CA

| Tuition & fees: $31,657 | Average undergraduate aid package: $23,671 |
|---|---|

**ABOUT THE INSTITUTION** Independent Roman Catholic, coed. *Awards:* certificates, associate, bachelor's, and master's degrees. 5 undergraduate majors. *Total enrollment:* 1,107. Undergraduates: 1,086. Freshmen: 314. Federal methodology is used as a basis for awarding need-based institutional aid.

**UNDERGRADUATE EXPENSES** for 2015–2016 *Application fee:* $50. *One-time required fee:* $275. *Comprehensive fee:* $44,655 includes full-time tuition ($31,112), mandatory fees ($545), and room and board ($12,998). *College room only:* $8200. Full-time tuition and fees vary according to degree level and location. Room and board charges vary according to board plan and housing facility. *Part-time tuition:* $1350 per credit hour. *Part-time fees:* $250 per year. Part-time tuition and fees vary according to degree level and location.

**FRESHMAN FINANCIAL AID (Fall 2014, est.)** 164 applied for aid; of those 96% were deemed to have need. 100% of freshmen with need received aid; of those 4% had need fully met. *Average percent of need met:* 89% (excluding resources awarded to replace EFC). *Average financial aid package:* $24,842 (excluding resources awarded to replace EFC). 5% of all full-time freshmen had no need and received non-need-based gift aid.

**UNDERGRADUATE FINANCIAL AID (Fall 2014, est.)** 587 applied for aid; of those 96% were deemed to have need. 100% of undergraduates with need received aid; of those 5% had need fully met. *Average percent of need met:* 75% (excluding resources awarded to replace EFC). *Average financial aid package:* $23,671 (excluding resources awarded to replace EFC). 5% of all full-time undergraduates had no need and received non-need-based gift aid.

**GIFT AID (NEED-BASED)** *Total amount:* $13,510,378 (15% federal, 16% state, 68% institutional, 1% external sources). *Receiving aid:* Freshmen: 49% (154); all full-time undergraduates: 54% (561). *Average award:* Freshmen: $22,788; Undergraduates: $22,417. *Scholarships, grants, and awards:* Federal Pell, FSEOG, state, private, college/university gift aid from institutional funds.

**GIFT AID (NON-NEED-BASED)** *Total amount:* $1,986,716 (22% federal, 77% institutional, 1% external sources). *Receiving aid:* Freshmen: 9% (28). Undergraduates: 7% (74). *Tuition waivers:* Full or partial for employees or children of employees, senior citizens.

**LOANS** *Student loans:* $4,976,434 (48% need-based, 52% non-need-based). 55% of past graduating class borrowed through all loan programs. *Average indebtedness per student:* $9421. *Average need-based loan:* Undergraduates: $5500. *Parent loans:* $1,813,052 (100% non-need-based). *Programs:* Federal Direct (Subsidized and Unsubsidized Stafford, PLUS), alternative loans.
**WORK-STUDY** *Federal work-study:* Total amount: $3000; jobs available.
**ATHLETIC AWARDS** Total amount: $1,016,314 (100% non-need-based).
**APPLYING FOR FINANCIAL AID** *Required financial aid form:* FAFSA. *Financial aid deadline:* 2/15. *Notification date:* Continuous beginning 3/1. Students must reply by 5/1 or within 3 weeks of notification.
**CONTACT** Ms. Alexis Gonzalez, Director of Financial Aid, Marymount California University, 30800 Palos Verdes Drive East, Rancho Palos Verdes, CA 90275, 310-303-7216. *Fax:* 310-303-7270. *E-mail:* agonzalez@marymountcalifornia.edu.
*Website:* http://www.marymountcalifornia.edu/.

# MARYMOUNT MANHATTAN COLLEGE
## New York, NY

| Tuition & fees: $27,636 | Average undergraduate aid package: $14,624 |
|---|---|

**ABOUT THE INSTITUTION** Independent, coed. *Awards:* associate and bachelor's degrees. 52 undergraduate majors. *Total enrollment:* 1,858. Undergraduates: 1,858. Freshmen: 514. Both federal and institutional methodology are used as a basis for awarding need-based institutional aid.
**UNDERGRADUATE EXPENSES for 2015–2016** *Application fee:* $60. *Comprehensive fee:* $42,636 includes full-time tuition ($26,352), mandatory fees ($1284), and room and board ($15,000). *College room only:* $13,000. Full-time tuition and fees vary according to course load and program. Room and board charges vary according to board plan. *Part-time tuition:* $880 per credit hour. *Part-time fees:* $467 per term. Part-time tuition and fees vary according to course load and program.
**FRESHMAN FINANCIAL AID (Fall 2013)** 332 applied for aid; of those 87% were deemed to have need. 100% of freshmen with need received aid; of those 4% had need fully met. *Average percent of need met:* 43% (excluding resources awarded to replace EFC). *Average financial aid package:* $15,264 (excluding resources awarded to replace EFC). 8% of all full-time freshmen had no need and received non-need-based gift aid.
**UNDERGRADUATE FINANCIAL AID (Fall 2013)** 1,230 applied for aid; of those 88% were deemed to have need. 100% of undergraduates with need received aid; of those 5% had need fully met. *Average percent of need met:* 44% (excluding resources awarded to replace EFC). *Average financial aid package:* $14,624 (excluding resources awarded to replace EFC). 7% of all full-time undergraduates had no need and received non-need-based gift aid.
**GIFT AID (NEED-BASED)** *Total amount:* $12,440,181 (18% federal, 7% state, 72% institutional, 3% external sources). *Receiving aid:* Freshmen: 73% (284); all full-time undergraduates: 68% (1,065). *Average award:* Freshmen: $12,334; Undergraduates: $10,840. *Scholarships, grants, and awards:* Federal Pell, FSEOG, state, private, college/university gift aid from institutional funds.
**GIFT AID (NON-NEED-BASED)** *Total amount:* $2,235,690 (15% federal, 83% institutional, 2% external sources). *Average award:* Freshmen: $7394. Undergraduates: $7665. *Scholarships, grants, and awards by category:* Academic interests/achievement: 719 awards ($5,063,700 total): biological sciences, general academic interests/achievements. *Creative arts/performance:* 312 awards ($607,750 total): art/fine arts, dance, performing arts. *Special achievements/activities:* 63 awards ($119,000 total): leadership. *Special characteristics:* 109 awards ($536,007 total): international students, local/state students, out-of-state students, veterans, veterans' children. *Tuition waivers:* Full or partial for employees or children of employees, senior citizens.
**LOANS** *Student loans:* $10,409,920 (37% need-based, 63% non-need-based). 73% of past graduating class borrowed through all loan programs. *Average indebtedness per student:* $29,419. *Average need-based loan:* Freshmen: $3342. Undergraduates: $4224. *Parent loans:* $9,970,384 (100% non-need-based). *Programs:* Federal Direct (Subsidized and Unsubsidized Stafford, PLUS).
**WORK-STUDY** *Federal work-study:* 134 jobs averaging $3124.
**APPLYING FOR FINANCIAL AID** *Required financial aid forms:* FAFSA, state aid form. *Financial aid deadline (priority):* 3/15. *Notification date:*

Continuous beginning 3/15. Students must reply by 5/1 or within 2 weeks of notification.
**CONTACT** Christina Bennett, Director of Financial Aid, Marymount Manhattan College, 221 East 71st Street, New York, NY 10021, 212-517-0556 or toll-free 800-627-9668. *E-mail:* cbennett@mmm.edu.
*Website:* http://www.mmm.edu/.

# MARYMOUNT UNIVERSITY
## Arlington, VA

| Tuition & fees: $27,470 | Average undergraduate aid package: $17,828 |
|---|---|

**ABOUT THE INSTITUTION** Independent Roman Catholic Church, coed. *Awards:* certificates, bachelor's, master's, and doctoral degrees. 28 undergraduate majors. *Total enrollment:* 3,441. Undergraduates: 2,363. Freshmen: 353. Federal methodology is used as a basis for awarding need-based institutional aid.
**UNDERGRADUATE EXPENSES for 2015–2016** *Application fee:* $40. *One-time required fee:* $410. *Comprehensive fee:* $39,480 includes full-time tuition ($27,100), mandatory fees ($370), and room and board ($12,010). Room and board charges vary according to housing facility. *Part-time tuition:* $885 per credit hour.
**FRESHMAN FINANCIAL AID (Fall 2014, est.)** 282 applied for aid; of those 88% were deemed to have need. 100% of freshmen with need received aid; of those 23% had need fully met. *Average percent of need met:* 67% (excluding resources awarded to replace EFC). *Average financial aid package:* $21,010 (excluding resources awarded to replace EFC). 23% of all full-time freshmen had no need and received non-need-based gift aid.
**UNDERGRADUATE FINANCIAL AID (Fall 2014, est.)** 1,515 applied for aid; of those 91% were deemed to have need. 100% of undergraduates with need received aid; of those 13% had need fully met. *Average percent of need met:* 54% (excluding resources awarded to replace EFC). *Average financial aid package:* $17,828 (excluding resources awarded to replace EFC). 18% of all full-time undergraduates had no need and received non-need-based gift aid.
**GIFT AID (NEED-BASED)** *Total amount:* $5,950,088 (51% federal, 1% state, 48% institutional). *Receiving aid:* Freshmen: 40% (140); all full-time undergraduates: 41% (875). *Average award:* Freshmen: $4382; Undergraduates: $6344. *Scholarships, grants, and awards:* Federal Pell, FSEOG, state, private, college/university gift aid from institutional funds.
**GIFT AID (NON-NEED-BASED)** *Total amount:* $18,067,062 (15% state, 84% institutional, 1% external sources). *Receiving aid:* Freshmen: 70% (246). Undergraduates: 54% (1,141). *Average award:* Freshmen: $13,904. Undergraduates: $12,302. *Scholarships, grants, and awards by category:* Academic interests/achievement: 1,351 awards ($13,367,596 total): biological sciences, business, communication, English, general academic interests/achievements, health fields, mathematics, religion/biblical studies, social sciences. *Special achievements/activities:* 388 awards ($1,053,305 total): community service, general special achievements/activities, leadership, memberships. *Special characteristics:* 899 awards ($2,681,590 total): children of current students, children of faculty/staff, general special characteristics, international students, local/state students, out-of-state students, religious affiliation, siblings of current students, veterans, veterans' children. *Tuition waivers:* Full or partial for employees or children of employees, senior citizens. *ROTC:* Army cooperative.
**LOANS** *Student loans:* $15,721,664 (32% need-based, 68% non-need-based). 74% of past graduating class borrowed through all loan programs. *Average indebtedness per student:* $26,528. *Average need-based loan:* Freshmen: $3409. Undergraduates: $4557. *Parent loans:* $8,526,641 (100% non-need-based). *Programs:* Federal Direct (Subsidized and Unsubsidized Stafford, PLUS), Perkins.
**WORK-STUDY** *Federal work-study:* Total amount: $1,393,055; 692 jobs averaging $2016.
**APPLYING FOR FINANCIAL AID** *Required financial aid form:* FAFSA. *Financial aid deadline (priority):* 3/1. *Notification date:* Continuous beginning 3/15.
**CONTACT** Mrs. Debbie A. Raines, Director of Financial Aid, Marymount University, 2807 North Glebe Road, Arlington, VA 22207-4299, 703-284-1530 or toll-free 800-548-7638. *Fax:* 703-516-4771. *E-mail:* debbie.raines@marymount.edu.
*Website:* http://www.marymount.edu/.

# MARYVILLE COLLEGE
## Maryville, TN

| Tuition & fees: $32,866 | Average undergraduate aid package: $31,239 |
|---|---|

**ABOUT THE INSTITUTION** Independent Presbyterian, coed. *Awards:* bachelor's degrees. 58 undergraduate majors. *Total enrollment:* 1,213. Undergraduates: 1,213. Freshmen: 334. Federal methodology is used as a basis for awarding need-based institutional aid.

**UNDERGRADUATE EXPENSES for 2015–2016 *Comprehensive fee:*** $43,308 includes full-time tuition ($32,104), mandatory fees ($762), and room and board ($10,442). *College room only:* $5182. Full-time tuition and fees vary according to course load. Room and board charges vary according to board plan and housing facility. *Part-time tuition:* $825 per credit hour. Part-time tuition and fees vary according to course load.

**FRESHMAN FINANCIAL AID (Fall 2014, est.)** 333 applied for aid; of those 86% were deemed to have need. 100% of freshmen with need received aid; of those 18% had need fully met. *Average percent of need met:* 75% (excluding resources awarded to replace EFC). *Average financial aid package:* $32,550 (excluding resources awarded to replace EFC). 13% of all full-time freshmen had no need and received non-need-based gift aid.

**UNDERGRADUATE FINANCIAL AID (Fall 2014, est.)** 1,162 applied for aid; of those 86% were deemed to have need. 100% of undergraduates with need received aid; of those 15% had need fully met. *Average percent of need met:* 71% (excluding resources awarded to replace EFC). *Average financial aid package:* $31,239 (excluding resources awarded to replace EFC). 13% of all full-time undergraduates had no need and received non-need-based gift aid.

**GIFT AID (NEED-BASED) *Total amount:*** $25,297,589 (12% federal, 12% state, 75% institutional, 1% external sources). *Receiving aid:* Freshmen: 86% (288); all full-time undergraduates: 86% (1,005). *Average award:* Freshmen: $26,623; Undergraduates: $25,219. *Scholarships, grants, and awards:* Federal Pell, FSEOG, state, private, college/university gift aid from institutional funds.

**GIFT AID (NON-NEED-BASED) *Total amount:*** $5,066,334 (9% federal, 13% state, 76% institutional, 2% external sources). *Receiving aid:* Freshmen: 16% (55). Undergraduates: 14% (169). *Average award:* Freshmen: $19,742. Undergraduates: $19,308. *Scholarships, grants, and awards by category:* Academic interests/achievement: general academic interests/achievements. Creative arts/performance: art/fine arts, music, theater/drama. Special achievements/activities: community service, leadership. Special characteristics: children and siblings of alumni, children of faculty/staff, members of minority groups, religious affiliation, veterans. *Tuition waivers:* Full or partial for employees or children of employees.

**LOANS *Student loans:*** $7,265,812 (83% need-based, 17% non-need-based). *Average need-based loan:* Freshmen: $5486. Undergraduates: $6000. *Parent loans:* $1,559,842 (47% need-based, 53% non-need-based). *Programs:* Federal Direct (Subsidized and Unsubsidized Stafford, PLUS), Perkins.

**WORK-STUDY *Federal work-study:*** Total amount: $1,223,151; 660 jobs averaging $1700. *State or other work-study/employment:* 11 part-time jobs averaging $1284.

**APPLYING FOR FINANCIAL AID *Required financial aid form:*** FAFSA. *Financial aid deadline (priority):* 3/1. *Notification date:* Continuous beginning 3/15. Students must reply within 4 weeks of notification.

**CONTACT** Ms. Melena Verity, Director of Financial Aid, Maryville College, 502 East Lamar Alexander Parkway, Maryville, TN 37804-5907, 865-981-8100 or toll-free 800-597-2687. *Fax:* 865-981-8084. *E-mail:* melena.verity@maryvillecollege.edu.
*Website:* http://www.maryvillecollege.edu/.

# MARYVILLE UNIVERSITY OF SAINT LOUIS
## St. Louis, MO

| Tuition & fees: $25,884 | Average undergraduate aid package: $22,812 |
|---|---|

**ABOUT THE INSTITUTION** Independent, coed. *Awards:* certificates, bachelor's, master's, and doctoral degrees. 53 undergraduate majors. *Total*

*enrollment:* 5,931. Undergraduates: 2,818. Freshmen: 412. Both federal and institutional methodology are used as a basis for awarding need-based institutional aid.

**UNDERGRADUATE EXPENSES for 2015–2016 *Application fee:*** $30. *Comprehensive fee:* $35,856 includes full-time tuition ($24,694), mandatory fees ($1190), and room and board ($9972). *College room only:* $7684. Full-time tuition and fees vary according to course load. Room and board charges vary according to board plan and housing facility. *Part-time tuition:* $740 per credit hour. *Part-time fees:* $297 per term. Part-time tuition and fees vary according to class time.

**FRESHMAN FINANCIAL AID (Fall 2014, est.)** 355 applied for aid; of those 87% were deemed to have need. 99% of freshmen with need received aid; of those 15% had need fully met. *Average percent of need met:* 75% (excluding resources awarded to replace EFC). *Average financial aid package:* $23,942 (excluding resources awarded to replace EFC). 25% of all full-time freshmen had no need and received non-need-based gift aid.

**UNDERGRADUATE FINANCIAL AID (Fall 2014, est.)** 1,428 applied for aid; of those 90% were deemed to have need. 100% of undergraduates with need received aid; of those 13% had need fully met. *Average percent of need met:* 70% (excluding resources awarded to replace EFC). *Average financial aid package:* $22,812 (excluding resources awarded to replace EFC). 26% of all full-time undergraduates had no need and received non-need-based gift aid.

**GIFT AID (NEED-BASED) *Total amount:*** $17,406,507 (17% federal, 4% state, 77% institutional, 2% external sources). *Receiving aid:* Freshmen: 75% (304); all full-time undergraduates: 67% (1,237). *Average award:* Freshmen: $17,127; Undergraduates: $14,323. *Scholarships, grants, and awards:* Federal Pell, FSEOG, state, private, college/university gift aid from institutional funds, Academic Competitiveness Grants, National SMART Grants, TEACH Grants.

**GIFT AID (NON-NEED-BASED) *Total amount:*** $5,678,120 (1% federal, 1% state, 95% institutional, 3% external sources). *Receiving aid:* Freshmen: 19% (78). Undergraduates: 13% (250). *Average award:* Freshmen: $10,834. Undergraduates: $9559. *Scholarships, grants, and awards by category:* Academic interests/achievement: 2,312 awards ($16,378,981 total): biological sciences, business, education, English, general academic interests/achievements, health fields, international studies, mathematics. Creative arts/performance: 73 awards ($194,197 total): art/fine arts, music. Special achievements/activities: 129 awards ($823,742 total): cheerleading/drum major, community service, general special achievements/activities, leadership, religious involvement. Special characteristics: 247 awards ($1,103,705 total): adult students, ethnic background, general special characteristics, international students, members of minority groups, out-of-state students, parents of current students. *Tuition waivers:* Full or partial for employees or children of employees, senior citizens. *ROTC:* Army cooperative.

**LOANS *Student loans:*** $13,702,754 (80% need-based, 20% non-need-based). 69% of past graduating class borrowed through all loan programs. *Average indebtedness per student:* $31,696. *Average need-based loan:* Freshmen: $2925. Undergraduates: $3958. *Parent loans:* $6,183,942 (49% need-based, 51% non-need-based). *Programs:* Federal Direct (Subsidized and Unsubsidized Stafford, PLUS), Perkins, private loans.

**WORK-STUDY *Federal work-study:*** Total amount: $264,390; 340 jobs averaging $618. *State or other work-study/employment:* Total amount: $1,007,899 (90% need-based, 10% non-need-based). 339 part-time jobs averaging $992.

**ATHLETIC AWARDS** Total amount: $2,113,494 (53% need-based, 47% non-need-based).

**APPLYING FOR FINANCIAL AID *Required financial aid form:*** FAFSA. *Financial aid deadline (priority):* 3/1. *Notification date:* Continuous beginning 3/15. Students must reply by 5/1 or within 2 weeks of notification.

**CONTACT** Ms. Martha Harbaugh, Director of Financial Aid, Maryville University of Saint Louis, 650 Maryville University Drive, St. Louis, MO 63141-7299, 800-627-9855 Ext. 9361 or toll-free 800-627-9855. *Fax:* 314-529-9199. *E-mail:* mharbaugh@maryville.edu.
*Website:* http://www.maryville.edu/.

# MARYWOOD UNIVERSITY
## Scranton, PA

| Tuition & fees: $32,692 | Average undergraduate aid package: $23,187 |
|---|---|

**ABOUT THE INSTITUTION** Independent Roman Catholic, coed. *Awards:* certificates, bachelor's, master's, and doctoral degrees. 70 undergraduate majors. *Total* *enrollment:* 3,056. Undergraduates: 2,003. Freshmen: 373. Federal methodology is used as a basis for awarding need-based institutional aid.

**UNDERGRADUATE EXPENSES for 2015–2016** *Application fee:* $35. *Comprehensive fee:* $46,592 includes full-time tuition ($30,942), mandatory fees ($1750), and room and board ($13,900). *College room only:* $7822. Full-time tuition and fees vary according to course load. Room and board charges vary according to board plan and housing facility. Part-time tuition and fees vary according to course load.

**FRESHMAN FINANCIAL AID (Fall 2014, est.)** 348 applied for aid; of those 87% were deemed to have need. 100% of freshmen with need received aid; of those 21% had need fully met. *Average percent of need met:* 79% (excluding resources awarded to replace EFC). *Average financial aid package:* $25,721 (excluding resources awarded to replace EFC). 16% of all full-time freshmen had no need and received non-need-based gift aid.

**UNDERGRADUATE FINANCIAL AID (Fall 2014, est.)** 1,660 applied for aid; of those 92% were deemed to have need. 100% of undergraduates with need received aid; of those 19% had need fully met. *Average percent of need met:* 73% (excluding resources awarded to replace EFC). *Average financial aid package:* $23,187 (excluding resources awarded to replace EFC). 13% of all full-time undergraduates had no need and received non-need-based gift aid.

**GIFT AID (NEED-BASED)** *Total amount:* $28,078,284 (11% federal, 9% state, 79% institutional, 1% external sources). *Receiving aid:* Freshmen: 69% (255); all full-time undergraduates: 70% (1,275). *Average award:* Freshmen: $23,630; Undergraduates: $20,072. *Scholarships, grants, and awards:* Federal Pell, FSEOG, state, private, college/university gift aid from institutional funds.

**GIFT AID (NON-NEED-BASED)** *Total amount:* $4,720,621 (93% institutional, 7% external sources). *Receiving aid:* Freshmen: 82% (301). Undergraduates: 84% (1,522). *Average award:* Freshmen: $15,280. Undergraduates: $14,015. *Scholarships, grants, and awards by category: Academic interests/achievement:* architecture, biological sciences, business, communication, computer science, education, English, foreign languages, general academic interests/achievements, health fields, home economics, mathematics, religion/biblical studies, social sciences. *Creative arts/performance:* art/fine arts, music. *Special achievements/activities:* community service, general special achievements/activities, leadership. *Tuition waivers:* Full or partial for employees or children of employees, senior citizens. *ROTC:* Army cooperative, Air Force cooperative.

**LOANS** *Student loans:* $14,763,151 (72% need-based, 28% non-need-based). 86% of past graduating class borrowed through all loan programs. *Average indebtedness per student:* $41,559. *Average need-based loan:* Freshmen: $3769. Undergraduates: $4481. *Parent loans:* $3,556,337 (42% need-based, 58% non-need-based). *Programs:* Federal Direct (Subsidized and Unsubsidized Stafford, PLUS), Perkins.

**WORK-STUDY** *Federal work-study:* Total amount: $1,301,398; 665 jobs averaging $1957.

**APPLYING FOR FINANCIAL AID** *Required financial aid forms:* FAFSA, state aid form. *Financial aid deadline (priority):* 2/15. *Notification date:* Continuous beginning 3/15. Students must reply by 5/1 or within 3 weeks of notification.

**CONTACT** Barbara Schmitt, Director of Financial Aid, Marywood University, 2300 Adams Avenue, Scranton, PA 18509-1598, 570-348-6225 or toll-free 866-279-9663. *Fax:* 570-961-4739. *E-mail:* schmitt@marywood.edu. *Website:* http://www.marywood.edu/.

# MASSACHUSETTS COLLEGE OF ART AND DESIGN
## Boston, MA

| Tuition & fees (MA res): $11,225 | Average undergraduate aid package: $10,544 |
|---|---|

**ABOUT THE INSTITUTION** State-supported, coed. *Awards:* certificates, bachelor's, and master's degrees. 17 undergraduate majors. *Total enrollment:* 2,100. Undergraduates: 1,965. Freshmen: 328. Federal methodology is used as a basis for awarding need-based institutional aid.

**UNDERGRADUATE EXPENSES for 2015–2016** *Application fee:* $50. *Tuition, state resident:* full-time $11,225. *Tuition, nonresident:* full-time $29,925. Part-time tuition and fees vary according to course load. *College room and board:* $13,000. Room and board charges vary according to board plan and housing facility.

**FRESHMAN FINANCIAL AID (Fall 2014, est.)** 298 applied for aid; of those 71% were deemed to have need. 100% of freshmen with need received aid. *Average financial aid package:* $12,642 (excluding resources awarded to replace EFC). 17% of all full-time freshmen had no need and received non-need-based gift aid.

**UNDERGRADUATE FINANCIAL AID (Fall 2014, est.)** 1,345 applied for aid; of those 74% were deemed to have need. 100% of undergraduates with need received aid. *Average financial aid package:* $10,544 (excluding resources awarded to replace EFC). 13% of all full-time undergraduates had no need and received non-need-based gift aid.

**GIFT AID (NEED-BASED)** *Total amount:* $5,715,844 (45% federal, 8% state, 47% institutional). *Receiving aid:* Freshmen: 55% (180); all full-time undergraduates: 45% (732). *Average award:* Freshmen: $7887; Undergraduates: $7198. *Scholarships, grants, and awards:* Federal Pell, FSEOG, state, private, college/university gift aid from institutional funds.

**GIFT AID (NON-NEED-BASED)** *Total amount:* $3,355,251 (4% federal, 82% institutional, 14% external sources). *Receiving aid:* Freshmen: 17% (56). Undergraduates: 13% (206). *Average award:* Freshmen: $6887. Undergraduates: $5737. *Scholarships, grants, and awards by category: Special characteristics:* children of faculty/staff, children of union members/company employees, veterans. *Tuition waivers:* Full or partial for employees or children of employees, senior citizens.

**LOANS** *Student loans:* $10,519,815 (39% need-based, 61% non-need-based). 76% of past graduating class borrowed through all loan programs. *Average indebtedness per student:* $26,792. *Average need-based loan:* Freshmen: $3562. Undergraduates: $4389. *Parent loans:* $3,760,951 (100% non-need-based). *Programs:* Federal Direct (Subsidized and Unsubsidized Stafford, PLUS), Perkins, state, alternative loans.

**WORK-STUDY** *Federal work-study:* Total amount: $263,049; 201 jobs averaging $1304. *State or other work-study/employment:* Part-time jobs available.

**APPLYING FOR FINANCIAL AID** *Required financial aid form:* FAFSA. *Financial aid deadline (priority):* 3/1. *Notification date:* Continuous beginning 3/15. Students must reply within 3 weeks of notification.

**CONTACT** Auelio Ramirez, Director of Student Financial Assistance, Massachusetts College of Art and Design, 621 Huntington Avenue, Boston, MA 02115-5882, 617-879-7850. *Fax:* 617-879-7880. *E-mail:* aurelio.ramirez@massart.edu. *Website:* http://www.massart.edu/.

# MASSACHUSETTS COLLEGE OF LIBERAL ARTS
## North Adams, MA

| Tuition & fees (MA res): $8975 | Average undergraduate aid package: $14,445 |
|---|---|

**ABOUT THE INSTITUTION** State-supported, coed. *Awards:* certificates, bachelor's, and master's degrees. 41 undergraduate majors. *Total enrollment:* 1,765. Undergraduates: 1,562. Freshmen: 352. Federal methodology is used as a basis for awarding need-based institutional aid.

**UNDERGRADUATE EXPENSES for 2015–2016** *Application fee:* $40. *Tuition, state resident:* full-time $1030; part-time $42.92 per credit. *Tuition, nonresident:* full-time $9975; part-time $415.63 per credit. *Required fees:* full-time $7945; $268.42 per credit. Part-time tuition and fees vary according to course load. *College room and board:* $9638. Room and board charges vary according to board plan and housing facility.

**FRESHMAN FINANCIAL AID (Fall 2014, est.)** 332 applied for aid; of those 81% were deemed to have need. 97% of freshmen with need received aid; of those 81% had need fully met. *Average percent of need met:* 79% (excluding resources awarded to replace EFC). *Average financial aid package:* $13,990 (excluding resources awarded to replace EFC). 7% of all full-time freshmen had no need and received non-need-based gift aid.

**UNDERGRADUATE FINANCIAL AID (Fall 2014, est.)** 1,252 applied for aid; of those 82% were deemed to have need. 98% of undergraduates with need received aid; of those 79% had need fully met. *Average percent of need met:* 79% (excluding resources awarded to replace EFC). *Average financial aid package:* $14,445 (excluding resources awarded to replace EFC). 4% of all full-time undergraduates had no need and received non-need-based gift aid.

**GIFT AID (NEED-BASED)** *Total amount:* $6,169,120 (52% federal, 16% state, 25% institutional, 7% external sources). *Receiving aid:* Freshmen: 63% (221); all full-time undergraduates: 60% (813). *Average award:* Freshmen: $6704; Undergraduates: $6370. **Scholarships, grants, and awards:** Federal Pell, FSEOG, state, private, college/university gift aid from institutional funds.

**GIFT AID (NON-NEED-BASED) Total amount:** $192,302 (15% state, 53% institutional, 32% external sources). **Receiving aid:** Freshmen: 29% (102). Undergraduates: 17% (238). **Average award:** Freshmen: $2042. Undergraduates: $2715. **Scholarships, grants, and awards by category:** Academic interests/achievement: biological sciences, business, communication, computer science, education, English, general academic interests/achievements, health fields, humanities, mathematics, physical sciences, social sciences. Creative arts/performance: applied art and design, art/fine arts, cinema/film/broadcasting, journalism/publications, music, performing arts, theater/drama. Special achievements/activities: general special achievements/activities, leadership, memberships. **Tuition waivers:** Full or partial for employees or children of employees, senior citizens.

**LOANS Student loans:** $9,150,549 (86% need-based, 14% non-need-based). 85% of past graduating class borrowed through all loan programs. Average indebtedness per student: $28,817. **Average need-based loan:** Freshmen: $3405. Undergraduates: $3978. **Parent loans:** $1,179,348 (86% need-based, 14% non-need-based). **Programs:** Federal Direct (Subsidized and Unsubsidized Stafford, PLUS), Perkins, state.

**WORK-STUDY Federal work-study:** Total amount: $324,143; jobs available. **State or other work-study/employment:** Total amount: $1500 (100% need-based). Part-time jobs available.

**APPLYING FOR FINANCIAL AID Required financial aid form:** FAFSA. **Financial aid deadline (priority):** 3/1. **Notification date:** Continuous beginning 3/1. Students must reply by 5/1 or within 2 weeks of notification.

**CONTACT** Mrs. Elizabeth M. Petri, Director of Financial Aid, Massachusetts College of Liberal Arts, 375 Church Street, North Adams, MA 01247, 413-662-5219 or toll-free 800-989-MCLA. Fax: 413-662-5105. E-mail: e.petri@mcla.edu. Website: http://www.mcla.edu/.

# MASSACHUSETTS INSTITUTE OF TECHNOLOGY
## Cambridge, MA

| Tuition & fees: $45,016 | Average undergraduate aid package: $40,118 |
|---|---|

**ABOUT THE INSTITUTION** Independent, coed. **Awards:** bachelor's, master's, and doctoral degrees. 36 undergraduate majors. **Total enrollment:** 11,319. Undergraduates: 4,512. Freshmen: 1,043. Institutional methodology is used as a basis for awarding need-based institutional aid.

**UNDERGRADUATE EXPENSES for 2015–2016 Application fee:** $75. **Comprehensive fee:** $58,240 includes full-time tuition ($44,720), mandatory fees ($296), and room and board ($13,224). **College room only:** $8330. Room and board charges vary according to board plan and housing facility. **Part-time tuition:** $699 per unit. Part-time tuition and fees vary according to course load.

**FRESHMAN FINANCIAL AID (Fall 2013)** 884 applied for aid; of those 78% were deemed to have need. 100% of freshmen with need received aid; of those 100% had need fully met. **Average percent of need met:** 100% (excluding resources awarded to replace EFC). **Average financial aid package:** $39,495 (excluding resources awarded to replace EFC).

**UNDERGRADUATE FINANCIAL AID (Fall 2013)** 2,965 applied for aid; of those 89% were deemed to have need. 100% of undergraduates with need received aid; of those 100% had need fully met. **Average percent of need met:** 100% (excluding resources awarded to replace EFC). **Average financial aid package:** $40,118 (excluding resources awarded to replace EFC).

**GIFT AID (NEED-BASED) Total amount:** $97,827,728 (6% federal, 90% institutional, 4% external sources). **Receiving aid:** Freshmen: 60% (669); all full-time undergraduates: 56% (2,547). **Average award:** Freshmen: $36,881; Undergraduates: $37,090. **Scholarships, grants, and awards:** Federal Pell, FSEOG, state, private, college/university gift aid from institutional funds.

**GIFT AID (NON-NEED-BASED) Total amount:** $8,842,815 (20% federal, 80% external sources). **Receiving aid:** Freshmen: 2% (24). Undergraduates: 1% (59). **Tuition waivers:** Full or partial for employees or children of employees. **ROTC:** Army, Naval, Air Force.

**LOANS Student loans:** $12,767,901 (53% need-based, 47% non-need-based). 40% of past graduating class borrowed through all loan programs. Average indebtedness

per student: $19,064. **Average need-based loan:** Freshmen: $2870. Undergraduates: $3005. **Parent loans:** $3,638,014 (5% need-based, 95% non-need-based). **Programs:** Federal Direct (Subsidized and Unsubsidized Stafford, PLUS), Perkins, college/university.

**WORK-STUDY Federal work-study:** 1,096 jobs averaging $2169. **State or other work-study/employment:** Total amount: $2,597,428 (67% need-based, 33% non-need-based). 963 part-time jobs averaging $2697.

**APPLYING FOR FINANCIAL AID Required financial aid forms:** FAFSA, CSS Financial Aid PROFILE, noncustodial (divorced/separated) parent's statement, business/farm supplement, federal income tax form(s), W-2 forms. **Financial aid deadline:** 2/15. **Notification date:** 3/14. Students must reply by 5/1.

**CONTACT** Elizabeth Hicks, Executive Director of Student Financial Services, Massachusetts Institute of Technology, 77 Massachusetts Avenue, Room 11-120, Cambridge, MA 02139-4307, 617-253-4090. Fax: 617-258-0700. E-mail: sfs@mit.edu. Website: http://web.mit.edu/.

# MASSACHUSETTS MARITIME ACADEMY
## Buzzards Bay, MA

| Tuition & fees (MA res): $7280 | Average undergraduate aid package: $12,158 |
|---|---|

**ABOUT THE INSTITUTION** State-supported, coed, primarily men. **Awards:** bachelor's and master's degrees. 10 undergraduate majors. **Total enrollment:** 1,497. Undergraduates: 1,401. Freshmen: 321. Federal methodology is used as a basis for awarding need-based institutional aid.

**UNDERGRADUATE EXPENSES for 2015–2016 Application fee:** $50. **Tuition, state resident:** full-time $1480; part-time $296.50 per credit. **Tuition, nonresident:** full-time $16,534; part-time $923.75 per credit. **Required fees:** full-time $5800. **College room and board:** $11,120; **Room only:** $6440.

**UNDERGRADUATE FINANCIAL AID (Fall 2014, est.)** 1,057 applied for aid; of those 71% were deemed to have need. 100% of undergraduates with need received aid; of those 38% had need fully met. **Average percent of need met:** 78% (excluding resources awarded to replace EFC). **Average financial aid package:** $12,158 (excluding resources awarded to replace EFC). 9% of all full-time undergraduates had no need and received non-need-based gift aid.

**GIFT AID (NEED-BASED) Total amount:** $4,453,035 (26% federal, 11% state, 63% institutional). **Receiving aid:** All full-time undergraduates: 44% (613). **Average award:** Undergraduates: $8844. **Scholarships, grants, and awards:** Federal Pell, FSEOG, state, private, college/university gift aid from institutional funds.

**GIFT AID (NON-NEED-BASED) Total amount:** $1,428,766 (14% federal, 5% state, 21% institutional, 60% external sources). **Receiving aid:** Undergraduates: 10% (141). **Average award:** Undergraduates: $4008. **Scholarships, grants, and awards by category:** Academic interests/achievement: general academic interests/achievements. Special achievements/activities: leadership. Special characteristics: children and siblings of alumni, children of faculty/staff, ethnic background, local/state students, members of minority groups. **ROTC:** Army cooperative, Naval.

**LOANS Student loans:** $9,795,211 (29% need-based, 71% non-need-based). 78% of past graduating class borrowed through all loan programs. Average indebtedness per student: $37,582. **Average need-based loan:** Undergraduates: $4180. **Parent loans:** $1,682,630 (100% non-need-based). **Programs:** Federal Direct (Subsidized and Unsubsidized Stafford, PLUS).

**WORK-STUDY Federal work-study:** Total amount: $160,000; 450 jobs averaging $1500.

**APPLYING FOR FINANCIAL AID Required financial aid forms:** FAFSA, institution's own form. **Financial aid deadline (priority):** 5/1. **Notification date:** Continuous beginning 3/20.

**CONTACT** Ms. Catherine Kedski, Director of Financial Aid, Massachusetts Maritime Academy, 101 Academy Drive, Buzzards Bay, MA 02532, 508-830-5042 or toll-free 800-544-3411. Fax: 508-830-5077. E-mail: ckedski@maritime.edu. Website: http://www.maritime.edu/.

# THE MASTER'S COLLEGE AND SEMINARY
## Santa Clarita, CA

**Tuition & fees:** $29,860 | **Average undergraduate aid package:** $21,043

**ABOUT THE INSTITUTION** Independent nondenominational, coed. *Awards:* bachelor's, master's, and doctoral degrees. 47 undergraduate majors. *Total enrollment:* 1,515. Undergraduates: 1,137. Freshmen: 195. Federal methodology is used as a basis for awarding need-based institutional aid.

**UNDERGRADUATE EXPENSES for 2015–2016** *Application fee:* $40. *Comprehensive fee:* $39,580 includes full-time tuition ($29,440), mandatory fees ($420), and room and board ($9720). Full-time tuition and fees vary according to course load, degree level, and program. Room and board charges vary according to board plan. *Part-time tuition:* $1235 per credit hour. Part-time tuition and fees vary according to course load, degree level, and program.

**FRESHMAN FINANCIAL AID (Fall 2013)** 187 applied for aid; of those 87% were deemed to have need. 98% of freshmen with need received aid; of those 13% had need fully met. *Average percent of need met:* 67% (excluding resources awarded to replace EFC). *Average financial aid package:* $22,662 (excluding resources awarded to replace EFC). 20% of all full-time freshmen had no need and received non-need-based gift aid.

**UNDERGRADUATE FINANCIAL AID (Fall 2013)** 908 applied for aid; of those 89% were deemed to have need. 98% of undergraduates with need received aid; of those 14% had need fully met. *Average percent of need met:* 66% (excluding resources awarded to replace EFC). *Average financial aid package:* $21,043 (excluding resources awarded to replace EFC). 15% of all full-time undergraduates had no need and received non-need-based gift aid.

**GIFT AID (NEED-BASED)** *Total amount:* $12,319,343 (14% federal, 15% state, 53% institutional, 18% external sources). *Receiving aid:* Freshmen: 70% (159); all full-time undergraduates: 76% (781). *Average award:* Freshmen: $18,899; Undergraduates: $16,745. *Scholarships, grants, and awards:* Federal Pell, FSEOG, state, private, college/university gift aid from institutional funds.

**GIFT AID (NON-NEED-BASED)** *Total amount:* $2,319,540 (70% institutional, 30% external sources). *Receiving aid:* Freshmen: 6% (14). Undergraduates: 7% (69). *Average award:* Freshmen: $9396. Undergraduates: $9106. *Scholarships, grants, and awards by category: Academic interests/achievement:* 699 awards ($3,728,878 total): biological sciences, business, education, general academic interests/achievements, mathematics, physical sciences, religion/biblical studies, social sciences. *Creative arts/performance:* 78 awards ($242,870 total): music. *Special achievements/activities:* 18 awards ($231,000 total): leadership. *Special characteristics:* 262 awards ($1,287,489 total): children and siblings of alumni, children of faculty/staff, general special characteristics, international students, relatives of clergy. *Tuition waivers:* Full or partial for employees or children of employees. *ROTC:* Army cooperative, Air Force cooperative.

**LOANS** *Student loans:* $7,385,618 (78% need-based, 22% non-need-based). 61% of past graduating class borrowed through all loan programs. *Average indebtedness per student:* $26,442. *Average need-based loan:* Freshmen: $3423. Undergraduates: $4327. *Parent loans:* $1,611,602 (63% need-based, 37% non-need-based). *Programs:* Federal Direct (Subsidized and Unsubsidized Stafford, PLUS), Perkins, alternative loans.

**WORK-STUDY** *Federal work-study:* 62 jobs averaging $2602. *State or other work-study/employment:* Total amount: $635,600 (74% need-based, 26% non-need-based). 183 part-time jobs averaging $2359.

**ATHLETIC AWARDS** Total amount: $1,978,723 (59% need-based, 41% non-need-based).

**APPLYING FOR FINANCIAL AID** *Required financial aid forms:* FAFSA, institution's own form, state aid form. *Financial aid deadline (priority):* 3/2. *Notification date:* Continuous beginning 2/1. Students must reply by 5/1 or within 2 weeks of notification.

**CONTACT** Mr. Gary Edwards, Director of Financial Aid, The Master's College and Seminary, 21726 Placerita Canyon Road, Santa Clarita, CA 91321-1200, 661-362-2291 or toll-free 800-568-6248. Fax: 661-362-2693. E-mail: gedwards@masters.edu. Website: http://www.masters.edu/.

# MATER ECCLESIAE COLLEGE
## Greenville, RI

**CONTACT** Financial Aid Office, Mater Ecclesiae College, 60 Austin Avenue, Greenville, RI 02828, 401-949-2820. *Website:* http://www.mecollege.edu/.

# MAYVILLE STATE UNIVERSITY
## Mayville, ND

**Tuition & fees (ND res):** $6489 | **Average undergraduate aid package:** $14,270

**ABOUT THE INSTITUTION** State-supported, coed. *Awards:* associate and bachelor's degrees. 36 undergraduate majors. *Total enrollment:* 1,081. Undergraduates: 1,056. Freshmen: 174. Federal methodology is used as a basis for awarding need-based institutional aid.

**UNDERGRADUATE EXPENSES for 2015–2016** *Application fee:* $35. *One-time required fee:* $35. *Tuition, state resident:* full-time $4810; part-time $200 per credit hour. *Tuition, nonresident:* full-time $7215; part-time $300 per credit hour. *Required fees:* full-time $1679; $70 per credit hour. Full-time tuition and fees vary according to course load and reciprocity agreements. Part-time tuition and fees vary according to course load and reciprocity agreements. *College room and board:* $5430; *Room only:* $2044. Room and board charges vary according to board plan and housing facility.

**FRESHMAN FINANCIAL AID (Fall 2014, est.)** 155 applied for aid; of those 74% were deemed to have need. 100% of freshmen with need received aid; of those 26% had need fully met. *Average percent of need met:* 75% (excluding resources awarded to replace EFC). *Average financial aid package:* $13,827 (excluding resources awarded to replace EFC). 34% of all full-time freshmen had no need and received non-need-based gift aid.

**UNDERGRADUATE FINANCIAL AID (Fall 2014, est.)** 536 applied for aid; of those 74% were deemed to have need. 99% of undergraduates with need received aid; of those 34% had need fully met. *Average percent of need met:* 67% (excluding resources awarded to replace EFC). *Average financial aid package:* $14,270 (excluding resources awarded to replace EFC). 28% of all full-time undergraduates had no need and received non-need-based gift aid.

**GIFT AID (NEED-BASED)** *Total amount:* $1,825,058 (73% federal, 14% state, 8% institutional, 5% external sources). *Receiving aid:* Freshmen: 59% (100); all full-time undergraduates: 52% (333). *Average award:* Freshmen: $5008; Undergraduates: $4902. *Scholarships, grants, and awards:* Federal Pell, FSEOG, state, private, college/university gift aid from institutional funds.

**GIFT AID (NON-NEED-BASED)** *Total amount:* $206,472 (6% federal, 20% state, 38% institutional, 36% external sources). *Receiving aid:* Freshmen: 19% (32). Undergraduates: 12% (78). *Average award:* Freshmen: $1180. Undergraduates: $1057. *Scholarships, grants, and awards by category: Academic interests/achievement:* 262 awards ($224,425 total): biological sciences, business, communication, computer science, education, English, general academic interests/achievements, health fields, library science, mathematics, physical sciences, premedicine, social sciences. *Creative arts/performance:* 81 awards ($33,500 total): music, theater/drama. *Special characteristics:* 112 awards ($164,010 total): children of faculty/staff, international students, local/state students, members of minority groups, out-of-state students, veterans' children. *Tuition waivers:* Full or partial for minority students, employees or children of employees, senior citizens. *ROTC:* Army cooperative, Air Force cooperative.

**LOANS** *Student loans:* $4,072,821 (60% need-based, 40% non-need-based). 75% of past graduating class borrowed through all loan programs. *Average indebtedness per student:* $31,681. *Average need-based loan:* Freshmen: $5844. Undergraduates: $6324. *Parent loans:* $339,548 (25% need-based, 75% non-need-based). *Programs:* Federal Direct (Subsidized and Unsubsidized Stafford, PLUS), Perkins, Federal Nursing, college/university.

**WORK-STUDY** *Federal work-study:* Total amount: $55,720; 66 jobs averaging $1096.

**ATHLETIC AWARDS** Total amount: $223,045 (71% need-based, 29% non-need-based).

**APPLYING FOR FINANCIAL AID** *Required financial aid form:* FAFSA. *Financial aid deadline (priority):* 2/15. *Notification date:* Continuous beginning 5/1. Students must reply within 2 weeks of notification.

**CONTACT** Ms. Shirley Hanson, Director of Financial Aid, Mayville State University, 330 3rd Street NE, Mayville, ND 58257-1299, 701-788-4767 or toll-free 800-437-4104. *Fax:* 701-788-4818. *E-mail:* shirley.m.hanson@mayvillestate.edu. *Website:* http://www.mayvillestate.edu/.

# McDANIEL COLLEGE
## Westminster, MD

| Tuition & fees: $38,350 | Average undergraduate aid package: $33,346 |
|---|---|

**ABOUT THE INSTITUTION** Independent, coed. *Awards:* certificates, bachelor's, and master's degrees. 34 undergraduate majors. *Total enrollment:* 3,187. Undergraduates: 1,706. Freshmen: 412. Federal methodology is used as a basis for awarding need-based institutional aid.

**UNDERGRADUATE EXPENSES for 2015–2016** *Application fee:* $50. *Comprehensive fee:* $47,450 includes full-time tuition ($38,350) and room and board ($9100). *College room only:* $4550. Full-time tuition and fees vary according to course load. Room and board charges vary according to board plan and housing facility. *Part-time tuition:* $1198 per credit hour. Part-time tuition and fees vary according to course load and reciprocity agreements. *Payment plan:* Tuition prepayment.

**FRESHMAN FINANCIAL AID (Fall 2014, est.)** 372 applied for aid; of those 88% were deemed to have need. 100% of freshmen with need received aid; of those 27% had need fully met. *Average percent of need met:* 90% (excluding resources awarded to replace EFC). *Average financial aid package:* $35,043 (excluding resources awarded to replace EFC). 20% of all full-time freshmen had no need and received non-need-based gift aid.

**UNDERGRADUATE FINANCIAL AID (Fall 2014, est.)** 1,353 applied for aid; of those 91% were deemed to have need. 100% of undergraduates with need received aid; of those 22% had need fully met. *Average percent of need met:* 86% (excluding resources awarded to replace EFC). *Average financial aid package:* $33,346 (excluding resources awarded to replace EFC). 23% of all full-time undergraduates had no need and received non-need-based gift aid.

**GIFT AID (NEED-BASED)** *Total amount:* $31,499,966 (8% federal, 7% state, 85% institutional). *Receiving aid:* Freshmen: 80% (328); all full-time undergraduates: 75% (1,231). *Average award:* Freshmen: $31,330; Undergraduates: $28,872. *Scholarships, grants, and awards:* Federal Pell, FSEOG, state, private, college/university gift aid from institutional funds.

**GIFT AID (NON-NEED-BASED)** *Total amount:* $8,065,065 (4% state, 93% institutional, 3% external sources). *Receiving aid:* Freshmen: 14% (58). Undergraduates: 11% (180). *Average award:* Freshmen: $18,040. Undergraduates: $17,988. *Scholarships, grants, and awards by category:* Academic interests/achievement: general academic interests/achievements. *Special achievements/activities:* junior miss, leadership. *Special characteristics:* general special characteristics, local/state students, previous college experience, siblings of current students, veterans. *Tuition waivers:* Full or partial for employees or children of employees. *ROTC:* Army.

**LOANS** *Student loans:* $9,897,948 (45% need-based, 55% non-need-based). 68% of past graduating class borrowed through all loan programs. *Average indebtedness per student:* $31,568. *Average need-based loan:* Freshmen: $3927. Undergraduates: $4747. *Parent loans:* $3,030,341 (100% non-need-based). *Programs:* Federal Direct (Subsidized and Unsubsidized Stafford, PLUS), Perkins, college/university.

**WORK-STUDY** *Federal work-study:* Total amount: $382,882; jobs available. *State or other work-study/employment:* Total amount: $210,882 (100% non-need-based). Part-time jobs available.

**APPLYING FOR FINANCIAL AID** *Required financial aid forms:* FAFSA, institution's own form, federal income tax form(s). *Financial aid deadline (priority):* 3/1. *Notification date:* Continuous beginning 3/1. Students must reply by 5/1 or within 2 weeks of notification.

**CONTACT** Ms. Caroline Bright, Financial Aid Office, McDaniel College, 2 College Hill, Westminster, MD 21157-4390, 410-857-2233 or toll-free 800-638-5005. *Fax:* 410-857-2729. *E-mail:* finaid@mcdaniel.edu. *Website:* http://www.mcdaniel.edu/.

# McKENDREE UNIVERSITY
## Lebanon, IL

| Tuition & fees: $27,930 | Average undergraduate aid package: $20,754 |
|---|---|

**ABOUT THE INSTITUTION** Independent United Methodist Church, coed. *Awards:* certificates, associate, bachelor's, master's, and doctoral degrees. 64 undergraduate majors. *Total enrollment:* 3,131. Undergraduates: 2,521. Freshmen: 421. Federal methodology is used as a basis for awarding need-based institutional aid.

**UNDERGRADUATE EXPENSES for 2015–2016** *Comprehensive fee:* $36,950 includes full-time tuition ($26,930), mandatory fees ($1000), and room and board ($9020). *College room only:* $4820. Full-time tuition and fees vary according to course load, degree level, and location. Room and board charges vary according to board plan and housing facility. *Part-time tuition:* $870 per credit hour. Part-time tuition and fees vary according to course load, degree level, and location.

**FRESHMAN FINANCIAL AID (Fall 2014, est.)** 384 applied for aid; of those 92% were deemed to have need. 100% of freshmen with need received aid; of those 24% had need fully met. *Average percent of need met:* 82% (excluding resources awarded to replace EFC). *Average financial aid package:* $24,083 (excluding resources awarded to replace EFC). 12% of all full-time freshmen had no need and received non-need-based gift aid.

**UNDERGRADUATE FINANCIAL AID (Fall 2014, est.)** 1,531 applied for aid; of those 92% were deemed to have need. 99% of undergraduates with need received aid; of those 20% had need fully met. *Average percent of need met:* 75% (excluding resources awarded to replace EFC). *Average financial aid package:* $20,754 (excluding resources awarded to replace EFC). 14% of all full-time undergraduates had no need and received non-need-based gift aid.

**GIFT AID (NEED-BASED)** *Total amount:* $21,915,195 (18% federal, 13% state, 64% institutional, 5% external sources). *Receiving aid:* Freshmen: 88% (352); all full-time undergraduates: 79% (1,336). *Average award:* Freshmen: $20,478; Undergraduates: $17,344. *Scholarships, grants, and awards:* Federal Pell, FSEOG, state, private, college/university gift aid from institutional funds.

**GIFT AID (NON-NEED-BASED)** *Total amount:* $3,456,334 (1% state, 88% institutional, 11% external sources). *Receiving aid:* Freshmen: 15% (59). Undergraduates: 10% (166). *Average award:* Freshmen: $13,347. Undergraduates: $11,109. *Scholarships, grants, and awards by category:* Academic interests/achievement: 1,026 awards ($7,699,645 total): biological sciences, business, general academic interests/achievements, religion/biblical studies. *Creative arts/performance:* 153 awards ($629,456 total): dance, debating, music. *Special achievements/activities:* 377 awards ($1,665,120 total): cheerleading/drum major, community service, leadership. *Special characteristics:* 237 awards ($644,498 total): children and siblings of alumni, children of faculty/staff, general special characteristics, international students, religious affiliation, veterans, veterans' children. *Tuition waivers:* Full or partial for children of alumni, employees or children of employees. *ROTC:* Army cooperative, Air Force cooperative.

**LOANS** *Student loans:* $12,228,101 (75% need-based, 25% non-need-based). 83% of past graduating class borrowed through all loan programs. *Average indebtedness per student:* $21,731. *Average need-based loan:* Freshmen: $3304. Undergraduates: $4165. *Parent loans:* $3,500,980 (32% need-based, 68% non-need-based). *Programs:* Federal Direct (Subsidized and Unsubsidized Stafford, PLUS), Perkins.

**WORK-STUDY** *Federal work-study:* Total amount: $1,120,920; 893 jobs averaging $1255. *State or other work-study/employment:* Total amount: $68,360 (100% non-need-based). 65 part-time jobs averaging $1052.

**ATHLETIC AWARDS** *Total amount:* $4,076,500 (54% need-based, 46% non-need-based).

**APPLYING FOR FINANCIAL AID** *Required financial aid form:* FAFSA. *Financial aid deadline (priority):* 5/31. *Notification date:* Continuous beginning 3/1.

**CONTACT** Elizabeth L. Juehne, Director of Financial Aid, McKendree University, 701 College Road, Lebanon, IL 62254-1299, 618-537-6532 or toll-free 800-232-7228. *Fax:* 618-537-6530. *E-mail:* bjuehne@mckendree.edu. *Website:* http://www.mckendree.edu/.

# McMURRY UNIVERSITY
## Abilene, TX

| Tuition & fees: $24,844 | Average undergraduate aid package: $19,729 |
|---|---|

**ABOUT THE INSTITUTION** Independent United Methodist, coed. *Awards:* bachelor's and master's degrees. 46 undergraduate majors. *Total enrollment:* 1,007. Undergraduates: 1,003. Freshmen: 208. Federal methodology is used as a basis for awarding need-based institutional aid.

**UNDERGRADUATE EXPENSES for 2015–2016** *Application fee:* $25. *One-time required fee:* $175. *Comprehensive fee:* $32,832 includes full-time tuition ($24,844) and room and board ($7988). *College room only:* $3886. Full-time tuition and fees vary according to course load. Room and board charges vary according to board plan and housing facility. *Part-time tuition:* $776 per credit hour. Part-time tuition and fees vary according to course load.

**FRESHMAN FINANCIAL AID (Fall 2013)** 218 applied for aid; of those 89% were deemed to have need. 100% of freshmen with need received aid; of those 14% had need fully met. *Average percent of need met:* 68% (excluding resources awarded to replace EFC). *Average financial aid package:* $20,495 (excluding resources awarded to replace EFC). 26% of all full-time freshmen had no need and received non-need-based gift aid.

**UNDERGRADUATE FINANCIAL AID (Fall 2013)** 982 applied for aid; of those 92% were deemed to have need. 100% of undergraduates with need received aid; of those 15% had need fully met. *Average percent of need met:* 64% (excluding resources awarded to replace EFC). *Average financial aid package:* $19,729 (excluding resources awarded to replace EFC). 10% of all full-time undergraduates had no need and received non-need-based gift aid.

**GIFT AID (NEED-BASED)** *Total amount:* $12,997,387 (19% federal, 12% state, 64% institutional, 5% external sources). *Receiving aid:* Freshmen: 78% (193); all full-time undergraduates: 74% (900). *Average award:* Freshmen: $16,909; Undergraduates: $14,809. *Scholarships, grants, and awards:* Federal Pell, FSEOG, state, private, college/university gift aid from institutional funds.

**GIFT AID (NON-NEED-BASED)** *Total amount:* $1,672,222 (96% institutional, 4% external sources). *Receiving aid:* Freshmen: 7% (17). Undergraduates: 7% (88). *Average award:* Freshmen: $8332. Undergraduates: $8503. *Scholarships, grants, and awards by category:* Academic interests/achievement: 428 awards ($2,777,208 total): biological sciences, business, computer science, education, English, foreign languages, general academic interests/achievements, mathematics, physical sciences, premedicine, religion/biblical studies, social sciences. *Creative arts/performance:* 54 awards ($110,400 total): art/fine arts, music, theater/drama. *Special achievements/activities:* 143 awards ($2,097,554 total): general special achievements/activities. *Special characteristics:* 294 awards ($1,828,865 total): children of faculty/staff, ethnic background, general special characteristics, international students, local/state students, out-of-state students, previous college experience, relatives of clergy, religious affiliation. *Tuition waivers:* Full or partial for employees or children of employees.

**LOANS** *Student loans:* $7,486,279 (51% need-based, 49% non-need-based). 90% of past graduating class borrowed through all loan programs. *Average indebtedness per student:* $34,742. *Average need-based loan:* Freshmen: $3323. Undergraduates: $4660. *Parent loans:* $876,425 (89% need-based, 11% non-need-based). *Programs:* Federal Direct (Subsidized and Unsubsidized Stafford, PLUS), Perkins, state, alternative loans, Bonner Price Loans, United Methodist Student Loans.

**WORK-STUDY** *Federal work-study:* 147 jobs averaging $1635. *State or other work-study/employment:* Total amount: $93,570 (12% need-based, 88% non-need-based). 56 part-time jobs averaging $1670.

**APPLYING FOR FINANCIAL AID** *Required financial aid form:* FAFSA. *Financial aid deadline (priority):* 3/15. *Notification date:* Continuous beginning 2/15. Students must reply within 3 weeks of notification.

**CONTACT** Mrs. Lori Eilene Herrick, Director of Financial Aid, McMurry University, #1 McMurry University Box 908, Abilene, TX 79697, 325-793-4978 or toll-free 800-460-2392. *Fax:* 325-793-4718. *E-mail:* herrick.lori@mcm.edu.
*Website:* http://www.mcm.edu/.

# McNALLY SMITH COLLEGE OF MUSIC
## Saint Paul, MN

| Tuition & fees: $25,210 | Average undergraduate aid package: $10,708 |
|---|---|

**ABOUT THE INSTITUTION** Proprietary, coed. *Awards:* diplomas, associate, bachelor's, and master's degrees. 9 undergraduate majors. *Total enrollment:* 568. Undergraduates: 548. Freshmen: 101. Federal methodology is used as a basis for awarding need-based institutional aid.

**UNDERGRADUATE EXPENSES for 2015–2016** *Application fee:* $75. *Comprehensive fee:* $30,310 includes full-time tuition ($24,310), mandatory fees ($900), and room and board ($5100). *College room only:* $3900. Full-time tuition and fees vary according to course load and program. Room and board charges vary according to board plan. *Part-time tuition:* $935 per credit. *Part-time fees:* $450 per term. Part-time tuition and fees vary according to course load and program. *Payment plan:* Tuition prepayment.

**FRESHMAN FINANCIAL AID (Fall 2013)** 67 applied for aid; of those 91% were deemed to have need. 95% of freshmen with need received aid. *Average percent of need met:* 33% (excluding resources awarded to replace EFC). *Average financial aid package:* $9112 (excluding resources awarded to replace EFC). 1% of all full-time freshmen had no need and received non-need-based gift aid.

**UNDERGRADUATE FINANCIAL AID (Fall 2013)** 331 applied for aid; of those 96% were deemed to have need. 95% of undergraduates with need received aid. *Average percent of need met:* 33% (excluding resources awarded to replace EFC). *Average financial aid package:* $10,708 (excluding resources awarded to replace EFC). 2% of all full-time undergraduates had no need and received non-need-based gift aid.

**GIFT AID (NEED-BASED)** *Total amount:* $1,555,296 (54% federal, 25% state, 21% institutional). *Receiving aid:* Freshmen: 35% (28); all full-time undergraduates: 33% (132). *Average award:* Freshmen: $7316; Undergraduates: $6703. *Scholarships, grants, and awards:* Federal Pell, FSEOG, state, private, college/university gift aid from institutional funds.

**GIFT AID (NON-NEED-BASED)** *Total amount:* $1,015,329 (26% federal, 68% institutional, 6% external sources). *Receiving aid:* Freshmen: 21% (17). Undergraduates: 23% (92). *Average award:* Freshmen: $7000. Undergraduates: $8927. *Scholarships, grants, and awards by category:* Creative arts/performance: 100 awards ($698,323 total): music. *Special characteristics:* 8 awards ($81,790 total): children of faculty/staff, veterans, veterans' children. *Tuition waivers:* Full or partial for employees or children of employees.

**LOANS** *Student loans:* $6,042,825 (29% need-based, 71% non-need-based). 88% of past graduating class borrowed through all loan programs. *Average indebtedness per student:* $46,230. *Average need-based loan:* Freshmen: $3530. Undergraduates: $4527. *Parent loans:* $1,846,769 (100% non-need-based). *Programs:* Federal Direct (Subsidized and Unsubsidized Stafford, PLUS), state, private loans.

**WORK-STUDY** *Federal work-study:* 31 jobs averaging $1954. *State or other work-study/employment:* Total amount: $31,935 (100% need-based). 21 part-time jobs averaging $1521.

**APPLYING FOR FINANCIAL AID** *Required financial aid form:* FAFSA. *Financial aid deadline:* 8/1 (priority: 5/1). *Notification date:* Continuous beginning 3/15. Students must reply by 5/1 or within 2 weeks of notification.

**CONTACT** Neil Leibundguth, Financial Aid Administrator, McNally Smith College of Music, 19 Exchange Street East, St. Paul, MN 55101-2220, 651-361-3324 or toll-free 800-594-9500. *Fax:* 651-291-0366. *E-mail:* neil.leibundguth@mcnallysmith.edu.
*Website:* http://www.mcnallysmith.edu/.

# McNEESE STATE UNIVERSITY
## Lake Charles, LA

**CONTACT** Ms. Taina J. Savoit, Director of Financial Aid, McNeese State University, PO Box 93260, Lake Charles, LA 70609-3260, 337-475-5065 or toll-free 800-622-3352. *Fax:* 337-475-5068. *E-mail:* financialaid@mcneese.edu.
*Website:* http://www.mcneese.edu/.

# McPHERSON COLLEGE
## McPherson, KS

**ABOUT THE INSTITUTION** Independent Church of the Brethren, coed. *Awards:* bachelor's and master's degrees. 28 undergraduate majors. *Total enrollment:* 656. Undergraduates: 637. Freshmen: 170.

**GIFT AID (NEED-BASED)** *Scholarships, grants, and awards:* Federal Pell, FSEOG, state, private, college/university gift aid from institutional funds.

**GIFT AID (NON-NEED-BASED)** *Scholarships, grants, and awards by category:* Academic interests/achievement: general academic interests/achievements. *Creative arts/performance:* art/fine arts, music, performing arts, theater/drama. *Special achievements/activities:* cheerleading/drum major, community service. *Special characteristics:* children and siblings of alumni, religious affiliation.

**LOANS** *Programs:* Federal Direct (Subsidized and Unsubsidized Stafford, PLUS), Perkins.

**APPLYING FOR FINANCIAL AID** *Required financial aid forms:* FAFSA, state aid form.

**CONTACT** Ms. Brenda Krehbiel, Director of Financial Aid, McPherson College, 1600 East Euclid, McPherson, KS 67460-1402, 620-242-0400 Ext. 2415 or toll-free 800-365-7402. *Fax:* 620-241-8443. *E-mail:* krehbieb2@mcpherson.edu. *Website:* http://www.mcpherson.edu/.

# MCPHS UNIVERSITY
## Boston, MA

| Tuition & fees: $30,530 | Average undergraduate aid package: $14,078 |
|---|---|

**ABOUT THE INSTITUTION** Independent, coed. *Awards:* certificates, bachelor's, master's, and doctoral degrees. 12 undergraduate majors. *Total enrollment:* 6,935. Undergraduates: 4,338. Freshmen: 875. Federal methodology is used as a basis for awarding need-based institutional aid.

**UNDERGRADUATE EXPENSES for 2015–2016** *Comprehensive fee:* $45,770 includes full-time tuition ($29,600), mandatory fees ($930), and room and board ($15,240). *College room only:* $12,100. Full-time tuition and fees vary according to course load, degree level, location, program, and student level. Room and board charges vary according to board plan, housing facility, and location. *Part-time tuition:* $1090 per credit. *Part-time fees:* $245 per term.

**FRESHMAN FINANCIAL AID (Fall 2013)** 768 applied for aid; of those 92% were deemed to have need. 98% of freshmen with need received aid; of those 6% had need fully met. *Average percent of need met:* 45% (excluding resources awarded to replace EFC). *Average financial aid package:* $16,330 (excluding resources awarded to replace EFC). 6% of all full-time freshmen had no need and received non-need-based gift aid.

**UNDERGRADUATE FINANCIAL AID (Fall 2013)** 3,046 applied for aid; of those 94% were deemed to have need. 99% of undergraduates with need received aid; of those 4% had need fully met. *Average percent of need met:* 33% (excluding resources awarded to replace EFC). *Average financial aid package:* $14,078 (excluding resources awarded to replace EFC). 4% of all full-time undergraduates had no need and received non-need-based gift aid.

**GIFT AID (NEED-BASED)** *Total amount:* $27,313,125 (10% federal, 4% state, 83% institutional, 3% external sources). *Receiving aid:* Freshmen: 50% (455); all full-time undergraduates: 69% (2,687). *Average award:* Freshmen: $8569; Undergraduates: $7540. *Scholarships, grants, and awards:* Federal Pell, FSEOG, state, private, college/university gift aid from institutional funds.

**GIFT AID (NON-NEED-BASED)** *Receiving aid:* Freshmen: 42% (381). Undergraduates: 41% (1,614). *Average award:* Freshmen: $10,621. Undergraduates: $8508. *Scholarships, grants, and awards by category:* Academic interests/achievement: general academic interests/achievements. *Special characteristics:* children of faculty/staff. *Tuition waivers:* Full or partial for employees or children of employees.

**LOANS** *Student loans:* $44,878,052 (33% need-based, 67% non-need-based). 78% of past graduating class borrowed through all loan programs. *Average indebtedness per student:* $14,618. *Average need-based loan:* Freshmen: $5767. Undergraduates: $5751. *Parent loans:* $13,487,161 (100% need-based). *Programs:* Federal Direct (Subsidized and Unsubsidized Stafford, PLUS), Perkins, Health Professions Student Loans (HPSL).

**WORK-STUDY** *Federal work-study:* jobs available.

**APPLYING FOR FINANCIAL AID** *Required financial aid form:* FAFSA. *Financial aid deadline (priority):* 3/15. *Notification date:* Continuous. Students must reply by 5/1 or within 2 weeks of notification.

**CONTACT** Elizabeth Goreham, Director of Student Financial Services, MCPHS University, 179 Longwood Avenue, Boston, MA 02115-5896, 617-879-5986. *E-mail:* elizabeth.goreham@mcphs.edu. *Website:* http://www.mcphs.edu/.

# MEDAILLE COLLEGE
## Buffalo, NY

**ABOUT THE INSTITUTION** Independent, coed. *Awards:* certificates, associate, bachelor's, master's, and doctoral degrees. 22 undergraduate majors. *Total enrollment:* 2,383. Undergraduates: 1,803. Freshmen: 438.

**GIFT AID (NEED-BASED)** *Scholarships, grants, and awards:* Federal Pell, FSEOG, state, private, college/university gift aid from institutional funds.

**GIFT AID (NON-NEED-BASED)** *Scholarships, grants, and awards by category:* Academic interests/achievement: biological sciences, business, communication, education, general academic interests/achievements, mathematics. *Creative arts/performance:* general creative arts/performance. *Special characteristics:* adult students, children of faculty/staff.

**LOANS** *Programs:* Federal Direct (Subsidized and Unsubsidized Stafford, PLUS), state.

**APPLYING FOR FINANCIAL AID** *Required financial aid forms:* FAFSA, institution's own form, state aid form.

**CONTACT** Ms. Catherine Buzanski, Director of Financial Aid, Medaille College, 18 Agassiz Circle, Buffalo, NY 14214-2695, 716-880-2179 or toll-free 800-292-1582. *Fax:* 716-884-0291. *E-mail:* cbuzanski@medaille.edu. *Website:* http://www.medaille.edu/.

# MEDGAR EVERS COLLEGE OF THE CITY UNIVERSITY OF NEW YORK
## Brooklyn, NY

| Tuition & fees (NY res): $6332 | Average undergraduate aid package: $6973 |
|---|---|

**ABOUT THE INSTITUTION** State and locally supported, coed. *Awards:* certificates, associate, and bachelor's degrees. 15 undergraduate majors. *Total enrollment:* 6,701. Undergraduates: 6,701. Freshmen: 1,100. Federal methodology is used as a basis for awarding need-based institutional aid.

**UNDERGRADUATE EXPENSES for 2015–2016** *Application fee:* $65. *Tuition, state resident:* full-time $6030; part-time $260 per credit. *Tuition, nonresident:* full-time $16,050; part-time $535 per credit. *Required fees:* full-time $302; $100.85 per term. Full-time tuition and fees vary according to course load. Part-time tuition and fees vary according to course load.

**FRESHMAN FINANCIAL AID (Fall 2013)** 879 applied for aid; of those 100% were deemed to have need. 100% of freshmen with need received aid. *Average financial aid package:* $7914 (excluding resources awarded to replace EFC).

**UNDERGRADUATE FINANCIAL AID (Fall 2013)** 3,741 applied for aid; of those 100% were deemed to have need. 100% of undergraduates with need received aid. *Average financial aid package:* $6973 (excluding resources awarded to replace EFC).

**GIFT AID (NEED-BASED)** *Total amount:* $27,266,320 (62% federal, 38% state). *Receiving aid:* Freshmen: 82% (858); all full-time undergraduates: 83% (3,558). *Average award:* Freshmen: $7459; Undergraduates: $6973. *Scholarships, grants, and awards:* Federal Pell, FSEOG, state, private, college/university gift aid from institutional funds, Thurgood Marshall Scholarship Fund.

**GIFT AID (NON-NEED-BASED)** *Scholarships, grants, and awards by category:* Academic interests/achievement: general academic interests/achievements.

**LOANS** *Student loans:* $4,445,006 (100% need-based). *Average need-based loan:* Freshmen: $3884. Undergraduates: $4665. *Programs:* Federal Direct (Subsidized and Unsubsidized Stafford, PLUS), Perkins.

**WORK-STUDY** *Federal work-study:* jobs available.

**APPLYING FOR FINANCIAL AID** *Required financial aid forms:* FAFSA, state aid form, University Financial Aid Information Supplemental Request (FASIR). *Financial aid deadline (priority):* 1/2. *Notification date:* Continuous beginning 4/1. Students must reply within 3 weeks of notification.

**CONTACT** Nigel Thompson, Director of Financial Aid, Medgar Evers College of the City University of New York, 1650 Bedford Avenue, Brooklyn, NY 11225, 718-270-6038. *Fax:* 718-270-6194. *E-mail:* nigel.thompson@mec.cuny.edu. *Website:* http://www.mec.cuny.edu/.

## MEDICAL UNIVERSITY OF SOUTH CAROLINA
### Charleston, SC

| Tuition & fees: N/R | Average undergraduate aid package: $8164 |
|---|---|

**ABOUT THE INSTITUTION** State-supported, coed. *Awards:* certificates, bachelor's, master's, and doctoral degrees. 2 undergraduate majors. *Total enrollment:* 2,775. Undergraduates: 205. Federal methodology is used as a basis for awarding need-based institutional aid.

**UNDERGRADUATE FINANCIAL AID (Fall 2014, est.)** 169 applied for aid; of those 92% were deemed to have need. 98% of undergraduates with need received aid; of those 1% had need fully met. *Average percent of need met:* 24% (excluding resources awarded to replace EFC). *Average financial aid package:* $8164 (excluding resources awarded to replace EFC).

**GIFT AID (NEED-BASED)** *Total amount:* $345,032 (21% federal, 5% state, 73% institutional, 1% external sources). *Receiving aid:* All full-time undergraduates: 31% (62). *Average award:* Undergraduates: $5067. *Scholarships, grants, and awards:* Federal Pell, FSEOG, state, private, college/university gift aid from institutional funds, Federal Nursing, Scholarships for Disadvantaged Students (SDS).

**GIFT AID (NON-NEED-BASED)** *Total amount:* $104,527 (27% federal, 57% state, 6% institutional, 10% external sources). *Receiving aid:* Undergraduates: 8% (17). *Scholarships, grants, and awards by category:* Academic interests/achievement: general academic interests/achievements, health fields. *Special characteristics:* ethnic background, general special characteristics, local/state students, members of minority groups. *ROTC:* Air Force cooperative.

**LOANS** *Student loans:* $3,563,211 (22% need-based, 78% non-need-based). *Average need-based loan:* Undergraduates: $5397. *Programs:* Federal Direct (Subsidized and Unsubsidized Stafford, PLUS), Perkins, Federal Nursing, state, alternative loans, Health Professions Student Loans (HPSL), Loans for Disadvantaged Students program, Primary Care Loans.

**WORK-STUDY** *Federal work-study:* Total amount: $16,078; jobs available.

**APPLYING FOR FINANCIAL AID** *Required financial aid form:* FAFSA. *Notification date:* Continuous.

**CONTACT** Mr. Joseph M. DuRant, Director for Financial Aid Services, Medical University of South Carolina, 45 Courtenay Drive, Charleston, SC 29425, 843-792-2252. *Fax:* 843-792-6356. *E-mail:* durantjm@musc.edu. *Website:* http://www.musc.edu/.

## MEMPHIS COLLEGE OF ART
### Memphis, TN

**ABOUT THE INSTITUTION** Independent, coed. *Awards:* bachelor's and master's degrees. 6 undergraduate majors. *Total enrollment:* 435. Undergraduates: 366. Freshmen: 100.

**GIFT AID (NEED-BASED)** *Scholarships, grants, and awards:* Federal Pell, FSEOG, state, private, college/university gift aid from institutional funds.

**GIFT AID (NON-NEED-BASED)** *Scholarships, grants, and awards by category:* Creative arts/performance: applied art and design, art/fine arts. *Special characteristics:* children of faculty/staff, previous college experience.

**LOANS** *Programs:* Federal Direct (Subsidized and Unsubsidized Stafford, PLUS), college/university.

**WORK-STUDY** *Federal work-study:* 117 jobs averaging $500. *State or other work-study/employment:* Total amount: $13,701 (12% need-based, 88% non-need-based). 32 part-time jobs averaging $500.

**APPLYING FOR FINANCIAL AID** *Required financial aid form:* FAFSA.

**CONTACT** Aaron White, Director of Financial Aid, Memphis College of Art, 1930 Poplar Avenue, Overton Park, Memphis, TN 38104, 901-272-5136 or toll-free 800-727-1088. *Fax:* 901-272-5134. *E-mail:* awhite@mca.edu. *Website:* http://www.mca.edu/.

## MENLO COLLEGE
### Atherton, CA

| Tuition & fees: $38,750 | Average undergraduate aid package: $28,874 |
|---|---|

**ABOUT THE INSTITUTION** Independent, coed. *Awards:* bachelor's degrees. 10 undergraduate majors. *Total enrollment:* 772. Undergraduates: 772. Freshmen: 194. Federal methodology is used as a basis for awarding need-based institutional aid.

**UNDERGRADUATE EXPENSES for 2015–2016** *Application fee:* $40. *Comprehensive fee:* $51,380 includes full-time tuition ($38,100), mandatory fees ($650), and room and board ($12,630). Room and board charges vary according to housing facility. *Part-time tuition:* $1588 per credit.

**FRESHMAN FINANCIAL AID (Fall 2014, est.)** 156 applied for aid; of those 87% were deemed to have need. 100% of freshmen with need received aid; of those 10% had need fully met. *Average percent of need met:* 64% (excluding resources awarded to replace EFC). *Average financial aid package:* $27,990 (excluding resources awarded to replace EFC). 26% of all full-time freshmen had no need and received non-need-based gift aid.

**UNDERGRADUATE FINANCIAL AID (Fall 2014, est.)** 522 applied for aid; of those 92% were deemed to have need. 99% of undergraduates with need received aid; of those 11% had need fully met. *Average percent of need met:* 66% (excluding resources awarded to replace EFC). *Average financial aid package:* $28,874 (excluding resources awarded to replace EFC). 22% of all full-time undergraduates had no need and received non-need-based gift aid.

**GIFT AID (NEED-BASED)** *Total amount:* $136,838,704 (1% federal, 95% state, 4% institutional). *Receiving aid:* Freshmen: 60% (136); all full-time undergraduates: 63% (473). *Average award:* Freshmen: $24,873; Undergraduates: $25,073. *Scholarships, grants, and awards:* Federal Pell, FSEOG, state, college/university gift aid from institutional funds.

**GIFT AID (NON-NEED-BASED)** *Total amount:* $2,459,602 (6% federal, 92% institutional, 2% external sources). *Receiving aid:* Freshmen: 5% (12). Undergraduates: 6% (46). *Average award:* Freshmen: $13,330. Undergraduates: $12,737. *Scholarships, grants, and awards by category:* Academic interests/achievement: 735 awards ($2,258,840 total): general academic interests/achievements. *Tuition waivers:* Full or partial for employees or children of employees.

**LOANS** *Student loans:* $3,884,777 (81% need-based, 19% non-need-based). 77% of past graduating class borrowed through all loan programs. *Average indebtedness per student:* $29,943. *Average need-based loan:* Freshmen: $2275. Undergraduates: $3741. *Parent loans:* $2,325,894 (57% need-based, 43% non-need-based). *Programs:* Federal Direct (Subsidized and Unsubsidized Stafford, PLUS).

**WORK-STUDY** *Federal work-study:* Total amount: $297,037; 345 jobs averaging $1024.

**ATHLETIC AWARDS** Total amount: $5,850,890 (73% need-based, 27% non-need-based).

**APPLYING FOR FINANCIAL AID** *Required financial aid forms:* FAFSA, state aid form. *Financial aid deadline (priority):* 3/2. *Notification date:* Continuous beginning 4/1.

**CONTACT** Jessica Ayers, Director of Financial Aid, Menlo College, 1000 El Camino Real, Atherton, CA 94027-4301, 650-543-3880 or toll-free 800-556-3656. *Fax:* 650-543-4103. *E-mail:* financialaid@menlo.edu. *Website:* http://www.menlo.edu/.

# MERCER UNIVERSITY
## Macon, GA

| Tuition & fees: $33,780 | Average undergraduate aid package: $32,468 |
|---|---|

**ABOUT THE INSTITUTION** Independent Baptist, coed. *Awards:* certificates, bachelor's, master's, and doctoral degrees. 55 undergraduate majors. *Total enrollment:* 6,729. Undergraduates: 2,747. Freshmen: 807. Federal methodology is used as a basis for awarding need-based institutional aid.

**UNDERGRADUATE EXPENSES for 2015–2016 Application fee:** $50. *Comprehensive fee:* $44,458 includes full-time tuition ($33,480), mandatory fees ($300), and room and board ($10,678). *College room only:* $4880. Full-time tuition and fees vary according to location. Room and board charges vary according to board plan, housing facility, location, and student level. *Part-time tuition:* $1116 per credit hour. *Part-time fees:* $10 per credit hour. Part-time tuition and fees vary according to course load and location.

**FRESHMAN FINANCIAL AID (Fall 2014, est.)** 804 applied for aid; of those 74% were deemed to have need. 100% of freshmen with need received aid; of those 42% had need fully met. *Average percent of need met:* 87% (excluding resources awarded to replace EFC). *Average financial aid package:* $34,847 (excluding resources awarded to replace EFC). 23% of all full-time freshmen had no need and received non-need-based gift aid.

**UNDERGRADUATE FINANCIAL AID (Fall 2014, est.)** 2,604 applied for aid; of those 74% were deemed to have need. 100% of undergraduates with need received aid; of those 35% had need fully met. *Average percent of need met:* 82% (excluding resources awarded to replace EFC). *Average financial aid package:* $32,468 (excluding resources awarded to replace EFC). 24% of all full-time undergraduates had no need and received non-need-based gift aid.

**GIFT AID (NEED-BASED) Total amount:** $42,591,151 (10% federal, 9% state, 79% institutional, 2% external sources). *Receiving aid:* Freshmen: 74% (596); all full-time undergraduates: 42% (1,092). *Average award:* Freshmen: $25,370; Undergraduates: $24,043. *Scholarships, grants, and awards:* Federal Pell, FSEOG, state, college/university gift aid from institutional funds, Federal Nursing.

**GIFT AID (NON-NEED-BASED) Total amount:** $17,486,596 (15% state, 84% institutional, 1% external sources). *Receiving aid:* Freshmen: 31% (252). Undergraduates: 25% (657). *Average award:* Freshmen: $19,406. Undergraduates: $19,145. *Scholarships, grants, and awards by category: Academic interests/ achievement:* biological sciences, business, education, engineering/technologies, English, foreign languages, general academic interests/achievements, international studies, military science, religion/biblical studies. *Creative arts/performance:* art/fine arts, debating, music, theater/drama. *Special achievements/activities:* community service, general special achievements/activities, leadership. *Special characteristics:* adult students, children of faculty/staff, children of public servants, general special characteristics, international students, relatives of clergy, siblings of current students. *Tuition waivers:* Full or partial for employees or children of employees. *ROTC:* Army.

**LOANS Student loans:** $11,419,447 (74% need-based, 26% non-need-based). 64% of past graduating class borrowed through all loan programs. *Average indebtedness per student:* $30,018. *Average need-based loan:* Freshmen: $9318. Undergraduates: $9226. *Parent loans:* $2,106,971 (39% need-based, 61% non-need-based). *Programs:* Federal Direct (Subsidized and Unsubsidized Stafford, PLUS), Perkins, Federal Nursing, college/university.

**WORK-STUDY Federal work-study:** Total amount: $113,000; jobs available.

**ATHLETIC AWARDS** Total amount: $6,548,448 (49% need-based, 51% non-need-based).

**APPLYING FOR FINANCIAL AID Required financial aid forms:** FAFSA, institution's own form, state aid form (GA residents only). *Financial aid deadline (priority):* 4/1. *Notification date:* Continuous. Students must reply within 2 weeks of notification.

**CONTACT** Ms. Maria Hammett, Associate Vice President, Mercer University, Office of Financial Planning, Macon, GA 31207-0003, 478-301-2226 or toll-free 800-MERCER-U. Fax: 478-301-2671. E-mail: hammett_ma@mercer.edu. *Website:* http://www.mercer.edu/.

# MERCY COLLEGE
## Dobbs Ferry, NY

| Tuition & fees: $17,766 | Average undergraduate aid package: $13,096 |
|---|---|

**ABOUT THE INSTITUTION** Independent, coed. *Awards:* certificates, associate, bachelor's, master's, and doctoral degrees. 59 undergraduate majors. *Total enrollment:* 11,272. Undergraduates: 7,939. Freshmen: 747. Federal methodology is used as a basis for awarding need-based institutional aid.

**UNDERGRADUATE EXPENSES for 2015–2016 Application fee:** $40. *Comprehensive fee:* $30,456 includes full-time tuition ($17,166), mandatory fees ($600), and room and board ($12,690). *College room only:* $8590. Full-time tuition and fees vary according to course load. Room and board charges vary according to board plan. *Part-time tuition:* $722 per credit. *Part-time fees:* $150 per term. Part-time tuition and fees vary according to course load.

**FRESHMAN FINANCIAL AID (Fall 2013)** 798 applied for aid; of those 95% were deemed to have need. 98% of freshmen with need received aid; of those 3% had need fully met. *Average percent of need met:* 61% (excluding resources awarded to replace EFC). *Average financial aid package:* $15,144 (excluding resources awarded to replace EFC). 3% of all full-time freshmen had no need and received non-need-based gift aid.

**UNDERGRADUATE FINANCIAL AID (Fall 2013)** 5,094 applied for aid; of those 95% were deemed to have need. 97% of undergraduates with need received aid; of those 2% had need fully met. *Average percent of need met:* 55% (excluding resources awarded to replace EFC). *Average financial aid package:* $13,096 (excluding resources awarded to replace EFC). 2% of all full-time undergraduates had no need and received non-need-based gift aid.

**GIFT AID (NEED-BASED) Total amount:** $41,015,200 (43% federal, 23% state, 34% institutional). *Receiving aid:* Freshmen: 83% (679); all full-time undergraduates: 78% (4,313). *Average award:* Freshmen: $10,789; Undergraduates: $9212. *Scholarships, grants, and awards:* Federal Pell, FSEOG, state, private, college/university gift aid from institutional funds.

**GIFT AID (NON-NEED-BASED) Total amount:** $4,920,687 (10% state, 85% institutional, 5% external sources). *Receiving aid:* Freshmen: 42% (348). Undergraduates: 22% (1,234). *Average award:* Freshmen: $5178. Undergraduates: $3889. *Scholarships, grants, and awards by category: Academic interests/ achievement:* 1,566 awards ($4,094,436 total): general academic interests/achievements. *Special characteristics:* 56 awards ($521,724 total): children of faculty/staff. *Tuition waivers:* Full or partial for employees or children of employees. *ROTC:* Army cooperative, Air Force cooperative.

**LOANS Student loans:** $41,120,608 (44% need-based, 56% non-need-based). 82% of past graduating class borrowed through all loan programs. *Average indebtedness per student:* $17,399. *Average need-based loan:* Freshmen: $3132. Undergraduates: $4062. *Parent loans:* $5,107,945 (100% non-need-based). *Programs:* Federal Direct (Subsidized and Unsubsidized Stafford, PLUS), Federal Nursing, state.

**WORK-STUDY Federal work-study:** 216 jobs averaging $2025.

**ATHLETIC AWARDS** Total amount: $1,173,389 (100% non-need-based).

**APPLYING FOR FINANCIAL AID Required financial aid forms:** FAFSA, state aid form. *Financial aid deadline (priority):* 2/15. *Notification date:* Continuous beginning 2/20. Students must reply by 5/1 or within 2 weeks of notification.

**CONTACT** Margaret McGrail, Vice President of Student Services, Mercy College, 555 Broadway, Dobbs Ferry, NY 10522, 877-637-2946 or toll-free 877-MERCY-GO (out-of-state). Fax: 914-674-7382. E-mail: admissions@mercy.edu. *Website:* http://www.mercy.edu/.

# MERCY COLLEGE OF HEALTH SCIENCES
## Des Moines, IA

| Tuition & fees: $15,642 | Average undergraduate aid package: N/A |
|---|---|

**ABOUT THE INSTITUTION** Independent Roman Catholic Church, coed. *Awards:* certificates, associate, and bachelor's degrees. 11 undergraduate majors.

**Total enrollment:** 774. Undergraduates: 774. Freshmen: 46. Federal methodology is used as a basis for awarding need-based institutional aid.

**UNDERGRADUATE EXPENSES for 2015–2016** *Tuition:* full-time $15,642; part-time $541 per credit hour. Full-time tuition and fees vary according to program. Part-time tuition and fees vary according to course load.

**GIFT AID (NEED-BASED)** *Scholarships, grants, and awards:* Federal Pell, FSEOG, state, private, college/university gift aid from institutional funds.

**GIFT AID (NON-NEED-BASED)** *Scholarships, grants, and awards by category: Academic interests/achievement:* general academic interests/achievements, health fields. *Special achievements/activities:* community service. *Special characteristics:* children of faculty/staff, children of union members/company employees, ethnic background.

**LOANS** *Programs:* Federal Direct (Subsidized and Unsubsidized Stafford, PLUS).

**WORK-STUDY** Federal work-study jobs available.

**APPLYING FOR FINANCIAL AID** *Required financial aid form:* FAFSA. *Financial aid deadline:* Continuous. *Notification date:* Continuous beginning 3/15. Students must reply within 3 weeks of notification.

**CONTACT** Lisa Croat, Financial Aid Director, Mercy College of Health Sciences, 921 Sixth Avenue, Des Moines, IA 50309, 515-643-6636 or toll-free 800-637-2994. *Fax:* 515-643-6747. *E-mail:* financialaid@mchs.edu.
*Website:* http://www.mchs.edu/.

# MERCY COLLEGE OF OHIO
## Toledo, OH

| Tuition & fees: N/R | Average undergraduate aid package: $6910 |
|---|---|

**ABOUT THE INSTITUTION** Independent Roman Catholic Church, coed, primarily women. *Awards:* certificates, associate, and bachelor's degrees. 8 undergraduate majors. *Total enrollment:* 1,195. Undergraduates: 1,195. Freshmen: 35. Federal methodology is used as a basis for awarding need-based institutional aid.

**FRESHMAN FINANCIAL AID (Fall 2013)** 26 applied for aid; of those 92% were deemed to have need. 96% of freshmen with need received aid; of those 4% had need fully met. *Average percent of need met:* 23% (excluding resources awarded to replace EFC). *Average financial aid package:* $4707 (excluding resources awarded to replace EFC). 6% of all full-time freshmen had no need and received non-need-based gift aid.

**UNDERGRADUATE FINANCIAL AID (Fall 2013)** 414 applied for aid; of those 93% were deemed to have need. 99% of undergraduates with need received aid; of those 3% had need fully met. *Average percent of need met:* 28% (excluding resources awarded to replace EFC). *Average financial aid package:* $6910 (excluding resources awarded to replace EFC). 1% of all full-time undergraduates had no need and received non-need-based gift aid.

**GIFT AID (NEED-BASED)** *Total amount:* $2,755,340 (79% federal, 17% state, 3% institutional, 1% external sources). *Receiving aid:* Freshmen: 42% (13); all full-time undergraduates: 48% (235). *Average award:* Freshmen: $3799; Undergraduates: $3133. *Scholarships, grants, and awards:* Federal Pell, FSEOG, state, private, college/university gift aid from institutional funds, Federal Nursing.

**GIFT AID (NON-NEED-BASED)** *Total amount:* $483,694 (6% state, 34% institutional, 60% external sources). *Receiving aid:* Freshmen: 29% (9). Undergraduates: 12% (61). *Average award:* Freshmen: $5049. Undergraduates: $3037. *Scholarships, grants, and awards by category: Academic interests/achievement:* health fields.

**LOANS** *Student loans:* $8,334,575 (41% need-based, 59% non-need-based). 77% of past graduating class borrowed through all loan programs. *Average indebtedness per student:* $28,842. *Average need-based loan:* Freshmen: $3098. Undergraduates: $3776. *Parent loans:* $502,740 (100% non-need-based). *Programs:* Federal Direct (Subsidized and Unsubsidized Stafford, PLUS), state, college/university.

**WORK-STUDY** *Federal work-study:* 28 jobs averaging $1517.

**APPLYING FOR FINANCIAL AID** *Required financial aid form:* FAFSA. *Financial aid deadline:* Continuous. *Notification date:* Continuous beginning 3/1. Students must reply by 8/15.

**CONTACT** Julie Leslie, Director of Financial Aid, Mercy College of Ohio, 2221 Madison Avenue, Toledo, OH 43604, 419-251-1598 or toll-free 888-80-MERCY. *Fax:* 419-251-0969. *E-mail:* julie.leslie@mercycollege.edu.
*Website:* http://www.mercycollege.edu/.

# MERCYHURST UNIVERSITY
## Erie, PA

| Tuition & fees: $31,485 | Average undergraduate aid package: $25,677 |
|---|---|

**ABOUT THE INSTITUTION** Independent Roman Catholic, coed. *Awards:* certificates, bachelor's, and master's degrees. 76 undergraduate majors. *Total enrollment:* 3,011. Undergraduates: 2,680. Freshmen: 602. Federal methodology is used as a basis for awarding need-based institutional aid.

**UNDERGRADUATE EXPENSES for 2015–2016** *Application fee:* $30. *Comprehensive fee:* $42,285 includes full-time tuition ($29,600), mandatory fees ($1885), and room and board ($10,800). *College room only:* $5474. Full-time tuition and fees vary according to class time, course load, degree level, location, and program. Room and board charges vary according to board plan, housing facility, and location. *Part-time tuition:* $2960 per course. *Part-time fees:* $65 per course. Part-time tuition and fees vary according to class time, course load, degree level, location, and program.

**FRESHMAN FINANCIAL AID (Fall 2014, est.)** 506 applied for aid; of those 92% were deemed to have need. 100% of freshmen with need received aid; of those 18% had need fully met. *Average percent of need met:* 48% (excluding resources awarded to replace EFC). *Average financial aid package:* $26,758 (excluding resources awarded to replace EFC). 22% of all full-time freshmen had no need and received non-need-based gift aid.

**UNDERGRADUATE FINANCIAL AID (Fall 2014, est.)** 2,022 applied for aid; of those 91% were deemed to have need. 100% of undergraduates with need received aid; of those 18% had need fully met. *Average percent of need met:* 49% (excluding resources awarded to replace EFC). *Average financial aid package:* $25,677 (excluding resources awarded to replace EFC). 22% of all full-time undergraduates had no need and received non-need-based gift aid.

**GIFT AID (NEED-BASED)** *Total amount:* $37,091,329 (10% federal, 6% state, 82% institutional, 2% external sources). *Receiving aid:* Freshmen: 73% (445); all full-time undergraduates: 70% (1,738). *Average award:* Freshmen: $16,072; Undergraduates: $16,240. *Scholarships, grants, and awards:* Federal Pell, FSEOG, state, private, college/university gift aid from institutional funds.

**GIFT AID (NON-NEED-BASED)** *Total amount:* $10,049,081 (5% federal, 95% institutional). *Receiving aid:* Freshmen: 63% (384). Undergraduates: 65% (1,608). *Average award:* Freshmen: $20,574. Undergraduates: $17,174. *Scholarships, grants, and awards by category: Academic interests/achievement:* general academic interests/achievements. *Creative arts/performance:* applied art and design, art/fine arts, dance, music. *Special achievements/activities:* community service, general special achievements/activities, leadership, religious involvement. *Special characteristics:* children and siblings of alumni, children of faculty/staff. *Tuition waivers:* Full or partial for employees or children of employees, adult students. *ROTC:* Army cooperative, Air Force cooperative.

**LOANS** *Student loans:* $19,401,177 (92% need-based, 8% non-need-based). 67% of past graduating class borrowed through all loan programs. *Average indebtedness per student:* $24,739. *Average need-based loan:* Freshmen: $3176. Undergraduates: $4371. *Parent loans:* $4,146,018 (96% need-based, 4% non-need-based). *Programs:* Federal Direct (Subsidized and Unsubsidized Stafford, PLUS), Perkins, college/university.

**WORK-STUDY** *Federal work-study:* Total amount: $730,068; jobs available. *State or other work-study/employment:* Total amount: $325,985 (40% need-based, 60% non-need-based). Part-time jobs available.

**ATHLETIC AWARDS** Total amount: $7,050,022 (48% need-based, 52% non-need-based).

**APPLYING FOR FINANCIAL AID** *Required financial aid form:* FAFSA. *Financial aid deadline:* 5/1 (priority: 3/1). *Notification date:* Continuous beginning 2/15. Students must reply within 2 weeks of notification.

**CONTACT** Carrie Newman, Director of Student Financial Services, Mercyhurst University, 501 East 38th Street, Erie, PA 16546, 814-824-2288 or toll-free 800-825-1926. *Fax:* 814-824-2300. *E-mail:* sfs@mercyhurst.edu.
*Website:* http://www.mercyhurst.edu/.

# MEREDITH COLLEGE
## Raleigh, NC

| Tuition & fees: $32,220 | Average undergraduate aid package: $23,739 |
|---|---|

**ABOUT THE INSTITUTION** Independent, undergraduate: women only; graduate: coed. *Awards:* certificates, bachelor's, and master's degrees. 39 undergraduate majors. *Total enrollment:* 1,885. Undergraduates: 1,644. Freshmen: 471. Federal methodology is used as a basis for awarding need-based institutional aid.

**UNDERGRADUATE EXPENSES for 2015–2016** *Application fee:* $40. *Comprehensive fee:* $41,736 includes full-time tuition ($32,140), mandatory fees ($80), and room and board ($9516). Full-time tuition and fees vary according to course load. Room and board charges vary according to board plan and housing facility. *Part-time tuition:* $795 per credit hour. *Part-time fees:* $80 per year. Part-time tuition and fees vary according to course load.

**FRESHMAN FINANCIAL AID (Fall 2014, est.)** 406 applied for aid; of those 87% were deemed to have need. 100% of freshmen with need received aid; of those 18% had need fully met. *Average percent of need met:* 75% (excluding resources awarded to replace EFC). *Average financial aid package:* $24,989 (excluding resources awarded to replace EFC). 11% of all full-time freshmen had no need and received non-need-based gift aid.

**UNDERGRADUATE FINANCIAL AID (Fall 2014, est.)** 1,326 applied for aid; of those 89% were deemed to have need. 100% of undergraduates with need received aid; of those 16% had need fully met. *Average percent of need met:* 72% (excluding resources awarded to replace EFC). *Average financial aid package:* $23,739 (excluding resources awarded to replace EFC). 9% of all full-time undergraduates had no need and received non-need-based gift aid.

**GIFT AID (NEED-BASED)** *Total amount:* $23,322,127 (13% federal, 16% state, 63% institutional, 8% external sources). *Receiving aid:* Freshmen: 75% (352); all full-time undergraduates: 75% (1,175). *Average award:* Freshmen: $21,423; Undergraduates: $19,763. *Scholarships, grants, and awards:* Federal Pell, FSEOG, state, private, college/university gift aid from institutional funds.

**GIFT AID (NON-NEED-BASED)** *Total amount:* $1,200,022 (3% federal, 3% state, 47% institutional, 47% external sources). *Average award:* Freshmen: $14,338. Undergraduates: $11,688. *Scholarships, grants, and awards by category:* Academic interests/achievement: biological sciences, business, computer science, education, English, foreign languages, general academic interests/achievements, mathematics, physical sciences, religion/biblical studies. *Creative arts/performance:* applied art and design, art/fine arts, creative writing, music. *Special achievements/activities:* community service, leadership. *Special characteristics:* adult students, children of faculty/staff, ethnic background, first-generation college students, international students, members of minority groups, out-of-state students, previous college experience, religious affiliation. *Tuition waivers:* Full or partial for employees or children of employees. *ROTC:* Army cooperative, Air Force cooperative.

**LOANS** *Student loans:* $15,908,471 (91% need-based, 9% non-need-based). 64% of past graduating class borrowed through all loan programs. *Average indebtedness per student:* $34,535. *Average need-based loan:* Freshmen: $3356. Undergraduates: $4303. *Parent loans:* $5,321,917 (49% need-based, 51% non-need-based). *Programs:* Federal Direct (Subsidized and Unsubsidized Stafford, PLUS), Perkins, college/university.

**WORK-STUDY** *Federal work-study:* Total amount: $440,838; jobs available. *State or other work-study/employment:* Part-time jobs available.

**APPLYING FOR FINANCIAL AID** *Required financial aid form:* FAFSA. *Financial aid deadline (priority):* 2/15. *Notification date:* Continuous beginning 3/15. Students must reply by 5/1 or within 2 weeks of notification.

**CONTACT** Mr. Kevin Michaelsen, Director of Financial Assistance, Meredith College, 3800 Hillsborough Street, Raleigh, NC 27607-5298, 919-760-8565 or toll-free 800-MEREDITH. *Fax:* 919-760-2375. *E-mail:* michaelsen@meredith.edu. *Website:* http://www.meredith.edu/.

# MERRIMACK COLLEGE
## North Andover, MA

| Tuition & fees: $36,215 | Average undergraduate aid package: $22,246 |
|---|---|

**ABOUT THE INSTITUTION** Independent Roman Catholic, coed. *Awards:* certificates, bachelor's, and master's degrees. 59 undergraduate majors. *Total enrollment:* 3,354. Undergraduates: 3,051. Freshmen: 858. Federal methodology is used as a basis for awarding need-based institutional aid.

**UNDERGRADUATE EXPENSES for 2015–2016** *Comprehensive fee:* $49,470 includes full-time tuition ($34,615), mandatory fees ($1600), and room and board ($13,255). Full-time tuition and fees vary according to degree level. Room and board charges vary according to board plan and housing facility. *Part-time tuition:* $1240 per credit. Part-time tuition and fees vary according to class time, course load, and degree level.

**FRESHMAN FINANCIAL AID (Fall 2014, est.)** 741 applied for aid; of those 88% were deemed to have need. 100% of freshmen with need received aid; of those 16% had need fully met. *Average percent of need met:* 64% (excluding resources awarded to replace EFC). *Average financial aid package:* $21,830 (excluding resources awarded to replace EFC). 19% of all full-time freshmen had no need and received non-need-based gift aid.

**UNDERGRADUATE FINANCIAL AID (Fall 2014, est.)** 2,298 applied for aid; of those 90% were deemed to have need. 100% of undergraduates with need received aid; of those 12% had need fully met. *Average percent of need met:* 64% (excluding resources awarded to replace EFC). *Average financial aid package:* $22,246 (excluding resources awarded to replace EFC). 19% of all full-time undergraduates had no need and received non-need-based gift aid.

**GIFT AID (NEED-BASED)** *Total amount:* $33,068,523 (10% federal, 3% state, 87% institutional). *Receiving aid:* Freshmen: 76% (653); all full-time undergraduates: 71% (2,043). *Average award:* Freshmen: $19,057; Undergraduates: $18,377. *Scholarships, grants, and awards:* Federal Pell, FSEOG, state, private, college/university gift aid from institutional funds.

**GIFT AID (NON-NEED-BASED)** *Total amount:* $6,282,034 (100% institutional). *Receiving aid:* Freshmen: 10% (90). Undergraduates: 7% (210). *Average award:* Freshmen: $11,519. Undergraduates: $9798. *Scholarships, grants, and awards by category:* Academic interests/achievement: general academic interests/achievements. *Special achievements/activities:* leadership. *Special characteristics:* children and siblings of alumni, children of faculty/staff, international students, relatives of clergy, religious affiliation, siblings of current students. *Tuition waivers:* Full or partial for employees or children of employees, senior citizens. *ROTC:* Air Force cooperative.

**LOANS** *Student loans:* $26,169,749 (68% need-based, 32% non-need-based). *Average need-based loan:* Freshmen: $3378. Undergraduates: $4635. *Parent loans:* $7,732,663 (47% need-based, 53% non-need-based). *Programs:* Federal Direct (Subsidized and Unsubsidized Stafford, PLUS), Perkins, state, college/university.

**WORK-STUDY** *Federal work-study:* Total amount: $130,862; jobs available. *State or other work-study/employment:* Part-time jobs available.

**ATHLETIC AWARDS** Total amount: $7,644,882 (51% need-based, 49% non-need-based).

**APPLYING FOR FINANCIAL AID** *Required financial aid forms:* FAFSA, business/farm supplement, sibling verification. *Financial aid deadline:* 2/15. *Notification date:* Continuous beginning 3/15. Students must reply by 5/1 or within 2 weeks of notification.

**CONTACT** Adrienne Montgomery, Director of Financial Aid, Merrimack College, 315 Turnpike Street, North Andover, MA 01845, 978-837-5186. *Fax:* 978-837-5067. *E-mail:* montgomerya@merrimack.edu. *Website:* http://www.merrimack.edu/.

# MESIVTA KESER TORAH
## Belmar, NJ

**CONTACT** Financial Aid Office, Mesivta Keser Torah, 503 Eleventh Avenue, Belmar, NJ 07719, 732-681-5656.

# MESIVTA OF EASTERN PARKWAY–YESHIVA ZICHRON MEILECH

### Brooklyn, NY

CONTACT Rabbi Joseph Halberstadt, Dean, Mesivta of Eastern Parkway–Yeshiva Zichron Meilech, 510 Dahill Road, Brooklyn, NY 11218-5559, 718-438-1002.

# MESIVTA TORAH VODAATH RABBINICAL SEMINARY

### Brooklyn, NY

CONTACT Mrs. Kayla Goldring, Director of Financial Aid, Mesivta Torah Vodaath Rabbinical Seminary, 425 East Ninth Street, Brooklyn, NY 11218-5209, 718-941-8000. *Website:* http://www.torahvodaath.org/.

# MESIVTHA TIFERETH JERUSALEM OF AMERICA

### New York, NY

CONTACT Rabbi Dickstein, Director of Financial Aid, Mesivtha Tifereth Jerusalem of America, 141 East Broadway, New York, NY 10002-6301, 212-964-2830.

# MESSENGER COLLEGE

### Euless, TX

CONTACT Patricia J. Pentecost, Director of Financial Aid, Messenger College, 300 East 50th Street, Joplin, MO 64804, 417-624-7070 Ext. 104 or toll-free 800-385-8940. *Fax:* 417-624-5070. *E-mail:* ppentecost@messengercollege.edu. *Website:* http://www.messengercollege.edu/.

# MESSIAH COLLEGE

### Mechanicsburg, PA

| Tuition & fees: $32,240 | Average undergraduate aid package: $22,327 |
| --- | --- |

ABOUT THE INSTITUTION Independent interdenominational, coed. *Awards:* certificates, bachelor's, and master's degrees. 77 undergraduate majors. *Total enrollment:* 3,234. Undergraduates: 2,789. Freshmen: 696. Federal methodology is used as a basis for awarding need-based institutional aid.

UNDERGRADUATE EXPENSES for 2015–2016 *Application fee:* $20. *Comprehensive fee:* $41,870 includes full-time tuition ($31,410), mandatory fees ($830), and room and board ($9630). *College room only:* $5100. Room and board charges vary according to board plan and housing facility. *Part-time tuition:* $1310 per credit hour.

FRESHMAN FINANCIAL AID (Fall 2014, est.) 596 applied for aid; of those 87% were deemed to have need. 100% of freshmen with need received aid; of those 21% had need fully met. *Average percent of need met:* 74% (excluding resources awarded to replace EFC). *Average financial aid package:* $23,466 (excluding resources awarded to replace EFC). 24% of all full-time freshmen had no need and received non-need-based gift aid.

UNDERGRADUATE FINANCIAL AID (Fall 2014, est.) 2,165 applied for aid; of those 88% were deemed to have need. 100% of undergraduates with need received aid; of those 18% had need fully met. *Average percent of need met:* 71% (excluding resources awarded to replace EFC). *Average financial aid package:* $22,327 (excluding resources awarded to replace EFC). 27% of all full-time undergraduates had no need and received non-need-based gift aid.

GIFT AID (NEED-BASED) *Total amount:* $31,445,474 (10% federal, 7% state, 80% institutional, 3% external sources). *Receiving aid:* Freshmen: 74% (516); all full-time undergraduates: 71% (1,884). *Average award:* Freshmen: $18,091; Undergrad-

uates: $16,642. *Scholarships, grants, and awards:* Federal Pell, FSEOG, state, private, college/university gift aid from institutional funds, Federal Nursing.

GIFT AID (NON-NEED-BASED) *Total amount:* $10,859,192 (3% federal, 94% institutional, 3% external sources). *Receiving aid:* Freshmen: 11% (73). Undergraduates: 8% (201). *Average award:* Freshmen: $14,700. Undergraduates: $12,925. *Scholarships, grants, and awards by category: Academic interests/achievement:* 2,153 awards ($21,150,121 total): general academic interests/achievements. *Creative arts/performance:* 122 awards ($862,520 total): art/fine arts, music, theater/drama. *Special achievements/activities:* 424 awards ($7,077,510 total): leadership. *Special characteristics:* 184 awards ($2,241,990 total): adult students, children of faculty/staff, local/state students, religious affiliation. *Tuition waivers:* Full or partial for employees or children of employees, adult students, senior citizens.

LOANS *Student loans:* $18,170,345 (69% need-based, 31% non-need-based). 71% of past graduating class borrowed through all loan programs. *Average indebtedness per student:* $34,301. *Average need-based loan:* Freshmen: $3855. Undergraduates: $4883. *Parent loans:* $4,271,058 (43% need-based, 57% non-need-based). *Programs:* Federal Direct (Subsidized and Unsubsidized Stafford, PLUS), Perkins, Federal Nursing.

WORK-STUDY *Federal work-study:* Total amount: $1,694,076; 852 jobs averaging $2134. *State or other work-study/employment:* Total amount: $2,298,709 (24% need-based, 76% non-need-based). 767 part-time jobs averaging $1926.

APPLYING FOR FINANCIAL AID *Required financial aid form:* FAFSA. *Financial aid deadline (priority):* 4/1. *Notification date:* Continuous beginning 3/15. Students must reply by 5/1 or within 4 weeks of notification.

CONTACT Mr. Michael Strite, Assistant Director of Financial Aid, Messiah College, One College Avenue, Suite 3006, Mechanicsburg, PA 17055, 717-691-6007 or toll-free 800-233-4220. *Fax:* 717-796-4791. *E-mail:* mstrite@messiah.edu. *Website:* http://www.messiah.edu/.

# METHODIST UNIVERSITY

### Fayetteville, NC

| Tuition & fees: N/R | Average undergraduate aid package: $18,364 |
| --- | --- |

ABOUT THE INSTITUTION Independent United Methodist, coed. 57 undergraduate majors. Federal methodology is used as a basis for awarding need-based institutional aid.

FRESHMAN FINANCIAL AID (Fall 2013) 493 applied for aid; of those 92% were deemed to have need. 100% of freshmen with need received aid; of those 9% had need fully met. *Average percent of need met:* 74% (excluding resources awarded to replace EFC). *Average financial aid package:* $22,085 (excluding resources awarded to replace EFC). 10% of all full-time freshmen had no need and received non-need-based gift aid.

UNDERGRADUATE FINANCIAL AID (Fall 2013) 1,625 applied for aid; of those 94% were deemed to have need. 99% of undergraduates with need received aid; of those 7% had need fully met. *Average percent of need met:* 64% (excluding resources awarded to replace EFC). *Average financial aid package:* $18,364 (excluding resources awarded to replace EFC). 10% of all full-time undergraduates had no need and received non-need-based gift aid.

GIFT AID (NEED-BASED) *Total amount:* $19,747,972 (19% federal, 15% state, 65% institutional, 1% external sources). *Receiving aid:* Freshmen: 82% (447); all full-time undergraduates: 74% (1,442). *Average award:* Freshmen: $21,175; Undergraduates: $14,977. *Scholarships, grants, and awards:* Federal Pell, FSEOG, state, private, college/university gift aid from institutional funds.

GIFT AID (NON-NEED-BASED) *Total amount:* $9,802,631 (4% federal, 69% institutional, 27% external sources). *Receiving aid:* Freshmen: 53% (289). Undergraduates: 44% (858). *Average award:* Freshmen: $14,429. Undergraduates: $14,022. *Scholarships, grants, and awards by category: Academic interests/achievement:* 591 awards ($2,574,127 total): business, education, English, foreign languages, general academic interests/achievements, international studies, military science, religion/biblical studies. *Creative arts/performance:* 88 awards ($141,075 total): dance, debating, music, theater/drama. *Special achievements/activities:* 33 awards ($30,050 total): cheerleading/drum major, leadership, religious involvement. *Special characteristics:* 530 awards ($3,024,165 total): children and siblings of alumni, children of faculty/staff, ethnic background, general special characteristics, local/state students, members of minority groups, relatives of clergy, religious affiliation, siblings of current students, veterans.

**LOANS** *Student loans:* $11,834,169 (41% need-based, 59% non-need-based). 71% of past graduating class borrowed through all loan programs. *Average indebtedness per student:* $35,525. *Average need-based loan:* Freshmen: $6469. Undergraduates: $7884. *Parent loans:* $3,994,558 (100% non-need-based). *Programs:* Federal Direct (Subsidized and Unsubsidized Stafford, PLUS), Perkins.

**WORK-STUDY** *Federal work-study:* 338 jobs averaging $666. *State or other work-study/employment:* Total amount: $225,150 (100% non-need-based). 144 part-time jobs averaging $1564.

**APPLYING FOR FINANCIAL AID** *Required financial aid form:* FAFSA. *Financial aid deadline (priority):* 8/1. *Notification date:* Continuous beginning 3/6. Students must reply within 2 weeks of notification.

**CONTACT** Bonnie Adamson, Financial Aid Office, Methodist University, 5400 Ramsey Street, Fayetteville, NC 28311-1420, 910-630-7307 or toll-free 800-488-7110 Ext. 7027. *Fax:* 910-630-7285. *E-mail:* adamson@methodist.edu. *Website:* http://www.methodist.edu/.

# METROPOLITAN COLLEGE OF NEW YORK
## New York, NY

**CONTACT** Rosibel Gomez, Financial Aid Director, Metropolitan College of New York, 75 Varick Street, New York, NY 10013-1919, 212-343-1234 Ext. 5004 or toll-free 800-33-THINK Ext. 5001. *Fax:* 212-343-7399. *Website:* http://www.metropolitan.edu/.

# METROPOLITAN STATE UNIVERSITY
## St. Paul, MN

| Tuition & fees (MN res): $6642 | Average undergraduate aid package: N/A |
|---|---|

**ABOUT THE INSTITUTION** State-supported, coed. *Awards:* certificates, bachelor's, master's, and doctoral degrees (offers primarily part-time evening degree programs). 49 undergraduate majors. *Total enrollment:* 8,354. Undergraduates: 7,593. Freshmen: 95. Federal methodology is used as a basis for awarding need-based institutional aid.

**UNDERGRADUATE EXPENSES for 2015–2016** *Application fee:* $20. *Tuition, state resident:* full-time $6329; part-time $210.97 per credit hour. *Tuition, nonresident:* full-time $12,914; part-time $430.45 per credit hour. *Required fees:* full-time $313; $10.43 per credit hour. Full-time tuition and fees vary according to degree level, program, and reciprocity agreements. Part-time tuition and fees vary according to degree level, program, and reciprocity agreements.

**GIFT AID (NEED-BASED)** *Total amount:* $20,528,085*Scholarships, grants, and awards:* Federal Pell, FSEOG, state, private, college/university gift aid from institutional funds.

**GIFT AID (NON-NEED-BASED)** *Scholarships, grants, and awards by category:* Academic interests/achievement: education, general academic interests/achievements. *Tuition waivers:* Full or partial for employees or children of employees, senior citizens.

**LOANS** *Programs:* Federal Direct (Subsidized and Unsubsidized Stafford, PLUS), state.

**WORK-STUDY** Federal work-study jobs available. *State or other work-study/employment:* Part-time jobs available.

**APPLYING FOR FINANCIAL AID** *Required financial aid form:* FAFSA. *Financial aid deadline (priority):* 6/1. *Notification date:* Continuous beginning 6/15. Students must reply within 2 weeks of notification.

**CONTACT** Dr. Lois Larson, Director of Financial Aid, Metropolitan State University, Founders Hall, Room 147A, 700 East 7th Street, St. Paul, MN 55106-5000, 651-793-1411. *Fax:* 651-793-1410. *E-mail:* finaid@metrostate.edu. *Website:* http://www.metrostate.edu/.

# METROPOLITAN STATE UNIVERSITY OF DENVER
## Denver, CO

| Tuition & fees: N/R | Average undergraduate aid package: $8176 |
|---|---|

**ABOUT THE INSTITUTION** State-supported, coed. 48 undergraduate majors. Federal methodology is used as a basis for awarding need-based institutional aid.

**FRESHMAN FINANCIAL AID (Fall 2014, est.)** 1,409 applied for aid; of those 78% were deemed to have need. 88% of freshmen with need received aid; of those 1% had need fully met. *Average percent of need met:* 51% (excluding resources awarded to replace EFC). *Average financial aid package:* $6517 (excluding resources awarded to replace EFC). 16% of all full-time freshmen had no need and received non-need-based gift aid.

**UNDERGRADUATE FINANCIAL AID (Fall 2014, est.)** 10,104 applied for aid; of those 85% were deemed to have need. 92% of undergraduates with need received aid; of those 2% had need fully met. *Average percent of need met:* 56% (excluding resources awarded to replace EFC). *Average financial aid package:* $8176 (excluding resources awarded to replace EFC). 19% of all full-time undergraduates had no need and received non-need-based gift aid.

**GIFT AID (NEED-BASED)** *Total amount:* $50,654,638 (60% federal, 22% state, 15% institutional, 3% external sources). *Receiving aid:* Freshmen: 41% (707); all full-time undergraduates: 44% (5,740). *Average award:* Freshmen: $5570; Undergraduates: $5868. *Scholarships, grants, and awards:* Federal Pell, FSEOG, state, private, college/university gift aid from institutional funds.

**GIFT AID (NON-NEED-BASED)** *Total amount:* $2,097,805 (1% federal, 77% institutional, 22% external sources). *Receiving aid:* Freshmen: 1% (12). Undergraduates: 1% (179). *Average award:* Freshmen: $2120. Undergraduates: $2562. *Scholarships, grants, and awards by category:* Academic interests/achievement: education, general academic interests/achievements. *Creative arts/performance:* music, performing arts, theater/drama. *Special achievements/activities:* leadership. *Special characteristics:* adult students, first-generation college students, local/state students, veterans.

**LOANS** *Student loans:* $79,262,875 (88% need-based, 12% non-need-based). 67% of past graduating class borrowed through all loan programs. *Average indebtedness per student:* $28,468. *Average need-based loan:* Freshmen: $2805. Undergraduates: $3942. *Parent loans:* $2,820,721 (51% need-based, 49% non-need-based). *Programs:* Federal Direct (Subsidized and Unsubsidized Stafford, PLUS), Perkins.

**WORK-STUDY** *Federal work-study:* Total amount: $489,719; 11 jobs averaging $1870. *State or other work-study/employment:* Total amount: $1,739,161 (84% need-based, 16% non-need-based). 32 part-time jobs averaging $2366.

**ATHLETIC AWARDS** Total amount: $1,503,935 (46% need-based, 54% non-need-based).

**APPLYING FOR FINANCIAL AID** *Required financial aid form:* FAFSA. *Financial aid deadline:* Continuous. *Notification date:* Continuous beginning 3/15.

**CONTACT** Office of Financial Aid, Metropolitan State University of Denver, PO Box 173362, Denver, CO 80217-3362, 303-556-8593. *Fax:* 303-556-4927. *Website:* http://www.msudenver.edu/.

# MIAMI INTERNATIONAL UNIVERSITY OF ART & DESIGN
## Miami, FL

Financial Aid Office, Miami International University of Art & Design, 1737 Bayshore Drive, Miami, FL 33132, 800-225-9023 Ext. 125 or toll-free 800-225-9023. *Fax:* 305-374-7946.

# MIAMI UNIVERSITY
## Oxford, OH

| Tuition & fees (OH res): $14,287 | Average undergraduate aid package: $11,902 |
|---|---|

**ABOUT THE INSTITUTION** State-related, coed. **Awards:** certificates, associate, bachelor's, master's, and doctoral degrees. 115 undergraduate majors. **Total enrollment:** 18,620. Undergraduates: 15,813. Freshmen: 3,644. Federal methodology is used as a basis for awarding need-based institutional aid.

**UNDERGRADUATE EXPENSES for 2015–2016 Application fee:** $50. **Tuition, state resident:** full-time $13,533; part-time $563.88 per credit hour. **Tuition, nonresident:** full-time $29,640; part-time $1235 per credit hour. **Required fees:** full-time $754. Full-time tuition and fees vary according to location and program. Part-time tuition and fees vary according to course load, location, and program. **College room and board:** $11,109; **Room only:** $5459. Room and board charges vary according to board plan and housing facility.

**FRESHMAN FINANCIAL AID (Fall 2013)** 2,689 applied for aid; of those 58% were deemed to have need. 96% of freshmen with need received aid; of those 24% had need fully met. **Average percent of need met:** 59% (excluding resources awarded to replace EFC). **Average financial aid package:** $12,599 (excluding resources awarded to replace EFC). 31% of all full-time freshmen had no need and received non-need-based gift aid.

**UNDERGRADUATE FINANCIAL AID (Fall 2013)** 8,571 applied for aid; of those 69% were deemed to have need. 98% of undergraduates with need received aid; of those 15% had need fully met. **Average percent of need met:** 56% (excluding resources awarded to replace EFC). **Average financial aid package:** $11,902 (excluding resources awarded to replace EFC). 29% of all full-time undergraduates had no need and received non-need-based gift aid.

**GIFT AID (NEED-BASED) Total amount:** $37,531,252 (29% federal, 3% state, 68% institutional). **Receiving aid:** Freshmen: 27% (978); all full-time undergraduates: 26% (3,898). **Average award:** Freshmen: $9511; Undergraduates: $8064. **Scholarships, grants, and awards:** Federal Pell, FSEOG, state, private, college/university gift aid from institutional funds.

**GIFT AID (NON-NEED-BASED) Total amount:** $33,543,933 (91% institutional, 9% external sources). **Receiving aid:** Freshmen: 8% (292). Undergraduates: 4% (614). **Average award:** Freshmen: $8174. Undergraduates: $6330. **Scholarships, grants, and awards by category:** Academic interests/achievement: architecture, education, engineering/technologies, general academic interests/achievements. Creative arts/performance: art/fine arts, music, theater/drama. Special achievements/activities: general special achievements/activities, leadership. Special characteristics: children of faculty/staff, local/state students, members of minority groups, out-of-state students. **Tuition waivers:** Full or partial for employees or children of employees. **ROTC:** Army cooperative, Naval, Air Force.

**LOANS Student loans:** $59,438,069 (33% need-based, 67% non-need-based). 54% of past graduating class borrowed through all loan programs. Average indebtedness per student: $27,181. **Average need-based loan:** Freshmen: $3599. Undergraduates: $4596. **Parent loans:** $29,150,409 (100% non-need-based). **Programs:** Federal Direct (Subsidized and Unsubsidized Stafford, PLUS), Perkins, college/university, private loans.

**WORK-STUDY Federal work-study:** 1,424 jobs averaging $1117.

**ATHLETIC AWARDS** Total amount: $8,954,928 (100% non-need-based).

**APPLYING FOR FINANCIAL AID Required financial aid form:** FAFSA. **Financial aid deadline (priority):** 2/15. **Notification date:** Continuous beginning 3/20. Students must reply by 5/1 or within 3 weeks of notification.

**CONTACT** Mr. Brent Shock, Office of Student Financial Aid, Miami University, Campus Avenue Building, Oxford, OH 45056-3427, 513-529-0001. Fax: 513-529-8713. E-mail: financialaid@miamioh.edu. Website: http://miamioh.edu/.

# MIAMI UNIVERSITY HAMILTON
## Hamilton, OH

**CONTACT** Financial Aid Office, Miami University Hamilton, 1601 Peck Boulevard, Hamilton, OH 45011-3399, 513-785-3000. Website: http://regionals.miamioh.edu/.

# MICHIGAN JEWISH INSTITUTE
## West Bloomfield, MI

**CONTACT** Financial Aid Office, Michigan Jewish Institute, 6890 Maple Road, West Bloomfield, MI 48322, 248-414-6900 or toll-free 888-INFO-MJI. Website: http://www.mji.edu/.

# MICHIGAN STATE UNIVERSITY
## East Lansing, MI

| Tuition & fees (MI res): $13,200 | Average undergraduate aid package: $12,712 |
|---|---|

**ABOUT THE INSTITUTION** State-supported, coed. **Awards:** certificates, bachelor's, master's, and doctoral degrees. 158 undergraduate majors. **Total enrollment:** 50,085. Undergraduates: 38,786. Freshmen: 8,055. Federal methodology is used as a basis for awarding need-based institutional aid.

**UNDERGRADUATE EXPENSES for 2015–2016 Application fee:** $50. **Tuition, state resident:** full-time $13,200; part-time $440 per credit hour. **Tuition, nonresident:** full-time $34,965; part-time $1166 per credit hour. Full-time tuition and fees vary according to course load, program, and student level. Part-time tuition and fees vary according to course load, program, and student level. **College room and board:** $9154; **Room only:** $3780. Room and board charges vary according to board plan and housing facility.

**FRESHMAN FINANCIAL AID (Fall 2014, est.)** 5,454 applied for aid; of those 70% were deemed to have need. 94% of freshmen with need received aid; of those 16% had need fully met. **Average percent of need met:** 63% (excluding resources awarded to replace EFC). **Average financial aid package:** $13,254 (excluding resources awarded to replace EFC). 9% of all full-time freshmen had no need and received non-need-based gift aid.

**UNDERGRADUATE FINANCIAL AID (Fall 2014, est.)** 21,555 applied for aid; of those 77% were deemed to have need. 96% of undergraduates with need received aid; of those 14% had need fully met. **Average percent of need met:** 62% (excluding resources awarded to replace EFC). **Average financial aid package:** $12,712 (excluding resources awarded to replace EFC). 7% of all full-time undergraduates had no need and received non-need-based gift aid.

**GIFT AID (NEED-BASED) Total amount:** $120,866,404 (33% federal, 3% state, 64% institutional). **Receiving aid:** Freshmen: 33% (2,566); all full-time undergraduates: 34% (11,829). **Average award:** Freshmen: $10,268; Undergraduates: $9587. **Scholarships, grants, and awards:** Federal Pell, FSEOG, state, private, college/university gift aid from institutional funds, United Negro College Fund.

**GIFT AID (NON-NEED-BASED) Total amount:** $63,018,441 (3% federal, 1% state, 66% institutional, 30% external sources). **Receiving aid:** Freshmen: 21% (1,655). Undergraduates: 13% (4,616). **Average award:** Freshmen: $9348. Undergraduates: $8241. **Scholarships, grants, and awards by category:** Academic interests/achievement: agriculture, biological sciences, business, communication, computer science, education, engineering/technologies, English, foreign languages, general academic interests/achievements, health fields, home economics, international studies, mathematics, military science, physical sciences, social sciences. Creative arts/performance: art/fine arts, creative writing, debating, journalism/publications, music, performing arts, theater/drama. Special achievements/activities: community service, general special achievements/activities, hobbies/interests, leadership, memberships, rodeo. Special characteristics: children and siblings of alumni, children of faculty/staff, children of union members/company employees, first-generation college students, handicapped students, international students, local/state students, out-of-state students, spouses of deceased or disabled public servants, veterans. **Tuition waivers:** Full or partial for employees or children of employees. **ROTC:** Army, Air Force.

**LOANS Student loans:** $132,177,265 (43% need-based, 57% non-need-based). 45% of past graduating class borrowed through all loan programs. Average indebtedness per student: $26,122. **Average need-based loan:** Freshmen: $3342. Undergraduates: $4166. **Parent loans:** $73,180,975 (100% non-need-based). **Programs:** Federal Direct (Subsidized and Unsubsidized Stafford, PLUS), Perkins, college/university.

**WORK-STUDY Federal work-study:** Total amount: $2,650,320; jobs available.

**ATHLETIC AWARDS** Total amount: $11,778,899 (53% need-based, 47% non-need-based).

**APPLYING FOR FINANCIAL AID** *Required financial aid form:* FAFSA. *Financial aid deadline:* Continuous. *Notification date:* Continuous beginning 3/15. Students must reply within 4 weeks of notification.

**CONTACT** Mr. Keith Williams, Associate Director of Financial Aid, Michigan State University, 252 Student Services Building, East Lansing, MI 48824-1113, 517-353-5940. *Fax:* 517-432-1155. *E-mail:* willi398@msu.edu.
*Website:* http://www.msu.edu/.

# MICHIGAN TECHNOLOGICAL UNIVERSITY
## Houghton, MI

| Tuition & fees (MI res): $14,040 | Average undergraduate aid package: $13,900 |
|---|---|

**ABOUT THE INSTITUTION** State-supported, coed. *Awards:* certificates, associate, bachelor's, master's, and doctoral degrees. 54 undergraduate majors. *Total enrollment:* 7,104. Undergraduates: 5,662. Freshmen: 1,199. Federal methodology is used as a basis for awarding need-based institutional aid.

**UNDERGRADUATE EXPENSES for 2015–2016** *Tuition, state resident:* full-time $13,740; part-time $520 per credit hour. *Tuition, nonresident:* full-time $29,220; part-time $1082 per credit hour. *Required fees:* full-time $300; $150 per term. Full-time tuition and fees vary according to program and student level. Part-time tuition and fees vary according to course load, program, and student level. *College room and board:* $9516; *Room only:* $5145. Room and board charges vary according to board plan and housing facility.

**FRESHMAN FINANCIAL AID (Fall 2014, est.)** 1,100 applied for aid; of those 75% were deemed to have need. 100% of freshmen with need received aid; of those 20% had need fully met. *Average percent of need met:* 79% (excluding resources awarded to replace EFC). *Average financial aid package:* $14,870 (excluding resources awarded to replace EFC). 26% of all full-time freshmen had no need and received non-need-based gift aid.

**UNDERGRADUATE FINANCIAL AID (Fall 2014, est.)** 4,157 applied for aid; of those 82% were deemed to have need. 99% of undergraduates with need received aid; of those 18% had need fully met. *Average percent of need met:* 72% (excluding resources awarded to replace EFC). *Average financial aid package:* $13,900 (excluding resources awarded to replace EFC). 24% of all full-time undergraduates had no need and received non-need-based gift aid.

**GIFT AID (NEED-BASED)** *Total amount:* $35,311,646 (19% federal, 10% state, 64% institutional, 7% external sources). *Receiving aid:* Freshmen: 57% (677); all full-time undergraduates: 50% (2,608). *Average award:* Freshmen: $8317; Undergraduates: $7198. *Scholarships, grants, and awards:* Federal Pell, FSEOG, state, private, college/university gift aid from institutional funds.

**GIFT AID (NON-NEED-BASED)** *Total amount:* $8,300,480 (1% state, 85% institutional, 14% external sources). *Receiving aid:* Freshmen: 58% (689). Undergraduates: 47% (2,481). *Average award:* Freshmen: $5136. Undergraduates: $5301. *Scholarships, grants, and awards by category:* Academic interests/achievement: 51 awards ($167,383 total): business, military science. *Creative arts/performance:* 12 awards ($39,000 total): art/fine arts, performing arts, theater/drama. *Special characteristics:* 612 awards ($187,447 total): children and siblings of alumni, veterans, veterans' children. *Tuition waivers:* Full or partial for children of alumni, employees or children of employees, senior citizens. *ROTC:* Army, Air Force.

**LOANS** *Student loans:* $36,901,027 (88% need-based, 12% non-need-based). 73% of past graduating class borrowed through all loan programs. *Average indebtedness per student:* $36,041. *Average need-based loan:* Freshmen: $3547. Undergraduates: $4800. *Parent loans:* $6,920,510 (83% need-based, 17% non-need-based). *Programs:* Federal Direct (Subsidized and Unsubsidized Stafford, PLUS), Perkins, college/university.

**WORK-STUDY** *Federal work-study:* Total amount: $343,215; 153 jobs averaging $866. *State or other work-study/employment:* Part-time jobs available.

**ATHLETIC AWARDS** Total amount: $3,050,538 (37% need-based, 63% non-need-based).

**APPLYING FOR FINANCIAL AID** *Required financial aid form:* FAFSA. *Financial aid deadline (priority):* 3/1. *Notification date:* Continuous beginning 3/15. Students must reply by 5/1.

**CONTACT** Mr. William Roberts, Director of Financial Aid, Michigan Technological University, 1400 Townsend Drive, Houghton, MI 49931-1295, 906-487-2622 or toll-free 888-MTU-1885. *Fax:* 906-487-3042. *E-mail:* wrrobert@mtu.edu.
*Website:* http://www.mtu.edu/.

# MID-AMERICA CHRISTIAN UNIVERSITY
## Oklahoma City, OK

**CONTACT** Mr. Todd Martin, Director of Financial Aid, Mid-America Christian University, 3500 Southwest 119th Street, Oklahoma City, OK 73170-4504, 405-691-3800 or toll-free 888-436-3035. *Fax:* 405-692-3165. *E-mail:* tmartin@mabc.edu.
*Website:* http://www.macu.edu/.

# MIDAMERICA NAZARENE UNIVERSITY
## Olathe, KS

**CONTACT** Rhonda L. Cole, Director of Student Financial Services, MidAmerica Nazarene University, 2030 East College Way, Olathe, KS 66062-1899, 913-791-3298 or toll-free 800-800-8887. *Fax:* 913-791-3482. *E-mail:* rcole@mnu.edu.
*Website:* http://www.mnu.edu/.

# MID-ATLANTIC CHRISTIAN UNIVERSITY
## Elizabeth City, NC

| Tuition & fees: $13,440 | Average undergraduate aid package: $12,224 |
|---|---|

**ABOUT THE INSTITUTION** Independent Christian, coed. *Awards:* certificates, associate, and bachelor's degrees. 10 undergraduate majors. *Total enrollment:* 196. Undergraduates: 196. Freshmen: 48. Federal methodology is used as a basis for awarding need-based institutional aid.

**UNDERGRADUATE EXPENSES for 2015–2016** *Application fee:* $50. *Comprehensive fee:* $21,640 includes full-time tuition ($13,440) and room and board ($8200). Full-time tuition and fees vary according to program. Room and board charges vary according to housing facility. *Part-time tuition:* $420 per credit. Part-time tuition and fees vary according to program.

**FRESHMAN FINANCIAL AID (Fall 2013)** 40 applied for aid; of those 98% were deemed to have need. 100% of freshmen with need received aid; of those 5% had need fully met. *Average percent of need met:* 60% (excluding resources awarded to replace EFC). *Average financial aid package:* $11,514 (excluding resources awarded to replace EFC). 3% of all full-time freshmen had no need and received non-need-based gift aid.

**UNDERGRADUATE FINANCIAL AID (Fall 2013)** 138 applied for aid; of those 96% were deemed to have need. 100% of undergraduates with need received aid; of those 4% had need fully met. *Average percent of need met:* 60% (excluding resources awarded to replace EFC). *Average financial aid package:* $12,224 (excluding resources awarded to replace EFC). 4% of all full-time undergraduates had no need and received non-need-based gift aid.

**GIFT AID (NEED-BASED)** *Total amount:* $1,259,274 (42% federal, 31% state, 25% institutional, 2% external sources). *Receiving aid:* Freshmen: 98% (39); all full-time undergraduates: 96% (132). *Average award:* Freshmen: $8812; Undergraduates: $8832. *Scholarships, grants, and awards:* Federal Pell, FSEOG, state, private, college/university gift aid from institutional funds.

**GIFT AID (NON-NEED-BASED)** *Total amount:* $45,795 (72% institutional, 28% external sources). *Receiving aid:* Undergraduates: 1% (1). *Average award:* Freshmen: $3000. Undergraduates: $5074. *Scholarships, grants, and awards by category:* Academic interests/achievement: 11 awards ($35,250 total): general academic interests/achievements, religion/biblical studies. *Special achievements/activities:* 15 awards ($15,520 total): general special achievements/activities, religious involvement. *Special characteristics:* 76 awards ($54,344 total): children and siblings of alumni, children of faculty/staff, general special characteristics, handicapped students, international students, married students, spouses of current students. *Tuition waivers:* Full or partial for children of alumni, employees or children of employees, senior citizens. *ROTC:* Army cooperative.

**LOANS** *Student loans:* $1,224,931 (93% need-based, 7% non-need-based). 90% of past graduating class borrowed through all loan programs. *Average indebtedness per student:* $33,980. *Average need-based loan:* Freshmen: $3011. Undergraduates: $3973. *Parent loans:* $60,478 (54% need-based, 46% non-need-based). *Programs:* Federal Direct (Subsidized and Unsubsidized Stafford, PLUS), private loans.

**WORK-STUDY** *Federal work-study:* 11 jobs averaging $674. *State or other work-study/employment:* Part-time jobs available.

**APPLYING FOR FINANCIAL AID** *Required financial aid forms:* FAFSA, institution's own form. *Financial aid deadline (priority):* 2/1. *Notification date:* Continuous beginning 4/1. Students must reply by 5/1 or within 2 weeks of notification.

**CONTACT** Lisa W. Pipkin, Financial Aid Administrator, Mid-Atlantic Christian University, 715 North Poindexter Street, Elizabeth City, NC 27909, 252-334-2020 or toll-free 866-996-MACU. *Fax:* 252-334-2064. *E-mail:* lisa.pipkin@macuniversity.edu. *Website:* http://www.macuniversity.edu/.

# MIDDLEBURY COLLEGE
## Middlebury, VT

| Tuition & fees: $46,044 | Average undergraduate aid package: $41,870 |
|---|---|

**ABOUT THE INSTITUTION** Independent, coed. *Awards:* bachelor's, master's, and doctoral degrees. 48 undergraduate majors. *Total enrollment:* 2,526. Undergraduates: 2,526. Freshmen: 580. Both federal and institutional methodology are used as a basis for awarding need-based institutional aid.

**UNDERGRADUATE EXPENSES for 2015–2016** *Application fee:* $65. *Comprehensive fee:* $59,160 includes full-time tuition ($45,637), mandatory fees ($407), and room and board ($13,116). *Payment plan:* Tuition prepayment.

**FRESHMAN FINANCIAL AID (Fall 2014, est.)** 304 applied for aid; of those 92% were deemed to have need. 100% of freshmen with need received aid; of those 100% had need fully met. *Average percent of need met:* 100% (excluding resources awarded to replace EFC). *Average financial aid package:* $43,346 (excluding resources awarded to replace EFC).

**UNDERGRADUATE FINANCIAL AID (Fall 2014, est.)** 1,202 applied for aid; of those 89% were deemed to have need. 100% of undergraduates with need received aid; of those 100% had need fully met. *Average percent of need met:* 100% (excluding resources awarded to replace EFC). *Average financial aid package:* $41,870 (excluding resources awarded to replace EFC).

**GIFT AID (NEED-BASED)** *Total amount:* $44,151,687 (5% federal, 93% institutional, 2% external sources). *Receiving aid:* Freshmen: 48% (276); all full-time undergraduates: 42% (1,044). *Average award:* Freshmen: $40,926; Undergraduates: $39,238. *Scholarships, grants, and awards:* Federal Pell, FSEOG, state, private, college/university gift aid from institutional funds.

**GIFT AID (NON-NEED-BASED)** *Tuition waivers:* Full or partial for employees or children of employees. *ROTC:* Army cooperative.

**LOANS** *Student loans:* $5,747,270 (47% need-based, 53% non-need-based). 44% of past graduating class borrowed through all loan programs. *Average indebtedness per student:* $17,975. *Average need-based loan:* Freshmen: $3248. Undergraduates: $3923. *Parent loans:* $2,500,000 (100% non-need-based). *Programs:* Federal Direct (Subsidized and Unsubsidized Stafford, PLUS), Perkins.

**WORK-STUDY** *Federal work-study:* Total amount: $305,425; jobs available. *State or other work-study/employment:* Total amount: $380,000 (100% need-based). Part-time jobs available.

**APPLYING FOR FINANCIAL AID** *Required financial aid forms:* FAFSA, CSS Financial Aid PROFILE, noncustodial (divorced/separated) parent's statement. *Financial aid deadline:* 2/1 (priority: 11/15). *Notification date:* 4/1. Students must reply by 5/1.

**CONTACT** Ms. Marguerite Corbin, Student Financial Services Counselor, Middlebury College, Service Building 104, Middlebury, VT 05753, 802-443-5158. *E-mail:* studentfinancialservices@middlebury.edu. *Website:* http://www.middlebury.edu/.

# MIDDLE GEORGIA STATE COLLEGE
## Cochran, GA

**CONTACT** Financial Aid Office, Middle Georgia State College, 1100 Second Street, SE, Cochran, GA 31014-1599, 478-934-6221. *Website:* http://www.mga.edu/.

# MIDDLE TENNESSEE STATE UNIVERSITY
## Murfreesboro, TN

| Tuition & fees (TN res): $7876 | Average undergraduate aid package: $9059 |
|---|---|

**ABOUT THE INSTITUTION** State-supported, coed. *Awards:* certificates, bachelor's, master's, and doctoral degrees. 61 undergraduate majors. *Total enrollment:* 22,729. Undergraduates: 20,262. Freshmen: 2,932. Federal methodology is used as a basis for awarding need-based institutional aid.

**UNDERGRADUATE EXPENSES for 2015–2016** *Application fee:* $25. *Tuition, state resident:* full-time $6240; part-time $260 per credit hour. *Tuition, nonresident:* full-time $22,488; part-time $937 per credit hour. *Required fees:* full-time $1636; $69 per credit hour. Full-time tuition and fees vary according to course load. Part-time tuition and fees vary according to course load. *College room and board:* $8302. Room and board charges vary according to board plan and housing facility.

**FRESHMAN FINANCIAL AID (Fall 2014, est.)** 2,673 applied for aid; of those 78% were deemed to have need. 99% of freshmen with need received aid; of those 14% had need fully met. *Average percent of need met:* 69% (excluding resources awarded to replace EFC). *Average financial aid package:* $10,518 (excluding resources awarded to replace EFC). 20% of all full-time freshmen had no need and received non-need-based gift aid.

**UNDERGRADUATE FINANCIAL AID (Fall 2014, est.)** 15,942 applied for aid; of those 81% were deemed to have need. 99% of undergraduates with need received aid; of those 9% had need fully met. *Average percent of need met:* 61% (excluding resources awarded to replace EFC). *Average financial aid package:* $9059 (excluding resources awarded to replace EFC). 13% of all full-time undergraduates had no need and received non-need-based gift aid.

**GIFT AID (NEED-BASED)** *Total amount:* $46,341,112 (82% federal, 16% state, 2% institutional). *Receiving aid:* Freshmen: 49% (1,338); all full-time undergraduates: 52% (8,768). *Average award:* Freshmen: $6063; Undergraduates: $5017. *Scholarships, grants, and awards:* Federal Pell, FSEOG, state, private, college/university gift aid from institutional funds.

**GIFT AID (NON-NEED-BASED)** *Total amount:* $51,549,494 (11% federal, 52% state, 19% institutional, 18% external sources). *Receiving aid:* Freshmen: 66% (1,824). Undergraduates: 43% (7,224). *Average award:* Freshmen: $7782. Undergraduates: $7444. *Scholarships, grants, and awards by category:* Academic interests/achievement: 871 awards ($1,279,422 total): agriculture, area/ethnic studies, biological sciences, business, communication, computer science, education, engineering/technologies, English, foreign languages, general academic interests/achievements, health fields, home economics, humanities, international studies, mathematics, military science, physical sciences, premedicine, social sciences. *Creative arts/performance:* 496 awards ($496,145 total): dance, debating, journalism/publications, music, theater/drama. *Special achievements/activities:* 2,462 awards ($6,410,387 total): cheerleading/drum major, general special achievements/activities, leadership. *Special characteristics:* 332 awards ($881,530 total): adult students, children and siblings of alumni, first-generation college students, general special characteristics, handicapped students, international students, local/state students, members of minority groups. *Tuition waivers:* Full or partial for employees or children of employees. *ROTC:* Army, Air Force cooperative.

**LOANS** *Student loans:* $84,062,894 (40% need-based, 60% non-need-based). 63% of past graduating class borrowed through all loan programs. *Average indebtedness per student:* $24,834. *Average need-based loan:* Freshmen: $3246. Undergraduates: $4050. *Parent loans:* $9,196,583 (100% non-need-based). *Programs:* Federal Direct (Subsidized and Unsubsidized Stafford, PLUS), Perkins, college/university.

**WORK-STUDY** *Federal work-study:* Total amount: $645,103; 280 jobs averaging $2304.

**ATHLETIC AWARDS** Total amount: $6,659,293 (100% non-need-based).

APPLYING FOR FINANCIAL AID *Required financial aid form:* FAFSA. *Financial aid deadline (priority):* 3/1. *Notification date:* Continuous beginning 4/15. Students must reply by 6/1.

APPLYING FOR FINANCIAL AID *Required financial aid form:* FAFSA. *Financial aid deadline (priority):* 3/1. *Notification date:* Continuous beginning 4/15. Students must reply by 6/1.

**CONTACT** Stephen White, Director of Financial Aid, Middle Tennessee State University, SSAC 260, 1301 East Main Street, Murfreesboro, TN 37132, 615-898-2830 or toll-free 800-331-MTSU. *Fax:* 615-898-5167.

*Website:* http://www.mtsu.edu/.

# MIDLAND COLLEGE
## Midland, TX

| Tuition & fees (area res): $2340 | Average undergraduate aid package: N/A |
| --- | --- |

**ABOUT THE INSTITUTION** State and locally supported, coed. *Awards:* certificates, associate, and bachelor's degrees. 23 undergraduate majors. *Total enrollment:* 5,233. Undergraduates: 5,233. Freshmen: 758. Federal methodology is used as a basis for awarding need-based institutional aid.

**UNDERGRADUATE EXPENSES for 2015–2016** *Tuition, area resident:* full-time $2340. *Tuition, state resident:* full-time $3750. *Tuition, nonresident:* full-time $4920. Full-time tuition and fees vary according to course level, course load, degree level, program, reciprocity agreements, and student level. Part-time tuition and fees vary according to student level. Room and board charges vary according to board plan and housing facility.

**GIFT AID (NEED-BASED)** *Total amount:* $3,525,000 (96% federal, 4% state). *Scholarships, grants, and awards:* Federal Pell, FSEOG, state, private, college/university gift aid from institutional funds.

**GIFT AID (NON-NEED-BASED)** *Total amount:* $300,000 (100% institutional). *Tuition waivers:* Full or partial for employees or children of employees, senior citizens.

**LOANS** *Student loans:* $300,000 (100% non-need-based).

**WORK-STUDY** Federal work-study jobs available. *State or other work-study/ employment:* Part-time jobs available.

**APPLYING FOR FINANCIAL AID** *Required financial aid form:* FAFSA. *Financial aid deadline (priority):* 5/1. *Notification date:* Continuous.

**CONTACT** Yolanda Ramos, Director of Financial Aid, Midland College, 3600 North Garfield, Midland, TX 79705, 432-685-5511. *Fax:* 432-685-6451. *E-mail:* finaid@midland.edu.

*Website:* http://www.midland.edu/.

# MIDLAND UNIVERSITY
## Fremont, NE

**CONTACT** Penny James, Director of Financial Aid, Midland University, 900 North Clarkson Street, Fremont, NE 68025-4200, 402-721-5480 Ext. 6520 or toll-free 800-642-8382 Ext. 6501. *Fax:* 402-721-0250. *E-mail:* finaid@mlc.edu.

*Website:* http://www.midlandu.edu/.

# MID-SOUTH CHRISTIAN COLLEGE
## Memphis, TN

**CONTACT** Financial Aid Office, Mid-South Christian College, 3097 Knight Road, Memphis, TN 38118-3151.

*Website:* http://www.midsouthcc.org/.

# MIDSTATE COLLEGE
## Peoria, IL

**CONTACT** Financial Aid Office, Midstate College, 411 West Northmoor Road, Peoria, IL 61614, 309-692-4092 or toll-free 800-251-4299.

*Website:* http://www.midstate.edu/.

# MIDWAY COLLEGE
## Midway, KY

**ABOUT THE INSTITUTION** Independent Christian Church (Disciples of Christ), coed, primarily women. 26 undergraduate majors.

**GIFT AID (NEED-BASED)** *Scholarships, grants, and awards:* Federal Pell, FSEOG, state, private, college/university gift aid from institutional funds.

**GIFT AID (NON-NEED-BASED)** *Scholarships, grants, and awards by category: Academic interests/achievement:* agriculture, business, general academic interests/achievements, health fields, premedicine. *Special achievements/activities:* general special achievements/activities, junior miss, leadership, religious involvement. *Special characteristics:* adult students, children and siblings of alumni, children of faculty/staff, members of minority groups, previous college experience, relatives of clergy, religious affiliation, veterans.

**LOANS** *Programs:* Federal Direct (Subsidized and Unsubsidized Stafford, PLUS), Perkins.

**APPLYING FOR FINANCIAL AID** *Required financial aid forms:* FAFSA, institution's own form.

**CONTACT** Kate Ware, Director of Student Financial Planning, Midway College, 512 East Stephens Street, Midway, KY 40347-1120, 859-846-5340 or toll-free 800-755-0031. *Fax:* 859-846-5751. *E-mail:* faid@midway.edu.

*Website:* http://www.midway.edu/.

# MIDWESTERN STATE UNIVERSITY
## Wichita Falls, TX

| Tuition & fees (TX res): $7753 | Average undergraduate aid package: $9339 |
| --- | --- |

**ABOUT THE INSTITUTION** State-supported, coed. *Awards:* certificates, associate, bachelor's, and master's degrees. 73 undergraduate majors. *Total enrollment:* 5,874. Undergraduates: 5,144. Freshmen: 843. Federal methodology is used as a basis for awarding need-based institutional aid.

**UNDERGRADUATE EXPENSES for 2015–2016** *Application fee:* $25. *Tuition, state resident:* full-time $5070; part-time $169 per credit hour. *Tuition, nonresident:* full-time $7020; part-time $234 per credit hour. *Required fees:* full-time $2683; $79.75 per credit hour or $185 per credit hour. Full-time tuition and fees vary according to course load, location, and program. Part-time tuition and fees vary according to course load, location, and program. *College room and board:* $6810. Room and board charges vary according to board plan and housing facility.

**FRESHMAN FINANCIAL AID (Fall 2014, est.)** 754 applied for aid; of those 72% were deemed to have need. 98% of freshmen with need received aid; of those 17% had need fully met. *Average percent of need met:* 69% (excluding resources awarded to replace EFC). *Average financial aid package:* $10,367 (excluding resources awarded to replace EFC). 18% of all full-time freshmen had no need and received non-need-based gift aid.

**UNDERGRADUATE FINANCIAL AID (Fall 2014, est.)** 3,341 applied for aid; of those 73% were deemed to have need. 94% of undergraduates with need received aid; of those 14% had need fully met. *Average percent of need met:* 64% (excluding resources awarded to replace EFC). *Average financial aid package:* $9339 (excluding resources awarded to replace EFC). 15% of all full-time undergraduates had no need and received non-need-based gift aid.

**GIFT AID (NEED-BASED)** *Total amount:* $15,321,894 (52% federal, 21% state, 23% institutional, 4% external sources). *Receiving aid:* Freshmen: 59% (486); all full-time undergraduates: 52% (1,997). *Average award:* Freshmen: $8369; Undergraduates: $6478. *Scholarships, grants, and awards:* Federal Pell, FSEOG, state, private, college/university gift aid from institutional funds, state nursing scholarships.

**GIFT AID (NON-NEED-BASED)** *Total amount:* $1,564,045 (1% federal, 1% state, 82% institutional, 16% external sources). *Receiving aid:* Freshmen: 28% (229). Undergraduates: 20% (774). *Average award:* Freshmen: $2001. Undergraduates: $1885. *Scholarships, grants, and awards by category: Academic interests/ achievement:* biological sciences, business, communication, computer science, education, engineering/technologies, English, foreign languages, general academic interests/achievements, health fields, humanities, international studies, mathematics, physical sciences, premedicine, social sciences. *Creative arts/performance:* art/fine arts, creative writing, general creative arts/performance, journalism/publications, music, theater/drama. *Special achievements/activities:* cheerleading/drum major, general special achievements/activities, leadership. *Special characteristics:* children and siblings of alumni, children of faculty/staff, children of union members/company employees, children of workers in trades, children with a deceased or disabled parent, first-generation college students, handicapped students, international students, members of minority groups, veterans, veterans' children. **Tuition waivers:** Full or partial for employees or children of employees, senior citizens. **ROTC:** Air Force cooperative.

**LOANS Student loans:** $25,763,737 (69% need-based, 31% non-need-based). 67% of past graduating class borrowed through all loan programs. *Average indebtedness per student:* $25,550. **Average need-based loan:** Freshmen: $5115. Undergraduates: $6533. **Parent loans:** $4,939,798 (49% need-based, 51% non-need-based). **Programs:** Federal Direct (Subsidized and Unsubsidized Stafford, PLUS), Perkins, state, college/university, private loans.

**WORK-STUDY Federal work-study:** Total amount: $100,978; 45 jobs averaging $2203. **State or other work-study/employment:** Total amount: $36,472 (100% need-based). 23 part-time jobs averaging $1585.

**ATHLETIC AWARDS** Total amount: $1,589,696 (49% need-based, 51% non-need-based).

**APPLYING FOR FINANCIAL AID Required financial aid forms:** FAFSA, institution's own form. **Financial aid deadline (priority):** 3/1. **Notification date:** Continuous beginning 4/15. Students must reply within 4 weeks of notification.

**CONTACT** Ms. Kathy Pennartz, Director of Financial Aid, Midwestern State University, 3410 Taft Boulevard, Wichita Falls, TX 76308, 940-397-4214 or toll-free 800-842-1922. *Fax:* 940-397-4852. *E-mail:* financial-aid@mwsu.edu. *Website:* http://www.mwsu.edu/.

---

# MIDWEST UNIVERSITY
## Wentzville, MO

**CONTACT** Financial Aid Office, Midwest University, 851 Parr Road, Wentzville, MO 63385, 636-327-4645.
*Website:* http://www.midwest.edu/.

---

# MIDWIVES COLLEGE OF UTAH
## Salt Lake City, UT

**CONTACT** Financial Aid Office, Midwives College of Utah, 1174 East 2700 South, Suite 2, Salt Lake City, UT 84106, 801-764-9068 or toll-free 866-680-2756.
*Website:* http://www.midwifery.edu/.

---

# MILES COLLEGE
## Fairfield, AL

**CONTACT** P. N. Lanier, Financial Aid Administrator, Miles College, PO Box 3800, Birmingham, AL 35208, 205-929-1663 or toll-free 800-445-0708 (out-of-state). *Fax:* 205-929-1668. *E-mail:* pnlani@netscape.net.
*Website:* http://www.miles.edu/.

---

# MILLENNIA ATLANTIC UNIVERSITY
## Doral, FL

**ABOUT THE INSTITUTION** Proprietary, coed. 8 undergraduate majors.

**GIFT AID (NEED-BASED) Scholarships, grants, and awards:** Federal Pell, FSEOG, state, college/university gift aid from institutional funds.

**LOANS Programs:** Federal Direct (Subsidized and Unsubsidized Stafford, PLUS), private loans.

**APPLYING FOR FINANCIAL AID Required financial aid forms:** FAFSA, institution's own form.

**CONTACT** Mrs. Karen S. Terry, Financial Aid Manager, Millennia Atlantic University, 3801 NW 97th Avenue, Suite 100, Doral, FL 33178, 785-331-1000 Ext. 202. *E-mail:* kterry@maufl.edu.
*Website:* http://www.maufl.edu/.

---

# MILLERSVILLE UNIVERSITY OF PENNSYLVANIA
## Millersville, PA

| Tuition & fees (PA res): $10,268 | Average undergraduate aid package: $8479 |
| --- | --- |

**ABOUT THE INSTITUTION** State-supported, coed. *Awards:* certificates, associate, bachelor's, and master's degrees. 36 undergraduate majors. **Total enrollment:** 8,047. Undergraduates: 7,171. Freshmen: 1,358. Federal methodology is used as a basis for awarding need-based institutional aid.

**UNDERGRADUATE EXPENSES for 2015–2016 Application fee:** $50. **Tuition, state resident:** full-time $7920; part-time $264 per credit. **Tuition, nonresident:** full-time $21,300; part-time $710 per credit. **Required fees:** full-time $2348; $80.25 per credit or $18 per credit. Full-time tuition and fees vary according to course load, location, and program. Part-time tuition and fees vary according to course load, location, and program. **College room and board:** $11,380; **Room only:** $7304. Room and board charges vary according to board plan, housing facility, and location. Mandatory fees differ for Non-Pennsylvania Residents.

**FRESHMAN FINANCIAL AID (Fall 2013)** 1,185 applied for aid; of those 74% were deemed to have need. 96% of freshmen with need received aid; of those 9% had need fully met. *Average percent of need met:* 79% (excluding resources awarded to replace EFC). *Average financial aid package:* $8025 (excluding resources awarded to replace EFC). 4% of all full-time freshmen had no need and received non-need-based gift aid.

**UNDERGRADUATE FINANCIAL AID (Fall 2013)** 5,578 applied for aid; of those 80% were deemed to have need. 97% of undergraduates with need received aid; of those 8% had need fully met. *Average percent of need met:* 69% (excluding resources awarded to replace EFC). *Average financial aid package:* $8479 (excluding resources awarded to replace EFC). 3% of all full-time undergraduates had no need and received non-need-based gift aid.

**GIFT AID (NEED-BASED) Total amount:** $19,233,187 (53% federal, 37% state, 5% institutional, 5% external sources). **Receiving aid:** Freshmen: 50% (639); all full-time undergraduates: 47% (3,109). *Average award:* Freshmen: $6026; Undergraduates: $5891. *Scholarships, grants, and awards:* Federal Pell, FSEOG, state, private, college/university gift aid from institutional funds, Schock Scholarships.

**GIFT AID (NON-NEED-BASED) Total amount:** $2,627,262 (1% federal, 10% state, 37% institutional, 52% external sources). **Receiving aid:** Freshmen: 11% (135). Undergraduates: 7% (452). *Average award:* Freshmen: $2053. Undergraduates: $2517. *Scholarships, grants, and awards by category:* Academic interests/achievement: 448 awards ($1,299,933 total): biological sciences, business, communication, computer science, education, English, foreign languages, general academic interests/achievements, health fields, humanities, mathematics, physical sciences, social sciences. *Creative arts/performance:* 40 awards ($37,426 total): art/fine arts, music. *Special achievements/activities:* 4 awards ($3678 total): community service. *Special characteristics:* 135 awards ($896,408 total): children of union members/company employees, international students. **Tuition waivers:** Full or partial for employees or children of employees, senior citizens. **ROTC:** Army.

**LOANS Student loans:** $35,790,461 (47% need-based, 53% non-need-based). 70% of past graduating class borrowed through all loan programs. *Average indebtedness per student:* $29,791. *Average need-based loan:* Freshmen: $3274. Undergraduates: $4192. **Parent loans:** $7,744,969 (100% non-need-based). **Programs:** Federal Direct (Subsidized and Unsubsidized Stafford, PLUS), Perkins, college/university, alternative loans.

**WORK-STUDY Federal work-study:** 308 jobs averaging $871. **State or other work-study/employment:** Total amount: $3,004,629 (100% non-need-based). 1,942 part-time jobs averaging $1547.

**ATHLETIC AWARDS** Total amount: $631,114 (28% need-based, 72% non-need-based).

**APPLYING FOR FINANCIAL AID Required financial aid form:** FAFSA. **Financial aid deadline (priority):** 3/15. **Notification date:** Continuous beginning 3/19. Students must reply within 2 weeks of notification.

**CONTACT** Mr. Dwight G. Horsey, Director of Financial Aid/Assistant Vice President for Enrollment Management, Millersville University of Pennsylvania, PO Box 1002, Millersville, PA 17551-0302, 717-871-5100 or toll-free 800-MU-ADMIT. *Fax:* 717-871-2248. *E-mail:* dwight.horsey@millersville.edu.
*Website:* http://www.millersville.edu/.

# MILLIGAN COLLEGE
## Milligan College, TN

| Tuition & fees: $29,830 | Average undergraduate aid package: $21,490 |
| --- | --- |

**ABOUT THE INSTITUTION** Independent Christian, coed. *Awards:* bachelor's and master's degrees. 30 undergraduate majors. *Total enrollment:* 1,191. Undergraduates: 979. Freshmen: 189. Federal methodology is used as a basis for awarding need-based institutional aid.

**UNDERGRADUATE EXPENSES for 2015–2016** *Application fee:* $30. *One-time required fee:* $75. *Comprehensive fee:* $36,330 includes full-time tuition ($28,800), mandatory fees ($1030), and room and board ($6500). Full-time tuition and fees vary according to course load and degree level. Room and board charges vary according to housing facility. *Part-time tuition:* $800 per credit hour. Part-time tuition and fees vary according to course load and degree level.

**FRESHMAN FINANCIAL AID (Fall 2014, est.)** 167 applied for aid; of those 84% were deemed to have need. 100% of freshmen with need received aid; of those 34% had need fully met. *Average percent of need met:* 82% (excluding resources awarded to replace EFC). *Average financial aid package:* $22,236 (excluding resources awarded to replace EFC). 18% of all full-time freshmen had no need and received non-need-based gift aid.

**UNDERGRADUATE FINANCIAL AID (Fall 2014, est.)** 752 applied for aid; of those 86% were deemed to have need. 100% of undergraduates with need received aid; of those 28% had need fully met. *Average percent of need met:* 77% (excluding resources awarded to replace EFC). *Average financial aid package:* $21,490 (excluding resources awarded to replace EFC). 15% of all full-time undergraduates had no need and received non-need-based gift aid.

**GIFT AID (NEED-BASED)** *Total amount:* $9,165,853 (15% federal, 13% state, 61% institutional, 11% external sources). *Receiving aid:* Freshmen: 77% (141); all full-time undergraduates: 79% (633). *Average award:* Freshmen: $19,003; Undergraduates: $18,088. *Scholarships, grants, and awards:* Federal Pell, FSEOG, state, private, college/university gift aid from institutional funds.

**GIFT AID (NON-NEED-BASED)** *Total amount:* $2,360,181 (22% state, 61% institutional, 17% external sources). *Receiving aid:* Freshmen: 18% (33). Undergraduates: 16% (128). *Average award:* Freshmen: $8148. Undergraduates: $9036. *Scholarships, grants, and awards by category: Academic interests/achievement:* 622 awards ($6,180,931 total): general academic interests/achievements, religion/biblical studies. *Creative arts/performance:* 56 awards ($213,950 total): art/fine arts, cinema/film/broadcasting, dance, music, theater/drama. *Special achievements/activities:* 87 awards ($273,700 total): cheerleading/drum major, community service. *Special characteristics:* 23 awards ($463,504 total): children of faculty/staff. *Tuition waivers:* Full or partial for employees or children of employees.

**LOANS** *Student loans:* $4,467,251 (75% need-based, 25% non-need-based). 71% of past graduating class borrowed through all loan programs. *Average indebtedness per student:* $25,626. *Average need-based loan:* Freshmen: $4576. Undergraduates: $4896. *Parent loans:* $973,296 (49% need-based, 51% non-need-based). *Programs:* Federal Direct (Subsidized and Unsubsidized Stafford, PLUS), Perkins, alternative loans.

**WORK-STUDY** *Federal work-study:* Total amount: $126,000; 105 jobs averaging $1200. *State or other work-study/employment:* Total amount: $319,250 (26% need-based, 74% non-need-based). 211 part-time jobs averaging $1494.

**ATHLETIC AWARDS** Total amount: $3,626,371 (62% need-based, 38% non-need-based).

**APPLYING FOR FINANCIAL AID** *Required financial aid form:* FAFSA. *Financial aid deadline (priority):* 3/1. *Notification date:* Continuous beginning 3/1. Students must reply within 2 weeks of notification.

**CONTACT** Diane Keasling, Coordinator of Financial Aid, Milligan College, PO Box 250, Milligan College, TN 37682, 423-461-8968 or toll-free 800-262-8337. *Fax:* 423-929-2368. *E-mail:* dlkeasling@milligan.edu. *Website:* http://www.milligan.edu/.

# MILLIKIN UNIVERSITY
## Decatur, IL

| Tuition & fees: $29,620 | Average undergraduate aid package: $23,190 |
| --- | --- |

**ABOUT THE INSTITUTION** Independent Presbyterian Church (U.S.A.), coed. *Awards:* bachelor's, master's, and doctoral degrees. 53 undergraduate majors. *Total enrollment:* 2,191. Undergraduates: 2,112. Freshmen: 477. Federal methodology is used as a basis for awarding need-based institutional aid.

**UNDERGRADUATE EXPENSES for 2015–2016** *Comprehensive fee:* $38,860 includes full-time tuition ($28,828), mandatory fees ($792), and room and board ($9240). *College room only:* $4820. Room and board charges vary according to board plan and housing facility. *Part-time tuition:* $964 per credit hour. *Part-time fees:* $22 per credit hour.

**FRESHMAN FINANCIAL AID (Fall 2013)** 434 applied for aid; of those 89% were deemed to have need. 100% of freshmen with need received aid; of those 30% had need fully met. *Average percent of need met:* 88% (excluding resources awarded to replace EFC). *Average financial aid package:* $24,593 (excluding resources awarded to replace EFC). 10% of all full-time freshmen had no need and received non-need-based gift aid.

**UNDERGRADUATE FINANCIAL AID (Fall 2013)** 1,898 applied for aid; of those 88% were deemed to have need. 100% of undergraduates with need received aid; of those 54% had need fully met. *Average percent of need met:* 92% (excluding resources awarded to replace EFC). *Average financial aid package:* $23,190 (excluding resources awarded to replace EFC). 10% of all full-time undergraduates had no need and received non-need-based gift aid.

**GIFT AID (NEED-BASED)** *Total amount:* $13,941,579 (27% federal, 26% state, 47% institutional). *Receiving aid:* Freshmen: 78% (351); all full-time undergraduates: 74% (1,502). *Average award:* Freshmen: $9371; Undergraduates: $9054. *Scholarships, grants, and awards:* Federal Pell, FSEOG, state, private, college/university gift aid from institutional funds.

**GIFT AID (NON-NEED-BASED)** *Total amount:* $22,241,959 (97% institutional, 3% external sources). *Receiving aid:* Freshmen: 86% (386). Undergraduates: 76% (1,541). *Average award:* Freshmen: $13,197. Undergraduates: $13,037. *Scholarships, grants, and awards by category: Academic interests/achievement:* 2,057 awards ($20,544,308 total): biological sciences, business, communication, education, English, foreign languages, general academic interests/achievements, health fields, humanities, international studies, mathematics, physical sciences, premedicine. *Creative arts/performance:* 523 awards ($1,173,468 total): art/fine arts, dance, music, theater/drama. *Special achievements/activities:* 67 awards ($123,139 total): community service, general special achievements/activities. *Special characteristics:* 242 awards ($821,624 total): children and siblings of alumni, children of faculty/staff, children of union members/company employees, children with a deceased or disabled parent, international students, parents of current students, relatives of clergy, siblings of current students, veterans. *Tuition waivers:* Full or partial for employees or children of employees.

**LOANS** *Student loans:* $14,641,679 (44% need-based, 56% non-need-based). 81% of past graduating class borrowed through all loan programs. *Average indebtedness per student:* $31,989. *Average need-based loan:* Freshmen: $4039. Undergraduates: $4599. *Parent loans:* $3,232,610 (100% non-need-based). *Programs:* Federal Direct (Subsidized and Unsubsidized Stafford, PLUS), Perkins, private loans.

**WORK-STUDY** *Federal work-study:* 496 jobs averaging $1027. *State or other work-study/employment:* Total amount: $280,083 (100% non-need-based). 344 part-time jobs averaging $814.

**APPLYING FOR FINANCIAL AID** *Required financial aid form:* FAFSA. *Financial aid deadline (priority):* 3/1. *Notification date:* Continuous beginning 3/1. Students must reply by 5/1 or within 4 weeks of notification.

**CONTACT** Cheryl Howerton, Director of Financial Aid, Millikin University, 1184 West Main Street, Decatur, IL 62522-2084, 217-424-6317 or toll-free 800-373-7733. *Fax:* 217-424-5070. *E-mail:* studentservicecenter@millikin.edu. *Website:* http://www.millikin.edu/.

# MILLSAPS COLLEGE
## Jackson, MS

| Tuition & fees: $33,982 | Average undergraduate aid package: $29,702 |
|---|---|

**ABOUT THE INSTITUTION** Independent United Methodist, coed. *Awards:* bachelor's and master's degrees. 31 undergraduate majors. *Total enrollment:* 845. Undergraduates: 771. Freshmen: 236. Federal methodology is used as a basis for awarding need-based institutional aid.

**UNDERGRADUATE EXPENSES for 2015–2016** *Comprehensive fee:* $45,860 includes full-time tuition ($31,872), mandatory fees ($2110), and room and board ($11,878). *College room only:* $6704. Room and board charges vary according to housing facility. *Part-time tuition:* $982 per semester hour. *Part-time fees:* $32 per semester hour. Part-time tuition and fees vary according to course load.

**FRESHMAN FINANCIAL AID (Fall 2014, est.)** 192 applied for aid; of those 83% were deemed to have need. 100% of freshmen with need received aid; of those 34% had need fully met. *Average percent of need met:* 87% (excluding resources awarded to replace EFC). *Average financial aid package:* $31,847 (excluding resources awarded to replace EFC). 31% of all full-time freshmen had no need and received non-need-based gift aid.

**UNDERGRADUATE FINANCIAL AID (Fall 2014, est.)** 528 applied for aid; of those 86% were deemed to have need. 100% of undergraduates with need received aid; of those 28% had need fully met. *Average percent of need met:* 80% (excluding resources awarded to replace EFC). *Average financial aid package:* $29,702 (excluding resources awarded to replace EFC). 38% of all full-time undergraduates had no need and received non-need-based gift aid.

**GIFT AID (NEED-BASED)** *Total amount:* $10,540,184 (8% federal, 3% state, 88% institutional, 1% external sources). *Receiving aid:* Freshmen: 68% (160); all full-time undergraduates: 60% (451). *Average award:* Freshmen: $25,280; Undergraduates: $23,363. *Scholarships, grants, and awards:* Federal Pell, FSEOG, state, private, college/university gift aid from institutional funds.

**GIFT AID (NON-NEED-BASED)** *Total amount:* $7,125,092 (3% state, 96% institutional, 1% external sources). *Receiving aid:* Freshmen: 18% (42). Undergraduates: 12% (89). *Average award:* Freshmen: $21,745. Undergraduates: $20,354. *Scholarships, grants, and awards by category: Academic interests/achievement:* business, general academic interests/achievements. *Creative arts/performance:* art/fine arts, music, theater/drama. *Special achievements/activities:* community service, general special achievements/activities, hobbies/interests, leadership, religious involvement. *Special characteristics:* adult students, children of faculty/staff, ethnic background, first-generation college students, local/state students, religious affiliation. *Tuition waivers:* Full or partial for employees or children of employees. *ROTC:* Army cooperative, Air Force cooperative.

**LOANS** *Student loans:* $3,863,801 (64% need-based, 36% non-need-based). 59% of past graduating class borrowed through all loan programs. *Average indebtedness per student:* $29,021. *Average need-based loan:* Freshmen: $3928. Undergraduates: $4993. *Parent loans:* $1,709,804 (31% need-based, 69% non-need-based). *Programs:* Federal Direct (Subsidized and Unsubsidized Stafford, PLUS), Perkins.

**WORK-STUDY** *Federal work-study:* Total amount: $446,995; 284 jobs averaging $807.

**APPLYING FOR FINANCIAL AID** *Required financial aid form:* FAFSA. *Financial aid deadline (priority):* 3/1. *Notification date:* Continuous beginning 3/15. Students must reply by 5/1 or within 2 weeks of notification.

**CONTACT** Isabelle Higbee, Interim Director of Financial Aid, Millsaps College, 1701 North State Street, Jackson, MS 39210-0001, 601-974-1220 or toll-free 800-352-1050. *Fax:* 601-974-1224. *E-mail:* isabelle.higbee@millsaps.edu.
*Website:* http://www.millsaps.edu/.

# MILLS COLLEGE
## Oakland, CA

| Tuition & fees: $42,918 | Average undergraduate aid package: $38,470 |
|---|---|

**ABOUT THE INSTITUTION** Independent, undergraduate: women only; graduate: coed. *Awards:* certificates, bachelor's, master's, and doctoral degrees. 38 under-

graduate majors. *Total enrollment:* 1,541. Undergraduates: 917. Freshmen: 188. Federal methodology is used as a basis for awarding need-based institutional aid.

**UNDERGRADUATE EXPENSES for 2015–2016** *Application fee:* $50. *Comprehensive fee:* $55,832 includes full-time tuition ($41,618), mandatory fees ($1300), and room and board ($12,914). Full-time tuition and fees vary according to course load. Room and board charges vary according to board plan and housing facility. *Part-time tuition:* $6936 per course. Part-time tuition and fees vary according to course load.

**FRESHMAN FINANCIAL AID (Fall 2014, est.)** 175 applied for aid; of those 93% were deemed to have need. 100% of freshmen with need received aid; of those 18% had need fully met. *Average percent of need met:* 86% (excluding resources awarded to replace EFC). *Average financial aid package:* $42,452 (excluding resources awarded to replace EFC). 18% of all full-time freshmen had no need and received non-need-based gift aid.

**UNDERGRADUATE FINANCIAL AID (Fall 2014, est.)** 782 applied for aid; of those 95% were deemed to have need. 100% of undergraduates with need received aid; of those 13% had need fully met. *Average percent of need met:* 78% (excluding resources awarded to replace EFC). *Average financial aid package:* $38,470 (excluding resources awarded to replace EFC). 13% of all full-time undergraduates had no need and received non-need-based gift aid.

**GIFT AID (NEED-BASED)** *Total amount:* $21,660,802 (10% federal, 13% state, 74% institutional, 3% external sources). *Receiving aid:* Freshmen: 87% (162); all full-time undergraduates: 81% (713). *Average award:* Freshmen: $24,841; Undergraduates: $20,610. *Scholarships, grants, and awards:* Federal Pell, FSEOG, state, private, college/university gift aid from institutional funds.

**GIFT AID (NON-NEED-BASED)** *Total amount:* $1,739,465 (98% institutional, 2% external sources). *Receiving aid:* Freshmen: 6% (12). Undergraduates: 4% (39). *Average award:* Freshmen: $14,501. Undergraduates: $14,565. *Scholarships, grants, and awards by category: Academic interests/achievement:* biological sciences, computer science, general academic interests/achievements, mathematics, physical sciences, premedicine. *Creative arts/performance:* music. *Special achievements/activities:* leadership. *Tuition waivers:* Full or partial for employees or children of employees. *ROTC:* Army cooperative.

**LOANS** *Student loans:* $5,414,726 (98% need-based, 2% non-need-based). 77% of past graduating class borrowed through all loan programs. *Average indebtedness per student:* $31,273. *Average need-based loan:* Freshmen: $5872. Undergraduates: $7758. *Parent loans:* $1,900,619 (94% need-based, 6% non-need-based). *Programs:* Federal Direct (Subsidized and Unsubsidized Stafford, PLUS), Perkins, college/university.

**WORK-STUDY** *Federal work-study:* Total amount: $851,821; jobs available. *State or other work-study/employment:* Total amount: $594,421 (94% need-based, 6% non-need-based). Part-time jobs available.

**APPLYING FOR FINANCIAL AID** *Required financial aid forms:* FAFSA, institution's own form, state aid form. *Financial aid deadline:* 2/15 (priority: 2/1). *Notification date:* Continuous beginning 3/1. Students must reply by 5/1 or within 2 weeks of notification.

**CONTACT** Mr. Larry Blair, Director of Financial Aid, Mills College, 5000 MacArthur Boulevard, Oakland, CA 94613, 510-430-2039 or toll-free 800-87-MILLS. *Fax:* 510-430-2003. *E-mail:* lblair@mills.edu.
*Website:* http://www.mills.edu/.

# MILWAUKEE INSTITUTE OF ART AND DESIGN
## Milwaukee, WI

**CONTACT** Carol Masse, Director of Financial Aid, Milwaukee Institute of Art and Design, 273 East Erie Street, Milwaukee, WI 53202-6003, 414-291-3272 or toll-free 888-749-MIAD. *Fax:* 414-291-8077. *E-mail:* carolmasse@miad.edu.
*Website:* http://www.miad.edu/.

# MILWAUKEE SCHOOL OF ENGINEERING
## Milwaukee, WI

| Tuition & fees: $36,540 | Average undergraduate aid package: $25,083 |
|---|---|

**ABOUT THE INSTITUTION** Independent, coed, primarily men. *Awards:* bachelor's and master's degrees. 19 undergraduate majors. *Total enrollment:* 2,810. Undergraduates: 2,596. Freshmen: 580. Federal methodology is used as a basis for awarding need-based institutional aid.

**UNDERGRADUATE EXPENSES for 2015–2016** *Comprehensive fee:* $45,153 includes full-time tuition ($34,890), mandatory fees ($1650), and room and board ($8613). *College room only:* $5439. Full-time tuition and fees vary according to course load. Room and board charges vary according to board plan and housing facility. *Part-time tuition:* $605 per credit. Part-time tuition and fees vary according to course load.

**FRESHMAN FINANCIAL AID (Fall 2013)** 463 applied for aid; of those 87% were deemed to have need. 100% of freshmen with need received; of those 24% had need fully met. *Average percent of need met:* 82% (excluding resources awarded to replace EFC). *Average financial aid package:* $26,284 (excluding resources awarded to replace EFC). 17% of all full-time freshmen had no need and received non-need-based gift aid.

**UNDERGRADUATE FINANCIAL AID (Fall 2013)** 1,882 applied for aid; of those 92% were deemed to have need. 100% of undergraduates with need received aid; of those 18% had need fully met. *Average percent of need met:* 73% (excluding resources awarded to replace EFC). *Average financial aid package:* $25,083 (excluding resources awarded to replace EFC). 14% of all full-time undergraduates had no need and received non-need-based gift aid.

**GIFT AID (NEED-BASED)** *Total amount:* $39,256,849 (7% federal, 6% state, 81% institutional, 6% external sources). *Receiving aid:* Freshmen: 75% (403); all full-time undergraduates: 76% (1,725). *Average award:* Freshmen: $23,994; Undergraduates: $21,887. *Scholarships, grants, and awards:* Federal Pell, FSEOG, state, private, college/university gift aid from institutional funds.

**GIFT AID (NON-NEED-BASED)** *Total amount:* $7,094,031 (1% state, 92% institutional, 7% external sources). *Receiving aid:* Freshmen: 15% (82). Undergraduates: 11% (243). *Average award:* Freshmen: $17,204. Undergraduates: $14,286. *Scholarships, grants, and awards by category:* Academic interests/achievement: 2,202 awards ($27,387,005 total): business, communication, computer science, engineering/technologies, health fields. *Special characteristics:* 37 awards ($887,568 total): children of faculty/staff. *Tuition waivers:* Full or partial for employees or children of employees. *ROTC:* Army cooperative, Naval cooperative, Air Force cooperative.

**LOANS** *Student loans:* $18,358,960 (69% need-based, 31% non-need-based). 84% of past graduating class borrowed through all loan programs. *Average indebtedness per student:* $37,243. *Average need-based loan:* Freshmen: $2848. Undergraduates: $3692. *Parent loans:* $3,115,466 (61% need-based, 39% non-need-based). *Programs:* Federal Direct (Subsidized and Unsubsidized Stafford, PLUS), Perkins, state, college/university.

**WORK-STUDY** *Federal work-study:* 253 jobs averaging $987.

**APPLYING FOR FINANCIAL AID** *Required financial aid form:* FAFSA. *Financial aid deadline (priority):* 3/15. *Notification date:* Continuous beginning 3/1. Students must reply within 2 weeks of notification.

**CONTACT** Steve Midthun, Director of Financial Aid, Milwaukee School of Engineering, 1025 North Broadway , Milwaukee, WI 53202-3109, 414-277-7223 or toll-free 800-332-6763. *Fax:* 414-277-6952. *E-mail:* finaid@msoe.edu. *Website:* http://www.msoe.edu/.

# MINNEAPOLIS COLLEGE OF ART AND DESIGN
## Minneapolis, MN

| Tuition & fees: $34,146 | Average undergraduate aid package: $22,825 |
|---|---|

**ABOUT THE INSTITUTION** Independent, coed. *Awards:* certificates, bachelor's, and master's degrees. 13 undergraduate majors. *Total enrollment:* 801. Undergraduates: 708. Freshmen: 119. Federal methodology is used as a basis for awarding need-based institutional aid.

**UNDERGRADUATE EXPENSES for 2015–2016** *Application fee:* $50. *Comprehensive fee:* $41,176 includes full-time tuition ($33,696), mandatory fees ($450), and room and board ($7030). *College room only:* $4960. Room and board charges vary according to housing facility. *Part-time tuition:* $1404 per credit hour. *Part-time fees:* $225 per hour. Part-time tuition and fees vary according to course load.

**FRESHMAN FINANCIAL AID (Fall 2014, est.)** 117 applied for aid; of those 88% were deemed to have need. 100% of freshmen with need received aid; of those 16% had need fully met. *Average percent of need met:* 70% (excluding resources awarded to replace EFC). *Average financial aid package:* $24,714 (excluding resources awarded to replace EFC). 15% of all full-time freshmen had no need and received non-need-based gift aid.

**UNDERGRADUATE FINANCIAL AID (Fall 2014, est.)** 546 applied for aid; of those 90% were deemed to have need. 100% of undergraduates with need received aid; of those 11% had need fully met. *Average percent of need met:* 68% (excluding resources awarded to replace EFC). *Average financial aid package:* $22,825 (excluding resources awarded to replace EFC). 18% of all full-time undergraduates had no need and received non-need-based gift aid.

**GIFT AID (NEED-BASED)** *Total amount:* $8,596,123 (13% federal, 9% state, 75% institutional, 3% external sources). *Receiving aid:* Freshmen: 85% (103); all full-time undergraduates: 78% (487). *Average award:* Freshmen: $19,635; Undergraduates: $17,718. *Scholarships, grants, and awards:* Federal Pell, FSEOG, state, private, college/university gift aid from institutional funds.

**GIFT AID (NON-NEED-BASED)** *Total amount:* $1,569,389 (88% institutional, 12% external sources). *Receiving aid:* Freshmen: 12% (14). Undergraduates: 7% (41). *Average award:* Freshmen: $13,166. Undergraduates: $11,165. *Scholarships, grants, and awards by category:* Creative arts/performance: applied art and design, art/fine arts, cinema/film/broadcasting, general creative arts/performance. *Tuition waivers:* Full or partial for children of alumni, employees or children of employees.

**LOANS** *Student loans:* $5,738,561 (78% need-based, 22% non-need-based). 88% of past graduating class borrowed through all loan programs. *Average indebtedness per student:* $33,400. *Average need-based loan:* Freshmen: $4543. Undergraduates: $4747. *Parent loans:* $1,382,259 (52% need-based, 48% non-need-based). *Programs:* Federal Direct (Subsidized and Unsubsidized Stafford, PLUS), Perkins, state.

**WORK-STUDY** *Federal work-study:* Total amount: $244,041; jobs available. *State or other work-study/employment:* Total amount: $351,500 (60% need-based, 40% non-need-based). Part-time jobs available.

**APPLYING FOR FINANCIAL AID** *Required financial aid form:* FAFSA. *Financial aid deadline:* 4/1 (priority: 3/1). *Notification date:* Continuous beginning 3/1. Students must reply by 5/1 or within 2 weeks of notification.

**CONTACT** Ms. Laura Link, Director of Financial Aid, Minneapolis College of Art and Design, 2501 Stevens Avenue South, Minneapolis, MN 55404-4347, 612-874-3733 or toll-free 800-874-6223. *Fax:* 612-874-3701. *E-mail:* laura_link@mead.edu. *Website:* http://www.mcad.edu/.

# MINNESOTA SCHOOL OF BUSINESS–BLAINE
## Blaine, MN

**CONTACT** Office of Financial Aid, Minnesota School of Business–Blaine, 3680 Pheasant Ridge Drive NE, Blaine, MN 55449, 763-225-8008. *Fax:* 763-225-8001. *E-mail:* lfourniea@msbcollege.edu. *Website:* http://www.msbcollege.edu/.

# MINNESOTA SCHOOL OF BUSINESS–ELK RIVER

## Elk River, MN

**CONTACT** Office of Financial Aid, Minnesota School of Business–Elk River, 11500 193rd Avenue, Elk River, MN 55330, 763-367-7000. *Website:* http://www.msbcollege.edu/.

# MINNESOTA SCHOOL OF BUSINESS–LAKEVILLE

## Lakeville, MN

**CONTACT** Office of Financial Aid, Minnesota School of Business–Lakeville, 17685 Juniper Path , Lakeville , MN 55044, 952-892-9000. *Fax:* 952-892-9001. *Website:* http://www.msbcollege.edu/.

# MINNESOTA SCHOOL OF BUSINESS–RICHFIELD

## Richfield, MN

**CONTACT** Office of Financial Aid, Minnesota School of Business–Richfield, 1401 West 76th Street, Richfield , MN 55423, 612-861-2000 or toll-free 800-752-4223. *Fax:* 612-861-5548. *Website:* http://www.msbcollege.edu/.

# MINNESOTA SCHOOL OF BUSINESS–ROCHESTER

## Rochester, MN

**CONTACT** Office of Financial Aid, Minnesota School of Business–Rochester, 2521 Pennington Drive NW , Rochester , MN 55901, 507-536-9500 or toll-free 888-662-8772. *Fax:* 507-536-8011. *Website:* http://www.msbcollege.edu/.

# MINNESOTA SCHOOL OF BUSINESS–ST. CLOUD

## Waite Park, MN

**CONTACT** Office of Financial Aid, Minnesota School of Business–St. Cloud, 1201 2nd Street South , Waite Park , MN 56387, 320-257-2000 or toll-free 866-403-3333. *Fax:* 320-257-0131. *Website:* http://www.msbcollege.edu/.

# MINNESOTA STATE UNIVERSITY MANKATO

## Mankato, MN

| Tuition & fees (MN res): $8481 | Average undergraduate aid package: $8960 |
| --- | --- |

**ABOUT THE INSTITUTION** State-supported, coed. *Awards:* certificates, associate, bachelor's, master's, and doctoral degrees. 108 undergraduate majors. *Total enrollment:* 15,407. Undergraduates: 13,459. Freshmen: 2,456. Federal methodology is used as a basis for awarding need-based institutional aid.

**UNDERGRADUATE EXPENSES** for 2015–2016 *Application fee:* $20. *Tuition, state resident:* full-time $7574; part-time $262.34 per credit hour. *Tuition, nonresident:* full-time $15,052; part-time $564.04 per credit hour. *Required fees:* full-time $907; $37.69 per credit hour. Full-time tuition and fees vary according to course load, location, program, and reciprocity agreements. Part-time tuition and fees vary according to course load, location, program, and reciprocity agreements. *College room and board:* $8042. Room and board charges vary according to board plan and housing facility.

**FRESHMAN FINANCIAL AID (Fall 2014, est.)** 1,986 applied for aid; of those 69% were deemed to have need. 99% of freshmen with need received aid; of those 20% had need fully met. *Average percent of need met:* 72% (excluding resources awarded to replace EFC). *Average financial aid package:* $9119 (excluding resources awarded to replace EFC). 7% of all full-time freshmen had no need and received non-need-based gift aid.

**UNDERGRADUATE FINANCIAL AID (Fall 2014, est.)** 8,721 applied for aid; of those 73% were deemed to have need. 99% of undergraduates with need received aid; of those 21% had need fully met. *Average percent of need met:* 72% (excluding resources awarded to replace EFC). *Average financial aid package:* $8960 (excluding resources awarded to replace EFC). 3% of all full-time undergraduates had no need and received non-need-based gift aid.

**GIFT AID (NEED-BASED)** *Total amount:* $25,800,752 (62% federal, 27% state, 4% institutional, 7% external sources). *Receiving aid:* Freshmen: 40% (919); all full-time undergraduates: 39% (4,269). *Average award:* Freshmen: $5457; Undergraduates: $5057. *Scholarships, grants, and awards:* Federal Pell, FSEOG, state, private, college/university gift aid from institutional funds.

**GIFT AID (NON-NEED-BASED)** *Total amount:* $5,658,136 (6% federal, 2% state, 33% institutional, 59% external sources). *Receiving aid:* Freshmen: 22% (505). Undergraduates: 13% (1,399). *Average award:* Freshmen: $2167. Undergraduates: $2940. *Scholarships, grants, and awards by category:* Academic interests/achievement: general academic interests/achievements. Creative arts/performance: art/fine arts, general creative arts/performance. Special achievements/activities: leadership. Special characteristics: members of minority groups. *Tuition waivers:* Full or partial for employees or children of employees, senior citizens. *ROTC:* Army.

**LOANS** *Student loans:* $78,377,815 (56% need-based, 44% non-need-based). 74% of past graduating class borrowed through all loan programs. *Average indebtedness per student:* $31,568. *Average need-based loan:* Freshmen: $3697. Undergraduates: $4245. *Parent loans:* $5,170,261 (23% need-based, 77% non-need-based). *Programs:* Federal Direct (Subsidized and Unsubsidized Stafford, PLUS), Perkins, state, college/university, alternative loans.

**WORK-STUDY** *Federal work-study:* Total amount: $1,496,055; jobs available. *State or other work-study/employment:* Total amount: $4,968,810 (37% need-based, 63% non-need-based). Part-time jobs available.

**ATHLETIC AWARDS** Total amount: $2,616,380 (32% need-based, 68% non-need-based).

**APPLYING FOR FINANCIAL AID** *Required financial aid form:* FAFSA. *Financial aid deadline (priority):* 3/15. *Notification date:* Continuous beginning 3/30.

**CONTACT** Sandra Loerts, Director of Financial Aid, Minnesota State University Mankato, 120 Wigley Administration Center, Mankato, MN 56001, 507-389-1866 or toll-free 800-722-0544. *Fax:* 507-389-2227. *E-mail:* campushub@mnsu.edu. *Website:* http://www.mnsu.edu/.

# MINNESOTA STATE UNIVERSITY MOORHEAD

## Moorhead, MN

| Tuition & fees (MN res): $7829 | Average undergraduate aid package: N/A |
| --- | --- |

**ABOUT THE INSTITUTION** State-supported, coed. *Awards:* certificates, associate, bachelor's, and master's degrees. 79 undergraduate majors. *Total enrollment:* 6,310. Undergraduates: 5,738. Freshmen: 894. Federal methodology is used as a basis for awarding need-based institutional aid.

**UNDERGRADUATE EXPENSES** for 2015–2016 *Application fee:* $20. *Tuition, state resident:* full-time $6898; part-time $222 per credit hour. *Tuition, nonresident:* full-time $13,796; part-time $445 per credit hour. *Required fees:* full-time $931; $465 per term. Full-time tuition and fees vary according to course load, program, and reciprocity agreements. Part-time tuition and fees vary according to course load, program, and reciprocity agreements. **College room and board:** $7398. Room and board charges vary according to board plan and housing facility.

**FRESHMAN FINANCIAL AID (Fall 2014, est.)** 758 applied for aid; of those 68% were deemed to have need. 99% of freshmen with need received aid.

**UNDERGRADUATE FINANCIAL AID (Fall 2014, est.)** 3,720 applied for aid; of those 73% were deemed to have need. 99% of undergraduates with need received aid.

**GIFT AID (NEED-BASED) Total amount:** $10,104,860 (68% federal, 29% state, 1% institutional, 2% external sources). **Receiving aid:** Freshmen: 38% (336); all full-time undergraduates: 39% (1,830). **Average award:** Freshmen: $2515; Undergraduates: $2665. **Scholarships, grants, and awards:** Federal Pell, FSEOG, state, private, college/university gift aid from institutional funds, TEACH Grants.

**GIFT AID (NON-NEED-BASED) Total amount:** $3,379,332 (19% federal, 2% state, 51% institutional, 28% external sources). **Receiving aid:** Freshmen: 33% (294). Undergraduates: 17% (809). **Scholarships, grants, and awards by category:** Academic interests/achievement: biological sciences, business, communication, computer science, education, engineering/technologies, English, general academic interests/achievements, health fields, international studies, mathematics, physical sciences, pre-medicine, social sciences. Creative arts/performance: art/fine arts, cinema/film/broadcasting, creative writing, music, theater/drama. Special achievements/activities: community service, general special achievements/activities. Special characteristics: adult students, children of faculty/staff, first-generation college students, members of minority groups, out-of-state students. **Tuition waivers:** Full or partial for employees or children of employees, senior citizens. **ROTC:** Army cooperative, Air Force cooperative.

**LOANS Student loans:** $29,071,146 (35% need-based, 65% non-need-based). **Average need-based loan:** Freshmen: $3147. Undergraduates: $3932. **Parent loans:** $622,052 (100% non-need-based). **Programs:** Federal Direct (Subsidized and Unsubsidized Stafford, PLUS), Perkins, state, private loans.

**WORK-STUDY Federal work-study:** Total amount: $626,141; 304 jobs averaging $2425. **State or other work-study/employment:** Total amount: $3,873,287 (11% need-based, 89% non-need-based). 208 part-time jobs averaging $2235.

**ATHLETIC AWARDS** Total amount: $774,809 (100% non-need-based).

**APPLYING FOR FINANCIAL AID Required financial aid form:** FAFSA. **Financial aid deadline (priority):** 2/15. **Notification date:** Continuous beginning 6/1. Students must reply within 2 weeks of notification.

**CONTACT** Ms. Carolyn Zehren, Director of Financial Aid, Minnesota State University Moorhead, 1104 7th Avenue South, Moorhead, MN 56563, 218-477-2251 or toll-free 800-593-7246. Fax: 218-477-2058. E-mail: finaid@mnstate.edu. Website: http://www.mnstate.edu/.

---

# MINOT STATE UNIVERSITY
## Minot, ND

| Tuition & fees (ND res): $6086 | Average undergraduate aid package: $9441 |
|---|---|

**ABOUT THE INSTITUTION** State-supported, coed. **Awards:** certificates, associate, bachelor's, and master's degrees. 58 undergraduate majors. **Total enrollment:** 3,410. Undergraduates: 3,116. Freshmen: 341. Federal methodology is used as a basis for awarding need-based institutional aid.

**UNDERGRADUATE EXPENSES for 2015–2016 Application fee:** $35. **Tuition, state resident:** full-time $4820; part-time $253.61 per credit hour. **Tuition, nonresident:** full-time $4820; part-time $253.61 per credit hour. **Required fees:** full-time $1266. Full-time tuition and fees vary according to class time, course load, degree level, location, program, and reciprocity agreements. Part-time tuition and fees vary according to class time, course load, degree level, location, program, and reciprocity agreements. **College room and board:** $5550. Room and board charges vary according to board plan and housing facility.

**FRESHMAN FINANCIAL AID (Fall 2013)** 261 applied for aid; of those 64% were deemed to have need. 100% of freshmen with need received aid; of those 31% had need fully met. **Average percent of need met:** 73% (excluding resources awarded to replace EFC). **Average financial aid package:** $8582 (excluding resources awarded to replace EFC). 22% of all full-time freshmen had no need and received non-need-based gift aid.

**UNDERGRADUATE FINANCIAL AID (Fall 2013)** 1,422 applied for aid; of those 72% were deemed to have need. 100% of undergraduates with need received aid; of those 33% had need fully met. **Average percent of need met:** 72% (excluding resources awarded to replace EFC). **Average financial aid package:**

$9441 (excluding resources awarded to replace EFC). 14% of all full-time undergraduates had no need and received non-need-based gift aid.

**GIFT AID (NEED-BASED) Total amount:** $4,216,549 (65% federal, 19% state, 7% institutional, 9% external sources). **Receiving aid:** Freshmen: 46% (162); all full-time undergraduates: 43% (912). **Average award:** Freshmen: $4860; Undergraduates: $4593. **Scholarships, grants, and awards:** Federal Pell, FSEOG, state, private, college/university gift aid from institutional funds.

**GIFT AID (NON-NEED-BASED) Total amount:** $1,086,766 (4% federal, 23% state, 32% institutional, 41% external sources). **Receiving aid:** Freshmen: 7% (26). Undergraduates: 3% (61). **Average award:** Freshmen: $820. Undergraduates: $1066. **Scholarships, grants, and awards by category:** Academic interests/achievement: biological sciences, business, communication, computer science, education, English, general academic interests/achievements, health fields, humanities, mathematics, social sciences. Creative arts/performance: art/fine arts, cinema/film/broadcasting, music, performing arts, theater/drama. Special characteristics: children and siblings of alumni, children of faculty/staff, ethnic background, international students, local/state students, members of minority groups, out-of-state students, veterans, veterans' children. **Tuition waivers:** Full or partial for minority students, children of alumni, employees or children of employees, senior citizens.

**LOANS Student loans:** $8,365,713 (63% need-based, 37% non-need-based). 56% of past graduating class borrowed through all loan programs. **Average indebtedness per student:** $24,856. **Average need-based loan:** Freshmen: $3871. Undergraduates: $5518. **Parent loans:** $94,894 (3% need-based, 97% non-need-based). **Programs:** Federal Direct (Subsidized and Unsubsidized Stafford, PLUS), Perkins, Federal Nursing.

**WORK-STUDY Federal work-study:** 97 jobs averaging $1681.

**ATHLETIC AWARDS** Total amount: $896,075 (38% need-based, 62% non-need-based).

**APPLYING FOR FINANCIAL AID Required financial aid forms:** FAFSA, institutional scholarship application form. **Financial aid deadline (priority):** 4/15. **Notification date:** Continuous beginning 4/15. Students must reply within 4 weeks of notification.

**CONTACT** Ms. Laurie Weber, Director of Financial Aid, Minot State University, 500 University Avenue, West, Minot, ND 58707-0002, 701-858-3875 or toll-free 800-777-0750 Ext. 3350. Fax: 701-858-4310. E-mail: laurie.weber@minotstateu.edu. Website: http://www.minotstateu.edu/.

---

# MIRRER YESHIVA
## Brooklyn, NY

**CONTACT** Financial Aid Office, Mirrer Yeshiva, 1795 Ocean Parkway, Brooklyn, NY 11223-2010, 718-645-0536.

---

# MISERICORDIA UNIVERSITY
## Dallas, PA

| Tuition & fees: $29,010 | Average undergraduate aid package: $20,002 |
|---|---|

**ABOUT THE INSTITUTION** Independent Roman Catholic, coed. **Awards:** certificates, bachelor's, master's, and doctoral degrees. 33 undergraduate majors. **Total enrollment:** 3,196. Undergraduates: 2,465. Freshmen: 438. Federal methodology is used as a basis for awarding need-based institutional aid.

**UNDERGRADUATE EXPENSES for 2015–2016 Application fee:** $35. **Comprehensive fee:** $41,060 includes full-time tuition ($27,470), mandatory fees ($1540), and room and board ($12,050). **College room only:** $7000. Full-time tuition and fees vary according to degree level. Room and board charges vary according to board plan and housing facility. **Part-time tuition:** $535 per credit. Part-time tuition and fees vary according to class time and location.

**FRESHMAN FINANCIAL AID (Fall 2014, est.)** 418 applied for aid; of those 81% were deemed to have need. 100% of freshmen with need received aid; of those 25% had need fully met. **Average percent of need met:** 76% (excluding resources awarded to replace EFC). **Average financial aid package:** $20,101 (excluding resources awarded to replace EFC). 18% of all full-time freshmen had no need and received non-need-based gift aid.

**UNDERGRADUATE FINANCIAL AID (Fall 2014, est.)** 1,629 applied for aid; of those 86% were deemed to have need. 100% of undergraduates with need received aid; of those 21% had need fully met. *Average percent of need met:* 74% (excluding resources awarded to replace EFC). *Average financial aid package:* $20,002 (excluding resources awarded to replace EFC). 12% of all full-time undergraduates had no need and received non-need-based gift aid.

**GIFT AID (NEED-BASED)** *Total amount:* $20,557,210 (15% federal, 10% state, 74% institutional, 1% external sources). *Receiving aid:* Freshmen: 77% (337); all full-time undergraduates: 79% (1,400). *Average award:* Freshmen: $13,733; Undergraduates: $14,030. *Scholarships, grants, and awards:* Federal Pell, FSEOG, state, private, college/university gift aid from institutional funds, Federal Nursing.

**GIFT AID (NON-NEED-BASED)** *Total amount:* $4,950,106 (98% institutional, 2% external sources). *Receiving aid:* Freshmen: 17% (73). Undergraduates: 12% (220). *Average award:* Freshmen: $11,688. Undergraduates: $10,709. *Scholarships, grants, and awards by category: Academic interests/achievement:* $12,574,230 total: business, computer science, education, general academic interests/achievements, health fields, physical sciences, social sciences. *Special achievements/activities:* $3,469,910 total: community service, general special achievements/activities, leadership. *Special characteristics:* $2,142,249 total: children and siblings of alumni, children of current students, children of faculty/staff, general special characteristics, members of minority groups, out-of-state students, previous college experience, relatives of clergy, siblings of current students. *Tuition waivers:* Full or partial for employees or children of employees. *ROTC:* Army cooperative, Air Force cooperative.

**LOANS** *Student loans:* $18,221,631 (70% need-based, 30% non-need-based). 88% of past graduating class borrowed through all loan programs. *Average indebtedness per student:* $35,140. *Average need-based loan:* Freshmen: $8526. Undergraduates: $9118. *Parent loans:* $5,119,722 (43% need-based, 57% non-need-based). *Programs:* Federal Direct (Subsidized and Unsubsidized Stafford, PLUS), Perkins, Federal Nursing, state.

**WORK-STUDY** *Federal work-study:* Total amount: $392,430; 254 jobs averaging $1545.

**APPLYING FOR FINANCIAL AID** *Required financial aid forms:* FAFSA, institution's own form. *Financial aid deadline (priority):* 3/1. *Notification date:* 3/15. Students must reply within 2 weeks of notification.

**CONTACT** Jane Dessoye, Executive Director of Enrollment Management, Misericordia University, 301 Lake Street, Dallas, PA 18612-1098, 570-674-6280 or toll-free 866-262-6363. *Fax:* 570-675-2441. *E-mail:* finaid@misericordia.edu. *Website:* http://www.misericordia.edu/.

# MISSISSIPPI COLLEGE
## Clinton, MS

| Tuition & fees: $15,458 | Average undergraduate aid package: $14,281 |
| --- | --- |

**ABOUT THE INSTITUTION** Independent Southern Baptist, coed. 61 undergraduate majors. Federal methodology is used as a basis for awarding need-based institutional aid.

**UNDERGRADUATE EXPENSES for 2015–2016** *Comprehensive fee:* $23,866 includes full-time tuition ($14,670), mandatory fees ($788), and room and board ($8408). *College room only:* $5548. Full-time tuition and fees vary according to course load. Room and board charges vary according to housing facility. *Part-time tuition:* $459 per semester hour. *Part-time fees:* $179 per term. Part-time tuition and fees vary according to course load.

**FRESHMAN FINANCIAL AID (Fall 2014, est.)** 483 applied for aid; of those 53% were deemed to have need. 100% of freshmen with need received aid; of those 11% had need fully met. *Average percent of need met:* 82% (excluding resources awarded to replace EFC). *Average financial aid package:* $15,863 (excluding resources awarded to replace EFC). 45% of all full-time freshmen had no need and received non-need-based gift aid.

**UNDERGRADUATE FINANCIAL AID (Fall 2014, est.)** 2,045 applied for aid; of those 70% were deemed to have need. 100% of undergraduates with need received aid; of those 10% had need fully met. *Average percent of need met:* 65% (excluding resources awarded to replace EFC). *Average financial aid package:* $14,281 (excluding resources awarded to replace EFC). 37% of all full-time undergraduates had no need and received non-need-based gift aid.

**GIFT AID (NEED-BASED)** *Total amount:* $15,909,776 (28% federal, 6% state, 62% institutional, 4% external sources). *Receiving aid:* Freshmen: 43% (248); all full-

time undergraduates: 52% (1,378). *Average award:* Freshmen: $11,239; Undergraduates: $9986. *Scholarships, grants, and awards:* Federal Pell, FSEOG, state, private, college/university gift aid from institutional funds, Federal Nursing.

**GIFT AID (NON-NEED-BASED)** *Total amount:* $8,279,993 (10% state, 89% institutional, 1% external sources). *Receiving aid:* Freshmen: 2% (13). Undergraduates: 1% (30). *Average award:* Freshmen: $7885. Undergraduates: $7420. *Scholarships, grants, and awards by category: Academic interests/achievement:* 1,526 awards ($10,734,658 total): general academic interests/achievements. *Creative arts/performance:* 93 awards ($210,940 total): applied art and design, art/fine arts, music. *Special achievements/activities:* 644 awards ($1,114,144 total): general special achievements/activities, leadership, religious involvement. *Special characteristics:* 1,211 awards ($2,904,756 total): children and siblings of alumni, children of faculty/staff, general special characteristics, relatives of clergy. *Tuition waivers:* Full or partial for employees or children of employees, adult students.

**LOANS** *Student loans:* $12,867,311 (79% need-based, 21% non-need-based). 56% of past graduating class borrowed through all loan programs. *Average indebtedness per student:* $29,189. *Average need-based loan:* Freshmen: $5671. Undergraduates: $7638. *Parent loans:* $1,071,732 (38% need-based, 62% non-need-based). *Programs:* Federal Direct (Subsidized and Unsubsidized Stafford, PLUS), Perkins, Federal Nursing, college/university.

**WORK-STUDY** *Federal work-study:* Total amount: $169,941; 229 jobs averaging $742.

**APPLYING FOR FINANCIAL AID** *Required financial aid forms:* FAFSA, state aid form. *Financial aid deadline (priority):* 3/1. *Notification date:* Continuous beginning 3/1. Students must reply by 5/1.

**CONTACT** Mrs. Karon Q. McMillan, Director of Financial Aid, Mississippi College, Box 4035, 200 South Capitol Street, Clinton, MS 39058-0001, 601-925-3249 or toll-free 800-738-1236. *Fax:* 601-925-3950. *E-mail:* kmcmilla@mc.edu. *Website:* http://www.mc.edu/.

# MISSISSIPPI STATE UNIVERSITY
## Mississippi State, MS

| Tuition & fees (MS res): $7140 | Average undergraduate aid package: $13,208 |
| --- | --- |

**ABOUT THE INSTITUTION** State-supported, coed. *Awards:* certificates, associate, bachelor's, master's, and doctoral degrees. 74 undergraduate majors. *Total enrollment:* 20,138. Undergraduates: 16,536. Freshmen: 2,974. Federal methodology is used as a basis for awarding need-based institutional aid.

**UNDERGRADUATE EXPENSES for 2015–2016** *Application fee:* $40. *Tuition, state resident:* full-time $7140; part-time $293.50 per credit hour. *Tuition, nonresident:* full-time $18,478; part-time $766 per credit hour. Full-time tuition and fees vary according to degree level and location. Part-time tuition and fees vary according to course load, degree level, and location. *College room and board:* $8954; *Room only:* $5404. Room and board charges vary according to board plan, housing facility, and student level. *Payment plan:* Tuition prepayment.

**FRESHMAN FINANCIAL AID (Fall 2013)** 2,584 applied for aid; of those 83% were deemed to have need. 99% of freshmen with need received aid; of those 29% had need fully met. *Average percent of need met:* 60% (excluding resources awarded to replace EFC). *Average financial aid package:* $15,020 (excluding resources awarded to replace EFC). 24% of all full-time freshmen had no need and received non-need-based gift aid.

**UNDERGRADUATE FINANCIAL AID (Fall 2013)** 10,902 applied for aid; of those 86% were deemed to have need. 98% of undergraduates with need received aid; of those 23% had need fully met. *Average percent of need met:* 60% (excluding resources awarded to replace EFC). *Average financial aid package:* $13,208 (excluding resources awarded to replace EFC). 18% of all full-time undergraduates had no need and received non-need-based gift aid.

**GIFT AID (NEED-BASED)** *Total amount:* $48,407,475 (52% federal, 12% state, 27% institutional, 9% external sources). *Receiving aid:* Freshmen: 62% (1,954); all full-time undergraduates: 54% (8,188). *Average award:* Freshmen: $5836; Undergraduates: $5435. *Scholarships, grants, and awards:* Federal Pell, FSEOG, state, private, college/university gift aid from institutional funds, United Negro College Fund.

**GIFT AID (NON-NEED-BASED)** *Total amount:* $17,214,380 (16% state, 75% institutional, 9% external sources). *Receiving aid:* Freshmen: 10% (323). Undergraduates: 4% (675). *Average award:* Freshmen: $4774. Undergraduates: $3930. *Scholarships, grants, and awards by category: Academic interests/achievement:*

agriculture, architecture, area/ethnic studies, biological sciences, business, communication, computer science, education, engineering/technologies, English, foreign languages, general academic interests/achievements, health fields, home economics, humanities, international studies, library science, mathematics, military science, physical sciences, premedicine, religion/biblical studies, social sciences. *Creative arts/performance:* applied art and design, art/fine arts, cinema/film/broadcasting, creative writing, dance, debating, general creative arts/performance, journalism/publications, music, performing arts, theater/drama. *Special achievements/activities:* cheerleading/drum major, general special achievements/activities, junior miss, leadership, memberships. *Special characteristics:* adult students, children and siblings of alumni, children of educators, children of faculty/staff, children of public servants, first-generation college students, handicapped students, local/state students, out-of-state students, previous college experience, spouses of deceased or disabled public servants. *Tuition waivers:* Full or partial for children of alumni, employees or children of employees, senior citizens. *ROTC:* Army, Air Force.

**LOANS** *Student loans:* $99,607,283 (84% need-based, 16% non-need-based). 53% of past graduating class borrowed through all loan programs. *Average indebtedness per student:* $29,365. *Average need-based loan:* Freshmen: $3344. Undergraduates: $3999. *Parent loans:* $11,661,168 (58% need-based, 42% non-need-based). *Programs:* Federal Direct (Subsidized and Unsubsidized Stafford, PLUS), Perkins, college/university.

**WORK-STUDY** *Federal work-study:* 713 jobs averaging $3741.

**ATHLETIC AWARDS** Total amount: $6,722,231 (100% non-need-based).

**APPLYING FOR FINANCIAL AID** *Required financial aid forms:* FAFSA, state aid form. *Financial aid deadline (priority):* 3/1. *Notification date:* Continuous beginning 12/1. Students must reply by 5/1.

**CONTACT** Mr. Kenneth Paul McKinney, Director of Financial Aid, Mississippi State University, PO Box 6035, Mississippi State, MS 39762, 662-325-7428. *Fax:* 662-325-0702. *E-mail:* financialaid@saffairs.msstate.edu.
*Website:* http://www.msstate.edu/.

# MISSISSIPPI UNIVERSITY FOR WOMEN
## Columbus, MS

| Tuition & fees (MS res): $5640 | Average undergraduate aid package: $8948 |
|---|---|

**ABOUT THE INSTITUTION** State-supported, coed. *Awards:* certificates, associate, bachelor's, master's, and doctoral degrees. 29 undergraduate majors. *Total enrollment:* 2,696. Undergraduates: 2,527. Freshmen: 243. Federal methodology is used as a basis for awarding need-based institutional aid.

**UNDERGRADUATE EXPENSES for 2015–2016** *Tuition, state resident:* full-time $5640; part-time $235 per credit hour. *Tuition, nonresident:* full-time $15,360; part-time $640 per credit hour. Part-time tuition and fees vary according to course load. *College room and board:* $6381. Room and board charges vary according to housing facility.

**FRESHMAN FINANCIAL AID (Fall 2013)** 159 applied for aid; of those 89% were deemed to have need. 99% of freshmen with need received aid; of those 16% had need fully met. *Average percent of need met:* 64% (excluding resources awarded to replace EFC). *Average financial aid package:* $10,534 (excluding resources awarded to replace EFC). 19% of all full-time freshmen had no need and received non-need-based gift aid.

**UNDERGRADUATE FINANCIAL AID (Fall 2013)** 1,651 applied for aid; of those 89% were deemed to have need. 99% of undergraduates with need received aid; of those 39% had need fully met. *Average percent of need met:* 74% (excluding resources awarded to replace EFC). *Average financial aid package:* $8948 (excluding resources awarded to replace EFC). 14% of all full-time undergraduates had no need and received non-need-based gift aid.

**GIFT AID (NEED-BASED)** *Total amount:* $5,306,551 (98% federal, 2% state). *Receiving aid:* Freshmen: 58% (105); all full-time undergraduates: 52% (1,018). *Average award:* Freshmen: $5242; Undergraduates: $5527. *Scholarships, grants, and awards:* Federal Pell, FSEOG, state, private, college/university gift aid from institutional funds.

**GIFT AID (NON-NEED-BASED)** *Total amount:* $6,806,852 (12% state, 84% institutional, 4% external sources). *Receiving aid:* Freshmen: 59% (107). Undergraduates: 45% (870). *Average award:* Freshmen: $6131. Undergraduates: $5458. *Scholarships, grants, and awards by category:* Academic interests/achievement: 755 awards ($2,257,680 total): biological sciences, business, communi-

cation, computer science, education, English, general academic interests/achievements, health fields, home economics, humanities, mathematics, physical sciences. *Creative arts/performance:* 90 awards ($42,400 total): art/fine arts, journalism/publications, music, performing arts, theater/drama. *Special achievements/activities:* 16 awards ($34,763 total): junior miss, leadership. *Special characteristics:* 181 awards ($901,227 total): adult students, children and siblings of alumni, children of faculty/staff, ethnic background, international students, members of minority groups, out-of-state students, parents of current students. *Tuition waivers:* Full or partial for employees or children of employees. *ROTC:* Army cooperative, Air Force cooperative.

**LOANS** *Student loans:* $12,520,216 (44% need-based, 56% non-need-based). 68% of past graduating class borrowed through all loan programs. *Average indebtedness per student:* $21,095. *Average need-based loan:* Freshmen: $3527. Undergraduates: $5194. *Parent loans:* $312,524 (100% non-need-based). *Programs:* Federal Direct (Subsidized and Unsubsidized Stafford, PLUS), Perkins.

**WORK-STUDY** *Federal work-study:* 88 jobs averaging $1690. *State or other work-study/employment:* Total amount: $440,294 (100% non-need-based). 243 part-time jobs averaging $1812.

**APPLYING FOR FINANCIAL AID** *Required financial aid forms:* FAFSA, institution's own form, state aid form. *Financial aid deadline (priority):* 3/1. *Notification date:* Continuous beginning 4/1. Students must reply within 2 weeks of notification.

**CONTACT** Ms. Nicole Patrick, Director of Financial Aid, Mississippi University for Women, 1100 College Street, MUW 1614, Columbus, MS 39701-4044, 662-329-7114 or toll-free 877-GO 2 THE W. *Fax:* 662-329-7325. *E-mail:* jnpatrick@muw.edu.
*Website:* http://www.muw.edu/.

# MISSISSIPPI VALLEY STATE UNIVERSITY
## Itta Bena, MS

**CONTACT** Margaret Sherrer, Director of Student Financial Aid, Mississippi Valley State University, 14000 Highway 82W #7268, Itta Bena, MS 38941-1400, 662-254-3335 or toll-free 800-844-6885 (in-state). *Fax:* 662-254-7900. *E-mail:* margaret.sherrer@mvsu.edu.
*Website:* http://www.mvsu.edu/.

# MISSOURI BAPTIST UNIVERSITY
## St. Louis, MO

| Tuition & fees: $22,760 | Average undergraduate aid package: $16,719 |
|---|---|

**ABOUT THE INSTITUTION** Independent Southern Baptist, coed. *Awards:* certificates, associate, bachelor's, master's, and doctoral degrees, 50 undergraduate majors. *Total enrollment:* 5,321. Undergraduates: 4,091. Freshmen: 224. Federal methodology is used as a basis for awarding need-based institutional aid.

**UNDERGRADUATE EXPENSES for 2015–2016** *Application fee:* $35. *Comprehensive fee:* $31,830 includes full-time tuition ($21,620), mandatory fees ($1140), and room and board ($9070). Full-time tuition and fees vary according to course load and location. Room and board charges vary according to board plan and housing facility. *Part-time tuition:* $745 per credit hour. *Part-time fees:* $24 per credit hour; $65 per term. Part-time tuition and fees vary according to course load and location.

**FRESHMAN FINANCIAL AID (Fall 2014, est.)** 204 applied for aid; of those 84% were deemed to have need. 100% of freshmen with need received aid; of those 22% had need fully met. *Average financial aid package:* $19,529 (excluding resources awarded to replace EFC). 3% of all full-time freshmen had no need and received non-need-based gift aid.

**UNDERGRADUATE FINANCIAL AID (Fall 2014, est.)** 1,224 applied for aid; of those 91% were deemed to have need. 100% of undergraduates with need received aid; of those 17% had need fully met. *Average financial aid package:* $16,719 (excluding resources awarded to replace EFC). 2% of all full-time undergraduates had no need and received non-need-based gift aid.

**GIFT AID (NEED-BASED)** *Total amount:* $6,877,454 (48% federal, 7% state, 35% institutional, 10% external sources). *Receiving aid:* Freshmen: 62% (137); all full-time undergraduates: 66% (906). *Average award:* Freshmen: $5181; Undergraduates: $4988. *Scholarships, grants, and awards:* Federal Pell, FSEOG, state, private, college/university gift aid from institutional funds.

**GIFT AID (NON-NEED-BASED)** *Total amount:* $278,938 (87% institutional, 13% external sources). *Receiving aid:* Freshmen: 77% (170). Undergraduates: 62% (861). *Average award:* Freshmen: $10,453. Undergraduates: $14,720. *Scholarships, grants, and awards by category:* Academic interests/achievement: general academic interests/achievements, religion/biblical studies. *Creative arts/performance:* music, theater/drama. *Special achievements/activities:* cheerleading/drum major, memberships, religious involvement. *Special characteristics:* adult students, children and siblings of alumni, children of current students, children of faculty/staff, first-generation college students, parents of current students, public servants, relatives of clergy, religious affiliation, siblings of current students, spouses of current students, veterans, veterans' children. *Tuition waivers:* Full or partial for children of alumni, employees or children of employees, senior citizens. *ROTC:* Army cooperative.

**LOANS** *Student loans:* $10,191,032 (96% need-based, 4% non-need-based). 94% of past graduating class borrowed through all loan programs. *Average indebtedness per student:* $25,337. *Average need-based loan:* Freshmen: $3031. Undergraduates: $4168. *Parent loans:* $1,261,726 (92% need-based, 8% non-need-based). *Programs:* Federal Direct (Subsidized and Unsubsidized Stafford, PLUS).

**WORK-STUDY** *Federal work-study:* Total amount: $1,125,957; 555 jobs averaging $1805. *State or other work-study/employment:* Part-time jobs available.

**ATHLETIC AWARDS** Total amount: $7,048,823 (89% need-based, 11% non-need-based).

**APPLYING FOR FINANCIAL AID** *Required financial aid forms:* FAFSA, institution's own form. *Financial aid deadline (priority):* 4/1. *Notification date:* Continuous beginning 4/15. Students must reply within 2 weeks of notification.

**CONTACT** Mr. John Brandt, Director of Student Financial Services, Missouri Baptist University, One College Park Drive, St. Louis, MO 63141, 314-744-7639 or toll-free 877-434-1115 Ext. 2290. *Fax:* 314-744-5320. *E-mail:* brandtJ@mobap.edu. *Website:* http://www.mobap.edu/.

# MISSOURI SOUTHERN STATE UNIVERSITY
## Joplin, MO

| Tuition & fees (MO res): $5762 | Average undergraduate aid package: $7413 |
| --- | --- |

**ABOUT THE INSTITUTION** State-supported, coed. *Awards:* certificates, associate, bachelor's, and master's degrees. 50 undergraduate majors. *Total enrollment:* 5,613. Undergraduates: 5,561. Freshmen: 856. Federal methodology is used as a basis for awarding need-based institutional aid.

**UNDERGRADUATE EXPENSES** for 2015–2016 *Application fee:* $25. *Tuition, state resident:* full-time $5196; part-time $173.20 per term. *Tuition, nonresident:* full-time $10,590; part-time $353 per term. *Required fees:* full-time $566. Full-time tuition and fees vary according to course load. *College room and board:* $6299. Room and board charges vary according to board plan and housing facility.

**FRESHMAN FINANCIAL AID (Fall 2013)** 624 applied for aid; of those 78% were deemed to have need. 97% of freshmen with need received aid; of those 8% had need fully met. *Average percent of need met:* 65% (excluding resources awarded to replace EFC). *Average financial aid package:* $8162 (excluding resources awarded to replace EFC). 15% of all full-time freshmen had no need and received non-need-based gift aid.

**UNDERGRADUATE FINANCIAL AID (Fall 2013)** 2,836 applied for aid; of those 82% were deemed to have need. 97% of undergraduates with need received aid; of those 7% had need fully met. *Average percent of need met:* 65% (excluding resources awarded to replace EFC). *Average financial aid package:* $7413 (excluding resources awarded to replace EFC). 9% of all full-time undergraduates had no need and received non-need-based gift aid.

**GIFT AID (NEED-BASED)** *Total amount:* $13,348,328 (90% federal, 10% state). *Receiving aid:* Freshmen: 65% (412); all full-time undergraduates: 65% (1,910). *Average award:* Freshmen: $4006; Undergraduates: $4121. *Scholarships, grants, and awards:* Federal Pell, FSEOG, state, private, college/university gift aid from institutional funds, TEACH Grants.

**GIFT AID (NON-NEED-BASED)** *Total amount:* $3,774,189 (3% state, 81% institutional, 16% external sources). *Receiving aid:* Freshmen: 47% (302). Under-

graduates: 31% (907). *Average award:* Freshmen: $2287. Undergraduates: $2105. *Scholarships, grants, and awards by category:* Academic interests/achievement: 957 awards ($1,145,706 total): general academic interests/achievements. *Creative arts/performance:* 242 awards ($454,111 total): art/fine arts, journalism/publications, music, theater/drama. *Special achievements/activities:* 30 awards ($30,505 total): cheerleading/drum major, general special achievements/activities, leadership. *Special characteristics:* veterans. *Tuition waivers:* Full or partial for employees or children of employees, senior citizens.

**LOANS** *Student loans:* $22,086,890 (50% need-based, 50% non-need-based). 69% of past graduating class borrowed through all loan programs. *Average indebtedness per student:* $29,405. *Average need-based loan:* Freshmen: $1000. Undergraduates: $2163. *Parent loans:* $204,626 (100% non-need-based). *Programs:* Federal Direct (Subsidized and Unsubsidized Stafford, PLUS), Perkins.

**WORK-STUDY** *Federal work-study:* 81 jobs averaging $2020. *State or other work-study/employment:* Total amount: $1,082,509 (100% non-need-based). 263 part-time jobs averaging $4116.

**ATHLETIC AWARDS** Total amount: $1,710,548 (100% non-need-based).

**APPLYING FOR FINANCIAL AID** *Required financial aid form:* FAFSA. *Financial aid deadline:* Continuous. *Notification date:* Continuous beginning 3/15. Students must reply by 5/1.

**CONTACT** Becca L. Diskin, Director of Financial Aid, Missouri Southern State University, 3950 Newman Road, Joplin, MO 64801-1595, 417-659-5422 or toll-free 866-818-MSSU. *Fax:* 417-659-4474. *E-mail:* diskin-b@mssu.edu. *Website:* http://www.mssu.edu/.

# MISSOURI STATE UNIVERSITY
## Springfield, MO

| Tuition & fees (MO res): $7796 | Average undergraduate aid package: $8892 |
| --- | --- |

**ABOUT THE INSTITUTION** State-supported, coed. *Awards:* certificates, bachelor's, master's, and doctoral degrees. 97 undergraduate majors. *Total enrollment:* 21,816. Undergraduates: 18,517. Freshmen: 2,870. Federal methodology is used as a basis for awarding need-based institutional aid.

**UNDERGRADUATE EXPENSES** for 2015–2016 *Application fee:* $35. *Tuition, state resident:* full-time $6908; part-time $204 per credit hour. *Tuition, nonresident:* full-time $13,668; part-time $426 per credit hour. *Required fees:* full-time $888. Full-time tuition and fees vary according to course level, course load, and program. Part-time tuition and fees vary according to course level, course load, and program. *College room and board:* $7678. Room and board charges vary according to board plan, housing facility, and location.

**FRESHMAN FINANCIAL AID (Fall 2014, est.)** 2,482 applied for aid; of those 71% were deemed to have need. 99% of freshmen with need received aid; of those 18% had need fully met. *Average percent of need met:* 64% (excluding resources awarded to replace EFC). *Average financial aid package:* $9457 (excluding resources awarded to replace EFC). 17% of all full-time freshmen had no need and received non-need-based gift aid.

**UNDERGRADUATE FINANCIAL AID (Fall 2014, est.)** 11,079 applied for aid; of those 79% were deemed to have need. 98% of undergraduates with need received aid; of those 15% had need fully met. *Average percent of need met:* 59% (excluding resources awarded to replace EFC). *Average financial aid package:* $8892 (excluding resources awarded to replace EFC). 10% of all full-time undergraduates had no need and received non-need-based gift aid.

**GIFT AID (NEED-BASED)** *Total amount:* $44,442,427 (62% federal, 17% state, 17% institutional, 4% external sources). *Receiving aid:* Freshmen: 55% (1,558); all full-time undergraduates: 52% (7,259). *Average award:* Freshmen: $6147; Undergraduates: $5632. *Scholarships, grants, and awards:* Federal Pell, FSEOG, state, private, college/university gift aid from institutional funds.

**GIFT AID (NON-NEED-BASED)** *Total amount:* $10,701,254 (7% federal, 13% state, 52% institutional, 28% external sources). *Receiving aid:* Freshmen: 5% (153). Undergraduates: 3% (434). *Average award:* Freshmen: $3235. Undergraduates: $3427. *Scholarships, grants, and awards by category:* Academic interests/achievement: general academic interests/achievements. *Creative arts/performance:* general creative arts/performance. *Special achievements/activities:* leadership. *Special characteristics:* children and siblings of alumni, local/state students, members of minority groups. *Tuition waivers:* Full or partial for children of alumni, employees or children of employees, senior citizens. *ROTC:* Army.

**LOANS** *Student loans:* $75,791,443 (69% need-based, 31% non-need-based). 62% of past graduating class borrowed through all loan programs. *Average indebtedness per student:* $24,655. *Average need-based loan:* Freshmen: $3471. Undergraduates: $4173. *Parent loans:* $9,089,453 (24% need-based, 76% non-need-based). *Programs:* Federal Direct (Subsidized and Unsubsidized Stafford, PLUS), Perkins.

**WORK-STUDY** *Federal work-study:* Total amount: $601,477; jobs available.

**ATHLETIC AWARDS** Total amount: $4,117,357 (26% need-based, 74% non-need-based).

**APPLYING FOR FINANCIAL AID** *Required financial aid form:* FAFSA. *Financial aid deadline (priority):* 3/31. *Notification date:* Continuous beginning 3/31.

**CONTACT** Vicki Mattocks, Director of Financial Aid, Missouri State University, 901 South National Avenue, Springfield, MO 65804, 417-836-5262 or toll-free 800-492-7900. *E-mail:* financialaid@missouristate.edu.

*Website:* http://www.missouristate.edu/.

# MISSOURI TECH
## St. Charles, MO

**ABOUT THE INSTITUTION** Proprietary, coed, primarily men. 7 undergraduate majors.

**GIFT AID (NEED-BASED)** *Scholarships, grants, and awards:* Federal Pell, private, college/university gift aid from institutional funds.

**LOANS** *Programs:* Federal Direct (Subsidized and Unsubsidized Stafford, PLUS).

**APPLYING FOR FINANCIAL AID** *Required financial aid forms:* FAFSA, institution's own form.

**CONTACT** Mrs. Cindy Ann Sinnott, Director of Financial Aid, Missouri Tech, 1690 Country Club Plaza Drive, St. Charles, MO 63303, 636-573-9300 or toll-free 800-960-TECH. *Fax:* 636-573-9398. *E-mail:* contact@motech.edu.

*Website:* http://www.motech.edu/.

# MISSOURI UNIVERSITY OF SCIENCE AND TECHNOLOGY
## Rolla, MO

| Tuition & fees (MO res): $9537 | Average undergraduate aid package: $15,253 |
| --- | --- |

**ABOUT THE INSTITUTION** State-supported, coed. *Awards:* certificates, bachelor's, master's, and doctoral degrees. 35 undergraduate majors. *Total enrollment:* 8,642. Undergraduates: 6,522. Freshmen: 1,288. Federal methodology is used as a basis for awarding need-based institutional aid.

**UNDERGRADUATE EXPENSES for 2015–2016** *Application fee:* $50. *Tuition, state resident:* full-time $8220; part-time $274 per credit hour. *Tuition, nonresident:* full-time $24,087; part-time $802.90 per credit hour. *Required fees:* full-time $1317; $146.31 per credit hour. Full-time tuition and fees vary according to course load, degree level, and program. Part-time tuition and fees vary according to course load, degree level, and program. *College room and board:* $9540; *Room only:* $6090. Room and board charges vary according to board plan, housing facility, and location.

**FRESHMAN FINANCIAL AID (Fall 2013)** 736 applied for aid; of those 95% were deemed to have need. 100% of freshmen with need received aid; of those 96% had need fully met. *Average percent of need met:* 28% (excluding resources awarded to replace EFC). *Average financial aid package:* $16,123 (excluding resources awarded to replace EFC). 20% of all full-time freshmen had no need and received non-need-based gift aid.

**UNDERGRADUATE FINANCIAL AID (Fall 2013)** 3,286 applied for aid; of those 97% were deemed to have need. 100% of undergraduates with need received aid; of those 94% had need fully met. *Average percent of need met:* 36% (excluding resources awarded to replace EFC). *Average financial aid package:* $15,253 (excluding resources awarded to replace EFC). 11% of all full-time undergraduates had no need and received non-need-based gift aid.

**GIFT AID (NEED-BASED)** *Total amount:* $23,062,164 (28% federal, 12% state, 53% institutional, 7% external sources). *Receiving aid:* Freshmen: 53% (665); all full-time undergraduates: 53% (2,899). *Average award:* Freshmen: $9488; Undergrad-

uates: $7460. *Scholarships, grants, and awards:* Federal Pell, FSEOG, state, private, college/university gift aid from institutional funds, ROTC (Army and Air Force) Scholarships.

**GIFT AID (NON-NEED-BASED)** *Total amount:* $13,821,550 (8% state, 72% institutional, 20% external sources). *Receiving aid:* Freshmen: 16% (196). Undergraduates: 19% (1,055). *Average award:* Freshmen: $5813. Undergraduates: $5080. *Scholarships, grants, and awards by category: Academic interests/achievement:* 3,653 awards ($16,482,284 total): biological sciences, business, computer science, education, engineering/technologies, English, general academic interests/achievements, humanities, mathematics, military science, physical sciences, premedicine, social sciences. *Creative arts/performance:* music, theater/drama. *Special characteristics:* 173 awards ($639,837 total): children and siblings of alumni, children of faculty/staff, children of union members/company employees, members of minority groups. *Tuition waivers:* Full or partial for employees or children of employees. *ROTC:* Army, Air Force.

**LOANS** *Student loans:* $34,805,332 (82% need-based, 18% non-need-based). 47% of past graduating class borrowed through all loan programs. *Average indebtedness per student:* $27,591. *Average need-based loan:* Freshmen: $6425. Undergraduates: $7776. *Parent loans:* $9,209,122 (80% need-based, 20% non-need-based). *Programs:* Federal Direct (Subsidized and Unsubsidized Stafford), Perkins, state, college/university, alternative loans.

**WORK-STUDY** *Federal work-study:* 226 jobs averaging $1176. *State or other work-study/employment:* Part-time jobs available.

**ATHLETIC AWARDS** Total amount: $2,742,504 (50% need-based, 50% non-need-based).

**APPLYING FOR FINANCIAL AID** *Required financial aid form:* FAFSA. *Financial aid deadline (priority):* 3/1. *Notification date:* Continuous beginning 4/1. Students must reply within 3 weeks of notification.

**CONTACT** Ms. Bridgette Betz, Director of Student Financial Assistance, Missouri University of Science and Technology, G1 Parker Hall, Rolla, MO 65409, 573-341-4282 or toll-free 800-522-0938. *Fax:* 573-341-4274. *E-mail:* berry@mst.edu.

*Website:* http://www.mst.edu/.

# MISSOURI VALLEY COLLEGE
## Marshall, MO

| Tuition & fees: $19,350 | Average undergraduate aid package: $12,850 |
| --- | --- |

**ABOUT THE INSTITUTION** Independent Presbyterian Church, coed. *Awards:* associate, bachelor's, and master's degrees. 38 undergraduate majors. *Total enrollment:* 1,659. Undergraduates: 1,653. Freshmen: 403. Federal methodology is used as a basis for awarding need-based institutional aid.

**UNDERGRADUATE EXPENSES for 2015–2016** *Application fee:* $15. *Comprehensive fee:* $27,450 includes full-time tuition ($18,200), mandatory fees ($1150), and room and board ($8100). *College room only:* $4300. *Part-time tuition:* $350 per credit hour.

**FRESHMAN FINANCIAL AID (Fall 2014, est.)** 309 applied for aid; of those 93% were deemed to have need. 100% of freshmen with need received aid; of those 40% had need fully met. *Average percent of need met:* 89% (excluding resources awarded to replace EFC). *Average financial aid package:* $13,450 (excluding resources awarded to replace EFC). 24% of all full-time freshmen had no need and received non-need-based gift aid.

**UNDERGRADUATE FINANCIAL AID (Fall 2014, est.)** 1,150 applied for aid; of those 98% were deemed to have need. 100% of undergraduates with need received aid; of those 40% had need fully met. *Average percent of need met:* 85% (excluding resources awarded to replace EFC). *Average financial aid package:* $12,850 (excluding resources awarded to replace EFC). 32% of all full-time undergraduates had no need and received non-need-based gift aid.

**GIFT AID (NEED-BASED)** *Total amount:* $6,089,171 (53% federal, 8% state, 39% institutional). *Receiving aid:* Freshmen: 79% (286); all full-time undergraduates: 79% (1,127). *Average award:* Freshmen: $13,450; Undergraduates: $12,850. *Scholarships, grants, and awards:* Federal Pell, FSEOG, state, private, college/university gift aid from institutional funds.

**GIFT AID (NON-NEED-BASED)** *Total amount:* $4,395,532 (94% institutional, 6% external sources). *Receiving aid:* Freshmen: 79% (286). Undergraduates: 79% (1,127). *Average award:* Freshmen: $13,450. Undergraduates: $12,850. *Scholarships, grants, and awards by category: Academic interests/achievement:* 89

awards ($118,150 total): biological sciences, business, communication, computer science, education, English, general academic interests/achievements, health fields, humanities, mathematics, military science, physical sciences, premedicine, social sciences. *Creative arts/performance:* 35 awards ($262,485 total): applied art and design, art/fine arts, cinema/film/broadcasting, dance, journalism/publications, music, performing arts, theater/drama. *Special achievements/activities:* 108 awards ($1,177,290 total): cheerleading/drum major, community service, general special achievements/activities, hobbies/interests, junior miss, leadership, rodeo. *Special characteristics:* 49 awards ($226,895 total): children and siblings of alumni, children of faculty/staff. *ROTC:* Army.

**LOANS** *Student loans:* $8,314,968 (42% need-based, 58% non-need-based). 76% of past graduating class borrowed through all loan programs. *Average indebtedness per student:* $25,200. *Average need-based loan:* Freshmen: $3500. Undergraduates: $3750. *Parent loans:* $1,468,595 (100% non-need-based). *Programs:* Federal Direct (Subsidized and Unsubsidized Stafford, PLUS), Perkins.

**WORK-STUDY** *Federal work-study:* Total amount: $138,044; 119 jobs averaging $1860. *State or other work-study/employment:* Total amount: $510,484 (100% non-need-based). 450 part-time jobs averaging $1860.

**ATHLETIC AWARDS** Total amount: $10,157,903 (100% need-based).

**APPLYING FOR FINANCIAL AID** *Required financial aid form:* FAFSA. *Financial aid deadline (priority):* 3/15. *Notification date:* Continuous beginning 10/1. Students must reply within 4 weeks of notification.

**CONTACT** Mrs. Rachel Kimberly Robinson, Director of Financial Aid, Missouri Valley College, 500 East College, Marshall, MO 65340-3197, 660-831-4176. *Fax:* 660-831-4003. *E-mail:* robinsonr@moval.edu. *Website:* http://www.moval.edu/.

# MISSOURI WESTERN STATE UNIVERSITY
## St. Joseph, MO

| Tuition & fees (MO res): $6498 | Average undergraduate aid package: $8428 |
| --- | --- |

**ABOUT THE INSTITUTION** State-supported, coed. *Awards:* certificates, associate, bachelor's, and master's degrees. 58 undergraduate majors. *Total enrollment:* 5,834. Undergraduates: 5,650. Freshmen: 1,042. Federal methodology is used as a basis for awarding need-based institutional aid.

**UNDERGRADUATE EXPENSES** for 2015–2016 *Tuition, state resident:* full-time $5780; part-time $192.65 per credit hour. *Tuition, nonresident:* full-time $11,771; part-time $392.36 per credit hour. *Required fees:* full-time $718. Full-time tuition and fees vary according to course load, location, and program. Part-time tuition and fees vary according to course load, location, and program. *College room and board:* $7346; *Room only:* $4248. Room and board charges vary according to board plan and housing facility.

**FRESHMAN FINANCIAL AID (Fall 2014, est.)** 856 applied for aid; of those 79% were deemed to have need. 99% of freshmen with need received aid; of those 14% had need fully met. *Average percent of need met:* 63% (excluding resources awarded to replace EFC). *Average financial aid package:* $8558 (excluding resources awarded to replace EFC). 15% of all full-time freshmen had no need and received non-need-based gift aid.

**UNDERGRADUATE FINANCIAL AID (Fall 2014, est.)** 3,534 applied for aid; of those 79% were deemed to have need. 99% of undergraduates with need received aid; of those 10% had need fully met. *Average percent of need met:* 62% (excluding resources awarded to replace EFC). *Average financial aid package:* $8428 (excluding resources awarded to replace EFC). 11% of all full-time undergraduates had no need and received non-need-based gift aid.

**GIFT AID (NEED-BASED)** *Receiving aid:* Freshmen: 75% (658); all full-time undergraduates: 67% (2,560). *Average award:* Freshmen: $6521; Undergraduates: $5596. *Scholarships, grants, and awards:* Federal Pell, FSEOG, state, private, college/university gift aid from institutional funds.

**GIFT AID (NON-NEED-BASED)** *Receiving aid:* Freshmen: 11% (92). Undergraduates: 7% (249). *Average award:* Freshmen: $3079. Undergraduates: $3189. *Scholarships, grants, and awards by category: Academic interests/achievement:* architecture, biological sciences, business, communication, computer science, education, engineering/technologies, English, foreign languages, general academic interests/achievements, health fields, humanities, mathematics, military science, physical sciences, premedicine, religion/biblical studies, social sciences. *Creative arts/*

*performance:* applied art and design, art/fine arts, cinema/film/broadcasting, dance, journalism/publications, music, performing arts, theater/drama. *Special achievements/activities:* cheerleading/drum major, community service, general special achievements/activities, hobbies/interests, leadership, religious involvement. *Special characteristics:* adult students, children and siblings of alumni, children of public servants, children of union members/company employees, children of workers in trades, first-generation college students, general special characteristics, international students, local/state students, out-of-state students, previous college experience, public servants, religious affiliation. *Tuition waivers:* Full or partial for employees or children of employees, senior citizens. *ROTC:* Army.

**LOANS** *Student loans:* 71% of past graduating class borrowed through all loan programs. *Average indebtedness per student:* $26,015. *Average need-based loan:* Freshmen: $2852. Undergraduates: $3636. *Programs:* Federal Direct (Subsidized and Unsubsidized Stafford, PLUS), Perkins.

**WORK-STUDY** *Federal work-study:* 354 jobs averaging $1328. *State or other work-study/employment:* 740 part-time jobs averaging $1502.

**APPLYING FOR FINANCIAL AID** *Required financial aid forms:* FAFSA, institutional scholarship application form. *Financial aid deadline:* Continuous. *Notification date:* Continuous beginning 4/15. Students must reply within 2 weeks of notification.

**CONTACT** Marilyn Baker, Director of Financial Aid, Missouri Western State University, 4525 Downs Drive, Saint Joseph, MO 64507-2294, 816-271-5986 or toll-free 800-662-7041. *Fax:* 816-271-5879. *E-mail:* mbaker3@missouriwestern.edu. *Website:* http://www.missouriwestern.edu/.

# MITCHELL COLLEGE
## New London, CT

**CONTACT** Jacklyn Stoltz, Director of Financial Aid, Mitchell College, 437 Pequot Avenue, New London, CT 06320-4498, 800-443-2811. *Fax:* 860-444-1209. *E-mail:* stoltz_j@mitchell.edu. *Website:* http://www.mitchell.edu/.

# MOLLOY COLLEGE
## Rockville Centre, NY

| Tuition & fees: $26,850 | Average undergraduate aid package: $14,394 |
| --- | --- |

**ABOUT THE INSTITUTION** Independent, coed. *Awards:* certificates, associate, bachelor's, master's, and doctoral degrees. 40 undergraduate majors. *Total enrollment:* 4,497. Undergraduates: 3,336. Freshmen: 492. Federal methodology is used as a basis for awarding need-based institutional aid.

**UNDERGRADUATE EXPENSES** for 2015–2016 *Application fee:* $40. *Comprehensive fee:* $40,440 includes full-time tuition ($25,800), mandatory fees ($1050), and room and board ($13,590). Full-time tuition and fees vary according to degree level. Room and board charges vary according to board plan. *Part-time tuition:* $850 per credit hour. Part-time tuition and fees vary according to degree level.

**FRESHMAN FINANCIAL AID (Fall 2013)** 469 applied for aid; of those 89% were deemed to have need. 100% of freshmen with need received aid; of those 8% had need fully met. *Average percent of need met:* 57% (excluding resources awarded to replace EFC). *Average financial aid package:* $18,217 (excluding resources awarded to replace EFC). 8% of all full-time freshmen had no need and received non-need-based gift aid.

**UNDERGRADUATE FINANCIAL AID (Fall 2013)** 2,473 applied for aid; of those 91% were deemed to have need. 100% of undergraduates with need received aid; of those 8% had need fully met. *Average percent of need met:* 45% (excluding resources awarded to replace EFC). *Average financial aid package:* $14,394 (excluding resources awarded to replace EFC). 6% of all full-time undergraduates had no need and received non-need-based gift aid.

**GIFT AID (NEED-BASED)** *Total amount:* $21,882,279 (21% federal, 15% state, 62% institutional, 2% external sources). *Receiving aid:* Freshmen: 81% (403); all full-time undergraduates: 78% (2,099). *Average award:* Freshmen: $14,762; Undergraduates: $11,180. *Scholarships, grants, and awards:* Federal Pell, FSEOG, state, private, college/university gift aid from institutional funds, Federal Nursing, TEACH Grants, TRiO Grants.

**GIFT AID (NON-NEED-BASED) Total amount:** $2,096,898 (1% federal, 5% state, 93% institutional, 1% external sources). **Receiving aid:** Freshmen: 6% (31). Undergraduates: 5% (141). **Average award:** Freshmen: $9956. Undergraduates: $8947. **Scholarships, grants, and awards by category:** Academic interests/achievement: 958 awards ($8,314,864 total): biological sciences, business, communication, education, English, general academic interests/achievements, health fields, humanities, international studies, mathematics, social sciences. Creative arts/performance: 77 awards ($185,422 total): art/fine arts, music, performing arts, theater/drama. Special achievements/activities: 466 awards ($1,645,260 total): community service, general special achievements/activities, leadership, memberships, religious involvement. Special characteristics: 105 awards ($174,604 total): ethnic background, members of minority groups, religious affiliation, siblings of current students, veterans. **Tuition waivers:** Full or partial for employees or children of employees, senior citizens. **ROTC:** Army cooperative, Naval cooperative.

**LOANS Student loans:** $26,119,470 (88% need-based, 12% non-need-based). 73% of past graduating class borrowed through all loan programs. **Average need-based loan:** Freshmen: $3297. Undergraduates: $4288. **Parent loans:** $7,913,102 (65% need-based, 35% non-need-based). **Programs:** Federal Direct (Subsidized and Unsubsidized Stafford, PLUS), Perkins, Federal Nursing, private loans.

**WORK-STUDY Federal work-study:** 174 jobs averaging $1638.

**ATHLETIC AWARDS** Total amount: $1,921,704 (75% need-based, 25% non-need-based).

**APPLYING FOR FINANCIAL AID Required financial aid forms:** FAFSA, state aid form. **Financial aid deadline:** 5/1 (priority: 4/15). **Notification date:** Continuous beginning 2/1. Students must reply within 5 weeks of notification.

**CONTACT** Ana C. Lockward, Director of Financial Aid, Molloy College, 1000 Hempstead Avenue, Rockville Centre, NY 11571, 516-323-4200 or toll-free 888-4MOLLOY. Fax: 516-323-4213. E-mail: alockward@molloy.edu. Website: http://www.molloy.edu/.

---

# MONMOUTH COLLEGE
## Monmouth, IL

| Tuition & fees: $34,200 | Average undergraduate aid package: $30,380 |
|---|---|

**ABOUT THE INSTITUTION** Independent Presbyterian Church, coed. **Awards:** bachelor's degrees. 36 undergraduate majors. **Total enrollment:** 1,300. Undergraduates: 1,300. Freshmen: 394. Both federal and institutional methodology are used as a basis for awarding need-based institutional aid.

**UNDERGRADUATE EXPENSES for 2015–2016 One-time required fee:** $190. **Comprehensive fee:** $42,260 includes full-time tuition ($34,200) and room and board ($8060). Full-time tuition and fees vary according to course load. Room and board charges vary according to board plan and housing facility.

**FRESHMAN FINANCIAL AID (Fall 2014, est.)** 370 applied for aid; of those 95% were deemed to have need. 100% of freshmen with need received aid; of those 16% had need fully met. **Average percent of need met:** 91% (excluding resources awarded to replace EFC). **Average financial aid package:** $33,263 (excluding resources awarded to replace EFC). 11% of all full-time freshmen had no need and received non-need-based gift aid.

**UNDERGRADUATE FINANCIAL AID (Fall 2014, est.)** 1,175 applied for aid; of those 94% were deemed to have need. 100% of undergraduates with need received aid; of those 18% had need fully met. **Average percent of need met:** 87% (excluding resources awarded to replace EFC). **Average financial aid package:** $30,380 (excluding resources awarded to replace EFC). 6% of all full-time undergraduates had no need and received non-need-based gift aid.

**GIFT AID (NEED-BASED) Total amount:** $27,320,301 (10% federal, 11% state, 79% institutional). **Receiving aid:** Freshmen: 89% (351); all full-time undergraduates: 86% (1,100). **Average award:** Freshmen: $28,992; Undergraduates: $25,285. **Scholarships, grants, and awards:** Federal Pell, FSEOG, state, private, college/university gift aid from institutional funds.

**GIFT AID (NON-NEED-BASED) Total amount:** $4,857,911 (86% institutional, 14% external sources). **Receiving aid:** Freshmen: 9% (36). Undergraduates: 10% (132). **Average award:** Freshmen: $22,988. Undergraduates: $15,703. **Scholarships, grants, and awards by category:** Academic interests/achievement: foreign languages, general academic interests/achievements. Creative arts/performance: art/fine arts, debating, music, theater/drama. Special achievements/activities: general special achievements/activities, religious involvement. Special characteristics: international students, veterans. **Tuition waivers:** Full or partial for employees or children of employees. **ROTC:** Army cooperative.

**LOANS Student loans:** $8,204,489 (48% need-based, 52% non-need-based). 89% of past graduating class borrowed through all loan programs. **Average indebtedness per student:** $31,154. **Average need-based loan:** Freshmen: $3654. Undergraduates: $4553. **Parent loans:** $3,848,017 (100% non-need-based). **Programs:** Federal Direct (Subsidized and Unsubsidized Stafford, PLUS), Perkins.

**WORK-STUDY Federal work-study:** Total amount: $769,620; jobs available. **State or other work-study/employment:** Part-time jobs available.

**APPLYING FOR FINANCIAL AID Required financial aid form:** FAFSA. **Financial aid deadline (priority):** 1/15. **Notification date:** Continuous beginning 2/15. Students must reply by 5/1.

**CONTACT** Mrs. Jayne Schreck, Director of Scholarships and Financial Aid, Monmouth College, 700 East Broadway, Monmouth, IL 61462-1998, 309-457-2129 or toll-free 800-747-2687. Fax: 309-457-2373. E-mail: jayne@monmouthcollege.edu. Website: http://www.monmouthcollege.edu/.

---

# MONMOUTH UNIVERSITY
## West Long Branch, NJ

| Tuition & fees: $32,310 | Average undergraduate aid package: $24,858 |
|---|---|

**ABOUT THE INSTITUTION** Independent, coed. **Awards:** certificates, associate, bachelor's, master's, and doctoral degrees. 34 undergraduate majors. **Total enrollment:** 6,395. Undergraduates: 4,634. Freshmen: 1,056. Federal methodology is used as a basis for awarding need-based institutional aid.

**UNDERGRADUATE EXPENSES for 2015–2016 Application fee:** $50. **One-time required fee:** $200. **Comprehensive fee:** $44,108 includes full-time tuition ($31,682), mandatory fees ($628), and room and board ($11,798). **College room only:** $6776. Room and board charges vary according to board plan and housing facility. **Part-time tuition:** $917 per credit hour. **Part-time fees:** $157 per term. Part-time tuition and fees vary according to course load.

**FRESHMAN FINANCIAL AID (Fall 2014, est.)** 961 applied for aid; of those 85% were deemed to have need. 100% of freshmen with need received aid; of those 15% had need fully met. **Average percent of need met:** 68% (excluding resources awarded to replace EFC). **Average financial aid package:** $24,607 (excluding resources awarded to replace EFC). 22% of all full-time freshmen had no need and received non-need-based gift aid.

**UNDERGRADUATE FINANCIAL AID (Fall 2014, est.)** 3,573 applied for aid; of those 87% were deemed to have need. 100% of undergraduates with need received aid; of those 14% had need fully met. **Average percent of need met:** 69% (excluding resources awarded to replace EFC). **Average financial aid package:** $24,858 (excluding resources awarded to replace EFC). 29% of all full-time undergraduates had no need and received non-need-based gift aid.

**GIFT AID (NEED-BASED) Total amount:** $19,602,610 (32% federal, 50% state, 15% institutional, 3% external sources). **Receiving aid:** Freshmen: 46% (489); all full-time undergraduates: 37% (1,621). **Average award:** Freshmen: $11,856; Undergraduates: $12,089. **Scholarships, grants, and awards:** Federal Pell, FSEOG, state, private, college/university gift aid from institutional funds, Federal Nursing.

**GIFT AID (NON-NEED-BASED) Total amount:** $35,937,694 (1% federal, 99% institutional). **Receiving aid:** Freshmen: 75% (795). Undergraduates: 67% (2,930). **Average award:** Freshmen: $9831. Undergraduates: $7856. **Scholarships, grants, and awards by category:** Academic interests/achievement: 4,075 awards ($32,471,226 total): business, communication, computer science, education, general academic interests/achievements, health fields, humanities, international studies, mathematics, social sciences. Special achievements/activities: 1 award ($2500 total): leadership. Special characteristics: 724 awards ($5,639,595 total): adult students, children and siblings of alumni, children of faculty/staff, children of public servants, first-generation college students, general special characteristics, international students, local/state students, members of minority groups, out-of-state students, previous college experience, veterans, veterans' children. **Tuition waivers:** Full or partial for employees or children of employees, senior citizens. **ROTC:** Army cooperative, Air Force cooperative.

**LOANS Student loans:** $26,265,305 (47% need-based, 53% non-need-based). 77% of past graduating class borrowed through all loan programs. Average indebtedness per student: $30,678. **Average need-based loan:** Freshmen: $3826. Undergraduates: $4751. **Parent loans:** $23,820,363 (100% non-need-based). **Programs:** Federal Direct (Subsidized and Unsubsidized Stafford, PLUS), Perkins, state, college/university, private loans.

**WORK-STUDY** Federal work-study: Total amount: $3,365,340; 930 jobs averaging $2003.

**ATHLETIC AWARDS** Total amount: $7,810,917 (100% non-need-based).

**APPLYING FOR FINANCIAL AID** Required financial aid form: FAFSA. **Financial aid deadline:** Continuous. **Notification date:** Continuous beginning 2/1. Students must reply within 2 weeks of notification.

**CONTACT** Ms. Claire Alasio, Associate Vice President of Enrollment Management/Director of Financial Aid, Monmouth University, 400 Cedar Avenue, West Long Branch, NJ 07764-1898, 732-571-3463 or toll-free 800-543-9671. Fax: 732-923-4791. E-mail: finaid@monmouth.edu.
Website: http://www.monmouth.edu/.

# MONROE COLLEGE
## Bronx, NY

| Tuition & fees: $13,740 | Average undergraduate aid package: $12,681 |
| --- | --- |

**ABOUT THE INSTITUTION** Proprietary, coed. **Awards:** certificates, associate, bachelor's, and master's degrees. 15 undergraduate majors. **Total enrollment:** 7,215. Undergraduates: 6,794. Freshmen: 1,202. Federal methodology is used as a basis for awarding need-based institutional aid.

**UNDERGRADUATE EXPENSES** for 2015–2016 Application fee: $35. **Comprehensive fee:** $22,940 includes full-time tuition ($12,840), mandatory fees ($900), and room and board ($9200). Room and board charges vary according to board plan and housing facility. **Part-time tuition:** $535 per credit. **Part-time fees:** $225 per term. **Payment plan:** Tuition prepayment.

**FRESHMAN FINANCIAL AID (Fall 2014, est.)** 806 applied for aid; of those 99% were deemed to have need. 100% of freshmen with need received aid; of those 64% had need fully met. **Average percent of need met:** 64% (excluding resources awarded to replace EFC). **Average financial aid package:** $14,334 (excluding resources awarded to replace EFC). 1% of all full-time freshmen had no need and received non-need-based gift aid.

**UNDERGRADUATE FINANCIAL AID (Fall 2014, est.)** 4,869 applied for aid; of those 99% were deemed to have need. 100% of undergraduates with need received aid; of those 64% had need fully met. **Average percent of need met:** 64% (excluding resources awarded to replace EFC). **Average financial aid package:** $12,681 (excluding resources awarded to replace EFC). 1% of all full-time undergraduates had no need and received non-need-based gift aid.

**GIFT AID (NEED-BASED) Total amount:** $51,507,536 (54% federal, 31% state, 14% institutional, 1% external sources). **Receiving aid:** Freshmen: 94% (793); all full-time undergraduates: 91% (4,696). **Average award:** Freshmen: $10,316; Undergraduates: $9241. **Scholarships, grants, and awards:** Federal Pell, FSEOG, state, private, college/university gift aid from institutional funds.

**GIFT AID (NON-NEED-BASED) Total amount:** $78,711 (71% institutional, 29% external sources). **Average award:** Freshmen: $6614. Undergraduates: $3580.

**LOANS Student loans:** $39,751,788 (99% need-based, 1% non-need-based). 84% of past graduating class borrowed through all loan programs. **Average indebtedness per student:** $27,986. **Average need-based loan:** Freshmen: $3122. Undergraduates: $4541. **Parent loans:** $3,534,973 (96% need-based, 4% non-need-based). **Programs:** Federal Direct (Subsidized and Unsubsidized Stafford, PLUS), state, college/university.

**WORK-STUDY** Federal work-study: Total amount: $650,000; 206 jobs averaging $3155.

**ATHLETIC AWARDS** Total amount: $1,695,337 (98% need-based, 2% non-need-based).

**APPLYING FOR FINANCIAL AID** Required financial aid forms: FAFSA, state aid form. **Financial aid deadline:** Continuous. **Notification date:** Continuous.

**CONTACT** Mr. Daniel Sharon, Director of Student Financial Services, Monroe College, 2501 Jerome Avenue, Bronx, NY 10468, 646-393-8257 or toll-free 800-55MONROE. Fax: 718-817-8401. E-mail: dsharon@monroecollege.edu.
Website: http://www.monroecollege.edu/.

# MONTANA BIBLE COLLEGE
## Bozeman, MT

**CONTACT** Financial Aid Office, Montana Bible College, 3625 South 19th Avenue, Bozeman, MT 59718, 406-586-3585 or toll-free 888-462-2463.
Website: http://www.montanabiblecollege.edu/.

# MONTANA STATE UNIVERSITY
## Bozeman, MT

| Tuition & fees (MT res): $5330 | Average undergraduate aid package: $12,022 |
| --- | --- |

**ABOUT THE INSTITUTION** State-supported, coed. **Awards:** certificates, associate, bachelor's, master's, and doctoral degrees. 59 undergraduate majors. **Total enrollment:** 15,421. Undergraduates: 13,371. Freshmen: 2,943. Federal methodology is used as a basis for awarding need-based institutional aid.

**UNDERGRADUATE EXPENSES** for 2015–2016 Application fee: $30. **Tuition, state resident:** full-time $5330; part-time $222 per credit hour. **Tuition, nonresident:** full-time $19,732; part-time $822 per credit hour. Full-time tuition and fees vary according to course load, degree level, location, and program. Part-time tuition and fees vary according to course load, degree level, location, and program. Room and board charges vary according to board plan and housing facility.

**FRESHMAN FINANCIAL AID (Fall 2013)** 1,730 applied for aid; of those 69% were deemed to have need. 97% of freshmen with need received aid; of those 7% had need fully met. **Average percent of need met:** 92% (excluding resources awarded to replace EFC). **Average financial aid package:** $11,948 (excluding resources awarded to replace EFC). 1% of all full-time freshmen had no need and received non-need-based gift aid.

**UNDERGRADUATE FINANCIAL AID (Fall 2013)** 7,302 applied for aid; of those 80% were deemed to have need. 97% of undergraduates with need received aid; of those 5% had need fully met. **Average percent of need met:** 74% (excluding resources awarded to replace EFC). **Average financial aid package:** $12,022 (excluding resources awarded to replace EFC). 3% of all full-time undergraduates had no need and received non-need-based gift aid.

**GIFT AID (NEED-BASED) Total amount:** $25,476,199 (58% federal, 5% state, 15% institutional, 22% external sources). **Receiving aid:** Freshmen: 43% (907); all full-time undergraduates: 39% (4,179). **Average award:** Freshmen: $5286; Undergraduates: $5226. **Scholarships, grants, and awards:** Federal Pell, FSEOG, state, private, college/university gift aid from institutional funds, Federal Nursing.

**GIFT AID (NON-NEED-BASED) Total amount:** $7,096,043 (5% state, 11% institutional, 84% external sources). **Receiving aid:** Freshmen: 2% (50). Undergraduates: 2% (187). **Average award:** Freshmen: $1689. Undergraduates: $1641. **Scholarships, grants, and awards by category:** Academic interests/achievement: agriculture, architecture, area/ethnic studies, biological sciences, business, communication, computer science, education, engineering/technologies, English, foreign languages, general academic interests/achievements, health fields, home economics, humanities, mathematics, military science, physical sciences, social sciences. Creative arts/performance: art/fine arts, cinema/film/broadcasting, dance, music, theater/drama. Special achievements/activities: general special achievements/activities, leadership. Special characteristics: children and siblings of alumni, general special characteristics, local/state students, members of minority groups. **Tuition waivers:** Full or partial for minority students, employees or children of employees, senior citizens. **ROTC:** Army, Air Force.

**LOANS Student loans:** $46,584,627 (80% need-based, 20% non-need-based). 64% of past graduating class borrowed through all loan programs. **Average indebtedness per student:** $27,200. **Average need-based loan:** Freshmen: $3587. Undergraduates: $4200. **Parent loans:** $16,042,345 (40% need-based, 60% non-need-based). **Programs:** Federal Direct (Subsidized and Unsubsidized Stafford, PLUS), Perkins, Federal Nursing, college/university.

**WORK-STUDY** Federal work-study: jobs available. **State or other work-study/employment:** Total amount: $293,105 (100% need-based). Part-time jobs available.

**ATHLETIC AWARDS** Total amount: $1,665,262 (60% need-based, 40% non-need-based).

**APPLYING FOR FINANCIAL AID** Required financial aid form: FAFSA. **Financial aid deadline (priority):** 3/1. **Notification date:** Continuous beginning 4/1.

**CONTACT** Brandi Payne, Director of Financial Aid, Montana State University, PO Box 174160, Bozeman, MT 59717-4160, 406-994-2845 or toll-free 888-MSU-CATS. *Fax:* 406-994-6962. *E-mail:* bpayne@montana.edu. *Website:* http://www.montana.edu/.

**CONTACT** Emily Williamson, Director of Financial Aid and Scholarships, Montana State University Billings, 1500 University Drive, Billings, MT 59101, 406-657-1617 or toll-free 800-565-6782. *Fax:* 406-657-1789. *E-mail:* finaid@msubillings.edu. *Website:* http://www.msubillings.edu/.

# MONTANA STATE UNIVERSITY BILLINGS
## Billings, MT

| Tuition & fees (MT res): $5780 | Average undergraduate aid package: $9981 |
|---|---|

**ABOUT THE INSTITUTION** State-supported, coed. *Awards:* certificates, associate, bachelor's, and master's degrees. 70 undergraduate majors. *Total enrollment:* 4,781. Undergraduates: 4,353. Freshmen: 782. Federal methodology is used as a basis for awarding need-based institutional aid.

**UNDERGRADUATE EXPENSES for 2015–2016** *Application fee:* $30. *Tuition, state resident:* full-time $4397; part-time $183.20 per credit hour. *Tuition, nonresident:* full-time $15,959; part-time $664.95 per credit hour. *Required fees:* full-time $1383. Full-time tuition and fees vary according to course load, degree level, and location. Part-time tuition and fees vary according to course load, degree level, and location. *College room and board:* $6980. Room and board charges vary according to board plan and housing facility.

**FRESHMAN FINANCIAL AID (Fall 2013)** 558 applied for aid; of those 83% were deemed to have need. 98% of freshmen with need received aid; of those 5% had need fully met. *Average percent of need met:* 65% (excluding resources awarded to replace EFC). *Average financial aid package:* $9210 (excluding resources awarded to replace EFC). 4% of all full-time freshmen had no need and received non-need-based gift aid.

**UNDERGRADUATE FINANCIAL AID (Fall 2013)** 2,399 applied for aid; of those 83% were deemed to have need. 98% of undergraduates with need received aid; of those 4% had need fully met. *Average percent of need met:* 67% (excluding resources awarded to replace EFC). *Average financial aid package:* $9981 (excluding resources awarded to replace EFC). 3% of all full-time undergraduates had no need and received non-need-based gift aid.

**GIFT AID (NEED-BASED)** *Total amount:* $9,664,858 (69% federal, 5% state, 11% institutional, 15% external sources). *Receiving aid:* Freshmen: 62% (404); all full-time undergraduates: 51% (1,622). *Average award:* Freshmen: $5132; Undergraduates: $5193. *Scholarships, grants, and awards:* Federal Pell, FSEOG, state, private, college/university gift aid from institutional funds.

**GIFT AID (NON-NEED-BASED)** *Total amount:* $2,318,505 (1% state, 20% institutional, 79% external sources). *Receiving aid:* Freshmen: 3% (18). Undergraduates: 2% (62). *Average award:* Freshmen: $2493. Undergraduates: $2278. *Scholarships, grants, and awards by category:* Academic interests/achievement: biological sciences, business, communication, computer science, education, engineering/technologies, English, foreign languages, general academic interests/achievements, health fields, humanities, mathematics, physical sciences, premedicine, social sciences. *Creative arts/performance:* art/fine arts, music, theater/drama. *Special achievements/activities:* cheerleading/drum major, general special achievements/activities. *Special characteristics:* adult students, children and siblings of alumni, children of faculty/staff, children of union members/company employees, ethnic background, first-generation college students, local/state students, members of minority groups, out-of-state students, veterans. *Tuition waivers:* Full or partial for employees or children of employees, senior citizens. *ROTC:* Army.

**LOANS** *Student loans:* $14,871,436 (81% need-based, 19% non-need-based). 78% of past graduating class borrowed through all loan programs. *Average indebtedness per student:* $27,225. *Average need-based loan:* Freshmen: $2768. Undergraduates: $3328. *Parent loans:* $842,585 (23% need-based, 77% non-need-based). *Programs:* Federal Direct (Subsidized and Unsubsidized Stafford, PLUS), Perkins, college/university.

**WORK-STUDY** *Federal work-study:* Total amount: $182,562; 1,302 jobs averaging $1881. *State or other work-study/employment:* Total amount: $169,229 (88% need-based, 12% non-need-based). 536 part-time jobs averaging $1762.

**ATHLETIC AWARDS** Total amount: $468,077 (23% need-based, 77% non-need-based).

**APPLYING FOR FINANCIAL AID** *Required financial aid form:* FAFSA. *Financial aid deadline:* Continuous. *Notification date:* Continuous beginning 3/15.

# MONTANA STATE UNIVERSITY– NORTHERN
## Havre, MT

**CONTACT** Cindy Small, Director of Financial Aid, Montana State University–Northern, PO Box 7751, Havre, MT 59501, 406-265-3787 or toll-free 800-662-6132. *Website:* http://www.msun.edu/.

# MONTANA TECH OF THE UNIVERSITY OF MONTANA
## Butte, MT

| Tuition & fees (MT res): $6752 | Average undergraduate aid package: $11,296 |
|---|---|

**ABOUT THE INSTITUTION** State-supported, coed. *Awards:* certificates, diplomas, associate, bachelor's, master's, and doctoral degrees. 36 undergraduate majors. *Total enrollment:* 2,945. Undergraduates: 2,751. Freshmen: 436. Federal methodology is used as a basis for awarding need-based institutional aid.

**UNDERGRADUATE EXPENSES for 2015–2016** *Application fee:* $30. *Tuition, state resident:* full-time $5177; part-time $216 per credit. *Tuition, nonresident:* full-time $18,493; part-time $767 per credit. *Required fees:* full-time $1575; $66 per credit. Full-time tuition and fees vary according to course load, degree level, location, program, and student level. Part-time tuition and fees vary according to course load, degree level, location, program, and student level. *College room and board:* $8238; *Room only:* $3658. Room and board charges vary according to board plan.

**FRESHMAN FINANCIAL AID (Fall 2013)** 372 applied for aid; of those 70% were deemed to have need. 100% of freshmen with need received aid; of those 21% had need fully met. *Average percent of need met:* 68% (excluding resources awarded to replace EFC). *Average financial aid package:* $9858 (excluding resources awarded to replace EFC). 13% of all full-time freshmen had no need and received non-need-based gift aid.

**UNDERGRADUATE FINANCIAL AID (Fall 2013)** 1,623 applied for aid; of those 81% were deemed to have need. 100% of undergraduates with need received aid; of those 12% had need fully met. *Average percent of need met:* 63% (excluding resources awarded to replace EFC). *Average financial aid package:* $11,296 (excluding resources awarded to replace EFC). 12% of all full-time undergraduates had no need and received non-need-based gift aid.

**GIFT AID (NEED-BASED)** *Total amount:* $6,854,326 (67% federal, 5% state, 23% institutional, 5% external sources). *Receiving aid:* Freshmen: 54% (235); all full-time undergraduates: 53% (1,163). *Average award:* Freshmen: $5678; Undergraduates: $5485. *Scholarships, grants, and awards:* Federal Pell, FSEOG, state, private, college/university gift aid from institutional funds.

**GIFT AID (NON-NEED-BASED)** *Total amount:* $1,689,951 (4% state, 74% institutional, 22% external sources). *Receiving aid:* Freshmen: 6% (27). Undergraduates: 3% (66). *Average award:* Freshmen: $4448. Undergraduates: $3817. *Scholarships, grants, and awards by category:* Academic interests/achievement: business, computer science, engineering/technologies, general academic interests/achievements, health fields, mathematics, physical sciences. *Special achievements/activities:* community service, general special achievements/activities, hobbies/interests, leadership, memberships. *Special characteristics:* children and siblings of alumni, children of faculty/staff, first-generation college students, general special characteristics, local/state students, married students, out-of-state students, veterans. *Tuition waivers:* Full or partial for minority students, employees or children of employees, senior citizens.

**LOANS** *Student loans:* $9,632,723 (81% need-based, 19% non-need-based). 57% of past graduating class borrowed through all loan programs. *Average indebtedness per student:* $24,448. *Average need-based loan:* Freshmen: $3048. Undergraduates: $3847. *Parent loans:* $1,777,357 (26% need-based, 74% non-need-based).

**Programs:** Federal Direct (Subsidized and Unsubsidized Stafford, PLUS), Perkins, college/university.
**WORK-STUDY** *Federal work-study:* jobs available. *State or other work-study/employment:* Total amount: $85,660 (100% need-based). Part-time jobs available.
**ATHLETIC AWARDS** Total amount: $856,946 (48% need-based, 52% non-need-based).
**APPLYING FOR FINANCIAL AID** *Required financial aid form:* FAFSA. *Financial aid deadline (priority):* 3/1. *Notification date:* Continuous beginning 3/15. Students must reply within 2 weeks of notification.
**CONTACT** Mike Richardson, Director of Financial Aid, Montana Tech of The University of Montana, 1300 West Park Street, Butte, MT 59701-8997, 406-496-4256 or toll-free 800-445-TECH. *Fax:* 406-496-4710. *E-mail:* mrichardson@mtech.edu. *Website:* http://www.mtech.edu/.

# MONTCLAIR STATE UNIVERSITY
## Montclair, NJ

| Tuition & fees (NJ res): $11,540 | Average undergraduate aid package: $9444 |
|---|---|

**ABOUT THE INSTITUTION** State-supported, coed. *Awards:* certificates, bachelor's, master's, and doctoral degrees. 59 undergraduate majors. *Total enrollment:* 20,022. Undergraduates: 15,885. Freshmen: 2,902. Federal methodology is used as a basis for awarding need-based institutional aid.
**UNDERGRADUATE EXPENSES for 2015–2016** *Application fee:* $65. *Tuition, state resident:* full-time $8346; part-time $278 per credit. *Tuition, non-resident:* full-time $17,060; part-time $569 per credit. *Required fees:* full-time $3194; $106.48 per credit. *College room and board:* $14,010. Room and board charges vary according to board plan and housing facility.
**FRESHMAN FINANCIAL AID (Fall 2013)** 2,736 applied for aid; of those 81% were deemed to have need. 90% of freshmen with need received aid; of those 1% had need fully met. *Average percent of need met:* 65% (excluding resources awarded to replace EFC). *Average financial aid package:* $8868 (excluding resources awarded to replace EFC). 4% of all full-time freshmen had no need and received non-need-based gift aid.
**UNDERGRADUATE FINANCIAL AID (Fall 2013)** 10,959 applied for aid; of those 85% were deemed to have need. 93% of undergraduates with need received aid; of those 2% had need fully met. *Average percent of need met:* 66% (excluding resources awarded to replace EFC). *Average financial aid package:* $9444 (excluding resources awarded to replace EFC). 4% of all full-time undergraduates had no need and received non-need-based gift aid.
**GIFT AID (NEED-BASED)** *Total amount:* $48,778,994 (55% federal, 45% state). *Receiving aid:* Freshmen: 43% (1,291); all full-time undergraduates: 36% (5,615). *Average award:* Freshmen: $9613; Undergraduates: $8541. *Scholarships, grants, and awards:* Federal Pell, FSEOG, state, private, college/university gift aid from institutional funds.
**GIFT AID (NON-NEED-BASED)** *Total amount:* $9,219,370 (2% state, 77% institutional, 21% external sources). *Receiving aid:* Freshmen: 4% (127). Undergraduates: 4% (589). *Average award:* Freshmen: $4664. Undergraduates: $6439. *Scholarships, grants, and awards by category:* Academic interests/achievement: biological sciences, business, communication, education, English, foreign languages, general academic interests/achievements, home economics, humanities, international studies, mathematics, physical sciences, religion/biblical studies, social sciences. *Creative arts/performance:* art/fine arts, cinema/film/broadcasting, dance, music, performing arts, theater/drama. *Special achievements/activities:* community service, general special achievements/activities, leadership. *Special characteristics:* children and siblings of alumni, international students. *Tuition waivers:* Full or partial for employees or children of employees, senior citizens. *ROTC:* Army, Naval, Air Force.
**LOANS** *Student loans:* $92,517,574 (38% need-based, 62% non-need-based). 71% of past graduating class borrowed through all loan programs. *Average indebtedness per student:* $28,070. *Average need-based loan:* Freshmen: $3514. Undergraduates: $3935. *Parent loans:* $13,983,552 (100% non-need-based). *Programs:* Federal Direct (Subsidized and Unsubsidized Stafford, PLUS), Perkins, state, private loans.
**WORK-STUDY** *Federal work-study:* 531 jobs averaging $1226. *State or other work-study/employment:* Total amount: $6,072,569 (100% non-need-based). Part-time jobs available.

**APPLYING FOR FINANCIAL AID** *Required financial aid form:* FAFSA. *Financial aid deadline (priority):* 3/15. *Notification date:* Continuous beginning 3/15. Students must reply within 2 weeks of notification.
**CONTACT** Mr. James T. Anderson, Director of Financial Aid, Montclair State University, College Hall, Room 222, Montclair, NJ 07043, 973-655-7022. *Fax:* 973-655-7712. *E-mail:* financialaid@montclair.edu. *Website:* http://www.montclair.edu/.

# MONTREAT COLLEGE
## Montreat, NC

| Tuition & fees: $24,240 | Average undergraduate aid package: $18,198 |
|---|---|

**ABOUT THE INSTITUTION** Independent Presbyterian Church (U.S.A.), coed. *Awards:* certificates, associate, bachelor's, and master's degrees. 19 undergraduate majors. *Total enrollment:* 933. Undergraduates: 735. Freshmen: 109. Federal methodology is used as a basis for awarding need-based institutional aid.
**UNDERGRADUATE EXPENSES for 2015–2016** *Comprehensive fee:* $32,506 includes full-time tuition ($24,040), mandatory fees ($200), and room and board ($8266). *College room only:* $4096. Full-time tuition and fees vary according to course load and degree level. Room and board charges vary according to board plan and housing facility. Part-time tuition and fees vary according to course load and degree level.
**FRESHMAN FINANCIAL AID (Fall 2014, est.)** 106 applied for aid; of those 80% were deemed to have need. 100% of freshmen with need received aid; of those 54% had need fully met. *Average percent of need met:* 82% (excluding resources awarded to replace EFC). *Average financial aid package:* $22,228 (excluding resources awarded to replace EFC). 7% of all full-time freshmen had no need and received non-need-based gift aid.
**UNDERGRADUATE FINANCIAL AID (Fall 2014, est.)** 398 applied for aid; of those 91% were deemed to have need. 100% of undergraduates with need received aid; of those 43% had need fully met. *Average percent of need met:* 72% (excluding resources awarded to replace EFC). *Average financial aid package:* $18,198 (excluding resources awarded to replace EFC). 7% of all full-time undergraduates had no need and received non-need-based gift aid.
**GIFT AID (NEED-BASED)** *Total amount:* $2,426,745 (66% federal, 33% state, 1% institutional). *Receiving aid:* Freshmen: 80% (85); all full-time undergraduates: 82% (363). *Average award:* Freshmen: $23,156; Undergraduates: $20,753. *Scholarships, grants, and awards:* Federal Pell, FSEOG, state, private, college/university gift aid from institutional funds.
**GIFT AID (NON-NEED-BASED)** *Total amount:* $174,162 (36% federal, 22% institutional, 42% external sources). *Receiving aid:* Freshmen: 63% (67). Undergraduates: 71% (315). *Average award:* Freshmen: $10,536. Undergraduates: $8240. *Scholarships, grants, and awards by category:* Academic interests/achievement: general academic interests/achievements. *Creative arts/performance:* music. *Special achievements/activities:* leadership. *Special characteristics:* children of faculty/staff, first-generation college students, international students, local/state students, relatives of clergy, religious affiliation, veterans, veterans' children. *Tuition waivers:* Full or partial for employees or children of employees, adult students.
**LOANS** *Student loans:* $4,883,604 (44% need-based, 56% non-need-based). 65% of past graduating class borrowed through all loan programs. *Average indebtedness per student:* $19,899. *Average need-based loan:* Freshmen: $3422. Undergraduates: $4156. *Parent loans:* $594,136 (100% non-need-based). *Programs:* Federal Direct (Subsidized and Unsubsidized Stafford, PLUS), Perkins.
**WORK-STUDY** *Federal work-study:* Total amount: $332,196; jobs available. *State or other work-study/employment:* Total amount: $264,677 (100% non-need-based). Part-time jobs available.
**ATHLETIC AWARDS** Total amount: $805,053 (100% non-need-based).
**APPLYING FOR FINANCIAL AID** *Required financial aid forms:* FAFSA, state aid form. *Financial aid deadline (priority):* 4/1. *Notification date:* Continuous beginning 4/1. Students must reply within 2 weeks of notification.
**CONTACT** Lisa Lounsbury, Financial Aid Awarding Specialist, Montreat College, PO Box 1267, Montreat, NC 28757, 828-669-8012 Ext. 3795 or toll-free 800-622-6968. *Fax:* 828-669-0120. *Website:* http://www.montreat.edu/.

# MONTSERRAT COLLEGE OF ART
## Beverly, MA

**Tuition & fees: $28,700**  **Average undergraduate aid package: N/A**

**ABOUT THE INSTITUTION** Independent, coed. 11 undergraduate majors. Federal methodology is used as a basis for awarding need-based institutional aid.

**UNDERGRADUATE EXPENSES for 2015–2016 *Comprehensive fee:*** $38,400 includes full-time tuition ($27,400), mandatory fees ($1300), and room and board ($9700). *College room only:* $8200. Full-time tuition and fees vary according to course load and student level. Room and board charges vary according to housing facility. *Part-time tuition:* $1145 per credit. *Part-time fees:* $50 per credit. Part-time tuition and fees vary according to course load and student level.

**GIFT AID (NEED-BASED)** *Scholarships, grants, and awards:* Federal Pell, FSEOG, state, private, college/university gift aid from institutional funds.

**GIFT AID (NON-NEED-BASED)** *Scholarships, grants, and awards by category: Creative arts/performance:* applied art and design, art/fine arts. *Special characteristics:* siblings of current students. *Tuition waivers:* Full or partial for employees or children of employees.

**LOANS** *Programs:* state, alternative loans.

**WORK-STUDY** Federal work-study jobs available.

**APPLYING FOR FINANCIAL AID** *Required financial aid form:* FAFSA. *Financial aid deadline (priority):* 3/1. *Notification date:* Continuous beginning 2/1. Students must reply within 2 weeks of notification.

**CONTACT** Emma Puglisi, Director of Financial Aid, Montserrat College of Art, 23 Essex Street, PO Box 26, Beverly, MA 01915, 978-922-8222 Ext. 1155 or toll-free 800-836-0487. *Fax:* 978-922-4268. *E-mail:* finaid@montserrat.edu. *Website:* http://www.montserrat.edu/.

# MOODY BIBLE INSTITUTE
## Chicago, IL

**ABOUT THE INSTITUTION** Independent nondenominational, coed. 8 undergraduate majors.

**GIFT AID (NEED-BASED)** *Scholarships, grants, and awards:* Federal Pell, FSEOG, private, college/university gift aid from institutional funds.

**LOANS** *Programs:* alternative loans.

**APPLYING FOR FINANCIAL AID** *Required financial aid forms:* FAFSA, institution's own form.

**CONTACT** Moody Central, Moody Bible Institute, 820 North LaSalle Boulevard, Chicago, IL 60610-3284, 312-329-4184 or toll-free 800-967-4MBI. *Fax:* 312-329-4274. *E-mail:* financial.aid@moody.edu. *Website:* http://www.moody.edu/.

# MOORE COLLEGE OF ART & DESIGN
## Philadelphia, PA

**ABOUT THE INSTITUTION** Independent, women only. *Awards:* certificates, bachelor's, and master's degrees. 10 undergraduate majors. *Total enrollment:* 453. Undergraduates: 412. Freshmen: 87.

**GIFT AID (NEED-BASED)** *Scholarships, grants, and awards:* Federal Pell, FSEOG, state, private, college/university gift aid from institutional funds.

**GIFT AID (NON-NEED-BASED)** *Scholarships, grants, and awards by category: Academic interests/achievement:* general academic interests/achievements. *Special achievements/activities:* leadership.

**LOANS** *Programs:* Perkins.

**WORK-STUDY** Federal work-study jobs available. *State or other work-study/employment:* Part-time jobs available.

**APPLYING FOR FINANCIAL AID** *Required financial aid form:* FAFSA.

**CONTACT** Michelle Shonleber, Director of Financial Aid, Moore College of Art & Design, 20th and the Parkway, Philadelphia, PA 19103-1179, 215-965-4042 or toll-free 800-523-2025. *Fax:* 215-568-1773. *E-mail:* mshonleber@moore.edu. *Website:* http://www.moore.edu/.

# MORAVIAN COLLEGE
## Bethlehem, PA

**Tuition & fees: $37,572**  **Average undergraduate aid package: $28,034**

**ABOUT THE INSTITUTION** Independent Moravian Church, coed. *Awards:* certificates, bachelor's, and master's degrees. 42 undergraduate majors. *Total enrollment:* 1,930. Undergraduates: 1,612. Freshmen: 386. Both federal and institutional methodology are used as a basis for awarding need-based institutional aid.

**UNDERGRADUATE EXPENSES for 2015–2016 *Comprehensive fee:*** $48,654 includes full-time tuition ($35,991), mandatory fees ($1581), and room and board ($11,082). *College room only:* $6248. Full-time tuition and fees vary according to student level. Room and board charges vary according to board plan and housing facility. *Part-time tuition:* $999.61 per credit. Part-time tuition and fees vary according to class time.

**FRESHMAN FINANCIAL AID (Fall 2014, est.)** 351 applied for aid; of those 91% were deemed to have need. 100% of freshmen with need received aid; of those 12% had need fully met. *Average percent of need met:* 76% (excluding resources awarded to replace EFC). *Average financial aid package:* $29,241 (excluding resources awarded to replace EFC). 12% of all full-time freshmen had no need and received non-need-based gift aid.

**UNDERGRADUATE FINANCIAL AID (Fall 2014, est.)** 1,299 applied for aid; of those 92% were deemed to have need. 100% of undergraduates with need received aid; of those 13% had need fully met. *Average percent of need met:* 73% (excluding resources awarded to replace EFC). *Average financial aid package:* $28,034 (excluding resources awarded to replace EFC). 13% of all full-time undergraduates had no need and received non-need-based gift aid.

**GIFT AID (NEED-BASED)** *Total amount:* $26,085,018 (9% federal, 7% state, 81% institutional, 3% external sources). *Receiving aid:* Freshmen: 83% (318); all full-time undergraduates: 83% (1,196). *Average award:* Freshmen: $23,499; Undergraduates: $21,958. *Scholarships, grants, and awards:* Federal Pell, FSEOG, state, private, college/university gift aid from institutional funds.

**GIFT AID (NON-NEED-BASED)** *Total amount:* $3,536,137 (91% institutional, 9% external sources). *Receiving aid:* Freshmen: 9% (33). Undergraduates: 7% (106). *Average award:* Freshmen: $16,214. Undergraduates: $13,540. *Scholarships, grants, and awards by category: Academic interests/achievement:* biological sciences, business, computer science, foreign languages, general academic interests/achievements, health fields, mathematics, physical sciences, premedicine. *Creative arts/performance:* 19 awards ($43,000 total): music. *Special achievements/activities:* 97 awards ($121,392 total): leadership, religious involvement. *Special characteristics:* 587 awards ($1,702,228 total): adult students, children and siblings of alumni, children of educators, children of faculty/staff, first-generation college students, international students, relatives of clergy, religious affiliation, siblings of current students. *Tuition waivers:* Full or partial for employees or children of employees. *ROTC:* Army cooperative.

**LOANS** *Student loans:* $14,334,537 (71% need-based, 29% non-need-based). *Average need-based loan:* Freshmen: $4146. Undergraduates: $4793. *Parent loans:* $5,162,813 (51% need-based, 49% non-need-based). *Programs:* Federal Direct (Subsidized and Unsubsidized Stafford, PLUS), Perkins.

**WORK-STUDY** *Federal work-study:* Total amount: $2,067,695; 1,032 jobs averaging $1978. *State or other work-study/employment:* Total amount: $107,000 (5% need-based, 95% non-need-based). 114 part-time jobs averaging $1135.

**APPLYING FOR FINANCIAL AID** *Required financial aid forms:* FAFSA, institution's own form. *Financial aid deadline (priority):* 3/1. *Notification date:* 3/15. Students must reply by 5/1 or within 2 weeks of notification.

**CONTACT** Mrs. Colby T. McCarthy, Director of Financial Aid, Moravian College, 1200 Main Street, Bethlehem, PA 18018-6650, 610-861-1330 or toll-free 800-441-3191. *Fax:* 610-861-1346. *E-mail:* cmccarthy@moravian.edu. *Website:* http://www.moravian.edu/.

# MOREHEAD STATE UNIVERSITY
## Morehead, KY

| Tuition & fees (KY res): $7866 | Average undergraduate aid package: $10,961 |
|---|---|

**ABOUT THE INSTITUTION** State-supported, coed. **Awards:** certificates, associate, bachelor's, master's, and doctoral degrees. 56 undergraduate majors. **Total enrollment:** 11,053. Undergraduates: 9,952. Freshmen: 1,513. Federal methodology is used as a basis for awarding need-based institutional aid.

**UNDERGRADUATE EXPENSES for 2015–2016 Application fee:** $30. **Tuition, state resident:** full-time $7866; part-time $328 per credit hour. **Tuition, nonresident:** full-time $19,666; part-time $820 per credit hour. Full-time tuition and fees vary according to course load, degree level, location, reciprocity agreements, and student level. Part-time tuition and fees vary according to course load, degree level, location, reciprocity agreements, and student level. **College room and board:** $7888; **Room only:** $4328. Room and board charges vary according to board plan and housing facility.

**FRESHMAN FINANCIAL AID (Fall 2014, est.)** 1,443 applied for aid; of those 84% were deemed to have need. 100% of freshmen with need received aid; of those 19% had need fully met. **Average percent of need met:** 63% (excluding resources awarded to replace EFC). **Average financial aid package:** $10,703 (excluding resources awarded to replace EFC). 14% of all full-time freshmen had no need and received non-need-based gift aid.

**UNDERGRADUATE FINANCIAL AID (Fall 2014, est.)** 5,481 applied for aid; of those 88% were deemed to have need. 99% of undergraduates with need received aid; of those 22% had need fully met. **Average percent of need met:** 64% (excluding resources awarded to replace EFC). **Average financial aid package:** $10,961 (excluding resources awarded to replace EFC). 14% of all full-time undergraduates had no need and received non-need-based gift aid.

**GIFT AID (NEED-BASED) Total amount:** $19,441,981 (82% federal, 18% state). **Receiving aid:** Freshmen: 54% (815); all full-time undergraduates: 53% (3,258). **Average award:** Freshmen: $5552; Undergraduates: $5421. **Scholarships, grants, and awards:** Federal Pell, FSEOG, state, private, college/university gift aid from institutional funds.

**GIFT AID (NON-NEED-BASED) Total amount:** $25,415,705 (24% state, 66% institutional, 10% external sources). **Receiving aid:** Freshmen: 75% (1,125). Undergraduates: 53% (3,272). **Average award:** Freshmen: $5211. Undergraduates: $6347. **Scholarships, grants, and awards by category:** Academic interests/achievement: 2,216 awards ($9,993,582 total): agriculture, biological sciences, business, communication, education, engineering/technologies, general academic interests/achievements, health fields, international studies, military science, physical sciences, social sciences. Creative arts/performance: 108 awards ($169,310 total): applied art and design, art/fine arts, journalism/publications, music, theater/drama. Special achievements/activities: 123 awards ($230,123 total): cheerleading/drum major, community service, general special achievements/activities, junior miss, leadership. Special characteristics: 1,243 awards ($5,666,287 total): adult students, children and siblings of alumni, ethnic background, general special characteristics, handicapped students, international students, local/state students, members of minority groups, out-of-state students, previous college experience, veterans, veterans' children. **Tuition waivers:** Full or partial for minority students, children of alumni, employees or children of employees, senior citizens. **ROTC:** Army.

**LOANS Student loans:** $35,510,310 (42% need-based, 58% non-need-based). 71% of past graduating class borrowed through all loan programs. **Average indebtedness per student:** $28,147. **Average need-based loan:** Freshmen: $3035. Undergraduates: $3644. **Parent loans:** $2,246,168 (100% non-need-based). **Programs:** Federal Direct (Subsidized and Unsubsidized Stafford, PLUS), Perkins, college/university.

**WORK-STUDY Federal work-study:** Total amount: $1,044,613; 526 jobs averaging $1927. **State or other work-study/employment:** Total amount: $1,935,993 (100% non-need-based). 768 part-time jobs averaging $2484.

**ATHLETIC AWARDS** Total amount: $2,550,083 (100% non-need-based).

**APPLYING FOR FINANCIAL AID Required financial aid form:** FAFSA. **Financial aid deadline (priority):** 3/15. **Notification date:** Continuous.

**CONTACT** Denise Trusty, Director of Financial Aid, Morehead State University, 100 Admissions Center, Morehead, KY 40351, 606-783-2000 or toll-free 800-585-6781. *Fax:* 606-783-2293. *E-mail:* dmtrusty@moreheadstate.edu. *Website:* http://www.moreheadstate.edu/.

# MOREHOUSE COLLEGE
## Atlanta, GA

**ABOUT THE INSTITUTION** Independent, men only. **Awards:** bachelor's degrees. 31 undergraduate majors. **Total enrollment:** 2,170. Undergraduates: 2,170. Freshmen: 486.

**GIFT AID (NEED-BASED) Scholarships, grants, and awards:** Federal Pell, FSEOG, state, private, college/university gift aid from institutional funds, United Negro College Fund.

**GIFT AID (NON-NEED-BASED) Scholarships, grants, and awards by category:** Academic interests/achievement: business, general academic interests/achievements, military science. Creative arts/performance: art/fine arts, music. Special achievements/activities: community service, leadership, religious involvement. Special characteristics: children and siblings of alumni, children of faculty/staff, local/state students.

**LOANS Programs:** Federal Direct (Subsidized and Unsubsidized Stafford, PLUS), Perkins, state, college/university.

**APPLYING FOR FINANCIAL AID Required financial aid forms:** FAFSA, institution's own form, CSS Financial Aid PROFILE, state aid form.

**CONTACT** Sheryl T. Spivey, Interim Director of Financial Aid, Morehouse College, 830 Westview Drive, SW, Atlanta, GA 30314, 404-215-2639 or toll-free 800-851-1254. *Fax:* 404-215-2711. *E-mail:* Sheryl.Spivey@morehouse.edu. *Website:* http://www.morehouse.edu/.

# MORGAN STATE UNIVERSITY
## Baltimore, MD

**ABOUT THE INSTITUTION** State-supported, coed. 55 undergraduate majors.

**GIFT AID (NEED-BASED) Scholarships, grants, and awards:** Federal Pell, FSEOG, state, private, college/university gift aid from institutional funds.

**GIFT AID (NON-NEED-BASED) Scholarships, grants, and awards by category:** Academic interests/achievement: general academic interests/achievements.

**LOANS Programs:** Federal Direct (Subsidized and Unsubsidized Stafford, PLUS), Perkins.

**WORK-STUDY Federal work-study:** 432 jobs averaging $2447. **State or other work-study/employment:** Total amount: $293,100 (100% need-based). 84 part-time jobs averaging $3489.

**APPLYING FOR FINANCIAL AID Required financial aid forms:** FAFSA, institution's own form, federal income tax form(s).

**CONTACT** Tanya Wilkerson, Director of Financial Aid, Morgan State University, 1700 East Cold Spring Lane, Baltimore, MD 21251, 443-885-3170 or toll-free 800-332-6674. *Fax:* 443-885-8272. *Website:* http://www.morgan.edu/.

# MORNINGSIDE COLLEGE
## Sioux City, IA

| Tuition & fees: $27,180 | Average undergraduate aid package: $21,392 |
|---|---|

**ABOUT THE INSTITUTION** Independent United Methodist Church, coed. **Awards:** bachelor's and master's degrees. 43 undergraduate majors. **Total enrollment:** 2,824. Undergraduates: 1,321. Freshmen: 353. Federal methodology is used as a basis for awarding need-based institutional aid.

**UNDERGRADUATE EXPENSES for 2015–2016 Comprehensive fee:** $35,430 includes full-time tuition ($25,710), mandatory fees ($1470), and room and board ($8250). **College room only:** $4220. Full-time tuition and fees vary according to program. Room and board charges vary according to housing facility. **Part-time tuition:** $820 per credit hour. Part-time tuition and fees vary according to course load and program.

**FRESHMAN FINANCIAL AID (Fall 2014, est.)** 338 applied for aid; of those 88% were deemed to have need. 100% of freshmen with need received aid; of those 39% had need fully met. **Average percent of need met:** 84% (excluding resources awarded to replace EFC). **Average financial aid package:** $23,119 (excluding resources awarded to replace EFC). 15% of all full-time freshmen had no need and received non-need-based gift aid.

**UNDERGRADUATE FINANCIAL AID (Fall 2014, est.)** 1,190 applied for aid; of those 90% were deemed to have need. 100% of undergraduates with need received aid; of those 34% had need fully met. *Average percent of need met:* 80% (excluding resources awarded to replace EFC). *Average financial aid package:* $21,392 (excluding resources awarded to replace EFC). 20% of all full-time undergraduates had no need and received non-need-based gift aid.

**GIFT AID (NEED-BASED)** *Total amount:* $4,947,774 (38% federal, 42% state, 20% institutional). *Receiving aid:* Freshmen: 57% (200); all full-time undergraduates: 60% (747). *Average award:* Freshmen: $6475; Undergraduates: $6562. *Scholarships, grants, and awards:* Federal Pell, FSEOG, state, college/university gift aid from institutional funds.

**GIFT AID (NON-NEED-BASED)** *Total amount:* $13,659,762 (6% federal, 2% state, 87% institutional, 5% external sources). *Receiving aid:* Freshmen: 84% (297). Undergraduates: 86% (1,075). *Average award:* Freshmen: $12,867. Undergraduates: $8821. *Scholarships, grants, and awards by category: Academic interests/achievement:* $8,533,976 total: computer science, general academic interests/achievements. *Creative arts/performance:* $875,083 total: art/fine arts, cinema/film/broadcasting, creative writing, dance, journalism/publications, music, theater/drama. *Special achievements/activities:* $296,400 total: cheerleading/drum major, community service, general special achievements/activities, leadership. *Special characteristics:* $1,531,948 total: children and siblings of alumni, children of faculty/staff, international students, local/state students, out-of-state students, religious affiliation. *Tuition waivers:* Full or partial for children of alumni, employees or children of employees, senior citizens. *ROTC:* Army cooperative.

**LOANS** *Student loans:* $9,698,951 (43% need-based, 57% non-need-based). 84% of past graduating class borrowed through all loan programs. *Average indebtedness per student:* $34,667. *Average need-based loan:* Freshmen: $4279. Undergraduates: $4609. *Parent loans:* $1,792,326 (100% non-need-based). *Programs:* Federal Direct (Subsidized and Unsubsidized Stafford, PLUS), Perkins, college/university, private loans.

**WORK-STUDY** *Federal work-study:* Total amount: $640,849; 560 jobs averaging $1112. *State or other work-study/employment:* Total amount: $511,683 (100% non-need-based). 310 part-time jobs averaging $1862.

**ATHLETIC AWARDS** Total amount: $2,628,378 (100% non-need-based).

**APPLYING FOR FINANCIAL AID** *Required financial aid form:* FAFSA. *Financial aid deadline (priority):* 3/1. *Notification date:* 3/15.

**CONTACT** Karen Gagnon, Director of Student Financial Planning, Morningside College, 1501 Morningside Avenue, Sioux City, IA 51106, 712-274-5272 or toll-free 800-831-0806 Ext. 5111. *Fax:* 712-274-5605. *E-mail:* gagnon@morningside.edu. *Website:* http://www.morningside.edu/.

# MORRIS COLLEGE
## Sumter, SC

**CONTACT** Ms. Sandra S. Gibson, Director of Financial Aid, Morris College, 100 West College Street, Sumter, SC 29150-3599, 803-934-3238 or toll-free 866-853-1345. *Fax:* 803-773-3687. *Website:* http://www.morris.edu/.

# MORRISVILLE STATE COLLEGE
## Morrisville, NY

| Tuition & fees (NY res): $7642 | Average undergraduate aid package: $9641 |
| --- | --- |

**ABOUT THE INSTITUTION** State-supported, coed. *Awards:* certificates, associate, and bachelor's degrees. 94 undergraduate majors. *Total enrollment:* 2,911. Undergraduates: 2,911. Freshmen: 779. Federal methodology is used as a basis for awarding need-based institutional aid.

**UNDERGRADUATE EXPENSES** for 2015–2016 *Application fee:* $50. *Tuition, state resident:* full-time $6170; part-time $257 per credit hour. *Tuition, nonresident:* full-time $10,640; part-time $443 per credit hour. *Required fees:* full-time $1472; $61.35 per credit hour. Full-time tuition and fees vary according to degree level and location. Part-time tuition and fees vary according to course load, degree level, and location. *College room and board:* $12,858; *Room only:*

$7868. Room and board charges vary according to board plan, housing facility, and location.

**FRESHMAN FINANCIAL AID (Fall 2014, est.)** 832 applied for aid; of those 91% were deemed to have need. 99% of freshmen with need received aid; of those .4% had need fully met. *Average percent of need met:* 52% (excluding resources awarded to replace EFC). *Average financial aid package:* $9746 (excluding resources awarded to replace EFC).

**UNDERGRADUATE FINANCIAL AID (Fall 2014, est.)** 2,532 applied for aid; of those 91% were deemed to have need. 99% of undergraduates with need received aid; of those .3% had need fully met. *Average percent of need met:* 52% (excluding resources awarded to replace EFC). *Average financial aid package:* $9641 (excluding resources awarded to replace EFC).

**GIFT AID (NEED-BASED)** *Total amount:* $14,312,878 (56% federal, 44% state). *Receiving aid:* Freshmen: 669; all full-time undergraduates: 2,011. *Average award:* Freshmen: $7223; Undergraduates: $6683. *Scholarships, grants, and awards:* Federal Pell, FSEOG, state, college/university gift aid from institutional funds.

**GIFT AID (NON-NEED-BASED)** *Total amount:* $1,234,401 (4% state, 42% institutional, 54% external sources). *Receiving aid:* Freshmen: 178. Undergraduates: 384. *Average award:* Freshmen: $1405. Undergraduates: $1531. *Scholarships, grants, and awards by category: Academic interests/achievement:* general academic interests/achievements. *Special achievements/activities:* leadership, memberships. *Special characteristics:* children of faculty/staff, local/state students, members of minority groups, out-of-state students. *Tuition waivers:* Full or partial for minority students, children of alumni, employees or children of employees, senior citizens. *ROTC:* Army cooperative, Air Force cooperative.

**LOANS** *Student loans:* $19,247,165 (45% need-based, 55% non-need-based). 87% of past graduating class borrowed through all loan programs. *Average indebtedness per student:* $29,023. *Average need-based loan:* Freshmen: $3339. Undergraduates: $3935. *Parent loans:* $6,403,665 (100% non-need-based). *Programs:* Federal Direct (Subsidized and Unsubsidized Stafford, PLUS), Perkins, Federal Nursing.

**WORK-STUDY** *Federal work-study:* Total amount: $112,898; jobs available.

**APPLYING FOR FINANCIAL AID** *Required financial aid forms:* FAFSA, state aid form. *Financial aid deadline (priority):* 3/1. *Notification date:* Continuous beginning 3/1.

**CONTACT** Financial Aid Office, Morrisville State College, PO Box 901, Morrisville, NY 13408-0901, 315-684-6289 or toll-free 800-258-0111. *Fax:* 315-684-6628. *Website:* http://www.morrisville.edu/.

# MOUNT ALOYSIUS COLLEGE
## Cresson, PA

| Tuition & fees: N/R | Average undergraduate aid package: $14,510 |
| --- | --- |

**ABOUT THE INSTITUTION** Independent Roman Catholic, coed. *Awards:* certificates, associate, bachelor's, and master's degrees. 25 undergraduate majors. *Total enrollment:* 1,867. Undergraduates: 1,794. Freshmen: 386. Federal methodology is used as a basis for awarding need-based institutional aid.

**FRESHMAN FINANCIAL AID (Fall 2014, est.)** 370 applied for aid; of those 91% were deemed to have need. 100% of freshmen with need received aid. *Average percent of need met:* 35% (excluding resources awarded to replace EFC). *Average financial aid package:* $15,525 (excluding resources awarded to replace EFC). 9% of all full-time freshmen had no need and received non-need-based gift aid.

**UNDERGRADUATE FINANCIAL AID (Fall 2014, est.)** 1,251 applied for aid; of those 92% were deemed to have need. 100% of undergraduates with need received aid. *Average percent of need met:* 38% (excluding resources awarded to replace EFC). *Average financial aid package:* $14,510 (excluding resources awarded to replace EFC). 8% of all full-time undergraduates had no need and received non-need-based gift aid.

**GIFT AID (NEED-BASED)** *Total amount:* $13,598,976 (24% federal, 18% state, 57% institutional, 1% external sources). *Receiving aid:* Freshmen: 91% (335); all full-time undergraduates: 92% (1,156). *Average award:* Freshmen: $6450; Undergraduates: $4650. *Scholarships, grants, and awards:* Federal Pell, FSEOG, state, private, college/university gift aid from institutional funds.

**GIFT AID (NON-NEED-BASED)** *Receiving aid:* Freshmen: 9% (35). Undergraduates: 8% (95). *Average award:* Freshmen: $5290. Undergraduates: $5310. *Scholarships, grants, and awards by category: Academic interests/achievement:* general academic interests/achievements. *Creative arts/performance:*

music, performing arts. *Special achievements/activities:* leadership. *Special characteristics:* children of current students, parents of current students, religious affiliation, siblings of current students, spouses of current students, twins.

**LOANS** *Student loans:* $10,968,049 (100% need-based). 90% of past graduating class borrowed through all loan programs. *Average need-based loan:* Freshmen: $3230. Undergraduates: $4020. *Parent loans:* $3,031,039 (100% need-based). *Programs:* Federal Direct (Subsidized and Unsubsidized Stafford, PLUS), Perkins, Federal Nursing, alternative loans.

**WORK-STUDY** *Federal work-study:* Total amount: $334,538; jobs available.

**APPLYING FOR FINANCIAL AID** *Required financial aid form:* FAFSA. *Financial aid deadline (priority):* 4/1. *Notification date:* Continuous beginning 3/15. Students must reply within 2 weeks of notification.

**CONTACT** Mrs. Stacy L. Schenk, Director of Financial Aid, Mount Aloysius College, 7373 Admiral Peary Highway, Cresson, PA 16630-1900, 814-886-6357 or toll-free 888-823-2220. *Fax:* 814-886-6463. *E-mail:* sschenk@mtaloy.edu.
*Website:* http://www.mtaloy.edu/.

---

# MOUNT ANGEL SEMINARY
## Saint Benedict, OR

**CONTACT** Dorene Preis, Director of Student Financial Aid/Registrar, Mount Angel Seminary, 1 Abbey Drive, Saint Benedict, OR 97373, 503-845-3951. *Fax:* 503-845-3126. *E-mail:* dpreis@mtangel.edu.
*Website:* http://www.mountangelabbey.org/seminary/.

---

# MOUNT CARMEL COLLEGE OF NURSING
## Columbus, OH

| Tuition & fees: $12,016 | Average undergraduate aid package: $7917 |
| --- | --- |

**ABOUT THE INSTITUTION** Independent, coed, primarily women. *Awards:* certificates, bachelor's, and master's degrees. 1 undergraduate major. *Total enrollment:* 1,084. Undergraduates: 927. Freshmen: 83. Federal methodology is used as a basis for awarding need-based institutional aid.

**UNDERGRADUATE EXPENSES** for 2015–2016 *Application fee:* $30. *One-time required fee:* $225. *Tuition:* full-time $11,284; part-time $364 per semester hour. *Required fees:* full-time $732; $858 per year. Full-time tuition and fees vary according to course level, course load, program, and student level. Part-time tuition and fees vary according to course level, course load, program, and student level.

**FRESHMAN FINANCIAL AID (Fall 2013)** 79 applied for aid; of those 82% were deemed to have need. 100% of freshmen with need received aid; of those 31% had need fully met. *Average percent of need met:* 39% (excluding resources awarded to replace EFC). *Average financial aid package:* $6036 (excluding resources awarded to replace EFC).

**UNDERGRADUATE FINANCIAL AID (Fall 2013)** 554 applied for aid; of those 82% were deemed to have need. 100% of undergraduates with need received aid; of those 28% had need fully met. *Average percent of need met:* 31% (excluding resources awarded to replace EFC). *Average financial aid package:* $7917 (excluding resources awarded to replace EFC).

**GIFT AID (NEED-BASED)** *Total amount:* $2,154,120 (50% federal, 16% state, 31% institutional, 3% external sources). *Receiving aid:* Freshmen: 46% (36); all full-time undergraduates: 35% (215). *Average award:* Freshmen: $5557; Undergraduates: $5470. *Scholarships, grants, and awards:* Federal Pell, FSEOG, state, private, college/university gift aid from institutional funds.

**GIFT AID (NON-NEED-BASED)** *Total amount:* $111,863 (100% external sources). *Scholarships, grants, and awards by category:* Academic interests/achievement: general academic interests/achievements. *Special achievements/activities:* community service. *Special characteristics:* children of faculty/staff, members of minority groups. *Tuition waivers:* Full or partial for employees or children of employees. *ROTC:* Army cooperative, Naval cooperative, Air Force cooperative.

**LOANS** *Student loans:* $6,715,663 (38% need-based, 62% non-need-based). 76% of past graduating class borrowed through all loan programs. *Average indebtedness per student:* $35,952. *Average need-based loan:* Freshmen: $3270. Undergrad-

uates: $4303. *Parent loans:* $1,512,782 (100% non-need-based). *Programs:* Federal Direct (Subsidized and Unsubsidized Stafford, PLUS), Federal Nursing, state, college/university.

**WORK-STUDY** *State or other work-study/employment:* Part-time jobs available.

**APPLYING FOR FINANCIAL AID** *Required financial aid form:* FAFSA. *Financial aid deadline:* Continuous. *Notification date:* Continuous beginning 5/31. Students must reply within 2 weeks of notification.

**CONTACT** Todd Everett, Director of Financial Aid, Mount Carmel College of Nursing, 127 South Davis Avenue, Columbus, OH 43222, 614-234-5800 Ext. 5177 or toll-free 800-556-6942. *Fax:* 614-234-5427. *E-mail:* teverett@mccn.edu.
*Website:* http://www.mccn.edu/.

---

# MOUNT HOLYOKE COLLEGE
## South Hadley, MA

| Tuition & fees: $43,886 | Average undergraduate aid package: $36,761 |
| --- | --- |

**ABOUT THE INSTITUTION** Independent, women only. *Awards:* certificates, bachelor's, and master's degrees. 50 undergraduate majors. *Total enrollment:* 2,255. Undergraduates: 2,189. Freshmen: 531. Both federal and institutional methodology are used as a basis for awarding need-based institutional aid.

**UNDERGRADUATE EXPENSES** for 2015–2016 *Application fee:* $60. *Comprehensive fee:* $56,746 includes full-time tuition ($43,700), mandatory fees ($186), and room and board ($12,860). *College room only:* $6280. *Part-time tuition:* $1370 per credit hour.

**FRESHMAN FINANCIAL AID (Fall 2014, est.)** 424 applied for aid; of those 85% were deemed to have need. 100% of freshmen with need received aid; of those 100% had need fully met. *Average percent of need met:* 100% (excluding resources awarded to replace EFC). *Average financial aid package:* $36,827 (excluding resources awarded to replace EFC). 12% of all full-time freshmen had no need and received non-need-based gift aid.

**UNDERGRADUATE FINANCIAL AID (Fall 2014, est.)** 1,729 applied for aid; of those 86% were deemed to have need. 100% of undergraduates with need received aid; of those 100% had need fully met. *Average percent of need met:* 100% (excluding resources awarded to replace EFC). *Average financial aid package:* $36,761 (excluding resources awarded to replace EFC). 13% of all full-time undergraduates had no need and received non-need-based gift aid.

**GIFT AID (NEED-BASED)** *Total amount:* $45,709,444 (5% federal, 1% state, 93% institutional, 1% external sources). *Receiving aid:* Freshmen: 68% (359); all full-time undergraduates: 67% (1,472). *Average award:* Freshmen: $32,155; Undergraduates: $30,707. *Scholarships, grants, and awards:* Federal Pell, FSEOG, state, private, college/university gift aid from institutional funds.

**GIFT AID (NON-NEED-BASED)** *Total amount:* $6,573,659 (89% institutional, 11% external sources). *Receiving aid:* Freshmen: 15% (81). Undergraduates: 12% (267). *Average award:* Freshmen: $17,727. Undergraduates: $16,888. *Scholarships, grants, and awards by category:* Academic interests/achievement: general academic interests/achievements. *Special characteristics:* general special characteristics. *Tuition waivers:* Full or partial for employees or children of employees. *ROTC:* Army cooperative, Air Force cooperative.

**LOANS** *Student loans:* $9,735,796 (87% need-based, 13% non-need-based). 73% of past graduating class borrowed through all loan programs. *Average indebtedness per student:* $23,914. *Average need-based loan:* Freshmen: $3755. Undergraduates: $5375. *Parent loans:* $3,880,511 (100% non-need-based). *Programs:* Federal Direct (Subsidized and Unsubsidized Stafford, PLUS), Perkins, state, college/university.

**WORK-STUDY** *Federal work-study:* Total amount: $1,515,363; 764 jobs averaging $1883. *State or other work-study/employment:* Total amount: $750,095 (100% need-based). 368 part-time jobs averaging $1959.

**APPLYING FOR FINANCIAL AID** *Required financial aid forms:* FAFSA, CSS Financial Aid PROFILE, noncustodial (divorced/separated) parent's statement, federal income tax form(s), W-2 forms. *Financial aid deadline:* 3/1 (priority: 2/15). *Notification date:* 4/1. Students must reply by 5/1.

**CONTACT** Ms. Kathryn Blaisdell, Director of Student Financial Services, Mount Holyoke College, 50 College Street, South Hadley, MA 01075-1492, 413-538-2291. *Fax:* 413-538-2512. *E-mail:* kblaisde@mtholyoke.edu.
*Website:* http://www.mtholyoke.edu/.

# MOUNT IDA COLLEGE
## Newton, MA

**CONTACT** David L. Goldman, Director of Financial Aid, Mount Ida College, 777 Dedham Street, Newton, MA 02459-3310, 617-928-4785. *Fax:* 617-332-7869. *E-mail:* finaid@mountida.edu.
*Website:* http://www.mountida.edu/.

# MOUNT MARTY COLLEGE
## Yankton, SD

| Tuition & fees: $22,892 | Average undergraduate aid package: $23,212 |
|---|---|

**ABOUT THE INSTITUTION** Independent Roman Catholic, coed. *Awards:* certificates, associate, bachelor's, and master's degrees. 32 undergraduate majors. *Total enrollment:* 1,236. Undergraduates: 1,108. Freshmen: 122. Federal methodology is used as a basis for awarding need-based institutional aid.

**UNDERGRADUATE EXPENSES for 2015–2016** *Application fee:* $35. *Comprehensive fee:* $29,870 includes full-time tuition ($21,062), mandatory fees ($1830), and room and board ($6978). Full-time tuition and fees vary according to degree level, location, and program. Room and board charges vary according to board plan. Part-time tuition and fees vary according to course load, degree level, location, and program.

**FRESHMAN FINANCIAL AID (Fall 2014, est.)** 107 applied for aid; of those 80% were deemed to have need. 100% of freshmen with need received aid; of those 49% had need fully met. *Average percent of need met:* 92% (excluding resources awarded to replace EFC). *Average financial aid package:* $27,730 (excluding resources awarded to replace EFC). 17% of all full-time freshmen had no need and received non-need-based gift aid.

**UNDERGRADUATE FINANCIAL AID (Fall 2014, est.)** 482 applied for aid; of those 86% were deemed to have need. 99% of undergraduates with need received aid; of those 54% had need fully met. *Average percent of need met:* 89% (excluding resources awarded to replace EFC). *Average financial aid package:* $23,212 (excluding resources awarded to replace EFC). 11% of all full-time undergraduates had no need and received non-need-based gift aid.

**GIFT AID (NEED-BASED)** *Total amount:* $4,640,651 (24% federal, 2% state, 71% institutional, 3% external sources). *Receiving aid:* Freshmen: 76% (85); all full-time undergraduates: 73% (384). *Average award:* Freshmen: $16,072; Undergraduates: $12,798. *Scholarships, grants, and awards:* Federal Pell, FSEOG, state, private, college/university gift aid from institutional funds.

**GIFT AID (NON-NEED-BASED)** *Total amount:* $630,977 (3% federal, 4% state, 87% institutional, 6% external sources). *Average award:* Freshmen: $10,624. Undergraduates: $9295. *Scholarships, grants, and awards by category:* Academic interests/achievement: 378 awards ($2,753,391 total): general academic interests/achievements. *Creative arts/performance:* 49 awards ($68,700 total): art/fine arts, music, performing arts, theater/drama. *Special achievements/activities:* community service, general special achievements/activities, leadership, religious involvement. *Special characteristics:* children of current students, children of faculty/staff, international students, parents of current students, religious affiliation, siblings of current students, spouses of current students. *Tuition waivers:* Full or partial for employees or children of employees. *ROTC:* Army cooperative.

**LOANS** *Student loans:* $2,363,726 (99% need-based, 1% non-need-based). 90% of past graduating class borrowed through all loan programs. *Average indebtedness per student:* $33,945. *Average need-based loan:* Freshmen: $4402. Undergraduates: $4992. *Parent loans:* $872,436 (94% need-based, 6% non-need-based). *Programs:* Federal Direct (Subsidized and Unsubsidized Stafford, PLUS), Perkins, Federal Nursing, state, college/university.

**WORK-STUDY** *Federal work-study:* Total amount: $305,136; 170 jobs averaging $1774. *State or other work-study/employment:* Total amount: $100,800 (41% need-based, 59% non-need-based). 55 part-time jobs averaging $1800.

**ATHLETIC AWARDS** Total amount: $851,314 (81% need-based, 19% non-need-based).

**APPLYING FOR FINANCIAL AID** *Required financial aid forms:* FAFSA, institution's own form. *Financial aid deadline (priority):* 3/1. *Notification date:* Continuous beginning 3/15. Students must reply within 2 weeks of notification.

**CONTACT** Mr. Ken Kocer, Director of Financial Assistance, Mount Marty College, 1105 West 8th Street, Yankton, SD 57078-3724, 605-668-1589 or toll-free 800-658-4552. *Fax:* 605-668-1585. *E-mail:* kkocer@mtmc.edu. *Website:* http://www.mtmc.edu/.

# MOUNT MARY UNIVERSITY
## Milwaukee, WI

| Tuition & fees: $25,852 | Average undergraduate aid package: $22,040 |
|---|---|

**ABOUT THE INSTITUTION** Independent Roman Catholic, undergraduate: women only; graduate: coed. *Awards:* certificates, bachelor's, master's, and doctoral degrees. 47 undergraduate majors. *Total enrollment:* 1,385. Undergraduates: 860. Freshmen: 155. Federal methodology is used as a basis for awarding need-based institutional aid.

**UNDERGRADUATE EXPENSES for 2015–2016** *Comprehensive fee:* $33,590 includes full-time tuition ($25,336), mandatory fees ($516), and room and board ($7738). Full-time tuition and fees vary according to degree level and program. Room and board charges vary according to board plan and housing facility. *Part-time tuition:* $768 per credit. *Part-time fees:* $320 per year. Part-time tuition and fees vary according to course load, degree level, and program.

**FRESHMAN FINANCIAL AID (Fall 2014, est.)** 111 applied for aid; of those 94% were deemed to have need. 100% of freshmen with need received aid; of those 11% had need fully met. *Average percent of need met:* 76% (excluding resources awarded to replace EFC). *Average financial aid package:* $24,121 (excluding resources awarded to replace EFC). 9% of all full-time freshmen had no need and received non-need-based gift aid.

**UNDERGRADUATE FINANCIAL AID (Fall 2014, est.)** 604 applied for aid; of those 93% were deemed to have need. 100% of undergraduates with need received aid; of those 9% had need fully met. *Average percent of need met:* 70% (excluding resources awarded to replace EFC). *Average financial aid package:* $22,040 (excluding resources awarded to replace EFC). 11% of all full-time undergraduates had no need and received non-need-based gift aid.

**GIFT AID (NEED-BASED)** *Total amount:* $11,288,951 (18% federal, 13% state, 68% institutional, 1% external sources). *Receiving aid:* Freshmen: 67% (103); all full-time undergraduates: 82% (559). *Average award:* Freshmen: $20,292; Undergraduates: $17,522. *Scholarships, grants, and awards:* Federal Pell, FSEOG, state, private, college/university gift aid from institutional funds.

**GIFT AID (NON-NEED-BASED)** *Total amount:* $1,143,926 (95% institutional, 5% external sources). *Receiving aid:* Freshmen: 7% (11). Undergraduates: 6% (39). *Average award:* Freshmen: $12,408. Undergraduates: $10,803. *Scholarships, grants, and awards by category:* Academic interests/achievement: 636 awards ($5,055,368 total): business, communication, education, English, general academic interests/achievements, humanities, mathematics, social sciences. *Creative arts/performance:* 43 awards ($44,850 total): applied art and design, art/fine arts, music. *Special achievements/activities:* 14 awards ($74,988 total): general special achievements/activities, leadership. *Special characteristics:* 29 awards ($117,398 total): children of faculty/staff, international students, parents of current students, siblings of current students, veterans. *Tuition waivers:* Full or partial for employees or children of employees, senior citizens. *ROTC:* Air Force cooperative.

**LOANS** *Student loans:* $5,448,074 (88% need-based, 12% non-need-based). 89% of past graduating class borrowed through all loan programs. *Average indebtedness per student:* $29,759. *Average need-based loan:* Freshmen: $3580. Undergraduates: $4501. *Parent loans:* $385,934 (52% need-based, 48% non-need-based). *Programs:* Federal Direct (Subsidized and Unsubsidized Stafford, PLUS), Perkins, state.

**WORK-STUDY** *Federal work-study:* Total amount: $156,248; 125 jobs averaging $1337. *State or other work-study/employment:* Total amount: $141,771 (100% non-need-based). 127 part-time jobs averaging $1302.

**APPLYING FOR FINANCIAL AID** *Required financial aid form:* FAFSA. *Financial aid deadline (priority):* 3/1. *Notification date:* Continuous. Students must reply within 2 weeks of notification.

**CONTACT** Debra Duff, Director of Financial Aid, Mount Mary University, 2900 North Menomonee River Parkway, Milwaukee, WI 53222-4597, 414-256-1258 or toll-free 800-321-6265. *Fax:* 414-443-3602. *E-mail:* finaid@mtmary.edu. *Website:* http://www.mtmary.edu/.

# MOUNT MERCY UNIVERSITY
## Cedar Rapids, IA

| Tuition & fees: $28,226 | Average undergraduate aid package: $19,750 |
|---|---|

**ABOUT THE INSTITUTION** Independent Roman Catholic, coed. *Awards:* bachelor's and master's degrees. 43 undergraduate majors. *Total enrollment:* 1,762. Undergraduates: 1,444. Freshmen: 134. Federal methodology is used as a basis for awarding need-based institutional aid.

**UNDERGRADUATE EXPENSES for 2015–2016** *Comprehensive fee:* $36,826 includes full-time tuition ($28,226) and room and board ($8600). Full-time tuition and fees vary according to course load. Room and board charges vary according to board plan and housing facility. *Part-time tuition:* $768 per credit. Part-time tuition and fees vary according to course load.

**FRESHMAN FINANCIAL AID (Fall 2013)** 123 applied for aid; of those 88% were deemed to have need. 100% of freshmen with need received aid; of those 15% had need fully met. *Average percent of need met:* 77% (excluding resources awarded to replace EFC). *Average financial aid package:* $22,057 (excluding resources awarded to replace EFC). 20% of all full-time freshmen had no need and received non-need-based gift aid.

**UNDERGRADUATE FINANCIAL AID (Fall 2013)** 666 applied for aid; of those 92% were deemed to have need. 99% of undergraduates with need received aid; of those 16% had need fully met. *Average percent of need met:* 71% (excluding resources awarded to replace EFC). *Average financial aid package:* $19,750 (excluding resources awarded to replace EFC). 16% of all full-time undergraduates had no need and received non-need-based gift aid.

**GIFT AID (NEED-BASED)** *Total amount:* $12,214,167 (14% federal, 20% state, 60% institutional, 6% external sources). *Receiving aid:* Freshmen: 81% (108); all full-time undergraduates: 74% (603). *Average award:* Freshmen: $18,987; Undergraduates: $15,859. *Scholarships, grants, and awards:* Federal Pell, FSEOG, state, private, college/university gift aid from institutional funds.

**GIFT AID (NON-NEED-BASED)** *Total amount:* $2,166,700 (1% federal, 1% state, 90% institutional, 8% external sources). *Receiving aid:* Freshmen: 11% (15). Undergraduates: 9% (70). *Average award:* Freshmen: $14,483. Undergraduates: $11,238. *Scholarships, grants, and awards by category:* Academic interests/achievement: general academic interests/achievements. Creative arts/performance: art/fine arts, music, theater/drama. Special achievements/activities: leadership. Special characteristics: previous college experience. *Tuition waivers:* Full or partial for employees or children of employees.

**LOANS** *Student loans:* $9,178,691 (74% need-based, 26% non-need-based). 84% of past graduating class borrowed through all loan programs. *Average indebtedness per student:* $27,442. *Average need-based loan:* Freshmen: $3172. Undergraduates: $4127. *Parent loans:* $9,622,351 (75% need-based, 25% non-need-based). *Programs:* Federal Direct (Subsidized and Unsubsidized Stafford, PLUS), Perkins, state, college/university.

**WORK-STUDY** *Federal work-study:* 246 jobs averaging $1453. *State or other work-study/employment:* Total amount: $176,459 (100% non-need-based). 225 part-time jobs averaging $998.

**ATHLETIC AWARDS** Total amount: $1,005,831 (59% need-based, 41% non-need-based).

**APPLYING FOR FINANCIAL AID** *Required financial aid form:* FAFSA. *Financial aid deadline (priority):* 3/1. *Notification date:* Continuous beginning 3/15. Students must reply by 5/1 or within 3 weeks of notification.

**CONTACT** Bethany Rinderknecht, Director of Financial Aid, Mount Mercy University, 1330 Elmhurst Drive NE, Cedar Rapids, IA 52402-4797, 319-368-6467 Ext. 1545 or toll-free 800-248-4504. *Fax:* 319-364-3546. *E-mail:* brinderknecht@mtmercy.edu.
*Website:* http://www.mtmercy.edu/.

# MOUNT ST. JOSEPH UNIVERSITY
## Cincinnati, OH

| Tuition & fees: $26,850 | Average undergraduate aid package: $18,934 |
|---|---|

**ABOUT THE INSTITUTION** Independent Roman Catholic, coed. *Awards:* certificates, associate, bachelor's, master's, and doctoral degrees. 33 undergraduate

majors. *Total enrollment:* 2,219. Undergraduates: 1,657. Freshmen: 297. Federal methodology is used as a basis for awarding need-based institutional aid.

**UNDERGRADUATE EXPENSES for 2015–2016** *Application fee:* $25. *One-time required fee:* $200. *Comprehensive fee:* $35,560 includes full-time tuition ($25,850), mandatory fees ($1000), and room and board ($8710). *College room only:* $4500. Full-time tuition and fees vary according to course load and reciprocity agreements. Room and board charges vary according to board plan and housing facility. *Part-time tuition:* $500 per credit hour. Part-time tuition and fees vary according to course load and reciprocity agreements.

**FRESHMAN FINANCIAL AID (Fall 2014, est.)** 275 applied for aid; of those 89% were deemed to have need. 100% of freshmen with need received aid; of those 23% had need fully met. *Average percent of need met:* 82% (excluding resources awarded to replace EFC). *Average financial aid package:* $20,464 (excluding resources awarded to replace EFC). 15% of all full-time freshmen had no need and received non-need-based gift aid.

**UNDERGRADUATE FINANCIAL AID (Fall 2014, est.)** 1,017 applied for aid; of those 89% were deemed to have need. 100% of undergraduates with need received aid; of those 20% had need fully met. *Average percent of need met:* 75% (excluding resources awarded to replace EFC). *Average financial aid package:* $18,934 (excluding resources awarded to replace EFC). 18% of all full-time undergraduates had no need and received non-need-based gift aid.

**GIFT AID (NEED-BASED)** *Total amount:* $14,481,187 (20% federal, 6% state, 72% institutional, 2% external sources). *Receiving aid:* Freshmen: 83% (243); all full-time undergraduates: 78% (892). *Average award:* Freshmen: $16,667; Undergraduates: $15,588. *Scholarships, grants, and awards:* Federal Pell, FSEOG, state, private, college/university gift aid from institutional funds.

**GIFT AID (NON-NEED-BASED)** *Total amount:* $2,669,744 (17% federal, 1% state, 81% institutional, 1% external sources). *Receiving aid:* Freshmen: 12% (34). Undergraduates: 10% (114). *Average award:* Freshmen: $12,561. Undergraduates: $12,578. *Scholarships, grants, and awards by category:* Academic interests/achievement: 189 awards ($1,880,345 total): general academic interests/achievements. Creative arts/performance: 18 awards ($37,250 total): art/fine arts, music. Special achievements/activities: 6 awards ($14,000 total): community service, leadership. Special characteristics: 31 awards ($702,993 total): adult students, children and siblings of alumni, children of faculty/staff. *Tuition waivers:* Full or partial for employees or children of employees, senior citizens. *ROTC:* Army cooperative, Air Force cooperative.

**LOANS** *Student loans:* $7,397,204 (93% need-based, 7% non-need-based). *Average need-based loan:* Freshmen: $3714. Undergraduates: $4352. *Parent loans:* $2,075,039 (90% need-based, 10% non-need-based). *Programs:* Perkins, Federal Nursing, state.

**WORK-STUDY** *Federal work-study:* Total amount: $145,810; 45 jobs averaging $1464. *State or other work-study/employment:* Total amount: $390,600 (96% need-based, 4% non-need-based). 92 part-time jobs averaging $1455.

**APPLYING FOR FINANCIAL AID** *Required financial aid form:* FAFSA. *Financial aid deadline (priority):* 3/1. *Notification date:* Continuous beginning 1/31. Students must reply by 5/1 or within 4 weeks of notification.

**CONTACT** Ms. Kathryn Kelly, Director of Student Administrative Services, Mount St. Joseph University, 5701 Delhi Road, Cincinnati, OH 45233-1670, 513-244-4418 or toll-free 800-654-9314. *Fax:* 513-244-4201. *E-mail:* kathy_kelly@mail.msj.edu. *Website:* http://www.msj.edu/.

# MOUNT SAINT MARY COLLEGE
## Newburgh, NY

| Tuition & fees: $27,312 | Average undergraduate aid package: $17,529 |
|---|---|

**ABOUT THE INSTITUTION** Independent, coed. *Awards:* certificates, bachelor's, and master's degrees. 24 undergraduate majors. *Total enrollment:* 2,479. Undergraduates: 2,123. Freshmen: 413. Federal methodology is used as a basis for awarding need-based institutional aid.

**UNDERGRADUATE EXPENSES for 2015–2016** *Application fee:* $45. *Comprehensive fee:* $40,868 includes full-time tuition ($26,312), mandatory fees ($1000), and room and board ($13,556). *College room only:* $7852. Full-time tuition and fees vary according to class time, location, and program. Room and board charges vary according to board plan and housing facility. *Part-time tuition:* $877 per credit. *Part-time fees:* $80 per term. Part-time tuition and fees vary according to class time, location, and program.

**FRESHMAN FINANCIAL AID (Fall 2014, est.)** 401 applied for aid; of those 84% were deemed to have need. 100% of freshmen with need received aid; of those 17% had need fully met. *Average percent of need met:* 63% (excluding resources awarded to replace EFC). *Average financial aid package:* $18,750 (excluding resources awarded to replace EFC). 17% of all full-time freshmen had no need and received non-need-based gift aid.

**UNDERGRADUATE FINANCIAL AID (Fall 2014, est.)** 1,577 applied for aid; of those 87% were deemed to have need. 100% of undergraduates with need received aid; of those 18% had need fully met. *Average percent of need met:* 60% (excluding resources awarded to replace EFC). *Average financial aid package:* $17,529 (excluding resources awarded to replace EFC). 12% of all full-time undergraduates had no need and received non-need-based gift aid.

**GIFT AID (NEED-BASED)** *Total amount:* $18,167,658 (19% federal, 11% state, 68% institutional, 2% external sources). *Receiving aid:* Freshmen: 82% (335); all full-time undergraduates: 79% (1,341). *Average award:* Freshmen: $15,140; Undergraduates: $13,517. *Scholarships, grants, and awards:* Federal Pell, FSEOG, state, private, college/university gift aid from institutional funds, Federal Nursing, Academic Competitiveness Grants, National SMART Grants.

**GIFT AID (NON-NEED-BASED)** *Total amount:* $3,804,096 (5% state, 91% institutional, 4% external sources). *Receiving aid:* Freshmen: 11% (46). Undergraduates: 10% (168). *Average award:* Freshmen: $10,220. Undergraduates: $9423. *Scholarships, grants, and awards by category:* Academic interests/achievement: 1,135 awards ($8,536,683 total): general academic interests/achievements. *Special achievements/activities:* 22 awards ($100,000 total): leadership. *Special characteristics:* children of faculty/staff. *Tuition waivers:* Full or partial for employees or children of employees. *ROTC:* Army cooperative.

**LOANS** *Student loans:* $17,440,487 (73% need-based, 27% non-need-based). 84% of past graduating class borrowed through all loan programs. *Average indebtedness per student:* $31,764. *Average need-based loan:* Freshmen: $3262. Undergraduates: $4388. *Parent loans:* $20,790,632 (35% need-based, 65% non-need-based). *Programs:* Federal Direct (Subsidized and Unsubsidized Stafford, PLUS), Perkins, Federal Nursing.

**WORK-STUDY** *Federal work-study:* Total amount: $696,005; 316 jobs averaging $1434. *State or other work-study/employment:* Part-time jobs available.

**APPLYING FOR FINANCIAL AID** *Required financial aid form:* FAFSA. *Financial aid deadline:* 3/1 (priority: 2/15). *Notification date:* Continuous beginning 3/15. Students must reply by 5/1.

**CONTACT** Barbara Winchell, Director of Financial Aid, Mount Saint Mary College, 330 Powell Avenue, Newburgh, NY 12550-3494, 845-561-3298 or toll-free 888-937-6762. Fax: 845-569-3302. E-mail: barbara.winchell@msmc.edu. *Website:* http://www.msmc.edu/.

# MOUNT SAINT MARY'S UNIVERSITY
## Los Angeles, CA

| Tuition & fees: $35,944 | Average undergraduate aid package: $25,295 |
|---|---|

**ABOUT THE INSTITUTION** Independent Roman Catholic, coed, primarily women. *Awards:* certificates, associate, bachelor's, master's, and doctoral degrees. 47 undergraduate majors. *Total enrollment:* 3,349. Undergraduates: 2,667. Freshmen: 494. Both federal and institutional methodology are used as a basis for awarding need-based institutional aid.

**UNDERGRADUATE EXPENSES** for 2015–2016 *Comprehensive fee:* $47,061 includes full-time tuition ($34,934), mandatory fees ($1010), and room and board ($11,117). Full-time tuition and fees vary according to course load, degree level, and program. Room and board charges vary according to board plan and housing facility. *Part-time tuition:* $1456 per unit. Part-time tuition and fees vary according to course load, degree level, and program.

**FRESHMAN FINANCIAL AID (Fall 2014, est.)** 450 applied for aid; of those 97% were deemed to have need. 100% of freshmen with need received aid; of those .2% had need fully met. *Average percent of need met:* 69% (excluding resources awarded to replace EFC). *Average financial aid package:* $29,525 (excluding resources awarded to replace EFC). 5% of all full-time freshmen had no need and received non-need-based gift aid.

**UNDERGRADUATE FINANCIAL AID (Fall 2014, est.)** 1,913 applied for aid; of those 97% were deemed to have need. 99% of undergraduates with need received aid; of those 1% had need fully met. *Average percent of need met:* 65% (excluding resources awarded to replace EFC). *Average financial aid package:* $25,295 (excluding resources awarded to replace EFC). 6% of all full-time undergraduates had no need and received non-need-based gift aid.

**GIFT AID (NEED-BASED)** *Total amount:* $42,143,592 (17% federal, 24% state, 59% institutional). *Receiving aid:* Freshmen: 92% (435); all full-time undergraduates: 86% (1,735). *Average award:* Freshmen: $16,136; Undergraduates: $13,528. *Scholarships, grants, and awards:* Federal Pell, FSEOG, state, private, college/university gift aid from institutional funds.

**GIFT AID (NON-NEED-BASED)** *Total amount:* $1,713,184 (98% institutional, 2% external sources). *Receiving aid:* Freshmen: 92% (435). Undergraduates: 41% (830). *Average award:* Freshmen: $14,769. Undergraduates: $13,539. *Scholarships, grants, and awards by category:* Academic interests/achievement: general academic interests/achievements. Creative arts/performance: music. Special achievements/activities: community service, leadership. Special characteristics: children and siblings of alumni. *Tuition waivers:* Full or partial for employees or children of employees.

**LOANS** *Student loans:* $16,950,921 (53% need-based, 47% non-need-based). 95% of past graduating class borrowed through all loan programs. *Average need-based loan:* Freshmen: $3509. Undergraduates: $4417. *Programs:* Federal Direct (Subsidized and Unsubsidized Stafford, PLUS), Federal Nursing, college/university.

**WORK-STUDY** *Federal work-study:* Total amount: $1,479,330; jobs available. *State or other work-study/employment:* Total amount: $398,045 (100% non-need-based). Part-time jobs available.

**APPLYING FOR FINANCIAL AID** *Required financial aid forms:* FAFSA, institution's own form. *Financial aid deadline:* Continuous. *Notification date:* Continuous beginning 3/1. Students must reply by 5/1.

**CONTACT** La Royce Housley, Director of Financial Aid, Mount Saint Mary's University, 12001 Chalon Road, Los Angeles, CA 90049, 310-954-4192 or toll-free 800-999-9893. *Website:* http://www.msmu.edu/.

# MOUNT ST. MARY'S UNIVERSITY
## Emmitsburg, MD

| Tuition & fees: $37,500 | Average undergraduate aid package: $24,665 |
|---|---|

**ABOUT THE INSTITUTION** Independent Roman Catholic, coed. *Awards:* certificates, bachelor's, and master's degrees. 31 undergraduate majors. *Total enrollment:* 2,305. Undergraduates: 1,810. Freshmen: 510. Federal methodology is used as a basis for awarding need-based institutional aid.

**UNDERGRADUATE EXPENSES** for 2015–2016 *Application fee:* $45. *Comprehensive fee:* $49,900 includes full-time tuition ($36,250), mandatory fees ($1250), and room and board ($12,400). *College room only:* $6070. Full-time tuition and fees vary according to location and program. Room and board charges vary according to housing facility. *Part-time tuition:* $1210 per credit. Part-time tuition and fees vary according to location and program.

**FRESHMAN FINANCIAL AID (Fall 2014, est.)** 448 applied for aid; of those 86% were deemed to have need. 100% of freshmen with need received aid; of those 27% had need fully met. *Average percent of need met:* 76% (excluding resources awarded to replace EFC). *Average financial aid package:* $26,271 (excluding resources awarded to replace EFC). 23% of all full-time freshmen had no need and received non-need-based gift aid.

**UNDERGRADUATE FINANCIAL AID (Fall 2014, est.)** 1,351 applied for aid; of those 88% were deemed to have need. 100% of undergraduates with need received aid; of those 24% had need fully met. *Average percent of need met:* 73% (excluding resources awarded to replace EFC). *Average financial aid package:* $24,665 (excluding resources awarded to replace EFC). 27% of all full-time undergraduates had no need and received non-need-based gift aid.

**GIFT AID (NEED-BASED)** *Total amount:* $22,143,122 (9% federal, 5% state, 83% institutional, 3% external sources). *Receiving aid:* Freshmen: 76% (387); all full-time undergraduates: 69% (1,181). *Average award:* Freshmen: $22,067; Undergraduates: $20,282. *Scholarships, grants, and awards:* Federal Pell, FSEOG, state, private, college/university gift aid from institutional funds.

**GIFT AID (NON-NEED-BASED)** *Total amount:* $10,139,947 (2% federal, 1% state, 90% institutional, 7% external sources). *Receiving aid:* Freshmen: 17% (88). Undergraduates: 13% (220). *Average award:* Freshmen: $18,406. Undergraduates: $15,923. *Scholarships, grants, and awards by category:* Academic interests/achievement: 1,533 awards ($23,956,795 total): general academic interests/achievements. *Creative arts/performance:* art/fine arts. *Special achievements/activities:* 31 awards ($137,000 total): religious involvement. *Special characteristics:* 222 awards ($1,147,362 total): children of educators, children of faculty/staff, members of minority groups, siblings of current students. *Tuition waivers:* Full or partial for employees or children of employees. *ROTC:* Army cooperative.

**LOANS** *Student loans:* $11,897,497 (63% need-based, 37% non-need-based). 72% of past graduating class borrowed through all loan programs. *Average indebtedness per student:* $36,130. *Average need-based loan:* Freshmen: $4298. Undergraduates: $4615. *Parent loans:* $5,892,901 (37% need-based, 63% non-need-based). *Programs:* Federal Direct (Subsidized and Unsubsidized Stafford, PLUS), Perkins.

**WORK-STUDY** *Federal work-study:* Total amount: $687,155; 130 jobs averaging $1800. *State or other work-study/employment:* Total amount: $495,902 (77% need-based, 23% non-need-based). 680 part-time jobs averaging $1200.

**ATHLETIC AWARDS** Total amount: $3,245,653 (50% need-based, 50% non-need-based).

**APPLYING FOR FINANCIAL AID** *Required financial aid form:* FAFSA. *Financial aid deadline:* 3/1. *Notification date:* Continuous beginning 2/15. Students must reply by 5/1.

**CONTACT** Mr. David C. Reeder, Director of Financial Aid, Mount St. Mary's University, 16300 Old Emmitsburg Road, Emmitsburg, MD 21727-7799, 301-447-5207 or toll-free 800-448-4347. *Fax:* 301-447-5915. *E-mail:* reeder@msmary.edu. *Website:* http://www.msmary.edu/.

---

# MT. SIERRA COLLEGE
## Monrovia, CA

**CONTACT** Financial Aid Office, Mt. Sierra College, 101 East Huntington Drive, Monrovia, CA 91016, 888-828-8800 or toll-free 888-828-8000. *Website:* http://www.mtsierra.edu/.

---

# MOUNT VERNON NAZARENE UNIVERSITY
## Mount Vernon, OH

**ABOUT THE INSTITUTION** Independent Nazarene, coed. *Awards:* associate, bachelor's, and master's degrees. 77 undergraduate majors. *Total enrollment:* 2,141. Undergraduates: 1,773. Freshmen: 311.

**GIFT AID (NEED-BASED)** *Scholarships, grants, and awards:* Federal Pell, FSEOG, state, private, college/university gift aid from institutional funds.

**GIFT AID (NON-NEED-BASED)** *Scholarships, grants, and awards by category:* Academic interests/achievement: general academic interests/achievements. *Creative arts/performance:* art/fine arts, music. *Special achievements/activities:* general special achievements/activities, religious involvement. *Special characteristics:* children of faculty/staff, international students, members of minority groups, relatives of clergy, religious affiliation.

**LOANS** *Programs:* Federal Direct (Subsidized and Unsubsidized Stafford, PLUS), Perkins, Federal Nursing, state, college/university, Schell Loans.

**WORK-STUDY** *Federal work-study:* 263 jobs averaging $1714. *State or other work-study/employment:* Total amount: $456,850 (35% need-based, 65% non-need-based). 335 part-time jobs averaging $1686.

**APPLYING FOR FINANCIAL AID** *Required financial aid form:* FAFSA.

**CONTACT** Jared M. Sponseller, Assistant Director of Student Financial Services, Mount Vernon Nazarene University, 800 Martinsburg Road, Mount Vernon, OH 43050-9500, 866-686-8243 or toll-free 866-462-6868. *Fax:* 740-399-8682. *E-mail:* finaid@mvnu.edu. *Website:* http://www.mvnu.edu/.

---

# MUHLENBERG COLLEGE
## Allentown, PA

| Tuition & fees: $44,145 | Average undergraduate aid package: $29,709 |
|---|---|

**ABOUT THE INSTITUTION** Independent Lutheran Church, coed. *Awards:* certificates, associate, and bachelor's degrees. 34 undergraduate majors. *Total enrollment:* 2,440. Undergraduates: 2,440. Freshmen: 589. Institutional methodology is used as a basis for awarding need-based institutional aid.

**UNDERGRADUATE EXPENSES** for 2015–2016 *Application fee:* $50. *Comprehensive fee:* $54,595 includes full-time tuition ($43,860), mandatory fees ($285), and room and board ($10,450). *College room only:* $5665. Room and board charges vary according to board plan, housing facility, and location. Part-time tuition and fees vary according to program.

**FRESHMAN FINANCIAL AID (Fall 2014, est.)** 439 applied for aid; of those 76% were deemed to have need. 99% of freshmen with need received aid; of those 86% had need fully met. *Average percent of need met:* 93% (excluding resources awarded to replace EFC). *Average financial aid package:* $31,900 (excluding resources awarded to replace EFC). 32% of all full-time freshmen had no need and received non-need-based gift aid.

**UNDERGRADUATE FINANCIAL AID (Fall 2014, est.)** 1,436 applied for aid; of those 82% were deemed to have need. 97% of undergraduates with need received aid; of those 90% had need fully met. *Average percent of need met:* 93% (excluding resources awarded to replace EFC). *Average financial aid package:* $29,709 (excluding resources awarded to replace EFC). 33% of all full-time undergraduates had no need and received non-need-based gift aid.

**GIFT AID (NEED-BASED)** *Total amount:* $29,944,000 (5% federal, 2% state, 92% institutional, 1% external sources). *Receiving aid:* Freshmen: 56% (329); all full-time undergraduates: 50% (1,125). *Average award:* Freshmen: $28,024; Undergraduates: $26,007. *Scholarships, grants, and awards:* Federal Pell, FSEOG, state, private, college/university gift aid from institutional funds, United Negro College Fund.

**GIFT AID (NON-NEED-BASED)** *Total amount:* $11,291,000 (98% institutional, 2% external sources). *Receiving aid:* Freshmen: 11% (65). Undergraduates: 9% (198). *Average award:* Freshmen: $12,459. Undergraduates: $11,792. *Scholarships, grants, and awards by category:* Academic interests/achievement: general academic interests/achievements. *Creative arts/performance:* art/fine arts, cinema/film/broadcasting, dance, music, performing arts, theater/drama. *Tuition waivers:* Full or partial for employees or children of employees. *ROTC:* Army cooperative.

**LOANS** *Student loans:* $10,790,000 (56% need-based, 44% non-need-based). 55% of past graduating class borrowed through all loan programs. *Average indebtedness per student:* $29,702. *Average need-based loan:* Freshmen: $4059. Undergraduates: $4766. *Parent loans:* $3,483,000 (17% need-based, 83% non-need-based). *Programs:* Federal Direct (Subsidized and Unsubsidized Stafford, PLUS), Perkins.

**WORK-STUDY** *Federal work-study:* Total amount: $225,000; jobs available. *State or other work-study/employment:* Total amount: $200,000 (20% need-based, 80% non-need-based). Part-time jobs available.

**APPLYING FOR FINANCIAL AID** *Required financial aid forms:* FAFSA, institution's own form, CSS Financial Aid PROFILE, noncustodial (divorced/separated) parent's statement, business/farm supplement. *Financial aid deadline:* 2/15. *Notification date:* 3/20. Students must reply by 5/1.

**CONTACT** Mr. Greg Mitton, Director of Financial Aid, Muhlenberg College, 2400 Chew Street, Allentown, PA 18104-5586, 484-664-3175. *Fax:* 484-664-3234. *E-mail:* mitton@muhlenberg.edu. *Website:* http://www.muhlenberg.edu/.

---

# MULTNOMAH UNIVERSITY
## Portland, OR

**CONTACT** Mrs. Mary J. McGlothlan, Director of Financial Aid, Multnomah University, 8435 NE Glisan Street, Portland, OR 97220-5898, 503-251-5337 or toll-free 877-251-6560. *Fax:* 503-445-5199. *E-mail:* mmcglothlan@multnomah.edu. *Website:* http://www.multnomah.edu/.

# MURRAY STATE UNIVERSITY
## Murray, KY

| Tuition & fees (KY res): $7392 | Average undergraduate aid package: $11,339 |
|---|---|

**ABOUT THE INSTITUTION** State-supported, coed. **Awards:** certificates, associate, bachelor's, master's, and doctoral degrees. 71 undergraduate majors. **Total enrollment:** 11,207. Undergraduates: 9,444. Freshmen: 1,508. Federal methodology is used as a basis for awarding need-based institutional aid.

**UNDERGRADUATE EXPENSES for 2015–2016 Application fee:** $40. **Tuition, state resident:** full-time $6360; part-time $265 per hour. **Tuition, nonresident:** full-time $19,080; part-time $795 per hour. **Required fees:** full-time $1032; $43 per hour. Full-time tuition and fees vary according to reciprocity agreements. Part-time tuition and fees vary according to reciprocity agreements. **College room and board:** $7912; **Room only:** $4576. Room and board charges vary according to board plan and housing facility.

**FRESHMAN FINANCIAL AID (Fall 2013)** 1,338 applied for aid; of those 78% were deemed to have need. 100% of freshmen with need received aid; of those 23% had need fully met. **Average percent of need met:** 34% (excluding resources awarded to replace EFC). **Average financial aid package:** $11,221 (excluding resources awarded to replace EFC). 11% of all full-time freshmen had no need and received non-need-based gift aid.

**UNDERGRADUATE FINANCIAL AID (Fall 2013)** 5,412 applied for aid; of those 86% were deemed to have need. 97% of undergraduates with need received aid; of those 26% had need fully met. **Average percent of need met:** 29% (excluding resources awarded to replace EFC). **Average financial aid package:** $11,339 (excluding resources awarded to replace EFC). 6% of all full-time undergraduates had no need and received non-need-based gift aid.

**GIFT AID (NEED-BASED) Total amount:** $24,925,010 (52% federal, 20% state, 20% institutional, 8% external sources). **Receiving aid:** Freshmen: 61% (959); all full-time undergraduates: 51% (3,568). **Average award:** Freshmen: $6208; Undergraduates: $5850. **Scholarships, grants, and awards:** Federal Pell, FSEOG, state, private, college/university gift aid from institutional funds.

**GIFT AID (NON-NEED-BASED) Total amount:** $10,491,264 (1% federal, 20% state, 48% institutional, 31% external sources). **Receiving aid:** Freshmen: 8% (131). Undergraduates: 5% (328). **Average award:** Freshmen: $4659. Undergraduates: $4381. **Scholarships, grants, and awards by category:** Academic interests/achievement: 1,868 awards ($3,859,555 total): agriculture, biological sciences, business, communication, computer science, education, engineering/technologies, English, general academic interests/achievements, health fields, home economics, humanities, international studies, mathematics, military science, physical sciences, premedicine. Creative arts/performance: 157 awards ($255,636 total): art/fine arts, dance, journalism/publications, music, theater/drama. Special achievements/activities: 281 awards ($1,015,212 total): memberships, rodeo. Special characteristics: 616 awards ($1,746,161 total): adult students, children of faculty/staff, general special characteristics, local/state students, members of minority groups, out-of-state students. **Tuition waivers:** Full or partial for children of alumni, employees or children of employees, senior citizens. **ROTC:** Army.

**LOANS Student loans:** $32,620,719 (80% need-based, 20% non-need-based). 47% of past graduating class borrowed through all loan programs. Average indebtedness per student: $24,554. **Average need-based loan:** Freshmen: $5180. Undergraduates: $6367. **Parent loans:** $3,601,302 (33% need-based, 67% non-need-based). **Programs:** Federal Direct (Subsidized and Unsubsidized Stafford, PLUS), Perkins, Federal Nursing, college/university.

**WORK-STUDY Federal work-study:** 339 jobs averaging $1625. **State or other work-study/employment:** Total amount: $4,154,056 (40% need-based, 60% non-need-based). 2,121 part-time jobs averaging $2138.

**ATHLETIC AWARDS** Total amount: $3,615,644 (47% need-based, 53% non-need-based).

**APPLYING FOR FINANCIAL AID Required financial aid forms:** FAFSA, institution's own form, general scholarship application form. **Financial aid deadline (priority):** 2/1. **Notification date:** Continuous beginning 3/15. Students must reply by 5/1.

**CONTACT** Lori Mitchum, Director of Financial Aid and Scholarships, Murray State University, 500 Sparks Hall, Murray, KY 42071-0009, 270-809-2546 or toll-free 800-272-4678. Fax: 270-809-3116. E-mail: lmitchum@murraystate.edu. Website: http://www.murraystate.edu/.

# MUSICIANS INSTITUTE
## Hollywood, CA

**CONTACT** Director of Financial Aid, Musicians Institute, 1655 North McCadden Place, Hollywood, CA 90028, 323-462-1384 or toll-free 800-255-PLAY. Website: http://www.mi.edu/.

# MUSKINGUM UNIVERSITY
## New Concord, OH

| Tuition & fees: N/R | Average undergraduate aid package: $24,104 |
|---|---|

**ABOUT THE INSTITUTION** Independent Presbyterian Church (U.S.A.), coed. 57 undergraduate majors. Federal methodology is used as a basis for awarding need-based institutional aid.

**FRESHMAN FINANCIAL AID (Fall 2014, est.)** 358 applied for aid; of those 96% were deemed to have need. 100% of freshmen with need received aid; of those 25% had need fully met. **Average percent of need met:** 86% (excluding resources awarded to replace EFC). **Average financial aid package:** $25,588 (excluding resources awarded to replace EFC). 10% of all full-time freshmen had no need and received non-need-based gift aid.

**UNDERGRADUATE FINANCIAL AID (Fall 2014, est.)** 1,218 applied for aid; of those 95% were deemed to have need. 100% of undergraduates with need received aid; of those 14% had need fully met. **Average percent of need met:** 81% (excluding resources awarded to replace EFC). **Average financial aid package:** $24,104 (excluding resources awarded to replace EFC). 15% of all full-time undergraduates had no need and received non-need-based gift aid.

**GIFT AID (NEED-BASED) Total amount:** $19,360,217 (17% federal, 7% state, 74% institutional, 2% external sources). **Receiving aid:** Freshmen: 89% (343); all full-time undergraduates: 84% (1,150). **Average award:** Freshmen: $18,284; Undergraduates: $16,507. **Scholarships, grants, and awards:** Federal Pell, FSEOG, state, private, college/university gift aid from institutional funds.

**GIFT AID (NON-NEED-BASED) Total amount:** $2,674,674 (1% state, 95% institutional, 4% external sources). **Receiving aid:** Freshmen: 79% (303). Undergraduates: 77% (1,052). **Average award:** Freshmen: $10,957. Undergraduates: $10,669. **Scholarships, grants, and awards by category:** Academic interests/achievement: 611 awards ($7,166,083 total): biological sciences, computer science, engineering/technologies, general academic interests/achievements, mathematics, physical sciences, premedicine. Creative arts/performance: 123 awards ($145,450 total): art/fine arts, debating, journalism/publications, music, theater/drama. Special achievements/activities: 195 awards ($146,500 total): community service, junior miss, leadership. Special characteristics: 801 awards ($887,281 total): children and siblings of alumni, ethnic background, local/state students, members of minority groups, relatives of clergy, religious affiliation, siblings of current students.

**LOANS Student loans:** $11,140,039 (81% need-based, 19% non-need-based). 79% of past graduating class borrowed through all loan programs. Average indebtedness per student: $33,488. **Average need-based loan:** Freshmen: $4186. Undergraduates: $4947. **Parent loans:** $2,756,010 (43% need-based, 57% non-need-based). **Programs:** Federal Direct (Subsidized and Unsubsidized Stafford, PLUS), Perkins, Federal Nursing, college/university.

**WORK-STUDY Federal work-study:** Total amount: $149,639; 490 jobs averaging $1000. **State or other work-study/employment:** Total amount: $500,000 (60% need-based, 40% non-need-based). 3 part-time jobs averaging $1000.

**APPLYING FOR FINANCIAL AID Required financial aid form:** FAFSA. **Financial aid deadline (priority):** 3/1. **Notification date:** Continuous beginning 3/1. Students must reply by 5/1 or within 2 weeks of notification.

**CONTACT** Mr. Jeff Zellers, Vice President of Enrollment, Muskingum University, 163 Stormont Street, New Concord, OH 43762, 740-826-8139 or toll-free 800-752-6082. Fax: 740-826-8100. E-mail: jzellers@muskingum.edu. Website: http://www.muskingum.edu/.

# NAROPA UNIVERSITY
## Boulder, CO

| Tuition & fees: $30,580 | Average undergraduate aid package: $35,101 |
|---|---|

**ABOUT THE INSTITUTION** Independent, coed. *Awards:* bachelor's and master's degrees. 13 undergraduate majors. *Total enrollment:* 945. Undergraduates: 386. Freshmen: 40. Federal methodology is used as a basis for awarding need-based institutional aid.

**UNDERGRADUATE EXPENSES for 2015–2016** *Application fee:* $50. *Comprehensive fee:* $40,184 includes full-time tuition ($30,400), mandatory fees ($180), and room and board ($9604). Full-time tuition and fees vary according to course load. *Part-time tuition:* $995 per credit. *Part-time fees:* $340 per term. Part-time tuition and fees vary according to course load.

**FRESHMAN FINANCIAL AID (Fall 2014, est.)** 32 applied for aid; of those 91% were deemed to have need. 100% of freshmen with need received aid; of those 10% had need fully met. *Average percent of need met:* 78% (excluding resources awarded to replace EFC). *Average financial aid package:* $23,370 (excluding resources awarded to replace EFC). 8% of all full-time freshmen had no need and received non-need-based gift aid.

**UNDERGRADUATE FINANCIAL AID (Fall 2014, est.)** 286 applied for aid; of those 95% were deemed to have need. 100% of undergraduates with need received aid; of those 1% had need fully met. *Average percent of need met:* 90% (excluding resources awarded to replace EFC). *Average financial aid package:* $35,101 (excluding resources awarded to replace EFC). 4% of all full-time undergraduates had no need and received non-need-based gift aid.

**GIFT AID (NEED-BASED)** *Total amount:* $6,302,919 (20% federal, 3% state, 72% institutional, 5% external sources). *Receiving aid:* Freshmen: 74% (29); all full-time undergraduates: 71% (257). *Average award:* Freshmen: $16,425; Undergraduates: $24,236. *Scholarships, grants, and awards:* Federal Pell, FSEOG, state, private, college/university gift aid from institutional funds.

**GIFT AID (NON-NEED-BASED)** *Total amount:* $97,050 (100% institutional). *Receiving aid:* Freshmen: 8% (3). Undergraduates: 4% (14). *Average award:* Freshmen: $5667. Undergraduates: $6738. *Tuition waivers:* Full or partial for employees or children of employees.

**LOANS** *Student loans:* $3,232,090 (94% need-based, 6% non-need-based). 75% of past graduating class borrowed through all loan programs. *Average indebtedness per student:* $23,755. *Average need-based loan:* Freshmen: $6609. Undergraduates: $11,070. *Parent loans:* $1,935,805 (100% need-based). *Programs:* Federal Direct (Subsidized and Unsubsidized Stafford, PLUS), Perkins.

**WORK-STUDY** *Federal work-study:* Total amount: $612,440; 160 jobs averaging $3013. *State or other work-study/employment:* Total amount: $36,000 (100% need-based). 12 part-time jobs averaging $2590.

**APPLYING FOR FINANCIAL AID** *Required financial aid form:* FAFSA. *Financial aid deadline (priority):* 3/1. *Notification date:* Continuous beginning 3/1. Students must reply within 4 weeks of notification.

**CONTACT** Ms. Nancy Morrell, Assistant Director of Financial Aid, Naropa University, 2130 Arapahoe Avenue, Boulder, CO 80302-6697, 303-546-3534 or toll-free 800-772-6951. *Fax:* 303-546-3536. *E-mail:* finaid@naropa.edu.
*Website:* http://www.naropa.edu/.

# NATIONAL AMERICAN UNIVERSITY
## Centennial, CO

**CONTACT** Financial Aid Office, National American University, 8242 S. University Boulevard, Suite 100, Centennial, CO 80122, 303-542-7000 or toll-free 877-593-0429.
*Website:* http://www.national.edu/.

# NATIONAL AMERICAN UNIVERSITY
## Colorado Springs, CO

**CONTACT** Financial Aid Office, National American University, 1079 Space Center Drive, Unit 140, Colorado Springs, CO 80915, 719-208-3800 or toll-free 877-593-0430.
*Website:* http://www.national.edu/.

# NATIONAL AMERICAN UNIVERSITY
## Colorado Springs, CO

**CONTACT** Financial Aid Coordinator, National American University, 2577 North Chelton Road, Colorado Springs, CO 80909, 719-471-4205.
*Website:* http://www.national.edu/.

# NATIONAL AMERICAN UNIVERSITY
## Denver, CO

**CONTACT** Cheryl Schunneman, Director of Financial Aid, National American University, 321 Kansas City Street, Rapid City, SD 57701, 605-394-4800.
*Website:* http://www.national.edu/.

# NATIONAL AMERICAN UNIVERSITY
## Burnsville, MN

**CONTACT** Financial Aid Office, National American University, 513 W. Travelers Trail, Burnsville, MN 55337, 952-563-1250 or toll-free 866-628-6387.
*Website:* http://www.national.edu/.

# NATIONAL AMERICAN UNIVERSITY
## Roseville, MN

**CONTACT** Financial Aid Office, National American University, 1500 West Highway 36, Roseville, MN 55113, 651-644-1265.
*Website:* http://www.national.edu/.

# NATIONAL AMERICAN UNIVERSITY
## Kansas City, MO

**CONTACT** Mary Anderson, Coordinator of Financial Aid, National American University, 4200 Blue Ridge, Kansas City, MO 64133, 816-353-4554. *Fax:* 816-353-1176.
*Website:* http://www.national.edu/.

# NATIONAL AMERICAN UNIVERSITY
## Lee's Summit, MO

**CONTACT** Financial Aid Office, National American University, 401 NW Murray Road, Lee's Summit, MO 64081, 816-600-3900 or toll-free 866-628-1288.
*Website:* http://www.national.edu/.

# NATIONAL AMERICAN UNIVERSITY
## Bellevue, NE

**CONTACT** Financial Aid Office, National American University, 3604 Summit Plaza Drive, Bellevue, NE 68123, 402-972-4250 or toll-free 800-609-1425.
*Website:* http://www.national.edu/.

## NATIONAL AMERICAN UNIVERSITY
### Albuquerque, NM

**CONTACT** Director of Financial Aid, National American University, 321 Kansas City Street, Rapid City, SD 57701, 605-394-4800 or toll-free 800-895-9904.
*Website:* http://www.national.edu/.

## NATIONAL AMERICAN UNIVERSITY
### Tulsa, OK

**CONTACT** Financial Aid Office, National American University, 8040 South Sheridan Road, Tulsa, OK 74133, 918-879-8400.
*Website:* http://www.national.edu/.

## NATIONAL AMERICAN UNIVERSITY
### Rapid City, SD

**CONTACT** Financial Aid Director, National American University, PO Box 1780, Rapid City, SD 57709-1780, 605-721-5213 or toll-free 800-209-0490 (in-state), 800-209-4090 (out-of-state).
*Website:* http://www.national.edu/.

## NATIONAL AMERICAN UNIVERSITY
### Sioux Falls, SD

**CONTACT** Ms. Rhonda Kohnen, Financial Aid Coordinator, National American University, 2801 South Kiwanis Avenue, Suite 100, Sioux Falls, SD 57105-4293, 605-334-5430 or toll-free 800-388-5430. *Fax:* 605-334-1575. *E-mail:* rkohnen@national.edu.
*Website:* http://www.national.edu/.

## NATIONAL AMERICAN UNIVERSITY
### Mesquite, TX

**CONTACT** Financial Aid Office, National American University, 18600 LBJ Freeway, Mesquite, TX 75150, 972-773-8800 or toll-free 800-548-0605.
*Website:* http://www.national.edu/.

## NATIONAL LOUIS UNIVERSITY
### Chicago, IL

**CONTACT** Janet Jazwiec, Assistant Director of Student Finance, National Louis University, 1000 Capitol Drive, Wheeling, IL 60090, 847-947-5453 or toll-free 888-658-8632. *Fax:* 847-947-5453. *E-mail:* jjazwiec@nl.edu.
*Website:* http://www.nl.edu/.

## NATIONAL PARALEGAL COLLEGE
### Phoenix, AZ

**CONTACT** Financial Aid Office, National Paralegal College, 717 East Maryland Avenue, Suite 115, Phoenix, AZ 85014, 845-371-9101 or toll-free 800-371-6105.
*Website:* http://nationalparalegal.edu/.

## NATIONAL UNIVERSITY
### La Jolla, CA

| Tuition & fees: N/R | Average undergraduate aid package: $8518 |
|---|---|

**ABOUT THE INSTITUTION** Independent, coed. *Awards:* certificates, associate, bachelor's, and master's degrees. 115 undergraduate majors. *Total enrollment:* 17,608. Undergraduates: 9,721. Freshmen: 170. Federal methodology is used as a basis for awarding need-based institutional aid.

**FRESHMAN FINANCIAL AID (Fall 2013)** 41 applied for aid; of those 100% were deemed to have need. 100% of freshmen with need received aid; of those 24% had need fully met. *Average percent of need met:* 72% (excluding resources awarded to replace EFC). *Average financial aid package:* $6207 (excluding resources awarded to replace EFC).

**UNDERGRADUATE FINANCIAL AID (Fall 2013)** 3,076 applied for aid; of those 75% were deemed to have need. 99% of undergraduates with need received aid; of those 3% had need fully met. *Average percent of need met:* 78% (excluding resources awarded to replace EFC). *Average financial aid package:* $8518 (excluding resources awarded to replace EFC).

**GIFT AID (NEED-BASED)** *Total amount:* $15,783,478 (79% federal, 18% state, 3% institutional). *Receiving aid:* Freshmen: 36% (24); all full-time undergraduates: 19% (1,043). *Average award:* Freshmen: $3594; Undergraduates: $8284. *Scholarships, grants, and awards:* Federal Pell, FSEOG, state, college/university gift aid from institutional funds.

**GIFT AID (NON-NEED-BASED)** *Total amount:* $1,261,195 (37% federal, 63% institutional). *Receiving aid:* Undergraduates: 1% (79). *Scholarships, grants, and awards by category:* Academic interests/achievement: general academic interests/achievements. Special achievements/activities: leadership. ROTC: Army cooperative, Air Force cooperative.

**LOANS** *Student loans:* $51,053,258 (48% need-based, 52% non-need-based). 74% of past graduating class borrowed through all loan programs. *Average indebtedness per student:* $12,076. *Average need-based loan:* Freshmen: $2146. Undergraduates: $10,480. *Parent loans:* $1,225,796 (100% need-based). *Programs:* Federal Direct (Subsidized and Unsubsidized Stafford, PLUS), Perkins, college/university.

**APPLYING FOR FINANCIAL AID** *Required financial aid forms:* FAFSA, institution's own form. *Financial aid deadline:* Continuous. *Notification date:* Continuous beginning 6/30.

**CONTACT** Valerie Ryan, Director of Financial Aid, National University, 9980 Carroll Canyon, San Diego, CA 92131, 858-642-8500 or toll-free 800-NAT-UNIV. *Fax:* 858-642-8720. *E-mail:* vryan@nu.edu.
*Website:* http://www.nu.edu/.

## NATIONAL UNIVERSITY COLLEGE
### Bayamón, PR

**CONTACT** Ms. Elizabeth Cruz, Institutional Director of Financial Aid, National University College, PO Box 2036, Bayamon, PR 00961, 787-780-5134 Ext. 4021 or toll-free 800-780-5134. *E-mail:* ecruz@nuc.edu.
*Website:* http://www.nuc.edu/.

## NATIONAL UNIVERSITY COLLEGE
### Caguas, PR

**CONTACT** Financial Aid Office, National University College, 190 Avenida Gautier Benitez Esquina Avenida Federico Degatau, Caguas, PR 00725, 787-653-4733 or toll-free 800-780-5134.
*Website:* http://www.nuc.edu/.

# NATIONAL UNIVERSITY COLLEGE
## Ponce, PR

**CONTACT** Financial Aid Office, National University College, PO Box 801243, Ponce, PR 00716, 787-840-4474.
*Website:* http://www.nuc.edu/.

# NATIONAL UNIVERSITY COLLEGE
## Rio Grande, PR

**CONTACT** Financial Aid Office, National University College, Carretera #3 Km. 22.1, Bo. Ciénaga Baja, Rio Grande, PR 00745, 787-809-5100 or toll-free 800-981-0812.
*Website:* http://www.nuc.edu/.

# NAVAJO TECHNICAL UNIVERSITY
## Crownpoint, NM

**CONTACT** Financial Aid Office, Navajo Technical University, PO Box 849, Crownpoint, NM 87313, 505-786-4100.
*Website:* http://www.navajotech.edu/.

# NAZARENE BIBLE COLLEGE
## Colorado Springs, CO

| Tuition & fees: $11,400 | Average undergraduate aid package: $7695 |
| --- | --- |

**ABOUT THE INSTITUTION** Independent Church of the Nazarene, coed. *Awards:* certificates, diplomas, associate, and bachelor's degrees. 9 undergraduate majors. *Total enrollment:* 762. Undergraduates: 762. Freshmen: 28. Federal methodology is used as a basis for awarding need-based institutional aid.
**UNDERGRADUATE EXPENSES for 2015–2016 Tuition:** full-time $10,800; part-time $450 per credit hour. *Required fees:* full-time $600; $25. Full-time tuition and fees vary according to program. Part-time tuition and fees vary according to program.
**FRESHMAN FINANCIAL AID (Fall 2014, est.)** 10 applied for aid; of those 100% were deemed to have need. 100% of freshmen with need received aid; of those 80% had need fully met. *Average percent of need met:* 92% (excluding resources awarded to replace EFC). *Average financial aid package:* $7940 (excluding resources awarded to replace EFC).
**UNDERGRADUATE FINANCIAL AID (Fall 2014, est.)** 122 applied for aid; of those 73% were deemed to have need. 100% of undergraduates with need received aid; of those 94% had need fully met. *Average percent of need met:* 96% (excluding resources awarded to replace EFC). *Average financial aid package:* $7695 (excluding resources awarded to replace EFC).
**GIFT AID (NEED-BASED) Total amount:** $1,107,947 (94% federal, 5% institutional, 1% external sources). *Receiving aid:* Freshmen: 64% (9); all full-time undergraduates: 72% (89). *Average award:* Freshmen: $3947; Undergraduates: $4527. *Scholarships, grants, and awards:* Federal Pell, FSEOG, college/university gift aid from institutional funds.
**GIFT AID (NON-NEED-BASED) Receiving aid:** Freshmen: 14% (2). *Tuition waivers:* Full or partial for employees or children of employees.
**LOANS Student loans:** $2,256,979 (100% need-based). 64% of past graduating class borrowed through all loan programs. *Average indebtedness per student:* $33,289. *Average need-based loan:* Freshmen: $3500. Undergraduates: $3337. *Parent loans:* $5000 (100% need-based). *Programs:* Federal Direct (Subsidized and Unsubsidized Stafford, PLUS), Perkins, college/university.
**WORK-STUDY Federal work-study:** Total amount: $15,000; jobs available.
**APPLYING FOR FINANCIAL AID Required financial aid form:** FAFSA. *Financial aid deadline:* Continuous. *Notification date:* Continuous beginning 2/1.

**CONTACT** Miss Jenny Madsen, Director of Financial Aid, Nazarene Bible College, 1111 Academy Park Loop, Colorado Springs, CO 80910-3717, 719-884-5051 or toll-free 800-873-3873. *Fax:* 719-884-5199.
*Website:* http://www.nbc.edu/.

# NAZARETH COLLEGE OF ROCHESTER
## Rochester, NY

| Tuition & fees: $30,562 | Average undergraduate aid package: $24,940 |
| --- | --- |

**ABOUT THE INSTITUTION** Independent, coed. *Awards:* certificates, bachelor's, master's, and doctoral degrees. 76 undergraduate majors. *Total enrollment:* 2,818. Undergraduates: 2,057. Freshmen: 476. Federal methodology is used as a basis for awarding need-based institutional aid.
**UNDERGRADUATE EXPENSES for 2015–2016 Application fee:** $45. *Comprehensive fee:* $43,160 includes full-time tuition ($29,244), mandatory fees ($1318), and room and board ($12,598). *College room only:* $6918. Full-time tuition and fees vary according to course load and program. Room and board charges vary according to board plan and housing facility. *Part-time tuition:* $697 per credit. *Part-time fees:* $100 per term.
**FRESHMAN FINANCIAL AID (Fall 2014, est.)** 454 applied for aid; of those 91% were deemed to have need. 100% of freshmen with need received aid; of those 26% had need fully met. *Average percent of need met:* 79% (excluding resources awarded to replace EFC). *Average financial aid package:* $25,715 (excluding resources awarded to replace EFC). 13% of all full-time freshmen had no need and received non-need-based gift aid.
**UNDERGRADUATE FINANCIAL AID (Fall 2014, est.)** 1,726 applied for aid; of those 91% were deemed to have need. 100% of undergraduates with need received aid; of those 24% had need fully met. *Average percent of need met:* 77% (excluding resources awarded to replace EFC). *Average financial aid package:* $24,940 (excluding resources awarded to replace EFC). 18% of all full-time undergraduates had no need and received non-need-based gift aid.
**GIFT AID (NEED-BASED) Total amount:** $24,247,647 (15% federal, 10% state, 74% institutional, 1% external sources). *Receiving aid:* Freshmen: 87% (412); all full-time undergraduates: 82% (1,565). *Average award:* Freshmen: $17,441; Undergraduates: $15,327. *Scholarships, grants, and awards:* Federal Pell, FSEOG, state, private, college/university gift aid from institutional funds, Federal Nursing.
**GIFT AID (NON-NEED-BASED) Total amount:** $4,879,952 (5% federal, 1% state, 89% institutional, 5% external sources). *Receiving aid:* Freshmen: 34% (160). Undergraduates: 26% (506). *Average award:* Freshmen: $16,265. Undergraduates: $15,594. *Scholarships, grants, and awards by category:* Academic interests/achievement: 1,820 awards ($14,495,250 total): general academic interests/achievements. Creative arts/performance: 255 awards ($565,750 total): art/fine arts, music, theater/drama. Special characteristics: 557 awards ($2,389,624 total): children and siblings of alumni, children of faculty/staff, ethnic background, out-of-state students, siblings of current students, veterans. *Tuition waivers:* Full or partial for minority students, children of alumni, employees or children of employees. *ROTC:* Army cooperative, Air Force cooperative.
**LOANS Student loans:** $16,062,601 (83% need-based, 17% non-need-based). 85% of past graduating class borrowed through all loan programs. *Average indebtedness per student:* $35,396. *Average need-based loan:* Freshmen: $3631. Undergraduates: $4640. *Parent loans:* $7,031,689 (53% need-based, 47% non-need-based). *Programs:* Federal Direct (Subsidized and Unsubsidized Stafford, PLUS), Perkins, Federal Nursing.
**WORK-STUDY Federal work-study:** Total amount: $2,309,860; 1,050 jobs averaging $2123.
**APPLYING FOR FINANCIAL AID Required financial aid forms:** FAFSA, state aid form. *Financial aid deadline (priority):* 2/15. *Notification date:* Continuous beginning 1/15. Students must reply by 5/1 or within 2 weeks of notification.

**CONTACT** Samantha Veeder, Director of Financial Aid, Nazareth College of Rochester, 4245 East Avenue, Rochester, NY 14618-3790, 585-389-2310 or toll-free 800-462-3944. *Fax:* 585-389-2317. *E-mail:* sveeder0@naz.edu.
*Website:* http://www.naz.edu/.

# NEBRASKA CHRISTIAN COLLEGE
## Papillion, NE

| Tuition & fees: $13,200 | Average undergraduate aid package: N/A |
| --- | --- |

**ABOUT THE INSTITUTION** Independent Christian Churches and Churches of Christ, coed. *Awards:* certificates, associate, and bachelor's degrees. 7 undergraduate majors. *Total enrollment:* 138. Undergraduates: 138. Federal methodology is used as a basis for awarding need-based institutional aid.

**UNDERGRADUATE EXPENSES for 2015–2016** *One-time required fee:* $300. *Comprehensive fee:* $20,900 includes full-time tuition ($13,200) and room and board ($7700). Full-time tuition and fees vary according to course load. Room and board charges vary according to board plan and housing facility. *Part-time tuition:* $550 per hour. Part-time tuition and fees vary according to course load.

**FRESHMAN FINANCIAL AID (Fall 2014, est.)** 65 applied for aid.

**UNDERGRADUATE FINANCIAL AID (Fall 2014, est.)** 119 applied for aid.

**GIFT AID (NEED-BASED)** *Total amount:* $810,030 (36% federal, 4% state, 46% institutional, 14% external sources). *Scholarships, grants, and awards:* Federal Pell, FSEOG, state, private, college/university gift aid from institutional funds.

**GIFT AID (NON-NEED-BASED)** *Scholarships, grants, and awards by category: Academic interests/achievement:* general academic interests/achievements, religion/biblical studies. *Special characteristics:* children of faculty/staff, international students, relatives of clergy. *Tuition waivers:* Full or partial for children of alumni, employees or children of employees.

**LOANS** *Student loans:* $770,898 (100% need-based). 90% of past graduating class borrowed through all loan programs. *Parent loans:* $48,940 (100% need-based).

**WORK-STUDY** *Federal work-study:* Total amount: $11,751; jobs available.

**APPLYING FOR FINANCIAL AID** *Required financial aid forms:* FAFSA, institution's own form. *Financial aid deadline (priority):* 6/1. *Notification date:* Continuous.

**CONTACT** Mrs. Sarah Nigro, Director of Financial Aid, Nebraska Christian College, 12550 South 114th Street, Papillion, NE 68046, 402-935-9400. *Fax:* 402-935-9500. *E-mail:* snigro@nechristian.edu.
*Website:* http://www.nechristian.edu/.

# NEBRASKA METHODIST COLLEGE
## Omaha, NE

| Tuition & fees: $18,109 | Average undergraduate aid package: N/A |
| --- | --- |

**ABOUT THE INSTITUTION** Independent United Methodist Church, coed. *Awards:* certificates, associate, bachelor's, master's, and doctoral degrees. 8 undergraduate majors. *Total enrollment:* 1,000. Undergraduates: 747. Freshmen: 38. Federal methodology is used as a basis for awarding need-based institutional aid.

**UNDERGRADUATE EXPENSES for 2015–2016** *Application fee:* $25. *Tuition:* full-time $16,560; part-time $552 per credit hour. Full-time tuition and fees vary according to degree level and program. Part-time tuition and fees vary according to degree level and program. Room and board charges vary according to housing facility.

**FRESHMAN FINANCIAL AID (Fall 2014, est.)** 34 applied for aid; of those 94% were deemed to have need. 100% of freshmen with need received aid; of those 3% had need fully met. *Average percent of need met:* 43% (excluding resources awarded to replace EFC). *Average financial aid package:* $9971 (excluding resources awarded to replace EFC). 5% of all full-time freshmen had no need and received non-need-based gift aid.

**GIFT AID (NEED-BASED)** *Total amount:* $2,512,696 (40% federal, 6% state, 47% institutional, 7% external sources). *Receiving aid:* Freshmen: 76% (29). *Average award:* Freshmen: $8323. *Scholarships, grants, and awards:* Federal Pell, FSEOG, state, private, college/university gift aid from institutional funds, Federal Nursing.

**GIFT AID (NON-NEED-BASED)** *Total amount:* $276,889 (93% institutional, 7% external sources). *Receiving aid:* Freshmen: 3% (1). *Average award:* Freshmen: $5000. *Scholarships, grants, and awards by category: Academic interests/achievement:* general academic interests/achievements, health fields. *Special characteristics:* children of faculty/staff. *Tuition waivers:* Full or partial for employees or children of employees. *ROTC:* Army cooperative, Air Force cooperative.

**LOANS** *Student loans:* $5,980,810 (86% need-based, 14% non-need-based). 91% of past graduating class borrowed through all loan programs. *Average indebtedness per student:* $31,591. *Average need-based loan:* Freshmen: $2784. *Parent loans:* $769,871 (52% need-based, 48% non-need-based). *Programs:* Federal Direct (Subsidized and Unsubsidized Stafford, PLUS), Perkins, Federal Nursing, college/university, private loans.

**WORK-STUDY** *Federal work-study:* Total amount: $56,142; 27 jobs averaging $2080.

**APPLYING FOR FINANCIAL AID** *Required financial aid forms:* FAFSA, institution's own form. *Financial aid deadline (priority):* 4/1. *Notification date:* Continuous beginning 3/15. Students must reply within 3 weeks of notification.

**CONTACT** Ms. Penny James, Director of Financial Aid, Nebraska Methodist College, The Josie Harper Campus, 720 North 87th Street, Omaha, NE 68114-3426, 402-354-7225 or toll-free 800-335-5510. *Fax:* 402-354-7020. *E-mail:* penny.james@methodistcollege.edu.
*Website:* http://www.methodistcollege.edu/.

# NEBRASKA WESLEYAN UNIVERSITY
## Lincoln, NE

**CONTACT** Mr. Thomas J. Ochsner, Director of Scholarships and Financial Aid, Nebraska Wesleyan University, 5000 Saint Paul Avenue, Lincoln, NE 68504, 402-465-2212 or toll-free 800-541-3818. *Fax:* 402-465-2194. *E-mail:* tjo@nebrwesleyan.edu. *Website:* http://www.nebrwesleyan.edu/.

# NER ISRAEL RABBINICAL COLLEGE
## Baltimore, MD

**CONTACT** Mr. Moshe Pelberg, Financial Aid Administrator , Ner Israel Rabbinical College, 400 Mount Wilson Lane, Baltimore, MD 21208, 410-484-7200.

# NEUMANN UNIVERSITY
## Aston, PA

**CONTACT** Deborah Cawley, Director of Financial Aid, Neumann University, One Neumann Drive, Aston, PA 19014-1298, 610-558-5519 or toll-free 800-963-8626. *E-mail:* cawleyd@neumann.edu.
*Website:* http://www.neumann.edu/.

# NEUMONT UNIVERSITY
## Salt Lake City, UT

| Tuition & fees: $24,000 | Average undergraduate aid package: N/A |
| --- | --- |

**ABOUT THE INSTITUTION** Proprietary, coed. *Awards:* bachelor's and master's degrees. 15 undergraduate majors. *Total enrollment:* 397. Undergraduates: 397. Freshmen: 136. Both federal and institutional methodology are used as a basis for awarding need-based institutional aid.

**UNDERGRADUATE EXPENSES for 2015–2016** *Application fee:* $35. *Tuition:* full-time $22,500; part-time $495 per credit hour. Room and board charges vary according to housing facility.

**GIFT AID (NEED-BASED)** *Total amount:* $711,287 (59% federal, 27% institutional, 14% external sources). *Scholarships, grants, and awards:* Federal Pell, FSEOG, college/university gift aid from institutional funds.

**GIFT AID (NON-NEED-BASED)** *Total amount:* $704,248 (24% federal, 76% institutional). *Scholarships, grants, and awards by category: Academic interests/achievement:* computer science. *Tuition waivers:* Full or partial for employees or children of employees.

**LOANS** *Student loans:* $1,627,033 (67% need-based, 33% non-need-based). *Parent loans:* $1,331,028 (100% need-based). *Programs:* Federal Direct (Subsidized and Unsubsidized Stafford, PLUS), college/university.

**APPLYING FOR FINANCIAL AID** *Required financial aid forms:* FAFSA, institution's own form. *Financial aid deadline (priority):* 4/1. *Notification date:* 5/1. Students must reply by 7/1.

**CONTACT** Mr. Nate Blanchard, Director of Financial Aid, Neumont University, 143 South Main Street, Salt Lake City, UT 84111, 801-302-2873 or toll-free 888-NEUMONT. *Fax:* 801-302-2834. *E-mail:* nate.blanchard@neumont.edu. *Website:* http://www.neumont.edu/.

# NEVADA STATE COLLEGE AT HENDERSON
## Henderson, NV

**CONTACT** Financial Aid Office, Nevada State College at Henderson, 1125 Nevada State Drive, Henderson, NV 89015, 702-992-2000. *Website:* http://www.nsc.nevada.edu/.

# NEWBERRY COLLEGE
## Newberry, SC

| Tuition & fees: $24,300 | Average undergraduate aid package: $21,948 |
|---|---|

**ABOUT THE INSTITUTION** Independent Evangelical Lutheran, coed. *Awards:* bachelor's degrees. 29 undergraduate majors. *Total enrollment:* 1,093. Undergraduates: 1,093. Freshmen: 277. Federal methodology is used as a basis for awarding need-based institutional aid.

**UNDERGRADUATE EXPENSES** for 2015–2016 *Application fee:* $30. *Comprehensive fee:* $33,600 includes full-time tuition ($22,500), mandatory fees ($1800), and room and board ($9300). *College room only:* $4700. Full-time tuition and fees vary according to course load and student level. Room and board charges vary according to board plan and housing facility. *Part-time tuition:* $525 per hour. *Part-time fees:* $125 per term. Part-time tuition and fees vary according to course load and student level. *Payment plan:* Guaranteed tuition.

**FRESHMAN FINANCIAL AID (Fall 2013)** 217 applied for aid; of those 91% were deemed to have need. 100% of freshmen with need received aid; of those 16% had need fully met. *Average percent of need met:* 71% (excluding resources awarded to replace EFC). *Average financial aid package:* $22,604 (excluding resources awarded to replace EFC). 11% of all full-time freshmen had no need and received non-need-based gift aid.

**UNDERGRADUATE FINANCIAL AID (Fall 2013)** 903 applied for aid; of those 93% were deemed to have need. 100% of undergraduates with need received aid; of those 17% had need fully met. *Average percent of need met:* 70% (excluding resources awarded to replace EFC). *Average financial aid package:* $21,948 (excluding resources awarded to replace EFC). 10% of all full-time undergraduates had no need and received non-need-based gift aid.

**GIFT AID (NEED-BASED)** *Total amount:* $14,565,995 (16% federal, 19% state, 57% institutional, 8% external sources). *Receiving aid:* Freshmen: 85% (197); all full-time undergraduates: 85% (831). *Average award:* Freshmen: $19,424; Undergraduates: $18,487. *Scholarships, grants, and awards:* Federal Pell, FSEOG, state, private, college/university gift aid from institutional funds.

**GIFT AID (NON-NEED-BASED)** *Total amount:* $2,184,915 (26% state, 64% institutional, 10% external sources). *Receiving aid:* Freshmen: 13% (29). Undergraduates: 14% (132). *Average award:* Freshmen: $9210. Undergraduates: $10,784. *Scholarships, grants, and awards by category: Academic interests/ achievement:* biological sciences, business, communication, education, foreign languages, general academic interests/achievements, humanities, mathematics, physical sciences, religion/biblical studies, social sciences. *Creative arts/performance:* music, theater/drama. *Special achievements/activities:* cheerleading/drum major, religious involvement. *Special characteristics:* children and siblings of alumni, children of faculty/ staff, international students, local/state students, relatives of clergy, religious affiliation, siblings of current students. *Tuition waivers:* Full or partial for employees or children of employees. *ROTC:* Army.

**LOANS** *Student loans:* $7,198,407 (80% need-based, 20% non-need-based). 77% of past graduating class borrowed through all loan programs. *Average indebtedness per student:* $26,908. *Average need-based loan:* Freshmen: $3996. Undergrad-

uates: $4577. *Parent loans:* $1,273,253 (100% non-need-based). *Programs:* Federal Direct (Subsidized and Unsubsidized Stafford, PLUS), Perkins.

**WORK-STUDY** *Federal work-study:* 93 jobs averaging $1100.

**ATHLETIC AWARDS** Total amount: $2,522,443 (100% non-need-based).

**APPLYING FOR FINANCIAL AID** *Required financial aid form:* FAFSA. *Financial aid deadline (priority):* 3/15. *Notification date:* Continuous beginning 3/15. Students must reply by 8/20.

**CONTACT** Danielle Bell, Director of Financial Aid, Newberry College, 2100 College Street, Newberry, SC 29108, 803-321-5128 or toll-free 800-845-4955. *Fax:* 803-321-5627. *E-mail:* danielle.bell@newberry.edu. *Website:* http://www.newberry.edu/.

# NEWBURY COLLEGE
## Brookline, MA

**ABOUT THE INSTITUTION** Independent, coed. *Awards:* certificates, associate, and bachelor's degrees. 23 undergraduate majors. *Total enrollment:* 873. Undergraduates: 873. Freshmen: 266.

**GIFT AID (NEED-BASED)** *Scholarships, grants, and awards:* Federal Pell, FSEOG, state, private, college/university gift aid from institutional funds.

**LOANS** *Programs:* Federal Direct (Subsidized and Unsubsidized Stafford, PLUS), Perkins, alternative loans, MEFA Loans, Signature Loans, Sallie Mae Loans.

**APPLYING FOR FINANCIAL AID** *Required financial aid form:* FAFSA.

**CONTACT** Elreo Campbell, Executive Director of Student Financial Services, Newbury College, 129 Fisher Avenue, Brookline, MA 02445-5796, 617-730-7100 or toll-free 800-NEWBURY. *Fax:* 617-730-7108. *Website:* http://www.newbury.edu/.

# NEW COLLEGE OF FLORIDA
## Sarasota, FL

| Tuition & fees (FL res): $7040 | Average undergraduate aid package: $12,940 |
|---|---|

**ABOUT THE INSTITUTION** State-supported, coed. *Awards:* bachelor's and master's degrees. 42 undergraduate majors. *Total enrollment:* 834. Undergraduates: 834. Freshmen: 236. Federal methodology is used as a basis for awarding need-based institutional aid.

**UNDERGRADUATE EXPENSES** for 2015–2016 *Application fee:* $30. *Tuition, state resident:* full-time $7040. *Tuition, nonresident:* full-time $30,069. Full-time tuition and fees vary according to course load. *College room and board:* $9009; *Room only:* $6348. Room and board charges vary according to board plan and housing facility.

**FRESHMAN FINANCIAL AID (Fall 2014, est.)** 215 applied for aid; of those 66% were deemed to have need. 100% of freshmen with need received aid; of those 42% had need fully met. *Average percent of need met:* 91% (excluding resources awarded to replace EFC). *Average financial aid package:* $14,178 (excluding resources awarded to replace EFC). 32% of all full-time freshmen had no need and received non-need-based gift aid.

**UNDERGRADUATE FINANCIAL AID (Fall 2014, est.)** 710 applied for aid; of those 65% were deemed to have need. 99% of undergraduates with need received aid; of those 33% had need fully met. *Average percent of need met:* 83% (excluding resources awarded to replace EFC). *Average financial aid package:* $12,940 (excluding resources awarded to replace EFC). 36% of all full-time undergraduates had no need and received non-need-based gift aid.

**GIFT AID (NEED-BASED)** *Total amount:* $3,753,208 (29% federal, 27% state, 39% institutional, 5% external sources). *Receiving aid:* Freshmen: 57% (135); all full-time undergraduates: 53% (442). *Average award:* Freshmen: $9765; Undergraduates: $8481. *Scholarships, grants, and awards:* Federal Pell, FSEOG, state, private, college/university gift aid from institutional funds.

**GIFT AID (NON-NEED-BASED)** *Total amount:* $1,775,997 (57% state, 40% institutional, 3% external sources). *Receiving aid:* Freshmen: 13% (31). Undergraduates: 8% (70). *Average award:* Freshmen: $1884. Undergraduates: $2293. *Scholarships, grants, and awards by category: Academic interests/achievement:* 872 awards ($2,875,607 total): general academic interests/achievements. *Special achieve-*

ments/activities: 43 awards ($149,250 total): general special achievements/activities. *Special characteristics:* 164 awards ($1,687,803 total): out-of-state students.
**LOANS** *Student loans:* $4,132,548 (46% need-based, 54% non-need-based). 38% of past graduating class borrowed through all loan programs. *Average indebtedness per student:* $17,553. *Average need-based loan:* Freshmen: $2292. Undergraduates: $3083. *Parent loans:* $131,651 (16% need-based, 84% non-need-based). *Programs:* Federal Direct (Subsidized and Unsubsidized Stafford, PLUS), alternative loans.
**WORK-STUDY** *Federal work-study:* Total amount: $53,151; 28 jobs averaging $2010. *State or other work-study/employment:* Part-time jobs available.
**APPLYING FOR FINANCIAL AID** *Required financial aid form:* FAFSA. *Financial aid deadline (priority):* 2/15. *Notification date:* Continuous beginning 3/15. Students must reply by 5/1 or within 2 weeks of notification.
**CONTACT** Tara Karas, Director of Financial Aid, New College of Florida, 5800 Bay Shore Road, Sarasota, FL 34243-2109, 941-487-5000. *Fax:* 941-487-5010. *E-mail:* tkaras@ncf.edu.
*Website:* http://www.ncf.edu/.

# NEW ENGLAND COLLEGE
## Henniker, NH

| Tuition & fees: $34,566 | Average undergraduate aid package: $22,768 |
| --- | --- |

**ABOUT THE INSTITUTION** Independent, coed. *Awards:* associate, bachelor's, master's, and doctoral degrees. 35 undergraduate majors. *Total enrollment:* 2,457. Undergraduates: 1,729. Freshmen: 420. Both federal and institutional methodology are used as a basis for awarding need-based institutional aid.
**UNDERGRADUATE EXPENSES** for 2015–2016 *Application fee:* $35. *Comprehensive fee:* $47,954 includes full-time tuition ($33,966), mandatory fees ($600), and room and board ($13,388). *College room only:* $6120. Full-time tuition and fees vary according to class time, course load, degree level, location, program, and reciprocity agreements. Room and board charges vary according to board plan and housing facility. *Part-time tuition:* $416 per credit. Part-time tuition and fees vary according to class time, course load, degree level, location, and program.
**FRESHMAN FINANCIAL AID (Fall 2014, est.)** 294 applied for aid; of those 96% were deemed to have need. 99% of freshmen with need received aid; of those 14% had need fully met. *Average percent of need met:* 70% (excluding resources awarded to replace EFC). *Average financial aid package:* $28,103 (excluding resources awarded to replace EFC). 3% of all full-time freshmen had no need and received non-need-based gift aid.
**UNDERGRADUATE FINANCIAL AID (Fall 2014, est.)** 1,377 applied for aid; of those 96% were deemed to have need. 99% of undergraduates with need received aid; of those 13% had need fully met. *Average percent of need met:* 68% (excluding resources awarded to replace EFC). *Average financial aid package:* $22,768 (excluding resources awarded to replace EFC). 6% of all full-time undergraduates had no need and received non-need-based gift aid.
**GIFT AID (NEED-BASED)** *Total amount:* $17,037,570 (25% federal, 1% state, 74% institutional). *Receiving aid:* Freshmen: 78% (275); all full-time undergraduates: 70% (1,167). *Average award:* Freshmen: $19,790; Undergraduates: $14,500. *Scholarships, grants, and awards:* Federal Pell, FSEOG, state, private, college/university gift aid from institutional funds.
**GIFT AID (NON-NEED-BASED)** *Total amount:* $1,535,327 (1% state, 99% institutional). *Receiving aid:* Freshmen: 3% (11). Undergraduates: 6% (94). *Average award:* Freshmen: $18,671. Undergraduates: $15,742. *Scholarships, grants, and awards by category:* Academic interests/achievement: 615 awards ($8,117,939 total): biological sciences, business, communication, computer science, education, engineering/technologies, English, general academic interests/achievements, health fields, humanities, international studies, mathematics, social sciences. *Creative arts/performance:* 3 awards ($37,000 total): applied art and design, art/fine arts, creative writing, theater/drama. *Special achievements/activities:* 208 awards ($848,878 total): community service, leadership. *Special characteristics:* 123 awards ($1,923,232 total): children and siblings of alumni, children of educators, children of faculty/staff, ethnic background, international students, local/state students, parents of current students, siblings of current students. *Tuition waivers:* Full or partial for children of alumni, employees or children of employees, adult students, senior citizens. *ROTC:* Army cooperative, Air Force cooperative.
**LOANS** *Student loans:* $12,477,698 (44% need-based, 56% non-need-based). 82% of past graduating class borrowed through all loan programs. *Average indebtedness*

per student: $31,073. *Average need-based loan:* Freshmen: $4160. Undergraduates: $4572. *Parent loans:* $3,782,086 (91% need-based, 9% non-need-based). *Programs:* Federal Direct (Subsidized and Unsubsidized Stafford, PLUS), Perkins, state.
**WORK-STUDY** *Federal work-study:* Total amount: $698,261; 369 jobs averaging $1892. *State or other work-study/employment:* Total amount: $26,383 (27% need-based, 73% non-need-based). 23 part-time jobs averaging $1147.
**APPLYING FOR FINANCIAL AID** *Required financial aid form:* FAFSA. *Financial aid deadline (priority):* 4/1. *Notification date:* Continuous beginning 2/1. Students must reply by 9/7 or within 2 weeks of notification.
**CONTACT** Kristen Blase, Student Financial Services Director, New England College, 15 Main Street, Henniker, NH 03242-3293, 603-428-2226 or toll-free 800-521-7642. *Fax:* 603-428-2404. *E-mail:* rstein@nec.edu.
*Website:* http://www.nec.edu/.

# NEW ENGLAND COLLEGE OF BUSINESS AND FINANCE
## Boston, MA

**CONTACT** Financial Aid Office, New England College of Business and Finance, 10 High Street, Suite 204, Boston, MA 02111-2645, 617-951-2350 or toll-free 800-997-1673.
*Website:* http://necb.edu/.

# NEW ENGLAND CONSERVATORY OF MUSIC
## Boston, MA

| Tuition & fees: $41,405 | Average undergraduate aid package: $25,463 |
| --- | --- |

**ABOUT THE INSTITUTION** Independent, coed. *Awards:* certificates, diplomas, bachelor's, master's, and doctoral degrees. 9 undergraduate majors. *Total enrollment:* 782. Undergraduates: 413. Freshmen: 75. Federal methodology is used as a basis for awarding need-based institutional aid.
**UNDERGRADUATE EXPENSES** for 2015–2016 *Application fee:* $115. *Comprehensive fee:* $54,255 includes full-time tuition ($40,950), mandatory fees ($455), and room and board ($12,850). Room and board charges vary according to board plan. *Part-time tuition:* $1310 per credit.
**FRESHMAN FINANCIAL AID (Fall 2014, est.)** 17 applied for aid; of those 79% were deemed to have need. 100% of freshmen with need received aid; of those 5% had need fully met. *Average percent of need met:* 57% (excluding resources awarded to replace EFC). *Average financial aid package:* $24,166 (excluding resources awarded to replace EFC). 56% of all full-time freshmen had no need and received non-need-based gift aid.
**UNDERGRADUATE FINANCIAL AID (Fall 2014, est.)** 244 applied for aid; of those 79% were deemed to have need. 100% of undergraduates with need received aid; of those 14% had need fully met. *Average percent of need met:* 59% (excluding resources awarded to replace EFC). *Average financial aid package:* $25,463 (excluding resources awarded to replace EFC). 49% of all full-time undergraduates had no need and received non-need-based gift aid.
**GIFT AID (NEED-BASED)** *Total amount:* $3,806,728 (11% federal, 79% institutional, 10% external sources). *Receiving aid:* Freshmen: 44% (37); all full-time undergraduates: 50% (192). *Average award:* Freshmen: $19,652; Undergraduates: $19,776. *Scholarships, grants, and awards:* Federal Pell, FSEOG, state, private, college/university gift aid from institutional funds.
**GIFT AID (NON-NEED-BASED)** *Total amount:* $3,174,039 (87% institutional, 13% external sources). *Receiving aid:* Freshmen: 6% (5). Undergraduates: 6% (22). *Average award:* Freshmen: $14,397. Undergraduates: $14,234. *Scholarships, grants, and awards by category:* Creative arts/performance: 348 awards ($3,024,562 total): music, theater/drama. *Tuition waivers:* Full or partial for employees or children of employees.
**LOANS** *Student loans:* $1,868,069 (76% need-based, 24% non-need-based). 47% of past graduating class borrowed through all loan programs. *Average indebtedness per student:* $25,288. *Average need-based loan:* Freshmen: $4166. Undergrad-

uates: $5112. *Parent loans:* $798,400 (69% need-based, 31% non-need-based). *Programs:* Federal Direct (Subsidized and Unsubsidized Stafford, PLUS), Perkins, state.
**WORK-STUDY** *Federal work-study:* Total amount: $259,312; 168 jobs averaging $1561. *State or other work-study/employment:* Total amount: $1,919,965 (87% need-based, 13% non-need-based). Part-time jobs available.
**APPLYING FOR FINANCIAL AID** *Required financial aid forms:* FAFSA, institution's own form. *Financial aid deadline (priority):* 2/15. *Notification date:* Continuous beginning 4/1. Students must reply by 5/1.
**CONTACT** Ms. Lauren G. Urbanek, Director of Financial Aid, New England Conservatory of Music, 290 Huntington Avenue, Boston, MA 02115, 617-585-1110. *Fax:* 617-585-1115. *E-mail:* finaid@necmusic.edu.
*Website:* http://necmusic.edu/.

# NEW ENGLAND INSTITUTE OF TECHNOLOGY
## East Greenwich, RI

**CONTACT** Financial Aid Office, New England Institute of Technology, One New England Tech Boulevard, East Greenwich, RI 02818, 401-467-7744 or toll-free 800-736-7744.
*Website:* http://www.neit.edu/.

# NEW HAMPSHIRE INSTITUTE OF ART
## Manchester, NH

**CONTACT** Linda Lavallee, Director of Financial Aid, New Hampshire Institute of Art, 148 Concord Street, Manchester, NH 03104-4858, 603-623-0313 Ext. 577 or toll-free 866-241-4918. *Fax:* 603-647-0658. *E-mail:* llavallee@nhia.edu.
*Website:* http://www.nhia.edu/.

# NEW HOPE CHRISTIAN COLLEGE
## Eugene, OR

**CONTACT** Nathan Icenhower, Financial Aid Administrator, New Hope Christian College, 2155 Bailey Hill Road, Eugene, OR 97405-1194, 541-485-1780 Ext. 3106 or toll-free 800-322-2638. *Fax:* 541-343-5801. *E-mail:* finaid@newhope.edu.
*Website:* http://www.newhope.edu/.

# NEW JERSEY CITY UNIVERSITY
## Jersey City, NJ

| Tuition & fees (NJ res): $10,852 | Average undergraduate aid package: $15,970 |
| --- | --- |

**ABOUT THE INSTITUTION** State-supported, coed. *Awards:* certificates, bachelor's, master's, and doctoral degrees. 30 undergraduate majors. *Total enrollment:* 8,136. Undergraduates: 6,229. Freshmen: 691. Federal methodology is used as a basis for awarding need-based institutional aid.
**UNDERGRADUATE EXPENSES** for 2015–2016 *Application fee:* $50. *Tuition, state resident:* full-time $7704; part-time $256.80 per credit hour. *Tuition, nonresident:* full-time $16,276; part-time $542.55 per credit hour. *Required fees:* full-time $3148. Part-time tuition and fees vary according to course load. *College room and board:* $10,604; *Room only:* $6816.
**FRESHMAN FINANCIAL AID (Fall 2013)** 550 applied for aid; of those 94% were deemed to have need. 97% of freshmen with need received aid; of those 7% had need fully met. *Average percent of need met:* 66% (excluding resources awarded to replace EFC). *Average financial aid package:* $14,864 (excluding resources awarded to replace EFC). 2% of all full-time freshmen had no need and received non-need-based gift aid.
**UNDERGRADUATE FINANCIAL AID (Fall 2013)** 4,355 applied for aid; of those 95% were deemed to have need. 96% of undergraduates with need received aid;

of those 92% had need fully met. *Average percent of need met:* 68% (excluding resources awarded to replace EFC). *Average financial aid package:* $15,970 (excluding resources awarded to replace EFC). 1% of all full-time undergraduates had no need and received non-need-based gift aid.
**GIFT AID (NEED-BASED)** *Total amount:* $27,196,615 (57% federal, 43% state). *Receiving aid:* Freshmen: 76% (433); all full-time undergraduates: 67% (3,196). *Average award:* Freshmen: $9556; Undergraduates: $8065. *Scholarships, grants, and awards:* Federal Pell, FSEOG, state, college/university gift aid from institutional funds.
**GIFT AID (NON-NEED-BASED)** *Total amount:* $1,762,589 (3% state, 97% institutional). *Receiving aid:* Freshmen: 18% (101). Undergraduates: 8% (364). *Average award:* Freshmen: $7774. Undergraduates: $6884. *Scholarships, grants, and awards by category: Academic interests/achievement:* general academic interests/achievements. *Tuition waivers:* Full or partial for employees or children of employees, senior citizens. *ROTC:* Army cooperative, Air Force cooperative.
**LOANS** *Student loans:* $67,451,227 (55% need-based, 45% non-need-based). 71% of past graduating class borrowed through all loan programs. *Average indebtedness per student:* $20,763. *Average need-based loan:* Freshmen: $3374. Undergraduates: $4080. *Parent loans:* $29,913,057 (100% non-need-based). *Programs:* Federal Direct (Subsidized and Unsubsidized Stafford, PLUS).
**WORK-STUDY** *Federal work-study:* jobs available.
**APPLYING FOR FINANCIAL AID** *Required financial aid form:* FAFSA. *Financial aid deadline (priority):* 4/15. *Notification date:* 5/15.
**CONTACT** Mr. Frank Cuozzo, Director of Financial Aid, New Jersey City University, 2039 Kennedy Boulevard, Jersey City, NJ 07305-1597, 201-200-3173 or toll-free 888-441-NJCU.
*Website:* http://www.njcu.edu/.

# NEW JERSEY INSTITUTE OF TECHNOLOGY
## Newark, NJ

| Tuition & fees (NJ res): $15,648 | Average undergraduate aid package: $14,123 |
| --- | --- |

**ABOUT THE INSTITUTION** State-supported, coed. *Awards:* certificates, bachelor's, master's, and doctoral degrees. 41 undergraduate majors. *Total enrollment:* 10,646. Undergraduates: 7,550. Freshmen: 1,053. Federal methodology is used as a basis for awarding need-based institutional aid.
**UNDERGRADUATE EXPENSES** for 2015–2016 *Application fee:* $70. *Tuition, state resident:* full-time $13,120; part-time $499 per credit. *Tuition, nonresident:* full-time $26,760; part-time $1144 per credit. *Required fees:* full-time $2528; $148 per credit. Full-time tuition and fees vary according to course load and degree level. Part-time tuition and fees vary according to course load and degree level. *College room and board:* $13,280. Room and board charges vary according to board plan and housing facility.
**FRESHMAN FINANCIAL AID (Fall 2013)** 804 applied for aid; of those 82% were deemed to have need. 100% of freshmen with need received aid; of those 15% had need fully met. *Average percent of need met:* 61% (excluding resources awarded to replace EFC). *Average financial aid package:* $14,728 (excluding resources awarded to replace EFC). 14% of all full-time freshmen had no need and received non-need-based gift aid.
**UNDERGRADUATE FINANCIAL AID (Fall 2013)** 4,419 applied for aid; of those 90% were deemed to have need. 100% of undergraduates with need received aid; of those 10% had need fully met. *Average percent of need met:* 60% (excluding resources awarded to replace EFC). *Average financial aid package:* $14,123 (excluding resources awarded to replace EFC). 9% of all full-time undergraduates had no need and received non-need-based gift aid.
**GIFT AID (NEED-BASED)** *Total amount:* $40,221,009 (31% federal, 44% state, 24% institutional, 1% external sources). *Receiving aid:* Freshmen: 60% (572); all full-time undergraduates: 60% (3,386). *Average award:* Freshmen: $13,675; Undergraduates: $11,799. *Scholarships, grants, and awards:* Federal Pell, FSEOG, state, private, college/university gift aid from institutional funds, United Negro College Fund.
**GIFT AID (NON-NEED-BASED)** *Total amount:* $1,061,159 (18% state, 75% institutional, 7% external sources). *Receiving aid:* Freshmen: 7% (71). Undergraduates: 3% (195). *Average award:* Freshmen: $13,735. Undergraduates: $12,290. *Scholarships, grants, and awards by category: Academic interests/achievement:* 699 awards ($11,315,202 total): architecture, area/ethnic studies, bio-

logical sciences, business, communication, computer science, education, engineering/technologies, general academic interests/achievements, humanities, international studies, mathematics, physical sciences, premedicine. *Creative arts/performance:* 133 awards ($2,065,720 total): applied art and design, art/fine arts, journalism/publications, performing arts, theater/drama. *Special achievements/activities:* community service, general special achievements/activities, hobbies/interests, leadership, religious involvement. *Special characteristics:* adult students, children of faculty/staff, children of union members/company employees, ethnic background, first-generation college students, general special characteristics, handicapped students, international students, local/state students, members of minority groups, out-of-state students, relatives of clergy, religious affiliation, siblings of current students, veterans, veterans' children. *Tuition waivers:* Full or partial for employees or children of employees. *ROTC:* Army cooperative, Air Force.

**LOANS** *Student loans:* $34,303,778 (40% need-based, 60% non-need-based). 59% of past graduating class borrowed through all loan programs. *Average need-based loan:* Freshmen: $3692. Undergraduates: $4586. *Parent loans:* $2,793,854 (100% non-need-based). *Programs:* Federal Direct (Subsidized and Unsubsidized Stafford, PLUS), Perkins, state, college/university, alternative loans.

**WORK-STUDY** *Federal work-study:* 239 jobs averaging $1363. *State or other work-study/employment:* Total amount: $1,785,906 (100% non-need-based). 813 part-time jobs averaging $2203.

**ATHLETIC AWARDS** Total amount: $3,544,654 (33% need-based, 67% non-need-based).

**APPLYING FOR FINANCIAL AID** *Required financial aid forms:* FAFSA, institution's own form. *Financial aid deadline (priority):* 3/15. *Notification date:* Continuous beginning 1/1. Students must reply by 5/1.

**CONTACT** Ivon Nunez, Director of Financial Aid Services, New Jersey Institute of Technology, Student Mall, University Heights, Newark, NJ 07102, 973-596-3476 or toll-free 800-925-NJIT. *Fax:* 973-596-6471. *E-mail:* ivon.nunez@njit.edu. *Website:* http://www.njit.edu/.

# NEWMAN UNIVERSITY
## Wichita, KS

| Tuition & fees: $24,730 | Average undergraduate aid package: $19,844 |
| --- | --- |

**ABOUT THE INSTITUTION** Independent Roman Catholic, coed. *Awards:* associate, bachelor's, and master's degrees. 42 undergraduate majors. *Total enrollment:* 3,687. Undergraduates: 2,732. Freshmen: 174. Federal methodology is used as a basis for awarding need-based institutional aid.

**UNDERGRADUATE EXPENSES** for 2015–2016 *Comprehensive fee:* $31,790 includes full-time tuition ($23,790), mandatory fees ($940), and room and board ($7060). Room and board charges vary according to board plan and housing facility. *Part-time tuition:* $793 per credit hour. *Part-time fees:* $17 per credit hour; $35 per term. Part-time tuition and fees vary according to course load.

**FRESHMAN FINANCIAL AID (Fall 2013)** 140 applied for aid; of those 78% were deemed to have need. 100% of freshmen with need received aid; of those 38% had need fully met. *Average percent of need met:* 79% (excluding resources awarded to replace EFC). *Average financial aid package:* $23,700 (excluding resources awarded to replace EFC). 12% of all full-time freshmen had no need and received non-need-based gift aid.

**UNDERGRADUATE FINANCIAL AID (Fall 2013)** 1,027 applied for aid; of those 85% were deemed to have need. 100% of undergraduates with need received aid; of those 26% had need fully met. *Average percent of need met:* 67% (excluding resources awarded to replace EFC). *Average financial aid package:* $19,844 (excluding resources awarded to replace EFC). 5% of all full-time undergraduates had no need and received non-need-based gift aid.

**GIFT AID (NEED-BASED)** *Total amount:* $3,889,987 (50% federal, 22% state, 28% institutional). *Receiving aid:* Freshmen: 66% (106); all full-time undergraduates: 70% (846). *Average award:* Freshmen: $5518; Undergraduates: $4844. *Scholarships, grants, and awards:* Federal Pell, FSEOG, state, private, college/university gift aid from institutional funds.

**GIFT AID (NON-NEED-BASED)** *Total amount:* $10,313,025 (92% institutional, 8% external sources). *Receiving aid:* Freshmen: 66% (105). Undergraduates: 66% (800). *Average award:* Freshmen: $9326. Undergraduates: $8927. *Scholarships, grants, and awards by category:* Academic interests/achievement: 884 awards ($7,438,830 total): general academic interests/achievements. *Creative arts/per-*

formance: 81 awards ($190,650 total): art/fine arts, journalism/publications, music, theater/drama. *Special achievements/activities:* 133 awards ($341,000 total): community service, leadership, memberships, religious involvement. *Special characteristics:* 140 awards ($647,926 total): children and siblings of alumni, children of current students, children of faculty/staff, international students, married students, siblings of current students, spouses of current students. *Tuition waivers:* Full or partial for employees or children of employees.

**LOANS** *Student loans:* $5,295,090 (47% need-based, 53% non-need-based). 77% of past graduating class borrowed through all loan programs. *Average indebtedness per student:* $23,843. *Average need-based loan:* Freshmen: $2807. Undergraduates: $4051. *Parent loans:* $509,865 (100% non-need-based). *Programs:* Federal Direct (Subsidized and Unsubsidized Stafford, PLUS), Perkins.

**WORK-STUDY** *Federal work-study:* 59 jobs averaging $2000. *State or other work-study/employment:* Total amount: $96,594 (100% non-need-based). 89 part-time jobs averaging $2000.

**ATHLETIC AWARDS** Total amount: $2,026,065 (100% non-need-based).

**APPLYING FOR FINANCIAL AID** *Required financial aid form:* FAFSA. *Financial aid deadline (priority):* 3/1. *Notification date:* Continuous beginning 3/1.

**CONTACT** Charly Smith, Director of Financial Aid, Newman University, 3100 McCormick Avenue, Wichita, KS 67213, 316-942-4291 Ext. 2132 or toll-free 877-NEWMANU. *Fax:* 316-942-4483. *E-mail:* smithc@newmanu.edu. *Website:* http://www.newmanu.edu/.

# NEW MEXICO HIGHLANDS UNIVERSITY
## Las Vegas, NM

| Tuition & fees (NM res): $4500 | Average undergraduate aid package: $1847 |
| --- | --- |

**ABOUT THE INSTITUTION** State-supported, coed. *Awards:* certificates, associate, bachelor's, and master's degrees. 44 undergraduate majors. *Total enrollment:* 3,546. Undergraduates: 2,275. Freshmen: 281. Both federal and institutional methodology are used as a basis for awarding need-based institutional aid.

**UNDERGRADUATE EXPENSES** for 2015–2016 *One-time required fee:* $20. *Tuition, state resident:* full-time $3192; part-time $133 per credit hour. *Tuition, nonresident:* full-time $5796; part-time $242 per credit hour. *Required fees:* full-time $1308; $54.50 per credit hour. Full-time tuition and fees vary according to course load and location. Part-time tuition and fees vary according to course load and location. *College room and board:* $7404. Room and board charges vary according to board plan and housing facility.

**FRESHMAN FINANCIAL AID (Fall 2013)** 314 applied for aid; of those 81% were deemed to have need. 98% of freshmen with need received aid; of those 6% had need fully met. *Average financial aid package:* $1573 (excluding resources awarded to replace EFC). 73% of all full-time freshmen had no need and received non-need-based gift aid.

**UNDERGRADUATE FINANCIAL AID (Fall 2013)** 1,433 applied for aid; of those 88% were deemed to have need. 97% of undergraduates with need received aid; of those 7% had need fully met. *Average financial aid package:* $1847 (excluding resources awarded to replace EFC). 39% of all full-time undergraduates had no need and received non-need-based gift aid.

**GIFT AID (NEED-BASED)** *Total amount:* $6,758,864 (86% federal, 10% state, 4% external sources). *Receiving aid:* Freshmen: 63% (221); all full-time undergraduates: 64% (1,054). *Average award:* Freshmen: $1769; Undergraduates: $1792. *Scholarships, grants, and awards:* Federal Pell, FSEOG, state, private, college/university gift aid from institutional funds.

**GIFT AID (NON-NEED-BASED)** *Total amount:* $1,940,079 (1% federal, 41% state, 43% institutional, 15% external sources). *Receiving aid:* Freshmen: 51% (177). Undergraduates: 39% (637). *Average award:* Freshmen: $2654. Undergraduates: $3953. *Scholarships, grants, and awards by category:* Academic interests/achievement: biological sciences, business, communication, computer science, education, engineering/technologies, English, foreign languages, general academic interests/achievements, health fields, humanities, mathematics, physical sciences, social sciences. *Creative arts/performance:* art/fine arts, music, performing arts. *Tuition waivers:* Full or partial for employees or children of employees, senior citizens.

**LOANS** *Student loans:* $1,893,330 (42% need-based, 58% non-need-based). 51% of past graduating class borrowed through all loan programs. *Average indebtedness per student:* $14,106. *Average need-based loan:* Freshmen: $1991. Undergraduates: $2489. *Parent loans:* $58,369 (100% non-need-based). *Programs:* Federal Direct (Subsidized and Unsubsidized Stafford, PLUS), Perkins.
**WORK-STUDY** *Federal work-study:* jobs available. *State or other work-study/employment:* Total amount: $163,089 (91% need-based, 9% non-need-based). Part-time jobs available.
**ATHLETIC AWARDS** Total amount: $600,241 (100% non-need-based).
**APPLYING FOR FINANCIAL AID** *Required financial aid form:* FAFSA. *Financial aid deadline:* Continuous. *Notification date:* Continuous beginning 3/15. Students must reply within 2 weeks of notification.
**CONTACT** Eileen Sedillo, Director of Financial Aid, New Mexico Highlands University, PO Box 9000, Las Vegas, NM 87701, 505-454-3430 or toll-free 800-338-6648. *Fax:* 505-454-3398. *E-mail:* sedillo_e@nmhu.edu. *Website:* http://www.nmhu.edu/.

# NEW MEXICO INSTITUTE OF MINING AND TECHNOLOGY
## Socorro, NM

| Tuition & fees (NM res): $6256 | Average undergraduate aid package: $10,821 |
| --- | --- |

**ABOUT THE INSTITUTION** State-supported, coed. *Awards:* associate, bachelor's, master's, and doctoral degrees. 22 undergraduate majors. *Total enrollment:* 2,127. Undergraduates: 1,633. Freshmen: 290. Federal methodology is used as a basis for awarding need-based institutional aid.
**UNDERGRADUATE EXPENSES** for 2015–2016 *Application fee:* $15. *Tuition, state resident:* full-time $5298; part-time $220.74 per credit hour. *Tuition, nonresident:* full-time $17,226; part-time $717.74 per credit hour. *Required fees:* full-time $958; $18 per credit hour or $258 per term. Full-time tuition and fees vary according to reciprocity agreements. Part-time tuition and fees vary according to course load. *College room and board:* $6740. Room and board charges vary according to board plan and housing facility.
**FRESHMAN FINANCIAL AID (Fall 2013)** 309 applied for aid; of those 59% were deemed to have need. 98% of freshmen with need received aid; of those 20% had need fully met. *Average percent of need met:* 70% (excluding resources awarded to replace EFC). *Average financial aid package:* $9972 (excluding resources awarded to replace EFC). 38% of all full-time freshmen had no need and received non-need-based gift aid.
**UNDERGRADUATE FINANCIAL AID (Fall 2013)** 1,286 applied for aid; of those 60% were deemed to have need. 97% of undergraduates with need received aid; of those 20% had need fully met. *Average percent of need met:* 74% (excluding resources awarded to replace EFC). *Average financial aid package:* $10,821 (excluding resources awarded to replace EFC). 34% of all full-time undergraduates had no need and received non-need-based gift aid.
**GIFT AID (NEED-BASED)** *Total amount:* $2,810,506 (84% federal, 12% state, 4% external sources). *Receiving aid:* Freshmen: 35% (112); all full-time undergraduates: 34% (485). *Average award:* Freshmen: $6005; Undergraduates: $5509. *Scholarships, grants, and awards:* Federal Pell, FSEOG, state, private, college/university gift aid from institutional funds.
**GIFT AID (NON-NEED-BASED)** *Total amount:* $6,448,986 (44% state, 45% institutional, 11% external sources). *Receiving aid:* Freshmen: 48% (152). Undergraduates: 39% (546). *Average award:* Freshmen: $7080. Undergraduates: $6651. *Scholarships, grants, and awards by category:* Academic interests/achievement: general academic interests/achievements. *Tuition waivers:* Full or partial for employees or children of employees, senior citizens.
**LOANS** *Student loans:* $3,980,378 (49% need-based, 51% non-need-based). 43% of past graduating class borrowed through all loan programs. *Average indebtedness per student:* $20,944. *Average need-based loan:* Freshmen: $2932. Undergraduates: $4151. *Parent loans:* $197,407 (100% non-need-based). *Programs:* Federal Direct (Subsidized and Unsubsidized Stafford, PLUS), Perkins.
**WORK-STUDY** *Federal work-study:* jobs available. *State or other work-study/employment:* Total amount: $70,658 (23% need-based, 77% non-need-based). Part-time jobs available.

**APPLYING FOR FINANCIAL AID** *Required financial aid form:* FAFSA. *Financial aid deadline (priority):* 5/1. *Notification date:* Continuous beginning 5/1. Students must reply within 2 weeks of notification.
**CONTACT** Ms. Marliss Monette, Director of Financial Aid, New Mexico Institute of Mining and Technology, 801 Leroy Place, Socorro, NM 87801, 575-835-5333 or toll-free 800-428-TECH. *Fax:* 575-835-5959. *E-mail:* mmonette@admin.nmt.edu. *Website:* http://www.nmt.edu/.

# NEW MEXICO STATE UNIVERSITY
## Las Cruces, NM

| Tuition & fees (NM res): $5950 | Average undergraduate aid package: $9089 |
| --- | --- |

**ABOUT THE INSTITUTION** State-supported, coed. *Awards:* certificates, associate, bachelor's, master's, and doctoral degrees. 86 undergraduate majors. *Total enrollment:* 15,829. Undergraduates: 12,784. Freshmen: 1,862. Federal methodology is used as a basis for awarding need-based institutional aid.
**UNDERGRADUATE EXPENSES** for 2015–2016 *Application fee:* $20. *One-time required fee:* $40. *Tuition, state resident:* full-time $4812; part-time $200.50 per credit hour. *Tuition, nonresident:* full-time $17,974; part-time $748.90 per credit hour. *Required fees:* full-time $1138; $47.40 per credit hour. Full-time tuition and fees vary according to course load. Part-time tuition and fees vary according to course load. *College room and board:* $8100; *Room only:* $4752. Room and board charges vary according to board plan and housing facility.
**FRESHMAN FINANCIAL AID (Fall 2013)** 1,676 applied for aid; of those 76% were deemed to have need. 100% of freshmen with need received aid; of those 12% had need fully met. *Average percent of need met:* 68% (excluding resources awarded to replace EFC). *Average financial aid package:* $8638 (excluding resources awarded to replace EFC). 22% of all full-time freshmen had no need and received non-need-based gift aid.
**UNDERGRADUATE FINANCIAL AID (Fall 2013)** 8,367 applied for aid; of those 85% were deemed to have need. 100% of undergraduates with need received aid; of those 9% had need fully met. *Average percent of need met:* 65% (excluding resources awarded to replace EFC). *Average financial aid package:* $9089 (excluding resources awarded to replace EFC). 11% of all full-time undergraduates had no need and received non-need-based gift aid.
**GIFT AID (NEED-BASED)** *Total amount:* $43,186,231 (56% federal, 29% state, 11% institutional, 4% external sources). *Receiving aid:* Freshmen: 66% (1,253); all full-time undergraduates: 60% (6,701). *Average award:* Freshmen: $9053; Undergraduates: $8714. *Scholarships, grants, and awards:* Federal Pell, FSEOG, state, private, college/university gift aid from institutional funds.
**GIFT AID (NON-NEED-BASED)** *Total amount:* $12,734,426 (4% federal, 59% state, 28% institutional, 9% external sources). *Receiving aid:* Freshmen: 8% (149). Undergraduates: 6% (619). *Average award:* Freshmen: $2898. Undergraduates: $2348. *Scholarships, grants, and awards by category:* Academic interests/achievement: 578 awards ($551,147 total): agriculture, area/ethnic studies, biological sciences, business, communication, computer science, education, engineering/technologies, English, foreign languages, general academic interests/achievements, health fields, home economics, humanities, mathematics, military science, physical sciences, social sciences. *Creative arts/performance:* 59 awards ($43,815 total): applied art and design, art/fine arts, cinema/film/broadcasting, creative writing, dance, general creative arts/performance, journalism/publications, music, performing arts, theater/drama. *Special achievements/activities:* 44 awards ($57,934 total): cheerleading/drum major, general special achievements/activities, hobbies/interests, junior miss, leadership, memberships, rodeo. *Special characteristics:* 484 awards ($867,639 total): adult students, children and siblings of alumni, children of current students, children of faculty/staff, children of public servants, children of union members/company employees, children of workers in trades, children with a deceased or disabled parent, ethnic background, handicapped students, international students, local/state students, married students, members of minority groups, out-of-state students, previous college experience, public servants, spouses of current students, spouses of deceased or disabled public servants, veterans, veterans' children. *Tuition waivers:* Full or partial for employees or children of employees, senior citizens. *ROTC:* Army, Air Force.
**LOANS** *Student loans:* $37,479,925 (79% need-based, 21% non-need-based). 58% of past graduating class borrowed through all loan programs. *Average indebtedness per student:* $18,628. *Average need-based loan:* Freshmen: $2927. Undergraduates: $3704. *Parent loans:* $856,691 (24% need-based, 76% non-need-based). *Pro-*

**grams:** Federal Direct (Subsidized and Unsubsidized Stafford, PLUS), Perkins, state, college/university.

**WORK-STUDY** *Federal work-study:* 341 jobs averaging $2718. *State or other work-study/employment:* Total amount: $1,977,260 (77% need-based, 23% non-need-based). 357 part-time jobs averaging $5642.

**ATHLETIC AWARDS** Total amount: $3,589,166 (19% need-based, 81% non-need-based).

**APPLYING FOR FINANCIAL AID** *Required financial aid form:* FAFSA. *Financial aid deadline:* 3/1 (priority: 1/1). *Notification date:* Continuous beginning 4/1.

**CONTACT** Ms. Janie Merchant, Director of Financial Aid, New Mexico State University, Box 30001, Department 5100, Las Cruces, NM 88003-8001, 575-646-4105 or toll-free 800-662-6678. *Fax:* 575-646-7381. *E-mail:* financialaid@nmsu.edu. *Website:* http://www.nmsu.edu/.

# NEW ORLEANS BAPTIST THEOLOGICAL SEMINARY
## New Orleans, LA

**CONTACT** Owen Nease, Financial Aid Office, New Orleans Baptist Theological Seminary, 3939 Gentilly Boulevard, New Orleans, LA 70126-4858, 504-282-4455 Ext. 3348 or toll-free 800-662-8701. *Fax:* 504-816-8437. *E-mail:* financialaid@nobts.edu. *Website:* http://www.nobts.edu/.

# NEW SAINT ANDREWS COLLEGE
## Moscow, ID

**CONTACT** Brenda Schlect, College Bursars Office, New Saint Andrews College, 405 South Main Street, PO Box 9025, Moscow, ID 83843, 208-882-1566 Ext. 113. *Fax:* 208-882-4297. *E-mail:* bschlect@nsa.edu. *Website:* http://www.nsa.edu/.

# THE NEW SCHOOL FOR DRAMA
## New York, NY

**ABOUT THE INSTITUTION** Independent, coed. *Awards:* bachelor's and master's degrees. 1 undergraduate major. *Total enrollment:* 132. Undergraduates: 50. Freshmen: 41.

**GIFT AID (NEED-BASED)** *Scholarships, grants, and awards:* Federal Pell, FSEOG, state, private, college/university gift aid from institutional funds.

**GIFT AID (NON-NEED-BASED)** *Scholarships, grants, and awards by category:* Academic interests/achievement: general academic interests/achievements.

**LOANS** *Programs:* Federal Direct (Subsidized and Unsubsidized Stafford, PLUS), Perkins.

**APPLYING FOR FINANCIAL AID** *Required financial aid forms:* FAFSA, state aid form.

**CONTACT** Student Financial Services, The New School for Drama, 66 West 12th Street, New York, NY 10011, 212-229-8930. *E-mail:* sfs@newschool.edu. *Website:* http://www.newschool.edu/drama/.

# THE NEW SCHOOL FOR JAZZ AND CONTEMPORARY MUSIC
## New York, NY

| Tuition & fees: N/R | Average undergraduate aid package: $18,661 |
|---|---|

**ABOUT THE INSTITUTION** Independent, coed. *Awards:* bachelor's degrees. 1 undergraduate major. *Total enrollment:* 243. Undergraduates: 243. Freshmen: 44. Federal methodology is used as a basis for awarding need-based institutional aid.

**FRESHMAN FINANCIAL AID (Fall 2013)** 25 applied for aid; of those 96% were deemed to have need. 100% of freshmen with need received aid; of those 25% had need fully met. *Average percent of need met:* 66% (excluding resources awarded to replace EFC). *Average financial aid package:* $18,152 (excluding resources awarded to replace EFC). 25% of all full-time freshmen had no need and received non-need-based gift aid.

**UNDERGRADUATE FINANCIAL AID (Fall 2013)** 107 applied for aid; of those 94% were deemed to have need. 100% of undergraduates with need received aid; of those 23% had need fully met. *Average percent of need met:* 67% (excluding resources awarded to replace EFC). *Average financial aid package:* $18,661 (excluding resources awarded to replace EFC). 31% of all full-time undergraduates had no need and received non-need-based gift aid.

**GIFT AID (NEED-BASED)** *Total amount:* $1,017,703 (22% federal; 3% state, 56% institutional, 19% external sources). *Receiving aid:* Freshmen: 34% (15); all full-time undergraduates: 34% (76). *Average award:* Freshmen: $11,340; Undergraduates: $8704. *Scholarships, grants, and awards:* Federal Pell, FSEOG, state, private, college/university gift aid from institutional funds.

**GIFT AID (NON-NEED-BASED)** *Total amount:* $2,017,170 (100% institutional). *Receiving aid:* Freshmen: 30% (13). Undergraduates: 25% (55). *Average award:* Freshmen: $15,707. Undergraduates: $16,403. *Scholarships, grants, and awards by category:* Academic interests/achievement: general academic interests/achievements. Creative arts/performance: music.

**LOANS** *Student loans:* $1,108,521 (72% need-based, 28% non-need-based). 66% of past graduating class borrowed through all loan programs. *Average indebtedness per student:* $28,966. *Average need-based loan:* Freshmen: $5863. Undergraduates: $7306. *Parent loans:* $832,253 (5% need-based, 95% non-need-based). *Programs:* Federal Direct (Subsidized and Unsubsidized Stafford, PLUS), Perkins.

**WORK-STUDY** *Federal work-study:* jobs available.

**APPLYING FOR FINANCIAL AID** *Required financial aid forms:* FAFSA, state aid form. *Financial aid deadline:* 3/1. *Notification date:* Continuous beginning 4/1. Students must reply within 4 weeks of notification.

**CONTACT** Office of Student Financial Services, The New School for Jazz and Contemporary Music, 72 Fifth Avenue, 2nd Floor, New York, NY 10011, 212-229-8930 or toll-free 800-292-3040 *E-mail:* sfs@newschool.edu. *Website:* http://www.newschool.edu/jazz/.

# THE NEW SCHOOL FOR PUBLIC ENGAGEMENT
## New York, NY

**ABOUT THE INSTITUTION** Independent, coed. *Awards:* certificates, bachelor's, master's, and doctoral degrees. 8 undergraduate majors. *Total enrollment:* 2,014. Undergraduates: 473. Freshmen: 15.

**GIFT AID (NEED-BASED)** *Scholarships, grants, and awards:* Federal Pell, FSEOG, state, private, college/university gift aid from institutional funds.

**GIFT AID (NON-NEED-BASED)** *Scholarships, grants, and awards by category:* Academic interests/achievement: general academic interests/achievements.

**LOANS** *Programs:* Federal Direct (Subsidized and Unsubsidized Stafford, PLUS), Perkins.

**APPLYING FOR FINANCIAL AID** *Required financial aid forms:* FAFSA, state aid form.

**CONTACT** Eileen F. Doyle, Assistant Vice President for Student Financial Services, The New School for Public Engagement, 65 Fifth Avenue, New York, NY 10003, 212-229-8930 or toll-free 800-292-3040. *Fax:* 212-229-5919. *E-mail:* sfs@newschool.edu. *Website:* http://www.newschool.edu/public-engagement/.

# NEWSCHOOL OF ARCHITECTURE AND DESIGN
## San Diego, CA

**CONTACT** Matt Wakeman, Director of Financial Aid, NewSchool of Architecture and Design, 1249 F Street, San Diego, CA 92101-6634, 619-235-4100 Ext. 103 or toll-free 800-490-7081. *Fax:* 619-235-4651. *Website:* http://www.newschoolarch.edu/.

# NEW WORLD SCHOOL OF THE ARTS
### Miami, FL

**CONTACT** Financial Aid Office, New World School of the Arts, 300 NE 2nd Avenue, Miami, FL 33132, 305-237-3135.
*Website:* http://www.mdc.edu/nwsa/.

# NEW YORK CITY COLLEGE OF TECHNOLOGY OF THE CITY UNIVERSITY OF NEW YORK
### Brooklyn, NY

**CONTACT** Sandra Higgins, Director of Financial Aid, New York City College of Technology of the City University of New York, 300 Jay Street, Namm Hall, Room G-13, Brooklyn, NY 11201, 718-260-5700. *Fax:* 718-254-8525. *E-mail:* financialaid@citytech.cuny.edu.
*Website:* http://www.citytech.cuny.edu/.

# NEW YORK COLLEGE OF HEALTH PROFESSIONS
### Syosset, NY

**CONTACT** Financial Aid Office, New York College of Health Professions, 6801 Jericho Turnpike, Syosset, NY 11791-4413, 516-364-0808 or toll-free 800-922-7337 Ext. 351.
*Website:* http://www.nycollege.edu/.

# NEW YORK FILM ACADEMY
### Los Angeles, CA

**CONTACT** Financial Aid Office, New York Film Academy, 3801 Barham Boulevard, Los Angeles, CA 90068, 818-733-2600.
*Website:* http://www.nyfa.com/.

# NEW YORK INSTITUTE OF TECHNOLOGY
### Old Westbury, NY

| Tuition & fees: $32,180 | Average undergraduate aid package: $19,693 |
|---|---|

**ABOUT THE INSTITUTION** Independent, coed. *Awards:* certificates, associate, bachelor's, master's, and doctoral degrees. 42 undergraduate majors. *Total enrollment:* 7,884. Undergraduates: 4,303. Freshmen: 712. Federal methodology is used as a basis for awarding need-based institutional aid.
**UNDERGRADUATE EXPENSES for 2015–2016** *Application fee:* $50. *Comprehensive fee:* $45,010 includes full-time tuition ($31,050), mandatory fees ($1130), and room and board ($12,830). *College room only:* $8280. Full-time tuition and fees vary according to program. Room and board charges vary according to location. *Part-time tuition:* $1050 per credit. *Part-time fees:* $470 per term. Part-time tuition and fees vary according to course load and program.
**FRESHMAN FINANCIAL AID (Fall 2014, est.)** 599 applied for aid; of those 88% were deemed to have need. 100% of freshmen with need received aid. *Average financial aid package:* $23,003 (excluding resources awarded to replace EFC). 15% of all full-time freshmen had no need and received non-need-based gift aid.
**UNDERGRADUATE FINANCIAL AID (Fall 2014, est.)** 2,763 applied for aid; of those 90% were deemed to have need. 100% of undergraduates with need received aid. *Average financial aid package:* $19,693 (excluding resources awarded to replace EFC). 14% of all full-time undergraduates had no need and received non-need-based gift aid.
**GIFT AID (NEED-BASED)** *Total amount:* $15,798,131 (42% federal, 26% state, 32% institutional). *Receiving aid:* Freshmen: 70% (474); all full-time undergraduates: 59% (2,107). *Average award:* Freshmen: $8107; Undergraduates: $7152. *Scholarships, grants, and awards:* Federal Pell, FSEOG, state, private, college/university gift aid from institutional funds.
**GIFT AID (NON-NEED-BASED)** *Total amount:* $30,141,436 (4% federal, 1% state, 92% institutional, 3% external sources). *Receiving aid:* Freshmen: 73% (495). Undergraduates: 54% (1,933). *Average award:* Freshmen: $14,178. Undergraduates: $11,493. *Scholarships, grants, and awards by category:* Academic interests/achievement: general academic interests/achievements. *Special characteristics:* children and siblings of alumni, children of faculty/staff, local/state students, previous college experience, veterans. *Tuition waivers:* Full or partial for employees or children of employees, senior citizens. *ROTC:* Army cooperative, Air Force cooperative.
**LOANS** *Student loans:* $18,944,625 (40% need-based, 60% non-need-based). *Average need-based loan:* Freshmen: $3322. Undergraduates: $4280. *Parent loans:* $12,460,887 (100% non-need-based). *Programs:* Federal Direct (Subsidized and Unsubsidized Stafford, PLUS), Perkins, alternative loans.
**WORK-STUDY** *Federal work-study:* Total amount: $653,563; jobs available. *State or other work-study/employment:* Total amount: $576,029 (100% non-need-based). Part-time jobs available.
**ATHLETIC AWARDS** Total amount: $2,908,182 (100% non-need-based).
**APPLYING FOR FINANCIAL AID** *Required financial aid form:* FAFSA. *Financial aid deadline (priority):* 3/1. *Notification date:* Continuous beginning 3/1. Students must reply within 4 weeks of notification.
**CONTACT** Ms. Doreen Meyer, Director of Financial Aid, New York Institute of Technology, PO Box 8000, Old Westbury, NY 11568-8000, 516-686-1083 or toll-free 800-345-NYIT. *Fax:* 516-686-7997. *E-mail:* dmeyer@nyit.edu.
*Website:* http://www.nyit.edu/.

# NEW YORK SCHOOL OF INTERIOR DESIGN
### New York, NY

| Tuition & fees: $30,790 | Average undergraduate aid package: $10,155 |
|---|---|

**ABOUT THE INSTITUTION** Independent, coed, primarily women. *Awards:* certificates, associate, bachelor's, and master's degrees. 1 undergraduate major. *Total enrollment:* 539. Undergraduates: 415. Freshmen: 21. Federal methodology is used as a basis for awarding need-based institutional aid.
**UNDERGRADUATE EXPENSES for 2015–2016** *Application fee:* $60. *Tuition:* full-time $30,195; part-time $915 per credit. Full-time tuition and fees vary according to course load. Part-time tuition and fees vary according to course load.
**FRESHMAN FINANCIAL AID (Fall 2013)** 11 applied for aid; of those 100% were deemed to have need. 100% of freshmen with need received aid. *Average percent of need met:* 33% (excluding resources awarded to replace EFC). *Average financial aid package:* $12,685 (excluding resources awarded to replace EFC). 15% of all full-time freshmen had no need and received non-need-based gift aid.
**UNDERGRADUATE FINANCIAL AID (Fall 2013)** 92 applied for aid; of those 95% were deemed to have need. 100% of undergraduates with need received aid; of those 3% had need fully met. *Average percent of need met:* 29% (excluding resources awarded to replace EFC). *Average financial aid package:* $10,155 (excluding resources awarded to replace EFC). 8% of all full-time undergraduates had no need and received non-need-based gift aid.
**GIFT AID (NEED-BASED)** *Total amount:* $767,839 (38% federal, 10% state, 48% institutional, 4% external sources). *Receiving aid:* Freshmen: 69% (9); all full-time undergraduates: 70% (69). *Average award:* Freshmen: $11,748; Undergraduates: $8332. *Scholarships, grants, and awards:* Federal Pell, FSEOG, state, private, college/university gift aid from institutional funds.
**GIFT AID (NON-NEED-BASED)** *Total amount:* $84,078 (3% state, 97% institutional). *Receiving aid:* Undergraduates: 2% (2). *Average award:* Freshmen: $13,000. Undergraduates: $8000. *Tuition waivers:* Full or partial for employees or children of employees.
**LOANS** *Student loans:* $1,458,236 (90% need-based, 10% non-need-based). 67% of past graduating class borrowed through all loan programs. *Average indebtedness*

per student: $33,146. **Average need-based loan:** Freshmen: $3500. Undergraduates: $3970. **Parent loans:** $643,891 (60% need-based, 40% non-need-based). **Programs:** Federal Direct (Subsidized and Unsubsidized Stafford, PLUS).
**WORK-STUDY** Federal work-study: 17 jobs averaging $2444.
**APPLYING FOR FINANCIAL AID** *Required financial aid forms:* FAFSA, state aid form. *Financial aid deadline (priority):* 8/1. *Notification date:* Continuous beginning 4/15. Students must reply within 2 weeks of notification.
**CONTACT** Mrs. Rashmi H. Wadhvani, Financial Aid Consultant, New York School of Interior Design, 170 East 70th Street, New York, NY 10021-5110, 212-472-1500 Ext. 204 or toll-free 800-336-9743 Ext. 204. *Fax:* 212-472-1867. *E-mail:* rwadhvani@nysid.edu.
*Website:* http://www.nysid.edu/.

# NEW YORK UNIVERSITY
## New York, NY

| Tuition & fees: $46,170 | Average undergraduate aid package: $29,271 |
|---|---|

**ABOUT THE INSTITUTION** Independent, coed. *Awards:* certificates, associate, bachelor's, master's, and doctoral degrees. 116 undergraduate majors. *Total enrollment:* 49,274. Undergraduates: 24,985. Freshmen: 5,913. Both federal and institutional methodology are used as a basis for awarding need-based institutional aid.
**UNDERGRADUATE EXPENSES** for 2015–2016 *Application fee:* $70. *Comprehensive fee:* $62,952 includes full-time tuition ($43,746), mandatory fees ($2424), and room and board ($16,782). *College room only:* $12,006. Full-time tuition and fees vary according to course load and program. Room and board charges vary according to board plan and housing facility. *Part-time tuition:* $1289 per credit hour. *Part-time fees:* $65 per credit; $461 per term. Part-time tuition and fees vary according to program. *Payment plan:* Tuition prepayment.
**FRESHMAN FINANCIAL AID (Fall 2013)** 3,687 applied for aid; of those 78% were deemed to have need. 97% of freshmen with need received aid; of those 11% had need fully met. *Average percent of need met:* 72% (excluding resources awarded to replace EFC). *Average financial aid package:* $33,980 (excluding resources awarded to replace EFC). 3% of all full-time freshmen had no need and received non-need-based gift aid.
**UNDERGRADUATE FINANCIAL AID (Fall 2013)** 14,469 applied for aid; of those 89% were deemed to have need. 95% of undergraduates with need received aid; of those 6% had need fully met. *Average percent of need met:* 58% (excluding resources awarded to replace EFC). *Average financial aid package:* $29,271 (excluding resources awarded to replace EFC). 5% of all full-time undergraduates had no need and received non-need-based gift aid.
**GIFT AID (NEED-BASED)** *Total amount:* $273,251,229 (9% federal, 4% state, 84% institutional, 3% external sources). *Receiving aid:* Freshmen: 46% (2,589); all full-time undergraduates: 49% (11,264). *Average award:* Freshmen: $31,488; Undergraduates: $24,246. *Scholarships, grants, and awards:* Federal Pell, FSEOG, state, private, college/university gift aid from institutional funds, Federal Nursing.
**GIFT AID (NON-NEED-BASED)** *Total amount:* $18,127,412 (1% federal, 1% state, 71% institutional, 27% external sources). *Receiving aid:* Freshmen: 14. Undergraduates: 53. *Average award:* Freshmen: $3692. Undergraduates: $7512. *Scholarships, grants, and awards by category: Academic interests/achievement:* general academic interests/achievements. *Creative arts/performance:* general creative arts/performance. *Tuition waivers:* Full or partial for employees or children of employees. *ROTC:* Army cooperative, Air Force cooperative.
**LOANS** *Student loans:* $108,622,146 (84% need-based, 16% non-need-based). 53% of past graduating class borrowed through all loan programs. *Average indebtedness per student:* $27,977. *Average need-based loan:* Freshmen: $5348. Undergraduates: $5788. *Parent loans:* $129,276,945 (63% need-based, 37% non-need-based). *Programs:* Federal Direct (Subsidized and Unsubsidized Stafford, PLUS), Perkins, Federal Nursing, college/university.
**WORK-STUDY** Federal work-study: jobs available.
**APPLYING FOR FINANCIAL AID** *Required financial aid forms:* FAFSA, CSS Financial Aid PROFILE, state aid form, noncustodial (divorced/separated) parent's statement. *Financial aid deadline:* 2/15. *Notification date:* 4/1. Students must reply by 5/1.

**CONTACT** Office of Financial Aid, New York University, 25 West Fourth Street, New York, NY 10012-1199, 212-998-4444. *Fax:* 212-995-4661. *E-mail:* financial.aid@nyu.edu.
*Website:* http://www.nyu.edu/.

# NIAGARA UNIVERSITY
## Niagara Falls, NY

| Tuition & fees: $29,060 | Average undergraduate aid package: $23,602 |
|---|---|

**ABOUT THE INSTITUTION** Independent Roman Catholic Church, coed. *Awards:* certificates, associate, bachelor's, master's, and doctoral degrees. 58 undergraduate majors. *Total enrollment:* 4,015. Undergraduates: 3,176. Freshmen: 618. Federal methodology is used as a basis for awarding need-based institutional aid.
**UNDERGRADUATE EXPENSES** for 2015–2016 *Comprehensive fee:* $41,010 includes full-time tuition ($27,700), mandatory fees ($1360), and room and board ($11,950). Room and board charges vary according to housing facility. *Part-time tuition:* $925 per credit hour.
**FRESHMAN FINANCIAL AID (Fall 2014, est.)** 562 applied for aid; of those 91% were deemed to have need. 99% of freshmen with need received aid; of those 51% had need fully met. *Average percent of need met:* 85% (excluding resources awarded to replace EFC). *Average financial aid package:* $25,245 (excluding resources awarded to replace EFC). 8% of all full-time freshmen had no need and received non-need-based gift aid.
**UNDERGRADUATE FINANCIAL AID (Fall 2014, est.)** 2,326 applied for aid; of those 92% were deemed to have need. 100% of undergraduates with need received aid; of those 51% had need fully met. *Average percent of need met:* 82% (excluding resources awarded to replace EFC). *Average financial aid package:* $23,602 (excluding resources awarded to replace EFC). 16% of all full-time undergraduates had no need and received non-need-based gift aid.
**GIFT AID (NEED-BASED)** *Total amount:* $42,154,659 (13% federal, 0% state, 78% institutional, 1% external sources). *Receiving aid:* Freshmen: 81% (502); all full-time undergraduates: 75% (2,116). *Average award:* Freshmen: $21,423; Undergraduates: $19,245. *Scholarships, grants, and awards:* Federal Pell, FSEOG, state, private, college/university gift aid from institutional funds.
**GIFT AID (NON-NEED-BASED)** *Total amount:* $6,639,227 (5% federal, 1% state, 93% institutional, 1% external sources). *Receiving aid:* Freshmen: 68% (419). Undergraduates: 58% (1,655). *Average award:* Freshmen: $14,448. Undergraduates: $13,104. *Scholarships, grants, and awards by category: Academic interests/achievement:* 2,589 awards ($31,414,363 total): general academic interests/achievements. *Creative arts/performance:* 67 awards ($344,483 total): theater/drama. *Special achievements/activities:* 11 awards ($55,000 total): community service. *Special characteristics:* 77 awards ($1,894,817 total): children of faculty/staff, relatives of clergy. *Tuition waivers:* Full or partial for employees or children of employees, senior citizens. *ROTC:* Army.
**LOANS** *Student loans:* $18,932,521 (95% need-based, 5% non-need-based). 72% of past graduating class borrowed through all loan programs. *Average indebtedness per student:* $30,289. *Average need-based loan:* Freshmen: $4460. Undergraduates: $4846. *Parent loans:* $4,592,524 (94% need-based, 6% non-need-based). *Programs:* Federal Direct (Subsidized and Unsubsidized Stafford, PLUS), Perkins, Federal Nursing, college/university.
**WORK-STUDY** Federal work-study: Total amount: $1,174,281; 408 jobs averaging $3096. *State or other work-study/employment:* Total amount: $273,358 (100% non-need-based). 61 part-time jobs averaging $4618.
**ATHLETIC AWARDS** Total amount: $4,011,930 (50% need-based, 50% non-need-based).
**APPLYING FOR FINANCIAL AID** *Required financial aid forms:* FAFSA, state aid form. *Financial aid deadline (priority):* 2/15. *Notification date:* Continuous beginning 3/15. Students must reply within 3 weeks of notification.
**CONTACT** Ms. Katie L. Kocsis, Director of Financial Aid, Niagara University, Niagara Falls, NY 14109, 716-286-8686 or toll-free 800-462-2111. *Fax:* 716-286-8678. *E-mail:* kkocsis@niagara.edu.
*Website:* http://www.niagara.edu/.

# NICHOLLS STATE UNIVERSITY
## Thibodaux, LA

| Tuition & fees (LA res): $7304 | Average undergraduate aid package: $8948 |
|---|---|

**ABOUT THE INSTITUTION** State-supported, coed. *Awards:* certificates, associate, bachelor's, and master's degrees. 37 undergraduate majors. *Total enrollment:* 6,298. Undergraduates: 5,695. Freshmen: 1,210. Federal methodology is used as a basis for awarding need-based institutional aid.

**UNDERGRADUATE EXPENSES** for 2015–2016 *Application fee:* $20. *Tuition, state resident:* full-time $4992. *Tuition, nonresident:* full-time $15,169. *Required fees:* full-time $2312. Full-time tuition and fees vary according to program. Part-time tuition and fees vary according to course load and program. *College room and board:* $8580; *Room only:* $5400. Room and board charges vary according to board plan, housing facility, and location.

**FRESHMAN FINANCIAL AID (Fall 2013)** 1,006 applied for aid; of those 67% were deemed to have need. 99% of freshmen with need received aid; of those 25% had need fully met. *Average percent of need met:* 65% (excluding resources awarded to replace EFC). *Average financial aid package:* $9919 (excluding resources awarded to replace EFC). 10% of all full-time freshmen had no need and received non-need-based gift aid.

**UNDERGRADUATE FINANCIAL AID (Fall 2013)** 4,119 applied for aid; of those 73% were deemed to have need. 99% of undergraduates with need received aid; of those 19% had need fully met. *Average percent of need met:* 59% (excluding resources awarded to replace EFC). *Average financial aid package:* $8948 (excluding resources awarded to replace EFC). 8% of all full-time undergraduates had no need and received non-need-based gift aid.

**GIFT AID (NEED-BASED)** *Total amount:* $18,814,660 (52% federal, 31% state, 10% institutional, 7% external sources). *Receiving aid:* Freshmen: 60% (638); all full-time undergraduates: 56% (2,634). *Average award:* Freshmen: $7751; Undergraduates: $6852. *Scholarships, grants, and awards:* Federal Pell, FSEOG, state, private, college/university gift aid from institutional funds.

**GIFT AID (NON-NEED-BASED)** *Total amount:* $6,963,411 (3% federal, 66% state, 24% institutional, 7% external sources). *Receiving aid:* Freshmen: 10% (101). Undergraduates: 7% (331). *Average award:* Freshmen: $3934. Undergraduates: $3824. *Scholarships, grants, and awards by category: Academic interests/achievement:* general academic interests/achievements. *Creative arts/performance:* dance, music. *Special achievements/activities:* cheerleading/drum major, leadership. *Special characteristics:* children of faculty/staff, general special characteristics, local/state students, members of minority groups, out-of-state students, previous college experience, public servants, veterans. *Tuition waivers:* Full or partial for employees or children of employees.

**LOANS** *Student loans:* $14,901,452 (71% need-based, 29% non-need-based). 47% of past graduating class borrowed through all loan programs. *Average indebtedness per student:* $24,250. *Average need-based loan:* Freshmen: $2550. Undergraduates: $3120. *Parent loans:* $1,066,754 (42% need-based, 58% non-need-based). *Programs:* Federal Direct (Subsidized and Unsubsidized Stafford, PLUS).

**WORK-STUDY** *Federal work-study:* jobs available. *State or other work-study/employment:* Total amount: $324,110 (60% need-based, 40% non-need-based). Part-time jobs available.

**ATHLETIC AWARDS** Total amount: $1,928,575 (50% need-based, 50% non-need-based).

**APPLYING FOR FINANCIAL AID** *Required financial aid forms:* FAFSA, institution's own form, state aid form, noncustodial (divorced/separated) parent's statement. *Financial aid deadline:* 6/30 (priority: 4/15). *Notification date:* Continuous.

**CONTACT** Casie Triche, Director of Financial Aid, Nicholls State University, PO Box 2005, Thibodaux, LA 70310, 985-448-4077 or toll-free 877-NICHOLLS. *Fax:* 985-448-4124. *E-mail:* finaid@nicholls.edu.
*Website:* http://www.nicholls.edu/.

# NICHOLS COLLEGE
## Dudley, MA

| Tuition & fees: $33,300 | Average undergraduate aid package: $25,024 |
|---|---|

**ABOUT THE INSTITUTION** Independent, coed. *Awards:* certificates, associate, bachelor's, and master's degrees. 18 undergraduate majors. *Total enrollment:* 1,695. Undergraduates: 1,330. Freshmen: 400. Federal methodology is used as a basis for awarding need-based institutional aid.

**UNDERGRADUATE EXPENSES** for 2015–2016 *Comprehensive fee:* $45,900 includes full-time tuition ($33,000), mandatory fees ($300), and room and board ($12,600). *College room only:* $7000. Room and board charges vary according to board plan, housing facility, and student level. *Part-time tuition:* $1100 per credit. *Part-time fees:* $150 per term.

**FRESHMAN FINANCIAL AID (Fall 2013)** 351 applied for aid; of those 91% were deemed to have need. 100% of freshmen with need received aid; of those 18% had need fully met. *Average percent of need met:* 74% (excluding resources awarded to replace EFC). *Average financial aid package:* $24,218 (excluding resources awarded to replace EFC). 9% of all full-time freshmen had no need and received non-need-based gift aid.

**UNDERGRADUATE FINANCIAL AID (Fall 2013)** 970 applied for aid; of those 93% were deemed to have need. 100% of undergraduates with need received aid; of those 17% had need fully met. *Average percent of need met:* 75% (excluding resources awarded to replace EFC). *Average financial aid package:* $25,024 (excluding resources awarded to replace EFC). 7% of all full-time undergraduates had no need and received non-need-based gift aid.

**GIFT AID (NEED-BASED)** *Total amount:* $17,734,000 (10% federal, 2% state, 86% institutional, 2% external sources). *Receiving aid:* Freshmen: 85% (318); all full-time undergraduates: 86% (898). *Average award:* Freshmen: $18,830; Undergraduates: $17,573. *Scholarships, grants, and awards:* Federal Pell, FSEOG, state, private, college/university gift aid from institutional funds.

**GIFT AID (NON-NEED-BASED)** *Total amount:* $915,850 (100% institutional). *Receiving aid:* Freshmen: 4% (15). Undergraduates: 2% (17). *Average award:* Freshmen: $15,093. Undergraduates: $14,120. *Scholarships, grants, and awards by category: Academic interests/achievement:* general academic interests/achievements. *Special achievements/activities:* community service, general special achievements/activities, leadership. *Special characteristics:* children and siblings of alumni, children of faculty/staff, siblings of current students. *Tuition waivers:* Full or partial for employees or children of employees. *ROTC:* Army cooperative, Air Force cooperative.

**LOANS** *Student loans:* $9,711,809 (95% need-based, 5% non-need-based). 82% of past graduating class borrowed through all loan programs. *Average indebtedness per student:* $32,747. *Average need-based loan:* Freshmen: $3195. Undergraduates: $4088. *Parent loans:* $3,938,240 (92% need-based, 8% non-need-based). *Programs:* Federal Direct (Subsidized and Unsubsidized Stafford, PLUS).

**WORK-STUDY** *Federal work-study:* 449 jobs averaging $1640.

**APPLYING FOR FINANCIAL AID** *Required financial aid form:* FAFSA. *Financial aid deadline (priority):* 3/1. *Notification date:* Continuous beginning 2/28. Students must reply within 2 weeks of notification.

**CONTACT** Ms. Denise Brindle, Director of Financial Assistance, Nichols College, PO Box 5000, Dudley, MA 01571, 508-213-2372 or toll-free 800-470-3379. *Fax:* 508-213-2118. *E-mail:* denise.brindle@nichols.edu.
*Website:* http://www.nichols.edu/.

# NORFOLK STATE UNIVERSITY
## Norfolk, VA

**CONTACT** Mr. Kevin Burns, Director of Financial Aid, Norfolk State University, 700 Park Avenue, Norfolk, VA 23504-3907, 757-823-8381 or toll-free 800-274-1821. *Fax:* 757-823-9059. *E-mail:* kburns@nsu.edu.
*Website:* http://www.nsu.edu/.

# NORTH AMERICAN UNIVERSITY
## Houston, TX

**CONTACT** Financial Aid Office, North American University, 3203 North Sam Houston Parkway W, Houston, TX 77038, 832-230-5555.
*Website:* http://www.na.edu/.

# NORTH CAROLINA AGRICULTURAL AND TECHNICAL STATE UNIVERSITY
## Greensboro, NC

| Tuition & fees (NC res): $5535 | Average undergraduate aid package: $14,160 |
|---|---|

**ABOUT THE INSTITUTION** State-supported, coed. **Awards:** bachelor's, master's, and doctoral degrees. 92 undergraduate majors. **Total enrollment:** 10,725. Undergraduates: 9,203. Freshmen: 1,722. Both federal and institutional methodology are used as a basis for awarding need-based institutional aid.

**UNDERGRADUATE EXPENSES for 2015–2016 Application fee:** $55. **Tuition, state resident:** full-time $3270. **Tuition, nonresident:** full-time $16,030. **Required fees:** full-time $2265. Full-time tuition and fees vary according to course load, degree level, and program. Part-time tuition and fees vary according to course load, degree level, and program. **College room and board:** $6755; **Room only:** $6755. Room and board charges vary according to board plan and housing facility.

**FRESHMAN FINANCIAL AID (Fall 2013)** 1,750 applied for aid; of those 90% were deemed to have need. 99% of freshmen with need received aid; of those 14% had need fully met. **Average percent of need met:** 83% (excluding resources awarded to replace EFC). **Average financial aid package:** $14,536 (excluding resources awarded to replace EFC). 2% of all full-time freshmen had no need and received non-need-based gift aid.

**UNDERGRADUATE FINANCIAL AID (Fall 2013)** 7,741 applied for aid; of those 91% were deemed to have need. 98% of undergraduates with need received aid; of those 13% had need fully met. **Average percent of need met:** 79% (excluding resources awarded to replace EFC). **Average financial aid package:** $14,160 (excluding resources awarded to replace EFC). 3% of all full-time undergraduates had no need and received non-need-based gift aid.

**GIFT AID (NEED-BASED) Total amount:** $47,326,582 (52% federal, 37% state, 7% institutional, 4% external sources). **Receiving aid:** Freshmen: 67% (1,190); all full-time undergraduates: 64% (5,213). **Average award:** Freshmen: $5377; Undergraduates: $5124. **Scholarships, grants, and awards:** Federal Pell, FSEOG, state, private, college/university gift aid from institutional funds.

**GIFT AID (NON-NEED-BASED) Total amount:** $3,076,149 (17% state, 48% institutional, 35% external sources). **Receiving aid:** Freshmen: 82% (1,460). Undergraduates: 71% (5,757). **Average award:** Freshmen: $5107. Undergraduates: $7013. **Scholarships, grants, and awards by category:** *Academic interests/achievement:* agriculture, business, engineering/technologies, general academic interests/achievements. *Creative arts/performance:* music. **ROTC:** Army, Air Force.

**LOANS Student loans:** $59,375,660 (91% need-based, 9% non-need-based). 76% of past graduating class borrowed through all loan programs. *Average indebtedness per student:* $26,265. **Average need-based loan:** Freshmen: $3361. Undergraduates: $4110. **Parent loans:** $4,663,164 (85% need-based, 15% non-need-based). **Programs:** Federal Direct (Subsidized and Unsubsidized Stafford, PLUS), Perkins.

**WORK-STUDY Federal work-study:** jobs available.

**ATHLETIC AWARDS** Total amount: $2,456,507 (77% need-based, 23% non-need-based).

**APPLYING FOR FINANCIAL AID Required financial aid form:** FAFSA. **Financial aid deadline (priority):** 3/1. **Notification date:** 4/15. Students must reply within 2 weeks of notification.

**CONTACT** Mrs. Sherri Avent, Director of Student Financial Aid, North Carolina Agricultural and Technical State University, Dowdy Administration Building, Room 100, 1601 East Market Street, Greensboro, NC 27411, 336-334-7973 or toll-free 800-443-8964 (in-state). *Fax:* 336-334-7954. *E-mail:* avent@ncat.edu.
*Website:* http://www.ncat.edu/.

# NORTH CAROLINA CENTRAL UNIVERSITY
## Durham, NC

| Tuition & fees (NC res): $5525 | Average undergraduate aid package: $11,764 |
|---|---|

**ABOUT THE INSTITUTION** State-supported, coed. **Awards:** bachelor's, master's, and doctoral degrees. 30 undergraduate majors. **Total enrollment:** 7,687. Undergraduates: 5,917. Freshmen: 925. Federal methodology is used as a basis for awarding need-based institutional aid.

**UNDERGRADUATE EXPENSES for 2015–2016 Application fee:** $40. **Tuition, state resident:** full-time $3455. **Tuition, nonresident:** full-time $14,870. **Required fees:** full-time $2070. Part-time tuition and fees vary according to course load. **College room and board:** $8165; **Room only:** $4663. Room and board charges vary according to board plan, housing facility, and location.

**FRESHMAN FINANCIAL AID (Fall 2013)** 942 applied for aid; of those 92% were deemed to have need. 100% of freshmen with need received aid; of those 6% had need fully met. **Average percent of need met:** 60% (excluding resources awarded to replace EFC). **Average financial aid package:** $11,804 (excluding resources awarded to replace EFC). 2% of all full-time freshmen had no need and received non-need-based gift aid.

**UNDERGRADUATE FINANCIAL AID (Fall 2013)** 4,841 applied for aid; of those 94% were deemed to have need. 100% of undergraduates with need received aid; of those 5% had need fully met. **Average percent of need met:** 59% (excluding resources awarded to replace EFC). **Average financial aid package:** $11,764 (excluding resources awarded to replace EFC). 1% of all full-time undergraduates had no need and received non-need-based gift aid.

**GIFT AID (NEED-BASED) Total amount:** $37,941,028 (51% federal, 22% state, 22% institutional, 5% external sources). **Receiving aid:** Freshmen: 75% (726); all full-time undergraduates: 77% (3,820). **Average award:** Freshmen: $8021; Undergraduates: $7727. **Scholarships, grants, and awards:** Federal Pell, FSEOG, state, private, college/university gift aid from institutional funds, Federal Nursing.

**GIFT AID (NON-NEED-BASED) Total amount:** $673,953 (1% state, 78% institutional, 21% external sources). **Receiving aid:** Freshmen: 24% (227). Undergraduates: 17% (868). **Average award:** Freshmen: $15,499. Undergraduates: $12,299. **Scholarships, grants, and awards by category:** *Academic interests/achievement:* biological sciences, business, computer science, education, English, general academic interests/achievements, library science, physical sciences, social sciences. *Creative arts/performance:* art/fine arts, music, theater/drama. *Special achievements/activities:* leadership. *Special characteristics:* children and siblings of alumni, general special characteristics. **Tuition waivers:** Full or partial for employees or children of employees. **ROTC:** Army, Air Force.

**LOANS Student loans:** $39,873,449 (98% need-based, 2% non-need-based). 96% of past graduating class borrowed through all loan programs. *Average indebtedness per student:* $31,747. **Average need-based loan:** Freshmen: $6605. Undergraduates: $4132. **Parent loans:** $6,423,217 (100% need-based). **Programs:** Federal Direct (Subsidized and Unsubsidized Stafford, PLUS), Perkins, Federal Nursing.

**WORK-STUDY Federal work-study:** jobs available. **State or other work-study/employment:** Total amount: $487,721 (83% need-based, 17% non-need-based). Part-time jobs available.

**ATHLETIC AWARDS** Total amount: $99,632 (100% need-based).

**APPLYING FOR FINANCIAL AID Required financial aid form:** FAFSA. **Financial aid deadline (priority):** 3/1. **Notification date:** Continuous.

**CONTACT** Mrs. Sharon J. Oliver, Director of Financial Aid, North Carolina Central University, 106 Student Services Building, Durham, NC 27707-3129, 919-530-5313 or toll-free 877-667-7533. *Fax:* 919-530-7959. *E-mail:* soliver@nccu.edu.
*Website:* http://www.nccu.edu/.

# NORTH CAROLINA STATE UNIVERSITY
## Raleigh, NC

| Tuition & fees (NC res): $8296 | Average undergraduate aid package: $13,174 |
|---|---|

**ABOUT THE INSTITUTION** State-supported, coed. *Awards:* certificates, associate, bachelor's, master's, and doctoral degrees. 101 undergraduate majors. *Total enrollment:* 33,989. Undergraduates: 24,473. Freshmen: 4,499. Federal methodology is used as a basis for awarding need-based institutional aid.

**UNDERGRADUATE EXPENSES for 2015–2016 Application fee:** $75. *Tuition, state resident:* full-time $6038. *Tuition, nonresident:* full-time $21,293. *Required fees:* full-time $2258. Full-time tuition and fees vary according to degree level, location, program, and reciprocity agreements. Part-time tuition and fees vary according to course load, degree level, location, program, and reciprocity agreements. *College room and board:* $10,030; *Room only:* $6244. Room and board charges vary according to board plan and housing facility.

**FRESHMAN FINANCIAL AID (Fall 2014, est.)** 3,401 applied for aid; of those 65% were deemed to have need. 98% of freshmen with need received aid; of those 26% had need fully met. *Average percent of need met:* 81% (excluding resources awarded to replace EFC). *Average financial aid package:* $13,773 (excluding resources awarded to replace EFC). 4% of all full-time freshmen had no need and received non-need-based gift aid.

**UNDERGRADUATE FINANCIAL AID (Fall 2014, est.)** 14,123 applied for aid; of those 75% were deemed to have need. 97% of undergraduates with need received aid; of those 23% had need fully met. *Average percent of need met:* 78% (excluding resources awarded to replace EFC). *Average financial aid package:* $13,174 (excluding resources awarded to replace EFC). 4% of all full-time undergraduates had no need and received non-need-based gift aid.

**GIFT AID (NEED-BASED) Total amount:** $98,837,477 (22% federal, 19% state, 55% institutional, 4% external sources). *Receiving aid:* Freshmen: 48% (2,077); all full-time undergraduates: 46% (9,653). *Average award:* Freshmen: $10,673; Undergraduates: $10,015. *Scholarships, grants, and awards:* Federal Pell, FSEOG, state, private, college/university gift aid from institutional funds, United Negro College Fund.

**GIFT AID (NON-NEED-BASED) Total amount:** $13,894,155 (4% state, 61% institutional, 35% external sources). *Receiving aid:* Freshmen: 9% (408). Undergraduates: 5% (1,148). *Average award:* Freshmen: $7718. Undergraduates: $6531. *Scholarships, grants, and awards by category: Academic interests/achievement:* agriculture, biological sciences, business, education, engineering/technologies, general academic interests/achievements, humanities, mathematics, military science, physical sciences, social sciences. *Special achievements/activities:* leadership. *Special characteristics:* children and siblings of alumni, local/state students. *Tuition waivers:* Full or partial for employees or children of employees. *ROTC:* Army, Naval, Air Force.

**LOANS Student loans:** $68,418,077 (66% need-based, 34% non-need-based). 57% of past graduating class borrowed through all loan programs. *Average indebtedness per student:* $20,482. *Average need-based loan:* Freshmen: $3368. Undergraduates: $4089. *Parent loans:* $11,470,567 (12% need-based, 88% non-need-based). *Programs:* Federal Direct (Subsidized and Unsubsidized Stafford, PLUS), Perkins, state, college/university.

**WORK-STUDY Federal work-study:** Total amount: $2,049,707; jobs available. *State or other work-study/employment:* Total amount: $2,323,755 (36% need-based, 64% non-need-based). Part-time jobs available.

**ATHLETIC AWARDS Total amount:** $7,448,057 (35% need-based, 65% non-need-based).

**APPLYING FOR FINANCIAL AID Required financial aid form:** FAFSA. *Financial aid deadline (priority):* 3/1. *Notification date:* Continuous beginning 4/1.

**CONTACT** Ms. Krista Ringler Domnick, Director of Scholarships and Financial Aid, North Carolina State University, 2016 Harris Hall, Box 7302, Raleigh, NC 27695-7302, 919-515-2866. *Fax:* 919-515-8422. *E-mail:* krista_domnick@ncsu.edu. *Website:* http://www.ncsu.edu/.

# NORTH CAROLINA WESLEYAN COLLEGE
## Rocky Mount, NC

**CONTACT** Leah Hill, Director of Financial Aid, North Carolina Wesleyan College, 3400 North Wesleyan Boulevard, Rocky Mount, NC 27804, 252-985-5200 or toll-free 800-488-6292. *Fax:* 252-985-5295. *E-mail:* lhill@ncwc.edu. *Website:* http://www.ncwc.edu/.

# NORTH CENTRAL COLLEGE
## Naperville, IL

| Tuition & fees: $34,230 | Average undergraduate aid package: $23,538 |
|---|---|

**ABOUT THE INSTITUTION** Independent United Methodist, coed. *Awards:* certificates, bachelor's, and master's degrees. 69 undergraduate majors. *Total enrollment:* 3,043. Undergraduates: 2,782. Freshmen: 576. Federal methodology is used as a basis for awarding need-based institutional aid.

**UNDERGRADUATE EXPENSES for 2015–2016 Application fee:** $25. *Comprehensive fee:* $44,025 includes full-time tuition ($34,050), mandatory fees ($180), and room and board ($9795). *College room only:* $6795. Room and board charges vary according to housing facility. *Part-time tuition:* $825 per credit hour. *Part-time fees:* $20 per term. Part-time tuition and fees vary according to course load.

**FRESHMAN FINANCIAL AID (Fall 2014, est.)** 537 applied for aid; of those 87% were deemed to have need. 100% of freshmen with need received aid; of those 24% had need fully met. *Average percent of need met:* 81% (excluding resources awarded to replace EFC). *Average financial aid package:* $26,156 (excluding resources awarded to replace EFC). 18% of all full-time freshmen had no need and received non-need-based gift aid.

**UNDERGRADUATE FINANCIAL AID (Fall 2014, est.)** 2,254 applied for aid; of those 89% were deemed to have need. 100% of undergraduates with need received aid; of those 20% had need fully met. *Average percent of need met:* 74% (excluding resources awarded to replace EFC). *Average financial aid package:* $23,538 (excluding resources awarded to replace EFC). 20% of all full-time undergraduates had no need and received non-need-based gift aid.

**GIFT AID (NEED-BASED) Total amount:** $37,518,583 (8% federal, 9% state, 81% institutional, 2% external sources). *Receiving aid:* Freshmen: 81% (469); all full-time undergraduates: 78% (2,009). *Average award:* Freshmen: $22,105; Undergraduates: $18,416. *Scholarships, grants, and awards:* Federal Pell, FSEOG, state, private, college/university gift aid from institutional funds.

**GIFT AID (NON-NEED-BASED) Total amount:** $9,564,256 (96% institutional, 4% external sources). *Receiving aid:* Freshmen: 13% (77). Undergraduates: 10% (264). *Average award:* Freshmen: $16,169. Undergraduates: $13,770. *Scholarships, grants, and awards by category: Academic interests/achievement:* biological sciences, business, communication, computer science, education, English, foreign languages, general academic interests/achievements, humanities, international studies, mathematics, physical sciences, premedicine, religion/biblical studies, social sciences. *Creative arts/performance:* art/fine arts, cinema/film/broadcasting, debating, journalism/publications, music, theater/drama. *Special achievements/activities:* community service, religious involvement. *Special characteristics:* adult students, children of faculty/staff, general special characteristics, international students, relatives of clergy. *Tuition waivers:* Full or partial for employees or children of employees, senior citizens. *ROTC:* Army cooperative, Air Force cooperative.

**LOANS Student loans:** $19,928,554 (68% need-based, 32% non-need-based). 86% of past graduating class borrowed through all loan programs. *Average indebtedness per student:* $32,086. *Average need-based loan:* Freshmen: $3338. Undergraduates: $4534. *Parent loans:* $5,861,499 (36% need-based, 64% non-need-based). *Programs:* Federal Direct (Subsidized and Unsubsidized Stafford, PLUS), Perkins, state, college/university.

**WORK-STUDY Federal work-study:** Total amount: $299,684; 1,397 jobs averaging $215. *State or other work-study/employment:* Total amount: $542,070 (43% need-based, 57% non-need-based). 54 part-time jobs averaging $10,038.

**APPLYING FOR FINANCIAL AID Required financial aid forms:** FAFSA, institution's own form, federal income tax form(s). *Financial aid deadline:* Continuous. *Notification date:* Continuous beginning 3/1. Students must reply within 4 weeks of notification.

**CONTACT** Martin R. Sauer, Vice President for Enrollment Management, North Central College, 30 North Brainard Street, Naperville, IL 60540, 630-637-5801 or toll-free 800-411-1861. *Fax:* 630-637-5608. *E-mail:* mrsauer@noctrl.edu. *Website:* http://www.northcentralcollege.edu/.

# NORTH CENTRAL UNIVERSITY
## Minneapolis, MN

**CONTACT** Mrs. Donna Jager, Director of Financial Aid, North Central University, 910 Elliot Avenue, Minneapolis, MN 55404-1322, 612-343-4485 or toll-free 800-289-6222. *Fax:* 612-343-8067. *E-mail:* finaid@northcentral.edu. *Website:* http://www.northcentral.edu/.

# NORTH DAKOTA STATE UNIVERSITY
## Fargo, ND

**CONTACT** Jeanne Enebo, Director of Financial Aid, North Dakota State University, PO Box 5315, Fargo, ND 58105, 701-231-7537 or toll-free 800-488-NDSU. *Fax:* 701-231-6126. *E-mail:* j.enebo@ndsu.edu. *Website:* http://www.ndsu.edu/.

# NORTHEAST CATHOLIC COLLEGE
## Warner, NH

**ABOUT THE INSTITUTION** Independent Roman Catholic, coed. 1 undergraduate major.
**GIFT AID (NEED-BASED)** *Scholarships, grants, and awards:* private, college/university gift aid from institutional funds.
**GIFT AID (NON-NEED-BASED)** *Scholarships, grants, and awards by category: Academic interests/achievement:* English, general academic interests/achievements, humanities, religion/biblical studies.
**LOANS** *Programs:* alternative loans.
**APPLYING FOR FINANCIAL AID** *Required financial aid forms:* institution's own form, business/farm supplement, federal income tax form(s).
**CONTACT** Marie A. Lasher, Financial Aid Director, Northeast Catholic College, 511 Kearsarge Mountain Road, Warner, NH 03278, 603-456-2656 Ext. 136 or toll-free 877-498-1723. *Fax:* 603-456-2660. *E-mail:* mlasher@northeastcatholic.edu. *Website:* http://www.magdalen.edu/.

# NORTHEASTERN ILLINOIS UNIVERSITY
## Chicago, IL

| Tuition & fees (IL res): $8612 | Average undergraduate aid package: $8284 |
|---|---|

**ABOUT THE INSTITUTION** State-supported, coed. *Awards:* bachelor's and master's degrees. 44 undergraduate majors. *Total enrollment:* 10,813. Undergraduates: 8,943. Freshmen: 805. Federal methodology is used as a basis for awarding need-based institutional aid.
**UNDERGRADUATE EXPENSES** for 2015–2016 *Application fee:* $30. *One-time required fee:* $10. *Tuition, state resident:* full-time $7296; part-time $304 per credit hour. *Tuition, nonresident:* full-time $14,592; part-time $608 per credit hour. *Required fees:* full-time $1316; $54.60 per credit hour or $3 per term. Full-time tuition and fees vary according to course load and degree level. Part-time tuition and fees vary according to course load and degree level. *Payment plan:* Guaranteed tuition.
**FRESHMAN FINANCIAL AID (Fall 2014, est.)** 646 applied for aid; of those 81% were deemed to have need. 91% of freshmen with need received aid; of those 2% had need fully met. *Average percent of need met:* 20% (excluding resources awarded to replace EFC). *Average financial aid package:* $8375 (excluding resources

awarded to replace EFC). 3% of all full-time freshmen had no need and received non-need-based gift aid.
**UNDERGRADUATE FINANCIAL AID (Fall 2014, est.)** 3,825 applied for aid; of those 88% were deemed to have need. 90% of undergraduates with need received aid; of those 4% had need fully met. *Average percent of need met:* 18% (excluding resources awarded to replace EFC). *Average financial aid package:* $8284 (excluding resources awarded to replace EFC). 2% of all full-time undergraduates had no need and received non-need-based gift aid.
**GIFT AID (NEED-BASED)** *Total amount:* $29,622,904 (68% federal, 28% state, 3% institutional, 1% external sources). *Receiving aid:* Freshmen: 64% (467); all full-time undergraduates: 57% (2,644). *Average award:* Freshmen: $7871; Undergraduates: $6730. *Scholarships, grants, and awards:* Federal Pell, FSEOG, state, private, college/university gift aid from institutional funds.
**GIFT AID (NON-NEED-BASED)** *Total amount:* $1,351,850 (64% state, 11% institutional, 25% external sources). *Receiving aid:* Freshmen: 6% (40). Undergraduates: 11% (518). *Average award:* Freshmen: $1636. Undergraduates: $1956. *Scholarships, grants, and awards by category: Academic interests/achievement:* biological sciences, business, communication, computer science, education, English, foreign languages, general academic interests/achievements, mathematics, physical sciences, social sciences. *Creative arts/performance:* art/fine arts, creative writing, dance, journalism/publications, music, performing arts, theater/drama. *Special achievements/activities:* general special achievements/activities, leadership. *Special characteristics:* adult students, children of faculty/staff, general special characteristics. *Tuition waivers:* Full or partial for employees or children of employees, senior citizens. *ROTC:* Army cooperative, Air Force cooperative.
**LOANS** *Student loans:* $18,553,419 (47% need-based, 53% non-need-based). 18% of past graduating class borrowed through all loan programs. *Average indebtedness per student:* $13,366. *Average need-based loan:* Freshmen: $2974. Undergraduates: $4278. *Parent loans:* $332,348 (100% non-need-based). *Programs:* Federal Direct (Subsidized and Unsubsidized Stafford, PLUS), Perkins.
**WORK-STUDY** *Federal work-study:* Total amount: $348,872; jobs available. *State or other work-study/employment:* Total amount: $278,925 (100% non-need-based). Part-time jobs available.
**APPLYING FOR FINANCIAL AID** *Required financial aid form:* FAFSA. *Financial aid deadline (priority):* 2/15. *Notification date:* Continuous beginning 3/15. Students must reply within 2 weeks of notification.
**CONTACT** Maureen T. Amos, Director, Office of Financial Aid, Northeastern Illinois University, 5500 North St. Louis Avenue, Chicago, IL 60625, 773-442-5010. *Fax:* 773-442-5040. *E-mail:* financial-aid@neiu.edu. *Website:* http://www.neiu.edu/.

# NORTHEASTERN STATE UNIVERSITY
## Tahlequah, OK

| Tuition & fees (OK res): $5284 | Average undergraduate aid package: $12,446 |
|---|---|

**ABOUT THE INSTITUTION** State-supported, coed. *Awards:* certificates, bachelor's, master's, and doctoral degrees. 58 undergraduate majors. *Total enrollment:* 8,332. Undergraduates: 7,117. Freshmen: 918. Federal methodology is used as a basis for awarding need-based institutional aid.
**UNDERGRADUATE EXPENSES** for 2015–2016 *Application fee:* $25. *Tuition, state resident:* full-time $4162; part-time $138.75 per credit hour. *Tuition, nonresident:* full-time $11,512; part-time $383.75 per credit hour. *Required fees:* full-time $1122; $37.40 per credit hour. Full-time tuition and fees vary according to course load and program. Part-time tuition and fees vary according to course load and program. *College room and board:* $6300; *Room only:* $2700. Room and board charges vary according to board plan and housing facility. *Payment plan:* Guaranteed tuition.
**FRESHMAN FINANCIAL AID (Fall 2014, est.)** 822 applied for aid; of those 71% were deemed to have need. 100% of freshmen with need received aid; of those 90% had need fully met. *Average percent of need met:* 99% (excluding resources awarded to replace EFC). *Average financial aid package:* $10,560 (excluding resources awarded to replace EFC). 8% of all full-time freshmen had no need and received non-need-based gift aid.
**UNDERGRADUATE FINANCIAL AID (Fall 2014, est.)** 4,362 applied for aid; of those 80% were deemed to have need. 99% of undergraduates with need received aid; of those 69% had need fully met. *Average percent of need met:* 95% (excluding

resources awarded to replace EFC). *Average financial aid package:* $12,446 (excluding resources awarded to replace EFC). 4% of all full-time undergraduates had no need and received non-need-based gift aid.

**GIFT AID (NEED-BASED)** *Total amount:* $22,342,099 (71% federal, 22% state, 1% institutional, 6% external sources). *Receiving aid:* Freshmen: 60% (533); all full-time undergraduates: 60% (3,051). *Average award:* Freshmen: $6856; Undergraduates: $6605. *Scholarships, grants, and awards:* Federal Pell, FSEOG, state, private, college/university gift aid from institutional funds.

**GIFT AID (NON-NEED-BASED)** *Total amount:* $1,985,408 (1% federal, 4% state, 33% institutional, 62% external sources). *Receiving aid:* Freshmen: 20% (177). Undergraduates: 10% (515). *Average award:* Freshmen: $2902. Undergraduates: $2862. *Scholarships, grants, and awards by category: Academic interests/ achievement:* biological sciences, business, communication, computer science, education, English, foreign languages, general academic interests/achievements, health fields, home economics, humanities, library science, mathematics, physical sciences, premedicine, social sciences. *Creative arts/performance:* applied art and design, art/ fine arts, dance, debating, journalism/publications, music, performing arts, theater/ drama. *Special achievements/activities:* cheerleading/drum major, community service, junior miss, leadership. *Special characteristics:* children and siblings of alumni, children of faculty/staff, children with a deceased or disabled parent, local/state students, members of minority groups, out-of-state students, religious affiliation, spouses of deceased or disabled public servants. *Tuition waivers:* Full or partial for employees or children of employees. **ROTC:** Army.

**LOANS** *Student loans:* $35,640,487 (77% need-based, 23% non-need-based). 67% of past graduating class borrowed through all loan programs. *Average indebtedness per student:* $24,431. *Average need-based loan:* Freshmen: $4905. Undergraduates: $7156. *Parent loans:* $7,859,858 (20% need-based, 80% non-need-based). *Programs:* Federal Direct (Subsidized and Unsubsidized Stafford, PLUS), Perkins.

**WORK-STUDY** *Federal work-study:* Total amount: $300,000; 230 jobs averaging $1350. *State or other work-study/employment:* Total amount: $1,300,000 (100% need-based). 733 part-time jobs averaging $2144.

**ATHLETIC AWARDS** Total amount: $1,050,306 (11% need-based, 89% non-need-based).

**APPLYING FOR FINANCIAL AID** *Required financial aid form:* FAFSA. *Financial aid deadline (priority):* 3/1. *Notification date:* Continuous beginning 3/1.

**CONTACT** Dr. Teri Cochran, Director of Student Financial Services, Northeastern State University, 715 North Grand Avenue, Tahlequah, OK 74464-2399, 918-444-3410 or toll-free 800-722-9614. *Fax:* 918-458-2510. *E-mail:* cochrant@nsuok.edu. *Website:* http://www.nsuok.edu/.

# NORTHEASTERN UNIVERSITY
## Boston, MA

| Tuition & fees: $43,440 | Average undergraduate aid package: $26,669 |
|---|---|

**ABOUT THE INSTITUTION** Independent, coed. *Awards:* certificates, bachelor's, master's, and doctoral degrees. 65 undergraduate majors. *Total enrollment:* 24,255. Undergraduates: 17,445. Freshmen: 2,944. Institutional methodology is used as a basis for awarding need-based institutional aid.

**UNDERGRADUATE EXPENSES** for 2015–2016 *Application fee:* $75. *Comprehensive fee:* $58,010 includes full-time tuition ($42,534), mandatory fees ($906), and room and board ($14,570). *College room only:* $7780. Room and board charges vary according to board plan and housing facility.

**FRESHMAN FINANCIAL AID (Fall 2014, est.)** 1,960 applied for aid; of those 65% were deemed to have need. 99% of freshmen with need received aid; of those 100% had need fully met. *Average percent of need met:* 100% (excluding resources awarded to replace EFC). *Average financial aid package:* $34,399 (excluding resources awarded to replace EFC). 26% of all full-time freshmen had no need and received non-need-based gift aid.

**UNDERGRADUATE FINANCIAL AID (Fall 2014, est.)** 8,877 applied for aid; of those 74% were deemed to have need. 99% of undergraduates with need received aid; of those 35% had need fully met. *Average percent of need met:* 81% (excluding resources awarded to replace EFC). *Average financial aid package:* $26,669 (excluding resources awarded to replace EFC). 25% of all full-time undergraduates had no need and received non-need-based gift aid.

**GIFT AID (NEED-BASED)** *Total amount:* $139,581,629 (9% federal, 1% state, 87% institutional, 3% external sources). *Receiving aid:* Freshmen: 42% (1,246); all

full-time undergraduates: 37% (6,214). *Average award:* Freshmen: $29,923; Undergraduates: $22,445. *Scholarships, grants, and awards:* Federal Pell, FSEOG, state, private, college/university gift aid from institutional funds.

**GIFT AID (NON-NEED-BASED)** *Total amount:* $81,963,960 (1% federal, 92% institutional, 7% external sources). *Receiving aid:* Freshmen: 22% (645). Undergraduates: 13% (2,215). *Average award:* Freshmen: $19,003. Undergraduates: $14,130. *Tuition waivers:* Full or partial for employees or children of employees. **ROTC:** Army, Naval cooperative, Air Force cooperative.

**LOANS** *Student loans:* $81,285,603 (53% need-based, 47% non-need-based). *Average need-based loan:* Freshmen: $4691. Undergraduates: $4880. *Parent loans:* $14,638,652 (26% need-based, 74% non-need-based). *Programs:* Federal Direct (Subsidized and Unsubsidized Stafford, PLUS), Perkins, Federal Nursing, state, college/university.

**WORK-STUDY** *Federal work-study:* Total amount: $6,671,508; jobs available.

**ATHLETIC AWARDS** Total amount: $11,272,299 (27% need-based, 73% non-need-based).

**APPLYING FOR FINANCIAL AID** *Required financial aid forms:* FAFSA, CSS Financial Aid PROFILE, noncustodial (divorced/separated) parent's statement. *Financial aid deadline (priority):* 2/15. *Notification date:* 4/1. Students must reply by 5/1.

**CONTACT** Mr. Anthony Erwin, Dean of Financial Aid, Northeastern University, 360 Huntington Avenue, Boston, MA 02115, 617-373-3190. *Fax:* 617-373-8735. *E-mail:* sfs@neu.edu. *Website:* http://www.northeastern.edu/.

# NORTHERN ARIZONA UNIVERSITY
## Flagstaff, AZ

| Tuition & fees (AZ res): $9990 | Average undergraduate aid package: $10,622 |
|---|---|

**ABOUT THE INSTITUTION** State-supported, coed. *Awards:* certificates, bachelor's, master's, and doctoral degrees. 67 undergraduate majors. *Total enrollment:* 27,715. Undergraduates: 23,845. Freshmen: 5,035. Federal methodology is used as a basis for awarding need-based institutional aid.

**UNDERGRADUATE EXPENSES** for 2015–2016 *Application fee:* $25. *Tuition, state resident:* full-time $9120. *Tuition, nonresident:* full-time $21,640. *Required fees:* full-time $870. Full-time tuition and fees vary according to course load, location, and reciprocity agreements. Part-time tuition and fees vary according to course load, location, and reciprocity agreements. *College room and board:* $9020; *Room only:* $4990. Room and board charges vary according to board plan and housing facility. *Payment plan:* Guaranteed tuition.

**FRESHMAN FINANCIAL AID (Fall 2013)** 3,746 applied for aid; of those 76% were deemed to have need. 96% of freshmen with need received aid; of those 14% had need fully met. *Average percent of need met:* 63% (excluding resources awarded to replace EFC). *Average financial aid package:* $11,167 (excluding resources awarded to replace EFC). 14% of all full-time freshmen had no need and received non-need-based gift aid.

**UNDERGRADUATE FINANCIAL AID (Fall 2013)** 14,219 applied for aid; of those 82% were deemed to have need. 96% of undergraduates with need received aid; of those 11% had need fully met. *Average percent of need met:* 63% (excluding resources awarded to replace EFC). *Average financial aid package:* $10,622 (excluding resources awarded to replace EFC). 12% of all full-time undergraduates had no need and received non-need-based gift aid.

**GIFT AID (NEED-BASED)** *Total amount:* $94,128,458 (40% federal, 4% state, 51% institutional, 5% external sources). *Receiving aid:* Freshmen: 45% (1,951); all full-time undergraduates: 44% (8,313). *Average award:* Freshmen: $6541; Undergraduates: $6226. *Scholarships, grants, and awards:* Federal Pell, FSEOG, state, private, college/university gift aid from institutional funds, Federal Nursing, TEACH Grants, tribal grants, LEAP Grants.

**GIFT AID (NON-NEED-BASED)** *Total amount:* $17,110,505 (4% federal, 90% institutional, 6% external sources). *Receiving aid:* Freshmen: 35% (1,527). Undergraduates: 27% (5,000). *Average award:* Freshmen: $6373. Undergraduates: $5658. *Scholarships, grants, and awards by category: Academic interests/ achievement:* general academic interests/achievements. *Creative arts/performance:* art/fine arts, music, theater/drama. *Special achievements/activities:* leadership. *Special characteristics:* children and siblings of alumni, local/state students, members of minority groups. *Tuition waivers:* Full or partial for employees or children of employees. *ROTC:* Army, Air Force.

**LOANS** *Student loans:* $94,739,765 (84% need-based, 16% non-need-based). 65% of past graduating class borrowed through all loan programs. *Average indebtedness per student:* $23,602. *Average need-based loan:* Freshmen: $3402. Undergraduates: $4239. *Parent loans:* $34,899,614 (72% need-based, 28% non-need-based). *Programs:* Federal Direct (Subsidized and Unsubsidized Stafford, PLUS), Perkins, Federal Nursing, state, college/university.

**WORK-STUDY** *Federal work-study:* jobs available. *State or other work-study/employment:* Total amount: $15,714,717 (68% need-based, 32% non-need-based). Part-time jobs available.

**ATHLETIC AWARDS** Total amount: $4,584,437 (45% need-based, 55% non-need-based).

**APPLYING FOR FINANCIAL AID** *Required financial aid form:* FAFSA. *Financial aid deadline (priority):* 2/1. *Notification date:* Continuous beginning 2/1.

**CONTACT** Office of Financial Aid, Northern Arizona University, PO Box 4108, Flagstaff, AZ 86011-4108, 928-523-4951 or toll-free 888-MORE-NAU. *Fax:* 928-523-1551. *E-mail:* financial.aid@nau.edu. *Website:* http://www.nau.edu/.

---

# NORTHERN ILLINOIS UNIVERSITY
## De Kalb, IL

| Tuition & fees (IL res): $11,992 | Average undergraduate aid package: $12,284 |
| --- | --- |

**ABOUT THE INSTITUTION** State-supported, coed. *Awards:* bachelor's, master's, and doctoral degrees. 66 undergraduate majors. *Total enrollment:* 20,611. Undergraduates: 15,435. Freshmen: 2,542. Federal methodology is used as a basis for awarding need-based institutional aid.

**UNDERGRADUATE EXPENSES** for 2015–2016 *Application fee:* $40. *Tuition, state resident:* full-time $9253. *Tuition, nonresident:* full-time $18,506. *Required fees:* full-time $2739. *College room and board:* $11,790. Room and board charges vary according to board plan and housing facility.

**FRESHMAN FINANCIAL AID (Fall 2013)** 2,469 applied for aid; of those 88% were deemed to have need. 100% of freshmen with need received aid; of those 6% had need fully met. *Average percent of need met:* 64% (excluding resources awarded to replace EFC). *Average financial aid package:* $14,581 (excluding resources awarded to replace EFC). 12% of all full-time freshmen had no need and received non-need-based gift aid.

**UNDERGRADUATE FINANCIAL AID (Fall 2013)** 12,180 applied for aid; of those 88% were deemed to have need. 99% of undergraduates with need received aid; of those 5% had need fully met. *Average percent of need met:* 59% (excluding resources awarded to replace EFC). *Average financial aid package:* $12,284 (excluding resources awarded to replace EFC). 7% of all full-time undergraduates had no need and received non-need-based gift aid.

**GIFT AID (NEED-BASED)** *Total amount:* $69,945,186 (44% federal, 32% state, 20% institutional, 4% external sources). *Receiving aid:* Freshmen: 76% (2,049); all full-time undergraduates: 59% (8,564). *Average award:* Freshmen: $9864; Undergraduates: $8067. *Scholarships, grants, and awards:* Federal Pell, FSEOG, state, private, college/university gift aid from institutional funds, TEACH Grants.

**GIFT AID (NON-NEED-BASED)** *Total amount:* $6,446,544 (13% state, 69% institutional, 18% external sources). *Receiving aid:* Freshmen: 3% (86). Undergraduates: 2% (233). *Average award:* Freshmen: $4670. Undergraduates: $3867. *Scholarships, grants, and awards by category: Academic interests/achievement:* biological sciences, business, communication, computer science, education, engineering/technologies, English, foreign languages, general academic interests/achievements, health fields, humanities, international studies, mathematics, physical sciences, social sciences. *Creative arts/performance:* applied art and design, art/fine arts, creative writing, dance, debating, journalism/publications, music, performing arts, theater/drama. *Special achievements/activities:* leadership. *Special characteristics:* adult students, children of faculty/staff, ethnic background, international students, members of minority groups, veterans. *ROTC:* Army, Air Force cooperative.

**LOANS** *Student loans:* $96,778,485 (82% need-based, 18% non-need-based). 77% of past graduating class borrowed through all loan programs. *Average indebtedness per student:* $33,234. *Average need-based loan:* Freshmen: $3558. Undergrad-

uates: $4418. *Parent loans:* $15,731,965 (48% need-based, 52% non-need-based). *Programs:* Federal Direct (Subsidized and Unsubsidized Stafford, PLUS).

**WORK-STUDY** *Federal work-study:* 7,082 jobs averaging $2689.

**ATHLETIC AWARDS** Total amount: $6,308,280 (35% need-based, 65% non-need-based).

**APPLYING FOR FINANCIAL AID** *Required financial aid form:* FAFSA. *Notification date:* Continuous beginning 3/15.

**CONTACT** Ms. Rebecca A. Babel, Director of Student Financial Aid, Northern Illinois University, Swen Parson Hall, Room 245, De Kalb, IL 60115, 815-753-1395 or toll-free 800-892-3050. *Fax:* 815-753-9475. *E-mail:* rbabel@niu.edu. *Website:* http://www.niu.edu/.

---

# NORTHERN KENTUCKY UNIVERSITY
## Highland Heights, KY

| Tuition & fees (KY res): $8856 | Average undergraduate aid package: $10,447 |
| --- | --- |

**ABOUT THE INSTITUTION** State-supported, coed. *Awards:* certificates, associate, bachelor's, master's, and doctoral degrees. 83 undergraduate majors. *Total enrollment:* 15,090. Undergraduates: 12,809. Freshmen: 2,193. Federal methodology is used as a basis for awarding need-based institutional aid.

**UNDERGRADUATE EXPENSES** for 2015–2016 *Application fee:* $40. *Tuition, state resident:* full-time $8472; part-time $353 per credit hour. *Tuition, nonresident:* full-time $16,944; part-time $706 per credit hour. *Required fees:* full-time $384; $353 per credit hour. Full-time tuition and fees vary according to course load and reciprocity agreements. Part-time tuition and fees vary according to course load and reciprocity agreements. *College room and board:* $8964. Room and board charges vary according to board plan and housing facility.

**FRESHMAN FINANCIAL AID (Fall 2013)** 1,912 applied for aid; of those 79% were deemed to have need. 99% of freshmen with need received aid; of those 30% had need fully met. *Average percent of need met:* 67% (excluding resources awarded to replace EFC). *Average financial aid package:* $11,120 (excluding resources awarded to replace EFC). 13% of all full-time freshmen had no need and received non-need-based gift aid.

**UNDERGRADUATE FINANCIAL AID (Fall 2013)** 7,820 applied for aid; of those 82% were deemed to have need. 98% of undergraduates with need received aid; of those 21% had need fully met. *Average percent of need met:* 59% (excluding resources awarded to replace EFC). *Average financial aid package:* $10,447 (excluding resources awarded to replace EFC). 9% of all full-time undergraduates had no need and received non-need-based gift aid.

**GIFT AID (NEED-BASED)** *Total amount:* $23,652,826 (84% federal, 13% state, 3% institutional). *Receiving aid:* Freshmen: 40% (870); all full-time undergraduates: 39% (3,792). *Average award:* Freshmen: $5869; Undergraduates: $5325. *Scholarships, grants, and awards:* Federal Pell, FSEOG, state, private, college/university gift aid from institutional funds.

**GIFT AID (NON-NEED-BASED)** *Total amount:* $26,429,994 (3% federal, 33% state, 46% institutional, 18% external sources). *Receiving aid:* Freshmen: 52% (1,135). Undergraduates: 33% (3,271). *Average award:* Freshmen: $5334. Undergraduates: $5039. *Scholarships, grants, and awards by category: Academic interests/achievement:* biological sciences, business, communication, computer science, education, engineering/technologies, English, foreign languages, general academic interests/achievements, health fields, international studies, mathematics, physical sciences, premedicine, social sciences. *Creative arts/performance:* art/fine arts, music, theater/drama. *Special achievements/activities:* cheerleading/drum major, community service, general special achievements/activities, leadership. *Special characteristics:* adult students, children and siblings of alumni, children of faculty/staff, children of public servants, children with a deceased or disabled parent, general special characteristics, handicapped students, local/state students, members of minority groups, spouses of deceased or disabled public servants, veterans, veterans' children. *Tuition waivers:* Full or partial for employees or children of employees, senior citizens. *ROTC:* Army cooperative, Air Force cooperative.

**LOANS** *Student loans:* $79,579,424 (39% need-based, 61% non-need-based). 71% of past graduating class borrowed through all loan programs. *Average indebtedness per student:* $27,594. *Average need-based loan:* Freshmen: $3388. Undergraduates: $4400. *Parent loans:* $52,834,069 (100% non-need-based). *Programs:* Federal Direct (Subsidized and Unsubsidized Stafford, PLUS), Perkins, Federal Nursing, college/university.

**WORK-STUDY** *Federal work-study:* jobs available. *State or other work-study/employment:* Total amount: $3,436,960 (100% non-need-based). Part-time jobs available.

**ATHLETIC AWARDS** Total amount: $2,612,966 (100% non-need-based).

**APPLYING FOR FINANCIAL AID** *Financial aid deadline (priority):* 2/1. *Notification date:* Continuous beginning 3/15.

**CONTACT** Leah Stewart, Director of Student Financial Assistance, Northern Kentucky University, 416 Administrative Center, Highland Heights, KY 41099, 859-572-5144 or toll-free 800-637-9948. *Fax:* 859-572-6997. *E-mail:* ofa@nku.edu. *Website:* http://www.nku.edu/.

# NORTHERN MICHIGAN UNIVERSITY
## Marquette, MI

| Tuition & fees (MI res): $9388 | Average undergraduate aid package: $9303 |
|---|---|

**ABOUT THE INSTITUTION** State-supported, coed. *Awards:* certificates, diplomas, associate, bachelor's, master's, and doctoral degrees. 146 undergraduate majors. *Total enrollment:* 8,781. Undergraduates: 8,001. Freshmen: 1,595. Federal methodology is used as a basis for awarding need-based institutional aid.

**UNDERGRADUATE EXPENSES for 2015–2016** *Application fee:* $35. *One-time required fee:* $235. *Tuition, state resident:* full-time $9324; part-time $361 per credit hour. *Tuition, nonresident:* full-time $14,556; part-time $579 per credit hour. *Required fees:* full-time $64. Full-time tuition and fees vary according to course level and program. Part-time tuition and fees vary according to course level, course load, and program. *College room and board:* $8954; *Room only:* $4566. Room and board charges vary according to board plan and housing facility.

**FRESHMAN FINANCIAL AID (Fall 2013)** 1,627 applied for aid; of those 73% were deemed to have need. 99% of freshmen with need received aid; of those 14% had need fully met. *Average percent of need met:* 58% (excluding resources awarded to replace EFC). *Average financial aid package:* $9229 (excluding resources awarded to replace EFC). 11% of all full-time freshmen had no need and received non-need-based gift aid.

**UNDERGRADUATE FINANCIAL AID (Fall 2013)** 6,864 applied for aid; of those 74% were deemed to have need. 98% of undergraduates with need received aid; of those 10% had need fully met. *Average percent of need met:* 58% (excluding resources awarded to replace EFC). *Average financial aid package:* $9303 (excluding resources awarded to replace EFC). 7% of all full-time undergraduates had no need and received non-need-based gift aid.

**GIFT AID (NEED-BASED)** *Total amount:* $17,924,125 (74% federal, 3% state, 22% institutional, 1% external sources). *Receiving aid:* Freshmen: 37% (700); all full-time undergraduates: 41% (3,043). *Average award:* Freshmen: $4217; Undergraduates: $5202. *Scholarships, grants, and awards:* Federal Pell, FSEOG, state, private, college/university gift aid from institutional funds.

**GIFT AID (NON-NEED-BASED)** *Total amount:* $13,755,241 (24% state, 64% institutional, 12% external sources). *Receiving aid:* Freshmen: 52% (978). Undergraduates: 33% (2,425). *Average award:* Freshmen: $3161. Undergraduates: $2970. *Scholarships, grants, and awards by category:* Academic interests/achievement: biological sciences, business, communication, computer science, education, engineering/technologies, English, foreign languages, general academic interests/achievements, health fields, international studies, mathematics, military science, physical sciences, premedicine, social sciences. *Creative arts/performance:* applied art and design, music, theater/drama. *Special achievements/activities:* cheerleading/drum major, leadership, memberships. *Special characteristics:* children of faculty/staff, children of union members/company employees, international students, members of minority groups, out-of-state students. *Tuition waivers:* Full or partial for employees or children of employees, senior citizens. *ROTC:* Army.

**LOANS** *Student loans:* $41,318,856 (42% need-based, 58% non-need-based). 70% of past graduating class borrowed through all loan programs. *Average indebtedness per student:* $29,618. *Average need-based loan:* Freshmen: $3243. Undergraduates: $4084. *Parent loans:* $5,063,119 (100% non-need-based). *Programs:* Federal Direct (Subsidized and Unsubsidized Stafford, PLUS), Perkins, state, alternative loans.

**WORK-STUDY** *Federal work-study:* 570 jobs averaging $1863.

**ATHLETIC AWARDS** Total amount: $2,459,717 (100% non-need-based).

**APPLYING FOR FINANCIAL AID** *Required financial aid form:* FAFSA. *Financial aid deadline (priority):* 3/1. *Notification date:* Continuous beginning 3/20. Students must reply within 2 weeks of notification.

**CONTACT** Michael Rotundo, Director of Financial Aid, Northern Michigan University, 1401 Presque Isle Avenue, Marquette, MI 49855, 906-227-1575 or toll-free 800-682-9797. *Fax:* 906-227-2321. *E-mail:* mrotundo@nmu.edu. *Website:* http://www.nmu.edu/.

# NORTHERN NEW MEXICO UNIVERSITY
## Espa&nnola, NM

**CONTACT** Financial Aid Office, Northern New Mexico University, 921 Paseo de O&nnate, Espa&nnola, NM 87532, 505-747-2100. *Website:* http://www.nnmc.edu/.

# NORTHERN STATE UNIVERSITY
## Aberdeen, SD

| Tuition & fees (SD res): $8043 | Average undergraduate aid package: $10,242 |
|---|---|

**ABOUT THE INSTITUTION** State-supported, coed. *Awards:* certificates, associate, bachelor's, and master's degrees. 46 undergraduate majors. *Total enrollment:* 3,531. Undergraduates: 3,001. Freshmen: 363. Federal methodology is used as a basis for awarding need-based institutional aid.

**UNDERGRADUATE EXPENSES for 2015–2016** *Application fee:* $20. *Tuition, state resident:* full-time $3993; part-time $133 per credit hour. *Tuition, nonresident:* full-time $5992; part-time $200 per credit hour. *Required fees:* full-time $4050. Full-time tuition and fees vary according to course level, course load, location, and reciprocity agreements. Part-time tuition and fees vary according to course level, course load, location, and reciprocity agreements. *College room and board:* $6942; *Room only:* $3155. Room and board charges vary according to board plan.

**FRESHMAN FINANCIAL AID (Fall 2014, est.)** 295 applied for aid; of those 79% were deemed to have need. 100% of freshmen with need received aid; of those 29% had need fully met. *Average percent of need met:* 75% (excluding resources awarded to replace EFC). *Average financial aid package:* $10,303 (excluding resources awarded to replace EFC). 12% of all full-time freshmen had no need and received non-need-based gift aid.

**UNDERGRADUATE FINANCIAL AID (Fall 2014, est.)** 1,139 applied for aid; of those 79% were deemed to have need. 99% of undergraduates with need received aid; of those 30% had need fully met. *Average percent of need met:* 69% (excluding resources awarded to replace EFC). *Average financial aid package:* $10,242 (excluding resources awarded to replace EFC). 8% of all full-time undergraduates had no need and received non-need-based gift aid.

**GIFT AID (NEED-BASED)** *Total amount:* $3,701,968 (72% federal, 3% state, 13% institutional, 12% external sources). *Receiving aid:* Freshmen: 62% (213); all full-time undergraduates: 53% (736). *Average award:* Freshmen: $4251; Undergraduates: $4342. *Scholarships, grants, and awards:* Federal Pell, FSEOG, state, private, college/university gift aid from institutional funds, South Dakota Education Access Foundation Grants.

**GIFT AID (NON-NEED-BASED)** *Total amount:* $769,855 (5% federal, 14% state, 55% institutional, 26% external sources). *Receiving aid:* Freshmen: 4% (15). Undergraduates: 3% (47). *Average award:* Freshmen: $1785. Undergraduates: $1751. *Scholarships, grants, and awards by category:* Academic interests/achievement: 580 awards ($818,313 total): biological sciences, business, communication, computer science, education, English, foreign languages, general academic interests/achievements, humanities, international studies, mathematics, physical sciences, social sciences. *Creative arts/performance:* 100 awards ($91,471 total): art/fine arts, music, theater/drama. *Special achievements/activities:* 10 awards ($3600 total): leadership. *Special characteristics:* 12 awards ($10,521 total): adult students, ethnic background, handicapped students, international students, local/state students, members of minority groups. *Tuition waivers:* Full or partial for senior citizens.

**LOANS** *Student loans:* $7,914,363 (69% need-based, 31% non-need-based). 80% of past graduating class borrowed through all loan programs. *Average indebtedness per student:* $27,487. *Average need-based loan:* Freshmen: $5259. Undergraduates: $5276. *Parent loans:* $565,204 (34% need-based, 66% non-need-based). *Pro-*

**grams:** Federal Direct (Subsidized and Unsubsidized Stafford, PLUS), Perkins, college/university, alternative loans.
**WORK-STUDY Federal work-study:** Total amount: $880,125; 399 jobs averaging $2206. **State or other work-study/employment:** Total amount: $490,844 (100% non-need-based). 371 part-time jobs averaging $1323.
**ATHLETIC AWARDS** Total amount: $1,074,799 (48% need-based, 52% non-need-based).
**APPLYING FOR FINANCIAL AID Required financial aid form:** FAFSA. **Financial aid deadline (priority):** 3/1. **Notification date:** 4/15. Students must reply within 2 weeks of notification.
**CONTACT** Ms. Sharon Kienow, Director of Financial Aid, Northern State University, 1200 South Jay Street, Aberdeen, SD 57401-7198, 605-626-2640 or toll-free 800-678-5330. *Fax:* 605-626-2587. *E-mail:* sharon.kienow@northern.edu.
*Website:* http://www.northern.edu/.

---

# NORTH GREENVILLE UNIVERSITY
## Tigerville, SC

**ABOUT THE INSTITUTION** Independent Southern Baptist, coed. **Awards:** bachelor's, master's, and doctoral degrees. 32 undergraduate majors. **Total enrollment:** 2,529. Undergraduates: 2,320. Freshmen: 575.
**GIFT AID (NEED-BASED) Scholarships, grants, and awards:** Federal Pell, FSEOG, state, private, college/university gift aid from institutional funds.
**GIFT AID (NON-NEED-BASED) Scholarships, grants, and awards by category:** Academic interests/achievement: biological sciences, communication, education, general academic interests/achievements, military science, religion/biblical studies. Creative arts/performance: journalism/publications, music, theater/drama. Special characteristics: children of faculty/staff.
**LOANS Programs:** Perkins, state.
**WORK-STUDY Federal work-study:** jobs available. **State or other work-study/employment:** Total amount: $242,400 (100% non-need-based). Part-time jobs available.
**APPLYING FOR FINANCIAL AID Required financial aid form:** FAFSA.
**CONTACT** Mike Jordan, Director of Financial Aid, North Greenville University, PO Box 1892, Tigerville, SC 29688, 864-977-7058 or toll-free 800-468-6642 Ext. 7001. *Fax:* 864-977-7177. *E-mail:* mjordan@ngu.edu.
*Website:* http://www.ngu.edu/.

---

# NORTHLAND COLLEGE
## Ashland, WI

| Tuition & fees: $31,480 | Average undergraduate aid package: $36,066 |
|---|---|

**ABOUT THE INSTITUTION** Independent United Church of Christ, coed. **Awards:** bachelor's degrees. 30 undergraduate majors. **Total enrollment:** 584. Undergraduates: 584. Freshmen: 150. Federal methodology is used as a basis for awarding need-based institutional aid.
**UNDERGRADUATE EXPENSES for 2015–2016 Comprehensive fee:** $39,338 includes full-time tuition ($30,450), mandatory fees ($1030), and room and board ($7858). **College room only:** $3468. Full-time tuition and fees vary according to course load. Room and board charges vary according to board plan and housing facility. **Part-time tuition:** $600 per credit hour. Part-time tuition and fees vary according to course load. **Payment plan:** Guaranteed tuition.
**FRESHMAN FINANCIAL AID (Fall 2014, est.)** 145 applied for aid; of those 91% were deemed to have need. 100% of freshmen with need received aid; of those 23% had need fully met. **Average percent of need met:** 86% (excluding resources awarded to replace EFC). **Average financial aid package:** $36,811 (excluding resources awarded to replace EFC). 12% of all full-time freshmen had no need and received non-need-based gift aid.
**UNDERGRADUATE FINANCIAL AID (Fall 2014, est.)** 543 applied for aid; of those 92% were deemed to have need. 100% of undergraduates with need received aid; of those 21% had need fully met. **Average percent of need met:** 82% (excluding resources awarded to replace EFC). **Average financial aid package:** $36,066 (excluding resources awarded to replace EFC). 11% of all full-time undergraduates had no need and received non-need-based gift aid.

**GIFT AID (NEED-BASED) Total amount:** $10,824,726 (11% federal, 5% state, 83% institutional, 1% external sources). **Receiving aid:** Freshmen: 88% (132); all full-time undergraduates: 87% (496). **Average award:** Freshmen: $24,150; Undergraduates: $21,714. **Scholarships, grants, and awards:** Federal Pell, FSEOG, state, private, college/university gift aid from institutional funds.
**GIFT AID (NON-NEED-BASED) Total amount:** $1,117,139 (99% institutional, 1% external sources). **Receiving aid:** Freshmen: 17% (25). Undergraduates: 15% (86). **Average award:** Freshmen: $17,647. Undergraduates: $17,530. **Scholarships, grants, and awards by category:** Academic interests/achievement: 527 awards ($7,570,366 total): general academic interests/achievements. Creative arts/performance: 42 awards ($79,500 total): art/fine arts, creative writing, music. Special achievements/activities: 213 awards ($593,250 total): leadership. Special characteristics: 39 awards ($72,958 total): children and siblings of alumni, ethnic background. **Tuition waivers:** Full or partial for employees or children of employees.
**LOANS Student loans:** $4,003,928 (47% need-based, 53% non-need-based). 82% of past graduating class borrowed through all loan programs. **Average indebtedness per student:** $30,637. **Average need-based loan:** Freshmen: $4358. Undergraduates: $4939. **Parent loans:** $721,790 (91% need-based, 9% non-need-based). **Programs:** Federal Direct (Subsidized and Unsubsidized Stafford, PLUS), Perkins, state.
**WORK-STUDY Federal work-study:** Total amount: $518,199; 292 jobs averaging $1772. **State or other work-study/employment:** Total amount: $449,010 (100% non-need-based). 251 part-time jobs averaging $1763.
**APPLYING FOR FINANCIAL AID Required financial aid form:** FAFSA. **Financial aid deadline (priority):** 3/15. **Notification date:** Continuous beginning 3/1. Students must reply by 5/1 or within 4 weeks of notification.
**CONTACT** Heather Shelly, Director of Financial Aid, Northland College, 1411 Ellis Avenue, Ashland, WI 54806, 715-682-1255 or toll-free 800-753-1840 (in-state), 800-753-1040 (out-of-state). *Fax:* 715-682-1368. *E-mail:* finaid@northland.edu.
*Website:* http://www.northland.edu/.

---

# NORTH PARK UNIVERSITY
## Chicago, IL

**CONTACT** Dr. Lucy Shaker, Director of Financial Aid , North Park University, 3225 West Foster Avenue, Chicago, IL 60625-4895, 773-244-5526 or toll-free 800-888-NPC8. *Fax:* 773-244-4953.
*Website:* http://www.northpark.edu/.

---

# NORTHPOINT BIBLE COLLEGE
## Haverhill, MA

**CONTACT** Financial Aid Office, Northpoint Bible College, 320 South Main Street, Haverhill, MA 01835, 978-478-3400 or toll-free 800-356-4014.
*Website:* http://northpoint.edu/.

---

# NORTHWEST CHRISTIAN UNIVERSITY
## Eugene, OR

| Tuition & fees: $26,180 | Average undergraduate aid package: $20,379 |
|---|---|

**ABOUT THE INSTITUTION** Independent Christian, coed. **Awards:** certificates, associate, bachelor's, and master's degrees. 27 undergraduate majors. **Total enrollment:** 705. Undergraduates: 490. Freshmen: 78. Federal methodology is used as a basis for awarding need-based institutional aid.
**UNDERGRADUATE EXPENSES for 2015–2016 Comprehensive fee:** $34,380 includes full-time tuition ($26,020), mandatory fees ($160), and room and board ($8200). Full-time tuition and fees vary according to course load. Room and board charges vary according to housing facility. **Part-time tuition:** $865 per credit hour. **Part-time fees:** $160 per year. Part-time tuition and fees vary according to course load.

**FRESHMAN FINANCIAL AID (Fall 2014, est.)** 76 applied for aid; of those 86% were deemed to have need. 100% of freshmen with need received aid; of those 25% had need fully met. *Average percent of need met:* 80% (excluding resources awarded to replace EFC). *Average financial aid package:* $21,760 (excluding resources awarded to replace EFC). 17% of all full-time freshmen had no need and received non-need-based gift aid.

**UNDERGRADUATE FINANCIAL AID (Fall 2014, est.)** 371 applied for aid; of those 92% were deemed to have need. 99% of undergraduates with need received aid; of those 17% had need fully met. *Average percent of need met:* 61% (excluding resources awarded to replace EFC). *Average financial aid package:* $20,379 (excluding resources awarded to replace EFC). 8% of all full-time undergraduates had no need and received non-need-based gift aid.

**GIFT AID (NEED-BASED)** *Total amount:* $5,031,909 (25% federal, 4% state, 56% institutional, 15% external sources). *Receiving aid:* Freshmen: 83% (65); all full-time undergraduates: 85% (336). *Average award:* Freshmen: $17,923; Undergraduates: $15,561. *Scholarships, grants, and awards:* Federal Pell, FSEOG, state, private, college/university gift aid from institutional funds.

**GIFT AID (NON-NEED-BASED)** *Total amount:* $503,480 (2% federal, 74% institutional, 24% external sources). *Receiving aid:* Freshmen: 9% (7). Undergraduates: 6% (24). *Average award:* Freshmen: $9791. Undergraduates: $9487. *Scholarships, grants, and awards by category:* Academic interests/achievement: 211 awards ($1,549,050 total): general academic interests/achievements. *Creative arts/performance:* 45 awards ($83,621 total): music. *Special achievements/activities:* 200 awards ($172,250 total): community service, leadership, religious involvement. *Special characteristics:* 88 awards ($319,942 total): children of faculty/staff, relatives of clergy, religious affiliation, siblings of current students. *Tuition waivers:* Full or partial for employees or children of employees.

**LOANS** *Student loans:* $3,514,961 (81% need-based, 19% non-need-based). 95% of past graduating class borrowed through all loan programs. *Average indebtedness per student:* $29,485. *Average need-based loan:* Freshmen: $2765. Undergraduates: $4269. *Parent loans:* $433,041 (68% need-based, 32% non-need-based). *Programs:* Federal Direct (Subsidized and Unsubsidized Stafford, PLUS), Perkins.

**WORK-STUDY** *Federal work-study:* Total amount: $150,000; 167 jobs averaging $2750. *State or other work-study/employment:* 3 part-time jobs averaging $2750.

**ATHLETIC AWARDS** Total amount: $783,139 (74% need-based, 26% non-need-based).

**APPLYING FOR FINANCIAL AID** *Required financial aid forms:* FAFSA, merit worksheet. *Financial aid deadline (priority):* 3/1. *Notification date:* Continuous beginning 3/1. Students must reply within 2 weeks of notification.

**CONTACT** Jocelyn Hubbs, Director of Financial Aid, Northwest Christian University, 828 East 11th Avenue, Eugene, OR 97401-3745, 541-684-7291 or toll-free 877-463-6622. *Fax:* 541-684-7300. *E-mail:* jhubbs@nwcu.edu. *Website:* http://www.nwcu.edu/.

# NORTHWEST COLLEGE OF ART & DESIGN
## Poulsbo, WA

| Tuition & fees: $19,050 | Average undergraduate aid package: $9940 |
|---|---|

**ABOUT THE INSTITUTION** Proprietary, coed. *Awards:* bachelor's degrees. 1 undergraduate major. Federal methodology is used as a basis for awarding need-based institutional aid.

**UNDERGRADUATE EXPENSES for 2015–2016** *One-time required fee:* $50. *Tuition:* full-time $18,200; part-time $800 per credit. Part-time tuition and fees vary according to course load.

**FRESHMAN FINANCIAL AID (Fall 2014, est.)** 34 applied for aid; of those 100% were deemed to have need. 100% of freshmen with need received aid. *Average percent of need met:* 55% (excluding resources awarded to replace EFC). *Average financial aid package:* $7940 (excluding resources awarded to replace EFC).

**UNDERGRADUATE FINANCIAL AID (Fall 2014, est.)** 84 applied for aid; of those 100% were deemed to have need. 100% of undergraduates with need received aid. *Average percent of need met:* 58% (excluding resources awarded to replace EFC). *Average financial aid package:* $9940 (excluding resources awarded to replace EFC).

**GIFT AID (NEED-BASED)** *Total amount:* $518,565 (41% federal, 54% state, 3% institutional, 2% external sources). *Receiving aid:* Freshmen: 54% (19); all full-time undergraduates: 48% (43). *Average award:* Freshmen: $4440; Undergraduates: $4440. *Scholarships, grants, and awards:* Federal Pell, state, private, college/university gift aid from institutional funds.

**GIFT AID (NON-NEED-BASED)** *Scholarships, grants, and awards by category:* Creative arts/performance: applied art and design, art/fine arts.

**LOANS** *Student loans:* $798,187 (100% need-based). 93% of past graduating class borrowed through all loan programs. *Average indebtedness per student:* $20,426. *Parent loans:* $230,035 (100% need-based). *Programs:* Federal Direct (Subsidized and Unsubsidized Stafford, PLUS), alternative loans.

**APPLYING FOR FINANCIAL AID** *Required financial aid form:* FAFSA. *Financial aid deadline:* Continuous. *Notification date:* Continuous.

**CONTACT** Mac Fox, Financial Aid Officer , Northwest College of Art & Design, 16301 Creative Drive NE, Poulsbo, WA 98370, 360-779-9993 or toll-free 800-769-ARTS. *Fax:* 360-779-9933. *E-mail:* mfox@ncad.edu. *Website:* http://www.ncad.edu/.

# NORTHWESTERN COLLEGE
## Orange City, IA

**CONTACT** Mr. Gerry Korver, Director of Financial Aid, Northwestern College, 101 Seventh Street, SW, Orange City, IA 51041-1996, 712-707-7131 or toll-free 800-747-4757. *Fax:* 712-707-7164. *Website:* http://www.nwciowa.edu/.

# NORTHWESTERN OKLAHOMA STATE UNIVERSITY
## Alva, OK

| Tuition & fees (OK res): $5843 | Average undergraduate aid package: N/A |
|---|---|

**ABOUT THE INSTITUTION** State-supported, coed. *Awards:* bachelor's and master's degrees. 40 undergraduate majors. *Total enrollment:* 2,165. Undergraduates: 1,947. Freshmen: 389. Both federal and institutional methodology are used as a basis for awarding need-based institutional aid.

**UNDERGRADUATE EXPENSES for 2015–2016** *Application fee:* $15. *Tuition, state resident:* full-time $4898. *Tuition, nonresident:* full-time $11,348. *Required fees:* full-time $945. Full-time tuition and fees vary according to course load, degree level, location, and program. Part-time tuition and fees vary according to course load, degree level, location, and program. *College room and board:* $4230; *Room only:* $1600. Room and board charges vary according to board plan.

**FRESHMAN FINANCIAL AID (Fall 2014, est.)** 264 applied for aid; of those 82% were deemed to have need. 99% of freshmen with need received aid.

**UNDERGRADUATE FINANCIAL AID (Fall 2014, est.)** 1,149 applied for aid; of those 83% were deemed to have need. 95% of undergraduates with need received aid.

**GIFT AID (NEED-BASED)** *Total amount:* $4,713,004 (70% federal, 30% state). *Receiving aid:* Freshmen: 55% (183); all full-time undergraduates: 48% (763). *Scholarships, grants, and awards:* Federal Pell, FSEOG, state, private, college/university gift aid from institutional funds.

**GIFT AID (NON-NEED-BASED)** *Total amount:* $878,207 (10% state, 90% external sources). *Scholarships, grants, and awards by category:* Academic interests/achievement: agriculture, biological sciences, business, communication, computer science, education, English, foreign languages, general academic interests/achievements, health fields, library science, mathematics, physical sciences, premedicine, social sciences. *Creative arts/performance:* art/fine arts, cinema/film/broadcasting, debating, general creative arts/performance, journalism/publications, music, theater/drama. *Special achievements/activities:* cheerleading/drum major, general special achievements/activities, leadership, memberships, rodeo. *Special characteristics:* children of faculty/staff. *Tuition waivers:* Full or partial for employees or children of employees, senior citizens.

**LOANS** *Student loans:* $5,298,979 (45% need-based, 55% non-need-based). 41% of past graduating class borrowed through all loan programs. *Average indebtedness per student:* $16,932. *Parent loans:* $139,726 (100% non-need-based). *Programs:* Federal Direct (Subsidized and Unsubsidized Stafford, PLUS).

**WORK-STUDY** *Federal work-study:* Total amount: $159,060; jobs available. *State or other work-study/employment:* Total amount: $280,435 (100% non-need-based). Part-time jobs available.

**APPLYING FOR FINANCIAL AID** *Required financial aid forms:* FAFSA, institution's own form. *Financial aid deadline:* Continuous. *Notification date:* Continuous beginning 3/1. Students must reply by 8/15.

**CONTACT** Rita J. Castleberry, Director of Financial Aid, Northwestern Oklahoma State University, 709 Oklahoma Boulevard, Alva, OK 73717-2799, 580-327-8542. *Fax:* 580-327-8177. *E-mail:* rjcastleberry@nwosu.edu. *Website:* http://www.nwosu.edu/.

# NORTHWESTERN STATE UNIVERSITY OF LOUISIANA
## Natchitoches, LA

**ABOUT THE INSTITUTION** State-supported, coed. *Awards:* certificates, associate, bachelor's, master's, and doctoral degrees. 34 undergraduate majors. *Total enrollment:* 8,944. Undergraduates: 7,836. Freshmen: 1,231.

**GIFT AID (NEED-BASED)** *Scholarships, grants, and awards:* Federal Pell, FSEOG, state, private, college/university gift aid from institutional funds.

**GIFT AID (NON-NEED-BASED)** *Scholarships, grants, and awards by category:* *Academic interests/achievement:* biological sciences, business, communication, education, engineering/technologies, English, general academic interests/achievements, health fields, humanities, mathematics, military science, social sciences. *Creative arts/performance:* art/fine arts, cinema/film/broadcasting, creative writing, dance, general creative arts/performance, music, performing arts, theater/drama. *Special achievements/activities:* cheerleading/drum major, general special achievements/activities, leadership, memberships. *Special characteristics:* adult students, children of faculty/staff, children of public servants, general special characteristics, international students, married students, out-of-state students, public servants, veterans, veterans' children.

**LOANS** *Programs:* Federal Direct (Subsidized and Unsubsidized Stafford), Perkins, Federal Nursing, state, college/university, alternative loans.

**APPLYING FOR FINANCIAL AID** *Required financial aid forms:* FAFSA, institution's own form.

**CONTACT** Ms. Lauren Jackson, Director of Financial Aid, Northwestern State University of Louisiana, 212 Student Services Center, Natchitoches, LA 71497, 318-357-5961 or toll-free 800-327-1903. *Fax:* 318-357-5488. *E-mail:* nsufinaid@nsula.edu. *Website:* http://www.nsula.edu/.

# NORTHWESTERN UNIVERSITY
## Evanston, IL

| Tuition & fees: $47,251 | Average undergraduate aid package: $40,978 |
| --- | --- |

**ABOUT THE INSTITUTION** Independent, coed. *Awards:* certificates, bachelor's, master's, and doctoral degrees. 112 undergraduate majors. *Total enrollment:* 21,108. Undergraduates: 9,177. Freshmen: 2,043. Both federal and institutional methodology are used as a basis for awarding need-based institutional aid.

**UNDERGRADUATE EXPENSES for 2015–2016** *Application fee:* $75. *Comprehensive fee:* $61,640 includes full-time tuition ($46,836), mandatory fees ($415), and room and board ($14,389). Room and board charges vary according to board plan and housing facility.

**FRESHMAN FINANCIAL AID (Fall 2013)** 1,076 applied for aid; of those 85% were deemed to have need. 100% of freshmen with need received aid; of those 100% had need fully met. *Average percent of need met:* 100% (excluding resources awarded to replace EFC). *Average financial aid package:* $41,952 (excluding resources awarded to replace EFC). 5% of all full-time freshmen had no need and received non-need-based gift aid.

**UNDERGRADUATE FINANCIAL AID (Fall 2013)** 4,109 applied for aid; of those 91% were deemed to have need. 100% of undergraduates with need received aid; of those 100% had need fully met. *Average percent of need met:* 100% (excluding resources awarded to replace EFC). *Average financial aid package:* $40,978 (excluding resources awarded to replace EFC). 5% of all full-time undergraduates had no need and received non-need-based gift aid.

**GIFT AID (NEED-BASED)** *Total amount:* $138,273,147 (5% federal, 1% state, 91% institutional, 3% external sources). *Receiving aid:* Freshmen: 44% (889); all full-time undergraduates: 43% (3,605). *Average award:* Freshmen: $39,101; Undergraduates: $37,674. *Scholarships, grants, and awards:* Federal Pell, FSEOG, state, college/university gift aid from institutional funds.

**GIFT AID (NON-NEED-BASED)** *Total amount:* $2,564,974 (66% institutional, 34% external sources). *Average award:* Freshmen: $2348. Undergraduates: $2480. *Scholarships, grants, and awards by category:* Creative arts/performance: music. *Special characteristics:* international students. *ROTC:* Army cooperative, Naval, Air Force cooperative.

**LOANS** *Student loans:* $15,205,217 (72% need-based, 28% non-need-based). 46% of past graduating class borrowed through all loan programs. *Average indebtedness per student:* $19,864. *Average need-based loan:* Freshmen: $4150. Undergraduates: $4926. *Parent loans:* $10,405,363 (100% non-need-based). *Programs:* Federal Direct (Subsidized and Unsubsidized Stafford, PLUS), Perkins, college/university.

**WORK-STUDY** *Federal work-study:* jobs available. *State or other work-study/employment:* Total amount: $2,356,583 (100% need-based). Part-time jobs available.

**ATHLETIC AWARDS** Total amount: $15,303,978 (100% non-need-based).

**APPLYING FOR FINANCIAL AID** *Required financial aid forms:* FAFSA, CSS Financial Aid PROFILE, noncustodial (divorced/separated) parent's statement, federal income tax form(s). *Financial aid deadline:* 3/5. *Notification date:* 4/15. Students must reply by 5/1 or within 2 weeks of notification.

**CONTACT** Office of Financial Aid, Northwestern University, 1801 Hinman Avenue, Evanston, IL 60204-1270, 847-491-7400. *E-mail:* undergradaid@u.northwestern.edu. *Website:* http://www.northwestern.edu/.

# NORTHWEST MISSOURI STATE UNIVERSITY
## Maryville, MO

| Tuition & fees (MO res): $8276 | Average undergraduate aid package: $9380 |
| --- | --- |

**ABOUT THE INSTITUTION** State-supported, coed. *Awards:* certificates, bachelor's, and master's degrees. 65 undergraduate majors. *Total enrollment:* 6,720. Undergraduates: 5,491. Freshmen: 1,379. Federal methodology is used as a basis for awarding need-based institutional aid.

**UNDERGRADUATE EXPENSES for 2015–2016** *Application fee:* $25. *Tuition, state resident:* full-time $5360; part-time $178.65 per credit hour. *Tuition, nonresident:* full-time $11,611; part-time $387.04 per credit hour. *Required fees:* full-time $2916; $97.20 per credit hour. Full-time tuition and fees vary according to course load, location, and reciprocity agreements. Part-time tuition and fees vary according to course load and location. *College room and board:* $9192; *Room only:* $5902. Room and board charges vary according to board plan and housing facility.

**FRESHMAN FINANCIAL AID (Fall 2013)** 1,209 applied for aid; of those 79% were deemed to have need. 100% of freshmen with need received aid; of those 70% had need fully met. *Average percent of need met:* 78% (excluding resources awarded to replace EFC). *Average financial aid package:* $11,121 (excluding resources awarded to replace EFC). 12% of all full-time freshmen had no need and received non-need-based gift aid.

**UNDERGRADUATE FINANCIAL AID (Fall 2013)** 4,268 applied for aid; of those 81% were deemed to have need. 99% of undergraduates with need received aid; of those 54% had need fully met. *Average percent of need met:* 68% (excluding resources awarded to replace EFC). *Average financial aid package:* $9380 (excluding resources awarded to replace EFC). 8% of all full-time undergraduates had no need and received non-need-based gift aid.

**GIFT AID (NEED-BASED)** *Total amount:* $13,367,609 (60% federal, 12% state, 26% institutional, 2% external sources). *Receiving aid:* Freshmen: 63% (831); all full-time undergraduates: 55% (2,730). *Average award:* Freshmen: $7028; Undergraduates: $5602. *Scholarships, grants, and awards:* Federal Pell, FSEOG, state, private, college/university gift aid from institutional funds.

**GIFT AID (NON-NEED-BASED)** *Total amount:* $4,223,365 (2% federal, 4% state, 86% institutional, 8% external sources). *Receiving aid:* Freshmen: 43% (560). Undergraduates: 24% (1,187). *Average award:* Freshmen: $3258. Undergraduates: $2759. *Scholarships, grants, and awards by category:* Academic interests/achievement: agriculture, biological sciences, business, communication, computer science, education, English, foreign languages, general academic interests/achievements, health fields, home economics, humanities, mathematics, physical sciences, social sciences. *Creative arts/performance:* art/fine arts, cinema/film/broadcasting, dance, debating, journalism/publications, music, theater/drama. *Special achievements/activities:* cheerleading/drum major, general special achievements/activities, leadership, memberships. *Special characteristics:* children and siblings of alumni, children of faculty/staff, general special characteristics, members of minority groups, out-of-state students, previous college experience. *Tuition waivers:* Full or partial for employees or children of employees, senior citizens. *ROTC:* Army.

**LOANS** *Student loans:* $28,915,567 (54% need-based, 46% non-need-based). 71% of past graduating class borrowed through all loan programs. *Average indebtedness per student:* $24,710. *Average need-based loan:* Freshmen: $3423. Undergraduates: $4021. *Parent loans:* $5,952,257 (17% need-based, 83% non-need-based). *Programs:* Federal Direct (Subsidized and Unsubsidized Stafford, PLUS), Perkins.

**WORK-STUDY** *Federal work-study:* 409 jobs averaging $1195. *State or other work-study/employment:* Total amount: $1,406,129 (16% need-based, 84% non-need-based). 1,153 part-time jobs averaging $1605.

**ATHLETIC AWARDS** Total amount: $1,954,139 (38% need-based, 62% non-need-based).

**APPLYING FOR FINANCIAL AID** *Required financial aid form:* FAFSA. *Financial aid deadline:* Continuous. *Notification date:* Continuous beginning 3/15.

**CONTACT** Mr. Del Morley, Director of Financial Assistance, Northwest Missouri State University, 800 University Drive, Maryville, MO 64468-6001, 660-562-1138 or toll-free 800-633-1175.
*Website:* http://www.nwmissouri.edu/.

# NORTHWEST NAZARENE UNIVERSITY
## Nampa, ID

| Tuition & fees: $27,950 | Average undergraduate aid package: $19,993 |
|---|---|

**ABOUT THE INSTITUTION** Independent Church of the Nazarene, coed. *Awards:* certificates, bachelor's, master's, and doctoral degrees. 72 undergraduate majors. *Total enrollment:* 2,249. Undergraduates: 1,524. Freshmen: 276. Federal methodology is used as a basis for awarding need-based institutional aid.

**UNDERGRADUATE EXPENSES for 2015–2016** *Application fee:* $25. *Comprehensive fee:* $34,550 includes full-time tuition ($27,750), mandatory fees ($200), and room and board ($6600). Full-time tuition and fees vary according to course load, degree level, program, and reciprocity agreements. Room and board charges vary according to board plan. *Payment plan:* Tuition prepayment.

**FRESHMAN FINANCIAL AID (Fall 2014, est.)** 265 applied for aid; of those 90% were deemed to have need. 100% of freshmen with need received aid; of those 19% had need fully met. *Average percent of need met:* 75% (excluding resources awarded to replace EFC). *Average financial aid package:* $21,426 (excluding resources awarded to replace EFC). 13% of all full-time freshmen had no need and received non-need-based gift aid.

**UNDERGRADUATE FINANCIAL AID (Fall 2014, est.)** 1,060 applied for aid; of those 92% were deemed to have need. 100% of undergraduates with need received aid; of those 17% had need fully met. *Average percent of need met:* 70% (excluding resources awarded to replace EFC). *Average financial aid package:* $19,993 (excluding resources awarded to replace EFC). 15% of all full-time undergraduates had no need and received non-need-based gift aid.

**GIFT AID (NEED-BASED)** *Total amount:* $13,017,701 (19% federal, 74% institutional, 7% external sources). *Receiving aid:* Freshmen: 86% (236); all full-time undergraduates: 64% (743). *Average award:* Freshmen: $7407; Undergraduates: $6512. *Scholarships, grants, and awards:* Federal Pell, FSEOG, state, private, college/university gift aid from institutional funds.

**GIFT AID (NON-NEED-BASED)** *Total amount:* $2,141,756 (1% state, 90% institutional, 9% external sources). *Receiving aid:* Freshmen: 10% (28). Undergraduates: 7% (78). *Average award:* Freshmen: $10,345. Undergraduates: $9729. *Schol-*arships, grants, and awards by category: Academic interests/achievement: 640 awards ($5,389,995 total): biological sciences, business, communication, computer science, education, engineering/technologies, English, general academic interests/achievements, health fields, mathematics, military science, physical sciences, premedicine, religion/biblical studies, social sciences. *Creative arts/performance:* 112 awards ($256,080 total): debating, music. *Special achievements/activities:* 124 awards ($359,230 total): leadership, religious involvement. *Special characteristics:* 556 awards ($2,801,941 total): children and siblings of alumni, children of faculty/staff, international students, relatives of clergy, religious affiliation. *Tuition waivers:* Full or partial for employees or children of employees. *ROTC:* Army.

**LOANS** *Student loans:* $8,566,664 (83% need-based, 17% non-need-based). 78% of past graduating class borrowed through all loan programs. *Average indebtedness per student:* $27,657. *Average need-based loan:* Freshmen: $3998. Undergraduates: $4813. *Parent loans:* $1,263,442 (48% need-based, 52% non-need-based). *Programs:* Federal Direct (Subsidized and Unsubsidized Stafford, PLUS), Perkins, college/university.

**WORK-STUDY** *Federal work-study:* Total amount: $120,000; 161 jobs averaging $987. *State or other work-study/employment:* 507 part-time jobs averaging $1401.

**ATHLETIC AWARDS** Total amount: $1,947,395 (49% need-based, 51% non-need-based).

**APPLYING FOR FINANCIAL AID** *Required financial aid form:* FAFSA. *Financial aid deadline (priority):* 3/1. *Notification date:* Continuous beginning 3/1. Students must reply within 3 weeks of notification.

**CONTACT** Mrs. Ann Crabb, Director of Financial Aid, Northwest Nazarene University, 623 South University Boulevard, Nampa, ID 83686, 208-467-8638 or toll-free 877-668-4968. *Fax:* 208-467-8375. *E-mail:* atcrabb@nnu.edu.
*Website:* http://www.nnu.edu/.

# NORTHWEST UNIVERSITY
## Kirkland, WA

| Tuition & fees: $27,700 | Average undergraduate aid package: $18,121 |
|---|---|

**ABOUT THE INSTITUTION** Independent Assemblies of God, coed. *Awards:* certificates, diplomas, associate, bachelor's, master's, and doctoral degrees. 43 undergraduate majors. *Total enrollment:* 1,634. Undergraduates: 1,376. Freshmen: 146. Federal methodology is used as a basis for awarding need-based institutional aid.

**UNDERGRADUATE EXPENSES for 2015–2016** *Application fee:* $30. *Comprehensive fee:* $35,490 includes full-time tuition ($27,700) and room and board ($7790). Full-time tuition and fees vary according to course load and program. Room and board charges vary according to housing facility. *Part-time tuition:* $1100 per credit. *Part-time fees:* $95 per term. Part-time tuition and fees vary according to course load.

**FRESHMAN FINANCIAL AID (Fall 2014, est.)** 180 applied for aid; of those 81% were deemed to have need. 99% of freshmen with need received aid; of those 17% had need fully met. *Average percent of need met:* 74% (excluding resources awarded to replace EFC). *Average financial aid package:* $17,773 (excluding resources awarded to replace EFC). 17% of all full-time freshmen had no need and received non-need-based gift aid.

**UNDERGRADUATE FINANCIAL AID (Fall 2014, est.)** 1,014 applied for aid; of those 90% were deemed to have need. 99% of undergraduates with need received aid; of those 14% had need fully met. *Average percent of need met:* 64% (excluding resources awarded to replace EFC). *Average financial aid package:* $18,121 (excluding resources awarded to replace EFC). 13% of all full-time undergraduates had no need and received non-need-based gift aid.

**GIFT AID (NEED-BASED)** *Total amount:* $12,317,284 (20% federal, 13% state, 64% institutional, 3% external sources). *Receiving aid:* Freshmen: 73% (139); all full-time undergraduates: 79% (871). *Average award:* Freshmen: $14,343; Undergraduates: $14,394. *Scholarships, grants, and awards:* Federal Pell, FSEOG, state, private, college/university gift aid from institutional funds.

**GIFT AID (NON-NEED-BASED)** *Total amount:* $1,746,327 (95% institutional, 5% external sources). *Receiving aid:* Freshmen: 7% (14). Undergraduates: 6% (67). *Average award:* Freshmen: $8283. Undergraduates: $9006. *Scholarships, grants, and awards by category:* Academic interests/achievement: general academic interests/achievements. *Creative arts/performance:* debating, music. *Special achievements/activities:* leadership, religious involvement. *Special characteristics:* children of current students, children of educators, children of faculty/staff, general special characteristics, international students, married students, parents of current students, relatives of clergy, religious affiliation, siblings of current students, spouses of current students. **Tuition waivers:** Full or partial for employees or children of employees. **ROTC:** Army cooperative, Air Force cooperative.

**LOANS Student loans:** $8,249,903 (76% need-based, 24% non-need-based). 83% of past graduating class borrowed through all loan programs. *Average indebtedness per student:* $27,479. **Average need-based loan:** Freshmen: $3113. Undergraduates: $3933. **Parent loans:** $1,261,951 (43% need-based, 57% non-need-based). **Programs:** Federal Direct (Subsidized and Unsubsidized Stafford, PLUS), Perkins, state, alternative loans.

**WORK-STUDY Federal work-study:** Total amount: $73,420; jobs available. **State or other work-study/employment:** Part-time jobs available.

**ATHLETIC AWARDS** Total amount: $935,114 (59% need-based, 41% non-need-based).

**APPLYING FOR FINANCIAL AID Required financial aid forms:** FAFSA, institution's own form. **Financial aid deadline:** 8/1 (priority: 2/15). **Notification date:** Continuous beginning 3/1. Students must reply within 4 weeks of notification.

**CONTACT** Mr. Roger Wilson, Director of Financial Aid, Northwest University, PO Box 579, Kirkland, WA 98083-0579, 425-889-5336 or toll-free 800-669-3781. *Fax:* 425-889-5224. *E-mail:* roger.wilson@northwestu.edu.

*Website:* http://www.northwestu.edu/.

# NORTHWOOD UNIVERSITY, MICHIGAN CAMPUS
## Midland, MI

**ABOUT THE INSTITUTION** Independent, coed. **Awards:** associate, bachelor's, and master's degrees. 13 undergraduate majors. **Total enrollment:** 1,669. Undergraduates: 1,416. Freshmen: 331.

**GIFT AID (NEED-BASED) Scholarships, grants, and awards:** Federal Pell, FSEOG, state, private, college/university gift aid from institutional funds.

**GIFT AID (NON-NEED-BASED) Scholarships, grants, and awards by category:** *Academic interests/achievement:* business, general academic interests/achievements. *Special achievements/activities:* cheerleading/drum major. *Special characteristics:* children and siblings of alumni, children of faculty/staff, siblings of current students.

**LOANS Programs:** Federal Direct (Subsidized and Unsubsidized Stafford, PLUS).

**WORK-STUDY Federal work-study:** 99 jobs averaging $1577.

**APPLYING FOR FINANCIAL AID Required financial aid form:** FAFSA.

**CONTACT** Terri Mieler, Director of Financial Aid, Northwood University, Michigan Campus, 4000 Whiting Drive, Midland, MI 48640-2398, 989-837-4301 or toll free 800-457-7878. *Fax:* 989-837-4130. *E-mail:* mieler@northwood.edu.

*Website:* http://www.northwood.edu/.

# NORTHWOOD UNIVERSITY, TEXAS CAMPUS
## Cedar Hill, TX

**ABOUT THE INSTITUTION** Independent, coed. **Awards:** bachelor's and master's degrees. 3 undergraduate majors. **Total enrollment:** 330. Undergraduates: 278. Freshmen: 3.

**GIFT AID (NEED-BASED) Scholarships, grants, and awards:** Federal Pell, FSEOG, state, private, college/university gift aid from institutional funds.

**GIFT AID (NON-NEED-BASED) Scholarships, grants, and awards by category:** *Academic interests/achievement:* business, general academic interests/achievements. *Special achievements/activities:* memberships. *Special characteristics:* children and siblings of alumni, children of faculty/staff, siblings of current students.

**LOANS Programs:** Federal Direct (Subsidized and Unsubsidized Stafford, PLUS).

**WORK-STUDY Federal work-study:** 21 jobs averaging $1857.

**APPLYING FOR FINANCIAL AID Required financial aid form:** FAFSA.

**CONTACT** Ms. Dawn Shestko, Director of Financial Aid, Northwood University, Texas Campus, 1114 West FM 1382, Cedar Hill, TX 75104, 972-293-5431 or toll-free 800-927-9663. *Fax:* 972-293-7196. *E-mail:* shestkod@northwood.edu.

*Website:* http://www.northwood.edu/.

# NORWICH UNIVERSITY
## Northfield, VT

| Tuition & fees: $32,812 | Average undergraduate aid package: $29,218 |
| --- | --- |

**ABOUT THE INSTITUTION** Independent, coed. **Awards:** certificates, bachelor's, and master's degrees. 28 undergraduate majors. **Total enrollment:** 3,672. Undergraduates: 2,649. Freshmen: 657. Federal methodology is used as a basis for awarding need-based institutional aid.

**UNDERGRADUATE EXPENSES for 2015–2016 Application fee:** $35. **Comprehensive fee:** $44,796 includes full-time tuition ($32,812) and room and board ($11,984). **Part-time tuition:** $962 per credit hour. Part-time tuition and fees vary according to course load.

**FRESHMAN FINANCIAL AID (Fall 2014, est.)** 601 applied for aid; of those 90% were deemed to have need. 100% of freshmen with need received aid; of those 20% had need fully met. **Average percent of need met:** 77% (excluding resources awarded to replace EFC). **Average financial aid package:** $30,302 (excluding resources awarded to replace EFC). 17% of all full-time freshmen had no need and received non-need-based gift aid.

**UNDERGRADUATE FINANCIAL AID (Fall 2014, est.)** 1,854 applied for aid; of those 100% were deemed to have need. 100% of undergraduates with need received aid; of those 21% had need fully met. **Average percent of need met:** 66% (excluding resources awarded to replace EFC). **Average financial aid package:** $29,218 (excluding resources awarded to replace EFC). 21% of all full-time undergraduates had no need and received non-need-based gift aid.

**GIFT AID (NEED-BASED) Total amount:** $42,635,805 (7% federal, 1% state, 78% institutional, 14% external sources). **Receiving aid:** Freshmen: 83% (541); all full-time undergraduates: 85% (1,854). **Average award:** Freshmen: $26,249; Undergraduates: $25,047. **Scholarships, grants, and awards:** Federal Pell, FSEOG, state, private, college/university gift aid from institutional funds.

**GIFT AID (NON-NEED-BASED) Total amount:** $15,708,407 (50% institutional, 50% external sources). **Receiving aid:** Freshmen: 14% (90). Undergraduates: 14% (313). **Average award:** Freshmen: $18,299. Undergraduates: $14,966. **Scholarships, grants, and awards by category:** *Academic interests/achievement:* general academic interests/achievements. *Special characteristics:* children of faculty/staff. **ROTC:** Army, Naval, Air Force.

**LOANS Student loans:** $14,701,611 (76% need-based, 24% non-need-based). 79% of past graduating class borrowed through all loan programs. *Average indebtedness per student:* $32,498. **Average need-based loan:** Freshmen: $4489. Undergraduates: $5003. **Parent loans:** $11,474,470 (46% need-based, 54% non-need-based). **Programs:** Federal Direct (Subsidized and Unsubsidized Stafford, PLUS), Perkins, private loans.

**WORK-STUDY Federal work-study:** Total amount: $566,939; jobs available.

**APPLYING FOR FINANCIAL AID Required financial aid form:** FAFSA. **Financial aid deadline (priority):** 3/1. **Notification date:** Continuous beginning 2/15.

**CONTACT** Ms. Jana Cox, Director of Student Financial Planning, Norwich University, 158 Harmon Drive, Northfield, VT 05663, 802-485-2015 or toll-free 800-468-6679. *Fax:* 802-485-2024. *E-mail:* jcox1@norwich.edu.

*Website:* http://www.norwich.edu/.

# NOSSI COLLEGE OF ART
## Nashville, TN

**CONTACT** Ms. Mary P. Kidd, Director of Financial Aid, Nossi College of Art, 590 Cheron Road, Nashville, TN 37115, 615-514-2787 or toll-free 888-986-ARTS. *Fax:* 615-514-2788. *E-mail:* financialaid@nossi.edu.

*Website:* http://www.nossi.edu/.

## NOTRE DAME COLLEGE
### South Euclid, OH

**CONTACT** Ms. Dianna Roberts, Assistant Director of Financial Aid, Notre Dame College, 4545 College Road, South Euclid, OH 44118, 216-373-5213 or toll-free 877-NDC-OHIO. *Fax:* 216-373-5243. *E-mail:* droberts@ndc.edu. *Website:* http://www.notredamecollege.edu/.

## NOTRE DAME DE NAMUR UNIVERSITY
### Belmont, CA

| Tuition & fees: $31,822 | Average undergraduate aid package: $24,678 |
|---|---|

**ABOUT THE INSTITUTION** Independent Roman Catholic, coed. *Awards:* certificates, bachelor's, master's, and doctoral degrees. 25 undergraduate majors. *Total enrollment:* 2,030. Undergraduates: 1,213. Freshmen: 172. Both federal and institutional methodology are used as a basis for awarding need-based institutional aid.

**UNDERGRADUATE EXPENSES for 2015–2016** *Application fee:* $50. *Comprehensive fee:* $44,316 includes full-time tuition ($31,422), mandatory fees ($400), and room and board ($12,494). *College room only:* $8114. Full-time tuition and fees vary according to degree level and program. Room and board charges vary according to board plan and housing facility. *Part-time tuition:* $1014 per unit. Part-time tuition and fees vary according to degree level and program.

**FRESHMAN FINANCIAL AID (Fall 2014, est.)** 169 applied for aid; of those 93% were deemed to have need. 100% of freshmen with need received aid; of those 8% had need fully met. *Average percent of need met:* 66% (excluding resources awarded to replace EFC). *Average financial aid package:* $27,813 (excluding resources awarded to replace EFC). 6% of all full-time freshmen had no need and received non-need-based gift aid.

**UNDERGRADUATE FINANCIAL AID (Fall 2014, est.)** 773 applied for aid; of those 94% were deemed to have need. 100% of undergraduates with need received aid; of those 6% had need fully met. *Average percent of need met:* 58% (excluding resources awarded to replace EFC). *Average financial aid package:* $24,678 (excluding resources awarded to replace EFC). 5% of all full-time undergraduates had no need and received non-need-based gift aid.

**GIFT AID (NEED-BASED)** *Total amount:* $14,895,673 (17% federal, 16% state, 65% institutional, 2% external sources). *Receiving aid:* Freshmen: 90% (157); all full-time undergraduates: 90% (723). *Average award:* Freshmen: $23,418; Undergraduates: $20,114. *Scholarships, grants, and awards:* Federal Pell, FSEOG, state, private, college/university gift aid from institutional funds.

**GIFT AID (NON-NEED-BASED)** *Total amount:* $493,604 (92% institutional, 8% external sources). *Receiving aid:* Freshmen: 5% (8). Undergraduates: 3% (24). *Average award:* Freshmen: $12,358. Undergraduates: $10,524. *Scholarships, grants, and awards by category:* Academic interests/achievement: general academic interests/achievements. Creative arts/performance: applied art and design, art/fine arts, creative writing, music, performing arts, theater/drama. Special achievements/activities: community service, general special achievements/activities, leadership. Special characteristics: children and siblings of alumni, children of faculty/staff, general special characteristics, religious affiliation. *Tuition waivers:* Full or partial for employees or children of employees, senior citizens. *ROTC:* Air Force cooperative.

**LOANS** *Student loans:* $8,331,056 (84% need-based, 16% non-need-based). 77% of past graduating class borrowed through all loan programs. *Average indebtedness per student:* $31,348. *Average need-based loan:* Freshmen: $3835. Undergraduates: $4921. *Parent loans:* $4,941,586 (55% need-based, 45% non-need-based). *Programs:* Federal Direct (Subsidized and Unsubsidized Stafford, PLUS), Perkins.

**WORK-STUDY** *Federal work-study:* Total amount: $370,000; jobs available. *State or other work-study/employment:* Total amount: $165,608 (99% need-based, 1% non-need-based). Part-time jobs available.

**ATHLETIC AWARDS** Total amount: $413,897 (82% need-based, 18% non-need-based).

**APPLYING FOR FINANCIAL AID** *Required financial aid form:* FAFSA. *Financial aid deadline (priority):* 3/2. *Notification date:* Continuous. Students must reply within 2 weeks of notification.

**CONTACT** Wilbert Lleses, Director of Financial Aid, Notre Dame de Namur University, 1500 Ralston Avenue, Belmont, CA 94002, 650-508-3441 or toll-free 800-263-0545. *Fax:* 650-508-3635. *E-mail:* wlleses@ndnu.edu. *Website:* http://www.ndnu.edu/.

## NOTRE DAME OF MARYLAND UNIVERSITY
### Baltimore, MD

| Tuition & fees: $33,670 | Average undergraduate aid package: $23,572 |
|---|---|

**ABOUT THE INSTITUTION** Independent Roman Catholic, coed, primarily women. *Awards:* certificates, bachelor's, master's, and doctoral degrees (offers coed undergraduate program for adult students). 33 undergraduate majors. *Total enrollment:* 2,764. Undergraduates: 1,169. Freshmen: 107. Federal methodology is used as a basis for awarding need-based institutional aid.

**UNDERGRADUATE EXPENSES for 2015–2016** *Application fee:* $45. *Comprehensive fee:* $44,600 includes full-time tuition ($32,548), mandatory fees ($1122), and room and board ($10,930). *Part-time tuition:* $485 per credit. *Part-time fees:* $130 per term. Part-time tuition and fees vary according to course load and reciprocity agreements.

**FRESHMAN FINANCIAL AID (Fall 2013)** 99 applied for aid; of those 86% were deemed to have need. 100% of freshmen with need received aid; of those 25% had need fully met. *Average percent of need met:* 79% (excluding resources awarded to replace EFC). *Average financial aid package:* $28,928 (excluding resources awarded to replace EFC). 18% of all full-time freshmen had no need and received non-need-based gift aid.

**UNDERGRADUATE FINANCIAL AID (Fall 2013)** 469 applied for aid; of those 94% were deemed to have need. 100% of undergraduates with need received aid; of those 15% had need fully met. *Average percent of need met:* 67% (excluding resources awarded to replace EFC). *Average financial aid package:* $23,572 (excluding resources awarded to replace EFC). 13% of all full-time undergraduates had no need and received non-need-based gift aid.

**GIFT AID (NEED-BASED)** *Total amount:* $8,356,491 (18% federal, 12% state, 67% institutional, 3% external sources). *Receiving aid:* Freshmen: 82% (85); all full-time undergraduates: 82% (431). *Average award:* Freshmen: $24,905; Undergraduates: $19,711. *Scholarships, grants, and awards:* Federal Pell, FSEOG, state, private, college/university gift aid from institutional funds, TEACH Grants.

**GIFT AID (NON-NEED-BASED)** *Total amount:* $2,093,416 (2% state, 82% institutional, 16% external sources). *Receiving aid:* Freshmen: 14% (15). Undergraduates: 10% (52). *Average award:* Freshmen: $18,367. Undergraduates: $16,044. *Scholarships, grants, and awards by category:* Academic interests/achievement: 265 awards ($3,750,883 total): general academic interests/achievements. Creative arts/performance: 6 awards ($20,000 total): art/fine arts, general creative arts/performance. Special achievements/activities: 378 awards ($2,205,324 total): community service, general special achievements/activities, leadership, memberships, religious involvement. Special characteristics: 47 awards ($168,872 total): general special characteristics, international students, siblings of current students. *Tuition waivers:* Full or partial for employees or children of employees. *ROTC:* Army cooperative.

**LOANS** *Student loans:* $5,368,508 (77% need-based, 23% non-need-based). 85% of past graduating class borrowed through all loan programs. *Average indebtedness per student:* $32,346. *Average need-based loan:* Freshmen: $3488. Undergraduates: $4401. *Parent loans:* $1,166,244 (10% need-based, 90% non-need-based). *Programs:* Federal Direct (Subsidized and Unsubsidized Stafford, PLUS), Perkins.

**WORK-STUDY** *Federal work-study:* 90 jobs averaging $1091.

**APPLYING FOR FINANCIAL AID** *Required financial aid form:* FAFSA. *Financial aid deadline (priority):* 2/15. *Notification date:* Continuous beginning 3/1. Students must reply by 5/1.

**CONTACT** Audrey Brooks, Director of Financial Aid, Notre Dame of Maryland University, 4701 North Charles Street, Baltimore, MD 21210-2404, 410-532-5369 or toll-free 800-435-0200. *Fax:* 410-532-6287. *E-mail:* finaid@ndm.edu. *Website:* http://www.ndm.edu/.

# NOVA SOUTHEASTERN UNIVERSITY
## Fort Lauderdale, FL

| Tuition & fees: $26,700 | Average undergraduate aid package: $25,774 |
|---|---|

**ABOUT THE INSTITUTION** Independent, coed. *Awards:* certificates, associate, bachelor's, master's, and doctoral degrees. 49 undergraduate majors. *Total enrollment:* 24,148. Undergraduates: 4,699. Freshmen: 602. Federal methodology is used as a basis for awarding need-based institutional aid.

**UNDERGRADUATE EXPENSES for 2015–2016** *Application fee:* $50. *Comprehensive fee:* $37,280 includes full-time tuition ($25,950), mandatory fees ($750), and room and board ($10,580). *College room only:* $7980. Full-time tuition and fees vary according to class time and program. Room and board charges vary according to board plan and housing facility. *Part-time tuition:* $865 per credit hour. Part-time tuition and fees vary according to class time, course load, and program.

**FRESHMAN FINANCIAL AID (Fall 2014, est.)** 519 applied for aid; of those 80% were deemed to have need. 100% of freshmen with need received aid; of those 19% had need fully met. *Average percent of need met:* 81% (excluding resources awarded to replace EFC). *Average financial aid package:* $26,886 (excluding resources awarded to replace EFC). 23% of all full-time freshmen had no need and received non-need-based gift aid.

**UNDERGRADUATE FINANCIAL AID (Fall 2014, est.)** 2,729 applied for aid; of those 88% were deemed to have need. 100% of undergraduates with need received aid; of those 11% had need fully met. *Average percent of need met:* 65% (excluding resources awarded to replace EFC). *Average financial aid package:* $25,774 (excluding resources awarded to replace EFC). 16% of all full-time undergraduates had no need and received non-need-based gift aid.

**GIFT AID (NEED-BASED)** *Total amount:* $37,047,873 (30% federal, 26% state, 40% institutional, 4% external sources). *Receiving aid:* Freshmen: 73% (412); all full-time undergraduates: 72% (2,278). *Average award:* Freshmen: $17,526; Undergraduates: $13,847. *Scholarships, grants, and awards:* Federal Pell, FSEOG, state, private, college/university gift aid from institutional funds, United Negro College Fund.

**GIFT AID (NON-NEED-BASED)** *Total amount:* $8,067,989 (14% state, 73% institutional, 13% external sources). *Receiving aid:* Freshmen: 9% (50). Undergraduates: 4% (130). *Average award:* Freshmen: $13,019. Undergraduates: $9515. *Scholarships, grants, and awards by category: Academic interests/achievement:* 2,033 awards ($23,808,160 total): general academic interests/achievements. *Creative arts/performance:* 49 awards ($94,000 total): music, performing arts. *Special achievements/activities:* 158 awards ($897,960 total): leadership, memberships. *Special characteristics:* 86 awards ($454,281 total): children of faculty/staff, veterans. *Tuition waivers:* Full or partial for employees or children of employees.

**LOANS** *Student loans:* $32,629,221 (95% need-based, 5% non-need-based). 56% of past graduating class borrowed through all loan programs. *Average indebtedness per student:* $31,022. *Average need-based loan:* Freshmen: $3153. Undergraduates: $4232. *Parent loans:* $6,036,530 (82% need-based, 18% non-need-based). *Programs:* Federal Direct (Subsidized and Unsubsidized Stafford, PLUS), Perkins.

**WORK-STUDY** *Federal work-study:* Total amount: $4,747,296; 966 jobs averaging $4914. *State or other work-study/employment:* Total amount: $493,349 (73% need-based, 27% non-need-based). 380 part-time jobs averaging $1298.

**ATHLETIC AWARDS** Total amount: $4,364,102 (56% need-based, 44% non-need-based).

**APPLYING FOR FINANCIAL AID** *Required financial aid forms:* FAFSA, state aid form. *Financial aid deadline (priority):* 4/15. *Notification date:* Continuous beginning 2/9.

**CONTACT** Dr. Stephanie G. Brown, Vice President for Enrollment and Student Services, Nova Southeastern University, 3301 College Avenue, Fort Lauderdale, FL 33314, 954-262-7456 or toll-free 800-541-NOVA. *Fax:* 954-262-3967. *E-mail:* browstep@nova.edu.
*Website:* http://www.nova.edu/.

# NYACK COLLEGE
## Nyack, NY

| Tuition & fees: $24,300 | Average undergraduate aid package: $19,219 |
|---|---|

**ABOUT THE INSTITUTION** Independent The Christian and Missionary Alliance, coed. *Awards:* associate, bachelor's, master's, and doctoral degrees. 36 undergraduate majors. *Total enrollment:* 2,896. Undergraduates: 1,705. Freshmen: 250. Federal methodology is used as a basis for awarding need-based institutional aid.

**UNDERGRADUATE EXPENSES for 2015–2016** *Application fee:* $25. *One-time required fee:* $100. *Comprehensive fee:* $33,250 includes full-time tuition ($24,000), mandatory fees ($300), and room and board ($8950). Room and board charges vary according to board plan and housing facility. *Part-time tuition:* $1000 per credit hour. *Part-time fees:* $75 per term. Part-time tuition and fees vary according to course load.

**FRESHMAN FINANCIAL AID (Fall 2013)** 235 applied for aid; of those 94% were deemed to have need. 100% of freshmen with need received aid; of those 5% had need fully met. *Average percent of need met:* 64% (excluding resources awarded to replace EFC). *Average financial aid package:* $20,158 (excluding resources awarded to replace EFC). 6% of all full-time freshmen had no need and received non-need-based gift aid.

**UNDERGRADUATE FINANCIAL AID (Fall 2013)** 1,399 applied for aid; of those 95% were deemed to have need. 100% of undergraduates with need received aid; of those 9% had need fully met. *Average percent of need met:* 62% (excluding resources awarded to replace EFC). *Average financial aid package:* $19,219 (excluding resources awarded to replace EFC). 4% of all full-time undergraduates had no need and received non-need-based gift aid.

**GIFT AID (NEED-BASED)** *Total amount:* $17,722,060 (26% federal, 12% state, 59% institutional, 3% external sources). *Receiving aid:* Freshmen: 88% (220); all full-time undergraduates: 82% (1,242). *Average award:* Freshmen: $10,891; Undergraduates: $9220. *Scholarships, grants, and awards:* Federal Pell, FSEOG, state, private, college/university gift aid from institutional funds.

**GIFT AID (NON-NEED-BASED)** *Total amount:* $1,881,945 (98% institutional, 2% external sources). *Receiving aid:* Freshmen: 82% (205). Undergraduates: 78% (1,180). *Average award:* Freshmen: $4930. Undergraduates: $9779. *Scholarships, grants, and awards by category: Academic interests/achievement:* $1,748,843 total: general academic interests/achievements. *Creative arts/performance:* $257,300 total: journalism/publications, music, performing arts, theater/drama. *Special achievements/activities:* $1,744,307 total: cheerleading/drum major, community service, general special achievements/activities, leadership, religious involvement. *Special characteristics:* $3,273,572 total: children and siblings of alumni, children of educators, children of faculty/staff, general special characteristics, international students, local/state students, out-of-state students, relatives of clergy, religious affiliation, siblings of current students, spouses of current students. *Tuition waivers:* Full or partial for employees or children of employees.

**LOANS** *Student loans:* $11,896,494 (87% need-based, 13% non-need-based). 89% of past graduating class borrowed through all loan programs. *Average indebtedness per student:* $37,577. *Average need-based loan:* Freshmen: $3307. Undergraduates: $3984. *Parent loans:* $2,347,277 (78% need-based, 22% non-need-based). *Programs:* Federal Direct (Subsidized and Unsubsidized Stafford, PLUS), Perkins.

**WORK-STUDY** *Federal work-study:* 163 jobs averaging $1137. *State or other work-study/employment:* Total amount: $944,843 (100% need-based). 60 part-time jobs averaging $1875.

**ATHLETIC AWARDS** Total amount: $2,130,384 (73% need-based, 27% non-need-based).

**APPLYING FOR FINANCIAL AID** *Required financial aid forms:* FAFSA, state aid form. *Financial aid deadline (priority):* 3/1. *Notification date:* Continuous beginning 3/1. Students must reply by 5/1 or within 4 weeks of notification.

**CONTACT** Steve Phillips, Director of Student Financial Services, Nyack College, 1 South Boulevard, Nyack, NY 10960-3698, 845-675-4747 or toll-free 800-33-NYACK. *Fax:* 845-358-7016. *E-mail:* nyacksfs@nyack.edu.
*Website:* http://www.nyack.edu/.

# OAK HILLS CHRISTIAN COLLEGE
## Bemidji, MN

**CONTACT** Daniel Hovestol, Financial Aid Director, Oak Hills Christian College, 1600 Oak Hills Road, SW, Bemidji, MN 56601-8832, 218-751-8671 Ext. 1220 or toll-free 888-751-8670 Ext. 1285. *Fax:* 218-444-1311. *E-mail:* ohfinaid@oakhills.edu. *Website:* http://www.oakhills.edu/.

# OAKLAND CITY UNIVERSITY
## Oakland City, IN

**CONTACT** Mrs. Caren K. Richeson, Director of Financial Aid, Oakland City University, 138 North Lucretia Street, Oakland City, IN 47660-1099, 812-749-1225 or toll-free 800-737-5125. *Fax:* 812-749-1438. *E-mail:* cricheson@oak.edu. *Website:* http://www.oak.edu/.

# OAKLAND UNIVERSITY
## Rochester, MI

| Tuition & fees (MI res): $10,613 | Average undergraduate aid package: $12,835 |
|---|---|

**ABOUT THE INSTITUTION** State-supported, coed. *Awards:* certificates, bachelor's, master's, and doctoral degrees. 88 undergraduate majors. *Total enrollment:* 20,519. Undergraduates: 16,935. Freshmen: 2,559. Federal methodology is used as a basis for awarding need-based institutional aid.
**UNDERGRADUATE EXPENSES for 2015–2016 *Tuition, state resident:*** full-time $10,613; part-time $353.75 per credit hour. *Tuition, nonresident:* full-time $23,873; part-time $795.38 per credit hour. Full-time tuition and fees vary according to student level. Part-time tuition and fees vary according to student level. *College room and board:* $8895. Room and board charges vary according to housing facility.
**FRESHMAN FINANCIAL AID (Fall 2013)** 2,060 applied for aid; of those 77% were deemed to have need. 98% of freshmen with need received aid; of those 8% had need fully met. *Average percent of need met:* 78% (excluding resources awarded to replace EFC). *Average financial aid package:* $13,567 (excluding resources awarded to replace EFC). 18% of all full-time freshmen had no need and received non-need-based gift aid.
**UNDERGRADUATE FINANCIAL AID (Fall 2013)** 9,522 applied for aid; of those 84% were deemed to have need. 97% of undergraduates with need received aid; of those 9% had need fully met. *Average percent of need met:* 70% (excluding resources awarded to replace EFC). *Average financial aid package:* $12,835 (excluding resources awarded to replace EFC). 13% of all full-time undergraduates had no need and received non-need-based gift aid.
**GIFT AID (NEED-BASED)** *Total amount:* $30,337,728 (69% federal, 2% state, 29% institutional). *Receiving aid:* Freshmen: 53% (1,295); all full-time undergraduates: 45% (5,519). *Average award:* Freshmen: $6647; Undergraduates: $5046. *Scholarships, grants, and awards:* Federal Pell, FSEOG, state, private, college/university gift aid from institutional funds.
**GIFT AID (NON-NEED-BASED)** *Total amount:* $25,468,940 (1% state, 77% institutional, 22% external sources). *Receiving aid:* Freshmen: 49% (1,190). Undergraduates: 32% (3,964). *Average award:* Freshmen: $4291. Undergraduates: $4112. *Scholarships, grants, and awards by category:* Academic interests/achievement: area/ethnic studies, biological sciences, business, education, engineering/technologies, English, foreign languages, general academic interests/achievements, health fields, humanities. Creative arts/performance: dance, music, performing arts. Special characteristics: adult students, ethnic background, out-of-state students. *Tuition waivers:* Full or partial for employees or children of employees, senior citizens. *ROTC:* Air Force cooperative.
**LOANS** *Student loans:* $65,154,652 (43% need-based, 57% non-need-based). 64% of past graduating class borrowed through all loan programs. *Average indebtedness per student:* $26,724. *Average need-based loan:* Freshmen: $2880. Undergraduates: $4069. *Parent loans:* $9,137,347 (100% need-based). *Programs:* Federal Direct (Subsidized and Unsubsidized Stafford, PLUS), Perkins, private loans.
**WORK-STUDY** *Federal work-study:* jobs available. *State or other work-study/employment:* Part-time jobs available.
**ATHLETIC AWARDS** Total amount: $3,494,772 (100% non-need-based).

**APPLYING FOR FINANCIAL AID** *Required financial aid form:* FAFSA. *Financial aid deadline (priority):* 2/15. *Notification date:* Continuous beginning 3/15.
**CONTACT** Ms. Cindy Hermsen, Director of Financial Aid, Oakland University, 120 North Foundation Hall, Rochester, MI 48309-4401, 248-370-2550 or toll-free 800-OAK-UNIV. *E-mail:* finaid@oakland.edu. *Website:* http://www.oakland.edu/.

# OAKWOOD UNIVERSITY
## Huntsville, AL

**CONTACT** Financial Aid Director, Oakwood University, 7000 Adventist Boulevard, Huntsville, AL 35896, 256-726-7210 or toll-free 800-824-5312. *Website:* http://www.oakwood.edu/.

# OBERLIN COLLEGE
## Oberlin, OH

| Tuition & fees: $50,564 | Average undergraduate aid package: $37,294 |
|---|---|

**ABOUT THE INSTITUTION** Independent, coed. *Awards:* certificates, diplomas, bachelor's, and master's degrees. 55 undergraduate majors. *Total enrollment:* 2,978. Undergraduates: 2,961. Freshmen: 797. Both federal and institutional methodology are used as a basis for awarding need-based institutional aid.
**UNDERGRADUATE EXPENSES for 2015–2016 *Comprehensive fee:*** $64,194 includes full-time tuition ($49,928), mandatory fees ($636), and room and board ($13,630). *College room only:* $7080. Room and board charges vary according to board plan and housing facility. *Part-time tuition:* $2040 per credit.
**FRESHMAN FINANCIAL AID (Fall 2014, est.)** 459 applied for aid; of those 83% were deemed to have need. 100% of freshmen with need received aid; of those 100% had need fully met. *Average percent of need met:* 100% (excluding resources awarded to replace EFC). *Average financial aid package:* $37,344 (excluding resources awarded to replace EFC). 35% of all full-time freshmen had no need and received non-need-based gift aid.
**UNDERGRADUATE FINANCIAL AID (Fall 2014, est.)** 1,663 applied for aid; of those 84% were deemed to have need. 100% of undergraduates with need received aid; of those 100% had need fully met. *Average percent of need met:* 100% (excluding resources awarded to replace EFC). *Average financial aid package:* $37,294 (excluding resources awarded to replace EFC). 36% of all full-time undergraduates had no need and received non-need-based gift aid.
**GIFT AID (NEED-BASED)** *Total amount:* $45,277,410 (4% federal, 93% institutional, 3% external sources). *Receiving aid:* Freshmen: 47% (377); all full-time undergraduates: 48% (1,391). *Average award:* Freshmen: $32,992; Undergraduates: $32,317. *Scholarships, grants, and awards:* Federal Pell, FSEOG, state, private, college/university gift aid from institutional funds.
**GIFT AID (NON-NEED-BASED)** *Total amount:* $16,222,285 (86% institutional, 14% external sources). *Receiving aid:* Freshmen: 39% (312). Undergraduates: 38% (1,103). *Average award:* Freshmen: $13,380. Undergraduates: $13,167. *Scholarships, grants, and awards by category:* Academic interests/achievement: 1,686 awards ($21,699,222 total): general academic interests/achievements, physical sciences. Creative arts/performance: 555 awards ($8,748,835 total): music. *Tuition waivers:* Full or partial for employees or children of employees.
**LOANS** *Student loans:* $8,733,155 (89% need-based, 11% non-need-based). 47% of past graduating class borrowed through all loan programs. *Average indebtedness per student:* $25,018. *Average need-based loan:* Freshmen: $3284. Undergraduates: $3861. *Parent loans:* $2,628,962 (79% need-based, 21% non-need-based). *Programs:* Federal Direct (Subsidized and Unsubsidized Stafford, PLUS), Perkins.
**WORK-STUDY** *Federal work-study:* Total amount: $1,867,172; 1,500 jobs averaging $2400. *State or other work-study/employment:* Total amount: $799,945 (86% need-based, 14% non-need-based). 600 part-time jobs averaging $2400.
**APPLYING FOR FINANCIAL AID** *Required financial aid forms:* FAFSA, CSS Financial Aid PROFILE, institution's own non-custodial form. *Financial aid deadline (priority):* 2/15. *Notification date:* 3/25. Students must reply by 5/1.

CONTACT Mr. Robert A. Reddy Jr., Director of Financial Aid, Oberlin College, Carnegie Building #123, 52 West Lorain Street, Oberlin, OH 44074, 440-775-8142 or toll-free 800-622-OBIE. *Fax:* 440-775-8249. *E-mail:* financial.aid@oberlin.edu. *Website:* http://www.oberlin.edu/.

# OCCIDENTAL COLLEGE
## Los Angeles, CA

| Tuition & fees: N/R | Average undergraduate aid package: $43,195 |
|---|---|

**ABOUT THE INSTITUTION** Independent, coed. *Awards:* bachelor's and master's degrees. 31 undergraduate majors. *Total enrollment:* 2,117. Undergraduates: 2,132. Freshmen: 546. Institutional methodology is used as a basis for awarding need-based institutional aid.
**FRESHMAN FINANCIAL AID (Fall 2013)** 386 applied for aid; of those 80% were deemed to have need. 100% of freshmen with need received aid; of those 100% had need fully met. *Average percent of need met:* 100% (excluding resources awarded to replace EFC). *Average financial aid package:* $42,608 (excluding resources awarded to replace EFC). 12% of all full-time freshmen had no need and received non-need-based gift aid.
**UNDERGRADUATE FINANCIAL AID (Fall 2013)** 1,348 applied for aid; of those 88% were deemed to have need. 99% of undergraduates with need received aid; of those 100% had need fully met. *Average percent of need met:* 100% (excluding resources awarded to replace EFC). *Average financial aid package:* $43,195 (excluding resources awarded to replace EFC). 13% of all full-time undergraduates had no need and received non-need-based gift aid.
**GIFT AID (NEED-BASED) Total amount:** $41,489,916 (6% federal, 6% state, 85% institutional, 3% external sources). *Receiving aid:* Freshmen: 52% (283); all full-time undergraduates: 49% (1,032). *Average award:* Freshmen: $36,924; Undergraduates: $35,661. *Scholarships, grants, and awards:* Federal Pell, FSEOG, state, private, college/university gift aid from institutional funds.
**GIFT AID (NON-NEED-BASED) Total amount:** $3,170,565 (1% state, 86% institutional, 13% external sources). *Receiving aid:* Freshmen: 8% (43). Undergraduates: 8% (169). *Average award:* Freshmen: $10,450. Undergraduates: $9928. *Scholarships, grants, and awards by category: Academic interests/achievement:* 225 awards ($2,313,878 total): general academic interests/achievements. *Creative arts/performance:* 21 awards ($12,628 total): music. *Special achievements/activities:* 3 awards ($45,000 total): leadership. *Special characteristics:* 14 awards ($567,031 total): children of educators, children of faculty/staff, veterans, veterans' children. *ROTC:* Army cooperative, Air Force cooperative.
**LOANS Student loans:** $10,026,750 (92% need-based, 8% non-need-based). 64% of past graduating class borrowed through all loan programs. *Average indebtedness per student:* $29,962. *Average need-based loan:* Freshmen: $4757. Undergraduates: $6282. *Parent loans:* $3,965,170 (74% need-based, 26% non-need-based). *Programs:* Federal Direct (Subsidized and Unsubsidized Stafford, PLUS), Perkins, college/university, alternative loans.
**WORK-STUDY Federal work-study:** 825 jobs averaging $2653. *State or other work-study/employment:* Total amount: $407,829 (95% need-based, 5% non-need-based). 273 part-time jobs averaging $1494.
**APPLYING FOR FINANCIAL AID Required financial aid forms:** FAFSA, CSS Financial Aid PROFILE, state aid form, noncustodial (divorced/separated) parent's statement. *Financial aid deadline:* 2/1. *Notification date:* 3/25. Students must reply by 5/1.
**CONTACT** Maureen McRae Goldberg, Director of Financial Aid, Occidental College, 1600 Campus Road, Los Angeles, CA 90041, 323-259-2548 or toll-free 800-825-5262. *Fax:* 323-341-4961. *E-mail:* finaid@oxy.edu. *Website:* http://www.oxy.edu/.

# OGLALA LAKOTA COLLEGE
## Kyle, SD

**CONTACT** Financial Aid Director, Oglala Lakota College, 490 Piya Wiconi Road, Kyle, SD 57752-0490, 605-455-6000. *Website:* http://www.olc.edu/.

# OGLETHORPE UNIVERSITY
## Atlanta, GA

| Tuition & fees: $32,500 | Average undergraduate aid package: $27,485 |
|---|---|

**ABOUT THE INSTITUTION** Independent, coed. *Awards:* bachelor's degrees. 32 undergraduate majors. *Total enrollment:* 1,095. Undergraduates: 1,095. Freshmen: 277. Federal methodology is used as a basis for awarding need-based institutional aid.
**UNDERGRADUATE EXPENSES for 2015–2016 Application fee:** $50. *Comprehensive fee:* $44,200 includes full-time tuition ($32,200), mandatory fees ($300), and room and board ($11,700). Full-time tuition and fees vary according to degree level. Room and board charges vary according to housing facility and location. *Part-time tuition:* $1350 per credit hour. Part-time tuition and fees vary according to class time, course load, and degree level. *Payment plan:* Tuition prepayment.
**FRESHMAN FINANCIAL AID (Fall 2014, est.)** 247 applied for aid; of those 89% were deemed to have need. 100% of freshmen with need received aid; of those 12% had need fully met. *Average percent of need met:* 74% (excluding resources awarded to replace EFC). *Average financial aid package:* $30,335 (excluding resources awarded to replace EFC). 19% of all full-time freshmen had no need and received non-need-based gift aid.
**UNDERGRADUATE FINANCIAL AID (Fall 2014, est.)** 797 applied for aid; of those 90% were deemed to have need. 100% of undergraduates with need received aid; of those 13% had need fully met. *Average percent of need met:* 71% (excluding resources awarded to replace EFC). *Average financial aid package:* $27,485 (excluding resources awarded to replace EFC). 27% of all full-time undergraduates had no need and received non-need-based gift aid.
**GIFT AID (NEED-BASED) Total amount:** $16,304,601 (13% federal, 8% state, 78% institutional, 1% external sources). *Receiving aid:* Freshmen: 79% (218); all full-time undergraduates: 69% (709). *Average award:* Freshmen: $26,145; Undergraduates: $22,888. *Scholarships, grants, and awards:* Federal Pell, FSEOG, state, private, college/university gift aid from institutional funds.
**GIFT AID (NON-NEED-BASED) Total amount:** $6,365,555 (6% state, 94% institutional). *Receiving aid:* Freshmen: 8% (22). Undergraduates: 7% (68). *Average award:* Freshmen: $20,818. Undergraduates: $20,540. *Scholarships, grants, and awards by category: Academic interests/achievement:* general academic interests/achievements. *Creative arts/performance:* art/fine arts, journalism/publications, music, performing arts, theater/drama. *Special achievements/activities:* community service, religious involvement. *Special characteristics:* children of faculty/staff, siblings of current students. *Tuition waivers:* Full or partial for employees or children of employees. *ROTC:* Air Force cooperative.
**LOANS Student loans:** $6,584,770 (81% need-based, 19% non-need-based). 76% of past graduating class borrowed through all loan programs. *Average indebtedness per student:* $24,058. *Average need-based loan:* Freshmen: $3891. Undergraduates: $4392. *Parent loans:* $1,229,335 (52% need-based, 48% non-need-based). *Programs:* Federal Direct (Subsidized and Unsubsidized Stafford, PLUS), Perkins, state.
**WORK-STUDY Federal work-study:** Total amount: $107,170; jobs available.
**APPLYING FOR FINANCIAL AID Required financial aid form:** FAFSA. *Financial aid deadline (priority):* 2/15. *Notification date:* Continuous beginning 3/15. Students must reply by 5/1 or within 2 weeks of notification.
**CONTACT** Mr. Chris Summers, Director of Financial Aid, Oglethorpe University, 4484 Peachtree Road NE, Atlanta, GA 30319, 404-364-8355 or toll-free 800-428-4484. *E-mail:* csummers@oglethorpe.edu. *Website:* http://www.oglethorpe.edu/.

# OHIO CHRISTIAN UNIVERSITY
## Circleville, OH

**CONTACT** Michael Fracassa, Assistant Vice President of Finance, Ohio Christian University, 1476 Lancaster Pike, PO Box 458, Circleville, OH 43113-9487, 740-477-7758 or toll-free 877-762-8669. *Fax:* 740-477-5921. *E-mail:* mfracassa@ohiochristian.edu. *Website:* http://www.ohiochristian.edu/.

# OHIO DOMINICAN UNIVERSITY
## Columbus, OH

**CONTACT** Ms. Cynthia A. Hahn, Director of Financial Aid, Ohio Dominican University, 1216 Sunbury Road, Columbus, OH 43219, 614-251-4778 or toll-free 800-955-6446. *Fax:* 614-251-4456. *E-mail:* fin-aid@ohiodominican.edu. *Website:* http://www.ohiodominican.edu/.

# OHIO NORTHERN UNIVERSITY
## Ada, OH

**CONTACT** Melanie Weaver, Director of Financial Aid, Ohio Northern University, 525 South Main Street, Ada, OH 45810, 419-772-2272 or toll-free 888-408-4ONU. *Fax:* 419-772-2313. *E-mail:* m-weaver.2@onu.edu. *Website:* http://www.onu.edu/.

# THE OHIO STATE UNIVERSITY
## Columbus, OH

| Tuition & fees (OH res): $10,037 | Average undergraduate aid package: $12,473 |
| --- | --- |

**ABOUT THE INSTITUTION** State-supported, coed. *Awards:* certificates, diplomas, bachelor's, master's, and doctoral degrees. 171 undergraduate majors. *Total enrollment:* 58,322. Undergraduates: 44,741. Freshmen: 7,079. Federal methodology is used as a basis for awarding need-based institutional aid.
**UNDERGRADUATE EXPENSES for 2015–2016 Tuition, state resident:** full-time $9615. *Tuition, nonresident:* full-time $26,115. *Required fees:* full-time $422. Full-time tuition and fees vary according to course load, location, program, and reciprocity agreements. Part-time tuition and fees vary according to course load, location, program, and reciprocity agreements. *College room and board:* $9850; *Room only:* $6250. Room and board charges vary according to board plan, housing facility, and location.
**FRESHMAN FINANCIAL AID (Fall 2014, est.)** 5,628 applied for aid; of those 63% were deemed to have need. 100% of freshmen with need received aid; of those 26% had need fully met. *Average percent of need met:* 71% (excluding resources awarded to replace EFC). *Average financial aid package:* $13,179 (excluding resources awarded to replace EFC). 31% of all full-time freshmen had no need and received non-need-based gift aid.
**UNDERGRADUATE FINANCIAL AID (Fall 2014, est.)** 27,308 applied for aid; of those 75% were deemed to have need. 99% of undergraduates with need received aid; of those 16% had need fully met. *Average percent of need met:* 65% (excluding resources awarded to replace EFC). *Average financial aid package:* $12,473 (excluding resources awarded to replace EFC). 17% of all full-time undergraduates had no need and received non-need-based gift aid.
**GIFT AID (NEED-BASED) Total amount:** $148,224,515 (28% federal, 6% state, 62% institutional, 4% external sources). *Receiving aid:* Freshmen: 45% (3,170); all full-time undergraduates: 40% (15,980). *Average award:* Freshmen: $10,107; Undergraduates: $9335. *Scholarships, grants, and awards:* Federal Pell, FSEOG, state, private, college/university gift aid from institutional funds.
**GIFT AID (NON-NEED-BASED) Total amount:** $66,847,656 (2% state, 93% institutional, 5% external sources). *Receiving aid:* Freshmen: 5% (338). Undergraduates: 2% (886). *Average award:* Freshmen: $6701. Undergraduates: $6418. *Scholarships, grants, and awards by category: Academic interests/achievement:* agriculture, architecture, area/ethnic studies, biological sciences, business, communication, computer science, education, engineering/technologies, English, foreign languages, general academic interests/achievements, health fields, home economics, humanities, international studies, mathematics, military science, physical sciences, premedicine, social sciences. *Creative arts/performance:* creative writing, dance, journalism/publications, music, performing arts, theater/drama. *Special achievements/activities:* cheerleading/drum major, hobbies/interests, leadership, memberships. *Special characteristics:* adult students, children and siblings of alumni, children of faculty/staff, children of public servants, children of union members/company employees, children of workers in trades, ethnic background, handicapped students, members of minority groups, out-of-state students, previous college experience.

**Tuition waivers:** Full or partial for employees or children of employees, senior citizens. **ROTC:** Army, Naval, Air Force.
**LOANS Student loans:** $204,843,562 (65% need-based, 35% non-need-based). 56% of past graduating class borrowed through all loan programs. *Average indebtedness per student:* $26,830. *Average need-based loan:* Freshmen: $3551. Undergraduates: $4565. *Parent loans:* $41,022,306 (100% non-need-based). *Programs:* Federal Direct (Subsidized and Unsubsidized Stafford, PLUS), Perkins, Federal Nursing, college/university.
**WORK-STUDY Federal work-study:** Total amount: $5,165,931; 1,857 jobs averaging $2782. *State or other work-study/employment:* Total amount: $174,735 (28% need-based, 72% non-need-based). 74 part-time jobs averaging $2361.
**ATHLETIC AWARDS** Total amount: $17,020,234 (100% non-need-based).
**APPLYING FOR FINANCIAL AID Required financial aid form:** FAFSA. *Financial aid deadline (priority):* 2/15. *Notification date:* 3/15. Students must reply by 5/1 or within 4 weeks of notification.
**CONTACT** Ms. Diane Stemper, Director of Student Financial Aid, The Ohio State University, 281 West Lane Avenue, 4th Floor, Columbus, OH 43210, 614-292-3600. *Fax:* 614-292-9264. *E-mail:* ssc@osu.edu. *Website:* http://www.osu.edu/.

# OHIO UNIVERSITY
## Athens, OH

| Tuition & fees (OH res): $10,602 | Average undergraduate aid package: $8397 |
| --- | --- |

**ABOUT THE INSTITUTION** State-supported, coed. *Awards:* certificates, associate, bachelor's, master's, and doctoral degrees. 124 undergraduate majors. *Total enrollment:* 29,217. Undergraduates: 23,571. Freshmen: 4,377. Federal methodology is used as a basis for awarding need-based institutional aid.
**UNDERGRADUATE EXPENSES for 2015–2016 Application fee:** $45. *Tuition, state resident:* full-time $10,602; part-time $502 per semester hour. *Tuition, nonresident:* full-time $19,566; part-time $944 per semester hour. Full-time tuition and fees vary according to degree level, location, program, and reciprocity agreements. Part-time tuition and fees vary according to course load, degree level, location, program, and reciprocity agreements. *College room and board:* $10,478; *Room only:* $6050. Room and board charges vary according to board plan. *Payment plan:* Guaranteed tuition.
**FRESHMAN FINANCIAL AID (Fall 2014, est.)** 3,623 applied for aid; of those 75% were deemed to have need. 100% of freshmen with need received aid; of those 28% had need fully met. *Average percent of need met:* 50% (excluding resources awarded to replace EFC). *Average financial aid package:* $8975 (excluding resources awarded to replace EFC). 8% of all full-time freshmen had no need and received non-need-based gift aid.
**UNDERGRADUATE FINANCIAL AID (Fall 2014, est.)** 12,640 applied for aid; of those 81% were deemed to have need. 100% of undergraduates with need received aid; of those 23% had need fully met. *Average percent of need met:* 43% (excluding resources awarded to replace EFC). *Average financial aid package:* $8397 (excluding resources awarded to replace EFC). 3% of all full-time undergraduates had no need and received non-need-based gift aid.
**GIFT AID (NEED-BASED) Total amount:** $59,361,192 (40% federal, 5% state, 50% institutional, 5% external sources). *Receiving aid:* Freshmen: 57% (2,485); all full-time undergraduates: 45% (7,581). *Average award:* Freshmen: $6234; Undergraduates: $6184. *Scholarships, grants, and awards:* Federal Pell, FSEOG, state, private, college/university gift aid from institutional funds.
**GIFT AID (NON-NEED-BASED) Total amount:** $3,896,447 (1% federal, 4% state, 83% institutional, 12% external sources). *Receiving aid:* Freshmen: 8% (345). Undergraduates: 3% (573). *Average award:* Freshmen: $3004. Undergraduates: $2942. *Scholarships, grants, and awards by category: Academic interests/achievement:* area/ethnic studies, biological sciences, business, communication, computer science, education, engineering/technologies, English, foreign languages, general academic interests/achievements, health fields, home economics, humanities, international studies, mathematics, military science, physical sciences, premedicine, social sciences. *Creative arts/performance:* applied art and design, art/fine arts, cinema/film/broadcasting, dance, debating, journalism/publications, music, performing arts, theater/drama. *Special characteristics:* children and siblings of alumni, children of faculty/staff, first-generation college students, members of minority groups. *Tuition waivers:* Full or partial for employees or children of employees, senior citizens. *ROTC:* Army, Air Force.

**LOANS** *Student loans:* $120,699,803 (85% need-based, 15% non-need-based). 66% of past graduating class borrowed through all loan programs. *Average indebtedness per student:* $27,645. *Average need-based loan:* Freshmen: $2988. Undergraduates: $3661. *Parent loans:* $34,291,637 (48% need-based, 52% non-need-based). *Programs:* Federal Direct (Subsidized and Unsubsidized Stafford, PLUS), Perkins, state, college/university.

**WORK-STUDY** *Federal work-study:* Total amount: $1,457,983; 720 jobs averaging $1871. *State or other work-study/employment:* Total amount: $15,354,992 (100% non-need-based). Part-time jobs available.

**ATHLETIC AWARDS** Total amount: $6,993,829 (41% need-based, 59% non-need-based).

**APPLYING FOR FINANCIAL AID** *Required financial aid form:* FAFSA. *Financial aid deadline (priority):* 3/15. *Notification date:* 3/15.

**CONTACT** Ms. Valerie K. Miller, Director of Financial Aid, Ohio University, 020 Chubb Hall, Athens, OH 45701-2979, 740-593-9853. *Fax:* 740-593-4140. *E-mail:* millerv@ohio.edu. *Website:* http://www.ohio.edu/.

# OHIO UNIVERSITY–CHILLICOTHE
## Chillicothe, OH

| Tuition & fees: N/R | Average undergraduate aid package: $7478 |
| --- | --- |

**ABOUT THE INSTITUTION** State-supported, coed. 22 undergraduate majors. Federal methodology is used as a basis for awarding need-based institutional aid.

**FRESHMAN FINANCIAL AID (Fall 2014, est.)** 315 applied for aid; of those 83% were deemed to have need. 100% of freshmen with need received aid; of those 8% had need fully met. *Average percent of need met:* 54% (excluding resources awarded to replace EFC). *Average financial aid package:* $6968 (excluding resources awarded to replace EFC). 1% of all full-time freshmen had no need and received non-need-based gift aid.

**UNDERGRADUATE FINANCIAL AID (Fall 2014, est.)** 1,036 applied for aid; of those 88% were deemed to have need. 100% of undergraduates with need received aid; of those 9% had need fully met. *Average percent of need met:* 49% (excluding resources awarded to replace EFC). *Average financial aid package:* $7478 (excluding resources awarded to replace EFC). 1% of all full-time undergraduates had no need and received non-need-based gift aid.

**GIFT AID (NEED-BASED)** *Total amount:* $5,501,495 (88% federal, 10% institutional, 2% external sources). *Receiving aid:* Freshmen: 64% (226); all full-time undergraduates: 70% (756). *Average award:* Freshmen: $5336; Undergraduates: $5284. *Scholarships, grants, and awards:* Federal Pell, FSEOG, state, private, college/university gift aid from institutional funds.

**GIFT AID (NON-NEED-BASED)** *Total amount:* $64,654 (6% federal, 23% state, 39% institutional, 32% external sources). *Receiving aid:* Freshmen: 1% (2). Undergraduates: 1% (14). *Average award:* Freshmen: $1000. Undergraduates: $2842. *Scholarships, grants, and awards by category: Academic interests/achievement:* area/ethnic studies, biological sciences, business, communication, computer science, education, engineering/technologies, English, foreign languages, general academic interests/achievements, health fields, home economics, humanities, international studies, mathematics, military science, physical sciences, premedicine, social sciences. *Creative arts/performance:* applied art and design, art/fine arts, cinema/film/broadcasting, dance, debating, journalism/publications, music, performing arts, theater/drama. *Special characteristics:* children and siblings of alumni, children of faculty/staff, first-generation college students, members of minority groups.

**LOANS** *Student loans:* $9,221,731 (99% need-based, 1% non-need-based). 66% of past graduating class borrowed through all loan programs. *Average indebtedness per student:* $27,645. *Average need-based loan:* Freshmen: $2357. Undergraduates: $3128. *Parent loans:* $76,414 (38% need-based, 62% non-need-based). *Programs:* Federal Direct (Subsidized and Unsubsidized Stafford, PLUS), Perkins, state, college/university.

**WORK-STUDY** *Federal work-study:* Total amount: $27,259; 12 jobs averaging $1638. *State or other work-study/employment:* Part-time jobs available.

**APPLYING FOR FINANCIAL AID** *Required financial aid form:* FAFSA. *Financial aid deadline (priority):* 3/15. *Notification date:* 3/15.

**CONTACT** Ms. Valerie K. Miller, Director of Financial Aid, Ohio University–Chillicothe, 020 Chubb Hall, Athens, OH 45701-2979, 740-593-4141 or toll-free 877-462-6824. *Fax:* 740-593-4140. *E-mail:* millerv@ohio.edu. *Website:* http://www.chillicothe.ohiou.edu/.

# OHIO UNIVERSITY–EASTERN
## St. Clairsville, OH

| Tuition & fees (OH res): $4872 | Average undergraduate aid package: $6039 |
| --- | --- |

**ABOUT THE INSTITUTION** State-supported, coed. 11 undergraduate majors. Federal methodology is used as a basis for awarding need-based institutional aid.

**UNDERGRADUATE EXPENSES for 2015–2016** *Tuition, state resident:* full-time $4806; part-time $219 per semester hour. *Tuition, nonresident:* full-time $6652; part-time $305 per semester hour. *Required fees:* full-time $66; $3 per semester hour. Full-time tuition and fees vary according to course load. Part-time tuition and fees vary according to course load.

**FRESHMAN FINANCIAL AID (Fall 2014, est.)** 77 applied for aid; of those 68% were deemed to have need. 100% of freshmen with need received aid; of those 17% had need fully met. *Average percent of need met:* 70% (excluding resources awarded to replace EFC). *Average financial aid package:* $5672 (excluding resources awarded to replace EFC). 4% of all full-time freshmen had no need and received non-need-based gift aid.

**UNDERGRADUATE FINANCIAL AID (Fall 2014, est.)** 303 applied for aid; of those 79% were deemed to have need. 100% of undergraduates with need received aid; of those 15% had need fully met. *Average percent of need met:* 51% (excluding resources awarded to replace EFC). *Average financial aid package:* $6039 (excluding resources awarded to replace EFC). 2% of all full-time undergraduates had no need and received non-need-based gift aid.

**GIFT AID (NEED-BASED)** *Total amount:* $1,194,113 (77% federal, 20% institutional, 3% external sources). *Receiving aid:* Freshmen: 50% (45); all full-time undergraduates: 54% (192). *Average award:* Freshmen: $5006; Undergraduates: $4533. *Scholarships, grants, and awards:* Federal Pell, FSEOG, state, college/university gift aid from institutional funds.

**GIFT AID (NON-NEED-BASED)** *Total amount:* $34,573 (9% state, 81% institutional, 10% external sources). *Receiving aid:* Freshmen: 4% (4). Undergraduates: 2% (7). *Average award:* Freshmen: $3796. Undergraduates: $2748. *Scholarships, grants, and awards by category: Academic interests/achievement:* area/ethnic studies, biological sciences, business, communication, computer science, education, engineering/technologies, English, foreign languages, general academic interests/achievements, health fields, home economics, humanities, international studies, mathematics, military science, physical sciences, premedicine, social sciences. *Creative arts/performance:* applied art and design, art/fine arts, cinema/film/broadcasting, dance, debating, journalism/publications, music, performing arts, theater/drama. *Special characteristics:* children of faculty/staff, members of minority groups. *Tuition waivers:* Full or partial for employees or children of employees, senior citizens.

**LOANS** *Student loans:* $1,931,259 (99% need-based, 1% non-need-based). 66% of past graduating class borrowed through all loan programs. *Average indebtedness per student:* $27,645. *Average need-based loan:* Freshmen: $1292. Undergraduates: $2389. *Parent loans:* $41,409 (58% need-based, 42% non-need-based). *Programs:* Federal Direct (Subsidized and Unsubsidized Stafford, PLUS), Perkins, state, college/university.

**WORK-STUDY** *Federal work-study:* Total amount: $23,750; 12 jobs averaging $1742. *State or other work-study/employment:* Part-time jobs available.

**APPLYING FOR FINANCIAL AID** *Required financial aid form:* FAFSA. *Financial aid deadline (priority):* 3/15. *Notification date:* 3/15.

**CONTACT** Ms. Valerie K. Miller, Director of Financial Aid, Ohio University–Eastern, 020 Chubb Hall, Athens, OH 45701-2979, 740-593-4141 or toll-free 800-648-3331. *Fax:* 740-593-4140. *E-mail:* millerv@ohio.edu. *Website:* http://www.eastern.ohiou.edu/.

# OHIO UNIVERSITY–LANCASTER
## Lancaster, OH

| Tuition & fees: N/R | Average undergraduate aid package: $6897 |
|---|---|

**ABOUT THE INSTITUTION** State-supported, coed. 14 undergraduate majors. Federal methodology is used as a basis for awarding need-based institutional aid.

**FRESHMAN FINANCIAL AID (Fall 2014, est.)** 353 applied for aid; of those 81% were deemed to have need. 100% of freshmen with need received aid; of those 16% had need fully met. *Average percent of need met:* 60% (excluding resources awarded to replace EFC). *Average financial aid package:* $6320 (excluding resources awarded to replace EFC). 3% of all full-time freshmen had no need and received non-need-based gift aid.

**UNDERGRADUATE FINANCIAL AID (Fall 2014, est.)** 1,013 applied for aid; of those 85% were deemed to have need. 100% of undergraduates with need received aid; of those 11% had need fully met. *Average percent of need met:* 49% (excluding resources awarded to replace EFC). *Average financial aid package:* $6897 (excluding resources awarded to replace EFC). 2% of all full-time undergraduates had no need and received non-need-based gift aid.

**GIFT AID (NEED-BASED)** *Total amount:* $4,884,411 (83% federal, 15% institutional, 2% external sources). *Receiving aid:* Freshmen: 58% (238); all full-time undergraduates: 60% (681). *Average award:* Freshmen: $5038; Undergraduates: $5096. *Scholarships, grants, and awards:* Federal Pell, FSEOG, state, private, college/university gift aid from institutional funds.

**GIFT AID (NON-NEED-BASED)** *Total amount:* $128,544 (7% state, 84% institutional, 9% external sources). *Receiving aid:* Freshmen: 3% (14). Undergraduates: 2% (23). *Average award:* Freshmen: $3318. Undergraduates: $3542. *Scholarships, grants, and awards by category: Academic interests/achievement:* area/ethnic studies, biological sciences, business, communication, computer science, education, engineering/technologies, English, foreign languages, general academic interests/achievements, health fields, home economics, humanities, international studies, mathematics, military science, physical sciences, premedicine, social sciences. *Creative arts/performance:* applied art and design, art/fine arts, cinema/film/broadcasting, dance, debating, journalism/publications, music, performing arts, theater/drama. *Special characteristics:* children and siblings of alumni, children of faculty/staff, first-generation college students, members of minority groups.

**LOANS** *Student loans:* $7,572,636 (99% need-based, 1% non-need-based). 66% of past graduating class borrowed through all loan programs. *Average indebtedness per student:* $27,645. *Average need-based loan:* Freshmen: $1990. Undergraduates: $2801. *Parent loans:* $43,898 (65% need-based, 35% non-need-based). *Programs:* Federal Direct (Subsidized and Unsubsidized Stafford, PLUS), Perkins, state, college/university.

**WORK-STUDY** *Federal work-study:* Total amount: $40,517; 20 jobs averaging $1741. *State or other work-study/employment:* Part-time jobs available.

**ATHLETIC AWARDS** Total amount: $13,379 (100% non-need-based).

**APPLYING FOR FINANCIAL AID** *Required financial aid form:* FAFSA. *Financial aid deadline (priority):* 3/15. *Notification date:* 3/15.

**CONTACT** Ms. Valerie K. Miller, Director of Financial Aid, Ohio University–Lancaster, 020 Chubb Hall, Athens, OH 45701-2979, 740-593-4141 or toll-free 888-446-4468. *Fax:* 740-593-4140. *E-mail:* millerv@ohio.edu. *Website:* http://www.ohiou.edu/lancaster/.

# OHIO UNIVERSITY–SOUTHERN CAMPUS
## Ironton, OH

| Tuition & fees: N/R | Average undergraduate aid package: $7729 |
|---|---|

**ABOUT THE INSTITUTION** State-supported, coed. 17 undergraduate majors. Federal methodology is used as a basis for awarding need-based institutional aid.

**FRESHMAN FINANCIAL AID (Fall 2014, est.)** 225 applied for aid; of those 92% were deemed to have need. 100% of freshmen with need received aid; of those 9% had need fully met. *Average percent of need met:* 53% (excluding resources awarded to replace EFC). *Average financial aid package:* $7448 (excluding resources awarded to replace EFC). 3% of all full-time freshmen had no need and received non-need-based gift aid.

**UNDERGRADUATE FINANCIAL AID (Fall 2014, est.)** 915 applied for aid; of those 92% were deemed to have need. 100% of undergraduates with need received aid; of those 8% had need fully met. *Average percent of need met:* 48% (excluding resources awarded to replace EFC). *Average financial aid package:* $7729 (excluding resources awarded to replace EFC). 2% of all full-time undergraduates had no need and received non-need-based gift aid.

**GIFT AID (NEED-BASED)** *Total amount:* $5,114,470 (86% federal, 13% institutional, 1% external sources). *Receiving aid:* Freshmen: 84% (190); all full-time undergraduates: 77% (744). *Average award:* Freshmen: $5453; Undergraduates: $5280. *Scholarships, grants, and awards:* Federal Pell, FSEOG, state, private, college/university gift aid from institutional funds.

**GIFT AID (NON-NEED-BASED)** *Total amount:* $79,334 (11% state, 82% institutional, 7% external sources). *Receiving aid:* Freshmen: 3% (6). Undergraduates: 2% (15). *Average award:* Freshmen: $2361. Undergraduates: $2779. *Scholarships, grants, and awards by category: Academic interests/achievement:* area/ethnic studies, biological sciences, business, communication, computer science, education, engineering/technologies, English, foreign languages, general academic interests/achievements, health fields, home economics, humanities, international studies, mathematics, military science, physical sciences, premedicine, social sciences. *Creative arts/performance:* applied art and design, art/fine arts, cinema/film/broadcasting, dance, debating, journalism/publications, music, performing arts, theater/drama. *Special characteristics:* children and siblings of alumni, children of faculty/staff, first-generation college students, members of minority groups.

**LOANS** *Student loans:* $7,779,097 (99% need-based, 1% non-need-based). 66% of past graduating class borrowed through all loan programs. *Average indebtedness per student:* $27,645. *Average need-based loan:* Freshmen: $2391. Undergraduates: $3114. *Parent loans:* $34,343 (76% need-based, 24% non-need-based). *Programs:* Federal Direct (Subsidized and Unsubsidized Stafford, PLUS), Perkins, state, college/university.

**WORK-STUDY** *Federal work-study:* Total amount: $13,300; 11 jobs averaging $1209. *State or other work-study/employment:* Part-time jobs available.

**APPLYING FOR FINANCIAL AID** *Required financial aid form:* FAFSA. *Financial aid deadline (priority):* 3/15. *Notification date:* 3/15.

**CONTACT** Ms. Valerie K. Miller, Director of Financial Aid, Ohio University–Southern Campus, 020 Chubb Hall, Athens, OH 45701-2979, 740-593-4141 or toll-free 800-626-0513. *Fax:* 740-593-4140. *E-mail:* millerv@ohio.edu. *Website:* http://www.ohiou.edu/.

# OHIO UNIVERSITY–ZANESVILLE
## Zanesville, OH

| Tuition & fees: N/R | Average undergraduate aid package: $6948 |
|---|---|

**ABOUT THE INSTITUTION** State-supported, coed. *Awards:* associate and bachelor's degrees (offers first 2 years of most bachelor's degree programs available at the main campus in Athens; also offers several bachelor's degree programs that can be completed at this campus; also offers some graduate courses). 7 undergraduate majors. *Total enrollment:* 2,042. Undergraduates: 2,042. Freshmen: 301. Federal methodology is used as a basis for awarding need-based institutional aid.

**FRESHMAN FINANCIAL AID (Fall 2014, est.)** 265 applied for aid; of those 78% were deemed to have need. 100% of freshmen with need received aid; of those 13% had need fully met. *Average percent of need met:* 67% (excluding resources awarded to replace EFC). *Average financial aid package:* $6724 (excluding resources awarded to replace EFC). 1% of all full-time freshmen had no need and received non-need-based gift aid.

**UNDERGRADUATE FINANCIAL AID (Fall 2014, est.)** 812 applied for aid; of those 83% were deemed to have need. 100% of undergraduates with need received aid; of those 11% had need fully met. *Average percent of need met:* 51% (excluding resources awarded to replace EFC). *Average financial aid package:* $6948 (excluding resources awarded to replace EFC). 1% of all full-time undergraduates had no need and received non-need-based gift aid.

**GIFT AID (NEED-BASED)** *Total amount:* $4,127,503 (74% federal, 22% institutional, 4% external sources). *Receiving aid:* Freshmen: 65% (188); all full-time undergraduates: 65% (564). *Average award:* Freshmen: $5574; Undergraduates: $5288. *Scholarships, grants, and awards:* Federal Pell, FSEOG, state, private, college/university gift aid from institutional funds.

**GIFT AID (NON-NEED-BASED)** *Total amount:* $102,198 (31% state, 56% institutional, 13% external sources). *Receiving aid:* Freshmen: 1% (3). Undergraduates: 2% (14). **Average award:** Freshmen: $5076. Undergraduates: $3405. **Scholarships, grants, and awards by category:** Academic interests/achievement: area/ethnic studies, biological sciences, business, communication, computer science, education, engineering/technologies, English, foreign languages, general academic interests/achievements, health fields, home economics, humanities, international studies, mathematics, military science, physical sciences, premedicine, social sciences. *Creative arts/performance:* applied art and design, art/fine arts, cinema/film/broadcasting, dance, debating, journalism/publications, music, performing arts, theater/drama. *Special characteristics:* children and siblings of alumni, children of faculty/staff, first-generation college students, members of minority groups.

**LOANS** *Student loans:* $5,607,691 (98% need-based, 2% non-need-based). 66% of past graduating class borrowed through all loan programs. *Average indebtedness per student:* $27,645. **Average need-based loan:** Freshmen: $1679. Undergraduates: $2562. **Parent loans:** $90,036 (49% need-based, 51% non-need-based). **Programs:** Federal Direct (Subsidized and Unsubsidized Stafford, PLUS), Perkins, state, college/university.

**WORK-STUDY** *Federal work-study:* Total amount: $22,734; 17 jobs averaging $1226. **State or other work-study/employment:** Part-time jobs available.

**APPLYING FOR FINANCIAL AID** *Required financial aid form:* FAFSA. *Financial aid deadline (priority):* 3/15. *Notification date:* 3/15.

**CONTACT** Ms. Valerie K. Miller, Director of Financial Aid, Ohio University–Zanesville, 020 Chubb Hall, Athens, OH 45701-2979, 740-593-4141. *Fax:* 740-593-4140. *E-mail:* millerv@ohio.edu. *Website:* http://www.zanesville.ohiou.edu/.

# OHIO VALLEY UNIVERSITY
## Vienna, WV

**ABOUT THE INSTITUTION** Independent Church of Christ, coed. *Awards:* certificates, associate, bachelor's, and master's degrees. 16 undergraduate majors. **Total enrollment:** 428. Undergraduates: 397. Freshmen: 88.

**GIFT AID (NEED-BASED)** *Scholarships, grants, and awards:* Federal Pell, FSEOG, state, private, college/university gift aid from institutional funds.

**GIFT AID (NON-NEED-BASED)** *Scholarships, grants, and awards by category:* Academic interests/achievement: education, English, general academic interests/achievements, religion/biblical studies. *Creative arts/performance:* general creative arts/performance, journalism/publications, music, performing arts, theater/drama. *Special achievements/activities:* community service, general special achievements/activities, leadership, religious involvement. *Special characteristics:* adult students, children of faculty/staff, ethnic background, general special characteristics, international students, local/state students, relatives of clergy, religious affiliation.

**LOANS** *Programs:* Federal Direct (Subsidized and Unsubsidized Stafford, PLUS), Perkins.

**APPLYING FOR FINANCIAL AID** *Required financial aid form:* FAFSA.

**CONTACT** Wes Wilson, Assistant Director of Financial Aid, Ohio Valley University, 1 Campus View Drive, Vienna, WV 26105-8000, 304-865-6207 or toll-free 877-446-8668. *Fax:* 304-865-6001. *E-mail:* wes.wilson@ovu.edu. *Website:* http://www.ovu.edu/.

# OHIO WESLEYAN UNIVERSITY
## Delaware, OH

| Tuition & fees: $41,920 | Average undergraduate aid package: $30,917 |
|---|---|

**ABOUT THE INSTITUTION** Independent United Methodist, coed. *Awards:* bachelor's degrees. 85 undergraduate majors. **Total enrollment:** 1,734. Undergraduates: 1,734. Freshmen: 458. Both federal and institutional methodology are used as a basis for awarding need-based institutional aid.

**UNDERGRADUATE EXPENSES for 2015–2016** *Comprehensive fee:* $53,130 includes full-time tuition ($41,660), mandatory fees ($260), and room and board ($11,210). **College room only:** $6050. Full-time tuition and fees vary according to course load. Room and board charges vary according to board plan and housing facility. *Part-time tuition:* $4523 per unit. Part-time tuition and fees vary according to course load.

**FRESHMAN FINANCIAL AID (Fall 2013)** 446 applied for aid; of those 89% were deemed to have need. 100% of freshmen with need received aid; of those 25% had need fully met. **Average percent of need met:** 79% (excluding resources awarded to replace EFC). **Average financial aid package:** $32,555 (excluding resources awarded to replace EFC). 25% of all full-time freshmen had no need and received non-need-based gift aid.

**UNDERGRADUATE FINANCIAL AID (Fall 2013)** 1,428 applied for aid; of those 89% were deemed to have need. 100% of undergraduates with need received aid; of those 24% had need fully met. **Average percent of need met:** 78% (excluding resources awarded to replace EFC). **Average financial aid package:** $30,917 (excluding resources awarded to replace EFC). 29% of all full-time undergraduates had no need and received non-need-based gift aid.

**GIFT AID (NEED-BASED)** *Total amount:* $32,662,374 (7% federal, 1% state, 91% institutional, 1% external sources). **Receiving aid:** Freshmen: 74% (399); all full-time undergraduates: 70% (1,260). *Average award:* Freshmen: $28,059; Undergraduates: $25,921. **Scholarships, grants, and awards:** Federal Pell, FSEOG, state, private, college/university gift aid from institutional funds.

**GIFT AID (NON-NEED-BASED)** *Total amount:* $14,322,370 (98% institutional, 2% external sources). **Receiving aid:** Freshmen: 18% (96). Undergraduates: 16% (283). *Average award:* Freshmen: $21,645. Undergraduates: $21,940. **Scholarships, grants, and awards by category:** Academic interests/achievement: business, education, general academic interests/achievements. *Creative arts/performance:* applied art and design, art/fine arts, dance, music, performing arts, theater/drama. *Special achievements/activities:* general special achievements/activities, leadership. *Special characteristics:* children and siblings of alumni, international students, local/state students, members of minority groups, relatives of clergy, religious affiliation, twins. **Tuition waivers:** Full or partial for employees or children of employees. *ROTC:* Army cooperative, Air Force cooperative.

**LOANS** *Student loans:* $12,903,229 (67% need-based, 33% non-need-based). 60% of past graduating class borrowed through all loan programs. *Average indebtedness per student:* $28,516. **Average need-based loan:** Freshmen: $3658. Undergraduates: $4582. **Parent loans:** $4,181,068 (43% need-based, 57% non-need-based). **Programs:** Federal Direct (Subsidized and Unsubsidized Stafford, PLUS), Perkins, college/university.

**WORK-STUDY** *Federal work-study:* jobs available. **State or other work-study/employment:** Total amount: $966,086 (14% need-based, 86% non-need-based). Part-time jobs available.

**APPLYING FOR FINANCIAL AID** *Required financial aid form:* FAFSA. *Financial aid deadline (priority):* 2/15. *Notification date:* Continuous beginning 2/15. Students must reply by 5/1 or within 2 weeks of notification.

**CONTACT** Mr. Kevin Paskvan, Director of Financial Aid, Ohio Wesleyan University, 61 South Sandusky Street, Delaware, OH 43015, 740-368-3050 or toll-free 800-922-8953. *Fax:* 740-368-3066. *E-mail:* financialaid@owu.edu . *Website:* http://www.owu.edu/.

# OHR HAMEIR THEOLOGICAL SEMINARY
## Cortlandt Manor, NY

**CONTACT** Financial Aid Office, Ohr Hameir Theological Seminary, Furnace Woods Road, Peekskill, NY 10566, 914-736-1500.

# OHR SOMAYACH/JOSEPH TANENBAUM EDUCATIONAL CENTER
## Monsey, NY

**CONTACT** Financial Aid Office, Ohr Somayach/Joseph Tanenbaum Educational Center, PO Box 334244, Route 306, Monsey, NY 10952-0334, 914-425-1370. *Website:* http://ohr.edu/.

# OKLAHOMA BAPTIST UNIVERSITY
### Shawnee, OK

**Tuition & fees: $24,000** | **Average undergraduate aid package: $19,312**

**ABOUT THE INSTITUTION** Independent Southern Baptist, coed. *Awards:* associate, bachelor's, and master's degrees. 67 undergraduate majors. *Total enrollment:* 1,979. Undergraduates: 1,921. Freshmen: 483. Federal methodology is used as a basis for awarding need-based institutional aid.

**UNDERGRADUATE EXPENSES for 2015–2016** *Comprehensive fee:* $30,780 includes full-time tuition ($21,630), mandatory fees ($2370), and room and board ($6780). Room and board charges vary according to housing facility. Part-time tuition and fees vary according to course load.

**FRESHMAN FINANCIAL AID (Fall 2013)** 520 applied for aid; of those 91% were deemed to have need. 100% of freshmen with need received aid; of those 26% had need fully met. *Average percent of need met:* 78% (excluding resources awarded to replace EFC). *Average financial aid package:* $19,822 (excluding resources awarded to replace EFC). 18% of all full-time freshmen had no need and received non-need-based gift aid.

**UNDERGRADUATE FINANCIAL AID (Fall 2013)** 1,482 applied for aid; of those 92% were deemed to have need. 100% of undergraduates with need received aid; of those 23% had need fully met. *Average percent of need met:* 75% (excluding resources awarded to replace EFC). *Average financial aid package:* $19,312 (excluding resources awarded to replace EFC). 26% of all full-time undergraduates had no need and received non-need-based gift aid.

**GIFT AID (NEED-BASED) *Total amount:*** $17,168,272 (17% federal, 12% state, 65% institutional, 6% external sources). *Receiving aid:* Freshmen: 67% (389); all full-time undergraduates: 63% (1,158). *Average award:* Freshmen: $7794; Undergraduates: $6907. *Scholarships, grants, and awards:* Federal Pell, FSEOG, state, private, college/university gift aid from institutional funds, TEACH Grants.

**GIFT AID (NON-NEED-BASED) *Total amount:*** $6,383,322 (6% federal, 1% state, 88% institutional, 5% external sources). *Receiving aid:* Freshmen: 80% (462). Undergraduates: 72% (1,318). *Average award:* Freshmen: $11,675. Undergraduates: $9752. *Scholarships, grants, and awards by category: Academic interests/achievement:* 1,859 awards ($10,275,111 total): biological sciences, business, computer science, education, English, foreign languages, general academic interests/achievements, health fields, humanities, mathematics, physical sciences, premedicine, religion/biblical studies, social sciences. *Creative arts/performance:* 329 awards ($484,737 total): applied art and design, art/fine arts, music, performing arts, theater/drama. *Special achievements/activities:* 49 awards ($35,420 total): cheerleading/drum major, leadership, religious involvement. *Special characteristics:* 961 awards ($1,689,073 total): adult students, children and siblings of alumni, children of faculty/staff, general special characteristics, international students, local/state students, members of minority groups, out-of-state students, relatives of clergy, religious affiliation, veterans. *Tuition waivers:* Full or partial for employees or children of employees, senior citizens. *ROTC:* Air Force cooperative.

**LOANS *Student loans:*** $8,835,875 (45% need-based, 55% non-need-based). 61% of past graduating class borrowed through all loan programs. *Average indebtedness per student:* $26,557. *Average need-based loan:* Freshmen: $3357. Undergraduates: $4101. *Parent loans:* $1,761,709 (55% need-based, 45% non-need-based). *Programs:* Federal Direct (Subsidized and Unsubsidized Stafford, PLUS), Perkins, college/university.

**WORK-STUDY** *Federal work-study:* 214 jobs averaging $1231. *State or other work-study/employment:* Total amount: $116,364 (100% non-need-based). Part-time jobs available.

**ATHLETIC AWARDS** Total amount: $3,978,023 (62% need-based, 38% non-need-based).

**APPLYING FOR FINANCIAL AID** *Financial aid deadline:* Continuous. *Notification date:* Continuous beginning 2/1.

**CONTACT** Jonna Raney, Director of Student Financial Services, Oklahoma Baptist University, 500 West University, Shawnee, OK 74804, 405-585-5020 or toll-free 800-654-3285. *Fax:* 405-585-5030. *E-mail:* jonna.raney@okbu.edu. *Website:* http://www.okbu.edu/.

# OKLAHOMA CHRISTIAN UNIVERSITY
### Oklahoma City, OK

**Tuition & fees: $19,890** | **Average undergraduate aid package: $21,652**

**ABOUT THE INSTITUTION** Independent Church of Christ, coed. *Awards:* bachelor's and master's degrees. 60 undergraduate majors. *Total enrollment:* 2,472. Undergraduates: 1,973. Freshmen: 505. Federal methodology is used as a basis for awarding need-based institutional aid.

**UNDERGRADUATE EXPENSES for 2015–2016** *Application fee:* $25. *Comprehensive fee:* $26,920 includes full-time tuition ($19,890) and room and board ($7030). *College room only:* $3870. Full-time tuition and fees vary according to course load, program, and reciprocity agreements. Room and board charges vary according to board plan and housing facility. *Part-time tuition:* $828 per credit hour. Part-time tuition and fees vary according to course load, program, and reciprocity agreements.

**FRESHMAN FINANCIAL AID (Fall 2013)** 443 applied for aid; of those 81% were deemed to have need. 100% of freshmen with need received aid; of those 46% had need fully met. *Average percent of need met:* 78% (excluding resources awarded to replace EFC). *Average financial aid package:* $21,135 (excluding resources awarded to replace EFC). 25% of all full-time freshmen had no need and received non-need-based gift aid.

**UNDERGRADUATE FINANCIAL AID (Fall 2013)** 1,418 applied for aid; of those 85% were deemed to have need. 100% of undergraduates with need received aid; of those 45% had need fully met. *Average percent of need met:* 83% (excluding resources awarded to replace EFC). *Average financial aid package:* $21,652 (excluding resources awarded to replace EFC). 25% of all full-time undergraduates had no need and received non-need-based gift aid.

**GIFT AID (NEED-BASED) *Total amount:*** $12,841,728 (21% federal, 5% state, 69% institutional, 5% external sources). *Receiving aid:* Freshmen: 44% (233); all full-time undergraduates: 41% (781). *Average award:* Freshmen: $3224; Undergraduates: $3078. *Scholarships, grants, and awards:* Federal Pell, FSEOG, state, private, college/university gift aid from institutional funds.

**GIFT AID (NON-NEED-BASED) *Total amount:*** $6,653,282 (1% federal, 2% state, 89% institutional, 8% external sources). *Receiving aid:* Freshmen: 56% (294). Undergraduates: 51% (970). *Average award:* Freshmen: $3914. Undergraduates: $5630. *Scholarships, grants, and awards by category: Academic interests/achievement:* engineering/technologies, general academic interests/achievements, religion/biblical studies. *Creative arts/performance:* 223 awards ($558,365 total): applied art and design, journalism/publications, music, theater/drama. *Special achievements/activities:* 11 awards ($12,750 total): cheerleading/drum major. *Special characteristics:* 71 awards ($809,902 total): children of faculty/staff, international students. *Tuition waivers:* Full or partial for employees or children of employees. *ROTC:* Army cooperative, Air Force cooperative.

**LOANS *Student loans:*** $8,089,675 (74% need-based, 26% non-need-based). 64% of past graduating class borrowed through all loan programs. *Average indebtedness per student:* $27,065. *Average need-based loan:* Freshmen: $2238. Undergraduates: $2042. *Parent loans:* $2,541,341 (30% need-based, 70% non-need-based). *Programs:* Federal Direct (Subsidized and Unsubsidized Stafford, PLUS), Perkins, alternative loans.

**WORK-STUDY** *Federal work-study:* 843 jobs averaging $1627.

**ATHLETIC AWARDS** Total amount: $2,573,259 (40% need-based, 60% non-need-based).

**APPLYING FOR FINANCIAL AID** *Required financial aid form:* FAFSA. *Financial aid deadline:* 8/31 (priority: 3/15). *Notification date:* Continuous beginning 2/15. Students must reply within 4 weeks of notification.

**CONTACT** Clint LaRue, Director of Financial Services, Oklahoma Christian University, Box 11000, Oklahoma City, OK 73136-1100, 405-425-5190 or toll-free 800-877-5010. *Fax:* 405-425-5197. *E-mail:* clint.larue@oc.edu. *Website:* http://www.oc.edu/.

# OKLAHOMA CITY UNIVERSITY
## Oklahoma City, OK

| Tuition & fees: $30,726 | Average undergraduate aid package: $20,762 |
|---|---|

**ABOUT THE INSTITUTION** Independent United Methodist, coed. *Awards:* bachelor's, master's, and doctoral degrees. 69 undergraduate majors. *Total enrollment:* 3,014. Undergraduates: 1,781. Freshmen: 297. Federal methodology is used as a basis for awarding need-based institutional aid.

**UNDERGRADUATE EXPENSES for 2015–2016** *Comprehensive fee:* $40,476 includes full-time tuition ($27,276), mandatory fees ($3450), and room and board ($9750). *College room only:* $5290. Full-time tuition and fees vary according to course level, course load, degree level, program, and student level. Room and board charges vary according to board plan and housing facility. *Part-time tuition:* $925 per credit hour. *Part-time fees:* $115 per credit hour. Part-time tuition and fees vary according to course level, degree level, program, and student level.

**FRESHMAN FINANCIAL AID (Fall 2014, est.)** 249 applied for aid; of those 85% were deemed to have need. 100% of freshmen with need received aid; of those 82% had need fully met. *Average percent of need met:* 65% (excluding resources awarded to replace EFC). *Average financial aid package:* $22,310 (excluding resources awarded to replace EFC). 14% of all full-time freshmen had no need and received non-need-based gift aid.

**UNDERGRADUATE FINANCIAL AID (Fall 2014, est.)** 1,123 applied for aid; of those 90% were deemed to have need. 99% of undergraduates with need received aid; of those 85% had need fully met. *Average percent of need met:* 62% (excluding resources awarded to replace EFC). *Average financial aid package:* $20,762 (excluding resources awarded to replace EFC). 21% of all full-time undergraduates had no need and received non-need-based gift aid.

**GIFT AID (NEED-BASED)** *Total amount:* $3,785,136 (43% federal, 18% state, 25% institutional, 14% external sources). *Receiving aid:* Freshmen: 72% (211); all full-time undergraduates: 59% (964). *Average award:* Freshmen: $17,572; Undergraduates: $16,114. *Scholarships, grants, and awards:* Federal Pell, FSEOG, state, private, college/university gift aid from institutional funds, United Negro College Fund, Federal Nursing, Native American Grants.

**GIFT AID (NON-NEED-BASED)** *Total amount:* $153,019 (20% state, 30% institutional, 50% external sources). *Receiving aid:* Freshmen: 13% (37). Undergraduates: 8% (138). *Average award:* Freshmen: $18,811. Undergraduates: $18,945. *Scholarships, grants, and awards by category:* Academic interests/achievement: business, communication, education, general academic interests/achievements, health fields, religion/biblical studies. Creative arts/performance: applied art and design, art/fine arts, dance, music, performing arts, theater/drama. Special achievements/activities: cheerleading/drum major, general special achievements/activities, junior miss, leadership, religious involvement. Special characteristics: children of faculty/staff, relatives of clergy, religious affiliation. *Tuition waivers:* Full or partial for employees or children of employees. *ROTC:* Army cooperative, Air Force cooperative.

**LOANS** *Student loans:* $6,651,791 (85% need-based, 15% non-need-based). 62% of past graduating class borrowed through all loan programs. *Average indebtedness per student:* $27,819. *Average need-based loan:* Freshmen: $3313. Undergraduates: $4480. *Parent loans:* $7,331,822 (46% need-based, 54% non-need-based). *Programs:* Federal Direct (Subsidized and Unsubsidized Stafford, PLUS), Perkins, Federal Nursing.

**WORK-STUDY** *Federal work-study:* Total amount: $630,718; 270 jobs averaging $1458. *State or other work-study/employment:* Total amount: $374,326 (100% non-need-based). 267 part-time jobs averaging $1383.

**ATHLETIC AWARDS** Total amount: $4,614,886 (88% need-based, 12% non-need-based).

**APPLYING FOR FINANCIAL AID** *Required financial aid form:* FAFSA. *Financial aid deadline (priority):* 3/1. *Notification date:* Continuous beginning 3/25. Students must reply within 4 weeks of notification.

**CONTACT** Denise Flis, Senior Director of Student Financial Services, Oklahoma City University, 2501 North Blackwelder, Oklahoma City, OK 73106-1493, 405-208-5848 or toll-free 800-633-7242. *Fax:* 405-208-5466. *E-mail:* dflis@okcu.edu. *Website:* http://www.okcu.edu/.

# OKLAHOMA PANHANDLE STATE UNIVERSITY
## Goodwell, OK

**CONTACT** Ms. Lori Ferguson, Director of Financial Aid, Oklahoma Panhandle State University, PO Box 430, Goodwell, OK 73939-0430, 580-349-1582 or toll-free 800-664-6778. *E-mail:* lorif@opsu.edu. *Website:* http://www.opsu.edu/.

# OKLAHOMA STATE UNIVERSITY
## Stillwater, OK

| Tuition & fees (OK res): $7441 | Average undergraduate aid package: $13,159 |
|---|---|

**ABOUT THE INSTITUTION** State-supported, coed. *Awards:* certificates, bachelor's, master's, and doctoral degrees. 85 undergraduate majors. *Total enrollment:* 25,854. Undergraduates: 20,821. Freshmen: 4,057. Federal methodology is used as a basis for awarding need-based institutional aid.

**UNDERGRADUATE EXPENSES for 2015–2016** *Application fee:* $40. *One-time required fee:* $95. *Tuition, state resident:* full-time $4425; part-time $147.50 per credit hour. *Tuition, nonresident:* full-time $17,010; part-time $567 per credit hour. *Required fees:* full-time $3016; $100.55 per credit hour. Full-time tuition and fees vary according to program. Part-time tuition and fees vary according to course load and program. *College room and board:* $7390; *Room only:* $3890. Room and board charges vary according to board plan and housing facility. *Payment plan:* Guaranteed tuition.

**FRESHMAN FINANCIAL AID (Fall 2013)** 2,915 applied for aid; of those 69% were deemed to have need. 97% of freshmen with need received aid; of those 17% had need fully met. *Average percent of need met:* 78% (excluding resources awarded to replace EFC). *Average financial aid package:* $13,284 (excluding resources awarded to replace EFC). 30% of all full-time freshmen had no need and received non-need-based gift aid.

**UNDERGRADUATE FINANCIAL AID (Fall 2013)** 11,957 applied for aid; of those 78% were deemed to have need. 98% of undergraduates with need received aid; of those 12% had need fully met. *Average percent of need met:* 76% (excluding resources awarded to replace EFC). *Average financial aid package:* $13,159 (excluding resources awarded to replace EFC). 27% of all full-time undergraduates had no need and received non-need-based gift aid.

**GIFT AID (NEED-BASED)** *Total amount:* $51,572,177 (47% federal, 26% state, 17% institutional, 10% external sources). *Receiving aid:* Freshmen: 42% (1,543); all full-time undergraduates: 40% (7,005). *Average award:* Freshmen: $7006; Undergraduates: $6615. *Scholarships, grants, and awards:* Federal Pell, FSEOG, state, private, college/university gift aid from institutional funds, TEACH Grants.

**GIFT AID (NON-NEED-BASED)** *Total amount:* $13,801,092 (5% federal, 12% state, 34% institutional, 49% external sources). *Receiving aid:* Freshmen: 5% (186). Undergraduates: 3% (488). *Average award:* Freshmen: $6461. Undergraduates: $5553. *Scholarships, grants, and awards by category:* Academic interests/achievement: agriculture, architecture, area/ethnic studies, biological sciences, business, communication, computer science, education, engineering/technologies, English, foreign languages, general academic interests/achievements, home economics, humanities, international studies, mathematics, military science, physical sciences, premedicine, social sciences. Creative arts/performance: art/fine arts, creative writing, general creative arts/performance, journalism/publications, music, theater/drama. Special achievements/activities: cheerleading/drum major, community service, general special achievements/activities, leadership, memberships, rodeo. Special characteristics: adult students, children and siblings of alumni, ethnic background, first-generation college students, general special characteristics, handicapped students, international students, local/state students, out-of-state students, previous college experience. *Tuition waivers:* Full or partial for children of alumni, employees or children of employees. *ROTC:* Army, Air Force.

**LOANS** *Student loans:* $64,228,139 (75% need-based, 25% non-need-based). 51% of past graduating class borrowed through all loan programs. *Average indebtedness per student:* $22,591. *Average need-based loan:* Freshmen: $3237. Undergraduates: $4093. *Parent loans:* $32,035,955 (32% need-based, 68% non-need-based). *Programs:* Federal Direct (Subsidized and Unsubsidized Stafford, PLUS), Perkins.

**WORK-STUDY** *Federal work-study:* 393 jobs averaging $2436. *State or other work-study/employment:* Total amount: $11,582,709 (100% non-need-based). 4,151 part-time jobs averaging $2790.
**ATHLETIC AWARDS** Total amount: $5,119,249 (33% need-based, 67% non-need-based).
**APPLYING FOR FINANCIAL AID** *Required financial aid form:* FAFSA. *Financial aid deadline (priority):* 2/1. *Notification date:* Continuous beginning 4/1. Students must reply by 5/1 or within 2 weeks of notification.
**CONTACT** Office of Scholarships and Financial Aid, Oklahoma State University, 119 Student Union, Stillwater, OK 74078-5061, 405-744-6604 or toll-free 800-233-5019. *Fax:* 405-744-6438. *E-mail:* finaid@okstate.edu.
*Website:* http://www.okstate.edu/.

# OKLAHOMA WESLEYAN UNIVERSITY
## Bartlesville, OK

| Tuition & fees: $23,180 | Average undergraduate aid package: $16,533 |
| --- | --- |

**ABOUT THE INSTITUTION** Independent Wesleyan Church, coed. *Awards:* associate, bachelor's, and master's degrees. 39 undergraduate majors. *Total enrollment:* 1,335. Undergraduates: 1,205. Freshmen: 197. Both federal and institutional methodology are used as a basis for awarding need-based institutional aid.
**UNDERGRADUATE EXPENSES for 2015–2016** *Application fee:* $25. *Comprehensive fee:* $30,668 includes full-time tuition ($21,930), mandatory fees ($1250), and room and board ($7488). *College room only:* $3858. Full-time tuition and fees vary according to course load. Room and board charges vary according to board plan and housing facility. *Part-time tuition:* $900 per credit.
**FRESHMAN FINANCIAL AID (Fall 2014, est.)** 148 applied for aid; of those 86% were deemed to have need. 100% of freshmen with need received aid; of those 13% had need fully met. *Average percent of need met:* 56% (excluding resources awarded to replace EFC). *Average financial aid package:* $15,264 (excluding resources awarded to replace EFC). 20% of all full-time freshmen had no need and received non-need-based gift aid.
**UNDERGRADUATE FINANCIAL AID (Fall 2014, est.)** 454 applied for aid; of those 89% were deemed to have need. 100% of undergraduates with need received aid; of those 19% had need fully met. *Average percent of need met:* 62% (excluding resources awarded to replace EFC). *Average financial aid package:* $16,533 (excluding resources awarded to replace EFC).
**GIFT AID (NEED-BASED)** *Total amount:* $5,006,983 (39% federal, 10% state, 41% institutional, 10% external sources). *Receiving aid:* Freshmen: 76% (127); all full-time undergraduates: 74% (400). *Average award:* Freshmen: $11,902; Undergraduates: $12,200. *Scholarships, grants, and awards:* Federal Pell, FSEOG, state, private, college/university gift aid from institutional funds.
**GIFT AID (NON-NEED-BASED)** *Total amount:* $1,132,780 (2% federal, 68% institutional, 30% external sources). *Receiving aid:* Freshmen: 8% (13). Undergraduates: 11% (57). *Average award:* Freshmen: $3980. Undergraduates: $5260. *Scholarships, grants, and awards by category: Academic interests/achievement:* biological sciences, business, computer science, education, general academic interests/achievements, health fields, religion/biblical studies. *Creative arts/performance:* music. *Special achievements/activities:* leadership, religious involvement. *Special characteristics:* children and siblings of alumni, children of educators, children of faculty/staff, international students, relatives of clergy, religious affiliation, siblings of current students. *Tuition waivers:* Full or partial for employees or children of employees, senior citizens.
**LOANS** *Student loans:* $7,296,399 (77% need-based, 23% non-need-based). 79% of past graduating class borrowed through all loan programs. *Average indebtedness per student:* $28,072. *Average need-based loan:* Freshmen: $3493. Undergraduates: $4694. *Parent loans:* $2,294,861 (45% need-based, 55% non-need-based). *Programs:* Federal Direct (Subsidized and Unsubsidized Stafford, PLUS), Perkins, college/university.
**WORK-STUDY** *Federal work-study:* Total amount: $222,552; jobs available. *State or other work-study/employment:* Total amount: $39,900 (36% need-based, 64% non-need-based). Part-time jobs available.
**ATHLETIC AWARDS** Total amount: $2,380,490 (45% need-based, 55% non-need-based).

**APPLYING FOR FINANCIAL AID** *Required financial aid forms:* FAFSA, institution's own form. *Financial aid deadline (priority):* 3/1. *Notification date:* Continuous beginning 1/15. Students must reply within 1 week of notification.
**CONTACT** Mrs. Kandi Lyn Molder, Director of Student Financial Services, Oklahoma Wesleyan University, 2201 Silver Lake Road, Bartlesville, OK 74006, 918-335-6282 or toll-free 866-222-8226. *Fax:* 918-335-6811. *E-mail:* financialaid@okwu.edu.
*Website:* http://www.okwu.edu/.

# OLD DOMINION UNIVERSITY
## Norfolk, VA

| Tuition & fees (VA res): $9250 | Average undergraduate aid package: $9681 |
| --- | --- |

**ABOUT THE INSTITUTION** State-supported, coed. *Awards:* certificates, bachelor's, master's, and doctoral degrees. 52 undergraduate majors. *Total enrollment:* 24,932. Undergraduates: 20,115. Freshmen: 2,795. Federal methodology is used as a basis for awarding need-based institutional aid.
**UNDERGRADUATE EXPENSES for 2015–2016** *Application fee:* $50. *Tuition, state resident:* full-time $8970; part-time $299 per credit hour. *Tuition, nonresident:* full-time $25,140; part-time $838 per credit hour. *Required fees:* full-time $280; $64 per term. Full-time tuition and fees vary according to location. Part-time tuition and fees vary according to location. *College room and board:* $10,233; *Room only:* $5689. Room and board charges vary according to board plan and housing facility.
**FRESHMAN FINANCIAL AID (Fall 2014, est.)** 2,420 applied for aid; of those 78% were deemed to have need. 98% of freshmen with need received aid; of those 15% had need fully met. *Average percent of need met:* 48% (excluding resources awarded to replace EFC). *Average financial aid package:* $10,504 (excluding resources awarded to replace EFC). 12% of all full-time freshmen had no need and received non-need-based gift aid.
**UNDERGRADUATE FINANCIAL AID (Fall 2014, est.)** 11,913 applied for aid; of those 83% were deemed to have need. 96% of undergraduates with need received aid; of those 11% had need fully met. *Average percent of need met:* 47% (excluding resources awarded to replace EFC). *Average financial aid package:* $9681 (excluding resources awarded to replace EFC). 7% of all full-time undergraduates had no need and received non-need-based gift aid.
**GIFT AID (NEED-BASED)** *Total amount:* $51,107,491 (63% federal, 29% state, 7% institutional, 1% external sources). *Receiving aid:* Freshmen: 56% (1,541); all full-time undergraduates: 49% (7,501). *Average award:* Freshmen: $6531; Undergraduates: $6049. *Scholarships, grants, and awards:* Federal Pell, FSEOG, state, private, college/university gift aid from institutional funds, United Negro College Fund, Federal Nursing.
**GIFT AID (NON-NEED-BASED)** *Total amount:* $10,558,991 (6% state, 77% institutional, 17% external sources). *Receiving aid:* Freshmen: 27% (745). Undergraduates: 13% (1,954). *Average award:* Freshmen: $3861. Undergraduates: $3902. *Scholarships, grants, and awards by category: Academic interests/achievement:* 1,545 awards ($4,265,250 total): area/ethnic studies, biological sciences, business, communication, computer science, education, engineering/technologies, English, foreign languages, general academic interests/achievements, health fields, humanities, international studies, mathematics, military science, physical sciences, social sciences. *Creative arts/performance:* 79 awards ($105,525 total): applied art and design, art/fine arts, cinema/film/broadcasting, creative writing, dance, general creative arts/performance, journalism/publications, music, performing arts, theater/drama. *Special achievements/activities:* 25 awards ($35,500 total): cheerleading/drum major, community service, leadership, memberships. *Special characteristics:* 154 awards ($284,250 total): children of faculty/staff, handicapped students, international students, local/state students, members of minority groups, previous college experience, veterans' children. *Tuition waivers:* Full or partial for employees or children of employees, senior citizens. *ROTC:* Army, Naval.
**LOANS** *Student loans:* $94,798,926 (42% need-based, 58% non-need-based). 69% of past graduating class borrowed through all loan programs. *Average indebtedness per student:* $29,357. *Average need-based loan:* Freshmen: $3514. Undergraduates: $4348. *Parent loans:* $12,165,279 (100% non-need-based). *Programs:* Federal Direct (Subsidized and Unsubsidized Stafford, PLUS), Perkins, Federal Nursing, college/university.
**WORK-STUDY** *Federal work-study:* Total amount: $2,441,751; 200 jobs averaging $2400.
**ATHLETIC AWARDS** Total amount: $6,847,083 (100% non-need-based).

APPLYING FOR FINANCIAL AID *Required financial aid form:* FAFSA. *Financial aid deadline:* 3/15 (priority: 2/15). *Notification date:* Continuous beginning 3/1. Students must reply within 2 weeks of notification.

CONTACT Office of Financial Aid, Old Dominion University, 121 Rollins Hall, Norfolk, VA 23529, 757-683-3683 or toll-free 800-348-7926. *Fax:* 757-683-5920. *E-mail:* finaid@odu.edu.

*Website:* http://www.odu.edu/.

# OLIVET COLLEGE
## Olivet, MI

| Tuition & fees: $23,801 | Average undergraduate aid package: $17,650 |
|---|---|

ABOUT THE INSTITUTION Independent Congregational Christian Church, coed. *Awards:* bachelor's and master's degrees. 43 undergraduate majors. *Total enrollment:* 1,059. Undergraduates: 1,456. Freshmen: 228. Federal methodology is used as a basis for awarding need-based institutional aid.

UNDERGRADUATE EXPENSES for 2015–2016 *Application fee:* $25. *Tuition:* full-time $22,950; part-time $750 per semester hour. Room and board charges vary according to board plan and housing facility.

FRESHMAN FINANCIAL AID (Fall 2013) 271 applied for aid; of those 92% were deemed to have need. 100% of freshmen with need received aid; of those 25% had need fully met. *Average percent of need met:* 78% (excluding resources awarded to replace EFC). *Average financial aid package:* $17,556 (excluding resources awarded to replace EFC). 17% of all full-time freshmen had no need and received non-need-based gift aid.

UNDERGRADUATE FINANCIAL AID (Fall 2013) 1,075 applied for aid; of those 94% were deemed to have need. 100% of undergraduates with need received aid; of those 20% had need fully met. *Average percent of need met:* 80% (excluding resources awarded to replace EFC). *Average financial aid package:* $17,650 (excluding resources awarded to replace EFC). 11% of all full-time undergraduates had no need and received non-need-based gift aid.

GIFT AID (NEED-BASED) *Total amount:* $10,929,541 (22% federal, 11% state, 65% institutional, 2% external sources). *Receiving aid:* Freshmen: 80% (223); all full-time undergraduates: 85% (955). *Average award:* Freshmen: $13,560; Undergraduates: $11,725. *Scholarships, grants, and awards:* Federal Pell, FSEOG, state, private, college/university gift aid from institutional funds.

GIFT AID (NON-NEED-BASED) *Total amount:* $1,656,414 (97% institutional, 3% external sources). *Receiving aid:* Freshmen: 15% (42). Undergraduates: 7% (81). *Average award:* Freshmen: $10,520. Undergraduates: $10,675. *Scholarships, grants, and awards by category:* Academic interests/achievement: 474 awards ($2,861,386 total): business, communication, education, English, foreign languages, general academic interests/achievements. *Creative arts/performance:* 10 awards ($12,550 total): art/fine arts, journalism/publications, music. *Special achievements/activities:* 321 awards ($573,981 total): community service, leadership, memberships. *Special characteristics:* 53 awards ($715,564 total): children and siblings of alumni, children of faculty/staff, international students, religious affiliation, siblings of current students. *ROTC:* Air Force cooperative.

LOANS *Student loans:* $8,892,792 (61% need-based, 39% non-need-based). 89% of past graduating class borrowed through all loan programs. *Average indebtedness per student:* $26,222. *Average need-based loan:* Freshmen: $2855. Undergraduates: $4612. *Parent loans:* $2,166,121 (39% need-based, 61% non-need-based). *Programs:* Perkins, state, alternative loans, CitiAssist Loans, Sallie Mae Smart Option Loans.

WORK-STUDY *Federal work-study:* 206 jobs averaging $864. *State or other work-study/employment:* Part-time jobs available.

APPLYING FOR FINANCIAL AID *Required financial aid form:* FAFSA. *Financial aid deadline:* Continuous. *Notification date:* Continuous beginning 3/1.

CONTACT Ms. Libby M. Jean, Director of Student Services, Olivet College, 320 South Main Street, Olivet, MI 49076-9701, 269-749-7655 or toll-free 800-456-7189. *Fax:* 269-749-3821. *E-mail:* ljean@olivetcollege.edu.

*Website:* http://www.olivetcollege.edu/.

# OLIVET NAZARENE UNIVERSITY
## Bourbonnais, IL

| Tuition & fees: $32,790 | Average undergraduate aid package: $24,719 |
|---|---|

ABOUT THE INSTITUTION Independent Church of the Nazarene, coed. *Awards:* associate, bachelor's, master's, and doctoral degrees. 57 undergraduate majors. *Total enrollment:* 4,861. Undergraduates: 3,521. Freshmen: 780. Federal methodology is used as a basis for awarding need-based institutional aid.

UNDERGRADUATE EXPENSES for 2015–2016 *Application fee:* $25. *Comprehensive fee:* $40,690 includes full-time tuition ($31,950), mandatory fees ($840), and room and board ($7900). Full-time tuition and fees vary according to course load. Room and board charges vary according to board plan. *Part-time tuition:* $1332 per semester hour. Part-time tuition and fees vary according to course load.

FRESHMAN FINANCIAL AID (Fall 2014, est.) 749 applied for aid; of those 90% were deemed to have need. 100% of freshmen with need received aid; of those 25% had need fully met. *Average percent of need met:* 80% (excluding resources awarded to replace EFC). *Average financial aid package:* $25,843 (excluding resources awarded to replace EFC). 13% of all full-time freshmen had no need and received non-need-based gift aid.

UNDERGRADUATE FINANCIAL AID (Fall 2014, est.) 2,698 applied for aid; of those 92% were deemed to have need. 99% of undergraduates with need received aid; of those 25% had need fully met. *Average percent of need met:* 80% (excluding resources awarded to replace EFC). *Average financial aid package:* $24,719 (excluding resources awarded to replace EFC). 17% of all full-time undergraduates had no need and received non-need-based gift aid.

GIFT AID (NEED-BASED) *Total amount:* $44,985,356 (11% federal, 8% state, 80% institutional, 1% external sources). *Receiving aid:* Freshmen: 87% (676); all full-time undergraduates: 82% (2,458). *Average award:* Freshmen: $20,261; Undergraduates: $19,925. *Scholarships, grants, and awards:* Federal Pell, FSEOG, state, private, college/university gift aid from institutional funds.

GIFT AID (NON-NEED-BASED) *Total amount:* $9,166,296 (5% federal, 93% institutional, 2% external sources). *Receiving aid:* Freshmen: 40% (312). Undergraduates: 36% (1,085). *Average award:* Freshmen: $14,783. Undergraduates: $12,655. *Scholarships, grants, and awards by category:* Academic interests/achievement: 2,830 awards ($32,710,165 total): general academic interests/achievements, military science. *Creative arts/performance:* 320 awards ($979,265 total): art/fine arts, music, performing arts, theater/drama. *Special achievements/activities:* 22 awards ($24,500 total): cheerleading/drum major, religious involvement. *Special characteristics:* 1,113 awards ($16,626,432 total): children of faculty/staff, general special characteristics, relatives of clergy, religious affiliation. *Tuition waivers:* Full or partial for employees or children of employees. *ROTC:* Army.

LOANS *Student loans:* $20,448,585 (69% need-based, 31% non-need-based). 76% of past graduating class borrowed through all loan programs. *Average indebtedness per student:* $32,906. *Average need-based loan:* Freshmen: $3490. Undergraduates: $4522. *Parent loans:* $5,621,056 (39% need-based, 61% non-need-based). *Programs:* Federal Direct (Subsidized and Unsubsidized Stafford, PLUS), Perkins, private loans.

WORK-STUDY *Federal work-study:* Total amount: $417,232; 353 jobs averaging $1380. *State or other work-study/employment:* Total amount: $1,187,139 (34% need-based, 66% non-need-based). 911 part-time jobs averaging $1302.

ATHLETIC AWARDS Total amount: $4,918,345 (56% need-based, 44% non-need-based).

APPLYING FOR FINANCIAL AID *Financial aid deadline (priority):* 3/1. *Notification date:* Continuous beginning 2/1. Students must reply by 5/1.

CONTACT Mr. Greg Bruner, Director of Financial Aid, Olivet Nazarene University, One University Avenue, Bourbonnais, IL 60914, 815-939-5249 or toll-free 800-648-1463. *Fax:* 815-939-5074. *E-mail:* gbruner@olivet.edu.

*Website:* http://www.olivet.edu/.

# O'MORE COLLEGE OF DESIGN
## Franklin, TN

| Tuition & fees: N/R | Average undergraduate aid package: N/A |
|---|---|

**ABOUT THE INSTITUTION** Independent, coed. 3 undergraduate majors. Federal methodology is used as a basis for awarding need-based institutional aid.

**GIFT AID (NEED-BASED) Scholarships, grants, and awards:** Federal Pell, FSEOG, state, college/university gift aid from institutional funds.

**GIFT AID (NON-NEED-BASED) Scholarships, grants, and awards by category:** Academic interests/achievement: general academic interests/achievements.

**LOANS Programs:** Federal Direct (Subsidized and Unsubsidized Stafford, PLUS).

**APPLYING FOR FINANCIAL AID Required financial aid forms:** FAFSA, institution's own form. **Financial aid deadline (priority):** 5/1. **Notification date:** Continuous.

**CONTACT** Lea Voigt, Director of Financial Assistance, O'More College of Design, 423 South Margin Street, Franklin, TN 37064-2816, 615-794-4254 Ext. 238 or toll-free 888-662-1970. E-mail: lvoigt@omorecollege.edu.
Website: http://www.omorecollege.edu/.

# ORAL ROBERTS UNIVERSITY
## Tulsa, OK

| Tuition & fees: $23,410 | Average undergraduate aid package: $22,392 |
|---|---|

**ABOUT THE INSTITUTION** Independent interdenominational, coed. **Awards:** certificates, bachelor's, master's, and doctoral degrees. 75 undergraduate majors. **Total enrollment:** 3,612. Undergraduates: 3,078. Freshmen: 408. Federal methodology is used as a basis for awarding need-based institutional aid.

**UNDERGRADUATE EXPENSES** for 2015–2016 **Application fee:** $35. **Comprehensive fee:** $33,175 includes full-time tuition ($22,564), mandatory fees ($846), and room and board ($9765). **College room only:** $4775. Full-time tuition and fees vary according to degree level. Room and board charges vary according to board plan and housing facility. **Part-time tuition:** $943 per credit hour. Part-time tuition and fees vary according to degree level.

**FRESHMAN FINANCIAL AID (Fall 2014, est.)** 319 applied for aid; of those 93% were deemed to have need. 100% of freshmen with need received aid; of those 35% had need fully met. **Average percent of need met:** 76% (excluding resources awarded to replace EFC). **Average financial aid package:** $24,133 (excluding resources awarded to replace EFC). 19% of all full-time freshmen had no need and received non-need-based gift aid.

**UNDERGRADUATE FINANCIAL AID (Fall 2014, est.)** 1,873 applied for aid; of those 93% were deemed to have need. 100% of undergraduates with need received aid; of those 32% had need fully met. **Average percent of need met:** 72% (excluding resources awarded to replace EFC). **Average financial aid package:** $22,392 (excluding resources awarded to replace EFC). 22% of all full-time undergraduates had no need and received non-need-based gift aid.

**GIFT AID (NEED-BASED) Receiving aid:** Freshmen: 73% (290); all full-time undergraduates: 70% (1,697). **Average award:** Freshmen: $15,988; Undergraduates: $14,335. **Scholarships, grants, and awards:** Federal Pell, FSEOG, state, private, college/university gift aid from institutional funds.

**GIFT AID (NON-NEED-BASED) Receiving aid:** Freshmen: 5% (21). Undergraduates: 5% (129). **Average award:** Freshmen: $10,297. Undergraduates: $11,030. **Scholarships, grants, and awards by category:** Academic interests/achievement: biological sciences, business, communication, education, engineering/technologies, general academic interests/achievements, health fields, religion/biblical studies. Creative arts/performance: applied art and design, art/fine arts, cinema/film/broadcasting, journalism/publications, music. Special achievements/activities: cheerleading/drum major, community service, general special achievements/activities, leadership, memberships, religious involvement. Special characteristics: children and siblings of alumni, children of faculty/staff, general special characteristics, international students, local/state students, relatives of clergy, siblings of current students. **Tuition waivers:** Full or partial for employees or children of employees. **ROTC:** Air Force cooperative.

**LOANS Student loans:** 66% of past graduating class borrowed through all loan programs. Average indebtedness per student: $32,750. **Average need-based loan:**

Freshmen: $5851. Undergraduates: $6293. **Programs:** Federal Direct (Subsidized and Unsubsidized Stafford, PLUS), Perkins.

**WORK-STUDY** Federal work-study jobs available. **State or other work-study/employment:** Part-time jobs available.

**APPLYING FOR FINANCIAL AID Required financial aid form:** FAFSA. **Financial aid deadline (priority):** 3/1. **Notification date:** Continuous beginning 3/5. Students must reply by 5/1 or within 3 weeks of notification.

**CONTACT** Office of Financial Aid, Oral Roberts University, 7777 South Lewis Avenue, Tulsa, OK 74171, 918-495-6510 or toll-free 800-678-8876. Fax: 918-495-6803.
Website: http://www.oru.edu/.

# OREGON COLLEGE OF ART & CRAFT
## Portland, OR

**CONTACT** Ms. Linda L. Anderson, Director of Financial Aid, Oregon College of Art & Craft, 8245 Southwest Barnes Road, Portland, OR 97225, 971-255-4224 or toll-free 800-390-0632, Fax: 503-297-9651. E-mail: landerson@ocac.edu.
Website: http://www.ocac.edu/.

# OREGON HEALTH & SCIENCE UNIVERSITY
## Portland, OR

| Tuition & fees: N/R | Average undergraduate aid package: $11,950 |
|---|---|

**ABOUT THE INSTITUTION** State-related, coed. **Awards:** certificates, bachelor's, master's, and doctoral degrees. 2 undergraduate majors. **Total enrollment:** 2,861. Undergraduates: 847. Federal methodology is used as a basis for awarding need-based institutional aid.

**UNDERGRADUATE FINANCIAL AID (Fall 2014, est.)** 301 applied for aid; of those 97% were deemed to have need. 96% of undergraduates with need received aid; of those 5% had need fully met. **Average percent of need met:** 34% (excluding resources awarded to replace EFC). **Average financial aid package:** $11,950 (excluding resources awarded to replace EFC).

**GIFT AID (NEED-BASED) Total amount:** $3,066,215 (50% federal, 31% state, 10% institutional, 9% external sources). **Receiving aid:** All full-time undergraduates: 53% (172). **Average award:** Undergraduates: $10,184. **Scholarships, grants, and awards:** Federal Pell, FSEOG, state, private, college/university gift aid from institutional funds.

**GIFT AID (NON-NEED-BASED) Total amount:** $20,515 (24% federal, 42% state, 34% external sources). **Receiving aid:** Undergraduates: 1. **Scholarships, grants, and awards by category:** Academic interests/achievement: 105 awards ($836,819 total): health fields.

**LOANS Student loans:** $14,233,092 (88% need-based, 12% non-need-based). **Average need-based loan:** Undergraduates: $6293. **Parent loans:** $545,227 (75% need-based, 25% non-need-based). **Programs:** Federal Direct (Subsidized and Unsubsidized Stafford, PLUS), Perkins, Federal Nursing, college/university, alternative loans.

**WORK-STUDY Federal work-study:** Total amount: $20,000; 20 jobs averaging $1000.

**APPLYING FOR FINANCIAL AID Notification date:** Continuous.

**CONTACT** Lea Pandozzi, Administrative Coordinator, Oregon Health & Science University, 3181 SW Sam Jackson Park Road, L-109, Portland, OR 97239-3089, 503-494-7323. Fax: 503-494-4629. E-mail: pandozzi@ohsu.edu.
Website: http://www.ohsu.edu/.

# OREGON INSTITUTE OF TECHNOLOGY
## Klamath Falls, OR

| Tuition & fees: N/R | Average undergraduate aid package: $8064 |
| --- | --- |

**ABOUT THE INSTITUTION** State-supported, coed. 19 undergraduate majors. Federal methodology is used as a basis for awarding need-based institutional aid.

**FRESHMAN FINANCIAL AID (Fall 2013)** 275 applied for aid; of those 80% were deemed to have need. 97% of freshmen with need received aid; of those 38% had need fully met. *Average percent of need met:* 22% (excluding resources awarded to replace EFC). *Average financial aid package:* $7246 (excluding resources awarded to replace EFC).

**UNDERGRADUATE FINANCIAL AID (Fall 2013)** 1,966 applied for aid; of those 88% were deemed to have need. 98% of undergraduates with need received aid; of those 30% had need fully met. *Average percent of need met:* 23% (excluding resources awarded to replace EFC). *Average financial aid package:* $8064 (excluding resources awarded to replace EFC).

**GIFT AID (NEED-BASED)** *Total amount:* $8,685,456 (71% federal, 14% state, 11% institutional, 4% external sources). *Receiving aid:* Freshmen: 54% (163); all full-time undergraduates: 50% (1,162). *Average award:* Freshmen: $6360; Undergraduates: $5912. *Scholarships, grants, and awards:* Federal Pell, FSEOG, state, private, college/university gift aid from institutional funds.

**GIFT AID (NON-NEED-BASED)** *Total amount:* $705,031 (5% federal, 95% institutional). *Receiving aid:* Freshmen: 40% (122). Undergraduates: 27% (631). *Scholarships, grants, and awards by category:* Academic interests/achievement: general academic interests/achievements. *Special achievements/activities:* general special achievements/activities, leadership.

**LOANS** *Student loans:* $16,567,705 (68% need-based, 32% non-need-based). 72% of past graduating class borrowed through all loan programs. *Average indebtedness per student:* $29,685. *Average need-based loan:* Freshmen: $3529. Undergraduates: $4613. *Parent loans:* $5,883,359 (50% need-based, 50% non-need-based). *Programs:* Federal Direct (Subsidized and Unsubsidized Stafford, PLUS), Perkins, college/university.

**WORK-STUDY** *Federal work-study:* jobs available. *State or other work-study/employment:* Part-time jobs available.

**ATHLETIC AWARDS** Total amount: $91,487 (37% need-based, 63% non-need-based).

**APPLYING FOR FINANCIAL AID** *Required financial aid form:* FAFSA. *Financial aid deadline (priority):* 2/1. *Notification date:* Continuous beginning 4/1. Students must reply within 3 weeks of notification.

**CONTACT** Tracey Lehman, Director of Financial Aid, Oregon Institute of Technology, 3201 Campus Drive, Klamath Falls, OR 97601, 541-885-1280 or toll-free 800-422-2017. *Fax:* 541-885-1024. *E-mail:* tracey.lehman@oit.edu. *Website:* http://www.oit.edu/.

# OREGON STATE UNIVERSITY
## Corvallis, OR

| Tuition & fees (OR res): $9122 | Average undergraduate aid package: $12,913 |
| --- | --- |

**ABOUT THE INSTITUTION** State-supported, coed. *Awards:* certificates, bachelor's, master's, and doctoral degrees. 80 undergraduate majors. *Total enrollment:* 28,886. Undergraduates: 23,903. Freshmen: 3,718. Federal methodology is used as a basis for awarding need-based institutional aid.

**UNDERGRADUATE EXPENSES for 2015–2016** *Application fee:* $60. *One-time required fee:* $300. *Tuition, state resident:* full-time $7650; part-time $189 per credit hour. *Tuition, nonresident:* full-time $24,822; part-time $613 per credit hour. *Required fees:* full-time $1472; $448.57 per term. Full-time tuition and fees vary according to course load, location, and program. Part-time tuition and fees vary according to course load, location, and program. *College room and board:* $11,151; *Room only:* $7650. Room and board charges vary according to board plan and housing facility.

**FRESHMAN FINANCIAL AID (Fall 2014, est.)** 2,937 applied for aid; of those 69% were deemed to have need. 99% of freshmen with need received aid; of those 9% had need fully met. *Average percent of need met:* 67% (excluding resources awarded to replace EFC). *Average financial aid package:* $11,695 (excluding resources awarded to replace EFC). 17% of all full-time freshmen had no need and received non-need-based gift aid.

**UNDERGRADUATE FINANCIAL AID (Fall 2014, est.)** 12,639 applied for aid; of those 81% were deemed to have need. 99% of undergraduates with need received aid; of those 8% had need fully met. *Average percent of need met:* 66% (excluding resources awarded to replace EFC). *Average financial aid package:* $12,913 (excluding resources awarded to replace EFC). 13% of all full-time undergraduates had no need and received non-need-based gift aid.

**GIFT AID (NEED-BASED)** *Total amount:* $71,015,385 (46% federal, 12% state, 32% institutional, 10% external sources). *Receiving aid:* Freshmen: 48% (1,650); all full-time undergraduates: 43% (7,764). *Average award:* Freshmen: $7392; Undergraduates: $6966. *Scholarships, grants, and awards:* Federal Pell, FSEOG, state, private, college/university gift aid from institutional funds.

**GIFT AID (NON-NEED-BASED)** *Total amount:* $10,731,702 (1% state, 87% institutional, 12% external sources). *Receiving aid:* Freshmen: 1% (30). Undergraduates: 1% (130). *Average award:* Freshmen: $4315. Undergraduates: $4123. *Scholarships, grants, and awards by category:* Academic interests/achievement: general academic interests/achievements. *Special achievements/activities:* leadership. *Special characteristics:* children and siblings of alumni, local/state students, members of minority groups. *Tuition waivers:* Full or partial for employees or children of employees. *ROTC:* Army, Naval, Air Force.

**LOANS** *Student loans:* $115,002,802 (86% need-based, 14% non-need-based). 58% of past graduating class borrowed through all loan programs. *Average indebtedness per student:* $21,955. *Average need-based loan:* Freshmen: $3827. Undergraduates: $4727. *Parent loans:* $34,321,544 (80% need-based, 20% non-need-based). *Programs:* Federal Direct (Subsidized and Unsubsidized Stafford, PLUS), Perkins, college/university.

**WORK-STUDY** *Federal work-study:* Total amount: $2,945,101; 1,422 jobs averaging $2071.

**ATHLETIC AWARDS** Total amount: $9,841,986 (37% need-based, 63% non-need-based).

**APPLYING FOR FINANCIAL AID** *Required financial aid form:* FAFSA. *Financial aid deadline (priority):* 2/28. *Notification date:* Continuous beginning 4/1. Students must reply within 4 weeks of notification.

**CONTACT** Doug Severs, Director of Financial Aid and Scholarships, Oregon State University, 218 Kerr Administration Building, Corvallis, OR 97331-2120, 541-737-4494 or toll-free 800-291-4192. *E-mail:* financial.aid@oregonstate.edu. *Website:* http://www.oregonstate.edu/.

# OREGON STATE UNIVERSITY–CASCADES
## Bend, OR

**CONTACT** Financial Aid Office, Oregon State University–Cascades, 2600 Northwest College Way, Bend, OR 97701, 541-322-3100. *Website:* http://www.osucascades.edu/.

# OTIS COLLEGE OF ART AND DESIGN
## Los Angeles, CA

| Tuition & fees: $37,380 | Average undergraduate aid package: $26,104 |
| --- | --- |

**ABOUT THE INSTITUTION** Independent, coed. *Awards:* bachelor's and master's degrees. 10 undergraduate majors. *Total enrollment:* 1,086. Undergraduates: 1,032. Freshmen: 160. Federal methodology is used as a basis for awarding need-based institutional aid.

**UNDERGRADUATE EXPENSES for 2015–2016** *Application fee:* $50. *Comprehensive fee:* $38,330 includes full-time tuition ($37,380) and room and board ($950).

**FRESHMAN FINANCIAL AID (Fall 2014, est.)** 156 applied for aid; of those 94% were deemed to have need. 100% of freshmen with need received aid; of those 10% had need fully met. *Average percent of need met:* 58% (excluding resources awarded to replace EFC). *Average financial aid package:* $24,098 (excluding resources awarded to replace EFC). 20% of all full-time freshmen had no need and received non-need-based gift aid.

**UNDERGRADUATE FINANCIAL AID (Fall 2014, est.)** 733 applied for aid; of those 96% were deemed to have need. 100% of undergraduates with need received aid; of those 7% had need fully met. *Average percent of need met:* 60% (excluding resources awarded to replace EFC). *Average financial aid package:* $26,104 (excluding resources awarded to replace EFC). 17% of all full-time undergraduates had no need and received non-need-based gift aid.

**GIFT AID (NEED-BASED)** *Total amount:* $14,663,219 (19% federal, 16% state, 64% institutional, 1% external sources). *Receiving aid:* Freshmen: 61% (146); all full-time undergraduates: 65% (696). *Average award:* Freshmen: $19,661; Undergraduates: $20,241. *Scholarships, grants, and awards:* Federal Pell, FSEOG, state, private, college/university gift aid from institutional funds.

**GIFT AID (NON-NEED-BASED)** *Total amount:* $2,222,937 (99% institutional, 1% external sources). *Receiving aid:* Freshmen: 23% (55). Undergraduates: 18% (197). *Average award:* Freshmen: $10,078. Undergraduates: $9919. *Scholarships, grants, and awards by category: Academic interests/achievement:* general academic interests/achievements. *Creative arts/performance:* applied art and design, art/fine arts.

**LOANS** *Student loans:* $5,833,184 (97% need-based, 3% non-need-based). 68% of past graduating class borrowed through all loan programs. *Average indebtedness per student:* $33,694. *Average need-based loan:* Freshmen: $3474. Undergraduates: $4696. *Parent loans:* $4,881,187 (90% need-based, 10% non-need-based). *Programs:* Federal Direct (Subsidized and Unsubsidized Stafford, PLUS), Perkins.

**WORK-STUDY** *Federal work-study:* Total amount: $114,089; jobs available. *State or other work-study/employment:* Total amount: $18,000 (100% non-need-based). Part-time jobs available.

**APPLYING FOR FINANCIAL AID** *Required financial aid form:* FAFSA. *Financial aid deadline (priority):* 2/15. *Notification date:* 3/1.

**CONTACT** Jessika Huerta, Director of Financial Aid, Otis College of Art and Design, 9045 Lincoln Boulevard, Los Angeles, CA 90045-9785, 310-665-6898 or toll-free 800-527-OTIS. *Fax:* 310-665-6884. *E-mail:* jhuerta@otis.edu. *Website:* http://www.otis.edu/.

---

# OTTAWA UNIVERSITY
## Ottawa, KS

**CONTACT** Financial Aid Coordinator, Ottawa University, 1001 South Cedar, Ottawa, KS 66067-3399, 785-242-5200 or toll-free 800-755-5200. *E-mail:* finaid@ottawa.edu. *Website:* http://www.ottawa.edu/.

---

# OTTERBEIN UNIVERSITY
## Westerville, OH

| Tuition & fees: $31,624 | Average undergraduate aid package: $23,051 |
| --- | --- |

**ABOUT THE INSTITUTION** Independent United Methodist, coed. *Awards:* certificates, bachelor's, master's, and doctoral degrees. 61 undergraduate majors. *Total enrollment:* 2,984. Undergraduates: 2,537. Freshmen: 564. Both federal and institutional methodology are used as a basis for awarding need-based institutional aid.

**UNDERGRADUATE EXPENSES for 2015–2016** *Application fee:* $25. *Comprehensive fee:* $41,084 includes full-time tuition ($31,424), mandatory fees ($200), and room and board ($9460). Full-time tuition and fees vary according to course load and program. Room and board charges vary according to board plan and housing facility. *Part-time tuition:* $564 per credit hour. Part-time tuition and fees vary according to course load and program.

**FRESHMAN FINANCIAL AID (Fall 2014, est.)** 530 applied for aid; of those 89% were deemed to have need. 100% of freshmen with need received aid; of those 21% had need fully met. *Average percent of need met:* 76% (excluding resources awarded to replace EFC). *Average financial aid package:* $23,871 (excluding

resources awarded to replace EFC). 15% of all full-time freshmen had no need and received non-need-based gift aid.

**UNDERGRADUATE FINANCIAL AID (Fall 2014, est.)** 1,841 applied for aid; of those 89% were deemed to have need. 100% of undergraduates with need received aid; of those 15% had need fully met. *Average percent of need met:* 75% (excluding resources awarded to replace EFC). *Average financial aid package:* $23,051 (excluding resources awarded to replace EFC). 22% of all full-time undergraduates had no need and received non-need-based gift aid.

**GIFT AID (NEED-BASED)** *Total amount:* $29,210,798 (10% federal, 4% state, 84% institutional, 2% external sources). *Receiving aid:* Freshmen: 83% (466); all full-time undergraduates: 76% (1,607). *Average award:* Freshmen: $18,614; Undergraduates: $17,629. *Scholarships, grants, and awards:* Federal Pell, FSEOG, state, private, college/university gift aid from institutional funds, Federal Nursing.

**GIFT AID (NON-NEED-BASED)** *Receiving aid:* Freshmen: 16% (89). Undergraduates: 10% (222). *Average award:* Freshmen: $18,077. Undergraduates: $16,204. *Scholarships, grants, and awards by category: Academic interests/achievement:* general academic interests/achievements. *Creative arts/performance:* art/fine arts, music, theater/drama. *Special achievements/activities:* community service, leadership. *Special characteristics:* children and siblings of alumni, children of faculty/staff, general special characteristics, international students, members of minority groups, previous college experience, relatives of clergy, siblings of current students, veterans. *Tuition waivers:* Full or partial for employees or children of employees. *ROTC:* Army cooperative.

**LOANS** *Student loans:* $16,073,040 (69% need-based, 31% non-need-based). 76% of past graduating class borrowed through all loan programs. *Average indebtedness per student:* $37,388. *Average need-based loan:* Freshmen: $5124. Undergraduates: $6531. *Parent loans:* $6,216,793 (39% need-based, 61% non-need-based). *Programs:* Federal Direct (Subsidized and Unsubsidized Stafford, PLUS), Perkins, Federal Nursing, state, college/university.

**WORK-STUDY** *Federal work-study:* Total amount: $1,026,467; 757 jobs averaging $1616. *State or other work-study/employment:* Total amount: $175,281 (100% non-need-based). 250 part-time jobs averaging $1500.

**APPLYING FOR FINANCIAL AID** *Required financial aid form:* FAFSA. *Financial aid deadline (priority):* 2/15. *Notification date:* Continuous beginning 3/1.

**CONTACT** Mr. Thomas V. Yarnell, Director of Financial Aid, Otterbein University, One Otterbein College, Westerville, OH 43081-2006, 614-823-1502 or toll-free 800-488-8144. *Fax:* 614-823-1200. *E-mail:* tyarnell@otterbein.edu. *Website:* http://www.otterbein.edu/.

---

# OUACHITA BAPTIST UNIVERSITY
## Arkadelphia, AR

| Tuition & fees: $23,320 | Average undergraduate aid package: $21,016 |
| --- | --- |

**ABOUT THE INSTITUTION** Independent Baptist, coed. *Awards:* associate and bachelor's degrees. 54 undergraduate majors. *Total enrollment:* 1,543. Undergraduates: 1,543. Freshmen: 393. Both federal and institutional methodology are used as a basis for awarding need-based institutional aid.

**UNDERGRADUATE EXPENSES for 2015–2016** *Comprehensive fee:* $30,220 includes full-time tuition ($22,800), mandatory fees ($520), and room and board ($6900). Full-time tuition and fees vary according to degree level. Room and board charges vary according to housing facility. *Part-time tuition:* $630 per semester hour. Part-time tuition and fees vary according to degree level.

**FRESHMAN FINANCIAL AID (Fall 2014, est.)** 382 applied for aid; of those 75% were deemed to have need. 100% of freshmen with need received aid; of those 31% had need fully met. *Average percent of need met:* 84% (excluding resources awarded to replace EFC). *Average financial aid package:* $20,358 (excluding resources awarded to replace EFC). 30% of all full-time freshmen had no need and received non-need-based gift aid.

**UNDERGRADUATE FINANCIAL AID (Fall 2014, est.)** 1,116 applied for aid; of those 81% were deemed to have need. 100% of undergraduates with need received aid; of those 36% had need fully met. *Average percent of need met:* 84% (excluding resources awarded to replace EFC). *Average financial aid package:* $21,016 (excluding resources awarded to replace EFC). 34% of all full-time undergraduates had no need and received non-need-based gift aid.

**GIFT AID (NEED-BASED)** *Total amount:* $12,471,314 (14% federal, 11% state, 70% institutional, 5% external sources). *Receiving aid:* Freshmen: 68% (284); all full-

time undergraduates: 60% (872). *Average award:* Freshmen: $14,158; Undergraduates: $14,241. *Scholarships, grants, and awards:* Federal Pell, FSEOG, state, private, college/university gift aid from institutional funds.

**GIFT AID (NON-NEED-BASED)** *Total amount:* $8,628,096 (19% state, 67% institutional, 14% external sources). *Receiving aid:* Freshmen: 14% (59). Undergraduates: 13% (188). *Average award:* Freshmen: $8716. Undergraduates: $9937. *Scholarships, grants, and awards by category:* Academic interests/achievement: area/ethnic studies, biological sciences, business, communication, computer science, education, engineering/technologies, English, foreign languages, general academic interests/achievements, health fields, home economics, humanities, international studies, mathematics, physical sciences, premedicine, religion/biblical studies, social sciences. *Creative arts/performance:* art/fine arts, journalism/publications, music, performing arts, theater/drama. *Special achievements/activities:* cheerleading/drum major, general special achievements/activities. *Special characteristics:* children and siblings of alumni, children of faculty/staff, ethnic background, first-generation college students, general special characteristics, handicapped students, international students, local/state students, married students, members of minority groups, out-of-state students, previous college experience, relatives of clergy, religious affiliation, twins. *Tuition waivers:* Full or partial for employees or children of employees. *ROTC:* Army.

**LOANS** *Student loans:* $6,488,327 (54% need-based, 46% non-need-based). 48% of past graduating class borrowed through all loan programs. *Average indebtedness per student:* $24,252. *Average need-based loan:* Freshmen: $3219. Undergraduates: $3855. *Parent loans:* $1,505,592 (37% need-based, 63% non-need-based). *Programs:* Federal Direct (Subsidized and Unsubsidized Stafford, PLUS), Perkins, college/university.

**WORK-STUDY** *Federal work-study:* Total amount: $583,813; 325 jobs averaging $1681. *State or other work-study/employment:* Total amount: $229,037 (56% need-based, 44% non-need-based). 141 part-time jobs averaging $1648.

**ATHLETIC AWARDS** Total amount: $2,515,455 (59% need-based, 41% non-need-based).

**APPLYING FOR FINANCIAL AID** *Required financial aid forms:* FAFSA, state aid form. *Financial aid deadline:* 6/1 (priority: 1/31). *Notification date:* Continuous beginning 11/1. Students must reply by 6/1.

**CONTACT** Ms. Susan Hurst, Director of Financial Aid, Ouachita Baptist University, PO Box 3774, Arkadelphia, AR 71998-0001, 870-245-5570 or toll-free 800-342-5628. *Fax:* 870-245-5318. *E-mail:* hursts@obu.edu.

*Website:* http://www.obu.edu/.

# OUR LADY OF HOLY CROSS COLLEGE
## New Orleans, LA

**ABOUT THE INSTITUTION** Independent Roman Catholic, coed. 17 undergraduate majors.

**GIFT AID (NEED-BASED)** *Scholarships, grants, and awards:* Federal Pell, FSEOG, state, private, college/university gift aid from institutional funds.

**GIFT AID (NON-NEED-BASED)** *Scholarships, grants, and awards by category:* Academic interests/achievement: education, general academic interests/achievements, health fields, religion/biblical studies. *Special characteristics:* children of faculty/staff, general special characteristics, relatives of clergy, religious affiliation.

**LOANS** *Programs:* Federal Direct (Subsidized and Unsubsidized Stafford, PLUS), private loans.

**WORK-STUDY** *Federal work-study:* 14 jobs averaging $3300.

**APPLYING FOR FINANCIAL AID** *Required financial aid form:* FAFSA.

**CONTACT** Miss Meredith Reed, Vice President for Enrollment Management, Our Lady of Holy Cross College, 4123 Woodland Drive, New Orleans, LA 70131-7399, 504-398-2185 or toll-free 800-259-7744. *Fax:* 504-394-1182. *E-mail:* mreed@olhcc.edu.

*Website:* http://www.olhcc.edu/.

# OUR LADY OF THE LAKE COLLEGE
## Baton Rouge, LA

**CONTACT** Tiffany D. Magee, Director of Financial Aid, Our Lady of the Lake College, 7434 Perkins Road, Baton Rouge, LA 70808, 225-768-1701. *Fax:* 225-490-1632. *E-mail:* tiffany.magee@ololcollege.edu.

*Website:* http://www.ololcollege.edu/.

# OUR LADY OF THE LAKE UNIVERSITY OF SAN ANTONIO
## San Antonio, TX

| Tuition & fees: $24,596 | Average undergraduate aid package: $19,688 |
|---|---|

**ABOUT THE INSTITUTION** Independent Roman Catholic, coed. *Awards:* bachelor's, master's, and doctoral degrees. 31 undergraduate majors. *Total enrollment:* 3,173. Undergraduates: 1,595. Freshmen: 357. Both federal and institutional methodology are used as a basis for awarding need-based institutional aid.

**UNDERGRADUATE EXPENSES for 2015–2016** *Comprehensive fee:* $32,032 includes full-time tuition ($23,868), mandatory fees ($728), and room and board ($7436). *College room only:* $4138. Full-time tuition and fees vary according to course load and location. Room and board charges vary according to board plan and housing facility. *Part-time tuition:* $765 per credit hour. *Part-time fees:* $208 per term. Part-time tuition and fees vary according to course load and location.

**FRESHMAN FINANCIAL AID (Fall 2013)** 326 applied for aid; of those 95% were deemed to have need. 100% of freshmen with need received aid; of those 19% had need fully met. *Average percent of need met:* 78% (excluding resources awarded to replace EFC). *Average financial aid package:* $21,174 (excluding resources awarded to replace EFC). 6% of all full-time freshmen had no need and received non-need-based gift aid.

**UNDERGRADUATE FINANCIAL AID (Fall 2013)** 1,231 applied for aid; of those 94% were deemed to have need. 100% of undergraduates with need received aid; of those 28% had need fully met. *Average percent of need met:* 77% (excluding resources awarded to replace EFC). *Average financial aid package:* $19,688 (excluding resources awarded to replace EFC). 7% of all full-time undergraduates had no need and received non-need-based gift aid.

**GIFT AID (NEED-BASED)** *Total amount:* $9,913,149 (43% federal, 27% state, 26% institutional, 4% external sources). *Receiving aid:* Freshmen: 86% (288); all full-time undergraduates: 80% (1,049). *Average award:* Freshmen: $9463; Undergraduates: $9091. *Scholarships, grants, and awards:* Federal Pell, FSEOG, state, private, college/university gift aid from institutional funds.

**GIFT AID (NON-NEED-BASED)** *Total amount:* $7,307,598 (100% institutional). *Receiving aid:* Freshmen: 90% (300). Undergraduates: 72% (949). *Average award:* Freshmen: $10,650. Undergraduates: $9182. *Scholarships, grants, and awards by category:* Academic interests/achievement: general academic interests/achievements. *Creative arts/performance:* music. *Special characteristics:* children of faculty/staff, religious affiliation. *Tuition waivers:* Full or partial for employees or children of employees. *ROTC:* Army cooperative.

**LOANS** *Student loans:* $10,947,666 (45% need-based, 55% non-need-based). 84% of past graduating class borrowed through all loan programs. *Average indebtedness per student:* $28,362. *Average need-based loan:* Freshmen: $3302. Undergraduates: $4423. *Parent loans:* $721,737 (100% non-need-based). *Programs:* Federal Direct (Subsidized and Unsubsidized Stafford, PLUS), Perkins, state.

**WORK-STUDY** *Federal work-study:* jobs available. *State or other work-study/employment:* Total amount: $14,287 (100% need-based). Part-time jobs available.

**ATHLETIC AWARDS** Total amount: $1,056,816 (1% need-based, 99% non-need-based).

**APPLYING FOR FINANCIAL AID** *Required financial aid forms:* FAFSA, institution's own form. *Financial aid deadline (priority):* 5/1. *Notification date:* Continuous beginning 4/1.

**CONTACT** Esmeralda Flores, Director of Financial Aid, Our Lady of the Lake University of San Antonio, 411 Southwest 24th Street, San Antonio, TX 78207-4689, 210-434-6711 Ext. 2558 or toll-free 800-436-6558. *Fax:* 210-431-3958. *E-mail:* emflores@lake.ollusa.edu.
*Website:* http://www.ollusa.edu/.

# OZARK CHRISTIAN COLLEGE
## Joplin, MO

**CONTACT** Jill Kaminsky, Application Processor, Ozark Christian College, 1111 North Main Street, Joplin, MO 64801-4804, 417-624-2518 Ext. 2017 or toll-free 800-299-4622. *Fax:* 417-624-0090. *E-mail:* finaid@occ.edu.
*Website:* http://www.occ.edu/.

# PACE UNIVERSITY
## New York, NY

| Tuition & fees: $39,697 | Average undergraduate aid package: $29,194 |
|---|---|

**ABOUT THE INSTITUTION** Independent, coed. *Awards:* certificates, associate, bachelor's, master's, and doctoral degrees. 74 undergraduate majors. *Total enrollment:* 12,857. Undergraduates: 8,694. Freshmen: 2,033. Federal methodology is used as a basis for awarding need-based institutional aid.
**UNDERGRADUATE EXPENSES for 2015–2016** *Application fee:* $50. *Comprehensive fee:* $55,471 includes full-time tuition ($38,200), mandatory fees ($1497), and room and board ($15,774). Full-time tuition and fees vary according to location. Room and board charges vary according to board plan, housing facility, location, and student level. *Part-time tuition:* $1096 per credit. Part-time tuition and fees vary according to course load and location.
**FRESHMAN FINANCIAL AID (Fall 2014, est.)** 1,632 applied for aid; of those 91% were deemed to have need. 100% of freshmen with need received aid; of those 13% had need fully met. *Average percent of need met:* 72% (excluding resources awarded to replace EFC). *Average financial aid package:* $31,015 (excluding resources awarded to replace EFC). 21% of all full-time freshmen had no need and received non-need-based gift aid.
**UNDERGRADUATE FINANCIAL AID (Fall 2014, est.)** 5,656 applied for aid; of those 93% were deemed to have need. 100% of undergraduates with need received aid; of those 11% had need fully met. *Average percent of need met:* 70% (excluding resources awarded to replace EFC). *Average financial aid package:* $29,194 (excluding resources awarded to replace EFC). 21% of all full-time undergraduates had no need and received non-need-based gift aid.
**GIFT AID (NEED-BASED)** *Total amount:* $124,476,935 (11% federal, 5% state, 82% institutional, 2% external sources). *Receiving aid:* Freshmen: 76% (1,476); all full-time undergraduates: 71% (5,176). *Average award:* Freshmen: $26,448; Undergraduates: $24,743. *Scholarships, grants, and awards:* Federal Pell, FSEOG, state, private, college/university gift aid from institutional funds.
**GIFT AID (NON-NEED-BASED)** *Total amount:* $30,412,447 (91% institutional, 9% external sources). *Receiving aid:* Freshmen: 8% (151). Undergraduates: 6% (431). *Average award:* Freshmen: $19,391. Undergraduates: $15,903. *Scholarships, grants, and awards by category:* Academic interests/achievement: 6,446 awards ($100,824,146 total): biological sciences, business, communication, computer science, education, English, foreign languages, general academic interests/achievements, health fields, humanities, mathematics, physical sciences, social sciences. *Creative arts/performance:* 47 awards ($137,120 total): dance, performing arts, theater/drama. *Special achievements/activities:* 491 awards ($6,254,108 total): community service, general special achievements/activities, leadership, memberships. *Special characteristics:* 398 awards ($3,408,379 total): children and siblings of alumni, children of faculty/staff, general special characteristics, spouses of deceased or disabled public servants, veterans. *Tuition waivers:* Full or partial for employees or children of employees, senior citizens. *ROTC:* Army cooperative, Air Force cooperative.
**LOANS** *Student loans:* $48,680,646 (79% need-based, 21% non-need-based). 74% of past graduating class borrowed through all loan programs. *Average indebtedness per student:* $35,442. *Average need-based loan:* Freshmen: $3736. Undergraduates: $4582. *Parent loans:* $41,345,978 (53% need-based, 47% non-need-based). *Programs:* Federal Direct (Subsidized and Unsubsidized Stafford, PLUS), Perkins, Federal Nursing.

**WORK-STUDY** *Federal work-study:* Total amount: $1,278,198; 1,123 jobs averaging $2241.
**ATHLETIC AWARDS** Total amount: $4,202,206 (67% need-based, 33% non-need-based).
**APPLYING FOR FINANCIAL AID** *Required financial aid forms:* FAFSA, state aid form. *Financial aid deadline (priority):* 2/15. *Notification date:* Continuous beginning 3/1. Students must reply by 5/1 or within 2 weeks of notification.
**CONTACT** Financial Aid Office, Pace University, 1 Pace Plaza, New York, NY 10038, 877-672-1830 or toll-free 800-874-7223. *Fax:* 212-346-1750. *E-mail:* financialaid@pace.edu.
*Website:* http://www.pace.edu/.

# PACIFIC COLLEGE
## Costa Mesa, CA

**CONTACT** Financial Aid Office, Pacific College, 3160 Red Hill Avenue, Costa Mesa, CA 92626, 714-662-4402.
*Website:* http://pacific-college.edu/.

# PACIFIC ISLANDS UNIVERSITY
## Mangilao, GU

**CONTACT** Financial Aid Office, Pacific Islands University, 172 Kinney's Road, Mangilao, GU 96913, 671-734-1812.
*Website:* http://www.piu.edu/.

# PACIFIC LUTHERAN UNIVERSITY
## Tacoma, WA

| Tuition & fees: $37,950 | Average undergraduate aid package: $33,960 |
|---|---|

**ABOUT THE INSTITUTION** Independent Evangelical Lutheran Church in America, coed. *Awards:* certificates, bachelor's, master's, and doctoral degrees. 42 undergraduate majors. *Total enrollment:* 3,275. Undergraduates: 2,959. Freshmen: 574. Federal methodology is used as a basis for awarding need-based institutional aid.
**UNDERGRADUATE EXPENSES for 2015–2016** *Application fee:* $40. *Comprehensive fee:* $48,280 includes full-time tuition ($37,600), mandatory fees ($350), and room and board ($10,330). *College room only:* $4870. Full-time tuition and fees vary according to course load. Room and board charges vary according to board plan and housing facility. *Part-time tuition:* $1175 per semester hour. Part-time tuition and fees vary according to course load.
**FRESHMAN FINANCIAL AID (Fall 2014, est.)** 541 applied for aid; of those 87% were deemed to have need. 100% of freshmen with need received aid; of those 29% had need fully met. *Average percent of need met:* 90% (excluding resources awarded to replace EFC). *Average financial aid package:* $35,650 (excluding resources awarded to replace EFC). 16% of all full-time freshmen had no need and received non-need-based gift aid.
**UNDERGRADUATE FINANCIAL AID (Fall 2014, est.)** 2,376 applied for aid; of those 89% were deemed to have need. 100% of undergraduates with need received aid; of those 21% had need fully met. *Average percent of need met:* 82% (excluding resources awarded to replace EFC). *Average financial aid package:* $33,960 (excluding resources awarded to replace EFC). 22% of all full-time undergraduates had no need and received non-need-based gift aid.
**GIFT AID (NEED-BASED)** *Total amount:* $44,762,010 (10% federal, 10% state, 78% institutional, 2% external sources). *Receiving aid:* Freshmen: 82% (471); all full-time undergraduates: 75% (2,112). *Average award:* Freshmen: $24,732; Undergraduates: $21,449. *Scholarships, grants, and awards:* Federal Pell, FSEOG, state, private, college/university gift aid from institutional funds, Federal Nursing.
**GIFT AID (NON-NEED-BASED)** *Total amount:* $12,355,819 (93% institutional, 7% external sources). *Receiving aid:* Freshmen: 68% (393). Undergraduates: 63% (1,777). *Average award:* Freshmen: $17,295. Undergraduates: $15,315. *Scholarships, grants, and awards by category:* Academic interests/achievement: 2,344 awards ($33,541,843 total): general academic interests/achievements. *Creative*

arts/performance: 249 awards ($1,455,176 total): art/fine arts, dance, debating, music, theater/drama. *Special achievements/activities:* 64 awards ($119,800 total): leadership. *Special characteristics:* 945 awards ($2,526,114 total): children and siblings of alumni, first-generation college students, international students, out-of-state students, relatives of clergy, religious affiliation. *Tuition waivers:* Full or partial for children of alumni, employees or children of employees. *ROTC:* Army.

**LOANS** *Student loans:* $16,491,923 (80% need-based, 20% non-need-based). 73% of past graduating class borrowed through all loan programs. *Average indebtedness per student:* $32,459. *Average need-based loan:* Freshmen: $3726. Undergraduates: $4963. *Parent loans:* $7,026,762 (40% need-based, 60% non-need-based). *Programs:* Federal Direct (Subsidized and Unsubsidized Stafford, PLUS), Perkins, Federal Nursing, state.

**WORK-STUDY** *Federal work-study:* Total amount: $5,741,495; 624 jobs averaging $3245. *State or other work-study/employment:* Total amount: $1,136,539 (100% need-based). 323 part-time jobs averaging $3786.

**APPLYING FOR FINANCIAL AID** *Required financial aid form:* FAFSA. *Financial aid deadline (priority):* 3/1. *Notification date:* Continuous beginning 2/15. Students must reply by 5/1 or within 3 weeks of notification.

**CONTACT** Kay W. Soltis, Office of Financial Aid, Pacific Lutheran University, Hauge Administration Building, Room 130, Tacoma, WA 98447, 253-535-7134 or toll-free 800-274-6758. *Fax:* 253-535-8406. *E-mail:* finaid@plu.edu. *Website:* http://www.plu.edu/.

# PACIFIC NORTHWEST COLLEGE OF ART
## Portland, OR

**CONTACT** Peggy Burgus, Director of Financial Aid, Pacific Northwest College of Art, 1241 Northwest Johnson Street, Portland, OR 97209, 503-821-8976. *Fax:* 503-821-8978. *Website:* http://www.pnca.edu/.

# PACIFIC OAKS COLLEGE
## Pasadena, CA

**CONTACT** Rosie Tristan, Financial Aid Specialist, Pacific Oaks College, 5 Westmoreland Place, Pasadena, CA 91103, 626-397-1350 or toll-free 877-314-2380. *Fax:* 626-577-6144. *E-mail:* financial@pacificoaks.edu. *Website:* http://www.pacificoaks.edu/.

# PACIFIC UNION COLLEGE
## Angwin, CA

**ABOUT THE INSTITUTION** Independent Seventh-day Adventist, coed. *Awards:* certificates, associate, bachelor's, and master's degrees. 40 undergraduate majors. *Total enrollment:* 1,647. Undergraduates: 1,645. Freshmen: 335.

**GIFT AID (NEED-BASED)** *Scholarships, grants, and awards:* Federal Pell, FSEOG, state, private, college/university gift aid from institutional funds.

**GIFT AID (NON-NEED-BASED)** *Scholarships, grants, and awards by category: Academic interests/achievement:* education, religion/biblical studies. *Creative arts/performance:* art/fine arts, music, theater/drama. *Special achievements/activities:* community service, general special achievements/activities, leadership, religious involvement. *Special characteristics:* religious affiliation, siblings of current students, spouses of current students, veterans.

**LOANS** *Programs:* Federal Direct (Subsidized and Unsubsidized Stafford, PLUS), Perkins, college/university.

**WORK-STUDY** *Federal work-study:* 225 jobs averaging $2916.

**APPLYING FOR FINANCIAL AID** *Required financial aid forms:* FAFSA, institution's own form.

**CONTACT** Laurie Wheeler, Director of Student Financial Services, Pacific Union College, One Angwin Avenue, Angwin, CA 94508, 707-965-7321 or toll-free 800-862-7080. *Fax:* 707-965-6595. *E-mail:* llwheeler@puc.edu. *Website:* http://www.puc.edu/.

# PACIFIC UNIVERSITY
## Forest Grove, OR

| Tuition & fees: $39,858 | Average undergraduate aid package: $32,277 |
| --- | --- |

**ABOUT THE INSTITUTION** Independent, coed. *Awards:* certificates, bachelor's, master's, and doctoral degrees. 50 undergraduate majors. *Total enrollment:* 3,640. Undergraduates: 1,840. Freshmen: 459. Federal methodology is used as a basis for awarding need-based institutional aid.

**UNDERGRADUATE EXPENSES for 2015–2016** *Application fee:* $40. *Comprehensive fee:* $51,306 includes full-time tuition ($38,950), mandatory fees ($908), and room and board ($11,448). *College room only:* $6154. Room and board charges vary according to board plan and housing facility. *Part-time tuition:* $1623 per credit hour. Part-time tuition and fees vary according to course load.

**FRESHMAN FINANCIAL AID (Fall 2014, est.)** 431 applied for aid; of those 90% were deemed to have need. 100% of freshmen with need received aid; of those 17% had need fully met. *Average percent of need met:* 77% (excluding resources awarded to replace EFC). *Average financial aid package:* $32,804 (excluding resources awarded to replace EFC). 15% of all full-time freshmen had no need and received non-need-based gift aid.

**UNDERGRADUATE FINANCIAL AID (Fall 2014, est.)** 1,558 applied for aid; of those 82% were deemed to have need. 100% of undergraduates with need received aid; of those 25% had need fully met. *Average percent of need met:* 75% (excluding resources awarded to replace EFC). *Average financial aid package:* $32,277 (excluding resources awarded to replace EFC). 17% of all full-time undergraduates had no need and received non-need-based gift aid.

**GIFT AID (NEED-BASED)** *Total amount:* $33,129,760 (8% federal, 2% state, 87% institutional, 3% external sources). *Receiving aid:* Freshmen: 59% (271); all full-time undergraduates: 61% (1,069). *Average award:* Freshmen: $10,785; Undergraduates: $10,833. *Scholarships, grants, and awards:* Federal Pell, FSEOG, state, private, college/university gift aid from institutional funds.

**GIFT AID (NON-NEED-BASED)** *Total amount:* $5,996,466 (98% institutional, 2% external sources). *Receiving aid:* Freshmen: 78% (357). Undergraduates: 67% (1,183). *Average award:* Freshmen: $17,712. Undergraduates: $17,030. *Scholarships, grants, and awards by category: Academic interests/achievement:* biological sciences, business, communication, education, English, foreign languages, general academic interests/achievements, health fields, humanities, mathematics, physical sciences, premedicine, social sciences. *Creative arts/performance:* art/fine arts, debating, journalism/publications, music, theater/drama. *Special achievements/activities:* community service, memberships, religious involvement. *Special characteristics:* children and siblings of alumni, children of faculty/staff, ethnic background, first-generation college students, general special characteristics, international students, relatives of clergy, veterans. *Tuition waivers:* Full or partial for employees or children of employees. *ROTC:* Army cooperative, Air Force cooperative.

**LOANS** *Student loans:* $16,309,443 (80% need-based, 20% non-need-based). 87% of past graduating class borrowed through all loan programs. *Average indebtedness per student:* $25,844. *Average need-based loan:* Freshmen: $4582. Undergraduates: $5502. *Parent loans:* $4,319,695 (43% need-based, 57% non-need-based). *Programs:* Federal Direct (Subsidized and Unsubsidized Stafford, PLUS), Perkins, private loans.

**WORK-STUDY** *Federal work-study:* Total amount: $1,849,055; jobs available. *State or other work-study/employment:* Total amount: $55,000 (8% need-based, 92% non-need-based). Part-time jobs available.

**APPLYING FOR FINANCIAL AID** *Required financial aid form:* FAFSA. *Financial aid deadline (priority):* 3/1. *Notification date:* Continuous beginning 3/1.

**CONTACT** Office of Financial Aid, Pacific University, 2043 College Way, Forest Grove, OR 97116-1797, 503-352-2222 or toll-free 877-722-8648. *E-mail:* financialaid@pacificu.edu. *Website:* http://www.pacificu.edu/.

# PAIER COLLEGE OF ART, INC.
## Hamden, CT

**CONTACT** Mr. John DeRose, Director of Financial Aid, Paier College of Art, Inc., 20 Gorham Avenue, Hamden, CT 06514-3902, 203-287-3034. *Fax:* 203-287-3021. *E-mail:* paier.art@snet.net.
*Website:* http://www.paiercollegeofart.edu/.

# PAINE COLLEGE
## Augusta, GA

**CONTACT** Ms. Gerri Bogan, Director of Financial Aid, Paine College, 1235 15th Street, Augusta, GA 30901, 706-821-8262 or toll-free 800-476-7703. *Fax:* 706-821-8691. *E-mail:* bogang@mail.paine.edu.
*Website:* http://www.paine.edu/.

# PALM BEACH ATLANTIC UNIVERSITY
## West Palm Beach, FL

| Tuition & fees: $26,274 | Average undergraduate aid package: $17,688 |
| --- | --- |

**ABOUT THE INSTITUTION** Independent nondenominational, coed. *Awards:* associate, bachelor's, master's, and doctoral degrees. 48 undergraduate majors. *Total enrollment:* 3,865. Undergraduates: 3,021. Freshmen: 524. Federal methodology is used as a basis for awarding need-based institutional aid.

**UNDERGRADUATE EXPENSES for 2015–2016** *Application fee:* $50. *One-time required fee:* $50. *Comprehensive fee:* $34,874 includes full-time tuition ($25,974), mandatory fees ($300), and room and board ($8600). *College room only:* $4430. Full-time tuition and fees vary according to course load, location, and program. Room and board charges vary according to board plan and housing facility. *Part-time tuition:* $625 per credit hour. *Part-time fees:* $99 per term. Part-time tuition and fees vary according to course load, location, and program. These charges are for the traditional day undergraduate program offered on the main campus in West Palm Beach, FL. Online and non-traditional evening undergraduate programs have other, per-credit-hour charges.

**FRESHMAN FINANCIAL AID (Fall 2014, est.)** 474 applied for aid; of those 81% were deemed to have need. 100% of freshmen with need received aid; of those 21% had need fully met. *Average percent of need met:* 66% (excluding resources awarded to replace EFC). *Average financial aid package:* $19,439 (excluding resources awarded to replace EFC). 26% of all full-time freshmen had no need and received non-need-based gift aid.

**UNDERGRADUATE FINANCIAL AID (Fall 2014, est.)** 2,112 applied for aid; of those 86% were deemed to have need. 100% of undergraduates with need received aid; of those 17% had need fully met. *Average percent of need met:* 61% (excluding resources awarded to replace EFC). *Average financial aid package:* $17,688 (excluding resources awarded to replace EFC). 24% of all full-time undergraduates had no need and received non-need-based gift aid.

**GIFT AID (NEED-BASED)** *Total amount:* $24,874,826 (18% federal, 17% state, 56% institutional, 9% external sources). *Receiving aid:* Freshmen: 73% (383); all full-time undergraduates: 74% (1,794). *Average award:* Freshmen: $17,244; Undergraduates: $14,721. *Scholarships, grants, and awards:* Federal Pell, FSEOG, state, private, college/university gift aid from institutional funds.

**GIFT AID (NON-NEED-BASED)** *Total amount:* $8,331,408 (20% state, 75% institutional, 5% external sources). *Receiving aid:* Freshmen: 13% (70). Undergraduates: 10% (244). *Average award:* Freshmen: $11,846. Undergraduates: $9594. *Scholarships, grants, and awards by category:* Academic interests/achievement: general academic interests/achievements. Creative arts/performance: dance, music, theater/drama. Special achievements/activities: leadership. Special characteristics: adult students, children and siblings of alumni, children of current students, children of educators, children of faculty/staff, international students, out-of-state students, previous college experience, siblings of current students, spouses of current students. *Tuition waivers:* Full or partial for employees or children of employees. *ROTC:* Army cooperative.

**LOANS** *Student loans:* $11,798,675 (79% need-based, 21% non-need-based). 68% of past graduating class borrowed through all loan programs. *Average indebtedness*

per student: $27,374. *Average need-based loan:* Freshmen: $3218. Undergraduates: $3910. *Parent loans:* $3,652,700 (50% need-based, 50% non-need-based). *Programs:* Federal Direct (Subsidized and Unsubsidized Stafford, PLUS), Perkins.

**WORK-STUDY** *Federal work-study:* Total amount: $475,982; 186 jobs averaging $2955. *State or other work-study/employment:* Total amount: $19,397 (100% need-based). 17 part-time jobs averaging $1441.

**ATHLETIC AWARDS** Total amount: $1,847,334 (45% need-based, 55% non-need-based).

**APPLYING FOR FINANCIAL AID** *Required financial aid forms:* FAFSA, state aid form. *Financial aid deadline:* 8/1 (priority: 5/1). *Notification date:* Continuous beginning 2/15. Students must reply within 4 weeks of notification.

**CONTACT** Mr. Joseph Bryan, Director of Financial Aid, Palm Beach Atlantic University, PO Box 24708, West Palm Beach, FL 33416-4708, 561-803-2000 or toll-free 888-GO-TO-PBA. *Fax:* 561-803-2130. *E-mail:* finaid@pba.edu.
*Website:* http://www.pba.edu/.

# PALM BEACH STATE COLLEGE
## Lake Worth, FL

**CONTACT** Financial Aid Office, Palm Beach State College, 4200 Congress Avenue, Lake Worth, FL 33461-4796, 561-967-7222.
*Website:* http://www.palmbeachstate.edu/.

# PARK UNIVERSITY
## Parkville, MO

| Tuition & fees: $10,600 | Average undergraduate aid package: $10,589 |
| --- | --- |

**ABOUT THE INSTITUTION** Independent, coed. *Awards:* certificates, associate, bachelor's, and master's degrees. 44 undergraduate majors. *Total enrollment:* 9,800. Undergraduates: 8,946. Freshmen: 165. Both federal and institutional methodology are used as a basis for awarding need-based institutional aid.

**UNDERGRADUATE EXPENSES for 2015–2016** *Application fee:* $25. *Comprehensive fee:* $18,580 includes full-time tuition ($10,500), mandatory fees ($100), and room and board ($7980). *College room only:* $3713. Full-time tuition and fees vary according to course load. Room and board charges vary according to housing facility. *Part-time tuition:* $369 per credit. Part-time tuition and fees vary according to course load.

**FRESHMAN FINANCIAL AID (Fall 2014, est.)** 138 applied for aid; of those 78% were deemed to have need. 99% of freshmen with need received aid; of those 22% had need fully met. *Average percent of need met:* 66% (excluding resources awarded to replace EFC). *Average financial aid package:* $11,544 (excluding resources awarded to replace EFC). 18% of all full-time freshmen had no need and received non-need-based gift aid.

**UNDERGRADUATE FINANCIAL AID (Fall 2014, est.)** 633 applied for aid; of those 77% were deemed to have need. 99% of undergraduates with need received aid; of those 19% had need fully met. *Average percent of need met:* 66% (excluding resources awarded to replace EFC). *Average financial aid package:* $10,589 (excluding resources awarded to replace EFC). 10% of all full-time undergraduates had no need and received non-need-based gift aid.

**GIFT AID (NEED-BASED)** *Total amount:* $17,686,346 (71% federal, 4% state, 8% institutional, 17% external sources). *Receiving aid:* Freshmen: 48% (78); all full-time undergraduates: 39% (348). *Average award:* Freshmen: $5084; Undergraduates: $4760. *Scholarships, grants, and awards:* Federal Pell, FSEOG, state, private, college/university gift aid from institutional funds.

**GIFT AID (NON-NEED-BASED)** *Total amount:* $3,814,975 (5% federal, 34% institutional, 61% external sources). *Receiving aid:* Freshmen: 51% (84). Undergraduates: 28% (247). *Average award:* Freshmen: $6706. Undergraduates: $7340. *Scholarships, grants, and awards by category:* Academic interests/achievement: general academic interests/achievements. Creative arts/performance: art/fine arts, music, theater/drama. Special characteristics: children of faculty/staff, religious affiliation, siblings of current students, veterans. *Tuition waivers:* Full or partial for employees or children of employees, senior citizens. *ROTC:* Army.

**LOANS** *Student loans:* $33,519,316 (82% need-based, 18% non-need-based). 33% of past graduating class borrowed through all loan programs. *Average indebtedness*

per student: $22,115. **Average need-based loan:** Freshmen: $3329. Undergraduates: $4574. **Parent loans:** $271,937 (6% need-based, 94% non-need-based). **Programs:** Federal Direct (Subsidized and Unsubsidized Stafford, PLUS), Perkins, college/university.
**WORK-STUDY** *Federal work-study:* Total amount: $41,488; 11 jobs averaging $3772. **State or other work-study/employment:** Total amount: $33,970 (100% non-need-based). 10 part-time jobs averaging $3397.
**ATHLETIC AWARDS** Total amount: $1,079,647 (42% need-based, 58% non-need-based).
**APPLYING FOR FINANCIAL AID** *Required financial aid forms:* FAFSA, institution's own form. **Financial aid deadline:** Continuous. **Notification date:** Continuous beginning 4/1. Students must reply by 8/1 or within 4 weeks of notification.
**CONTACT** Cathy Colapietro, Executive Director of Student Financial Services, Park University, 8700 NW River Park Drive, Parkville, MO 64152, 816-584-6728 or toll-free 800-745-7275. *E-mail:* cathy.colapietro@park.edu.
*Website:* http://www.park.edu/.

# PARSONS THE NEW SCHOOL FOR DESIGN
### New York, NY

**ABOUT THE INSTITUTION** Independent, coed. *Awards:* certificates, associate, bachelor's, and master's degrees. 12 undergraduate majors. **Total enrollment:** 5,134. Undergraduates: 4,372. Freshmen: 614.
**GIFT AID (NEED-BASED)** *Scholarships, grants, and awards:* Federal Pell, FSEOG, state, private, college/university gift aid from institutional funds.
**GIFT AID (NON-NEED-BASED)** *Scholarships, grants, and awards by category:* Academic interests/achievement: general academic interests/achievements. Creative arts/performance: general creative arts/performance. Special achievements/activities: leadership. Special characteristics: members of minority groups.
**LOANS** *Programs:* Federal Direct (Subsidized and Unsubsidized Stafford, PLUS), Perkins.
**APPLYING FOR FINANCIAL AID** *Required financial aid forms:* FAFSA, state aid form.
**CONTACT** Office of Student Financial Services, Parsons The New School for Design, 72 Fifth Avenue, New York, NY 10011, 212-229-8930 or toll-free 800-292-3040. *E-mail:* sfs@newschool.edu.
*Website:* http://www.newschool.edu/parsons/.

# PATRICK HENRY COLLEGE
### Purcellville, VA

| Tuition & fees: $27,098 | Average undergraduate aid package: $11,200 |
|---|---|

**ABOUT THE INSTITUTION** Independent nondenominational, coed. *Awards:* bachelor's degrees. 6 undergraduate majors. **Total enrollment:** 338. Undergraduates: 338. Freshmen: 80. Institutional methodology is used as a basis for awarding need-based institutional aid.
**UNDERGRADUATE EXPENSES for 2015–2016** *Application fee:* $20. **Comprehensive fee:** $37,826 includes full-time tuition ($26,848), mandatory fees ($250), and room and board ($10,728). Full-time tuition and fees vary according to course load. Room and board charges vary according to board plan and housing facility. **Part-time tuition:** $1118 per credit hour. Part-time tuition and fees vary according to course level and course load.
**FRESHMAN FINANCIAL AID (Fall 2013)** 58 applied for aid; of those 66% were deemed to have need. 100% of freshmen with need received aid. **Average percent of need met:** 35% (excluding resources awarded to replace EFC). **Average financial aid package:** $10,600 (excluding resources awarded to replace EFC). 53% of all full-time freshmen had no need and received non-need-based gift aid.
**UNDERGRADUATE FINANCIAL AID (Fall 2013)** 143 applied for aid; of those 80% were deemed to have need. 100% of undergraduates with need received aid. **Average percent of need met:** 37% (excluding resources awarded to replace EFC). **Average financial aid package:** $11,200 (excluding resources awarded to

replace EFC). 55% of all full-time undergraduates had no need and received non-need-based gift aid.
**GIFT AID (NEED-BASED)** *Total amount:* $649,036 (100% institutional). **Receiving aid:** Freshmen: 43% (38); all full-time undergraduates: 37% (115). **Average award:** Freshmen: $5200; Undergraduates: $5600. **Scholarships, grants, and awards:** private, college/university gift aid from institutional funds.
**GIFT AID (NON-NEED-BASED)** *Total amount:* $2,608,533 (94% institutional, 6% external sources). **Receiving aid:** Freshmen: 27% (24). Undergraduates: 27% (83). **Average award:** Freshmen: $10,600. Undergraduates: $10,380. **Scholarships, grants, and awards by category:** Academic interests/achievement: communication, general academic interests/achievements. Creative arts/performance: debating, journalism/publications, music. Special achievements/activities: community service, leadership, memberships, religious involvement. Special characteristics: children of faculty/staff, children of public servants, public servants, relatives of clergy, veterans. **Tuition waivers:** Full or partial for employees or children of employees.
**LOANS** *Student loans:* $2,100,382 (100% need-based). 43% of past graduating class borrowed through all loan programs. *Average indebtedness per student:* $35,400. **Average need-based loan:** Freshmen: $11,600. Undergraduates: $12,500. **Programs:** college/university, private loans.
**APPLYING FOR FINANCIAL AID** *Required financial aid form:* CSS Financial Aid PROFILE. **Financial aid deadline:** 6/15 (priority: 3/15). **Notification date:** Continuous beginning 3/1. Students must reply within 4 weeks of notification.
**CONTACT** Mrs. Christine W. Guenard, Associate Director of Financial Aid, Patrick Henry College, 10 Patrick Henry Circle, Purcellville, VA 20132, 540-441-8140 or toll-free 888-338-1776. *Fax:* 540-441-8149. *E-mail:* financialaid@phc.edu.
*Website:* http://www.phc.edu/.

# PATTEN UNIVERSITY
### Oakland, CA

**CONTACT** Mr. Robert A. Olivera, Dean of Enrollment Services, Patten University, 2433 Coolidge Avenue, Oakland, CA 94601-2699, 510-261-8500 Ext. 783 or toll-free 877-4PATTEN. *Fax:* 510-534-8969. *E-mail:* oliverob@patten.edu.
*Website:* http://patten.edu/.

# PAUL QUINN COLLEGE
### Dallas, TX

**CONTACT** Khaleelah Ali, Assistant Director of Financial Aid, Paul Quinn College, 3837 Simpson Stuart Road, Dallas, TX 75241, 214-302-3530 or toll-free 877-346-1063. *Fax:* 214-302-3535. *E-mail:* kali@pqc.edu.
*Website:* http://www.pqc.edu/.

# PAUL SMITH'S COLLEGE
### Paul Smiths, NY

**CONTACT** Mary Ellen Chamberlain, Director of Financial Aid, Paul Smith's College, Routes 86 and 30, Paul Smiths, NY 12970, 518-327-6119 or toll-free 800-421-2605. *Fax:* 518-327-6055. *E-mail:* mchamberlain@paulsmiths.edu.
*Website:* http://www.paulsmiths.edu/.

# PEABODY CONSERVATORY OF THE JOHNS HOPKINS UNIVERSITY
### Baltimore, MD

| Tuition & fees: $41,870 | Average undergraduate aid package: $16,252 |
|---|---|

**ABOUT THE INSTITUTION** Independent, coed. *Awards:* certificates, diplomas, bachelor's, master's, and doctoral degrees. 10 undergraduate majors. **Total**

**enrollment:** 567. Undergraduates: 269. Freshmen: 54. Federal methodology is used as a basis for awarding need-based institutional aid.

**UNDERGRADUATE EXPENSES for 2015–2016** *Application fee:* $100. *One-time required fee:* $700. *Comprehensive fee:* $55,390 includes full-time tuition ($41,190), mandatory fees ($680), and room and board ($13,520). Full-time tuition and fees vary according to program. Room and board charges vary according to board plan. *Part-time tuition:* $1175 per semester hour. Part-time tuition and fees vary according to course load.

**FRESHMAN FINANCIAL AID (Fall 2013)** 66 applied for aid; of those 74% were deemed to have need. 96% of freshmen with need received aid; of those 15% had need fully met. *Average percent of need met:* 63% (excluding resources awarded to replace EFC). *Average financial aid package:* $17,739 (excluding resources awarded to replace EFC). 25% of all full-time freshmen had no need and received non-need-based gift aid.

**UNDERGRADUATE FINANCIAL AID (Fall 2013)** 226 applied for aid; of those 98% were deemed to have need. 91% of undergraduates with need received aid; of those 21% had need fully met. *Average percent of need met:* 66% (excluding resources awarded to replace EFC). *Average financial aid package:* $16,252 (excluding resources awarded to replace EFC). 22% of all full-time undergraduates had no need and received non-need-based gift aid.

**GIFT AID (NEED-BASED)** *Total amount:* $3,630,873 (10% federal, 2% state, 86% institutional, 2% external sources). *Receiving aid:* Freshmen: 56% (41); all full-time undergraduates: 39% (147). *Average award:* Freshmen: $13,679; Undergraduates: $12,722. *Scholarships, grants, and awards:* Federal Pell, FSEOG, state, private, college/university gift aid from institutional funds.

**GIFT AID (NON-NEED-BASED)** *Total amount:* $1,455,527 (99% institutional, 1% external sources). *Receiving aid:* Freshmen: 25% (18). Undergraduates: 22% (83). *Average award:* Freshmen: $12,173. Undergraduates: $16,429. *Scholarships, grants, and awards by category:* Creative arts/performance: music.

**LOANS** *Student loans:* $2,175,674 (89% need-based, 11% non-need-based). 77% of past graduating class borrowed through all loan programs. *Average indebtedness per student:* $32,489. *Average need-based loan:* Freshmen: $4399. Undergraduates: $5220. *Parent loans:* $992,753 (100% need-based). *Programs:* Federal Direct (Subsidized and Unsubsidized Stafford, PLUS), Perkins, college/university.

**WORK-STUDY** *Federal work-study:* jobs available.

**APPLYING FOR FINANCIAL AID** *Required financial aid form:* FAFSA. *Financial aid deadline (priority):* 3/1. *Notification date:* 4/1. Students must reply by 5/1.

**CONTACT** Rebecca Polgar, Director of Financial Aid, Peabody Conservatory of The Johns Hopkins University, 1 East Mount Vernon Place, Baltimore, MD 21202-2397, 410-234-4900 or toll-free 800-368-2521 (out-of-state). *Fax:* 410-659-8102. *E-mail:* finaid@peabody.jhu.edu.
*Website:* http://www.peabody.jhu.edu/.

# PEIRCE COLLEGE
## Philadelphia, PA

| Tuition & fees: $13,800 | Average undergraduate aid package: $10,981 |
|---|---|

**ABOUT THE INSTITUTION** Independent, coed, primarily women. *Awards:* certificates, associate, bachelor's, and master's degrees. 10 undergraduate majors. *Total enrollment:* 1,833. Undergraduates: 1,771. Freshmen: 116. Federal methodology is used as a basis for awarding need-based institutional aid.

**UNDERGRADUATE EXPENSES for 2015–2016** *Application fee:* $50. *Tuition:* full-time $13,200; part-time $550 per credit hour. *Required fees:* full-time $600; $600 per term. Full-time tuition and fees vary according to course load and reciprocity agreements. Part-time tuition and fees vary according to course load and reciprocity agreements.

**FRESHMAN FINANCIAL AID (Fall 2013)** 12 applied for aid; of those 100% were deemed to have need. 100% of freshmen with need received aid. *Average percent of need met:* 44% (excluding resources awarded to replace EFC). *Average financial aid package:* $14,150 (excluding resources awarded to replace EFC).

**UNDERGRADUATE FINANCIAL AID (Fall 2013)** 326 applied for aid; of those 98% were deemed to have need. 99% of undergraduates with need received aid. *Average percent of need met:* 40% (excluding resources awarded to replace EFC). *Average financial aid package:* $10,981 (excluding resources awarded to replace EFC). 1% of all full-time undergraduates had no need and received non-need-based gift aid.

**GIFT AID (NEED-BASED)** *Total amount:* $7,452,339 (63% federal, 18% state, 18% institutional, 1% external sources). *Receiving aid:* Freshmen: 100% (12); all full-time undergraduates: 77% (274). *Average award:* Freshmen: $5856; Undergraduates: $6595. *Scholarships, grants, and awards:* Federal Pell, FSEOG, state, private, college/university gift aid from institutional funds.

**GIFT AID (NON-NEED-BASED)** *Total amount:* $29,815 (100% institutional). *Receiving aid:* Freshmen: 83% (10). Undergraduates: 41% (146). *Average award:* Undergraduates: $2250. *Scholarships, grants, and awards by category:* Academic interests/achievement: business, computer science, general academic interests/achievements, health fields. *Special achievements/activities:* leadership, memberships. *Special characteristics:* children and siblings of alumni, children of faculty/staff, children of public servants, international students, public servants, siblings of current students, veterans, veterans' children. *Tuition waivers:* Full or partial for children of alumni, employees or children of employees.

**LOANS** *Student loans:* $15,199,520 (98% need-based, 2% non-need-based). *Average need-based loan:* Freshmen: $4012. Undergraduates: $4713. *Parent loans:* $153,359 (100% need-based). *Programs:* Federal Direct (Subsidized and Unsubsidized Stafford, PLUS).

**WORK-STUDY** *Federal work-study:* jobs available.

**APPLYING FOR FINANCIAL AID** *Required financial aid form:* FAFSA. *Financial aid deadline:* Continuous. *Notification date:* Continuous beginning 5/1.

**CONTACT** Chanel Greene, Manager of Financial Aid, Peirce College, 1420 Pine Street, Philadelphia, PA 19102, 215-670-9330 or toll-free 888-467-3472. *Fax:* 215-545-3671. *E-mail:* cgreen1@peirce.edu.
*Website:* http://www.peirce.edu/.

# PENN STATE ABINGTON
## Abington, PA

| Tuition & fees (PA res): $13,942 | Average undergraduate aid package: $10,802 |
|---|---|

**ABOUT THE INSTITUTION** State-related, coed. *Awards:* certificates, associate, and bachelor's degrees (enrollment figures include students enrolled at The Graduate School at Penn State who are taking courses at this location). 118 undergraduate majors. *Total enrollment:* 3,952. Undergraduates: 3,947. Freshmen: 896. Federal methodology is used as a basis for awarding need-based institutional aid.

**UNDERGRADUATE EXPENSES for 2015–2016** *Application fee:* $50. *Tuition, state resident:* full-time $13,012; part-time $535 per credit hour. *Tuition, nonresident:* full-time $19,848; part-time $827 per credit hour. *Required fees:* full-time $930. Full-time tuition and fees vary according to course level, degree level, location, program, and student level. Part-time tuition and fees vary according to course level, course load, degree level, location, program, and student level.

**FRESHMAN FINANCIAL AID (Fall 2013)** 798 applied for aid; of those 82% were deemed to have need. 99% of freshmen with need received aid; of those 3% had need fully met. *Average percent of need met:* 61% (excluding resources awarded to replace EFC). *Average financial aid package:* $11,384 (excluding resources awarded to replace EFC). 9% of all full-time freshmen had no need and received non-need-based gift aid.

**UNDERGRADUATE FINANCIAL AID (Fall 2013)** 2,414 applied for aid; of those 85% were deemed to have need. 99% of undergraduates with need received aid; of those 3% had need fully met. *Average percent of need met:* 60% (excluding resources awarded to replace EFC). *Average financial aid package:* $10,802 (excluding resources awarded to replace EFC). 5% of all full-time undergraduates had no need and received non-need-based gift aid.

**GIFT AID (NEED-BASED)** *Total amount:* $15,429,475 (49% federal, 31% state, 18% institutional, 2% external sources). *Receiving aid:* Freshmen: 59% (541); all full-time undergraduates: 60% (1,687). *Average award:* Freshmen: $7978; Undergraduates: $7421. *Scholarships, grants, and awards:* Federal Pell, FSEOG, state, private, college/university gift aid from institutional funds.

**GIFT AID (NON-NEED-BASED)** *Total amount:* $928,100 (21% federal, 1% state, 61% institutional, 17% external sources). *Receiving aid:* Freshmen: 32% (295). Undergraduates: 19% (524). *Average award:* Freshmen: $4150. Undergraduates: $3383. *Scholarships, grants, and awards by category:* Academic interests/achievement: general academic interests/achievements. *Special characteristics:* children and siblings of alumni, general special characteristics. *Tuition waivers:* Full or partial for employees or children of employees, senior citizens. *ROTC:* Army cooperative, Air Force cooperative.

**LOANS** *Student loans:* $16,937,516 (86% need-based, 14% non-need-based). 63% of past graduating class borrowed through all loan programs. *Average indebtedness per student:* $36,935. *Average need-based loan:* Freshmen: $3365. Undergraduates: $4084. *Parent loans:* $1,593,928 (73% need-based, 27% non-need-based). *Programs:* Federal Direct (Subsidized and Unsubsidized Stafford, PLUS), Perkins, college/university, private loans.

**WORK-STUDY** *Federal work-study:* jobs available.

**APPLYING FOR FINANCIAL AID** *Required financial aid form:* FAFSA. *Financial aid deadline (priority):* 2/15. *Notification date:* Continuous.

**CONTACT** Student Aid Office, Penn State Abington, 1600 Woodland Road, Abington, PA 19001-3990, 215-881-7348. *Fax:* 215-881-7655. *Website:* http://www.abington.psu.edu/.

# PENN STATE ALTOONA
### Altoona, PA

| Tuition & fees (PA res): $14,588 | Average undergraduate aid package: $10,438 |
| --- | --- |

**ABOUT THE INSTITUTION** State-related, coed. *Awards:* certificates, associate, and bachelor's degrees (enrollment figures include students enrolled at The Graduate School at Penn State who are taking courses at this location). 125 undergraduate majors. *Total enrollment:* 3,903. Undergraduates: 3,903. Freshmen: 1,487. Federal methodology is used as a basis for awarding need-based institutional aid.

**UNDERGRADUATE EXPENSES** for 2015–2016 *Application fee:* $50. *Tuition, state resident:* full-time $13,658; part-time $569 per credit hour. *Tuition, nonresident:* full-time $20,890; part-time $870 per credit hour. *Required fees:* full-time $930. Full-time tuition and fees vary according to course level, degree level, location, program, and student level. Part-time tuition and fees vary according to course level, course load, degree level, location, program, and student level. *College room and board:* $10,520; *Room only:* $5460. Room and board charges vary according to board plan, housing facility, and location.

**FRESHMAN FINANCIAL AID (Fall 2013)** 1,185 applied for aid; of those 83% were deemed to have need. 97% of freshmen with need received aid; of those 7% had need fully met. *Average percent of need met:* 57% (excluding resources awarded to replace EFC). *Average financial aid package:* $10,875 (excluding resources awarded to replace EFC). 12% of all full-time freshmen had no need and received non-need-based gift aid.

**UNDERGRADUATE FINANCIAL AID (Fall 2013)** 2,993 applied for aid; of those 86% were deemed to have need. 98% of undergraduates with need received aid; of those 6% had need fully met. *Average percent of need met:* 57% (excluding resources awarded to replace EFC). *Average financial aid package:* $10,438 (excluding resources awarded to replace EFC). 7% of all full-time undergraduates had no need and received non-need-based gift aid.

**GIFT AID (NEED-BASED)** *Total amount:* $15,636,615 (42% federal, 25% state, 28% institutional, 5% external sources). *Receiving aid:* Freshmen: 42% (592); all full-time undergraduates: 44% (1,595). *Average award:* Freshmen: $6543; Undergraduates: $6395. *Scholarships, grants, and awards:* Federal Pell, FSEOG, state, private, college/university gift aid from institutional funds.

**GIFT AID (NON-NEED-BASED)** *Total amount:* $1,618,599 (26% federal, 1% state, 59% institutional, 14% external sources). *Receiving aid:* Freshmen: 42% (600). Undergraduates: 31% (1,122). *Average award:* Freshmen: $4726. Undergraduates: $3639. *Scholarships, grants, and awards by category:* Academic interests/achievement: general academic interests/achievements. *Special characteristics:* children and siblings of alumni, general special characteristics. *Tuition waivers:* Full or partial for employees or children of employees, senior citizens. *ROTC:* Army, Air Force.

**LOANS** *Student loans:* $25,800,800 (89% need-based, 11% non-need-based). 63% of past graduating class borrowed through all loan programs. *Average indebtedness per student:* $36,935. *Average need-based loan:* Freshmen: $3465. Undergraduates: $4061. *Parent loans:* $7,504,972 (87% need-based, 13% non-need-based). *Programs:* Federal Direct (Subsidized and Unsubsidized Stafford, PLUS), Perkins, college/university, private loans.

**WORK-STUDY** *Federal work-study:* jobs available.

**APPLYING FOR FINANCIAL AID** *Required financial aid form:* FAFSA. *Financial aid deadline (priority):* 2/15. *Notification date:* Continuous beginning 3/1.

**CONTACT** Mr. David Pearlman, Director of Student Aid, Penn State Altoona, W113 Smith Building, Altoona, PA 16601-3760, 814-949-5055 or toll-free 800-848-9843. *Fax:* 814-949-5536. *E-mail:* dpp1@psu.edu. *Website:* http://www.altoona.psu.edu/.

# PENN STATE BEAVER
### Monaca, PA

| Tuition & fees (PA res): $13,636 | Average undergraduate aid package: $11,645 |
| --- | --- |

**ABOUT THE INSTITUTION** State-related, coed. *Awards:* certificates and bachelor's degrees. 118 undergraduate majors. *Total enrollment:* 720. Undergraduates: 720. Freshmen: 218. Federal methodology is used as a basis for awarding need-based institutional aid.

**UNDERGRADUATE EXPENSES** for 2015–2016 *Application fee:* $50. *Tuition, state resident:* full-time $12,718; part-time $524 per credit hour. *Tuition, nonresident:* full-time $19,404; part-time $809 per credit hour. *Required fees:* full-time $918. Full-time tuition and fees vary according to course level, degree level, location, program, and student level. Part-time tuition and fees vary according to course level, course load, degree level, location, program, and student level. *College room and board:* $10,520; *Room only:* $5460. Room and board charges vary according to board plan, housing facility, and location.

**FRESHMAN FINANCIAL AID (Fall 2013)** 212 applied for aid; of those 82% were deemed to have need. 98% of freshmen with need received aid; of those 5% had need fully met. *Average percent of need met:* 62% (excluding resources awarded to replace EFC). *Average financial aid package:* $11,363 (excluding resources awarded to replace EFC). 17% of all full-time freshmen had no need and received non-need-based gift aid.

**UNDERGRADUATE FINANCIAL AID (Fall 2013)** 543 applied for aid; of those 85% were deemed to have need. 99% of undergraduates with need received aid; of those 4% had need fully met. *Average percent of need met:* 62% (excluding resources awarded to replace EFC). *Average financial aid package:* $11,645 (excluding resources awarded to replace EFC). 11% of all full-time undergraduates had no need and received non-need-based gift aid.

**GIFT AID (NEED-BASED)** *Total amount:* $3,471,359 (45% federal, 25% state, 27% institutional, 3% external sources). *Receiving aid:* Freshmen: 50% (121); all full-time undergraduates: 56% (341). *Average award:* Freshmen: $7039; Undergraduates: $6916. *Scholarships, grants, and awards:* Federal Pell, FSEOG, state, private, college/university gift aid from institutional funds.

**GIFT AID (NON-NEED-BASED)** *Total amount:* $369,529 (29% federal, 2% state, 44% institutional, 25% external sources). *Receiving aid:* Freshmen: 51% (123). Undergraduates: 40% (246). *Average award:* Freshmen: $2930. Undergraduates: $2505. *Scholarships, grants, and awards by category:* Academic interests/achievement: general academic interests/achievements. *Special characteristics:* children and siblings of alumni. *Tuition waivers:* Full or partial for employees or children of employees, senior citizens.

**LOANS** *Student loans:* $3,768,967 (90% need-based, 10% non-need-based). 63% of past graduating class borrowed through all loan programs. *Average indebtedness per student:* $36,935. *Average need-based loan:* Freshmen: $3771. Undergraduates: $4335. *Parent loans:* $941,309 (88% need-based, 12% non-need-based). *Programs:* Federal Direct (Subsidized and Unsubsidized Stafford, PLUS), Perkins, college/university, private loans.

**WORK-STUDY** *Federal work-study:* jobs available. *State or other work-study/employment:* Part-time jobs available.

**APPLYING FOR FINANCIAL AID** *Required financial aid form:* FAFSA. *Financial aid deadline (priority):* 2/15. *Notification date:* Continuous beginning 3/1.

**CONTACT** Gail Gray, Student Aid and Veterans Coordinator, Penn State Beaver, 113 Student Union Building, 100 University Drive, Monaca, PA 15061, 724-773-3803. *E-mail:* gailgray@psu.edu. *Website:* http://www.br.psu.edu/.

# PENN STATE BERKS
## Reading, PA

| Tuition & fees (PA res): $14,588 | Average undergraduate aid package: $10,208 |
|---|---|

**ABOUT THE INSTITUTION** State-related, coed. **Awards:** certificates, associate, and bachelor's degrees (enrollment figures include students enrolled at The Graduate School at Penn State who are taking courses at this location). 129 undergraduate majors. **Total enrollment:** 2,839. Undergraduates: 2,828. Freshmen: 855. Federal methodology is used as a basis for awarding need-based institutional aid.

**UNDERGRADUATE EXPENSES for 2015–2016 Application fee:** $50. **Tuition, state resident:** full-time $13,658; part-time $569 per credit hour. **Tuition, nonresident:** full-time $20,890; part-time $870 per credit hour. **Required fees:** full-time $930. Full-time tuition and fees vary according to course level, degree level, location, program, and student level. Part-time tuition and fees vary according to course level, course load, degree level, location, program, and student level. **College room and board:** $11,500; **Room only:** $6440. Room and board charges vary according to board plan, housing facility, and location.

**FRESHMAN FINANCIAL AID (Fall 2013)** 710 applied for aid; of those 84% were deemed to have need. 96% of freshmen with need received aid; of those 2% had need fully met. **Average percent of need met:** 56% (excluding resources awarded to replace EFC). **Average financial aid package:** $9863 (excluding resources awarded to replace EFC). 7% of all full-time freshmen had no need and received non-need-based gift aid.

**UNDERGRADUATE FINANCIAL AID (Fall 2013)** 1,987 applied for aid; of those 84% were deemed to have need. 98% of undergraduates with need received aid; of those 4% had need fully met. **Average percent of need met:** 58% (excluding resources awarded to replace EFC). **Average financial aid package:** $10,208 (excluding resources awarded to replace EFC). 5% of all full-time undergraduates had no need and received non-need-based gift aid.

**GIFT AID (NEED-BASED) Total amount:** $10,649,769 (45% federal, 30% state, 21% institutional, 4% external sources). **Receiving aid:** Freshmen: 51% (404); all full-time undergraduates: 49% (1,168). **Average award:** Freshmen: $6798; Undergraduates: $6815. **Scholarships, grants, and awards:** Federal Pell, FSEOG, state, private, college/university gift aid from institutional funds.

**GIFT AID (NON-NEED-BASED) Total amount:** $850,154 (38% federal, 2% state, 40% institutional, 20% external sources). **Receiving aid:** Freshmen: 30% (236). Undergraduates: 22% (523). **Average award:** Freshmen: $3285. Undergraduates: $2703. **Scholarships, grants, and awards by category:** Academic interests/achievement: general academic interests/achievements. **Special characteristics:** children and siblings of alumni. **Tuition waivers:** Full or partial for employees or children of employees, senior citizens. **ROTC:** Army cooperative.

**LOANS Student loans:** $16,135,579 (88% need-based, 12% non-need-based). 63% of past graduating class borrowed through all loan programs. **Average indebtedness per student:** $36,935. **Average need-based loan:** Freshmen: $3390. Undergraduates: $4194. **Parent loans:** $4,866,609 (87% need-based, 13% non-need-based). **Programs:** Federal Direct (Subsidized and Unsubsidized Stafford, PLUS), Perkins, college/university, private loans.

**WORK-STUDY Federal work-study:** jobs available.

**APPLYING FOR FINANCIAL AID Required financial aid form:** FAFSA. **Financial aid deadline (priority):** 2/15. **Notification date:** Continuous beginning 3/1.

**CONTACT** Judith A. Rile, Financial Aid Coordinator, Penn State Berks, Perkins Student Center, Room 6, Reading, PA 19610-6009, 610-396-6070. Fax: 610-396-6316. E-mail: jar38@psu.edu. Website: http://www.bk.psu.edu/.

# PENN STATE BRANDYWINE
## Media, PA

| Tuition & fees (PA res): $13,942 | Average undergraduate aid package: $9961 |
|---|---|

**ABOUT THE INSTITUTION** State-related, coed. **Awards:** certificates, associate, and bachelor's degrees. 120 undergraduate majors. **Total enrollment:** 1,488. Undergraduates: 1,488. Freshmen: 389. Federal methodology is used as a basis for awarding need-based institutional aid.

**UNDERGRADUATE EXPENSES for 2015–2016 Application fee:** $50. **Tuition, state resident:** full-time $13,012; part-time $535 per credit hour. **Tuition, nonresident:** full-time $19,848; part-time $827 per credit hour. **Required fees:** full-time $930. Full-time tuition and fees vary according to course level, degree level, location, program, and student level. Part-time tuition and fees vary according to course level, course load, degree level, location, program, and student level.

**FRESHMAN FINANCIAL AID (Fall 2013)** 290 applied for aid; of those 70% were deemed to have need. 99% of freshmen with need received aid; of those 8% had need fully met. **Average percent of need met:** 60% (excluding resources awarded to replace EFC). **Average financial aid package:** $9841 (excluding resources awarded to replace EFC). 23% of all full-time freshmen had no need and received non-need-based gift aid.

**UNDERGRADUATE FINANCIAL AID (Fall 2013)** 974 applied for aid; of those 79% were deemed to have need. 99% of undergraduates with need received aid; of those 6% had need fully met. **Average percent of need met:** 59% (excluding resources awarded to replace EFC). **Average financial aid package:** $9961 (excluding resources awarded to replace EFC). 11% of all full-time undergraduates had no need and received non-need-based gift aid.

**GIFT AID (NEED-BASED) Total amount:** $5,189,644 (44% federal, 29% state, 24% institutional, 3% external sources). **Receiving aid:** Freshmen: 47% (152); all full-time undergraduates: 49% (573). **Average award:** Freshmen: $6566; Undergraduates: $6694. **Scholarships, grants, and awards:** Federal Pell, FSEOG, state, private, college/university gift aid from institutional funds.

**GIFT AID (NON-NEED-BASED) Total amount:** $744,227 (21% federal, 2% state, 63% institutional, 14% external sources). **Receiving aid:** Freshmen: 32% (104). Undergraduates: 22% (258). **Average award:** Freshmen: $4693. Undergraduates: $3729. **Scholarships, grants, and awards by category:** Academic interests/achievement: general academic interests/achievements. **Special characteristics:** children and siblings of alumni. **Tuition waivers:** Full or partial for employees or children of employees, senior citizens. **ROTC:** Army cooperative, Air Force cooperative.

**LOANS Student loans:** $6,577,233 (82% need-based, 18% non-need-based). 63% of past graduating class borrowed through all loan programs. **Average indebtedness per student:** $36,935. **Average need-based loan:** Freshmen: $3150. Undergraduates: $4026. **Parent loans:** $649,242 (71% need-based, 29% non-need-based). **Programs:** Federal Direct (Subsidized and Unsubsidized Stafford, PLUS), Perkins, college/university, private loans.

**WORK-STUDY Federal work-study:** jobs available. **State or other work-study/employment:** Part-time jobs available.

**APPLYING FOR FINANCIAL AID Required financial aid form:** FAFSA. **Financial aid deadline (priority):** 2/15. **Notification date:** Continuous beginning 3/1.

**CONTACT** Student Financial Aid Office, Penn State Brandywine, 105 Main Building, 25 Yearsley Mill Road, Media, PA 19063, 610-892-1260. E-mail: bw-financial@psu.edu. Website: http://www.brandywine.psu.edu/.

# PENN STATE ERIE, THE BEHREND COLLEGE
## Erie, PA

| Tuition & fees (PA res): $14,588 | Average undergraduate aid package: $10,689 |
|---|---|

**ABOUT THE INSTITUTION** State-related, coed. **Awards:** certificates, associate, bachelor's, and master's degrees. 129 undergraduate majors. **Total enrollment:** 4,138. Undergraduates: 4,001. Freshmen: 1,186. Federal methodology is used as a basis for awarding need-based institutional aid.

**UNDERGRADUATE EXPENSES for 2015–2016 Application fee:** $50. **Tuition, state resident:** full-time $13,658; part-time $569 per credit hour. **Tuition, nonresident:** full-time $20,890; part-time $870 per credit hour. **Required fees:** full-time $930. Full-time tuition and fees vary according to course level, degree level, location, program, and student level. Part-time tuition and fees vary according to course level, course load, degree level, location, program, and student level. **College room and board:** $10,520; **Room only:** $5460. Room and board charges vary according to board plan, housing facility, and location.

**FRESHMAN FINANCIAL AID (Fall 2013)** 959 applied for aid; of those 83% were deemed to have need. 98% of freshmen with need received aid; of those 3% had need fully met. **Average percent of need met:** 61% (excluding resources awarded to replace EFC). *Average financial aid package:* $10,811 (excluding resources awarded to replace EFC). 11% of all full-time freshmen had no need and received non-need-based gift aid.

**UNDERGRADUATE FINANCIAL AID (Fall 2013)** 3,050 applied for aid; of those 86% were deemed to have need. 98% of undergraduates with need received aid; of those 4% had need fully met. *Average percent of need met:* 59% (excluding resources awarded to replace EFC). *Average financial aid package:* $10,689 (excluding resources awarded to replace EFC). 6% of all full-time undergraduates had no need and received non-need-based gift aid.

**GIFT AID (NEED-BASED)** *Total amount:* $17,012,756 (37% federal, 27% state, 29% institutional, 7% external sources). *Receiving aid:* Freshmen: 47% (522); all full-time undergraduates: 47% (1,694). *Average award:* Freshmen: $7058; Undergraduates: $6711. *Scholarships, grants, and awards:* Federal Pell, FSEOG, state, private, college/university gift aid from institutional funds.

**GIFT AID (NON-NEED-BASED)** *Total amount:* $1,239,531 (14% federal, 57% institutional, 29% external sources). *Receiving aid:* Freshmen: 46% (505). Undergraduates: 31% (1,109). *Average award:* Freshmen: $3035. Undergraduates: $3236. *Scholarships, grants, and awards by category:* Academic interests/achievement: general academic interests/achievements. *Special characteristics:* children and siblings of alumni. *Tuition waivers:* Full or partial for employees or children of employees, senior citizens. *ROTC:* Army.

**LOANS** *Student loans:* $26,247,676 (90% need-based, 10% non-need-based). 63% of past graduating class borrowed through all loan programs. *Average indebtedness per student:* $36,935. *Average need-based loan:* Freshmen: $3570. Undergraduates: $4342. *Parent loans:* $7,695,949 (87% need-based, 13% non-need-based). *Programs:* Federal Direct (Subsidized and Unsubsidized Stafford, PLUS), Perkins, college/university, private loans.

**WORK-STUDY** *Federal work-study:* jobs available.

**APPLYING FOR FINANCIAL AID** *Required financial aid form:* FAFSA. *Financial aid deadline (priority):* 2/15. *Notification date:* Continuous beginning 3/1.

**CONTACT** Ms. Jane Brady, Associate Director of Financial Aid, Penn State Erie, The Behrend College, 4851 College Drive, Metzgar Admissions and Alumni Center, Erie, PA 16563, 814-898-6162 or toll-free 866-374-3378. *Fax:* 814-898-7595. *E-mail:* jub9@psu.edu.
*Website:* http://www.pserie.psu.edu/.

# PENN STATE GREATER ALLEGHENY
## McKeesport, PA

| Tuition & fees (PA res): $13,648 | Average undergraduate aid package: $12,299 |
|---|---|

**ABOUT THE INSTITUTION** State-related, coed. *Awards:* certificates, associate, bachelor's, and master's degrees. 119 undergraduate majors. *Total enrollment:* 604. Undergraduates: 604. Freshmen: 183. Federal methodology is used as a basis for awarding need-based institutional aid.

**UNDERGRADUATE EXPENSES for 2015–2016** *Application fee:* $50. *Tuition, state resident:* full-time $12,718; part-time $524 per credit hour. *Tuition, nonresident:* full-time $19,404; part-time $809 per credit hour. *Required fees:* full-time $930. Full-time tuition and fees vary according to course level, degree level, location, program, and student level. Part-time tuition and fees vary according to course level, course load, degree level, location, program, and student level. *College room and board:* $10,520; *Room only:* $5460. Room and board charges vary according to board plan, housing facility, and location.

**FRESHMAN FINANCIAL AID (Fall 2013)** 163 applied for aid; of those 83% were deemed to have need. 98% of freshmen with need received aid; of those 7% had need fully met. *Average percent of need met:* 66% (excluding resources awarded to replace EFC). *Average financial aid package:* $13,069 (excluding resources awarded to replace EFC). 10% of all full-time freshmen had no need and received non-need-based gift aid.

**UNDERGRADUATE FINANCIAL AID (Fall 2013)** 474 applied for aid; of those 89% were deemed to have need. 98% of undergraduates with need received aid; of those 6% had need fully met. *Average percent of need met:* 63% (excluding resources awarded to replace EFC). *Average financial aid package:* $12,299 (excluding resources awarded to replace EFC). 9% of all full-time undergraduates had no need and received non-need-based gift aid.

**GIFT AID (NEED-BASED)** *Total amount:* $3,636,832 (42% federal, 22% state, 24% institutional, 12% external sources). *Receiving aid:* Freshmen: 59% (113); all full-time undergraduates: 60% (334). *Average award:* Freshmen: $7231; Undergraduates: $6998. *Scholarships, grants, and awards:* Federal Pell, FSEOG, state, private, college/university gift aid from institutional funds.

**GIFT AID (NON-NEED-BASED)** *Total amount:* $267,897 (23% federal, 59% institutional, 18% external sources). *Receiving aid:* Freshmen: 45% (86). Undergraduates: 38% (212). *Average award:* Freshmen: $4060. Undergraduates: $3257. *Tuition waivers:* Full or partial for employees or children of employees, senior citizens.

**LOANS** *Student loans:* $3,303,089 (93% need-based, 7% non-need-based). 63% of past graduating class borrowed through all loan programs. *Average indebtedness per student:* $36,935. *Average need-based loan:* Freshmen: $3334. Undergraduates: $4124. *Parent loans:* $587,290 (89% need-based, 11% non-need-based). *Programs:* Federal Direct (Subsidized and Unsubsidized Stafford, PLUS), Perkins, college/university, private loans.

**WORK-STUDY** *Federal work-study:* jobs available. *State or other work-study/employment:* Part-time jobs available.

**APPLYING FOR FINANCIAL AID** *Required financial aid form:* FAFSA. *Financial aid deadline (priority):* 2/15. *Notification date:* Continuous beginning 3/1.

**CONTACT** Student Aid Office, Penn State Greater Allegheny, 4000 University Drive, McKeesport, PA 15132-7698, 412-675-9160. *Fax:* 412-675-9036.
*Website:* http://www.ga.psu.edu/.

# PENN STATE HARRISBURG
## Middletown, PA

| Tuition & fees (PA res): $14,588 | Average undergraduate aid package: $10,873 |
|---|---|

**ABOUT THE INSTITUTION** State-related, coed. *Awards:* certificates, associate, bachelor's, master's, and doctoral degrees. 29 undergraduate majors. *Total enrollment:* 4,519. Undergraduates: 3,691. Freshmen: 794. Federal methodology is used as a basis for awarding need-based institutional aid.

**UNDERGRADUATE EXPENSES for 2015–2016** *Application fee:* $50. *Tuition, state resident:* full-time $13,658; part-time $569 per credit hour. *Tuition, nonresident:* full-time $20,890; part-time $870 per credit hour. *Required fees:* full-time $930. Full-time tuition and fees vary according to course level, degree level, location, program, and student level. Part-time tuition and fees vary according to course level, course load, degree level, location, program, and student level. *College room and board:* $11,980; *Room only:* $6920. Room and board charges vary according to board plan, housing facility, and location.

**FRESHMAN FINANCIAL AID (Fall 2013)** 539 applied for aid; of those 85% were deemed to have need. 98% of freshmen with need received aid; of those 7% had need fully met. *Average percent of need met:* 54% (excluding resources awarded to replace EFC). *Average financial aid package:* $10,644 (excluding resources awarded to replace EFC). 13% of all full-time freshmen had no need and received non-need-based gift aid.

**UNDERGRADUATE FINANCIAL AID (Fall 2013)** 2,390 applied for aid; of those 87% were deemed to have need. 98% of undergraduates with need received aid; of those 5% had need fully met. *Average percent of need met:* 56% (excluding resources awarded to replace EFC). *Average financial aid package:* $10,873 (excluding resources awarded to replace EFC). 7% of all full-time undergraduates had no need and received non-need-based gift aid.

**GIFT AID (NEED-BASED)** *Total amount:* $13,614,756 (49% federal, 25% state, 22% institutional, 4% external sources). *Receiving aid:* Freshmen: 38% (281); all full-time undergraduates: 45% (1,383). *Average award:* Freshmen: $6729; Undergraduates: $6638. *Scholarships, grants, and awards:* Federal Pell, FSEOG, state, private, college/university gift aid from institutional funds.

**GIFT AID (NON-NEED-BASED)** *Total amount:* $1,572,993 (49% federal, 2% state, 30% institutional, 19% external sources). *Receiving aid:* Freshmen: 44% (329). Undergraduates: 27% (847). *Average award:* Freshmen: $2765. Undergraduates: $2068. *Scholarships, grants, and awards by category:* Academic interests/achievement: general academic interests/achievements. *Special characteristics:* children and siblings of alumni, general special characteristics. *Tuition waivers:* Full or partial for employees or children of employees, senior citizens. *ROTC:* Army cooperative.

**LOANS** *Student loans:* $22,442,233 (88% need-based, 12% non-need-based). 63% of past graduating class borrowed through all loan programs. *Average indebtedness per student:* $36,935. *Average need-based loan:* Freshmen: $3465. Undergraduates: $4525. *Parent loans:* $5,556,158 (84% need-based, 16% non-need-based). **Programs:** Federal Direct (Subsidized and Unsubsidized Stafford, PLUS), Perkins, college/university, private loans.

**WORK-STUDY** *Federal work-study:* jobs available.

**APPLYING FOR FINANCIAL AID** *Required financial aid form:* FAFSA. *Financial aid deadline (priority):* 2/15. *Notification date:* Continuous beginning 3/1.

**CONTACT** Student Aid Office, Penn State Harrisburg, 777 West Harrisburg Pike, Middletown, PA 17057-4898, 717-948-6307 or toll-free 800-222-2056. *Fax:* 717-948-6008. *E-mail:* hbgfinaid@psu.edu.
*Website:* http://www.hbg.psu.edu/.

---

# PENN STATE HAZLETON
## Hazleton, PA

| Tuition & fees (PA res): $13,882 | Average undergraduate aid package: $11,189 |
|---|---|

**ABOUT THE INSTITUTION** State-related, coed. *Awards:* certificates, associate, and bachelor's degrees. 125 undergraduate majors. *Total enrollment:* 850. Undergraduates: 850. Freshmen: 304. Federal methodology is used as a basis for awarding need-based institutional aid.

**UNDERGRADUATE EXPENSES** for 2015–2016 *Application fee:* $50. *Tuition, state resident:* full-time $13,012; part-time $535 per credit hour. *Tuition, nonresident:* full-time $19,848; part-time $827 per credit hour. *Required fees:* full-time $870. Full-time tuition and fees vary according to course level, degree level, location, program, and student level. Part-time tuition and fees vary according to course level, course load, degree level, location, program, and student level. *College room and board:* $10,520; *Room only:* $5460. Room and board charges vary according to board plan, housing facility, and location.

**FRESHMAN FINANCIAL AID (Fall 2013)** 338 applied for aid; of those 89% were deemed to have need. 98% of freshmen with need received aid; of those 3% had need fully met. *Average percent of need met:* 59% (excluding resources awarded to replace EFC). *Average financial aid package:* $10,929 (excluding resources awarded to replace EFC). 7% of all full-time freshmen had no need and received non-need-based gift aid.

**UNDERGRADUATE FINANCIAL AID (Fall 2013)** 799 applied for aid; of those 92% were deemed to have need. 98% of undergraduates with need received aid; of those 3% had need fully met. *Average percent of need met:* 59% (excluding resources awarded to replace EFC). *Average financial aid package:* $11,189 (excluding resources awarded to replace EFC). 6% of all full-time undergraduates had no need and received non-need-based gift aid.

**GIFT AID (NEED-BASED)** *Total amount:* $5,469,294 (43% federal, 22% state, 32% institutional, 3% external sources). *Receiving aid:* Freshmen: 60% (217); all full-time undergraduates: 62% (539). *Average award:* Freshmen: $7181; Undergraduates: $6949. *Scholarships, grants, and awards:* Federal Pell, FSEOG, state, private, college/university gift aid from institutional funds.

**GIFT AID (NON-NEED-BASED)** *Total amount:* $180,504 (1% federal, 94% institutional, 5% external sources). *Receiving aid:* Freshmen: 47% (168). Undergraduates: 40% (350). *Average award:* Freshmen: $3556. Undergraduates: $3375. *Scholarships, grants, and awards by category: Academic interests/achievement:* general academic interests/achievements. *Special characteristics:* children and siblings of alumni. *Tuition waivers:* Full or partial for employees or children of employees, senior citizens. *ROTC:* Army, Air Force cooperative.

**LOANS** *Student loans:* $6,238,769 (94% need-based, 6% non-need-based). 63% of past graduating class borrowed through all loan programs. *Average indebtedness per student:* $36,935. *Average need-based loan:* Freshmen: $3378. Undergraduates: $3964. *Parent loans:* $1,955,725 (93% need-based, 7% non-need-based). **Programs:** Federal Direct (Subsidized and Unsubsidized Stafford, PLUS), Perkins, college/university, private loans.

**WORK-STUDY** *Federal work-study:* jobs available. *State or other work-study/employment:* Part-time jobs available.

**APPLYING FOR FINANCIAL AID** *Required financial aid form:* FAFSA. *Financial aid deadline (priority):* 2/15. *Notification date:* Continuous beginning 3/1.

**CONTACT** Mrs. Sarah Evancho, Student Aid Coordinator, Penn State Hazleton, Administration Building, Room 222, Hazleton, PA 18201-1291, 570-450-3163 or toll-free 800-279-8495. *E-mail:* sjw37@psu.edu.
*Website:* http://www.hn.psu.edu/.

---

# PENN STATE LEHIGH VALLEY
## Center Valley, PA

| Tuition & fees (PA res): $13,930 | Average undergraduate aid package: $9964 |
|---|---|

**ABOUT THE INSTITUTION** State-related, coed. *Awards:* certificates, associate, and bachelor's degrees (enrollment figures include students enrolled at The Graduate School at Penn State who are taking courses at this location). 119 undergraduate majors. *Total enrollment:* 913. Undergraduates: 881. Freshmen: 215. Federal methodology is used as a basis for awarding need-based institutional aid.

**UNDERGRADUATE EXPENSES** for 2015–2016 *Application fee:* $50. *Tuition, state resident:* full-time $13,012; part-time $535 per credit hour. *Tuition, nonresident:* full-time $19,848; part-time $827 per credit hour. *Required fees:* full-time $918. Full-time tuition and fees vary according to course level, degree level, location, program, and student level. Part-time tuition and fees vary according to course level, course load, degree level, location, program, and student level.

**FRESHMAN FINANCIAL AID (Fall 2013)** 206 applied for aid; of those 83% were deemed to have need. 96% of freshmen with need received aid; of those 3% had need fully met. *Average percent of need met:* 58% (excluding resources awarded to replace EFC). *Average financial aid package:* $9310 (excluding resources awarded to replace EFC). 11% of all full-time freshmen had no need and received non-need-based gift aid.

**UNDERGRADUATE FINANCIAL AID (Fall 2013)** 594 applied for aid; of those 83% were deemed to have need. 97% of undergraduates with need received aid; of those 4% had need fully met. *Average percent of need met:* 59% (excluding resources awarded to replace EFC). *Average financial aid package:* $9964 (excluding resources awarded to replace EFC). 8% of all full-time undergraduates had no need and received non-need-based gift aid.

**GIFT AID (NEED-BASED)** *Total amount:* $3,175,964 (49% federal, 28% state, 20% institutional, 3% external sources). *Receiving aid:* Freshmen: 55% (126); all full-time undergraduates: 54% (379). *Average award:* Freshmen: $6464; Undergraduates: $6422. *Scholarships, grants, and awards:* Federal Pell, FSEOG, state, private, college/university gift aid from institutional funds.

**GIFT AID (NON-NEED-BASED)** *Total amount:* $256,161 (32% federal, 4% state, 53% institutional, 11% external sources). *Receiving aid:* Freshmen: 37% (85). Undergraduates: 23% (160). *Average award:* Freshmen: $3398. Undergraduates: $2518. *Scholarships, grants, and awards by category: Academic interests/achievement:* general academic interests/achievements. *Special characteristics:* general special characteristics. *Tuition waivers:* Full or partial for employees or children of employees, senior citizens. *ROTC:* Army cooperative.

**LOANS** *Student loans:* $4,013,647 (84% need-based, 16% non-need-based). 63% of past graduating class borrowed through all loan programs. *Average indebtedness per student:* $36,935. *Average need-based loan:* Freshmen: $3290. Undergraduates: $4093. *Parent loans:* $300,290 (83% need-based, 17% non-need-based). **Programs:** Federal Direct (Subsidized and Unsubsidized Stafford, PLUS), Perkins, college/university, private loans.

**WORK-STUDY** *Federal work-study:* jobs available. *State or other work-study/employment:* Part-time jobs available.

**APPLYING FOR FINANCIAL AID** *Required financial aid form:* FAFSA. *Financial aid deadline:* Continuous. *Notification date:* Continuous beginning 3/1.

**CONTACT** Maryann Hubick, Student Aid Coordinator, Penn State Lehigh Valley, 8380 Mohr Lane, Fogelsville, PA 18051, 610-285-5033. *Fax:* 610-285-5220. *E-mail:* mxh61@psu.edu.
*Website:* http://www.lv.psu.edu/.

# PENN STATE NEW KENSINGTON
## New Kensington, PA

| Tuition & fees (PA res): $13,588 | Average undergraduate aid package: $9942 |
|---|---|

**ABOUT THE INSTITUTION** State-related, coed. *Awards:* certificates, associate, bachelor's, and master's degrees. 124 undergraduate majors. *Total enrollment:* 665. Undergraduates: 665. Freshmen: 185. Federal methodology is used as a basis for awarding need-based institutional aid.

**UNDERGRADUATE EXPENSES for 2015–2016** *Application fee:* $50. *Tuition, state resident:* full-time $12,718; part-time $524 per credit hour. *Tuition, nonresident:* full-time $19,404; part-time $809 per credit hour. *Required fees:* full-time $870. Full-time tuition and fees vary according to course level, degree level, location, program, and student level. Part-time tuition and fees vary according to course level, course load, degree level, location, program, and student level.

**FRESHMAN FINANCIAL AID (Fall 2013)** 143 applied for aid; of those 83% were deemed to have need. 100% of freshmen with need received aid; of those 6% had need fully met. *Average percent of need met:* 68% (excluding resources awarded to replace EFC). *Average financial aid package:* $10,761 (excluding resources awarded to replace EFC). 12% of all full-time freshmen had no need and received non-need-based gift aid.

**UNDERGRADUATE FINANCIAL AID (Fall 2013)** 448 applied for aid; of those 86% were deemed to have need. 100% of undergraduates with need received aid; of those 7% had need fully met. *Average percent of need met:* 63% (excluding resources awarded to replace EFC). *Average financial aid package:* $9942 (excluding resources awarded to replace EFC). 8% of all full-time undergraduates had no need and received non-need-based gift aid.

**GIFT AID (NEED-BASED)** *Total amount:* $2,477,826 (38% federal, 31% state, 25% institutional, 6% external sources). *Receiving aid:* Freshmen: 60% (97); all full-time undergraduates: 57% (288). *Average award:* Freshmen: $6527; Undergraduates: $6075. *Scholarships, grants, and awards:* Federal Pell, FSEOG, state, private, college/university gift aid from institutional funds.

**GIFT AID (NON-NEED-BASED)** *Total amount:* $316,345 (43% federal, 37% institutional, 20% external sources). *Receiving aid:* Freshmen: 48% (78). Undergraduates: 31% (159). *Average award:* Freshmen: $3325. Undergraduates: $2728. *Scholarships, grants, and awards by category:* Academic interests/achievement: general academic interests/achievements. *Special characteristics:* children and siblings of alumni. *Tuition waivers:* Full or partial for employees or children of employees, senior citizens. *ROTC:* Air Force cooperative.

**LOANS** *Student loans:* $3,517,905 (90% need-based, 10% non-need-based). 63% of past graduating class borrowed through all loan programs. *Average indebtedness per student:* $36,935. *Average need-based loan:* Freshmen: $3326. Undergraduates: $4102. *Parent loans:* $592,629 (72% need-based, 28% non-need-based). *Programs:* Federal Direct (Subsidized and Unsubsidized Stafford, PLUS), Perkins, college/university, private loans.

**WORK-STUDY** *Federal work-study:* jobs available. *State or other work-study/employment:* Part-time jobs available.

**APPLYING FOR FINANCIAL AID** *Required financial aid form:* FAFSA. *Financial aid deadline (priority):* 2/15. *Notification date:* Continuous beginning 3/1.

**CONTACT** Office of Student Aid, Penn State New Kensington, Administrative Building, 3550 Seventh Street Road, New Kensington, PA 15068, 724-334-6047 or toll-free 888-968-7297. *Fax:* 724-334-6111. *E-mail:* nk-finaid@psu.edu. *Website:* http://www.nk.psu.edu/.

# PENN STATE SCHUYLKILL
## Schuylkill Haven, PA

| Tuition & fees (PA res): $13,870 | Average undergraduate aid package: $12,576 |
|---|---|

**ABOUT THE INSTITUTION** State-related, coed. *Awards:* certificates, associate, and bachelor's degrees (bachelor's degree programs completed at the Harrisburg campus). 124 undergraduate majors. *Total enrollment:* 796. Undergraduates: 796. Freshmen: 250. Federal methodology is used as a basis for awarding need-based institutional aid.

**UNDERGRADUATE EXPENSES for 2015–2016** *Application fee:* $50. *Tuition, state resident:* full-time $13,012; part-time $535 per credit hour. *Tuition, nonresident:* full-time $19,848; part-time $827 per credit hour. *Required fees:* full-time $858. Full-time tuition and fees vary according to course level, degree level, location, program, and student level. Part-time tuition and fees vary according to course level, course load, degree level, location, program, and student level. *College room and board:* $7886; *Room only:* $5886. Room and board charges vary according to board plan, housing facility, and location.

**FRESHMAN FINANCIAL AID (Fall 2013)** 241 applied for aid; of those 94% were deemed to have need. 100% of freshmen with need received aid; of those 8% had need fully met. *Average percent of need met:* 63% (excluding resources awarded to replace EFC). *Average financial aid package:* $13,076 (excluding resources awarded to replace EFC). 5% of all full-time freshmen had no need and received non-need-based gift aid.

**UNDERGRADUATE FINANCIAL AID (Fall 2013)** 600 applied for aid; of those 94% were deemed to have need. 99% of undergraduates with need received aid; of those 5% had need fully met. *Average percent of need met:* 62% (excluding resources awarded to replace EFC). *Average financial aid package:* $12,576 (excluding resources awarded to replace EFC). 3% of all full-time undergraduates had no need and received non-need-based gift aid.

**GIFT AID (NEED-BASED)** *Total amount:* $4,997,446 (43% federal, 23% state, 27% institutional, 7% external sources). *Receiving aid:* Freshmen: 74% (190); all full-time undergraduates: 74% (476). *Average award:* Freshmen: $7034; Undergraduates: $6954. *Scholarships, grants, and awards:* Federal Pell, FSEOG, state, private, college/university gift aid from institutional funds.

**GIFT AID (NON-NEED-BASED)** *Total amount:* $128,813 (29% federal, 42% institutional, 29% external sources). *Receiving aid:* Freshmen: 62% (160). Undergraduates: 45% (285). *Average award:* Freshmen: $3078. Undergraduates: $2571. *Scholarships, grants, and awards by category:* Academic interests/achievement: general academic interests/achievements. *Special characteristics:* general special characteristics. *Tuition waivers:* Full or partial for employees or children of employees, senior citizens.

**LOANS** *Student loans:* $4,926,410 (94% need-based, 6% non-need-based). 63% of past graduating class borrowed through all loan programs. *Average indebtedness per student:* $36,935. *Average need-based loan:* Freshmen: $3682. Undergraduates: $4179. *Parent loans:* $919,810 (90% need-based, 10% non-need-based). *Programs:* Federal Direct (Subsidized and Unsubsidized Stafford, PLUS), Perkins, college/university, private loans.

**WORK-STUDY** *Federal work-study:* jobs available. *State or other work-study/employment:* Part-time jobs available.

**APPLYING FOR FINANCIAL AID** *Required financial aid form:* FAFSA. *Financial aid deadline (priority):* 2/15. *Notification date:* Continuous beginning 3/1.

**CONTACT** Student Aid and Admissions Office, Penn State Schuylkill, 200 University Drive, Schuylkill Haven, PA 17972-2208, 570-385-6244. *Fax:* 570-385-6272. *E-mail:* sl-financialaid@psu.edu. *Website:* http://www.sl.psu.edu/.

# PENN STATE UNIVERSITY PARK
## State College, PA

| Tuition & fees (PA res): $17,502 | Average undergraduate aid package: $10,875 |
|---|---|

**ABOUT THE INSTITUTION** State-related, coed. *Awards:* certificates, associate, bachelor's, master's, and doctoral degrees. 125 undergraduate majors. *Total enrollment:* 47,040. Undergraduates: 40,541. Freshmen: 8,183. Federal methodology is used as a basis for awarding need-based institutional aid.

**UNDERGRADUATE EXPENSES for 2015–2016** *Application fee:* $50. *Tuition, state resident:* full-time $16,572; part-time $691 per credit hour. *Tuition, nonresident:* full-time $29,522; part-time $1230 per credit hour. *Required fees:* full-time $930. Full-time tuition and fees vary according to course level, degree level, location, program, and student level. Part-time tuition and fees vary according to course level, course load, degree level, location, program, and student level. *College room and board:* $10,520; *Room only:* $5460. Room and board charges vary according to board plan, housing facility, and location.

**FRESHMAN FINANCIAL AID (Fall 2013)** 5,809 applied for aid; of those 66% were deemed to have need. 92% of freshmen with need received aid; of those 8% had need fully met. **Average percent of need met:** 54% (excluding resources awarded to replace EFC). **Average financial aid package:** $10,039 (excluding resources awarded to replace EFC). 12% of all full-time freshmen had no need and received non-need-based gift aid.

**UNDERGRADUATE FINANCIAL AID (Fall 2013)** 24,601 applied for aid; of those 79% were deemed to have need. 96% of undergraduates with need received aid; of those 7% had need fully met. **Average percent of need met:** 57% (excluding resources awarded to replace EFC). **Average financial aid package:** $10,875 (excluding resources awarded to replace EFC). 10% of all full-time undergraduates had no need and received non-need-based gift aid.

**GIFT AID (NEED-BASED) Total amount:** $109,526,628 (37% federal, 20% state, 35% institutional, 8% external sources). **Receiving aid:** Freshmen: 20% (1,599); all full-time undergraduates: 26% (9,829). **Average award:** Freshmen: $6984; Undergraduates: $6987. **Scholarships, grants, and awards:** Federal Pell, FSEOG, state, private, college/university gift aid from institutional funds.

**GIFT AID (NON-NEED-BASED) Total amount:** $49,240,954 (17% federal, 28% institutional, 55% external sources). **Receiving aid:** Freshmen: 22% (1,776). Undergraduates: 17% (6,494). **Average award:** Freshmen: $5557. Undergraduates: $3757. **Scholarships, grants, and awards by category:** Academic interests/achievement: general academic interests/achievements. **Tuition waivers:** Full or partial for employees or children of employees, senior citizens. **ROTC:** Army, Naval, Air Force.

**LOANS Student loans:** $220,603,876 (84% need-based, 16% non-need-based). 63% of past graduating class borrowed through all loan programs. **Average indebtedness per student:** $36,935. **Average need-based loan:** Freshmen: $3500. Undergraduates: $4681. **Parent loans:** $107,551,148 (86% need-based, 14% non-need-based). **Programs:** Federal Direct (Subsidized and Unsubsidized Stafford, PLUS), Perkins, college/university, private loans.

**WORK-STUDY Federal work-study:** 976 jobs averaging $1824.

**ATHLETIC AWARDS** Total amount: $14,904,258 (40% need-based, 60% non-need-based).

**APPLYING FOR FINANCIAL AID Required financial aid form:** FAFSA. **Financial aid deadline (priority):** 2/15. **Notification date:** Continuous.

**CONTACT** Ms. Anna M. Griswold, Assistant Vice President for Undergraduate Education/Executive Director for Student Aid, Penn State University Park, 311 Shields Building, University Park, PA 16802, 814-863-0507. Fax: 814-863-0322. Website: http://www.psu.edu/.

---

# PENN STATE WILKES-BARRE
## Lehman, PA

| Tuition & fees (PA res): $13,588 | Average undergraduate aid package: $10,174 |
| --- | --- |

**ABOUT THE INSTITUTION** State-related, coed. **Awards:** certificates, associate, and bachelor's degrees (enrollment figures include students enrolled at The Graduate School at Penn State who are taking courses at this location). 122 undergraduate majors. **Total enrollment:** 545. Undergraduates: 536. Freshmen: 137. Federal methodology is used as a basis for awarding need-based institutional aid.

**UNDERGRADUATE EXPENSES for 2015–2016 Application fee:** $50. **Tuition, state resident:** full-time $12,718; part-time $524 per credit hour. **Tuition, nonresident:** full-time $19,404; part-time $809 per credit hour. **Required fees:** full-time $870. Full-time tuition and fees vary according to course level, degree level, location, program, and student level. Part-time tuition and fees vary according to course level, course load, degree level, location, program, and student level.

**FRESHMAN FINANCIAL AID (Fall 2013)** 158 applied for aid; of those 78% were deemed to have need. 98% of freshmen with need received aid; of those 8% had need fully met. **Average percent of need met:** 62% (excluding resources awarded to replace EFC). **Average financial aid package:** $9949 (excluding resources awarded to replace EFC). 16% of all full-time freshmen had no need and received non-need-based gift aid.

**UNDERGRADUATE FINANCIAL AID (Fall 2013)** 457 applied for aid; of those 83% were deemed to have need. 98% of undergraduates with need received aid; of those 5% had need fully met. **Average percent of need met:** 63% (excluding resources awarded to replace EFC). **Average financial aid package:** $10,174 (excluding resources awarded to replace EFC). 9% of all full-time undergraduates had no need and received non-need-based gift aid.

**GIFT AID (NEED-BASED) Total amount:** $2,497,382 (41% federal, 27% state, 31% institutional, 1% external sources). **Receiving aid:** Freshmen: 55% (92); all full-

time undergraduates: 55% (279). **Average award:** Freshmen: $6513; Undergraduates: $6576. **Scholarships, grants, and awards:** Federal Pell, FSEOG, state, private, college/university gift aid from institutional funds.

**GIFT AID (NON-NEED-BASED) Total amount:** $210,999 (43% federal, 54% institutional, 3% external sources). **Receiving aid:** Freshmen: 45% (75). Undergraduates: 33% (167). **Average award:** Freshmen: $2513. Undergraduates: $2405. **Tuition waivers:** Full or partial for employees or children of employees, senior citizens. **ROTC:** Army cooperative, Air Force cooperative.

**LOANS Student loans:** $2,945,688 (86% need-based, 14% non-need-based). 63% of past graduating class borrowed through all loan programs. **Average indebtedness per student:** $36,935. **Average need-based loan:** Freshmen: $3308. Undergraduates: $4196. **Parent loans:** $688,050 (75% need-based, 25% non-need-based). **Programs:** Federal Direct (Subsidized and Unsubsidized Stafford, PLUS), Perkins, college/university, private loans.

**WORK-STUDY Federal work-study:** jobs available. **State or other work-study/employment:** Part-time jobs available.

**APPLYING FOR FINANCIAL AID Required financial aid form:** FAFSA. **Financial aid deadline (priority):** 2/15. **Notification date:** Continuous beginning 3/1.

**CONTACT** Stacey Zelinka, Financial Aid Coordinator, Penn State Wilkes-Barre, Old Route 115, PO Box PSU, Lehman, PA 18627, 570-675-9238. Fax: 570-675-9113. E-mail: saz3@psu.edu. Website: http://www.wb.psu.edu/.

---

# PENN STATE WORTHINGTON SCRANTON
## Dunmore, PA

| Tuition & fees (PA res): $13,882 | Average undergraduate aid package: $9902 |
| --- | --- |

**ABOUT THE INSTITUTION** State-related, coed. **Awards:** certificates, associate, and bachelor's degrees. 119 undergraduate majors. **Total enrollment:** 1,126. Undergraduates: 1,126. Freshmen: 268. Federal methodology is used as a basis for awarding need-based institutional aid.

**UNDERGRADUATE EXPENSES for 2015–2016 Application fee:** $50. **Tuition, state resident:** full-time $13,012; part-time $535 per credit hour. **Tuition, nonresident:** full-time $19,848; part-time $827 per credit hour. **Required fees:** full-time $870. Full-time tuition and fees vary according to course level, degree level, location, program, and student level. Part-time tuition and fees vary according to course level, course load, degree level, location, program, and student level.

**FRESHMAN FINANCIAL AID (Fall 2013)** 236 applied for aid; of those 86% were deemed to have need. 96% of freshmen with need received aid; of those 6% had need fully met. **Average percent of need met:** 61% (excluding resources awarded to replace EFC). **Average financial aid package:** $9957 (excluding resources awarded to replace EFC). 4% of all full-time freshmen had no need and received non-need-based gift aid.

**UNDERGRADUATE FINANCIAL AID (Fall 2013)** 831 applied for aid; of those 88% were deemed to have need. 98% of undergraduates with need received aid; of those 4% had need fully met. **Average percent of need met:** 59% (excluding resources awarded to replace EFC). **Average financial aid package:** $9902 (excluding resources awarded to replace EFC). 3% of all full-time undergraduates had no need and received non-need-based gift aid.

**GIFT AID (NEED-BASED) Total amount:** $4,966,867 (49% federal, 32% state, 16% institutional, 3% external sources). **Receiving aid:** Freshmen: 68% (169); all full-time undergraduates: 67% (608). **Average award:** Freshmen: $6742; Undergraduates: $6386. **Scholarships, grants, and awards:** Federal Pell, FSEOG, state, private, college/university gift aid from institutional funds.

**GIFT AID (NON-NEED-BASED) Total amount:** $174,419 (40% federal, 53% institutional, 7% external sources). **Receiving aid:** Freshmen: 24% (60). Undergraduates: 16% (144). **Average award:** Freshmen: $5792. Undergraduates: $3410. **Tuition waivers:** Full or partial for employees or children of employees, senior citizens. **ROTC:** Army cooperative, Air Force cooperative.

**LOANS Student loans:** $6,806,349 (91% need-based, 9% non-need-based). 63% of past graduating class borrowed through all loan programs. **Average indebtedness per student:** $36,935. **Average need-based loan:** Freshmen: $3372. Undergraduates: $4100. **Parent loans:** $598,911 (85% need-based, 15% non-need-based). **Programs:**

Federal Direct (Subsidized and Unsubsidized Stafford, PLUS), Perkins, college/university, private loans.
**WORK-STUDY** *Federal work-study:* jobs available. *State or other work-study/employment:* Part-time jobs available.
**APPLYING FOR FINANCIAL AID** *Required financial aid form:* FAFSA. *Financial aid deadline:* Continuous. *Notification date:* Continuous beginning 3/1.
**CONTACT** Financial Aid Office, Penn State Worthington Scranton, Room 21, Study Learning Center, 120 Ridge View Drive, Dunmore, PA 18512, 570-963-2690. *Fax:* 570-963-2683.
*Website:* http://www.sn.psu.edu/.

# PENN STATE YORK
## York, PA

| Tuition & fees (PA res): $13,930 | Average undergraduate aid package: $10,669 |
| --- | --- |

**ABOUT THE INSTITUTION** State-related, coed. *Awards:* certificates, associate, bachelor's, and master's degrees (also offers up to 2 years of most bachelor's degree programs offered at University Park campus). 126 undergraduate majors. *Total enrollment:* 1,172. Undergraduates: 1,126. Freshmen: 310. Federal methodology is used as a basis for awarding need-based institutional aid.
**UNDERGRADUATE EXPENSES** for 2015–2016 *Application fee:* $50. *Tuition, state resident:* full-time $13,012; part-time $535 per credit hour. *Tuition, nonresident:* full-time $19,848; part-time $827 per credit hour. *Required fees:* full-time $918. Full-time tuition and fees vary according to course level, degree level, location, program, and student level. Part-time tuition and fees vary according to course level, course load, degree level, location, program, and student level.
**FRESHMAN FINANCIAL AID (Fall 2013)** 227 applied for aid; of those 82% were deemed to have need. 97% of freshmen with need received aid; of those 8% had need fully met. *Average percent of need met:* 60% (excluding resources awarded to replace EFC). *Average financial aid package:* $10,442 (excluding resources awarded to replace EFC). 11% of all full-time freshmen had no need and received non-need-based gift aid.
**UNDERGRADUATE FINANCIAL AID (Fall 2013)** 627 applied for aid; of those 83% were deemed to have need. 98% of undergraduates with need received aid; of those 8% had need fully met. *Average percent of need met:* 61% (excluding resources awarded to replace EFC). *Average financial aid package:* $10,669 (excluding resources awarded to replace EFC). 9% of all full-time undergraduates had no need and received non-need-based gift aid.
**GIFT AID (NEED-BASED)** *Total amount:* $3,802,238 (47% federal, 26% state, 24% institutional, 3% external sources). *Receiving aid:* Freshmen: 50% (143); all full-time undergraduates: 50% (395). *Average award:* Freshmen: $6657; Undergraduates: $6430. *Scholarships, grants, and awards:* Federal Pell, FSEOG, state, private, college/university gift aid from institutional funds.
**GIFT AID (NON-NEED-BASED)** *Total amount:* $541,894 (46% federal, 39% institutional, 15% external sources). *Receiving aid:* Freshmen: 32% (92). Undergraduates: 26% (206). *Average award:* Freshmen: $3496. Undergraduates: $2893. *Scholarships, grants, and awards by category:* Academic interests/achievement: general academic interests/achievements. *Special characteristics:* children and siblings of alumni. *Tuition waivers:* Full or partial for employees or children of employees, senior citizens.
**LOANS** *Student loans:* $4,864,494 (85% need-based, 15% non-need-based). 63% of past graduating class borrowed through all loan programs. *Average indebtedness per student:* $36,935. *Average need-based loan:* Freshmen: $3284. Undergraduates: $4033. *Parent loans:* $585,533 (81% need-based, 19% non-need-based). *Programs:* Federal Direct (Subsidized and Unsubsidized Stafford, PLUS), Perkins, college/university, private loans.
**WORK-STUDY** *Federal work-study:* jobs available. *State or other work-study/employment:* Part-time jobs available.
**APPLYING FOR FINANCIAL AID** *Required financial aid form:* FAFSA. *Financial aid deadline (priority):* 2/15. *Notification date:* Continuous beginning 3/1.
**CONTACT** Financial Aid Office, Penn State York, 1031 Edgecomb Avenue, York, PA 17403-3326, 717-771-4045 or toll-free 800-778-6227. *E-mail:* yorkfinaid@yk.psu.edu. *Website:* http://www.yk.psu.edu/.

# PENNSYLVANIA ACADEMY OF THE FINE ARTS
## Philadelphia, PA

| Tuition & fees: N/R | Average undergraduate aid package: N/A |
| --- | --- |

**ABOUT THE INSTITUTION** Independent, coed. 1 undergraduate major. Federal methodology is used as a basis for awarding need-based institutional aid.
**GIFT AID (NEED-BASED)** *Total amount:* $1,395,834 (31% federal, 8% state, 54% institutional, 7% external sources). *Scholarships, grants, and awards:* Federal Pell, FSEOG, state.
**GIFT AID (NON-NEED-BASED)** *Total amount:* $975,764 (85% institutional, 15% external sources).
**LOANS** *Student loans:* $1,003,454 (50% need-based, 50% non-need-based). *Parent loans:* $319,638 (100% non-need-based). *Programs:* Federal Direct (Subsidized and Unsubsidized Stafford, PLUS).
**WORK-STUDY** *Federal work-study:* jobs available.
**APPLYING FOR FINANCIAL AID** *Notification date:* Continuous.
**CONTACT** Dana Moore, Director of Financial Aid, Pennsylvania Academy of the Fine Arts, 128 North Broad Street, Philadelphia, PA 19102, 215-972-2019. *Fax:* 215-972-0839. *E-mail:* dmoore@pafa.edu.
*Website:* http://www.pafa.edu/.

# PENNSYLVANIA COLLEGE OF ART & DESIGN
## Lancaster, PA

**CONTACT** J. David Hershey, Registrar/Director of Financial Aid, Pennsylvania College of Art & Design, 204 North Prince Street, PO Box 59, Lancaster, PA 17608-0059, 717-396-7833 Ext. 13 or toll free 800-689-0379 Ext. 1001. *Fax:* 717-396-1339. *E-mail:* finaid@pcad.edu.
*Website:* http://www.pcad.edu/.

# PENNSYLVANIA COLLEGE OF HEALTH SCIENCES
## Lancaster, PA

**CONTACT** Financial Aid Office, Pennsylvania College of Health Sciences, 410 North Lime Street, Lancaster, PA 17602, 717-544-4912 or toll-free 800-622-5443.
*Website:* http://www.pacollege.edu/.

# PENNSYLVANIA COLLEGE OF TECHNOLOGY
## Williamsport, PA

| Tuition & fees (PA res): $15,450 | Average undergraduate aid package: $11,920 |
| --- | --- |

**ABOUT THE INSTITUTION** State-related, coed. *Awards:* certificates, associate, and bachelor's degrees. 78 undergraduate majors. *Total enrollment:* 5,623. Undergraduates: 5,623. Freshmen: 1,287. Federal methodology is used as a basis for awarding need-based institutional aid.
**UNDERGRADUATE EXPENSES** for 2015–2016 *Application fee:* $50. *Tuition, state resident:* full-time $12,960; part-time $432 per credit hour. *Tuition, nonresident:* full-time $19,440; part-time $648 per credit hour. *Required fees:* full-time $2490; $83 per credit hour. Full-time tuition and fees vary according to course load and program. Part-time tuition and fees vary according to course load and program. *College room and board:* $10,836; *Room only:* $6236. Room and board charges vary according to board plan and housing facility.

**FRESHMAN FINANCIAL AID (Fall 2013)** 1,421 applied for aid; of those 92% were deemed to have need. 100% of freshmen with need received aid. *Average financial aid package:* $11,579 (excluding resources awarded to replace EFC).
**UNDERGRADUATE FINANCIAL AID (Fall 2013)** 4,649 applied for aid; of those 95% were deemed to have need. 100% of undergraduates with need received aid. *Average financial aid package:* $11,920 (excluding resources awarded to replace EFC).
**GIFT AID (NEED-BASED)** *Total amount:* $31,816,651 (32% federal, 23% state, 3% institutional, 42% external sources). *Receiving aid:* Freshmen: 67% (1,027); all full-time undergraduates: 67% (3,348). *Average award:* Freshmen: $6891; Undergraduates: $7637. *Scholarships, grants, and awards:* Federal Pell, FSEOG, state, private, college/university gift aid from institutional funds.
**GIFT AID (NON-NEED-BASED)** *Tuition waivers:* Full or partial for employees or children of employees. *ROTC:* Army.
**LOANS** *Student loans:* $45,437,192 (100% need-based). *Average need-based loan:* Freshmen: $3143. Undergraduates: $3738. *Parent loans:* $15,578,903 (100% need-based). *Programs:* Federal Direct (Subsidized and Unsubsidized Stafford, PLUS).
**WORK-STUDY** *Federal work-study:* 127 jobs averaging $1711.
**APPLYING FOR FINANCIAL AID** *Required financial aid forms:* FAFSA, institution's own form. *Financial aid deadline (priority):* 4/15. *Notification date:* Continuous beginning 6/1. Students must reply within 2 weeks of notification.
**CONTACT** Candace Baran, Director of Financial Aid, Pennsylvania College of Technology, One College Avenue, Williamsport, PA 17701, 570-326-4766 or toll-free 800-367-9222. *Fax:* 570-321-5552. *E-mail:* cbaran@pct.edu.
*Website:* http://www.pct.edu/.

# PEPPERDINE UNIVERSITY
## Malibu, CA

| Tuition & fees: $46,692 | Average undergraduate aid package: $40,131 |
|---|---|

**ABOUT THE INSTITUTION** Independent Church of Christ, coed. *Awards:* bachelor's, master's, and doctoral degrees. 61 undergraduate majors. *Total enrollment:* 7,417. Undergraduates: 3,451. Freshmen: 656. Federal methodology is used as a basis for awarding need-based institutional aid.
**UNDERGRADUATE EXPENSES for 2015–2016** *Application fee:* $65. *Comprehensive fee:* $60,082 includes full-time tuition ($46,440), mandatory fees ($252), and room and board ($13,390). Room and board charges vary according to board plan and housing facility. *Part-time tuition:* $1455 per credit hour.
**FRESHMAN FINANCIAL AID (Fall 2014, est.)** 636 applied for aid; of those 63% were deemed to have need. 100% of freshmen with need received aid; of those 28% had need fully met. *Average percent of need met:* 77% (excluding resources awarded to replace EFC). *Average financial aid package:* $34,868 (excluding resources awarded to replace EFC). 13% of all full-time freshmen had no need and received non-need-based gift aid.
**UNDERGRADUATE FINANCIAL AID (Fall 2014, est.)** 2,627 applied for aid; of those 67% were deemed to have need. 99% of undergraduates with need received aid; of those 21% had need fully met. *Average percent of need met:* 79% (excluding resources awarded to replace EFC). *Average financial aid package:* $40,131 (excluding resources awarded to replace EFC). 16% of all full-time undergraduates had no need and received non-need-based gift aid.
**GIFT AID (NEED-BASED)** *Total amount:* $61,603,610 (6% federal, 6% state, 85% institutional, 3% external sources). *Receiving aid:* Freshmen: 60% (395); all full-time undergraduates: 54% (1,696). *Average award:* Freshmen: $32,949; Undergraduates: $37,394. *Scholarships, grants, and awards:* Federal Pell, FSEOG, state, private, college/university gift aid from institutional funds, United Negro College Fund, Academic Competitiveness Grants, National SMART Grants.
**GIFT AID (NON-NEED-BASED)** *Total amount:* $10,402,519 (2% federal, 93% institutional, 5% external sources). *Average award:* Freshmen: $17,127. Undergraduates: $18,784. *Tuition waivers:* Full or partial for employees or children of employees. *ROTC:* Army cooperative, Air Force cooperative.
**LOANS** *Student loans:* $13,773,284 (89% need-based, 11% non-need-based). 63% of past graduating class borrowed through all loan programs. *Average indebtedness per student:* $31,884. *Average need-based loan:* Freshmen: $4035. Undergraduates: $5460. *Parent loans:* $14,636,425 (83% need-based, 17% non-need-based). *Programs:* Federal Direct (Subsidized and Unsubsidized Stafford, PLUS), Perkins, college/university.

**WORK-STUDY** *Federal work-study:* Total amount: $318,287; jobs available. *State or other work-study/employment:* Total amount: $92,691 (73% need-based, 27% non-need-based). Part-time jobs available.
**ATHLETIC AWARDS** Total amount: $5,353,198 (21% need-based, 79% non-need-based).
**APPLYING FOR FINANCIAL AID** *Required financial aid form:* FAFSA. *Financial aid deadline (priority):* 2/15. *Notification date:* 4/15. Students must reply by 5/1.
**CONTACT** Ms. Janet Lockhart, Director of Financial Assistance, Pepperdine University, 24255 Pacific Coast Highway, Malibu, CA 90263-4301, 310-506-4301. *Fax:* 310-506-4746. *E-mail:* janet.lockhart@pepperdine.edu.
*Website:* http://www.pepperdine.edu/.

# PERU STATE COLLEGE
## Peru, NE

**CONTACT** Diana Lind, Director of Financial Aid, Peru State College, PO Box 10, Peru, NE 68421, 402-872-2228 or toll-free 800-742-4412 (in-state), 800-741-4412 (out-of-state). *Fax:* 402-872-2419. *E-mail:* finaid@oakmail.peru.edu.
*Website:* http://www.peru.edu/.

# PFEIFFER UNIVERSITY
## Misenheimer, NC

**CONTACT** Amy Brown, Director of Financial Aid, Pfeiffer University, PO Box 960, Misenheimer, NC 28109, 704-463-1360 Ext. 3046 or toll-free 800-338-2060. *Fax:* 704-463-1363. *E-mail:* amy.brown@pfeiffer.edu.
*Website:* http://www.pfeiffer.edu/.

# PHILADELPHIA UNIVERSITY
## Philadelphia, PA

| Tuition & fees: $35,080 | Average undergraduate aid package: $25,116 |
|---|---|

**ABOUT THE INSTITUTION** Independent, coed. *Awards:* certificates, associate, bachelor's, master's, and doctoral degrees. 32 undergraduate majors. *Total enrollment:* 3,757. Undergraduates: 2,906. Freshmen: 661. Federal methodology is used as a basis for awarding need-based institutional aid.
**UNDERGRADUATE EXPENSES for 2015–2016** *Application fee:* $40. *Comprehensive fee:* $46,690 includes full-time tuition ($34,280), mandatory fees ($800), and room and board ($11,610). *College room only:* $5420. Full-time tuition and fees vary according to course load, degree level, and program. Room and board charges vary according to board plan and housing facility. *Part-time tuition:* $595 per credit hour. Part-time tuition and fees vary according to class time, course load, degree level, program, and reciprocity agreements.
**FRESHMAN FINANCIAL AID (Fall 2014, est.)** 564 applied for aid; of those 88% were deemed to have need. 100% of freshmen with need received aid; of those 28% had need fully met. *Average percent of need met:* 75% (excluding resources awarded to replace EFC). *Average financial aid package:* $28,420 (excluding resources awarded to replace EFC). 15% of all full-time freshmen had no need and received non-need-based gift aid.
**UNDERGRADUATE FINANCIAL AID (Fall 2014, est.)** 2,204 applied for aid; of those 90% were deemed to have need. 100% of undergraduates with need received aid; of those 15% had need fully met. *Average percent of need met:* 68% (excluding resources awarded to replace EFC). *Average financial aid package:* $25,116 (excluding resources awarded to replace EFC). 17% of all full-time undergraduates had no need and received non-need-based gift aid.
**GIFT AID (NEED-BASED)** *Total amount:* $35,420,236 (12% federal, 6% state, 81% institutional, 1% external sources). *Receiving aid:* Freshmen: 83% (499); all full-time undergraduates: 78% (1,990). *Average award:* Freshmen: $24,292; Undergraduates: $19,786. *Scholarships, grants, and awards:* Federal Pell, FSEOG, state, private, college/university gift aid from institutional funds, university-chosen non-endowed scholarships from outside sources.

**GIFT AID (NON-NEED-BASED)** *Total amount:* $5,943,857 (2% federal, 96% institutional, 2% external sources). *Receiving aid:* Freshmen: 20% (118). Undergraduates: 8% (206). *Average award:* Freshmen: $12,738. Undergraduates: $9652. *Scholarships, grants, and awards by category:* Academic interests/achievement: engineering/technologies, general academic interests/achievements. *Tuition waivers:* Full or partial for employees or children of employees.

**LOANS** *Student loans:* $20,549,134 (73% need-based, 27% non-need-based). 79% of past graduating class borrowed through all loan programs. *Average indebtedness per student:* $40,101. *Average need-based loan:* Freshmen: $3588. Undergraduates: $4373. *Parent loans:* $10,429,573 (46% need-based, 54% non-need-based). *Programs:* Federal Direct (Subsidized and Unsubsidized Stafford, PLUS), Perkins, private loans.

**WORK-STUDY** *Federal work-study:* Total amount: $2,504,624; jobs available. *State or other work-study/employment:* Total amount: $551,022 (82% need-based, 18% non-need-based). Part-time jobs available.

**ATHLETIC AWARDS** Total amount: $2,874,935 (47% need-based, 53% non-need-based).

**APPLYING FOR FINANCIAL AID** *Required financial aid form:* FAFSA. *Financial aid deadline:* 4/15 (priority: 3/1). *Notification date:* Continuous beginning 2/20. Students must reply by 5/1.

**CONTACT** Ms. Lisa J. Cooper, Director of Financial Aid, Philadelphia University, School House Lane and Henry Avenue, Philadelphia, PA 19144, 215-951-2940. *Fax:* 215-951-2941. *E-mail:* cooperl@philau.edu. *Website:* http://www.philau.edu/.

# PHILANDER SMITH COLLEGE
## Little Rock, AR

| Tuition & fees: $12,414 | Average undergraduate aid package: $13,369 |
| --- | --- |

**ABOUT THE INSTITUTION** Independent United Methodist, coed. *Awards:* bachelor's degrees. 18 undergraduate majors. *Total enrollment:* 567. Undergraduates: 567. Freshmen: 112. Federal methodology is used as a basis for awarding need-based institutional aid.

**UNDERGRADUATE EXPENSES** for 2015–2016 *Application fee:* $25. *One-time required fee:* $150. *Comprehensive fee:* $21,478 includes full-time tuition ($11,804), mandatory fees ($610), and room and board ($9064). *College room only:* $5908. Full-time tuition and fees vary according to course load, program, and student level. *Part-time tuition:* $495 per credit hour. Part-time tuition and fees vary according to course load, program, and student level.

**FRESHMAN FINANCIAL AID (Fall 2013)** 125 applied for aid; of those 95% were deemed to have need. 100% of freshmen with need received aid; of those 8% had need fully met. *Average percent of need met:* 61% (excluding resources awarded to replace EFC). *Average financial aid package:* $14,611 (excluding resources awarded to replace EFC). 10% of all full-time freshmen had no need and received non-need-based gift aid.

**UNDERGRADUATE FINANCIAL AID (Fall 2013)** 477 applied for aid; of those 96% were deemed to have need. 99% of undergraduates with need received aid; of those 7% had need fully met. *Average percent of need met:* 54% (excluding resources awarded to replace EFC). *Average financial aid package:* $13,369 (excluding resources awarded to replace EFC). 9% of all full-time undergraduates had no need and received non-need-based gift aid.

**GIFT AID (NEED-BASED)** *Total amount:* $5,177,782 (39% federal, 5% state, 47% institutional, 9% external sources). *Receiving aid:* Freshmen: 87% (118); all full-time undergraduates: 83% (437). *Average award:* Freshmen: $11,565; Undergraduates: $9858. *Scholarships, grants, and awards:* Federal Pell, FSEOG, state, private, college/university gift aid from institutional funds, United Negro College Fund.

**GIFT AID (NON-NEED-BASED)** *Receiving aid:* Freshmen: 4% (6). Undergraduates: 3% (15). *Average award:* Freshmen: $16,340. Undergraduates: $15,490. *Scholarships, grants, and awards by category:* Academic interests/achievement: 251 awards ($2,646,644 total): general academic interests/achievements. Creative arts/performance: 24 awards ($32,750 total): music. *Special characteristics:* 3 awards ($17,811 total). *Tuition waivers:* Full or partial for employees or children of employees. *ROTC:* Army cooperative.

**LOANS** *Student loans:* $4,061,943 (94% need-based, 6% non-need-based). 81% of past graduating class borrowed through all loan programs. *Average indebtedness per*

---

*student:* $35,968. *Average need-based loan:* Freshmen: $3279. Undergraduates: $4009. *Parent loans:* $488,752 (100% non-need-based). *Programs:* Federal Direct (Subsidized and Unsubsidized Stafford, PLUS), state.

**WORK-STUDY** *Federal work-study:* 82 jobs averaging $2600.

**ATHLETIC AWARDS** Total amount: $230,104 (100% non-need-based).

**APPLYING FOR FINANCIAL AID** *Required financial aid forms:* FAFSA, institution's own form. *Financial aid deadline (priority):* 3/1. *Notification date:* Continuous beginning 3/1.

**CONTACT** Kisa L. Hinton, Interim Director, Philander Smith College, 900 Daisy Bates Drive, Little Rock, AR 72202-3799, 501-370-5367 or toll-free 800-446-6772. *Fax:* 501-370-5357. *E-mail:* khinton@philander.edu. *Website:* http://www.philander.edu/.

# PIEDMONT COLLEGE
## Demorest, GA

| Tuition & fees: $21,350 | Average undergraduate aid package: $18,169 |
| --- | --- |

**ABOUT THE INSTITUTION** Independent United Church of Christ, coed. *Awards:* certificates, bachelor's, master's, and doctoral degrees. 46 undergraduate majors. *Total enrollment:* 2,120. Undergraduates: 1,286. Freshmen: 271. Both federal and institutional methodology are used as a basis for awarding need-based institutional aid.

**UNDERGRADUATE EXPENSES** for 2015–2016 *Comprehensive fee:* $30,136 includes full-time tuition ($21,350) and room and board ($8786). *College room only:* $4886. Full-time tuition and fees vary according to course load, degree level, location, and program. Room and board charges vary according to board plan. *Part-time tuition:* $890 per credit. Part-time tuition and fees vary according to course load, degree level, location, and program.

**FRESHMAN FINANCIAL AID (Fall 2014, est.)** 243 applied for aid; of those 88% were deemed to have need. 100% of freshmen with need received aid; of those 20% had need fully met. *Average percent of need met:* 75% (excluding resources awarded to replace EFC). *Average financial aid package:* $19,080 (excluding resources awarded to replace EFC). 19% of all full-time freshmen had no need and received non-need-based gift aid.

**UNDERGRADUATE FINANCIAL AID (Fall 2014, est.)** 1,102 applied for aid; of those 82% were deemed to have need. 99% of undergraduates with need received aid; of those 16% had need fully met. *Average percent of need met:* 70% (excluding resources awarded to replace EFC). *Average financial aid package:* $18,169 (excluding resources awarded to replace EFC). 18% of all full-time undergraduates had no need and received non-need-based gift aid.

**GIFT AID (NEED-BASED)** *Total amount:* $13,010,421 (20% federal, 18% state, 61% institutional, 1% external sources). *Receiving aid:* Freshmen: 81% (215); all full-time undergraduates: 80% (903). *Average award:* Freshmen: $15,852; Undergraduates: $14,047. *Scholarships, grants, and awards:* Federal Pell, FSEOG, state, private, college/university gift aid from institutional funds.

**GIFT AID (NON-NEED-BASED)** *Total amount:* $3,167,206 (15% state, 83% institutional, 2% external sources). *Receiving aid:* Freshmen: 14% (38). Undergraduates: 9% (105). *Average award:* Freshmen: $12,068. Undergraduates: $11,292. *Scholarships, grants, and awards by category:* Academic interests/achievement: 1,423 awards ($7,626,370 total): biological sciences, business, education, English, foreign languages, general academic interests/achievements, health fields, humanities, mathematics, premedicine, religion/biblical studies, social sciences. Creative arts/performance: 156 awards ($201,950 total): art/fine arts, debating, journalism/publications, music, theater/drama. *Special achievements/activities:* 30 awards ($104,165 total): community service, leadership, religious involvement. *Special characteristics:* 154 awards ($1,187,048 total): adult students, children of faculty/staff, international students, out-of-state students. *Tuition waivers:* Full or partial for employees or children of employees.

**LOANS** *Student loans:* $7,062,527 (80% need-based, 20% non-need-based). 84% of past graduating class borrowed through all loan programs. *Average indebtedness per student:* $23,481. *Average need-based loan:* Freshmen: $3099. Undergraduates: $4196. *Parent loans:* $1,241,194 (35% need-based, 65% non-need-based). *Programs:* Federal Direct (Subsidized and Unsubsidized Stafford, PLUS), state.

**WORK-STUDY** *Federal work-study:* Total amount: $213,729; 82 jobs averaging $2606. *State or other work-study/employment:* Total amount: $1,074,324 (44% need-based, 56% non-need-based). 343 part-time jobs averaging $3132.

**APPLYING FOR FINANCIAL AID** *Required financial aid forms:* FAFSA, state aid form. *Financial aid deadline (priority):* 3/1. *Notification date:* Continuous beginning 1/15. Students must reply within 2 weeks of notification.

**CONTACT** Mr. David Richmond McMillion, Director of Financial Aid, Piedmont College, PO Box 10, Demorest, GA 30535-0010, 706-778-3000 Ext. 1191 or toll-free 800-277-7020. *Fax:* 706-778-0708. *E-mail:* dmcmillion@piedmont.edu. *Website:* http://www.piedmont.edu/.

---

# PIEDMONT INTERNATIONAL UNIVERSITY
## Winston-Salem, NC

**ABOUT THE INSTITUTION** Independent Baptist, coed. *Awards:* certificates, associate, bachelor's, master's, and doctoral degrees. 13 undergraduate majors. *Total enrollment:* 384. Undergraduates: 197. Freshmen: 33.

**GIFT AID (NEED-BASED)** *Scholarships, grants, and awards:* Federal Pell, FSEOG.

**GIFT AID (NON-NEED-BASED)** *Scholarships, grants, and awards by category:* Academic interests/achievement: general academic interests/achievements. Special characteristics: children of faculty/staff, ethnic background, international students, relatives of clergy, spouses of current students, veterans.

**LOANS** *Programs:* Federal Direct (Subsidized and Unsubsidized Stafford, PLUS).

**APPLYING FOR FINANCIAL AID** *Required financial aid forms:* FAFSA, institution's own form.

**CONTACT** Bethany M. Sarazen, Director of Financial Assistance, Piedmont International University, 420 South Broad Street, Winston-Salem, NC 27101-5197, 336-714-7926 or toll-free 800-937-5097. *Fax:* 336-714-8022. *E-mail:* sarazenb@piedmontu.edu. *Website:* http://www.piedmontu.edu/.

---

# PILLAR COLLEGE
## Newark, NJ

**CONTACT** Financial Aid Office, Pillar College, 60 Park Place, Suite 701, Newark, NJ 07102, 973-803-5000 or toll-free 800-234-9305. *Website:* http://www.pillar.edu/.

---

# PINE MANOR COLLEGE
## Chestnut Hill, MA

| Tuition & fees: $25,516 | Average undergraduate aid package: $25,405 |
| --- | --- |

**ABOUT THE INSTITUTION** Independent, coed. *Awards:* associate, bachelor's, and master's degrees. 12 undergraduate majors. *Total enrollment:* 442. Undergraduates: 403. Freshmen: 122. Federal methodology is used as a basis for awarding need-based institutional aid.

**UNDERGRADUATE EXPENSES** for 2015–2016 *Application fee:* $25. *One-time required fee:* $664. *Comprehensive fee:* $38,336 includes full-time tuition ($25,516) and room and board ($12,820). Full-time tuition and fees vary according to course load. Room and board charges vary according to housing facility. *Part-time tuition:* $760 per credit. Part-time tuition and fees vary according to course load.

**FRESHMAN FINANCIAL AID (Fall 2014, est.)** 117 applied for aid; of those 99% were deemed to have need. 100% of freshmen with need received aid; of those 3% had need fully met. *Average percent of need met:* 73% (excluding resources awarded to replace EFC). *Average financial aid package:* $24,347 (excluding resources awarded to replace EFC). 9% of all full-time freshmen had no need and received non-need-based gift aid.

**UNDERGRADUATE FINANCIAL AID (Fall 2014, est.)** 263 applied for aid; of those 98% were deemed to have need. 100% of undergraduates with need received aid; of those 3% had need fully met. *Average percent of need met:* 74% (excluding resources awarded to replace EFC). *Average financial aid package:* $25,405 (excluding resources awarded to replace EFC). 9% of all full-time undergraduates had no need and received non-need-based gift aid.

**GIFT AID (NEED-BASED)** *Total amount:* $5,251,822 (20% federal, 4% state, 67% institutional, 9% external sources). *Receiving aid:* Freshmen: 95% (116); all full-time undergraduates: 89% (259). *Average award:* Freshmen: $20,371; Undergraduates: $20,316. *Scholarships, grants, and awards:* Federal Pell, FSEOG, state, private, college/university gift aid from institutional funds.

**GIFT AID (NON-NEED-BASED)** *Total amount:* $363,361 (92% institutional, 8% external sources). *Receiving aid:* Freshmen: 2% (3). Undergraduates: 2% (6). *Average award:* Freshmen: $8494. Undergraduates: $11,770. *Scholarships, grants, and awards by category:* Academic interests/achievement: biological sciences, education, general academic interests/achievements. Special achievements/activities: general special achievements/activities, leadership. Special characteristics: children and siblings of alumni, members of minority groups, siblings of current students. Tuition waivers: Full or partial for children of alumni, employees or children of employees.

**LOANS** *Student loans:* $2,035,190 (96% need-based, 4% non-need-based). 81% of past graduating class borrowed through all loan programs. *Average indebtedness per student:* $32,975. *Average need-based loan:* Freshmen: $3343. Undergraduates: $4511. *Parent loans:* $723,901 (87% need-based, 13% non-need-based). *Programs:* Federal Direct (Subsidized and Unsubsidized Stafford, PLUS), state, alternative loans.

**WORK-STUDY** *Federal work-study:* Total amount: $184,771; 210 jobs averaging $988.

**APPLYING FOR FINANCIAL AID** *Required financial aid form:* FAFSA. *Financial aid deadline (priority):* 5/1. *Notification date:* Continuous beginning 4/1. Students must reply by 5/1 or within 2 weeks of notification.

**CONTACT** Elizabeth M. Gorra, Director of Financial Aid, Pine Manor College, 400 Heath Street, Chestnut Hill, MA 02467, 617-731-7000 or toll-free 800-762-1357. *Fax:* 617-731-7102. *E-mail:* egorra@pmc.edu. *Website:* http://www.pmc.edu/.

---

# PIONEER PACIFIC COLLEGE
## Wilsonville, OR

**CONTACT** Financial Aid Office, Pioneer Pacific College, 27501 Southwest Parkway Avenue, Wilsonville, OR 97070, 503-682-3903 or toll-free 866-PPC-INFO. *Website:* http://www.pioneerpacific.edu/.

---

# PIONEER PACIFIC COLLEGE–EUGENE/ SPRINGFIELD BRANCH
## Springfield, OR

**CONTACT** Financial Aid Office, Pioneer Pacific College–Eugene/Springfield Branch, 3800 Sports Way, Springfield, OR 97477 or toll-free 866-772-4636. *Website:* http://www.pioneerpacific.edu/.

---

# PITTSBURG STATE UNIVERSITY
## Pittsburg, KS

| Tuition & fees (KS res): $6230 | Average undergraduate aid package: $6505 |
| --- | --- |

**ABOUT THE INSTITUTION** State-supported, coed. *Awards:* certificates, associate, bachelor's, and master's degrees. 62 undergraduate majors. *Total enrollment:* 7,479. Undergraduates: 6,270. Freshmen: 1,027. Federal methodology is used as a basis for awarding need-based institutional aid.

**UNDERGRADUATE EXPENSES** for 2015–2016 *Application fee:* $30. *Tuition, state resident:* full-time $4936; part-time $165 per credit hour. *Tuition, nonresident:* full-time $15,042; part-time $502 per credit hour. *Required fees:* full-time $1294; $56 per credit hour. Part-time tuition and fees vary according to course load. *College room and board:* $6936. Room and board charges vary according to board plan and housing facility.

**FRESHMAN FINANCIAL AID (Fall 2014, est.)** 957 applied for aid; of those 75% were deemed to have need. 100% of freshmen with need received aid; of those 21% had need fully met. *Average percent of need met:* 2% (excluding resources awarded to replace EFC). *Average financial aid package:* $5866 (excluding resources awarded to replace EFC). 13% of all full-time freshmen had no need and received non-need-based gift aid.

**UNDERGRADUATE FINANCIAL AID (Fall 2014, est.)** 4,411 applied for aid; of those 81% were deemed to have need. 100% of undergraduates with need received aid; of those 12% had need fully met. *Average percent of need met:* 6% (excluding resources awarded to replace EFC). *Average financial aid package:* $6505 (excluding resources awarded to replace EFC). 7% of all full-time undergraduates had no need and received non-need-based gift aid.

**GIFT AID (NEED-BASED)** *Total amount:* $11,542,035 (91% federal, 6% state, 3% institutional). *Receiving aid:* Freshmen: 41% (455); all full-time undergraduates: 43% (2,443). *Average award:* Freshmen: $4540; Undergraduates: $4422. *Scholarships, grants, and awards:* Federal Pell, FSEOG, state, private, college/university gift aid from institutional funds.

**GIFT AID (NON-NEED-BASED)** *Total amount:* $7,267,572 (9% federal, 2% state, 72% institutional, 17% external sources). *Receiving aid:* Freshmen: 63% (697). Undergraduates: 44% (2,446). *Average award:* Freshmen: $2010. Undergraduates: $2094. *Scholarships, grants, and awards by category: Academic interests/achievement:* biological sciences, business, communication, computer science, education, engineering/technologies, English, foreign languages, general academic interests/achievements, health fields, home economics, mathematics, military science, physical sciences, social sciences. *Creative arts/performance:* music. *Special characteristics:* children and siblings of alumni, general special characteristics. *Tuition waivers:* Full or partial for employees or children of employees. *ROTC:* Army.

**LOANS** *Student loans:* $30,117,793 (40% need-based, 60% non-need-based). 68% of past graduating class borrowed through all loan programs. *Average indebtedness per student:* $23,307. *Average need-based loan:* Freshmen: $3290. Undergraduates: $3973. *Parent loans:* $1,387,239 (100% non-need-based). *Programs:* Federal Direct (Subsidized and Unsubsidized Stafford, PLUS), Perkins, Federal Nursing, college/university.

**WORK-STUDY** *Federal work-study:* Total amount: $453,576; 270 jobs averaging $1680. *State or other work-study/employment:* Total amount: $11,381 (100% non-need-based). 8 part-time jobs averaging $1423.

**ATHLETIC AWARDS** Total amount: $319,687 (100% non-need-based).

**APPLYING FOR FINANCIAL AID** *Required financial aid forms:* FAFSA, state aid form. *Financial aid deadline (priority):* 3/1. *Notification date:* Continuous beginning 3/1. Students must reply within 2 weeks of notification.

**CONTACT** Tammy Higgins, Director of Student Financial Assistance, Pittsburg State University, 1701 South Broadway Street, Pittsburg, KS 66762-7534, 620-235-4238 or toll-free 800-854-7488. *Fax:* 620-235-4078. *E-mail:* thiggins@pittstate.edu. *Website:* http://www.pittstate.edu/.

# PITZER COLLEGE
## Claremont, CA

| Tuition & fees: $46,992 | Average undergraduate aid package: $40,250 |
| --- | --- |

**ABOUT THE INSTITUTION** Independent, coed. *Awards:* bachelor's degrees. 37 undergraduate majors. *Total enrollment:* 1,081. Undergraduates: 1,081. Freshmen: 266. Both federal and institutional methodology are used as a basis for awarding need-based institutional aid.

**UNDERGRADUATE EXPENSES for 2015–2016** *Application fee:* $60. *Comprehensive fee:* $61,750 includes full-time tuition ($46,720), mandatory fees ($272), and room and board ($14,758). *College room only:* $8538. Room and board charges vary according to board plan. *Part-time tuition:* $5840 per course. Part-time tuition and fees vary according to course load.

**FRESHMAN FINANCIAL AID (Fall 2014, est.)** 129 applied for aid; of those 74% were deemed to have need. 100% of freshmen with need received aid; of those 100% had need fully met. *Average percent of need met:* 100% (excluding resources awarded to replace EFC). *Average financial aid package:* $44,719 (excluding resources awarded to replace EFC). 2% of all full-time freshmen had no need and received non-need-based gift aid.

**UNDERGRADUATE FINANCIAL AID (Fall 2014, est.)** 460 applied for aid; of those 78% were deemed to have need. 100% of undergraduates with need received aid; of those 100% had need fully met. *Average percent of need met:* 100% (excluding resources awarded to replace EFC). *Average financial aid package:*

$40,250 (excluding resources awarded to replace EFC). 1% of all full-time undergraduates had no need and received non-need-based gift aid.

**GIFT AID (NEED-BASED)** *Total amount:* $13,742,115 (6% federal, 4% state, 86% institutional, 4% external sources). *Receiving aid:* Freshmen: 36% (95); all full-time undergraduates: 34% (357). *Average award:* Freshmen: $40,248; Undergraduates: $35,293. *Scholarships, grants, and awards:* Federal Pell, FSEOG, state, private, college/university gift aid from institutional funds.

**GIFT AID (NON-NEED-BASED)** *Total amount:* $522,260 (13% institutional, 87% external sources). *Receiving aid:* Freshmen: 1% (4). Undergraduates: 1% (6). *Average award:* Freshmen: $5000. Undergraduates: $4687. *Scholarships, grants, and awards by category: Academic interests/achievement:* general academic interests/achievements. *Special achievements/activities:* community service, leadership. *Tuition waivers:* Full or partial for employees or children of employees. *ROTC:* Army cooperative, Air Force cooperative.

**LOANS** *Student loans:* $1,579,145 (80% need-based, 20% non-need-based). 44% of past graduating class borrowed through all loan programs. *Average indebtedness per student:* $19,422. *Average need-based loan:* Freshmen: $2542. Undergraduates: $3393. *Parent loans:* $1,219,700 (100% non-need-based). *Programs:* Federal Direct (Subsidized and Unsubsidized Stafford, PLUS), Perkins, college/university.

**WORK-STUDY** *Federal work-study:* Total amount: $794,940; jobs available.

**APPLYING FOR FINANCIAL AID** *Required financial aid forms:* FAFSA, CSS Financial Aid PROFILE, state aid form, noncustodial (divorced/separated) parent's statement. *Financial aid deadline:* 2/1. *Notification date:* 4/1. Students must reply by 5/1.

**CONTACT** Robin Thompson, Director of Financial Aid, Pitzer College, 1050 North Mills Avenue, Claremont, CA 91711-6101, 909-621-8208 or toll-free 800-748-9371. *Fax:* 909-607-1205. *E-mail:* robin_thompson@pitzer.edu. *Website:* http://www.pitzer.edu/.

# PLATT COLLEGE
## Riverside, CA

**CONTACT** Financial Aid Office, Platt College, 6465 Sycamore Canyon Boulevard, Suite 100, Riverside, CA 92507, 951-572-4300 or toll-free 888-807-5288. *Website:* http://www.plattcollege.edu/.

# PLATT COLLEGE
## Aurora, CO

| Tuition & fees: N/R | Average undergraduate aid package: $7500 |
| --- | --- |

**ABOUT THE INSTITUTION** Proprietary, coed. 2 undergraduate majors. Federal methodology is used as a basis for awarding need-based institutional aid.

**FRESHMAN FINANCIAL AID (Fall 2013)** 3 applied for aid; of those 100% were deemed to have need. 100% of freshmen with need received aid. *Average percent of need met:* 72% (excluding resources awarded to replace EFC). *Average financial aid package:* $7500 (excluding resources awarded to replace EFC).

**UNDERGRADUATE FINANCIAL AID (Fall 2013)** 180 applied for aid; of those 100% were deemed to have need. 100% of undergraduates with need received aid. *Average percent of need met:* 76% (excluding resources awarded to replace EFC). *Average financial aid package:* $7500 (excluding resources awarded to replace EFC).

**GIFT AID (NEED-BASED)** *Total amount:* $561,557 (100% federal). *Receiving aid:* Freshmen: 67% (2); all full-time undergraduates: 57% (118). *Average award:* Freshmen: $1492; Undergraduates: $2492. *Scholarships, grants, and awards:* Federal Pell, FSEOG.

**LOANS** *Student loans:* $2,980,201 (53% need-based, 47% non-need-based). *Average need-based loan:* Freshmen: $3683. Undergraduates: $4352. *Parent loans:* $165,266 (100% need-based). *Programs:* Federal Direct (Subsidized and Unsubsidized Stafford, PLUS), Perkins.

**APPLYING FOR FINANCIAL AID** *Financial aid deadline:* Continuous. *Notification date:* Continuous beginning 1/1.

**CONTACT** Ms. Margie Rose, Office of Financial Aid, Platt College, 3100 South Parker Road, #200, Aurora, CO 80014, 303-369-5151 Ext. 233. *Fax:* 303-745-1433. *Website:* http://www.plattcolorado.edu/.

---

# PLATT COLLEGE
## Oklahoma City, OK

**CONTACT** Financial Aid Office, Platt College, 2727 West Memorial Road, Oklahoma City, OK 73134-8034.
*Website:* http://www.plattcolleges.edu/.

---

# PLATT COLLEGE SAN DIEGO
## San Diego, CA

**ABOUT THE INSTITUTION** Proprietary, coed. *Awards:* certificates, diplomas, and bachelor's degrees. 8 undergraduate majors. *Total enrollment:* 369. Undergraduates: 369. Freshmen: 72.

**GIFT AID (NEED-BASED)** *Scholarships, grants, and awards:* Federal Pell, FSEOG.

**LOANS** *Programs:* Federal Direct (Subsidized and Unsubsidized Stafford).

**APPLYING FOR FINANCIAL AID** *Required financial aid forms:* FAFSA, institution's own form.

**CONTACT** Matilde Aguilar, Student Accounts Coordinator, Platt College San Diego, 6250 El Cajon Boulevard, San Diego, CA 92115, 619-265-0107 Ext. 12 or toll-free 866-752-8826. *Fax:* 619-265-8655. *E-mail:* maguilar@platt.edu.
*Website:* http://www.platt.edu/.

---

# PLYMOUTH STATE UNIVERSITY
## Plymouth, NH

| Tuition & fees (NH res): $12,677 | Average undergraduate aid package: $10,571 |
|---|---|

**ABOUT THE INSTITUTION** State-supported, coed. *Awards:* certificates, bachelor's, master's, and doctoral degrees. 54 undergraduate majors. *Total enrollment:* 4,887. Undergraduates: 3,787. Freshmen: 751. Federal methodology is used as a basis for awarding need-based institutional aid.

**UNDERGRADUATE EXPENSES** for 2015–2016 *Application fee:* $50. *Tuition, state resident:* full-time $10,410; part-time $435 per credit hour. *Tuition, nonresident:* full-time $18,320; part-time $763 per credit hour. *Required fees:* full-time $2267; $96 per credit hour. Full-time tuition and fees vary according to reciprocity agreements. Part-time tuition and fees vary according to reciprocity agreements. *College room and board:* $10,728; *Room only:* $6750. Room and board charges vary according to board plan and housing facility.

**FRESHMAN FINANCIAL AID (Fall 2013)** 834 applied for aid; of those 80% were deemed to have need. 99% of freshmen with need received aid; of those 17% had need fully met. *Average percent of need met:* 60% (excluding resources awarded to replace EFC). *Average financial aid package:* $9906 (excluding resources awarded to replace EFC). 10% of all full-time freshmen had no need and received non-need-based gift aid.

**UNDERGRADUATE FINANCIAL AID (Fall 2013)** 3,249 applied for aid; of those 80% were deemed to have need. 99% of undergraduates with need received aid; of those 14% had need fully met. *Average percent of need met:* 57% (excluding resources awarded to replace EFC). *Average financial aid package:* $10,571 (excluding resources awarded to replace EFC). 8% of all full-time undergraduates had no need and received non-need-based gift aid.

**GIFT AID (NEED-BASED)** *Total amount:* $9,746,040 (50% federal, 6% state, 44% institutional). *Receiving aid:* Freshmen: 51% (470); all full-time undergraduates: 41% (1,560). *Average award:* Freshmen: $6376; Undergraduates: $6126. *Scholarships, grants, and awards:* Federal Pell, FSEOG, state, private, college/university gift aid from institutional funds.

**GIFT AID (NON-NEED-BASED)** *Total amount:* $6,033,797 (87% institutional, 13% external sources). *Receiving aid:* Freshmen: 43% (401). Undergraduates: 32% (1,227). *Average award:* Freshmen: $4492. Undergraduates: $3930. *Scholarships, grants, and awards by category: Academic interests/achievement:* 896 awards ($3,844,365 total): general academic interests/achievements. *Creative arts/performance:* 47 awards ($76,800 total): creative writing, dance, music, theater/drama. *Special characteristics:* 64 awards ($271,307 total): children of faculty/staff, international students. *Tuition waivers:* Full or partial for employees or children of employees, senior citizens. *ROTC:* Army cooperative, Air Force cooperative.

**LOANS** *Student loans:* $30,018,654 (37% need-based, 63% non-need-based). 85% of past graduating class borrowed through all loan programs. *Average indebtedness per student:* $32,327. *Average need-based loan:* Freshmen: $3499. Undergraduates: $4239. *Parent loans:* $8,434,833 (100% non-need-based). *Programs:* Federal Direct (Subsidized and Unsubsidized Stafford, PLUS), Perkins.

**WORK-STUDY** *Federal work-study:* jobs available.

**APPLYING FOR FINANCIAL AID** *Required financial aid form:* FAFSA. *Financial aid deadline (priority):* 3/1. *Notification date:* Continuous beginning 3/1. Students must reply by 5/1.

**CONTACT** Crystal Gaff, Director of Financial Aid, Plymouth State University, 17 High Street, Plymouth, NH 03264-1595, 603-535-2338 or toll-free 800-842-6900. *Fax:* 603-535-2627. *E-mail:* clgaff@plymouth.edu.
*Website:* http://www.plymouth.edu/.

---

# POINT LOMA NAZARENE UNIVERSITY
## San Diego, CA

| Tuition & fees: $31,406 | Average undergraduate aid package: $21,589 |
|---|---|

**ABOUT THE INSTITUTION** Independent Nazarene, coed. *Awards:* certificates, bachelor's, and master's degrees. 65 undergraduate majors. *Total enrollment:* 3,374. Undergraduates: 2,568. Freshmen: 588. Federal methodology is used as a basis for awarding need-based institutional aid.

**UNDERGRADUATE EXPENSES** for 2015–2016 *Application fee:* $50. *Comprehensive fee:* $41,006 includes full-time tuition ($30,800), mandatory fees ($606), and room and board ($9600). Full-time tuition and fees vary according to course load. Room and board charges vary according to board plan. *Part-time tuition:* $1285 per credit hour. Part-time tuition and fees vary according to course load.

**FRESHMAN FINANCIAL AID (Fall 2013)** 560 applied for aid; of those 80% were deemed to have need. 100% of freshmen with need received aid; of those 16% had need fully met. *Average percent of need met:* 63% (excluding resources awarded to replace EFC). *Average financial aid package:* $20,692 (excluding resources awarded to replace EFC). 18% of all full-time freshmen had no need and received non-need-based gift aid.

**UNDERGRADUATE FINANCIAL AID (Fall 2013)** 2,023 applied for aid; of those 85% were deemed to have need. 100% of undergraduates with need received aid; of those 15% had need fully met. *Average percent of need met:* 63% (excluding resources awarded to replace EFC). *Average financial aid package:* $21,589 (excluding resources awarded to replace EFC). 16% of all full-time undergraduates had no need and received non-need-based gift aid.

**GIFT AID (NEED-BASED)** *Total amount:* $23,502,546 (14% federal, 20% state, 53% institutional, 13% external sources). *Receiving aid:* Freshmen: 65% (422); all full-time undergraduates: 64% (1,596). *Average award:* Freshmen: $15,639; Undergraduates: $15,892. *Scholarships, grants, and awards:* Federal Pell, FSEOG, state, private, college/university gift aid from institutional funds, Federal Nursing.

**GIFT AID (NON-NEED-BASED)** *Total amount:* $4,797,463 (83% institutional, 17% external sources). *Receiving aid:* Freshmen: 7% (43). Undergraduates: 5% (133). *Average award:* Freshmen: $9827. Undergraduates: $8656. *Scholarships, grants, and awards by category: Academic interests/achievement:* biological sciences, business, communication, education, engineering/technologies, general academic interests/achievements, health fields, home economics, humanities, mathematics, religion/biblical studies, social sciences. *Creative arts/performance:* art/fine arts, debating, music, theater/drama. *Tuition waivers:* Full or partial for employees or children of employees, senior citizens. *ROTC:* Army cooperative, Naval cooperative, Air Force cooperative.

**LOANS** *Student loans:* $19,080,101 (72% need-based, 28% non-need-based). 74% of past graduating class borrowed through all loan programs. *Average indebtedness per student:* $32,649. *Average need-based loan:* Freshmen: $3582. Undergraduates: $4802. *Parent loans:* $7,959,711 (48% need-based, 52% non-need-based). *Programs:* Federal Direct (Subsidized and Unsubsidized Stafford, PLUS), Perkins, Federal Nursing.

**WORK-STUDY** *Federal work-study:* jobs available.
**ATHLETIC AWARDS** Total amount: $2,124,837 (55% need-based, 45% non-need-based).
**APPLYING FOR FINANCIAL AID** *Required financial aid form:* FAFSA. *Financial aid deadline (priority):* 3/2. *Notification date:* Continuous beginning 12/15. Students must reply by 5/15.
**CONTACT** Pam Macias, Director of Financial Aid, Point Loma Nazarene University, 3900 Lomaland Drive, San Diego, CA 92106, 619-849-2538 or toll-free 800-733-7770. *Fax:* 619-849-7078. *E-mail:* sfs@pointloma.edu.
*Website:* http://www.pointloma.edu/.

---

## POINT PARK UNIVERSITY
### Pittsburgh, PA

**ABOUT THE INSTITUTION** Independent, coed. *Awards:* certificates, associate, bachelor's, and master's degrees. 51 undergraduate majors. *Total enrollment:* 3,841. Undergraduates: 3,226. Freshmen: 548.
**GIFT AID (NEED-BASED)** *Scholarships, grants, and awards:* Federal Pell, FSEOG, state, private, college/university gift aid from institutional funds.
**GIFT AID (NON-NEED-BASED)** *Scholarships, grants, and awards by category:* *Academic interests/achievement:* biological sciences, business, communication, computer science, education, engineering/technologies, English, general academic interests/achievements, health fields, humanities, international studies, mathematics, physical sciences, premedicine, social sciences. *Creative arts/performance:* cinema/film/broadcasting, dance, performing arts, theater/drama. *Special achievements/activities:* community service, memberships. *Special characteristics:* children and siblings of alumni, children of faculty/staff, international students, members of minority groups, previous college experience, siblings of current students.
**LOANS** *Programs:* Federal Direct (Subsidized and Unsubsidized Stafford, PLUS), Perkins.
**WORK-STUDY** *Federal work-study:* 286 jobs averaging $1843. *State or other work-study/employment:* Total amount: $2,551,574 (62% need-based, 38% non-need-based). 202 part-time jobs averaging $3342.
**APPLYING FOR FINANCIAL AID** *Required financial aid form:* FAFSA.
**CONTACT** Sheila Nelson-Hensley, Director of Financial Aid, Point Park University, 201 Wood Street, Pittsburgh, PA 15222-1984, 412-392-3930 or toll-free 800-321-0129. *E-mail:* snelsonhensley@pointpark.edu.
*Website:* http://www.pointpark.edu/.

---

## POINT UNIVERSITY
### West Point, GA

**CONTACT** Blair Walker, Director of Financial Aid, Point University, 2605 Ben Hill Road, East Point, GA 30344, 404-761-8861 or toll-free 855-37-POINT. *Fax:* 404-669-2024. *E-mail:* blairw@acc.edu.
*Website:* http://point.edu/.

---

## POLK STATE COLLEGE
### Winter Haven, FL

**CONTACT** Lenora Burnett, Financial Aid Supervisor, Polk State College, 999 Avenue H, NE, Winter Haven, FL 33881, 863-297-5269. *E-mail:* lburnett@polk.edu.
*Website:* http://www.polk.edu/.

---

## POLYTECHNIC UNIVERSITY OF PUERTO RICO
### Hato Rey, PR

**ABOUT THE INSTITUTION** Independent, coed. *Awards:* associate, bachelor's, master's, and doctoral degrees. 21 undergraduate majors. *Total enrollment:* 4,507. Undergraduates: 3,788. Freshmen: 438.

**GIFT AID (NEED-BASED)** *Scholarships, grants, and awards:* Federal Pell, FSEOG, state, college/university gift aid from institutional funds.
**GIFT AID (NON-NEED-BASED)** *Scholarships, grants, and awards by category:* *Academic interests/achievement:* architecture, business, engineering/technologies.
**WORK-STUDY** Federal work-study jobs available.
**APPLYING FOR FINANCIAL AID** *Required financial aid form:* FAFSA.
**CONTACT** Sergio E. Villoldo, Financial Aid Director, Polytechnic University of Puerto Rico, 377 Ponce de Leon Avenue, Hato Rey, PR 00919, 787-754-8000 Ext. 253. *Fax:* 787-766-1163.
*Website:* http://www.pupr.edu/.

---

## POLYTECHNIC UNIVERSITY OF PUERTO RICO, MIAMI CAMPUS
### Miami, FL

**CONTACT** Maria Victoria Shehadeh, Administrative Affairs Coordinator/Financial Aid Officer, Polytechnic University of Puerto Rico, Miami Campus, 8180 Northwest 36th Street, Suite 401, Miami, FL 33166, 305-418-8000 Ext. 204 or toll-free 888-729-7659. *E-mail:* mshehadeh@pupr.edu.
*Website:* http://www.pupr.edu/miami/.

---

## POLYTECHNIC UNIVERSITY OF PUERTO RICO, ORLANDO CAMPUS
### Winter Park, FL

**ABOUT THE INSTITUTION** Independent, coed. 4 undergraduate majors.
**GIFT AID (NEED-BASED)** *Scholarships, grants, and awards:* Federal Pell, FSEOG, state.
**LOANS** *Programs:* Federal Direct (Subsidized and Unsubsidized Stafford, PLUS), private loans.
**APPLYING FOR FINANCIAL AID** *Required financial aid form:* FAFSA.
**CONTACT** Mrs. Ileana Diaz, Financial Aid Officer, Polytechnic University of Puerto Rico, Orlando Campus, 550 North Econlockhatchee Trail, Orlando, FL 32825, 407-677-7000 Ext. 806 or toll-free 888-577-POLY. *Fax:* 407-677-5082. *E-mail:* idiaz@pupr.edu.
*Website:* http://www.pupr.edu/orlando/.

---

## POMONA COLLEGE
### Claremont, CA

| Tuition & fees: $45,832 | Average undergraduate aid package: $43,395 |
| --- | --- |

**ABOUT THE INSTITUTION** Independent, coed. *Awards:* bachelor's degrees. 49 undergraduate majors. *Total enrollment:* 1,650. Undergraduates: 1,650. Freshmen: 450. Both federal and institutional methodology are used as a basis for awarding need-based institutional aid.
**UNDERGRADUATE EXPENSES** for 2015–2016 *Application fee:* $70. *Comprehensive fee:* $60,532 includes full-time tuition ($45,500), mandatory fees ($332), and room and board ($14,700). Room and board charges vary according to board plan.
**FRESHMAN FINANCIAL AID (Fall 2013)** 281 applied for aid; of those 81% were deemed to have need. 100% of freshmen with need received aid; of those 100% had need fully met. *Average percent of need met:* 100% (excluding resources awarded to replace EFC). *Average financial aid package:* $43,912 (excluding resources awarded to replace EFC).
**UNDERGRADUATE FINANCIAL AID (Fall 2013)** 1,135 applied for aid; of those 79% were deemed to have need. 100% of undergraduates with need received aid; of those 100% had need fully met. *Average percent of need met:* 100% (excluding resources awarded to replace EFC). *Average financial aid package:* $43,395 (excluding resources awarded to replace EFC).
**GIFT AID (NEED-BASED)** Total amount: $36,943,453 (5% federal, 3% state, 90% institutional, 2% external sources). *Receiving aid:* Freshmen: 58% (229); all full-

time undergraduates: 56% (894). *Average award:* Freshmen: $42,080; Undergraduates: $41,443. *Scholarships, grants, and awards:* Federal Pell, FSEOG, state, private, college/university gift aid from institutional funds.

**GIFT AID (NON-NEED-BASED)** *Total amount:* $502,305 (100% external sources). *Tuition waivers:* Full or partial for employees or children of employees. **ROTC:** Army cooperative, Air Force cooperative.

**LOANS** *Student loans:* $2,247,520 (11% need-based, 89% non-need-based). 34% of past graduating class borrowed through all loan programs. *Average indebtedness per student:* $16,273. *Parent loans:* $928,437 (100% non-need-based). *Programs:* Federal Direct (Subsidized and Unsubsidized Stafford, PLUS), Perkins, college/university.

**WORK-STUDY** *Federal work-study:* 150 jobs averaging $1598. *State or other work-study/employment:* Total amount: $1,553,080 (68% need-based, 32% non-need-based). 836 part-time jobs averaging $1857.

**APPLYING FOR FINANCIAL AID** *Required financial aid forms:* FAFSA, CSS Financial Aid PROFILE, state aid form, noncustodial (divorced/separated) parent's statement, business/farm supplement. *Financial aid deadline:* 3/1. *Notification date:* 4/10. Students must reply by 5/1.

**CONTACT** Mary Booker, Director of Financial Aid, Pomona College, 333 North College Way, Sumner Hall, 2nd Floor, Claremont, CA 91711, 909-621-8205. *Fax:* 909-607-7941. *E-mail:* financial_aid@pomadm.pomona.edu. *Website:* http://www.pomona.edu/.

# PONTIFICAL CATHOLIC UNIVERSITY OF PUERTO RICO
## Ponce, PR

**CONTACT** Mrs. Rosalia Martinez, Director of Financial Aid, Pontifical Catholic University of Puerto Rico, 2250 Las Americas Avenue, Suite 549, Ponce, PR 00717-9777, 787-841-2000 Ext. 1065 or toll-free 800-961-7696. *Fax:* 787-651-2041. *E-mail:* rosalia.martinez@email.pucpr.edu. *Website:* http://www.pucpr.edu/.

# PONTIFICAL COLLEGE JOSEPHINUM
## Columbus, OH

**CONTACT** Marky Leichtnam, Financial Aid Director, Pontifical College Josephinum, 7625 North High Street, Columbus, OH 43235-1498, 614-985-2212 or toll-free 888-252-5812. *Fax:* 614-885-2307. *E-mail:* mleichtnam@pcj.edu. *Website:* http://www.pcj.edu/.

# PORTLAND STATE UNIVERSITY
## Portland, OR

| Tuition & fees (OR res): $7794 | Average undergraduate aid package: $9509 |
| --- | --- |

**ABOUT THE INSTITUTION** State-supported, coed. *Awards:* certificates, bachelor's, master's, and doctoral degrees. 79 undergraduate majors. *Total enrollment:* 27,696. Undergraduates: 22,136. Freshmen: 1,644. Federal methodology is used as a basis for awarding need-based institutional aid.

**UNDERGRADUATE EXPENSES** for 2015–2016 *Application fee:* $50. *Tuition, state resident:* full-time $6525; part-time $145 per credit. *Tuition, nonresident:* full-time $220,520; part-time $490 per credit. *Required fees:* full-time $1269. Full-time tuition and fees vary according to program and reciprocity agreements. Part-time tuition and fees vary according to program. *College room and board:* $11,349. Room and board charges vary according to board plan and housing facility.

**FRESHMAN FINANCIAL AID (Fall 2014, est.)** 1,406 applied for aid; of those 71% were deemed to have need. 98% of freshmen with need received aid; of those 8% had need fully met. *Average percent of need met:* 66% (excluding resources awarded to replace EFC). *Average financial aid package:* $10,078 (excluding

resources awarded to replace EFC). 1% of all full-time freshmen had no need and received non-need-based gift aid.

**UNDERGRADUATE FINANCIAL AID (Fall 2014, est.)** 11,724 applied for aid; of those 83% were deemed to have need. 97% of undergraduates with need received aid; of those 5% had need fully met. *Average percent of need met:* 65% (excluding resources awarded to replace EFC). *Average financial aid package:* $9509 (excluding resources awarded to replace EFC). 1% of all full-time undergraduates had no need and received non-need-based gift aid.

**GIFT AID (NEED-BASED)** *Total amount:* $53,106,927 (77% federal, 16% state, 3% institutional, 4% external sources). *Receiving aid:* Freshmen: 51% (775); all full-time undergraduates: 53% (7,702). *Average award:* Freshmen: $6220; Undergraduates: $5840. *Scholarships, grants, and awards:* Federal Pell, FSEOG, state, private, college/university gift aid from institutional funds, United Negro College Fund.

**GIFT AID (NON-NEED-BASED)** *Total amount:* $629,245 (8% federal, 46% institutional, 46% external sources). *Receiving aid:* Freshmen: 1% (14). Undergraduates: 36. *Average award:* Freshmen: $2586. Undergraduates: $2785. *Scholarships, grants, and awards by category: Academic interests/achievement:* architecture, area/ethnic studies, business, computer science, education, engineering/technologies, foreign languages, general academic interests/achievements, humanities, international studies, physical sciences, social sciences. *Creative arts/performance:* art/fine arts, general creative arts/performance, music, theater/drama. *Special achievements/activities:* community service, general special achievements/activities, leadership, memberships. *Special characteristics:* adult students, ethnic background, handicapped students, international students, members of minority groups, out-of-state students, veterans. *Tuition waivers:* Full or partial for employees or children of employees, senior citizens. **ROTC:** Air Force cooperative.

**LOANS** *Student loans:* $98,790,192 (91% need-based, 9% non-need-based). 62% of past graduating class borrowed through all loan programs. *Average indebtedness per student:* $28,410. *Average need-based loan:* Freshmen: $3445. Undergraduates: $4395. *Parent loans:* $7,597,176 (53% need-based, 47% non-need-based). *Programs:* Federal Direct (Subsidized and Unsubsidized Stafford, PLUS), Perkins.

**WORK-STUDY** *Federal work-study:* Total amount: $1,717,367; jobs available. *State or other work-study/employment:* Total amount: $287,803 (73% need-based, 27% non-need-based). Part-time jobs available.

**ATHLETIC AWARDS** Total amount: $1,253,137 (44% need-based, 56% non-need-based).

**APPLYING FOR FINANCIAL AID** *Required financial aid form:* FAFSA. *Financial aid deadline:* Continuous. *Notification date:* Continuous beginning 3/15.

**CONTACT** G. Michael Johnson, Director of Financial Aid, Portland State University, PO Box 851, Portland, OR 97207, 800-547-8887. *Fax:* 503-725-5965. *E-mail:* askfa@pdx.edu. *Website:* http://www.pdx.edu/.

# POST UNIVERSITY
## Waterbury, CT

| Tuition & fees: $27,350 | Average undergraduate aid package: $19,779 |
| --- | --- |

**ABOUT THE INSTITUTION** Independent, coed. *Awards:* certificates, associate, bachelor's, and master's degrees. 24 undergraduate majors. *Total enrollment:* 731. Undergraduates: 731. Freshmen: 185. Federal methodology is used as a basis for awarding need-based institutional aid.

**UNDERGRADUATE EXPENSES** for 2015–2016 *Application fee:* $40. *Comprehensive fee:* $37,850 includes full-time tuition ($26,250), mandatory fees ($1100), and room and board ($10,500). Room and board charges vary according to housing facility. *Part-time tuition:* $875 per credit. Part-time tuition and fees vary according to class time. *Payment plan:* Tuition prepayment.

**FRESHMAN FINANCIAL AID (Fall 2013)** 238 applied for aid; of those 94% were deemed to have need. 100% of freshmen with need received aid; of those 13% had need fully met. *Average percent of need met:* 59% (excluding resources awarded to replace EFC). *Average financial aid package:* $18,898 (excluding resources awarded to replace EFC). 4% of all full-time freshmen had no need and received non-need-based gift aid.

**UNDERGRADUATE FINANCIAL AID (Fall 2013)** 647 applied for aid; of those 95% were deemed to have need. 100% of undergraduates with need received aid; of those 13% had need fully met. *Average percent of need met:* 59% (excluding resources awarded to replace EFC). *Average financial aid package:* $19,779

PRATT INSTITUTE

(excluding resources awarded to replace EFC). 3% of all full-time undergraduates had no need and received non-need-based gift aid.
**GIFT AID (NEED-BASED)** *Total amount:* $10,021,398 (20% federal, 77% institutional, 3% external sources). *Receiving aid:* Freshmen: 85% (220); all full-time undergraduates: 85% (607). *Average award:* Freshmen: $15,628; Undergraduates: $15,419. *Scholarships, grants, and awards:* Federal Pell, FSEOG, state, private, college/university gift aid from institutional funds.
**GIFT AID (NON-NEED-BASED)** *Total amount:* $249,750 (69% institutional, 31% external sources). *Receiving aid:* Freshmen: 31% (81). Undergraduates: 28% (197). *Average award:* Freshmen: $7700. Undergraduates: $8425. *Scholarships, grants, and awards by category: Academic interests/achievement:* agriculture, biological sciences, business, communication, computer science, education, general academic interests/achievements, humanities, international studies, social sciences. *Special characteristics:* children and siblings of alumni, local/state students, siblings of current students. *Tuition waivers:* Full or partial for employees or children of employees, senior citizens.
**LOANS** *Student loans:* $5,319,490 (46% need-based, 54% non-need-based). 82% of past graduating class borrowed through all loan programs. *Average indebtedness per student:* $15,995. *Average need-based loan:* Freshmen: $3419. Undergraduates: $4443. *Parent loans:* $2,196,550 (100% non-need-based). *Programs:* Federal Direct (Subsidized and Unsubsidized Stafford, PLUS), Perkins, college/university.
**WORK-STUDY** *Federal work-study:* jobs available. *State or other work-study/employment:* Part-time jobs available.
**ATHLETIC AWARDS** Total amount: $1,627,339 (100% non-need-based).
**APPLYING FOR FINANCIAL AID** *Required financial aid form:* FAFSA. *Financial aid deadline (priority):* 3/1. *Notification date:* Continuous beginning 4/1. Students must reply within 2 weeks of notification.
**CONTACT** Ms. Michelle Gambacini, Director of Financial Aid, Post University, 800 Country Club Road, Waterbury, CT 06723-2540, 203-591-5615 or toll-free 800-345-2562. *Fax:* 203-596-4599. *E-mail:* mgambacini@post.edu.
*Website:* http://www.post.edu/.

# PRAIRIE VIEW A&M UNIVERSITY
## Prairie View, TX

| Tuition & fees (TX res): $8098 | Average undergraduate aid package: $14,265 |
| --- | --- |

**ABOUT THE INSTITUTION** State-supported, coed. *Awards:* certificates, bachelor's, master's, and doctoral degrees. 39 undergraduate majors. *Total enrollment:* 8,429. Undergraduates: 6,905. Freshmen: 1,609. Federal methodology is used as a basis for awarding need-based institutional aid.
**UNDERGRADUATE EXPENSES** for 2015–2016 *Application fee:* $25. *Tuition, state resident:* full-time $5393; part-time $217 per credit hour. *Tuition, nonresident:* full-time $16,013; part-time $599 per credit hour. *Required fees:* full-time $2705. Full-time tuition and fees vary according to course load, degree level, program, and reciprocity agreements. Part-time tuition and fees vary according to course load, degree level, program, and reciprocity agreements. *College room and board:* $7467; *Room only:* $5144. Room and board charges vary according to board plan, housing facility, and student level. *Payment plan:* Guaranteed tuition.
**FRESHMAN FINANCIAL AID (Fall 2013)** 1,475 applied for aid; of those 81% were deemed to have need. 83% of freshmen with need received aid; of those 1% had need fully met. *Average percent of need met:* 87% (excluding resources awarded to replace EFC). *Average financial aid package:* $14,745 (excluding resources awarded to replace EFC). 2% of all full-time freshmen had no need and received non-need-based gift aid.
**UNDERGRADUATE FINANCIAL AID (Fall 2013)** 5,939 applied for aid; of those 75% were deemed to have need. 83% of undergraduates with need received aid; of those 1% had need fully met. *Average percent of need met:* 85% (excluding resources awarded to replace EFC). *Average financial aid package:* $14,265 (excluding resources awarded to replace EFC). 9% of all full-time undergraduates had no need and received non-need-based gift aid.
**GIFT AID (NEED-BASED)** *Total amount:* $38,579,209 (56% federal, 16% state, 20% institutional, 8% external sources). *Receiving aid:* Freshmen: 62% (929); all full-time undergraduates: 53% (3,308). *Average award:* Freshmen: $4120; Undergraduates: $4120. *Scholarships, grants, and awards:* Federal Pell, FSEOG, state, private, college/university gift aid from institutional funds, United Negro College Fund, Federal Nursing.

**GIFT AID (NON-NEED-BASED)** *Total amount:* $361,249 (100% external sources). *Receiving aid:* Freshmen: 23% (352). Undergraduates: 11% (663). *Average award:* Freshmen: $2510. Undergraduates: $2645. *Tuition waivers:* Full or partial for senior citizens. *ROTC:* Army, Naval.
**LOANS** *Student loans:* $71,490,276 (42% need-based, 58% non-need-based). 76% of past graduating class borrowed through all loan programs. *Average indebtedness per student:* $27,500. *Average need-based loan:* Freshmen: $3875. Undergraduates: $3875. *Parent loans:* $4,279,379 (100% non-need-based). *Programs:* Federal Direct (Subsidized and Unsubsidized Stafford, PLUS), state, alternative loans.
**WORK-STUDY** *Federal work-study:* jobs available. *State or other work-study/employment:* Total amount: $50,972 (100% need-based). Part-time jobs available.
**ATHLETIC AWARDS** Total amount: $2,708,150 (100% non-need-based).
**APPLYING FOR FINANCIAL AID** *Required financial aid form:* FAFSA. *Financial aid deadline (priority):* 3/15. *Notification date:* 6/1. Students must reply by 8/1 or within 2 weeks of notification.
**CONTACT** Mr. Ralph Perri, Director of Student Financial Aid and Scholarships, Prairie View A&M University, PO Box 519, Mail Stop 1005, Prairie View, TX 77446, 936-261-1205. *E-mail:* rrperri@pvamu.edu.
*Website:* http://www.pvamu.edu/.

# PRATT INSTITUTE
## Brooklyn, NY

| Tuition & fees: $46,586 | Average undergraduate aid package: $23,884 |
| --- | --- |

**ABOUT THE INSTITUTION** Independent, coed. *Awards:* certificates, associate, bachelor's, and master's degrees. 25 undergraduate majors. *Total enrollment:* 4,556. Undergraduates: 3,145. Freshmen: 640. Federal methodology is used as a basis for awarding need-based institutional aid.
**UNDERGRADUATE EXPENSES** for 2015–2016 *Application fee:* $50. *Comprehensive fee:* $58,082 includes full-time tuition ($44,580), mandatory fees ($2006), and room and board ($11,496). *College room only:* $7430. Full-time tuition and fees vary according to program. Room and board charges vary according to board plan and housing facility. *Part-time tuition:* $1438 per credit hour. Part-time tuition and fees vary according to program.
**FRESHMAN FINANCIAL AID (Fall 2014, est.)** 636 applied for aid; of those 78% were deemed to have need. 100% of freshmen with need received aid. *Average percent of need met:* 47% (excluding resources awarded to replace EFC). *Average financial aid package:* $22,466 (excluding resources awarded to replace EFC). 35% of all full-time freshmen had no need and received non-need-based gift aid.
**UNDERGRADUATE FINANCIAL AID (Fall 2014, est.)** 2,713 applied for aid; of those 88% were deemed to have need. 100% of undergraduates with need received aid. *Average percent of need met:* 49% (excluding resources awarded to replace EFC). *Average financial aid package:* $23,884 (excluding resources awarded to replace EFC). 20% of all full-time undergraduates had no need and received non-need-based gift aid.
**GIFT AID (NEED-BASED)** *Total amount:* $10,694,835 (33% federal, 9% state, 58% institutional). *Receiving aid:* Freshmen: 55% (420); all full-time undergraduates: 78% (2,344). *Average award:* Freshmen: $11,612; Undergraduates: $12,550. *Scholarships, grants, and awards:* Federal Pell, FSEOG, state, college/university gift aid from institutional funds.
**GIFT AID (NON-NEED-BASED)** *Total amount:* $34,839,298 (95% institutional, 5% external sources). *Receiving aid:* Freshmen: 56% (422). Undergraduates: 46% (1,388). *Average award:* Freshmen: $15,000. Undergraduates: $13,000. *Scholarships, grants, and awards by category: Academic interests/achievement:* general academic interests/achievements. *ROTC:* Army cooperative.
**LOANS** *Student loans:* $10,559,093 (62% need-based, 38% non-need-based). 47% of past graduating class borrowed through all loan programs. *Average indebtedness per student:* $34,877. *Parent loans:* $19,180,378 (100% non-need-based). *Programs:* Federal Direct (Subsidized and Unsubsidized Stafford, PLUS), Perkins.
**WORK-STUDY** *Federal work-study:* Total amount: $957,883; jobs available. *State or other work-study/employment:* Part-time jobs available.
**APPLYING FOR FINANCIAL AID** *Required financial aid forms:* FAFSA, state aid form. *Financial aid deadline:* 3/1. *Notification date:* Continuous beginning 4/15. Students must reply within 2 weeks of notification.

CONTACT Nedzad Goga, Director of Financial Aid, Pratt Institute, 200 Willoughby Avenue, Myrtle Hall, Room 6E-9, Brooklyn, NY 11205-3899, 718-636-3563 or toll-free 800-331-0834. *Fax:* 718-636-3739. *E-mail:* finaid@pratt.edu. *Website:* http://www.pratt.edu/.

## PRESBYTERIAN COLLEGE
### Clinton, SC

| Tuition & fees: $34,828 | Average undergraduate aid package: $33,373 |
|---|---|

**ABOUT THE INSTITUTION** Independent Presbyterian Church (U.S.A.), coed. **Awards:** bachelor's and doctoral degrees. 31 undergraduate majors. **Total enrollment:** 1,460. Undergraduates: 1,146. Freshmen: 275. Federal methodology is used as a basis for awarding need-based institutional aid.

**UNDERGRADUATE EXPENSES** for 2015–2016 **Comprehensive fee:** $44,172 includes full-time tuition ($32,076), mandatory fees ($2752), and room and board ($9344). **College room only:** $4542. Full-time tuition and fees vary according to course load and reciprocity agreements. Room and board charges vary according to board plan and housing facility. **Part-time tuition:** $1337 per credit hour. **Part-time fees:** $52 per term. Part-time tuition and fees vary according to course load and program.

**FRESHMAN FINANCIAL AID (Fall 2014, est.)** 258 applied for aid; of those 88% were deemed to have need. 100% of freshmen with need received aid; of those 38% had need fully met. **Average percent of need met:** 87% (excluding resources awarded to replace EFC). **Average financial aid package:** $32,936 (excluding resources awarded to replace EFC). 16% of all full-time freshmen had no need and received non-need-based gift aid.

**UNDERGRADUATE FINANCIAL AID (Fall 2014, est.)** 916 applied for aid; of those 89% were deemed to have need. 100% of undergraduates with need received aid; of those 44% had need fully met. **Average percent of need met:** 88% (excluding resources awarded to replace EFC). **Average financial aid package:** $33,373 (excluding resources awarded to replace EFC). 18% of all full-time undergraduates had no need and received non-need-based gift aid.

**GIFT AID (NEED-BASED) Total amount:** $18,152,821 (6% federal, 22% state, 70% institutional, 2% external sources). **Receiving aid:** Freshmen: 82% (226); all full-time undergraduates: 79% (810). **Average award:** Freshmen: $30,439; Undergraduates: $30,703. **Scholarships, grants, and awards:** Federal Pell, FSEOG, state, private, college/university gift aid from institutional funds.

**GIFT AID (NON-NEED-BASED) Total amount:** $5,962,753 (8% state, 86% institutional, 6% external sources). **Receiving aid:** Freshmen: 28% (76). Undergraduates: 29% (301). **Average award:** Freshmen: $17,241. Undergraduates: $15,692. **Scholarships, grants, and awards by category:** *Academic interests/achievement:* general academic interests/achievements. *Creative arts/performance:* music. *Special achievements/activities:* leadership, religious involvement. *Special characteristics:* children of faculty/staff, relatives of clergy, religious affiliation. **Tuition waivers:** Full or partial for employees or children of employees, senior citizens. **ROTC:** Army.

**LOANS Student loans:** $14,571,659 (88% need-based, 12% non-need-based). 90% of past graduating class borrowed through all loan programs. *Average indebtedness per student:* $30,835. **Average need-based loan:** Freshmen: $3984. Undergraduates: $4299. **Parent loans:** $6,361,368 (74% need-based, 26% non-need-based). **Programs:** Federal Direct (Subsidized and Unsubsidized Stafford, PLUS), Perkins, state.

**WORK-STUDY Federal work-study:** Total amount: $216,815; jobs available. **State or other work-study/employment:** Part-time jobs available.

**ATHLETIC AWARDS Total amount:** $6,256,108 (52% need-based, 48% non-need-based).

**APPLYING FOR FINANCIAL AID Required financial aid form:** FAFSA. **Financial aid deadline:** 6/30 (priority: 3/15). **Notification date:** 3/1. Students must reply by 5/1.

**CONTACT** Ms. Linda J. McAnnally, Director of Financial Aid, Presbyterian College, 503 South Broad Street, Clinton, SC 29325, 864-833-8287 or toll-free 800-960-7583. *E-mail:* lmmcannally@presby.edu. *Website:* http://www.presby.edu/.

## PRESCOTT COLLEGE
### Prescott, AZ

| Tuition & fees: N/R | Average undergraduate aid package: $19,456 |
|---|---|

**ABOUT THE INSTITUTION** Independent, coed. **Awards:** certificates, bachelor's, master's, and doctoral degrees. 30 undergraduate majors. **Total enrollment:** 848. Undergraduates: 464. Freshmen: 41. Federal methodology is used as a basis for awarding need-based institutional aid.

**FRESHMAN FINANCIAL AID (Fall 2014, est.)** 37 applied for aid; of those 84% were deemed to have need. 100% of freshmen with need received aid; of those 3% had need fully met. **Average percent of need met:** 65% (excluding resources awarded to replace EFC). **Average financial aid package:** $21,076 (excluding resources awarded to replace EFC). 21% of all full-time freshmen had no need and received non-need-based gift aid.

**UNDERGRADUATE FINANCIAL AID (Fall 2014, est.)** 270 applied for aid; of those 91% were deemed to have need. 99% of undergraduates with need received aid; of those 6% had need fully met. **Average percent of need met:** 59% (excluding resources awarded to replace EFC). **Average financial aid package:** $19,456 (excluding resources awarded to replace EFC). 29% of all full-time undergraduates had no need and received non-need-based gift aid.

**GIFT AID (NEED-BASED) Total amount:** $3,756,442 (27% federal, 72% institutional, 1% external sources). **Receiving aid:** Freshmen: 79% (31); all full-time undergraduates: 66% (245). **Average award:** Freshmen: $16,564; Undergraduates: $14,231. **Scholarships, grants, and awards:** Federal Pell, FSEOG, state, private, college/university gift aid from institutional funds.

**GIFT AID (NON-NEED-BASED) Total amount:** $834,468 (1% federal, 98% institutional, 1% external sources). **Receiving aid:** Freshmen: 3% (1). Undergraduates: 2% (7). **Average award:** Freshmen: $5837. Undergraduates: $6984. **Scholarships, grants, and awards by category:** *Academic interests/achievement:* general academic interests/achievements. *Special achievements/activities:* general special achievements/activities, leadership.

**LOANS Student loans:** $2,884,175 (87% need-based, 13% non-need-based). 60% of past graduating class borrowed through all loan programs. *Average indebtedness per student:* $24,651. **Average need-based loan:** Freshmen: $3437. Undergraduates: $4572. **Parent loans:** $340,490 (59% need-based, 41% non-need-based). **Programs:** Federal Direct (Subsidized and Unsubsidized Stafford, PLUS).

**WORK-STUDY Federal work-study:** Total amount: $232,224; jobs available. **State or other work-study/employment:** Part-time jobs available.

**APPLYING FOR FINANCIAL AID Required financial aid form:** FAFSA. **Financial aid deadline (priority):** 3/1. **Notification date:** Continuous beginning 3/15.

**CONTACT** Mary Frances Causey, Director of Financial Aid, Prescott College, 220 Grove Avenue, Prescott, AZ 86301, 928-350-1111 or toll-free 877-350-2100. *Fax:* 928-350-1120. *E-mail:* finaid@prescott.edu. *Website:* http://www.prescott.edu/.

## PRESENTATION COLLEGE
### Aberdeen, SD

**CONTACT** Ms. Janel Wagner, Director of Financial Aid, Presentation College, 1500 North Main Street, Aberdeen, SD 57401-1299, 605-229-8427 or toll-free 800-437-6060. *Fax:* 605-229-8537. *E-mail:* janel.wagner@presentation.edu. *Website:* http://www.presentation.edu/.

## PRINCETON UNIVERSITY
### Princeton, NJ

| Tuition & fees: $43,450 | Average undergraduate aid package: $44,047 |
|---|---|

**ABOUT THE INSTITUTION** Independent, coed. **Awards:** bachelor's, master's, and doctoral degrees. 36 undergraduate majors. **Total enrollment:** 8,088. Under-

PROVIDENCE COLLEGE

graduates: 5,391. Freshmen: 1,310. Both federal and institutional methodology are used as a basis for awarding need-based institutional aid.

**UNDERGRADUATE EXPENSES for 2015–2016** *Application fee:* $65. *Comprehensive fee:* $57,610 includes full-time tuition ($43,450) and room and board ($14,160). *College room only:* $7920. Room and board charges vary according to board plan.

**FRESHMAN FINANCIAL AID (Fall 2014, est.)** 882 applied for aid; of those 87% were deemed to have need. 100% of freshmen with need received aid; of those 100% had need fully met. *Average percent of need met:* 100% (excluding resources awarded to replace EFC). *Average financial aid package:* $45,467 (excluding resources awarded to replace EFC).

**UNDERGRADUATE FINANCIAL AID (Fall 2014, est.)** 3,312 applied for aid; of those 94% were deemed to have need. 100% of undergraduates with need received aid; of those 100% had need fully met. *Average percent of need met:* 100% (excluding resources awarded to replace EFC). *Average financial aid package:* $44,047 (excluding resources awarded to replace EFC).

**GIFT AID (NEED-BASED)** *Total amount:* $130,500,000 (3% federal, 94% institutional, 3% external sources). *Receiving aid:* Freshmen: 59% (770); all full-time undergraduates: 59% (3,100). *Average award:* Freshmen: $44,115; Undergraduates: $42,097. *Scholarships, grants, and awards:* Federal Pell, FSEOG, state, private, college/university gift aid from institutional funds.

**GIFT AID (NON-NEED-BASED)** *Tuition waivers:* Full or partial for employees or children of employees. *ROTC:* Army, Naval cooperative, Air Force cooperative.

**LOANS** *Student loans:* 17% of past graduating class borrowed through all loan programs. *Average indebtedness per student:* $6600. *Parent loans:* $525,000 (100% non-need-based). *Programs:* Federal Direct (Subsidized and Unsubsidized Stafford, PLUS), Perkins, college/university.

**WORK-STUDY** *Federal work-study:* Total amount: $700,000; 688 jobs averaging $1017. *State or other work-study/employment:* Total amount: $2,000,000 (100% need-based). 1,366 part-time jobs averaging $1464.

**APPLYING FOR FINANCIAL AID** *Required financial aid forms:* FAFSA, institution's own form. *Financial aid deadline (priority):* 2/1. *Notification date:* 4/1. Students must reply by 5/1.

**CONTACT** Robin Moscato, Director of Financial Aid, Princeton University, PO Box 591, Princeton, NJ 08542, 609-258-3330. *Fax:* 609-258-3558. *E-mail:* moscato@princeton.edu. *Website:* http://www.princeton.edu/.

# PRINCIPIA COLLEGE
## Elsah, IL

| Tuition & fees: $27,440 | Average undergraduate aid package: $28,728 |
| --- | --- |

**ABOUT THE INSTITUTION** Independent Christian Science, coed. *Awards:* bachelor's degrees. 24 undergraduate majors. *Total enrollment:* 495. Undergraduates: 495. Freshmen: 117. Institutional methodology is used as a basis for awarding need-based institutional aid.

**UNDERGRADUATE EXPENSES for 2015–2016** *Comprehensive fee:* $38,250 includes full-time tuition ($26,940), mandatory fees ($500), and room and board ($10,810). *College room only:* $5130. Full-time tuition and fees vary according to course load. Room and board charges vary according to board plan. Part-time tuition and fees vary according to course load.

**FRESHMAN FINANCIAL AID (Fall 2014, est.)** 90 applied for aid; of those 84% were deemed to have need. 100% of freshmen with need received aid; of those 42% had need fully met. *Average percent of need met:* 99% (excluding resources awarded to replace EFC). *Average financial aid package:* $29,677 (excluding resources awarded to replace EFC). 33% of all full-time freshmen had no need and received non-need-based gift aid.

**UNDERGRADUATE FINANCIAL AID (Fall 2014, est.)** 382 applied for aid; of those 91% were deemed to have need. 100% of undergraduates with need received aid; of those 52% had need fully met. *Average percent of need met:* 91% (excluding resources awarded to replace EFC). *Average financial aid package:* $28,728 (excluding resources awarded to replace EFC). 27% of all full-time undergraduates had no need and received non-need-based gift aid.

**GIFT AID (NEED-BASED)** *Total amount:* $8,548,892 (100% institutional). *Receiving aid:* Freshmen: 63% (76); all full-time undergraduates: 71% (349).

*Average award:* Freshmen: $24,771; Undergraduates: $24,591. *Scholarships, grants, and awards:* private, college/university gift aid from institutional funds.

**GIFT AID (NON-NEED-BASED)** *Total amount:* $2,731,682 (100% institutional). *Receiving aid:* Freshmen: 40% (49). Undergraduates: 35% (174). *Average award:* Freshmen: $24,197. Undergraduates: $22,664. *Scholarships, grants, and awards by category:* Academic interests/achievement: 98 awards ($1,824,635 total): general academic interests/achievements. Special achievements/activities: 195 awards ($2,784,689 total): community service, general special achievements/activities, leadership, religious involvement. Special characteristics: 24 awards ($86,250 total): children and siblings of alumni, children of faculty/staff.

**LOANS** *Student loans:* $1,490,400 (97% need-based, 3% non-need-based). 55% of past graduating class borrowed through all loan programs. *Average indebtedness per student:* $23,732. *Average need-based loan:* Freshmen: $5841. Undergraduates: $5536. *Programs:* college/university.

**APPLYING FOR FINANCIAL AID** *Required financial aid forms:* CSS Financial Aid PROFILE, noncustodial (divorced/separated) parent's statement, federal income tax form(s). *Financial aid deadline (priority):* 3/1. *Notification date:* Continuous beginning 3/1. Students must reply by 5/1 or within 4 weeks of notification.

**CONTACT** Tami Gavaletz, Director of Financial Aid, Principia College, 1 Maybeck Place, Elsah, IL 62028-9799, 618-374-5187 or toll-free 800-277-4648 Ext. 2804. *Fax:* 618-374-4000. *E-mail:* tami.gavaletz@principia.edu. *Website:* http://www.principiacollege.edu/.

# PROVIDENCE CHRISTIAN COLLEGE
## Pasadena, CA

**CONTACT** Financial Aid Office, Providence Christian College, 1539 East Howard Street, Pasadena, CA 91124, 626-696-4000. *Website:* http://www.providencecc.edu/.

# PROVIDENCE COLLEGE
## Providence, RI

| Tuition & fees: $44,323 | Average undergraduate aid package: $27,800 |
| --- | --- |

**ABOUT THE INSTITUTION** Independent Roman Catholic, coed. *Awards:* certificates, associate, bachelor's, and master's degrees. 61 undergraduate majors. *Total enrollment:* 4,687. Undergraduates: 4,176. Freshmen: 1,032. Both federal and institutional methodology are used as a basis for awarding need-based institutional aid.

**UNDERGRADUATE EXPENSES for 2015–2016** *Comprehensive fee:* $57,383 includes full-time tuition ($43,443), mandatory fees ($880), and room and board ($13,060). *College room only:* $7530. Full-time tuition and fees vary according to class time and degree level. Room and board charges vary according to board plan and housing facility. *Part-time tuition:* $1551 per credit hour. Part-time tuition and fees vary according to class time and degree level.

**FRESHMAN FINANCIAL AID (Fall 2014, est.)** 748 applied for aid; of those 77% were deemed to have need. 90% of freshmen with need received aid; of those 25% had need fully met. *Average percent of need met:* 86% (excluding resources awarded to replace EFC). *Average financial aid package:* $28,448 (excluding resources awarded to replace EFC). 19% of all full-time freshmen had no need and received non-need-based gift aid.

**UNDERGRADUATE FINANCIAL AID (Fall 2014, est.)** 2,595 applied for aid; of those 82% were deemed to have need. 100% of undergraduates with need received aid; of those 22% had need fully met. *Average percent of need met:* 84% (excluding resources awarded to replace EFC). *Average financial aid package:* $27,800 (excluding resources awarded to replace EFC). 17% of all full-time undergraduates had no need and received non-need-based gift aid.

**GIFT AID (NEED-BASED)** *Total amount:* $49,059,018 (7% federal, 91% institutional, 2% external sources). *Receiving aid:* Freshmen: 50% (515); all full-time undergraduates: 52% (2,022). *Average award:* Freshmen: $24,420; Undergraduates: $22,860. *Scholarships, grants, and awards:* Federal Pell, FSEOG, state, private, college/university gift aid from institutional funds, Academic Competitiveness Grants, National SMART Grants.

**GIFT AID (NON-NEED-BASED)** *Total amount:* $13,328,434 (89% institutional, 11% external sources). *Receiving aid:* Freshmen: 12% (121). Undergraduates:

7% (268). **Average award:** Freshmen: $19,990. Undergraduates: $20,050. **Scholarships, grants, and awards by category:** Academic interests/achievement: 400 awards ($1,500,000 total): business, general academic interests/achievements, military science, premedicine. Creative arts/performance: 5 awards ($15,000 total): theater/drama. Special achievements/activities: 20 awards ($100,000 total): community service. Special characteristics: 111 awards ($110,000 total): siblings of current students. **Tuition waivers:** Full or partial for employees or children of employees. **ROTC:** Army.

**LOANS Student loans:** $22,367,808 (62% need-based, 38% non-need-based). 72% of past graduating class borrowed through all loan programs. **Average indebtedness per student:** $32,475. **Average need-based loan:** Freshmen: $4892. Undergraduates: $5143. **Parent loans:** $7,696,018 (22% need-based, 78% non-need-based). **Programs:** Federal Direct (Subsidized and Unsubsidized Stafford, PLUS), Perkins.

**WORK-STUDY Federal work-study:** Total amount: $1,450,000; 1,250 jobs averaging $1750. **State or other work-study/employment:** Total amount: $900,000 (100% non-need-based). Part-time jobs available.

**ATHLETIC AWARDS** Total amount: $7,862,987 (13% need-based, 87% non-need-based).

**APPLYING FOR FINANCIAL AID Required financial aid forms:** FAFSA, CSS Financial Aid PROFILE, federal income tax form(s). **Financial aid deadline:** 2/1. **Notification date:** 3/15. Students must reply by 5/1.

**CONTACT** Ms. Sandra J. Oliveira, Executive Director of Financial Aid, Providence College, One Cunningham Square, Providence, RI 02918, 401-865-2286 or toll-free 800-721-6444. Fax: 401-865-1186. E-mail: solivei6@providence.edu. Website: http://www.providence.edu/.

# PURCHASE COLLEGE, STATE UNIVERSITY OF NEW YORK
## Purchase, NY

| Tuition & fees (NY res): $7933 | Average undergraduate aid package: $10,095 |
|---|---|

**ABOUT THE INSTITUTION** State-supported, coed. **Awards:** certificates, bachelor's, and master's degrees. 43 undergraduate majors. **Total enrollment:** 4,289. Undergraduates: 4,188. Freshmen: 758. Federal methodology is used as a basis for awarding need-based institutional aid.

**UNDERGRADUATE EXPENSES for 2015–2016 Application fee:** $50. **One-time required fee:** $210. **Tuition, state resident:** full-time $6170; part-time $257 per credit. **Tuition, nonresident:** full-time $15,820. **Required fees:** full-time $1763; $68 per credit. Full-time tuition and fees vary according to program. Part-time tuition and fees vary according to course load and program. **College room and board:** $12,232; **Room only:** $7960. Room and board charges vary according to board plan and housing facility.

**FRESHMAN FINANCIAL AID (Fall 2013)** 681 applied for aid; of those 75% were deemed to have need. 100% of freshmen with need received aid; of those 4% had need fully met. **Average percent of need met:** 32% (excluding resources awarded to replace EFC). **Average financial aid package:** $9476 (excluding resources awarded to replace EFC). 7% of all full-time freshmen had no need and received non-need-based gift aid.

**UNDERGRADUATE FINANCIAL AID (Fall 2013)** 2,998 applied for aid; of those 81% were deemed to have need. 100% of undergraduates with need received aid; of those 4% had need fully met. **Average percent of need met:** 47% (excluding resources awarded to replace EFC). **Average financial aid package:** $10,095 (excluding resources awarded to replace EFC). 6% of all full-time undergraduates had no need and received non-need-based gift aid.

**GIFT AID (NEED-BASED) Total amount:** $13,134,995 (48% federal, 38% state, 10% institutional, 4% external sources). **Receiving aid:** Freshmen: 54% (414); all full-time undergraduates: 52% (1,984). **Average award:** Freshmen: $7039; Undergraduates: $6514. **Scholarships, grants, and awards:** Federal Pell, FSEOG, state, private, college/university gift aid from institutional funds.

**GIFT AID (NON-NEED-BASED) Total amount:** $993,335 (22% state, 52% institutional, 26% external sources). **Receiving aid:** Freshmen: 1% (10). Undergraduates: 1% (28). **Average award:** Freshmen: $2350. Undergraduates: $2040. **Scholarships, grants, and awards by category:** Academic interests/achievement: area/ethnic studies, biological sciences, computer science, English, general academic interests/achievements, humanities, mathematics, social sciences. Creative arts/performance: art/fine arts, cinema/film/broadcasting, creative writing, dance, general creative arts/performance, music, performing arts, theater/drama. **Tuition waivers:** Full or partial for employees or children of employees.

**LOANS Student loans:** $23,801,554 (75% need-based, 25% non-need-based). 60% of past graduating class borrowed through all loan programs. **Average indebtedness per student:** $26,348. **Average need-based loan:** Freshmen: $3800. Undergraduates: $4686. **Parent loans:** $29,147,149 (35% need-based, 65% non-need-based). **Programs:** Federal Direct (Subsidized and Unsubsidized Stafford, PLUS), Perkins.

**WORK-STUDY Federal work-study:** jobs available. **State or other work-study/employment:** Total amount: $640,235 (51% need-based, 49% non-need-based). Part-time jobs available.

**APPLYING FOR FINANCIAL AID Required financial aid forms:** FAFSA, state aid form. **Financial aid deadline (priority):** 2/1. **Notification date:** Continuous beginning 3/1.

**CONTACT** Ms. Corey York, Director of Student Financial Services, Purchase College, State University of New York, 735 Anderson Hill Road, Purchase, NY 10577-1400, 914-251-6085. Fax: 914-251-6099. E-mail: corey.york@purchase.edu. Website: http://www.purchase.edu/.

# PURDUE UNIVERSITY
## West Lafayette, IN

| Tuition & fees (IN res): $10,002 | Average undergraduate aid package: $13,076 |
|---|---|

**ABOUT THE INSTITUTION** State-supported, coed. **Awards:** certificates, associate, bachelor's, master's, and doctoral degrees. 137 undergraduate majors. **Total enrollment:** 38,770. Undergraduates: 29,255. Freshmen: 6,422. Federal methodology is used as a basis for awarding need-based institutional aid.

**UNDERGRADUATE EXPENSES for 2015–2016 Application fee:** $60. **Tuition, state resident:** full-time $9208; part-time $348 per credit hour. **Tuition, nonresident:** full-time $28,010; part-time $948 per credit hour. **Required fees:** full-time $794. Full-time tuition and fees vary according to course load and program. Part-time tuition and fees vary according to course load. **College room and board:** $10,030; **Room only:** $4860. Room and board charges vary according to board plan and housing facility.

**FRESHMAN FINANCIAL AID (Fall 2014, est.)** 4,412 applied for aid; of those 67% were deemed to have need. 100% of freshmen with need received aid; of those 48% had need fully met. **Average percent of need met:** 81% (excluding resources awarded to replace EFC). **Average financial aid package:** $12,530 (excluding resources awarded to replace EFC). 10% of all full-time freshmen had no need and received non-need-based gift aid.

**UNDERGRADUATE FINANCIAL AID (Fall 2014, est.)** 16,551 applied for aid; of those 73% were deemed to have need. 100% of undergraduates with need received aid; of those 39% had need fully met. **Average percent of need met:** 85% (excluding resources awarded to replace EFC). **Average financial aid package:** $13,076 (excluding resources awarded to replace EFC). 11% of all full-time undergraduates had no need and received non-need-based gift aid.

**GIFT AID (NEED-BASED) Total amount:** $83,602,106 (29% federal, 25% state, 43% institutional, 3% external sources). **Receiving aid:** Freshmen: 29% (1,895); all full-time undergraduates: 30% (8,354). **Average award:** Freshmen: $12,536; Undergraduates: $11,744. **Scholarships, grants, and awards:** Federal Pell, FSEOG, state, private, college/university gift aid from institutional funds.

**GIFT AID (NON-NEED-BASED) Total amount:** $45,465,138 (14% federal, 5% state, 64% institutional, 17% external sources). **Receiving aid:** Freshmen: 21% (1,361). Undergraduates: 16% (4,419). **Average award:** Freshmen: $6683. Undergraduates: $6697. **Scholarships, grants, and awards by category:** Academic interests/achievement: agriculture, computer science, education, engineering/technologies, general academic interests/achievements, health fields, humanities, mathematics, military science, physical sciences. Creative arts/performance: music. Special achievements/activities: leadership. Special characteristics: children of faculty/staff. **Tuition waivers:** Full or partial for employees or children of employees, senior citizens. **ROTC:** Army, Naval, Air Force.

**LOANS Student loans:** $114,053,512 (59% need-based, 41% non-need-based). 52% of past graduating class borrowed through all loan programs. **Average indebtedness per student:** $28,343. **Average need-based loan:** Freshmen: $3699. Undergraduates: $4543. **Parent loans:** $111,688,168 (24% need-based, 76% non-need-based). **Programs:** Federal Direct (Subsidized and Unsubsidized Stafford, PLUS), Perkins, college/university.

**WORK-STUDY** *Federal work-study:* Total amount: $4,583,427; 1,975 jobs averaging $2321. *State or other work-study/employment:* Total amount: $2,482,425 (31% need-based, 69% non-need-based). Part-time jobs available.

**ATHLETIC AWARDS** Total amount: $8,701,165 (31% need-based, 69% non-need-based).

**APPLYING FOR FINANCIAL AID** *Required financial aid form:* FAFSA. *Financial aid deadline (priority):* 3/1. *Notification date:* 4/15.

**CONTACT** Theodore E. Malone, Division of Financial Aid, Purdue University, Schleman Hall of Student Services, Room 305, West Lafayette, IN 47907-2050, 765-494-5056. *Fax:* 765-496-3918.
*Website:* http://www.purdue.edu/.

# PURDUE UNIVERSITY CALUMET
## Hammond, IN

| Tuition & fees (IN res): $6758 | Average undergraduate aid package: $7282 |
|---|---|

**ABOUT THE INSTITUTION** State-supported, coed. *Awards:* certificates, associate, bachelor's, and master's degrees. 42 undergraduate majors. *Total enrollment:* 9,501. Undergraduates: 8,491. Freshmen: 945. Federal methodology is used as a basis for awarding need-based institutional aid.

**UNDERGRADUATE EXPENSES** for 2015–2016 *Application fee:* $25. *Tuition, state resident:* full-time $6758; part-time $241.35 per credit hour. *Tuition, nonresident:* full-time $15,266; part-time $545.20 per credit hour. Full-time tuition and fees vary according to course load and program. Part-time tuition and fees vary according to course load and program. *Room only:* $5485. Room and board charges vary according to housing facility.

**FRESHMAN FINANCIAL AID (Fall 2013)** 709 applied for aid; of those 82% were deemed to have need. 92% of freshmen with need received aid; of those 4% had need fully met. *Average percent of need met:* 11% (excluding resources awarded to replace EFC). *Average financial aid package:* $4008 (excluding resources awarded to replace EFC). 7% of all full-time freshmen had no need and received non-need-based gift aid.

**UNDERGRADUATE FINANCIAL AID (Fall 2013)** 4,173 applied for aid; of those 88% were deemed to have need. 94% of undergraduates with need received aid; of those 2% had need fully met. *Average percent of need met:* 10% (excluding resources awarded to replace EFC). *Average financial aid package:* $7282 (excluding resources awarded to replace EFC). 3% of all full-time undergraduates had no need and received non-need-based gift aid.

**GIFT AID (NEED-BASED)** *Total amount:* $14,690,091 (71% federal, 27% state, 2% institutional). *Receiving aid:* Freshmen: 41% (342); all full-time undergraduates: 44% (2,395). *Average award:* Freshmen: $3181; Undergraduates: $5378. *Scholarships, grants, and awards:* Federal Pell, FSEOG, state, private, college/university gift aid from institutional funds.

**GIFT AID (NON-NEED-BASED)** *Total amount:* $4,574,698 (1% state, 59% institutional, 40% external sources). *Receiving aid:* Freshmen: 24% (201). Undergraduates: 15% (815). *Average award:* Freshmen: $1603. Undergraduates: $4570. *Scholarships, grants, and awards by category:* Academic interests/achievement: 669 awards ($2,633,873 total): general academic interests/achievements. *Tuition waivers:* Full or partial for employees or children of employees. *ROTC:* Army.

**LOANS** *Student loans:* $26,203,879 (97% need-based, 3% non-need-based). 64% of past graduating class borrowed through all loan programs. *Average indebtedness per student:* $28,600. *Average need-based loan:* Freshmen: $1876. Undergraduates: $3507. *Parent loans:* $2,625,403 (100% need-based). *Programs:* Federal Direct (Subsidized and Unsubsidized Stafford, PLUS), Perkins.

**WORK-STUDY** *Federal work-study:* 111 jobs averaging $1853.

**ATHLETIC AWARDS** Total amount: $297,552 (100% non-need-based).

**APPLYING FOR FINANCIAL AID** *Required financial aid form:* FAFSA. *Financial aid deadline (priority):* 3/10. *Notification date:* Continuous beginning 4/15. Students must reply within 2 weeks of notification.

**CONTACT** Ms. Sharon Sweeney, Director of Student Financial Services, Purdue University Calumet, 2200 169th Street, Hammond, IN 46323-2094, 219-989-2301 or toll-free 800-447-8738. *Fax:* 219-989-2141. *E-mail:* finaid2@purduecal.edu.
*Website:* http://www.purduecal.edu/.

# PURDUE UNIVERSITY NORTH CENTRAL
## Westville, IN

**CONTACT** Brad Remmenga, Director of Financial Aid and Compliance, Purdue University North Central, 1401 South US Highway 421, Westville, IN 46391-9528, 219-785-5749 or toll-free 800-872-1231 (in-state). *Fax:* 219-785-5538. *E-mail:* remmenga@pnc.edu.
*Website:* http://www.pnc.edu/.

# QUEENS COLLEGE OF THE CITY UNIVERSITY OF NEW YORK
## Flushing, NY

| Tuition & fees (NY res): $6638 | Average undergraduate aid package: $7469 |
|---|---|

**ABOUT THE INSTITUTION** State and locally supported, coed. *Awards:* certificates, bachelor's, and master's degrees. 58 undergraduate majors. *Total enrollment:* 19,310. Undergraduates: 15,773. Freshmen: 1,544. Federal methodology is used as a basis for awarding need-based institutional aid.

**UNDERGRADUATE EXPENSES** for 2015–2016 *Application fee:* $65. *Tuition, state resident:* full-time $6030; part-time $260 per credit. *Tuition, nonresident:* full-time $16,050; part-time $535 per credit. *Required fees:* full-time $608; $260 per credit or $208.85 per term. Part-time tuition and fees vary according to course load. *Room only:* $11,000. Room and board charges vary according to board plan and housing facility.

**FRESHMAN FINANCIAL AID (Fall 2014, est.)** 1,378 applied for aid; of those 90% were deemed to have need. 71% of freshmen with need received aid; of those 72% had need fully met. *Average percent of need met:* 95% (excluding resources awarded to replace EFC). *Average financial aid package:* $6800 (excluding resources awarded to replace EFC). 3% of all full-time freshmen had no need and received non-need-based gift aid.

**UNDERGRADUATE FINANCIAL AID (Fall 2014, est.)** 10,652 applied for aid; of those 76% were deemed to have need. 83% of undergraduates with need received aid; of those 98% had need fully met. *Average percent of need met:* 95% (excluding resources awarded to replace EFC). *Average financial aid package:* $7469 (excluding resources awarded to replace EFC). 3% of all full-time undergraduates had no need and received non-need-based gift aid.

**GIFT AID (NEED-BASED)** *Total amount:* $44,794,908 (58% federal, 42% state). *Receiving aid:* Freshmen: 44% (668); all full-time undergraduates: 56% (6,160). *Average award:* Freshmen: $5100; Undergraduates: $6512. *Scholarships, grants, and awards:* Federal Pell, FSEOG, state, college/university gift aid from institutional funds.

**GIFT AID (NON-NEED-BASED)** *Total amount:* $631,956 (100% institutional). *Receiving aid:* Freshmen: 2% (28). Undergraduates: 3% (319). *Average award:* Freshmen: $7800. Undergraduates: $7800. *Scholarships, grants, and awards by category:* Academic interests/achievement: general academic interests/achievements. Creative arts/performance: music, theater/drama. Special characteristics: local/state students. *Tuition waivers:* Full or partial for senior citizens. *ROTC:* Army cooperative, Naval cooperative.

**LOANS** *Student loans:* $12,306,852 (55% need-based, 45% non-need-based). *Average need-based loan:* Freshmen: $4870. Undergraduates: $3045. *Programs:* Federal Direct (Subsidized and Unsubsidized Stafford, PLUS), Perkins.

**WORK-STUDY** *Federal work-study:* Total amount: $1,302,296; 1,067 jobs averaging $1220. *State or other work-study/employment:* Part-time jobs available.

**ATHLETIC AWARDS** Total amount: $1,070,425 (15% need-based, 85% non-need-based).

**APPLYING FOR FINANCIAL AID** *Required financial aid forms:* FAFSA, institution's own form, state aid form. *Financial aid deadline (priority):* 2/15. *Notification date:* Continuous beginning 5/1. Students must reply within 3 weeks of notification.

**CONTACT** Rena Smith-Kiawu, Director of Financial Aid, Queens College of the City University of New York, 65-30 Kissena Boulevard, Flushing, NY 11367-1597, 718-997-5100.
*Website:* http://www.qc.cuny.edu/.

# QUEENS UNIVERSITY OF CHARLOTTE
## Charlotte, NC

| Tuition & fees: N/R | Average undergraduate aid package: $22,563 |
| --- | --- |

**ABOUT THE INSTITUTION** Independent Presbyterian, coed. 44 undergraduate majors. Federal methodology is used as a basis for awarding need-based institutional aid.

**FRESHMAN FINANCIAL AID (Fall 2014, est.)** 228 applied for aid; of those 85% were deemed to have need. 100% of freshmen with need received aid; of those 17% had need fully met. *Average percent of need met:* 69% (excluding resources awarded to replace EFC). *Average financial aid package:* $24,788 (excluding resources awarded to replace EFC). 24% of all full-time freshmen had no need and received non-need-based gift aid.

**UNDERGRADUATE FINANCIAL AID (Fall 2014, est.)** 915 applied for aid; of those 89% were deemed to have need. 100% of undergraduates with need received aid; of those 18% had need fully met. *Average percent of need met:* 67% (excluding resources awarded to replace EFC). *Average financial aid package:* $22,563 (excluding resources awarded to replace EFC). 28% of all full-time undergraduates had no need and received non-need-based gift aid.

**GIFT AID (NEED-BASED)** *Total amount:* $14,038,481 (13% federal, 12% state, 72% institutional, 3% external sources). *Receiving aid:* Freshmen: 72% (193); all full-time undergraduates: 69% (808). *Average award:* Freshmen: $21,031; Undergraduates: $18,578. *Scholarships, grants, and awards:* Federal Pell, FSEOG, state, private, college/university gift aid from institutional funds.

**GIFT AID (NON-NEED-BASED)** *Total amount:* $4,872,180 (1% state, 96% institutional, 3% external sources). *Receiving aid:* Freshmen: 8% (22). Undergraduates: 9% (101). *Average award:* Freshmen: $14,000. Undergraduates: $12,475. *Scholarships, grants, and awards by category: Academic interests/ achievement:* communication, education, general academic interests/achievements, health fields. *Creative arts/performance:* art/fine arts, music, theater/drama. *Special achievements/activities:* community service, general special achievements/activities, leadership, religious involvement. *Special characteristics:* adult students, children of current students, children of faculty/staff, first-generation college students, international students, relatives of clergy, religious affiliation, siblings of current students, veterans, veterans' children.

**LOANS** *Student loans:* $8,943,889 (76% need-based, 24% non-need-based). 68% of past graduating class borrowed through all loan programs. *Average indebtedness per student:* $28,359. *Average need-based loan:* Freshmen: $3206. Undergraduates: $4323. *Parent loans:* $3,395,140 (46% need-based, 54% non-need-based). *Programs:* Federal Direct (Subsidized and Unsubsidized Stafford, PLUS), Perkins, state.

**WORK-STUDY** *Federal work-study:* Total amount: $398,430; 243 jobs averaging $1700.

**ATHLETIC AWARDS** Total amount: $3,765,111 (46% need-based, 54% non-need-based).

**APPLYING FOR FINANCIAL AID** *Required financial aid form:* FAFSA. *Financial aid deadline:* Continuous. *Notification date:* Continuous beginning 3/1.

**CONTACT** Nancy Buchanan, Director of Financial Aid, Queens University of Charlotte, 1900 Selwyn Avenue, Charlotte, NC 28274-0002, 704-337-2713 or toll-free 800-849-0202. *Fax:* 704-337-2416. *E-mail:* buchanann@queens.edu. *Website:* http://www.queens.edu/.

# QUINCY UNIVERSITY
## Quincy, IL

| Tuition & fees: $26,998 | Average undergraduate aid package: $24,349 |
| --- | --- |

**ABOUT THE INSTITUTION** Independent Roman Catholic, coed. *Awards:* associate, bachelor's, and master's degrees. 40 undergraduate majors. *Total enrollment:* 1,279. Undergraduates: 1,097. Freshmen: 214. Federal methodology is used as a basis for awarding need-based institutional aid.

**UNDERGRADUATE EXPENSES for 2015–2016** *Application fee:* $25. *Comprehensive fee:* $36,998 includes full-time tuition ($25,998), mandatory fees ($1000), and room and board ($10,000). *College room only:* $5500. Room and board charges vary according to board plan, housing facility, and student level. *Part-time tuition:* $700 per semester hour. *Part-time fees:* $30 per semester hour. Part-time tuition and fees vary according to course load.

**FRESHMAN FINANCIAL AID (Fall 2014, est.)** 202 applied for aid; of those 91% were deemed to have need. 100% of freshmen with need received aid; of those 28% had need fully met. *Average percent of need met:* 81% (excluding resources awarded to replace EFC). *Average financial aid package:* $25,268 (excluding resources awarded to replace EFC). 8% of all full-time freshmen had no need and received non-need-based gift aid.

**UNDERGRADUATE FINANCIAL AID (Fall 2014, est.)** 944 applied for aid; of those 93% were deemed to have need. 95% of undergraduates with need received aid; of those 90% had need fully met. *Average percent of need met:* 79% (excluding resources awarded to replace EFC). *Average financial aid package:* $24,349 (excluding resources awarded to replace EFC). 6% of all full-time undergraduates had no need and received non-need-based gift aid.

**GIFT AID (NEED-BASED)** *Total amount:* $14,982,548 (15% federal, 10% state, 74% institutional, 1% external sources). *Receiving aid:* Freshmen: 85% (181); all full-time undergraduates: 80% (812). *Average award:* Freshmen: $19,626; Undergraduates: $18,114. *Scholarships, grants, and awards:* Federal Pell, FSEOG, state, private, college/university gift aid from institutional funds.

**GIFT AID (NON-NEED-BASED)** *Total amount:* $1,335,412 (6% federal, 2% state, 91% institutional, 1% external sources). *Receiving aid:* Freshmen: 20% (42). Undergraduates: 14% (141). *Average award:* Freshmen: $15,167. Undergraduates: $14,220. *Scholarships, grants, and awards by category: Academic interests/ achievement:* 1,074 awards ($10,643,526 total): biological sciences, business, communication, computer science, education, English, general academic interests/achievements, health fields, humanities, international studies, mathematics, physical sciences, premedicine, religion/biblical studies, social sciences. *Creative arts/performance:* 50 awards ($81,191 total): art/fine arts, cinema/film/broadcasting, music. *Special achievements/activities:* 184 awards ($193,940 total): cheerleading/drum major, community service, general special achievements/activities, hobbies/interests, leadership, memberships. *Special characteristics:* 122 awards ($233,701 total): adult students, children and siblings of alumni, children of faculty/staff, first-generation college students, general special characteristics, local/state students, members of minority groups. *Tuition waivers:* Full or partial for employees or children of employees, senior citizens.

**LOANS** *Student loans:* $5,998,897 (76% need-based, 24% non-need-based). 87% of past graduating class borrowed through all loan programs. *Average indebtedness per student:* $27,857. *Average need-based loan:* Freshmen: $3244. Undergraduates: $4243. *Parent loans:* $907,750 (42% need-based, 58% non-need-based). *Programs:* Federal Direct (Subsidized and Unsubsidized Stafford, PLUS).

**WORK-STUDY** *Federal work-study:* Total amount: $513,995; 279 jobs averaging $2000. *State or other work-study/employment:* Total amount: $199,565 (100% non-need-based). 153 part-time jobs averaging $1104.

**ATHLETIC AWARDS** Total amount: $3,173,413 (77% need-based, 23% non-need-based).

**APPLYING FOR FINANCIAL AID** *Required financial aid form:* FAFSA. *Financial aid deadline (priority):* 3/21. *Notification date:* Continuous beginning 3/1. Students must reply by 5/1 or within 2 weeks of notification.

**CONTACT** Lisa Flack, Director of Financial Aid, Quincy University, 1800 College Avenue, Quincy, IL 62301-2699, 217-228-5260 or toll-free 800-688-4295. *Fax:* 217-228-5635. *E-mail:* financialaid@quincy.edu. *Website:* http://www.quincy.edu/.

# QUINNIPIAC UNIVERSITY
## Hamden, CT

| Tuition & fees: $42,270 | Average undergraduate aid package: $25,571 |
| --- | --- |

**ABOUT THE INSTITUTION** Independent, coed. *Awards:* certificates, bachelor's, master's, and doctoral degrees. 67 undergraduate majors. *Total enrollment:* 9,035. Undergraduates: 6,553. Freshmen: 1,656. Both federal and institutional methodology are used as a basis for awarding need-based institutional aid.

**UNDERGRADUATE EXPENSES for 2015–2016** *Application fee:* $65. *Comprehensive fee:* $57,090 includes full-time tuition ($42,270) and room and board ($14,820). Room and board charges vary according to housing facility. *Part-time tuition:* $965 per credit. *Part-time fees:* $38 per credit. Part-time tuition and fees vary according to class time and course load.

**FRESHMAN FINANCIAL AID (Fall 2014, est.)** 1,352 applied for aid; of those 82% were deemed to have need. 99% of freshmen with need received aid; of those 15% had need fully met. *Average percent of need met:* 68% (excluding resources awarded to replace EFC). *Average financial aid package:* $26,791 (excluding resources awarded to replace EFC). 22% of all full-time freshmen had no need and received non-need-based gift aid.

**UNDERGRADUATE FINANCIAL AID (Fall 2014, est.)** 4,595 applied for aid; of those 85% were deemed to have need. 99% of undergraduates with need received aid; of those 14% had need fully met. *Average percent of need met:* 65% (excluding resources awarded to replace EFC). *Average financial aid package:* $25,571 (excluding resources awarded to replace EFC). 21% of all full-time undergraduates had no need and received non-need-based gift aid.

**GIFT AID (NEED-BASED)** *Total amount:* $69,291,791 (7% federal, 2% state, 87% institutional, 4% external sources). *Receiving aid:* Freshmen: 65% (1,073); all full-time undergraduates: 59% (3,762). *Average award:* Freshmen: $21,508; Undergraduates: $19,741. *Scholarships, grants, and awards:* Federal Pell, FSEOG, state, private, college/university gift aid from institutional funds.

**GIFT AID (NON-NEED-BASED)** *Total amount:* $24,567,872 (97% institutional, 3% external sources). *Receiving aid:* Freshmen: 41% (680). Undergraduates: 34% (2,185). *Average award:* Freshmen: $14,973. Undergraduates: $14,155. *Scholarships, grants, and awards by category:* Academic interests/achievement: 3,370 awards ($45,841,770 total): general academic interests/achievements. *Special characteristics:* 417 awards ($5,861,837 total): children of faculty/staff, international students, siblings of current students. *Tuition waivers:* Full or partial for employees or children of employees. *ROTC:* Army cooperative, Air Force cooperative.

**LOANS** *Student loans:* $52,266,749 (71% need-based, 29% non-need-based). 71% of past graduating class borrowed through all loan programs. *Average indebtedness per student:* $45,711. *Average need-based loan:* Freshmen: $3685. Undergraduates: $4667. *Parent loans:* $24,349,211 (100% non-need-based). *Programs:* Federal Direct (Subsidized and Unsubsidized Stafford, PLUS), Perkins.

**WORK-STUDY** *Federal work-study:* Total amount: $3,575,370; 1,713 jobs averaging $2047.

**ATHLETIC AWARDS** Total amount: $10,915,149 (100% non-need-based).

**APPLYING FOR FINANCIAL AID** *Required financial aid forms:* FAFSA, CSS Financial Aid PROFILE. *Financial aid deadline (priority):* 3/1. *Notification date:* Continuous beginning 3/1. Students must reply by 5/1 or within 2 weeks of notification.

**CONTACT** Mr. Dominic Yoia, Associate Vice President and University Director of Financial Aid, Quinnipiac University, 275 Mount Carmel Avenue, Hamden, CT 06518, 203-582-5224 or toll-free 800-462-1944. *Fax:* 203-582-5238. *E-mail:* finaid@quinnipiac.edu.
*Website:* http://www.quinnipiac.edu/.

# RABBI JACOB JOSEPH SCHOOL
## Edison, NJ

**CONTACT** Financial Aid Office, Rabbi Jacob Joseph School, One Plainfield Ave, Edison, NJ 08817, 732-985-6533.

# RABBINICAL ACADEMY MESIVTA RABBI CHAIM BERLIN
## Brooklyn, NY

**CONTACT** Office of Financial Aid, Rabbinical Academy Mesivta Rabbi Chaim Berlin, 1605 Coney Island Avenue, Brooklyn, NY 11230-4715, 718-377-0777.

# RABBINICAL COLLEGE BETH SHRAGA
## Monsey, NY

**CONTACT** Financial Aid Office, Rabbinical College Beth Shraga, 28 Saddle River Road, Monsey, NY 10952-3035, 914-356-1980.

# RABBINICAL COLLEGE BOBOVER YESHIVA B'NEI ZION
## Brooklyn, NY

**CONTACT** Financial Aid Office, Rabbinical College Bobover Yeshiva B'nei Zion, 1577 48th Street, Brooklyn, NY 11219, 718-438-2018.

# RABBINICAL COLLEGE CH'SAN SOFER
## Brooklyn, NY

**CONTACT** Financial Aid Office, Rabbinical College Ch'san Sofer, 1876 50th Street, Brooklyn, NY 11204, 718-236-1171.

# RABBINICAL COLLEGE OF AMERICA
## Morristown, NJ

**CONTACT** Financial Aid Office , Rabbinical College of America, 226 Sussex Avenue, Morristown, NJ 07960, 973-267-9404. *Fax:* 973-267-5208.
*Website:* http://www.rca.edu/.

# RABBINICAL COLLEGE OF LONG ISLAND
## Long Beach, NY

**CONTACT** Rabbi Cone, Financial Aid Administrator, Rabbinical College of Long Island, 201 Magnolia Boulevard, Long Beach, NY 11561-3305, 516-431-7114.

# RABBINICAL COLLEGE OF OHR SHIMON YISROEL
## Brooklyn, NY

**CONTACT** Financial Aid Office, Rabbinical College of Ohr Shimon Yisroel, 215-217 Hewes Street, Brooklyn, NY 11211, 718-855-4092.

# RABBINICAL COLLEGE OF TELSHE
## Wickliffe, OH

**CONTACT** Financial Aid Office, Rabbinical College of Telshe, 28400 Euclid Avenue, Wickliffe, OH 44092-2523, 216-943-5300.

# RABBINICAL SEMINARY OF AMERICA
## Flushing, NY

**CONTACT** Ms. Leah Eisenstein, Director of Financial Aid, Rabbinical Seminary of America, 92-15 69th Avenue, Forest Hills, NY 11375, 718-268-4700. *Fax:* 718-268-4684.

# RADFORD UNIVERSITY
## Radford, VA

| Tuition & fees (VA res): $9360 | Average undergraduate aid package: $9421 |
|---|---|

**ABOUT THE INSTITUTION** State-supported, coed. *Awards:* certificates, bachelor's, master's, and doctoral degrees. 38 undergraduate majors. *Total enrollment:* 9,798. Undergraduates: 8,885. Freshmen: 2,015. Federal methodology is used as a basis for awarding need-based institutional aid.

**UNDERGRADUATE EXPENSES for 2015–2016** *Application fee:* $50. *Tuition, state resident:* full-time $6386; part-time $266 per credit hour. *Tuition, nonresident:* full-time $18,626; part-time $776 per credit hour. *Required fees:* full-time $2974; $125 per credit hour. Part-time tuition and fees vary according to course load. *College room and board:* $8406; *Room only:* $4632. Room and board charges vary according to board plan and housing facility.

**FRESHMAN FINANCIAL AID (Fall 2014, est.)** 1,654 applied for aid; of those 70% were deemed to have need. 95% of freshmen with need received aid; of those 26% had need fully met. *Average percent of need met:* 79% (excluding resources awarded to replace EFC). *Average financial aid package:* $8776 (excluding resources awarded to replace EFC). 4% of all full-time freshmen had no need and received non-need-based gift aid.

**UNDERGRADUATE FINANCIAL AID (Fall 2014, est.)** 6,256 applied for aid; of those 76% were deemed to have need. 96% of undergraduates with need received aid; of those 28% had need fully met. *Average percent of need met:* 80% (excluding resources awarded to replace EFC). *Average financial aid package:* $9421 (excluding resources awarded to replace EFC). 4% of all full-time undergraduates had no need and received non-need-based gift aid.

**GIFT AID (NEED-BASED)** *Total amount:* $23,950,893 (50% federal, 32% state, 15% institutional, 3% external sources). *Receiving aid:* Freshmen: 34% (691); all full-time undergraduates: 35% (2,995). *Average award:* Freshmen: $7235; Undergraduates: $6998. *Scholarships, grants, and awards:* Federal Pell, FSEOG, state, private, college/university gift aid from institutional funds.

**GIFT AID (NON-NEED-BASED)** *Total amount:* $1,912,636 (16% federal, 3% state, 59% institutional, 22% external sources). *Receiving aid:* Freshmen: 15% (302). Undergraduates: 11% (940). *Average award:* Freshmen: $5246. Undergraduates: $3637. *Scholarships, grants, and awards by category: Academic interests/achievement:* 670 awards ($2,117,330 total): general academic interests/achievements. *Tuition waivers:* Full or partial for employees or children of employees, senior citizens. *ROTC:* Army.

**LOANS** *Student loans:* $45,607,430 (79% need-based, 21% non-need-based). 62% of past graduating class borrowed through all loan programs. *Average indebtedness per student:* $26,333. *Average need-based loan:* Freshmen: $3329. Undergraduates: $4186. *Parent loans:* $11,128,181 (68% need-based, 32% non-need-based). *Programs:* Federal Direct (Subsidized and Unsubsidized Stafford, PLUS), Perkins, Federal Nursing, state, college/university.

**WORK-STUDY** *Federal work-study:* Total amount: $728,989; 295 jobs averaging $2471. *State or other work-study/employment:* Total amount: $1,302,039 (58% need-based, 42% non-need-based). 544 part-time jobs averaging $2393.

**ATHLETIC AWARDS** Total amount: $2,730,452 (52% need-based, 48% non-need-based).

**APPLYING FOR FINANCIAL AID** *Required financial aid form:* FAFSA. *Financial aid deadline (priority):* 2/15. *Notification date:* 4/15. Students must reply within 4 weeks of notification.

**CONTACT** Mrs. Barbara Porter, Director of Financial Aid, Radford University, PO Box 6905, Radford, VA 24142, 540-831-5408. *Fax:* 540-831-5138. *E-mail:* bporter@radford.edu.
*Website:* http://www.radford.edu/.

# RAMAPO COLLEGE OF NEW JERSEY
## Mahwah, NJ

| Tuition & fees (NJ res): $8650 | Average undergraduate aid package: $11,637 |
|---|---|

**ABOUT THE INSTITUTION** State-supported, coed. *Awards:* certificates, bachelor's, and master's degrees. 36 undergraduate majors. *Total enrollment:* 6,003. Undergraduates: 5,710. Freshmen: 965. Federal methodology is used as a basis for awarding need-based institutional aid.

**UNDERGRADUATE EXPENSES for 2015–2016** *Application fee:* $60. *Tuition, state resident:* full-time $8650. *Tuition, nonresident:* full-time $17,300. *College room and board:* $11,550; *Room only:* $8020. Room and board charges vary according to board plan and housing facility.

**FRESHMAN FINANCIAL AID (Fall 2014, est.)** 825 applied for aid; of those 73% were deemed to have need. 94% of freshmen with need received aid; of those 13% had need fully met. *Average percent of need met:* 66% (excluding resources awarded to replace EFC). *Average financial aid package:* $13,850 (excluding resources awarded to replace EFC). 11% of all full-time freshmen had no need and received non-need-based gift aid.

**UNDERGRADUATE FINANCIAL AID (Fall 2014, est.)** 3,929 applied for aid; of those 77% were deemed to have need. 96% of undergraduates with need received aid; of those 14% had need fully met. *Average percent of need met:* 58% (excluding resources awarded to replace EFC). *Average financial aid package:* $11,637 (excluding resources awarded to replace EFC). 8% of all full-time undergraduates had no need and received non-need-based gift aid.

**GIFT AID (NEED-BASED)** *Total amount:* $13,648,803 (48% federal, 43% state, 9% institutional). *Receiving aid:* Freshmen: 27% (259); all full-time undergraduates: 30% (1,482). *Average award:* Freshmen: $13,168; Undergraduates: $9129. *Scholarships, grants, and awards:* Federal Pell, FSEOG, state, private, college/university gift aid from institutional funds, Federal Nursing.

**GIFT AID (NON-NEED-BASED)** *Total amount:* $9,244,133 (1% state, 91% institutional, 8% external sources). *Receiving aid:* Freshmen: 18% (171). Undergraduates: 16% (774). *Average award:* Freshmen: $10,871. Undergraduates: $10,921. *Scholarships, grants, and awards by category: Academic interests/achievement:* 788 awards ($7,888,417 total): general academic interests/achievements. *Special characteristics:* 152 awards ($669,902 total): children of faculty/staff, international students, out-of-state students. *Tuition waivers:* Full or partial for employees or children of employees, senior citizens. *ROTC:* Army cooperative, Air Force cooperative.

**LOANS** *Student loans:* $34,369,710 (32% need-based, 68% non-need-based). 69% of past graduating class borrowed through all loan programs. *Average indebtedness per student:* $29,972. *Average need-based loan:* Freshmen: $3334. Undergraduates: $4312. *Parent loans:* $654,219 (100% non-need-based). *Programs:* Federal Direct (Subsidized and Unsubsidized Stafford, PLUS), Perkins, state.

**WORK-STUDY** *Federal work-study:* Total amount: $245,012; 146 jobs averaging $1774. *State or other work-study/employment:* Total amount: $1,486,744 (100% non-need-based). 716 part-time jobs averaging $2076.

**APPLYING FOR FINANCIAL AID** *Required financial aid form:* FAFSA. *Financial aid deadline (priority):* 3/1. *Notification date:* Continuous beginning 4/1. Students must reply by 5/1 or within 2 weeks of notification.

**CONTACT** Bernice Mulch, Assistant Director of Financial Aid, Ramapo College of New Jersey, 505 Ramapo Valley Road, Mahwah, NJ 07430-1680, 201-684-7252 or toll-free 800-9RAMAPO. *Fax:* 201-684-7085. *E-mail:* finaid@ramapo.edu.
*Website:* http://www.ramapo.edu/.

# RANDOLPH COLLEGE
## Lynchburg, VA

| Tuition & fees: $34,110 | Average undergraduate aid package: $28,783 |
|---|---|

**ABOUT THE INSTITUTION** Independent Methodist, coed. *Awards:* bachelor's and master's degrees. 37 undergraduate majors. *Total enrollment:* 693. Undergraduates: 675. Freshmen: 191. Both federal and institutional methodology are used as a basis for awarding need-based institutional aid.

**UNDERGRADUATE EXPENSES for 2015–2016** *Comprehensive fee:* $45,760 includes full-time tuition ($33,500), mandatory fees ($610), and room and board ($11,650). *Part-time tuition:* $1400 per credit hour. *Part-time fees:* $52.50 per term. Part-time tuition and fees vary according to course load.

**FRESHMAN FINANCIAL AID (Fall 2014, est.)** 158 applied for aid; of those 90% were deemed to have need. 100% of freshmen with need received aid; of those 33% had need fully met. *Average percent of need met:* 83% (excluding resources awarded to replace EFC). *Average financial aid package:* $28,259 (excluding resources awarded to replace EFC). 24% of all full-time freshmen had no need and received non-need-based gift aid.

**UNDERGRADUATE FINANCIAL AID (Fall 2014, est.)** 509 applied for aid; of those 91% were deemed to have need. 100% of undergraduates with need received aid; of those 26% had need fully met. *Average percent of need met:* 80% (excluding resources awarded to replace EFC). *Average financial aid package:* $28,783 (excluding resources awarded to replace EFC). 28% of all full-time undergraduates had no need and received non-need-based gift aid.

**GIFT AID (NEED-BASED)** *Total amount:* $10,691,271 (10% federal, 6% state, 83% institutional, 1% external sources). *Receiving aid:* Freshmen: 74% (142); all full-time undergraduates: 70% (457). *Average award:* Freshmen: $24,330; Undergraduates: $23,875. *Scholarships, grants, and awards:* Federal Pell, FSEOG, state, private, college/university gift aid from institutional funds.

**GIFT AID (NON-NEED-BASED)** *Total amount:* $4,638,576 (8% state, 91% institutional, 1% external sources). *Receiving aid:* Freshmen: 19% (36). Undergraduates: 13% (86). *Average award:* Freshmen: $27,741. Undergraduates: $20,074. *Scholarships, grants, and awards by category: Academic interests/achievement:* biological sciences, education, English, general academic interests/achievements, mathematics, physical sciences, premedicine, social sciences. *Special achievements/activities:* community service, general special achievements/activities, leadership. *Special characteristics:* adult students, children of faculty/staff, international students, local/state students, relatives of clergy, religious affiliation, twins. *Tuition waivers:* Full or partial for employees or children of employees, adult students.

**LOANS** *Student loans:* $4,797,942 (67% need-based, 33% non-need-based). 68% of past graduating class borrowed through all loan programs. *Average indebtedness per student:* $33,854. *Average need-based loan:* Freshmen: $4704. Undergraduates: $5614. *Parent loans:* $1,399,960 (40% need-based, 60% non-need-based). *Programs:* Federal Direct (Subsidized and Unsubsidized Stafford, PLUS), Perkins, college/university.

**WORK-STUDY** *Federal work-study:* Total amount: $191,622; jobs available. *State or other work-study/employment:* Total amount: $226,000 (12% need-based, 88% non-need-based). Part-time jobs available.

**APPLYING FOR FINANCIAL AID** *Required financial aid forms:* FAFSA, noncustodial (divorced/separated) parent's statement. *Financial aid deadline (priority):* 4/1. *Notification date:* Continuous beginning 3/1. Students must reply by 5/1 or within 2 weeks of notification.

**CONTACT** Debi Woodall-Stevens, Director of Student Financial Services, Randolph College, 2500 Rivermont Avenue, Lynchburg, VA 24503, 434-947-8128 or toll-free 800-745-7692. *Fax:* 434-947-8996. *E-mail:* dwstevens@randolphcollege.edu . *Website:* http://www.randolphcollege.edu/.

# RANDOLPH-MACON COLLEGE
## Ashland, VA

| Tuition & fees: $36,340 | Average undergraduate aid package: $26,925 |
| --- | --- |

**ABOUT THE INSTITUTION** Independent United Methodist, coed. *Awards:* bachelor's degrees. 33 undergraduate majors. *Total enrollment:* 1,394. Undergraduates: 1,394. Freshmen: 427. Federal methodology is used as a basis for awarding need-based institutional aid.

**UNDERGRADUATE EXPENSES for 2015–2016** *Application fee:* $30. *Comprehensive fee:* $47,090 includes full-time tuition ($35,360), mandatory fees ($980), and room and board ($10,750). *College room only:* $6100. Full-time tuition and fees vary according to reciprocity agreements. Room and board charges vary according to board plan and housing facility. *Part-time tuition:* $3930 per course.

**FRESHMAN FINANCIAL AID (Fall 2014, est.)** 407 applied for aid; of those 80% were deemed to have need. 100% of freshmen with need received aid; of those 29% had need fully met. *Average percent of need met:* 83% (excluding resources awarded to replace EFC). *Average financial aid package:* $28,144 (excluding resources awarded to replace EFC). 24% of all full-time freshmen had no need and received non-need-based gift aid.

**UNDERGRADUATE FINANCIAL AID (Fall 2014, est.)** 1,206 applied for aid; of those 84% were deemed to have need. 100% of undergraduates with need received aid; of those 27% had need fully met. *Average percent of need met:* 80% (excluding resources awarded to replace EFC). *Average financial aid package:* $26,925 (excluding resources awarded to replace EFC). 25% of all full-time undergraduates had no need and received non-need-based gift aid.

**GIFT AID (NEED-BASED)** *Total amount:* $22,993,177 (6% federal, 9% state, 81% institutional, 4% external sources). *Receiving aid:* Freshmen: 76% (324); all full-time undergraduates: 74% (1,009). *Average award:* Freshmen: $24,424; Undergraduates: $22,944. *Scholarships, grants, and awards:* Federal Pell, FSEOG, state, private, college/university gift aid from institutional funds.

**GIFT AID (NON-NEED-BASED)** *Total amount:* $8,725,309 (12% state, 79% institutional, 9% external sources). *Receiving aid:* Freshmen: 18% (75). Undergraduates: 15% (210). *Average award:* Freshmen: $17,059. Undergraduates: $16,330. *Scholarships, grants, and awards by category: Academic interests/achievement:* general academic interests/achievements, religion/biblical studies. *Special achievements/activities:* general special achievements/activities, religious involvement. *Special characteristics:* children and siblings of alumni, children of faculty/staff, ethnic background, out-of-state students, relatives of clergy, siblings of current students, veterans, veterans' children. *Tuition waivers:* Full or partial for employees or children of employees. *ROTC:* Army cooperative.

**LOANS** *Student loans:* $10,455,725 (60% need-based, 40% non-need-based). *Average need-based loan:* Freshmen: $4595. Undergraduates: $4779. *Parent loans:* $5,202,369 (32% need-based, 68% non-need-based). *Programs:* Federal Direct (Subsidized and Unsubsidized Stafford, PLUS), Perkins, college/university.

**WORK-STUDY** *Federal work-study:* Total amount: $237,183; jobs available.

**APPLYING FOR FINANCIAL AID** *Required financial aid forms:* FAFSA, state aid form. *Financial aid deadline (priority):* 2/15. *Notification date:* 3/1. Students must reply by 5/1 or within 2 weeks of notification.

**CONTACT** Ms. Mary Neal, Director of Financial Aid, Randolph-Macon College, PO Box 5005, Ashland, VA 23005-5505, 804-752-7259 or toll-free 800-888-1762. *Fax:* 804-752-3719. *E-mail:* mneal@rmc.edu. *Website:* http://www.rmc.edu/.

# RASMUSSEN COLLEGE APPLETON
## Appleton, WI

**CONTACT** Financial Aid Office, Rasmussen College Appleton, 3500 E. Destination Drive, Appleton, WI 54915, 920-750-5900 or toll-free 888-549-6755. *Website:* http://www.rasmussen.edu/.

# RASMUSSEN COLLEGE AURORA
## Aurora, IL

**CONTACT** Financial Aid Office, Rasmussen College Aurora, 2363 Sequoia Drive, Aurora, IL 60506, 630-888-3500 or toll free 888-549-6755. *Website:* http://www.rasmussen.edu/.

# RASMUSSEN COLLEGE BISMARCK
## Bismarck, ND

**CONTACT** Financial Aid Office, Rasmussen College Bismarck, 1701 East Century Avenue, Bismarck, ND 58503, 701-530-9600 or toll-free 888-549-6755. *Website:* http://www.rasmussen.edu/.

# RASMUSSEN COLLEGE BLAINE
## Blaine, MN

**CONTACT** Financial Aid Office, Rasmussen College Blaine, 3629 95th Avenue NE, Blaine, MN 55014, 763-795-4720 or toll-free 888-549-6755. *Website:* http://www.rasmussen.edu/.

## RASMUSSEN COLLEGE BLOOMINGTON

### Bloomington, MN

**CONTACT** Financial Aid Office, Rasmussen College Bloomington, 4400 West 78th Street, Bloomington, MN 55435, 952-545-2000 or toll-free 888-549-6755. *Website:* http://www.rasmussen.edu/.

## RASMUSSEN COLLEGE EAGAN

### Eagan, MN

**CONTACT** Financial Aid Office, Rasmussen College Eagan, 3500 Federal Drive, Eagan, MN 55122-1346, 651-687-9000 or toll-free 888-549-6755. *Website:* http://www.rasmussen.edu/.

## RASMUSSEN COLLEGE FARGO

### Fargo, ND

**CONTACT** Financial Aid Office, Rasmussen College Fargo, 4012 19th Avenue SW, Fargo, ND 58103, 701-277-3889 or toll-free 888-549-6755. *Website:* http://www.rasmussen.edu/.

## RASMUSSEN COLLEGE FORT MYERS

### Fort Myers, FL

**CONTACT** Financial Aid Office, Rasmussen College Fort Myers, 9160 Forum Corporate Parkway, Suite 100, Fort Myers, FL 33905, 239-477-2100 or toll-free 888-549-6755. *Website:* http://www.rasmussen.edu/.

## RASMUSSEN COLLEGE GREEN BAY

### Green Bay, WI

**CONTACT** Financial Aid Office, Rasmussen College Green Bay, 940 South Taylor Street, Suite 100, Green Bay, WI 54303, 920-593-8400 or toll-free 888-549-6755. *Website:* http://www.rasmussen.edu/.

## RASMUSSEN COLLEGE KANSAS CITY/ OVERLAND PARK

### Overland Park, KS

**CONTACT** Financial Aid Office, Rasmussen College Kansas City/Overland Park, 11600 College Boulevard, Overland Park, KS 66210, 913-491-7870 or toll-free 888-549-6755. *Website:* http://www.rasmussen.edu/.

## RASMUSSEN COLLEGE LAKE ELMO/ WOODBURY

### Lake Elmo, MN

**CONTACT** Financial Aid Office, Rasmussen College Lake Elmo/Woodbury, 8565 Eagle Point Circle, Lake Elmo, MN 55042, 651-259-6600 or toll-free 888-549-6755. *Website:* http://www.rasmussen.edu/.

## RASMUSSEN COLLEGE LAND O' LAKES

### Land O' Lakes, FL

**CONTACT** Financial Aid Office, Rasmussen College Land O' Lakes, 18600 Fernview Street, Land O' Lakes, FL 34638, 813-435-3601 or toll-free 888-549-6755. *Website:* http://www.rasmussen.edu/.

## RASMUSSEN COLLEGE MANKATO

### Mankato, MN

**CONTACT** Financial Aid Office, Rasmussen College Mankato, 130 Saint Andrews Drive, Mankato, MN 56001, 507-625-6556 or toll-free 888-549-6755. *Website:* http://www.rasmussen.edu/.

## RASMUSSEN COLLEGE MOKENA/ TINLEY PARK

### Mokena, IL

**CONTACT** Financial Aid Office, Rasmussen College Mokena/Tinley Park, 8650 West Spring Lake Road, Mokena, IL 60448, 815-534-3300 or toll-free 888-549-6755. *Website:* http://www.rasmussen.edu/.

## RASMUSSEN COLLEGE MOORHEAD

### Moorhead, MN

**CONTACT** Financial Aid Office, Rasmussen College Moorhead, 1250 29th Avenue South, Moorhead, MN 56560, 218-304-6200 or toll-free 888-549-6755. *Website:* http://www.rasmussen.edu/.

## RASMUSSEN COLLEGE NEW PORT RICHEY

### New Port Richey, FL

**CONTACT** Financial Aid Office, Rasmussen College New Port Richey, 8661 Citizens Drive, New Port Richey, FL 34654, 727-942-0069 or toll-free 888-549-6755. *Website:* http://www.rasmussen.edu/.

## RASMUSSEN COLLEGE OCALA

### Ocala, FL

**CONTACT** Financial Aid Office, Rasmussen College Ocala, 4755 SW 46th Court, Ocala, FL 34471, 352-629-1941 or toll-free 888-549-6755. *Website:* http://www.rasmussen.edu/.

## RASMUSSEN COLLEGE OCALA SCHOOL OF NURSING

### Ocala, FL

**CONTACT** Financial Aid Office, Rasmussen College Ocala School of Nursing, 2100 SW 22nd Place, Ocala, FL 34471, 352-291-8560 or toll-free 888-549-6755. *Website:* http://www.rasmussen.edu/.

# RASMUSSEN COLLEGE ROMEOVILLE/ JOLIET

### Romeoville, IL

**CONTACT** Financial Aid Office, Rasmussen College Romeoville/Joliet, 1400 W. Normantown Road, Romeoville, IL 60446, 815-306-2600 or toll-free 888-549-6755. *Website:* http://www.rasmussen.edu/.

# RASMUSSEN COLLEGE ST. CLOUD

### St. Cloud, MN

**CONTACT** Financial Aid Office, Rasmussen College St. Cloud, 226 Park Avenue South, St. Cloud, MN 56301-3713, 320-251-5600 or toll-free 888-549-6755. *Website:* http://www.rasmussen.edu/.

# RASMUSSEN COLLEGE TAMPA/ BRANDON

### Tampa, FL

**CONTACT** Financial Aid Office, Rasmussen College Tampa/Brandon, 4042 Park Oaks Boulevard, Tampa, FL 33610, 813-246-7600 or toll-free 888-549-6755. *Website:* http://www.rasmussen.edu/.

# RASMUSSEN COLLEGE TOPEKA

### Topeka, KS

**CONTACT** Financial Aid Office, Rasmussen College Topeka, 620 SW Governor View, Topeka, KS 66606, 785-228-7320 or toll-free 888-549-6755. *Website:* http://www.rasmussen.edu/.

# RASMUSSEN COLLEGE WAUSAU

### Wausau, WI

**CONTACT** Financial Aid Office, Rasmussen College Wausau, 1101 Westwood Drive, Wausau, WI 54401, 715-841-8000 or toll-free 888-549-6755. *Website:* http://www.rasmussen.edu/.

# REED COLLEGE

### Portland, OR

| Tuition & fees: $47,760 | Average undergraduate aid package: $44,147 |
| --- | --- |

**ABOUT THE INSTITUTION** Independent, coed. *Awards:* bachelor's and master's degrees. 32 undergraduate majors. *Total enrollment:* 1,394. Undergraduates: 1,374. Freshmen: 347. Both federal and institutional methodology are used as a basis for awarding need-based institutional aid.

**UNDERGRADUATE EXPENSES for 2015–2016** *Comprehensive fee:* $59,960 includes full-time tuition ($47,500), mandatory fees ($260), and room and board ($12,200). *College room only:* $6350. Full-time tuition and fees vary according to degree level. Room and board charges vary according to board plan and housing facility. *Part-time tuition:* $8060 per unit. Part-time tuition and fees vary according to course load and degree level.

**FRESHMAN FINANCIAL AID (Fall 2014, est.)** 212 applied for aid; of those 73% were deemed to have need. 100% of freshmen with need received aid; of those 99% had need fully met. *Average percent of need met:* 100% (excluding resources awarded to replace EFC). *Average financial aid package:* $47,253 (excluding resources awarded to replace EFC).

**UNDERGRADUATE FINANCIAL AID (Fall 2014, est.)** 783 applied for aid; of those 84% were deemed to have need. 100% of undergraduates with need received aid; of those 100% had need fully met. *Average percent of need met:* 100% (excluding resources awarded to replace EFC). *Average financial aid package:* $44,147 (excluding resources awarded to replace EFC).

**GIFT AID (NEED-BASED)** *Total amount:* $26,095,117 (5% federal, 93% institutional, 2% external sources). *Receiving aid:* Freshmen: 44% (151); all full-time undergraduates: 49% (653). *Average award:* Freshmen: $43,617; Undergraduates: $39,329. *Scholarships, grants, and awards:* Federal Pell, FSEOG, state, private, college/university gift aid from institutional funds.

**GIFT AID (NON-NEED-BASED)** *Total amount:* $45,100 (100% external sources). *Tuition waivers:* Full or partial for employees or children of employees. *ROTC:* Air Force cooperative.

**LOANS** *Student loans:* $3,123,233 (84% need-based, 16% non-need-based). 53% of past graduating class borrowed through all loan programs. *Average indebtedness per student:* $19,151. *Average need-based loan:* Freshmen: $2980. Undergraduates: $4311. *Parent loans:* $1,277,900 (100% non-need-based). *Programs:* Federal Direct (Subsidized and Unsubsidized Stafford, PLUS), Perkins, college/university.

**WORK-STUDY** *Federal work-study:* Total amount: $563,576; jobs available. *State or other work-study/employment:* Total amount: $218,000 (100% need-based). Part-time jobs available.

**APPLYING FOR FINANCIAL AID** *Required financial aid forms:* FAFSA, CSS Financial Aid PROFILE, noncustodial (divorced/separated) parent's statement. *Financial aid deadline:* 2/1. *Notification date:* 4/1. Students must reply by 5/1 or within 2 weeks of notification.

**CONTACT** Leslie Limper, Director of Financial Aid, Reed College, 3203 Southeast Woodstock Boulevard, Portland, OR 97202-8199, 503-777-7223 or toll-free 800-547-4750. *Fax:* 503-788-6682. *E-mail:* financial.aid@reed.edu. *Website:* http://www.reed.edu/.

# REGENT UNIVERSITY

### Virginia Beach, VA

| Tuition & fees: $17,150 | Average undergraduate aid package: $11,678 |
| --- | --- |

**ABOUT THE INSTITUTION** Independent Christian, coed. *Awards:* certificates, associate, bachelor's, master's, and doctoral degrees. 21 undergraduate majors. *Total enrollment:* 6,154. Undergraduates: 2,410. Freshmen: 223. Federal methodology is used as a basis for awarding need-based institutional aid.

**UNDERGRADUATE EXPENSES for 2015–2016** *Application fee:* $50. *Comprehensive fee:* $25,400 includes full-time tuition ($16,350), mandatory fees ($800), and room and board ($8250). *College room only:* $5730. Full-time tuition and fees vary according to course level, course load, program, and student level. Room and board charges vary according to board plan and housing facility. *Part-time tuition:* $545 per credit hour. *Part-time fees:* $545 per credit hour; $400 per term. Part-time tuition and fees vary according to course level, course load, program, and student level.

**FRESHMAN FINANCIAL AID (Fall 2014, est.)** 184 applied for aid; of those 83% were deemed to have need. 99% of freshmen with need received aid; of those 16% had need fully met. *Average percent of need met:* 52% (excluding resources awarded to replace EFC). *Average financial aid package:* $11,974 (excluding resources awarded to replace EFC). 23% of all full-time freshmen had no need and received non-need-based gift aid.

**UNDERGRADUATE FINANCIAL AID (Fall 2014, est.)** 1,278 applied for aid; of those 89% were deemed to have need. 100% of undergraduates with need received aid; of those 10% had need fully met. *Average percent of need met:* 53% (excluding resources awarded to replace EFC). *Average financial aid package:* $11,678 (excluding resources awarded to replace EFC). 13% of all full-time undergraduates had no need and received non-need-based gift aid.

**GIFT AID (NEED-BASED)** *Total amount:* $10,369,403 (46% federal, 14% state, 38% institutional, 2% external sources). *Receiving aid:* Freshmen: 73% (149); all full-time undergraduates: 71% (1,058). *Average award:* Freshmen: $7935; Undergraduates: $7870. *Scholarships, grants, and awards:* Federal Pell, state, private, college/university gift aid from institutional funds.

**GIFT AID (NON-NEED-BASED)** *Total amount:* $2,201,272 (24% state, 74% institutional, 2% external sources). *Receiving aid:* Freshmen: 12% (24). Undergraduates: 6% (83). *Average award:* Freshmen: $7772. Undergraduates: $7508. *Scholarships, grants, and awards by category: Academic interests/achievement: business, communication, computer science, education, English, foreign languages, humanities, mathematics, religion/biblical studies, social sciences. Creative arts/performance: cinema/film/broadcasting, journalism/publications. Special achievements/activities: leadership, memberships. Special characteristics: children and siblings of alumni, children of faculty/staff, public servants, siblings of current students, veterans. Tuition waivers: Full or partial for employees or children of employees. ROTC: Army cooperative, Naval cooperative.

LOANS Student loans: $20,280,339 (31% need-based, 69% non-need-based). 82% of past graduating class borrowed through all loan programs. Average indebtedness per student: $36,564. Average need-based loan: Freshmen: $3341. Undergraduates: $3841. Parent loans: $8,307,801 (38% need-based, 62% non-need-based). Programs: Federal Direct (Subsidized and Unsubsidized Stafford, PLUS).

APPLYING FOR FINANCIAL AID Required financial aid forms: FAFSA, institution's own form, state aid form. Financial aid deadline: Continuous. Notification date: Continuous beginning 3/1. Students must reply within 2 weeks of notification.

CONTACT Mrs. Dorothy Davidson, Director of Central Financial Aid, Regent University, 1000 Regent University Drive, Student Center 251, Virginia Beach, VA 23464, 757-352-4108 or toll-free 800-373-5504. Fax: 757-352-4118. E-mail: finaid@regent.edu.
Website: http://www.regent.edu/.

# REGIS COLLEGE
## Weston, MA

CONTACT Dee J. Ludwick, Director of Financial Aid, Regis College, Box 81, Weston, MA 02493, 781-768-7180 or toll-free 866-438-7344. Fax: 781-768-7225. E-mail: finaid@regiscollege.edu.
Website: http://www.regiscollege.edu/.

# REGIS UNIVERSITY
## Denver, CO

| Tuition & fees: $33,710 | Average undergraduate aid package: $26,920 |
|---|---|

ABOUT THE INSTITUTION Independent Roman Catholic (Jesuit), coed. Awards: certificates, bachelor's, master's, and doctoral degrees. 44 undergraduate majors. Total enrollment: 9,208. Undergraduates: 5,009. Freshmen: 481. Federal methodology is used as a basis for awarding need-based institutional aid.

UNDERGRADUATE EXPENSES for 2015–2016 Application fee: $50. Comprehensive fee: $43,540 includes full-time tuition ($33,110), mandatory fees ($600), and room and board ($9830). College room only: $5400. Full-time tuition and fees vary according to course load, location, program, and reciprocity agreements. Room and board charges vary according to board plan and housing facility. Part-time tuition: $1035 per credit hour. Part-time fees: $150 per term. Part-time tuition and fees vary according to course load, location, program, and reciprocity agreements.

FRESHMAN FINANCIAL AID (Fall 2013) 330 applied for aid; of those 82% were deemed to have need. 99% of freshmen with need received aid; of those 16% had need fully met. Average percent of need met: 81% (excluding resources awarded to replace EFC). Average financial aid package: $30,557 (excluding resources awarded to replace EFC). 28% of all full-time freshmen had no need and received non-need-based gift aid.

UNDERGRADUATE FINANCIAL AID (Fall 2013) 1,992 applied for aid; of those 87% were deemed to have need. 98% of undergraduates with need received aid; of those 12% had need fully met. Average percent of need met: 77% (excluding resources awarded to replace EFC). Average financial aid package: $26,920 (excluding resources awarded to replace EFC). 19% of all full-time undergraduates had no need and received non-need-based gift aid.

GIFT AID (NEED-BASED) Total amount: $26,189,876 (21% federal, 6% state, 69% institutional, 4% external sources). Receiving aid: Freshmen: 68% (263); all full-time undergraduates: 56% (1,399). Average award: Freshmen: $20,662; Undergraduates: $16,998. Scholarships, grants, and awards: Federal Pell, FSEOG, state, private, college/university gift aid from institutional funds.

GIFT AID (NON-NEED-BASED) Total amount: $6,476,325 (94% institutional, 6% external sources). Receiving aid: Freshmen: 9% (34). Undergraduates: 5% (119). Average award: Freshmen: $11,765. Undergraduates: $11,479. Scholarships, grants, and awards by category: Academic interests/achievement: 677 awards ($7,891,592 total): biological sciences, general academic interests/achievements, mathematics, physical sciences. Creative arts/performance: 30 awards ($142,947 total): debating, music. Special achievements/activities: 45 awards ($197,241 total): leadership. Special characteristics: 41 awards ($409,692 total): adult students, children of faculty/staff, local/state students, public servants. Tuition waivers: Full or partial for employees or children of employees. ROTC: Army cooperative, Naval cooperative, Air Force cooperative.

LOANS Student loans: $30,164,242 (83% need-based, 17% non-need-based). 68% of past graduating class borrowed through all loan programs. Average indebtedness per student: $28,461. Average need-based loan: Freshmen: $3886. Undergraduates: $4504. Parent loans: $4,522,651 (41% need-based, 59% non-need-based). Programs: Federal Direct (Subsidized and Unsubsidized Stafford, PLUS), Perkins, Federal Nursing.

WORK-STUDY Federal work-study: 410 jobs averaging $1635. State or other work-study/employment: Total amount: $1,039,902 (37% need-based, 63% non-need-based). 422 part-time jobs averaging $1829.

ATHLETIC AWARDS Total amount: $2,566,472 (39% need-based, 61% non-need-based).

APPLYING FOR FINANCIAL AID Required financial aid form: FAFSA. Financial aid deadline (priority): 5/31. Notification date: Continuous beginning 3/15.

CONTACT Ellie Miller, Director of Financial Aid, Regis University, 3333 Regis Boulevard, Denver, CO 80221-1099, 303-964-5758 or toll-free 800-388-2366 Ext. 4900. Fax: 303-964-5449. E-mail: emiller@regis.edu.
Website: http://www.regis.edu/.

# REINHARDT UNIVERSITY
## Waleska, GA

| Tuition & fees: $20,266 | Average undergraduate aid package: $14,124 |
|---|---|

ABOUT THE INSTITUTION Independent United Methodist Church, coed. Awards: associate, bachelor's, and master's degrees. 32 undergraduate majors. Total enrollment: 1,422. Undergraduates: 1,334. Freshmen: 310. Federal methodology is used as a basis for awarding need-based institutional aid.

UNDERGRADUATE EXPENSES for 2015–2016 Comprehensive fee: $27,834 includes full-time tuition ($19,946), mandatory fees ($320), and room and board ($7568). Part-time tuition: $665 per credit hour.

FRESHMAN FINANCIAL AID (Fall 2013) 285 applied for aid; of those 88% were deemed to have need. 100% of freshmen with need received aid; of those 11% had need fully met. Average percent of need met: 57% (excluding resources awarded to replace EFC). Average financial aid package: $13,914 (excluding resources awarded to replace EFC). 15% of all full-time freshmen had no need and received non-need-based gift aid.

UNDERGRADUATE FINANCIAL AID (Fall 2013) 884 applied for aid; of those 88% were deemed to have need. 100% of undergraduates with need received aid; of those 10% had need fully met. Average percent of need met: 60% (excluding resources awarded to replace EFC). Average financial aid package: $14,124 (excluding resources awarded to replace EFC). 20% of all full-time undergraduates had no need and received non-need-based gift aid.

GIFT AID (NEED-BASED) Total amount: $7,367,959 (30% federal, 22% state, 46% institutional, 2% external sources). Receiving aid: Freshmen: 83% (251); all full-time undergraduates: 76% (774). Average award: Freshmen: $11,201; Undergraduates: $10,899. Scholarships, grants, and awards: Federal Pell, FSEOG, state, private, college/university gift aid from institutional funds.

GIFT AID (NON-NEED-BASED) Total amount: $2,845,169 (49% state, 49% institutional, 2% external sources). Receiving aid: Freshmen: 9% (28). Undergraduates: 8% (77). Average award: Freshmen: $4771. Undergraduates: $5829. Scholarships, grants, and awards by category: Academic interests/achievement: general academic interests/achievements. Creative arts/performance: art/fine arts, music. Special achievements/activities: leadership. Special characteristics: religious affiliation.

**LOANS** *Student loans:* $6,001,767 (82% need-based, 18% non-need-based). 63% of past graduating class borrowed through all loan programs. *Average indebtedness per student:* $23,235. *Average need-based loan:* Freshmen: $3672. Undergraduates: $4122. *Parent loans:* $996,007 (68% need-based, 32% non-need-based). *Programs:* Federal Direct (Subsidized and Unsubsidized Stafford, PLUS).

**WORK-STUDY** *Federal work-study:* jobs available. *State or other work-study/employment:* Part-time jobs available.

**ATHLETIC AWARDS** Total amount: $2,436,154 (69% need-based, 31% non-need-based).

**APPLYING FOR FINANCIAL AID** *Required financial aid forms:* FAFSA, state aid form. *Financial aid deadline:* Continuous. *Notification date:* Continuous beginning 1/1. Students must reply by 6/1.

**CONTACT** Angela D. Harlow, Director of Financial Aid, Reinhardt University, 7300 Reinhardt College Circle, Waleska, GA 30183-2981, 770-720-5603. *Fax:* 770-720-9126.

*Website:* http://www.reinhardt.edu/.

# RENSSELAER POLYTECHNIC INSTITUTE
## Troy, NY

| Tuition & fees: $47,908 | Average undergraduate aid package: $34,359 |
| --- | --- |

**ABOUT THE INSTITUTION** Independent, coed. *Awards:* bachelor's, master's, and doctoral degrees. 40 undergraduate majors. *Total enrollment:* 7,028. Undergraduates: 5,618. Freshmen: 1,331. Both federal and institutional methodology are used as a basis for awarding need-based institutional aid.

**UNDERGRADUATE EXPENSES for 2015–2016** *Application fee:* $70. *Comprehensive fee:* $61,528 includes full-time tuition ($46,700), mandatory fees ($1208), and room and board ($13,620). *College room only:* $7740. Room and board charges vary according to board plan and location. *Part-time tuition:* $1945 per credit hour.

**FRESHMAN FINANCIAL AID (Fall 2014, est.)** 1,057 applied for aid; of those 82% were deemed to have need. 100% of freshmen with need received aid; of those 26% had need fully met. *Average percent of need met:* 85% (excluding resources awarded to replace EFC). *Average financial aid package:* $37,760 (excluding resources awarded to replace EFC). 23% of all full-time freshmen had no need and received non-need-based gift aid.

**UNDERGRADUATE FINANCIAL AID (Fall 2014, est.)** 3,893 applied for aid; of those 90% were deemed to have need. 100% of undergraduates with need received aid; of those 21% had need fully met. *Average percent of need met:* 77% (excluding resources awarded to replace EFC). *Average financial aid package:* $34,359 (excluding resources awarded to replace EFC). 27% of all full-time undergraduates had no need and received non-need-based gift aid.

**GIFT AID (NEED-BASED)** *Total amount:* $100,016,954 (12% federal, 2% state, 84% institutional, 2% external sources). *Receiving aid:* Freshmen: 65% (862); all full-time undergraduates: 63% (3,486). *Average award:* Freshmen: $32,205; Undergraduates: $28,527. *Scholarships, grants, and awards:* Federal Pell, FSEOG, state, private, college/university gift aid from institutional funds, Academic Competitiveness Grants, National SMART Grants, Gates Millennium Scholarships.

**GIFT AID (NON-NEED-BASED)** *Total amount:* $30,462,706 (4% federal, 1% state, 92% institutional, 3% external sources). *Receiving aid:* Freshmen: 15% (203). Undergraduates: 9% (516). *Average award:* Freshmen: $17,440. Undergraduates: $15,860. *Scholarships, grants, and awards by category:* Academic interests/achievement: general academic interests/achievements, humanities, mathematics, military science. *Creative arts/performance:* general creative arts/performance. *Special achievements/activities:* general special achievements/activities. *Special characteristics:* children and siblings of alumni, children of faculty/staff, ethnic background, general special characteristics, members of minority groups. *Tuition waivers:* Full or partial for employees or children of employees. *ROTC:* Army, Naval, Air Force.

**LOANS** *Student loans:* $40,375,308 (60% need-based, 40% non-need-based). 66% of past graduating class borrowed through all loan programs. *Average indebtedness per student:* $41,814. *Average need-based loan:* Freshmen: $4811. Undergraduates: $5610. *Parent loans:* $8,794,998 (24% need-based, 76% non-need-based). *Programs:* Federal Direct (Subsidized and Unsubsidized Stafford, PLUS), Perkins, college/university.

**WORK-STUDY** *Federal work-study:* Total amount: $1,300,260; 809 jobs averaging $1854.

**ATHLETIC AWARDS** Total amount: $2,234,768 (100% non-need-based).

**APPLYING FOR FINANCIAL AID** *Required financial aid forms:* FAFSA, CSS Financial Aid PROFILE. *Financial aid deadline (priority):* 2/1. *Notification date:* 3/15.

**CONTACT** Mr. Larry Chambers, Director of Financial Aid, Rensselaer Polytechnic Institute, Academy Hall, Troy, NY 12180-3590, 518-276-6813. *Fax:* 518-276-4797. *E-mail:* financial_aid@rpi.edu.

*Website:* http://www.rpi.edu/.

# RESEARCH COLLEGE OF NURSING
## Kansas City, MO

**ABOUT THE INSTITUTION** Independent, coed, primarily women. *Awards:* certificates, bachelor's, and master's degrees (bachelor's degree offered jointly with Rockhurst College). 1 undergraduate major. *Total enrollment:* 474. Undergraduates: 340. Freshmen: 78.

**GIFT AID (NEED-BASED)** *Scholarships, grants, and awards:* Federal Pell, FSEOG, state, private, college/university gift aid from institutional funds.

**GIFT AID (NON-NEED-BASED)** *Scholarships, grants, and awards by category:* Academic interests/achievement: general academic interests/achievements, health fields. *Special characteristics:* children and siblings of alumni, children of educators, children of faculty/staff, siblings of current students.

**LOANS** *Programs:* Federal Direct (Subsidized and Unsubsidized Stafford, PLUS), Federal Nursing.

**APPLYING FOR FINANCIAL AID** *Required financial aid form:* FAFSA.

**CONTACT** Ms. Stacie Withers, Director of Financial Aid, Research College of Nursing, 2525 East Meyer Boulevard, Kansas City, MO 64132, 816-995-2832. *Fax:* 816-995-2833. *E-mail:* stacie.withers@researchcollege.edu.

*Website:* http://www.researchcollege.edu/.

# RESURRECTION UNIVERSITY
## Chicago, IL

**ABOUT THE INSTITUTION** Independent, coed. *Awards:* certificates, bachelor's, and master's degrees. 2 undergraduate majors. *Total enrollment:* 476. Undergraduates: 339.

**GIFT AID (NEED-BASED)** *Scholarships, grants, and awards:* Federal Pell, FSEOG, state, private, college/university gift aid from institutional funds.

**LOANS** *Programs:* Federal Direct (Subsidized and Unsubsidized Stafford, PLUS).

**WORK-STUDY** *Federal work-study:* 11 jobs averaging $3000.

**CONTACT** Ms. Shirley Howell, Financial Aid Officer, Resurrection University, 1431 North Claremont Avenue, Chicago, IL 60622, 773-252-5125. *Fax:* 773-227-3838. *E-mail:* shirley.howell@resu.edu.

*Website:* http://www.resu.edu/.

# RHODE ISLAND COLLEGE
## Providence, RI

| Tuition & fees (RI res): $7602 | Average undergraduate aid package: $8999 |
| --- | --- |

**ABOUT THE INSTITUTION** State-supported, coed. *Awards:* certificates, bachelor's, master's, and doctoral degrees. 103 undergraduate majors. *Total enrollment:* 8,641. Undergraduates: 7,518. Freshmen: 1,094. Institutional methodology is used as a basis for awarding need-based institutional aid.

**UNDERGRADUATE EXPENSES for 2015–2016** *Application fee:* $50. *Tuition, state resident:* full-time $6530; part-time $272 per credit. *Tuition, nonresident:* full-time $17,228; part-time $670 per credit. *Required fees:* full-time $1072; $32 per credit or $72 per term. Part-time tuition and fees vary according to course load. *College room and board:* $10,094; *Room only:* $5744. Room and board charges vary according to housing facility.

**FRESHMAN FINANCIAL AID (Fall 2014, est.)** 987 applied for aid; of those 80% were deemed to have need. 97% of freshmen with need received aid; of those 14% had need fully met. *Average percent of need met:* 72% (excluding resources awarded to replace EFC). *Average financial aid package:* $9501 (excluding resources awarded to replace EFC). 4% of all full-time freshmen had no need and received non-need-based gift aid.

**UNDERGRADUATE FINANCIAL AID (Fall 2014, est.)** 4,682 applied for aid; of those 82% were deemed to have need. 95% of undergraduates with need received aid; of those 15% had need fully met. *Average percent of need met:* 70% (excluding resources awarded to replace EFC). *Average financial aid package:* $8999 (excluding resources awarded to replace EFC). 2% of all full-time undergraduates had no need and received non-need-based gift aid.

**GIFT AID (NEED-BASED)** *Total amount:* $20,981,050 (66% federal, 6% state, 25% institutional, 3% external sources). *Receiving aid:* Freshmen: 63% (677); all full-time undergraduates: 58% (3,193). *Average award:* Freshmen: $7143; Undergraduates: $5731. *Scholarships, grants, and awards:* Federal Pell, FSEOG, state, private, college/university gift aid from institutional funds.

**GIFT AID (NON-NEED-BASED)** *Total amount:* $484,548 (80% institutional, 20% external sources). *Receiving aid:* Freshmen: 1% (12). Undergraduates: 1% (42). *Average award:* Freshmen: $2754. Undergraduates: $2572. *Scholarships, grants, and awards by category:* Academic interests/achievement: general academic interests/achievements. Creative arts/performance: art/fine arts, cinema/film/broadcasting, dance, journalism/publications, music, theater/drama. Special characteristics: children and siblings of alumni. *Tuition waivers:* Full or partial for employees or children of employees. ROTC: Army cooperative.

**LOANS** *Student loans:* $36,399,980 (72% need-based, 28% non-need-based). 71% of past graduating class borrowed through all loan programs. *Average indebtedness per student:* $25,567. *Average need-based loan:* Freshmen: $3368. Undergraduates: $4000. *Parent loans:* $1,275,319 (32% need-based, 68% non-need-based). *Programs:* Federal Direct (Subsidized and Unsubsidized Stafford, PLUS), Perkins, state, private loans.

**WORK-STUDY** *Federal work-study:* Total amount: $1,659,138; jobs available.

**APPLYING FOR FINANCIAL AID** *Required financial aid forms:* FAFSA, institution's own form. *Financial aid deadline (priority):* 3/1. *Notification date:* Continuous beginning 3/15. Students must reply by 5/1 or within 3 weeks of notification.

**CONTACT** Mr. James T. Hanbury, Director of Financial Aid, Rhode Island College, 600 Mount Pleasant Avenue, Providence, RI 02908, 401-456-8033 or toll-free 800-669-5760. Fax: 401-456-8686. *E-mail:* jhanbury@ric.edu.
*Website:* http://www.ric.edu/.

# RHODE ISLAND SCHOOL OF DESIGN
## Providence, RI

| Tuition & fees: $44,594 | Average undergraduate aid package: $28,778 |
| --- | --- |

**ABOUT THE INSTITUTION** Independent, coed. *Awards:* bachelor's and master's degrees. 16 undergraduate majors. *Total enrollment:* 2,449. Undergraduates: 2,014. Freshmen: 462. Both federal and institutional methodology are used as a basis for awarding need-based institutional aid.

**UNDERGRADUATE EXPENSES for 2015–2016** *Application fee:* $60. *Comprehensive fee:* $57,234 includes full-time tuition ($44,284), mandatory fees ($310), and room and board ($12,640). *College room only:* $7167. Room and board charges vary according to board plan and housing facility.

**FRESHMAN FINANCIAL AID (Fall 2013)** 244 applied for aid; of those 76% were deemed to have need. 100% of freshmen with need received aid; of those 3% had need fully met. *Average percent of need met:* 65% (excluding resources awarded to replace EFC). *Average financial aid package:* $27,500 (excluding resources awarded to replace EFC). 1% of all full-time freshmen had no need and received non-need-based gift aid.

**UNDERGRADUATE FINANCIAL AID (Fall 2013)** 919 applied for aid; of those 85% were deemed to have need. 100% of undergraduates with need received aid; of those 3% had need fully met. *Average percent of need met:* 62% (excluding resources awarded to replace EFC). *Average financial aid package:* $28,778 (excluding resources awarded to replace EFC). 1% of all full-time undergraduates had no need and received non-need-based gift aid.

**GIFT AID (NEED-BASED)** *Total amount:* $18,326,280 (10% federal, 87% institutional, 3% external sources). *Receiving aid:* Freshmen: 30% (135); all full-time undergraduates: 31% (623). *Average award:* Freshmen: $21,000; Undergraduates: $24,337. *Scholarships, grants, and awards:* Federal Pell, FSEOG, state, private, college/university gift aid from institutional funds.

**GIFT AID (NON-NEED-BASED)** *Total amount:* $200,000 (100% institutional). *Receiving aid:* Freshmen: 1% (5). Undergraduates: 1% (20). *Average award:* Freshmen: $10,000. Undergraduates: $10,000. *Scholarships, grants, and awards by category:* Academic interests/achievement: general academic interests/achievements. Creative arts/performance: applied art and design, art/fine arts. Special characteristics: children of faculty/staff. *Tuition waivers:* Full or partial for employees or children of employees. ROTC: Army cooperative.

**LOANS** *Student loans:* $10,000,000 (100% need-based). 48% of past graduating class borrowed through all loan programs. *Average indebtedness per student:* $30,376. *Average need-based loan:* Freshmen: $3500. Undergraduates: $5500. *Parent loans:* $5,500,000 (100% need-based). *Programs:* Federal Direct (Subsidized and Unsubsidized Stafford, PLUS), Perkins, college/university.

**WORK-STUDY** *Federal work-study:* jobs available. *State or other work-study/employment:* Total amount: $500,000 (100% need-based). Part-time jobs available.

**ATHLETIC AWARDS** Total amount: $455 (100% non-need-based).

**APPLYING FOR FINANCIAL AID** *Required financial aid forms:* FAFSA, CSS Financial Aid PROFILE. *Financial aid deadline (priority):* 2/15. *Notification date:* 4/1. Students must reply by 5/1 or within 4 weeks of notification.

**CONTACT** Anthony Gallonio, Director of Student Financial Services, Rhode Island School of Design, 2 College Street, Providence, RI 02903-2784, 401-454-6661 or toll-free 800-364-7473. Fax: 401-454-6412.
*Website:* http://www.risd.edu/.

# RHODES COLLEGE
## Memphis, TN

| Tuition & fees: $43,224 | Average undergraduate aid package: $34,455 |
| --- | --- |

**ABOUT THE INSTITUTION** Independent, coed. *Awards:* bachelor's and master's degrees (master's degree in accounting only). 33 undergraduate majors. *Total enrollment:* 2,054. Undergraduates: 2,031. Freshmen: 507. Institutional methodology is used as a basis for awarding need-based institutional aid.

**UNDERGRADUATE EXPENSES for 2015–2016** *Comprehensive fee:* $53,970 includes full-time tuition ($42,914), mandatory fees ($310), and room and board ($10,746). *College room only:* $5373. Room and board charges vary according to board plan and housing facility. *Part-time tuition:* $1800 per credit hour.

**FRESHMAN FINANCIAL AID (Fall 2014, est.)** 429 applied for aid; of those 61% were deemed to have need. 100% of freshmen with need received aid; of those 56% had need fully met. *Average percent of need met:* 93% (excluding resources awarded to replace EFC). *Average financial aid package:* $34,061 (excluding resources awarded to replace EFC). 40% of all full-time freshmen had no need and received non-need-based gift aid.

**UNDERGRADUATE FINANCIAL AID (Fall 2014, est.)** 1,351 applied for aid; of those 61% were deemed to have need. 100% of undergraduates with need received aid; of those 47% had need fully met. *Average percent of need met:* 90% (excluding resources awarded to replace EFC). *Average financial aid package:* $34,455 (excluding resources awarded to replace EFC). 50% of all full-time undergraduates had no need and received non-need-based gift aid.

**GIFT AID (NEED-BASED)** *Total amount:* $21,574,506 (7% federal, 5% state, 87% institutional, 1% external sources). *Receiving aid:* Freshmen: 52% (262); all full-time undergraduates: 41% (818). *Average award:* Freshmen: $26,578; Undergraduates: $26,183. *Scholarships, grants, and awards:* Federal Pell, FSEOG, state, private, college/university gift aid from institutional funds.

**GIFT AID (NON-NEED-BASED)** *Total amount:* $23,099,539 (5% state, 90% institutional, 5% external sources). *Receiving aid:* Freshmen: 24% (120). Undergraduates: 14% (274). *Average award:* Freshmen: $19,113. Undergraduates: $18,642. *Scholarships, grants, and awards by category:* Academic interests/achievement: general academic interests/achievements, physical sciences. Creative arts/performance: art/fine arts, general creative arts/performance, music, theater/drama. Special characteristics: children of faculty/staff, members of minority groups, relatives of clergy, religious affiliation. *Tuition waivers:* Full or partial for employees or children of employees. ROTC: Army cooperative, Air Force cooperative.

**LOANS** *Student loans:* $7,173,125 (40% need-based, 60% non-need-based). 55% of past graduating class borrowed through all loan programs. *Average indebtedness per student:* $27,077. *Average need-based loan:* Freshmen: $2984. Undergraduates: $5056. *Parent loans:* $2,319,305 (12% need-based, 88% non-need-based). *Programs:* Federal Direct (Subsidized and Unsubsidized Stafford, PLUS), Perkins.
**WORK-STUDY** *Federal work-study:* Total amount: $783,282; jobs available. *State or other work-study/employment:* Total amount: $908,325 (15% need-based, 85% non-need-based). Part-time jobs available.
**APPLYING FOR FINANCIAL AID** *Required financial aid forms:* FAFSA, CSS Financial Aid PROFILE, noncustodial (divorced/separated) parent's statement. *Financial aid deadline:* 3/1. *Notification date:* 4/15. Students must reply by 5/1.
**CONTACT** Mr. Michael Morgan, Director of Financial Aid, Rhodes College, 2000 North Parkway, Memphis, TN 38112-1690, 901-843-3808 or toll-free 800-844-5969. *Fax:* 901-843-3435. *E-mail:* morganm@rhodes.edu.
*Website:* http://www.rhodes.edu/.

# RICE UNIVERSITY
## Houston, TX

| Tuition & fees: $40,566 | Average undergraduate aid package: $39,201 |
|---|---|

**ABOUT THE INSTITUTION** Independent, coed. *Awards:* bachelor's, master's, and doctoral degrees. 58 undergraduate majors. *Total enrollment:* 6,621. Undergraduates: 3,926. Freshmen: 949. Both federal and institutional methodology are used as a basis for awarding need-based institutional aid.
**UNDERGRADUATE EXPENSES for 2015–2016** *Application fee:* $75. *One-time required fee:* $575. *Comprehensive fee:* $53,966 includes full-time tuition ($39,880), mandatory fees ($686), and room and board ($13,400). *College room only:* $9100. *Part-time tuition:* $1662 per credit hour.
**FRESHMAN FINANCIAL AID (Fall 2014, est.)** 822 applied for aid; of those 46% were deemed to have need. 99% of freshmen with need received aid; of those 100% had need fully met. *Average percent of need met:* 100% (excluding resources awarded to replace EFC). *Average financial aid package:* $38,034 (excluding resources awarded to replace EFC). 7% of all full-time freshmen had no need and received non-need-based gift aid.
**UNDERGRADUATE FINANCIAL AID (Fall 2014, est.)** 2,990 applied for aid; of those 52% were deemed to have need. 99% of undergraduates with need received aid; of those 100% had need fully met. *Average percent of need met:* 100% (excluding resources awarded to replace EFC). *Average financial aid package:* $39,201 (excluding resources awarded to replace EFC). 13% of all full-time undergraduates had no need and received non-need-based gift aid.
**GIFT AID (NEED-BASED)** *Total amount:* $53,422,739 (5% federal, 4% state, 91% institutional). *Receiving aid:* Freshmen: 39% (366); all full-time undergraduates: 39% (1,526). *Average award:* Freshmen: $33,235; Undergraduates: $34,954. *Scholarships, grants, and awards:* Federal Pell, FSEOG, state, private, college/university gift aid from institutional funds.
**GIFT AID (NON-NEED-BASED)** *Total amount:* $10,832,515 (4% federal, 67% institutional, 29% external sources). *Receiving aid:* Freshmen: 2% (16). Undergraduates: 1% (59). *Average award:* Freshmen: $22,748. Undergraduates: $13,730. *Scholarships, grants, and awards by category:* Academic interests/achievement: engineering/technologies, general academic interests/achievements. Creative arts/performance: art/fine arts, music. Special achievements/activities: general special achievements/activities, leadership. Special characteristics: local/state students, members of minority groups. *Tuition waivers:* Full or partial for employees or children of employees. *ROTC:* Army cooperative, Naval, Air Force cooperative.
**LOANS** *Student loans:* $5,501,926 (35% need-based, 65% non-need-based). 29% of past graduating class borrowed through all loan programs. *Average indebtedness per student:* $22,241. *Average need-based loan:* Freshmen: $3201. Undergraduates: $3593. *Parent loans:* $2,588,737 (100% non-need-based). *Programs:* Federal Direct (Subsidized and Unsubsidized Stafford, PLUS), Perkins, state.
**WORK-STUDY** *Federal work-study:* Total amount: $2,357,765; jobs available. *State or other work-study/employment:* Total amount: $14,895 (100% need-based). Part-time jobs available.
**ATHLETIC AWARDS** Total amount: $11,607,096 (3% need-based, 97% non-need-based).
**APPLYING FOR FINANCIAL AID** *Required financial aid forms:* FAFSA, CSS Financial Aid PROFILE, noncustodial (divorced/separated) parent's statement, business/farm supplement, federal income tax form(s), W-2 forms. *Financial aid deadline (priority):* 3/1. *Notification date:* Continuous beginning 4/1. Students must reply by 5/1.
**CONTACT** Ms. Anne Walker, Director of Student Financial Services, Rice University, 116 Allen Center, MS 12, Houston, TX 77005, 713-348-4958. *Fax:* 713-348-2139. *E-mail:* fina@rice.edu.
*Website:* http://www.rice.edu/.

# RIDER UNIVERSITY
## Lawrenceville, NJ

| Tuition & fees: $36,830 | Average undergraduate aid package: $25,946 |
|---|---|

**ABOUT THE INSTITUTION** Independent, coed. *Awards:* certificates, associate, bachelor's, and master's degrees. 66 undergraduate majors. *Total enrollment:* 5,326. Undergraduates: 4,324. Freshmen: 1,000. Federal methodology is used as a basis for awarding need-based institutional aid.
**UNDERGRADUATE EXPENSES for 2015–2016** *Application fee:* $50. *Comprehensive fee:* $50,160 includes full-time tuition ($36,120), mandatory fees ($710), and room and board ($13,330). *College room only:* $8570. Room and board charges vary according to board plan and housing facility. *Part-time tuition:* $1060 per credit. *Part-time fees:* $13.33 per credit. Part-time tuition and fees vary according to program.
**FRESHMAN FINANCIAL AID (Fall 2014, est.)** 922 applied for aid; of those 89% were deemed to have need. 100% of freshmen with need received aid; of those 14% had need fully met. *Average percent of need met:* 75% (excluding resources awarded to replace EFC). *Average financial aid package:* $29,235 (excluding resources awarded to replace EFC). 18% of all full-time freshmen had no need and received non-need-based gift aid.
**UNDERGRADUATE FINANCIAL AID (Fall 2014, est.)** 3,080 applied for aid; of those 90% were deemed to have need. 100% of undergraduates with need received aid; of those 15% had need fully met. *Average percent of need met:* 72% (excluding resources awarded to replace EFC). *Average financial aid package:* $25,946 (excluding resources awarded to replace EFC). 22% of all full-time undergraduates had no need and received non-need-based gift aid.
**GIFT AID (NEED-BASED)** *Total amount:* $56,012,258 (10% federal, 14% state, 75% institutional, 1% external sources). *Receiving aid:* Freshmen: 82% (816); all full-time undergraduates: 72% (2,736). *Average award:* Freshmen: $24,590; Undergraduates: $21,742. *Scholarships, grants, and awards:* Federal Pell, state, college/university gift aid from institutional funds.
**GIFT AID (NON-NEED-BASED)** *Total amount:* $15,549,624 (3% federal, 96% institutional, 1% external sources). *Receiving aid:* Freshmen: 11% (107). Undergraduates: 10% (387). *Average award:* Freshmen: $16,233. Undergraduates: $14,955. *Scholarships, grants, and awards by category:* Academic interests/achievement: general academic interests/achievements. Creative arts/performance: theater/drama. Special characteristics: members of minority groups. *ROTC:* Army cooperative.
**LOANS** *Student loans:* $28,353,728 (100% need-based). 73% of past graduating class borrowed through all loan programs. *Average indebtedness per student:* $28,080. *Average need-based loan:* Freshmen: $2906. Undergraduates: $3701. *Parent loans:* $10,202,642 (55% need-based, 45% non-need-based). *Programs:* Federal Direct (Subsidized and Unsubsidized Stafford, PLUS), Perkins, state, alternative loans.
**WORK-STUDY** *Federal work-study:* Total amount: $3,807,609; jobs available. *State or other work-study/employment:* Part-time jobs available.
**ATHLETIC AWARDS** Total amount: $3,820,444 (47% need-based, 53% non-need-based).
**APPLYING FOR FINANCIAL AID** *Required financial aid form:* FAFSA. *Financial aid deadline (priority):* 3/1. *Notification date:* Continuous beginning 2/20.
**CONTACT** Dr. Dennis Levy, Director of Financial Aid, Rider University, 2083 Lawrenceville Road, Lawrenceville, NJ 08648-3001, 609-896-5360 or toll-free 800-257-9026. *Fax:* 609-219-4487. *E-mail:* finaid@rider.edu.
*Website:* http://www.rider.edu/.

# RINGLING COLLEGE OF ART AND DESIGN
### Sarasota, FL

| Tuition & fees: $40,040 | Average undergraduate aid package: $20,276 |
|---|---|

**ABOUT THE INSTITUTION** Independent, coed. *Awards:* bachelor's degrees. 10 undergraduate majors. *Total enrollment:* 1,219. Undergraduates: 1,219. Freshmen: 270. Federal methodology is used as a basis for awarding need-based institutional aid.

**UNDERGRADUATE EXPENSES for 2015–2016** *Application fee:* $70. *Comprehensive fee:* $53,620 includes full-time tuition ($36,880), mandatory fees ($3160), and room and board ($13,580). *College room only:* $7220. Full-time tuition and fees vary according to course load, program, and student level. Room and board charges vary according to board plan and housing facility. *Part-time tuition:* $1720 per credit hour. Part-time tuition and fees vary according to course load, program, and student level.

**FRESHMAN FINANCIAL AID (Fall 2014, est.)** 188 applied for aid; of those 90% were deemed to have need. 100% of freshmen with need received aid; of those 8% had need fully met. *Average percent of need met:* 44% (excluding resources awarded to replace EFC). *Average financial aid package:* $19,564 (excluding resources awarded to replace EFC). 24% of all full-time freshmen had no need and received non-need-based gift aid.

**UNDERGRADUATE FINANCIAL AID (Fall 2014, est.)** 790 applied for aid; of those 90% were deemed to have need. 100% of undergraduates with need received aid; of those 5% had need fully met. *Average percent of need met:* 43% (excluding resources awarded to replace EFC). *Average financial aid package:* $20,276 (excluding resources awarded to replace EFC). 14% of all full-time undergraduates had no need and received non-need-based gift aid.

**GIFT AID (NEED-BASED)** *Total amount:* $9,985,914 (17% federal, 15% state, 59% institutional, 9% external sources). *Receiving aid:* Freshmen: 73% (168); all full-time undergraduates: 59% (694). *Average award:* Freshmen: $15,063; Undergraduates: $13,591. *Scholarships, grants, and awards:* Federal Pell, FSEOG, state, private, college/university gift aid from institutional funds.

**GIFT AID (NON-NEED-BASED)** *Total amount:* $2,917,884 (4% state, 90% institutional, 6% external sources). *Receiving aid:* Freshmen: 4% (9). Undergraduates: 2% (20). *Average award:* Freshmen: $13,585. Undergraduates: $15,603. *Scholarships, grants, and awards by category: Academic interests/achievement:* general academic interests/achievements. *Creative arts/performance:* applied art and design, art/fine arts. *Special achievements/activities:* community service. *Tuition waivers:* Full or partial for employees or children of employees.

**LOANS** *Student loans:* $8,083,382 (86% need-based, 14% non-need-based). 67% of past graduating class borrowed through all loan programs. *Average indebtedness per student:* $43,685. *Average need-based loan:* Freshmen: $5194. Undergraduates: $7648. *Parent loans:* $10,708,860 (73% need-based, 27% non-need-based). *Programs:* Federal Direct (Subsidized and Unsubsidized Stafford, PLUS), alternative loans.

**WORK-STUDY** *Federal work-study:* Total amount: $234,235; jobs available. *State or other work-study/employment:* Part-time jobs available.

**APPLYING FOR FINANCIAL AID** *Required financial aid form:* FAFSA. *Financial aid deadline (priority):* 3/1. *Notification date:* Continuous beginning 3/15. Students must reply within 4 weeks of notification.

**CONTACT** Mr. Lee Harrell, Director of Financial Aid, Ringling College of Art and Design, 2700 North Tamiami Trail, Sarasota, FL 34243, 941-359-7532 or toll-free 800-255-7695. *Fax:* 941-359-6107. *E-mail:* lharrell@ringling.edu. *Website:* http://www.ringling.edu/.

# RIO GRANDE BIBLE INSTITUTE
### Edinburg, TX

**CONTACT** Financial Aid Office, Rio Grande Bible Institute, 4300 S US Hwy 281, Edinburg, TX 78539, 956-380-8100. *Website:* http://www.riogrande.edu/.

# RIPON COLLEGE
### Ripon, WI

**CONTACT** Mr. Leigh D. Mlodzik, Dean of Admission and Financial Aid, Ripon College, 300 Seward Street, Ripon, WI 54971, 920-748-8704 or toll-free 800-947-4766. *Fax:* 920-748-8335. *E-mail:* financialaid@ripon.edu. *Website:* http://www.ripon.edu/.

# RIVIER UNIVERSITY
### Nashua, NH

**CONTACT** Valerie Patnaude, Director of Financial Aid, Rivier University, 420 Main Street, Nashua, NH 03060-5086, 603-897-8533 or toll-free 800-44RIVIER. *Fax:* 603-897-8810. *E-mail:* vpatnaude@rivier.edu. *Website:* http://www.rivier.edu/.

# ROANOKE COLLEGE
### Salem, VA

| Tuition & fees: $39,666 | Average undergraduate aid package: $30,036 |
|---|---|

**ABOUT THE INSTITUTION** Independent Evangelical Lutheran Church in America, coed. *Awards:* bachelor's degrees. 32 undergraduate majors. *Total enrollment:* 2,054. Undergraduates: 2,054. Freshmen: 562. Federal methodology is used as a basis for awarding need-based institutional aid.

**UNDERGRADUATE EXPENSES for 2015–2016** *One-time required fee:* $125. *Comprehensive fee:* $52,036 includes full-time tuition ($38,302), mandatory fees ($1364), and room and board ($12,370). *College room only:* $5746. Full-time tuition and fees vary according to reciprocity agreements. Room and board charges vary according to board plan and housing facility. *Part-time tuition:* $1832 per course. *Part-time fees:* $38 per term. Part-time tuition and fees vary according to course load and reciprocity agreements.

**FRESHMAN FINANCIAL AID (Fall 2014, est.)** 487 applied for aid; of those 88% were deemed to have need. 100% of freshmen with need received aid; of those 22% had need fully met. *Average percent of need met:* 80% (excluding resources awarded to replace EFC). *Average financial aid package:* $31,100 (excluding resources awarded to replace EFC). 24% of all full-time freshmen had no need and received non-need-based gift aid.

**UNDERGRADUATE FINANCIAL AID (Fall 2014, est.)** 1,655 applied for aid; of those 88% were deemed to have need. 100% of undergraduates with need received aid; of those 20% had need fully met. *Average percent of need met:* 79% (excluding resources awarded to replace EFC). *Average financial aid package:* $30,036 (excluding resources awarded to replace EFC). 25% of all full-time undergraduates had no need and received non-need-based gift aid.

**GIFT AID (NEED-BASED)** *Total amount:* $36,313,300 (6% federal, 7% state, 83% institutional, 4% external sources). *Receiving aid:* Freshmen: 76% (427); all full-time undergraduates: 72% (1,442). *Average award:* Freshmen: $26,367; Undergraduates: $24,298. *Scholarships, grants, and awards:* Federal Pell, FSEOG, state, private, college/university gift aid from institutional funds.

**GIFT AID (NON-NEED-BASED)** *Total amount:* $8,898,137 (7% state, 86% institutional, 7% external sources). *Receiving aid:* Freshmen: 75% (424). Undergraduates: 71% (1,416). *Average award:* Freshmen: $16,635. Undergraduates: $15,554. *Scholarships, grants, and awards by category: Academic interests/achievement:* general academic interests/achievements. *Creative arts/performance:* art/fine arts, music. *Tuition waivers:* Full or partial for employees or children of employees, adult students, senior citizens.

**LOANS** *Student loans:* $14,371,451 (91% need-based, 9% non-need-based). 76% of past graduating class borrowed through all loan programs. *Average indebtedness per student:* $34,320. *Average need-based loan:* Freshmen: $4185. Undergraduates: $4854. *Parent loans:* $3,801,697 (90% need-based, 10% non-need-based). *Programs:* Federal Direct (Subsidized and Unsubsidized Stafford, PLUS), Perkins, college/university, alternative loans.

**WORK-STUDY** *Federal work-study:* Total amount: $1,567,685; jobs available.

**APPLYING FOR FINANCIAL AID** *Required financial aid forms:* FAFSA, state aid form. *Financial aid deadline (priority):* 3/1. *Notification date:* Continuous beginning 10/1. Students must reply within 2 weeks of notification.

**CONTACT** Mr. Thomas S. Blair Jr., Director of Financial Aid, Roanoke College, 221 College Lane, Salem, VA 24153-3794, 540-375-2235 or toll-free 800-388-2276. *E-mail:* finaid@roanoke.edu.
*Website:* http://www.roanoke.edu/.

# THE ROBERT B. MILLER COLLEGE
### Battle Creek, MI

**CONTACT** Mrs. Kimberly Cvitkovic, Dean of Student Services and Director of Financial Aid, The Robert B. Miller College, 450 North Avenue, Battle Creek, MI 49017, 269-660-8021 Ext. 2926. *Fax:* 269-565-2180. *E-mail:* cvitkovick@millercollege.edu .
*Website:* http://www.millercollege.edu/.

# ROBERT MORRIS UNIVERSITY
### Moon Township, PA

Tuition & fees: $26,054 — Average undergraduate aid package: $20,822

**ABOUT THE INSTITUTION** Independent, coed. *Awards:* certificates, bachelor's, master's, and doctoral degrees. 30 undergraduate majors. *Total enrollment:* 5,555. Undergraduates: 4,574. Freshmen: 864. Federal methodology is used as a basis for awarding need-based institutional aid.

**UNDERGRADUATE EXPENSES for 2015–2016** *Application fee:* $30. *Comprehensive fee:* $37,864 includes full-time tuition ($25,380), mandatory fees ($674), and room and board ($11,810). *College room only:* $5640. Full-time tuition and fees vary according to degree level and program. Room and board charges vary according to board plan and housing facility. *Part-time tuition:* $820 per credit hour. *Part-time fees:* $40 per credit hour. Part-time tuition and fees vary according to course load, degree level, and program.

**FRESHMAN FINANCIAL AID (Fall 2014, est.)** 727 applied for aid; of those 90% were deemed to have need. 100% of freshmen with need received aid; of those 13% had need fully met. *Average percent of need met:* 75% (excluding resources awarded to replace EFC). *Average financial aid package:* $22,315 (excluding resources awarded to replace EFC). 15% of all full-time freshmen had no need and received non-need-based gift aid.

**UNDERGRADUATE FINANCIAL AID (Fall 2014, est.)** 2,644 applied for aid; of those 91% were deemed to have need. 100% of undergraduates with need received aid; of those 12% had need fully met. *Average percent of need met:* 73% (excluding resources awarded to replace EFC). *Average financial aid package:* $20,822 (excluding resources awarded to replace EFC). 15% of all full-time undergraduates had no need and received non-need-based gift aid.

**GIFT AID (NEED-BASED)** *Total amount:* $37,508,868 (19% federal, 16% state, 61% institutional, 4% external sources). *Receiving aid:* Freshmen: 76% (655); all full-time undergraduates: 74% (2,319). *Average award:* Freshmen: $16,939; Undergraduates: $14,359. *Scholarships, grants, and awards:* Federal Pell, FSEOG, state, private, college/university gift aid from institutional funds.

**GIFT AID (NON-NEED-BASED)** *Total amount:* $15,758,282 (8% federal, 1% state, 48% institutional, 43% external sources). *Receiving aid:* Freshmen: 8% (67). Undergraduates: 7% (208). *Average award:* Freshmen: $11,944. Undergraduates: $10,733. *Scholarships, grants, and awards by category:* Academic interests/achievement: general academic interests/achievements. *Special characteristics:* children of faculty/staff, veterans. *Tuition waivers:* Full or partial for employees or children of employees. *ROTC:* Army, Air Force cooperative.

**LOANS** *Student loans:* $33,253,114 (74% need-based, 26% non-need-based). 85% of past graduating class borrowed through all loan programs. *Average indebtedness per student:* $37,531. *Average need-based loan:* Freshmen: $4650. Undergraduates: $5981. *Parent loans:* $11,061,061 (51% need-based, 49% non-need-based). *Programs:* Federal Direct (Subsidized and Unsubsidized Stafford, PLUS), Perkins, private loans.

**WORK-STUDY** *Federal work-study:* Total amount: $4,601,901; jobs available. *State or other work-study/employment:* Part-time jobs available.
**ATHLETIC AWARDS** Total amount: $3,809,201 (45% need-based, 55% non-need-based).
**APPLYING FOR FINANCIAL AID** *Required financial aid form:* FAFSA. *Financial aid deadline:* Continuous. *Notification date:* Continuous beginning 3/1. Students must reply within 2 weeks of notification.
**CONTACT** Ms. Stephanie Hendershot, Director of Financial Aid, Robert Morris University, 6001 University Boulevard, Moon Township, PA 15108-1189, 412-397-6250 or toll-free 800-762-0097. *Fax:* 412-397-2200. *E-mail:* finaid@rmu.edu.
*Website:* http://www.rmu.edu/.

# ROBERT MORRIS UNIVERSITY ILLINOIS
### Chicago, IL

Tuition & fees: $25,200 — Average undergraduate aid package: $16,097

**ABOUT THE INSTITUTION** Independent, coed. *Awards:* associate, bachelor's, and master's degrees. 15 undergraduate majors. *Total enrollment:* 3,205. Undergraduates: 2,779. Freshmen: 727. Federal methodology is used as a basis for awarding need-based institutional aid.

**UNDERGRADUATE EXPENSES for 2015–2016** *Application fee:* $20. *Comprehensive fee:* $37,800 includes full-time tuition ($25,200) and room and board ($12,600). *Part-time tuition:* $700 per credit hour. Part-time tuition and fees vary according to course load.

**FRESHMAN FINANCIAL AID (Fall 2014, est.)** 835 applied for aid; of those 97% were deemed to have need. 96% of freshmen with need received aid; of those 5% had need fully met. *Average percent of need met:* 51% (excluding resources awarded to replace EFC). *Average financial aid package:* $16,234 (excluding resources awarded to replace EFC). 5% of all full-time freshmen had no need and received non-need-based gift aid.

**UNDERGRADUATE FINANCIAL AID (Fall 2014, est.)** 3,380 applied for aid; of those 96% were deemed to have need. 92% of undergraduates with need received aid; of those 4% had need fully met. *Average percent of need met:* 49% (excluding resources awarded to replace EFC). *Average financial aid package:* $16,097 (excluding resources awarded to replace EFC). 2% of all full-time undergraduates had no need and received non-need-based gift aid.

**GIFT AID (NEED-BASED)** *Total amount:* $20,455,003 (52% federal, 27% state, 21% institutional). *Receiving aid:* Freshmen: 87% (762); all full-time undergraduates: 83% (2,931). *Average award:* Freshmen: $12,301; Undergraduates: $12,298. *Scholarships, grants, and awards:* Federal Pell, FSEOG, state, private, college/university gift aid from institutional funds.

**GIFT AID (NON-NEED-BASED)** *Total amount:* $12,450,686 (98% institutional, 2% external sources). *Receiving aid:* Freshmen: 59% (512). Undergraduates: 76% (2,703). *Average award:* Freshmen: $10,909. Undergraduates: $11,374. *Scholarships, grants, and awards by category:* Academic interests/achievement: architecture, business, computer science, general academic interests/achievements, health fields. *Creative arts/performance:* applied art and design, dance, journalism/publications, music, performing arts. *Special achievements/activities:* cheerleading/drum major, community service, general special achievements/activities, leadership. *Special characteristics:* adult students, children of faculty/staff, children of public servants, general special characteristics, local/state students, out-of-state students, veterans. *Tuition waivers:* Full or partial for employees or children of employees. *ROTC:* Army cooperative.

**LOANS** *Student loans:* $21,073,105 (95% need-based, 5% non-need-based). 98% of past graduating class borrowed through all loan programs. *Average indebtedness per student:* $31,562. *Average need-based loan:* Freshmen: $3855. Undergraduates: $4152. *Parent loans:* $3,458,389 (89% need-based, 11% non-need-based). *Programs:* Federal Direct (Subsidized and Unsubsidized Stafford, PLUS), Perkins.
**WORK-STUDY** *Federal work-study:* Total amount: $187,398; 164 jobs averaging $1168.
**ATHLETIC AWARDS** Total amount: $6,555,903 (87% need-based, 13% non-need-based).
**APPLYING FOR FINANCIAL AID** *Required financial aid form:* FAFSA. *Financial aid deadline:* Continuous. *Notification date:* Continuous.

**CONTACT** Leigh Brinson, Vice President of Financial Services, Robert Morris University Illinois, 401 South State Street, Suite 122, Chicago, IL 60605, 312-935-4408 or toll-free 800-762-5960. *Fax:* 312-935-4415. *E-mail:* lbrinson@robertmorris.edu. *Website:* http://www.robertmorris.edu/.

---

# ROBERTS WESLEYAN COLLEGE
### Rochester, NY

| Tuition & fees: $28,068 | Average undergraduate aid package: $21,535 |
|---|---|

**ABOUT THE INSTITUTION** Independent Free Methodist Church of North America, coed. *Awards:* bachelor's and master's degrees. 57 undergraduate majors. *Total enrollment:* 1,762. Undergraduates: 1,336. Freshmen: 256. Federal methodology is used as a basis for awarding need-based institutional aid.

**UNDERGRADUATE EXPENSES for 2015–2016 One-time required fee:** $398. *Comprehensive fee:* $37,908 includes full-time tuition ($27,036), mandatory fees ($1032), and room and board ($9840). *College room only:* $6290. Room and board charges vary according to board plan and housing facility. Part-time tuition and fees vary according to course load.

**FRESHMAN FINANCIAL AID (Fall 2014, est.)** 219 applied for aid; of those 92% were deemed to have need. 100% of freshmen with need received aid; of those 17% had need fully met. *Average percent of need met:* 80% (excluding resources awarded to replace EFC). *Average financial aid package:* $25,944 (excluding resources awarded to replace EFC). 13% of all full-time freshmen had no need and received non-need-based gift aid.

**UNDERGRADUATE FINANCIAL AID (Fall 2014, est.)** 1,008 applied for aid; of those 95% were deemed to have need. 100% of undergraduates with need received aid; of those 13% had need fully met. *Average percent of need met:* 71% (excluding resources awarded to replace EFC). *Average financial aid package:* $21,535 (excluding resources awarded to replace EFC). 14% of all full-time undergraduates had no need and received non-need-based gift aid.

**GIFT AID (NEED-BASED) Total amount:** $15,439,778 (16% federal, 9% state, 64% institutional, 11% external sources). *Receiving aid:* Freshmen: 86% (202); all full-time undergraduates: 83% (928). *Average award:* Freshmen: $20,753; Undergraduates: $16,339. *Scholarships, grants, and awards:* Federal Pell, FSEOG, state, private, college/university gift aid from institutional funds, Academic Competitiveness Grants, National SMART Grants, TEACH Grants.

**GIFT AID (NON-NEED-BASED) Total amount:** $2,689,801 (1% state, 76% institutional, 23% external sources). *Receiving aid:* Freshmen: 12% (29). Undergraduates: 8% (94). *Average award:* Freshmen: $12,875. Undergraduates: $9673. *Scholarships, grants, and awards by category:* Academic interests/achievement: 444 awards ($3,165,650 total): general academic interests/achievements. *Creative arts/performance:* 104 awards ($249,739 total): art/fine arts, music. *Special achievements/activities:* 322 awards ($1,126,325 total): general special achievements/activities, junior miss. *Special characteristics:* 426 awards ($1,333,678 total): children and siblings of alumni, children of faculty/staff, international students, out-of-state students, relatives of clergy, religious affiliation, siblings of current students. *Tuition waivers:* Full or partial for employees or children of employees, senior citizens. *ROTC:* Army cooperative, Air Force cooperative.

**LOANS Student loans:** $9,501,004 (83% need-based, 17% non-need-based). 88% of past graduating class borrowed through all loan programs. *Average indebtedness per student:* $35,461. *Average need-based loan:* Freshmen: $4934. Undergraduates: $5435. *Parent loans:* $2,890,048 (41% need-based, 59% non-need-based). *Programs:* Federal Direct (Subsidized and Unsubsidized Stafford, PLUS), Perkins.

**WORK-STUDY Federal work-study:** Total amount: $281,700; 723 jobs averaging $390. *State or other work-study/employment:* Total amount: $70,000 (100% non-need-based). 36 part-time jobs averaging $1944.

**ATHLETIC AWARDS** Total amount: $1,457,685 (64% need-based, 36% non-need-based).

**APPLYING FOR FINANCIAL AID Required financial aid forms:** FAFSA, state aid form. *Financial aid deadline (priority):* 3/15. *Notification date:* Continuous beginning 3/15. Students must reply by 5/1 or within 2 weeks of notification.

**CONTACT** Office of Financial Aid, Roberts Wesleyan College, 2301 Westside Drive, Rochester, NY 14624-1997, 585-594-6150 or toll-free 800-777-4RWC. *Fax:* 585-594-6036. *E-mail:* finaid@roberts.edu. *Website:* http://www.roberts.edu/.

---

# ROCHESTER COLLEGE
### Rochester Hills, MI

| Tuition & fees: N/R | Average undergraduate aid package: N/A |
|---|---|

**ABOUT THE INSTITUTION** Independent Church of Christ, coed. 30 undergraduate majors. Both federal and institutional methodology are used as a basis for awarding need-based institutional aid.

**GIFT AID (NEED-BASED) Total amount:** $6,056,512 (32% federal, 11% state, 50% institutional, 7% external sources). *Scholarships, grants, and awards:* Federal Pell, FSEOG, state, private, college/university gift aid from institutional funds.

**GIFT AID (NON-NEED-BASED) Scholarships, grants, and awards by category:** *Academic interests/achievement:* business, computer science, education, general academic interests/achievements, mathematics, religion/biblical studies. *Creative arts/performance:* journalism/publications, music, theater/drama. *Special achievements/activities:* general special achievements/activities, leadership. *Special characteristics:* adult students, children and siblings of alumni, children of faculty/staff, first-generation college students, general special characteristics, local/state students, out-of-state students, previous college experience, relatives of clergy, religious affiliation, siblings of current students.

**LOANS Student loans:** $7,284,485 (100% need-based). *Parent loans:* $837,093 (100% need-based). *Programs:* Federal Direct (Subsidized and Unsubsidized Stafford, PLUS), Perkins.

**WORK-STUDY Federal work-study:** jobs available. *State or other work-study/employment:* Part-time jobs available.

**ATHLETIC AWARDS** Total amount: $838,493 (100% need-based).

**APPLYING FOR FINANCIAL AID Required financial aid form:** FAFSA. *Financial aid deadline:* Continuous. *Notification date:* Continuous beginning 1/1.

**CONTACT** Student Financial Services, Rochester College, 800 West Avon Road, Rochester Hills, MI 48307, 248-218-2038 or toll-free 800-521-6010. *Fax:* 248-218-2065. *Website:* http://www.rc.edu/.

---

# ROCHESTER INSTITUTE OF TECHNOLOGY
### Rochester, NY

| Tuition & fees: $36,038 | Average undergraduate aid package: $24,000 |
|---|---|

**ABOUT THE INSTITUTION** Independent, coed. *Awards:* certificates, associate, bachelor's, master's, and doctoral degrees. 113 undergraduate majors. *Total enrollment:* 16,320. Undergraduates: 13,460. Freshmen: 2,678. Both federal and institutional methodology are used as a basis for awarding need-based institutional aid.

**UNDERGRADUATE EXPENSES for 2015–2016 Application fee:** $60. *Comprehensive fee:* $47,606 includes full-time tuition ($35,526), mandatory fees ($512), and room and board ($11,568). *College room only:* $6758. Full-time tuition and fees vary according to course load. Room and board charges vary according to board plan and housing facility. *Part-time tuition:* $1259 per credit hour. *Part-time fees:* $65 per term. Part-time tuition and fees vary according to class time and course load. *Payment plan:* Tuition prepayment.

**FRESHMAN FINANCIAL AID (Fall 2013)** 2,447 applied for aid; of those 86% were deemed to have need. 100% of freshmen with need received aid; of those 81% had need fully met. *Average percent of need met:* 87% (excluding resources awarded to replace EFC). *Average financial aid package:* $24,500 (excluding resources awarded to replace EFC). 17% of all full-time freshmen had no need and received non-need-based gift aid.

**UNDERGRADUATE FINANCIAL AID (Fall 2013)** 10,068 applied for aid; of those 91% were deemed to have need. 99% of undergraduates with need received aid; of those 83% had need fully met. *Average percent of need met:* 87% (excluding resources awarded to replace EFC). *Average financial aid package:* $24,000 (excluding resources awarded to replace EFC). 13% of all full-time undergraduates had no need and received non-need-based gift aid.

**GIFT AID (NEED-BASED) Total amount:** $141,175,669 (13% federal, 5% state, 82% institutional). *Receiving aid:* Freshmen: 72% (1,999); all full-time undergraduates: 7% (820). *Average award:* Freshmen: $20,500; Undergraduates: $19,000.

**Scholarships, grants, and awards:** Federal Pell, FSEOG, state, private, college/university gift aid from institutional funds, United Negro College Fund, NACME Scholarships, National Science Foundation Grants.

**GIFT AID (NON-NEED-BASED) Total amount:** $43,565,050 (19% federal, 24% state, 49% institutional, 8% external sources). **Receiving aid:** Freshmen: 22% (606). Undergraduates: 22% (2,606). **Average award:** Freshmen: $12,000. Undergraduates: $10,000. **Scholarships, grants, and awards by category:** Academic interests/achievement: biological sciences, business, communication, computer science, engineering/technologies, general academic interests/achievements, health fields, international studies, mathematics, military science, physical sciences, premedicine, social sciences. Creative arts/performance: applied art and design, art/fine arts, cinema/film/broadcasting. Special achievements/activities: community service, leadership. Special characteristics: children of faculty/staff, veterans. **Tuition waivers:** Full or partial for employees or children of employees. **ROTC:** Army, Naval cooperative, Air Force.

**LOANS Student loans:** $81,917,893 (55% need-based, 45% non-need-based). 68% of past graduating class borrowed through all loan programs. Average indebtedness per student: $26,000. **Average need-based loan:** Freshmen: $3600. Undergraduates: $5500. **Parent loans:** $24,017,344 (41% need-based, 59% non-need-based). **Programs:** Federal Direct (Subsidized and Unsubsidized Stafford, PLUS), Perkins.

**WORK-STUDY Federal work-study:** 1,800 jobs averaging $2600. **State or other work-study/employment:** Total amount: $12,064,346 (100% non-need-based). Part-time jobs available.

**APPLYING FOR FINANCIAL AID Required financial aid forms:** FAFSA, state aid form. **Financial aid deadline (priority):** 3/1. **Notification date:** Continuous beginning 3/15. Students must reply by 5/1.

**CONTACT** Mrs. Verna Hazen, Associate Vice President for Financial Aid and Scholarships, Rochester Institute of Technology, 56 Lomb Memorial Drive, Rochester, NY 14623-5604, 585-475-2186. Fax: 585-475-7270. E-mail: verna.hazen@rit.edu. Website: http://www.rit.edu/.

# ROCKFORD UNIVERSITY
## Rockford, IL

| Tuition & fees: $27,530 | Average undergraduate aid package: $18,844 |
|---|---|

**ABOUT THE INSTITUTION** Independent, coed. **Awards:** certificates, bachelor's, and master's degrees. 51 undergraduate majors. **Total enrollment:** 1,284. Undergraduates: 1,032. Freshmen: 147. Federal methodology is used as a basis for awarding need-based institutional aid.

**UNDERGRADUATE EXPENSES for 2015-2016 Comprehensive fee:** $35,240 includes full-time tuition ($27,400), mandatory fees ($130), and room and board ($7710). **College room only:** $4190. Full-time tuition and fees vary according to course load. Room and board charges vary according to board plan and housing facility. **Part-time tuition:** $735 per credit. Part-time tuition and fees vary according to course load.

**FRESHMAN FINANCIAL AID (Fall 2013)** 98 applied for aid; of those 96% were deemed to have need. 100% of freshmen with need received aid; of those 15% had need fully met. **Average percent of need met:** 69% (excluding resources awarded to replace EFC). **Average financial aid package:** $19,248 (excluding resources awarded to replace EFC). 8% of all full-time freshmen had no need and received non-need-based gift aid.

**UNDERGRADUATE FINANCIAL AID (Fall 2013)** 723 applied for aid; of those 96% were deemed to have need. 100% of undergraduates with need received aid; of those 11% had need fully met. **Average percent of need met:** 66% (excluding resources awarded to replace EFC). **Average financial aid package:** $18,844 (excluding resources awarded to replace EFC). 7% of all full-time undergraduates had no need and received non-need-based gift aid.

**GIFT AID (NEED-BASED) Total amount:** $10,525,297 (19% federal, 17% state, 62% institutional, 2% external sources). **Receiving aid:** Freshmen: 90% (93); all full-time undergraduates: 91% (686). **Average award:** Freshmen: $15,881; Undergraduates: $13,997. **Scholarships, grants, and awards:** Federal Pell, FSEOG, state, private, college/university gift aid from institutional funds.

**GIFT AID (NON-NEED-BASED) Total amount:** $1,096,087 (89% institutional, 11% external sources). **Receiving aid:** Freshmen: 14% (14). Undergraduates: 10% (78). **Average award:** Freshmen: $10,476. Undergraduates: $9444. **Scholarships, grants, and awards by category:** Academic interests/achievement: 846 awards

($6,183,501 total): biological sciences, business, computer science, education, English, foreign languages, general academic interests/achievements, mathematics, physical sciences, premedicine, social sciences. Creative arts/performance: 25 awards ($72,375 total): art/fine arts, dance, music, performing arts, theater/drama. Special achievements/activities: 3 awards ($4069 total): community service, leadership. Special characteristics: 165 awards ($648,818 total): children and siblings of alumni, children of current students, children of educators, children of faculty/staff, general special characteristics, international students, out-of-state students, parents of current students, siblings of current students. **Tuition waivers:** Full or partial for employees or children of employees.

**LOANS Student loans:** $8,312,317 (86% need-based, 14% non-need-based). 86% of past graduating class borrowed through all loan programs. Average indebtedness per student: $39,619. **Average need-based loan:** Freshmen: $3780. Undergraduates: $5191. **Parent loans:** $1,214,133 (49% need-based, 51% non-need-based). **Programs:** Federal Direct (Subsidized and Unsubsidized Stafford, PLUS), Perkins, college/university, alternative loans.

**WORK-STUDY Federal work-study:** 120 jobs averaging $734. **State or other work-study/employment:** Total amount: $127,040 (35% need-based, 65% non-need-based). 172 part-time jobs averaging $771.

**APPLYING FOR FINANCIAL AID Required financial aid form:** FAFSA. **Financial aid deadline (priority):** 3/1. **Notification date:** Continuous beginning 3/15. Students must reply within 4 weeks of notification.

**CONTACT** Todd M. Fischer-Free, Assistant Vice President of Student Administrative Services, Rockford University, 5050 East State Street, Rockford, IL 61108, 815-226-3385 or toll-free 800-892-2984. Fax: 815-394-5174. E-mail: tfree@rockford.edu. Website: http://www.rockford.edu/.

# ROCKHURST UNIVERSITY
## Kansas City, MO

| Tuition & fees: $32,865 | Average undergraduate aid package: $24,834 |
|---|---|

**ABOUT THE INSTITUTION** Independent Roman Catholic (Jesuit), coed. **Awards:** certificates, bachelor's, master's, and doctoral degrees. 30 undergraduate majors. **Total enrollment:** 3,002. Undergraduates: 2,276. Freshmen: 399. Federal methodology is used as a basis for awarding need-based institutional aid.

**UNDERGRADUATE EXPENSES for 2015-2016 Application fee:** $25. **Comprehensive fee:** $41,945 includes full-time tuition ($32,075), mandatory fees ($790), and room and board ($9080). **College room only:** $5480. Full-time tuition and fees vary according to class time and course load. Room and board charges vary according to board plan and housing facility. **Part-time tuition:** $535 per credit hour. **Part-time fees:** $25 per credit hour. Part-time tuition and fees vary according to class time and course load.

**FRESHMAN FINANCIAL AID (Fall 2013)** 403 applied for aid; of those 66% were deemed to have need. 100% of freshmen with need received aid; of those 30% had need fully met. **Average percent of need met:** 83% (excluding resources awarded to replace EFC). **Average financial aid package:** $25,848 (excluding resources awarded to replace EFC). 27% of all full-time freshmen had no need and received non-need-based gift aid.

**UNDERGRADUATE FINANCIAL AID (Fall 2013)** 1,287 applied for aid; of those 76% were deemed to have need. 100% of undergraduates with need received aid; of those 18% had need fully met. **Average percent of need met:** 77% (excluding resources awarded to replace EFC). **Average financial aid package:** $24,834 (excluding resources awarded to replace EFC). 17% of all full-time undergraduates had no need and received non-need-based gift aid.

**GIFT AID (NEED-BASED) Total amount:** $22,147,273 (7% federal, 4% state, 88% institutional, 1% external sources). **Receiving aid:** Freshmen: 42% (182); all full-time undergraduates: 47% (726). **Average award:** Freshmen: $2695; Undergraduates: $3209. **Scholarships, grants, and awards:** Federal Pell, FSEOG, state, private, college/university gift aid from institutional funds, United Negro College Fund.

**GIFT AID (NON-NEED-BASED) Total amount:** $8,215,160 (1% state, 98% institutional, 1% external sources). **Receiving aid:** Freshmen: 61% (266). Undergraduates: 63% (975). **Average award:** Freshmen: $23,434. Undergraduates: $20,636. **Scholarships, grants, and awards by category:** Academic interests/achievement: biological sciences, business, communication, computer science, education, engineering/technologies, English, foreign languages, general academic interests/achievements, health fields, humanities, international studies, mathematics, physical sciences, premedicine, religion/biblical studies, social sciences. *Creative arts/performance:* creative writing, music, performing arts, theater/drama. *Special achievements/activities:* community service, leadership. *Special characteristics:* children of faculty/staff, siblings of current students. *Tuition waivers:* Full or partial for employees or children of employees, senior citizens. *ROTC:* Army cooperative.

**LOANS** *Student loans:* $7,753,127 (74% need-based, 26% non-need-based). 70% of past graduating class borrowed through all loan programs. *Average indebtedness per student:* $24,852. *Average need-based loan:* Freshmen: $5667. Undergraduates: $5561. *Parent loans:* $2,044,825 (52% need-based, 48% non-need-based). *Programs:* Federal Direct (Subsidized and Unsubsidized Stafford, PLUS), Perkins.

**WORK-STUDY** *Federal work-study:* jobs available. *State or other work-study/employment:* Part-time jobs available.

**ATHLETIC AWARDS** Total amount: $2,669,736 (43% need-based, 57% non-need-based).

**APPLYING FOR FINANCIAL AID** *Required financial aid form:* FAFSA. *Financial aid deadline (priority):* 3/1. *Notification date:* Continuous beginning 3/1. Students must reply by 6/1 or within 4 weeks of notification.

**CONTACT** Maureen McKinnon, Director of Financial Aid, Rockhurst University, 1100 Rockhurst Road, Kansas City, MO 64110-2561, 816-501-4831 or toll-free 800-842-6776. *Fax:* 816-501-3139. *E-mail:* maureen.mckinnon@rockhurst.edu. *Website:* http://www.rockhurst.edu/.

# ROCKY MOUNTAIN COLLEGE
## Billings, MT

| Tuition & fees: $25,252 | Average undergraduate aid package: $22,121 |
| --- | --- |

**ABOUT THE INSTITUTION** Independent interdenominational, coed. *Awards:* associate, bachelor's, and master's degrees. 51 undergraduate majors. *Total enrollment:* 1,031. Undergraduates: 939. Freshmen: 229. Federal methodology is used as a basis for awarding need-based institutional aid.

**UNDERGRADUATE EXPENSES for 2015–2016** *Application fee:* $35. *Comprehensive fee:* $33,196 includes full-time tuition ($24,762), mandatory fees ($490), and room and board ($7944). *College room only:* $3692. Full-time tuition and fees vary according to course load, degree level, and program. Room and board charges vary according to board plan and housing facility. *Part-time tuition:* $1052 per credit. Part-time tuition and fees vary according to course load, degree level, and program.

**FRESHMAN FINANCIAL AID (Fall 2014, est.)** 199 applied for aid; of those 91% were deemed to have need. 100% of freshmen with need received aid; of those 27% had need fully met. *Average percent of need met:* 73% (excluding resources awarded to replace EFC). *Average financial aid package:* $21,481 (excluding resources awarded to replace EFC). 8% of all full-time freshmen had no need and received non-need-based gift aid.

**UNDERGRADUATE FINANCIAL AID (Fall 2014, est.)** 728 applied for aid; of those 89% were deemed to have need. 100% of undergraduates with need received aid; of those 28% had need fully met. *Average percent of need met:* 74% (excluding resources awarded to replace EFC). *Average financial aid package:* $22,121 (excluding resources awarded to replace EFC). 8% of all full-time undergraduates had no need and received non-need-based gift aid.

**GIFT AID (NEED-BASED)** *Total amount:* $10,056,376 (15% federal, 81% institutional, 4% external sources). *Receiving aid:* Freshmen: 79% (181); all full-time undergraduates: 68% (642). *Average award:* Freshmen: $17,537; Undergraduates: $16,829. *Scholarships, grants, and awards:* Federal Pell, FSEOG, state, private, college/university gift aid from institutional funds.

**GIFT AID (NON-NEED-BASED)** *Total amount:* $1,240,672 (92% institutional, 8% external sources). *Receiving aid:* Freshmen: 19% (43). Undergraduates: 17% (155). *Average award:* Freshmen: $11,556. Undergraduates: $10,651. *Scholarships, grants, and awards by category:* Special achievements/activities: 16 awards ($29,200 total): cheerleading/drum major. *Tuition waivers:* Full or partial for employees or children of employees. *ROTC:* Army cooperative.

**LOANS** *Student loans:* $5,538,785 (71% need-based, 29% non-need-based). 69% of past graduating class borrowed through all loan programs. *Average indebtedness per student:* $29,206. *Average need-based loan:* Freshmen: $3337. Undergraduates: $4236. *Parent loans:* $1,195,556 (40% need-based, 60% non-need-based). *Programs:* Federal Direct (Subsidized and Unsubsidized Stafford, PLUS), Perkins.

**WORK-STUDY** *Federal work-study:* Total amount: $142,254; 345 jobs averaging $416. *State or other work-study/employment:* Total amount: $137,560 (66% need-based, 34% non-need-based). 168 part-time jobs averaging $819.

**ATHLETIC AWARDS** Total amount: $2,464,329 (85% need-based, 15% non-need-based).

**APPLYING FOR FINANCIAL AID** *Required financial aid form:* FAFSA. *Financial aid deadline:* Continuous. *Notification date:* Continuous beginning 2/15. Students must reply within 4 weeks of notification.

**CONTACT** Jessica Francischetti, Financial Aid Director, Rocky Mountain College, 1511 Poly Drive, Billings, MT 59102-1796, 406-657-1031 or toll-free 800-877-6259. *Fax:* 406-657-1169. *E-mail:* finaid@rocky.edu. *Website:* http://www.rocky.edu/.

# ROCKY MOUNTAIN COLLEGE OF ART + DESIGN
## Lakewood, CO

**ABOUT THE INSTITUTION** Proprietary, coed. *Awards:* certificates, bachelor's, and master's degrees. 10 undergraduate majors. *Total enrollment:* 1,045. Undergraduates: 1,018. Freshmen: 53.

**GIFT AID (NEED-BASED)** *Scholarships, grants, and awards:* Federal Pell, FSEOG, state, college/university gift aid from institutional funds.

**GIFT AID (NON-NEED-BASED)** *Scholarships, grants, and awards by category:* Academic interests/achievement: general academic interests/achievements. *Creative arts/performance:* applied art and design, art/fine arts. *Special characteristics:* children of faculty/staff.

**LOANS** *Programs:* Federal Direct (Subsidized and Unsubsidized Stafford, PLUS), alternative loans.

**WORK-STUDY** *Federal work-study:* 20 jobs averaging $2984. *State or other work-study/employment:* Total amount: $115,755 (93% need-based, 7% non-need-based). 30 part-time jobs averaging $3606.

**APPLYING FOR FINANCIAL AID** *Required financial aid form:* FAFSA.

**CONTACT** Tammy Dybdahl, Director of Financial Aid, Rocky Mountain College of Art + Design, 1600 Pierce Street, Lakewood, CO 80214, 303-225-8551 or toll-free 800-888-ARTS. *Fax:* 303-567-7280. *E-mail:* tdybdahl@rmcad.edu. *Website:* http://www.rmcad.edu/.

# ROGERS STATE UNIVERSITY
## Claremore, OK

| Tuition & fees (OK res): $5321 | Average undergraduate aid package: $9637 |
| --- | --- |

**ABOUT THE INSTITUTION** State-supported, coed. *Awards:* associate and bachelor's degrees. 25 undergraduate majors. *Total enrollment:* 4,289. Undergraduates: 4,289. Freshmen: 785. Federal methodology is used as a basis for awarding need-based institutional aid.

**UNDERGRADUATE EXPENSES for 2015–2016** *Tuition, state resident:* full-time $3327; part-time $110.90 per hour. *Tuition, nonresident:* full-time $9981; part-time $332.70 per hour. *Required fees:* full-time $1994; $66.45 per hour or $15 per term. Full-time tuition and fees vary according to course level, course load, location, program, and student level. Part-time tuition and fees vary according to course level, course load, location, program, and student level. *College room and board:* $8830. Room and board charges vary according to housing facility.

**FRESHMAN FINANCIAL AID (Fall 2014, est.)** 435 applied for aid; of those 75% were deemed to have need. 98% of freshmen with need received aid; of those 7% had need fully met. *Average percent of need met:* 51% (excluding resources awarded to replace EFC). *Average financial aid package:* $9469 (excluding resources awarded to replace EFC). 3% of all full-time freshmen had no need and received non-need-based gift aid.

**UNDERGRADUATE FINANCIAL AID (Fall 2014, est.)** 1,663 applied for aid; of those 81% were deemed to have need. 98% of undergraduates with need received aid; of those 8% had need fully met. *Average percent of need met:* 50% (excluding resources awarded to replace EFC). *Average financial aid package:* $9637 (excluding resources awarded to replace EFC). 3% of all full-time undergraduates had no need and received non-need-based gift aid.

**GIFT AID (NEED-BASED)** *Total amount:* $12,313,489 (62% federal, 24% state, 4% institutional, 10% external sources). *Receiving aid:* Freshmen: 54% (262); all full-time undergraduates: 55% (1,097). *Average award:* Freshmen: $6333; Undergraduates: $5914. *Scholarships, grants, and awards:* Federal Pell, FSEOG, state, private, college/university gift aid from institutional funds.

**GIFT AID (NON-NEED-BASED)** *Total amount:* $2,115,633 (48% state, 32% institutional, 20% external sources). *Receiving aid:* Freshmen: 26% (128). Undergraduates: 20% (406). *Average award:* Freshmen: $8668. Undergraduates: $8750. *Scholarships, grants, and awards by category:* Academic interests/achievement: 37 awards ($25,123 total): general academic interests/achievements. Creative arts/performance: 21 awards ($22,710 total): music, theater/drama. Special achievements/activities: 51 awards ($226,491 total): cheerleading/drum major, leadership. Special characteristics: 192 awards ($1,116,502 total): adult students, out-of-state students. *Tuition waivers:* Full or partial for employees or children of employees, senior citizens.

**LOANS** *Student loans:* $9,820,990 (89% need-based, 11% non-need-based). 51% of past graduating class borrowed through all loan programs. *Average indebtedness per student:* $13,403. *Average need-based loan:* Freshmen: $3328. Undergraduates: $4081. *Parent loans:* $309,303 (61% need-based, 39% non-need-based). *Programs:* Federal Direct (Subsidized and Unsubsidized Stafford, PLUS), alternative loans.

**WORK-STUDY** *Federal work-study:* Total amount: $123,601; 62 jobs averaging $1994. *State or other work-study/employment:* Total amount: $540,236 (39% need-based, 61% non-need-based). 258 part-time jobs averaging $1934.

**ATHLETIC AWARDS** Total amount: $1,107,463 (45% need-based, 55% non-need-based).

**APPLYING FOR FINANCIAL AID** *Required financial aid form:* FAFSA. *Financial aid deadline (priority):* 6/1. *Notification date:* Continuous beginning 4/1. Students must reply within 2 weeks of notification.

**CONTACT** Ms. Kelly Hicks, Director of Financial Aid, Rogers State University, 1701 West Will Rogers Boulevard, Claremore, OK 74017-3252, 918-343-7553 or toll-free 800-256-7511. *Fax:* 918-343-7598. *E-mail:* finaid@rsu.edu. *Website:* http://www.rsu.edu/.

# ROGER WILLIAMS UNIVERSITY
## Bristol, RI

| Tuition & fees: $31,750 | Average undergraduate aid package: $20,466 |
|---|---|

**ABOUT THE INSTITUTION** Independent, coed. *Awards:* certificates, associate, bachelor's, master's, and doctoral degrees. 55 undergraduate majors. *Total enrollment:* 4,884. Undergraduates: 4,610. Freshmen: 1,152. Both federal and institutional methodology are used as a basis for awarding need-based institutional aid.

**UNDERGRADUATE EXPENSES** for 2015–2016 *Application fee:* $50. *Comprehensive fee:* $46,296 includes full-time tuition ($29,976), mandatory fees ($1774), and room and board ($14,546). Full-time tuition and fees vary according to class time, course load, and program. Room and board charges vary according to board plan and housing facility. *Part-time tuition:* $966 per course. Part-time tuition and fees vary according to class time. *Payment plan:* Guaranteed tuition.

**FRESHMAN FINANCIAL AID (Fall 2014, est.)** 962 applied for aid; of those 79% were deemed to have need. 100% of freshmen with need received aid; of those 9% had need fully met. *Average percent of need met:* 83% (excluding resources awarded to replace EFC). *Average financial aid package:* $20,071 (excluding resources awarded to replace EFC). 16% of all full-time freshmen had no need and received non-need-based gift aid.

**UNDERGRADUATE FINANCIAL AID (Fall 2014, est.)** 2,990 applied for aid; of those 82% were deemed to have need. 99% of undergraduates with need received aid; of those 10% had need fully met. *Average percent of need met:* 89% (excluding resources awarded to replace EFC). *Average financial aid package:* $20,466 (excluding resources awarded to replace EFC). 12% of all full-time undergraduates had no need and received non-need-based gift aid.

**GIFT AID (NEED-BASED)** *Total amount:* $34,680,475 (7% federal, 1% state, 90% institutional, 2% external sources). *Receiving aid:* Freshmen: 50% (577); all full-time undergraduates: 40% (1,604). *Average award:* Freshmen: $14,310; Undergraduates: $13,501. *Scholarships, grants, and awards:* Federal Pell, FSEOG, state, private, college/university gift aid from institutional funds.

**GIFT AID (NON-NEED-BASED)** *Total amount:* $5,668,168 (99% institutional, 1% external sources). *Receiving aid:* Freshmen: 59% (681). Undergraduates: 46%

(1,837). *Average award:* Freshmen: $11,831. Undergraduates: $11,527. *Scholarships, grants, and awards by category:* Academic interests/achievement: 2,956 awards ($32,503,393 total): general academic interests/achievements. *Tuition waivers:* Full or partial for employees or children of employees. *ROTC:* Army cooperative.

**LOANS** *Student loans:* $16,244,915 (86% need-based, 14% non-need-based). 68% of past graduating class borrowed through all loan programs. *Average indebtedness per student:* $40,612. *Average need-based loan:* Freshmen: $3486. Undergraduates: $4752. *Parent loans:* $10,582,544 (91% need-based, 9% non-need-based). *Programs:* Federal Direct (Subsidized and Unsubsidized Stafford, PLUS), Perkins, state.

**WORK-STUDY** *Federal work-study:* Total amount: $497,457; 1,554 jobs averaging $2104. *State or other work-study/employment:* Part-time jobs available.

**APPLYING FOR FINANCIAL AID** *Required financial aid forms:* FAFSA, CSS Financial Aid PROFILE. *Financial aid deadline:* 2/1 (priority: 1/1). *Notification date:* Continuous beginning 3/15. Students must reply within 2 weeks of notification.

**CONTACT** Diane Usher, Associate Director of Student Financial Aid and Planning, Roger Williams University, One Old Ferry Road, Bristol, RI 02809, 800-458-7144 Ext. 3100 or toll-free 800-458-7144. *Fax:* 401-254-3356 . *E-mail:* finaid@rwu.edu . *Website:* http://www.rwu.edu/.

# ROLLINS COLLEGE
## Winter Park, FL

| Tuition & fees: $43,080 | Average undergraduate aid package: $31,352 |
|---|---|

**ABOUT THE INSTITUTION** Independent, coed. *Awards:* bachelor's, master's, and doctoral degrees. 32 undergraduate majors. *Total enrollment:* 2,469. Undergraduates: 1,932. Freshmen: 540. Federal methodology is used as a basis for awarding need-based institutional aid.

**UNDERGRADUATE EXPENSES** for 2015–2016 *Application fee:* $40. *Comprehensive fee:* $56,550 includes full-time tuition ($43,080) and room and board ($13,470). *College room only:* $7920. Room and board charges vary according to housing facility.

**FRESHMAN FINANCIAL AID (Fall 2014, est.)** 334 applied for aid; of those 82% were deemed to have need. 99% of freshmen with need received aid; of those 29% had need fully met. *Average percent of need met:* 77% (excluding resources awarded to replace EFC). *Average financial aid package:* $31,655 (excluding resources awarded to replace EFC). 30% of all full-time freshmen had no need and received non-need-based gift aid.

**UNDERGRADUATE FINANCIAL AID (Fall 2014, est.)** 1,135 applied for aid; of those 86% were deemed to have need. 99% of undergraduates with need received aid; of those 26% had need fully met. *Average percent of need met:* 78% (excluding resources awarded to replace EFC). *Average financial aid package:* $31,352 (excluding resources awarded to replace EFC). 27% of all full-time undergraduates had no need and received non-need-based gift aid.

**GIFT AID (NEED-BASED)** *Total amount:* $25,688,995 (7% federal, 13% state, 79% institutional, 1% external sources). *Receiving aid:* Freshmen: 51% (273); all full-time undergraduates: 50% (964). *Average award:* Freshmen: $26,828; Undergraduates: $26,635. *Scholarships, grants, and awards:* Federal Pell, FSEOG, state, private, college/university gift aid from institutional funds.

**GIFT AID (NON-NEED-BASED)** *Total amount:* $12,738,466 (14% state, 85% institutional, 1% external sources). *Receiving aid:* Freshmen: 7% (37). Undergraduates: 5% (104). *Average award:* Freshmen: $19,788. Undergraduates: $19,134. *Scholarships, grants, and awards by category:* Academic interests/achievement: 105 awards ($519,953 total): computer science, engineering/technologies, general academic interests/achievements, mathematics, physical sciences. Creative arts/performance: 62 awards ($371,300 total): art/fine arts, music, theater/drama. *Tuition waivers:* Full or partial for employees or children of employees.

**LOANS** *Student loans:* $5,934,165 (80% need-based, 20% non-need-based). 56% of past graduating class borrowed through all loan programs. *Average indebtedness per student:* $26,689. *Average need-based loan:* Freshmen: $4835. Undergraduates: $4721. *Parent loans:* $3,277,159 (40% need-based, 60% non-need-based). *Programs:* Federal Direct (Subsidized and Unsubsidized Stafford, PLUS), Perkins.

**WORK-STUDY** *Federal work-study:* Total amount: $401,369; 240 jobs averaging $1705. *State or other work-study/employment:* Total amount: $7982 (100% need-based). 2 part-time jobs averaging $2762.

**ATHLETIC AWARDS** Total amount: $3,772,435 (35% need-based, 65% non-need-based).

**APPLYING FOR FINANCIAL AID** *Required financial aid form:* FAFSA. *Financial aid deadline (priority):* 3/1. *Notification date:* Continuous beginning 3/1. Students must reply by 5/1.

**CONTACT** Mr. Steve Booker, Director of Financial Aid, Rollins College, 1000 Holt Avenue, #2721, Winter Park, FL 32789-4499, 407-646-2395. *Fax:* 407-646-2173. *E-mail:* sbooker@rollins.edu. *Website:* http://www.rollins.edu/.

## ROOSEVELT UNIVERSITY
### Chicago, IL

| Tuition & fees: $27,300 | Average undergraduate aid package: $22,678 |
|---|---|

**ABOUT THE INSTITUTION** Independent, coed. *Awards:* certificates, bachelor's, master's, and doctoral degrees. 57 undergraduate majors. *Total enrollment:* 6,113. Undergraduates: 3,793. Freshmen: 607. Federal methodology is used as a basis for awarding need-based institutional aid.

**UNDERGRADUATE EXPENSES** for 2015–2016 *Application fee:* $25. *Comprehensive fee:* $39,832 includes full-time tuition ($27,300) and room and board ($12,532). Full-time tuition and fees vary according to program. *Part-time tuition:* $737 per credit. Part-time tuition and fees vary according to program.

**FRESHMAN FINANCIAL AID (Fall 2013)** 420 applied for aid; of those 88% were deemed to have need. 96% of freshmen with need received aid; of those 22% had need fully met. *Average percent of need met:* 75% (excluding resources awarded to replace EFC). *Average financial aid package:* $24,450 (excluding resources awarded to replace EFC). 19% of all full-time freshmen had no need and received non-need-based gift aid.

**UNDERGRADUATE FINANCIAL AID (Fall 2013)** 2,608 applied for aid; of those 85% were deemed to have need. 97% of undergraduates with need received aid; of those 8% had need fully met. *Average percent of need met:* 75% (excluding resources awarded to replace EFC). *Average financial aid package:* $22,678 (excluding resources awarded to replace EFC). 18% of all full-time undergraduates had no need and received non-need-based gift aid.

**GIFT AID (NEED-BASED)** *Total amount:* $19,485,091 (32% federal, 25% state, 43% institutional). *Receiving aid:* Freshmen: 71% (305); all full-time undergraduates: 77% (2,100). *Average award:* Freshmen: $12,000; Undergraduates: $9000. *Scholarships, grants, and awards:* Federal Pell, FSEOG, state, private, college/university gift aid from institutional funds.

**GIFT AID (NON-NEED-BASED)** *Total amount:* $22,592,136 (75% institutional, 25% external sources). *Receiving aid:* Freshmen: 83% (356). Undergraduates: 80% (2,156). *Average award:* Freshmen: $11,000. Undergraduates: $7000. *Scholarships, grants, and awards by category:* Academic interests/achievement: general academic interests/achievements. Creative arts/performance: music, theater/drama. Special achievements/activities: general special achievements/activities. Special characteristics: general special characteristics.

**LOANS** *Student loans:* $26,699,042 (100% need-based). *Average need-based loan:* Freshmen: $7000. Undergraduates: $8900. *Parent loans:* $6,503,193 (100% need-based).

**WORK-STUDY** *Federal work-study:* jobs available.

**APPLYING FOR FINANCIAL AID** *Required financial aid forms:* FAFSA, institution's own form. *Financial aid deadline (priority):* 3/1. *Notification date:* Continuous beginning 2/15. Students must reply within 3 weeks of notification.

**CONTACT** Office of Financial Aid, Roosevelt University, 430 South Michigan Avenue, Chicago, IL 60605-1394, 866-421-0935 or toll-free 877-APPLYRU. *Fax:* 312-341-3545. *E-mail:* fao@roosevelt.edu. *Website:* http://www.roosevelt.edu/.

## ROSE-HULMAN INSTITUTE OF TECHNOLOGY
### Terre Haute, IN

| Tuition & fees: $41,283 | Average undergraduate aid package: $28,720 |
|---|---|

**ABOUT THE INSTITUTION** Independent, coed, primarily men. *Awards:* bachelor's and master's degrees. 16 undergraduate majors. *Total enrollment:* 2,388. Undergraduates: 2,280. Freshmen: 582. Federal methodology is used as a basis for awarding need-based institutional aid.

**UNDERGRADUATE EXPENSES** for 2015–2016 *Application fee:* $40. *One-time required fee:* $2400. *Comprehensive fee:* $53,340 includes full-time tuition ($40,449), mandatory fees ($834), and room and board ($12,057). *College room only:* $7392. Full-time tuition and fees vary according to course load. Room and board charges vary according to board plan. *Part-time tuition:* $1181 per credit hour. Part-time tuition and fees vary according to course load. *Payment plan:* Tuition prepayment.

**FRESHMAN FINANCIAL AID (Fall 2014, est.)** 452 applied for aid; of those 84% were deemed to have need. 100% of freshmen with need received aid; of those 20% had need fully met. *Average percent of need met:* 76% (excluding resources awarded to replace EFC). *Average financial aid package:* $29,661 (excluding resources awarded to replace EFC). 34% of all full-time freshmen had no need and received non-need-based gift aid.

**UNDERGRADUATE FINANCIAL AID (Fall 2014, est.)** 1,587 applied for aid; of those 87% were deemed to have need. 100% of undergraduates with need received aid; of those 18% had need fully met. *Average percent of need met:* 74% (excluding resources awarded to replace EFC). *Average financial aid package:* $28,720 (excluding resources awarded to replace EFC). 36% of all full-time undergraduates had no need and received non-need-based gift aid.

**GIFT AID (NEED-BASED)** *Total amount:* $34,280,309 (5% federal, 3% state, 85% institutional, 7% external sources). *Receiving aid:* Freshmen: 57% (334); all full-time undergraduates: 55% (1,207). *Average award:* Freshmen: $25,201; Undergraduates: $23,950. *Scholarships, grants, and awards:* Federal Pell, FSEOG, state, college/university gift aid from institutional funds.

**GIFT AID (NON-NEED-BASED)** *Total amount:* $10,800,007 (81% institutional, 19% external sources). *Receiving aid:* Freshmen: 65% (379). Undergraduates: 62% (1,369). *Average award:* Freshmen: $9295. Undergraduates: $11,295. *Tuition waivers:* Full or partial for employees or children of employees. *ROTC:* Army, Air Force.

**LOANS** *Student loans:* $13,527,349 (94% need-based, 6% non-need-based). 64% of past graduating class borrowed through all loan programs. *Average indebtedness per student:* $35,420. *Average need-based loan:* Freshmen: $5189. Undergraduates: $5288. *Parent loans:* $6,468,443 (93% need-based, 7% non-need-based). *Programs:* Federal Direct (Subsidized and Unsubsidized Stafford, PLUS), Perkins.

**WORK-STUDY** *Federal work-study:* Total amount: $534,674; 417 jobs averaging $1257. *State or other work-study/employment:* Total amount: $637,461 (100% need-based). 487 part-time jobs averaging $1266.

**APPLYING FOR FINANCIAL AID** *Required financial aid form:* FAFSA. *Financial aid deadline (priority):* 3/1. *Notification date:* 3/10. Students must reply by 5/1.

**CONTACT** Melinda L. Middleton, Director of Financial Aid, Rose-Hulman Institute of Technology, 5500 Wabash Avenue, CM 5, Terre Haute, IN 47803, 812-877-8259 or toll-free 800-248-7448. *Fax:* 812-877-8746. *E-mail:* melinda.middleton@rose-hulman.edu. *Website:* http://www.rose-hulman.edu/.

## ROSEMONT COLLEGE
### Rosemont, PA

| Tuition & fees: $31,580 | Average undergraduate aid package: $31,781 |
|---|---|

**ABOUT THE INSTITUTION** Independent Roman Catholic, coed. *Awards:* certificates, bachelor's, and master's degrees. 21 undergraduate majors. *Total enrollment:* 890. Undergraduates: 522. Freshmen: 124. Federal methodology is used as a basis for awarding need-based institutional aid.

**UNDERGRADUATE EXPENSES** for 2015–2016 *Comprehensive fee:* $44,460 includes full-time tuition ($30,600), mandatory fees ($980), and room and board ($12,880). Full-time tuition and fees vary according to course load and program. Room and board charges vary according to board plan and housing facility. *Part-time tuition:* $1165 per credit hour. *Part-time fees:* $340 per term. Part-time tuition and fees vary according to course load and program.

**FRESHMAN FINANCIAL AID (Fall 2014, est.)** 122 applied for aid; of those 90% were deemed to have need. 100% of freshmen with need received aid; of those 14% had need fully met. *Average percent of need met:* 86% (excluding resources awarded to replace EFC). *Average financial aid package:* $35,709 (excluding resources awarded to replace EFC). 11% of all full-time freshmen had no need and received non-need-based gift aid.

**UNDERGRADUATE FINANCIAL AID (Fall 2014, est.)** 351 applied for aid; of those 94% were deemed to have need. 100% of undergraduates with need received aid; of those 14% had need fully met. *Average percent of need met:* 82% (excluding resources awarded to replace EFC). *Average financial aid package:* $31,781 (excluding resources awarded to replace EFC). 10% of all full-time undergraduates had no need and received non-need-based gift aid.

**GIFT AID (NEED-BASED)** *Total amount:* $9,815,019 (12% federal, 8% state, 78% institutional, 2% external sources). *Receiving aid:* Freshmen: 89% (109); all full-time undergraduates: 86% (327). *Average award:* Freshmen: $30,566; Undergraduates: $25,806. *Scholarships, grants, and awards:* Federal Pell, FSEOG, state, private, college/university gift aid from institutional funds, Academic Competitiveness Grants, National SMART Grants.

**GIFT AID (NON-NEED-BASED)** *Total amount:* $842,844 (1% state, 95% institutional, 4% external sources). *Receiving aid:* Freshmen: 9% (11). Undergraduates: 10% (39). *Average award:* Freshmen: $14,808. Undergraduates: $13,047. *Scholarships, grants, and awards by category: Academic interests/achievement:* general academic interests/achievements. *Creative arts/performance:* art/fine arts. *Special achievements/activities:* community service, general special achievements/activities, leadership, religious involvement. *Special characteristics:* children and siblings of alumni, children of educators, children of faculty/staff, relatives of clergy, siblings of current students. *Tuition waivers:* Full or partial for employees or children of employees, senior citizens.

**LOANS** *Student loans:* $3,974,646 (79% need-based, 21% non-need-based). 90% of past graduating class borrowed through all loan programs. *Average indebtedness per student:* $40,792. *Average need-based loan:* Freshmen: $3320. Undergraduates: $4570. *Parent loans:* $1,044,186 (27% need-based, 73% non-need-based). *Programs:* Federal Direct (Subsidized and Unsubsidized Stafford, PLUS), Perkins, alternative loans.

**WORK-STUDY** *Federal work-study:* Total amount: $104,003; 126 jobs averaging $825. *State or other work-study/employment:* Total amount: $11,778 (100% need-based). 6 part-time jobs averaging $1963.

**APPLYING FOR FINANCIAL AID** *Required financial aid form:* FAFSA. *Financial aid deadline (priority):* 2/15. *Notification date:* Continuous beginning 3/15. Students must reply by 5/1 or within 4 weeks of notification.

**CONTACT** Ms. Laverne Glenn, Director of Financial Aid, Rosemont College, 1400 Montgomery Avenue, Rosemont, PA 19010, 610-527-0200 Ext. 2236 or toll-free 888-2-ROSEMONT. *Fax:* 610-526-2971. *E-mail:* laverne.glenn@rosemont.edu. *Website:* http://www.rosemont.edu/.

# ROWAN UNIVERSITY
## Glassboro, NJ

| Tuition & fees (NJ res): $12,616 | Average undergraduate aid package: $9086 |
|---|---|

**ABOUT THE INSTITUTION** State-supported, coed. *Awards:* certificates, bachelor's, master's, and doctoral degrees. 62 undergraduate majors. *Total enrollment:* 14,778. Undergraduates: 12,022. Freshmen: 1,920. Both federal and institutional methodology are used as a basis for awarding need-based institutional aid.

**UNDERGRADUATE EXPENSES** for 2015–2016 *Application fee:* $65. *Tuition, state resident:* full-time $9076; part-time $348 per credit hour. *Tuition, nonresident:* full-time $17,030; part-time $656 per credit hour. *Required fees:* full-time $3540; $151 per credit hour. Full-time tuition and fees vary according to course load, degree level, location, and program. Part-time tuition and fees vary according to course load, degree level, location, and program. *College room and board:* $11,406; *Room only:* $7206. Room and board charges vary according to board plan and housing facility.

**FRESHMAN FINANCIAL AID (Fall 2013)** 1,348 applied for aid; of those 73% were deemed to have need. 95% of freshmen with need received aid; of those 30% had need fully met. *Average percent of need met:* 84% (excluding resources awarded to replace EFC). *Average financial aid package:* $8681 (excluding resources awarded to replace EFC). 16% of all full-time freshmen had no need and received non-need-based gift aid.

**UNDERGRADUATE FINANCIAL AID (Fall 2013)** 7,627 applied for aid; of those 80% were deemed to have need. 96% of undergraduates with need received aid; of those 29% had need fully met. *Average percent of need met:* 79% (excluding resources awarded to replace EFC). *Average financial aid package:* $9086 (excluding resources awarded to replace EFC). 8% of all full-time undergraduates had no need and received non-need-based gift aid.

**GIFT AID (NEED-BASED)** *Total amount:* $37,428,222 (37% federal, 37% state, 24% institutional, 2% external sources). *Receiving aid:* Freshmen: 30% (448); all full-time undergraduates: 34% (3,213). *Average award:* Freshmen: $10,191; Undergraduates: $8551. *Scholarships, grants, and awards:* Federal Pell, FSEOG, state, private, college/university gift aid from institutional funds.

**GIFT AID (NON-NEED-BASED)** *Total amount:* $6,618,468 (91% institutional, 9% external sources). *Receiving aid:* Freshmen: 31% (472). Undergraduates: 14% (1,335). *Average award:* Freshmen: $7835. Undergraduates: $7811. *Scholarships, grants, and awards by category: Academic interests/achievement:* general academic interests/achievements. *Creative arts/performance:* general creative arts/performance, music. *Tuition waivers:* Full or partial for employees or children of employees. *ROTC:* Army cooperative.

**LOANS** *Student loans:* $59,524,710 (93% need-based, 7% non-need-based). 73% of past graduating class borrowed through all loan programs. *Average indebtedness per student:* $31,759. *Average need-based loan:* Freshmen: $3197. Undergraduates: $4328. *Parent loans:* $19,426,511 (78% need-based, 22% non-need-based). *Programs:* Federal Direct (Subsidized and Unsubsidized Stafford, PLUS), state.

**WORK-STUDY** *Federal work-study:* 426 jobs averaging $1267. *State or other work-study/employment:* Total amount: $1,774,247 (67% need-based, 33% non-need-based). Part-time jobs available.

**APPLYING FOR FINANCIAL AID** *Required financial aid form:* FAFSA. *Financial aid deadline (priority):* 3/16. *Notification date:* Continuous beginning 3/16. Students must reply by 5/1.

**CONTACT** Jeff Hand, Associate Provost for Enrollment Management, Rowan University, 201 Mullica Hill Road, Glassboro, NJ 08028-1701, 856-256-5186 or toll-free 800-447-1165 (in-state), 800-447-1165N (out-of-state). *Fax:* 856-256-4413. *E-mail:* handj@rowan.edu. *Website:* http://www.rowan.edu/.

# RUSH UNIVERSITY
## Chicago, IL

**CONTACT** Mike Frechette, Director of Student Financial Aid, Rush University, 600 South Paulina Street, Suite 440, Chicago, IL 60612-3832, 312-942-6256. *Fax:* 312-942-2732. *E-mail:* michael_frechette@rush.edu. *Website:* http://www.rushu.rush.edu/.

# RUST COLLEGE
## Holly Springs, MS

**CONTACT** Mrs. Helen L. Street, Director of Financial Aid, Rust College, 150 Rust Avenue, Holly Springs, MS 38635, 662-252-8000 Ext. 4061 or toll-free 888-886-8492 Ext. 4065. *Fax:* 662-252-8895. *Website:* http://www.rustcollege.edu/.

# RUTGERS, THE STATE UNIVERSITY OF NEW JERSEY, CAMDEN
## Camden, NJ

| Tuition & fees (NJ res): $13,683 | Average undergraduate aid package: $12,618 |
|---|---|

**ABOUT THE INSTITUTION** State-supported, coed. *Awards:* bachelor's, master's, and doctoral degrees. 33 undergraduate majors. *Total enrollment:* 6,321. Undergraduates: 4,857. Freshmen: 431. Federal methodology is used as a basis for awarding need-based institutional aid.

**UNDERGRADUATE EXPENSES for 2015–2016** *Application fee:* $65. *Tuition, state resident:* full-time $10,954; part-time $353 per credit. *Tuition, nonresident:* full-time $25,249; part-time $835 per credit. *Required fees:* full-time $2729; $459 per term. Part-time tuition and fees vary according to course load. *College room and board:* $11,438; *Room only:* $7938. Room and board charges vary according to board plan and housing facility.

**FRESHMAN FINANCIAL AID (Fall 2014, est.)** 380 applied for aid; of those 83% were deemed to have need. 100% of freshmen with need received aid; of those 4% had need fully met. *Average percent of need met:* 61% (excluding resources awarded to replace EFC). *Average financial aid package:* $14,858 (excluding resources awarded to replace EFC). 11% of all full-time freshmen had no need and received non-need-based gift aid.

**UNDERGRADUATE FINANCIAL AID (Fall 2014, est.)** 3,457 applied for aid; of those 90% were deemed to have need. 100% of undergraduates with need received aid; of those 2% had need fully met. *Average percent of need met:* 54% (excluding resources awarded to replace EFC). *Average financial aid package:* $12,618 (excluding resources awarded to replace EFC). 3% of all full-time undergraduates had no need and received non-need-based gift aid.

**GIFT AID (NEED-BASED)** *Total amount:* $24,601,179 (40% federal, 46% state, 14% institutional). *Receiving aid:* Freshmen: 57% (238); all full-time undergraduates: 58% (2,327). *Average award:* Freshmen: $12,440; Undergraduates: $10,275. *Scholarships, grants, and awards:* Federal Pell, FSEOG, state, private, college/university gift aid from institutional funds, Federal Nursing.

**GIFT AID (NON-NEED-BASED)** *Total amount:* $2,490,872 (91% institutional, 9% external sources). *Receiving aid:* Freshmen: 32% (133). Undergraduates: 15% (615). *Average award:* Freshmen: $4196. Undergraduates: $3185. *Tuition waivers:* Full or partial for employees or children of employees. *ROTC:* Army cooperative, Air Force cooperative.

**LOANS** *Student loans:* $31,527,987 (42% need-based, 58% non-need-based). 77% of past graduating class borrowed through all loan programs. *Average indebtedness per student:* $28,651. *Average need-based loan:* Freshmen: $3987. Undergraduates: $4741. *Parent loans:* $2,748,656 (100% non-need-based). *Programs:* Federal Direct (Subsidized and Unsubsidized Stafford, PLUS), Perkins, Federal Nursing, state, college/university, alternative loans.

**WORK-STUDY** *Federal work-study:* Total amount: $523,489; 279 jobs averaging $1876. *State or other work-study/employment:* Total amount: $708,399 (100% non-need-based). 452 part-time jobs averaging $1567.

**APPLYING FOR FINANCIAL AID** *Required financial aid form:* FAFSA. *Financial aid deadline (priority):* 3/15. *Notification date:* Continuous beginning 3/1. Students must reply within 2 weeks of notification.

**CONTACT** Ms. Carolann Pierre, Senior Funds Management Specialist, Rutgers, The State University of New Jersey, Camden, 620 George Street, New Brunswick, NJ 08901, 848-932-2603. *Fax:* 732-932-0516. *E-mail:* carolann.pierre@ofa.rutgers.edu. *Website:* http://www.camden.rutgers.edu/.

# RUTGERS, THE STATE UNIVERSITY OF NEW JERSEY, NEWARK
## Newark, NJ

| Tuition & fees (NJ res): $13,297 | Average undergraduate aid package: $13,705 |
|---|---|

**ABOUT THE INSTITUTION** State-supported, coed. *Awards:* associate, bachelor's, master's, and doctoral degrees. 59 undergraduate majors. *Total enrollment:* 11,314. Undergraduates: 7,408. Freshmen: 1,017. Federal methodology is used as a basis for awarding need-based institutional aid.

**UNDERGRADUATE EXPENSES for 2015–2016** *Application fee:* $65. *Tuition, state resident:* full-time $10,954; part-time $353 per credit. *Tuition, nonresident:* full-time $25,732; part-time $835 per credit. *Required fees:* full-time $2343; $441 per term. Part-time tuition and fees vary according to course load. *College room and board:* $12,509; *Room only:* $7743. Room and board charges vary according to board plan and housing facility.

**FRESHMAN FINANCIAL AID (Fall 2014, est.)** 856 applied for aid; of those 92% were deemed to have need. 100% of freshmen with need received aid; of those 2% had need fully met. *Average percent of need met:* 63% (excluding resources awarded to replace EFC). *Average financial aid package:* $14,912 (excluding resources awarded to replace EFC). 1% of all full-time freshmen had no need and received non-need-based gift aid.

**UNDERGRADUATE FINANCIAL AID (Fall 2014, est.)** 5,238 applied for aid; of those 94% were deemed to have need. 100% of undergraduates with need received aid; of those 2% had need fully met. *Average percent of need met:* 57% (excluding resources awarded to replace EFC). *Average financial aid package:* $13,705 (excluding resources awarded to replace EFC). 1% of all full-time undergraduates had no need and received non-need-based gift aid.

**GIFT AID (NEED-BASED)** *Total amount:* $47,071,595 (39% federal, 47% state, 14% institutional). *Receiving aid:* Freshmen: 66% (665); all full-time undergraduates: 71% (4,226). *Average award:* Freshmen: $12,327; Undergraduates: $10,938. *Scholarships, grants, and awards:* Federal Pell, FSEOG, state, private, college/university gift aid from institutional funds.

**GIFT AID (NON-NEED-BASED)** *Total amount:* $2,685,947 (83% institutional, 17% external sources). *Receiving aid:* Freshmen: 12% (123). Undergraduates: 7% (394). *Average award:* Freshmen: $8000. Undergraduates: $7255. *Tuition waivers:* Full or partial for employees or children of employees. *ROTC:* Army, Naval, Air Force.

**LOANS** *Student loans:* $37,239,221 (50% need-based, 50% non-need-based). 65% of past graduating class borrowed through all loan programs. *Average indebtedness per student:* $26,993. *Average need-based loan:* Freshmen: $4273. Undergraduates: $4811. *Parent loans:* $3,474,964 (100% non-need-based). *Programs:* Federal Direct (Subsidized and Unsubsidized Stafford, PLUS), Perkins, state, college/university, alternative loans.

**WORK-STUDY** *Federal work-study:* Total amount: $1,080,496; 655 jobs averaging $1650. *State or other work-study/employment:* Total amount: $858,959 (100% non-need-based). 710 part-time jobs averaging $1210.

**APPLYING FOR FINANCIAL AID** *Required financial aid form:* FAFSA. *Financial aid deadline (priority):* 3/15. *Notification date:* Continuous beginning 3/1. Students must reply within 4 weeks of notification.

**CONTACT** Ms. Carolann Pierre, Senior Funds Management Specialist, Rutgers, The State University of New Jersey, Newark, 620 George Street, New Brunswick, NJ 08901, 848-932-2603. *Fax:* 732-932-0516. *E-mail:* carolann.pierre@ofa.rutgers.edu. *Website:* http://www.newark.rutgers.edu/.

# RUTGERS, THE STATE UNIVERSITY OF NEW JERSEY, NEW BRUNSWICK
## Piscataway, NJ

| Tuition & fees (NJ res): $13,813 | Average undergraduate aid package: $13,376 |
|---|---|

**ABOUT THE INSTITUTION** State-supported, coed. *Awards:* certificates, associate, bachelor's, master's, and doctoral degrees. 137 undergraduate majors. *Total enrollment:* 48,378. Undergraduates: 34,544. Freshmen: 6,412. Federal methodology is used as a basis for awarding need-based institutional aid.

**UNDERGRADUATE EXPENSES for 2015–2016** *Application fee:* $65. *Tuition, state resident:* full-time $10,954; part-time $353 per credit. *Tuition, nonresident:* full-time $25,732; part-time $835 per credit. *Required fees:* full-time $2859; $299.25 per term. Part-time tuition and fees vary according to course load. *College room and board:* $11,749; *Room only:* $7163. Room and board charges vary according to board plan and housing facility.

**FRESHMAN FINANCIAL AID (Fall 2014, est.)** 4,499 applied for aid; of those 78% were deemed to have need. 100% of freshmen with need received aid; of those 5% had need fully met. *Average percent of need met:* 57% (excluding resources awarded to replace EFC). *Average financial aid package:* $14,880 (excluding resources awarded to replace EFC). 5% of all full-time freshmen had no need and received non-need-based gift aid.

**UNDERGRADUATE FINANCIAL AID (Fall 2014, est.)** 21,161 applied for aid; of those 85% were deemed to have need. 100% of undergraduates with need received aid; of those 4% had need fully met. *Average percent of need met:* 52% (excluding resources awarded to replace EFC). *Average financial aid package:* $13,376 (excluding resources awarded to replace EFC). 2% of all full-time undergraduates had no need and received non-need-based gift aid.

**GIFT AID (NEED-BASED)** *Total amount:* $139,818,922 (36% federal, 45% state, 19% institutional). *Receiving aid:* Freshmen: 37% (2,348); all full-time undergraduates: 38% (12,473). *Average award:* Freshmen: $12,594; Undergraduates: $10,995. *Scholarships, grants, and awards:* Federal Pell, FSEOG, state, private, college/university gift aid from institutional funds, Federal Nursing.

**GIFT AID (NON-NEED-BASED)** *Total amount:* $35,902,492 (87% institutional, 13% external sources). *Receiving aid:* Freshmen: 15% (946). Undergraduates: 9% (2,877). *Average award:* Freshmen: $9586. Undergraduates: $8276. *Tuition waivers:* Full or partial for employees or children of employees. *ROTC:* Army, Naval, Air Force.

**LOANS** *Student loans:* $175,964,232 (41% need-based, 59% non-need-based). 62% of past graduating class borrowed through all loan programs. *Average indebtedness per student:* $25,228. *Average need-based loan:* Freshmen: $4031. Undergraduates: $4684. *Parent loans:* $36,465,776 (100% non-need-based). *Programs:* Federal Direct (Subsidized and Unsubsidized Stafford, PLUS), Perkins, Federal Nursing, state, college/university, alternative loans.

**WORK-STUDY** *Federal work-study:* Total amount: $5,790,913; 2,954 jobs averaging $1952. *State or other work-study/employment:* Total amount: $6,603,806 (100% non-need-based). 5,610 part-time jobs averaging $1177.

**ATHLETIC AWARDS** Total amount: $9,910,035 (100% non-need-based).

**APPLYING FOR FINANCIAL AID** *Required financial aid form:* FAFSA. *Financial aid deadline (priority):* 3/15. *Notification date:* Continuous beginning 3/1. Students must reply within 4 weeks of notification.

**CONTACT** Ms. Carolann Pierre, Senior Funds Management Specialist, Rutgers, The State University of New Jersey, New Brunswick, 620 George Street, New Brunswick, NJ 08901, 848-932-2603. *Fax:* 732-932-0516. *E-mail:* carolann.pierre@ofa.rutgers.edu. *Website:* http://newbrunswick.rutgers.edu/.

---

# SACRED HEART MAJOR SEMINARY
## Detroit, MI

**ABOUT THE INSTITUTION** Independent Roman Catholic, coed. 3 undergraduate majors.

**GIFT AID (NEED-BASED)** *Scholarships, grants, and awards:* Federal Pell, FSEOG, state, private, college/university gift aid from institutional funds.

**GIFT AID (NON-NEED-BASED)** *Scholarships, grants, and awards by category:* Academic interests/achievement: religion/biblical studies. Special achievements/activities: religious involvement. Special characteristics: local/state students, religious affiliation.

**LOANS** *Programs:* Federal Direct (Subsidized and Unsubsidized Stafford).

**APPLYING FOR FINANCIAL AID** *Required financial aid forms:* FAFSA, institution's own form.

**CONTACT** Financial Aid Office, Sacred Heart Major Seminary, 2701 Chicago Boulevard, Detroit, MI 48206-1799, 313-883-8534. *Fax:* 313-868-7025. *E-mail:* financialaid@shms.edu. *Website:* http://www.shms.edu/.

---

# SACRED HEART UNIVERSITY
## Fairfield, CT

| Tuition & fees: $35,750 | Average undergraduate aid package: $19,052 |
| --- | --- |

**ABOUT THE INSTITUTION** Independent Roman Catholic, coed. *Awards:* certificates, bachelor's, master's, and doctoral degrees (also offers part-time program with significant enrollment not reflected in profile). 56 undergraduate majors. *Total enrollment:* 7,781. Undergraduates: 4,997. Freshmen: 1,385. Both federal and institutional methodology are used as a basis for awarding need-based institutional aid.

**UNDERGRADUATE EXPENSES for 2015–2016** *Application fee:* $50. *Comprehensive fee:* $49,264 includes full-time tuition ($35,500), mandatory fees ($250),

and room and board ($13,514). *College room only:* $9474. Full-time tuition and fees vary according to location and program. Room and board charges vary according to board plan and housing facility. *Part-time tuition:* $545 per credit hour. *Part-time fees:* $115 per term. Part-time tuition and fees vary according to course load, location, and program.

**FRESHMAN FINANCIAL AID (Fall 2013)** 1,147 applied for aid; of those 80% were deemed to have need. 100% of freshmen with need received aid; of those 15% had need fully met. *Average percent of need met:* 56% (excluding resources awarded to replace EFC). *Average financial aid package:* $19,402 (excluding resources awarded to replace EFC). 25% of all full-time freshmen had no need and received non-need-based gift aid.

**UNDERGRADUATE FINANCIAL AID (Fall 2013)** 3,596 applied for aid; of those 72% were deemed to have need. 98% of undergraduates with need received aid; of those 15% had need fully met. *Average percent of need met:* 57% (excluding resources awarded to replace EFC). *Average financial aid package:* $19,052 (excluding resources awarded to replace EFC). 20% of all full-time undergraduates had no need and received non-need-based gift aid.

**GIFT AID (NEED-BASED)** *Total amount:* $37,283,669 (11% federal, 4% state, 78% institutional, 7% external sources). *Receiving aid:* Freshmen: 57% (724); all full-time undergraduates: 54% (2,028). *Average award:* Freshmen: $15,798; Undergraduates: $15,037. *Scholarships, grants, and awards:* Federal Pell, FSEOG, state, private, college/university gift aid from institutional funds.

**GIFT AID (NON-NEED-BASED)** *Total amount:* $10,067,833 (4% federal, 78% institutional, 18% external sources). *Receiving aid:* Freshmen: 9% (113). Undergraduates: 8% (293). *Average award:* Freshmen: $11,335. Undergraduates: $8572. *Scholarships, grants, and awards by category:* Academic interests/achievement: 2,254 awards ($13,727,543 total): biological sciences, business, computer science, education, English, general academic interests/achievements, health fields, humanities, mathematics, physical sciences, premedicine. Creative arts/performance: 565 awards ($1,825,712 total): applied art and design, art/fine arts, cinema/film/broadcasting, creative writing, dance, music, performing arts, theater/drama. Special achievements/activities: 674 awards ($1,025,744 total): community service, general special achievements/activities, hobbies/interests, leadership, memberships, religious involvement. Special characteristics: 513 awards ($2,705,892 total): adult students, children and siblings of alumni, children of current students, children of faculty/staff, children of union members/company employees, ethnic background, general special characteristics, handicapped students, international students, local/state students, members of minority groups, out-of-state students, religious affiliation, siblings of current students, twins, veterans, veterans' children. *Tuition waivers:* Full or partial for employees or children of employees. *ROTC:* Army cooperative.

**LOANS** *Student loans:* $31,059,747 (70% need-based, 30% non-need-based). 80% of past graduating class borrowed through all loan programs. *Average indebtedness per student:* $45,746. *Average need-based loan:* Freshmen: $4351. Undergraduates: $5003. *Parent loans:* $17,782,107 (46% need-based, 54% non-need-based). *Programs:* Federal Direct (Subsidized and Unsubsidized Stafford, PLUS), Perkins, state.

**WORK-STUDY** *Federal work-study:* 933 jobs averaging $732. *State or other work-study/employment:* Total amount: $335,596 (4% need-based, 96% non-need-based). 562 part-time jobs averaging $597.

**ATHLETIC AWARDS** Total amount: $7,594,342 (46% need-based, 54% non-need-based).

**APPLYING FOR FINANCIAL AID** *Required financial aid forms:* FAFSA, CSS Financial Aid PROFILE, noncustodial (divorced/separated) parent's statement. *Financial aid deadline (priority):* 2/15. *Notification date:* Continuous beginning 3/1. Students must reply within 2 weeks of notification.

**CONTACT** Ms. Julie B. Savino, Executive Director of University Financial Assistance, Sacred Heart University, 5151 Park Avenue, Fairfield, CT 06825, 203-371-7980. *Fax:* 203-365-7608. *E-mail:* savinoj@sacredheart.edu. *Website:* http://www.sacredheart.edu/.

---

# THE SAGE COLLEGES
## Troy, NY

| Tuition & fees: $28,200 | Average undergraduate aid package: N/A |
| --- | --- |

**ABOUT THE INSTITUTION** Independent, coed. *Awards:* certificates, bachelor's, master's, and doctoral degrees. 33 undergraduate majors. *Total* *enrollment:* 2,877. Undergraduates: 1,704. Freshmen: 283. Federal methodology is used as a basis for awarding need-based institutional aid.

**UNDERGRADUATE EXPENSES** for 2015–2016 *Application fee:* $30. *Comprehensive fee:* $40,030 includes full-time tuition ($27,000), mandatory fees ($1200), and room and board ($11,830). *College room only:* $6200. Room and board charges vary according to board plan. *Part-time tuition:* $900 per credit hour.

**FRESHMAN FINANCIAL AID (Fall 2014, est.)** 281 applied for aid; of those 97% were deemed to have need. 100% of freshmen with need received aid. 3% of all full-time freshmen had no need and received non-need-based gift aid.

**UNDERGRADUATE FINANCIAL AID (Fall 2014, est.)** 1,407 applied for aid; of those 95% were deemed to have need. 100% of undergraduates with need received aid. 4% of all full-time undergraduates had no need and received non-need-based gift aid.

**GIFT AID (NEED-BASED)** *Total amount:* $16,658,459 (21% federal, 15% state, 63% institutional, 1% external sources). *Receiving aid:* Freshmen: 84% (238); all full-time undergraduates: 79% (1,154). *Average award:* Freshmen: $17,080; Undergraduates: $14,404. *Scholarships, grants, and awards:* Federal Pell, FSEOG, state, private, college/university gift aid from institutional funds, Federal Nursing.

**GIFT AID (NON-NEED-BASED)** *Total amount:* $10,704,295 (1% state, 98% institutional, 1% external sources). *Receiving aid:* Freshmen: 73% (208). Undergraduates: 71% (1,033). *Average award:* Freshmen: $16,625. Undergraduates: $11,790. *Scholarships, grants, and awards by category: Academic interests/achievement:* 1,024 awards ($9,398,986 total): general academic interests/achievements. *Creative arts/performance:* 14 awards ($186,726 total): art/fine arts, theater/drama. *Special achievements/activities:* 109 awards ($121,431 total): community service, general special achievements/activities, leadership. *Special characteristics:* 283 awards ($492,693 total): adult students, children and siblings of alumni, ethnic background, first-generation college students, general special characteristics, members of minority groups, veterans. *Tuition waivers:* Full or partial for employees or children of employees. *ROTC:* Army, Air Force.

**LOANS** *Student loans:* $10,909,034 (47% need-based, 53% non-need-based). 85% of past graduating class borrowed through all loan programs. *Average indebtedness per student:* $26,534. *Average need-based loan:* Freshmen: $1658. Undergraduates: $3366. *Parent loans:* $2,162,760 (100% non-need-based). *Programs:* Federal Direct (Subsidized and Unsubsidized Stafford, PLUS), Perkins.

**WORK-STUDY** *Federal work-study:* Total amount: $975,357; 500 jobs averaging $1951. *State or other work-study/employment:* Total amount: $167,546 (100% non-need-based). 30 part-time jobs averaging $5585.

**APPLYING FOR FINANCIAL AID** *Required financial aid forms:* FAFSA, state aid form. *Financial aid deadline (priority):* 3/1. *Notification date:* Continuous beginning 3/1. Students must reply within 2 weeks of notification.

**CONTACT** Kelley Robinson, Director of Financial Aid, The Sage Colleges, 65 First Street, Troy, NY 12180, 518-244-2062. *Fax:* 518-244-2460. *E-mail:* robink3@sage.edu. *Website:* http://www.sage.edu/.

---

# SAGINAW VALLEY STATE UNIVERSITY
## University Center, MI

| Tuition & fees (MI res): $8691 | Average undergraduate aid package: N/A |
|---|---|

**ABOUT THE INSTITUTION** State-supported, coed. *Awards:* certificates, bachelor's, master's, and doctoral degrees. 81 undergraduate majors. *Total enrollment:* 9,829. Undergraduates: 8,797. Freshmen: 1,507. Federal methodology is used as a basis for awarding need-based institutional aid.

**UNDERGRADUATE EXPENSES** for 2015–2016 *Application fee:* $30. *Tuition, state resident:* full-time $8253; part-time $275.10 per credit hour. *Tuition, nonresident:* full-time $19,971; part-time $665.70 per credit hour. *Required fees:* full-time $438; $14.60 per credit hour. Full-time tuition and fees vary according to course level, degree level, location, and program. Part-time tuition and fees vary according to course level, degree level, location, and program. *College room and board:* $8400; *Room only:* $4750. Room and board charges vary according to board plan and housing facility.

**FRESHMAN FINANCIAL AID (Fall 2014, est.)** 1,060 applied for aid; of those 99% were deemed to have need. 92% of freshmen with need received aid.

**UNDERGRADUATE FINANCIAL AID (Fall 2014, est.)** 4,908 applied for aid; of those 99% were deemed to have need. 96% of undergraduates with need received aid.

**GIFT AID (NEED-BASED)** *Total amount:* $17,617,228 (84% federal, 5% state, 9% institutional, 2% external sources). *Receiving aid:* Freshmen: 50% (746); all full-time undergraduates: 48% (3,465). *Scholarships, grants, and awards:* Federal Pell, FSEOG, state, private, college/university gift aid from institutional funds.

**GIFT AID (NON-NEED-BASED)** *Total amount:* $19,282,849 (1% federal, 1% state, 57% institutional, 41% external sources). *Scholarships, grants, and awards by category: Academic interests/achievement:* biological sciences, business, computer science, education, engineering/technologies, general academic interests/achievements, health fields, mathematics, physical sciences. *Creative arts/performance:* art/fine arts, music, theater/drama. *Special achievements/activities:* community service, leadership. *Special characteristics:* adult students, local/state students, members of minority groups, veterans, veterans' children. *Tuition waivers:* Full or partial for employees or children of employees.

**LOANS** *Student loans:* $51,356,067 (91% need-based, 9% non-need-based). *Programs:* Federal Direct (Subsidized and Unsubsidized Stafford, PLUS), CitiAssist Loans, Chase Select loans, Charter One TruFit Student Loans, Discover Private Educational Loans.

**WORK-STUDY** *Federal work-study:* Total amount: $302,324; jobs available. *State or other work-study/employment:* Part-time jobs available.

**APPLYING FOR FINANCIAL AID** *Required financial aid form:* FAFSA. *Financial aid deadline:* Continuous. *Notification date:* Continuous beginning 3/1.

**CONTACT** Robert Lemuel, Director of Scholarships and Financial Aid, Saginaw Valley State University, 7400 Bay Road, University Center, MI 48710, 989-964-4900 or toll-free 800-968-9500. *Fax:* 989-790-0180. *E-mail:* cfsc@svsu.edu. *Website:* http://www.svsu.edu/.

---

# ST. AMBROSE UNIVERSITY
## Davenport, IA

| Tuition & fees: N/R | Average undergraduate aid package: $20,016 |
|---|---|

**ABOUT THE INSTITUTION** Independent Roman Catholic, coed. 71 undergraduate majors. Federal methodology is used as a basis for awarding need-based institutional aid.

**FRESHMAN FINANCIAL AID (Fall 2014, est.)** 472 applied for aid; of those 87% were deemed to have need. 100% of freshmen with need received aid; of those 24% had need fully met. *Average percent of need met:* 71% (excluding resources awarded to replace EFC). *Average financial aid package:* $21,117 (excluding resources awarded to replace EFC). 20% of all full-time freshmen had no need and received non-need-based gift aid.

**UNDERGRADUATE FINANCIAL AID (Fall 2014, est.)** 1,971 applied for aid; of those 88% were deemed to have need. 100% of undergraduates with need received aid; of those 25% had need fully met. *Average percent of need met:* 69% (excluding resources awarded to replace EFC). *Average financial aid package:* $20,016 (excluding resources awarded to replace EFC). 21% of all full-time undergraduates had no need and received non-need-based gift aid.

**GIFT AID (NEED-BASED)** *Total amount:* $24,161,969 (11% federal, 9% state, 79% institutional, 1% external sources). *Receiving aid:* Freshmen: 79% (410); all full-time undergraduates: 71% (1,712). *Average award:* Freshmen: $15,536; Undergraduates: $14,379. *Scholarships, grants, and awards:* Federal Pell, FSEOG, state, private, college/university gift aid from institutional funds.

**GIFT AID (NON-NEED-BASED)** *Total amount:* $5,903,098 (98% institutional, 2% external sources). *Receiving aid:* Freshmen: 43% (222). Undergraduates: 29% (691). *Average award:* Freshmen: $11,754. Undergraduates: $11,711. *Scholarships, grants, and awards by category: Academic interests/achievement:* 1,857 awards: biological sciences, communication, engineering/technologies, foreign languages, general academic interests/achievements, health fields, international studies, religion/biblical studies. *Creative arts/performance:* 93 awards: art/fine arts, dance, journalism/publications, music, theater/drama. *Special achievements/activities:* 23 awards: cheerleading/drum major, leadership. *Special characteristics:* 278 awards: adult students, children and siblings of alumni, children of educators, children of faculty/staff, international students, members of minority groups, out-of-state students, previous college experience, religious affiliation, veterans.

**LOANS** *Student loans:* $19,002,854 (89% need-based, 11% non-need-based). 78% of past graduating class borrowed through all loan programs. *Average indebtedness per student:* $34,937. *Average need-based loan:* Freshmen: $3371. Undergraduates: $4283. *Parent loans:* $4,561,843 (90% need-based, 10% non-need-based).

**Programs:** Federal Direct (Subsidized and Unsubsidized Stafford, PLUS), Perkins, private loans.
**WORK-STUDY** *Federal work-study:* Total amount: $1,000,588; 311 jobs averaging $1840. *State or other work-study/employment:* Total amount: $429,270 (86% need-based, 14% non-need-based). 156 part-time jobs averaging $1839.
**ATHLETIC AWARDS** Total amount: $2,550,182 (73% need-based, 27% non-need-based).
**APPLYING FOR FINANCIAL AID** *Required financial aid form:* FAFSA. *Financial aid deadline (priority):* 3/15. *Notification date:* Continuous beginning 2/15. Students must reply within 2 weeks of notification.
**CONTACT** Ms. Julie Haack, Director of Financial Aid, St. Ambrose University, 518 West Locust Street, Davenport, IA 52803, 563-333-6314 or toll-free 800-383-2627. *Fax:* 563-333-6243. *E-mail:* haackjuliea@sau.edu.
*Website:* http://www.sau.edu/.

# ST. ANDREWS UNIVERSITY
## Laurinburg, NC

| Tuition & fees: $23,682 | Average undergraduate aid package: $20,896 |
| --- | --- |

**ABOUT THE INSTITUTION** Independent Presbyterian, coed. **Awards:** diplomas, bachelor's, and master's degrees. 16 undergraduate majors. **Total enrollment:** 650. Undergraduates: 617. Freshmen: 153. Federal methodology is used as a basis for awarding need-based institutional aid.
**UNDERGRADUATE EXPENSES for 2015–2016** *Application fee:* $35. *Comprehensive fee:* $33,580 includes full-time tuition ($23,682) and room and board ($9898). Full-time tuition and fees vary according to course load and location. Room and board charges vary according to housing facility. *Part-time tuition:* $274 per credit hour. Part-time tuition and fees vary according to location.
**FRESHMAN FINANCIAL AID (Fall 2014, est.)** 128 applied for aid; of those 90% were deemed to have need. 98% of freshmen with need received aid; of those 4% had need fully met. *Average percent of need met:* 68% (excluding resources awarded to replace EFC). *Average financial aid package:* $22,338 (excluding resources awarded to replace EFC). 14% of all full-time freshmen had no need and received non-need-based gift aid.
**UNDERGRADUATE FINANCIAL AID (Fall 2014, est.)** 456 applied for aid; of those 91% were deemed to have need. 99% of undergraduates with need received aid; of those 10% had need fully met. *Average percent of need met:* 68% (excluding resources awarded to replace EFC). *Average financial aid package:* $20,896 (excluding resources awarded to replace EFC). 18% of all full-time undergraduates had no need and received non-need-based gift aid.
**GIFT AID (NEED-BASED)** *Total amount:* $5,264,986 (21% federal, 14% state, 57% institutional, 8% external sources). *Receiving aid:* Freshmen: 66% (113); all full-time undergraduates: 70% (401). *Average award:* Freshmen: $18,609; Undergraduates: $17,209. *Scholarships, grants, and awards:* Federal Pell, FSEOG, state, private, college/university gift aid from institutional funds.
**GIFT AID (NON-NEED-BASED)** *Total amount:* $1,141,588 (87% institutional, 13% external sources). *Receiving aid:* Freshmen: 3% (5). Undergraduates: 5% (27). *Average award:* Freshmen: $10,018. Undergraduates: $9290. *Scholarships, grants, and awards by category:* Academic interests/achievement: business, general academic interests/achievements. Creative arts/performance: general creative arts/performance, performing arts, theater/drama. Special achievements/activities: community service, general special achievements/activities, leadership. *Tuition waivers:* Full or partial for employees or children of employees, adult students, senior citizens.
**LOANS** *Student loans:* $3,319,925 (82% need-based, 18% non-need-based). 76% of past graduating class borrowed through all loan programs. *Average indebtedness per student:* $27,760. *Average need-based loan:* Freshmen: $3902. Undergraduates: $4645. *Parent loans:* $1,509,503 (48% need-based, 52% non-need-based).
**Programs:** Federal Direct (Subsidized and Unsubsidized Stafford, PLUS), state.
**WORK-STUDY** *Federal work-study:* Total amount: $101,315; 61 jobs averaging $1800. *State or other work-study/employment:* 40 part-time jobs averaging $1200.
**ATHLETIC AWARDS** Total amount: $2,388,660 (70% need-based, 30% non-need-based).

**APPLYING FOR FINANCIAL AID** *Required financial aid forms:* FAFSA, state aid form. *Financial aid deadline:* Continuous. *Notification date:* Continuous beginning 2/1. Students must reply within 2 weeks of notification.
**CONTACT** Kimberly Driggers, Director of Financial Aid, St. Andrews University, 1700 Dogwood Mile, Laurinburg, NC 28352, 910-277-5562 or toll-free 800-763-0198. *Fax:* 910-277-5206.
*Website:* http://www.sapc.edu/.

# SAINT ANSELM COLLEGE
## Manchester, NH

| Tuition & fees: N/R | Average undergraduate aid package: $27,727 |
| --- | --- |

**ABOUT THE INSTITUTION** Independent Roman Catholic, coed. **Awards:** bachelor's degrees. 40 undergraduate majors. **Total enrollment:** 1,968. Undergraduates: 1,968. Freshmen: 523. Both federal and institutional methodology are used as a basis for awarding need-based institutional aid.
**FRESHMAN FINANCIAL AID (Fall 2014, est.)** 470 applied for aid; of those 82% were deemed to have need. 100% of freshmen with need received aid; of those 24% had need fully met. *Average percent of need met:* 83% (excluding resources awarded to replace EFC). *Average financial aid package:* $27,051 (excluding resources awarded to replace EFC). 22% of all full-time freshmen had no need and received non-need-based gift aid.
**UNDERGRADUATE FINANCIAL AID (Fall 2014, est.)** 1,614 applied for aid; of those 86% were deemed to have need. 100% of undergraduates with need received aid; of those 22% had need fully met. *Average percent of need met:* 83% (excluding resources awarded to replace EFC). *Average financial aid package:* $27,727 (excluding resources awarded to replace EFC). 22% of all full-time undergraduates had no need and received non-need-based gift aid.
**GIFT AID (NEED-BASED)** *Total amount:* $27,165,581 (6% federal, 92% institutional, 2% external sources). *Receiving aid:* Freshmen: 73% (383); all full-time undergraduates: 72% (1,378). *Average award:* Freshmen: $21,382; Undergraduates: $21,255. *Scholarships, grants, and awards:* Federal Pell, FSEOG, state, private, college/university gift aid from institutional funds.
**GIFT AID (NON-NEED-BASED)** *Total amount:* $6,198,860 (91% institutional, 9% external sources). *Receiving aid:* Freshmen: 12% (64). Undergraduates: 10% (194). *Average award:* Freshmen: $12,111. Undergraduates: $11,563. *Scholarships, grants, and awards by category:* Academic interests/achievement: 1,243 awards ($12,798,250 total): general academic interests/achievements. Creative arts/performance: 343 awards ($4,760,000 total): general creative arts/performance. Special characteristics: 155 awards ($2,743,749 total): children of educators, children of faculty/staff, siblings of current students. ROTC: Army cooperative.
**LOANS** *Student loans:* $16,947,510 (56% need-based, 44% non-need-based). 82% of past graduating class borrowed through all loan programs. *Average indebtedness per student:* $35,601. *Average need-based loan:* Freshmen: $5412. Undergraduates: $6326. *Parent loans:* $4,720,640 (30% need-based, 70% non-need-based). *Programs:* Federal Direct (Subsidized and Unsubsidized Stafford, PLUS), Perkins.
**WORK-STUDY** *Federal work-study:* Total amount: $1,651,417; 1,116 jobs averaging $1481. *State or other work-study/employment:* Total amount: $18,000 (100% need-based). 9 part-time jobs averaging $2000.
**ATHLETIC AWARDS** Total amount: $15,872,017 (7% need-based, 93% non-need-based).
**APPLYING FOR FINANCIAL AID** *Required financial aid forms:* FAFSA, CSS Financial Aid PROFILE, noncustodial (divorced/separated) parent's statement. *Financial aid deadline:* 3/15. *Notification date:* Continuous beginning 3/1. Students must reply by 5/1 or within 2 weeks of notification.
**CONTACT** Elizabeth Keuffel, Director of Financial Aid, Saint Anselm College, 100 Saint Anselm Drive, Manchester, NH 03102-1310, 603-641-7110 or toll-free 888-4ANSELM. *Fax:* 603-656-6015. *E-mail:* financial_aid@anselm.edu.
*Website:* http://www.anselm.edu/.

# SAINT ANTHONY COLLEGE OF NURSING
## Rockford, IL

| Tuition & fees: $22,890 | Average undergraduate aid package: $8775 |
|---|---|

**ABOUT THE INSTITUTION** Independent Roman Catholic, coed, primarily women. **Awards:** certificates, bachelor's, master's, and doctoral degrees. 1 undergraduate major. **Total enrollment:** 310. Undergraduates: 235. Federal methodology is used as a basis for awarding need-based institutional aid.

**UNDERGRADUATE EXPENSES for 2015–2016 Application fee:** $50. **Tuition:** full-time $22,144; part-time $692 per credit hour. **Required fees:** full-time $746; $403 per year. Full-time tuition and fees vary according to course load and student level. Part-time tuition and fees vary according to course load and student level.

**UNDERGRADUATE FINANCIAL AID (Fall 2013)** 144 applied for aid; of those 96% were deemed to have need. 99% of undergraduates with need received aid; of those 2% had need fully met. **Average percent of need met:** 36% (excluding resources awarded to replace EFC). **Average financial aid package:** $8775 (excluding resources awarded to replace EFC). 1% of all full-time undergraduates had no need and received non-need-based gift aid.

**GIFT AID (NEED-BASED) Total amount:** $705,266 (46% federal, 43% state, 8% institutional, 3% external sources). **Receiving aid:** All full-time undergraduates: 58% (89). **Average award:** Undergraduates: $6475. **Scholarships, grants, and awards:** Federal Pell, state, private, college/university gift aid from institutional funds.

**GIFT AID (NON-NEED-BASED) Total amount:** $16,104 (67% federal, 6% institutional, 27% external sources). **Receiving aid:** Undergraduates: 2% (3). **Average award:** Undergraduates: $1000.

**LOANS Student loans:** $2,224,952 (86% need-based, 14% non-need-based). **Average need-based loan:** Undergraduates: $4457. **Parent loans:** $168,949 (60% need-based, 40% non-need-based). **Programs:** Federal Direct (Subsidized and Unsubsidized Stafford, PLUS), alternative loans.

**WORK-STUDY State or other work-study/employment:** Total amount: $187,180 (75% need-based, 25% non-need-based). 42 part-time jobs averaging $4457.

**APPLYING FOR FINANCIAL AID Notification date:** Continuous.

**CONTACT** Serrita Woods, Financial Aid Officer, Saint Anthony College of Nursing, 5658 East State Street, Rockford, IL 61108-2468, 815-395-5089. Fax: 815-227-2730. E-mail: serritawoods@sacn.edu.
**Website:** http://www.sacn.edu/.

# ST. AUGUSTINE COLLEGE
## Chicago, IL

**CONTACT** Mrs. Maria Zambonino, Director of Financial Aid, St. Augustine College, 1345 W Angyle, Chicago, IL 60640, 773-878-3813. Fax: 773-878-9032. E-mail: mzambonino@hotmail.com.
**Website:** http://www.staugustine.edu/.

# SAINT AUGUSTINE'S UNIVERSITY
## Raleigh, NC

| Tuition & fees: N/R | Average undergraduate aid package: $5134 |
|---|---|

**ABOUT THE INSTITUTION** Independent Episcopal, coed. **Awards:** bachelor's degrees. 25 undergraduate majors. **Total enrollment:** 1,016. Undergraduates: 1,016. Freshmen: 268. Federal methodology is used as a basis for awarding need-based institutional aid.

**UNDERGRADUATE EXPENSES for 2015–2016 Application fee:** $50. **Tuition:** part-time $537 per credit hour. **Required fees:** $208 per credit hour. Full-time tuition and fees vary according to course load. Part-time tuition and fees vary according to course load. Room and board charges vary according to housing facility.

**FRESHMAN FINANCIAL AID (Fall 2014, est.)** 319 applied for aid; of those 97% were deemed to have need. 100% of freshmen with need received aid; of those 37%

had need fully met. **Average percent of need met:** 65% (excluding resources awarded to replace EFC). **Average financial aid package:** $4813 (excluding resources awarded to replace EFC).

**UNDERGRADUATE FINANCIAL AID (Fall 2014, est.)** 906 applied for aid; of those 92% were deemed to have need. 100% of undergraduates with need received aid; of those 52% had need fully met. **Average percent of need met:** 80% (excluding resources awarded to replace EFC). **Average financial aid package:** $5134 (excluding resources awarded to replace EFC). 1% of all full-time undergraduates had no need and received non-need-based gift aid.

**GIFT AID (NEED-BASED) Total amount:** $4,919,748 (100% federal). **Receiving aid:** Freshmen: 94% (309); all full-time undergraduates: 64% (831). **Average award:** Freshmen: $4769; Undergraduates: $5190. **Scholarships, grants, and awards:** Federal Pell, FSEOG, state, private, college/university gift aid from institutional funds, United Negro College Fund.

**GIFT AID (NON-NEED-BASED) Total amount:** $5,242,093 (42% state, 45% institutional, 13% external sources). **Receiving aid:** Freshmen: 88% (289). Undergraduates: 64% (826). **Average award:** Undergraduates: $5528. **Scholarships, grants, and awards by category:** Academic interests/achievement: biological sciences, general academic interests/achievements, military science. Creative arts/performance: music, performing arts. Special characteristics: children of faculty/staff, local/state students. **Tuition waivers:** Full or partial for employees or children of employees. **ROTC:** Army, Air Force cooperative.

**LOANS Student loans:** $8,565,733 (44% need-based, 56% non-need-based). 93% of past graduating class borrowed through all loan programs. Average indebtedness per student: $19,500. **Average need-based loan:** Freshmen: $6160. Undergraduates: $5682. **Parent loans:** $1,816,874 (100% non-need-based). **Programs:** Federal Direct (Subsidized and Unsubsidized Stafford, PLUS), Perkins.

**WORK-STUDY Federal work-study:** Total amount: $749,243; jobs available. **State or other work-study/employment:** Total amount: $10,000 (100% non-need-based). Part-time jobs available.

**ATHLETIC AWARDS** Total amount: $1,419,462 (100% non-need-based).

**APPLYING FOR FINANCIAL AID Required financial aid forms:** FAFSA, institution's own form. **Financial aid deadline (priority):** 3/15. **Notification date:** Continuous beginning 3/1. Students must reply within 2 weeks of notification.

**CONTACT** Ms. Nadine Y. Ford, Director of Financial Aid, Saint Augustine's University, 1315 Oakwood Avenue, Raleigh, NC 27610-2298, 919-516-4131 or toll-free 800-948-1126. Fax: 919-516-4431. E-mail: nford@st-aug.edu.
**Website:** http://www.st-aug.edu/.

# ST. BONAVENTURE UNIVERSITY
## St. Bonaventure, NY

| Tuition & fees: $30,475 | Average undergraduate aid package: $26,368 |
|---|---|

**ABOUT THE INSTITUTION** Independent Roman Catholic Church, coed. **Awards:** certificates, bachelor's, and master's degrees. 41 undergraduate majors. **Total enrollment:** 2,147. Undergraduates: 1,771. Freshmen: 435. Federal methodology is used as a basis for awarding need-based institutional aid.

**UNDERGRADUATE EXPENSES for 2015–2016 One-time required fee:** $100. **Comprehensive fee:** $41,575 includes full-time tuition ($29,510), mandatory fees ($965), and room and board ($11,100). **College room only:** $5400. Room and board charges vary according to board plan and housing facility. **Part-time tuition:** $880 per credit hour. Part-time tuition and fees vary according to course load.

**FRESHMAN FINANCIAL AID (Fall 2013)** 404 applied for aid; of those 90% were deemed to have need. 100% of freshmen with need received aid; of those 20% had need fully met. **Average percent of need met:** 85% (excluding resources awarded to replace EFC). **Average financial aid package:** $26,138 (excluding resources awarded to replace EFC). 15% of all full-time freshmen had no need and received non-need-based gift aid.

**UNDERGRADUATE FINANCIAL AID (Fall 2013)** 1,511 applied for aid; of those 91% were deemed to have need. 100% of undergraduates with need received aid; of those 19% had need fully met. **Average percent of need met:** 86% (excluding resources awarded to replace EFC). **Average financial aid package:** $26,368 (excluding resources awarded to replace EFC). 20% of all full-time undergraduates had no need and received non-need-based gift aid.

**GIFT AID (NEED-BASED) Total amount:** $23,111,007 (14% federal, 8% state, 77% institutional, 1% external sources). **Receiving aid:** Freshmen: 83% (364); all full-

time undergraduates: 77% (1,369). *Average award:* Freshmen: $20,524; Undergraduates: $18,899. *Scholarships, grants, and awards:* Federal Pell, FSEOG, state, private, college/university gift aid from institutional funds.

**GIFT AID (NON-NEED-BASED)** *Total amount:* $5,311,749 (8% federal, 1% state, 89% institutional, 2% external sources). *Receiving aid:* Freshmen: 78% (342). Undergraduates: 73% (1,293). *Average award:* Freshmen: $13,931. Undergraduates: $12,572. *Scholarships, grants, and awards by category: Academic interests/ achievement:* 1,530 awards ($17,024,575 total): business, education, general academic interests/achievements. *Creative arts/performance:* 40 awards ($38,713 total): journalism/publications, music, performing arts. *Special characteristics:* 560 awards ($2,504,529 total): children of faculty/staff, local/state students, members of minority groups, out-of-state students, relatives of clergy, religious affiliation, siblings of current students. *Tuition waivers:* Full or partial for employees or children of employees, senior citizens. *ROTC:* Army.

**LOANS** *Student loans:* $12,730,855 (95% need-based, 5% non-need-based). 80% of past graduating class borrowed through all loan programs. *Average indebtedness per student:* $35,627. *Average need-based loan:* Freshmen: $4235. Undergraduates: $4660. *Parent loans:* $4,780,520 (94% need-based, 6% non-need-based). *Programs:* Federal Direct (Subsidized and Unsubsidized Stafford, PLUS), Perkins, college/university.

**WORK-STUDY** *Federal work-study:* 335 jobs averaging $894. *State or other work-study/employment:* Total amount: $264,480 (100% non-need-based). 398 part-time jobs averaging $665.

**ATHLETIC AWARDS** Total amount: $2,912,695 (53% need-based, 47% non-need-based).

**APPLYING FOR FINANCIAL AID** *Required financial aid forms:* FAFSA, state aid form. *Financial aid deadline (priority):* 2/15. *Notification date:* Continuous beginning 3/1. Students must reply by 5/1 or within 2 weeks of notification.

**CONTACT** Mr. Troy R. Martin, Director of Financial Aid, St. Bonaventure University, 3261 West State Road, St. Bonaventure, NY 14778-2284, 716-375-2373 or toll-free 800-462-5050. *Fax:* 716-375-2087. *E-mail:* tmartin@sbu.edu. *Website:* http://www.sbu.edu/.

---

# ST. CATHARINE COLLEGE
## St. Catharine, KY

**CONTACT** Financial Aid Office, St. Catharine College, 2735 Bardstown Road, St. Catharine, KY 40061-9499, 859-336-5082. *Website:* http://www.sccky.edu/.

---

# ST. CATHERINE UNIVERSITY
## St. Paul, MN

| Tuition & fees: $36,420 | Average undergraduate aid package: $32,615 |
| --- | --- |

**ABOUT THE INSTITUTION** Independent Roman Catholic, undergraduate: women only; graduate: coed. *Awards:* certificates, associate, bachelor's, master's, and doctoral degrees. 80 undergraduate majors. *Total enrollment:* 5,055. Undergraduates: 3,491. Freshmen: 478. Federal methodology is used as a basis for awarding need-based institutional aid.

**UNDERGRADUATE EXPENSES** for 2015–2016 *One-time required fee:* $100. *Comprehensive fee:* $45,314 includes full-time tuition ($35,840), mandatory fees ($580), and room and board ($8894). *College room only:* $5000. Full-time tuition and fees vary according to class time and degree level. Room and board charges vary according to board plan and housing facility. *Part-time tuition:* $1120 per credit hour. *Part-time fees:* $290 per term. Part-time tuition and fees vary according to class time and degree level.

**FRESHMAN FINANCIAL AID (Fall 2014, est.)** 413 applied for aid; of those 90% were deemed to have need. 100% of freshmen with need received aid; of those 24% had need fully met. *Average percent of need met:* 92% (excluding resources awarded to replace EFC). *Average financial aid package:* $35,807 (excluding resources awarded to replace EFC). 10% of all full-time freshmen had no need and received non-need-based gift aid.

**UNDERGRADUATE FINANCIAL AID (Fall 2014, est.)** 1,778 applied for aid; of those 86% were deemed to have need. 100% of undergraduates with need received

aid; of those 26% had need fully met. *Average percent of need met:* 87% (excluding resources awarded to replace EFC). *Average financial aid package:* $32,615 (excluding resources awarded to replace EFC). 14% of all full-time undergraduates had no need and received non-need-based gift aid.

**GIFT AID (NEED-BASED)** *Total amount:* $15,726,901 (36% federal, 23% state, 32% institutional, 9% external sources). *Receiving aid:* Freshmen: 77% (320); all full-time undergraduates: 69% (1,229). *Average award:* Freshmen: $10,014; Undergraduates: $10,136. *Scholarships, grants, and awards:* Federal Pell, FSEOG, state, private, college/university gift aid from institutional funds.

**GIFT AID (NON-NEED-BASED)** *Total amount:* $23,472,818 (100% institutional). *Receiving aid:* Freshmen: 89% (372). Undergraduates: 73% (1,306). *Average award:* Freshmen: $18,106. Undergraduates: $15,889. *Scholarships, grants, and awards by category: Academic interests/achievement:* business, education, English, foreign languages, general academic interests/achievements, health fields, home economics, humanities, mathematics, physical sciences, premedicine, social sciences. *Creative arts/performance:* art/fine arts, music. *Special achievements/activities:* community service, general special achievements/activities, leadership, memberships. *Special characteristics:* adult students, children and siblings of alumni, children of current students, children of educators, children of faculty/staff, ethnic background, general special characteristics, international students, local/state students, out-of-state students, religious affiliation, siblings of current students, spouses of current students. *Tuition waivers:* Full or partial for employees or children of employees, senior citizens. *ROTC:* Army cooperative, Air Force cooperative.

**LOANS** *Student loans:* $23,809,334 (42% need-based, 58% non-need-based). 87% of past graduating class borrowed through all loan programs. *Average indebtedness per student:* $39,748. *Average need-based loan:* Freshmen: $4040. Undergraduates: $5137. *Parent loans:* $4,153,919 (100% non-need-based). *Programs:* Federal Direct (Subsidized and Unsubsidized Stafford, PLUS), Perkins, Federal Nursing, state, alternative loans.

**WORK-STUDY** *Federal work-study:* Total amount: $438,546; jobs available. *State or other work-study/employment:* Total amount: $412,795 (100% need-based). Part-time jobs available.

**APPLYING FOR FINANCIAL AID** *Required financial aid forms:* FAFSA, institution's own form. *Financial aid deadline (priority):* 4/15. *Notification date:* Continuous. Students must reply within 2 weeks of notification.

**CONTACT** Beth Stevens, Director of Financial Aid, St. Catherine University, 2004 Randolph Avenue, Derham Hall, Suite 208, St. Paul, MN 55105, 651-690-6540 or toll-free 800-945-4599. *Fax:* 651-690-6765. *E-mail:* finaid@stkate.edu. *Website:* http://www.stkate.edu/.

---

# SAINT CHARLES BORROMEO SEMINARY, OVERBROOK
## Wynnewood, PA

**CONTACT** Ms. Nora M. Downey, Coordinator of Financial Aid, Saint Charles Borromeo Seminary, Overbrook, 100 East Wynnewood Road, Wynnewood, PA 19096-3099, 610-785-6582. *Fax:* 610-667-3971. *E-mail:* ndowney@scs.edu. *Website:* http://www.scs.edu/.

---

# ST. CLOUD STATE UNIVERSITY
## St. Cloud, MN

| Tuition & fees (MN res): $7554 | Average undergraduate aid package: $9605 |
| --- | --- |

**ABOUT THE INSTITUTION** State-supported, coed. *Awards:* certificates, diplomas, associate, bachelor's, master's, and doctoral degrees. 128 undergraduate majors. *Total enrollment:* 16,245. Undergraduates: 14,641. Freshmen: 1,703. Federal methodology is used as a basis for awarding need-based institutional aid.

**UNDERGRADUATE EXPENSES** for 2015–2016 *Application fee:* $20. *Tuition, state resident:* full-time $6584; part-time $219.45 per credit hour. *Tuition, nonresident:* full-time $14,226; part-time $474.20 per credit hour. *Required fees:* full-time $970; $38.89 per credit hour. Full-time tuition and fees vary according to course load, location, and reciprocity agreements. Part-time tuition and fees vary according to course load, location, and reciprocity agreements. *College* *room and board:* $7560; *Room only:* $4700. Room and board charges vary according to board plan and housing facility.

**FRESHMAN FINANCIAL AID (Fall 2014, est.)** 1,410 applied for aid; of those 73% were deemed to have need. 100% of freshmen with need received aid; of those 12% had need fully met. *Average percent of need met:* 61% (excluding resources awarded to replace EFC). *Average financial aid package:* $9406 (excluding resources awarded to replace EFC). 23% of all full-time freshmen had no need and received non-need-based gift aid.

**UNDERGRADUATE FINANCIAL AID (Fall 2014, est.)** 7,066 applied for aid; of those 78% were deemed to have need. 100% of undergraduates with need received aid; of those 13% had need fully met. *Average percent of need met:* 62% (excluding resources awarded to replace EFC). *Average financial aid package:* $9605 (excluding resources awarded to replace EFC). 17% of all full-time undergraduates had no need and received non-need-based gift aid.

**GIFT AID (NEED-BASED)** *Total amount:* $27,209,441 (70% federal, 29% state, 1% institutional). *Receiving aid:* Freshmen: 46% (763); all full-time undergraduates: 47% (4,222). *Average award:* Freshmen: $5739; Undergraduates: $5448. *Scholarships, grants, and awards:* Federal Pell, FSEOG, state, private, college/university gift aid from institutional funds.

**GIFT AID (NON-NEED-BASED)** *Total amount:* $10,607,975 (11% federal, 3% state, 60% institutional, 26% external sources). *Receiving aid:* Freshmen: 29% (480). Undergraduates: 16% (1,413). *Average award:* Freshmen: $9473. Undergraduates: $9542. *Scholarships, grants, and awards by category: Academic interests/achievement:* biological sciences, business, communication, computer science, education, engineering/technologies, English, general academic interests/achievements, health fields, international studies, mathematics, physical sciences, social sciences. *Creative arts/performance:* applied art and design, art/fine arts, cinema/film/broadcasting, creative writing, journalism/publications, music, performing arts, theater/drama. *Special achievements/activities:* community service, general special achievements/activities, leadership. *Special characteristics:* children of faculty/staff, children of union members/company employees, out-of-state students. *Tuition waivers:* Full or partial for employees or children of employees, senior citizens. *ROTC:* Army.

**LOANS** *Student loans:* $67,020,696 (39% need-based, 61% non-need-based). 74% of past graduating class borrowed through all loan programs. *Average indebtedness per student:* $31,953. *Average need-based loan:* Freshmen: $3544. Undergraduates: $4131. *Parent loans:* $1,566,668 (100% non-need-based). *Programs:* Federal Direct (Subsidized and Unsubsidized Stafford, PLUS), Perkins, state.

**WORK-STUDY** *Federal work-study:* Total amount: $1,704,028; jobs available. *State or other work-study/employment:* Total amount: $1,864,017 (84% need-based, 16% non-need-based). Part-time jobs available.

**ATHLETIC AWARDS** Total amount: $1,998,582 (100% non-need-based).

**APPLYING FOR FINANCIAL AID** *Required financial aid forms:* FAFSA, institution's own form. *Financial aid deadline:* Continuous. *Notification date:* Continuous beginning 6/1.

**CONTACT** Financial Aid Office, St. Cloud State University, 720 4th Avenue South, AS106, St. Cloud, MN 56301-4498, 320-308-2047 or toll-free 877-654-7278. *Fax:* 320-308-5424. *E-mail:* financialaid@stcloudstate.edu.

*Website:* http://www.stcloudstate.edu/.

---

# ST. EDWARD'S UNIVERSITY
## Austin, TX

| Tuition & fees: $38,720 | Average undergraduate aid package: $28,906 |
|---|---|

**ABOUT THE INSTITUTION** Independent Roman Catholic, coed. *Awards:* certificates, bachelor's, and master's degrees. 58 undergraduate majors. *Total enrollment:* 4,686. Undergraduates: 4,003. Freshmen: 811. Federal methodology is used as a basis for awarding need-based institutional aid.

**UNDERGRADUATE EXPENSES for 2015–2016** *Application fee:* $50. *Comprehensive fee:* $50,384 includes full-time tuition ($38,320), mandatory fees ($400), and room and board ($11,664). *College room only:* $6734. Full-time tuition and fees vary according to course load and degree level. Room and board charges vary according to board plan and housing facility. *Part-time tuition:* $1278 per credit hour. Part-time tuition and fees vary according to course load and degree level.

**FRESHMAN FINANCIAL AID (Fall 2014, est.)** 665 applied for aid; of those 88% were deemed to have need. 100% of freshmen with need received aid; of those 10% had need fully met. *Average percent of need met:* 74% (excluding resources

awarded to replace EFC). *Average financial aid package:* $32,068 (excluding resources awarded to replace EFC). 6% of all full-time freshmen had no need and received non-need-based gift aid.

**UNDERGRADUATE FINANCIAL AID (Fall 2014, est.)** 2,508 applied for aid; of those 89% were deemed to have need. 99% of undergraduates with need received aid; of those 10% had need fully met. *Average percent of need met:* 67% (excluding resources awarded to replace EFC). *Average financial aid package:* $28,906 (excluding resources awarded to replace EFC). 4% of all full-time undergraduates had no need and received non-need-based gift aid.

**GIFT AID (NEED-BASED)** *Total amount:* $39,987,577 (16% federal, 11% state, 73% institutional). *Receiving aid:* Freshmen: 67% (540); all full-time undergraduates: 60% (2,045). *Average award:* Freshmen: $21,458; Undergraduates: $18,539. *Scholarships, grants, and awards:* Federal Pell, FSEOG, state, private, college/university gift aid from institutional funds.

**GIFT AID (NON-NEED-BASED)** *Total amount:* $23,459,173 (6% federal, 91% institutional, 3% external sources). *Receiving aid:* Freshmen: 49% (395). Undergraduates: 45% (1,555). *Average award:* Freshmen: $15,642. Undergraduates: $11,337. *Scholarships, grants, and awards by category: Academic interests/achievement:* 1,830 awards ($19,698,653 total): biological sciences, business, communication, computer science, education, English, foreign languages, general academic interests/achievements, health fields, humanities, international studies, mathematics, military science, physical sciences, premedicine, religion/biblical studies, social sciences. *Creative arts/performance:* 25 awards ($69,000 total): art/fine arts, journalism/publications, theater/drama. *Special achievements/activities:* 53 awards ($102,500 total): cheerleading/drum major, community service, general special achievements/activities, leadership. *Special characteristics:* 68 awards ($1,443,491 total): adult students, children of faculty/staff, religious affiliation, veterans. *Tuition waivers:* Full or partial for employees or children of employees. *ROTC:* Army cooperative, Air Force cooperative.

**LOANS** *Student loans:* $22,676,504 (39% need-based, 61% non-need-based). 73% of past graduating class borrowed through all loan programs. *Average indebtedness per student:* $34,444. *Average need-based loan:* Freshmen: $3393. Undergraduates: $4523. *Parent loans:* $3,518,902 (100% non-need-based). *Programs:* Federal Direct (Subsidized and Unsubsidized Stafford, PLUS), Perkins, state.

**WORK-STUDY** *Federal work-study:* Total amount: $430,470; 217 jobs averaging $1984. *State or other work-study/employment:* Total amount: $33,000 (100% need-based). 16 part-time jobs averaging $2063.

**ATHLETIC AWARDS** Total amount: $3,237,453 (100% non-need-based).

**APPLYING FOR FINANCIAL AID** *Required financial aid form:* FAFSA. *Financial aid deadline (priority):* 3/1. *Notification date:* Continuous beginning 2/1. Students must reply by 5/1 or within 2 weeks of notification.

**CONTACT** Office of Student Financial Services, St. Edward's University, 3001 South Congress Avenue, Austin, TX 78704-6489, 512-448-8523 or toll-free 800-555-0164. *Fax:* 512-416-5837. *E-mail:* seu.finaid@stedwards.edu.

*Website:* http://www.stedwards.edu/.

---

# ST. FRANCIS COLLEGE
## Brooklyn Heights, NY

| Tuition & fees: $22,300 | Average undergraduate aid package: $14,255 |
|---|---|

**ABOUT THE INSTITUTION** Independent Roman Catholic, coed. *Awards:* certificates, associate, bachelor's, and master's degrees. 36 undergraduate majors. *Total enrollment:* 2,749. Undergraduates: 2,671. Freshmen: 516. Both federal and institutional methodology are used as a basis for awarding need-based institutional aid.

**UNDERGRADUATE EXPENSES for 2015–2016** *Tuition:* full-time $21,400; part-time $10,700 per term. *Required fees:* full-time $900; $725 per credit hour or $275 per term. Full-time tuition and fees vary according to course load and degree level. Part-time tuition and fees vary according to course load and degree level.

**FRESHMAN FINANCIAL AID (Fall 2014, est.)** 434 applied for aid; of those 91% were deemed to have need. 100% of freshmen with need received aid; of those 8% had need fully met. *Average percent of need met:* 61% (excluding resources awarded to replace EFC). *Average financial aid package:* $14,280 (excluding resources awarded to replace EFC). 19% of all full-time freshmen had no need and received non-need-based gift aid.

**UNDERGRADUATE FINANCIAL AID (Fall 2014, est.)** 1,917 applied for aid; of those 92% were deemed to have need. 100% of undergraduates with need received aid; of those 11% had need fully met. *Average percent of need met:* 61%

(excluding resources awarded to replace EFC). *Average financial aid package:* $14,255 (excluding resources awarded to replace EFC). 20% of all full-time undergraduates had no need and received non-need-based gift aid.

**GIFT AID (NEED-BASED) *Total amount:*** $24,905,818 (22% federal, 14% state, 64% institutional). *Receiving aid:* Freshmen: 77% (392); all full-time undergraduates: 72% (1,727). *Average award:* Freshmen: $11,890; Undergraduates: $10,675. *Scholarships, grants, and awards:* Federal Pell, FSEOG, state, private, college/university gift aid from institutional funds.

**GIFT AID (NON-NEED-BASED) *Receiving aid:*** Freshmen: 68% (349). Undergraduates: 56% (1,363). *Average award:* Freshmen: $8953. Undergraduates: $9300. *Scholarships, grants, and awards by category:* Academic interests/achievement: general academic interests/achievements. *Special characteristics:* children of public servants, handicapped students, public servants. *ROTC:* Army cooperative, Air Force cooperative.

**LOANS *Student loans:*** $9,907,300 (100% need-based). 44% of past graduating class borrowed through all loan programs. *Average indebtedness per student:* $23,835. *Average need-based loan:* Freshmen: $3370. Undergraduates: $4170. *Parent loans:* $3,792,500 (100% need-based). *Programs:* Federal Direct (Subsidized and Unsubsidized Stafford, PLUS), Perkins.

**WORK-STUDY *Federal work-study:*** Total amount: $145,000; 125 jobs averaging $2000.

**ATHLETIC AWARDS *Total amount:*** $2,394,000 (100% need-based).

**APPLYING FOR FINANCIAL AID *Required financial aid forms:*** FAFSA, state aid form. *Financial aid deadline (priority):* 2/15. *Notification date:* Continuous. Students must reply within 2 weeks of notification.

**CONTACT** Ms. Hellitz Lopez, Director of Student Financial Services, St. Francis College, 180 Remsen Street, Brooklyn Heights, NY 11201-4398, 718-489-5346. *Fax:* 718-643-0076. *E-mail:* hlopez@sfc.edu.
*Website:* http://www.sfc.edu/.

---

# SAINT FRANCIS MEDICAL CENTER COLLEGE OF NURSING
## Peoria, IL

| Tuition & fees: $18,881 | Average undergraduate aid package: $9346 |
|---|---|

**ABOUT THE INSTITUTION** Independent Roman Catholic, coed, primarily women. *Awards:* certificates, bachelor's, master's, and doctoral degrees. 1 undergraduate major. *Total enrollment:* 682. Undergraduates: 405. Federal methodology is used as a basis for awarding need-based institutional aid.

**UNDERGRADUATE EXPENSES for 2015–2016 *Application fee:*** $50. *Tuition:* full-time $18,016; part-time $563 per hour. Full-time tuition and fees vary according to course load, degree level, and student level. Part-time tuition and fees vary according to course load, degree level, and student level.

**UNDERGRADUATE FINANCIAL AID (Fall 2014, est.)** 254 applied for aid; of those 79% were deemed to have need. 100% of undergraduates with need received aid; of those 7% had need fully met. *Average percent of need met:* 41% (excluding resources awarded to replace EFC). *Average financial aid package:* $9346 (excluding resources awarded to replace EFC). 6% of all full-time undergraduates had no need and received non-need-based gift aid.

**GIFT AID (NEED-BASED) *Total amount:*** $942,535 (35% federal, 46% state, 13% institutional, 6% external sources). *Receiving aid:* All full-time undergraduates: 48% (146). *Average award:* Undergraduates: $6526. *Scholarships, grants, and awards:* Federal Pell, state, private, college/university gift aid from institutional funds.

**GIFT AID (NON-NEED-BASED) *Total amount:*** $65,236 (16% state, 53% institutional, 31% external sources). *Receiving aid:* Undergraduates: 1% (2). *Average award:* Undergraduates: $1547. *Scholarships, grants, and awards by category:* Academic interests/achievement: 23 awards ($23,000 total): general academic interests/achievements, health fields. *Tuition waivers:* Full or partial for employees or children of employees.

**LOANS *Student loans:*** $2,193,439 (78% need-based, 22% non-need-based). *Average need-based loan:* Undergraduates: $4924. *Parent loans:* $272,358 (45% need-based, 55% non-need-based). *Programs:* Federal Direct (Subsidized and Unsubsidized Stafford, PLUS), college/university.

**APPLYING FOR FINANCIAL AID *Required financial aid forms:*** FAFSA, institution's own form. *Financial aid deadline (priority):* 3/1. *Notification date:* Continuous beginning 5/1.

**CONTACT** Ms. Nancy Perryman, Coordinator for Student Financial Assistance, Saint Francis Medical Center College of Nursing, 511 Northeast Greenleaf Street, Peoria, IL 61603-3783, 309-655-4119. *Fax:* 309-655-3962. *E-mail:* nancy.s.perryman@osfhealthcare.org.
*Website:* http://www.sfmccon.edu/.

---

# SAINT FRANCIS UNIVERSITY
## Loretto, PA

| Tuition & fees: $32,128 | Average undergraduate aid package: $19,008 |
|---|---|

**ABOUT THE INSTITUTION** Independent Roman Catholic, coed. *Awards:* certificates, associate, bachelor's, master's, and doctoral degrees. 68 undergraduate majors. *Total enrollment:* 2,387. Undergraduates: 1,722. Freshmen: 389. Federal methodology is used as a basis for awarding need-based institutional aid.

**UNDERGRADUATE EXPENSES for 2015–2016 *Application fee:*** $30. *One-time required fee:* $100. *Comprehensive fee:* $43,210 includes full-time tuition ($31,078), mandatory fees ($1050), and room and board ($11,082). Full-time tuition and fees vary according to course load, degree level, program, and student level. Room and board charges vary according to board plan and housing facility. *Part-time tuition:* $971 per credit hour. Part-time tuition and fees vary according to class time, degree level, and program.

**FRESHMAN FINANCIAL AID (Fall 2014, est.)** 396 applied for aid; of those 86% were deemed to have need. 100% of freshmen with need received aid; of those 20% had need fully met. *Average percent of need met:* 72% (excluding resources awarded to replace EFC). *Average financial aid package:* $22,960 (excluding resources awarded to replace EFC). 10% of all full-time freshmen had no need and received non-need-based gift aid.

**UNDERGRADUATE FINANCIAL AID (Fall 2014, est.)** 1,483 applied for aid; of those 82% were deemed to have need. 100% of undergraduates with need received aid; of those 23% had need fully met. *Average percent of need met:* 43% (excluding resources awarded to replace EFC). *Average financial aid package:* $19,008 (excluding resources awarded to replace EFC). 10% of all full-time undergraduates had no need and received non-need-based gift aid.

**GIFT AID (NEED-BASED) *Total amount:*** $17,703,064 (10% federal, 11% state, 78% institutional, 1% external sources). *Receiving aid:* Freshmen: 47% (189); all full-time undergraduates: 45% (678). *Average award:* Freshmen: $11,063; Undergraduates: $15,978. *Scholarships, grants, and awards:* Federal Pell, FSEOG, state, private, college/university gift aid from institutional funds.

**GIFT AID (NON-NEED-BASED) *Total amount:*** $4,010,254 (99% institutional, 1% external sources). *Receiving aid:* Freshmen: 85% (342). Undergraduates: 14% (216). *Average award:* Freshmen: $16,134. Undergraduates: $16,641. *Scholarships, grants, and awards by category:* Academic interests/achievement: 833 awards ($3,530,037 total): biological sciences, business, communication, computer science, education, engineering/technologies, English, general academic interests/achievements, health fields, humanities, international studies, mathematics, religion/biblical studies, social sciences. *Creative arts/performance:* 55 awards ($60,000 total): art/fine arts. *Special achievements/activities:* 52 awards ($112,022 total): cheerleading/drum major, leadership, religious involvement. *Special characteristics:* 654 awards ($3,830,293 total): adult students, children and siblings of alumni, children of current students, children of educators, children of faculty/staff, international students, out-of-state students, previous college experience, religious affiliation, siblings of current students, spouses of current students. *Tuition waivers:* Full or partial for employees or children of employees. *ROTC:* Army.

**LOANS *Student loans:*** $13,826,700 (94% need-based, 6% non-need-based). 91% of past graduating class borrowed through all loan programs. *Average indebtedness per student:* $36,656. *Average need-based loan:* Freshmen: $3537. Undergraduates: $4412. *Parent loans:* $2,959,289 (94% need-based, 6% non-need-based). *Programs:* Federal Direct (Subsidized and Unsubsidized Stafford, PLUS), Perkins, private loans.

**WORK-STUDY *Federal work-study:*** Total amount: $412,191; 283 jobs averaging $1000. *State or other work-study/employment:* Total amount: $405,000 (93% need-based, 7% non-need-based). 755 part-time jobs averaging $1000.

**ATHLETIC AWARDS** Total amount: $5,325,409 (85% need-based, 15% non-need-based).

**APPLYING FOR FINANCIAL AID** *Required financial aid form:* FAFSA. *Financial aid deadline (priority):* 5/1. *Notification date:* Continuous beginning 3/1. Students must reply by 5/1.

**CONTACT** Mr. Jamie Kosh, Director of Financial Aid, Saint Francis University, PO Box 600, Loretto, PA 15931, 814-472-3010 or toll-free 866-DIAL-SFU. *Fax:* 814-472-3999. *E-mail:* jkosh@francis.edu. *Website:* http://www.francis.edu/.

# ST. GREGORY'S UNIVERSITY
## Shawnee, OK

**CONTACT** Matt McCoin, Director of Financial Aid, St. Gregory's University, 1900 West MacArthur Drive, Shawnee, OK 74804, 405-878-5412 or toll-free 888-STGREGS. *Fax:* 405-878-5403. *E-mail:* mdmccoin@stgregorys.edu. *Website:* http://www.stgregorys.edu/.

# ST. GREGORY THE GREAT SEMINARY
## Seward, NE

**CONTACT** Financial Aid Office, St. Gregory the Great Seminary, 800 Fletcher Road, Seward, NE 67434, 402-643-4052. *Website:* http://www.stgregoryseminary.edu/.

# ST. JOHN FISHER COLLEGE
## Rochester, NY

| Tuition & fees: $29,550 | Average undergraduate aid package: $20,935 |
|---|---|

**ABOUT THE INSTITUTION** Independent Roman Catholic Church, coed. *Awards:* certificates, bachelor's, master's, and doctoral degrees. 40 undergraduate majors. *Total enrollment:* 3,856. Undergraduates: 2,857. Freshmen: 597. Federal methodology is used as a basis for awarding need-based institutional aid.

**UNDERGRADUATE EXPENSES for 2015–2016** *Comprehensive fee:* $40,708 includes full-time tuition ($28,970), mandatory fees ($580), and room and board ($11,158). *College room only:* $7230. Full-time tuition and fees vary according to program. Room and board charges vary according to board plan. *Part-time tuition:* $790 per credit hour. *Part-time fees:* $10 per credit hour. Part-time tuition and fees vary according to course load and program.

**FRESHMAN FINANCIAL AID (Fall 2014, est.)** 575 applied for aid; of those 88% were deemed to have need. 100% of freshmen with need received aid; of those 37% had need fully met. *Average percent of need met:* 73% (excluding resources awarded to replace EFC). *Average financial aid package:* $22,096 (excluding resources awarded to replace EFC). 16% of all full-time freshmen had no need and received non-need-based gift aid.

**UNDERGRADUATE FINANCIAL AID (Fall 2014, est.)** 2,368 applied for aid; of those 92% were deemed to have need. 100% of undergraduates with need received aid; of those 35% had need fully met. *Average percent of need met:* 71% (excluding resources awarded to replace EFC). *Average financial aid package:* $20,935 (excluding resources awarded to replace EFC). 18% of all full-time undergraduates had no need and received non-need-based gift aid.

**GIFT AID (NEED-BASED)** *Total amount:* $35,073,415 (13% federal, 9% state, 76% institutional, 2% external sources). *Receiving aid:* Freshmen: 84% (504); all full-time undergraduates: 81% (2,159). *Average award:* Freshmen: $18,180; Undergraduates: $16,063. *Scholarships, grants, and awards:* Federal Pell, FSEOG, state, private, college/university gift aid from institutional funds, Federal Nursing.

**GIFT AID (NON-NEED-BASED)** *Total amount:* $5,185,963 (2% federal, 95% institutional, 3% external sources). *Receiving aid:* Freshmen: 65% (388). Undergraduates: 60% (1,604). *Average award:* Freshmen: $11,360. Undergraduates: $10,658. *Scholarships, grants, and awards by category: Academic interests/achievement:* 1,309 awards ($14,712,475 total): biological sciences, business, English, foreign languages, general academic interests/achievements, humanities, mathematics,

physical sciences. *Special achievements/activities:* 93 awards ($1,441,815 total): community service. *Special characteristics:* 159 awards ($2,332,475 total): children and siblings of alumni, children of faculty/staff, ethnic background, first-generation college students, local/state students, members of minority groups. *Tuition waivers:* Full or partial for employees or children of employees. *ROTC:* Army cooperative, Naval cooperative, Air Force cooperative.

**LOANS** *Student loans:* $22,219,282 (93% need-based, 7% non-need-based). 85% of past graduating class borrowed through all loan programs. *Average indebtedness per student:* $32,982. *Average need-based loan:* Freshmen: $3737. Undergraduates: $4745. *Parent loans:* $13,105,269 (89% need-based, 11% non-need-based). *Programs:* Federal Direct (Subsidized and Unsubsidized Stafford, PLUS), Perkins.

**WORK-STUDY** *Federal work-study:* Total amount: $1,924,235; 1,280 jobs averaging $1494.

**APPLYING FOR FINANCIAL AID** *Required financial aid forms:* FAFSA, state aid form. *Financial aid deadline (priority):* 2/15. *Notification date:* Continuous beginning 3/21. Students must reply by 5/1 or within 3 weeks of notification.

**CONTACT** Mrs. Angela Monnat, Director of Financial Aid, St. John Fisher College, 3690 East Avenue, Rochester, NY 14618-3597, 585-385-8042 or toll-free 800-444-4640. *Fax:* 585-385-8044. *E-mail:* amonnat@sjfc.edu. *Website:* http://www.sjfc.edu/.

# ST. JOHN'S COLLEGE
## Springfield, IL

**CONTACT** Mary M. Deatherage, Financial Aid Officer, St. John's College, 421 North Ninth Street, Springfield, IL 62702, 217-544-6464 Ext. 44705. *Fax:* 217-757-6870. *E-mail:* mdeather@st-johns.org. *Website:* http://www.stjohnscollegespringfield.edu/.

# ST. JOHN'S COLLEGE
## Annapolis, MD

| Tuition & fees: $450 | Average undergraduate aid package: $35,892 |
|---|---|

**ABOUT THE INSTITUTION** Independent, coed. *Awards:* bachelor's and master's degrees. 1 undergraduate major. *Total enrollment:* 472. Undergraduates: 426. Freshmen: 133. Both federal and institutional methodology are used as a basis for awarding need-based institutional aid.

**UNDERGRADUATE EXPENSES for 2015–2016** Room and board charges vary according to board plan and housing facility. *Payment plan:* Tuition prepayment.

**FRESHMAN FINANCIAL AID (Fall 2014, est.)** 99 applied for aid; of those 82% were deemed to have need. 100% of freshmen with need received aid; of those 36% had need fully met. *Average percent of need met:* 84% (excluding resources awarded to replace EFC). *Average financial aid package:* $35,999 (excluding resources awarded to replace EFC). 31% of all full-time freshmen had no need and received non-need-based gift aid.

**UNDERGRADUATE FINANCIAL AID (Fall 2014, est.)** 348 applied for aid; of those 90% were deemed to have need. 100% of undergraduates with need received aid; of those 21% had need fully met. *Average percent of need met:* 81% (excluding resources awarded to replace EFC). *Average financial aid package:* $35,892 (excluding resources awarded to replace EFC). 19% of all full-time undergraduates had no need and received non-need-based gift aid.

**GIFT AID (NEED-BASED)** *Total amount:* $9,383,171 (6% federal, 1% state, 89% institutional, 4% external sources). *Receiving aid:* Freshmen: 59% (79); all full-time undergraduates: 72% (307). *Average award:* Freshmen: $32,562; Undergraduates: $30,564. *Scholarships, grants, and awards:* Federal Pell, FSEOG, state, private, college/university gift aid from institutional funds.

**GIFT AID (NON-NEED-BASED)** *Total amount:* $2,315,254 (83% institutional, 17% external sources). *Receiving aid:* Freshmen: 18% (24). Undergraduates: 12% (53). *Average award:* Freshmen: $21,737. Undergraduates: $19,258. *Scholarships, grants, and awards by category: Academic interests/achievement:* general academic interests/achievements. *Tuition waivers:* Full or partial for employees or children of employees.

**LOANS** *Student loans:* $2,677,344 (79% need-based, 21% non-need-based). 72% of past graduating class borrowed through all loan programs. *Average indebtedness per student:* $28,730. *Average need-based loan:* Freshmen: $3619. Undergraduates: $4855. *Parent loans:* $1,037,847 (33% need-based, 67% non-need-based). *Programs:* Federal Direct (Subsidized and Unsubsidized Stafford, PLUS), Perkins, college/university.

**WORK-STUDY** *Federal work-study:* Total amount: $258,899; 101 jobs averaging $2712. *State or other work-study/employment:* 95 part-time jobs averaging $2668.

**APPLYING FOR FINANCIAL AID** *Required financial aid forms:* FAFSA, CSS Financial Aid PROFILE, noncustodial (divorced/separated) parent's statement, business/farm supplement. *Financial aid deadline (priority):* 2/15. *Notification date:* Continuous beginning 2/15. Students must reply by 5/1.

**CONTACT** Ms. Dana Kennedy, Director of Financial Aid, St. John's College, 60 College Avenue, Annapolis, MD 21401, 410-626-2502 or toll-free 800-727-9238. *Fax:* 410-626-2885. *E-mail:* dana.kennedy@sjc.edu. *Website:* http://www.stjohnscollege.edu/.

# ST. JOHN'S COLLEGE
## Santa Fe, NM

| Tuition & fees: $48,994 | Average undergraduate aid package: $33,590 |
|---|---|

**ABOUT THE INSTITUTION** Independent, coed. *Awards:* bachelor's and master's degrees. 3 undergraduate majors. *Total enrollment:* 404. Undergraduates: 342. Freshmen: 76. Both federal and institutional methodology are used as a basis for awarding need-based institutional aid.

**UNDERGRADUATE EXPENSES for 2015–2016** *Comprehensive fee:* $59,884 includes full-time tuition ($48,544), mandatory fees ($450), and room and board ($10,890). Room and board charges vary according to board plan. *Part-time tuition:* $1428 per credit.

**FRESHMAN FINANCIAL AID (Fall 2013)** 84 applied for aid; of those 100% were deemed to have need. 100% of freshmen with need received aid; of those 95% had need fully met. *Average percent of need met:* 92% (excluding resources awarded to replace EFC). *Average financial aid package:* $36,485 (excluding resources awarded to replace EFC). 42% of all full-time freshmen had no need and received non-need-based gift aid.

**UNDERGRADUATE FINANCIAL AID (Fall 2013)** 328 applied for aid; of those 100% were deemed to have need. 100% of undergraduates with need received aid; of those 89% had need fully met. *Average percent of need met:* 94% (excluding resources awarded to replace EFC). *Average financial aid package:* $33,590 (excluding resources awarded to replace EFC). 10% of all full-time undergraduates had no need and received non-need-based gift aid.

**GIFT AID (NEED-BASED)** *Total amount:* $9,327,799 (8% federal, 92% institutional). *Receiving aid:* Freshmen: 80% (67); all full-time undergraduates: 92% (318). *Average award:* Freshmen: $31,280; Undergraduates: $29,288. *Scholarships, grants, and awards:* Federal Pell, FSEOG, state, private, college/university gift aid from institutional funds.

**GIFT AID (NON-NEED-BASED)** *Total amount:* $396,447 (70% institutional, 30% external sources). *Receiving aid:* Freshmen: 20% (17). Undergraduates: 8% (28). *Average award:* Freshmen: $10,771. Undergraduates: $10,805. *Scholarships, grants, and awards by category:* Special characteristics: children of faculty/staff, veterans. *Tuition waivers:* Full or partial for employees or children of employees.

**LOANS** *Student loans:* $1,977,685 (69% need-based, 31% non-need-based). 80% of past graduating class borrowed through all loan programs. *Average indebtedness per student:* $25,570. *Average need-based loan:* Freshmen: $5500. Undergraduates: $6750. *Parent loans:* $773,348 (100% non-need-based). *Programs:* Federal Direct (Subsidized and Unsubsidized Stafford, PLUS), Perkins, college/university.

**WORK-STUDY** *Federal work-study:* jobs available. *State or other work-study/employment:* Total amount: $101,890 (100% need-based). Part-time jobs available.

**APPLYING FOR FINANCIAL AID** *Required financial aid forms:* FAFSA, CSS Financial Aid PROFILE, noncustodial (divorced/separated) parent's statement, business/farm supplement. *Financial aid deadline (priority):* 2/15. *Notification date:* Continuous beginning 12/15. Students must reply by 5/1 or within 2 weeks of notification.

**CONTACT** Michael R. Rodriguez, Director of Financial Aid, St. John's College, 1160 Camino Cruz Blanca, Santa Fe, NM 87505, 505-984-6058 or toll-free 800-331-5232. *Fax:* 505-984-6164. *E-mail:* mrodriguez@sjc.edu. *Website:* http://www.stjohnscollege.edu/.

# SAINT JOHN'S UNIVERSITY
## Collegeville, MN

| Tuition & fees: $38,704 | Average undergraduate aid package: $30,327 |
|---|---|

**ABOUT THE INSTITUTION** Independent Roman Catholic, undergraduate: men only; graduate: coed. *Awards:* bachelor's and master's degrees (coordinate with College of Saint Benedict for women). 50 undergraduate majors. *Total enrollment:* 1,895. Undergraduates: 1,789. Freshmen: 450. Federal methodology is used as a basis for awarding need-based institutional aid.

**UNDERGRADUATE EXPENSES for 2015–2016** *Comprehensive fee:* $47,984 includes full-time tuition ($38,024), mandatory fees ($680), and room and board ($9280). *College room only:* $4640. Room and board charges vary according to board plan and housing facility. *Part-time tuition:* $1584 per credit hour. Part-time tuition and fees vary according to course load.

**FRESHMAN FINANCIAL AID (Fall 2014, est.)** 387 applied for aid; of those 85% were deemed to have need. 100% of freshmen with need received aid; of those 43% had need fully met. *Average percent of need met:* 95% (excluding resources awarded to replace EFC). *Average financial aid package:* $32,415 (excluding resources awarded to replace EFC). 21% of all full-time freshmen had no need and received non-need-based gift aid.

**UNDERGRADUATE FINANCIAL AID (Fall 2014, est.)** 1,354 applied for aid; of those 86% were deemed to have need. 100% of undergraduates with need received aid; of those 38% had need fully met. *Average percent of need met:* 89% (excluding resources awarded to replace EFC). *Average financial aid package:* $30,327 (excluding resources awarded to replace EFC). 26% of all full-time undergraduates had no need and received non-need-based gift aid.

**GIFT AID (NEED-BASED)** *Total amount:* $30,007,344 (7% federal, 6% state, 85% institutional, 2% external sources). *Receiving aid:* Freshmen: 73% (328); all full-time undergraduates: 66% (1,156). *Average award:* Freshmen: $28,121; Undergraduates: $25,274. *Scholarships, grants, and awards:* Federal Pell, FSEOG, state, private, college/university gift aid from institutional funds.

**GIFT AID (NON-NEED-BASED)** *Total amount:* $10,397,474 (88% institutional, 12% external sources). *Receiving aid:* Freshmen: 70% (317). Undergraduates: 64% (1,112). *Average award:* Freshmen: $16,482. Undergraduates: $15,184. *Scholarships, grants, and awards by category:* Academic interests/achievement: general academic interests/achievements. Creative arts/performance: art/fine arts, music, theater/drama. Special characteristics: 444 awards ($3,305,274 total): International students, out-of-state students. *Tuition waivers:* Full or partial for employees or children of employees. *ROTC:* Army.

**LOANS** *Student loans:* $11,863,873 (90% need-based, 10% non-need-based). 70% of past graduating class borrowed through all loan programs. *Average indebtedness per student:* $38,089. *Average need-based loan:* Freshmen: $3282. Undergraduates: $3935. *Parent loans:* $915,154 (86% need-based, 14% non-need-based). *Programs:* Federal Direct (Subsidized and Unsubsidized Stafford, PLUS), Perkins, state, alternative loans.

**WORK-STUDY** *Federal work-study:* Total amount: $566,844; jobs available. *State or other work-study/employment:* Total amount: $2,289,678 (77% need-based, 23% non-need-based). Part-time jobs available.

**APPLYING FOR FINANCIAL AID** *Required financial aid forms:* FAFSA, institution's own form, federal income tax form(s). *Financial aid deadline (priority):* 3/15. *Notification date:* Continuous beginning 3/15. Students must reply by 5/1 or within 3 weeks of notification.

**CONTACT** Ms. Mary Dehler, Senior Associate Director of Financial Aid, Saint John's University, PO Box 5000, Collegeville, MN 56321-5000, 320-363-3664 or toll-free 800-544-1489. *Fax:* 320-363-3102. *E-mail:* mdehler@csbsju.edu. *Website:* http://www.csbsju.edu/.

## ST. JOHN'S UNIVERSITY
### Queens, NY

| Tuition & fees: $38,680 | Average undergraduate aid package: $27,001 |
|---|---|

**ABOUT THE INSTITUTION** Independent Roman Catholic Church, coed. *Awards:* certificates, associate, bachelor's, master's, and doctoral degrees. 67 undergraduate majors. *Total enrollment:* 20,445. Undergraduates: 15,765. Freshmen: 2,795. Federal methodology is used as a basis for awarding need-based institutional aid.

**UNDERGRADUATE EXPENSES for 2015–2016** *Application fee:* $50. *Comprehensive fee:* $55,070 includes full-time tuition ($37,870), mandatory fees ($810), and room and board ($16,390). *College room only:* $10,260. Full-time tuition and fees vary according to course load, program, and student level. Room and board charges vary according to board plan, housing facility, and location. *Part-time tuition:* $1262 per credit. *Part-time fees:* $302.50 per term. Part-time tuition and fees vary according to course load, program, and student level.

**FRESHMAN FINANCIAL AID (Fall 2013)** 2,534 applied for aid; of those 92% were deemed to have need. 100% of freshmen with need received aid; of those 12% had need fully met. *Average percent of need met:* 98% (excluding resources awarded to replace EFC). *Average financial aid package:* $28,262 (excluding resources awarded to replace EFC). 7% of all full-time freshmen had no need and received non-need-based gift aid.

**UNDERGRADUATE FINANCIAL AID (Fall 2013)** 9,391 applied for aid; of those 94% were deemed to have need. 100% of undergraduates with need received aid; of those 11% had need fully met. *Average percent of need met:* 80% (excluding resources awarded to replace EFC). *Average financial aid package:* $27,001 (excluding resources awarded to replace EFC). 2% of all full-time undergraduates had no need and received non-need-based gift aid.

**GIFT AID (NEED-BASED) Total amount:** $91,665,337 (26% federal, 13% state, 61% institutional). *Receiving aid:* Freshmen: 72% (2,009); all full-time undergraduates: 70% (7,684). *Average award:* Freshmen: $11,201; Undergraduates: $12,101. *Scholarships, grants, and awards:* Federal Pell, FSEOG, state, private, college/university gift aid from institutional funds.

**GIFT AID (NON-NEED-BASED) Total amount:** $118,558,760 (1% state, 91% institutional, 8% external sources). *Receiving aid:* Freshmen: 79% (2,218). Undergraduates: 69% (7,493). *Average award:* Freshmen: $18,658. Undergraduates: $16,330. *Scholarships, grants, and awards by category: Academic interests/ achievement:* 6,459 awards ($78,867,131 total): biological sciences, business, communication, computer science, education, English, foreign languages, general academic interests/achievements, health fields, humanities, mathematics, military science, physical sciences, premedicine, social sciences. *Creative arts/performance:* 122 awards ($449,606 total): art/fine arts, cinema/film/broadcasting, creative writing, dance, debating, journalism/publications, music. *Special achievements/activities:* 438 awards ($1,388,950 total): cheerleading/drum major, community service, general special achievements/activities, hobbies/interests, leadership, religious involvement. *Special characteristics:* 3,649 awards ($16,264,866 total): children of faculty/staff, general special characteristics, local/state students, relatives of clergy, religious affiliation. *Tuition waivers:* Full or partial for employees or children of employees, adult students, senior citizens. *ROTC:* Army.

**LOANS Student loans:** $66,280,750 (42% need-based, 58% non-need-based). 75% of past graduating class borrowed through all loan programs. *Average indebtedness per student:* $32,950. *Average need-based loan:* Freshmen: $3762. Undergraduates: $4718. *Parent loans:* $67,559,227 (100% non-need-based). *Programs:* Federal Direct (Subsidized and Unsubsidized Stafford, PLUS), Perkins, Health Professions Student Loans (HPSL).

**WORK-STUDY Federal work-study:** 850 jobs averaging $2415. *State or other work-study/employment:* Total amount: $12,134,300 (95% need-based, 5% non-need-based). Part-time jobs available.

**ATHLETIC AWARDS Total amount:** $6,409,675 (100% non-need-based).

**APPLYING FOR FINANCIAL AID** *Required financial aid form:* FAFSA. *Financial aid deadline (priority):* 2/1. *Notification date:* 3/1. Students must reply by 5/1 or within 2 weeks of notification.

**CONTACT** Mr. Jorge Rodriguez, Associate Vice President for Student Financial Services, St. John's University, 8000 Utopia Parkway, Queens, NY 11439, 718-990-2000 or toll-free 888-9STJOHNS. *Fax:* 718-990-5945. *E-mail:* studentfinancialserv@stjohns.edu. *Website:* http://www.stjohns.edu/.

## ST. JOHN VIANNEY COLLEGE SEMINARY
### Miami, FL

**CONTACT** Ms. Bonnie DeAngulo, Director of Financial Aid, St. John Vianney College Seminary, 2900 Southwest 87th Avenue, Miami, FL 33165-3244, 305-223-4561 Ext. 10. *Website:* http://www.sjvcs.edu/.

## SAINT JOSEPH'S COLLEGE
### Rensselaer, IN

| Tuition & fees: $27,485 | Average undergraduate aid package: $27,622 |
|---|---|

**ABOUT THE INSTITUTION** Independent Roman Catholic, coed. *Awards:* diplomas, associate, bachelor's, and master's degrees. 33 undergraduate majors. *Total enrollment:* 1,166. Undergraduates: 1,142. Freshmen: 216. Federal methodology is used as a basis for awarding need-based institutional aid.

**UNDERGRADUATE EXPENSES for 2015–2016** *Application fee:* $25. *Comprehensive fee:* $36,095 includes full-time tuition ($27,295), mandatory fees ($190), and room and board ($8610). *College room only:* $4180. Full-time tuition and fees vary according to reciprocity agreements and student level. Room and board charges vary according to board plan and housing facility. *Part-time tuition:* $925 per credit. Part-time tuition and fees vary according to course load and reciprocity agreements. *Payment plan:* Guaranteed tuition.

**FRESHMAN FINANCIAL AID (Fall 2013)** 273 applied for aid; of those 92% were deemed to have need. 100% of freshmen with need received aid; of those 23% had need fully met. *Average percent of need met:* 83% (excluding resources awarded to replace EFC). *Average financial aid package:* $26,472 (excluding resources awarded to replace EFC). 8% of all full-time freshmen had no need and received non-need-based gift aid.

**UNDERGRADUATE FINANCIAL AID (Fall 2013)** 825 applied for aid; of those 87% were deemed to have need. 100% of undergraduates with need received aid; of those 33% had need fully met. *Average percent of need met:* 85% (excluding resources awarded to replace EFC). *Average financial aid package:* $27,622 (excluding resources awarded to replace EFC). 11% of all full-time undergraduates had no need and received non-need-based gift aid.

**GIFT AID (NEED-BASED) Total amount:** $11,696,223 (13% federal, 10% state, 75% institutional, 2% external sources). *Receiving aid:* Freshmen: 92% (250); all full-time undergraduates: 84% (709). *Average award:* Freshmen: $19,227; Undergraduates: $19,209. *Scholarships, grants, and awards:* Federal Pell, FSEOG, state, private, college/university gift aid from institutional funds.

**GIFT AID (NON-NEED-BASED) Total amount:** $2,849,573 (94% institutional, 6% external sources). *Receiving aid:* Freshmen: 25% (68). Undergraduates: 25% (212). *Average award:* Freshmen: $18,372. Undergraduates: $16,896. *Scholarships, grants, and awards by category: Academic interests/achievement:* general academic interests/achievements. *Creative arts/performance:* cinema/film/broadcasting, dance, music, theater/drama. *Special achievements/activities:* cheerleading/drum major. *Special characteristics:* children and siblings of alumni, children of faculty/staff, siblings of current students. *Tuition waivers:* Full or partial for minority students, children of alumni, employees or children of employees.

**LOANS Student loans:** $5,635,603 (84% need-based, 16% non-need-based). 84% of past graduating class borrowed through all loan programs. *Average indebtedness per student:* $30,899. *Average need-based loan:* Freshmen: $4286. Undergraduates: $4607. *Parent loans:* $1,232,481 (68% need-based, 32% non-need-based). *Programs:* Federal Direct (Subsidized and Unsubsidized Stafford, PLUS), Perkins.

**WORK-STUDY Federal work-study:** 229 jobs averaging $1441.

**ATHLETIC AWARDS Total amount:** $2,741,316 (62% need-based, 38% non-need-based).

**APPLYING FOR FINANCIAL AID** *Required financial aid form:* FAFSA. *Financial aid deadline (priority):* 3/1. *Notification date:* Continuous beginning 3/1. Students must reply by 5/1 or within 2 weeks of notification.

**CONTACT** Debra Sizemore, Director of Student Financial Services, Saint Joseph's College, 1498 South College Avenue, PO Box 971, Rensselaer, IN 47978, 219-866-6163 or toll-free 800-447-8781. *Fax:* 219-866-6144. *E-mail:* debbie@saintjoe.edu. *Website:* http://www.saintjoe.edu/.

# ST. JOSEPH'S COLLEGE, LONG ISLAND CAMPUS
## Patchogue, NY

**Tuition & fees: $24,130**     **Average undergraduate aid package: $12,522**

**ABOUT THE INSTITUTION** Independent, coed. *Awards:* certificates, bachelor's, and master's degrees. 35 undergraduate majors. *Total enrollment:* 3,623. Undergraduates: 3,023. Freshmen: 321. Federal methodology is used as a basis for awarding need-based institutional aid.

**UNDERGRADUATE EXPENSES for 2015–2016** *Application fee:* $25. *Tuition:* full-time $23,500; part-time $760 per credit. Full-time tuition and fees vary according to course load and program. Part-time tuition and fees vary according to course load and program.

**FRESHMAN FINANCIAL AID (Fall 2013)** 375 applied for aid; of those 81% were deemed to have need. 99% of freshmen with need received aid; of those 34% had need fully met. *Average percent of need met:* 68% (excluding resources awarded to replace EFC). *Average financial aid package:* $15,995 (excluding resources awarded to replace EFC). 18% of all full-time freshmen had no need and received non-need-based gift aid.

**UNDERGRADUATE FINANCIAL AID (Fall 2013)** 2,558 applied for aid; of those 80% were deemed to have need. 99% of undergraduates with need received aid; of those 34% had need fully met. *Average percent of need met:* 61% (excluding resources awarded to replace EFC). *Average financial aid package:* $12,522 (excluding resources awarded to replace EFC). 15% of all full-time undergraduates had no need and received non-need-based gift aid.

**GIFT AID (NEED-BASED)** *Total amount:* $19,694,137 (19% federal, 14% state, 67% institutional). *Receiving aid:* Freshmen: 62% (238); all full-time undergraduates: 72% (1,920). *Average award:* Freshmen: $15,318; Undergraduates: $10,256. *Scholarships, grants, and awards:* Federal Pell, FSEOG, state, private, college/university gift aid from institutional funds.

**GIFT AID (NON-NEED-BASED)** *Total amount:* $4,123,733 (3% state, 91% institutional, 6% external sources). *Receiving aid:* Freshmen: 71% (271). Undergraduates: 59% (1,584). *Average award:* Freshmen: $9272. Undergraduates: $8684. *Scholarships, grants, and awards by category:* Academic interests/achievement: 1,913 awards ($14,754,196 total): general academic interests/achievements. Special achievements/activities: 10 awards ($23,750 total): community service, leadership. Special characteristics: 195 awards ($657,970 total): children and siblings of alumni, children of faculty/staff, parents of current students, public servants, siblings of current students, spouses of current students, twins. *Tuition waivers:* Full or partial for employees or children of employees, senior citizens.

**LOANS** *Student loans:* $15,825,291 (86% need-based, 14% non-need-based). 66% of past graduating class borrowed through all loan programs. *Average indebtedness per student:* $23,603. *Average need-based loan:* Freshmen: $3287. Undergraduates: $4333. *Parent loans:* $5,139,980 (83% need-based, 17% non-need-based). *Programs:* Federal Direct (Subsidized and Unsubsidized Stafford, PLUS), Perkins, state.

**WORK-STUDY** *Federal work-study:* 85 jobs averaging $2467. *State or other work-study/employment:* Total amount: $266,716 (63% need-based, 37% non-need-based). 89 part-time jobs averaging $3001.

**APPLYING FOR FINANCIAL AID** *Required financial aid forms:* FAFSA, state aid form. *Financial aid deadline (priority):* 2/25. *Notification date:* Continuous beginning 3/15. Students must reply by 5/1 or within 2 weeks of notification.

**CONTACT** Amy Thompson, Director of Financial Aid, St. Joseph's College, Long Island Campus, 155 West Roe Boulevard, Patchogue, NY 11772-2399, 631-687-2611. *Fax:* 631-650-2525. *E-mail:* althompson@sjcny.edu.
*Website:* http://www.sjcny.edu/.

# ST. JOSEPH'S COLLEGE, NEW YORK
## Brooklyn, NY

**Tuition & fees: $24,130**     **Average undergraduate aid package: $14,871**

**ABOUT THE INSTITUTION** Independent, coed. *Awards:* certificates, bachelor's, and master's degrees. 35 undergraduate majors. *Total enrollment:* 1,356. Undergraduates: 1,115. Freshmen: 190. Federal methodology is used as a basis for awarding need-based institutional aid.

**UNDERGRADUATE EXPENSES for 2015–2016** *Application fee:* $25. *Tuition:* full-time $23,500; part-time $760 per credit. Full-time tuition and fees vary according to course load and program. Part-time tuition and fees vary according to course load and program.

**FRESHMAN FINANCIAL AID (Fall 2013)** 159 applied for aid; of those 82% were deemed to have need. 100% of freshmen with need received aid; of those 21% had need fully met. *Average percent of need met:* 62% (excluding resources awarded to replace EFC). *Average financial aid package:* $17,588 (excluding resources awarded to replace EFC). 17% of all full-time freshmen had no need and received non-need-based gift aid.

**UNDERGRADUATE FINANCIAL AID (Fall 2013)** 883 applied for aid; of those 81% were deemed to have need. 100% of undergraduates with need received aid; of those 23% had need fully met. *Average percent of need met:* 63% (excluding resources awarded to replace EFC). *Average financial aid package:* $14,871 (excluding resources awarded to replace EFC). 17% of all full-time undergraduates had no need and received non-need-based gift aid.

**GIFT AID (NEED-BASED)** *Total amount:* $9,133,508 (25% federal, 15% state, 60% institutional). *Receiving aid:* Freshmen: 80% (130); all full-time undergraduates: 77% (704). *Average award:* Freshmen: $12,938; Undergraduates: $13,287. *Scholarships, grants, and awards:* Federal Pell, FSEOG, state, private, college/university gift aid from institutional funds.

**GIFT AID (NON-NEED-BASED)** *Total amount:* $2,014,470 (2% state, 93% institutional, 5% external sources). *Receiving aid:* Freshmen: 73% (119). Undergraduates: 66% (603). *Average award:* Freshmen: $11,995. Undergraduates: $11,389. *Scholarships, grants, and awards by category:* Academic interests/achievement: 532 awards ($4,720,252 total): general academic interests/achievements. Special achievements/activities: 8 awards ($20,000 total): community service, leadership. Special characteristics: 80 awards ($299,587 total): children and siblings of alumni, children of faculty/staff, parents of current students, public servants, siblings of current students, spouses of current students, twins. *Tuition waivers:* Full or partial for employees or children of employees, senior citizens.

**LOANS** *Student loans:* $4,830,845 (90% need-based, 10% non-need-based). 56% of past graduating class borrowed through all loan programs. *Average indebtedness per student:* $23,772. *Average need-based loan:* Freshmen: $3228. Undergraduates: $4341. *Parent loans:* $1,198,002 (78% need-based, 22% non-need-based). *Programs:* Federal Direct (Subsidized and Unsubsidized Stafford, PLUS), Perkins, state.

**WORK-STUDY** *Federal work-study:* 88 jobs averaging $1692. *State or other work-study/employment:* Total amount: $31,478 (74% need-based, 26% non-need-based). 14 part-time jobs averaging $1544.

**APPLYING FOR FINANCIAL AID** *Required financial aid forms:* FAFSA, state aid form. *Financial aid deadline (priority):* 2/25. *Notification date:* Continuous beginning 3/15. Students must reply by 5/1 or within 2 weeks of notification.

**CONTACT** Ms. Amy Thompson, Director of Financial Aid, St. Joseph's College, New York, 245 Clinton Avenue, Brooklyn, NY 11205-3688, 718-940-5713. *Fax:* 718-636-6827. *E-mail:* althompson@sjcny.edu.
*Website:* http://www.sjcny.edu/.

# SAINT JOSEPH'S COLLEGE OF MAINE
## Standish, ME

**ABOUT THE INSTITUTION** Independent Roman Catholic Church, coed. 52 undergraduate majors.

**GIFT AID (NEED-BASED)** *Scholarships, grants, and awards:* Federal Pell, FSEOG, state, private, college/university gift aid from institutional funds, Federal Nursing.

**GIFT AID (NON-NEED-BASED)** *Scholarships, grants, and awards by category:* *Academic interests/achievement:* general academic interests/achievements. *Special characteristics:* children of faculty/staff, siblings of current students, spouses of current students.

**LOANS** *Programs:* Federal Direct (Subsidized and Unsubsidized Stafford, PLUS), Perkins, Federal Nursing, state.

**APPLYING FOR FINANCIAL AID** *Required financial aid form:* FAFSA.

**CONTACT** Office of Financial Aid, Saint Joseph's College of Maine, 278 Whites Bridge Road, Standish, ME 04084-5263, 800-752-1266 or toll-free 800-338-7057. *Fax:* 207-893-6699. *E-mail:* finaid@sjcme.edu. *Website:* http://www.sjcme.edu/.

# SAINT JOSEPH SEMINARY COLLEGE
## Saint Benedict, LA

| Tuition & fees: $16,240 | Average undergraduate aid package: N/A |
| --- | --- |

**ABOUT THE INSTITUTION** Independent Roman Catholic, men only. *Awards:* bachelor's degrees (Religious Studies Institute is coed). 1 undergraduate major. *Total enrollment:* 107. Undergraduates: 107. Freshmen: 11. Federal methodology is used as a basis for awarding need-based institutional aid.

**UNDERGRADUATE EXPENSES for 2015–2016** *One-time required fee:* $350. *Comprehensive fee:* $30,070 includes full-time tuition ($14,320), mandatory fees ($1920), and room and board ($13,830). *College room only:* $7266. Full-time tuition and fees vary according to student level. *Part-time tuition:* $260 per semester hour. *Part-time fees:* $600 per year. Part-time tuition and fees vary according to course load.

**GIFT AID (NEED-BASED)** *Total amount:* $294,965 (50% federal, 50% state). *Scholarships, grants, and awards:* Federal Pell, state, private, college/university gift aid from institutional funds.

**LOANS** *Student loans:* $83,040 (62% need-based, 38% non-need-based). *Parent loans:* $5613 (100% need-based). *Programs:* Federal Direct (Subsidized and Unsubsidized Stafford, PLUS).

**APPLYING FOR FINANCIAL AID** *Required financial aid form:* FAFSA. *Financial aid deadline (priority):* 8/15. *Notification date:* Continuous beginning 7/1. Students must reply within 4 weeks of notification.

**CONTACT** Katie F. Plude, Director of Student Financial Aid, Saint Joseph Seminary College, 75376 River Road, Saint Benedict, LA 70457, 985-867-2248. *Fax:* 985-867-2270. *E-mail:* kplude@sjasc.edu. *Website:* http://www.sjasc.edu/.

# SAINT JOSEPH'S UNIVERSITY
## Philadelphia, PA

| Tuition & fees: $40,580 | Average undergraduate aid package: $25,302 |
| --- | --- |

**ABOUT THE INSTITUTION** Independent Roman Catholic (Jesuit), coed. *Awards:* certificates, associate, bachelor's, master's, and doctoral degrees. 70 undergraduate majors. *Total enrollment:* 8,974. Undergraduates: 5,512. Freshmen: 1,353. Federal methodology is used as a basis for awarding need-based institutional aid.

**UNDERGRADUATE EXPENSES for 2015–2016** *Application fee:* $60. *Comprehensive fee:* $55,006 includes full-time tuition ($40,420), mandatory fees ($160), and room and board ($14,426). *College room only:* $9397. Full-time tuition and fees vary according to course load. Room and board charges vary according to board plan and housing facility. *Part-time tuition:* $541 per credit. Part-time tuition and fees vary according to course load.

**FRESHMAN FINANCIAL AID (Fall 2014, est.)** 1,133 applied for aid; of those 75% were deemed to have need. 100% of freshmen with need received aid; of those 22% had need fully met. *Average percent of need met:* 76% (excluding resources awarded to replace EFC). *Average financial aid package:* $26,081 (excluding resources awarded to replace EFC). 35% of all full-time freshmen had no need and received non-need-based gift aid.

**UNDERGRADUATE FINANCIAL AID (Fall 2014, est.)** 3,311 applied for aid; of those 81% were deemed to have need. 100% of undergraduates with need received aid; of those 23% had need fully met. *Average percent of need met:* 73%

(excluding resources awarded to replace EFC). *Average financial aid package:* $25,302 (excluding resources awarded to replace EFC). 33% of all full-time undergraduates had no need and received non-need-based gift aid.

**GIFT AID (NEED-BASED)** *Total amount:* $55,940,319 (6% federal, 3% state, 90% institutional, 1% external sources). *Receiving aid:* Freshmen: 61% (821); all full-time undergraduates: 56% (2,594). *Average award:* Freshmen: $20,785; Undergraduates: $19,065. *Scholarships, grants, and awards:* Federal Pell, FSEOG, state, private, college/university gift aid from institutional funds.

**GIFT AID (NON-NEED-BASED)** *Total amount:* $22,259,947 (98% institutional, 2% external sources). *Receiving aid:* Freshmen: 10% (135). Undergraduates: 8% (389). *Average award:* Freshmen: $11,200. Undergraduates: $11,276. *Scholarships, grants, and awards by category:* *Academic interests/achievement:* general academic interests/achievements. *Creative arts/performance:* debating, general creative arts/performance, theater/drama. *Special achievements/activities:* community service, general special achievements/activities. *Special characteristics:* children and siblings of alumni, children of faculty/staff, first-generation college students, international students, members of minority groups, veterans, veterans' children. *Tuition waivers:* Full or partial for employees or children of employees. *ROTC:* Army cooperative, Naval cooperative, Air Force.

**LOANS** *Student loans:* $31,488,616 (62% need-based, 38% non-need-based). *Average need-based loan:* Freshmen: $3568. Undergraduates: $4423. *Parent loans:* $17,761,367 (41% need-based, 59% non-need-based). *Programs:* Federal Direct (Subsidized and Unsubsidized Stafford, PLUS), Perkins.

**WORK-STUDY** *Federal work-study:* Total amount: $1,426,932; jobs available.

**ATHLETIC AWARDS** Total amount: $6,262,832 (41% need-based, 59% non-need-based).

**APPLYING FOR FINANCIAL AID** *Required financial aid form:* FAFSA. *Financial aid deadline (priority):* 2/15. *Notification date:* Continuous beginning 3/31. Students must reply by 5/1.

**CONTACT** Eileen M. Tucker, Director of Financial Assistance, Saint Joseph's University, 5600 City Avenue, Philadelphia, PA 19131-1395, 610-660-1555 or toll-free 888-BE-A-HAWK (in-state), 800-BE-A-HAWK (out-of-state). *Fax:* 610-660-1342. *E-mail:* finaid@sju.edu. *Website:* http://www.sju.edu/.

# ST. LAWRENCE UNIVERSITY
## Canton, NY

| Tuition & fees: $47,686 | Average undergraduate aid package: $38,322 |
| --- | --- |

**ABOUT THE INSTITUTION** Independent, coed. *Awards:* certificates, bachelor's, and master's degrees. 32 undergraduate majors. *Total enrollment:* 2,508. Undergraduates: 3,017. Freshmen: 596. Both federal and institutional methodology are used as a basis for awarding need-based institutional aid.

**UNDERGRADUATE EXPENSES for 2015–2016** *Application fee:* $60. *Comprehensive fee:* $59,972 includes full-time tuition ($47,350), mandatory fees ($336), and room and board ($12,286). *College room only:* $6166. Room and board charges vary according to board plan. *Payment plan:* Tuition prepayment.

**FRESHMAN FINANCIAL AID (Fall 2014, est.)** 424 applied for aid; of those 84% were deemed to have need. 100% of freshmen with need received aid; of those 22% had need fully met. *Average percent of need met:* 86% (excluding resources awarded to replace EFC). *Average financial aid package:* $39,913 (excluding resources awarded to replace EFC). 32% of all full-time freshmen had no need and received non-need-based gift aid.

**UNDERGRADUATE FINANCIAL AID (Fall 2014, est.)** 1,508 applied for aid; of those 87% were deemed to have need. 100% of undergraduates with need received aid; of those 26% had need fully met. *Average percent of need met:* 84% (excluding resources awarded to replace EFC). *Average financial aid package:* $38,322 (excluding resources awarded to replace EFC). 35% of all full-time undergraduates had no need and received non-need-based gift aid.

**GIFT AID (NEED-BASED)** *Total amount:* $41,671,320 (5% federal, 3% state, 92% institutional). *Receiving aid:* Freshmen: 59% (355); all full-time undergraduates: 55% (1,310). *Average award:* Freshmen: $33,908; Undergraduates: $31,636. *Scholarships, grants, and awards:* Federal Pell, FSEOG, state, private, college/university gift aid from institutional funds.

**GIFT AID (NON-NEED-BASED)** *Total amount:* $19,819,516 (94% institutional, 6% external sources). *Receiving aid:* Freshmen: 42% (254). Undergraduates:

37% (878). *Average award:* Freshmen: $19,843. Undergraduates: $20,225. *Scholarships, grants, and awards by category:* Academic interests/achievement: 1,081 awards ($24,071,167 total): general academic interests/achievements. *Special achievements/activities:* 72 awards ($712,500 total): community service, leadership. *Special characteristics:* 393 awards ($981,250 total): children and siblings of alumni, siblings of current students, veterans' children. *Tuition waivers:* Full or partial for employees or children of employees. *ROTC:* Army cooperative, Air Force cooperative.

**LOANS** *Student loans:* $10,938,546 (43% need-based, 57% non-need-based). 66% of past graduating class borrowed through all loan programs. *Average indebtedness per student:* $26,792. *Average need-based loan:* Freshmen: $3390. Undergraduates: $4535. *Parent loans:* $4,686,117 (100% non-need-based). *Programs:* Federal Direct (Subsidized and Unsubsidized Stafford, PLUS), Perkins, college/university.

**WORK-STUDY** *Federal work-study:* Total amount: $1,315,933; 842 jobs averaging $1597. *State or other work-study/employment:* Total amount: $523,389 (100% non-need-based). 319 part-time jobs averaging $1640.

**ATHLETIC AWARDS** Total amount: $2,110,595 (100% non-need-based).

**APPLYING FOR FINANCIAL AID** *Required financial aid forms:* FAFSA, CSS Financial Aid PROFILE, noncustodial (divorced/separated) parent's statement. *Financial aid deadline:* 2/1. *Notification date:* 3/30. Students must reply by 5/1 or within 2 weeks of notification.

**CONTACT** Mrs. Patricia J.B. Farmer, Director of Financial Aid, St. Lawrence University, Payson Hall, 23 Romoda Drive, Canton, NY 13617-1455, 315-229-5265 or toll-free 800-285-1856. *Fax:* 315-229-7418. *E-mail:* pfarmer@stlawu.edu. *Website:* http://www.stlawu.edu/.

# SAINT LEO UNIVERSITY
## Saint Leo, FL

| Tuition & fees: $20,520 | Average undergraduate aid package: $19,034 |
|---|---|

**ABOUT THE INSTITUTION** Independent Roman Catholic, coed. *Awards:* certificates, associate, bachelor's, master's, and doctoral degrees. 35 undergraduate majors. *Total enrollment:* 6,058. Undergraduates: 2,290. Freshmen: 617. Federal methodology is used as a basis for awarding need-based institutional aid.

**UNDERGRADUATE EXPENSES for 2015–2016** *Application fee:* $40. *Comprehensive fee:* $30,390 includes full-time tuition ($20,150), mandatory fees ($370), and room and board ($9870). *College room only:* $5250. Room and board charges vary according to board plan and housing facility.

**FRESHMAN FINANCIAL AID (Fall 2014, est.)** 560 applied for aid; of those 88% were deemed to have need. 100% of freshmen with need received aid; of those 12% had need fully met. *Average percent of need met:* 67% (excluding resources awarded to replace EFC). *Average financial aid package:* $18,548 (excluding resources awarded to replace EFC). 19% of all full-time freshmen had no need and received non-need-based gift aid.

**UNDERGRADUATE FINANCIAL AID (Fall 2014, est.)** 1,783 applied for aid; of those 87% were deemed to have need. 100% of undergraduates with need received aid; of those 17% had need fully met. *Average percent of need met:* 69% (excluding resources awarded to replace EFC). *Average financial aid package:* $19,034 (excluding resources awarded to replace EFC). 7% of all full-time undergraduates had no need and received non-need-based gift aid.

**GIFT AID (NEED-BASED)** *Total amount:* $21,232,725 (22% federal, 20% state, 56% institutional, 2% external sources). *Receiving aid:* Freshmen: 80% (492); all full-time undergraduates: 71% (1,549). *Average award:* Freshmen: $14,155; Undergraduates: $14,433. *Scholarships, grants, and awards:* Federal Pell, FSEOG, state, private, college/university gift aid from institutional funds, United Negro College Fund.

**GIFT AID (NON-NEED-BASED)** *Total amount:* $4,099,267 (19% state, 76% institutional, 5% external sources). *Receiving aid:* Freshmen: 4% (22). Undergraduates: 5% (117). *Average award:* Freshmen: $5302. Undergraduates: $5911. *Scholarships, grants, and awards by category:* Academic interests/achievement: general academic interests/achievements. *Tuition waivers:* Full or partial for employees or children of employees. *ROTC:* Army.

**LOANS** *Student loans:* $13,165,154 (77% need-based, 23% non-need-based). 70% of past graduating class borrowed through all loan programs. *Average indebtedness per student:* $27,436. *Average need-based loan:* Freshmen: $3408. Undergraduates: $3941. *Parent loans:* $3,205,521 (69% need-based, 31% non-need-based). *Programs:* Federal Direct (Subsidized and Unsubsidized Stafford, PLUS).

**WORK-STUDY** *Federal work-study:* Total amount: $1,431,595; 419 jobs averaging $3417. *State or other work-study/employment:* Total amount: $14,000 (100% need-based). 4 part-time jobs averaging $3500.

**ATHLETIC AWARDS** Total amount: $2,683,768 (41% need-based, 59% non-need-based).

**APPLYING FOR FINANCIAL AID** *Required financial aid form:* FAFSA. *Financial aid deadline (priority):* 3/1. *Notification date:* Continuous beginning 1/1.

**CONTACT** Ms. Melinda Clark, Assistant Vice President of Financial Aid, Saint Leo University, PO Box 6665, MC 2228, Saint Leo, FL 33574-6665, 800-240-7658 or toll-free 800-334-5532. *Fax:* 866-708-7770. *E-mail:* finaid@saintleo.edu. *Website:* http://www.saintleo.edu/.

# SAINT LOUIS CHRISTIAN COLLEGE
## Florissant, MO

| Tuition & fees: $10,075 | Average undergraduate aid package: $7966 |
|---|---|

**ABOUT THE INSTITUTION** Independent Christian, coed. *Awards:* associate and bachelor's degrees. 5 undergraduate majors. *Total enrollment:* 179. Undergraduates: 179. Freshmen: 14. Federal methodology is used as a basis for awarding need-based institutional aid.

**UNDERGRADUATE EXPENSES for 2015–2016** *Comprehensive fee:* $14,675 includes full-time tuition ($10,075) and room and board ($4600). Room and board charges vary according to housing facility.

**FRESHMAN FINANCIAL AID (Fall 2014, est.)** 10 applied for aid; of those 90% were deemed to have need. 100% of freshmen with need received aid; of those 11% had need fully met. *Average percent of need met:* 58% (excluding resources awarded to replace EFC). *Average financial aid package:* $7486 (excluding resources awarded to replace EFC). 18% of all full-time freshmen had no need and received non-need-based gift aid.

**UNDERGRADUATE FINANCIAL AID (Fall 2014, est.)** 122 applied for aid; of those 93% were deemed to have need. 100% of undergraduates with need received aid; of those 4% had need fully met. *Average percent of need met:* 59% (excluding resources awarded to replace EFC). *Average financial aid package:* $7966 (excluding resources awarded to replace EFC). 3% of all full-time undergraduates had no need and received non-need-based gift aid.

**GIFT AID (NEED-BASED)** *Total amount:* $445,043 (84% federal, 14% institutional, 2% external sources). *Receiving aid:* Freshmen: 73% (8); all full-time undergraduates: 78% (101). *Average award:* Freshmen: $4476; Undergraduates: $4828. *Scholarships, grants, and awards:* Federal Pell, FSEOG, private, college/university gift aid from institutional funds.

**GIFT AID (NON-NEED-BASED)** *Total amount:* $54,192 (24% institutional, 76% external sources). *Average award:* Freshmen: $1025. Undergraduates: $3257. *Tuition waivers:* Full or partial for employees or children of employees.

**LOANS** *Student loans:* $956,764 (93% need-based, 7% non-need-based). 92% of past graduating class borrowed through all loan programs. *Average indebtedness per student:* $32,975. *Average need-based loan:* Freshmen: $3386. Undergraduates: $3797. *Parent loans:* $50,160 (67% need-based, 33% non-need-based). *Programs:* Federal Direct (Subsidized and Unsubsidized Stafford, PLUS), private loans.

**WORK-STUDY** *Federal work-study:* Total amount: $13,700; jobs available. *State or other work-study/employment:* Total amount: $130,000 (100% non-need-based). Part-time jobs available.

**APPLYING FOR FINANCIAL AID** *Required financial aid form:* FAFSA. *Financial aid deadline:* Continuous. *Notification date:* Continuous.

**CONTACT** Mrs. Catherine Wilhoit, Director of Financial Aid, Saint Louis Christian College, 1360 Grandview Drive, Florissant, MO 63033-6499, 314-837-6777 Ext. 1101 or toll-free 800-887-SLCC. *Fax:* 314-837-8291. *Website:* http://www.slcconline.edu/.

# ST. LOUIS COLLEGE OF PHARMACY
## St. Louis, MO

| Tuition & fees: $28,264 | Average undergraduate aid package: $13,868 |
| --- | --- |

**ABOUT THE INSTITUTION** Independent, coed. *Awards:* doctoral degrees. 1 undergraduate major. *Total enrollment:* 1,366. Undergraduates: 698. Freshmen: 193. Federal methodology is used as a basis for awarding need-based institutional aid.

**UNDERGRADUATE EXPENSES for 2015–2016** *Application fee:* $55. *Comprehensive fee:* $38,047 includes full-time tuition ($27,502), mandatory fees ($762), and room and board ($9783). Full-time tuition and fees vary according to student level. Room and board charges vary according to board plan and housing facility. *Part-time tuition:* $908 per credit.

**FRESHMAN FINANCIAL AID (Fall 2013)** 179 applied for aid; of those 85% were deemed to have need. 100% of freshmen with need received aid; of those 7% had need fully met. *Average percent of need met:* 50% (excluding resources awarded to replace EFC). *Average financial aid package:* $13,826 (excluding resources awarded to replace EFC). 21% of all full-time freshmen had no need and received non-need-based gift aid.

**UNDERGRADUATE FINANCIAL AID (Fall 2013)** 499 applied for aid; of those 88% were deemed to have need. 100% of undergraduates with need received aid; of those 7% had need fully met. *Average percent of need met:* 45% (excluding resources awarded to replace EFC). *Average financial aid package:* $13,868 (excluding resources awarded to replace EFC). 20% of all full-time undergraduates had no need and received non-need-based gift aid.

**GIFT AID (NEED-BASED)** *Total amount:* $4,646,384 (17% federal, 8% state, 67% institutional, 8% external sources). *Receiving aid:* Freshmen: 78% (153); all full-time undergraduates: 69% (397). *Average award:* Freshmen: $9567; Undergraduates: $9351. *Scholarships, grants, and awards:* Federal Pell, FSEOG, state, private, college/university gift aid from institutional funds.

**GIFT AID (NON-NEED-BASED)** *Total amount:* $1,132,004 (2% state, 88% institutional, 10% external sources). *Receiving aid:* Freshmen: 4% (7). Undergraduates: 3% (17). *Average award:* Freshmen: $6302. Undergraduates: $6712. *Scholarships, grants, and awards by category: Academic interests/achievement:* 637 awards ($4,265,092 total): general academic interests/achievements. *Special achievements/activities:* 23 awards ($55,750 total): community service, leadership. *Special characteristics:* children of faculty/staff, local/state students. *Tuition waivers:* Full or partial for employees or children of employees. *ROTC:* Army cooperative, Naval cooperative, Air Force cooperative.

**LOANS** *Student loans:* $7,671,177 (81% need-based, 19% non-need-based). 88% of past graduating class borrowed through all loan programs. *Average indebtedness per student:* $104,713. *Average need-based loan:* Freshmen: $4649. Undergraduates: $5669. *Parent loans:* $2,793,845 (61% need-based, 39% non-need-based). *Programs:* Federal Direct (Subsidized and Unsubsidized Stafford, PLUS), Perkins, Health Professions Student Loans (HPSL).

**WORK-STUDY** *Federal work-study:* 285 jobs averaging $431.

**ATHLETIC AWARDS** Total amount: $143,350 (73% need-based, 27% non-need-based).

**APPLYING FOR FINANCIAL AID** *Required financial aid form:* FAFSA. *Financial aid deadline (priority):* 3/15. *Notification date:* Continuous beginning 3/15. Students must reply within 2 weeks of notification.

**CONTACT** Mr. Dan Stiffler, Director of Financial Aid, St. Louis College of Pharmacy, 4588 Parkview Place, St. Louis, MO 63110, 314-446-8321 or toll-free 800-278-5267. *Fax:* 314-446-8310. *E-mail:* daniel.stiffler@stlcop.edu. *Website:* http://www.stlcop.edu/.

# SAINT LOUIS UNIVERSITY
## St. Louis, MO

| Tuition & fees: $37,966 | Average undergraduate aid package: $25,135 |
| --- | --- |

**ABOUT THE INSTITUTION** Independent Roman Catholic (Jesuit), coed. *Awards:* certificates, bachelor's, master's, and doctoral degrees. 73 undergraduate majors. *Total enrollment:* 13,287. Undergraduates: 8,564. Freshmen: 1,691. Federal methodology is used as a basis for awarding need-based institutional aid.

**UNDERGRADUATE EXPENSES for 2015–2016** *Comprehensive fee:* $48,346 includes full-time tuition ($37,350), mandatory fees ($616), and room and board ($10,380). *College room only:* $5676. Full-time tuition and fees vary according to course level, course load, degree level, location, program, and reciprocity agreements. Room and board charges vary according to board plan, housing facility, and location. *Part-time tuition:* $1305 per credit hour. *Part-time fees:* $153 per term. Part-time tuition and fees vary according to course level, course load, degree level, location, program, and reciprocity agreements.

**FRESHMAN FINANCIAL AID (Fall 2013)** 1,303 applied for aid; of those 80% were deemed to have need. 100% of freshmen with need received aid; of those 24% had need fully met. *Average percent of need met:* 73% (excluding resources awarded to replace EFC). *Average financial aid package:* $26,055 (excluding resources awarded to replace EFC). 30% of all full-time freshmen had no need and received non-need-based gift aid.

**UNDERGRADUATE FINANCIAL AID (Fall 2013)** 5,183 applied for aid; of those 87% were deemed to have need. 100% of undergraduates with need received aid; of those 18% had need fully met. *Average percent of need met:* 69% (excluding resources awarded to replace EFC). *Average financial aid package:* $25,135 (excluding resources awarded to replace EFC). 27% of all full-time undergraduates had no need and received non-need-based gift aid.

**GIFT AID (NEED-BASED)** *Total amount:* $91,212,743 (10% federal, 3% state, 85% institutional, 2% external sources). *Receiving aid:* Freshmen: 64% (1,008); all full-time undergraduates: 55% (4,304). *Average award:* Freshmen: $21,750; Undergraduates: $20,291. *Scholarships, grants, and awards:* Federal Pell, FSEOG, state, private, college/university gift aid from institutional funds, Federal Nursing.

**GIFT AID (NON-NEED-BASED)** *Total amount:* $27,527,888 (1% state, 87% institutional, 12% external sources). *Receiving aid:* Freshmen: 9% (136). Undergraduates: 6% (469). *Average award:* Freshmen: $15,691. Undergraduates: $13,880. *Scholarships, grants, and awards by category: Academic interests/ achievement:* area/ethnic studies, biological sciences, business, communication, computer science, education, engineering/technologies, English, foreign languages, general academic interests/achievements, health fields, humanities, international studies, mathematics, military science, physical sciences, premedicine, religion/biblical studies, social sciences. *Creative arts/performance:* art/fine arts, music, performing arts, theater/ drama. *Special achievements/activities:* cheerleading/drum major, community service, general special achievements/activities, leadership, memberships, religious involvement. *Special characteristics:* children of faculty/staff, first-generation college students, general special characteristics, international students, members of minority groups, previous college experience, religious affiliation, siblings of current students. *Tuition waivers:* Full or partial for children of alumni, employees or children of employees. *ROTC:* Army cooperative, Air Force.

**LOANS** *Student loans:* $46,922,464 (40% need-based, 60% non-need-based). 61% of past graduating class borrowed through all loan programs. *Average indebtedness per student:* $35,615. *Average need-based loan:* Freshmen: $3786. Undergraduates: $5010. *Parent loans:* $14,360,659 (100% non-need-based). *Programs:* Federal Direct (Subsidized and Unsubsidized Stafford, PLUS), Perkins, Federal Nursing, state, college/university.

**WORK-STUDY** *Federal work-study:* jobs available. *State or other work-study/employment:* Total amount: $356,899 (100% non-need-based). Part-time jobs available.

**ATHLETIC AWARDS** Total amount: $4,317,663 (36% need-based, 64% non-need-based).

**APPLYING FOR FINANCIAL AID** *Required financial aid form:* FAFSA. *Financial aid deadline (priority):* 3/1. *Notification date:* Continuous beginning 3/15. Students must reply by 5/1 or within 4 weeks of notification.

**CONTACT** Cari S. Wickliffe, Assistant Vice President and Director of Student Financial Services, Saint Louis University, 221 North Grand Boulevard, DuBourg Hall, Room 121, St. Louis, MO 63103-2097, 314-977-2350 or toll-free 800-758-3678. *Fax:* 314-977-3437. *E-mail:* sfs@slu.edu. *Website:* http://www.slu.edu/.

# SAINT LUKE'S COLLEGE OF HEALTH SCIENCES
## Kansas City, MO

| Tuition & fees: N/R | Average undergraduate aid package: $13,000 |
|---|---|

**ABOUT THE INSTITUTION** Independent Episcopal, coed, primarily women. 1 undergraduate major. Both federal and institutional methodology are used as a basis for awarding need-based institutional aid.

**UNDERGRADUATE FINANCIAL AID (Fall 2014, est.)** 373 applied for aid; of those 93% were deemed to have need. 100% of undergraduates with need received aid; of those 7% had need fully met. *Average percent of need met:* 60% (excluding resources awarded to replace EFC). *Average financial aid package:* $13,000 (excluding resources awarded to replace EFC). 1% of all full-time undergraduates had no need and received non-need-based gift aid.

**GIFT AID (NEED-BASED)** *Total amount:* $976,774 (62% federal, 9% state, 29% institutional). *Receiving aid:* All full-time undergraduates: 64% (302). *Average award:* Undergraduates: $2000. *Scholarships, grants, and awards:* Federal Pell, FSEOG, state, private, college/university gift aid from institutional funds.

**GIFT AID (NON-NEED-BASED)** *Total amount:* $190,475 (20% institutional, 80% external sources). *Receiving aid:* Undergraduates: 19% (91). *Average award:* Undergraduates: $2500.

**LOANS** *Student loans:* $3,868,778 (37% need-based, 63% non-need-based). *Average need-based loan:* Undergraduates: $5500. *Parent loans:* $553,062 (100% non-need-based). *Programs:* Federal Direct (Subsidized and Unsubsidized Stafford, PLUS), Perkins, Federal Nursing, college/university.

**WORK-STUDY** *Federal work-study:* Total amount: $15,085; 5 jobs averaging $3016.

**APPLYING FOR FINANCIAL AID** *Notification date:* Continuous.

**CONTACT** Jennifer Wright, Financial Aid Administrator, Saint Luke's College of Health Sciences, 624 Westport Road, Kansas City, MO 64111, 816-932-6749. *Fax:* 816-932-6760. *E-mail:* jrwright@saintlukescollege.edu. *Website:* http://www.saintlukescollege.edu/.

# SAINT MARTIN'S UNIVERSITY
## Lacey, WA

| Tuition & fees: $31,688 | Average undergraduate aid package: $25,247 |
|---|---|

**ABOUT THE INSTITUTION** Independent Roman Catholic, coed. *Awards:* certificates, bachelor's, and master's degrees. 25 undergraduate majors. *Total enrollment:* 1,760. Undergraduates: 1,415. Freshmen: 153. Federal methodology is used as a basis for awarding need-based institutional aid.

**UNDERGRADUATE EXPENSES** for **2015–2016** *Comprehensive fee:* $41,678 includes full-time tuition ($31,300), mandatory fees ($388), and room and board ($9990). *College room only:* $5000. Full-time tuition and fees vary according to course load, degree level, location, and program. Room and board charges vary according to board plan and housing facility. *Part-time tuition:* $1045 per credit. Part-time tuition and fees vary according to degree level, location, and program.

**FRESHMAN FINANCIAL AID (Fall 2013)** 103 applied for aid; of those 88% were deemed to have need. 100% of freshmen with need received aid; of those 29% had need fully met. *Average percent of need met:* 83% (excluding resources awarded to replace EFC). *Average financial aid package:* $26,115 (excluding resources awarded to replace EFC). 12% of all full-time freshmen had no need and received non-need-based gift aid.

**UNDERGRADUATE FINANCIAL AID (Fall 2013)** 766 applied for aid; of those 90% were deemed to have need. 100% of undergraduates with need received aid; of those 22% had need fully met. *Average percent of need met:* 79% (excluding resources awarded to replace EFC). *Average financial aid package:* $25,247 (excluding resources awarded to replace EFC). 9% of all full-time undergraduates had no need and received non-need-based gift aid.

**GIFT AID (NEED-BASED)** *Total amount:* $15,731,077 (14% federal, 15% state, 58% institutional, 13% external sources). *Receiving aid:* Freshmen: 88% (91); all full-time undergraduates: 89% (688). *Average award:* Freshmen: $22,539; Undergraduates: $20,971. *Scholarships, grants, and awards:* Federal Pell, FSEOG, state, private, college/university gift aid from institutional funds.

**GIFT AID (NON-NEED-BASED)** *Total amount:* $1,607,750 (1% state, 77% institutional, 22% external sources). *Receiving aid:* Freshmen: 19% (20). Undergraduates: 12% (93). *Average award:* Freshmen: $14,000. Undergraduates: $12,176. *Scholarships, grants, and awards by category: Academic interests/achievement:* business, education, engineering/technologies, general academic interests/achievements, humanities, international studies, premedicine. *Creative arts/performance:* music, theater/drama. *Special achievements/activities:* community service, general special achievements/activities, hobbies/interests, leadership, religious involvement. *Special characteristics:* children and siblings of alumni, children of faculty/staff, ethnic background, general special characteristics, international students, local/state students, members of minority groups, out-of-state students, siblings of current students, veterans, veterans' children. *Tuition waivers:* Full or partial for children of alumni, employees or children of employees. *ROTC:* Army cooperative, Air Force cooperative.

**LOANS** *Student loans:* $8,535,050 (75% need-based, 25% non-need-based). 79% of past graduating class borrowed through all loan programs. *Average indebtedness per student:* $27,944. *Average need-based loan:* Freshmen: $3496. Undergraduates: $4519. *Parent loans:* $1,528,363 (39% need-based, 61% non-need-based). *Programs:* Federal Direct (Subsidized and Unsubsidized Stafford, PLUS), Perkins, state, alternative loans.

**WORK-STUDY** *Federal work-study:* 173 jobs averaging $2045. *State or other work-study/employment:* Total amount: $210,038 (100% need-based). 59 part-time jobs averaging $5064.

**ATHLETIC AWARDS** Total amount: $1,261,319 (74% need-based, 26% non-need-based).

**APPLYING FOR FINANCIAL AID** *Required financial aid form:* FAFSA. *Financial aid deadline (priority):* 4/15. *Notification date:* Continuous beginning 2/15. Students must reply within 3 weeks of notification.

**CONTACT** Mr. Michael Grosso, Director of Financial Aid, Saint Martin's University, 5000 Abbey Way SE, Lacey, WA 98503-7500, 360-438-4389 or toll-free 800-368-8803. *Fax:* 360-412-6190. *E-mail:* finaid@stmartin.edu. *Website:* http://www.stmartin.edu/.

# SAINT MARY-OF-THE-WOODS COLLEGE
## Saint Mary of the Woods, IN

**ABOUT THE INSTITUTION** Independent Roman Catholic, coed, primarily women. *Awards:* certificates, associate, bachelor's, and master's degrees (also offers external degree program with significant enrollment not reflected in profile). 37 undergraduate majors. *Total enrollment:* 930. Undergraduates: 746. Freshmen: 94.

**GIFT AID (NEED-BASED)** *Scholarships, grants, and awards:* Federal Pell, FSEOG, state, private, college/university gift aid from institutional funds.

**GIFT AID (NON-NEED-BASED)** *Scholarships, grants, and awards by category: Academic interests/achievement:* general academic interests/achievements. *Creative arts/performance:* applied art and design, art/fine arts, creative writing, dance, general creative arts/performance, journalism/publications, music, performing arts, theater/drama. *Special achievements/activities:* community service, general special achievements/activities, leadership, memberships, religious involvement. *Special characteristics:* adult students, children and siblings of alumni, children of current students, children of faculty/staff, ethnic background, first-generation college students, general special characteristics, international students, local/state students, members of minority groups, out-of-state students, parents of current students, religious affiliation, siblings of current students, spouses of current students.

**LOANS** *Programs:* Federal Direct (Subsidized and Unsubsidized Stafford, PLUS), Perkins, college/university, private loans.

**APPLYING FOR FINANCIAL AID** *Required financial aid form:* FAFSA.

**CONTACT** Ms. Darla Hopper, Director of Financial Aid, Saint Mary-of-the-Woods College, 226 Guerin Hall, Saint Mary-of-the-Woods, IN 47876, 812-535-5110 or toll-free 800-926-SMWC. *Fax:* 812-535-4900. *E-mail:* dhopper@smwc.edu. *Website:* http://www.smwc.edu/.

# SAINT MARY'S COLLEGE
## Notre Dame, IN

| Tuition & fees: $35,970 | Average undergraduate aid package: $29,773 |
|---|---|

**ABOUT THE INSTITUTION** Independent Roman Catholic, women only. *Awards:* bachelor's degrees. 35 undergraduate majors. *Total enrollment:* 1,519. Undergraduates: 1,519. Freshmen: 378. Both federal and institutional methodology are used as a basis for awarding need-based institutional aid.

**UNDERGRADUATE EXPENSES for 2015–2016** *Comprehensive fee:* $46,900 includes full-time tuition ($35,210), mandatory fees ($760), and room and board ($10,930). *College room only:* $6760. Room and board charges vary according to board plan and housing facility. *Part-time tuition:* $1390 per credit hour. *Part-time fees:* $380 per term.

**FRESHMAN FINANCIAL AID (Fall 2014, est.)** 337 applied for aid; of those 80% were deemed to have need. 100% of freshmen with need received aid; of those 20% had need fully met. *Average percent of need met:* 85% (excluding resources awarded to replace EFC). *Average financial aid package:* $29,530 (excluding resources awarded to replace EFC). 28% of all full-time freshmen had no need and received non-need-based gift aid.

**UNDERGRADUATE FINANCIAL AID (Fall 2014, est.)** 1,138 applied for aid; of those 76% were deemed to have need. 100% of undergraduates with need received aid; of those 19% had need fully met. *Average percent of need met:* 84% (excluding resources awarded to replace EFC). *Average financial aid package:* $29,773 (excluding resources awarded to replace EFC). 38% of all full-time undergraduates had no need and received non-need-based gift aid.

**GIFT AID (NEED-BASED)** *Total amount:* $21,932,344 (7% federal, 3% state, 87% institutional, 3% external sources). *Receiving aid:* Freshmen: 69% (261); all full-time undergraduates: 57% (854). *Average award:* Freshmen: $26,237; Undergraduates: $25,675. *Scholarships, grants, and awards:* Federal Pell, FSEOG, state, private, college/university gift aid from institutional funds.

**GIFT AID (NON-NEED-BASED)** *Total amount:* $8,012,309 (1% federal, 98% institutional, 1% external sources). *Receiving aid:* Freshmen: 67% (255). Undergraduates: 53% (791). *Average award:* Freshmen: $13,498. Undergraduates: $13,874. *Tuition waivers:* Full or partial for employees or children of employees. *ROTC:* Army cooperative, Naval cooperative, Air Force cooperative.

**LOANS** *Student loans:* $8,013,624 (80% need-based, 20% non-need-based). 69% of past graduating class borrowed through all loan programs. *Average indebtedness per student:* $30,910. *Average need-based loan:* Freshmen: $4316. Undergraduates: $4937. *Parent loans:* $2,628,777 (70% need-based, 30% non-need-based). *Programs:* Federal Direct (Subsidized and Unsubsidized Stafford, PLUS), Perkins.

**WORK-STUDY** *Federal work-study:* Total amount: $559,900; jobs available. *State or other work-study/employment:* Part-time jobs available.

**APPLYING FOR FINANCIAL AID** *Required financial aid forms:* FAFSA, CSS Financial Aid PROFILE, noncustodial (divorced/separated) parent's statement. *Financial aid deadline:* 3/1. *Notification date:* Continuous beginning 3/15. Students must reply within 3 weeks of notification.

**CONTACT** Kathleen M. Brown, Director of Financial Aid, Saint Mary's College, 141 Le Mans Hall, Notre Dame, IN 46556, 574-284-4557 or toll-free 800-551-7621. *Fax:* 574-284-4818. *E-mail:* kbrown@saintmarys.edu. *Website:* http://www.saintmarys.edu/.

# SAINT MARY'S COLLEGE OF CALIFORNIA
## Moraga, CA

| Tuition & fees: $41,380 | Average undergraduate aid package: $29,383 |
|---|---|

**ABOUT THE INSTITUTION** Independent Roman Catholic, coed. *Awards:* bachelor's, master's, and doctoral degrees. 67 undergraduate majors. *Total enrollment:* 4,257. Undergraduates: 3,055. Entering class: 114. Federal methodology is used as a basis for awarding need-based institutional aid.

**UNDERGRADUATE EXPENSES for 2015–2016** *Application fee:* $55. *Comprehensive fee:* $55,520 includes full-time tuition ($41,230), mandatory fees ($150), and room and board ($14,140). *College room only:* $7710. Room and board charges vary according to board plan and housing facility. *Part-time tuition:* $5160 per credit hour. Part-time tuition and fees vary according to course load and program. *Payment plan:* Tuition prepayment.

**UNDERGRADUATE FINANCIAL AID (Fall 2014, est.)** 2,439 applied for aid; of those 81% were deemed to have need. 99% of undergraduates with need received aid; of those 8% had need fully met. *Average percent of need met:* 61% (excluding resources awarded to replace EFC). *Average financial aid package:* $29,383 (excluding resources awarded to replace EFC). 11% of all full-time undergraduates had no need and received non-need-based gift aid.

**GIFT AID (NEED-BASED)** *Total amount:* $42,451,230 (9% federal, 12% state, 78% institutional, 1% external sources). *Receiving aid:* Entering class: 75% (438); all full-time undergraduates: 68% (1,895). *Average award:* Freshmen: $27,125; Undergraduates: $23,443. *Scholarships, grants, and awards:* Federal Pell, FSEOG, state, private, college/university gift aid from institutional funds.

**GIFT AID (NON-NEED-BASED)** *Total amount:* $4,722,296 (94% institutional, 6% external sources). *Receiving aid:* Freshmen: 45% (260). Undergraduates: 36% (1,009). *Average award:* Freshmen: $14,429. Undergraduates: $13,188. *Scholarships, grants, and awards by category:* Academic interests/achievement: 1,271 awards ($11,717,262 total): English, general academic interests/achievements, humanities, international studies, mathematics, physical sciences, religion/biblical studies. *Creative arts/performance:* 46 awards ($575,500 total): cinema/film/broadcasting, dance, debating, music, performing arts, theater/drama. *Special achievements/activities:* 121 awards ($1,355,083 total): leadership, memberships. *Special characteristics:* 83 awards ($1,985,798 total): children and siblings of alumni, children of educators, children of faculty/staff, general special characteristics, relatives of clergy, veterans, veterans' children. *Tuition waivers:* Full or partial for employees or children of employees. *ROTC:* Army cooperative, Air Force cooperative.

**LOANS** *Student loans:* $18,074,750 (93% need-based, 7% non-need-based). 75% of past graduating class borrowed through all loan programs. *Average indebtedness per student:* $32,803. *Average need-based loan:* Freshmen: $2876. Undergraduates: $3986. *Parent loans:* $9,826,341 (93% need-based, 7% non-need-based). *Programs:* Federal Direct (Subsidized and Unsubsidized Stafford, PLUS), Perkins.

**WORK-STUDY** *Federal work-study:* Total amount: $704,817; 375 jobs averaging $2250.

**ATHLETIC AWARDS** Total amount: $5,387,092 (37% need-based, 63% non-need-based).

**APPLYING FOR FINANCIAL AID** *Required financial aid form:* FAFSA. *Financial aid deadline (priority):* 2/15. *Notification date:* Continuous beginning 2/1. Students must reply by 5/1 or within 2 weeks of notification.

**CONTACT** Priscilla Muha, Director of Financial Aid, Saint Mary's College of California, 1928 St. Mary's Road, PMB 4530, Moraga, CA 94575, 925-631-4370 or toll-free 800-800-4SMC. *Fax:* 925-376-2965. *E-mail:* finaid@stmarys-ca.edu. *Website:* http://www.stmarys-ca.edu/.

# ST. MARY'S COLLEGE OF MARYLAND
## St. Mary's City, MD

| Tuition & fees (MD res): $13,824 | Average undergraduate aid package: $14,332 |
|---|---|

**ABOUT THE INSTITUTION** State-supported, coed. *Awards:* bachelor's and master's degrees. 23 undergraduate majors. *Total enrollment:* 1,804. Undergraduates: 1,771. Freshmen: 379. Federal methodology is used as a basis for awarding need-based institutional aid.

**UNDERGRADUATE EXPENSES for 2015–2016** *Application fee:* $50. *Tuition, state resident:* full-time $11,195; part-time $195 per credit hour. *Tuition, nonresident:* full-time $26,045; part-time $195 per credit hour. *Required fees:* full-time $2629. Full-time tuition and fees vary according to course load. Part-time tuition and fees vary according to course load. *College room and board:* $11,930; *Room only:* $6770. Room and board charges vary according to board plan and housing facility.

**FRESHMAN FINANCIAL AID (Fall 2013)** 327 applied for aid; of those 61% were deemed to have need. 98% of freshmen with need received aid; of those 12% had need fully met. *Average percent of need met:* 75% (excluding resources awarded to replace EFC). *Average financial aid package:* $15,694 (excluding resources awarded to replace EFC). 17% of all full-time freshmen had no need and received non-need-based gift aid.

**UNDERGRADUATE FINANCIAL AID (Fall 2013)** 1,226 applied for aid; of those 67% were deemed to have need. 97% of undergraduates with need received aid;

of those 8% had need fully met. *Average percent of need met:* 70% (excluding resources awarded to replace EFC). *Average financial aid package:* $14,332 (excluding resources awarded to replace EFC). 16% of all full-time undergraduates had no need and received non-need-based gift aid.

**GIFT AID (NEED-BASED)** *Total amount:* $3,981,114 (37% federal, 50% state, 5% institutional, 8% external sources). *Receiving aid:* Freshmen: 46% (177); all full-time undergraduates: 37% (655). *Average award:* Freshmen: $12,278; Undergraduates: $10,944. *Scholarships, grants, and awards:* Federal Pell, FSEOG, state, private, college/university gift aid from institutional funds.

**GIFT AID (NON-NEED-BASED)** *Total amount:* $764,372 (24% state, 51% institutional, 25% external sources). *Receiving aid:* Freshmen: 23% (87). Undergraduates: 21% (375). *Average award:* Freshmen: $4634. Undergraduates: $4021. *Scholarships, grants, and awards by category: Academic interests/achievement:* education, general academic interests/achievements. *Special characteristics:* children of faculty/staff. *Tuition waivers:* Full or partial for employees or children of employees, senior citizens.

**LOANS** *Student loans:* $5,544,050 (73% need-based, 27% non-need-based). 53% of past graduating class borrowed through all loan programs. *Average indebtedness per student:* $24,621. *Average need-based loan:* Freshmen: $3349. Undergraduates: $4198. *Parent loans:* $4,358,074 (56% need-based, 44% non-need-based). *Programs:* Federal Direct (Subsidized and Unsubsidized Stafford, PLUS).

**WORK-STUDY** *Federal work-study:* 117 jobs averaging $861.

**APPLYING FOR FINANCIAL AID** *Required financial aid form:* FAFSA. *Financial aid deadline (priority):* 2/28. *Notification date:* 3/15. Students must reply by 5/1.

**CONTACT** Ms. Nadine Hutton, Director of Financial Aid, St. Mary's College of Maryland, 18952 East Fisher Road, St. Mary's City, MD 20686-3001, 240-895-3000 or toll-free 800-492-7181. *Fax:* 240-895-4959. *E-mail:* nlhutton@smcm.edu. *Website:* http://www.smcm.edu/.

---

# ST. MARY'S UNIVERSITY
## San Antonio, TX

**CONTACT** Mr. David R. Krause, Director of Financial Assistance, St. Mary's University, One Camino Santa Maria, San Antonio, TX 78228-8541, 210-436-3141 or toll-free 800-FOR-STMU. *Fax:* 210-431-2221. *E-mail:* dkrause@alvin.stmarytx.edu. *Website:* http://www.stmarytx.edu/.

---

# SAINT MARY'S UNIVERSITY OF MINNESOTA
## Winona, MN

| Tuition & fees: $31,335 | Average undergraduate aid package: $23,158 |
| --- | --- |

**ABOUT THE INSTITUTION** Independent Roman Catholic, coed. *Awards:* certificates, diplomas, bachelor's, master's, and doctoral degrees. 56 undergraduate majors. *Total enrollment:* 5,825. Undergraduates: 1,904. Freshmen: 334. Federal methodology is used as a basis for awarding need-based institutional aid.

**UNDERGRADUATE EXPENSES for 2015–2016** *Application fee:* $25. *Comprehensive fee:* $39,575 includes full-time tuition ($30,830), mandatory fees ($505), and room and board ($8240). *College room only:* $4610. Full-time tuition and fees vary according to course load. Room and board charges vary according to board plan and housing facility. *Part-time tuition:* $1026 per credit. *Part-time fees:* $505 per year. Part-time tuition and fees vary according to course load.

**FRESHMAN FINANCIAL AID (Fall 2014, est.)** 304 applied for aid; of those 87% were deemed to have need. 100% of freshmen with need received aid; of those 28% had need fully met. *Average percent of need met:* 90% (excluding resources awarded to replace EFC). *Average financial aid package:* $26,200 (excluding resources awarded to replace EFC). 20% of all full-time freshmen had no need and received non-need-based gift aid.

**UNDERGRADUATE FINANCIAL AID (Fall 2014, est.)** 1,072 applied for aid; of those 90% were deemed to have need. 100% of undergraduates with need received aid; of those 19% had need fully met. *Average percent of need met:* 73% (excluding resources awarded to replace EFC). *Average financial aid package:*

---

$23,158 (excluding resources awarded to replace EFC). 21% of all full-time undergraduates had no need and received non-need-based gift aid.

**GIFT AID (NEED-BASED)** *Total amount:* $20,895,764 (10% federal, 6% state, 82% institutional, 2% external sources). *Receiving aid:* Freshmen: 79% (265); all full-time undergraduates: 73% (938). *Average award:* Freshmen: $22,626; Undergraduates: $18,700. *Scholarships, grants, and awards:* Federal Pell, FSEOG, state, college/university gift aid from institutional funds.

**GIFT AID (NON-NEED-BASED)** *Average award:* Freshmen: $16,460. Undergraduates: $13,667. *Scholarships, grants, and awards by category: Academic interests/achievement:* 930 awards ($10,165,000 total): general academic interests/achievements. *Creative arts/performance:* 134 awards ($228,500 total): art/fine arts, music, theater/drama. *Special achievements/activities:* 117 awards ($320,000 total): leadership. *Special characteristics:* 301 awards ($1,386,166 total): children and siblings of alumni, children of faculty/staff, ethnic background, international students, members of minority groups. *Tuition waivers:* Full or partial for employees or children of employees. *ROTC:* Army cooperative.

**LOANS** *Student loans:* $10,661,528 (100% need-based). 81% of past graduating class borrowed through all loan programs. *Average indebtedness per student:* $33,216. *Average need-based loan:* Freshmen: $4087. Undergraduates: $4822. *Parent loans:* $1,501,557 (100% need-based). *Programs:* Federal Direct (Subsidized and Unsubsidized Stafford, PLUS), Perkins, state.

**WORK-STUDY** *Federal work-study:* Total amount: $300,311; 175 jobs averaging $1716. *State or other work-study/employment:* Total amount: $464,175 (100% need-based). 256 part-time jobs averaging $1813.

**APPLYING FOR FINANCIAL AID** *Required financial aid form:* FAFSA. *Financial aid deadline (priority):* 3/15. *Notification date:* Continuous beginning 2/1. Students must reply within 3 weeks of notification.

**CONTACT** Ms. Jayne P. Wobig, Director of Financial Aid, Saint Mary's University of Minnesota, 700 Terrace Heights, #5, Winona, MN 55987-1399, 507-457-1437 or toll-free 800-635-5987. *Fax:* 507-457-6698. *E-mail:* jwobig@smumn.edu. *Website:* http://www.smumn.edu/.

---

# SAINT MICHAEL'S COLLEGE
## Colchester, VT

| Tuition & fees: $40,750 | Average undergraduate aid package: $28,612 |
| --- | --- |

**ABOUT THE INSTITUTION** Independent Roman Catholic, coed. *Awards:* certificates, bachelor's, and master's degrees. 39 undergraduate majors. *Total enrollment:* 2,617. Undergraduates: 2,123. Freshmen: 574. Federal methodology is used as a basis for awarding need-based institutional aid.

**UNDERGRADUATE EXPENSES for 2015–2016** *Application fee:* $50. *Comprehensive fee:* $51,725 includes full-time tuition ($40,425), mandatory fees ($325), and room and board ($10,975). Full-time tuition and fees vary according to course load. Room and board charges vary according to board plan and housing facility. *Part-time tuition:* $1300 per credit hour. Part-time tuition and fees vary according to course load.

**FRESHMAN FINANCIAL AID (Fall 2014, est.)** 483 applied for aid; of those 83% were deemed to have need. 100% of freshmen with need received aid; of those 33% had need fully met. *Average percent of need met:* 82% (excluding resources awarded to replace EFC). *Average financial aid package:* $30,604 (excluding resources awarded to replace EFC). 29% of all full-time freshmen had no need and received non-need-based gift aid.

**UNDERGRADUATE FINANCIAL AID (Fall 2014, est.)** 1,447 applied for aid; of those 86% were deemed to have need. 100% of undergraduates with need received aid; of those 28% had need fully met. *Average percent of need met:* 78% (excluding resources awarded to replace EFC). *Average financial aid package:* $28,612 (excluding resources awarded to replace EFC). 28% of all full-time undergraduates had no need and received non-need-based gift aid.

**GIFT AID (NEED-BASED)** *Total amount:* $26,491,856 (6% federal, 2% state, 90% institutional, 2% external sources). *Receiving aid:* Freshmen: 70% (402); all full-time undergraduates: 62% (1,250). *Average award:* Freshmen: $23,557; Undergraduates: $21,999. *Scholarships, grants, and awards:* Federal Pell, FSEOG, state, private, college/university gift aid from institutional funds.

**GIFT AID (NON-NEED-BASED)** *Total amount:* $10,712,854 (97% institutional, 3% external sources). *Receiving aid:* Freshmen: 17% (100). Undergraduates: 13% (257). *Average award:* Freshmen: $15,974. Undergraduates: $14,525. *Schol-*

---

arships, grants, and awards by category: *Academic interests/achievement:* computer science, general academic interests/achievements, mathematics. *Creative arts/performance:* art/fine arts, performing arts, theater/drama. *Special characteristics:* local/state students, members of minority groups, out-of-state students, religious affiliation, siblings of current students, veterans, veterans' children. *Tuition waivers:* Full or partial for employees or children of employees. *ROTC:* Army cooperative, Air Force cooperative.

**LOANS** *Student loans:* $14,261,933 (59% need-based, 41% non-need-based). 75% of past graduating class borrowed through all loan programs. *Average indebtedness per student:* $36,967. *Average need-based loan:* Freshmen: $5027. Undergraduates: $5334. *Parent loans:* $3,355,028 (37% need-based, 63% non-need-based). *Programs:* Federal Direct (Subsidized and Unsubsidized Stafford, PLUS), Perkins.

**WORK-STUDY** *Federal work-study:* Total amount: $397,236; 229 jobs averaging $1650. *State or other work-study/employment:* Total amount: $467,315 (96% need-based, 4% non-need-based). 249 part-time jobs averaging $1650.

**ATHLETIC AWARDS** Total amount: $798,665 (17% need-based, 83% non-need-based).

**APPLYING FOR FINANCIAL AID** *Required financial aid forms:* FAFSA, federal income tax form(s). *Financial aid deadline (priority):* 2/1. *Notification date:* 4/1. Students must reply by 5/1 or within 2 weeks of notification.

**CONTACT** Mr. Daniel Couture, Director of Student Financial Services, Saint Michael's College, Winooski Park, Colchester, VT 05439, 802-654-3243 or toll-free 800-762-8000. *Fax:* 802-654-2591. *E-mail:* finaid@smcvt.edu. *Website:* http://www.smcvt.edu/.

# ST. NORBERT COLLEGE
## De Pere, WI

| Tuition & fees: $33,023 | Average undergraduate aid package: $23,755 |
| --- | --- |

**ABOUT THE INSTITUTION** Independent Roman Catholic, coed. *Awards:* bachelor's and master's degrees. 35 undergraduate majors. *Total enrollment:* 2,169. Undergraduates: 2,112. Freshmen: 536. Federal methodology is used as a basis for awarding need-based institutional aid.

**UNDERGRADUATE EXPENSES** for 2015–2016 *Application fee:* $10. *Comprehensive fee:* $41,478 includes full-time tuition ($32,408), mandatory fees ($615), and room and board ($8455). *College room only:* $4514. Full-time tuition and fees vary according to course load. Room and board charges vary according to board plan and housing facility. *Part-time tuition:* $1013 per credit. Part-time tuition and fees vary according to course load.

**FRESHMAN FINANCIAL AID (Fall 2013)** 482 applied for aid; of those 84% were deemed to have need. 100% of freshmen with need received aid; of those 23% had need fully met. *Average percent of need met:* 84% (excluding resources awarded to replace EFC). *Average financial aid package:* $24,600 (excluding resources awarded to replace EFC). 23% of all full-time freshmen had no need and received non-need-based gift aid.

**UNDERGRADUATE FINANCIAL AID (Fall 2013)** 1,725 applied for aid; of those 87% were deemed to have need. 100% of undergraduates with need received aid; of those 26% had need fully met. *Average percent of need met:* 83% (excluding resources awarded to replace EFC). *Average financial aid package:* $23,755 (excluding resources awarded to replace EFC). 24% of all full-time undergraduates had no need and received non-need-based gift aid.

**GIFT AID (NEED-BASED)** *Total amount:* $28,150,685 (7% federal, 8% state, 81% institutional, 4% external sources). *Receiving aid:* Freshmen: 74% (398); all full-time undergraduates: 70% (1,468). *Average award:* Freshmen: $20,342; Undergraduates: $18,342. *Scholarships, grants, and awards:* Federal Pell, FSEOG, state, private, college/university gift aid from institutional funds.

**GIFT AID (NON-NEED-BASED)** *Total amount:* $6,192,736 (1% federal, 92% institutional, 7% external sources). *Receiving aid:* Freshmen: 2% (13). Undergraduates: 3% (55). *Average award:* Freshmen: $10,778. Undergraduates: $11,107. *Scholarships, grants, and awards by category:* *Academic interests/achievement:* general academic interests/achievements. *Creative arts/performance:* art/fine arts, music, theater/drama. *Special characteristics:* children of faculty/staff, international students. *Tuition waivers:* Full or partial for employees or children of employees. *ROTC:* Army.

**LOANS** *Student loans:* $15,214,777 (95% need-based, 5% non-need-based). 78% of past graduating class borrowed through all loan programs. *Average indebtedness*

per student: $31,438. *Average need-based loan:* Freshmen: $3714. Undergraduates: $4661. *Parent loans:* $3,167,209 (90% need-based, 10% non-need-based). *Programs:* Federal Direct (Subsidized and Unsubsidized Stafford, PLUS), Perkins, state, college/university.

**WORK-STUDY** *Federal work-study:* 375 jobs averaging $1194. *State or other work-study/employment:* Part-time jobs available.

**APPLYING FOR FINANCIAL AID** *Required financial aid form:* FAFSA. *Financial aid deadline (priority):* 3/1. *Notification date:* Continuous beginning 3/15. Students must reply within 2 weeks of notification.

**CONTACT** Ms. Jessica Rafeld, Director of Financial Aid, St. Norbert College, 100 Grant Street, De Pere, WI 54115-2099, 920-403-3071 or toll-free 800-236-4878. *Fax:* 920-403-3062. *E-mail:* financialaid@snc.edu. *Website:* http://www.snc.edu/.

# ST. OLAF COLLEGE
## Northfield, MN

| Tuition & fees: $42,940 | Average undergraduate aid package: $33,883 |
| --- | --- |

**ABOUT THE INSTITUTION** Independent Lutheran, coed. *Awards:* bachelor's degrees. 44 undergraduate majors. *Total enrollment:* 3,034. Undergraduates: 3,034. Freshmen: 765. Both federal and institutional methodology are used as a basis for awarding need-based institutional aid.

**UNDERGRADUATE EXPENSES** for 2015–2016 *Comprehensive fee:* $52,730 includes full-time tuition ($42,940) and room and board ($9790). *College room only:* $4720. Full-time tuition and fees vary according to course load. Room and board charges vary according to board plan. Part-time tuition and fees vary according to course load.

**FRESHMAN FINANCIAL AID (Fall 2014, est.)** 618 applied for aid; of those 87% were deemed to have need. 100% of freshmen with need received aid; of those 88% had need fully met. *Average percent of need met:* 99% (excluding resources awarded to replace EFC). *Average financial aid package:* $36,286 (excluding resources awarded to replace EFC). 19% of all full-time freshmen had no need and received non-need-based gift aid.

**UNDERGRADUATE FINANCIAL AID (Fall 2014, est.)** 2,165 applied for aid; of those 91% were deemed to have need. 100% of undergraduates with need received aid; of those 84% had need fully met. *Average percent of need met:* 97% (excluding resources awarded to replace EFC). *Average financial aid package:* $33,883 (excluding resources awarded to replace EFC). 22% of all full-time undergraduates had no need and received non-need-based gift aid.

**GIFT AID (NEED-BASED)** *Total amount:* $56,159,170 (4% federal, 3% state, 89% institutional, 4% external sources). *Receiving aid:* Freshmen: 70% (535); all full-time undergraduates: 66% (1,954). *Average award:* Freshmen: $31,519; Undergraduates: $28,644. *Scholarships, grants, and awards:* Federal Pell, FSEOG, state, private, college/university gift aid from institutional funds.

**GIFT AID (NON-NEED-BASED)** *Total amount:* $9,609,950 (93% institutional, 7% external sources). *Receiving aid:* Freshmen: 18% (138). Undergraduates: 16% (475). *Average award:* Freshmen: $15,130. Undergraduates: $13,290. *Scholarships, grants, and awards by category:* *Academic interests/achievement:* 554 awards ($7,114,671 total): general academic interests/achievements. *Creative arts/performance:* 123 awards ($855,640 total): art/fine arts, dance, music, theater/drama. *Special achievements/activities:* 124 awards ($687,299 total): community service, religious involvement. *Tuition waivers:* Full or partial for employees or children of employees, senior citizens.

**LOANS** *Student loans:* $15,003,168 (45% need-based, 55% non-need-based). 60% of past graduating class borrowed through all loan programs. *Average indebtedness per student:* $28,396. *Average need-based loan:* Freshmen: $3858. Undergraduates: $4149. *Parent loans:* $2,409,404 (100% non-need-based). *Programs:* Federal Direct (Subsidized and Unsubsidized Stafford, PLUS), Perkins, Federal Nursing, state, college/university.

**WORK-STUDY** *Federal work-study:* Total amount: $625,682; 294 jobs averaging $2120. *State or other work-study/employment:* Total amount: $3,645,401 (95% need-based, 5% non-need-based). 1,600 part-time jobs averaging $2100.

**APPLYING FOR FINANCIAL AID** *Required financial aid forms:* FAFSA, CSS Financial Aid PROFILE, noncustodial (divorced/separated) parent's statement. *Financial aid deadline:* 3/1 (priority: 2/1). *Notification date:* 4/1. Students must reply by 5/1.

**CONTACT** Ms. Sandy Sundstrom, Director of Student Financial Aid, St. Olaf College, 1520 Saint Olaf Avenue, Northfield, MN 55057-1098, 507-786-3019 or toll-free 800-800-3025. *Fax:* 507-786-6688. *E-mail:* sundstro@stolaf.edu. *Website:* http://www.stolaf.edu/.

---

# ST. PETERSBURG COLLEGE
## St. Petersburg, FL

**CONTACT** Financial Aid Office, St. Petersburg College, PO Box 13489, St. Petersburg, FL 33733-3489, 727-341-3600. *Website:* http://www.spcollege.edu/.

---

# SAINT PETER'S UNIVERSITY
## Jersey City, NJ

**CONTACT** Jennifer Ragsdale, Acting Director of Financial Aid, Saint Peter's University, 2641 Kennedy Boulevard, Jersey City, NJ 07306, 201-761-6071 or toll-free 888-SPC-9933. *Fax:* 201-761-6073. *E-mail:* jragsdale@spc.edu. *Website:* http://www.saintpeters.edu/.

---

# ST. THOMAS AQUINAS COLLEGE
## Sparkill, NY

| Tuition & fees: $28,130 | Average undergraduate aid package: $15,315 |
|---|---|

**ABOUT THE INSTITUTION** Independent, coed. *Awards:* certificates, associate, bachelor's, and master's degrees. 43 undergraduate majors. *Total enrollment:* 1,942. Undergraduates: 1,780. Freshmen: 209. Federal methodology is used as a basis for awarding need-based institutional aid.

**UNDERGRADUATE EXPENSES** for 2015–2016 *Application fee:* $30. *Comprehensive fee:* $39,810 includes full-time tuition ($27,130), mandatory fees ($1000), and room and board ($11,680). *College room only:* $6300. Room and board charges vary according to board plan and housing facility. *Part-time tuition:* $865 per credit.

**FRESHMAN FINANCIAL AID (Fall 2013)** 215 applied for aid; of those 85% were deemed to have need. 95% of freshmen with need received aid; of those 15% had need fully met. *Average percent of need met:* 34% (excluding resources awarded to replace EFC). *Average financial aid package:* $13,815 (excluding resources awarded to replace EFC). 20% of all full-time freshmen had no need and received non-need-based gift aid.

**UNDERGRADUATE FINANCIAL AID (Fall 2013)** 1,063 applied for aid; of those 82% were deemed to have need. 97% of undergraduates with need received aid; of those 18% had need fully met. *Average percent of need met:* 37% (excluding resources awarded to replace EFC). *Average financial aid package:* $15,315 (excluding resources awarded to replace EFC). 18% of all full-time undergraduates had no need and received non-need-based gift aid.

**GIFT AID (NEED-BASED)** *Total amount:* $4,643,718 (42% federal, 29% state, 26% institutional, 3% external sources). *Receiving aid:* Freshmen: 70% (164); all full-time undergraduates: 72% (821). *Average award:* Freshmen: $10,315; Undergraduates: $10,315. *Scholarships, grants, and awards:* Federal Pell, FSEOG, state, private, college/university gift aid from institutional funds.

**GIFT AID (NON-NEED-BASED)** *Total amount:* $7,979,188 (1% state, 99% institutional). *Receiving aid:* Freshmen: 52% (121). Undergraduates: 52% (592). *Average award:* Freshmen: $11,911. Undergraduates: $10,195. *Scholarships, grants, and awards by category:* Academic interests/achievement: business, communication, computer science, education, engineering/technologies, English, foreign languages, general academic interests/achievements, humanities, mathematics, religion/biblical studies, social sciences. *Creative arts/performance:* creative writing. *Special achievements/activities:* community service, leadership. *Special characteristics:* siblings of current students, spouses of current students, twins, veterans. *Tuition waivers:* Full or partial for employees or children of employees. *ROTC:* Air Force cooperative.

**LOANS** *Student loans:* $6,339,553 (43% need-based, 57% non-need-based). 78% of past graduating class borrowed through all loan programs. *Average indebtedness per student:* $28,750. *Average need-based loan:* Freshmen: $3300. Undergraduates: $4800. *Parent loans:* $4,938,165 (88% need-based, 12% non-need-based). *Programs:* Federal Direct (Subsidized and Unsubsidized Stafford, PLUS), Perkins, state, alternative loans.

**WORK-STUDY** *Federal work-study:* 119 jobs averaging $1142.

**ATHLETIC AWARDS** Total amount: $1,813,277 (100% non-need-based).

**APPLYING FOR FINANCIAL AID** *Required financial aid forms:* FAFSA, state aid form. *Financial aid deadline (priority):* 2/15. *Notification date:* Continuous beginning 3/1. Students must reply by 5/1 or within 2 weeks of notification.

**CONTACT** Mrs. Jean Marie Mohr, Director of Financial Aid, St. Thomas Aquinas College, 125 Route 340, Sparkill, NY 10976, 845-398-4098 or toll-free 800-999-STAC. *Fax:* 845-398-4114. *E-mail:* jmohr@stac.edu. *Website:* http://www.stac.edu/.

---

# ST. THOMAS UNIVERSITY
## Miami Gardens, FL

| Tuition & fees: $27,150 | Average undergraduate aid package: N/A |
|---|---|

**ABOUT THE INSTITUTION** Independent Roman Catholic, coed. *Awards:* certificates, bachelor's, master's, and doctoral degrees. 39 undergraduate majors. *Total enrollment:* 2,225. Undergraduates: 936. Freshmen: 163. Federal methodology is used as a basis for awarding need-based institutional aid.

**UNDERGRADUATE EXPENSES** for 2015–2016 *Application fee:* $40. *Comprehensive fee:* $32,300 includes full-time tuition ($27,150) and room and board ($5150). *College room only:* $4120. Full-time tuition and fees vary according to course load and program. Room and board charges vary according to board plan and housing facility. *Part-time tuition:* $543 per credit hour. Part-time tuition and fees vary according to course load and program.

**FRESHMAN FINANCIAL AID (Fall 2014, est.)** 142 applied for aid; of those 88% were deemed to have need. 100% of freshmen with need received aid; of those 23% had need fully met. 20% of all full-time freshmen had no need and received non-need-based gift aid.

**UNDERGRADUATE FINANCIAL AID (Fall 2014, est.)** 712 applied for aid; of those 87% were deemed to have need. 100% of undergraduates with need received aid; of those 21% had need fully met. 20% of all full-time undergraduates had no need and received non-need-based gift aid.

**GIFT AID (NEED-BASED)** *Total amount:* $13,150,145 (15% federal, 14% state, 70% institutional, 1% external sources). *Receiving aid:* Freshmen: 46% (74); all full-time undergraduates: 50% (443). *Average award:* Freshmen: $3506; Undergraduates: $3482. *Scholarships, grants, and awards:* Federal Pell, FSEOG, state, private, college/university gift aid from institutional funds.

**GIFT AID (NON-NEED-BASED)** *Receiving aid:* Freshmen: 73% (118). Undergraduates: 68% (599). *Average award:* Freshmen: $10,392. Undergraduates: $8000. *Scholarships, grants, and awards by category:* Academic interests/achievement: general academic interests/achievements. *Special achievements/activities:* leadership. *Tuition waivers:* Full or partial for employees or children of employees.

**LOANS** *Student loans:* $9,934,721 (43% need-based, 57% non-need-based). *Average need-based loan:* Freshmen: $3706. Undergraduates: $4416. *Parent loans:* $725,126 (100% need-based). *Programs:* Federal Direct (Subsidized and Unsubsidized Stafford, PLUS), Perkins.

**WORK-STUDY** *Federal work-study:* Total amount: $395,750; jobs available.

**ATHLETIC AWARDS** Total amount: $1,170,696 (100% need-based).

**APPLYING FOR FINANCIAL AID** *Required financial aid form:* FAFSA. *Financial aid deadline (priority):* 4/1. *Notification date:* Continuous beginning 3/1.

**CONTACT** Ms. Yaidani Rivero, Associate Director of Financial Aid, St. Thomas University, 16401 Northwest 37th Avenue, Miami Gardens, FL 33054, 305-474-6900 or toll-free 800-367-9010. *Fax:* 305-474-6930. *E-mail:* yrivero@stu.edu. *Website:* http://www.stu.edu/.

# SAINT VINCENT COLLEGE
## Latrobe, PA

| Tuition & fees: $30,706 | Average undergraduate aid package: $27,394 |
|---|---|

**ABOUT THE INSTITUTION** Independent Roman Catholic, coed. *Awards:* certificates, bachelor's, master's, and doctoral degrees. 49 undergraduate majors. *Total enrollment:* 1,829. Undergraduates: 1,626. Freshmen: 449. Federal methodology is used as a basis for awarding need-based institutional aid.

**UNDERGRADUATE EXPENSES for 2015–2016** *Application fee:* $25. *Comprehensive fee:* $40,244 includes full-time tuition ($29,540), mandatory fees ($1166), and room and board ($9538). *College room only:* $4884. Full-time tuition and fees vary according to course load and degree level. Room and board charges vary according to board plan and housing facility. *Part-time fees:* $955 per credit hour. Part-time tuition and fees vary according to course load and degree level.

**FRESHMAN FINANCIAL AID (Fall 2014, est.)** 413 applied for aid; of those 88% were deemed to have need. 100% of freshmen with need received aid; of those 24% had need fully met. *Average percent of need met:* 83% (excluding resources awarded to replace EFC). *Average financial aid package:* $28,780 (excluding resources awarded to replace EFC). 19% of all full-time freshmen had no need and received non-need-based gift aid.

**UNDERGRADUATE FINANCIAL AID (Fall 2014, est.)** 1,336 applied for aid; of those 91% were deemed to have need. 100% of undergraduates with need received aid; of those 18% had need fully met. *Average percent of need met:* 81% (excluding resources awarded to replace EFC). *Average financial aid package:* $27,394 (excluding resources awarded to replace EFC). 14% of all full-time undergraduates had no need and received non-need-based gift aid.

**GIFT AID (NEED-BASED)** *Total amount:* $4,184,021 (46% federal, 54% state). *Receiving aid:* Freshmen: 53% (233); all full-time undergraduates: 47% (732). *Average award:* Freshmen: $6100; Undergraduates: $6068. *Scholarships, grants, and awards:* Federal Pell, FSEOG, state, private, college/university gift aid from institutional funds, United Negro College Fund.

**GIFT AID (NON-NEED-BASED)** *Total amount:* $19,638,413 (98% institutional, 2% external sources). *Receiving aid:* Freshmen: 80% (353). Undergraduates: 75% (1,171). *Average award:* Freshmen: $18,570. Undergraduates: $17,680. *Scholarships, grants, and awards by category:* Academic interests/achievement: general academic interests/achievements. *Special characteristics:* children and siblings of alumni, children of faculty/staff, first-generation college students, general special characteristics, out-of-state students, religious affiliation. *Tuition waivers:* Full or partial for employees or children of employees. *ROTC:* Army cooperative, Air Force cooperative.

**LOANS** *Student loans:* $9,751,203 (37% need-based, 63% non-need-based). 98% of past graduating class borrowed through all loan programs. *Average indebtedness per student:* $29,464. *Average need-based loan:* Freshmen: $3430. Undergraduates: $4228. *Parent loans:* $3,187,720 (100% non-need-based). *Programs:* Federal Direct (Subsidized and Unsubsidized Stafford, PLUS), Perkins.

**WORK-STUDY** *Federal work-study:* Total amount: $193,027; 302 jobs averaging $1493. *State or other work-study/employment:* Total amount: $257,967 (100% non-need-based). Part-time jobs available.

**APPLYING FOR FINANCIAL AID** *Required financial aid forms:* FAFSA, state aid form. *Financial aid deadline (priority):* 5/1. *Notification date:* Continuous beginning 3/5.

**CONTACT** Mrs. Mary Gazal, Director of Financial Aid, Saint Vincent College, 300 Fraser Purchase Road, Latrobe, PA 15650, 724-805-2627 or toll-free 800-782-5549. *Fax:* 724-805-2953. *E-mail:* mary.gazal@stvincent.edu. *Website:* http://www.stvincent.edu/.

# SAINT XAVIER UNIVERSITY
## Chicago, IL

| Tuition & fees: N/R | Average undergraduate aid package: $23,760 |
|---|---|

**ABOUT THE INSTITUTION** Independent Roman Catholic, coed. 39 undergraduate majors. Federal methodology is used as a basis for awarding need-based institutional aid.

**FRESHMAN FINANCIAL AID (Fall 2014, est.)** 553 applied for aid; of those 95% were deemed to have need. 100% of freshmen with need received aid; of those 10% had need fully met. *Average percent of need met:* 79% (excluding resources awarded to replace EFC). *Average financial aid package:* $26,245 (excluding resources awarded to replace EFC). 4% of all full-time freshmen had no need and received non-need-based gift aid.

**UNDERGRADUATE FINANCIAL AID (Fall 2014, est.)** 2,384 applied for aid; of those 95% were deemed to have need. 100% of undergraduates with need received aid; of those 14% had need fully met. *Average percent of need met:* 76% (excluding resources awarded to replace EFC). *Average financial aid package:* $23,760 (excluding resources awarded to replace EFC). 9% of all full-time undergraduates had no need and received non-need-based gift aid.

**GIFT AID (NEED-BASED)** *Receiving aid:* Freshmen: 80% (453); all full-time undergraduates: 68% (1,751). *Average award:* Freshmen: $21,191; Undergraduates: $18,178. *Scholarships, grants, and awards:* Federal Pell, FSEOG, state, private, college/university gift aid from institutional funds, United Negro College Fund, Federal Nursing.

**GIFT AID (NON-NEED-BASED)** *Receiving aid:* Freshmen: 78% (441). Undergraduates: 72% (1,835). *Average award:* Freshmen: $15,785. Undergraduates: $11,244. *Scholarships, grants, and awards by category:* Academic interests/achievement: general academic interests/achievements. Creative arts/performance: art/fine arts, music. *Special achievements/activities:* religious involvement. *Special characteristics:* children of faculty/staff.

**LOANS** *Average need-based loan:* Freshmen: $3569. Undergraduates: $4443. *Programs:* Federal Direct (Subsidized and Unsubsidized Stafford, PLUS), Perkins.

**WORK-STUDY** Federal work-study jobs available. *State or other work-study/employment:* Part-time jobs available.

**APPLYING FOR FINANCIAL AID** *Required financial aid form:* FAFSA. *Financial aid deadline (priority):* 3/1. *Notification date:* Continuous beginning 3/1. Students must reply by 5/1 or within 2 weeks of notification.

**CONTACT** Ms. Susan Swisher, Director of Financial Aid, Saint Xavier University, 3700 West 103rd Street, Chicago, IL 60655-3105, 773-298-3073 or toll-free 800-462-9288. *Fax:* 773-298-3033. *E-mail:* swisher@sxu.edu. *Website:* http://www.sxu.edu/.

# SALEM COLLEGE
## Winston-Salem, NC

| Tuition & fees: $25,356 | Average undergraduate aid package: N/A |
|---|---|

**ABOUT THE INSTITUTION** Independent Moravian, coed, primarily women. *Awards:* certificates, bachelor's, and master's degrees (only students age 23 or over are eligible to enroll part-time). 32 undergraduate majors. *Total enrollment:* 1,118. Undergraduates: 945. Freshmen: 202. Federal methodology is used as a basis for awarding need-based institutional aid.

**UNDERGRADUATE EXPENSES for 2015–2016** *Application fee:* $30. *Comprehensive fee:* $37,120 includes full-time tuition ($24,990), mandatory fees ($366), and room and board ($11,764). Room and board charges vary according to housing facility. *Part-time tuition:* $1440 per course. *Part-time fees:* $150 per year.

**GIFT AID (NEED-BASED)** *Total amount:* $2,431,301 (19% federal, 17% state, 64% institutional). *Scholarships, grants, and awards:* Federal Pell, FSEOG, state, private, college/university gift aid from institutional funds.

**GIFT AID (NON-NEED-BASED)** *Total amount:* $1,964,078 (96% institutional, 4% external sources). *Scholarships, grants, and awards by category:* Academic interests/achievement: general academic interests/achievements. Creative arts/performance: music. *Special achievements/activities:* leadership. *Special characteristics:* children of educators, children of faculty/staff, relatives of clergy. *ROTC:* Army cooperative, Air Force cooperative.

**LOANS** *Student loans:* $894,919 (51% need-based, 49% non-need-based). *Parent loans:* $314,116 (100% non-need-based). *Programs:* Federal Direct (Subsidized and Unsubsidized Stafford, PLUS), Perkins.

**WORK-STUDY** *Federal work-study:* jobs available. *State or other work-study/employment:* Total amount: $105,600 (100% need-based). Part-time jobs available.

**APPLYING FOR FINANCIAL AID** *Required financial aid forms:* FAFSA, institution's own form. *Financial aid deadline (priority):* 3/1. *Notification date:* Continuous beginning 3/1. Students must reply by 5/1 or within 2 weeks of notification.

**CONTACT** Lori A. Lewis, Director of Financial Aid, Salem College, 601 South Church Street, Winston-Salem, NC 27101, 336-917-5577 or toll-free 800-327-2536. *Fax:* 336-917-5584. *E-mail:* lori.lewis@salem.edu. *Website:* http://www.salem.edu/.

# SALEM INTERNATIONAL UNIVERSITY
## Salem, WV

**CONTACT** Pat Zinsmeister, Vice President for Financial Aid and Compliance, Salem International University, 223 West Main Street, Salem, WV 26426-0500, 304-326-1299 or toll-free 888-235-5024. *Fax:* 304-326-1509. *E-mail:* pzinsmeister@salemu.edu. *Website:* http://www.salemu.edu/.

# SALEM STATE UNIVERSITY
## Salem, MA

**CONTACT** Mary Benda, Director of Financial Aid, Salem State University, 352 Lafayette Street, Salem, MA 01970-5353, 978-542-6139. *Fax:* 978-542-6876. *Website:* http://www.salemstate.edu/.

# SALISBURY UNIVERSITY
## Salisbury, MD

| Tuition & fees (MD res): $8560 | Average undergraduate aid package: $8174 |
| --- | --- |

**ABOUT THE INSTITUTION** State-supported, coed. *Awards:* certificates, bachelor's, master's, and doctoral degrees. 46 undergraduate majors. *Total enrollment:* 8,770. Undergraduates: 7,997. Freshmen: 1,157. Federal methodology is used as a basis for awarding need-based institutional aid.
**UNDERGRADUATE EXPENSES for 2015–2016 Application fee:** $50. *Tuition, state resident:* full-time $6268; part-time $258 per credit hour. *Tuition, nonresident:* full-time $14,614; part-time $605 per credit hour. *Required fees:* full-time $2292; $76 per credit hour. Full-time tuition and fees vary according to course load and degree level. Part-time tuition and fees vary according to course load and degree level. *College room and board:* $10,620; *Room only:* $6150. Room and board charges vary according to board plan and housing facility.
**FRESHMAN FINANCIAL AID (Fall 2013)** 1,076 applied for aid; of those 62% were deemed to have need. 96% of freshmen with need received aid; of those 15% had need fully met. *Average percent of need met:* 57% (excluding resources awarded to replace EFC). *Average financial aid package:* $8111 (excluding resources awarded to replace EFC). 22% of all full-time freshmen had no need and received non-need-based gift aid.
**UNDERGRADUATE FINANCIAL AID (Fall 2013)** 5,417 applied for aid; of those 72% were deemed to have need. 98% of undergraduates with need received aid; of those 12% had need fully met. *Average percent of need met:* 53% (excluding resources awarded to replace EFC). *Average financial aid package:* $8174 (excluding resources awarded to replace EFC). 12% of all full-time undergraduates had no need and received non-need-based gift aid.
**GIFT AID (NEED-BASED) Total amount:** $18,146,102 (40% federal, 31% state, 24% institutional, 5% external sources). *Receiving aid:* Freshmen: 46% (575); all full-time undergraduates: 42% (3,113). *Average award:* Freshmen: $6637; Undergraduates: $5881. *Scholarships, grants, and awards:* Federal Pell, FSEOG, state, private, college/university gift aid from institutional funds.
**GIFT AID (NON-NEED-BASED) Total amount:** $3,016,316 (14% state, 75% institutional, 11% external sources). *Average award:* Freshmen: $2328. Undergraduates: $2322. *Scholarships, grants, and awards by category:* Academic interests/achievement: 1,626 awards ($3,792,223 total): business, education, general academic interests/achievements, health fields, humanities, physical sciences, social sciences. *Creative arts/performance:* 31 awards ($17,700 total): applied art and design, music, theater/drama. *Special characteristics:* 15 awards ($16,500 total): adult students, children and siblings of alumni, first-generation college students. *Tuition waivers:* Full or partial for employees or children of employees, senior citizens. *ROTC:* Army, Air Force cooperative.

**LOANS Student loans:** $34,380,921 (76% need-based, 24% non-need-based). 57% of past graduating class borrowed through all loan programs. *Average indebtedness per student:* $24,567. *Average need-based loan:* Freshmen: $3102. Undergraduates: $4297. *Parent loans:* $13,157,337 (66% need-based, 34% non-need-based). *Programs:* Federal Direct (Subsidized and Unsubsidized Stafford, PLUS), Perkins.
**WORK-STUDY Federal work-study:** 73 jobs averaging $1779.
**APPLYING FOR FINANCIAL AID Required financial aid form:** FAFSA. *Financial aid deadline:* 12/31 (priority: 3/1). *Notification date:* 3/15. Students must reply by 5/1.
**CONTACT** Ms. Elizabeth Zimmerman, Director of Financial Aid, Salisbury University, 1101 Camden Avenue, Salisbury, MD 21801, 410-543-6165 or toll-free 888-543-0148. *Fax:* 410-543-6138. *E-mail:* finaid@salisbury.edu. *Website:* http://www.salisbury.edu/.

# SALVE REGINA UNIVERSITY
## Newport, RI

| Tuition & fees: $35,690 | Average undergraduate aid package: $24,568 |
| --- | --- |

**ABOUT THE INSTITUTION** Independent Roman Catholic, coed. *Awards:* certificates, associate, bachelor's, master's, and doctoral degrees. 51 undergraduate majors. *Total enrollment:* 2,739. Undergraduates: 2,121. Freshmen: 623. Federal methodology is used as a basis for awarding need-based institutional aid.
**UNDERGRADUATE EXPENSES for 2015–2016 Application fee:** $50. *Comprehensive fee:* $48,550 includes full-time tuition ($35,140), mandatory fees ($550), and room and board ($12,860). Full-time tuition and fees vary according to location. Room and board charges vary according to board plan and housing facility. *Part-time tuition:* $1171 per credit. *Part-time fees:* $50 per term. Part-time tuition and fees vary according to course load and location.
**FRESHMAN FINANCIAL AID (Fall 2014, est.)** 575 applied for aid; of those 88% were deemed to have need. 99% of freshmen with need received aid; of those 13% had need fully met. *Average percent of need met:* 76% (excluding resources awarded to replace EFC). *Average financial aid package:* $27,310 (excluding resources awarded to replace EFC). 39% of all full-time freshmen had no need and received non-need-based gift aid.
**UNDERGRADUATE FINANCIAL AID (Fall 2014, est.)** 1,782 applied for aid; of those 90% were deemed to have need. 96% of undergraduates with need received aid; of those 11% had need fully met. *Average percent of need met:* 70% (excluding resources awarded to replace EFC). *Average financial aid package:* $24,568 (excluding resources awarded to replace EFC). 17% of all full-time undergraduates had no need and received non-need-based gift aid.
**GIFT AID (NEED-BASED) Total amount:** $29,699,963 (7% federal, 1% state, 89% institutional, 3% external sources). *Receiving aid:* Freshmen: 81% (502); all full-time undergraduates: 77% (1,518). *Average award:* Freshmen: $22,906; Undergraduates: $19,724. *Scholarships, grants, and awards:* Federal Pell, FSEOG, state, private, college/university gift aid from institutional funds.
**GIFT AID (NON-NEED-BASED) Total amount:** $5,112,370 (1% federal, 93% institutional, 6% external sources). *Receiving aid:* Freshmen: 10% (60). Undergraduates: 7% (133). *Average award:* Freshmen: $12,436. Undergraduates: $11,958. *Scholarships, grants, and awards by category:* Academic interests/achievement: general academic interests/achievements. *Creative arts/performance:* art/fine arts. *Special characteristics:* children and siblings of alumni. *Tuition waivers:* Full or partial for employees or children of employees. *ROTC:* Army cooperative.
**LOANS Student loans:** $16,203,126 (71% need-based, 29% non-need-based). 83% of past graduating class borrowed through all loan programs. *Average indebtedness per student:* $38,425. *Average need-based loan:* Freshmen: $3930. Undergraduates: $4607. *Parent loans:* $5,675,849 (46% need-based, 54% non-need-based). *Programs:* Federal Direct (Subsidized and Unsubsidized Stafford, PLUS), Perkins, Federal Nursing, college/university, alternative loans.
**WORK-STUDY Federal work-study:** Total amount: $293,205; jobs available. *State or other work-study/employment:* Part-time jobs available.
**APPLYING FOR FINANCIAL AID Required financial aid form:** FAFSA. *Financial aid deadline (priority):* 3/1. *Notification date:* Continuous beginning 1/1. Students must reply by 5/1 or within 2 weeks of notification.

CONTACT Mrs. Anne McDermott, Director of Financial Aid, Salve Regina University, 100 Ochre Point Avenue, Newport, RI 02840-4192, 401-341-2901 or toll-free 888-GO SALVE. *Fax:* 401-341-2928. *E-mail:* financial_aid@salve.edu. *Website:* http://www.salve.edu/.

CONTACT Lane Smith, Director of Financial Aid, Samford University, 800 Lakeshore Drive, Birmingham, AL 35229, 205-726-2905 or toll-free 800-888-7218. *Fax:* 205-726-2738. *E-mail:* lsmith1@samford.edu. *Website:* http://www.samford.edu/.

# SAMFORD UNIVERSITY
## Birmingham, AL

| Tuition & fees: $28,370 | Average undergraduate aid package: $17,866 |
| --- | --- |

**ABOUT THE INSTITUTION** Independent Baptist, coed. *Awards:* certificates, bachelor's, master's, and doctoral degrees. 71 undergraduate majors. *Total enrollment:* 4,933. Undergraduates: 3,051. Freshmen: 730. Federal methodology is used as a basis for awarding need-based institutional aid.

**UNDERGRADUATE EXPENSES for 2015–2016** *Application fee:* $40. *Comprehensive fee:* $38,604 includes full-time tuition ($27,520), mandatory fees ($850), and room and board ($10,234). *College room only:* $5694. Full-time tuition and fees vary according to course load and program. Room and board charges vary according to board plan, housing facility, and student level. *Part-time tuition:* $920 per credit hour. *Part-time fees:* $320 per credit hour. Part-time tuition and fees vary according to course load and program.

**FRESHMAN FINANCIAL AID (Fall 2013)** 567 applied for aid; of those 65% were deemed to have need. 100% of freshmen with need received aid; of those 23% had need fully met. *Average percent of need met:* 69% (excluding resources awarded to replace EFC). *Average financial aid package:* $17,470 (excluding resources awarded to replace EFC). 43% of all full-time freshmen had no need and received non-need-based gift aid.

**UNDERGRADUATE FINANCIAL AID (Fall 2013)** 1,681 applied for aid; of those 73% were deemed to have need. 100% of undergraduates with need received aid; of those 22% had need fully met. *Average percent of need met:* 66% (excluding resources awarded to replace EFC). *Average financial aid package:* $17,866 (excluding resources awarded to replace EFC). 43% of all full-time undergraduates had no need and received non-need-based gift aid.

**GIFT AID (NEED-BASED)** *Total amount:* $13,044,180 (15% federal, 1% state, 79% institutional, 5% external sources). *Receiving aid:* Freshmen: 49% (368); all full-time undergraduates: 41% (1,177). *Average award:* Freshmen: $13,841; Undergraduates: $14,046. *Scholarships, grants, and awards:* Federal Pell, FSEOG, state, private, college/university gift aid from institutional funds, United Negro College Fund, Federal Nursing.

**GIFT AID (NON-NEED-BASED)** *Total amount:* $13,571,584 (1% state, 94% institutional, 5% external sources). *Receiving aid:* Freshmen: 10% (76). Undergraduates: 8% (227). *Average award:* Freshmen: $10,686. Undergraduates: $9636. *Scholarships, grants, and awards by category:* Academic interests/achievement: 2,099 awards ($16,179,250 total): biological sciences, business, computer science, education, English, foreign languages, general academic interests/achievements, health fields, home economics, humanities, international studies, mathematics, physical sciences, premedicine, religion/biblical studies, social sciences. Creative arts/performance: 274 awards ($1,368,987 total): debating, journalism/publications, music, performing arts, theater/drama. Special achievements/activities: 779 awards ($1,251,325 total): cheerleading/drum major, leadership. Special characteristics: 179 awards ($2,172,193 total): children of faculty/staff, members of minority groups, relatives of clergy, siblings of current students, spouses of current students, veterans. *Tuition waivers:* Full or partial for employees or children of employees. *ROTC:* Army cooperative, Air Force cooperative.

**LOANS** *Student loans:* $14,556,298 (65% need-based, 35% non-need-based). 39% of past graduating class borrowed through all loan programs. *Average indebtedness per student:* $26,543. *Average need-based loan:* Freshmen: $3166. Undergraduates: $3687. *Parent loans:* $14,310,019 (33% need-based, 67% non-need-based). *Programs:* Federal Direct (Subsidized and Unsubsidized Stafford, PLUS), Perkins, Federal Nursing, college/university.

**WORK-STUDY** *Federal work-study:* 356 jobs averaging $1744. *State or other work-study/employment:* Total amount: $882,990 (18% need-based, 82% non-need-based). 602 part-time jobs averaging $1523.

**ATHLETIC AWARDS** Total amount: $7,179,419 (46% need-based, 54% non-need-based).

**APPLYING FOR FINANCIAL AID** *Required financial aid forms:* FAFSA, state aid form. *Financial aid deadline (priority):* 3/1. *Notification date:* 4/1. Students must reply by 5/1.

# SAM HOUSTON STATE UNIVERSITY
## Huntsville, TX

| Tuition & fees (TX res): $8932 | Average undergraduate aid package: $11,573 |
| --- | --- |

**ABOUT THE INSTITUTION** State-supported, coed. *Awards:* certificates, bachelor's, master's, and doctoral degrees. 66 undergraduate majors. *Total enrollment:* 19,573. Undergraduates: 16,819. Freshmen: 2,542. Federal methodology is used as a basis for awarding need-based institutional aid.

**UNDERGRADUATE EXPENSES for 2015–2016** *Application fee:* $45. *Tuition, state resident:* full-time $6120. *Tuition, nonresident:* full-time $16,980. *Required fees:* full-time $2812. Full-time tuition and fees vary according to course load and location. Part-time tuition and fees vary according to course load and location. *College room and board:* $8324. Room and board charges vary according to board plan and housing facility. *Payment plan:* Guaranteed tuition.

**FRESHMAN FINANCIAL AID (Fall 2013)** 1,957 applied for aid; of those 80% were deemed to have need. 100% of freshmen with need received aid; of those 19% had need fully met. *Average percent of need met:* 67% (excluding resources awarded to replace EFC). *Average financial aid package:* $12,173 (excluding resources awarded to replace EFC). 9% of all full-time freshmen had no need and received non-need-based gift aid.

**UNDERGRADUATE FINANCIAL AID (Fall 2013)** 10,235 applied for aid; of those 85% were deemed to have need. 99% of undergraduates with need received aid; of those 14% had need fully met. *Average percent of need met:* 60% (excluding resources awarded to replace EFC). *Average financial aid package:* $11,573 (excluding resources awarded to replace EFC). 8% of all full-time undergraduates had no need and received non-need-based gift aid.

**GIFT AID (NEED-BASED)** *Total amount:* $54,099,436 (51% federal, 39% state, 5% institutional, 5% external sources). *Receiving aid:* Freshmen: 61% (1,366); all full-time undergraduates: 56% (7,442). *Average award:* Freshmen: $8940; Undergraduates: $6900. *Scholarships, grants, and awards:* Federal Pell, FSEOG, state, college/university gift aid from institutional funds.

**GIFT AID (NON-NEED-BASED)** *Total amount:* $3,697,936 (1% federal, 53% institutional, 46% external sources). *Receiving aid:* Freshmen: 6% (144). Undergraduates: 3% (412). *Average award:* Freshmen: $2836. Undergraduates: $2422. *Scholarships, grants, and awards by category:* Academic interests/achievement: agriculture, biological sciences, business, communication, computer science, education, engineering/technologies, English, foreign languages, general academic interests/achievements, home economics, humanities, library science, mathematics, military science, physical sciences, social sciences. Creative arts/performance: art/fine arts, dance, music, theater/drama. Special achievements/activities: cheerleading/drum major, general special achievements/activities, leadership, rodeo. Special characteristics: general special characteristics. *Tuition waivers:* Full or partial for employees or children of employees. *ROTC:* Army.

**LOANS** *Student loans:* $106,370,382 (77% need-based, 23% non-need-based). 71% of past graduating class borrowed through all loan programs. *Average indebtedness per student:* $31,433. *Average need-based loan:* Freshmen: $3127. Undergraduates: $4554. *Parent loans:* $39,090,310 (43% need-based, 57% non-need-based). *Programs:* Federal Direct (Subsidized and Unsubsidized Stafford, PLUS), Perkins, state, college/university.

**WORK-STUDY** *Federal work-study:* 630 jobs averaging $2337. *State or other work-study/employment:* Total amount: $193,546 (100% need-based). 212 part-time jobs averaging $1479.

**ATHLETIC AWARDS** Total amount: $3,514,020 (45% need-based, 55% non-need-based).

**APPLYING FOR FINANCIAL AID** *Required financial aid forms:* FAFSA, Texas Application for State Financial Aid (TASFA). *Financial aid deadline (priority):* 3/15. *Notification date:* Continuous beginning 3/15. Students must reply within 4 weeks of notification.

**CONTACT** Lydia Hall, Director of Financial Aid, Sam Houston State University, 1903 University, Estill 201, Box 2328, Huntsville, TX 77341-2328, 936-294-1750 or toll-free 866-232-7528 Ext. 1828. *Fax:* 936-294-3668. *E-mail:* lth003@shsu.edu. *Website:* http://www.shsu.edu/.

# SAMUEL MERRITT UNIVERSITY
## Oakland, CA

**CONTACT** Adel Mareghni, Financial Aid Counselor, Samuel Merritt University, 450 30th Street, Oakland, CA 94609, 510-869-6193 or toll-free 800-607-6377. *Fax:* 510-869-1529. *E-mail:* amareghni@samuelmerritt.edu. *Website:* http://www.samuelmerritt.edu/.

# SAN DIEGO CHRISTIAN COLLEGE
## Santee, CA

**ABOUT THE INSTITUTION** Independent nondenominational, coed. *Awards:* certificates, associate, and bachelor's degrees. 25 undergraduate majors. *Total enrollment:* 965. Undergraduates: 939. Freshmen: 129.

**GIFT AID (NEED-BASED)** *Scholarships, grants, and awards:* Federal Pell, FSEOG, state, private, college/university gift aid from institutional funds.

**GIFT AID (NON-NEED-BASED)** *Scholarships, grants, and awards by category:* Academic interests/achievement: general academic interests/achievements. *Creative arts/performance:* debating, music, performing arts, theater/drama. *Special achievements/activities:* leadership, religious involvement. *Special characteristics:* children and siblings of alumni, children of faculty/staff, international students, out-of-state students, relatives of clergy, religious affiliation, siblings of current students.

**LOANS** *Programs:* Federal Direct (Subsidized and Unsubsidized Stafford, PLUS), Perkins.

**WORK-STUDY** *Federal work-study:* 20 jobs averaging $2158. *State or other work-study/employment:* Total amount: $19,800 (100% need-based). 9 part-time jobs averaging $2200.

**APPLYING FOR FINANCIAL AID** *Required financial aid forms:* FAFSA, institution's own form, state aid form.

**CONTACT** Erin Neill, Financial Aid Specialist, San Diego Christian College, 200 Riverview Parkway, Santee, CA 92071, 619-201-8731 or toll-free 800-676-2242. *Fax:* 619-201-8797. *E-mail:* eneill@sdcc.edu. *Website:* http://www.sdcc.edu/.

# SAN DIEGO STATE UNIVERSITY
## San Diego, CA

| Tuition & fees (CA res): $6866 | Average undergraduate aid package: $10,800 |
|---|---|

**ABOUT THE INSTITUTION** State-supported, coed. *Awards:* certificates, bachelor's, master's, and doctoral degrees. 105 undergraduate majors. *Total enrollment:* 33,483. Undergraduates: 28,362. Freshmen: 5,054. Federal methodology is used as a basis for awarding need-based institutional aid.

**UNDERGRADUATE EXPENSES** for 2015–2016 *Application fee:* $55. *Tuition, state resident:* full-time $5472. *Tuition, nonresident:* full-time $16,632. *Required fees:* full-time $1394. Full-time tuition and fees vary according to course load, degree level, location, and program. Part-time tuition and fees vary according to course load, degree level, location, and program. *College room and board:* $14,745. Room and board charges vary according to board plan and housing facility.

**FRESHMAN FINANCIAL AID (Fall 2014, est.)** 3,700 applied for aid; of those 73% were deemed to have need. 96% of freshmen with need received aid; of those 4% had need fully met. *Average percent of need met:* 66% (excluding resources awarded to replace EFC). *Average financial aid package:* $10,300 (excluding resources awarded to replace EFC). 2% of all full-time freshmen had no need and received non-need-based gift aid.

**UNDERGRADUATE FINANCIAL AID (Fall 2014, est.)** 17,300 applied for aid; of those 84% were deemed to have need. 97% of undergraduates with need received aid; of those 11% had need fully met. *Average percent of need met:* 70%

(excluding resources awarded to replace EFC). *Average financial aid package:* $10,800 (excluding resources awarded to replace EFC). 4% of all full-time undergraduates had no need and received non-need-based gift aid.

**GIFT AID (NEED-BASED)** *Total amount:* $115,285,000 (43% federal, 28% state, 29% institutional). *Receiving aid:* Freshmen: 38% (1,800); all full-time undergraduates: 43% (10,700). *Average award:* Freshmen: $10,500; Undergraduates: $9900. *Scholarships, grants, and awards:* Federal Pell, FSEOG, state, private, college/university gift aid from institutional funds, Federal Nursing.

**GIFT AID (NON-NEED-BASED)** *Total amount:* $5,483,500 (49% institutional, 51% external sources). *Receiving aid:* Freshmen: 15% (700). Undergraduates: 10% (2,500). *Average award:* Freshmen: $4200. Undergraduates: $2300. *Scholarships, grants, and awards by category:* Academic interests/achievement: area/ethnic studies, biological sciences, business, communication, computer science, education, engineering/technologies, English, foreign languages, general academic interests/achievements, health fields, humanities, international studies, mathematics, military science, physical sciences, religion/biblical studies, social sciences. *Creative arts/performance:* applied art and design, art/fine arts, cinema/film/broadcasting, creative writing, dance, debating, journalism/publications, music, performing arts, theater/drama. *Special achievements/activities:* cheerleading/drum major, hobbies/interests, leadership, memberships. *Special characteristics:* adult students, children and siblings of alumni, children of faculty/staff, children of workers in trades, first-generation college students, handicapped students, local/state students, previous college experience, veterans, veterans' children. *Tuition waivers:* Full or partial for employees or children of employees. *ROTC:* Army, Naval, Air Force.

**LOANS** *Student loans:* $132,582,000 (70% need-based, 30% non-need-based). 49% of past graduating class borrowed through all loan programs. *Average indebtedness per student:* $18,400. *Average need-based loan:* Freshmen: $3200. Undergraduates: $4100. *Parent loans:* $83,424,000 (21% need-based, 79% non-need-based). *Programs:* Federal Direct (Subsidized and Unsubsidized Stafford, PLUS), Perkins, college/university.

**WORK-STUDY** *Federal work-study:* Total amount: $1,311,000; 650 jobs averaging $1900.

**ATHLETIC AWARDS** Total amount: $7,274,000 (100% non-need-based).

**APPLYING FOR FINANCIAL AID** *Required financial aid forms:* FAFSA, state aid form. *Financial aid deadline:* 3/2. *Notification date:* Continuous beginning 3/9.

**CONTACT** Mrs. Rose Pasenelli, Director of Financial Aid and Scholarships, San Diego State University, 5500 Campanile Drive, SSW-3605, San Diego, CA 92182-7436, 619-594-6323 or toll-free 855-594-6336 (in-state), 855-594-3983 (out-of-state). *Website:* http://www.sdsu.edu/.

# SAN FRANCISCO ART INSTITUTE
## San Francisco, CA

| Tuition & fees: $40,096 | Average undergraduate aid package: $36,909 |
|---|---|

**ABOUT THE INSTITUTION** Independent, coed. *Awards:* certificates, bachelor's, and master's degrees. 8 undergraduate majors. *Total enrollment:* 699. Undergraduates: 467. Freshmen: 81. Federal methodology is used as a basis for awarding need-based institutional aid.

**UNDERGRADUATE EXPENSES** for 2015–2016 *Application fee:* $75. *Comprehensive fee:* $55,762 includes full-time tuition ($39,226), mandatory fees ($870), and room and board ($15,666). *College room only:* $11,500. Full-time tuition and fees vary according to degree level. Room and board charges vary according to housing facility. *Part-time tuition:* $1718 per unit. Part-time tuition and fees vary according to degree level.

**FRESHMAN FINANCIAL AID (Fall 2013)** 50 applied for aid; of those 94% were deemed to have need. 100% of freshmen with need received aid; of those 15% had need fully met. *Average percent of need met:* 45% (excluding resources awarded to replace EFC). *Average financial aid package:* $36,933 (excluding resources awarded to replace EFC). 37% of all full-time freshmen had no need and received non-need-based gift aid.

**UNDERGRADUATE FINANCIAL AID (Fall 2013)** 278 applied for aid; of those 92% were deemed to have need. 100% of undergraduates with need received aid; of those 14% had need fully met. *Average percent of need met:* 47% (excluding resources awarded to replace EFC). *Average financial aid package:* $36,909

(excluding resources awarded to replace EFC). 36% of all full-time undergraduates had no need and received non-need-based gift aid.

**GIFT AID (NEED-BASED) Total amount:** $6,823,795 (13% federal, 7% state, 77% institutional, 3% external sources). **Receiving aid:** Freshmen: 53% (42); all full-time undergraduates: 55% (236). **Average award:** Freshmen: $17,398; Undergraduates: $16,370. **Scholarships, grants, and awards:** Federal Pell, FSEOG, state, private, college/university gift aid from institutional funds.

**GIFT AID (NON-NEED-BASED) Total amount:** $1,183,358 (100% institutional). **Receiving aid:** Freshmen: 43% (34). Undergraduates: 47% (201). **Average award:** Freshmen: $8810. Undergraduates: $9084. **Scholarships, grants, and awards by category:** Academic interests/achievement: general academic interests/achievements. Creative arts/performance: art/fine arts. **Tuition waivers:** Full or partial for employees or children of employees.

**LOANS Student loans:** $3,183,479 (68% need-based, 32% non-need-based). 68% of past graduating class borrowed through all loan programs. Average indebtedness per student: $25,931. **Average need-based loan:** Freshmen: $4294. Undergraduates: $4598. **Parent loans:** $2,015,820 (100% need-based). **Programs:** Federal Direct (Subsidized and Unsubsidized Stafford, PLUS), state, college/university.

**WORK-STUDY Federal work-study:** jobs available. **State or other work-study/employment:** Total amount: $87,637 (100% need-based). Part-time jobs available.

**APPLYING FOR FINANCIAL AID Required financial aid forms:** FAFSA, Cal Grant forms, GPA verification form (CA residents only). **Financial aid deadline:** 5/31 (priority: 3/1). **Notification date:** Continuous beginning 4/15. Students must reply within 3 weeks of notification.

**CONTACT** Annita Alldredge, Director of Financial Aid, San Francisco Art Institute, 800 Chestnut Street, San Francisco, CA 94133, 415-749-4560 or toll-free 800-345-SFAI. Fax: 415-351-3503. E-mail: aalldredge@sfai.edu.
Website: http://www.sfai.edu/.

# SAN FRANCISCO CONSERVATORY OF MUSIC
## San Francisco, CA

| Tuition & fees: $40,992 | Average undergraduate aid package: $30,600 |
|---|---|

**ABOUT THE INSTITUTION** Independent, coed. **Awards:** certificates, diplomas, bachelor's, and master's degrees. 7 undergraduate majors. **Total enrollment:** 389. Undergraduates: 171. Freshmen: 41. Both federal and institutional methodology are used as a basis for awarding need-based institutional aid.

**UNDERGRADUATE EXPENSES for 2015–2016 Tuition:** full-time $40,000; part-time $1764 per credit. **Required fees:** full-time $992; $992 per year. Part-time tuition and fees vary according to course load. Room and board charges vary according to housing facility.

**FRESHMAN FINANCIAL AID (Fall 2014, est.)** 38 applied for aid; of those 100% were deemed to have need. 100% of freshmen with need received aid; of those 16% had need fully met. **Average percent of need met:** 49% (excluding resources awarded to replace EFC). **Average financial aid package:** $31,825 (excluding resources awarded to replace EFC). 22% of all full-time freshmen had no need and received non-need-based gift aid.

**UNDERGRADUATE FINANCIAL AID (Fall 2014, est.)** 157 applied for aid; of those 100% were deemed to have need. 100% of undergraduates with need received aid; of those 13% had need fully met. **Average percent of need met:** 59% (excluding resources awarded to replace EFC). **Average financial aid package:** $30,600 (excluding resources awarded to replace EFC). 7% of all full-time undergraduates had no need and received non-need-based gift aid.

**GIFT AID (NEED-BASED) Total amount:** $3,466,164 (8% federal, 6% state, 86% institutional). **Receiving aid:** Freshmen: 93% (38); all full-time undergraduates: 92% (157). **Average award:** Freshmen: $25,000; Undergraduates: $22,360. **Scholarships, grants, and awards:** Federal Pell, FSEOG, state, private, college/university gift aid from institutional funds.

**GIFT AID (NON-NEED-BASED) Total amount:** $312,500 (97% institutional, 3% external sources). **Receiving aid:** Freshmen: 15% (6). Undergraduates: 12% (20). **Average award:** Freshmen: $13,700. Undergraduates: $12,450. **Scholarships, grants, and awards by category:** Creative arts/performance: 21 awards ($254,000 total): music. **Tuition waivers:** Full or partial for employees or children of employees.

**LOANS Student loans:** $452,707 (70% need-based, 30% non-need-based). 70% of past graduating class borrowed through all loan programs. Average indebtedness per student: $24,500. **Average need-based loan:** Freshmen: $5700. Undergraduates: $12,970. **Parent loans:** $519,226 (49% need-based, 51% non-need-based). **Programs:** Federal Direct (Subsidized and Unsubsidized Stafford, PLUS), Perkins.

**WORK-STUDY Federal work-study:** Total amount: $60,000; 24 jobs averaging $2500. **State or other work-study/employment:** 5 part-time jobs averaging $1500.

**APPLYING FOR FINANCIAL AID Required financial aid forms:** FAFSA, institution's own form, CSS Financial Aid PROFILE, noncustodial (divorced/separated) parent's statement. **Financial aid deadline (priority):** 2/15. **Notification date:** Continuous beginning 3/15. Students must reply by 5/1 or within 2 weeks of notification.

**CONTACT** Doris Howard, Director of Financial Aid, San Francisco Conservatory of Music, 50 Oak Street, San Francisco, CA 94102-6011, 415-503-6214. Fax: 415-503-6299. E-mail: dbh@sfcm.edu.
Website: http://www.sfcm.edu/.

# SAN FRANCISCO STATE UNIVERSITY
## San Francisco, CA

| Tuition & fees (CA res): $6468 | Average undergraduate aid package: $11,297 |
|---|---|

**ABOUT THE INSTITUTION** State-supported, coed. **Awards:** certificates, bachelor's, master's, and doctoral degrees. 91 undergraduate majors. **Total enrollment:** 29,465. Undergraduates: 25,938. Freshmen: 3,754. Federal methodology is used as a basis for awarding need-based institutional aid.

**UNDERGRADUATE EXPENSES for 2015–2016 Application fee:** $55. **Tuition, state resident:** full-time $5472. **Tuition, nonresident:** full-time $16,632. **Required fees:** full-time $996. Full-time tuition and fees vary according to course load. Part-time tuition and fees vary according to course load. Room and board charges vary according to board plan and housing facility.

**FRESHMAN FINANCIAL AID (Fall 2014, est.)** 3,127 applied for aid; of those 88% were deemed to have need. 98% of freshmen with need received aid; of those 31% had need fully met. **Average percent of need met:** 73% (excluding resources awarded to replace EFC). **Average financial aid package:** $11,564 (excluding resources awarded to replace EFC). 1% of all full-time freshmen had no need and received non-need-based gift aid.

**UNDERGRADUATE FINANCIAL AID (Fall 2014, est.)** 16,688 applied for aid; of those 90% were deemed to have need. 98% of undergraduates with need received aid; of those 26% had need fully met. **Average percent of need met:** 72% (excluding resources awarded to replace EFC). **Average financial aid package:** $11,297 (excluding resources awarded to replace EFC). 1% of all full-time undergraduates had no need and received non-need-based gift aid.

**GIFT AID (NEED-BASED) Total amount:** $116,943,335 (47% federal, 52% state, 1% external sources). **Receiving aid:** Freshmen: 69% (2,592); all full-time undergraduates: 67% (14,326). **Average award:** Freshmen: $8239; Undergraduates: $8236. **Scholarships, grants, and awards:** Federal Pell, FSEOG, state, private, college/university gift aid from institutional funds.

**GIFT AID (NON-NEED-BASED) Total amount:** $69,623 (11% institutional, 89% external sources). **Receiving aid:** Freshmen: 5% (197). Undergraduates: 3% (579). **Average award:** Freshmen: $1890. Undergraduates: $1738. **Tuition waivers:** Full or partial for employees or children of employees, senior citizens. **ROTC:** Army cooperative, Air Force cooperative.

**LOANS Student loans:** $67,251,233 (96% need-based, 4% non-need-based). 48% of past graduating class borrowed through all loan programs. Average indebtedness per student: $22,741. **Average need-based loan:** Freshmen: $3583. Undergraduates: $4530. **Parent loans:** $23,554,204 (67% need-based, 33% non-need-based). **Programs:** Federal Direct (Subsidized and Unsubsidized Stafford, PLUS), Perkins.

**WORK-STUDY Federal work-study:** Total amount: $1,826,024; jobs available. **ATHLETIC AWARDS** Total amount: $326,390 (100% need-based).

**APPLYING FOR FINANCIAL AID Required financial aid form:** FAFSA. **Financial aid deadline (priority):** 3/2. **Notification date:** Continuous beginning 4/15. Students must reply within 2 weeks of notification.

**CONTACT** Barbara Hubler, Director of Financial Aid, San Francisco State University, 1600 Holloway Avenue, San Francisco, CA 94132-1722, 415-338-7000. *Fax:* 415-338-0949. *E-mail:* finaid@sfsu.edu. *Website:* http://www.sfsu.edu/.

# SAN JOSE STATE UNIVERSITY
## San Jose, CA

| Tuition & fees (CA res): $7323 | Average undergraduate aid package: $14,235 |
|---|---|

**ABOUT THE INSTITUTION** State-supported, coed. *Awards:* bachelor's and master's degrees. 88 undergraduate majors. *Total enrollment:* 32,697. Undergraduates: 26,664. Freshmen: 3,486. Federal methodology is used as a basis for awarding need-based institutional aid.

**UNDERGRADUATE EXPENSES for 2015–2016** *Application fee:* $55. *Tuition, state resident:* full-time $0. *Tuition, nonresident:* full-time $11,600. *Required fees:* full-time $7323. *College room and board:* $11,810; *Room only:* $7150.

**FRESHMAN FINANCIAL AID (Fall 2013)** 2,889 applied for aid; of those 86% were deemed to have need. 93% of freshmen with need received aid; of those 26% had need fully met. *Average percent of need met:* 76% (excluding resources awarded to replace EFC). *Average financial aid package:* $14,881 (excluding resources awarded to replace EFC). 1% of all full-time freshmen had no need and received non-need-based gift aid.

**UNDERGRADUATE FINANCIAL AID (Fall 2013)** 16,248 applied for aid; of those 91% were deemed to have need. 95% of undergraduates with need received aid; of those 24% had need fully met. *Average percent of need met:* 75% (excluding resources awarded to replace EFC). *Average financial aid package:* $14,235 (excluding resources awarded to replace EFC). 1% of all full-time undergraduates had no need and received non-need-based gift aid.

**GIFT AID (NEED-BASED)** *Total amount:* $108,230,132 (44% federal, 54% state, 1% institutional, 1% external sources). *Receiving aid:* Freshmen: 48% (1,716); all full-time undergraduates: 51% (10,597). *Average award:* Freshmen: $8402; Undergraduates: $7500. *Scholarships, grants, and awards:* Federal Pell, FSEOG, state, private, college/university gift aid from institutional funds.

**GIFT AID (NON-NEED-BASED)** *Total amount:* $176,425 (37% institutional, 63% external sources). *Receiving aid:* Freshmen: 1% (34). Undergraduates: 78. *Average award:* Freshmen: $1714. Undergraduates: $1863. *Scholarships, grants, and awards by category:* Academic interests/achievement: general academic interests/achievements. Creative arts/performance: art/fine arts, general creative arts/performance. Special achievements/activities: leadership. Special characteristics: local/state students. *ROTC:* Army cooperative, Air Force.

**LOANS** *Student loans:* $58,764,893 (90% need-based, 10% non-need-based). 45% of past graduating class borrowed through all loan programs. *Average indebtedness per student:* $23,467. *Average need-based loan:* Freshmen: $3433. Undergraduates: $7271. *Parent loans:* $9,016,661 (73% need-based, 27% non-need-based). *Programs:* Federal Direct (Subsidized and Unsubsidized Stafford, PLUS), Perkins.

**WORK-STUDY** *Federal work-study:* jobs available.

**ATHLETIC AWARDS** Total amount: $5,311,738 (81% need-based, 19% non-need-based).

**APPLYING FOR FINANCIAL AID** *Required financial aid form:* FAFSA. *Financial aid deadline:* 6/15 (priority: 3/2). *Notification date:* Continuous beginning 4/1.

**CONTACT** Coleetta McElroy, Director of Financial Aid and Scholarship Office, San Jose State University, One Washington Square, San Jose, CA 95192-0036, 408-924-6086. *E-mail:* coleetta.mcelroy@sjsu.edu. *Website:* http://www.sjsu.edu/.

# SANTA BARBARA BUSINESS COLLEGE
## Ventura, CA

**CONTACT** Financial Aid Office, Santa Barbara Business College, 4839 Market Street, Ventura, CA 93003, 805-339-2999. *Website:* http://www.sbbcollege.com/.

# SANTA CLARA UNIVERSITY
## Santa Clara, CA

| Tuition & fees: $43,812 | Average undergraduate aid package: $30,016 |
|---|---|

**ABOUT THE INSTITUTION** Independent Roman Catholic (Jesuit), coed. *Awards:* certificates, bachelor's, master's, and doctoral degrees. 47 undergraduate majors. *Total enrollment:* 9,015. Undergraduates: 5,486. Freshmen: 1,319. Both federal and institutional methodology are used as a basis for awarding need-based institutional aid.

**UNDERGRADUATE EXPENSES for 2015–2016** *Application fee:* $55. *Comprehensive fee:* $56,733 includes full-time tuition ($43,812) and room and board ($12,921). Room and board charges vary according to board plan, housing facility, location, and student level. *Part-time tuition:* $1217 per unit. Part-time tuition and fees vary according to course load.

**FRESHMAN FINANCIAL AID (Fall 2014, est.)** 818 applied for aid; of those 67% were deemed to have need. 98% of freshmen with need received aid; of those 45% had need fully met. *Average percent of need met:* 81% (excluding resources awarded to replace EFC). *Average financial aid package:* $32,665 (excluding resources awarded to replace EFC). 25% of all full-time freshmen had no need and received non-need-based gift aid.

**UNDERGRADUATE FINANCIAL AID (Fall 2014, est.)** 3,421 applied for aid; of those 78% were deemed to have need. 81% of undergraduates with need received aid; of those 37% had need fully met. *Average percent of need met:* 72% (excluding resources awarded to replace EFC). *Average financial aid package:* $30,016 (excluding resources awarded to replace EFC). 26% of all full-time undergraduates had no need and received non-need-based gift aid.

**GIFT AID (NEED-BASED)** *Total amount:* $54,656,064 (6% federal, 8% state, 84% institutional, 2% external sources). *Receiving aid:* Freshmen: 35% (461); all full-time undergraduates: 33% (1,823). *Average award:* Freshmen: $25,536; Undergraduates: $23,155. *Scholarships, grants, and awards:* Federal Pell, FSEOG, state, private, college/university gift aid from institutional funds.

**GIFT AID (NON-NEED-BASED)** *Total amount:* $22,637,263 (95% institutional, 5% external sources). *Receiving aid:* Freshmen: 20% (260). Undergraduates: 17% (919). *Average award:* Freshmen: $12,975. Undergraduates: $13,120. *Scholarships, grants, and awards by category:* Academic interests/achievement: 2,555 awards ($34,276,043 total): business, engineering/technologies, general academic interests/achievements, military science. Creative arts/performance: 90 awards ($292,294 total): dance, debating, music, theater/drama. Special characteristics: 93 awards ($3,468,348 total): children and siblings of alumni, children of faculty/staff, children with a deceased or disabled parent, handicapped students. *Tuition waivers:* Full or partial for employees or children of employees. *ROTC:* Army, Air Force cooperative.

**LOANS** *Student loans:* $12,129,355 (87% need-based, 13% non-need-based). 56% of past graduating class borrowed through all loan programs. *Average indebtedness per student:* $26,759. *Average need-based loan:* Freshmen: $3328. Undergraduates: $5003. *Parent loans:* $10,979,843 (82% need-based, 18% non-need-based). *Programs:* Federal Direct (Subsidized and Unsubsidized Stafford, PLUS), Perkins, private loans.

**WORK-STUDY** *Federal work-study:* Total amount: $481,572; 258 jobs averaging $2961. *State or other work-study/employment:* Total amount: $4,069,909 (66% need-based, 34% non-need-based). Part-time jobs available.

**ATHLETIC AWARDS** Total amount: $5,464,667 (23% need-based, 77% non-need-based).

**APPLYING FOR FINANCIAL AID** *Required financial aid forms:* FAFSA, CSS Financial Aid PROFILE. *Financial aid deadline (priority):* 2/1. *Notification date:* 4/1. Students must reply by 5/1 or within 2 weeks of notification.

**CONTACT** Marta I. Murchison, Associate Director of Systems and Data Analysis, Santa Clara University, 500 El Camino Real, Santa Clara, CA 95053, 408-551-6088. *Fax:* 408-554-2154. *E-mail:* mmurchison@scu.edu. *Website:* http://www.scu.edu/.

# SANTA FE COLLEGE
### Gainesville, FL

**CONTACT** Financial Aid Office, Santa Fe College, 3000 Northwest 83rd Street, Gainesville, FL 32606, 352-395-5000.
*Website:* http://www.sfcollege.edu/.

# SANTA FE UNIVERSITY OF ART AND DESIGN
### Sànta Fe, NM

| Tuition & fees: N/R | Average undergraduate aid package: $22,375 |
|---|---|

**ABOUT THE INSTITUTION** Independent, coed. *Awards:* certificates and bachelor's degrees. 10 undergraduate majors. *Total enrollment:* 950. Undergraduates: 950. Freshmen: 251. Federal methodology is used as a basis for awarding need-based institutional aid.
**FRESHMAN FINANCIAL AID (Fall 2013)** 182 applied for aid; of those 83% were deemed to have need. 100% of freshmen with need received aid; of those 9% had need fully met. *Average percent of need met:* 61% (excluding resources awarded to replace EFC). *Average financial aid package:* $20,013 (excluding resources awarded to replace EFC). 21% of all full-time freshmen had no need and received non-need-based gift aid.
**UNDERGRADUATE FINANCIAL AID (Fall 2013)** 561 applied for aid; of those 88% were deemed to have need. 100% of undergraduates with need received aid; of those 11% had need fully met. *Average percent of need met:* 66% (excluding resources awarded to replace EFC). *Average financial aid package:* $22,375 (excluding resources awarded to replace EFC). 15% of all full-time undergraduates had no need and received non-need-based gift aid.
**GIFT AID (NEED-BASED)** *Total amount:* $8,918,038 (18% federal, 81% institutional, 1% external sources). *Receiving aid:* Freshmen: 75% (151); all full-time undergraduates: 60% (495). *Average award:* Freshmen: $16,696; Undergraduates: $18,023. *Scholarships, grants, and awards:* Federal Pell, FSEOG, private.
**GIFT AID (NON-NEED-BASED)** *Total amount:* $1,860,240 (99% institutional, 1% external sources). *Receiving aid:* Freshmen: 5% (11). Undergraduates: 5% (38). *Average award:* Freshmen: $12,124. Undergraduates: $12,987. *Scholarships, grants, and awards by category:* Academic interests/achievement: general academic interests/achievements. Creative arts/performance: applied art and design, art/fine arts, cinema/film/broadcasting, creative writing, dance, general creative arts/performance, music, performing arts, theater/drama. Special characteristics: children of faculty/staff, general special characteristics, local/state students.
**LOANS** *Student loans:* $4,236,422 (82% need-based, 18% non-need-based). *Average need-based loan:* Freshmen: $3371. Undergraduates: $4187. *Parent loans:* $1,847,045 (54% need-based, 46% non-need-based). *Programs:* Federal Direct (Subsidized and Unsubsidized Stafford, PLUS), Perkins.
**WORK-STUDY** *Federal work-study:* 194 jobs averaging $1471.
**APPLYING FOR FINANCIAL AID** *Required financial aid form:* FAFSA. *Financial aid deadline:* Continuous. *Notification date:* Continuous beginning 3/1. Students must reply within 2 weeks of notification.
**CONTACT** Krystina Hines, Interim Director of Financial Aid, Santa Fe University of Art and Design, 1600 St. Michael's Drive, Santa Fe, NM 87505-7634, 505-473-6454 or toll-free 800-456-2673. *Fax:* 505-473-6318. *E-mail:* krystina.hines@santafeuniversity.edu.
*Website:* http://www.santafeuniversity.edu/.

# SARAH LAWRENCE COLLEGE
### Bronxville, NY

| Tuition & fees: $50,736 | Average undergraduate aid package: $35,368 |
|---|---|

**ABOUT THE INSTITUTION** Independent, coed. *Awards:* bachelor's and master's degrees. 25 undergraduate majors. *Total enrollment:* 1,761. Undergraduates: 1,437. Freshmen: 356. Both federal and institutional methodology are used as a basis for awarding need-based institutional aid.
**UNDERGRADUATE EXPENSES for 2015–2016** *Application fee:* $60. *Comprehensive fee:* $65,240 includes full-time tuition ($49,680), mandatory fees ($1056), and room and board ($14,504). *College room only:* $9314. Full-time tuition and fees vary according to course load. Room and board charges vary according to board plan. *Part-time tuition:* $1656 per credit. *Part-time fees:* $275 per term. Part-time tuition and fees vary according to course load.
**FRESHMAN FINANCIAL AID (Fall 2014, est.)** 321 applied for aid; of those 82% were deemed to have need. 100% of freshmen with need received aid; of those 40% had need fully met. *Average percent of need met:* 91% (excluding resources awarded to replace EFC). *Average financial aid package:* $28,307 (excluding resources awarded to replace EFC). 8% of all full-time freshmen had no need and received non-need-based gift aid.
**UNDERGRADUATE FINANCIAL AID (Fall 2014, est.)** 1,127 applied for aid; of those 88% were deemed to have need. 100% of undergraduates with need received aid; of those 75% had need fully met. *Average percent of need met:* 89% (excluding resources awarded to replace EFC). *Average financial aid package:* $35,368 (excluding resources awarded to replace EFC). 21% of all full-time undergraduates had no need and received non-need-based gift aid.
**GIFT AID (NEED-BASED)** *Total amount:* $26,703,488 (4% federal, 1% state, 92% institutional, 3% external sources). *Receiving aid:* Freshmen: 53% (190); all full-time undergraduates: 61% (820). *Average award:* Freshmen: $27,447; Undergraduates: $34,650. *Scholarships, grants, and awards:* Federal Pell, FSEOG, state, private, college/university gift aid from institutional funds.
**GIFT AID (NON-NEED-BASED)** *Total amount:* $5,611,805 (100% institutional). *Receiving aid:* Freshmen: 8% (27). Undergraduates: 21% (283). *Average award:* Freshmen: $16,319. Undergraduates: $16,582. *Scholarships, grants, and awards by category:* Academic interests/achievement: 284 awards ($4,627,647 total): general academic interests/achievements. *Tuition waivers:* Full or partial for employees or children of employees.
**LOANS** *Student loans:* $3,058,344 (95% need-based, 5% non-need-based). 78% of past graduating class borrowed through all loan programs. *Average indebtedness per student:* $18,483. *Average need-based loan:* Freshmen: $2567. Undergraduates: $3241. *Parent loans:* $3,575,644 (87% need-based, 13% non-need-based). *Programs:* Federal Direct (Subsidized and Unsubsidized Stafford, PLUS), Perkins, private loans.
**WORK-STUDY** *Federal work-study:* Total amount: $1,007,395; 616 jobs averaging $1617. *State or other work-study/employment:* Total amount: $86,600 (100% non-need-based). 53 part-time jobs averaging $1638.
**APPLYING FOR FINANCIAL AID** *Required financial aid forms:* FAFSA, CSS Financial Aid PROFILE, state aid form, noncustodial (divorced/separated) parent's statement. *Financial aid deadline:* 2/1. *Notification date:* 4/1. Students must reply by 5/1.
**CONTACT** Ms. Heather McDonnell, Director of Financial Aid, Sarah Lawrence College, One Mead Way, Bronxville, NY 10708, 914-395-2570 or toll-free 800-888-2858. *Fax:* 914-395-2676. *E-mail:* hmcdonn@sarahlawrence.edu.
*Website:* http://www.sarahlawrence.edu/.

# SAVANNAH COLLEGE OF ART AND DESIGN
### Savannah, GA

| Tuition & fees: $34,295 | Average undergraduate aid package: $27,795 |
|---|---|

**ABOUT THE INSTITUTION** Independent, coed. *Awards:* certificates, bachelor's, and master's degrees. 31 undergraduate majors. *Total enrollment:* 11,973. Undergraduates: 9,695. Freshmen: 1,925. Federal methodology is used as a basis for awarding need-based institutional aid.
**UNDERGRADUATE EXPENSES for 2015–2016** *Application fee:* $40. *Comprehensive fee:* $48,005 includes full-time tuition ($33,795), mandatory fees ($500), and room and board ($13,710). *College room only:* $8715. Full-time tuition and fees vary according to course load and degree level. Room and board charges vary according to board plan, housing facility, and location. *Part-time tuition:* $751 per quarter hour. Part-time tuition and fees vary according to course load and degree level.
**FRESHMAN FINANCIAL AID (Fall 2014, est.)** 1,236 applied for aid; of those 83% were deemed to have need. 100% of freshmen with need received aid; of those

10% had need fully met. *Average percent of need met:* 15% (excluding resources awarded to replace EFC). *Average financial aid package:* $31,001 (excluding resources awarded to replace EFC). 41% of all full-time freshmen had no need and received non-need-based gift aid.

**UNDERGRADUATE FINANCIAL AID (Fall 2014, est.)** 4,837 applied for aid; of those 87% were deemed to have need. 100% of undergraduates with need received aid; of those 8% had need fully met. *Average percent of need met:* 18% (excluding resources awarded to replace EFC). *Average financial aid package:* $27,795 (excluding resources awarded to replace EFC). 38% of all full-time undergraduates had no need and received non-need-based gift aid.

**GIFT AID (NEED-BASED) Total amount:** $17,259,060 (64% federal, 5% state, 31% institutional). *Receiving aid:* Freshmen: 35% (628); all full-time undergraduates: 34% (2,672). *Average award:* Freshmen: $5641; Undergraduates: $6013. *Scholarships, grants, and awards:* Federal Pell, FSEOG, state, private, college/university gift aid from institutional funds.

**GIFT AID (NON-NEED-BASED) Total amount:** $83,016,196 (5% state, 93% institutional, 2% external sources). *Receiving aid:* Freshmen: 57% (1,025). Undergraduates: 48% (3,765). *Average award:* Freshmen: $10,479. Undergraduates: $9891. *Scholarships, grants, and awards by category: Academic interests/achievement:* architecture, general academic interests/achievements. *Creative arts/performance:* applied art and design, art/fine arts, cinema/film/broadcasting, creative writing, dance, debating, general creative arts/performance, journalism/publications, music, performing arts, theater/drama. *Special achievements/activities:* general special achievements/activities. *Special characteristics:* general special characteristics, veterans, veterans' children. *Tuition waivers:* Full or partial for employees or children of employees.

**LOANS Student loans:** $55,946,466 (88% need-based, 12% non-need-based). 61% of past graduating class borrowed through all loan programs. *Average indebtedness per student:* $36,088. *Average need-based loan:* Freshmen: $3124. Undergraduates: $4097. *Parent loans:* $57,542,418 (86% need-based, 14% non-need-based). *Programs:* Federal Direct (Subsidized and Unsubsidized Stafford, PLUS), state.

**WORK-STUDY Federal work-study:** Total amount: $506,057; jobs available. *State or other work-study/employment:* Total amount: $1,118,086 (100% need-based). Part-time jobs available.

**ATHLETIC AWARDS** Total amount: $4,813,062 (45% need-based, 55% non-need-based).

**APPLYING FOR FINANCIAL AID** *Required financial aid forms:* FAFSA, state aid form. *Financial aid deadline:* Continuous. *Notification date:* Continuous beginning 3/15. Students must reply within 4 weeks of notification.

**CONTACT** Ms. Kim Beveridge, Director of Financial Aid, Savannah College of Art and Design, PO Box 3146, Savannah, GA 31402-3146, 800-859-7223 or toll-free 800-869-7223. *E-mail:* admission@scad.edu. *Website:* http://www.scad.edu/.

# SAVANNAH STATE UNIVERSITY
## Savannah, GA

| Tuition & fees (GA res): $6498 | Average undergraduate aid package: N/A |
| --- | --- |

**ABOUT THE INSTITUTION** State-supported, coed. *Awards:* certificates, associate, bachelor's, and master's degrees. 30 undergraduate majors. *Total enrollment:* 4,915. Undergraduates: 4,769. Freshmen: 1,204. Federal methodology is used as a basis for awarding need-based institutional aid.

**UNDERGRADUATE EXPENSES for 2015–2016** *One-time required fee:* $125. *Tuition, state resident:* full-time $4740; part-time $158 per credit hour. *Tuition, nonresident:* full-time $17,246; part-time $547.87 per credit hour. *Required fees:* full-time $1758; $879 per term. Full-time tuition and fees vary according to course load and program. Part-time tuition and fees vary according to course load and program. *College room and board:* $7330; *Room only:* $3386. Room and board charges vary according to board plan and housing facility.

**GIFT AID (NEED-BASED) Total amount:** $18,929,086 (98% federal, 2% institutional). *Scholarships, grants, and awards:* Federal Pell, FSEOG, state, private, college/university gift aid from institutional funds.

**GIFT AID (NON-NEED-BASED) Total amount:** $6,367,125 (56% state, 27% institutional, 17% external sources). *Scholarships, grants, and awards by category: Academic interests/achievement:* biological sciences, business, computer science, engineering/technologies, English, general academic interests/achievements,

humanities, mathematics, military science, physical sciences, social sciences. *Tuition waivers:* Full or partial for employees or children of employees, senior citizens. *ROTC:* Army, Naval.

**LOANS Student loans:** $35,588,394 (42% need-based, 58% non-need-based). *Parent loans:* $5,301,268 (100% need-based). *Programs:* Federal Direct (Subsidized and Unsubsidized Stafford, PLUS), Perkins, state, college/university.

**WORK-STUDY Federal work-study:** Total amount: $390,654; jobs available.

**ATHLETIC AWARDS** Total amount: $941,325 (100% need-based).

**APPLYING FOR FINANCIAL AID** *Required financial aid form:* FAFSA. *Financial aid deadline:* 7/31. *Notification date:* Continuous beginning 4/1. Students must reply within 8 weeks of notification.

**CONTACT** Kenneth Wilson, Director of Financial Aid, Savannah State University, PO Box 20523, Savannah, GA 31404, 912-358-4162 or toll-free 800-788-0478. *Fax:* 912-358-3167. *E-mail:* finaid@savannahstate.edu. *Website:* http://www.savannahstate.edu/.

# SCHILLER INTERNATIONAL UNIVERSITY
## Largo, FL

**CONTACT** Financial Aid Office, Schiller International University, 8560 Ulmerton Road, Largo, FL 33771, 727-736-5082 or toll-free 800-261-9571 (in-state), 800-261-9751 (out-of-state). *Website:* http://www.schiller.edu/.

# SCHOOL OF THE ART INSTITUTE OF CHICAGO
## Chicago, IL

| Tuition & fees: $42,230 | Average undergraduate aid package: $31,573 |
| --- | --- |

**ABOUT THE INSTITUTION** Independent, coed. *Awards:* certificates, bachelor's, and master's degrees. 33 undergraduate majors. *Total enrollment:* 3,522. Undergraduates: 2,783. Freshmen: 604. Federal methodology is used as a basis for awarding need-based institutional aid.

**UNDERGRADUATE EXPENSES for 2015–2016** *Application fee:* $65. *One-time required fee:* $150. *Comprehensive fee:* $54,730 includes full-time tuition ($41,430), mandatory fees ($800), and room and board ($12,500) *College room only:* $11,000. Full-time tuition and fees vary according to course load, degree level, and program. Room and board charges vary according to board plan. *Part-time tuition:* $1381 per credit hour. *Part-time fees:* $265 per term. Part-time tuition and fees vary according to course load, degree level, and program.

**FRESHMAN FINANCIAL AID (Fall 2013)** 332 applied for aid; of those 85% were deemed to have need. 100% of freshmen with need received aid; of those 9% had need fully met. *Average percent of need met:* 75% (excluding resources awarded to replace EFC). *Average financial aid package:* $30,276 (excluding resources awarded to replace EFC). 50% of all full-time freshmen had no need and received non-need-based gift aid.

**UNDERGRADUATE FINANCIAL AID (Fall 2013)** 1,367 applied for aid; of those 90% were deemed to have need. 100% of undergraduates with need received aid; of those 7% had need fully met. *Average percent of need met:* 74% (excluding resources awarded to replace EFC). *Average financial aid package:* $31,573 (excluding resources awarded to replace EFC). 47% of all full-time undergraduates had no need and received non-need-based gift aid.

**GIFT AID (NEED-BASED) Total amount:** $20,951,990 (15% federal, 4% state, 80% institutional, 1% external sources). *Receiving aid:* Freshmen: 49% (279); all full-time undergraduates: 49% (1,215). *Average award:* Freshmen: $15,912; Undergraduates: $16,633. *Scholarships, grants, and awards:* Federal Pell, FSEOG, state, private, college/university gift aid from institutional funds.

**GIFT AID (NON-NEED-BASED) Total amount:** $9,639,978 (97% institutional, 3% external sources). *Receiving aid:* Freshmen: 4% (21). Undergraduates: 3% (68). *Average award:* Freshmen: $7942. Undergraduates: $7766. *Scholarships, grants, and awards by category: Academic interests/achievement:* general academic interests/achievements. *Creative arts/performance:* art/fine arts. *Tuition waivers:* Full or partial for employees or children of employees.

**LOANS** *Student loans:* $13,555,765 (86% need-based, 14% non-need-based). 54% of past graduating class borrowed through all loan programs. *Average indebtedness per student:* $42,097. *Average need-based loan:* Freshmen: $4198. Undergraduates: $5233. *Parent loans:* $8,889,684 (65% need-based, 35% non-need-based). *Programs:* Federal Direct (Subsidized and Unsubsidized Stafford, PLUS), Perkins.

**WORK-STUDY** *Federal work-study:* jobs available. *State or other work-study/employment:* Total amount: $801,853 (53% need-based, 47% non-need-based). Part-time jobs available.

**APPLYING FOR FINANCIAL AID** *Required financial aid form:* FAFSA. *Financial aid deadline (priority):* 3/1. *Notification date:* Continuous beginning 4/1.

**CONTACT** Mr. Patrick James, Student Financial Services Office, School of the Art Institute of Chicago, 36 South Wabash, Suite 1218, Chicago, IL 60603-3103, 312-629-6600 or toll-free 800-232-SAIC. *Fax:* 312-629-6601. *E-mail:* finaid@saic.edu. *Website:* http://www.saic.edu/.

# SCHOOL OF THE MUSEUM OF FINE ARTS, BOSTON
## Boston, MA

| Tuition & fees: $40,348 | Average undergraduate aid package: $23,317 |
| --- | --- |

**ABOUT THE INSTITUTION** Independent, coed. *Awards:* certificates, diplomas, bachelor's, and master's degrees. 19 undergraduate majors. *Total enrollment:* 560. Undergraduates: 235. Freshmen: 70. Federal methodology is used as a basis for awarding need-based institutional aid.

**UNDERGRADUATE EXPENSES** for 2015–2016 *Application fee:* $65. *Tuition:* full-time $39,068; part-time $1452 per credit hour. Full-time tuition and fees vary according to course load, degree level, program, and student level. Part-time tuition and fees vary according to class time, course load, program, and student level. Room and board charges vary according to board plan and housing facility.

**FRESHMAN FINANCIAL AID (Fall 2014, est.)** 49 applied for aid; of those 90% were deemed to have need. 100% of freshmen with need received aid; of those 5% had need fully met. *Average percent of need met:* 65% (excluding resources awarded to replace EFC). *Average financial aid package:* $26,948 (excluding resources awarded to replace EFC). 8% of all full-time freshmen had no need and received non-need-based gift aid.

**UNDERGRADUATE FINANCIAL AID (Fall 2014, est.)** 267 applied for aid; of those 94% were deemed to have need. 100% of undergraduates with need received aid; of those 8% had need fully met. *Average percent of need met:* 57% (excluding resources awarded to replace EFC). *Average financial aid package:* $23,317 (excluding resources awarded to replace EFC). 4% of all full-time undergraduates had no need and received non-need-based gift aid.

**GIFT AID (NEED-BASED)** *Total amount:* $1,993,611 (26% federal, 2% state, 68% institutional, 4% external sources). *Receiving aid:* Freshmen: 71% (44); all full-time undergraduates: 71% (252). *Average award:* Freshmen: $8222; Undergraduates: $7351. *Scholarships, grants, and awards:* Federal Pell, FSEOG, state, private, college/university gift aid from institutional funds.

**GIFT AID (NON-NEED-BASED)** *Total amount:* $2,755,417 (100% institutional). *Receiving aid:* Freshmen: 71% (44). Undergraduates: 71% (252). *Average award:* Freshmen: $7200. Undergraduates: $7786. *Scholarships, grants, and awards by category:* Creative arts/performance: art/fine arts. *Special characteristics:* general special characteristics. *Tuition waivers:* Full or partial for employees or children of employees.

**LOANS** *Student loans:* $2,072,529 (100% need-based). 42% of past graduating class borrowed through all loan programs. *Average indebtedness per student:* $34,081. *Average need-based loan:* Freshmen: $4507. Undergraduates: $4966. *Parent loans:* $1,891,602 (100% need-based). *Programs:* Federal Direct (Subsidized and Unsubsidized Stafford, PLUS), state.

**WORK-STUDY** *Federal work-study:* Total amount: $59,820; jobs available.

**APPLYING FOR FINANCIAL AID** *Required financial aid form:* FAFSA. *Financial aid deadline (priority):* 3/15. *Notification date:* Continuous beginning 3/31. Students must reply by 5/1 or within 2 weeks of notification.

**CONTACT** Mr. Shaun Thomas, Director of Financial Aid, School of the Museum of Fine Arts, Boston, 230 The Fenway, Boston, MA 02115, 617-369-3684 or toll-free 800-643-6078 (in-state). *Fax:* 617-369-3041. *Website:* http://www.smfa.edu/.

# SCHOOL OF VISUAL ARTS
## New York, NY

| Tuition & fees: N/R | Average undergraduate aid package: $16,039 |
| --- | --- |

**ABOUT THE INSTITUTION** Proprietary, coed. *Awards:* bachelor's and master's degrees. 15 undergraduate majors. *Total enrollment:* 4,397. Undergraduates: 3,678. Freshmen: 623. Federal methodology is used as a basis for awarding need-based institutional aid.

**FRESHMAN FINANCIAL AID (Fall 2014, est.)** 373 applied for aid; of those 87% were deemed to have need. 95% of freshmen with need received aid; of those 3% had need fully met. *Average percent of need met:* 39% (excluding resources awarded to replace EFC). *Average financial aid package:* $15,651 (excluding resources awarded to replace EFC). 6% of all full-time freshmen had no need and received non-need-based gift aid.

**UNDERGRADUATE FINANCIAL AID (Fall 2014, est.)** 1,603 applied for aid; of those 91% were deemed to have need. 96% of undergraduates with need received aid; of those 1% had need fully met. *Average percent of need met:* 31% (excluding resources awarded to replace EFC). *Average financial aid package:* $16,039 (excluding resources awarded to replace EFC). 6% of all full-time undergraduates had no need and received non-need-based gift aid.

**GIFT AID (NEED-BASED)** *Total amount:* $15,920,215 (28% federal, 9% state, 60% institutional, 3% external sources). *Receiving aid:* Freshmen: 39% (243); all full-time undergraduates: 32% (1,087). *Average award:* Freshmen: $12,523; Undergraduates: $12,205. *Scholarships, grants, and awards:* Federal Pell, FSEOG, state, private, college/university gift aid from institutional funds.

**GIFT AID (NON-NEED-BASED)** *Total amount:* $2,402,858 (1% federal, 85% institutional, 14% external sources). *Receiving aid:* Freshmen: 16% (102). Undergraduates: 11% (377). *Average award:* Freshmen: $12,986. Undergraduates: $11,362. *Scholarships, grants, and awards by category:* Creative arts/performance: art/fine arts.

**LOANS** *Student loans:* $19,250,544 (93% need-based, 7% non-need-based). 54% of past graduating class borrowed through all loan programs. *Average indebtedness per student:* $33,172. *Average need-based loan:* Freshmen: $3584. Undergraduates: $4591. *Parent loans:* $14,015,517 (93% need-based, 7% non-need-based). *Programs:* Federal Direct (Subsidized and Unsubsidized Stafford, PLUS), Perkins, alternative loans.

**WORK-STUDY** *Federal work-study:* Total amount: $868,831; jobs available. *State or other work-study/employment:* Total amount: $627,458 (81% need-based, 19% non-need-based). Part-time jobs available.

**APPLYING FOR FINANCIAL AID** *Required financial aid forms:* FAFSA, state aid form. *Financial aid deadline:* 3/1 (priority: 2/1). *Notification date:* Continuous beginning 2/15. Students must reply within 4 weeks of notification.

**CONTACT** Mr. William Berrios, Financial Aid Office, School of Visual Arts, 209 East 23rd Street, New York, NY 10010, 212-592-2030 or toll-free 800-436-4204. *Fax:* 212-592-2029. *E-mail:* fa@sva.edu. *Website:* http://www.sva.edu/.

# SCHREINER UNIVERSITY
## Kerrville, TX

| Tuition & fees: $24,360 | Average undergraduate aid package: $18,278 |
| --- | --- |

**ABOUT THE INSTITUTION** Independent Presbyterian, coed. *Awards:* certificates, associate, bachelor's, and master's degrees. 35 undergraduate majors. *Total enrollment:* 1,136. Undergraduates: 1,065. Freshmen: 299. Federal methodology is used as a basis for awarding need-based institutional aid.

**UNDERGRADUATE EXPENSES** for 2015–2016 *Application fee:* $25. *Comprehensive fee:* $34,970 includes full-time tuition ($22,760), mandatory fees

($1600), and room and board ($10,610). Room and board charges vary according to board plan and housing facility. *Part-time tuition:* $972 per credit hour.

**FRESHMAN FINANCIAL AID (Fall 2013)** 280 applied for aid; of those 83% were deemed to have need. 100% of freshmen with need received aid; of those 20% had need fully met. *Average percent of need met:* 74% (excluding resources awarded to replace EFC). *Average financial aid package:* $18,367 (excluding resources awarded to replace EFC). 13% of all full-time freshmen had no need and received non-need-based gift aid.

**UNDERGRADUATE FINANCIAL AID (Fall 2013)** 850 applied for aid; of those 88% were deemed to have need. 100% of undergraduates with need received aid; of those 17% had need fully met. *Average percent of need met:* 71% (excluding resources awarded to replace EFC). *Average financial aid package:* $18,278 (excluding resources awarded to replace EFC). 9% of all full-time undergraduates had no need and received non-need-based gift aid.

**GIFT AID (NEED-BASED)** *Total amount:* $12,282,808 (15% federal, 14% state, 52% institutional, 19% external sources). *Receiving aid:* Freshmen: 82% (231); all full-time undergraduates: 88% (746). *Average award:* Freshmen: $15,812; Undergraduates: $14,969. *Scholarships, grants, and awards:* Federal Pell, FSEOG, state, private, college/university gift aid from institutional funds.

**GIFT AID (NON-NEED-BASED)** *Total amount:* $1,586,250 (2% state, 61% institutional, 37% external sources). *Receiving aid:* Freshmen: 14% (40). Undergraduates: 11% (97). *Average award:* Freshmen: $8065. Undergraduates: $8152. *Scholarships, grants, and awards by category:* Academic interests/achievement: biological sciences, business, education, English, general academic interests/achievements, mathematics, physical sciences, premedicine, religion/biblical studies, social sciences. Creative arts/performance: applied art and design, art/fine arts, journalism/publications, music, theater/drama. Special achievements/activities: community service, leadership, memberships, religious involvement. Special characteristics: children of faculty/staff, general special characteristics, international students, relatives of clergy, religious affiliation, siblings of current students, veterans. *Tuition waivers:* Full or partial for employees or children of employees.

**LOANS** *Student loans:* $7,481,065 (70% need-based, 30% non-need-based). 87% of past graduating class borrowed through all loan programs. *Average indebtedness per student:* $29,364. *Average need-based loan:* Freshmen: $3078. Undergraduates: $3836. *Parent loans:* $1,175,869 (40% need-based, 60% non-need-based). *Programs:* Federal Direct (Subsidized and Unsubsidized Stafford, PLUS), state.

**WORK-STUDY** *Federal work-study:* jobs available. *State or other work-study/employment:* Total amount: $227,396 (48% need-based, 52% non-need-based). Part-time jobs available.

**APPLYING FOR FINANCIAL AID** *Required financial aid form:* FAFSA. *Financial aid deadline (priority):* 5/1. *Notification date:* Continuous beginning 2/15. Students must reply within 2 weeks of notification.

**CONTACT** Toni Bryant, Director of Financial Aid, Schreiner University, 2100 Memorial Boulevard, Kerrville, TX 78028, 830-792-7217 or toll-free 800-343-4919. *Fax:* 830-792-7226. *E-mail:* finaid@schreiner.edu. *Website:* http://www.schreiner.edu/.

# SCRIPPS COLLEGE
## Claremont, CA

| Tuition & fees: $47,378 | Average undergraduate aid package: $40,179 |
| --- | --- |

**ABOUT THE INSTITUTION** Independent, women only. *Awards:* certificates and bachelor's degrees. 62 undergraduate majors. *Total enrollment:* 988. Undergraduates: 972. Freshmen: 250. Both federal and institutional methodology are used as a basis for awarding need-based institutional aid.

**UNDERGRADUATE EXPENSES for 2015–2016** *Application fee:* $60. *Comprehensive fee:* $61,940 includes full-time tuition ($47,164), mandatory fees ($214), and room and board ($14,562). *College room only:* $7934. Full-time tuition and fees vary according to course load and degree level. Room and board charges vary according to board plan. *Part-time tuition:* $5896 per course. Part-time tuition and fees vary according to course load and degree level. *Payment plan:* Tuition prepayment.

**FRESHMAN FINANCIAL AID (Fall 2013)** 163 applied for aid; of those 68% were deemed to have need. 100% of freshmen with need received aid; of those 100% had need fully met. *Average percent of need met:* 100% (excluding resources awarded to replace EFC). *Average financial aid package:* $37,680 (excluding

resources awarded to replace EFC). 18% of all full-time freshmen had no need and received non-need-based gift aid.

**UNDERGRADUATE FINANCIAL AID (Fall 2013)** 511 applied for aid; of those 82% were deemed to have need. 100% of undergraduates with need received aid; of those 100% had need fully met. *Average percent of need met:* 100% (excluding resources awarded to replace EFC). *Average financial aid package:* $40,179 (excluding resources awarded to replace EFC). 13% of all full-time undergraduates had no need and received non-need-based gift aid.

**GIFT AID (NEED-BASED)** *Total amount:* $14,447,332 (5% federal, 3% state, 90% institutional, 2% external sources). *Receiving aid:* Freshmen: 41% (111); all full-time undergraduates: 43% (415). *Average award:* Freshmen: $33,021; Undergraduates: $34,792. *Scholarships, grants, and awards:* Federal Pell, FSEOG, state, private, college/university gift aid from institutional funds.

**GIFT AID (NON-NEED-BASED)** *Total amount:* $2,813,303 (90% institutional, 10% external sources). *Receiving aid:* Freshmen: 3% (9). Undergraduates: 1% (12). *Average award:* Freshmen: $13,611. Undergraduates: $19,712. *Scholarships, grants, and awards by category:* Academic interests/achievement: general academic interests/achievements. *Tuition waivers:* Full or partial for employees or children of employees. *ROTC:* Army cooperative, Air Force cooperative.

**LOANS** *Student loans:* $2,386,997 (82% need-based, 18% non-need-based). 50% of past graduating class borrowed through all loan programs. *Average indebtedness per student:* $20,060. *Average need-based loan:* Freshmen: $3237. Undergraduates: $3541. *Parent loans:* $1,471,277 (56% need-based, 44% non-need-based). *Programs:* Federal Direct (Subsidized and Unsubsidized Stafford, PLUS), Perkins, college/university.

**WORK-STUDY** *Federal work-study:* jobs available. *State or other work-study/employment:* Total amount: $20,000 (78% need-based, 22% non-need-based). Part-time jobs available.

**APPLYING FOR FINANCIAL AID** *Required financial aid forms:* FAFSA, CSS Financial Aid PROFILE, state aid form, noncustodial (divorced/separated) parent's statement, business/farm supplement. *Financial aid deadline:* 2/1. *Notification date:* 4/1. Students must reply by 5/1.

**CONTACT** Victoria Romero, Office of Financial Aid, Scripps College, 1030 Columbia Avenue, Claremont, CA 91711-3948, 909-621-8275 or toll-free 800-770-1333. *Fax:* 909-607-7742. *E-mail:* finaid@scrippscollege.edu. *Website:* http://www.scrippscollege.edu/.

# SEATTLE PACIFIC UNIVERSITY
## Seattle, WA

| Tuition & fees: $35,472 | Average undergraduate aid package: $30,933 |
| --- | --- |

**ABOUT THE INSTITUTION** Independent Free Methodist, coed. *Awards:* certificates, bachelor's, master's, and doctoral degrees. 51 undergraduate majors. *Total enrollment:* 4,217. Undergraduates: 3,264. Freshmen: 685. Federal methodology is used as a basis for awarding need-based institutional aid.

**UNDERGRADUATE EXPENSES for 2015–2016** *Application fee:* $50. *Comprehensive fee:* $45,558 includes full-time tuition ($35,100), mandatory fees ($372), and room and board ($10,086). *College room only:* $5553. Room and board charges vary according to board plan and housing facility. *Part-time tuition:* $975 per credit hour. *Part-time fees:* $6 per credit hour. Part-time tuition and fees vary according to course load.

**FRESHMAN FINANCIAL AID (Fall 2014, est.)** 606 applied for aid; of those 81% were deemed to have need. 100% of freshmen with need received aid; of those 9% had need fully met. *Average percent of need met:* 81% (excluding resources awarded to replace EFC). *Average financial aid package:* $31,276 (excluding resources awarded to replace EFC). 23% of all full-time freshmen had no need and received non-need-based gift aid.

**UNDERGRADUATE FINANCIAL AID (Fall 2014, est.)** 2,557 applied for aid; of those 86% were deemed to have need. 100% of undergraduates with need received aid; of those 6% had need fully met. *Average percent of need met:* 80% (excluding resources awarded to replace EFC). *Average financial aid package:* $30,933 (excluding resources awarded to replace EFC). 22% of all full-time undergraduates had no need and received non-need-based gift aid.

**GIFT AID (NEED-BASED)** *Total amount:* $51,347,411 (10% federal, 7% state, 78% institutional, 5% external sources). *Receiving aid:* Freshmen: 73% (489); all full-time undergraduates: 71% (2,193). *Average award:* Freshmen: $26,838; Undergrad-

uates: $26,101. **Scholarships, grants, and awards:** Federal Pell, FSEOG, state, private, college/university gift aid from institutional funds.

**GIFT AID (NON-NEED-BASED) Total amount:** $12,783,568 (79% institutional, 21% external sources). **Average award:** Freshmen: $20,698. Undergraduates: $18,566. **Scholarships, grants, and awards by category:** Academic interests/achievement: 619 awards ($7,380,419 total): engineering/technologies, general academic interests/achievements. Creative arts/performance: 36 awards ($47,501 total): art/fine arts, performing arts. Special characteristics: 237 awards ($894,724 total): children and siblings of alumni, children of faculty/staff, general special characteristics, international students, relatives of clergy, religious affiliation, veterans, veterans' children. **Tuition waivers:** Full or partial for employees or children of employees, senior citizens. **ROTC:** Army cooperative, Naval cooperative, Air Force cooperative.

**LOANS Student loans:** $17,862,592 (93% need-based, 7% non-need-based). 71% of past graduating class borrowed through all loan programs. Average indebtedness per student: $28,844. **Average need-based loan:** Freshmen: $5118. Undergraduates: $5278. **Parent loans:** $8,673,576 (85% need-based, 15% non-need-based). **Programs:** Federal Direct (Subsidized and Unsubsidized Stafford, PLUS), Perkins, Federal Nursing, state, college/university.

**WORK-STUDY Federal work-study:** Total amount: $525,958; 299 jobs averaging $1759. **State or other work-study/employment:** Total amount: $311,642 (100% need-based). 160 part-time jobs averaging $1948.

**ATHLETIC AWARDS** Total amount: $2,072,224 (46% need-based, 54% non-need-based).

**APPLYING FOR FINANCIAL AID Required financial aid form:** FAFSA. **Financial aid deadline (priority):** 2/1. **Notification date:** Continuous beginning 3/15. Students must reply by 5/1 or within 4 weeks of notification.

**CONTACT** Mr. Jordan Grant, Director of Student Financial Services, Seattle Pacific University, 3307 Third Avenue West, Seattle, WA 98119-1997, 206-281-2469 or toll-free 800-366-3344. E-mail: grantj@spu.edu.

Website: http://www.spu.edu/.

# SEATTLE UNIVERSITY
## Seattle, WA

| Tuition & fees: $38,205 | Average undergraduate aid package: $30,502 |
| --- | --- |

**ABOUT THE INSTITUTION** Independent Roman Catholic, coed. **Awards:** certificates, bachelor's, master's, and doctoral degrees. 68 undergraduate majors. **Total enrollment:** 7,273. Undergraduates: 4,511. Freshmen: 927. Federal methodology is used as a basis for awarding need-based institutional aid.

**UNDERGRADUATE EXPENSES for 2015–2016 Application fee:** $50. **Comprehensive fee:** $49,035 includes full-time tuition ($37,485), mandatory fees ($720), and room and board ($10,830). Full-time tuition and fees vary according to course load. Room and board charges vary according to board plan and housing facility. **Part-time tuition:** $833 per credit hour. Part-time tuition and fees vary according to course load.

**FRESHMAN FINANCIAL AID (Fall 2014, est.)** 769 applied for aid; of those 79% were deemed to have need. 100% of freshmen with need received aid; of those 11% had need fully met. **Average percent of need met:** 67% (excluding resources awarded to replace EFC). **Average financial aid package:** $29,590 (excluding resources awarded to replace EFC). 9% of all full-time freshmen had no need and received non-need-based gift aid.

**UNDERGRADUATE FINANCIAL AID (Fall 2014, est.)** 2,969 applied for aid; of those 83% were deemed to have need. 100% of undergraduates with need received aid; of those 12% had need fully met. **Average percent of need met:** 67% (excluding resources awarded to replace EFC). **Average financial aid package:** $30,502 (excluding resources awarded to replace EFC). 4% of all full-time undergraduates had no need and received non-need-based gift aid.

**GIFT AID (NEED-BASED) Total amount:** $61,086,632 (11% federal, 6% state, 79% institutional, 4% external sources). **Receiving aid:** Freshmen: 59% (545); all full-time undergraduates: 53% (2,278). **Average award:** Freshmen: $21,732; Undergraduates: $20,689. **Scholarships, grants, and awards:** Federal Pell, FSEOG, state, private, college/university gift aid from institutional funds, Federal Nursing.

**GIFT AID (NON-NEED-BASED) Total amount:** $12,719,795 (21% federal, 77% institutional, 2% external sources). **Receiving aid:** Freshmen: 39% (358). Undergraduates: 25% (1,079). **Average award:** Freshmen: $11,665. Undergraduates: $10,810. **Scholarships, grants, and awards by category:** Academic interests/

achievement: general academic interests/achievements. Creative arts/performance: art/fine arts, music, theater/drama. Special achievements/activities: leadership. Special characteristics: children and siblings of alumni, children of educators, children of faculty/staff, members of minority groups, religious affiliation. **Tuition waivers:** Full or partial for employees or children of employees. **ROTC:** Army, Naval cooperative, Air Force cooperative.

**LOANS Student loans:** $21,993,755 (68% need-based, 32% non-need-based). 73% of past graduating class borrowed through all loan programs. Average indebtedness per student: $29,044. **Average need-based loan:** Freshmen: $3818. Undergraduates: $5781. **Parent loans:** $10,015,951 (9% need-based, 91% non-need-based). **Programs:** Federal Direct (Subsidized and Unsubsidized Stafford, PLUS), Perkins, Federal Nursing.

**WORK-STUDY Federal work-study:** Total amount: $1,360,520; 462 jobs averaging $3755. **State or other work-study/employment:** Total amount: $625,826 (100% need-based). 237 part-time jobs averaging $6009.

**ATHLETIC AWARDS** Total amount: $4,875,134 (100% non-need-based).

**APPLYING FOR FINANCIAL AID Required financial aid form:** FAFSA. **Financial aid deadline (priority):** 2/1. **Notification date:** 3/1. Students must reply by 5/1 or within 2 weeks of notification.

**CONTACT** Mr. Jeff Scofield, Director of Student Financial Services, Seattle University, 901 12th Avenue, PO Box 222000, Seattle, WA 98122-1090, 206-296-2000 or toll-free 800-542-0833 (in-state), 800-426-7123 (out-of-state). Fax: 206-296-5755. E-mail: financial-aid@seattleu.edu.

Website: http://www.seattleu.edu/.

# SELMA UNIVERSITY
## Selma, AL

**CONTACT** Financial Aid Office, Selma University, 1501 Lapsley Street, Selma, AL 36701-5299, 334-872-2533.

Website: http://www.selmauniversity.edu/.

# SENTARA COLLEGE OF HEALTH SCIENCES
## Chesapeake, VA

**CONTACT** Financial Aid Office, Sentara College of Health Sciences, 1441 Crossways Boulevard, Crossways I, Suite 105, Chesapeake, VA 23320, 757-388-2900.

Website: http://www.sentara.edu/.

# SETON HALL UNIVERSITY
## South Orange, NJ

**CONTACT** Office of Enrollment Services, Seton Hall University, 400 South Orange Avenue, South Orange, NJ 07079, 973-761-9350 or toll-free 800-THE HALL. Fax: 973-275-2040. E-mail: thehall@shu.edu.

Website: http://www.shu.edu/.

# SETON HILL UNIVERSITY
## Greensburg, PA

| Tuition & fees: $32,037 | Average undergraduate aid package: $24,777 |
| --- | --- |

**ABOUT THE INSTITUTION** Independent Roman Catholic, coed. **Awards:** certificates, bachelor's, and master's degrees. 74 undergraduate majors. **Total enrollment:** 1,959. Undergraduates: 1,582. Freshmen: 335. Federal methodology is used as a basis for awarding need-based institutional aid.

**UNDERGRADUATE EXPENSES for 2015–2016 Application fee:** $35. **Comprehensive fee:** $42,776 includes full-time tuition ($31,037), mandatory fees ($1000), and room and board ($10,739). Full-time tuition and fees vary according to course load, degree level, and program. Room and board charges vary according to board plan and housing facility. **Part-time tuition:** $832 per credit hour. **Part-time fees:** $25 per credit hour. Part-time tuition and fees vary according to course load, degree level, and program.

**FRESHMAN FINANCIAL AID (Fall 2014, est.)** 294 applied for aid; of those 92% were deemed to have need. 100% of freshmen with need received aid; of those 22% had need fully met. **Average percent of need met:** 77% (excluding resources awarded to replace EFC). **Average financial aid package:** $25,414 (excluding resources awarded to replace EFC). 14% of all full-time freshmen had no need and received non-need-based gift aid.

**UNDERGRADUATE FINANCIAL AID (Fall 2014, est.)** 1,155 applied for aid; of those 94% were deemed to have need. 99% of undergraduates with need received aid; of those 18% had need fully met. **Average percent of need met:** 74% (excluding resources awarded to replace EFC). **Average financial aid package:** $24,777 (excluding resources awarded to replace EFC). 14% of all full-time undergraduates had no need and received non-need-based gift aid.

**GIFT AID (NEED-BASED) Total amount:** $19,081,529 (12% federal, 10% state, 76% institutional, 2% external sources). **Receiving aid:** Freshmen: 84% (270); all full-time undergraduates: 84% (1,070). **Average award:** Freshmen: $20,195; Undergraduates: $19,198. **Scholarships, grants, and awards:** Federal Pell, FSEOG, state, private, college/university gift aid from institutional funds.

**GIFT AID (NON-NEED-BASED) Total amount:** $2,945,597 (1% state, 95% institutional, 4% external sources). **Receiving aid:** Freshmen: 16% (52). Undergraduates: 12% (148). **Average award:** Freshmen: $13,524. Undergraduates: $12,333. **Scholarships, grants, and awards by category:** Academic interests/achievement: 860 awards ($8,328,639 total): biological sciences, business, communication, computer science, education, English, foreign languages, general academic interests/achievements, home economics, humanities, mathematics, physical sciences, religion/biblical studies, social sciences. Creative arts/performance: 52 awards ($103,900 total): applied art and design, art/fine arts, music, performing arts, theater/drama. Special achievements/activities: 72 awards ($56,750 total): cheerleading/drum major. Special characteristics: 112 awards ($715,978 total): children and siblings of alumni, children of faculty/staff, siblings of current students. **Tuition waivers:** Full or partial for employees or children of employees. **ROTC:** Army cooperative.

**LOANS Student loans:** $10,178,045 (76% need-based, 24% non-need-based). 85% of past graduating class borrowed through all loan programs. Average indebtedness per student: $36,295. **Average need-based loan:** Freshmen: $5913. Undergraduates: $5906. **Parent loans:** $2,821,993 (53% need-based, 47% non-need-based). **Programs:** Federal Direct (Subsidized and Unsubsidized Stafford, PLUS), Perkins, college/university.

**WORK-STUDY Federal work-study:** Total amount: $856,530; 687 jobs averaging $868. **State or other work-study/employment:** Total amount: $230,931 (12% need-based, 88% non-need-based). 93 part-time jobs averaging $351.

**ATHLETIC AWARDS** Total amount: $4,104,523 (56% need-based, 44% non-need-based).

**APPLYING FOR FINANCIAL AID Required financial aid forms:** FAFSA, institution's own form. **Financial aid deadline:** Continuous. **Notification date:** Continuous beginning 11/20. Students must reply by 5/1.

**CONTACT** Tracey Snyder de Baez, Director of Financial Aid, Seton Hill University, 1 Seton Hill Drive, Greensburg, PA 15601, 724-838-4293 or toll-free 800-826-6234. Fax: 724-830-1194. E-mail: snyderdebaez@setonhill.edu.
Website: http://www.setonhill.edu/.

# SEWANEE: THE UNIVERSITY OF THE SOUTH
## Sewanee, TN

| Tuition & fees: $38,700 | Average undergraduate aid package: $31,602 |
|---|---|

**ABOUT THE INSTITUTION** Independent Episcopal, coed. **Awards:** certificates, bachelor's, master's, and doctoral degrees. 37 undergraduate majors. **Total enrollment:** 1,714. Undergraduates: 1,631. Freshmen: 466. Both federal and institutional methodology are used as a basis for awarding need-based institutional aid.

**UNDERGRADUATE EXPENSES for 2015–2016 Comprehensive fee:** $49,750 includes full-time tuition ($38,428), mandatory fees ($272), and room and board ($11,050). **College room only:** $5730. Full-time tuition and fees vary

according to student level. Room and board charges vary according to student level. **Part-time tuition:** $1350 per credit hour. Part-time tuition and fees vary according to student level. **Payment plan:** Guaranteed tuition.

**FRESHMAN FINANCIAL AID (Fall 2014, est.)** 326 applied for aid; of those 71% were deemed to have need. 100% of freshmen with need received aid; of those 36% had need fully met. **Average percent of need met:** 95% (excluding resources awarded to replace EFC). **Average financial aid package:** $31,889 (excluding resources awarded to replace EFC). 33% of all full-time freshmen had no need and received non-need-based gift aid.

**UNDERGRADUATE FINANCIAL AID (Fall 2014, est.)** 1,013 applied for aid; of those 77% were deemed to have need. 100% of undergraduates with need received aid; of those 41% had need fully met. **Average percent of need met:** 96% (excluding resources awarded to replace EFC). **Average financial aid package:** $31,602 (excluding resources awarded to replace EFC). 25% of all full-time undergraduates had no need and received non-need-based gift aid.

**GIFT AID (NEED-BASED) Total amount:** $20,352,085 (7% federal, 5% state, 87% institutional, 1% external sources). **Receiving aid:** Freshmen: 49% (228); all full-time undergraduates: 48% (771). **Average award:** Freshmen: $26,181; Undergraduates: $26,247. **Scholarships, grants, and awards:** Federal Pell, FSEOG, state, private, college/university gift aid from institutional funds.

**GIFT AID (NON-NEED-BASED) Total amount:** $5,966,510 (9% state, 87% institutional, 4% external sources). **Receiving aid:** Freshmen: 17% (79). Undergraduates: 14% (223). **Average award:** Freshmen: $10,319. Undergraduates: $10,883. **Scholarships, grants, and awards by category:** Academic interests/achievement: general academic interests/achievements. Creative arts/performance: general creative arts/performance. Special achievements/activities: general special achievements/activities. Special characteristics: general special characteristics. **Tuition waivers:** Full or partial for employees or children of employees.

**LOANS Student loans:** $3,391,155 (72% need-based, 28% non-need-based). 39% of past graduating class borrowed through all loan programs. Average indebtedness per student: $21,277. **Average need-based loan:** Freshmen: $4234. Undergraduates: $4062. **Parent loans:** $2,733,717 (7% need-based, 93% non-need-based). **Programs:** Federal Direct (Subsidized and Unsubsidized Stafford, PLUS), Perkins, alternative loans.

**WORK-STUDY Federal work-study:** Total amount: $665,535; jobs available. **State or other work-study/employment:** Total amount: $425,598 (28% need-based, 72% non-need-based). Part-time jobs available.

**APPLYING FOR FINANCIAL AID Required financial aid forms:** FAFSA, CSS Financial Aid PROFILE. **Financial aid deadline:** 2/1. **Notification date:** Continuous beginning 3/1. Students must reply by 5/1.

**CONTACT** Ms. Beth A. Cragar, Associate Dean of Admission for Financial Aid, Sewanee: The University of the South, 735 University Avenue, Sewanee, TN 37383-1000, 931-598-1312 or toll-free 800-522-2234. Fax: 931-598-3273. E-mail: finaid@sewanee.edu.
Website: http://www.sewanee.edu/.

# SHASTA BIBLE COLLEGE
## Redding, CA

**CONTACT** Linda Iles, Financial Aid Administrator, Shasta Bible College, 2951 Goodwater Avenue, Redding, CA 96002, 530-221-4275 or toll-free 800-800-4SBC. Fax: 530-221-6929. E-mail: finaid@shasta.edu.
Website: http://www.shasta.edu/.

# SHAWNEE STATE UNIVERSITY
## Portsmouth, OH

| Tuition & fees (OH res): $7364 | Average undergraduate aid package: N/A |
|---|---|

**ABOUT THE INSTITUTION** State-supported, coed. **Awards:** certificates, associate, bachelor's, and master's degrees. 48 undergraduate majors. **Total enrollment:** 4,247. Undergraduates: 4,114. Freshmen: 955. Both federal and institutional methodology are used as a basis for awarding need-based institutional aid.

**UNDERGRADUATE EXPENSES for 2015–2016 Tuition, state resident:** full-time $6251; part-time $260 per credit hour. **Tuition, nonresident:** full-time

$11,504; part-time $479 per credit hour. **Required fees:** full-time $1113; $46 per credit hour. Full-time tuition and fees vary according to course load and reciprocity agreements. Part-time tuition and fees vary according to course load and reciprocity agreements. **College room and board:** $9552; **Room only:** $6024. Room and board charges vary according to board plan and housing facility.

**GIFT AID (NEED-BASED) Scholarships, grants, and awards:** Federal Pell, FSEOG, state, private, college/university gift aid from institutional funds.

**GIFT AID (NON-NEED-BASED) Scholarships, grants, and awards by category: Academic interests/achievement:** general academic interests/achievements. **Creative arts/performance:** art/fine arts, performing arts. **Special achievements/activities:** memberships. **Special characteristics:** ethnic background, first-generation college students, handicapped students, local/state students, members of minority groups, veterans. **Tuition waivers:** Full or partial for employees or children of employees, senior citizens.

**LOANS Programs:** Federal Direct (Subsidized and Unsubsidized Stafford).

**WORK-STUDY** Federal work-study jobs available.

**APPLYING FOR FINANCIAL AID Required financial aid form:** FAFSA. **Financial aid deadline:** Continuous. **Notification date:** Continuous beginning 3/15.

**CONTACT** Ms. Nicole Neal, Director of Financial Aid, Shawnee State University, 940 Second Street, Portsmouth, OH 45662-4344, 740-351-3140 or toll-free 800-959-2SSU. *E-mail:* nneal@shawnee.edu.
*Website:* http://www.shawnee.edu/.

---

# SHAW UNIVERSITY
## Raleigh, NC

**CONTACT** Rochelle King, Director of Financial Aid, Shaw University, 118 East South Street, Raleigh, NC 27601-2399, 919-546-8565 or toll-free 800-214-6683. *Fax:* 919-546-8356. *E-mail:* rking@shawu.edu.
*Website:* http://www.shawu.edu/.

---

# SHENANDOAH UNIVERSITY
## Winchester, VA

| Tuition & fees: $30,760 | Average undergraduate aid package: $29,205 |
|---|---|

**ABOUT THE INSTITUTION** Independent United Methodist, coed. **Awards:** certificates, bachelor's, master's, and doctoral degrees. 36 undergraduate majors. **Total enrollment:** 3,693. Undergraduates: 1,892. Freshmen: 417. Federal methodology is used as a basis for awarding need-based institutional aid.

**UNDERGRADUATE EXPENSES for 2015–2016 Comprehensive fee:** $40,680 includes full-time tuition ($29,570), mandatory fees ($1190), and room and board ($9920). Full-time tuition and fees vary according to course load and program. Room and board charges vary according to board plan and housing facility. **Part-time tuition:** $860 per credit. **Part-time fees:** $515 per term. Part-time tuition and fees vary according to course load and program.

**FRESHMAN FINANCIAL AID (Fall 2014, est.)** 394 applied for aid; of those 86% were deemed to have need. 100% of freshmen with need received aid; of those 42% had need fully met. **Average percent of need met:** 31% (excluding resources awarded to replace EFC). **Average financial aid package:** $29,611 (excluding resources awarded to replace EFC). 23% of all full-time freshmen had no need and received non-need-based gift aid.

**UNDERGRADUATE FINANCIAL AID (Fall 2014, est.)** 1,590 applied for aid; of those 85% were deemed to have need. 100% of undergraduates with need received aid; of those 21% had need fully met. **Average percent of need met:** 30% (excluding resources awarded to replace EFC). **Average financial aid package:** $29,205 (excluding resources awarded to replace EFC). 14% of all full-time undergraduates had no need and received non-need-based gift aid.

**GIFT AID (NEED-BASED) Total amount:** $3,944,675 (72% federal, 28% institutional). **Receiving aid:** Freshmen: 35% (146); all full-time undergraduates: 32% (581). **Average award:** Freshmen: $4980; Undergraduates: $5821. **Scholarships, grants, and awards:** Federal Pell, FSEOG, state, college/university gift aid from institutional funds.

**GIFT AID (NON-NEED-BASED) Total amount:** $21,748,478 (15% state, 84% institutional, 1% external sources). **Receiving aid:** Freshmen: 81% (339). Undergrad-

---

uates: 74% (1,350). **Average award:** Freshmen: $11,083. Undergraduates: $9461. **Scholarships, grants, and awards by category: Academic interests/achievement:** 1,687 awards ($10,245,915 total): business, general academic interests/achievements. **Creative arts/performance:** 159 awards ($1,564,587 total): dance, music, performing arts, theater/drama. **Special achievements/activities:** 54 awards ($54,129 total): religious involvement. **Special characteristics:** 51 awards ($653,051 total): children of faculty/staff, local/state students, relatives of clergy, religious affiliation. **Tuition waivers:** Full or partial for employees or children of employees.

**LOANS Student loans:** $9,681,998 (50% need-based, 50% non-need-based). 85% of past graduating class borrowed through all loan programs. **Average indebtedness per student:** $28,831. **Average need-based loan:** Freshmen: $2833. Undergraduates: $4913. **Parent loans:** $8,041,415 (100% non-need-based). **Programs:** Federal Direct (Subsidized and Unsubsidized Stafford, PLUS), Perkins, Federal Nursing.

**WORK-STUDY Federal work-study:** Total amount: $1,972,736; 883 jobs averaging $2300. **State or other work-study/employment:** Total amount: $873,300 (100% non-need-based). 467 part-time jobs averaging $2300.

**APPLYING FOR FINANCIAL AID Required financial aid forms:** FAFSA, state aid form. **Financial aid deadline:** Continuous. **Notification date:** Continuous beginning 3/15. Students must reply within 4 weeks of notification.

**CONTACT** Ms. Nancy Bragg, Director of Financial Aid, Shenandoah University, 1460 University Drive, Winchester, VA 22601-5195, 540-665-4538 or toll-free 800-432-2266. *Fax:* 540-665-4939. *E-mail:* nbragg@su.edu.
*Website:* http://www.su.edu/.

---

# SHEPHERD UNIVERSITY
## Los Angeles, CA

**CONTACT** Financial Aid Office, Shepherd University, 3200 North San Fernando Road, Los Angeles, CA 90065, 323-550-8888.
*Website:* http://www.shepherduniversity.edu/.

---

# SHEPHERD UNIVERSITY
## Shepherdstown, WV

| Tuition & fees (WV res): $6830 | Average undergraduate aid package: $11,874 |
|---|---|

**ABOUT THE INSTITUTION** State-supported, coed. **Awards:** bachelor's and master's degrees. 26 undergraduate majors. **Total enrollment:** 4,041. Undergraduates: 3,776. Freshmen: 642. Federal methodology is used as a basis for awarding need-based institutional aid.

**UNDERGRADUATE EXPENSES for 2015–2016 Application fee:** $45. **Tuition, state resident:** full-time $6830; part-time $286 per credit hour. **Tuition, nonresident:** full-time $16,628; part-time $693 per credit hour. Full-time tuition and fees vary according to program and reciprocity agreements. Part-time tuition and fees vary according to program. **College room and board:** $9682. Room and board charges vary according to board plan and housing facility.

**FRESHMAN FINANCIAL AID (Fall 2014, est.)** 618 applied for aid; of those 69% were deemed to have need. 97% of freshmen with need received aid; of those 35% had need fully met. **Average percent of need met:** 82% (excluding resources awarded to replace EFC). **Average financial aid package:** $11,773 (excluding resources awarded to replace EFC). 23% of all full-time freshmen had no need and received non-need-based gift aid.

**UNDERGRADUATE FINANCIAL AID (Fall 2014, est.)** 2,861 applied for aid; of those 71% were deemed to have need. 98% of undergraduates with need received aid; of those 32% had need fully met. **Average percent of need met:** 78% (excluding resources awarded to replace EFC). **Average financial aid package:** $11,874 (excluding resources awarded to replace EFC). 21% of all full-time undergraduates had no need and received non-need-based gift aid.

**GIFT AID (NEED-BASED) Total amount:** $7,363,484 (73% federal, 25% state, 2% institutional). **Receiving aid:** Freshmen: 43% (274); all full-time undergraduates: 44% (1,365). **Average award:** Freshmen: $5154; Undergraduates: $5076. **Scholarships, grants, and awards:** Federal Pell, FSEOG, state, private, college/university gift aid from institutional funds.

**GIFT AID (NON-NEED-BASED) Total amount:** $5,689,585 (40% state, 54% institutional, 6% external sources). **Receiving aid:** Freshmen: 36% (231). Undergrad-

---

uates: 22% (696). **Average award:** Freshmen: $9970. Undergraduates: $10,377. **Scholarships, grants, and awards by category:** *Academic interests/ achievement:* 651 awards ($2,397,306 total): biological sciences, business, communication, computer science, education, engineering/technologies, English, general academic interests/achievements, health fields, home economics, humanities, mathematics, physical sciences, premedicine, social sciences. *Creative arts/performance:* 33 awards ($279,363 total): applied art and design, art/fine arts, music, performing arts, theater/ drama. *Special achievements/activities:* 222 awards ($764,000 total): leadership. *Special characteristics:* 113 awards ($174,789 total): ethnic background, handicapped students, local/state students, members of minority groups, out-of-state students, previous college experience. **Tuition waivers:** Full or partial for minority students, employees or children of employees, senior citizens. **ROTC:** Air Force cooperative.

**LOANS Student loans:** $16,082,045 (40% need-based, 60% non-need-based). 68% of past graduating class borrowed through all loan programs. *Average indebtedness per student:* $27,938. **Average need-based loan:** Freshmen: $3446. Undergraduates: $4150. **Parent loans:** $5,099,877 (100% non-need-based). **Programs:** Federal Direct (Subsidized and Unsubsidized Stafford, PLUS), Perkins.

**WORK-STUDY Federal work-study:** Total amount: $200,506; 109 jobs averaging $661. **State or other work-study/employment:** Total amount: $1,319,718 (100% non-need-based). 535 part-time jobs averaging $2467.

**ATHLETIC AWARDS** Total amount: $1,284,778 (100% non-need-based).

**APPLYING FOR FINANCIAL AID Required financial aid forms:** FAFSA, state aid form. **Financial aid deadline (priority):** 3/1. **Notification date:** Continuous beginning 2/28. Students must reply within 2 weeks of notification.

**CONTACT** Mr. Brian De Young, Director of Financial Aid, Shepherd University, PO Box 5000, Shepherdstown, WV 25443-5000, 304-876-5470 or toll-free 800-344-5231. *Fax:* 304-876-5238. *E-mail:* faoweb@shepherd.edu. *Website:* http://www.shepherd.edu/.

# SHILOH UNIVERSITY
## Kalona, IA

**CONTACT** Financial Aid Office, Shiloh University, 100 Shiloh Drive, Kalona, IA 52247, 319-656-2447.
*Website:* http://www.shilohuniversity.edu/.

# SHIMER COLLEGE
## Chicago, IL

| Tuition & fees: $32,499 | Average undergraduate aid package: $22,684 |
|---|---|

**ABOUT THE INSTITUTION** Independent, coed. **Awards:** bachelor's degrees. 7 undergraduate majors. **Total enrollment:** 77. Undergraduates: 77. Freshmen: 11. Both federal and institutional methodology are used as a basis for awarding need-based institutional aid.

**UNDERGRADUATE EXPENSES for 2015–2016 Application fee:** $25. **Comprehensive fee:** $43,303 includes full-time tuition ($28,454), mandatory fees ($4045), and room and board ($10,804). Room and board charges vary according to board plan and housing facility. **Part-time tuition:** $1035 per credit hour. **Part-time fees:** $1700 per year.

**FRESHMAN FINANCIAL AID (Fall 2013)** 8 applied for aid; of those 88% were deemed to have need. 100% of freshmen with need received aid; of those 29% had need fully met. **Average percent of need met:** 61% (excluding resources awarded to replace EFC). **Average financial aid package:** $13,902 (excluding resources awarded to replace EFC). 13% of all full-time freshmen had no need and received non-need-based gift aid.

**UNDERGRADUATE FINANCIAL AID (Fall 2013)** 67 applied for aid; of those 84% were deemed to have need. 100% of undergraduates with need received aid; of those 5% had need fully met. **Average percent of need met:** 64% (excluding resources awarded to replace EFC). **Average financial aid package:** $22,684 (excluding resources awarded to replace EFC). 16% of all full-time undergraduates had no need and received non-need-based gift aid.

**GIFT AID (NEED-BASED) Total amount:** $1,087,820 (22% federal, 8% state, 67% institutional, 3% external sources). **Receiving aid:** Freshmen: 62% (5); all full-time undergraduates: 76% (56). **Average award:** Freshmen: $13,789; Undergrad-

uates: $14,257. **Scholarships, grants, and awards:** Federal Pell, FSEOG, state, private, college/university gift aid from institutional funds.

**GIFT AID (NON-NEED-BASED) Total amount:** $199,756 (96% institutional, 4% external sources). **Receiving aid:** Freshmen: 62% (5). Undergraduates: 57% (42). **Average award:** Freshmen: $2000. Undergraduates: $8775. **Scholarships, grants, and awards by category:** *Academic interests/achievement:* general academic interests/achievements. *Special characteristics:* children and siblings of alumni. **Tuition waivers:** Full or partial for employees or children of employees, senior citizens.

**LOANS Student loans:** $821,751 (94% need-based, 6% non-need-based). 100% of past graduating class borrowed through all loan programs. *Average indebtedness per student:* $25,125. **Average need-based loan:** Freshmen: $3150. Undergraduates: $5428. **Parent loans:** $103,161 (100% need-based). **Programs:** Federal Direct (Subsidized and Unsubsidized Stafford, PLUS), Perkins.

**WORK-STUDY Federal work-study:** jobs available. **State or other work-study/employment:** Part-time jobs available.

**APPLYING FOR FINANCIAL AID Required financial aid forms:** FAFSA, institution's own form. **Financial aid deadline:** Continuous. **Notification date:** Continuous beginning 3/15. Students must reply by 5/1 or within 3 weeks of notification.

**CONTACT** Janet Henthorn, Director of Financial Aid, Shimer College, 3424 South State Street, Chicago, IL 60616, 312-235-3507 or toll-free 800-215-7173. *Fax:* 312-235-3502. *E-mail:* j.henthorn@shimer.edu. *Website:* http://www.shimer.edu/.

# SHIPPENSBURG UNIVERSITY OF PENNSYLVANIA
## Shippensburg, PA

| Tuition & fees (PA res): $9774 | Average undergraduate aid package: $8351 |
|---|---|

**ABOUT THE INSTITUTION** State-supported, coed. **Awards:** certificates, bachelor's, master's, and doctoral degrees. 39 undergraduate majors. **Total enrollment:** 7,355. Undergraduates: 6,305. Freshmen: 1,484. Federal methodology is used as a basis for awarding need-based institutional aid.

**UNDERGRADUATE EXPENSES for 2015–2016 Application fee:** $45. *Tuition, state resident:* full-time $6820; part-time $284 per credit hour. *Tuition, nonresident:* full-time $15,346; part-time $639 per credit hour. **Required fees:** full-time $2954; $123 per credit hour. **College room and board:** $11,160; **Room only:** $7314. Room and board charges vary according to board plan and housing facility.

**FRESHMAN FINANCIAL AID (Fall 2014, est.)** 1,349 applied for aid; of those 79% were deemed to have need. 97% of freshmen with need received aid; of those 8% had need fully met. **Average percent of need met:** 52% (excluding resources awarded to replace EFC). **Average financial aid package:** $8221 (excluding resources awarded to replace EFC). 7% of all full-time freshmen had no need and received non-need-based gift aid.

**UNDERGRADUATE FINANCIAL AID (Fall 2014, est.)** 5,086 applied for aid; of those 81% were deemed to have need. 98% of undergraduates with need received aid; of those 10% had need fully met. **Average percent of need met:** 55% (excluding resources awarded to replace EFC). **Average financial aid package:** $8351 (excluding resources awarded to replace EFC). 7% of all full-time undergraduates had no need and received non-need-based gift aid.

**GIFT AID (NEED-BASED) Total amount:** $16,717,179 (51% federal, 37% state, 4% institutional, 8% external sources). **Receiving aid:** Freshmen: 52% (774); all full-time undergraduates: 48% (2,862). **Average award:** Freshmen: $6387; Undergraduates: $6151. **Scholarships, grants, and awards:** Federal Pell, FSEOG, state, private, college/university gift aid from institutional funds.

**GIFT AID (NON-NEED-BASED) Total amount:** $1,099,084 (14% state, 16% institutional, 70% external sources). **Receiving aid:** Freshmen: 2% (30). Undergraduates: 2% (118). **Average award:** Freshmen: $3248. Undergraduates: $4378. **Scholarships, grants, and awards by category:** *Academic interests/achievement:* biological sciences, business, communication, computer science, education, English, foreign languages, general academic interests/achievements, humanities, mathematics, physical sciences, social sciences. *Creative arts/performance:* art/fine arts, music, theater/drama. *Special achievements/activities:* community service, general special achievements/activities, leadership. *Special characteristics:* children and siblings of alumni, general special characteristics, handicapped students, local/state students. *Tuition waivers:* Full or partial for employees or children of employees, senior citizens. *ROTC:* Army.

**LOANS** *Student loans:* $42,221,105 (68% need-based, 32% non-need-based). 80% of past graduating class borrowed through all loan programs. *Average indebtedness per student:* $29,988. *Average need-based loan:* Freshmen: $3542. Undergraduates: $3949. *Parent loans:* $10,820,392 (42% need-based, 58% non-need-based). *Programs:* Federal Direct (Subsidized and Unsubsidized Stafford, PLUS), Perkins, alternative loans.

**WORK-STUDY** *Federal work-study:* Total amount: $238,234; 126 jobs averaging $1891. *State or other work-study/employment:* Total amount: $1,307,666 (38% need-based, 62% non-need-based). 595 part-time jobs averaging $2198.

**ATHLETIC AWARDS** Total amount: $999,977 (64% need-based, 36% non-need-based).

**APPLYING FOR FINANCIAL AID** *Required financial aid form:* FAFSA. *Financial aid deadline (priority):* 3/15. *Notification date:* Continuous. Students must reply within 2 weeks of notification.

**CONTACT** Dr. Sandra L. Tarbox, Director of Financial Aid and Scholarships, Shippensburg University of Pennsylvania, 1871 Old Main Drive, Shippensburg, PA 17257-2299, 717-477-1131 or toll-free 800-822-8028 (in-state). *Fax:* 717-477-4028. *E-mail:* finaid@ship.edu.
*Website:* http://www.ship.edu/.

---

# SHORTER UNIVERSITY
## Rome, GA

**CONTACT** Ms. Tara Jones, Director of Financial Aid, Shorter University, 315 Shorter Avenue, Rome, GA 30165, 706-233-7227 or toll-free 800-868-6980. *Fax:* 706-233-7314. *E-mail:* tjones@shorter.edu.
*Website:* http://www.shorter.edu/.

---

# SH'OR YOSHUV RABBINICAL COLLEGE
## Lawrence, NY

**CONTACT** Office of Financial Aid, Sh'or Yoshuv Rabbinical College, 1526 Central Avenue, Far Rockaway, NY 11691-4002, 718-327-2048.
*Website:* http://www.shoryoshuv.org/.

---

# SIENA COLLEGE
## Loudonville, NY

| Tuition & fees: $33,415 | Average undergraduate aid package: $24,015 |
| --- | --- |

**ABOUT THE INSTITUTION** Independent Roman Catholic, coed. *Awards:* certificates, bachelor's, and master's degrees. 27 undergraduate majors. *Total enrollment:* 3,184. Undergraduates: 3,139. Freshmen: 709. Federal methodology is used as a basis for awarding need-based institutional aid.

**UNDERGRADUATE EXPENSES** for 2015–2016 *Application fee:* $50. *Comprehensive fee:* $47,010 includes full-time tuition ($33,165), mandatory fees ($250), and room and board ($13,595). *College room only:* $8015. Full-time tuition and fees vary according to course load, program, and student level. Room and board charges vary according to board plan and housing facility. *Part-time tuition:* $600 per credit. Part-time tuition and fees vary according to course load, program, and student level.

**FRESHMAN FINANCIAL AID (Fall 2013)** 711 applied for aid; of those 90% were deemed to have need. 100% of freshmen with need received aid; of those 24% had need fully met. *Average percent of need met:* 76% (excluding resources awarded to replace EFC). *Average financial aid package:* $27,232 (excluding resources awarded to replace EFC). 13% of all full-time freshmen had no need and received non-need-based gift aid.

**UNDERGRADUATE FINANCIAL AID (Fall 2013)** 2,462 applied for aid; of those 90% were deemed to have need. 100% of undergraduates with need received aid; of those 22% had need fully met. *Average percent of need met:* 70% (excluding resources awarded to replace EFC). *Average financial aid package:* $24,015 (excluding resources awarded to replace EFC). 17% of all full-time undergraduates had no need and received non-need-based gift aid.

**GIFT AID (NEED-BASED)** *Total amount:* $41,169,260 (8% federal, 9% state, 83% institutional). *Receiving aid:* Freshmen: 83% (637); all full-time undergraduates: 73% (2,199). *Average award:* Freshmen: $21,438; Undergraduates: $17,423. *Scholarships, grants, and awards:* Federal Pell, FSEOG, state, private, college/university gift aid from institutional funds, Siena Grants, Franciscan Community Grants.

**GIFT AID (NON-NEED-BASED)** *Total amount:* $5,771,080 (2% federal, 2% state, 82% institutional, 14% external sources). *Receiving aid:* Freshmen: 76% (584). Undergraduates: 68% (2,033). *Average award:* Freshmen: $8360. Undergraduates: $7106. *Scholarships, grants, and awards by category:* Academic interests/ achievement: biological sciences, business, communication, computer science, education, English, foreign languages, general academic interests/achievements, health fields, humanities, international studies, mathematics, military science, physical sciences, premedicine, religion/biblical studies, social sciences. *Creative arts/performance:* creative writing, general creative arts/performance, journalism/publications, music, performing arts, theater/drama. *Special achievements/activities:* community service, general special achievements/activities, hobbies/interests, leadership, memberships, religious involvement. *Special characteristics:* adult students, children and siblings of alumni, children of faculty/staff, children of public servants, children of union members/company employees, children of workers in trades, children with a deceased or disabled parent, ethnic background, general special characteristics, local/state students, out-of-state students, previous college experience, relatives of clergy, religious affiliation, veterans' children. *Tuition waivers:* Full or partial for employees or children of employees. *ROTC:* Army, Air Force cooperative.

**LOANS** *Student loans:* $21,052,675 (84% need-based, 16% non-need-based). 77% of past graduating class borrowed through all loan programs. *Average indebtedness per student:* $32,678. *Average need-based loan:* Freshmen: $3353. Undergraduates: $4421. *Parent loans:* $8,182,838 (75% need-based, 25% non-need-based). *Programs:* Federal Direct (Subsidized and Unsubsidized Stafford, PLUS), Perkins.

**WORK-STUDY** *Federal work-study:* jobs available.

**ATHLETIC AWARDS** Total amount: $4,580,282 (40% need-based, 60% non-need-based).

**APPLYING FOR FINANCIAL AID** *Required financial aid forms:* FAFSA, state aid form. *Financial aid deadline:* 5/1 (priority: 2/15). *Notification date:* 4/1. Students must reply by 5/1.

**CONTACT** Mary Lawyer, Associate Vice President for Enrollment Management, Siena College, 515 Loudon Road, Loudonville, NY 12211-1462, 518-783-2427 or toll-free 888-AT-SIENA. *Fax:* 518-783-2410. *E-mail:* aid@siena.edu.
*Website:* http://www.siena.edu/.

---

# SIENA HEIGHTS UNIVERSITY
## Adrian, MI

**CONTACT** Office of Financial Aid, Siena Heights University, 1247 East Siena Heights Drive, Adrian, MI 49221, 517-264-7130 or toll-free 800-521-0009.
*Website:* http://www.sienaheights.edu/.

---

# SIERRA NEVADA COLLEGE
## Incline Village, NV

| Tuition & fees: $29,149 | Average undergraduate aid package: N/A |
| --- | --- |

**ABOUT THE INSTITUTION** Independent, coed. *Awards:* certificates, diplomas, bachelor's, and master's degrees. 24 undergraduate majors. *Total enrollment:* 972. Undergraduates: 547. Freshmen: 91. Federal methodology is used as a basis for awarding need-based institutional aid.

**UNDERGRADUATE EXPENSES** for 2015–2016 *Comprehensive fee:* $41,215 includes full-time tuition ($28,170), mandatory fees ($979), and room and board ($12,066). *College room only:* $5900. Full-time tuition and fees vary according to course load and program. Room and board charges vary according to board plan. *Part-time tuition:* $1198 per credit hour. Part-time tuition and fees vary according to course load and program.

**GIFT AID (NEED-BASED)** *Scholarships, grants, and awards:* Federal Pell, FSEOG, state, private, college/university gift aid from institutional funds.

**GIFT AID (NON-NEED-BASED)** *Scholarships, grants, and awards by category:* Academic interests/achievement: English, general academic interests/achievements. *Creative arts/performance:* art/fine arts. *Special characteristics:* veterans. *Tuition waivers:* Full or partial for employees or children of employees.

**LOANS** *Programs:* Federal Direct (Subsidized and Unsubsidized Stafford, PLUS), alternative loans.

**APPLYING FOR FINANCIAL AID** *Required financial aid form:* FAFSA. *Financial aid deadline (priority):* 1/1. *Notification date:* Continuous beginning 4/1. Students must reply by 8/20 or within 4 weeks of notification.

**CONTACT** Nicole D. Ferguson, Director of Financial Aid, Sierra Nevada College, 999 Tahoe Boulevard, Incline Village, NV 89451, 775-831-1314 Ext. 7404. *Fax:* 775-832-1678 . *E-mail:* nferguson@sierranevada.edu.
*Website:* http://www.sierranevada.edu/.

# SILICON VALLEY UNIVERSITY
### San Jose, CA

**CONTACT** Financial Aid Office, Silicon Valley University, 2160 Lundy Avenue, Suite 110, San Jose, CA 95131, 408-435-8989.
*Website:* http://www.svuca.edu/.

# SILVER LAKE COLLEGE OF THE HOLY FAMILY
### Manitowoc, WI

**CONTACT** Ms. Michelle Leider, Associate Director of Financial Aid, Silver Lake College of the Holy Family, 2406 South Alverno Road, Manitowoc, WI 54220-9319, 920-686-6122 or toll-free 800-236-4752 Ext. 175. *Fax:* 920-684-7082. *E-mail:* financialaid@sl.edu.
*Website:* http://www.sl.edu/.

# SIMMONS COLLEGE
### Boston, MA

| Tuition & fees: $36,230 | Average undergraduate aid package: $27,978 |
|---|---|

**ABOUT THE INSTITUTION** Independent, undergraduate: women only; graduate: coed. *Awards:* certificates, bachelor's, master's, and doctoral degrees. 45 undergraduate majors. *Total enrollment:* 4,800. Undergraduates: 1,622. Freshmen: 303. Federal methodology is used as a basis for awarding need-based institutional aid.

**UNDERGRADUATE EXPENSES** for 2015–2016 *Application fee:* $55. *Comprehensive fee:* $49,966 includes full-time tuition ($35,200), mandatory fees ($1030), and room and board ($13,736). Full-time tuition and fees vary according to course load and program. Room and board charges vary according to location. *Part-time tuition:* $1100 per credit hour. *Part-time fees:* $260 per term. Part-time tuition and fees vary according to course load and program.

**FRESHMAN FINANCIAL AID (Fall 2014, est.)** 270 applied for aid; of those 91% were deemed to have need. 100% of freshmen with need received aid; of those 15% had need fully met. *Average percent of need met:* 77% (excluding resources awarded to replace EFC). *Average financial aid package:* $28,999 (excluding resources awarded to replace EFC). 17% of all full-time freshmen had no need and received non-need-based gift aid.

**UNDERGRADUATE FINANCIAL AID (Fall 2014, est.)** 1,220 applied for aid; of those 94% were deemed to have need. 100% of undergraduates with need received aid; of those 10% had need fully met. *Average percent of need met:* 72% (excluding resources awarded to replace EFC). *Average financial aid package:* $27,978 (excluding resources awarded to replace EFC). 16% of all full-time undergraduates had no need and received non-need-based gift aid.

**GIFT AID (NEED-BASED)** *Total amount:* $28,461,210 (8% federal, 2% state, 88% institutional, 2% external sources). *Receiving aid:* Freshmen: 81% (246); all full-time undergraduates: 77% (1,142). *Average award:* Freshmen: $25,225; Undergraduates: $23,636. *Scholarships, grants, and awards:* Federal Pell, FSEOG, state, private, college/university gift aid from institutional funds.

**GIFT AID (NON-NEED-BASED)** *Total amount:* $3,766,122 (99% institutional, 1% external sources). *Receiving aid:* Freshmen: 8% (25). Undergraduates: 4% (57). *Average award:* Freshmen: $15,366. Undergraduates: $14,030. *Scholarships, grants, and awards by category:* Academic interests/achievement: general academic interests/achievements. *Special achievements/activities:* community service, general special achievements/activities. *Special characteristics:* children and siblings of alumni, general special characteristics. *Tuition waivers:* Full or partial for employees or children of employees. *ROTC:* Army cooperative.

**LOANS** *Student loans:* $13,679,313 (38% need-based, 62% non-need-based). *Average need-based loan:* Freshmen: $3332. Undergraduates: $4602. *Parent loans:* $3,965,679 (100% non-need-based). *Programs:* Federal Direct (Subsidized and Unsubsidized Stafford, PLUS), Perkins, college/university.

**WORK-STUDY** *Federal work-study:* Total amount: $2,033,573; 860 jobs averaging $2365.

**APPLYING FOR FINANCIAL AID** *Required financial aid forms:* FAFSA, institution's own form. *Financial aid deadline (priority):* 3/1. *Notification date:* Continuous beginning 3/15.

**CONTACT** Heather Patenaude, Director of Financial Aid, Simmons College, 300 The Fenway, Boston, MA 02115, 617-521-2001 or toll-free 800-345-8468. *Fax:* 617-521-3195. *E-mail:* heather.patenaude@simmons.edu.
*Website:* http://www.simmons.edu/.

# SIMMONS COLLEGE OF KENTUCKY
### Louisville, KY

**CONTACT** Financial Aid Office, Simmons College of Kentucky, 1018 South 7th Street, Louisville, KY 40203, 502-776-1443.
*Website:* http://www.simmonscollegeky.edu/.

# SIMPSON COLLEGE
### Indianola, IA

| Tuition & fees: $32,550 | Average undergraduate aid package: $29,037 |
|---|---|

**ABOUT THE INSTITUTION** Independent United Methodist, coed. *Awards:* certificates, bachelor's, and master's degrees. 58 undergraduate majors. *Total enrollment:* 1,725. Undergraduates: 1,660. Freshmen: 345. Federal methodology is used as a basis for awarding need based institutional aid.

**UNDERGRADUATE EXPENSES** for 2015–2016 *One-time required fee:* $200. *Comprehensive fee:* $40,513 includes full-time tuition ($31,935), mandatory fees ($615), and room and board ($7963). *College room only:* $3860. Full-time tuition and fees vary according to class time, course load, degree level, and program. Room and board charges vary according to board plan and housing facility. *Part-time tuition:* $365 per credit hour. Part-time tuition and fees vary according to class time, course load, degree level, and program.

**FRESHMAN FINANCIAL AID (Fall 2014, est.)** 344 applied for aid; of those 86% were deemed to have need. 100% of freshmen with need received aid; of those 24% had need fully met. *Average percent of need met:* 89% (excluding resources awarded to replace EFC). *Average financial aid package:* $31,544 (excluding resources awarded to replace EFC). 14% of all full-time freshmen had no need and received non-need-based gift aid.

**UNDERGRADUATE FINANCIAL AID (Fall 2014, est.)** 1,459 applied for aid; of those 83% were deemed to have need. 100% of undergraduates with need received aid; of those 23% had need fully met. *Average percent of need met:* 86% (excluding resources awarded to replace EFC). *Average financial aid package:* $29,037 (excluding resources awarded to replace EFC). 16% of all full-time undergraduates had no need and received non-need-based gift aid.

**GIFT AID (NEED-BASED)** *Total amount:* $24,154,695 (10% federal, 13% state, 75% institutional, 2% external sources). *Receiving aid:* Freshmen: 86% (295); all full-

time undergraduates: 82% (1,198). *Average award:* Freshmen: $23,160; Undergraduates: $19,883. *Scholarships, grants, and awards:* Federal Pell, FSEOG, state, private, college/university gift aid from institutional funds.
**GIFT AID (NON-NEED-BASED)** *Total amount:* $6,021,767 (2% federal, 94% institutional, 4% external sources). *Receiving aid:* Freshmen: 14% (49). Undergraduates: 12% (175). *Average award:* Freshmen: $19,590. Undergraduates: $18,070. *Scholarships, grants, and awards by category:* Academic interests/achievement: $14,704,629 total: general academic interests/achievements. Creative arts/performance: $486,400 total: art/fine arts, music, theater/drama. Special achievements/activities: $181,300 total: community service, leadership, religious involvement. Special characteristics: $2,995,981 total: adult students, children and siblings of alumni, children of educators, children of faculty/staff, ethnic background, international students, members of minority groups, relatives of clergy, religious affiliation, siblings of current students, twins. *Tuition waivers:* Full or partial for children of alumni, employees or children of employees, senior citizens.
**LOANS** *Student loans:* $11,559,879 (69% need-based, 31% non-need-based). 87% of past graduating class borrowed through all loan programs. *Average indebtedness per student:* $35,205. *Average need-based loan:* Freshmen: $3669. Undergraduates: $3845. *Parent loans:* $1,952,687 (40% need-based, 60% non-need-based). *Programs:* Federal Direct (Subsidized and Unsubsidized Stafford, PLUS), Perkins, state, college/university, alternative loans.
**WORK-STUDY** *Federal work-study:* Total amount: $327,181; 408 jobs averaging $1047. *State or other work-study/employment:* Total amount: $477,721 (28% need-based, 72% non-need-based). 409 part-time jobs averaging $1369.
**APPLYING FOR FINANCIAL AID** *Required financial aid form:* FAFSA. *Financial aid deadline:* Continuous. *Notification date:* Continuous beginning 3/20. Students must reply by 5/1 or within 3 weeks of notification.
**CONTACT** Tracie Lynn Pavon, Assistant Vice President for Enrollment and Financial Assistance, Simpson College, 701 North C Street, Indianola, IA 50125-1297, 515-961-1630 Ext. 1596 or toll-free 800-362-2454. *Fax:* 515-961-1300. *E-mail:* tracie.pavon@simpson.edu.
*Website:* http://www.simpson.edu/.

# SIMPSON UNIVERSITY
## Redding, CA

| Tuition & fees: $24,300 | Average undergraduate aid package: $19,571 |
| --- | --- |

**ABOUT THE INSTITUTION** Independent The Christian and Missionary Alliance, coed. *Awards:* certificates, associate, bachelor's, and master's degrees. 29 undergraduate majors. *Total enrollment:* 1,267. Undergraduates: 1,068. Freshmen: 127. Federal methodology is used as a basis for awarding need-based institutional aid.
**UNDERGRADUATE EXPENSES for 2015–2016** *Application fee:* $25. *Comprehensive fee:* $32,200 includes full-time tuition ($24,300) and room and board ($7900). Full-time tuition and fees vary according to course load. Room and board charges vary according to board plan. Part-time tuition and fees vary according to course load.
**FRESHMAN FINANCIAL AID (Fall 2014, est.)** 121 applied for aid; of those 91% were deemed to have need. 100% of freshmen with need received aid; of those 14% had need fully met. *Average percent of need met:* 58% (excluding resources awarded to replace EFC). *Average financial aid package:* $20,111 (excluding resources awarded to replace EFC). 9% of all full-time freshmen had no need and received non-need-based gift aid.
**UNDERGRADUATE FINANCIAL AID (Fall 2014, est.)** 731 applied for aid; of those 92% were deemed to have need. 100% of undergraduates with need received aid; of those 9% had need fully met. *Average percent of need met:* 55% (excluding resources awarded to replace EFC). *Average financial aid package:* $19,571 (excluding resources awarded to replace EFC). 6% of all full-time undergraduates had no need and received non-need-based gift aid.
**GIFT AID (NEED-BASED)** *Total amount:* $8,510,340 (15% federal, 34% state, 49% institutional, 2% external sources). *Receiving aid:* Freshmen: 87% (110); all full-time undergraduates: 88% (673). *Average award:* Freshmen: $15,977; Undergraduates: $14,678. *Scholarships, grants, and awards:* Federal Pell, FSEOG, state, private, college/university gift aid from institutional funds.
**GIFT AID (NON-NEED-BASED)** *Total amount:* $630,894 (98% institutional, 2% external sources). *Receiving aid:* Freshmen: 14% (18). Undergraduates: 4% (31). *Average award:* Freshmen: $10,027. Undergraduates: $9673. *Scholarships, grants, and awards by category:* Academic interests/achievement: 389 awards

($1,241,412 total): communication, general academic interests/achievements. *Creative arts/performance:* 97 awards ($118,875 total): music. Special achievements/activities: 88 awards ($124,708 total): community service, leadership, religious involvement. Special characteristics: 253 awards ($696,971 total): children of faculty/staff, general special characteristics, members of minority groups, out-of-state students, relatives of clergy, religious affiliation, siblings of current students. *Tuition waivers:* Full or partial for employees or children of employees.
**LOANS** *Student loans:* $8,192,821 (93% need-based, 7% non-need-based). 79% of past graduating class borrowed through all loan programs. *Average indebtedness per student:* $28,161. *Average need-based loan:* Freshmen: $7713. Undergraduates: $8281. *Parent loans:* $1,538,910 (53% need-based, 47% non-need-based). *Programs:* Federal Direct (Subsidized and Unsubsidized Stafford, PLUS), Perkins, alternative loans.
**WORK-STUDY** *Federal work-study:* Total amount: $232,792; 65 jobs averaging $1490.
**ATHLETIC AWARDS** Total amount: $2,499,369 (75% need-based, 25% non-need-based).
**APPLYING FOR FINANCIAL AID** *Required financial aid forms:* FAFSA, state aid form. *Financial aid deadline (priority):* 3/2. *Notification date:* Continuous beginning 3/15. Students must reply within 3 weeks of notification.
**CONTACT** Melissa Hudson, Director of Student Financial Services, Simpson University, 2211 College View Drive, Redding, CA 96003-8606, 530-226-4974 or toll-free 888-9-SIMPSON. *Fax:* 530-226-4855. *E-mail:* financialaid@simpsonu.edu. *Website:* http://www.simpsonu.edu/.

# SINTE GLESKA UNIVERSITY
## Mission, SD

**ABOUT THE INSTITUTION** Independent, coed. 32 undergraduate majors.
**GIFT AID (NEED-BASED)** *Scholarships, grants, and awards:* Federal Pell, FSEOG.
**GIFT AID (NON-NEED-BASED)** *Scholarships, grants, and awards by category:* Academic interests/achievement: business, education. Creative arts/performance: art/fine arts. Special achievements/activities: general special achievements/activities, rodeo.
**APPLYING FOR FINANCIAL AID** *Required financial aid forms:* FAFSA, institution's own form.
**CONTACT** Office of Financial Aid, Sinte Gleska University, PO Box 105, Mission, SD 5755504105, 605-856-8197 Ext. 8477. *Fax:* 605-856-5874. *E-mail:* bhay@sintegleska.edu.
*Website:* http://www.sintegleska.edu/.

# SITTING BULL COLLEGE
## Fort Yates, ND

**ABOUT THE INSTITUTION** Independent, coed. 15 undergraduate majors.
**GIFT AID (NEED-BASED)** *Scholarships, grants, and awards:* Federal Pell, FSEOG, state, private, college/university gift aid from institutional funds, BIA Grants, JTPA Scholarships, American Indian College Fund, Gates Millennium Scholarships.
**APPLYING FOR FINANCIAL AID** *Required financial aid forms:* FAFSA, institution's own form.
**CONTACT** Donna M. Seaboy, Financial Aid Director, Sitting Bull College, 9299 Highway 24, Fort Yates, ND 58538, 701-854-8013. *Fax:* 701-854-3403. *E-mail:* donnas@sbci.edu.
*Website:* http://www.sittingbull.edu/.

# SKIDMORE COLLEGE
## Saratoga Springs, NY

| Tuition & fees: $47,314 | Average undergraduate aid package: $41,800 |
| --- | --- |

**ABOUT THE INSTITUTION** Independent, coed. *Awards:* bachelor's and master's degrees. 42 undergraduate majors. *Total enrollment:* 2,646. Undergraduates: 2,632. Freshmen: 724. Both federal and institutional methodology are used as a basis for awarding need-based institutional aid.

**UNDERGRADUATE EXPENSES** for 2015–2016 *Application fee:* $65. *One-time required fee:* $150. *Comprehensive fee:* $59,942 includes full-time tuition ($46,390), mandatory fees ($924), and room and board ($12,628). *College room only:* $7466. Full-time tuition and fees vary according to course load. Room and board charges vary according to board plan and housing facility. *Part-time tuition:* $1546 per credit. *Part-time fees:* $25 per term. Part-time tuition and fees vary according to course load. *Payment plan:* Tuition prepayment.

**FRESHMAN FINANCIAL AID (Fall 2014, est.)** 411 applied for aid; of those 82% were deemed to have need. 100% of freshmen with need received aid; of those 100% had need fully met. *Average percent of need met:* 100% (excluding resources awarded to replace EFC). *Average financial aid package:* $40,200 (excluding resources awarded to replace EFC). 1% of all full-time freshmen had no need and received non-need-based gift aid.

**UNDERGRADUATE FINANCIAL AID (Fall 2014, est.)** 1,350 applied for aid; of those 86% were deemed to have need. 99% of undergraduates with need received aid; of those 92% had need fully met. *Average percent of need met:* 94% (excluding resources awarded to replace EFC). *Average financial aid package:* $41,800 (excluding resources awarded to replace EFC). 1% of all full-time undergraduates had no need and received non-need-based gift aid.

**GIFT AID (NEED-BASED)** *Total amount:* $43,660,000 (4% federal, 3% state, 93% institutional). *Receiving aid:* Freshmen: 46% (336); all full-time undergraduates: 44% (1,146). *Average award:* Freshmen: $37,300; Undergraduates: $38,400. *Scholarships, grants, and awards:* Federal Pell, FSEOG, state, private, college/university gift aid from institutional funds.

**GIFT AID (NON-NEED-BASED)** *Total amount:* $1,960,000 (5% state, 55% institutional, 40% external sources). *Receiving aid:* Freshmen: 3% (22). Undergraduates: 4% (99). *Average award:* Freshmen: $14,000. Undergraduates: $12,000. *Scholarships, grants, and awards by category: Academic interests/achievement:* biological sciences, computer science, mathematics, physical sciences. *Creative arts/performance:* music. *Special characteristics:* children of faculty/staff. *Tuition waivers:* Full or partial for employees or children of employees, senior citizens. *ROTC:* Army cooperative, Air Force cooperative.

**LOANS** *Student loans:* $6,574,000 (45% need-based, 55% non-need-based). 46% of past graduating class borrowed through all loan programs. *Average indebtedness per student:* $22,887. *Average need-based loan:* Freshmen: $3010. Undergraduates: $4100. *Parent loans:* $2,700,000 (100% non-need-based). *Programs:* Federal Direct (Subsidized and Unsubsidized Stafford, PLUS), Perkins, state.

**WORK-STUDY** *Federal work-study:* Total amount: $1,150,000; jobs available. *State or other work-study/employment:* Total amount: $1,180,000 (100% non-need-based). Part-time jobs available.

**APPLYING FOR FINANCIAL AID** *Required financial aid forms:* CSS Financial Aid PROFILE, noncustodial (divorced/separated) parent's statement. *Financial aid deadline:* 2/1. *Notification date:* 4/1. Students must reply by 5/1.

**CONTACT** Ms. Beth A. Post-Lundquist, Director of Financial Aid, Skidmore College, 815 North Broadway, Saratoga Springs, NY 12866-1632, 518-580-5750 or toll-free 800-867-6007. *Fax:* 518-580-5752. *E-mail:* finaid@skidmore.edu. *Website:* http://www.skidmore.edu/.

# SKYLINE COLLEGE
### Roanoke, VA

**CONTACT** Ms. Amanda Little, Director of Financial Aid, Skyline College, 5234 Airport Road, Roanoke, VA 24012, 540-563-8080 or toll-free 866-708-6178. *E-mail:* alittle@ecpi.edu. *Website:* http://www.skyline.edu/.

# SLIPPERY ROCK UNIVERSITY OF PENNSYLVANIA
### Slippery Rock, PA

| Tuition & fees (PA res): $9309 | Average undergraduate aid package: $8831 |
|---|---|

**ABOUT THE INSTITUTION** State-supported, coed. *Awards:* certificates, bachelor's, master's, and doctoral degrees. 65 undergraduate majors. *Total enrollment:* 8,495. Undergraduates: 7,587. Freshmen: 1,586. Federal methodology is used as a basis for awarding need-based institutional aid.

**UNDERGRADUATE EXPENSES** for 2015–2016 *Application fee:* $30. *Tuition, state resident:* full-time $6820; part-time $284 per credit hour. *Tuition, nonresident:* full-time $10,230; part-time $426 per credit hour. *Required fees:* full-time $2489; $104.16 per credit hour. Full-time tuition and fees vary according to course load. Part-time tuition and fees vary according to course load. *College room and board:* $9794; *Room only:* $6490. Room and board charges vary according to board plan and housing facility.

**FRESHMAN FINANCIAL AID (Fall 2014, est.)** 1,494 applied for aid; of those 79% were deemed to have need. 99% of freshmen with need received aid; of those 13% had need fully met. *Average percent of need met:* 57% (excluding resources awarded to replace EFC). *Average financial aid package:* $8314 (excluding resources awarded to replace EFC). 9% of all full-time freshmen had no need and received non-need-based gift aid.

**UNDERGRADUATE FINANCIAL AID (Fall 2014, est.)** 6,169 applied for aid; of those 80% were deemed to have need. 98% of undergraduates with need received aid; of those 13% had need fully met. *Average percent of need met:* 60% (excluding resources awarded to replace EFC). *Average financial aid package:* $8831 (excluding resources awarded to replace EFC). 6% of all full-time undergraduates had no need and received non-need-based gift aid.

**GIFT AID (NEED-BASED)** *Total amount:* $18,316,097 (55% federal, 40% state, 5% institutional). *Receiving aid:* Freshmen: 46% (722); all full-time undergraduates: 43% (3,040). *Average award:* Freshmen: $5998; Undergraduates: $5859. *Scholarships, grants, and awards:* Federal Pell, FSEOG, state, private, college/university gift aid from institutional funds.

**GIFT AID (NON-NEED-BASED)** *Total amount:* $4,856,397 (10% state, 45% institutional, 45% external sources). *Receiving aid:* Freshmen: 28% (438). Undergraduates: 15% (1,079). *Average award:* Freshmen: $2383. Undergraduates: $2734. *Scholarships, grants, and awards by category: Academic interests/achievement:* biological sciences, business, communication, computer science, education, English, general academic interests/achievements, health fields, physical sciences, social sciences. *Creative arts/performance:* applied art and design, art/fine arts, dance, music, performing arts, theater/drama. *Special achievements/activities:* community service, general special achievements/activities, leadership. *Special characteristics:* children and siblings of alumni, children of faculty/staff, children of union members/company employees, ethnic background, general special characteristics, local/state students, members of minority groups, out-of-state students, previous college experience. *Tuition waivers:* Full or partial for minority students, employees or children of employees, senior citizens. *ROTC:* Army.

**LOANS** *Student loans:* $50,395,838 (40% need-based, 60% non-need-based). 86% of past graduating class borrowed through all loan programs. *Average indebtedness per student:* $30,458. *Average need-based loan:* Freshmen: $3570. Undergraduates: $4354. *Parent loans:* $10,689,783 (100% non-need-based). *Programs:* Federal Direct (Subsidized and Unsubsidized Stafford, PLUS), Perkins.

**WORK-STUDY** *Federal work-study:* Total amount: $824,486; 556 jobs averaging $1725. *State or other work-study/employment:* Total amount: $1,726,388 (100% non-need-based). 887 part-time jobs averaging $1981.

**ATHLETIC AWARDS** Total amount: $1,081,689 (100% non-need-based).

**APPLYING FOR FINANCIAL AID** *Required financial aid form:* FAFSA. *Financial aid deadline (priority):* 5/1. *Notification date:* Continuous beginning 3/15.

**CONTACT** Ms. Michelle Jackson, Director of Financial Aid, Slippery Rock University of Pennsylvania, 1 Morrow Way, Slippery Rock, PA 16057, 724-738-2044 or toll-free 800-SRU-9111. *Fax:* 724-738-2922. *E-mail:* financial.aid@sru.edu. *Website:* http://www.sru.edu/.

# SMITH COLLEGE
### Northampton, MA

| Tuition & fees: $44,724 | Average undergraduate aid package: $43,182 |
|---|---|

**ABOUT THE INSTITUTION** Independent, undergraduate: women only; graduate: coed. *Awards:* certificates, bachelor's, master's, and doctoral degrees. 53 undergraduate majors. *Total enrollment:* 2,989. Undergraduates: 2,563. Freshmen: 616. Both federal and institutional methodology are used as a basis for awarding need-based institutional aid.

**UNDERGRADUATE EXPENSES** for 2015–2016 *Application fee:* $60. *Comprehensive fee:* $59,674 includes full-time tuition ($44,450), mandatory fees ($274), and room and board ($14,950). *College room only:* $7480. *Part-time tuition:* $1390 per credit hour. *Payment plan:* Tuition prepayment.

**FRESHMAN FINANCIAL AID (Fall 2014, est.)** 459 applied for aid; of those 83% were deemed to have need. 100% of freshmen with need received aid; of those 100% had need fully met. *Average percent of need met:* 100% (excluding resources awarded to replace EFC). *Average financial aid package:* $42,078 (excluding resources awarded to replace EFC). 7% of all full-time freshmen had no need and received non-need-based gift aid.

**UNDERGRADUATE FINANCIAL AID (Fall 2014, est.)** 1,772 applied for aid; of those 90% were deemed to have need. 100% of undergraduates with need received aid; of those 100% had need fully met. *Average percent of need met:* 100% (excluding resources awarded to replace EFC). *Average financial aid package:* $43,182 (excluding resources awarded to replace EFC). 5% of all full-time undergraduates had no need and received non-need-based gift aid.

**GIFT AID (NEED-BASED)** *Total amount:* $60,314,405 (5% federal, 1% state, 91% institutional, 3% external sources). *Receiving aid:* Freshmen: 58% (358); all full-time undergraduates: 59% (1,501). *Average award:* Freshmen: $40,117; Undergraduates: $38,417. *Scholarships, grants, and awards:* Federal Pell, FSEOG, state, private, college/university gift aid from institutional funds.

**GIFT AID (NON-NEED-BASED)** *Total amount:* $1,867,760 (1% federal, 89% institutional, 10% external sources). *Receiving aid:* Freshmen: 1% (7). Undergraduates: 12. *Average award:* Freshmen: $13,152. Undergraduates: $15,982. *Scholarships, grants, and awards by category:* Academic interests/achievement: general academic interests/achievements. *Special characteristics:* local/state students. *Tuition waivers:* Full or partial for employees or children of employees. *ROTC:* Army cooperative, Air Force cooperative.

**LOANS** *Student loans:* $8,532,923 (69% need-based, 31% non-need-based). 65% of past graduating class borrowed through all loan programs. *Average indebtedness per student:* $24,758. *Average need-based loan:* Freshmen: $3213. Undergraduates: $4960. *Parent loans:* $3,544,084 (100% non-need-based). *Programs:* Federal Direct (Subsidized and Unsubsidized Stafford, PLUS), Perkins, college/university.

**WORK-STUDY** *Federal work-study:* Total amount: $2,433,846; jobs available. *State or other work-study/employment:* Total amount: $1,139,774 (82% need-based, 18% non-need-based). Part-time jobs available.

**APPLYING FOR FINANCIAL AID** *Required financial aid forms:* FAFSA, institution's own form, CSS Financial Aid PROFILE, noncustodial (divorced/separated) parent's statement, federal income tax form(s). *Financial aid deadline:* 2/15. *Notification date:* 4/1. Students must reply by 5/1.

**CONTACT** David Belanger, Director of Student Financial Services, Smith College, College Hall 106, 10 Elm Street, Northampton, MA 01063, 413-585-2530 or toll-free 800-383-3232. *Fax:* 413-585-2566. *E-mail:* sfs@smith.edu. *Website:* http://www.smith.edu/.

# SOKA UNIVERSITY OF AMERICA
### Aliso Viejo, CA

| Tuition & fees: $30,642 | Average undergraduate aid package: $34,356 |
|---|---|

**ABOUT THE INSTITUTION** Independent, coed. *Awards:* bachelor's and master's degrees. 1 undergraduate major. *Total enrollment:* 418. Undergraduates: 412. Freshmen: 100. Both federal and institutional methodology are used as a basis for awarding need-based institutional aid.

**UNDERGRADUATE EXPENSES** for 2015–2016 *Application fee:* $45. *Comprehensive fee:* $42,110 includes full-time tuition ($28,938), mandatory fees ($1704), and room and board ($11,468). Full-time tuition and fees vary according to class time, course load, and program. Room and board charges vary according to board plan. *Part-time tuition:* $1206 per credit. Part-time tuition and fees vary according to class time, course load, and program.

**FRESHMAN FINANCIAL AID (Fall 2014, est.)** 95 applied for aid; of those 92% were deemed to have need. 100% of freshmen with need received aid; of those 31% had need fully met. *Average percent of need met:* 100% (excluding resources awarded to replace EFC). *Average financial aid package:* $34,486 (excluding resources awarded to replace EFC). 8% of all full-time freshmen had no need and received non-need-based gift aid.

**UNDERGRADUATE FINANCIAL AID (Fall 2014, est.)** 395 applied for aid; of those 94% were deemed to have need. 100% of undergraduates with need received aid; of those 34% had need fully met. *Average percent of need met:* 100% (excluding resources awarded to replace EFC). *Average financial aid package:* $34,356 (excluding resources awarded to replace EFC). 6% of all full-time undergraduates had no need and received non-need-based gift aid.

**GIFT AID (NEED-BASED)** *Total amount:* $9,560,156 (6% federal, 6% state, 88% institutional). *Receiving aid:* Freshmen: 87% (87); all full-time undergraduates: 88% (364). *Average award:* Freshmen: $27,127; Undergraduates: $26,716. *Scholarships, grants, and awards:* Federal Pell, FSEOG, state, private, college/university gift aid from institutional funds.

**GIFT AID (NON-NEED-BASED)** *Total amount:* $3,291,141 (99% institutional, 1% external sources). *Receiving aid:* Freshmen: 87% (87). Undergraduates: 89% (365). *Average award:* Freshmen: $5812. Undergraduates: $9984. *Scholarships, grants, and awards by category:* Special characteristics: children of faculty/staff. *Tuition waivers:* Full or partial for employees or children of employees.

**LOANS** *Student loans:* $1,310,290 (29% need-based, 71% non-need-based). 61% of past graduating class borrowed through all loan programs. *Average indebtedness per student:* $19,563. *Average need-based loan:* Freshmen: $1732. Undergraduates: $2956. *Parent loans:* $342,316 (100% non-need-based). *Programs:* Federal Direct (Subsidized and Unsubsidized Stafford, PLUS), college/university.

**WORK-STUDY** *Federal work-study:* Total amount: $89,140; jobs available. *State or other work-study/employment:* Part-time jobs available.

**ATHLETIC AWARDS** Total amount: $464,250 (100% non-need-based).

**APPLYING FOR FINANCIAL AID** *Required financial aid forms:* FAFSA, state aid form. *Financial aid deadline:* 3/2 (priority: 2/15). *Notification date:* Continuous beginning 3/15. Students must reply by 5/1 or within 4 weeks of notification.

**CONTACT** Mrs. Stacey Choi Fung, Manager of Financial Aid, Soka University of America, 1 University Drive, Aliso Viejo, CA 92656, 949-480-4048 or toll-free 888-600-SOKA. *Fax:* 949-480-4151. *E-mail:* schoi@soka.edu . *Website:* http://www.soka.edu/.

# SONOMA STATE UNIVERSITY
### Rohnert Park, CA

| Tuition & fees (CA res): $7276 | Average undergraduate aid package: $10,349 |
|---|---|

**ABOUT THE INSTITUTION** State-supported, coed. *Awards:* bachelor's and master's degrees. 63 undergraduate majors. *Total enrollment:* 9,120. Undergraduates: 8,351. Freshmen: 1,807. Federal methodology is used as a basis for awarding need-based institutional aid.

**UNDERGRADUATE EXPENSES** for 2015–2016 *Application fee:* $55. *Tuition, state resident:* full-time $5472. *Tuition, nonresident:* full-time $16,632. *Required fees:* full-time $1804. Full-time tuition and fees vary according to course load and degree level. Part-time tuition and fees vary according to course load and degree level. *College room and board:* $11,799. Room and board charges vary according to housing facility.

**FRESHMAN FINANCIAL AID (Fall 2013)** 969 applied for aid; of those 70% were deemed to have need. 89% of freshmen with need received aid; of those 14% had need fully met. *Average percent of need met:* 58% (excluding resources awarded to replace EFC). *Average financial aid package:* $10,384 (excluding resources awarded to replace EFC). 1% of all full-time freshmen had no need and received non-need-based gift aid.

**UNDERGRADUATE FINANCIAL AID (Fall 2013)** 5,077 applied for aid; of those 79% were deemed to have need. 90% of undergraduates with need received aid; of those 4% had need fully met. *Average percent of need met:* 66% (excluding resources awarded to replace EFC). *Average financial aid package:* $10,349

(excluding resources awarded to replace EFC). 3% of all full-time undergraduates had no need and received non-need-based gift aid.

**GIFT AID (NEED-BASED)** *Total amount:* $27,788,774 (41% federal, 59% state). *Receiving aid:* Freshmen: 25% (442); all full-time undergraduates: 35% (2,670). *Average award:* Freshmen: $9942; Undergraduates: $9541. *Scholarships, grants, and awards:* Federal Pell, FSEOG, state, private, college/university gift aid from institutional funds.

**GIFT AID (NON-NEED-BASED)** *Total amount:* $1,824,379 (2% federal, 11% state, 38% institutional, 49% external sources). *Receiving aid:* Freshmen: 7% (132). Undergraduates: 8% (582). *Average award:* Freshmen: $1042. Undergraduates: $1280. *Scholarships, grants, and awards by category: Academic interests/achievement:* 162 awards ($147,180 total): area/ethnic studies, biological sciences, business, communication, computer science, education, engineering/technologies, English, foreign languages, general academic interests/achievements, health fields, humanities, mathematics, physical sciences, premedicine, social sciences. *Creative arts/performance:* 95 awards ($109,953 total): applied art and design, art/fine arts, cinema/film/broadcasting, creative writing, dance, journalism/publications, music, performing arts, theater/drama. *Special achievements/activities:* 39 awards ($47,350 total): community service, leadership, memberships. *Special characteristics:* 364 awards ($368,775 total): adult students, children and siblings of alumni, children of educators, children of faculty/staff, children of public servants, children of union members/company employees, children of workers in trades, ethnic background, first-generation college students, general special characteristics, handicapped students, international students, local/state students, married students, members of minority groups, out-of-state students, previous college experience, veterans. *Tuition waivers:* Full or partial for employees or children of employees. *ROTC:* Army cooperative, Air Force cooperative.

**LOANS** *Student loans:* $24,309,365 (47% need-based, 53% non-need-based). 62% of past graduating class borrowed through all loan programs. *Average indebtedness per student:* $20,744. *Average need-based loan:* Freshmen: $3169. Undergraduates: $4034. *Parent loans:* $10,214,297 (100% non-need-based). *Programs:* Federal Direct (Subsidized and Unsubsidized Stafford, PLUS), Perkins.

**WORK-STUDY** *Federal work-study:* 224 jobs averaging $2882. *State or other work-study/employment:* Total amount: $1,600,000 (100% non-need-based). 592 part-time jobs averaging $2700.

**ATHLETIC AWARDS** Total amount: $500,970 (100% non-need-based).

**APPLYING FOR FINANCIAL AID** *Required financial aid form:* FAFSA. *Financial aid deadline (priority):* 1/31. *Notification date:* Continuous beginning 3/15. Students must reply within 2 weeks of notification.

**CONTACT** Susan Gutierrez, Director of Financial Aid, Sonoma State University, 1801 East Cotati Avenue, Rohnert Park, CA 94928-3609, 707-664-2287. *Fax:* 707-664-4242. *E-mail:* susan.gutierrez@sonoma.edu. *Website:* http://www.sonoma.edu/.

# SOUTH CAROLINA STATE UNIVERSITY
## Orangeburg, SC

**CONTACT** Sandra S. Davis, Director of Financial Aid, South Carolina State University, 300 College Street Northeast, Orangeburg, SC 29117, 803-536-7067 or toll-free 800-260-5956. *Fax:* 803-536-8420. *E-mail:* sdavis@scsu.edu. *Website:* http://www.scsu.edu/.

# SOUTH COLLEGE
## Knoxville, TN

**CONTACT** Financial Aid Office, South College, 720 North Fifth Avenue, Knoxville, TN 37917, 865-524-3043. *Website:* http://www.southcollegetn.edu/.

# SOUTH DAKOTA SCHOOL OF MINES AND TECHNOLOGY
## Rapid City, SD

| Tuition & fees (SD res): $10,040 | Average undergraduate aid package: $13,722 |
|---|---|

**ABOUT THE INSTITUTION** State-supported, coed. *Awards:* certificates, associate, bachelor's, master's, and doctoral degrees. 17 undergraduate majors. *Total enrollment:* 2,798. Undergraduates: 2,471. Freshmen: 599. Both federal and institutional methodology are used as a basis for awarding need-based institutional aid.

**UNDERGRADUATE EXPENSES for 2015–2016** *Application fee:* $20. *Tuition, state resident:* full-time $4170; part-time $138.80 per credit hour. *Tuition, nonresident:* full-time $7000; part-time $233.20 per credit hour. *Required fees:* full-time $5870; $202.35 per credit hour. Full-time tuition and fees vary according to course load, program, and reciprocity agreements. Part-time tuition and fees vary according to course load, program, and reciprocity agreements. *College room and board:* $6370; *Room only:* $3350. Room and board charges vary according to board plan and housing facility.

**FRESHMAN FINANCIAL AID (Fall 2013)** 523 applied for aid; of those 60% were deemed to have need. 100% of freshmen with need received aid; of those 46% had need fully met. *Average percent of need met:* 79% (excluding resources awarded to replace EFC). *Average financial aid package:* $13,500 (excluding resources awarded to replace EFC). 27% of all full-time freshmen had no need and received non-need-based gift aid.

**UNDERGRADUATE FINANCIAL AID (Fall 2013)** 1,767 applied for aid; of those 61% were deemed to have need. 100% of undergraduates with need received aid; of those 38% had need fully met. *Average percent of need met:* 76% (excluding resources awarded to replace EFC). *Average financial aid package:* $13,722 (excluding resources awarded to replace EFC). 20% of all full-time undergraduates had no need and received non-need-based gift aid.

**GIFT AID (NEED-BASED)** *Total amount:* $4,359,949 (57% federal, 20% institutional, 23% external sources). *Receiving aid:* Freshmen: 42% (230); all full-time undergraduates: 37% (718). *Average award:* Freshmen: $4301; Undergraduates: $4482. *Scholarships, grants, and awards:* Federal Pell, FSEOG, state, private, college/university gift aid from institutional funds.

**GIFT AID (NON-NEED-BASED)** *Total amount:* $1,290,952 (56% institutional, 44% external sources). *Receiving aid:* Freshmen: 34% (184). Undergraduates: 22% (417). *Average award:* Freshmen: $2596. Undergraduates: $2829. *Scholarships, grants, and awards by category: Academic interests/achievement:* 591 awards ($693,515 total): biological sciences, computer science, engineering/technologies, mathematics, military science, physical sciences. *Special characteristics:* 600 awards ($871,149 total): adult students, ethnic background, international students, local/state students, married students, members of minority groups, out-of-state students. *Tuition waivers:* Full or partial for employees or children of employees, senior citizens. *ROTC:* Army.

**LOANS** *Student loans:* $8,251,066 (100% need-based). 72% of past graduating class borrowed through all loan programs. *Average indebtedness per student:* $22,810. *Average need-based loan:* Freshmen: $3512. Undergraduates: $4300. *Parent loans:* $2,068,091 (75% need-based, 25% non-need-based). *Programs:* Federal Direct (Subsidized and Unsubsidized Stafford, PLUS), Perkins.

**WORK-STUDY** *Federal work-study:* 127 jobs averaging $1899.

**ATHLETIC AWARDS** Total amount: $783,884 (64% need-based, 36% non-need-based).

**APPLYING FOR FINANCIAL AID** *Required financial aid form:* FAFSA. *Financial aid deadline:* Continuous. *Notification date:* Continuous beginning 4/15. Students must reply within 3 weeks of notification.

**CONTACT** David W. Martin, Director of Financial Aid, South Dakota School of Mines and Technology, 501 East Saint Joseph Street, Rapid City, SD 57701-3995, 605-394-2274 or toll-free 800-544-8162. *Fax:* 605-394-1979. *E-mail:* david.martin@sdsmt.edu. *Website:* http://www.sdsmt.edu/.

# SOUTH DAKOTA STATE UNIVERSITY
## Brookings, SD

| Tuition & fees (SD res): $7713 | Average undergraduate aid package: $12,474 |
|---|---|

**ABOUT THE INSTITUTION** State-supported, coed. *Awards:* certificates, associate, bachelor's, master's, and doctoral degrees. 83 undergraduate majors. *Total enrollment:* 12,557. Undergraduates: 10,951. Freshmen: 2,283. Federal methodology is used as a basis for awarding need-based institutional aid.

**UNDERGRADUATE EXPENSES for 2015–2016** *Application fee:* $20. *Tuition, state resident:* full-time $4164; part-time $138.80 per credit hour. *Tuition, nonresident:* full-time $6246; part-time $208.20 per credit hour. *Required fees:* full-time $3549. Full-time tuition and fees vary according to course level, course load, degree level, location, program, and reciprocity agreements. Part-time tuition and fees vary according to course level, course load, degree level, location, program, and reciprocity agreements. *College room and board:* $6985; *Room only:* $3214. Room and board charges vary according to board plan and housing facility.

**FRESHMAN FINANCIAL AID (Fall 2013)** 1,847 applied for aid; of those 70% were deemed to have need. 100% of freshmen with need received aid; of those 37% had need fully met. *Average percent of need met:* 70% (excluding resources awarded to replace EFC). *Average financial aid package:* $11,975 (excluding resources awarded to replace EFC). 20% of all full-time freshmen had no need and received non-need-based gift aid.

**UNDERGRADUATE FINANCIAL AID (Fall 2013)** 6,787 applied for aid; of those 75% were deemed to have need. 100% of undergraduates with need received aid; of those 32% had need fully met. *Average percent of need met:* 68% (excluding resources awarded to replace EFC). *Average financial aid package:* $12,474 (excluding resources awarded to replace EFC). 16% of all full-time undergraduates had no need and received non-need-based gift aid.

**GIFT AID (NEED-BASED)** *Total amount:* $11,522,875 (100% federal). *Receiving aid:* Freshmen: 28% (604); all full-time undergraduates: 27% (2,366). *Average award:* Freshmen: $3922; Undergraduates: $4031. *Scholarships, grants, and awards:* Federal Pell, FSEOG, state, private, college/university gift aid from institutional funds, United Negro College Fund, Federal Nursing, TEACH Grants, TRiO Scholarships, South Dakota Education Access Foundation.

**GIFT AID (NON-NEED-BASED)** *Total amount:* $13,220,051 (5% federal, 14% state, 48% institutional, 33% external sources). *Receiving aid:* Freshmen: 58% (1,264). Undergraduates: 56% (4,801). *Average award:* Freshmen: $1773. Undergraduates: $1904. *Scholarships, grants, and awards by category: Academic interests/achievement:* agriculture, area/ethnic studies, biological sciences, business, communication, computer science, education, engineering/technologies, English, foreign languages, general academic interests/achievements, health fields, home economics, humanities, international studies, mathematics, military science, physical sciences, premedicine, social sciences. *Creative arts/performance:* art/fine arts, debating, general creative arts/performance, journalism/publications, music, performing arts, theater/drama. *Special achievements/activities:* community service, general special achievements/activities, hobbies/interests, junior miss, leadership, memberships, rodeo. *Special characteristics:* adult students, children of faculty/staff, children of workers in trades, ethnic background, first-generation college students, general special characteristics, handicapped students, international students, members of minority groups, veterans, veterans' children. *Tuition waivers:* Full or partial for employees or children of employees, senior citizens. *ROTC:* Army, Air Force.

**LOANS** *Student loans:* $384,637,158 (6% need-based, 94% non-need-based). 59% of past graduating class borrowed through all loan programs. *Average indebtedness per student:* $23,183. *Average need-based loan:* Freshmen: $3454. Undergraduates: $4384. *Parent loans:* $3,423,777 (100% non-need-based). *Programs:* Federal Direct (Subsidized and Unsubsidized Stafford, PLUS), Perkins, Federal Nursing, college/university, alternative loans, Health Professions Student Loans (HPSL).

**WORK-STUDY** *Federal work-study:* jobs available. *State or other work-study/employment:* Part-time jobs available.

**ATHLETIC AWARDS** Total amount: $3,620,000 (100% non-need-based).

**APPLYING FOR FINANCIAL AID** *Required financial aid form:* FAFSA. *Financial aid deadline (priority):* 3/10. *Notification date:* Continuous beginning 4/1. Students must reply within 3 weeks of notification.

**CONTACT** Carolyn Halgerson, Director of Financial Aid, South Dakota State University, Administration 100, PO Box 2201, Brookings, SD 57007, 605-688-4695 or toll-free 800-952-3541. *Fax:* 605-688-5882. *E-mail:* carolyn.halgerson@sdstate.edu. *Website:* http://www.sdstate.edu/.

# SOUTHEASTERN BAPTIST COLLEGE
## Laurel, MS

**CONTACT** Financial Aid Officer, Southeastern Baptist College, 4229 Highway 15 North, Laurel, MS 39440-1096, 601-426-6346. *Website:* http://www.southeasternbaptist.edu/.

# SOUTHEASTERN BAPTIST THEOLOGICAL SEMINARY
## Wake Forest, NC

**CONTACT** Financial Aid Office, Southeastern Baptist Theological Seminary, PO Box 1889, Wake Forest, NC 27588-1889, 919-556-3101 or toll-free 800-284-6317. *Website:* http://www.sebts.edu/.

# SOUTHEASTERN BIBLE COLLEGE
## Birmingham, AL

**ABOUT THE INSTITUTION** Independent nondenominational, coed. *Awards:* diplomas, associate, and bachelor's degrees. 2 undergraduate majors. *Total enrollment:* 173. Undergraduates: 173.

**GIFT AID (NEED-BASED)** *Scholarships, grants, and awards:* Federal Pell, FSEOG, college/university gift aid from institutional funds.

**GIFT AID (NON-NEED-BASED)** *Scholarships, grants, and awards by category: Academic interests/achievement:* general academic interests/achievements. *Creative arts/performance:* music. *Special characteristics:* children of faculty/staff, local/state students, veterans.

**LOANS** *Programs:* Federal Direct (Subsidized and Unsubsidized Stafford, PLUS).

**WORK-STUDY** *Federal work-study:* jobs available. *State or other work-study/employment:* Part-time jobs available.

**APPLYING FOR FINANCIAL AID** *Required financial aid forms:* FAFSA, institution's own form.

**CONTACT** Mr. Jay Powell, Financial Aid Administrator, Southeastern Bible College, 2545 Valleydale Road, Birmingham, AL 35244-2083, 205-970-9216 or toll-free 800-749-8878. *Fax:* 205-970-9207. *E-mail:* finaid@sebc.edu. *Website:* http://www.sebc.edu/.

# SOUTHEASTERN LOUISIANA UNIVERSITY
## Hammond, LA

| Tuition & fees (LA res): $6547 | Average undergraduate aid package: $9093 |
|---|---|

**ABOUT THE INSTITUTION** State-supported, coed. *Awards:* certificates, associate, bachelor's, master's, and doctoral degrees. 37 undergraduate majors. *Total enrollment:* 14,498. Undergraduates: 13,376. Freshmen: 2,428. Both federal and institutional methodology are used as a basis for awarding need-based institutional aid.

**UNDERGRADUATE EXPENSES for 2015–2016** *Application fee:* $20. *Tuition, state resident:* full-time $4798; part-time $273 per credit hour. *Tuition, nonresident:* full-time $17,362; part-time $796 per credit hour. *Required fees:* full-time $1749; $273 per credit hour. Full-time tuition and fees vary according to course load. Part-time tuition and fees vary according to course load. *College room and board:* $7100; *Room only:* $4520. Room and board charges vary according to board plan and housing facility.

**FRESHMAN FINANCIAL AID (Fall 2013)** 2,170 applied for aid; of those 73% were deemed to have need. 99% of freshmen with need received aid; of those 13% had need fully met. *Average financial aid package:* $8358 (excluding resources awarded to replace EFC). 9% of all full-time freshmen had no need and received non-need-based gift aid.

**UNDERGRADUATE FINANCIAL AID (Fall 2013)** 7,976 applied for aid; of those 76% were deemed to have need. 99% of undergraduates with need received aid;

of those 16% had need fully met. **Average financial aid package:** $9093 (excluding resources awarded to replace EFC). 9% of all full-time undergraduates had no need and received non-need-based gift aid.
**GIFT AID (NEED-BASED) Total amount:** $21,817,687 (87% federal, 13% state). **Receiving aid:** Freshmen: 42% (1,007); all full-time undergraduates: 41% (4,054). **Average award:** Freshmen: $3581; Undergraduates: $4916. **Scholarships, grants, and awards:** Federal Pell, FSEOG, state, private, college/university gift aid from institutional funds.
**GIFT AID (NON-NEED-BASED) Total amount:** $28,240,230 (1% federal, 65% state, 31% institutional, 3% external sources). **Receiving aid:** Freshmen: 44% (1,051). Undergraduates: 30% (3,010). **Average award:** Freshmen: $2526. Undergraduates: $3210. **Scholarships, grants, and awards by category:** Academic interests/achievement: business, communication, computer science, education, English, foreign languages, general academic interests/achievements, humanities, mathematics, premedicine, social sciences. Creative arts/performance: art/fine arts, music, theater/drama. Special achievements/activities: cheerleading/drum major, leadership, memberships. Special characteristics: adult students, children and siblings of alumni, children of faculty/staff, first-generation college students, out-of-state students, veterans, veterans' children. **Tuition waivers:** Full or partial for employees or children of employees.
**ROTC:** Army cooperative.
**LOANS Student loans:** $31,480,374 (48% need-based, 52% non-need-based). 57% of past graduating class borrowed through all loan programs. **Average need-based loan:** Freshmen: $3055. Undergraduates: $3778. **Parent loans:** $1,877,143 (100% non-need-based). **Programs:** Federal Direct (Subsidized and Unsubsidized Stafford, PLUS), Perkins, college/university.
**WORK-STUDY Federal work-study:** 165 jobs averaging $2045. **State or other work-study/employment:** Total amount: $2,246,839 (100% non-need-based). 1,074 part-time jobs averaging $2163.
**ATHLETIC AWARDS** Total amount: $2,423,157 (100% non-need-based).
**APPLYING FOR FINANCIAL AID Required financial aid form:** FAFSA. **Financial aid deadline (priority):** 5/1. **Notification date:** Continuous beginning 4/1. Students must reply within 2 weeks of notification.
**CONTACT** Mrs. Mary Lacour, Director of Financial Aid, Southeastern Louisiana University, SLU 10768, Hammond, LA 70402, 985-549-2244 or toll-free 800-222-7350. Fax: 985-549-5077. E-mail: finaid@selu.edu.
Website: http://www.selu.edu/.

(excluding resources awarded to replace EFC). 1% of all full-time undergraduates had no need and received non-need-based gift aid.
**GIFT AID (NEED-BASED) Total amount:** $10,845,275 (74% federal, 26% state). **Receiving aid:** Freshmen: 57% (268); all full-time undergraduates: 56% (1,333). **Average award:** Freshmen: $1766; Undergraduates: $1840. **Scholarships, grants, and awards:** Federal Pell, FSEOG, state, private, college/university gift aid from institutional funds.
**GIFT AID (NON-NEED-BASED) Total amount:** $2,387,315 (4% state, 13% institutional, 83% external sources). **Receiving aid:** Freshmen: 32% (151). Undergraduates: 23% (554). **Average award:** Freshmen: $444. Undergraduates: $646. **Scholarships, grants, and awards by category:** Academic interests/achievement: 499 awards ($461,005 total): biological sciences, business, communication, computer science, education, engineering/technologies, English, general academic interests/achievements, mathematics, physical sciences, social sciences. Creative arts/performance: 197 awards ($151,067 total): art/fine arts, dance, debating, music, performing arts, theater/drama. Special achievements/activities: 735 awards ($1,419,591 total): cheerleading/drum major, leadership, rodeo. Special characteristics: 2,654 awards ($6,922,537 total): children and siblings of alumni, out-of-state students. **Tuition waivers:** Full or partial for minority students, children of alumni, employees or children of employees, adult students, senior citizens.
**LOANS Student loans:** $11,499,687 (45% need-based, 55% non-need-based). 56% of past graduating class borrowed through all loan programs. **Average indebtedness per student:** $19,368. **Average need-based loan:** Freshmen: $1311. Undergraduates: $1920. **Parent loans:** $495,252 (100% non-need-based). **Programs:** Federal Direct (Subsidized and Unsubsidized Stafford, PLUS).
**WORK-STUDY Federal work-study:** 736 jobs averaging $1832. **State or other work-study/employment:** Part-time jobs available.
**ATHLETIC AWARDS** Total amount: $1,561,178 (100% non-need-based).
**APPLYING FOR FINANCIAL AID Required financial aid forms:** FAFSA, institution's own form. **Financial aid deadline (priority):** 3/1. **Notification date:** Continuous beginning 4/15. Students must reply within 2 weeks of notification.
**CONTACT** Tony Lehrling, Director of Student Financial Aid, Southeastern Oklahoma State University, 1405 North 4th Avenue, Durant, OK 74701-0609, 580-745-2186 or toll-free 800-435-1327. Fax: 580-745-7469. E-mail: shudson@se.edu.
Website: http://www.se.edu/.

# SOUTHEASTERN OKLAHOMA STATE UNIVERSITY
### Durant, OK

| Tuition & fees (OK res): $5688 | Average undergraduate aid package: $10,559 |
|---|---|

**ABOUT THE INSTITUTION** State-supported, coed. **Awards:** certificates, bachelor's, and master's degrees. 43 undergraduate majors. **Total enrollment:** 3,877. Undergraduates: 3,468. Freshmen: 502. Federal methodology is used as a basis for awarding need-based institutional aid.
**UNDERGRADUATE EXPENSES for 2015–2016 Application fee:** $20. **Tuition, state resident:** full-time $5055; part-time $168.50 per credit hour. **Tuition, nonresident:** full-time $15,100; part-time $445.30 per credit hour. **Required fees:** full-time $633; $21.10 per credit hour. Full-time tuition and fees vary according to course level, degree level, location, and program. Part-time tuition and fees vary according to course level, course load, degree level, location, and program. **College room and board:** $6143; **Room only:** $3773. Room and board charges vary according to board plan, housing facility, and student level. **Payment plan:** Guaranteed tuition.
**FRESHMAN FINANCIAL AID (Fall 2013)** 423 applied for aid; of those 88% were deemed to have need. 99% of freshmen with need received aid; of those 9% had need fully met. **Average percent of need met:** 7% (excluding resources awarded to replace EFC). **Average financial aid package:** $10,410 (excluding resources awarded to replace EFC). 1% of all full-time freshmen had no need and received non-need-based gift aid.
**UNDERGRADUATE FINANCIAL AID (Fall 2013)** 1,937 applied for aid; of those 91% were deemed to have need. 98% of undergraduates with need received aid; of those 7% had need fully met. **Average percent of need met:** 13% (excluding resources awarded to replace EFC). **Average financial aid package:** $10,559

# SOUTHEASTERN UNIVERSITY
### Lakeland, FL

**CONTACT** Ms. Carol B. Bradley, Director of Student Financial Services, Southeastern University, 1000 Longfellow Boulevard, Lakeland, FL 33801-6099, 863-667-5000 or toll-free 800-500-8760. Fax: 863-667-5200. E-mail: cbradley@seu.edu.
Website: http://www.seu.edu/.

# SOUTHEAST MISSOURI STATE UNIVERSITY
### Cape Girardeau, MO

| Tuition & fees (MO res): $6938 | Average undergraduate aid package: $8388 |
|---|---|

**ABOUT THE INSTITUTION** State-supported, coed. **Awards:** certificates, associate, bachelor's, and master's degrees. 70 undergraduate majors. **Total enrollment:** 12,087. Undergraduates: 10,848. Freshmen: 1,849. Both federal and institutional methodology are used as a basis for awarding need-based institutional aid.
**UNDERGRADUATE EXPENSES for 2015–2016 Application fee:** $30. **Tuition, state resident:** full-time $5927; part-time $197.55 per credit hour. **Tuition, nonresident:** full-time $11,259; part-time $375.30 per credit hour. **Required fees:** full-time $1011; $33.70 per credit hour. Full-time tuition and fees vary according to course load and location. Part-time tuition and fees vary according to course load and location. **College room and board:** $8432. Room and board charges vary according to board plan and housing facility.
**FRESHMAN FINANCIAL AID (Fall 2013)** 1,387 applied for aid; of those 76% were deemed to have need. 99% of freshmen with need received aid; of those 13% had need fully met. **Average percent of need met:** 59% (excluding resources awarded

to replace EFC). **Average financial aid package:** $8788 (excluding resources awarded to replace EFC). 22% of all full-time freshmen had no need and received non-need-based gift aid.

**UNDERGRADUATE FINANCIAL AID (Fall 2013)** 6,146 applied for aid; of those 80% were deemed to have need. 98% of undergraduates with need received aid; of those 12% had need fully met. **Average percent of need met:** 56% (excluding resources awarded to replace EFC). **Average financial aid package:** $8388 (excluding resources awarded to replace EFC). 17% of all full-time undergraduates had no need and received non-need-based gift aid.

**GIFT AID (NEED-BASED) Total amount:** $25,335,413 (59% federal, 11% state, 26% institutional, 4% external sources). **Receiving aid:** Freshmen: 63% (992); all full-time undergraduates: 54% (4,279). **Average award:** Freshmen: $6322; Undergraduates: $5365. **Scholarships, grants, and awards:** Federal Pell, FSEOG, state, private, college/university gift aid from institutional funds.

**GIFT AID (NON-NEED-BASED) Total amount:** $6,807,740 (1% federal, 5% state, 88% institutional, 6% external sources). **Receiving aid:** Freshmen: 6% (96). Undergraduates: 4% (283). **Average award:** Freshmen: $3970. Undergraduates: $3944. **Scholarships, grants, and awards by category:** Academic interests/achievement: 2,528 awards ($8,063,811 total): agriculture, biological sciences, business, communication, computer science, education, engineering/technologies, English, foreign languages, general academic interests/achievements, health fields, home economics, humanities, international studies, mathematics, military science, physical sciences, premedicine, religion/biblical studies, social sciences. Creative arts/performance: 322 awards ($336,428 total): music, performing arts, theater/drama. Special achievements/activities: 1,418 awards ($3,740,158 total): cheerleading/drum major, general special achievements/activities, leadership, memberships. Special characteristics: 1,129 awards ($3,061,080 total): children of faculty/staff, first-generation college students, general special characteristics, international students, members of minority groups, out-of-state students, previous college experience, veterans. **Tuition waivers:** Full or partial for employees or children of employees, senior citizens. **ROTC:** Air Force.

**LOANS Student loans:** $37,255,015 (75% need-based, 25% non-need-based). 65% of past graduating class borrowed through all loan programs. **Average indebtedness per student:** $26,508. **Average need-based loan:** Freshmen: $3235. Undergraduates: $4066. **Parent loans:** $5,500,127 (28% need-based, 72% non-need-based). **Programs:** Federal Direct (Subsidized and Unsubsidized Stafford, PLUS), Perkins.

**WORK-STUDY Federal work-study:** 219 jobs averaging $1556. **State or other work-study/employment:** 1,642 part-time jobs averaging $1935.

**ATHLETIC AWARDS** Total amount: $3,193,625 (44% need-based, 56% non-need-based).

**APPLYING FOR FINANCIAL AID Required financial aid form:** FAFSA. **Financial aid deadline (priority):** 3/1. **Notification date:** Continuous beginning 4/1. Students must reply within 3 weeks of notification.

**CONTACT** Ms. Karen Walker, Director of Financial Aid, Southeast Missouri State University, One University Plaza, Cape Girardeau, MO 63701, 573-651-2253. Fax: 573-986-6431. E-mail: sfs@semo.edu. Website: http://www.semo.edu/.

# SOUTHERN ADVENTIST UNIVERSITY
## Collegedale, TN

**CONTACT** Mr. Marc Grundy, Vice President of Enrollment Services, Southern Adventist University, PO Box 370, Collegedale, TN 37315-0370, 423-236-2875 or toll-free 800-768-8437. Fax: 423-236-1835.
Website: http://www.southern.edu/.

# SOUTHERN ARKANSAS UNIVERSITY–MAGNOLIA
## Magnolia, AR

**CONTACT** Ms. Bronwyn C. Sneed, Director of Student Aid, Southern Arkansas University–Magnolia, PO Box 9344, Magnolia, AR 71754-9344, 870-235-4023 or toll-free 800-332-7286. Fax: 870-235-4913. E-mail: bcsneed@saumag.edu. Website: http://www.saumag.edu/.

# SOUTHERN BAPTIST THEOLOGICAL SEMINARY
## Louisville, KY

**CONTACT** Mrs. Erin Joiner, Manager of Financial Aid, Southern Baptist Theological Seminary, 2825 Lexington Road, Louisville, KY 40280, 502-897-4206. Fax: 502-897-4031. E-mail: financialaid@sbts.edu.
Website: http://www.sbts.edu/.

# SOUTHERN CALIFORNIA INSTITUTE OF ARCHITECTURE
## Los Angeles, CA

| Tuition & fees: $2450 | Average undergraduate aid package: $18,567 |
|---|---|

**ABOUT THE INSTITUTION** Independent, coed. **Awards:** bachelor's and master's degrees. 1 undergraduate major. **Total enrollment:** 526. Undergraduates: 263. Freshmen: 33. Federal methodology is used as a basis for awarding need-based institutional aid.

**UNDERGRADUATE EXPENSES for 2015–2016 Application fee:** $85. **Tuition:** full-time . Full-time tuition and fees vary according to course load.

**FRESHMAN FINANCIAL AID (Fall 2014, est.)** 6 applied for aid; of those 100% were deemed to have need. 100% of freshmen with need received aid. **Average percent of need met:** 33% (excluding resources awarded to replace EFC). **Average financial aid package:** $20,942 (excluding resources awarded to replace EFC).

**UNDERGRADUATE FINANCIAL AID (Fall 2014, est.)** 110 applied for aid; of those 95% were deemed to have need. 100% of undergraduates with need received aid. **Average percent of need met:** 29% (excluding resources awarded to replace EFC). **Average financial aid package:** $18,567 (excluding resources awarded to replace EFC). 14% of all full-time undergraduates had no need and received non-need-based gift aid.

**GIFT AID (NEED-BASED) Total amount:** $1,487,380 (31% federal, 23% state, 43% institutional, 3% external sources). **Receiving aid:** Freshmen: 83% (5); all full-time undergraduates: 72% (89). **Average award:** Freshmen: $21,131; Undergraduates: $16,237. **Scholarships, grants, and awards:** Federal Pell, FSEOG, state, private, college/university gift aid from institutional funds.

**GIFT AID (NON-NEED-BASED) Total amount:** $298,850 (50% institutional, 50% external sources). **Average award:** Undergraduates: $8705. **Scholarships, grants, and awards by category:** Academic interests/achievement: architecture.

**LOANS Student loans:** $1,846,770 (96% need-based, 4% non-need-based). 87% of past graduating class borrowed through all loan programs. **Average indebtedness per student:** $39,287. **Average need-based loan:** Freshmen: $2800. Undergraduates: $4527. **Programs:** Federal Direct (Subsidized and Unsubsidized Stafford, PLUS), alternative loans.

**WORK-STUDY Federal work-study:** Total amount: $68,276; jobs available (averaging $3000). **State or other work-study/employment:** Part-time jobs available (averaging $3000).

**APPLYING FOR FINANCIAL AID Required financial aid forms:** FAFSA, institution's own form. **Financial aid deadline (priority):** 3/2. **Notification date:** 4/1. Students must reply within 4 weeks of notification.

**CONTACT** Marisela De La Torre, Financial Aid Counselor, Southern California Institute of Architecture, 960 East 3rd Street, Los Angeles, CA 90013, 213-613-2200 Ext. 376. Fax: 213-613-2260. E-mail: financialaid@sciarc.edu.
Website: http://www.sciarc.edu/.

# SOUTHERN CALIFORNIA INSTITUTE OF TECHNOLOGY

## Anaheim, CA

**CONTACT** Financial Aid Office, Southern California Institute of Technology, 525 North Muller Street, Anaheim, CA 92801, 714-520-5552.
*Website:* http://www.scitech.edu/.

# SOUTHERN CALIFORNIA SEMINARY

## El Cajon, CA

**CONTACT** Financial Aid Office, Southern California Seminary, 2075 East Madison Avenue, El Cajon, CA 92019, 619-442-9841 or toll-free 888-389-7244 (out-of-state).
*Website:* http://www.socalsem.edu/.

# SOUTHERN CONNECTICUT STATE UNIVERSITY

## New Haven, CT

| Tuition & fees (CT res): $9157 | Average undergraduate aid package: $13,602 |
|---|---|

**ABOUT THE INSTITUTION** State-supported, coed. *Awards:* certificates, bachelor's, master's, and doctoral degrees. 43 undergraduate majors. *Total enrollment:* 10,825. Undergraduates: 8,133. Freshmen: 1,286. Federal methodology is used as a basis for awarding need-based institutional aid.
**UNDERGRADUATE EXPENSES for 2015–2016 Application fee:** $50. *Tuition, state resident:* full-time $4600; part-time $457 per credit hour. *Tuition, nonresident:* full-time $14,886; part-time $471 per credit hour. *Required fees:* full-time $4557; $55 per term. Full-time tuition and fees vary according to course load and reciprocity agreements. Part-time tuition and fees vary according to course load. *College room and board:* $11,289; *Room only:* $6216. Room and board charges vary according to board plan and housing facility.
**FRESHMAN FINANCIAL AID (Fall 2014, est.)** 1,082 applied for aid; of those 84% were deemed to have need. 100% of freshmen with need received aid; of those 21% had need fully met. *Average percent of need met:* 70% (excluding resources awarded to replace EFC). *Average financial aid package:* $13,690 (excluding resources awarded to replace EFC). 5% of all full-time freshmen had no need and received non-need-based gift aid.
**UNDERGRADUATE FINANCIAL AID (Fall 2014, est.)** 5,465 applied for aid; of those 84% were deemed to have need. 100% of undergraduates with need received aid; of those 16% had need fully met. *Average percent of need met:* 69% (excluding resources awarded to replace EFC). *Average financial aid package:* $13,602 (excluding resources awarded to replace EFC). 4% of all full-time undergraduates had no need and received non-need-based gift aid.
**GIFT AID (NEED-BASED) Total amount:** $22,856,951 (60% federal, 13% state, 26% institutional, 1% external sources). *Receiving aid:* Freshmen: 54% (684); all full-time undergraduates: 48% (3,277). *Average award:* Freshmen: $6098; Undergraduates: $6592. *Scholarships, grants, and awards:* Federal Pell, FSEOG, state, private, college/university gift aid from institutional funds.
**GIFT AID (NON-NEED-BASED) Total amount:** $3,515,632 (1% federal, 18% state, 49% institutional, 32% external sources). *Receiving aid:* Freshmen: 18% (235). Undergraduates: 11% (746). *Average award:* Freshmen: $4801. Undergraduates: $5796. *Scholarships, grants, and awards by category: Special characteristics:* children of faculty/staff, veterans. *Tuition waivers:* Full or partial for employees or children of employees, senior citizens. *ROTC:* Army cooperative, Air Force cooperative.
**LOANS Student loans:** $40,610,378 (51% need-based, 49% non-need-based). 78% of past graduating class borrowed through all loan programs. *Average indebtedness per student:* $23,781. *Average need-based loan:* Freshmen: $5620. Undergraduates: $4829. *Parent loans:* $10,104,595 (100% non-need-based). *Programs:* Federal Direct (Subsidized and Unsubsidized Stafford, PLUS), Perkins.
**WORK-STUDY Federal work-study:** Total amount: $447,196; 128 jobs averaging $3420. *State or other work-study/employment:* Part-time jobs available.

**ATHLETIC AWARDS** Total amount: $1,642,419 (100% non-need-based).
**APPLYING FOR FINANCIAL AID Required financial aid form:** FAFSA. *Financial aid deadline:* 3/9 (priority: 3/5). *Notification date:* Continuous beginning 4/11. Students must reply within 2 weeks of notification.
**CONTACT** Mrs. Gloria Lee, Director of Financial Aid, Southern Connecticut State University, Wintergreen Building, New Haven, CT 06515-1355, 203-392-5445. *Fax:* 203-392-5229. *E-mail:* leeg1@southernct.edu.
*Website:* http://www.southernct.edu/.

# SOUTHERN ILLINOIS UNIVERSITY CARBONDALE

## Carbondale, IL

| Tuition & fees (IL res): $12,248 | Average undergraduate aid package: $14,366 |
|---|---|

**ABOUT THE INSTITUTION** State-supported, coed. *Awards:* certificates, associate, bachelor's, master's, and doctoral degrees. 85 undergraduate majors. *Total enrollment:* 17,989. Undergraduates: 13,461. Freshmen: 2,775. Federal methodology is used as a basis for awarding need-based institutional aid.
**UNDERGRADUATE EXPENSES for 2015–2016 Application fee:** $40. *Tuition, state resident:* full-time $8415; part-time $281 per credit hour. *Tuition, nonresident:* full-time $21,038; part-time $701 per credit hour. *Required fees:* full-time $3833; $172 per credit hour. Full-time tuition and fees vary according to course load, program, reciprocity agreements, and student level. Part-time tuition and fees vary according to course load, program, reciprocity agreements, and student level. *College room and board:* $9694. Room and board charges vary according to board plan and housing facility. *Payment plan:* Guaranteed tuition.
**FRESHMAN FINANCIAL AID (Fall 2014, est.)** 2,550 applied for aid; of those 83% were deemed to have need. 99% of freshmen with need received aid; of those 8% had need fully met. *Average percent of need met:* 61% (excluding resources awarded to replace EFC). *Average financial aid package:* $16,057 (excluding resources awarded to replace EFC). 9% of all full-time freshmen had no need and received non-need-based gift aid.
**UNDERGRADUATE FINANCIAL AID (Fall 2014, est.)** 9,681 applied for aid; of those 86% were deemed to have need. 99% of undergraduates with need received aid; of those 6% had need fully met. *Average percent of need met:* 60% (excluding resources awarded to replace EFC). *Average financial aid package:* $14,366 (excluding resources awarded to replace EFC). 4% of all full-time undergraduates had no need and received non-need-based gift aid.
**GIFT AID (NEED-BASED) Total amount:** $58,444,974 (49% federal, 29% state, 18% institutional, 4% external sources). *Receiving aid:* Freshmen: 55% (1,478); all full-time undergraduates: 49% (5,641). *Average award:* Freshmen: $8592; Undergraduates: $7931. *Scholarships, grants, and awards:* Federal Pell, FSEOG, state, private, college/university gift aid from institutional funds.
**GIFT AID (NON-NEED-BASED) Total amount:** $11,702,435 (9% federal, 1% state, 39% institutional, 51% external sources). *Receiving aid:* Freshmen: 31% (825). Undergraduates: 20% (2,360). *Average award:* Freshmen: $6455. Undergraduates: $6057. *Scholarships, grants, and awards by category: Academic interests/achievement:* agriculture, architecture, area/ethnic studies, biological sciences, business, communication, computer science, education, engineering/technologies, English, foreign languages, general academic interests/achievements, health fields, home economics, humanities, international studies, mathematics, military science, physical sciences, premedicine, religion/biblical studies, social sciences. *Creative arts/performance:* applied art and design, art/fine arts, cinema/film/broadcasting, creative writing, dance, debating, general creative arts/performance, journalism/publications, music, performing arts, theater/drama. *Special achievements/activities:* cheerleading/drum major, community service, general special achievements/activities, leadership. *Special characteristics:* children and siblings of alumni, children of educators, children of faculty/staff, children of public servants, children with a deceased or disabled parent, first-generation college students, general special characteristics, handicapped students, international students, local/state students, members of minority groups, public servants, spouses of deceased or disabled public servants, veterans, veterans' children. *Tuition waivers:* Full or partial for children of alumni, employees or children of employees, senior citizens. *ROTC:* Army, Air Force.
**LOANS Student loans:** $71,067,146 (79% need-based, 21% non-need-based). 70% of past graduating class borrowed through all loan programs. *Average indebtedness*

per student: $30,138. **Average need-based loan:** Freshmen: $3351. Undergraduates: $4368. **Parent loans:** $7,855,443 (28% need-based, 72% non-need-based).
**Programs:** Federal Direct (Subsidized and Unsubsidized Stafford, PLUS), Perkins.
**WORK-STUDY** *Federal work-study:* Total amount: $2,174,996; 1,633 jobs averaging $1165.
**ATHLETIC AWARDS** Total amount: $3,193,086 (42% need-based, 58% non-need-based).
**APPLYING FOR FINANCIAL AID** *Required financial aid form:* FAFSA. *Financial aid deadline (priority):* 3/1. *Notification date:* Continuous beginning 3/15.
**CONTACT** Terri R. Harfst, Director of Financial Aid, Southern Illinois University Carbondale, Student Services Building, 1263 Lincoln Drive, 2nd Floor, Carbondale, IL 62901-4702, 618-453-3102. *Fax:* 618-453-4606. *E-mail:* fao@siu.edu.
*Website:* http://www.siuc.edu/.

# SOUTHERN ILLINOIS UNIVERSITY EDWARDSVILLE
## Edwardsville, IL

| Tuition & fees (IL res): $9738 | Average undergraduate aid package: $11,179 |
|---|---|

**ABOUT THE INSTITUTION** State-supported, coed. **Awards:** certificates, bachelor's, master's, and doctoral degrees. 42 undergraduate majors. **Total enrollment:** 13,972. Undergraduates: 11,421. Freshmen: 2,126. Federal methodology is used as a basis for awarding need-based institutional aid.
**UNDERGRADUATE EXPENSES for 2015–2016 Application fee:** $30. Tuition, state resident: full-time $7296; part-time $243.20 per credit hour. Tuition, nonresident: full-time $18,240; part-time $608 per credit hour. **Required fees:** full-time $2442; $872 per term. Full-time tuition and fees vary according to course load. Part-time tuition and fees vary according to course load. **College room and board:** $8781. Room and board charges vary according to board plan and housing facility. **Payment plan:** Guaranteed tuition.
**FRESHMAN FINANCIAL AID (Fall 2013)** 1,825 applied for aid; of those 81% were deemed to have need. 98% of freshmen with need received aid; of those 24% had need fully met. **Average percent of need met:** 56% (excluding resources awarded to replace EFC). **Average financial aid package:** $11,911 (excluding resources awarded to replace EFC). 1% of all full-time freshmen had no need and received non-need-based gift aid.
**UNDERGRADUATE FINANCIAL AID (Fall 2013)** 7,968 applied for aid; of those 84% were deemed to have need. 97% of undergraduates with need received aid; of those 23% had need fully met. **Average percent of need met:** 53% (excluding resources awarded to replace EFC). **Average financial aid package:** $11,179 (excluding resources awarded to replace EFC). 1% of all full-time undergraduates had no need and received non-need-based gift aid.
**GIFT AID (NEED-BASED) Total amount:** $34,453,488 (56% federal, 28% state, 13% institutional, 3% external sources). **Receiving aid:** Freshmen: 62% (1,197); all full-time undergraduates: 48% (4,606). **Average award:** Freshmen: $8373; Undergraduates: $8502. **Scholarships, grants, and awards:** Federal Pell, FSEOG, state, private, college/university gift aid from institutional funds, Federal Nursing.
**GIFT AID (NON-NEED-BASED) Total amount:** $4,261,266 (23% federal, 22% state, 45% institutional, 10% external sources). **Receiving aid:** Freshmen: 36% (704). Undergraduates: 19% (1,807). **Average award:** Freshmen: $10,082. Undergraduates: $6712. **Scholarships, grants, and awards by category:** Academic interests/achievement: business, education, general academic interests/achievements, health fields. Creative arts/performance: art/fine arts, dance, music, theater/drama. Special characteristics: children of faculty/staff. **Tuition waivers:** Full or partial for employees or children of employees, senior citizens. **ROTC:** Army, Air Force cooperative.
**LOANS Student loans:** $45,041,187 (82% need-based, 18% non-need-based). 52% of past graduating class borrowed through all loan programs. *Average indebtedness per student:* $27,681. **Average need-based loan:** Freshmen: $3477. Undergraduates: $4346. **Parent loans:** $20,592,761 (29% need-based, 71% non-need-based).
**Programs:** Federal Direct (Subsidized and Unsubsidized Stafford, PLUS), Perkins, Federal Nursing, college/university, alternative loans.

**WORK-STUDY** *Federal work-study:* jobs available. **State or other work-study/employment:** Total amount: $51,370,472 (82% need-based, 18% non-need-based). Part-time jobs available.
**ATHLETIC AWARDS** Total amount: $836,544 (45% need-based, 55% non-need-based).
**APPLYING FOR FINANCIAL AID** *Required financial aid form:* FAFSA. *Financial aid deadline (priority):* 3/1. *Notification date:* Continuous beginning 3/15. Students must reply within 2 weeks of notification.
**CONTACT** Sally Mullen, Acting Director of Financial Aid, Southern Illinois University Edwardsville, Campus Box 1060, Edwardsville, IL 62026-1060, 618-650-3834 or toll-free 800-447-SIUE. *Fax:* 618-650-3885. *E-mail:* smullen@siue.edu.
*Website:* http://www.siue.edu/.

# SOUTHERN METHODIST UNIVERSITY
## Dallas, TX

| Tuition & fees: $48,190 | Average undergraduate aid package: $37,976 |
|---|---|

**ABOUT THE INSTITUTION** Independent United Methodist Church, coed. **Awards:** certificates, bachelor's, master's, and doctoral degrees. 66 undergraduate majors. **Total enrollment:** 11,272. Undergraduates: 6,391. Freshmen: 1,459. Both federal and institutional methodology are used as a basis for awarding need-based institutional aid.
**UNDERGRADUATE EXPENSES for 2015–2016 Application fee:** $60. **Comprehensive fee:** $63,765 includes full-time tuition ($42,770), mandatory fees ($5420), and room and board ($15,575). Room and board charges vary according to board plan and housing facility. **Part-time tuition:** $1787 per credit hour. Part-time tuition and fees vary according to course load. **Payment plan:** Tuition prepayment.
**FRESHMAN FINANCIAL AID (Fall 2014, est.)** 696 applied for aid; of those 73% were deemed to have need. 99% of freshmen with need received aid; of those 41% had need fully met. **Average percent of need met:** 88% (excluding resources awarded to replace EFC). **Average financial aid package:** $38,600 (excluding resources awarded to replace EFC). 37% of all full-time freshmen had no need and received non-need-based gift aid.
**UNDERGRADUATE FINANCIAL AID (Fall 2014, est.)** 2,659 applied for aid; of those 84% were deemed to have need. 99% of undergraduates with need received aid; of those 32% had need fully met. **Average percent of need met:** 86% (excluding resources awarded to replace EFC). **Average financial aid package:** $37,976 (excluding resources awarded to replace EFC). 33% of all full-time undergraduates had no need and received non-need-based gift aid.
**GIFT AID (NEED-BASED) Total amount:** $59,746,063 (8% federal, 5% state, 86% institutional, 1% external sources). **Receiving aid:** Freshmen: 24% (347); all full-time undergraduates: 27% (1,680). **Average award:** Freshmen: $19,444; Undergraduates: $19,674. **Scholarships, grants, and awards:** Federal Pell, FSEOG, state, private, college/university gift aid from institutional funds.
**GIFT AID (NON-NEED-BASED) Total amount:** $37,221,493 (97% institutional, 3% external sources). **Receiving aid:** Freshmen: 26% (379). Undergraduates: 23% (1,430). **Average award:** Freshmen: $19,568. Undergraduates: $20,479. **Tuition waivers:** Full or partial for employees or children of employees. **ROTC:** Army, Air Force cooperative.
**LOANS Student loans:** $23,860,596 (56% need-based, 44% non-need-based). 42% of past graduating class borrowed through all loan programs. *Average indebtedness per student:* $34,671. **Average need-based loan:** Freshmen: $3265. Undergraduates: $4373. **Parent loans:** $11,636,791 (27% need-based, 73% non-need-based).
**Programs:** Federal Direct (Subsidized and Unsubsidized Stafford, PLUS), Perkins, state, college/university.
**WORK-STUDY** *Federal work-study:* Total amount: $5,768,471; jobs available. **State or other work-study/employment:** Total amount: $33,989 (14% need-based, 86% non-need-based). Part-time jobs available.
**ATHLETIC AWARDS** Total amount: $14,034,243 (37% need-based, 63% non-need-based).
**APPLYING FOR FINANCIAL AID** *Required financial aid forms:* FAFSA, CSS Financial Aid PROFILE, noncustodial (divorced/separated) parent's statement. *Financial aid deadline (priority):* 2/15. *Notification date:* Continuous beginning 4/1. Students must reply within 3 weeks of notification.

**CONTACT** Marc Peterson, Director of Financial Aid, Southern Methodist University, PO Box 750181, Dallas, TX 75275, 214-768-3417 or toll-free 800-323-0672. *Fax:* 214-768-3878. *E-mail:* enrol_serv@smu.edu. *Website:* http://www.smu.edu/.

# SOUTHERN NAZARENE UNIVERSITY
## Bethany, OK

**CONTACT** Diana Lee, Director of Financial Assistance, Southern Nazarene University, 6729 Northwest 39th Expressway, Bethany, OK 73008, 405-491-6310 or toll-free 800-648-9899. *Fax:* 405-717-6271. *E-mail:* dlee@snu.edu. *Website:* http://www.snu.edu/.

# SOUTHERN NEW HAMPSHIRE UNIVERSITY
## Manchester, NH

**CONTACT** Financial Aid Office, Southern New Hampshire University, 2500 North River Road, Manchester, NH 03106, 603-645-9645 or toll-free 888-327-7648. *Fax:* 603-645-9639. *E-mail:* finaid@snhu.edu. *Website:* http://www.snhu.edu/.

# SOUTHERN OREGON UNIVERSITY
## Ashland, OR

| Tuition & fees (OR res): $7720 | Average undergraduate aid package: $9483 |
|---|---|

**ABOUT THE INSTITUTION** State-supported, coed. *Awards:* certificates, bachelor's, and master's degrees. 38 undergraduate majors. *Total enrollment:* 5,913. Undergraduates: 5,247. Freshmen: 629. Federal methodology is used as a basis for awarding need-based institutional aid.

**UNDERGRADUATE EXPENSES for 2015–2016** *Application fee:* $50. *Tuition, state resident:* full-time $6307; part-time $140.15 per credit hour. *Tuition, nonresident:* full-time $19,883; part-time $441.84 per credit hour. *Required fees:* full-time $1413; $56 per credit hour Full-time tuition and fees vary according to course load, program, and reciprocity agreements. Part-time tuition and fees vary according to course load, program, and reciprocity agreements. *College room and board:* $11,397; *Room only:* $6402. Room and board charges vary according to board plan and housing facility.

**FRESHMAN FINANCIAL AID (Fall 2013)** 571 applied for aid; of those 78% were deemed to have need. 99% of freshmen with need received aid; of those 9% had need fully met. *Average percent of need met:* 52% (excluding resources awarded to replace EFC). *Average financial aid package:* $8560 (excluding resources awarded to replace EFC). 2% of all full-time freshmen had no need and received non-need-based gift aid.

**UNDERGRADUATE FINANCIAL AID (Fall 2013)** 3,263 applied for aid; of those 87% were deemed to have need. 98% of undergraduates with need received aid; of those 7% had need fully met. *Average percent of need met:* 52% (excluding resources awarded to replace EFC). *Average financial aid package:* $9483 (excluding resources awarded to replace EFC). 2% of all full-time undergraduates had no need and received non-need-based gift aid.

**GIFT AID (NEED-BASED)** *Total amount:* $13,173,231 (73% federal, 12% state, 5% institutional, 10% external sources). *Receiving aid:* Freshmen: 59% (373); all full-time undergraduates: 70% (2,410). *Average award:* Freshmen: $6728; Undergraduates: $6262. *Scholarships, grants, and awards:* Federal Pell, FSEOG, state, private, college/university gift aid from institutional funds.

**GIFT AID (NON-NEED-BASED)** *Total amount:* $465,289 (1% federal, 3% state, 39% institutional, 57% external sources). *Receiving aid:* Freshmen: 4% (26). Undergraduates: 2% (78). *Average award:* Freshmen: $3560. Undergraduates: $2088. *Scholarships, grants, and awards by category:* Academic interests/achievement: 632 awards ($797,870 total): biological sciences, business, education, English, foreign languages, general academic interests/achievements, health fields, mathematics, physical sciences, social sciences. *Creative arts/performance:* 135 awards ($135,647 total): art/fine arts, creative writing, journalism/publications, music, theater/drama. *Special achievements/activities:* 14 awards ($16,365 total): community service, general special achievements/activities, hobbies/interests, leadership, memberships. *Special characteristics:* 97 awards ($413,821 total): adult students, international students, members of minority groups. *Tuition waivers:* Full or partial for employees or children of employees, senior citizens. *ROTC:* Army.

**LOANS** *Student loans:* $25,792,375 (85% need-based, 15% non-need-based). 88% of past graduating class borrowed through all loan programs. *Average indebtedness per student:* $30,936. *Average need-based loan:* Freshmen: $3047. Undergraduates: $4264. *Parent loans:* $14,472,414 (36% need-based, 64% non-need-based). *Programs:* Federal Direct (Subsidized and Unsubsidized Stafford, PLUS), Perkins, college/university.

**WORK-STUDY** *Federal work-study:* 240 jobs averaging $2006.

**ATHLETIC AWARDS** Total amount: $511,987 (61% need-based, 39% non-need-based).

**APPLYING FOR FINANCIAL AID** *Required financial aid form:* FAFSA. *Financial aid deadline (priority):* 3/1. *Notification date:* Continuous beginning 3/2. Students must reply within 4 weeks of notification.

**CONTACT** Enrollment Services Center, Southern Oregon University, 1250 Siskiyou Boulevard, Ashland, OR 97520, 541-552-6600 or toll-free 855-470-3377 (out-of-state). *Fax:* 541-552-6614. *E-mail:* esc@sou.edu. *Website:* http://www.sou.edu/.

# SOUTHERN POLYTECHNIC STATE UNIVERSITY
## Marietta, GA

**CONTACT** Mr. Gary L. Mann, Director of Financial Aid, Southern Polytechnic State University, 1100 South Marietta Parkway, Marietta, GA 30060-2896, 678-915-7290 or toll-free 800-635-3204. *Fax:* 678 915 4227. *E-mail:* gmann@spsu.edu. *Website:* http://www.spsu.edu/.

# SOUTHERN TECHNICAL COLLEGE
## Fort Myers, FL

**CONTACT** Financial Aid Office, Southern Technical College, 1685 Medical Lane, Fort Myers, FL 33907, 239-939-4766 or toll-free 877 347 5492. *Website:* http://www.southerntech.edu/locations/ft-myers/.

# SOUTHERN UNIVERSITY AND AGRICULTURAL AND MECHANICAL COLLEGE
## Baton Rouge, LA

**CONTACT** Mr. Phillip Rodgers Sr., Director of Financial Aid, Southern University and Agricultural and Mechanical College, PO Box 9961, Baton Rouge, LA 70813, 225-771-2790. *Fax:* 225-771-5898. *E-mail:* phillip_rodgers@cxs.subr.edu. *Website:* http://www.subr.edu/.

# SOUTHERN UNIVERSITY AT NEW ORLEANS
## New Orleans, LA

**ABOUT THE INSTITUTION** State-supported, coed, primarily women. 16 undergraduate majors.

**GIFT AID (NEED-BASED)** *Scholarships, grants, and awards:* Federal Pell, FSEOG, state, private, college/university gift aid from institutional funds.

**GIFT AID (NON-NEED-BASED)** *Scholarships, grants, and awards by category: Academic interests/achievement:* area/ethnic studies, biological sciences, business, communication, education, engineering/technologies, general academic interests/achievements, humanities, international studies, library science, mathematics, physical sciences, social sciences. *Creative arts/performance:* music. *Special achievements/activities:* leadership, memberships. *Special characteristics:* first-generation college students.

**LOANS** *Programs:* Federal Direct (Subsidized and Unsubsidized Stafford, PLUS).

**APPLYING FOR FINANCIAL AID** *Required financial aid form:* FAFSA.

**CONTACT** La'Charlotte C. Garrett, Director of Financial Aid, Southern University at New Orleans, 6400 Press Drive, New Orleans, LA 70126, 504-286-5435. *Fax:* 504-286-5213. *E-mail:* lgarrett@suno.edu.
*Website:* http://www.suno.edu/.

# SOUTHERN UTAH UNIVERSITY
## Cedar City, UT

| Tuition & fees (UT res): $6138 | Average undergraduate aid package: $8272 |
|---|---|

**ABOUT THE INSTITUTION** State-supported, coed. **Awards:** certificates, diplomas, associate, bachelor's, and master's degrees. 66 undergraduate majors. **Total enrollment:** 7,656. Undergraduates: 6,953. Freshmen: 1,198. Federal methodology is used as a basis for awarding need-based institutional aid.

**UNDERGRADUATE EXPENSES for 2015–2016** *Application fee:* $50. *Tuition, state resident:* full-time $5416; part-time $254 per credit hour. *Tuition, nonresident:* full-time $17,874; part-time $842 per credit hour. *Required fees:* full-time $722; $361 per term. Full-time tuition and fees vary according to program. Part-time tuition and fees vary according to course load and program. *Room only:* $3100. Room and board charges vary according to board plan and housing facility.

**FRESHMAN FINANCIAL AID (Fall 2013)** 857 applied for aid; of those 86% were deemed to have need. 98% of freshmen with need received aid; of those 9% had need fully met. *Average percent of need met:* 46% (excluding resources awarded to replace EFC). *Average financial aid package:* $8630 (excluding resources awarded to replace EFC). 27% of all full-time freshmen had no need and received non-need-based gift aid.

**UNDERGRADUATE FINANCIAL AID (Fall 2013)** 3,667 applied for aid; of those 90% were deemed to have need. 98% of undergraduates with need received aid; of those 5% had need fully met. *Average percent of need met:* 45% (excluding resources awarded to replace EFC). *Average financial aid package:* $8272 (excluding resources awarded to replace EFC). 16% of all full-time undergraduates had no need and received non-need-based gift aid.

**GIFT AID (NEED-BASED)** *Total amount:* $12,691,284 (98% federal, 1% state, 1% external sources). *Receiving aid:* Freshmen: 59% (716); all full-time undergraduates: 64% (3,215). *Average award:* Freshmen: $7344; Undergraduates: $6413. *Scholarships, grants, and awards:* Federal Pell, FSEOG, state, private, college/university gift aid from institutional funds.

**GIFT AID (NON-NEED-BASED)** *Total amount:* $9,971,588 (4% state, 87% institutional, 9% external sources). *Receiving aid:* Freshmen: 23% (274). Undergraduates: 12% (593). *Average award:* Freshmen: $5031. Undergraduates: $4704. *Scholarships, grants, and awards by category: Academic interests/achievement:* general academic interests/achievements. *Creative arts/performance:* art/fine arts, music, theater/drama. *Special achievements/activities:* general special achievements/activities, leadership. *Special characteristics:* children and siblings of alumni, local/state students, members of minority groups. *Tuition waivers:* Full or partial for children of alumni, employees or children of employees, senior citizens. *ROTC:* Army.

**LOANS** *Student loans:* $18,713,494 (48% need-based, 52% non-need-based). 53% of past graduating class borrowed through all loan programs. *Average indebtedness per student:* $14,978. *Average need-based loan:* Freshmen: $3125. Undergraduates: $3843. *Parent loans:* $933,990 (100% non-need-based). *Programs:* Federal Direct (Subsidized and Unsubsidized Stafford, PLUS), Perkins.

**WORK-STUDY** *Federal work-study:* jobs available. *State or other work-study/employment:* Total amount: $90,137 (100% need-based). Part-time jobs available.

**ATHLETIC AWARDS** Total amount: $2,708,200 (100% non-need-based).

**APPLYING FOR FINANCIAL AID** *Required financial aid form:* FAFSA. *Financial aid deadline (priority):* 12/1. *Notification date:* Continuous beginning 11/1. Students must reply by 5/1.

**CONTACT** Jan Carey-McDonald, Director of Financial Aid and Scholarships, Southern Utah University, 351 West University Boulevard, Cedar City, UT 84720-2498, 435-586-7735. *Fax:* 435-586-7736. *E-mail:* careymcdonald@suu.edu. *Website:* http://www.suu.edu/.

# SOUTHERN VERMONT COLLEGE
## Bennington, VT

**ABOUT THE INSTITUTION** Independent, coed. **Awards:** certificates, associate, and bachelor's degrees. 14 undergraduate majors. **Total enrollment:** 457. Undergraduates: 455. Freshmen: 90.

**GIFT AID (NEED-BASED)** *Scholarships, grants, and awards:* Federal Pell, FSEOG, state, private, college/university gift aid from institutional funds.

**GIFT AID (NON-NEED-BASED)** *Scholarships, grants, and awards by category: Academic interests/achievement:* general academic interests/achievements. *Special achievements/activities:* community service, leadership.

**LOANS** *Programs:* Federal Direct (Subsidized and Unsubsidized Stafford, PLUS).

**WORK-STUDY** *Federal work-study:* 91 jobs averaging $849.

**APPLYING FOR FINANCIAL AID** *Required financial aid forms:* FAFSA, institution's own form.

**CONTACT** Susan Rochette, Director of Student Financial Services, Southern Vermont College, 982 Mansion Drive, Bennington, VT 05201, 802-447-6339. *Fax:* 802-447-6329. *E-mail:* financialaid@svc.edu.
*Website:* http://www.svc.edu/.

# SOUTHERN VIRGINIA UNIVERSITY
## Buena Vista, VA

**CONTACT** Darin Hassell, Financial Aid Specialist, Southern Virginia University, One University Hill Drive, Buena Vista, VA 24416, 540-261-4351 or toll-free 800-229-8420. *Fax:* 540-261-8559. *E-mail:* finaid@svu.edu.
*Website:* http://www.svu.edu/.

# SOUTHERN WESLEYAN UNIVERSITY
## Central, SC

**ABOUT THE INSTITUTION** Independent Wesleyan Church, coed. 35 undergraduate majors.

**GIFT AID (NEED-BASED)** *Scholarships, grants, and awards:* Federal Pell, FSEOG, state, private, college/university gift aid from institutional funds.

**GIFT AID (NON-NEED-BASED)** *Scholarships, grants, and awards by category: Academic interests/achievement:* biological sciences, business, computer science, education, English, general academic interests/achievements, humanities, mathematics, physical sciences, premedicine, religion/biblical studies, social sciences. *Creative arts/performance:* art/fine arts, creative writing, journalism/publications, music, theater/drama. *Special achievements/activities:* community service, leadership, religious involvement. *Special characteristics:* children of faculty/staff, ethnic background, members of minority groups, relatives of clergy, religious affiliation.

**LOANS** *Programs:* Federal Direct (Subsidized and Unsubsidized Stafford, PLUS), Perkins, state.

**APPLYING FOR FINANCIAL AID** *Required financial aid forms:* FAFSA, state aid form.

**CONTACT** Mrs. Amanda Stewart, Financial Aid Associate, Southern Wesleyan University, 907 Wesleyan Drive, Central, SC 29630-1020, 800-289-8798 Ext. 5517 or toll-free 800-CU-AT-SWU. *Fax:* 864-644-5970. *E-mail:* finaid@swu.edu.
*Website:* http://www.swu.edu/.

# SOUTH FLORIDA BIBLE COLLEGE AND THEOLOGICAL SEMINARY
## Deerfield Beach, FL

**CONTACT** Financial Aid Office, South Florida Bible College and Theological Seminary, 1100 South Federal Highway, Deerfield Beach, FL 33441, 954-428-8980. *Website:* http://www.sfbc.edu/.

# SOUTH UNIVERSITY
## Montgomery, AL

**CONTACT** Financial Aid Office, South University, 5355 Vaughn Road, Montgomery, AL 36116-1120, 334-395-8800 or toll-free 866-629-2962. *Website:* http://www.southuniversity.edu/montgomery/.

# SOUTH UNIVERSITY
## Royal Palm Beach, FL

Financial Aid Office, South University, University Centre, 9801 Belvedere Road, Royal Palm Beach, FL 33411, 561-697-9200 or toll-free 866-629-2902.

# SOUTH UNIVERSITY
## Tampa, FL

**CONTACT** Financial Aid Office, South University, 4401 North Himes Avenue, Suite 175, Tampa, FL 33614, 813-393-3800 or toll-free 800-846-1472. *Website:* http://www.southuniversity.edu/tampa/.

# SOUTH UNIVERSITY
## Savannah, GA

**CONTACT** Financial Aid Office, South University, 709 Mall Boulevard, Savannah, GA 31406, 912-201-8000 or toll-free 866-629-2901. *Website:* http://www.southuniversity.edu/savannah/.

# SOUTH UNIVERSITY
## Novi, MI

**CONTACT** Financial Aid Office, South University, 41555 Twelve Mile Road, Novi, MI 48377, 248-675-0200 or toll-free 877-693-2085. *Website:* http://www.southuniversity.edu/novi.aspx.

# SOUTH UNIVERSITY
## High Point, NC

**CONTACT** Financial Aid Office, South University, 3975 Premier Drive, High Point, NC 27265, 336-812-7200 or toll-free 855-268-2187. *Website:* http://www.southuniversity.edu/high-point.aspx.

# SOUTH UNIVERSITY
## Cleveland, OH

**CONTACT** Financial Aid Office, South University, 4743 Richmond Road, Cleveland, OH 44128, 216-755-5000 or toll-free 855-398-9280. *Website:* http://www.southuniversity.edu/cleveland.aspx.

# SOUTH UNIVERSITY
## Columbia, SC

**CONTACT** Financial Aid Office, South University, 9 Science Court, Columbia, SC 29203, 803-799-9082 or toll-free 866-629-3031. *Website:* http://www.southuniversity.edu/columbia/.

# SOUTH UNIVERSITY
## Austin, TX

**CONTACT** Financial Aid Office, South University, 7700 West Parmer Lane, Building A, Suite A100, Austin, TX 78729, 512-516-8800 or toll-free 877-659-5706. *Website:* http://www.southuniversity.edu/austin.aspx.

# SOUTH UNIVERSITY
## Glen Allen, VA

**CONTACT** Financial Aid Office, South University, 2151 Old Brick Road, Glen Allen, VA 23060, 804-727-6800 or toll-free 888-422-5076. *Website:* http://www.southuniversity.edu/richmond.

# SOUTH UNIVERSITY
## Virginia Beach, VA

**CONTACT** Financial Aid Office, South University, 301 Bendix Road, Suite 100, Virginia Beach, VA 23452, 757-493-6900 or toll-free 877-206-1845. *Website:* http://www.southuniversity.edu/virginia-beach.

# SOUTHWEST BAPTIST UNIVERSITY
## Bolivar, MO

| Tuition & fees: $20,840 | Average undergraduate aid package: $16,305 |
|---|---|

**ABOUT THE INSTITUTION** Independent Southern Baptist, coed. *Awards:* certificates, associate, bachelor's, master's, and doctoral degrees. 56 undergraduate majors. *Total enrollment:* 3,696. Undergraduates: 2,952. Freshmen: 439. Federal methodology is used as a basis for awarding need-based institutional aid.

**UNDERGRADUATE EXPENSES for 2015–2016** *Application fee:* $30. *Comprehensive fee:* $27,640 includes full-time tuition ($20,000), mandatory fees ($840), and room and board ($6800). *College room only:* $3300. Full-time tuition and fees vary according to course load and location. Room and board charges vary according to board plan and housing facility. *Part-time tuition:* $775 per credit hour. *Part-time fees:* $145 per term. Part-time tuition and fees vary according to course load and location.

**FRESHMAN FINANCIAL AID (Fall 2014, est.)** 401 applied for aid; of those 90% were deemed to have need. 99% of freshmen with need received aid; of those 27% had need fully met. *Average percent of need met:* 78% (excluding resources awarded to replace EFC). *Average financial aid package:* $19,540 (excluding resources awarded to replace EFC). 15% of all full-time freshmen had no need and received non-need-based gift aid.

**UNDERGRADUATE FINANCIAL AID (Fall 2014, est.)** 1,748 applied for aid; of those 91% were deemed to have need. 99% of undergraduates with need received aid; of those 17% had need fully met. *Average percent of need met:* 68% (excluding resources awarded to replace EFC). *Average financial aid package:* $16,305 (excluding resources awarded to replace EFC). 15% of all full-time undergraduates had no need and received non-need-based gift aid.

**GIFT AID (NEED-BASED)** *Total amount:* $7,194,720 (69% federal, 14% state, 17% institutional). *Receiving aid:* Freshmen: 60% (256); all full-time undergraduates: 57% (1,150). *Average award:* Freshmen: $4682; Undergraduates: $4885. *Scholarships, grants, and awards:* Federal Pell, FSEOG, state, private, college/university gift aid from institutional funds.

**GIFT AID (NON-NEED-BASED)** *Total amount:* $14,532,236 (5% state, 90% institutional, 5% external sources). *Receiving aid:* Freshmen: 77% (330). Undergraduates: 61% (1,229). *Average award:* Freshmen: $11,872. Undergraduates: $9934. *Scholarships, grants, and awards by category: Academic interests/achievement:* 1,716 awards ($10,946,099 total): general academic interests/achievements. *Creative arts/performance:* 140 awards ($304,047 total): art/fine arts, debating, general creative arts/performance, music, theater/drama. *Special achievements/activities:* 141 awards ($276,000 total): religious involvement. *Special characteristics:* 292 awards ($188,700 total): general special characteristics, local/state students, relatives of clergy, religious affiliation. *Tuition waivers:* Full or partial for employees or children of employees. *ROTC:* Army cooperative.

**LOANS** *Student loans:* $12,186,659 (49% need-based, 51% non-need-based). 77% of past graduating class borrowed through all loan programs. *Average indebtedness per student:* $26,615. *Average need-based loan:* Freshmen: $3869. Undergraduates: $4367. *Parent loans:* $883,719 (100% non-need-based). *Programs:* Federal Direct (Subsidized and Unsubsidized Stafford, PLUS), Perkins, Federal Nursing, state, alternative loans.

**WORK-STUDY** *Federal work-study:* Total amount: $717,600; 382 jobs averaging $1878.

**ATHLETIC AWARDS** Total amount: $2,764,064 (100% non-need-based).

**APPLYING FOR FINANCIAL AID** *Required financial aid forms:* FAFSA, institution's own form. *Financial aid deadline (priority):* 3/15. *Notification date:* Continuous beginning 3/1. Students must reply within 2 weeks of notification.

**CONTACT** Mr. Brad Gamble, Director of Financial Aid, Southwest Baptist University, 1600 University Avenue, Bolivar, MO 65613-2597, 417-328-1823 or toll-free 800-526-5859. *Fax:* 417-328-1514. *E-mail:* bgamble@sbuniv.edu.
*Website:* http://www.sbuniv.edu/.

---

# SOUTHWESTERN ADVENTIST UNIVERSITY
## Keene, TX

**CONTACT** Student Financial Services, Southwestern Adventist University, PO Box 567, Keene, TX 76059, 817-645-3921 Ext. 262 or toll-free 800-433-2240. *Fax:* 817-556-4744.
*Website:* http://www.swau.edu/.

---

# SOUTHWESTERN ASSEMBLIES OF GOD UNIVERSITY
## Waxahachie, TX

**CONTACT** Financial Aid Office, Southwestern Assemblies of God University, 1200 Sycamore Street, Waxahachie, TX 75165-2397, 972-825-4730 or toll-free 888-937-7248. *Fax:* 972-937-4001. *E-mail:* finaid@sagu.edu.
*Website:* http://www.sagu.edu/.

---

# SOUTHWESTERN CHRISTIAN COLLEGE
## Terrell, TX

| Tuition & fees: N/R | Average undergraduate aid package: $9370 |
|---|---|

**ABOUT THE INSTITUTION** Independent Church of Christ, coed. 2 undergraduate majors. Federal methodology is used as a basis for awarding need-based institutional aid.

**FRESHMAN FINANCIAL AID (Fall 2014, est.)** 57 applied for aid; of those 100% were deemed to have need. 100% of freshmen with need received aid; of those 49% had need fully met. *Average financial aid package:* $14,370 (excluding resources awarded to replace EFC).

**UNDERGRADUATE FINANCIAL AID (Fall 2014, est.)** 145 applied for aid; of those 97% were deemed to have need. 100% of undergraduates with need received aid; of those 43% had need fully met. *Average financial aid package:* $9370 (excluding resources awarded to replace EFC). 3% of all full-time undergraduates had no need and received non-need-based gift aid.

**GIFT AID (NEED-BASED)** *Total amount:* $1,019,529 (72% federal, 7% state, 18% institutional, 3% external sources). *Receiving aid:* Freshmen: 39% (22); all full-time undergraduates: 57% (83). *Average award:* Freshmen: $12,964; Undergraduates: $9370. *Scholarships, grants, and awards:* Federal Pell, FSEOG, state, college/university gift aid from institutional funds.

**GIFT AID (NON-NEED-BASED)** *Average award:* Undergraduates: $12,964. *Scholarships, grants, and awards by category: Academic interests/achievement:* general academic interests/achievements. *Creative arts/performance:* music. *Special characteristics:* children of faculty/staff, local/state students.

**LOANS** *Student loans:* $357,169 (60% need-based, 40% non-need-based). *Average need-based loan:* Freshmen: $4000. Undergraduates: $4500. *Parent loans:* $3830 (100% non-need-based). *Programs:* Federal Direct (Subsidized and Unsubsidized Stafford, PLUS).

**WORK-STUDY** *Federal work-study:* Total amount: $98,154; 111 jobs averaging $1400. *State or other work-study/employment:* Total amount: $934 (100% need-based). 1 part-time job averaging $934.

**ATHLETIC AWARDS** Total amount: $361,451 (83% need-based, 17% non-need-based).

**APPLYING FOR FINANCIAL AID** *Required financial aid form:* FAFSA. *Financial aid deadline (priority):* 6/1. *Notification date:* Continuous.

**CONTACT** Mrs. Tonya Dean, Financial Aid Office, Southwestern Christian College, PO Box 10, 200 Bowser Circle, Terrell, TX 75160, 972-524-3341 Ext. 124. *Fax:* 972-563-7133. *E-mail:* tdean@swcc.edu.
*Website:* http://www.swcc.edu/.

---

# SOUTHWESTERN CHRISTIAN UNIVERSITY
## Bethany, OK

**CONTACT** Mrs. Billie Stewart, Financial Aid Director, Southwestern Christian University, PO Box 340, Bethany, OK 73008, 405-789-7661 Ext. 3456. *Fax:* 405-495-0078. *E-mail:* billie.stewart@swcu.edu.
*Website:* http://www.swcu.edu/.

---

# SOUTHWESTERN COLLEGE
## Winfield, KS

| Tuition & fees: $25,946 | Average undergraduate aid package: $20,531 |
|---|---|

**ABOUT THE INSTITUTION** Independent United Methodist, coed. *Awards:* certificates, bachelor's, master's, and doctoral degrees. 45 undergraduate majors. *Total enrollment:* 1,627. Undergraduates: 1,323. Freshmen: 123. Federal methodology is used as a basis for awarding need-based institutional aid.

**UNDERGRADUATE EXPENSES for 2015–2016** *Application fee:* $25. *Comprehensive fee:* $33,026 includes full-time tuition ($25,796), mandatory fees ($150), and room and board ($7080). *College room only:* $3200. Full-time tuition and fees vary according to class time, course load, degree level, location, and program. Room and board charges vary according to board plan and housing facility. *Part-time tuition:* $1075 per credit hour. Part-time tuition and fees vary according to class time, course load, degree level, location, and program.

**FRESHMAN FINANCIAL AID (Fall 2013)** 111 applied for aid; of those 93% were deemed to have need. 100% of freshmen with need received aid; of those 14% had need fully met. *Average percent of need met:* 75% (excluding resources awarded to replace EFC). *Average financial aid package:* $20,635 (excluding resources awarded to replace EFC). 14% of all full-time freshmen had no need and received non-need-based gift aid.

**UNDERGRADUATE FINANCIAL AID (Fall 2013)** 479 applied for aid; of those 92% were deemed to have need. 100% of undergraduates with need received aid; of those 15% had need fully met. *Average percent of need met:* 71% (excluding resources awarded to replace EFC). *Average financial aid package:* $20,531 (excluding resources awarded to replace EFC). 17% of all full-time undergraduates had no need and received non-need-based gift aid.

**GIFT AID (NEED-BASED)** *Total amount:* $6,253,793 (34% federal, 9% state, 53% institutional, 4% external sources). *Receiving aid:* Freshmen: 80% (103); all full-time undergraduates: 79% (437). *Average award:* Freshmen: $15,683; Undergraduates: $14,101. *Scholarships, grants, and awards:* Federal Pell, FSEOG, state, private, college/university gift aid from institutional funds.

**GIFT AID (NON-NEED-BASED)** *Total amount:* $889,679 (95% institutional, 5% external sources). *Receiving aid:* Freshmen: 10% (13). Undergraduates: 8% (44). *Average award:* Freshmen: $7361. Undergraduates: $7729. *Scholarships, grants, and awards by category:* Academic interests/achievement: 554 awards ($2,792,100 total): biological sciences, business, communication, computer science, general academic interests/achievements, health fields, physical sciences, religion/biblical studies, social sciences. *Creative arts/performance:* 61 awards ($235,800 total): cinema/film/broadcasting, dance, journalism/publications, music, performing arts, theater/drama. *Special achievements/activities:* 71 awards ($278,100 total): cheerleading/drum major, community service, general special achievements/activities, leadership, memberships, religious involvement. *Special characteristics:* 269 awards ($493,625 total): children of faculty/staff, international students, members of minority groups, religious affiliation. *Tuition waivers:* Full or partial for employees or children of employees, senior citizens.

**LOANS** *Student loans:* $7,044,380 (88% need-based, 12% non-need-based). 75% of past graduating class borrowed through all loan programs. *Average indebtedness per student:* $33,478. *Average need-based loan:* Freshmen: $5326. Undergraduates: $6337. *Parent loans:* $1,780,523 (39% need-based, 61% non-need-based). *Programs:* Federal Direct (Subsidized and Unsubsidized Stafford, PLUS), Perkins.

**WORK-STUDY** *Federal work-study:* 140 jobs averaging $1640. *State or other work-study/employment:* Total amount: $120,276 (38% need-based, 62% non-need-based). 91 part-time jobs averaging $1322.

**ATHLETIC AWARDS** Total amount: $1,265,800 (77% need-based, 23% non-need-based).

**APPLYING FOR FINANCIAL AID** *Required financial aid forms:* FAFSA, institution's own form. *Financial aid deadline:* 8/15 (priority: 4/1). *Notification date:* Continuous beginning 2/1. Students must reply within 2 weeks of notification.

**CONTACT** Mrs. Brenda D. Hicks, Director of Financial Aid, Southwestern College, 100 College Street, Winfield, KS 67156-2499, 620-229-6215 or toll-free 800-846-1543. *Fax:* 620-229-6363. *E-mail:* finaid@sckans.edu. *Website:* http://www.sckans.edu/.

# SOUTHWESTERN OKLAHOMA STATE UNIVERSITY
## Weatherford, OK

| Tuition & fees: N/R | Average undergraduate aid package: $5568 |
| --- | --- |

**ABOUT THE INSTITUTION** State-supported, coed. *Awards:* certificates, associate, bachelor's, master's, and doctoral degrees. 53 undergraduate majors. *Total enrollment:* 4,942. Undergraduates: 4,162. Freshmen: 898. Both federal and institutional methodology are used as a basis for awarding need-based institutional aid.

**FRESHMAN FINANCIAL AID (Fall 2014, est.)** 712 applied for aid; of those 77% were deemed to have need. 97% of freshmen with need received aid; of those 27% had need fully met. *Average percent of need met:* 93% (excluding resources awarded to replace EFC). *Average financial aid package:* $5631 (excluding resources awarded to replace EFC). 10% of all full-time freshmen had no need and received non-need-based gift aid.

**UNDERGRADUATE FINANCIAL AID (Fall 2014, est.)** 2,548 applied for aid; of those 82% were deemed to have need. 97% of undergraduates with need received aid; of those 30% had need fully met. *Average percent of need met:* 93% (excluding resources awarded to replace EFC). *Average financial aid package:* $5568 (excluding resources awarded to replace EFC). 38% of all full-time undergraduates had no need and received non-need-based gift aid.

**GIFT AID (NEED-BASED)** *Total amount:* $11,100,881 (61% federal, 7% state, 32% external sources). *Receiving aid:* Freshmen: 55% (472); all full-time undergraduates: 55% (1,883). *Average award:* Freshmen: $1568; Undergraduates: $1707. *Scholarships, grants, and awards:* Federal Pell, FSEOG, state, private, college/university gift aid from institutional funds.

**GIFT AID (NON-NEED-BASED)** *Total amount:* $3,277,412 (19% federal, 15% state, 31% institutional, 35% external sources). *Receiving aid:* Freshmen: 38% (322). Undergraduates: 22% (756). *Average award:* Freshmen: $530. Undergraduates: $573. *Scholarships, grants, and awards by category:* Academic interests/achievement: biological sciences, business, communication, computer science, education, engineering/technologies, English, foreign languages, general academic interests/achievements, health fields, mathematics, physical sciences, social sciences. *Creative arts/performance:* applied art and design, art/fine arts, music, theater/drama. *Special achievements/activities:* cheerleading/drum major, leadership, rodeo. *Special characteristics:* children and siblings of alumni, local/state students, out-of-state students.

**LOANS** *Student loans:* $15,833,541 (41% need-based, 59% non-need-based). 79% of past graduating class borrowed through all loan programs. *Average indebtedness per student:* $16,262. *Average need-based loan:* Freshmen: $1232. Undergraduates: $1658. *Parent loans:* $8,425,406 (100% non-need-based). *Programs:* Federal Direct (Subsidized and Unsubsidized Stafford, PLUS).

**WORK-STUDY** *Federal work-study:* Total amount: $1,963,624; jobs available.

**ATHLETIC AWARDS** Total amount: $1,618,673 (100% non-need-based).

**APPLYING FOR FINANCIAL AID** *Required financial aid forms:* FAFSA, institution's own form. *Financial aid deadline:* 3/1. *Notification date:* 3/15.

**CONTACT** Mr. Jerome Wichert, Director of Student Financial Services, Southwestern Oklahoma State University, 100 Campus Drive, Weatherford, OK 73096, 580-774-6003. *Fax:* 580-774-7066. *E-mail:* jerome.wichert@swosu.edu. *Website:* http://www.swosu.edu/.

# SOUTHWESTERN UNIVERSITY
## Georgetown, TX

| Tuition & fees: $37,560 | Average undergraduate aid package: $31,865 |
| --- | --- |

**ABOUT THE INSTITUTION** Independent Methodist, coed. *Awards:* bachelor's degrees. 37 undergraduate majors. *Total enrollment:* 1,538. Undergraduates: 1,538. Freshmen: 382. Federal methodology is used as a basis for awarding need-based institutional aid.

**UNDERGRADUATE EXPENSES for 2015–2016** *Comprehensive fee:* $49,668 includes full-time tuition ($37,560) and room and board ($12,108). *College room only:* $5960. Room and board charges vary according to board plan and housing facility. *Part-time tuition:* $1565 per credit hour. Part-time tuition and fees vary according to course load.

**FRESHMAN FINANCIAL AID (Fall 2014, est.)** 312 applied for aid; of those 80% were deemed to have need. 100% of freshmen with need received aid; of those 26% had need fully met. *Average percent of need met:* 90% (excluding resources awarded to replace EFC). *Average financial aid package:* $32,220 (excluding resources awarded to replace EFC). 34% of all full-time freshmen had no need and received non-need-based gift aid.

**UNDERGRADUATE FINANCIAL AID (Fall 2014, est.)** 1,093 applied for aid; of those 87% were deemed to have need. 100% of undergraduates with need received aid; of those 27% had need fully met. *Average percent of need met:* 88% (excluding resources awarded to replace EFC). *Average financial aid package:* $31,865 (excluding resources awarded to replace EFC). 35% of all full-time undergraduates had no need and received non-need-based gift aid.

**GIFT AID (NEED-BASED)** *Total amount:* $24,382,320 (8% federal, 6% state, 82% institutional, 4% external sources). *Receiving aid:* Freshmen: 65% (250); all full-time undergraduates: 63% (947). *Average award:* Freshmen: $27,629; Undergraduates: $26,126. *Scholarships, grants, and awards:* Federal Pell, FSEOG, state, private, college/university gift aid from institutional funds.

**GIFT AID (NON-NEED-BASED)** *Total amount:* $10,543,234 (96% institutional, 4% external sources). *Receiving aid:* Freshmen: 65% (248). Undergraduates: 60% (915). *Average award:* Freshmen: $19,801. Undergraduates: $18,514. *Scholarships, grants, and awards by category:* Academic interests/achievement: 2,404 awards ($25,976,439 total): business, general academic interests/achievements, humanities, international studies, mathematics, premedicine, social sciences. *Creative arts/performance:* 117 awards ($701,074 total): art/fine arts, music, theater/drama. *Special achievements/activities:* 4 awards ($4000 total): leadership. *Special characteristics:* 57 awards ($1,115,715 total): children of faculty/staff, ethnic background, general special characteristics, relatives of clergy, religious affiliation. *Tuition waivers:* Full or partial for employees or children of employees.

**LOANS** *Student loans:* $8,192,701 (91% need-based, 9% non-need-based). 60% of past graduating class borrowed through all loan programs. *Average indebtedness per student:* $30,935. *Average need-based loan:* Freshmen: $4225. Undergraduates: $5018. *Parent loans:* $10,765,848 (79% need-based, 21% non-need-based). *Programs:* Federal Direct (Subsidized and Unsubsidized Stafford, PLUS), Perkins, state, college/university.

**WORK-STUDY** *Federal work-study:* Total amount: $440,517; 233 jobs averaging $1996. *State or other work-study/employment:* Total amount: $1,134,780 (60% need-based, 40% non-need-based). 569 part-time jobs averaging $2396.

**APPLYING FOR FINANCIAL AID** *Required financial aid form:* FAFSA. *Financial aid deadline (priority):* 3/1. *Notification date:* Continuous beginning 3/1. Students must reply by 5/1 or within 2 weeks of notification.

**CONTACT** Mr. James P. Gaeta, Director of Financial Aid, Southwestern University, PO Box 770, Georgetown, TX 78627-0770, 512-863-1259 or toll-free 800-252-3166. *Fax:* 512-863-1507. *E-mail:* gaetaj@southwestern.edu. *Website:* http://www.southwestern.edu/.

# SOUTHWEST MINNESOTA STATE UNIVERSITY
## Marshall, MN

**ABOUT THE INSTITUTION** State-supported, coed. *Awards:* certificates, associate, bachelor's, and master's degrees. 56 undergraduate majors. *Total enrollment:* 6,896. Undergraduates: 6,451. Freshmen: 467.

**GIFT AID (NEED-BASED)** *Scholarships, grants, and awards:* Federal Pell, FSEOG, state, private, college/university gift aid from institutional funds.

**GIFT AID (NON-NEED-BASED)** *Scholarships, grants, and awards by category:* Academic interests/achievement: agriculture, biological sciences, business, communication, computer science, education, English, foreign languages, general academic interests/achievements, mathematics, physical sciences, premedicine, social sciences. *Creative arts/performance:* art/fine arts, creative writing, debating, journalism/publications, music, performing arts, theater/drama. *Special achievements/activities:* general special achievements/activities, hobbies/interests, leadership. *Special characteristics:* children and siblings of alumni, children of union members/company employees, ethnic background, first-generation college students, general special characteristics, handicapped students, international students, local/state students, members of minority groups, previous college experience, veterans, veterans' children.

**LOANS** *Programs:* Federal Direct (Subsidized and Unsubsidized Stafford, PLUS), Perkins, state, private loans.

**WORK-STUDY** *Federal work-study:* 93 jobs averaging $2203. *State or other work-study/employment:* Total amount: $364,975 (100% need-based). 154 part-time jobs averaging $2325.

**APPLYING FOR FINANCIAL AID** *Required financial aid forms:* FAFSA, institution's own form.

**CONTACT** Mr. David Vikander, Director of Financial Aid, Southwest Minnesota State University, 1501 State Street, Marshall, MN 56258, 507-537-6281 or toll-free 800-642-0684. *Fax:* 507-537-6275. *E-mail:* vikander@smsu.edu. *Website:* http://www.smsu.edu/.

# SOUTHWEST UNIVERSITY
## Kenner, LA

**CONTACT** Financial Aid Office, Southwest University, 2200 Veterans Memorial Boulevard, Kenner, LA 70062, 504-468-2900 or toll-free 800-433-5923. *Website:* http://www.southwest.edu/.

# SOUTHWEST UNIVERSITY AT EL PASO
## El Paso, TX

**CONTACT** Financial Aid Office, Southwest University at El Paso, 1414 Geronimo Drive, El Paso, TX 79925, 915-778-4001. *Website:* http://southwestuniversity.edu/.

# SOUTHWEST UNIVERSITY OF VISUAL ARTS
## Tucson, AZ

**CONTACT** Financial Aid Office, Southwest University of Visual Arts, 2525 North Country Club Road, Tucson, AZ 85716-2505, 520-325-0123 or toll-free 800-825-8753. *Website:* http://www.suva.edu/.

# SPALDING UNIVERSITY
## Louisville, KY

**CONTACT** Director of Student Financial Services, Spalding University, 851 South Fourth Street, Louisville, KY 40203, 502-588-7185 or toll-free 800-896-8941. *Fax:* 502-585-7128. *E-mail:* onestop@spalding.edu. *Website:* http://www.spalding.edu/.

# SPELMAN COLLEGE
## Atlanta, GA

| Tuition & fees: $25,496 | Average undergraduate aid package: $18,184 |
| --- | --- |

**ABOUT THE INSTITUTION** Independent, women only. *Awards:* bachelor's degrees. 27 undergraduate majors. *Total enrollment:* 2,135. Undergraduates: 2,135. Freshmen: 552. Federal methodology is used as a basis for awarding need-based institutional aid.

**UNDERGRADUATE EXPENSES for 2015–2016** *Application fee:* $35. *Comprehensive fee:* $37,441 includes full-time tuition ($22,055), mandatory fees ($3441), and room and board ($11,945). Full-time tuition and fees vary according to course load. Room and board charges vary according to board plan and housing facility. Part-time tuition and fees vary according to course load.

**FRESHMAN FINANCIAL AID (Fall 2013)** 525 applied for aid; of those 91% were deemed to have need. 97% of freshmen with need received aid; of those 11% had need fully met. *Average percent of need met:* 34% (excluding resources awarded to replace EFC). *Average financial aid package:* $15,611 (excluding resources awarded to replace EFC).

**UNDERGRADUATE FINANCIAL AID (Fall 2013)** 1,878 applied for aid; of those 92% were deemed to have need. 98% of undergraduates with need received aid; of those 15% had need fully met. *Average percent of need met:* 44% (excluding resources awarded to replace EFC). *Average financial aid package:* $18,184 (excluding resources awarded to replace EFC).

**GIFT AID (NEED-BASED)** *Total amount:* $23,138,959 (21% federal, 6% state, 55% institutional, 18% external sources). *Receiving aid:* Freshmen: 72% (401); all full-time undergraduates: 70% (1,434). *Average award:* Freshmen: $12,056; Undergraduates: $13,427. **Scholarships, grants, and awards:** Federal Pell, FSEOG, state, private, college/university gift aid from institutional funds, United Negro College Fund.

**GIFT AID (NON-NEED-BASED) Tuition waivers:** Full or partial for employees or children of employees. **ROTC:** Army cooperative, Naval cooperative, Air Force cooperative.

**LOANS Student loans:** $15,849,978 (77% need-based, 23% non-need-based). 60% of past graduating class borrowed through all loan programs. **Average indebtedness per student:** $35,516. **Average need-based loan:** Freshmen: $6584. Undergraduates: $7666. **Parent loans:** $31,273,278 (100% non-need-based). **Programs:** Federal Direct (Subsidized and Unsubsidized Stafford, PLUS), Perkins, state.

**WORK-STUDY Federal work-study:** 181 jobs averaging $1280.

**APPLYING FOR FINANCIAL AID Required financial aid forms:** FAFSA, institution's own form. **Financial aid deadline (priority):** 2/1. **Notification date:** Continuous beginning 2/15. Students must reply within 2 weeks of notification.

**CONTACT** Ms. Lenora Jackson, Director of Financial Aid, Spelman College, 350 Spelman Lane, SW, Atlanta, GA 30314-4399, 404-270-5212 or toll-free 800-982-2411. **Fax:** 404-270-5220. **E-mail:** lenoraj@spelman.edu.
**Website:** http://www.spelman.edu/.

# SPRING ARBOR UNIVERSITY
## Spring Arbor, MI

| Tuition & fees: $24,350 | Average undergraduate aid package: $21,899 |
|---|---|

**ABOUT THE INSTITUTION** Independent Free Methodist, coed. **Awards:** certificates, associate, bachelor's, and master's degrees. 62 undergraduate majors. **Total enrollment:** 3,961. Undergraduates: 2,967. Freshmen: 368. Federal methodology is used as a basis for awarding need-based institutional aid.

**UNDERGRADUATE EXPENSES for 2015–2016 Application fee:** $30. **Comprehensive fee:** $32,810 includes full-time tuition ($23,750), mandatory fees ($600), and room and board ($8460). **College room only:** $3940. Full-time tuition and fees vary according to course load, degree level, and program. Room and board charges vary according to board plan and housing facility. **Part-time tuition:** $575 per credit hour. **Part-time fees:** $280 per term. Part-time tuition and fees vary according to course load, degree level, program, and reciprocity agreements.

**FRESHMAN FINANCIAL AID (Fall 2014, est.)** 327 applied for aid; of those 90% were deemed to have need. 100% of freshmen with need received aid; of those 20% had need fully met. **Average percent of need met:** 82% (excluding resources awarded to replace EFC). **Average financial aid package:** $22,184 (excluding resources awarded to replace EFC).

**UNDERGRADUATE FINANCIAL AID (Fall 2014, est.)** 1,262 applied for aid; of those 92% were deemed to have need. 100% of undergraduates with need received aid; of those 17% had need fully met. **Average percent of need met:** 79% (excluding resources awarded to replace EFC). **Average financial aid package:** $21,899 (excluding resources awarded to replace EFC). 1% of all full-time undergraduates had no need and received non-need-based gift aid.

**GIFT AID (NEED-BASED) Total amount:** $20,867,158 (24% federal, 10% state, 66% institutional). **Receiving aid:** Freshmen: 85% (292); all full-time undergraduates: 85% (1,147). **Average award:** Freshmen: $15,799; Undergraduates: $14,364. **Scholarships, grants, and awards:** Federal Pell, FSEOG, private, college/university gift aid from institutional funds.

**GIFT AID (NON-NEED-BASED) Total amount:** $212,461 (76% state, 24% external sources). **Receiving aid:** Freshmen: 7% (25). Undergraduates: 8% (108). **Average award:** Undergraduates: $1212. **Scholarships, grants, and awards by category:** Academic interests/achievement: general academic interests/achievements. Creative arts/performance: art/fine arts. Special achievements/activities: junior miss. Special characteristics: adult students, children of faculty/staff, general special characteristics, international students, members of minority groups, relatives of clergy, religious affiliation. **Tuition waivers:** Full or partial for employees or children of employees. **ROTC:** Army, Air Force cooperative.

**LOANS Student loans:** $30,820,220 (28% need-based, 72% non-need-based). 87% of past graduating class borrowed through all loan programs. **Average indebtedness per student:** $30,580. **Average need-based loan:** Freshmen: $3717. Undergraduates: $4713. **Parent loans:** $2,241,204 (100% need-based). **Programs:** Federal Direct (Subsidized and Unsubsidized Stafford, PLUS), Perkins.

**WORK-STUDY Federal work-study:** Total amount: $192,803; jobs available.
**ATHLETIC AWARDS** Total amount: $1,908,583 (100% need-based).
**APPLYING FOR FINANCIAL AID Required financial aid form:** FAFSA. **Financial aid deadline (priority):** 3/1. **Notification date:** Continuous. Students must reply within 2 weeks of notification.

**CONTACT** Herbert Rotich, Director of Financial Aid, Spring Arbor University, 106 East Main Street, Spring Arbor, MI 49283-9799, 517-750-6463 or toll-free 800-968-0011. **Fax:** 517-750-6620. **E-mail:** hrotich@arbor.edu.
**Website:** http://www.arbor.edu/.

# SPRINGFIELD COLLEGE
## Springfield, MA

| Tuition & fees: $33,455 | Average undergraduate aid package: $24,673 |
|---|---|

**ABOUT THE INSTITUTION** Independent, coed. **Awards:** certificates, bachelor's, master's, and doctoral degrees. 38 undergraduate majors. **Total enrollment:** 3,286. Undergraduates: 2,204. Freshmen: 510. Institutional methodology is used as a basis for awarding need-based institutional aid.

**UNDERGRADUATE EXPENSES for 2015–2016 Application fee:** $50. **Comprehensive fee:** $44,665 includes full-time tuition ($32,980), mandatory fees ($475), and room and board ($11,210). **College room only:** $6100. Room and board charges vary according to board plan and housing facility. **Part-time tuition:** $992 per credit hour.

**FRESHMAN FINANCIAL AID (Fall 2014, est.)** 533 applied for aid; of those 91% were deemed to have need. 100% of freshmen with need received aid; of those 8% had need fully met. **Average percent of need met:** 77% (excluding resources awarded to replace EFC). **Average financial aid package:** $25,584 (excluding resources awarded to replace EFC). 9% of all full-time freshmen had no need and received non-need-based gift aid.

**UNDERGRADUATE FINANCIAL AID (Fall 2014, est.)** 1,814 applied for aid; of those 91% were deemed to have need. 100% of undergraduates with need received aid; of those 9% had need fully met. **Average percent of need met:** 74% (excluding resources awarded to replace EFC). **Average financial aid package:** $24,673 (excluding resources awarded to replace EFC). 11% of all full-time undergraduates had no need and received non-need-based gift aid.

**GIFT AID (NEED-BASED) Total amount:** $32,553,867 (6% federal, 2% state, 88% institutional, 4% external sources). **Receiving aid:** Freshmen: 79% (487); all full-time undergraduates: 82% (1,655). **Average award:** Freshmen: $20,954; Undergraduates: $19,321. **Scholarships, grants, and awards:** Federal Pell, FSEOG, state, private, college/university gift aid from institutional funds.

**GIFT AID (NON-NEED-BASED) Total amount:** $3,170,271 (84% institutional, 16% external sources). **Receiving aid:** Freshmen: 6% (36). Undergraduates: 5% (103). **Average award:** Freshmen: $9931. Undergraduates: $9333. **Scholarships, grants, and awards by category:** Academic interests/achievement: general academic interests/achievements. Special characteristics: children of faculty/staff, siblings of current students. **Tuition waivers:** Full or partial for employees or children of employees. **ROTC:** Army cooperative, Air Force cooperative.

**LOANS Student loans:** $20,251,102 (70% need-based, 30% non-need-based). 90% of past graduating class borrowed through all loan programs. **Average indebtedness per student:** $41,659. **Average need-based loan:** Freshmen: $4111. Undergraduates: $4566. **Parent loans:** $7,081,672 (40% need-based, 60% non-need-based). **Programs:** Federal Direct (Subsidized and Unsubsidized Stafford, PLUS), Perkins, state, alternative loans.

**WORK-STUDY Federal work-study:** Total amount: $1,355,712; jobs available. **State or other work-study/employment:** Total amount: $734,902 (85% need-based, 15% non-need-based). Part-time jobs available.

**APPLYING FOR FINANCIAL AID Required financial aid forms:** FAFSA, institution's own form, state aid form, federal income tax form(s). **Financial aid deadline (priority):** 3/15. **Notification date:** Continuous beginning 2/7. Students must reply within 2 weeks of notification.

**CONTACT** Ms. Kinser Cancelmo, Assistant Director of Financial Aid, Springfield College, 263 Alden Street, Springfield, MA 01109-3797, 413-748-3108 or toll-free 800-343-1257. **Fax:** 413-748-3462. **E-mail:** financialaid@springfieldcollege.edu.
**Website:** http://www.springfieldcollege.edu/.

# SPRING HILL COLLEGE
## Mobile, AL

| Tuition & fees: $32,468 | Average undergraduate aid package: $26,574 |
|---|---|

**ABOUT THE INSTITUTION** Independent Roman Catholic (Jesuit), coed. *Awards:* certificates, bachelor's, and master's degrees. 45 undergraduate majors. *Total enrollment:* 1,412. Undergraduates: 1,274. Freshmen: 360. Federal methodology is used as a basis for awarding need-based institutional aid.

**UNDERGRADUATE EXPENSES for 2015–2016** *Application fee:* $25. *Comprehensive fee:* $44,164 includes full-time tuition ($30,506), mandatory fees ($1962), and room and board ($11,696). *College room only:* $6300. Room and board charges vary according to board plan and housing facility. *Part-time tuition:* $975 per credit hour. *Part-time fees:* $50 per credit hour.

**FRESHMAN FINANCIAL AID (Fall 2014, est.)** 317 applied for aid; of those 85% were deemed to have need. 100% of freshmen with need received aid; of those 16% had need fully met. *Average percent of need met:* 90% (excluding resources awarded to replace EFC). *Average financial aid package:* $28,172 (excluding resources awarded to replace EFC). 22% of all full-time freshmen had no need and received non-need-based gift aid.

**UNDERGRADUATE FINANCIAL AID (Fall 2014, est.)** 963 applied for aid; of those 88% were deemed to have need. 100% of undergraduates with need received aid; of those 14% had need fully met. *Average percent of need met:* 88% (excluding resources awarded to replace EFC). *Average financial aid package:* $26,574 (excluding resources awarded to replace EFC). 26% of all full-time undergraduates had no need and received non-need-based gift aid.

**GIFT AID (NEED-BASED)** *Total amount:* $20,280,966 (10% federal, 1% state, 88% institutional, 1% external sources). *Receiving aid:* Freshmen: 72% (265); all full-time undergraduates: 68% (831). *Average award:* Freshmen: $24,187; Undergraduates: $23,568. *Scholarships, grants, and awards:* Federal Pell, FSEOG, state, private, college/university gift aid from institutional funds, TEACH Grants.

**GIFT AID (NON-NEED-BASED)** *Total amount:* $6,585,418 (1% state, 99% institutional). *Receiving aid:* Freshmen: 72% (265). Undergraduates: 68% (831). *Average award:* Freshmen: $20,705. Undergraduates: $18,148. *Scholarships, grants, and awards by category:* Academic interests/achievement: general academic interests/achievements. Special achievements/activities: community service. Special characteristics: children of faculty/staff, siblings of current students. *Tuition waivers:* Full or partial for employees or children of employees. *ROTC:* Army cooperative, Air Force cooperative.

**LOANS** *Student loans:* $7,273,302 (75% need-based, 25% non-need-based). 71% of past graduating class borrowed through all loan programs. *Average indebtedness per student:* $31,855. *Average need-based loan:* Freshmen: $2230. Undergraduates: $2124. *Parent loans:* $1,986,628 (31% need-based, 69% non-need-based). *Programs:* Federal Direct (Subsidized and Unsubsidized Stafford, PLUS), Perkins, alternative loans.

**WORK-STUDY** *Federal work-study:* Total amount: $330,383; jobs available. *State or other work-study/employment:* Total amount: $74,800 (100% non-need-based). Part-time jobs available.

**ATHLETIC AWARDS** Total amount: $1,318,757 (44% need-based, 56% non-need-based).

**APPLYING FOR FINANCIAL AID** *Required financial aid forms:* FAFSA, state aid form. *Financial aid deadline (priority):* 3/1. *Notification date:* Continuous beginning 2/15. Students must reply by 5/1 or within 2 weeks of notification.

**CONTACT** Mr. Jim V. Love, Director of Student Financial Services Operations and Processing, Spring Hill College, 4000 Dauphin Street, Mobile, AL 36608, 251-380-3460 or toll-free 800-SHC-6704. *Fax:* 251-460-2176. *E-mail:* jvlove@shc.edu. *Website:* http://www.shc.edu/.

# STANFORD UNIVERSITY
## Stanford, CA

| Tuition & fees: $45,729 | Average undergraduate aid package: $44,043 |
|---|---|

**ABOUT THE INSTITUTION** Independent, coed. *Awards:* bachelor's, master's, and doctoral degrees. 75 undergraduate majors. *Total enrollment:* 18,469. Undergraduates: 7,089. Freshmen: 1,677. Both federal and institutional methodology are used as a basis for awarding need-based institutional aid.

**UNDERGRADUATE EXPENSES for 2015–2016** *Application fee:* $90. *One-time required fee:* $591. *Comprehensive fee:* $59,836 includes full-time tuition ($45,729) and room and board ($14,107). Room and board charges vary according to board plan.

**FRESHMAN FINANCIAL AID (Fall 2013)** 979 applied for aid; of those 80% were deemed to have need. 100% of freshmen with need received aid; of those 95% had need fully met. *Average percent of need met:* 100% (excluding resources awarded to replace EFC). *Average financial aid package:* $44,790 (excluding resources awarded to replace EFC).

**UNDERGRADUATE FINANCIAL AID (Fall 2013)** 3,814 applied for aid; of those 90% were deemed to have need. 100% of undergraduates with need received aid; of those 88% had need fully met. *Average percent of need met:* 100% (excluding resources awarded to replace EFC). *Average financial aid package:* $44,043 (excluding resources awarded to replace EFC). 1% of all full-time undergraduates had no need and received non-need-based gift aid.

**GIFT AID (NEED-BASED)** *Total amount:* $139,026,653 (5% federal, 2% state, 90% institutional, 3% external sources). *Receiving aid:* Freshmen: 46% (771); all full-time undergraduates: 48% (3,342). *Average award:* Freshmen: $42,815; Undergraduates: $41,620. *Scholarships, grants, and awards:* Federal Pell, FSEOG, state, private, college/university gift aid from institutional funds.

**GIFT AID (NON-NEED-BASED)** *Total amount:* $6,772,101 (11% federal, 1% state, 11% institutional, 77% external sources). *Receiving aid:* Freshmen: 1% (25). Undergraduates: 2% (108). *Average award:* Undergraduates: $8980. *Tuition waivers:* Full or partial for employees or children of employees. *ROTC:* Army cooperative, Naval cooperative, Air Force cooperative.

**LOANS** *Student loans:* $7,399,698 (28% need-based, 72% non-need-based). 23% of past graduating class borrowed through all loan programs. *Average indebtedness per student:* $19,230. *Average need-based loan:* Freshmen: $2500. Undergraduates: $3026. *Parent loans:* $6,370,912 (100% non-need-based). *Programs:* Federal Direct (Subsidized and Unsubsidized Stafford, PLUS), Perkins.

**WORK-STUDY** *Federal work-study:* 588 jobs averaging $2316. *State or other work-study/employment:* Total amount: $3,963,557 (85% need-based, 15% non-need-based). 1,785 part-time jobs averaging $2219.

**ATHLETIC AWARDS** Total amount: $19,830,622 (12% need-based, 88% non-need-based).

**APPLYING FOR FINANCIAL AID** *Required financial aid forms:* FAFSA, CSS Financial Aid PROFILE. *Financial aid deadline (priority):* 2/15. *Notification date:* Continuous beginning 4/1. Students must reply by 5/1.

**CONTACT** Financial Aid Office, Stanford University, Montag Hall, 355 Galvez Street, Stanford, CA 94305-3021, 650-723-3058. *Fax:* 650-725-0540. *E-mail:* financialaid@stanford.edu. *Website:* http://www.stanford.edu/.

# STATE COLLEGE OF FLORIDA MANATEE-SARASOTA
## Bradenton, FL

**CONTACT** Financial Aid Office, State College of Florida Manatee-Sarasota, 5840 26th Street West, PO Box 1849, Bradenton, FL 34206-7046, 941-752-5000. *Website:* http://www.scf.edu/.

# STATE UNIVERSITY OF NEW YORK AT FREDONIA
## Fredonia, NY

| Tuition & fees (NY res): $7740 | Average undergraduate aid package: $10,689 |
|---|---|

**ABOUT THE INSTITUTION** State-supported, coed. *Awards:* certificates, bachelor's, and master's degrees. 72 undergraduate majors. *Total enrollment:* 5,214. Undergraduates: 4,941. Freshmen: 1,072. Federal methodology is used as a basis for awarding need-based institutional aid.

**UNDERGRADUATE EXPENSES** for 2015–2016 *Application fee:* $50. *Tuition, state resident:* full-time $6170; part-time $257 per credit hour. *Tuition, nonresident:* full-time $15,820; part-time $659 per credit hour. *Required fees:* full-time $1570; $65.25 per credit hour. *College room and board:* $12,100; *Room only:* $7200. Room and board charges vary according to board plan and housing facility.
**FRESHMAN FINANCIAL AID (Fall 2014, est.)** 983 applied for aid; of those 77% were deemed to have need. 98% of freshmen with need received aid; of those 15% had need fully met. *Average percent of need met:* 65% (excluding resources awarded to replace EFC). *Average financial aid package:* $11,456 (excluding resources awarded to replace EFC). 11% of all full-time freshmen had no need and received non-need-based gift aid.
**UNDERGRADUATE FINANCIAL AID (Fall 2014, est.)** 4,062 applied for aid; of those 80% were deemed to have need. 98% of undergraduates with need received aid; of those 13% had need fully met. *Average percent of need met:* 62% (excluding resources awarded to replace EFC). *Average financial aid package:* $10,689 (excluding resources awarded to replace EFC). 8% of all full-time undergraduates had no need and received non-need-based gift aid.
**GIFT AID (NEED-BASED)** *Total amount:* $19,087,022 (43% federal, 41% state, 12% institutional, 4% external sources). *Receiving aid:* Freshmen: 54% (571); all full-time undergraduates: 52% (2,458). *Average award:* Freshmen: $5755; Undergraduates: $5489. *Scholarships, grants, and awards:* Federal Pell, FSEOG, state, private, college/university gift aid from institutional funds, TEACH Grants.
**GIFT AID (NON-NEED-BASED)** *Total amount:* $386,426 (100% federal). *Receiving aid:* Freshmen: 29% (304). Undergraduates: 17% (785). *Average award:* Freshmen: $3217. Undergraduates: $3292. *Scholarships, grants, and awards by category:* Academic interests/achievement: 400 awards ($517,612 total): biological sciences, business, communication, computer science, education, English, foreign languages, general academic interests/achievements, humanities, international studies, mathematics, physical sciences, social sciences. *Creative arts/performance:* 126 awards ($123,073 total): applied art and design, art/fine arts, dance, music, performing arts, theater/drama. *Special achievements/activities:* 19 awards ($64,250 total): general special achievements/activities, leadership. *Special characteristics:* 152 awards ($390,263 total): children and siblings of alumni, ethnic background, general special characteristics, international students, local/state students, members of minority groups, out-of-state students, parents of current students, previous college experience.
**LOANS** *Student loans:* $35,009,242 (41% need-based, 59% non-need-based). 86% of past graduating class borrowed through all loan programs. *Average indebtedness per student:* $28,900. *Average need-based loan:* Freshmen: $5561. Undergraduates: $5404. *Parent loans:* $4,679,904 (100% non-need-based). *Programs:* Federal Direct (Subsidized and Unsubsidized Stafford, PLUS), Perkins, alternative loans.
**WORK-STUDY** *Federal work-study:* Total amount: $340,107; 220 jobs averaging $1900.
**APPLYING FOR FINANCIAL AID** *Required financial aid forms:* FAFSA, state aid form. *Financial aid deadline:* Continuous. *Notification date:* Continuous beginning 3/1. Students must reply by 5/1.
**CONTACT** Mark Zaffalon, Financial Aid Counselor, State University of New York at Fredonia, 209 Maytum Hall, Fredonia, NY 14063, 716-673-3253 or toll-free 800-252-1212. *Fax:* 716-673-3785. *E-mail:* mark.zaffalon@fredonia.edu.
*Website:* http://www.fredonia.edu/.

# STATE UNIVERSITY OF NEW YORK AT NEW PALTZ
## New Paltz, NY

| Tuition & fees (NY res): $7418 | Average undergraduate aid package: $10,590 |
| --- | --- |

**ABOUT THE INSTITUTION** State-supported, coed. *Awards:* certificates, bachelor's, and master's degrees. 67 undergraduate majors. *Total enrollment:* 7,692. Undergraduates: 6,642. Freshmen: 1,079. Federal methodology is used as a basis for awarding need-based institutional aid.
**UNDERGRADUATE EXPENSES** for 2015–2016 *Application fee:* $50. *Tuition, state resident:* full-time $6170; part-time $257 per credit hour. *Tuition, nonresident:* full-time $15,820; part-time $659 per credit hour. *Required fees:* full-time $1248; $35.70 per credit hour or $193 per term. *College room and*

board: $10,896; *Room only:* $7220. Room and board charges vary according to board plan.
**FRESHMAN FINANCIAL AID (Fall 2014, est.)** 979 applied for aid; of those 66% were deemed to have need. 99% of freshmen with need received aid; of those 5% had need fully met. *Average percent of need met:* 59% (excluding resources awarded to replace EFC). *Average financial aid package:* $11,227 (excluding resources awarded to replace EFC). 1% of all full-time freshmen had no need and received non-need-based gift aid.
**UNDERGRADUATE FINANCIAL AID (Fall 2014, est.)** 4,702 applied for aid; of those 74% were deemed to have need. 99% of undergraduates with need received aid; of those 7% had need fully met. *Average percent of need met:* 58% (excluding resources awarded to replace EFC). *Average financial aid package:* $10,590 (excluding resources awarded to replace EFC). 1% of all full-time undergraduates had no need and received non-need-based gift aid.
**GIFT AID (NEED-BASED)** *Total amount:* $19,017,212 (52% federal, 48% state). *Receiving aid:* Freshmen: 35% (378); all full-time undergraduates: 33% (2,000). *Average award:* Freshmen: $5179; Undergraduates: $4840. *Scholarships, grants, and awards:* Federal Pell, FSEOG, state, private, college/university gift aid from institutional funds.
**GIFT AID (NON-NEED-BASED)** *Total amount:* $1,501,712 (2% federal, 39% state, 8% institutional, 51% external sources). *Receiving aid:* Freshmen: 6% (69). Undergraduates: 3% (205). *Average award:* Freshmen: $1600. Undergraduates: $1830. *Scholarships, grants, and awards by category:* Academic interests/achievement: area/ethnic studies, biological sciences, business, communication, education, engineering/technologies, English, foreign languages, general academic interests/achievements, international studies, mathematics, physical sciences. *Creative arts/performance:* art/fine arts, music, theater/drama. *Special characteristics:* children of faculty/staff, ethnic background, first-generation college students, local/state students, members of minority groups.
**LOANS** *Student loans:* $27,477,516 (48% need-based, 52% non-need-based). 63% of past graduating class borrowed through all loan programs. *Average indebtedness per student:* $25,874. *Average need-based loan:* Freshmen: $3355. Undergraduates: $4387. *Parent loans:* $18,327,522 (100% non-need-based). *Programs:* Federal Direct (Subsidized and Unsubsidized Stafford, PLUS), Perkins, state, private loans.
**WORK-STUDY** *Federal work-study:* Total amount: $1,436,688; jobs available. *State or other work-study/employment:* Total amount: $866,940 (100% non-need-based). Part-time jobs available.
**APPLYING FOR FINANCIAL AID** *Required financial aid forms:* FAFSA, state aid form. *Financial aid deadline (priority):* 3/15. *Notification date:* Continuous beginning 4/1. Students must reply within 6 weeks of notification.
**CONTACT** Mr. Daniel Sistarenik, Director of Financial Aid, State University of New York at New Paltz, 200 Hawk Drive, New Paltz, NY 12561-2437, 845-257-3250 or toll-free 877-MY-NP-411 (in-state). *Fax:* 845-257-3568. *E-mail:* sistared@newpaltz.edu.
*Website:* http://www.newpaltz.edu/.

# STATE UNIVERSITY OF NEW YORK AT OSWEGO
## Oswego, NY

| Tuition & fees (NY res): $7581 | Average undergraduate aid package: $10,616 |
| --- | --- |

**ABOUT THE INSTITUTION** State-supported, coed. *Awards:* certificates, bachelor's, and master's degrees. 67 undergraduate majors. *Total enrollment:* 8,034. Undergraduates: 7,193. Freshmen: 1,417. Federal methodology is used as a basis for awarding need-based institutional aid.
**UNDERGRADUATE EXPENSES** for 2015–2016 *Application fee:* $50. *Tuition, state resident:* full-time $6170; part-time $257 per credit hour. *Tuition, nonresident:* full-time $15,820; part-time $659 per credit hour. *Required fees:* full-time $1411; $44.30 per credit hour. Part-time tuition and fees vary according to course load. *College room and board:* $12,690. Room and board charges vary according to board plan and housing facility.
**FRESHMAN FINANCIAL AID (Fall 2014, est.)** 1,270 applied for aid; of those 76% were deemed to have need. 99% of freshmen with need received aid; of those 10% had need fully met. *Average percent of need met:* 86% (excluding resources awarded to replace EFC). *Average financial aid package:* $11,391 (excluding

resources awarded to replace EFC). 23% of all full-time freshmen had no need and received non-need-based gift aid.

**UNDERGRADUATE FINANCIAL AID (Fall 2014, est.)** 5,651 applied for aid; of those 79% were deemed to have need. 99% of undergraduates with need received aid; of those 11% had need fully met. *Average percent of need met:* 84% (excluding resources awarded to replace EFC). *Average financial aid package:* $10,616 (excluding resources awarded to replace EFC). 12% of all full-time undergraduates had no need and received non-need-based gift aid.

**GIFT AID (NEED-BASED)** *Total amount:* $27,661,984 (46% federal, 41% state, 12% institutional, 1% external sources). *Receiving aid:* Freshmen: 64% (902); all full-time undergraduates: 57% (3,869). *Average award:* Freshmen: $7764; Undergraduates: $6966. *Scholarships, grants, and awards:* Federal Pell, FSEOG, state, private, college/university gift aid from institutional funds.

**GIFT AID (NON-NEED-BASED)** *Total amount:* $2,156,390 (1% federal, 5% state, 88% institutional, 6% external sources). *Receiving aid:* Freshmen: 47% (661). Undergraduates: 22% (1,523). *Average award:* Freshmen: $1865. Undergraduates: $2371. *Scholarships, grants, and awards by category: Academic interests/ achievement:* area/ethnic studies, biological sciences, business, communication, computer science, education, English, foreign languages, general academic interests/achievements, humanities, international studies, mathematics, physical sciences, premedicine, social sciences. *ROTC:* Army cooperative, Air Force cooperative.

**LOANS** *Student loans:* $46,985,278 (81% need-based, 19% non-need-based). 77% of past graduating class borrowed through all loan programs. *Average indebtedness per student:* $28,362. *Average need-based loan:* Freshmen: $3989. Undergraduates: $4495. *Parent loans:* $14,733,374 (72% need-based, 28% non-need-based). *Programs:* Federal Direct (Subsidized and Unsubsidized Stafford, PLUS), Perkins.

**WORK-STUDY** *Federal work-study:* Total amount: $630,199; 510 jobs averaging $1156. *State or other work-study/employment:* Total amount: $858,380 (59% need-based, 41% non-need-based). 1,586 part-time jobs averaging $1959.

**APPLYING FOR FINANCIAL AID** *Required financial aid forms:* FAFSA, state aid form. *Financial aid deadline (priority):* 2/15. *Notification date:* Continuous beginning 2/15. Students must reply by 5/1 or within 3 weeks of notification.

**CONTACT** Mark C. Humbert, Director of Financial Aid, State University of New York at Oswego, 206 Culkin Hall, Oswego, NY 13126, 315-312-2248. *Fax:* 315-312-3696. *E-mail:* finaid@oswego.edu. *Website:* http://www.oswego.edu/.

# STATE UNIVERSITY OF NEW YORK AT PLATTSBURGH
## Plattsburgh, NY

| Tuition & fees (NY res): $7497 | Average undergraduate aid package: $12,581 |
|---|---|

**ABOUT THE INSTITUTION** State-supported, coed. *Awards:* certificates, bachelor's, and master's degrees. 58 undergraduate majors. *Total enrollment:* 5,968. Undergraduates: 5,565. Freshmen: 1,036. Both federal and institutional methodology are used as a basis for awarding need-based institutional aid.

**UNDERGRADUATE EXPENSES** for 2015–2016 *Application fee:* $50. *Tuition, state resident:* full-time $6170; part-time $257 per credit hour. *Tuition, nonresident:* full-time $15,820; part-time $659 per credit hour. *Required fees:* full-time $1327; $55.80 per credit hour. Full-time tuition and fees vary according to course load and location. Part-time tuition and fees vary according to course load and location. *College room and board:* $11,304; *Room only:* $7158. Room and board charges vary according to board plan and housing facility.

**FRESHMAN FINANCIAL AID (Fall 2014, est.)** 920 applied for aid; of those 73% were deemed to have need. 97% of freshmen with need received aid; of those 22% had need fully met. *Average percent of need met:* 79% (excluding resources awarded to replace EFC). *Average financial aid package:* $12,168 (excluding resources awarded to replace EFC). 19% of all full-time freshmen had no need and received non-need-based gift aid.

**UNDERGRADUATE FINANCIAL AID (Fall 2014, est.)** 4,168 applied for aid; of those 79% were deemed to have need. 98% of undergraduates with need received aid; of those 19% had need fully met. *Average percent of need met:* 78% (excluding resources awarded to replace EFC). *Average financial aid package:* $12,581 (excluding resources awarded to replace EFC). 14% of all full-time undergraduates had no need and received non-need-based gift aid.

**GIFT AID (NEED-BASED)** *Total amount:* $19,569,902 (46% federal, 34% state, 18% institutional, 2% external sources). *Receiving aid:* Freshmen: 57% (585); all full-time undergraduates: 54% (2,769). *Average award:* Freshmen: $7818; Undergraduates: $7067. *Scholarships, grants, and awards:* Federal Pell, FSEOG, state, private, college/university gift aid from institutional funds.

**GIFT AID (NON-NEED-BASED)** *Total amount:* $3,194,948 (3% federal, 8% state, 85% institutional, 4% external sources). *Receiving aid:* Freshmen: 20% (207). Undergraduates: 15% (792). *Average award:* Freshmen: $3451. Undergraduates: $3643. *Scholarships, grants, and awards by category: Academic interests/ achievement:* 4,758 awards ($5,515,630 total): area/ethnic studies, biological sciences, business, communication, computer science, education, engineering/technologies, English, general academic interests/achievements, health fields, home economics, humanities, international studies, mathematics, physical sciences, premedicine, social sciences. *Creative arts/performance:* 393 awards ($441,175 total): art/fine arts, journalism/publications, music, theater/drama. *Special achievements/activities:* 16 awards ($17,100 total): community service, general special achievements/activities, leadership. *Special characteristics:* 1,045 awards ($2,174,755 total): international students, out-of-state students. *Tuition waivers:* Full or partial for employees or children of employees.

**LOANS** *Student loans:* $26,568,982 (80% need-based, 20% non-need-based). 79% of past graduating class borrowed through all loan programs. *Average indebtedness per student:* $28,125. *Average need-based loan:* Freshmen: $6427. Undergraduates: $7712. *Parent loans:* $4,894,564 (70% need-based, 30% non-need-based). *Programs:* Federal Direct (Subsidized and Unsubsidized Stafford, PLUS), Perkins, Federal Nursing, private loans.

**WORK-STUDY** *Federal work-study:* Total amount: $544,485; 303 jobs averaging $2165. *State or other work-study/employment:* Part-time jobs available.

**APPLYING FOR FINANCIAL AID** *Required financial aid forms:* FAFSA, state aid form. *Financial aid deadline (priority):* 2/15. *Notification date:* Continuous beginning 3/1. Students must reply within 8 weeks of notification.

**CONTACT** Mr. Todd Moravec, Director of Financial Aid, State University of New York at Plattsburgh, 101 Broad Street, Plattsburgh, NY 12901-2681, 518-564-2072 or toll-free 888-673-0012. *Fax:* 518-564-4079. *E-mail:* todd.moravec@plattsburgh.edu. *Website:* http://www.plattsburgh.edu/.

# STATE UNIVERSITY OF NEW YORK COLLEGE AT CORTLAND
## Cortland, NY

| Tuition & fees (NY res): $7719 | Average undergraduate aid package: $13,587 |
|---|---|

**ABOUT THE INSTITUTION** State-supported, coed. *Awards:* certificates, bachelor's, and master's degrees. 57 undergraduate majors. *Total enrollment:* 6,958. Undergraduates: 6,317. Freshmen: 1,196. Federal methodology is used as a basis for awarding need-based institutional aid.

**UNDERGRADUATE EXPENSES** for 2015–2016 *Application fee:* $50. *Tuition, state resident:* full-time $6170; part-time $258 per credit hour. *Tuition, nonresident:* full-time $15,820; part-time $660 per credit hour. *Required fees:* full-time $1549. Full-time tuition and fees vary according to degree level. Part-time tuition and fees vary according to degree level. *College room and board:* $12,040; *Room only:* $7660. Room and board charges vary according to board plan and housing facility.

**FRESHMAN FINANCIAL AID (Fall 2013)** 1,100 applied for aid; of those 69% were deemed to have need. 95% of freshmen with need received aid; of those 11% had need fully met. *Average percent of need met:* 67% (excluding resources awarded to replace EFC). *Average financial aid package:* $13,607 (excluding resources awarded to replace EFC). 4% of all full-time freshmen had no need and received non-need-based gift aid.

**UNDERGRADUATE FINANCIAL AID (Fall 2013)** 5,192 applied for aid; of those 76% were deemed to have need. 97% of undergraduates with need received aid; of those 8% had need fully met. *Average percent of need met:* 68% (excluding resources awarded to replace EFC). *Average financial aid package:* $13,587 (excluding resources awarded to replace EFC). 3% of all full-time undergraduates had no need and received non-need-based gift aid.

**GIFT AID (NEED-BASED)** *Total amount:* $13,811,934 (55% federal, 45% state). *Receiving aid:* Freshmen: 40% (486); all full-time undergraduates: 44% (2,739). *Average award:* Freshmen: $5399; Undergraduates: $5825. *Scholarships, grants,* and awards: Federal Pell, FSEOG, state, private, college/university gift aid from institutional funds.

**GIFT AID (NON-NEED-BASED)** *Total amount:* $4,920,261 (26% federal, 36% institutional, 38% external sources). *Receiving aid:* Freshmen: 23% (276). Undergraduates: 15% (961). *Average award:* Freshmen: $3896. Undergraduates: $3947. *Scholarships, grants, and awards by category:* Academic interests/achievement: education, general academic interests/achievements, international studies, mathematics, physical sciences. *Creative arts/performance:* art/fine arts, music. *Special achievements/activities:* community service, general special achievements/activities, hobbies/interests, leadership. *Special characteristics:* adult students, local/state students, members of minority groups. *ROTC:* Army cooperative, Air Force cooperative.

**LOANS** *Student loans:* $34,641,042 (41% need-based, 59% non-need-based). 76% of past graduating class borrowed through all loan programs. *Average indebtedness per student:* $27,472. *Average need-based loan:* Freshmen: $3526. Undergraduates: $4335. *Parent loans:* $7,417,150 (100% non-need-based). *Programs:* Federal Direct (Subsidized and Unsubsidized Stafford, PLUS), Perkins.

**WORK-STUDY** *Federal work-study:* jobs available. *State or other work-study/employment:* Total amount: $1,053,659 (100% non-need-based). Part-time jobs available.

**APPLYING FOR FINANCIAL AID** *Required financial aid forms:* FAFSA, state aid form. *Financial aid deadline (priority):* 3/1. *Notification date:* Continuous beginning 3/15. Students must reply by 5/1 or within 4 weeks of notification.

**CONTACT** Karen Gallagher, Director of Financial Advisement, State University of New York College at Cortland, PO Box 2000, Cortland, NY 13045, 607-753-4717. *Fax:* 607-753-5990. *E-mail:* finaid@cortland.edu. *Website:* http://www.cortland.edu/.

# STATE UNIVERSITY OF NEW YORK COLLEGE AT GENESEO
## Geneseo, NY

| Tuition & fees (NY res): $7774 | Average undergraduate aid package: $10,672 |
|---|---|

**ABOUT THE INSTITUTION** State-supported, coed. *Awards:* bachelor's and master's degrees. 41 undergraduate majors. *Total enrollment:* 5,658. Undergraduates: 5,553. Freshmen: 1,236. Federal methodology is used as a basis for awarding need-based institutional aid.

**UNDERGRADUATE EXPENSES for 2015–2016** *Application fee:* $50. *Tuition, state resident:* full-time $6170; part-time $257 per credit hour. *Tuition, nonresident:* full-time $15,820; part-time $659 per credit hour. *Required fees:* full-time $1604; $66.65 per credit hour. Part-time tuition and fees vary according to course load. *College room and board:* $11,518; *Room only:* $7220. Room and board charges vary according to board plan and housing facility.

**FRESHMAN FINANCIAL AID (Fall 2014, est.)** 1,055 applied for aid; of those 60% were deemed to have need. 100% of freshmen with need received aid; of those 60% had need fully met. *Average percent of need met:* 60% (excluding resources awarded to replace EFC). *Average financial aid package:* $10,911 (excluding resources awarded to replace EFC). 6% of all full-time freshmen had no need and received non-need-based gift aid.

**UNDERGRADUATE FINANCIAL AID (Fall 2014, est.)** 3,921 applied for aid; of those 69% were deemed to have need. 100% of undergraduates with need received aid; of those 60% had need fully met. *Average percent of need met:* 60% (excluding resources awarded to replace EFC). *Average financial aid package:* $10,672 (excluding resources awarded to replace EFC). 11% of all full-time undergraduates had no need and received non-need-based gift aid.

**GIFT AID (NEED-BASED)** *Total amount:* $12,052,875 (47% federal, 53% state). *Receiving aid:* Freshmen: 40% (487); all full-time undergraduates: 39% (2,108). *Average award:* Freshmen: $6494; Undergraduates: $5718. *Scholarships, grants, and awards:* Federal Pell, FSEOG, state.

**GIFT AID (NON-NEED-BASED)** *Total amount:* $3,858,832 (2% federal, 15% state, 61% institutional, 22% external sources). *Receiving aid:* Freshmen: 11% (134). Undergraduates: 12% (650). *Average award:* Freshmen: $3952. Undergraduates: $2790. *Scholarships, grants, and awards by category:* Academic interests/achievement: area/ethnic studies, biological sciences, business, communication, computer science, education, English, foreign languages, general academic interests/achieve-

ments, humanities, international studies, mathematics, physical sciences, premedicine, social sciences. *Creative arts/performance:* applied art and design, art/fine arts, creative writing, dance, general creative arts/performance, journalism/publications, music, performing arts, theater/drama. *Special achievements/activities:* community service, leadership, memberships. *Special characteristics:* adult students, ethnic background, local/state students, members of minority groups, religious affiliation. *ROTC:* Army cooperative, Air Force cooperative.

**LOANS** *Student loans:* $21,455,500 (46% need-based, 54% non-need-based). 63% of past graduating class borrowed through all loan programs. *Average indebtedness per student:* $23,308. *Average need-based loan:* Freshmen: $4170. Undergraduates: $4844. *Parent loans:* $7,688,342 (100% non-need-based). *Programs:* Federal Direct (Subsidized and Unsubsidized Stafford, PLUS), Perkins.

**WORK-STUDY** *Federal work-study:* Total amount: $673,417; jobs available. *State or other work-study/employment:* Total amount: $744,200 (100% non-need-based). Part-time jobs available.

**APPLYING FOR FINANCIAL AID** *Required financial aid forms:* FAFSA, state aid form. *Financial aid deadline (priority):* 2/15. *Notification date:* Continuous beginning 3/15. Students must reply by 5/1.

**CONTACT** Archie Cureton, Director of Financial Aid, State University of New York College at Geneseo, 1 College Circle, Erwin Hall 104, Geneseo, NY 14454, 585-245-5731 or toll-free 866-245-5211. *Fax:* 585-245-5717. *E-mail:* finaid@geneseo.edu. *Website:* http://www.geneseo.edu/.

# STATE UNIVERSITY OF NEW YORK COLLEGE AT OLD WESTBURY
## Old Westbury, NY

| Tuition & fees (NY res): $7323 | Average undergraduate aid package: N/A |
|---|---|

**ABOUT THE INSTITUTION** State-supported, coed. *Awards:* certificates, bachelor's, and master's degrees. 42 undergraduate majors. *Total enrollment:* 4,504. Undergraduates: 4,317. Freshmen: 457. Both federal and institutional methodology are used as a basis for awarding need-based institutional aid.

**UNDERGRADUATE EXPENSES for 2015–2016** *Application fee:* $50. *Tuition, state resident:* full-time $6190; part-time $257 per credit hour. *Tuition, nonresident:* full-time $15,820; part-time $659 per credit hour. *Required fees:* full-time $1133; $22.35 per credit hour or $158 per term. Part-time tuition and fees vary according to course load. *College room and board:* $10,390; *Room only:* $7000. Room and board charges vary according to board plan.

**GIFT AID (NEED-BASED)** *Scholarships, grants, and awards:* Federal Pell, FSEOG, state, private, college/university gift aid from institutional funds.

**GIFT AID (NON-NEED-BASED)** *Scholarships, grants, and awards by category:* Academic interests/achievement: biological sciences, health fields, physical sciences. *Tuition waivers:* Full or partial for senior citizens. *ROTC:* Army cooperative, Air Force cooperative.

**LOANS** *Programs:* Federal Direct (Subsidized and Unsubsidized Stafford, PLUS), Perkins.

**WORK-STUDY** Federal work-study jobs available.

**APPLYING FOR FINANCIAL AID** *Required financial aid forms:* FAFSA, institution's own form, state aid form, verification worksheet. *Financial aid deadline (priority):* 4/15. *Notification date:* Continuous beginning 4/25. Students must reply within 2 weeks of notification.

**CONTACT** Ms. Dee Darrell, Financial Aid Assistant, State University of New York College at Old Westbury, PO Box 210, Old Westbury, NY 11568-0210, 516-876-3224. *Fax:* 516-876-3008. *E-mail:* finaid@oldwestbury.edu. *Website:* http://www.oldwestbury.edu/.

# STATE UNIVERSITY OF NEW YORK COLLEGE AT ONEONTA

### Oneonta, NY

**CONTACT** Mr. Bill Goodhue, Director of Financial Aid, State University of New York College at Oneonta, 108 Ravine Parkway, Oneonta, NY 13820, 607-436-2992 or toll-free 800-SUNY-123. *Fax:* 607-436-2659. *E-mail:* bill.goodhue@oneonta.edu. *Website:* http://www.oneonta.edu/.

# STATE UNIVERSITY OF NEW YORK COLLEGE AT POTSDAM

### Potsdam, NY

| Tuition & fees (NY res): $7553 | Average undergraduate aid package: $14,253 |
|---|---|

**ABOUT THE INSTITUTION** State-supported, coed. **Awards:** bachelor's and master's degrees. 46 undergraduate majors. **Total enrollment:** 3,979. Undergraduates: 3,681. Freshmen: 830. Federal methodology is used as a basis for awarding need-based institutional aid.

**UNDERGRADUATE EXPENSES for 2015–2016 Application fee:** $50. **Tuition, state resident:** full-time $6170; part-time $257 per credit hour. **Tuition, nonresident:** full-time $15,820; part-time $659 per credit hour. **Required fees:** full-time $1383. **College room and board:** $10,920; **Room only:** $6420. Room and board charges vary according to board plan and housing facility.

**FRESHMAN FINANCIAL AID (Fall 2014, est.)** 781 applied for aid; of those 80% were deemed to have need. 99% of freshmen with need received aid; of those 44% had need fully met. **Average percent of need met:** 90% (excluding resources awarded to replace EFC). **Average financial aid package:** $15,189 (excluding resources awarded to replace EFC). 9% of all full-time freshmen had no need and received non-need-based gift aid.

**UNDERGRADUATE FINANCIAL AID (Fall 2014, est.)** 3,297 applied for aid; of those 80% were deemed to have need. 99% of undergraduates with need received aid; of those 46% had need fully met. **Average percent of need met:** 88% (excluding resources awarded to replace EFC). **Average financial aid package:** $14,253 (excluding resources awarded to replace EFC). 8% of all full-time undergraduates had no need and received non-need-based gift aid.

**GIFT AID (NEED-BASED) Total amount:** $18,725,123 (43% federal, 42% state, 12% institutional, 3% external sources). **Receiving aid:** Freshmen: 67% (552); all full-time undergraduates: 65% (2,333). **Average award:** Freshmen: $8737; Undergraduates: $7614. **Scholarships, grants, and awards:** Federal Pell, FSEOG, state, private, college/university gift aid from institutional funds, TEACH Grants.

**GIFT AID (NON-NEED-BASED) Total amount:** $1,097,618 (3% federal, 5% state, 80% institutional, 12% external sources). **Receiving aid:** Freshmen: 29% (240). Undergraduates: 24% (865). **Average award:** Freshmen: $2798. Undergraduates: $2591. **Scholarships, grants, and awards by category:** Academic interests/achievement: 262 awards ($331,580 total): biological sciences, business, communication, computer science, education, engineering/technologies, English, foreign languages, general academic interests/achievements, humanities, mathematics, physical sciences, social sciences. Creative arts/performance: 171 awards ($229,565 total): art/fine arts, dance, music, performing arts, theater/drama. Special achievements/activities: 759 awards ($1,684,472 total): community service, general special achievements/activities, leadership. Special characteristics: 70 awards ($88,240 total): adult students, children and siblings of alumni, children of faculty/staff, ethnic background, handicapped students, local/state students, members of minority groups, previous college experience. **Tuition waivers:** Full or partial for employees or children of employees. **ROTC:** Army cooperative, Air Force cooperative.

**LOANS Student loans:** $21,503,788 (74% need-based, 26% non-need-based). 75% of past graduating class borrowed through all loan programs. *Average indebtedness per student:* $21,531. **Average need-based loan:** Freshmen: $3893. Undergraduates: $4653. **Parent loans:** $11,219,090 (31% need-based, 69% non-need-based). **Programs:** Federal Direct (Subsidized and Unsubsidized Stafford, PLUS), Perkins, alternative loans.

**WORK-STUDY Federal work-study:** Total amount: $367,676; 260 jobs averaging $1091.

**APPLYING FOR FINANCIAL AID Required financial aid forms:** FAFSA, state aid form. **Financial aid deadline:** 5/1 (priority: 3/1). **Notification date:** Continuous beginning 2/1. Students must reply by 5/1 or within 4 weeks of notification. **CONTACT** Susan C. Merchant, Director of Financial Aid, State University of New York College at Potsdam, 44 Pierrepont Avenue, Potsdam, NY 13676, 315-267-2162 or toll-free 877-POTSDAM. *Fax:* 315-267-3067. *E-mail:* finaid@potsdam.edu. *Website:* http://www.potsdam.edu/.

# STATE UNIVERSITY OF NEW YORK COLLEGE OF AGRICULTURE AND TECHNOLOGY AT COBLESKILL

### Cobleskill, NY

| Tuition & fees (NY res): $7609 | Average undergraduate aid package: $8250 |
|---|---|

**ABOUT THE INSTITUTION** State-supported, coed. **Awards:** certificates, associate, and bachelor's degrees. 49 undergraduate majors. **Total enrollment:** 2,532. Undergraduates: 2,532. Freshmen: 779. Federal methodology is used as a basis for awarding need-based institutional aid.

**UNDERGRADUATE EXPENSES for 2015–2016 Application fee:** $50. **Tuition, state resident:** full-time $6170; part-time $257 per credit hour. **Tuition, nonresident:** full-time $15,820; part-time $638 per credit hour. **Required fees:** full-time $1439; $57.26 per credit hour. Full-time tuition and fees vary according to degree level. Part-time tuition and fees vary according to degree level. **College room and board:** $12,140; **Room only:** $7280. Room and board charges vary according to board plan.

**FRESHMAN FINANCIAL AID (Fall 2013)** 748 applied for aid; of those 86% were deemed to have need. 99% of freshmen with need received aid; of those 1% had need fully met. **Average percent of need met:** 66% (excluding resources awarded to replace EFC). **Average financial aid package:** $8606 (excluding resources awarded to replace EFC). 13% of all full-time freshmen had no need and received non-need-based gift aid.

**UNDERGRADUATE FINANCIAL AID (Fall 2013)** 2,223 applied for aid; of those 88% were deemed to have need. 99% of undergraduates with need received aid; of those 3% had need fully met. **Average percent of need met:** 63% (excluding resources awarded to replace EFC). **Average financial aid package:** $8250 (excluding resources awarded to replace EFC). 10% of all full-time undergraduates had no need and received non-need-based gift aid.

**GIFT AID (NEED-BASED) Total amount:** $11,135,366 (53% federal, 47% state). **Receiving aid:** Freshmen: 81% (642); all full-time undergraduates: 75% (1,939). **Average award:** Freshmen: $5700; Undergraduates: $5231. **Scholarships, grants, and awards:** Federal Pell, FSEOG, state, private, college/university gift aid from institutional funds.

**GIFT AID (NON-NEED-BASED) Total amount:** $1,340,003 (25% institutional, 75% external sources). **Receiving aid:** Freshmen: 21% (163). Undergraduates: 14% (368). **Average award:** Freshmen: $635. Undergraduates: $410. **Scholarships, grants, and awards by category:** Academic interests/achievement: general academic interests/achievements. Special achievements/activities: leadership. Special characteristics: children and siblings of alumni, local/state students, members of minority groups. **Tuition waivers:** Full or partial for employees or children of employees, senior citizens.

**LOANS Student loans:** $13,033,177 (45% need-based, 55% non-need-based). 84% of past graduating class borrowed through all loan programs. *Average indebtedness per student:* $24,952. **Average need-based loan:** Freshmen: $3322. Undergraduates: $3705. **Parent loans:** $4,192,973 (100% need-based). **Programs:** Federal Direct (Subsidized and Unsubsidized Stafford, PLUS), Perkins.

**WORK-STUDY Federal work-study:** jobs available. **State or other work-study/employment:** Part-time jobs available.

**APPLYING FOR FINANCIAL AID Required financial aid forms:** FAFSA, institution's own form, state aid form. **Financial aid deadline:** Continuous. **Notification date:** Continuous beginning 3/1. Students must reply within 4 weeks of notification.

**CONTACT** Office of Financial Aid, State University of New York College of Agriculture and Technology at Cobleskill, 118B Knapp Hall, Cobleskill, NY 12043, 518-255-5623 or toll-free 800-295-8988. *Fax:* 518-255-5844. *E-mail:* financialaid@cobleskill.edu. *Website:* http://www.cobleskill.edu/.

**CONTACT** Mr. Mark J. Hill, Director of Financial Aid, State University of New York College of Environmental Science and Forestry, One Forestry Drive, Syracuse, NY 13210-2779, 315-470-6673. *Fax:* 315-470-4734. *E-mail:* mjhill@esf.edu. *Website:* http://www.esf.edu/.

# STATE UNIVERSITY OF NEW YORK COLLEGE OF ENVIRONMENTAL SCIENCE AND FORESTRY
## Syracuse, NY

| Tuition & fees (NY res): $7398 | Average undergraduate aid package: $15,000 |
|---|---|

**ABOUT THE INSTITUTION** State-supported, coed. *Awards:* certificates, associate, bachelor's, master's, and doctoral degrees. 55 undergraduate majors. *Total enrollment:* 2,457. Undergraduates: 1,856. Freshmen: 331. Federal methodology is used as a basis for awarding need-based institutional aid.
**UNDERGRADUATE EXPENSES for 2015–2016 Application fee:** $50. *Tuition, state resident:* full-time $6170; part-time $270 per credit hour. *Tuition, nonresident:* full-time $15,820; part-time $680 per credit hour. *Required fees:* full-time $1228; $60 per term. Full-time tuition and fees vary according to location. Part-time tuition and fees vary according to course load and location. *College room and board:* $15,120. Room and board charges vary according to board plan, housing facility, and location.
**FRESHMAN FINANCIAL AID (Fall 2014, est.)** 300 applied for aid; of those 85% were deemed to have need. 100% of freshmen with need received aid; of those 45% had need fully met. *Average percent of need met:* 83% (excluding resources awarded to replace EFC). *Average financial aid package:* $14,600 (excluding resources awarded to replace EFC). 15% of all full-time freshmen had no need and received non-need-based gift aid.
**UNDERGRADUATE FINANCIAL AID (Fall 2014, est.)** 1,348 applied for aid; of those 87% were deemed to have need. 100% of undergraduates with need received aid; of those 69% had need fully met. *Average percent of need met:* 86% (excluding resources awarded to replace EFC). *Average financial aid package:* $15,000 (excluding resources awarded to replace EFC). 8% of all full-time undergraduates had no need and received non-need-based gift aid.
**GIFT AID (NEED-BASED) Total amount:** $7,030,889 (30% federal, 24% state, 41% institutional, 5% external sources). *Receiving aid:* Freshmen: 69% (227); all full-time undergraduates: 65% (1,083). *Average award:* Freshmen: $6200; Undergraduates: $4720. *Scholarships, grants, and awards:* Federal Pell, FSEOG, state, private, college/university gift aid from institutional funds.
**GIFT AID (NON-NEED-BASED) Total amount:** $846,563 (4% federal, 11% state, 57% institutional, 28% external sources). *Receiving aid:* Freshmen: 41% (136). Undergraduates: 32% (541). *Average award:* Freshmen: $3091. Undergraduates: $3158. *Scholarships, grants, and awards by category:* Academic interests/achievement: agriculture, architecture, biological sciences, engineering/technologies, general academic interests/achievements, physical sciences, premedicine. *Special achievements/activities:* community service, general special achievements/activities, leadership, memberships. *Special characteristics:* children and siblings of alumni, general special characteristics, international students, local/state students, members of minority groups, out-of-state students. *ROTC:* Army cooperative, Air Force cooperative.
**LOANS Student loans:** $7,347,203 (45% need-based, 55% non-need-based). 70% of past graduating class borrowed through all loan programs. *Average indebtedness per student:* $25,399. *Average need-based loan:* Freshmen: $4000. Undergraduates: $4400. *Parent loans:* $2,702,437 (30% need-based, 70% non-need-based). *Programs:* Federal Direct (Subsidized and Unsubsidized Stafford, PLUS), Perkins.
**WORK-STUDY Federal work-study:** Total amount: $320,000; 192 jobs averaging $1622. *State or other work-study/employment:* Total amount: $354,089 (47% need-based, 53% non-need-based). 336 part-time jobs averaging $1054.
**APPLYING FOR FINANCIAL AID Required financial aid forms:** FAFSA, state aid form. *Financial aid deadline (priority):* 3/1. *Notification date:* Continuous beginning 3/15. Students must reply by 5/1.

# STATE UNIVERSITY OF NEW YORK COLLEGE OF TECHNOLOGY AT CANTON
## Canton, NY

| Tuition & fees (NY res): $7509 | Average undergraduate aid package: $10,516 |
|---|---|

**ABOUT THE INSTITUTION** State-supported, coed. *Awards:* certificates, associate, and bachelor's degrees. 35 undergraduate majors. *Total enrollment:* 3,278. Undergraduates: 3,278. Freshmen: 733. Federal methodology is used as a basis for awarding need-based institutional aid.
**UNDERGRADUATE EXPENSES for 2015–2016 Application fee:** $50. *One-time required fee:* $60. *Tuition, state resident:* full-time $6170; part-time $257 per credit hour. *Tuition, nonresident:* full-time $10,340; part-time $431 per credit hour. *Required fees:* full-time $1339; $59.40 per credit hour or $5 per term. Full-time tuition and fees vary according to degree level. Part-time tuition and fees vary according to degree level. *College room and board:* $11,300; *Room only:* $6700. Room and board charges vary according to board plan and housing facility.
**FRESHMAN FINANCIAL AID (Fall 2014, est.)** 705 applied for aid; of those 89% were deemed to have need. 99% of freshmen with need received aid; of those 17% had need fully met. *Average percent of need met:* 17% (excluding resources awarded to replace EFC). *Average financial aid package:* $10,622 (excluding resources awarded to replace EFC). 2% of all full-time freshmen had no need and received non-need-based gift aid.
**UNDERGRADUATE FINANCIAL AID (Fall 2014, est.)** 2,627 applied for aid; of those 90% were deemed to have need. 99% of undergraduates with need received aid; of those 16% had need fully met. *Average percent of need met:* 16% (excluding resources awarded to replace EFC). *Average financial aid package:* $10,516 (excluding resources awarded to replace EFC). 2% of all full-time undergraduates had no need and received non-need-based gift aid.
**GIFT AID (NEED-BASED) Total amount:** $17,478,669 (52% federal, 44% state, 4% institutional). *Receiving aid:* Freshmen: 78% (565); all full-time undergraduates: 73% (2,049). *Average award:* Freshmen: $8060; Undergraduates: $7648. *Scholarships, grants, and awards:* Federal Pell, FSEOG, state, private, college/university gift aid from institutional funds, Bureau of Indian Affairs Grants.
**GIFT AID (NON-NEED-BASED) Receiving aid:** Freshmen: 10% (73). Undergraduates: 8% (222). *Average award:* Freshmen: $922. Undergraduates: $1254. *Tuition waivers:* Full or partial for employees or children of employees. *ROTC:* Army cooperative, Air Force cooperative.
**LOANS Student loans:** $16,589,158 (51% need-based, 49% non-need-based). 88% of past graduating class borrowed through all loan programs. *Average indebtedness per student:* $30,905. *Average need-based loan:* Freshmen: $3461. Undergraduates: $3953. *Parent loans:* $4,735,374 (100% need-based). *Programs:* Federal Direct (Subsidized and Unsubsidized Stafford, PLUS), Perkins, alternative loans.
**WORK-STUDY Federal work-study:** Total amount: $173,871; 145 jobs averaging $1199. *State or other work-study/employment:* Total amount: $5972 (100% need-based). 5 part-time jobs averaging $1194.
**APPLYING FOR FINANCIAL AID Required financial aid forms:** FAFSA, state aid form. *Financial aid deadline (priority):* 3/1. *Notification date:* Continuous beginning 2/15. Students must reply within 4 weeks of notification.
**CONTACT** Ms. Kerrie Cooper, Director of Financial Aid, State University of New York College of Technology at Canton, Student Service Center, Canton, NY 13617, 315-386-7616 or toll-free 800-388-7123. *Fax:* 315-386-7930. *E-mail:* cooper@canton.edu. *Website:* http://www.canton.edu/.

# STATE UNIVERSITY OF NEW YORK COLLEGE OF TECHNOLOGY AT DELHI
### Delhi, NY

| Tuition & fees (NY res): $7530 | Average undergraduate aid package: N/A |
|---|---|

**ABOUT THE INSTITUTION** State-supported, coed. *Awards:* certificates, associate, bachelor's, and master's degrees. 36 undergraduate majors. *Total enrollment:* 3,616. Undergraduates: 3,614. Freshmen: 965. Federal methodology is used as a basis for awarding need-based institutional aid.

**UNDERGRADUATE EXPENSES for 2015–2016 Application fee:** $50. *Tuition, state resident:* full-time $6170; part-time $257 per credit hour. *Tuition, nonresident:* full-time $10,340; part-time $431 per credit hour. *Required fees:* full-time $1360; $65.66 per credit hour or $65.66 per credit hour. Full-time tuition and fees vary according to degree level. Part-time tuition and fees vary according to degree level. *College room and board:* $10,970; *Room only:* $6310. Room and board charges vary according to board plan and housing facility.

**FRESHMAN FINANCIAL AID (Fall 2013)** 917 applied for aid; of those 95% were deemed to have need. 98% of freshmen with need received aid.

**UNDERGRADUATE FINANCIAL AID (Fall 2013)** 2,620 applied for aid; of those 97% were deemed to have need. 92% of undergraduates with need received aid.

**GIFT AID (NEED-BASED) Total amount:** $13,303,499 (53% federal, 38% state, 4% institutional, 5% external sources). *Receiving aid:* Freshmen: 77% (741); all full-time undergraduates: 72% (1,950). *Scholarships, grants, and awards:* Federal Pell, FSEOG, state, private, college/university gift aid from institutional funds.

**GIFT AID (NON-NEED-BASED) Scholarships, grants, and awards by category:** *Academic interests/achievement:* general academic interests/achievements. *Special achievements/activities:* community service.

**LOANS Student loans:** $15,868,362 (100% need-based). 87% of past graduating class borrowed through all loan programs. *Parent loans:* $4,598,477 (100% need-based). *Programs:* Federal Direct (Subsidized and Unsubsidized Stafford, PLUS), Perkins.

**WORK-STUDY Federal work-study:** jobs available. *State or other work-study/employment:* Total amount: $439,981 (100% need-based). Part-time jobs available.

**APPLYING FOR FINANCIAL AID Required financial aid forms:** FAFSA, state aid form. *Financial aid deadline (priority):* 2/15. *Notification date:* Continuous beginning 3/15.

**CONTACT** Nancy B. Hughes, Director of Financial Aid, State University of New York College of Technology at Delhi, 158 Bush Hall, Delhi, NY 13753, 607-746-4570 or toll-free 800-96-DELHI. *Fax:* 607-746-4104. *Website:* http://www.delhi.edu/.

# STATE UNIVERSITY OF NEW YORK DOWNSTATE MEDICAL CENTER
### Brooklyn, NY

**CONTACT** Financial Aid Office, State University of New York Downstate Medical Center, 450 Clarkson Avenue, Brooklyn, NY 11203-2098, 718-270-2488. *Fax:* 718-270-7592. *E-mail:* finaid1@downstate.edu. *Website:* http://www.downstate.edu/.

# STATE UNIVERSITY OF NEW YORK MARITIME COLLEGE
### Throggs Neck, NY

| Tuition & fees (NY res): $7446 | Average undergraduate aid package: $7520 |
|---|---|

**ABOUT THE INSTITUTION** State-supported, coed. *Awards:* associate, bachelor's, and master's degrees. 6 undergraduate majors. *Total enrollment:* 1,799. Undergraduates: 1,641. Freshmen: 349. Federal methodology is used as a basis for awarding need-based institutional aid.

**UNDERGRADUATE EXPENSES for 2015–2016 Application fee:** $50. *Tuition, state resident:* full-time $6170; part-time $257 per credit hour. *Tuition, nonresident:* full-time $15,820; part-time $659 per credit hour. *Required fees:* full-time $1276. Full-time tuition and fees vary according to course load. Part-time tuition and fees vary according to course load. *College room and board:* $11,040; *Room only:* $7132. Room and board charges vary according to board plan and housing facility.

**FRESHMAN FINANCIAL AID (Fall 2013)** 194 applied for aid; of those 94% were deemed to have need. 86% of freshmen with need received aid; of those 4% had need fully met. *Average percent of need met:* 45% (excluding resources awarded to replace EFC). *Average financial aid package:* $6226 (excluding resources awarded to replace EFC). 7% of all full-time freshmen had no need and received non-need-based gift aid.

**UNDERGRADUATE FINANCIAL AID (Fall 2013)** 826 applied for aid; of those 96% were deemed to have need. 92% of undergraduates with need received aid; of those 2% had need fully met. *Average percent of need met:* 44% (excluding resources awarded to replace EFC). *Average financial aid package:* $7520 (excluding resources awarded to replace EFC). 3% of all full-time undergraduates had no need and received non-need-based gift aid.

**GIFT AID (NEED-BASED) Total amount:** $4,025,505 (50% federal, 34% state, 7% institutional, 9% external sources). *Receiving aid:* Freshmen: 30% (100); all full-time undergraduates: 34% (518). *Average award:* Freshmen: $5231; Undergraduates: $5232. *Scholarships, grants, and awards:* Federal Pell, FSEOG, state, private, college/university gift aid from institutional funds, Educational Opportunity Program (EOP).

**GIFT AID (NON-NEED-BASED) Total amount:** $1,235,414 (27% federal, 29% state, 17% institutional, 27% external sources). *Receiving aid:* Freshmen: 16% (53). Undergraduates: 15% (233). *Average award:* Freshmen: $2711. Undergraduates: $2255. *Scholarships, grants, and awards by category:* Academic interests/achievement: 104 awards ($235,155 total): general academic interests/achievements. *Special achievements/activities:* leadership. *ROTC:* Army cooperative, Naval.

**LOANS Student loans:** $8,067,834 (55% need-based, 45% non-need-based). *Average need-based loan:* Freshmen: $3152. Undergraduates: $4282. *Parent loans:* $2,823,553 (2% need-based, 98% non-need-based). *Programs:* Federal Direct (Subsidized and Unsubsidized Stafford, PLUS), Perkins, alternative loans.

**WORK-STUDY Federal work-study:** 33 jobs averaging $420.

**APPLYING FOR FINANCIAL AID Required financial aid form:** FAFSA. *Financial aid deadline:* 7/15 (priority: 3/15). *Notification date:* 3/1. Students must reply by 5/1.

**CONTACT** Ms. Wen Huang, Acting Director of Financial Aid, State University of New York Maritime College, 6 Pennyfield Avenue, Throgs Neck, NY 10465-4198, 718-409-7268. *Fax:* 718-409-7275. *E-mail:* whuang@sunymaritime.edu. *Website:* http://www.sunymaritime.edu/.

# STATE UNIVERSITY OF NEW YORK POLYTECHNIC INSTITUTE
### Utica, NY

| Tuition & fees (NY res): $7440 | Average undergraduate aid package: $9820 |
|---|---|

**ABOUT THE INSTITUTION** State-supported, coed. *Awards:* certificates, bachelor's, and master's degrees. 21 undergraduate majors. *Total enrollment:* 2,737. Undergraduates: 2,034. Freshmen: 347. Federal methodology is used as a basis for awarding need-based institutional aid.

**UNDERGRADUATE EXPENSES for 2015–2016 Application fee:** $50. *Tuition, state resident:* full-time $6170; part-time $257 per credit hour. *Tuition, nonresident:* full-time $15,820; part-time $659 per credit hour. *Required fees:* full-time $1270; $52.80 per credit hour. Part-time tuition and fees vary according to course load. *College room and board:* $11,236. Room and board charges vary according to board plan.

**FRESHMAN FINANCIAL AID (Fall 2014, est.)** 336 applied for aid; of those 70% were deemed to have need. 100% of freshmen with need received aid; of those 99% had need fully met. *Average percent of need met:* 99% (excluding resources awarded to replace EFC). *Average financial aid package:* $9845 (excluding resources awarded to replace EFC). 22% of all full-time freshmen had no need and received non-need-based gift aid.

**UNDERGRADUATE FINANCIAL AID (Fall 2014, est.)** 1,468 applied for aid; of those 79% were deemed to have need. 100% of undergraduates with need received aid; of those 99% had need fully met. **Average percent of need met:** 99% (excluding resources awarded to replace EFC). **Average financial aid package:** $9820 (excluding resources awarded to replace EFC). 3% of all full-time undergraduates had no need and received non-need-based gift aid.

**GIFT AID (NEED-BASED) Total amount:** $7,223,420 (49% federal, 33% state, 15% institutional, 3% external sources). **Receiving aid:** Freshmen: 61% (212); all full-time undergraduates: 62% (1,017). **Average award:** Freshmen: $7472; Undergraduates: $6910. **Scholarships, grants, and awards:** Federal Pell, FSEOG, state, private, college/university gift aid from institutional funds.

**GIFT AID (NON-NEED-BASED) Total amount:** $758,190 (7% state, 46% institutional, 47% external sources). **Receiving aid:** Freshmen: 43% (148). Undergraduates: 21% (351). **Average award:** Freshmen: $2518. Undergraduates: $2308. **Scholarships, grants, and awards by category:** Academic interests/achievement: computer science, engineering/technologies, general academic interests/achievements. Special characteristics: local/state students, members of minority groups, previous college experience. ROTC: Army cooperative, Air Force cooperative.

**LOANS Student loans:** $10,524,155 (85% need-based, 15% non-need-based). **Average need-based loan:** Freshmen: $2981. Undergraduates: $3731. **Parent loans:** $4,275,576 (67% need-based, 33% non-need-based). **Programs:** Federal Direct (Subsidized and Unsubsidized Stafford, PLUS), Perkins, Federal Nursing.

**WORK-STUDY Federal work-study:** Total amount: $189,528; jobs available. **State or other work-study/employment:** Total amount: $193,250 (86% need-based, 14% non-need-based). Part-time jobs available.

**APPLYING FOR FINANCIAL AID Required financial aid forms:** FAFSA, state aid form. **Financial aid deadline (priority):** 3/1. **Notification date:** Continuous beginning 3/15. Students must reply within 2 weeks of notification.

**CONTACT** Office of Financial Aid, State University of New York Polytechnic Institute, 100 Seymour Road, Utica, NY 13502, 315-792-7210 or toll-free 866-278-6948. Fax: 315-792-7220. E-mail: finaid@sunyIt.edu. Website: http://www.sunypoly.edu/.

# STATE UNIVERSITY OF NEW YORK UPSTATE MEDICAL UNIVERSITY
### Syracuse, NY

**ABOUT THE INSTITUTION** State-supported, coed. 6 undergraduate majors.
**GIFT AID (NEED-BASED) Scholarships, grants, and awards:** Federal Pell, FSEOG, state, college/university gift aid from institutional funds.
**GIFT AID (NON-NEED-BASED) Scholarships, grants, and awards by category:** Academic interests/achievement: health fields.
**LOANS Programs:** Federal Direct (Subsidized and Unsubsidized Stafford, PLUS), Perkins.
**WORK-STUDY Federal work-study:** 45 jobs averaging $1568.
**APPLYING FOR FINANCIAL AID Required financial aid form:** FAFSA.

**CONTACT** Michael Pede, Office of Financial Aid, State University of New York Upstate Medical University, Weiskotten Hall, Room 1213, 766 Irving Avenue, Syracuse, NY 13210-2375, 315-464-4329 or toll-free 800-736-2171. E-mail: finaid@upstate.edu. Website: http://www.upstate.edu/.

# STEPHEN F. AUSTIN STATE UNIVERSITY
### Nacogdoches, TX

| Tuition & fees (TX res): $8892 | Average undergraduate aid package: $11,487 |
| --- | --- |

**ABOUT THE INSTITUTION** State-supported, coed. **Awards:** bachelor's, master's, and doctoral degrees. 65 undergraduate majors. **Total enrollment:** 12,801. Undergraduates: 11,024. Freshmen: 2,013. Federal methodology is used as a basis for awarding need-based institutional aid.

**UNDERGRADUATE EXPENSES for 2015–2016 Application fee:** $45. **Tuition, state resident:** full-time $6630; part-time $221 per credit hour. **Tuition, nonresident:** full-time $17,490; part-time $583 per credit hour. **Required fees:** full-time $2262; $157 per credit hour. Full-time tuition and fees vary according to course load, degree level, and location. Part-time tuition and fees vary according to course load, degree level, and location. **College room and board:** $8868. Room and board charges vary according to board plan and housing facility. **Payment plan:** Guaranteed tuition.

**FRESHMAN FINANCIAL AID (Fall 2013)** 1,737 applied for aid; of those 80% were deemed to have need. 100% of freshmen with need received aid; of those 14% had need fully met. **Average percent of need met:** 58% (excluding resources awarded to replace EFC). **Average financial aid package:** $11,783 (excluding resources awarded to replace EFC). 9% of all full-time freshmen had no need and received non-need-based gift aid.

**UNDERGRADUATE FINANCIAL AID (Fall 2013)** 7,974 applied for aid; of those 84% were deemed to have need. 100% of undergraduates with need received aid; of those 14% had need fully met. **Average percent of need met:** 58% (excluding resources awarded to replace EFC). **Average financial aid package:** $11,487 (excluding resources awarded to replace EFC). 7% of all full-time undergraduates had no need and received non-need-based gift aid.

**GIFT AID (NEED-BASED) Total amount:** $32,075,995 (63% federal, 22% state, 15% institutional). **Receiving aid:** Freshmen: 50% (1,011); all full-time undergraduates: 50% (5,050). **Average award:** Freshmen: $8799; Undergraduates: $6537. **Scholarships, grants, and awards:** Federal Pell, FSEOG, state, private, college/university gift aid from institutional funds, Academic Competitiveness Grants, National SMART Grants, TEACH Grants.

**GIFT AID (NON-NEED-BASED) Total amount:** $12,018,444 (4% federal, 4% state, 69% institutional, 23% external sources). **Receiving aid:** Freshmen: 33% (670). Undergraduates: 22% (2,250). **Average award:** Freshmen: $3245. Undergraduates: $2795. **Scholarships, grants, and awards by category:** Academic interests/achievement: agriculture, biological sciences, business, communication, computer science, education, general academic interests/achievements, health fields, home economics, mathematics, military science, physical sciences, premedicine. Creative arts/performance: journalism/publications, music, theater/drama. Special achievements/activities: cheerleading/drum major, general special achievements/activities, hobbies/interests, leadership, rodeo. Special characteristics: adult students, children and siblings of alumni, children of faculty/staff, children of union members/company employees, first-generation college students, general special characteristics, local/state students, previous college experience, veterans, veterans' children. **Tuition waivers:** Full or partial for employees or children of employees, senior citizens. **ROTC:** Army.

**LOANS Student loans:** $72,661,419 (35% need-based, 65% non-need-based). 66% of past graduating class borrowed through all loan programs. Average indebtedness per student: $27,278. **Average need-based loan:** Freshmen: $3630. Undergraduates: $4798. **Parent loans:** $16,206,097 (100% non-need-based). **Programs:** Federal Direct (Subsidized and Unsubsidized Stafford, PLUS), Perkins, state, college/university, short-term emergency loans.

**WORK-STUDY Federal work-study:** jobs available. **State or other work-study/employment:** Total amount: $90,154 (100% need-based). Part-time jobs available.

**ATHLETIC AWARDS** Total amount: $3,723,587 (100% non-need-based).
**APPLYING FOR FINANCIAL AID Required financial aid form:** FAFSA. **Financial aid deadline:** Continuous. **Notification date:** Continuous beginning 4/1.

**CONTACT** H. Rachele Garrett, Office of Financial Aid, Stephen F. Austin State University, PO Box 13052, Nacogdoches, TX 75962, 936-468-2403 or toll-free 800-731-2902. Fax: 936-468-1048. E-mail: finaid@sfasu.edu. Website: http://www.sfasu.edu/.

# STEPHENS COLLEGE
### Columbia, MO

| Tuition & fees: $28,510 | Average undergraduate aid package: $24,002 |
| --- | --- |

**ABOUT THE INSTITUTION** Independent, women only. **Awards:** certificates, associate, bachelor's, and master's degrees. 25 undergraduate majors. **Total enrollment:** 865. Undergraduates: 668. Freshmen: 184. Federal methodology is used as a basis for awarding need-based institutional aid.

**UNDERGRADUATE EXPENSES for 2015–2016** *Application fee:* $25. *Comprehensive fee:* $38,042 includes full-time tuition ($28,310), mandatory fees ($200), and room and board ($9532). *College room only:* $6065. Full-time tuition and fees vary according to course load, degree level, program, and reciprocity agreements. Room and board charges vary according to board plan and housing facility. *Part-time tuition:* $700 per credit hour. Part-time tuition and fees vary according to course load, degree level, and program.

**FRESHMAN FINANCIAL AID (Fall 2014, est.)** 146 applied for aid; of those 97% were deemed to have need. 100% of freshmen with need received aid; of those 10% had need fully met. *Average percent of need met:* 70% (excluding resources awarded to replace EFC). *Average financial aid package:* $24,869 (excluding resources awarded to replace EFC). 7% of all full-time freshmen had no need and received non-need-based gift aid.

**UNDERGRADUATE FINANCIAL AID (Fall 2014, est.)** 447 applied for aid; of those 97% were deemed to have need. 100% of undergraduates with need received aid; of those 12% had need fully met. *Average percent of need met:* 70% (excluding resources awarded to replace EFC). *Average financial aid package:* $24,002 (excluding resources awarded to replace EFC). 7% of all full-time undergraduates had no need and received non-need-based gift aid.

**GIFT AID (NEED-BASED)** *Total amount:* $3,705,278 (35% federal, 7% state, 58% institutional). *Receiving aid:* Freshmen: 66% (121); all full-time undergraduates: 69% (386). *Average award:* Freshmen: $8148; Undergraduates: $9175. *Scholarships, grants, and awards:* Federal Pell, FSEOG, state, private, college/university gift aid from institutional funds, Academic Competitiveness Grants, National SMART Grants.

**GIFT AID (NON-NEED-BASED)** *Total amount:* $3,670,079 (1% state, 92% institutional, 7% external sources). *Receiving aid:* Freshmen: 75% (138). Undergraduates: 74% (412). *Average award:* Freshmen: $7371. Undergraduates: $7264. *Scholarships, grants, and awards by category:* Academic interests/achievement: 622 awards ($2,922,712 total): English, general academic interests/achievements. Creative arts/performance: 85 awards ($192,875 total): dance, music, performing arts, theater/drama. Special achievements/activities: 108 awards ($665,840 total): leadership, memberships. Special characteristics: 27 awards ($220,060 total): children of faculty/staff, children of union members/company employees, parents of current students, siblings of current students, veterans, veterans' children. *Tuition waivers:* Full or partial for employees or children of employees. *ROTC:* Army cooperative, Naval cooperative, Air Force cooperative.

**LOANS** *Student loans:* $4,717,474 (43% need-based, 57% non-need-based). 77% of past graduating class borrowed through all loan programs. *Average indebtedness per student:* $26,824. *Average need-based loan:* Freshmen: $3370. Undergraduates: $4360. *Parent loans:* $984,124 (100% non-need-based). *Programs:* Federal Direct (Subsidized and Unsubsidized Stafford, PLUS), Perkins, alternative loans.

**WORK-STUDY** *Federal work-study:* Total amount: $83,500; 54 jobs averaging $1546. *State or other work-study/employment:* Total amount: $220,491 (100% non-need-based). 150 part-time jobs averaging $1475.

**ATHLETIC AWARDS** Total amount: $662,170 (100% non-need-based).

**APPLYING FOR FINANCIAL AID** *Required financial aid form:* FAFSA. *Financial aid deadline (priority):* 3/15. *Notification date:* Continuous beginning 3/1.

**CONTACT** Mrs. Kim Stonecipher-Fisher, Director of Financial Aid, Stephens College, 1200 East Broadway, Columbia, MO 65215-0002, 800-876-7207. *Fax:* 573-876-2320. *E-mail:* finaid@stephens.edu.
*Website:* http://www.stephens.edu/.

---

# STERLING COLLEGE
## Sterling, KS

| Tuition & fees: $21,990 | Average undergraduate aid package: $21,107 |
| --- | --- |

**ABOUT THE INSTITUTION** Independent Presbyterian, coed. *Awards:* bachelor's degrees. 20 undergraduate majors. *Total enrollment:* 718. Undergraduates: 718. Freshmen: 188. Federal methodology is used as a basis for awarding need-based institutional aid.

**UNDERGRADUATE EXPENSES for 2015–2016** *Application fee:* $25. *Comprehensive fee:* $29,921 includes full-time tuition ($21,700), mandatory fees ($290), and room and board ($7931). Room and board charges vary according to board plan and housing facility. *Part-time tuition:* $406 per credit.

**FRESHMAN FINANCIAL AID (Fall 2013)** 127 applied for aid; of those 97% were deemed to have need. 100% of freshmen with need received aid; of those 24% had need fully met. *Average percent of need met:* 83% (excluding resources awarded to replace EFC). *Average financial aid package:* $19,893 (excluding resources awarded to replace EFC). 4% of all full-time freshmen had no need and received non-need-based gift aid.

**UNDERGRADUATE FINANCIAL AID (Fall 2013)** 588 applied for aid; of those 87% were deemed to have need. 100% of undergraduates with need received aid; of those 32% had need fully met. *Average percent of need met:* 89% (excluding resources awarded to replace EFC). *Average financial aid package:* $21,107 (excluding resources awarded to replace EFC). 13% of all full-time undergraduates had no need and received non-need-based gift aid.

**GIFT AID (NEED-BASED)** *Total amount:* $5,486,389 (25% federal, 7% state, 68% institutional). *Receiving aid:* Freshmen: 90% (116); all full-time undergraduates: 82% (487). *Average award:* Freshmen: $11,066; Undergraduates: $11,050. *Scholarships, grants, and awards:* Federal Pell, FSEOG, state, private, college/university gift aid from institutional funds.

**GIFT AID (NON-NEED-BASED)** *Total amount:* $786,711 (74% institutional, 26% external sources). *Average award:* Freshmen: $12,330. Undergraduates: $9778. *Scholarships, grants, and awards by category:* Academic interests/achievement: 529 awards ($3,363,496 total): general academic interests/achievements. Creative arts/performance: 139 awards ($260,464 total): art/fine arts, dance, debating, general creative arts/performance, music, theater/drama. Special achievements/activities: 21 awards ($36,088 total): cheerleading/drum major, religious involvement. Special characteristics: 50 awards ($142,341 total): children and siblings of alumni, twins. *Tuition waivers:* Full or partial for employees or children of employees, senior citizens.

**LOANS** *Student loans:* $4,360,580 (59% need-based, 41% non-need-based). 81% of past graduating class borrowed through all loan programs. *Average indebtedness per student:* $28,221. *Average need-based loan:* Freshmen: $4179. Undergraduates: $5297. *Parent loans:* $976,082 (100% non-need-based). *Programs:* Federal Direct (Subsidized and Unsubsidized Stafford, PLUS), Perkins, college/university.

**WORK-STUDY** *Federal work-study:* 206 jobs averaging $712.

**ATHLETIC AWARDS** Total amount: $1,677,185 (89% need-based, 11% non-need-based).

**APPLYING FOR FINANCIAL AID** *Required financial aid form:* FAFSA. *Financial aid deadline (priority):* 3/15. *Notification date:* Continuous beginning 2/1. Students must reply within 2 weeks of notification.

**CONTACT** Ms. Mitzi Suhler, Director of Financial Aid, Sterling College, 125 W. Cooper, Sterling, KS 67579, 620-278-4226 or toll-free 800-346-1017. *Fax:* 620-278-4416. *E-mail:* msuhler@sterling.edu.
*Website:* http://www.sterling.edu/.

---

# STERLING COLLEGE
## Craftsbury Common, VT

**ABOUT THE INSTITUTION** Independent, coed. *Awards:* bachelor's degrees. 11 undergraduate majors. *Total enrollment:* 119. Undergraduates: 119. Freshmen: 20.

**GIFT AID (NEED-BASED)** *Scholarships, grants, and awards:* Federal Pell, FSEOG, state, private, college/university gift aid from institutional funds, Veterans Administration Benefits, Yellow Ribbon Grant Program.

**GIFT AID (NON-NEED-BASED)** *Scholarships, grants, and awards by category:* Academic interests/achievement: general academic interests/achievements. Special achievements/activities: general special achievements/activities, leadership. Special characteristics: general special characteristics, previous college experience.

**LOANS** *Programs:* Federal Direct (Subsidized and Unsubsidized Stafford, PLUS).

**WORK-STUDY** *Federal work-study:* jobs available. *State or other work-study/employment:* Part-time jobs available.

**APPLYING FOR FINANCIAL AID** *Required financial aid forms:* FAFSA, institution's own form.

**CONTACT** Barbara Stuart, Director of Financial Aid, Sterling College, PO Box 72, Craftsbury Common, VT 05827, 800-648-3591 Ext. 3 or toll-free 800-648-3591 Ext. 100. *Fax:* 802-586-2596. *E-mail:* bstuart@sterlingcollege.edu.
*Website:* http://www.sterlingcollege.edu/.

# STETSON UNIVERSITY
## DeLand, FL

| Tuition & fees: $41,590 | Average undergraduate aid package: $33,033 |
|---|---|

**ABOUT THE INSTITUTION** Independent, coed. **Awards:** certificates, bachelor's, master's, and doctoral degrees. 55 undergraduate majors. **Total enrollment:** 4,137. Undergraduates: 2,841. Freshmen: 773. Federal methodology is used as a basis for awarding need-based institutional aid.

**UNDERGRADUATE EXPENSES for 2015–2016 Application fee:** $50. **Tuition:** full-time $41,240; part-time $4274 per course. Part-time tuition and fees vary according to course load. Room and board charges vary according to board plan and housing facility.

**FRESHMAN FINANCIAL AID (Fall 2014, est.)** 683 applied for aid; of those 89% were deemed to have need. 100% of freshmen with need received aid; of those 22% had need fully met. **Average percent of need met:** 79% (excluding resources awarded to replace EFC). **Average financial aid package:** $34,219 (excluding resources awarded to replace EFC). 17% of all full-time freshmen had no need and received non-need-based gift aid.

**UNDERGRADUATE FINANCIAL AID (Fall 2014, est.)** 2,326 applied for aid; of those 88% were deemed to have need. 100% of undergraduates with need received aid; of those 20% had need fully met. **Average percent of need met:** 76% (excluding resources awarded to replace EFC). **Average financial aid package:** $33,033 (excluding resources awarded to replace EFC). 21% of all full-time undergraduates had no need and received non-need-based gift aid.

**GIFT AID (NEED-BASED) Total amount:** $51,162,448 (9% federal, 12% state, 78% institutional, 1% external sources). **Receiving aid:** Freshmen: 78% (604); all full-time undergraduates: 73% (2,036). **Average award:** Freshmen: $27,487; Undergraduates: $26,057. **Scholarships, grants, and awards:** Federal Pell, FSEOG, state, private, college/university gift aid from institutional funds.

**GIFT AID (NON-NEED-BASED) Total amount:** $17,707,242 (13% state, 86% institutional, 1% external sources). **Receiving aid:** Freshmen: 16% (122). Undergraduates: 12% (339). **Average award:** Freshmen: $21,120. Undergraduates: $19,811. **Scholarships, grants, and awards by category:** Academic interests/achievement: area/ethnic studies, biological sciences, business, communication, computer science, education, English, foreign languages, general academic interests/achievements, humanities, mathematics, military science, physical sciences, premedicine, religion/biblical studies, social sciences. Creative arts/performance: applied art and design, art/fine arts, music, theater/drama. Special achievements/activities: cheerleading/drum major, community service, general special achievements/activities, junior miss, leadership, religious involvement. Special characteristics: children and siblings of alumni, children of faculty/staff, ethnic background, first-generation college students, general special characteristics, international students, local/state students, members of minority groups, out-of-state students, veterans, veterans' children. **Tuition waivers:** Full or partial for employees or children of employees. **ROTC:** Army cooperative.

**LOANS Student loans:** $15,867,632 (78% need-based, 22% non-need-based). 70% of past graduating class borrowed through all loan programs. **Average indebtedness per student:** $32,302. **Average need-based loan:** Freshmen: $3798. Undergraduates: $5082. **Parent loans:** $6,025,716 (55% need-based, 45% non-need-based). **Programs:** Federal Direct (Subsidized and Unsubsidized Stafford, PLUS), Perkins.

**WORK-STUDY Federal work-study:** Total amount: $2,206,958; 904 jobs averaging $2444. **State or other work-study/employment:** Total amount: $685,405 (11% need-based, 89% non-need-based). 277 part-time jobs averaging $2465.

**ATHLETIC AWARDS** Total amount: $4,772,080 (42% need-based, 58% non-need-based).

**APPLYING FOR FINANCIAL AID Required financial aid form:** FAFSA. **Financial aid deadline (priority):** 2/15. **Notification date:** Continuous beginning 2/15. Students must reply within 2 weeks of notification.

**CONTACT** Sean View, Interim Director of Financial Aid, Stetson University, 421 North Woodland Boulevard, DeLand, FL 32723, 386-822-7120 or toll-free 800-688-0101. *Fax:* 386-822-7126. *E-mail:* finaid@stetson.edu. *Website:* http://www.stetson.edu/.

# STEVENS-HENAGER COLLEGE
## Idaho Falls, ID

**CONTACT** Financial Aid Office, Stevens-Henager College, 901 Pier View Drive, Suite 105, Idaho Falls, ID 83402, 208-522-0887 or toll-free 800-622-2640. *Website:* http://www.stevenshenager.edu/.

# STEVENS-HENAGER COLLEGE
## St. George, UT

**CONTACT** Financial Aid Office, Stevens-Henager College, 720 South River Road, Suite C-130, St. George, UT 84790, 435-628-9150 or toll-free 800-622-2640. *Website:* http://www.stevenshenager.edu/.

# STEVENS-HENAGER COLLEGE–BOISE
## Boise, ID

**CONTACT** Ms. Jaime L. Davis, Training and Project Development, Stevens-Henager College–Boise, 1444 South Entertainment Avenue, Boise, ID 83709, 208-383-4540 Ext. 1875 or toll-free 800-622-2670 (in-state), 800-622-2640 (out-of-state). *Fax:* 208-345-6999. *E-mail:* jaime.davis@stevenshenager.edu. *Website:* http://www.stevenshenager.edu/.

# STEVENS-HENAGER COLLEGE–OGDEN/WEST HAVEN
## Ogden, UT

**CONTACT** Financial Aid Office, Stevens-Henager College–Ogden/West Haven, 1890 South 1350 West, Ogden, UT 84401, 801-394-7791 or toll-free 800-622-2640. *Website:* http://www.stevenshenager.edu/.

# STEVENS INSTITUTE OF TECHNOLOGY
## Hoboken, NJ

**CONTACT** Ms. Adrienne Hynek, Associate Director of Financial Aid, Stevens Institute of Technology, Castle Point on Hudson, Hoboken, NJ 07030, 201-216-5555 or toll-free 800-458-5323. *Fax:* 201-216-8050. *E-mail:* ahynek@stevens.edu. *Website:* http://www.stevens.edu/.

# STEVENSON UNIVERSITY
## Stevenson, MD

| Tuition & fees: $28,980 | Average undergraduate aid package: $19,286 |
|---|---|

**ABOUT THE INSTITUTION** Independent, coed. **Awards:** bachelor's and master's degrees. 35 undergraduate majors. **Total enrollment:** 4,323. Undergraduates: 3,808. Freshmen: 690. Federal methodology is used as a basis for awarding need-based institutional aid.

**UNDERGRADUATE EXPENSES for 2015–2016 Application fee:** $40. **Comprehensive fee:** $41,470 includes full-time tuition ($26,976), mandatory fees ($2004), and room and board ($12,490). **College room only:** $8718. Full-time tuition and fees vary according to degree level. Room and board charges vary according to board plan and housing facility. **Part-time tuition:** $682 per credit hour. **Part-time fees:** $75 per credit. Part-time tuition and fees vary according to course load and degree level.

**FRESHMAN FINANCIAL AID (Fall 2014, est.)** 655 applied for aid; of those 88% were deemed to have need. 100% of freshmen with need received aid; of those 10% had need fully met. *Average percent of need met:* 61% (excluding resources awarded to replace EFC). *Average financial aid package:* $20,739 (excluding resources awarded to replace EFC). 14% of all full-time freshmen had no need and received non-need-based gift aid.

**UNDERGRADUATE FINANCIAL AID (Fall 2014, est.)** 2,763 applied for aid; of those 89% were deemed to have need. 100% of undergraduates with need received aid; of those 8% had need fully met. *Average percent of need met:* 59% (excluding resources awarded to replace EFC). *Average financial aid package:* $19,286 (excluding resources awarded to replace EFC). 19% of all full-time undergraduates had no need and received non-need-based gift aid.

**GIFT AID (NEED-BASED) Total amount:** $37,380,817 (14% federal, 11% state, 72% institutional, 3% external sources). *Receiving aid:* Freshmen: 85% (579); all full-time undergraduates: 75% (2,373). *Average award:* Freshmen: $17,771; Undergraduates: $15,755. *Scholarships, grants, and awards:* Federal Pell, FSEOG, state, private, college/university gift aid from institutional funds.

**GIFT AID (NON-NEED-BASED) Total amount:** $7,450,417 (2% state, 92% institutional, 6% external sources). *Receiving aid:* Freshmen: 10% (71). Undergraduates: 4% (135). *Average award:* Freshmen: $10,805. Undergraduates: $9354. *Scholarships, grants, and awards by category: Academic interests/achievement:* 2,716 awards ($25,450,826 total): general academic interests/achievements. *Creative arts/performance:* 8 awards ($17,500 total): art/fine arts. *Tuition waivers:* Full or partial for employees or children of employees. *ROTC:* Army cooperative, Air Force cooperative.

**LOANS Student loans:** $24,503,280 (75% need-based, 25% non-need-based). 75% of past graduating class borrowed through all loan programs. *Average indebtedness per student:* $32,503. *Average need-based loan:* Freshmen: $3298. Undergraduates: $4230. *Parent loans:* $14,942,435 (47% need-based, 53% non-need-based). *Programs:* Federal Direct (Subsidized and Unsubsidized Stafford, PLUS), Perkins.

**WORK-STUDY Federal work-study:** Total amount: $421,007; 146 jobs averaging $2904.

**APPLYING FOR FINANCIAL AID Required financial aid form:** FAFSA. *Financial aid deadline (priority):* 2/15. *Notification date:* Continuous beginning 3/15. Students must reply by 5/1 or within 2 weeks of notification.

**CONTACT** Ms. Barbara L. Miller, Office of Financial Aid, Stevenson University, 100 Campus Circle, Owings Mills, MD 21117, 443-352-4369 or toll-free 877-468-6852 (in-state), 877-468-3852 (out-of-state). *Fax:* 443-352-4370. *E-mail:* blmiller@stevenson.edu.
*Website:* http://www.stevenson.edu/.

# STEVENS–THE INSTITUTE OF BUSINESS & ARTS
## St. Louis, MO

**CONTACT** Financial Aid Office, Stevens–The Institute of Business & Arts, 1521 Washington Avenue, St. Louis, MO 63102, 314-421-0949 or toll-free 800-871-0949. *Website:* http://www.siba.edu/.

# STILLMAN COLLEGE
## Tuscaloosa, AL

**CONTACT** Jacqueline S. Morris, Director of Financial Aid, Stillman College, PO Box 1430, Tuscaloosa, AL 35403, 205-366-8950 or toll-free 800-841-5722. *Fax:* 205-247-8106. *E-mail:* jmorris@stillman.edu.
*Website:* http://www.stillman.edu/.

# STOCKTON UNIVERSITY
## Galloway, NJ

| Tuition & fees (NJ res): $12,568 | Average undergraduate aid package: $15,871 |
| --- | --- |

**ABOUT THE INSTITUTION** State-supported, coed. *Awards:* certificates, bachelor's, master's, and doctoral degrees. 32 undergraduate majors. *Total enrollment:* 8,570. Undergraduates: 7,714. Freshmen: 1,186. Federal methodology is used as a basis for awarding need-based institutional aid.

**UNDERGRADUATE EXPENSES for 2015–2016 Application fee:** $50. *Tuition, state resident:* full-time $8107; part-time $312 per credit. *Tuition, non-resident:* full-time $14,628; part-time $563 per credit. *Required fees:* full-time $4461; $171.59 per credit or $80 per credit. Part-time tuition and fees vary according to course load. *College room and board:* $11,164; *Room only:* $7604. Room and board charges vary according to board plan and housing facility.

**FRESHMAN FINANCIAL AID (Fall 2014, est.)** 1,078 applied for aid; of those 76% were deemed to have need. 97% of freshmen with need received aid; of those 40% had need fully met. *Average percent of need met:* 76% (excluding resources awarded to replace EFC). *Average financial aid package:* $17,072 (excluding resources awarded to replace EFC). 11% of all full-time freshmen had no need and received non-need-based gift aid.

**UNDERGRADUATE FINANCIAL AID (Fall 2014, est.)** 6,087 applied for aid; of those 84% were deemed to have need. 97% of undergraduates with need received aid; of those 30% had need fully met. *Average percent of need met:* 68% (excluding resources awarded to replace EFC). *Average financial aid package:* $15,871 (excluding resources awarded to replace EFC). 7% of all full-time undergraduates had no need and received non-need-based gift aid.

**GIFT AID (NEED-BASED) Total amount:** $33,487,965 (38% federal, 32% state, 28% institutional, 2% external sources). *Receiving aid:* Freshmen: 47% (555); all full-time undergraduates: 41% (2,929). *Average award:* Freshmen: $9595; Undergraduates: $8507. *Scholarships, grants, and awards:* Federal Pell, FSEOG, state, private, college/university gift aid from institutional funds.

**GIFT AID (NON-NEED-BASED) Total amount:** $2,802,938 (2% state, 86% institutional, 12% external sources). *Receiving aid:* Freshmen: 27% (315). Undergraduates: 20% (1,399). *Average award:* Freshmen: $6991. Undergraduates: $6265. *Scholarships, grants, and awards by category: Academic interests/achievement:* area/ethnic studies, biological sciences, business, computer science, education, general academic interests/achievements, health fields, humanities, mathematics, physical sciences, social sciences. *Creative arts/performance:* applied art and design, art/fine arts, creative writing, dance, journalism/publications, music, performing arts, theater/drama. *Special achievements/activities:* community service, general special achievements/activities, leadership. *Special characteristics:* adult students, children of faculty/staff, children of union members/company employees, ethnic background, first-generation college students, general special characteristics, international students, local/state students, members of minority groups, previous college experience. *Tuition waivers:* Full or partial for employees or children of employees, senior citizens. *ROTC:* Army cooperative.

**LOANS Student loans:** $57,604,134 (74% need-based, 26% non-need-based). 76% of past graduating class borrowed through all loan programs. *Average indebtedness per student:* $33,543. *Average need-based loan:* Freshmen: $3414. Undergraduates: $4525. *Parent loans:* $7,406,259 (73% need-based, 27% non-need-based). *Programs:* Federal Direct (Subsidized and Unsubsidized Stafford, PLUS), Perkins, state.

**WORK-STUDY Federal work-study:** Total amount: $446,850; 199 jobs averaging $2022. *State or other work-study/employment:* Total amount: $1,559,371 (100% non-need-based). 885 part-time jobs averaging $1762.

**APPLYING FOR FINANCIAL AID Required financial aid forms:** FAFSA, state aid form. *Financial aid deadline (priority):* 3/1. *Notification date:* Continuous beginning 4/1. Students must reply within 2 weeks of notification.

**CONTACT** Mrs. Jeanne S. Lewis, Director of Financial Aid, Stockton University, 101 Vera King Farris Drive, Galloway, NJ 08205-9441, 609-652-4203. *Fax:* 609-626-5517. *E-mail:* jeanne.lewis@stockton.edu.
*Website:* http://www.stockton.edu/.

# STONEHILL COLLEGE
Easton, MA

| Tuition & fees: $37,426 | Average undergraduate aid package: $28,514 |
|---|---|

**ABOUT THE INSTITUTION** Independent Roman Catholic, coed. *Awards:* bachelor's degrees. 36 undergraduate majors. *Total enrollment:* 2,401. Undergraduates: 2,401. Freshmen: 610. Institutional methodology is used as a basis for awarding need-based institutional aid.

**UNDERGRADUATE EXPENSES for 2015–2016** *Application fee:* $60. *Comprehensive fee:* $51,716 includes full-time tuition ($37,426) and room and board ($14,290). Room and board charges vary according to board plan. *Part-time tuition:* $1247 per credit. Part-time tuition and fees vary according to course load. *Payment plan:* Tuition prepayment.

**FRESHMAN FINANCIAL AID (Fall 2014, est.)** 562 applied for aid; of those 86% were deemed to have need. 100% of freshmen with need received aid; of those 57% had need fully met. *Average percent of need met:* 93% (excluding resources awarded to replace EFC). *Average financial aid package:* $31,183 (excluding resources awarded to replace EFC). 15% of all full-time freshmen had no need and received non-need-based gift aid.

**UNDERGRADUATE FINANCIAL AID (Fall 2014, est.)** 1,969 applied for aid; of those 86% were deemed to have need. 99% of undergraduates with need received aid; of those 48% had need fully met. *Average percent of need met:* 91% (excluding resources awarded to replace EFC). *Average financial aid package:* $28,514 (excluding resources awarded to replace EFC). 19% of all full-time undergraduates had no need and received non-need-based gift aid.

**GIFT AID (NEED-BASED)** *Total amount:* $34,873,104 (7% federal, 2% state, 89% institutional, 2% external sources). *Receiving aid:* Freshmen: 78% (476); all full-time undergraduates: 68% (1,616). *Average award:* Freshmen: $26,233; Undergraduates: $23,001. *Scholarships, grants, and awards:* Federal Pell, FSEOG, state, private, college/university gift aid from institutional funds.

**GIFT AID (NON-NEED-BASED)** *Total amount:* $8,569,542 (3% federal, 95% institutional, 2% external sources). *Receiving aid:* Freshmen: 16% (97). Undergraduates: 13% (303). *Average award:* Freshmen: $13,619. Undergraduates: $13,797. *Scholarships, grants, and awards by category: Academic interests/achievement:* general academic interests/achievements. *Special characteristics:* children of faculty/staff, children of union members/company employees, relatives of clergy, siblings of current students, veterans, veterans' children. *Tuition waivers:* Full or partial for employees or children of employees. *ROTC:* Army.

**LOANS** *Student loans:* $15,645,322 (52% need-based, 48% non-need-based). 78% of past graduating class borrowed through all loan programs. *Average indebtedness per student:* $31,622. *Average need-based loan:* Freshmen: $3923. Undergraduates: $4732. *Parent loans:* $8,994,519 (14% need-based, 86% non-need-based). *Programs:* Federal Direct (Subsidized and Unsubsidized Stafford, PLUS), Perkins, state.

**WORK-STUDY** *Federal work-study:* Total amount: $1,324,596; jobs available. *State or other work-study/employment:* Total amount: $308,150 (2% need-based, 98% non-need-based). Part-time jobs available.

**ATHLETIC AWARDS** Total amount: $2,695,159 (28% need-based, 72% non-need-based).

**APPLYING FOR FINANCIAL AID** *Required financial aid forms:* FAFSA, CSS Financial Aid PROFILE, noncustodial (divorced/separated) parent's statement. *Financial aid deadline (priority):* 12/1. *Notification date:* 4/1. Students must reply by 5/1.

**CONTACT** Rhonda Nickley, Office Manager, Stonehill College, 320 Washington Street, Easton, MA 02357, 508-565-1088. *Fax:* 508-565-1426. *E-mail:* finaid@stonehill.edu. *Website:* http://www.stonehill.edu/.

# STONY BROOK UNIVERSITY, STATE UNIVERSITY OF NEW YORK
Stony Brook, NY

| Tuition & fees (NY res): $8430 | Average undergraduate aid package: $12,087 |
|---|---|

**ABOUT THE INSTITUTION** State-supported, coed. *Awards:* certificates, bachelor's, master's, and doctoral degrees. 64 undergraduate majors. *Total enrollment:* 24,607. Undergraduates: 16,480. Freshmen: 2,855. Federal methodology is used as a basis for awarding need-based institutional aid.

**UNDERGRADUATE EXPENSES for 2015–2016** *Application fee:* $50. *Tuition, state resident:* full-time $6170; part-time $257 per credit hour. *Tuition, nonresident:* full-time $19,590; part-time $816 per credit hour. *Required fees:* full-time $2260; $112.60 per credit hour. Full-time tuition and fees vary according to course load. Part-time tuition and fees vary according to course load. *College room and board:* $11,648; *Room only:* $7552. Room and board charges vary according to board plan and housing facility.

**FRESHMAN FINANCIAL AID (Fall 2013)** 2,186 applied for aid; of those 69% were deemed to have need. 99% of freshmen with need received aid; of those 21% had need fully met. *Average percent of need met:* 73% (excluding resources awarded to replace EFC). *Average financial aid package:* $12,474 (excluding resources awarded to replace EFC). 14% of all full-time freshmen had no need and received non-need-based gift aid.

**UNDERGRADUATE FINANCIAL AID (Fall 2013)** 10,486 applied for aid; of those 83% were deemed to have need. 99% of undergraduates with need received aid; of those 19% had need fully met. *Average percent of need met:* 70% (excluding resources awarded to replace EFC). *Average financial aid package:* $12,087 (excluding resources awarded to replace EFC). 5% of all full-time undergraduates had no need and received non-need-based gift aid.

**GIFT AID (NEED-BASED)** *Total amount:* $52,751,641 (47% federal, 35% state, 17% institutional, 1% external sources). *Receiving aid:* Freshmen: 49% (1,329); all full-time undergraduates: 49% (7,132). *Average award:* Freshmen: $8526; Undergraduates: $7261. *Scholarships, grants, and awards:* Federal Pell, FSEOG, state, private, college/university gift aid from institutional funds.

**GIFT AID (NON-NEED-BASED)** *Total amount:* $8,170,670 (4% federal, 4% state, 78% institutional, 14% external sources). *Receiving aid:* Freshmen: 7% (183). Undergraduates: 4% (536). *Average award:* Freshmen: $4953. Undergraduates: $4230. *Scholarships, grants, and awards by category: Academic interests/achievement:* area/ethnic studies, biological sciences, business, computer science, engineering/technologies, English, foreign languages, general academic interests/achievements, health fields, international studies, mathematics, physical sciences, social sciences. *Creative arts/performance:* cinema/film/broadcasting, journalism/publications, music. *Special achievements/activities:* community service, leadership. *Special characteristics:* ethnic background, general special characteristics. *ROTC:* Army, Naval cooperative, Air Force cooperative.

**LOANS** *Student loans:* $92,354,421 (71% need-based, 29% non-need-based). 58% of past graduating class borrowed through all loan programs. *Average indebtedness per student:* $24,884. *Average need-based loan:* Freshmen: $3982. Undergraduates: $4936. *Parent loans:* $8,940,856 (32% need-based, 68% non-need-based). *Programs:* Federal Direct (Subsidized and Unsubsidized Stafford, PLUS), Perkins.

**WORK-STUDY** *Federal work-study:* 491 jobs averaging $1951. *State or other work-study/employment:* Total amount: $8,071,619 (29% need-based, 71% non-need-based). 2,276 part-time jobs averaging $3548.

**ATHLETIC AWARDS** Total amount: $5,758,168 (42% need-based, 58% non-need-based).

**APPLYING FOR FINANCIAL AID** *Required financial aid forms:* FAFSA, state aid form, . *Financial aid deadline (priority):* 3/1. *Notification date:* Continuous beginning 4/1. Students must reply by 5/1.

**CONTACT** Office of Student Financial Aid and Scholarship Services, Stony Brook University, State University of New York, Administration Building, Room 180, Stony Brook, NY 11794, 631-632-6840. *Fax:* 631-632-9525. *E-mail:* finaid@stonybrook.edu. *Website:* http://www.stonybrook.edu/.

## STRATFORD UNIVERSITY
### Baltimore, MD

**Tuition & fees:** N/R     **Average undergraduate aid package:** N/A

**ABOUT THE INSTITUTION** Proprietary, coed. *Awards:* certificates, associate, bachelor's, and master's degrees. 4 undergraduate majors. *Total enrollment:* 353. Undergraduates: 347. Federal methodology is used as a basis for awarding need-based institutional aid.

**UNDERGRADUATE EXPENSES for 2015–2016** *Application fee:* $50. *Tuition:* part-time $370 per quarter hour. *Required fees:* $100 per degree program. Full-time tuition and fees vary according to course level, degree level, and program. Part-time tuition and fees vary according to course level, degree level, and program.

**GIFT AID (NEED-BASED)** *Total amount:* $6,662,324 (100% federal). *Scholarships, grants, and awards:* Federal Pell, FSEOG.

**GIFT AID (NON-NEED-BASED)** *Scholarships, grants, and awards by category: Academic interests/achievement:* general academic interests/achievements. *Tuition waivers:* Full or partial for employees or children of employees.

**LOANS** *Student loans:* $17,746,732 (100% need-based). *Parent loans:* $117,306 (100% need-based). *Programs:* Federal Direct (Subsidized and Unsubsidized Stafford, PLUS).

**APPLYING FOR FINANCIAL AID** *Required financial aid form:* FAFSA. *Financial aid deadline:* Continuous. *Notification date:* Continuous beginning 1/1.

**CONTACT** Lesley Otterbein, Student Accounts Manager, Stratford University, 17 Commerce Street, Baltimore, MD 21202, 410-752-0490 or toll-free 800-624-9926 (in-state), 800-624-9926 Ext. 120 (out-of-state). *Fax:* 410-752-3730. *E-mail:* studentaccounts@stratford.edu.
*Website:* http://www.stratford.edu/.

## STRATFORD UNIVERSITY
### Falls Church, VA

**Tuition & fees:** N/R     **Average undergraduate aid package:** N/A

**ABOUT THE INSTITUTION** Proprietary, coed. *Awards:* certificates, diplomas, associate, bachelor's, and master's degrees. 12 undergraduate majors. *Total enrollment:* 955. Undergraduates: 604. Freshmen: 211. Federal methodology is used as a basis for awarding need-based institutional aid.

**UNDERGRADUATE EXPENSES for 2015–2016** *Application fee:* $50. *Tuition:* part-time $370 per quarter hour. *Required fees:* $100 per degree program. Full-time tuition and fees vary according to course level, degree level, and program. Part-time tuition and fees vary according to course level, degree level, and program.

**GIFT AID (NEED-BASED)** *Total amount:* $6,662,324 (100% federal). *Scholarships, grants, and awards:* Federal Pell, FSEOG, state, private, college/university gift aid from institutional funds.

**GIFT AID (NON-NEED-BASED)** *Scholarships, grants, and awards by category: Academic interests/achievement:* general academic interests/achievements. *Tuition waivers:* Full or partial for employees or children of employees.

**LOANS** *Student loans:* $17,746,732 (100% need-based). *Parent loans:* $117,306 (100% need-based). *Programs:* Federal Direct (Subsidized and Unsubsidized Stafford, PLUS).

**WORK-STUDY** Federal work-study jobs available.

**APPLYING FOR FINANCIAL AID** *Required financial aid form:* FAFSA. *Financial aid deadline:* Continuous. *Notification date:* Continuous beginning 1/1.

**CONTACT** Imane Babsiri, Student Account Manager, Stratford University, 7777 Leesburg Pike, Falls Church, VA 22043, 703-821-8570 Ext. 3401 or toll-free 800-444-0804. *E-mail:* ibabsiri@stratford.edu.
*Website:* http://www.stratford.edu/.

## STRATFORD UNIVERSITY
### Glen Allen, VA

**Tuition & fees:** N/R     **Average undergraduate aid package:** N/A

**ABOUT THE INSTITUTION** Proprietary, coed. *Awards:* certificates, diplomas, associate, bachelor's, and master's degrees. 14 undergraduate majors. *Total enrollment:* 486. Undergraduates: 363. Freshmen: 233. Federal methodology is used as a basis for awarding need-based institutional aid.

**UNDERGRADUATE EXPENSES for 2015–2016** *Tuition:* part-time $370 per quarter hour. *Required fees:* $100 per degree program. Full-time tuition and fees vary according to course level, degree level, and program. Part-time tuition and fees vary according to course level, degree level, and program.

**GIFT AID (NEED-BASED)** *Total amount:* $6,662,324 (100% federal). *Scholarships, grants, and awards:* Federal Pell, FSEOG.

**GIFT AID (NON-NEED-BASED)** *Scholarships, grants, and awards by category: Academic interests/achievement:* general academic interests/achievements. *Tuition waivers:* Full or partial for employees or children of employees.

**LOANS** *Student loans:* $17,746,732 (100% need-based). *Parent loans:* $117,306 (100% need-based). *Programs:* Federal Direct (Subsidized and Unsubsidized Stafford, PLUS).

**APPLYING FOR FINANCIAL AID** *Required financial aid form:* FAFSA. *Financial aid deadline:* Continuous. *Notification date:* Continuous beginning 1/1.

**CONTACT** Noshuo Rivers, Student Account Manager, Stratford University, 11104 West Broad Street, Glen Allen, VA 23060, 804-290-4231 or toll-free 877-373-5173. *E-mail:* studentaccounts@stratford.edu.
*Website:* http://www.stratford.edu/.

## STRATFORD UNIVERSITY
### Newport News, VA

**Tuition & fees:** N/R     **Average undergraduate aid package:** N/A

**ABOUT THE INSTITUTION** Proprietary, coed. *Awards:* certificates, diplomas, associate, bachelor's, and master's degrees. 14 undergraduate majors. *Total enrollment:* 158. Undergraduates: 152. Freshmen: 75. Federal methodology is used as a basis for awarding need-based institutional aid.

**UNDERGRADUATE EXPENSES for 2015–2016** *Tuition:* part-time $370 per credit. *Required fees:* $100 per degree program. Full-time tuition and fees vary according to course level, degree level, and program. Part-time tuition and fees vary according to course level, degree level, and program.

**GIFT AID (NEED-BASED)** *Total amount:* $6,662,324 (100% federal). *Scholarships, grants, and awards:* Federal Pell, FSEOG.

**GIFT AID (NON-NEED-BASED)** *Scholarships, grants, and awards by category: Academic interests/achievement:* general academic interests/achievements. *Tuition waivers:* Full or partial for employees or children of employees.

**LOANS** *Student loans:* $17,746,732 (100% need-based). *Parent loans:* $117,306 (100% need-based). *Programs:* Federal Direct (Subsidized and Unsubsidized Stafford, PLUS).

**APPLYING FOR FINANCIAL AID** *Required financial aid form:* FAFSA. *Financial aid deadline:* Continuous. *Notification date:* Continuous beginning 1/1.

**CONTACT** Sheryl Kimberly, Student Accounts Manager, Stratford University, 836 J. Clyde Morris Boulevard, Newport News, VA 23601, 757-873-4235 or toll-free 855-873-4235. *E-mail:* skimberly@stratford.edu.
*Website:* http://www.stratford.edu/.

# STRATFORD UNIVERSITY
## Woodbridge, VA

| Tuition & fees: N/R | Average undergraduate aid package: N/A |
|---|---|

**ABOUT THE INSTITUTION** Proprietary, coed. *Awards:* certificates, diplomas, associate, bachelor's, and master's degrees. 15 undergraduate majors. *Total enrollment:* 728. Undergraduates: 694. Freshmen: 132. Federal methodology is used as a basis for awarding need-based institutional aid.

**UNDERGRADUATE EXPENSES for 2015–2016** *Application fee:* $50. *Tuition:* part-time $370 per quarter hour. *Required fees:* $100 per degree program. Full-time tuition and fees vary according to course level, degree level, and program. Part-time tuition and fees vary according to course level, degree level, and program.

**GIFT AID (NEED-BASED)** *Total amount:* $6,662,324 (100% federal). *Scholarships, grants, and awards:* Federal Pell, FSEOG.

**GIFT AID (NON-NEED-BASED)** *Scholarships, grants, and awards by category:* Academic interests/achievement: general academic interests/achievements. *Tuition waivers:* Full or partial for employees or children of employees.

**LOANS** *Student loans:* $17,746,732 (100% need-based). *Parent loans:* $117,306 (100% need-based). *Programs:* Federal Direct (Subsidized and Unsubsidized Stafford, PLUS).

**APPLYING FOR FINANCIAL AID** *Required financial aid form:* FAFSA. *Financial aid deadline:* Continuous. *Notification date:* Continuous beginning 1/1.

**CONTACT** Sherrese Whiting, Student Account Manager, Stratford University, 14349 Gideon Drive, Woodbridge, VA 22192, 703-897-1982 or toll-free 888-546-1250. *E-mail:* studentaccounts@stratford.edu. *Website:* http://www.stratford.edu/.

# STRAYER UNIVERSITY–ALEXANDRIA CAMPUS
## Alexandria, VA

**CONTACT** Financial Aid Office, Strayer University–Alexandria Campus, 2730 Eisenhower Avenue, Alexandria, VA 22314, 703-317-2626. *Website:* http://www.strayer.edu/virginia/alexandria/.

# STRAYER UNIVERSITY–ALLENTOWN CAMPUS
## Center Valley, PA

**CONTACT** Financial Aid Office, Strayer University–Allentown Campus, 3800 Sierra Circle, Suite 300, Center Valley, PA 18034, 484-809-7770. *Website:* http://www.strayer.edu/pennsylvania/allentown/.

# STRAYER UNIVERSITY–ANNE ARUNDEL CAMPUS
## Millersville, MD

**CONTACT** Financial Aid Office, Strayer University–Anne Arundel Campus, 1520 Jabez Run, Millersville, MD 21108, 410-923-4500. *Website:* http://www.strayer.edu/maryland/anne-arundel/.

# STRAYER UNIVERSITY–ARLINGTON CAMPUS
## Arlington, VA

**CONTACT** Financial Aid Office, Strayer University–Arlington Campus, 2121 15th Street North, Arlington, VA 22201, 703-892-5100. *Website:* http://www.strayer.edu/virginia/arlington/.

# STRAYER UNIVERSITY–AUGUSTA CAMPUS
## Augusta, GA

**CONTACT** Financial Aid Office, Strayer University–Augusta Campus, 1330 Augusta West Parkway, Augusta, GA 30909, 706-855-8233. *Website:* http://www.strayer.edu/georgia/augusta/.

# STRAYER UNIVERSITY–BAYMEADOWS CAMPUS
## Jacksonville, FL

**CONTACT** Financial Aid Office, Strayer University–Baymeadows Campus, 8375 Dix Ellis Trail, Suite 200, Jacksonville, FL 32256, 904-538-1000. *Website:* http://www.strayer.edu/florida/baymeadows/.

# STRAYER UNIVERSITY–BIRMINGHAM CAMPUS
## Birmingham, AL

**CONTACT** Financial Aid Office, Strayer University–Birmingham Campus, 3570 Grandview Parkway, Suite 200, Birmingham, AL 35243, 205-453-6300. *Website:* http://www.strayer.edu/alabama/birmingham/.

# STRAYER UNIVERSITY–BRICKELL CAMPUS
## Miami, FL

**CONTACT** Financial Aid Office, Strayer University–Brickell Campus, 1201 Brickell Avenue, Suite 700, Miami, FL 33131, 305-507-5800. *Website:* http://www.strayer.edu/florida/brickell/.

# STRAYER UNIVERSITY–CENTER CITY CAMPUS
## Philadelphia, PA

**CONTACT** Financial Aid Office, Strayer University–Center City Campus, 1601 Cherry Street, Suite 100, Philadelphia, PA 19102, 267-256-0200. *Website:* http://www.strayer.edu/pennsylvania/center-city/.

## STRAYER UNIVERSITY–CHAMBLEE CAMPUS
### Atlanta, GA

CONTACT Financial Aid Office, Strayer University–Chamblee Campus, 3355 Northeast Expressway, Suite 100, Atlanta, GA 30341, 770-454-9270. *Website:* http://www.strayer.edu/georgia/chamblee/.

## STRAYER UNIVERSITY–CHARLESTON CAMPUS
### North Charleston, SC

CONTACT Financial Aid Office, Strayer University–Charleston Campus, 5010 Wetland Crossing, North Charleston, SC 29418, 843-746-5100. *Website:* http://www.strayer.edu/south-carolina/charleston/.

## STRAYER UNIVERSITY–CHERRY HILL CAMPUS
### Cherry Hill, NJ

CONTACT Financial Aid Office, Strayer University–Cherry Hill Campus, 2201 Route 38, Suite 100, Cherry Hill, NJ 08002, 856-482-4200. *Website:* http://www.strayer.edu/new-jersey/cherry-hill/.

## STRAYER UNIVERSITY–CHESAPEAKE CAMPUS
### Chesapeake, VA

CONTACT Financial Aid Office, Strayer University–Chesapeake Campus, 676 Independence Parkway, Suite 300, Chesapeake, VA 23320, 757-382-9900. *Website:* http://www.strayer.edu/virginia/chesapeake/.

## STRAYER UNIVERSITY–CHESTERFIELD CAMPUS
### Midlothian, VA

CONTACT Financial Aid Office, Strayer University–Chesterfield Campus, 2820 Waterford Lake Drive, Suite 100, Midlothian, VA 23112, 804-763-6300. *Website:* http://www.strayer.edu/virginia/chesterfield/.

## STRAYER UNIVERSITY–CHRISTIANA CAMPUS
### Newark, DE

CONTACT Financial Aid Office, Strayer University–Christiana Campus, 240 Continental Drive, Suite 108, Newark, DE 19713, 302-292-6100. *Website:* http://www.strayer.edu/delaware/christiana/.

## STRAYER UNIVERSITY–COBB COUNTY CAMPUS
### Atlanta, GA

CONTACT Financial Aid Office, Strayer University–Cobb County Campus, 3101 Towercreek Parkway, SE, Suite 700, Atlanta, GA 30339-3256, 770-612-2170. *Website:* http://www.strayer.edu/georgia/cobb-county/.

## STRAYER UNIVERSITY–COLUMBIA CAMPUS
### Columbia, SC

CONTACT Financial Aid Office, Strayer University–Columbia Campus, 200 Center Point Circle, Suite 300, Columbia, SC 29210, 803-750-2500. *Website:* http://www.strayer.edu/south-carolina/columbia/.

## STRAYER UNIVERSITY–CORAL SPRINGS CAMPUS
### Pompano Beach, FL

CONTACT Financial Aid Office, Strayer University–Coral Springs Campus, 5830 Coral Ridge Drive, Suite 300, Pompano Beach, FL 33076, 954-369-0700. *Website:* http://www.strayer.edu/florida/coral-springs/.

## STRAYER UNIVERSITY–DELAWARE COUNTY CAMPUS
### Springfield, PA

CONTACT Financial Aid Office, Strayer University–Delaware County Campus, 760 West Sproul Road, Suite 200, Springfield, PA 19064-1215, 610-604-7700. *Website:* http://www.strayer.edu/pennsylvania/delaware-county/.

## STRAYER UNIVERSITY–DORAL CAMPUS
### Miami, FL

CONTACT Financial Aid Office, Strayer University–Doral Campus, 11430 Northwest 20th Street, Suite 150, Miami, FL 33172, 305-507-5700. *Website:* http://www.strayer.edu/florida/doral/.

## STRAYER UNIVERSITY–DOUGLASVILLE CAMPUS
### Douglasville, GA

CONTACT Financial Aid Office, Strayer University–Douglasville Campus, 4655 Timber Ridge Drive, Douglasville, GA 30135, 678-715-2200. *Website:* http://www.strayer.edu/georgia/douglasville/.

## STRAYER UNIVERSITY–FORT LAUDERDALE CAMPUS
### Fort Lauderdale, FL

CONTACT Financial Aid Office, Strayer University–Fort Lauderdale Campus, 2307 West Broward Boulevard, Suite 100, Fort Lauderdale, FL 33312, 954-745-6960.
*Website:* http://www.strayer.edu/florida/fort-lauderdale/.

## STRAYER UNIVERSITY–FREDERICKSBURG CAMPUS
### Fredericksburg, VA

CONTACT Financial Aid Office, Strayer University–Fredericksburg Campus, 150 Riverside Parkway, Suite 100, Fredericksburg, VA 22406, 540-374-4300.
*Website:* http://www.strayer.edu/virginia/fredericksburg/.

## STRAYER UNIVERSITY–GREENSBORO CAMPUS
### Greensboro, NC

CONTACT Financial Aid Office, Strayer University–Greensboro Campus, 4900 Koger Boulevard, Suite 400, Greensboro, NC 27407, 336-315.7800.
*Website:* http://www.strayer.edu/north-carolina/greensboro/.

## STRAYER UNIVERSITY–GREENVILLE CAMPUS
### Greenville, SC

CONTACT Financial Aid Office, Strayer University–Greenville Campus, 555 North Pleasantburg Drive, Suite 300, Greenville, SC 29607, 864-250-7000.
*Website:* http://www.strayer.edu/south-carolina/greenville/.

## STRAYER UNIVERSITY–HENRICO CAMPUS
### Glen Allen, VA

CONTACT Financial Aid Office, Strayer University–Henrico Campus, 11501 Nuckols Road, Glen Allen, VA 23059, 804-527-1000.
*Website:* http://www.strayer.edu/virginia/henrico/.

## STRAYER UNIVERSITY–HUNTERSVILLE CAMPUS
### Huntersville, NC

CONTACT Financial Aid Office, Strayer University–Huntersville Campus, 13620 Reese Boulevard, Suite 130, Huntersville, NC 28078, 704-379-6800.
*Website:* http://www.strayer.edu/north-carolina/huntersville/.

## STRAYER UNIVERSITY–HUNTSVILLE CAMPUS
### Huntsville, AL

CONTACT Financial Aid Office, Strayer University–Huntsville Campus, 4955 Corporate Drive, NW, Suite 200, Huntsville, AL 35805, 256-665-9800.
*Website:* http://www.strayer.edu/alabama/huntsville/.

## STRAYER UNIVERSITY–IRVING CAMPUS
### Irving, TX

CONTACT Financial Aid Office, Strayer University–Irving Campus, 7701 Las Colinas Ridge, Suite 450, Irving, TX 75063, 214-429-3900.
*Website:* http://www.strayer.edu/texas/irving/.

## STRAYER UNIVERSITY–JACKSON CAMPUS
### Jackson, MS

CONTACT Financial Aid Office, Strayer University–Jackson Campus, 460 Briarwood Drive, Suite 200, Jackson, MS 39206, 601-718-5900.
*Website:* http://www.strayer.edu/mississippi/jackson/.

## STRAYER UNIVERSITY–KING OF PRUSSIA CAMPUS
### King of Prussia, PA

CONTACT Financial Aid Office, Strayer University–King of Prussia Campus, 234 Mall Boulevard, Suite G-50, King of Prussia, PA 19406, 610-992-1700.
*Website:* http://www.strayer.edu/pennsylvania/king-prussia/.

## STRAYER UNIVERSITY–KNOXVILLE CAMPUS
### Knoxville, TN

CONTACT Financial Aid Office, Strayer University–Knoxville Campus, 10118 Parkside Drive, Suite 200, Knoxville, TN 37922, 865-288-6000.
*Website:* http://www.strayer.edu/tennessee/knoxville/.

## STRAYER UNIVERSITY–LAWRENCEVILLE CAMPUS
### Lawrenceville, NJ

CONTACT Financial Aid Office, Strayer University–Lawrenceville Campus, 3150 Brunswick Pike, Suite 100, Lawrenceville, NJ 08648, 609-406-7600.
*Website:* http://www.strayer.edu/new-jersey/lawrenceville/.

## STRAYER UNIVERSITY–LITHONIA CAMPUS

### Lithonia, GA

**CONTACT** Financial Aid Office, Strayer University–Lithonia Campus, 3120 Stonecrest Boulevard, Suite 200, Lithonia, GA 30038, 678-323-7700. *Website:* http://www.strayer.edu/georgia/lithonia/.

## STRAYER UNIVERSITY–LITTLE ROCK CAMPUS

### Little Rock, AR

**CONTACT** Financial Aid Office, Strayer University–Little Rock Campus, 10825 Financial Centre Parkway, Suite 131, Little Rock, AR 72211. *Website:* http://www.strayer.edu/arkansas/little-rock/.

## STRAYER UNIVERSITY–LOUDOUN CAMPUS

### Ashburn, VA

**CONTACT** Financial Aid Office, Strayer University–Loudoun Campus, 45150 Russell Branch Parkway, Suite 200, Ashburn, VA 20147, 703-729-8800. *Website:* http://www.strayer.edu/virginia/loudoun/.

## STRAYER UNIVERSITY–LOWER BUCKS COUNTY CAMPUS

### Trevose, PA

**CONTACT** Financial Aid Office, Strayer University–Lower Bucks County Campus, 3800 Horizon Boulevard, Suite 100, Trevose, PA 19053, 215-953-5999. *Website:* http://www.strayer.edu/pennsylvania/lower-bucks-county/.

## STRAYER UNIVERSITY–MAITLAND CAMPUS

### Maitland, FL

**CONTACT** Financial Aid Office, Strayer University–Maitland Campus, 850 Trafalgar Court, Suite 360, Maitland, FL 32751, 407-618-5900. *Website:* http://www.strayer.edu/florida/maitland/.

## STRAYER UNIVERSITY–MANASSAS CAMPUS

### Manassas, VA

**CONTACT** Financial Aid Office, Strayer University–Manassas Campus, 9990 Battleview Parkway, Manassas, VA 20109, 703-330-8400. *Website:* http://www.strayer.edu/virginia/manassas/.

## STRAYER UNIVERSITY–METAIRIE CAMPUS

### Metairie, LA

**CONTACT** Financial Aid Office, Strayer University–Metairie Campus, 111 Veterans Memorial Boulevard, Suite 420, Metairie, LA 70005, 504-799-1700. *Website:* http://www.strayer.edu/louisiana/metairie/.

## STRAYER UNIVERSITY–MIRAMAR CAMPUS

### Miramar, FL

**CONTACT** Financial Aid Office, Strayer University–Miramar Campus, 15620 Southwest 29th Street, Miramar, FL 33027, 954-378-2400. *Website:* http://www.strayer.edu/florida/miramar/.

## STRAYER UNIVERSITY–MORROW CAMPUS

### Morrow, GA

**CONTACT** Financial Aid Office, Strayer University–Morrow Campus, 3000 Corporate Center Drive, Suite 100, Morrow, GA 30260, 678-422-4100. *Website:* http://www.strayer.edu/georgia/morrow/.

## STRAYER UNIVERSITY–NASHVILLE CAMPUS

### Nashville, TN

**CONTACT** Financial Aid Office, Strayer University–Nashville Campus, 1809 Dabbs Avenue, Nashville, TN 37210, 615-871-2260. *Website:* http://www.strayer.edu/tennessee/nashville/.

## STRAYER UNIVERSITY–NEWPORT NEWS CAMPUS

### Newport News, VA

**CONTACT** Financial Aid Office, Strayer University–Newport News Campus, 99 Old Oyster Point Road, Unit 1, Newport News, VA 23602, 757-873-3100. *Website:* http://www.strayer.edu/virginia/newport-news/.

## STRAYER UNIVERSITY–NORTH AUSTIN CAMPUS

### Austin, TX

**CONTACT** Financial Aid Office, Strayer University–North Austin Campus, 8501 North Mopac Expressway, Suite 100, Austin, TX 78759, 512-568-3300. *Website:* http://www.strayer.edu/texas/north-austin/.

## STRAYER UNIVERSITY–NORTH CHARLOTTE CAMPUS
### Concord, NC

**CONTACT** Financial Aid Office, Strayer University–North Charlotte Campus, 7870 Commons Park Circle NW, Concord, NC 28027, 704-886-6500.
*Website:* http://www.strayer.edu/north-carolina/north-charlotte/.

## STRAYER UNIVERSITY–NORTH RALEIGH CAMPUS
### Raleigh, NC

**CONTACT** Financial Aid Office, Strayer University–North Raleigh Campus, 8701 Wadford Drive, Raleigh, NC 27616, 919-878-9900.
*Website:* http://www.strayer.edu/north-carolina/north-raleigh/.

## STRAYER UNIVERSITY–NORTHWEST HOUSTON CAMPUS
### Houston, TX

**CONTACT** Financial Aid Office, Strayer University–Northwest Houston Campus, 10940 W. Sam Houston Parkway N., Suite 200, Houston, TX 77064, 281-949-1800.
*Website:* http://www.strayer.edu/texas/northwest-houston/.

## STRAYER UNIVERSITY–ORLANDO EAST CAMPUS
### Orlando, FL

**CONTACT** Financial Aid Office, Strayer University–Orlando East Campus, 2200 North Alafaya Trail, Suite 500, Orlando, FL 32826, 407-926-2000.
*Website:* http://www.strayer.edu/florida/orlando-east/.

## STRAYER UNIVERSITY–OWINGS MILLS CAMPUS
### Owings Mills, MD

**CONTACT** Financial Aid Office, Strayer University–Owings Mills Campus, 500 Redland Court, Suite 100, Owings Mills, MD 21117, 443-394-3339.
*Website:* http://www.strayer.edu/maryland/owings-mills/.

## STRAYER UNIVERSITY–PALM BEACH GARDENS CAMPUS
### West Palm Beach, FL

**CONTACT** Financial Aid Office, Strayer University–Palm Beach Gardens Campus, 11025 RCA Center Drive, Suite 200, West Palm Beach, FL 33410, 561-904-3000.
*Website:* http://www.strayer.edu/florida/palm-beach-gardens/.

## STRAYER UNIVERSITY–PISCATAWAY CAMPUS
### Piscataway, NJ

**CONTACT** Financial Aid Office, Strayer University–Piscataway Campus, 242 Old New Brunswick Road, Suite 220, Piscataway, NJ 08854, 732-743-3800.
*Website:* http://www.strayer.edu/new-jersey/piscataway/.

## STRAYER UNIVERSITY–PLANO CAMPUS
### Plano, TX

**CONTACT** Financial Aid Office, Strayer University–Plano Campus, 2701 North Dallas Parkway, Suite 300, Plano, TX 75093, 972-535-3700.
*Website:* http://www.strayer.edu/texas/plano/.

## STRAYER UNIVERSITY–PRINCE GEORGE'S CAMPUS
### Suitland, MD

**CONTACT** Financial Aid Office, Strayer University–Prince George's Campus, 4710 Auth Place, First Floor, Suitland, MD 20746, 301-423-3600.
*Website:* http://www.strayer.edu/maryland/prince-georges/.

## STRAYER UNIVERSITY–ROCKVILLE CAMPUS
### Rockville, MD

**CONTACT** Financial Aid Office, Strayer University–Rockville Campus, 4 Research Place, Suite 100, Rockville, MD 20850, 301-548-5500.
*Website:* http://www.strayer.edu/maryland/rockville/.

## STRAYER UNIVERSITY–ROSWELL CAMPUS
### Roswell, GA

**CONTACT** Financial Aid Office, Strayer University–Roswell Campus, 100 Mansell Court East, Suite 100, Roswell, GA 30076, 770-650-3000.
*Website:* http://www.strayer.edu/georgia/roswell/.

## STRAYER UNIVERSITY–RTP CAMPUS
### Morrisville, NC

**CONTACT** Financial Aid Office, Strayer University–RTP Campus, 4 Copley Parkway, Morrisville, NC 27560, 919-466-4400.
*Website:* http://www.strayer.edu/north-carolina/rtp/.

# STRAYER UNIVERSITY–SAND LAKE CAMPUS
### Orlando, FL

**CONTACT** Financial Aid Office, Strayer University–Sand Lake Campus, 8541 South Park Circle, Building 900, Orlando, FL 32819, 407-264-9400.
*Website:* http://www.strayer.edu/florida/sand-lake/.

# STRAYER UNIVERSITY–SAVANNAH CAMPUS
### Savannah, GA

**CONTACT** Financial Aid Office, Strayer University–Savannah Campus, 20 Martin Court, Savannah, GA 31419, 912-921-2900.
*Website:* http://www.strayer.edu/georgia/savannah/.

# STRAYER UNIVERSITY–SHELBY CAMPUS
### Memphis, TN

**CONTACT** Financial Aid Office, Strayer University–Shelby Campus, 7275 Appling Farms Parkway, Memphis, TN 38133, 901-383-6750.
*Website:* http://www.strayer.edu/tennessee/shelby/.

# STRAYER UNIVERSITY–SOUTH CHARLOTTE CAMPUS
### Charlotte, NC

**CONTACT** Financial Aid Office, Strayer University–South Charlotte Campus, 9101 Kings Parade Boulevard, Suite 200, Charlotte, NC 28273, 704-499-9200.
*Website:* http://www.strayer.edu/north-carolina/south-charlotte/.

# STRAYER UNIVERSITY–SOUTH RALEIGH CAMPUS
### Raleigh, NC

**CONTACT** Financial Aid Office, Strayer University–South Raleigh Campus, 3421 Olympia Drive, Raleigh, NC 27603, 919-890-7500.
*Website:* http://www.strayer.edu/north-carolina/south-raleigh/.

# STRAYER UNIVERSITY–TAKOMA PARK CAMPUS
### Washington, DC

**CONTACT** Financial Aid Office, Strayer University–Takoma Park Campus, 6830 Laurel Street, NW, Washington, DC 20012, 202-722-8100.
*Website:* http://www.strayer.edu/district-columbia/takoma-park/.

# STRAYER UNIVERSITY–TAMPA EAST CAMPUS
### Tampa, FL

**CONTACT** Financial Aid Office, Strayer University–Tampa East Campus, 5650 Breckenridge Park Drive, Suite 300, Tampa, FL 33610, 813-663-0100.
*Website:* http://www.strayer.edu/florida/tampa-east/.

# STRAYER UNIVERSITY–TAMPA WESTSHORE CAMPUS
### Tampa, FL

**CONTACT** Financial Aid Office, Strayer University–Tampa Westshore Campus, 4902 Eisenhower Boulevard, Suite 100, Tampa, FL 33634, 813-882-0100.
*Website:* http://www.strayer.edu/florida/tampa-westshore/.

# STRAYER UNIVERSITY–TEAYS VALLEY CAMPUS
### Scott Depot, WV

**CONTACT** Financial Aid Office, Strayer University–Teays Valley Campus, 100 Corporate Center Drive, Scott Depot, WV 25560, 304-760-1700.
*Website:* http://www.strayer.edu/west-virginia/teays-valley/.

# STRAYER UNIVERSITY–THOUSAND OAKS CAMPUS
### Memphis, TN

**CONTACT** Financial Aid Office, Strayer University–Thousand Oaks Campus, 2620 Thousand Oaks Boulevard, Suite 1100, Memphis, TN 38118, 901-369-0835.
*Website:* http://www.strayer.edu/tennessee/thousand-oaks/.

# STRAYER UNIVERSITY–VIRGINIA BEACH CAMPUS
### Virginia Beach, VA

**CONTACT** Financial Aid Office, Strayer University–Virginia Beach Campus, 249 Central Park Avenue, Suite 350, Virginia Beach, VA 23462, 757-493-6000.
*Website:* http://www.strayer.edu/virginia/virginia-beach/.

# STRAYER UNIVERSITY–WARRENDALE CAMPUS
### Warrendale, PA

**CONTACT** Financial Aid Office, Strayer University–Warrendale Campus, 802 Warrendale Village Drive, Warrendale, PA 15086, 724-799-2900.
*Website:* http://www.strayer.edu/pennsylvania/warrendale/.

# STRAYER UNIVERSITY–WASHINGTON CAMPUS
## Washington, DC

**CONTACT** Financial Aid Office, Strayer University–Washington Campus, 1133 15th Street, NW, Washington, DC 20025, 202-408-2400.
*Website:* http://www.strayer.edu/district-columbia/washington/.

# STRAYER UNIVERSITY–WHITE MARSH CAMPUS
## Nottingham, MD

**CONTACT** Financial Aid Office, Strayer University–White Marsh Campus, 9920 Franklin Square Drive, Suite 200, Nottingham, MD 21236, 410-238-9000.
*Website:* http://www.strayer.edu/maryland/white-marsh/.

# STRAYER UNIVERSITY–WILLINGBORO CAMPUS
## Willingboro, NJ

**CONTACT** Financial Aid Office, Strayer University–Willingboro Campus, 300 Willingboro Parkway, Willingboro Town Center, Suite 125, Willingboro, NJ 08046, 609-835-6000.
*Website:* http://www.strayer.edu/new-jersey/willingboro/.

# STRAYER UNIVERSITY–WOODBRIDGE CAMPUS
## Woodbridge, VA

**CONTACT** Financial Aid Office, Strayer University–Woodbridge Campus, 13385 Minnieville Road, Woodbridge, VA 22192, 703-878-2800.
*Website:* http://www.strayer.edu/virginia/woodbridge/.

# SUFFOLK UNIVERSITY
## Boston, MA

| Tuition & fees: $32,660 | Average undergraduate aid package: $26,333 |
| --- | --- |

**ABOUT THE INSTITUTION** Independent, coed. *Awards:* certificates, diplomas, associate, bachelor's, master's, and doctoral degrees (doctoral degree in law). 47 undergraduate majors. *Total enrollment:* 8,321. Undergraduates: 5,496. Freshmen: 1,113. Federal methodology is used as a basis for awarding need-based institutional aid.
**UNDERGRADUATE EXPENSES for 2015–2016** *Application fee:* $50. *One-time required fee:* $200. *Comprehensive fee:* $47,298 includes full-time tuition ($32,530), mandatory fees ($130), and room and board ($14,638). Full-time tuition and fees vary according to reciprocity agreements. Room and board charges vary according to board plan and housing facility. *Part-time tuition:* $798 per credit hour. Part-time tuition and fees vary according to course load and reciprocity agreements.
**FRESHMAN FINANCIAL AID (Fall 2014, est.)** 767 applied for aid; of those 90% were deemed to have need. 100% of freshmen with need received aid; of those 14% had need fully met. *Average percent of need met:* 66% (excluding resources awarded to replace EFC). *Average financial aid package:* $24,081 (excluding resources awarded to replace EFC). 31% of all full-time freshmen had no need and received non-need-based gift aid.
**UNDERGRADUATE FINANCIAL AID (Fall 2014, est.)** 3,299 applied for aid; of those 93% were deemed to have need. 100% of undergraduates with need received aid; of those 16% had need fully met. *Average percent of need met:* 72% (excluding resources awarded to replace EFC). *Average financial aid package:*

$26,333 (excluding resources awarded to replace EFC). 16% of all full-time undergraduates had no need and received non-need-based gift aid.
**GIFT AID (NEED-BASED)** *Total amount:* $37,028,411 (20% federal, 5% state, 73% institutional, 2% external sources). *Receiving aid:* Freshmen: 51% (565); all full-time undergraduates: 53% (2,720). *Average award:* Freshmen: $6486; Undergraduates: $13,106. *Scholarships, grants, and awards:* Federal Pell, FSEOG, state, private, college/university gift aid from institutional funds.
**GIFT AID (NON-NEED-BASED)** *Total amount:* $27,802,031 (100% institutional). *Receiving aid:* Freshmen: 57% (632). Undergraduates: 33% (1,667). *Average award:* Freshmen: $11,815. Undergraduates: $10,647. *Scholarships, grants, and awards by category: Academic interests/achievement:* 2,794 awards ($26,371,308 total): business, engineering/technologies, foreign languages, general academic interests/achievements, mathematics. *Creative arts/performance:* 2 awards ($2800 total): general creative arts/performance, journalism/publications. *Special achievements/activities:* 798 awards ($188,048 total): community service, general special achievements/activities, leadership. *Special characteristics:* 187 awards ($251,368 total): children and siblings of alumni, children of faculty/staff, general special characteristics, siblings of current students, veterans. *Tuition waivers:* Full or partial for children of alumni, employees or children of employees, senior citizens. *ROTC:* Army cooperative.
**LOANS** *Student loans:* $25,018,402 (47% need-based, 53% non-need-based). 75% of past graduating class borrowed through all loan programs. *Average indebtedness per student:* $29,535. *Average need-based loan:* Freshmen: $2214. Undergraduates: $3954. *Parent loans:* $6,994,490 (100% non-need-based). *Programs:* Federal Direct (Subsidized and Unsubsidized Stafford, PLUS), Perkins, state, college/university.
**WORK-STUDY** *Federal work-study:* Total amount: $1,945,367; 855 jobs averaging $2275. *State or other work-study/employment:* Total amount: $1,762,852 (100% non-need-based). 579 part-time jobs averaging $3049.
**APPLYING FOR FINANCIAL AID** *Required financial aid form:* FAFSA. *Financial aid deadline:* 3/1. *Notification date:* Continuous beginning 2/5. Students must reply by 5/1 or within 2 weeks of notification.
**CONTACT** Ms. Christine A. Perry, Director of Student Financial Services, Suffolk University, 8 Ashburton Place, Boston, MA 02108, 617-573-8470 or toll-free 800-6-SUFFOLK. *Fax:* 617-720-3579. *E-mail:* finaid@suffolk.edu.
*Website:* http://www.suffolk.edu/.

# SULLIVAN UNIVERSITY
## Louisville, KY

**CONTACT** Charlene Geiser, Financial Planning Office, Sullivan University, 3101 Bardstown Road, Louisville, KY 40205, 502-456-6504 Ext. 311 or toll-free 800-844-1354. *Fax:* 502-456-0040. *E-mail:* cgeiser@sullivan.edu.
*Website:* http://www.sullivan.edu/.

# SUL ROSS STATE UNIVERSITY
## Alpine, TX

| Tuition & fees (TX res): $6900 | Average undergraduate aid package: N/A |
| --- | --- |

**ABOUT THE INSTITUTION** State-supported, coed. *Awards:* certificates, associate, bachelor's, and master's degrees. 22 undergraduate majors. *Total enrollment:* 2,906. Undergraduates: 2,031. Freshmen: 332. Federal methodology is used as a basis for awarding need-based institutional aid.
**UNDERGRADUATE EXPENSES for 2015–2016** *Application fee:* $25. *Tuition, state resident:* full-time $4980; part-time $166 per credit hour. *Tuition, nonresident:* full-time $15,840; part-time $528 per credit hour. *Required fees:* full-time $1920; $167 per credit hour. *College room and board:* $7416. Room and board charges vary according to board plan and housing facility.
**FRESHMAN FINANCIAL AID (Fall 2013)** 273 applied for aid; of those 88% were deemed to have need. 100% of freshmen with need received aid.
**UNDERGRADUATE FINANCIAL AID (Fall 2013)** 1,060 applied for aid; of those 87% were deemed to have need. 100% of undergraduates with need received aid.
**GIFT AID (NEED-BASED)** *Total amount:* $6,408,056 (74% federal, 26% state). *Receiving aid:* Freshmen: 83% (240); all full-time undergraduates: 80% (921). *Schol-*

arships, grants, and awards: Federal Pell, FSEOG, state, private, college/university gift aid from institutional funds.

GIFT AID (NON-NEED-BASED) Total amount: $475,832 (97% state, 3% institutional). Scholarships, grants, and awards by category: Academic interests/achievement: agriculture, biological sciences, business, education, English, foreign languages, general academic interests/achievements, health fields. Creative arts/performance: art/fine arts, cinema/film/broadcasting, journalism/publications, music, theater/drama. Special achievements/activities: leadership. Special characteristics: children and siblings of alumni, local/state students. Tuition waivers: Full or partial for employees or children of employees.

LOANS Student loans: $6,651,445 (61% need-based, 39% non-need-based). Parent loans: $381,215 (100% non-need-based). Programs: Federal Direct (Subsidized and Unsubsidized Stafford, PLUS), state, college/university.

WORK-STUDY Federal work-study: 126 jobs averaging $1626. State or other work-study/employment: Total amount: $253,036 (100% need-based). 156 part-time jobs averaging $1622.

APPLYING FOR FINANCIAL AID Required financial aid forms: FAFSA, institution's own form, business/farm supplement. Financial aid deadline: 4/1 (priority: 3/1). Notification date: Continuous beginning 3/20.

CONTACT Mickey Corbett, Director of Financial Aid, Sul Ross State University, Box C-2, Lawrence Hall, Alpine, TX 79832, 432-837-8055 or toll-free 888-722-7778. Fax: 432-837-8411. E-mail: fa@sulross.edu. Website: http://www.sulross.edu/.

---

# SUMMIT UNIVERSITY
## Clarks Summit, PA

ABOUT THE INSTITUTION Independent Baptist, coed. Awards: certificates, associate, bachelor's, master's, and doctoral degrees. 28 undergraduate majors. Total enrollment: 1,001. Undergraduates: 722. Freshmen: 115.

GIFT AID (NEED-BASED) Scholarships, grants, and awards: Federal Pell, FSEOG, state, private, college/university gift aid from institutional funds.

GIFT AID (NON-NEED-BASED) Scholarships, grants, and awards by category: Academic interests/achievement: education, general academic interests/achievements, religion/biblical studies. Creative arts/performance: general creative arts/performance, music. Special achievements/activities: general special achievements/activities, leadership, religious involvement. Special characteristics: children of faculty/staff, general special characteristics, married students.

LOANS Programs: Federal Direct (Subsidized and Unsubsidized Stafford, PLUS), alternative loans.

WORK-STUDY Federal work-study: 63 jobs averaging $1475. State or other work-study/employment: Part-time jobs available.

APPLYING FOR FINANCIAL AID Required financial aid form: FAFSA.

CONTACT Mr. Steven E. Brown, Director of Student Financial Services, Summit University, 538 Venard Road, Clarks Summit, PA 18411, 570-586-2400 Ext. 9206 or toll-free 800-451-7664. Fax: 570-587-8045. E-mail: sbrown@bbc.edu. Website: http://www.summitu.edu/.

---

# SUSQUEHANNA UNIVERSITY
## Selinsgrove, PA

| Tuition & fees: $40,350 | Average undergraduate aid package: $30,817 |
|---|---|

ABOUT THE INSTITUTION Independent Evangelical Lutheran Church in America, coed. Awards: bachelor's degrees (also offers evening associate degree program limited to local adult students). 44 undergraduate majors. Total enrollment: 2,093. Undergraduates: 2,084. Freshmen: 575. Both federal and institutional methodology are used as a basis for awarding need-based institutional aid.

UNDERGRADUATE EXPENSES for 2015–2016 Comprehensive fee: $51,150 includes full-time tuition ($39,830), mandatory fees ($520), and room and board ($10,800). College room only: $5650. Room and board charges vary according to board plan. Part-time tuition: $1265 per semester hour. Payment plan: Tuition prepayment.

FRESHMAN FINANCIAL AID (Fall 2014, est.) 521 applied for aid; of those 88% were deemed to have need. 98% of freshmen with need received aid; of those 24% had

need fully met. Average percent of need met: 82% (excluding resources awarded to replace EFC). Average financial aid package: $30,922 (excluding resources awarded to replace EFC). 19% of all full-time freshmen had no need and received non-need-based gift aid.

UNDERGRADUATE FINANCIAL AID (Fall 2014, est.) 1,720 applied for aid; of those 90% were deemed to have need. 100% of undergraduates with need received aid; of those 20% had need fully met. Average percent of need met: 80% (excluding resources awarded to replace EFC). Average financial aid package: $30,817 (excluding resources awarded to replace EFC). 22% of all full-time undergraduates had no need and received non-need-based gift aid.

GIFT AID (NEED-BASED) Total amount: $39,842,254 (7% federal, 4% state, 87% institutional, 2% external sources). Receiving aid: Freshmen: 78% (450); all full-time undergraduates: 75% (1,551). Average award: Freshmen: $27,465; Undergraduates: $26,103. Scholarships, grants, and awards: Federal Pell, FSEOG, state, private, college/university gift aid from institutional funds.

GIFT AID (NON-NEED-BASED) Total amount: $8,772,849 (93% institutional, 7% external sources). Receiving aid: Freshmen: 15% (87). Undergraduates: 11% (222). Average award: Freshmen: $16,381. Undergraduates: $15,094. Scholarships, grants, and awards by category: Academic interests/achievement: business, general academic interests/achievements. Creative arts/performance: creative writing, music, theater/drama. Special achievements/activities: general special achievements/activities, leadership. Special characteristics: children and siblings of alumni, children of faculty/staff, relatives of clergy, veterans. Tuition waivers: Full or partial for employees or children of employees. ROTC: Army cooperative.

LOANS Student loans: $13,691,805 (69% need-based, 31% non-need-based). 72% of past graduating class borrowed through all loan programs. Average indebtedness per student: $29,734. Average need-based loan: Freshmen: $3029. Undergraduates: $4307. Parent loans: $6,546,940 (41% need-based, 59% non-need-based). Programs: Federal Direct (Subsidized and Unsubsidized Stafford, PLUS), Perkins, college/university.

WORK-STUDY Federal work-study: Total amount: $1,650,688; 1,115 jobs averaging $2143. State or other work-study/employment: Total amount: $597,166 (41% need-based, 59% non-need-based). 93 part-time jobs averaging $6293.

APPLYING FOR FINANCIAL AID Required financial aid forms: FAFSA, CSS Financial Aid PROFILE, federal income tax form(s). Financial aid deadline (priority): 3/1. Notification date: 3/15. Students must reply by 5/1.

CONTACT Ms. Erin M. Wolfe, Director of Financial Aid, Susquehanna University, 514 University Avenue, Selinsgrove, PA 17870, 570-372-4450 or toll-free 800-326-9672. Fax: 570-372-2722. E-mail: wolfeerin@susqu.edu. Website: http://www.susqu.edu/.

---

# SWARTHMORE COLLEGE
## Swarthmore, PA

| Tuition & fees: $46,060 | Average undergraduate aid package: $41,989 |
|---|---|

ABOUT THE INSTITUTION Independent, coed. Awards: bachelor's degrees. 48 undergraduate majors. Total enrollment: 1,534. Undergraduates: 1,534. Freshmen: 388. Institutional methodology is used as a basis for awarding need-based institutional aid.

UNDERGRADUATE EXPENSES for 2015–2016 Application fee: $60. Comprehensive fee: $59,610 includes full-time tuition ($45,700), mandatory fees ($360), and room and board ($13,550). College room only: $6950. Room and board charges vary according to board plan.

FRESHMAN FINANCIAL AID (Fall 2014, est.) 269 applied for aid; of those 78% were deemed to have need. 100% of freshmen with need received aid; of those 100% had need fully met. Average percent of need met: 100% (excluding resources awarded to replace EFC). Average financial aid package: $43,934 (excluding resources awarded to replace EFC). 1% of all full-time freshmen had no need and received non-need-based gift aid.

UNDERGRADUATE FINANCIAL AID (Fall 2014, est.) 891 applied for aid; of those 87% were deemed to have need. 100% of undergraduates with need received aid; of those 100% had need fully met. Average percent of need met: 100% (excluding resources awarded to replace EFC). Average financial aid package: $41,989 (excluding resources awarded to replace EFC). 1% of all full-time undergraduates had no need and received non-need-based gift aid.

**GIFT AID (NEED-BASED)** *Total amount:* $31,150,060 (4% federal, 93% institutional, 3% external sources). *Receiving aid:* Freshmen: 51% (209); all full-time undergraduates: 51% (777). *Average award:* Freshmen: $42,195; Undergraduates: $40,314. *Scholarships, grants, and awards:* Federal Pell, FSEOG, state, private, college/university gift aid from institutional funds.

**GIFT AID (NON-NEED-BASED)** *Total amount:* $850,516 (70% institutional, 30% external sources). *Average award:* Freshmen: $45,700. Undergraduates: $37,474. *Scholarships, grants, and awards by category:* Special characteristics: 13 awards ($586,990 total): local/state students. *ROTC:* Army cooperative, Naval cooperative, Air Force cooperative.

**LOANS** *Student loans:* $1,856,787 (100% non-need-based). 33% of past graduating class borrowed through all loan programs. *Average indebtedness per student:* $21,866. *Parent loans:* $1,549,782 (100% non-need-based). *Programs:* Federal Direct (Subsidized and Unsubsidized Stafford, PLUS), Perkins, college/university.

**WORK-STUDY** *Federal work-study:* Total amount: $866,135; 713 jobs averaging $1826. *State or other work-study/employment:* Total amount: $638,400 (89% need-based, 11% non-need-based). Part-time jobs available.

**APPLYING FOR FINANCIAL AID** *Required financial aid forms:* FAFSA, institution's own form, CSS Financial Aid PROFILE, state aid form, noncustodial (divorced/separated) parent's statement, business/farm supplement, federal income tax form(s), W-2 forms, year-end paycheck stub. *Financial aid deadline:* 2/15. *Notification date:* 4/1. Students must reply by 5/1.

**CONTACT** Varo L. Duffins, Director of Financial Aid, Swarthmore College, 500 College Avenue, Swarthmore, PA 19081-1397, 610-328-8358 or toll-free 800-667-3110. *Fax:* 610-690-5751. *E-mail:* finaid@swarthmore.edu.
*Website:* http://www.swarthmore.edu/.

# SWEDISH INSTITUTE, COLLEGE OF HEALTH SCIENCES
## New York, NY

**CONTACT** Financial Aid Office, Swedish Institute, College of Health Sciences, 226 West 26th Street, New York, NY 10001-6700, 212-924-5900.
*Website:* http://www.swedishinstitute.edu/.

# SYRACUSE UNIVERSITY
## Syracuse, NY

| Tuition & fees: $41,886 | Average undergraduate aid package: $34,620 |
|---|---|

**ABOUT THE INSTITUTION** Independent, coed. *Awards:* certificates, bachelor's, master's, and doctoral degrees. 135 undergraduate majors. *Total enrollment:* 21,492. Undergraduates: 15,224. Freshmen: 3,470. Institutional methodology is used as a basis for awarding need-based institutional aid.

**UNDERGRADUATE EXPENSES** for 2015–2016 *Application fee:* $75. *Comprehensive fee:* $56,346 includes full-time tuition ($40,380), mandatory fees ($1506), and room and board ($14,460). *College room only:* $7640. Full-time tuition and fees vary according to course load. Room and board charges vary according to board plan and housing facility. *Part-time tuition:* $1757 per credit hour. Part-time tuition and fees vary according to course load. *Payment plan:* Tuition prepayment.

**FRESHMAN FINANCIAL AID (Fall 2014, est.)** 2,508 applied for aid; of those 75% were deemed to have need. 100% of freshmen with need received aid; of those 42% had need fully met. *Average percent of need met:* 96% (excluding resources awarded to replace EFC). *Average financial aid package:* $35,510 (excluding resources awarded to replace EFC). 12% of all full-time freshmen had no need and received non-need-based gift aid.

**UNDERGRADUATE FINANCIAL AID (Fall 2014, est.)** 9,518 applied for aid; of those 85% were deemed to have need. 100% of undergraduates with need received aid; of those 35% had need fully met. *Average percent of need met:* 90% (excluding resources awarded to replace EFC). *Average financial aid package:* $34,620 (excluding resources awarded to replace EFC). 11% of all full-time undergraduates had no need and received non-need-based gift aid.

**GIFT AID (NEED-BASED)** *Total amount:* $233,265,127 (10% federal, 4% state, 84% institutional, 2% external sources). *Receiving aid:* Freshmen: 50% (1,725); all full-time undergraduates: 52% (7,352). *Average award:* Freshmen: $27,980; Undergraduates: $26,770. *Scholarships, grants, and awards:* Federal Pell, FSEOG, state, private, college/university gift aid from institutional funds.

**GIFT AID (NON-NEED-BASED)** *Total amount:* $16,709,207 (9% federal, 86% institutional, 5% external sources). *Receiving aid:* Freshmen: 5% (160). Undergraduates: 4% (512). *Average award:* Freshmen: $11,110. Undergraduates: $10,290. *Scholarships, grants, and awards by category:* Academic interests/achievement: general academic interests/achievements. Creative arts/performance: art/fine arts, music, theater/drama. *Tuition waivers:* Full or partial for employees or children of employees. *ROTC:* Army, Air Force.

**LOANS** *Student loans:* $81,016,049 (91% need-based, 9% non-need-based). 66% of past graduating class borrowed through all loan programs. *Average indebtedness per student:* $34,584. *Average need-based loan:* Freshmen: $4600. Undergraduates: $5400. *Parent loans:* $37,932,327 (88% need-based, 12% non-need-based). *Programs:* Federal Direct (Subsidized and Unsubsidized Stafford, PLUS), Perkins.

**WORK-STUDY** *Federal work-study:* Total amount: $13,207,766; 5,011 jobs averaging $2600.

**ATHLETIC AWARDS** Total amount: $15,833,612 (50% need-based, 50% non-need-based).

**APPLYING FOR FINANCIAL AID** *Required financial aid forms:* FAFSA, CSS Financial Aid PROFILE, noncustodial (divorced/separated) parent's statement. *Financial aid deadline:* 2/1. *Notification date:* 3/15. Students must reply by 5/1.

**CONTACT** Office of Financial Aid, Syracuse University, 200 Archbold North, Syracuse, NY 13244-1140, 315-443-1513. *E-mail:* finmail@syr.edu.
*Website:* http://www.syr.edu/.

# TABOR COLLEGE
## Hillsboro, KS

| Tuition & fees: $23,900 | Average undergraduate aid package: $19,268 |
|---|---|

**ABOUT THE INSTITUTION** Independent Mennonite Brethren, coed. *Awards:* associate, bachelor's, and master's degrees. 53 undergraduate majors. *Total enrollment:* 766. Undergraduates: 735. Freshmen: 159. Federal methodology is used as a basis for awarding need-based institutional aid.

**UNDERGRADUATE EXPENSES** for 2015–2016 *Application fee:* $30. *Comprehensive fee:* $32,520 includes full-time tuition ($23,100), mandatory fees ($800), and room and board ($8620). Full-time tuition and fees vary according to course load and program. Room and board charges vary according to housing facility and location. *Part-time tuition:* $482 per hour. *Part-time fees:* $480 per term. Part-time tuition and fees vary according to course load and program.

**FRESHMAN FINANCIAL AID (Fall 2013)** 157 applied for aid; of those 86% were deemed to have need. 100% of freshmen with need received aid; of those 7% had need fully met. *Average percent of need met:* 71% (excluding resources awarded to replace EFC). *Average financial aid package:* $18,638 (excluding resources awarded to replace EFC). 15% of all full-time freshmen had no need and received non-need-based gift aid.

**UNDERGRADUATE FINANCIAL AID (Fall 2013)** 581 applied for aid; of those 86% were deemed to have need. 100% of undergraduates with need received aid; of those 12% had need fully met. *Average percent of need met:* 72% (excluding resources awarded to replace EFC). *Average financial aid package:* $19,268 (excluding resources awarded to replace EFC). 14% of all full-time undergraduates had no need and received non-need-based gift aid.

**GIFT AID (NEED-BASED)** *Total amount:* $1,755,386 (74% federal, 26% state). *Receiving aid:* Freshmen: 66% (104); all full-time undergraduates: 64% (382). *Average award:* Freshmen: $4917; Undergraduates: $4696. *Scholarships, grants, and awards:* Federal Pell, FSEOG, state, private, college/university gift aid from institutional funds.

**GIFT AID (NON-NEED-BASED)** *Total amount:* $5,235,659 (94% institutional, 6% external sources). *Receiving aid:* Freshmen: 85% (135). Undergraduates: 82% (486). *Average award:* Freshmen: $9874. Undergraduates: $9458. *Scholarships, grants, and awards by category:* Academic interests/achievement: biological sciences, communication, general academic interests/achievements, humanities. Creative arts/performance: journalism/publications, music, performing arts, theater/drama.

Special achievements/activities: cheerleading/drum major, general special achievements/activities, religious involvement. Special characteristics: children and siblings of alumni, children of faculty/staff, general special characteristics, international students, local/state students, out-of-state students, religious affiliation. Tuition waivers: Full or partial for employees or children of employees.

**LOANS** *Student loans:* $2,656,528 (100% need-based). 80% of past graduating class borrowed through all loan programs. *Average indebtedness per student:* $26,588. *Average need-based loan:* Freshmen: $3584. Undergraduates: $4656. *Parent loans:* $748,285 (100% need-based). *Programs:* Federal Direct (Subsidized and Unsubsidized Stafford, PLUS), Perkins.

**WORK-STUDY** *Federal work-study:* 235 jobs averaging $914. *State or other work-study/employment:* Part-time jobs available.

**ATHLETIC AWARDS** Total amount: $1,816,521 (100% non-need-based).

**APPLYING FOR FINANCIAL AID** *Required financial aid forms:* FAFSA, state aid form. *Financial aid deadline:* 8/15 (priority: 3/1). *Notification date:* Continuous beginning 3/15. Students must reply within 5 weeks of notification.

**CONTACT** Mr. Scott Franz, Director of Student Financial Assistance, Tabor College, 400 South Jefferson, Hillsboro, KS 67063, 620-947-3121 Ext. 1726 or toll-free 800-822-6799. *Fax:* 620-947-6276. *E-mail:* scottf@tabor.edu. *Website:* http://www.tabor.edu/.

# TALLADEGA COLLEGE
## Talladega, AL

**CONTACT** K. Michael Francois, Director of Financial Aid, Talladega College, 627 West Battle Street, Talladega, AL 35160, 256-761-6341 or toll-free 866-540-3956. *Fax:* 256-761-6462.
*Website:* http://www.talladega.edu/.

# TALMUDICAL ACADEMY OF NEW JERSEY
## Adelphia, NJ

**CONTACT** Office of Financial Aid, Talmudical Academy of New Jersey, Route 524, Adelphia, NJ 07710, 732-431-1600.

# TALMUDICAL INSTITUTE OF UPSTATE NEW YORK
## Rochester, NY

**CONTACT** Mrs. Ella Berenstein, Financial Aid Administrator, Talmudical Institute of Upstate New York, 769 Park Avenue, Rochester, NY 14607-3046, 585-473-2810.
*Website:* http://www.tiuny.org/.

# TALMUDICAL SEMINARY OF BOBOV
## Brooklyn, NY

**CONTACT** Financial Aid Office, Talmudical Seminary of Bobov, 5120 New Utrecht Avenue, Brooklyn, NY 11219, 718-436-2122.

# TALMUDICAL SEMINARY OHOLEI TORAH
## Brooklyn, NY

**CONTACT** Financial Aid Administrator, Talmudical Seminary Oholei Torah, 667 Eastern Parkway, Brooklyn, NY 11213-3310, 718-774-5050.

# TALMUDICAL YESHIVA OF PHILADELPHIA
## Philadelphia, PA

**CONTACT** Director of Student Financial Aid/Registrar, Talmudical Yeshiva of Philadelphia, 6063 Drexel Road, Philadelphia, PA 19131-1296, 215-473-1212.

# TALMUDIC COLLEGE OF FLORIDA
## Miami Beach, FL

**CONTACT** Rabbi Ira Hill, Director of Financial Aid, Talmudic College of Florida, 1910 Alton Road, Miami Beach, FL 33139, 305-534-7050. *Fax:* 305-534-8444. *Website:* http://www.talmudicu.edu/.

# TARLETON STATE UNIVERSITY
## Stephenville, TX

| Tuition & fees (TX res): $8246 | Average undergraduate aid package: $8940 |
| --- | --- |

**ABOUT THE INSTITUTION** State-supported, coed. *Awards:* associate, bachelor's, master's, and doctoral degrees. 101 undergraduate majors. *Total enrollment:* 11,697. Undergraduates: 10,277. Freshmen: 1,971. Federal methodology is used as a basis for awarding need-based institutional aid.

**UNDERGRADUATE EXPENSES for 2015–2016** *Application fee:* $30. *Tuition, state resident:* full-time $4922; part-time $154 per credit. *Tuition, nonresident:* full-time $15,782; part-time $516 per hour. *Required fees:* full-time $3324. Full-time tuition and fees vary according to course load and degree level. Part-time tuition and fees vary according to course load and degree level. *College room and board:* $9042; *Room only:* $5400. Room and board charges vary according to board plan and housing facility. *Payment plan:* Guaranteed tuition.

**FRESHMAN FINANCIAL AID (Fall 2013)** 1,544 applied for aid; of those 79% were deemed to have need. 97% of freshmen with need received aid; of those 6% had need fully met. *Average percent of need met:* 56% (excluding resources awarded to replace EFC). *Average financial aid package:* $9001 (excluding resources awarded to replace EFC).

**UNDERGRADUATE FINANCIAL AID (Fall 2013)** 5,763 applied for aid; of those 84% were deemed to have need. 97% of undergraduates with need received aid; of those 3% had need fully met. *Average percent of need met:* 51% (excluding resources awarded to replace EFC). *Average financial aid package:* $8940 (excluding resources awarded to replace EFC).

**GIFT AID (NEED-BASED)** *Total amount:* $31,861,977 (53% federal, 25% state, 14% institutional, 8% external sources). *Receiving aid:* Freshmen: 61% (1,111); all full-time undergraduates: 58% (4,290). *Average award:* Freshmen: $7265; Undergraduates: $6305. *Scholarships, grants, and awards:* Federal Pell, FSEOG, state, college/university gift aid from institutional funds.

**GIFT AID (NON-NEED-BASED)** *Total amount:* $272,000 (100% state). *Receiving aid:* Freshmen: 6% (114). Undergraduates: 3% (216). *Scholarships, grants, and awards by category:* Academic interests/achievement: general academic interests/achievements. Creative arts/performance: music, theater/drama. *ROTC:* Army.

**LOANS** *Student loans:* $43,641,689 (42% need-based, 58% non-need-based). 64% of past graduating class borrowed through all loan programs. *Average indebtedness per student:* $26,267. *Average need-based loan:* Freshmen: $3229. Undergraduates: $4173. *Parent loans:* $10,300,260 (100% non-need-based). *Programs:* Federal Direct (Subsidized and Unsubsidized Stafford, PLUS), state.

**WORK-STUDY** *Federal work-study:* jobs available. *State or other work-study/employment:* Total amount: $172,866 (100% need-based). Part-time jobs available.

**ATHLETIC AWARDS** Total amount: $1,626,693 (67% need-based, 33% non-need-based).

**APPLYING FOR FINANCIAL AID** *Required financial aid form:* FAFSA. *Financial aid deadline:* 11/1 (priority: 3/15). *Notification date:* Continuous beginning 3/1. Students must reply within 2 weeks of notification.

**CONTACT** Ms. Kathy Purvis, Executive Director, Tarleton State University, Box T-0310, Stephenville, TX 76402, 254-968-9070 or toll-free 800-687-8236. *Fax:* 254-968-9600. *E-mail:* finaid@tarleton.edu. *Website:* http://www.tarleton.edu/.

# TAYLOR UNIVERSITY
## Upland, IN

| Tuition & fees: $29,538 | Average undergraduate aid package: $19,626 |
| --- | --- |

**ABOUT THE INSTITUTION** Independent interdenominational, coed. *Awards:* certificates, diplomas, associate, bachelor's, and master's degrees. 59 undergraduate majors. *Total enrollment:* 2,209. Undergraduates: 2,103. Freshmen: 438. Federal methodology is used as a basis for awarding need-based institutional aid.

**UNDERGRADUATE EXPENSES for 2015–2016 Application fee:** $25. *Comprehensive fee:* $37,821 includes full-time tuition ($29,298), mandatory fees ($240), and room and board ($8283). *College room only:* $4346. Full-time tuition and fees vary according to course load. Room and board charges vary according to board plan and housing facility. *Part-time tuition:* $1032 per credit hour. *Part-time fees:* $37.50 per term. Part-time tuition and fees vary according to course load.

**FRESHMAN FINANCIAL AID (Fall 2014, est.)** 358 applied for aid; of those 82% were deemed to have need. 100% of freshmen with need received aid; of those 25% had need fully met. *Average percent of need met:* 74% (excluding resources awarded to replace EFC). *Average financial aid package:* $20,074 (excluding resources awarded to replace EFC). 25% of all full-time freshmen had no need and received non-need-based gift aid.

**UNDERGRADUATE FINANCIAL AID (Fall 2014, est.)** 1,310 applied for aid; of those 83% were deemed to have need. 100% of undergraduates with need received aid; of those 23% had need fully met. *Average percent of need met:* 72% (excluding resources awarded to replace EFC). *Average financial aid package:* $19,626 (excluding resources awarded to replace EFC). 28% of all full-time undergraduates had no need and received non-need-based gift aid.

**GIFT AID (NEED-BASED) Total amount:** $14,189,454 (13% federal, 6% state, 74% institutional, 7% external sources). *Receiving aid:* Freshmen: 67% (294); all full-time undergraduates: 59% (1,072). *Average award:* Freshmen: $16,153; Undergraduates: $15,416. *Scholarships, grants, and awards:* Federal Pell, FSEOG, state, private, college/university gift aid from institutional funds, Academic Competitiveness Grants, National SMART Grants.

**GIFT AID (NON-NEED-BASED) Total amount:** $6,974,282 (90% institutional, 10% external sources). *Receiving aid:* Freshmen: 12% (52). Undergraduates: 9% (166). *Average award:* Freshmen: $10,049. Undergraduates: $9342. *Scholarships, grants, and awards by category: Academic interests/achievement:* 1,388 awards ($9,286,212 total): general academic interests/achievements. *Creative arts/performance:* 109 awards ($287,500 total): music, theater/drama. *Special achievements/activities:* 440 awards ($1,090,688 total): leadership. *Special characteristics:* 744 awards ($3,878,379 total): children and siblings of alumni, children of faculty/staff, ethnic background, international students, religious affiliation. *Tuition waivers:* Full or partial for employees or children of employees, senior citizens.

**LOANS Student loans:** $10,333,461 (65% need-based, 35% non-need-based). 63% of past graduating class borrowed through all loan programs. *Average indebtedness per student:* $25,125. *Average need-based loan:* Freshmen: $4424. Undergraduates: $4681. *Parent loans:* $20,228,860 (28% need-based, 72% non-need-based). *Programs:* Federal Direct (Subsidized and Unsubsidized Stafford, PLUS), Perkins, college/university.

**WORK-STUDY Federal work-study:** Total amount: $443,033; 819 jobs averaging $541.

**ATHLETIC AWARDS** Total amount: $2,162,960 (56% need-based, 44% non-need-based).

**APPLYING FOR FINANCIAL AID Required financial aid form:** FAFSA. *Financial aid deadline:* 3/10. *Notification date:* Continuous beginning 3/1. Students must reply by 5/1.

**CONTACT** Mr. Timothy A. Nace, Director of Financial Aid, Taylor University, 236 West Reade Avenue, Upland, IN 46989-1001, 765-998-5358 or toll-free 800-882-3456. *Fax:* 765-998-4910. *E-mail:* tmnace@taylor.edu. *Website:* http://www.taylor.edu/.

# TELSHE YESHIVA–CHICAGO
## Chicago, IL

**CONTACT** Office of Financial Aid, Telshe Yeshiva–Chicago, 3535 West Foster Avenue, Chicago, IL 60625-5598, 773-463-7738.

# TEMPLE UNIVERSITY
## Philadelphia, PA

| Tuition & fees (PA res): $15,096 | Average undergraduate aid package: $16,385 |
| --- | --- |

**ABOUT THE INSTITUTION** State-related, coed. *Awards:* certificates, diplomas, associate, bachelor's, master's, and doctoral degrees. 116 undergraduate majors. *Total enrollment:* 37,788. Undergraduates: 28,408. Freshmen: 4,485. Federal methodology is used as a basis for awarding need-based institutional aid.

**UNDERGRADUATE EXPENSES for 2015–2016 Application fee:** $55. *Tuition, state resident:* full-time $14,406; part-time $554 per credit hour. *Tuition, nonresident:* full-time $24,432; part-time $834 per credit hour. *Required fees:* full-time $690. Full-time tuition and fees vary according to course load, degree level, location, program, reciprocity agreements, and student level. Part-time tuition and fees vary according to course load, degree level, location, program, reciprocity agreements, and student level. *College room and board:* $10,738; *Room only:* $7150. Room and board charges vary according to board plan and housing facility.

**FRESHMAN FINANCIAL AID (Fall 2013)** 3,832 applied for aid; of those 82% were deemed to have need. 99% of freshmen with need received aid; of those 30% had need fully met. *Average percent of need met:* 70% (excluding resources awarded to replace EFC). *Average financial aid package:* $16,444 (excluding resources awarded to replace EFC). 14% of all full-time freshmen had no need and received non-need-based gift aid.

**UNDERGRADUATE FINANCIAL AID (Fall 2013)** 20,373 applied for aid; of those 86% were deemed to have need. 99% of undergraduates with need received aid; of those 25% had need fully met. *Average percent of need met:* 66% (excluding resources awarded to replace EFC). *Average financial aid package:* $16,385 (excluding resources awarded to replace EFC). 10% of all full-time undergraduates had no need and received non-need-based gift aid.

**GIFT AID (NEED-BASED) Total amount:** $101,577,271 (41% federal, 28% state, 31% institutional). *Receiving aid:* Freshmen: 61% (2,657); all full-time undergraduates: 61% (15,042). *Average award:* Freshmen: $6638; Undergraduates: $6335. *Scholarships, grants, and awards:* Federal Pell, FSEOG, state, private, college/university gift aid from institutional funds, Federal Nursing.

**GIFT AID (NON-NEED-BASED) Total amount:** $48,426,614 (74% institutional, 26% external sources). *Receiving aid:* Freshmen: 38% (1,655). Undergraduates: 26% (6,495). *Average award:* Freshmen: $8181. Undergraduates: $5871. *Scholarships, grants, and awards by category: Academic interests/achievement:* 6,990 awards ($29,346,502 total): general academic interests/achievements. *Creative arts/performance:* 162 awards ($536,038 total): art/fine arts, general creative arts/performance, music, performing arts. *Special achievements/activities:* 238 awards ($330,940 total): cheerleading/drum major. *Special characteristics:* 2,236 awards ($13,419,174 total): children of faculty/staff, general special characteristics, veterans. *Tuition waivers:* Full or partial for employees or children of employees. *ROTC:* Army, Naval cooperative, Air Force cooperative.

**LOANS Student loans:** $188,225,738 (77% need-based, 23% non-need-based). 77% of past graduating class borrowed through all loan programs. *Average indebtedness per student:* $35,760. *Average need-based loan:* Freshmen: $3606. Undergraduates: $4580. *Parent loans:* $41,681,143 (100% non-need-based). *Programs:* Federal Direct (Subsidized and Unsubsidized Stafford, PLUS), Perkins, Federal Nursing, state, college/university.

**WORK-STUDY Federal work-study:** 2,419 jobs averaging $1130.

**ATHLETIC AWARDS** Total amount: $8,488,692 (100% non-need-based).

**APPLYING FOR FINANCIAL AID Required financial aid form:** FAFSA. *Financial aid deadline (priority):* 3/1. *Notification date:* Continuous beginning 2/15. Students must reply by 5/1 or within 3 weeks of notification.

**CONTACT** Mr. Craig Fennell, Director of Student Financial Services, Temple University, Conwell Hall, Ground Floor, Philadelphia, PA 19122-6096, 215-204-8760 or toll-free 888-340-2222. *Fax:* 215-204-2016. *E-mail:* craig.fennell@temple.edu. *Website:* http://www.temple.edu/.

# TENNESSEE STATE UNIVERSITY
## Nashville, TN

| Tuition & fees (TN res): $6930 | Average undergraduate aid package: $10,704 |
|---|---|

**ABOUT THE INSTITUTION** State-supported, coed. **Awards:** certificates, associate, bachelor's, master's, and doctoral degrees. 58 undergraduate majors. **Total enrollment:** 9,027. Undergraduates: 7,073. Freshmen: 1,377. Federal methodology is used as a basis for awarding need-based institutional aid.

**UNDERGRADUATE EXPENSES for 2015–2016 Application fee:** $25. **Tuition, state resident:** full-time $6930; part-time $310 per hour. **Tuition, nonresident:** full-time $19,650; part-time $840 per hour. **College room and board:** $6240; **Room only:** $3560.

**FRESHMAN FINANCIAL AID (Fall 2014, est.)** 1,375 applied for aid; of those 95% were deemed to have need. 100% of freshmen with need received aid; of those 9% had need fully met. **Average percent of need met:** 59% (excluding resources awarded to replace EFC). **Average financial aid package:** $11,434 (excluding resources awarded to replace EFC). 3% of all full-time freshmen had no need and received non-need-based gift aid.

**UNDERGRADUATE FINANCIAL AID (Fall 2014, est.)** 5,529 applied for aid; of those 94% were deemed to have need. 100% of undergraduates with need received aid; of those 7% had need fully met. **Average percent of need met:** 57% (excluding resources awarded to replace EFC). **Average financial aid package:** $10,704 (excluding resources awarded to replace EFC). 3% of all full-time undergraduates had no need and received non-need-based gift aid.

**GIFT AID (NEED-BASED) Total amount:** $25,500,573 (89% federal, 11% state). **Receiving aid:** Freshmen: 73% (1,090); all full-time undergraduates: 68% (4,172). **Average award:** Freshmen: $5666; Undergraduates: $5376. **Scholarships, grants, and awards:** Federal Pell, FSEOG, state, private, college/university gift aid from institutional funds.

**GIFT AID (NON-NEED-BASED) Total amount:** $22,737,046 (15% state, 45% institutional, 40% external sources). **Receiving aid:** Freshmen: 47% (704). Undergraduates: 36% (2,219). **Average award:** Freshmen: $14,884. Undergraduates: $13,455. **Scholarships, grants, and awards by category:** Academic interests/achievement: general academic interests/achievements. Creative arts/performance: music. Special achievements/activities: general special achievements/activities. Special characteristics: local/state students, members of minority groups. **ROTC:** Army cooperative, Naval cooperative, Air Force.

**LOANS Student loans:** $41,536,976 (44% need-based, 56% non-need-based). 86% of past graduating class borrowed through all loan programs. **Average indebtedness per student:** $35,645. **Average need-based loan:** Freshmen: $3430. Undergraduates: $4030. **Parent loans:** $5,526,507 (100% non-need-based). **Programs:** Federal Direct (Subsidized and Unsubsidized Stafford, PLUS), Perkins.

**WORK-STUDY Federal work-study:** Total amount: $1,473,313; 781 jobs averaging $1926. **State or other work-study/employment:** Total amount: $1,473,313 (100% need-based). Part-time jobs available.

**APPLYING FOR FINANCIAL AID Required financial aid form:** FAFSA. **Financial aid deadline (priority):** 4/1. **Notification date:** Continuous beginning 4/25. Students must reply within 3 weeks of notification.

**CONTACT** Amy Wood, Director of Financial Aid, Tennessee State University, 3500 John Merritt Boulevard, Nashville, TN 37209-1561, 615-963-7548. *Fax:* 615-963-7540. *E-mail:* finaid@tnstate.edu. *Website:* http://www.tnstate.edu/.

---

**UNDERGRADUATE EXPENSES for 2015–2016 Application fee:** $25. **Tuition, state resident:** full-time $7317; part-time $352 per credit hour. **Tuition, nonresident:** full-time $22,317; part-time $976 per credit hour. **Required fees:** full-time $181. Full-time tuition and fees vary according to course load and program. Part-time tuition and fees vary according to course load and program. **College room and board:** $8296; **Room only:** $4370. Room and board charges vary according to board plan and housing facility.

**FRESHMAN FINANCIAL AID (Fall 2013)** 1,929 applied for aid; of those 80% were deemed to have need. 100% of freshmen with need received aid; of those 10% had need fully met. **Average percent of need met:** 65% (excluding resources awarded to replace EFC). **Average financial aid package:** $10,292 (excluding resources awarded to replace EFC). 28% of all full-time freshmen had no need and received non-need-based gift aid.

**UNDERGRADUATE FINANCIAL AID (Fall 2013)** 8,180 applied for aid; of those 81% were deemed to have need. 98% of undergraduates with need received aid; of those 8% had need fully met. **Average percent of need met:** 60% (excluding resources awarded to replace EFC). **Average financial aid package:** $9271 (excluding resources awarded to replace EFC). 24% of all full-time undergraduates had no need and received non-need-based gift aid.

**GIFT AID (NEED-BASED) Total amount:** $19,909,681 (79% federal, 20% state, 1% institutional). **Receiving aid:** Freshmen: 37% (811); all full-time undergraduates: 41% (3,744). **Average award:** Freshmen: $5832; Undergraduates: $5163. **Scholarships, grants, and awards:** Federal Pell, FSEOG, state, private, college/university gift aid from institutional funds, United Negro College Fund.

**GIFT AID (NON-NEED-BASED) Total amount:** $31,560,468 (72% state, 21% institutional, 7% external sources). **Receiving aid:** Freshmen: 66% (1,428). Undergraduates: 50% (4,601). **Average award:** Freshmen: $11,214. Undergraduates: $12,252. **Scholarships, grants, and awards by category:** Academic interests/achievement: 2,121 awards ($5,215,349 total): agriculture, biological sciences, business, communication, computer science, education, engineering/technologies, English, foreign languages, general academic interests/achievements, health fields, home economics, humanities, international studies, mathematics, military science, physical sciences, premedicine, social sciences. Creative arts/performance: 257 awards ($537,189 total): art/fine arts, debating, music. Special achievements/activities: 86 awards ($111,935 total): cheerleading/drum major, general special achievements/activities. Special characteristics: 399 awards ($937,507 total): children and siblings of alumni, children of educators, children of faculty/staff, children of public servants, ethnic background, first-generation college students, local/state students, members of minority groups, out-of-state students, public servants. **Tuition waivers:** Full or partial for employees or children of employees, senior citizens. **ROTC:** Army, Air Force cooperative.

**LOANS Student loans:** $28,626,734 (55% need-based, 45% non-need-based). 53% of past graduating class borrowed through all loan programs. **Average indebtedness per student:** $18,467. **Average need-based loan:** Freshmen: $2946. Undergraduates: $3836. **Parent loans:** $1,884,095 (100% non-need-based). **Programs:** Federal Direct (Subsidized and Unsubsidized Stafford, PLUS), Perkins, college/university.

**WORK-STUDY Federal work-study:** 1,315 jobs averaging $1401. **State or other work-study/employment:** Part-time jobs available.

**ATHLETIC AWARDS** Total amount: $3,556,950 (100% non-need-based).

**APPLYING FOR FINANCIAL AID Required financial aid form:** FAFSA. **Financial aid deadline (priority):** 3/15. **Notification date:** Continuous beginning 4/1. Students must reply within 2 weeks of notification.

**CONTACT** Lester C. McKenzie III, Director of Financial Aid, Tennessee Technological University, PO Box 5076, 1000 North Dixie Avenue, Cookeville, TN 38501, 931-372-3073 or toll-free 800-255-8881. *Fax:* 931-372-6309. *E-mail:* lmckenzie@tntech.edu. *Website:* http://www.tntech.edu/.

---

# TENNESSEE TECHNOLOGICAL UNIVERSITY
## Cookeville, TN

| Tuition & fees (TN res): $7498 | Average undergraduate aid package: $9271 |
|---|---|

**ABOUT THE INSTITUTION** State-supported, coed. **Awards:** certificates, bachelor's, master's, and doctoral degrees. 67 undergraduate majors. **Total enrollment:** 11,118. Undergraduates: 10,083. Freshmen: 2,176. Federal methodology is used as a basis for awarding need-based institutional aid.

---

# TENNESSEE WESLEYAN COLLEGE
## Athens, TN

| Tuition & fees: $22,900 | Average undergraduate aid package: $16,283 |
|---|---|

**ABOUT THE INSTITUTION** Independent United Methodist, coed. **Awards:** bachelor's and master's degrees (profile includes information for both the main and branch campuses). 42 undergraduate majors. **Total enrollment:** 1,034. Undergraduates: 1,019. Freshmen: 192. Federal methodology is used as a basis for awarding need-based institutional aid.

**UNDERGRADUATE EXPENSES for 2015–2016** *Application fee:* $30. *Comprehensive fee:* $30,210 includes full-time tuition ($22,000), mandatory fees ($900), and room and board ($7310). Full-time tuition and fees vary according to class time and degree level. Room and board charges vary according to board plan and housing facility. *Part-time tuition:* $570 per credit. Part-time tuition and fees vary according to class time, course load, degree level, location, and program.
**FRESHMAN FINANCIAL AID (Fall 2013)** 183 applied for aid; of those 92% were deemed to have need. 98% of freshmen with need received aid; of those 18% had need fully met. *Average percent of need met:* 68% (excluding resources awarded to replace EFC). *Average financial aid package:* $18,112 (excluding resources awarded to replace EFC). 6% of all full-time freshmen had no need and received non-need-based gift aid.
**UNDERGRADUATE FINANCIAL AID (Fall 2013)** 903 applied for aid; of those 89% were deemed to have need. 94% of undergraduates with need received aid; of those 16% had need fully met. *Average percent of need met:* 60% (excluding resources awarded to replace EFC). *Average financial aid package:* $16,283 (excluding resources awarded to replace EFC). 7% of all full-time undergraduates had no need and received non-need-based gift aid.
**GIFT AID (NEED-BASED)** *Total amount:* $9,374,641 (23% federal, 23% state, 49% institutional, 5% external sources). *Receiving aid:* Freshmen: 81% (164); all full-time undergraduates: 75% (728). *Average award:* Freshmen: $16,035; Undergraduates: $13,930. *Scholarships, grants, and awards:* Federal Pell, FSEOG, state, private, college/university gift aid from institutional funds.
**GIFT AID (NON-NEED-BASED)** *Total amount:* $1,540,439 (29% state, 62% institutional, 9% external sources). *Receiving aid:* Freshmen: 11% (22). Undergraduates: 9% (87). *Average award:* Freshmen: $12,184. Undergraduates: $9675. *Scholarships, grants, and awards by category:* Academic interests/achievement: general academic interests/achievements. Creative arts/performance: music. Special achievements/activities: cheerleading/drum major, general special achievements/activities, junior miss, memberships, religious involvement. Special characteristics: children and siblings of alumni, children of faculty/staff, general special characteristics, international students, members of minority groups, relatives of clergy, religious affiliation. *Tuition waivers:* Full or partial for employees or children of employees.
**LOANS** *Student loans:* $5,603,314 (81% need-based, 19% non-need-based). 84% of past graduating class borrowed through all loan programs. *Average indebtedness per student:* $21,280. *Average need-based loan:* Freshmen: $2981. Undergraduates: $3899. *Parent loans:* $728,573 (40% need-based, 60% non-need-based). *Programs:* Federal Direct (Subsidized and Unsubsidized Stafford, PLUS).
**WORK-STUDY** *Federal work-study:* jobs available. *State or other work-study/employment:* Total amount: $11,774 (20% need-based, 80% non-need-based). Part-time jobs available.
**ATHLETIC AWARDS** Total amount: $3,391,142 (62% need-based, 38% non-need-based).
**APPLYING FOR FINANCIAL AID** *Required financial aid forms:* FAFSA, institution's own form. *Financial aid deadline:* Continuous. *Notification date:* Continuous beginning 2/15.
**CONTACT** Mrs. Lacey Weese, Director of Financial Aid, Tennessee Wesleyan College, 204 East College Street, Athens, TN 37303, 423-746-5209 or toll-free 800-PICK-TWC. *Fax:* 423-744-9968. *E-mail:* lweese@twcnet.edu.
*Website:* http://www.twcnet.edu/.

# TEXAS A&M INTERNATIONAL UNIVERSITY
## Laredo, TX

| Tuition & fees (TX res): $7558 | Average undergraduate aid package: $8502 |
|---|---|

**ABOUT THE INSTITUTION** State-supported, coed. *Awards:* bachelor's, master's, and doctoral degrees. 40 undergraduate majors. *Total enrollment:* 7,554. Undergraduates: 6,741. Freshmen: 903. Federal methodology is used as a basis for awarding need-based institutional aid.
**UNDERGRADUATE EXPENSES for 2015–2016** *Tuition, state resident:* full-time $7558. *Tuition, nonresident:* full-time $18,652. Full-time tuition and fees vary according to course load. Part-time tuition and fees vary according to course load and reciprocity agreements. *College room and board:* $8028. Room and board charges vary according to board plan and housing facility.

**FRESHMAN FINANCIAL AID (Fall 2013)** 819 applied for aid; of those 94% were deemed to have need. 100% of freshmen with need received aid; of those 3% had need fully met. *Average percent of need met:* 60% (excluding resources awarded to replace EFC). *Average financial aid package:* $10,131 (excluding resources awarded to replace EFC). 4% of all full-time freshmen had no need and received non-need-based gift aid.
**UNDERGRADUATE FINANCIAL AID (Fall 2013)** 3,964 applied for aid; of those 90% were deemed to have need. 100% of undergraduates with need received aid; of those 6% had need fully met. *Average percent of need met:* 51% (excluding resources awarded to replace EFC). *Average financial aid package:* $8502 (excluding resources awarded to replace EFC). 4% of all full-time undergraduates had no need and received non-need-based gift aid.
**GIFT AID (NEED-BASED)** *Total amount:* $24,272,046 (63% federal, 27% state, 10% institutional). *Receiving aid:* Freshmen: 87% (750); all full-time undergraduates: 65% (3,494). *Average award:* Freshmen: $8041; Undergraduates: $6343. *Scholarships, grants, and awards:* Federal Pell, FSEOG, state, college/university gift aid from institutional funds, Federal Nursing.
**GIFT AID (NON-NEED-BASED)** *Total amount:* $3,296,951 (13% state, 78% institutional, 9% external sources). *Receiving aid:* Freshmen: 34% (295). Undergraduates: 24% (1,307). *Average award:* Freshmen: $3171. Undergraduates: $3413. *Scholarships, grants, and awards by category:* Academic interests/achievement: business, communication, education, engineering/technologies, English, foreign languages, general academic interests/achievements, health fields, international studies, mathematics, physical sciences, premedicine, social sciences. Creative arts/performance: art/fine arts, dance, music, performing arts. *Tuition waivers:* Full or partial for senior citizens. *ROTC:* Army.
**LOANS** *Student loans:* $13,105,912 (71% need-based, 29% non-need-based). 74% of past graduating class borrowed through all loan programs. *Average indebtedness per student:* $17,394. *Average need-based loan:* Freshmen: $2560. Undergraduates: $3758. *Parent loans:* $110,822 (100% non-need-based). *Programs:* Federal Direct (Subsidized and Unsubsidized Stafford, PLUS), state, college/university, Hinson-Hazelwood Loan Program.
**WORK-STUDY** *Federal work-study:* 91 jobs averaging $2232. *State or other work-study/employment:* Total amount: $59,751 (100% need-based). 33 part-time jobs averaging $1924.
**ATHLETIC AWARDS** Total amount: $730,735 (100% non-need-based).
**APPLYING FOR FINANCIAL AID** *Required financial aid form:* FAFSA. *Financial aid deadline:* 7/30 (priority: 3/15). *Notification date:* Continuous beginning 4/5. Students must reply within 6 weeks of notification.
**CONTACT** Mrs. Laura Elizondo, Director of Financial Aid, Texas A&M International University, 5201 University Boulevard, Laredo, TX 78041, 956-326-2225 or toll-free 888-489-2648. *Fax:* 956-326-2224. *E-mail:* laura@tamiu.edu.
*Website:* http://www.tamiu.edu/.

# TEXAS A&M UNIVERSITY
## College Station, TX

| Tuition & fees (TX res): $9180 | Average undergraduate aid package: $15,337 |
|---|---|

**ABOUT THE INSTITUTION** State-supported, coed. *Awards:* certificates, bachelor's, master's, and doctoral degrees. 109 undergraduate majors. *Total enrollment:* 61,263. Undergraduates: 47,093. Freshmen: 10,835. Both federal and institutional methodology are used as a basis for awarding need-based institutional aid.
**UNDERGRADUATE EXPENSES for 2015–2016** *Application fee:* $75. *Tuition, state resident:* full-time $5971; part-time $199 per credit hour. *Tuition, nonresident:* full-time $23,147; part-time $772 per credit hour. *Required fees:* full-time $3209. Full-time tuition and fees vary according to program. Part-time tuition and fees vary according to program. *College room and board:* $9522. Room and board charges vary according to board plan, housing facility, and location. *Payment plan:* Guaranteed tuition.
**FRESHMAN FINANCIAL AID (Fall 2013)** 6,975 applied for aid; of those 61% were deemed to have need. 97% of freshmen with need received aid; of those 48% had need fully met. *Average percent of need met:* 75% (excluding resources awarded to replace EFC). *Average financial aid package:* $16,417 (excluding resources awarded to replace EFC). 12% of all full-time freshmen had no need and received non-need-based gift aid.

**UNDERGRADUATE FINANCIAL AID (Fall 2013)** 24,520 applied for aid; of those 70% were deemed to have need. 96% of undergraduates with need received aid; of those 42% had need fully met. *Average percent of need met:* 69% (excluding resources awarded to replace EFC). *Average financial aid package:* $15,337 (excluding resources awarded to replace EFC). 7% of all full-time undergraduates had no need and received non-need-based gift aid.
**GIFT AID (NEED-BASED)** *Total amount:* $151,379,903 (27% federal, 25% state, 36% institutional, 12% external sources). *Receiving aid:* Freshmen: 44% (3,998); all full-time undergraduates: 37% (14,575). *Average award:* Freshmen: $11,833; Undergraduates: $9572. *Scholarships, grants, and awards:* Federal Pell, FSEOG, state, private, college/university gift aid from institutional funds.
**GIFT AID (NON-NEED-BASED)** *Total amount:* $22,529,333 (4% federal, 8% state, 52% institutional, 36% external sources). *Receiving aid:* Freshmen: 9% (780). Undergraduates: 5% (1,941). *Average award:* Freshmen: $3693. Undergraduates: $3502. *Scholarships, grants, and awards by category:* Academic interests/achievement: agriculture, architecture, biological sciences, business, computer science, education, engineering/technologies, general academic interests/achievements, health fields, mathematics, physical sciences, premedicine. Creative arts/performance: journalism/publications, performing arts, theater/drama. Special achievements/activities: community service, general special achievements/activities, leadership, memberships, rodeo. Special characteristics: children of faculty/staff, first-generation college students, general special characteristics, international students, local/state students, veterans, veterans' children. ROTC: Army, Naval, Air Force.
**LOANS** *Student loans:* $115,465,832 (59% need-based, 41% non-need-based). 47% of past graduating class borrowed through all loan programs. *Average indebtedness per student:* $23,703. *Average need-based loan:* Freshmen: $4996. Undergraduates: $6671. *Parent loans:* $36,137,511 (17% need-based, 83% non-need-based). *Programs:* Federal Direct (Subsidized and Unsubsidized Stafford, PLUS), Perkins, Federal Nursing, state, college/university.
**WORK-STUDY** *Federal work-study:* 748 jobs averaging $2967. *State or other work-study/employment:* Total amount: $450,798 (100% need-based). 189 part-time jobs averaging $2385.
**ATHLETIC AWARDS** Total amount: $3,176,631 (78% need-based, 22% non-need-based).
**APPLYING FOR FINANCIAL AID** *Required financial aid forms:* FAFSA, scholarships section of the ApplyTexas application. *Financial aid deadline (priority):* 3/15. *Notification date:* Continuous beginning 4/1. Students must reply within 4 weeks of notification.
**CONTACT** Scholarships and Financial Aid Office, Texas A&M University, The Pavilion 200, Spence Street, 1252 TAMU, College Station, TX 77842-3016, 979-845-3236. Fax: 979-847-9061. E-mail: financialaid@tamu.edu.
*Website:* http://www.tamu.edu/.

# TEXAS A&M UNIVERSITY–COMMERCE
## Commerce, TX

| Tuition & fees (TX res): $7096 | Average undergraduate aid package: $10,814 |
|---|---|

**ABOUT THE INSTITUTION** State-supported, coed. *Awards:* bachelor's, master's, and doctoral degrees. 41 undergraduate majors. *Total enrollment:* 11,490. Undergraduates: 7,148. Freshmen: 960. Federal methodology is used as a basis for awarding need-based institutional aid.
**UNDERGRADUATE EXPENSES for 2015–2016** *Tuition, state resident:* full-time $4790; part-time $160 per credit hour. *Tuition, nonresident:* full-time $15,650; part-time $522 per credit hour. *Required fees:* full-time $2306. Full-time tuition and fees vary according to course load, location, program, and reciprocity agreements. Part-time tuition and fees vary according to course load, location, program, and reciprocity agreements. *College room and board:* $8106. Room and board charges vary according to board plan and housing facility. *Payment plan:* Guaranteed tuition.
**FRESHMAN FINANCIAL AID (Fall 2014, est.)** 891 applied for aid; of those 85% were deemed to have need. 97% of freshmen with need received aid; of those 12% had need fully met. *Average percent of need met:* 76% (excluding resources awarded to replace EFC). *Average financial aid package:* $12,948 (excluding resources awarded to replace EFC). 7% of all full-time freshmen had no need and received non-need-based gift aid.
**UNDERGRADUATE FINANCIAL AID (Fall 2014, est.)** 4,533 applied for aid; of those 90% were deemed to have need. 96% of undergraduates with need received aid;

of those 6% had need fully met. *Average percent of need met:* 61% (excluding resources awarded to replace EFC). *Average financial aid package:* $10,814 (excluding resources awarded to replace EFC). 3% of all full-time undergraduates had no need and received non-need-based gift aid.
**GIFT AID (NEED-BASED)** *Total amount:* $27,990,753 (63% federal, 20% state, 15% institutional, 2% external sources). *Receiving aid:* Freshmen: 75% (684); all full-time undergraduates: 68% (3,574). *Average award:* Freshmen: $10,732; Undergraduates: $7885. *Scholarships, grants, and awards:* Federal Pell, FSEOG, state, private, college/university gift aid from institutional funds.
**GIFT AID (NON-NEED-BASED)** *Total amount:* $2,124,202 (3% federal, 90% institutional, 7% external sources). *Average award:* Freshmen: $1599. Undergraduates: $1814. *Scholarships, grants, and awards by category:* Academic interests/achievement: agriculture, biological sciences, business, communication, computer science, education, engineering/technologies, English, foreign languages, general academic interests/achievements, health fields, humanities, international studies, mathematics, physical sciences, premedicine, social sciences. Creative arts/performance: applied art and design, art/fine arts, journalism/publications, music, performing arts, theater/drama. Special achievements/activities: cheerleading/drum major, general special achievements/activities, junior miss, leadership, rodeo. Special characteristics: adult students, children and siblings of alumni, ethnic background, first-generation college students, members of minority groups, out-of-state students, previous college experience, veterans, veterans' children. *Tuition waivers:* Full or partial for employees or children of employees, senior citizens. ROTC: Air Force cooperative.
**LOANS** *Student loans:* $38,511,981 (91% need-based, 9% non-need-based). *Average need-based loan:* Freshmen: $3581. Undergraduates: $4057. *Parent loans:* $2,932,279 (73% need-based, 27% non-need-based). *Programs:* Federal Direct (Subsidized and Unsubsidized Stafford, PLUS), Perkins, state.
**WORK-STUDY** *Federal work-study:* Total amount: $355,926; jobs available. *State or other work-study/employment:* Total amount: $173,194 (100% need-based). Part-time jobs available.
**ATHLETIC AWARDS** Total amount: $1,573,447 (62% need-based, 38% non-need-based).
**APPLYING FOR FINANCIAL AID** *Required financial aid form:* FAFSA. *Financial aid deadline (priority):* 3/20. *Notification date:* Continuous beginning 4/15. Students must reply within 2 weeks of notification.
**CONTACT** Ms. Maria Ramos, Director of Financial Aid and Scholarships, Texas A&M University–Commerce, PO Box 3011, Commerce, TX 75429, 903-886-5091 or toll-free 888-868-2682. Fax: 903-886-5098. E-mail: maria.ramos@tamuc.edu. *Website:* http://www.tamuc.edu/.

# TEXAS A&M UNIVERSITY–CORPUS CHRISTI
## Corpus Christi, TX

| Tuition & fees (TX res): $7591 | Average undergraduate aid package: $9542 |
|---|---|

**ABOUT THE INSTITUTION** State-supported, coed. *Awards:* bachelor's, master's, and doctoral degrees. 27 undergraduate majors. *Total enrollment:* 11,234. Undergraduates: 9,058. Freshmen: 1,948. Federal methodology is used as a basis for awarding need-based institutional aid.
**UNDERGRADUATE EXPENSES for 2015–2016** *Application fee:* $50. *Tuition, state resident:* full-time $4623; part-time $174 per credit hour. *Tuition, nonresident:* full-time $13,255; part-time $532 per credit hour. *Required fees:* full-time $2968. Full-time tuition and fees vary according to course load, degree level, location, program, and student level. Part-time tuition and fees vary according to course load, degree level, location, program, and student level. *College room and board:* $8583; *Room only:* $5283. Room and board charges vary according to board plan and housing facility. *Payment plan:* Guaranteed tuition.
**FRESHMAN FINANCIAL AID (Fall 2014, est.)** 1,420 applied for aid; of those 85% were deemed to have need. 95% of freshmen with need received aid; of those 19% had need fully met. *Average percent of need met:* 53% (excluding resources awarded to replace EFC). *Average financial aid package:* $9823 (excluding resources awarded to replace EFC). 6% of all full-time freshmen had no need and received non-need-based gift aid.
**UNDERGRADUATE FINANCIAL AID (Fall 2014, est.)** 4,915 applied for aid; of those 88% were deemed to have need. 97% of undergraduates with need received aid; of those 18% had need fully met. *Average percent of need met:* 48% (excluding

resources awarded to replace EFC). **Average financial aid package:** $9542 (excluding resources awarded to replace EFC). 7% of all full-time undergraduates had no need and received non-need-based gift aid.

**GIFT AID (NEED-BASED) Total amount:** $25,793,426 (65% federal, 25% state, 10% institutional). **Receiving aid:** Freshmen: 58% (954); all full-time undergraduates: 52% (3,413). **Average award:** Freshmen: $6755; Undergraduates: $5738. **Scholarships, grants, and awards:** Federal Pell, FSEOG, state, college/university gift aid from institutional funds.

**GIFT AID (NON-NEED-BASED) Total amount:** $4,397,428 (73% institutional, 27% external sources). **Receiving aid:** Freshmen: 21% (350). Undergraduates: 15% (952). **Average award:** Freshmen: $3494. Undergraduates: $2592. **Scholarships, grants, and awards by category:** Academic interests/achievement: general academic interests/achievements. Creative arts/performance: art/fine arts, general creative arts/performance. Special characteristics: first-generation college students, international students. **Tuition waivers:** Full or partial for senior citizens. **ROTC:** Army.

**LOANS Student loans:** $36,958,918 (42% need-based, 58% non-need-based). 69% of past graduating class borrowed through all loan programs. Average indebtedness per student: $26,445. **Average need-based loan:** Freshmen: $3236. Undergraduates: $3802. **Parent loans:** $9,893,867 (100% non-need-based). **Programs:** Federal Direct (Subsidized and Unsubsidized Stafford, PLUS), Perkins, state, college/university.

**WORK-STUDY Federal work-study:** Total amount: $393,722; 149 jobs averaging $2416. **State or other work-study/employment:** Total amount: $272,427 (100% need-based). 115 part-time jobs averaging $1981.

**ATHLETIC AWARDS** Total amount: $2,051,501 (100% non-need-based).

**APPLYING FOR FINANCIAL AID Required financial aid form:** FAFSA. **Financial aid deadline (priority):** 3/31. **Notification date:** Continuous beginning 4/1. Students must reply within 2 weeks of notification.

**CONTACT** Jeannie Gage, Director of Financial Assistance, Texas A&M University–Corpus Christi, 6300 Ocean Drive, Corpus Christi, TX 78412-5503, 361-825-2338 or toll-free 800-482-6822. Fax: 361-825-6095. E-mail: faoweb@tamucc.edu. Website: http://www.tamucc.edu/.

# TEXAS A&M UNIVERSITY–KINGSVILLE
## Kingsville, TX

**CONTACT** Ralph Perri, Director, Financial Aid, Texas A&M University–Kingsville, 700 University Boulevard, Kingsville, TX 78363, 361-593-2883 or toll-free 800-687-6000. Fax: 361-593-3036. E-mail: financial.aid@tamuk.edu. Website: http://www.tamuk.edu/.

# TEXAS A&M UNIVERSITY– SAN ANTONIO
## San Antonio, TX

**CONTACT** Financial Aid Office, Texas A&M University–San Antonio, One University Way, San Antonio, TX 78224, 210-784-1000. Website: http://www.tamusa.tamus.edu/.

# TEXAS A&M UNIVERSITY– TEXARKANA
## Texarkana, TX

**CONTACT** Alyssa Haley, Director of Financial Aid and Veterans Services, Texas A&M University–Texarkana, 7101 University Avenue, Texarkana, TX 75503, 903-223-3060. Fax: 903-223-3140. E-mail: ahaley@tamut.edu. Website: http://www.tamut.edu/.

# TEXAS CHRISTIAN UNIVERSITY
## Fort Worth, TX

| Tuition & fees: $38,600 | Average undergraduate aid package: $24,785 |
|---|---|

**ABOUT THE INSTITUTION** Independent Christian Church (Disciples of Christ), coed. **Awards:** certificates, diplomas, bachelor's, master's, and doctoral degrees. 95 undergraduate majors. **Total enrollment:** 10,033. Undergraduates: 8,647. Freshmen: 1,891. Both federal and institutional methodology are used as a basis for awarding need-based institutional aid.

**UNDERGRADUATE EXPENSES for 2015–2016 Application fee:** $40. **Comprehensive fee:** $49,980 includes full-time tuition ($38,510), mandatory fees ($90), and room and board ($11,380). **College room only:** $6900. Room and board charges vary according to board plan and housing facility. **Part-time tuition:** $1625 per credit hour. **Part-time fees:** $45 per term. Part-time tuition and fees vary according to course load.

**FRESHMAN FINANCIAL AID (Fall 2014, est.)** 1,083 applied for aid; of those 63% were deemed to have need. 99% of freshmen with need received aid; of those 26% had need fully met. **Average percent of need met:** 66% (excluding resources awarded to replace EFC). **Average financial aid package:** $24,644 (excluding resources awarded to replace EFC). 29% of all full-time freshmen had no need and received non-need-based gift aid.

**UNDERGRADUATE FINANCIAL AID (Fall 2014, est.)** 4,218 applied for aid; of those 76% were deemed to have need. 98% of undergraduates with need received aid; of those 24% had need fully met. **Average percent of need met:** 63% (excluding resources awarded to replace EFC). **Average financial aid package:** $24,785 (excluding resources awarded to replace EFC). 25% of all full-time undergraduates had no need and received non-need-based gift aid.

**GIFT AID (NEED-BASED) Total amount:** $59,635,276 (8% federal, 6% state, 83% institutional, 3% external sources). **Receiving aid:** Freshmen: 33% (631); all full-time undergraduates: 35% (2,953). **Average award:** Freshmen: $22,677; Undergraduates: $21,732. **Scholarships, grants, and awards:** Federal Pell, FSEOG, state, private, college/university gift aid from institutional funds.

**GIFT AID (NON-NEED-BASED) Total amount:** $34,899,675 (98% institutional, 2% external sources). **Receiving aid:** Freshmen: 23% (428). Undergraduates: 22% (1,831). **Average award:** Freshmen: $15,404. Undergraduates: $14,330. **Scholarships, grants, and awards by category:** Academic interests/achievement: 3,168 awards ($36,719,570 total): agriculture, biological sciences, business, communication, education, engineering/technologies, English, foreign languages, general academic interests/achievements, health fields, humanities, international studies, mathematics, military science, physical sciences, premedicine, religion/biblical studies, social sciences. Creative arts/performance: 455 awards ($4,019,763 total): applied art and design, art/fine arts, cinema/film/broadcasting, creative writing, dance, general creative arts/performance, journalism/publications, music, performing arts, theater/drama. Special achievements/activities: 512 awards ($5,898,450 total): general special achievements/activities, leadership, memberships, religious involvement. Special characteristics: 742 awards ($15,425,267 total): adult students, children of educators, children of faculty/staff, children of union members/company employees, children of workers in trades, ethnic background, general special characteristics, handicapped students, international students, local/state students, members of minority groups, previous college experience, relatives of clergy, religious affiliation, veterans, veterans' children. **Tuition waivers:** Full or partial for employees or children of employees. **ROTC:** Army, Air Force.

**LOANS Student loans:** $43,273,196 (56% need-based, 44% non-need-based). 43% of past graduating class borrowed through all loan programs. Average indebtedness per student: $39,584. **Average need-based loan:** Freshmen: $3460. Undergraduates: $4691. **Parent loans:** $21,118,391 (28% need-based, 72% non-need-based). **Programs:** Federal Direct (Subsidized and Unsubsidized Stafford, PLUS), Perkins, Federal Nursing, state.

**WORK-STUDY Federal work-study:** Total amount: $2,473,463; 1,246 jobs averaging $1900. **State or other work-study/employment:** Total amount: $5000 (100% need-based). 30 part-time jobs averaging $1583.

**ATHLETIC AWARDS** Total amount: $13,777,138 (39% need-based, 61% non-need-based).

**APPLYING FOR FINANCIAL AID Required financial aid forms:** FAFSA, CSS Financial Aid PROFILE, noncustodial (divorced/separated) parent's statement. **Financial aid deadline:** 5/1. **Notification date:** Continuous beginning 3/15. Students must reply by 5/1.

CONTACT Michael Scott, Director of Scholarships and Student Financial Aid, Texas Christian University, PO Box 297012, Fort Worth, TX 76129-0002, 817-257-7858 or toll-free 800-828-3764. *Fax:* 817-257-7462. *E-mail:* m.scott@tcu.edu. *Website:* http://www.tcu.edu/.

# TEXAS COLLEGE
## Tyler, TX

CONTACT Ms. Cecelia K. Jones, Director of Financial Aid, Texas College, 2404 North Grand Avenue, Tyler, TX 75702, 903-593-8311 Ext. 2241 or toll-free 800-306-6299. *Fax:* 903-593-9607. *E-mail:* ckjones@texascollege.edu. *Website:* http://www.texascollege.edu/.

# TEXAS LUTHERAN UNIVERSITY
## Seguin, TX

| Tuition & fees: $26,800 | Average undergraduate aid package: $22,525 |
| --- | --- |

**ABOUT THE INSTITUTION** Independent Evangelical Lutheran Church, coed. *Awards:* bachelor's and master's degrees. 39 undergraduate majors. *Total enrollment:* 1,320. Undergraduates: 1,306. Freshmen: 309. Federal methodology is used as a basis for awarding need-based institutional aid.

**UNDERGRADUATE EXPENSES for 2015–2016** *Comprehensive fee:* $36,040 includes full-time tuition ($26,670), mandatory fees ($130), and room and board ($9240). *College room only:* $5400. Full-time tuition and fees vary according to course load. Room and board charges vary according to board plan and housing facility. *Part-time tuition:* $885 per semester hour.

**FRESHMAN FINANCIAL AID (Fall 2014, est.)** 284 applied for aid; of those 88% were deemed to have need. 100% of freshmen with need received aid; of those 33% had need fully met. *Average percent of need met:* 84% (excluding resources awarded to replace EFC). *Average financial aid package:* $23,262 (excluding resources awarded to replace EFC). 17% of all full-time freshmen had no need and received non-need-based gift aid.

**UNDERGRADUATE FINANCIAL AID (Fall 2014, est.)** 1,108 applied for aid; of those 91% were deemed to have need. 100% of undergraduates with need received aid; of those 26% had need fully met. *Average percent of need met:* 80% (excluding resources awarded to replace EFC). *Average financial aid package:* $22,525 (excluding resources awarded to replace EFC). 17% of all full-time undergraduates had no need and received non-need-based gift aid.

**GIFT AID (NEED-BASED)** *Total amount:* $17,066,428 (14% federal, 11% state, 73% institutional, 2% external sources). *Receiving aid:* Freshmen: 82% (251); all full-time undergraduates: 82% (999). *Average award:* Freshmen: $19,388; Undergraduates: $17,431. *Scholarships, grants, and awards:* Federal Pell, FSEOG, state, college/university gift aid from institutional funds, TEACH Grants.

**GIFT AID (NON-NEED-BASED)** *Total amount:* $3,706,170 (95% institutional, 5% external sources). *Receiving aid:* Freshmen: 21% (63). Undergraduates: 12% (153). *Average award:* Freshmen: $14,371. Undergraduates: $12,993. *Scholarships, grants, and awards by category:* Academic interests/achievement: biological sciences, business, education, general academic interests/achievements, mathematics, physical sciences, premedicine. *Creative arts/performance:* journalism/publications, music, theater/drama. *Special achievements/activities:* general special achievements/activities, junior miss, leadership, memberships, religious involvement. *Special characteristics:* children and siblings of alumni, children of faculty/staff, first-generation college students, religious affiliation, veterans, veterans' children. *Tuition waivers:* Full or partial for children of alumni, employees or children of employees. *ROTC:* Army cooperative, Air Force cooperative.

**LOANS** *Student loans:* $9,756,715 (70% need-based, 30% non-need-based). 82% of past graduating class borrowed through all loan programs. *Average indebtedness per student:* $31,576. *Average need-based loan:* Freshmen: $4093. Undergraduates: $5056. *Parent loans:* $1,190,568 (39% need-based, 61% non-need-based). *Programs:* Federal Direct (Subsidized and Unsubsidized Stafford, PLUS), Perkins, state, alternative loans.

**WORK-STUDY** *Federal work-study:* Total amount: $1,059,792; 145 jobs averaging $2063. *State or other work-study/employment:* 9 part-time jobs averaging $1344.

**APPLYING FOR FINANCIAL AID** *Required financial aid form:* FAFSA. *Financial aid deadline (priority):* 3/1. *Notification date:* Continuous beginning 3/1. Students must reply by 8/15.

CONTACT Bonnie Trevino, Director of Financial Aid, Texas Lutheran University, 1000 West Court Street, Seguin, TX 78155-5999, 830-372-8075 or toll-free 800-771-8521. *Fax:* 830-372-8096. *E-mail:* ytrevino@tlu.edu. *Website:* http://www.tlu.edu/.

# TEXAS SOUTHERN UNIVERSITY
## Houston, TX

| Tuition & fees (TX res): $8126 | Average undergraduate aid package: $18,986 |
| --- | --- |

**ABOUT THE INSTITUTION** State-supported, coed. *Awards:* certificates, bachelor's, master's, and doctoral degrees. 49 undergraduate majors. *Total enrollment:* 9,233. Undergraduates: 6,915. Freshmen: 1,532. Federal methodology is used as a basis for awarding need-based institutional aid.

**UNDERGRADUATE EXPENSES for 2015–2016** *Application fee:* $42. *Tuition, state resident:* full-time $8126; part-time $263 per credit hour. *Tuition, nonresident:* full-time $18,986; part-time $362 per credit hour. Full-time tuition and fees vary according to course level, course load, degree level, and program. Part-time tuition and fees vary according to course level, course load, degree level, and program. *College room and board:* $9438. Room and board charges vary according to board plan, housing facility, and location. *Payment plan:* Guaranteed tuition.

**FRESHMAN FINANCIAL AID (Fall 2014, est.)** 1,427 applied for aid; of those 76% were deemed to have need. 100% of freshmen with need received aid; of those 94% had need fully met. *Average percent of need met:* 94% (excluding resources awarded to replace EFC). *Average financial aid package:* $19,711 (excluding resources awarded to replace EFC).

**UNDERGRADUATE FINANCIAL AID (Fall 2014, est.)** 5,338 applied for aid; of those 81% were deemed to have need. 100% of undergraduates with need received aid; of those 92% had need fully met. *Average percent of need met:* 92% (excluding resources awarded to replace EFC). *Average financial aid package:* $18,986 (excluding resources awarded to replace EFC).

**GIFT AID (NEED-BASED)** *Total amount:* $33,918,785 (57% federal, 22% state, 19% institutional, 2% external sources). *Receiving aid:* Freshmen: 72% (1,024); all full-time undergraduates: 69% (4,050). *Average award:* Freshmen: $4355; Undergraduates: $6262. *Scholarships, grants, and awards:* Federal Pell, FSEOG, state, private, college/university gift aid from institutional funds, United Negro College Fund, Federal Nursing.

**GIFT AID (NON-NEED-BASED)** *Tuition waivers:* Full or partial for minority students, senior citizens. *ROTC:* Army, Naval cooperative, Air Force cooperative.

**LOANS** *Student loans:* $34,921,610 (100% need-based). 95% of past graduating class borrowed through all loan programs. *Average indebtedness per student:* $43,600. *Average need-based loan:* Freshmen: $3340. Undergraduates: $4133. *Parent loans:* $4,404,042 (100% need-based). *Programs:* Federal Direct (Subsidized and Unsubsidized Stafford, PLUS), state, college/university.

**WORK-STUDY** *Federal work-study:* Total amount: $450,298; 303 jobs averaging $4000. *State or other work-study/employment:* Total amount: $34,457 (100% need-based). 20 part-time jobs averaging $4000.

**ATHLETIC AWARDS** Total amount: $2,874,133 (100% need-based).

**APPLYING FOR FINANCIAL AID** *Required financial aid forms:* FAFSA, institution's own form. *Financial aid deadline (priority):* 4/15. *Notification date:* Continuous beginning 4/15.

CONTACT Office of Financial Aid, Texas Southern University, 3100 Cleburne Street, Houston, TX 77004-4584, 713-313-7011. *Fax:* 713-313-1858. *Website:* http://www.tsu.edu/.

# TEXAS STATE UNIVERSITY
## San Marcos, TX

| Tuition & fees (TX res): $9516 | Average undergraduate aid package: $11,301 |
| --- | --- |

**ABOUT THE INSTITUTION** State-supported, coed. *Awards:* certificates, bachelor's, master's, and doctoral degrees. 93 undergraduate majors. *Total enrollment:* 36,739. Undergraduates: 32,177. Freshmen: 5,357. Federal methodology is used as a basis for awarding need-based institutional aid.

**UNDERGRADUATE EXPENSES for 2015–2016** *Application fee:* $75. *Tuition, state resident:* full-time $7160; part-time $239 per credit hour. *Tuition, nonresident:* full-time $18,020; part-time $601 per credit hour. *Required fees:* full-time $2356; $54 per credit hour or $413 per term. Full-time tuition and fees vary according to course load and degree level. Part-time tuition and fees vary according to course load and degree level. *College room and board:* $7612; *Room only:* $5050. Room and board charges vary according to board plan and housing facility. *Payment plan:* Guaranteed tuition.

**FRESHMAN FINANCIAL AID (Fall 2014, est.)** 5,035 applied for aid; of those 64% were deemed to have need. 95% of freshmen with need received aid; of those 7% had need fully met. *Average percent of need met:* 75% (excluding resources awarded to replace EFC). *Average financial aid package:* $11,472 (excluding resources awarded to replace EFC). 4% of all full-time freshmen had no need and received non-need-based gift aid.

**UNDERGRADUATE FINANCIAL AID (Fall 2014, est.)** 21,651 applied for aid; of those 70% were deemed to have need. 97% of undergraduates with need received aid; of those 7% had need fully met. *Average percent of need met:* 73% (excluding resources awarded to replace EFC). *Average financial aid package:* $11,301 (excluding resources awarded to replace EFC). 2% of all full-time undergraduates had no need and received non-need-based gift aid.

**GIFT AID (NEED-BASED)** *Total amount:* $94,296,862 (51% federal, 47% state, 1% institutional, 1% external sources). *Receiving aid:* Freshmen: 52% (2,629); all full-time undergraduates: 48% (12,651). *Average award:* Freshmen: $7699; Undergraduates: $6867. *Scholarships, grants, and awards:* Federal Pell, FSEOG, state, private, college/university gift aid from institutional funds.

**GIFT AID (NON-NEED-BASED)** *Total amount:* $11,740,578 (9% federal, 28% institutional, 63% external sources). *Receiving aid:* Freshmen: 15% (739). Undergraduates: 9% (2,369). *Average award:* Freshmen: $3823. Undergraduates: $3305. *Scholarships, grants, and awards by category: Academic interests/achievement:* 687 awards ($4,067,721 total): agriculture, business, education, English, general academic interests/achievements, home economics, international studies, military science. *Creative arts/performance:* 335 awards ($1,211,394 total): applied art and design, art/fine arts, journalism/publications, music, theater/drama. *Special achievements/activities:* 71 awards ($147,845 total): leadership. *Special characteristics:* children and siblings of alumni, first-generation college students, handicapped students, local/state students. *Tuition waivers:* Full or partial for employees or children of employees. *ROTC:* Army, Air Force.

**LOANS** *Student loans:* $137,839,326 (51% need-based, 49% non-need-based). 64% of past graduating class borrowed through all loan programs. *Average indebtedness per student:* $26,031. *Average need-based loan:* Freshmen: $3852. Undergraduates: $4963. *Parent loans:* $47,565,057 (2% need-based, 98% non-need-based). *Programs:* Federal Direct (Subsidized and Unsubsidized Stafford, PLUS), Perkins, state, college/university, short-term emergency loans.

**WORK-STUDY** *Federal work-study:* Total amount: $4,782,889; 1,437 jobs averaging $3219. *State or other work-study/employment:* Total amount: $378,313 (100% need-based). 171 part-time jobs averaging $2130.

**ATHLETIC AWARDS** *Total amount:* $3,488,570 (2% need-based, 98% non-need-based).

**APPLYING FOR FINANCIAL AID** *Required financial aid form:* FAFSA. *Financial aid deadline (priority):* 4/1. *Notification date:* Continuous beginning 5/1. Students must reply within 3 weeks of notification.

**CONTACT** Mr. Chris Murr, Director of Financial Aid, Texas State University, 601 University Drive, San Marcos, TX 78666-4602, 512-245-2315. *Fax:* 512-245-7920. *E-mail:* cm18@txstate.edu. *Website:* http://www.txstate.edu/.

# TEXAS TECH UNIVERSITY
## Lubbock, TX

| Tuition & fees (TX res): $9308 | Average undergraduate aid package: $14,063 |
| --- | --- |

**ABOUT THE INSTITUTION** State-supported, coed. *Awards:* certificates, bachelor's, master's, and doctoral degrees. 90 undergraduate majors. *Total enrollment:* 35,158. Undergraduates: 28,632. Freshmen: 5,619. Federal methodology is used as a basis for awarding need-based institutional aid.

**UNDERGRADUATE EXPENSES for 2015–2016** *Application fee:* $60. *Tuition, state resident:* full-time $6388; part-time $213 per credit hour. *Tuition, nonresident:* full-time $17,248; part-time $575 per credit hour. *Required fees:* full-time $2920; $37 per credit hour or $909 per term. Full-time tuition and fees vary according to course level, course load, degree level, location, program, reciprocity agreements, and student level. Part-time tuition and fees vary according to course level, course load, degree level, location, program, reciprocity agreements, and student level. *College room and board:* $8405; *Room only:* $4510. Room and board charges vary according to board plan and housing facility.

**FRESHMAN FINANCIAL AID (Fall 2013)** 3,196 applied for aid; of those 74% were deemed to have need. 100% of freshmen with need received aid; of those 17% had need fully met. *Average percent of need met:* 77% (excluding resources awarded to replace EFC). *Average financial aid package:* $14,231 (excluding resources awarded to replace EFC). 12% of all full-time freshmen had no need and received non-need-based gift aid.

**UNDERGRADUATE FINANCIAL AID (Fall 2013)** 14,923 applied for aid; of those 82% were deemed to have need. 100% of undergraduates with need received aid; of those 9% had need fully met. *Average percent of need met:* 71% (excluding resources awarded to replace EFC). *Average financial aid package:* $14,063 (excluding resources awarded to replace EFC). 10% of all full-time undergraduates had no need and received non-need-based gift aid.

**GIFT AID (NEED-BASED)** *Total amount:* $74,878,640 (42% federal, 23% state, 27% institutional, 8% external sources). *Receiving aid:* Freshmen: 44% (2,100); all full-time undergraduates: 43% (10,354). *Average award:* Freshmen: $8644; Undergraduates: $7187. *Scholarships, grants, and awards:* Federal Pell, FSEOG, state, private, college/university gift aid from institutional funds.

**GIFT AID (NON-NEED-BASED)** *Total amount:* $10,618,967 (74% institutional, 26% external sources). *Receiving aid:* Freshmen: 28% (1,308). Undergraduates: 16% (4,000). *Average award:* Freshmen: $3790. Undergraduates: $3289. *Scholarships, grants, and awards by category: Academic interests/achievement:* agriculture, architecture, biological sciences, business, communication, computer science, education, engineering/technologies, English, foreign languages, general academic interests/achievements, home economics, humanities, international studies, mathematics, military science, physical sciences, premedicine, social sciences. *Creative arts/performance:* applied art and design, art/fine arts, dance, journalism/publications, music, performing arts, theater/drama. *Special achievements/activities:* community service, general special achievements/activities, hobbies/interests, leadership, memberships, rodeo. *Special characteristics:* children of faculty/staff, first-generation college students, handicapped students, out-of-state students, veterans, veterans' children. *Tuition waivers:* Full or partial for employees or children of employees, senior citizens. *ROTC:* Army, Air Force.

**LOANS** *Student loans:* $111,647,475 (82% need-based, 18% non-need-based). 56% of past graduating class borrowed through all loan programs. *Average indebtedness per student:* $25,306. *Average need-based loan:* Freshmen: $4152. Undergraduates: $4781. *Parent loans:* $18,587,037 (74% need-based, 26% non-need-based). *Programs:* Federal Direct (Subsidized and Unsubsidized Stafford, PLUS), Perkins, state, college/university, private loans.

**WORK-STUDY** *Federal work-study:* jobs available. *State or other work-study/employment:* Part-time jobs available.

**ATHLETIC AWARDS** *Total amount:* $4,653,856 (56% need-based, 44% non-need-based).

**APPLYING FOR FINANCIAL AID** *Required financial aid form:* FAFSA. *Financial aid deadline (priority):* 3/15. *Notification date:* Continuous. Students must reply within 2 weeks of notification.

**CONTACT** Becky Wilson, Director of Student Financial Aid, Texas Tech University, PO Box 45011, Lubbock, TX 79409-5011, 806-742-3681. *Fax:* 806-742-0880. *Website:* http://www.ttu.edu/.

# TEXAS WESLEYAN UNIVERSITY
## Fort Worth, TX

| Tuition & fees: $23,144 | Average undergraduate aid package: $20,304 |
|---|---|

**ABOUT THE INSTITUTION** Independent United Methodist, coed. **Awards:** bachelor's, master's, and doctoral degrees. 39 undergraduate majors. **Total enrollment:** 2,606. Undergraduates: 1,917. Freshmen: 313. Federal methodology is used as a basis for awarding need-based institutional aid.

**UNDERGRADUATE EXPENSES for 2015–2016 Comprehensive fee:** $31,382 includes full-time tuition ($20,642), mandatory fees ($2502), and room and board ($8238). **College room only:** $4830. Full-time tuition and fees vary according to course level, course load, degree level, program, and student level. Room and board charges vary according to housing facility. **Part-time tuition:** $700 per credit hour. Part-time tuition and fees vary according to course level, course load, degree level, program, and student level.

**FRESHMAN FINANCIAL AID (Fall 2013)** 171 applied for aid; of those 92% were deemed to have need. 100% of freshmen with need received aid; of those 22% had need fully met. **Average percent of need met:** 76% (excluding resources awarded to replace EFC). **Average financial aid package:** $23,424 (excluding resources awarded to replace EFC). 35% of all full-time freshmen had no need and received non-need-based gift aid.

**UNDERGRADUATE FINANCIAL AID (Fall 2013)** 972 applied for aid; of those 89% were deemed to have need. 100% of undergraduates with need received aid; of those 16% had need fully met. **Average percent of need met:** 67% (excluding resources awarded to replace EFC). **Average financial aid package:** $20,304 (excluding resources awarded to replace EFC). 17% of all full-time undergraduates had no need and received non-need-based gift aid.

**GIFT AID (NEED-BASED) Total amount:** $11,654,988 (28% federal, 20% state, 51% institutional, 1% external sources). **Receiving aid:** Freshmen: 59% (157); all full-time undergraduates: 59% (844). **Average award:** Freshmen: $18,180; Undergraduates: $13,732. **Scholarships, grants, and awards:** Federal Pell, FSEOG, state, private, college/university gift aid from institutional funds.

**GIFT AID (NON-NEED-BASED) Total amount:** $3,479,370 (3% federal, 5% state, 90% institutional, 2% external sources). **Receiving aid:** Freshmen: 26% (69). Undergraduates: 20% (292). **Average award:** Freshmen: $8676. Undergraduates: $8623. **Scholarships, grants, and awards by category:** Academic interests/achievement: 840 awards ($5,918,226 total): biological sciences, business, communication, education, English, foreign languages, general academic interests/achievements, health fields, humanities, international studies, mathematics, military science, physical sciences, premedicine, religion/biblical studies, social sciences. Creative arts/performance: art/fine arts, creative writing, dance, debating, journalism/publications, music, performing arts, theater/drama. Special achievements/activities: 37 awards ($100,000 total): cheerleading/drum major, community service, leadership, memberships, religious involvement. Special characteristics: adult students, children and siblings of alumni, children of current students, children of educators, children of faculty/staff, children of public servants, children of union members/company employees, children with a deceased or disabled parent, ethnic background, first-generation college students, general special characteristics, handicapped students, international students, local/state students, married students, members of minority groups, out-of-state students, parents of current students, previous college experience, public servants, relatives of clergy, religious affiliation, siblings of current students, spouses of current students, spouses of deceased or disabled public servants, twins, veterans, veterans' children. **Tuition waivers:** Full or partial for employees or children of employees. **ROTC:** Army cooperative, Air Force cooperative.

**LOANS Student loans:** $12,086,956 (83% need-based, 17% non-need-based). 92% of past graduating class borrowed through all loan programs. Average indebtedness per student: $37,014. **Average need-based loan:** Freshmen: $3278. Undergraduates: $4145. **Parent loans:** $974,382 (48% need-based, 52% non-need-based). **Programs:** Federal Direct (Subsidized and Unsubsidized Stafford, PLUS), state.

**WORK-STUDY Federal work-study:** 125 jobs averaging $4000. **State or other work-study/employment:** Total amount: $38,038 (96% need-based, 4% non-need-based). 12 part-time jobs averaging $4000.

**ATHLETIC AWARDS** Total amount: $1,456,348 (55% need-based, 45% non-need-based).

**APPLYING FOR FINANCIAL AID Required financial aid form:** FAFSA. **Financial aid deadline (priority):** 3/1. **Notification date:** Continuous beginning 3/1. Students must reply by 3/1.

**CONTACT** Laurie Rosenkrantz, Office of Financial Aid, Texas Wesleyan University, 1201 Wesleyan Street, Fort Worth, TX 76105-1536, 817-531-4420 or toll-free 800-580-8980. Fax: 817-531-4231. E-mail: financialaid@txwes.edu. Website: http://www.txwes.edu/.

# TEXAS WOMAN'S UNIVERSITY
## Denton, TX

| Tuition & fees (TX res): $7995 | Average undergraduate aid package: $8249 |
|---|---|

**ABOUT THE INSTITUTION** State-supported, coed, primarily women. **Awards:** certificates, bachelor's, master's, and doctoral degrees. 38 undergraduate majors. **Total enrollment:** 15,070. Undergraduates: 9,679. Freshmen: 1,134. Both federal and institutional methodology are used as a basis for awarding need-based institutional aid.

**UNDERGRADUATE EXPENSES for 2015–2016 Application fee:** $50. **Tuition, state resident:** full-time $5650; part-time $188.32 per credit hour. **Tuition, nonresident:** full-time $16,510; part-time $550.32 per credit hour. **Required fees:** full-time $2345. Full-time tuition and fees vary according to course load, program, and reciprocity agreements. Part-time tuition and fees vary according to course load, program, and reciprocity agreements. **College room and board:** $6780; **Room only:** $3690. Room and board charges vary according to board plan and housing facility.

**FRESHMAN FINANCIAL AID (Fall 2013)** 1,052 applied for aid; of those 83% were deemed to have need. 100% of freshmen with need received aid; of those 31% had need fully met. **Average percent of need met:** 84% (excluding resources awarded to replace EFC). **Average financial aid package:** $9976 (excluding resources awarded to replace EFC). 4% of all full-time freshmen had no need and received non-need-based gift aid.

**UNDERGRADUATE FINANCIAL AID (Fall 2013)** 5,567 applied for aid; of those 88% were deemed to have need. 99% of undergraduates with need received aid; of those 28% had need fully met. **Average percent of need met:** 82% (excluding resources awarded to replace EFC). **Average financial aid package:** $8249 (excluding resources awarded to replace EFC). 1% of all full-time undergraduates had no need and received non-need-based gift aid.

**GIFT AID (NEED-BASED) Total amount:** $35,111,599 (49% federal, 32% state, 16% institutional, 3% external sources). **Receiving aid:** Freshmen: 70% (814); all full-time undergraduates: 66% (4,449). **Average award:** Freshmen: $8758; Undergraduates: $6466. **Scholarships, grants, and awards:** Federal Pell, FSEOG, state, private, college/university gift aid from institutional funds, United Negro College Fund.

**GIFT AID (NON-NEED-BASED) Total amount:** $6,926,744 (100% institutional). **Receiving aid:** Freshmen: 22% (257). Undergraduates: 18% (1,198). **Average award:** Freshmen: $1748. Undergraduates: $2287. **Scholarships, grants, and awards by category:** Academic interests/achievement: biological sciences, business, communication, computer science, education, English, foreign languages, general academic interests/achievements, health fields, home economics, humanities, library science, mathematics, physical sciences, premedicine, social sciences. Creative arts/performance: applied art and design, art/fine arts, cinema/film/broadcasting, dance, journalism/publications, music, theater/drama. Special characteristics: international students. **Tuition waivers:** Full or partial for senior citizens. **ROTC:** Army cooperative, Air Force cooperative.

**LOANS Student loans:** $31,627,467 (100% need-based). **Average need-based loan:** Freshmen: $2913. Undergraduates: $3843. **Parent loans:** $619,488 (100% need-based). **Programs:** Federal Direct (Subsidized and Unsubsidized Stafford, PLUS), Perkins, Federal Nursing, state, college/university, alternative loans.

**WORK-STUDY Federal work-study:** jobs available. **State or other work-study/employment:** Total amount: $2,480,980 (4% need-based, 96% non-need-based). Part-time jobs available.

**ATHLETIC AWARDS** Total amount: $497,141 (100% need-based).

**APPLYING FOR FINANCIAL AID Required financial aid forms:** FAFSA, institution's own form. **Financial aid deadline (priority):** 3/15. **Notification date:** 5/1.

**CONTACT** Mr. Governor Jackson, Director of Financial Aid, Texas Woman's University, PO Box 425408, Denton, TX 76204-5408, 940-898-3051 or toll-free 866-809-6130. Fax: 940-898-3068. E-mail: gjackson@twu.edu. Website: http://www.twu.edu/.

# THIEL COLLEGE
## Greenville, PA

| Tuition & fees: $27,828 | Average undergraduate aid package: $23,041 |
|---|---|

**ABOUT THE INSTITUTION** Independent Evangelical Lutheran Church in America, coed. *Awards:* associate and bachelor's degrees. 43 undergraduate majors. *Total enrollment:* 1,074. Undergraduates: 1,074. Freshmen: 280. Federal methodology is used as a basis for awarding need-based institutional aid.

**UNDERGRADUATE EXPENSES for 2015–2016** *Comprehensive fee:* $38,728 includes full-time tuition ($25,998), mandatory fees ($1830), and room and board ($10,900). *College room only:* $5450. Full-time tuition and fees vary according to course load. Room and board charges vary according to housing facility. *Part-time tuition:* $850 per credit hour. *Part-time fees:* $915 per term. Part-time tuition and fees vary according to course load.

**FRESHMAN FINANCIAL AID (Fall 2014, est.)** 237 applied for aid; of those 94% were deemed to have need. 100% of freshmen with need received aid; of those 9% had need fully met. *Average percent of need met:* 71% (excluding resources awarded to replace EFC). *Average financial aid package:* $23,644 (excluding resources awarded to replace EFC). 6% of all full-time freshmen had no need and received non-need-based gift aid.

**UNDERGRADUATE FINANCIAL AID (Fall 2014, est.)** 913 applied for aid; of those 95% were deemed to have need. 100% of undergraduates with need received aid; of those 11% had need fully met. *Average percent of need met:* 70% (excluding resources awarded to replace EFC). *Average financial aid package:* $23,041 (excluding resources awarded to replace EFC). 8% of all full-time undergraduates had no need and received non-need-based gift aid.

**GIFT AID (NEED-BASED)** *Total amount:* $15,879,174 (13% federal, 9% state, 74% institutional, 4% external sources). *Receiving aid:* Freshmen: 80% (223); all full-time undergraduates: 86% (865). *Average award:* Freshmen: $20,090; Undergraduates: $18,846. *Scholarships, grants, and awards:* Federal Pell, FSEOG, state, private, college/university gift aid from institutional funds.

**GIFT AID (NON-NEED-BASED)** *Total amount:* $1,405,857 (89% institutional, 11% external sources). *Receiving aid:* Freshmen: 7% (19). Undergraduates: 7% (75). *Average award:* Freshmen: $14,117. Undergraduates: $11,816. *Scholarships, grants, and awards by category: Academic interests/achievement:* biological sciences, business, computer science, education, English, general academic interests/achievements, mathematics, physical sciences, religion/biblical studies. *Creative arts/performance:* 101 awards ($89,450 total): music, theater/drama. *Special achievements/activities:* 124 awards ($131,970 total): leadership. *Special characteristics:* 180 awards ($641,642 total): children and siblings of alumni, children of faculty/staff, international students, local/state students, relatives of clergy, religious affiliation, siblings of current students, veterans. *Tuition waivers:* Full or partial for employees or children of employees.

**LOANS** *Student loans:* $8,757,242 (79% need-based, 21% non-need-based). 88% of past graduating class borrowed through all loan programs. *Average indebtedness per student:* $37,932. *Average need-based loan:* Freshmen: $4064. Undergraduates: $4654. *Parent loans:* $3,161,816 (49% need-based, 51% non-need-based). *Programs:* Federal Direct (Subsidized and Unsubsidized Stafford, PLUS), Perkins.

**WORK-STUDY** *Federal work-study:* Total amount: $88,730; 60 jobs averaging $1475. *State or other work-study/employment:* Total amount: $618,876 (89% need-based, 11% non-need-based). 300 part-time jobs averaging $2063.

**APPLYING FOR FINANCIAL AID** *Required financial aid forms:* FAFSA, state aid form. *Financial aid deadline:* Continuous. *Notification date:* Continuous beginning 3/15. Students must reply within 2 weeks of notification.

**CONTACT** Ms. Cynthia H. Farrell, Director of Financial Aid, Thiel College, 75 College Avenue, Greenville, PA 16125-2181, 724-589-2178 or toll-free 800-248-4435. *Fax:* 724-589-2790. *E-mail:* cfarrell@thiel.edu. *Website:* http://www.thiel.edu/.

# THOMAS AQUINAS COLLEGE
## Santa Paula, CA

| Tuition & fees: $24,500 | Average undergraduate aid package: $22,171 |
|---|---|

**ABOUT THE INSTITUTION** Independent Roman Catholic, coed. *Awards:* bachelor's degrees. 1 undergraduate major. *Total enrollment:* 378. Undergraduates: 378. Freshmen: 89. Both federal and institutional methodology are used as a basis for awarding need-based institutional aid.

**UNDERGRADUATE EXPENSES for 2015–2016** *Comprehensive fee:* $32,450 includes full-time tuition ($24,500) and room and board ($7950).

**FRESHMAN FINANCIAL AID (Fall 2014, est.)** 72 applied for aid; of those 99% were deemed to have need. 100% of freshmen with need received aid; of those 100% had need fully met. *Average percent of need met:* 100% (excluding resources awarded to replace EFC). *Average financial aid package:* $21,178 (excluding resources awarded to replace EFC).

**UNDERGRADUATE FINANCIAL AID (Fall 2014, est.)** 293 applied for aid; of those 98% were deemed to have need. 100% of undergraduates with need received aid; of those 100% had need fully met. *Average percent of need met:* 100% (excluding resources awarded to replace EFC). *Average financial aid package:* $22,171 (excluding resources awarded to replace EFC).

**GIFT AID (NEED-BASED)** *Total amount:* $4,174,948 (15% federal, 10% state, 74% institutional, 1% external sources). *Receiving aid:* Freshmen: 65% (66); all full-time undergraduates: 70% (265). *Average award:* Freshmen: $15,178; Undergraduates: $15,755. *Scholarships, grants, and awards:* Federal Pell, state, private, college/university gift aid from institutional funds, Canadian federal and provincial grants.

**GIFT AID (NON-NEED-BASED)** *Total amount:* $11,500 (100% external sources). *Receiving aid:* Undergraduates: 1.

**LOANS** *Student loans:* $1,383,249 (86% need-based, 14% non-need-based). 85% of past graduating class borrowed through all loan programs. *Average indebtedness per student:* $16,263. *Average need-based loan:* Freshmen: $3278. Undergraduates: $5753. *Parent loans:* $239,308 (100% non-need-based). *Programs:* Federal Direct (Subsidized and Unsubsidized Stafford, PLUS), college/university, Canadian federal and provincial loans.

**WORK-STUDY** *State or other work-study/employment:* Total amount: $1,019,351 (100% need-based). 256 part-time jobs averaging $3982.

**APPLYING FOR FINANCIAL AID** *Required financial aid forms:* FAFSA, institution's own form, state aid form, federal income tax form(s), W-2 forms, institution's own Non-custodial Parent Statement. *Financial aid deadline:* 3/2. *Notification date:* Continuous beginning 3/1. Students must reply by 5/1 or within 2 weeks of notification.

**CONTACT** Mr. Gregory Becher, Director of Financial Aid, Thomas Aquinas College, 10000 Ojai Road, Santa Paula, CA 93060-9980, 805-525-4419 Ext. 5936 or toll-free 800-634-9797. *Fax:* 805-525-9342. *E-mail:* gbecher@thomasaquinas.edu. *Website:* http://www.thomasaquinas.edu/.

# THOMAS COLLEGE
## Waterville, ME

| Tuition & fees: N/R | Average undergraduate aid package: $20,385 |
|---|---|

**ABOUT THE INSTITUTION** Independent, coed. 15 undergraduate majors. Federal methodology is used as a basis for awarding need-based institutional aid.

**FRESHMAN FINANCIAL AID (Fall 2014, est.)** 188 applied for aid; of those 91% were deemed to have need. 100% of freshmen with need received aid; of those 9% had need fully met. *Average percent of need met:* 85% (excluding resources awarded to replace EFC). *Average financial aid package:* $22,785 (excluding resources awarded to replace EFC). 5% of all full-time freshmen had no need and received non-need-based gift aid.

**UNDERGRADUATE FINANCIAL AID (Fall 2014, est.)** 712 applied for aid; of those 94% were deemed to have need. 98% of undergraduates with need received aid; of those 14% had need fully met. *Average percent of need met:* 85% (excluding resources awarded to replace EFC). *Average financial aid package:* $20,385 (excluding resources awarded to replace EFC). 7% of all full-time undergraduates had no need and received non-need-based gift aid.

**GIFT AID (NEED-BASED) Total amount:** $9,770,997 (22% federal, 3% state, 75% institutional). **Receiving aid:** Freshmen: 85% (172); all full-time undergraduates: 83% (650). **Average award:** Freshmen: $17,774; Undergraduates: $15,342. **Scholarships, grants, and awards:** Federal Pell, FSEOG, state, private, college/university gift aid from institutional funds.

**GIFT AID (NON-NEED-BASED) Total amount:** $1,080,184 (77% institutional, 23% external sources). **Receiving aid:** Freshmen: 26% (52). Undergraduates: 13% (103). **Average award:** Freshmen: $9500. Undergraduates: $8526. **Scholarships, grants, and awards by category:** *Academic interests/achievement:* general academic interests/achievements. *Special characteristics:* children of faculty/staff, international students, local/state students, out-of-state students, veterans, veterans' children.

**LOANS Student loans:** $6,742,488 (42% need-based, 58% non-need-based). 95% of past graduating class borrowed through all loan programs. **Average indebtedness per student:** $36,278. **Average need-based loan:** Freshmen: $3946. Undergraduates: $4513. **Parent loans:** $776,484 (100% non-need-based). **Programs:** Federal Direct (Subsidized and Unsubsidized Stafford, PLUS), Perkins.

**WORK-STUDY Federal work-study:** Total amount: $198,931; 102 jobs averaging $1950.

**APPLYING FOR FINANCIAL AID Required financial aid form:** FAFSA. **Financial aid deadline (priority):** 2/15. **Notification date:** Continuous beginning 3/15. Students must reply within 2 weeks of notification.

**CONTACT** Jeannine Bosse, Director of Student Financial Services, Thomas College, 180 West River Road, Waterville, ME 04901-5097, 800-339-7001. *Fax:* 207-859-1115. *E-mail:* sfsdir@thomas.edu.
*Website:* http://www.thomas.edu/.

# THOMAS EDISON STATE COLLEGE
### Trenton, NJ

| Tuition & fees: N/R | Average undergraduate aid package: N/A |
|---|---|

**ABOUT THE INSTITUTION** State-supported, coed. 74 undergraduate majors. Federal methodology is used as a basis for awarding need-based institutional aid.

**GIFT AID (NEED-BASED) Total amount:** $5,879,000 (95% federal, 5% state). **Scholarships, grants, and awards:** Federal Pell, state, private.

**LOANS Student loans:** $23,687,000 (100% need-based). **Parent loans:** $32,000 (100% need-based). **Programs:** state, private loans.

**APPLYING FOR FINANCIAL AID Required financial aid forms:** FAFSA, institution's own form. **Financial aid deadline:** Continuous. **Notification date:** Continuous. Students must reply within 4 weeks of notification.

**CONTACT** Mr. James Owens, Director of Financial Aid, Thomas Edison State College, 101 West State Street, Trenton, NJ 08608, 609-633-9658 or toll-free 888-442-8372. *Fax:* 609-633-6489. *E-mail:* finaid@tesc.edu.
*Website:* http://www.tesc.edu/.

# THOMAS JEFFERSON UNIVERSITY
### Philadelphia, PA

| Tuition & fees: N/R | Average undergraduate aid package: N/A |
|---|---|

**ABOUT THE INSTITUTION** Independent, coed. 7 undergraduate majors. Institutional methodology is used as a basis for awarding need-based institutional aid.

**GIFT AID (NEED-BASED) Total amount:** $1,531,933 (57% federal, 23% state, 18% institutional, 2% external sources). **Scholarships, grants, and awards:** Federal Pell, FSEOG, state, private, college/university gift aid from institutional funds, HHS Grants.

**GIFT AID (NON-NEED-BASED) Total amount:** $1,354,835 (4% federal, 91% institutional, 5% external sources). **Scholarships, grants, and awards by category:** *Academic interests/achievement:* general academic interests/achievements, health fields. *Special characteristics:* members of minority groups, veterans.

**LOANS Student loans:** $14,932,305 (26% need-based, 74% non-need-based). *Average indebtedness per student:* $55,363. **Parent loans:** $1,851,779 (100% non-need-based). **Programs:** Federal Direct (Subsidized and Unsubsidized Stafford, PLUS), Perkins, Federal Nursing, college/university.

**WORK-STUDY Federal work-study:** Total amount: $23,000; jobs available.

**APPLYING FOR FINANCIAL AID Required financial aid form:** FAFSA. **Financial aid deadline (priority):** 4/1. **Notification date:** Continuous beginning 4/1. Students must reply within 2 weeks of notification.

**CONTACT** Susan McFadden, University Director of Financial Aid, Thomas Jefferson University, 1015 Walnut Street, Suite 115, Philadelphia, PA 19107, 215-955-2867 or toll-free 877-533-3247. *Fax:* 215-923-6974. *E-mail:* financial.aid@jefferson.edu.
*Website:* http://www.jefferson.edu/university.html.

# THOMAS MORE COLLEGE
### Crestview Hills, KY

| Tuition & fees: $29,153 | Average undergraduate aid package: $20,151 |
|---|---|

**ABOUT THE INSTITUTION** Independent Roman Catholic, coed. **Awards:** certificates, associate, bachelor's, and master's degrees. 44 undergraduate majors. **Total enrollment:** 1,655. Undergraduates: 1,497. Freshmen: 276. Federal methodology is used as a basis for awarding need-based institutional aid.

**UNDERGRADUATE EXPENSES for 2015–2016 Application fee:** $25. **Comprehensive fee:** $36,923 includes full-time tuition ($27,628), mandatory fees ($1525), and room and board ($7770). **College room only:** $3570. Room and board charges vary according to board plan and housing facility. **Part-time tuition:** $605 per semester hour. **Part-time fees:** $70 per semester hour.

**FRESHMAN FINANCIAL AID (Fall 2013)** 255 applied for aid; of those 85% were deemed to have need. 100% of freshmen with need received aid; of those 28% had need fully met. **Average percent of need met:** 76% (excluding resources awarded to replace EFC). **Average financial aid package:** $19,660 (excluding resources awarded to replace EFC). 12% of all full-time freshmen had no need and received non-need-based gift aid.

**UNDERGRADUATE FINANCIAL AID (Fall 2013)** 973 applied for aid; of those 68% were deemed to have need. 100% of undergraduates with need received aid; of those 25% had need fully met. **Average percent of need met:** 74% (excluding resources awarded to replace EFC). **Average financial aid package:** $20,151 (excluding resources awarded to replace EFC). 12% of all full-time undergraduates had no need and received non-need-based gift aid.

**GIFT AID (NEED-BASED) Total amount:** $11,214,203 (15% federal, 10% state, 73% institutional, 2% external sources). **Receiving aid:** Freshmen: 83% (217); all full-time undergraduates: 53% (661). **Average award:** Freshmen: $15,710; Undergraduates: $15,681. **Scholarships, grants, and awards:** Federal Pell, FSEOG, state, private, college/university gift aid from institutional funds, Federal Nursing.

**GIFT AID (NON-NEED-BASED) Total amount:** $3,001,924 (4% state, 94% institutional, 2% external sources). **Receiving aid:** Freshmen: 15% (39). Undergraduates: 9% (113). **Average award:** Freshmen: $15,126. Undergraduates: $14,474. **Scholarships, grants, and awards by category:** *Academic interests/achievement:* 594 awards ($6,868,334 total): biological sciences, business, communication, computer science, education, English, general academic interests/achievements, mathematics, physical sciences, premedicine, religion/biblical studies, social sciences. *Creative arts/performance:* 16 awards ($19,065 total): art/fine arts, theater/drama. *Special achievements/activities:* 56 awards ($99,900 total): community service, leadership, memberships, religious involvement. *Special characteristics:* 435 awards ($2,785,792 total): adult students, children and siblings of alumni, children of faculty/staff, children of union members/company employees, international students, members of minority groups, out-of-state students, religious affiliation, siblings of current students, veterans, veterans' children. *Tuition waivers:* Full or partial for employees or children of employees, senior citizens. *ROTC:* Army cooperative, Air Force cooperative.

**LOANS Student loans:** $7,228,946 (42% need-based, 58% non-need-based). 72% of past graduating class borrowed through all loan programs. *Average indebtedness per student:* $31,014. **Average need-based loan:** Freshmen: $3578. Undergraduates: $4544. **Parent loans:** $1,546,490 (100% non-need-based). **Programs:** Federal Direct (Subsidized and Unsubsidized Stafford, PLUS), Perkins, Federal Nursing, college/university.

**WORK-STUDY Federal work-study:** 139 jobs averaging $916. **State or other work-study/employment:** 205 part-time jobs averaging $858.

**APPLYING FOR FINANCIAL AID Required financial aid form:** FAFSA. **Financial aid deadline (priority):** 3/15. **Notification date:** Continuous beginning 3/1. Students must reply by 5/1.

**CONTACT** Ms. Mary Givhan, Director of Financial Aid, Thomas More College, 333 Thomas More Parkway, Crestview Hills, KY 41017-3495, 859-344-3531 or toll-free 800-825-4557. *Fax:* 859-344-3638. *E-mail:* givhanm@thomasmore.edu. *Website:* http://www.thomasmore.edu/.

# THOMAS MORE COLLEGE OF LIBERAL ARTS
## Merrimack, NH

**ABOUT THE INSTITUTION** Independent Roman Catholic Church, coed. 1 undergraduate major.

**GIFT AID (NEED-BASED)** *Scholarships, grants, and awards:* Federal Pell, FSEOG, state, private, college/university gift aid from institutional funds.

**GIFT AID (NON-NEED-BASED)** *Scholarships, grants, and awards by category:* Academic interests/achievement: general academic interests/achievements.

**LOANS** *Programs:* Federal Direct (Subsidized and Unsubsidized Stafford, PLUS).

**WORK-STUDY** *State or other work-study/employment:* Total amount: $85,801 (93% need-based, 7% non-need-based). 47 part-time jobs averaging $1455.

**APPLYING FOR FINANCIAL AID** *Required financial aid form:* FAFSA.

**CONTACT** Clinton A. Hanson Jr., Director of Financial Aid, Thomas More College of Liberal Arts, 6 Manchester Street, Merrimack, NH 03054-4818, 603-880-8308 Ext. 23 or toll-free 800-880-8308. *Fax:* 603-880-9280. *E-mail:* chanson@ thomasmorecollege.edu. *Website:* http://www.thomasmorecollege.edu/.

# THOMAS UNIVERSITY
## Thomasville, GA

| Tuition & fees: N/R | Average undergraduate aid package: N/A |
|---|---|

**ABOUT THE INSTITUTION** Independent, coed. 23 undergraduate majors. Federal methodology is used as a basis for awarding need-based institutional aid.

**GIFT AID (NEED-BASED)** *Total amount:* $1,840,552 (97% federal, 3% institutional). *Scholarships, grants, and awards:* Federal Pell, FSEOG, state, private, college/university gift aid from institutional funds.

**GIFT AID (NON-NEED-BASED)** *Total amount:* $903,982 (2% federal, 40% state, 54% institutional, 4% external sources). *Scholarships, grants, and awards by category:* Academic interests/achievement: biological sciences, business, education, English, general academic interests/achievements, health fields, humanities, international studies, mathematics, physical sciences, premedicine, social sciences. *Creative arts/performance:* art/fine arts, music. *Special characteristics:* children and siblings of alumni, children of faculty/staff, ethnic background, out-of-state students, veterans.

**LOANS** *Student loans:* $5,694,689 (100% non-need-based). *Parent loans:* $120,387 (100% non-need-based). *Programs:* Federal Direct (Subsidized and Unsubsidized Stafford, PLUS), state, alternative loans.

**WORK-STUDY** *Federal work-study:* jobs available.

**ATHLETIC AWARDS** Total amount: $1,617,640 (100% non-need-based).

**APPLYING FOR FINANCIAL AID** *Required financial aid forms:* FAFSA, state aid form. *Financial aid deadline (priority):* 5/1. *Notification date:* Continuous beginning 5/1.

**CONTACT** Ms. Christina J. Gainous, Director of Financial Aid, Thomas University, 1501 Millpond Road, Thomasville, GA 31792-7499, 229-226-1621 Ext. 1002 or toll-free 800-538-9784. *Fax:* 229-227-6888. *E-mail:* cgainous@thomasu.edu. *Website:* http://www.thomasu.edu/.

# TIFFIN UNIVERSITY
## Tiffin, OH

| Tuition & fees: $21,560 | Average undergraduate aid package: $17,005 |
|---|---|

**ABOUT THE INSTITUTION** Independent, coed. *Awards:* certificates, associate, bachelor's, and master's degrees. 39 undergraduate majors. *Total enrollment:* 4,098. Undergraduates: 3,014. Freshmen: 514. Federal methodology is used as a basis for awarding need-based institutional aid.

**UNDERGRADUATE EXPENSES for 2015–2016** *Application fee:* $20. *Comprehensive fee:* $31,430 includes full-time tuition ($21,510), mandatory fees ($50), and room and board ($9870). *College room only:* $5120. Full-time tuition and fees vary according to course load, degree level, location, and program. Room and board charges vary according to board plan and housing facility. *Part-time tuition:* $717 per credit. Part-time tuition and fees vary according to course load, degree level, location, and program.

**FRESHMAN FINANCIAL AID (Fall 2014, est.)** 441 applied for aid; of those 92% were deemed to have need. 100% of freshmen with need received aid; of those 11% had need fully met. *Average percent of need met:* 67% (excluding resources awarded to replace EFC). *Average financial aid package:* $18,639 (excluding resources awarded to replace EFC).

**UNDERGRADUATE FINANCIAL AID (Fall 2014, est.)** 1,690 applied for aid; of those 93% were deemed to have need. 100% of undergraduates with need received aid; of those 14% had need fully met. *Average percent of need met:* 68% (excluding resources awarded to replace EFC). *Average financial aid package:* $17,005 (excluding resources awarded to replace EFC).

**GIFT AID (NEED-BASED)** *Total amount:* $21,389,627 (29% federal, 9% state, 61% institutional, 1% external sources). *Receiving aid:* Freshmen: 90% (403); all full-time undergraduates: 86% (1,522). *Average award:* Freshmen: $14,266; Undergraduates: $12,701. *Scholarships, grants, and awards:* Federal Pell, FSEOG, state, private, college/university gift aid from institutional funds.

**GIFT AID (NON-NEED-BASED)** *Receiving aid:* Freshmen: 7% (30). Undergraduates: 7% (122). *Scholarships, grants, and awards by category:* Academic interests/achievement: general academic interests/achievements. *Creative arts/performance:* music, performing arts, theater/drama. *Special achievements/activities:* cheerleading/drum major. *Special characteristics:* children of faculty/staff. *Tuition waivers:* Full or partial for employees or children of employees, senior citizens. *ROTC:* Army cooperative, Air Force cooperative.

**LOANS** *Student loans:* $18,521,195 (100% need-based). 88% of past graduating class borrowed through all loan programs. *Average indebtedness per student:* $32,679. *Average need-based loan:* Freshmen: $3350. Undergraduates: $4133. *Parent loans:* $2,502,501 (100% need-based). *Programs:* Federal Direct (Subsidized and Unsubsidized Stafford, PLUS), Perkins, college/university.

**WORK-STUDY** *Federal work-study:* Total amount: $1,857,711; jobs available.

**ATHLETIC AWARDS** Total amount: $3,645,056 (100% need-based).

**APPLYING FOR FINANCIAL AID** *Required financial aid form:* FAFSA. *Financial aid deadline:* Continuous. *Notification date:* Continuous beginning 2/1. Students must reply within 2 weeks of notification.

**CONTACT** Ms. Cindy Little, Director of Financial Aid Operations, Tiffin University, 155 Miami Street, Tiffin, OH 44883, 419-448-3415 or toll-free 800-968-6446. *Fax:* 419-443-5006. *E-mail:* clittle@tiffin.edu. *Website:* http://www.tiffin.edu/.

# TOCCOA FALLS COLLEGE
## Toccoa Falls, GA

**CONTACT** Vince Welch, Director of Financial Aid, Toccoa Falls College, PO Box 800900, Toccoa Falls, GA 30598, 706-886-7299 Ext. 5234 or toll-free 888-785-5624. *Fax:* 706-282-6041. *E-mail:* vwelch@tfc.edu. *Website:* http://www.tfc.edu/.

# TORAH TEMIMAH TALMUDICAL SEMINARY

### Brooklyn, NY

**CONTACT** Financial Aid Office, Torah Temimah Talmudical Seminary, 507 Ocean Parkway, Brooklyn, NY 11218-5913, 718-853-8500.

# TOUGALOO COLLEGE

### Tougaloo, MS

**CONTACT** Director of Financial Aid, Tougaloo College, 500 West County Line Road, Tougaloo, MS 39174, 601-977-6134 or toll-free 888-42GALOO. *Fax:* 601-977-6164.
*Website:* http://www.tougaloo.edu/.

# TOURO COLLEGE

### New York, NY

**ABOUT THE INSTITUTION** Independent, coed. 26 undergraduate majors.
**GIFT AID (NEED-BASED)** *Scholarships, grants, and awards:* Federal Pell, FSEOG, state, private, college/university gift aid from institutional funds.
**GIFT AID (NON-NEED-BASED)** *Scholarships, grants, and awards by category:* Academic interests/achievement: general academic interests/achievements. *Special characteristics:* children of faculty/staff.
**LOANS** *Programs:* Federal Direct (Subsidized and Unsubsidized Stafford, PLUS), Perkins, alternative loans.
**WORK-STUDY** *Federal work-study:* jobs available.
**APPLYING FOR FINANCIAL AID** *Required financial aid forms:* FAFSA, institution's own form.
**CONTACT** Karyn Wright-Moore, Office of Financial Aid, Touro College, 27 West 23rd Street, New York, NY 10010, 212-463-0400 Ext. 5108. *E-mail:* karyn.wright-moore4@touro.edu.
*Website:* http://www.touro.edu/.

# TOURO COLLEGE LOS ANGELES

### West Hollywood, CA

**CONTACT** Financial Aid Office, Touro College Los Angeles, 1317 North Crescent Heights Boulevard, West Hollywood, CA 90046, 323-822-9700.
*Website:* http://www.touro.edu/losangeles/.

# TOURO UNIVERSITY WORLDWIDE

### Los Alamitos, CA

**CONTACT** Financial Aid Office, Touro University Worldwide, 10601 Calle Lee, Suite 179, Los Alamitos, CA 90720, 818-575-6800.
*Website:* http://www.tuw.edu/.

# TOWSON UNIVERSITY

### Towson, MD

| Tuition & fees (MD res): $8650 | Average undergraduate aid package: $9675 |
| --- | --- |

**ABOUT THE INSTITUTION** State-supported, coed. *Awards:* certificates, bachelor's, master's, and doctoral degrees. 62 undergraduate majors. *Total enrollment:* 22,285. Undergraduates: 18,807. Freshmen: 2,712. Federal methodology is used as a basis for awarding need-based institutional aid.

**UNDERGRADUATE EXPENSES** for 2015–2016 *Application fee:* $45. *Tuition, state resident:* full-time $6064; part-time $260 per credit hour. *Tuition, nonresident:* full-time $17,742; part-time $740 per credit hour. *Required fees:* full-time $2586; $111 per credit hour. Full-time tuition and fees vary according to course load. Part-time tuition and fees vary according to course load. *College room and board:* $11,260; *Room only:* $6238. Room and board charges vary according to board plan and housing facility.
**FRESHMAN FINANCIAL AID** (Fall 2014, est.) 2,286 applied for aid; of those 67% were deemed to have need. 91% of freshmen with need received aid; of those 14% had need fully met. *Average percent of need met:* 56% (excluding resources awarded to replace EFC). *Average financial aid package:* $9196 (excluding resources awarded to replace EFC). 7% of all full-time freshmen had no need and received non-need-based gift aid.
**UNDERGRADUATE FINANCIAL AID** (Fall 2014, est.) 11,899 applied for aid; of those 75% were deemed to have need. 95% of undergraduates with need received aid; of those 12% had need fully met. *Average percent of need met:* 60% (excluding resources awarded to replace EFC). *Average financial aid package:* $9675 (excluding resources awarded to replace EFC). 6% of all full-time undergraduates had no need and received non-need-based gift aid.
**GIFT AID (NEED-BASED)** *Total amount:* $51,412,920 (42% federal, 22% state, 35% institutional, 1% external sources). *Receiving aid:* Freshmen: 29% (780); all full-time undergraduates: 35% (5,708). *Average award:* Freshmen: $8725; Undergraduates: $8316. *Scholarships, grants, and awards:* Federal Pell, FSEOG, state, private, college/university gift aid from institutional funds.
**GIFT AID (NON-NEED-BASED)** *Total amount:* $10,896,717 (2% federal, 8% state, 71% institutional, 19% external sources). *Receiving aid:* Freshmen: 20% (533). Undergraduates: 13% (2,139). *Average award:* Freshmen: $5421. Undergraduates: $4867. *Scholarships, grants, and awards by category:* Academic interests/achievement: 1,852 awards ($8,966,589 total): biological sciences, business, communication, computer science, education, English, foreign languages, general academic interests/achievements, health fields, mathematics, physical sciences. *Creative arts/performance:* 145 awards ($462,416 total): art/fine arts, cinema/film/broadcasting, dance, debating, music, performing arts, theater/drama. *Special achievements/activities:* 245 awards ($356,611 total): community service, memberships. *Special characteristics:* 568 awards ($1,791,430 total): adult students, children and siblings of alumni, children of faculty/staff, ethnic background, first-generation college students, handicapped students, international students, members of minority groups, previous college experience, veterans. *Tuition waivers:* Full or partial for employees or children of employees, senior citizens. *ROTC:* Army cooperative, Air Force cooperative.
**LOANS** *Student loans:* $70,068,920 (46% need-based, 54% non-need-based). 63% of past graduating class borrowed through all loan programs. *Average indebtedness per student:* $25,926. *Average need-based loan:* Freshmen: $3207. Undergraduates: $4010. *Parent loans:* $34,875,830 (1% need-based, 99% non-need-based). *Programs:* Federal Direct (Subsidized and Unsubsidized Stafford, PLUS), Perkins.
**WORK-STUDY** *Federal work-study:* Total amount: $966,060; 544 jobs averaging $1704.
**ATHLETIC AWARDS** Total amount: $5,616,931 (3% need-based, 97% non-need-based).
**APPLYING FOR FINANCIAL AID** *Required financial aid forms:* FAFSA, state aid form. *Financial aid deadline (priority):* 2/15. *Notification date:* Continuous beginning 3/21. Students must reply by 5/1 or within 2 weeks of notification.
**CONTACT** Mr. David Horne, Director of Financial Aid, Towson University, 8000 York Road, Towson, MD 21252-0001, 410-704-4236. *E-mail:* finaid@towson.edu.
*Website:* http://www.towson.edu/.

# TRANSYLVANIA UNIVERSITY

### Lexington, KY

| Tuition & fees: $33,360 | Average undergraduate aid package: $27,365 |
| --- | --- |

**ABOUT THE INSTITUTION** Independent Christian Church (Disciples of Christ), coed. *Awards:* bachelor's degrees. 36 undergraduate majors. *Total enrollment:* 1,014. Undergraduates: 1,014. Freshmen: 261. Federal methodology is used as a basis for awarding need-based institutional aid.
**UNDERGRADUATE EXPENSES** for 2015–2016 *Comprehensive fee:* $42,660 includes full-time tuition ($32,010), mandatory fees ($1350), and room and board ($9300). Room and board charges vary according to board plan and housing

facility. *Part-time tuition:* $3560 per course. Part-time tuition and fees vary according to course load.

**FRESHMAN FINANCIAL AID (Fall 2014, est.)** 214 applied for aid; of those 80% were deemed to have need. 100% of freshmen with need received aid; of those 29% had need fully met. *Average percent of need met:* 87% (excluding resources awarded to replace EFC). *Average financial aid package:* $27,367 (excluding resources awarded to replace EFC). 29% of all full-time freshmen had no need and received non-need-based gift aid.

**UNDERGRADUATE FINANCIAL AID (Fall 2014, est.)** 785 applied for aid; of those 86% were deemed to have need. 100% of undergraduates with need received aid; of those 25% had need fully met. *Average percent of need met:* 82% (excluding resources awarded to replace EFC). *Average financial aid package:* $27,365 (excluding resources awarded to replace EFC). 31% of all full-time undergraduates had no need and received non-need-based gift aid.

**GIFT AID (NEED-BASED)** *Total amount:* $15,374,596 (8% federal, 15% state, 74% institutional, 3% external sources). *Receiving aid:* Freshmen: 66% (172); all full-time undergraduates: 67% (677). *Average award:* Freshmen: $23,628; Undergraduates: $22,883. *Scholarships, grants, and awards:* Federal Pell, FSEOG, state, private, college/university gift aid from institutional funds.

**GIFT AID (NON-NEED-BASED)** *Total amount:* $6,339,642 (9% state, 88% institutional, 3% external sources). *Receiving aid:* Freshmen: 13% (34). Undergraduates: 12% (116). *Average award:* Freshmen: $16,172. Undergraduates: $15,372. *Scholarships, grants, and awards by category:* Academic interests/achievement: $11,169,646 total: general academic interests/achievements. Creative arts/performance: $332,750 total: art/fine arts, music, theater/drama. Special achievements/activities: $4,123,791 total: general special achievements/activities. Special characteristics: $1,446,472 total: children of faculty/staff, members of minority groups, out-of-state students, relatives of clergy, religious affiliation. *Tuition waivers:* Full or partial for employees or children of employees. *ROTC:* Army cooperative, Air Force cooperative.

**LOANS** *Student loans:* $5,410,533 (67% need-based, 33% non-need-based). 70% of past graduating class borrowed through all loan programs. *Average indebtedness per student:* $28,079. *Average need-based loan:* Freshmen: $4040, Undergraduates: $4921. *Parent loans:* $1,447,746 (35% need-based, 65% non-need-based). *Programs:* Federal Direct (Subsidized and Unsubsidized Stafford, PLUS), Perkins.

**WORK-STUDY** *Federal work-study:* Total amount: $471,197; 377 jobs averaging $1719. *State or other work-study/employment:* Total amount: $239,960 (28% need-based, 72% non-need-based). 44 part-time jobs averaging $5453.

**APPLYING FOR FINANCIAL AID** *Required financial aid form:* FAFSA. *Financial aid deadline (priority):* 1/15. *Notification date:* Continuous beginning 3/15. Students must reply within 2 weeks of notification.

**CONTACT** Mr. Dave Cecil, Associate Vice President for Financial Aid, Transylvania University, 300 North Broadway, Lexington, KY 40508-1797, 859-233-8239 or toll-free 800-872-6798. *Fax:* 859-281-3650. *E-mail:* dcecil@transy.edu. *Website:* http://www.transy.edu/.

# TREVECCA NAZARENE UNIVERSITY
## Nashville, TN

| Tuition & fees: $23,126 | Average undergraduate aid package: N/A |
| --- | --- |

**ABOUT THE INSTITUTION** Independent Nazarene, coed. *Awards:* certificates, associate, bachelor's, master's, and doctoral degrees. 68 undergraduate majors. *Total enrollment:* 2,606. Undergraduates: 1,677. Freshmen: 320. Federal methodology is used as a basis for awarding need-based institutional aid.

**UNDERGRADUATE EXPENSES for 2015–2016** *Application fee:* $25. *Comprehensive fee:* $31,186 includes full-time tuition ($22,626), mandatory fees ($500), and room and board ($8060). *College room only:* $4030. Full-time tuition and fees vary according to course load and program. Room and board charges vary according to board plan. *Part-time tuition:* $874 per credit hour. Part-time tuition and fees vary according to course load and program. *Payment plan:* Tuition prepayment.

**GIFT AID (NEED-BASED)** *Total amount:* $3,501,538 (69% federal, 10% state, 21% institutional). *Scholarships, grants, and awards:* Federal Pell, FSEOG, state, private, college/university gift aid from institutional funds.

**GIFT AID (NON-NEED-BASED)** *Total amount:* $7,765,277 (20% state, 77% institutional, 3% external sources). *Scholarships, grants, and awards by category:* Academic interests/achievement: biological sciences, business, communi-

cation, education, English, general academic interests/achievements, physical sciences, religion/biblical studies, social sciences. *Creative arts/performance:* cinema/film/broadcasting, music. *Special achievements/activities:* general special achievements/activities. *Special characteristics:* children of faculty/staff, general special characteristics, relatives of clergy, religious affiliation. *Tuition waivers:* Full or partial for employees or children of employees, senior citizens. *ROTC:* Army cooperative.

**LOANS** *Student loans:* $8,159,261 (48% need-based, 52% non-need-based). 76% of past graduating class borrowed through all loan programs. *Average indebtedness per student:* $28,430. *Parent loans:* $1,218,313 (100% non-need-based). *Programs:* Federal Direct (Subsidized and Unsubsidized Stafford, PLUS), Perkins.

**WORK-STUDY** *Federal work-study:* jobs available. *State or other work-study/employment:* Total amount: $673,300 (100% non-need-based). Part-time jobs available.

**ATHLETIC AWARDS** Total amount: $1,847,996 (100% non-need-based).

**APPLYING FOR FINANCIAL AID** *Required financial aid form:* FAFSA. *Financial aid deadline (priority):* 2/1. *Notification date:* Continuous beginning 3/1.

**CONTACT** Eddie White, Director of Financial Aid, Trevecca Nazarene University, 333 Murfreesboro Road, Nashville, TN 37210-2834, 615-248-1242 or toll-free 888-210-4TNU. *Fax:* 615-248-7728. *E-mail:* ewhite@trevecca.edu. *Website:* http://www.trevecca.edu/.

# TRIDENT UNIVERSITY INTERNATIONAL
## Cypress, CA

**CONTACT** Taisha Azlin, Director of Financial Aid, Trident University International, 5665 Plaza Drive, Third Floor, Cypress, CA 90630, 800-375-9878 Ext. 1061. *Fax:* 714-484-7621. *E-mail:* financialaid@tuiu.edu. *Website:* http://www.trident.edu/.

# TRINE UNIVERSITY
## Angola, IN

| Tuition & fees: $30,350 | Average undergraduate aid package: $25,519 |
| --- | --- |

**ABOUT THE INSTITUTION** Independent, coed. *Awards:* associate, bachelor's, and master's degrees. 35 undergraduate majors. *Total enrollment:* 2,832. Undergraduates: 2,791. Freshmen: 523. Federal methodology is used as a basis for awarding need-based institutional aid.

**UNDERGRADUATE EXPENSES for 2015–2016** *Comprehensive fee:* $40,550 includes full-time tuition ($29,900), mandatory fees ($450), and room and board ($10,200). Full-time tuition and fees vary according to degree level, location, and program. Room and board charges vary according to board plan and housing facility. *Part-time tuition:* $935 per credit hour. Part-time tuition and fees vary according to degree level, location, and program.

**FRESHMAN FINANCIAL AID (Fall 2014, est.)** 485 applied for aid; of those 91% were deemed to have need. 100% of freshmen with need received aid; of those 11% had need fully met. *Average percent of need met:* 80% (excluding resources awarded to replace EFC). *Average financial aid package:* $27,189 (excluding resources awarded to replace EFC). 14% of all full-time freshmen had no need and received non-need-based gift aid.

**UNDERGRADUATE FINANCIAL AID (Fall 2014, est.)** 1,442 applied for aid; of those 90% were deemed to have need. 99% of undergraduates with need received aid; of those 16% had need fully met. *Average percent of need met:* 78% (excluding resources awarded to replace EFC). *Average financial aid package:* $25,519 (excluding resources awarded to replace EFC). 11% of all full-time undergraduates had no need and received non-need-based gift aid.

**GIFT AID (NEED-BASED)** *Total amount:* $8,140,440 (23% federal, 23% state, 54% institutional). *Receiving aid:* Freshmen: 84% (441); all full-time undergraduates: 78% (1,293). *Average award:* Freshmen: $5796; Undergraduates: $4596. *Scholarships, grants, and awards:* Federal Pell, FSEOG, state, private, college/university gift aid from institutional funds.

**GIFT AID (NON-NEED-BASED)** *Total amount:* $20,579,624 (91% institutional, 9% external sources). *Receiving aid:* Freshmen: 84% (442). Undergraduates: 78% (1,295). *Average award:* Freshmen: $11,230. Undergraduates: $12,318. *Scholarships, grants, and awards by category:* Academic interests/achievement: 21 awards ($41,000 total): general academic interests/achievements, premedicine. *Creative arts/performance:* 120 awards ($130,542 total): dance, music. *Special achievements/activities:* 12 awards ($11,500 total): cheerleading/drum major. *Special characteristics:* 160 awards ($312,522 total): children and siblings of alumni, children of educators, children of faculty/staff, members of minority groups, siblings of current students, twins. *Tuition waivers:* Full or partial for employees or children of employees, senior citizens. *ROTC:* Air Force cooperative.

**LOANS** *Student loans:* $7,839,319 (56% need-based, 44% non-need-based). 86% of past graduating class borrowed through all loan programs. *Average indebtedness per student:* $32,641. *Average need-based loan:* Freshmen: $4533. Undergraduates: $5572. *Parent loans:* $4,287,457 (100% non-need-based). *Programs:* Federal Direct (Subsidized and Unsubsidized Stafford, PLUS), alternative loans.

**WORK-STUDY** *Federal work-study:* Total amount: $151,678; 990 jobs averaging $1861. *State or other work-study/employment:* Part-time jobs available.

**APPLYING FOR FINANCIAL AID** *Required financial aid form:* FAFSA. *Financial aid deadline (priority):* 3/1. *Notification date:* Continuous beginning 3/10. Students must reply by 5/1.

**CONTACT** Kim Bennett, Assistant Vice President of Enrollment Management, Trine University, 1 University Avenue, Angola, IN 46703-1764, 260-665-4438 or toll-free 800-347-4878. *Fax:* 260-665-4511. *E-mail:* bennettk@trine.edu. *Website:* http://www.trine.edu/.

---

# TRINITY BAPTIST COLLEGE
## Jacksonville, FL

**ABOUT THE INSTITUTION** Independent Baptist, coed. 10 undergraduate majors.

**GIFT AID (NEED-BASED)** *Scholarships, grants, and awards:* Federal Pell, FSEOG, state, private, college/university gift aid from institutional funds.

**GIFT AID (NON-NEED-BASED)** *Scholarships, grants, and awards by category:* Academic interests/achievement: education, general academic interests/achievements, religion/biblical studies. *Special achievements/activities:* leadership, religious involvement. *Special characteristics:* relatives of clergy, religious affiliation, spouses of current students.

**APPLYING FOR FINANCIAL AID** *Required financial aid forms:* FAFSA, institution's own form, state aid form.

**CONTACT** Mr. Mark Elkins, Financial Aid Administrator, Trinity Baptist College, 800 Hammond Boulevard, Jacksonville, FL 32221, 904-596-2445 or toll-free 800-786-2206. *Fax:* 904-596-2531. *E-mail:* melkins@tbc.edu. *Website:* http://www.tbc.edu/.

---

# TRINITY BIBLE COLLEGE
## Ellendale, ND

**ABOUT THE INSTITUTION** Independent Assemblies of God, coed. 12 undergraduate majors.

**GIFT AID (NEED-BASED)** *Scholarships, grants, and awards:* Federal Pell, FSEOG, state, private, college/university gift aid from institutional funds.

**GIFT AID (NON-NEED-BASED)** *Scholarships, grants, and awards by category:* Academic interests/achievement: business, education, general academic interests/achievements, religion/biblical studies. *Creative arts/performance:* art/fine arts, creative writing, music, theater/drama. *Special achievements/activities:* community service, general special achievements/activities, leadership, religious involvement. *Special characteristics:* children and siblings of alumni, children of current students, children of faculty/staff, general special characteristics, international students, married students, parents of current students, relatives of clergy, siblings of current students, spouses of current students.

**LOANS** *Programs:* Federal Direct (Subsidized and Unsubsidized Stafford, PLUS), Perkins, alternative loans.

**WORK-STUDY** Federal work-study jobs available.

**APPLYING FOR FINANCIAL AID** *Required financial aid form:* FAFSA.

**CONTACT** Mary Anne Whitman, Director of Financial Aid, Trinity Bible College, 50 South 6th Avenue, Ellendale, ND 58436-7150, 701-349-5403 or toll-free 800-523-1603. *Fax:* 701-349-5786. *E-mail:* mwhitman@trinitybiblecollege.edu. *Website:* http://www.trinitybiblecollege.edu/.

---

# TRINITY CHRISTIAN COLLEGE
## Palos Heights, IL

| Tuition & fees: $25,290 | Average undergraduate aid package: $17,489 |
| --- | --- |

**ABOUT THE INSTITUTION** Independent Christian Reformed, coed. *Awards:* bachelor's and master's degrees. 46 undergraduate majors. *Total enrollment:* 1,406. Undergraduates: 1,337. Freshmen: 190. Federal methodology is used as a basis for awarding need-based institutional aid.

**UNDERGRADUATE EXPENSES** for 2015–2016 *Application fee:* $30. *One-time required fee:* $225. *Comprehensive fee:* $34,680 includes full-time tuition ($25,060), mandatory fees ($230), and room and board ($9390). *College room only:* $4960. Room and board charges vary according to board plan. *Part-time tuition:* $836 per credit hour.

**FRESHMAN FINANCIAL AID (Fall 2014, est.)** 163 applied for aid; of those 89% were deemed to have need. 100% of freshmen with need received aid; of those 16% had need fully met. *Average percent of need met:* 74% (excluding resources awarded to replace EFC). *Average financial aid package:* $22,143 (excluding resources awarded to replace EFC). 11% of all full-time freshmen had no need and received non-need-based gift aid.

**UNDERGRADUATE FINANCIAL AID (Fall 2014, est.)** 840 applied for aid; of those 91% were deemed to have need. 100% of undergraduates with need received aid; of those 13% had need fully met. *Average percent of need met:* 68% (excluding resources awarded to replace EFC). *Average financial aid package:* $17,489 (excluding resources awarded to replace EFC). 10% of all full-time undergraduates had no need and received non-need-based gift aid.

**GIFT AID (NEED-BASED)** *Total amount:* $9,151,066 (21% federal, 16% state, 61% institutional, 2% external sources). *Receiving aid:* Freshmen: 76% (145); all full-time undergraduates: 68% (738). *Average award:* Freshmen: $17,580; Undergraduates: $13,796. *Scholarships, grants, and awards:* Federal Pell, FSEOG, state, private, college/university gift aid from institutional funds, Federal Nursing.

**GIFT AID (NON-NEED-BASED)** *Total amount:* $1,305,220 (6% federal, 91% institutional, 3% external sources). *Receiving aid:* Freshmen: 9% (17). Undergraduates: 6% (64). *Average award:* Freshmen: $10,473. Undergraduates: $8260. *Scholarships, grants, and awards by category:* Academic interests/achievement: 592 awards ($4,951,806 total): biological sciences, business, communication, computer science, education, engineering/technologies, English, general academic interests/achievements, health fields, humanities, international studies, mathematics, physical sciences, premedicine, religion/biblical studies, social sciences. *Creative arts/performance:* 83 awards ($115,588 total): applied art and design, art/fine arts, general creative arts/performance, journalism/publications, music, performing arts, theater/drama. *Special achievements/activities:* 4 awards ($8400 total): community service, general special achievements/activities, leadership, religious involvement. *Special characteristics:* 265 awards ($540,646 total): adult students, children and siblings of alumni, children of faculty/staff, ethnic background, first-generation college students, local/state students, members of minority groups, out-of-state students, religious affiliation, veterans. *Tuition waivers:* Full or partial for employees or children of employees.

**LOANS** *Student loans:* $8,664,925 (44% need-based, 56% non-need-based). 83% of past graduating class borrowed through all loan programs. *Average indebtedness per student:* $30,996. *Average need-based loan:* Freshmen: $3756. Undergraduates: $4679. *Parent loans:* $1,081,491 (100% non-need-based). *Programs:* Federal Direct (Subsidized and Unsubsidized Stafford, PLUS), Perkins, Federal Nursing.

**WORK-STUDY** *Federal work-study:* Total amount: $93,071; 76 jobs averaging $1426. *State or other work-study/employment:* Total amount: $518,501 (100% non-need-based). 367 part-time jobs averaging $1190.

**ATHLETIC AWARDS** Total amount: $1,312,851 (66% need-based, 34% non-need-based).

**APPLYING FOR FINANCIAL AID** *Required financial aid form:* FAFSA. *Financial aid deadline (priority):* 2/15. *Notification date:* Continuous beginning 3/1. Students must reply by 5/1 or within 2 weeks of notification.

**CONTACT** Ryan P. Zantingh, Director of Financial Aid, Trinity Christian College, 6601 West College Drive, Palos Heights, IL 60463-0929, 708-239-4872 or toll-free 866-TRIN-4-ME. *Fax:* 708-239-4814. *E-mail:* ryan.zantingh@trnty.edu. *Website:* http://www.trnty.edu/.

# TRINITY COLLEGE
## Hartford, CT

| Tuition & fees: $50,776 | Average undergraduate aid package: $44,424 |
|---|---|

**ABOUT THE INSTITUTION** Independent, coed. *Awards:* bachelor's and master's degrees. 48 undergraduate majors. *Total enrollment:* 2,350. Undergraduates: 2,255. Freshmen: 611. Both federal and institutional methodology are used as a basis for awarding need-based institutional aid.

**UNDERGRADUATE EXPENSES for 2015–2016** *Application fee:* $60. *One-time required fee:* $25. *Comprehensive fee:* $63,920 includes full-time tuition ($48,446), mandatory fees ($2330), and room and board ($13,144). *College room only:* $8550. Full-time tuition and fees vary according to course load and program. Room and board charges vary according to board plan. Part-time tuition and fees vary according to course load and program.

**FRESHMAN FINANCIAL AID (Fall 2014, est.)** 320 applied for aid; of those 82% were deemed to have need. 100% of freshmen with need received aid; of those 100% had need fully met. *Average percent of need met:* 100% (excluding resources awarded to replace EFC). *Average financial aid package:* $43,931 (excluding resources awarded to replace EFC). 6% of all full-time freshmen had no need and received non-need-based gift aid.

**UNDERGRADUATE FINANCIAL AID (Fall 2014, est.)** 989 applied for aid; of those 92% were deemed to have need. 100% of undergraduates with need received aid; of those 100% had need fully met. *Average percent of need met:* 100% (excluding resources awarded to replace EFC). *Average financial aid package:* $44,424 (excluding resources awarded to replace EFC). 4% of all full-time undergraduates had no need and received non-need-based gift aid.

**GIFT AID (NEED-BASED)** *Total amount:* $37,486,338 (4% federal, 1% state, 93% institutional, 2% external sources). *Receiving aid:* Freshmen: 41% (252); all full-time undergraduates: 39% (867). *Average award:* Freshmen: $40,557; Undergraduates: $41,684. *Scholarships, grants, and awards:* Federal Pell, FSEOG, state, private, college/university gift aid from institutional funds, Academic Competitiveness Grants, National SMART Grants, Yellow Ribbon Grant Program.

**GIFT AID (NON-NEED-BASED)** *Total amount:* $2,776,115 (1% federal, 92% institutional, 7% external sources). *Receiving aid:* Freshmen: 6% (37). Undergraduates: 3% (67). *Average award:* Freshmen: $23,591. Undergraduates: $24,836. *Scholarships, grants, and awards by category:* Academic interests/achievement: 22 awards ($1,019,401 total): general academic interests/achievements. *Special achievements/activities:* 216 awards ($7,383,213 total): leadership. *Tuition waivers:* Full or partial for employees or children of employees, adult students. *ROTC:* Army cooperative.

**LOANS** *Student loans:* $6,622,282 (50% need-based, 50% non-need-based). 43% of past graduating class borrowed through all loan programs. *Average indebtedness per student:* $28,237. *Average need-based loan:* Freshmen: $3720. Undergraduates: $4583. *Parent loans:* $3,286,775 (100% non-need-based). *Programs:* Federal Direct (PLUS), Perkins, college/university, alternative loans.

**WORK-STUDY** *Federal work-study:* Total amount: $917,894; 791 jobs averaging $1797. *State or other work-study/employment:* Part-time jobs available.

**APPLYING FOR FINANCIAL AID** *Required financial aid forms:* FAFSA, CSS Financial Aid PROFILE, noncustodial (divorced/separated) parent's statement, business/farm supplement, federal income tax form(s). *Financial aid deadline:* 3/1 (priority: 2/1). *Notification date:* 4/1. Students must reply by 5/1 or within 2 weeks of notification.

**CONTACT** Ms. Kelly O'Brien, Director of Financial Aid, Trinity College, 300 Summit Street, Hartford, CT 06106-3100, 860-297-2046. *Fax:* 860-987-6296. *Website:* http://www.trincoll.edu/.

# TRINITY COLLEGE OF FLORIDA
## Trinity, FL

| Tuition & fees: $15,650 | Average undergraduate aid package: $14,321 |
|---|---|

**ABOUT THE INSTITUTION** Independent nondenominational, coed. *Awards:* certificates, associate, and bachelor's degrees. 10 undergraduate majors. *Total enrollment:* 229. Undergraduates: 219. Freshmen: 31. Both federal and institutional methodology are used as a basis for awarding need-based institutional aid.

**UNDERGRADUATE EXPENSES for 2015–2016** *Application fee:* $35. *Comprehensive fee:* $22,100 includes full-time tuition ($14,850), mandatory fees ($800), and room and board ($6450). Full-time tuition and fees vary according to program. *Part-time tuition:* $495 per credit hour. *Part-time fees:* $400 per term. Part-time tuition and fees vary according to program.

**FRESHMAN FINANCIAL AID (Fall 2014, est.)** 30 applied for aid; of those 90% were deemed to have need. 100% of freshmen with need received aid; of those 7% had need fully met. *Average percent of need met:* 69% (excluding resources awarded to replace EFC). *Average financial aid package:* $15,210 (excluding resources awarded to replace EFC). 13% of all full-time freshmen had no need and received non-need-based gift aid.

**UNDERGRADUATE FINANCIAL AID (Fall 2014, est.)** 175 applied for aid; of those 97% were deemed to have need. 100% of undergraduates with need received aid; of those 12% had need fully met. *Average percent of need met:* 59% (excluding resources awarded to replace EFC). *Average financial aid package:* $14,321 (excluding resources awarded to replace EFC). 7% of all full-time undergraduates had no need and received non-need-based gift aid.

**GIFT AID (NEED-BASED)** *Total amount:* $1,170,286 (60% federal, 7% state, 31% institutional, 2% external sources). *Receiving aid:* Freshmen: 84% (27); all full-time undergraduates: 81% (166). *Average award:* Freshmen: $8482; Undergraduates: $6747. *Scholarships, grants, and awards:* Federal Pell, FSEOG, state, private, college/university gift aid from institutional funds.

**GIFT AID (NON-NEED-BASED)** *Total amount:* $28,233 (14% state, 86% institutional). *Receiving aid:* Freshmen: 6% (2). Undergraduates: 2% (5). *Average award:* Freshmen: $1875. Undergraduates: $1596. *Scholarships, grants, and awards by category:* Academic interests/achievement: 68 awards ($156,320 total): general academic interests/achievements, religion/biblical studies. *Creative arts/performance:* theater/drama. *Special achievements/activities:* 10 awards ($59,150 total): community service, leadership, religious involvement. *Special characteristics:* 2 awards ($1200 total): children of faculty/staff, relatives of clergy, spouses of current students. *Tuition waivers:* Full or partial for employees or children of employees, senior citizens.

**LOANS** *Student loans:* $1,447,100 (94% need-based, 6% non-need-based). 90% of past graduating class borrowed through all loan programs. *Average indebtedness per student:* $28,201. *Average need-based loan:* Freshmen: $3013. Undergraduates: $8915. *Parent loans:* $21,200 (73% need-based, 27% non-need-based). *Programs:* Federal Direct (Subsidized and Unsubsidized Stafford, PLUS).

**WORK-STUDY** *Federal work-study:* Total amount: $48,882; 16 jobs averaging $3055. *State or other work-study/employment:* Total amount: $1903 (100% need-based). 1 part-time job averaging $1903.

**APPLYING FOR FINANCIAL AID** *Required financial aid forms:* FAFSA, institution's own form. *Financial aid deadline:* Continuous. *Notification date:* Continuous beginning 1/1. Students must reply within 6 weeks of notification.

**CONTACT** Sue Wayne, Director of Financial Aid, Trinity College of Florida, 2430 Welbilt Boulevard, New Port Richey, FL 34655, 727-569-1413 or toll-free 800-388-0869. *Fax:* 727-376-0781. *E-mail:* swayne@trinitycollege.edu. *Website:* http://www.trinitycollege.edu/.

# TRINITY COLLEGE OF NURSING AND HEALTH SCIENCES
## Rock Island, IL

| Tuition & fees: N/R | Average undergraduate aid package: $2534 |
|---|---|

**ABOUT THE INSTITUTION** Independent, coed. 8 undergraduate majors. Federal methodology is used as a basis for awarding need-based institutional aid.

**UNDERGRADUATE FINANCIAL AID (Fall 2013)** 101 applied for aid; of those 100% were deemed to have need. 100% of undergraduates with need received aid. *Average percent of need met:* 76% (excluding resources awarded to replace EFC). *Average financial aid package:* $2534 (excluding resources awarded to replace EFC).

**GIFT AID (NEED-BASED)** *Total amount:* $545,148 (56% federal, 19% state, 21% institutional, 4% external sources). *Receiving aid:* All full-time undergraduates: 85% (88). *Average award:* Undergraduates: $1231. *Scholarships, grants, and awards:* Federal Pell, FSEOG, state, private, college/university gift aid from institutional funds.

**LOANS** *Student loans:* $1,329,968 (46% need-based, 54% non-need-based). *Parent loans:* $192,065 (100% non-need-based). *Programs:* Federal Direct (Subsidized and Unsubsidized Stafford, PLUS), Federal Nursing.

**WORK-STUDY** *Federal work-study:* 2 jobs averaging $9518.

**APPLYING FOR FINANCIAL AID** *Required financial aid forms:* FAFSA, institution's own form. *Financial aid deadline:* Continuous. *Notification date:* Continuous beginning 1/1. Students must reply within 8 weeks of notification.

**CONTACT** Mrs. Christine Carol Christopherson, Financial Aid Specialist, Trinity College of Nursing and Health Sciences, 2122 25th Avenue, Rock Island, IL 61201, 309-779-7740. *Fax:* 309-779-7748. *E-mail:* c.christopherson@trinitycollegeqc.edu. *Website:* http://www.trinitycollegeqc.edu/.

---

# TRINITY INTERNATIONAL UNIVERSITY
## Deerfield, IL

**CONTACT** Pat Coles, Interim Director of Financial Aid, Trinity International University, 2065 Half Day Road, Deerfield, IL 60015-1284, 847-317-8060 or toll-free 800-822-3225. *Fax:* 847-317-7081. *E-mail:* finaid@tiu.edu. *Website:* http://www.tiu.edu/.

---

# TRINITY LUTHERAN COLLEGE
## Issaquah, WA

**CONTACT** Ms. Shanna Pyzer, Director of Financial Aid, Trinity Lutheran College, 2802 Wetmore Avenue, Everett, WA 98201, 425-249-4800 or toll-free 800-843-5659. *Fax:* 425-249-4801. *E-mail:* fin_aid@tlc.edu. *Website:* http://www.tlc.edu/.

---

# TRINITY UNIVERSITY
## San Antonio, TX

| Tuition & fees: $36,214 | Average undergraduate aid package: $34,073 |
| --- | --- |

**ABOUT THE INSTITUTION** Independent Presbyterian Church, coed. *Awards:* bachelor's and master's degrees. 59 undergraduate majors. *Total enrollment:* 2,488. Undergraduates: 2,297. Freshmen: 655. Both federal and institutional methodology are used as a basis for awarding need-based institutional aid.

**UNDERGRADUATE EXPENSES** for 2015–2016 *Comprehensive fee:* $48,150 includes full-time tuition ($35,688), mandatory fees ($526), and room and board ($11,936). *College room only:* $7714. Full-time tuition and fees vary according to course load. Room and board charges vary according to board plan. *Part-time tuition:* $1487 per credit hour. Part-time tuition and fees vary according to course load.

**FRESHMAN FINANCIAL AID (Fall 2014, est.)** 438 applied for aid; of those 69% were deemed to have need. 100% of freshmen with need received aid; of those 88% had need fully met. *Average percent of need met:* 99% (excluding resources awarded to replace EFC). *Average financial aid package:* $36,648 (excluding resources awarded to replace EFC). 50% of all full-time freshmen had no need and received non-need-based gift aid.

**UNDERGRADUATE FINANCIAL AID (Fall 2014, est.)** 1,235 applied for aid; of those 81% were deemed to have need. 100% of undergraduates with need received aid; of those 56% had need fully met. *Average percent of need met:* 93%

(excluding resources awarded to replace EFC). *Average financial aid package:* $34,073 (excluding resources awarded to replace EFC). 47% of all full-time undergraduates had no need and received non-need-based gift aid.

**GIFT AID (NEED-BASED)** *Total amount:* $25,582,746 (9% federal, 6% state, 82% institutional, 3% external sources). *Receiving aid:* Freshmen: 46% (302); all full-time undergraduates: 44% (998). *Average award:* Freshmen: $28,171; Undergraduates: $25,809. *Scholarships, grants, and awards:* Federal Pell, FSEOG, state, private, college/university gift aid from institutional funds.

**GIFT AID (NON-NEED-BASED)** *Total amount:* $19,893,093 (94% institutional, 6% external sources). *Receiving aid:* Freshmen: 28% (185). Undergraduates: 11% (254). *Average award:* Freshmen: $19,506. Undergraduates: $16,583. *Scholarships, grants, and awards by category:* Academic interests/achievement: general academic interests/achievements. *Creative arts/performance:* art/fine arts, debating, music, theater/drama. *Special characteristics:* children and siblings of alumni, children of educators, international students, veterans, veterans' children. *Tuition waivers:* Full or partial for employees or children of employees. *ROTC:* Army cooperative, Air Force cooperative.

**LOANS** *Student loans:* $9,129,660 (59% need-based, 41% non-need-based). 50% of past graduating class borrowed through all loan programs. *Average indebtedness per student:* $35,318. *Average need-based loan:* Freshmen: $4166. Undergraduates: $5577. *Parent loans:* $1,753,223 (15% need-based, 85% non-need-based). *Programs:* Federal Direct (Subsidized and Unsubsidized Stafford, PLUS), Perkins, state, college/university.

**WORK-STUDY** *Federal work-study:* Total amount: $1,542,291; 687 jobs averaging $2245. *State or other work-study/employment:* Part-time jobs available.

**APPLYING FOR FINANCIAL AID** *Required financial aid forms:* FAFSA, CSS Financial Aid PROFILE. *Financial aid deadline (priority):* 2/15. *Notification date:* 3/15. Students must reply by 5/1.

**CONTACT** Financial Aid Office, Trinity University, One Trinity Place, San Antonio, TX 78212-7200, 210-999-8898 or toll-free 800-TRINITY. *Fax:* 210-999-8316. *E-mail:* financialaid@trinity.edu. *Website:* http://www.trinity.edu/.

---

# TRINITY WASHINGTON UNIVERSITY
## Washington, DC

**CONTACT** Catherine H. Geier, Director of Student Financial Services, Trinity Washington University, 125 Michigan Avenue, NE, Washington, DC 20017-1094, 202-884-9530 or toll-free 800-IWANTTC. *Fax:* 202-884-9524. *E-mail:* financialaid@trinitydc.edu. *Website:* http://www.trinitydc.edu/.

---

# TRI-STATE BIBLE COLLEGE
## South Point, OH

**CONTACT** Mrs. Roberta Mercer, Financial Aid Director, Tri-State Bible College, 506 Margaret Street, PO Box 445, South Point, OH 45680, 740-377-2520 Ext. 23. *Fax:* 740-377-0001. *E-mail:* tsbc@zoominternet.net. *Website:* http://www.tsbc.edu/.

---

# TROY UNIVERSITY
## Troy, AL

| Tuition & fees (AL res): $7564 | Average undergraduate aid package: $4497 |
| --- | --- |

**ABOUT THE INSTITUTION** State-supported, coed. *Awards:* certificates, associate, bachelor's, master's, and doctoral degrees. 48 undergraduate majors. *Total enrollment:* 19,041. Undergraduates: 15,115. Freshmen: 1,900. Federal methodology is used as a basis for awarding need-based institutional aid.

**UNDERGRADUATE EXPENSES** for 2015–2016 *Application fee:* $30. *Tuition, state resident:* full-time $6528; part-time $264 per credit hour. *Tuition, nonresident:* full-time $13,056; part-time $528 per credit hour. *Required fees:*

full-time $1036; $35 per credit hour or $50 per term. Full-time tuition and fees vary according to location and program. Part-time tuition and fees vary according to location and program. **College room and board:** $6498; **Room only:** $3724. Room and board charges vary according to board plan and housing facility.
**FRESHMAN FINANCIAL AID (Fall 2014, est.)** 1,108 applied for aid; of those 100% were deemed to have need. 100% of freshmen with need received aid. **Average financial aid package:** $3640 (excluding resources awarded to replace EFC). 29% of all full-time freshmen had no need and received non-need-based gift aid.
**UNDERGRADUATE FINANCIAL AID (Fall 2014, est.)** 6,342 applied for aid; of those 100% were deemed to have need. 100% of undergraduates with need received aid. **Average financial aid package:** $4497 (excluding resources awarded to replace EFC). 25% of all full-time undergraduates had no need and received non-need-based gift aid.
**GIFT AID (NEED-BASED) Total amount:** $36,894,388 (100% federal). **Receiving aid:** Freshmen: 43% (639); all full-time undergraduates: 46% (4,187). **Average award:** Freshmen: $4574; Undergraduates: $4659. **Scholarships, grants, and awards:** Federal Pell, FSEOG, state, private, college/university gift aid from institutional funds.
**GIFT AID (NON-NEED-BASED) Total amount:** $52,742,465 (62% institutional, 38% external sources). **Receiving aid:** Freshmen: 46% (698). Undergraduates: 26% (2,336). **Average award:** Freshmen: $5118. Undergraduates: $5844. **Scholarships, grants, and awards by category:** Academic interests/achievement: general academic interests/achievements. Creative arts/performance: music, theater/drama. Special achievements/activities: leadership. Special characteristics: general special characteristics. **Tuition waivers:** Full or partial for employees or children of employees. **ROTC:** Army, Air Force.
**LOANS Student loans:** $156,181,852 (100% need-based). **Average need-based loan:** Freshmen: $3359. Undergraduates: $4470. **Parent loans:** $7,717,365 (100% need-based). **Programs:** Perkins.
**WORK-STUDY Federal work-study:** Total amount: $935,200; jobs available.
**ATHLETIC AWARDS** Total amount: $4,984,661 (100% non-need-based).
**APPLYING FOR FINANCIAL AID Required financial aid forms:** FAFSA, institution's own form. **Financial aid deadline (priority):** 3/1. **Notification date:** Continuous beginning 6/1. Students must reply within 2 weeks of notification.
**CONTACT** Ms. Carol Ballard, Associate Vice Chancellor of Financial Aid, Troy University, 131 Adams Administration Building, Troy, AL 36082, 334-670-3186 or toll-free 800-551-9716. Fax: 334-670-3702. E-mail: csupri@troy.edu.
Website: http://www.troy.edu/.

# TRUETT-MCCONNELL COLLEGE
## Cleveland, GA

| Tuition & fees: $17,300 | Average undergraduate aid package: $14,314 |
| --- | --- |

**ABOUT THE INSTITUTION** Independent Baptist, coed. **Awards:** bachelor's and master's degrees. 14 undergraduate majors. **Total enrollment:** 1,681. Undergraduates: 1,663. Freshmen: 209. Federal methodology is used as a basis for awarding need-based institutional aid.
**UNDERGRADUATE EXPENSES for 2015–2016 Application fee:** $25. **Comprehensive fee:** $24,420 includes full-time tuition ($16,650), mandatory fees ($650), and room and board ($7120). Full-time tuition and fees vary according to course load and location. Room and board charges vary according to housing facility. **Part-time tuition:** $555 per credit hour. Part-time tuition and fees vary according to course load and location.
**FRESHMAN FINANCIAL AID (Fall 2014, est.)** 202 applied for aid; of those 90% were deemed to have need. 100% of freshmen with need received aid; of those 13% had need fully met. **Average percent of need met:** 67% (excluding resources awarded to replace EFC). **Average financial aid package:** $14,546 (excluding resources awarded to replace EFC). 14% of all full-time freshmen had no need and received non-need-based gift aid.
**UNDERGRADUATE FINANCIAL AID (Fall 2014, est.)** 642 applied for aid; of those 91% were deemed to have need. 100% of undergraduates with need received aid; of those 11% had need fully met. **Average percent of need met:** 65% (excluding resources awarded to replace EFC). **Average financial aid package:** $14,314 (excluding resources awarded to replace EFC). 13% of all full-time undergraduates had no need and received non-need-based gift aid.

**GIFT AID (NEED-BASED) Total amount:** $5,945,695 (27% federal, 22% state, 41% institutional, 10% external sources). **Receiving aid:** Freshmen: 87% (182); all full-time undergraduates: 86% (586). **Average award:** Freshmen: $11,496; Undergraduates: $11,309. **Scholarships, grants, and awards:** Federal Pell, FSEOG, state, private, college/university gift aid from institutional funds.
**GIFT AID (NON-NEED-BASED) Total amount:** $1,038,737 (37% state, 52% institutional, 11% external sources). **Receiving aid:** Freshmen: 10% (21). Undergraduates: 9% (62). **Average award:** Freshmen: $4729. Undergraduates: $6015. **Scholarships, grants, and awards by category:** Academic interests/achievement: 564 awards ($1,579,707 total): education, general academic interests/achievements, health fields, religion/biblical studies. Creative arts/performance: 70 awards ($155,491 total): music. Special achievements/activities: 244 awards ($211,421 total): general special achievements/activities, leadership, religious involvement. Special characteristics: 259 awards ($754,641 total): children of current students, children of faculty/staff, general special characteristics, international students, local/state students, married students, out-of-state students, parents of current students, relatives of clergy, religious affiliation, siblings of current students, spouses of current students. **Tuition waivers:** Full or partial for employees or children of employees.
**LOANS Student loans:** $3,899,879 (79% need-based, 21% non-need-based). 62% of past graduating class borrowed through all loan programs. **Average indebtedness per student:** $13,508. **Average need-based loan:** Freshmen: $4051. Undergraduates: $4236. **Parent loans:** $556,557 (62% need-based, 38% non-need-based). **Programs:** Federal Direct (Subsidized and Unsubsidized Stafford, PLUS), state, alternative loans.
**WORK-STUDY Federal work-study:** Total amount: $29,889; 32 jobs averaging $1059.
**ATHLETIC AWARDS** Total amount: $975,980 (72% need-based, 28% non-need-based).
**APPLYING FOR FINANCIAL AID Required financial aid forms:** FAFSA, institution's own form. **Financial aid deadline:** Continuous. **Notification date:** Continuous beginning 3/15. Students must reply within 4 weeks of notification.
**CONTACT** Ms. Kaye Church, Assistant Director of Financial Aid , Truett-McConnell College, 100 Alumni Drive, Cleveland, GA 30528, 706-865-2134 Ext. 144 or toll-free 800-226-8621. Fax: 706-243-4642. E-mail: kchurch@truett.edu.
Website: http://www.truett.edu/.

# TRUMAN STATE UNIVERSITY
## Kirksville, MO

| Tuition & fees (MO res): $7374 | Average undergraduate aid package: $11,407 |
| --- | --- |

**ABOUT THE INSTITUTION** State-supported, coed. **Awards:** bachelor's and master's degrees. 37 undergraduate majors. **Total enrollment:** 6,248. Undergraduates: 5,910. Freshmen: 1,320. Federal methodology is used as a basis for awarding need-based institutional aid.
**UNDERGRADUATE EXPENSES for 2015–2016 One-time required fee:** $315. **Tuition, state resident:** full-time $7096; part-time $295.50 per credit hour. **Tuition, nonresident:** full-time $13,160; part-time $548 per credit hour. **Required fees:** full-time $278; $278 per year. Full-time tuition and fees vary according to course load, degree level, and program. Part-time tuition and fees vary according to course load, degree level, and program. Room and board charges vary according to housing facility.
**FRESHMAN FINANCIAL AID (Fall 2013)** 1,143 applied for aid; of those 68% were deemed to have need. 100% of freshmen with need received aid; of those 41% had need fully met. **Average percent of need met:** 87% (excluding resources awarded to replace EFC). **Average financial aid package:** $12,466 (excluding resources awarded to replace EFC). 40% of all full-time freshmen had no need and received non-need-based gift aid.
**UNDERGRADUATE FINANCIAL AID (Fall 2013)** 3,840 applied for aid; of those 73% were deemed to have need. 100% of undergraduates with need received aid; of those 33% had need fully met. **Average percent of need met:** 81% (excluding resources awarded to replace EFC). **Average financial aid package:** $11,407 (excluding resources awarded to replace EFC). 35% of all full-time undergraduates had no need and received non-need-based gift aid.
**GIFT AID (NEED-BASED) Total amount:** $17,504,027 (30% federal, 11% state, 54% institutional, 5% external sources). **Receiving aid:** Freshmen: 58% (772); all full-time undergraduates: 50% (2,635). **Average award:** Freshmen: $7767; Undergrad-

uates: $6794. *Scholarships, grants, and awards:* Federal Pell, FSEOG, state, private, college/university gift aid from institutional funds, TEACH Grants.

**GIFT AID (NON-NEED-BASED)** *Total amount:* $13,969,165 (2% federal, 11% state, 80% institutional, 7% external sources). *Receiving aid:* Freshmen: 58% (762). Undergraduates: 42% (2,217). *Average award:* Freshmen: $5209. Undergraduates: $5322. *Scholarships, grants, and awards by category:* Academic interests/achievement: 8,988 awards ($20,933,823 total): agriculture, biological sciences, business, communication, computer science, education, English, foreign languages, general academic interests/achievements, health fields, humanities, mathematics, military science, physical sciences, premedicine, social sciences. *Creative arts/performance:* 144 awards ($161,668 total): art/fine arts, debating, music, theater/drama. *Special achievements/activities:* 511 awards ($2,394,530 total): leadership. *Special characteristics:* 552 awards ($1,437,036 total): children and siblings of alumni, children of faculty/staff, ethnic background, first-generation college students, international students, out-of-state students, previous college experience. *Tuition waivers:* Full or partial for children of alumni, employees or children of employees, senior citizens. *ROTC:* Army.

**LOANS** *Student loans:* $26,078,662 (52% need-based, 48% non-need-based). 54% of past graduating class borrowed through all loan programs. *Average indebtedness per student:* $23,585. *Average need-based loan:* Freshmen: $3587. Undergraduates: $4386. *Parent loans:* $1,475,290 (15% need-based, 85% non-need-based). *Programs:* Federal Direct (Subsidized and Unsubsidized Stafford, PLUS), Perkins, Federal Nursing, college/university.

**WORK-STUDY** *Federal work-study:* 442 jobs averaging $1673. *State or other work-study/employment:* Total amount: $1,803,935 (2% need-based, 98% non-need-based). 1,461 part-time jobs averaging $1212.

**ATHLETIC AWARDS** Total amount: $1,392,461 (34% need-based, 66% non-need-based).

**APPLYING FOR FINANCIAL AID** *Required financial aid form:* FAFSA. *Financial aid deadline (priority):* 4/1. *Notification date:* Continuous beginning 3/1.

**CONTACT** Kathy Elsea, Director of Financial Aid, Truman State University, 103 McClain Hall, Kirksville, MO 63501-4221, 660-785-4130 or toll-free 800-892-7792. *Fax:* 660-785-7389. *E-mail:* kelsea@truman.edu. *Website:* http://www.truman.edu/.

# TUFTS UNIVERSITY
## Medford, MA

| Tuition & fees: $48,643 | Average undergraduate aid package: $40,168 |
| --- | --- |

**ABOUT THE INSTITUTION** Independent, coed. *Awards:* certificates, bachelor's, master's, and doctoral degrees. 96 undergraduate majors. *Total enrollment:* 10,917. Undergraduates: 5,177. Freshmen: 1,347. Both federal and institutional methodology are used as a basis for awarding need-based institutional aid.

**UNDERGRADUATE EXPENSES** for 2015–2016 *Application fee:* $70. *Comprehensive fee:* $61,277 includes full-time tuition ($47,596), mandatory fees ($1047), and room and board ($12,634). *College room only:* $6876. Room and board charges vary according to board plan. *Payment plan:* Tuition prepayment.

**FRESHMAN FINANCIAL AID (Fall 2014, est.)** 716 applied for aid; of those 80% were deemed to have need. 98% of freshmen with need received aid; of those 100% had need fully met. *Average percent of need met:* 100% (excluding resources awarded to replace EFC). *Average financial aid package:* $42,770 (excluding resources awarded to replace EFC). 2% of all full-time freshmen had no need and received non-need-based gift aid.

**UNDERGRADUATE FINANCIAL AID (Fall 2014, est.)** 2,337 applied for aid; of those 87% were deemed to have need. 98% of undergraduates with need received aid; of those 100% had need fully met. *Average percent of need met:* 100% (excluding resources awarded to replace EFC). *Average financial aid package:* $40,168 (excluding resources awarded to replace EFC). 2% of all full-time undergraduates had no need and received non-need-based gift aid.

**GIFT AID (NEED-BASED)** *Total amount:* $74,849,538 (4% federal, 1% state, 92% institutional, 3% external sources). *Receiving aid:* Freshmen: 40% (544); all full-time undergraduates: 37% (1,889). *Average award:* Freshmen: $40,300; Undergraduates: $37,147. *Scholarships, grants, and awards:* Federal Pell, FSEOG, state, private, college/university gift aid from institutional funds.

**GIFT AID (NON-NEED-BASED)** *Total amount:* $1,286,749 (14% federal, 5% institutional, 81% external sources). *Receiving aid:* Freshmen: 2% (30). Undergraduates: 2% (100). *Average award:* Freshmen: $500. Undergraduates: $500. *Scholarships, grants, and awards by category:* Academic interests/achievement: 100 awards ($50,000 total): general academic interests/achievements. *Tuition waivers:* Full or partial for employees or children of employees. *ROTC:* Army cooperative, Naval cooperative, Air Force cooperative.

**LOANS** *Student loans:* $11,993,065 (59% need-based, 41% non-need-based). 40% of past graduating class borrowed through all loan programs. *Average indebtedness per student:* $26,616. *Average need-based loan:* Freshmen: $2813. Undergraduates: $3869. *Parent loans:* $5,606,699 (100% non-need-based). *Programs:* Federal Direct (Subsidized and Unsubsidized Stafford, PLUS), Perkins, college/university.

**WORK-STUDY** *Federal work-study:* Total amount: $2,880,768; 1,537 jobs averaging $1866. *State or other work-study/employment:* Total amount: $210,800 (100% need-based). 125 part-time jobs averaging $1782.

**APPLYING FOR FINANCIAL AID** *Required financial aid forms:* FAFSA, CSS Financial Aid PROFILE, noncustodial (divorced/separated) parent's statement, federal income tax form(s). *Financial aid deadline:* 2/15. *Notification date:* 4/5. Students must reply by 5/1.

**CONTACT** Patricia C. Reilly, Director of Financial Aid, Tufts University, Dowling Hall, Medford, MA 02155, 617-627-2000. *Fax:* 617-627-3987. *E-mail:* patricia.reilly@tufts.edu. *Website:* http://www.tufts.edu/.

# TULANE UNIVERSITY
## New Orleans, LA

| Tuition & fees: $48,306 | Average undergraduate aid package: $34,605 |
| --- | --- |

**ABOUT THE INSTITUTION** Independent, coed. *Awards:* certificates, associate, bachelor's, master's, and doctoral degrees. 82 undergraduate majors. *Total enrollment:* 13,531. Undergraduates: 8,353. Freshmen: 1,647. Both federal and institutional methodology are used as a basis for awarding need-based institutional aid.

**UNDERGRADUATE EXPENSES** for 2015–2016 *Comprehensive fee:* $60,862 includes full-time tuition ($44,426), mandatory fees ($3880), and room and board ($12,556). *College room only:* $7206. Room and board charges vary according to board plan and housing facility. *Payment plan:* Tuition prepayment.

**FRESHMAN FINANCIAL AID (Fall 2013)** 998 applied for aid; of those 63% were deemed to have need. 99% of freshmen with need received aid; of those 69% had need fully met. *Average percent of need met:* 95% (excluding resources awarded to replace EFC). *Average financial aid package:* $32,424 (excluding resources awarded to replace EFC). 30% of all full-time freshmen had no need and received non-need-based gift aid.

**UNDERGRADUATE FINANCIAL AID (Fall 2013)** 3,278 applied for aid; of those 75% were deemed to have need. 99% of undergraduates with need received aid; of those 69% had need fully met. *Average percent of need met:* 93% (excluding resources awarded to replace EFC). *Average financial aid package:* $34,605 (excluding resources awarded to replace EFC). 33% of all full-time undergraduates had no need and received non-need-based gift aid.

**GIFT AID (NEED-BASED)** *Total amount:* $63,665,079 (8% federal, 2% state, 89% institutional, 1% external sources). *Receiving aid:* Freshmen: 37% (603); all full-time undergraduates: 36% (2,366). *Average award:* Freshmen: $27,030; Undergraduates: $28,233. *Scholarships, grants, and awards:* Federal Pell, FSEOG, state, private, college/university gift aid from institutional funds.

**GIFT AID (NON-NEED-BASED)** *Total amount:* $54,380,616 (1% federal, 3% state, 94% institutional, 2% external sources). *Receiving aid:* Freshmen: 14% (224). Undergraduates: 9% (619). *Average award:* Freshmen: $22,660. Undergraduates: $21,325. *Scholarships, grants, and awards by category:* Creative arts/performance: 89 awards ($211,170 total): music. *Special achievements/activities:* 52 awards ($454,249 total): community service. *Special characteristics:* 274 awards ($11,318,232 total): children of faculty/staff, international students, local/state students. *Tuition waivers:* Full or partial for employees or children of employees. *ROTC:* Army, Naval, Air Force.

**LOANS** *Student loans:* $37,582,178 (59% need-based, 41% non-need-based). 45% of past graduating class borrowed through all loan programs. *Average indebtedness per student:* $31,653. *Average need-based loan:* Freshmen: $7995. Undergrad-

uates: $8600. **Parent loans:** $9,504,824 (10% need-based, 90% non-need-based). **Programs:** Federal Direct (Subsidized and Unsubsidized Stafford, PLUS), Perkins.
**WORK-STUDY Federal work-study:** 1,083 jobs averaging $2440. **State or other work-study/employment:** Total amount: $1,026,376 (13% need-based, 87% non-need-based). Part-time jobs available.
**ATHLETIC AWARDS** Total amount: $10,971,710 (39% need-based, 61% non-need-based).

**APPLYING FOR FINANCIAL AID Required financial aid forms:** FAFSA, CSS Financial Aid PROFILE, noncustodial (divorced/separated) parent's statement, business/farm supplement. **Financial aid deadline (priority):** 2/15. **Notification date:** Continuous beginning 3/15. Students must reply within 2 weeks of notification.

**CONTACT** Mr. Michael T. Goodman, Director of Financial Aid, Tulane University, 6823 St. Charles Avenue, New Orleans, LA 70118-5669, 504-865-5723 or toll-free 800-873-9283. **Fax:** 504-862-8750. **E-mail:** finaid@tulane.edu.
**Website:** http://www.tulane.edu/.

# TUSCULUM COLLEGE
## Greeneville, TN

| Tuition & fees: $22,670 | Average undergraduate aid package: $16,213 |
|---|---|

**ABOUT THE INSTITUTION** Independent Presbyterian, coed. **Awards:** bachelor's and master's degrees. 38 undergraduate majors. **Total enrollment:** 1,921. Undergraduates: 1,746. Freshmen: 287. Federal methodology is used as a basis for awarding need-based institutional aid.
**UNDERGRADUATE EXPENSES for 2015–2016 Comprehensive fee:** $31,170 includes full-time tuition ($22,670) and room and board ($8500). **College room only:** $5610. **Part-time tuition:** $704 per credit hour.
**FRESHMAN FINANCIAL AID (Fall 2013)** 300 applied for aid; of those 95% were deemed to have need. 100% of freshmen with need received aid; of those 14% had need fully met. **Average percent of need met:** 70% (excluding resources awarded to replace EFC). **Average financial aid package:** $20,448 (excluding resources awarded to replace EFC). 10% of all full-time freshmen had no need and received non-need-based gift aid.
**UNDERGRADUATE FINANCIAL AID (Fall 2013)** 1,596 applied for aid; of those 95% were deemed to have need. 99% of undergraduates with need received aid; of those 8% had need fully met. **Average percent of need met:** 61% (excluding resources awarded to replace EFC). **Average financial aid package:** $16,213 (excluding resources awarded to replace EFC). 13% of all full-time undergraduates had no need and received non-need-based gift aid.
**GIFT AID (NEED-BASED) Total amount:** $9,355,911 (53% federal, 17% state, 30% institutional). **Receiving aid:** Freshmen: 77% (244); all full-time undergraduates: 69% (1,209). **Average award:** Freshmen: $9339; Undergraduates: $7572. **Scholarships, grants, and awards:** Federal Pell, FSEOG, state, private, college/university gift aid from institutional funds.
**GIFT AID (NON-NEED-BASED) Total amount:** $8,341,833 (1% federal, 25% state, 70% institutional, 4% external sources). **Receiving aid:** Freshmen: 87% (275). Undergraduates: 59% (1,026). **Average award:** Freshmen: $7963. Undergraduates: $7682. **Scholarships, grants, and awards by category:** Academic interests/achievement: general academic interests/achievements. Creative arts/performance: general creative arts/performance, music. Special achievements/activities: cheerleading/drum major, community service, leadership. Special characteristics: adult students, children of faculty/staff, local/state students.
**LOANS Student loans:** $15,230,404 (41% need-based, 59% non-need-based). 83% of past graduating class borrowed through all loan programs. **Average indebtedness per student:** $29,162. **Average need-based loan:** Freshmen: $3423. Undergraduates: $4368. **Programs:** Perkins.
**WORK-STUDY Federal work-study:** jobs available. **State or other work-study/employment:** Part-time jobs available.
**ATHLETIC AWARDS** Total amount: $2,349,398 (100% non-need-based).
**APPLYING FOR FINANCIAL AID Required financial aid form:** FAFSA. **Financial aid deadline (priority):** 2/15. **Notification date:** Continuous beginning 3/1. Students must reply within 3 weeks of notification.
**CONTACT** Karen Sartain, Director of Financial Aid, Tusculum College, PO Box 5049, 60 Shiloh Road, Greeneville, TN 37743-9997, 423-636-7377 or toll-free 800-729-0256. **Fax:** 615-250-4968. **E-mail:** ksartain@tusculum.edu.
**Website:** http://www.tusculum.edu/.

# TUSKEGEE UNIVERSITY
## Tuskegee, AL

| Tuition & fees: $19,120 | Average undergraduate aid package: $19,250 |
|---|---|

**ABOUT THE INSTITUTION** Independent, coed. **Awards:** bachelor's, master's, and doctoral degrees. 43 undergraduate majors. **Total enrollment:** 3,118. Undergraduates: 2,584. Freshmen: 647. Federal methodology is used as a basis for awarding need-based institutional aid.
**UNDERGRADUATE EXPENSES for 2015–2016 Application fee:** $25. **Comprehensive fee:** $28,224 includes full-time tuition ($18,560), mandatory fees ($560), and room and board ($9104). **College room only:** $4300. Full-time tuition and fees vary according to course level, course load, degree level, and program. Room and board charges vary according to board plan and housing facility. Part-time tuition and fees vary according to course level, course load, degree level, and program.
**FRESHMAN FINANCIAL AID (Fall 2013)** 635 applied for aid; of those 85% were deemed to have need. 94% of freshmen with need received aid; of those 68% had need fully met. **Average percent of need met:** 85% (excluding resources awarded to replace EFC). **Average financial aid package:** $19,250 (excluding resources awarded to replace EFC). 28% of all full-time freshmen had no need and received non-need-based gift aid.
**UNDERGRADUATE FINANCIAL AID (Fall 2013)** 2,519 applied for aid; of those 85% were deemed to have need. 92% of undergraduates with need received aid; of those 70% had need fully met. **Average percent of need met:** 85% (excluding resources awarded to replace EFC). **Average financial aid package:** $19,250 (excluding resources awarded to replace EFC). 22% of all full-time undergraduates had no need and received non-need-based gift aid.
**GIFT AID (NEED-BASED) Total amount:** $6,963,035 (97% federal, 1% state, 2% institutional). **Receiving aid:** Freshmen: 58% (434); all full-time undergraduates: 61% (1,675). **Average award:** Freshmen: $800; Undergraduates: $800. **Scholarships, grants, and awards:** Federal Pell, FSEOG, state, private, college/university gift aid from institutional funds, United Negro College Fund.
**GIFT AID (NON-NEED-BASED) Total amount:** $3,999,178 (50% institutional, 50% external sources). **Receiving aid:** Freshmen: 38% (284). Undergraduates: 35% (951). **Average award:** Freshmen: $6000. Undergraduates: $6000. **Scholarships, grants, and awards by category:** Academic interests/achievement: 1,704 awards ($1,498,210 total): agriculture, architecture, business, computer science, engineering/technologies, general academic interests/achievements. Creative arts/performance: 150 awards ($220,000 total): music. Special characteristics: 36 awards ($612,000 total): children of faculty/staff, local/state students. **Tuition waivers:** Full or partial for employees or children of employees. **ROTC:** Army, Naval, Air Force.
**LOANS Student loans:** $38,940,368 (27% need-based, 73% non-need-based). 92% of past graduating class borrowed through all loan programs. **Average indebtedness per student:** $26,500. **Average need-based loan:** Freshmen: $5625. Undergraduates: $6006. **Parent loans:** $7,655,210 (100% non-need-based). **Programs:** Federal Direct (Subsidized and Unsubsidized Stafford, PLUS), Perkins.
**WORK-STUDY Federal work-study:** 620 jobs averaging $2014. **State or other work-study/employment:** Total amount: $695,000 (100% non-need-based). 416 part-time jobs averaging $4755.
**ATHLETIC AWARDS** Total amount: $1,765,210 (100% non-need-based).
**APPLYING FOR FINANCIAL AID Required financial aid forms:** FAFSA, institution's own form. **Financial aid deadline (priority):** 3/31. **Notification date:** Continuous beginning 2/15. Students must reply within 2 weeks of notification.
**CONTACT** Mr. A. D. James Jr., Executive Director of Student Financial Services, Tuskegee University, Carnegie Hall, 2nd Floor, Tuskegee, AL 36088, 334-727-8088 or toll-free 800-622-6531. **Fax:** 334-724-4078. **E-mail:** jamesad@mytu.tuskegee.edu.
**Website:** http://www.tuskegee.edu/.

# UNION COLLEGE
## Barbourville, KY

| Tuition & fees: $24,075 | Average undergraduate aid package: $21,434 |
|---|---|

**ABOUT THE INSTITUTION** Independent United Methodist, coed. **Awards:** certificates, bachelor's, and master's degrees. 34 undergraduate majors. **Total**

*enrollment:* 1,139. Undergraduates: 870. Freshmen: 240. Federal methodology is used as a basis for awarding need-based institutional aid.

**UNDERGRADUATE EXPENSES for 2015–2016** *Application fee:* $10. *Comprehensive fee:* $31,075 includes full-time tuition ($22,720), mandatory fees ($1355), and room and board ($7000). *College room only:* $3100. Room and board charges vary according to housing facility. *Part-time tuition:* $340 per credit. *Part-time fees:* $25 per credit hour.

**FRESHMAN FINANCIAL AID (Fall 2014, est.)** 220 applied for aid; of those 97% were deemed to have need. 96% of freshmen with need received aid; of those 12% had need fully met. *Average percent of need met:* 70% (excluding resources awarded to replace EFC). *Average financial aid package:* $21,953 (excluding resources awarded to replace EFC). 10% of all full-time freshmen had no need and received non-need-based gift aid.

**UNDERGRADUATE FINANCIAL AID (Fall 2014, est.)** 767 applied for aid; of those 95% were deemed to have need. 94% of undergraduates with need received aid; of those 15% had need fully met. *Average percent of need met:* 68% (excluding resources awarded to replace EFC). *Average financial aid package:* $21,434 (excluding resources awarded to replace EFC). 10% of all full-time undergraduates had no need and received non-need-based gift aid.

**GIFT AID (NEED-BASED)** *Total amount:* $10,931,487 (21% federal, 17% state, 61% institutional, 1% external sources). *Receiving aid:* Freshmen: 87% (206); all full-time undergraduates: 83% (683). *Average award:* Freshmen: $18,625; Undergraduates: $17,682. *Scholarships, grants, and awards:* Federal Pell, FSEOG, state, private, college/university gift aid from institutional funds.

**GIFT AID (NON-NEED-BASED)** *Total amount:* $116,642 (100% state). *Receiving aid:* Freshmen: 7% (17). Undergraduates: 8% (68). *Average award:* Freshmen: $15,413. Undergraduates: $15,252. *Scholarships, grants, and awards by category:* Academic interests/achievement: 711 awards ($5,637,852 total): biological sciences, general academic interests/achievements, health fields, mathematics, physical sciences. Creative arts/performance: 56 awards ($113,500 total): music, theater/drama. Special achievements/activities: 122 awards ($540,255 total): cheerleading/drum major, community service, general special achievements/activities, hobbies/interests, leadership, memberships, religious involvement. Special characteristics: 95 awards ($223,810 total): adult students, children and siblings of alumni, children of current students, children of faculty/staff, members of minority groups, religious affiliation, siblings of current students, veterans, veterans' children. *Tuition waivers:* Full or partial for employees or children of employees.

**LOANS** *Student loans:* $4,196,650 (54% need-based, 46% non-need-based). 84% of past graduating class borrowed through all loan programs. *Average indebtedness per student:* $32,691. *Average need-based loan:* Freshmen: $3699. Undergraduates: $4316. *Parent loans:* $959,251 (45% need-based, 55% non-need-based). *Programs:* Federal Direct (Subsidized and Unsubsidized Stafford, PLUS), Perkins, college/university.

**WORK-STUDY** *Federal work-study:* Total amount: $166,581; 111 jobs averaging $1500. *State or other work-study/employment:* Total amount: $16,019 (100% need-based). 33 part-time jobs averaging $1500.

**ATHLETIC AWARDS** Total amount: $2,790,895 (100% need-based).

**APPLYING FOR FINANCIAL AID** *Required financial aid form:* FAFSA. *Financial aid deadline (priority):* 2/1. *Notification date:* Continuous beginning 2/25. Students must reply within 2 weeks of notification.

**CONTACT** Mrs. Andra Butler, Director of Financial Aid, Union College, 310 College Street, Barbourville, KY 40906-1499, 606-546-1224 or toll-free 800-489-8646. *Fax:* 606-546-1264. *E-mail:* abutler@unionky.edu. *Website:* http://www.unionky.edu/.

---

# UNION COLLEGE
## Lincoln, NE

| Tuition & fees: $21,970 | Average undergraduate aid package: $15,499 |
| --- | --- |

**ABOUT THE INSTITUTION** Independent Seventh-day Adventist, coed. *Awards:* associate, bachelor's, and master's degrees. 64 undergraduate majors. *Total enrollment:* 886. Undergraduates: 797. Freshmen: 156. Federal methodology is used as a basis for awarding need-based institutional aid.

**UNDERGRADUATE EXPENSES for 2015–2016** *Comprehensive fee:* $28,700 includes full-time tuition ($20,928), mandatory fees ($1042), and room and board ($6730). *College room only:* $3800. Full-time tuition and fees vary according

to course load, degree level, and program. Room and board charges vary according to housing facility. *Part-time tuition:* $872 per credit hour. Part-time tuition and fees vary according to program.

**FRESHMAN FINANCIAL AID (Fall 2014, est.)** 128 applied for aid; of those 87% were deemed to have need. 100% of freshmen with need received aid; of those 25% had need fully met. *Average percent of need met:* 72% (excluding resources awarded to replace EFC). *Average financial aid package:* $17,604 (excluding resources awarded to replace EFC). 27% of all full-time freshmen had no need and received non-need-based gift aid.

**UNDERGRADUATE FINANCIAL AID (Fall 2014, est.)** 581 applied for aid; of those 88% were deemed to have need. 100% of undergraduates with need received aid; of those 14% had need fully met. *Average percent of need met:* 62% (excluding resources awarded to replace EFC). *Average financial aid package:* $15,499 (excluding resources awarded to replace EFC). 26% of all full-time undergraduates had no need and received non-need-based gift aid.

**GIFT AID (NEED-BASED)** *Total amount:* $5,909,283 (23% federal, 1% state, 55% institutional, 21% external sources). *Receiving aid:* Freshmen: 71% (111); all full-time undergraduates: 72% (512). *Average award:* Freshmen: $14,909; Undergraduates: $11,502. *Scholarships, grants, and awards:* Federal Pell, FSEOG, state, private, college/university gift aid from institutional funds, United Negro College Fund.

**GIFT AID (NON-NEED-BASED)** *Total amount:* $1,719,885 (74% institutional, 26% external sources). *Receiving aid:* Freshmen: 12% (18). Undergraduates: 7% (48). *Average award:* Freshmen: $8878. Undergraduates: $6294. *Scholarships, grants, and awards by category:* Academic interests/achievement: general academic interests/achievements. Creative arts/performance: music. Special achievements/activities: community service, leadership, religious involvement. *Tuition waivers:* Full or partial for employees or children of employees.

**LOANS** *Student loans:* $4,027,941 (83% need-based, 17% non-need-based). 69% of past graduating class borrowed through all loan programs. *Average indebtedness per student:* $29,020. *Average need-based loan:* Freshmen: $3837. Undergraduates: $4867. *Parent loans:* $290,403 (11% need-based, 89% non-need-based). *Programs:* Federal Direct (Subsidized and Unsubsidized Stafford, PLUS), Perkins, Federal Nursing, college/university.

**WORK-STUDY** *Federal work-study:* Total amount: $181,727; jobs available.

**APPLYING FOR FINANCIAL AID** *Required financial aid forms:* FAFSA, institution's own form. *Financial aid deadline:* Continuous. *Notification date:* Continuous beginning 12/1. Students must reply by 9/1.

**CONTACT** Mrs. Taryn A. Rouse, Director of Student Financial Services, Union College, 3800 South 48th Street, Lincoln, NE 68506-4300, 402-486-2600 Ext. 2505 or toll-free 800-228-4600. *Fax:* 402-486-2952. *E-mail:* sfs@ucollege.edu. *Website:* http://www.ucollege.edu/.

---

# UNION COLLEGE
## Schenectady, NY

| Tuition & fees: $48,384 | Average undergraduate aid package: $39,479 |
| --- | --- |

**ABOUT THE INSTITUTION** Independent, coed. *Awards:* bachelor's degrees. 40 undergraduate majors. *Total enrollment:* 2,242. Undergraduates: 2,242. Freshmen: 570. Both federal and institutional methodology are used as a basis for awarding need-based institutional aid.

**UNDERGRADUATE EXPENSES for 2015–2016** *Comprehensive fee:* $60,240 includes full-time tuition ($47,913), mandatory fees ($471), and room and board ($11,856). *College room only:* $6501.

**FRESHMAN FINANCIAL AID (Fall 2014, est.)** 369 applied for aid; of those 81% were deemed to have need. 100% of freshmen with need received aid; of those 100% had need fully met. *Average percent of need met:* 100% (excluding resources awarded to replace EFC). *Average financial aid package:* $37,631 (excluding resources awarded to replace EFC). 31% of all full-time freshmen had no need and received non-need-based gift aid.

**UNDERGRADUATE FINANCIAL AID (Fall 2014, est.)** 1,313 applied for aid; of those 86% were deemed to have need. 100% of undergraduates with need received aid; of those 99% had need fully met. *Average percent of need met:* 99% (excluding resources awarded to replace EFC). *Average financial aid package:* $39,479 (excluding resources awarded to replace EFC). 27% of all full-time undergraduates had no need and received non-need-based gift aid.

**GIFT AID (NEED-BASED)** *Total amount:* $38,131,848 (5% federal, 2% state, 92% institutional, 1% external sources). *Receiving aid:* Freshmen: 50% (286); all full-time undergraduates: 50% (1,093). *Average award:* Freshmen: $33,255; Undergraduates: $33,915. *Scholarships, grants, and awards:* Federal Pell, FSEOG, state, private, college/university gift aid from institutional funds.

**GIFT AID (NON-NEED-BASED)** *Total amount:* $5,923,009 (4% federal, 2% state, 90% institutional, 4% external sources). *Receiving aid:* Freshmen: 4% (20). Undergraduates: 5% (105). *Average award:* Freshmen: $9148. Undergraduates: $9025. *Scholarships, grants, and awards by category: Academic interests/achievement:* general academic interests/achievements. *Special characteristics:* children of faculty/staff. *Tuition waivers:* Full or partial for employees or children of employees, senior citizens. *ROTC:* Army cooperative, Naval cooperative, Air Force cooperative.

**LOANS** *Student loans:* $10,681,684 (47% need-based, 53% non-need-based). 69% of past graduating class borrowed through all loan programs. *Average indebtedness per student:* $29,586. *Average need-based loan:* Freshmen: $3834. Undergraduates: $5036. *Parent loans:* $3,541,676 (100% non-need-based). *Programs:* Federal Direct (Subsidized and Unsubsidized Stafford, PLUS), Perkins, college/university.

**WORK-STUDY** *Federal work-study:* Total amount: $815,472; jobs available. *State or other work-study/employment:* Total amount: $270,000 (100% need-based). Part-time jobs available.

**APPLYING FOR FINANCIAL AID** *Required financial aid forms:* FAFSA, CSS Financial Aid PROFILE, state aid form, noncustodial (divorced/separated) parent's statement. *Financial aid deadline:* 2/1. *Notification date:* 3/25. Students must reply by 5/1.

**CONTACT** Ms. Linda Parker, Director of Financial Aid, Union College, Grant Hall, 807 Union Street, Schenectady, NY 12308-2311, 518-388-6123 or toll-free 888-843-6688. *Fax:* 518-388-8052. *E-mail:* finaid@union.edu. *Website:* http://www.union.edu/.

# UNION INSTITUTE & UNIVERSITY
## Cincinnati, OH

**CONTACT** Ms. Lisa Perdomo, Director of Financial Aid, Union Institute & University, 440 East McMillan Street, Cincinnati, OH 45206-1925, 513-861-6400 Ext. 1261 or toll-free 800-486-3116. *Fax:* 513-487-1078. *Website:* http://www.myunion.edu/.

# UNION UNIVERSITY
## Jackson, TN

| Tuition & fees: $28,190 | Average undergraduate aid package: $18,840 |
|---|---|

**ABOUT THE INSTITUTION** Independent Southern Baptist, coed. *Awards:* certificates, diplomas, associate, bachelor's, master's, and doctoral degrees. 66 undergraduate majors. *Total enrollment:* 3,846. Undergraduates: 2,717. Freshmen: 387. Federal methodology is used as a basis for awarding need-based institutional aid.

**UNDERGRADUATE EXPENSES for 2015–2016** *Application fee:* $35. *Comprehensive fee:* $36,620 includes full-time tuition ($27,470), mandatory fees ($720), and room and board ($8430). Full-time tuition and fees vary according to class time, course load, degree level, location, and program. Room and board charges vary according to board plan and housing facility. *Part-time tuition:* $915 per credit hour. *Part-time fees:* $295 per term. Part-time tuition and fees vary according to class time, course load, degree level, location, and program.

**FRESHMAN FINANCIAL AID (Fall 2014, est.)** 311 applied for aid; of those 88% were deemed to have need. 100% of freshmen with need received aid; of those 15% had need fully met. *Average percent of need met:* 66% (excluding resources awarded to replace EFC). *Average financial aid package:* $23,634 (excluding resources awarded to replace EFC). 18% of all full-time freshmen had no need and received non-need-based gift aid.

**UNDERGRADUATE FINANCIAL AID (Fall 2014, est.)** 1,768 applied for aid; of those 89% were deemed to have need. 100% of undergraduates with need received aid; of those 15% had need fully met. *Average percent of need met:* 59% (excluding resources awarded to replace EFC). *Average financial aid package:*

$18,840 (excluding resources awarded to replace EFC). 19% of all full-time undergraduates had no need and received non-need-based gift aid.

**GIFT AID (NEED-BASED)** *Total amount:* $7,290,272 (43% federal, 16% state, 41% institutional). *Receiving aid:* Freshmen: 66% (211); all full-time undergraduates: 54% (1,075). *Average award:* Freshmen: $6621; Undergraduates: $5886. *Scholarships, grants, and awards:* Federal Pell, FSEOG, state, private, college/university gift aid from institutional funds, Federal Nursing.

**GIFT AID (NON-NEED-BASED)** *Total amount:* $21,665,657 (2% federal, 15% state, 79% institutional, 4% external sources). *Receiving aid:* Freshmen: 85% (270). Undergraduates: 60% (1,190). *Average award:* Freshmen: $11,729. Undergraduates: $12,889. *Scholarships, grants, and awards by category: Academic interests/achievement:* $10,098,401 total: biological sciences, business, communication, computer science, education, engineering/technologies, English, foreign languages, general academic interests/achievements, health fields, humanities, international studies, mathematics, military science, physical sciences, premedicine, religion/biblical studies, social sciences. *Creative arts/performance:* $507,989 total: art/fine arts, cinema/film/broadcasting, debating, journalism/publications, music, theater/drama. *Special achievements/activities:* $2,190,506 total: cheerleading/drum major, community service, general special achievements/activities, leadership, memberships, religious involvement. *Special characteristics:* $3,420,362 total: children and siblings of alumni, children of current students, children of educators, children of faculty/staff, ethnic background, first-generation college students, general special characteristics, handicapped students, international students, members of minority groups, relatives of clergy, religious affiliation, siblings of current students, spouses of current students, twins, veterans, veterans' children. *Tuition waivers:* Full or partial for children of alumni, employees or children of employees. *ROTC:* Army cooperative.

**LOANS** *Student loans:* $14,554,881 (37% need-based, 63% non-need-based). 61% of past graduating class borrowed through all loan programs. *Average indebtedness per student:* $29,187. *Average need-based loan:* Freshmen: $3438. Undergraduates: $4434. *Parent loans:* $2,465,420 (100% non-need-based). *Programs:* Federal Direct (Subsidized and Unsubsidized Stafford, PLUS), Perkins, alternative loans.

**WORK-STUDY** *Federal work-study:* Total amount: $154,669; 98 jobs averaging $1827. *State or other work-study/employment:* Total amount: $333,560 (100% non-need-based). 191 part-time jobs averaging $1744.

**ATHLETIC AWARDS** Total amount: $2,215,495 (100% non-need-based).

**APPLYING FOR FINANCIAL AID** *Required financial aid forms:* FAFSA, institution's own form. *Financial aid deadline (priority):* 2/1. *Notification date:* Continuous beginning 12/1. Students must reply by 5/1 or within 2 weeks of notification.

**CONTACT** Mr. John Windham, Director of Student Financial Planning, Union University, 1050 Union University Drive, Jackson, TN 38305-3697, 731-661-5015 or toll-free 800-33-UNION. *Fax:* 731-661-5570. *E-mail:* jwindham@uu.edu. *Website:* http://www.uu.edu/.

# UNITED STATES SPORTS ACADEMY
## Daphne, AL

**CONTACT** Financial Aid Office, United States Sports Academy, One Academy Drive, Daphne, AL 36526-7055, 251-626-3303 or toll-free 800-223-2668. *Website:* http://www.ussa.edu/.

# UNITED STATES UNIVERSITY
## Chula Vista, CA

**CONTACT** Financial Aid Office, United States University, 830 Bay Boulevard, Chula Vista, CA 91911, 619-477-6310 or toll-free 888-422-3381. *Website:* http://www.usuniversity.edu/.

# UNITED STATES UNIVERSITY
## Cypress, CA

**CONTACT** Financial Aid Office, United States University, 6251 Katella Avenue, Cypress, CA 90630, 714-252-8592 or toll-free 888-422-3381.
*Website:* http://www.usuniversity.edu/.

# UNITED TALMUDICAL SEMINARY
## Brooklyn, NY

**CONTACT** Financial Aid Office, United Talmudical Seminary, 82 Lee Avenue, Brooklyn, NY 11211-7900, 718-963-9770 Ext. 309.

# UNITY COLLEGE
## Unity, ME

| Tuition & fees: $25,820 | Average undergraduate aid package: $19,914 |
|---|---|

**ABOUT THE INSTITUTION** Independent, coed. *Awards:* associate and bachelor's degrees. 15 undergraduate majors. *Total enrollment:* 577. Undergraduates: 577. Freshmen: 183. Federal methodology is used as a basis for awarding need-based institutional aid.

**UNDERGRADUATE EXPENSES for 2015–2016** *Comprehensive fee:* $35,150 includes full-time tuition ($24,620), mandatory fees ($1200), and room and board ($9330). Room and board charges vary according to board plan and housing facility. *Part-time tuition:* $890 per credit hour. Part-time tuition and fees vary according to course load.

**FRESHMAN FINANCIAL AID (Fall 2014, est.)** 176 applied for aid; of those 93% were deemed to have need. 100% of freshmen with need received aid; of those 6% had need fully met. *Average percent of need met:* 72% (excluding resources awarded to replace EFC). *Average financial aid package:* $21,137 (excluding resources awarded to replace EFC). 10% of all full-time freshmen had no need and received non-need-based gift aid.

**UNDERGRADUATE FINANCIAL AID (Fall 2014, est.)** 544 applied for aid; of those 92% were deemed to have need. 100% of undergraduates with need received aid; of those 7% had need fully met. *Average percent of need met:* 72% (excluding resources awarded to replace EFC). *Average financial aid package:* $19,914 (excluding resources awarded to replace EFC). 11% of all full-time undergraduates had no need and received non-need-based gift aid.

**GIFT AID (NEED-BASED)** *Total amount:* $7,081,044 (18% federal, 2% state, 75% institutional, 5% external sources). *Receiving aid:* Freshmen: 90% (163); all full-time undergraduates: 87% (501). *Average award:* Freshmen: $16,079; Undergraduates: $13,915. *Scholarships, grants, and awards:* Federal Pell, FSEOG, state, private, college/university gift aid from institutional funds.

**GIFT AID (NON-NEED-BASED)** *Total amount:* $634,540 (84% institutional, 16% external sources). *Receiving aid:* Freshmen: 4% (7). Undergraduates: 5% (26). *Average award:* Freshmen: $9812. Undergraduates: $6955. *Scholarships, grants, and awards by category:* Academic interests/achievement: 415 awards ($3,234,740 total): general academic interests/achievements. *Special achievements/ activities:* 31 awards ($32,850 total): community service, leadership. *Special characteristics:* 94 awards ($165,425 total): children of educators, general special characteristics, local/state students, members of minority groups. *Tuition waivers:* Full or partial for employees or children of employees. *ROTC:* Army cooperative.

**LOANS** *Student loans:* $5,157,683 (77% need-based, 23% non-need-based). *Average need-based loan:* Freshmen: $4691. Undergraduates: $5739. *Parent loans:* $1,754,876 (59% need-based, 41% non-need-based). *Programs:* Federal Direct (Subsidized and Unsubsidized Stafford, PLUS), Perkins.

**WORK-STUDY** *Federal work-study:* Total amount: $502,017; 411 jobs averaging $1221. *State or other work-study/employment:* Total amount: $19,350 (100% non-need-based). 11 part-time jobs averaging $1286.

**APPLYING FOR FINANCIAL AID** *Required financial aid form:* FAFSA. *Financial aid deadline:* Continuous. *Notification date:* Continuous beginning 3/10. Students must reply within 2 weeks of notification.

**CONTACT** Mr. Rand E. Newell, Director of Financial Aid, Unity College, 90 Quaker Hill Road, Unity, ME 04988, 207-509-7201. *Fax:* 207-512-1168. *E-mail:* rnewell@unity.edu.
*Website:* http://www.unity.edu/.

# UNIVERSIDAD ADVENTISTA DE LAS ANTILLAS
## Mayagüez, PR

**ABOUT THE INSTITUTION** Independent Seventh-day Adventist, coed. 18 undergraduate majors.

**GIFT AID (NEED-BASED)** *Scholarships, grants, and awards:* Federal Pell, FSEOG, state, college/university gift aid from institutional funds.

**GIFT AID (NON-NEED-BASED)** *Scholarships, grants, and awards by category:* Special achievements/activities: community service. Special characteristics: relatives of clergy, veterans.

**LOANS** *Programs:* Federal Direct (Subsidized and Unsubsidized Stafford, PLUS).

**WORK-STUDY** *Federal work-study:* 179 jobs averaging $756. *State or other work-study/employment:* Total amount: $267,241 (100% need-based). 278 part-time jobs averaging $961.

**APPLYING FOR FINANCIAL AID** *Required financial aid forms:* FAFSA, institution's own form.

**CONTACT** Mrs. Awilda Matos, Director of Financial Aid, Universidad Adventista de las Antillas, Box 118, Mayaguez, PR 00681-0118, 787-834-9595 Ext. 2263. *Fax:* 787-834-9597. *E-mail:* amatos@uaa.edu .
*Website:* http://www.uaa.edu/.

# UNIVERSIDAD DEL ESTE
## Carolina, PR

| Tuition & fees: N/R | Average undergraduate aid package: N/A |
|---|---|

**ABOUT THE INSTITUTION** Independent, coed. 49 undergraduate majors.

**LOANS** *Programs:* Federal Direct (Subsidized and Unsubsidized Stafford, PLUS).

**WORK-STUDY** Federal work-study jobs available.

**APPLYING FOR FINANCIAL AID** *Required financial aid form:* FAFSA. *Financial aid deadline:* Continuous. *Notification date:* Continuous beginning 2/1.

**CONTACT** Mrs. Eigna De Jess Molinari, Director of Financial Aid , Universidad del Este, Apartado 2010, Carolina, PR 00928, 787-257-7373 Ext. 3301. *E-mail:* eidejesus@suagm.edu.
*Website:* http://www.suagm.edu/une/.

# UNIVERSIDAD DEL TURABO
## Gurabo, PR

**ABOUT THE INSTITUTION** Independent, coed. *Awards:* certificates, associate, bachelor's, master's, and doctoral degrees. 63 undergraduate majors. *Total enrollment:* 17,325. Undergraduates: 14,596. Freshmen: 2,553.

**GIFT AID (NEED-BASED)** *Scholarships, grants, and awards:* Federal Pell, FSEOG, state, private, college/university gift aid from institutional funds, Federal Nursing.

**LOANS** *Programs:* Federal Direct (Subsidized and Unsubsidized Stafford).

**WORK-STUDY** *Federal work-study:* 493 jobs averaging $634.

**APPLYING FOR FINANCIAL AID** *Required financial aid form:* FAFSA.

**CONTACT** Ms. Carmen J. Rivera Lopez, Directora de la Oficina de Asistencia Economica, Universidad del Turabo, Apartado 3030, Gurabo, PR 00778-3030, 787-743-7979 Ext. 4352. *Fax:* 787-746-6777.
*Website:* http://www.suagm.edu/ut/.

# UNIVERSIDAD METROPOLITANA
## San Juan, PR

**CONTACT** Economic Assistant Director, Universidad Metropolitana, Call Box 21150, Rio Piedras, PR 00928-1150, 787-766-1717 Ext. 6586 or toll-free 800-747-8362 (out-of-state).
*Website:* http://www.suagm.edu/umet/.

# UNIVERSIDAD PENTECOSTAL MIZPA
## San Juan, PR

**CONTACT** Mrs. Myriam Juarbe, Director of Financial Aid, Universidad Pentecostal Mizpa, PO Box 20966, San Juan, PR 00928, 787-720-4476. *Fax:* 787-720-2012. *E-mail:* asistenciaeconomica@colmizpa.edu .
*Website:* http://www.mizpa.edu/.

# UNIVERSIDAD TEOLGICA DEL CARIBE
## St. Just, PR

| Tuition & fees: $4448 | Average undergraduate aid package: N/A |
|---|---|

**ABOUT THE INSTITUTION** Independent Pentecostal, coed. *Awards:* certificates, diplomas, bachelor's, master's, and doctoral degrees. 3 undergraduate majors. *Total enrollment:* 250. Undergraduates: 209. Freshmen: 10. Federal methodology is used as a basis for awarding need-based institutional aid.
**UNDERGRADUATE EXPENSES for 2015–2016** *Application fee:* $25. *One-time required fee:* $13. *Comprehensive fee:* $6848 includes full-time tuition ($3784), mandatory fees ($664), and room and board ($2400). *College room only:* $1200. Full-time tuition and fees vary according to course load. Room and board charges vary according to board plan. *Part-time tuition:* $18 per credit hour. *Part-time fees:* $130 per credit hour; $3004 per term. Part-time tuition and fees vary according to course load.
**FRESHMAN FINANCIAL AID (Fall 2013)** 13 applied for aid; of those 100% were deemed to have need. 100% of freshmen with need received aid.
**UNDERGRADUATE FINANCIAL AID (Fall 2013)** 112 applied for aid; of those 100% were deemed to have need. 100% of undergraduates with need received aid.
**GIFT AID (NEED-BASED)** *Total amount:* $719,219 (100% federal). *Receiving aid:* Freshmen: 100% (13); all full-time undergraduates: 100% (112). *Scholarships, grants, and awards:* Federal Pell, state.
**GIFT AID (NON-NEED-BASED)** *Tuition waivers:* Full or partial for employees or children of employees.
**LOANS** *Student loans:* $242,836 (100% need-based). 30% of past graduating class borrowed through all loan programs. *Programs:* Federal Direct (Subsidized and Unsubsidized Stafford).
**WORK-STUDY** Federal work-study jobs available. *State or other work-study/employment:* Part-time jobs available.
**APPLYING FOR FINANCIAL AID** *Required financial aid form:* FAFSA. *Financial aid deadline:* 6/30 (priority: 1/1). *Notification date:* Continuous.
**CONTACT** Mrs. Claudia M. Rodriguez, Financial Aid Office, Universidad Teolgica del Caribe, PO Box 901, Saint Just, PR 00978-0901, 787-761-0640 Ext. 224. *Fax:* 787-748-9220. *E-mail:* asistenciaeconomica@utcpr.edu.
*Website:* http://www.utcpr.edu/.

# UNIVERSITY AT ALBANY, STATE UNIVERSITY OF NEW YORK
## Albany, NY

| Tuition & fees (NY res): $8527 | Average undergraduate aid package: $10,639 |
|---|---|

**ABOUT THE INSTITUTION** State-supported, coed. *Awards:* certificates, bachelor's, master's, and doctoral degrees. 57 undergraduate majors. *Total enrollment:* 17,273. Undergraduates: 12,929. Freshmen: 2,548. Federal methodology is used as a basis for awarding need-based institutional aid.
**UNDERGRADUATE EXPENSES for 2015–2016** *Application fee:* $50. *Tuition, state resident:* full-time $6170; part-time $257 per credit hour. *Tuition, nonresident:* full-time $17,810; part-time $742 per credit hour. *Required fees:* full-time $2357; $60.90 per credit hour or $242.75 per term. Part-time tuition and fees vary according to course load. *College room and board:* $11,986; *Room only:* $7436. Room and board charges vary according to board plan and housing facility.
**FRESHMAN FINANCIAL AID (Fall 2014, est.)** 2,172 applied for aid; of those 74% were deemed to have need. 96% of freshmen with need received aid; of those 8% had need fully met. *Average percent of need met:* 59% (excluding resources awarded to replace EFC). *Average financial aid package:* $10,235 (excluding resources awarded to replace EFC). 8% of all full-time freshmen had no need and received non-need-based gift aid.
**UNDERGRADUATE FINANCIAL AID (Fall 2014, est.)** 9,595 applied for aid; of those 81% were deemed to have need. 97% of undergraduates with need received aid; of those 7% had need fully met. *Average percent of need met:* 61% (excluding resources awarded to replace EFC). *Average financial aid package:* $10,639 (excluding resources awarded to replace EFC). 5% of all full-time undergraduates had no need and received non-need-based gift aid.
**GIFT AID (NEED-BASED)** *Total amount:* $48,332,219 (48% federal, 37% state, 13% institutional, 2% external sources). *Receiving aid:* Freshmen: 52% (1,340); all full-time undergraduates: 54% (6,514). *Average award:* Freshmen: $8194; Undergraduates: $7358. *Scholarships, grants, and awards:* Federal Pell, FSEOG, state, private, college/university gift aid from institutional funds.
**GIFT AID (NON-NEED-BASED)** *Total amount:* $3,634,862 (7% federal, 20% state, 63% institutional, 10% external sources). *Receiving aid:* Freshmen: 2% (44). Undergraduates: 1% (140). *Average award:* Freshmen: $4343. Undergraduates: $3682. *Scholarships, grants, and awards by category:* Academic interests/achievement: general academic interests/achievements. *ROTC:* Army, Air Force cooperative.
**LOANS** *Student loans:* $59,599,707 (47% need-based, 53% non-need-based). 70% of past graduating class borrowed through all loan programs. *Average indebtedness per student:* $24,779. *Average need-based loan:* Freshmen: $3851 Undergraduates: $4553. *Parent loans:* $16,331,559 (100% non-need-based). *Programs:* Federal Direct (Subsidized and Unsubsidized Stafford, PLUS), Perkins.
**WORK-STUDY** *Federal work-study:* Total amount: $867,965; jobs available. *State or other work-study/employment:* Total amount: $1,637,548 (85% need-based, 15% non-need-based). Part-time jobs available.
**ATHLETIC AWARDS** Total amount: $5,917,914 (5% need-based, 95% non-need-based).
**APPLYING FOR FINANCIAL AID** *Required financial aid forms:* FAFSA, Tuition Assistance Program (TAP) for NY State residents. *Financial aid deadline (priority):* 3/15. *Notification date:* Continuous beginning 3/20.
**CONTACT** Stephen Kudzin, Director of Financial Aid, University at Albany, State University of New York, Student Financial Center, Campus Center G-26, 1400 Washington Avenue, Albany, NY 12222-0001, 518-442-3202. *Fax:* 518-442-5295. *E-mail:* sfc@albany.edu.
*Website:* http://www.albany.edu/.

# UNIVERSITY AT BUFFALO, THE STATE UNIVERSITY OF NEW YORK
## Buffalo, NY

| Tuition & fees (NY res): $8871 | Average undergraduate aid package: $9494 |
|---|---|

**ABOUT THE INSTITUTION** State-supported, coed. *Awards:* certificates, bachelor's, master's, and doctoral degrees. 75 undergraduate majors. *Total enrollment:* 29,944. Undergraduates: 19,829. Freshmen: 3,517. Federal methodology is used as a basis for awarding need-based institutional aid.
**UNDERGRADUATE EXPENSES for 2015–2016** *Application fee:* $50. *Tuition, state resident:* full-time $6170; part-time $257 per credit hour. *Tuition, nonresident:* full-time $19,590; part-time $816 per credit hour. *Required fees:* full-time $2701; $223.80 per credit hour. Part-time tuition and fees vary according to course load. *College room and board:* $12,400; *Room only:* $7210. Room and board charges vary according to board plan and housing facility.

**FRESHMAN FINANCIAL AID (Fall 2013)** 2,948 applied for aid; of those 81% were deemed to have need. 88% of freshmen with need received aid; of those 54% had need fully met. *Average percent of need met:* 65% (excluding resources awarded to replace EFC). *Average financial aid package:* $9558 (excluding resources awarded to replace EFC). 3% of all full-time freshmen had no need and received non-need-based gift aid.

**UNDERGRADUATE FINANCIAL AID (Fall 2013)** 15,950 applied for aid; of those 86% were deemed to have need. 84% of undergraduates with need received aid; of those 43% had need fully met. *Average percent of need met:* 64% (excluding resources awarded to replace EFC). *Average financial aid package:* $9494 (excluding resources awarded to replace EFC). 1% of all full-time undergraduates had no need and received non-need-based gift aid.

**GIFT AID (NEED-BASED) Total amount:** $60,740,649 (47% federal, 42% state, 8% institutional, 3% external sources). *Receiving aid:* Freshmen: 57% (2,057); all full-time undergraduates: 52% (9,204). *Average award:* Freshmen: $5840; Undergraduates: $5427. *Scholarships, grants, and awards:* Federal Pell, FSEOG, state, private, college/university gift aid from institutional funds, Federal Nursing.

**GIFT AID (NON-NEED-BASED) Total amount:** $13,390,064 (100% institutional). *Receiving aid:* Freshmen: 12% (452). Undergraduates: 22% (3,847). *Average award:* Freshmen: $5805. Undergraduates: $6158. *Tuition waivers:* Full or partial for minority students. *ROTC:* Army cooperative.

**LOANS Student loans:** $70,077,538 (100% need-based). 45% of past graduating class borrowed through all loan programs. *Average need-based loan:* Freshmen: $3625. Undergraduates: $4478. *Parent loans:* $11,052,693 (100% non-need-based). *Programs:* Federal Direct (Subsidized and Unsubsidized Stafford, PLUS), Perkins, Federal Nursing, college/university.

**WORK-STUDY Federal work-study:** 1,451 jobs averaging $1189. *State or other work-study/employment:* Total amount: $15,614,690 (100% need-based). 962 part-time jobs averaging $3889.

**ATHLETIC AWARDS** Total amount: $7,570,681 (100% non-need-based).

**APPLYING FOR FINANCIAL AID Required financial aid form:** FAFSA. *Financial aid deadline (priority):* 3/1. *Notification date:* Continuous beginning 2/1. Students must reply by 5/1.

**CONTACT** John Gottardy, Director of Financial Aid, University at Buffalo, the State University of New York, 232 Capen Hall, Buffalo, NY 14260, 716-645-8232 or toll-free 888-UB-ADMIT. *Fax:* 716-645-7760. *E-mail:* pollardj@buffalo.edu. *Website:* http://www.buffalo.edu/.

# UNIVERSITY OF ADVANCING TECHNOLOGY
## Tempe, AZ

**CONTACT** Financial Aid Office, University of Advancing Technology, 2625 West Baseline Road, Tempe, AZ 85283-1042, 602-383-8228 or toll-free 800-658-5744. *Fax:* 602-383-8222. *E-mail:* fa@uat.edu. *Website:* http://www.uat.edu/.

# THE UNIVERSITY OF AKRON
## Akron, OH

| Tuition & fees (OH res): $10,260 | Average undergraduate aid package: $7118 |
| --- | --- |

**ABOUT THE INSTITUTION** State-supported, coed. *Awards:* certificates, associate, bachelor's, master's, and doctoral degrees. 153 undergraduate majors. *Total enrollment:* 23,976. Undergraduates: 19,723. Freshmen: 3,780. Federal methodology is used as a basis for awarding need-based institutional aid.

**UNDERGRADUATE EXPENSES for 2015–2016 Application fee:** $45. *Tuition, state resident:* full-time $8618; part-time $359 per credit hour. *Tuition, nonresident:* full-time $17,149; part-time $714 per credit hour. *Required fees:* full-time $1642. Full-time tuition and fees vary according to course load, degree level, location, and program. Part-time tuition and fees vary according to course load, degree level, location, and program. *College room and board:* $10,968; *Room only:* $7020. Room and board charges vary according to board plan and housing facility.

**FRESHMAN FINANCIAL AID (Fall 2013)** 3,298 applied for aid; of those 86% were deemed to have need. 100% of freshmen with need received aid; of those 9% had

need fully met. *Average percent of need met:* 48% (excluding resources awarded to replace EFC). *Average financial aid package:* $7825 (excluding resources awarded to replace EFC). 10% of all full-time freshmen had no need and received non-need-based gift aid.

**UNDERGRADUATE FINANCIAL AID (Fall 2013)** 13,592 applied for aid; of those 89% were deemed to have need. 100% of undergraduates with need received aid; of those 7% had need fully met. *Average percent of need met:* 46% (excluding resources awarded to replace EFC). *Average financial aid package:* $7118 (excluding resources awarded to replace EFC). 6% of all full-time undergraduates had no need and received non-need-based gift aid.

**GIFT AID (NEED-BASED) Total amount:** $38,595,417 (88% federal, 12% state). *Receiving aid:* Freshmen: 43% (1,552); all full-time undergraduates: 41% (6,393). *Average award:* Freshmen: $5996; Undergraduates: $5711. *Scholarships, grants, and awards:* Federal Pell, FSEOG.

**GIFT AID (NON-NEED-BASED) Total amount:** $33,950,509 (6% state, 77% institutional, 17% external sources). *Receiving aid:* Freshmen: 49% (1,746). Undergraduates: 41% (6,339). *Average award:* Freshmen: $4629. Undergraduates: $4300. *Scholarships, grants, and awards by category:* Academic interests/achievement: 3,147 awards ($8,494,034 total): biological sciences, business, communication, computer science, education, engineering/technologies, English, foreign languages, general academic interests/achievements, health fields, home economics, humanities, international studies, mathematics, military science, physical sciences, premedicine, social sciences. Creative arts/performance: 114 awards ($122,193 total): applied art and design, art/fine arts, creative writing, dance, debating, general creative arts/performance, journalism/publications, music, performing arts, theater/drama. Special achievements/activities: 91 awards ($260,656 total): community service, general special achievements/activities, leadership, memberships. Special characteristics: 3,058 awards ($10,891,794 total): adult students, general special characteristics, handicapped students, international students, local/state students, members of minority groups, out-of-state students. *Tuition waivers:* Full or partial for employees or children of employees, senior citizens. *ROTC:* Army, Air Force cooperative.

**LOANS Student loans:** $51,904,565 (88% need-based, 12% non-need-based). 70% of past graduating class borrowed through all loan programs. *Average indebtedness per student:* $23,124. *Average need-based loan:* Freshmen: $4104. Undergraduates: $4535. *Parent loans:* $17,038,823 (100% non-need-based). *Programs:* Federal Direct (Subsidized and Unsubsidized Stafford, PLUS), Perkins, Federal Nursing, college/university.

**WORK-STUDY Federal work-study:** 540 jobs averaging $2147. *State or other work-study/employment:* Total amount: $9,033,876 (100% non-need-based). 3,563 part-time jobs averaging $2716.

**ATHLETIC AWARDS** Total amount: $4,661,348 (100% non-need-based).

**APPLYING FOR FINANCIAL AID Required financial aid forms:** FAFSA, institution's own form. *Financial aid deadline (priority):* 3/1. *Notification date:* Continuous beginning 3/15. Students must reply within 2 weeks of notification.

**CONTACT** Ms. Michelle Ellis, Director of Student Financial Aid, The University of Akron, 302 Buchtel Mall, Akron, OH 44325-6211, 330-972-5860 or toll-free 800-655-4884. *Fax:* 330-972-7139. *E-mail:* mellis@uakron.edu. *Website:* http://www.uakron.edu/.

# THE UNIVERSITY OF ALABAMA
## Tuscaloosa, AL

| Tuition & fees (AL res): $9826 | Average undergraduate aid package: $11,617 |
| --- | --- |

**ABOUT THE INSTITUTION** State-supported, coed. *Awards:* certificates, bachelor's, master's, and doctoral degrees. 72 undergraduate majors. *Total enrollment:* 36,047. Undergraduates: 30,752. Freshmen: 6,824. Federal methodology is used as a basis for awarding need-based institutional aid.

**UNDERGRADUATE EXPENSES for 2015–2016 Application fee:** $40. *Tuition, state resident:* full-time $9826. *Tuition, nonresident:* full-time $24,950. Full-time tuition and fees vary according to course load. Part-time tuition and fees vary according to course load. *College room and board:* $8866; *Room only:* $5600. Room and board charges vary according to board plan and housing facility.

**FRESHMAN FINANCIAL AID (Fall 2013)** 4,170 applied for aid; of those 71% were deemed to have need. 95% of freshmen with need received aid; of those 25% had need fully met. *Average percent of need met:* 55% (excluding resources awarded to replace EFC). *Average financial aid package:* $13,271 (excluding resources

awarded to replace EFC). 26% of all full-time freshmen had no need and received non-need-based gift aid.

**UNDERGRADUATE FINANCIAL AID (Fall 2013)** 14,389 applied for aid; of those 79% were deemed to have need. 97% of undergraduates with need received aid; of those 15% had need fully met. *Average percent of need met:* 50% (excluding resources awarded to replace EFC). *Average financial aid package:* $11,617 (excluding resources awarded to replace EFC). 22% of all full-time undergraduates had no need and received non-need-based gift aid.

**GIFT AID (NEED-BASED)** *Total amount:* $67,935,553 (38% federal, 4% state, 55% institutional, 3% external sources). *Receiving aid:* Freshmen: 35% (2,246); all full-time undergraduates: 31% (8,112). *Average award:* Freshmen: $11,495; Undergraduates: $9178. *Scholarships, grants, and awards:* Federal Pell, FSEOG, state, private, college/university gift aid from institutional funds, Federal Nursing.

**GIFT AID (NON-NEED-BASED)** *Total amount:* $93,535,206 (1% federal, 10% state, 85% institutional, 4% external sources). *Receiving aid:* Freshmen: 27% (1,736). Undergraduates: 19% (4,934). *Average award:* Freshmen: $12,186. Undergraduates: $12,209. *Scholarships, grants, and awards by category: Academic interests/achievement:* area/ethnic studies, biological sciences, business, communication, computer science, education, engineering/technologies, English, foreign languages, general academic interests/achievements, home economics, library science, mathematics, military science, physical sciences, premedicine, social sciences. *Creative arts/performance:* art/fine arts, cinema/film/broadcasting, creative writing, dance, debating, journalism/publications, music, theater/drama. *Special achievements/activities:* cheerleading/drum major, community service, general special achievements/activities, hobbies/interests, junior miss. *Special characteristics:* children of union members/company employees, general special characteristics, international students, out-of-state students, spouses of deceased or disabled public servants. *Tuition waivers:* Full or partial for employees or children of employees. *ROTC:* Army, Air Force.

**LOANS** *Student loans:* $119,773,128 (69% need-based, 31% non-need-based). 45% of past graduating class borrowed through all loan programs. *Average indebtedness per student:* $29,320. *Average need-based loan:* Freshmen: $3524. Undergraduates: $4328. *Parent loans:* $49,856,795 (49% need-based, 51% non-need-based). *Programs:* Federal Direct (Subsidized and Unsubsidized Stafford, PLUS), Perkins, college/university, private loans.

**WORK-STUDY** *Federal work-study:* jobs available.

**ATHLETIC AWARDS** Total amount: $11,115,349 (7% need-based, 93% non-need-based).

**APPLYING FOR FINANCIAL AID** *Required financial aid form:* FAFSA. *Financial aid deadline (priority):* 3/1. *Notification date:* 4/1. Students must reply within 3 weeks of notification.

**CONTACT** Helen Allen, Director of Financial Aid, The University of Alabama, Box 870162, Tuscaloosa, AL 35487-0162, 205-348-6756 or toll-free 800-933-BAMA. *Fax:* 205-348-2989. *E-mail:* helen.leathers@ua.edu. *Website:* http://www.ua.edu/.

# THE UNIVERSITY OF ALABAMA AT BIRMINGHAM
## Birmingham, AL

| Tuition & fees (AL res): $9280 | Average undergraduate aid package: $9148 |
|---|---|

**ABOUT THE INSTITUTION** State-supported, coed. *Awards:* certificates, bachelor's, master's, and doctoral degrees. 46 undergraduate majors. *Total enrollment:* 18,698. Undergraduates: 11,679. Freshmen: 1,748. Federal methodology is used as a basis for awarding need-based institutional aid.

**UNDERGRADUATE EXPENSES for 2015–2016** *Application fee:* $30. *Tuition, state resident:* full-time $9280; part-time $295 per credit hour. *Tuition, nonresident:* full-time $21,220; part-time $693 per credit hour. Full-time tuition and fees vary according to course load, program, and reciprocity agreements. Part-time tuition and fees vary according to course load, program, and reciprocity agreements. *Room only:* $5720. Room and board charges vary according to board plan and housing facility.

**FRESHMAN FINANCIAL AID (Fall 2014, est.)** 1,397 applied for aid; of those 76% were deemed to have need. 98% of freshmen with need received aid; of those 9% had need fully met. *Average percent of need met:* 54% (excluding resources awarded to replace EFC). *Average financial aid package:* $10,685 (excluding

resources awarded to replace EFC). 26% of all full-time freshmen had no need and received non-need-based gift aid.

**UNDERGRADUATE FINANCIAL AID (Fall 2014, est.)** 6,197 applied for aid; of those 84% were deemed to have need. 98% of undergraduates with need received aid; of those 4% had need fully met. *Average percent of need met:* 47% (excluding resources awarded to replace EFC). *Average financial aid package:* $9148 (excluding resources awarded to replace EFC). 17% of all full-time undergraduates had no need and received non-need-based gift aid.

**GIFT AID (NEED-BASED)** *Total amount:* $18,293,451 (98% federal, 1% institutional, 1% external sources). *Receiving aid:* Freshmen: 38% (650); all full-time undergraduates: 39% (3,293). *Average award:* Freshmen: $5197; Undergraduates: $4658. *Scholarships, grants, and awards:* Federal Pell, FSEOG, state, private, college/university gift aid from institutional funds, United Negro College Fund.

**GIFT AID (NON-NEED-BASED)** *Total amount:* $22,558,870 (93% institutional, 7% external sources). *Receiving aid:* Freshmen: 43% (742). Undergraduates: 24% (2,050). *Average award:* Freshmen: $6799. Undergraduates: $6939. *Scholarships, grants, and awards by category: Academic interests/achievement:* business, communication, computer science, engineering/technologies, general academic interests/achievements, health fields, mathematics. *Creative arts/performance:* art/fine arts, music, performing arts, theater/drama. *Special achievements/activities:* cheerleading/drum major, junior miss, leadership, memberships, religious involvement. *Special characteristics:* adult students, children and siblings of alumni, children of current students, children of educators, children of faculty/staff, children of public servants, children of union members/company employees, children of workers in trades, children with a deceased or disabled parent, ethnic background, first-generation college students, general special characteristics, handicapped students, international students, married students, members of minority groups, out-of-state students, parents of current students, previous college experience, public servants, relatives of clergy, siblings of current students, spouses of current students, spouses of deceased or disabled public servants, twins, veterans, veterans' children. *Tuition waivers:* Full or partial for employees or children of employees. *ROTC:* Army, Air Force cooperative.

**LOANS** *Student loans:* $51,108,157 (47% need-based, 53% non-need-based). 60% of past graduating class borrowed through all loan programs. *Average indebtedness per student:* $30,642. *Average need-based loan:* Freshmen: $3789. Undergraduates: $4141. *Parent loans:* $6,215,867 (100% non-need-based). *Programs:* Federal Direct (Subsidized and Unsubsidized Stafford, PLUS), Perkins, state, college/university.

**WORK-STUDY** *Federal work-study:* Total amount: $2,372,616; jobs available.

**ATHLETIC AWARDS** Total amount: $6,813,961 (100% non-need-based).

**APPLYING FOR FINANCIAL AID** *Required financial aid form:* FAFSA. *Financial aid deadline (priority):* 3/1. *Notification date:* Continuous beginning 3/15. Students must reply within 4 weeks of notification.

**CONTACT** Ms. Helen M. McIntyre, Office of Student Financial Aid, The University of Alabama at Birmingham, LHL 120, 1720 2nd Avenue South, Birmingham, AL 35294-0013, 205-934-8132 or toll-free 800-421-8743. *E-mail:* finaid@uab.edu. *Website:* http://www.uab.edu/.

# THE UNIVERSITY OF ALABAMA IN HUNTSVILLE
## Huntsville, AL

| Tuition & fees (AL res): $9158 | Average undergraduate aid package: $9868 |
|---|---|

**ABOUT THE INSTITUTION** State-supported, coed. *Awards:* certificates, bachelor's, master's, and doctoral degrees. 35 undergraduate majors. *Total enrollment:* 7,348. Undergraduates: 5,618. Freshmen: 724. Both federal and institutional methodology are used as a basis for awarding need-based institutional aid.

**UNDERGRADUATE EXPENSES for 2015–2016** *Application fee:* $30. *Tuition, state resident:* full-time $9158; part-time $355 per credit hour. *Tuition, nonresident:* full-time $21,232; part-time $815 per credit hour. Full-time tuition and fees vary according to course load and program. Part-time tuition and fees vary according to course load and program. *College room and board:* $8433; *Room only:* $5753. Room and board charges vary according to board plan and housing facility.

**FRESHMAN FINANCIAL AID (Fall 2014, est.)** 679 applied for aid; of those 57% were deemed to have need. 100% of freshmen with need received aid; of those 28% had need fully met. *Average percent of need met:* 71% (excluding resources awarded to replace EFC). **Average financial aid package:** $12,556 (excluding resources awarded to replace EFC). 33% of all full-time freshmen had no need and received non-need-based gift aid.

**UNDERGRADUATE FINANCIAL AID (Fall 2014, est.)** 3,616 applied for aid; of those 64% were deemed to have need. 99% of undergraduates with need received aid; of those 12% had need fully met. **Average percent of need met:** 56% (excluding resources awarded to replace EFC). **Average financial aid package:** $9868 (excluding resources awarded to replace EFC). 19% of all full-time undergraduates had no need and received non-need-based gift aid.

**GIFT AID (NEED-BASED) Total amount:** $13,537,472 (62% federal, 35% institutional, 3% external sources). **Receiving aid:** Freshmen: 48% (342); all full-time undergraduates: 43% (1,858). **Average award:** Freshmen: $9367; Undergraduates: $6814. **Scholarships, grants, and awards:** Federal Pell, FSEOG, state, private, college/university gift aid from institutional funds, Federal Nursing.

**GIFT AID (NON-NEED-BASED) Total amount:** $8,075,055 (95% institutional, 5% external sources). **Receiving aid:** Freshmen: 12% (84). Undergraduates: 4% (155). **Average award:** Freshmen: $9104. Undergraduates: $8291. **Scholarships, grants, and awards by category:** Academic interests/achievement: biological sciences, business, communication, computer science, education, engineering/technologies, English, foreign languages, general academic interests/achievements, health fields, humanities, mathematics, physical sciences, social sciences. Creative arts/performance: art/fine arts, music. Special achievements/activities: cheerleading/drum major, community service, general special achievements/activities, junior miss, leadership. Special characteristics: general special characteristics, local/state students, members of minority groups. **Tuition waivers:** Full or partial for employees or children of employees. **ROTC:** Army cooperative.

**LOANS Student loans:** $24,514,842 (83% need-based, 17% non-need-based). 52% of past graduating class borrowed through all loan programs. Average indebtedness per student: $29,421. **Average need-based loan:** Freshmen: $5565. Undergraduates: $7858. **Parent loans:** $1,778,043 (44% need-based, 56% non-need-based). **Programs:** Federal Direct (Subsidized and Unsubsidized Stafford, PLUS).

**WORK-STUDY Federal work-study:** Total amount: $312,580; jobs available.

**ATHLETIC AWARDS** Total amount: $2,534,762 (25% need-based, 75% non-need-based).

**APPLYING FOR FINANCIAL AID Required financial aid form:** FAFSA. **Financial aid deadline:** 7/31 (priority: 4/1). **Notification date:** Continuous beginning 4/1. Students must reply within 2 weeks of notification.

**CONTACT** Mr. Andrew Weaver, Director of Student Financial Services, The University of Alabama in Huntsville, 301 Sparkman Drive, UC Room 212, Huntsville, AL 35899, 256-824-6241 or toll-free 800-UAH-CALL. Fax: 256-824-6212. E-mail: finaid@uah.edu. Website: http://www.uah.edu/.

# UNIVERSITY OF ALASKA ANCHORAGE
## Anchorage, AK

| Tuition & fees (AK res): $6074 | Average undergraduate aid package: $8793 |
| --- | --- |

**ABOUT THE INSTITUTION** State-supported, coed. **Awards:** certificates, associate, bachelor's, master's, and doctoral degrees. 107 undergraduate majors. **Total enrollment:** 17,321. Undergraduates: 16,463. Freshmen: 1,903. Federal methodology is used as a basis for awarding need-based institutional aid.

**UNDERGRADUATE EXPENSES for 2015–2016 Application fee:** $50. **Tuition, state resident:** full-time $5220; part-time $174 per credit. **Tuition, nonresident:** full-time $18,540; part-time $618 per credit. **Required fees:** full-time $854. Full-time tuition and fees vary according to course level and location. Part-time tuition and fees vary according to course level and location. **College room and board:** $11,179. Room and board charges vary according to board plan and housing facility.

**FRESHMAN FINANCIAL AID (Fall 2014, est.)** 1,204 applied for aid; of those 65% were deemed to have need. 98% of freshmen with need received aid; of those 31% had need fully met. **Average percent of need met:** 74% (excluding resources awarded to replace EFC). **Average financial aid package:** $8423 (excluding resources awarded to replace EFC). 8% of all full-time freshmen had no need and received non-need-based gift aid.

**UNDERGRADUATE FINANCIAL AID (Fall 2014, est.)** 5,196 applied for aid; of those 72% were deemed to have need. 96% of undergraduates with need received aid; of those 24% had need fully met. **Average percent of need met:** 70% (excluding resources awarded to replace EFC). **Average financial aid package:** $8793 (excluding resources awarded to replace EFC). 7% of all full-time undergraduates had no need and received non-need-based gift aid.

**GIFT AID (NEED-BASED) Total amount:** $29,182,214 (61% federal, 18% state, 10% institutional, 11% external sources). **Receiving aid:** Freshmen: 49% (677); all full-time undergraduates: 44% (3,063). **Average award:** Freshmen: $2818; Undergraduates: $2950. **Scholarships, grants, and awards:** Federal Pell, FSEOG, state, private, college/university gift aid from institutional funds.

**GIFT AID (NON-NEED-BASED) Total amount:** $6,584,068 (47% state, 23% institutional, 30% external sources). **Average award:** Freshmen: $2696. Undergraduates: $2546. **Scholarships, grants, and awards by category:** Academic interests/achievement: biological sciences, business, communication, computer science, education, engineering/technologies, English, general academic interests/achievements, health fields, humanities, mathematics, social sciences. Creative arts/performance: art/fine arts, dance, debating, music, performing arts. Special achievements/activities: general special achievements/activities, leadership. Special characteristics: children and siblings of alumni, children of current students, children of educators, children of faculty/staff. **ROTC:** Army, Air Force.

**LOANS Student loans:** $46,823,054 (73% need-based, 27% non-need-based). 49% of past graduating class borrowed through all loan programs. Average indebtedness per student: $26,569. **Average need-based loan:** Freshmen: $3134. Undergraduates: $3940. **Parent loans:** $14,664,632 (47% need-based, 53% non-need-based). **Programs:** Federal Direct (Subsidized and Unsubsidized Stafford, PLUS), state.

**WORK-STUDY Federal work-study:** Total amount: $1,425,002; jobs available.

**ATHLETIC AWARDS** Total amount: $1,433,746 (24% need-based, 76% non-need-based).

**APPLYING FOR FINANCIAL AID Financial aid deadline:** Continuous. **Notification date:** Continuous beginning 3/15. Students must reply within 4 weeks of notification.

**CONTACT** Sonya F. Stein, Director of Student Financial Assistance, University of Alaska Anchorage, PO Box 141608, Anchorage, AK 99514-1608, 907-786-1517. Fax: 907-786-6122. E-mail: sefisher@uaa.alaska.edu. Website: http://www.uaa.alaska.edu/.

# UNIVERSITY OF ALASKA FAIRBANKS
## Fairbanks, AK

| Tuition & fees (AK res): $7370 | Average undergraduate aid package: $7745 |
| --- | --- |

**ABOUT THE INSTITUTION** State-supported, coed. **Awards:** certificates, associate, bachelor's, master's, and doctoral degrees. 73 undergraduate majors. **Total enrollment:** 8,700. Undergraduates: 7,563. Freshmen: 942. Federal methodology is used as a basis for awarding need-based institutional aid.

**UNDERGRADUATE EXPENSES for 2015–2016 Application fee:** $50. **Tuition, state resident:** full-time $6060; part-time $183 per credit. **Tuition, nonresident:** full-time $20,040; part-time $649 per credit. **Required fees:** full-time $1310. Full-time tuition and fees vary according to course level, course load, location, and reciprocity agreements. Part-time tuition and fees vary according to course level, course load, location, and reciprocity agreements. **College room and board:** $8242; Room only: $3922. Room and board charges vary according to board plan, housing facility, and location.

**FRESHMAN FINANCIAL AID (Fall 2013)** 724 applied for aid; of those 59% were deemed to have need. 96% of freshmen with need received aid; of those 21% had need fully met. **Average percent of need met:** 58% (excluding resources awarded to replace EFC). **Average financial aid package:** $7630 (excluding resources awarded to replace EFC). 18% of all full-time freshmen had no need and received non-need-based gift aid.

**UNDERGRADUATE FINANCIAL AID (Fall 2013)** 2,873 applied for aid; of those 68% were deemed to have need. 96% of undergraduates with need received aid; of those 12% had need fully met. **Average percent of need met:** 53% (excluding resources awarded to replace EFC). **Average financial aid package:** $7745 (excluding resources awarded to replace EFC). 14% of all full-time undergraduates had no need and received non-need-based gift aid.

**GIFT AID (NEED-BASED)** *Total amount:* $12,410,867 (54% federal, 16% state, 16% institutional, 14% external sources). *Receiving aid:* Freshmen: 49% (379); all full-time undergraduates: 46% (1,649). *Average award:* Freshmen: $6694; Undergraduates: $6262. *Scholarships, grants, and awards:* Federal Pell, FSEOG, state, private, college/university gift aid from institutional funds.

**GIFT AID (NON-NEED-BASED)** *Total amount:* $4,842,611 (39% state, 37% institutional, 24% external sources). *Receiving aid:* Freshmen: 7% (56). Undergraduates: 4% (137). *Average award:* Freshmen: $3614. Undergraduates: $3519. *Scholarships, grants, and awards by category:* Academic interests/achievement: agriculture, biological sciences, engineering/technologies, general academic interests/achievements, mathematics, physical sciences. *Creative arts/performance:* applied art and design, art/fine arts, creative writing, music, theater/drama. *Special achievements/activities:* community service, general special achievements/activities. *Special characteristics:* local/state students. *Tuition waivers:* Full or partial for children of alumni, employees or children of employees, senior citizens. *ROTC:* Army.

**LOANS** *Student loans:* $15,476,604 (82% need-based, 18% non-need-based). 51% of past graduating class borrowed through all loan programs. *Average indebtedness per student:* $29,906. *Average need-based loan:* Freshmen: $2926. Undergraduates: $3833. *Parent loans:* $1,842,414 (46% need-based, 54% non-need-based). *Programs:* Federal Direct (Subsidized and Unsubsidized Stafford, PLUS), state.

**WORK-STUDY** *Federal work-study:* 50 jobs averaging $5332.

**ATHLETIC AWARDS** Total amount: $1,000,689 (26% need-based, 74% non-need-based).

**APPLYING FOR FINANCIAL AID** *Required financial aid form:* FAFSA. *Financial aid deadline:* 7/1 (priority: 2/15). *Notification date:* Continuous beginning 3/1. Students must reply within 2 weeks of notification.

**CONTACT** Deanna Dieringer, Director of Financial Aid, University of Alaska Fairbanks, PO Box 756360, Fairbanks, AK 99775-6360, 907-474-7256 or toll-free 800-478-1823. *Fax:* 907-474-7065. *E-mail:* uaf-financialaid@alaska.edu. *Website:* http://www.uaf.edu/.

# UNIVERSITY OF ALASKA SOUTHEAST
## Juneau, AK

**ABOUT THE INSTITUTION** State-supported, coed. 27 undergraduate majors.

**GIFT AID (NEED-BASED)** *Scholarships, grants, and awards:* Federal Pell, FSEOG, state, private, college/university gift aid from institutional funds.

**GIFT AID (NON-NEED-BASED)** *Scholarships, grants, and awards by category:* Academic interests/achievement: general academic interests/achievements. *Creative arts/performance:* general creative arts/performance. *Special achievements/activities:* leadership. *Special characteristics:* local/state students.

**LOANS** *Programs:* Federal Direct (Subsidized and Unsubsidized Stafford, PLUS), state.

**APPLYING FOR FINANCIAL AID** *Required financial aid form:* FAFSA.

**CONTACT** Ms. Corinne Soltis, Director of Financial Aid, University of Alaska Southeast, 11120 Glacier Highway, Juneau, AK 99801-8680, 907-796-6255 or toll-free 877-465-4827. *Fax:* 907-796-6250. *E-mail:* casoltis@uas.alaska.edu. *Website:* http://www.uas.alaska.edu/.

# UNIVERSITY OF ANTELOPE VALLEY
## Lancaster, CA

**CONTACT** Financial Aid Office, University of Antelope Valley, 44055 North Sierra Highway, Lancaster, CA 93534, 661-726-1911. *Website:* http://www.uav.edu/.

# THE UNIVERSITY OF ARIZONA
## Tucson, AZ

| Tuition & fees (AZ res): $10,581 | Average undergraduate aid package: $12,790 |
|---|---|

**ABOUT THE INSTITUTION** State-supported, coed. *Awards:* certificates, bachelor's, master's, and doctoral degrees. 109 undergraduate majors. *Total enrollment:* 42,236. Undergraduates: 32,987. Freshmen: 7,744. Both federal and institutional methodology are used as a basis for awarding need-based institutional aid.

**UNDERGRADUATE EXPENSES for 2015–2016** *Application fee:* $50. *Tuition, state resident:* full-time $9576; part-time $684 per credit hour. *Tuition, nonresident:* full-time $27,374; part-time $1141 per credit hour. *Required fees:* full-time $1005; $87 per credit hour. Full-time tuition and fees vary according to course level, course load, degree level, location, program, reciprocity agreements, and student level. Part-time tuition and fees vary according to course level, course load, degree level, location, program, reciprocity agreements, and student level. *College room and board:* $9700; *Room only:* $7000. Room and board charges vary according to board plan and housing facility. *Payment plan:* Guaranteed tuition.

**FRESHMAN FINANCIAL AID (Fall 2014, est.)** 4,762 applied for aid; of those 76% were deemed to have need. 98% of freshmen with need received aid; of those 12% had need fully met. *Average percent of need met:* 62% (excluding resources awarded to replace EFC). *Average financial aid package:* $12,564 (excluding resources awarded to replace EFC). 26% of all full-time freshmen had no need and received non-need-based gift aid.

**UNDERGRADUATE FINANCIAL AID (Fall 2014, est.)** 18,554 applied for aid; of those 84% were deemed to have need. 97% of undergraduates with need received aid; of those 9% had need fully met. *Average percent of need met:* 60% (excluding resources awarded to replace EFC). *Average financial aid package:* $12,790 (excluding resources awarded to replace EFC). 19% of all full-time undergraduates had no need and received non-need-based gift aid.

**GIFT AID (NEED-BASED)** *Total amount:* $155,450,236 (33% federal, 57% institutional, 10% external sources). *Receiving aid:* Freshmen: 54% (3,393); all full-time undergraduates: 49% (13,961). *Average award:* Freshmen: $11,041; Undergraduates: $10,726. *Scholarships, grants, and awards:* Federal Pell, FSEOG, state, private, college/university gift aid from institutional funds, Federal Nursing.

**GIFT AID (NON-NEED-BASED)** *Total amount:* $59,862,268 (4% federal, 74% institutional, 22% external sources). *Receiving aid:* Freshmen: 6% (392). Undergraduates: 4% (1,092). *Average award:* Freshmen: $7129. Undergraduates: $8099. *Scholarships, grants, and awards by category:* Academic interests/achievement: agriculture, architecture, biological sciences, business, education, engineering/technologies, general academic interests/achievements, humanities, military science, physical sciences, religion/biblical studies. *Creative arts/performance:* art/fine arts, dance, music, performing arts, theater/drama. *Special characteristics:* children of faculty/staff, ethnic background, international students. *Tuition waivers:* Full or partial for employees or children of employees. *ROTC:* Army, Naval, Air Force.

**LOANS** *Student loans:* $100,303,978 (88% need-based, 12% non-need-based). 52% of past graduating class borrowed through all loan programs. *Average indebtedness per student:* $22,761. *Average need-based loan:* Freshmen: $3277. Undergraduates: $4293. *Parent loans:* $45,025,932 (74% need-based, 26% non-need-based). *Programs:* Federal Direct (Subsidized and Unsubsidized Stafford, PLUS), Perkins, Federal Nursing, college/university.

**WORK-STUDY** *Federal work-study:* Total amount: $2,147,457; jobs available. *State or other work-study/employment:* Total amount: $20,143,438 (67% need-based, 33% non-need-based). Part-time jobs available.

**ATHLETIC AWARDS** Total amount: $7,297,785 (44% need-based, 56% non-need-based).

**APPLYING FOR FINANCIAL AID** *Required financial aid form:* FAFSA. *Financial aid deadline:* Continuous. *Notification date:* Continuous.

**CONTACT** Elizabeth Acree, Registrar, The University of Arizona, PO Box 210067, Tucson, AZ 85721-0067, 520-621-3432. *Fax:* 520-621-9473. *E-mail:* askaid@arizona.edu. *Website:* http://www.arizona.edu/.

# UNIVERSITY OF ARKANSAS
## Fayetteville, AR

| Tuition & fees (AR res): $8210 | Average undergraduate aid package: $9264 |
|---|---|

**ABOUT THE INSTITUTION** State-supported, coed. *Awards:* certificates, bachelor's, master's, and doctoral degrees. 78 undergraduate majors. *Total enrollment:* 26,237. Undergraduates: 21,836. Freshmen: 4,571. Federal methodology is used as a basis for awarding need-based institutional aid.

**UNDERGRADUATE EXPENSES** for 2015–2016 *Application fee:* $40. *Tuition, state resident:* full-time $6824; part-time $227.44 per credit hour. *Tuition, nonresident:* full-time $18,914; part-time $630.45 per credit hour. *Required fees:* full-time $1386. Full-time tuition and fees vary according to course load, location, and program. Part-time tuition and fees vary according to course load, location, and program. *College room and board:* $9454; *Room only:* $6014. Room and board charges vary according to board plan, housing facility, and location.

**FRESHMAN FINANCIAL AID (Fall 2014, est.)** 3,631 applied for aid; of those 60% were deemed to have need. 96% of freshmen with need received aid; of those 17% had need fully met. *Average percent of need met:* 58% (excluding resources awarded to replace EFC). *Average financial aid package:* $8941 (excluding resources awarded to replace EFC). 16% of all full-time freshmen had no need and received non-need-based gift aid.

**UNDERGRADUATE FINANCIAL AID (Fall 2014, est.)** 12,335 applied for aid; of those 70% were deemed to have need. 95% of undergraduates with need received aid; of those 14% had need fully met. *Average percent of need met:* 57% (excluding resources awarded to replace EFC). *Average financial aid package:* $9264 (excluding resources awarded to replace EFC). 14% of all full-time undergraduates had no need and received non-need-based gift aid.

**GIFT AID (NEED-BASED)** *Total amount:* $44,263,396 (48% federal, 27% state, 19% institutional, 6% external sources). *Receiving aid:* Freshmen: 39% (1,765); all full-time undergraduates: 35% (6,647). *Average award:* Freshmen: $6662; Undergraduates: $6706. *Scholarships, grants, and awards:* Federal Pell, FSEOG, state, private, college/university gift aid from institutional funds.

**GIFT AID (NON-NEED-BASED)** *Total amount:* $32,014,334 (48% state, 45% institutional, 7% external sources). *Receiving aid:* Freshmen: 6% (259). Undergraduates: 4% (710). *Average award:* Freshmen: $4056. Undergraduates: $4895. *Scholarships, grants, and awards by category: Academic interests/achievement:* agriculture, architecture, area/ethnic studies, biological sciences, business, communication, computer science, education, engineering/technologies, English, foreign languages, general academic interests/achievements, health fields, home economics, humanities, international studies, mathematics, military science, physical sciences, pre-medicine, social sciences. *Creative arts/performance:* art/fine arts, journalism/publications, music, theater/drama. *Special achievements/activities:* cheerleading/drum major, community service, general special achievements/activities, leadership. *Special characteristics:* adult students, children and siblings of alumni, children of faculty/staff, children of union members/company employees, children of workers in trades, children with a deceased or disabled parent, ethnic background, first-generation college students, handicapped students, international students, local/state students, married students, members of minority groups, out-of-state students, previous college experience, veterans, veterans' children. *Tuition waivers:* Full or partial for employees or children of employees, senior citizens. *ROTC:* Army, Air Force.

**LOANS** *Student loans:* $68,747,354 (66% need-based, 34% non-need-based). 44% of past graduating class borrowed through all loan programs. *Average indebtedness per student:* $24,120. *Average need-based loan:* Freshmen: $3475. Undergraduates: $4362. *Parent loans:* $16,883,687 (30% need-based, 70% non-need-based). *Programs:* Federal Direct (Subsidized and Unsubsidized Stafford, PLUS), Perkins, Federal Nursing, state, college/university, alternative loans.

**WORK-STUDY** *Federal work-study:* Total amount: $3,055,391; 1,092 jobs averaging $2797.

**ATHLETIC AWARDS** Total amount: $5,769,361 (37% need-based, 63% non-need-based).

**APPLYING FOR FINANCIAL AID** *Required financial aid form:* FAFSA. *Financial aid deadline (priority):* 3/15. *Notification date:* Continuous beginning 4/1. Students must reply within 4 weeks of notification.

**CONTACT** Wendy Stouffer, Executive Director of Financial Aid and Academic Scholarships, University of Arkansas, 114 Silas H. Hunt Hall, Fayetteville, AR 72701-1201, 479-575-3078 or toll-free 800-377-8632. *Fax:* 479-575-7790. *E-mail:* wstouff@uark.edu. *Website:* http://www.uark.edu/.

# UNIVERSITY OF ARKANSAS AT LITTLE ROCK
## Little Rock, AR

**CONTACT** Financial Aid Office, University of Arkansas at Little Rock, 2801 South University Avenue, Little Rock, AR 72204-1099, 501-569-3035 or toll-free 800-482-8892. *E-mail:* financialaid@ualr.edu. *Website:* http://www.ualr.edu/.

# UNIVERSITY OF ARKANSAS AT MONTICELLO
## Monticello, AR

**CONTACT** Susan Brewer, Director of Financial Aid, University of Arkansas at Monticello, PO Box 3470, Monticello, AR 71656, 870-460-1050 or toll-free 800-844-1826. *Fax:* 870-460-1450. *E-mail:* brewers@uamont.edu. *Website:* http://www.uamont.edu/.

# UNIVERSITY OF ARKANSAS AT PINE BLUFF
## Pine Bluff, AR

**CONTACT** Mrs. Carolyn Iverson, Director of Financial Aid, University of Arkansas at Pine Bluff, 1200 North University Drive, PO Box 4985, Pine Bluff, AR 71601, 870-575-8303 or toll-free 800-264-6585. *Fax:* 870-575-4622. *E-mail:* iverson_c@uapb.edu. *Website:* http://www.uapb.edu/.

# UNIVERSITY OF ARKANSAS FOR MEDICAL SCIENCES
## Little Rock, AR

**CONTACT** Mr. Paul Carter, Director of Financial Aid, University of Arkansas for Medical Sciences, 4301 West Markham Street, MS 601, Little Rock, AR 72205, 501-686-5451. *Fax:* 501-686-5661. *E-mail:* pvcarter@uams.edu. *Website:* http://www.uams.edu/.

# UNIVERSITY OF ARKANSAS–FORT SMITH
## Fort Smith, AR

**CONTACT** Tammy Malone, Interim Financial Aid Director, University of Arkansas–Fort Smith, 5210 Grand Avenue, Fort Smith, AR 72913, 479-788-7099 or toll-free 888-512-5466. *Fax:* 479-788-7095. *E-mail:* tmalone@uafortsmith.edu. *Website:* http://uafs.edu/.

# UNIVERSITY OF BALTIMORE
## Baltimore, MD

**CONTACT** Financial Aid Office, University of Baltimore, 1420 North Charles Street, CH 123, Baltimore, MD 21201-5779, 410-837-4763. *Fax:* 410-837-5493. *E-mail:* financial-aid@ubalt.edu. *Website:* http://www.ubalt.edu/.

# UNIVERSITY OF BRIDGEPORT
## Bridgeport, CT

| Tuition & fees: $29,920 | Average undergraduate aid package: $25,487 |
|---|---|

**ABOUT THE INSTITUTION** Independent, coed. *Awards:* certificates, associate, bachelor's, master's, and doctoral degrees. 37 undergraduate majors. *Total enrollment:* 5,191. Undergraduates: 3,021. Freshmen: 537. Federal methodology is used as a basis for awarding need-based institutional aid.

**UNDERGRADUATE EXPENSES for 2015–2016 *Application fee:* $25. *Comprehensive fee:* $42,630 includes full-time tuition ($27,900), mandatory fees ($2020), and room and board ($12,710). Full-time tuition and fees vary according to course load and program. Room and board charges vary according to board plan and housing facility. *Part-time tuition:* $930 per credit hour. *Part-time fees:* $200 per term. Part-time tuition and fees vary according to course load and program.

**FRESHMAN FINANCIAL AID (Fall 2014, est.)** 485 applied for aid; of those 97% were deemed to have need. 99% of freshmen with need received aid; of those 5% had need fully met. *Average percent of need met:* 62% (excluding resources awarded to replace EFC). *Average financial aid package:* $26,551 (excluding resources awarded to replace EFC). 9% of all full-time freshmen had no need and received non-need-based gift aid.

**UNDERGRADUATE FINANCIAL AID (Fall 2014, est.)** 1,893 applied for aid; of those 96% were deemed to have need. 99% of undergraduates with need received aid; of those 4% had need fully met. *Average percent of need met:* 59% (excluding resources awarded to replace EFC). *Average financial aid package:* $25,487 (excluding resources awarded to replace EFC). 13% of all full-time undergraduates had no need and received non-need-based gift aid.

**GIFT AID (NEED-BASED) *Total amount:* $15,444,098 (45% federal, 7% state, 48% institutional). *Receiving aid:* Freshmen: 75% (400); all full-time undergraduates: 80% (1,803). *Average award:* Freshmen: $6015; Undergraduates: $5625. *Scholarships, grants, and awards:* Federal Pell, FSEOG, state, private, college/university gift aid from institutional funds.

**GIFT AID (NON-NEED-BASED) *Total amount:* $21,320,579 (99% institutional, 1% external sources). *Receiving aid:* Freshmen: 87% (464). Undergraduates: 74% (1,668). *Average award:* Freshmen: $14,000. Undergraduates: $9000. *Scholarships, grants, and awards by category:* Academic interests/achievement: general academic interests/achievements. Creative arts/performance: applied art and design, music. Special characteristics: children of faculty/staff, international students, local/state students, previous college experience. *Tuition waivers:* Full or partial for employees or children of employees, senior citizens.

**LOANS *Student loans:* $18,212,107 (51% need-based, 49% non-need-based). 68% of past graduating class borrowed through all loan programs. *Average indebtedness per student:* $21,200. *Average need-based loan:* Freshmen: $3245. Undergraduates: $4224. *Parent loans:* $5,067,970 (100% non-need-based). *Programs:* Federal Direct (Subsidized and Unsubsidized Stafford, PLUS), Perkins.

**WORK-STUDY *Federal work-study:* Total amount: $401,693; jobs available. *State or other work-study/employment:* Part-time jobs available.

**ATHLETIC AWARDS** Total amount: $4,121,676 (100% non-need-based).

**APPLYING FOR FINANCIAL AID *Required financial aid form:* FAFSA. *Financial aid deadline (priority):* 3/1. *Notification date:* Continuous beginning 3/1. Students must reply by 5/15 or within 4 weeks of notification.

**CONTACT** Ms. Christine E. Falzerano, Director of Student Financial Services, University of Bridgeport, 126 Park Avenue, Bridgeport, CT 06604, 203-576-4568 or toll-free 800-EXCEL-UB. *Fax:* 203-576-4570. *E-mail:* finaid@bridgeport.edu. *Website:* http://www.bridgeport.edu/.

# UNIVERSITY OF CALIFORNIA, BERKELEY
## Berkeley, CA

| Tuition & fees (CA res): $12,972 | Average undergraduate aid package: $23,345 |
|---|---|

**ABOUT THE INSTITUTION** State-supported, coed. *Awards:* certificates, bachelor's, master's, and doctoral degrees. 90 undergraduate majors. *Total enrollment:* 37,565. Undergraduates: 27,126. Freshmen: 5,466. Federal methodology is used as a basis for awarding need-based institutional aid.

**UNDERGRADUATE EXPENSES for 2015–2016 *Application fee:* $70. *Tuition, state resident:* full-time $11,220. *Tuition, nonresident:* full-time $35,850. *Required fees:* full-time $1752. *College room and board:* $15,438. Room and board charges vary according to board plan and housing facility.

**FRESHMAN FINANCIAL AID (Fall 2014, est.)** 4,018 applied for aid; of those 68% were deemed to have need. 100% of freshmen with need received aid; of those 74% had need fully met. *Average percent of need met:* 89% (excluding resources awarded to replace EFC). *Average financial aid package:* $26,871 (excluding resources awarded to replace EFC). 2% of all full-time freshmen had no need and received non-need-based gift aid.

**UNDERGRADUATE FINANCIAL AID (Fall 2014, est.)** 16,463 applied for aid; of those 82% were deemed to have need. 100% of undergraduates with need received aid; of those 78% had need fully met. *Average percent of need met:* 85% (excluding resources awarded to replace EFC). *Average financial aid package:* $23,345 (excluding resources awarded to replace EFC). 2% of all full-time undergraduates had no need and received non-need-based gift aid.

**GIFT AID (NEED-BASED) *Total amount:* $248,118,938 (17% federal, 32% state, 49% institutional, 2% external sources). *Receiving aid:* Freshmen: 50% (2,713); all full-time undergraduates: 51% (13,358). *Average award:* Freshmen: $26,442; Undergraduates: $22,135. *Scholarships, grants, and awards:* Federal Pell, FSEOG, state, private, college/university gift aid from institutional funds.

**GIFT AID (NON-NEED-BASED) *Total amount:* $12,415,029 (5% federal, 2% state, 57% institutional, 36% external sources). *Receiving aid:* Freshmen: 2% (115). Undergraduates: 3% (668). *Average award:* Freshmen: $5596. Undergraduates: $5925. *Scholarships, grants, and awards by category:* Academic interests/achievement: general academic interests/achievements. *ROTC:* Army, Naval, Air Force.

**LOANS *Student loans:* $41,976,041 (76% need-based, 24% non-need-based). 39% of past graduating class borrowed through all loan programs. *Average indebtedness per student:* $17,584. *Average need-based loan:* Freshmen: $4374. Undergraduates: $4640. *Parent loans:* $19,506,883 (26% need-based, 74% non-need-based). *Programs:* Federal Direct (Subsidized and Unsubsidized Stafford, PLUS), Perkins.

**WORK-STUDY *Federal work-study:* Total amount: $4,691,282; jobs available. *State or other work-study/employment:* Total amount: $2,612,896 (100% need-based). Part-time jobs available.

**ATHLETIC AWARDS** Total amount: $10,636,396 (28% need-based, 72% non-need-based).

**APPLYING FOR FINANCIAL AID *Required financial aid forms:* FAFSA, Cal Grant forms, GPA verification form (CA residents only). *Financial aid deadline:* 3/2. *Notification date:* 3/31. Students must reply by 5/1.

**CONTACT** Kathy Bradley, Administrative Specialist, University of California, Berkeley, 225 Sproul Hall, Berkeley, CA 94720-1960, 510-642-0649. *Fax:* 510-643-5526. *E-mail:* kbradley@berkeley.edu. *Website:* http://www.berkeley.edu/.

# UNIVERSITY OF CALIFORNIA, DAVIS
## Davis, CA

| Tuition & fees (CA res): $13,896 | Average undergraduate aid package: $20,093 |
|---|---|

**ABOUT THE INSTITUTION** State-supported, coed. *Awards:* certificates, bachelor's, master's, and doctoral degrees. 83 undergraduate majors. *Total enrollment:* 34,508. Undergraduates: 27,728. Freshmen: 5,398. Both federal and institutional methodology are used as a basis for awarding need-based institutional aid.

**UNDERGRADUATE EXPENSES for 2015–2016 *Application fee:* $70. *Tuition, state resident:* full-time $11,220. *Tuition, nonresident:* full-time $34,098. *Required fees:* full-time $2676. *College room and board:* $14,218. Room and board charges vary according to board plan.

**FRESHMAN FINANCIAL AID (Fall 2014, est.)** 4,313 applied for aid; of those 79% were deemed to have need. 98% of freshmen with need received aid; of those 16% had need fully met. *Average percent of need met:* 81% (excluding resources awarded to replace EFC). *Average financial aid package:* $22,899 (excluding resources awarded to replace EFC). 5% of all full-time freshmen had no need and received non-need-based gift aid.

**UNDERGRADUATE FINANCIAL AID (Fall 2014, est.)** 20,007 applied for aid; of those 87% were deemed to have need. 99% of undergraduates with need received aid; of those 15% had need fully met. **Average percent of need met:** 78% (excluding resources awarded to replace EFC). **Average financial aid package:** $20,093 (excluding resources awarded to replace EFC). 4% of all full-time undergraduates had no need and received non-need-based gift aid.

**GIFT AID (NEED-BASED) Total amount:** $292,735,011 (20% federal, 35% state, 43% institutional, 2% external sources). **Receiving aid:** Freshmen: 62% (3,312); all full-time undergraduates: 63% (16,915). **Average award:** Freshmen: $19,277; Undergraduates: $16,993. **Scholarships, grants, and awards:** Federal Pell, FSEOG, state, private, college/university gift aid from institutional funds.

**GIFT AID (NON-NEED-BASED) Total amount:** $14,234,330 (16% federal, 6% state, 41% institutional, 37% external sources). **Receiving aid:** Freshmen: 1% (74). Undergraduates: 1% (226). **Average award:** Freshmen: $4080. Undergraduates: $5626. **Scholarships, grants, and awards by category:** Academic interests/achievement: agriculture, area/ethnic studies, biological sciences, business, communication, computer science, engineering/technologies, English, foreign languages, general academic interests/achievements, health fields, home economics, humanities, international studies, mathematics, premedicine, religion/biblical studies, social sciences. **ROTC:** Army, Naval cooperative, Air Force cooperative.

**LOANS Student loans:** $59,914,063 (84% need-based, 16% non-need-based). 56% of past graduating class borrowed through all loan programs. **Average indebtedness per student:** $19,705. **Average need-based loan:** Freshmen: $5684. Undergraduates: $5401. **Parent loans:** $24,575,884 (20% need-based, 80% non-need-based). **Programs:** Federal Direct (Subsidized and Unsubsidized Stafford, PLUS), Perkins, college/university.

**WORK-STUDY Federal work-study:** Total amount: $2,660,306; jobs available. **State or other work-study/employment:** Total amount: $65,000 (100% need-based). Part-time jobs available.

**ATHLETIC AWARDS** Total amount: $4,231,340 (6% need-based, 94% non-need-based).

**APPLYING FOR FINANCIAL AID Required financial aid forms:** FAFSA, state aid form. **Financial aid deadline (priority):** 3/2. **Notification date:** Continuous beginning 3/16.

**CONTACT** Deborah G. Agee, Director of Financial Aid and Scholarships, University of California, Davis, One Shields Avenue, 2116 Dutton Hall, Davis, CA 95616, 530-752-2396. Fax: 530-752-7339. E-mail: dgagee@ucdavis.edu.
Website: http://www.ucdavis.edu/.

Undergraduates: $17,317. **Scholarships, grants, and awards:** Federal Pell, FSEOG, state, private, college/university gift aid from institutional funds.

**GIFT AID (NON-NEED-BASED) Total amount:** $8,079,032 (6% federal, 11% state, 54% institutional, 29% external sources). **Receiving aid:** Freshmen: 1% (43). Undergraduates: 1% (161). **Average award:** Freshmen: $9593. Undergraduates: $8541. **Scholarships, grants, and awards by category:** Academic interests/achievement: 546 awards ($1,539,273 total): area/ethnic studies, biological sciences, business, communication, computer science, education, engineering/technologies, English, foreign languages, general academic interests/achievements, health fields, humanities, international studies, mathematics, physical sciences, premedicine, social sciences. Creative arts/performance: 32 awards ($129,200 total): art/fine arts, cinema/film/broadcasting, creative writing, dance, general creative arts/performance, music, performing arts, theater/drama. Special achievements/activities: 3 awards ($3000 total): community service, general special achievements/activities, leadership. Special characteristics: 135 awards ($1,001,666 total): international students, out-of-state students. **Tuition waivers:** Full or partial for employees or children of employees. **ROTC:** Army, Air Force cooperative.

**LOANS Student loans:** $66,396,052 (85% need-based, 15% non-need-based). 55% of past graduating class borrowed through all loan programs. **Average indebtedness per student:** $20,319. **Average need-based loan:** Freshmen: $6384. Undergraduates: $6741. **Parent loans:** $32,791,877 (28% need-based, 72% non-need-based). **Programs:** Federal Direct (Subsidized and Unsubsidized Stafford, PLUS), Perkins, college/university, private loans.

**WORK-STUDY Federal work-study:** Total amount: $3,726,047; 3,053 jobs averaging $1628. **State or other work-study/employment:** Total amount: $3,770,353 (100% need-based). 2,503 part-time jobs averaging $1840.

**ATHLETIC AWARDS** Total amount: $3,271,395 (29% need-based, 71% non-need-based).

**APPLYING FOR FINANCIAL AID Required financial aid forms:** FAFSA, state aid form. **Financial aid deadline:** 6/20 (priority: 3/3). **Notification date:** Continuous beginning 4/1.

**CONTACT** Ms. Lindsay Crowell, Senior Associate Director, University of California, Irvine, 102 Aldrich Hall, Irvine, CA 92697-2825, 949-824-4898. Fax: 949-824-2820. E-mail: finaid@uci.edu.
Website: http://www.uci.edu/.

# UNIVERSITY OF CALIFORNIA, IRVINE
## Irvine, CA

| Tuition & fees (CA res): $14,757 | Average undergraduate aid package: $21,475 |
| --- | --- |

**ABOUT THE INSTITUTION** State-supported, coed. **Awards:** certificates, bachelor's, master's, and doctoral degrees. 85 undergraduate majors. **Total enrollment:** 30,051. Undergraduates: 24,489. Freshmen: 5,435. Federal methodology is used as a basis for awarding need-based institutional aid.

**UNDERGRADUATE EXPENSES for 2015–2016 Application fee:** $70. **Tuition, state resident:** full-time $11,220. **Tuition, nonresident:** full-time $34,098. **Required fees:** full-time $3537. **College room and board:** $12,638. Room and board charges vary according to board plan and housing facility.

**FRESHMAN FINANCIAL AID (Fall 2014, est.)** 4,320 applied for aid; of those 84% were deemed to have need. 98% of freshmen with need received aid; of those 26% had need fully met. **Average percent of need met:** 85% (excluding resources awarded to replace EFC). **Average financial aid package:** $23,303 (excluding resources awarded to replace EFC). 1% of all full-time freshmen had no need and received non-need-based gift aid.

**UNDERGRADUATE FINANCIAL AID (Fall 2014, est.)** 18,687 applied for aid; of those 89% were deemed to have need. 98% of undergraduates with need received aid; of those 21% had need fully met. **Average percent of need met:** 81% (excluding resources awarded to replace EFC). **Average financial aid package:** $21,475 (excluding resources awarded to replace EFC). 2% of all full-time undergraduates had no need and received non-need-based gift aid.

**GIFT AID (NEED-BASED) Total amount:** $279,263,351 (21% federal, 46% state, 32% institutional, 1% external sources). **Receiving aid:** Freshmen: 65% (3,523); all full-time undergraduates: 67% (16,078). **Average award:** Freshmen: $18,619;

# UNIVERSITY OF CALIFORNIA, LOS ANGELES
## Los Angeles, CA

| Tuition & fees (CA res): $13,029 | Average undergraduate aid package: $22,405 |
| --- | --- |

**ABOUT THE INSTITUTION** State-supported, coed. **Awards:** bachelor's, master's, and doctoral degrees. 99 undergraduate majors. **Total enrollment:** 43,239. Undergraduates: 29,633. Freshmen: 5,764. Both federal and institutional methodology are used as a basis for awarding need-based institutional aid.

**UNDERGRADUATE EXPENSES for 2015–2016 Application fee:** $70. **One-time required fee:** $165. **Tuition, state resident:** full-time $11,220. **Tuition, nonresident:** full-time $34,098. **Required fees:** full-time $1809. **College room and board:** $13,135. Room and board charges vary according to board plan and housing facility.

**FRESHMAN FINANCIAL AID (Fall 2014, est.)** 3,558 applied for aid; of those 86% were deemed to have need. 100% of freshmen with need received aid; of those 25% had need fully met. **Average percent of need met:** 83% (excluding resources awarded to replace EFC). **Average financial aid package:** $23,903 (excluding resources awarded to replace EFC). 2% of all full-time freshmen had no need and received non-need-based gift aid.

**UNDERGRADUATE FINANCIAL AID (Fall 2014, est.)** 17,699 applied for aid; of those 91% were deemed to have need. 100% of undergraduates with need received aid; of those 25% had need fully met. **Average percent of need met:** 83% (excluding resources awarded to replace EFC). **Average financial aid package:** $22,405 (excluding resources awarded to replace EFC). 3% of all full-time undergraduates had no need and received non-need-based gift aid.

**GIFT AID (NEED-BASED) Total amount:** $293,324,653 (16% federal, 35% state, 47% institutional, 2% external sources). **Receiving aid:** Freshmen: 52% (2,975); all full-time undergraduates: 54% (15,644). **Average award:** Freshmen: $20,255; Undergraduates: $18,806. **Scholarships, grants, and awards:** Federal Pell,

FSEOG, state, private, college/university gift aid from institutional funds, United Negro College Fund, Federal Nursing.

**GIFT AID (NON-NEED-BASED)** *Total amount:* $6,873,343 (8% federal, 10% state, 62% institutional, 20% external sources). *Receiving aid:* Freshmen: 1% (70). Undergraduates: 1% (209). *Average award:* Freshmen: $4494. Undergraduates: $4539. *Scholarships, grants, and awards by category: Academic interests/ achievement:* general academic interests/achievements. *Special achievements/activities:* general special achievements/activities. *ROTC:* Army, Naval, Air Force.

**LOANS** *Student loans:* $68,673,048 (80% need-based, 20% non-need-based). 48% of past graduating class borrowed through all loan programs. *Average indebtedness per student:* $20,759. *Average need-based loan:* Freshmen: $7168. Undergraduates: $6771. *Parent loans:* $34,974,399 (24% need-based, 76% non-need-based). *Programs:* Federal Direct (Subsidized and Unsubsidized Stafford, PLUS), Perkins, Federal Nursing, state, college/university.

**WORK-STUDY** *Federal work-study:* Total amount: $5,763,461; 2,463 jobs averaging $1818. *State or other work-study/employment:* Total amount: $835,223 (100% need-based). 743 part-time jobs averaging $1113.

**ATHLETIC AWARDS** Total amount: $11,108,209 (31% need-based, 69% non-need-based).

**APPLYING FOR FINANCIAL AID** *Required financial aid form:* FAFSA. *Financial aid deadline (priority):* 3/2. *Notification date:* Continuous beginning 3/15.

**CONTACT** Ms. Carolyn Turpin, Budget Officer, University of California, Los Angeles, A-129 Murphy Hall, Los Angeles, CA 90095-1435, 310-206-0407. *E-mail:* finaid@saonet.ucla.edu.

*Website:* http://www.ucla.edu/.

# UNIVERSITY OF CALIFORNIA, MERCED
## Merced, CA

| Tuition & fees (CA res): $14,813 | Average undergraduate aid package: $22,919 |
|---|---|

**ABOUT THE INSTITUTION** State-supported, coed. *Awards:* bachelor's, master's, and doctoral degrees. 24 undergraduate majors. *Total enrollment:* 6,268. Undergraduates: 5,884. Freshmen: 1,551. Both federal and institutional methodology are used as a basis for awarding need-based institutional aid.

**UNDERGRADUATE EXPENSES** for 2015–2016 *Application fee:* $70. *Tuition, state resident:* full-time $13,070. *Tuition, nonresident:* full-time $35,948. *Required fees:* full-time $1743. *College room and board:* $14,718. Room and board charges vary according to board plan.

**FRESHMAN FINANCIAL AID (Fall 2014, est.)** 1,496 applied for aid; of those 93% were deemed to have need. 99% of freshmen with need received aid; of those 35% had need fully met. *Average percent of need met:* 88% (excluding resources awarded to replace EFC). *Average financial aid package:* $26,712 (excluding resources awarded to replace EFC). 1% of all full-time freshmen had no need and received non-need-based gift aid.

**UNDERGRADUATE FINANCIAL AID (Fall 2014, est.)** 5,410 applied for aid; of those 93% were deemed to have need. 99% of undergraduates with need received aid; of those 32% had need fully met. *Average percent of need met:* 85% (excluding resources awarded to replace EFC). *Average financial aid package:* $22,919 (excluding resources awarded to replace EFC). 1% of all full-time undergraduates had no need and received non-need-based gift aid.

**GIFT AID (NEED-BASED)** *Total amount:* $91,448,681 (20% federal, 44% state, 35% institutional, 1% external sources). *Receiving aid:* Freshmen: 89% (1,373); all full-time undergraduates: 85% (4,952). *Average award:* Freshmen: $21,477; Undergraduates: $18,409. *Scholarships, grants, and awards:* Federal Pell, FSEOG, state, private, college/university gift aid from institutional funds.

**GIFT AID (NON-NEED-BASED)** *Total amount:* $958,277 (7% federal, 12% state, 67% institutional, 14% external sources). *Receiving aid:* Freshmen: 5. Undergraduates: 25. *Average award:* Freshmen: $10,521. Undergraduates: $11,300. *Scholarships, grants, and awards by category: Academic interests/ achievement:* general academic interests/achievements. *Tuition waivers:* Full or partial for employees or children of employees.

**LOANS** *Student loans:* $18,578,977 (83% need-based, 17% non-need-based). 70% of past graduating class borrowed through all loan programs. *Average indebtedness per student:* $20,408. *Average need-based loan:* Freshmen: $4771. Undergraduates: $5366. *Parent loans:* $6,497,878 (12% need-based, 88% non-need-based). *Programs:* Federal Direct (Subsidized and Unsubsidized Stafford, PLUS), alternative loans.

**WORK-STUDY** *Federal work-study:* Total amount: $7,312,161; jobs available.

**ATHLETIC AWARDS** Total amount: $38,050 (83% need-based, 17% non-need-based).

**APPLYING FOR FINANCIAL AID** *Required financial aid form:* FAFSA. *Financial aid deadline (priority):* 3/2. *Notification date:* Continuous beginning 3/2.

**CONTACT** Ms. Diana M. Ralls, Director of Financial Aid, University of California, Merced, Kolligian Library, Room 122, 5200 North Lake Road, Merced, CA 95343, 209-228-7178. *Fax:* 209-228-7861. *E-mail:* finaid@ucmerced.edu.

*Website:* http://www.ucmerced.edu/.

# UNIVERSITY OF CALIFORNIA, RIVERSIDE
## Riverside, CA

| Tuition & fees (CA res): $13,307 | Average undergraduate aid package: $21,068 |
|---|---|

**ABOUT THE INSTITUTION** State-supported, coed. *Awards:* certificates, bachelor's, master's, and doctoral degrees. 56 undergraduate majors. *Total enrollment:* 21,569. Undergraduates: 18,782. Freshmen: 4,279. Federal methodology is used as a basis for awarding need-based institutional aid.

**UNDERGRADUATE EXPENSES** for 2015–2016 *Application fee:* $70. *Tuition, state resident:* full-time $11,220; part-time $5610 per year. *Tuition, nonresident:* full-time $34,098; part-time $17,049 per year. *Required fees:* full-time $2087. Full-time tuition and fees vary according to course load. Part-time tuition and fees vary according to course load. *College room and board:* $15,000. Room and board charges vary according to board plan and housing facility.

**FRESHMAN FINANCIAL AID (Fall 2014, est.)** 3,869 applied for aid; of those 85% were deemed to have need. 99% of freshmen with need received aid; of those 29% had need fully met. *Average percent of need met:* 88% (excluding resources awarded to replace EFC). *Average financial aid package:* $24,523 (excluding resources awarded to replace EFC). 8% of all full-time freshmen had no need and received non-need-based gift aid.

**UNDERGRADUATE FINANCIAL AID (Fall 2014, est.)** 16,039 applied for aid; of those 90% were deemed to have need. 99% of undergraduates with need received aid; of those 23% had need fully met. *Average percent of need met:* 82% (excluding resources awarded to replace EFC). *Average financial aid package:* $21,068 (excluding resources awarded to replace EFC). 3% of all full-time undergraduates had no need and received non-need-based gift aid.

**GIFT AID (NEED-BASED)** *Total amount:* $242,242,205 (21% federal, 44% state, 34% institutional, 1% external sources). *Receiving aid:* Freshmen: 75% (3,217); all full-time undergraduates: 76% (14,091). *Average award:* Freshmen: $19,858; Undergraduates: $16,766. *Scholarships, grants, and awards:* Federal Pell, FSEOG, state, private, college/university gift aid from institutional funds.

**GIFT AID (NON-NEED-BASED)** *Total amount:* $11,950,636 (6% federal, 88% institutional, 6% external sources). *Receiving aid:* Freshmen: 2% (91). Undergraduates: 2% (280). *Average award:* Freshmen: $10,122. Undergraduates: $12,155. *Scholarships, grants, and awards by category: Academic interests/ achievement:* agriculture, area/ethnic studies, biological sciences, business, education, engineering/technologies, English, general academic interests/achievements, humanities, mathematics, physical sciences, premedicine, social sciences. *Creative arts/performance:* art/fine arts, creative writing, dance, music, theater/drama. *Special characteristics:* religious affiliation, veterans, veterans' children. *ROTC:* Army cooperative, Air Force cooperative.

**LOANS** *Student loans:* $62,915,504 (87% need-based, 13% non-need-based). 70% of past graduating class borrowed through all loan programs. *Average indebtedness per student:* $21,166. *Average need-based loan:* Freshmen: $6054. Undergraduates: $6345. *Parent loans:* $19,435,628 (31% need-based, 69% non-need-based). *Programs:* Federal Direct (Subsidized and Unsubsidized Stafford, PLUS), Perkins, college/university.

**WORK-STUDY** *Federal work-study:* Total amount: $4,419,039; 2,929 jobs averaging $1508.

**ATHLETIC AWARDS** Total amount: $3,210,012 (38% need-based, 62% non-need-based).

**APPLYING FOR FINANCIAL AID** *Required financial aid forms:* FAFSA, state aid form. *Financial aid deadline:* 3/2. *Notification date:* Continuous beginning 3/1. Students must reply by 5/15 or within 3 weeks of notification.

**CONTACT** Mr. Jose A. Aguilar, Director of Financial Aid, University of California, Riverside, 2106 Student Services Building, Riverside, CA 92521-0209, 951-827-7249. *Fax:* 951-827-5619. *E-mail:* finaid@ucr.edu.
*Website:* http://www.ucr.edu/.

# UNIVERSITY OF CALIFORNIA, SAN DIEGO
## La Jolla, CA

| Tuition & fees (CA res): $13,456 | Average undergraduate aid package: $22,196 |
|---|---|

**ABOUT THE INSTITUTION** State-supported, coed. 68 undergraduate majors. Both federal and institutional methodology are used as a basis for awarding need-based institutional aid.

**UNDERGRADUATE EXPENSES for 2015–2016** *Tuition, state resident:* full-time $13,456. *Tuition, nonresident:* full-time $36,334. *College room and board:* $12,254. Room and board charges vary according to board plan and housing facility.

**FRESHMAN FINANCIAL AID (Fall 2014, est.)** 3,542 applied for aid; of those 79% were deemed to have need. 96% of freshmen with need received aid; of those 33% had need fully met. *Average percent of need met:* 87% (excluding resources awarded to replace EFC). *Average financial aid package:* $23,076 (excluding resources awarded to replace EFC). 1% of all full-time freshmen had no need and received non-need-based gift aid.

**UNDERGRADUATE FINANCIAL AID (Fall 2014, est.)** 16,589 applied for aid; of those 89% were deemed to have need. 97% of undergraduates with need received aid; of those 31% had need fully met. *Average percent of need met:* 85% (excluding resources awarded to replace EFC). *Average financial aid package:* $22,196 (excluding resources awarded to replace EFC). 2% of all full-time undergraduates had no need and received non-need-based gift aid.

**GIFT AID (NEED-BASED)** *Total amount:* $250,915,742 (19% federal, 36% state, 43% institutional, 2% external sources). *Receiving aid:* Freshmen: 54% (2,656); all full-time undergraduates: 58% (14,072). *Average award:* Freshmen: $18,427; Undergraduates: $17,624. *Scholarships, grants, and awards:* Federal Pell, FSEOG, state, private, college/university gift aid from institutional funds, TEACH Grants.

**GIFT AID (NON-NEED-BASED)** *Total amount:* $8,061,718 (19% federal, 6% state, 59% institutional, 16% external sources). *Receiving aid:* Freshmen: 1% (54). Undergraduates: 1% (149). *Average award:* Freshmen: $9550. Undergraduates: $9195. *Scholarships, grants, and awards by category: Academic interests/achievement:* biological sciences, business, communication, computer science, engineering/technologies, general academic interests/achievements, mathematics, physical sciences, premedicine, social sciences. *Creative arts/performance:* applied art and design, cinema/film/broadcasting, dance, journalism/publications, performing arts. *Special achievements/activities:* community service, leadership. *Special characteristics:* ethnic background, first-generation college students, handicapped students, members of minority groups, veterans' children.

**LOANS** *Student loans:* $63,200,520 (81% need-based, 19% non-need-based). 60% of past graduating class borrowed through all loan programs. *Average indebtedness per student:* $21,790. *Average need-based loan:* Freshmen: $5063. Undergraduates: $5833. *Parent loans:* $11,792,124 (14% need-based, 86% non-need-based). *Programs:* Federal Direct (Subsidized and Unsubsidized Stafford, PLUS), Perkins, college/university, alternative loans.

**WORK-STUDY** *Federal work-study:* Total amount: $16,605,873; jobs available. *State or other work-study/employment:* Total amount: $831,150 (100% need-based). Part-time jobs available.

**ATHLETIC AWARDS** Total amount: $235,101 (40% need-based, 60% non-need-based).

**APPLYING FOR FINANCIAL AID** *Required financial aid forms:* FAFSA, state aid form. *Financial aid deadline (priority):* 3/2. *Notification date:* Continuous beginning 3/15.

**CONTACT** Ann Klein, Director of Financial Aid, University of California, San Diego, 9500 Gilman Drive, Mail Code 0013, La Jolla, CA 92093-0013, 858-534-4480. *Fax:* 858-534-5459. *E-mail:* aklein@ucsd.edu.
*Website:* http://www.ucsd.edu/.

# UNIVERSITY OF CALIFORNIA, SANTA BARBARA
## Santa Barbara, CA

| Tuition & fees (CA res): $13,860 | Average undergraduate aid package: $22,572 |
|---|---|

**ABOUT THE INSTITUTION** State-supported, coed. *Awards:* certificates, bachelor's, master's, and doctoral degrees. 74 undergraduate majors. *Total enrollment:* 23,051. Undergraduates: 20,238. Freshmen: 4,738. Both federal and institutional methodology are used as a basis for awarding need-based institutional aid.

**UNDERGRADUATE EXPENSES for 2015–2016** *Application fee:* $70. *Tuition, state resident:* full-time $11,220. *Tuition, nonresident:* full-time $34,098. *Required fees:* full-time $2640. *College room and board:* $14,128. Room and board charges vary according to board plan and housing facility.

**FRESHMAN FINANCIAL AID (Fall 2014, est.)** 3,872 applied for aid; of those 79% were deemed to have need. 97% of freshmen with need received aid; of those 29% had need fully met. *Average percent of need met:* 83% (excluding resources awarded to replace EFC). *Average financial aid package:* $25,326 (excluding resources awarded to replace EFC). 2% of all full-time freshmen had no need and received non-need-based gift aid.

**UNDERGRADUATE FINANCIAL AID (Fall 2014, est.)** 14,437 applied for aid; of those 85% were deemed to have need. 97% of undergraduates with need received aid; of those 26% had need fully met. *Average percent of need met:* 82% (excluding resources awarded to replace EFC). *Average financial aid package:* $22,572 (excluding resources awarded to replace EFC). 2% of all full-time undergraduates had no need and received non-need-based gift aid.

**GIFT AID (NEED-BASED)** *Total amount:* $211,060,986 (18% federal, 43% state, 38% institutional, 1% external sources). *Receiving aid:* Freshmen: 62% (2,915); all full-time undergraduates: 59% (11,739). *Average award:* Freshmen: $20,515; Undergraduates: $17,948. *Scholarships, grants, and awards:* Federal Pell, FSEOG, state, private, college/university gift aid from institutional funds, endowed and restricted scholarships and grants.

**GIFT AID (NON-NEED-BASED)** *Total amount:* $6,636,398 (6% federal, 15% state, 73% institutional, 6% external sources). *Receiving aid:* Freshmen: 1% (24). Undergraduates: 1% (107). *Average award:* Freshmen: $12,062. Undergraduates: $12,066. *Scholarships, grants, and awards by category: Academic interests/achievement:* general academic interests/achievements. *ROTC:* Army, Air Force cooperative.

**LOANS** *Student loans:* $48,225,644 (85% need-based, 15% non-need-based). 57% of past graduating class borrowed through all loan programs. *Average indebtedness per student:* $21,045. *Average need-based loan:* Freshmen: $6130. Undergraduates: $6250. *Parent loans:* $25,009,151 (19% need-based, 81% non-need-based). *Programs:* Federal Direct (Subsidized and Unsubsidized Stafford, PLUS), Perkins.

**WORK-STUDY** *Federal work-study:* Total amount: $13,128,522; jobs available.

**ATHLETIC AWARDS** Total amount: $3,845,472 (34% need-based, 66% non-need-based).

**APPLYING FOR FINANCIAL AID** *Required financial aid form:* FAFSA. *Financial aid deadline (priority):* 3/2. *Notification date:* Continuous beginning 3/15. Students must reply within 2 weeks of notification.

**CONTACT** Mike Miller, Office of Financial Aid, University of California, Santa Barbara, 2103 SAASB, Santa Barbara, CA 93106-3180, 805-893-2432. *Fax:* 805-893-8793.
*Website:* http://www.ucsb.edu/.

# UNIVERSITY OF CALIFORNIA, SANTA CRUZ
## Santa Cruz, CA

| Tuition & fees (CA res): $13,398 | Average undergraduate aid package: $23,134 |
|---|---|

**ABOUT THE INSTITUTION** State-supported, coed. **Awards:** certificates, bachelor's, master's, and doctoral degrees. 57 undergraduate majors. **Total enrollment:** 17,866. Undergraduates: 16,277. Freshmen: 4,035. Both federal and institutional methodology are used as a basis for awarding need-based institutional aid.

**UNDERGRADUATE EXPENSES for 2015–2016 Application fee:** $70. **Tuition, state resident:** full-time $12,192. **Tuition, nonresident:** full-time $35,070. **Required fees:** full-time $1206. Part-time tuition and fees vary according to course load. **College room and board:** $14,730. Room and board charges vary according to board plan and housing facility.

**FRESHMAN FINANCIAL AID (Fall 2014, est.)** 3,368 applied for aid; of those 82% were deemed to have need. 97% of freshmen with need received aid; of those 18% had need fully met. **Average percent of need met:** 81% (excluding resources awarded to replace EFC). **Average financial aid package:** $24,303 (excluding resources awarded to replace EFC). 9% of all full-time freshmen had no need and received non-need-based gift aid.

**UNDERGRADUATE FINANCIAL AID (Fall 2014, est.)** 12,682 applied for aid; of those 88% were deemed to have need. 98% of undergraduates with need received aid; of those 21% had need fully met. **Average percent of need met:** 82% (excluding resources awarded to replace EFC). **Average financial aid package:** $23,134 (excluding resources awarded to replace EFC). 5% of all full-time undergraduates had no need and received non-need-based gift aid.

**GIFT AID (NEED-BASED) Total amount:** $194,139,167 (18% federal, 42% state, 39% institutional, 1% external sources). **Receiving aid:** Freshmen: 65% (2,622); all full-time undergraduates: 67% (10,569). **Average award:** Freshmen: $19,339; Undergraduates: $18,125. **Scholarships, grants, and awards:** Federal Pell, FSEOG, state, private, college/university gift aid from institutional funds.

**GIFT AID (NON-NEED-BASED) Total amount:** $5,321,872 (2% federal, 9% state, 85% institutional, 4% external sources). **Receiving aid:** Freshmen: 1% (23). Undergraduates: 75. **Average award:** Freshmen: $4860. Undergraduates: $5887. **Scholarships, grants, and awards by category:** Academic interests/achievement: 177 awards ($669,673 total): computer science, general academic interests/achievements, humanities, mathematics, physical sciences, social sciences. Creative arts/performance: 104 awards ($67,455 total): art/fine arts, cinema/film/broadcasting, creative writing, music, theater/drama. Special achievements/activities: 2 awards ($1000 total): leadership. Special characteristics: 652 awards ($2,540,819 total): first-generation college students, international students, out-of-state students, veterans. **ROTC:** Army cooperative, Naval cooperative, Air Force cooperative.

**LOANS Student loans:** $55,328,114 (84% need-based, 16% non-need-based). 63% of past graduating class borrowed through all loan programs. Average indebtedness per student: $22,583. **Average need-based loan:** Freshmen: $6477. Undergraduates: $6572. **Parent loans:** $23,701,045 (20% need-based, 80% non-need-based). **Programs:** Federal Direct (Subsidized and Unsubsidized Stafford, PLUS), Perkins.

**WORK-STUDY Federal work-study:** Total amount: $8,167,288; 4,336 jobs averaging $1955. **State or other work-study/employment:** Part-time jobs available.

**APPLYING FOR FINANCIAL AID Required financial aid forms:** FAFSA, state aid form. **Financial aid deadline:** 6/3 (priority: 4/14). **Notification date:** Continuous beginning 4/1. Students must reply within 4 weeks of notification.

**CONTACT** John Patrick Register, Director of Financial Aid, University of California, Santa Cruz, 201 Hahn Student Services Building, Santa Cruz, CA 95064, 831-459-4404. Fax: 831-459-3628. E-mail: jpregis@ucsc.edu. Website: http://www.ucsc.edu/.

# UNIVERSITY OF CENTRAL ARKANSAS
## Conway, AR

| Tuition & fees (AR res): $7889 | Average undergraduate aid package: N/A |
|---|---|

**ABOUT THE INSTITUTION** State-supported, coed. **Awards:** certificates, associate, bachelor's, master's, and doctoral degrees. 61 undergraduate majors. **Total**

**enrollment:** 11,698. Undergraduates: 9,842. Freshmen: 2,232. Federal methodology is used as a basis for awarding need-based institutional aid.

**UNDERGRADUATE EXPENSES for 2015–2016 Application fee:** $25. **Tuition, state resident:** full-time $5918; part-time $197.25 per credit hour. **Tuition, nonresident:** full-time $11,835; part-time $394.50 per credit hour. **Required fees:** full-time $1971. Full-time tuition and fees vary according to course load. Part-time tuition and fees vary according to course load. **College room and board:** $5778. Room and board charges vary according to board plan and housing facility.

**GIFT AID (NEED-BASED) Scholarships, grants, and awards:** Federal Pell, FSEOG, state, private, college/university gift aid from institutional funds, Federal Nursing.

**GIFT AID (NON-NEED-BASED) Scholarships, grants, and awards by category:** Academic interests/achievement: general academic interests/achievements. **Tuition waivers:** Full or partial for employees or children of employees, senior citizens. **ROTC:** Army.

**LOANS Programs:** Perkins, Federal Nursing, state, alternative loans.

**APPLYING FOR FINANCIAL AID Required financial aid form:** FAFSA. **Financial aid deadline:** 7/1 (priority: 4/15). **Notification date:** Continuous.

**CONTACT** Cheryl Lyons, Director of Student Aid, University of Central Arkansas, 201 Donaghey Avenue, Conway, AR 72035, 501-450-3140 or toll-free 800-243-8245. Fax: 501-450-5168. E-mail: clyons@uca.edu. Website: http://www.uca.edu/.

# UNIVERSITY OF CENTRAL FLORIDA
## Orlando, FL

| Tuition & fees (FL res): $6368 | Average undergraduate aid package: $8295 |
|---|---|

**ABOUT THE INSTITUTION** State-supported, coed. **Awards:** certificates, associate, bachelor's, master's, and doctoral degrees. 82 undergraduate majors. **Total enrollment:** 60,810. Undergraduates: 52,532. Freshmen: 6,467. Federal methodology is used as a basis for awarding need-based institutional aid.

**UNDERGRADUATE EXPENSES for 2015–2016 Application fee:** $30. **Tuition, state resident:** full-time $6368; part-time $212.28 per credit hour. **Tuition, nonresident:** full-time $22,467; part-time $748.89 per credit hour. Full-time tuition and fees vary according to course load. Part-time tuition and fees vary according to course load. **College room and board:** $9300; **Room only:** $5400. Room and board charges vary according to board plan and housing facility. **Payment plan:** Tuition prepayment.

**FRESHMAN FINANCIAL AID (Fall 2013)** 5,501 applied for aid; of those 67% were deemed to have need. 99% of freshmen with need received aid; of those 10% had need fully met. **Average percent of need met:** 57% (excluding resources awarded to replace EFC). **Average financial aid package:** $8213 (excluding resources awarded to replace EFC). 8% of all full-time freshmen had no need and received non-need-based gift aid.

**UNDERGRADUATE FINANCIAL AID (Fall 2013)** 31,410 applied for aid; of those 75% were deemed to have need. 97% of undergraduates with need received aid; of those 7% had need fully met. **Average percent of need met:** 57% (excluding resources awarded to replace EFC). **Average financial aid package:** $8295 (excluding resources awarded to replace EFC). 4% of all full-time undergraduates had no need and received non-need-based gift aid.

**GIFT AID (NEED-BASED) Total amount:** $115,141,849 (73% federal, 8% state, 19% institutional). **Receiving aid:** Freshmen: 41% (2,393); all full-time undergraduates: 48% (17,159). **Average award:** Freshmen: $4961; Undergraduates: $4953. **Scholarships, grants, and awards:** Federal Pell, FSEOG, state, private, college/university gift aid from institutional funds.

**GIFT AID (NON-NEED-BASED) Total amount:** $64,758,846 (70% state, 21% institutional, 9% external sources). **Receiving aid:** Freshmen: 56% (3,239). Undergraduates: 36% (13,005). **Average award:** Freshmen: $3491. Undergraduates: $3459. **Scholarships, grants, and awards by category:** Academic interests/achievement: general academic interests/achievements. Creative arts/performance: cinema/film/broadcasting, music, theater/drama. Special achievements/activities: general special achievements/activities, leadership. Special characteristics: first-generation college students. **Tuition waivers:** Full or partial for employees or children of employees, senior citizens. **ROTC:** Army, Air Force.

**LOANS** *Student loans:* $184,767,449 (51% need-based, 49% non-need-based). 50% of past graduating class borrowed through all loan programs. *Average indebtedness per student:* $23,378. *Average need-based loan:* Freshmen: $3499. Undergraduates: $4584. *Parent loans:* $7,890,154 (100% non-need-based). *Programs:* Federal Direct (Subsidized and Unsubsidized Stafford, PLUS), Perkins.

**WORK-STUDY** *Federal work-study:* 563 jobs averaging $3445. *State or other work-study/employment:* Part-time jobs available.

**ATHLETIC AWARDS** Total amount: $4,399,340 (100% non-need-based).

**APPLYING FOR FINANCIAL AID** *Required financial aid form:* FAFSA. *Financial aid deadline:* 6/30 (priority: 3/1). *Notification date:* Continuous beginning 3/15. Students must reply within 3 weeks of notification.

**CONTACT** Ms. Inez Ford, Associate Director of Student Financial Assistance, University of Central Florida, 4000 Central Florida Boulevard, Orlando, FL 32816-0113, 407-823-2827. Fax: 407-823-5241. E-mail: inez.ford@ucf.edu. Website: http://www.ucf.edu/.

# UNIVERSITY OF CENTRAL MISSOURI
## Warrensburg, MO

| Tuition & fees (MO res): $7264 | Average undergraduate aid package: $8314 |
| --- | --- |

**ABOUT THE INSTITUTION** State-supported, coed. *Awards:* certificates, bachelor's, and master's degrees. 63 undergraduate majors. *Total enrollment:* 13,379. Undergraduates: 9,838. Freshmen: 1,710. Federal methodology is used as a basis for awarding need-based institutional aid.

**UNDERGRADUATE EXPENSES for 2015–2016** *Application fee:* $30. *Tuition, state resident:* full-time $6394; part-time $213.15 per credit hour. *Tuition, nonresident:* full-time $12,789; part-time $426.20 per credit hour. *Required fees:* full-time $870; $29 per credit hour. Full-time tuition and fees vary according to course load and location. Part-time tuition and fees vary according to location. *College room and board:* $7828; *Room only:* $5034. Room and board charges vary according to board plan, housing facility, and student level.

**FRESHMAN FINANCIAL AID (Fall 2013)** 1,599 applied for aid; of those 72% were deemed to have need. 100% of freshmen with need received aid; of those 13% had need fully met. *Average percent of need met:* 63% (excluding resources awarded to replace EFC). *Average financial aid package:* $8531 (excluding resources awarded to replace EFC). 22% of all full-time freshmen had no need and received non-need-based gift aid.

**UNDERGRADUATE FINANCIAL AID (Fall 2013)** 6,950 applied for aid; of those 74% were deemed to have need. 100% of undergraduates with need received aid; of those 8% had need fully met. *Average percent of need met:* 59% (excluding resources awarded to replace EFC). *Average financial aid package:* $8314 (excluding resources awarded to replace EFC). 20% of all full-time undergraduates had no need and received non-need-based gift aid.

**GIFT AID (NEED-BASED)** *Total amount:* $27,199,711 (59% federal, 15% state, 6% institutional, 20% external sources). *Receiving aid:* Freshmen: 40% (701); all full-time undergraduates: 39% (3,234). *Average award:* Freshmen: $4289; Undergraduates: $4212. *Scholarships, grants, and awards:* Federal Pell, FSEOG, state, private, college/university gift aid from institutional funds.

**GIFT AID (NON-NEED-BASED)** *Total amount:* $5,039,149 (13% federal, 5% state, 81% institutional, 1% external sources). *Receiving aid:* Freshmen: 65% (1,139). Undergraduates: 59% (4,924). *Average award:* Freshmen: $3407. Undergraduates: $3144. *Scholarships, grants, and awards by category:* Academic interests/achievement: social sciences. *Tuition waivers:* Full or partial for employees or children of employees. *ROTC:* Army, Air Force cooperative.

**LOANS** *Student loans:* $44,590,669 (45% need-based, 55% non-need-based). 78% of past graduating class borrowed through all loan programs. *Average indebtedness per student:* $27,424. *Parent loans:* $8,904,865 (100% non-need-based). *Programs:* Federal Direct (Subsidized and Unsubsidized Stafford, PLUS), Perkins, private loans.

**WORK-STUDY** *Federal work-study:* 211 jobs averaging $1120. *State or other work-study/employment:* Total amount: $2,854,881 (100% non-need-based). 1,415 part-time jobs averaging $1930.

**ATHLETIC AWARDS** Total amount: $2,289,937 (100% non-need-based).

**APPLYING FOR FINANCIAL AID** *Required financial aid forms:* FAFSA, institution's own form. *Financial aid deadline (priority):* 4/1. *Notification date:* Continuous beginning 3/20. Students must reply within 3 weeks of notification.

**CONTACT** Ms. Angela Karlin, Director of Student Financial Assistance, University of Central Missouri, Ward Edwards Building 1100, Warrensburg, MO 64093, 660-543-4177 or toll-free 800-729-8266. Fax: 660-543-8080. E-mail: sfs@ucmo.edu. Website: http://www.ucmo.edu/.

# UNIVERSITY OF CENTRAL OKLAHOMA
## Edmond, OK

| Tuition & fees (OK res): $6686 | Average undergraduate aid package: $8722 |
| --- | --- |

**ABOUT THE INSTITUTION** State-supported, coed. *Awards:* certificates, associate, bachelor's, and master's degrees. 137 undergraduate majors. *Total enrollment:* 16,840. Undergraduates: 14,998. Freshmen: 2,149. Federal methodology is used as a basis for awarding need-based institutional aid.

**UNDERGRADUATE EXPENSES for 2015–2016** *Application fee:* $40. *Tuition, state resident:* full-time $5807; part-time $164.25 per credit hour. *Tuition, nonresident:* full-time $14,286; part-time $446.90 per credit hour. *Required fees:* full-time $879; $181 per credit hour. Full-time tuition and fees vary according to course load, degree level, and program. Part-time tuition and fees vary according to course load, degree level, and program. *College room and board:* $9862; *Room only:* $6992. Room and board charges vary according to board plan and housing facility. *Payment plan:* Guaranteed tuition.

**FRESHMAN FINANCIAL AID (Fall 2014, est.)** 1,590 applied for aid; of those 78% were deemed to have need. 96% of freshmen with need received aid; of those 22% had need fully met. *Average percent of need met:* 62% (excluding resources awarded to replace EFC). *Average financial aid package:* $8588 (excluding resources awarded to replace EFC). 5% of all full-time freshmen had no need and received non-need-based gift aid.

**UNDERGRADUATE FINANCIAL AID (Fall 2014, est.)** 7,264 applied for aid; of those 85% were deemed to have need. 96% of undergraduates with need received aid; of those 14% had need fully met. *Average percent of need met:* 54% (excluding resources awarded to replace EFC). *Average financial aid package:* $8722 (excluding resources awarded to replace EFC). 3% of all full-time undergraduates had no need and received non-need-based gift aid.

**GIFT AID (NEED-BASED)** *Total amount:* $32,408,165 (67% federal, 32% state, 1% institutional). *Receiving aid:* Freshmen: 50% (977); all full-time undergraduates: 43% (4,550). *Average award:* Freshmen: $5556; Undergraduates: $6075. *Scholarships, grants, and awards:* Federal Pell, FSEOG, state, private, college/university gift aid from institutional funds.

**GIFT AID (NON-NEED-BASED)** *Total amount:* $14,394,403 (7% federal, 2% state, 9% institutional, 82% external sources). *Receiving aid:* Freshmen: 34% (670). Undergraduates: 35% (3,684). *Average award:* Freshmen: $2730. Undergraduates: $2715. *Scholarships, grants, and awards by category:* Academic interests/achievement: 595 awards ($681,489 total): biological sciences, business, communication, computer science, education, English, foreign languages, general academic interests/achievements, health fields, home economics, humanities, mathematics, military science, physical sciences, social sciences. *Creative arts/performance:* 465 awards ($789,944 total): applied art and design, art/fine arts, journalism/publications, music, theater/drama. *Special achievements/activities:* 1,224 awards ($2,448,430 total): general special achievements/activities, junior miss, leadership. *Special characteristics:* 707 awards ($1,034,192 total): children of faculty/staff, ethnic background, international students, members of minority groups. *Tuition waivers:* Full or partial for employees or children of employees. *ROTC:* Army.

**LOANS** *Student loans:* $44,479,275 (46% need-based, 54% non-need-based). 53% of past graduating class borrowed through all loan programs. *Average indebtedness per student:* $24,530. *Average need-based loan:* Freshmen: $3106. Undergraduates: $3978. *Parent loans:* $2,968,558 (100% non-need-based). *Programs:* Federal Direct (Subsidized and Unsubsidized Stafford, PLUS).

**WORK-STUDY** *Federal work-study:* Total amount: $11,593,399; 2,593 jobs averaging $4471. *State or other work-study/employment:* Total amount: $4,267,520 (100% non-need-based). 1,339 part-time jobs averaging $2361.

**ATHLETIC AWARDS** Total amount: $2,225,645 (100% non-need-based).

**APPLYING FOR FINANCIAL AID** *Required financial aid forms:* FAFSA, institution's own form. *Financial aid deadline:* Continuous. *Notification date:* Continuous beginning 5/1. Students must reply within 4 weeks of notification.

**CONTACT** Ms. Kerry Housley, Assistant Director of Technical Services, University of Central Oklahoma, 100 North University Drive, Edmond, OK 73034-5209, 405-974-5325. *Fax:* 405-340-7658. *E-mail:* khousley@uco.edu. *Website:* http://www.uco.edu/.

# UNIVERSITY OF CHARLESTON
## Charleston, WV

| Tuition & fees: $24,200 | Average undergraduate aid package: $19,375 |
|---|---|

**ABOUT THE INSTITUTION** Independent, coed. *Awards:* associate, bachelor's, master's, and doctoral degrees. 32 undergraduate majors. *Total enrollment:* 2,111. Undergraduates: 1,549. Freshmen: 335. Both federal and institutional methodology are used as a basis for awarding need-based institutional aid.

**UNDERGRADUATE EXPENSES for 2015–2016** *Application fee:* $25. *Comprehensive fee:* $33,300 includes full-time tuition ($23,000), mandatory fees ($1200), and room and board ($9100). Full-time tuition and fees vary according to location, program, and student level. Room and board charges vary according to board plan, housing facility, and location. Part-time tuition and fees vary according to course load, location, and program.

**FRESHMAN FINANCIAL AID (Fall 2014, est.)** 323 applied for aid; of those 64% were deemed to have need. 100% of freshmen with need received aid; of those 7% had need fully met. *Average percent of need met:* 59% (excluding resources awarded to replace EFC). *Average financial aid package:* $20,712 (excluding resources awarded to replace EFC). 8% of all full-time freshmen had no need and received non-need-based gift aid.

**UNDERGRADUATE FINANCIAL AID (Fall 2014, est.)** 1,295 applied for aid; of those 66% were deemed to have need. 100% of undergraduates with need received aid; of those 4% had need fully met. *Average percent of need met:* 53% (excluding resources awarded to replace EFC). *Average financial aid package:* $19,375 (excluding resources awarded to replace EFC). 5% of all full-time undergraduates had no need and received non-need-based gift aid.

**GIFT AID (NEED-BASED)** *Receiving aid:* Freshmen: 47% (156); all full-time undergraduates: 49% (656). *Average award:* Freshmen: $4915; Undergraduates: $5074. *Scholarships, grants, and awards:* Federal Pell, FSEOG, state, private, college/university gift aid from institutional funds.

**GIFT AID (NON-NEED-BASED)** *Receiving aid:* Freshmen: 57% (190). Undergraduates: 62% (837). *Average award:* Freshmen: $9459. Undergraduates: $9479. *Scholarships, grants, and awards by category:* Academic interests/achievement: general academic interests/achievements. *Creative arts/performance:* music. *Special achievements/activities:* community service, general special achievements/activities, leadership. *Special characteristics:* international students. *Tuition waivers:* Full or partial for children of alumni, employees or children of employees, senior citizens. *ROTC:* Army.

**LOANS** *Average need-based loan:* Freshmen: $3500. Undergraduates: $5500. *Programs:* Federal Direct (Subsidized and Unsubsidized Stafford, PLUS), Perkins, Federal Nursing, private loans.

**WORK-STUDY** Federal work-study jobs available. *State or other work-study/employment:* Part-time jobs available.

**APPLYING FOR FINANCIAL AID** *Required financial aid forms:* FAFSA, institution's own form, state aid form. *Financial aid deadline:* 8/15 (priority: 3/1). *Notification date:* Continuous beginning 3/1. Students must reply by 5/1 or within 4 weeks of notification.

**CONTACT** Ms. Nina Morton, Director of Financial Aid, University of Charleston, 2300 MacCorkle Avenue SE, Charleston, WV 25304-1099, 304-357-4947 or toll-free 800-995-GOUC. *E-mail:* ninamorton@ucwv.edu. *Website:* http://www.ucwv.edu/.

# UNIVERSITY OF CHICAGO
## Chicago, IL

| Tuition & fees: $48,253 | Average undergraduate aid package: $43,220 |
|---|---|

**ABOUT THE INSTITUTION** Independent, coed. *Awards:* bachelor's, master's, and doctoral degrees. 49 undergraduate majors. *Total enrollment:* 12,558. Undergraduates: 5,681. Freshmen: 1,445. Both federal and institutional methodology are used as a basis for awarding need-based institutional aid.

**UNDERGRADUATE EXPENSES for 2015–2016** *Application fee:* $75. *One-time required fee:* $1128. *Comprehensive fee:* $62,458 includes full-time tuition ($47,139), mandatory fees ($1114), and room and board ($14,205). Full-time tuition and fees vary according to course load and program. Room and board charges vary according to board plan and housing facility. Part-time tuition and fees vary according to course load and program. *Payment plan:* Tuition prepayment.

**FRESHMAN FINANCIAL AID (Fall 2014, est.)** 906 applied for aid; of those 79% were deemed to have need. 100% of freshmen with need received aid; of those 100% had need fully met. *Average percent of need met:* 100% (excluding resources awarded to replace EFC). *Average financial aid package:* $43,402 (excluding resources awarded to replace EFC).

**UNDERGRADUATE FINANCIAL AID (Fall 2014, est.)** 3,032 applied for aid; of those 85% were deemed to have need. 100% of undergraduates with need received aid; of those 100% had need fully met. *Average percent of need met:* 100% (excluding resources awarded to replace EFC). *Average financial aid package:* $43,220 (excluding resources awarded to replace EFC).

**GIFT AID (NEED-BASED)** *Total amount:* $103,459,781 (4% federal, 1% state, 93% institutional, 2% external sources). *Receiving aid:* Freshmen: 49% (712); all full-time undergraduates: 45% (2,540). *Average award:* Freshmen: $40,705; Undergraduates: $39,784. *Scholarships, grants, and awards:* Federal Pell, FSEOG, state, private, college/university gift aid from institutional funds.

**GIFT AID (NON-NEED-BASED)** *Total amount:* $11,326,014 (80% institutional, 20% external sources). *Receiving aid:* Freshmen: 19% (280). Undergraduates: 14% (790). *Scholarships, grants, and awards by category:* Academic interests/achievement: general academic interests/achievements. *Special achievements/activities:* community service, leadership. *Tuition waivers:* Full or partial for employees or children of employees. *ROTC:* Army cooperative, Air Force cooperative.

**LOANS** *Student loans:* $9,412,040 (63% need-based, 37% non-need-based). 41% of past graduating class borrowed through all loan programs. *Average indebtedness per student:* $23,223. *Average need-based loan:* Freshmen: $2849. Undergraduates: $4196. *Parent loans:* $4,760,466 (100% non-need-based). *Programs:* Federal Direct (Subsidized and Unsubsidized Stafford, PLUS), Perkins.

**WORK-STUDY** *Federal work-study:* Total amount: $2,158,450; jobs available. *State or other work-study/employment:* Part-time jobs available.

**APPLYING FOR FINANCIAL AID** *Required financial aid forms:* FAFSA, CSS Financial Aid PROFILE, noncustodial (divorced/separated) parent's statement, federal income tax form(s). *Financial aid deadline (priority):* 2/1. *Notification date:* 4/1. Students must reply by 5/1.

**CONTACT** Office of College Aid, University of Chicago, 1101 East 58th Street, Chicago, IL 60637, 773-702-8666. *Fax:* 773-834-4300. *E-mail:* college-aid@uchicago.edu. *Website:* http://www.uchicago.edu/.

# UNIVERSITY OF CINCINNATI
## Cincinnati, OH

| Tuition & fees (OH res): $3318 | Average undergraduate aid package: $8470 |
|---|---|

**ABOUT THE INSTITUTION** State-supported, coed. *Awards:* certificates, associate, bachelor's, master's, and doctoral degrees. 139 undergraduate majors. *Total enrollment:* 35,421. Undergraduates: 24,407. Freshmen: 4,618. Federal methodology is used as a basis for awarding need-based institutional aid.

**UNDERGRADUATE EXPENSES for 2015–2016** *Application fee:* $50. *Tuition, state resident:* full-time $1100; part-time $398 per credit hour. *Tuition, nonresident:* full-time $26,334; part-time $1098 per credit hour. *Required fees:* full-time $2218; $70 per credit hour. Full-time tuition and fees vary according to

course load, degree level, location, program, and reciprocity agreements. Part-time tuition and fees vary according to course load, degree level, location, program, and reciprocity agreements. **College room and board:** $10,750; **Room only:** $6430. Room and board charges vary according to board plan and housing facility.
**FRESHMAN FINANCIAL AID (Fall 2014, est.)** 3,865 applied for aid; of those 70% were deemed to have need. 93% of freshmen with need received aid; of those 7% had need fully met. **Average percent of need met:** 46% (excluding resources awarded to replace EFC). **Average financial aid package:** $8662 (excluding resources awarded to replace EFC). 18% of all full-time freshmen had no need and received non-need-based gift aid.
**UNDERGRADUATE FINANCIAL AID (Fall 2014, est.)** 14,579 applied for aid; of those 79% were deemed to have need. 94% of undergraduates with need received aid; of those 4% had need fully met. **Average percent of need met:** 43% (excluding resources awarded to replace EFC). **Average financial aid package:** $8470 (excluding resources awarded to replace EFC). 15% of all full-time undergraduates had no need and received non-need-based gift aid.
**GIFT AID (NEED-BASED) Total amount:** $52,893,488 (52% federal, 8% state, 33% institutional, 7% external sources). **Receiving aid:** Freshmen: 22% (1,023); all full-time undergraduates: 24% (4,997). **Average award:** Freshmen: $6107; Undergraduates: $5710. **Scholarships, grants, and awards:** Federal Pell, FSEOG, state, private, college/university gift aid from institutional funds, United Negro College Fund, Federal Nursing, TEACH Grants.
**GIFT AID (NON-NEED-BASED) Total amount:** $18,428,655 (86% institutional, 14% external sources). **Receiving aid:** Freshmen: 30% (1,392). Undergraduates: 20% (4,129). **Average award:** Freshmen: $5395. Undergraduates: $5026. **Tuition waivers:** Full or partial for employees or children of employees. **ROTC:** Army, Air Force.
**LOANS Student loans:** $96,552,527 (88% need-based, 12% non-need-based). 66% of past graduating class borrowed through all loan programs. *Average indebtedness per student:* $28,228. **Average need-based loan:** Freshmen: $3798. Undergraduates: $4588. **Parent loans:** $48,413,905 (80% need-based, 20% non-need-based). **Programs:** Federal Direct (Subsidized and Unsubsidized Stafford, PLUS), Perkins, Federal Nursing, state, college/university.
**WORK-STUDY Federal work-study:** Total amount: $2,879,554; 922 jobs averaging $3072.
**ATHLETIC AWARDS** Total amount: $4,218,121 (51% need-based, 49% non-need-based).
**APPLYING FOR FINANCIAL AID Required financial aid form:** FAFSA. **Financial aid deadline:** Continuous. **Notification date:** Continuous beginning 3/10. Students must reply within 2 weeks of notification.
**CONTACT** Mr. Randy Ulses, Director, Scholarships and Enrollment, University of Cincinnati, PO Box 210125, Cincinnati, OH 45221-0125, 513-556-1000. *Fax:* 513-556-9171. *E-mail:* financeaid@uc.edu.
*Website:* http://www.uc.edu/.

**UNDERGRADUATE FINANCIAL AID (Fall 2014, est.)** 12,446 applied for aid; of those 74% were deemed to have need. 97% of undergraduates with need received aid; of those 40% had need fully met. **Average percent of need met:** 80% (excluding resources awarded to replace EFC). **Average financial aid package:** $16,269 (excluding resources awarded to replace EFC). 24% of all full-time undergraduates had no need and received non-need-based gift aid.
**GIFT AID (NEED-BASED) Total amount:** $74,046,402 (29% federal, 9% state, 57% institutional, 5% external sources). **Receiving aid:** Freshmen: 32% (1,831); all full-time undergraduates: 29% (6,893). **Average award:** Freshmen: $10,775; Undergraduates: $10,380. **Scholarships, grants, and awards:** Federal Pell, FSEOG, state, private, college/university gift aid from institutional funds.
**GIFT AID (NON-NEED-BASED) Total amount:** $32,398,052 (9% federal, 1% state, 51% institutional, 39% external sources). **Receiving aid:** Freshmen: 2% (98). Undergraduates: 1% (262). **Average award:** Freshmen: $9676. Undergraduates: $10,019. **Scholarships, grants, and awards by category:** *Academic interests/achievement:* architecture, area/ethnic studies, biological sciences, business, communication, computer science, education, engineering/technologies, English, foreign languages, general academic interests/achievements, health fields, humanities, international studies, mathematics, military science, physical sciences, premedicine, social sciences. *Creative arts/performance:* art/fine arts, cinema/film/broadcasting, creative writing, dance, journalism/publications, music, performing arts, theater/drama. *Special achievements/activities:* community service, general special achievements/activities, leadership. *Special characteristics:* first-generation college students, general special characteristics, local/state students. **Tuition waivers:** Full or partial for employees or children of employees, senior citizens. **ROTC:** Army, Naval, Air Force.
**LOANS Student loans:** $88,941,227 (60% need-based, 40% non-need-based). 46% of past graduating class borrowed through all loan programs. *Average indebtedness per student:* $25,126. **Average need-based loan:** Freshmen: $5387. Undergraduates: $6418. **Parent loans:** $84,838,221 (33% need-based, 67% non-need-based). **Programs:** Federal Direct (Subsidized and Unsubsidized Stafford, PLUS), Perkins, college/university, private loans.
**WORK-STUDY Federal work-study:** Total amount: $757,289; 1,127 jobs averaging $1743. **State or other work-study/employment:** Total amount: $3,804,510 (96% need-based, 4% non-need-based). 708 part-time jobs averaging $2600.
**ATHLETIC AWARDS** Total amount: $8,241,827 (32% need-based, 68% non-need-based).
**APPLYING FOR FINANCIAL AID Required financial aid forms:** FAFSA, federal income tax form(s). **Financial aid deadline (priority):** 3/1. **Notification date:** Continuous beginning 3/15. Students must reply within 3 weeks of notification.
**CONTACT** Gwen E. Pomper, Director of Financial Aid, University of Colorado Boulder, 556 UCB, Boulder, CO 80309-0077, 303-492-5091. *Fax:* 303-492-0838. *E-mail:* finaid@colorado.edu.
*Website:* http://www.colorado.edu/.

# UNIVERSITY OF COLORADO BOULDER
## Boulder, CO

| Tuition & fees (CO res): $10,789 | Average undergraduate aid package: $16,269 |
| --- | --- |

**ABOUT THE INSTITUTION** State-supported, coed. **Awards:** certificates, bachelor's, master's, and doctoral degrees. 70 undergraduate majors. **Total enrollment:** 32,080. Undergraduates: 26,426. Freshmen: 5,869. Federal methodology is used as a basis for awarding need-based institutional aid.
**UNDERGRADUATE EXPENSES for 2015–2016 Application fee:** $50. **One-time required fee:** $182. **Tuition, state resident:** full-time $9048. **Tuition, nonresident:** full-time $31,410. **Required fees:** full-time $1741. Full-time tuition and fees vary according to program. Part-time tuition and fees vary according to course load and program. **College room and board:** $12,810. Room and board charges vary according to board plan, housing facility, and location.
**FRESHMAN FINANCIAL AID (Fall 2014, est.)** 3,747 applied for aid; of those 65% were deemed to have need. 97% of freshmen with need received aid; of those 43% had need fully met. **Average percent of need met:** 81% (excluding resources awarded to replace EFC). **Average financial aid package:** $15,782 (excluding resources awarded to replace EFC). 30% of all full-time freshmen had no need and received non-need-based gift aid.

# UNIVERSITY OF COLORADO COLORADO SPRINGS
## Colorado Springs, CO

| Tuition & fees (CO res): $9143 | Average undergraduate aid package: $7805 |
| --- | --- |

**ABOUT THE INSTITUTION** State-supported, coed. **Awards:** certificates, bachelor's, master's, and doctoral degrees. 31 undergraduate majors. **Total enrollment:** 11,463. Undergraduates: 9,489. Freshmen: 1,722. Federal methodology is used as a basis for awarding need-based institutional aid.
**UNDERGRADUATE EXPENSES for 2015–2016 Application fee:** $50. **One-time required fee:** $100. **Tuition, state resident:** full-time $7710; part-time $332 per credit hour. **Tuition, nonresident:** full-time $20,250; part-time $675 per credit hour. **Required fees:** full-time $1433; $388 per term or $388 per term. Full-time tuition and fees vary according to course level, course load, degree level, location, program, reciprocity agreements, and student level. Part-time tuition and fees vary according to course level, course load, degree level, location, program, reciprocity agreements, and student level. **College room and board:** $9150. Room and board charges vary according to board plan and housing facility.
**FRESHMAN FINANCIAL AID (Fall 2013)** 1,238 applied for aid; of those 72% were deemed to have need. 91% of freshmen with need received aid; of those 3% had need fully met. **Average percent of need met:** 42% (excluding resources awarded to replace EFC). **Average financial aid package:** $7865 (excluding resources

awarded to replace EFC). 5% of all full-time freshmen had no need and received non-need-based gift aid.

**UNDERGRADUATE FINANCIAL AID (Fall 2013)** 5,536 applied for aid; of those 75% were deemed to have need. 91% of undergraduates with need received aid; of those 4% had need fully met. *Average percent of need met:* 46% (excluding resources awarded to replace EFC). *Average financial aid package:* $7805 (excluding resources awarded to replace EFC). 4% of all full-time undergraduates had no need and received non-need-based gift aid.

**GIFT AID (NEED-BASED)** *Total amount:* $22,449,376 (51% federal, 11% state, 28% institutional, 10% external sources). *Receiving aid:* Freshmen: 35% (508); all full-time undergraduates: 35% (2,449). *Average award:* Freshmen: $3421; Undergraduates: $5481. *Scholarships, grants, and awards:* Federal Pell, FSEOG, state, private, college/university gift aid from institutional funds.

**GIFT AID (NON-NEED-BASED)** *Receiving aid:* Freshmen: 15% (217). Undergraduates: 12% (832). *Average award:* Freshmen: $2711. Undergraduates: $3750. *Scholarships, grants, and awards by category:* Academic interests/achievement: general academic interests/achievements. *Special achievements/activities:* leadership. *Tuition waivers:* Full or partial for employees or children of employees. *ROTC:* Army.

**LOANS** *Student loans:* $33,865,234 (100% need-based). 69% of past graduating class borrowed through all loan programs. *Average indebtedness per student:* $19,780. *Average need-based loan:* Freshmen: $3895. Undergraduates: $4203. *Parent loans:* $9,597,460 (100% need-based). *Programs:* Federal Direct (Subsidized and Unsubsidized Stafford, PLUS), Perkins.

**WORK-STUDY** *Federal work-study:* 190 jobs averaging $2385. *State or other work-study/employment:* Total amount: $570,237 (89% need-based, 11% non-need-based). 237 part-time jobs averaging $3004.

**ATHLETIC AWARDS** Total amount: $793,220 (100% need-based).

**APPLYING FOR FINANCIAL AID** *Required financial aid form:* FAFSA. *Financial aid deadline (priority):* 3/1. *Notification date:* Continuous beginning 4/15.

**CONTACT** Jevita Rogers, Director of Financial Aid, University of Colorado Colorado Springs, 1420 Austin Bluffs Parkway, Colorado Springs, CO 80918, 719-255-3460 or toll-free 800-990-8227 Ext. 3383. *Fax:* 719-255-3650. *E-mail:* finaidse@uccs.edu.
*Website:* http://www.uccs.edu/.

**GIFT AID (NEED-BASED)** *Total amount:* $28,304,524 (50% federal, 14% state, 29% institutional, 7% external sources). *Receiving aid:* Freshmen: 51% (547); all full-time undergraduates: 46% (3,533). *Average award:* Freshmen: $7333; Undergraduates: $6907. *Scholarships, grants, and awards:* Federal Pell, FSEOG, state, private, college/university gift aid from institutional funds, College Access Challenge Grants, TEACH Grants, Armed Services Scholarships.

**GIFT AID (NON-NEED-BASED)** *Total amount:* $2,172,590 (1% state, 79% institutional, 20% external sources). *Receiving aid:* Freshmen: 1% (15). Undergraduates: 1% (51). *Average award:* Freshmen: $2271. Undergraduates: $3114. *Scholarships, grants, and awards by category:* Academic interests/achievement: 964 awards ($1,739,529 total): biological sciences, business, communication, education, engineering/technologies, English, general academic interests/achievements, humanities, international studies, mathematics, physical sciences, premedicine, social sciences. *Creative arts/performance:* 12 awards ($6950 total): applied art and design, art/fine arts, general creative arts/performance, music, performing arts, theater/drama. *Special characteristics:* 333 awards ($1,626,829 total): children of faculty/staff, first-generation college students, general special characteristics, handicapped students, international students, out-of-state students, veterans. *Tuition waivers:* Full or partial for employees or children of employees. *ROTC:* Army cooperative, Air Force cooperative.

**LOANS** *Student loans:* $37,759,488 (79% need-based, 21% non-need-based). 51% of past graduating class borrowed through all loan programs. *Average indebtedness per student:* $21,502. *Average need-based loan:* Freshmen: $3188. Undergraduates: $4333. *Parent loans:* $7,165,397 (14% need-based, 86% non-need-based). *Programs:* Federal Direct (Subsidized and Unsubsidized Stafford, PLUS), Perkins, Federal Nursing.

**WORK-STUDY** *Federal work-study:* 266 jobs averaging $3140. *State or other work-study/employment:* Total amount: $751,676 (98% need-based, 2% non-need-based). 200 part-time jobs averaging $3758.

**APPLYING FOR FINANCIAL AID** *Required financial aid form:* FAFSA. *Financial aid deadline:* Continuous. *Notification date:* Continuous beginning 4/1.

**CONTACT** Justin Jaramillo, Interim Director of Financial Aid, University of Colorado Denver, PO Box 173364, Denver, CO 80217-3364, 303-315-1835. *Fax:* 303-556-2325. *E-mail:* financial.aid@ucdenver.edu.
*Website:* http://www.ucdenver.edu/.

# UNIVERSITY OF COLORADO DENVER
## Denver, CO

| Tuition & fees (CO res): $9985 | Average undergraduate aid package: $9059 |
|---|---|

**ABOUT THE INSTITUTION** State-supported, coed. *Awards:* certificates, bachelor's, master's, and doctoral degrees. 35 undergraduate majors. *Total enrollment:* 22,791. Undergraduates: 13,509. Freshmen: 1,367. Federal methodology is used as a basis for awarding need-based institutional aid.

**UNDERGRADUATE EXPENSES for 2015–2016** *Application fee:* $50. *Tuition, state resident:* full-time $8760; part-time $292 per credit hour. *Tuition, nonresident:* full-time $27,030; part-time $901 per credit hour. *Required fees:* full-time $1225; $1225 per year. Full-time tuition and fees vary according to course level, course load, degree level, location, program, reciprocity agreements, and student level. Part-time tuition and fees vary according to course level, course load, degree level, location, program, reciprocity agreements, and student level. *College room and board:* $11,140; *Room only:* $7640. Room and board charges vary according to board plan.

**FRESHMAN FINANCIAL AID (Fall 2013)** 928 applied for aid; of those 76% were deemed to have need. 91% of freshmen with need received aid; of those 4% had need fully met. *Average percent of need met:* 52% (excluding resources awarded to replace EFC). *Average financial aid package:* $8565 (excluding resources awarded to replace EFC). 9% of all full-time freshmen had no need and received non-need-based gift aid.

**UNDERGRADUATE FINANCIAL AID (Fall 2013)** 5,489 applied for aid; of those 85% were deemed to have need. 94% of undergraduates with need received aid; of those 4% had need fully met. *Average percent of need met:* 51% (excluding resources awarded to replace EFC). *Average financial aid package:* $9059 (excluding resources awarded to replace EFC). 6% of all full-time undergraduates had no need and received non-need-based gift aid.

# UNIVERSITY OF CONNECTICUT
## Storrs, CT

| Tuition & fees: $2842 | Average undergraduate aid package: $13,545 |
|---|---|

**ABOUT THE INSTITUTION** State-supported, coed. *Awards:* certificates, associate, bachelor's, master's, and doctoral degrees. 101 undergraduate majors. *Total enrollment:* 26,541. Undergraduates: 18,395. Freshmen: 3,588. Federal methodology is used as a basis for awarding need-based institutional aid.

**UNDERGRADUATE EXPENSES for 2015–2016** *Application fee:* $70. *College room only:* $6660. Room and board charges vary according to board plan and housing facility. Part-time tuition and fees vary according to course load.

**FRESHMAN FINANCIAL AID (Fall 2014, est.)** 2,949 applied for aid; of those 69% were deemed to have need. 98% of freshmen with need received aid; of those 14% had need fully met. *Average percent of need met:* 60% (excluding resources awarded to replace EFC). *Average financial aid package:* $14,256 (excluding resources awarded to replace EFC). 13% of all full-time freshmen had no need and received non-need-based gift aid.

**UNDERGRADUATE FINANCIAL AID (Fall 2014, est.)** 12,722 applied for aid; of those 78% were deemed to have need. 98% of undergraduates with need received aid; of those 13% had need fully met. *Average percent of need met:* 61% (excluding resources awarded to replace EFC). *Average financial aid package:* $13,545 (excluding resources awarded to replace EFC). 11% of all full-time undergraduates had no need and received non-need-based gift aid.

**GIFT AID (NEED-BASED)** *Total amount:* $80,158,401 (21% federal, 11% state, 63% institutional, 5% external sources). *Receiving aid:* Freshmen: 39% (1,384); all full-time undergraduates: 41% (7,154). *Average award:* Freshmen: $9827; Undergraduates: $8754. *Scholarships, grants, and awards:* Federal Pell, FSEOG, state, private, college/university gift aid from institutional funds.

**GIFT AID (NON-NEED-BASED)** *Total amount:* $19,699,233 (86% institutional, 14% external sources). *Receiving aid:* Freshmen: 28% (1,016). Undergraduates: 20% (3,521). *Average award:* Freshmen: $7535. Undergraduates: $6519. *Scholarships, grants, and awards by category: Academic interests/achievement:* 6,039 awards ($26,000,257 total): agriculture, biological sciences, business, communication, computer science, education, engineering/technologies, English, foreign languages, general academic interests/achievements, health fields, humanities, international studies, mathematics, physical sciences, premedicine, religion/biblical studies, social sciences. *Creative arts/performance:* 178 awards ($325,376 total): art/fine arts, music, theater/drama. *Special achievements/activities:* 918 awards ($6,777,496 total): community service, leadership. *Special characteristics:* 781 awards ($8,015,426 total): adult students, children of faculty/staff, children of union members/company employees, handicapped students, local/state students, out-of-state students, spouses of deceased or disabled public servants, veterans. *Tuition waivers:* Full or partial for employees or children of employees, senior citizens. *ROTC:* Army, Air Force.

**LOANS** *Student loans:* $79,148,774 (85% need-based, 15% non-need-based). 64% of past graduating class borrowed through all loan programs. *Average indebtedness per student:* $24,999. *Average need-based loan:* Freshmen: $3456. Undergraduates: $4443. *Parent loans:* $49,045,457 (39% need-based, 61% non-need-based). *Programs:* Federal Direct (Subsidized and Unsubsidized Stafford, PLUS), Perkins, Federal Nursing.

**WORK-STUDY** *Federal work-study:* Total amount: $1,085,918; 631 jobs averaging $2040. *State or other work-study/employment:* Total amount: $16,271,579 (32% need-based, 68% non-need-based). 4,295 part-time jobs averaging $2392.

**ATHLETIC AWARDS** Total amount: $11,616,930 (29% need-based, 71% non-need-based).

**APPLYING FOR FINANCIAL AID** *Required financial aid form:* FAFSA. *Financial aid deadline (priority):* 3/1. *Notification date:* Continuous beginning 3/1.

**CONTACT** Mona L. Lucas, Director of Financial Aid, University of Connecticut, 233 Glenbrook Road, Unit 4116, Storrs, CT 06269-4116, 860-486-2819. *Fax:* 860-486-6629. *E-mail:* financialaid@uconn.edu. *Website:* http://www.uconn.edu/.

# UNIVERSITY OF DALLAS
## Irving, TX

| Tuition & fees: $35,800 | Average undergraduate aid package: $28,690 |
|---|---|

**ABOUT THE INSTITUTION** Independent Roman Catholic, coed. *Awards:* certificates, bachelor's, master's, and doctoral degrees. 33 undergraduate majors. *Total enrollment:* 2,548. Undergraduates: 1,327. Freshmen: 342. Federal methodology is used as a basis for awarding need-based institutional aid.

**UNDERGRADUATE EXPENSES for 2015–2016** *Application fee:* $50. *Comprehensive fee:* $47,100 includes full-time tuition ($33,360), mandatory fees ($2440), and room and board ($11,300). *College room only:* $6450. Full-time tuition and fees vary according to course load. Room and board charges vary according to board plan and housing facility. *Part-time tuition:* $1330 per credit. *Part-time fees:* $2440 per year. Part-time tuition and fees vary according to course load.

**FRESHMAN FINANCIAL AID (Fall 2014, est.)** 279 applied for aid; of those 84% were deemed to have need. 100% of freshmen with need received aid; of those 22% had need fully met. *Average percent of need met:* 82% (excluding resources awarded to replace EFC). *Average financial aid package:* $30,165 (excluding resources awarded to replace EFC). 30% of all full-time freshmen had no need and received non-need-based gift aid.

**UNDERGRADUATE FINANCIAL AID (Fall 2014, est.)** 906 applied for aid; of those 89% were deemed to have need. 100% of undergraduates with need received aid; of those 22% had need fully met. *Average percent of need met:* 79% (excluding resources awarded to replace EFC). *Average financial aid package:* $28,690 (excluding resources awarded to replace EFC). 49% of all full-time undergraduates had no need and received non-need-based gift aid.

**GIFT AID (NEED-BASED)** *Total amount:* $18,846,668 (7% federal, 5% state, 87% institutional, 1% external sources). *Receiving aid:* Freshmen: 68% (232); all full-time undergraduates: 60% (790). *Average award:* Freshmen: $25,881; Undergraduates: $23,392. *Scholarships, grants, and awards:* Federal Pell, FSEOG, state, private, college/university gift aid from institutional funds.

**GIFT AID (NON-NEED-BASED)** *Total amount:* $7,736,726 (99% institutional, 1% external sources). *Receiving aid:* Freshmen: 14% (47). Undergraduates: 10% (134). *Average award:* Freshmen: $18,949. Undergraduates: $16,730. *Scholarships, grants, and awards by category: Academic interests/achievement:* 1,583 awards ($20,309,529 total): biological sciences, business, education, foreign languages, general academic interests/achievements, mathematics, physical sciences, premedicine. *Creative arts/performance:* 37 awards ($81,000 total): art/fine arts, theater/drama. *Special achievements/activities:* 12 awards ($14,000 total). *Special characteristics:* 30 awards ($541,225 total): children of faculty/staff, ethnic background, religious affiliation, siblings of current students. *Tuition waivers:* Full or partial for employees or children of employees. *ROTC:* Army cooperative, Air Force cooperative.

**LOANS** *Student loans:* $6,749,016 (81% need-based, 19% non-need-based). 61% of past graduating class borrowed through all loan programs. *Average indebtedness per student:* $36,561. *Average need-based loan:* Freshmen: $4873. Undergraduates: $5929. *Parent loans:* $1,536,721 (100% non-need-based). *Programs:* Federal Direct (Subsidized and Unsubsidized Stafford, PLUS), Perkins, state.

**WORK-STUDY** *Federal work-study:* Total amount: $391,474; 274 jobs averaging $1522. *State or other work-study/employment:* Total amount: $111,800 (92% need-based, 8% non-need-based). 73 part-time jobs averaging $1587.

**APPLYING FOR FINANCIAL AID** *Required financial aid form:* FAFSA. *Financial aid deadline:* 11/15 (priority: 3/1). *Notification date:* Continuous beginning 3/1. Students must reply by 5/1 or within 2 weeks of notification.

**CONTACT** Mrs. Taryn Anderson, Director of Financial Aid, University of Dallas, 1845 East Northgate Drive, Irving, TX 75062, 972-721-5266 or toll-free 800-628-6999. *Fax:* 972-721-5017. *E-mail:* ugadmis@udallas.edu. *Website:* http://www.udallas.edu/.

# UNIVERSITY OF DAYTON
## Dayton, OH

| Tuition & fees: $37,230 | Average undergraduate aid package: $23,498 |
|---|---|

**ABOUT THE INSTITUTION** Independent Roman Catholic, coed. *Awards:* certificates, bachelor's, master's, and doctoral degrees. 74 undergraduate majors. *Total enrollment:* 11,343. Undergraduates: 8,529. Freshmen: 2,173. Federal methodology is used as a basis for awarding need-based institutional aid.

**UNDERGRADUATE EXPENSES for 2015–2016** *Application fee:* $50. *Comprehensive fee:* $49,070 includes full-time tuition ($37,230) and room and board ($11,840). *College room only:* $7100. Full-time tuition and fees vary according to degree level. Room and board charges vary according to board plan and housing facility. *Part-time tuition:* $1241 per credit hour. Part-time tuition and fees vary according to course load and degree level. *Payment plan:* Tuition prepayment.

**FRESHMAN FINANCIAL AID (Fall 2014, est.)** 1,899 applied for aid; of those 70% were deemed to have need. 100% of freshmen with need received aid; of those 31% had need fully met. *Average percent of need met:* 86% (excluding resources awarded to replace EFC). *Average financial aid package:* $26,436 (excluding resources awarded to replace EFC). 24% of all full-time freshmen had no need and received non-need-based gift aid.

**UNDERGRADUATE FINANCIAL AID (Fall 2014, est.)** 5,729 applied for aid; of those 71% were deemed to have need. 100% of undergraduates with need received aid; of those 35% had need fully met. *Average percent of need met:* 84% (excluding resources awarded to replace EFC). *Average financial aid package:* $23,498 (excluding resources awarded to replace EFC). 35% of all full-time undergraduates had no need and received non-need-based gift aid.

**GIFT AID (NEED-BASED)** *Total amount:* $75,037,899 (6% federal, 1% state, 92% institutional, 1% external sources). *Receiving aid:* Freshmen: 62% (1,337); all full-time undergraduates: 51% (4,048). *Average award:* Freshmen: $23,610; Undergraduates: $20,508. *Scholarships, grants, and awards:* Federal Pell, FSEOG, state, private, college/university gift aid from institutional funds.

**GIFT AID (NON-NEED-BASED)** *Total amount:* $46,984,755 (98% institutional, 2% external sources). *Receiving aid:* Freshmen: 12% (257). Undergraduates: 10% (821). *Average award:* Freshmen: $13,572. Undergraduates: $12,540. *Scholarships, grants, and awards by category: Academic interests/achievement:* biological sciences, business, communication, computer science, education, engineering/technologies, English, foreign languages, general academic interests/achievements, health fields, humanities, international studies, mathematics, military science, physical sciences, premedicine, religion/biblical studies, social sciences. *Creative arts/performance:* art/fine arts, music. *Special achievements/activities:* leadership. *Special characteristics:* children and siblings of alumni, children of faculty/staff, local/state students, members of minority groups, religious affiliation. *Tuition waivers:* Full or partial for employees or children of employees, adult students, senior citizens. *ROTC:* Army, Air Force cooperative.

**LOANS** *Student loans:* $38,801,052 (57% need-based, 43% non-need-based). 60% of past graduating class borrowed through all loan programs. *Average indebtedness per student:* $35,278. *Average need-based loan:* Freshmen: $2909. Undergraduates: $4895. *Parent loans:* $15,504,456 (35% need-based, 65% non-need-based). *Programs:* Federal Direct (Subsidized and Unsubsidized Stafford, PLUS), Perkins.

**WORK-STUDY** *Federal work-study:* Total amount: $2,500,000; jobs available. *State or other work-study/employment:* Total amount: $9,500,000 (26% need-based, 74% non-need-based). Part-time jobs available.

**ATHLETIC AWARDS** Total amount: $4,719,568 (9% need-based, 91% non-need-based).

**APPLYING FOR FINANCIAL AID** *Required financial aid form:* FAFSA. *Financial aid deadline (priority):* 3/1. *Notification date:* Continuous beginning 3/20. Students must reply within 2 weeks of notification.

**CONTACT** Kathy Harmon, Dean of Admission and Financial Aid, University of Dayton, 300 College Park, Dayton, OH 45469-1668, 937-229-4311 or toll-free 800-837-7433. *Fax:* 937-229-4338. *E-mail:* kharmon@udayton.edu. *Website:* http://www.udayton.edu/.

# UNIVERSITY OF DELAWARE
## Newark, DE

| Tuition & fees (DE res): $12,342 | Average undergraduate aid package: $15,854 |
|---|---|

**ABOUT THE INSTITUTION** State-related, coed. *Awards:* associate, bachelor's, master's, and doctoral degrees. 126 undergraduate majors. *Total enrollment:* 21,895. Undergraduates: 18,141. Freshmen: 4,179. Federal methodology is used as a basis for awarding need-based institutional aid.

**UNDERGRADUATE EXPENSES for 2015–2016** *Application fee:* $75. *Tuition, state resident:* full-time $10,900; part-time $454 per credit hour. *Tuition, nonresident:* full-time $29,250; part-time $1219 per credit hour. *Required fees:* full-time $1442. *College room and board:* $11,558; *Room only:* $7014. Room and board charges vary according to board plan, housing facility, and student level.

**FRESHMAN FINANCIAL AID (Fall 2014, est.)** 3,694 applied for aid; of those 64% were deemed to have need. 95% of freshmen with need received aid; of those 51% had need fully met. *Average percent of need met:* 76% (excluding resources awarded to replace EFC). *Average financial aid package:* $15,989 (excluding resources awarded to replace EFC). 28% of all full-time freshmen had no need and received non-need-based gift aid.

**UNDERGRADUATE FINANCIAL AID (Fall 2014, est.)** 12,076 applied for aid; of those 69% were deemed to have need. 98% of undergraduates with need received aid; of those 47% had need fully met. *Average percent of need met:* 75% (excluding resources awarded to replace EFC). *Average financial aid package:* $15,854 (excluding resources awarded to replace EFC). 23% of all full-time undergraduates had no need and received non-need-based gift aid.

**GIFT AID (NEED-BASED)** *Total amount:* $63,400,803 (19% federal, 12% state, 63% institutional, 6% external sources). *Receiving aid:* Freshmen: 52% (2,164); all full-time undergraduates: 41% (6,875). *Average award:* Freshmen: $9756; Undergraduates: $8991. *Scholarships, grants, and awards:* Federal Pell, FSEOG, state, private, college/university gift aid from institutional funds.

**GIFT AID (NON-NEED-BASED)** *Total amount:* $33,987,366 (5% state, 79% institutional, 16% external sources). *Receiving aid:* Freshmen: 35% (1,460). Undergraduates: 27% (4,571). *Average award:* Freshmen: $7349. Undergraduates: $7037. *Scholarships, grants, and awards by category:* Academic interests/achievement: agriculture, biological sciences, business, communication, computer science, education, engineering/technologies, English, foreign languages, general academic interests/achievements, health fields, humanities, international studies, mathematics, military science, physical sciences, premedicine, religion/biblical studies, social sciences. *Creative arts/performance:* applied art and design, art/fine arts, music, theater/drama. *Special achievements/activities:* cheerleading/drum major, community service, general special achievements/activities, leadership. *Special characteristics:* children and siblings of alumni, children of faculty/staff, children of public servants, ethnic background, first-generation college students, general special characteristics, local/state students, members of minority groups. *Tuition waivers:* Full or partial for employees or children of employees, senior citizens. *ROTC:* Army, Air Force.

**LOANS** *Student loans:* $94,514,735 (57% need-based, 43% non-need-based). 58% of past graduating class borrowed through all loan programs. *Average indebtedness per student:* $32,705. *Average need-based loan:* Freshmen: $6605. Undergraduates: $7904. *Parent loans:* $34,104,912 (33% need-based, 67% non-need-based). *Programs:* Federal Direct (Subsidized and Unsubsidized Stafford, PLUS), Perkins, Federal Nursing.

**WORK-STUDY** *Federal work-study:* Total amount: $525,000; jobs available. *State or other work-study/employment:* Total amount: $127,525 (100% need-based). Part-time jobs available.

**ATHLETIC AWARDS** Total amount: $9,851,434 (30% need-based, 70% non-need-based).

**APPLYING FOR FINANCIAL AID** *Required financial aid form:* FAFSA. *Financial aid deadline:* 3/15 (priority: 2/1). *Notification date:* Continuous beginning 3/15. Students must reply by 5/1 or within 3 weeks of notification.

**CONTACT** Mr. James Holloway, Manager of Student Financial Services Compliance, University of Delaware, 140 Student Services Building, Newark, DE 19716, 302-831-0520. *Fax:* 302-831-4334. *E-mail:* holloway@udel.edu. *Website:* http://www.udel.edu/.

# UNIVERSITY OF DENVER
## Denver, CO

| Tuition & fees: $42,090 | Average undergraduate aid package: $34,455 |
|---|---|

**ABOUT THE INSTITUTION** Independent, coed. *Awards:* certificates, bachelor's, master's, and doctoral degrees. 72 undergraduate majors. *Total enrollment:* 11,808. Undergraduates: 5,643. Freshmen: 1,424. Institutional methodology is used as a basis for awarding need-based institutional aid.

**UNDERGRADUATE EXPENSES for 2015–2016** *Application fee:* $60. *Comprehensive fee:* $53,199 includes full-time tuition ($41,112), mandatory fees ($978), and room and board ($11,109). *College room only:* $6723. Full-time tuition and fees vary according to course load and program. Room and board charges vary according to board plan and housing facility. *Part-time tuition:* $1142 per credit hour. Part-time tuition and fees vary according to course load and program.

**FRESHMAN FINANCIAL AID (Fall 2014, est.)** 964 applied for aid; of those 71% were deemed to have need. 99% of freshmen with need received aid; of those 37% had need fully met. *Average percent of need met:* 86% (excluding resources awarded to replace EFC). *Average financial aid package:* $34,610 (excluding resources awarded to replace EFC). 33% of all full-time freshmen had no need and received non-need-based gift aid.

**UNDERGRADUATE FINANCIAL AID (Fall 2014, est.)** 2,826 applied for aid; of those 78% were deemed to have need. 100% of undergraduates with need received aid; of those 39% had need fully met. *Average percent of need met:* 86% (excluding resources awarded to replace EFC). *Average financial aid package:* $34,455 (excluding resources awarded to replace EFC). 38% of all full-time undergraduates had no need and received non-need-based gift aid.

**GIFT AID (NEED-BASED)** *Total amount:* $59,538,129 (7% federal, 1% state, 87% institutional, 5% external sources). *Receiving aid:* Freshmen: 48% (678); all full-time undergraduates: 41% (2,163). *Average award:* Freshmen: $29,496; Undergraduates: $28,597. *Scholarships, grants, and awards:* Federal Pell, FSEOG, state, private, college/university gift aid from institutional funds.

**GIFT AID (NON-NEED-BASED)** *Total amount:* $34,182,242 (1% federal, 94% institutional, 5% external sources). *Receiving aid:* Freshmen: 12% (176). Undergraduates: 10% (528). *Average award:* Freshmen: $16,218. Undergraduates: $14,724. *Scholarships, grants, and awards by category:* Academic interests/achievement: biological sciences, business, communication, computer science, engineering/technologies, general academic interests/achievements, humanities, international studies, mathematics, physical sciences, social sciences. *Creative arts/performance:* art/fine arts, debating, music, theater/drama. *Special achievements/activities:* community service, leadership. *Tuition waivers:* Full or partial for employees or children of employees, senior citizens. *ROTC:* Army cooperative, Air Force cooperative.

**LOANS** *Student loans:* $18,035,654 (54% need-based, 46% non-need-based). 45% of past graduating class borrowed through all loan programs. *Average indebtedness per student:* $29,050. *Average need-based loan:* Freshmen: $3346. Undergraduates: $4181. *Parent loans:* $9,432,972 (19% need-based, 81% non-need-based).
**Programs:** Federal Direct (Subsidized and Unsubsidized Stafford, PLUS), Perkins, college/university.
**WORK-STUDY** *Federal work-study:* Total amount: $1,145,381; 380 jobs averaging $2993. *State or other work-study/employment:* Total amount: $592,014 (81% need-based, 19% non-need-based). 197 part-time jobs averaging $3119.
**ATHLETIC AWARDS** Total amount: $9,316,885 (21% need-based, 79% non-need-based).
**APPLYING FOR FINANCIAL AID** *Required financial aid forms:* FAFSA, CSS Financial Aid PROFILE, noncustodial (divorced/separated) parent's statement. *Financial aid deadline:* 5/1 (priority: 2/15). *Notification date:* 3/20. Students must reply by 5/1 or within 4 weeks of notification.
**CONTACT** Ms. Karen Woodrum, Interim Director of Financial Aid, University of Denver, University Hall, 2197 South University Boulevard, Denver, CO 80208, 303-871-4020 or toll-free 800-525-9495. *Fax:* 303-871-2341. *E-mail:* finaid@du.edu. *Website:* http://www.du.edu/.

---

# UNIVERSITY OF DETROIT MERCY
## Detroit, MI

**CONTACT** Sandy Ross, Director of Financial Aid and Scholarships, University of Detroit Mercy, 4001 West McNichols Road, Detroit, MI 48221-3038, 313-993-3350 or toll-free 800-635-5020. *Fax:* 313-993-3347.
*Website:* http://www.udmercy.edu/.

---

# UNIVERSITY OF DUBUQUE
## Dubuque, IA

| Tuition & fees: $26,950 | Average undergraduate aid package: $22,959 |
| --- | --- |

**ABOUT THE INSTITUTION** Independent Presbyterian, coed. *Awards:* associate, bachelor's, and master's degrees. 32 undergraduate majors. *Total enrollment:* 2,118. Undergraduates: 1,764. Freshmen: 447. Federal methodology is used as a basis for awarding need-based institutional aid.
**UNDERGRADUATE EXPENSES** for 2015–2016 *Application fee:* $25. *Comprehensive fee:* $35,440 includes full-time tuition ($25,730), mandatory fees ($1220), and room and board ($8490). *College room only:* $4230. Room and board charges vary according to board plan, housing facility, and location. *Part-time fees:* $570 per credit hour.
**FRESHMAN FINANCIAL AID (Fall 2014, est.)** 371 applied for aid; of those 92% were deemed to have need. 100% of freshmen with need received aid; of those 18% had need fully met. *Average percent of need met:* 79% (excluding resources awarded to replace EFC). *Average financial aid package:* $24,189 (excluding resources awarded to replace EFC). 12% of all full-time freshmen had no need and received non-need-based gift aid.
**UNDERGRADUATE FINANCIAL AID (Fall 2014, est.)** 1,401 applied for aid; of those 93% were deemed to have need. 100% of undergraduates with need received aid; of those 17% had need fully met. *Average percent of need met:* 71% (excluding resources awarded to replace EFC). *Average financial aid package:* $22,959 (excluding resources awarded to replace EFC). 11% of all full-time undergraduates had no need and received non-need-based gift aid.
**GIFT AID (NEED-BASED)** *Total amount:* $22,530,659 (15% federal, 9% state, 54% institutional, 22% external sources). *Receiving aid:* Freshmen: 88% (343); all full-time undergraduates: 88% (1,297). *Average award:* Freshmen: $18,109; Undergraduates: $16,807. *Scholarships, grants, and awards:* Federal Pell, FSEOG, state, private, college/university gift aid from institutional funds.
**GIFT AID (NON-NEED-BASED)** *Total amount:* $4,673,140 (41% institutional, 59% external sources). *Receiving aid:* Freshmen: 14% (53). Undergraduates: 11% (168). *Average award:* Freshmen: $10,777. Undergraduates: $9822. *Scholarships, grants, and awards by category:* Academic interests/achievement: general academic interests/achievements. Creative arts/performance: 50 awards: dance, music, performing arts, theater/drama. Special characteristics: children and siblings of alumni,

---

children of educators, children of faculty/staff, out-of-state students, relatives of clergy, religious affiliation, siblings of current students, spouses of current students. *Tuition waivers:* Full or partial for employees or children of employees. *ROTC:* Army.
**LOANS** *Student loans:* $15,022,147 (77% need-based, 23% non-need-based). 89% of past graduating class borrowed through all loan programs. *Average indebtedness per student:* $22,894. *Average need-based loan:* Freshmen: $6847. Undergraduates: $6843. *Parent loans:* $2,563,592 (56% need-based, 44% non-need-based).
**Programs:** Federal Direct (Subsidized and Unsubsidized Stafford, PLUS), Perkins, state, college/university.
**WORK-STUDY** *Federal work-study:* Total amount: $617,799; 185 jobs averaging $2000. *State or other work-study/employment:* Total amount: $177,710 (30% need-based, 70% non-need-based). 150 part-time jobs averaging $2000.
**APPLYING FOR FINANCIAL AID** *Required financial aid form:* FAFSA. *Financial aid deadline (priority):* 4/1. *Notification date:* Continuous beginning 3/1. Students must reply within 3 weeks of notification.
**CONTACT** Mr. Timothy Kremer, Dean of Student Financial Planning, University of Dubuque, 2000 University Avenue, Dubuque, IA 52001-5050, 563-589-3170 or toll-free 800-722-5583. *Fax:* 563-589-3690. *E-mail:* tkremer@dbq.edu.
*Website:* http://www.dbq.edu/.

---

# UNIVERSITY OF EVANSVILLE
## Evansville, IN

| Tuition & fees: $31,776 | Average undergraduate aid package: $26,090 |
| --- | --- |

**ABOUT THE INSTITUTION** Independent United Methodist Church, coed. *Awards:* associate, bachelor's, master's, and doctoral degrees. 80 undergraduate majors. *Total enrollment:* 2,567. Undergraduates: 2,420. Freshmen: 532. Federal methodology is used as a basis for awarding need-based institutional aid.
**UNDERGRADUATE EXPENSES** for 2015–2016 *Comprehensive fee:* $42,656 includes full-time tuition ($30,900), mandatory fees ($876), and room and board ($10,880). *College room only:* $5690. Room and board charges vary according to board plan and housing facility. *Part-time tuition:* $860 per credit hour. *Part-time fees:* $130 per term. Part-time tuition and fees vary according to course load.
**FRESHMAN FINANCIAL AID (Fall 2014, est.)** 442 applied for aid; of those 84% were deemed to have need. 100% of freshmen with need received aid; of those 25% had need fully met. *Average percent of need met:* 85% (excluding resources awarded to replace EFC). *Average financial aid package:* $27,491 (excluding resources awarded to replace EFC). 22% of all full-time freshmen had no need and received non-need-based gift aid.
**UNDERGRADUATE FINANCIAL AID (Fall 2014, est.)** 1,632 applied for aid; of those 89% were deemed to have need. 100% of undergraduates with need received aid; of those 27% had need fully met. *Average percent of need met:* 83% (excluding resources awarded to replace EFC). *Average financial aid package:* $26,090 (excluding resources awarded to replace EFC). 26% of all full-time undergraduates had no need and received non-need-based gift aid.
**GIFT AID (NEED-BASED)** *Total amount:* $30,837,703 (9% federal, 8% state, 79% institutional, 4% external sources). *Receiving aid:* Freshmen: 70% (370); all full-time undergraduates: 64% (1,431). *Average award:* Freshmen: $24,598; Undergraduates: $22,778. *Scholarships, grants, and awards:* Federal Pell, FSEOG, state, private, college/university gift aid from institutional funds.
**GIFT AID (NON-NEED-BASED)** *Total amount:* $9,944,216 (91% institutional, 9% external sources). *Receiving aid:* Freshmen: 70% (370). Undergraduates: 63% (1,398). *Average award:* Freshmen: $18,204. Undergraduates: $17,045. *Scholarships, grants, and awards by category:* Academic interests/achievement: 1,975 awards ($20,293,676 total): biological sciences, business, communication, computer science, education, engineering/technologies, English, foreign languages, general academic interests/achievements, health fields, humanities, international studies, mathematics, physical sciences, premedicine, religion/biblical studies, social sciences. *Creative arts/performance:* 164 awards ($2,179,080 total): art/fine arts, music, theater/drama. *Special achievements/activities:* 346 awards ($408,825 total): general special achievements/activities, leadership, memberships. *Special characteristics:* 311 awards ($3,304,726 total): children and siblings of alumni, children of faculty/staff, international students, members of minority groups, religious affiliation, siblings of current students, veterans. *Tuition waivers:* Full or partial for minority students, children of alumni, employees or children of employees, adult students, senior citizens. *ROTC:* Army cooperative.

**LOANS** *Student loans:* $8,724,533 (95% need-based, 5% non-need-based). 75% of past graduating class borrowed through all loan programs. *Average indebtedness per student:* $29,441. *Average need-based loan:* Freshmen: $3934. Undergraduates: $4962. *Parent loans:* $3,580,390 (92% need-based, 8% non-need-based). *Programs:* Federal Direct (Subsidized and Unsubsidized Stafford, PLUS), Perkins, Federal Nursing, college/university.

**WORK-STUDY** *Federal work-study:* Total amount: $469,240; 310 jobs averaging $1514. *State or other work-study/employment:* Total amount: $22,875 (20% need-based, 80% non-need-based). 15 part-time jobs averaging $1525.

**ATHLETIC AWARDS** Total amount: $4,439,934 (46% need-based, 54% non-need-based).

**APPLYING FOR FINANCIAL AID** *Required financial aid form:* FAFSA. *Financial aid deadline (priority):* 3/1. *Notification date:* Continuous beginning 3/1. Students must reply within 3 weeks of notification.

**CONTACT** Ms. Cathleen Wright, Director of Financial Aid, University of Evansville, 1800 Lincoln Avenue, Evansville, IN 47722, 812-488-2364 or toll-free 800-423-8633 Ext. 2468. *Fax:* 812-488-2028. *E-mail:* financialaid@evansville.edu. *Website:* http://www.evansville.edu/.

# THE UNIVERSITY OF FINDLAY
## Findlay, OH

| Tuition & fees: $30,640 | Average undergraduate aid package: $17,685 |
|---|---|

**ABOUT THE INSTITUTION** Independent Church of God, coed. *Awards:* certificates, associate, bachelor's, master's, and doctoral degrees. 60 undergraduate majors. *Total enrollment:* 5,170. Undergraduates: 3,967. Freshmen: 619. Both federal and institutional methodology are used as a basis for awarding need-based institutional aid.

**UNDERGRADUATE EXPENSES for 2015–2016** *Comprehensive fee:* $39,990 includes full-time tuition ($29,716), mandatory fees ($924), and room and board ($9350). *College room only:* $4666. Room and board charges vary according to board plan and housing facility. *Part-time tuition:* $659 per semester hour. *Part-time fees:* $397 per term. Part-time tuition and fees vary according to course load and program.

**FRESHMAN FINANCIAL AID (Fall 2013)** 442 applied for aid; of those 93% were deemed to have need. 100% of freshmen with need received aid; of those 18% had need fully met. *Average percent of need met:* 59% (excluding resources awarded to replace EFC). *Average financial aid package:* $20,543 (excluding resources awarded to replace EFC). 15% of all full-time freshmen had no need and received non-need-based gift aid.

**UNDERGRADUATE FINANCIAL AID (Fall 2013)** 2,031 applied for aid; of those 85% were deemed to have need. 100% of undergraduates with need received aid; of those 18% had need fully met. *Average percent of need met:* 45% (excluding resources awarded to replace EFC). *Average financial aid package:* $17,685 (excluding resources awarded to replace EFC). 15% of all full-time undergraduates had no need and received non-need-based gift aid.

**GIFT AID (NEED-BASED)** *Total amount:* $30,561,545 (11% federal, 3% state, 84% institutional, 2% external sources). *Receiving aid:* Freshmen: 71% (410); all full-time undergraduates: 69% (1,734). *Average award:* Freshmen: $17,043; Undergraduates: $14,670. *Scholarships, grants, and awards:* Federal Pell, FSEOG, state, college/university gift aid from institutional funds.

**GIFT AID (NON-NEED-BASED)** *Total amount:* $7,106,805 (1% federal, 6% state, 90% institutional, 3% external sources). *Receiving aid:* Freshmen: 71% (410). Undergraduates: 69% (1,734). *Average award:* Freshmen: $13,292. Undergraduates: $12,083. *Scholarships, grants, and awards by category:* Academic interests/achievement: general academic interests/achievements. Creative arts/performance: music, theater/drama. Special characteristics: children of faculty/staff. *Tuition waivers:* Full or partial for children of alumni, employees or children of employees, senior citizens. *ROTC:* Army cooperative, Air Force cooperative.

**LOANS** *Student loans:* $32,300,754 (84% need-based, 16% non-need-based). 75% of past graduating class borrowed through all loan programs. *Average indebtedness per student:* $34,434. *Average need-based loan:* Freshmen: $2866. Undergraduates: $4502. *Parent loans:* $5,279,069 (60% need-based, 40% non-need-based). *Programs:* Federal Direct (Subsidized and Unsubsidized Stafford, PLUS), Perkins, college/university.

**WORK-STUDY** *Federal work-study:* jobs available. *State or other work-study/employment:* Total amount: $1,247,499 (100% non-need-based). Part-time jobs available.

**ATHLETIC AWARDS** Total amount: $4,511,330 (80% need-based, 20% non-need-based).

**APPLYING FOR FINANCIAL AID** *Required financial aid form:* FAFSA. *Financial aid deadline:* 9/1 (priority: 8/1). *Notification date:* Continuous beginning 3/1. Students must reply within 2 weeks of notification.

**CONTACT** Mr. Edward R. Recker, Director of Financial Aid, The University of Findlay, 1000 North Main Street, Findlay, OH 45840-3695, 419-434-5678 or toll-free 800-548-0932. *Fax:* 419-434-4344. *E-mail:* reckere1@findlay.edu. *Website:* http://www.findlay.edu/.

# UNIVERSITY OF FLORIDA
## Gainesville, FL

| Tuition & fees (FL res): $4477 | Average undergraduate aid package: $11,597 |
|---|---|

**ABOUT THE INSTITUTION** State-supported, coed. *Awards:* certificates, bachelor's, master's, and doctoral degrees. 98 undergraduate majors. *Total enrollment:* 50,350. Undergraduates: 33,720. Freshmen: 6,524. Federal methodology is used as a basis for awarding need-based institutional aid.

**UNDERGRADUATE EXPENSES for 2015–2016** *Application fee:* $30. *Tuition, state resident:* full-time $4477; part-time $149.24 per credit hour. *Tuition, nonresident:* full-time $25,694; part-time $856.45 per credit hour. Full-time tuition and fees vary according to course level, location, and program. Part-time tuition and fees vary according to course level, location, and program. *College room and board:* $9630; *Room only:* $5340. Room and board charges vary according to board plan and housing facility.

**FRESHMAN FINANCIAL AID (Fall 2013)** 5,965 applied for aid; of those 58% were deemed to have need. 99% of freshmen with need received aid; of those 23% had need fully met. *Average percent of need met:* 99% (excluding resources awarded to replace EFC). *Average financial aid package:* $11,875 (excluding resources awarded to replace EFC). 4% of all full-time freshmen had no need and received non-need-based gift aid.

**UNDERGRADUATE FINANCIAL AID (Fall 2013)** 27,502 applied for aid; of those 68% were deemed to have need. 98% of undergraduates with need received aid; of those 20% had need fully met. *Average percent of need met:* 96% (excluding resources awarded to replace EFC). *Average financial aid package:* $11,597 (excluding resources awarded to replace EFC). 5% of all full-time undergraduates had no need and received non-need-based gift aid.

**GIFT AID (NEED-BASED)** *Total amount:* $78,360,471 (60% federal, 8% state, 32% institutional). *Receiving aid:* Freshmen: 34% (2,144); all full-time undergraduates: 34% (11,540). *Average award:* Freshmen: $7346; Undergraduates: $6778. *Scholarships, grants, and awards:* Federal Pell, FSEOG, state, private, college/university gift aid from institutional funds.

**GIFT AID (NON-NEED-BASED)** *Total amount:* $98,004,125 (2% federal, 67% state, 19% institutional, 12% external sources). *Receiving aid:* Freshmen: 51% (3,238). Undergraduates: 43% (14,743). *Average award:* Freshmen: $1717. Undergraduates: $2437. *Scholarships, grants, and awards by category:* Academic interests/achievement: agriculture, architecture, business, communication, computer science, education, engineering/technologies, general academic interests/achievements, health fields, military science. Creative arts/performance: art/fine arts, dance, general creative arts/performance, journalism/publications, music, performing arts, theater/drama. Special achievements/activities: community service, general special achievements/activities, leadership. Special characteristics: children of faculty/staff, members of minority groups, out-of-state students. *Tuition waivers:* Full or partial for employees or children of employees, senior citizens. *ROTC:* Army, Naval, Air Force.

**LOANS** *Student loans:* $70,643,428 (52% need-based, 48% non-need-based). 44% of past graduating class borrowed through all loan programs. *Average indebtedness per student:* $20,642. *Average need-based loan:* Freshmen: $3701. Undergraduates: $4592. *Parent loans:* $10,725,312 (100% non-need-based). *Programs:* Federal Direct (Subsidized and Unsubsidized Stafford, PLUS), Perkins, college/university.

**WORK-STUDY** *Federal work-study:* 659 jobs averaging $2277. *State or other work-study/employment:* Total amount: $10,414,044 (1% need-based, 99% non-need-based). 4,308 part-time jobs averaging $2043.

**ATHLETIC AWARDS** Total amount: $9,095,942 (100% non-need-based).
**APPLYING FOR FINANCIAL AID** *Required financial aid form:* FAFSA. *Financial aid deadline (priority):* 3/15. *Notification date:* Continuous beginning 4/15.
**CONTACT** Mr. Richard D. Wilder, Director of Student Financial Affairs, University of Florida, S-107 Criser Hall, Gainesville, FL 32611-4025, 352-294-3220. *Fax:* 352-392-2861. *E-mail:* rwilder@ufl.edu.
*Website:* http://www.ufl.edu/.

# UNIVERSITY OF FORT LAUDERDALE
## Lauderhill, FL

**CONTACT** Financial Aid Office, University of Fort Lauderdale, 4093 NW 16th Street, Lauderhill, FL 33313, 954-486-7728.
*Website:* http://uftl.edu/.

# UNIVERSITY OF GEORGIA
## Athens, GA

| Tuition & fees (GA res): $10,836 | Average undergraduate aid package: $11,395 |
| --- | --- |

**ABOUT THE INSTITUTION** State-supported, coed. *Awards:* certificates, bachelor's, master's, and doctoral degrees. 125 undergraduate majors. *Total enrollment:* 35,197. Undergraduates: 26,882. Freshmen: 5,348. Federal methodology is used as a basis for awarding need-based institutional aid.
**UNDERGRADUATE EXPENSES** for 2015–2016 *Application fee:* $60. *Tuition, state resident:* full-time $8590. *Tuition, nonresident:* full-time $26,800. *Required fees:* full-time $2246. Full-time tuition and fees vary according to course load, location, and program. Part-time tuition and fees vary according to course load, location, and program. *College room and board:* $9246; *Room only:* $5290. Room and board charges vary according to board plan and housing facility.
**FRESHMAN FINANCIAL AID (Fall 2014, est.)** 4,184 applied for aid; of those 53% were deemed to have need. 99% of freshmen with need received aid; of those 31% had need fully met. *Average percent of need met:* 82% (excluding resources awarded to replace EFC). *Average financial aid package:* $12,795 (excluding resources awarded to replace EFC). 6% of all full-time freshmen had no need and received non-need-based gift aid.
**UNDERGRADUATE FINANCIAL AID (Fall 2014, est.)** 18,161 applied for aid; of those 61% were deemed to have need. 98% of undergraduates with need received aid; of those 24% had need fully met. *Average percent of need met:* 75% (excluding resources awarded to replace EFC). *Average financial aid package:* $11,395 (excluding resources awarded to replace EFC). 6% of all full-time undergraduates had no need and received non-need-based gift aid.
**GIFT AID (NEED-BASED)** *Total amount:* $85,771,017 (33% federal, 59% state, 5% institutional, 3% external sources). *Receiving aid:* Freshmen: 44% (2,160); all full-time undergraduates: 40% (10,168). *Average award:* Freshmen: $9864; Undergraduates: $8623. *Scholarships, grants, and awards:* Federal Pell, FSEOG, state, private, college/university gift aid from institutional funds.
**GIFT AID (NON-NEED-BASED)** *Total amount:* $83,527,220 (1% federal, 92% state, 4% institutional, 3% external sources). *Receiving aid:* Freshmen: 10% (509). Undergraduates: 7% (1,830). *Average award:* Freshmen: $2405. Undergraduates: $2141. *Scholarships, grants, and awards by category: Academic interests/achievement:* 23,990 awards ($139,620,515 total): agriculture, business, education, general academic interests/achievements. *Creative arts/performance:* 132 awards ($120,520 total): music. *Special characteristics:* 215 awards ($300,500 total): local/state students. *Tuition waivers:* Full or partial for senior citizens. *ROTC:* Army, Air Force.
**LOANS** *Student loans:* $73,565,705 (58% need-based, 42% non-need-based). 46% of past graduating class borrowed through all loan programs. *Average indebtedness per student:* $21,638. *Average need-based loan:* Freshmen: $3339. Undergraduates: $4154. *Parent loans:* $24,974,329 (25% need-based, 75% non-need-based). *Programs:* Federal Direct (Subsidized and Unsubsidized Stafford, PLUS), Perkins, state, college/university.
**WORK-STUDY** *Federal work-study:* Total amount: $1,043,582; 378 jobs averaging $2640.

**ATHLETIC AWARDS** Total amount: $8,322,417 (31% need-based, 69% non-need-based).
**APPLYING FOR FINANCIAL AID** *Required financial aid form:* FAFSA. *Financial aid deadline (priority):* 3/15. *Notification date:* Continuous beginning 4/1. Students must reply within 2 weeks of notification.
**CONTACT** Ms. Bonnie C. Joerschke, Director of Financial Aid, University of Georgia, 220 Holmes/Hunter Academic Building, Athens, GA 30602-6114, 706-542-6147. *Fax:* 706-542-8217. *E-mail:* osfa@uga.edu.
*Website:* http://www.uga.edu/.

# UNIVERSITY OF GREAT FALLS
## Great Falls, MT

| Tuition & fees: $21,556 | Average undergraduate aid package: $18,476 |
| --- | --- |

**ABOUT THE INSTITUTION** Independent Roman Catholic, coed. *Awards:* certificates, associate, bachelor's, and master's degrees. 73 undergraduate majors. *Total enrollment:* 1,100. Undergraduates: 1,043. Freshmen: 152. Federal methodology is used as a basis for awarding need-based institutional aid.
**UNDERGRADUATE EXPENSES** for 2015–2016 *Application fee:* $35. *Comprehensive fee:* $28,356 includes full-time tuition ($20,456), mandatory fees ($1100), and room and board ($6800). *College room only:* $3900. Full-time tuition and fees vary according to course load. Room and board charges vary according to housing facility. *Part-time tuition:* $647 per credit hour. Part-time tuition and fees vary according to course load, location, and program.
**FRESHMAN FINANCIAL AID (Fall 2014, est.)** 144 applied for aid; of those 90% were deemed to have need. 100% of freshmen with need received aid; of those 2% had need fully met. *Average percent of need met:* 73% (excluding resources awarded to replace EFC). *Average financial aid package:* $20,158 (excluding resources awarded to replace EFC). 10% of all full-time freshmen had no need and received non-need-based gift aid.
**UNDERGRADUATE FINANCIAL AID (Fall 2014, est.)** 531 applied for aid; of those 90% were deemed to have need. 100% of undergraduates with need received aid; of those 2% had need fully met. *Average percent of need met:* 69% (excluding resources awarded to replace EFC). *Average financial aid package:* $18,476 (excluding resources awarded to replace EFC). 14% of all full-time undergraduates had no need and received non-need-based gift aid.
**GIFT AID (NEED-BASED)** *Total amount:* $6,503,432 (25% federal, 75% institutional). *Receiving aid:* Freshmen: 79% (119); all full-time undergraduates: 68% (428). *Average award:* Freshmen: $12,220; Undergraduates: $10,773. *Scholarships, grants, and awards:* Federal Pell, FSEOG, private, college/university gift aid from institutional funds.
**GIFT AID (NON-NEED-BASED)** *Total amount:* $1,121,111 (100% institutional). *Receiving aid:* Freshmen: 4% (6). Undergraduates: 4% (26). *Average award:* Freshmen: $9515. Undergraduates: $7114. *Scholarships, grants, and awards by category: Academic interests/achievement:* biological sciences, business, computer science, education, general academic interests/achievements, humanities, mathematics, physical sciences, premedicine, religion/biblical studies, social sciences. *Creative arts/performance:* dance, general creative arts/performance. *Special achievements/activities:* cheerleading/drum major, religious involvement. *Special characteristics:* children and siblings of alumni, children of current students, children of faculty/staff, ethnic background, first-generation college students, international students, local/state students, parents of current students, religious affiliation, siblings of current students, spouses of current students. *Tuition waivers:* Full or partial for employees or children of employees.
**LOANS** *Student loans:* $4,909,901 (83% need-based, 17% non-need-based). 88% of past graduating class borrowed through all loan programs. *Average indebtedness per student:* $23,340. *Average need-based loan:* Freshmen: $3520. Undergraduates: $4400. *Parent loans:* $595,257 (65% need-based, 35% non-need-based). *Programs:* Federal Direct (Subsidized and Unsubsidized Stafford, PLUS), Perkins.
**WORK-STUDY** *Federal work-study:* Total amount: $63,519; jobs available. *State or other work-study/employment:* Total amount: $147,000 (100% need-based). Part-time jobs available.
**ATHLETIC AWARDS** Total amount: $2,984,295 (65% need-based, 35% non-need-based).
**APPLYING FOR FINANCIAL AID** *Required financial aid form:* FAFSA. *Financial aid deadline (priority):* 3/1. *Notification date:* Continuous beginning 3/1.

**CONTACT** Kelli Engelhardt, Director of Financial Aid, University of Great Falls, 1301 20th Street South, Great Falls, MT 59405, 406-791-5237 or toll-free 800-856-9544. *Fax:* 406-791-5242. *E-mail:* kengelhardt01@ugf.edu. *Website:* http://www.ugf.edu/.

# UNIVERSITY OF GUAM
## Mangilao, GU

**CONTACT** Office of Financial Aid, University of Guam, UOG Station, Mangilao, GU 96923, 671-735-2288. *Fax:* 671-734-2907. *Website:* http://www.uog.edu/.

# UNIVERSITY OF HARTFORD
## West Hartford, CT

| Tuition & fees: $36,460 | Average undergraduate aid package: $23,883 |
|---|---|

**ABOUT THE INSTITUTION** Independent, coed. *Awards:* certificates, diplomas, associate, bachelor's, master's, and doctoral degrees. 81 undergraduate majors. *Total enrollment:* 6,817. Undergraduates: 5,180. Freshmen: 1,217. Federal methodology is used as a basis for awarding need-based institutional aid.

**UNDERGRADUATE EXPENSES for 2015–2016 Application fee:** $40. *Comprehensive fee:* $48,098 includes full-time tuition ($33,740), mandatory fees ($2720), and room and board ($11,638). *College room only:* $7548. Full-time tuition and fees vary according to program. Room and board charges vary according to board plan and housing facility. *Part-time tuition:* $500 per credit. Part-time tuition and fees vary according to course load and program. *Payment plan:* Tuition prepayment.

**FRESHMAN FINANCIAL AID (Fall 2014, est.)** 1,054 applied for aid; of those 92% were deemed to have need. 100% of freshmen with need received aid; of those 13% had need fully met. *Average percent of need met:* 65% (excluding resources awarded to replace EFC). *Average financial aid package:* $24,135 (excluding resources awarded to replace EFC). 16% of all full-time freshmen had no need and received non-need-based gift aid.

**UNDERGRADUATE FINANCIAL AID (Fall 2014, est.)** 3,612 applied for aid; of those 93% were deemed to have need. 100% of undergraduates with need received aid; of those 12% had need fully met. *Average percent of need met:* 65% (excluding resources awarded to replace EFC). *Average financial aid package:* $23,883 (excluding resources awarded to replace EFC). 17% of all full-time undergraduates had no need and received non-need-based gift aid.

**GIFT AID (NEED-BASED)** *Total amount:* $59,636,698 (12% federal, 3% state, 84% institutional, 1% external sources). *Receiving aid:* Freshmen: 79% (946); all full-time undergraduates: 73% (3,270). *Average award:* Freshmen: $20,026; Undergraduates: $18,654. *Scholarships, grants, and awards:* Federal Pell, FSEOG, state, private, college/university gift aid from institutional funds.

**GIFT AID (NON-NEED-BASED)** *Total amount:* $10,511,842 (98% institutional, 2% external sources). *Receiving aid:* Freshmen: 9% (102). Undergraduates: 6% (277). *Average award:* Freshmen: $12,055. Undergraduates: $11,707. *Scholarships, grants, and awards by category: Academic interests/achievement:* engineering/technologies, general academic interests/achievements, health fields, premedicine. *Creative arts/performance:* art/fine arts, dance, music, performing arts, theater/drama. *Special achievements/activities:* community service. *Special characteristics:* adult students, children of current students, children of faculty/staff, children of union members/company employees, children with a deceased or disabled parent, ethnic background, first-generation college students, handicapped students, international students, local/state students, members of minority groups, parents of current students, previous college experience, religious affiliation, siblings of current students, twins. *Tuition waivers:* Full or partial for employees or children of employees, senior citizens. *ROTC:* Army cooperative, Air Force cooperative.

**LOANS** *Student loans:* $39,619,161 (74% need-based, 26% non-need-based). *Average need-based loan:* Freshmen: $3551. Undergraduates: $4641. *Parent loans:* $14,510,295 (60% need-based, 40% non-need-based). *Programs:* Federal Direct (Subsidized and Unsubsidized Stafford, PLUS), Perkins.

**WORK-STUDY** *Federal work-study:* Total amount: $684,644; 611 jobs averaging $1121. *State or other work-study/employment:* Total amount: $1,502,000 (75% need-based, 25% non-need-based). Part-time jobs available.

**ATHLETIC AWARDS** Total amount: $5,255,909 (36% need-based, 64% non-need-based).

**APPLYING FOR FINANCIAL AID** *Required financial aid form:* FAFSA. *Financial aid deadline (priority):* 2/1. *Notification date:* Continuous beginning 3/1. Students must reply by 5/1 or within 2 weeks of notification.

**CONTACT** Jennifer Horner, Office of Financial Aid, University of Hartford, 200 Bloomfield Avenue, West Hartford, CT 06117-1599, 860-768-4296 or toll-free 800-947-4303. *Fax:* 860-768-4961. *E-mail:* finaid@hartford.edu. *Website:* http://www.hartford.edu/.

# UNIVERSITY OF HAWAII AT HILO
## Hilo, HI

**ABOUT THE INSTITUTION** State-supported, coed. *Awards:* certificates, bachelor's, master's, and doctoral degrees. 33 undergraduate majors. *Total enrollment:* 3,924. Undergraduates: 3,362. Freshmen: 432.

**GIFT AID (NEED-BASED)** *Scholarships, grants, and awards:* Federal Pell, FSEOG, state, private, college/university gift aid from institutional funds.

**GIFT AID (NON-NEED-BASED)** *Scholarships, grants, and awards by category: Academic interests/achievement:* business, computer science, English, general academic interests/achievements, health fields, social sciences. *Creative arts/performance:* art/fine arts, music, performing arts, theater/drama. *Special achievements/activities:* community service, general special achievements/activities, leadership. *Special characteristics:* general special characteristics, local/state students.

**LOANS** *Programs:* Federal Direct (Subsidized and Unsubsidized Stafford, PLUS), Perkins, state.

**WORK-STUDY** *Federal work-study:* jobs available. *State or other work-study/employment:* Total amount: $1,236,084 (100% non-need-based). Part-time jobs available.

**APPLYING FOR FINANCIAL AID** *Required financial aid form:* FAFSA.

**CONTACT** Financial Aid Office, University of Hawaii at Hilo, 200 West Kawili Street, Hilo, HI 96720-4091, 808-932-7449 or toll-free 800-897-4456. *Fax:* 808-932-7459. *E-mail:* uhhfao@hawaii.edu. *Website:* http://hilo.hawaii.edu/.

# UNIVERSITY OF HAWAII AT MANOA
## Honolulu, HI

| Tuition & fees (HI res): $10,584 | Average undergraduate aid package: $13,718 |
|---|---|

**ABOUT THE INSTITUTION** State-supported, coed. *Awards:* certificates, bachelor's, master's, and doctoral degrees. 90 undergraduate majors. *Total enrollment:* 19,507. Undergraduates: 14,126. Freshmen: 1,841. Federal methodology is used as a basis for awarding need-based institutional aid.

**UNDERGRADUATE EXPENSES for 2015–2016 Application fee:** $70. *Tuition, state resident:* full-time $10,584; part-time $410 per credit hour. *Tuition, nonresident:* full-time $30,696; part-time $1193 per credit hour. Full-time tuition and fees vary according to class time, course level, course load, degree level, program, reciprocity agreements, and student level. Part-time tuition and fees vary according to class time, course level, course load, degree level, program, reciprocity agreements, and student level. Room and board charges vary according to board plan and housing facility.

**FRESHMAN FINANCIAL AID (Fall 2014, est.)** 1,303 applied for aid; of those 67% were deemed to have need. 99% of freshmen with need received aid; of those 35% had need fully met. *Average percent of need met:* 76% (excluding resources awarded to replace EFC). *Average financial aid package:* $14,615 (excluding resources awarded to replace EFC). 20% of all full-time freshmen had no need and received non-need-based gift aid.

**UNDERGRADUATE FINANCIAL AID (Fall 2014, est.)** 9,514 applied for aid; of those 72% were deemed to have need. 97% of undergraduates with need received aid; of those 30% had need fully met. *Average percent of need met:* 71% (excluding resources awarded to replace EFC). *Average financial aid package:* $13,718

(excluding resources awarded to replace EFC). 19% of all full-time undergraduates had no need and received non-need-based gift aid.

**GIFT AID (NEED-BASED)** *Total amount:* $43,395,240 (44% federal, 5% state, 45% institutional, 6% external sources). *Receiving aid:* Freshmen: 55% (849); all full-time undergraduates: 51% (6,229). *Average award:* Freshmen: $9620; Undergraduates: $8846. *Scholarships, grants, and awards:* Federal Pell, FSEOG, state, private, college/university gift aid from institutional funds.

**GIFT AID (NON-NEED-BASED)** *Total amount:* $14,937,093 (53% institutional, 47% external sources). *Receiving aid:* Freshmen: 15% (229). Undergraduates: 12% (1,427). *Average award:* Freshmen: $11,058. Undergraduates: $10,405. *Scholarships, grants, and awards by category:* Academic interests/achievement: general academic interests/achievements. Creative arts/performance: general creative arts/performance. Special achievements/activities: general special achievements/activities. Special characteristics: general special characteristics. *Tuition waivers:* Full or partial for minority students, employees or children of employees, adult students, senior citizens. *ROTC:* Army, Air Force.

**LOANS** *Student loans:* $44,734,631 (53% need-based, 47% non-need-based). 45% of past graduating class borrowed through all loan programs. *Average indebtedness per student:* $24,277. *Average need-based loan:* Freshmen: $4008. Undergraduates: $4829. *Parent loans:* $26,022,615 (100% non-need-based). *Programs:* Federal Direct (Subsidized and Unsubsidized Stafford, PLUS), Perkins, state.

**WORK-STUDY** *Federal work-study:* Total amount: $1,312,074; 479 jobs averaging $2739.

**ATHLETIC AWARDS** Total amount: $6,901,540 (1% need-based, 99% non-need-based).

**APPLYING FOR FINANCIAL AID** *Required financial aid form:* FAFSA. *Financial aid deadline (priority):* 3/1. *Notification date:* Continuous beginning 4/1. Students must reply by 5/1 or within 4 weeks of notification.

**CONTACT** Jodie Kuba, Director of Financial Aid Services, University of Hawaii at Manoa, 2600 Campus Road, Suite 112, Honolulu, HI 96822, 808-956-7251 or toll-free 800-823-9771. *Fax:* 808-956-3985. *E-mail:* finaid@hawaii.edu. *Website:* http://manoa.hawaii.edu/.

# UNIVERSITY OF HAWAII–WEST OAHU
## Kapolei, HI

| Tuition & fees (HI res): $7380 | Average undergraduate aid package: $11,308 |
|---|---|

**ABOUT THE INSTITUTION** State-supported, coed. *Awards:* certificates and bachelor's degrees. 21 undergraduate majors. *Total enrollment:* 2,661. Undergraduates: 2,658. Freshmen: 266. Federal methodology is used as a basis for awarding need-based institutional aid.

**UNDERGRADUATE EXPENSES** for 2015–2016 *Application fee:* $50. *Tuition, state resident:* full-time $7128; part-time $297 per credit. *Tuition, nonresident:* full-time $19,368; part-time $807 per credit. *Required fees:* full-time $252; $252 per term.

**FRESHMAN FINANCIAL AID (Fall 2013)** 126 applied for aid; of those 100% were deemed to have need. 100% of freshmen with need received aid. *Average percent of need met:* 50% (excluding resources awarded to replace EFC). *Average financial aid package:* $6580 (excluding resources awarded to replace EFC).

**UNDERGRADUATE FINANCIAL AID (Fall 2013)** 678 applied for aid; of those 100% were deemed to have need. 100% of undergraduates with need received aid. *Average percent of need met:* 50% (excluding resources awarded to replace EFC). *Average financial aid package:* $11,308 (excluding resources awarded to replace EFC).

**GIFT AID (NEED-BASED)** *Total amount:* $3,937,931 (78% federal, 21% institutional, 1% external sources). *Receiving aid:* Freshmen: 28% (59); all full-time undergraduates: 42% (435). *Average award:* Freshmen: $4250; Undergraduates: $7760. *Scholarships, grants, and awards:* Federal Pell, FSEOG, state, private, college/university gift aid from institutional funds.

**GIFT AID (NON-NEED-BASED)** *Total amount:* $79,526 (100% external sources). *Receiving aid:* Freshmen: 3% (7). Undergraduates: 5% (56). *Tuition waivers:* Full or partial for employees or children of employees. *ROTC:* Army cooperative, Air Force cooperative.

**LOANS** *Student loans:* $4,848,145 (100% need-based). *Average need-based loan:* Freshmen: $591. Undergraduates: $1768. *Parent loans:* $16,909 (100% need-based). *Programs:* Federal Direct (Subsidized and Unsubsidized Stafford, PLUS).

**WORK-STUDY** *Federal work-study:* jobs available. *State or other work-study/employment:* Part-time jobs available.

**APPLYING FOR FINANCIAL AID** *Required financial aid form:* FAFSA. *Financial aid deadline (priority):* 4/1. *Notification date:* Continuous. Students must reply within 2 weeks of notification.

**CONTACT** Lester Ishimoto, Office of Financial Aid, University of Hawaii–West Oahu, 91-1001 Farrington Highway, Kapolei, HI 96707, 808-689-2689 or toll-free 866-299-8656. *Fax:* 808-689-2691. *E-mail:* uhwo-finaid-l@lists.hawaii.edu. *Website:* http://www.uhwo.hawaii.edu/.

# UNIVERSITY OF HOUSTON
## Houston, TX

| Tuition & fees (TX res): $10,518 | Average undergraduate aid package: $12,119 |
|---|---|

**ABOUT THE INSTITUTION** State-supported, coed. *Awards:* bachelor's, master's, and doctoral degrees. 87 undergraduate majors. *Total enrollment:* 40,914. Undergraduates: 32,915. Freshmen: 4,048. Federal methodology is used as a basis for awarding need-based institutional aid.

**UNDERGRADUATE EXPENSES** for 2015–2016 *Application fee:* $50. *Tuition, state resident:* full-time $9564; part-time $319 per credit hour. *Tuition, nonresident:* full-time $23,424; part-time $781 per credit hour. *Required fees:* full-time $954. Full-time tuition and fees vary according to course level, course load, degree level, program, and student level. Part-time tuition and fees vary according to course level, course load, degree level, program, and student level. *College room and board:* $9278. Room and board charges vary according to board plan and housing facility. *Payment plan:* Guaranteed tuition.

**FRESHMAN FINANCIAL AID (Fall 2014, est.)** 3,089 applied for aid; of those 80% were deemed to have need. 96% of freshmen with need received aid; of those 19% had need fully met. *Average percent of need met:* 68% (excluding resources awarded to replace EFC). *Average financial aid package:* $13,138 (excluding resources awarded to replace EFC). 10% of all full-time freshmen had no need and received non-need-based gift aid.

**UNDERGRADUATE FINANCIAL AID (Fall 2014, est.)** 16,692 applied for aid; of those 89% were deemed to have need. 95% of undergraduates with need received aid; of those 13% had need fully met. *Average percent of need met:* 60% (excluding resources awarded to replace EFC). *Average financial aid package:* $12,119 (excluding resources awarded to replace EFC). 3% of all full-time undergraduates had no need and received non-need-based gift aid.

**GIFT AID (NEED-BASED)** *Total amount:* $112,577,157 (49% federal, 19% state, 26% institutional, 6% external sources). *Receiving aid:* Freshmen: 56% (2,190); all full-time undergraduates: 50% (11,943). *Average award:* Freshmen: $10,369; Undergraduates: $8089. *Scholarships, grants, and awards:* Federal Pell, FSEOG, state, private, college/university gift aid from institutional funds.

**GIFT AID (NON-NEED-BASED)** *Total amount:* $6,283,472 (1% state, 79% institutional, 20% external sources). *Receiving aid:* Freshmen: 5% (204). Undergraduates: 2% (509). *Average award:* Freshmen: $5731. Undergraduates: $5075. *Scholarships, grants, and awards by category:* Academic interests/achievement: architecture, area/ethnic studies, biological sciences, business, communication, computer science, education, engineering/technologies, English, foreign languages, general academic interests/achievements, health fields, humanities, international studies, library science, mathematics, military science, physical sciences, premedicine, social sciences. Creative arts/performance: art/fine arts, creative writing, dance, journalism/publications, music, performing arts, theater/drama. Special achievements/activities: cheerleading/drum major, community service, general special achievements/activities, hobbies/interests, leadership. Special characteristics: children and siblings of alumni, first-generation college students, handicapped students, international students, local/state students, out-of-state students, previous college experience. *ROTC:* Army, Naval cooperative, Air Force.

**LOANS** *Student loans:* $105,663,817 (85% need-based, 15% non-need-based). 48% of past graduating class borrowed through all loan programs. *Average indebtedness per student:* $18,453. *Average need-based loan:* Freshmen: $5511. Undergraduates: $7429. *Parent loans:* $6,614,786 (38% need-based, 62% non-need-based). *Programs:* Federal Direct (Subsidized and Unsubsidized Stafford, PLUS), Perkins, state.

**WORK-STUDY** *Federal work-study:* Total amount: $2,013,359; 515 jobs averaging $3909. *State or other work-study/employment:* Part-time jobs available.
**ATHLETIC AWARDS** Total amount: $5,072,455 (86% need-based, 14% non-need-based).
**APPLYING FOR FINANCIAL AID** *Required financial aid form:* FAFSA. *Financial aid deadline (priority):* 4/1. *Notification date:* Continuous beginning 5/1.
**CONTACT** Office of Scholarships and Financial Aid, University of Houston, 4800 Calhoun Road, Houston, TX 77204, 713-743-1010. *Fax:* 713-743-9098.
*Website:* http://www.uh.edu/.

# UNIVERSITY OF HOUSTON–CLEAR LAKE
### Houston, TX

| Tuition & fees (TX res): $6936 | Average undergraduate aid package: $8882 |
|---|---|

**ABOUT THE INSTITUTION** State-supported, coed. *Awards:* certificates, bachelor's, master's, and doctoral degrees. 33 undergraduate majors. *Total enrollment:* 8,665. Undergraduates: 5,077. Freshmen: 201. Federal methodology is used as a basis for awarding need-based institutional aid.
**UNDERGRADUATE EXPENSES for 2015–2016** *Application fee:* $45. *Tuition, state resident:* full-time $5670; part-time $189 per credit hour. *Tuition, nonresident:* full-time $18,630; part-time $621 per credit hour. *Required fees:* full-time $1266; $462 per term. Full-time tuition and fees vary according to course load, degree level, and program. Part-time tuition and fees vary according to course load, degree level, and program. *Room only:* $9682. Room and board charges vary according to housing facility.
**UNDERGRADUATE FINANCIAL AID (Fall 2013)** 1,573 applied for aid; of those 93% were deemed to have need. 96% of undergraduates with need received aid, of those 6% had need fully met. *Average percent of need met:* 55% (excluding resources awarded to replace EFC). *Average financial aid package:* $8882 (excluding resources awarded to replace EFC). 13% of all full-time undergraduates had no need and received non-need-based gift aid.
**GIFT AID (NEED-BASED)** *Total amount:* $11,355,753 (64% federal, 15% state, 19% institutional, 2% external sources). *Receiving aid:* All full-time undergraduates: 53% (1,095). *Average award:* Undergraduates: $6350. *Scholarships, grants, and awards:* Federal Pell, FSEOG, state, private, college/university gift aid from institutional funds.
**GIFT AID (NON-NEED-BASED)** *Total amount:* $1,461,849 (15% federal, 69% institutional, 16% external sources). *Receiving aid:* Undergraduates: 28% (576). *Average award:* Undergraduates: $1115. *Scholarships, grants, and awards by category:* Academic interests/achievement: biological sciences, business, computer science, education, humanities, mathematics, social sciences. *Creative arts/performance:* art/fine arts. *Special achievements/activities:* community service, general special achievements/activities, leadership. *Special characteristics:* local/state students, veterans, veterans' children. *Tuition waivers:* Full or partial for senior citizens.
**LOANS** *Student loans:* $16,361,803 (47% need-based, 53% non-need-based). *Average need-based loan:* Undergraduates: $4507. *Parent loans:* $44,047 (100% non-need-based). *Programs:* Federal Direct (Subsidized and Unsubsidized Stafford, PLUS), Perkins, state, college/university.
**WORK-STUDY** *Federal work-study:* jobs available. *State or other work-study/employment:* Total amount: $44,645 (100% need-based). Part-time jobs available.
**APPLYING FOR FINANCIAL AID** *Required financial aid form:* FAFSA. *Financial aid deadline (priority):* 3/15. *Notification date:* Continuous beginning 5/1. Students must reply within 2 weeks of notification.
**CONTACT** Dr. Billy Satterfield, Executive Director of Student Financial Aid, University of Houston–Clear Lake, 2700 Bay Area Boulevard, Houston, TX 77058-1098, 281-283-2480. *Fax:* 281-283-2502. *E-mail:* satterfield@uhcl.edu.
*Website:* http://www.uhcl.edu/.

# UNIVERSITY OF HOUSTON–DOWNTOWN
### Houston, TX

| Tuition & fees (TX res): $6614 | Average undergraduate aid package: $10,289 |
|---|---|

**ABOUT THE INSTITUTION** State-supported, coed. *Awards:* certificates, bachelor's, and master's degrees. 37 undergraduate majors. *Total enrollment:* 14,439. Undergraduates: 13,830. Freshmen: 993. Federal methodology is used as a basis for awarding need-based institutional aid.
**UNDERGRADUATE EXPENSES for 2015–2016** *Application fee:* $35. *Tuition, state resident:* full-time $5490; part-time $183 per credit hour. *Tuition, nonresident:* full-time $16,350; part-time $545 per credit hour. *Required fees:* full-time $1124; $456 per term. Full-time tuition and fees vary according to course load and program. Part-time tuition and fees vary according to course load and program.
**FRESHMAN FINANCIAL AID (Fall 2014, est.)** 807 applied for aid; of those 87% were deemed to have need. 91% of freshmen with need received aid; of those 99% had need fully met. *Average percent of need met:* 47% (excluding resources awarded to replace EFC). *Average financial aid package:* $8032 (excluding resources awarded to replace EFC). 2% of all full-time freshmen had no need and received non-need-based gift aid.
**UNDERGRADUATE FINANCIAL AID (Fall 2014, est.)** 5,621 applied for aid; of those 92% were deemed to have need. 93% of undergraduates with need received aid; of those 95% had need fully met. *Average percent of need met:* 57% (excluding resources awarded to replace EFC). *Average financial aid package:* $10,289 (excluding resources awarded to replace EFC). 2% of all full-time undergraduates had no need and received non-need-based gift aid.
**GIFT AID (NEED-BASED)** *Total amount:* $36,309,920 (79% federal, 10% state, 11% institutional). *Receiving aid:* Freshmen: 66% (604); all full-time undergraduates: 62% (4,402). *Average award:* Freshmen: $6721; Undergraduates: $5573. *Scholarships, grants, and awards:* Federal Pell, FSEOG, state, private, college/university gift aid from institutional funds.
**GIFT AID (NON-NEED-BASED)** *Total amount:* $2,578,566 (20% state, 60% institutional, 20% external sources). *Receiving aid:* Freshmen: 19% (177). Undergraduates: 6% (449). *Average award:* Freshmen: $2837. Undergraduates: $2705. *Scholarships, grants, and awards by category:* Academic interests/achievement: business, general academic interests/achievements. *Special achievements/activities:* community service, general special achievements/activities, leadership. *Special characteristics:* general special characteristics. *Tuition waivers:* Full or partial for senior citizens. *ROTC:* Army cooperative, Air Force cooperative.
**LOANS** *Student loans:* $47,891,692 (99% need-based, 1% non-need-based). 57% of past graduating class borrowed through all loan programs. *Average indebtedness per student:* $23,249. *Average need-based loan:* Freshmen: $4709. Undergraduates: $8156. *Parent loans:* $132,022 (100% need-based). *Programs:* Federal Direct (Subsidized and Unsubsidized Stafford, PLUS), state.
**WORK-STUDY** *Federal work-study:* Total amount: $427,734; jobs available. *State or other work-study/employment:* Total amount: $77,986 (100% need-based). Part-time jobs available.
**APPLYING FOR FINANCIAL AID** *Required financial aid form:* FAFSA. *Financial aid deadline (priority):* 4/1. *Notification date:* Continuous beginning 4/15. Students must reply within 4 weeks of notification.
**CONTACT** Office of Scholarships and Financial Aid, University of Houston–Downtown, One Main Street, Houston, TX 77002, 713-221-8041. *Fax:* 713-221-7483. *E-mail:* uhdfinaid@uhd.edu.
*Website:* http://www.uhd.edu/.

# UNIVERSITY OF HOUSTON–VICTORIA
### Victoria, TX

**CONTACT** Carolyn Mallory, Financial Aid Director, University of Houston–Victoria, 3007 North Ben Wilson, Victoria, TX 77901-5731, 361-570-4131 or toll-free 877-970-4848 Ext. 110. *Fax:* 361-580-5555. *E-mail:* malloryc@uhv.edu.
*Website:* http://www.uhv.edu/.

# UNIVERSITY OF IDAHO
Moscow, ID

| Tuition & fees (ID res): $6784 | Average undergraduate aid package: $13,279 |
|---|---|

**ABOUT THE INSTITUTION** State-supported, coed. *Awards:* certificates, bachelor's, master's, and doctoral degrees. 95 undergraduate majors. *Total enrollment:* 11,702. Undergraduates: 9,388. Freshmen: 1,590. Federal methodology is used as a basis for awarding need-based institutional aid.

**UNDERGRADUATE EXPENSES for 2015–2016** *Application fee:* $60. *Tuition, state resident:* full-time $4784; part-time $280.50 per credit hour. *Tuition, nonresident:* full-time $18,314; part-time $957.50 per credit hour. *Required fees:* full-time $2000; $58.50 per credit hour. Full-time tuition and fees vary according to degree level and program. Part-time tuition and fees vary according to degree level and program. *College room and board:* $8022. Room and board charges vary according to board plan and housing facility.

**FRESHMAN FINANCIAL AID (Fall 2013)** 1,481 applied for aid; of those 77% were deemed to have need. 99% of freshmen with need received aid; of those 42% had need fully met. *Average percent of need met:* 80% (excluding resources awarded to replace EFC). *Average financial aid package:* $13,573 (excluding resources awarded to replace EFC). 25% of all full-time freshmen had no need and received non-need-based gift aid.

**UNDERGRADUATE FINANCIAL AID (Fall 2013)** 6,809 applied for aid; of those 83% were deemed to have need. 98% of undergraduates with need received aid; of those 30% had need fully met. *Average percent of need met:* 75% (excluding resources awarded to replace EFC). *Average financial aid package:* $13,279 (excluding resources awarded to replace EFC). 18% of all full-time undergraduates had no need and received non-need-based gift aid.

**GIFT AID (NEED-BASED)** *Total amount:* $19,637,700 (82% federal, 2% state, 16% institutional). *Receiving aid:* Freshmen: 49% (832); all full-time undergraduates: 50% (4,289). *Average award:* Freshmen: $4681; Undergraduates: $4753. *Scholarships, grants, and awards:* Federal Pell, FSEOG, state, private, college/university gift aid from institutional funds.

**GIFT AID (NON-NEED-BASED)** *Total amount:* $11,855,636 (10% state, 72% institutional, 18% external sources). *Receiving aid:* Freshmen: 59% (1,009). Undergraduates: 39% (3,328). *Average award:* Freshmen: $4009. Undergraduates: $3910. *Scholarships, grants, and awards by category:* Academic interests/achievement: agriculture, architecture, biological sciences, business, communication, computer science, education, engineering/technologies, English, foreign languages, general academic interests/achievements, health fields, home economics, humanities, library science, mathematics, military science, physical sciences, premedicine, social sciences. Creative arts/performance: applied art and design, art/fine arts, creative writing, dance, general creative arts/performance, journalism/publications, music, performing arts, theater/drama. Special achievements/activities: cheerleading/drum major, general special achievements/activities, junior miss, leadership, rodeo. Special characteristics: adult students, children and siblings of alumni, children of faculty/staff, ethnic background, first-generation college students, general special characteristics, handicapped students, international students, local/state students, members of minority groups, out-of-state students, veterans, veterans' children. *Tuition waivers:* Full or partial for employees or children of employees, senior citizens. *ROTC:* Army, Naval, Air Force cooperative.

**LOANS** *Student loans:* $39,490,131 (48% need-based, 52% non-need-based). 68% of past graduating class borrowed through all loan programs. *Average indebtedness per student:* $25,753. *Average need-based loan:* Freshmen: $5290. Undergraduates: $6931. *Parent loans:* $90,522,273 (100% non-need-based). *Programs:* Federal Direct (Subsidized and Unsubsidized Stafford, PLUS), Perkins, college/university.

**WORK-STUDY** *Federal work-study:* 374 jobs averaging $1783. *State or other work-study/employment:* Total amount: $329,373 (100% need-based). 185 part-time jobs averaging $1889.

**ATHLETIC AWARDS** Total amount: $5,352,747 (100% non-need-based).

**APPLYING FOR FINANCIAL AID** *Required financial aid form:* FAFSA. *Financial aid deadline (priority):* 2/15. *Notification date:* Continuous beginning 3/30. Students must reply within 4 weeks of notification.

**CONTACT** Mr. Dan D. Davenport, Director of Student Financial Aid Services, University of Idaho, 875 Perimeter Drive, MS-4291, Moscow, ID 83844-4291, 208-885-6312 or toll-free 888-884-3246. *Fax:* 208-885-5592. *E-mail:* dand@uidaho.edu. *Website:* http://www.uidaho.edu/.

# UNIVERSITY OF ILLINOIS AT CHICAGO
Chicago, IL

| Tuition & fees (IL res): $13,634 | Average undergraduate aid package: $14,024 |
|---|---|

**ABOUT THE INSTITUTION** State-supported, coed. *Awards:* certificates, bachelor's, master's, and doctoral degrees. 86 undergraduate majors. *Total enrollment:* 27,563. Undergraduates: 16,707. Freshmen: 3,030. Federal methodology is used as a basis for awarding need-based institutional aid.

**UNDERGRADUATE EXPENSES for 2015–2016** *Application fee:* $50. *Tuition, state resident:* full-time $10,584. *Tuition, nonresident:* full-time $22,974. *Required fees:* full-time $3050. Full-time tuition and fees vary according to degree level and program. Part-time tuition and fees vary according to course load, degree level, and program. *College room and board:* $10,871; *Room only:* $7808. Room and board charges vary according to board plan and housing facility. *Payment plan:* Guaranteed tuition.

**FRESHMAN FINANCIAL AID (Fall 2013)** 2,792 applied for aid; of those 87% were deemed to have need. 95% of freshmen with need received aid; of those 7% had need fully met. *Average percent of need met:* 59% (excluding resources awarded to replace EFC). *Average financial aid package:* $14,240 (excluding resources awarded to replace EFC). 3% of all full-time freshmen had no need and received non-need-based gift aid.

**UNDERGRADUATE FINANCIAL AID (Fall 2013)** 12,920 applied for aid; of those 91% were deemed to have need. 96% of undergraduates with need received aid; of those 8% had need fully met. *Average percent of need met:* 60% (excluding resources awarded to replace EFC). *Average financial aid package:* $14,024 (excluding resources awarded to replace EFC). 3% of all full-time undergraduates had no need and received non-need-based gift aid.

**GIFT AID (NEED-BASED)** *Total amount:* $115,606,816 (33% federal, 27% state, 38% institutional, 2% external sources). *Receiving aid:* Freshmen: 65% (1,989); all full-time undergraduates: 61% (9,313). *Average award:* Freshmen: $13,768; Undergraduates: $12,863. *Scholarships, grants, and awards:* Federal Pell, FSEOG, state, private, college/university gift aid from institutional funds.

**GIFT AID (NON-NEED-BASED)** *Total amount:* $2,164,189 (26% state, 50% institutional, 24% external sources). *Receiving aid:* Freshmen: 3% (87). Undergraduates: 2% (253). *Average award:* Freshmen: $5041. Undergraduates: $5027. *Scholarships, grants, and awards by category:* Academic interests/achievement: 1,352 awards ($5,753,217 total): architecture, business, general academic interests/achievements. Creative arts/performance: 184 awards ($675,000 total): applied art and design, art/fine arts, music, performing arts, theater/drama. *Tuition waivers:* Full or partial for employees or children of employees, senior citizens. *ROTC:* Army, Naval cooperative, Air Force cooperative.

**LOANS** *Student loans:* $67,440,532 (90% need-based, 10% non-need-based). 65% of past graduating class borrowed through all loan programs. *Average indebtedness per student:* $23,158. *Average need-based loan:* Freshmen: $3569. Undergraduates: $4592. *Parent loans:* $15,965,555 (84% need-based, 16% non-need-based). *Programs:* Federal Direct (Subsidized and Unsubsidized Stafford, PLUS), Perkins, Federal Nursing, college/university, private loans.

**WORK-STUDY** *Federal work-study:* 1,041 jobs averaging $2000. *State or other work-study/employment:* Total amount: $8,931,628 (78% need-based, 22% non-need-based). 2,602 part-time jobs averaging $2500.

**ATHLETIC AWARDS** Total amount: $3,784,037 (38% need-based, 62% non-need-based).

**APPLYING FOR FINANCIAL AID** *Required financial aid form:* FAFSA. *Financial aid deadline (priority):* 3/1. *Notification date:* Continuous beginning 3/15. Students must reply by 5/1.

**CONTACT** Deidre Rush, Associate Director of Financial Aid, University of Illinois at Chicago, 1200 West Harrison, M/C 334, Chicago, IL 60607-7128, 312-996-5563. *Fax:* 312-996-3385. *E-mail:* deidreb@uic.edu. *Website:* http://www.uic.edu/.

# UNIVERSITY OF ILLINOIS AT SPRINGFIELD
## Springfield, IL

| Tuition & fees (IL res): $11,413 | Average undergraduate aid package: $12,320 |
| --- | --- |

**ABOUT THE INSTITUTION** State-supported, coed. **Awards:** certificates, bachelor's, master's, and doctoral degrees. 25 undergraduate majors. **Total enrollment:** 5,431. Undergraduates: 3,038. Freshmen: 305. Federal methodology is used as a basis for awarding need-based institutional aid.

**UNDERGRADUATE EXPENSES** for 2015–2016 **Application fee:** $50. **Tuition, state resident:** full-time $9405; part-time $313.50 per credit hour. **Tuition, nonresident:** full-time $18,930; part-time $631 per credit hour. **Required fees:** full-time $2008; $18.40 per credit hour or $1004 per term. Full-time tuition and fees vary according to course load. Part-time tuition and fees vary according to course load. **College room and board:** $11,550; **Room only:** $7350. Room and board charges vary according to board plan and housing facility. **Payment plan:** Guaranteed tuition.

**FRESHMAN FINANCIAL AID (Fall 2013)** 298 applied for aid; of those 82% were deemed to have need. 100% of freshmen with need received aid; of those 23% had need fully met. **Average percent of need met:** 82% (excluding resources awarded to replace EFC). **Average financial aid package:** $16,291 (excluding resources awarded to replace EFC). 17% of all full-time freshmen had no need and received non-need-based gift aid.

**UNDERGRADUATE FINANCIAL AID (Fall 2013)** 1,656 applied for aid; of those 85% were deemed to have need. 99% of undergraduates with need received aid; of those 10% had need fully met. **Average percent of need met:** 68% (excluding resources awarded to replace EFC). **Average financial aid package:** $12,320 (excluding resources awarded to replace EFC). 13% of all full-time undergraduates had no need and received non-need-based gift aid.

**GIFT AID (NEED-BASED) Total amount:** $11,598,887 (40% federal, 29% state, 28% institutional, 3% external sources). **Receiving aid:** Freshmen: 77% (239), all full-time undergraduates: 62% (1,226). **Average award:** Freshmen: $13,908; Undergraduates: $9451. **Scholarships, grants, and awards:** Federal Pell, FSEOG, state, private, college/university gift aid from institutional funds.

**GIFT AID (NON-NEED-BASED) Total amount:** $1,855,422 (13% federal, 24% state, 48% institutional, 15% external sources). **Receiving aid:** Freshmen: 15% (48). Undergraduates: 8% (160). **Average award:** Freshmen: $8132. Undergraduates: $5932. **Scholarships, grants, and awards by category:** Academic interests/achievement: biological sciences, business, communication, computer science, education, English, general academic interests/achievements, humanities, international studies, library science, mathematics, social sciences. Creative arts/performance: art/fine arts, music, theater/drama. Special achievements/activities: community service, leadership. Special characteristics: children and siblings of alumni, children of faculty/staff, children of union members/company employees, ethnic background, first-generation college students, handicapped students, out-of-state students, veterans, veterans' children. **Tuition waivers:** Full or partial for employees or children of employees, senior citizens.

**LOANS Student loans:** $13,308,676 (90% need-based, 10% non-need-based). 70% of past graduating class borrowed through all loan programs. **Average indebtedness per student:** $23,507. **Average need-based loan:** Freshmen: $3244. Undergraduates: $4250. **Parent loans:** $1,459,437 (75% need-based, 25% non-need-based). **Programs:** Federal Direct (Subsidized and Unsubsidized Stafford, PLUS), Perkins, college/university.

**WORK-STUDY Federal work-study:** jobs available. **State or other work-study/employment:** Total amount: $1,200,327 (77% need-based, 23% non-need-based). Part-time jobs available.

**ATHLETIC AWARDS** Total amount: $657,609 (61% need-based, 39% non-need-based).

**APPLYING FOR FINANCIAL AID Required financial aid form:** FAFSA. **Financial aid deadline:** 11/15 (priority: 3/1). **Notification date:** Continuous beginning 1/1. Students must reply within 3 weeks of notification.

**CONTACT** Ms. Carolyn Schloemann, Acting Director, Financial Assistance, University of Illinois at Springfield, One University Plaza, MS UHB 1015, Springfield, IL 62703-5407, 217-206-6724 or toll-free 888-977-4847. Fax: 217-206-7376. E-mail: finaid@uis.edu. Website: http://www.uis.edu/.

# UNIVERSITY OF ILLINOIS AT URBANA–CHAMPAIGN
## Champaign, IL

**CONTACT** Daniel Mann, Director of Student Financial Aid, University of Illinois at Urbana–Champaign, Student Services Arcade Building, 620 East John Street, Champaign, IL 61820-5711, 217-333-0100. Website: http://www.illinois.edu/.

# UNIVERSITY OF INDIANAPOLIS
## Indianapolis, IN

| Tuition & fees: $26,170 | Average undergraduate aid package: $17,983 |
| --- | --- |

**ABOUT THE INSTITUTION** Independent United Methodist Church, coed. **Awards:** associate, bachelor's, master's, and doctoral degrees. 62 undergraduate majors. **Total enrollment:** 5,442. Undergraduates: 4,169. Freshmen: 992. Federal methodology is used as a basis for awarding need-based institutional aid.

**UNDERGRADUATE EXPENSES** for 2015–2016 **Application fee:** $25. **Comprehensive fee:** $35,494 includes full-time tuition ($25,910), mandatory fees ($260), and room and board ($9324). **College room only:** $5340. Full-time tuition and fees vary according to class time. Room and board charges vary according to board plan and housing facility. **Part-time tuition:** $1080 per credit hour. Part-time tuition and fees vary according to class time and course load.

**FRESHMAN FINANCIAL AID (Fall 2014, est.)** 878 applied for aid; of those 88% were deemed to have need. 100% of freshmen with need received aid; of those 14% had need fully met. **Average percent of need met:** 71% (excluding resources awarded to replace EFC). **Average financial aid package:** $19,556 (excluding resources awarded to replace EFC). 13% of all full-time freshmen had no need and received non-need-based gift aid.

**UNDERGRADUATE FINANCIAL AID (Fall 2014, est.)** 3,261 applied for aid; of those 88% were deemed to have need. 99% of undergraduates with need received aid; of those 14% had need fully met. **Average percent of need met:** 66% (excluding resources awarded to replace EFC). **Average financial aid package:** $17,983 (excluding resources awarded to replace EFC). 14% of all full-time undergraduates had no need and received non-need-based gift aid.

**GIFT AID (NEED-BASED) Total amount:** $15,022,774 (42% federal, 44% state, 14% institutional). **Receiving aid:** Freshmen: 50% (485); all full-time undergraduates: 46% (1,823). **Average award:** Freshmen: $8343; Undergraduates: $7968. **Scholarships, grants, and awards:** Federal Pell, FSEOG, state, private, college/university gift aid from institutional funds.

**GIFT AID (NON-NEED-BASED) Total amount:** $24,811,429 (1% federal, 99% institutional). **Receiving aid:** Freshmen: 79% (760). Undergraduates: 57% (2,290). **Average award:** Freshmen: $11,467. Undergraduates: $9629. **Scholarships, grants, and awards by category:** Academic interests/achievement: business, communication, general academic interests/achievements, health fields, physical sciences, religion/biblical studies. Creative arts/performance: art/fine arts, debating, music, theater/drama. Special achievements/activities: community service, religious involvement. Special characteristics: children of faculty/staff, international students, out-of-state students, relatives of clergy, religious affiliation, veterans. **Tuition waivers:** Full or partial for employees or children of employees. **ROTC:** Army cooperative.

**LOANS Student loans:** $35,725,644 (100% need-based). 81% of past graduating class borrowed through all loan programs. **Average indebtedness per student:** $35,689. **Average need-based loan:** Freshmen: $3641. Undergraduates: $4249. **Parent loans:** $7,989,853 (100% non-need-based). **Programs:** Federal Direct (Subsidized and Unsubsidized Stafford, PLUS), Perkins.

**WORK-STUDY Federal work-study:** Total amount: $279,974; 379 jobs averaging $739. **State or other work-study/employment:** Total amount: $1,079,514 (100% need-based). 147 part-time jobs averaging $7344.

**ATHLETIC AWARDS** Total amount: $5,728,486 (100% non-need-based).

**APPLYING FOR FINANCIAL AID Required financial aid forms:** FAFSA, institution's own form. **Financial aid deadline (priority):** 3/10. **Notification date:** Continuous beginning 3/1.

**CONTACT** Ms. Linda B. Handy, Associate Vice President of Financial Aid, University of Indianapolis, 1400 East Hanna Avenue, Indianapolis, IN 46227-3697, 317-788-3217 or toll-free 800-232-8634 Ext. 3216. *Fax:* 317-788-6136. *E-mail:* handy@uindy.edu. *Website:* http://www.uindy.edu/.

# THE UNIVERSITY OF IOWA
## Iowa City, IA

| Tuition & fees (IA res): $8104 | Average undergraduate aid package: $13,515 |
|---|---|

**ABOUT THE INSTITUTION** State-supported, coed. *Awards:* certificates, bachelor's, master's, and doctoral degrees. 138 undergraduate majors. *Total enrollment:* 31,387. Undergraduates: 22,354. Freshmen: 4,666. Federal methodology is used as a basis for awarding need-based institutional aid.

**UNDERGRADUATE EXPENSES** for 2015–2016 *Application fee:* $40. *Tuition, state resident:* full-time $6678; part-time $279 per semester hour. *Tuition, nonresident:* full-time $26,464; part-time $1101 per semester hour. *Required fees:* full-time $1426; $73 per semester hour. Full-time tuition and fees vary according to program and student level. Part-time tuition and fees vary according to course load, program, and student level. *College room and board:* $9728. Room and board charges vary according to board plan and housing facility.

**FRESHMAN FINANCIAL AID (Fall 2013)** 3,159 applied for aid; of those 65% were deemed to have need. 100% of freshmen with need received aid; of those 32% had need fully met. *Average percent of need met:* 71% (excluding resources awarded to replace EFC). *Average financial aid package:* $14,888 (excluding resources awarded to replace EFC). 18% of all full-time freshmen had no need and received non-need-based gift aid.

**UNDERGRADUATE FINANCIAL AID (Fall 2013)** 12,619 applied for aid; of those 71% were deemed to have need. 100% of undergraduates with need received aid; of those 24% had need fully met. *Average percent of need met:* 60% (excluding resources awarded to replace EFC). *Average financial aid package:* $13,515 (excluding resources awarded to replace EFC). 16% of all full-time undergraduates had no need and received non-need-based gift aid.

**GIFT AID (NEED-BASED)** *Total amount:* $53,179,536 (34% federal, 3% state, 58% institutional, 5% external sources). *Receiving aid:* Freshmen: 35% (1,461); all full-time undergraduates: 32% (6,082). *Average award:* Freshmen: $8409; Undergraduates: $7623. *Scholarships, grants, and awards:* Federal Pell, FSEOG, state, private, college/university gift aid from institutional funds.

**GIFT AID (NON-NEED-BASED)** *Total amount:* $45,426,210 (1% federal, 1% state, 87% institutional, 11% external sources). *Receiving aid:* Freshmen: 33% (1,373). Undergraduates: 21% (4,125). *Average award:* Freshmen: $4610. Undergraduates: $4739. *Scholarships, grants, and awards by category:* Academic interests/achievement: business, engineering/technologies, general academic interests/achievements, military science. *Creative arts/performance:* general creative arts/performance, music. *Special achievements/activities:* general special achievements/activities, leadership. *Special characteristics:* children and siblings of alumni, ethnic background, first-generation college students, handicapped students, local/state students, out-of-state students, veterans. *ROTC:* Army, Air Force.

**LOANS** *Student loans:* $92,861,467 (52% need-based, 48% non-need-based). 56% of past graduating class borrowed through all loan programs. *Average indebtedness per student:* $28,716. *Average need-based loan:* Freshmen: $4534. Undergraduates: $5147. *Parent loans:* $44,882,092 (100% non-need-based). *Programs:* Federal Direct (Subsidized and Unsubsidized Stafford, PLUS), Perkins, Federal Nursing, college/university.

**WORK-STUDY** *Federal work-study:* jobs available.

**ATHLETIC AWARDS** Total amount: $11,114,369 (100% non-need-based).

**APPLYING FOR FINANCIAL AID** *Required financial aid forms:* FAFSA, institution's own form. *Financial aid deadline:* Continuous. *Notification date:* Continuous beginning 3/15. Students must reply by 5/1 or within 2 weeks of notification.

**CONTACT** Mark Warner, Director of Student Financial Aid, The University of Iowa, 208 Calvin Hall, Iowa City, IA 52242, 319-335-3127 or toll-free 800-553-4692. *Website:* http://www.uiowa.edu/.

# UNIVERSITY OF JAMESTOWN
## Jamestown, ND

| Tuition & fees: $19,870 | Average undergraduate aid package: $13,893 |
|---|---|

**ABOUT THE INSTITUTION** Independent Presbyterian, coed. *Awards:* bachelor's, master's, and doctoral degrees. 44 undergraduate majors. *Total enrollment:* 970. Undergraduates: 892. Freshmen: 210. Federal methodology is used as a basis for awarding need-based institutional aid.

**UNDERGRADUATE EXPENSES** for 2015–2016 *Comprehensive fee:* $26,730 includes full-time tuition ($19,350), mandatory fees ($520), and room and board ($6860). *College room only:* $3235. Full-time tuition and fees vary according to course load, degree level, and program. Room and board charges vary according to housing facility. *Part-time tuition:* $435 per credit. *Part-time fees:* $60 per term. Part-time tuition and fees vary according to course load, degree level, and program.

**FRESHMAN FINANCIAL AID (Fall 2013)** 224 applied for aid; of those 79% were deemed to have need. 100% of freshmen with need received aid; of those 27% had need fully met. *Average percent of need met:* 73% (excluding resources awarded to replace EFC). *Average financial aid package:* $14,330 (excluding resources awarded to replace EFC). 31% of all full-time freshmen had no need and received non-need-based gift aid.

**UNDERGRADUATE FINANCIAL AID (Fall 2013)** 692 applied for aid; of those 84% were deemed to have need. 100% of undergraduates with need received aid; of those 23% had need fully met. *Average percent of need met:* 69% (excluding resources awarded to replace EFC). *Average financial aid package:* $13,893 (excluding resources awarded to replace EFC). 31% of all full-time undergraduates had no need and received non-need-based gift aid.

**GIFT AID (NEED-BASED)** *Total amount:* $4,892,762 (26% federal, 7% state, 64% institutional, 3% external sources). *Receiving aid:* Freshmen: 69% (177); all full-time undergraduates: 67% (579). *Average award:* Freshmen: $11,680; Undergraduates: $10,563. *Scholarships, grants, and awards:* Federal Pell, FSEOG, state, private, college/university gift aid from institutional funds.

**GIFT AID (NON-NEED-BASED)** *Total amount:* $2,346,887 (6% state, 87% institutional, 7% external sources). *Receiving aid:* Freshmen: 16% (41). Undergraduates: 12% (106). *Average award:* Freshmen: $7908. Undergraduates: $6797. *Scholarships, grants, and awards by category:* Academic interests/achievement: 824 awards ($4,256,701 total): general academic interests/achievements, physical sciences. *Creative arts/performance:* 43 awards ($85,625 total): art/fine arts, music, theater/drama. *Special achievements/activities:* 356 awards ($415,667 total): community service, leadership. *Special characteristics:* 215 awards ($523,904 total): children and siblings of alumni, children of faculty/staff, relatives of clergy, religious affiliation, siblings of current students, spouses of current students, veterans. *Tuition waivers:* Full or partial for employees or children of employees.

**LOANS** *Student loans:* $5,537,935 (61% need-based, 39% non-need-based). 71% of past graduating class borrowed through all loan programs. *Average indebtedness per student:* $26,530. *Average need-based loan:* Freshmen: $3499. Undergraduates: $4025. *Parent loans:* $481,935 (38% need-based, 62% non-need-based). *Programs:* Federal Direct (Subsidized and Unsubsidized Stafford, PLUS), Perkins, alternative loans.

**WORK-STUDY** *Federal work-study:* jobs available. *State or other work-study/employment:* Total amount: $6892 (100% non-need-based). Part-time jobs available.

**ATHLETIC AWARDS** Total amount: $2,043,851 (60% need-based, 40% non-need-based).

**APPLYING FOR FINANCIAL AID** *Required financial aid form:* FAFSA. *Financial aid deadline (priority):* 3/15. *Notification date:* Continuous beginning 9/1. Students must reply by 5/1.

**CONTACT** Judy Hager, Director of Financial Aid, University of Jamestown, 6085 College Lane, Jamestown, ND 58405, 701-252-3467 Ext. 5548 or toll-free 800-336-2554. *Fax:* 701-253-4318. *E-mail:* jhager@uj.edu. *Website:* http://www.uj.edu/.

# THE UNIVERSITY OF KANSAS
## Lawrence, KS

| Tuition & fees (KS res): $9706 | Average undergraduate aid package: $8965 |
|---|---|

**ABOUT THE INSTITUTION** State-supported, coed. *Awards:* certificates, bachelor's, master's, and doctoral degrees (University of Kansas is a single institution with academic programs and facilities at two primary locations: Lawrence and Kansas City). 114 undergraduate majors. *Total enrollment:* 27,180. Undergraduates: 19,343. Freshmen: 4,084. Federal methodology is used as a basis for awarding need-based institutional aid.

**UNDERGRADUATE EXPENSES for 2015–2016** *Application fee:* $30. *Tuition, state resident:* full-time $8806; part-time $293.55 per credit hour. *Tuition, nonresident:* full-time $22,947; part-time $764.90 per credit hour. *Required fees:* full-time $900; $75.01 per credit hour. Full-time tuition and fees vary according to program, reciprocity agreements, and student level. Part-time tuition and fees vary according to program, reciprocity agreements, and student level. *College room and board:* $7896; *Room only:* $4262. Room and board charges vary according to board plan and housing facility. *Payment plan:* Guaranteed tuition.

**FRESHMAN FINANCIAL AID (Fall 2013)** 3,070 applied for aid; of those 68% were deemed to have need. 96% of freshmen with need received aid; of those 13% had need fully met. *Average percent of need met:* 52% (excluding resources awarded to replace EFC). *Average financial aid package:* $9160 (excluding resources awarded to replace EFC). 19% of all full-time freshmen had no need and received non-need-based gift aid.

**UNDERGRADUATE FINANCIAL AID (Fall 2013)** 11,117 applied for aid; of those 74% were deemed to have need. 97% of undergraduates with need received aid; of those 10% had need fully met. *Average percent of need met:* 50% (excluding resources awarded to replace EFC). *Average financial aid package:* $8965 (excluding resources awarded to replace EFC). 12% of all full-time undergraduates had no need and received non-need-based gift aid.

**GIFT AID (NEED-BASED)** *Total amount:* $25,882,313 (69% federal, 8% state, 23% institutional). *Receiving aid:* Freshmen: 29% (1,135); all full-time undergraduates: 29% (4,852). *Average award:* Freshmen: $5529; Undergraduates: $5096. *Scholarships, grants, and awards:* Federal Pell, FSEOG, state, private, college/university gift aid from institutional funds, Federal Nursing.

**GIFT AID (NON-NEED-BASED)** *Total amount:* $19,194,809 (1% state, 77% institutional, 22% external sources). *Receiving aid:* Freshmen: 26% (1,000). Undergraduates: 16% (2,651). *Average award:* Freshmen: $3327. Undergraduates: $3744. *Scholarships, grants, and awards by category:* Academic interests/achievement: architecture, area/ethnic studies, biological sciences, business, communication, computer science, education, engineering/technologies, English, foreign languages, general academic interests/achievements, health fields, humanities, international studies, mathematics, military science, physical sciences, premedicine, religion/biblical studies, social sciences. *Creative arts/performance:* applied art and design, art/fine arts, cinema/film/broadcasting, creative writing, dance, debating, general creative arts/performance, journalism/publications, music, performing arts, theater/drama. *Special achievements/activities:* community service, general special achievements/activities, leadership. *Special characteristics:* adult students, children and siblings of alumni, children of faculty/staff, ethnic background, first-generation college students, general special characteristics, international students, local/state students, married students, members of minority groups, out-of-state students, previous college experience, veterans. *Tuition waivers:* Full or partial for employees or children of employees. *ROTC:* Army, Naval, Air Force.

**LOANS** *Student loans:* $71,821,048 (40% need-based, 60% non-need-based). 53% of past graduating class borrowed through all loan programs. *Average indebtedness per student:* $25,268. *Average need-based loan:* Freshmen: $3272. Undergraduates: $4253. *Parent loans:* $37,528,462 (100% non-need-based). *Programs:* Federal Direct (Subsidized and Unsubsidized Stafford, PLUS), Perkins, Federal Nursing, college/university.

**WORK-STUDY** *Federal work-study:* 440 jobs averaging $2136. *State or other work-study/employment:* Total amount: $259,622 (100% non-need-based). 63 part-time jobs averaging $4121.

**ATHLETIC AWARDS** Total amount: $8,937,318 (100% non-need-based).

**APPLYING FOR FINANCIAL AID** *Required financial aid form:* FAFSA. *Financial aid deadline (priority):* 3/1. *Notification date:* Continuous beginning 4/1. Students must reply within 4 weeks of notification.

**CONTACT** Ms. Brenda Maigaard, Assistant Vice Provost of Financial Aid and Scholarships, The University of Kansas, KU Visitor Center, 1502 Iowa Street, Lawrence, KS 66045-7576, 785-864-4700 or toll-free 888-686-7323 (in-state). *Fax:* 785-864-5469. *E-mail:* financialaid@ku.edu. *Website:* http://www.ku.edu/.

# UNIVERSITY OF KENTUCKY
## Lexington, KY

**ABOUT THE INSTITUTION** State-supported, coed. *Awards:* certificates, bachelor's, master's, and doctoral degrees. 101 undergraduate majors. *Total enrollment:* 29,199. Undergraduates: 22,223. Freshmen: 5,185.

**GIFT AID (NEED-BASED)** *Scholarships, grants, and awards:* Federal Pell, FSEOG, state, private, college/university gift aid from institutional funds.

**GIFT AID (NON-NEED-BASED)** *Scholarships, grants, and awards by category:* Academic interests/achievement: agriculture, architecture, area/ethnic studies, biological sciences, business, communication, computer science, education, engineering/technologies, English, foreign languages, general academic interests/achievements, health fields, home economics, international studies, mathematics, military science, physical sciences. *Creative arts/performance:* applied art and design, art/fine arts, cinema/film/broadcasting, creative writing, dance, debating, general creative arts/performance, journalism/publications, music, performing arts, theater/drama. *Special achievements/activities:* cheerleading/drum major, general special achievements/activities, leadership. *Special characteristics:* adult students, children and siblings of alumni, children of educators, children of faculty/staff, children of public servants, children of union members/company employees, children of workers in trades, children with a deceased or disabled parent, ethnic background, first-generation college students, general special characteristics, handicapped students, international students, members of minority groups, public servants, spouses of deceased or disabled public servants, veterans, veterans' children.

**LOANS** *Programs:* Federal Direct (Subsidized and Unsubsidized Stafford, PLUS), Perkins, college/university.

**WORK-STUDY** *Federal work-study:* jobs available. *State or other work-study/employment:* Part-time jobs available.

**APPLYING FOR FINANCIAL AID** *Required financial aid form:* FAFSA.

**CONTACT** Ms. Lynda S. George, Director of Financial Aid, University of Kentucky, 128 Funkhouser Building, Lexington, KY 40506-0054, 859-257-3172 Ext. 241 or toll-free 866-900-GO-UK. *Fax:* 859-257-4398. *E-mail:* lgeorge@email.uky.edu. *Website:* http://www.uky.edu/.

# UNIVERSITY OF LA VERNE
## La Verne, CA

| Tuition & fees: $38,560 | Average undergraduate aid package: $29,286 |
|---|---|

**ABOUT THE INSTITUTION** Independent, coed. *Awards:* certificates, bachelor's, master's, and doctoral degrees (also offers continuing education program with significant enrollment not reflected in profile). 46 undergraduate majors. *Total enrollment:* 4,876. Undergraduates: 2,713. Freshmen: 563. Federal methodology is used as a basis for awarding need-based institutional aid.

**UNDERGRADUATE EXPENSES for 2015–2016** *Application fee:* $50. *Comprehensive fee:* $51,070 includes full-time tuition ($37,100), mandatory fees ($1460), and room and board ($12,510). *College room only:* $6580. Full-time tuition and fees vary according to location. Room and board charges vary according to board plan and housing facility. *Part-time tuition:* $1083 per semester hour. Part-time tuition and fees vary according to location.

**FRESHMAN FINANCIAL AID (Fall 2014, est.)** 520 applied for aid; of those 94% were deemed to have need. 100% of freshmen with need received aid; of those 9% had need fully met. *Average percent of need met:* 50% (excluding resources awarded to replace EFC). *Average financial aid package:* $30,662 (excluding resources awarded to replace EFC). 13% of all full-time freshmen had no need and received non-need-based gift aid.

**UNDERGRADUATE FINANCIAL AID (Fall 2014, est.)** 2,297 applied for aid; of those 94% were deemed to have need. 100% of undergraduates with need received aid; of those 9% had need fully met. *Average percent of need met:* 43% (excluding

resources awarded to replace EFC). **Average financial aid package:** $29,286 (excluding resources awarded to replace EFC). 14% of all full-time undergraduates had no need and received non-need-based gift aid.

**GIFT AID (NEED-BASED) Total amount:** $53,984,415 (12% federal, 18% state, 70% institutional). **Receiving aid:** Freshmen: 85% (476); all full-time undergraduates: 72% (1,903). **Average award:** Freshmen: $14,493; Undergraduates: $10,923. **Scholarships, grants, and awards:** Federal Pell, FSEOG, state, private, college/university gift aid from institutional funds.

**GIFT AID (NON-NEED-BASED) Total amount:** $5,027,130 (99% institutional, 1% external sources). **Receiving aid:** Freshmen: 86% (481). Undergraduates: 81% (2,134). **Average award:** Freshmen: $16,896. Undergraduates: $20,664. **Scholarships, grants, and awards by category:** Academic interests/achievement: 2,532 awards ($43,718,684 total): general academic interests/achievements. Creative arts/performance: 37 awards ($969,408 total): art/fine arts, cinema/film/broadcasting, journalism/publications, music, performing arts, theater/drama. Special achievements/activities: 15 awards ($75,000 total): community service, leadership. **Tuition waivers:** Full or partial for employees or children of employees. **ROTC:** Army cooperative.

**LOANS Student loans:** $16,804,760 (94% need-based, 6% non-need-based). 80% of past graduating class borrowed through all loan programs. Average indebtedness per student: $28,215. **Average need-based loan:** Freshmen: $4004. Undergraduates: $4974. **Parent loans:** $9,135,460 (82% need-based, 18% non-need-based). **Programs:** Federal Direct (Subsidized and Unsubsidized Stafford), Perkins, college/university, alternative loans.

**WORK-STUDY Federal work-study:** Total amount: $687,600; 311 jobs averaging $2246. **State or other work-study/employment:** 1,070 part-time jobs averaging $8857.

**APPLYING FOR FINANCIAL AID Required financial aid forms:** FAFSA, state aid form. **Financial aid deadline (priority):** 3/2. **Notification date:** Continuous beginning 4/1. Students must reply within 2 weeks of notification.

**CONTACT** Diane A. Anchundia , Director of Financial Aid, University of La Verne, 1950 3rd Street, La Verne, CA 91750-4443, 800-649-0160 or toll-free 800-876-4858. Fax: 909-392-2751. E-mail: finaid@laverne.edu. Website: http://www.laverne.edu/.

# UNIVERSITY OF LOUISIANA AT LAFAYETTE
### Lafayette, LA

| Tuition & fees (LA res): $6948 | Average undergraduate aid package: $8507 |
| --- | --- |

**ABOUT THE INSTITUTION** State-supported, coed. **Awards:** certificates, bachelor's, master's, and doctoral degrees. 60 undergraduate majors. **Total enrollment:** 17,195. Undergraduates: 15,574. Freshmen: 2,922. Federal methodology is used as a basis for awarding need-based institutional aid.

**UNDERGRADUATE EXPENSES for 2015–2016 Application fee:** $25. **Tuition, state resident:** full-time $4915; part-time $289.50 per credit hour. **Tuition, nonresident:** full-time $17,315; part-time $763.82 per credit hour. **Required fees:** full-time $2033. Full-time tuition and fees vary according to course load. Part-time tuition and fees vary according to course load. **College room and board:** $8566. Room and board charges vary according to board plan and housing facility.

**FRESHMAN FINANCIAL AID (Fall 2013)** 2,534 applied for aid; of those 65% were deemed to have need. 99% of freshmen with need received aid; of those 15% had need fully met. **Average percent of need met:** 62% (excluding resources awarded to replace EFC). **Average financial aid package:** $9048 (excluding resources awarded to replace EFC). 16% of all full-time freshmen had no need and received non-need-based gift aid.

**UNDERGRADUATE FINANCIAL AID (Fall 2013)** 9,951 applied for aid; of those 70% were deemed to have need. 98% of undergraduates with need received aid; of those 10% had need fully met. **Average percent of need met:** 52% (excluding resources awarded to replace EFC). **Average financial aid package:** $8507 (excluding resources awarded to replace EFC). 9% of all full-time undergraduates had no need and received non-need-based gift aid.

**GIFT AID (NEED-BASED) Total amount:** $22,857,379 (90% federal, 10% state). **Receiving aid:** Freshmen: 59% (1,579); all full-time undergraduates: 50% (6,157). **Average award:** Freshmen: $7203; Undergraduates: $6609. **Scholarships, grants,**

and awards: Federal Pell, FSEOG, state, college/university gift aid from institutional funds.

**GIFT AID (NON-NEED-BASED) Total amount:** $34,589,579 (75% state, 23% institutional, 2% external sources). **Receiving aid:** Freshmen: 9% (247). Undergraduates: 5% (639). **Average award:** Freshmen: $2824. Undergraduates: $3050. **Scholarships, grants, and awards by category:** Academic interests/achievement: general academic interests/achievements. Creative arts/performance: general creative arts/performance. Special achievements/activities: general special achievements/activities. **Tuition waivers:** Full or partial for children of alumni, employees or children of employees. **ROTC:** Army.

**LOANS Student loans:** $28,043,998 (50% need-based, 50% non-need-based). **Average need-based loan:** Freshmen: $3157. Undergraduates: $3697. **Parent loans:** $2,355,534 (100% non-need-based). **Programs:** Federal Direct (Subsidized and Unsubsidized Stafford, PLUS), Perkins, Federal Nursing.

**WORK-STUDY Federal work-study:** 510 jobs averaging $1574. **State or other work-study/employment:** Total amount: $429,907 (100% non-need-based). 303 part-time jobs averaging $1419.

**ATHLETIC AWARDS** Total amount: $3,349,606 (100% non-need-based).

**APPLYING FOR FINANCIAL AID Required financial aid form:** FAFSA. **Financial aid deadline (priority):** 5/1. **Notification date:** Continuous beginning 4/1. Students must reply within 2 weeks of notification.

**CONTACT** Cindy S. Perez, Director of Financial Aid, University of Louisiana at Lafayette, PO Box 41206, Lafayette, LA 70504-1206, 337-482-6497 or toll-free 800-752-6553. Fax: 337-482-6502. E-mail: cperez@louisiana.edu. Website: http://www.louisiana.edu/.

# UNIVERSITY OF LOUISIANA AT MONROE
### Monroe, LA

**CONTACT** Ms. Teresa Smith, Director, Financial Aid, University of Louisiana at Monroe, 700 University Avenue, Monroe, LA 71209, 318-342-5320 or toll-free 800-372-5127. Fax: 318-342-3539. E-mail: tsmith@ulm.edu. Website: http://www.ulm.edu/.

# UNIVERSITY OF LOUISVILLE
### Louisville, KY

| Tuition & fees (KY res): $10,236 | Average undergraduate aid package: $11,342 |
| --- | --- |

**ABOUT THE INSTITUTION** State-supported, coed. **Awards:** certificates, associate, bachelor's, master's, and doctoral degrees. 54 undergraduate majors. **Total enrollment:** 21,559. Undergraduates: 15,959. Freshmen: 2,887. Federal methodology is used as a basis for awarding need-based institutional aid.

**UNDERGRADUATE EXPENSES for 2015–2016 Application fee:** $50. **Tuition, state resident:** full-time $10,236; part-time $427 per credit hour. **Tuition, nonresident:** full-time $24,124; part-time $1006 per credit hour. Full-time tuition and fees vary according to reciprocity agreements. Part-time tuition and fees vary according to reciprocity agreements. **College room and board:** $7710; **Room only:** $4790. Room and board charges vary according to board plan and housing facility.

**FRESHMAN FINANCIAL AID (Fall 2014, est.)** 2,487 applied for aid; of those 76% were deemed to have need. 99% of freshmen with need received aid; of those 28% had need fully met. **Average percent of need met:** 63% (excluding resources awarded to replace EFC). **Average financial aid package:** $12,078 (excluding resources awarded to replace EFC). 16% of all full-time freshmen had no need and received non-need-based gift aid.

**UNDERGRADUATE FINANCIAL AID (Fall 2014, est.)** 9,455 applied for aid; of those 81% were deemed to have need. 96% of undergraduates with need received aid; of those 22% had need fully met. **Average percent of need met:** 61% (excluding resources awarded to replace EFC). **Average financial aid package:** $11,342 (excluding resources awarded to replace EFC). 14% of all full-time undergraduates had no need and received non-need-based gift aid.

**GIFT AID (NEED-BASED) Total amount:** $58,988,690 (33% federal, 19% state, 36% institutional, 12% external sources). **Receiving aid:** Freshmen: 64% (1,816); all full-time undergraduates: 55% (6,837). *Average award:* Freshmen: $9156; Undergraduates: $8705. *Scholarships, grants, and awards:* Federal Pell, FSEOG, state, private, college/university gift aid from institutional funds.

**GIFT AID (NON-NEED-BASED)** *Total amount:* $28,837,192 (23% state, 61% institutional, 16% external sources). *Receiving aid:* Freshmen: 13% (372). Undergraduates: 8% (972). *Average award:* Freshmen: $7654. Undergraduates: $7908. *Scholarships, grants, and awards by category:* Academic interests/achievement: biological sciences, business, education, engineering/technologies, English, foreign languages, general academic interests/achievements, health fields, mathematics, military science, premedicine. *Creative arts/performance:* art/fine arts, creative writing, dance, debating, general creative arts/performance, music, theater/drama. *Special achievements/activities:* cheerleading/drum major, community service, general special achievements/activities, hobbies/interests, junior miss, leadership, memberships. *Special characteristics:* adult students, children and siblings of alumni, children of faculty/staff, children of union members/company employees, children with a deceased or disabled parent, ethnic background, general special characteristics, local/state students, members of minority groups, out-of-state students, previous college experience, veterans, veterans' children. *Tuition waivers:* Full or partial for employees or children of employees, senior citizens. *ROTC:* Army, Air Force.

**LOANS** *Student loans:* $49,783,022 (71% need-based, 29% non-need-based). 57% of past graduating class borrowed through all loan programs. *Average indebtedness per student:* $23,375. *Average need-based loan:* Freshmen: $3347. Undergraduates: $4074. *Parent loans:* $7,109,985 (32% need-based, 68% non-need-based). *Programs:* Federal Direct (Subsidized and Unsubsidized Stafford, PLUS), Perkins, Federal Nursing.

**WORK-STUDY** *Federal work-study:* Total amount: $1,134,513; 375 jobs averaging $3196.

**ATHLETIC AWARDS** Total amount: $9,463,556 (34% need-based, 66% non-need-based).

**APPLYING FOR FINANCIAL AID** *Required financial aid form:* FAFSA. *Financial aid deadline (priority):* 3/15. *Notification date:* Continuous beginning 4/1. Students must reply by 5/1.

**CONTACT** Ms. Patricia O. Arauz, Director of Financial Aid, University of Louisville, 2301 South Third Street, Louisville, KY 40292-0001, 502-852-6145 or toll-free 800-334-8635. *Fax:* 502-852-0182. *E-mail:* finaid@louisville.edu. *Website:* http://www.louisville.edu/.

# UNIVERSITY OF MAINE
## Orono, ME

| Tuition & fees (ME res): $10,606 | Average undergraduate aid package: $16,083 |
|---|---|

**ABOUT THE INSTITUTION** State-supported, coed. *Awards:* certificates, bachelor's, master's, and doctoral degrees. 77 undergraduate majors. *Total enrollment:* 11,286. Undergraduates: 9,339. Freshmen: 2,068. Federal methodology is used as a basis for awarding need-based institutional aid.

**UNDERGRADUATE EXPENSES for 2015-2016** *Application fee:* $40. *Tuition, state resident:* full-time $8370; part-time $279 per credit hour. *Tuition, nonresident:* full-time $26,250; part-time $875 per credit hour. *Required fees:* full-time $2236. Full-time tuition and fees vary according to course load. Part-time tuition and fees vary according to course load. *College room and board:* $9296; *Room only:* $4858. Room and board charges vary according to board plan and housing facility.

**FRESHMAN FINANCIAL AID (Fall 2014, est.)** 1,910 applied for aid; of those 81% were deemed to have need. 100% of freshmen with need received aid; of those 18% had need fully met. *Average percent of need met:* 83% (excluding resources awarded to replace EFC). *Average financial aid package:* $18,106 (excluding resources awarded to replace EFC). 13% of all full-time freshmen had no need and received non-need-based gift aid.

**UNDERGRADUATE FINANCIAL AID (Fall 2014, est.)** 6,887 applied for aid; of those 83% were deemed to have need. 98% of undergraduates with need received aid; of those 15% had need fully met. *Average percent of need met:* 80% (excluding resources awarded to replace EFC). *Average financial aid package:* $16,083 (excluding resources awarded to replace EFC). 7% of all full-time undergraduates had no need and received non-need-based gift aid.

**GIFT AID (NEED-BASED)** *Total amount:* $44,427,673 (34% federal, 6% state, 53% institutional, 7% external sources). *Receiving aid:* Freshmen: 72% (1,479); all

full-time undergraduates: 61% (4,897). *Average award:* Freshmen: $10,133; Undergraduates: $8332. *Scholarships, grants, and awards:* Federal Pell, FSEOG, state, private, college/university gift aid from institutional funds, Federal Nursing, Academic Competitiveness Grants, National SMART Grants.

**GIFT AID (NON-NEED-BASED)** *Total amount:* $4,539,293 (1% federal, 76% institutional, 23% external sources). *Receiving aid:* Freshmen: 6% (130). Undergraduates: 4% (302). *Average award:* Freshmen: $4608. Undergraduates: $4679. *Scholarships, grants, and awards by category:* Academic interests/achievement: general academic interests/achievements. *Creative arts/performance:* art/fine arts, general creative arts/performance. *Special achievements/activities:* leadership. *Special characteristics:* children and siblings of alumni, local/state students, members of minority groups. *Tuition waivers:* Full or partial for employees or children of employees, senior citizens. *ROTC:* Army, Naval cooperative.

**LOANS** *Student loans:* $58,236,924 (71% need-based, 29% non-need-based). 77% of past graduating class borrowed through all loan programs. *Average indebtedness per student:* $33,875. *Average need-based loan:* Freshmen: $3973. Undergraduates: $4569. *Parent loans:* $6,129,062 (44% need-based, 56% non-need-based). *Programs:* Federal Direct (Subsidized and Unsubsidized Stafford, PLUS), Perkins, state, college/university, private loans.

**WORK-STUDY** *Federal work-study:* Total amount: $3,116,642; 1,330 jobs averaging $2343.

**ATHLETIC AWARDS** Total amount: $5,603,694 (89% need-based, 11% non-need-based).

**APPLYING FOR FINANCIAL AID** *Required financial aid form:* FAFSA. *Financial aid deadline:* 5/15 (priority: 3/1). *Notification date:* Continuous beginning 3/15.

**CONTACT** Ms. Gianna Marrs, Interim Director of Student Financial Aid, University of Maine, 5781 Wingate Hall, Orono, ME 04469-5781, 207-581-1324 or toll-free 877-486-2364. *Fax:* 207-581-3261. *Website:* http://www.umaine.edu/.

# UNIVERSITY OF MAINE AT AUGUSTA
## Augusta, ME

| Tuition & fees (ME res): $7448 | Average undergraduate aid package: $9172 |
|---|---|

**ABOUT THE INSTITUTION** State-supported, coed. *Awards:* certificates, associate, and bachelor's degrees (also offers some graduate courses and continuing education programs with significant enrollment not reflected in profile). 21 undergraduate majors. *Total enrollment:* 4,664. Undergraduates: 4,664. Freshmen: 405. Federal methodology is used as a basis for awarding need-based institutional aid.

**UNDERGRADUATE EXPENSES for 2015-2016** *Application fee:* $40. *Tuition, state resident:* full-time $6510; part-time $217 per credit hour. *Tuition, nonresident:* full-time $15,750; part-time $525 per credit hour. *Required fees:* full-time $938; $31.25 per credit hour. Full-time tuition and fees vary according to course load, location, program, and reciprocity agreements. Part-time tuition and fees vary according to course load, location, program, and reciprocity agreements.

**FRESHMAN FINANCIAL AID (Fall 2014, est.)** 245 applied for aid; of those 94% were deemed to have need. 97% of freshmen with need received aid; of those 1% had need fully met. *Average percent of need met:* 51% (excluding resources awarded to replace EFC). *Average financial aid package:* $7976 (excluding resources awarded to replace EFC).

**UNDERGRADUATE FINANCIAL AID (Fall 2014, est.)** 1,609 applied for aid; of those 95% were deemed to have need. 98% of undergraduates with need received aid; of those 3% had need fully met. *Average percent of need met:* 52% (excluding resources awarded to replace EFC). *Average financial aid package:* $9172 (excluding resources awarded to replace EFC). 1% of all full-time undergraduates had no need and received non-need-based gift aid.

**GIFT AID (NEED-BASED)** *Total amount:* $12,651,584 (79% federal, 15% state, 6% institutional). *Receiving aid:* Freshmen: 81% (211); all full-time undergraduates: 75% (1,325). *Average award:* Freshmen: $5303; Undergraduates: $5749. *Scholarships, grants, and awards:* Federal Pell, FSEOG, state, private, college/university gift aid from institutional funds.

**GIFT AID (NON-NEED-BASED)** *Total amount:* $4833 (52% state, 48% institutional). *Receiving aid:* Freshmen: 1% (2). Undergraduates: 4% (65). *Average award:* Undergraduates: $1000. *Scholarships, grants, and awards by category:* Academic interests/achievement: biological sciences, business, general academic interests/achievements, mathematics. *Creative arts/performance:* music. *Special achievements/activities:* general special achievements/activities, leadership. *Special characteristics:* children of faculty/staff, ethnic background, international students, local/state students, veterans' children. *Tuition waivers:* Full or partial for minority students, employees or children of employees, senior citizens. *ROTC:* Army cooperative.

**LOANS** *Student loans:* $21,286,775 (89% need-based, 11% non-need-based). 79% of past graduating class borrowed through all loan programs. *Average indebtedness per student:* $30,827. *Average need-based loan:* Freshmen: $6253. Undergraduates: $7755. *Parent loans:* $74,602 (85% need-based, 15% non-need-based). *Programs:* Federal Direct (Subsidized and Unsubsidized Stafford, PLUS), Perkins, Federal Nursing.

**WORK-STUDY** *Federal work-study:* Total amount: $303,384; jobs available. *State or other work-study/employment:* Total amount: $57,106 (100% non-need-based). Part-time jobs available.

**ATHLETIC AWARDS** Total amount: $21,085 (50% need-based, 50% non-need-based).

**APPLYING FOR FINANCIAL AID** *Required financial aid form:* FAFSA. *Financial aid deadline (priority):* 3/1. *Notification date:* Continuous beginning 3/15. Students must reply within 2 weeks of notification.

**CONTACT** UMA Financial Aid, University of Maine at Augusta, 46 University Drive, Augusta, ME 04330-9410, 207-621-3185 or toll-free 877-862-1234 Ext. 3185 (in-state), 877-862-1234 (out-of-state). *Fax:* 207-621-3116. *E-mail:* umafa@maine.edu. *Website:* http://www.uma.maine.edu/.

# UNIVERSITY OF MAINE AT FARMINGTON
## Farmington, ME

| Tuition & fees (ME res): $9217 | Average undergraduate aid package: $13,342 |
|---|---|

**ABOUT THE INSTITUTION** State-supported, coed. *Awards:* certificates, bachelor's, and master's degrees. 36 undergraduate majors. *Total enrollment:* 1,960. Undergraduates: 1,773. Freshmen: 412. Federal methodology is used as a basis for awarding need-based institutional aid.

**UNDERGRADUATE EXPENSES** for 2015–2016 *Tuition, state resident:* full-time $8352; part-time $261 per credit hour. *Tuition, nonresident:* full-time $17,440; part-time $545 per credit hour. *Required fees:* full-time $865. Full-time tuition and fees vary according to course load and reciprocity agreements. Part-time tuition and fees vary according to course load and reciprocity agreements. *College room and board:* $8970; *Room only:* $4750. Room and board charges vary according to board plan and housing facility.

**FRESHMAN FINANCIAL AID (Fall 2013)** 423 applied for aid; of those 87% were deemed to have need. 100% of freshmen with need received aid; of those 41% had need fully met. *Average percent of need met:* 87% (excluding resources awarded to replace EFC). *Average financial aid package:* $14,320 (excluding resources awarded to replace EFC). 8% of all full-time freshmen had no need and received non-need-based gift aid.

**UNDERGRADUATE FINANCIAL AID (Fall 2013)** 1,663 applied for aid; of those 87% were deemed to have need. 100% of undergraduates with need received aid; of those 42% had need fully met. *Average percent of need met:* 83% (excluding resources awarded to replace EFC). *Average financial aid package:* $13,342 (excluding resources awarded to replace EFC). 2% of all full-time undergraduates had no need and received non-need-based gift aid.

**GIFT AID (NEED-BASED)** *Total amount:* $8,722,236 (49% federal, 10% state, 32% institutional, 9% external sources). *Receiving aid:* Freshmen: 80% (351); all full-time undergraduates: 73% (1,290). *Average award:* Freshmen: $8190; Undergraduates: $6502. *Scholarships, grants, and awards:* Federal Pell, FSEOG, state, private, college/university gift aid from institutional funds.

**GIFT AID (NON-NEED-BASED)** *Total amount:* $157,208 (98% institutional, 2% external sources). *Receiving aid:* Freshmen: 3% (15). Undergraduates: 1% (16). *Average award:* Freshmen: $2499. Undergraduates: $2528. *Scholarships, grants, and awards by category:* Academic interests/achievement: general academic interests/achievements. Creative arts/performance: music, theater/drama. Special achievements/activities: leadership. Special characteristics: children of faculty/staff, members of minority groups, out-of-state students, veterans' children. *Tuition*

*waivers:* Full or partial for minority students, employees or children of employees, senior citizens.

**LOANS** *Student loans:* $12,331,696 (77% need-based, 23% non-need-based). 86% of past graduating class borrowed through all loan programs. *Average indebtedness per student:* $31,792. *Average need-based loan:* Freshmen: $5817. Undergraduates: $6888. *Parent loans:* $1,162,509 (38% need-based, 62% non-need-based). *Programs:* Federal Direct (Subsidized and Unsubsidized Stafford, PLUS), Perkins, state, college/university.

**WORK-STUDY** *Federal work-study:* jobs available. *State or other work-study/employment:* Total amount: $223,694 (51% need-based, 49% non-need-based). Part-time jobs available.

**APPLYING FOR FINANCIAL AID** *Required financial aid form:* FAFSA. *Financial aid deadline (priority):* 3/1. *Notification date:* Continuous beginning 3/15.

**CONTACT** Mr. Ronald P. Milliken, Director of Financial Aid, University of Maine at Farmington, 224 Main Street, Farmington, ME 04938-1990, 207-778-7105. *Fax:* 207-778-8178. *E-mail:* milliken@maine.edu. *Website:* http://www.umf.maine.edu/.

# UNIVERSITY OF MAINE AT FORT KENT
## Fort Kent, ME

| Tuition & fees (ME res): $7575 | Average undergraduate aid package: $11,455 |
|---|---|

**ABOUT THE INSTITUTION** State-supported, coed. *Awards:* certificates, associate, and bachelor's degrees. 19 undergraduate majors. *Total enrollment:* 1,327. Undergraduates: 1,327. Freshmen: 138. Both federal and institutional methodology are used as a basis for awarding need-based institutional aid.

**UNDERGRADUATE EXPENSES** for 2015–2016 *Application fee:* $40. *Tuition, state resident:* full-time $6600; part-time $220 per credit. *Tuition, nonresident:* full-time $9900; part-time $330 per credit. *Required fees:* full-time $975; $32.50 per credit. Full-time tuition and fees vary according to program. Part-time tuition and fees vary according to program. *College room and board:* $7720; *Room only:* $4150. Room and board charges vary according to board plan and housing facility.

**FRESHMAN FINANCIAL AID (Fall 2013)** 139 applied for aid; of those 86% were deemed to have need. 100% of freshmen with need received aid; of those 54% had need fully met. *Average percent of need met:* 80% (excluding resources awarded to replace EFC). *Average financial aid package:* $11,198 (excluding resources awarded to replace EFC). 3% of all full-time freshmen had no need and received non-need-based gift aid.

**UNDERGRADUATE FINANCIAL AID (Fall 2013)** 524 applied for aid; of those 87% were deemed to have need. 100% of undergraduates with need received aid; of those 57% had need fully met. *Average percent of need met:* 80% (excluding resources awarded to replace EFC). *Average financial aid package:* $11,455 (excluding resources awarded to replace EFC). 3% of all full-time undergraduates had no need and received non-need-based gift aid.

**GIFT AID (NEED-BASED)** *Total amount:* $3,312,234 (55% federal, 6% state, 33% institutional, 6% external sources). *Receiving aid:* Freshmen: 77% (118); all full-time undergraduates: 73% (432). *Average award:* Freshmen: $5792; Undergraduates: $5670. *Scholarships, grants, and awards:* Federal Pell, FSEOG, state, private, college/university gift aid from institutional funds, Federal Nursing.

**GIFT AID (NON-NEED-BASED)** *Total amount:* $71,229 (100% institutional). *Receiving aid:* Freshmen: 3% (5). Undergraduates: 2% (11). *Average award:* Freshmen: $1200. Undergraduates: $2675. *Scholarships, grants, and awards by category:* Academic interests/achievement: 630 awards ($1,149,244 total): biological sciences, business, communication, computer science, education, English, foreign languages, general academic interests/achievements, health fields, humanities, mathematics, social sciences. Creative arts/performance: general creative arts/performance, performing arts. Special achievements/activities: general special achievements/activities. Special characteristics: 22 awards ($8600 total): adult students, children of faculty/staff, ethnic background, general special characteristics, international students, members of minority groups. *Tuition waivers:* Full or partial for employees or children of employees, senior citizens.

**LOANS** *Student loans:* $4,153,454 (77% need-based, 23% non-need-based). 79% of past graduating class borrowed through all loan programs. *Average indebtedness*

per student: $24,028. **Average need-based loan:** Freshmen: $5315. Undergraduates: $6278. **Parent loans:** $218,931 (49% need-based, 51% non-need-based). **Programs:** Federal Direct (Subsidized and Unsubsidized Stafford, PLUS), Perkins, Federal Nursing, state, college/university.

**WORK-STUDY** *Federal work-study:* 80 jobs averaging $680. **State or other work-study/employment:** Part-time jobs available.

**APPLYING FOR FINANCIAL AID** *Required financial aid forms:* FAFSA, institution's own form, CSS Financial Aid PROFILE, state aid form. *Financial aid deadline (priority):* 3/1. *Notification date:* Continuous beginning 3/1.

**CONTACT** Lisa Lipe, Associate Director of Financial Aid, University of Maine at Fort Kent, 23 University Drive, Fort Kent, ME 04743-1292, 207-834-7607 or toll-free 888-TRY-UMFK. *Fax:* 207-834-7841. *E-mail:* lisa.lipe@maine.edu.
*Website:* http://www.umfk.maine.edu/.

# UNIVERSITY OF MAINE AT MACHIAS
## Machias, ME

| Tuition & fees (ME res): $7480 | Average undergraduate aid package: $14,267 |
|---|---|

**ABOUT THE INSTITUTION** State-supported, coed. *Awards:* certificates, associate, and bachelor's degrees. 37 undergraduate majors. *Total enrollment:* 810. Undergraduates: 810. Freshmen: 118. Federal methodology is used as a basis for awarding need-based institutional aid.

**UNDERGRADUATE EXPENSES** for 2015–2016 *Application fee:* $40. *Tuition, state resident:* full-time $6660; part-time $222 per credit. *Tuition, nonresident:* full-time $18,480; part-time $616 per credit. *Required fees:* full-time $820. *College room and board:* $8178.

**FRESHMAN FINANCIAL AID (Fall 2013)** 94 applied for aid; of those 93% were deemed to have need. 100% of freshmen with need received aid; of those 69% had need fully met. *Average percent of need met:* 87% (excluding resources awarded to replace EFC). *Average financial aid package:* $13,737 (excluding resources awarded to replace EFC).

**UNDERGRADUATE FINANCIAL AID (Fall 2013)** 413 applied for aid; of those 92% were deemed to have need. 100% of undergraduates with need received aid; of those 66% had need fully met. *Average percent of need met:* 86% (excluding resources awarded to replace EFC). *Average financial aid package:* $14,267 (excluding resources awarded to replace EFC). 1% of all full-time undergraduates had no need and received non-need-based gift aid.

**GIFT AID (NEED-BASED)** *Total amount:* $3,743,303 (51% federal, 7% state, 36% institutional, 6% external sources). *Receiving aid:* Freshmen: 86% (84); all full-time undergraduates: 81% (361). *Average award:* Freshmen: $9271; Undergraduates: $8782. *Scholarships, grants, and awards:* Federal Pell, FSEOG, state, private, college/university gift aid from institutional funds.

**GIFT AID (NON-NEED-BASED)** *Total amount:* $11,300 (100% institutional). *Receiving aid:* Undergraduates: 2% (7). *Average award:* Undergraduates: $916. *Scholarships, grants, and awards by category:* Academic interests/achievement: general academic interests/achievements.

**LOANS** *Student loans:* $2,828,153 (79% need-based, 21% non-need-based). 85% of past graduating class borrowed through all loan programs. *Average indebtedness per student:* $29,146. *Average need-based loan:* Freshmen: $5187. Undergraduates: $6307. *Parent loans:* $171,147 (13% need-based, 87% non-need-based). *Programs:* Federal Direct (Subsidized and Unsubsidized Stafford, PLUS), Perkins, state.

**WORK-STUDY** *Federal work-study:* jobs available. *State or other work-study/employment:* Part-time jobs available.

**APPLYING FOR FINANCIAL AID** *Required financial aid form:* FAFSA. *Financial aid deadline (priority):* 3/1. *Notification date:* Continuous.

**CONTACT** Ms. Stephanie Larrabee, Director of Financial Aid, University of Maine at Machias, 9 O'Brien Avenue, Machias, ME 04654, 207-255-1203 or toll-free 888-GOTOUMM (in-state), 888-468-6866 (out-of-state). *Fax:* 207-255-4864.
*Website:* http://umm.maine.edu/.

# UNIVERSITY OF MAINE AT PRESQUE ISLE
## Presque Isle, ME

| Tuition & fees (ME res): $7435 | Average undergraduate aid package: $11,575 |
|---|---|

**ABOUT THE INSTITUTION** State-supported, coed. *Awards:* certificates, associate, and bachelor's degrees. 26 undergraduate majors. *Total enrollment:* 1,138. Undergraduates: 1,138. Freshmen: 197. Federal methodology is used as a basis for awarding need-based institutional aid.

**UNDERGRADUATE EXPENSES** for 2015–2016 *Tuition, state resident:* full-time $6600; part-time $220 per credit hour. *Tuition, nonresident:* full-time $9900; part-time $330 per credit hour. *Required fees:* full-time $835. Full-time tuition and fees vary according to course load, location, and reciprocity agreements. Part-time tuition and fees vary according to course load, location, and reciprocity agreements. *College room and board:* $7656. Room and board charges vary according to board plan and housing facility.

**FRESHMAN FINANCIAL AID (Fall 2014, est.)** 170 applied for aid; of those 88% were deemed to have need. 100% of freshmen with need received aid; of those 63% had need fully met. *Average percent of need met:* 90% (excluding resources awarded to replace EFC). *Average financial aid package:* $11,418 (excluding resources awarded to replace EFC). 8% of all full-time freshmen had no need and received non-need-based gift aid.

**UNDERGRADUATE FINANCIAL AID (Fall 2014, est.)** 575 applied for aid; of those 90% were deemed to have need. 100% of undergraduates with need received aid; of those 63% had need fully met. *Average percent of need met:* 88% (excluding resources awarded to replace EFC). *Average financial aid package:* $11,575 (excluding resources awarded to replace EFC). 5% of all full-time undergraduates had no need and received non-need-based gift aid.

**GIFT AID (NEED-BASED)** *Total amount:* $3,868,830 (63% federal, 10% state, 20% institutional, 7% external sources). *Receiving aid:* Freshmen: 82% (150); all full-time undergraduates: 75% (508). *Average award:* Freshmen: $6955; Undergraduates: $6568. *Scholarships, grants, and awards:* Federal Pell, FSEOG, state, private, college/university gift aid from institutional funds.

**GIFT AID (NON-NEED-BASED)** *Total amount:* $122,726 (71% institutional, 29% external sources). *Receiving aid:* Freshmen: 5% (9). Undergraduates: 3% (20). *Average award:* Freshmen: $2734. Undergraduates: $2344. *Scholarships, grants, and awards by category:* Academic interests/achievement: general academic interests/achievements. Special achievements/activities: community service. Special characteristics: children of faculty/staff, ethnic background, international students, local/state students, out-of-state students, veterans' children. *Tuition waivers:* Full or partial for minority students, employees or children of employees, senior citizens.

**LOANS** *Student loans:* $3,212,106 (70% need-based, 30% non-need-based). 80% of past graduating class borrowed through all loan programs. *Average indebtedness per student:* $23,777. *Average need-based loan:* Freshmen: $4383. Undergraduates: $5019. *Parent loans:* $41,871 (4% need-based, 96% non-need-based). *Programs:* Federal Direct (Subsidized and Unsubsidized Stafford, PLUS), Perkins, state, college/university.

**WORK-STUDY** *Federal work-study:* Total amount: $653,645; 232 jobs averaging $2573.

**APPLYING FOR FINANCIAL AID** *Required financial aid form:* FAFSA. *Financial aid deadline (priority):* 3/1. *Notification date:* Continuous beginning 3/1. Students must reply within 2 weeks of notification.

**CONTACT** Christopher A.R. Bell, Director of Financial Aid, University of Maine at Presque Isle, 181 Main Street, Presque Isle, ME 04769-2888, 207-768-9511. *Fax:* 207-768-9509. *E-mail:* chris@maine.edu.
*Website:* http://www.umpi.edu/.

# UNIVERSITY OF MANAGEMENT AND TECHNOLOGY
## Arlington, VA

| Tuition & fees: N/R | Average undergraduate aid package: N/A |
| --- | --- |

**ABOUT THE INSTITUTION** Proprietary, coed. 5 undergraduate majors. Both federal and institutional methodology are used as a basis for awarding need-based institutional aid.

**FRESHMAN FINANCIAL AID (Fall 2013)** 4 applied for aid; of those 100% were deemed to have need. 100% of freshmen with need received aid.

**UNDERGRADUATE FINANCIAL AID (Fall 2013)** 109 applied for aid; of those 98% were deemed to have need. 100% of undergraduates with need received aid.

**GIFT AID (NEED-BASED) Total amount:** $367,481 (100% federal). **Receiving aid:** Freshmen: 100% (4); all full-time undergraduates: 98% (107). **Average award:** Undergraduates: $2747. **Scholarships, grants, and awards:** Federal Pell.

**GIFT AID (NON-NEED-BASED) Total amount:** $2865 (100% external sources). **Receiving aid:** Freshmen: 100% (4). Undergraduates: 2% (2).

**LOANS Student loans:** $397,507 (50% need-based, 50% non-need-based). **Average need-based loan:** Undergraduates: $1616. **Parent loans:** $7057 (100% non-need-based). **Programs:** Federal Direct (Subsidized and Unsubsidized Stafford, PLUS).

**APPLYING FOR FINANCIAL AID Required financial aid forms:** FAFSA, institution's own form. **Financial aid deadline:** Continuous. **Notification date:** Continuous.

**CONTACT** Ms. Margo Jacobs, Financial Aid Administrator, University of Management and Technology, 1901 North Fort Myer Drive, Arlington, VA 22209, 703-516-0035 Ext. 2014 or toll-free 800-924-4883. Fax: 703-516-0985. E-mail: info@umtweb.edu. Website: http://www.umtweb.edu/.

# UNIVERSITY OF MARY
## Bismarck, ND

**ABOUT THE INSTITUTION** Independent Roman Catholic, coed. 47 undergraduate majors.

**GIFT AID (NEED-BASED) Scholarships, grants, and awards:** Federal Pell, FSEOG, state, private, college/university gift aid from institutional funds, TEACH Grants.

**GIFT AID (NON-NEED-BASED) Scholarships, grants, and awards by category:** Academic interests/achievement: general academic interests/achievements. Creative arts/performance: music. Special achievements/activities: general special achievements/activities. Special characteristics: children of faculty/staff, general special characteristics, local/state students, religious affiliation, veterans.

**LOANS Programs:** Federal Direct (Subsidized and Unsubsidized Stafford, PLUS), Perkins, Federal Nursing, private loans.

**APPLYING FOR FINANCIAL AID Required financial aid form:** FAFSA.

**CONTACT** Brenda Zastoupil, Financial Assistance Director, University of Mary, 7500 University Drive, Bismarck, ND 58504-9652, 701-355-8244 or toll-free 800-288-6279. Fax: 701-255-7687. E-mail: brendaz@umary.edu. Website: http://www.umary.edu/.

# UNIVERSITY OF MARY HARDIN-BAYLOR
## Belton, TX

| Tuition & fees: $24,460 | Average undergraduate aid package: $15,833 |
| --- | --- |

**ABOUT THE INSTITUTION** Independent Southern Baptist, coed. **Awards:** certificates, bachelor's, master's, and doctoral degrees. 61 undergraduate majors. **Total enrollment:** 3,740. Undergraduates: 3,110. Freshmen: 711. Federal methodology is used as a basis for awarding need-based institutional aid.

**UNDERGRADUATE EXPENSES** for 2015–2016 **Application fee:** $35. **Comprehensive fee:** $31,480 includes full-time tuition ($22,260), mandatory fees ($2200), and room and board ($7020). Full-time tuition and fees vary according to course load and degree level. Room and board charges vary according to housing facility. **Part-time tuition:** $795 per credit hour. Part-time tuition and fees vary according to course load and degree level.

**FRESHMAN FINANCIAL AID (Fall 2014, est.)** 666 applied for aid; of those 86% were deemed to have need. 100% of freshmen with need received aid; of those 7% had need fully met. **Average percent of need met:** 64% (excluding resources awarded to replace EFC). **Average financial aid package:** $17,835 (excluding resources awarded to replace EFC). 12% of all full-time freshmen had no need and received non-need-based gift aid.

**UNDERGRADUATE FINANCIAL AID (Fall 2014, est.)** 2,643 applied for aid; of those 84% were deemed to have need. 100% of undergraduates with need received aid; of those 8% had need fully met. **Average percent of need met:** 56% (excluding resources awarded to replace EFC). **Average financial aid package:** $15,833 (excluding resources awarded to replace EFC). 12% of all full-time undergraduates had no need and received non-need-based gift aid.

**GIFT AID (NEED-BASED) Total amount:** $27,247,347 (20% federal, 15% state, 63% institutional, 2% external sources). **Receiving aid:** Freshmen: 70% (495); all full-time undergraduates: 71% (2,021). **Average award:** Freshmen: $14,015; Undergraduates: $11,562. **Scholarships, grants, and awards:** Federal Pell, FSEOG, state, private, college/university gift aid from institutional funds.

**GIFT AID (NON-NEED-BASED) Total amount:** $3,200,121 (96% institutional, 4% external sources). **Receiving aid:** Freshmen: 4% (26). Undergraduates: 3% (78). **Average award:** Freshmen: $5286. Undergraduates: $5823. **Scholarships, grants, and awards by category:** Academic interests/achievement: biological sciences, business, communication, computer science, education, English, foreign languages, general academic interests/achievements, health fields, humanities, international studies, mathematics, physical sciences, premedicine, religion/biblical studies, social sciences. Creative arts/performance: art/fine arts, music. Special achievements/activities: cheerleading/drum major, community service, leadership, religious involvement. Special characteristics: children and siblings of alumni, children of faculty/staff, ethnic background, handicapped students, international students, local/state students, members of minority groups, out-of-state students, relatives of clergy, religious affiliation. **Tuition waivers:** Full or partial for employees or children of employees. **ROTC:** Army, Air Force cooperative.

**LOANS Student loans:** $19,797,475 (82% need-based, 18% non-need-based). 90% of past graduating class borrowed through all loan programs. **Average indebtedness per student:** $37,048. **Average need-based loan:** Freshmen: $394. Undergraduates: $4602. **Parent loans:** $6,067,297 (44% need-based, 56% non-need-based). **Programs:** Federal Direct (Subsidized and Unsubsidized Stafford, PLUS), Perkins, state.

**WORK-STUDY Federal work-study:** Total amount: $489,532; jobs available. **State or other work-study/employment:** Total amount: $553,047 (46% need-based, 54% non-need-based). Part-time jobs available.

**APPLYING FOR FINANCIAL AID Required financial aid form:** FAFSA. **Financial aid deadline (priority):** 3/1. **Notification date:** Continuous beginning 2/1. Students must reply within 2 weeks of notification.

**CONTACT** Mr. David Orsag, Associate Director of Financial Aid, University of Mary Hardin-Baylor, 900 College Street, Box 8080, Belton, TX 76513, 254-295-4517 or toll-free 800-727-8642. Fax: 254-295-5009. E-mail: dorsag@umhb.edu. Website: http://www.umhb.edu/.

# UNIVERSITY OF MARYLAND, BALTIMORE COUNTY
## Baltimore, MD

| Tuition & fees (MD res): $10,384 | Average undergraduate aid package: $10,641 |
| --- | --- |

**ABOUT THE INSTITUTION** State-supported, coed. **Awards:** certificates, bachelor's, master's, and doctoral degrees. 48 undergraduate majors. **Total enrollment:** 13,979. Undergraduates: 11,379. Freshmen: 1,629. Federal methodology is used as a basis for awarding need-based institutional aid.

**UNDERGRADUATE EXPENSES** for 2015–2016 **Application fee:** $50. **One-time required fee:** $125. **Tuition, state resident:** full-time $7518; part-time $313 per credit hour. **Tuition, nonresident:** full-time $19,816; part-time $823 per credit hour. **Required fees:** full-time $2866; $122 per credit hour. Full-time tuition and fees vary according to location and program. Part-time tuition and fees vary according to location and program. **College room and board:** $10,562; **Room only:** $6376. Room and board charges vary according to board plan and housing facility.

**FRESHMAN FINANCIAL AID (Fall 2014, est.)** 1,245 applied for aid; of those 66% were deemed to have need. 92% of freshmen with need received aid; of those 22% had need fully met. **Average percent of need met:** 63% (excluding resources awarded to replace EFC). **Average financial aid package:** $10,494 (excluding resources awarded to replace EFC). 20% of all full-time freshmen had no need and received non-need-based gift aid.

**UNDERGRADUATE FINANCIAL AID (Fall 2014, est.)** 6,363 applied for aid; of those 80% were deemed to have need. 94% of undergraduates with need received aid; of those 13% had need fully met. **Average percent of need met:** 58% (excluding resources awarded to replace EFC). **Average financial aid package:** $10,641 (excluding resources awarded to replace EFC). 13% of all full-time undergraduates had no need and received non-need-based gift aid.

**GIFT AID (NEED-BASED) Total amount:** $34,200,168 (45% federal, 23% state, 27% institutional, 5% external sources). **Receiving aid:** Freshmen: 38% (612); all full-time undergraduates: 40% (3,893). **Average award:** Freshmen: $9154; Undergraduates: $8292. **Scholarships, grants, and awards:** Federal Pell, FSEOG, state, private, college/university gift aid from institutional funds.

**GIFT AID (NON-NEED-BASED) Total amount:** $11,068,807 (8% federal, 3% state, 79% institutional, 10% external sources). **Receiving aid:** Freshmen: 13% (214). Undergraduates: 5% (511). **Average award:** Freshmen: $8523. Undergraduates: $8555. **Scholarships, grants, and awards by category:** Academic interests/achievement: 2,426 awards ($16,392,624 total): biological sciences, computer science, education, engineering/technologies, English, foreign languages, general academic interests/achievements, humanities, mathematics, physical sciences, social sciences. Creative arts/performance: 29 awards ($34,150 total): art/fine arts, cinema/film/broadcasting, creative writing, dance, music, performing arts, theater/drama. **Tuition waivers:** Full or partial for employees or children of employees, senior citizens. **ROTC:** Army cooperative, Air Force cooperative.

**LOANS Student loans:** $40,966,620 (40% need-based, 60% non-need-based). 49% of past graduating class borrowed through all loan programs. Average indebtedness per student: $25,925. **Average need-based loan:** Freshmen: $3448. Undergraduates: $4377. **Parent loans:** $5,946,882 (68% need-based, 32% non-need-based). **Programs:** Federal Direct (Subsidized and Unsubsidized Stafford, PLUS), Perkins.

**WORK-STUDY Federal work-study:** Total amount: $179,540; 89 jobs averaging $2017. **State or other work-study/employment:** Total amount: $906,895 (61% need-based, 39% non-need-based). 94 part-time jobs averaging $9647.

**ATHLETIC AWARDS** Total amount: $2,776,207 (40% need-based, 60% non-need-based).

**APPLYING FOR FINANCIAL AID Required financial aid form:** FAFSA. **Financial aid deadline (priority):** 2/15. **Notification date:** Continuous beginning 3/15.

**CONTACT** Jane Hickey, Director, University of Maryland, Baltimore County, 1000 Hilltop Circle, Baltimore, MD 21250, 410-455-2387 or toll-free 800-UMBC-4U2 (in-state), 800-862-2402 (out-of-state). Fax: 410-455-3322.
Website: http://www.umbc.edu/.

---

# UNIVERSITY OF MARYLAND, COLLEGE PARK

## College Park, MD

| Tuition & fees (MD res): $9427 | Average undergraduate aid package: $13,531 |
|---|---|

**ABOUT THE INSTITUTION** State-supported, coed. **Awards:** certificates, bachelor's, master's, and doctoral degrees. 90 undergraduate majors. **Total enrollment:** 37,610. Undergraduates: 27,056. Freshmen: 4,129. Federal methodology is used as a basis for awarding need-based institutional aid.

**UNDERGRADUATE EXPENSES for 2015–2016 Application fee:** $65. **Tuition, state resident:** full-time $7612; part-time $317 per credit hour. **Tuition, nonresident:** full-time $27,905; part-time $1163 per credit hour. **Required fees:** full-time $1815; $420.04 per term. Part-time tuition and fees vary according to course load. **College room and board:** $10,633; **Room only:** $6424. Room and board charges vary according to board plan and housing facility.

---

**FRESHMAN FINANCIAL AID (Fall 2013)** 3,112 applied for aid; of those 55% were deemed to have need. 99% of freshmen with need received aid; of those 29% had need fully met. **Average percent of need met:** 76% (excluding resources awarded to replace EFC). **Average financial aid package:** $13,672 (excluding resources awarded to replace EFC). 19% of all full-time freshmen had no need and received non-need-based gift aid.

**UNDERGRADUATE FINANCIAL AID (Fall 2013)** 14,560 applied for aid; of those 72% were deemed to have need. 99% of undergraduates with need received aid; of those 25% had need fully met. **Average percent of need met:** 75% (excluding resources awarded to replace EFC). **Average financial aid package:** $13,531 (excluding resources awarded to replace EFC). 13% of all full-time undergraduates had no need and received non-need-based gift aid.

**GIFT AID (NEED-BASED) Total amount:** $70,480,632 (32% federal, 24% state, 39% institutional, 5% external sources). **Receiving aid:** Freshmen: 36% (1,436); all full-time undergraduates: 35% (8,609). **Average award:** Freshmen: $9655; Undergraduates: $8656. **Scholarships, grants, and awards:** Federal Pell, FSEOG, state, private, college/university gift aid from institutional funds.

**GIFT AID (NON-NEED-BASED) Total amount:** $29,537,108 (5% state, 78% institutional, 17% external sources). **Receiving aid:** Freshmen: 5% (201). Undergraduates: 3% (633). **Average award:** Freshmen: $6430. Undergraduates: $6657. **Scholarships, grants, and awards by category:** Academic interests/achievement: agriculture, architecture, biological sciences, business, communication, computer science, education, engineering/technologies, English, foreign languages, general academic interests/achievements, health fields, humanities, international studies, library science, mathematics, military science, physical sciences, premedicine, social sciences. Creative arts/performance: applied art and design, art/fine arts, dance, music, performing arts, theater/drama. Special achievements/activities: cheerleading/drum major. Special characteristics: adult students, out-of-state students. **Tuition waivers:** Full or partial for employees or children of employees. **ROTC:** Army, Naval cooperative, Air Force.

**LOANS Student loans:** $124,434,191 (51% need-based, 49% non-need-based). 45% of past graduating class borrowed through all loan programs. Average indebtedness per student: $25,131. **Average need-based loan:** Freshmen: $5027. Undergraduates: $6379. **Parent loans:** $31,307,744 (44% need-based, 56% non-need-based). **Programs:** Federal Direct (Subsidized and Unsubsidized Stafford, PLUS), Perkins, private loans.

**WORK-STUDY Federal work-study:** jobs available.

**ATHLETIC AWARDS** Total amount: $11,916,630 (40% need-based, 60% non-need-based).

**APPLYING FOR FINANCIAL AID Required financial aid form:** FAFSA. **Financial aid deadline (priority):** 2/15. **Notification date:** Continuous beginning 4/1. Students must reply by 5/1.

**CONTACT** Barbara Gill, Assistant Vice President for Undergraduate Admissions and Enrollment Planning, University of Maryland, College Park, 0102 Lee Building, College Park, MD 20742, 301-314-8279 or toll-free 800-422-5867. Fax: 301-314-9587. E-mail: bgill@umd.edu.
Website: http://www.maryland.edu/.

---

# UNIVERSITY OF MARYLAND EASTERN SHORE

## Princess Anne, MD

| Tuition & fees (MD res): $9807 | Average undergraduate aid package: $10,259 |
|---|---|

**ABOUT THE INSTITUTION** State-supported, coed. 51 undergraduate majors. Federal methodology is used as a basis for awarding need-based institutional aid.

**UNDERGRADUATE EXPENSES for 2015–2016 Tuition, state resident:** full-time $7287; part-time $198 per credit hour. **Tuition, nonresident:** full-time $16,311; part-time $508 per credit hour. **Required fees:** full-time $2520; $43 per term. Full-time tuition and fees vary according to course load. Part-time tuition and fees vary according to course load. **College room and board:** $8994; **Room only:** $4994. Room and board charges vary according to board plan and housing facility.

**FRESHMAN FINANCIAL AID (Fall 2013)** 589 applied for aid; of those 87% were deemed to have need. 93% of freshmen with need received aid; of those .2% had need fully met. **Average percent of need met:** 33% (excluding resources awarded to replace EFC). **Average financial aid package:** $9968 (excluding resources

awarded to replace EFC). 2% of all full-time freshmen had no need and received non-need-based gift aid.

**UNDERGRADUATE FINANCIAL AID (Fall 2013)** 3,051 applied for aid; of those 86% were deemed to have need. 95% of undergraduates with need received aid; of those 1% had need fully met. *Average percent of need met:* 29% (excluding resources awarded to replace EFC). *Average financial aid package:* $10,259 (excluding resources awarded to replace EFC). 5% of all full-time undergraduates had no need and received non-need-based gift aid.

**GIFT AID (NEED-BASED)** *Total amount:* $14,683,789 (58% federal, 31% state, 11% institutional). *Receiving aid:* Freshmen: 68% (408); all full-time undergraduates: 64% (2,043). *Average award:* Freshmen: $7581; Undergraduates: $7055. *Scholarships, grants, and awards:* Federal Pell, FSEOG, state, college/university gift aid from institutional funds.

**GIFT AID (NON-NEED-BASED)** *Total amount:* $4,601,895 (1% federal, 6% state, 74% institutional, 19% external sources). *Receiving aid:* Freshmen: 32% (193). Undergraduates: 24% (747). *Average award:* Freshmen: $2191. Undergraduates: $6247. *Scholarships, grants, and awards by category:* Academic interests/achievement: agriculture, business, computer science, education, engineering/technologies, English, general academic interests/achievements, health fields, home economics, mathematics, physical sciences, social sciences. *Creative arts/performance:* art/fine arts, music, performing arts, theater/drama. *Special characteristics:* adult students, children of faculty/staff, first-generation college students, veterans. *Tuition waivers:* Full or partial for employees or children of employees, senior citizens.

**LOANS** *Student loans:* $12,886,863 (54% need-based, 46% non-need-based). 77% of past graduating class borrowed through all loan programs. *Average indebtedness per student:* $27,562. *Average need-based loan:* Freshmen: $3276. Undergraduates: $4030. *Parent loans:* $4,393,359 (100% non-need-based). *Programs:* Federal Direct (Subsidized and Unsubsidized Stafford, PLUS), Perkins.

**WORK-STUDY** *Federal work-study:* jobs available. *State or other work-study/employment:* Part-time jobs available.

**ATHLETIC AWARDS** Total amount: $1,745,444 (100% non-need-based).

**APPLYING FOR FINANCIAL AID** *Required financial aid form:* FAFSA. *Financial aid deadline:* 4/1 (priority: 3/1). *Notification date:* Continuous beginning 4/15.

**CONTACT** Mr. James W. Kellam, Director of Financial Aid, University of Maryland Eastern Shore, Backbone Road, SDC, Suite 1100, Princess Anne, MD 21853-1299, 410-651-6172. *Fax:* 410-651-7670. *E-mail:* jwkellam@umes.edu. *Website:* http://www.umes.edu/.

# UNIVERSITY OF MARYLAND UNIVERSITY COLLEGE
## Adelphi, MD

| Tuition & fees (MD res): $6744 | Average undergraduate aid package: $7752 |
|---|---|

**ABOUT THE INSTITUTION** State-supported, coed. *Awards:* certificates, associate, bachelor's, master's, and doctoral degrees (offers primarily part-time evening and weekend degree programs at more than 30 off-campus locations in Maryland and the Washington, DC area, and more than 180 military communities in Europe and Asia with military enrollment not reflected in this profile; associate of arts program available to military students only). 28 undergraduate majors. *Total enrollment:* 47,906. Undergraduates: 35,154. Freshmen: 1,143. Federal methodology is used as a basis for awarding need-based institutional aid.

**UNDERGRADUATE EXPENSES** for 2015–2016 *Application fee:* $50. *Tuition, state resident:* full-time $6384; part-time $266 per credit hour. *Tuition, nonresident:* full-time $11,976; part-time $499 per credit hour. *Required fees:* full-time $360.

**FRESHMAN FINANCIAL AID (Fall 2013)** 74 applied for aid; of those 99% were deemed to have need. 88% of freshmen with need received aid. *Average percent of need met:* 17% (excluding resources awarded to replace EFC). *Average financial aid package:* $5271 (excluding resources awarded to replace EFC).

**UNDERGRADUATE FINANCIAL AID (Fall 2013)** 3,742 applied for aid; of those 96% were deemed to have need. 88% of undergraduates with need received aid; of those 1% had need fully met. *Average percent of need met:* 28% (excluding resources awarded to replace EFC). *Average financial aid package:* $7752 (excluding resources awarded to replace EFC).

**GIFT AID (NEED-BASED)** *Total amount:* $26,530,940 (82% federal, 10% state, 8% institutional). *Receiving aid:* Freshmen: 58% (51); all full-time undergraduates: 38% (2,255). *Average award:* Freshmen: $2695; Undergraduates: $4741. *Scholarships, grants, and awards:* Federal Pell, FSEOG, state, private, college/university gift aid from institutional funds.

**GIFT AID (NON-NEED-BASED)** *Total amount:* $2,364,309 (11% state, 77% institutional, 12% external sources). *Receiving aid:* Undergraduates: 8% (453). *Scholarships, grants, and awards by category:* Academic interests/achievement: general academic interests/achievements. Special achievements/activities: general special achievements/activities. *Tuition waivers:* Full or partial for employees or children of employees, senior citizens.

**LOANS** *Student loans:* $84,894,786 (41% need-based, 59% non-need-based). *Average need-based loan:* Freshmen: $2976. Undergraduates: $4451. *Parent loans:* $267,512 (100% non-need-based). *Programs:* Federal Direct (Subsidized and Unsubsidized Stafford, PLUS), Perkins.

**WORK-STUDY** *Federal work-study:* jobs available. *State or other work-study/employment:* Part-time jobs available.

**APPLYING FOR FINANCIAL AID** *Required financial aid form:* FAFSA. *Financial aid deadline (priority):* 6/1. *Notification date:* Continuous beginning 5/1. Students must reply within 2 weeks of notification.

**CONTACT** Cheryl Storie, Associate Vice President of Financial Aid, University of Maryland University College, 3501 University Boulevard East, Adelphi, MD 20783, 301-985-7847 or toll-free 800-888-8682. *Fax:* 301-985-7462. *E-mail:* finaid@umuc.edu. *Website:* http://www.umuc.edu/.

# UNIVERSITY OF MARY WASHINGTON
## Fredericksburg, VA

| Tuition & fees (VA res): $10,252 | Average undergraduate aid package: $8575 |
|---|---|

**ABOUT THE INSTITUTION** State-supported, coed. *Awards:* certificates, bachelor's, and master's degrees. 28 undergraduate majors. *Total enrollment:* 4,535. Undergraduates: 4,167. Freshmen: 853. Federal methodology is used as a basis for awarding need-based institutional aid.

**UNDERGRADUATE EXPENSES** for 2015–2016 *Application fee:* $50. *One-time required fee:* $60. *Tuition, state resident:* full-time $5190; part-time $222 per credit hour. *Tuition, nonresident:* full-time $18,476; part-time $774 per credit hour. *Required fees:* full-time $5062; $144 per credit hour or $30 per term. Full-time tuition and fees vary according to course load, degree level, and location. Part-time tuition and fees vary according to course load, degree level, and location. *College room and board:* $9430; *Room only:* $5766. Room and board charges vary according to board plan and housing facility.

**FRESHMAN FINANCIAL AID (Fall 2014, est.)** 664 applied for aid; of those 55% were deemed to have need. 96% of freshmen with need received aid; of those 15% had need fully met. *Average percent of need met:* 50% (excluding resources awarded to replace EFC). *Average financial aid package:* $8466 (excluding resources awarded to replace EFC). 30% of all full-time freshmen had no need and received non-need-based gift aid.

**UNDERGRADUATE FINANCIAL AID (Fall 2014, est.)** 2,298 applied for aid; of those 66% were deemed to have need. 95% of undergraduates with need received aid; of those 13% had need fully met. *Average percent of need met:* 50% (excluding resources awarded to replace EFC). *Average financial aid package:* $8575 (excluding resources awarded to replace EFC). 12% of all full-time undergraduates had no need and received non-need-based gift aid.

**GIFT AID (NEED-BASED)** *Total amount:* $6,018,920 (49% federal, 30% state, 21% institutional). *Receiving aid:* Freshmen: 29% (246); all full-time undergraduates: 23% (825). *Average award:* Freshmen: $3850; Undergraduates: $3695. *Scholarships, grants, and awards:* Federal Pell, FSEOG, state, private, college/university gift aid from institutional funds.

**GIFT AID (NON-NEED-BASED)** *Total amount:* $3,179,801 (1% state, 78% institutional, 21% external sources). *Receiving aid:* Freshmen: 17% (144). Undergraduates: 9% (334). *Average award:* Freshmen: $2391. Undergraduates: $2803. *Scholarships, grants, and awards by category:* Academic interests/achievement: 50 awards ($120,000 total): biological sciences, business, computer science, education, English, foreign languages, general academic interests/achievements, humanities, international studies, mathematics, physical sciences, religion/biblical studies, social sciences. *Creative arts/performance:* 60 awards ($120,000 total): art/

fine arts, dance, journalism/publications, music, theater/drama. *Special achievements/activities:* 3 awards ($18,000 total): leadership. *Special characteristics:* 15 awards ($3500 total): adult students, children and siblings of alumni, children of faculty/staff, local/state students. *Tuition waivers:* Full or partial for senior citizens. *ROTC:* Army cooperative.

**LOANS** *Student loans:* $12,733,999 (44% need-based, 56% non-need-based). 48% of past graduating class borrowed through all loan programs. *Average indebtedness per student:* $17,460. *Average need-based loan:* Freshmen: $3492. Undergraduates: $4255. *Parent loans:* $3,966,981 (100% non-need-based). *Programs:* Federal Direct (Subsidized and Unsubsidized Stafford, PLUS), Perkins.

**WORK-STUDY** *Federal work-study:* Total amount: $72,574; 37 jobs averaging $1881. *State or other work-study/employment:* Total amount: $670,030 (100% non-need-based). 802 part-time jobs averaging $1724.

**APPLYING FOR FINANCIAL AID** *Required financial aid forms:* FAFSA, UMW scholarship application form. *Financial aid deadline:* 6/1 (priority: 3/1). *Notification date:* 3/15. Students must reply by 5/1 or within 2 weeks of notification.

**CONTACT** Ms. Heidi Hunter-Goldsworthy, Director of Financial Aid, University of Mary Washington, 1301 College Avenue, Fredericksburg, VA 22401-5358, 540-654-2468 or toll-free 800-468-5614. *Fax:* 540-654-1858. *E-mail:* hhunterg@umw.edu. *Website:* http://www.umw.edu/.

# UNIVERSITY OF MASSACHUSETTS AMHERST
## Amherst, MA

| Tuition & fees (MA res): $1714 | Average undergraduate aid package: $15,526 |
|---|---|

**ABOUT THE INSTITUTION** State-supported, coed. *Awards:* certificates, associate, bachelor's, master's, and doctoral degrees. 85 undergraduate majors. *Total enrollment:* 28,635. Undergraduates: 22,252. Freshmen: 4,694. Federal methodology is used as a basis for awarding need-based institutional aid.

**UNDERGRADUATE EXPENSES** for 2015–2016 *Application fee:* $75. *One-time required fee:* $185. *Tuition, state resident:* full-time $1714; part-time $71.50 per credit hour. *Tuition, nonresident:* full-time $9937; part-time $414 per credit hour. Full-time tuition and fees vary according to class time, course load, location, program, reciprocity agreements, and student level. Part-time tuition and fees vary according to class time, course load, location, program, reciprocity agreements, and student level. *College room and board:* $6137; *Room only:* $5320. Room and board charges vary according to board plan and housing facility. Mandatory fees: $11,729 for first-year state residents; $19,061 for first year out-of-state students.

**FRESHMAN FINANCIAL AID (Fall 2013)** 4,128 applied for aid; of those 66% were deemed to have need. 98% of freshmen with need received aid; of those 13% had need fully met. *Average percent of need met:* 80% (excluding resources awarded to replace EFC). *Average financial aid package:* $14,887 (excluding resources awarded to replace EFC). 14% of all full-time freshmen had need and received non-need-based gift aid.

**UNDERGRADUATE FINANCIAL AID (Fall 2013)** 16,961 applied for aid; of those 72% were deemed to have need. 98% of undergraduates with need received aid; of those 12% had need fully met. *Average percent of need met:* 81% (excluding resources awarded to replace EFC). *Average financial aid package:* $15,526 (excluding resources awarded to replace EFC). 10% of all full-time undergraduates had no need and received non-need-based gift aid.

**GIFT AID (NEED-BASED)** *Total amount:* $88,656,943 (28% federal, 7% state, 61% institutional, 4% external sources). *Receiving aid:* Freshmen: 52% (2,445); all full-time undergraduates: 51% (10,477). *Average award:* Freshmen: $9936; Undergraduates: $9653. *Scholarships, grants, and awards:* Federal Pell, FSEOG, state, private, college/university gift aid from institutional funds.

**GIFT AID (NON-NEED-BASED)** *Total amount:* $12,408,992 (1% state, 79% institutional, 20% external sources). *Receiving aid:* Freshmen: 5% (222). Undergraduates: 3% (609). *Average award:* Freshmen: $5662. Undergraduates: $4310. *Scholarships, grants, and awards by category:* Academic interests/achievement: agriculture, architecture, biological sciences, business, communication, computer science, education, engineering/technologies, English, health fields, humanities, mathematics, military science, physical sciences, premedicine, social sciences. *Creative arts/performance:* art/fine arts, dance, journalism/publications, music, theater/drama.

*Special achievements/activities:* cheerleading/drum major, general special achievements/activities, leadership. *Special characteristics:* children and siblings of alumni, children of faculty/staff, handicapped students, veterans. *Tuition waivers:* Full or partial for employees or children of employees, senior citizens. *ROTC:* Army, Air Force.

**LOANS** *Student loans:* $118,022,235 (66% need-based, 34% non-need-based). 72% of past graduating class borrowed through all loan programs. *Average indebtedness per student:* $30,453. *Average need-based loan:* Freshmen: $3682. Undergraduates: $4642. *Parent loans:* $28,083,496 (32% need-based, 68% non-need-based). *Programs:* Federal Direct (Subsidized and Unsubsidized Stafford, PLUS), Perkins.

**WORK-STUDY** *Federal work-study:* 2,254 jobs averaging $1244.

**ATHLETIC AWARDS** Total amount: $8,567,941 (35% need-based, 65% non-need-based).

**APPLYING FOR FINANCIAL AID** *Required financial aid form:* FAFSA. *Financial aid deadline (priority):* 3/1. *Notification date:* Continuous beginning 4/1. Students must reply by 5/1.

**CONTACT** Office of Financial Aid Services, University of Massachusetts Amherst, 255 Whitmore Administration Building, 181 Presidents Drive, Amherst, MA 01003, 413-545-0801. *Fax:* 413-545-1700. *Website:* http://www.umass.edu/.

# UNIVERSITY OF MASSACHUSETTS BOSTON
## Boston, MA

| Tuition & fees (MA res): $11,966 | Average undergraduate aid package: $15,227 |
|---|---|

**ABOUT THE INSTITUTION** State-supported, coed. *Awards:* certificates, bachelor's, master's, and doctoral degrees. 41 undergraduate majors. *Total enrollment:* 16,756. Undergraduates: 12,700. Freshmen: 1,542. Federal methodology is used as a basis for awarding need-based institutional aid.

**UNDERGRADUATE EXPENSES** for 2015–2016 *Application fee:* $60. *Tuition, state resident:* full-time $11,966. *Tuition, nonresident:* full-time $28,390. Full-time tuition and fees vary according to program. Part-time tuition and fees vary according to program.

**FRESHMAN FINANCIAL AID (Fall 2013)** 1,004 applied for aid; of those 86% were deemed to have need. 100% of freshmen with need received aid; of those 58% had need fully met. *Average percent of need met:* 91% (excluding resources awarded to replace FFC). *Average financial aid package:* $14,002 (excluding resources awarded to replace EFC). 6% of all full-time freshmen had no need and received non-need-based gift aid.

**UNDERGRADUATE FINANCIAL AID (Fall 2013)** 6,448 applied for aid; of those 89% were deemed to have need. 100% of undergraduates with need received aid; of those 51% had need fully met. *Average percent of need met:* 90% (excluding resources awarded to replace EFC). *Average financial aid package:* $15,227 (excluding resources awarded to replace EFC). 3% of all full-time undergraduates had no need and received non-need-based gift aid.

**GIFT AID (NEED-BASED)** *Total amount:* $48,167,169 (44% federal, 11% state, 43% institutional, 2% external sources). *Receiving aid:* Freshmen: 62% (815); all full-time undergraduates: 61% (5,274). *Average award:* Freshmen: $9554; Undergraduates: $8901. *Scholarships, grants, and awards:* Federal Pell, FSEOG, state, private, college/university gift aid from institutional funds, TEACH Grants.

**GIFT AID (NON-NEED-BASED)** *Total amount:* $2,461,766 (3% federal, 4% state, 80% institutional, 13% external sources). *Receiving aid:* Freshmen: 4% (55). Undergraduates: 2% (175). *Average award:* Freshmen: $5817. Undergraduates: $4846. *Scholarships, grants, and awards by category:* Academic interests/achievement: general academic interests/achievements, health fields. *Special achievements/activities:* general special achievements/activities, leadership. *Special characteristics:* adult students, children of faculty/staff, children of union members/company employees, first-generation college students, veterans. *ROTC:* Army cooperative, Naval cooperative, Air Force cooperative.

**LOANS** *Student loans:* $54,227,269 (76% need-based, 24% non-need-based). 73% of past graduating class borrowed through all loan programs. *Average indebtedness per student:* $27,229. *Average need-based loan:* Freshmen: $3641. Undergraduates: $4360. *Parent loans:* $3,115,957 (22% need-based, 78% non-need-based). *Programs:* Federal Direct (Subsidized and Unsubsidized Stafford, PLUS), Perkins.

**WORK-STUDY** *Federal work-study:* 554 jobs averaging $3529.
**APPLYING FOR FINANCIAL AID** *Required financial aid form:* FAFSA. *Financial aid deadline (priority):* 3/1. *Notification date:* Continuous beginning 3/1.
**CONTACT** Judy L. Keyes, Director of Financial Aid Services, University of Massachusetts Boston, 100 Morrissey Boulevard, Boston, MA 02125-3393, 617-287-6300. *Fax:* 617-287-6323. *E-mail:* judy.keyes@umb.edu.
*Website:* http://www.umb.edu/.

# UNIVERSITY OF MASSACHUSETTS DARTMOUTH
## North Dartmouth, MA

| Tuition & fees (MA res): $11,681 | Average undergraduate aid package: $16,379 |
|---|---|

**ABOUT THE INSTITUTION** State-supported, coed. *Awards:* certificates, bachelor's, master's, and doctoral degrees. 55 undergraduate majors. *Total enrollment:* 9,111. Undergraduates: 7,454. Freshmen: 1,509. Federal methodology is used as a basis for awarding need-based institutional aid.
**UNDERGRADUATE EXPENSES** for 2015–2016 *Application fee:* $60. *One-time required fee:* $100. *Tuition, state resident:* full-time $1417; part-time $59.04 per credit. *Tuition, nonresident:* full-time $8099; part-time $337.46 per credit. *Required fees:* full-time $10,264; $427.66 per credit. Full-time tuition and fees vary according to class time and reciprocity agreements. Part-time tuition and fees vary according to class time, course load, and reciprocity agreements. *College room and board:* $11,435; *Room only:* $7247. Room and board charges vary according to board plan and housing facility. Out-of-state mandatory fees $16,520.
**FRESHMAN FINANCIAL AID (Fall 2014, est.)** 1,350 applied for aid; of those 85% were deemed to have need. 100% of freshmen with need received aid; of those 39% had need fully met. *Average percent of need met:* 89% (excluding resources awarded to replace EFC). *Average financial aid package:* $16,523 (excluding resources awarded to replace EFC). 9% of all full-time freshmen had no need and received non-need-based gift aid.
**UNDERGRADUATE FINANCIAL AID (Fall 2014, est.)** 5,451 applied for aid; of those 85% were deemed to have need. 100% of undergraduates with need received aid; of those 51% had need fully met. *Average percent of need met:* 90% (excluding resources awarded to replace EFC). *Average financial aid package:* $16,379 (excluding resources awarded to replace EFC). 6% of all full-time undergraduates had no need and received non-need-based gift aid.
**GIFT AID (NEED-BASED)** *Total amount:* $36,370,000 (35% federal, 12% state, 51% institutional, 2% external sources). *Receiving aid:* Freshmen: 71% (1,061); all full-time undergraduates: 64% (4,006). *Average award:* Freshmen: $10,057; Undergraduates: $9550. *Scholarships, grants, and awards:* Federal Pell, FSEOG, state, private, college/university gift aid from institutional funds.
**GIFT AID (NON-NEED-BASED)** *Total amount:* $4,700,000 (1% state, 96% institutional, 3% external sources). *Receiving aid:* Freshmen: 3% (38). Undergraduates: 3% (159). *Average award:* Freshmen: $3328. Undergraduates: $4542. *Scholarships, grants, and awards by category:* Academic interests/achievement: biological sciences, business, computer science, education, engineering/technologies, foreign languages, general academic interests/achievements, health fields, humanities, mathematics, physical sciences, religion/biblical studies, social sciences. *Creative arts/performance:* applied art and design, art/fine arts. *Special achievements/activities:* community service. *Special characteristics:* adult students, children of faculty/staff, children of union members/company employees, children with a deceased or disabled parent, ethnic background, first-generation college students, local/state students, members of minority groups, previous college experience, public servants, veterans. *Tuition waivers:* Full or partial for employees or children of employees, senior citizens. *ROTC:* Army cooperative.
**LOANS** *Student loans:* $44,500,000 (70% need-based, 30% non-need-based). 81% of past graduating class borrowed through all loan programs. *Average indebtedness per student:* $31,070. *Average need-based loan:* Freshmen: $3344. Undergraduates: $4157. *Parent loans:* $9,600,000 (40% need-based, 60% non-need-based). *Programs:* Federal Direct (Subsidized and Unsubsidized Stafford, PLUS), Perkins, Federal Nursing, state.
**WORK-STUDY** *Federal work-study:* Total amount: $1,500,000; 1,150 jobs averaging $1304. *State or other work-study/employment:* Part-time jobs available.

**APPLYING FOR FINANCIAL AID** *Required financial aid form:* FAFSA. *Financial aid deadline (priority):* 3/1. *Notification date:* Continuous beginning 3/25. Students must reply within 3 weeks of notification.
**CONTACT** Ms. Audra Callahan, Director of Financial Aid, University of Massachusetts Dartmouth, 285 Old Westport Road, North Dartmouth, MA 02747-2300, 508-999-8643. *Fax:* 508-999-8935. *E-mail:* financialaid@umassd.edu.
*Website:* http://www.umassd.edu/.

# UNIVERSITY OF MASSACHUSETTS LOWELL
## Lowell, MA

| Tuition & fees (MA res): $12,447 | Average undergraduate aid package: $14,453 |
|---|---|

**ABOUT THE INSTITUTION** State-supported, coed. *Awards:* certificates, associate, bachelor's, master's, and doctoral degrees. 45 undergraduate majors. *Total enrollment:* 17,184. Undergraduates: 12,986. Freshmen: 1,642. Federal methodology is used as a basis for awarding need-based institutional aid.
**UNDERGRADUATE EXPENSES** for 2015–2016 *Application fee:* $60. *One-time required fee:* $200. *Tuition, state resident:* full-time $1454; part-time $61 per credit hour. *Tuition, nonresident:* full-time $8567; part-time $357 per credit hour. *Required fees:* full-time $10,993; $458 per credit hour. Part-time tuition and fees vary according to course load. *College room and board:* $11,278; *Room only:* $7450. Room and board charges vary according to board plan and housing facility.
**FRESHMAN FINANCIAL AID (Fall 2013)** 1,403 applied for aid; of those 75% were deemed to have need. 100% of freshmen with need received aid; of those 48% had need fully met. *Average percent of need met:* 91% (excluding resources awarded to replace EFC). *Average financial aid package:* $14,771 (excluding resources awarded to replace EFC). 14% of all full-time freshmen had no need and received non-need-based gift aid.
**UNDERGRADUATE FINANCIAL AID (Fall 2013)** 7,003 applied for aid; of those 80% were deemed to have need. 100% of undergraduates with need received aid; of those 50% had need fully met. *Average percent of need met:* 90% (excluding resources awarded to replace EFC). *Average financial aid package:* $14,453 (excluding resources awarded to replace EFC). 7% of all full-time undergraduates had no need and received non-need-based gift aid.
**GIFT AID (NEED-BASED)** *Total amount:* $36,011,260 (41% federal, 11% state, 45% institutional, 3% external sources). *Receiving aid:* Freshmen: 60% (981); all full-time undergraduates: 55% (4,922). *Average award:* Freshmen: $8688; Undergraduates: $7700. *Scholarships, grants, and awards:* Federal Pell, FSEOG, state, private, college/university gift aid from institutional funds.
**GIFT AID (NON-NEED-BASED)** *Total amount:* $5,857,624 (8% state, 84% institutional, 8% external sources). *Receiving aid:* Freshmen: 4% (64). Undergraduates: 2% (213). *Average award:* Freshmen: $4338. Undergraduates: $4286. *Scholarships, grants, and awards by category:* Academic interests/achievement: biological sciences, business, computer science, education, engineering/technologies, English, general academic interests/achievements, health fields, humanities, mathematics. *Creative arts/performance:* art/fine arts, music. *Special achievements/activities:* community service, general special achievements/activities. *Special characteristics:* children and siblings of alumni, children of faculty/staff, children of public servants, children of union members/company employees, general special characteristics, out-of-state students, veterans. *Tuition waivers:* Full or partial for employees or children of employees, senior citizens. *ROTC:* Army, Air Force.
**LOANS** *Student loans:* $66,559,557 (67% need-based, 33% non-need-based). 81% of past graduating class borrowed through all loan programs. *Average indebtedness per student:* $30,505. *Average need-based loan:* Freshmen: $3450. Undergraduates: $4388. *Parent loans:* $8,336,750 (27% need-based, 73% non-need-based). *Programs:* Federal Direct (Subsidized and Unsubsidized Stafford, PLUS), Perkins, Federal Nursing.
**WORK-STUDY** *Federal work-study:* jobs available. *State or other work-study/employment:* Total amount: $2,227,610 (96% need-based, 4% non-need-based). Part-time jobs available.
**ATHLETIC AWARDS** Total amount: $2,259,779 (45% need-based, 55% non-need-based).

# UNIVERSITY OF MEMPHIS
## Memphis, TN

| Tuition & fees (TN res): $8973 | Average undergraduate aid package: $9087 |
|---|---|

**ABOUT THE INSTITUTION** State-supported, coed. *Awards:* certificates, bachelor's, master's, and doctoral degrees. 67 undergraduate majors. *Total enrollment:* 21,059. Undergraduates: 17,068. Freshmen: 2,365. Federal methodology is used as a basis for awarding need-based institutional aid.

**UNDERGRADUATE EXPENSES for 2015–2016 Application fee:** $25. *Tuition, state resident:* full-time $7410; part-time $294 per credit hour. *Tuition, nonresident:* full-time $19,122; part-time $488 per credit hour. *Required fees:* full-time $1563; $93.50 per credit hour. Full-time tuition and fees vary according to course load, degree level, program, and reciprocity agreements. Part-time tuition and fees vary according to course load, degree level, and program. *College room and board:* $8976; *Room only:* $5386. Room and board charges vary according to board plan, housing facility, and location.

**FRESHMAN FINANCIAL AID (Fall 2014, est.)** 2,193 applied for aid; of those 82% were deemed to have need. 84% of freshmen with need received aid; of those 25% had need fully met. *Average percent of need met:* 77% (excluding resources awarded to replace EFC). *Average financial aid package:* $10,415 (excluding resources awarded to replace EFC). 17% of all full-time freshmen had no need and received non-need-based gift aid.

**UNDERGRADUATE FINANCIAL AID (Fall 2014, est.)** 11,446 applied for aid; of those 85% were deemed to have need. 88% of undergraduates with need received aid; of those 15% had need fully met. *Average percent of need met:* 72% (excluding resources awarded to replace EFC). *Average financial aid package:* $9087 (excluding resources awarded to replace EFC). 10% of all full-time undergraduates had no need and received non-need-based gift aid.

**GIFT AID (NEED-BASED) Total amount:** $43,897,744 (82% federal, 17% state, 1% institutional). *Receiving aid:* Freshmen: 54% (1,227); all full-time undergraduates: 55% (6,772). *Average award:* Freshmen: $6519; Undergraduates: $5647. *Scholarships, grants, and awards:* Federal Pell, FSEOG, state, private, college/university gift aid from institutional funds.

**GIFT AID (NON-NEED-BASED) Total amount:** $33,813,618 (55% state, 42% institutional, 3% external sources). *Receiving aid:* Freshmen: 39% (894). Undergraduates: 43% (5,350). *Average award:* Freshmen: $7855. Undergraduates: $6410. *Scholarships, grants, and awards by category:* Academic interests/achievement: biological sciences, business, communication, education, engineering/technologies, English, general academic interests/achievements, health fields, humanities, international studies, mathematics, military science, physical sciences, premedicine, social sciences. *Creative arts/performance:* art/fine arts, cinema/film/broadcasting, dance, journalism/publications, music. *Special achievements/activities:* cheerleading/drum major, general special achievements/activities, leadership. *Special characteristics:* adult students, children of educators, children of faculty/staff, children of public servants, handicapped students, members of minority groups, public servants. *Tuition waivers:* Full or partial for employees or children of employees, senior citizens. *ROTC:* Army, Naval, Air Force.

**LOANS Student loans:** $81,065,064 (47% need-based, 53% non-need-based). 68% of past graduating class borrowed through all loan programs. *Average indebtedness per student:* $25,244. *Average need-based loan:* Freshmen: $3342. Undergraduates: $3187. *Parent loans:* $5,335,437 (100% non-need-based). *Programs:* Federal Direct (Subsidized and Unsubsidized Stafford, PLUS), Perkins, college/university.

**WORK-STUDY Federal work-study:** Total amount: $352,374; 152 jobs averaging $2318. *State or other work-study/employment:* Total amount: $3,516,818 (100% non-need-based). Part-time jobs available.

**ATHLETIC AWARDS** Total amount: $4,323,194 (100% non-need-based).

# UNIVERSITY OF MIAMI
## Coral Gables, FL

| Tuition & fees: $44,350 | Average undergraduate aid package: $33,539 |
|---|---|

**ABOUT THE INSTITUTION** Independent, coed. *Awards:* certificates, bachelor's, master's, and doctoral degrees. 129 undergraduate majors. *Total enrollment:* 16,774. Undergraduates: 11,273. Freshmen: 2,076. Both federal and institutional methodology are used as a basis for awarding need-based institutional aid.

**UNDERGRADUATE EXPENSES for 2015–2016 Application fee:** $70. *Comprehensive fee:* $57,034 includes full-time tuition ($43,040), mandatory fees ($1310), and room and board ($12,684). *College room only:* $7336. Full-time tuition and fees vary according to course load. Room and board charges vary according to board plan and housing facility. *Part-time tuition:* $1790 per credit hour. Part-time tuition and fees vary according to course load and program.

**FRESHMAN FINANCIAL AID (Fall 2014, est.)** 1,306 applied for aid; of those 76% were deemed to have need. 100% of freshmen with need received aid; of those 28% had need fully met. *Average percent of need met:* 78% (excluding resources awarded to replace EFC). *Average financial aid package:* $35,536 (excluding resources awarded to replace EFC). 33% of all full-time freshmen had no need and received non-need-based gift aid.

**UNDERGRADUATE FINANCIAL AID (Fall 2014, est.)** 5,629 applied for aid; of those 81% were deemed to have need. 99% of undergraduates with need received aid; of those 30% had need fully met. *Average percent of need met:* 75% (excluding resources awarded to replace EFC). *Average financial aid package:* $33,539 (excluding resources awarded to replace EFC). 23% of all full-time undergraduates had no need and received non-need-based gift aid.

**GIFT AID (NEED-BASED) Total amount:** $99,402,147 (10% federal, 10% state, 78% institutional, 2% external sources). *Receiving aid:* Freshmen: 48% (975); all full-time undergraduates: 41% (4,283). *Average award:* Freshmen: $29,028; Undergraduates: $25,950. *Scholarships, grants, and awards:* Federal Pell, FSEOG, state, private, college/university gift aid from institutional funds.

**GIFT AID (NON-NEED-BASED) Total amount:** $63,926,820 (14% state, 84% institutional, 2% external sources). *Receiving aid:* Freshmen: 12% (241). Undergraduates: 12% (1,239). *Average award:* Freshmen: $17,507. Undergraduates: $18,846. *Scholarships, grants, and awards by category:* Academic interests/achievement: general academic interests/achievements, military science. *Creative arts/performance:* music, performing arts, theater/drama. *Special achievements/activities:* cheerleading/drum major, leadership. *Special characteristics:* children of faculty/staff, first-generation college students, international students, veterans, veterans' children. *Tuition waivers:* Full or partial for employees or children of employees. *ROTC:* Army, Air Force.

**LOANS Student loans:** $46,666,806 (66% need-based, 34% non-need-based). 43% of past graduating class borrowed through all loan programs. *Average indebtedness per student:* $26,793. *Average need-based loan:* Freshmen: $4201. Undergraduates: $5770. *Parent loans:* $14,749,273 (44% need-based, 56% non-need-based). *Programs:* Federal Direct (Subsidized and Unsubsidized Stafford, PLUS), Perkins, Federal Nursing, college/university, private loans.

**WORK-STUDY Federal work-study:** Total amount: $5,411,125; 2,010 jobs averaging $3000. *State or other work-study/employment:* Total amount: $2,094,090 (30% need-based, 70% non-need-based). 1,700 part-time jobs averaging $3000.

**ATHLETIC AWARDS** Total amount: $12,745,208 (42% need-based, 58% non-need-based).

**CONTACT** Mr. Raymond Nault-Hix, Executive Director for Financial Assistance Services, University of Miami, 1306 Stanford Drive, University Center, Suite 2275, Coral Gables, FL 33146, 305-284-5212. *Fax:* 305-284-8641. *E-mail:* rnaulthix@miami.edu.
*Website:* http://www.miami.edu/.

# UNIVERSITY OF MICHIGAN
## Ann Arbor, MI

| Tuition & fees (MI res): $13,486 | Average undergraduate aid package: $21,422 |
|---|---|

**ABOUT THE INSTITUTION** State-supported, coed. **Awards:** certificates, bachelor's, master's, and doctoral degrees. 128 undergraduate majors. **Total enrollment:** 43,625. Undergraduates: 28,413. Freshmen: 6,523. Both federal and institutional methodology are used as a basis for awarding need-based institutional aid.

**UNDERGRADUATE EXPENSES for 2015–2016 Application fee:** $75. **Tuition, state resident:** full-time $13,158; part-time $519 per credit hour. **Tuition, nonresident:** full-time $41,578; part-time $1703 per credit hour. **Required fees:** full-time $328; $164 per term. Full-time tuition and fees vary according to course load, program, and student level. Part-time tuition and fees vary according to course load, program, and student level. **College room and board:** $10,246. Room and board charges vary according to board plan and housing facility.

**FRESHMAN FINANCIAL AID (Fall 2013)** 3,453 applied for aid; of those 68% were deemed to have need. 100% of freshmen with need received aid; of those 78% had need fully met. **Average percent of need met:** 85% (excluding resources awarded to replace EFC). **Average financial aid package:** $20,207 (excluding resources awarded to replace EFC). 20% of all full-time freshmen had no need and received non-need-based gift aid.

**UNDERGRADUATE FINANCIAL AID (Fall 2013)** 13,311 applied for aid; of those 78% were deemed to have need. 100% of undergraduates with need received aid; of those 79% had need fully met. **Average percent of need met:** 82% (excluding resources awarded to replace EFC). **Average financial aid package:** $21,422 (excluding resources awarded to replace EFC). 16% of all full-time undergraduates had no need and received non-need-based gift aid.

**GIFT AID (NEED-BASED) Total amount:** $126,183,188 (17% federal, 83% institutional). **Receiving aid:** Freshmen: 29% (1,771); all full-time undergraduates: 30% (8,162). **Average award:** Freshmen: $14,124; Undergraduates: $15,050. **Scholarships, grants, and awards:** Federal Pell, FSEOG, state, private, college/university gift aid from institutional funds, TEACH Grants, Iraq and Afghanistan Service Grants.

**GIFT AID (NON-NEED-BASED) Total amount:** $74,159,922 (11% federal, 3% state, 65% institutional, 21% external sources). **Receiving aid:** Freshmen: 29% (1,818). Undergraduates: 25% (6,706). **Average award:** Freshmen: $5742. Undergraduates: $7536. **Scholarships, grants, and awards by category:** *Academic interests/achievement:* architecture, area/ethnic studies, biological sciences, business, communication, computer science, education, engineering/technologies, English, foreign languages, general academic interests/achievements, health fields, humanities, international studies, library science, mathematics, military science, physical sciences, premedicine, social sciences. *Creative arts/performance:* art/fine arts, cinema/film/broadcasting, creative writing, dance, journalism/publications, music, performing arts, theater/drama. *Special achievements/activities:* community service, general special achievements/activities, leadership. *Special characteristics:* children of faculty/staff, children of workers in trades, handicapped students, international students, local/state students, members of minority groups, out-of-state students. **ROTC:** Army, Naval, Air Force.

**LOANS Student loans:** $75,173,928 (56% need-based, 44% non-need-based). 45% of past graduating class borrowed through all loan programs. *Average indebtedness per student:* $26,510. *Average need-based loan:* Freshmen: $3985. Undergraduates: $5205. **Parent loans:** $29,681,225 (100% non-need-based). **Programs:** Federal Direct (Subsidized and Unsubsidized Stafford, PLUS), Perkins, Federal Nursing, college/university, Health Professions Student Loans (HPSL).

**WORK-STUDY Federal work-study:** 2,864 jobs averaging $1602.

**ATHLETIC AWARDS** Total amount: $17,700,928 (100% non-need-based).

**APPLYING FOR FINANCIAL AID Required financial aid forms:** FAFSA, CSS Financial Aid PROFILE. **Financial aid deadline:** 4/30. **Notification date:** Continuous beginning 3/15.

**CONTACT** Office of Financial Aid, University of Michigan, 2500 Student Activities Building, 515 East Jefferson Street, Ann Arbor, MI 48109-1316, 734-763-6600. *Fax:* 734-647-3081. *E-mail:* financial.aid@umich.edu.
*Website:* http://www.umich.edu/.

# UNIVERSITY OF MICHIGAN–DEARBORN
## Dearborn, MI

| Tuition & fees (MI res): $11,222 | Average undergraduate aid package: $9427 |
|---|---|

**ABOUT THE INSTITUTION** State-supported, coed. **Awards:** bachelor's, master's, and doctoral degrees. 53 undergraduate majors. **Total enrollment:** 8,923. Undergraduates: 7,171. Freshmen: 951. Federal methodology is used as a basis for awarding need-based institutional aid.

**UNDERGRADUATE EXPENSES for 2015–2016 Application fee:** $30. **One-time required fee:** $75. **Tuition, state resident:** full-time $10,542; part-time $417 per credit hour. **Tuition, nonresident:** full-time $22,740; part-time $905 per credit hour. **Required fees:** full-time $680; $323 per term. Full-time tuition and fees vary according to course level, course load, degree level, program, and student level. Part-time tuition and fees vary according to course level, course load, degree level, program, and student level.

**FRESHMAN FINANCIAL AID (Fall 2013)** 778 applied for aid; of those 78% were deemed to have need. 100% of freshmen with need received aid; of those 11% had need fully met. **Average percent of need met:** 62% (excluding resources awarded to replace EFC). **Average financial aid package:** $9692 (excluding resources awarded to replace EFC). 19% of all full-time freshmen had no need and received non-need-based gift aid.

**UNDERGRADUATE FINANCIAL AID (Fall 2013)** 3,762 applied for aid; of those 85% were deemed to have need. 100% of undergraduates with need received aid; of those 6% had need fully met. **Average percent of need met:** 55% (excluding resources awarded to replace EFC). **Average financial aid package:** $9427 (excluding resources awarded to replace EFC). 11% of all full-time undergraduates had no need and received non-need-based gift aid.

**GIFT AID (NEED-BASED) Total amount:** $19,683,314 (62% federal, 2% state, 35% institutional, 1% external sources). **Receiving aid:** Freshmen: 49% (446); all full-time undergraduates: 50% (2,351). **Average award:** Freshmen: $5570; Undergraduates: $5344. **Scholarships, grants, and awards:** Federal Pell, FSEOG, state, private, college/university gift aid from institutional funds.

**GIFT AID (NON-NEED-BASED) Total amount:** $3,201,108 (94% institutional, 6% external sources). **Receiving aid:** Freshmen: 39% (355). Undergraduates: 23% (1,112). **Average award:** Freshmen: $5184. Undergraduates: $5038. **Scholarships, grants, and awards by category:** *Academic interests/achievement:* 1,788 awards ($5,516,264 total): biological sciences, business, communication, computer science, education, engineering/technologies, foreign languages, general academic interests/achievements, international studies, mathematics, physical sciences, social sciences. *Creative arts/performance:* 54 awards ($35,426 total): art/fine arts, cinema/film/broadcasting, creative writing, debating, general creative arts/performance, journalism/publications. *Special achievements/activities:* 162 awards ($384,549 total): community service, general special achievements/activities, leadership, memberships. *Special characteristics:* 345 awards ($1,883,444 total): adult students, children and siblings of alumni, children of faculty/staff, ethnic background, general special characteristics, handicapped students, international students, members of minority groups, out-of-state students, previous college experience, public servants. **Tuition waivers:** Full or partial for employees or children of employees, senior citizens. **ROTC:** Army, Naval, Air Force.

**LOANS Student loans:** $29,166,650 (87% need-based, 13% non-need-based). 58% of past graduating class borrowed through all loan programs. *Average indebtedness per student:* $22,168. *Average need-based loan:* Freshmen: $3402. Undergraduates: $4571. **Parent loans:** $2,996,880 (36% need-based, 64% non-need-based). **Programs:** Federal Direct (Subsidized and Unsubsidized Stafford, PLUS), Perkins, alternative loans.

**WORK-STUDY Federal work-study:** 152 jobs averaging $1309. **State or other work-study/employment:** 703 part-time jobs averaging $1517.

**ATHLETIC AWARDS** Total amount: $160,718 (49% need-based, 51% non-need-based).

APPLYING FOR FINANCIAL AID *Required financial aid form:* FAFSA. *Financial aid deadline (priority):* 3/1. *Notification date:* Continuous beginning 3/5. Students must reply within 5 weeks of notification.

CONTACT Ms. Katherine M. Allen, Director of Financial Aid and Scholarships, University of Michigan–Dearborn, 4901 Evergreen Road, 1183 UC, Dearborn, MI 48128-2406, 313-593-5300. *Fax:* 313-593-5313. *E-mail:* umd.ask.ofa@umich.edu. *Website:* http://www.umdearborn.edu/.

# UNIVERSITY OF MICHIGAN–FLINT
## Flint, MI

| Tuition & fees (MI res): $10,138 | Average undergraduate aid package: $12,405 |
|---|---|

**ABOUT THE INSTITUTION** State-supported, coed. *Awards:* certificates, bachelor's, master's, and doctoral degrees. 76 undergraduate majors. *Total enrollment:* 8,574. Undergraduates: 7,078. Freshmen: 662. Federal methodology is used as a basis for awarding need-based institutional aid.

**UNDERGRADUATE EXPENSES for 2015–2016 Application fee:** $30. *Tuition, state resident:* full-time $9720; part-time $383.75 per credit hour. *Tuition, nonresident:* full-time $18,942; part-time $765.50 per credit hour. *Required fees:* full-time $418; $160 per term. Full-time tuition and fees vary according to course level, course load, degree level, program, and student level. Part-time tuition and fees vary according to course level, course load, degree level, program, and student level. *College room and board:* $7911; *Room only:* $4978. Room and board charges vary according to housing facility.

**FRESHMAN FINANCIAL AID (Fall 2013)** 546 applied for aid; of those 87% were deemed to have need. 95% of freshmen with need received aid; of those 3% had need fully met. *Average percent of need met:* 67% (excluding resources awarded to replace EFC). *Average financial aid package:* $10,759 (excluding resources awarded to replace EFC). 3% of all full-time freshmen had no need and received non-need-based gift aid.

**UNDERGRADUATE FINANCIAL AID (Fall 2013)** 3,673 applied for aid; of those 89% were deemed to have need. 97% of undergraduates with need received aid; of those 4% had need fully met. *Average percent of need met:* 72% (excluding resources awarded to replace EFC). *Average financial aid package:* $12,405 (excluding resources awarded to replace EFC). 2% of all full-time undergraduates had no need and received non-need-based gift aid.

**GIFT AID (NEED-BASED) Total amount:** $16,934,517 (69% federal, 2% state, 29% institutional). *Receiving aid:* Freshmen: 53% (344); all full-time undergraduates: 55% (2,436). *Average award:* Freshmen: $6044; Undergraduates: $5780. *Scholarships, grants, and awards:* Federal Pell, FSEOG, state, private, college/university gift aid from institutional funds.

**GIFT AID (NON-NEED-BASED) Total amount:** $3,435,150 (1% federal, 1% state, 83% institutional, 15% external sources). *Receiving aid:* Freshmen: 21% (139). Undergraduates: 14% (629). *Average award:* Freshmen: $3674. Undergraduates: $3755. *Scholarships, grants, and awards by category:* Academic interests/achievement: biological sciences, business, communication, computer science, education, engineering/technologies, English, foreign languages, general academic interests/achievements, health fields, humanities, international studies, mathematics, physical sciences, premedicine, social sciences. *Creative arts/performance:* art/fine arts, journalism/publications, music, performing arts, theater/drama. *Special achievements/activities:* community service, general special achievements/activities, hobbies/interests, leadership. *Special characteristics:* adult students, children and siblings of alumni, children of faculty/staff, children of union members/company employees, first-generation college students, general special characteristics, handicapped students, international students, local/state students, members of minority groups, veterans, veterans' children. *Tuition waivers:* Full or partial for senior citizens. *ROTC:* Army cooperative.

**LOANS Student loans:** $35,767,466 (94% need-based, 6% non-need-based). 68% of past graduating class borrowed through all loan programs. *Average indebtedness per student:* $32,107. *Average need-based loan:* Freshmen: $3200. Undergraduates: $4193. *Parent loans:* $1,431,317 (100% non-need-based). *Programs:* Federal Direct (Subsidized and Unsubsidized Stafford, PLUS), Perkins.

**WORK-STUDY Federal work-study:** 231 jobs averaging $2355.

**APPLYING FOR FINANCIAL AID Required financial aid forms:** FAFSA, institution's own financial aid form (for spring and summer applicants only). *Financial aid deadline (priority):* 3/1. *Notification date:* Continuous beginning 3/15.

CONTACT Lori Vedder, Office of Financial Aid, University of Michigan–Flint, Room 277 Pavilion, 303 East Kearsley Street, Flint, MI 48502-1950, 810-762-3444 or toll-free 800-942-5636. *Fax:* 810-766-6757. *E-mail:* financial_aid@list.flint.umich.edu. *Website:* http://www.umflint.edu/.

# UNIVERSITY OF MINNESOTA, CROOKSTON
## Crookston, MN

| Tuition & fees (MN res): $11,468 | Average undergraduate aid package: $11,205 |
|---|---|

**ABOUT THE INSTITUTION** State-supported, coed. *Awards:* bachelor's degrees. 43 undergraduate majors. *Total enrollment:* 2,850. Undergraduates: 2,850. Freshmen: 274. Federal methodology is used as a basis for awarding need-based institutional aid.

**UNDERGRADUATE EXPENSES for 2015–2016 Application fee:** $30. *Tuition, state resident:* full-time $10,030; part-time $385.77 per credit. *Tuition, nonresident:* full-time $10,030; part-time $385.77 per credit. *Required fees:* full-time $1438; $718.75 per term. Full-time tuition and fees vary according to course load and location. Part-time tuition and fees vary according to course load and location. *College room and board:* $7350; *Room only:* $3480. Room and board charges vary according to board plan and housing facility.

**FRESHMAN FINANCIAL AID (Fall 2013)** 228 applied for aid; of those 87% were deemed to have need. 98% of freshmen with need received aid; of those 18% had need fully met. *Average percent of need met:* 75% (excluding resources awarded to replace EFC). *Average financial aid package:* $11,793 (excluding resources awarded to replace EFC). 6% of all full-time freshmen had no need and received non-need-based gift aid.

**UNDERGRADUATE FINANCIAL AID (Fall 2013)** 1,021 applied for aid; of those 85% were deemed to have need. 97% of undergraduates with need received aid; of those 10% had need fully met. *Average percent of need met:* 73% (excluding resources awarded to replace EFC). *Average financial aid package:* $11,205 (excluding resources awarded to replace EFC). 6% of all full-time undergraduates had no need and received non-need-based gift aid.

**GIFT AID (NEED-BASED) Total amount:** $6,800,257 (40% federal, 23% state, 32% institutional, 5% external sources). *Receiving aid:* Freshmen: 73% (191); all full-time undergraduates: 64% (795). *Average award:* Freshmen: $9171; Undergraduates: $8130. *Scholarships, grants, and awards:* Federal Pell, FSEOG, state, private, college/university gift aid from institutional funds, Academic Competitiveness Grants.

**GIFT AID (NON-NEED-BASED) Total amount:** $350,279 (7% state, 70% institutional, 23% external sources). *Receiving aid:* Freshmen: 8% (20). Undergraduates: 4% (53). *Average award:* Freshmen: $3632. Undergraduates: $2369. *Scholarships, grants, and awards by category:* Academic interests/achievement: agriculture, biological sciences, general academic interests/achievements. *Creative arts/performance:* general creative arts/performance. *Special achievements/activities:* leadership. *Special characteristics:* children and siblings of alumni, children of faculty/staff, ethnic background, first-generation college students, general special characteristics, local/state students, members of minority groups. *Tuition waivers:* Full or partial for senior citizens. *ROTC:* Air Force cooperative.

**LOANS Student loans:** $9,432,284 (61% need-based, 39% non-need-based). 77% of past graduating class borrowed through all loan programs. *Average indebtedness per student:* $23,621. *Average need-based loan:* Freshmen: $3275. Undergraduates: $4177. *Parent loans:* $1,187,837 (27% need-based, 73% non-need-based). *Programs:* Federal Direct (Subsidized and Unsubsidized Stafford, PLUS), Perkins, state, private loans.

**WORK-STUDY Federal work-study:** jobs available. *State or other work-study/employment:* Total amount: $119,344 (100% need-based). Part-time jobs available.

**ATHLETIC AWARDS Total amount:** $1,166,136 (80% need-based, 20% non-need-based).

**APPLYING FOR FINANCIAL AID Required financial aid form:** FAFSA. *Financial aid deadline (priority):* 3/1. *Notification date:* Continuous beginning 3/1. Students must reply within 8 weeks of notification.

**CONTACT** Melissa Dingmann, Director of Financial Aid, University of Minnesota, Crookston, 170 Owen Hall, 2900 University Avenue, Crookston, MN 56716-5001, 218-281-8576 or toll-free 800-862-6466. *Fax:* 218-281-8575. *E-mail:* dingmann@umn.edu.
*Website:* http://www.umcrookston.edu/.

# UNIVERSITY OF MINNESOTA, DULUTH
## Duluth, MN

| Tuition & fees (MN res): $12,802 | Average undergraduate aid package: $11,043 |
|---|---|

**ABOUT THE INSTITUTION** State-supported, coed. *Awards:* certificates, bachelor's, master's, and doctoral degrees. 83 undergraduate majors. *Total enrollment:* 11,093. Undergraduates: 9,987. Freshmen: 2,196. Federal methodology is used as a basis for awarding need-based institutional aid.
**UNDERGRADUATE EXPENSES for 2015–2016 Application fee:** $35. *Tuition, state resident:* full-time $11,720; part-time $450.76 per credit. *Tuition, nonresident:* full-time $15,385; part-time $591.73 per credit. *Required fees:* full-time $1082. Full-time tuition and fees vary according to course load, program, and reciprocity agreements. Part-time tuition and fees vary according to course load, program, and reciprocity agreements. *College room and board:* $7004. Room and board charges vary according to board plan and housing facility.
**FRESHMAN FINANCIAL AID (Fall 2013)** 1,834 applied for aid; of those 69% were deemed to have need. 98% of freshmen with need received aid; of those 17% had need fully met. *Average percent of need met:* 67% (excluding resources awarded to replace EFC). *Average financial aid package:* $10,790 (excluding resources awarded to replace EFC). 9% of all full-time freshmen had no need and received non-need-based aid.
**UNDERGRADUATE FINANCIAL AID (Fall 2013)** 7,242 applied for aid; of those 74% were deemed to have need. 98% of undergraduates with need received aid; of those 21% had need fully met. *Average percent of need met:* 68% (excluding resources awarded to replace EFC). *Average financial aid package:* $11,043 (excluding resources awarded to replace EFC). 10% of all full-time undergraduates had no need and received non-need-based gift aid.
**GIFT AID (NEED-BASED)** *Total amount:* $36,281,480 (27% federal, 31% state, 34% institutional, 8% external sources). *Receiving aid:* Freshmen: 53% (1,090); all full-time undergraduates: 52% (4,636). *Average award:* Freshmen: $8221; Undergraduates: $7686. *Scholarships, grants, and awards:* Federal Pell, FSEOG, state, private, college/university gift aid from institutional funds.
**GIFT AID (NON-NEED-BASED)** *Total amount:* $2,482,723 (67% institutional, 33% external sources). *Receiving aid:* Freshmen: 9% (175). Undergraduates: 9% (793). *Average award:* Freshmen: $2680. Undergraduates: $2655. *Scholarships, grants, and awards by category:* Academic interests/achievement: general academic interests/achievements. *Tuition waivers:* Full or partial for children of alumni. *ROTC:* Air Force.
**LOANS** *Student loans:* $49,363,072 (78% need-based, 22% non-need-based). 76% of past graduating class borrowed through all loan programs. *Average indebtedness per student:* $31,244. *Average need-based loan:* Freshmen: $4114. Undergraduates: $4772. *Parent loans:* $16,777,581 (65% need-based, 35% non-need-based). *Programs:* Federal Direct (Subsidized and Unsubsidized Stafford, PLUS), Perkins, Federal Nursing, state, college/university.
**WORK-STUDY** *Federal work-study:* 348 jobs averaging $1819. *State or other work-study/employment:* Total amount: $955,268 (100% need-based). 734 part-time jobs averaging $1301.
**ATHLETIC AWARDS** Total amount: $1,962,266 (85% need-based, 15% non-need-based).
**APPLYING FOR FINANCIAL AID** *Required financial aid form:* FAFSA. *Financial aid deadline:* Continuous. *Notification date:* Continuous beginning 3/1.
**CONTACT** Ms. Brenda Herzig, Director of Financial Aid, University of Minnesota, Duluth, 10 University Drive, 184 Darland Administration Building, Duluth, MN 55812-2496, 218-726-8000 or toll-free 800-232-1339. *Fax:* 218-726-8219.
*Website:* http://www.d.umn.edu/.

# UNIVERSITY OF MINNESOTA, MORRIS
## Morris, MN

**ABOUT THE INSTITUTION** State-supported, coed. *Awards:* bachelor's degrees. 43 undergraduate majors. *Total enrollment:* 1,899. Undergraduates: 1,899. Freshmen: 413.
**GIFT AID (NEED-BASED)** *Scholarships, grants, and awards:* Federal Pell, FSEOG, state, private, college/university gift aid from institutional funds.
**GIFT AID (NON-NEED-BASED)** *Scholarships, grants, and awards by category:* Academic interests/achievement: general academic interests/achievements. Creative arts/performance: music. Special achievements/activities: general special achievements/activities. Special characteristics: ethnic background, international students, members of minority groups, veterans, veterans' children.
**LOANS** *Programs:* Federal Direct (Subsidized and Unsubsidized Stafford, PLUS), Perkins, state.
**WORK-STUDY** *Federal work-study:* jobs available. *State or other work-study/employment:* Total amount: $162,226 (100% need-based). Part-time jobs available.
**APPLYING FOR FINANCIAL AID** *Required financial aid form:* FAFSA.
**CONTACT** Ms. Jill Beauregard, Director of Financial Aid, University of Minnesota, Morris, 600 East 4th Street, Morris, MN 56267, 320-589-6046 or toll-free 888-866-3382. *Fax:* 320-589-1673. *E-mail:* morrisfa@morris.umn.edu.
*Website:* http://www.morris.umn.edu/.

# UNIVERSITY OF MINNESOTA, TWIN CITIES CAMPUS
## Minneapolis, MN

| Tuition & fees (MN res): $13,626 | Average undergraduate aid package: $12,397 |
|---|---|

**ABOUT THE INSTITUTION** State-supported, coed. *Awards:* certificates, diplomas, bachelor's, master's, and doctoral degrees. 219 undergraduate majors. *Total enrollment:* 51,147. Undergraduates: 34,351. Freshmen: 5,530. Federal methodology is used as a basis for awarding need-based institutional aid.
**UNDERGRADUATE EXPENSES for 2015–2016 Application fee:** $55. *Tuition, state resident:* full-time $12,060; part-time $463.85 per credit. *Tuition, nonresident:* full-time $19,310; part-time $742.69 per credit. *Required fees:* full-time $1566. Full-time tuition and fees vary according to program and reciprocity agreements. Part-time tuition and fees vary according to course load, program, and reciprocity agreements. *College room and board:* $8920; *Room only:* $4920. Room and board charges vary according to board plan, housing facility, and location.
**FRESHMAN FINANCIAL AID (Fall 2014, est.)** 4,513 applied for aid; of those 63% were deemed to have need. 98% of freshmen with need received aid; of those 29% had need fully met. *Average percent of need met:* 77% (excluding resources awarded to replace EFC). *Average financial aid package:* $12,815 (excluding resources awarded to replace EFC). 13% of all full-time freshmen had no need and received non-need-based gift aid.
**UNDERGRADUATE FINANCIAL AID (Fall 2014, est.)** 19,106 applied for aid; of those 73% were deemed to have need. 98% of undergraduates with need received aid; of those 23% had need fully met. *Average percent of need met:* 72% (excluding resources awarded to replace EFC). *Average financial aid package:* $12,397 (excluding resources awarded to replace EFC). 7% of all full-time undergraduates had no need and received non-need-based gift aid.
**GIFT AID (NEED-BASED)** *Total amount:* $125,258,730 (25% federal, 24% state, 42% institutional, 9% external sources). *Receiving aid:* Freshmen: 44% (2,411); all full-time undergraduates: 42% (11,773). *Average award:* Freshmen: $10,335; Undergraduates: $9388. *Scholarships, grants, and awards:* Federal Pell, FSEOG, state, private, college/university gift aid from institutional funds, Federal Nursing, ROTC Scholarships.
**GIFT AID (NON-NEED-BASED)** *Total amount:* $15,873,202 (1% state, 79% institutional, 20% external sources). *Receiving aid:* Freshmen: 5% (292). Undergraduates: 3% (942). *Average award:* Freshmen: $5282. Undergraduates: $4992. *Scholarships, grants, and awards by category:* Academic interests/achievement: agriculture, architecture, area/ethnic studies, biological sciences, business, communication, computer science, education, engineering/technologies, English, foreign languages, general academic interests/achievements, health fields, home economics, humanities, international studies, library science, mathematics, military science,

physical sciences, premedicine, religion/biblical studies, social sciences. *Creative arts/ performance:* art/fine arts, general creative arts/performance. *Special achievements/ activities:* hobbies/interests, leadership. *Special characteristics:* general special characteristics, local/state students, members of minority groups. *Tuition waivers:* Full or partial for senior citizens. *ROTC:* Army, Naval, Air Force.

**LOANS** *Student loans:* $120,426,507 (65% need-based, 35% non-need-based). 61% of past graduating class borrowed through all loan programs. *Average indebtedness per student:* $26,796. *Average need-based loan:* Freshmen: $3526. Undergraduates: $4624. *Parent loans:* $45,921,302 (24% need-based, 76% non-need-based). *Programs:* Federal Direct (Subsidized and Unsubsidized Stafford, PLUS), Perkins, Federal Nursing, state, college/university, Health Professions Student Loans (HPSL).

**WORK-STUDY** *Federal work-study:* Total amount: $3,605,788; jobs available. *State or other work-study/employment:* Total amount: $10,151,349 (100% need-based). Part-time jobs available.

**ATHLETIC AWARDS** Total amount: $8,557,613 (86% need-based, 14% non-need-based).

**APPLYING FOR FINANCIAL AID** *Required financial aid forms:* FAFSA, institution's own form. *Financial aid deadline (priority):* 3/1. *Notification date:* Continuous beginning 2/15.

**CONTACT** Office of Student Finance, University of Minnesota, Twin Cities Campus, 200 Fraser Hall, 106 Pleasant Street SE, Minneapolis, MN 55455, 612-624-1111 or toll-free 800-752-1000. *Fax:* 612-624-9584. *E-mail:* onestop@umn.edu. *Website:* http://www.umn.edu/tc/.

# UNIVERSITY OF MISSISSIPPI
## Oxford, MS

| Tuition & fees (MS res): $7096 | Average undergraduate aid package: $8728 |
|---|---|

**ABOUT THE INSTITUTION** State-supported, coed. *Awards:* certificates, bachelor's, master's, and doctoral degrees. 65 undergraduate majors. *Total enrollment:* 22,503. Undergraduates: 18,101. Freshmen: 3,809. Federal methodology is used as a basis for awarding need-based institutional aid.

**UNDERGRADUATE EXPENSES** for 2015–2016 *Application fee:* $40. *Tuition, state resident:* full-time $6996; part-time $291.50 per credit hour. *Tuition, nonresident:* full-time $19,044; part-time $793.50 per credit hour. *Required fees:* full-time $100; $4.16 per credit hour. Full-time tuition and fees vary according to course load and program. Part-time tuition and fees vary according to course load and program. *College room and board:* $9908. Room and board charges vary according to board plan and housing facility.

**FRESHMAN FINANCIAL AID (Fall 2013)** 2,664 applied for aid; of those 69% were deemed to have need. 98% of freshmen with need received aid; of those 15% had need fully met. *Average percent of need met:* 74% (excluding resources awarded to replace EFC). *Average financial aid package:* $10,956 (excluding resources awarded to replace EFC). 29% of all full-time freshmen had no need and received non-need-based gift aid.

**UNDERGRADUATE FINANCIAL AID (Fall 2013)** 10,475 applied for aid; of those 79% were deemed to have need. 97% of undergraduates with need received aid; of those 11% had need fully met. *Average percent of need met:* 72% (excluding resources awarded to replace EFC). *Average financial aid package:* $8728 (excluding resources awarded to replace EFC). 21% of all full-time undergraduates had no need and received non-need-based gift aid.

**GIFT AID (NEED-BASED)** *Total amount:* $48,647,631 (44% federal, 9% state, 44% institutional, 3% external sources). *Receiving aid:* Freshmen: 45% (1,619); all full-time undergraduates: 44% (6,924). *Average award:* Freshmen: $8339; Undergraduates: $7563. *Scholarships, grants, and awards:* Federal Pell, FSEOG, state, private, college/university gift aid from institutional funds.

**GIFT AID (NON-NEED-BASED)** *Total amount:* $31,238,750 (9% state, 86% institutional, 5% external sources). *Receiving aid:* Freshmen: 8% (269). Undergraduates: 5% (754). *Average award:* Freshmen: $7080. Undergraduates: $7363. *Scholarships, grants, and awards by category:* Academic interests/achievement: 14,817 awards ($36,938,935 total): biological sciences, business, communication, computer science, education, engineering/technologies, English, foreign languages, general academic interests/achievements, health fields, humanities, international studies, mathematics, military science, physical sciences, premedicine, religion/biblical studies, social sciences. *Creative arts/performance:* 734 awards ($1,335,352 total): art/fine arts, cinema/film/broadcasting, creative writing, debating, journalism/publications, music,

performing arts, theater/drama. *Special achievements/activities:* 4,943 awards ($9,850,177 total): cheerleading/drum major, community service, general special achievements/activities, junior miss, leadership, memberships. *Special characteristics:* 5,795 awards ($17,156,677 total): adult students, children and siblings of alumni, children of faculty/staff, ethnic background, first-generation college students, general special characteristics, handicapped students, international students, local/state students, members of minority groups, out-of-state students, previous college experience, spouses of current students, veterans. *Tuition waivers:* Full or partial for children of alumni, employees or children of employees, senior citizens. *ROTC:* Army, Naval, Air Force.

**LOANS** *Student loans:* $68,970,096 (75% need-based, 25% non-need-based). 49% of past graduating class borrowed through all loan programs. *Average indebtedness per student:* $26,443. *Average need-based loan:* Freshmen: $3539. Undergraduates: $4604. *Parent loans:* $23,172,847 (42% need-based, 58% non-need-based). *Programs:* Federal Direct (Subsidized and Unsubsidized Stafford, PLUS), Perkins, college/university, alternative loans, Health Professions Student Loans (HPSL).

**WORK-STUDY** *Federal work-study:* 388 jobs averaging $1389.

**ATHLETIC AWARDS** Total amount: $6,885,815 (49% need-based, 51% non-need-based).

**APPLYING FOR FINANCIAL AID** *Required financial aid form:* FAFSA. *Financial aid deadline (priority):* 3/1. *Notification date:* Continuous beginning 4/1. Students must reply within 4 weeks of notification.

**CONTACT** Ms. Laura Diven-Brown, Director of Financial Aid, University of Mississippi, 257 Martindale Center, University, MS 38677, 662-915-5788 or toll-free 800-653-6477 (in-state). *Fax:* 662-915-1164. *E-mail:* ldivenbr@olemiss.edu. *Website:* http://www.olemiss.edu/.

# UNIVERSITY OF MISSISSIPPI MEDICAL CENTER
## Jackson, MS

**CONTACT** Minetta Veazey, Administrative Secretary, University of Mississippi Medical Center, 2500 North State Street, Jackson, MS 39216, 601-984-1117. *Fax:* 601-984-6984. *E-mail:* mveazey@registrar.umsmed.edu. *Website:* http://www.umc.edu/.

# UNIVERSITY OF MISSOURI
## Columbia, MO

| Tuition & fees (MO res): $9433 | Average undergraduate aid package: $14,571 |
|---|---|

**ABOUT THE INSTITUTION** State-supported, coed. *Awards:* certificates, bachelor's, master's, and doctoral degrees. 115 undergraduate majors. *Total enrollment:* 35,441. Undergraduates: 27,654. Freshmen: 6,515. Federal methodology is used as a basis for awarding need-based institutional aid.

**UNDERGRADUATE EXPENSES** for 2015–2016 *Application fee:* $50. *Tuition, state resident:* full-time $8220. *Tuition, nonresident:* full-time $23,247. *Required fees:* full-time $1213. Full-time tuition and fees vary according to course load, program, and reciprocity agreements. Part-time tuition and fees vary according to course load, program, and reciprocity agreements. *College room and board:* $9386; *Room only:* $6530. Room and board charges vary according to board plan and housing facility.

**FRESHMAN FINANCIAL AID (Fall 2014, est.)** 5,102 applied for aid; of those 67% were deemed to have need. 96% of freshmen with need received aid; of those 17% had need fully met. *Average percent of need met:* 79% (excluding resources awarded to replace EFC). *Average financial aid package:* $15,678 (excluding resources awarded to replace EFC). 23% of all full-time freshmen had no need and received non-need-based gift aid.

**UNDERGRADUATE FINANCIAL AID (Fall 2014, est.)** 17,491 applied for aid; of those 72% were deemed to have need. 97% of undergraduates with need received aid; of those 14% had need fully met. *Average percent of need met:* 76% (excluding resources awarded to replace EFC). *Average financial aid package:* $14,571 (excluding resources awarded to replace EFC). 17% of all full-time undergraduates had no need and received non-need-based gift aid.

**GIFT AID (NEED-BASED)** *Total amount:* $79,225,451 (31% federal, 12% state, 50% institutional, 7% external sources). *Receiving aid:* Freshmen: 45% (2,863); all full-time undergraduates: 39% (10,148). *Average award:* Freshmen: $9877; Undergraduates: $8783. *Scholarships, grants, and awards:* Federal Pell, FSEOG, state, private, college/university gift aid from institutional funds, Federal Nursing.

**GIFT AID (NON-NEED-BASED)** *Total amount:* $28,837,572 (1% federal, 11% state, 66% institutional, 22% external sources). *Receiving aid:* Freshmen: 4% (267). Undergraduates: 2% (561). *Average award:* Freshmen: $6099. Undergraduates: $5065. *Scholarships, grants, and awards by category: Academic interests/ achievement:* agriculture, area/ethnic studies, biological sciences, business, communication, computer science, education, engineering/technologies, English, foreign languages, general academic interests/achievements, health fields, home economics, humanities, international studies, library science, mathematics, physical sciences, premedicine, religion/biblical studies, social sciences. *Creative arts/performance:* art/fine arts, cinema/film/broadcasting, creative writing, journalism/publications, music, theater/drama. *Special achievements/activities:* cheerleading/drum major, general special achievements/activities, memberships. *Special characteristics:* adult students, children and siblings of alumni, children of faculty/staff, ethnic background, first-generation college students, international students, local/state students, members of minority groups, out-of-state students. *Tuition waivers:* Full or partial for employees or children of employees, senior citizens. *ROTC:* Army, Naval, Air Force.

**LOANS** *Student loans:* $98,417,147 (68% need-based, 32% non-need-based). 55% of past graduating class borrowed through all loan programs. *Average indebtedness per student:* $25,321. *Average need-based loan:* Freshmen: $3540. Undergraduates: $4425. *Parent loans:* $48,249,871 (43% need-based, 57% non-need-based). *Programs:* Federal Direct (Subsidized and Unsubsidized Stafford, PLUS), Perkins, Federal Nursing, state, college/university, alternative loans.

**WORK-STUDY** *Federal work-study:* Total amount: $1,471,802; jobs available.

**ATHLETIC AWARDS** Total amount: $7,584,606 (39% need-based, 61% non-need-based).

**APPLYING FOR FINANCIAL AID** *Required financial aid form:* FAFSA. *Financial aid deadline (priority):* 3/1. *Notification date:* Continuous beginning 4/1. Students must reply within 4 weeks of notification.

**CONTACT** Nicholas Prewett, Director of Student Financial Aid, University of Missouri, 11 Jesse Hall, Columbia, MO 65211, 573-882-7506 or toll-free 800-225-6075 (in-state). *Fax:* 573-884-5335. *E-mail:* finaidinfo@missouri.edu. *Website:* http://www.missouri.edu/.

# UNIVERSITY OF MISSOURI–KANSAS CITY
## Kansas City, MO

| Tuition & fees (MO res): $9475 | Average undergraduate aid package: $9709 |
|---|---|

**ABOUT THE INSTITUTION** State-supported, coed. *Awards:* certificates, bachelor's, master's, and doctoral degrees. 52 undergraduate majors. *Total enrollment:* 16,160. Undergraduates: 10,462. Freshmen: 1,073. Federal methodology is used as a basis for awarding need-based institutional aid.

**UNDERGRADUATE EXPENSES** for 2015–2016 *Application fee:* $45. *Tuition, state resident:* full-time $8102; part-time $270.10 per credit hour. *Tuition, nonresident:* full-time $21,162; part-time $705.40 per credit hour. *Required fees:* full-time $1373; $98.62 per credit hour. Full-time tuition and fees vary according to course load and program. Part-time tuition and fees vary according to course load and program. *College room and board:* $9815; *Room only:* $6769. Room and board charges vary according to board plan and housing facility.

**FRESHMAN FINANCIAL AID (Fall 2014, est.)** 930 applied for aid; of those 77% were deemed to have need. 97% of freshmen with need received aid; of those 12% had need fully met. *Average percent of need met:* 60% (excluding resources awarded to replace EFC). *Average financial aid package:* $10,863 (excluding resources awarded to replace EFC). 19% of all full-time freshmen had no need and received non-need-based gift aid.

**UNDERGRADUATE FINANCIAL AID (Fall 2014, est.)** 5,198 applied for aid; of those 85% were deemed to have need. 97% of undergraduates with need received aid; of those 8% had need fully met. *Average percent of need met:* 53% (excluding resources awarded to replace EFC). *Average financial aid package:* $9709 (excluding resources awarded to replace EFC). 13% of all full-time undergraduates had no need and received non-need-based gift aid.

**GIFT AID (NEED-BASED)** *Total amount:* $27,044,268 (56% federal, 8% state, 30% institutional, 6% external sources). *Receiving aid:* Freshmen: 63% (664); all full-time undergraduates: 60% (3,974). *Average award:* Freshmen: $8584; Undergraduates: $7093. *Scholarships, grants, and awards:* Federal Pell, FSEOG, state, private, college/university gift aid from institutional funds, United Negro College Fund, Federal Nursing.

**GIFT AID (NON-NEED-BASED)** *Total amount:* $7,001,710 (5% state, 63% institutional, 32% external sources). *Receiving aid:* Freshmen: 3% (36). Undergraduates: 1% (83). *Average award:* Freshmen: $5473. Undergraduates: $4828. *Scholarships, grants, and awards by category: Academic interests/achievement:* 6,661 awards ($17,983,985 total): general academic interests/achievements. *Creative arts/performance:* 339 awards ($910,805 total): art/fine arts, debating, general creative arts/performance, music, performing arts. *Special achievements/activities:* 288 awards ($376,228 total): general special achievements/activities, leadership. *Special characteristics:* 2,661 awards ($7,252,869 total): children and siblings of alumni, ethnic background, local/state students, members of minority groups, out-of-state students. *Tuition waivers:* Full or partial for employees or children of employees. *ROTC:* Army, Air Force cooperative.

**LOANS** *Student loans:* $35,877,274 (86% need-based, 14% non-need-based). 60% of past graduating class borrowed through all loan programs. *Average indebtedness per student:* $29,464. *Average need-based loan:* Freshmen: $6099. Undergraduates: $8046. *Parent loans:* $7,907,758 (60% need-based, 40% non-need-based). *Programs:* Federal Direct (Subsidized and Unsubsidized Stafford, PLUS), Perkins, Federal Nursing, state, college/university.

**WORK-STUDY** *Federal work-study:* Total amount: $1,898,170; 487 jobs averaging $4134.

**ATHLETIC AWARDS** Total amount: $3,207,886 (34% need-based, 66% non-need-based).

**APPLYING FOR FINANCIAL AID** *Required financial aid form:* FAFSA. *Financial aid deadline (priority):* 3/1. *Notification date:* Continuous beginning 4/15. Students must reply within 2 weeks of notification.

**CONTACT** Scott Young, Director of Financial Aid and Scholarships, University of Missouri–Kansas City, 5100 Rockhill Road, Kansas City, MO 64110-2499, 816-235-1154 or toll-free 800-775-8652. *Fax:* 816-235-5511. *E-mail:* youngsc@umkc.edu. *Website:* http://www.umkc.edu/.

# UNIVERSITY OF MISSOURI–ST. LOUIS
## St. Louis, MO

| Tuition & fees (MO res): $10,065 | Average undergraduate aid package: $10,702 |
|---|---|

**ABOUT THE INSTITUTION** State-supported, coed. *Awards:* certificates, bachelor's, master's, and doctoral degrees. 39 undergraduate majors. *Total enrollment:* 17,085. Undergraduates: 13,887. Freshmen: 513. Federal methodology is used as a basis for awarding need-based institutional aid.

**UNDERGRADUATE EXPENSES** for 2015–2016 *Application fee:* $35. *Tuition, state resident:* full-time $10,065; part-time $335.50 per credit hour. *Tuition, nonresident:* full-time $25,512; part-time $850.40 per credit hour. Full-time tuition and fees vary according to course level, course load, program, and reciprocity agreements. Part-time tuition and fees vary according to course level, course load, program, and reciprocity agreements. *College room and board:* $9052; *Room only:* $5280. Room and board charges vary according to board plan and housing facility.

**FRESHMAN FINANCIAL AID (Fall 2014, est.)** 421 applied for aid; of those 81% were deemed to have need. 99% of freshmen with need received aid; of those 22% had need fully met. *Average percent of need met:* 73% (excluding resources awarded to replace EFC). *Average financial aid package:* $12,727 (excluding resources awarded to replace EFC). 17% of all full-time freshmen had no need and received non-need-based gift aid.

**UNDERGRADUATE FINANCIAL AID (Fall 2014, est.)** 4,760 applied for aid; of those 88% were deemed to have need. 99% of undergraduates with need received aid; of those 12% had need fully met. *Average percent of need met:* 61% (excluding resources awarded to replace EFC). *Average financial aid package:* $10,702 (excluding resources awarded to replace EFC). 9% of all full-time undergraduates had no need and received non-need-based gift aid.

**GIFT AID (NEED-BASED)** *Total amount:* $31,333,031 (53% federal, 10% state, 33% institutional, 4% external sources). *Receiving aid:* Freshmen: 66% (330); all full-

time undergraduates: 62% (3,600). *Average award:* Freshmen: $10,340; Undergraduates: $7462. *Scholarships, grants, and awards:* Federal Pell, FSEOG, state, private, college/university gift aid from institutional funds, United Negro College Fund, Federal Nursing, TEACH Grants.

**GIFT AID (NON-NEED-BASED)** *Total amount:* $5,924,951 (3% federal, 4% state, 70% institutional, 23% external sources). *Receiving aid:* Freshmen: 11% (55). Undergraduates: 4% (231). *Average award:* Freshmen: $6994. Undergraduates: $5680. *Scholarships, grants, and awards by category: Academic interests/ achievement:* biological sciences, business, communication, computer science, education, engineering/technologies, English, foreign languages, general academic interests/achievements, health fields, humanities, international studies, mathematics, physical sciences, premedicine, social sciences. *Creative arts/performance:* art/fine arts, creative writing, dance, music, theater/drama. *Special achievements/activities:* cheerleading/drum major, community service, memberships. *Special characteristics:* adult students, children and siblings of alumni, children of faculty/staff, ethnic background, general special characteristics, international students, local/state students, members of minority groups, out-of-state students, previous college experience, veterans. *Tuition waivers:* Full or partial for employees or children of employees, senior citizens. *ROTC:* Army, Air Force cooperative.

**LOANS** *Student loans:* $53,356,969 (86% need-based, 14% non-need-based). 66% of past graduating class borrowed through all loan programs. *Average indebtedness per student:* $25,208. *Average need-based loan:* Freshmen: $3305. Undergraduates: $4588. *Parent loans:* $1,558,536 (32% need-based, 68% non-need-based). *Programs:* Federal Direct (Subsidized and Unsubsidized Stafford, PLUS), Perkins, Federal Nursing, state.

**WORK-STUDY** *Federal work-study:* Total amount: $176,647; 53 jobs averaging $3333.

**ATHLETIC AWARDS** Total amount: $2,071,054 (38% need-based, 62% non-need-based).

**APPLYING FOR FINANCIAL AID** *Required financial aid form:* FAFSA. *Financial aid deadline (priority):* 3/1. *Notification date:* Continuous beginning 4/1. Students must reply within 2 weeks of notification.

**CONTACT** Mr. Jason Bornhop, Associate Director, University of Missouri–St. Louis, One University Boulevard, 327 Millennium Student Center, St. Louis, MO 63121-4400, 314-516-5526 or toll-free 888-GO2-UMSL (in-state), 888-GO2-USML (out-of-state). *Fax:* 314-516-5408. *E-mail:* financialaid@umsl.edu. *Website:* http://www.umsl.edu/.

# UNIVERSITY OF MOBILE
## Mobile, AL

| Tuition & fees: $19,700 | Average undergraduate aid package: $17,569 |
| --- | --- |

**ABOUT THE INSTITUTION** Independent Southern Baptist, coed. *Awards:* associate, bachelor's, and master's degrees. 38 undergraduate majors. *Total enrollment:* 1,600. Undergraduates: 1,466. Freshmen: 275. Federal methodology is used as a basis for awarding need-based institutional aid.

**UNDERGRADUATE EXPENSES for 2015–2016** *Application fee:* $25. *Comprehensive fee:* $29,250 includes full-time tuition ($18,720), mandatory fees ($980), and room and board ($9550). *College room only:* $5710. Full-time tuition and fees vary according to course load. Room and board charges vary according to housing facility. *Part-time tuition:* $667 per credit hour. *Part-time fees:* $356 per year. Part-time tuition and fees vary according to course load.

**FRESHMAN FINANCIAL AID (Fall 2014, est.)** 248 applied for aid; of those 91% were deemed to have need. 100% of freshmen with need received aid; of those 100% had need fully met. *Average percent of need met:* 70% (excluding resources awarded to replace EFC). *Average financial aid package:* $18,602 (excluding resources awarded to replace EFC). 8% of all full-time freshmen had no need and received non-need-based gift aid.

**UNDERGRADUATE FINANCIAL AID (Fall 2014, est.)** 919 applied for aid; of those 94% were deemed to have need. 100% of undergraduates with need received aid; of those 100% had need fully met. *Average percent of need met:* 68% (excluding resources awarded to replace EFC). *Average financial aid package:* $17,569 (excluding resources awarded to replace EFC). 11% of all full-time undergraduates had no need and received non-need-based gift aid.

**GIFT AID (NEED-BASED)** *Total amount:* $10,701,335 (28% federal, 3% state, 64% institutional, 5% external sources). *Receiving aid:* Freshmen: 58% (159); all full-

time undergraduates: 45% (532). *Average award:* Freshmen: $5389; Undergraduates: $5219. *Scholarships, grants, and awards:* Federal Pell, FSEOG, state, private, college/university gift aid from institutional funds, Federal Nursing.

**GIFT AID (NON-NEED-BASED)** *Total amount:* $358,680 (100% external sources). *Receiving aid:* Freshmen: 82% (225). Undergraduates: 70% (817). *Average award:* Freshmen: $9377. Undergraduates: $9728. *Scholarships, grants, and awards by category: Academic interests/achievement:* general academic interests/achievements. *Creative arts/performance:* art/fine arts, music, performing arts. *Special achievements/activities:* religious involvement. *Special characteristics:* children of faculty/staff, relatives of clergy. *Tuition waivers:* Full or partial for employees or children of employees. *ROTC:* Army cooperative, Air Force cooperative.

**LOANS** *Student loans:* $10,791,436 (34% need-based, 66% non-need-based). 90% of past graduating class borrowed through all loan programs. *Average indebtedness per student:* $28,250. *Average need-based loan:* Freshmen: $3735. Undergraduates: $4571. *Parent loans:* $1,123,783 (100% non-need-based). *Programs:* Federal Direct (Subsidized and Unsubsidized Stafford, PLUS), Perkins, Federal Nursing, college/university.

**WORK-STUDY** *Federal work-study:* Total amount: $136,444; 63 jobs averaging $2175.

**ATHLETIC AWARDS** Total amount: $4,087,901 (100% non-need-based).

**APPLYING FOR FINANCIAL AID** *Required financial aid forms:* FAFSA, institution's own form, state aid form. *Financial aid deadline:* Continuous. *Notification date:* Continuous beginning 2/1. Students must reply within 2 weeks of notification.

**CONTACT** Mrs. Marie Thomas Batson, Associate Vice President for Campus Life and Enrollment Management Services, University of Mobile, 5735 College Parkway, Mobile, AL 36613, 251-442-2370 or toll-free 800-946-7267. *Fax:* 251-442-2498. *E-mail:* mbatson@umobile.edu. *Website:* http://www.umobile.edu/.

# THE UNIVERSITY OF MONTANA
## Missoula, MT

| Tuition & fees (MT res): $6330 | Average undergraduate aid package: $10,458 |
| --- | --- |

**ABOUT THE INSTITUTION** State-supported, coed. *Awards:* certificates, associate, bachelor's, master's, and doctoral degrees. 116 undergraduate majors. *Total enrollment:* 13,952. Undergraduates: 11,692. Freshmen: 2,027. Federal methodology is used as a basis for awarding need-based institutional aid.

**UNDERGRADUATE EXPENSES for 2015–2016** *Application fee:* $36. *Tuition, state resident:* full-time $4604; part-time $192 per credit hour. *Tuition, nonresident:* full-time $21,420; part-time $889 per credit hour. *Required fees:* full-time $1726. Full-time tuition and fees vary according to degree level, location, program, reciprocity agreements, and student level. Part-time tuition and fees vary according to course load, degree level, location, and student level. *College room and board:* $8006; *Room only:* $3494. Room and board charges vary according to board plan and housing facility.

**FRESHMAN FINANCIAL AID (Fall 2014, est.)** 1,508 applied for aid; of those 75% were deemed to have need. 100% of freshmen with need received aid; of those 12% had need fully met. *Average percent of need met:* 71% (excluding resources awarded to replace EFC). *Average financial aid package:* $10,836 (excluding resources awarded to replace EFC). 14% of all full-time freshmen had no need and received non-need-based gift aid.

**UNDERGRADUATE FINANCIAL AID (Fall 2014, est.)** 6,740 applied for aid; of those 83% were deemed to have need. 99% of undergraduates with need received aid; of those 8% had need fully met. *Average percent of need met:* 65% (excluding resources awarded to replace EFC). *Average financial aid package:* $10,458 (excluding resources awarded to replace EFC). 6% of all full-time undergraduates had no need and received non-need-based gift aid.

**GIFT AID (NEED-BASED)** *Total amount:* $23,441,836 (92% federal, 5% state, 3% institutional). *Receiving aid:* Freshmen: 43% (770); all full-time undergraduates: 41% (3,833). *Average award:* Freshmen: $4789; Undergraduates: $4914. *Scholarships, grants, and awards:* Federal Pell, FSEOG, state, private, college/university gift aid from institutional funds.

**GIFT AID (NON-NEED-BASED)** *Total amount:* $14,477,685 (96% institutional, 4% external sources). *Receiving aid:* Freshmen: 36% (652). Undergraduates:

24% (2,235). *Average award:* Freshmen: $4346. Undergraduates: $3659. *Scholarships, grants, and awards by category: Academic interests/achievement:* biological sciences, business, computer science, education, English, foreign languages, general academic interests/achievements, health fields, humanities, international studies, mathematics, military science, physical sciences, premedicine, social sciences. *Creative arts/performance:* creative writing, dance, journalism/publications, music, performing arts, theater/drama. *Special achievements/activities:* cheerleading/drum major, leadership, rodeo. *Special characteristics:* children and siblings of alumni, children with a deceased or disabled parent, general special characteristics, international students, local/state students, out-of-state students, veterans. *Tuition waivers:* Full or partial for minority students, employees or children of employees, senior citizens. *ROTC:* Army.

**LOANS** *Student loans:* $67,729,608 (100% need-based). 66% of past graduating class borrowed through all loan programs. *Average indebtedness per student:* $27,203. *Average need-based loan:* Freshmen: $4482. Undergraduates: $5113. *Parent loans:* $12,039,948 (7% need-based, 93% non-need-based). *Programs:* Federal Direct (Subsidized and Unsubsidized Stafford, PLUS), Perkins.

**WORK-STUDY** *Federal work-study:* Total amount: $5,333,200; 1,637 jobs averaging $2922. *State or other work-study/employment:* Total amount: $1,574,907 (100% need-based). 110 part-time jobs averaging $2941.

**ATHLETIC AWARDS** Total amount: $1,905,092 (100% non-need-based).

**APPLYING FOR FINANCIAL AID** *Required financial aid forms:* FAFSA, UM Supplemental Information Sheet. *Financial aid deadline (priority):* 2/15. *Notification date:* Continuous beginning 3/15. Students must reply within 4 weeks of notification.

**CONTACT** Mr. Kent McGowan, Director of Financial Aid, The University of Montana, Lommasson Center 218, Missoula, MT 59812, 406-243-5373 or toll-free 800-462-8636. *Fax:* 406-243-4930. *E-mail:* faid@mso.umt.edu. *Website:* http://www.umt.edu/.

# THE UNIVERSITY OF MONTANA WESTERN
## Dillon, MT

| Tuition & fees (MT res): $4797 | Average undergraduate aid package: N/A |
| --- | --- |

**ABOUT THE INSTITUTION** State-supported, coed. *Awards:* certificates, associate, and bachelor's degrees. 31 undergraduate majors. *Total enrollment:* 1,470. Undergraduates: 1,470. Freshmen: 293. Federal methodology is used as a basis for awarding need-based institutional aid.

**UNDERGRADUATE EXPENSES** for 2015–2016 *Application fee:* $30. *Tuition, state resident:* full-time $3699; part-time $153 per hour. *Tuition, nonresident:* full-time $14,356; part-time $597 per hour. *Required fees:* full-time $1098; $141 per credit. Full-time tuition and fees vary according to course load, location, program, reciprocity agreements, and student level. Part-time tuition and fees vary according to course load, location, program, reciprocity agreements, and student level. *College room and board:* $6536; *Room only:* $2404. Room and board charges vary according to housing facility.

**FRESHMAN FINANCIAL AID (Fall 2013)** 255 applied for aid; of those 81% were deemed to have need.

**UNDERGRADUATE FINANCIAL AID (Fall 2013)** 971 applied for aid; of those 81% were deemed to have need.

**GIFT AID (NEED-BASED)** *Scholarships, grants, and awards:* Federal Pell, FSEOG, state, private, college/university gift aid from institutional funds, TEACH Grants, Western Undergraduate Exchange (WUE) Scholarships.

**GIFT AID (NON-NEED-BASED)** *Scholarships, grants, and awards by category: Academic interests/achievement:* biological sciences, business, education, English, general academic interests/achievements, humanities, mathematics, physical sciences, premedicine, social sciences. *Creative arts/performance:* art/fine arts. *Special achievements/activities:* general special achievements/activities, rodeo. *Special characteristics:* children of faculty/staff, first-generation college students, international students, members of minority groups, out-of-state students, veterans. *Tuition waivers:* Full or partial for minority students, employees or children of employees, senior citizens.

**LOANS** *Programs:* Federal Direct (Subsidized and Unsubsidized Stafford, PLUS), Perkins, college/university.

**WORK-STUDY** Federal work-study jobs available. *State or other work-study/employment:* Part-time jobs available.

**APPLYING FOR FINANCIAL AID** *Required financial aid form:* FAFSA. *Financial aid deadline (priority):* 3/1. *Notification date:* Continuous beginning 4/1. Students must reply within 4 weeks of notification.

**CONTACT** Erica L. Jones, Director of Financial Aid, The University of Montana Western, 710 South Atlantic Street, Dillon, MT 59725, 406-683-7511 or toll-free 877-683-7331. *Fax:* 406-683-7510. *E-mail:* erica.jones@umwestern.edu. *Website:* http://www.umwestern.edu/.

# UNIVERSITY OF MONTEVALLO
## Montevallo, AL

| Tuition & fees (AL res): $10,660 | Average undergraduate aid package: $10,076 |
| --- | --- |

**ABOUT THE INSTITUTION** State-supported, coed. *Awards:* certificates, bachelor's, and master's degrees. 26 undergraduate majors. *Total enrollment:* 3,066. Undergraduates: 2,620. Freshmen: 531. Federal methodology is used as a basis for awarding need-based institutional aid.

**UNDERGRADUATE EXPENSES** for 2015–2016 *Application fee:* $30. *Tuition, state resident:* full-time $9990; part-time $333 per credit hour. *Tuition, nonresident:* full-time $20,550; part-time $685 per credit hour. *Required fees:* full-time $670. *College room and board:* $6400; *Room only:* $4000. Room and board charges vary according to housing facility.

**FRESHMAN FINANCIAL AID (Fall 2014, est.)** 518 applied for aid; of those 68% were deemed to have need. 99% of freshmen with need received aid; of those 13% had need fully met. *Average percent of need met:* 56% (excluding resources awarded to replace EFC). *Average financial aid package:* $10,495 (excluding resources awarded to replace EFC). 24% of all full-time freshmen had no need and received non-need-based gift aid.

**UNDERGRADUATE FINANCIAL AID (Fall 2014, est.)** 1,735 applied for aid; of those 88% were deemed to have need. 99% of undergraduates with need received aid; of those 11% had need fully met. *Average percent of need met:* 53% (excluding resources awarded to replace EFC). *Average financial aid package:* $10,076 (excluding resources awarded to replace EFC). 22% of all full-time undergraduates had no need and received non-need-based gift aid.

**GIFT AID (NEED-BASED)** *Total amount:* $10,426,564 (50% federal, 9% state, 37% institutional, 4% external sources). *Receiving aid:* Freshmen: 59% (314); all full-time undergraduates: 56% (1,320). *Average award:* Freshmen: $8001; Undergraduates: $6475. *Scholarships, grants, and awards:* Federal Pell, FSEOG, state, private, college/university gift aid from institutional funds.

**GIFT AID (NON-NEED-BASED)** *Total amount:* $3,582,299 (12% state, 86% institutional, 2% external sources). *Receiving aid:* Freshmen: 9% (47). Undergraduates: 5% (129). *Average award:* Freshmen: $9204. Undergraduates: $9307. *Scholarships, grants, and awards by category: Academic interests/achievement:* 958 awards ($6,073,040 total): biological sciences, business, communication, education, English, foreign languages, general academic interests/achievements, mathematics, physical sciences, social sciences. *Creative arts/performance:* 141 awards ($321,136 total): art/fine arts, cinema/film/broadcasting, creative writing, journalism/publications, music, theater/drama. *Special achievements/activities:* 264 awards ($1,135,657 total): junior miss, leadership. *Special characteristics:* 149 awards ($1,537,928 total): children of faculty/staff, international students, out-of-state students. *Tuition waivers:* Full or partial for employees or children of employees. *ROTC:* Army cooperative, Air Force cooperative.

**LOANS** *Student loans:* $11,645,333 (45% need-based, 55% non-need-based). 69% of past graduating class borrowed through all loan programs. *Average indebtedness per student:* $27,090. *Average need-based loan:* Freshmen: $3224. Undergraduates: $4132. *Parent loans:* $1,242,090 (83% need-based, 17% non-need-based). *Programs:* Federal Direct (Subsidized and Unsubsidized Stafford, PLUS), Perkins.

**WORK-STUDY** *Federal work-study:* Total amount: $265,207; 102 jobs averaging $1800.

**ATHLETIC AWARDS** Total amount: $1,885,574 (38% need-based, 62% non-need-based).

**APPLYING FOR FINANCIAL AID** *Required financial aid form:* FAFSA. *Financial aid deadline (priority):* 3/1. *Notification date:* Continuous beginning 3/25. Students must reply within 2 weeks of notification.

**CONTACT** Ms. Maria Parker, Director of Student Financial Aid, University of Montevallo, Station 6050, Montevallo, AL 35115, 205-665-6050 or toll-free 800-292-4349. *E-mail:* finaid@montevallo.edu. *Website:* http://www.montevallo.edu/.

# UNIVERSITY OF MOUNT OLIVE
## Mount Olive, NC

| Tuition & fees: $17,800 | Average undergraduate aid package: $13,988 |
|---|---|

**ABOUT THE INSTITUTION** Independent Free Will Baptist, coed. 24 undergraduate majors. Federal methodology is used as a basis for awarding need-based institutional aid.

**UNDERGRADUATE EXPENSES** for 2015–2016 *Comprehensive fee:* $25,000 includes full-time tuition ($17,800) and room and board ($7200).

**FRESHMAN FINANCIAL AID (Fall 2013)** 154 applied for aid; of those 88% were deemed to have need. 99% of freshmen with need received aid; of those 20% had need fully met. *Average percent of need met:* 74% (excluding resources awarded to replace EFC). *Average financial aid package:* $15,647 (excluding resources awarded to replace EFC). 1% of all full-time freshmen had no need and received non-need-based gift aid.

**UNDERGRADUATE FINANCIAL AID (Fall 2013)** 848 applied for aid; of those 88% were deemed to have need. 99% of undergraduates with need received aid; of those 22% had need fully met. *Average percent of need met:* 71% (excluding resources awarded to replace EFC). *Average financial aid package:* $13,988 (excluding resources awarded to replace EFC). 1% of all full-time undergraduates had no need and received non-need-based gift aid.

**GIFT AID (NEED-BASED)** *Total amount:* $12,138,072 (57% federal, 24% state, 1% institutional, 18% external sources). *Receiving aid:* Freshmen: 70% (132); all full-time undergraduates: 66% (677). *Average award:* Freshmen: $12,958; Undergraduates: $11,517. *Scholarships, grants, and awards:* Federal Pell, FSEOG, state, private, college/university gift aid from institutional funds.

**GIFT AID (NON-NEED-BASED)** *Total amount:* $1,060,759 (15% state, 4% institutional, 81% external sources). *Receiving aid:* Freshmen: 13% (25). Undergraduates: 15% (150). *Average award:* Freshmen: $1750. Undergraduates: $2064. *Scholarships, grants, and awards by category:* Academic interests/achievement: general academic interests/achievements. Creative arts/performance: art/fine arts, general creative arts/performance. Special achievements/activities: general special achievements/activities, leadership. Special characteristics: children of faculty/staff, local/state students, religious affiliation, veterans, veterans' children.

**LOANS** *Student loans:* $21,537,117 (87% need-based, 13% non-need-based). 92% of past graduating class borrowed through all loan programs. *Average indebtedness per student:* $28,241. *Average need-based loan:* Freshmen: $3429. Undergraduates: $4018. *Parent loans:* $628,400 (38% need-based, 62% non-need-based). *Programs:* Federal Direct (Subsidized and Unsubsidized Stafford, PLUS), Perkins, state.

**WORK-STUDY** *Federal work-study:* jobs available.

**ATHLETIC AWARDS** Total amount: $933,809 (100% need-based).

**APPLYING FOR FINANCIAL AID** *Required financial aid forms:* FAFSA, institution's own form, state aid form. *Financial aid deadline:* Continuous. *Notification date:* Continuous beginning 3/1. Students must reply within 2 weeks of notification.

**CONTACT** Mrs. Katrina K. Lee, Director of Financial Aid, University of Mount Olive, 634 Henderson Street, Mount Olive, NC 28365, 919-658-2502 or toll-free 800-653-0854. *Fax:* 919-658-9816. *E-mail:* klee@umo.edu. *Website:* http://www.umo.edu/.

# UNIVERSITY OF MOUNT UNION
## Alliance, OH

| Tuition & fees: $27,990 | Average undergraduate aid package: $21,420 |
|---|---|

**ABOUT THE INSTITUTION** Independent United Methodist, coed. *Awards:* bachelor's and master's degrees. 66 undergraduate majors. *Total enrollment:* 2,262.

Undergraduates: 2,174. Freshmen: 635. Federal methodology is used as a basis for awarding need-based institutional aid.

**UNDERGRADUATE EXPENSES** for 2015–2016 *Comprehensive fee:* $37,190 includes full-time tuition ($27,670), mandatory fees ($320), and room and board ($9200). Full-time tuition and fees vary according to course load and degree level. Room and board charges vary according to board plan and housing facility. *Part-time tuition:* $1170 per credit hour. Part-time tuition and fees vary according to course load. *Payment plan:* Tuition prepayment.

**FRESHMAN FINANCIAL AID (Fall 2013)** 498 applied for aid; of those 89% were deemed to have need. 100% of freshmen with need received aid; of those 10% had need fully met. *Average percent of need met:* 76% (excluding resources awarded to replace EFC). *Average financial aid package:* $21,906 (excluding resources awarded to replace EFC). 15% of all full-time freshmen had no need and received non-need-based gift aid.

**UNDERGRADUATE FINANCIAL AID (Fall 2013)** 1,811 applied for aid; of those 90% were deemed to have need. 100% of undergraduates with need received aid; of those 12% had need fully met. *Average percent of need met:* 77% (excluding resources awarded to replace EFC). *Average financial aid package:* $21,420 (excluding resources awarded to replace EFC). 17% of all full-time undergraduates had no need and received non-need-based gift aid.

**GIFT AID (NEED-BASED)** *Total amount:* $25,035,428 (12% federal, 4% state, 81% institutional, 3% external sources). *Receiving aid:* Freshmen: 74% (444); all full-time undergraduates: 78% (1,627). *Average award:* Freshmen: $16,539; Undergraduates: $15,660. *Scholarships, grants, and awards:* Federal Pell, FSEOG, state, private, college/university gift aid from institutional funds.

**GIFT AID (NON-NEED-BASED)** *Total amount:* $4,510,806 (95% institutional, 5% external sources). *Receiving aid:* Freshmen: 8% (45). Undergraduates: 7% (148). *Average award:* Freshmen: $10,978. Undergraduates: $10,032. *Scholarships, grants, and awards by category:* Academic interests/achievement: general academic interests/achievements. Creative arts/performance: art/fine arts, cinema/film/broadcasting, journalism/publications, music, theater/drama. Special characteristics: children and siblings of alumni, children of faculty/staff, ethnic background, international students, members of minority groups, relatives of clergy, veterans. *Tuition waivers:* Full or partial for children of alumni, employees or children of employees, senior citizens. *ROTC:* Army, Air Force cooperative.

**LOANS** *Student loans:* $17,657,094 (70% need-based, 30% non-need-based). 93% of past graduating class borrowed through all loan programs. *Average indebtedness per student:* $34,586. *Average need-based loan:* Freshmen: $5131. Undergraduates: $5733. *Parent loans:* $4,687,231 (47% need-based, 53% non-need-based). *Programs:* Federal Direct (Subsidized and Unsubsidized Stafford, PLUS), Perkins, state, private loans.

**WORK-STUDY** *Federal work-study:* 467 jobs averaging $1311. *State or other work-study/employment:* Total amount: $401,313 (22% need-based, 78% non-need-based). 39 part-time jobs averaging $1319.

**APPLYING FOR FINANCIAL AID** *Required financial aid form:* FAFSA. *Financial aid deadline:* Continuous. *Notification date:* Continuous beginning 3/15. Students must reply by 8/24.

**CONTACT** Mrs. Emily J. Mattison, Director of Student Financial Services, University of Mount Union, 1972 Clark Avenue, Alliance, OH 44601-3993, 330-823-2674 or toll-free 800-334-6682. *Fax:* 330-829-2814. *E-mail:* mattisej@mountunion.edu. *Website:* http://www.mountunion.edu/.

# UNIVERSITY OF NEBRASKA AT KEARNEY
## Kearney, NE

| Tuition & fees (NE res): $6584 | Average undergraduate aid package: $10,376 |
|---|---|

**ABOUT THE INSTITUTION** State-supported, coed. *Awards:* certificates, bachelor's, and master's degrees. 38 undergraduate majors. *Total enrollment:* 6,902. Undergraduates: 5,274. Freshmen: 990. Federal methodology is used as a basis for awarding need-based institutional aid.

**UNDERGRADUATE EXPENSES** for 2015–2016 *Application fee:* $45. *Tuition, state resident:* full-time $5235; part-time $174.50 per credit hour. *Tuition, nonresident:* full-time $11,393; part-time $380 per credit hour. *Required fees:* full-time $1349; $25 per credit hour or $299.50 per term. Full-time tuition and fees vary according to course level, course load, degree level, location, and program. Part-time tuition and fees vary according to course level, course load, degree level, location, and program. **College room and board:** $8850; **Room only:** $4524. Room and board charges vary according to board plan and housing facility.

**FRESHMAN FINANCIAL AID (Fall 2013)** 826 applied for aid; of those 79% were deemed to have need. 100% of freshmen with need received aid; of those 24% had need fully met. **Average percent of need met:** 68% (excluding resources awarded to replace EFC). **Average financial aid package:** $11,904 (excluding resources awarded to replace EFC). 4% of all full-time freshmen had no need and received non-need-based gift aid.

**UNDERGRADUATE FINANCIAL AID (Fall 2013)** 3,639 applied for aid; of those 83% were deemed to have need. 100% of undergraduates with need received aid; of those 5% had need fully met. **Average percent of need met:** 63% (excluding resources awarded to replace EFC). **Average financial aid package:** $10,376 (excluding resources awarded to replace EFC). 3% of all full-time undergraduates had no need and received non-need-based gift aid.

**GIFT AID (NEED-BASED) Total amount:** $16,901,496 (43% federal, 6% state, 24% institutional, 27% external sources). **Receiving aid:** Freshmen: 59% (590); all full-time undergraduates: 51% (2,399). **Average award:** Freshmen: $7354; Undergraduates: $6300. **Scholarships, grants, and awards:** Federal Pell, FSEOG, state, private, college/university gift aid from institutional funds.

**GIFT AID (NON-NEED-BASED) Total amount:** $1,140,993 (1% state, 57% institutional, 42% external sources). **Receiving aid:** Freshmen: 5% (46). Undergraduates: 3% (150). **Average award:** Freshmen: $1857. Undergraduates: $2066. **Scholarships, grants, and awards by category:** Academic interests/achievement: communication, general academic interests/achievements. Creative arts/performance: applied art and design, art/fine arts, debating, journalism/publications, music. Special achievements/activities: cheerleading/drum major, leadership. Special characteristics: children and siblings of alumni, children of faculty/staff, ethnic background, first-generation college students, international students, local/state students, members of minority groups, out-of-state students, veterans, veterans' children. **Tuition waivers:** Full or partial for employees or children of employees. **ROTC:** Army.

**LOANS Student loans:** $18,400,495 (76% need-based, 24% non-need-based). 59% of past graduating class borrowed through all loan programs. **Average indebtedness per student:** $23,229. **Average need-based loan:** Freshmen: $3313. Undergraduates: $4172. **Parent loans:** $4,579,817 (34% need-based, 66% non-need-based). **Programs:** Federal Direct (Subsidized and Unsubsidized Stafford, PLUS), Perkins, college/university.

**WORK-STUDY Federal work-study:** jobs available.

**ATHLETIC AWARDS** Total amount: $1,205,645 (66% need-based, 34% non-need-based).

**APPLYING FOR FINANCIAL AID Required financial aid forms:** FAFSA, institution's own form. **Financial aid deadline (priority):** 4/1. **Notification date:** Continuous beginning 3/15.

**CONTACT** Financial Aid Office, University of Nebraska at Kearney, Memorial Student Affairs Building, 905 West 25th Street, Kearney, NE 68849-0001, 308-865-8520 or toll-free 800-532-7639. Fax: 308-865-8096. E-mail: finaid1@unk.edu. Website: http://www.unk.edu/.

# UNIVERSITY OF NEBRASKA AT OMAHA
## Omaha, NE

| Tuition & fees (NE res): $6750 | Average undergraduate aid package: $11,854 |
|---|---|

**ABOUT THE INSTITUTION** State-supported, coed. **Awards:** certificates, bachelor's, master's, and doctoral degrees. 83 undergraduate majors. **Total enrollment:** 15,227. Undergraduates: 12,335. Freshmen: 1,889. Federal methodology is used as a basis for awarding need-based institutional aid.

**UNDERGRADUATE EXPENSES for 2015–2016 Application fee:** $45. **Tuition, state resident:** full-time $5312; part-time $197 per credit hour. **Tuition, nonresident:** full-time $16,632; part-time $598 per credit hour. **Required fees:** full-time $1438. **College room and board:** $8408. Room and board charges vary according to board plan and housing facility.

**FRESHMAN FINANCIAL AID (Fall 2013)** 1,461 applied for aid; of those 82% were deemed to have need. 95% of freshmen with need received aid; of those 28% had need fully met. **Average percent of need met:** 65% (excluding resources awarded

to replace EFC). **Average financial aid package:** $10,637 (excluding resources awarded to replace EFC). 6% of all full-time freshmen had no need and received non-need-based gift aid.

**UNDERGRADUATE FINANCIAL AID (Fall 2013)** 6,764 applied for aid; of those 86% were deemed to have need. 95% of undergraduates with need received aid; of those 28% had need fully met. **Average percent of need met:** 68% (excluding resources awarded to replace EFC). **Average financial aid package:** $11,854 (excluding resources awarded to replace EFC). 5% of all full-time undergraduates had no need and received non-need-based gift aid.

**GIFT AID (NEED-BASED) Total amount:** $36,783,505 (45% federal, 7% state, 21% institutional, 27% external sources). **Receiving aid:** Freshmen: 39% (715); all full-time undergraduates: 39% (3,633). **Average award:** Freshmen: $5865; Undergraduates: $5503. **Scholarships, grants, and awards:** Federal Pell, FSEOG, state, private, college/university gift aid from institutional funds.

**GIFT AID (NON-NEED-BASED) Receiving aid:** Freshmen: 7% (122). Undergraduates: 7% (617). **Average award:** Freshmen: $1929. Undergraduates: $2220. **Scholarships, grants, and awards by category:** Academic interests/achievement: biological sciences, business, communication, computer science, education, engineering/technologies, English, foreign languages, general academic interests/achievements, home economics, mathematics, physical sciences, premedicine, social sciences. Creative arts/performance: art/fine arts, creative writing, debating, journalism/publications, music, performing arts, theater/drama. Special achievements/activities: general special achievements/activities, leadership, memberships. Special characteristics: adult students, children and siblings of alumni, children of faculty/staff, ethnic background, first-generation college students, handicapped students, international students, members of minority groups, out-of-state students, veterans' children. **Tuition waivers:** Full or partial for children of alumni, employees or children of employees. **ROTC:** Army cooperative, Air Force.

**LOANS Student loans:** $38,372,606 (43% need-based, 57% non-need-based). 64% of past graduating class borrowed through all loan programs. **Average indebtedness per student:** $26,866. **Average need-based loan:** Freshmen: $3395. Undergraduates: $3996. **Parent loans:** $6,637,729 (100% non-need-based). **Programs:** Perkins, college/university.

**WORK-STUDY Federal work-study:** jobs available.

**ATHLETIC AWARDS** Total amount: $1,340,504 (100% need-based).

**APPLYING FOR FINANCIAL AID Required financial aid form:** FAFSA. **Financial aid deadline (priority):** 4/1. **Notification date:** Continuous beginning 4/15. Students must reply within 2 weeks of notification.

**CONTACT** Marty Habrock, Office of Financial Aid, University of Nebraska at Omaha, 103 Eppley Administration Building, Omaha, NE 68182-0187, 402-554-2327 or toll-free 800-858-8648 (in-state). Fax: 402-554-3472. E-mail: finaid@unomaha.edu. Website: http://www.unomaha.edu/.

# UNIVERSITY OF NEBRASKA–LINCOLN
## Lincoln, NE

| Tuition & fees (NE res): $8070 | Average undergraduate aid package: $12,825 |
|---|---|

**ABOUT THE INSTITUTION** State-supported, coed. **Awards:** certificates, bachelor's, master's, and doctoral degrees. 124 undergraduate majors. **Total enrollment:** 25,006. Undergraduates: 19,979. Freshmen: 4,652. Both federal and institutional methodology are used as a basis for awarding need-based institutional aid.

**UNDERGRADUATE EXPENSES for 2015–2016 Application fee:** $45. **Tuition, state resident:** full-time $6480; part-time $216 per credit hour. **Tuition, nonresident:** full-time $20,400; part-time $680 per credit hour. **Required fees:** full-time $1590; $13.25 per credit hour or $340 per term. Full-time tuition and fees vary according to course load, program, and reciprocity agreements. Part-time tuition and fees vary according to course load, program, and reciprocity agreements. **College room and board:** $9961. Room and board charges vary according to board plan and housing facility.

**FRESHMAN FINANCIAL AID (Fall 2013)** 3,493 applied for aid; of those 73% were deemed to have need. 97% of freshmen with need received aid; of those 21% had need fully met. **Average percent of need met:** 81% (excluding resources awarded to replace EFC). **Average financial aid package:** $13,753 (excluding resources awarded to replace EFC). 12% of all full-time freshmen had no need and received non-need-based gift aid.

**UNDERGRADUATE FINANCIAL AID (Fall 2013)** 11,180 applied for aid; of those 76% were deemed to have need. 97% of undergraduates with need received aid;

of those 16% had need fully met. *Average percent of need met:* 77% (excluding resources awarded to replace EFC). *Average financial aid package:* $12,825 (excluding resources awarded to replace EFC). 6% of all full-time undergraduates had no need and received non-need-based gift aid.

**GIFT AID (NEED-BASED)** *Total amount:* $57,828,804 (32% federal, 5% state, 42% institutional, 21% external sources). *Receiving aid:* Freshmen: 47% (2,066); all full-time undergraduates: 35% (6,401). *Average award:* Freshmen: $7569; Undergraduates: $7097. *Scholarships, grants, and awards:* Federal Pell, FSEOG, state, private, college/university gift aid from institutional funds.

**GIFT AID (NON-NEED-BASED)** *Total amount:* $28,394,589 (90% institutional, 10% external sources). *Receiving aid:* Freshmen: 9% (384). Undergraduates: 4% (664). *Average award:* Freshmen: $6821. Undergraduates: $6399. *Scholarships, grants, and awards by category: Academic interests/achievement:* agriculture, architecture, biological sciences, business, computer science, education, engineering/technologies, English, foreign languages, general academic interests/achievements, health fields, home economics, humanities, international studies, mathematics, physical sciences, premedicine, social sciences. *Creative arts/performance:* art/fine arts, cinema/film/broadcasting, dance, journalism/publications, music, performing arts, theater/drama. *Special achievements/activities:* cheerleading/drum major, community service, leadership. *Special characteristics:* children and siblings of alumni, ethnic background, handicapped students, international students, members of minority groups, out-of-state students, veterans' children. *Tuition waivers:* Full or partial for employees or children of employees. *ROTC:* Army, Naval, Air Force.

**LOANS** *Student loans:* $52,178,066 (75% need-based, 25% non-need-based). 59% of past graduating class borrowed through all loan programs. *Average indebtedness per student:* $23,395. *Average need-based loan:* Freshmen: $3586. Undergraduates: $4196. *Parent loans:* $32,217,873 (52% need-based, 48% non-need-based). *Programs:* Federal Direct (Subsidized and Unsubsidized Stafford, PLUS), Perkins, college/university.

**WORK-STUDY** *Federal work-study:* 1,481 jobs averaging $2234.

**ATHLETIC AWARDS** Total amount: $8,406,874 (100% non-need-based).

**APPLYING FOR FINANCIAL AID** *Required financial aid form:* FAFSA. *Financial aid deadline (priority):* 4/1. *Notification date:* Continuous beginning 4/1.

**CONTACT** Ms. Jo Tederman, Assistant Director of Scholarships and Financial Aid, University of Nebraska–Lincoln, 17 Canfield Administration Building, Lincoln, NE 68588-0411, 402-472-2030 or toll-free 800-742-8800. *Fax:* 402-472-9826. *Website:* http://www.unl.edu/.

# UNIVERSITY OF NEBRASKA MEDICAL CENTER
## Omaha, NE

**CONTACT** Judy D. Walker, Director of Financial Aid, University of Nebraska Medical Center, 984265 Nebraska Medical Center, Omaha, NE 68198-4265, 402-559-6409 or toll-free 800-626-8431 Ext. 6468. *Fax:* 402-559-6796. *E-mail:* jdwalker@unmc.edu. *Website:* http://www.unmc.edu/.

# UNIVERSITY OF NEVADA, LAS VEGAS
## Las Vegas, NV

| Tuition & fees (NV res): $6590 | Average undergraduate aid package: $11,044 |
| --- | --- |

**ABOUT THE INSTITUTION** State-supported, coed. *Awards:* certificates, bachelor's, master's, and doctoral degrees. 85 undergraduate majors. *Total enrollment:* 28,525. Undergraduates: 23,813. Freshmen: 3,865. Federal methodology is used as a basis for awarding need-based institutional fund.

**UNDERGRADUATE EXPENSES** for 2015–2016 *Application fee:* $60. *One-time required fee:* $120. *Tuition, state resident:* full-time $6044; part-time $191.50 per credit hour. *Tuition, nonresident:* full-time $19,954; part-time $402.25 per credit hour. *Required fees:* full-time $546; $9.97 per credit hour or $273 per term. Full-time tuition and fees vary according to course level, program, and reciprocity agreements. Part-time tuition and fees vary according to course level, program,

and reciprocity agreements. *College room and board:* $10,730; *Room only:* $5880. Room and board charges vary according to board plan.

**FRESHMAN FINANCIAL AID (Fall 2014, est.)** 3,157 applied for aid; of those 81% were deemed to have need. 95% of freshmen with need received aid; of those 10% had need fully met. *Average percent of need met:* 65% (excluding resources awarded to replace EFC). *Average financial aid package:* $11,374 (excluding resources awarded to replace EFC). 12% of all full-time freshmen had no need and received non-need-based gift aid.

**UNDERGRADUATE FINANCIAL AID (Fall 2014, est.)** 12,839 applied for aid; of those 85% were deemed to have need. 96% of undergraduates with need received aid; of those 13% had need fully met. *Average percent of need met:* 69% (excluding resources awarded to replace EFC). *Average financial aid package:* $11,044 (excluding resources awarded to replace EFC). 7% of all full-time undergraduates had no need and received non-need-based gift aid.

**GIFT AID (NEED-BASED)** *Total amount:* $71,545,050 (58% federal, 19% state, 20% institutional, 3% external sources). *Receiving aid:* Freshmen: 47% (1,741); all full-time undergraduates: 44% (7,622). *Average award:* Freshmen: $5959; Undergraduates: $5616. *Scholarships, grants, and awards:* Federal Pell, FSEOG, state, private, college/university gift aid from institutional funds.

**GIFT AID (NON-NEED-BASED)** *Total amount:* $7,084,240 (27% federal, 37% state, 28% institutional, 8% external sources). *Receiving aid:* Freshmen: 44% (1,649). Undergraduates: 27% (4,707). *Average award:* Freshmen: $3647. Undergraduates: $3450. *Scholarships, grants, and awards by category: Academic interests/achievement:* architecture, biological sciences, business, communication, computer science, education, engineering/technologies, English, foreign languages, general academic interests/achievements, health fields, humanities, international studies, mathematics, physical sciences, premedicine, social sciences. *Creative arts/performance:* applied art and design, art/fine arts, cinema/film/broadcasting, creative writing, dance, debating, general creative arts/performance, journalism/publications, music, performing arts, theater/drama. *Special achievements/activities:* cheerleading/drum major, community service, general special achievements/activities, leadership, rodeo. *Special characteristics:* adult students, children and siblings of alumni, children of faculty/staff, children of public servants, children of union members/company employees, children with a deceased or disabled parent, ethnic background, first-generation college students, general special characteristics, handicapped students, international students, local/state students, members of minority groups, out-of-state students, previous college experience, veterans, veterans' children. *Tuition waivers:* Full or partial for employees or children of employees. *ROTC:* Army, Air Force.

**LOANS** *Student loans:* $142,190,280 (82% need-based, 18% non-need-based). 46% of past graduating class borrowed through all loan programs. *Average indebtedness per student:* $18,542. *Average need-based loan:* Freshmen: $3254. Undergraduates: $4085. *Parent loans:* $13,970,487 (63% need-based, 37% non-need-based). *Programs:* Federal Direct (Subsidized and Unsubsidized Stafford, PLUS), Perkins, Federal Nursing, state, college/university.

**WORK-STUDY** *Federal work-study:* Total amount: $1,213,888; jobs available. *State or other work-study/employment:* Total amount: $603,006 (100% need-based). Part-time jobs available.

**ATHLETIC AWARDS** Total amount: $6,803,609 (86% need-based, 14% non-need-based).

**APPLYING FOR FINANCIAL AID** *Required financial aid form:* FAFSA. *Financial aid deadline (priority):* 2/1. *Notification date:* Continuous beginning 3/15.

**CONTACT** Norm Bedford, Director of Financial Aid and Scholarships, University of Nevada, Las Vegas, 4505 South Maryland Parkway, Las Vegas, NV 89154-2016, 702-895-3424. *Fax:* 702-895-1353. *Website:* http://www.unlv.edu/.

# UNIVERSITY OF NEVADA, RENO
## Reno, NV

| Tuition & fees (NV res): $6872 | Average undergraduate aid package: $9160 |
| --- | --- |

**ABOUT THE INSTITUTION** State-supported, coed. *Awards:* certificates, bachelor's, master's, and doctoral degrees. 69 undergraduate majors. *Total enrollment:* 19,934. Undergraduates: 16,839. Freshmen: 3,283. Federal methodology is used as a basis for awarding need-based institutional fund.

**UNDERGRADUATE EXPENSES for 2015–2016** *Application fee:* $60. *Tuition, area resident:* part-time $211.25 per credit hour. *Tuition, state resident:* full-time $6338. *Tuition, nonresident:* full-time $20,248. *Required fees:* full-time $534. Full-time tuition and fees vary according to course level, course load, degree level, and program. Part-time tuition and fees vary according to course level, course load, degree level, and program. *College room and board:* $10,868; *Room only:* $6100. Room and board charges vary according to board plan and housing facility.

**FRESHMAN FINANCIAL AID (Fall 2013)** 2,330 applied for aid; of those 72% were deemed to have need. 100% of freshmen with need received aid; of those 12% had need fully met. *Average percent of need met:* 62% (excluding resources awarded to replace EFC). *Average financial aid package:* $8508 (excluding resources awarded to replace EFC). 33% of all full-time freshmen had no need and received non-need-based gift aid.

**UNDERGRADUATE FINANCIAL AID (Fall 2013)** 8,524 applied for aid; of those 81% were deemed to have need. 100% of undergraduates with need received aid; of those 11% had need fully met. *Average percent of need met:* 62% (excluding resources awarded to replace EFC). *Average financial aid package:* $9160 (excluding resources awarded to replace EFC). 24% of all full-time undergraduates had no need and received non-need-based gift aid.

**GIFT AID (NEED-BASED)** *Total amount:* $37,442,877 (49% federal, 21% state, 26% institutional, 4% external sources). *Receiving aid:* Freshmen: 40% (1,183); all full-time undergraduates: 41% (5,261). *Average award:* Freshmen: $5131; Undergraduates: $5127. *Scholarships, grants, and awards:* Federal Pell, FSEOG, state, private, college/university gift aid from institutional funds.

**GIFT AID (NON-NEED-BASED)** *Total amount:* $11,751,079 (1% federal, 57% state, 29% institutional, 13% external sources). *Receiving aid:* Freshmen: 46% (1,356). Undergraduates: 33% (4,221). *Average award:* Freshmen: $2683. Undergraduates: $2569. *Scholarships, grants, and awards by category:* Academic interests/achievement: 2,049 awards ($3,923,000 total): agriculture, biological sciences, business, communication, computer science, education, engineering/technologies, English, foreign languages, general academic interests/achievements, health fields, mathematics, physical sciences. *Creative arts/performance:* 130 awards ($190,000 total): art/fine arts, general creative arts/performance, journalism/publications, music, theater/drama. *Special characteristics:* adult students, children and siblings of alumni, ethnic background, first-generation college students, married students. *Tuition waivers:* Full or partial for employees or children of employees, senior citizens. *ROTC:* Army.

**LOANS** *Student loans:* $44,237,464 (70% need-based, 30% non-need-based). 46% of past graduating class borrowed through all loan programs. *Average indebtedness per student:* $22,500. *Average need-based loan:* Freshmen: $3334. Undergraduates: $4435. *Parent loans:* $7,496,604 (11% need-based, 89% non-need-based). *Programs:* Federal Direct (Subsidized and Unsubsidized Stafford, PLUS), Perkins, Federal Nursing, college/university, private loans.

**WORK-STUDY** *Federal work-study:* jobs available. *State or other work-study/employment:* Total amount: $435,648 (46% need-based, 54% non-need-based). Part-time jobs available.

**ATHLETIC AWARDS** Total amount: $5,625,398 (21% need-based, 79% non-need-based).

**APPLYING FOR FINANCIAL AID** *Required financial aid form:* FAFSA. *Financial aid deadline (priority):* 3/1. *Notification date:* Continuous beginning 3/1. Students must reply within 4 weeks of notification.

**CONTACT** Tim Wolfe, Director of Student Financial Aid, University of Nevada, Reno, Mail Stop 076, Reno, NV 89557, 775-784-4666 or toll-free 866-263-8232. *Fax:* 775-784-1025. *E-mail:* tawolfe@unr.edu. *Website:* http://www.unr.edu/.

# UNIVERSITY OF NEW ENGLAND
## Biddeford, ME

| Tuition & fees: $34,080 | Average undergraduate aid package: N/A |
|---|---|

**ABOUT THE INSTITUTION** Independent, coed. *Awards:* certificates, bachelor's, master's, and doctoral degrees. 37 undergraduate majors. *Total enrollment:* 6,429. Undergraduates: 2,749. Freshmen: 576. Federal methodology is used as a basis for awarding need-based institutional aid.

**UNDERGRADUATE EXPENSES for 2015–2016** *Application fee:* $40. *Comprehensive fee:* $46,750 includes full-time tuition ($32,880), mandatory fees ($1200), and room and board ($12,670). Full-time tuition and fees vary according to course load and program. Room and board charges vary according to board plan and housing facility. *Part-time tuition:* $1160 per credit hour. Part-time tuition and fees vary according to course load and program.

**GIFT AID (NEED-BASED)** *Scholarships, grants, and awards:* Federal Pell, FSEOG, state, private, college/university gift aid from institutional funds.

**GIFT AID (NON-NEED-BASED)** *Scholarships, grants, and awards by category:* Academic interests/achievement: general academic interests/achievements. Special achievements/activities: leadership. Special characteristics: children and siblings of alumni, siblings of current students. *Tuition waivers:* Full or partial for children of alumni, employees or children of employees. *ROTC:* Army cooperative.

**LOANS** *Programs:* Federal Direct (Subsidized and Unsubsidized Stafford, PLUS), Perkins, Federal Nursing, state.

**APPLYING FOR FINANCIAL AID** *Required financial aid form:* FAFSA. *Financial aid deadline (priority):* 5/1. *Notification date:* Continuous.

**CONTACT** Paul Henderson, Director of Financial Aid, University of New England, 11 Hills Beach Road, Biddeford, ME 04005, 207-602-2342 or toll-free 800-477-4UNE. *Fax:* 207-602-5968. *E-mail:* finaid@une.edu. *Website:* http://www.une.edu/.

# UNIVERSITY OF NEW HAMPSHIRE
## Durham, NH

| Tuition & fees (NH res): $16,552 | Average undergraduate aid package: $22,877 |
|---|---|

**ABOUT THE INSTITUTION** State-supported, coed. *Awards:* certificates, associate, bachelor's, master's, and doctoral degrees. 84 undergraduate majors. *Total enrollment:* 15,169. Undergraduates: 12,840. Freshmen: 3,227. Federal methodology is used as a basis for awarding need-based institutional aid.

**UNDERGRADUATE EXPENSES for 2015–2016** *Application fee:* $50. *Tuition, state resident:* full-time $13,670; part-time $570 per credit hour. *Tuition, nonresident:* full-time $26,650; part-time $1110 per credit hour. *Required fees:* full-time $2882; $1441 per year. Full-time tuition and fees vary according to program. Part-time tuition and fees vary according to course load and program. *College room and board:* $10,360; *Room only:* $6460. Room and board charges vary according to board plan and housing facility.

**FRESHMAN FINANCIAL AID (Fall 2013)** 2,431 applied for aid; of those 81% were deemed to have need. 98% of freshmen with need received aid; of those 18% had need fully met. *Average percent of need met:* 79% (excluding resources awarded to replace EFC). *Average financial aid package:* $23,716 (excluding resources awarded to replace EFC). 13% of all full-time freshmen had no need and received non-need-based gift aid.

**UNDERGRADUATE FINANCIAL AID (Fall 2013)** 9,477 applied for aid; of those 84% were deemed to have need. 98% of undergraduates with need received aid; of those 16% had need fully met. *Average percent of need met:* 77% (excluding resources awarded to replace EFC). *Average financial aid package:* $22,877 (excluding resources awarded to replace EFC). 16% of all full-time undergraduates had no need and received non-need-based gift aid.

**GIFT AID (NEED-BASED)** *Total amount:* $67,861,381 (21% federal, 1% state, 69% institutional, 9% external sources). *Receiving aid:* Freshmen: 54% (1,464); all full-time undergraduates: 47% (5,487). *Average award:* Freshmen: $5789; Undergraduates: $4643. *Scholarships, grants, and awards:* Federal Pell, FSEOG, state, private, college/university gift aid from institutional funds, Veterans Education Benefits (GI Bill).

**GIFT AID (NON-NEED-BASED)** *Total amount:* $15,210,554 (100% institutional). *Receiving aid:* Freshmen: 4% (96). Undergraduates: 3% (340). *Average award:* Freshmen: $9418. Undergraduates: $9467. *Scholarships, grants, and awards by category:* Academic interests/achievement: agriculture, biological sciences, business, computer science, education, engineering/technologies, English, foreign languages, general academic interests/achievements, health fields, humanities, mathematics, military science, physical sciences. *Creative arts/performance:* art/fine arts, dance, music, performing arts, theater/drama. *Special achievements/activities:* community service, leadership. *Special characteristics:* children and siblings of alumni, children of faculty/staff, handicapped students, international students, local/state students. *Tuition waivers:* Full or partial for employees or children of employees. *ROTC:* Army, Air Force.

**LOANS** *Student loans:* $103,820,849 (33% need-based, 67% non-need-based). 79% of past graduating class borrowed through all loan programs. *Average indebtedness per student:* $36,965. *Average need-based loan:* Freshmen: $2658. Undergraduates: $3318. *Parent loans:* $25,677,810 (100% non-need-based). *Programs:* Federal Direct (Subsidized and Unsubsidized Stafford, PLUS), Perkins, state, college/university.

**WORK-STUDY** *Federal work-study:* 5,596 jobs averaging $2507. *State or other work-study/employment:* Total amount: $7,039,893 (100% non-need-based). 3,926 part-time jobs averaging $1634.

**ATHLETIC AWARDS** Total amount: $8,494,670 (100% non-need-based).

**APPLYING FOR FINANCIAL AID** *Required financial aid form:* FAFSA. *Financial aid deadline (priority):* 3/1. *Notification date:* Continuous beginning 3/1.

**CONTACT** Susan K. Allen, Director of Financial Aid, University of New Hampshire, 11 Garrison Avenue, Durham, NH 03824, 603-862-3600. *Fax:* 603-862-1947. *E-mail:* financial.aid@unh.edu.

*Website:* http://www.unh.edu/.

# UNIVERSITY OF NEW HAMPSHIRE AT MANCHESTER
## Manchester, NH

| Tuition & fees (NH res): $13,757 | Average undergraduate aid package: $12,837 |
| --- | --- |

**ABOUT THE INSTITUTION** State-supported, coed. *Awards:* associate, bachelor's, and master's degrees. 11 undergraduate majors. *Total enrollment:* 719. Undergraduates: 719. Freshmen: 81. Federal methodology is used as a basis for awarding need-based institutional aid.

**UNDERGRADUATE EXPENSES** for 2015–2016 *Application fee:* $60. *Tuition, state resident:* full-time $13,350. *Tuition, nonresident:* full-time $26,330. *Required fees:* full-time $407. Full-time tuition and fees vary according to course load and program. Part-time tuition and fees vary according to course load and program.

**FRESHMAN FINANCIAL AID (Fall 2013)** 78 applied for aid; of those 72% were deemed to have need. 100% of freshmen with need received aid; of those 11% had need fully met. *Average percent of need met:* 66% (excluding resources awarded to replace EFC). *Average financial aid package:* $10,821 (excluding resources awarded to replace EFC). 15% of all full-time freshmen had no need and received non-need-based gift aid.

**UNDERGRADUATE FINANCIAL AID (Fall 2013)** 616 applied for aid; of those 84% were deemed to have need. 98% of undergraduates with need received aid; of those 8% had need fully met. *Average percent of need met:* 58% (excluding resources awarded to replace EFC). *Average financial aid package:* $12,837 (excluding resources awarded to replace EFC). 2% of all full-time undergraduates had no need and received non-need-based gift aid.

**GIFT AID (NEED-BASED)** *Total amount:* $1,523,566 (69% federal, 23% institutional, 8% external sources). *Receiving aid:* Freshmen: 28% (26); all full-time undergraduates: 31% (242). *Average award:* Freshmen: $1384; Undergraduates: $853. *Scholarships, grants, and awards:* Federal Pell, FSEOG, state, private, college/university gift aid from institutional funds.

**GIFT AID (NON-NEED-BASED)** *Total amount:* $332,693 (100% institutional). *Receiving aid:* Freshmen: 15% (14). Undergraduates: 2% (18). *Average award:* Freshmen: $1964. Undergraduates: $1946. *Scholarships, grants, and awards by category: Academic interests/achievement:* biological sciences, business, communication, computer science, engineering/technologies, English, general academic interests/achievements, humanities. *Special characteristics:* children of faculty/staff. *Tuition waivers:* Full or partial for employees or children of employees, senior citizens. *ROTC:* Army cooperative, Air Force cooperative.

**LOANS** *Student loans:* $4,679,422 (42% need-based, 58% non-need-based). 79% of past graduating class borrowed through all loan programs. *Average indebtedness per student:* $29,393. *Average need-based loan:* Freshmen: $2386. Undergraduates: $3797. *Parent loans:* $461,056 (100% non-need-based). *Programs:* Federal Direct (Subsidized and Unsubsidized Stafford, PLUS), Perkins, state, college/university.

**WORK-STUDY** *Federal work-study:* 163 jobs averaging $2450.

**APPLYING FOR FINANCIAL AID** *Required financial aid form:* FAFSA. *Financial aid deadline (priority):* 3/1. *Notification date:* Continuous beginning 4/1.

**CONTACT** Sharon Eaton, Assistant Director of Financial Aid, University of New Hampshire at Manchester, 400 Commercial Street, Student Services Suite, 2nd Floor, Manchester, NH 03101-1113, 603-641-4114. *Fax:* 603-641-4125. *Website:* http://www.manchester.unh.edu/.

# UNIVERSITY OF NEW HAVEN
## West Haven, CT

| Tuition & fees: $34,630 | Average undergraduate aid package: $21,989 |
| --- | --- |

**ABOUT THE INSTITUTION** Independent, coed. *Awards:* certificates, associate, bachelor's, master's, and doctoral degrees. 62 undergraduate majors. *Total enrollment:* 6,811. Undergraduates: 5,048. Freshmen: 1,221. Both federal and institutional methodology are used as a basis for awarding need-based institutional aid.

**UNDERGRADUATE EXPENSES** for 2015–2016 *Application fee:* $50. *Comprehensive fee:* $49,040 includes full-time tuition ($33,330), mandatory fees ($1300), and room and board ($14,410). *College room only:* $9160. Full-time tuition and fees vary according to course load and program. Room and board charges vary according to board plan and housing facility. *Part-time tuition:* $1110 per credit. Part-time tuition and fees vary according to class time, course load, and program.

**FRESHMAN FINANCIAL AID (Fall 2014, est.)** 1,030 applied for aid; of those 91% were deemed to have need. 100% of freshmen with need received aid; of those 13% had need fully met. *Average percent of need met:* 62% (excluding resources awarded to replace EFC). *Average financial aid package:* $23,035 (excluding resources awarded to replace EFC). 13% of all full-time freshmen had no need and received non-need-based gift aid.

**UNDERGRADUATE FINANCIAL AID (Fall 2014, est.)** 3,710 applied for aid; of those 92% were deemed to have need. 100% of undergraduates with need received aid; of those 16% had need fully met. *Average percent of need met:* 61% (excluding resources awarded to replace EFC). *Average financial aid package:* $21,989 (excluding resources awarded to replace EFC). 13% of all full-time undergraduates had no need and received non-need-based gift aid.

**GIFT AID (NEED-BASED)** *Total amount:* $59,629,171 (10% federal, 3% state, 85% institutional, 2% external sources). *Receiving aid:* Freshmen: 77% (934); all full-time undergraduates: 73% (3,429). *Average award:* Freshmen: $20,088; Undergraduates: $18,345. *Scholarships, grants, and awards:* Federal Pell, FSEOG, state, private, college/university gift aid from institutional funds.

**GIFT AID (NON-NEED-BASED)** *Total amount:* $10,401,558 (1% state, 99% institutional). *Receiving aid:* Freshmen: 8% (103). Undergraduates: 9% (403). *Average award:* Freshmen: $15,781. Undergraduates: $13,014. *Tuition waivers:* Full or partial for employees or children of employees, senior citizens. *ROTC:* Army, Air Force cooperative.

**LOANS** *Student loans:* $41,950,438 (70% need-based, 30% non-need-based). 84% of past graduating class borrowed through all loan programs. *Average indebtedness per student:* $43,472. *Average need-based loan:* Freshmen: $3481. Undergraduates: $4371. *Parent loans:* $17,557,675 (100% non-need-based). *Programs:* Federal Direct (Subsidized and Unsubsidized Stafford, PLUS), Perkins.

**WORK-STUDY** *Federal work-study:* Total amount: $221,575; jobs available.

**ATHLETIC AWARDS** Total amount: $2,814,364 (66% need-based, 34% non-need-based).

**APPLYING FOR FINANCIAL AID** *Required financial aid form:* FAFSA. *Financial aid deadline (priority):* 3/1. *Notification date:* Continuous beginning 3/1. Students must reply by 5/1 or within 2 weeks of notification.

**CONTACT** Mrs. Karen Flynn, Associate Vice President for Financial Aid, University of New Haven, 300 Boston Post Road, West Haven, CT 06516-1916, 203-932-7315 or toll-free 800-342-5864. *Fax:* 203-931-6050. *E-mail:* financialaid@newhaven.edu. *Website:* http://www.newhaven.edu/.

# UNIVERSITY OF NEW MEXICO
## Albuquerque, NM

**CONTACT** Brian Malone, Office of Student Financial Aid, University of New Mexico, MSC 11 6315, 1 University of New Mexico, Albuquerque, NM 87131, 505-277-8900 or toll-free 800-CALL-UNM. *Fax:* 505-277-6326. *E-mail:* finaid@unm.edu. *Website:* http://www.unm.edu/.

# UNIVERSITY OF NEW ORLEANS
## New Orleans, LA

| Tuition & fees (LA res): $7482 | Average undergraduate aid package: $9359 |
| --- | --- |

**ABOUT THE INSTITUTION** State-supported, coed. *Awards:* certificates, bachelor's, master's, and doctoral degrees. 37 undergraduate majors. *Total enrollment:* 9,234. Undergraduates: 7,152. Freshmen: 865. Federal methodology is used as a basis for awarding need-based institutional aid.

**UNDERGRADUATE EXPENSES** for 2015–2016 *Application fee:* $20. *Tuition, state resident:* full-time $5537. *Tuition, nonresident:* full-time $19,147. *Required fees:* full-time $1945. Full-time tuition and fees vary according to course load. Part-time tuition and fees vary according to course load. *College room and board:* $9274. Room and board charges vary according to board plan and housing facility.

**FRESHMAN FINANCIAL AID (Fall 2014, est.)** 812 applied for aid; of those 83% were deemed to have need. 96% of freshmen with need received aid; of those 11% had need fully met. *Average percent of need met:* 66% (excluding resources awarded to replace EFC). *Average financial aid package:* $11,563 (excluding resources awarded to replace EFC). 1% of all full-time freshmen had no need and received non-need-based gift aid.

**UNDERGRADUATE FINANCIAL AID (Fall 2014, est.)** 4,410 applied for aid; of those 86% were deemed to have need. 92% of undergraduates with need received aid; of those 6% had need fully met. *Average percent of need met:* 57% (excluding resources awarded to replace EFC). *Average financial aid package:* $9359 (excluding resources awarded to replace EFC). 1% of all full-time undergraduates had no need and received non-need-based gift aid.

**GIFT AID (NEED-BASED)** *Total amount:* $14,604,951 (69% federal, 7% state, 24% institutional). *Receiving aid:* Freshmen: 60% (509); all full-time undergraduates: 49% (2,539). *Average award:* Freshmen: $6048; Undergraduates: $5575. *Scholarships, grants, and awards:* Federal Pell, FSEOG, state, private, college/university gift aid from institutional funds.

**GIFT AID (NON-NEED-BASED)** *Total amount:* $9,543,580 (95% state, 2% institutional, 3% external sources). *Receiving aid:* Freshmen: 53% (448). Undergraduates: 30% (1,537). *Average award:* Freshmen: $650. Undergraduates: $1450. *Scholarships, grants, and awards by category: Academic interests/ achievement:* 1,761 awards ($8,736,342 total): biological sciences, business, education, engineering/technologies, English, foreign languages, general academic interests/ achievements, mathematics, physical sciences, social sciences. *Creative arts/performance:* 16 awards ($5100 total): general creative arts/performance, music, theater/ drama. *Special achievements/activities:* 132 awards ($594,015 total): community service, general special achievements/activities, leadership. *Special characteristics:* 1,809 awards ($9,505,758 total): adult students, children and siblings of alumni, children of public servants, children with a deceased or disabled parent, general special characteristics, international students, local/state students, members of minority groups, out-of-state students, public servants, veterans. *Tuition waivers:* Full or partial for employees or children of employees, senior citizens. *ROTC:* Army cooperative, Naval cooperative, Air Force cooperative.

**LOANS** *Student loans:* $17,255,399 (44% need-based, 56% non-need-based). 53% of past graduating class borrowed through all loan programs. *Average indebtedness per student:* $18,850. *Average need-based loan:* Freshmen: $3507. Undergraduates: $4079. *Parent loans:* $387,985 (100% non-need-based). *Programs:* Federal Direct (Subsidized and Unsubsidized Stafford, PLUS), Perkins.

**WORK-STUDY** *Federal work-study:* Total amount: $404,185; 202 jobs averaging $2001. *State or other work-study/employment:* Total amount: $528,184 (100% non-need-based). 317 part-time jobs averaging $1666.

**ATHLETIC AWARDS** Total amount: $1,247,339 (56% need-based, 44% non-need-based).

**APPLYING FOR FINANCIAL AID** *Required financial aid form:* FAFSA. *Financial aid deadline (priority):* 1/15. *Notification date:* Continuous beginning 3/15.

**CONTACT** Ann Lockridge, Associate Director of Financial Aid, University of New Orleans, Privateer Enrollment Center, 2000 Lakeshore Drive, 105 Earl K. Long Library, New Orleans, LA 70148, 504-280-6603 or toll-free 800-256-5866. *Fax:* 504-280-3973. *E-mail:* finaid@uno.edu. *Website:* http://www.uno.edu/.

# UNIVERSITY OF NORTH ALABAMA
## Florence, AL

| Tuition & fees (AL res): $9073 | Average undergraduate aid package: $7409 |
| --- | --- |

**ABOUT THE INSTITUTION** State-supported, coed. *Awards:* certificates, bachelor's, and master's degrees. 36 undergraduate majors. *Total enrollment:* 6,841. Undergraduates: 5,885. Freshmen: 944. Federal methodology is used as a basis for awarding need-based institutional aid.

**UNDERGRADUATE EXPENSES** for 2015–2016 *Application fee:* $25. *Tuition, state resident:* full-time $7320; part-time $244 per credit hour. *Tuition, nonresident:* full-time $14,640; part-time $488 per credit hour. *Required fees:* full-time $1753. Full-time tuition and fees vary according to course load and program. Part-time tuition and fees vary according to course load and program. *College room and board:* $6327. Room and board charges vary according to board plan and housing facility.

**FRESHMAN FINANCIAL AID (Fall 2013)** 775 applied for aid; of those 86% were deemed to have need. 95% of freshmen with need received aid; of those 12% had need fully met. *Average percent of need met:* 61% (excluding resources awarded to replace EFC). *Average financial aid package:* $6666 (excluding resources awarded to replace EFC). 13% of all full-time freshmen had no need and received non-need-based gift aid.

**UNDERGRADUATE FINANCIAL AID (Fall 2013)** 2,796 applied for aid; of those 88% were deemed to have need. 97% of undergraduates with need received aid; of those 17% had need fully met. *Average percent of need met:* 63% (excluding resources awarded to replace EFC). *Average financial aid package:* $7409 (excluding resources awarded to replace EFC). 13% of all full-time undergraduates had no need and received non-need-based gift aid.

**GIFT AID (NEED-BASED)** *Total amount:* $9,769,251 (100% federal). *Receiving aid:* Freshmen: 48% (460); all full-time undergraduates: 35% (1,706). *Average award:* Freshmen: $4210; Undergraduates: $4096. *Scholarships, grants, and awards:* Federal Pell, FSEOG, state, private, Academic Competitiveness Grants, Project OPEN.

**GIFT AID (NON-NEED-BASED)** *Total amount:* $6,726,476 (84% institutional, 16% external sources). *Receiving aid:* Freshmen: 22% (205). Undergraduates: 16% (760). *Average award:* Freshmen: $4339. Undergraduates: $3970. *Scholarships, grants, and awards by category: Academic interests/achievement:* 613 awards ($2,818,690 total): general academic interests/achievements. *Creative arts/performance:* 266 awards ($599,619 total): art/fine arts, dance, journalism/publications, music. *Special achievements/activities:* 224 awards ($709,210 total): cheerleading/ drum major, general special achievements/activities, leadership. *Special characteristics:* 11 awards ($11,592 total): children and siblings of alumni, children of faculty/staff, first-generation college students, general special characteristics, handicapped students, out-of-state students. *Tuition waivers:* Full or partial for employees or children of employees, senior citizens. *ROTC:* Army.

**LOANS** *Student loans:* $19,879,005 (49% need-based, 51% non-need-based). 72% of past graduating class borrowed through all loan programs. *Average indebtedness per student:* $29,839. *Average need-based loan:* Freshmen: $2834. Undergraduates: $3603. *Parent loans:* $1,603,798 (100% non-need-based). *Programs:* Federal Direct (Subsidized and Unsubsidized Stafford, PLUS).

**WORK-STUDY** *Federal work-study:* 171 jobs averaging $1603. *State or other work-study/employment:* Total amount: $771,426 (100% non-need-based). 476 part-time jobs averaging $1621.

**ATHLETIC AWARDS** Total amount: $2,298,416 (100% non-need-based).

**APPLYING FOR FINANCIAL AID** *Required financial aid form:* FAFSA. *Financial aid deadline (priority):* 6/1. *Notification date:* 4/1. Students must reply within 2 weeks of notification.

**CONTACT** Dr. Laura B. Bozovic, Interim Director of Student Financial Services, University of North Alabama, UNA Box 5014, Florence, AL 35632-0001, 256-765-5795 or toll-free 800-TALK-UNA. *E-mail:* lbozovic@una.edu. *Website:* http://www.una.edu/.

**CONTACT** Financial Aid Office, University of North Carolina at Asheville, One University Heights, 215 Brown Hall, CPO 1330, Asheville, NC 28804, 828-251-6535 or toll-free 800-531-9842. *Fax:* 828-232-2294. *E-mail:* finaid@unca.edu. *Website:* http://www.unca.edu/.

# UNIVERSITY OF NORTH CAROLINA AT ASHEVILLE
## Asheville, NC

| Tuition & fees (NC res): $6392 | Average undergraduate aid package: $11,633 |
|---|---|

**ABOUT THE INSTITUTION** State-supported, coed. *Awards:* certificates, bachelor's, and master's degrees. 32 undergraduate majors. *Total enrollment:* 3,845. Undergraduates: 3,804. Freshmen: 633. Federal methodology is used as a basis for awarding need-based institutional aid.

**UNDERGRADUATE EXPENSES for 2015–2016** *Application fee:* $60. *Tuition, state resident:* full-time $3817. *Tuition, nonresident:* full-time $18,688. *Required fees:* full-time $2575. Full-time tuition and fees vary according to course load. Part-time tuition and fees vary according to course load. *College room and board:* $8332. Room and board charges vary according to housing facility.

**FRESHMAN FINANCIAL AID (Fall 2013)** 523 applied for aid; of those 65% were deemed to have need. 99% of freshmen with need received aid; of those 21% had need fully met. *Average percent of need met:* 71% (excluding resources awarded to replace EFC). *Average financial aid package:* $10,787 (excluding resources awarded to replace EFC). 7% of all full-time freshmen had no need and received non-need-based gift aid.

**UNDERGRADUATE FINANCIAL AID (Fall 2013)** 2,424 applied for aid; of those 76% were deemed to have need. 99% of undergraduates with need received aid; of those 21% had need fully met. *Average percent of need met:* 71% (excluding resources awarded to replace EFC). *Average financial aid package:* $11,633 (excluding resources awarded to replace EFC). 6% of all full-time undergraduates had no need and received non-need-based gift aid.

**GIFT AID (NEED-BASED)** *Total amount:* $11,593,925 (46% federal, 26% state, 28% institutional). *Receiving aid:* Freshmen: 50% (317); all full-time undergraduates: 53% (1,652). *Average award:* Freshmen: $5983; Undergraduates: $6628. *Scholarships, grants, and awards:* Federal Pell, FSEOG, state, private, college/university gift aid from institutional funds.

**GIFT AID (NON-NEED-BASED)** *Total amount:* $661,747 (2% federal, 13% state, 85% institutional). *Receiving aid:* Freshmen: 7% (42). Undergraduates: 6% (199). *Average award:* Freshmen: $2145. Undergraduates: $2654. *Scholarships, grants, and awards by category:* Academic interests/achievement: biological sciences, business, communication, computer science, education, engineering/technologies, English, general academic interests/achievements, health fields, mathematics, physical sciences, premedicine, social sciences. *Creative arts/performance:* art/fine arts, general creative arts/performance, music, theater/drama. *Special achievements/activities:* community service, general special achievements/activities, junior miss, leadership. *Special characteristics:* adult students, children and siblings of alumni, children of faculty/staff, ethnic background, first-generation college students, general special characteristics, handicapped students, international students, local/state students, veterans, veterans' children. *Tuition waivers:* Full or partial for employees or children of employees.

**LOANS** *Student loans:* $11,684,539 (75% need-based, 25% non-need-based). 53% of past graduating class borrowed through all loan programs. *Average indebtedness per student:* $21,105. *Average need-based loan:* Freshmen: $4201. Undergraduates: $4568. *Programs:* Federal Direct (Subsidized and Unsubsidized Stafford, PLUS), Perkins, state, college/university.

**WORK-STUDY** *Federal work-study:* jobs available. *State or other work-study/employment:* Total amount: $1,501,821 (22% need-based, 78% non-need-based). Part-time jobs available.

**ATHLETIC AWARDS** Total amount: $1,573,550 (36% need-based, 64% non-need-based).

**APPLYING FOR FINANCIAL AID** *Required financial aid form:* FAFSA. *Financial aid deadline (priority):* 3/1. *Notification date:* Continuous beginning 3/1.

# THE UNIVERSITY OF NORTH CAROLINA AT CHAPEL HILL
## Chapel Hill, NC

| Tuition & fees (NC res): $8336 | Average undergraduate aid package: $17,946 |
|---|---|

**ABOUT THE INSTITUTION** State-supported, coed. *Awards:* certificates, bachelor's, master's, and doctoral degrees. 61 undergraduate majors. *Total enrollment:* 29,135. Undergraduates: 18,350. Freshmen: 3,976. Both federal and institutional methodology are used as a basis for awarding need-based institutional aid.

**UNDERGRADUATE EXPENSES for 2015–2016** *Application fee:* $80. *Tuition, state resident:* full-time $6423. *Tuition, nonresident:* full-time $31,505. *Required fees:* full-time $1913. Full-time tuition and fees vary according to program. Part-time tuition and fees vary according to course load and program. *College room and board:* $10,592; *Room only:* $5928. Room and board charges vary according to board plan, housing facility, and location.

**FRESHMAN FINANCIAL AID (Fall 2013)** 2,960 applied for aid; of those 61% were deemed to have need. 100% of freshmen with need received aid; of those 78% had need fully met. *Average percent of need met:* 100% (excluding resources awarded to replace EFC). *Average financial aid package:* $17,797 (excluding resources awarded to replace EFC). 4% of all full-time freshmen had no need and received non-need-based gift aid.

**UNDERGRADUATE FINANCIAL AID (Fall 2013)** 10,259 applied for aid; of those 77% were deemed to have need. 100% of undergraduates with need received aid; of those 85% had need fully met. *Average percent of need met:* 100% (excluding resources awarded to replace EFC). *Average financial aid package:* $17,946 (excluding resources awarded to replace EFC). 5% of all full-time undergraduates had no need and received non-need-based gift aid.

**GIFT AID (NEED-BASED)** *Total amount:* $108,443,697 (16% federal, 12% state, 66% institutional, 6% external sources). *Receiving aid:* Freshmen: 43% (1,680); all full-time undergraduates: 43% (7,509). *Average award:* Freshmen: $15,609; Undergraduates: $14,791. *Scholarships, grants, and awards:* Federal Pell, FSEOG, state, private, college/university gift aid from institutional funds.

**GIFT AID (NON-NEED-BASED)** *Total amount:* $14,009,176 (8% state, 32% institutional, 60% external sources). *Receiving aid:* Freshmen: 4% (145). Undergraduates: 2% (404). *Average award:* Freshmen: $9054. Undergraduates: $6784. *Scholarships, grants, and awards by category:* Academic interests/achievement: business, communication, education, English, general academic interests/achievements, health fields, mathematics. *Creative arts/performance:* applied art and design, art/fine arts, journalism/publications, music, theater/drama. *Special achievements/activities:* community service, general special achievements/activities, leadership. *Special characteristics:* children of faculty/staff, international students, out-of-state students, relatives of clergy, religious affiliation. *Tuition waivers:* Full or partial for employees or children of employees. *ROTC:* Army, Naval, Air Force.

**LOANS** *Student loans:* $46,740,645 (64% need-based, 36% non-need-based). 41% of past graduating class borrowed through all loan programs. *Average indebtedness per student:* $18,945. *Average need-based loan:* Freshmen: $4667. Undergraduates: $5202. *Parent loans:* $8,771,005 (6% need-based, 94% non-need-based). *Programs:* Federal Direct (Subsidized and Unsubsidized Stafford, PLUS), Perkins, state, college/university, alternative loans.

**WORK-STUDY** *Federal work-study:* 1,837 jobs averaging $1796.

**ATHLETIC AWARDS** Total amount: $12,257,950 (23% need-based, 77% non-need-based).

**APPLYING FOR FINANCIAL AID** *Required financial aid forms:* FAFSA, CSS Financial Aid PROFILE. *Financial aid deadline (priority):* 3/1. *Notification date:* Continuous beginning 3/15. Students must reply by 5/1.

**CONTACT** Ms. Shirley A. Ort, Associate Provost/Director of Scholarships and Student Aid, The University of North Carolina at Chapel Hill, CB # 2300, 111 Pettigrew Hall, Chapel Hill, NC 27599, 919-962-8396. *Fax:* 919-962-2716. *E-mail:* aidinfo@unc.edu. *Website:* http://www.unc.edu/.

# THE UNIVERSITY OF NORTH CAROLINA AT CHARLOTTE
### Charlotte, NC

| Tuition & fees (NC res): $6277 | Average undergraduate aid package: $9861 |
|---|---|

**ABOUT THE INSTITUTION** State-supported, coed. *Awards:* certificates, bachelor's, master's, and doctoral degrees. 64 undergraduate majors. *Total enrollment:* 27,238. Undergraduates: 22,216. Freshmen: 3,319. Federal methodology is used as a basis for awarding need-based institutional aid.

**UNDERGRADUATE EXPENSES for 2015–2016** *Application fee:* $60. *Tuition, state resident:* full-time $3522. *Tuition, nonresident:* full-time $16,693. *Required fees:* full-time $2755. Full-time tuition and fees vary according to course load and program. Part-time tuition and fees vary according to course load and program. *College room and board:* $9270; *Room only:* $5200. Room and board charges vary according to board plan and housing facility.

**FRESHMAN FINANCIAL AID (Fall 2014, est.)** 2,826 applied for aid; of those 58% were deemed to have need. 100% of freshmen with need received; of those 15% had need fully met. *Average percent of need met:* 72% (excluding resources awarded to replace EFC). *Average financial aid package:* $10,645 (excluding resources awarded to replace EFC). 1% of all full-time freshmen had no need and received non-need-based gift aid.

**UNDERGRADUATE FINANCIAL AID (Fall 2014, est.)** 15,671 applied for aid; of those 71% were deemed to have need. 99% of undergraduates with need received aid; of those 13% had need fully met. *Average percent of need met:* 67% (excluding resources awarded to replace EFC). *Average financial aid package:* $9861 (excluding resources awarded to replace EFC). 1% of all full-time undergraduates had no need and received non-need-based gift aid.

**GIFT AID (NEED-BASED)** *Total amount:* $73,663,863 (60% federal, 18% state, 21% institutional, 1% external sources). *Receiving aid:* Freshmen: 43% (1,439); all full-time undergraduates: 48% (9,565). *Average award:* Freshmen: $9551; Undergraduates: $6416. *Scholarships, grants, and awards:* Federal Pell, FSEOG, state, private, college/university gift aid from institutional funds.

**GIFT AID (NON-NEED-BASED)** *Total amount:* $2,356,383 (8% state, 25% institutional, 67% external sources). *Receiving aid:* Freshmen: 10% (323). Undergraduates: 5% (1,085). *Average award:* Freshmen: $3685. Undergraduates: $4184. *Scholarships, grants, and awards by category:* Academic interests/ achievement: 138 awards ($530,631 total): architecture, business, computer science, education, engineering/technologies, general academic interests/achievements, health fields, humanities, mathematics, military science. *Creative arts/performance:* 60 awards ($50,850 total): music, performing arts. *Special achievements/activities:* religious involvement. *Special characteristics:* ethnic background, handicapped students, members of minority groups. *Tuition waivers:* Full or partial for employees or children of employees, senior citizens. *ROTC:* Army, Air Force.

**LOANS** *Student loans:* $142,903,503 (98% need-based, 2% non-need-based). 67% of past graduating class borrowed through all loan programs. *Average indebtedness per student:* $26,488. *Average need-based loan:* Freshmen: $4074. Undergraduates: $4931. *Parent loans:* $18,376,691 (100% need-based). *Programs:* Federal Direct (Subsidized and Unsubsidized Stafford, PLUS), Perkins, state, college/university.

**WORK-STUDY** *Federal work-study:* Total amount: $1,953,079; 467 jobs averaging $2552.

**ATHLETIC AWARDS** Total amount: $4,403,508 (100% non-need-based).

**APPLYING FOR FINANCIAL AID** *Required financial aid form:* FAFSA. *Financial aid deadline (priority):* 3/1. *Notification date:* Continuous beginning 3/1. Students must reply by 7/1.

**CONTACT** Mr. Bruce Blackmon, Office of Financial Aid, The University of North Carolina at Charlotte, 9201 University City Boulevard, Charlotte, NC 28223-0001, 704-687-7010. *Fax:* 704-687-1461. *E-mail:* ablackm8@uncc.edu. *Website:* http://www.uncc.edu/.

# THE UNIVERSITY OF NORTH CAROLINA AT GREENSBORO
### Greensboro, NC

| Tuition & fees (NC res): $6442 | Average undergraduate aid package: $9757 |
|---|---|

**ABOUT THE INSTITUTION** State-supported, coed. *Awards:* certificates, bachelor's, master's, and doctoral degrees. 70 undergraduate majors. *Total enrollment:* 18,647. Undergraduates: 15,173. Freshmen: 2,608. Federal methodology is used as a basis for awarding need-based institutional aid.

**UNDERGRADUATE EXPENSES for 2015–2016** *Application fee:* $55. *Tuition, state resident:* full-time $3932; part-time $491.50 per credit hour. *Tuition, nonresident:* full-time $18,794; part-time $2349.25 per credit hour. *Required fees:* full-time $2510; $93 per credit hour. Part-time tuition and fees vary according to course load. *College room and board:* $7688; *Room only:* $4586. Room and board charges vary according to board plan and housing facility.

**FRESHMAN FINANCIAL AID (Fall 2014, est.)** 1,782 applied for aid; of those 99% were deemed to have need. 97% of freshmen with need received aid; of those 22% had need fully met. *Average percent of need met:* 69% (excluding resources awarded to replace EFC). *Average financial aid package:* $9951 (excluding resources awarded to replace EFC). 1% of all full-time freshmen had no need and received non-need-based gift aid.

**UNDERGRADUATE FINANCIAL AID (Fall 2014, est.)** 9,462 applied for aid; of those 99% were deemed to have need. 97% of undergraduates with need received aid; of those 26% had need fully met. *Average percent of need met:* 70% (excluding resources awarded to replace EFC). *Average financial aid package:* $9757 (excluding resources awarded to replace EFC). 2% of all full-time undergraduates had no need and received non-need-based gift aid.

**GIFT AID (NEED-BASED)** *Total amount:* $60,086,945 (50% federal, 29% state, 21% institutional). *Receiving aid:* Freshmen: 66% (1,565); all full-time undergraduates: 60% (7,560). *Average award:* Freshmen: $8089; Undergraduates: $7619. *Scholarships, grants, and awards:* Federal Pell, FSEOG, state, private, college/university gift aid from institutional funds.

**GIFT AID (NON-NEED-BASED)** *Total amount:* $3,781,228 (12% state, 73% institutional, 15% external sources). *Receiving aid:* Freshmen: 55% (1,304). Undergraduates: 45% (5,625). *Average award:* Freshmen: $3974. Undergraduates: $3482. *Scholarships, grants, and awards by category:* Academic interests/ achievement: biological sciences, business, communication, computer science, education, English, foreign languages, general academic interests/achievements, health fields, home economics, humanities, international studies, library science, mathematics, physical sciences, premedicine, religion/biblical studies, social sciences. *Creative arts/performance:* art/fine arts, cinema/film/broadcasting, dance, music, performing arts, theater/drama. *Special achievements/activities:* community service, general special achievements/activities, junior miss, leadership, religious involvement. *Special characteristics:* adult students, children and siblings of alumni, children of faculty/staff, general special characteristics, handicapped students, international students, local/state students, out-of-state students, religious affiliation, veterans, veterans' children. *Tuition waivers:* Full or partial for employees or children of employees. *ROTC:* Army cooperative, Air Force cooperative.

**LOANS** *Student loans:* $66,327,234 (50% need-based, 50% non-need-based). 73% of past graduating class borrowed through all loan programs. *Average indebtedness per student:* $23,265. *Average need-based loan:* Freshmen: $3257. Undergraduates: $4145. *Parent loans:* $10,388,656 (100% non-need-based). *Programs:* Federal Direct (Subsidized and Unsubsidized Stafford, PLUS), Perkins, state, college/university.

**WORK-STUDY** *Federal work-study:* Total amount: $539,180; jobs available.

**ATHLETIC AWARDS** Total amount: $2,882,809 (100% non-need-based).

**APPLYING FOR FINANCIAL AID** *Required financial aid form:* FAFSA. *Financial aid deadline (priority):* 3/1. *Notification date:* Continuous beginning 3/15. Students must reply within 3 weeks of notification.

**CONTACT** Mr. Bruce Cabiness, Associate Director of Financial Aid, The University of North Carolina at Greensboro, PO Box 26170, Greensboro, NC 27402-6170, 336-334-5702. *Fax:* 336-334-3010. *E-mail:* bruce_cabiness@uncg.edu. *Website:* http://www.uncg.edu/.

# THE UNIVERSITY OF NORTH CAROLINA AT PEMBROKE
## Pembroke, NC

| Tuition & fees (NC res): $5287 | Average undergraduate aid package: $9948 |
| --- | --- |

**ABOUT THE INSTITUTION** State-supported, coed. *Awards:* bachelor's and master's degrees. 46 undergraduate majors. *Total enrollment:* 6,269. Undergraduates: 5,511. Freshmen: 1,074. Federal methodology is used as a basis for awarding need-based institutional aid.

**UNDERGRADUATE EXPENSES for 2015–2016 Application fee:** $45. *Tuition, state resident:* full-time $3211. *Tuition, nonresident:* full-time $13,162. *Required fees:* full-time $2076. Full-time tuition and fees vary according to course load and location. Part-time tuition and fees vary according to course load and location. *College room and board:* $8101; *Room only:* $5620. Room and board charges vary according to board plan, housing facility, and location.

**FRESHMAN FINANCIAL AID (Fall 2014, est.)** 1,020 applied for aid; of those 96% were deemed to have need. 87% of freshmen with need received aid; of those 6% had need fully met. *Average percent of need met:* 62% (excluding resources awarded to replace EFC). *Average financial aid package:* $9233 (excluding resources awarded to replace EFC). 1% of all full-time freshmen had no need and received non-need-based gift aid.

**UNDERGRADUATE FINANCIAL AID (Fall 2014, est.)** 3,987 applied for aid; of those 91% were deemed to have need. 98% of undergraduates with need received aid; of those 7% had need fully met. *Average percent of need met:* 66% (excluding resources awarded to replace EFC). *Average financial aid package:* $9948 (excluding resources awarded to replace EFC). 1% of all full-time undergraduates had no need and received non-need-based gift aid.

**GIFT AID (NEED-BASED) Total amount:** $22,571,616 (65% federal, 28% state, 7% institutional). *Receiving aid:* Freshmen: 68% (736); all full-time undergraduates: 68% (2,995). *Average award:* Freshmen: $6945; Undergraduates: $6907. *Scholarships, grants, and awards:* Federal Pell, FSEOG, state, private, college/university gift aid from institutional funds.

**GIFT AID (NON-NEED-BASED) Total amount:** $796,532 (2% institutional, 98% external sources). *Receiving aid:* Freshmen: 14% (150). Undergraduates: 12% (540). *Average award:* Freshmen: $932. Undergraduates: $1090. *Scholarships, grants, and awards by category:* Academic interests/achievement: 170 awards ($151,811 total): education, general academic interests/achievements. *Creative arts/performance:* 1 award ($300 total): art/fine arts, cinema/film/broadcasting. *Special characteristics:* 1 award ($500 total): children and siblings of alumni. *Tuition waivers:* Full or partial for employees or children of employees. *ROTC:* Army, Air Force.

**LOANS Student loans:** $25,087,498 (96% need-based, 4% non-need-based). 81% of past graduating class borrowed through all loan programs. *Average indebtedness per student:* $24,860. *Average need-based loan:* Freshmen: $3361. Undergraduates: $4237. *Parent loans:* $2,938,977 (72% need-based, 28% non-need-based). *Programs:* Federal Direct (Subsidized and Unsubsidized Stafford, PLUS), Perkins, college/university.

**WORK-STUDY Federal work-study:** Total amount: $210,976; 108 jobs averaging $1953. *State or other work-study/employment:* Part-time jobs available.

**ATHLETIC AWARDS** Total amount: $1,560,640 (100% need-based).

**APPLYING FOR FINANCIAL AID Required financial aid form:** FAFSA. *Financial aid deadline:* Continuous. *Notification date:* Continuous beginning 4/15.

**CONTACT** Mildred Weber, Associate Director of Financial Aid, The University of North Carolina at Pembroke, PO Box 1510, Pembroke, NC 28372, 910-521-6612 or toll-free 800-949-UNCP. *Fax:* 910-775-4159. *E-mail:* mildred.weber@uncp.edu. *Website:* http://www.uncp.edu/.

# UNIVERSITY OF NORTH CAROLINA SCHOOL OF THE ARTS
## Winston-Salem, NC

| Tuition & fees (NC res): $8363 | Average undergraduate aid package: $13,157 |
| --- | --- |

**ABOUT THE INSTITUTION** State-supported, coed. *Awards:* certificates, bachelor's, and master's degrees. 6 undergraduate majors. *Total enrollment:* 958. Undergraduates: 854. Freshmen: 219. Federal methodology is used as a basis for awarding need-based institutional aid.

**UNDERGRADUATE EXPENSES for 2015–2016 Tuition, state resident:** full-time $5870; part-time $244.75 per credit hour. *Tuition, nonresident:* full-time $21,240; part-time $889.75 per credit hour. *Required fees:* full-time $2493; $98 per credit hour. *College room and board:* $8570; *Room only:* $4178. Room and board charges vary according to board plan and housing facility.

**FRESHMAN FINANCIAL AID (Fall 2014, est.)** 189 applied for aid; of those 74% were deemed to have need. 99% of freshmen with need received aid; of those 7% had need fully met. *Average percent of need met:* 58% (excluding resources awarded to replace EFC). *Average financial aid package:* $12,273 (excluding resources awarded to replace EFC). 5% of all full-time freshmen had no need and received non-need-based gift aid.

**UNDERGRADUATE FINANCIAL AID (Fall 2014, est.)** 658 applied for aid; of those 82% were deemed to have need. 99% of undergraduates with need received aid; of those 9% had need fully met. *Average percent of need met:* 63% (excluding resources awarded to replace EFC). *Average financial aid package:* $13,157 (excluding resources awarded to replace EFC). 3% of all full-time undergraduates had no need and received non-need-based gift aid.

**GIFT AID (NEED-BASED) Total amount:** $5,057,057 (25% federal, 45% state, 26% institutional, 4% external sources). *Receiving aid:* Freshmen: 57% (122); all full-time undergraduates: 56% (475). *Average award:* Freshmen: $7421; Undergraduates: $7900. *Scholarships, grants, and awards:* Federal Pell, FSEOG, state, private, college/university gift aid from institutional funds.

**GIFT AID (NON-NEED-BASED) Total amount:** $21,150 (81% institutional, 19% external sources). *Receiving aid:* Freshmen: 35% (74). Undergraduates: 31% (264). *Average award:* Freshmen: $5225. Undergraduates: $3739. *Scholarships, grants, and awards by category:* Creative arts/performance: applied art and design, cinema/film/broadcasting, dance, music, performing arts, theater/drama. *Tuition waivers:* Full or partial for employees or children of employees.

**LOANS Student loans:** $5,039,936 (91% need-based, 9% non-need-based). 62% of past graduating class borrowed through all loan programs. *Average indebtedness per student:* $22,697. *Average need-based loan:* Freshmen: $3692. Undergraduates: $4459. *Parent loans:* $2,242,186 (65% need-based, 35% non-need-based). *Programs:* Federal Direct (Subsidized and Unsubsidized Stafford, PLUS), Perkins.

**WORK-STUDY Federal work-study:** Total amount: $200,246; jobs available.

**APPLYING FOR FINANCIAL AID Required financial aid form:** FAFSA. *Financial aid deadline (priority):* 3/1. *Notification date:* Continuous beginning 4/10. Students must reply within 2 weeks of notification.

**CONTACT** Jane C. Kamlab, Director of Financial Aid, University of North Carolina School of the Arts, 1533 South Main Street, Winston-Salem, NC 27127, 336-770-3297. *Fax:* 336-770-1489. *Website:* http://www.uncsa.edu/.

# THE UNIVERSITY OF NORTH CAROLINA WILMINGTON
## Wilmington, NC

| Tuition & fees (NC res): $6392 | Average undergraduate aid package: $10,163 |
| --- | --- |

**ABOUT THE INSTITUTION** State-supported, coed. *Awards:* certificates, bachelor's, master's, and doctoral degrees. 57 undergraduate majors. *Total enrollment:* 14,570. Undergraduates: 12,952. Freshmen: 2,159. Federal methodology is used as a basis for awarding need-based institutional aid.

**UNDERGRADUATE EXPENSES for 2015–2016 Application fee:** $75. *Tuition, state resident:* full-time $4026; part-time $154.13 per credit hour.

*Tuition, nonresident:* full-time $18,054; part-time $691.18 per credit hour. *Required fees:* full-time $2366; $75.35 per credit hour. Full-time tuition and fees vary according to course load and location. Part-time tuition and fees vary according to course load and location. *College room and board:* $9124; *Room only:* $5594. Room and board charges vary according to board plan and housing facility.

**FRESHMAN FINANCIAL AID (Fall 2013)** 1,578 applied for aid; of those 68% were deemed to have need. 96% of freshmen with need received aid; of those 11% had need fully met. *Average percent of need met:* 57% (excluding resources awarded to replace EFC). *Average financial aid package:* $9380 (excluding resources awarded to replace EFC). 1% of all full-time freshmen had no need and received non-need-based gift aid.

**UNDERGRADUATE FINANCIAL AID (Fall 2013)** 8,111 applied for aid; of those 79% were deemed to have need. 97% of undergraduates with need received aid; of those 12% had need fully met. *Average percent of need met:* 58% (excluding resources awarded to replace EFC). *Average financial aid package:* $10,163 (excluding resources awarded to replace EFC). 1% of all full-time undergraduates had no need and received non-need-based gift aid.

**GIFT AID (NEED-BASED)** *Total amount:* $42,824,419 (40% federal, 21% state, 32% institutional, 7% external sources). *Receiving aid:* Freshmen: 47% (912); all full-time undergraduates: 47% (5,382). *Average award:* Freshmen: $2490; Undergraduates: $2427. *Scholarships, grants, and awards:* Federal Pell, FSEOG, state, private, college/university gift aid from institutional funds.

**GIFT AID (NON-NEED-BASED)** *Total amount:* $1,819,432 (1% federal, 65% institutional, 34% external sources). *Receiving aid:* Freshmen: 4% (78). Undergraduates: 6% (665). *Average award:* Freshmen: $3333. Undergraduates: $3853. *Scholarships, grants, and awards by category:* Academic interests/achievement: biological sciences, business, communication, computer science, education, engineering/technologies, English, foreign languages, general academic interests/achievements, health fields, humanities, international studies, mathematics, physical sciences, premedicine, social sciences. *Creative arts/performance:* art/fine arts, cinema/film/broadcasting, creative writing, music, theater/drama. *Special achievements/activities:* cheerleading/drum major, general special achievements/activities, leadership. *Special characteristics:* local/state students, married students. *Tuition waivers:* Full or partial for employees or children of employees.

**LOANS** *Student loans:* $104,489,279 (62% need-based, 38% non-need-based). 40% of past graduating class borrowed through all loan programs. *Average indebtedness per student:* $6630. *Average need-based loan:* Freshmen: $3213. Undergraduates: $4276. *Parent loans:* $11,636,956 (100% non-need-based). *Programs:* Federal Direct (Subsidized and Unsubsidized Stafford, PLUS), Perkins.

**WORK-STUDY** *Federal work-study:* jobs available.

**ATHLETIC AWARDS** Total amount: $1,683,505 (78% need-based, 22% non-need-based).

**APPLYING FOR FINANCIAL AID** *Required financial aid form:* FAFSA. *Financial aid deadline (priority):* 3/1. *Notification date:* Continuous beginning 3/15. Students must reply within 3 weeks of notification.

**CONTACT** Dr. Ixchel Baker-Tate, Director of Financial Aid and Veterans Services, The University of North Carolina Wilmington, 601 South College Road, Wilmington, NC 28403-5951, 910-962-3177. *Fax:* 910-962-3851. *E-mail:* finaid@uncw.edu. *Website:* http://www.uncw.edu/.

# UNIVERSITY OF NORTH DAKOTA
## Grand Forks, ND

**CONTACT** Janelle Kilgore, Interim Director of Student Financial Aid, University of North Dakota, 264 Centennial Drive Stop 8371, Grand Forks, ND 58202, 701-777-3121 or toll-free 800-CALL-UND. *Fax:* 701-777-2040. *E-mail:* janelle.kilgore@und.edu. *Website:* http://www.und.edu/.

# UNIVERSITY OF NORTHERN COLORADO
## Greeley, CO

| Tuition & fees (CO res): $7733 | Average undergraduate aid package: $6601 |
| --- | --- |

**ABOUT THE INSTITUTION** State-supported, coed. *Awards:* bachelor's, master's, and doctoral degrees. 46 undergraduate majors. *Total enrollment:* 11,784. Undergraduates: 9,424. Freshmen: 1,905. Federal methodology is used as a basis for awarding need-based institutional aid.

**UNDERGRADUATE EXPENSES for 2015–2016** *Application fee:* $45. *Tuition, state resident:* full-time $6024; part-time $238.50 per credit hour. *Tuition, nonresident:* full-time $17,568; part-time $707 per credit hour. *Required fees:* full-time $1709; $78.36 per credit hour. Full-time tuition and fees vary according to location and program. Part-time tuition and fees vary according to location and program. *College room and board:* $10,360; *Room only:* $4800. Room and board charges vary according to board plan and housing facility.

**FRESHMAN FINANCIAL AID (Fall 2013)** 1,561 applied for aid; of those 89% were deemed to have need. 98% of freshmen with need received aid; of those 39% had need fully met. *Average percent of need met:* 78% (excluding resources awarded to replace EFC). *Average financial aid package:* $7114 (excluding resources awarded to replace EFC). 21% of all full-time freshmen had no need and received non-need-based gift aid.

**UNDERGRADUATE FINANCIAL AID (Fall 2013)** 6,582 applied for aid; of those 86% were deemed to have need. 98% of undergraduates with need received aid; of those 34% had need fully met. *Average percent of need met:* 75% (excluding resources awarded to replace EFC). *Average financial aid package:* $6601 (excluding resources awarded to replace EFC). 13% of all full-time undergraduates had no need and received non-need-based gift aid.

**GIFT AID (NEED-BASED)** *Total amount:* $32,630,953 (44% federal, 10% state, 33% institutional, 13% external sources). *Receiving aid:* Freshmen: 64% (1,255); all full-time undergraduates: 58% (4,580). *Average award:* Freshmen: $5175; Undergraduates: $3996. *Scholarships, grants, and awards:* Federal Pell, FSEOG, state, private, college/university gift aid from institutional funds.

**GIFT AID (NON-NEED-BASED)** *Total amount:* $5,877,382 (5% federal, 47% institutional, 48% external sources). *Receiving aid:* Freshmen: 2% (48). Undergraduates: 2% (188). *Average award:* Freshmen: $301. Undergraduates: $230. *Scholarships, grants, and awards by category:* Academic interests/achievement: biological sciences, business, communication, education, English, general academic interests/achievements, health fields, home economics, mathematics, military science, physical sciences, social sciences. *Creative arts/performance:* dance, music, performing arts, theater/drama. *Special characteristics:* adult students, children of faculty/staff, children of union members/company employees, ethnic background, general special characteristics, handicapped students, international students, out-of-state students, veterans. *Tuition waivers:* Full or partial for employees or children of employees. *ROTC:* Army, Air Force.

**LOANS** *Student loans:* $41,434,682 (84% need-based, 16% non-need-based). 47% of past graduating class borrowed through all loan programs. *Average indebtedness per student:* $25,446. *Average need-based loan:* Freshmen: $2986. Undergraduates: $3827. *Parent loans:* $16,941,689 (76% need-based, 24% non-need-based). *Programs:* Federal Direct (Subsidized and Unsubsidized Stafford, PLUS), Perkins, Federal Nursing.

**WORK-STUDY** *Federal work-study:* 185 jobs averaging $2967. *State or other work-study/employment:* Total amount: $1,363,212 (95% need-based, 5% non-need-based). 493 part-time jobs averaging $2842.

**ATHLETIC AWARDS** Total amount: $4,053,645 (44% need-based, 56% non-need-based).

**APPLYING FOR FINANCIAL AID** *Required financial aid form:* FAFSA. *Financial aid deadline (priority):* 3/1. *Notification date:* Continuous beginning 3/1. Students must reply within 4 weeks of notification.

**CONTACT** Marty Somero, Director of Financial Aid, University of Northern Colorado, Carter Hall 1005, Greeley, CO 80639, 970-351-2502 or toll-free 888-700-4UNC. *Fax:* 970-351-3737. *E-mail:* ofa@unco.edu. *Website:* http://www.unco.edu/.

# UNIVERSITY OF NORTHERN IOWA
## Cedar Falls, IA

| Tuition & fees (IA res): $7749 | Average undergraduate aid package: $7352 |
| --- | --- |

**ABOUT THE INSTITUTION** State-supported, coed. *Awards:* bachelor's, master's, and doctoral degrees. 89 undergraduate majors. *Total enrollment:* 11,928. Undergraduates: 10,142. Freshmen: 1,797. Federal methodology is used as a basis for awarding need-based institutional aid.

**UNDERGRADUATE EXPENSES for 2015–2016 Application fee:** $40. *Tuition, state resident:* full-time $6648; part-time $277 per credit hour. *Tuition, nonresident:* full-time $16,546; part-time $689 per credit hour. *Required fees:* full-time $1101. Full-time tuition and fees vary according to course load and program. Part-time tuition and fees vary according to course load and program. *College room and board:* $8046; *Room only:* $3962. Room and board charges vary according to board plan and housing facility.

**FRESHMAN FINANCIAL AID (Fall 2013)** 1,480 applied for aid; of those 71% were deemed to have need. 97% of freshmen with need received aid; of those 26% had need fully met. *Average percent of need met:* 76% (excluding resources awarded to replace EFC). *Average financial aid package:* $7548 (excluding resources awarded to replace EFC). 18% of all full-time freshmen had no need and received non-need-based gift aid.

**UNDERGRADUATE FINANCIAL AID (Fall 2013)** 7,267 applied for aid; of those 80% were deemed to have need. 96% of undergraduates with need received aid; of those 18% had need fully met. *Average percent of need met:* 73% (excluding resources awarded to replace EFC). *Average financial aid package:* $7352 (excluding resources awarded to replace EFC). 9% of all full-time undergraduates had no need and received non-need-based gift aid.

**GIFT AID (NEED-BASED) Total amount:** $24,676,966 (49% federal, 5% state, 39% institutional, 7% external sources). *Receiving aid:* Freshmen: 34% (574); all full-time undergraduates: 36% (3,316). *Average award:* Freshmen: $4510; Undergraduates: $4351. *Scholarships, grants, and awards:* Federal Pell, FSEOG, state, private, college/university gift aid from institutional funds, TEACH Grants.

**GIFT AID (NON-NEED-BASED) Total amount:** $2,814,132 (15% federal, 2% state, 67% institutional, 16% external sources). *Receiving aid:* Freshmen: 42% (702). Undergraduates: 26% (2,371). *Average award:* Freshmen: $3463. Undergraduates: $3378. *Scholarships, grants, and awards by category: Academic interests/achievement:* biological sciences, business, communication, computer science, education, general academic interests/achievements, mathematics, physical sciences, social sciences. *Creative arts/performance:* applied art and design, art/fine arts, debating, music, theater/drama. *Special achievements/activities:* leadership. *Special characteristics:* general special characteristics, members of minority groups, veterans. **ROTC:** Army.

**LOANS Student loans:** $45,050,554 (44% need-based, 56% non-need-based). 75% of past graduating class borrowed through all loan programs. *Average indebtedness per student:* $23,163. *Average need-based loan:* Freshmen: $3354. Undergraduates: $4205. *Parent loans:* $11,687,382 (100% non-need-based). *Programs:* Federal Direct (Subsidized and Unsubsidized Stafford, PLUS), Perkins, private loans.

**WORK-STUDY Federal work-study:** 418 jobs averaging $1504. *State or other work-study/employment:* Part-time jobs available.

**ATHLETIC AWARDS** Total amount: $3,380,605 (86% need-based, 14% non-need-based).

**APPLYING FOR FINANCIAL AID Required financial aid form:** FAFSA. *Financial aid deadline:* Continuous. *Notification date:* Continuous beginning 3/15.

**CONTACT** Heather Soesbe, Associate Director of Student Financial Aid, University of Northern Iowa, 105 Gilchrist Hall, Cedar Falls, IA 50614-0024, 319-273-2700 or toll-free 800-772-2037. *Fax:* 319-273-6950. *E-mail:* heather.soesbe@uni.edu. *Website:* http://www.uni.edu/.

# UNIVERSITY OF NORTH FLORIDA
## Jacksonville, FL

| Tuition & fees (FL res): $6385 | Average undergraduate aid package: $8668 |
| --- | --- |

**ABOUT THE INSTITUTION** State-supported, coed. *Awards:* certificates, associate, bachelor's, master's, and doctoral degrees (doctoral degree in education only). 54 undergraduate majors. *Total enrollment:* 15,984. Undergraduates: 14,121. Freshmen: 1,859. Federal methodology is used as a basis for awarding need-based institutional aid.

**UNDERGRADUATE EXPENSES for 2015–2016 Application fee:** $30. *Tuition, state resident:* full-time $4281; part-time $142.70 per credit hour. *Tuition, nonresident:* full-time $17,999; part-time $599.97 per credit hour. *Required fees:* full-time $2104; $70.14 per credit hour. Full-time tuition and fees vary according to course load. Part-time tuition and fees vary according to course load. *College room and board:* $9204. Room and board charges vary according to board plan and housing facility.

**FRESHMAN FINANCIAL AID (Fall 2014, est.)** 1,495 applied for aid; of those 69% were deemed to have need. 95% of freshmen with need received aid; of those 13% had need fully met. *Average percent of need met:* 91% (excluding resources awarded to replace EFC). *Average financial aid package:* $9199 (excluding resources awarded to replace EFC). 8% of all full-time freshmen had no need and received non-need-based gift aid.

**UNDERGRADUATE FINANCIAL AID (Fall 2014, est.)** 7,324 applied for aid; of those 77% were deemed to have need. 95% of undergraduates with need received aid; of those 9% had need fully met. *Average percent of need met:* 91% (excluding resources awarded to replace EFC). *Average financial aid package:* $8668 (excluding resources awarded to replace EFC). 14% of all full-time undergraduates had no need and received non-need-based gift aid.

**GIFT AID (NEED-BASED) Total amount:** $36,122,941 (58% federal, 17% state, 24% institutional, 1% external sources). *Receiving aid:* Freshmen: 40% (712); all full-time undergraduates: 40% (3,925). *Average award:* Freshmen: $7030; Undergraduates: $6060. *Scholarships, grants, and awards:* Federal Pell, FSEOG, state, private, college/university gift aid from institutional funds, 2+2 Scholarships.

**GIFT AID (NON-NEED-BASED) Total amount:** $9,762,137 (59% state, 37% institutional, 4% external sources). *Receiving aid:* Freshmen: 29% (518). Undergraduates: 25% (2,427). *Average award:* Freshmen: $3258. Undergraduates: $2970. *Scholarships, grants, and awards by category: Academic interests/achievement:* 621 awards ($1,675,874 total): business, computer science, education, engineering/technologies, general academic interests/achievements, health fields, international studies. *Creative arts/performance:* 43 awards ($83,070 total): art/fine arts, music. *Special achievements/activities:* 54 awards ($67,745 total): community service, general special achievements/activities, leadership. *Special characteristics:* 24 awards ($32,000 total): first-generation college students, general special characteristics, international students, members of minority groups, out-of-state students. *Tuition waivers:* Full or partial for employees or children of employees, senior citizens. **ROTC:** Army, Naval cooperative.

**LOANS Student loans:** $41,130,472 (66% need-based, 34% non-need-based). 49% of past graduating class borrowed through all loan programs. *Average indebtedness per student:* $19,253. *Average need-based loan:* Freshmen: $3244. Undergraduates: $4762. *Parent loans:* $2,792,919 (43% need-based, 57% non-need-based). *Programs:* Federal Direct (Subsidized and Unsubsidized Stafford, PLUS).

**WORK-STUDY Federal work-study:** Total amount: $408,079; 184 jobs averaging $2921.

**ATHLETIC AWARDS** Total amount: $682,770 (50% need-based, 50% non-need-based).

**APPLYING FOR FINANCIAL AID Required financial aid form:** FAFSA. *Financial aid deadline (priority):* 4/1. *Notification date:* Continuous beginning 3/15. Students must reply within 2 weeks of notification.

**CONTACT** Ms. Anissa Agne, Director of Financial Aid, University of North Florida, 1 UNF Drive, Jacksonville, FL 32224-7699, 904-620-2604. *E-mail:* anissa.agne@unf.edu. *Website:* http://www.unf.edu/.

# UNIVERSITY OF NORTH GEORGIA
### Dahlonega, GA

| Tuition & fees (GA res): $6816 | Average undergraduate aid package: $13,652 |
| --- | --- |

**ABOUT THE INSTITUTION** State-supported, coed. *Awards:* certificates, associate, bachelor's, master's, and doctoral degrees. 39 undergraduate majors. *Total enrollment:* 16,064. Undergraduates: 15,507. Freshmen: 3,261. Federal methodology is used as a basis for awarding need-based institutional aid.

**UNDERGRADUATE EXPENSES for 2015–2016 *Application fee:*** $30. *Tuition, state resident:* full-time $5098; part-time $193.93 per credit hour. *Tuition, nonresident:* full-time $17,994; part-time $599.80 per credit hour. *Required fees:* full-time $1718. Full-time tuition and fees vary according to course load, degree level, and location. Part-time tuition and fees vary according to course load, degree level, and location. *College room and board:* $9162; *Room only:* $5090. Room and board charges vary according to board plan and housing facility.

**FRESHMAN FINANCIAL AID (Fall 2013)** 2,672 applied for aid; of those 67% were deemed to have need. 95% of freshmen with need received aid; of those 62% had need fully met. *Average percent of need met:* 68% (excluding resources awarded to replace EFC). *Average financial aid package:* $9450 (excluding resources awarded to replace EFC). 9% of all full-time freshmen had no need and received non-need-based gift aid.

**UNDERGRADUATE FINANCIAL AID (Fall 2013)** 10,100 applied for aid; of those 65% were deemed to have need. 99% of undergraduates with need received aid; of those 56% had need fully met. *Average percent of need met:* 66% (excluding resources awarded to replace EFC). *Average financial aid package:* $13,652 (excluding resources awarded to replace EFC). 5% of all full-time undergraduates had no need and received non-need-based gift aid.

**GIFT AID (NEED-BASED) *Total amount:*** $25,783,386 (90% federal, 7% state, 2% institutional, 1% external sources). *Receiving aid:* Freshmen: 36% (1,054); all full-time undergraduates: 36% (3,830). *Average award:* Freshmen: $5945; Undergraduates: $5800. *Scholarships, grants, and awards:* Federal Pell, FSEOG, state, private, college/university gift aid from institutional funds.

**GIFT AID (NON-NEED-BASED) *Total amount:*** $20,765,879 (1% federal, 91% state, 4% institutional, 4% external sources). *Receiving aid:* Freshmen: 58% (1,690). Undergraduates: 41% (4,444). *Average award:* Freshmen: $1100. Undergraduates: $1205. *Scholarships, grants, and awards by category: Academic interests/achievement:* biological sciences, business, education, English, general academic interests/achievements, health fields, humanities, mathematics, military science, physical sciences, premedicine. *Creative arts/performance:* applied art and design, general creative arts/performance, music. *Special achievements/activities:* cheerleading/drum major, community service, general special achievements/activities, leadership. *Special characteristics:* general special characteristics. *Tuition waivers:* Full or partial for employees or children of employees, senior citizens. *ROTC:* Army.

**LOANS *Student loans:*** $46,510,770 (40% need-based, 60% non-need-based). 51% of past graduating class borrowed through all loan programs. *Average indebtedness per student:* $12,892. *Average need-based loan:* Freshmen: $3775. Undergraduates: $5245. *Parent loans:* $1,820,316 (23% need-based, 77% non-need-based). *Programs:* Federal Direct (Subsidized and Unsubsidized Stafford, PLUS), Perkins, state, college/university.

**WORK-STUDY *Federal work-study:*** jobs available. *State or other work-study/employment:* Total amount: $985,400 (100% non-need-based). Part-time jobs available.

**ATHLETIC AWARDS** Total amount: $1,336,684 (26% need-based, 74% non-need-based).

**APPLYING FOR FINANCIAL AID *Required financial aid form:*** FAFSA. *Financial aid deadline (priority):* 3/17. *Notification date:* Continuous beginning 4/1. Students must reply within 4 weeks of notification.

**CONTACT** Jill Rayner, Director of Financial Aid, University of North Georgia, 82 College Circle, Dahlonega, GA 30597-1001, 706-864-1688 or toll-free 800-498-9581. *Fax:* 706-864-1411. *E-mail:* jill.rayner@ung.edu. *Website:* http://www.ung.edu/.

# UNIVERSITY OF NORTH TEXAS
### Denton, TX

| Tuition & fees (TX res): $9706 | Average undergraduate aid package: $11,039 |
| --- | --- |

**ABOUT THE INSTITUTION** State-supported, coed. *Awards:* certificates, bachelor's, master's, and doctoral degrees. 87 undergraduate majors. *Total enrollment:* 36,166. Undergraduates: 29,724. Freshmen: 4,373. Federal methodology is used as a basis for awarding need-based institutional aid.

**UNDERGRADUATE EXPENSES for 2015–2016 *Application fee:*** $75. *Tuition, state resident:* full-time $7204; part-time $240.13 per credit hour. *Tuition, nonresident:* full-time $18,064; part-time $602.13 per credit hour. *Required fees:* full-time $2502. *College room and board:* $7760. Room and board charges vary according to board plan and housing facility. *Payment plan:* Guaranteed tuition.

**FRESHMAN FINANCIAL AID (Fall 2014, est.)** 3,497 applied for aid; of those 77% were deemed to have need. 97% of freshmen with need received aid; of those 20% had need fully met. *Average percent of need met:* 72% (excluding resources awarded to replace EFC). *Average financial aid package:* $13,107 (excluding resources awarded to replace EFC). 13% of all full-time freshmen had no need and received non-need-based gift aid.

**UNDERGRADUATE FINANCIAL AID (Fall 2014, est.)** 17,584 applied for aid; of those 83% were deemed to have need. 95% of undergraduates with need received aid; of those 14% had need fully met. *Average percent of need met:* 58% (excluding resources awarded to replace EFC). *Average financial aid package:* $11,039 (excluding resources awarded to replace EFC). 11% of all full-time undergraduates had no need and received non-need-based gift aid.

**GIFT AID (NEED-BASED) *Total amount:*** $111,727,845 (43% federal, 21% state, 26% institutional, 10% external sources). *Receiving aid:* Freshmen: 48% (1,950); all full-time undergraduates: 42% (9,923). *Average award:* Freshmen: $10,260; Undergraduates: $7619. *Scholarships, grants, and awards:* Federal Pell, FSEOG, state, private, college/university gift aid from institutional funds.

**GIFT AID (NON-NEED-BASED) *Total amount:*** $9,082,041 (42% institutional, 58% external sources). *Receiving aid:* Freshmen: 27% (1,102). Undergraduates: 16% (3,736). *Average award:* Freshmen: $5549. Undergraduates: $5289. *Tuition waivers:* Full or partial for employees or children of employees, senior citizens. *ROTC:* Army, Air Force.

**LOANS *Student loans:*** $133,755,751 (86% need-based, 14% non-need-based). *Average need-based loan:* Freshmen: $3326. Undergraduates: $4447. *Parent loans:* $83,015,807 (71% need-based, 29% non-need-based). *Programs:* Federal Direct (Subsidized and Unsubsidized Stafford, PLUS), Perkins, state.

**WORK-STUDY *Federal work-study:*** Total amount: $5,916,404; jobs available. *State or other work-study/employment:* Total amount: $851,936 (100% need-based). Part-time jobs available.

**ATHLETIC AWARDS** Total amount: $3,688,085 (54% need-based, 46% non-need-based).

**APPLYING FOR FINANCIAL AID *Required financial aid form:*** FAFSA. *Financial aid deadline (priority):* 3/15. *Notification date:* Continuous beginning 4/1.

**CONTACT** Mrs. Zelma DeLeon, Director of Student Financial Aid and Scholarships, University of North Texas, 1155 Union Circle #311370, Denton, TX 76203-5017, 940-565-2302 or toll-free 800-868-8211. *Fax:* 940-565-2738. *E-mail:* zelma.deleon@unt.edu. *Website:* http://www.unt.edu/.

# UNIVERSITY OF NORTHWESTERN OHIO
### Lima, OH

**CONTACT** Financial Aid Office, University of Northwestern Ohio, 1441 North Cable Road, Lima, OH 45805-1498, 419-227-3141. *Website:* http://www.unoh.edu/.

# UNIVERSITY OF NORTHWESTERN–ST. PAUL
## St. Paul, MN

**CONTACT** Mr. Richard L. Blatchley, Director of Financial Aid, University of Northwestern–St. Paul, 3003 Snelling Avenue North, St. Paul, MN 55113-1598, 651-631-5321 or toll-free 800-827-6827. *Fax:* 651-628-3332. *E-mail:* rlb@nwc.edu. *Website:* http://www.unwsp.edu/.

# UNIVERSITY OF NOTRE DAME
## Notre Dame, IN

| Tuition & fees: $46,237 | Average undergraduate aid package: $41,932 |
| --- | --- |

**ABOUT THE INSTITUTION** Independent Roman Catholic, coed. *Awards:* bachelor's, master's, and doctoral degrees. 57 undergraduate majors. *Total enrollment:* 12,179. Undergraduates: 8,448. Freshmen: 2,011. Both federal and institutional methodology are used as a basis for awarding need-based institutional aid.

**UNDERGRADUATE EXPENSES for 2015–2016** *Application fee:* $75. *Comprehensive fee:* $59,461 includes full-time tuition ($45,730), mandatory fees ($507), and room and board ($13,224). *Part-time tuition:* $1905 per credit hour.

**FRESHMAN FINANCIAL AID (Fall 2014, est.)** 1,346 applied for aid; of those 66% were deemed to have need. 100% of freshmen with need received aid; of those 99% had need fully met. *Average percent of need met:* 100% (excluding resources awarded to replace EFC). *Average financial aid package:* $42,499 (excluding resources awarded to replace EFC). 5% of all full-time freshmen had no need and received non-need-based gift aid.

**UNDERGRADUATE FINANCIAL AID (Fall 2014, est.)** 4,945 applied for aid; of those 77% were deemed to have need. 100% of undergraduates with need received aid; of those 99% had need fully met. *Average percent of need met:* 100% (excluding resources awarded to replace EFC). *Average financial aid package:* $41,932 (excluding resources awarded to replace EFC). 7% of all full-time undergraduates had no need and received non-need-based gift aid.

**GIFT AID (NEED-BASED)** *Total amount:* $119,447,329 (5% federal, 93% institutional, 2% external sources). *Receiving aid:* Freshmen: 41% (820); all full-time undergraduates: 43% (3,613). *Average award:* Freshmen: $35,998; Undergraduates: $33,025. *Scholarships, grants, and awards:* Federal Pell, FSEOG, state, private, college/university gift aid from institutional funds.

**GIFT AID (NON-NEED-BASED)** *Total amount:* $27,516,198 (22% federal, 60% institutional, 18% external sources). *Receiving aid:* Freshmen: 22% (436). Undergraduates: 22% (1,828). *Average award:* Freshmen: $21,979. Undergraduates: $15,804. *Scholarships, grants, and awards by category:* Special characteristics: children of faculty/staff. *Tuition waivers:* Full or partial for employees or children of employees. *ROTC:* Army, Naval, Air Force.

**LOANS** *Student loans:* $33,768,551 (50% need-based, 50% non-need-based). 50% of past graduating class borrowed through all loan programs. *Average indebtedness per student:* $26,674. *Average need-based loan:* Freshmen: $3622. Undergraduates: $5496. *Parent loans:* $10,928,698 (100% non-need-based). *Programs:* Federal Direct (Subsidized and Unsubsidized Stafford, PLUS), Perkins, college/university, private loans.

**WORK-STUDY** *Federal work-study:* Total amount: $4,000,939; 1,681 jobs averaging $2526. *State or other work-study/employment:* Total amount: $9,948,314 (8% need-based, 92% non-need-based). 3,073 part-time jobs averaging $3237.

**ATHLETIC AWARDS** Total amount: $19,254,805 (4% need-based, 96% non-need-based).

**APPLYING FOR FINANCIAL AID** *Required financial aid forms:* FAFSA, CSS Financial Aid PROFILE, noncustodial (divorced/separated) parent's statement, business/farm supplement, federal income tax form(s), W-2 forms. *Financial aid deadline (priority):* 2/15. *Notification date:* Continuous beginning 3/28. Students must reply by 5/1.

**CONTACT** Dr. Thomas Bear, Executive Director of Student Financial Services, University of Notre Dame, 115 Main Building, Notre Dame, IN 46556, 574-631-6436. *Fax:* 574-631-6899. *E-mail:* finaid.1@nd.edu. *Website:* http://www.nd.edu/.

# UNIVERSITY OF OKLAHOMA
## Norman, OK

| Tuition & fees (OK res): $7695 | Average undergraduate aid package: $12,210 |
| --- | --- |

**ABOUT THE INSTITUTION** State-supported, coed. *Awards:* certificates, bachelor's, master's, and doctoral degrees. 99 undergraduate majors. *Total enrollment:* 27,261. Undergraduates: 21,011. Freshmen: 4,176. Federal methodology is used as a basis for awarding need-based institutional aid.

**UNDERGRADUATE EXPENSES for 2015–2016** *Application fee:* $40. *Tuition, state resident:* full-time $4128; part-time $137.60 per credit hour. *Tuition, nonresident:* full-time $16,902; part-time $563.40 per credit hour. *Required fees:* full-time $3567; $110.45 per credit hour or $126.50 per term. Full-time tuition and fees vary according to course load, location, program, and reciprocity agreements. Part-time tuition and fees vary according to course load, location, program, and reciprocity agreements. *College room and board:* $9126; *Room only:* $5022. Room and board charges vary according to board plan and housing facility. *Payment plan:* Guaranteed tuition.

**FRESHMAN FINANCIAL AID (Fall 2013)** 2,740 applied for aid; of those 67% were deemed to have need. 95% of freshmen with need received aid; of those 82% had need fully met. *Average percent of need met:* 83% (excluding resources awarded to replace EFC). *Average financial aid package:* $11,633 (excluding resources awarded to replace EFC). 13% of all full-time freshmen had no need and received non-need-based gift aid.

**UNDERGRADUATE FINANCIAL AID (Fall 2013)** 10,801 applied for aid; of those 77% were deemed to have need. 97% of undergraduates with need received aid; of those 86% had need fully met. *Average percent of need met:* 86% (excluding resources awarded to replace EFC). *Average financial aid package:* $12,210 (excluding resources awarded to replace EFC). 11% of all full-time undergraduates had no need and received non-need-based gift aid.

**GIFT AID (NEED-BASED)** *Total amount:* $46,116,317 (45% federal, 27% state, 14% institutional, 14% external sources). *Receiving aid:* Freshmen: 26% (978); all full-time undergraduates: 30% (5,144). *Average award:* Freshmen: $6614; Undergraduates: $5995. *Scholarships, grants, and awards:* Federal Pell, FSEOG, state, private, college/university gift aid from institutional funds, United Negro College Fund.

**GIFT AID (NON-NEED-BASED)** *Total amount:* $10,168,962 (35% state, 33% institutional, 32% external sources). *Receiving aid:* Freshmen: 36% (1,340). Undergraduates: 29% (5,031). *Average award:* Freshmen: $2023. Undergraduates: $2108. *Scholarships, grants, and awards by category:* Academic interests/achievement: 5,461 awards ($26,430,102 total): architecture, area/ethnic studies, biological sciences, business, communication, computer science, education, engineering/technologies, English, foreign languages, general academic interests/achievements, humanities, international studies, mathematics, military science, physical sciences, social sciences. *Creative arts/performance:* 320 awards ($1,194,764 total): art/fine arts, cinema/film/broadcasting, dance, debating, journalism/publications, music, performing arts, theater/drama. *Special achievements/activities:* 212 awards ($217,177 total): leadership. *Special characteristics:* 424 awards ($410,692 total): children and siblings of alumni, members of minority groups, previous college experience, public servants. *Tuition waivers:* Full or partial for employees or children of employees, senior citizens. *ROTC:* Army, Naval, Air Force.

**LOANS** *Student loans:* $62,580,478 (84% need-based, 16% non-need-based). 49% of past graduating class borrowed through all loan programs. *Average indebtedness per student:* $23,151. *Average need-based loan:* Freshmen: $3610. Undergraduates: $4286. *Parent loans:* $16,310,244 (73% need-based, 27% non-need-based). *Programs:* Federal Direct (Subsidized and Unsubsidized Stafford, PLUS), Perkins, college/university, alternative loans.

**WORK-STUDY** *Federal work-study:* 520 jobs averaging $2598. *State or other work-study/employment:* Total amount: $976,374 (58% need-based, 42% non-need-based). 129 part-time jobs averaging $8535.

**ATHLETIC AWARDS** Total amount: $9,963,108 (48% need-based, 52% non-need-based).

**APPLYING FOR FINANCIAL AID** *Required financial aid form:* FAFSA. *Financial aid deadline:* Continuous. *Notification date:* Continuous beginning 3/15. Students must reply within 6 weeks of notification.

**CONTACT** Office of Financial Aid, University of Oklahoma, 1000 Asp Avenue, Room 216, Norman, OK 73019-4078, 405-325-4521 or toll-free 800-234-6868. *Fax:* 405-325-0819. *E-mail:* financialaid@ou.edu. *Website:* http://www.ou.edu/.

# UNIVERSITY OF OREGON
## Eugene, OR

| Tuition & fees (OR res): $9918 | Average undergraduate aid package: $10,046 |
|---|---|

**ABOUT THE INSTITUTION** State-supported, coed. **Awards:** certificates, bachelor's, master's, and doctoral degrees. 77 undergraduate majors. **Total enrollment:** 24,096. Undergraduates: 20,559. Freshmen: 3,961. Federal methodology is used as a basis for awarding need-based institutional aid.

**UNDERGRADUATE EXPENSES for 2015–2016 Application fee:** $50. **One-time required fee:** $375. **Tuition, state resident:** full-time $8190; part-time $182 per credit hour. **Tuition, nonresident:** full-time $29,160; part-time $648 per credit hour. **Required fees:** full-time $1728. Full-time tuition and fees vary according to course load. Part-time tuition and fees vary according to course load. **College room and board:** $11,442. Room and board charges vary according to board plan and housing facility.

**FRESHMAN FINANCIAL AID (Fall 2013)** 2,893 applied for aid; of those 68% were deemed to have need. 92% of freshmen with need received aid; of those 12% had need fully met. **Average percent of need met:** 60% (excluding resources awarded to replace EFC). **Average financial aid package:** $10,187 (excluding resources awarded to replace EFC). 14% of all full-time freshmen had no need and received non-need-based gift aid.

**UNDERGRADUATE FINANCIAL AID (Fall 2013)** 11,336 applied for aid; of those 77% were deemed to have need. 95% of undergraduates with need received aid; of those 8% had need fully met. **Average percent of need met:** 60% (excluding resources awarded to replace EFC). **Average financial aid package:** $10,046 (excluding resources awarded to replace EFC). 14% of all full-time undergraduates had no need and received non-need-based gift aid.

**GIFT AID (NEED-BASED) Total amount:** $50,265,281 (48% federal, 10% state, 31% institutional, 11% external sources). **Receiving aid:** Freshmen: 36% (1,393); all full-time undergraduates: 33% (6,285). **Average award:** Freshmen: $8501; Undergraduates: $7493. **Scholarships, grants, and awards:** Federal Pell, FSEOG, state, private, college/university gift aid from institutional funds.

**GIFT AID (NON-NEED-BASED) Total amount:** $12,483,835 (100% institutional). **Receiving aid:** Freshmen: 4% (148). Undergraduates: 1% (231). **Average award:** Freshmen: $6023. Undergraduates: $4014. **Scholarships, grants, and awards by category:** Academic interests/achievement: 6,888 awards ($21,190,458 total): architecture, biological sciences, business, education, English, foreign languages, general academic interests/achievements, health fields, humanities, international studies, mathematics, military science, physical sciences, premedicine, social sciences. Creative arts/performance: 244 awards ($546,749 total): applied art and design, art/fine arts, creative writing, dance, debating, journalism/publications, music, performing arts, theater/drama. Special characteristics: 381 awards ($1,876,016 total): children of faculty/staff, general special characteristics, international students, local/state students, veterans, veterans' children. **Tuition waivers:** Full or partial for employees or children of employees. **ROTC:** Army, Air Force cooperative.

**LOANS Student loans:** $69,486,382 (68% need-based, 32% non-need-based). 50% of past graduating class borrowed through all loan programs. Average indebtedness per student: $24,508. **Average need-based loan:** Freshmen: $4015. Undergraduates: $4744. **Parent loans:** $53,875,600 (39% need-based, 61% non-need-based). **Programs:** Federal Direct (Subsidized and Unsubsidized Stafford, PLUS), Perkins, college/university.

**WORK-STUDY Federal work-study:** 1,314 jobs averaging $1474. **State or other work-study/employment:** Total amount: $135,783 (100% non-need-based). 57 part-time jobs averaging $2294.

**ATHLETIC AWARDS** Total amount: $9,465,807 (22% need-based, 78% non-need-based).

**APPLYING FOR FINANCIAL AID Required financial aid form:** FAFSA. **Financial aid deadline (priority):** 3/1. **Notification date:** Continuous beginning 4/1. Students must reply within 4 weeks of notification.

**CONTACT** Jim Brooks, Director of Financial Aid and Scholarships, University of Oregon, Eugene, OR 97403, 800-760-6953 or toll-free 800-232-3825. Fax: 541-346-1175. E-mail: financialaid@uoregon.edu.
Website: http://www.uoregon.edu/.

# UNIVERSITY OF PENNSYLVANIA
## Philadelphia, PA

| Tuition & fees: $47,668 | Average undergraduate aid package: $42,419 |
|---|---|

**ABOUT THE INSTITUTION** Independent, coed. **Awards:** certificates, associate, bachelor's, master's, and doctoral degrees (also offers evening program with significant enrollment not reflected in profile). 96 undergraduate majors. **Total enrollment:** 21,296. Undergraduates: 9,746. Freshmen: 2,350. Both federal and institutional methodology are used as a basis for awarding need-based institutional aid.

**UNDERGRADUATE EXPENSES for 2015–2016 Application fee:** $75. **Comprehensive fee:** $61,132 includes full-time tuition ($42,176), mandatory fees ($5492), and room and board ($13,464). **College room only:** $8688. Room and board charges vary according to board plan and housing facility. **Part-time tuition:** $1346 per credit hour. Part-time tuition and fees vary according to course load. **Payment plan:** Tuition prepayment.

**FRESHMAN FINANCIAL AID (Fall 2013)** 1,356 applied for aid; of those 83% were deemed to have need. 100% of freshmen with need received aid; of those 100% had need fully met. **Average percent of need met:** 100% (excluding resources awarded to replace EFC). **Average financial aid package:** $43,166 (excluding resources awarded to replace EFC).

**UNDERGRADUATE FINANCIAL AID (Fall 2013)** 4,904 applied for aid; of those 92% were deemed to have need. 100% of undergraduates with need received aid; of those 100% had need fully met. **Average percent of need met:** 100% (excluding resources awarded to replace EFC). **Average financial aid package:** $42,419 (excluding resources awarded to replace EFC).

**GIFT AID (NEED-BASED) Total amount:** $183,265,778 (6% federal, 1% state, 91% institutional, 2% external sources). **Receiving aid:** Freshmen: 47% (1,115); all full-time undergraduates: 47% (4,445). **Average award:** Freshmen: $41,149; Undergraduates: $40,044. **Scholarships, grants, and awards:** Federal Pell, FSEOG, state, private, college/university gift aid from institutional funds.

**GIFT AID (NON-NEED-BASED) Total amount:** $6,719,258 (4% federal, 96% external sources). **Tuition waivers:** Full or partial for employees or children of employees. **ROTC:** Army cooperative, Naval, Air Force cooperative.

**LOANS Student loans:** $18,966,510 (7% need-based, 93% non-need-based). 36% of past graduating class borrowed through all loan programs. Average indebtedness per student: $19,442. **Average need-based loan:** Freshmen: $82. Undergraduates: $355. **Parent loans:** $10,413,379 (100% non-need-based). **Programs:** Federal Direct (Subsidized and Unsubsidized Stafford, PLUS), Perkins, Federal Nursing, college/university, supplemental third-party loans (guaranteed by institution).

**WORK-STUDY Federal work-study:** 3,897 jobs averaging $2988. **State or other work-study/employment:** Total amount: $3,313,868 (100% need-based). 1,454 part-time jobs averaging $2234.

**APPLYING FOR FINANCIAL AID Required financial aid forms:** FAFSA, institution's own form, CSS Financial Aid PROFILE, noncustodial (divorced/separated) parent's statement, business/farm supplement, federal income tax form(s). **Financial aid deadline (priority):** 2/15. **Notification date:** 4/1. Students must reply by 5/1.

**CONTACT** Mr. Joel Carstens, Director of Financial Aid, University of Pennsylvania, 3451 Walnut Streeet, 100 Franklin Building, Philadelphia, PA 19104-6270, 215-898-1988. Fax: 215-573-2208. E-mail: carstens@sfs.upenn.edu.
Website: http://www.upenn.edu/.

# UNIVERSITY OF PHOENIX–ATLANTA CAMPUS
## Sandy Springs, GA

**CONTACT** ACS/AFS, University of Phoenix–Atlanta Campus, 875 West Elliot Road, Tempe, AZ 85284, 480-735-3000 or toll-free 866-766-0766. Fax: 480-940-2060.
Website: http://www.phoenix.edu/.

# UNIVERSITY OF PHOENIX–BAY AREA CAMPUS
### San Jose, CA

**CONTACT** ACS/AFS, University of Phoenix–Bay Area Campus, 875 West Elliot Road, Tempe, AZ 85284, 480-735-3000 or toll-free 866-766-0766. *Fax:* 480-940-2060. *Website:* http://www.phoenix.edu/.

# UNIVERSITY OF PHOENIX–BIRMINGHAM CAMPUS
### Birmingham, AL

**CONTACT** Financial Aid Office, University of Phoenix–Birmingham Campus, 100 Corporate Parkway, Suite 250, Birmingham, AL 35242 or toll-free 866-766-0766. *Website:* http://www.phoenix.edu/.

# UNIVERSITY OF PHOENIX–BOSTON CAMPUS
### Braintree, MA

**CONTACT** ACS/AFS, University of Phoenix–Boston Campus, 875 West Elliot Road, Tempe, AZ 85284, 480-735-3000 or toll-free 866-766-0766. *Fax:* 480-940-2060. *Website:* http://www.phoenix.edu/.

# UNIVERSITY OF PHOENIX–CENTRAL FLORIDA CAMPUS
### Orlando, FL

**CONTACT** ACS/AFS, University of Phoenix–Central Florida Campus, 875 West Elliot Road, Tempe, AZ 85284, 480-735-3000 or toll-free 866-766-0766. *Fax:* 480-940-2060. *Website:* http://www.phoenix.edu/.

# UNIVERSITY OF PHOENIX–CENTRAL VALLEY CAMPUS
### Fresno, CA

**CONTACT** ACS/AFS, University of Phoenix–Central Valley Campus, 875 West Elliot Road, Tempe, AZ 85284, 480-735-3000 or toll-free 866-766-0766. *Fax:* 480-940-2060. *Website:* http://www.phoenix.edu/.

# UNIVERSITY OF PHOENIX–CHARLOTTE CAMPUS
### Charlotte, NC

**CONTACT** ACS/AFS, University of Phoenix–Charlotte Campus, 875 West Elliot Road, Tempe, AZ 85284, 480-735-3000 or toll-free 866-766-0766. *Fax:* 480-940-2060. *Website:* http://www.phoenix.edu/.

# UNIVERSITY OF PHOENIX–CHICAGO CAMPUS
### Schaumburg, IL

**CONTACT** Office of Financial Aid, University of Phoenix–Chicago Campus, 1500 McConner Parkway, Suite 700, Schaumburg, IL 60173-4399, 866-766-0766. *Website:* http://www.phoenix.edu/.

# UNIVERSITY OF PHOENIX–CLEVELAND CAMPUS
### Beachwood, OH

**CONTACT** ACS/AFS, University of Phoenix–Cleveland Campus, 875 West Elliot Road, Tempe, AZ 85284, 480-735-3000 or toll-free 866-766-0766. *Fax:* 480-940-2060. *Website:* http://www.phoenix.edu/.

# UNIVERSITY OF PHOENIX–COLORADO CAMPUS
### Lone Tree, CO

**CONTACT** ACS/AFS, University of Phoenix–Colorado Campus, 875 West Elliot Road, Tempe, AZ 85284, 480-735-3000 or toll-free 866-766-0766. *Fax:* 480-940-2060. *Website:* http://www.phoenix.edu/.

# UNIVERSITY OF PHOENIX–COLORADO SPRINGS DOWNTOWN CAMPUS
### Colorado Springs, CO

**CONTACT** ACS/AFS, University of Phoenix–Colorado Springs Downtown Campus, 875 West Elliot Road, Tempe, AZ 85284, 480-735-3000 or toll-free 866-766-0766. *Fax:* 480-940-2060. *Website:* http://www.phoenix.edu/.

# UNIVERSITY OF PHOENIX–COLUMBIA CAMPUS
### Columbia, SC

**CONTACT** Financial Aid Office, University of Phoenix–Columbia Campus, 1001 Pinnacle Point Drive, Suite 200, Columbia, SC 29223, 803-699-5096 or toll-free 866-766-0766. *Website:* http://www.phoenix.edu/.

# UNIVERSITY OF PHOENIX–COLUMBUS GEORGIA CAMPUS
### Columbus, GA

**CONTACT** ACS/AFS, University of Phoenix–Columbus Georgia Campus, 875 West Elliot Road, Tempe, AZ 85284, 480-735-3000 or toll-free 866-766-0766. *Fax:* 480-940-2060. *Website:* http://www.phoenix.edu/.

## UNIVERSITY OF PHOENIX–DALLAS CAMPUS
### Dallas, TX

**CONTACT** ACS/AFS, University of Phoenix–Dallas Campus, 875 West Elliot Road, Tempe, AZ 85284, 480-735-3000 or toll-free 866-766-0766. *Fax:* 480-940-2060. *Website:* http://www.phoenix.edu/.

## UNIVERSITY OF PHOENIX–DETROIT CAMPUS
### Southfield, MI

**CONTACT** ACS/AFS, University of Phoenix–Detroit Campus, 875 West Elliot Road, Tempe, AZ 85284, 480-735-3000 or toll-free 866-766-0766. *Fax:* 480-940-2060. *Website:* http://www.phoenix.edu/.

## UNIVERSITY OF PHOENIX–HAWAII CAMPUS
### Honolulu, HI

**CONTACT** ACS/AFS, University of Phoenix–Hawaii Campus, 875 West Elliot Road, Tempe, AZ 85284, 480-735-3000 or toll-free 866-766-0766. *Fax:* 480-940-2060. *Website:* http://www.phoenix.edu/.

## UNIVERSITY OF PHOENIX–HOUSTON CAMPUS
### Houston, TX

**CONTACT** ACS/AFS, University of Phoenix–Houston Campus, 875 West Elliot Road, Tempe, AZ 85284, 480-735-3000 or toll-free 866-766-0766. *Fax:* 480-940-2060. *Website:* http://www.phoenix.edu/.

## UNIVERSITY OF PHOENIX–IDAHO CAMPUS
### Meridian, ID

**CONTACT** ACS/AFS, University of Phoenix–Idaho Campus, 875 West Elliot Road, Tempe, AZ 85284, 480-735-3000 or toll-free 866-766-0766. *Fax:* 480-940-2060. *Website:* http://www.phoenix.edu/.

## UNIVERSITY OF PHOENIX–INDIANAPOLIS CAMPUS
### Indianapolis, IN

**CONTACT** ACS/AFS, University of Phoenix–Indianapolis Campus, 875 West Elliot Road, Tempe, AZ 85284, 480-735-3000 or toll-free 866-766-0766. *Fax:* 480-940-2060. *Website:* http://www.phoenix.edu/.

## UNIVERSITY OF PHOENIX–JACKSON CAMPUS
### Flowood, MS

**CONTACT** Financial Aid Office, University of Phoenix–Jackson Campus, 120 Stone Creek Boulevard, Suite 200, Flowood, MS 39232, 601-664-9500 or toll-free 866-766-0766. *Website:* http://www.phoenix.edu/.

## UNIVERSITY OF PHOENIX–KANSAS CITY CAMPUS
### Kansas City, MO

**CONTACT** ACS/AFS, University of Phoenix–Kansas City Campus, 875 West Elliot Road, Tempe, AZ 85284, 480-735-3000 or toll-free 866-766-0766. *Fax:* 480-940-2060. *Website:* http://www.phoenix.edu/.

## UNIVERSITY OF PHOENIX–LAS VEGAS CAMPUS
### Las Vegas, NV

**CONTACT** ACS/AFS, University of Phoenix–Las Vegas Campus, 875 West Elliot Road, Tempe, AZ 85284, 480-735-3000 or toll-free 866-766-0766. *Fax:* 480-940-2060. *Website:* http://www.phoenix.edu/.

## UNIVERSITY OF PHOENIX–LITTLE ROCK CAMPUS
### Little Rock, AR

**CONTACT** ACS/AFS, University of Phoenix–Little Rock Campus, 875 West Elliot Road, Tempe, AZ 85284, 480-735-3000 or toll-free 866-766-0766. *Fax:* 480-940-2060. *Website:* http://www.phoenix.edu/.

## UNIVERSITY OF PHOENIX–MARYLAND CAMPUS
### Columbia, MD

**CONTACT** Office of Financial Aid, University of Phoenix–Maryland Campus, 8830 Stanford Boulevard, Suite 100, Columbia, MD 21045-5424, 866-766-0766. *Website:* http://www.phoenix.edu/.

## UNIVERSITY OF PHOENIX–MILWAUKEE CAMPUS
### Milwaukee, WI

**CONTACT** Financial Aid Office, University of Phoenix–Milwaukee Campus, 10850 West Park Place, Milwaukee, WI 53224, 262-785-0608 or toll-free 866-766-0766. *Website:* http://www.phoenix.edu/.

## UNIVERSITY OF PHOENIX–NASHVILLE CAMPUS
### Nashville, TN

**CONTACT** ACS/AFS, University of Phoenix–Nashville Campus, 875 West Elliot Road, Tempe, AZ 85284, 480-735-3000 or toll-free 866-766-0766. *Fax:* 480-940-2060. *Website:* http://www.phoenix.edu/.

## UNIVERSITY OF PHOENIX–NEW MEXICO CAMPUS
### Albuquerque, NM

**CONTACT** ACS/AFS, University of Phoenix–New Mexico Campus, 875 West Elliot Road, Tempe, AZ 85284, 480-735-3000 or toll-free 866-766-0766. *Fax:* 480-940-2060. *Website:* http://www.phoenix.edu/.

## UNIVERSITY OF PHOENIX–NORTH FLORIDA CAMPUS
### Jacksonville, FL

**CONTACT** ACS/AFS, University of Phoenix–North Florida Campus, 875 West Elliot Road, Tempe, AZ 85284, 480-735-3000 or toll-free 866-766-0766. *Fax:* 480-940-2060. *Website:* http://www.phoenix.edu/.

## UNIVERSITY OF PHOENIX–OKLAHOMA CITY CAMPUS
### Oklahoma City, OK

**CONTACT** ACS/AFS, University of Phoenix–Oklahoma City Campus, 875 West Elliot Road, Tempe, AZ 85284, 480-735-3000 or toll-free 866-766-0766. *Fax:* 480-940-2060. *Website:* http://www.phoenix.edu/.

## UNIVERSITY OF PHOENIX–ONLINE CAMPUS
### Phoenix, AZ

**CONTACT** Office of Financial Aid, University of Phoenix–Online Campus, 3157 East Elwood Street, Phoenix, AZ 85034-7209, 866-766-0766. *Website:* http://www.uopxonline.com/.

## UNIVERSITY OF PHOENIX–OREGON CAMPUS
### Tigard, OR

**CONTACT** ACS/AFS, University of Phoenix–Oregon Campus, 875 West Elliot Road, Tempe, AZ 85284, 480-735-3000 or toll-free 866-766-0766. *Fax:* 480-940-2060. *Website:* http://www.phoenix.edu/.

## UNIVERSITY OF PHOENIX–PHILADELPHIA CAMPUS
### Wayne, PA

**CONTACT** ACS/AFS, University of Phoenix–Philadelphia Campus, 875 West Elliot Road, Tempe, AZ 85284, 480-735-3000 or toll-free 866-766-0766. *Fax:* 480-940-2060. *Website:* http://www.phoenix.edu/.

## UNIVERSITY OF PHOENIX–PHOENIX CAMPUS
### Tempe, AZ

**CONTACT** Office of Financial Aid, University of Phoenix–Phoenix Campus, 1625 West Fountainhead Parkway, Tempe, AZ 85282-2371, 866-766-0766. *Website:* http://www.phoenix.edu/.

## UNIVERSITY OF PHOENIX–PUERTO RICO CAMPUS
### Guaynabo, PR

**CONTACT** ACS/AFS, University of Phoenix–Puerto Rico Campus, 875 West Elliot Road, Tempe, AZ 85284, 480-735-3000 or toll-free 866-766-0766. *Fax:* 480-940-2060. *Website:* http://www.phoenix.edu/.

## UNIVERSITY OF PHOENIX–RICHMOND-VIRGINIA BEACH CAMPUS
### Glen Allen, VA

**CONTACT** ACS/AFS, University of Phoenix–Richmond-Virginia Beach Campus, 875 West Elliot Road, Tempe, AZ 85284, 480-735-3000 or toll-free 866-766-0766. *Fax:* 480-940-2060. *Website:* http://www.phoenix.edu/.

## UNIVERSITY OF PHOENIX–SACRAMENTO VALLEY CAMPUS
### Sacramento, CA

**CONTACT** ACS/AFS, University of Phoenix–Sacramento Valley Campus, 875 West Elliot Road, Tempe, AZ 85284, 480-735-3000 or toll-free 866-766-0766. *Fax:* 480-940-2060. *Website:* http://www.phoenix.edu/.

## UNIVERSITY OF PHOENIX–ST. LOUIS CAMPUS
### St. Louis, MO

**CONTACT** ACS/AFS, University of Phoenix–St. Louis Campus, 875 West Elliot Road, Tempe, AZ 85284, 480-735-3000 or toll-free 866-766-0766. *Fax:* 480-940-2060. *Website:* http://www.phoenix.edu/.

## UNIVERSITY OF PHOENIX–SAN DIEGO CAMPUS
### San Diego, CA

**CONTACT** ACS/AFS, University of Phoenix–San Diego Campus, 875 West Elliot Road, Tempe, AZ 85284, 480-735-3000 or toll-free 866-766-0766. *Fax:* 480-940-2060. *Website:* http://www.phoenix.edu/.

## UNIVERSITY OF PHOENIX–SOUTHERN ARIZONA CAMPUS
### Tucson, AZ

**CONTACT** ACS/AFS, University of Phoenix–Southern Arizona Campus, 875 West Elliot Road, Tempe, AZ 85284, 480-735-3000 or toll-free 866-766-0766. *Fax:* 480-940-2060. *Website:* http://www.phoenix.edu/.

## UNIVERSITY OF PHOENIX–SOUTHERN CALIFORNIA CAMPUS
### Costa Mesa, CA

**CONTACT** Office of Financial Aid, University of Phoenix–Southern California Campus, 3090 Bristol Street, Costa Mesa, CA 92626, 866-766-0766. *Website:* http://www.phoenix.edu/.

## UNIVERSITY OF PHOENIX–SOUTH FLORIDA CAMPUS
### Miramar, FL

**CONTACT** ACS/AFS, University of Phoenix–South Florida Campus, 875 West Elliot Road, Tempe, AZ 85284, 480-735-3000 or toll-free 866-766-0766. *Fax:* 480-940-2060. *Website:* http://www.phoenix.edu/.

## UNIVERSITY OF PHOENIX–UTAH CAMPUS
### Salt Lake City, UT

**CONTACT** ACS/AFS, University of Phoenix–Utah Campus, 875 West Elliot Road, Tempe, AZ 85284, 480-735-3000 or toll-free 866-766-0766. *Fax:* 480-940-2060. *Website:* http://www.phoenix.edu/.

## UNIVERSITY OF PHOENIX–WASHINGTON D.C. CAMPUS
### Washington, DC

**CONTACT** Financial Aid Office, University of Phoenix–Washington D.C. Campus, 25 Massachusetts Avenue NW, Suite 150, Washington, DC 20001 or toll-free 866-766-0766. *Website:* http://www.phoenix.edu/.

## UNIVERSITY OF PHOENIX–WESTERN WASHINGTON CAMPUS
### Tukwila, WA

**CONTACT** ACS/AFS, University of Phoenix–Western Washington Campus, 875 West Elliot Road, Tempe, AZ 85284, 480-735-3000 or toll-free 866-766-0766. *Fax:* 480-940-2060. *Website:* http://www.phoenix.edu/.

## UNIVERSITY OF PIKEVILLE
### Pikeville, KY

| Tuition & fees: $18,840 | Average undergraduate aid package: $20,661 |
|---|---|

**ABOUT THE INSTITUTION** Independent Presbyterian Church (U.S.A.), coed. *Awards:* associate, bachelor's, master's, and doctoral degrees. 21 undergraduate majors. *Total enrollment:* 2,457. Undergraduates: 1,929. Freshmen: 352. Federal methodology is used as a basis for awarding need-based institutional aid.

**UNDERGRADUATE EXPENSES** for 2015–2016 *Comprehensive fee:* $26,050 includes full-time tuition ($18,840) and room and board ($7210). Full-time tuition and fees vary according to course load. Room and board charges vary according to housing facility. *Part-time tuition:* $785 per semester hour. Part-time tuition and fees vary according to course load.

**FRESHMAN FINANCIAL AID (Fall 2014, est.)** 349 applied for aid; of those 100% were deemed to have need. 100% of freshmen with need received aid; of those 36% had need fully met. *Average percent of need met:* 83% (excluding resources awarded to replace EFC). *Average financial aid package:* $20,993 (excluding resources awarded to replace EFC).

**UNDERGRADUATE FINANCIAL AID (Fall 2014, est.)** 1,283 applied for aid; of those 100% were deemed to have need. 100% of undergraduates with need received aid; of those 42% had need fully met. *Average percent of need met:* 84% (excluding resources awarded to replace EFC). *Average financial aid package:* $20,661 (excluding resources awarded to replace EFC).

**GIFT AID (NEED-BASED)** *Total amount:* $19,501,528 (22% federal, 27% state, 49% institutional, 2% external sources). *Receiving aid:* Freshmen: 99% (349); all full-time undergraduates: 99% (1,280). *Average award:* Freshmen: $18,038; Undergraduates: $17,286. *Scholarships, grants, and awards:* Federal Pell, FSEOG, state, private, college/university gift aid from institutional funds.

**GIFT AID (NON-NEED-BASED)** *Receiving aid:* Freshmen: 53% (185). Undergraduates: 46% (599). *Tuition waivers:* Full or partial for employees or children of employees, senior citizens. *ROTC:* Army.

**LOANS** *Student loans:* $9,252,879 (100% need-based). 70% of past graduating class borrowed through all loan programs. *Average indebtedness per student:* $20,087. *Average need-based loan:* Freshmen: $3415. Undergraduates: $4104. *Parent loans:* $251,300 (100% need-based). *Programs:* Federal Direct (Subsidized and Unsubsidized Stafford, PLUS), Perkins, college/university.

**WORK-STUDY** *Federal work-study:* Total amount: $341,975; 176 jobs averaging $1943.

**ATHLETIC AWARDS** Total amount: $2,650,235 (100% need-based).

**APPLYING FOR FINANCIAL AID** *Required financial aid form:* FAFSA. *Financial aid deadline (priority):* 2/1. *Notification date:* Continuous. Students must reply by 5/1.

**CONTACT** Mrs. Judy Vance Bradley, Assistant Dean of Student Financial Services, University of Pikeville, 147 Sycamore Street, Pikeville, KY 41501, 606-218-5254 or toll-free 866-232-7700. *Fax:* 606-218-5255. *E-mail:* judybradley@upike.edu. *Website:* http://www.upike.edu/.

# UNIVERSITY OF PITTSBURGH
## Pittsburgh, PA

| Tuition & fees (PA res): $17,772 | Average undergraduate aid package: $12,394 |
| --- | --- |

**ABOUT THE INSTITUTION** State-related, coed. **Awards:** certificates, bachelor's, master's, and doctoral degrees. 94 undergraduate majors. **Total enrollment:** 28,617. Undergraduates: 18,757. Freshmen: 3,847. Federal methodology is used as a basis for awarding need-based institutional aid.

**UNDERGRADUATE EXPENSES for 2015–2016 Application fee:** $45. **Tuition, state resident:** full-time $16,872; part-time $703 per credit hour. **Tuition, nonresident:** full-time $27,268; part-time $1136 per credit hour. **Required fees:** full-time $900; $214 per term. Full-time tuition and fees vary according to location and program. Part-time tuition and fees vary according to location and program. **College room and board:** $10,800; **Room only:** $6200. Room and board charges vary according to board plan, housing facility, and location.

**FRESHMAN FINANCIAL AID (Fall 2013)** 3,182 applied for aid; of those 70% were deemed to have need. 96% of freshmen with need received aid; of those 11% had need fully met. **Average percent of need met:** 58% (excluding resources awarded to replace EFC). **Average financial aid package:** $14,031 (excluding resources awarded to replace EFC). 6% of all full-time freshmen had no need and received non-need-based gift aid.

**UNDERGRADUATE FINANCIAL AID (Fall 2013)** 12,348 applied for aid; of those 79% were deemed to have need. 97% of undergraduates with need received aid; of those 9% had need fully met. **Average percent of need met:** 54% (excluding resources awarded to replace EFC). **Average financial aid package:** $12,394 (excluding resources awarded to replace EFC). 3% of all full-time undergraduates had no need and received non-need-based gift aid.

**GIFT AID (NEED-BASED) Total amount:** $51,809,986 (24% federal, 22% state, 43% institutional, 11% external sources). **Receiving aid:** Freshmen: 44% (1,705); all full-time undergraduates: 38% (6,662). **Average award:** Freshmen: $9457; Undergraduates: $8085. **Scholarships, grants, and awards:** Federal Pell, FSEOG, state, private, college/university gift aid from institutional funds, Federal Nursing.

**GIFT AID (NON-NEED-BASED) Total amount:** $30,440,309 (75% institutional, 25% external sources). **Receiving aid:** Freshmen: 4% (147). Undergraduates: 2% (419). **Average award:** Freshmen: $12,286. Undergraduates: $11,460. **Scholarships, grants, and awards by category:** Academic interests/achievement: general academic interests/achievements. **Special characteristics:** children of faculty/staff, children of union members/company employees. **Tuition waivers:** Full or partial for employees or children of employees. **ROTC:** Army, Naval cooperative, Air Force.

**LOANS Student loans:** $106,866,707 (69% need-based, 31% non-need-based). 67% of past graduating class borrowed through all loan programs. **Average indebtedness per student:** $36,466. **Average need-based loan:** Freshmen: $4758. Undergraduates: $5182. **Parent loans:** $29,570,733 (46% need-based, 54% non-need-based). **Programs:** Federal Direct (Subsidized and Unsubsidized Stafford, PLUS), Perkins, Federal Nursing, state, college/university.

**WORK-STUDY Federal work-study:** jobs available.

**ATHLETIC AWARDS** Total amount: $9,159,761 (41% need-based, 59% non-need-based).

**APPLYING FOR FINANCIAL AID Required financial aid form:** FAFSA. **Financial aid deadline (priority):** 3/1. **Notification date:** Continuous beginning 3/15.

**CONTACT** Mr. Marc L. Harding, Chief Enrollment Officer, University of Pittsburgh, 4227 Fifth Avenue, First Floor, Pittsburgh, PA 15260, 412-624-7488. *Fax:* 412-648-8815. *E-mail:* oafa@pitt.edu. *Website:* http://www.pitt.edu/.

# UNIVERSITY OF PITTSBURGH AT BRADFORD
## Bradford, PA

| Tuition & fees (PA res): $13,322 | Average undergraduate aid package: $14,244 |
| --- | --- |

**ABOUT THE INSTITUTION** State-related, coed. **Awards:** associate and bachelor's degrees. 33 undergraduate majors. **Total enrollment:** 1,499. Undergraduates: 1,499. Freshmen: 398. Federal methodology is used as a basis for awarding need-based institutional aid.

**UNDERGRADUATE EXPENSES for 2015–2016 Application fee:** $45. **One-time required fee:** $90. **Tuition, state resident:** full-time $12,452; part-time $518 per credit hour. **Tuition, nonresident:** full-time $23,268; part-time $969 per credit hour. **Required fees:** full-time $870; $155 per term. Full-time tuition and fees vary according to course load and program. Part-time tuition and fees vary according to course load and program. **College room and board:** $8480; **Room only:** $5160. Room and board charges vary according to board plan and housing facility.

**FRESHMAN FINANCIAL AID (Fall 2013)** 369 applied for aid; of those 93% were deemed to have need. 99% of freshmen with need received aid; of those 10% had need fully met. **Average percent of need met:** 64% (excluding resources awarded to replace EFC). **Average financial aid package:** $14,106 (excluding resources awarded to replace EFC). 4% of all full-time freshmen had no need and received non-need-based gift aid.

**UNDERGRADUATE FINANCIAL AID (Fall 2013)** 1,238 applied for aid; of those 92% were deemed to have need. 99% of undergraduates with need received aid; of those 13% had need fully met. **Average percent of need met:** 66% (excluding resources awarded to replace EFC). **Average financial aid package:** $14,244 (excluding resources awarded to replace EFC). 4% of all full-time undergraduates had no need and received non-need-based gift aid.

**GIFT AID (NEED-BASED) Total amount:** $9,221,365 (30% federal, 26% state, 39% institutional, 5% external sources). **Receiving aid:** Freshmen: 83% (321); all full-time undergraduates: 78% (1,053). **Average award:** Freshmen: $9314; Undergraduates: $8559. **Scholarships, grants, and awards:** Federal Pell, FSEOG, state, private, college/university gift aid from institutional funds, Academic Competitiveness Grants, National SMART Grants.

**GIFT AID (NON-NEED-BASED) Total amount:** $1,121,092 (4% state, 86% institutional, 10% external sources). **Receiving aid:** Freshmen: 3% (13). Undergraduates: 4% (55). **Average award:** Freshmen: $6656. Undergraduates: $5504. **Scholarships, grants, and awards by category:** Academic interests/achievement: 156 awards ($148,775 total): biological sciences, business, communication, computer science, education, engineering/technologies, English, general academic interests/achievements, health fields, humanities, mathematics, physical sciences, premedicine, social sciences. Creative arts/performance: 6 awards ($1500 total): cinema/film/broadcasting. **Special characteristics:** 1,048 awards ($4,412,611 total): adult students, children of faculty/staff, children of union members/company employees, local/state students, out-of-state students, veterans. **Tuition waivers:** Full or partial for employees or children of employees. **ROTC:** Army cooperative.

**LOANS Student loans:** $31,650,938 (25% need-based, 75% non-need-based). 89% of past graduating class borrowed through all loan programs. **Average indebtedness per student:** $37,157. **Average need-based loan:** Freshmen: $4009. Undergraduates: $4691. **Parent loans:** $2,075,512 (46% need-based, 54% non-need-based). **Programs:** Federal Direct (Subsidized and Unsubsidized Stafford, PLUS), Perkins.

**WORK-STUDY Federal work-study:** 201 jobs averaging $1740. **State or other work-study/employment:** 2 part-time jobs averaging $1740.

**APPLYING FOR FINANCIAL AID Required financial aid form:** FAFSA. **Financial aid deadline (priority):** 3/1. **Notification date:** Continuous beginning 4/1. Students must reply within 2 weeks of notification.

**CONTACT** Melissa Ibanez, Director of Financial Aid, University of Pittsburgh at Bradford, 300 Campus Drive, Bradford, PA 16701-2812, 814-362-7550 or toll-free 800-872-1787. *Fax:* 814-362-7578. *E-mail:* ibanez@pitt.edu. *Website:* http://www.upb.pitt.edu/.

# UNIVERSITY OF PITTSBURGH AT GREENSBURG
## Greensburg, PA

| Tuition & fees (PA res): $13,372 | Average undergraduate aid package: $10,936 |
|---|---|

**ABOUT THE INSTITUTION** State-related, coed. *Awards:* certificates and bachelor's degrees. 25 undergraduate majors. *Total enrollment:* 1,578. Undergraduates: 1,578. Freshmen: 423. Federal methodology is used as a basis for awarding need-based institutional aid.

**UNDERGRADUATE EXPENSES for 2015–2016 Application fee:** $45. *Tuition, state resident:* full-time $12,452; part-time $518 per credit hour. *Tuition, nonresident:* full-time $23,268; part-time $969 per credit hour. *Required fees:* full-time $920. *College room and board:* $9490; *Room only:* $5860. Room and board charges vary according to board plan and housing facility.

**FRESHMAN FINANCIAL AID (Fall 2013)** 348 applied for aid; of those 84% were deemed to have need. 98% of freshmen with need received aid; of those 15% had need fully met. *Average percent of need met:* 64% (excluding resources awarded to replace EFC). *Average financial aid package:* $11,753 (excluding resources awarded to replace EFC). 6% of all full-time freshmen had no need and received non-need-based gift aid.

**UNDERGRADUATE FINANCIAL AID (Fall 2013)** 1,339 applied for aid; of those 88% were deemed to have need. 98% of undergraduates with need received aid; of those 13% had need fully met. *Average percent of need met:* 61% (excluding resources awarded to replace EFC). *Average financial aid package:* $10,936 (excluding resources awarded to replace EFC). 3% of all full-time undergraduates had no need and received non-need-based gift aid.

**GIFT AID (NEED-BASED) Total amount:** $6,423,148 (38% federal, 37% state, 16% institutional, 9% external sources). *Receiving aid:* Freshmen: 63% (242); all full-time undergraduates: 59% (926). *Average award:* Freshmen: $8136; Undergraduates: $6822. *Scholarships, grants, and awards:* Federal Pell, FSEOG, state, private, college/university gift aid from institutional funds, United Negro College Fund.

**GIFT AID (NON-NEED-BASED) Total amount:** $668,575 (6% state, 71% institutional, 23% external sources). *Receiving aid:* Freshmen: 6% (23). Undergraduates: 3% (49). *Average award:* Freshmen: $4821. Undergraduates: $4939. *Tuition waivers:* Full or partial for employees or children of employees, senior citizens. *ROTC:* Army cooperative, Air Force cooperative.

**LOANS Student loans:** $10,030,385 (74% need-based, 26% non-need-based). 82% of past graduating class borrowed through all loan programs. *Average indebtedness per student:* $34,451. *Average need-based loan:* Freshmen: $3765. Undergraduates: $4638. *Parent loans:* $1,512,154 (50% need-based, 50% non-need-based). *Programs:* Federal Direct (Subsidized and Unsubsidized Stafford, PLUS), Perkins.

**WORK-STUDY Federal work-study:** jobs available.

**APPLYING FOR FINANCIAL AID Required financial aid forms:** FAFSA, state aid form. *Financial aid deadline (priority):* 2/15. *Notification date:* Continuous beginning 3/15. Students must reply within 3 weeks of notification.

**CONTACT** Ms. Brandi S. Darr, Director of Financial Aid, University of Pittsburgh at Greensburg, 150 Finoli Drive, Greensburg, PA 15601-5898, 724-836-7167. *E-mail:* upgfnaid@pitt.edu. *Website:* http://www.greensburg.pitt.edu/.

# UNIVERSITY OF PITTSBURGH AT JOHNSTOWN
## Johnstown, PA

| Tuition & fees (PA res): $13,374 | Average undergraduate aid package: $10,830 |
|---|---|

**ABOUT THE INSTITUTION** State-related, coed. 50 undergraduate majors. Federal methodology is used as a basis for awarding need-based institutional aid.

**UNDERGRADUATE EXPENSES for 2015–2016 Tuition, state resident:** full-time $12,452; part-time $518 per credit hour. *Tuition, nonresident:* full-time $23,268; part-time $969 per credit hour. *Required fees:* full-time $922. Full-time tuition and fees vary according to program. Part-time tuition and fees vary according to program. *College room and board:* $9080; *Room only:* $5340. Room and board charges vary according to board plan and housing facility.

**FRESHMAN FINANCIAL AID (Fall 2014, est.)** 645 applied for aid; of those 82% were deemed to have need. 99% of freshmen with need received aid; of those 15% had need fully met. *Average percent of need met:* 63% (excluding resources awarded to replace EFC). *Average financial aid package:* $11,154 (excluding resources awarded to replace EFC). 9% of all full-time freshmen had no need and received non-need-based gift aid.

**UNDERGRADUATE FINANCIAL AID (Fall 2014, est.)** 2,435 applied for aid; of those 86% were deemed to have need. 98% of undergraduates with need received aid; of those 13% had need fully met. *Average percent of need met:* 61% (excluding resources awarded to replace EFC). *Average financial aid package:* $10,830 (excluding resources awarded to replace EFC). 5% of all full-time undergraduates had no need and received non-need-based gift aid.

**GIFT AID (NEED-BASED) Total amount:** $9,832,063 (35% federal, 36% state, 18% institutional, 11% external sources). *Receiving aid:* Freshmen: 64% (438); all full-time undergraduates: 58% (1,584). *Average award:* Freshmen: $6347; Undergraduates: $6155. *Scholarships, grants, and awards:* Federal Pell, FSEOG, state, private, college/university gift aid from institutional funds.

**GIFT AID (NON-NEED-BASED) Total amount:** $1,099,265 (2% state, 64% institutional, 34% external sources). *Receiving aid:* Freshmen: 5% (33). Undergraduates: 3% (81). *Average award:* Freshmen: $2751. Undergraduates: $2749. *Scholarships, grants, and awards by category:* Academic interests/achievement: biological sciences, business, communication, computer science, education, engineering/technologies, English, general academic interests/achievements, health fields, humanities, mathematics, physical sciences, premedicine, social sciences. *Creative arts/performance:* journalism/publications, theater/drama. *Special achievements/activities:* leadership. *Special characteristics:* children of faculty/staff. *Tuition waivers:* Full or partial for employees or children of employees.

**LOANS Student loans:** $19,454,065 (69% need-based, 31% non-need-based). 85% of past graduating class borrowed through all loan programs. *Average indebtedness per student:* $34,162. *Average need-based loan:* Freshmen: $3746. Undergraduates: $4533. *Parent loans:* $4,758,060 (42% need-based, 58% non-need-based). *Programs:* Federal Direct (Subsidized and Unsubsidized Stafford, PLUS), Perkins.

**WORK-STUDY Federal work-study:** Total amount: $1,708,317; jobs available. *State or other work-study/employment:* Total amount: $43,066 (67% need-based, 33% non-need-based). Part-time jobs available.

**ATHLETIC AWARDS** Total amount: $708,209 (62% need-based, 38% non-need-based).

**APPLYING FOR FINANCIAL AID Required financial aid forms:** FAFSA, state aid form. *Financial aid deadline (priority):* 4/1. *Notification date:* Continuous beginning 4/1. Students must reply within 2 weeks of notification.

**CONTACT** Ms. Joni L. Trovato, Director of Student Financial Aid, University of Pittsburgh at Johnstown, 450 Schoolhouse Road, 114 Blackington Hall, Johnstown, PA 15904-2990, 814-269-7045 or toll-free 800-765-4875. *Fax:* 814-269-7061. *E-mail:* jtrovato@pitt.edu. *Website:* http://www.upj.pitt.edu/.

# UNIVERSITY OF PORTLAND
## Portland, OR

| Tuition & fees: $38,520 | Average undergraduate aid package: $28,700 |
|---|---|

**ABOUT THE INSTITUTION** Independent Roman Catholic, coed. *Awards:* certificates, bachelor's, master's, and doctoral degrees. 38 undergraduate majors. *Total enrollment:* 4,169. Undergraduates: 3,680. Freshmen: 1,082. Federal methodology is used as a basis for awarding need-based institutional aid.

**UNDERGRADUATE EXPENSES for 2015–2016 Application fee:** $50. *Comprehensive fee:* $49,964 includes full-time tuition ($38,350), mandatory fees ($170), and room and board ($11,444). Full-time tuition and fees vary according to program. Room and board charges vary according to board plan and housing facility. *Part-time tuition:* $1200 per credit hour. Part-time tuition and fees vary according to course load and program.

**FRESHMAN FINANCIAL AID (Fall 2014, est.)** 936 applied for aid; of those 76% were deemed to have need. 100% of freshmen with need received aid; of those 8% had need fully met. *Average percent of need met:* 71% (excluding resources awarded to replace EFC). *Average financial aid package:* $28,002 (excluding resources

awarded to replace EFC). 31% of all full-time freshmen had no need and received non-need-based gift aid.

**UNDERGRADUATE FINANCIAL AID (Fall 2014, est.)** 2,718 applied for aid; of those 83% were deemed to have need. 100% of undergraduates with need received aid; of those 7% had need fully met. *Average percent of need met:* 71% (excluding resources awarded to replace EFC). *Average financial aid package:* $28,700 (excluding resources awarded to replace EFC). 33% of all full-time undergraduates had no need and received non-need-based gift aid.

**GIFT AID (NEED-BASED)** *Total amount:* $51,221,981 (7% federal, 1% state, 88% institutional, 4% external sources). *Receiving aid:* Freshmen: 53% (572); all full-time undergraduates: 50% (1,811). *Average award:* Freshmen: $24,178; Undergraduates: $21,981. *Scholarships, grants, and awards:* Federal Pell, FSEOG, state, private, college/university gift aid from institutional funds, United Negro College Fund, Federal Nursing.

**GIFT AID (NON-NEED-BASED)** *Total amount:* $19,158,942 (99% institutional, 1% external sources). *Receiving aid:* Freshmen: 63% (678). Undergraduates: 57% (2,056). *Average award:* Freshmen: $16,959. Undergraduates: $14,965. *Scholarships, grants, and awards by category: Academic interests/achievement:* 2,179 awards ($33,964,141 total): biological sciences, business, communication, computer science, education, engineering/technologies, English, foreign languages, general academic interests/achievements, health fields, humanities, mathematics, military science, physical sciences, premedicine, religion/biblical studies, social sciences. *Creative arts/performance:* 88 awards ($231,875 total): music, performing arts, theater/drama. *Special achievements/activities:* 32 awards ($23,132 total): general special achievements/activities. *Special characteristics:* 77 awards ($2,876,698 total): children of faculty/staff, married students, relatives of clergy, religious affiliation. *Tuition waivers:* Full or partial for employees or children of employees. *ROTC:* Army, Air Force.

**LOANS** *Student loans:* $18,731,936 (88% need-based, 12% non-need-based). 68% of past graduating class borrowed through all loan programs. *Average indebtedness per student:* $26,557. *Average need-based loan:* Freshmen: $3675. Undergraduates: $5012. *Parent loans:* $21,545,215 (82% need-based, 18% non-need-based). *Programs:* Federal Direct (Subsidized and Unsubsidized Stafford, PLUS), Perkins, Federal Nursing.

**WORK-STUDY** *Federal work-study:* Total amount: $471,906; 366 jobs averaging $1474. *State or other work-study/employment:* Total amount: $2,500,000 (100% non-need-based). 1,468 part-time jobs averaging $1437.

**ATHLETIC AWARDS** Total amount: $4,963,364 (36% need-based, 64% non-need-based).

**APPLYING FOR FINANCIAL AID** *Required financial aid form:* FAFSA. *Financial aid deadline (priority):* 3/1. *Notification date:* Continuous beginning 3/1. Students must reply by 5/1.

**CONTACT** Ms. Janet Turner, Director of Financial Aid, University of Portland, 5000 North Willamette Boulevard, Portland, OR 97203-5798, 503-943-7311 or toll-free 888-627-5601. *Fax:* 503-943-7508. *E-mail:* turnerj@up.edu.
*Website:* http://www.up.edu/.

# UNIVERSITY OF PUERTO RICO IN AGUADILLA
## Aguadilla, PR

**CONTACT** Director of Financial Aid, University of Puerto Rico in Aguadilla, PO Box 250-160, Aguadilla, PR 00604-0160, 787-890-2681 Ext. 273.
*Website:* http://www.uprag.edu/.

# UNIVERSITY OF PUERTO RICO IN ARECIBO
## Arecibo, PR

**CONTACT** Myrta F. Salcedo-Ortiz, Director of Financial Aid, University of Puerto Rico in Arecibo, PO Box 4010, Arecibo, PR 00613, 787-878-2830 Ext. 2008. *E-mail:* myrta.ortiz@upr.edu.
*Website:* http://www.upra.edu/.

# UNIVERSITY OF PUERTO RICO IN BAYAMÓN
## Bayamón, PR

**ABOUT THE INSTITUTION** Commonwealth-supported, coed. *Awards:* associate and bachelor's degrees. 16 undergraduate majors. *Total enrollment:* 5,075. Undergraduates: 5,075. Freshmen: 1,134.

**GIFT AID (NEED-BASED)** *Scholarships, grants, and awards:* Federal Pell, FSEOG, state, college/university gift aid from institutional funds.

**GIFT AID (NON-NEED-BASED)** *Scholarships, grants, and awards by category: Academic interests/achievement:* general academic interests/achievements. *Creative arts/performance:* dance, music, theater/drama. *Special achievements/activities:* cheerleading/drum major. *Special characteristics:* veterans, veterans' children.

**LOANS** *Programs:* Federal Direct (Unsubsidized Stafford, PLUS), Perkins.

**APPLYING FOR FINANCIAL AID** *Required financial aid forms:* FAFSA, state income tax form(s).

**CONTACT** Mr. Hector Cuadrado, Financial Aid Director, University of Puerto Rico in Bayamón, Street 174 #170 Minillas Industrial Park, Bayamon, PR 00959-1911, 787-993-8953 Ext. 4033. *E-mail:* hector.cuadrado@upr.edu.
*Website:* http://www.uprb.edu/.

# UNIVERSITY OF PUERTO RICO IN CAROLINA
## Carolina, PR

**CONTACT** Financial Aid Office, University of Puerto Rico in Carolina, PO Box 4800, Carolina, PR 00984-4800, 787-257-0000.
*Website:* http://www.uprc.edu/.

# UNIVERSITY OF PUERTO RICO IN CAYEY
## Cayey, PR

**CONTACT** Mr. Hector Maldonado Otero, Director of Financial Aid, University of Puerto Rico in Cayey, Antonio Barcelo, Cayey, PR 00736, 787-738-2161. *Fax:* 787-263-0676.
*Website:* http://www.cayey.upr.edu/.

# UNIVERSITY OF PUERTO RICO IN HUMACAO
## Humacao, PR

**CONTACT** Alfredo Aponte Serrano, Director of Financial Aid, University of Puerto Rico in Humacao, HUC Station, Humacao, PR 00791-4300, 787-850-9362. *E-mail:* alfredo.aponte@upr.edu.
*Website:* http://www.uprh.edu/.

# UNIVERSITY OF PUERTO RICO IN PONCE
## Ponce, PR

**CONTACT** Carmelo Vega Montes, Director of Financial Aid, University of Puerto Rico in Ponce, Box 7186, Ponce, PR 00732-7186, 787-844-8181. *Fax:* 787-840-8108.
*Website:* http://www.uprp.edu/.

# UNIVERSITY OF PUERTO RICO IN UTUADO

## Utuado, PR

**CONTACT** Edgar Salv, Director of Financial Assistance, University of Puerto Rico in Utuado, PO Box 2500, Utuado, PR 00641, 787-894-2828 Ext. 2603. *Fax:* 787-894-3810. *E-mail:* esalva@uprutuado.edu. *Website:* http://www.uprutuado.edu/.

# UNIVERSITY OF PUERTO RICO, MAYAGÜEZ CAMPUS

## Mayagüez, PR

**CONTACT** Ms. Ana I. Rodriguez, Director of Financial Aid, University of Puerto Rico, Mayagüez Campus, PO Box 9000, Mayagüez, PR 00681-9000, 787-265-3863. *Fax:* 787-265-1920. *E-mail:* a_rodriguez@rumad.uprm.edu. *Website:* http://www.uprm.edu/.

# UNIVERSITY OF PUERTO RICO, MEDICAL SCIENCES CAMPUS

## San Juan, PR

**CONTACT** Mrs. Zoraida Figueroa, Financial Aid Director, University of Puerto Rico, Medical Sciences Campus, Terreno Centro Medico-Edificio Decanato Farmacia y Estudiantes, San Juan, PR 00936-5067, 787-763-2525. *Fax:* 787-282-7117. *E-mail:* zoraida.figueroa@upr.edu. *Website:* http://www.rcm.upr.edu/.

# UNIVERSITY OF PUERTO RICO, RÍO PIEDRAS CAMPUS

## San Juan, PR

**CONTACT** Mr. Efraim Williams, EDP Manager, University of Puerto Rico, Río Piedras Campus, PO Box 23300, San Juan, PR 00931-3300, 787-764-0000 Ext. 5573. *Website:* http://www.uprrp.edu/.

# UNIVERSITY OF PUGET SOUND

## Tacoma, WA

| Tuition & fees: $43,428 | Average undergraduate aid package: $29,668 |
| --- | --- |

**ABOUT THE INSTITUTION** Independent, coed. *Awards:* bachelor's, master's, and doctoral degrees. 40 undergraduate majors. *Total enrollment:* 2,826. Undergraduates: 2,554. Freshmen: 663. Federal methodology is used as a basis for awarding need-based institutional aid.

**UNDERGRADUATE EXPENSES** for 2015–2016 *Application fee:* $50. *Comprehensive fee:* $54,608 includes full-time tuition ($43,200), mandatory fees ($228), and room and board ($11,180). *College room only:* $6150. Full-time tuition and fees vary according to course load. Room and board charges vary according to board plan and housing facility. *Part-time tuition:* $5450 per unit. Part-time tuition and fees vary according to course load.

**FRESHMAN FINANCIAL AID (Fall 2014, est.)** 507 applied for aid; of those 75% were deemed to have need. 100% of freshmen with need received aid; of those 19% had need fully met. *Average percent of need met:* 75% (excluding resources awarded to replace EFC). *Average financial aid package:* $28,459 (excluding resources awarded to replace EFC). 42% of all full-time freshmen had no need and received non-need-based gift aid.

**UNDERGRADUATE FINANCIAL AID (Fall 2014, est.)** 1,641 applied for aid; of those 86% were deemed to have need. 100% of undergraduates with need received aid; of those 15% had need fully met. *Average percent of need met:* 73% (excluding resources awarded to replace EFC). *Average financial aid package:* $29,668 (excluding resources awarded to replace EFC). 42% of all full-time undergraduates had no need and received non-need-based gift aid.

**GIFT AID (NEED-BASED)** *Total amount:* $31,993,552 (8% federal, 3% state, 85% institutional, 4% external sources). *Receiving aid:* Freshmen: 56% (372); all full-time undergraduates: 55% (1,390). *Average award:* Freshmen: $24,168; Undergraduates: $23,410. *Scholarships, grants, and awards:* Federal Pell, FSEOG, state, private, college/university gift aid from institutional funds.

**GIFT AID (NON-NEED-BASED)** *Total amount:* $16,775,443 (95% institutional, 5% external sources). *Receiving aid:* Freshmen: 11% (72). Undergraduates: 7% (168). *Average award:* Freshmen: $13,755. Undergraduates: $14,886. *Scholarships, grants, and awards by category:* Academic interests/achievement: 1,145 awards ($14,568,541 total): biological sciences, business, communication, computer science, English, foreign languages, general academic interests/achievements, humanities, international studies, mathematics, physical sciences, premedicine, social sciences. Creative arts/performance: 76 awards ($463,050 total): art/fine arts, debating, music, theater/drama. Special achievements/activities: 6 awards ($16,500 total): community service, leadership, religious involvement. Special characteristics: 27 awards ($638,608 total): children of faculty/staff, international students, veterans, veterans' children. *Tuition waivers:* Full or partial for employees or children of employees. *ROTC:* Army cooperative.

**LOANS** *Student loans:* $11,867,264 (91% need-based, 9% non-need-based). 62% of past graduating class borrowed through all loan programs. *Average indebtedness per student:* $27,776. *Average need-based loan:* Freshmen: $5019. Undergraduates: $6276. *Parent loans:* $6,566,355 (89% need-based, 11% non-need-based). *Programs:* Federal Direct (Subsidized and Unsubsidized Stafford, PLUS), Perkins.

**WORK-STUDY** *Federal work-study:* Total amount: $1,768,240; 567 jobs averaging $2730. *State or other work-study/employment:* Total amount: $2,305,936 (100% need-based). 842 part-time jobs averaging $2487.

**APPLYING FOR FINANCIAL AID** *Required financial aid form:* FAFSA. *Financial aid deadline (priority):* 2/1. *Notification date:* Continuous beginning 3/15. Students must reply by 5/1.

**CONTACT** Maggie A. Mittuch, Associate Vice President for Student Financial Services, University of Puget Sound, 1500 North Warner Street #1039, Tacoma, WA 98416-1039, 253-879-3214 or toll-free 800-396-7191. *Fax:* 253-879-8508. *E-mail:* mmittuch@pugetsound.edu. *Website:* http://www.pugetsound.edu/.

# UNIVERSITY OF REDLANDS

## Redlands, CA

| Tuition & fees: $43,186 | Average undergraduate aid package: N/A |
| --- | --- |

**ABOUT THE INSTITUTION** Independent, coed. *Awards:* certificates, bachelor's, master's, and doctoral degrees. 45 undergraduate majors. *Total enrollment:* 5,147. Undergraduates: 3,609. Freshmen: 663. Federal methodology is used as a basis for awarding need-based institutional aid.

**UNDERGRADUATE EXPENSES** for 2015–2016 *Application fee:* $30. *One-time required fee:* $150. *Comprehensive fee:* $55,896 includes full-time tuition ($42,836), mandatory fees ($350), and room and board ($12,710). Full-time tuition and fees vary according to program. Room and board charges vary according to board plan and housing facility. *Part-time tuition:* $1339 per credit hour. *Part-time fees:* $116 per year. Part-time tuition and fees vary according to course load and program.

**GIFT AID (NEED-BASED)** *Total amount:* $60,084,744 (8% federal, 11% state, 80% institutional, 1% external sources). *Scholarships, grants, and awards:* Federal Pell, FSEOG, state, private, college/university gift aid from institutional funds.

**GIFT AID (NON-NEED-BASED)** *Total amount:* $11,154,932 (98% institutional, 2% external sources). *Scholarships, grants, and awards by category:* Academic interests/achievement: general academic interests/achievements. Creative arts/performance: art/fine arts, creative writing, debating, music. Special achievements/activities: general special achievements/activities. Special characteristics: international students. *Tuition waivers:* Full or partial for employees or children of employees. *ROTC:* Army cooperative, Air Force cooperative.

**LOANS** *Student loans:* $22,465,835 (65% need-based, 35% non-need-based). **Parent loans:** $6,210,192 (100% non-need-based). **Programs:** Perkins, college/university.
**WORK-STUDY** *Federal work-study:* Total amount: $2,318,900; jobs available. **State or other work-study/employment:** Total amount: $2,111,100 (58% need-based, 42% non-need-based). Part-time jobs available.
**APPLYING FOR FINANCIAL AID** *Required financial aid forms:* FAFSA, state aid form. **Financial aid deadline (priority):** 2/15. **Notification date:** Continuous beginning 2/28. Students must reply by 5/1.
**CONTACT** Alisha Aguilar, Director of Financial Aid, University of Redlands, 1200 East Colton Avenue, PO Box 3080, Redlands, CA 92373-0999, 909-748-8047 or toll-free 800-455-5064. *Fax:* 909-335-4089. *E-mail:* financialaid@redlands.edu.
*Website:* http://www.redlands.edu/.

# UNIVERSITY OF RHODE ISLAND
## Kingston, RI

| Tuition & fees (RI res): $12,506 | Average undergraduate aid package: $15,819 |
|---|---|

**ABOUT THE INSTITUTION** State-supported, coed. **Awards:** certificates, bachelor's, master's, and doctoral degrees. 83 undergraduate majors. **Total enrollment:** 16,571. Undergraduates: 13,580. Freshmen: 3,145. Federal methodology is used as a basis for awarding need-based institutional aid.
**UNDERGRADUATE EXPENSES for 2015–2016** *Application fee:* $65. **Tuition, state resident:** full-time $10,878; part-time $453 per credit hour. **Tuition, nonresident:** full-time $26,444; part-time $1102 per credit hour. **Required fees:** full-time $1628; $3 per credit hour or $58 per term. Full-time tuition and fees vary according to course load, location, and reciprocity agreements. Part-time tuition and fees vary according to course load, location, and reciprocity agreements. **College room and board:** $7256; *Room only:* $4240. Room and board charges vary according to board plan and housing facility.
**FRESHMAN FINANCIAL AID (Fall 2014, est.)** 2,601 applied for aid; of those 79% were deemed to have need. 94% of freshmen with need received aid; of those 99% had need fully met. *Average percent of need met:* 62% (excluding resources awarded to replace EFC). *Average financial aid package:* $16,091 (excluding resources awarded to replace EFC). 10% of all full-time freshmen had no need and received non-need-based gift aid.
**UNDERGRADUATE FINANCIAL AID (Fall 2014, est.)** 11,732 applied for aid; of those 85% were deemed to have need. 87% of undergraduates with need received aid; of those 97% had need fully met. *Average percent of need met:* 59% (excluding resources awarded to replace EFC). *Average financial aid package:* $15,819 (excluding resources awarded to replace EFC). 7% of all full-time undergraduates had no need and received non-need-based gift aid.
**GIFT AID (NEED-BASED)** *Total amount:* $87,916,660 (19% federal, 2% state, 76% institutional, 3% external sources). **Receiving aid:** Freshmen: 55% (1,731); all full-time undergraduates: 67% (8,004). *Average award:* Freshmen: $10,183; Undergraduates: $9713. **Scholarships, grants, and awards:** Federal Pell, FSEOG, state, private, college/university gift aid from institutional funds.
**GIFT AID (NON-NEED-BASED)** *Total amount:* $5,729,243 (94% institutional, 6% external sources). **Receiving aid:** Freshmen: 11% (337). Undergraduates: 8% (943). *Average award:* Freshmen: $6704. Undergraduates: $6564. **Scholarships, grants, and awards by category:** Academic interests/achievement: general academic interests/achievements. Creative arts/performance: art/fine arts, music, theater/drama. Special characteristics: children and siblings of alumni. **Tuition waivers:** Full or partial for minority students, employees or children of employees, senior citizens. **ROTC:** Army.
**LOANS** *Student loans:* $76,501,802 (77% need-based, 23% non-need-based). 71% of past graduating class borrowed through all loan programs. *Average indebtedness per student:* $30,731. *Average need-based loan:* Freshmen: $5155. Undergraduates: $5636. **Parent loans:** $31,249,663 (62% need-based, 38% non-need-based). **Programs:** Federal Direct (Subsidized and Unsubsidized Stafford, PLUS), Perkins, Federal Nursing, college/university.
**WORK-STUDY** *Federal work-study:* Total amount: $1,174,969; jobs available.
**ATHLETIC AWARDS** Total amount: $8,057,735 (94% need-based, 6% non-need-based).

**APPLYING FOR FINANCIAL AID** *Required financial aid form:* FAFSA. **Financial aid deadline (priority):** 3/1. **Notification date:** Continuous beginning 3/15. Students must reply by 5/1.
**CONTACT** Office of Enrollment Services, University of Rhode Island, Green Hall, 35 Campus Avenue, Kingston, RI 02881, 401-874-9500.
*Website:* http://www.uri.edu/.

# UNIVERSITY OF RICHMOND
## Richmond, VA

| Tuition & fees: $46,680 | Average undergraduate aid package: $43,016 |
|---|---|

**ABOUT THE INSTITUTION** Independent, coed. **Awards:** bachelor's, master's, and doctoral degrees. 54 undergraduate majors. **Total enrollment:** 3,514. Undergraduates: 2,984. Freshmen: 816. Institutional methodology is used as a basis for awarding need-based institutional aid.
**UNDERGRADUATE EXPENSES for 2015–2016** *Application fee:* $50. **Comprehensive fee:** $57,470 includes full-time tuition ($46,680) and room and board ($10,790). *College room only:* $4870. Full-time tuition and fees vary according to course load. Room and board charges vary according to board plan and housing facility. **Part-time tuition:** $2334 per credit hour. Part-time tuition and fees vary according to course load.
**FRESHMAN FINANCIAL AID (Fall 2014, est.)** 500 applied for aid; of those 73% were deemed to have need. 100% of freshmen with need received aid; of those 89% had need fully met. *Average percent of need met:* 100% (excluding resources awarded to replace EFC). *Average financial aid package:* $44,626 (excluding resources awarded to replace EFC). 8% of all full-time freshmen had no need and received non-need-based gift aid.
**UNDERGRADUATE FINANCIAL AID (Fall 2014, est.)** 1,568 applied for aid; of those 82% were deemed to have need. 100% of undergraduates with need received aid; of those 85% had need fully met. *Average percent of need met:* 100% (excluding resources awarded to replace EFC). *Average financial aid package:* $43,016 (excluding resources awarded to replace EFC). 15% of all full-time undergraduates had no need and received non-need-based gift aid.
**GIFT AID (NEED-BASED)** *Total amount:* $44,063,674 (5% federal, 2% state, 91% institutional, 2% external sources). **Receiving aid:** Freshmen: 44% (359); all full-time undergraduates: 40% (1,255). *Average award:* Freshmen: $39,262; Undergraduates: $37,199. **Scholarships, grants, and awards:** Federal Pell, FSEOG, state, private, college/university gift aid from institutional funds.
**GIFT AID (NON-NEED-BASED)** *Total amount:* $14,794,081 (4% federal, 5% state, 83% institutional, 8% external sources). **Receiving aid:** Freshmen: 11% (86). Undergraduates: 7% (218). *Average award:* Freshmen: $33,250. Undergraduates: $23,692. **Scholarships, grants, and awards by category:** Academic interests/achievement: 178 awards ($7,361,335 total): biological sciences, computer science, general academic interests/achievements, mathematics, physical sciences. *Creative arts/performance:* 40 awards ($1,353,500 total): art/fine arts, dance, music, performing arts, theater/drama. Special achievements/activities: 92 awards ($230,000 total): community service. **Tuition waivers:** Full or partial for employees or children of employees. **ROTC:** Army.
**LOANS** *Student loans:* $11,347,813 (35% need-based, 65% non-need-based). 44% of past graduating class borrowed through all loan programs. *Average indebtedness per student:* $22,550. *Average need-based loan:* Freshmen: $2969. Undergraduates: $3656. **Parent loans:** $3,707,162 (3% need-based, 97% non-need-based). **Programs:** Federal Direct (Subsidized and Unsubsidized Stafford, PLUS), Perkins.
**WORK-STUDY** *Federal work-study:* Total amount: $770,398; 529 jobs averaging $1390.
**ATHLETIC AWARDS** Total amount: $9,740,903 (20% need-based, 80% non-need-based).
**APPLYING FOR FINANCIAL AID** *Required financial aid forms:* FAFSA, CSS Financial Aid PROFILE, noncustodial (divorced/separated) parent's statement, federal income tax form(s). **Financial aid deadline:** 2/15. **Notification date:** 4/1. Students must reply within 4 weeks of notification.
**CONTACT** Office of Financial Aid, University of Richmond, Brunet Hall, 28 Westhampton Way, University of Richmond, VA 23173, 804-289-8438 or toll-free 800-700-1662. *Fax:* 804-484-1650. *E-mail:* finaid@richmond.edu.
*Website:* http://www.richmond.edu/.

# UNIVERSITY OF RIO GRANDE
## Rio Grande, OH

**Tuition & fees:** $21,930 | **Average undergraduate aid package:** $7030

**ABOUT THE INSTITUTION** Independent, coed. *Awards:* certificates, associate, bachelor's, and master's degrees. 71 undergraduate majors. *Total enrollment:* 2,161. Undergraduates: 2,106. Freshmen: 359. Both federal and institutional methodology are used as a basis for awarding need-based institutional aid.

**UNDERGRADUATE EXPENSES for 2015–2016 Application fee:** $25. *Comprehensive fee:* $31,380 includes full-time tuition ($21,540), mandatory fees ($390), and room and board ($9450). Full-time tuition and fees vary according to course level, course load, degree level, and program. *Part-time tuition:* $900 per credit hour. Part-time tuition and fees vary according to course level, course load, degree level, and program.

**FRESHMAN FINANCIAL AID (Fall 2014, est.)** 320 applied for aid; of those 100% were deemed to have need. 94% of freshmen with need received aid; of those 74% had need fully met. *Average percent of need met:* 82% (excluding resources awarded to replace EFC). *Average financial aid package:* $5555 (excluding resources awarded to replace EFC). 86% of all full-time freshmen had no need and received non-need-based gift aid.

**UNDERGRADUATE FINANCIAL AID (Fall 2014, est.)** 1,035 applied for aid; of those 100% were deemed to have need. 97% of undergraduates with need received aid; of those 73% had need fully met. *Average percent of need met:* 87% (excluding resources awarded to replace EFC). *Average financial aid package:* $7030 (excluding resources awarded to replace EFC). 2% of all full-time undergraduates had no need and received non-need-based gift aid.

**GIFT AID (NEED-BASED) Total amount:** $1,415,800 (88% federal, 8% institutional, 4% external sources). *Receiving aid:* Freshmen: 66% (219); all full-time undergraduates: 66% (721). *Average award:* Freshmen: $2838; Undergraduates: $3778. *Scholarships, grants, and awards:* Federal Pell, FSEOG, state, private, college/university gift aid from institutional funds.

**GIFT AID (NON-NEED-BASED) Total amount:** $3,378,626 (3% federal, 8% state, 82% institutional, 7% external sources). *Receiving aid:* Freshmen: 61% (204). Undergraduates: 66% (720). *Average award:* Freshmen: $4024. Undergraduates: $11,067. *Scholarships, grants, and awards by category:* Academic interests/achievement: biological sciences, business, communication, computer science, education, English, general academic interests/achievements, health fields, humanities, mathematics, physical sciences, social sciences. *Creative arts/performance:* art/fine arts, music. *Special achievements/activities:* cheerleading/drum major. *Special characteristics:* children and siblings of alumni, children of faculty/staff, local/state students, out-of-state students. *Tuition waivers:* Full or partial for employees or children of employees, senior citizens.

**LOANS Student loans:** $7,862,880 (1% need-based, 99% non-need-based). 86% of past graduating class borrowed through all loan programs. *Average indebtedness per student:* $28,617. *Average need-based loan:* Freshmen: $2594. Undergraduates: $3191. *Parent loans:* $230,793 (100% non-need-based). *Programs:* Federal Direct (Subsidized and Unsubsidized Stafford, PLUS), Perkins.

**WORK-STUDY Federal work-study:** Total amount: $164,183; jobs available. *State or other work-study/employment:* Part-time jobs available.

**ATHLETIC AWARDS** Total amount: $1,078,020 (100% non-need-based).

**APPLYING FOR FINANCIAL AID Required financial aid forms:** FAFSA, institution's own form. *Financial aid deadline:* Continuous. *Notification date:* Continuous beginning 1/15. Students must reply within 3 weeks of notification.

**CONTACT** Ms. Meghann Fraley, Assistant Director of Financial Aid, University of Rio Grande, PO Box 500, 218 North College Avenue, Rio Grande, OH 45674, 740-245-7218 or toll-free 800-282-7201. *Fax:* 740-245-7102.
*Website:* http://www.rio.edu/.

# UNIVERSITY OF ROCHESTER
## Rochester, NY

**Tuition & fees:** $46,960 | **Average undergraduate aid package:** $40,149

**ABOUT THE INSTITUTION** Independent, coed. *Awards:* certificates, bachelor's, master's, and doctoral degrees. 66 undergraduate majors. *Total enrollment:* 11,060. Undergraduates: 6,266. Freshmen: 1,436. Institutional methodology is used as a basis for awarding need-based institutional aid.

**UNDERGRADUATE EXPENSES for 2015–2016 Application fee:** $50. *Comprehensive fee:* $60,668 includes full-time tuition ($46,150), mandatory fees ($810), and room and board ($13,708). *College room only:* $8416. Full-time tuition and fees vary according to student level. Room and board charges vary according to board plan. *Part-time tuition:* $1442 per credit hour. Part-time tuition and fees vary according to course load. *Payment plan:* Tuition prepayment.

**FRESHMAN FINANCIAL AID (Fall 2014, est.)** 982 applied for aid; of those 79% were deemed to have need. 100% of freshmen with need received aid; of those 91% had need fully met. *Average percent of need met:* 97% (excluding resources awarded to replace EFC). *Average financial aid package:* $42,161 (excluding resources awarded to replace EFC). 30% of all full-time freshmen had no need and received non-need-based gift aid.

**UNDERGRADUATE FINANCIAL AID (Fall 2014, est.)** 3,569 applied for aid; of those 83% were deemed to have need. 100% of undergraduates with need received aid; of those 90% had need fully met. *Average percent of need met:* 95% (excluding resources awarded to replace EFC). *Average financial aid package:* $40,149 (excluding resources awarded to replace EFC). 30% of all full-time undergraduates had no need and received non-need-based gift aid.

**GIFT AID (NEED-BASED) Total amount:** $99,834,220 (6% federal, 2% state, 90% institutional, 2% external sources). *Receiving aid:* Freshmen: 53% (768); all full-time undergraduates: 51% (2,938). *Average award:* Freshmen: $37,908; Undergraduates: $35,076. *Scholarships, grants, and awards:* Federal Pell, FSEOG, state, college/university gift aid from institutional funds.

**GIFT AID (NON-NEED-BASED) Total amount:** $28,522,485 (1% state, 90% institutional, 9% external sources). *Receiving aid:* Freshmen: 10% (141). Undergraduates: 7% (412). *Average award:* Freshmen: $13,573. Undergraduates: $13,617. *Scholarships, grants, and awards by category:* Academic interests/achievement: engineering/technologies, general academic interests/achievements, military science. *Creative arts/performance:* general creative arts/performance, music, performing arts. *Special achievements/activities:* general special achievements/activities, leadership. *Special characteristics:* children and siblings of alumni, children of faculty/staff, general special characteristics, international students, veterans. *Tuition waivers:* Full or partial for employees or children of employees. *ROTC:* Army cooperative, Naval, Air Force cooperative.

**LOANS Student loans:** $22,909,418 (65% need-based, 35% non-need-based). 58% of past graduating class borrowed through all loan programs. *Average indebtedness per student:* $30,604. *Average need-based loan:* Freshmen: $4336. Undergraduates: $4990. *Parent loans:* $8,952,006 (13% need-based, 87% non-need-based). *Programs:* Federal Direct (Subsidized and Unsubsidized Stafford, PLUS), Perkins.

**WORK-STUDY Federal work-study:** Total amount: $5,730,791; 2,099 jobs averaging $2730. *State or other work-study/employment:* Total amount: $1,366,854 (41% need-based, 59% non-need-based). Part-time jobs available.

**APPLYING FOR FINANCIAL AID Required financial aid forms:** FAFSA, CSS Financial Aid PROFILE, state aid form, noncustodial (divorced/separated) parent's statement. *Financial aid deadline (priority):* 2/15. *Notification date:* 4/1. Students must reply by 5/1.

**CONTACT** Jonathan Burdick, Vice Provost for Enrollment Initiatives, University of Rochester, Wallis Hall, PO Box 270250, Rochester, NY 14627-0250, 585-275-6805 or toll-free 888-822-2256. *Fax:* 585-756-7664. *E-mail:* deanafa@admissions.rochester.edu.
*Website:* http://www.rochester.edu/.

# UNIVERSITY OF ST. FRANCIS
## Joliet, IL

**Tuition & fees:** $29,950 | **Average undergraduate aid package:** $22,972

**ABOUT THE INSTITUTION** Independent Roman Catholic, coed. *Awards:* certificates, bachelor's, master's, and doctoral degrees. 52 undergraduate majors. *Total enrollment:* 2,414. Undergraduates: 1,381. Freshmen: 216. Federal methodology is used as a basis for awarding need-based institutional aid.

**UNDERGRADUATE EXPENSES for 2015–2016 Tuition:** full-time $29,630; part-time $825 per credit hour. *Required fees:* full-time $320; $75 per term. Full-time tuition and fees vary according to degree level, location, and program. Part-time tuition and fees vary according to degree level and program. Room and board charges vary according to housing facility.

**FRESHMAN FINANCIAL AID (Fall 2014, est.)** 209 applied for aid; of those 92% were deemed to have need. 100% of freshmen with need received aid; of those 72% had need fully met. **Average percent of need met:** 85% (excluding resources awarded to replace EFC). **Average financial aid package:** $25,881 (excluding resources awarded to replace EFC). 9% of all full-time freshmen had no need and received non-need-based gift aid.

**UNDERGRADUATE FINANCIAL AID (Fall 2014, est.)** 1,221 applied for aid; of those 92% were deemed to have need. 100% of undergraduates with need received aid; of those 64% had need fully met. **Average percent of need met:** 74% (excluding resources awarded to replace EFC). **Average financial aid package:** $22,972 (excluding resources awarded to replace EFC). 13% of all full-time undergraduates had no need and received non-need-based gift aid.

**GIFT AID (NEED-BASED) Total amount:** $13,732,514 (20% federal, 19% state, 60% institutional, 1% external sources). **Receiving aid:** Freshmen: 62% (134); all full-time undergraduates: 63% (820). **Average award:** Freshmen: $9629; Undergraduates: $8742. **Scholarships, grants, and awards:** Federal Pell, FSEOG, state, private, college/university gift aid from institutional funds, Federal Nursing.

**GIFT AID (NON-NEED-BASED) Total amount:** $5,780,706 (9% federal, 89% institutional, 2% external sources). **Receiving aid:** Freshmen: 84% (182). Undergraduates: 84% (1,093). **Average award:** Freshmen: $10,201. Undergraduates: $10,119. **Scholarships, grants, and awards by category:** Academic interests/achievement: 1,228 awards ($8,393,473 total): biological sciences, communication, education, general academic interests/achievements, health fields, international studies, premedicine, social sciences. Creative arts/performance: 41 awards ($41,100 total): applied art and design, art/fine arts, general creative arts/performance, music, performing arts. Special achievements/activities: 554 awards ($3,924,371 total): cheerleading/drum major, community service, general special achievements/activities, leadership, religious involvement. Special characteristics: 492 awards ($1,978,368 total): adult students, children and siblings of alumni, children of educators, ethnic background, first-generation college students, general special characteristics, religious affiliation, siblings of current students, veterans, veterans' children. **Tuition waivers:** Full or partial for children of alumni, employees or children of employees. **ROTC:** Army cooperative.

**LOANS Student loans:** $9,639,789 (67% need-based, 33% non-need-based). 78% of past graduating class borrowed through all loan programs. **Average indebtedness per student:** $29,418. **Average need-based loan:** Freshmen: $3797. Undergraduates: $4742. **Parent loans:** $2,883,820 (88% need-based, 12% non-need-based). **Programs:** Federal Direct (Subsidized and Unsubsidized Stafford, PLUS), Perkins, alternative loans.

**WORK-STUDY Federal work-study:** Total amount: $270,822; 182 jobs averaging $1488. **State or other work-study/employment:** Total amount: $458,297 (100% non-need-based). 322 part-time jobs averaging $1423.

**ATHLETIC AWARDS** Total amount: $4,024,183 (82% need-based, 18% non-need-based).

**APPLYING FOR FINANCIAL AID Required financial aid forms:** FAFSA, institution's own form. **Financial aid deadline (priority):** 2/15. **Notification date:** Continuous beginning 2/15. Students must reply within 4 weeks of notification.

**CONTACT** Mrs. Mary V. Shaw, Director of Financial Aid Services, University of St. Francis, 500 North Wilcox Street, Joliet, IL 60435-6188, 815-740-3403 or toll-free 800-735-7500. Fax: 815-740-3822. E-mail: mshaw@stfrancis.edu. Website: http://www.stfrancis.edu/.

# UNIVERSITY OF SAINT FRANCIS
## Fort Wayne, IN

**CONTACT** Office of Financial Aid, University of Saint Francis, 2701 Spring Street, Fort Wayne, IN 46808, 260-399-8003 or toll-free 800-729-4732. Fax: 260-399-8162. E-mail: finaid@sf.edu. Website: http://www.sf.edu/.

# UNIVERSITY OF SAINT JOSEPH
## West Hartford, CT

| Tuition & fees: $36,140 | Average undergraduate aid package: $24,930 |
| --- | --- |

**ABOUT THE INSTITUTION** Independent Roman Catholic, coed, primarily women. **Awards:** certificates, bachelor's, master's, and doctoral degrees. 24 undergraduate majors. **Total enrollment:** 2,565. Undergraduates: 987. Freshmen: 150. Federal methodology is used as a basis for awarding need-based institutional aid.

**UNDERGRADUATE EXPENSES for 2015–2016 Application fee:** $50. **Comprehensive fee:** $50,990 includes full-time tuition ($34,530), mandatory fees ($1610), and room and board ($14,850). **College room only:** $6850. Full-time tuition and fees vary according to course load, degree level, location, program, and student level. Room and board charges vary according to board plan and housing facility. **Part-time tuition:** $751 per credit hour. **Part-time fees:** $55 per credit hour. Part-time tuition and fees vary according to course load, degree level, location, program, and student level.

**FRESHMAN FINANCIAL AID (Fall 2014, est.)** 145 applied for aid; of those 94% were deemed to have need. 100% of freshmen with need received aid; of those 12% had need fully met. **Average percent of need met:** 77% (excluding resources awarded to replace EFC). **Average financial aid package:** $28,540 (excluding resources awarded to replace EFC). 7% of all full-time freshmen had no need and received non-need-based gift aid.

**UNDERGRADUATE FINANCIAL AID (Fall 2014, est.)** 720 applied for aid; of those 95% were deemed to have need. 100% of undergraduates with need received aid; of those 12% had need fully met. **Average percent of need met:** 68% (excluding resources awarded to replace EFC). **Average financial aid package:** $24,930 (excluding resources awarded to replace EFC). 8% of all full-time undergraduates had no need and received non-need-based gift aid.

**GIFT AID (NEED-BASED) Total amount:** $13,905,085 (12% federal, 7% state, 78% institutional, 3% external sources). **Receiving aid:** Freshmen: 91% (136); all full-time undergraduates: 86% (658). **Average award:** Freshmen: $24,912; Undergraduates: $20,175. **Scholarships, grants, and awards:** Federal Pell, FSEOG, state, private, college/university gift aid from institutional funds.

**GIFT AID (NON-NEED-BASED) Total amount:** $799,612 (97% institutional, 3% external sources). **Receiving aid:** Freshmen: 8% (12). Undergraduates: 6% (45). **Average award:** Freshmen: $12,636. Undergraduates: $12,380. **Scholarships, grants, and awards by category:** Academic interests/achievement: 571 awards ($6,359,290 total): general academic interests/achievements. Special characteristics: 21 awards ($21,000 total): siblings of current students. **Tuition waivers:** Full or partial for employees or children of employees.

**LOANS Student loans:** $8,223,731 (81% need-based, 19% non-need-based). 90% of past graduating class borrowed through all loan programs. **Average indebtedness per student:** $37,557. **Average need-based loan:** Freshmen: $4020. Undergraduates: $5878. **Parent loans:** $3,032,821 (48% need-based, 52% non-need-based). **Programs:** Federal Direct (Subsidized and Unsubsidized Stafford, PLUS), Perkins, private loans.

**WORK-STUDY** Federal work-study jobs available. **State or other work-study/employment:** Total amount: $106,500 (53% need-based, 47% non-need-based). 50 part-time jobs averaging $1806.

**APPLYING FOR FINANCIAL AID Required financial aid form:** FAFSA. **Financial aid deadline (priority):** 2/15. **Notification date:** Continuous beginning 2/15.

**CONTACT** Financial Aid Office, University of Saint Joseph, 1678 Asylum Avenue, West Hartford, CT 06117, 860-231-5223 or toll-free 866-442-8752. E-mail: financialaid@usj.edu. Website: http://www.usj.edu/.

# UNIVERSITY OF SAINT MARY
## Leavenworth, KS

**CONTACT** Mrs. Judy Wiedower, Financial Aid Director, University of Saint Mary, 4100 South Fourth Street, Leavenworth, KS 66048, 913-758-6314 or toll-free 800-752-7043. Fax: 913-758-6146. E-mail: wiedower@hub.smcks.edu. Website: http://www.stmary.edu/.

# UNIVERSITY OF ST. THOMAS
## St. Paul, MN

| Tuition & fees: $36,682 | Average undergraduate aid package: $24,513 |
| --- | --- |

**ABOUT THE INSTITUTION** Independent Roman Catholic, coed. *Awards:* certificates, bachelor's, master's, and doctoral degrees. 59 undergraduate majors. *Total enrollment:* 10,226. Undergraduates: 6,234. Freshmen: 1,409. Federal methodology is used as a basis for awarding need-based institutional aid.

**UNDERGRADUATE EXPENSES for 2015–2016** Tuition: full-time $35,872; part-time $1121 per credit hour. Room and board charges vary according to board plan and housing facility.

**FRESHMAN FINANCIAL AID (Fall 2014, est.)** 1,165 applied for aid; of those 77% were deemed to have need. 100% of freshmen with need received aid; of those 17% had need fully met. *Average percent of need met:* 87% (excluding resources awarded to replace EFC). *Average financial aid package:* $26,552 (excluding resources awarded to replace EFC). 19% of all full-time freshmen had no need and received non-need-based gift aid.

**UNDERGRADUATE FINANCIAL AID (Fall 2014, est.)** 4,178 applied for aid; of those 82% were deemed to have need. 100% of undergraduates with need received aid; of those 15% had need fully met. *Average percent of need met:* 82% (excluding resources awarded to replace EFC). *Average financial aid package:* $24,513 (excluding resources awarded to replace EFC). 11% of all full-time undergraduates had no need and received non-need-based gift aid.

**GIFT AID (NEED-BASED)** *Total amount:* $61,046,500 (9% federal, 9% state, 80% institutional, 2% external sources). *Receiving aid:* Freshmen: 62% (878); all full-time undergraduates: 56% (3,308). *Average award:* Freshmen: $20,661; Undergraduates: $18,352. *Scholarships, grants, and awards:* Federal Pell, FSEOG, state, private, college/university gift aid from institutional funds.

**GIFT AID (NON-NEED-BASED)** *Total amount:* $14,125,573 (95% institutional, 5% external sources). *Receiving aid:* Freshmen: 12% (169). Undergraduates: 7% (414). *Average award:* Freshmen: $17,723. Undergraduates: $15,098. *Scholarships, grants, and awards by category: Academic interests/achievement:* 1,807 awards ($28,879,903 total): biological sciences, business, education, English, general academic interests/achievements, humanities, international studies, mathematics, physical sciences, religion/biblical studies, social sciences. *Creative arts/performance:* 51 awards ($145,226 total): journalism/publications, music. *Special characteristics:* 172 awards ($3,266,691 total): children of educators, children of faculty/staff, general special characteristics. *Tuition waivers:* Full or partial for employees or children of employees, senior citizens. *ROTC:* Army cooperative, Naval cooperative, Air Force.

**LOANS** *Student loans:* $36,677,788 (64% need-based, 36% non-need-based). 65% of past graduating class borrowed through all loan programs. *Average indebtedness per student:* $37,131. *Average need-based loan:* Freshmen: $7139. Undergraduates: $8135. *Parent loans:* $5,158,306 (49% need-based, 51% non-need-based). *Programs:* Federal Direct (Subsidized and Unsubsidized Stafford, PLUS), Perkins, state, alternative loans.

**WORK-STUDY** *Federal work-study:* Total amount: $3,914,444; 1,348 jobs averaging $2904. *State or other work-study/employment:* Total amount: $3,212,623 (56% need-based, 44% non-need-based). 810 part-time jobs averaging $2671.

**APPLYING FOR FINANCIAL AID** *Required financial aid form:* FAFSA. *Financial aid deadline (priority):* 4/1. *Notification date:* Continuous beginning 3/1. Students must reply within 3 weeks of notification.

**CONTACT** Ms. Paula Benson, Associate Director of Student Financial Services, University of St. Thomas, 2115 Summit Avenue, MHC 152, St. Paul, MN 55105-1096, 651-962-6547 or toll-free 800-328-6819. *Fax:* 651-962-6599. *E-mail:* paula.benson@stthomas.edu.
*Website:* http://www.stthomas.edu/.

*enrollment:* 3,522. Undergraduates: 1,645. Freshmen: 227. Federal methodology is used as a basis for awarding need-based institutional aid.

**UNDERGRADUATE EXPENSES for 2015–2016** *Comprehensive fee:* $37,690 includes full-time tuition ($29,100), mandatory fees ($340), and room and board ($8250). *College room only:* $5000. Full-time tuition and fees vary according to course load. Room and board charges vary according to board plan and housing facility. *Part-time tuition:* $970 per credit hour. Part-time tuition and fees vary according to course load.

**FRESHMAN FINANCIAL AID (Fall 2014, est.)** 168 applied for aid; of those 90% were deemed to have need. 99% of freshmen with need received aid; of those 15% had need fully met. *Average percent of need met:* 68% (excluding resources awarded to replace EFC). *Average financial aid package:* $23,529 (excluding resources awarded to replace EFC). 26% of all full-time freshmen had no need and received non-need-based gift aid.

**UNDERGRADUATE FINANCIAL AID (Fall 2014, est.)** 816 applied for aid; of those 93% were deemed to have need. 99% of undergraduates with need received aid; of those 9% had need fully met. *Average percent of need met:* 59% (excluding resources awarded to replace EFC). *Average financial aid package:* $21,618 (excluding resources awarded to replace EFC). 27% of all full-time undergraduates had no need and received non-need-based gift aid.

**GIFT AID (NEED-BASED)** *Total amount:* $13,591,369 (19% federal, 14% state, 64% institutional, 3% external sources). *Receiving aid:* Freshmen: 65% (146); all full-time undergraduates: 58% (738). *Average award:* Freshmen: $18,997; Undergraduates: $17,466. *Scholarships, grants, and awards:* Federal Pell, FSEOG, state, private, college/university gift aid from institutional funds, Academic Competitiveness Grants, National SMART Grants.

**GIFT AID (NON-NEED-BASED)** *Total amount:* $3,779,757 (98% institutional, 2% external sources). *Receiving aid:* Freshmen: 7% (16). Undergraduates: 3% (38). *Average award:* Freshmen: $11,794. Undergraduates: $10,520. *Scholarships, grants, and awards by category: Academic interests/achievement:* biological sciences, business, communication, computer science, education, English, foreign languages, general academic interests/achievements, health fields, humanities, international studies, mathematics, physical sciences, premedicine, religion/biblical studies, social sciences. *Creative arts/performance:* applied art and design, art/fine arts, general creative arts/performance, music, performing arts, theater/drama. *Special achievements/activities:* general special achievements/activities, leadership, religious involvement. *Special characteristics:* children of faculty/staff, general special characteristics, previous college experience, religious affiliation. *Tuition waivers:* Full or partial for employees or children of employees, senior citizens. *ROTC:* Army cooperative, Air Force cooperative.

**LOANS** *Student loans:* $3,446,539 (90% need-based, 10% non-need-based). 57% of past graduating class borrowed through all loan programs. *Average indebtedness per student:* $36,497. *Average need-based loan:* Freshmen: $5084. Undergraduates: $5085. *Parent loans:* $1,329,455 (42% need-based, 58% non-need-based). *Programs:* Federal Direct (Subsidized and Unsubsidized Stafford, PLUS), Perkins, state, private loans.

**WORK-STUDY** *Federal work-study:* Total amount: $386,513; 79 jobs averaging $3880. *State or other work-study/employment:* 2 part-time jobs averaging $4000.

**ATHLETIC AWARDS** Total amount: $506,000 (37% need-based, 63% non-need-based).

**APPLYING FOR FINANCIAL AID** *Required financial aid form:* FAFSA. *Financial aid deadline (priority):* 4/15. *Notification date:* Continuous beginning 2/15. Students must reply within 2 weeks of notification.

**CONTACT** Lynda McKendree, Dean of Scholarships and Financial Aid, University of St. Thomas, 3800 Montrose Boulevard, Houston, TX 77006-4696, 713-525-2170 or toll-free 800-856-8565. *Fax:* 713-525-2142. *E-mail:* finaid@stthom.edu.
*Website:* http://www.stthom.edu/.

# UNIVERSITY OF ST. THOMAS
## Houston, TX

| Tuition & fees: $29,440 | Average undergraduate aid package: $21,618 |
| --- | --- |

**ABOUT THE INSTITUTION** Independent Roman Catholic, coed. *Awards:* diplomas, bachelor's, master's, and doctoral degrees. 37 undergraduate majors. *Total*

# UNIVERSITY OF SAN DIEGO
## San Diego, CA

| Tuition & fees: $42,908 | Average undergraduate aid package: $31,056 |
| --- | --- |

**ABOUT THE INSTITUTION** Independent Roman Catholic, coed. *Awards:* certificates, bachelor's, master's, and doctoral degrees. 42 undergraduate majors. *Total enrollment:* 8,349. Undergraduates: 5,741. Freshmen: 1,129. Federal methodology is used as a basis for awarding need-based institutional aid.

UNDERGRADUATE EXPENSES for 2015–2016 *Application fee:* $55. *Comprehensive fee:* $54,818 includes full-time tuition ($42,330), mandatory fees ($578), and room and board ($11,910). Room and board charges vary according to board plan and housing facility. *Part-time tuition:* $1460 per unit. Part-time tuition and fees vary according to course load.

FRESHMAN FINANCIAL AID (Fall 2013) 940 applied for aid; of those 81% were deemed to have need. 99% of freshmen with need received aid; of those 15% had need fully met. *Average percent of need met:* 73% (excluding resources awarded to replace EFC). *Average financial aid package:* $32,328 (excluding resources awarded to replace EFC). 16% of all full-time freshmen had no need and received non-need-based gift aid.

UNDERGRADUATE FINANCIAL AID (Fall 2013) 3,432 applied for aid; of those 88% were deemed to have need. 98% of undergraduates with need received aid; of those 14% had need fully met. *Average percent of need met:* 70% (excluding resources awarded to replace EFC). *Average financial aid package:* $31,056 (excluding resources awarded to replace EFC). 14% of all full-time undergraduates had no need and received non-need-based gift aid.

GIFT AID (NEED-BASED) *Total amount:* $68,991,133 (13% federal, 7% state, 78% institutional, 2% external sources). *Receiving aid:* Freshmen: 60% (745); all full-time undergraduates: 53% (2,872). *Average award:* Freshmen: $26,405; Undergraduates: $24,438. *Scholarships, grants, and awards:* Federal Pell, FSEOG, state, private, college/university gift aid from institutional funds, Federal Nursing, TEACH Grants.

GIFT AID (NON-NEED-BASED) *Total amount:* $15,322,529 (19% federal, 77% institutional, 4% external sources). *Receiving aid:* Freshmen: 35% (439). Undergraduates: 25% (1,376). *Average award:* Freshmen: $17,729. Undergraduates: $14,025. *Scholarships, grants, and awards by category:* Academic interests/achievement: 1,670 awards ($23,900,654 total): general academic interests/achievements. Creative arts/performance: 14 awards ($114,750 total): music. Special achievements/activities: 79 awards: leadership, religious involvement. Special characteristics: 84 awards ($3,138,066 total): children of faculty/staff, religious affiliation. *Tuition waivers:* Full or partial for employees or children of employees. *ROTC:* Army cooperative, Naval, Air Force cooperative.

LOANS *Student loans:* $23,129,016 (91% need-based, 9% non-need-based). 54% of past graduating class borrowed through all loan programs. *Average indebtedness per student:* $30,225. *Average need-based loan:* Freshmen: $6602. Undergraduates: $7862. *Parent loans:* $26,874,807 (51% need-based, 49% non-need-based). *Programs:* Federal Direct (Subsidized and Unsubsidized Stafford, PLUS), Perkins, college/university.

WORK-STUDY *Federal work-study:* 505 jobs averaging $1973. *State or other work-study/employment:* Total amount: $1,153,887 (42% need-based, 58% non-need-based). Part-time jobs available.

ATHLETIC AWARDS Total amount: $6,511,563 (29% need-based, 71% non-need-based).

APPLYING FOR FINANCIAL AID *Required financial aid form:* FAFSA. *Financial aid deadline (priority):* 3/2. *Notification date:* Continuous beginning 3/1. Students must reply by 5/1 or within 3 weeks of notification.

CONTACT Judith Lewis Logue, Director of Financial Aid Services, University of San Diego, 5998 Alcalá Park, San Diego, CA 92110-2492, 619-260-2700 or toll-free 800-248-4873. *E-mail:* jllogue@sandiego.edu. *Website:* http://www.sandiego.edu/.

# UNIVERSITY OF SAN FRANCISCO
## San Francisco, CA

| Tuition & fees: $42,634 | Average undergraduate aid package: $37,283 |
| --- | --- |

ABOUT THE INSTITUTION Independent Roman Catholic (Jesuit), coed. *Awards:* certificates, bachelor's, master's, and doctoral degrees. 79 undergraduate majors. *Total enrollment:* 10,701. Undergraduates: 6,845. Freshmen: 1,502. Federal methodology is used as a basis for awarding need-based institutional aid.

UNDERGRADUATE EXPENSES for 2015–2016 *Application fee:* $55. *Comprehensive fee:* $56,284 includes full-time tuition ($42,180), mandatory fees ($454), and room and board ($13,650). *College room only:* $9170. Full-time tuition and fees vary according to course load, degree level, location, program, and reciprocity agreements. Room and board charges vary according to board plan and housing facility. *Part-time tuition:* $1500 per credit. *Part-time fees:* $454 per year. Part-time

tuition and fees vary according to course load, degree level, location, program, and reciprocity agreements.

FRESHMAN FINANCIAL AID (Fall 2014, est.) 1,179 applied for aid; of those 73% were deemed to have need. 98% of freshmen with need received aid; of those 11% had need fully met. *Average percent of need met:* 66% (excluding resources awarded to replace EFC). *Average financial aid package:* $38,481 (excluding resources awarded to replace EFC). 16% of all full-time freshmen had no need and received non-need-based gift aid.

UNDERGRADUATE FINANCIAL AID (Fall 2014, est.) 4,596 applied for aid; of those 78% were deemed to have need. 98% of undergraduates with need received aid; of those 11% had need fully met. *Average percent of need met:* 59% (excluding resources awarded to replace EFC). *Average financial aid package:* $37,283 (excluding resources awarded to replace EFC). 10% of all full-time undergraduates had no need and received non-need-based gift aid.

GIFT AID (NEED-BASED) *Total amount:* $79,346,644 (11% federal, 11% state, 76% institutional, 2% external sources). *Receiving aid:* Freshmen: 55% (817); all full-time undergraduates: 50% (3,248). *Average award:* Freshmen: $26,104; Undergraduates: $22,199. *Scholarships, grants, and awards:* Federal Pell, FSEOG, state, private, college/university gift aid from institutional funds, Federal Nursing.

GIFT AID (NON-NEED-BASED) *Total amount:* $8,817,817 (1% federal, 98% institutional, 1% external sources). *Receiving aid:* Freshmen: 5% (70). Undergraduates: 11% (727). *Average award:* Freshmen: $12,953. Undergraduates: $11,198. *Scholarships, grants, and awards by category:* Academic interests/achievement: 2,430 awards ($24,517,195 total): general academic interests/achievements, military science. *Tuition waivers:* Full or partial for employees or children of employees. *ROTC:* Army, Air Force cooperative.

LOANS *Student loans:* $37,312,605 (80% need-based, 20% non-need-based). 59% of past graduating class borrowed through all loan programs. *Average indebtedness per student:* $31,098. *Average need-based loan:* Freshmen: $4195. Undergraduates: $4955. *Parent loans:* $12,265,104 (48% need-based, 52% non-need-based). *Programs:* Federal Direct (Subsidized and Unsubsidized Stafford, PLUS), Perkins, Federal Nursing, college/university.

WORK-STUDY *Federal work-study:* Total amount: $1,971,578; 580 jobs averaging $3402. *State or other work-study/employment:* Total amount: $4,354,681 (99% need-based, 1% non-need-based). 1,063 part-time jobs averaging $4053.

ATHLETIC AWARDS Total amount: $5,958,194 (32% need-based, 68% non-need-based).

APPLYING FOR FINANCIAL AID *Required financial aid form:* FAFSA. *Financial aid deadline (priority):* 2/1. *Notification date:* Continuous beginning 4/1. Students must reply within 4 weeks of notification.

CONTACT Ms. Susan Murphy, Senior Associate Dean/Director of Enrollment and Financial Services, University of San Francisco, 2130 Fulton Street, LM 257, San Francisco, CA 94117-1080, 415-422-2620 or toll-free 800-CALL-USF. *Fax:* 415-422-6084. *E-mail:* murphy@usfca.edu. *Website:* http://www.usfca.edu/.

# UNIVERSITY OF SCIENCE AND ARTS OF OKLAHOMA
## Chickasha, OK

| Tuition & fees (OK res): $6270 | Average undergraduate aid package: $10,607 |
| --- | --- |

ABOUT THE INSTITUTION State-supported, coed. *Awards:* bachelor's degrees. 24 undergraduate majors. *Total enrollment:* 904. Undergraduates: 902. Freshmen: 170. Federal methodology is used as a basis for awarding need-based institutional aid.

UNDERGRADUATE EXPENSES for 2015–2016 *Application fee:* $40. *Tuition, state resident:* full-time $5100; part-time $170 per credit hour. *Tuition, nonresident:* full-time $14,040; part-time $468 per credit hour. *Required fees:* full-time $1170; $39 per credit hour. Full-time tuition and fees vary according to course load. Part-time tuition and fees vary according to course load. *College room and board:* $5470; *Room only:* $2760. Room and board charges vary according to board plan and housing facility. *Payment plan:* Guaranteed tuition.

FRESHMAN FINANCIAL AID (Fall 2014, est.) 145 applied for aid; of those 85% were deemed to have need. 99% of freshmen with need received aid; of those 25% had need fully met. *Average percent of need met:* 74% (excluding resources awarded to replace EFC). *Average financial aid package:* $10,779 (excluding resources awarded to replace EFC). 10% of all full-time freshmen had no need and received non-need-based gift aid.

**UNDERGRADUATE FINANCIAL AID (Fall 2014, est.)** 617 applied for aid; of those 85% were deemed to have need. 96% of undergraduates with need received aid; of those 18% had need fully met. *Average percent of need met:* 62% (excluding resources awarded to replace EFC). *Average financial aid package:* $10,607 (excluding resources awarded to replace EFC). 13% of all full-time undergraduates had no need and received non-need-based gift aid.

**GIFT AID (NEED-BASED)** *Total amount:* $3,198,983 (57% federal, 25% state, 12% institutional, 6% external sources). *Receiving aid:* Freshmen: 71% (120); all full-time undergraduates: 60% (482). *Average award:* Freshmen: $8911; Undergraduates: $8191. *Scholarships, grants, and awards:* Federal Pell, FSEOG, state, private, college/university gift aid from institutional funds, USAO Foundation Grants.

**GIFT AID (NON-NEED-BASED)** *Total amount:* $510,034 (25% state, 60% institutional, 15% external sources). *Receiving aid:* Freshmen: 11% (19). Undergraduates: 5% (44). *Average award:* Freshmen: $3132. Undergraduates: $2779. *Scholarships, grants, and awards by category:* Academic interests/achievement: 503 awards ($1,008,799 total): general academic interests/achievements. *Creative arts/performance:* 4 awards ($4600 total): art/fine arts, music, theater/drama. *Special achievements/activities:* 9 awards ($8000 total): cheerleading/drum major. *Special characteristics:* 81 awards ($263,501 total): children of faculty/staff, international students, out-of-state students, previous college experience. *Tuition waivers:* Full or partial for employees or children of employees, senior citizens.

**LOANS** *Student loans:* $2,361,862 (76% need-based, 24% non-need-based). 61% of past graduating class borrowed through all loan programs. *Average indebtedness per student:* $20,074. *Average need-based loan:* Freshmen: $2727. Undergraduates: $3304. *Parent loans:* $80,857 (20% need-based, 80% non-need-based). *Programs:* Federal Direct (Subsidized and Unsubsidized Stafford, PLUS), Perkins, college/university.

**WORK-STUDY** *Federal work-study:* Total amount: $221,035; 171 jobs averaging $1374.

**ATHLETIC AWARDS** Total amount: $1,581,658 (30% need-based, 70% non-need-based).

**APPLYING FOR FINANCIAL AID** *Required financial aid forms:* FAFSA, institution's own form. *Financial aid deadline (priority):* 3/1. *Notification date:* Continuous beginning 3/1. Students must reply within 4 weeks of notification.

**CONTACT** Laura D. Coponiti, Director of Financial Aid, University of Science and Arts of Oklahoma, 1727 West Alabama, Chickasha, OK 73018-5322, 405-574-1350 or toll-free 800-933-8726. *Fax:* 405-574-1220. *E-mail:* lcoponiti@usao.edu. *Website:* http://www.usao.edu/.

# THE UNIVERSITY OF SCRANTON
## Scranton, PA

| Tuition & fees: $39,956 | Average undergraduate aid package: $24,187 |
| --- | --- |

**ABOUT THE INSTITUTION** Independent Roman Catholic (Jesuit), coed. *Awards:* certificates, bachelor's, master's, and doctoral degrees. 66 undergraduate majors. *Total enrollment:* 5,589. Undergraduates: 3,998. Freshmen: 1,067. Federal methodology is used as a basis for awarding need-based institutional aid.

**UNDERGRADUATE EXPENSES for 2015–2016** *Comprehensive fee:* $53,522 includes full-time tuition ($39,556), mandatory fees ($400), and room and board ($13,566). *College room only:* $7954. Room and board charges vary according to board plan and housing facility.

**FRESHMAN FINANCIAL AID (Fall 2013)** 794 applied for aid; of those 85% were deemed to have need. 99% of freshmen with need received aid; of those 12% had need fully met. *Average percent of need met:* 68% (excluding resources awarded to replace EFC). *Average financial aid package:* $24,093 (excluding resources awarded to replace EFC). 17% of all full-time freshmen had no need and received non-need-based gift aid.

**UNDERGRADUATE FINANCIAL AID (Fall 2013)** 3,104 applied for aid; of those 89% were deemed to have need. 99% of undergraduates with need received aid; of those 10% had need fully met. *Average percent of need met:* 67% (excluding resources awarded to replace EFC). *Average financial aid package:* $24,187 (excluding resources awarded to replace EFC). 17% of all full-time undergraduates had no need and received non-need-based gift aid.

**GIFT AID (NEED-BASED)** *Total amount:* $51,922,636 (7% federal, 5% state, 85% institutional, 3% external sources). *Receiving aid:* Freshmen: 75% (655); all full-time undergraduates: 71% (2,645). *Average award:* Freshmen: $21,056; Undergraduates: $20,140. *Scholarships, grants, and awards:* Federal Pell, FSEOG, state, private, college/university gift aid from institutional funds.

**GIFT AID (NON-NEED-BASED)** *Total amount:* $10,888,407 (3% federal, 86% institutional, 11% external sources). *Receiving aid:* Freshmen: 8% (66). Undergraduates: 5% (190). *Average award:* Freshmen: $13,007. Undergraduates: $12,620. *Scholarships, grants, and awards by category:* Academic interests/achievement: general academic interests/achievements, military science. *Special characteristics:* children of educators, children of faculty/staff, ethnic background, members of minority groups, religious affiliation, siblings of current students, veterans, veterans' children. *Tuition waivers:* Full or partial for employees or children of employees, senior citizens. *ROTC:* Army, Air Force cooperative.

**LOANS** *Student loans:* $30,110,771 (67% need-based, 33% non-need-based). 75% of past graduating class borrowed through all loan programs. *Average indebtedness per student:* $38,640. *Average need-based loan:* Freshmen: $7103. Undergraduates: $8310. *Parent loans:* $13,515,029 (43% need-based, 57% non-need-based). *Programs:* Federal Direct (Subsidized and Unsubsidized Stafford, PLUS), Perkins.

**WORK-STUDY** *Federal work-study:* jobs available. *State or other work-study/employment:* Total amount: $997,820 (55% need-based, 45% non-need-based). Part-time jobs available.

**APPLYING FOR FINANCIAL AID** *Required financial aid form:* FAFSA. *Financial aid deadline (priority):* 2/15. *Notification date:* Continuous beginning 3/15. Students must reply by 5/1.

**CONTACT** Mr. William R. Burke, Director of Financial Aid, The University of Scranton, St. Thomas Hall 401, Scranton, PA 18510, 570-941-7887 or toll-free 888-SCRANTON. *Fax:* 570-941-4370. *E-mail:* finaid@scranton.edu. *Website:* http://www.scranton.edu/.

# UNIVERSITY OF SIOUX FALLS
## Sioux Falls, SD

**CONTACT** Rachel Gunn, Financial Aid Counselor, University of Sioux Falls, 1101 West 22nd Street, Sioux Falls, SD 57105-1699, 605-331-6623 or toll-free 800-888-1047. *Fax:* 605-331-6615. *E-mail:* rachel.gunn@usiouxfalls.edu. *Website:* http://www.usiouxfalls.edu/.

# UNIVERSITY OF SOUTH ALABAMA
## Mobile, AL

| Tuition & fees (AL res): $8610 | Average undergraduate aid package: $9405 |
| --- | --- |

**ABOUT THE INSTITUTION** State-supported, coed. *Awards:* certificates, bachelor's, master's, and doctoral degrees. 53 undergraduate majors. *Total enrollment:* 15,805. Undergraduates: 11,479. Freshmen: 2,073. Federal methodology is used as a basis for awarding need-based institutional aid.

**UNDERGRADUATE EXPENSES for 2015–2016** *Application fee:* $35. *Tuition, state resident:* full-time $8610; part-time $287 per credit hour. *Tuition, nonresident:* full-time $17,220; part-time $554 per credit hour. Full-time tuition and fees vary according to course load and program. Part-time tuition and fees vary according to course load and program. *College room and board:* $7100; *Room only:* $3800. Room and board charges vary according to board plan and housing facility.

**FRESHMAN FINANCIAL AID (Fall 2013)** 1,626 applied for aid; of those 75% were deemed to have need. 100% of freshmen with need received aid; of those 14% had need fully met. *Average percent of need met:* 59% (excluding resources awarded to replace EFC). *Average financial aid package:* $9665 (excluding resources awarded to replace EFC). 20% of all full-time freshmen had no need and received non-need-based gift aid.

**UNDERGRADUATE FINANCIAL AID (Fall 2013)** 6,671 applied for aid; of those 83% were deemed to have need. 100% of undergraduates with need received aid; of those 11% had need fully met. *Average percent of need met:* 54% (excluding resources awarded to replace EFC). *Average financial aid package:*

$9405 (excluding resources awarded to replace EFC). 11% of all full-time undergraduates had no need and received non-need-based gift aid.

**GIFT AID (NEED-BASED)** *Total amount:* $19,943,476 (99% federal, 1% state). *Receiving aid:* Freshmen: 60% (1,097); all full-time undergraduates: 51% (4,482). *Average award:* Freshmen: $7062; Undergraduates: $6433. *Scholarships, grants, and awards:* Federal Pell, FSEOG, state, private, college/university gift aid from institutional funds.

**GIFT AID (NON-NEED-BASED)** *Total amount:* $11,002,695 (91% institutional, 9% external sources). *Receiving aid:* Freshmen: 60% (1,097). Undergraduates: 51% (4,482). *Average award:* Freshmen: $5222. Undergraduates: $5186. *Scholarships, grants, and awards by category: Academic interests/achievement:* business, computer science, general academic interests/achievements, humanities, international studies, military science. *Creative arts/performance:* art/fine arts, journalism/publications, music, theater/drama. *Special achievements/activities:* general special achievements/activities, hobbies/interests, junior miss, leadership. *Special characteristics:* children and siblings of alumni, children of faculty/staff, local/state students, members of minority groups. *Tuition waivers:* Full or partial for employees or children of employees. *ROTC:* Army, Air Force.

**LOANS** *Student loans:* $46,658,024 (42% need-based, 58% non-need-based). *Average need-based loan:* Freshmen: $3464. Undergraduates: $4323. *Parent loans:* $10,063,024 (100% non-need-based). *Programs:* Federal Direct (Subsidized and Unsubsidized Stafford, PLUS), Perkins, college/university.

**WORK-STUDY** *Federal work-study:* jobs available. *State or other work-study/employment:* Part-time jobs available.

**ATHLETIC AWARDS** Total amount: $4,744,091 (100% non-need-based).

**APPLYING FOR FINANCIAL AID** *Required financial aid forms:* FAFSA, institution's own form. *Financial aid deadline (priority):* 5/31. *Notification date:* Continuous beginning 4/15.

**CONTACT** Financial Aid Office, University of South Alabama, 390 Alumni Circle, Meisler Hall, Suite 1200, Mobile, AL 36688-0001, 800-305-6828 or toll-free 800-872-5247. *Fax:* 251-460-6517. *E-mail:* finaid@southalabama.edu. *Website:* http://www.southalabama.edu/.

# UNIVERSITY OF SOUTH CAROLINA
## Columbia, SC

| Tuition & fees (SC res): $11,158 | Average undergraduate aid package: $10,147 |
| --- | --- |

**ABOUT THE INSTITUTION** State-supported, coed. *Awards:* certificates, associate, bachelor's, master's, and doctoral degrees. 76 undergraduate majors. *Total enrollment:* 32,971. Undergraduates: 24,863. Freshmen: 4,980. Federal methodology is used as a basis for awarding need-based institutional aid.

**UNDERGRADUATE EXPENSES** for 2015–2016 *Application fee:* $50. *Tuition, state resident:* full-time $10,758; part-time $448.25 per credit hour. *Tuition, nonresident:* full-time $29,040; part-time $1210 per credit hour. *Required fees:* full-time $400. Full-time tuition and fees vary according to program and reciprocity agreements. Part-time tuition and fees vary according to course load. *College room and board:* $9248; *Room only:* $6216. Room and board charges vary according to board plan, housing facility, and location.

**FRESHMAN FINANCIAL AID (Fall 2014, est.)** 3,819 applied for aid; of those 62% were deemed to have need. 100% of freshmen with need received aid; of those 23% had need fully met. *Average percent of need met:* 65% (excluding resources awarded to replace EFC). *Average financial aid package:* $9411 (excluding resources awarded to replace EFC). 45% of all full-time freshmen had no need and received non-need-based gift aid.

**UNDERGRADUATE FINANCIAL AID (Fall 2014, est.)** 14,747 applied for aid; of those 72% were deemed to have need. 100% of undergraduates with need received aid; of those 20% had need fully met. *Average percent of need met:* 71% (excluding resources awarded to replace EFC). *Average financial aid package:* $10,147 (excluding resources awarded to replace EFC). 36% of all full-time undergraduates had no need and received non-need-based gift aid.

**GIFT AID (NEED-BASED)** *Total amount:* $77,034,956 (33% federal, 40% state, 13% institutional, 14% external sources). *Receiving aid:* Freshmen: 22% (975); all full-time undergraduates: 27% (5,361). *Average award:* Freshmen: $5356; Undergraduates: $5092. *Scholarships, grants, and awards:* Federal Pell, FSEOG, state, private, college/university gift aid from institutional funds, United Negro College Fund, Federal Nursing, USC Opportunity Grants, Gamecock Guarantee.

**GIFT AID (NON-NEED-BASED)** *Total amount:* $47,050,303 (52% state, 31% institutional, 17% external sources). *Receiving aid:* Freshmen: 47% (2,136). Undergraduates: 34% (6,868). *Average award:* Freshmen: $4274. Undergraduates: $4924. *Scholarships, grants, and awards by category: Academic interests/achievement:* area/ethnic studies, biological sciences, business, communication, computer science, education, engineering/technologies, English, foreign languages, general academic interests/achievements, health fields, humanities, international studies, library science, mathematics, military science, physical sciences, premedicine, religion/biblical studies, social sciences. *Creative arts/performance:* art/fine arts, dance, debating, journalism/publications, music, theater/drama. *Special achievements/activities:* cheerleading/drum major, community service, general special achievements/activities, leadership, memberships, religious involvement. *Special characteristics:* adult students, children and siblings of alumni, children of faculty/staff, children of union members/company employees, children of workers in trades, children with a deceased or disabled parent, ethnic background, first-generation college students, general special characteristics, handicapped students, international students, local/state students, members of minority groups, out-of-state students, religious affiliation, spouses of deceased or disabled public servants. *Tuition waivers:* Full or partial for employees or children of employees, senior citizens. *ROTC:* Army, Naval, Air Force.

**LOANS** *Student loans:* $107,679,151 (66% need-based, 34% non-need-based). 54% of past graduating class borrowed through all loan programs. *Average indebtedness per student:* $28,233. *Average need-based loan:* Freshmen: $3442. Undergraduates: $4545. *Parent loans:* $28,861,630 (42% need-based, 58% non-need-based). *Programs:* Federal Direct (Subsidized and Unsubsidized Stafford, PLUS), Perkins, Federal Nursing.

**WORK-STUDY** *Federal work-study:* Total amount: $1,477,099; jobs available. *State or other work-study/employment:* Part-time jobs available.

**ATHLETIC AWARDS** Total amount: $7,131,122 (35% need-based, 65% non-need-based).

**APPLYING FOR FINANCIAL AID** *Required financial aid form:* FAFSA. *Financial aid deadline (priority):* 4/1. *Notification date:* Continuous beginning 4/1.

**CONTACT** Dr. Ed Miller, Director of Financial Aid, University of South Carolina, 1714 College Street, Columbia, SC 29208, 803 777 8134 or toll-free 800-868-5872. *Fax:* 803-777-0941. *E-mail:* ewmiller@mailbox.sc.edu. *Website:* http://www.sc.edu/.

# UNIVERSITY OF SOUTH CAROLINA AIKEN
## Aiken, SC

| Tuition & fees (SC res): $9602 | Average undergraduate aid package: $10,374 |
| --- | --- |

**ABOUT THE INSTITUTION** State-supported, coed. *Awards:* bachelor's and master's degrees. 20 undergraduate majors. *Total enrollment:* 3,444. Undergraduates: 3,256. Freshmen: 643. Federal methodology is used as a basis for awarding need-based institutional aid.

**UNDERGRADUATE EXPENSES** for 2015–2016 *Application fee:* $45. *Tuition, state resident:* full-time $9312; part-time $388 per credit hour. *Tuition, nonresident:* full-time $18,636; part-time $777 per credit hour. *Required fees:* full-time $290; $9 per credit hour or $25 per term. Full-time tuition and fees vary according to reciprocity agreements. Part-time tuition and fees vary according to course load and reciprocity agreements. *College room and board:* $7110. Room and board charges vary according to board plan and housing facility.

**FRESHMAN FINANCIAL AID (Fall 2013)** 584 applied for aid; of those 76% were deemed to have need. 100% of freshmen with need received aid; of those 13% had need fully met. *Average percent of need met:* 63% (excluding resources awarded to replace EFC). *Average financial aid package:* $9999 (excluding resources awarded to replace EFC). 5% of all full-time freshmen had no need and received non-need-based gift aid.

**UNDERGRADUATE FINANCIAL AID (Fall 2013)** 2,267 applied for aid; of those 65% were deemed to have need. 98% of undergraduates with need received aid; of those 13% had need fully met. *Average percent of need met:* 62% (excluding resources awarded to replace EFC). *Average financial aid package:* $10,374 (excluding resources awarded to replace EFC). 10% of all full-time undergraduates had no need and received non-need-based gift aid.

**GIFT AID (NEED-BASED)** *Total amount:* $8,935,762 (59% federal, 35% state, 6% institutional). *Receiving aid:* Freshmen: 69% (411); all full-time undergraduates: 51% (1,228). *Average award:* Freshmen: $7082; Undergraduates: $6547. *Scholarships, grants, and awards:* Federal Pell, FSEOG, state, college/university gift aid from institutional funds.

**GIFT AID (NON-NEED-BASED)** *Total amount:* $4,060,565 (25% federal, 60% state, 14% institutional, 1% external sources). *Receiving aid:* Freshmen: 5% (31). Undergraduates: 4% (103). *Average award:* Freshmen: $3479. Undergraduates: $2213. *Scholarships, grants, and awards by category: Academic interests/achievement:* biological sciences, business, communication, computer science, education, engineering/technologies, English, general academic interests/achievements, humanities, mathematics, physical sciences, social sciences. *Creative arts/performance:* art/fine arts, journalism/publications, music, theater/drama. *Special achievements/activities:* cheerleading/drum major, community service, leadership. *Special characteristics:* adult students, first-generation college students, handicapped students, international students, members of minority groups. *Tuition waivers:* Full or partial for employees or children of employees, senior citizens.

**LOANS** *Student loans:* $14,995,348 (69% need-based, 31% non-need-based). 67% of past graduating class borrowed through all loan programs. *Average indebtedness per student:* $28,104. *Average need-based loan:* Freshmen: $3344. Undergraduates: $4267. *Parent loans:* $1,604,267 (46% need-based, 54% non-need-based). *Programs:* Federal Direct (Subsidized and Unsubsidized Stafford, PLUS), Perkins.

**WORK-STUDY** *Federal work-study:* 54 jobs averaging $1655. *State or other work-study/employment:* Total amount: $693,817 (30% need-based, 70% non-need-based). 351 part-time jobs averaging $1806.

**ATHLETIC AWARDS** Total amount: $761,281 (36% need-based, 64% non-need-based).

**APPLYING FOR FINANCIAL AID** *Required financial aid form:* FAFSA. *Financial aid deadline (priority):* 3/15. *Notification date:* Continuous beginning 4/20. Students must reply within 2 weeks of notification.

**CONTACT** Mrs. Linda Aubrey-Higgins, Director of Financial Aid, University of South Carolina Aiken, 471 University Parkway, Aiken, SC 29801, 803-641-3476 or toll-free 888-WOW-USCA. *Fax:* 803-643-6840. *E-mail:* lindahi@usca.edu. *Website:* http://www.usca.edu/.

# UNIVERSITY OF SOUTH CAROLINA BEAUFORT
### Bluffton, SC

**CONTACT** Jamella Taylor, Financial Aid Administrative Assistant, University of South Carolina Beaufort, 801 Carteret Street, Beaufort, SC 29902, 843-521-3104. *Fax:* 843-521-3194. *E-mail:* uscbfina@uscb.edu. *Website:* http://www.uscb.edu/.

# UNIVERSITY OF SOUTH CAROLINA UPSTATE
### Spartanburg, SC

| Tuition & fees (SC res): $10,518 | Average undergraduate aid package: $8693 |
| --- | --- |

**ABOUT THE INSTITUTION** State-supported, coed. *Awards:* certificates, bachelor's, and master's degrees. 31 undergraduate majors. *Total enrollment:* 5,509. Undergraduates: 5,334. Freshmen: 791. Federal methodology is used as a basis for awarding need-based institutional aid.

**UNDERGRADUATE EXPENSES** for 2015–2016 *Application fee:* $40. *One-time required fee:* $75. *Tuition, state resident:* full-time $10,068; part-time $419.50 per semester hour. *Tuition, nonresident:* full-time $20,418; part-time $850.75 per semester hour. *Required fees:* full-time $450. Full-time tuition and fees vary according to course load and program. Part-time tuition and fees vary according to course load and program. *College room and board:* $7682; *Room only:* $4732. Room and board charges vary according to board plan and housing facility.

**FRESHMAN FINANCIAL AID (Fall 2014, est.)** 690 applied for aid; of those 83% were deemed to have need. 100% of freshmen with need received aid; of those 13% had need fully met. *Average percent of need met:* 57% (excluding resources

awarded to replace EFC). *Average financial aid package:* $9434 (excluding resources awarded to replace EFC). 5% of all full-time freshmen had no need and received non-need-based gift aid.

**UNDERGRADUATE FINANCIAL AID (Fall 2014, est.)** 3,585 applied for aid; of those 89% were deemed to have need. 99% of undergraduates with need received aid; of those 7% had need fully met. *Average percent of need met:* 51% (excluding resources awarded to replace EFC). *Average financial aid package:* $8693 (excluding resources awarded to replace EFC). 3% of all full-time undergraduates had no need and received non-need-based gift aid.

**GIFT AID (NEED-BASED)** *Total amount:* $13,742,597 (91% federal, 9% state). *Receiving aid:* Freshmen: 56% (410); all full-time undergraduates: 55% (2,216). *Average award:* Freshmen: $4944; Undergraduates: $4715. *Scholarships, grants, and awards:* Federal Pell, FSEOG, state, private, college/university gift aid from institutional funds.

**GIFT AID (NON-NEED-BASED)** *Total amount:* $10,186,678 (87% state, 7% institutional, 6% external sources). *Receiving aid:* Freshmen: 70% (509). Undergraduates: 38% (1,508). *Average award:* Freshmen: $2086. Undergraduates: $2200. *Scholarships, grants, and awards by category: Academic interests/achievement:* 525 awards ($702,679 total): general academic interests/achievements. *Special characteristics:* first-generation college students. *Tuition waivers:* Full or partial for senior citizens. *ROTC:* Army cooperative.

**LOANS** *Student loans:* $30,294,412 (45% need-based, 55% non-need-based). 67% of past graduating class borrowed through all loan programs. *Average indebtedness per student:* $22,660. *Average need-based loan:* Freshmen: $2552. Undergraduates: $3467. *Parent loans:* $2,572,036 (100% non-need-based). *Programs:* Federal Direct (Subsidized and Unsubsidized Stafford, PLUS), Perkins, state, private loans.

**WORK-STUDY** *Federal work-study:* Total amount: $104,836; 126 jobs averaging $846. *State or other work-study/employment:* Total amount: $722,237 (100% non-need-based). Part-time jobs available.

**ATHLETIC AWARDS** Total amount: $1,577,957 (100% non-need-based).

**APPLYING FOR FINANCIAL AID** *Required financial aid form:* FAFSA. *Financial aid deadline (priority):* 3/1. *Notification date:* Continuous beginning 4/1. Students must reply within 2 weeks of notification.

**CONTACT** Bonnie Carson-Durham, Director of Financial Aid, University of South Carolina Upstate, 800 University Way, Spartanburg, SC 29303, 864-503-5340 or toll-free 800-277-8727. *Fax:* 864-503-5974. *E-mail:* bcarson@uscupstate.edu. *Website:* http://www.uscupstate.edu/.

# THE UNIVERSITY OF SOUTH DAKOTA
### Vermillion, SD

| Tuition & fees (SD res): $8022 | Average undergraduate aid package: $6507 |
| --- | --- |

**ABOUT THE INSTITUTION** State-supported, coed. *Awards:* certificates, associate, bachelor's, master's, and doctoral degrees. 60 undergraduate majors. *Total enrollment:* 10,061. Undergraduates: 7,541. Freshmen: 1,247. Federal methodology is used as a basis for awarding need-based institutional aid.

**UNDERGRADUATE EXPENSES** for 2015–2016 *Application fee:* $20. *Tuition, state resident:* full-time $4164; part-time $138.80 per credit hour. *Tuition, nonresident:* full-time $6246; part-time $208.20 per credit hour. *Required fees:* full-time $3858; $128.60 per credit hour. Full-time tuition and fees vary according to course load. Part-time tuition and fees vary according to course load. *College room and board:* $7089; *Room only:* $3785. Room and board charges vary according to board plan and housing facility.

**FRESHMAN FINANCIAL AID (Fall 2013)** 1,088 applied for aid; of those 72% were deemed to have need. 86% of freshmen with need received aid; of those 68% had need fully met. *Average percent of need met:* 78% (excluding resources awarded to replace EFC). *Average financial aid package:* $5867 (excluding resources awarded to replace EFC). 27% of all full-time freshmen had no need and received non-need-based gift aid.

**UNDERGRADUATE FINANCIAL AID (Fall 2013)** 4,413 applied for aid; of those 78% were deemed to have need. 91% of undergraduates with need received aid; of those 65% had need fully met. *Average percent of need met:* 77% (excluding resources awarded to replace EFC). *Average financial aid package:* $6507 (excluding resources awarded to replace EFC). 20% of all full-time undergraduates had no need and received non-need-based gift aid.

**GIFT AID (NEED-BASED)** *Total amount:* $9,351,071 (100% federal). *Receiving aid:* Freshmen: 30% (370); all full-time undergraduates: 32% (1,704).

**Average award:** Freshmen: $4444; Undergraduates: $4192. **Scholarships, grants, and awards:** Federal Pell, FSEOG, private, college/university gift aid from institutional funds, Federal Nursing.

**GIFT AID (NON-NEED-BASED) Total amount:** $8,565,012 (6% federal, 12% state, 49% institutional, 33% external sources). **Receiving aid:** Freshmen: 49% (599). Undergraduates: 35% (1,835). **Average award:** Freshmen: $4062. Undergraduates: $4513. **Scholarships, grants, and awards by category:** Academic interests/achievement: 2,456 awards ($4,436,462 total): biological sciences, business, communication, computer science, education, English, foreign languages, general academic interests/achievements, humanities, mathematics, military science, premedicine, social sciences. Creative arts/performance: 258 awards ($456,815 total): art/fine arts, creative writing, debating, music, theater/drama. Special achievements/activities: 198 awards ($425,816 total): leadership. Special characteristics: 38 awards ($108,245 total): members of minority groups. **Tuition waivers:** Full or partial for children of alumni, employees or children of employees, senior citizens. **ROTC:** Army.

**LOANS Student loans:** $32,318,281 (48% need-based, 52% non-need-based). 75% of past graduating class borrowed through all loan programs. Average indebtedness per student: $25,554. **Average need-based loan:** Freshmen: $3582. Undergraduates: $4234. **Parent loans:** $5,370,259 (100% non-need-based). **Programs:** Federal Direct (Subsidized and Unsubsidized Stafford, PLUS), Perkins, Federal Nursing, college/university.

**WORK-STUDY Federal work-study:** jobs available.

**ATHLETIC AWARDS** Total amount: $3,135,653 (100% non-need-based).

**APPLYING FOR FINANCIAL AID Required financial aid form:** FAFSA. **Financial aid deadline (priority):** 3/15. **Notification date:** Continuous beginning 3/1.

**CONTACT** Julie Pier, Director of Student Financial Aid, The University of South Dakota, Belbas Center, 414 East Clark Street, Vermillion, SD 57069, 605-677-5446 or toll-free 877-269-6837. Fax: 605-677-5238.

Website: http://www.usd.edu/.

---

# UNIVERSITY OF SOUTHERN CALIFORNIA
## Los Angeles, CA

| Tuition & fees: $48,280 | Average undergraduate aid package: $43,170 |
| --- | --- |

**ABOUT THE INSTITUTION** Independent, coed. **Awards:** certificates, bachelor's, master's, and doctoral degrees. 106 undergraduate majors. **Total enrollment:** 42,469. Undergraduates: 18,740. Freshmen: 3,098. Both federal and institutional methodology are used as a basis for awarding need-based institutional aid.

**UNDERGRADUATE EXPENSES for 2015–2016 Application fee:** $80. **One-time required fee:** $350. **Comprehensive fee:** $61,614 includes full-time tuition ($47,562), mandatory fees ($718), and room and board ($13,334). **College room only:** $8034. Full-time tuition and fees vary according to program. Room and board charges vary according to board plan and housing facility. **Part-time tuition:** $1602 per unit. Part-time tuition and fees vary according to course load and program. **Payment plan:** Tuition prepayment.

**FRESHMAN FINANCIAL AID (Fall 2013)** 1,786 applied for aid; of those 59% were deemed to have need. 100% of freshmen with need received aid; of those 98% had need fully met. **Average percent of need met:** 100% (excluding resources awarded to replace EFC). **Average financial aid package:** $45,044 (excluding resources awarded to replace EFC). 22% of all full-time freshmen had no need and received non-need-based gift aid.

**UNDERGRADUATE FINANCIAL AID (Fall 2013)** 9,559 applied for aid; of those 76% were deemed to have need. 100% of undergraduates with need received aid; of those 92% had need fully met. **Average percent of need met:** 100% (excluding resources awarded to replace EFC). **Average financial aid package:** $43,170 (excluding resources awarded to replace EFC). 18% of all full-time undergraduates had no need and received non-need-based gift aid.

**GIFT AID (NEED-BASED) Total amount:** $242,969,108 (9% federal, 9% state, 79% institutional, 3% external sources). **Receiving aid:** Freshmen: 31% (909); all full-time undergraduates: 37% (6,554). **Average award:** Freshmen: $31,692; Undergraduates: $30,656. **Scholarships, grants, and awards:** Federal Pell, FSEOG, state, private, college/university gift aid from institutional funds.

**GIFT AID (NON-NEED-BASED) Total amount:** $68,461,933 (86% institutional, 14% external sources). **Receiving aid:** Freshmen: 22% (657). Undergraduates: 19% (3,264). **Average award:** Freshmen: $21,460. Undergraduates: $19,014. **Scholarships, grants, and awards by category:** Academic interests/achievement: general academic interests/achievements. Creative arts/performance: art/fine arts, debating, music, theater/drama. Special achievements/activities: leadership. Special characteristics: children and siblings of alumni, children of faculty/staff. **Tuition waivers:** Full or partial for employees or children of employees. **ROTC:** Army, Naval, Air Force.

**LOANS Student loans:** $73,530,658 (63% need-based, 37% non-need-based). 45% of past graduating class borrowed through all loan programs. Average indebtedness per student: $28,541. **Average need-based loan:** Freshmen: $5019. Undergraduates: $6606. **Parent loans:** $61,695,622 (100% non-need-based). **Programs:** Federal Direct (Subsidized and Unsubsidized Stafford, PLUS), Perkins, college/university, private loans.

**WORK-STUDY Federal work-study:** jobs available.

**ATHLETIC AWARDS** Total amount: $17,342,559 (91% need-based, 9% non-need-based).

**APPLYING FOR FINANCIAL AID Required financial aid forms:** FAFSA, CSS Financial Aid PROFILE, noncustodial (divorced/separated) parent's statement, federal income tax form(s). **Financial aid deadline (priority):** 2/13. **Notification date:** 4/1. Students must reply by 5/1.

**CONTACT** Thomas McWhorter, Office of Financial Aid, University of Southern California, 700 Childs Way, Los Angeles, CA 90089-0914, 213-740-5445. Fax: 213-821-3796. E-mail: faodean@usc.edu.

Website: http://www.usc.edu/.

---

# UNIVERSITY OF SOUTHERN INDIANA
## Evansville, IN

| Tuition & fees (IN res): $6957 | Average undergraduate aid package: $9015 |
| --- | --- |

**ABOUT THE INSTITUTION** State-supported, coed. **Awards:** certificates, associate, bachelor's, master's, and doctoral degrees. 58 undergraduate majors. **Total enrollment:** 9,364. Undergraduates: 8,414. Freshmen: 1,613. Federal methodology is used as a basis for awarding need-based institutional aid.

**UNDERGRADUATE EXPENSES for 2015–2016 Application fee:** $40. **One-time required fee:** $100. **Tuition, state resident:** full-time $6637, part-time $221.22 per credit hour. **Tuition, nonresident:** full-time $15,977; part-time $532.56 per credit hour. **Required fees:** full-time $320; $22.75 per term. Full-time tuition and fees vary according to course load, program, and reciprocity agreements. Part-time tuition and fees vary according to course load, program, and reciprocity agreements. **College room and board:** $7928; **Room only:** $4140. Room and board charges vary according to board plan and housing facility.

**FRESHMAN FINANCIAL AID (Fall 2014, est.)** 1,481 applied for aid; of those 75% were deemed to have need. 99% of freshmen with need received aid; of those 7% had need fully met. **Average percent of need met:** 77% (excluding resources awarded to replace EFC). **Average financial aid package:** $8781 (excluding resources awarded to replace EFC). 15% of all full-time freshmen had no need and received non-need-based gift aid.

**UNDERGRADUATE FINANCIAL AID (Fall 2014, est.)** 6,347 applied for aid; of those 70% were deemed to have need. 99% of undergraduates with need received aid; of those 6% had need fully met. **Average percent of need met:** 76% (excluding resources awarded to replace EFC). **Average financial aid package:** $9015 (excluding resources awarded to replace EFC). 12% of all full-time undergraduates had no need and received non-need-based gift aid.

**GIFT AID (NEED-BASED) Total amount:** $23,750,436 (52% federal, 35% state, 11% institutional, 2% external sources). **Receiving aid:** Freshmen: 43% (688); all full-time undergraduates: 39% (2,693). **Average award:** Freshmen: $7595; Undergraduates: $7062. **Scholarships, grants, and awards:** Federal Pell, FSEOG, state, private, college/university gift aid from institutional funds, Federal Nursing.

**GIFT AID (NON-NEED-BASED) Total amount:** $3,677,001 (77% institutional, 23% external sources). **Receiving aid:** Freshmen: 28% (440). Undergraduates: 20% (1,424). **Average award:** Freshmen: $2026. Undergraduates: $1970. **Scholarships, grants, and awards by category:** Academic interests/achievement: 1,488 awards ($2,486,529 total): biological sciences, business, education, engineering/technologies, general academic interests/achievements, health fields, humanities, mathematics, premedicine, social sciences. *Creative arts/performance:* 42 awards ($91,190 total): art/fine arts, creative writing, theater/drama. *Special achievements/activities:* 59 awards ($93,930 total): leadership. *Special characteristics:* 628 awards ($3,495,343 total): children of faculty/staff, members of minority groups, out-of-state students, spouses of current students, veterans' children. *Tuition waivers:* Full or partial for employees or children of employees. *ROTC:* Army.

**LOANS** *Student loans:* $42,823,546 (88% need-based, 12% non-need-based). 69% of past graduating class borrowed through all loan programs. *Average indebtedness per student:* $25,732. *Average need-based loan:* Freshmen: $3249. Undergraduates: $4019. *Parent loans:* $3,027,877 (92% need-based, 8% non-need-based). *Programs:* Federal Direct (Subsidized and Unsubsidized Stafford, PLUS).

**WORK-STUDY** *Federal work-study:* Total amount: $182,033; 119 jobs averaging $1210.

**ATHLETIC AWARDS** Total amount: $1,104,780 (28% need-based, 72% non-need-based).

**APPLYING FOR FINANCIAL AID** *Required financial aid form:* FAFSA. *Financial aid deadline:* Continuous. *Notification date:* Continuous beginning 4/1.

**CONTACT** Mrs. Mary Harper, Financial Aid Office, University of Southern Indiana, 8600 University Boulevard, Evansville, IN 47712-3590, 812-464-1767 or toll-free 800-467-1965. *Fax:* 812-461-5305. *E-mail:* finaid@usi.edu. *Website:* http://www.usi.edu/.

# UNIVERSITY OF SOUTHERN MAINE
## Portland, ME

| Tuition & fees (ME res): $8920 | Average undergraduate aid package: $13,146 |
| --- | --- |

**ABOUT THE INSTITUTION** State-supported, coed. *Awards:* certificates, bachelor's, master's, and doctoral degrees. 48 undergraduate majors. *Total enrollment:* 8,428. Undergraduates: 6,628. Freshmen: 737. Federal methodology is used as a basis for awarding need-based institutional aid.

**UNDERGRADUATE EXPENSES for 2015–2016** *Application fee:* $40. *Tuition, state resident:* full-time $7590; part-time $253 per credit hour. *Tuition, nonresident:* full-time $19,950; part-time $665 per credit hour. *Required fees:* full-time $1330. Full-time tuition and fees vary according to course load, degree level, and reciprocity agreements. Part-time tuition and fees vary according to course load, degree level, and reciprocity agreements. *College room and board:* $9150; *Room only:* $4700. Room and board charges vary according to board plan, housing facility, and location.

**FRESHMAN FINANCIAL AID (Fall 2013)** 689 applied for aid; of those 85% were deemed to have need. 100% of freshmen with need received aid; of those 41% had need fully met. *Average percent of need met:* 74% (excluding resources awarded to replace EFC). *Average financial aid package:* $12,911 (excluding resources awarded to replace EFC). 8% of all full-time freshmen had no need and received non-need-based gift aid.

**UNDERGRADUATE FINANCIAL AID (Fall 2013)** 3,751 applied for aid; of those 87% were deemed to have need. 100% of undergraduates with need received aid; of those 48% had need fully met. *Average percent of need met:* 75% (excluding resources awarded to replace EFC). *Average financial aid package:* $13,146 (excluding resources awarded to replace EFC). 3% of all full-time undergraduates had no need and received non-need-based gift aid.

**GIFT AID (NEED-BASED)** *Total amount:* $20,744,916 (57% federal, 10% state, 23% institutional, 10% external sources). *Receiving aid:* Freshmen: 73% (540); all full-time undergraduates: 63% (2,704). *Average award:* Freshmen: $3940; Undergraduates: $6385. *Scholarships, grants, and awards:* Federal Pell, FSEOG, state, private, college/university gift aid from institutional funds.

**GIFT AID (NON-NEED-BASED)** *Total amount:* $601,444 (100% institutional). *Receiving aid:* Freshmen: 4% (32). Undergraduates: 2% (103). *Average award:* Freshmen: $4312. Undergraduates: $3934. *Scholarships, grants, and awards by category:* Academic interests/achievement: general academic interests/achievements. *Creative arts/performance:* music, theater/drama. *Special achievements/activities:* community service. *ROTC:* Army cooperative, Air Force cooperative.

**LOANS** *Student loans:* $33,057,096 (79% need-based, 21% non-need-based). 82% of past graduating class borrowed through all loan programs. *Average need-based loan:* Freshmen: $5953. Undergraduates: $7479. *Parent loans:* $2,963,673 (34%

need-based, 66% non-need-based). *Programs:* Federal Direct (Subsidized and Unsubsidized Stafford, PLUS), Perkins, Federal Nursing, college/university.

**WORK-STUDY** *Federal work-study:* jobs available.

**APPLYING FOR FINANCIAL AID** *Required financial aid form:* FAFSA. *Financial aid deadline (priority):* 2/15. *Notification date:* Continuous beginning 3/15. Students must reply within 2 weeks of notification.

**CONTACT** Mr. Keith P. Dubois, Director of Financial Aid, University of Southern Maine, 37 College Avenue, 107 Baily Hall, Gorham, ME 04038, 207-780-5122 or toll-free 800-800-4USM Ext. 5670. *Fax:* 207-780-5143. *E-mail:* dubois@maine.edu. *Website:* http://www.usm.maine.edu/.

# UNIVERSITY OF SOUTHERN MISSISSIPPI
## Hattiesburg, MS

| Tuition & fees (MS res): $7224 | Average undergraduate aid package: $10,338 |
| --- | --- |

**ABOUT THE INSTITUTION** State-supported, coed. *Awards:* certificates, bachelor's, master's, and doctoral degrees. 74 undergraduate majors. *Total enrollment:* 14,792. Undergraduates: 12,005. Freshmen: 1,607. Federal methodology is used as a basis for awarding need-based institutional aid.

**UNDERGRADUATE EXPENSES for 2015–2016** *Application fee:* $35. *Tuition, state resident:* full-time $7224; part-time $291 per credit hour. *Tuition, nonresident:* full-time $16,094; part-time $358 per credit hour. Part-time tuition and fees vary according to course load and degree level. *College room and board:* $7640; *Room only:* $4646. Room and board charges vary according to board plan and housing facility.

**FRESHMAN FINANCIAL AID (Fall 2013)** 1,587 applied for aid; of those 86% were deemed to have need. 99% of freshmen with need received aid; of those 29% had need fully met. *Average percent of need met:* 76% (excluding resources awarded to replace EFC). *Average financial aid package:* $12,046 (excluding resources awarded to replace EFC). 11% of all full-time freshmen had no need and received non-need-based gift aid.

**UNDERGRADUATE FINANCIAL AID (Fall 2013)** 9,243 applied for aid; of those 89% were deemed to have need. 98% of undergraduates with need received aid; of those 19% had need fully met. *Average percent of need met:* 68% (excluding resources awarded to replace EFC). *Average financial aid package:* $10,338 (excluding resources awarded to replace EFC). 55% of all full-time undergraduates had no need and received non-need-based gift aid.

**GIFT AID (NEED-BASED)** *Total amount:* $35,683,587 (74% federal, 8% state, 15% institutional, 3% external sources). *Receiving aid:* Freshmen: 54% (907); all full-time undergraduates: 51% (5,528). *Average award:* Freshmen: $4753; Undergraduates: $4500. *Scholarships, grants, and awards:* Federal Pell, FSEOG, state, private, college/university gift aid from institutional funds.

**GIFT AID (NON-NEED-BASED)** *Total amount:* $18,414,216 (15% federal, 16% state, 62% institutional, 7% external sources). *Receiving aid:* Freshmen: 57% (959). Undergraduates: 39% (4,201). *Average award:* Freshmen: $5143. Undergraduates: $4702. *Scholarships, grants, and awards by category:* Academic interests/achievement: general academic interests/achievements. *Creative arts/performance:* art/fine arts, dance, music, theater/drama. *Special achievements/activities:* cheerleading/drum major, leadership. *Special characteristics:* children and siblings of alumni, children of faculty/staff, ethnic background, local/state students, out-of-state students, veterans. *Tuition waivers:* Full or partial for children of alumni, employees or children of employees, senior citizens. *ROTC:* Army cooperative, Air Force.

**LOANS** *Student loans:* $66,463,352 (47% need-based, 53% non-need-based). 67% of past graduating class borrowed through all loan programs. *Average indebtedness per student:* $17,806. *Average need-based loan:* Freshmen: $4207. Undergraduates: $4542. *Parent loans:* $4,677,305 (31% need-based, 69% non-need-based). *Programs:* Federal Direct (Subsidized and Unsubsidized Stafford, PLUS).

**WORK-STUDY** *Federal work-study:* jobs available.

**ATHLETIC AWARDS** Total amount: $4,598,204 (44% need-based, 56% non-need-based).

**APPLYING FOR FINANCIAL AID** *Required financial aid forms:* FAFSA, institution's own form. *Financial aid deadline (priority):* 3/15. *Notification date:* Continuous. Students must reply within 2 weeks of notification.

**CONTACT** Mr. David Williamson, Director of Financial Aid, University of Southern Mississippi, 118 College Drive #5101, Hattiesburg, MS 39406-0001, 601-266-4774. *Fax:* 601-266-5769. *E-mail:* financial.aid@usm.edu.
*Website:* http://www.usm.edu/.

# UNIVERSITY OF SOUTH FLORIDA
## Tampa, FL

| Tuition & fees (FL res): $6410 | Average undergraduate aid package: $9309 |
|---|---|

**ABOUT THE INSTITUTION** State-supported, coed. *Awards:* associate, bachelor's, master's, and doctoral degrees. 83 undergraduate majors. *Total enrollment:* 41,938. Undergraduates: 31,067. Freshmen: 4,116. Federal methodology is used as a basis for awarding need-based institutional aid.

**UNDERGRADUATE EXPENSES for 2015–2016 Application fee:** $30. *Tuition, state resident:* full-time $4559; part-time $211 per credit hour. *Tuition, nonresident:* full-time $15,474; part-time $575 per credit hour. *Required fees:* full-time $1851; $37 per credit hour. Full-time tuition and fees vary according to course level, course load, and location. Part-time tuition and fees vary according to course level, course load, and location. *College room and board:* $9400; *Room only:* $5750. Room and board charges vary according to board plan, housing facility, and location.

**FRESHMAN FINANCIAL AID (Fall 2013)** 4,174 applied for aid; of those 76% were deemed to have need. 98% of freshmen with need received aid; of those 8% had need fully met. *Average percent of need met:* 60% (excluding resources awarded to replace EFC). *Average financial aid package:* $10,581 (excluding resources awarded to replace EFC). 14% of all full-time freshmen had no need and received non-need-based gift aid.

**UNDERGRADUATE FINANCIAL AID (Fall 2013)** 23,523 applied for aid; of those 82% were deemed to have need. 96% of undergraduates with need received aid; of those 4% had need fully met. *Average percent of need met:* 50% (excluding resources awarded to replace EFC). *Average financial aid package:* $9309 (excluding resources awarded to replace EFC). 6% of all full-time undergraduates had no need and received non-need-based gift aid.

**GIFT AID (NEED-BASED) Total amount:** $121,857,559 (50% federal, 24% state, 23% institutional, 3% external sources). *Receiving aid:* Freshmen: 67% (3,030); all full-time undergraduates: 63% (17,065). *Average award:* Freshmen: $8801; Undergraduates: $6757. *Scholarships, grants, and awards:* Federal Pell, FSEOG, state, private, college/university gift aid from institutional funds.

**GIFT AID (NON-NEED-BASED) Total amount:** $15,098,002 (61% state, 32% institutional, 7% external sources). *Receiving aid:* Freshmen: 5% (217). Undergraduates: 2% (648). *Average award:* Freshmen: $2634. Undergraduates: $2576. *Scholarships, grants, and awards by category: Academic interests/achievement:* architecture, biological sciences, business, communication, computer science, education, engineering/technologies, English, foreign languages, general academic interests/achievements, health fields, humanities, international studies, library science, mathematics, military science, physical sciences, premedicine, religion/biblical studies, social sciences. *Creative arts/performance:* applied art and design, art/fine arts, cinema/film/broadcasting, creative writing, dance, debating, journalism/publications, music, performing arts, theater/drama. *Special achievements/activities:* general special achievements/activities. *Special characteristics:* general special characteristics. *Tuition waivers:* Full or partial for senior citizens. *ROTC:* Army, Naval, Air Force.

**LOANS Student loans:** $127,146,824 (88% need-based, 12% non-need-based). 60% of past graduating class borrowed through all loan programs. *Average indebtedness per student:* $22,611. *Average need-based loan:* Freshmen: $4844. Undergraduates: $6987. *Parent loans:* $10,425,905 (41% need-based, 59% non-need-based). *Programs:* Federal Direct (Subsidized and Unsubsidized Stafford, PLUS), Perkins, college/university.

**WORK-STUDY Federal work-study:** 704 jobs averaging $3180. *State or other work-study/employment:* Total amount: $551,005 (100% need-based). 311 part-time jobs averaging $1772.

**ATHLETIC AWARDS** Total amount: $4,555,331 (49% need-based, 51% non-need-based).

**APPLYING FOR FINANCIAL AID Required financial aid form:** FAFSA. *Financial aid deadline:* Continuous. *Notification date:* Continuous beginning 3/1. Students must reply within 4 weeks of notification.

**CONTACT** Ms. Billie Jo Hamilton, Director of Student Financial Aid, University of South Florida, 4202 East Fowler Avenue, SVC 1102, Tampa, FL 33620-6960, 813-974-4700. *Fax:* 813-974-5144. *E-mail:* bjhamilton@admin.usf.edu.
*Website:* http://www.usf.edu/.

# UNIVERSITY OF SOUTH FLORIDA, ST. PETERSBURG
## St. Petersburg, FL

**CONTACT** Financial Aid Office, University of South Florida, St. Petersburg, 140 Seventh Ave S., St. Petersburg, FL 33701, 727-873-7748.
*Website:* http://www.stpt.usf.edu/.

# UNIVERSITY OF SOUTH FLORIDA SARASOTA-MANATEE
## Sarasota, FL

**CONTACT** Financial Aid Office, University of South Florida Sarasota-Manatee, 8350 N Tamiami Trail, Sarasota, FL 34243, 941-359-4200.
*Website:* http://www.usfsm.edu/.

# THE UNIVERSITY OF TAMPA
## Tampa, FL

| Tuition & fees: $26,330 | Average undergraduate aid package: $16,667 |
|---|---|

**ABOUT THE INSTITUTION** Independent, coed. *Awards:* certificates, associate, bachelor's, and master's degrees. 49 undergraduate majors. *Total enrollment:* 7,683. Undergraduates: 8,045. Freshmen: 1,753. Federal methodology is used as a basis for awarding need-based institutional aid.

**UNDERGRADUATE EXPENSES for 2015–2016 Application fee:** $40. *One-time required fee:* $85. *Comprehensive fee:* $35,954 includes full-time tuition ($24,528), mandatory fees ($1802), and room and board ($9624). *College room only:* $5100. Full-time tuition and fees vary according to class time, course load, and program. Room and board charges vary according to board plan and housing facility. *Part-time tuition:* $522 per credit hour. *Part-time fees:* $40 per term. Part-time tuition and fees vary according to class time, course load, and program.

**FRESHMAN FINANCIAL AID (Fall 2014, est.)** 1,415 applied for aid; of those 78% were deemed to have need. 100% of freshmen with need received aid; of those 10% had need fully met. *Average percent of need met:* 64% (excluding resources awarded to replace EFC). *Average financial aid package:* $16,395 (excluding resources awarded to replace EFC). 27% of all full-time freshmen had no need and received non-need-based gift aid.

**UNDERGRADUATE FINANCIAL AID (Fall 2014, est.)** 4,769 applied for aid; of those 82% were deemed to have need. 100% of undergraduates with need received aid; of those 9% had need fully met. *Average percent of need met:* 64% (excluding resources awarded to replace EFC). *Average financial aid package:* $16,667 (excluding resources awarded to replace EFC). 28% of all full-time undergraduates had no need and received non-need-based gift aid.

**GIFT AID (NEED-BASED) Total amount:** $45,880,529 (16% federal, 10% state, 72% institutional, 2% external sources). *Receiving aid:* Freshmen: 63% (1,105); all full-time undergraduates: 59% (3,864). *Average award:* Freshmen: $13,534; Undergraduates: $13,058. *Scholarships, grants, and awards:* Federal Pell, FSEOG, state, private, college/university gift aid from institutional funds.

**GIFT AID (NON-NEED-BASED) Total amount:** $14,665,584 (11% state, 88% institutional, 1% external sources). *Receiving aid:* Freshmen: 63% (1,105). Undergraduates: 59% (3,837). *Average award:* Freshmen: $7893. Undergraduates: $7249. *Scholarships, grants, and awards by category: Academic interests/achievement:* 5,141 awards ($37,609,176 total): biological sciences, English, general academic interests/achievements, international studies, military science, social sciences. *Creative arts/performance:* 165 awards ($362,500 total): art/fine arts, creative writing,

journalism/publications, music, performing arts, theater/drama. *Special achievements/ activities:* 197 awards ($268,000 total): general special achievements/activities, leadership, memberships. *Special characteristics:* 415 awards ($2,526,565 total): children and siblings of alumni, children of faculty/staff, international students, veterans. *Tuition waivers:* Full or partial for employees or children of employees. *ROTC:* Army, Naval cooperative, Air Force cooperative.
**LOANS** *Student loans:* $33,311,727 (87% need-based, 13% non-need-based). 60% of past graduating class borrowed through all loan programs. *Average indebtedness per student:* $33,673. *Average need-based loan:* Freshmen: $3381. Undergraduates: $4368. *Parent loans:* $19,723,845 (87% need-based, 13% non-need-based). *Programs:* Federal Direct (Subsidized and Unsubsidized Stafford, PLUS), Perkins, college/university.
**WORK-STUDY** *Federal work-study:* Total amount: $136,261; 301 jobs averaging $2000. *State or other work-study/employment:* Total amount: $50,064 (1% need-based, 99% non-need-based). 4 part-time jobs averaging $2000.
**ATHLETIC AWARDS** Total amount: $2,193,180 (64% need-based, 36% non-need-based).
**APPLYING FOR FINANCIAL AID** *Required financial aid form:* FAFSA. *Financial aid deadline:* Continuous. *Notification date:* Continuous beginning 2/1. Students must reply by 5/1.
**CONTACT** Jacqueline M. LaTorella, Office of Financial Aid, The University of Tampa, 401 West Kennedy Boulevard, Box E, Tampa, FL 33606-1490, 813-253-6219 or toll-free 888-646-2738 (in-state), 888-MINARET (out-of-state). *Fax:* 813-258-7439. *E-mail:* finaid@ut.edu.
*Website:* http://www.ut.edu/.

# THE UNIVERSITY OF TENNESSEE
## Knoxville, TN

| Tuition & fees (TN res): $11,876 | Average undergraduate aid package: $12,313 |
| --- | --- |

**ABOUT THE INSTITUTION** State-supported, coed. *Awards:* certificates, bachelor's, master's, and doctoral degrees. 79 undergraduate majors. *Total enrollment:* 30,386. Undergraduates: 21,664. Freshmen: 4,701. Federal methodology is used as a basis for awarding need-based institutional aid.
**UNDERGRADUATE EXPENSES for 2015–2016** *Application fee:* $40. *Tuition, state resident:* full-time $10,366; part-time $346 per hour. *Tuition, nonresident:* full-time $28,556; part-time $1105 per hour. *Required fees:* full-time $1510; $71 per hour. Full-time tuition and fees vary according to course level, location, program, and reciprocity agreements. Part-time tuition and fees vary according to course level, location, program, and reciprocity agreements. *College room and board:* $10,296. Room and board charges vary according to board plan and housing facility.
**FRESHMAN FINANCIAL AID (Fall 2014, est.)** 4,437 applied for aid; of those 65% were deemed to have need. 100% of freshmen with need received aid; of those 29% had need fully met. *Average percent of need met:* 65% (excluding resources awarded to replace EFC). *Average financial aid package:* $13,793 (excluding resources awarded to replace EFC). 13% of all full-time freshmen had no need and received non-need-based gift aid.
**UNDERGRADUATE FINANCIAL AID (Fall 2014, est.)** 17,831 applied for aid; of those 68% were deemed to have need. 99% of undergraduates with need received aid; of those 21% had need fully met. *Average percent of need met:* 57% (excluding resources awarded to replace EFC). *Average financial aid package:* $12,313 (excluding resources awarded to replace EFC). 12% of all full-time undergraduates had no need and received non-need-based gift aid.
**GIFT AID (NEED-BASED)** *Total amount:* $127,577,443 (21% federal, 43% state, 33% institutional, 3% external sources). *Receiving aid:* Freshmen: 59% (2,744); all full-time undergraduates: 53% (10,683). *Average award:* Freshmen: $11,207; Undergraduates: $8961. *Scholarships, grants, and awards:* Federal Pell, FSEOG, state, private, college/university gift aid from institutional funds.
**GIFT AID (NON-NEED-BASED)** *Average award:* Freshmen: $5042. Undergraduates: $3685. *Scholarships, grants, and awards by category: Academic interests/achievement:* 1,916 awards ($4,644,297 total): agriculture, architecture, business, communication, computer science, education, engineering/technologies, general academic interests/achievements, health fields, humanities, international studies, library science, military science, social sciences. *Creative arts/performance:* 202 awards ($367,100 total): art/fine arts. *Tuition waivers:* Full or partial for employees or children of employees, senior citizens. *ROTC:* Army, Air Force.

**LOANS** *Student loans:* $73,498,146 (84% need-based, 16% non-need-based). 51% of past graduating class borrowed through all loan programs. *Average indebtedness per student:* $23,870. *Average need-based loan:* Freshmen: $5093. Undergraduates: $6414. *Parent loans:* $19,543,493 (100% need-based). *Programs:* Federal Direct (Subsidized and Unsubsidized Stafford, PLUS), Perkins, state, college/university.
**WORK-STUDY** *Federal work-study:* Total amount: $856,267; 657 jobs averaging $2294.
**ATHLETIC AWARDS** Total amount: $7,479,513 (100% need-based).
**APPLYING FOR FINANCIAL AID** *Required financial aid form:* FAFSA. *Financial aid deadline (priority):* 2/15. *Notification date:* Continuous beginning 3/15. Students must reply within 3 weeks of notification.
**CONTACT** Jeffery Gerkin, Office of Financial Aid and Scholarships, The University of Tennessee, 115 Student Services Building, Knoxville, TN 37996-0210, 865-974-3131. *Fax:* 865-974-2175. *E-mail:* finaid@utk.edu.
*Website:* http://www.utk.edu/.

# THE UNIVERSITY OF TENNESSEE AT CHATTANOOGA
## Chattanooga, TN

| Tuition & fees (TN res): $8138 | Average undergraduate aid package: $9765 |
| --- | --- |

**ABOUT THE INSTITUTION** State-supported, coed. *Awards:* certificates, bachelor's, master's, and doctoral degrees. 48 undergraduate majors. *Total enrollment:* 11,670. Undergraduates: 10,315. Freshmen: 2,160. Federal methodology is used as a basis for awarding need-based institutional aid.
**UNDERGRADUATE EXPENSES for 2015–2016** *Application fee:* $30. *Tuition, state resident:* full-time $6430; part-time $268 per credit hour. *Tuition, nonresident:* full-time $22,548; part-time $940 per credit hour. *Required fees:* full-time $1708; $252 per credit hour. Full-time tuition and fees vary according to degree level. Part-time tuition and fees vary according to course load and degree level. *College room and board:* $8110; *Room only:* $4910. Room and board charges vary according to board plan and housing facility.
**FRESHMAN FINANCIAL AID (Fall 2014, est.)** 2,051 applied for aid; of those 69% were deemed to have need. 99% of freshmen with need received aid; of those 18% had need fully met. *Average percent of need met:* 74% (excluding resources awarded to replace EFC). *Average financial aid package:* $10,611 (excluding resources awarded to replace EFC). 12% of all full-time freshmen had no need and received non-need-based gift aid.
**UNDERGRADUATE FINANCIAL AID (Fall 2014, est.)** 8,096 applied for aid; of those 70% were deemed to have need. 99% of undergraduates with need received aid; of those 14% had need fully met. *Average percent of need met:* 66% (excluding resources awarded to replace EFC). *Average financial aid package:* $9765 (excluding resources awarded to replace EFC). 9% of all full-time undergraduates had no need and received non-need-based gift aid.
**GIFT AID (NEED-BASED)** *Total amount:* $36,018,602 (44% federal, 43% state, 11% institutional, 2% external sources). *Receiving aid:* Freshmen: 62% (1,334); all full-time undergraduates: 54% (4,818). *Average award:* Freshmen: $8558; Undergraduates: $7720. *Scholarships, grants, and awards:* Federal Pell, FSEOG, state, private, college/university gift aid from institutional funds.
**GIFT AID (NON-NEED-BASED)** *Total amount:* $11,273,273 (68% state, 28% institutional, 4% external sources). *Receiving aid:* Freshmen: 1% (29). Undergraduates: 2% (183). *Average award:* Freshmen: $3107. Undergraduates: $3094. *Scholarships, grants, and awards by category: Academic interests/achievement:* biological sciences, business, communication, education, engineering/technologies, English, general academic interests/achievements, home economics, mathematics, military science, physical sciences. *Creative arts/performance:* art/fine arts, cinema/film/broadcasting, journalism/publications, music, performing arts, theater/drama. *Special achievements/activities:* cheerleading/drum major, community service, memberships, religious involvement. *Special characteristics:* children and siblings of alumni, children of faculty/staff, children of union members/company employees, children with a deceased or disabled parent, ethnic background, handicapped students, religious affiliation. *Tuition waivers:* Full or partial for employees or children of employees, senior citizens. *ROTC:* Army.
**LOANS** *Student loans:* $51,242,335 (62% need-based, 38% non-need-based). 57% of past graduating class borrowed through all loan programs. *Average indebtedness per student:* $21,420. *Average need-based loan:* Freshmen: $3293. Undergrad-

uates: $3967. **Parent loans:** $4,083,428 (31% need-based, 69% non-need-based). **Programs:** Federal Direct (Subsidized and Unsubsidized Stafford, PLUS), Perkins, private loans.
**WORK-STUDY** *Federal work-study:* Total amount: $425,858; jobs available. **State or other work-study/employment:** Total amount: $353,052 (23% need-based, 77% non-need-based). Part-time jobs available.
**ATHLETIC AWARDS** Total amount: $4,692,225 (47% need-based, 53% non-need-based).
**APPLYING FOR FINANCIAL AID** *Required financial aid forms:* FAFSA, institutional scholarship application form. **Financial aid deadline:** 5/1. **Notification date:** Continuous beginning 3/1. Students must reply within 4 weeks of notification.
**CONTACT** Dianne Cox, Director of Financial Aid, The University of Tennessee at Chattanooga, 615 McCallie Avenue, Chattanooga, TN 37403-2598, 423-425-4677 or toll-free 800-UTC-MOCS (in-state), 800-UTC.MOCS (out-of-state). *Fax:* 423-425-2292. *E-mail:* dianne-cox@utc.edu.
*Website:* http://www.utc.edu/.

# THE UNIVERSITY OF TENNESSEE AT MARTIN
## Martin, TN

| Tuition & fees (TN res): $8024 | Average undergraduate aid package: $13,437 |
|---|---|

**ABOUT THE INSTITUTION** State-supported, coed. **Awards:** bachelor's and master's degrees. 85 undergraduate majors. **Total enrollment:** 7,042. Undergraduates: 6,677. Freshmen: 1,181. Federal methodology is used as a basis for awarding need-based institutional aid.
**UNDERGRADUATE EXPENSES for 2015–2016** *Application fee:* $30. *Tuition, state resident:* full-time $6716; part-time $280 per credit hour. *Tuition, nonresident:* full-time $20,660; part-time $861 per credit hour. *Required fees:* full-time $1308; $54 per credit hour. Part-time tuition and fees vary according to course load. **College room and board:** $5786; **Room only:** $2780. Room and board charges vary according to board plan and housing facility.
**FRESHMAN FINANCIAL AID (Fall 2014, est.)** 1,156 applied for aid; of those 79% were deemed to have need. 99% of freshmen with need received aid; of those 24% had need fully met. **Average percent of need met:** 77% (excluding resources awarded to replace EFC). **Average financial aid package:** $13,637 (excluding resources awarded to replace EFC). 20% of all full-time freshmen had no need and received non-need-based gift aid.
**UNDERGRADUATE FINANCIAL AID (Fall 2014, est.)** 5,463 applied for aid; of those 81% were deemed to have need. 97% of undergraduates with need received aid; of those 21% had need fully met. **Average percent of need met:** 73% (excluding resources awarded to replace EFC). **Average financial aid package:** $13,437 (excluding resources awarded to replace EFC). 14% of all full-time undergraduates had no need and received non-need-based gift aid.
**GIFT AID (NEED-BASED)** *Total amount:* $20,195,117 (77% federal, 20% state, 3% institutional). **Receiving aid:** Freshmen: 52% (611); all full-time undergraduates: 54% (3,091). **Average award:** Freshmen: $6408; Undergraduates: $6029. **Scholarships, grants, and awards:** Federal Pell, FSEOG, state, private, college/university gift aid from institutional funds.
**GIFT AID (NON-NEED-BASED)** *Total amount:* $15,218,122 (68% state, 24% institutional, 8% external sources). **Receiving aid:** Freshmen: 70% (826). Undergraduates: 43% (2,437). **Average award:** Freshmen: $6671. Undergraduates: $6787. **Scholarships, grants, and awards by category:** Academic interests/achievement: 801 awards ($1,377,004 total): agriculture, biological sciences, business, communication, computer science, education, engineering/technologies, English, general academic interests/achievements, health fields, home economics, humanities, mathematics, military science, physical sciences, premedicine, social sciences. *Creative arts/performance:* 210 awards ($209,725 total): art/fine arts, cinema/film/broadcasting, creative writing, journalism/publications, music, theater/drama. *Special achievements/activities:* 121 awards ($314,456 total): cheerleading/drum major, general special achievements/activities, leadership, rodeo. *Special characteristics:* 207 awards ($325,008 total): adult students, children and siblings of alumni, children of educators, children of faculty/staff, children of union members/company employees, ethnic background, handicapped students, members of minority groups, out-of-state students.

**Tuition waivers:** Full or partial for employees or children of employees, senior citizens. **ROTC:** Army.
**LOANS** *Student loans:* $27,042,299 (50% need-based, 50% non-need-based). 63% of past graduating class borrowed through all loan programs. *Average indebtedness per student:* $28,701. **Average need-based loan:** Freshmen: $3288. Undergraduates: $4342. **Parent loans:** $1,867,361 (100% non-need-based). **Programs:** Federal Direct (Subsidized and Unsubsidized Stafford, PLUS), Perkins.
**WORK-STUDY** *Federal work-study:* Total amount: $536,252; 252 jobs averaging $2269.
**ATHLETIC AWARDS** Total amount: $3,923,808 (100% non-need-based).
**APPLYING FOR FINANCIAL AID** *Required financial aid form:* FAFSA. **Financial aid deadline (priority):** 2/15. **Notification date:** Continuous beginning 4/1. Students must reply within 2 weeks of notification.
**CONTACT** Amy J. Mistric, Coordinator III, The University of Tennessee at Martin, 205 Administration Building, Martin, TN 38238-1000, 731-881-7040 or toll-free 800-829-8861. *Fax:* 731-881-7036. *E-mail:* sfrazier@utm.edu.
*Website:* http://www.utm.edu/.

# THE UNIVERSITY OF TEXAS AT ARLINGTON
## Arlington, TX

| Tuition & fees (TX res): $8878 | Average undergraduate aid package: $12,559 |
|---|---|

**ABOUT THE INSTITUTION** State-supported, coed. **Awards:** certificates, bachelor's, master's, and doctoral degrees. 66 undergraduate majors. **Total enrollment:** 39,740. Undergraduates: 29,883. Freshmen: 2,736. Federal methodology is used as a basis for awarding need-based institutional aid.
**UNDERGRADUATE EXPENSES for 2015–2016** *Application fee:* $60. *Tuition, state resident:* full-time $8878. *Tuition, nonresident:* full-time $20,274. *College room and board:* $8156; *Room only:* $4408. Room and board charges vary according to board plan and housing facility. **Payment plan:** Guaranteed tuition.
**FRESHMAN FINANCIAL AID (Fall 2014, est.)** 2,056 applied for aid; of those 100% were deemed to have need. 82% of freshmen with need received aid; of those 22% had need fully met. **Average percent of need met:** 76% (excluding resources awarded to replace EFC). **Average financial aid package:** $12,229 (excluding resources awarded to replace EFC). 6% of all full-time freshmen had no need and received non-need-based gift aid.
**UNDERGRADUATE FINANCIAL AID (Fall 2014, est.)** 12,273 applied for aid; of those 96% were deemed to have need. 93% of undergraduates with need received aid; of those 12% had need fully met. **Average percent of need met:** 68% (excluding resources awarded to replace EFC). **Average financial aid package:** $12,559 (excluding resources awarded to replace EFC). 1% of all full-time undergraduates had no need and received non-need-based gift aid.
**GIFT AID (NEED-BASED)** *Total amount:* $92,479,937 (47% federal, 18% state, 29% institutional, 6% external sources). **Receiving aid:** Freshmen: 67% (1,670); all full-time undergraduates: 67% (10,383). **Average award:** Freshmen: $7856; Undergraduates: $7033. **Scholarships, grants, and awards:** Federal Pell, FSEOG, state, private, college/university gift aid from institutional funds, United Negro College Fund.
**GIFT AID (NON-NEED-BASED)** *Total amount:* $4,840,853 (1% state, 84% institutional, 15% external sources). **Receiving aid:** Freshmen: 38% (937). Undergraduates: 23% (3,568). **Average award:** Freshmen: $5149. Undergraduates: $4819. **Scholarships, grants, and awards by category:** Academic interests/achievement: 4,048 awards ($16,971,413 total): architecture, biological sciences, business, communication, computer science, education, engineering/technologies, English, foreign languages, general academic interests/achievements, health fields, humanities, international studies, mathematics, military science, physical sciences, social sciences. *Creative arts/performance:* journalism/publications, music, theater/drama. *Special achievements/activities:* cheerleading/drum major, community service, general special achievements/activities, leadership. *Special characteristics:* children with a deceased or disabled parent, first-generation college students, general special characteristics, handicapped students, public servants. **Tuition waivers:** Full or partial for employees or children of employees. **ROTC:** Army, Air Force cooperative.
**LOANS** *Student loans:* $96,305,170 (82% need-based, 18% non-need-based). 58% of past graduating class borrowed through all loan programs. *Average indebtedness per student:* $23,210. **Average need-based loan:** Freshmen: $3252. Undergrad-

uates: $4235. *Parent loans:* $4,188,367 (44% need-based, 56% non-need-based). *Programs:* Federal Direct (Subsidized and Unsubsidized Stafford, PLUS), Perkins, state.

**WORK-STUDY** *Federal work-study:* Total amount: $5,780,359; 1,822 jobs averaging $3178. *State or other work-study/employment:* Total amount: $246,136 (100% need-based). 20 part-time jobs averaging $560.

**ATHLETIC AWARDS** Total amount: $2,486,901 (90% need-based, 10% non-need-based).

**APPLYING FOR FINANCIAL AID** *Required financial aid form:* FAFSA. *Financial aid deadline (priority):* 4/15. *Notification date:* Continuous beginning 4/1. Students must reply within 3 weeks of notification.

**CONTACT** Karen Krause, Director of Financial Aid, The University of Texas at Arlington, UTA Box 19199, Arlington, TX 76019, 817-272-3561. *Fax:* 817-272-3555. *E-mail:* kkrause@uta.edu.
*Website:* http://www.uta.edu/.

# THE UNIVERSITY OF TEXAS AT AUSTIN
## Austin, TX

| Tuition & fees (TX res): $9830 | Average undergraduate aid package: $12,935 |
| --- | --- |

**ABOUT THE INSTITUTION** State-supported, coed. *Awards:* certificates, bachelor's, master's, and doctoral degrees. 102 undergraduate majors. *Total enrollment:* 51,313. Undergraduates: 39,523. Freshmen: 7,285. Federal methodology is used as a basis for awarding need-based institutional aid.

**UNDERGRADUATE EXPENSES for 2015–2016** *Tuition, state resident:* full-time $9830. *Tuition, nonresident:* full-time $34,836. Full-time tuition and fees vary according to course load, degree level, and program. Part-time tuition and fees vary according to course load, degree level, and program. *College room and board:* $11,456. Room and board charges vary according to housing facility. *Payment plan:* Guaranteed tuition.

**FRESHMAN FINANCIAL AID (Fall 2014, est.)** 5,304 applied for aid; of those 56% were deemed to have need. 100% of freshmen with need received aid; of those 27% had need fully met. *Average percent of need met:* 77% (excluding resources awarded to replace EFC). *Average financial aid package:* $13,209 (excluding resources awarded to replace EFC). 1% of all full-time freshmen had no need and received non-need-based gift aid.

**UNDERGRADUATE FINANCIAL AID (Fall 2014, est.)** 21,734 applied for aid; of those 71% were deemed to have need. 100% of undergraduates with need received aid; of those 17% had need fully met. *Average percent of need met:* 67% (excluding resources awarded to replace EFC). *Average financial aid package:* $12,935 (excluding resources awarded to replace EFC). 1% of all full-time undergraduates had no need and received non-need-based gift aid.

**GIFT AID (NEED-BASED)** *Total amount:* $143,552,783 (32% federal, 23% state, 36% institutional, 9% external sources). *Receiving aid:* Freshmen: 37% (2,714); all full-time undergraduates: 35% (12,458). *Average award:* Freshmen: $8529; Undergraduates: $9118. *Scholarships, grants, and awards:* Federal Pell, FSEOG, state, private, college/university gift aid from institutional funds.

**GIFT AID (NON-NEED-BASED)** *Total amount:* $6,644,682 (31% institutional, 69% external sources). *Receiving aid:* Freshmen: 19% (1,370). Undergraduates: 12% (4,175). *Average award:* Freshmen: $7273. Undergraduates: $6047. *Scholarships, grants, and awards by category:* Academic interests/achievement: general academic interests/achievements. Creative arts/performance: art/fine arts, general creative arts/performance. Special achievements/activities: leadership. Special characteristics: local/state students. *Tuition waivers:* Full or partial for employees or children of employees, senior citizens. *ROTC:* Army, Naval, Air Force.

**LOANS** *Student loans:* $107,536,120 (76% need-based, 24% non-need-based). 55% of past graduating class borrowed through all loan programs. *Average indebtedness per student:* $27,207. *Average need-based loan:* Freshmen: $4099. Undergraduates: $4987. *Parent loans:* $74,440,127 (29% need-based, 71% non-need-based). *Programs:* Federal Direct (Subsidized and Unsubsidized Stafford, PLUS), Perkins, state.

**WORK-STUDY** *Federal work-study:* Total amount: $3,834,519; jobs available. *State or other work-study/employment:* Total amount: $166,028 (100% need-based). Part-time jobs available.

**APPLYING FOR FINANCIAL AID** *Required financial aid forms:* FAFSA, institution's own form. *Financial aid deadline (priority):* 3/31. *Notification date:* Continuous beginning 3/15. Students must reply by 5/1 or within 3 weeks of notification.

**CONTACT** Dr. Tom Melecki, Director of Student Financial Services, The University of Texas at Austin, PO Box 7758, Student Services Building, Suite 3.214, Austin, TX 78713-7758, 512-475-6203. *Fax:* 512-475-6349. *E-mail:* ask@finaid.utexas.edu. *Website:* http://www.utexas.edu/.

# THE UNIVERSITY OF TEXAS AT BROWNSVILLE
## Brownsville, TX

| Tuition & fees: N/R | Average undergraduate aid package: $9352 |
| --- | --- |

**ABOUT THE INSTITUTION** State-supported, coed. *Awards:* certificates, bachelor's, master's, and doctoral degrees. 38 undergraduate majors. *Total enrollment:* 8,612. Undergraduates: 7,547. Freshmen: 921. Federal methodology is used as a basis for awarding need-based institutional aid.

**FRESHMAN FINANCIAL AID (Fall 2013)** 768 applied for aid; of those 93% were deemed to have need. 98% of freshmen with need received aid. *Average percent of need met:* 42% (excluding resources awarded to replace EFC). *Average financial aid package:* $10,261 (excluding resources awarded to replace EFC). 2% of all full-time freshmen had no need and received non-need-based gift aid.

**UNDERGRADUATE FINANCIAL AID (Fall 2013)** 3,342 applied for aid; of those 94% were deemed to have need. 99% of undergraduates with need received aid. *Average percent of need met:* 49% (excluding resources awarded to replace EFC). *Average financial aid package:* $9352 (excluding resources awarded to replace EFC). 1% of all full-time undergraduates had no need and received non-need-based gift aid.

**GIFT AID (NEED-BASED)** *Total amount:* $26,689,075 (74% federal, 26% state). *Receiving aid:* Freshmen: 75% (633); all full-time undergraduates: 72% (2,823). *Average award:* Freshmen: $4169; Undergraduates: $6757. *Scholarships, grants, and awards:* Federal Pell, FSEOG, state, private, college/university gift aid from institutional funds.

**GIFT AID (NON-NEED-BASED)** *Total amount:* $3,091,653 (14% state, 70% institutional, 16% external sources). *Receiving aid:* Freshmen: 27% (232). Undergraduates: 33% (1,312). *Average award:* Freshmen: $8490. Undergraduates: $7458. *Scholarships, grants, and awards by category:* Academic interests/achievement: biological sciences, business, communication, computer science, education, engineering/technologies, English, foreign languages, general academic interests/achievements, health fields, international studies, mathematics, physical sciences, social sciences. Creative arts/performance: art/fine arts, music, performing arts. Special characteristics: children of faculty/staff, first-generation college students, general special characteristics, international students. *ROTC:* Army.

**LOANS** *Student loans:* $20,839,020 (61% need-based, 39% non-need-based). *Average need-based loan:* Freshmen: $3011. Undergraduates: $3906. *Parent loans:* $72,294 (100% non-need-based). *Programs:* Federal Direct (Subsidized and Unsubsidized Stafford, PLUS), state, college/university.

**WORK-STUDY** *Federal work-study:* jobs available. *State or other work-study/employment:* Total amount: $46,319 (100% need-based). Part-time jobs available.

**ATHLETIC AWARDS** Total amount: $499,608 (100% non-need-based).

**APPLYING FOR FINANCIAL AID** *Required financial aid form:* FAFSA. *Financial aid deadline:* 7/1 (priority: 3/1). *Notification date:* 5/1. Students must reply by 7/1 or within 12 weeks of notification.

**CONTACT** Mr. Arnold Trejo, Director of Financial Aid, The University of Texas at Brownsville, 80 Fort Brown, Brownsville, TX 78520-4991, 956-882-8277 or toll-free 877-UTBTSC1. *Fax:* 956-882-8229. *E-mail:* arnold.trejo@utb.edu. *Website:* http://www.utb.edu/.

# THE UNIVERSITY OF TEXAS AT DALLAS
### Richardson, TX

| Tuition & fees (TX res): $11,806 | Average undergraduate aid package: $12,488 |
|---|---|

**ABOUT THE INSTITUTION** State-supported, coed. **Awards:** certificates, bachelor's, master's, and doctoral degrees. 42 undergraduate majors. **Total enrollment:** 23,095. Undergraduates: 14,300. Freshmen: 2,520. Both federal and institutional methodology are used as a basis for awarding need-based institutional aid.

**UNDERGRADUATE EXPENSES for 2015–2016 Application fee:** $50. **Tuition, state resident:** full-time $11,806; part-time $393.53 per credit hour. **Tuition, nonresident:** full-time $31,328; part-time $1044.27 per credit hour. Full-time tuition and fees vary according to course load and degree level. Part-time tuition and fees vary according to course load and degree level. **College room and board:** $9542. Room and board charges vary according to board plan and housing facility. **Payment plan:** Guaranteed tuition.

**FRESHMAN FINANCIAL AID (Fall 2013)** 1,612 applied for aid; of those 73% were deemed to have need. 98% of freshmen with need received aid; of those 34% had need fully met. **Average percent of need met:** 76% (excluding resources awarded to replace EFC). **Average financial aid package:** $15,278 (excluding resources awarded to replace EFC). 27% of all full-time freshmen had no need and received non-need-based gift aid.

**UNDERGRADUATE FINANCIAL AID (Fall 2013)** 6,810 applied for aid; of those 86% were deemed to have need. 96% of undergraduates with need received aid; of those 18% had need fully met. **Average percent of need met:** 64% (excluding resources awarded to replace EFC). **Average financial aid package:** $12,488 (excluding resources awarded to replace EFC). 22% of all full-time undergraduates had no need and received non-need-based gift aid.

**GIFT AID (NEED-BASED) Total amount:** $68,919,411 (25% federal, 10% state, 61% institutional, 4% external sources). **Receiving aid:** Freshmen: 47% (1,040); all full-time undergraduates: 48% (5,008). **Average award:** Freshmen: $11,391; Undergraduates: $8592. **Scholarships, grants, and awards:** Federal Pell, FSEOG, state, private, college/university gift aid from institutional funds.

**GIFT AID (NON-NEED-BASED) Total amount:** $8,602,470 (89% institutional, 11% external sources). **Receiving aid:** Freshmen: 9% (207). Undergraduates: 4% (408). **Average award:** Freshmen: $13,544. Undergraduates: $11,813. **Scholarships, grants, and awards by category:** Academic interests/achievement: biological sciences, business, computer science, engineering/technologies, general academic interests/achievements, mathematics, physical sciences. Special achievements/activities: general special achievements/activities, leadership. Special characteristics: adult students, children of public servants, general special characteristics, handicapped students, international students, local/state students, members of minority groups, out-of-state students, public servants, veterans, veterans' children. **Tuition waivers:** Full or partial for employees or children of employees, senior citizens. **ROTC:** Army cooperative, Air Force cooperative.

**LOANS Student loans:** $38,071,053 (81% need-based, 19% non-need-based). 48% of past graduating class borrowed through all loan programs. **Average indebtedness per student:** $19,613. **Average need-based loan:** Freshmen: $3290. Undergraduates: $4395. **Parent loans:** $4,553,584 (29% need-based, 71% non-need-based). **Programs:** Federal Direct (Subsidized and Unsubsidized Stafford, PLUS), Perkins, state, college/university.

**WORK-STUDY Federal work-study:** 203 jobs averaging $2702. **State or other work-study/employment:** Total amount: $100,062 (100% need-based). 32 part-time jobs averaging $3127.

**APPLYING FOR FINANCIAL AID Required financial aid form:** FAFSA. **Financial aid deadline (priority):** 3/31. **Notification date:** Continuous beginning 3/1. Students must reply within 2 weeks of notification.

**CONTACT** M. Beth N. Tolan, Director of Financial Aid, The University of Texas at Dallas, 800 West Campbell Road, SS22, Richardson, TX 75080-3021, 972-883-2941 or toll-free 800-889-2443. *Fax:* 972-883-2947. *E-mail:* bnt031000@utdallas.edu. *Website:* http://www.utdallas.edu/.

# THE UNIVERSITY OF TEXAS AT EL PASO
### El Paso, TX

| Tuition & fees (TX res): $7255 | Average undergraduate aid package: $11,957 |
|---|---|

**ABOUT THE INSTITUTION** State-supported, coed. **Awards:** certificates, bachelor's, master's, and doctoral degrees. 61 undergraduate majors. **Total enrollment:** 8,036. Undergraduates: 5,849. Freshmen: 692. Federal methodology is used as a basis for awarding need-based institutional aid.

**UNDERGRADUATE EXPENSES for 2015–2016 Application fee:** $40. **Tuition, state resident:** full-time $5606; part-time $187 per credit hour. **Tuition, nonresident:** full-time $17,456; part-time $582 per credit hour. **Required fees:** full-time $1649. **College room and board:** $9180.

**FRESHMAN FINANCIAL AID (Fall 2013)** 2,812 applied for aid; of those 85% were deemed to have need. 98% of freshmen with need received aid; of those 14% had need fully met. **Average percent of need met:** 67% (excluding resources awarded to replace EFC). **Average financial aid package:** $11,537 (excluding resources awarded to replace EFC). 4% of all full-time freshmen had no need and received non-need-based gift aid.

**UNDERGRADUATE FINANCIAL AID (Fall 2013)** 11,653 applied for aid; of those 88% were deemed to have need. 97% of undergraduates with need received aid; of those 11% had need fully met. **Average percent of need met:** 64% (excluding resources awarded to replace EFC). **Average financial aid package:** $11,957 (excluding resources awarded to replace EFC). 4% of all full-time undergraduates had no need and received non-need-based gift aid.

**GIFT AID (NEED-BASED) Total amount:** $82,864,769 (66% federal, 21% state, 13% institutional). **Receiving aid:** Freshmen: 69% (2,035); all full-time undergraduates: 67% (8,674). **Average award:** Freshmen: $9225; Undergraduates: $7569. **Scholarships, grants, and awards:** Federal Pell, FSEOG, state, private, college/university gift aid from institutional funds, United Negro College Fund, Federal Nursing.

**GIFT AID (NON-NEED-BASED) Total amount:** $7,032,307 (3% federal, 14% state, 62% institutional, 21% external sources). **Receiving aid:** Freshmen: 15% (439). Undergraduates: 11% (1,420). **Average award:** Freshmen: $4854. Undergraduates: $4654. **Scholarships, grants, and awards by category:** Academic interests/achievement: biological sciences, business, communication, computer science, education, engineering/technologies, English, general academic interests/achievements, health fields, humanities, international studies, mathematics, military science, physical sciences. Creative arts/performance: applied art and design, art/fine arts, journalism/publications, music, performing arts, theater/drama. Special achievements/activities: cheerleading/drum major, leadership. Special characteristics: ethnic background, international students, local/state students, members of minority groups, out-of-state students.

**LOANS Student loans:** $70,530,145 (98% need-based, 2% non-need-based). 67% of past graduating class borrowed through all loan programs. **Average indebtedness per student:** $24,000. **Average need-based loan:** Freshmen: $4178. Undergraduates: $6171. **Parent loans:** $5,583,401 (100% non-need-based). **Programs:** Federal Direct (Subsidized and Unsubsidized Stafford, PLUS), Perkins, Federal Nursing, state, college/university.

**WORK-STUDY Federal work-study:** 287 jobs averaging $3321. **State or other work-study/employment:** Total amount: $1,287,410 (100% need-based). 100 part-time jobs averaging $2053.

**ATHLETIC AWARDS** Total amount: $4,488,611 (100% non-need-based).

**APPLYING FOR FINANCIAL AID Required financial aid forms:** FAFSA, institution's own form. **Financial aid deadline (priority):** 3/15. **Notification date:** Continuous beginning 6/30. Students must reply within 2 weeks of notification.

**CONTACT** Mr. Ron Williams, Interim Director of Financial Aid, The University of Texas at El Paso, 500 West University Avenue, El Paso, TX 79968-0001, 915-747-5204 or toll-free 877-74MINER. *Fax:* 915-747-5631. *E-mail:* rwilliams@utep.edu. *Website:* http://www.utep.edu/.

# THE UNIVERSITY OF TEXAS AT SAN ANTONIO
## San Antonio, TX

| Tuition & fees (TX res): $8737 | Average undergraduate aid package: $9553 |
|---|---|

**ABOUT THE INSTITUTION** State-supported, coed. **Awards:** bachelor's, master's, and doctoral degrees. 73 undergraduate majors. **Total enrollment:** 28,628. Undergraduates: 24,492. Freshmen: 4,983. Federal methodology is used as a basis for awarding need-based institutional aid.

**UNDERGRADUATE EXPENSES for 2015–2016 Application fee:** $60. **Tuition, state resident:** full-time $5982; part-time $199.41 per credit hour. **Tuition, nonresident:** full-time $17,295; part-time $576.50 per credit hour. **Required fees:** full-time $2755. Full-time tuition and fees vary according to course load and degree level. Part-time tuition and fees vary according to course load and degree level. **College room and board:** $7624; **Room only:** $4690. Room and board charges vary according to board plan and housing facility.

**FRESHMAN FINANCIAL AID (Fall 2013)** 2,966 applied for aid; of those 78% were deemed to have need. 96% of freshmen with need received aid; of those 20% had need fully met. **Average percent of need met:** 61% (excluding resources awarded to replace EFC). **Average financial aid package:** $10,677 (excluding resources awarded to replace EFC). 2% of all full-time freshmen had no need and received non-need-based gift aid.

**UNDERGRADUATE FINANCIAL AID (Fall 2013)** 15,178 applied for aid; of those 86% were deemed to have need. 97% of undergraduates with need received aid; of those 12% had need fully met. **Average percent of need met:** 51% (excluding resources awarded to replace EFC). **Average financial aid package:** $9553 (excluding resources awarded to replace EFC). 2% of all full-time undergraduates had no need and received non-need-based gift aid.

**GIFT AID (NEED-BASED) Total amount:** $63,073,026 (69% federal, 31% state). **Receiving aid:** Freshmen: 57% (2,019); all full-time undergraduates: 55% (11,092). **Average award:** Freshmen: $8036; Undergraduates: $6263. **Scholarships, grants, and awards:** Federal Pell, FSEOG, state, private, college/university gift aid from institutional funds.

**GIFT AID (NON-NEED-BASED) Total amount:** $20,421,212 (76% institutional, 24% external sources). **Receiving aid:** Freshmen: 24% (860). Undergraduates: 13% (2,628). **Average award:** Freshmen: $2879. Undergraduates: $3300. **Scholarships, grants, and awards by category:** Academic interests/achievement: agriculture, architecture, area/ethnic studies, biological sciences, business, communication, computer science, education, engineering/technologies, English, foreign languages, general academic interests/achievements, humanities, international studies, mathematics, physical sciences, social sciences. Creative arts/performance: art/fine arts, creative writing, debating, music. Special achievements/activities: cheerleading/drum major, general special achievements/activities. Special characteristics: ethnic background, first-generation college students, general special characteristics, handicapped students, local/state students, members of minority groups, out-of-state students. **Tuition waivers:** Full or partial for employees or children of employees. **ROTC:** Army, Air Force.

**LOANS Student loans:** $93,001,497 (48% need-based, 52% non-need-based). 66% of past graduating class borrowed through all loan programs. Average indebtedness per student: $27,337. Average need-based loan: Freshmen: $3223. Undergraduates: $4167. **Parent loans:** $9,197,236 (100% non-need-based). **Programs:** Federal Direct (Subsidized and Unsubsidized Stafford, PLUS), Perkins, state, college/university.

**WORK-STUDY Federal work-study:** 304 jobs averaging $2831. **State or other work-study/employment:** Total amount: $1,906,707 (100% need-based). 797 part-time jobs averaging $2481.

**ATHLETIC AWARDS** Total amount: $4,688,397 (100% need-based).

**APPLYING FOR FINANCIAL AID Required financial aid form:** FAFSA. **Financial aid deadline (priority):** 3/15. **Notification date:** Continuous beginning 3/1. Students must reply within 4 weeks of notification.

**CONTACT** Kim Canady, Associate Director of Student Financial Aid, The University of Texas at San Antonio, One UTSA Circle, San Antonio, TX 78249, 210-458-8000 or toll-free 800-669-0919. Fax: 210-458-4638. E-mail: financialaid@utsa.edu. Website: http://www.utsa.edu/.

# THE UNIVERSITY OF TEXAS AT TYLER
## Tyler, TX

**ABOUT THE INSTITUTION** State-supported, coed. **Awards:** certificates, bachelor's, master's, and doctoral degrees. 41 undergraduate majors. **Total enrollment:** 8,036. Undergraduates: 5,849. Freshmen: 692.

**GIFT AID (NEED-BASED) Scholarships, grants, and awards:** Federal Pell, FSEOG, state, private, college/university gift aid from institutional funds, Texas Grants, Institutional Grants (Education Affordability Program).

**GIFT AID (NON-NEED-BASED) Scholarships, grants, and awards by category:** Academic interests/achievement: communication, engineering/technologies, general academic interests/achievements, health fields. Creative arts/performance: art/fine arts, music. Special characteristics: children of faculty/staff.

**LOANS Programs:** Federal Direct (Subsidized and Unsubsidized Stafford, PLUS).

**APPLYING FOR FINANCIAL AID Required financial aid forms:** FAFSA, institution's own form.

**CONTACT** Candice A. Lindsey, Assistant Vice President for Enrollment Management, Marketing and Customer Relations, The University of Texas at Tyler, 3900 University Boulevard, Tyler, TX 75799, 903-566-7221 or toll-free 800-UTTYLER. Fax: 903-566-7183. E-mail: enroll@uttyler.edu. Website: http://www.uttyler.edu/.

# THE UNIVERSITY OF TEXAS HEALTH SCIENCE CENTER AT HOUSTON
## Houston, TX

| Tuition & fees (TX res): $6507 | Average undergraduate aid package: $8299 |
|---|---|

**ABOUT THE INSTITUTION** State-supported, coed. **Awards:** certificates, bachelor's, master's, and doctoral degrees. 2 undergraduate majors. **Total enrollment:** 4,556. Undergraduates: 657. Entering class: 387. Federal methodology is used as a basis for awarding need-based institutional aid.

**UNDERGRADUATE EXPENSES for 2015–2016 Application fee:** $60. **Tuition, state resident:** full-time $5520. **Tuition, nonresident:** full-time $24,180. **Required fees:** full-time $987. Full-time tuition and fees vary according to course load. Part-time tuition and fees vary according to course load.

**UNDERGRADUATE FINANCIAL AID (Fall 2014, est.)** 636 applied for aid; of those 93% were deemed to have need. 100% of undergraduates with need received aid; of those 37% had need fully met. **Average percent of need met:** 36% (excluding resources awarded to replace EFC). **Average financial aid package:** $8299 (excluding resources awarded to replace EFC). 1% of all full-time undergraduates had no need and received non-need-based gift aid.

**GIFT AID (NEED-BASED) Total amount:** $1,476,359 (66% federal, 29% institutional, 5% external sources). **Receiving aid:** All full-time undergraduates: 47% (310). **Average award:** Undergraduates: $4762. **Scholarships, grants, and awards:** Federal Pell, FSEOG, state, private, college/university gift aid from institutional funds.

**GIFT AID (NON-NEED-BASED) Average award:** Undergraduates: $1000. **Scholarships, grants, and awards by category:** Academic interests/achievement: health fields. **ROTC:** Army cooperative.

**LOANS Student loans:** $5,915,232 (100% need-based). **Average need-based loan:** Undergraduates: $5966. **Parent loans:** $1,862,109 (100% need-based). **Programs:** Federal Direct (Subsidized and Unsubsidized Stafford, PLUS), Perkins, Federal Nursing, state, college/university, alternative loans.

**APPLYING FOR FINANCIAL AID Notification date:** Continuous.

**CONTACT** Ms. Araceli Alvarez, Director of Student Financial Services, The University of Texas Health Science Center at Houston, PO Box 20036, Houston, TX 77225, 713-500-3860. Fax: 713-500-3863. E-mail: araceli.alvarez@uth.tmc.edu. Website: http://www.uthouston.edu/.

# THE UNIVERSITY OF TEXAS HEALTH SCIENCE CENTER AT SAN ANTONIO
### San Antonio, TX

**CONTACT** Robert T. Lawson, Financial Aid Administrator, The University of Texas Health Science Center at San Antonio, 7703 Floyd Curl Drive, MSC 7708, San Antonio, TX 78284, 210-567-0025. *Fax:* 210-567-6643. *Website:* http://www.uthscsa.edu/.

# THE UNIVERSITY OF TEXAS MEDICAL BRANCH
### Galveston, TX

**CONTACT** Mrs. Carol A. Cromie, University Financial Aid Officer, The University of Texas Medical Branch, 301 University Boulevard, Galveston, TX 77555-1305, 409-772-9795. *Fax:* 409-772-4466. *E-mail:* cacromie@umtb.edu. *Website:* http://www.utmb.edu/.

# THE UNIVERSITY OF TEXAS OF THE PERMIAN BASIN
### Odessa, TX

**ABOUT THE INSTITUTION** State-supported, coed. *Awards:* certificates, bachelor's, and master's degrees. 32 undergraduate majors. *Total enrollment:* 5,560. Undergraduates: 4,661. Freshmen: 405.

**GIFT AID (NEED-BASED)** *Scholarships, grants, and awards:* Federal Pell, FSEOG, state, private, college/university gift aid from institutional funds.

**GIFT AID (NON-NEED-BASED)** *Scholarships, grants, and awards by category:* Academic interests/achievement: general academic interests/achievements. *Creative arts/performance:* art/fine arts, dance, general creative arts/performance, music, theater/drama. *Special achievements/activities:* cheerleading/drum major, leadership.

**LOANS** *Programs:* Federal Direct (Subsidized and Unsubsidized Stafford, PLUS), state.

**WORK-STUDY** *Federal work-study:* jobs available. *State or other work-study/employment:* Total amount: $19,500 (100% need-based). Part-time jobs available.

**APPLYING FOR FINANCIAL AID** *Required financial aid forms:* FAFSA, institution's own form.

**CONTACT** Jennifer Marie Taveras, Director of Financial Aid, The University of Texas of the Permian Basin, 4901 East University Boulevard, Odessa, TX 79762, 432-552-2620 or toll-free 866-552-UTPB. *Fax:* 432-552-2621. *E-mail:* finaid@utpb.edu. *Website:* http://www.utpb.edu/.

# THE UNIVERSITY OF TEXAS–PAN AMERICAN
### Edinburg, TX

| Tuition & fees (TX res): $5173 | Average undergraduate aid package: $9468 |
|---|---|

**ABOUT THE INSTITUTION** State-supported, coed. *Awards:* certificates, bachelor's, master's, and doctoral degrees. 50 undergraduate majors. *Total enrollment:* 21,015. Undergraduates: 18,200. Freshmen: 3,483. Federal methodology is used as a basis for awarding need-based institutional aid.

**UNDERGRADUATE EXPENSES** for 2015–2016 *Tuition, state resident:* full-time $4176; part-time $174 per credit hour. *Tuition, nonresident:* full-time $13,026; part-time $542.74 per credit hour. *Required fees:* full-time $997. Full-time tuition and fees vary according to course load and degree level. Part-time tuition and fees vary according to course load and degree level. *College room and board:* $5952; *Room only:* $3580. Room and board charges vary according to board plan and housing facility.

**FRESHMAN FINANCIAL AID (Fall 2013)** 2,916 applied for aid; of those 95% were deemed to have need. 100% of freshmen with need received aid; of those 3% had need fully met. *Average percent of need met:* 68% (excluding resources awarded to replace EFC). *Average financial aid package:* $9796 (excluding resources awarded to replace EFC). 3% of all full-time freshmen had no need and received non-need-based gift aid.

**UNDERGRADUATE FINANCIAL AID (Fall 2013)** 11,358 applied for aid; of those 96% were deemed to have need. 100% of undergraduates with need received aid; of those 3% had need fully met. *Average percent of need met:* 63% (excluding resources awarded to replace EFC). *Average financial aid package:* $9468 (excluding resources awarded to replace EFC). 2% of all full-time undergraduates had no need and received non-need-based gift aid.

**GIFT AID (NEED-BASED)** *Total amount:* $90,450,837 (56% federal, 31% state, 12% institutional, 1% external sources). *Receiving aid:* Freshmen: 83% (2,715); all full-time undergraduates: 79% (10,423). *Average award:* Freshmen: $10,016; Undergraduates: $10,224. *Scholarships, grants, and awards:* Federal Pell, FSEOG, state, private, college/university gift aid from institutional funds.

**GIFT AID (NON-NEED-BASED)** *Total amount:* $1,600,135 (4% federal, 5% state, 74% institutional, 17% external sources). *Receiving aid:* Freshmen: 1% (31). Undergraduates: 1% (101). *Average award:* Freshmen: $4696. Undergraduates: $3385. *Scholarships, grants, and awards by category: Academic interests/achievement:* 1,503 awards ($4,266,087 total): biological sciences, business, communication, computer science, education, engineering/technologies, English, general academic interests/achievements, health fields, mathematics, military science, premedicine, social sciences. *Creative arts/performance:* 143 awards ($102,573 total): art/fine arts, dance, journalism/publications, music, theater/drama. *Special achievements/activities:* 28 awards ($25,500 total): cheerleading/drum major, community service, general special achievements/activities, leadership, memberships. *Special characteristics:* 81 awards ($104,006 total): ethnic background, general special characteristics, international students, local/state students, out-of-state students, veterans, veterans' children. *ROTC:* Army.

**LOANS** *Student loans:* $37,218,610 (90% need-based, 10% non-need-based). 61% of past graduating class borrowed through all loan programs. *Average indebtedness per student:* $14,900. *Average need-based loan:* Freshmen: $3067. Undergraduates: $4830. *Parent loans:* $267,262 (8% need-based, 92% non-need-based). *Programs:* Federal Direct (Subsidized and Unsubsidized Stafford, PLUS), Perkins, state.

**WORK-STUDY** *Federal work-study:* 644 jobs averaging $2529. *State or other work-study/employment:* Total amount: $368,764 (100% need-based). 149 part-time jobs averaging $2474.

**ATHLETIC AWARDS** Total amount: $1,289,885 (42% need-based, 58% non-need-based).

**APPLYING FOR FINANCIAL AID** *Required financial aid form:* FAFSA. *Financial aid deadline (priority):* 3/15. *Notification date:* Continuous beginning 3/15. Students must reply within 2 weeks of notification.

**CONTACT** Mr. Elias Ozuna, Executive Director of Student Financial Services, The University of Texas–Pan American, 1201 West University Drive, Edinburg, TX 78541, 956-665-5372 or toll-free 866-441-8872 (in-state). *Fax:* 956-665-2396. *E-mail:* cozuna@utpa.edu. *Website:* http://www.utpa.edu/.

# THE UNIVERSITY OF THE ARTS
### Philadelphia, PA

**CONTACT** Office of Financial Aid, The University of the Arts, 320 South Broad Street, Philadelphia, PA 19102-4944, 800-616-ARTS Ext. 6170 or toll-free 800-616-ARTS. *E-mail:* finaid@uarts.edu. *Website:* http://www.uarts.edu/.

# UNIVERSITY OF THE CUMBERLANDS
## Williamsburg, KY

| Tuition & fees: $22,000 | Average undergraduate aid package: $19,233 |
|---|---|

**ABOUT THE INSTITUTION** Independent Kentucky Baptist, coed. **Awards:** certificates, associate, bachelor's, master's, and doctoral degrees. 40 undergraduate majors. **Total enrollment:** 5,736. Undergraduates: 2,655. Freshmen: 405. Federal methodology is used as a basis for awarding need-based institutional aid.

**UNDERGRADUATE EXPENSES for 2015–2016 Application fee:** $30. **Comprehensive fee:** $30,500 includes full-time tuition ($21,640), mandatory fees ($360), and room and board ($8500). **Part-time tuition:** $690 per credit. Part-time tuition and fees vary according to course load. **Payment plan:** Guaranteed tuition.

**FRESHMAN FINANCIAL AID (Fall 2014, est.)** 390 applied for aid; of those 93% were deemed to have need. 100% of freshmen with need received aid; of those 22% had need fully met. **Average percent of need met:** 79% (excluding resources awarded to replace EFC). **Average financial aid package:** $21,032 (excluding resources awarded to replace EFC). 12% of all full-time freshmen had no need and received non-need-based gift aid.

**UNDERGRADUATE FINANCIAL AID (Fall 2014, est.)** 1,441 applied for aid; of those 93% were deemed to have need. 100% of undergraduates with need received aid; of those 17% had need fully met. **Average percent of need met:** 77% (excluding resources awarded to replace EFC). **Average financial aid package:** $19,233 (excluding resources awarded to replace EFC). 11% of all full-time undergraduates had no need and received non-need-based gift aid.

**GIFT AID (NEED-BASED) Total amount:** $19,125,498 (24% federal, 21% state, 54% institutional, 1% external sources). **Receiving aid:** Freshmen: 88% (363); all full-time undergraduates: 82% (1,315). **Average award:** Freshmen: $17,165; Undergraduates: $15,543. **Scholarships, grants, and awards:** Federal Pell, FSEOG, state, private, college/university gift aid from institutional funds.

**GIFT AID (NON-NEED-BASED) Total amount:** $2,697,404 (2% federal, 11% state, 85% institutional, 2% external sources). **Receiving aid:** Freshmen: 15% (63). Undergraduates: 9% (147). **Average award:** Freshmen: $9675. Undergraduates: $9564. **Scholarships, grants, and awards by category:** Academic interests/achievement: 1,327 awards ($9,126,191 total): general academic interests/achievements. Creative arts/performance: 23 awards ($31,175 total): music. Special achievements/activities: 197 awards ($395,776 total): cheerleading/drum major, community service, leadership, religious involvement. Special characteristics: 193 awards ($960,902 total): children and siblings of alumni, children of faculty/staff, general special characteristics, local/state students, relatives of clergy, religious affiliation, siblings of current students. **Tuition waivers:** Full or partial for employees or children of employees, senior citizens.

**LOANS Student loans:** $7,201,619 (82% need-based, 18% non-need-based). 75% of past graduating class borrowed through all loan programs. Average indebtedness per student: $18,777. **Average need-based loan:** Freshmen: $3178. Undergraduates: $3622. **Parent loans:** $977,532 (27% need-based, 73% non-need-based). **Programs:** Federal Direct (Subsidized and Unsubsidized Stafford, PLUS), Perkins, college/university.

**WORK-STUDY Federal work-study:** Total amount: $1,699,796; 830 jobs averaging $1954. **State or other work-study/employment:** Total amount: $24,288 (23% need-based, 77% non-need-based). 11 part-time jobs averaging $2095.

**ATHLETIC AWARDS** Total amount: $3,216,305 (67% need-based, 33% non-need-based).

**APPLYING FOR FINANCIAL AID Required financial aid form:** FAFSA. **Financial aid deadline (priority):** 2/1. **Notification date:** Continuous beginning 3/1. Students must reply within 2 weeks of notification.

**CONTACT** Mr. Steve Allen, Vice President for Student Financial Planning, University of the Cumberlands, 6190 College Station Drive, Williamsburg, KY 40769-1372, 606-549-2200 or toll-free 800-343-1609. Fax: 606-539-4515. E-mail: finplan@ucumberlands.edu.
Website: http://www.ucumberlands.edu/.

# UNIVERSITY OF THE DISTRICT OF COLUMBIA
## Washington, DC

| Tuition & fees (DC res): $5128 | Average undergraduate aid package: $8200 |
|---|---|

**ABOUT THE INSTITUTION** District-supported, coed. **Awards:** associate, bachelor's, master's, and doctoral degrees. 85 undergraduate majors. **Total enrollment:** 4,803. Undergraduates: 4,491. Freshmen: 521. Federal methodology is used as a basis for awarding need-based institutional aid.

**UNDERGRADUATE EXPENSES for 2015–2016 Application fee:** $35. **Tuition, state resident:** full-time $4518; part-time $188.25 per credit hour. **Tuition, nonresident:** full-time $10,354; part-time $431.41 per credit hour. **Required fees:** full-time $610; $30 per credit hour. Full-time tuition and fees vary according to course load and location. Part-time tuition and fees vary according to course load. **College room and board:** $10,300; **Room only:** $8400.

**FRESHMAN FINANCIAL AID (Fall 2014, est.)** 175 applied for aid; of those 100% were deemed to have need. 97% of freshmen with need received aid; of those 31% had need fully met. **Average percent of need met:** 52% (excluding resources awarded to replace EFC). **Average financial aid package:** $8000 (excluding resources awarded to replace EFC).

**UNDERGRADUATE FINANCIAL AID (Fall 2014, est.)** 1,503 applied for aid; of those 93% were deemed to have need. 100% of undergraduates with need received aid; of those 19% had need fully met. **Average percent of need met:** 58% (excluding resources awarded to replace EFC). **Average financial aid package:** $8200 (excluding resources awarded to replace EFC). 1% of all full-time undergraduates had no need and received non-need-based gift aid.

**GIFT AID (NEED-BASED) Total amount:** $9,961,706 (97% federal, 2% state, 1% institutional). **Receiving aid:** Freshmen: 77% (158); all full-time undergraduates: 60% (1,206). **Average award:** Freshmen: $5150; Undergraduates: $5500. **Scholarships, grants, and awards:** Federal Pell, FSEOG, state, private, college/university gift aid from institutional funds, United Negro College Fund, Federal Nursing.

**GIFT AID (NON-NEED-BASED) Total amount:** $1,989,505 (7% institutional, 93% external sources). **Receiving aid:** Freshmen: 11% (22). Undergraduates: 8% (163). **Average award:** Undergraduates: $3200. **Scholarships, grants, and awards by category:** Academic interests/achievement: agriculture, education, health fields. Special achievements/activities: general special achievements/activities, junior miss. Special characteristics: children of faculty/staff. **Tuition waivers:** Full or partial for employees or children of employees, senior citizens. **ROTC:** Army cooperative, Air Force cooperative.

**LOANS Student loans:** $17,436,836 (40% need-based, 60% non-need-based). **Average need-based loan:** Freshmen: $3000. Undergraduates: $4200. **Parent loans:** $275,003 (100% non-need-based). **Programs:** Federal Direct (Subsidized and Unsubsidized Stafford, PLUS), private loans.

**WORK-STUDY Federal work-study:** Total amount: $105,855; 45 jobs averaging $2500. **State or other work-study/employment:** Total amount: $168,000 (100% non-need-based). 53 part-time jobs averaging $3000.

**ATHLETIC AWARDS** Total amount: $1,586,616 (100% non-need-based).

**APPLYING FOR FINANCIAL AID Required financial aid form:** FAFSA. **Financial aid deadline (priority):** 6/30. **Notification date:** Continuous beginning 5/20. Students must reply within 2 weeks of notification.

**CONTACT** Mr. James O. Contreras, Director of Financial Aid, University of the District of Columbia, 4200 Connecticut Avenue NW, Washington, DC 20008-1175, 202-274-6053. Fax: 202-274-6060. E-mail: finaid@udc.edu.
Website: http://www.udc.edu/.

# UNIVERSITY OF THE INCARNATE WORD
## San Antonio, TX

| Tuition & fees: $27,798 | Average undergraduate aid package: $20,598 |
|---|---|

**ABOUT THE INSTITUTION** Independent Roman Catholic, coed. **Awards:** diplomas, associate, bachelor's, master's, and doctoral degrees. 67 undergraduate majors. **Total enrollment:** 8,745. Undergraduates: 6,496. Freshmen: 946. Federal methodology is used as a basis for awarding need-based institutional aid.

**UNDERGRADUATE EXPENSES for 2015–2016 *Application fee:*** $20. ***Comprehensive fee:*** $39,162 includes full-time tuition ($25,900), mandatory fees ($1898), and room and board ($11,364). ***College room only:*** $6600. Full-time tuition and fees vary according to course load, degree level, location, program, and reciprocity agreements. Room and board charges vary according to board plan and housing facility. ***Part-time tuition:*** $850 per credit hour. Part-time tuition and fees vary according to course load, degree level, location, program, and reciprocity agreements.

**FRESHMAN FINANCIAL AID (Fall 2013)** 911 applied for aid; of those 92% were deemed to have need. 100% of freshmen with need received aid; of those 32% had need fully met. ***Average percent of need met:*** 76% (excluding resources awarded to replace EFC). ***Average financial aid package:*** $19,939 (excluding resources awarded to replace EFC). 15% of all full-time freshmen had no need and received non-need-based gift aid.

**UNDERGRADUATE FINANCIAL AID (Fall 2013)** 3,459 applied for aid; of those 94% were deemed to have need. 100% of undergraduates with need received aid; of those 27% had need fully met. ***Average percent of need met:*** 80% (excluding resources awarded to replace EFC). ***Average financial aid package:*** $20,598 (excluding resources awarded to replace EFC). 19% of all full-time undergraduates had no need and received non-need-based gift aid.

**GIFT AID (NEED-BASED) *Total amount:*** $46,293,991 (25% federal, 10% state, 62% institutional, 3% external sources). ***Receiving aid:*** Freshmen: 80% (799); all full-time undergraduates: 76% (3,154). ***Average award:*** Freshmen: $17,053; Undergraduates: $15,277. ***Scholarships, grants, and awards:*** Federal Pell, FSEOG, state, private, college/university gift aid from institutional funds, United Negro College Fund, Federal Nursing.

**GIFT AID (NON-NEED-BASED) *Total amount:*** $7,720,189 (98% institutional, 2% external sources). ***Receiving aid:*** Freshmen: 4% (43). Undergraduates: 4% (163). ***Average award:*** Freshmen: $7778. Undergraduates: $7720. ***Scholarships, grants, and awards by category:*** Academic interests/achievement: general academic interests/achievements. Creative arts/performance: art/fine arts, music, theater/drama. Special achievements/activities: leadership, religious involvement. Special characteristics: children and siblings of alumni, children of faculty/staff. ***Tuition waivers:*** Full or partial for employees or children of employees, senior citizens. ***ROTC:*** Army cooperative, Air Force cooperative.

**LOANS *Student loans:*** $37,461,825 (93% need-based, 7% non-need-based). 82% of past graduating class borrowed through all loan programs. ***Average indebtedness per student:*** $29,744. ***Average need-based loan:*** Freshmen: $7658. Undergraduates: $4509. ***Parent loans:*** $5,362,951 (86% need-based, 14% non-need-based). ***Programs:*** Federal Direct (Subsidized and Unsubsidized Stafford, PLUS), Perkins, Federal Nursing, state, alternative loans.

**WORK-STUDY *Federal work-study:*** jobs available. ***State or other work-study/employment:*** Total amount: $53,350 (100% need-based). Part-time jobs available.

**ATHLETIC AWARDS** Total amount: $6,257,790 (54% need-based, 46% non-need-based).

**APPLYING FOR FINANCIAL AID *Required financial aid form:*** FAFSA. ***Financial aid deadline (priority):*** 4/1. ***Notification date:*** Continuous beginning 2/15. Students must reply within 2 weeks of notification.

**CONTACT** Ms. Amy Carcanagues, Director of Financial Assistance, University of the Incarnate Word, 4301 Broadway, San Antonio, TX 78209, 210-829-6008 or toll-free 800-749-WORD. *Fax:* 210-283-5053. *E-mail:* finaid@uiwtx.edu.
*Website:* http://www.uiw.edu/.

# UNIVERSITY OF THE OZARKS
## Clarksville, AR

**ABOUT THE INSTITUTION** Independent Presbyterian, coed. ***Awards:*** bachelor's degrees. 30 undergraduate majors. ***Total enrollment:*** 178. Undergraduates: 178. Freshmen: 178.

**GIFT AID (NEED-BASED) *Scholarships, grants, and awards:*** Federal Pell, FSEOG, state, private, college/university gift aid from institutional funds, United Negro College Fund, Federal Nursing.

**GIFT AID (NON-NEED-BASED) *Scholarships, grants, and awards by category:*** Academic interests/achievement: biological sciences, business, communication, education, English, general academic interests/achievements, humanities,

mathematics, premedicine, religion/biblical studies, social sciences. Creative arts/performance: art/fine arts, music, theater/drama. Special achievements/activities: leadership. Special characteristics: children and siblings of alumni, children of faculty/staff, ethnic background, general special characteristics, international students, members of minority groups, relatives of clergy, religious affiliation, siblings of current students.

**LOANS *Programs:*** Federal Direct (Subsidized and Unsubsidized Stafford, PLUS), Perkins, college/university.

**WORK-STUDY *Federal work-study:*** jobs available. ***State or other work-study/employment:*** Part-time jobs available.

**APPLYING FOR FINANCIAL AID *Required financial aid form:*** FAFSA.

**CONTACT** Ms. Jana D. Hart, Director of Financial Aid, University of the Ozarks, 415 North College Avenue, Clarksville, AR 72830-2880, 479-979-1221 or toll-free 800-264-8636. *Fax:* 479-979-1417. *E-mail:* jhart@ozarks.edu.
*Website:* http://www.ozarks.edu/.

# UNIVERSITY OF THE PACIFIC
## Stockton, CA

| Tuition & fees: $41,342 | Average undergraduate aid package: $31,221 |
|---|---|

**ABOUT THE INSTITUTION** Independent, coed. ***Awards:*** bachelor's, master's, and doctoral degrees. 54 undergraduate majors. ***Total enrollment:*** 6,304. Undergraduates: 3,810. Freshmen: 924. Federal methodology is used as a basis for awarding need-based institutional aid.

**UNDERGRADUATE EXPENSES for 2015–2016 *Application fee:*** $35. ***Comprehensive fee:*** $53,924 includes full-time tuition ($40,822), mandatory fees ($520), and room and board ($12,582). Room and board charges vary according to board plan and housing facility. ***Part-time tuition:*** $1408 per credit hour. Part-time tuition and fees vary according to course load.

**FRESHMAN FINANCIAL AID (Fall 2014, est.)** 744 applied for aid; of those 86% were deemed to have need. 100% of freshmen with need received aid; of those 17% had need fully met. ***Average financial aid package:*** $29,594 (excluding resources awarded to replace EFC). 22% of all full-time freshmen had no need and received non-need-based gift aid.

**UNDERGRADUATE FINANCIAL AID (Fall 2014, est.)** 2,844 applied for aid; of those 92% were deemed to have need. 100% of undergraduates with need received aid; of those 11% had need fully met. ***Average financial aid package:*** $31,221 (excluding resources awarded to replace EFC). 15% of all full-time undergraduates had no need and received non-need-based gift aid.

**GIFT AID (NEED-BASED) *Total amount:*** $58,787,410 (12% federal, 19% state, 69% institutional). ***Receiving aid:*** Freshmen: 68% (631); all full-time undergraduates: 69% (2,546). ***Average award:*** Freshmen: $23,737; Undergraduates: $22,930. ***Scholarships, grants, and awards:*** Federal Pell, FSEOG, state, private, college/university gift aid from institutional funds.

**GIFT AID (NON-NEED-BASED) *Total amount:*** $5,767,154 (100% institutional). ***Average award:*** Freshmen: $10,310. Undergraduates: $10,364. ***Scholarships, grants, and awards by category:*** Academic interests/achievement: general academic interests/achievements. Creative arts/performance: debating, music. Special achievements/activities: leadership, religious involvement. Special characteristics: religious affiliation. ***Tuition waivers:*** Full or partial for employees or children of employees. ***ROTC:*** Air Force cooperative.

**LOANS *Student loans:*** $21,764,558 (95% need-based, 5% non-need-based). ***Average need-based loan:*** Freshmen: $6070. Undergraduates: $8451. ***Parent loans:*** $51,105,379 (86% need-based, 14% non-need-based). ***Programs:*** Federal Direct (Subsidized and Unsubsidized Stafford, PLUS), Perkins.

**WORK-STUDY *Federal work-study:*** Total amount: $2,320,303; jobs available.

**ATHLETIC AWARDS** Total amount: $7,761,690 (33% need-based, 67% non-need-based).

**APPLYING FOR FINANCIAL AID *Required financial aid form:*** FAFSA. ***Financial aid deadline (priority):*** 2/15. ***Notification date:*** Continuous beginning 3/1.

**CONTACT** Lynn Fox, Director of Financial Aid, University of the Pacific, 3601 Pacific Avenue, Stockton, CA 95211-0197, 209-946-2421.
*Website:* http://www.pacific.edu/.

# UNIVERSITY OF THE POTOMAC
## Washington, DC

**CONTACT** Phyllis Crews, Financial Aid Counselor, University of the Potomac, 4000 Chesapeake Street NW, Washington, DC 20016, 202-686-0876 or toll-free 888-686-0876. *Fax:* 202-686-0818. *E-mail:* pcrews@potomac.edu. *Website:* http://www.potomac.edu/.

# UNIVERSITY OF THE SACRED HEART
## San Juan, PR

**CONTACT** Ms. Maria Torres, Director of Financial Aid, University of the Sacred Heart, PO Box 12383, San Juan, PR 00914-0383, 787-728-1515 Ext. 3605. *Website:* http://www.sagrado.edu/.

# UNIVERSITY OF THE SCIENCES
## Philadelphia, PA

| Tuition & fees: $36,096 | Average undergraduate aid package: $22,967 |
|---|---|

**ABOUT THE INSTITUTION** Independent, coed. *Awards:* certificates, bachelor's, master's, and doctoral degrees. 18 undergraduate majors. *Total enrollment:* 2,748. Undergraduates: 2,339. Freshmen: 360. Federal methodology is used as a basis for awarding need-based institutional aid.

**UNDERGRADUATE EXPENSES for 2015–2016 *Application fee:* $45. *Comprehensive fee:*** $50,204 includes full-time tuition ($34,336), mandatory fees ($1760), and room and board ($14,108). *College room only:* $8620.

**FRESHMAN FINANCIAL AID (Fall 2013)** 340 applied for aid; of those 91% were deemed to have need. 100% of freshmen with need received aid; of those 43% had need fully met. *Average percent of need met:* 20% (excluding resources awarded to replace EFC). *Average financial aid package:* $20,894 (excluding resources awarded to replace EFC). 13% of all full-time freshmen had no need and received non-need-based gift aid.

**UNDERGRADUATE FINANCIAL AID (Fall 2013)** 1,552 applied for aid; of those 94% were deemed to have need. 100% of undergraduates with need received aid; of those 36% had need fully met. *Average percent of need met:* 32% (excluding resources awarded to replace EFC). *Average financial aid package:* $22,967 (excluding resources awarded to replace EFC). 5% of all full-time undergraduates had no need and received non-need-based gift aid.

**GIFT AID (NEED-BASED) *Total amount:*** $19,407,127 (13% federal, 7% state, 80% institutional). *Receiving aid:* Freshmen: 71% (262); all full-time undergraduates: 76% (1,325). *Average award:* Freshmen: $9159; Undergraduates: $13,322. *Scholarships, grants, and awards:* Federal Pell, FSEOG, state, private, college/university gift aid from institutional funds.

**GIFT AID (NON-NEED-BASED) *Total amount:*** $10,118,906 (95% institutional, 5% external sources). *Receiving aid:* Freshmen: 83% (307). Undergraduates: 55% (972). *Average award:* Freshmen: $14,907. Undergraduates: $14,035. *Scholarships, grants, and awards by category:* Academic interests/achievement: general academic interests/achievements. *Tuition waivers:* Full or partial for employees or children of employees. *ROTC:* Army cooperative; Air Force cooperative.

**LOANS *Student loans:*** $9,268,951 (64% need-based, 36% non-need-based). *Average need-based loan:* Freshmen: $3602. Undergraduates: $4820. *Parent loans:* $5,521,291 (100% non-need-based). *Programs:* Federal Direct (Subsidized and Unsubsidized Stafford, PLUS), Perkins, college/university, Health Professions Student Loans (HPSL), Loans for Disadvantaged Students.

**WORK-STUDY *Federal work-study:*** jobs available. *State or other work-study/employment:* Part-time jobs available.

**ATHLETIC AWARDS** Total amount: $1,113,522 (100% non-need-based).

**APPLYING FOR FINANCIAL AID *Required financial aid form:*** FAFSA. *Financial aid deadline:* 3/15. *Notification date:* Continuous beginning 2/15. Students must reply by 5/1 or within 2 weeks of notification.

**CONTACT** Ms. Paula Lehrberger, Director of Financial Aid, University of the Sciences, 600 South 43rd Street, Philadelphia, PA 19104, 215-596-8894 or toll-free 888-996-8747. *Fax:* 215-596-8554. *Website:* http://www.usciences.edu/.

# UNIVERSITY OF THE SOUTHWEST
## Hobbs, NM

**CONTACT** Kerrie Mitchell, Director of Financial Aid, University of the Southwest, 6610 North Lovington Highway, Hobbs, NM 88240-9129, 575-492-2114 or toll-free 800-530-4400. *Fax:* 575-392-6006. *E-mail:* kmitchell@usw.edu. *Website:* http://www.usw.edu/.

# UNIVERSITY OF THE VIRGIN ISLANDS
## Saint Thomas, VI

**CONTACT** Mavis M. Gilchrist, Director of Financial Aid, University of the Virgin Islands, RR #2, Box 10,000, Kingshill, St. Thomas, VI 00850, 340-692-4186. *Fax:* 340-692-4145. *E-mail:* mgilchr@uvi.edu. *Website:* http://www.uvi.edu/.

# UNIVERSITY OF THE WEST
## Rosemead, CA

**CONTACT** Jamie Johnston, Financial Aid Officer, University of the West, 1409 Walnut Grove Avenue, Rosemead, CA 91770, 626-571-8811 Ext. 122. *Fax:* 626-571-1413. *E-mail:* jamiej@uwest.edu. *Website:* http://www.uwest.edu/.

# THE UNIVERSITY OF TOLEDO
## Toledo, OH

| Tuition & fees (OH res): $9463 | Average undergraduate aid package: $11,172 |
|---|---|

**ABOUT THE INSTITUTION** State-supported, coed. *Awards:* certificates, associate, bachelor's, master's, and doctoral degrees. 148 undergraduate majors. *Total enrollment:* 20,626. Undergraduates: 16,090. Freshmen: 3,436. Federal methodology is used as a basis for awarding need-based institutional aid.

**UNDERGRADUATE EXPENSES for 2015–2016 *Application fee:*** $40. *Tuition, state resident:* full-time $8052; part-time $335.49 per credit hour. *Tuition, nonresident:* full-time $17,390; part-time $724.57 per credit hour. *Required fees:* full-time $1411; $57.80 per credit hour. Full-time tuition and fees vary according to course load, program, reciprocity agreements, and student level. Part-time tuition and fees vary according to course load, program, reciprocity agreements, and student level. *College room and board:* $10,304; *Room only:* $6632. Room and board charges vary according to board plan and housing facility.

**FRESHMAN FINANCIAL AID (Fall 2014, est.)** 3,099 applied for aid; of those 82% were deemed to have need. 96% of freshmen with need received aid; of those 17% had need fully met. *Average percent of need met:* 63% (excluding resources awarded to replace EFC). *Average financial aid package:* $11,753 (excluding resources awarded to replace EFC). 25% of all full-time freshmen had no need and received non-need-based gift aid.

**UNDERGRADUATE FINANCIAL AID (Fall 2014, est.)** 10,515 applied for aid; of those 82% were deemed to have need. 98% of undergraduates with need received aid; of those 15% had need fully met. *Average percent of need met:* 57% (excluding resources awarded to replace EFC). *Average financial aid package:* $11,172 (excluding resources awarded to replace EFC). 22% of all full-time undergraduates had no need and received non-need-based gift aid.

**GIFT AID (NEED-BASED) *Total amount:*** $67,935,279 (38% federal, 7% state, 52% institutional, 3% external sources). *Receiving aid:* Freshmen: 71% (2,403); all full-time undergraduates: 59% (7,732). *Average award:* Freshmen: $9290; Undergraduates: $8683. **Scholarships, grants, and awards:** Federal Pell, FSEOG, state, private, college/university gift aid from institutional funds, Federal Nursing, Academic Competitiveness Grants, National SMART Grants, TEACH Grants.

**GIFT AID (NON-NEED-BASED) Total amount:** $26,114,799 (2% federal, 2% state, 76% institutional, 20% external sources). **Receiving aid:** Freshmen: 18% (617). Undergraduates: 12% (1,535). **Average award:** Freshmen: $6392. Undergraduates: $6234. **Scholarships, grants, and awards by category:** Academic interests/achievement: 5,646 awards ($13,918,364 total): biological sciences, business, communication, education, engineering/technologies, English, foreign languages, general academic interests/achievements, health fields, humanities, international studies, library science, mathematics, physical sciences, premedicine, social sciences. Creative arts/performance: 140 awards ($90,024 total): art/fine arts, general creative arts/performance, music, performing arts, theater/drama. Special achievements/activities: 264 awards ($518,509 total): cheerleading/drum major, community service, general special achievements/activities, hobbies/interests, leadership, memberships, religious involvement. Special characteristics: 2,124 awards ($6,309,651 total): adult students, children and siblings of alumni, children of faculty/staff, children of public servants, children of union members/company employees, ethnic background, first-generation college students, general special characteristics, handicapped students, international students, members of minority groups, out-of-state students, previous college experience, public servants, religious affiliation, veterans, veterans' children. **Tuition waivers:** Full or partial for children of alumni, employees or children of employees. **ROTC:** Army, Air Force cooperative.

**LOANS Student loans:** $69,146,118 (89% need-based, 11% non-need-based). 70% of past graduating class borrowed through all loan programs. Average indebtedness per student: $27,928. **Average need-based loan:** Freshmen: $3701. Undergraduates: $4287. **Parent loans:** $16,550,623 (86% need-based, 14% non-need-based). **Programs:** Federal Direct (Subsidized and Unsubsidized Stafford, PLUS), Perkins, Federal Nursing, college/university, alternative loans.

**WORK-STUDY Federal work-study:** Total amount: $711,209; 170 jobs averaging $1362.

**ATHLETIC AWARDS** Total amount: $6,154,089 (46% need-based, 54% non-need-based).

**APPLYING FOR FINANCIAL AID Required financial aid form:** FAFSA. **Financial aid deadline (priority):** 3/1. **Notification date:** Continuous beginning 4/1. Students must reply within 8 weeks of notification.

**CONTACT** Stephen Schissler, Director, The University of Toledo, 2801 West Bancroft Street, MS-314, Toledo, OH 43606, 419-530-5812 or toll-free 800-5TOLEDO. Fax: 419-530-5835. E-mail: stephen.schissler@utoledo.edu. Website: http://www.utoledo.edu/.

# THE UNIVERSITY OF TULSA
## Tulsa, OK

| Tuition & fees: $39,036 | Average undergraduate aid package: $26,493 |
| --- | --- |

**ABOUT THE INSTITUTION** Independent, coed. **Awards:** certificates, bachelor's, master's, and doctoral degrees. 69 undergraduate majors. **Total enrollment:** 4,682. Undergraduates: 3,473. Freshmen: 764. Federal methodology is used as a basis for awarding need-based institutional aid.

**UNDERGRADUATE EXPENSES for 2015–2016 Application fee:** $50. **One-time required fee:** $485. **Comprehensive fee:** $49,716 includes full-time tuition ($38,556), mandatory fees ($480), and room and board ($10,680). **College room only:** $6140. Full-time tuition and fees vary according to course load. Room and board charges vary according to board plan and housing facility. **Part-time tuition:** $1384 per credit. Part-time tuition and fees vary according to course load.

**FRESHMAN FINANCIAL AID (Fall 2014, est.)** 536 applied for aid; of those 74% were deemed to have need. 100% of freshmen with need received aid; of those 56% had need fully met. **Average percent of need met:** 86% (excluding resources awarded to replace EFC). **Average financial aid package:** $28,252 (excluding resources awarded to replace EFC). 39% of all full-time freshmen had no need and received non-need-based gift aid.

**UNDERGRADUATE FINANCIAL AID (Fall 2014, est.)** 1,645 applied for aid; of those 82% were deemed to have need. 99% of undergraduates with need received aid; of those 51% had need fully met. **Average percent of need met:** 81% (excluding resources awarded to replace EFC). **Average financial aid package:** $26,493

(excluding resources awarded to replace EFC). 41% of all full-time undergraduates had no need and received non-need-based gift aid.

**GIFT AID (NEED-BASED) Total amount:** $5,437,517 (47% federal, 25% state, 28% institutional). **Receiving aid:** Freshmen: 16% (118); all full-time undergraduates: 15% (493). **Average award:** Freshmen: $7305; Undergraduates: $5862. **Scholarships, grants, and awards:** Federal Pell, FSEOG, state, private, college/university gift aid from institutional funds.

**GIFT AID (NON-NEED-BASED) Total amount:** $45,029,028 (3% state, 93% institutional, 4% external sources). **Receiving aid:** Freshmen: 49% (373). Undergraduates: 36% (1,201). **Average award:** Freshmen: $19,048. Undergraduates: $17,829. **Scholarships, grants, and awards by category:** Academic interests/achievement: biological sciences, business, communication, computer science, education, engineering/technologies, English, foreign languages, general academic interests/achievements, health fields, international studies, mathematics, physical sciences, premedicine, religion/biblical studies, social sciences. Creative arts/performance: art/fine arts, music, performing arts, theater/drama. Special achievements/activities: cheerleading/drum major, community service, leadership. Special characteristics: children and siblings of alumni, children of faculty/staff, relatives of clergy, religious affiliation, siblings of current students. **Tuition waivers:** Full or partial for employees or children of employees. **ROTC:** Air Force cooperative.

**LOANS Student loans:** $9,902,993 (43% need-based, 57% non-need-based). 49% of past graduating class borrowed through all loan programs. Average indebtedness per student: $29,161. **Average need-based loan:** Freshmen: $4897. Undergraduates: $6003. **Parent loans:** $4,171,226 (100% non-need-based). **Programs:** Federal Direct (Subsidized and Unsubsidized Stafford, PLUS), Perkins.

**WORK-STUDY Federal work-study:** Total amount: $631,414; 246 jobs averaging $2531. **State or other work-study/employment:** Total amount: $14,602 (100% non-need-based). 2 part-time jobs averaging $4575.

**ATHLETIC AWARDS** Total amount: $11,463,864 (100% non-need-based).

**APPLYING FOR FINANCIAL AID Required financial aid form:** FAFSA. **Financial aid deadline (priority):** 3/1. **Notification date:** Continuous. Students must reply by 5/1 or within 2 weeks of notification.

**CONTACT** Ms. Vicki Hendrickson, Director of Student Financial Services, The University of Tulsa, 800 South Tucker Drive, Tulsa, OK 74104, 918-631-2526 or toll-free 800-331-3050. Fax: 918-631-5105. E-mail: vicki-hendrickson@utulsa.edu. Website: http://www.utulsa.edu/.

# UNIVERSITY OF UTAH
## Salt Lake City, UT

| Tuition & fees (UT res): $7835 | Average undergraduate aid package: $18,259 |
| --- | --- |

**ABOUT THE INSTITUTION** State-supported, coed. **Awards:** certificates, bachelor's, master's, and doctoral degrees. 98 undergraduate majors. **Total enrollment:** 31,515. Undergraduates: 23,907. Freshmen: 3,151. Federal methodology is used as a basis for awarding need-based institutional aid.

**UNDERGRADUATE EXPENSES for 2015–2016 Application fee:** $45. **Tuition, state resident:** full-time $6889; part-time $193.52 per credit hour. **Tuition, nonresident:** full-time $24,111; part-time $665.33 per credit hour. **Required fees:** full-time $946. Full-time tuition and fees vary according to course level, course load, degree level, program, and student level. Part-time tuition and fees vary according to course level, course load, degree level, program, and student level. **College room and board:** $8528; **Room only:** $4338. Room and board charges vary according to board plan, housing facility, and location.

**FRESHMAN FINANCIAL AID (Fall 2014, est.)** 1,952 applied for aid; of those 70% were deemed to have need. 98% of freshmen with need received aid; of those 14% had need fully met. **Average percent of need met:** 62% (excluding resources awarded to replace EFC). **Average financial aid package:** $18,997 (excluding resources awarded to replace EFC). 12% of all full-time freshmen had no need and received non-need-based gift aid.

**UNDERGRADUATE FINANCIAL AID (Fall 2014, est.)** 9,297 applied for aid; of those 83% were deemed to have need. 99% of undergraduates with need received aid; of those 8% had need fully met. **Average percent of need met:** 61% (excluding resources awarded to replace EFC). **Average financial aid package:** $18,259 (excluding resources awarded to replace EFC). 11% of all full-time undergraduates had no need and received non-need-based gift aid.

**GIFT AID (NEED-BASED)** *Total amount:* $46,791,926 (77% federal, 2% state, 7% institutional, 14% external sources). *Receiving aid:* Freshmen: 41% (1,189); all full-time undergraduates: 12% (2,043). *Average award:* Freshmen: $8398; Undergraduates: $4618. *Scholarships, grants, and awards:* Federal Pell, FSEOG, state, private, college/university gift aid from institutional funds, Federal Nursing, TEACH Grants.

**GIFT AID (NON-NEED-BASED)** *Total amount:* $23,656,043 (20% state, 61% institutional, 19% external sources). *Receiving aid:* Freshmen: 5% (138). Undergraduates: 20. *Average award:* Freshmen: $5834. Undergraduates: $4661. *Scholarships, grants, and awards by category:* Academic interests/achievement: architecture, area/ethnic studies, biological sciences, business, communication, computer science, education, engineering/technologies, English, foreign languages, general academic interests/achievements, health fields, humanities, international studies, mathematics, military science, physical sciences, social sciences. *Creative arts/performance:* art/fine arts, cinema/film/broadcasting, creative writing, dance, journalism/publications, music, performing arts, theater/drama. *Special achievements/activities:* cheerleading/drum major, general special achievements/activities, leadership. *Special characteristics:* children of faculty/staff, children of public servants, children with a deceased or disabled parent, ethnic background, first-generation college students, handicapped students, out-of-state students, spouses of deceased or disabled public servants. *Tuition waivers:* Full or partial for employees or children of employees, senior citizens. *ROTC:* Army, Naval, Air Force.

**LOANS** *Student loans:* $48,673,008 (54% need-based, 46% non-need-based). 39% of past graduating class borrowed through all loan programs. *Average indebtedness per student:* $20,019. *Average need-based loan:* Freshmen: $3246. Undergraduates: $4322. *Parent loans:* $2,924,036 (42% need-based, 58% non-need-based). *Programs:* Federal Direct (Subsidized and Unsubsidized Stafford, PLUS), Perkins, Federal Nursing, college/university, private loans.

**WORK-STUDY** *Federal work-study:* Total amount: $1,717,344; 357 jobs averaging $4662.

**ATHLETIC AWARDS** Total amount: $9,329,515 (36% need-based, 64% non-need-based).

**APPLYING FOR FINANCIAL AID** *Required financial aid forms:* FAFSA, institution's own form. *Financial aid deadline (priority):* 4/1. *Notification date:* Continuous beginning 4/15. Students must reply within 6 weeks of notification.

**CONTACT** Amy Capps, Assistant Director, University of Utah, 201 South 1460 East, Room 105, Salt Lake City, UT 84112-9055, 801-581-6211 or toll-free 800-685-8856. *Fax:* 801-585-6350. *E-mail:* financialaid@sa.utah.edu. *Website:* http://www.utah.edu/.

# UNIVERSITY OF VALLEY FORGE
## Phoenixville, PA

| Tuition & fees: $20,364 | Average undergraduate aid package: $13,598 |
| --- | --- |

**ABOUT THE INSTITUTION** Independent Assemblies of God, coed. *Awards:* associate, bachelor's, and master's degrees. 34 undergraduate majors. *Total enrollment:* 931. Undergraduates: 895. Freshmen: 149. Federal methodology is used as a basis for awarding need-based institutional aid.

**UNDERGRADUATE EXPENSES for 2015–2016** *Application fee:* $25. *Comprehensive fee:* $28,480 includes full-time tuition ($18,644), mandatory fees ($1720), and room and board ($8116). Full-time tuition and fees vary according to course load and location. Room and board charges vary according to board plan and housing facility. Part-time tuition and fees vary according to course load and location.

**FRESHMAN FINANCIAL AID (Fall 2014, est.)** 117 applied for aid; of those 91% were deemed to have need. 100% of freshmen with need received aid; of those 12% had need fully met. *Average percent of need met:* 52% (excluding resources awarded to replace EFC). *Average financial aid package:* $13,286 (excluding resources awarded to replace EFC). 21% of all full-time freshmen had no need and received non-need-based gift aid.

**UNDERGRADUATE FINANCIAL AID (Fall 2014, est.)** 510 applied for aid; of those 92% were deemed to have need. 100% of undergraduates with need received aid; of those 11% had need fully met. *Average percent of need met:* 55% (excluding resources awarded to replace EFC). *Average financial aid package:* $13,598 (excluding resources awarded to replace EFC). 11% of all full-time undergraduates had no need and received non-need-based gift aid.

**GIFT AID (NEED-BASED)** *Total amount:* $5,872,435 (28% federal, 9% state, 58% institutional, 5% external sources). *Receiving aid:* Freshmen: 74% (106); all full-time undergraduates: 85% (456). *Average award:* Freshmen: $10,439; Undergraduates: $10,123. *Scholarships, grants, and awards:* Federal Pell, FSEOG, state, private, college/university gift aid from institutional funds.

**GIFT AID (NON-NEED-BASED)** *Total amount:* $606,540 (89% institutional, 11% external sources). *Receiving aid:* Freshmen: 8% (11). Undergraduates: 6% (34). *Average award:* Freshmen: $5081. Undergraduates: $5757. *Scholarships, grants, and awards by category:* Academic interests/achievement: $482,407 total: general academic interests/achievements. *Creative arts/performance:* $950,598 total: art/fine arts, music. *Special achievements/activities:* $253,726 total: community service, general special achievements/activities, leadership, religious involvement. *Special characteristics:* $1,864,620 total: children of current students, children of faculty/staff, general special characteristics, local/state students, married students, parents of current students, relatives of clergy, siblings of current students, spouses of current students. *Tuition waivers:* Full or partial for employees or children of employees.

**LOANS** *Student loans:* $5,656,284 (83% need-based, 17% non-need-based). 87% of past graduating class borrowed through all loan programs. *Average indebtedness per student:* $31,570. *Average need-based loan:* Freshmen: $3493. Undergraduates: $4286. *Parent loans:* $1,691,873 (69% need-based, 31% non-need-based). *Programs:* Federal Direct (Subsidized and Unsubsidized Stafford, PLUS), Perkins.

**WORK-STUDY** *Federal work-study:* Total amount: $43,767; 33 jobs averaging $1326.

**APPLYING FOR FINANCIAL AID** *Required financial aid form:* FAFSA. *Financial aid deadline (priority):* 5/1. *Notification date:* Continuous beginning 3/1. Students must reply within 3 weeks of notification.

**CONTACT** Mrs. Linda Stein, Director of Financial Aid, University of Valley Forge, 1401 Charlestown Road, Phoenixville, PA 19460-2399, 610-917-1416 or toll-free 800-432-8322. *Fax:* 610-917-2069. *E-mail:* llstein@vfcc.edu. *Website:* http://www.valleyforge.edu/.

# UNIVERSITY OF VALLEY FORGE VIRGINIA CAMPUS
## Woodbridge, VA

**CONTACT** Christiana Bruwaa-Frimpong, Student Accounts/Financial Aid Counselor, University of Valley Forge Virginia Campus, 13909 Smoketown Road, Woodbridge, VA 22192, 703-580-4810 Ext. 172 or toll-free 800-432-8322. *Fax:* 703-580-4806. *Website:* http://www.valleyforge.edu/.

# UNIVERSITY OF VERMONT
## Burlington, VT

| Tuition & fees (VT res): $16,226 | Average undergraduate aid package: $21,989 |
| --- | --- |

**ABOUT THE INSTITUTION** State-supported, coed. *Awards:* certificates, bachelor's, master's, and doctoral degrees. 99 undergraduate majors. *Total enrollment:* 12,856. Undergraduates: 10,994. Freshmen: 2,310. Federal methodology is used as a basis for awarding need-based institutional aid.

**UNDERGRADUATE EXPENSES for 2015–2016** *Application fee:* $55. *Tuition, state resident:* full-time $14,184. *Tuition, nonresident:* full-time $35,832. *Required fees:* full-time $2042. Part-time tuition and fees vary according to course load. *College room and board:* $10,780; *Room only:* $7116. Room and board charges vary according to board plan and housing facility.

**FRESHMAN FINANCIAL AID (Fall 2013)** 1,889 applied for aid; of those 78% were deemed to have need. 99% of freshmen with need received aid; of those 15% had need fully met. *Average percent of need met:* 70% (excluding resources awarded to replace EFC). *Average financial aid package:* $24,308 (excluding resources awarded to replace EFC). 30% of all full-time freshmen had no need and received non-need-based gift aid.

**UNDERGRADUATE FINANCIAL AID (Fall 2013)** 6,587 applied for aid; of those 82% were deemed to have need. 99% of undergraduates with need received aid; of those 10% had need fully met. *Average percent of need met:* 65% (excluding resources awarded to replace EFC). *Average financial aid package:* $21,989 (excluding resources awarded to replace EFC). 26% of all full-time undergraduates had no need and received non-need-based gift aid.

**GIFT AID (NEED-BASED)** *Total amount:* $79,021,760 (13% federal, 5% state, 79% institutional, 3% external sources). *Receiving aid:* Freshmen: 61% (1,428); all full-time undergraduates: 56% (5,186). *Average award:* Freshmen: $16,693; Undergraduates: $14,736. *Scholarships, grants, and awards:* Federal Pell, FSEOG, state, private, college/university gift aid from institutional funds, Federal Nursing.

**GIFT AID (NON-NEED-BASED)** *Total amount:* $17,694,423 (2% state, 89% institutional, 9% external sources). *Receiving aid:* Freshmen: 8% (177). Undergraduates: 4% (406). *Average award:* Freshmen: $10,293. Undergraduates: $8658. *Scholarships, grants, and awards by category: Academic interests/achievement:* agriculture, area/ethnic studies, business, computer science, education, engineering/technologies, English, foreign languages, general academic interests/achievements, health fields, home economics, humanities, international studies, mathematics, military science, physical sciences, premedicine, social sciences. *Creative arts/performance:* debating, music, theater/drama. *Special achievements/activities:* community service, leadership, memberships. *Special characteristics:* adult students, ethnic background, first-generation college students. *Tuition waivers:* Full or partial for employees or children of employees. *ROTC:* Army.

**LOANS** *Student loans:* $43,484,379 (42% need-based, 58% non-need-based). 63% of past graduating class borrowed through all loan programs. *Average indebtedness per student:* $27,276. *Average need-based loan:* Freshmen: $3565. Undergraduates: $4494. *Parent loans:* $30,720,623 (100% non-need-based). *Programs:* Federal Direct (Subsidized and Unsubsidized Stafford, PLUS), Perkins, Federal Nursing, college/university.

**WORK-STUDY** *Federal work-study:* 1,527 jobs averaging $1600.

**ATHLETIC AWARDS** Total amount: $6,422,874 (25% need-based, 75% non-need-based).

**APPLYING FOR FINANCIAL AID** *Required financial aid form:* FAFSA. *Financial aid deadline (priority):* 2/10. *Notification date:* Continuous beginning 3/31. Students must reply within 4 weeks of notification.

**CONTACT** Office of Student Financial Services, University of Vermont, 223 Waterman Building, Burlington, VT 05405-0160, 802-656-5700. *Fax:* 802-656-4076. *E-mail:* sfs@uvm.edu. *Website:* http://www.uvm.cdu/.

# UNIVERSITY OF VIRGINIA
## Charlottesville, VA

| Tuition & fees (VA res): $12,998 | Average undergraduate aid package: $24,427 |
|---|---|

**ABOUT THE INSTITUTION** State-supported, coed. *Awards:* certificates, bachelor's, master's, and doctoral degrees. 50 undergraduate majors. *Total enrollment:* 23,732. Undergraduates: 16,483. Freshmen: 3,709. Both federal and institutional methodology are used as a basis for awarding need-based institutional aid.

**UNDERGRADUATE EXPENSES** for 2015–2016 *Application fee:* $60. *Tuition, state resident:* full-time $10,484; part-time $349 per credit hour. *Tuition, nonresident:* full-time $38,988; part-time $1300 per credit hour. *Required fees:* full-time $2514; $2541 per year. Full-time tuition and fees vary according to program and student level. *College room and board:* $10,052; *Room only:* $5492. Room and board charges vary according to board plan and housing facility.

**FRESHMAN FINANCIAL AID (Fall 2014, est.)** 2,752 applied for aid; of those 46% were deemed to have need. 100% of freshmen with need received aid; of those 100% had need fully met. *Average percent of need met:* 100% (excluding resources awarded to replace EFC). *Average financial aid package:* $24,920 (excluding resources awarded to replace EFC). 2% of all full-time freshmen had no need and received non-need-based gift aid.

**UNDERGRADUATE FINANCIAL AID (Fall 2014, est.)** 8,782 applied for aid; of those 57% were deemed to have need. 100% of undergraduates with need received aid; of those 100% had need fully met. *Average percent of need met:* 100% (excluding resources awarded to replace EFC). *Average financial aid package:* $24,427 (excluding resources awarded to replace EFC). 3% of all full-time undergraduates had no need and received non-need-based gift aid.

**GIFT AID (NEED-BASED)** *Total amount:* $76,151,880 (14% federal, 8% state, 71% institutional, 7% external sources). *Receiving aid:* Freshmen: 28% (1,042); all full-time undergraduates: 27% (4,046). *Average award:* Freshmen: $18,723; Undergraduates: $19,406. *Scholarships, grants, and awards:* Federal Pell, FSEOG, state, private, college/university gift aid from institutional funds, Federal Nursing.

**GIFT AID (NON-NEED-BASED)** *Total amount:* $20,945,643 (16% federal, 17% institutional, 67% external sources). *Receiving aid:* Freshmen: 3% (122). Undergraduates: 2% (371). *Average award:* Freshmen: $8701. Undergraduates: $7277. *Scholarships, grants, and awards by category: Academic interests/achievement:* general academic interests/achievements. *Creative arts/performance:* music. *Tuition waivers:* Full or partial for employees or children of employees, senior citizens. *ROTC:* Army, Naval, Air Force.

**LOANS** *Student loans:* $34,079,276 (58% need-based, 42% non-need-based). 36% of past graduating class borrowed through all loan programs. *Average indebtedness per student:* $22,933. *Average need-based loan:* Freshmen: $5806. Undergraduates: $6466. *Parent loans:* $9,619,811 (13% need-based, 87% non-need-based). *Programs:* Perkins, Federal Nursing, college/university, private loans.

**WORK-STUDY** *Federal work-study:* Total amount: $2,928,409; jobs available.

**ATHLETIC AWARDS** Total amount: $13,000,016 (28% need-based, 72% non-need-based).

**APPLYING FOR FINANCIAL AID** *Required financial aid forms:* FAFSA, CSS Financial Aid PROFILE. *Financial aid deadline (priority):* 3/1. *Notification date:* 4/5. Students must reply by 5/1.

**CONTACT** Mr. Steve Kimata, Assistant Vice President for Student Financial Services, University of Virginia, PO Box 400194, Charlottesville, VA 22904-4194, 434-924-4241. *Fax:* 434-982-2315. *E-mail:* faid@virginia.edu. *Website:* http://www.virginia.edu/.

# THE UNIVERSITY OF VIRGINIA'S COLLEGE AT WISE
## Wise, VA

| Tuition & fees (VA res): $8868 | Average undergraduate aid package: $13,141 |
|---|---|

**ABOUT THE INSTITUTION** State-supported, coed. *Awards:* bachelor's degrees. 25 undergraduate majors. *Total enrollment:* 2,182. Undergraduates: 2,183. Freshmen: 309. Federal methodology is used as a basis for awarding need-based institutional aid.

**UNDERGRADUATE EXPENSES** for 2015–2016 *Application fee:* $25. *Tuition, state resident:* full-time $4862; part-time $208 per credit hour. *Tuition, nonresident:* full-time $19,864; part-time $840 per credit hour. *Required fees:* full-time $4006; $254 per credit hour. Part-time tuition and fees vary according to course load. *College room and board:* $10,340. Room and board charges vary according to board plan and housing facility.

**FRESHMAN FINANCIAL AID (Fall 2013)** 318 applied for aid; of those 79% were deemed to have need. 100% of freshmen with need received aid; of those 43% had need fully met. *Average percent of need met:* 87% (excluding resources awarded to replace EFC). *Average financial aid package:* $14,275 (excluding resources awarded to replace EFC). 4% of all full-time freshmen had no need and received non-need-based gift aid.

**UNDERGRADUATE FINANCIAL AID (Fall 2013)** 1,209 applied for aid; of those 91% were deemed to have need. 100% of undergraduates with need received aid; of those 27% had need fully met. *Average percent of need met:* 83% (excluding resources awarded to replace EFC). *Average financial aid package:* $13,141 (excluding resources awarded to replace EFC). 11% of all full-time undergraduates had no need and received non-need-based gift aid.

**GIFT AID (NEED-BASED)** *Total amount:* $5,977,989 (59% federal, 37% state, 4% institutional). *Receiving aid:* Freshmen: 71% (235); all full-time undergraduates: 71% (1,010). *Average award:* Freshmen: $8320; Undergraduates: $6898. *Scholarships, grants, and awards:* Federal Pell, FSEOG, state, private, college/university gift aid from institutional funds.

**GIFT AID (NON-NEED-BASED)** *Total amount:* $3,385,685 (2% federal, 5% state, 75% institutional, 18% external sources). *Receiving aid:* Freshmen: 55% (180). Undergraduates: 42% (598). *Average award:* Freshmen: $5685. Undergraduates: $5077. *Scholarships, grants, and awards by category: Academic interests/achievement:* agriculture, biological sciences, business, computer science, education, English, general academic interests/achievements, health fields, humanities, mathematics, physical sciences, premedicine, social sciences. *Creative arts/performance:* creative writing, general creative arts/performance, journalism/publications, music, performing arts, theater/drama. *Special achievements/activities:* community service, religious involvement. *Special characteristics:* children with a deceased or disabled

parent, ethnic background, local/state students, veterans, veterans' children. **Tuition waivers:** Full or partial for employees or children of employees, senior citizens. **ROTC:** Army.
**LOANS Student loans:** $5,926,824 (50% need-based, 50% non-need-based). 68% of past graduating class borrowed through all loan programs. *Average indebtedness per student:* $12,662. **Average need-based loan:** Freshmen: $2626. Undergraduates: $3996. **Parent loans:** $807,216 (100% non-need-based). **Programs:** Perkins, state, college/university.
**WORK-STUDY Federal work-study:** jobs available.
**ATHLETIC AWARDS** Total amount: $617,589 (100% non-need-based).
**APPLYING FOR FINANCIAL AID Required financial aid form:** FAFSA. *Financial aid deadline (priority):* 4/1. *Notification date:* Continuous. Students must reply within 4 weeks of notification.
**CONTACT** Mrs. Rebecca Huffman, Director of Financial Aid, The University of Virginia's College at Wise, 1 College Avenue, Wise, VA 24293, 276-328-0277 or toll-free 888-282-9324. *Fax:* 276-328-0251. *E-mail:* reg5a@uvawise.edu.
*Website:* http://www.uvawise.edu/.

# UNIVERSITY OF WASHINGTON
## Seattle, WA

| Tuition & fees (WA res): $12,394 | Average undergraduate aid package: $18,500 |
| --- | --- |

**ABOUT THE INSTITUTION** State-supported, coed. **Awards:** certificates, bachelor's, master's, and doctoral degrees. 154 undergraduate majors. **Total enrollment:** 44,784. Undergraduates: 30,672. Freshmen: 6,360. Federal methodology is used as a basis for awarding need-based institutional aid.
**UNDERGRADUATE EXPENSES for 2015–2016 Application fee:** $60. **Tuition, state resident:** full-time $11,305; part-time $377 per credit. **Tuition, nonresident:** full-time $32,424; part-time $1081 per credit. **Required fees:** full-time $1089; $29 per credit or $76 per term. Full-time tuition and fees vary according to course load and location. Part-time tuition and fees vary according to course load and location. **College room and board:** $10,833. Room and board charges vary according to board plan and housing facility.
**FRESHMAN FINANCIAL AID (Fall 2014, est.)** 4,375 applied for aid; of those 63% were deemed to have need. 93% of freshmen with need received aid; of those 39% had need fully met. **Average percent of need met:** 82% (excluding resources awarded to replace EFC). **Average financial aid package:** $17,500 (excluding resources awarded to replace EFC). 5% of all full-time freshmen had no need and received non-need-based gift aid.
**UNDERGRADUATE FINANCIAL AID (Fall 2014, est.)** 17,700 applied for aid; of those 76% were deemed to have need. 86% of undergraduates with need received aid; of those 23% had need fully met. **Average percent of need met:** 82% (excluding resources awarded to replace EFC). **Average financial aid package:** $18,500 (excluding resources awarded to replace EFC). 5% of all full-time undergraduates had no need and received non-need-based gift aid.
**GIFT AID (NEED-BASED) Total amount:** $156,600,000 (27% federal, 31% state, 40% institutional, 2% external sources). **Receiving aid:** Freshmen: 33% (2,050); all full-time undergraduates: 37% (9,800). **Average award:** Freshmen: $14,000; Undergraduates: $15,000. **Scholarships, grants, and awards:** Federal Pell, FSEOG, state, private, college/university gift aid from institutional funds, Federal Nursing.
**GIFT AID (NON-NEED-BASED) Total amount:** $21,200,000 (1% state, 76% institutional, 23% external sources). **Receiving aid:** Freshmen: 5% (300). Undergraduates: 3% (700). **Average award:** Freshmen: $6400. Undergraduates: $5500. **Scholarships, grants, and awards by category:** *Academic interests/achievement:* architecture, business, computer science, education, engineering/technologies, general academic interests/achievements, health fields. *Creative arts/performance:* art/fine arts, general creative arts/performance, music, performing arts. *Special achievements/activities:* general special achievements/activities, leadership, memberships. **Tuition waivers:** Full or partial for employees or children of employees, senior citizens. **ROTC:** Army, Naval, Air Force.
**LOANS Student loans:** $83,000,000 (76% need-based, 24% non-need-based). 46% of past graduating class borrowed through all loan programs. *Average indebtedness per student:* $21,532. **Average need-based loan:** Freshmen: $5500. Undergraduates: $7000. **Parent loans:** $42,000,000 (100% non-need-based). **Programs:** Federal Direct (Subsidized and Unsubsidized Stafford, PLUS), Perkins, Federal Nursing.

**WORK-STUDY Federal work-study:** Total amount: $2,600,000; 1,500 jobs averaging $2800. **State or other work-study/employment:** Total amount: $466,300 (100% need-based). 200 part-time jobs averaging $3200.
**ATHLETIC AWARDS** Total amount: $8,100,000 (100% non-need-based).
**APPLYING FOR FINANCIAL AID Required financial aid form:** FAFSA. *Financial aid deadline (priority):* 2/28. *Notification date:* 4/1. Students must reply by 5/1 or within 3 weeks of notification.
**CONTACT** Office of Student Financial Aid, University of Washington, Box 355880, Seattle, WA 98195-5880, 206-543-6101. *Fax:* 206-685-1338. *E-mail:* osfa@u.washington.edu.
*Website:* http://www.washington.edu/.

# UNIVERSITY OF WASHINGTON, BOTHELL
## Bothell, WA

| Tuition & fees (WA res): $12,517 | Average undergraduate aid package: $18,500 |
| --- | --- |

**ABOUT THE INSTITUTION** State-supported, coed. **Awards:** bachelor's and master's degrees. 31 undergraduate majors. **Total enrollment:** 4,962. Undergraduates: 4,405. Freshmen: 639. Federal methodology is used as a basis for awarding need-based institutional aid.
**UNDERGRADUATE EXPENSES for 2015–2016 Application fee:** $60. **Tuition, state resident:** full-time $11,911; part-time $377 per credit. **Tuition, nonresident:** full-time $33,030; part-time $1081 per credit. **Required fees:** full-time $606; $20.20 per credit. Full-time tuition and fees vary according to course load. Part-time tuition and fees vary according to course load. **College room and board:** $10,833. Room and board charges vary according to board plan, housing facility, and location.
**FRESHMAN FINANCIAL AID (Fall 2014, est.)** 493 applied for aid; of those 81% were deemed to have need. 94% of freshmen with need received aid; of those 13% had need fully met. **Average percent of need met:** 81% (excluding resources awarded to replace EFC). **Average financial aid package:** $17,000 (excluding resources awarded to replace EFC). 6% of all full-time freshmen had no need and received non-need-based gift aid.
**UNDERGRADUATE FINANCIAL AID (Fall 2014, est.)** 2,525 applied for aid; of those 87% were deemed to have need. 95% of undergraduates with need received aid; of those 12% had need fully met. **Average percent of need met:** 79% (excluding resources awarded to replace EFC). **Average financial aid package:** $18,500 (excluding resources awarded to replace EFC). 2% of all full-time undergraduates had no need and received non-need-based gift aid.
**GIFT AID (NEED-BASED) Total amount:** $28,050,000 (31% federal, 34% state, 34% institutional, 1% external sources). **Receiving aid:** Freshmen: 54% (344); all full-time undergraduates: 49% (1,832). **Average award:** Freshmen: $14,000; Undergraduates: $15,000. **Scholarships, grants, and awards:** Federal Pell, FSEOG, state, private, college/university gift aid from institutional funds, Federal Nursing.
**GIFT AID (NON-NEED-BASED) Total amount:** $840,000 (71% institutional, 29% external sources). **Receiving aid:** Freshmen: 2% (10). Undergraduates: 1% (20). **Average award:** Freshmen: $5500. Undergraduates: $5000. **Scholarships, grants, and awards by category:** *Academic interests/achievement:* general academic interests/achievements. **Tuition waivers:** Full or partial for employees or children of employees, senior citizens. **ROTC:** Army cooperative, Naval cooperative, Air Force cooperative.
**LOANS Student loans:** $14,200,000 (77% need-based, 23% non-need-based). 51% of past graduating class borrowed through all loan programs. *Average indebtedness per student:* $19,536. **Average need-based loan:** Freshmen: $5500. Undergraduates: $7000. **Parent loans:** $4,500,000 (100% non-need-based). **Programs:** Federal Direct (Subsidized and Unsubsidized Stafford, PLUS), Perkins, Federal Nursing.
**WORK-STUDY Federal work-study:** Total amount: $500,000; 280 jobs averaging $2800. **State or other work-study/employment:** Total amount: $100,000 (100% need-based). 40 part-time jobs averaging $3400.
**APPLYING FOR FINANCIAL AID Required financial aid form:** FAFSA. *Financial aid deadline (priority):* 2/28. *Notification date:* 4/1. Students must reply by 5/1 or within 3 weeks of notification.

CONTACT Office of Financial Aid and Scholarships, University of Washington, Bothell, Box 358500, 18115 Campus Way NE, Bothell, WA 98011-8246, 425-352-5240. *Fax:* 425-352-3217. *E-mail:* finaid@uwb.edu.
*Website:* http://www.uwb.edu/.

# UNIVERSITY OF WASHINGTON, TACOMA
## Tacoma, WA

| Tuition & fees (WA res): $12,262 | Average undergraduate aid package: $18,500 |
|---|---|

**ABOUT THE INSTITUTION** State-supported, coed. *Awards:* bachelor's, master's, and doctoral degrees. 32 undergraduate majors. *Total enrollment:* 4,477. Undergraduates: 3,809. Freshmen: 435. Federal methodology is used as a basis for awarding need-based institutional aid.
**UNDERGRADUATE EXPENSES for 2015–2016** *Application fee:* $60. *Tuition, state resident:* full-time $11,305; part-time $377 per credit. *Tuition, nonresident:* full-time $32,424; part-time $1081 per credit. *Required fees:* full-time $957; $20 per credit. Full-time tuition and fees vary according to course load. Part-time tuition and fees vary according to course load. *College room and board:* $10,833. Room and board charges vary according to housing facility and location.
**FRESHMAN FINANCIAL AID (Fall 2014, est.)** 396 applied for aid; of those 87% were deemed to have need. 93% of freshmen with need received aid; of those 22% had need fully met. *Average percent of need met:* 81% (excluding resources awarded to replace EFC). *Average financial aid package:* $17,000 (excluding resources awarded to replace EFC). 7% of all full-time freshmen had no need and received non-need-based gift aid.
**UNDERGRADUATE FINANCIAL AID (Fall 2014, est.)** 2,715 applied for aid; of those 92% were deemed to have need. 95% of undergraduates with need received aid; of those 19% had need fully met. *Average percent of need met:* 79% (excluding resources awarded to replace EFC). *Average financial aid package:* $18,500 (excluding resources awarded to replace EFC). 6% of all full-time undergraduates had no need and received non-need-based gift aid.
**GIFT AID (NEED-BASED) *Total amount:*** $36,575,000 (31% federal, 34% state, 34% institutional, 1% external sources). *Receiving aid:* Freshmen: 73% (313); all full-time undergraduates: 67% (2,221). *Average award:* Freshmen: $14,000; Undergraduates: $15,000. *Scholarships, grants, and awards:* Federal Pell, FSEOG, state, private, college/university gift aid from institutional funds, Federal Nursing.
**GIFT AID (NON-NEED-BASED) *Total amount:*** $1,050,000 (76% institutional, 24% external sources). *Receiving aid:* Freshmen: 2% (10). Undergraduates: 1% (30). *Average award:* Freshmen: $3300. Undergraduates: $2400. *Scholarships, grants, and awards by category:* Academic interests/achievement: general academic interests/achievements. *Tuition waivers:* Full or partial for employees or children of employees, senior citizens. *ROTC:* Army cooperative, Naval cooperative, Air Force cooperative.
**LOANS *Student loans:*** $16,650,000 (91% need-based, 9% non-need-based). 62% of past graduating class borrowed through all loan programs. *Average indebtedness per student:* $23,396. *Average need-based loan:* Freshmen: $5500. Undergraduates: $7000. *Parent loans:* $2,800,000 (100% non-need-based). *Programs:* Federal Direct (Subsidized and Unsubsidized Stafford, PLUS), Perkins, Federal Nursing.
**WORK-STUDY *Federal work-study:*** Total amount: $700,000; 360 jobs averaging $2600. *State or other work-study/employment:* Total amount: $40,000 (100% need-based). 20 part-time jobs averaging $3800.
**APPLYING FOR FINANCIAL AID *Required financial aid form:*** FAFSA. *Financial aid deadline (priority):* 2/28. *Notification date:* 4/1. Students must reply by 5/1 or within 3 weeks of notification.
**CONTACT** Office of Student Financial Aid, University of Washington, Tacoma, 1900 Commerce Street, Box 358400, Tacoma, WA 98402-3100, 253-692-4374 or toll-free 800-736-7750. *Fax:* 253-692-4788. *E-mail:* uwtfa@uw.edu.
*Website:* http://www.tacoma.washington.edu/.

# THE UNIVERSITY OF WEST ALABAMA
## Livingston, AL

| Tuition & fees (AL res): $8018 | Average undergraduate aid package: $10,803 |
|---|---|

**ABOUT THE INSTITUTION** State-supported, coed. *Awards:* certificates, associate, bachelor's, and master's degrees. 27 undergraduate majors. *Total enrollment:* 3,989. Undergraduates: 1,922. Freshmen: 350. Federal methodology is used as a basis for awarding need-based institutional aid.
**UNDERGRADUATE EXPENSES for 2015–2016** *Application fee:* $35. *Tuition, state resident:* full-time $6868; part-time $292 per credit hour. *Tuition, nonresident:* full-time $13,736; part-time $584 per credit hour. *Required fees:* full-time $1150. Full-time tuition and fees vary according to course load, degree level, and program. Part-time tuition and fees vary according to course load, degree level, and program. *College room and board:* $6256; *Room only:* $3800. Room and board charges vary according to board plan and housing facility.
**FRESHMAN FINANCIAL AID (Fall 2013)** 311 applied for aid; of those 97% were deemed to have need. 100% of freshmen with need received aid; of those .3% had need fully met. *Average percent of need met:* 21% (excluding resources awarded to replace EFC). *Average financial aid package:* $10,159 (excluding resources awarded to replace EFC). 1% of all full-time freshmen had no need and received non-need-based gift aid.
**UNDERGRADUATE FINANCIAL AID (Fall 2013)** 1,434 applied for aid; of those 94% were deemed to have need. 99% of undergraduates with need received aid; of those 1% had need fully met. *Average percent of need met:* 21% (excluding resources awarded to replace EFC). *Average financial aid package:* $10,803 (excluding resources awarded to replace EFC). 1% of all full-time undergraduates had no need and received non-need-based gift aid.
**GIFT AID (NEED-BASED) *Total amount:*** $4,650,898 (99% federal, 1% state). *Receiving aid:* Freshmen: 62% (220); all full-time undergraduates: 57% (973). *Average award:* Freshmen: $5130; Undergraduates: $4965. *Scholarships, grants, and awards:* Federal Pell, FSEOG, state, private, college/university gift aid from institutional funds, United Negro College Fund.
**GIFT AID (NON-NEED-BASED) *Total amount:*** $2,058,450 (89% institutional, 11% external sources). *Receiving aid:* Freshmen: 48% (172). Undergraduates: 32% (535). *Average award:* Freshmen: $3425. Undergraduates: $2588. *Scholarships, grants, and awards by category:* Academic interests/achievement: English, general academic interests/achievements. *Creative arts/performance:* dance, music, theater/drama. *Special achievements/activities:* cheerleading/drum major, general special achievements/activities, junior miss, leadership, memberships, rodeo. *Special characteristics:* children and siblings of alumni, children of faculty/staff, first-generation college students, previous college experience. *Tuition waivers:* Full or partial for employees or children of employees. *ROTC:* Air Force cooperative.
**LOANS *Student loans:*** $10,440,780 (46% need-based, 54% non-need-based). 73% of past graduating class borrowed through all loan programs. *Average indebtedness per student:* $31,901. *Parent loans:* $1,714,438 (100% non-need-based). *Programs:* Federal Direct (Subsidized and Unsubsidized Stafford, PLUS), Perkins.
**WORK-STUDY *Federal work-study:*** 157 jobs averaging $2475. *State or other work-study/employment:* 34 part-time jobs averaging $1920.
**ATHLETIC AWARDS** Total amount: $1,692,707 (100% non-need-based).
**APPLYING FOR FINANCIAL AID *Required financial aid form:*** FAFSA. *Financial aid deadline (priority):* 3/1. *Notification date:* Continuous beginning 4/15. Students must reply within 2 weeks of notification.
**CONTACT** Mr. Don Rainer, Director of Financial Aid, The University of West Alabama, Station 3, Livingston, AL 35470, 205-652-3576 or toll-free 888-636-8800. *Fax:* 205-652-3847. *E-mail:* drainer@uwa.edu.
*Website:* http://www.uwa.edu/.

# UNIVERSITY OF WEST FLORIDA
## Pensacola, FL

| Tuition & fees (FL res): $8400 | Average undergraduate aid package: $8868 |
|---|---|

**ABOUT THE INSTITUTION** State-supported, coed. *Awards:* certificates, associate, bachelor's, master's, and doctoral degrees. 56 undergraduate majors. *Total* *enrollment:* 12,602. Undergraduates: 10,072. Freshmen: 1,237. Federal methodology is used as a basis for awarding need-based institutional aid.

**UNDERGRADUATE EXPENSES for 2015–2016 Application fee:** $30. *Tuition, state resident:* full-time $6359; part-time $212 per semester hour. *Tuition, nonresident:* full-time $19,241; part-time $642 per semester hour. *Required fees:* full-time $2041. Full-time tuition and fees vary according to location and reciprocity agreements. Part-time tuition and fees vary according to location and reciprocity agreements. *College room and board:* $9912. Room and board charges vary according to board plan, housing facility, and student level. *Payment plan:* Tuition prepayment.

**FRESHMAN FINANCIAL AID (Fall 2013)** 1,002 applied for aid; of those 74% were deemed to have need. 97% of freshmen with need received aid; of those 18% had need fully met. *Average percent of need met:* 66% (excluding resources awarded to replace EFC). *Average financial aid package:* $9078 (excluding resources awarded to replace EFC). 5% of all full-time freshmen had no need and received non-need-based gift aid.

**UNDERGRADUATE FINANCIAL AID (Fall 2013)** 6,202 applied for aid; of those 80% were deemed to have need. 97% of undergraduates with need received aid; of those 14% had need fully met. *Average percent of need met:* 60% (excluding resources awarded to replace EFC). *Average financial aid package:* $8868 (excluding resources awarded to replace EFC). 6% of all full-time undergraduates had no need and received non-need-based gift aid.

**GIFT AID (NEED-BASED) Total amount:** $29,316,860 (56% federal, 20% state, 22% institutional, 2% external sources). *Receiving aid:* Freshmen: 53% (602); all full-time undergraduates: 52% (3,870). *Average award:* Freshmen: $6229; Undergraduates: $5563. *Scholarships, grants, and awards:* Federal Pell, FSEOG, state, private, college/university gift aid from institutional funds.

**GIFT AID (NON-NEED-BASED) Total amount:** $4,201,030 (2% federal, 53% state, 30% institutional, 15% external sources). *Receiving aid:* Freshmen: 35% (402). Undergraduates: 28% (2,057). *Average award:* Freshmen: $3694. Undergraduates: $2891. *Scholarships, grants, and awards by category: Academic interests/achievement:* biological sciences, business, communication, computer science, education, engineering/technologies, general academic interests/achievements, mathematics, military science, physical sciences, social sciences. *Creative arts/performance:* applied art and design, art/fine arts, music, theater/drama. *Special achievements/activities:* leadership. *Special characteristics:* children and siblings of alumni, children of faculty/staff, handicapped students, international students, out-of-state students, veterans. *Tuition waivers:* Full or partial for employees or children of employees, senior citizens. *ROTC:* Army, Air Force.

**LOANS Student loans:** $36,944,886 (76% need-based, 24% non-need-based). *Average need-based loan:* Freshmen: $3134. Undergraduates: $4203. *Parent loans:* $1,113,832 (32% need-based, 68% non-need-based). *Programs:* Federal Direct (Subsidized and Unsubsidized Stafford, PLUS), Perkins.

**WORK-STUDY Federal work-study:** 369 jobs averaging $1943. *State or other work-study/employment:* Part-time jobs available.

**ATHLETIC AWARDS** Total amount: $1,952,286 (33% need-based, 67% non-need-based).

**APPLYING FOR FINANCIAL AID Required financial aid form:** FAFSA. *Financial aid deadline:* Continuous. *Notification date:* Continuous beginning 2/1.

**CONTACT** Ms. Shana Gore, Coordinator of Financial Aid, University of West Florida, 11000 University Parkway, Pensacola, FL 32514-5750, 850-474-2398 or toll-free 800-263-1074. *E-mail:* sgore1@uwf.edu. *Website:* http://www.uwf.edu/.

# UNIVERSITY OF WEST GEORGIA
## Carrollton, GA

| Tuition & fees (GA res): $6956 | Average undergraduate aid package: $8242 |
|---|---|

**ABOUT THE INSTITUTION** State-supported, coed. *Awards:* certificates, bachelor's, master's, and doctoral degrees. 39 undergraduate majors. *Total enrollment:* 12,206. Undergraduates: 10,249. Freshmen: 2,231. Federal methodology is used as a basis for awarding need-based institutional aid.

**UNDERGRADUATE EXPENSES for 2015–2016 Application fee:** $40. *Tuition, state resident:* full-time $5098; part-time $169.93 per semester hour. *Tuition, nonresident:* full-time $17,994; part-time $599.80 per semester hour.

*Required fees:* full-time $1858; $83.40 per semester hour or $512 per term. Full-time tuition and fees vary according to course load and location. Part-time tuition and fees vary according to course load and location. *College room and board:* $8532; *Room only:* $4700. Room and board charges vary according to board plan and housing facility.

**FRESHMAN FINANCIAL AID (Fall 2014, est.)** 2,057 applied for aid; of those 82% were deemed to have need. 99% of freshmen with need received aid; of those 53% had need fully met. *Average percent of need met:* 43% (excluding resources awarded to replace EFC). *Average financial aid package:* $7704 (excluding resources awarded to replace EFC). 4% of all full-time freshmen had no need and received non-need-based gift aid.

**UNDERGRADUATE FINANCIAL AID (Fall 2014, est.)** 7,618 applied for aid; of those 85% were deemed to have need. 99% of undergraduates with need received aid; of those 46% had need fully met. *Average percent of need met:* 45% (excluding resources awarded to replace EFC). *Average financial aid package:* $8242 (excluding resources awarded to replace EFC). 3% of all full-time undergraduates had no need and received non-need-based gift aid.

**GIFT AID (NEED-BASED) Total amount:** $24,542,243 (99% federal, 1% institutional). *Receiving aid:* Freshmen: 51% (1,125); all full-time undergraduates: 52% (4,418). *Average award:* Freshmen: $4880; Undergraduates: $4875. *Scholarships, grants, and awards:* Federal Pell, FSEOG, state, private, college/university gift aid from institutional funds, United Negro College Fund, Federal Nursing.

**GIFT AID (NON-NEED-BASED) Total amount:** $16,809,032 (1% federal, 92% state, 4% institutional, 3% external sources). *Receiving aid:* Freshmen: 13% (289). Undergraduates: 9% (783). *Average award:* Freshmen: $2021. Undergraduates: $2200. *Scholarships, grants, and awards by category: Academic interests/achievement:* biological sciences, business, communication, computer science, education, English, foreign languages, general academic interests/achievements, health fields, humanities, mathematics, physical sciences, premedicine, social sciences. *Creative arts/performance:* applied art and design, art/fine arts, debating, general creative arts/performance, journalism/publications, music, performing arts, theater/drama. *Special achievements/activities:* community service, leadership, memberships, religious involvement. *Special characteristics:* adult students, children and siblings of alumni, general special characteristics, handicapped students, international students, local/state students, members of minority groups. *Tuition waivers:* Full or partial for employees or children of employees, senior citizens. *ROTC:* Air Force cooperative.

**LOANS Student loans:** $50,619,919 (45% need-based, 55% non-need-based). 76% of past graduating class borrowed through all loan programs. *Average indebtedness per student:* $27,494. *Average need-based loan:* Freshmen: $3270. Undergraduates: $3933. *Parent loans:* $10,645,453 (100% non-need-based). *Programs:* Federal Direct (Subsidized and Unsubsidized Stafford, PLUS), Perkins, Federal Nursing, state.

**WORK-STUDY Federal work-study:** Total amount: $450,000; jobs available. *State or other work-study/employment:* Part-time jobs available.

**ATHLETIC AWARDS** Total amount: $1,211,480 (100% non-need-based).

**APPLYING FOR FINANCIAL AID Required financial aid form:** FAFSA. *Financial aid deadline (priority):* 4/1. *Notification date:* 5/1.

**CONTACT** Dr. Philip Hawkins, Director of Financial Aid, University of West Georgia, 1601 Maple Street, Aycock Hall, Carrollton, GA 30118, 678-839-6421. *Fax:* 678-839-6422. *E-mail:* finaid@westga.edu. *Website:* http://www.westga.edu/.

# UNIVERSITY OF WISCONSIN–EAU CLAIRE
## Eau Claire, WI

| Tuition & fees (WI res): $8744 | Average undergraduate aid package: $9751 |
|---|---|

**ABOUT THE INSTITUTION** State-supported, coed. *Awards:* certificates, associate, bachelor's, master's, and doctoral degrees. 51 undergraduate majors. *Total enrollment:* 10,689. Undergraduates: 10,164. Freshmen: 2,020. Federal methodology is used as a basis for awarding need-based institutional aid.

**UNDERGRADUATE EXPENSES for 2015–2016 Application fee:** $44. *Tuition, state resident:* full-time $7361; part-time $307 per credit. *Tuition, nonresident:* full-time $14,934; part-time $622 per credit. *Required fees:* full-time $1383; $58 per credit. Full-time tuition and fees vary according to reciprocity agreements. Part-time tuition and fees vary according to reciprocity agreements. *College* room and board: $6986; Room only: $3656. Room and board charges vary according to board plan and housing facility.

**FRESHMAN FINANCIAL AID (Fall 2013)** 1,777 applied for aid; of those 66% were deemed to have need. 99% of freshmen with need received aid; of those 76% had need fully met. **Average percent of need met:** 85% (excluding resources awarded to replace EFC). **Average financial aid package:** $9260 (excluding resources awarded to replace EFC). 5% of all full-time freshmen had no need and received non-need-based gift aid.

**UNDERGRADUATE FINANCIAL AID (Fall 2013)** 7,308 applied for aid; of those 73% were deemed to have need. 99% of undergraduates with need received aid; of those 76% had need fully met. **Average percent of need met:** 86% (excluding resources awarded to replace EFC). **Average financial aid package:** $9751 (excluding resources awarded to replace EFC). 5% of all full-time undergraduates had no need and received non-need-based gift aid.

**GIFT AID (NEED-BASED) Total amount:** $23,623,316 (49% federal, 24% state, 17% institutional, 10% external sources). **Receiving aid:** Freshmen: 46% (917); all full-time undergraduates: 43% (4,041). **Average award:** Freshmen: $5742; Undergraduates: $5887. **Scholarships, grants, and awards:** Federal Pell, FSEOG, state, private, college/university gift aid from institutional funds, Federal Nursing, Bureau of Indian Affairs Grants, Student Support Services Grants.

**GIFT AID (NON-NEED-BASED) Total amount:** $1,769,209 (22% state, 27% institutional, 51% external sources). **Receiving aid:** Freshmen: 2% (39). Undergraduates: 1% (109). **Average award:** Freshmen: $1680. Undergraduates: $1840. **Scholarships, grants, and awards by category:** Academic interests/achievement: area/ethnic studies, biological sciences, business, communication, computer science, education, English, foreign languages, general academic interests/achievements, health fields, humanities, international studies, library science, mathematics, physical sciences, premedicine, religion/biblical studies, social sciences. Creative arts/performance: art/fine arts, debating, journalism/publications, music, performing arts, theater/drama. Special achievements/activities: community service, general special achievements/activities, hobbies/interests, leadership, memberships. Special characteristics: adult students, ethnic background, first-generation college students, general special characteristics, international students, local/state students, members of minority groups, previous college experience. **ROTC:** Army.

**LOANS Student loans:** $44,136,229 (60% need-based, 40% non-need-based). 68% of past graduating class borrowed through all loan programs. Average indebtedness per student: $26,210. **Average need-based loan:** Freshmen: $4124. Undergraduates: $4644. **Parent loans:** $2,488,030 (61% need-based, 39% non-need-based). **Programs:** Federal Direct (Subsidized and Unsubsidized Stafford, PLUS), Perkins, state, college/university, private loans.

**WORK-STUDY Federal work-study:** 4,569 jobs averaging $1517.

**APPLYING FOR FINANCIAL AID Required financial aid form:** FAFSA. **Financial aid deadline (priority):** 4/15. **Notification date:** Continuous beginning 4/15.

**CONTACT** Ms. Kathleen Sahlhoff, Director of Financial Aid, University of Wisconsin–Eau Claire, 115 Schofield Hall, Eau Claire, WI 54701, 715-836-3373. Fax: 715-836-3846. E-mail: sahlhoka@uwec.edu.
Website: http://www.uwec.edu/.

$7224; Room only: $4116. Room and board charges vary according to board plan and housing facility.

**FRESHMAN FINANCIAL AID (Fall 2014, est.)** 657 applied for aid; of those 79% were deemed to have need. 100% of freshmen with need received aid; of those 23% had need fully met. **Average percent of need met:** 71% (excluding resources awarded to replace EFC). **Average financial aid package:** $9414 (excluding resources awarded to replace EFC). 4% of all full-time freshmen had no need and received non-need-based gift aid.

**UNDERGRADUATE FINANCIAL AID (Fall 2014, est.)** 3,458 applied for aid; of those 84% were deemed to have need. 100% of undergraduates with need received aid; of those 29% had need fully met. **Average percent of need met:** 75% (excluding resources awarded to replace EFC). **Average financial aid package:** $10,258 (excluding resources awarded to replace EFC). 2% of all full-time undergraduates had no need and received non-need-based gift aid.

**GIFT AID (NEED-BASED) Total amount:** $13,858,338 (55% federal, 29% state, 3% institutional, 13% external sources). **Receiving aid:** Freshmen: 52% (390); all full-time undergraduates: 50% (2,067). **Average award:** Freshmen: $5253; Undergraduates: $5713. **Scholarships, grants, and awards:** Federal Pell, FSEOG, state, private, college/university gift aid from institutional funds.

**GIFT AID (NON-NEED-BASED) Total amount:** $416,003 (1% federal, 5% state, 25% institutional, 69% external sources). **Receiving aid:** Freshmen: 2% (18). Undergraduates: 1% (45). **Average award:** Freshmen: $2749. Undergraduates: $2177. **Scholarships, grants, and awards by category:** Academic interests/achievement: area/ethnic studies, biological sciences, business, communication, education, engineering/technologies, general academic interests/achievements, health fields, humanities, physical sciences, premedicine, social sciences. Creative arts/performance: art/fine arts, dance, journalism/publications, music, theater/drama. Special achievements/activities: community service, general special achievements/activities, leadership. Special characteristics: adult students, children of public servants, ethnic background, handicapped students, members of minority groups, veterans. **Tuition waivers:** Full or partial for senior citizens. **ROTC:** Army cooperative.

**LOANS Student loans:** $23,652,761 (70% need-based, 30% non-need-based). 78% of past graduating class borrowed through all loan programs. Average indebtedness per student: $27,239. **Average need-based loan:** Freshmen: $5141. Undergraduates: $5878. **Parent loans:** $1,515,788 (28% need-based, 72% non-need-based). **Programs:** Federal Direct (Subsidized and Unsubsidized Stafford, PLUS), Perkins.

**WORK-STUDY Federal work-study:** Total amount: $541,957; 219 jobs averaging $1071. **State or other work-study/employment:** 219 part-time jobs averaging $357.

**ATHLETIC AWARDS** Total amount: $2,452,127 (81% need-based, 19% non-need-based).

**APPLYING FOR FINANCIAL AID Required financial aid form:** FAFSA. **Financial aid deadline (priority):** 1/1. **Notification date:** Continuous beginning 1/1. Students must reply within 3 weeks of notification.

**CONTACT** Mr. James Rohan, Director of Financial Aid, University of Wisconsin–Green Bay, 2420 Nicolet Drive, Green Bay, WI 54311-7001, 920-465-2073. E-mail: rohanj@uwgb.edu.
Website: http://www.uwgb.edu/.

# UNIVERSITY OF WISCONSIN–GREEN BAY
## Green Bay, WI

**Tuition & fees (WI res):** $7758    **Average undergraduate aid package:** $10,258

**ABOUT THE INSTITUTION** State-supported, coed. **Awards:** associate, bachelor's, and master's degrees. 45 undergraduate majors. **Total enrollment:** 6,921. Undergraduates: 6,668. Freshmen: 770. Federal methodology is used as a basis for awarding need-based institutional aid.

**UNDERGRADUATE EXPENSES for 2015–2016 Application fee:** $44. **One-time required fee:** $212. **Tuition, state resident:** full-time $6298; part-time $262 per credit hour. **Tuition, nonresident:** full-time $13,871; part-time $578 per credit hour. **Required fees:** full-time $1460; $57 per credit hour. Full-time tuition and fees vary according to course load and reciprocity agreements. Part-time tuition and fees vary according to reciprocity agreements. **College room and board:**

# UNIVERSITY OF WISCONSIN–LA CROSSE
## La Crosse, WI

**Tuition & fees (WI res):** $8795    **Average undergraduate aid package:** $7188

**ABOUT THE INSTITUTION** State-supported, coed. **Awards:** certificates, associate, bachelor's, master's, and doctoral degrees. 50 undergraduate majors. **Total enrollment:** 10,536. Undergraduates: 9,755. Freshmen: 1,980. Federal methodology is used as a basis for awarding need-based institutional aid.

**UNDERGRADUATE EXPENSES for 2015–2016 Application fee:** $44. **Tuition, state resident:** full-time $7585. **Tuition, nonresident:** full-time $15,158. **Required fees:** full-time $1210. Full-time tuition and fees vary according to program and reciprocity agreements. Part-time tuition and fees vary according to course load, program, and reciprocity agreements. **College room and board:** $5910; **Room only:** $3500. Room and board charges vary according to board plan and housing facility.

**FRESHMAN FINANCIAL AID (Fall 2013)** 1,734 applied for aid; of those 62% were deemed to have need. 99% of freshmen with need received aid; of those 18% had need fully met. *Average percent of need met:* 67% (excluding resources awarded to replace EFC). *Average financial aid package:* $7060 (excluding resources awarded to replace EFC). 5% of all full-time freshmen had no need and received non-need-based gift aid.

**UNDERGRADUATE FINANCIAL AID (Fall 2013)** 6,895 applied for aid; of those 69% were deemed to have need. 99% of undergraduates with need received aid; of those 16% had need fully met. *Average percent of need met:* 67% (excluding resources awarded to replace EFC). *Average financial aid package:* $7188 (excluding resources awarded to replace EFC). 2% of all full-time undergraduates had no need and received non-need-based gift aid.

**GIFT AID (NEED-BASED)** *Total amount:* $13,473,609 (65% federal, 25% state, 4% institutional, 6% external sources). *Receiving aid:* Freshmen: 22% (443); all full-time undergraduates: 25% (2,296). *Average award:* Freshmen: $6155; Undergraduates: $5715. *Scholarships, grants, and awards:* Federal Pell, FSEOG, state, private, college/university gift aid from institutional funds.

**GIFT AID (NON-NEED-BASED)** *Total amount:* $5,421,845 (3% federal, 25% state, 23% institutional, 49% external sources). *Receiving aid:* Freshmen: 33% (650). Undergraduates: 18% (1,673). *Average award:* Freshmen: $2006. Undergraduates: $1583. *Scholarships, grants, and awards by category:* Academic interests/achievement: area/ethnic studies, biological sciences, business, communication, computer science, education, English, foreign languages, general academic interests/achievements, health fields, humanities, international studies, mathematics, military science, physical sciences, social sciences. *Creative arts/performance:* art/fine arts, music, theater/drama. *Special achievements/activities:* community service, leadership, memberships. *Special characteristics:* adult students, children and siblings of alumni, children of union members/company employees, ethnic background, first-generation college students, general special characteristics, international students, local/state students, members of minority groups, out-of-state students, veterans, veterans' children. *Tuition waivers:* Full or partial for minority students. *ROTC:* Army.

**LOANS** *Student loans:* $90,073,656 (19% need-based, 81% non-need-based). 67% of past graduating class borrowed through all loan programs. *Average indebtedness per student:* $25,932. *Average need-based loan:* Freshmen: $3369. Undergraduates: $4192. *Parent loans:* $4,813,924 (100% non-need-based). *Programs:* Federal Direct (Subsidized and Unsubsidized Stafford, PLUS), Perkins.

**WORK-STUDY** *Federal work-study:* jobs available. *State or other work-study/employment:* Part-time jobs available.

**APPLYING FOR FINANCIAL AID** *Required financial aid form:* FAFSA. *Financial aid deadline (priority):* 3/15. *Notification date:* Continuous beginning 4/1.

**CONTACT** Louise Janke, Director of Financial Aid, University of Wisconsin–La Crosse, 1725 State Street, La Crosse, WI 54601-3742, 608-785-8604. *Fax:* 608-785-8843. *E-mail:* finaid@uwlax.edu. *Website:* http://www.uwlax.edu/.

# UNIVERSITY OF WISCONSIN–MADISON
## Madison, WI

| Tuition & fees (WI res): $10,410 | Average undergraduate aid package: $14,015 |
| --- | --- |

**ABOUT THE INSTITUTION** State-supported, coed. *Awards:* certificates, bachelor's, master's, and doctoral degrees. 121 undergraduate majors. *Total enrollment:* 43,193. Undergraduates: 31,289. Freshmen: 6,264. Federal methodology is used as a basis for awarding need-based institutional aid.

**UNDERGRADUATE EXPENSES for 2015–2016** *Application fee:* $44. *Tuition, state resident:* full-time $9273; part-time $386.39 per credit hour. *Tuition, nonresident:* full-time $25,523; part-time $1063.46 per credit hour. *Required fees:* full-time $1137; $94.12 per credit hour. Full-time tuition and fees vary according to program and reciprocity agreements. Part-time tuition and fees vary according to course load, program, and reciprocity agreements. *College room and board:* $8600. Room and board charges vary according to board plan and housing facility.

**FRESHMAN FINANCIAL AID (Fall 2014, est.)** 4,368 applied for aid; of those 57% were deemed to have need. 95% of freshmen with need received aid; of those 37% had need fully met. *Average percent of need met:* 78% (excluding resources

awarded to replace EFC). *Average financial aid package:* $13,229 (excluding resources awarded to replace EFC). 8% of all full-time freshmen had no need and received non-need-based gift aid.

**UNDERGRADUATE FINANCIAL AID (Fall 2014, est.)** 15,549 applied for aid; of those 69% were deemed to have need. 96% of undergraduates with need received aid; of those 40% had need fully met. *Average percent of need met:* 80% (excluding resources awarded to replace EFC). *Average financial aid package:* $14,015 (excluding resources awarded to replace EFC). 7% of all full-time undergraduates had no need and received non-need-based gift aid.

**GIFT AID (NEED-BASED)** *Total amount:* $77,839,828 (26% federal, 13% state, 55% institutional, 6% external sources). *Receiving aid:* Freshmen: 31% (1,961); all full-time undergraduates: 30% (8,303). *Average award:* Freshmen: $9486; Undergraduates: $9890. *Scholarships, grants, and awards:* Federal Pell, FSEOG, state, private, college/university gift aid from institutional funds.

**GIFT AID (NON-NEED-BASED)** *Total amount:* $15,962,515 (2% federal, 17% state, 56% institutional, 25% external sources). *Receiving aid:* Freshmen: 3% (176). Undergraduates: 3% (783). *Average award:* Freshmen: $3551. Undergraduates: $3876. *Scholarships, grants, and awards by category:* Academic interests/achievement: general academic interests/achievements. *Creative arts/performance:* general creative arts/performance. *Special achievements/activities:* general special achievements/activities. *Special characteristics:* general special characteristics. *ROTC:* Army, Naval, Air Force.

**LOANS** *Student loans:* $93,234,317 (58% need-based, 42% non-need-based). 51% of past graduating class borrowed through all loan programs. *Average indebtedness per student:* $26,579. *Average need-based loan:* Freshmen: $5200. Undergraduates: $5995. *Parent loans:* $14,581,886 (23% need-based, 77% non-need-based). *Programs:* Federal Direct (Subsidized and Unsubsidized Stafford, PLUS), Perkins, Federal Nursing.

**WORK-STUDY** *Federal work-study:* Total amount: $7,406,895; jobs available. *State or other work-study/employment:* Part-time jobs available.

**ATHLETIC AWARDS** Total amount: $10,810,924 (13% need-based, 87% non-need-based).

**APPLYING FOR FINANCIAL AID** *Required financial aid form:* FAFSA. *Financial aid deadline:* Continuous. *Notification date:* Continuous beginning 4/1. Students must reply within 3 weeks of notification.

**CONTACT** Office of Student Financial Aid, University of Wisconsin–Madison, 333 East Campus Mall #9701, Madison, WI 53715-1382, 608-262-3060. *Fax:* 608-262-9068. *E-mail:* finaid@wisc.edu. *Website:* http://www.wisc.edu/.

# UNIVERSITY OF WISCONSIN–MILWAUKEE
## Milwaukee, WI

| Tuition & fees (WI res): $9391 | Average undergraduate aid package: $8062 |
| --- | --- |

**ABOUT THE INSTITUTION** State-supported, coed. *Awards:* certificates, bachelor's, master's, and doctoral degrees. 83 undergraduate majors. *Total enrollment:* 28,013. Undergraduates: 23,079. Freshmen: 3,453. Federal methodology is used as a basis for awarding need-based institutional aid.

**UNDERGRADUATE EXPENSES for 2015–2016** *Application fee:* $44. *Tuition, state resident:* full-time $8091; part-time $337.13 per credit. *Tuition, nonresident:* full-time $17,820; part-time $742.48 per credit. *Required fees:* full-time $1300; $1300 per year. Full-time tuition and fees vary according to course load, degree level, location, program, and reciprocity agreements. Part-time tuition and fees vary according to course load, degree level, location, program, and reciprocity agreements. *College room and board:* $9126; *Room only:* $6126. Room and board charges vary according to board plan, housing facility, and location.

**FRESHMAN FINANCIAL AID (Fall 2014, est.)** 2,935 applied for aid; of those 82% were deemed to have need. 97% of freshmen with need received aid; of those 28% had need fully met. *Average percent of need met:* 41% (excluding resources awarded to replace EFC). *Average financial aid package:* $7133 (excluding resources awarded to replace EFC). 1% of all full-time freshmen had no need and received non-need-based gift aid.

**UNDERGRADUATE FINANCIAL AID (Fall 2014, est.)** 18,104 applied for aid; of those 86% were deemed to have need. 83% of undergraduates with need received aid; of those 22% had need fully met. *Average percent of need met:* 50%

(excluding resources awarded to replace EFC). *Average financial aid package:* $8062 (excluding resources awarded to replace EFC). 1% of all full-time undergraduates had no need and received non-need-based gift aid.

**GIFT AID (NEED-BASED)** *Total amount:* $59,544,485 (64% federal, 30% state, 4% institutional, 2% external sources). *Receiving aid:* Freshmen: 43% (1,393); all full-time undergraduates: 45% (8,800). *Average award:* Freshmen: $6731; Undergraduates: $6017. *Scholarships, grants, and awards:* Federal Pell, FSEOG, state, private, college/university gift aid from institutional funds, Federal Nursing.

**GIFT AID (NON-NEED-BASED)** *Total amount:* $13,408,627 (50% federal, 14% state, 9% institutional, 27% external sources). *Receiving aid:* Freshmen: 19% (624). Undergraduates: 12% (2,338). *Average award:* Freshmen: $2172. Undergraduates: $2371. *Scholarships, grants, and awards by category:* Academic interests/achievement: general academic interests/achievements. *Creative arts/performance:* general creative arts/performance. *Special achievements/activities:* general special achievements/activities. *Special characteristics:* general special characteristics. *Tuition waivers:* Full or partial for senior citizens. *ROTC:* Army cooperative, Naval cooperative, Air Force cooperative.

**LOANS** *Student loans:* $114,374,348 (44% need-based, 56% non-need-based). 73% of past graduating class borrowed through all loan programs. *Average indebtedness per student:* $33,234. *Average need-based loan:* Freshmen: $3633. Undergraduates: $4321. *Parent loans:* $12,853,561 (100% non-need-based). *Programs:* Federal Direct (Subsidized and Unsubsidized Stafford, PLUS), Perkins, Federal Nursing, state, alternative loans.

**WORK-STUDY** *Federal work-study:* Total amount: $423,409; jobs available.

**ATHLETIC AWARDS** Total amount: $518,730 (100% non-need-based).

**APPLYING FOR FINANCIAL AID** *Required financial aid form:* FAFSA. *Financial aid deadline (priority):* 3/1. *Notification date:* Continuous beginning 3/10. Students must reply within 2 weeks of notification.

**CONTACT** Ms. Jane Hojan-Clark, Director of Financial Aid and Student Employment Services, University of Wisconsin–Milwaukee, Mellencamp Hall 162, Milwaukee, WI 53201, 414-229-6300. *E-mail:* jhojan@uwm.edu. *Website:* http://www.uwm.edu/.

# UNIVERSITY OF WISCONSIN–OSHKOSH

### Oshkosh, WI

| Tuition & fees (WI res): $7437 | Average undergraduate aid package: $8369 |
| --- | --- |

**ABOUT THE INSTITUTION** State-supported, coed. *Awards:* certificates, associate, bachelor's, master's, and doctoral degrees. 56 undergraduate majors. *Total enrollment:* 14,411. Undergraduates: 13,194. Freshmen: 1,691. Federal methodology is used as a basis for awarding need-based institutional aid.

**UNDERGRADUATE EXPENSES** for 2015–2016 *Application fee:* $44. *Tuition, state resident:* full-time $7437; part-time $309.89 per credit. *Tuition, nonresident:* full-time $15,010; part-time $625.43 per credit. *College room and board:* $7386.

**FRESHMAN FINANCIAL AID (Fall 2014, est.)** 1,492 applied for aid; of those 70% were deemed to have need. 94% of freshmen with need received aid; of those 40% had need fully met. *Average percent of need met:* 35% (excluding resources awarded to replace EFC). *Average financial aid package:* $6414 (excluding resources awarded to replace EFC). 30% of all full-time freshmen had no need and received non-need-based gift aid.

**UNDERGRADUATE FINANCIAL AID (Fall 2014, est.)** 7,278 applied for aid; of those 77% were deemed to have need. 95% of undergraduates with need received aid; of those 36% had need fully met. *Average percent of need met:* 46% (excluding resources awarded to replace EFC). *Average financial aid package:* $8369 (excluding resources awarded to replace EFC). 8% of all full-time undergraduates had no need and received non-need-based gift aid.

**GIFT AID (NEED-BASED)** *Total amount:* $23,702,275 (60% federal, 31% state, 2% institutional, 7% external sources). *Receiving aid:* Freshmen: 31% (517); all full-time undergraduates: 36% (3,252). *Average award:* Freshmen: $5777; Undergraduates: $5410. *Scholarships, grants, and awards:* Federal Pell, FSEOG, state, private, college/university gift aid from institutional funds, United Negro College Fund, Federal Nursing.

**GIFT AID (NON-NEED-BASED)** *Total amount:* $640,818 (22% federal, 22% state, 18% institutional, 38% external sources). *Receiving aid:* Freshmen: 26% (432). Undergraduates: 14% (1,275). *Average award:* Freshmen: $588. Undergraduates: $713. *Scholarships, grants, and awards by category:* Academic interests/achievement: general academic interests/achievements. *Creative arts/performance:* art/fine arts, general creative arts/performance. *Special achievements/activities:* leadership. *Special characteristics:* local/state students, members of minority groups. *ROTC:* Army.

**LOANS** *Student loans:* $50,606,625 (83% need-based, 17% non-need-based). 78% of past graduating class borrowed through all loan programs. *Average indebtedness per student:* $23,989. *Average need-based loan:* Freshmen: $2124. Undergraduates: $2024. *Parent loans:* $6,436,333 (66% need-based, 34% non-need-based). *Programs:* Federal Direct (Subsidized and Unsubsidized Stafford, PLUS), Perkins, Federal Nursing, state, college/university.

**WORK-STUDY** *Federal work-study:* Total amount: $2,354,100; jobs available. *State or other work-study/employment:* Part-time jobs available.

**APPLYING FOR FINANCIAL AID** *Required financial aid form:* FAFSA. *Financial aid deadline (priority):* 3/15. *Notification date:* 4/15.

**CONTACT** Ms. Stacy Drews, Financial Aid Counselor, University of Wisconsin–Oshkosh, 800 Algoma Boulevard, Oshkosh, WI 54901, 920-424-3379. *E-mail:* drewss@uwosh.edu. *Website:* http://www.uwosh.edu/.

# UNIVERSITY OF WISCONSIN–PARKSIDE

### Kenosha, WI

| Tuition & fees (WI res): $8334 | Average undergraduate aid package: N/A |
| --- | --- |

**ABOUT THE INSTITUTION** State-supported, coed. *Awards:* certificates, bachelor's, and master's degrees. 37 undergraduate majors. *Total enrollment:* 4,584. Undergraduates: 4,448. Freshmen: 618. Federal methodology is used as a basis for awarding need-based institutional aid.

**UNDERGRADUATE EXPENSES** for 2015–2016 *Application fee:* $44. *Tuition, state resident:* full-time $7316. *Tuition, nonresident:* full-time $14,889. *Required fees:* full-time $1018. Full-time tuition and fees vary according to course load and program. Part-time tuition and fees vary according to course load and program. *College room and board:* $6572; *Room only:* $4276. Room and board charges vary according to board plan.

**FRESHMAN FINANCIAL AID (Fall 2013)** 559 applied for aid; of those 79% were deemed to have need. 95% of freshmen with need received aid.

**UNDERGRADUATE FINANCIAL AID (Fall 2013)** 2,624 applied for aid; of those 85% were deemed to have need. 96% of undergraduates with need received aid.

**GIFT AID (NEED-BASED)** *Total amount:* $12,755,596 (68% federal, 29% state, 3% external sources). *Receiving aid:* Freshmen: 46% (313); all full-time undergraduates: 51% (1,696). *Average award:* Freshmen: $6350; Undergraduates: $6264. *Scholarships, grants, and awards:* Federal Pell, FSEOG, state, private, college/university gift aid from institutional funds.

**GIFT AID (NON-NEED-BASED)** *Total amount:* $405,059 (24% state, 76% external sources). *Receiving aid:* Freshmen: 14% (98). Undergraduates: 9% (287). *Scholarships, grants, and awards by category:* Academic interests/achievement: biological sciences, business, communication, education, engineering/technologies, English, foreign languages, general academic interests/achievements, health fields, mathematics, physical sciences, premedicine. *Creative arts/performance:* applied art and design, art/fine arts, music, theater/drama. *Special achievements/activities:* community service, leadership. *Special characteristics:* adult students, children of union members/company employees, children of workers in trades, ethnic background, general special characteristics, international students, local/state students, members of minority groups. *ROTC:* Army cooperative.

**LOANS** *Student loans:* $20,871,287 (42% need-based, 58% non-need-based). *Parent loans:* $1,312,456 (100% non-need-based). *Programs:* Federal Direct (Subsidized and Unsubsidized Stafford, PLUS), Perkins.

**WORK-STUDY** *Federal work-study:* jobs available.

**ATHLETIC AWARDS** Total amount: $334,857 (100% non-need-based).

**APPLYING FOR FINANCIAL AID** *Required financial aid form:* FAFSA. *Financial aid deadline (priority):* 3/15. *Notification date:* Continuous beginning 3/15.

**CONTACT** Kristina Klemens, Interim Director of Student Financial Aid, University of Wisconsin–Parkside, 900 Wood Road, Kenosha, WI 53141-2000, 262-595-2004. *Fax:* 262-595-2216. *E-mail:* klemens@uwp.edu.
*Website:* http://www.uwp.edu/.

# UNIVERSITY OF WISCONSIN–PLATTEVILLE
## Platteville, WI

**CONTACT** Elizabeth Tucker, Director of Financial Aid, University of Wisconsin–Platteville, 1 University Plaza, Platteville, WI 53818-3099, 608-342-1836 or toll-free 800-362-5515. *Fax:* 608-342-1281. *E-mail:* tucker@uwplatt.edu.
*Website:* http://www.uwplatt.edu/.

# UNIVERSITY OF WISCONSIN–RIVER FALLS
## River Falls, WI

| Tuition & fees (WI res): $7751 | Average undergraduate aid package: $6846 |
| --- | --- |

**ABOUT THE INSTITUTION** State-supported, coed. *Awards:* certificates, bachelor's, and master's degrees. 95 undergraduate majors. *Total enrollment:* 6,184. Undergraduates: 5,721. Freshmen: 978. Federal methodology is used as a basis for awarding need-based institutional aid.
**UNDERGRADUATE EXPENSES for 2015–2016 Application fee:** $44. *Tuition, state resident:* full-time $6428; part-time $267.85 per credit hour. *Tuition, nonresident:* full-time $14,001; part-time $583.39 per credit hour. *Required fees:* full-time $1323. Full-time tuition and fees vary according to course load, degree level, and reciprocity agreements. Part-time tuition and fees vary according to course load, degree level, and reciprocity agreements. *College room and board:* $6435. Room and board charges vary according to board plan and housing facility.
**FRESHMAN FINANCIAL AID (Fall 2013)** 810 applied for aid; of those 77% were deemed to have need. 91% of freshmen with need received aid; of those 1% had need fully met. *Average percent of need met:* 51% (excluding resources awarded to replace EFC). *Average financial aid package:* $6524 (excluding resources awarded to replace EFC). 3% of all full-time freshmen had no need and received non-need-based gift aid.
**UNDERGRADUATE FINANCIAL AID (Fall 2013)** 4,096 applied for aid; of those 79% were deemed to have need. 93% of undergraduates with need received aid; of those 1% had need fully met. *Average percent of need met:* 54% (excluding resources awarded to replace EFC). *Average financial aid package:* $6846 (excluding resources awarded to replace EFC). 3% of all full-time undergraduates had no need and received non-need-based gift aid.
**GIFT AID (NEED-BASED) Total amount:** $9,758,668 (75% federal, 23% state, 2% external sources). *Receiving aid:* Freshmen: 38% (332); all full-time undergraduates: 36% (1,729). *Average award:* Freshmen: $4909; Undergraduates: $4906. *Scholarships, grants, and awards:* Federal Pell, FSEOG, state, private, college/university gift aid from institutional funds.
**GIFT AID (NON-NEED-BASED) Total amount:** $862,464 (9% state, 91% institutional). *Receiving aid:* Freshmen: 12% (110). Undergraduates: 12% (559). *Average award:* Freshmen: $1196. Undergraduates: $1275. *Scholarships, grants, and awards by category:* Academic interests/achievement: agriculture, area/ethnic studies, biological sciences, business, communication, computer science, education, English, foreign languages, general academic interests/achievements, health fields, humanities, international studies, mathematics, physical sciences, premedicine, social sciences. Creative arts/performance: art/fine arts, music, theater/drama. Special achievements/activities: leadership. Special characteristics: local/state students, members of minority groups. ROTC: Army.
**LOANS Student loans:** $26,889,799 (90% need-based, 10% non-need-based). 76% of past graduating class borrowed through all loan programs. *Average indebtedness per student:* $27,134. *Average need-based loan:* Freshmen: $3758. Undergraduates: $4194. *Parent loans:* $1,134,399 (100% need-based). *Programs:* Federal Direct (Subsidized and Unsubsidized Stafford, PLUS), Perkins, state, alternative loans.

**WORK-STUDY Federal work-study:** 452 jobs averaging $1031. *State or other work-study/employment:* Part-time jobs available.
**APPLYING FOR FINANCIAL AID Required financial aid form:** FAFSA. *Financial aid deadline:* Continuous. *Notification date:* Continuous beginning 4/15.
**CONTACT** Ms. Barbara J. Stinson, Director of Financial Aid, University of Wisconsin–River Falls, 410 South Third Street, River Falls, WI 54022-5001, 715-425-4111. *Fax:* 715-425-0708.
*Website:* http://www.uwrf.edu/.

# UNIVERSITY OF WISCONSIN–STEVENS POINT
## Stevens Point, WI

| Tuition & fees (WI res): $7669 | Average undergraduate aid package: $8513 |
| --- | --- |

**ABOUT THE INSTITUTION** State-supported, coed. *Awards:* associate, bachelor's, master's, and doctoral degrees. 69 undergraduate majors. *Total enrollment:* 9,292. Undergraduates: 8,975. Freshmen: 1,616. Federal methodology is used as a basis for awarding need-based institutional aid.
**UNDERGRADUATE EXPENSES for 2015–2016 Application fee:** $44. *Tuition, state resident:* full-time $7669; part-time $378.46 per credit. *Tuition, nonresident:* full-time $15,242; part-time $694 per credit. Full-time tuition and fees vary according to course load, program, and reciprocity agreements. Part-time tuition and fees vary according to course load, program, and reciprocity agreements. *College room and board:* $6786; *Room only:* $3660. Room and board charges vary according to board plan and housing facility.
**FRESHMAN FINANCIAL AID (Fall 2013)** 1,412 applied for aid; of those 67% were deemed to have need. 100% of freshmen with need received aid; of those 6% had need fully met. *Average percent of need met:* 67% (excluding resources awarded to replace EFC). *Average financial aid package:* $7209 (excluding resources awarded to replace EFC). 5% of all full-time freshmen had no need and received non-need-based gift aid.
**UNDERGRADUATE FINANCIAL AID (Fall 2013)** 7,291 applied for aid; of those 75% were deemed to have need. 100% of undergraduates with need received aid; of those 6% had need fully met. *Average percent of need met:* 70% (excluding resources awarded to replace EFC). *Average financial aid package:* $8513 (excluding resources awarded to replace EFC). 5% of all full-time undergraduates had no need and received non-need-based gift aid.
**GIFT AID (NEED-BASED) Total amount:** $20,574,573 (68% federal, 27% state, 3% institutional, 2% external sources). *Receiving aid:* Freshmen: 39% (633); all full-time undergraduates: 42% (3,756). *Average award:* Freshmen: $5155; Undergraduates: $5189. *Scholarships, grants, and awards:* Federal Pell, FSEOG, state, private, college/university gift aid from institutional funds.
**GIFT AID (NON-NEED-BASED) Total amount:** $1,404,860 (2% state, 65% institutional, 33% external sources). *Receiving aid:* Freshmen: 5% (88). Undergraduates: 5% (491). *Average award:* Freshmen: $1801. Undergraduates: $1559. *Scholarships, grants, and awards by category:* Academic interests/achievement: 8 awards ($11,322 total): agriculture, architecture, biological sciences, business, communication, computer science, education, engineering/technologies, English, foreign languages, general academic interests/achievements, health fields, home economics, humanities, international studies, mathematics, military science, physical sciences, premedicine, social sciences. Creative arts/performance: applied art and design, creative writing, dance, music, performing arts, theater/drama. Special achievements/activities: general special achievements/activities, leadership. Special characteristics: 4 awards ($1698 total): adult students, ethnic background, general special characteristics, international students, members of minority groups, out-of-state students, veterans. ROTC: Army.
**LOANS Student loans:** $41,966,930 (64% need-based, 36% non-need-based). 76% of past graduating class borrowed through all loan programs. *Average indebtedness per student:* $25,871. *Average need-based loan:* Freshmen: $4030. Undergraduates: $5208. *Parent loans:* $6,996,784 (20% need-based, 80% non-need-based). *Programs:* Federal Direct (Subsidized and Unsubsidized Stafford, PLUS), Perkins.
**WORK-STUDY Federal work-study:** jobs available. *State or other work-study/employment:* Part-time jobs available.

**APPLYING FOR FINANCIAL AID** *Required financial aid form:* FAFSA. *Financial aid deadline:* 5/1 (priority: 3/15). *Notification date:* Continuous beginning 3/1. Students must reply within 4 weeks of notification.

**CONTACT** Ms. Mandy Slowinski, Director of Financial Aid, University of Wisconsin–Stevens Point, 106 Student Services Center, Stevens Point, WI 54481-3897, 715-346-4771. *Fax:* 715-346-3526. *E-mail:* finaid@uwsp.edu.

*Website:* http://www.uwsp.edu/.

# UNIVERSITY OF WISCONSIN–STOUT
## Menomonie, WI

| Tuition & fees (WI res): $9025 | Average undergraduate aid package: $10,638 |
|---|---|

**ABOUT THE INSTITUTION** State-supported, coed. *Awards:* certificates, bachelor's, master's, and doctoral degrees. 43 undergraduate majors. *Total enrollment:* 9,371. Undergraduates: 8,254. Freshmen: 1,441. Federal methodology is used as a basis for awarding need-based institutional aid.

**UNDERGRADUATE EXPENSES** for 2015–2016 *Application fee:* $44. *Tuition, state resident:* full-time $7014; part-time $234 per credit hour. *Tuition, nonresident:* full-time $14,760; part-time $492 per credit hour. *Required fees:* full-time $2011. Full-time tuition and fees vary according to degree level and reciprocity agreements. Part-time tuition and fees vary according to degree level and reciprocity agreements. *College room and board:* $6434; *Room only:* $3890. Room and board charges vary according to board plan and housing facility.

**FRESHMAN FINANCIAL AID (Fall 2014, est.)** 1,236 applied for aid; of those 69% were deemed to have need. 99% of freshmen with need received aid; of those 14% had need fully met. *Average percent of need met:* 84% (excluding resources awarded to replace EFC). *Average financial aid package:* $10,101 (excluding resources awarded to replace EFC). 4% of all full-time freshmen had no need and received non-need-based gift aid.

**UNDERGRADUATE FINANCIAL AID (Fall 2014, est.)** 5,410 applied for aid; of those 75% were deemed to have need. 98% of undergraduates with need received aid; of those 14% had need fully met. *Average percent of need met:* 82% (excluding resources awarded to replace EFC). *Average financial aid package:* $10,638 (excluding resources awarded to replace EFC). 2% of all full-time undergraduates had no need and received non-need-based gift aid.

**GIFT AID (NEED-BASED)** *Total amount:* $14,127,659 (72% federal, 24% state, 4% external sources). *Receiving aid:* Freshmen: 31% (439); all full-time undergraduates: 33% (2,260). *Average award:* Freshmen: $5621; Undergraduates: $5646. *Scholarships, grants, and awards:* Federal Pell, FSEOG, state, private, college/university gift aid from institutional funds, Bureau of Indian Affairs Grants, GEAR UP Scholarships.

**GIFT AID (NON-NEED-BASED)** *Total amount:* $3,507,158 (1% federal, 16% state, 42% institutional, 41% external sources). *Receiving aid:* Freshmen: 25% (354). Undergraduates: 16% (1,059). *Average award:* Freshmen: $2827. Undergraduates: $2389. *Scholarships, grants, and awards by category:* Academic interests/achievement: 267 awards ($417,725 total): business, computer science, education, engineering/technologies, general academic interests/achievements, home economics, international studies, mathematics, physical sciences. *Creative arts/performance:* 12 awards ($12,500 total): applied art and design, art/fine arts, music. *Special achievements/activities:* 39 awards ($41,050 total): community service, general special achievements/activities, leadership, memberships, religious involvement. *Special characteristics:* 42 awards ($38,100 total): adult students, first-generation college students, handicapped students, international students, local/state students, members of minority groups, out-of-state students, previous college experience, veterans, veterans' children. *ROTC:* Army, Air Force cooperative.

**LOANS** *Student loans:* $43,388,524 (42% need-based, 58% non-need-based). 76% of past graduating class borrowed through all loan programs. *Average indebtedness per student:* $27,397. *Average need-based loan:* Freshmen: $4055. Undergraduates: $4639. *Parent loans:* $2,339,681 (100% non-need-based). *Programs:* Federal Direct (Subsidized and Unsubsidized Stafford, PLUS), Perkins, alternative loans.

**WORK-STUDY** *Federal work-study:* Total amount: $2,243,921; 1,537 jobs averaging $1468.

**APPLYING FOR FINANCIAL AID** *Required financial aid form:* FAFSA. *Financial aid deadline (priority):* 3/15. *Notification date:* Continuous beginning 3/29. Students must reply within 4 weeks of notification.

**CONTACT** Beth Boisen, Director of Financial Aid, University of Wisconsin–Stout, 210 Bowman Hall, Menomonie, WI 54751, 715-232-1363 or toll-free 800-HI-STOUT. *Fax:* 715-232-5246. *E-mail:* boisenb@uwstout.edu.

*Website:* http://www.uwstout.edu/.

# UNIVERSITY OF WISCONSIN–SUPERIOR
## Superior, WI

| Tuition & fees (WI res): $7994 | Average undergraduate aid package: $11,623 |
|---|---|

**ABOUT THE INSTITUTION** State-supported, coed. *Awards:* certificates, associate, bachelor's, and master's degrees. 68 undergraduate majors. *Total enrollment:* 2,589. Undergraduates: 2,455. Freshmen: 330. Federal methodology is used as a basis for awarding need-based institutional aid.

**UNDERGRADUATE EXPENSES** for 2015–2016 *Application fee:* $44. *Tuition, state resident:* full-time $6535; part-time $272.31 per credit hour. *Tuition, nonresident:* full-time $14,108; part-time $587.85 per credit hour. *Required fees:* full-time $1459. Full-time tuition and fees vary according to course load and reciprocity agreements. Part-time tuition and fees vary according to course load and reciprocity agreements. *College room and board:* $6320; *Room only:* $3400. Room and board charges vary according to board plan and housing facility.

**FRESHMAN FINANCIAL AID (Fall 2014, est.)** 272 applied for aid; of those 79% were deemed to have need. 97% of freshmen with need received aid; of those 13% had need fully met. *Average percent of need met:* 80% (excluding resources awarded to replace EFC). *Average financial aid package:* $10,574 (excluding resources awarded to replace EFC). 5% of all full-time freshmen had no need and received non-need-based gift aid.

**UNDERGRADUATE FINANCIAL AID (Fall 2014, est.)** 1,591 applied for aid; of those 84% were deemed to have need. 98% of undergraduates with need received aid; of those 12% had need fully met. *Average percent of need met:* 82% (excluding resources awarded to replace EFC). *Average financial aid package:* $11,623 (excluding resources awarded to replace EFC). 3% of all full-time undergraduates had no need and received non-need-based gift aid.

**GIFT AID (NEED-BASED)** *Total amount:* $6,396,309 (68% federal, 19% state, 12% institutional, 1% external sources). *Receiving aid:* Freshmen: 36% (116); all full-time undergraduates: 48% (914). *Average award:* Freshmen: $5797; Undergraduates: $5360. *Scholarships, grants, and awards:* Federal Pell, FSEOG, state, private, college/university gift aid from institutional funds.

**GIFT AID (NON-NEED-BASED)** *Total amount:* $616,816 (17% state, 8% institutional, 75% external sources). *Receiving aid:* Freshmen: 33% (108). Undergraduates: 18% (347). *Average award:* Freshmen: $1424. Undergraduates: $1813. *Scholarships, grants, and awards by category:* Academic interests/achievement: biological sciences, business, communication, computer science, education, English, general academic interests/achievements, health fields, humanities, mathematics, physical sciences, social sciences. *Creative arts/performance:* general creative arts/performance. *Special characteristics:* general special characteristics, international students, members of minority groups, veterans. *ROTC:* Air Force cooperative.

**LOANS** *Student loans:* $12,096,333 (44% need-based, 56% non-need-based). 72% of past graduating class borrowed through all loan programs. *Average indebtedness per student:* $29,410. *Average need-based loan:* Freshmen: $3545. Undergraduates: $4298. *Parent loans:* $341,647 (100% non-need-based). *Programs:* Federal Direct (Subsidized and Unsubsidized Stafford, PLUS), Perkins, state, college/university.

**WORK-STUDY** *Federal work-study:* Total amount: $315,000; jobs available. *State or other work-study/employment:* Total amount: $1,579,846 (9% need-based, 91% non-need-based). Part-time jobs available.

**APPLYING FOR FINANCIAL AID** *Required financial aid form:* FAFSA. *Financial aid deadline (priority):* 4/1. *Notification date:* Continuous beginning 4/1. Students must reply by 5/1 or within 4 weeks of notification.

**CONTACT** Tammi Reijo, Financial Aid Information Manager, University of Wisconsin–Superior, Belknap and Catlin, Old Main 110, PO Box 2000, Superior, WI 54880, 715-394-8148. *Fax:* 715-394-8027. *E-mail:* finaid@uwsuper.edu.

*Website:* http://www.uwsuper.edu/.

# UNIVERSITY OF WISCONSIN–WHITEWATER
## Whitewater, WI

| Tuition & fees (WI res): $7600 | Average undergraduate aid package: $8047 |
| --- | --- |

**ABOUT THE INSTITUTION** State-supported, coed. **Awards:** associate, bachelor's, and master's degrees. 53 undergraduate majors. **Total enrollment:** 12,159. Undergraduates: 10,971. Freshmen: 2,151. Federal methodology is used as a basis for awarding need-based institutional aid.

**UNDERGRADUATE EXPENSES for 2015–2016 Application fee:** $44. **Tuition, state resident:** full-time $6519. **Tuition, nonresident:** full-time $14,092. **Required fees:** full-time $1081. Full-time tuition and fees vary according to degree level and reciprocity agreements. **College room and board:** $6144; **Room only:** $3744. Room and board charges vary according to board plan and housing facility.

**FRESHMAN FINANCIAL AID (Fall 2014, est.)** 2,050 applied for aid; of those 71% were deemed to have need. 96% of freshmen with need received aid; of those 41% had need fully met. **Average percent of need met:** 56% (excluding resources awarded to replace EFC). **Average financial aid package:** $7236 (excluding resources awarded to replace EFC). 6% of all full-time freshmen had no need and received non-need-based gift aid.

**UNDERGRADUATE FINANCIAL AID (Fall 2014, est.)** 8,097 applied for aid; of those 75% were deemed to have need. 97% of undergraduates with need received aid; of those 42% had need fully met. **Average percent of need met:** 60% (excluding resources awarded to replace EFC). **Average financial aid package:** $8047 (excluding resources awarded to replace EFC). 4% of all full-time undergraduates had no need and received non-need-based gift aid.

**GIFT AID (NEED-BASED) Total amount:** $21,374,000 (66% federal, 31% state, 3% external sources). **Receiving aid:** Freshmen: 37% (802); all full-time undergraduates: 37% (3,616). **Average award:** Freshmen: $5548; Undergraduates: $5511. **Scholarships, grants, and awards:** Federal Pell, FSEOG, state, private, college/university gift aid from institutional funds.

**GIFT AID (NON-NEED-BASED) Total amount:** $3,854,000 (3% federal, 2% state, 37% institutional, 58% external sources). **Receiving aid:** Freshmen: 14% (305). Undergraduates: 11% (1,075). **Average award:** Freshmen: $1904. Undergraduates: $1862. **Scholarships, grants, and awards by category:** Academic interests/achievement: biological sciences, business, communication, computer science, education, English, foreign languages, general academic interests/achievements, humanities, mathematics, physical sciences, premedicine, social sciences. **Creative arts/performance:** art/fine arts, cinema/film/broadcasting, creative writing, journalism/publications, music, theater/drama. **Special achievements/activities:** leadership. **Special characteristics:** adult students, ethnic background, handicapped students, international students, local/state students, members of minority groups, out-of-state students. **Tuition waivers:** Full or partial for children of alumni, senior citizens. **ROTC:** Army, Air Force.

**LOANS Student loans:** $64,659,000 (37% need-based, 63% non-need-based). 75% of past graduating class borrowed through all loan programs. **Average indebtedness per student:** $27,623. **Average need-based loan:** Freshmen: $3470. Undergraduates: $4264. **Parent loans:** $10,320,000 (100% non-need-based). **Programs:** Federal Direct (Subsidized and Unsubsidized Stafford, PLUS), Perkins.

**WORK-STUDY Federal work-study:** Total amount: $625,000; 742 jobs averaging $1281. **State or other work-study/employment:** Total amount: $5,635,600 (2% need-based, 98% non-need-based). 2,273 part-time jobs averaging $1910.

**APPLYING FOR FINANCIAL AID Required financial aid form:** FAFSA. **Financial aid deadline (priority):** 3/1. **Notification date:** Continuous beginning 4/1. Students must reply within 3 weeks of notification.

**CONTACT** Ms. Carol Miller, Director of Financial Aid, University of Wisconsin–Whitewater, 800 West Main Street, Whitewater, WI 53190-1790, 262-472-1130. Fax: 262-472-5655. E-mail: millerc@uww.edu. Website: http://www.uww.edu/.

# UNIVERSITY OF WYOMING
## Laramie, WY

| Tuition & fees (WY res): $4646 | Average undergraduate aid package: $9422 |
| --- | --- |

**ABOUT THE INSTITUTION** State-supported, coed. **Awards:** certificates, bachelor's, master's, and doctoral degrees. 81 undergraduate majors. **Total enrollment:** 12,820. Undergraduates: 10,124. Freshmen: 1,567. Federal methodology is used as a basis for awarding need-based institutional aid.

**UNDERGRADUATE EXPENSES for 2015–2016 Application fee:** $40. **One-time required fee:** $40. **Tuition, state resident:** full-time $3390; part-time $113 per credit hour. **Tuition, nonresident:** full-time $13,620; part-time $454 per credit hour. **Required fees:** full-time $1256; $293.33 per term. Full-time tuition and fees vary according to course load, location, and reciprocity agreements. Part-time tuition and fees vary according to course load, location, and reciprocity agreements. **College room and board:** $9755; **Room only:** $4160. Room and board charges vary according to board plan and housing facility.

**FRESHMAN FINANCIAL AID (Fall 2013)** 1,264 applied for aid; of those 63% were deemed to have need. 99% of freshmen with need received aid; of those 25% had need fully met. **Average percent of need met:** 65% (excluding resources awarded to replace EFC). **Average financial aid package:** $9864 (excluding resources awarded to replace EFC). 29% of all full-time freshmen had no need and received non-need-based gift aid.

**UNDERGRADUATE FINANCIAL AID (Fall 2013)** 5,423 applied for aid; of those 73% were deemed to have need. 97% of undergraduates with need received aid; of those 15% had need fully met. **Average percent of need met:** 60% (excluding resources awarded to replace EFC). **Average financial aid package:** $9422 (excluding resources awarded to replace EFC). 21% of all full-time undergraduates had no need and received non-need-based gift aid.

**GIFT AID (NEED-BASED) Total amount:** $17,172,503 (59% federal, 32% state, 5% institutional, 4% external sources). **Receiving aid:** Freshmen: 31% (481); all full-time undergraduates: 33% (2,690). **Average award:** Freshmen: $4734; Undergraduates: $4918. **Scholarships, grants, and awards:** Federal Pell, FSEOG, state, private, college/university gift aid from institutional funds.

**GIFT AID (NON-NEED-BASED) Total amount:** $27,219,553 (2% federal, 32% state, 57% institutional, 9% external sources). **Receiving aid:** Freshmen: 43% (677). Undergraduates: 32% (2,631). **Average award:** Freshmen: $4524. Undergraduates: $4815. **Scholarships, grants, and awards by category:** Academic interests/achievement: agriculture, architecture, area/ethnic studies, biological sciences, business, communication, computer science, education, general academic interests/achievements. **Creative arts/performance:** applied art and design, art/fine arts, cinema/film/broadcasting, creative writing, dance, debating, general creative arts/performance, journalism/publications, music, performing arts, theater/drama. **Special achievements/activities:** cheerleading/drum major, junior miss, leadership, rodeo. **Special characteristics:** adult students, children and siblings of alumni, children of public servants, ethnic background, first-generation college students, handicapped students, international students, local/state students, members of minority groups, out-of-state students, spouses of current students, veterans, veterans' children. **Tuition waivers:** Full or partial for children of alumni, employees or children of employees, senior citizens. **ROTC:** Army, Air Force.

**LOANS Student loans:** $29,821,577 (41% need-based, 59% non-need-based). 46% of past graduating class borrowed through all loan programs. **Average indebtedness per student:** $23,708. **Average need-based loan:** Freshmen: $3706. Undergraduates: $4518. **Parent loans:** $2,921,341 (100% non-need-based). **Programs:** Federal Direct (Subsidized and Unsubsidized Stafford, PLUS), Perkins.

**WORK-STUDY Federal work-study:** 289 jobs averaging $1771.

**ATHLETIC AWARDS** Total amount: $4,441,627 (82% need-based, 18% non-need-based).

**APPLYING FOR FINANCIAL AID Required financial aid form:** FAFSA. **Financial aid deadline (priority):** 3/1. **Notification date:** Continuous beginning 4/25.

**CONTACT** Kathy Bobbitt, Interim Director of Student Financial Aid, University of Wyoming, Department 3335, 1000 East University Avenue, Laramie, WY 82071, 307-766-2116 or toll-free 800-342-5996. Fax: 307-766-3800. E-mail: finaid@uwyo.edu. Website: http://www.uwyo.edu/.

# UPPER IOWA UNIVERSITY
## Fayette, IA

| Tuition & fees: $28,073 | Average undergraduate aid package: $12,097 |
| --- | --- |

**ABOUT THE INSTITUTION** Independent, coed. *Awards:* certificates, associate, bachelor's, and master's degrees (enrollment figures include extended learning centers and online and distance education programs). 39 undergraduate majors. *Total enrollment:* 5,162. Undergraduates: 4,439. Freshmen: 355. Federal methodology is used as a basis for awarding need-based institutional aid.

**UNDERGRADUATE EXPENSES for 2015–2016** *Comprehensive fee:* $35,983 includes full-time tuition ($27,323), mandatory fees ($750), and room and board ($7910). *College room only:* $3213. Full-time tuition and fees vary according to degree level, location, and program. Room and board charges vary according to board plan, housing facility, and location.

**FRESHMAN FINANCIAL AID (Fall 2014, est.)** 354 applied for aid; of those 100% were deemed to have need. 100% of freshmen with need received aid. *Average percent of need met:* 42% (excluding resources awarded to replace EFC). *Average financial aid package:* $16,256 (excluding resources awarded to replace EFC). 1% of all full-time freshmen had no need and received non-need-based gift aid.

**UNDERGRADUATE FINANCIAL AID (Fall 2014, est.)** 2,459 applied for aid; of those 100% were deemed to have need. 100% of undergraduates with need received aid; of those .1% had need fully met. *Average percent of need met:* 54% (excluding resources awarded to replace EFC). *Average financial aid package:* $12,097 (excluding resources awarded to replace EFC). 1% of all full-time undergraduates had no need and received non-need-based gift aid.

**GIFT AID (NEED-BASED)** *Total amount:* $20,440,699 (39% federal, 14% state, 47% institutional). *Receiving aid:* Freshmen: 97% (346); all full-time undergraduates: 79% (2,120). *Average award:* Freshmen: $15,144; Undergraduates: $10,426. *Scholarships, grants, and awards:* Federal Pell, FSEOG, state, private, college/university gift aid from institutional funds.

**GIFT AID (NON-NEED-BASED)** *Total amount:* $3,309,216 (94% institutional, 6% external sources). *Receiving aid:* Freshmen: 3% (12). Undergraduates: 2% (51). *Average award:* Freshmen: $500. Undergraduates: $1000. *Scholarships, grants, and awards by category:* Special achievements/activities: 216 awards ($2,608,773 total): general special achievements/activities. Special characteristics: 25 awards ($14,250 total): children and siblings of alumni, children of current students, parents of current students, spouses of current students. *Tuition waivers:* Full or partial for employees or children of employees.

**LOANS** *Student loans:* $24,828,461 (42% need-based, 58% non-need-based). 62% of past graduating class borrowed through all loan programs. *Average indebtedness per student:* $30,401. *Average need-based loan:* Freshmen: $2697. Undergraduates: $2764. *Parent loans:* $1,667,766 (100% non-need-based). *Programs:* Federal Direct (Subsidized and Unsubsidized Stafford, PLUS), Perkins, college/university, alternative loans.

**WORK-STUDY** *Federal work-study:* Total amount: $345,870; 213 jobs averaging $1930. *State or other work-study/employment:* Part-time jobs available.

**ATHLETIC AWARDS** Total amount: $2,709,850 (100% non-need-based).

**APPLYING FOR FINANCIAL AID** *Required financial aid form:* FAFSA. *Financial aid deadline (priority):* 3/1. *Notification date:* Continuous beginning 3/1. Students must reply within 3 weeks of notification.

**CONTACT** Jeannie Barness, Director of Financial Aid, Upper Iowa University, Garbee Hall, Box 1859, Fayette, IA 52142-1859, 563-425-5276 or toll-free 800-553-4150. *Fax:* 563-425-5277. *E-mail:* barnessj@uiu.edu.
*Website:* http://www.uiu.edu/.

# URBANA UNIVERSITY
## Urbana, OH

**CONTACT** Mrs. Amy M. Barnhart, Director of Financial Aid, Urbana University, 579 College Way, Urbana, OH 43078-2091, 937-484-1359 or toll-free 800-7-URBANA. *Fax:* 937-652-6870. *E-mail:* abarnhart@urbana.edu.
*Website:* http://www.urbana.edu/.

# URSINUS COLLEGE
## Collegeville, PA

| Tuition & fees: $46,080 | Average undergraduate aid package: $34,458 |
| --- | --- |

**ABOUT THE INSTITUTION** Independent, coed. *Awards:* bachelor's degrees. 51 undergraduate majors. *Total enrollment:* 1,681. Undergraduates: 1,681. Freshmen: 497. Both federal and institutional methodology are used as a basis for awarding need-based institutional aid.

**UNDERGRADUATE EXPENSES for 2015–2016** *Comprehensive fee:* $57,580 includes full-time tuition ($45,890), mandatory fees ($190), and room and board ($11,500). *Part-time tuition:* $1434 per credit hour.

**FRESHMAN FINANCIAL AID (Fall 2014, est.)** 429 applied for aid; of those 87% were deemed to have need. 100% of freshmen with need received aid; of those 24% had need fully met. *Average percent of need met:* 83% (excluding resources awarded to replace EFC). *Average financial aid package:* $36,276 (excluding resources awarded to replace EFC). 24% of all full-time freshmen had no need and received non-need-based gift aid.

**UNDERGRADUATE FINANCIAL AID (Fall 2014, est.)** 1,367 applied for aid; of those 87% were deemed to have need. 100% of undergraduates with need received aid; of those 20% had need fully met. *Average percent of need met:* 79% (excluding resources awarded to replace EFC). *Average financial aid package:* $34,458 (excluding resources awarded to replace EFC). 26% of all full-time undergraduates had no need and received non-need-based gift aid.

**GIFT AID (NEED-BASED)** *Total amount:* $35,736,917 (5% federal, 3% state, 89% institutional, 3% external sources). *Receiving aid:* Freshmen: 75% (374); all full-time undergraduates: 72% (1,192). *Average award:* Freshmen: $32,511; Undergraduates: $29,968. *Scholarships, grants, and awards:* Federal Pell, FSEOG, state, private, college/university gift aid from institutional funds, Academic Competitiveness Grants, National SMART Grants.

**GIFT AID (NON-NEED-BASED)** *Total amount:* $10,495,961 (89% institutional, 11% external sources). *Receiving aid:* Freshmen: 16% (80). Undergraduates: 12% (194). *Average award:* Freshmen: $21,420. Undergraduates: $17,949. *Scholarships, grants, and awards by category:* Academic interests/achievement: general academic interests/achievements. Creative arts/performance: creative writing. Special achievements/activities: general special achievements/activities, leadership. Special characteristics: children and siblings of alumni, children of faculty/staff, general special characteristics, international students, siblings of current students. *Tuition waivers:* Full or partial for employees or children of employees.

**LOANS** *Student loans:* $11,628,976 (66% need-based, 34% non-need-based). 79% of past graduating class borrowed through all loan programs. *Average indebtedness per student:* $35,360. *Average need-based loan:* Freshmen: $3705. Undergraduates: $4558. *Parent loans:* $4,955,669 (39% need-based, 61% non-need-based). *Programs:* Federal Direct (Subsidized and Unsubsidized Stafford, PLUS), Perkins.

**WORK-STUDY** *Federal work-study:* Total amount: $1,010,199; 773 jobs averaging $1834. *State or other work-study/employment:* Total amount: $5322 (100% non-need-based). 2 part-time jobs averaging $5322.

**APPLYING FOR FINANCIAL AID** *Required financial aid forms:* FAFSA, institution's own form, CSS Financial Aid PROFILE. *Financial aid deadline (priority):* 2/15. *Notification date:* 4/1. Students must reply by 5/1.

**CONTACT** Mr. Andrew Sturgill, Assistant Director of Scholarships and Financial Aid, Ursinus College, 601 East Main Street, Collegeville, PA 19426-1000, 610-409-3600. *Fax:* 610-409-3662. *E-mail:* finaid@ursinus.edu.
*Website:* http://www.ursinus.edu/.

# URSULINE COLLEGE
## Pepper Pike, OH

| Tuition & fees: $28,520 | Average undergraduate aid package: $20,128 |
| --- | --- |

**ABOUT THE INSTITUTION** Independent Roman Catholic, coed, primarily women. *Awards:* certificates, bachelor's, master's, and doctoral degrees (applications from men are also accepted). 41 undergraduate majors. *Total enrollment:* 1,236. Undergraduates: 706. Freshmen: 92. Federal methodology is used as a basis for awarding need-based institutional aid.

**UNDERGRADUATE EXPENSES** for 2015–2016 *Application fee:* $25. *Comprehensive fee:* $38,010 includes full-time tuition ($28,230), mandatory fees ($290), and room and board ($9490). *College room only:* $4848. Full-time tuition and fees vary according to location. Room and board charges vary according to board plan and housing facility. *Part-time tuition:* $565 per credit. *Part-time fees:* $100 per term. Part-time tuition and fees vary according to location.

**FRESHMAN FINANCIAL AID (Fall 2013)** 95 applied for aid; of those 96% were deemed to have need. 100% of freshmen with need received aid; of those 19% had need fully met. *Average percent of need met:* 85% (excluding resources awarded to replace EFC). *Average financial aid package:* $24,288 (excluding resources awarded to replace EFC). 12% of all full-time freshmen had no need and received non-need-based gift aid.

**UNDERGRADUATE FINANCIAL AID (Fall 2013)** 393 applied for aid; of those 95% were deemed to have need. 99% of undergraduates with need received aid; of those 12% had need fully met. *Average percent of need met:* 67% (excluding resources awarded to replace EFC). *Average financial aid package:* $20,128 (excluding resources awarded to replace EFC). 9% of all full-time undergraduates had no need and received non-need-based gift aid.

**GIFT AID (NEED-BASED)** *Total amount:* $6,122,784 (25% federal, 8% state, 64% institutional, 3% external sources). *Receiving aid:* Freshmen: 89% (91); all full-time undergraduates: 80% (339). *Average award:* Freshmen: $20,480; Undergraduates: $15,872. *Scholarships, grants, and awards:* Federal Pell, FSEOG, state, private, college/university gift aid from institutional funds, United Negro College Fund.

**GIFT AID (NON-NEED-BASED)** *Total amount:* $339,494 (1% federal, 87% institutional, 12% external sources). *Receiving aid:* Freshmen: 16% (16). Undergraduates: 9% (38). *Average award:* Freshmen: $9708. Undergraduates: $7119. *Scholarships, grants, and awards by category:* Academic interests/achievement: general academic interests/achievements. *Creative arts/performance:* general creative arts/performance. *Special achievements/activities:* community service, leadership. *Special characteristics:* children and siblings of alumni, children of faculty/staff, relatives of clergy, religious affiliation, siblings of current students, veterans. *Tuition waivers:* Full or partial for employees or children of employees. *ROTC:* Army cooperative.

**LOANS** *Student loans:* $7,038,110 (86% need-based, 14% non-need-based). 87% of past graduating class borrowed through all loan programs. *Average indebtedness per student:* $29,542. *Average need-based loan:* Freshmen: $3999. Undergraduates: $5886. *Parent loans:* $618,243 (61% need-based, 39% non-need-based). *Programs:* Federal Direct (Subsidized and Unsubsidized Stafford, PLUS), Perkins, state, college/university.

**WORK-STUDY** *Federal work-study:* jobs available.

**ATHLETIC AWARDS** Total amount: $1,611,844 (59% need-based, 41% non-need-based).

**APPLYING FOR FINANCIAL AID** *Required financial aid form:* FAFSA. *Financial aid deadline:* Continuous. *Notification date:* Continuous beginning 3/1. Students must reply within 3 weeks of notification.

**CONTACT** Ms. Mary Lynn Perri, Director of Financial Aid and Enrollment Services, Ursuline College, 2550 Lander Road, Pepper Pike, OH 44124-4398, 440-646-8330 or toll-free 888-URSULINE. *Fax:* 440-684-6114. *E-mail:* mperri@ursuline.edu. *Website:* http://www.ursuline.edu/.

had need fully met. *Average percent of need met:* 75% (excluding resources awarded to replace EFC). *Average financial aid package:* $8600 (excluding resources awarded to replace EFC). 26% of all full-time freshmen had no need and received non-need-based gift aid.

**UNDERGRADUATE FINANCIAL AID (Fall 2014, est.)** 10,447 applied for aid; of those 87% were deemed to have need. 97% of undergraduates with need received aid; of those 4% had need fully met. *Average percent of need met:* 60% (excluding resources awarded to replace EFC). *Average financial aid package:* $8100 (excluding resources awarded to replace EFC). 22% of all full-time undergraduates had no need and received non-need-based gift aid.

**GIFT AID (NEED-BASED)** *Total amount:* $37,131,072 (95% federal, 5% state). *Receiving aid:* Freshmen: 34% (1,263); all full-time undergraduates: 57% (6,842). *Average award:* Freshmen: $4264; Undergraduates: $4400. *Scholarships, grants, and awards:* Federal Pell, FSEOG, state, private, college/university gift aid from institutional funds.

**GIFT AID (NON-NEED-BASED)** *Total amount:* $15,134,000 (79% institutional, 21% external sources). *Receiving aid:* Freshmen: 33% (1,213). Undergraduates: 30% (3,642). *Average award:* Freshmen: $6300. Undergraduates: $6800. *Scholarships, grants, and awards by category:* Academic interests/achievement: agriculture, architecture, biological sciences, business, communication, computer science, education, engineering/technologies, English, foreign languages, general academic interests/achievements, health fields, home economics, humanities, international studies, library science, mathematics, physical sciences, premedicine, social sciences. *Creative arts/performance:* applied art and design, art/fine arts, general creative arts/performance, journalism/publications, music, performing arts, theater/drama. *Special achievements/activities:* leadership. *Special characteristics:* children and siblings of alumni, children of faculty/staff, international students, local/state students, members of minority groups, religious affiliation. *Tuition waivers:* Full or partial for minority students, children of alumni, employees or children of employees, adult students, senior citizens. *ROTC:* Army, Air Force.

**LOANS** *Student loans:* $46,390,100 (57% need-based, 43% non-need-based). 49% of past graduating class borrowed through all loan programs. *Average indebtedness per student:* $21,200. *Average need-based loan:* Freshmen: $2800. Undergraduates: $3800. *Parent loans:* $1,457,800 (100% non-need-based). *Programs:* Federal Direct (Subsidized and Unsubsidized Stafford, PLUS), Perkins, college/university.

**WORK-STUDY** *Federal work-study:* Total amount: $600,000; jobs available. *State or other work-study/employment:* Total amount: $356,900 (100% need-based). Part-time jobs available.

**ATHLETIC AWARDS** Total amount: $4,840,040 (100% non-need-based).

**APPLYING FOR FINANCIAL AID** *Required financial aid form:* FAFSA. *Financial aid deadline:* Continuous. *Notification date:* Continuous beginning 4/1. Students must reply within 4 weeks of notification.

**CONTACT** Associate Director of Financial Aid, Utah State University, 1800 Old Main Hill, Logan, UT 84322-1800, 435-797-0173 or toll-free 800-488-8108. *Fax:* 435-797-0654. *E-mail:* finaid@usu.edu. *Website:* http://www.usu.edu/.

# UTAH STATE UNIVERSITY
## Logan, UT

| Tuition & fees (UT res): $6384 | Average undergraduate aid package: $8100 |
| --- | --- |

**ABOUT THE INSTITUTION** State-supported, coed. *Awards:* certificates, associate, bachelor's, master's, and doctoral degrees. 115 undergraduate majors. *Total enrollment:* 27,662. Undergraduates: 24,271. Freshmen: 4,071. Federal methodology is used as a basis for awarding need-based institutional aid.

**UNDERGRADUATE EXPENSES** for 2015–2016 *Application fee:* $40. *Tuition, state resident:* full-time $5454. *Tuition, nonresident:* full-time $17,561. *Required fees:* full-time $930. Full-time tuition and fees vary according to course level, course load, program, and reciprocity agreements. Part-time tuition and fees vary according to course level, course load, program, and reciprocity agreements. *College room and board:* $5680; *Room only:* $1980. Room and board charges vary according to board plan and housing facility.

**FRESHMAN FINANCIAL AID (Fall 2014, est.)** 2,461 applied for aid; of those 80% were deemed to have need. 96% of freshmen with need received aid; of those 8%

# UTAH VALLEY UNIVERSITY
## Orem, UT

| Tuition & fees (UT res): $5270 | Average undergraduate aid package: $7777 |
| --- | --- |

**ABOUT THE INSTITUTION** State-supported, coed. *Awards:* certificates, diplomas, associate, bachelor's, and master's degrees. 83 undergraduate majors. *Total enrollment:* 31,332. Undergraduates: 31,163. Freshmen: 3,528. Federal methodology is used as a basis for awarding need-based institutional aid.

**UNDERGRADUATE EXPENSES** for 2015–2016 *Application fee:* $35. *Tuition, state resident:* full-time $4542; part-time $189.25 per credit. *Tuition, nonresident:* full-time $14,074; part-time $586.41 per credit. *Required fees:* full-time $728; $364 per term or $364 per term. Full-time tuition and fees vary according to course load and degree level. Part-time tuition and fees vary according to course load and degree level.

**FRESHMAN FINANCIAL AID (Fall 2014, est.)** 1,664 applied for aid; of those 82% were deemed to have need. 95% of freshmen with need received aid; of those 12% had need fully met. *Average percent of need met:* 66% (excluding resources awarded to replace EFC). *Average financial aid package:* $7375 (excluding resources awarded to replace EFC). 1% of all full-time freshmen had no need and received non-need-based gift aid.

**UNDERGRADUATE FINANCIAL AID (Fall 2014, est.)** 11,104 applied for aid; of those 91% were deemed to have need. 97% of undergraduates with need received aid; of those 7% had need fully met. *Average percent of need met:* 63% (excluding resources awarded to replace EFC). *Average financial aid package:* $7777 (excluding resources awarded to replace EFC). 1% of all full-time undergraduates had no need and received non-need-based gift aid.

**GIFT AID (NEED-BASED)** *Total amount:* $54,703,527 (94% federal, 4% state, 1% institutional, 1% external sources). *Receiving aid:* Freshmen: 35% (901); all full-time undergraduates: 51% (7,864). *Average award:* Freshmen: $4669; Undergraduates: $4814. *Scholarships, grants, and awards:* Federal Pell, FSEOG, state, private, college/university gift aid from institutional funds.

**GIFT AID (NON-NEED-BASED)** *Total amount:* $2,368,893 (1% federal, 57% state, 16% institutional, 26% external sources). *Receiving aid:* Freshmen: 17% (437). Undergraduates: 12% (1,865). *Average award:* Freshmen: $1821. Undergraduates: $1841. *Tuition waivers:* Full or partial for employees or children of employees. *ROTC:* Army, Air Force cooperative.

**LOANS** *Student loans:* $74,952,030 (86% need-based, 14% non-need-based). 87% of past graduating class borrowed through all loan programs. *Average indebtedness per student:* $16,784. *Average need-based loan:* Freshmen: $2244. Undergraduates: $3087. *Parent loans:* $514,925 (45% need-based, 55% non-need-based). *Programs:* Federal Direct (Subsidized and Unsubsidized Stafford, PLUS), Perkins, state, college/university.

**WORK-STUDY** *Federal work-study:* Total amount: $794,548; jobs available. *State or other work-study/employment:* Part-time jobs available.

**ATHLETIC AWARDS** Total amount: $1,924,059 (45% need-based, 55% non-need-based).

**APPLYING FOR FINANCIAL AID** *Required financial aid forms:* FAFSA, institution's own form. *Financial aid deadline:* Continuous. *Notification date:* Continuous beginning 1/1. Students must reply by 6/15.

**CONTACT** Trish Howard, Director of Financial Aid and Scholarships, Utah Valley University, 800 West University Parkway, Orem, UT 84058, 801-863-8442. *Fax:* 801-863-8448. *E-mail:* howardpa@uvu.edu.
*Website:* http://www.uvu.edu/.

---

# U.T.A. MESIVTA OF KIRYAS JOEL
## Monroe, NY

**CONTACT** Financial Aid Office, U.T.A. Mesivta of Kiryas Joel, 9 Nickelsburg Road, Unit 312, Monroe, NY 10950, 845-873-9901.

---

# UTICA COLLEGE
## Utica, NY

| Tuition & fees: $33,736 | Average undergraduate aid package: $25,627 |
|---|---|

**ABOUT THE INSTITUTION** Independent, coed. *Awards:* certificates, bachelor's, master's, and doctoral degrees. 47 undergraduate majors. *Total enrollment:* 4,249. Undergraduates: 2,921. Freshmen: 472. Federal methodology is used as a basis for awarding need-based institutional aid.

**UNDERGRADUATE EXPENSES for 2015–2016** *Application fee:* $40. *Comprehensive fee:* $45,670 includes full-time tuition ($33,216), mandatory fees ($520), and room and board ($11,934). Room and board charges vary according to board plan. *Part-time tuition:* $1107 per credit hour. *Part-time fees:* $50 per term.

**FRESHMAN FINANCIAL AID (Fall 2014, est.)** 446 applied for aid; of those 97% were deemed to have need. 100% of freshmen with need received aid; of those 10% had need fully met. *Average percent of need met:* 77% (excluding resources awarded to replace EFC). *Average financial aid package:* $30,140 (excluding resources awarded to replace EFC). 7% of all full-time freshmen had no need and received non-need-based gift aid.

**UNDERGRADUATE FINANCIAL AID (Fall 2014, est.)** 2,034 applied for aid; of those 95% were deemed to have need. 100% of undergraduates with need received aid; of those 9% had need fully met. *Average percent of need met:* 68% (excluding resources awarded to replace EFC). *Average financial aid package:* $25,627 (excluding resources awarded to replace EFC). 9% of all full-time undergraduates had no need and received non-need-based gift aid.

**GIFT AID (NEED-BASED)** *Total amount:* $39,800,270 (13% federal, 9% state, 77% institutional, 1% external sources). *Receiving aid:* Freshmen: 92% (431); all full-time undergraduates: 84% (1,843). *Average award:* Freshmen: $8708; Undergraduates: $7481. *Scholarships, grants, and awards:* Federal Pell, FSEOG, state, private, college/university gift aid from institutional funds.

**GIFT AID (NON-NEED-BASED)** *Total amount:* $3,479,466 (2% state, 95% institutional, 3% external sources). *Receiving aid:* Freshmen: 3% (12). Undergraduates: 4% (91). *Average award:* Freshmen: $23,409. Undergraduates: $17,168. *Scholarships, grants, and awards by category:* Academic interests/achievement: general academic interests/achievements. *Tuition waivers:* Full or partial for employees or children of employees. *ROTC:* Army, Air Force cooperative.

**LOANS** *Student loans:* $24,951,309 (92% need-based, 8% non-need-based). 93% of past graduating class borrowed through all loan programs. *Average indebtedness per student:* $42,083. *Average need-based loan:* Freshmen: $3419. Undergraduates: $4434. *Parent loans:* $4,411,051 (95% need-based, 5% non-need-based). *Programs:* Federal Direct (Subsidized and Unsubsidized Stafford, PLUS), Perkins.

**WORK-STUDY** *Federal work-study:* Total amount: $828,083; jobs available. *State or other work-study/employment:* Part-time jobs available.

**APPLYING FOR FINANCIAL AID** *Required financial aid form:* FAFSA. *Financial aid deadline (priority):* 2/15. *Notification date:* Continuous. Students must reply by 5/1 or within 4 weeks of notification.

**CONTACT** Laura Bedford, Director of Student Financial Services, Utica College, 1600 Burrstone Road, Utica, NY 13502-4892, 315-792-3179 or toll-free 800-782-8884. *Fax:* 315-792-3368. *E-mail:* lbedford@utica.edu.
*Website:* http://www.utica.edu/.

---

# VALDOSTA STATE UNIVERSITY
## Valdosta, GA

| Tuition & fees (GA res): $6142 | Average undergraduate aid package: $17,136 |
|---|---|

**ABOUT THE INSTITUTION** State-supported, coed. *Awards:* certificates, associate, bachelor's, master's, and doctoral degrees. 52 undergraduate majors. *Total enrollment:* 11,563. Undergraduates: 9,328. Freshmen: 1,555. Federal methodology is used as a basis for awarding need-based institutional aid.

**UNDERGRADUATE EXPENSES for 2015–2016** *Application fee:* $40. *Tuition, state resident:* full-time $4078; part-time $169.93 per credit hour. *Tuition, nonresident:* full-time $14,395; part-time $599.80 per credit hour. *Required fees:* full-time $2064; $1032 per term. Full-time tuition and fees vary according to course load, location, program, and reciprocity agreements. Part-time tuition and fees vary according to course load, location, program, and reciprocity agreements. *College room and board:* $7864; *Room only:* $4072. Room and board charges vary according to board plan and housing facility.

**FRESHMAN FINANCIAL AID (Fall 2013)** 1,550 applied for aid; of those 81% were deemed to have need. 100% of freshmen with need received aid; of those 22% had need fully met. *Average percent of need met:* 99% (excluding resources awarded to replace EFC). *Average financial aid package:* $16,069 (excluding resources awarded to replace EFC). 1% of all full-time freshmen had no need and received non-need-based gift aid.

**UNDERGRADUATE FINANCIAL AID (Fall 2013)** 7,243 applied for aid; of those 85% were deemed to have need. 99% of undergraduates with need received aid; of those 19% had need fully met. *Average percent of need met:* 94% (excluding resources awarded to replace EFC). *Average financial aid package:* $17,136 (excluding resources awarded to replace EFC). 1% of all full-time undergraduates had no need and received non-need-based gift aid.

**GIFT AID (NEED-BASED)** *Total amount:* $33,118,727 (64% federal, 33% state, 1% institutional, 2% external sources). *Receiving aid:* Freshmen: 69% (1,130); all full-time undergraduates: 62% (5,128). *Average award:* Freshmen: $6650; Undergraduates: $6131. *Scholarships, grants, and awards:* Federal Pell, FSEOG, state, private, college/university gift aid from institutional funds, Federal Nursing.

**GIFT AID (NON-NEED-BASED)** *Total amount:* $4,926,409 (3% federal, 88% state, 4% institutional, 5% external sources). *Receiving aid:* Freshmen: 4% (66). Undergraduates: 3% (224). *Average award:* Freshmen: $1625. Undergraduates: $1776. *Scholarships, grants, and awards by category:* Academic interests/achievement: biological sciences, communication, education, general academic interests/achievements, health fields, library science, mathematics, physical sciences, social sciences. *Creative arts/performance*: art/fine arts, general creative arts/performance, journalism/publications, music, performing arts, theater/drama. *Special achievements/activities*: general special achievements/activities, religious involvement. *Special characteristics*: general special characteristics, local/state students, members of minority groups. *Tuition waivers*: Full or partial for employees or children of employees. *ROTC*: Air Force.

**LOANS** *Student loans*: $63,159,514 (79% need-based, 21% non-need-based). 71% of past graduating class borrowed through all loan programs. *Average indebtedness per student*: $27,308. *Average need-based loan*: Freshmen: $3394. Undergraduates: $4288. *Parent loans*: $52,369,787 (39% need-based, 61% non-need-based). *Programs*: Federal Direct (Subsidized and Unsubsidized Stafford, PLUS).

**WORK-STUDY** *Federal work-study*: jobs available.

**ATHLETIC AWARDS** Total amount: $1,425,739 (56% need-based, 44% non-need-based).

**APPLYING FOR FINANCIAL AID** *Required financial aid form*: FAFSA. *Financial aid deadline (priority)*: 3/1. *Notification date*: Continuous beginning 3/15.

**CONTACT** Mr. Douglas R. Tanner, Director of Financial Aid, Valdosta State University, 1500 North Patterson Street, Valdosta, GA 31698, 229-333-5935 or toll-free 800-618-1878. *Fax*: 229-333-5430.
*Website*: http://www.valdosta.edu/.

---

# VALENCIA COLLEGE
## Orlando, FL

**CONTACT** College Answer Center Specialists, Valencia College, PO Box 3028, Orlando, FL 32802-3028, 407-299-5000.
*Website*: http://valenciacollege.edu/.

---

# VALLEY CITY STATE UNIVERSITY
## Valley City, ND

| Tuition & fees (ND res): $6674 | Average undergraduate aid package: $9366 |
|---|---|

**ABOUT THE INSTITUTION** State-supported, coed. *Awards*: bachelor's and master's degrees. 45 undergraduate majors. *Total enrollment*: 1,378. Undergraduates: 1,234. Freshmen: 190. Federal methodology is used as a basis for awarding need-based institutional aid.

**UNDERGRADUATE EXPENSES for 2015–2016** *Application fee*: $35. *Tuition, state resident*: full-time $5027; part-time $168 per semester hour. *Tuition, nonresident*: full-time $13,423; part-time $448 per semester hour. *Required fees*: full-time $1647; $68.61 per semester hour. Full-time tuition and fees vary according to course load, location, program, and reciprocity agreements. Part-time tuition and fees vary according to course load, location, program, and reciprocity agreements. *College room and board*: $5938; *Room only*: $3070. Room and board charges vary according to board plan and housing facility.

**FRESHMAN FINANCIAL AID (Fall 2014, est.)** 163 applied for aid; of those 72% were deemed to have need. 99% of freshmen with need received aid; of those 32% had need fully met. *Average percent of need met*: 77% (excluding resources awarded to replace EFC). *Average financial aid package*: $8641 (excluding resources awarded to replace EFC). 38% of all full-time freshmen had no need and received non-need-based gift aid.

**UNDERGRADUATE FINANCIAL AID (Fall 2014, est.)** 639 applied for aid; of those 75% were deemed to have need. 99% of undergraduates with need received aid; of those 50% had need fully met. *Average percent of need met*: 70% (excluding resources awarded to replace EFC). *Average financial aid package*: $9366 (excluding resources awarded to replace EFC). 24% of all full-time undergraduates had no need and received non-need-based gift aid.

**GIFT AID (NEED-BASED)** *Total amount*: $1,940,103 (60% federal, 19% state, 16% institutional, 5% external sources). *Receiving aid*: Freshmen: 64% (107); all full-time undergraduates: 56% (403). *Average award*: Freshmen: $5709; Undergraduates: $4851. *Scholarships, grants, and awards*: Federal Pell, FSEOG, state, private, college/university gift aid from institutional funds.

**GIFT AID (NON-NEED-BASED)** *Total amount*: $336,249 (4% federal, 18% state, 54% institutional, 24% external sources). *Receiving aid*: Freshmen: 49% (82).

Undergraduates: 46% (331). *Average award*: Freshmen: $2590. Undergraduates: $2920. *Scholarships, grants, and awards by category*: Academic interests/achievement: biological sciences, business, communication, computer science, education, engineering/technologies, English, general academic interests/achievements, humanities, library science, mathematics, physical sciences, social sciences. *Creative arts/performance*: applied art and design, art/fine arts, journalism/publications, music, theater/drama. *Special achievements/activities*: general special achievements/activities. *Special characteristics*: children and siblings of alumni, children of faculty/staff, ethnic background, general special characteristics, international students, members of minority groups. *Tuition waivers*: Full or partial for employees or children of employees.

**LOANS** *Student loans*: $4,113,296 (57% need-based, 43% non-need-based). 69% of past graduating class borrowed through all loan programs. *Average indebtedness per student*: $27,756. *Average need-based loan*: Freshmen: $3379. Undergraduates: $3702. *Parent loans*: $96,801 (14% need-based, 86% non-need-based). *Programs*: Federal Direct (Subsidized and Unsubsidized Stafford, PLUS), Perkins.

**WORK-STUDY** *Federal work-study*: Total amount: $76,103; 42 jobs averaging $1850. *State or other work-study/employment*: Part-time jobs available.

**ATHLETIC AWARDS** Total amount: $234,123 (64% need-based, 36% non-need-based).

**APPLYING FOR FINANCIAL AID** *Required financial aid form*: FAFSA. *Financial aid deadline (priority)*: 4/15. *Notification date*: Continuous beginning 2/15. Students must reply within 4 weeks of notification.

**CONTACT** Ms. Betty Kuss Schumacher, Director of Student Financial Aid, Valley City State University, 101 College Street SW, Valley City, ND 58072, 701-845-7412 or toll-free 800-532-8641 Ext. 7101. *Fax*: 701-845-7410. *E-mail*: betty.schumacher@vcsu.edu. *Website*: http://www.vcsu.edu/.

---

# VALPARAISO UNIVERSITY
## Valparaiso, IN

| Tuition & fees: $34,760 | Average undergraduate aid package: $29,768 |
|---|---|

**ABOUT THE INSTITUTION** Independent Lutheran Church, coed. *Awards*: certificates, associate, bachelor's, master's, and doctoral degrees. 86 undergraduate majors. *Total enrollment*: 4,516. Undergraduates: 3,260. Freshmen: 714. Both federal and institutional methodology are used as a basis for awarding need-based institutional aid.

**UNDERGRADUATE EXPENSES for 2015–2016** *Comprehensive fee*: $44,940 includes full-time tuition ($33,680), mandatory fees ($1080), and room and board ($10,180). *College room only*: $6200. Full-time tuition and fees vary according to course load and program. Room and board charges vary according to housing facility and student level. *Part-time tuition*: $1505 per credit hour. *Part-time fees*: $96 per term. Part-time tuition and fees vary according to course load and program. *Payment plan*: Tuition prepayment.

**FRESHMAN FINANCIAL AID (Fall 2013)** 782 applied for aid; of those 87% were deemed to have need. 100% of freshmen with need received aid; of those 42% had need fully met. *Average percent of need met*: 89% (excluding resources awarded to replace EFC). *Average financial aid package*: $31,026 (excluding resources awarded to replace EFC). 18% of all full-time freshmen had no need and received non-need-based gift aid.

**UNDERGRADUATE FINANCIAL AID (Fall 2013)** 2,552 applied for aid; of those 90% were deemed to have need. 100% of undergraduates with need received aid; of those 37% had need fully met. *Average percent of need met*: 84% (excluding resources awarded to replace EFC). *Average financial aid package*: $29,768 (excluding resources awarded to replace EFC). 19% of all full-time undergraduates had no need and received non-need-based gift aid.

**GIFT AID (NEED-BASED)** *Total amount*: $41,241,936 (11% federal, 4% state, 82% institutional, 3% external sources). *Receiving aid*: Freshmen: 77% (673); all full-time undergraduates: 73% (2,268). *Average award*: Freshmen: $23,073; Undergraduates: $22,433. *Scholarships, grants, and awards*: Federal Pell, FSEOG, state, private, college/university gift aid from institutional funds.

**GIFT AID (NON-NEED-BASED)** *Total amount*: $14,062,470 (3% federal, 92% institutional, 5% external sources). *Receiving aid*: Freshmen: 12% (103). Undergraduates: 8% (264). *Average award*: Freshmen: $14,235. Undergraduates: $13,003. *Scholarships, grants, and awards by category*: Academic interests/achievement: business, engineering/technologies, foreign languages, general academic interests/achievements, health fields, physical sciences, religion/biblical studies. *Creative arts/performance:* art/fine arts, music, performing arts, theater/drama. *Special characteristics:* children and siblings of alumni, children of faculty/staff, international students, relatives of clergy, religious affiliation. *Tuition waivers:* Full or partial for employees or children of employees. *ROTC:* Army cooperative, Air Force cooperative.

**LOANS** *Student loans:* $21,005,862 (82% need-based, 18% non-need-based). 74% of past graduating class borrowed through all loan programs. *Average indebtedness per student:* $35,449. *Average need-based loan:* Freshmen: $5019. Undergraduates: $5330. *Parent loans:* $6,285,072 (40% need-based, 60% non-need-based). *Programs:* Federal Direct (Subsidized and Unsubsidized Stafford, PLUS), Perkins, college/university, private loans.

**WORK-STUDY** *Federal work-study:* 546 jobs averaging $1245. *State or other work-study/employment:* Total amount: $1,309,826 (72% need-based, 28% non-need-based). 779 part-time jobs averaging $1698.

**ATHLETIC AWARDS** Total amount: $3,964,349 (33% need-based, 67% non-need-based).

**APPLYING FOR FINANCIAL AID** *Required financial aid form:* FAFSA. *Financial aid deadline (priority):* 3/1. *Notification date:* Continuous beginning 3/1.

**CONTACT** Ms. Karen Klimczyk, Director of Financial Aid, Valparaiso University, 1700 Chapel Drive, Valparaiso, IN 46383-6493, 219-464-5015 or toll-free 888-GO-VALPO. *Fax:* 219-464-5012. *E-mail:* karen.klimczyk@valpo.edu. *Website:* http://www.valpo.edu/.

# VANDERBILT UNIVERSITY
## Nashville, TN

| Tuition & fees: $43,838 | Average undergraduate aid package: $45,477 |
|---|---|

**ABOUT THE INSTITUTION** Independent, coed. *Awards:* bachelor's, master's, and doctoral degrees. 69 undergraduate majors. *Total enrollment:* 12,686. Undergraduates: 6,851. Freshmen: 1,605. Both federal and institutional methodology are used as a basis for awarding need-based institutional aid.

**UNDERGRADUATE EXPENSES** for 2015–2016 *Application fee:* $50. *Comprehensive fee:* $58,220 includes full-time tuition ($42,768), mandatory fees ($1070), and room and board ($14,382). *College room only:* $9392. Room and board charges vary according to board plan. *Part-time tuition:* $1782 per credit hour. *Payment plan:* Tuition prepayment.

**FRESHMAN FINANCIAL AID (Fall 2014, est.)** 1,055 applied for aid; of those 81% were deemed to have need. 99% of freshmen with need received aid; of those 100% had need fully met. *Average percent of need met:* 100% (excluding resources awarded to replace EFC). *Average financial aid package:* $45,640 (excluding resources awarded to replace EFC). 8% of all full-time freshmen had no need and received non-need-based gift aid.

**UNDERGRADUATE FINANCIAL AID (Fall 2014, est.)** 3,764 applied for aid; of those 88% were deemed to have need. 99% of undergraduates with need received aid; of those 100% had need fully met. *Average percent of need met:* 100% (excluding resources awarded to replace EFC). *Average financial aid package:* $45,477 (excluding resources awarded to replace EFC). 10% of all full-time undergraduates had no need and received non-need-based gift aid.

**GIFT AID (NEED-BASED)** *Total amount:* $138,863,601 (4% federal, 1% state, 94% institutional, 1% external sources). *Receiving aid:* Freshmen: 48% (773); all full-time undergraduates: 45% (3,061). *Average award:* Freshmen: $40,331; Undergraduates: $39,953. *Scholarships, grants, and awards:* Federal Pell, FSEOG, state, private, college/university gift aid from institutional funds.

**GIFT AID (NON-NEED-BASED)** *Total amount:* $22,270,130 (9% federal, 4% state, 79% institutional, 8% external sources). *Receiving aid:* Freshmen: 30% (480). Undergraduates: 21% (1,413). *Average award:* Freshmen: $16,325. Undergraduates: $22,372. *Scholarships, grants, and awards by category:* Academic interests/achievement: general academic interests/achievements. *Creative arts/performance:* general creative arts/performance. *Special achievements/activities:* community service, general special achievements/activities, leadership. *Special characteristics:* general special characteristics, local/state students, members of minority groups. *Tuition waivers:* Full or partial for employees or children of employees. *ROTC:* Army, Naval, Air Force cooperative.

**LOANS** *Student loans:* $7,961,840 (16% need-based, 84% non-need-based). 24% of past graduating class borrowed through all loan programs. *Average indebtedness per student:* $20,790. *Average need-based loan:* Freshmen: $3096. Undergraduates: $3520. *Parent loans:* $5,495,576 (100% non-need-based). *Programs:* Federal Direct (Subsidized and Unsubsidized Stafford, PLUS), Perkins, Federal Nursing, college/university.

**WORK-STUDY** *Federal work-study:* Total amount: $3,394,778; 1,407 jobs averaging $2319. *State or other work-study/employment:* Total amount: $908,234 (100% need-based). Part-time jobs available.

**ATHLETIC AWARDS** Total amount: $11,355,425 (30% need-based, 70% non-need-based).

**APPLYING FOR FINANCIAL AID** *Required financial aid forms:* FAFSA, CSS Financial Aid PROFILE. *Financial aid deadline (priority):* 2/2. *Notification date:* 4/1. Students must reply by 5/1.

**CONTACT** Mr. Brent Tener, Director, Student Financial Aid, Vanderbilt University, 2309 West End Avenue, Nashville, TN 37203, 615-322-3591 or toll-free 800-288-0432. *Fax:* 615-343-8512. *E-mail:* finaid@vanderbilt.edu. *Website:* http://www.vanderbilt.edu/.

# VANDERCOOK COLLEGE OF MUSIC
## Chicago, IL

| Tuition & fees: $25,690 | Average undergraduate aid package: $16,671 |
|---|---|

**ABOUT THE INSTITUTION** Independent, coed. *Awards:* bachelor's and master's degrees. 1 undergraduate major. *Total enrollment:* 246. Undergraduates: 148. Freshmen: 25. Federal methodology is used as a basis for awarding need-based institutional aid.

**UNDERGRADUATE EXPENSES** for 2015–2016 *Comprehensive fee:* $36,870 includes full-time tuition ($24,150), mandatory fees ($1540), and room and board ($11,180). *College room only:* $5712. Full-time tuition and fees vary according to course level, course load, degree level, and program. Room and board charges vary according to board plan and housing facility. *Part-time tuition:* $1000 per semester hour. *Part-time fees:* $1190 per year. Part-time tuition and fees vary according to course level, course load, degree level, and program.

**FRESHMAN FINANCIAL AID (Fall 2013)** 15 applied for aid; of those 87% were deemed to have need. 100% of freshmen with need received aid. *Average financial aid package:* $16,596 (excluding resources awarded to replace EFC). 13% of all full-time freshmen had no need and received non-need-based gift aid.

**UNDERGRADUATE FINANCIAL AID (Fall 2013)** 97 applied for aid; of those 89% were deemed to have need. 100% of undergraduates with need received aid. *Average financial aid package:* $16,671 (excluding resources awarded to replace EFC). 11% of all full-time undergraduates had no need and received non-need-based gift aid.

**GIFT AID (NEED-BASED)** *Total amount:* $458,919 (52% federal, 41% state, 7% institutional). *Receiving aid:* Freshmen: 87% (13); all full-time undergraduates: 86% (86). *Average award:* Freshmen: $7869; Undergraduates: $9722. *Scholarships, grants, and awards:* Federal Pell, FSEOG, state, private, college/university gift aid from institutional funds.

**GIFT AID (NON-NEED-BASED)** *Total amount:* $757,821 (9% federal, 19% state, 68% institutional, 4% external sources). *Receiving aid:* Freshmen: 87% (13). Undergraduates: 85% (85). *Average award:* Freshmen: $5350. Undergraduates: $5550. *Scholarships, grants, and awards by category:* Academic interests/achievement: 89 awards ($245,400 total): education, general academic interests/achievements. *Creative arts/performance:* 99 awards ($182,250 total): music. *Special characteristics:* 10 awards ($8250 total): ethnic background, out-of-state students, religious affiliation. *Tuition waivers:* Full or partial for employees or children of employees.

**LOANS** *Student loans:* $877,688 (46% need-based, 54% non-need-based). 71% of past graduating class borrowed through all loan programs. *Average indebtedness per student:* $38,861. *Average need-based loan:* Freshmen: $3409. Undergraduates: $4699. *Parent loans:* $530,108 (100% non-need-based). *Programs:* Federal Direct (Subsidized and Unsubsidized Stafford, PLUS).

**WORK-STUDY** *Federal work-study:* 18 jobs averaging $706. *State or other work-study/employment:* Total amount: $16,219 (100% non-need-based). 15 part-time jobs averaging $1026.

**APPLYING FOR FINANCIAL AID** *Required financial aid form:* FAFSA. *Financial aid deadline (priority):* 2/15. *Notification date:* Continuous beginning 5/1. Students must reply within 2 weeks of notification.

**CONTACT** Ms. Sirena Covington, Director of Financial Aid, VanderCook College of Music, 3140 South Federal Street, Chicago, IL 60616-3731, 312-788-1146. *Fax:* 312-225-5211. *E-mail:* scovington@vandercook.edu. *Website:* http://www.vandercook.edu/.

# VANGUARD UNIVERSITY OF SOUTHERN CALIFORNIA
## Costa Mesa, CA

| Tuition & fees: $30,050 | Average undergraduate aid package: $13,017 |
|---|---|

**ABOUT THE INSTITUTION** Independent Assemblies of God, coed. *Awards:* certificates, associate, bachelor's, and master's degrees. 46 undergraduate majors. *Total enrollment:* 2,255. Undergraduates: 1,987. Freshmen: 318. Federal methodology is used as a basis for awarding need-based institutional aid.

**UNDERGRADUATE EXPENSES** for 2015–2016 *Application fee:* $45. *Comprehensive fee:* $39,470 includes full-time tuition ($29,980), mandatory fees ($70), and room and board ($9420). *College room only:* $4870. Full-time tuition and fees vary according to course load. Room and board charges vary according to board plan and housing facility. *Part-time tuition:* $1250 per credit hour. Part-time tuition and fees vary according to course load.

**FRESHMAN FINANCIAL AID (Fall 2014, est.)** 304 applied for aid; of those 91% were deemed to have need. 100% of freshmen with need received aid; of those 16% had need fully met. *Average percent of need met:* 30% (excluding resources awarded to replace EFC). *Average financial aid package:* $12,944 (excluding resources awarded to replace EFC). 8% of all full-time freshmen had no need and received non-need-based gift aid.

**UNDERGRADUATE FINANCIAL AID (Fall 2014, est.)** 1,397 applied for aid; of those 91% were deemed to have need. 100% of undergraduates with need received aid; of those 12% had need fully met. *Average percent of need met:* 33% (excluding resources awarded to replace EFC). *Average financial aid package:* $13,017 (excluding resources awarded to replace EFC). 7% of all full-time undergraduates had no need and received non-need-based gift aid.

**GIFT AID (NEED-BASED)** *Total amount:* $26,193,415 (14% federal, 17% state, 67% institutional, 2% external sources). *Receiving aid:* Freshmen: 53% (176); all full-time undergraduates: 53% (799). *Average award:* Freshmen: $4441; Undergraduates: $6070. *Scholarships, grants, and awards:* Federal Pell, FSEOG, state, private, college/university gift aid from institutional funds.

**GIFT AID (NON-NEED-BASED)** *Receiving aid:* Freshmen: 80% (264). Undergraduates: 75% (1,131). *Average award:* Freshmen: $7480. Undergraduates: $6850. *Scholarships, grants, and awards by category:* Academic interests/achievement: general academic interests/achievements. *Creative arts/performance:* debating, music, theater/drama. *Special characteristics:* children of faculty/staff, religious affiliation. *Tuition waivers:* Full or partial for employees or children of employees. *ROTC:* Air Force cooperative.

**LOANS** *Student loans:* $17,882,104 (38% need-based, 62% non-need-based). *Parent loans:* $3,288,526 (100% non-need-based). *Programs:* Federal Direct (Subsidized and Unsubsidized Stafford, PLUS), Perkins.

**WORK-STUDY** *Federal work-study:* Total amount: $218,391; jobs available.

**ATHLETIC AWARDS** Total amount: $1,824,745 (100% need-based).

**APPLYING FOR FINANCIAL AID** *Required financial aid forms:* FAFSA, state aid form. *Financial aid deadline:* 3/2. *Notification date:* Continuous beginning 3/15. Students must reply within 3 weeks of notification.

**CONTACT** Financial Aid Office, Vanguard University of Southern California, 55 Fair Drive, Costa Mesa, CA 92626-6597, 714-619-5490 or toll-free 800-722-6279. *Fax:* 714-619-6655. *E-mail:* financialaid@vanguard.edu. *Website:* http://www.vanguard.edu/.

# VASSAR COLLEGE
## Poughkeepsie, NY

| Tuition & fees: $49,570 | Average undergraduate aid package: $47,836 |
|---|---|

**ABOUT THE INSTITUTION** Independent, coed. *Awards:* bachelor's and master's degrees. 51 undergraduate majors. *Total enrollment:* 2,418. Undergraduates: 2,418. Freshmen: 663. Institutional methodology is used as a basis for awarding need-based institutional aid.

**UNDERGRADUATE EXPENSES** for 2015–2016 *Application fee:* $70. *One-time required fee:* $80. *Comprehensive fee:* $61,140 includes full-time tuition ($48,840), mandatory fees ($730), and room and board ($11,570). *College room only:* $6280. Room and board charges vary according to board plan and housing facility. *Part-time tuition:* $5800 per unit.

**FRESHMAN FINANCIAL AID (Fall 2014, est.)** 469 applied for aid; of those 88% were deemed to have need. 100% of freshmen with need received aid; of those 100% had need fully met. *Average percent of need met:* 100% (excluding resources awarded to replace EFC). *Average financial aid package:* $48,398 (excluding resources awarded to replace EFC).

**UNDERGRADUATE FINANCIAL AID (Fall 2014, est.)** 1,581 applied for aid; of those 90% were deemed to have need. 100% of undergraduates with need received aid; of those 100% had need fully met. *Average percent of need met:* 100% (excluding resources awarded to replace EFC). *Average financial aid package:* $47,836 (excluding resources awarded to replace EFC).

**GIFT AID (NEED-BASED)** *Total amount:* $64,182,183 (5% federal, 1% state, 90% institutional, 4% external sources). *Receiving aid:* Freshmen: 62% (409); all full-time undergraduates: 58% (1,416). *Average award:* Freshmen: $45,154; Undergraduates: $43,094. *Scholarships, grants, and awards:* Federal Pell, FSEOG, state, private, college/university gift aid from institutional funds.

**GIFT AID (NON-NEED-BASED)** *Total amount:* $186,530 (4% federal, 12% state, 84% external sources). *Tuition waivers:* Full or partial for employees or children of employees.

**LOANS** *Student loans:* $5,531,040 (55% need-based, 45% non-need-based). 57% of past graduating class borrowed through all loan programs. *Average indebtedness per student:* $17,476. *Average need-based loan:* Freshmen: $1860. Undergraduates: $3479. *Parent loans:* $3,453,471 (100% non-need-based). *Programs:* Federal Direct (Subsidized and Unsubsidized Stafford, PLUS), Perkins.

**WORK-STUDY** *Federal work-study:* Total amount: $2,455,829; 1,033 jobs averaging $2297. *State or other work-study/employment:* Total amount: $801,040 (100% need-based). 366 part-time jobs averaging $2262.

**APPLYING FOR FINANCIAL AID** *Required financial aid forms:* FAFSA, CSS Financial Aid PROFILE, noncustodial (divorced/separated) parent's statement. *Financial aid deadline:* 2/15. *Notification date:* 3/30. Students must reply by 5/1.

**CONTACT** Ms. Jessica L. Bernier, Director of Student Financial Services, Vassar College, 124 Raymond Avenue, Box 8, Poughkeepsie, NY 12604, 845-437-5320 or toll-free 800-827-7270. *Fax:* 845-437-5325. *E-mail:* jebernier@vassar.edu. *Website:* http://www.vassar.edu/.

# VAUGHN COLLEGE OF AERONAUTICS AND TECHNOLOGY
## Flushing, NY

**CONTACT** Dorothy Martin, Director of Financial Aid, Vaughn College of Aeronautics and Technology, 86-01 23rd Avenue, Flushing, NY 11369, 718-429-6600 Ext. 187 or toll-free 866-6VAUGHN. *Fax:* 718-779-2231. *E-mail:* dorothy.martin@vaughn.edu. *Website:* http://www.vaughn.edu/.

# VERMONT TECHNICAL COLLEGE
## Randolph Center, VT

| Tuition & fees (VT res): $13,200 | Average undergraduate aid package: $10,716 |
|---|---|

**ABOUT THE INSTITUTION** State-supported, coed. *Awards:* certificates, associate, and bachelor's degrees. 24 undergraduate majors. *Total enrollment:* 1,544. Undergraduates: 1,544. Freshmen: 543. Federal methodology is used as a basis for awarding need-based institutional aid.
**UNDERGRADUATE EXPENSES for 2015–2016** *Application fee:* $40. *Tuition, state resident:* full-time $11,856; part-time $494 per credit. *Tuition, nonresident:* full-time $22,704; part-time $946 per credit. *Required fees:* full-time $1344. Full-time tuition and fees vary according to course load and program. Part-time tuition and fees vary according to program. *College room and board:* $9414; *Room only:* $5606. Room and board charges vary according to board plan.
**FRESHMAN FINANCIAL AID (Fall 2014, est.)** 440 applied for aid; of those 91% were deemed to have need. 99% of freshmen with need received aid; of those 4% had need fully met. *Average percent of need met:* 44% (excluding resources awarded to replace EFC). *Average financial aid package:* $9322 (excluding resources awarded to replace EFC). 1% of all full-time freshmen had no need and received non-need-based gift aid.
**UNDERGRADUATE FINANCIAL AID (Fall 2014, est.)** 840 applied for aid; of those 91% were deemed to have need. 99% of undergraduates with need received aid; of those 8% had need fully met. *Average percent of need met:* 50% (excluding resources awarded to replace EFC). *Average financial aid package:* $10,716 (excluding resources awarded to replace EFC). 1% of all full-time undergraduates had no need and received non-need-based gift aid.
**GIFT AID (NEED-BASED)** *Total amount:* $5,401,598 (44% federal, 23% state, 21% institutional, 12% external sources). *Receiving aid:* Freshmen: 61% (309); all full-time undergraduates: 64% (636). *Average award:* Freshmen: $6028; Undergraduates: $6530. *Scholarships, grants, and awards:* Federal Pell, FSEOG, state, private, college/university gift aid from institutional funds.
**GIFT AID (NON-NEED-BASED)** *Total amount:* $382,478 (71% institutional, 29% external sources). *Receiving aid:* Freshmen: 13% (66). Undergraduates: 8% (81). *Average award:* Freshmen: $6952. Undergraduates: $4606. *Scholarships, grants, and awards by category: Academic interests/achievement:* 123 awards ($396,228 total): agriculture, general academic interests/achievements. *Tuition waivers:* Full or partial for employees or children of employees. *ROTC:* Army cooperative.
**LOANS** *Student loans:* $10,220,153 (91% need-based, 9% non-need-based). 80% of past graduating class borrowed through all loan programs. *Average indebtedness per student:* $23,530. *Average need-based loan:* Freshmen: $3528. Undergraduates: $3982. *Parent loans:* $1,377,302 (94% need-based, 6% non-need-based). *Programs:* Federal Direct (Subsidized and Unsubsidized Stafford, PLUS), Perkins.
**WORK-STUDY** *Federal work-study:* Total amount: $162,198; 154 jobs averaging $1000.
**APPLYING FOR FINANCIAL AID** *Required financial aid forms:* FAFSA, state aid form. *Financial aid deadline (priority):* 3/1. *Notification date:* Continuous beginning 2/24.
**CONTACT** Catherine R. McCullough, Director of Financial Aid, Vermont Technical College, PO Box 500, Randolph Center, VT 05061-0500, 802-728-1248 or toll-free 800-442-VTCI. *Fax:* 802-728-1390.
*Website:* http://www.vtc.edu/.

# VILLA MARIA COLLEGE
## Buffalo, NY

| Tuition & fees: $19,170 | Average undergraduate aid package: $8012 |
|---|---|

**ABOUT THE INSTITUTION** Independent Roman Catholic Church, coed. *Awards:* certificates, associate, and bachelor's degrees. 19 undergraduate majors. *Total enrollment:* 465. Undergraduates: 524. Freshmen: 124. Federal methodology is used as a basis for awarding need-based institutional aid.
**UNDERGRADUATE EXPENSES for 2015–2016** *Tuition:* full-time $18,520; part-time $620 per credit hour. *Required fees:* full-time $650; $230 per term. Full-

time tuition and fees vary according to program. Part-time tuition and fees vary according to course load and program.
**FRESHMAN FINANCIAL AID (Fall 2013)** 101 applied for aid; of those 87% were deemed to have need. 100% of freshmen with need received aid; of those 57% had need fully met. *Average percent of need met:* 50% (excluding resources awarded to replace EFC). *Average financial aid package:* $14,358 (excluding resources awarded to replace EFC). 33% of all full-time freshmen had no need and received non-need-based gift aid.
**UNDERGRADUATE FINANCIAL AID (Fall 2013)** 321 applied for aid; of those 99% were deemed to have need. 100% of undergraduates with need received aid; of those 16% had need fully met. *Average percent of need met:* 50% (excluding resources awarded to replace EFC). *Average financial aid package:* $8012 (excluding resources awarded to replace EFC). 50% of all full-time undergraduates had no need and received non-need-based gift aid.
**GIFT AID (NEED-BASED)** *Total amount:* $2,111,142 (65% federal, 1% state, 34% institutional). *Receiving aid:* Freshmen: 85% (88); all full-time undergraduates: 97% (316). *Average award:* Freshmen: $8286; Undergraduates: $5662. *Scholarships, grants, and awards:* Federal Pell, FSEOG, state, private, college/university gift aid from institutional funds.
**GIFT AID (NON-NEED-BASED)** *Total amount:* $667,295 (16% federal, 1% state, 68% institutional, 15% external sources). *Receiving aid:* Freshmen: 41% (43). Undergraduates: 15% (49). *Average award:* Freshmen: $1953. Undergraduates: $1902. *Tuition waivers:* Full or partial for employees or children of employees.
**LOANS** *Student loans:* $1,569,260 (89% need-based, 11% non-need-based). 91% of past graduating class borrowed through all loan programs. *Average indebtedness per student:* $22,658. *Average need-based loan:* Freshmen: $3385. Undergraduates: $3756. *Parent loans:* $187,520 (100% need-based). *Programs:* Federal Direct (Subsidized and Unsubsidized Stafford, PLUS), private loans.
**WORK-STUDY** *Federal work-study:* jobs available. *State or other work-study/employment:* Part-time jobs available.
**APPLYING FOR FINANCIAL AID** *Required financial aid forms:* FAFSA, state aid form. *Financial aid deadline:* Continuous. *Notification date:* Continuous beginning 5/1. Students must reply within 2 weeks of notification.
**CONTACT** Aimee Murch, Director of Financial Aid, Villa Maria College, 240 Pine Ridge Road, Buffalo, NY 14225, 716-961-1828. *Fax:* 716-896-0705. *E-mail:* murcha@villa.edu.
*Website:* http://www.villa.edu/.

# VILLANOVA UNIVERSITY
## Villanova, PA

| Tuition & fees: $45,966 | Average undergraduate aid package: $33,845 |
|---|---|

**ABOUT THE INSTITUTION** Independent Roman Catholic, coed. *Awards:* certificates, bachelor's, master's, and doctoral degrees. 51 undergraduate majors. *Total enrollment:* 10,735. Undergraduates: 7,118. Freshmen: 1,669. Both federal and institutional methodology are used as a basis for awarding need-based institutional aid.
**UNDERGRADUATE EXPENSES for 2015–2016** *Application fee:* $80. *One-time required fee:* $150. *Comprehensive fee:* $58,244 includes full-time tuition ($45,376), mandatory fees ($590), and room and board ($12,278). *College room only:* $6508. Room and board charges vary according to board plan and housing facility. *Part-time tuition:* $1894 per credit hour. *Part-time fees:* $845 per credit hour. Part-time tuition and fees vary according to class time, course load, and program.
**FRESHMAN FINANCIAL AID (Fall 2014, est.)** 1,172 applied for aid; of those 73% were deemed to have need. 99% of freshmen with need received aid; of those 19% had need fully met. *Average percent of need met:* 81% (excluding resources awarded to replace EFC). *Average financial aid package:* $35,413 (excluding resources awarded to replace EFC). 4% of all full-time freshmen had no need and received non-need-based gift aid.
**UNDERGRADUATE FINANCIAL AID (Fall 2014, est.)** 3,805 applied for aid; of those 83% were deemed to have need. 98% of undergraduates with need received aid; of those 17% had need fully met. *Average percent of need met:* 80% (excluding resources awarded to replace EFC). *Average financial aid package:* $33,845 (excluding resources awarded to replace EFC). 7% of all full-time undergraduates had no need and received non-need-based gift aid.
**GIFT AID (NEED-BASED)** *Total amount:* $79,305,365 (9% federal, 1% state, 89% institutional, 1% external sources). *Receiving aid:* Freshmen: 48% (800); all full-

time undergraduates: 45% (2,829). *Average award:* Freshmen: $31,227; Undergraduates: $29,629. *Scholarships, grants, and awards:* Federal Pell, FSEOG, state, private, college/university gift aid from institutional funds, endowed and restricted scholarships and grants.

**GIFT AID (NON-NEED-BASED)** *Total amount:* $10,289,082 (29% federal, 61% institutional, 10% external sources). *Receiving aid:* Freshmen: 8% (130). Undergraduates: 12% (777). *Average award:* Freshmen: $12,280. Undergraduates: $13,416. *Scholarships, grants, and awards by category: Academic interests/achievement:* 885 awards ($9,257,619 total): general academic interests/achievements, international studies, military science. *Special achievements/activities:* 21 awards ($52,000 total): general special achievements/activities. *Special characteristics:* 285 awards ($9,650,622 total): children of educators, children of faculty/staff, general special characteristics, religious affiliation. *Tuition waivers:* Full or partial for employees or children of employees, senior citizens. *ROTC:* Army, Naval, Air Force cooperative.

**LOANS** *Student loans:* $31,916,523 (84% need-based, 16% non-need-based). 53% of past graduating class borrowed through all loan programs. *Average indebtedness per student:* $35,122. *Average need-based loan:* Freshmen: $3817. Undergraduates: $4965. *Parent loans:* $12,386,019 (77% need-based, 23% non-need-based). *Programs:* Federal Direct (Subsidized and Unsubsidized Stafford, PLUS), Perkins, Federal Nursing, alternative loans.

**WORK-STUDY** *Federal work-study:* Total amount: $7,032,315; 2,344 jobs averaging $2837. *State or other work-study/employment:* Total amount: $99,000 (100% need-based). 31 part-time jobs averaging $3000.

**ATHLETIC AWARDS** Total amount: $11,441,831 (24% need-based, 76% non-need-based).

**APPLYING FOR FINANCIAL AID** *Required financial aid forms:* FAFSA, CSS Financial Aid PROFILE, noncustodial (divorced/separated) parent's statement, federal income tax form(s), W-2 forms. *Financial aid deadline:* 2/7. *Notification date:* 4/1. Students must reply by 5/1.

**CONTACT** Bonnie Lee Behm, Director of Financial Assistance, Villanova University, 800 Lancaster Avenue, Villanova, PA 19085-1699, 610-519-4010. *Fax:* 610-519-7599. *E-mail:* bonnie.behm@villanova.edu. *Website:* http://www.villanova.edu/.

# VIRGINIA COLLEGE IN BIRMINGHAM
## Birmingham, AL

**CONTACT** Vice President, Campus Administration, Virginia College in Birmingham, 65 Bagby Drive, Birmingham, AL 35209, 205-802-1200. *Fax:* 205-271-8273. *Website:* http://www.vc.edu/.

# VIRGINIA COMMONWEALTH UNIVERSITY
## Richmond, VA

| Tuition & fees (VA res): $14,573 | Average undergraduate aid package: $10,527 |
| --- | --- |

**ABOUT THE INSTITUTION** State-supported, coed. *Awards:* certificates, bachelor's, master's, and doctoral degrees. 60 undergraduate majors. *Total enrollment:* 31,163. Undergraduates: 23,962. Freshmen: 3,586. Federal methodology is used as a basis for awarding need-based institutional aid.

**UNDERGRADUATE EXPENSES for 2015–2016** *Application fee:* $50. *Tuition, state resident:* full-time $12,398; part-time $352.50 per credit hour. *Tuition, nonresident:* full-time $30,459; part-time $954.19 per credit hour. *Required fees:* full-time $2175. *College room and board:* $9318. Room and board charges vary according to board plan and housing facility.

**FRESHMAN FINANCIAL AID (Fall 2013)** 2,775 applied for aid; of those 77% were deemed to have need. 96% of freshmen with need received aid; of those 7% had need fully met. *Average percent of need met:* 52% (excluding resources awarded to replace EFC). *Average financial aid package:* $11,283 (excluding resources awarded to replace EFC). 12% of all full-time freshmen had no need and received non-need-based gift aid.

**UNDERGRADUATE FINANCIAL AID (Fall 2013)** 13,866 applied for aid; of those 83% were deemed to have need. 97% of undergraduates with need received aid; of those 7% had need fully met. *Average percent of need met:* 52% (excluding resources awarded to replace EFC). *Average financial aid package:* $10,527 (excluding resources awarded to replace EFC). 10% of all full-time undergraduates had no need and received non-need-based gift aid.

**GIFT AID (NEED-BASED)** *Total amount:* $74,168,289 (37% federal, 29% state, 24% institutional, 10% external sources). *Receiving aid:* Freshmen: 49% (1,753); all full-time undergraduates: 45% (8,911). *Average award:* Freshmen: $8271; Undergraduates: $7211. *Scholarships, grants, and awards:* Federal Pell, FSEOG, state, private, college/university gift aid from institutional funds, United Negro College Fund.

**GIFT AID (NON-NEED-BASED)** *Total amount:* $20,938,367 (1% state, 37% institutional, 62% external sources). *Receiving aid:* Freshmen: 17% (607). Undergraduates: 10% (1,958). *Average award:* Freshmen: $9390. Undergraduates: $10,354. *Scholarships, grants, and awards by category: Academic interests/achievement:* 5,938 awards ($23,129,101 total): biological sciences, business, computer science, education, engineering/technologies, foreign languages, general academic interests/achievements, health fields, humanities, mathematics, military science, physical sciences. *Creative arts/performance:* 212 awards ($327,000 total): art/fine arts, dance, music, performing arts, theater/drama. *Special characteristics:* veterans' children. *Tuition waivers:* Full or partial for employees or children of employees. *ROTC:* Army cooperative.

**LOANS** *Student loans:* $87,204,648 (89% need-based, 11% non-need-based). 66% of past graduating class borrowed through all loan programs. *Average indebtedness per student:* $32,411. *Average need-based loan:* Freshmen: $3551. Undergraduates: $4444. *Parent loans:* $15,243,766 (79% need-based, 21% non-need-based). *Programs:* Federal Direct (Subsidized and Unsubsidized Stafford, PLUS), Perkins, Federal Nursing, college/university.

**WORK-STUDY** *Federal work-study:* 827 jobs averaging $1803. *State or other work-study/employment:* Total amount: $12,564 (100% non-need-based). Part-time jobs available.

**ATHLETIC AWARDS** Total amount: $3,548,625 (34% need-based, 66% non-need-based).

**APPLYING FOR FINANCIAL AID** *Required financial aid form:* FAFSA. *Financial aid deadline (priority):* 3/1. *Notification date:* Continuous beginning 4/1. Students must reply within 2 weeks of notification.

**CONTACT** Brenda Burke, Director for Financial Aid, Virginia Commonwealth University, PO Box 843026, Richmond, VA 23284-3026, 804-828-6669 or toll-free 800-841-3638. *Fax:* 804-827-0060. *E-mail:* faidmail@vcu.edu. *Website:* http://www.vcu.edu/.

# VIRGINIA INTERNATIONAL UNIVERSITY
## Fairfax, VA

**CONTACT** Financial Aid Office, Virginia International University, 11200 Waples Mill Road, Fairfax, VA 22030, 703-591-7042 or toll-free 800-514-6848. *Website:* http://www.viu.edu/.

# VIRGINIA MILITARY INSTITUTE
## Lexington, VA

| Tuition & fees (VA res): $15,518 | Average undergraduate aid package: $15,481 |
| --- | --- |

**ABOUT THE INSTITUTION** State-supported, coed, primarily men. *Awards:* bachelor's degrees. 14 undergraduate majors. *Total enrollment:* 1,700. Undergraduates: 1,700. Freshmen: 452. Federal methodology is used as a basis for awarding need-based institutional aid.

**UNDERGRADUATE EXPENSES for 2015–2016** *Application fee:* $40. *Tuition, state resident:* full-time $7498. *Tuition, nonresident:* full-time $29,554. *Required fees:* full-time $8020. *College room and board:* $8372.

**FRESHMAN FINANCIAL AID (Fall 2013)** 350 applied for aid; of those 70% were deemed to have need. 96% of freshmen with need received aid; of those 45% had need fully met. *Average percent of need met:* 89% (excluding resources awarded to replace EFC). *Average financial aid package:* $17,430 (excluding resources

awarded to replace EFC). 7% of all full-time freshmen had no need and received non-need-based gift aid.

**UNDERGRADUATE FINANCIAL AID (Fall 2013)** 1,145 applied for aid; of those 75% were deemed to have need. 99% of undergraduates with need received aid; of those 52% had need fully met. *Average percent of need met:* 88% (excluding resources awarded to replace EFC). *Average financial aid package:* $15,481 (excluding resources awarded to replace EFC). 14% of all full-time undergraduates had no need and received non-need-based gift aid.

**GIFT AID (NEED-BASED)** *Total amount:* $8,891,195 (12% federal, 10% state, 75% institutional, 3% external sources). *Receiving aid:* Freshmen: 47% (211); all full-time undergraduates: 43% (730). *Average award:* Freshmen: $16,738; Undergraduates: $14,402. *Scholarships, grants, and awards:* Federal Pell, FSEOG, state, private, college/university gift aid from institutional funds.

**GIFT AID (NON-NEED-BASED)** *Total amount:* $9,145,109 (84% federal, 3% state, 11% institutional, 2% external sources). *Receiving aid:* Freshmen: 21% (92). Undergraduates: 18% (309). *Average award:* Freshmen: $6606. Undergraduates: $4195. *Scholarships, grants, and awards by category: Academic interests/achievement:* 489 awards ($887,524 total): biological sciences, business, computer science, engineering/technologies, English, foreign languages, general academic interests/achievements, humanities, international studies, mathematics, military science, physical sciences, premedicine. *Creative arts/performance:* 11 awards ($8570 total): music. *Special achievements/activities:* general special achievements/activities, leadership. *Special characteristics:* 50 awards ($115,000 total): children and siblings of alumni, children of faculty/staff, general special characteristics, local/state students, out-of-state students. *ROTC:* Army, Naval, Air Force.

**LOANS** *Student loans:* $6,882,747 (37% need-based, 63% non-need-based). 59% of past graduating class borrowed through all loan programs. *Average indebtedness per student:* $26,720. *Average need-based loan:* Freshmen: $3920. Undergraduates: $4393. *Parent loans:* $2,526,405 (100% non-need-based). *Programs:* Federal Direct (Subsidized and Unsubsidized Stafford, PLUS), Perkins.

**ATHLETIC AWARDS** Total amount: $3,473,322 (37% need-based, 63% non-need-based).

**APPLYING FOR FINANCIAL AID** *Required financial aid forms:* FAFSA, institution's own form. *Financial aid deadline (priority):* 3/1. *Notification date:* Continuous beginning 3/1. Students must reply by 5/1.

**CONTACT** Col. Timothy P. Golden, Director of Financial Aid, Virginia Military Institute, 306 Carroll Hall, Lexington, VA 24450, 540-464-7208 or toll-free 800-767-4207. *Fax:* 540-464-7629. *E-mail:* goldentp@vmi.edu. *Website:* http://www.vmi.edu/.

# VIRGINIA POLYTECHNIC INSTITUTE AND STATE UNIVERSITY
## Blacksburg, VA

| Tuition & fees: N/R | Average undergraduate aid package: $16,455 |
| --- | --- |

**ABOUT THE INSTITUTION** State-supported, coed. *Awards:* certificates, associate, bachelor's, master's, and doctoral degrees. 70 undergraduate majors. *Total enrollment:* 31,224. Undergraduates: 24,247. Freshmen: 5,494. Federal methodology is used as a basis for awarding need-based institutional aid.

**FRESHMAN FINANCIAL AID (Fall 2013)** 4,177 applied for aid; of those 58% were deemed to have need. 93% of freshmen with need received aid; of those 16% had need fully met. *Average percent of need met:* 62% (excluding resources awarded to replace EFC). *Average financial aid package:* $16,745 (excluding resources awarded to replace EFC). 11% of all full-time freshmen had no need and received non-need-based gift aid.

**UNDERGRADUATE FINANCIAL AID (Fall 2013)** 15,673 applied for aid; of those 68% were deemed to have need. 95% of undergraduates with need received aid; of those 18% had need fully met. *Average percent of need met:* 64% (excluding resources awarded to replace EFC). *Average financial aid package:* $16,455 (excluding resources awarded to replace EFC). 12% of all full-time undergraduates had no need and received non-need-based gift aid.

**GIFT AID (NEED-BASED)** *Total amount:* $36,603,659 (49% federal, 42% state, 9% institutional). *Receiving aid:* Freshmen: 30% (1,594); all full-time undergraduates: 32% (7,384). *Average award:* Freshmen: $8413; Undergraduates: $6736. *Scholar-*

ships, grants, and awards: Federal Pell, FSEOG, state, private, college/university gift aid from institutional funds, United Negro College Fund.

**GIFT AID (NON-NEED-BASED)** *Total amount:* $35,967,174 (36% federal, 28% institutional, 36% external sources). *Receiving aid:* Freshmen: 20% (1,077). Undergraduates: 15% (3,579). *Average award:* Freshmen: $3453. Undergraduates: $3526. *Scholarships, grants, and awards by category: Academic interests/achievement:* general academic interests/achievements, library science. *Creative arts/performance:* applied art and design, art/fine arts, cinema/film/broadcasting, creative writing, journalism/publications, music, performing arts, theater/drama. *Special achievements/activities:* cheerleading/drum major, community service, general special achievements/activities, leadership, memberships, religious involvement. *Special characteristics:* children of faculty/staff, first-generation college students, local/state students, members of minority groups, out-of-state students, twins, veterans' children. *ROTC:* Army, Naval, Air Force.

**LOANS** *Student loans:* $93,021,080 (39% need-based, 61% non-need-based). 53% of past graduating class borrowed through all loan programs. *Average indebtedness per student:* $27,865. *Average need-based loan:* Freshmen: $4008. Undergraduates: $4711. *Parent loans:* $27,298,837 (100% non-need-based). *Programs:* Federal Direct (Subsidized and Unsubsidized Stafford, PLUS), Perkins, state, college/university.

**WORK-STUDY** *Federal work-study:* jobs available. *State or other work-study/employment:* Total amount: $12,124,568 (100% non-need-based). Part-time jobs available.

**ATHLETIC AWARDS** Total amount: $9,588,221 (100% non-need-based).

**APPLYING FOR FINANCIAL AID** *Required financial aid forms:* FAFSA, general scholarship application form. *Financial aid deadline (priority):* 3/1. *Notification date:* 4/1. Students must reply by 5/1 or within 4 weeks of notification.

**CONTACT** Miss Beth Armstrong, Director of Student Financial Services, Virginia Polytechnic Institute and State University, 300 Student Service Building, Blacksburg, VA 24061, 540-231-5179. *Fax:* 540-231-9139. *E-mail:* simmonsb@vt.edu. *Website:* http://www.vt.edu/.

# VIRGINIA STATE UNIVERSITY
## Petersburg, VA

| Tuition & fees (VA res): $8002 | Average undergraduate aid package: $11,487 |
| --- | --- |

**ABOUT THE INSTITUTION** State-supported, coed. *Awards:* certificates, associate, bachelor's, master's, and doctoral degrees. 35 undergraduate majors. *Total enrollment:* 5,025. Undergraduates: 4,498. Freshmen: 907. Federal methodology is used as a basis for awarding need-based institutional aid.

**UNDERGRADUATE EXPENSES for 2015–2016** *Application fee:* $25. *Tuition, state resident:* full-time $4876; part-time $348 per credit hour. *Tuition, nonresident:* full-time $14,132; part-time $770 per credit hour. *Required fees:* full-time $3126; $10 per credit hour. Full-time tuition and fees vary according to course load and program. Part-time tuition and fees vary according to course load and program. *College room and board:* $10,128; *Room only:* $5990. Room and board charges vary according to board plan and housing facility.

**FRESHMAN FINANCIAL AID (Fall 2013)** 1,045 applied for aid; of those 100% were deemed to have need. 100% of freshmen with need received aid; of those 34% had need fully met. *Average percent of need met:* 70% (excluding resources awarded to replace EFC). *Average financial aid package:* $10,834 (excluding resources awarded to replace EFC). 18% of all full-time freshmen had no need and received non-need-based gift aid.

**UNDERGRADUATE FINANCIAL AID (Fall 2013)** 4,566 applied for aid; of those 100% were deemed to have need. 100% of undergraduates with need received aid; of those 15% had need fully met. *Average percent of need met:* 65% (excluding resources awarded to replace EFC). *Average financial aid package:* $11,487 (excluding resources awarded to replace EFC). 10% of all full-time undergraduates had no need and received non-need-based gift aid.

**GIFT AID (NEED-BASED)** *Total amount:* $25,730,938 (62% federal, 24% state, 14% institutional). *Receiving aid:* Freshmen: 74% (835); all full-time undergraduates: 72% (3,653). *Average award:* Freshmen: $5708; Undergraduates: $6708. *Scholarships, grants, and awards:* Federal Pell, FSEOG, state, private, college/university gift aid from institutional funds.

**GIFT AID (NON-NEED-BASED)** *Total amount:* $7,248,996 (35% state, 55% institutional, 10% external sources). *Receiving aid:* Freshmen: 31% (356). Undergraduates: 20% (1,004). *Average award:* Freshmen: $500. Undergraduates: $1000. *Scholarships, grants, and awards by category:* Academic interests/achievement: 105 awards ($929,605 total): biological sciences, computer science, engineering/technologies, mathematics, physical sciences, premedicine. *Creative arts/performance:* 29 awards ($40,100 total): applied art and design, art/fine arts, dance, music, performing arts. *Special achievements/activities:* 26 awards ($97,693 total): cheerleading/drum major, community service, hobbies/interests, leadership, religious involvement. *Tuition waivers:* Full or partial for senior citizens. *ROTC:* Army.

**LOANS** *Student loans:* $37,652,901 (91% need-based, 9% non-need-based). 92% of past graduating class borrowed through all loan programs. *Average indebtedness per student:* $28,250. *Average need-based loan:* Freshmen: $3500. Undergraduates: $5500. *Parent loans:* $8,575,592 (100% non-need-based). *Programs:* Federal Direct (Subsidized and Unsubsidized Stafford, PLUS), Perkins, college/university.

**WORK-STUDY** *Federal work-study:* 300 jobs averaging $2000. *State or other work-study/employment:* Total amount: $113,430 (100% need-based). Part-time jobs available.

**ATHLETIC AWARDS** Total amount: $1,278,209 (100% non-need-based).

**APPLYING FOR FINANCIAL AID** *Required financial aid forms:* FAFSA, institution's own form. *Financial aid deadline (priority):* 3/31. *Notification date:* Continuous beginning 3/15. Students must reply within 2 weeks of notification.

**CONTACT** Most Rev. Sheila Allen, Scholarship Manager, Virginia State University, PO Box 9031, Petersburg, VA 23806-2096, 804-524-6854 or toll-free 800-871-7611. *Fax:* 804-524-6818. *E-mail:* sallen@vsu.edu. *Website:* http://www.vsu.edu/.

# VIRGINIA UNION UNIVERSITY
### Richmond, VA

| Tuition & fees: $14,930 | Average undergraduate aid package: $13,322 |
| --- | --- |

**ABOUT THE INSTITUTION** Independent Baptist, coed. *Awards:* bachelor's, master's, and doctoral degrees. 23 undergraduate majors. *Total enrollment:* 1,715. Undergraduates: 1,323. Freshmen: 421. Federal methodology is used as a basis for awarding need-based institutional aid.

**UNDERGRADUATE EXPENSES for 2015–2016** *Application fee:* $25. *One-time required fee:* $200. *Comprehensive fee:* $23,004 includes full-time tuition ($13,614), mandatory fees ($1316), and room and board ($8074). *College room only:* $3690. Full-time tuition and fees vary according to course level, course load, and reciprocity agreements. Room and board charges vary according to housing facility. *Part-time tuition:* $422 per credit hour. *Part-time fees:* $40 per credit hour. Part-time tuition and fees vary according to course level, course load, and reciprocity agreements.

**FRESHMAN FINANCIAL AID (Fall 2014, est.)** 404 applied for aid; of those 95% were deemed to have need. 100% of freshmen with need received aid; of those 7% had need fully met. *Average percent of need met:* 49% (excluding resources awarded to replace EFC). *Average financial aid package:* $12,238 (excluding resources awarded to replace EFC). 5% of all full-time freshmen had no need and received non-need-based gift aid.

**UNDERGRADUATE FINANCIAL AID (Fall 2014, est.)** 1,110 applied for aid; of those 96% were deemed to have need. 100% of undergraduates with need received aid; of those 6% had need fully met. *Average percent of need met:* 53% (excluding resources awarded to replace EFC). *Average financial aid package:* $13,322 (excluding resources awarded to replace EFC). 3% of all full-time undergraduates had no need and received non-need-based gift aid.

**GIFT AID (NEED-BASED)** *Total amount:* $9,818,955 (50% federal, 17% state, 30% institutional, 3% external sources). *Receiving aid:* Freshmen: 89% (372); all full-time undergraduates: 84% (1,040). *Average award:* Freshmen: $9512; Undergraduates: $9590. *Scholarships, grants, and awards:* Federal Pell, FSEOG, state, private, college/university gift aid from institutional funds.

**GIFT AID (NON-NEED-BASED)** *Total amount:* $495,515 (1% federal, 24% state, 67% institutional, 8% external sources). *Receiving aid:* Freshmen: 5% (19). Undergraduates: 3% (41). *Average award:* Freshmen: $6477. Undergraduates: $5046. *Scholarships, grants, and awards by category:* Academic interests/achievement: general academic interests/achievements. *Creative arts/performance:* music. *Special characteristics:* children of faculty/staff. *Tuition waivers:* Full or partial for employees or children of employees. *ROTC:* Army cooperative.

**LOANS** *Student loans:* $9,626,739 (92% need-based, 8% non-need-based). 98% of past graduating class borrowed through all loan programs. *Average indebtedness per student:* $33,286. *Average need-based loan:* Freshmen: $3165. Undergraduates: $3899. *Parent loans:* $4,454,554 (68% need-based, 32% non-need-based). *Programs:* Federal Direct (Subsidized and Unsubsidized Stafford).

**WORK-STUDY** *Federal work-study:* Total amount: $436,038; 303 jobs averaging $1912.

**ATHLETIC AWARDS** Total amount: $1,387,207 (77% need-based, 23% non-need-based).

**APPLYING FOR FINANCIAL AID** *Required financial aid forms:* FAFSA, state aid form. *Financial aid deadline (priority):* 5/1. *Notification date:* Continuous beginning 3/15. Students must reply within 2 weeks of notification.

**CONTACT** Mrs. Karen Gee, Director of Financial Aid, Virginia Union University, 1500 North Lombardy Street, Richmond, VA 23220-1170, 804-257-5882 or toll-free 800-368-3227. *E-mail:* klgee@vuu.edu. *Website:* http://www.vuu.edu/.

# VIRGINIA UNIVERSITY OF LYNCHBURG
### Lynchburg, VA

**CONTACT** Mrs. Charlene P. Scruggs, Financial Aid Director, Virginia University of Lynchburg, 2058 Garfield Avenue, Lynchburg, VA 24572, 434-528-5276. *Fax:* 434-455-5958. *E-mail:* cscruggs@vul.edu. *Website:* http://www.vul.edu/.

# VIRGINIA WESLEYAN COLLEGE
### Norfolk, VA

| Tuition & fees: $34,428 | Average undergraduate aid package: $21,869 |
| --- | --- |

**ABOUT THE INSTITUTION** Independent United Methodist, coed. *Awards:* bachelor's degrees. 50 undergraduate majors. *Total enrollment:* 1,502. Undergraduates: 1,502. Freshmen: 406. Federal methodology is used as a basis for awarding need-based institutional aid.

**UNDERGRADUATE EXPENSES for 2015–2016** *Application fee:* $40. *One-time required fee:* $350. *Comprehensive fee:* $43,108 includes full-time tuition ($33,778), mandatory fees ($650), and room and board ($8680). Full-time tuition and fees vary according to course load. Room and board charges vary according to board plan and housing facility. *Part-time tuition:* $1408 per credit hour. Part-time tuition and fees vary according to course load.

**FRESHMAN FINANCIAL AID (Fall 2013)** 453 applied for aid; of those 89% were deemed to have need. 100% of freshmen with need received aid; of those 18% had need fully met. *Average percent of need met:* 70% (excluding resources awarded to replace EFC). *Average financial aid package:* $23,272 (excluding resources awarded to replace EFC). 11% of all full-time freshmen had no need and received non-need-based gift aid.

**UNDERGRADUATE FINANCIAL AID (Fall 2013)** 1,394 applied for aid; of those 83% were deemed to have need. 100% of undergraduates with need received aid; of those 14% had need fully met. *Average percent of need met:* 66% (excluding resources awarded to replace EFC). *Average financial aid package:* $21,869 (excluding resources awarded to replace EFC). 17% of all full-time undergraduates had no need and received non-need-based gift aid.

**GIFT AID (NEED-BASED)** *Total amount:* $21,629,592 (19% federal, 9% state, 70% institutional, 2% external sources). *Receiving aid:* Freshmen: 89% (403); all full-time undergraduates: 82% (1,148). *Average award:* Freshmen: $19,469; Undergraduates: $18,774. *Scholarships, grants, and awards:* Federal Pell, FSEOG, state, private, college/university gift aid from institutional funds, United Negro College Fund.

**GIFT AID (NON-NEED-BASED)** *Total amount:* $5,399,284 (27% federal, 11% state, 61% institutional, 1% external sources). *Receiving aid:* Freshmen: 17% (76). Undergraduates: 14% (198). *Average award:* Freshmen: $17,137. Undergraduates: $18,893. *Scholarships, grants, and awards by category:* Academic interests/achievement: general academic interests/achievements. *Creative arts/performance:* art/fine arts, music, theater/drama. *Special achievements/activities:* community service, leadership, religious involvement. *Special characteristics:* children of faculty/

staff, relatives of clergy, religious affiliation. *Tuition waivers:* Full or partial for employees or children of employees, adult students, senior citizens. *ROTC:* Army cooperative.

**LOANS** *Student loans:* $8,400,989 (81% need-based, 19% non-need-based). 84% of past graduating class borrowed through all loan programs. *Average indebtedness per student:* $31,891. *Average need-based loan:* Freshmen: $6428. Undergraduates: $7142. *Parent loans:* $4,302,513 (56% need-based, 44% non-need-based). *Programs:* Federal Direct (Subsidized and Unsubsidized Stafford, PLUS), Perkins, alternative loans.

**WORK-STUDY** *Federal work-study:* 209 jobs averaging $968.

**APPLYING FOR FINANCIAL AID** *Required financial aid forms:* FAFSA, state aid form. *Financial aid deadline (priority):* 3/1. *Notification date:* Continuous beginning 2/15. Students must reply by 5/1 or within 2 weeks of notification.

**CONTACT** Mrs. Teresa Rhyne, Director of Financial Aid, Virginia Wesleyan College, 1584 Wesleyan Drive, Norfolk, VA 23502-5599, 757-455-3345 or toll-free 800-737-8684. *Fax:* 757-455-6779. *E-mail:* finaid@vwc.edu.
*Website:* http://www.vwc.edu/.

---

# VISIBLE MUSIC COLLEGE
## Memphis, TN

**CONTACT** Financial Aid Office, Visible Music College, 200 Madison Avenue, Memphis, TN 38103, 901-381-3939.
*Website:* http://visible.edu/.

---

# VITERBO UNIVERSITY
## La Crosse, WI

**CONTACT** Ms. Terry Norman, Director of Financial Aid, Viterbo University, 900 Viterbo Drive, La Crosse, WI 54601-4797, 608-796-3900 or toll-free 800-VITERBO. *Fax:* 608-796-3050. *E-mail:* twnorman@viterbo.edu.
*Website:* http://www.viterbo.edu/.

---

# VOORHEES COLLEGE
## Denmark, SC

**CONTACT** Augusta L. Kitchen, Director of Financial Aid, Voorhees College, PO Box 678, Denmark, SC 29042, 803-703-7109 Ext. 7106 or toll-free 866-237-4570. *Fax:* 803-793-0831. *E-mail:* akitchen@voorhees.edu.
*Website:* http://www.voorhees.edu/.

---

# WABASH COLLEGE
## Crawfordsville, IN

| Tuition & fees: $37,750 | Average undergraduate aid package: $31,886 |
| --- | --- |

**ABOUT THE INSTITUTION** Independent, men only. *Awards:* bachelor's degrees. 22 undergraduate majors. *Total enrollment:* 926. Undergraduates: 926. Freshmen: 256. Both federal and institutional methodology are used as a basis for awarding need-based institutional aid.

**UNDERGRADUATE EXPENSES** for 2015–2016 *Application fee:* $40. *Comprehensive fee:* $46,880 includes full-time tuition ($37,100), mandatory fees ($650), and room and board ($9130). *College room only:* $4530. Room and board charges vary according to board plan and housing facility. *Part-time tuition:* $6183 per course. Part-time tuition and fees vary according to course load. *Payment plan:* Tuition prepayment.

**FRESHMAN FINANCIAL AID (Fall 2014, est.)** 247 applied for aid; of those 85% were deemed to have need. 100% of freshmen with need received aid; of those 63% had need fully met. *Average percent of need met:* 88% (excluding resources awarded to replace EFC). *Average financial aid package:* $32,745 (excluding

resources awarded to replace EFC). 16% of all full-time freshmen had no need and received non-need-based gift aid.

**UNDERGRADUATE FINANCIAL AID (Fall 2014, est.)** 882 applied for aid; of those 83% were deemed to have need. 100% of undergraduates with need received aid; of those 64% had need fully met. *Average percent of need met:* 88% (excluding resources awarded to replace EFC). *Average financial aid package:* $31,886 (excluding resources awarded to replace EFC). 18% of all full-time undergraduates had no need and received non-need-based gift aid.

**GIFT AID (NEED-BASED)** *Total amount:* $17,456,855 (7% federal, 6% state, 84% institutional, 3% external sources). *Receiving aid:* Freshmen: 81% (209); all full-time undergraduates: 78% (722). *Average award:* Freshmen: $25,485; Undergraduates: $23,621. *Scholarships, grants, and awards:* Federal Pell, FSEOG, state, private, college/university gift aid from institutional funds.

**GIFT AID (NON-NEED-BASED)** *Total amount:* $3,243,569 (91% institutional, 9% external sources). *Receiving aid:* Freshmen: 15% (38). Undergraduates: 11% (100). *Average award:* Freshmen: $20,966. Undergraduates: $19,235. *Scholarships, grants, and awards by category:* Academic interests/achievement: 748 awards ($10,604,606 total): general academic interests/achievements. Creative arts/performance: 72 awards ($313,962 total): art/fine arts, creative writing, journalism/publications, music, theater/drama. Special achievements/activities: 115 awards ($753,331 total): community service, leadership. Special characteristics: 13 awards ($476,210 total): children of faculty/staff. *Tuition waivers:* Full or partial for employees or children of employees.

**LOANS** *Student loans:* $7,456,738 (68% need-based, 32% non-need-based). 92% of past graduating class borrowed through all loan programs. *Average indebtedness per student:* $30,734. *Average need-based loan:* Freshmen: $3540. Undergraduates: $5919. *Parent loans:* $2,051,598 (22% need-based, 78% non-need-based). *Programs:* Federal Direct (Subsidized and Unsubsidized Stafford, PLUS), college/university.

**WORK-STUDY** *Federal work-study:* Total amount: $221,780; 75 jobs averaging $2943. *State or other work-study/employment:* Total amount: $1,314,220 (100% need-based). 550 part-time jobs averaging $2672.

**APPLYING FOR FINANCIAL AID** *Required financial aid forms:* FAFSA, CSS Financial Aid PROFILE, federal income tax form(s), W-2 forms. *Financial aid deadline:* 3/1 (priority: 2/15). *Notification date:* 3/31. Students must reply by 5/1 or within 2 weeks of notification.

**CONTACT** Ms. Heidi Carl, Director of Financial Aid, Wabash College, PO Box 352, Crawfordsville, IN 47933-0352, 800-718-9746 or toll-free 800-345-5385. *Fax:* 765-361-6166. *E-mail:* financialaid@wabash.edu.
*Website:* http://www.wabash.edu/.

---

# WAGNER COLLEGE
## Staten Island, NY

| Tuition & fees: $40,750 | Average undergraduate aid package: $27,083 |
| --- | --- |

**ABOUT THE INSTITUTION** Independent, coed. *Awards:* certificates, bachelor's, master's, and doctoral degrees. 38 undergraduate majors. *Total enrollment:* 2,217. Undergraduates: 1,809. Freshmen: 443. Federal methodology is used as a basis for awarding need-based institutional aid.

**UNDERGRADUATE EXPENSES** for 2015–2016 *Comprehensive fee:* $53,200 includes full-time tuition ($40,450), mandatory fees ($300), and room and board ($12,450). *Part-time tuition:* $5056 per unit.

**FRESHMAN FINANCIAL AID (Fall 2014, est.)** 368 applied for aid; of those 87% were deemed to have need. 100% of freshmen with need received aid; of those 25% had need fully met. *Average percent of need met:* 78% (excluding resources awarded to replace EFC). *Average financial aid package:* $30,510 (excluding resources awarded to replace EFC). 19% of all full-time freshmen had no need and received non-need-based gift aid.

**UNDERGRADUATE FINANCIAL AID (Fall 2014, est.)** 1,342 applied for aid; of those 84% were deemed to have need. 100% of undergraduates with need received aid; of those 26% had need fully met. *Average percent of need met:* 70% (excluding resources awarded to replace EFC). *Average financial aid package:* $27,083 (excluding resources awarded to replace EFC). 25% of all full-time undergraduates had no need and received non-need-based gift aid.

**GIFT AID (NEED-BASED)** *Total amount:* $20,404,928 (8% federal, 5% state, 86% institutional, 1% external sources). *Receiving aid:* Freshmen: 72% (319); all full-

time undergraduates: 64% (1,119). *Average award:* Freshmen: $16,829; Undergraduates: $21,020. *Scholarships, grants, and awards:* Federal Pell, FSEOG, state, private, college/university gift aid from institutional funds.

**GIFT AID (NON-NEED-BASED)** *Total amount:* $9,247,986 (99% institutional, 1% external sources). *Average award:* Freshmen: $16,318. Undergraduates: $15,248. *Scholarships, grants, and awards by category: Academic interests/achievement:* general academic interests/achievements. *Creative arts/performance:* music, theater/drama. *Special characteristics:* children of faculty/staff, siblings of current students. *Tuition waivers:* Full or partial for employees or children of employees. *ROTC:* Army cooperative.

**LOANS** *Student loans:* $13,553,541 (83% need-based, 17% non-need-based). *Average need-based loan:* Freshmen: $3784. Undergraduates: $4488. *Parent loans:* $4,495,717 (82% need-based, 18% non-need-based). *Programs:* Federal Direct (Subsidized and Unsubsidized Stafford, PLUS), Perkins, Federal Nursing, alternative loans.

**WORK-STUDY** *Federal work-study:* Total amount: $605,850; jobs available.

**ATHLETIC AWARDS** Total amount: $6,929,665 (62% need-based, 38% non-need-based).

**APPLYING FOR FINANCIAL AID** *Required financial aid forms:* FAFSA, state aid form. *Financial aid deadline (priority):* 2/15. *Notification date:* 3/1. Students must reply within 3 weeks of notification.

**CONTACT** Ms. Theresa Weimer, Director of Financial Aid, Wagner College, One Campus Road, Staten Island, NY 10301, 718-390-3122 or toll-free 800-221-1010. *Fax:* 718-390-3203. *E-mail:* tweimer@wagner.edu.
*Website:* http://www.wagner.edu/.

---

# WAKE FOREST UNIVERSITY
## Winston-Salem, NC

| Tuition & fees: $47,682 | Average undergraduate aid package: $40,534 |
| --- | --- |

**ABOUT THE INSTITUTION** Independent, coed. *Awards:* bachelor's, master's, and doctoral degrees. 38 undergraduate majors. *Total enrollment:* 7,788. Undergraduates: 4,867. Freshmen: 1,287. Institutional methodology is used as a basis for awarding need-based institutional aid.

**UNDERGRADUATE EXPENSES** for 2015–2016 *Application fee:* $50. *Comprehensive fee:* $60,678 includes full-time tuition ($47,120), mandatory fees ($562), and room and board ($12,996). *College room only:* $8496. *Part-time tuition:* $1892 per credit hour.

**FRESHMAN FINANCIAL AID (Fall 2014, est.)** 593 applied for aid; of those 72% were deemed to have need. 100% of freshmen with need received aid; of those 80% had need fully met. *Average percent of need met:* 99% (excluding resources awarded to replace EFC). *Average financial aid package:* $41,169 (excluding resources awarded to replace EFC). 3% of all full-time freshmen had no need and received non-need-based gift aid.

**UNDERGRADUATE FINANCIAL AID (Fall 2014, est.)** 2,027 applied for aid; of those 84% were deemed to have need. 100% of undergraduates with need received aid; of those 77% had need fully met. *Average percent of need met:* 99% (excluding resources awarded to replace EFC). *Average financial aid package:* $40,534 (excluding resources awarded to replace EFC). 6% of all full-time undergraduates had no need and received non-need-based gift aid.

**GIFT AID (NEED-BASED)** *Total amount:* $49,223,451 (7% federal, 3% state, 86% institutional, 4% external sources). *Receiving aid:* Freshmen: 31% (397); all full-time undergraduates: 33% (1,570). *Average award:* Freshmen: $38,182; Undergraduates: $35,551. *Scholarships, grants, and awards:* Federal Pell, FSEOG, state, private, college/university gift aid from institutional funds.

**GIFT AID (NON-NEED-BASED)** *Total amount:* $8,063,460 (17% federal, 64% institutional, 19% external sources). *Receiving aid:* Freshmen: 18% (235). Undergraduates: 18% (846). *Average award:* Freshmen: $30,763. Undergraduates: $16,055. *Scholarships, grants, and awards by category: Academic interests/achievement:* general academic interests/achievements. *Creative arts/performance:* art/fine arts, general creative arts/performance. *Special achievements/activities:* leadership. *Special characteristics:* children and siblings of alumni, local/state students, religious affiliation. *ROTC:* Army.

**LOANS** *Student loans:* $21,724,519 (85% need-based, 15% non-need-based). 41% of past graduating class borrowed through all loan programs. *Average indebtedness per student:* $34,745. *Average need-based loan:* Freshmen: $9825. Undergrad-

---

uates: $11,386. *Parent loans:* $7,347,851 (69% need-based, 31% non-need-based). *Programs:* Federal Direct (Subsidized and Unsubsidized Stafford, PLUS), Perkins, state, college/university.

**WORK-STUDY** *Federal work-study:* Total amount: $1,152,645; jobs available. *State or other work-study/employment:* Part-time jobs available.

**ATHLETIC AWARDS** Total amount: $12,381,806 (43% need-based, 57% non-need-based).

**APPLYING FOR FINANCIAL AID** *Required financial aid forms:* FAFSA, CSS Financial Aid PROFILE, state aid form, noncustodial (divorced/separated) parent's statement. *Financial aid deadline:* 3/1 (priority: 2/15). *Notification date:* Continuous beginning 4/1. Students must reply by 5/1 or within 4 weeks of notification.

**CONTACT** Bill Wells, Director of Student Financial Aid, Wake Forest University, PO Box 7246, Winston-Salem, NC 27109-7246, 336-758-5154. *Fax:* 336-758-4924. *E-mail:* financial-aid@wfu.edu.
*Website:* http://www.wfu.edu/.

---

# WALDEN UNIVERSITY
## Minneapolis, MN

**CONTACT** Office of Financial Aid, Walden University, 100 Washington South, Suite 900, Minneapolis, MN 55401, 800-444-6795 or toll-free 866-492-5336. *Fax:* 410-843-6211. *E-mail:* finaid@waldenu.edu.
*Website:* http://www.waldenu.edu/.

---

# WALDORF COLLEGE
## Forest City, IA

| Tuition & fees: $20,884 | Average undergraduate aid package: $13,082 |
| --- | --- |

**ABOUT THE INSTITUTION** Independent Lutheran, coed. *Awards:* associate and bachelor's degrees. 22 undergraduate majors. *Total enrollment:* 1,457. Undergraduates: 1,425. Freshmen: 146. Federal methodology is used as a basis for awarding need-based institutional aid.

**UNDERGRADUATE EXPENSES** for 2015–2016 *Comprehensive fee:* $27,878 includes full-time tuition ($19,804), mandatory fees ($1080), and room and board ($6994). Full-time tuition and fees vary according to class time, course load, and program. Room and board charges vary according to board plan and housing facility.

**FRESHMAN FINANCIAL AID (Fall 2014, est.)** 157 applied for aid; of those 77% were deemed to have need. 95% of freshmen with need received aid; of those 10% had need fully met. *Average percent of need met:* 58% (excluding resources awarded to replace EFC). *Average financial aid package:* $15,664 (excluding resources awarded to replace EFC). 20% of all full-time freshmen had no need and received non-need-based gift aid.

**UNDERGRADUATE FINANCIAL AID (Fall 2014, est.)** 947 applied for aid; of those 82% were deemed to have need. 97% of undergraduates with need received aid; of those 11% had need fully met. *Average percent of need met:* 60% (excluding resources awarded to replace EFC). *Average financial aid package:* $13,082 (excluding resources awarded to replace EFC). 11% of all full-time undergraduates had no need and received non-need-based gift aid.

**GIFT AID (NEED-BASED)** *Total amount:* $5,321,709 (47% federal, 4% state, 42% institutional, 7% external sources). *Receiving aid:* Freshmen: 60% (113); all full-time undergraduates: 64% (665). *Average award:* Freshmen: $11,832; Undergraduates: $9802. *Scholarships, grants, and awards:* Federal Pell, FSEOG, state, private, college/university gift aid from institutional funds.

**GIFT AID (NON-NEED-BASED)** *Total amount:* $1,042,223 (1% federal, 1% state, 83% institutional, 15% external sources). *Receiving aid:* Freshmen: 5% (9). Undergraduates: 4% (39). *Average award:* Freshmen: $7844. Undergraduates: $6833. *Scholarships, grants, and awards by category: Academic interests/achievement:* communication, general academic interests/achievements. *Creative arts/performance:* music, theater/drama. *Special achievements/activities:* cheerleading/drum major, junior miss, leadership. *Special characteristics:* children of faculty/staff, religious affiliation. *Tuition waivers:* Full or partial for employees or children of employees.

**LOANS** *Student loans:* $8,321,266 (79% need-based, 21% non-need-based). 100% of past graduating class borrowed through all loan programs. *Average indebtedness*

---

per student: $33,494. **Average need-based loan:** Freshmen: $4092. Undergraduates: $4488. **Parent loans:** $2,328,457 (36% need-based, 64% non-need-based). **Programs:** Federal Direct (Subsidized and Unsubsidized Stafford, PLUS), Perkins, state, alternative loans.

**WORK-STUDY Federal work-study:** Total amount: $363,372; jobs available. **State or other work-study/employment:** Part-time jobs available.

**ATHLETIC AWARDS** Total amount: $1,966,888 (79% need-based, 21% non-need-based).

**APPLYING FOR FINANCIAL AID Required financial aid form:** FAFSA. **Financial aid deadline (priority):** 3/1. **Notification date:** Continuous beginning 3/1. Students must reply within 2 weeks of notification.

**CONTACT** Duane Polsdofer, Director of Financial Aid, Waldorf College, 106 South 6th Street, Forest City, IA 50436, 641-585-8120 or toll-free 800-292-1903. Fax: 641-585-8125. E-mail: polsdofed@waldorf.edu.

Website: http://www.waldorf.edu/.

---

# WALLA WALLA UNIVERSITY
## College Place, WA

| Tuition & fees: $25,866 | Average undergraduate aid package: $20,874 |
| --- | --- |

**ABOUT THE INSTITUTION** Independent Seventh-day Adventist, coed. **Awards:** diplomas, associate, bachelor's, and master's degrees. 80 undergraduate majors. **Total enrollment:** 1,887. Undergraduates: 1,689. Freshmen: 364. Both federal and institutional methodology are used as a basis for awarding need-based institutional aid.

**UNDERGRADUATE EXPENSES for 2015–2016 Application fee:** $40. **Comprehensive fee:** $32,721 includes full-time tuition ($25,296), mandatory fees ($570), and room and board ($6855). **College room only:** $3735. Room and board charges vary according to board plan and housing facility.

**FRESHMAN FINANCIAL AID (Fall 2013)** 301 applied for aid; of those 84% were deemed to have need. 100% of freshmen with need received aid; of those 31% had need fully met. **Average percent of need met:** 90% (excluding resources awarded to replace EFC). **Average financial aid package:** $20,779 (excluding resources awarded to replace EFC). 32% of all full-time freshmen had no need and received non-need-based gift aid.

**UNDERGRADUATE FINANCIAL AID (Fall 2013)** 1,163 applied for aid; of those 86% were deemed to have need. 99% of undergraduates with need received aid; of those 25% had need fully met. **Average percent of need met:** 90% (excluding resources awarded to replace EFC). **Average financial aid package:** $20,874 (excluding resources awarded to replace EFC). 27% of all full-time undergraduates had no need and received non-need-based gift aid.

**GIFT AID (NEED-BASED) Total amount:** $14,258,067 (19% federal, 5% state, 57% institutional, 19% external sources). **Receiving aid:** Freshmen: 52% (191); all full-time undergraduates: 52% (777). **Average award:** Freshmen: $4242; Undergraduates: $5864. **Scholarships, grants, and awards:** Federal Pell, FSEOG, state, private, college/university gift aid from institutional funds, Federal Nursing.

**GIFT AID (NON-NEED-BASED) Total amount:** $5,714,184 (2% federal, 60% institutional, 38% external sources). **Receiving aid:** Freshmen: 67% (246). Undergraduates: 56% (831). **Average award:** Freshmen: $9691. Undergraduates: $7870. **Scholarships, grants, and awards by category:** Academic interests/achievement: biological sciences, business, communication, education, engineering/technologies, English, foreign languages, general academic interests/achievements, humanities, mathematics, religion/biblical studies. Creative arts/performance: general creative arts/performance, music, theater/drama. Special achievements/activities: leadership. Special characteristics: children of faculty/staff, veterans.

**LOANS Student loans:** $10,071,122 (73% need-based, 27% non-need-based). 67% of past graduating class borrowed through all loan programs. Average indebtedness per student: $38,778. **Average need-based loan:** Freshmen: $3363. Undergraduates: $4195. **Parent loans:** $1,256,760 (31% need-based, 69% non-need-based). **Programs:** Federal Direct (Subsidized and Unsubsidized Stafford, PLUS), Perkins, Federal Nursing, college/university.

**WORK-STUDY Federal work-study:** jobs available. **State or other work-study/employment:** Total amount: $111,139 (100% need-based). Part-time jobs available.

**APPLYING FOR FINANCIAL AID Required financial aid forms:** FAFSA, institution's own form. **Financial aid deadline (priority):** 4/30. **Notification date:** Continuous beginning 2/15.

**CONTACT** Ms. Cassie Ragenovich, Director of Student Financial Services, Walla Walla University, 204 South College Avenue, College Place, WA 99324-1198, 509-527-2315 or toll-free 800-541-8900. Fax: 509-527-2556. E-mail: financial.aid@wallawalla.edu.

Website: http://www.wallawalla.edu/.

---

# WALSH COLLEGE OF ACCOUNTANCY AND BUSINESS ADMINISTRATION
## Troy, MI

**CONTACT** Howard Thomas, Director of Student Financial Resources, Walsh College of Accountancy and Business Administration, 3838 Livernois Road, PO Box 7006, Troy, MI 48007-7006, 248-823-1285 or toll-free 800-925-7401. Fax: 248-524-2520. E-mail: hthomas@walshcollege.edu.

Website: http://www.walshcollege.edu/.

---

# WALSH UNIVERSITY
## North Canton, OH

**CONTACT** Holly Van Gilder, Director of Financial Aid, Walsh University, 2020 East Maple NW, North Canton, OH 44720-3396, 330-490-7147 or toll-free 800-362-9846 (in-state), 800-362-8846 (out-of-state). Fax: 330-490-7372. E-mail: hvangilder@walsh.edu.

Website: http://www.walsh.edu/.

---

# WARNER PACIFIC COLLEGE
## Portland, OR

| Tuition & fees: $20,300 | Average undergraduate aid package: $17,590 |
| --- | --- |

**ABOUT THE INSTITUTION** Independent Church of God, coed. **Awards:** certificates, associate, bachelor's, and master's degrees. 30 undergraduate majors. **Total enrollment:** 554. Undergraduates: 552. Freshmen: 142. Federal methodology is used as a basis for awarding need-based institutional aid.

**UNDERGRADUATE EXPENSES for 2015–2016 Comprehensive fee:** $28,530 includes full-time tuition ($19,640), mandatory fees ($660), and room and board ($8230). **College room only:** $3340. Room and board charges vary according to board plan and housing facility. **Part-time tuition:** $900 per credit hour. **Part-time fees:** $660 per term. Part-time tuition and fees vary according to course load.

**FRESHMAN FINANCIAL AID (Fall 2014, est.)** 122 applied for aid; of those 92% were deemed to have need. 100% of freshmen with need received aid; of those 16% had need fully met. **Average percent of need met:** 72% (excluding resources awarded to replace EFC). **Average financial aid package:** $18,796 (excluding resources awarded to replace EFC). 15% of all full-time freshmen had no need and received non-need-based gift aid.

**UNDERGRADUATE FINANCIAL AID (Fall 2014, est.)** 471 applied for aid; of those 91% were deemed to have need. 100% of undergraduates with need received aid; of those 14% had need fully met. **Average percent of need met:** 68% (excluding resources awarded to replace EFC). **Average financial aid package:** $17,590 (excluding resources awarded to replace EFC). 12% of all full-time undergraduates had no need and received non-need-based gift aid.

**GIFT AID (NEED-BASED) Total amount:** $3,696,038 (38% federal, 8% state, 50% institutional, 4% external sources). **Receiving aid:** Freshmen: 54% (72); all full-time undergraduates: 64% (334). **Average award:** Freshmen: $7462; Undergraduates: $6462. **Scholarships, grants, and awards:** Federal Pell, FSEOG, state, private, college/university gift aid from institutional funds.

**GIFT AID (NON-NEED-BASED)** *Total amount:* $422,149 (95% institutional, 5% external sources). *Receiving aid:* Freshmen: 83% (111). Undergraduates: 77% (403). *Average award:* Freshmen: $8499. Undergraduates: $5777. *Scholarships, grants, and awards by category: Academic interests/achievement:* 386 awards ($1,302,986 total): area/ethnic studies, biological sciences, business, communication, education, English, general academic interests/achievements, health fields, humanities, mathematics, physical sciences, religion/biblical studies, social sciences. *Creative arts/performance:* 56 awards ($114,253 total): music, theater/drama. *Special achievements/activities:* 67 awards ($69,167 total): leadership, memberships. *Special characteristics:* 165 awards ($238,062 total): children and siblings of alumni, international students, local/state students, members of minority groups, religious affiliation. *Tuition waivers:* Full or partial for children of alumni, employees or children of employees. *ROTC:* Air Force cooperative.

**LOANS** *Student loans:* $3,134,208 (86% need-based, 14% non-need-based). 89% of past graduating class borrowed through all loan programs. *Average indebtedness per student:* $31,338. *Average need-based loan:* Freshmen: $3800. Undergraduates: $4181. *Parent loans:* $773,468 (37% need-based, 63% non-need-based). *Programs:* Federal Direct (Subsidized and Unsubsidized Stafford, PLUS), Perkins.

**WORK-STUDY** *Federal work-study:* Total amount: $693,246; 384 jobs averaging $1929.

**ATHLETIC AWARDS** Total amount: $1,536,130 (76% need-based, 24% non-need-based).

**APPLYING FOR FINANCIAL AID** *Required financial aid form:* FAFSA. *Financial aid deadline:* Continuous. *Notification date:* Continuous beginning 3/1. Students must reply within 2 weeks of notification.

**CONTACT** Cynthia D. Pollard, Director of Student Financial Services and Financial Aid, Warner Pacific College, 2219 Southeast 68th Avenue, Portland, OR 97215-4099, 503-517-1018 or toll-free 800-804-1510. *Fax:* 503-517-1352. *E-mail:* cpollard@warnerpacific.edu.
*Website:* http://www.warnerpacific.edu/.

# WARNER UNIVERSITY
## Lake Wales, FL

**CONTACT** Student Financial Services, Warner University, 13895 Highway 27, Lake Wales, FL 33859, 863-638-7202 or toll-free 800-309-9563. *Fax:* 863-638-7603. *E-mail:* financialaid@warner.edu.
*Website:* http://www.warner.edu/.

# WARREN WILSON COLLEGE
## Swannanoa, NC

| Tuition & fees: $32,560 | Average undergraduate aid package: $28,482 |
|---|---|

**ABOUT THE INSTITUTION** Independent Presbyterian Church (U.S.A.), coed. *Awards:* bachelor's and master's degrees. 19 undergraduate majors. *Total enrollment:* 886. Undergraduates: 824. Freshmen: 234. Both federal and institutional methodology are used as a basis for awarding need-based institutional aid.

**UNDERGRADUATE EXPENSES** for 2015–2016 *Comprehensive fee:* $42,460 includes full-time tuition ($31,980), mandatory fees ($580), and room and board ($9900). Full-time tuition and fees vary according to course load. Room and board charges vary according to board plan. *Part-time tuition:* $1334 per credit hour. *Part-time fees:* $100 per term. Part-time tuition and fees vary according to course load.

**FRESHMAN FINANCIAL AID (Fall 2014, est.)** 211 applied for aid; of those 91% were deemed to have need. 100% of freshmen with need received aid; of those 15% had need fully met. *Average percent of need met:* 82% (excluding resources awarded to replace EFC). *Average financial aid package:* $29,801 (excluding resources awarded to replace EFC). 18% of all full-time freshmen had no need and received non-need-based gift aid.

**UNDERGRADUATE FINANCIAL AID (Fall 2014, est.)** 669 applied for aid; of those 92% were deemed to have need. 100% of undergraduates with need received aid; of those 11% had need fully met. *Average percent of need met:* 79% (excluding resources awarded to replace EFC). *Average financial aid package:* $28,482 (excluding resources awarded to replace EFC). 18% of all full-time undergraduates had no need and received non-need-based gift aid.

**GIFT AID (NEED-BASED)** *Total amount:* $12,208,126 (12% federal, 5% state, 80% institutional, 3% external sources). *Receiving aid:* Freshmen: 71% (166); all full-time undergraduates: 71% (576). *Average award:* Freshmen: $23,381; Undergraduates: $20,991. *Scholarships, grants, and awards:* Federal Pell, FSEOG, state, college/university gift aid from institutional funds.

**GIFT AID (NON-NEED-BASED)** *Total amount:* $1,264,274 (88% institutional, 12% external sources). *Receiving aid:* Freshmen: 11% (25). Undergraduates: 5% (42). *Average award:* Freshmen: $9654. Undergraduates: $7386. *Scholarships, grants, and awards by category: Academic interests/achievement:* 259 awards ($1,522,065 total): general academic interests/achievements. *Creative arts/performance:* 3 awards ($5000 total): art/fine arts, creative writing. *Special achievements/activities:* 78 awards ($283,058 total): community service, leadership. *Special characteristics:* 153 awards ($859,953 total): children of faculty/staff, general special characteristics, local/state students, previous college experience, relatives of clergy, religious affiliation. *Tuition waivers:* Full or partial for employees or children of employees.

**LOANS** *Student loans:* $5,000,398 (93% need-based, 7% non-need-based). 64% of past graduating class borrowed through all loan programs. *Average indebtedness per student:* $24,839. *Average need-based loan:* Freshmen: $3004. Undergraduates: $4581. *Parent loans:* $1,126,622 (91% need-based, 9% non-need-based). *Programs:* Federal Direct (Subsidized and Unsubsidized Stafford, PLUS).

**WORK-STUDY** *Federal work-study:* Total amount: $1,869,244; 556 jobs averaging $3362. *State or other work-study/employment:* Total amount: $490,026 (29% need-based, 71% non-need-based). 145 part-time jobs averaging $3379.

**APPLYING FOR FINANCIAL AID** *Required financial aid forms:* FAFSA, state aid form. *Financial aid deadline (priority):* 3/15. *Notification date:* Continuous beginning 2/15. Students must reply by 5/1 or within 3 weeks of notification.

**CONTACT** Financial Aid Office, Warren Wilson College, PO Box 9000, Asheville, NC 28815-9000, 828-771-2082 or toll-free 800-934-3536. *Fax:* 828-771-2030. *E-mail:* finaid@warren-wilson.edu.
*Website:* http://www.warren-wilson.edu/.

# WARTBURG COLLEGE
## Waverly, IA

| Tuition & fees: $37,190 | Average undergraduate aid package: $25,732 |
|---|---|

**ABOUT THE INSTITUTION** Independent Lutheran, coed. *Awards:* bachelor's degrees. 59 undergraduate majors. *Total enrollment:* 1,661. Undergraduates: 1,661. Freshmen: 464. Federal methodology is used as a basis for awarding need-based institutional aid.

**UNDERGRADUATE EXPENSES** for 2015–2016 *Comprehensive fee:* $46,200 includes full-time tuition ($36,210), mandatory fees ($980), and room and board ($9010). *College room only:* $4325. Room and board charges vary according to board plan and housing facility. Part-time tuition and fees vary according to course load.

**FRESHMAN FINANCIAL AID (Fall 2013)** 384 applied for aid; of those 91% were deemed to have need. 100% of freshmen with need received aid; of those 24% had need fully met. *Average percent of need met:* 84% (excluding resources awarded to replace EFC). *Average financial aid package:* $27,396 (excluding resources awarded to replace EFC). 22% of all full-time freshmen had no need and received non-need-based gift aid.

**UNDERGRADUATE FINANCIAL AID (Fall 2013)** 1,392 applied for aid; of those 89% were deemed to have need. 100% of undergraduates with need received aid; of those 19% had need fully met. *Average percent of need met:* 81% (excluding resources awarded to replace EFC). *Average financial aid package:* $25,732 (excluding resources awarded to replace EFC). 24% of all full-time undergraduates had no need and received non-need-based gift aid.

**GIFT AID (NEED-BASED)** *Total amount:* $25,802,063 (7% federal, 9% state, 75% institutional, 9% external sources). *Receiving aid:* Freshmen: 77% (349); all full-time undergraduates: 75% (1,235). *Average award:* Freshmen: $22,936; Undergraduates: $20,830. *Scholarships, grants, and awards:* Federal Pell, FSEOG, state, private, college/university gift aid from institutional funds.

**GIFT AID (NON-NEED-BASED)** *Total amount:* $10,929,891 (1% federal, 79% institutional, 20% external sources). *Receiving aid:* Freshmen: 17% (78). Undergraduates: 13% (221). *Average award:* Freshmen: $19,900. Undergraduates: $18,077. *Scholarships, grants, and awards by category: Academic interests/*

*achievement:* 1,383 awards ($17,455,379 total): biological sciences, business, communication, computer science, education, engineering/technologies, English, foreign languages, general academic interests/achievements, humanities, mathematics, physical sciences, premedicine, religion/biblical studies, social sciences. *Creative arts/performance:* 324 awards ($1,078,400 total): art/fine arts, cinema/film/broadcasting, journalism/publications, music, performing arts, theater/drama. *Special achievements/activities:* 30 awards ($28,000 total): junior miss, leadership. *Special characteristics:* 869 awards ($5,646,307 total): children and siblings of alumni, children of faculty/staff, international students, previous college experience, religious affiliation, siblings of current students. *Tuition waivers:* Full or partial for employees or children of employees.

**LOANS** *Student loans:* $12,198,937 (61% need-based, 39% non-need-based). 80% of past graduating class borrowed through all loan programs. *Average indebtedness per student:* $39,414. *Average need-based loan:* Freshmen: $4160. Undergraduates: $5055. *Parent loans:* $1,855,249 (59% need-based, 41% non-need-based). *Programs:* Federal Direct (Subsidized and Unsubsidized Stafford, PLUS), Perkins, college/university, private loans.

**WORK-STUDY** *Federal work-study:* 423 jobs averaging $1230. *State or other work-study/employment:* 900 part-time jobs averaging $1668.

**APPLYING FOR FINANCIAL AID** *Required financial aid form:* FAFSA. *Financial aid deadline (priority):* 3/1. *Notification date:* Continuous beginning 3/1. Students must reply within 2 weeks of notification.

**CONTACT** Ms. Jennifer Sassman, Director of Financial Aid, Wartburg College, 100 Wartburg Boulevard, PO Box 1003, Waverly, IA 50677-0903, 319-352-8262 or toll-free 800-772-2085. *Fax:* 319-352-8514. *E-mail:* jennifer.sassman@wartburg.edu. *Website:* http://www.wartburg.edu/.

# WASHBURN UNIVERSITY
## Topeka, KS

| Tuition & fees (KS res): $6038 | Average undergraduate aid package: $9613 |
| --- | --- |

**ABOUT THE INSTITUTION** City-supported, coed. *Awards:* certificates, associate, bachelor's, master's, and doctoral degrees. 89 undergraduate majors. *Total enrollment:* 6,722. Undergraduates: 5,901. Freshmen: 801. Federal methodology is used as a basis for awarding need-based institutional aid.

**UNDERGRADUATE EXPENSES** for 2015–2016 *Application fee:* $20. *Tuition, state resident:* full-time $5952; part-time $248 per credit hour. *Tuition, nonresident:* full-time $13,440; part-time $560 per credit hour. *Required fees:* full-time $86; $21 per term. Full-time tuition and fees vary according to program. Part-time tuition and fees vary according to program. *College room and board:* $6541; *Room only:* $3701. Room and board charges vary according to board plan and housing facility.

**FRESHMAN FINANCIAL AID (Fall 2014, est.)** 718 applied for aid; of those 70% were deemed to have need. 100% of freshmen with need received aid; of those 18% had need fully met. *Average percent of need met:* 43% (excluding resources awarded to replace EFC). *Average financial aid package:* $9767 (excluding resources awarded to replace EFC). 21% of all full-time freshmen had no need and received non-need-based gift aid.

**UNDERGRADUATE FINANCIAL AID (Fall 2014, est.)** 3,462 applied for aid; of those 70% were deemed to have need. 100% of undergraduates with need received aid; of those 14% had need fully met. *Average percent of need met:* 43% (excluding resources awarded to replace EFC). *Average financial aid package:* $9613 (excluding resources awarded to replace EFC). 15% of all full-time undergraduates had no need and received non-need-based gift aid.

**GIFT AID (NEED-BASED)** *Total amount:* $12,894,933 (76% federal, 4% state, 15% institutional, 5% external sources). *Receiving aid:* Freshmen: 43% (325); all full-time undergraduates: 41% (1,552). *Average award:* Freshmen: $5081; Undergraduates: $5090. *Scholarships, grants, and awards:* Federal Pell, FSEOG, state, private, college/university gift aid from institutional funds.

**GIFT AID (NON-NEED-BASED)** *Total amount:* $3,073,250 (1% federal, 2% state, 70% institutional, 27% external sources). *Receiving aid:* Freshmen: 43% (324). Undergraduates: 31% (1,160). *Average award:* Freshmen: $3474. Undergraduates: $3111. *Scholarships, grants, and awards by category: Academic interests/achievement:* 2,317 awards ($3,412,455 total): biological sciences, business, communication, computer science, education, engineering/technologies, English, foreign languages, general academic interests/achievements, health fields, humanities,

international studies, mathematics, physical sciences, premedicine, religion/biblical studies, social sciences. *Creative arts/performance:* 368 awards ($334,807 total): art/fine arts, cinema/film/broadcasting, debating, general creative arts/performance, journalism/publications, music, performing arts, theater/drama. *Special achievements/activities:* 720 awards ($1,799,581 total): cheerleading/drum major, community service, leadership. *Special characteristics:* 342 awards ($699,570 total): adult students, children and siblings of alumni, children of faculty/staff, ethnic background, international students, local/state students. *Tuition waivers:* Full or partial for employees or children of employees, senior citizens. *ROTC:* Army, Naval cooperative, Air Force cooperative.

**LOANS** *Student loans:* $21,859,418 (59% need-based, 41% non-need-based). 70% of past graduating class borrowed through all loan programs. *Average indebtedness per student:* $27,383. *Average need-based loan:* Freshmen: $3272. Undergraduates: $4216. *Parent loans:* $3,412,149 (52% need-based, 48% non-need-based). *Programs:* Federal Direct (Subsidized and Unsubsidized Stafford, PLUS), Perkins, college/university, private loans.

**WORK-STUDY** *Federal work-study:* Total amount: $1,797,477; 707 jobs averaging $2601. *State or other work-study/employment:* Total amount: $28,050 (100% need-based). 16 part-time jobs averaging $1753.

**ATHLETIC AWARDS** Total amount: $1,675,538 (63% need-based, 37% non-need-based).

**APPLYING FOR FINANCIAL AID** *Required financial aid forms:* FAFSA, institution's own form. *Financial aid deadline (priority):* 2/15. *Notification date:* Continuous beginning 3/15. Students must reply within 2 weeks of notification.

**CONTACT** Gail Palmer, Director of Financial Aid, Washburn University, 1700 SW College Avenue, Topeka, KS 66621, 785-670-1151 or toll-free 800-332-0291. *Fax:* 785-670-1079. *E-mail:* gail.palmer@washburn.edu. *Website:* http://www.washburn.edu/.

# WASHINGTON ADVENTIST UNIVERSITY
## Takoma Park, MD

**CONTACT** Sharon Conway, Director of Student Financial Services, Washington Adventist University, 7600 Flower Avenue, Takoma Park, MD 20912, 301-891-4005 or toll-free 800-835-4212. *Fax:* 301-891-4167. *E-mail:* sconway@wau.edu. *Website:* http://www.wau.edu/.

# WASHINGTON & JEFFERSON COLLEGE
## Washington, PA

| Tuition & fees: $41,282 | Average undergraduate aid package: $31,274 |
| --- | --- |

**ABOUT THE INSTITUTION** Independent, coed. *Awards:* bachelor's degrees. 31 undergraduate majors. *Total enrollment:* 1,362. Undergraduates: 1,362. Freshmen: 399. Both federal and institutional methodology are used as a basis for awarding need-based institutional aid.

**UNDERGRADUATE EXPENSES** for 2015–2016 *Application fee:* $25. *Comprehensive fee:* $52,166 includes full-time tuition ($40,722), mandatory fees ($560), and room and board ($10,884). *College room only:* $6390. Full-time tuition and fees vary according to reciprocity agreements. Room and board charges vary according to board plan and housing facility. *Part-time tuition:* $1022 per credit hour. Part-time tuition and fees vary according to course load. *Payment plan:* Tuition prepayment.

**FRESHMAN FINANCIAL AID (Fall 2014, est.)** 365 applied for aid; of those 90% were deemed to have need. 100% of freshmen with need received aid; of those 15% had need fully met. *Average percent of need met:* 83% (excluding resources awarded to replace EFC). *Average financial aid package:* $34,720 (excluding resources awarded to replace EFC). 18% of all full-time freshmen had no need and received non-need-based gift aid.

**UNDERGRADUATE FINANCIAL AID (Fall 2014, est.)** 1,145 applied for aid; of those 90% were deemed to have need. 100% of undergraduates with need received

aid; of those 17% had need fully met. **Average percent of need met:** 79% (excluding resources awarded to replace EFC). **Average financial aid package:** $31,274 (excluding resources awarded to replace EFC). 20% of all full-time undergraduates had no need and received non-need-based gift aid.

**GIFT AID (NEED-BASED) Total amount:** $26,114,956 (6% federal, 6% state, 86% institutional, 2% external sources). **Receiving aid:** Freshmen: 73% (291); all full-time undergraduates: 68% (897). **Average award:** Freshmen: $14,950; Undergraduates: $13,270. **Scholarships, grants, and awards:** Federal Pell, FSEOG, state, private, college/university gift aid from institutional funds.

**GIFT AID (NON-NEED-BASED) Total amount:** $4,130,117 (97% institutional, 3% external sources). **Receiving aid:** Freshmen: 80% (320). Undergraduates: 71% (931). **Average award:** Freshmen: $16,428. Undergraduates: $15,129. **Scholarships, grants, and awards by category:** Academic interests/achievement: 1,166 awards ($16,920,226 total): business, general academic interests/achievements, humanities. **Special characteristics:** 75 awards ($1,871,100 total): children and siblings of alumni, children of faculty/staff, international students, local/state students, members of minority groups, veterans, veterans' children. **Tuition waivers:** Full or partial for employees or children of employees. **ROTC:** Army, Air Force cooperative.

**LOANS Student loans:** $11,655,079 (67% need-based, 33% non-need-based). 83% of past graduating class borrowed through all loan programs. **Average need-based loan:** Freshmen: $3470. Undergraduates: $4440. **Parent loans:** $4,373,524 (66% need-based, 34% non-need-based). **Programs:** Federal Direct (Subsidized and Unsubsidized Stafford, PLUS), Perkins, college/university.

**WORK-STUDY Federal work-study:** Total amount: $814,880; 519 jobs averaging $1570. **State or other work-study/employment:** Total amount: $250,000 (100% non-need-based). 180 part-time jobs averaging $1000.

**APPLYING FOR FINANCIAL AID Required financial aid form:** FAFSA. **Financial aid deadline (priority):** 2/15. **Notification date:** Continuous beginning 3/1. Students must reply by 5/1.

**CONTACT** Ms. Michelle Anderson, Director of Financial Aid, Washington & Jefferson College, 60 South Lincoln Street, Washington, PA 15301-4801, 724-503-1001 Ext. 6019 or toll-free 888-WANDJAY. Fax: 724-250-3340. E-mail: manderson@washjeff.edu.
Website: http://www.washjeff.edu/.

# WASHINGTON AND LEE UNIVERSITY
## Lexington, VA

| Tuition & fees: $45,617 | Average undergraduate aid package: $46,604 |
|---|---|

**ABOUT THE INSTITUTION** Independent, coed. **Awards:** bachelor's, master's, and doctoral degrees. 35 undergraduate majors. **Total enrollment:** 2,264. Undergraduates: 1,890. Freshmen: 471. Both federal and institutional methodology are used as a basis for awarding need-based institutional aid.

**UNDERGRADUATE EXPENSES for 2015–2016 Application fee:** $50. **Comprehensive fee:** $56,262 includes full-time tuition ($44,660), mandatory fees ($957), and room and board ($10,645). **College room only:** $4750. Full-time tuition and fees vary according to degree level. Room and board charges vary according to board plan and housing facility. **Part-time tuition:** $1595 per credit hour. Part-time tuition and fees vary according to degree level.

**FRESHMAN FINANCIAL AID (Fall 2014, est.)** 239 applied for aid; of those 81% were deemed to have need. 100% of freshmen with need received aid; of those 100% had need fully met. **Average percent of need met:** 100% (excluding resources awarded to replace EFC). **Average financial aid package:** $47,862 (excluding resources awarded to replace EFC). 7% of all full-time freshmen had no need and received non-need-based gift aid.

**UNDERGRADUATE FINANCIAL AID (Fall 2014, est.)** 872 applied for aid; of those 90% were deemed to have need. 100% of undergraduates with need received aid; of those 100% had need fully met. **Average percent of need met:** 100% (excluding resources awarded to replace EFC). **Average financial aid package:** $46,604 (excluding resources awarded to replace EFC). 8% of all full-time undergraduates had no need and received non-need-based gift aid.

**GIFT AID (NEED-BASED) Total amount:** $32,661,543 (3% federal, 1% state, 95% institutional, 1% external sources). **Receiving aid:** Freshmen: 41% (193); all full-time undergraduates: 41% (779). **Average award:** Freshmen: $42,766; Undergraduates: $41,472. **Scholarships, grants, and awards:** Federal Pell, FSEOG, state, private, college/university gift aid from institutional funds.

**GIFT AID (NON-NEED-BASED) Total amount:** $8,825,720 (5% federal, 6% state, 86% institutional, 3% external sources). **Receiving aid:** Freshmen: 12% (57). Undergraduates: 10% (197). **Average award:** Freshmen: $45,042. Undergraduates: $36,293. **Scholarships, grants, and awards by category:** Academic interests/achievement: 268 awards ($7,553,943 total): general academic interests/achievements. **Tuition waivers:** Full or partial for employees or children of employees. **ROTC:** Army cooperative.

**LOANS Student loans:** $2,537,553 (36% need-based, 64% non-need-based). 32% of past graduating class borrowed through all loan programs. **Average indebtedness per student:** $23,224. **Average need-based loan:** Freshmen: $908. Undergraduates: $973. **Parent loans:** $5,108,797 (100% non-need-based). **Programs:** Federal Direct (Subsidized and Unsubsidized Stafford, PLUS), Perkins, college/university.

**WORK-STUDY Federal work-study:** Total amount: $480,187; 212 jobs averaging $2000. **State or other work-study/employment:** Total amount: $718,378 (45% need-based, 55% non-need-based). 371 part-time jobs averaging $2000.

**APPLYING FOR FINANCIAL AID Required financial aid forms:** FAFSA, CSS Financial Aid PROFILE, noncustodial (divorced/separated) parent's statement, federal income tax form(s). **Financial aid deadline:** 2/15. **Notification date:** 4/1. Students must reply by 5/1.

**CONTACT** James D. Kaster, Director of Financial Aid, Washington and Lee University, 204 West Washington Street, Lexington, VA 24450, 540-458-8720. Fax: 540-458-8614. E-mail: financialaid@wlu.edu.
Website: http://www.wlu.edu/.

# WASHINGTON COLLEGE
## Chestertown, MD

| Tuition & fees: $43,840 | Average undergraduate aid package: $29,263 |
|---|---|

**ABOUT THE INSTITUTION** Independent, coed. **Awards:** bachelor's and master's degrees. 35 undergraduate majors. **Total enrollment:** 1,481. Undergraduates: 1,463. Freshmen: 388. Both federal and institutional methodology are used as a basis for awarding need-based institutional aid.

**UNDERGRADUATE EXPENSES for 2015–2016 Application fee:** $50. **Comprehensive fee:** $54,452 includes full-time tuition ($42,844), mandatory fees ($996), and room and board ($10,612). **College room only:** $5390. Room and board charges vary according to board plan, housing facility, and location. Part-time tuition and fees vary according to course load. **Payment plan:** Tuition prepayment.

**FRESHMAN FINANCIAL AID (Fall 2014, est.)** 285 applied for aid; of those 88% were deemed to have need. 100% of freshmen with need received aid; of those 23% had need fully met. **Average percent of need met:** 84% (excluding resources awarded to replace EFC). **Average financial aid package:** $32,294 (excluding resources awarded to replace EFC). 30% of all full-time freshmen had no need and received non-need-based gift aid.

**UNDERGRADUATE FINANCIAL AID (Fall 2014, est.)** 921 applied for aid; of those 89% were deemed to have need. 100% of undergraduates with need received aid; of those 20% had need fully met. **Average percent of need met:** 79% (excluding resources awarded to replace EFC). **Average financial aid package:** $29,263 (excluding resources awarded to replace EFC). 33% of all full-time undergraduates had no need and received non-need-based gift aid.

**GIFT AID (NEED-BASED) Total amount:** $18,036,105 (6% federal, 6% state, 88% institutional). **Receiving aid:** Freshmen: 65% (252); all full-time undergraduates: 58% (814). **Average award:** Freshmen: $26,039; Undergraduates: $23,935. **Scholarships, grants, and awards:** Federal Pell, FSEOG, state, private, college/university gift aid from institutional funds.

**GIFT AID (NON-NEED-BASED) Total amount:** $10,967,062 (86% institutional, 14% external sources). **Receiving aid:** Freshmen: 9% (33). Undergraduates: 6% (89). **Average award:** Freshmen: $19,045. Undergraduates: $16,794. **Scholarships, grants, and awards by category:** Academic interests/achievement: general academic interests/achievements. **Creative arts/performance:** art/fine arts, creative writing, music, performing arts, theater/drama. **Special characteristics:** 30 awards ($891,348 total): children of faculty/staff. **Tuition waivers:** Full or partial for employees or children of employees.

**LOANS Student loans:** $8,560,672 (38% need-based, 62% non-need-based). 73% of past graduating class borrowed through all loan programs. **Average indebtedness per student:** $35,833. **Average need-based loan:** Freshmen: $3500. Undergrad-

uates: $4481. **Parent loans:** $5,338,034 (100% non-need-based). **Programs:** Federal Direct (Subsidized and Unsubsidized Stafford, PLUS).
**WORK-STUDY** **Federal work-study:** Total amount: $176,350; 138 jobs averaging $1200.
**APPLYING FOR FINANCIAL AID** **Required financial aid form:** FAFSA. **Financial aid deadline (priority):** 3/1. **Notification date:** Continuous beginning 1/20. Students must reply by 5/1.
**CONTACT** Ms. Jeani M. Narcum, Director of Financial Aid, Washington College, 300 Washington Avenue, Chestertown, MD 21620-1197, 410-778-7214 or toll-free 800-422-1782. Fax: 410-778-7287. E-mail: jnarcum2@washcoll.edu.
*Website:* http://www.washcoll.edu/.

# WASHINGTON STATE UNIVERSITY
## Pullman, WA

| Tuition & fees (WA res): $12,428 | Average undergraduate aid package: $12,737 |
|---|---|

**ABOUT THE INSTITUTION** State-supported, coed. **Awards:** certificates, bachelor's, master's, and doctoral degrees. 137 undergraduate majors. **Total enrollment:** 28,686. Undergraduates: 23,867. Freshmen: 4,457. Federal methodology is used as a basis for awarding need-based institutional aid.
**UNDERGRADUATE EXPENSES** for 2015–2016 **Application fee:** $50. **Tuition, state resident:** full-time $10,874; part-time $571 per credit hour. **Tuition, nonresident:** full-time $23,956; part-time $1225 per credit hour. **Required fees:** full-time $1554. Full-time tuition and fees vary according to location and reciprocity agreements. Part-time tuition and fees vary according to course load, location, and reciprocity agreements. **College room and board:** $11,276; **Room only:** $6858. Room and board charges vary according to board plan, housing facility, and location.
**FRESHMAN FINANCIAL AID (Fall 2013)** 3,639 applied for aid; of those 77% were deemed to have need. 94% of freshmen with need received aid; of those 19% had need fully met. **Average percent of need met:** 68% (excluding resources awarded to replace EFC). **Average financial aid package:** $12,786 (excluding resources awarded to replace EFC). 4% of all full-time freshmen had no need and received non-need-based gift aid.
**UNDERGRADUATE FINANCIAL AID (Fall 2013)** 16,469 applied for aid; of those 84% were deemed to have need. 96% of undergraduates with need received aid; of those 24% had need fully met. **Average percent of need met:** 71% (excluding resources awarded to replace EFC). **Average financial aid package:** $12,737 (excluding resources awarded to replace EFC). 2% of all full-time undergraduates had no need and received non-need-based gift aid.
**GIFT AID (NEED-BASED)** **Total amount:** $97,730,558 (35% federal, 51% state, 14% institutional). **Receiving aid:** Freshmen: 52% (2,119); all full-time undergraduates: 49% (9,883). **Average award:** Freshmen: $10,381; Undergraduates: $10,397. **Scholarships, grants, and awards:** Federal Pell, FSEOG, state, private, college/university gift aid from institutional funds, United Negro College Fund, Federal Nursing.
**GIFT AID (NON-NEED-BASED)** **Total amount:** $21,266,345 (5% state, 60% institutional, 35% external sources). **Receiving aid:** Freshmen: 31% (1,251). Undergraduates: 23% (4,646). **Average award:** Freshmen: $3019. Undergraduates: $3229. **Scholarships, grants, and awards by category:** Academic interests/achievement: agriculture, architecture, area/ethnic studies, biological sciences, business, communication, computer science, education, engineering/technologies, English, foreign languages, general academic interests/achievements, health fields, home economics, humanities, international studies, mathematics, military science, physical sciences, premedicine, social sciences. Creative arts/performance: applied art and design, art/fine arts, cinema/film/broadcasting, creative writing, general creative arts/performance, journalism/publications, music, performing arts, theater/drama. Special achievements/activities: community service, general special achievements/activities, junior miss, leadership, memberships, religious involvement, rodeo. Special characteristics: children and siblings of alumni, children of faculty/staff, children of public servants, children with a deceased or disabled parent, first-generation college students, handicapped students, international students, out-of-state students, public servants, religious affiliation, veterans, veterans' children. **Tuition waivers:** Full or partial for employees or children of employees, senior citizens. **ROTC:** Army, Naval cooperative, Air Force.
**LOANS** **Student loans:** $92,488,119 (45% need-based, 55% non-need-based). 58% of past graduating class borrowed through all loan programs. *Average indebtedness*

per student: $24,298. **Average need-based loan:** Freshmen: $3482. Undergraduates: $4312. **Parent loans:** $35,817,738 (100% non-need-based). **Programs:** Federal Direct (Subsidized and Unsubsidized Stafford, PLUS), Perkins, Federal Nursing, alternative loans.
**WORK-STUDY** **Federal work-study:** jobs available. **State or other work-study/employment:** Total amount: $1,100,649 (100% need-based). Part-time jobs available.
**ATHLETIC AWARDS** Total amount: $7,293,527 (100% non-need-based).
**APPLYING FOR FINANCIAL AID** **Required financial aid form:** FAFSA. **Financial aid deadline (priority):** 2/15. **Notification date:** Continuous beginning 4/15. Students must reply within 2 weeks of notification.
**CONTACT** Office of Financial Aid and Scholarships, Washington State University, PO Box 641068, Pullman, WA 99164-1068, 509-335-9711 or toll-free 888-468-6978. Fax: 509-335-1385. E-mail: finaid@wsu.edu.
*Website:* http://www.wsu.edu/.

# WASHINGTON UNIVERSITY IN ST. LOUIS
## St. Louis, MO

| Tuition & fees: $48,093 | Average undergraduate aid package: $37,928 |
|---|---|

**ABOUT THE INSTITUTION** Independent, coed. **Awards:** certificates, bachelor's, master's, and doctoral degrees. 173 undergraduate majors. **Total enrollment:** 14,348. Undergraduates: 7,401. Freshmen: 1,734. Institutional methodology is used as a basis for awarding need-based institutional aid.
**UNDERGRADUATE EXPENSES** for 2015–2016 **Application fee:** $75. **Comprehensive fee:** $63,373 includes full-time tuition ($47,300), mandatory fees ($793), and room and board ($15,280). **College room only:** $10,486. Room and board charges vary according to board plan and housing facility. **Payment plan:** Tuition prepayment.
**FRESHMAN FINANCIAL AID (Fall 2014, est.)** 913 applied for aid; of those 73% were deemed to have need. 97% of freshmen with need received aid; of those 100% had need fully met. **Average percent of need met:** 100% (excluding resources awarded to replace EFC). **Average financial aid package:** $38,410 (excluding resources awarded to replace EFC). 15% of all full-time freshmen had no need and received non-need-based gift aid.
**UNDERGRADUATE FINANCIAL AID (Fall 2014, est.)** 3,194 applied for aid; of those 84% were deemed to have need. 99% of undergraduates with need received aid; of those 100% had need fully met. **Average percent of need met:** 100% (excluding resources awarded to replace EFC). **Average financial aid package:** $37,928 (excluding resources awarded to replace EFC). 13% of all full-time undergraduates had no need and received non-need-based gift aid.
**GIFT AID (NEED-BASED)** **Total amount:** $90,413,553 (3% federal, 1% state, 92% institutional, 4% external sources). **Receiving aid:** Freshmen: 36% (619); all full-time undergraduates: 39% (2,596). **Average award:** Freshmen: $34,708; Undergraduates: $35,555. **Scholarships, grants, and awards:** Federal Pell, FSEOG, state, private, college/university gift aid from institutional funds.
**GIFT AID (NON-NEED-BASED)** **Total amount:** $7,217,022 (7% state, 75% institutional, 18% external sources). **Receiving aid:** Freshmen: 3% (60). Undergraduates: 2% (158). **Average award:** Freshmen: $11,455. Undergraduates: $8665. **Scholarships, grants, and awards by category:** Academic interests/achievement: architecture, biological sciences, business, communication, computer science, education, engineering/technologies, English, foreign languages, general academic interests/achievements, health fields, humanities, international studies, mathematics, military science, physical sciences, premedicine, religion/biblical studies, social sciences. Creative arts/performance: applied art and design, art/fine arts, creative writing. **Tuition waivers:** Full or partial for employees or children of employees. **ROTC:** Army, Air Force cooperative.
**LOANS** **Student loans:** $10,532,495 (91% need-based, 9% non-need-based). 30% of past graduating class borrowed through all loan programs. *Average indebtedness per student:* $23,858. **Average need-based loan:** Freshmen: $5124. Undergraduates: $6006. **Parent loans:** $2,421,905 (62% need-based, 38% non-need-based). **Programs:** Federal Direct (Subsidized and Unsubsidized Stafford, PLUS), Perkins, state, college/university.

**WORK-STUDY** *Federal work-study:* Total amount: $2,510,194; 1,139 jobs averaging $2204.
**APPLYING FOR FINANCIAL AID** *Required financial aid forms:* FAFSA, institution's own form, CSS Financial Aid PROFILE, noncustodial (divorced/separated) parent's statement. *Financial aid deadline:* 2/1. *Notification date:* 4/1. Students must reply by 5/1.
**CONTACT** Mr. Michael Runiewicz, Director of Financial Aid, Washington University in St. Louis, Campus Box 1041, St. Louis, MO 63130-4899, 314-935-5900 or toll-free 800-638-0700. *Fax:* 314-935-4037. *E-mail:* financial@wustl.edu.
*Website:* http://www.wustl.edu/.

# WATKINS COLLEGE OF ART, DESIGN, & FILM
## Nashville, TN

**CONTACT** Lyle Jones, Financial Aid Coordinator, Watkins College of Art, Design, & Film, 2298 Rosa L. Parks Boulevard, Nashville, TN 37228, 615-383-4848 Ext. 7421. *Fax:* 615-383-4849. *E-mail:* financialaid@watkins.edu.
*Website:* http://www.watkins.edu/.

# WAYLAND BAPTIST UNIVERSITY
## Plainview, TX

| Tuition & fees: $16,980 | Average undergraduate aid package: $13,512 |
| --- | --- |

**ABOUT THE INSTITUTION** Independent Baptist, coed. *Awards:* associate, bachelor's, and master's degrees (branch locations in Anchorage, AK; Amarillo, TX; Luke Air Force Base, AZ; Glorieta, NM; Aiea, HI; Lubbock, TX; San Antonio, TX; Wichita Falls, TX). 45 undergraduate majors. *Total enrollment:* 5,534. Undergraduates: 3,980. Freshmen: 315. Federal methodology is used as a basis for awarding need-based institutional aid.
**UNDERGRADUATE EXPENSES for 2015–2016** *Application fee:* $35. *Comprehensive fee:* $23,670 includes full-time tuition ($15,750), mandatory fees ($1230), and room and board ($6690). *College room only:* $2638. Full-time tuition and fees vary according to course load and location. Room and board charges vary according to board plan and housing facility. *Part-time tuition:* $525 per credit hour. Part-time tuition and fees vary according to course load and location.
**FRESHMAN FINANCIAL AID (Fall 2014, est.)** 213 applied for aid; of those 86% were deemed to have need. 100% of freshmen with need received aid; of those 13% had need fully met. *Average percent of need met:* 66% (excluding resources awarded to replace EFC). *Average financial aid package:* $13,775 (excluding resources awarded to replace EFC). 12% of all full-time freshmen had no need and received non-need-based gift aid.
**UNDERGRADUATE FINANCIAL AID (Fall 2014, est.)** 821 applied for aid; of those 88% were deemed to have need. 100% of undergraduates with need received aid; of those 12% had need fully met. *Average percent of need met:* 65% (excluding resources awarded to replace EFC). *Average financial aid package:* $13,512 (excluding resources awarded to replace EFC). 8% of all full-time undergraduates had no need and received non-need-based gift aid.
**GIFT AID (NEED-BASED)** *Total amount:* $9,942,442 (58% federal, 14% state, 20% institutional, 8% external sources). *Receiving aid:* Freshmen: 62% (181); all full-time undergraduates: 37% (706). *Average award:* Freshmen: $10,972; Undergraduates: $10,113. *Scholarships, grants, and awards:* Federal Pell, FSEOG, state, private, college/university gift aid from institutional funds.
**GIFT AID (NON-NEED-BASED)** *Total amount:* $1,174,567 (1% federal, 1% state, 89% institutional, 9% external sources). *Receiving aid:* Freshmen: 7% (20). Undergraduates: 3% (65). *Average award:* Freshmen: $5078. Undergraduates: $5469. *Scholarships, grants, and awards by category:* Academic interests/achievement: 387 awards ($1,090,933 total): biological sciences, business, communication, education, English, general academic interests/achievements, mathematics, physical sciences, religion/biblical studies, social sciences. Creative arts/performance: 194 awards ($387,300 total): art/fine arts, journalism/publications, music, theater/drama. Special achievements/activities: 50 awards ($82,413 total): cheerleading/drum major, leadership, memberships, religious involvement. Special characteristics: 147 awards ($406,989 total): children and siblings of alumni, children of faculty/staff, ethnic

background, general special characteristics, international students, local/state students, members of minority groups, relatives of clergy, religious affiliation. *Tuition waivers:* Full or partial for employees or children of employees. *ROTC:* Army cooperative, Air Force cooperative.
**LOANS** *Student loans:* $15,639,112 (89% need-based, 11% non-need-based). 71% of past graduating class borrowed through all loan programs. *Average indebtedness per student:* $25,725. *Average need-based loan:* Freshmen: $4189. Undergraduates: $4410. *Parent loans:* $692,244 (34% need-based, 66% non-need-based). *Programs:* Federal Direct (Subsidized and Unsubsidized Stafford, PLUS), Perkins, state, private loans.
**WORK-STUDY** *Federal work-study:* Total amount: $140,354; 138 jobs averaging $1374. *State or other work-study/employment:* Total amount: $121,647 (42% need-based, 58% non-need-based). 138 part-time jobs averaging $1775.
**ATHLETIC AWARDS** Total amount: $2,851,731 (50% need-based, 50% non-need-based).
**APPLYING FOR FINANCIAL AID** *Required financial aid forms:* FAFSA, institution's own form. *Financial aid deadline (priority):* 5/1. *Notification date:* Continuous beginning 1/1. Students must reply within 3 weeks of notification.
**CONTACT** Karen LaQuey, Director of Financial Aid, Wayland Baptist University, 1900 West 7th Street, Plainview, TX 79072-6998, 806-291-3520 or toll-free 800-588-1928. *Fax:* 806-291-1956. *E-mail:* laquey@wbu.edu.
*Website:* http://www.wbu.edu/.

# WAYNESBURG UNIVERSITY
## Waynesburg, PA

| Tuition & fees: $21,290 | Average undergraduate aid package: $16,597 |
| --- | --- |

**ABOUT THE INSTITUTION** Independent Presbyterian Church (U.S.A.), coed. *Awards:* bachelor's, master's, and doctoral degrees. 54 undergraduate majors. *Total enrollment:* 2,039. Undergraduates: 1,528. Freshmen: 335. Federal methodology is used as a basis for awarding need-based institutional aid.
**UNDERGRADUATE EXPENSES for 2015–2016** *Application fee:* $20. *Comprehensive fee:* $30,150 includes full-time tuition ($20,890), mandatory fees ($400), and room and board ($8860). *College room only:* $4480. Full-time tuition and fees vary according to class time. Room and board charges vary according to board plan and housing facility. *Part-time tuition:* $870 per credit hour. *Part-time fees:* $16 per credit hour. Part-time tuition and fees vary according to class time, course load, and location.
**FRESHMAN FINANCIAL AID (Fall 2014, est.)** 307 applied for aid; of those 87% were deemed to have need. 100% of freshmen with need received aid; of those 26% had need fully met. *Average percent of need met:* 80% (excluding resources awarded to replace EFC). *Average financial aid package:* $17,898 (excluding resources awarded to replace EFC). 14% of all full-time freshmen had no need and received non-need-based gift aid.
**UNDERGRADUATE FINANCIAL AID (Fall 2014, est.)** 1,316 applied for aid; of those 89% were deemed to have need. 100% of undergraduates with need received aid; of those 28% had need fully met. *Average percent of need met:* 76% (excluding resources awarded to replace EFC). *Average financial aid package:* $16,597 (excluding resources awarded to replace EFC). 13% of all full-time undergraduates had no need and received non-need-based gift aid.
**GIFT AID (NEED-BASED)** *Total amount:* $14,532,681 (14% federal, 13% state, 66% institutional, 7% external sources). *Receiving aid:* Freshmen: 83% (268); all full-time undergraduates: 82% (1,142). *Average award:* Freshmen: $14,305; Undergraduates: $12,596. *Scholarships, grants, and awards:* Federal Pell, FSEOG, state, private, college/university gift aid from institutional funds, United Negro College Fund.
**GIFT AID (NON-NEED-BASED)** *Total amount:* $2,370,080 (1% state, 84% institutional, 15% external sources). *Receiving aid:* Freshmen: 11% (35). Undergraduates: 9% (123). *Average award:* Freshmen: $8308. Undergraduates: $8743. *Scholarships, grants, and awards by category:* Academic interests/achievement: biological sciences, business, communication, computer science, education, English, general academic interests/achievements, health fields, humanities, international studies, mathematics, physical sciences, religion/biblical studies, social sciences. Creative arts/performance: art/fine arts, music, theater/drama. Special achievements/activities: community service. Special characteristics: 60 awards ($550,000 total): children of faculty/staff, siblings of current students. *Tuition waivers:* Full or partial for employees or children of employees. *ROTC:* Army cooperative.

**LOANS** *Student loans:* $11,907,392 (58% need-based, 42% non-need-based). 93% of past graduating class borrowed through all loan programs. *Average indebtedness per student:* $30,250. *Average need-based loan:* Freshmen: $3625. Undergraduates: $4875. *Parent loans:* $3,234,639 (60% need-based, 40% non-need-based). *Programs:* Federal Direct (Subsidized and Unsubsidized Stafford, PLUS), Perkins, Federal Nursing.

**WORK-STUDY** *Federal work-study:* Total amount: $156,008; 200 jobs averaging $1500.

**APPLYING FOR FINANCIAL AID** *Required financial aid form:* FAFSA. *Financial aid deadline:* Continuous. *Notification date:* Continuous beginning 2/15. Students must reply within 2 weeks of notification.

**CONTACT** Matthew C. Stokan, Director of Financial Aid, Waynesburg University, 51 West College Street, Waynesburg, PA 15370-1222, 724-852-3208 or toll-free 800-225-7393. *Fax:* 724-852-6312. *E-mail:* mstokan@waynesburg.edu.
*Website:* http://www.waynesburg.edu/.

# WAYNE STATE COLLEGE
## Wayne, NE

| Tuition & fees (NE res): $5604 | Average undergraduate aid package: $8034 |
| --- | --- |

**ABOUT THE INSTITUTION** State-supported, coed. *Awards:* certificates, bachelor's, and master's degrees. 53 undergraduate majors. *Total enrollment:* 3,470. Undergraduates: 2,969. Freshmen: 685. Federal methodology is used as a basis for awarding need-based institutional aid.

**UNDERGRADUATE EXPENSES for 2015–2016** *Tuition, state resident:* full-time $4200; part-time $140 per credit hour. *Tuition, nonresident:* full-time $8400; part-time $280 per credit hour. *Required fees:* full-time $1404; $55.75 per credit hour. Full-time tuition and fees vary according to course level and course load. Part-time tuition and fees vary according to course level and course load. *College room and board:* $6420; *Room only:* $3120. Room and board charges vary according to board plan and housing facility.

**FRESHMAN FINANCIAL AID (Fall 2014, est.)** 591 applied for aid; of those 74% were deemed to have need. 98% of freshmen with need received aid; of those 47% had need fully met. *Average percent of need met:* 54% (excluding resources awarded to replace EFC). *Average financial aid package:* $8660 (excluding resources awarded to replace EFC). 11% of all full-time freshmen had no need and received non-need-based gift aid.

**UNDERGRADUATE FINANCIAL AID (Fall 2014, est.)** 2,346 applied for aid; of those 78% were deemed to have need. 97% of undergraduates with need received aid; of those 41% had need fully met. *Average percent of need met:* 56% (excluding resources awarded to replace EFC). *Average financial aid package:* $8034 (excluding resources awarded to replace EFC). 7% of all full-time undergraduates had no need and received non-need-based gift aid.

**GIFT AID (NEED-BASED)** *Total amount:* $5,693,589 (82% federal, 15% state, 3% institutional). *Receiving aid:* Freshmen: 49% (336); all full-time undergraduates: 46% (1,236). *Average award:* Freshmen: $4375; Undergraduates: $4381. *Scholarships, grants, and awards:* Federal Pell, FSEOG, state, private, college/university gift aid from institutional funds.

**GIFT AID (NON-NEED-BASED)** *Total amount:* $3,096,192 (1% federal, 36% institutional, 63% external sources). *Receiving aid:* Freshmen: 44% (299). Undergraduates: 39% (1,052). *Average award:* Freshmen: $2282. Undergraduates: $2768. *Scholarships, grants, and awards by category:* Academic interests/achievement: biological sciences, business, communication, computer science, education, English, foreign languages, general academic interests/achievements, health fields, home economics, humanities, mathematics, physical sciences, premedicine, social sciences. *Creative arts/performance:* applied art and design, art/fine arts, creative writing, general creative arts/performance, journalism/publications, music, performing arts, theater/drama. *Special achievements/activities:* general special achievements/activities, leadership. *Special characteristics:* children of faculty/staff, ethnic background, general special characteristics, local/state students, members of minority groups, out-of-state students, veterans, veterans' children. *Tuition waivers:* Full or partial for employees or children of employees. *ROTC:* Army.

**LOANS** *Student loans:* $10,883,319 (46% need-based, 54% non-need-based). *Average need-based loan:* Freshmen: $3384. Undergraduates: $3892. *Parent loans:* $768,847 (100% non-need-based). *Programs:* Federal Direct (Subsidized and Unsubsidized Stafford, PLUS), Perkins.

**WORK-STUDY** *Federal work-study:* Total amount: $112,326; jobs available.

**ATHLETIC AWARDS** Total amount: $470,057 (100% non-need-based).

**APPLYING FOR FINANCIAL AID** *Required financial aid form:* FAFSA. *Financial aid deadline (priority):* 4/1. *Notification date:* Continuous beginning 3/1. Students must reply within 4 weeks of notification.

**CONTACT** Annette Kaus, Director of Financial Aid, Wayne State College, 1111 Main Street, Wayne, NE 68787, 402-375-7230 or toll-free 866-WSC-CATS. *Fax:* 402-375-7067. *E-mail:* ankaus1@wsc.edu .
*Website:* http://www.wsc.edu/.

# WAYNE STATE UNIVERSITY
## Detroit, MI

| Tuition & fees (MI res): $12,349 | Average undergraduate aid package: $10,291 |
| --- | --- |

**ABOUT THE INSTITUTION** State-supported, coed. *Awards:* certificates, bachelor's, master's, and doctoral degrees. 88 undergraduate majors. *Total enrollment:* 27,578. Undergraduates: 18,347. Freshmen: 2,195. Federal methodology is used as a basis for awarding need-based institutional aid.

**UNDERGRADUATE EXPENSES for 2015–2016** *Application fee:* $25. *One-time required fee:* $250. *Tuition, state resident:* full-time $10,995; part-time $336.45 per credit hour. *Tuition, nonresident:* full-time $25,237; part-time $841.23 per credit hour. *Required fees:* full-time $1354; $30.25 per credit hour or $223.50 per term. Full-time tuition and fees vary according to course load, program, reciprocity agreements, and student level. Part-time tuition and fees vary according to course load, program, reciprocity agreements, and student level. *College room and board:* $9713; *Room only:* $5723. Room and board charges vary according to board plan and housing facility.

**FRESHMAN FINANCIAL AID (Fall 2013)** 1,853 applied for aid; of those 85% were deemed to have need. 98% of freshmen with need received aid; of those 8% had need fully met. *Average percent of need met:* 62% (excluding resources awarded to replace EFC). *Average financial aid package:* $11,527 (excluding resources awarded to replace EFC). 10% of all full-time freshmen had no need and received non-need-based gift aid.

**UNDERGRADUATE FINANCIAL AID (Fall 2013)** 10,093 applied for aid; of those 92% were deemed to have need. 98% of undergraduates with need received aid; of those 4% had need fully met. *Average percent of need met:* 50% (excluding resources awarded to replace EFC). *Average financial aid package:* $10,291 (excluding resources awarded to replace EFC). 9% of all full-time undergraduates had no need and received non-need-based gift aid.

**GIFT AID (NEED-BASED)** *Total amount:* $56,206,957 (68% federal, 32% institutional). *Receiving aid:* Freshmen: 60% (1,255); all full-time undergraduates: 58% (7,089). *Average award:* Freshmen: $7493; Undergraduates: $6496. *Scholarships, grants, and awards:* Federal Pell, FSEOG, state, private, college/university gift aid from institutional funds, United Negro College Fund.

**GIFT AID (NON-NEED-BASED)** *Total amount:* $22,273,786 (4% state, 91% institutional, 5% external sources). *Receiving aid:* Freshmen: 46% (947). Undergraduates: 30% (3,607). *Average award:* Freshmen: $5847. Undergraduates: $6556. *Scholarships, grants, and awards by category:* Academic interests/achievement: 3,248 awards ($15,403,331 total): area/ethnic studies, biological sciences, business, communication, computer science, education, engineering/technologies, English, foreign languages, general academic interests/achievements, health fields, humanities, international studies, library science, mathematics, military science, physical sciences, premedicine, social sciences. *Creative arts/performance:* 513 awards ($1,260,159 total): art/fine arts, dance, debating, general creative arts/performance, journalism/publications, music, performing arts, theater/drama. *Special achievements/activities:* 40 awards ($19,700 total): leadership. *Special characteristics:* 176 awards ($889,817 total): children of faculty/staff. *Tuition waivers:* Full or partial for employees or children of employees, senior citizens. *ROTC:* Army, Air Force cooperative.

**LOANS** *Student loans:* $90,587,835 (93% need-based, 7% non-need-based). 64% of past graduating class borrowed through all loan programs. *Average indebtedness per student:* $23,785. *Average need-based loan:* Freshmen: $3439. Undergraduates: $4348. *Parent loans:* $7,388,908 (100% non-need-based). *Programs:* Federal Direct (Subsidized and Unsubsidized Stafford, PLUS), Perkins, Federal Nursing, college/university.

**WORK-STUDY** *Federal work-study:* 361 jobs averaging $2577. *State or other work-study/employment:* Part-time jobs available.
**ATHLETIC AWARDS** Total amount: $3,464,410 (100% non-need-based).
**APPLYING FOR FINANCIAL AID** *Required financial aid forms:* FAFSA, federal income tax form(s), W-2 forms. *Financial aid deadline (priority):* 3/31. *Notification date:* Continuous beginning 3/31.
**CONTACT** Gabriela Garfield, Acting Senior Director of Financial Aid, Wayne State University, 3W HNJ Student Services Building, Detroit, MI 48202, 313-577-3378 or toll-free 877-WSU-INFO. *Fax:* 313-577-6648. *E-mail:* financialaid@wayne.edu.
*Website:* http://www.wayne.edu/.

# WEBBER INTERNATIONAL UNIVERSITY
## Babson Park, FL

| Tuition & fees: $23,816 | Average undergraduate aid package: $19,410 |
|---|---|

**ABOUT THE INSTITUTION** Independent, coed. *Awards:* associate, bachelor's, and master's degrees. 13 undergraduate majors. *Total enrollment:* 681. Undergraduates: 681. Freshmen: 178. Federal methodology is used as a basis for awarding need-based institutional aid.
**UNDERGRADUATE EXPENSES** for 2015–2016 *Application fee:* $35. *Comprehensive fee:* $32,278 includes full-time tuition ($21,686), mandatory fees ($2130), and room and board ($8462). *College room only:* $5432. Full-time tuition and fees vary according to class time and course load. Room and board charges vary according to board plan, gender, and housing facility. *Part-time tuition:* $316 per credit hour. Part-time tuition and fees vary according to course load.
**FRESHMAN FINANCIAL AID (Fall 2014, est.)** 122 applied for aid; of those 91% were deemed to have need. 98% of freshmen with need received aid; of those 6% had need fully met. *Average percent of need met:* 58% (excluding resources awarded to replace EFC). *Average financial aid package:* $18,991 (excluding resources awarded to replace EFC). 27% of all full-time freshmen had no need and received non-need-based gift aid.
**UNDERGRADUATE FINANCIAL AID (Fall 2014, est.)** 502 applied for aid; of those 92% were deemed to have need. 98% of undergraduates with need received aid; of those 8% had need fully met. *Average percent of need met:* 62% (excluding resources awarded to replace EFC). *Average financial aid package:* $19,410 (excluding resources awarded to replace EFC). 25% of all full-time undergraduates had no need and received non-need-based gift aid.
**GIFT AID (NEED-BASED)** *Total amount:* $4,691,354 (31% federal, 29% state, 38% institutional, 2% external sources). *Receiving aid:* Freshmen: 54% (109); all full-time undergraduates: 61% (448). *Average award:* Freshmen: $16,068; Undergraduates: $16,117. *Scholarships, grants, and awards:* Federal Pell, FSEOG, state, private, college/university gift aid from institutional funds.
**GIFT AID (NON-NEED-BASED)** *Total amount:* $1,804,898 (9% state, 91% institutional). *Receiving aid:* Freshmen: 2% (5). Undergraduates: 4% (28). *Average award:* Freshmen: $11,334. Undergraduates: $10,302. *Scholarships, grants, and awards by category:* Academic interests/achievement: 390 awards ($2,072,236 total): business, general academic interests/achievements. *Creative arts/performance:* 8 awards ($44,000 total): journalism/publications, music. *Special achievements/activities:* 37 awards ($22,625 total): cheerleading/drum major, general special achievements/activities, leadership, memberships. *Special characteristics:* 97 awards ($1,203,694 total): children and siblings of alumni, children of faculty/staff, general special characteristics, international students, local/state students, siblings of current students, veterans. *Tuition waivers:* Full or partial for children of alumni, employees or children of employees, adult students, senior citizens.
**LOANS** *Student loans:* $3,191,168 (88% need-based, 12% non-need-based). 47% of past graduating class borrowed through all loan programs. *Average indebtedness per student:* $24,578. *Average need-based loan:* Freshmen: $3445. Undergraduates: $4132. *Parent loans:* $905,830 (65% need-based, 35% non-need-based). *Programs:* Federal Direct (Subsidized and Unsubsidized Stafford, PLUS), Perkins.
**WORK-STUDY** *Federal work-study:* Total amount: $31,131; 35 jobs averaging $1066. *State or other work-study/employment:* Total amount: $46,615 (35% need-based, 65% non-need-based). 38 part-time jobs averaging $952.
**ATHLETIC AWARDS** Total amount: $2,985,674 (80% need-based, 20% non-need-based).

**APPLYING FOR FINANCIAL AID** *Required financial aid forms:* FAFSA, state aid form. *Financial aid deadline:* 8/1 (priority: 4/1). *Notification date:* Continuous beginning 3/1. Students must reply within 4 weeks of notification.
**CONTACT** Ms. Kathleen Wilson, Vice President, Student Record Services, Webber International University, PO Box 96, 1201 Scenic Highway, Babson Park, FL 33827-0096, 863-638-2930 or toll-free 800-741-1844. *Fax:* 863-638-1513. *E-mail:* wilsonka@webber.edu.
*Website:* http://www.webber.edu/.

# WEBB INSTITUTE
## Glen Cove, NY

| Tuition & fees: $46,000 | Average undergraduate aid package: $47,255 |
|---|---|

**ABOUT THE INSTITUTION** Independent, coed. *Awards:* bachelor's degrees. 1 undergraduate major. *Total enrollment:* 90. Undergraduates: 90. Freshmen: 24. Both federal and institutional methodology are used as a basis for awarding need-based institutional aid.
**UNDERGRADUATE EXPENSES** for 2015–2016 *Application fee:* $25. *One-time required fee:* $2850. *Comprehensive fee:* $60,050 includes full-time tuition ($45,500), mandatory fees ($500), and room and board ($14,050). Webb provides scholarships that will fully cover the tuition expenses of U.S. citizens and permanent residents. One-time required fee is for a laptop charged in the first year only.
**FRESHMAN FINANCIAL AID (Fall 2013)** 6 applied for aid; of those 100% were deemed to have need. 100% of freshmen with need received aid. *Average percent of need met:* 80% (excluding resources awarded to replace EFC). *Average financial aid package:* $46,250 (excluding resources awarded to replace EFC). 73% of all full-time freshmen had no need and received non-need-based gift aid.
**UNDERGRADUATE FINANCIAL AID (Fall 2013)** 15 applied for aid; of those 100% were deemed to have need. 100% of undergraduates with need received aid. *Average percent of need met:* 79% (excluding resources awarded to replace EFC). *Average financial aid package:* $47,255 (excluding resources awarded to replace EFC). 78% of all full-time undergraduates had no need and received non-need-based gift aid.
**GIFT AID (NEED-BASED)** *Total amount:* $961,925 (2% federal, 6% state, 87% institutional, 5% external sources). *Receiving aid:* Freshmen: 23% (6); all full-time undergraduates: 18% (15). *Average award:* Freshmen: $2000; Undergraduates: $2000. *Scholarships, grants, and awards:* Federal Pell, state, private, college/university gift aid from institutional funds.
**GIFT AID (NON-NEED-BASED)** *Total amount:* $2,543,625 (100% institutional). *Receiving aid:* Freshmen: 8% (2). Undergraduates: 10% (8). *Average award:* Freshmen: $42,750. Undergraduates: $43,740. *Scholarships, grants, and awards by category:* Academic interests/achievement: 57 awards ($2,436,750 total): engineering/technologies, general academic interests/achievements. *Special achievements/activities:* 4 awards ($15,000 total): community service, leadership.
**LOANS** *Student loans:* $138,100 (100% need-based). 20% of past graduating class borrowed through all loan programs. *Average indebtedness per student:* $10,000. *Average need-based loan:* Freshmen: $3258. Undergraduates: $4505. *Parent loans:* $26,570 (100% need-based). *Programs:* Federal Direct (Subsidized and Unsubsidized Stafford, PLUS).
**APPLYING FOR FINANCIAL AID** *Required financial aid form:* FAFSA. *Financial aid deadline (priority):* 7/1. *Notification date:* Continuous beginning 5/25. Students must reply by 7/1.
**CONTACT** Lauri D'Ambra, Director of Financial Aid, Webb Institute, 298 Crescent Beach Road, Glen Cove, NY 11542-1398, 516-671-8355 Ext. 1107. *Fax:* 516-674-9838. *E-mail:* ldambra@webb.edu.
*Website:* http://www.webb.edu/.

# WEBER STATE UNIVERSITY
## Ogden, UT

| Tuition & fees (UT res): $5184 | Average undergraduate aid package: $3282 |
|---|---|

**ABOUT THE INSTITUTION** State-supported, coed. *Awards:* certificates, associate, bachelor's, and master's degrees. 135 undergraduate majors. *Total enrollment:* 25,954. Undergraduates: 25,335. Freshmen: 2,865. Both federal and institutional methodology are used as a basis for awarding need-based institutional aid.

**UNDERGRADUATE EXPENSES for 2015–2016** *Application fee:* $30. *Tuition, state resident:* full-time $4326; part-time $180 per credit hour. *Tuition, nonresident:* full-time $12,980; part-time $540 per credit hour. *Required fees:* full-time $858; $36 per credit hour. Full-time tuition and fees vary according to course level and course load. Part-time tuition and fees vary according to course level and course load. *College room and board:* $8400. Room and board charges vary according to board plan and housing facility.

**FRESHMAN FINANCIAL AID (Fall 2014, est.)** 1,532 applied for aid; of those 85% were deemed to have need. 97% of freshmen with need received aid; of those 48% had need fully met. *Average financial aid package:* $2865 (excluding resources awarded to replace EFC).

**UNDERGRADUATE FINANCIAL AID (Fall 2014, est.)** 7,573 applied for aid; of those 88% were deemed to have need. 91% of undergraduates with need received aid; of those 36% had need fully met. *Average financial aid package:* $3282 (excluding resources awarded to replace EFC).

**GIFT AID (NEED-BASED)** *Total amount:* $36,135,006 (95% federal, 3% state, 2% external sources). *Receiving aid:* Freshmen: 40% (865); all full-time undergraduates: 44% (4,824). *Average award:* Freshmen: $2381; Undergraduates: $2347. *Scholarships, grants, and awards:* Federal Pell, FSEOG, state, private, college/university gift aid from institutional funds.

**GIFT AID (NON-NEED-BASED)** *Total amount:* $3,236,914 (100% institutional). *Receiving aid:* Freshmen: 8% (180). Undergraduates: 13% (1,392). *Tuition waivers:* Full or partial for employees or children of employees, senior citizens. *ROTC:* Army, Naval cooperative, Air Force cooperative.

**LOANS** *Student loans:* $81,413,500 (43% need-based, 57% non-need-based). *Average need-based loan:* Freshmen: $1469. Undergraduates: $1934. *Parent loans:* $272,610 (100% non-need-based). *Programs:* Federal Direct (Subsidized and Unsubsidized Stafford, PLUS), Perkins, college/university.

**WORK-STUDY** *Federal work-study:* Total amount: $1,399,800; jobs available. *State or other work-study/employment:* Total amount: $1,189,000 (100% need-based). Part-time jobs available.

**ATHLETIC AWARDS** Total amount: $2,269,356 (73% need-based, 27% non-need-based).

**APPLYING FOR FINANCIAL AID** *Required financial aid forms:* FAFSA, institution's own form. *Financial aid deadline (priority):* 3/1. *Notification date:* Continuous beginning 3/15. Students must reply within 2 weeks of notification.

**CONTACT** Mr. Jed Spencer, Financial Aid Director, Weber State University, Student Service Center, Suite 120, 3885 West Campus Drive, Dept 1136, Ogden, UT 84408-1136, 801-626-7569 or toll-free 800-848-7700 (in-state), 800-848-7770 (out-of-state). *E-mail:* finaid@weber.edu. *Website:* http://www.weber.edu/.

# WEBSTER UNIVERSITY
## St. Louis, MO

| Tuition & fees: $24,500 | Average undergraduate aid package: $25,134 |
|---|---|

**ABOUT THE INSTITUTION** Independent, coed. *Awards:* certificates, bachelor's, master's, and doctoral degrees. 67 undergraduate majors. *Total enrollment:* 4,692. Undergraduates: 2,928. Freshmen: 463. Federal methodology is used as a basis for awarding need-based institutional aid.

**UNDERGRADUATE EXPENSES for 2015–2016** *Application fee:* $35. *Comprehensive fee:* $35,100 includes full-time tuition ($24,500) and room and board ($10,600). *College room only:* $5850. Full-time tuition and fees vary according to program. Room and board charges vary according to board plan and housing facility. *Part-time tuition:* $630 per credit hour.

**FRESHMAN FINANCIAL AID (Fall 2014, est.)** 431 applied for aid; of those 82% were deemed to have need. 100% of freshmen with need received aid; of those 2% had need fully met. *Average percent of need met:* 34% (excluding resources awarded to replace EFC). *Average financial aid package:* $27,757 (excluding resources awarded to replace EFC). 20% of all full-time freshmen had no need and received non-need-based gift aid.

**UNDERGRADUATE FINANCIAL AID (Fall 2014, est.)** 2,180 applied for aid; of those 83% were deemed to have need. 100% of undergraduates with need received aid; of those 3% had need fully met. *Average percent of need met:* 33% (excluding resources awarded to replace EFC). *Average financial aid package:* $25,134 (excluding resources awarded to replace EFC). 12% of all full-time undergraduates had no need and received non-need-based gift aid.

**GIFT AID (NEED-BASED)** *Total amount:* $26,010,860 (19% federal, 5% state, 74% institutional, 2% external sources). *Receiving aid:* Freshmen: 70% (319); all full-time undergraduates: 66% (1,611). *Average award:* Freshmen: $10,046; Undergraduates: $8640. *Scholarships, grants, and awards:* Federal Pell, FSEOG, state, private, college/university gift aid from institutional funds.

**GIFT AID (NON-NEED-BASED)** *Total amount:* $6,041,422 (1% state, 94% institutional, 5% external sources). *Receiving aid:* Freshmen: 40% (181). Undergraduates: 27% (660). *Average award:* Freshmen: $4085. Undergraduates: $5820. *Scholarships, grants, and awards by category:* Academic interests/achievement: biological sciences, business, communication, computer science, education, English, foreign languages, general academic interests/achievements, humanities, international studies. Creative arts/performance: art/fine arts, creative writing, debating, music, theater/drama. Special achievements/activities: community service, leadership. Special characteristics: children and siblings of alumni, children of faculty/staff, ethnic background, international students, members of minority groups, out-of-state students, veterans' children. *Tuition waivers:* Full or partial for employees or children of employees. *ROTC:* Army cooperative, Air Force cooperative.

**LOANS** *Student loans:* $18,571,874 (83% need-based, 17% non-need-based). 48% of past graduating class borrowed through all loan programs. *Average indebtedness per student:* $30,413. *Average need-based loan:* Freshmen: $3685. Undergraduates: $4616. *Parent loans:* $2,758,401 (80% need-based, 20% non-need-based). *Programs:* Federal Direct (Subsidized and Unsubsidized Stafford, PLUS), Perkins.

**WORK-STUDY** *Federal work-study:* Total amount: $2,203,101; 1,008 jobs averaging $2186. *State or other work-study/employment:* Total amount: $750,684 (1% need-based, 99% non-need-based). 475 part-time jobs averaging $1571.

**APPLYING FOR FINANCIAL AID** *Required financial aid forms:* FAFSA, institution's own form. *Financial aid deadline (priority):* 4/1. *Notification date:* Continuous beginning 2/1.

**CONTACT** Office of Financial Aid, Webster University, 470 East Lockwood Avenue, St. Louis, MO 63119, 314-968-6992 or toll-free 800-75-ENROL. *Fax:* 314-968-7125. *E-mail:* financialaid@webster.edu. *Website:* http://www.webster.edu/.

# WELCH COLLEGE
## Nashville, TN

**CONTACT** Angie Edgmon, Financial Aid Coordinator, Welch College, 3606 West End Avenue, Nashville, TN 37205, 615-844-5000 Ext. 5249 or toll-free 800-763-9222. *Fax:* 615-269-6028. *E-mail:* finaid@fwbbc.edu. *Website:* http://www.welch.edu/.

# WELLESLEY COLLEGE
## Wellesley, MA

| Tuition & fees: $45,078 | Average undergraduate aid package: $42,400 |
|---|---|

**ABOUT THE INSTITUTION** Independent, women only. *Awards:* bachelor's degrees (double bachelor's degree with Massachusetts Institute of Technology). 58 undergraduate majors. *Total enrollment:* 2,474. Undergraduates: 2,474. Freshmen: 593. Both federal and institutional methodology are used as a basis for awarding need-based institutional aid.

**UNDERGRADUATE EXPENSES** for 2015–2016 *Comprehensive fee:* $59,038 includes full-time tuition ($44,802), mandatory fees ($276), and room and board ($13,960). *College room only:* $7086. *Part-time tuition:* $5411 per course. Part-time tuition and fees vary according to course load. *Payment plan:* Tuition prepayment.

**FRESHMAN FINANCIAL AID (Fall 2014, est.)** 416 applied for aid; of those 86% were deemed to have need. 100% of freshmen with need received aid; of those 100% had need fully met. *Average percent of need met:* 100% (excluding resources awarded to replace EFC). *Average financial aid package:* $40,932 (excluding resources awarded to replace EFC).

**UNDERGRADUATE FINANCIAL AID (Fall 2014, est.)** 1,532 applied for aid; of those 91% were deemed to have need. 100% of undergraduates with need received aid; of those 100% had need fully met. *Average percent of need met:* 100% (excluding resources awarded to replace EFC). *Average financial aid package:* $42,400 (excluding resources awarded to replace EFC).

**GIFT AID (NEED-BASED)** *Total amount:* $54,575,934 (4% federal, 94% institutional, 2% external sources). *Receiving aid:* Freshmen: 58% (341); all full-time undergraduates: 62% (1,345). *Average award:* Freshmen: $39,129; Undergraduates: $39,988. *Scholarships, grants, and awards:* Federal Pell, FSEOG, state, private, college/university gift aid from institutional funds.

**GIFT AID (NON-NEED-BASED)** *Total amount:* $296,581 (100% external sources). *Tuition waivers:* Full or partial for employees or children of employees. *ROTC:* Army cooperative, Air Force cooperative.

**LOANS** *Student loans:* $4,204,284 (69% need-based, 31% non-need-based). 52% of past graduating class borrowed through all loan programs. *Average indebtedness per student:* $12,956. *Average need-based loan:* Freshmen: $2786. Undergraduates: $3352. *Parent loans:* $2,494,646 (100% non-need-based). *Programs:* Federal Direct (Subsidized and Unsubsidized Stafford, PLUS), Perkins, state, college/university.

**WORK-STUDY** *Federal work-study:* Total amount: $1,730,594; 856 jobs averaging $2022. *State or other work-study/employment:* Total amount: $643,673 (100% need-based). 311 part-time jobs averaging $2070.

**APPLYING FOR FINANCIAL AID** *Required financial aid forms:* FAFSA, CSS Financial Aid PROFILE, noncustodial (divorced/separated) parent's statement, federal income tax form(s), W-2 forms. *Financial aid deadline (priority):* 2/13. *Notification date:* 4/1. Students must reply by 5/1.

**CONTACT** Mr. Scott J. Juedes, Director of Student Financial Services, Wellesley College, 106 Central Street, Wellesley, MA 02481-8203, 781-283-2360. *Fax:* 781-283-3946. *E-mail:* sfs@wellesley.edu.
*Website:* http://www.wellesley.edu/.

---

# WELLS COLLEGE
## Aurora, NY

| Tuition & fees: $37,500 | Average undergraduate aid package: $31,365 |
| --- | --- |

**ABOUT THE INSTITUTION** Independent, coed. *Awards:* bachelor's degrees. 34 undergraduate majors. *Total enrollment:* 551. Undergraduates: 552. Freshmen: 163. Federal methodology is used as a basis for awarding need-based institutional aid.

**UNDERGRADUATE EXPENSES** for 2015–2016 *Application fee:* $40. *Comprehensive fee:* $50,500 includes full-time tuition ($36,000), mandatory fees ($1500), and room and board ($13,000). Room and board charges vary according to housing facility.

**FRESHMAN FINANCIAL AID (Fall 2014, est.)** 161 applied for aid; of those 96% were deemed to have need. 100% of freshmen with need received aid; of those 10% had need fully met. *Average percent of need met:* 82% (excluding resources awarded to replace EFC). *Average financial aid package:* $33,910 (excluding resources awarded to replace EFC). 4% of all full-time freshmen had no need and received non-need-based gift aid.

**UNDERGRADUATE FINANCIAL AID (Fall 2014, est.)** 515 applied for aid; of those 95% were deemed to have need. 100% of undergraduates with need received aid; of those 10% had need fully met. *Average percent of need met:* 77% (excluding resources awarded to replace EFC). *Average financial aid package:* $31,365 (excluding resources awarded to replace EFC). 7% of all full-time undergraduates had no need and received non-need-based gift aid.

**GIFT AID (NEED-BASED)** *Total amount:* $13,337,435 (9% federal, 6% state, 83% institutional, 2% external sources). *Receiving aid:* Freshmen: 85% (139); all full-time undergraduates: 87% (462). *Average award:* Freshmen: $29,886; Undergraduates: $31,797. *Scholarships, grants, and awards:* Federal Pell, FSEOG, state, private, college/university gift aid from institutional funds.

**GIFT AID (NON-NEED-BASED)** *Total amount:* $685,410 (98% institutional, 2% external sources). *Receiving aid:* Freshmen: 83% (136). Undergraduates: 77% (411). *Average award:* Freshmen: $22,071. Undergraduates: $19,183. *Scholarships, grants, and awards by category:* Academic interests/achievement: 423 awards ($6,642,400 total): general academic interests/achievements. Special achievements/activities: 82 awards ($883,500 total): leadership. Special characteristics: 19 awards ($59,250 total): children and siblings of alumni, international students. *Tuition waivers:* Full or partial for employees or children of employees, senior citizens.

**LOANS** *Student loans:* $4,335,549 (40% need-based, 60% non-need-based). 88% of past graduating class borrowed through all loan programs. *Average indebtedness per student:* $36,498. *Average need-based loan:* Freshmen: $3232. Undergraduates: $3912. *Parent loans:* $1,306,920 (100% non-need-based). *Programs:* Federal Direct (Subsidized and Unsubsidized Stafford, PLUS), Perkins, state.

**WORK-STUDY** *Federal work-study:* Total amount: $100,000; 55 jobs averaging $1850. *State or other work-study/employment:* Total amount: $701,590 (95% need-based, 5% non-need-based). 240 part-time jobs averaging $1850.

**APPLYING FOR FINANCIAL AID** *Required financial aid form:* FAFSA. *Financial aid deadline (priority):* 2/15. *Notification date:* 3/1. Students must reply by 5/1.

**CONTACT** Ms. Laura Burns, Director of Financial Aid, Wells College, Route 90, Aurora, NY 13026, 315-364-3289 or toll-free 800-952-9355. *Fax:* 315-364-3445. *E-mail:* lburns@wells.edu.
*Website:* http://www.wells.edu/.

---

# WENTWORTH INSTITUTE OF TECHNOLOGY
## Boston, MA

| Tuition & fees: $30,765 | Average undergraduate aid package: N/A |
| --- | --- |

**ABOUT THE INSTITUTION** Independent, coed. *Awards:* certificates, associate, bachelor's, and master's degrees. 23 undergraduate majors. *Total enrollment:* 4,558. Undergraduates: 4,329. Freshmen: 1,085. Federal methodology is used as a basis for awarding need-based institutional aid.

**UNDERGRADUATE EXPENSES** for 2015–2016 *Application fee:* $50. *Comprehensive fee:* $43,605 includes full-time tuition ($29,320), mandatory fees ($1445), and room and board ($12,840). Room and board charges vary according to board plan and housing facility. *Part-time tuition:* $915 per credit hour. *Part-time fees:* $465 per credit hour. Part-time tuition and fees vary according to course load and degree level.

**GIFT AID (NEED-BASED)** *Total amount:* $14,300,086 (32% federal, 5% state, 63% institutional). *Scholarships, grants, and awards:* Federal Pell, FSEOG, state, private, college/university gift aid from institutional funds.

**GIFT AID (NON-NEED-BASED)** *Total amount:* $28,329,006 (97% institutional, 3% external sources). *Tuition waivers:* Full or partial for employees or children of employees. *ROTC:* Army cooperative, Air Force cooperative.

**LOANS** *Student loans:* $33,153,715 (25% need-based, 75% non-need-based). *Parent loans:* $7,111,742 (100% non-need-based). *Programs:* Federal Direct (Subsidized and Unsubsidized Stafford, PLUS), Perkins, state.

**WORK-STUDY** *Federal work-study:* Total amount: $296,817; jobs available. *State or other work-study/employment:* Total amount: $201,789 (100% need-based). Part-time jobs available.

**APPLYING FOR FINANCIAL AID** *Required financial aid form:* FAFSA. *Financial aid deadline (priority):* 3/1. *Notification date:* Continuous beginning 3/15. Students must reply within 2 weeks of notification.

**CONTACT** Anne-Marie Caruso, Director of Financial Aid, Wentworth Institute of Technology, 550 Huntington Avenue, Boston, MA 02115-5998, 617-989-4174 or toll-free 800-556-0610. *Fax:* 617-989-4201. *E-mail:* carusoa@wit.edu.
*Website:* http://www.wit.edu/.

# WESLEYAN COLLEGE
## Macon, GA

| Tuition & fees: $19,900 | Average undergraduate aid package: $19,067 |
|---|---|

**ABOUT THE INSTITUTION** Independent United Methodist, undergraduate: women only; graduate: coed. *Awards:* bachelor's and master's degrees. 31 undergraduate majors. *Total enrollment:* 715. Undergraduates: 665. Freshmen: 106. Federal methodology is used as a basis for awarding need-based institutional aid.

**UNDERGRADUATE EXPENSES for 2015–2016** *Application fee:* $30. *One-time required fee:* $250. *Comprehensive fee:* $28,700 includes full-time tuition ($19,750), mandatory fees ($150), and room and board ($8800). Full-time tuition and fees vary according to degree level, program, and reciprocity agreements. Room and board charges vary according to board plan and housing facility. *Part-time tuition:* $470 per credit hour. *Part-time fees:* $5 per credit hour. Part-time tuition and fees vary according to class time, degree level, program, and reciprocity agreements.

**FRESHMAN FINANCIAL AID (Fall 2013)** 68 applied for aid; of those 87% were deemed to have need. 93% of freshmen with need received aid; of those 11% had need fully met. *Average percent of need met:* 69% (excluding resources awarded to replace EFC). *Average financial aid package:* $17,453 (excluding resources awarded to replace EFC). 40% of all full-time freshmen had no need and received non-need-based gift aid.

**UNDERGRADUATE FINANCIAL AID (Fall 2013)** 277 applied for aid; of those 94% were deemed to have need. 98% of undergraduates with need received aid; of those 11% had need fully met. *Average percent of need met:* 71% (excluding resources awarded to replace EFC). *Average financial aid package:* $19,067 (excluding resources awarded to replace EFC). 32% of all full-time undergraduates had no need and received non-need-based gift aid.

**GIFT AID (NEED-BASED)** *Total amount:* $4,370,744 (28% federal, 13% state, 56% institutional, 3% external sources). *Receiving aid:* Freshmen: 36% (45); all full-time undergraduates: 61% (253). *Average award:* Freshmen: $13,660; Undergraduates: $14,845. *Scholarships, grants, and awards:* Federal Pell, FSEOG, state, private, college/university gift aid from institutional funds.

**GIFT AID (NON-NEED-BASED)** *Total amount:* $1,971,847 (1% federal, 8% state, 89% institutional, 2% external sources). *Receiving aid:* Freshmen: 5% (6). Undergraduates: 5% (21). *Average award:* Freshmen: $9526. Undergraduates: $11,617. *Scholarships, grants, and awards by category: Academic interests/ achievement:* biological sciences, English, general academic interests/achievements, religion/biblical studies. *Creative arts/performance:* art/fine arts, music, theater/drama. *Special achievements/activities:* community service, general special achievements/ activities, leadership, memberships, religious involvement. *Special characteristics:* adult students, children and siblings of alumni, children of current students, children of faculty/staff, ethnic background, first-generation college students, general special characteristics, handicapped students, international students, parents of current students, relatives of clergy, religious affiliation, siblings of current students, spouses of current students, veterans. *Tuition waivers:* Full or partial for employees or children of employees, senior citizens. *ROTC:* Army cooperative.

**LOANS** *Student loans:* $2,773,919 (87% need-based, 13% non-need-based). 52% of past graduating class borrowed through all loan programs. *Average indebtedness per student:* $32,755. *Average need-based loan:* Freshmen: $4531. Undergraduates: $4771. *Parent loans:* $332,675 (72% need-based, 28% non-need-based). *Programs:* Federal Direct (Subsidized and Unsubsidized Stafford, PLUS), Perkins, state, college/university, alternative loans.

**WORK-STUDY** *Federal work-study:* 25 jobs averaging $1472. *State or other work-study/employment:* Total amount: $247,041 (46% need-based, 54% non-need-based). 172 part-time jobs averaging $1433.

**APPLYING FOR FINANCIAL AID** *Required financial aid forms:* FAFSA, institution's own form, state aid form. *Financial aid deadline:* 6/15 (priority: 4/15). *Notification date:* Continuous beginning 3/1. Students must reply by 5/1 or within 3 weeks of notification.

**CONTACT** Danielle Lodge, Director of Financial Aid, Wesleyan College, 4760 Forsyth Road, Macon, GA 31210-4462, 478-757-5205 or toll-free 800-447-6610. *Fax:* 478-757-3780. *E-mail:* financialaid@wesleyancollege.edu. *Website:* http://www.wesleyancollege.edu/.

# WESLEYAN UNIVERSITY
## Middletown, CT

| Tuition & fees: $48,974 | Average undergraduate aid package: $45,507 |
|---|---|

**ABOUT THE INSTITUTION** Independent, coed. *Awards:* certificates, bachelor's, master's, and doctoral degrees. 45 undergraduate majors. *Total enrollment:* 3,224. Undergraduates: 2,928. Freshmen: 750. Institutional methodology is used as a basis for awarding need-based institutional aid.

**UNDERGRADUATE EXPENSES for 2015–2016** *Application fee:* $55. *Comprehensive fee:* $62,478 includes full-time tuition ($48,704), mandatory fees ($270), and room and board ($13,504). Room and board charges vary according to board plan, housing facility, and student level.

**FRESHMAN FINANCIAL AID (Fall 2014, est.)** 381 applied for aid; of those 90% were deemed to have need. 100% of freshmen with need received aid; of those 100% had need fully met. *Average percent of need met:* 100% (excluding resources awarded to replace EFC). *Average financial aid package:* $45,001 (excluding resources awarded to replace EFC). 1% of all full-time freshmen had no need and received non-need-based gift aid.

**UNDERGRADUATE FINANCIAL AID (Fall 2014, est.)** 1,430 applied for aid; of those 94% were deemed to have need. 100% of undergraduates with need received aid; of those 100% had need fully met. *Average percent of need met:* 100% (excluding resources awarded to replace EFC). *Average financial aid package:* $45,507 (excluding resources awarded to replace EFC). 1% of all full-time undergraduates had no need and received non-need-based gift aid.

**GIFT AID (NEED-BASED)** *Total amount:* $52,500,010 (7% federal, 91% institutional, 2% external sources). *Receiving aid:* Freshmen: 43% (323); all full-time undergraduates: 44% (1,268). *Average award:* Freshmen: $42,797; Undergraduates: $41,532. *Scholarships, grants, and awards:* Federal Pell, FSEOG, state, private, college/university gift aid from institutional funds.

**GIFT AID (NON-NEED-BASED)** *Total amount:* $1,592,375 (63% institutional, 37% external sources). *Average award:* Freshmen: $48,282. Undergraduates: $48,032. *Scholarships, grants, and awards by category: Special characteristics:* international students. *ROTC:* Air Force cooperative.

**LOANS** *Student loans:* $8,245,125 (65% need-based, 35% non-need-based). 39% of past graduating class borrowed through all loan programs. *Average indebtedness per student:* $22,959. *Average need-based loan:* Freshmen: $3328. Undergraduates: $4688. *Parent loans:* $3,811,062 (100% non-need-based). *Programs:* Federal Direct (Subsidized and Unsubsidized Stafford, PLUS), Perkins, college/university.

**WORK-STUDY** *Federal work-study:* Total amount: $2,739,930; jobs available. *State or other work-study/employment:* Total amount: $256,731 (100% need-based). Part-time jobs available.

**APPLYING FOR FINANCIAL AID** *Required financial aid forms:* FAFSA, CSS Financial Aid PROFILE, noncustodial (divorced/separated) parent's statement, parent and student tax forms, W-2 forms, business tax returns. *Financial aid deadline:* 2/15. *Notification date:* 4/1. Students must reply by 5/1.

**CONTACT** John Gudvangen, Director of Financial Aid, Wesleyan University, 237 High Street, Middletown, CT 06459-0260, 860-685-2800. *Fax:* 860-685-2801. *E-mail:* finaid@wesleyan.edu. *Website:* http://www.wesleyan.edu/.

# WESLEY COLLEGE
## Dover, DE

**CONTACT** Mr. Michael Hall, Director of Student Financial Planning, Wesley College, 120 North State Street, Dover, DE 19901-3875, 302-736-2334 or toll-free 800-937-5398. *Fax:* 302-736-2594. *E-mail:* halljmic@wesley.edu. *Website:* http://www.wesley.edu/.

# WEST CHESTER UNIVERSITY OF PENNSYLVANIA
## West Chester, PA

| Tuition & fees (PA res): $9054 | Average undergraduate aid package: $7669 |
|---|---|

**ABOUT THE INSTITUTION** State-supported, coed. *Awards:* certificates, bachelor's, master's, and doctoral degrees. 50 undergraduate majors. *Total enrollment:* 16,086. Undergraduates: 13,844. Freshmen: 2,351. Federal methodology is used as a basis for awarding need-based institutional aid.

**UNDERGRADUATE EXPENSES** for 2015–2016 *Application fee:* $45. *Tuition, state resident:* full-time $6820; part-time $284 per credit. *Tuition, nonresident:* full-time $17,050; part-time $710 per credit. *Required fees:* full-time $2234; $97.24 per credit. Full-time tuition and fees vary according to course load. Part-time tuition and fees vary according to course load. *College room and board:* $8042; *Room only:* $4848. Room and board charges vary according to board plan and housing facility.

**FRESHMAN FINANCIAL AID (Fall 2013)** 2,062 applied for aid; of those 72% were deemed to have need. 100% of freshmen with need received aid; of those 7% had need fully met. *Average percent of need met:* 41% (excluding resources awarded to replace EFC). *Average financial aid package:* $6983 (excluding resources awarded to replace EFC). 2% of all full-time freshmen had no need and received non-need-based gift aid.

**UNDERGRADUATE FINANCIAL AID (Fall 2013)** 9,757 applied for aid; of those 78% were deemed to have need. 100% of undergraduates with need received aid; of those 9% had need fully met. *Average percent of need met:* 50% (excluding resources awarded to replace EFC). *Average financial aid package:* $7669 (excluding resources awarded to replace EFC). 1% of all full-time undergraduates had no need and received non-need-based gift aid.

**GIFT AID (NEED-BASED)** *Total amount:* $27,553,757 (50% federal, 33% state, 9% institutional, 8% external sources). *Receiving aid:* Freshmen: 30% (694); all full-time undergraduates: 32% (4,011). *Average award:* Freshmen: $5827; Undergraduates: $5562. *Scholarships, grants, and awards:* Federal Pell, FSEOG, state, private, college/university gift aid from institutional funds.

**GIFT AID (NON-NEED-BASED)** *Total amount:* $1,785,571 (2% state, 43% institutional, 55% external sources). *Receiving aid:* Freshmen: 14% (329). Undergraduates: 9% (1,096). *Average award:* Freshmen: $4595. Undergraduates: $4128. *Scholarships, grants, and awards by category:* Academic interests/achievement: business, general academic interests/achievements, mathematics, social sciences. Creative arts/performance: art/fine arts, music, theater/drama. Special achievements/activities: leadership. Special characteristics: children of faculty/staff. *Tuition waivers:* Full or partial for employees or children of employees, senior citizens. *ROTC:* Army, Air Force cooperative.

**LOANS** *Student loans:* $96,675,606 (79% need-based, 21% non-need-based). 74% of past graduating class borrowed through all loan programs. *Average indebtedness per student:* $30,881. *Average need-based loan:* Freshmen: $3769. Undergraduates: $4425. *Parent loans:* $18,952,460 (100% non-need-based). *Programs:* Federal Direct (Subsidized and Unsubsidized Stafford, PLUS), Perkins, Federal Nursing.

**WORK-STUDY** *Federal work-study:* jobs available. *State or other work-study/employment:* Part-time jobs available.

**ATHLETIC AWARDS** Total amount: $1,022,173 (81% need-based, 19% non-need-based).

**APPLYING FOR FINANCIAL AID** *Required financial aid form:* FAFSA. *Financial aid deadline:* Continuous. *Notification date:* Continuous beginning 4/1. Students must reply within 4 weeks of notification.

**CONTACT** Mr. Dana Parker, Financial Aid Director, West Chester University of Pennsylvania, 25 University Avenue, Suite 030, West Chester, PA 19383, 610-436-2627 or toll-free 877-315-2165 (in-state). *Fax:* 610-436-2574. *E-mail:* finaid@wcupa.edu. *Website:* http://www.wcupa.edu/.

# WEST COAST UNIVERSITY
## Anaheim, CA

**CONTACT** Financial Aid Office, West Coast University, 1477 S. Manchester Avenue, Anaheim, CA 92802, 714-782-1700. *Website:* http://westcoastuniversity.edu/.

# WEST COAST UNIVERSITY
## North Hollywood, CA

**CONTACT** Financial Aid Office, West Coast University, 12215 Victory Boulevard, North Hollywood, CA 91606, 323-315-5207 or toll-free 866-508-2684. *Website:* http://www.westcoastuniversity.edu/.

# WEST COAST UNIVERSITY
## Ontario, CA

**CONTACT** Financial Aid Office, West Coast University, 2855 E. Guasti Road, Ontario, CA 91761, 909-467-6100. *Website:* http://westcoastuniversity.edu/.

# WEST COAST UNIVERSITY
## Dallas, TX

**CONTACT** Financial Aid Office, West Coast University, 8435 N. Stemmons Freeway, Dallas, TX 75247, 214-453-4533 or toll-free 866-508-2684. *Website:* http://www.westcoastuniversity.edu/.

# WESTERN CAROLINA UNIVERSITY
## Cullowhee, NC

| Tuition & fees (NC res): $6531 | Average undergraduate aid package: $9507 |
|---|---|

**ABOUT THE INSTITUTION** State-supported, coed. *Awards:* certificates, bachelor's, master's, and doctoral degrees. 68 undergraduate majors. *Total enrollment:* 10,382. Undergraduates: 8,787. Freshmen: 1,756. Federal methodology is used as a basis for awarding need-based institutional aid.

**UNDERGRADUATE EXPENSES** for 2015–2016 *Application fee:* $55. *Tuition, state resident:* full-time $3669. *Tuition, nonresident:* full-time $14,062. *Required fees:* full-time $2862. Full-time tuition and fees vary according to degree level. Part-time tuition and fees vary according to course load and degree level. *College room and board:* $8016. Room and board charges vary according to board plan and housing facility.

**FRESHMAN FINANCIAL AID (Fall 2013)** 1,420 applied for aid; of those 75% were deemed to have need. 99% of freshmen with need received aid; of those 11% had need fully met. *Average percent of need met:* 62% (excluding resources awarded to replace EFC). *Average financial aid package:* $8709 (excluding resources awarded to replace EFC). 5% of all full-time freshmen had no need and received non-need-based gift aid.

**UNDERGRADUATE FINANCIAL AID (Fall 2013)** 5,882 applied for aid; of those 82% were deemed to have need. 98% of undergraduates with need received aid; of those 13% had need fully met. *Average percent of need met:* 66% (excluding resources awarded to replace EFC). *Average financial aid package:* $9507 (excluding resources awarded to replace EFC). 4% of all full-time undergraduates had no need and received non-need-based gift aid.

**GIFT AID (NEED-BASED)** *Total amount:* $28,805,081 (47% federal, 30% state, 18% institutional, 5% external sources). *Receiving aid:* Freshmen: 64% (1,030); all full-time undergraduates: 64% (4,540). *Average award:* Freshmen: $6141; Undergraduates: $6158. *Scholarships, grants, and awards:* Federal Pell, FSEOG, state, private, college/university gift aid from institutional funds.

**GIFT AID (NON-NEED-BASED)** *Total amount:* $1,712,734 (1% federal, 28% state, 38% institutional, 33% external sources). *Receiving aid:* Freshmen: 2% (36). Undergraduates: 2% (119). *Average award:* Freshmen: $2074. Undergraduates: $1780. *Scholarships, grants, and awards by category:* Academic interests/achievement: biological sciences, business, communication, education, English, general academic interests/achievements, mathematics. Creative arts/performance: art/fine arts, music, theater/drama. Special characteristics: ethnic background, handicapped students, local/state students, members of minority groups.

**LOANS** *Student loans:* $34,694,447 (79% need-based, 21% non-need-based). 73% of past graduating class borrowed through all loan programs. *Average indebtedness*

*per student:* $23,806. *Average need-based loan:* Freshmen: $3315. Undergraduates: $3726. *Parent loans:* $12,236,045 (50% need-based, 50% non-need-based). *Programs:* Federal Direct (Subsidized and Unsubsidized Stafford, PLUS), Perkins.

**WORK-STUDY** *Federal work-study:* jobs available.

**ATHLETIC AWARDS** Total amount: $2,750,693 (60% need-based, 40% non-need-based).

**APPLYING FOR FINANCIAL AID** *Required financial aid forms:* FAFSA, institution's own form. *Financial aid deadline (priority):* 3/15. *Notification date:* Continuous beginning 4/1.

**CONTACT** Ms. Trina F. Orr, Director of Financial Aid, Western Carolina University, 123 Killian Annex, Cullowhee, NC 28723, 828-227-7292 or toll-free 877-WCU4YOU. *Fax:* 828-227-7042. *E-mail:* torr@email.wcu.edu. *Website:* http://www.wcu.edu/.

# WESTERN CONNECTICUT STATE UNIVERSITY
## Danbury, CT

| Tuition & fees (CT res): $9077 | Average undergraduate aid package: N/A |
|---|---|

**ABOUT THE INSTITUTION** State-supported, coed. *Awards:* certificates, associate, bachelor's, master's, and doctoral degrees. 37 undergraduate majors. *Total enrollment:* 6,025. Undergraduates: 5,492. Freshmen: 797. Federal methodology is used as a basis for awarding need-based institutional aid.

**UNDERGRADUATE EXPENSES** for 2015–2016 *Application fee:* $50. *Tuition, state resident:* full-time $4600; part-time $192 per credit. *Tuition, nonresident:* full-time $14,886; part-time $196 per credit. *Required fees:* full-time $4477; $226 per credit. Full-time tuition and fees vary according to course load, program, and reciprocity agreements. *College room and board:* $11,311; *Room only:* $6637. Room and board charges vary according to board plan and housing facility.

**GIFT AID (NEED-BASED)** *Total amount:* $14,693,540 (46% federal, 8% state, 43% institutional, 3% external sources). *Scholarships, grants, and awards:* Federal Pell, FSEOG, state, private, college/university gift aid from institutional funds, Federal Nursing.

**GIFT AID (NON-NEED-BASED)** *Total amount:* $757,940 (100% institutional). *Scholarships, grants, and awards by category:* Academic interests/achievement: general academic interests/achievements. *Tuition walvers:* Full or partial for employees or children of employees, senior citizens. *ROTC:* Army cooperative, Air Force cooperative.

**LOANS** *Student loans:* $24,083,765 (100% need-based). *Parent loans:* $3,248,442 (100% need-based). *Programs:* Federal Direct (Subsidized and Unsubsidized Stafford, PLUS), Perkins.

**WORK-STUDY** *Federal work-study:* jobs available. *State or other work-study/employment:* Part-time jobs available.

**APPLYING FOR FINANCIAL AID** *Required financial aid form:* FAFSA. *Financial aid deadline:* 3/15 (priority: 3/1). *Notification date:* Continuous beginning 3/20. Students must reply by 5/1 or within 3 weeks of notification.

**CONTACT** Melissa Stephens, Director of Student Financial Services, Western Connecticut State University, 181 White Street, Danbury, CT 06810-6860, 203-837-8582 or toll-free 877-837-WCSU. *Fax:* 203-837-8528. *E-mail:* stephensm@wcsu.edu. *Website:* http://www.wcsu.edu/.

# WESTERN GOVERNORS UNIVERSITY
## Salt Lake City, UT

| Tuition & fees: $6070 | Average undergraduate aid package: $5127 |
|---|---|

**ABOUT THE INSTITUTION** Independent, coed. *Awards:* certificates, bachelor's, and master's degrees. 6 undergraduate majors. *Total enrollment:* 57,821. Undergraduates: 44,499. Freshmen: 92. Federal methodology is used as a basis for awarding need-based institutional aid.

**UNDERGRADUATE EXPENSES** for 2015–2016 *Application fee:* $65. *One-time required fee:* $65. *Tuition:* full-time $5780. Full-time tuition and fees vary according to program.

**FRESHMAN FINANCIAL AID (Fall 2013)** 35 applied for aid; of those 86% were deemed to have need. 97% of freshmen with need received aid. *Average percent of need met:* 58% (excluding resources awarded to replace EFC). *Average financial aid package:* $5115 (excluding resources awarded to replace EFC).

**UNDERGRADUATE FINANCIAL AID (Fall 2013)** 23,111 applied for aid; of those 84% were deemed to have need. 96% of undergraduates with need received aid; of those 1% had need fully met. *Average percent of need met:* 55% (excluding resources awarded to replace EFC). *Average financial aid package:* $5127 (excluding resources awarded to replace EFC).

**GIFT AID (NEED-BASED)** *Total amount:* $34,157,831 (95% federal, 3% state, 2% institutional). *Receiving aid:* Freshmen: 56% (29); all full-time undergraduates: 43% (15,172). *Average award:* Freshmen: $3669; Undergraduates: $3673. *Scholarships, grants, and awards:* Federal Pell, FSEOG, state, private, college/university gift aid from institutional funds.

**GIFT AID (NON-NEED-BASED)** *Receiving aid:* Undergraduates: 129.

**LOANS** *Student loans:* $174,066,241 (24% need-based, 76% non-need-based). 81% of past graduating class borrowed through all loan programs. *Average indebtedness per student:* $19,880. *Average need-based loan:* Freshmen: $5471. Undergraduates: $5471. *Parent loans:* $76,855 (100% non-need-based). *Programs:* Federal Direct (Subsidized and Unsubsidized Stafford, PLUS).

**APPLYING FOR FINANCIAL AID** *Required financial aid form:* FAFSA. *Financial aid deadline:* Continuous. *Notification date:* Continuous.

**CONTACT** Robert Collins, Vice President of Financial Aid, Western Governors University, 4001 South 700 East, Suite 700, Salt Lake City, UT 84107, 877-435-7948 or toll-free 866-225-5948. *Fax:* 801-907-7727. *E-mail:* robert.collins@wgu.edu. *Website:* http://www.wgu.edu/.

# WESTERN ILLINOIS UNIVERSITY
## Macomb, IL

| Tuition & fees (IL res): $11,282 | Average undergraduate aid package: $11,221 |
|---|---|

**ABOUT THE INSTITUTION** State-supported, coed. *Awards:* certificates, bachelor's, master's, and doctoral degrees. 67 undergraduate majors. *Total enrollment:* 11,458. Undergraduates: 9,645. Freshmen: 1,605. Federal methodology is used as a basis for awarding need-based institutional aid.

**UNDERGRADUATE EXPENSES** for 2015–2016 *Application fee:* $30. *Tuition, state resident:* full-time $8632; part-time $287.74 per credit hour. *Tuition, nonresident:* full-time $12,948; part-time $431.60 per credit hour. *Required fees:* full-time $2650; $88.30 per credit hour. Full-time tuition and fees vary according to course load and student level. Part-time tuition and fees vary according to course load and student level. *College room and board:* $9450; *Room only:* $5800. Room and board charges vary according to board plan, housing facility, and student level. *Payment plan:* Guaranteed tuition.

**FRESHMAN FINANCIAL AID (Fall 2014, est.)** 1,457 applied for aid; of those 88% were deemed to have need. 99% of freshmen with need received aid; of those 26% had need fully met. *Average percent of need met:* 60% (excluding resources awarded to replace EFC). *Average financial aid package:* $12,206 (excluding resources awarded to replace EFC). 4% of all full-time freshmen had no need and received non-need-based gift aid.

**UNDERGRADUATE FINANCIAL AID (Fall 2014, est.)** 7,363 applied for aid; of those 88% were deemed to have need. 98% of undergraduates with need received aid; of those 29% had need fully met. *Average percent of need met:* 59% (excluding resources awarded to replace EFC). *Average financial aid package:* $11,221 (excluding resources awarded to replace EFC). 2% of all full-time undergraduates had no need and received non-need-based gift aid.

**GIFT AID (NEED-BASED)** *Total amount:* $43,710,678 (46% federal, 37% state, 15% institutional, 2% external sources). *Receiving aid:* Freshmen: 73% (1,151); all full-time undergraduates: 60% (5,174). *Average award:* Freshmen: $9595; Undergraduates: $8595. *Scholarships, grants, and awards:* Federal Pell, FSEOG, state, private, college/university gift aid from institutional funds.

**GIFT AID (NON-NEED-BASED)** *Total amount:* $3,507,747 (1% federal, 32% state, 54% institutional, 13% external sources). *Average award:* Freshmen: $3172. Undergraduates: $2851. *Scholarships, grants, and awards by category:* Academic interests/achievement: 4,928 awards ($5,254,890 total): agriculture, area/ethnic studies, biological sciences, business, communication, computer science, education, engineering/technologies, English, foreign languages, general academic interests/achievements, health fields, home economics, international studies, library science, mathematics, military science, physical sciences, religion/biblical studies, social sciences. Creative arts/performance: 631 awards ($886,926 total): applied art and design, art/fine arts, cinema/film/broadcasting, creative writing, dance, debating, general creative arts/performance, journalism/publications, music, performing arts, theater/drama. Special achievements/activities: 225 awards ($161,022 total): community service, general special achievements/activities, leadership. Special characteristics: 1,820 awards ($2,950,440 total): children of faculty/staff, general special characteristics, international students, members of minority groups, veterans' children. Tuition waivers: Full or partial for employees or children of employees, senior citizens. ROTC: Army.

LOANS Student loans: $61,760,370 (50% need-based, 50% non-need-based). 80% of past graduating class borrowed through all loan programs. Average indebtedness per student: $28,785. Average need-based loan: Freshmen: $3575. Undergraduates: $4316. Parent loans: $11,816,972 (81% need-based, 19% non-need-based). Programs: Federal Direct (Subsidized and Unsubsidized Stafford, PLUS), Perkins, college/university.

WORK-STUDY Federal work-study: Total amount: $401,617; jobs available. State or other work-study/employment: Total amount: $2,107,505 (84% need-based, 16% non-need-based). Part-time jobs available.

ATHLETIC AWARDS Total amount: $3,532,907 (51% need-based, 49% non-need-based).

APPLYING FOR FINANCIAL AID Required financial aid form: FAFSA. Financial aid deadline (priority): 2/15. Notification date: Continuous beginning 1/15.

CONTACT Office of Financial Aid, Western Illinois University, 1 University Circle, Macomb, IL 61455-1390, 309-298-2446 or toll-free 877-742-5948. Fax: 309-298-2353. E-mail: finaid@wiu.edu. Website: http://www.wiu.edu/.

# WESTERN INTERNATIONAL UNIVERSITY
## Phoenix, AZ

CONTACT Ms. Ella Owen, Compliance Officer, Western International University, 9215 North Black Canyon Highway, Phoenix, AZ 85021, 602-429-1056. Fax: 602-383-9812. E-mail: ella.owen@west.edu. Website: http://www.west.edu/.

# WESTERN KENTUCKY UNIVERSITY
## Bowling Green, KY

| Tuition & fees (KY res): $9140 | Average undergraduate aid package: $13,904 |
| --- | --- |

ABOUT THE INSTITUTION State-supported, coed. Awards: certificates, associate, bachelor's, master's, and doctoral degrees. 99 undergraduate majors. Total enrollment: 20,171. Undergraduates: 17,452. Freshmen: 3,136. Federal methodology is used as a basis for awarding need-based institutional aid.

UNDERGRADUATE EXPENSES for 2015–2016 Application fee: $40. Tuition, state resident: full-time $9140; part-time $381 per credit hour. Tuition, nonresident: full-time $23,352; part-time $973 per credit hour. Full-time tuition and fees vary according to course load, location, program, and reciprocity agreements. Part-time tuition and fees vary according to course load, location, program, and reciprocity agreements. College room and board: $7171; Room only: $4180. Room and board charges vary according to board plan and housing facility.

FRESHMAN FINANCIAL AID (Fall 2013) 2,636 applied for aid; of those 78% were deemed to have need. 99% of freshmen with need received aid; of those 29% had need fully met. Average percent of need met: 29% (excluding resources awarded to replace EFC). Average financial aid package: $13,575 (excluding resources awarded to replace EFC). 10% of all full-time freshmen had no need and received non-need-based gift aid.

UNDERGRADUATE FINANCIAL AID (Fall 2013) 10,622 applied for aid; of those 82% were deemed to have need. 99% of undergraduates with need received aid; of those 28% had need fully met. Average percent of need met: 28% (excluding resources awarded to replace EFC). Average financial aid package: $13,904 (excluding resources awarded to replace EFC). 10% of all full-time undergraduates had no need and received non-need-based gift aid.

GIFT AID (NEED-BASED) Total amount: $33,443,535 (79% federal, 14% state, 7% institutional). Receiving aid: Freshmen: 43% (1,308); all full-time undergraduates: 44% (5,831). Average award: Freshmen: $5161; Undergraduates: $4941. Scholarships, grants, and awards: Federal Pell, FSEOG, state, private, college/university gift aid from institutional funds, United Negro College Fund.

GIFT AID (NON-NEED-BASED) Total amount: $35,437,648 (9% federal, 32% state, 54% institutional, 5% external sources). Receiving aid: Freshmen: 58% (1,764). Undergraduates: 41% (5,441). Average award: Freshmen: $6418. Undergraduates: $5812. Scholarships, grants, and awards by category: Academic interests/achievement: 3,089 awards ($13,446,403 total): agriculture, biological sciences, business, communication, education, engineering/technologies, English, foreign languages, general academic interests/achievements, health fields, home economics, library science, mathematics, military science, physical sciences, premedicine, social sciences. Creative arts/performance: 525 awards ($1,427,717 total): art/fine arts, cinema/film/broadcasting, dance, debating, general creative arts/performance, journalism/publications, music, theater/drama. Special achievements/activities: 980 awards ($1,496,996 total): general special achievements/activities, leadership, memberships. Special characteristics: 2,771 awards ($4,745,804 total): adult students, children of union members/company employees, ethnic background, general special characteristics, handicapped students, international students, local/state students, members of minority groups, out-of-state students, religious affiliation, veterans, veterans' children. Tuition waivers: Full or partial for children of alumni, employees or children of employees, senior citizens. ROTC: Army, Air Force cooperative.

LOANS Student loans: $69,243,676 (42% need-based, 58% non-need-based). 62% of past graduating class borrowed through all loan programs. Average indebtedness per student: $26,768. Average need-based loan: Freshmen: $3055. Undergraduates: $3937. Parent loans: $12,725,121 (100% non-need-based). Programs: Federal Direct (Subsidized and Unsubsidized Stafford, PLUS), Perkins.

WORK-STUDY Federal work-study: 751 jobs averaging $2648. State or other work-study/employment: Total amount: $4,565,281 (100% non-need-based). 1,787 part-time jobs averaging $2563.

ATHLETIC AWARDS Total amount: $6,094,231 (100% non-need-based).

APPLYING FOR FINANCIAL AID Required financial aid form: FAFSA. Financial aid deadline (priority): 2/15. Notification date: Continuous beginning 3/1.

CONTACT Cindy Burnette, Director of Student Financial Assistance, Western Kentucky University, Potter Hall, Room 317, Bowling Green, KY 42101-1018, 270-745-2758 or toll-free 800-495-8463. Fax: 270-745-6586. E-mail: cindy.burnette@wku.edu. Website: http://www.wku.edu/.

# WESTERN MICHIGAN UNIVERSITY
## Kalamazoo, MI

| Tuition & fees (MI res): $10,685 | Average undergraduate aid package: $14,400 |
| --- | --- |

ABOUT THE INSTITUTION State-supported, coed. Awards: certificates, bachelor's, master's, and doctoral degrees. 139 undergraduate majors. Total enrollment: 23,914. Undergraduates: 18,889. Freshmen: 3,012. Federal methodology is used as a basis for awarding need-based institutional aid.

UNDERGRADUATE EXPENSES for 2015–2016 Application fee: $40. One-time required fee: $300. Tuition, state resident: full-time $9794; part-time $338.70 per credit hour. Tuition, nonresident: full-time $24,026; part-time $830.90 per credit hour. Required fees: full-time $891; $242.50 per term. Full-time tuition and fees vary according to course load, location, program, and student level. Part-time tuition and fees vary according to course load, location, program, and student level. College room and board: $8943; Room only: $4613. Room and board charges vary according to board plan.

FRESHMAN FINANCIAL AID (Fall 2013) 2,750 applied for aid; of those 77% were deemed to have need. 100% of freshmen with need received aid; of those 25% had need fully met. Average percent of need met: 79% (excluding resources awarded to replace EFC). Average financial aid package: $15,300 (excluding resources awarded to replace EFC). 5% of all full-time freshmen had no need and received non-need-based gift aid.

**UNDERGRADUATE FINANCIAL AID (Fall 2013)** 14,150 applied for aid; of those 83% were deemed to have need. 100% of undergraduates with need received aid; of those 20% had need fully met. *Average percent of need met:* 75% (excluding resources awarded to replace EFC). *Average financial aid package:* $14,400 (excluding resources awarded to replace EFC). 3% of all full-time undergraduates had no need and received non-need-based gift aid.

**GIFT AID (NEED-BASED)** *Total amount:* $44,414,459 (68% federal, 2% state, 30% institutional). *Receiving aid:* Freshmen: 44% (1,475); all full-time undergraduates: 42% (8,150). *Average award:* Freshmen: $5000; Undergraduates: $5300. *Scholarships, grants, and awards:* Federal Pell, FSEOG, state, private, college/university gift aid from institutional funds.

**GIFT AID (NON-NEED-BASED)** *Total amount:* $24,444,731 (70% institutional, 30% external sources). *Receiving aid:* Freshmen: 39% (1,325). Undergraduates: 23% (4,400). *Average award:* Freshmen: $4100. Undergraduates: $3300. *Scholarships, grants, and awards by category:* Academic interests/achievement: general academic interests/achievements. Creative arts/performance: art/fine arts, dance, general creative arts/performance, music, theater/drama. Special characteristics: children and siblings of alumni, children of faculty/staff, international students, local/state students, out-of-state students, previous college experience, veterans. *Tuition waivers:* Full or partial for employees or children of employees, senior citizens. *ROTC:* Army.

**LOANS** *Student loans:* $114,646,201 (61% need-based, 39% non-need-based). 64% of past graduating class borrowed through all loan programs. *Average indebtedness per student:* $32,720. *Average need-based loan:* Freshmen: $2600. Undergraduates: $3700. *Parent loans:* $22,552,816 (50% need-based, 50% non-need-based). *Programs:* Federal Direct (Subsidized and Unsubsidized Stafford, PLUS), Perkins, private loans.

**WORK-STUDY** *Federal work-study:* jobs available. *State or other work-study/employment:* Part-time jobs available.

**ATHLETIC AWARDS** Total amount: $7,205,843 (100% non-need-based).

**APPLYING FOR FINANCIAL AID** *Required financial aid form:* FAFSA. *Financial aid deadline (priority):* 3/1. *Notification date:* Continuous beginning 3/15.

**CONTACT** Mr. Mark Delorey, Director of Financial Aid, Western Michigan University, Faunce Student Services Building, Room 3306, 1903 West Michigan Avenue, Kalamazoo, MI 49008-5337, 269-387-6000. *E-mail:* finaid-info@wmich.edu. *Website:* http://www.wmich.edu/.

# WESTERN NEW ENGLAND UNIVERSITY
## Springfield, MA

| Tuition & fees: $33,466 | Average undergraduate aid package: $23,667 |
|---|---|

**ABOUT THE INSTITUTION** Independent, coed. *Awards:* certificates, associate, bachelor's, master's, and doctoral degrees. 48 undergraduate majors. *Total enrollment:* 3,966. Undergraduates: 2,732. Freshmen: 757. Federal methodology is used as a basis for awarding need-based institutional aid.

**UNDERGRADUATE EXPENSES for 2015–2016** *Application fee:* $40. *Comprehensive fee:* $46,154 includes full-time tuition ($31,200), mandatory fees ($2266), and room and board ($12,688). Full-time tuition and fees vary according to course load and program. Room and board charges vary according to board plan and housing facility. *Part-time tuition:* $588 per credit hour. Part-time tuition and fees vary according to course load and program. *Payment plan:* Tuition prepayment.

**FRESHMAN FINANCIAL AID (Fall 2014, est.)** 696 applied for aid; of those 90% were deemed to have need. 100% of freshmen with need received aid; of those 11% had need fully met. *Average percent of need met:* 73% (excluding resources awarded to replace EFC). *Average financial aid package:* $25,375 (excluding resources awarded to replace EFC). 13% of all full-time freshmen had no need and received non-need-based gift aid.

**UNDERGRADUATE FINANCIAL AID (Fall 2014, est.)** 2,474 applied for aid; of those 83% were deemed to have need. 99% of undergraduates with need received aid; of those 11% had need fully met. *Average percent of need met:* 70% (excluding resources awarded to replace EFC). *Average financial aid package:* $23,667 (excluding resources awarded to replace EFC). 15% of all full-time undergraduates had no need and received non-need-based gift aid.

**GIFT AID (NEED-BASED)** *Total amount:* $36,252,616 (13% federal, 2% state, 83% institutional, 2% external sources). *Receiving aid:* Freshmen: 84% (628); all full-time undergraduates: 80% (2,042). *Average award:* Freshmen: $20,212; Undergraduates: $18,377. *Scholarships, grants, and awards:* Federal Pell, FSEOG, state, private, college/university gift aid from institutional funds.

**GIFT AID (NON-NEED-BASED)** *Total amount:* $3,553,150 (8% federal, 90% institutional, 2% external sources). *Receiving aid:* Freshmen: 6% (42). Undergraduates: 5% (133). *Average award:* Freshmen: $12,114. Undergraduates: $11,817. *Scholarships, grants, and awards by category:* Academic interests/achievement: general academic interests/achievements. Creative arts/performance: music. Special characteristics: children of faculty/staff, children of union members/company employees, siblings of current students. *Tuition waivers:* Full or partial for employees or children of employees, senior citizens. *ROTC:* Army, Air Force cooperative.

**LOANS** *Student loans:* $23,098,285 (94% need-based, 6% non-need-based). *Average need-based loan:* Freshmen: $3505. Undergraduates: $4184. *Parent loans:* $8,152,256 (94% need-based, 6% non-need-based). *Programs:* Federal Direct (Subsidized and Unsubsidized Stafford, PLUS), Perkins.

**WORK-STUDY** *Federal work-study:* Total amount: $2,263,567; 894 jobs averaging $1548. *State or other work-study/employment:* Total amount: $700,000 (100% non-need-based). 590 part-time jobs averaging $1068.

**APPLYING FOR FINANCIAL AID** *Required financial aid forms:* FAFSA, IRS Data Retrieval. *Financial aid deadline (priority):* 4/15. *Notification date:* Continuous beginning 3/1. Students must reply by 5/1 or within 2 weeks of notification.

**CONTACT** Mrs. Kathy M. Chambers, Director of Financial Aid, Western New England University, 1215 Wilbraham Road, Springfield, MA 01119-2684, 413-796-2080 or toll-free 800-325-1122 Ext. 1321. *Fax:* 413-796-2081. *E-mail:* finaid@wne.edu. *Website:* http://www.wne.edu/.

# WESTERN NEW MEXICO UNIVERSITY
## Silver City, NM

| Tuition & fees: N/R | Average undergraduate aid package: $2893 |
|---|---|

**ABOUT THE INSTITUTION** State-supported, coed. 58 undergraduate majors. Federal methodology is used as a basis for awarding need-based institutional aid.

**FRESHMAN FINANCIAL AID (Fall 2014, est.)** 289 applied for aid; of those 96% were deemed to have need. 90% of freshmen with need received aid; of those 11% had need fully met. *Average percent of need met:* 36% (excluding resources awarded to replace EFC). *Average financial aid package:* $2759 (excluding resources awarded to replace EFC). 4% of all full-time freshmen had no need and received non-need-based gift aid.

**UNDERGRADUATE FINANCIAL AID (Fall 2014, est.)** 1,283 applied for aid; of those 99% were deemed to have need. 95% of undergraduates with need received aid; of those 13% had need fully met. *Average percent of need met:* 38% (excluding resources awarded to replace EFC). *Average financial aid package:* $2893 (excluding resources awarded to replace EFC). 2% of all full-time undergraduates had no need and received non-need-based gift aid.

**GIFT AID (NEED-BASED)** *Total amount:* $7,614,652 (95% federal, 4% state, 1% institutional). *Receiving aid:* Freshmen: 63% (207); all full-time undergraduates: 60% (1,002). *Average award:* Freshmen: $2688; Undergraduates: $2789. *Scholarships, grants, and awards:* Federal Pell, FSEOG, state, private, college/university gift aid from institutional funds.

**GIFT AID (NON-NEED-BASED)** *Total amount:* $939,575 (23% federal, 42% state, 19% institutional, 16% external sources). *Receiving aid:* Freshmen: 43% (139). Undergraduates: 43% (715). *Average award:* Freshmen: $2527. Undergraduates: $2810. *Scholarships, grants, and awards by category:* Academic interests/achievement: general academic interests/achievements. Creative arts/performance: performing arts. Special achievements/activities: general special achievements/activities. Special characteristics: general special characteristics, veterans.

**LOANS** *Student loans:* $4,341,170 (97% need-based, 3% non-need-based). 62% of past graduating class borrowed through all loan programs. *Average indebtedness per student:* $29,758. *Average need-based loan:* Freshmen: $1690. Undergraduates: $2089. *Parent loans:* $118,133 (100% non-need-based). *Programs:* Federal Direct (Subsidized and Unsubsidized Stafford, PLUS), Perkins, state, college/university.

**WORK-STUDY** *Federal work-study:* Total amount: $71,608; jobs available. *State or other work-study/employment:* Total amount: $208,092 (32% need-based, 68% non-need-based). Part-time jobs available.
**ATHLETIC AWARDS** Total amount: $644,627 (100% non-need-based).
**APPLYING FOR FINANCIAL AID** *Required financial aid forms:* FAFSA, institution's own form. *Financial aid deadline (priority):* 3/1. *Notification date:* Continuous beginning 3/1. Students must reply within 2 weeks of notification.
**CONTACT** Debra Reyes, Assistant Director, Western New Mexico University, PO Box 680, Silver City, NM 88062, 575-538-6173 or toll-free 800-872-WNMU. *Fax:* 575-538-6189. *E-mail:* reyesd@wnmu.edu.
*Website:* http://www.wnmu.edu/.

# WESTERN OREGON UNIVERSITY
## Monmouth, OR

| Tuition & fees (OR res): $8723 | Average undergraduate aid package: $9853 |
|---|---|

**ABOUT THE INSTITUTION** State-supported, coed. *Awards:* certificates, bachelor's, and master's degrees. 35 undergraduate majors. *Total enrollment:* 5,996. Undergraduates: 4,930. Freshmen: 872. Federal methodology is used as a basis for awarding need-based institutional aid.
**UNDERGRADUATE EXPENSES** for 2015–2016 *Application fee:* $60. *Tuition, state resident:* full-time $8723. *Tuition, nonresident:* full-time $22,257. Full-time tuition and fees vary according to course load. Part-time tuition and fees vary according to course load. *College room and board:* $9416; *Room only:* $7766. Room and board charges vary according to board plan and housing facility. *Payment plan:* Guaranteed tuition.
**FRESHMAN FINANCIAL AID (Fall 2014, est.)** 686 applied for aid; of those 83% were deemed to have need. 95% of freshmen with need received aid; of those 10% had need fully met. *Average percent of need met:* 55% (excluding resources awarded to replace EFC). *Average financial aid package:* $9866 (excluding resources awarded to replace EFC). 4% of all full-time freshmen had no need and received non-need-based gift aid.
**UNDERGRADUATE FINANCIAL AID (Fall 2014, est.)** 3,688 applied for aid; of those 85% were deemed to have need. 92% of undergraduates with need received aid; of those 9% had need fully met. *Average percent of need met:* 52% (excluding resources awarded to replace EFC). *Average financial aid package:* $9853 (excluding resources awarded to replace EFC). 3% of all full-time undergraduates had no need and received non-need-based gift aid.
**GIFT AID (NEED-BASED)** *Total amount:* $15,376,424 (65% federal, 18% state, 5% institutional, 12% external sources). *Receiving aid:* Freshmen: 66% (467); all full-time undergraduates: 63% (2,427). *Average award:* Freshmen: $7836; Undergraduates: $7030. *Scholarships, grants, and awards:* Federal Pell, FSEOG, state, private, college/university gift aid from institutional funds, TEACH Grants.
**GIFT AID (NON-NEED-BASED)** *Total amount:* $728,769 (2% federal, 47% institutional, 51% external sources). *Receiving aid:* Freshmen: 4% (26). Undergraduates: 2% (73). *Average award:* Freshmen: $1262. Undergraduates: $2172. *Scholarships, grants, and awards by category:* Academic interests/achievement: biological sciences, business, computer science, education, English, foreign languages, general academic interests/achievements, humanities, mathematics, physical sciences, premedicine, social sciences. *Creative arts/performance:* art/fine arts, dance, music, performing arts, theater/drama. *Special achievements/activities:* community service, general special achievements/activities, leadership. *Special characteristics:* adult students, children of workers in trades, ethnic background, handicapped students, international students, local/state students, out-of-state students, veterans, veterans' children.
**ROTC:** Army, Naval cooperative.
**LOANS** *Student loans:* $23,254,697 (80% need-based, 20% non-need-based). 68% of past graduating class borrowed through all loan programs. *Average indebtedness per student:* $28,331. *Average need-based loan:* Freshmen: $3290. Undergraduates: $4126. *Parent loans:* $6,190,575 (33% need-based, 67% non-need-based). *Programs:* Federal Direct (Subsidized and Unsubsidized Stafford, PLUS), Perkins, college/university.
**WORK-STUDY** *Federal work-study:* Total amount: $971,570; 1,044 jobs averaging $978.
**ATHLETIC AWARDS** Total amount: $643,559 (56% need-based, 44% non-need-based).

**APPLYING FOR FINANCIAL AID** *Required financial aid form:* FAFSA. *Financial aid deadline (priority):* 2/1. *Notification date:* Continuous beginning 3/15. Students must reply within 3 weeks of notification.
**CONTACT** Ms. Donna Kirk, Director of Financial Aid, Western Oregon University, 345 North Monmouth Avenue, Monmouth, OR 97361, 503-838-8475 or toll-free 877-877-1593. *Fax:* 503-838-8200. *E-mail:* finaid@wou.edu.
*Website:* http://www.wou.edu/.

# WESTERN STATE COLORADO UNIVERSITY
## Gunnison, CO

| Tuition & fees (CO res): $7874 | Average undergraduate aid package: $12,202 |
|---|---|

**ABOUT THE INSTITUTION** State-supported, coed. *Awards:* certificates, bachelor's, and master's degrees. 70 undergraduate majors. *Total enrollment:* 2,581. Undergraduates: 2,338. Freshmen: 454. Federal methodology is used as a basis for awarding need-based institutional aid.
**UNDERGRADUATE EXPENSES** for 2015–2016 *Application fee:* $30. *Tuition, state resident:* full-time $5539; part-time $230.80 per credit hour. *Tuition, nonresident:* full-time $15,984; part-time $666 per credit hour. *Required fees:* full-time $2335. Full-time tuition and fees vary according to course load and reciprocity agreements. Part-time tuition and fees vary according to course load and reciprocity agreements. *College room and board:* $9050; *Room only:* $4794. Room and board charges vary according to board plan and housing facility.
**FRESHMAN FINANCIAL AID (Fall 2014, est.)** 376 applied for aid; of those 70% were deemed to have need. 100% of freshmen with need received aid; of those 21% had need fully met. *Average percent of need met:* 68% (excluding resources awarded to replace EFC). *Average financial aid package:* $13,054 (excluding resources awarded to replace EFC). 25% of all full-time freshmen had no need and received non-need-based gift aid.
**UNDERGRADUATE FINANCIAL AID (Fall 2014, est.)** 1,372 applied for aid; of those 77% were deemed to have need. 100% of undergraduates with need received aid; of those 18% had need fully met. *Average percent of need met:* 56% (excluding resources awarded to replace EFC). *Average financial aid package:* $12,202 (excluding resources awarded to replace EFC). 17% of all full-time undergraduates had no need and received non-need-based gift aid.
**GIFT AID (NEED-BASED)** *Total amount:* $6,257,197 (42% federal, 12% state, 38% institutional, 8% external sources). *Receiving aid:* Freshmen: 55% (245); all full-time undergraduates: 53% (961). *Average award:* Freshmen: $5909; Undergraduates: $5748. *Scholarships, grants, and awards:* Federal Pell, FSEOG, state, private, college/university gift aid from institutional funds.
**GIFT AID (NON-NEED-BASED)** *Total amount:* $1,646,730 (1% state, 85% institutional, 14% external sources). *Average award:* Freshmen: $3762. Undergraduates: $4104. *Scholarships, grants, and awards by category:* Academic interests/achievement: general academic interests/achievements. *Creative arts/performance:* art/fine arts, music, performing arts. *Special achievements/activities:* leadership. *Special characteristics:* children and siblings of alumni. *Tuition waivers:* Full or partial for employees or children of employees, senior citizens.
**LOANS** *Student loans:* $9,322,548 (80% need-based, 20% non-need-based). 60% of past graduating class borrowed through all loan programs. *Average indebtedness per student:* $21,251. *Average need-based loan:* Freshmen: $3029. Undergraduates: $3578. *Parent loans:* $6,750,035 (64% need-based, 36% non-need-based). *Programs:* Federal Direct (Subsidized and Unsubsidized Stafford, PLUS), Perkins.
**WORK-STUDY** *Federal work-study:* Total amount: $407,882; 173 jobs averaging $1443. *State or other work-study/employment:* Total amount: $407,880 (99% need-based, 1% non-need-based). 176 part-time jobs averaging $1679.
**ATHLETIC AWARDS** Total amount: $1,432,649 (56% need-based, 44% non-need-based).
**APPLYING FOR FINANCIAL AID** *Required financial aid form:* FAFSA. *Financial aid deadline (priority):* 3/1. *Notification date:* Continuous beginning 3/1. Students must reply within 3 weeks of notification.
**CONTACT** Jerry Martinez, Director of Financial Aid, Western State Colorado University, Taylor Hall , Gunnison, CO 81231, 970-943-3026 or toll-free 800-876-5309. *Fax:* 970-943-3086. *E-mail:* jmartinez@western.edu.
*Website:* http://www.western.edu/.

# WESTERN WASHINGTON UNIVERSITY
## Bellingham, WA

| Tuition & fees (WA res): $8965 | Average undergraduate aid package: $14,092 |
| --- | --- |

**ABOUT THE INSTITUTION** State-supported, coed. *Awards:* certificates, bachelor's, and master's degrees. 112 undergraduate majors. *Total enrollment:* 15,060. Undergraduates: 14,152. Freshmen: 2,786. Federal methodology is used as a basis for awarding need-based institutional aid.

**UNDERGRADUATE EXPENSES for 2015–2016** *Application fee:* $55. *Tuition, state resident:* full-time $7503; part-time $270 per credit hour. *Tuition, nonresident:* full-time $18,945; part-time $651 per credit hour. *Required fees:* full-time $1462. Full-time tuition and fees vary according to course load, location, and reciprocity agreements. Part-time tuition and fees vary according to course load, location, and reciprocity agreements. *College room and board:* $10,042. Room and board charges vary according to board plan, housing facility, and location.

**FRESHMAN FINANCIAL AID (Fall 2014, est.)** 2,323 applied for aid; of those 66% were deemed to have need. 98% of freshmen with need received aid; of those 22% had need fully met. *Average percent of need met:* 88% (excluding resources awarded to replace EFC). *Average financial aid package:* $14,590 (excluding resources awarded to replace EFC). 2% of all full-time freshmen had no need and received non-need-based gift aid.

**UNDERGRADUATE FINANCIAL AID (Fall 2014, est.)** 8,834 applied for aid; of those 75% were deemed to have need. 98% of undergraduates with need received aid; of those 19% had need fully met. *Average percent of need met:* 85% (excluding resources awarded to replace EFC). *Average financial aid package:* $14,092 (excluding resources awarded to replace EFC). 2% of all full-time undergraduates had no need and received non-need-based gift aid.

**GIFT AID (NEED-BASED)** *Total amount:* $39,046,965 (43% federal, 39% state, 14% institutional, 4% external sources). *Receiving aid:* Freshmen: 47% (1,301); all full-time undergraduates: 38% (5,002). *Average award:* Freshmen: $9603; Undergraduates: $9063. *Scholarships, grants, and awards:* Federal Pell, FSEOG, state, private, college/university gift aid from institutional funds.

**GIFT AID (NON-NEED-BASED)** *Total amount:* $1,999,122 (10% federal, 4% state, 38% institutional, 48% external sources). *Receiving aid:* Freshmen: 4% (104). Undergraduates: 2% (196). *Average award:* Freshmen: $2176. Undergraduates: $2020. *Scholarships, grants, and awards by category:* Academic interests/achievement: biological sciences, business, communication, computer science, education, engineering/technologies, English, foreign languages, general academic interests/achievements, health fields, humanities, library science, mathematics, physical sciences, premedicine, social sciences. *Creative arts/performance:* applied art and design, art/fine arts, cinema/film/broadcasting, creative writing, dance, general creative arts/performance, journalism/publications, music, performing arts, theater/drama. *Special achievements/activities:* community service, leadership, memberships. *Special characteristics:* children of public servants, children of union members/company employees, ethnic background, general special characteristics, international students, local/state students, members of minority groups, previous college experience, veterans. *Tuition waivers:* Full or partial for minority students, employees or children of employees.

**LOANS** *Student loans:* $50,960,901 (69% need-based, 31% non-need-based). 57% of past graduating class borrowed through all loan programs. *Average indebtedness per student:* $21,520. *Average need-based loan:* Freshmen: $3822. Undergraduates: $4544. *Parent loans:* $40,297,825 (24% need-based, 76% non-need-based). *Programs:* Federal Direct (Subsidized and Unsubsidized Stafford, PLUS), Perkins, college/university, alternative loans.

**WORK-STUDY** *Federal work-study:* Total amount: $445,839; 132 jobs averaging $3378. *State or other work-study/employment:* Total amount: $2,199,553 (100% need-based). 624 part-time jobs averaging $3525.

**ATHLETIC AWARDS** Total amount: $1,392,278 (37% need-based, 63% non-need-based).

**APPLYING FOR FINANCIAL AID** *Required financial aid form:* FAFSA. *Financial aid deadline (priority):* 2/15. *Notification date:* Continuous beginning 3/15. Students must reply within 3 weeks of notification.

**CONTACT** Ms. Barbara Luton, Office Support Supervisor for Financial Aid, Western Washington University, Old Main 255, MS 9006, 516 High Street, Bellingham, WA 98225-9006, 360-650-3470. *E-mail:* financialaid@wwu.edu.
*Website:* http://www.wwu.edu/.

# WESTFIELD STATE UNIVERSITY
## Westfield, MA

| Tuition & fees (MA res): $8682 | Average undergraduate aid package: $6893 |
| --- | --- |

**ABOUT THE INSTITUTION** State-supported, coed. *Awards:* certificates, bachelor's, and master's degrees. 31 undergraduate majors. *Total enrollment:* 6,321. Undergraduates: 5,590. Freshmen: 1,224. Federal methodology is used as a basis for awarding need-based institutional aid.

**UNDERGRADUATE EXPENSES for 2015–2016** *Application fee:* $50. *Tuition, state resident:* full-time $970; part-time $260 per credit hour. *Tuition, nonresident:* full-time $7050; part-time $260 per credit hour. *Required fees:* full-time $7712; $75 per term. Full-time tuition and fees vary according to program and reciprocity agreements. Part-time tuition and fees vary according to course load. *College room and board:* $10,236. Room and board charges vary according to board plan and housing facility.

**FRESHMAN FINANCIAL AID (Fall 2013)** 1,141 applied for aid; of those 74% were deemed to have need. 100% of freshmen with need received aid; of those 51% had need fully met. *Average percent of need met:* 67% (excluding resources awarded to replace EFC). *Average financial aid package:* $6673 (excluding resources awarded to replace EFC). 1% of all full-time freshmen had no need and received non-need-based gift aid.

**UNDERGRADUATE FINANCIAL AID (Fall 2013)** 4,549 applied for aid; of those 68% were deemed to have need. 100% of undergraduates with need received aid; of those 6% had need fully met. *Average percent of need met:* 66% (excluding resources awarded to replace EFC). *Average financial aid package:* $6893 (excluding resources awarded to replace EFC). 2% of all full-time undergraduates had no need and received non-need-based gift aid.

**GIFT AID (NEED-BASED)** *Total amount:* $13,284,238 (56% federal, 25% state, 13% institutional, 6% external sources). *Receiving aid:* Freshmen: 48% (615); all full-time undergraduates: 44% (2,195). *Average award:* Freshmen: $5055; Undergraduates: $4621. *Scholarships, grants, and awards:* Federal Pell, FSEOG, state, private, college/university gift aid from institutional funds.

**GIFT AID (NON-NEED-BASED)** *Total amount:* $620,252 (36% state, 27% institutional, 37% external sources). *Receiving aid:* Freshmen: 23% (301). Undergraduates: 13% (668). *Average award:* Freshmen: $4303. Undergraduates: $3277. *Scholarships, grants, and awards by category:* Academic interests/achievement: general academic interests/achievements. *Tuition waivers:* Full or partial for employees or children of employees, senior citizens. *ROTC:* Army cooperative, Air Force cooperative.

**LOANS** *Student loans:* $30,870,745 (69% need-based, 31% non-need-based). 79% of past graduating class borrowed through all loan programs. *Average indebtedness per student:* $26,326. *Average need-based loan:* Freshmen: $3201. Undergraduates: $4047. *Parent loans:* $5,249,459 (27% need-based, 73% non-need-based). *Programs:* Federal Direct (Subsidized and Unsubsidized Stafford, PLUS), Perkins.

**WORK-STUDY** *Federal work-study:* 332 jobs averaging $1304.

**APPLYING FOR FINANCIAL AID** *Required financial aid form:* FAFSA. *Financial aid deadline (priority):* 3/1. *Notification date:* 4/15.

**CONTACT** Catherine Ryan, Director of Financial Aid, Westfield State University, 333 Western Avenue, Westfield, MA 01086, 413-572-5218.
*Website:* http://www.wsc.ma.edu/.

# WEST LIBERTY UNIVERSITY
## West Liberty, WV

**CONTACT** Christ Taskalines, Financial Aid Manager, West Liberty University, PO Box 295, West Liberty, WV 26074-0295, 304-336-8016 or toll-free 800-732-6204 (in-state), 866-WESTLIB (out-of-state). *Fax:* 304-336-8088. *E-mail:* taskalic@westliberty.edu.
*Website:* http://www.westliberty.edu/.

# WESTMINSTER COLLEGE
## Fulton, MO

| Tuition & fees: $22,560 | Average undergraduate aid package: $20,800 |
|---|---|

**ABOUT THE INSTITUTION** Independent Presbyterian Church, coed. *Awards:* bachelor's degrees. 30 undergraduate majors. *Total enrollment:* 944. Undergraduates: 944. Freshmen: 212. Federal methodology is used as a basis for awarding need-based institutional aid.

**UNDERGRADUATE EXPENSES for 2015–2016** *Comprehensive fee:* $31,720 includes full-time tuition ($21,360), mandatory fees ($1200), and room and board ($9160). *College room only:* $4940. Full-time tuition and fees vary according to reciprocity agreements. Room and board charges vary according to board plan and housing facility. *Part-time tuition:* $800 per credit.

**FRESHMAN FINANCIAL AID (Fall 2014, est.)** 179 applied for aid; of those 81% were deemed to have need. 100% of freshmen with need received aid; of those 69% had need fully met. *Average percent of need met:* 92% (excluding resources awarded to replace EFC). *Average financial aid package:* $22,339 (excluding resources awarded to replace EFC). 34% of all full-time freshmen had no need and received non-need-based gift aid.

**UNDERGRADUATE FINANCIAL AID (Fall 2014, est.)** 717 applied for aid; of those 77% were deemed to have need. 100% of undergraduates with need received aid; of those 77% had need fully met. *Average percent of need met:* 91% (excluding resources awarded to replace EFC). *Average financial aid package:* $20,800 (excluding resources awarded to replace EFC). 39% of all full-time undergraduates had no need and received non-need-based gift aid.

**GIFT AID (NEED-BASED)** *Total amount:* $14,937,521 (9% federal, 3% state, 74% institutional, 14% external sources). *Receiving aid:* Freshmen: 68% (145); all full-time undergraduates: 59% (554). *Average award:* Freshmen: $18,575; Undergraduates: $16,309. *Scholarships, grants, and awards:* Federal Pell, FSEOG, state, private, college/university gift aid from institutional funds.

**GIFT AID (NON-NEED-BASED)** *Total amount:* $261,338 (100% federal). *Average award:* Freshmen: $12,864. Undergraduates: $11,477. *Scholarships, grants, and awards by category:* Academic interests/achievement: 398 awards ($3,705,647 total): general academic interests/achievements. Creative arts/performance: 10 awards ($17,500 total): music. Special achievements/activities: 476 awards ($1,568,613 total): general special achievements/activities, leadership. Special characteristics: 310 awards ($2,642,084 total): children and siblings of alumni, children of faculty/staff, ethnic background, international students, local/state students, relatives of clergy, religious affiliation, siblings of current students, twins. *Tuition waivers:* Full or partial for children of alumni, employees or children of employees. *ROTC:* Army cooperative, Air Force cooperative.

**LOANS** *Student loans:* $3,867,618 (48% need-based, 52% non-need-based). 61% of past graduating class borrowed through all loan programs. *Average indebtedness per student:* $29,004. *Average need-based loan:* Freshmen: $2881. Undergraduates: $3714. *Parent loans:* $1,358,407 (100% non-need-based). *Programs:* Federal Direct (Subsidized and Unsubsidized Stafford, PLUS), Perkins.

**WORK-STUDY** *Federal work-study:* Total amount: $620,497; 443 jobs averaging $1401. *State or other work-study/employment:* Total amount: $383,836 (100% non-need-based). 188 part-time jobs averaging $2042.

**APPLYING FOR FINANCIAL AID** *Required financial aid form:* FAFSA. *Financial aid deadline (priority):* 2/15. *Notification date:* Continuous beginning 3/15. Students must reply within 3 weeks of notification.

**CONTACT** Ms. Aimee Bristow, Director of Financial Aid, Westminster College, 501 Westminster Avenue, Fulton, MO 65251-1299, 800-475-3361. *Fax:* 573-592-5255. *E-mail:* aimee.bristow@westminster-mo.edu. *Website:* http://www.westminster-mo.edu/.

# WESTMINSTER COLLEGE
## New Wilmington, PA

| Tuition & fees: $33,410 | Average undergraduate aid package: $25,855 |
|---|---|

**ABOUT THE INSTITUTION** Independent Presbyterian Church (U.S.A.), coed. 52 undergraduate majors. Federal methodology is used as a basis for awarding need-based institutional aid.

**UNDERGRADUATE EXPENSES for 2015–2016** *Comprehensive fee:* $43,570 includes full-time tuition ($32,170), mandatory fees ($1240), and room and board ($10,160). Room and board charges vary according to board plan and housing facility. *Part-time tuition:* $1030 per semester hour. *Part-time fees:* $200 per semester hour.

**FRESHMAN FINANCIAL AID (Fall 2013)** 295 applied for aid; of those 94% were deemed to have need. 100% of freshmen with need received aid; of those 15% had need fully met. *Average percent of need met:* 76% (excluding resources awarded to replace EFC). *Average financial aid package:* $26,945 (excluding resources awarded to replace EFC). 10% of all full-time freshmen had no need and received non-need-based gift aid.

**UNDERGRADUATE FINANCIAL AID (Fall 2013)** 1,125 applied for aid; of those 93% were deemed to have need. 100% of undergraduates with need received aid; of those 16% had need fully met. *Average percent of need met:* 77% (excluding resources awarded to replace EFC). *Average financial aid package:* $25,855 (excluding resources awarded to replace EFC). 15% of all full-time undergraduates had no need and received non-need-based gift aid.

**GIFT AID (NEED-BASED)** *Total amount:* $21,930,699 (9% federal, 9% state, 78% institutional, 4% external sources). *Receiving aid:* Freshmen: 90% (276); all full-time undergraduates: 79% (1,034). *Average award:* Freshmen: $22,708; Undergraduates: $21,129. *Scholarships, grants, and awards:* Federal Pell, FSEOG, state, private, college/university gift aid from institutional funds.

**GIFT AID (NON-NEED-BASED)** *Total amount:* $3,353,345 (1% federal, 98% institutional, 1% external sources). *Receiving aid:* Freshmen: 88% (271). Undergraduates: 77% (1,016). *Average award:* Freshmen: $18,800. Undergraduates: $16,519. *Scholarships, grants, and awards by category:* Academic interests/achievement: 1,127 awards ($15,037,280 total): general academic interests/achievements. Creative arts/performance: 105 awards ($96,775 total): cinema/film/broadcasting, general creative arts/performance, music, theater/drama. Special characteristics: 558 awards ($4,738,470 total): children and siblings of alumni, general special characteristics, international students, religious affiliation. *Tuition waivers:* Full or partial for employees or children of employees.

**LOANS** *Student loans:* $10,045,131 (95% need-based, 5% non-need-based). 83% of past graduating class borrowed through all loan programs. *Average indebtedness per student:* $35,333. *Average need-based loan:* Freshmen: $4027. Undergraduates: $4665. *Parent loans:* $3,097,045 (95% need-based, 5% non-need-based). *Programs:* Federal Direct (Subsidized and Unsubsidized Stafford, PLUS), Perkins, alternative loans.

**WORK-STUDY** *Federal work-study:* 364 jobs averaging $1693. *State or other work-study/employment:* Total amount: $106,582 (64% need-based, 36% non-need-based). 69 part-time jobs averaging $1561.

**APPLYING FOR FINANCIAL AID** *Required financial aid forms:* FAFSA, W-2 forms. *Financial aid deadline (priority):* 5/1. *Notification date:* Continuous beginning 3/1. Students must reply by 5/1 or within 3 weeks of notification.

**CONTACT** Mrs. Cheryl A. Gerber, Director of Financial Aid, Westminster College, 319 South Market Street, New Wilmington, PA 16172-0001, 724-946-7102 or toll-free 800-942-8033. *Fax:* 724-946-6171. *E-mail:* gerberca@westminster.edu. *Website:* http://www.westminster.edu/.

# WESTMINSTER COLLEGE
## Salt Lake City, UT

| Tuition & fees: $30,364 | Average undergraduate aid package: $23,513 |
|---|---|

**ABOUT THE INSTITUTION** Independent, coed. *Awards:* certificates, bachelor's, and master's degrees. 36 undergraduate majors. *Total enrollment:* 2,992. Undergraduates: 2,233. Freshmen: 485. Federal methodology is used as a basis for awarding need-based institutional aid.

**UNDERGRADUATE EXPENSES for 2015–2016** *Application fee:* $50. *Comprehensive fee:* $38,820 includes full-time tuition ($29,856), mandatory fees ($508), and room and board ($8456). Full-time tuition and fees vary according to course load and program. Room and board charges vary according to board plan. *Part-time tuition:* $1244 per credit hour. Part-time tuition and fees vary according to course load and program.

**FRESHMAN FINANCIAL AID (Fall 2014, est.)** 383 applied for aid; of those 83% were deemed to have need. 100% of freshmen with need received aid; of those 28% had need fully met. *Average percent of need met:* 83% (excluding resources awarded to replace EFC). *Average financial aid package:* $24,900 (excluding

resources awarded to replace EFC). 27% of all full-time freshmen had no need and received non-need-based gift aid.

**UNDERGRADUATE FINANCIAL AID (Fall 2014, est.)** 1,417 applied for aid; of those 86% were deemed to have need. 100% of undergraduates with need received aid; of those 21% had need fully met. *Average percent of need met:* 76% (excluding resources awarded to replace EFC). *Average financial aid package:* $23,513 (excluding resources awarded to replace EFC). 31% of all full-time undergraduates had no need and received non-need-based gift aid.

**GIFT AID (NEED-BASED)** *Total amount:* $20,032,787 (13% federal, 83% institutional, 4% external sources). *Receiving aid:* Freshmen: 66% (318); all full-time undergraduates: 58% (1,198). *Average award:* Freshmen: $20,475; Undergraduates: $18,811. *Scholarships, grants, and awards:* Federal Pell, FSEOG, state, private, college/university gift aid from institutional funds.

**GIFT AID (NON-NEED-BASED)** *Total amount:* $9,261,147 (93% institutional, 7% external sources). *Receiving aid:* Freshmen: 16% (76). Undergraduates: 13% (261). *Average award:* Freshmen: $14,286. Undergraduates: $13,176. *Tuition waivers:* Full or partial for employees or children of employees. *ROTC:* Army cooperative, Naval cooperative, Air Force cooperative.

**LOANS** *Student loans:* $12,716,741 (91% need-based, 9% non-need-based). 60% of past graduating class borrowed through all loan programs. *Average indebtedness per student:* $27,523. *Average need-based loan:* Freshmen: $3710. Undergraduates: $4833. *Parent loans:* $1,577,379 (81% need-based, 19% non-need-based). *Programs:* Federal Direct (Subsidized and Unsubsidized Stafford, PLUS), Perkins.

**WORK-STUDY** *Federal work-study:* Total amount: $1,037,079; 410 jobs averaging $2514. *State or other work-study/employment:* Total amount: $600,000 (100% non-need-based). Part-time jobs available.

**ATHLETIC AWARDS** Total amount: $908,818 (57% need-based, 43% non-need-based).

**APPLYING FOR FINANCIAL AID** *Required financial aid form:* FAFSA. *Financial aid deadline (priority):* 4/15. *Notification date:* Continuous beginning 3/1. Students must reply by 5/1 or within 3 weeks of notification.

**CONTACT** Jenny Ryan, Director of Financial Aid, Westminster College, 1840 South 1300 East, Salt Lake City, UT 84105, 801-832-2500 or toll-free 800-748-4753. *Fax:* 801-832-2501. *E-mail:* jryan@westminstercollege.edu. *Website:* http://www.westminstercollege.edu/.

# WESTMONT COLLEGE
## Santa Barbara, CA

| Tuition & fees: $39,990 | Average undergraduate aid package: $30,373 |
| --- | --- |

**ABOUT THE INSTITUTION** Independent nondenominational, coed. 43 undergraduate majors. Federal methodology is used as a basis for awarding need-based institutional aid.

**UNDERGRADUATE EXPENSES for 2015–2016** *Comprehensive fee:* $52,570 includes full-time tuition ($38,960), mandatory fees ($1030), and room and board ($12,580). *College room only:* $7820. Room and board charges vary according to board plan.

**FRESHMAN FINANCIAL AID (Fall 2014, est.)** 289 applied for aid; of those 82% were deemed to have need. 100% of freshmen with need received aid; of those 13% had need fully met. *Average percent of need met:* 76% (excluding resources awarded to replace EFC). *Average financial aid package:* $30,188 (excluding resources awarded to replace EFC). 25% of all full-time freshmen had no need and received non-need-based gift aid.

**UNDERGRADUATE FINANCIAL AID (Fall 2014, est.)** 941 applied for aid; of those 86% were deemed to have need. 100% of undergraduates with need received aid; of those 16% had need fully met. *Average percent of need met:* 78% (excluding resources awarded to replace EFC). *Average financial aid package:* $30,373 (excluding resources awarded to replace EFC). 26% of all full-time undergraduates had no need and received non-need-based gift aid.

**GIFT AID (NEED-BASED)** *Total amount:* $18,492,155 (7% federal, 10% state, 80% institutional, 3% external sources). *Receiving aid:* Freshmen: 69% (234); all full-time undergraduates: 66% (808). *Average award:* Freshmen: $25,157; Undergraduates: $24,089. *Scholarships, grants, and awards:* Federal Pell, FSEOG, state, private, college/university gift aid from institutional funds.

**GIFT AID (NON-NEED-BASED)** *Total amount:* $5,135,950 (97% institutional, 3% external sources). *Receiving aid:* Freshmen: 7% (23). Undergraduates: 8% (104).

*Average award:* Freshmen: $13,717. Undergraduates: $13,634. *Scholarships, grants, and awards by category:* Academic interests/achievement: general academic interests/achievements. Creative arts/performance: art/fine arts, dance, music, theater/drama. Special achievements/activities: general special achievements/activities, leadership. Special characteristics: children of faculty/staff, ethnic background, international students.

**LOANS** *Student loans:* $9,049,443 (72% need-based, 28% non-need-based). 61% of past graduating class borrowed through all loan programs. *Average indebtedness per student:* $34,428. *Average need-based loan:* Freshmen: $4165. Undergraduates: $5948. *Parent loans:* $3,654,656 (37% need-based, 63% non-need-based). *Programs:* Federal Direct (Subsidized and Unsubsidized Stafford, PLUS), Perkins, college/university, alternative loans.

**WORK-STUDY** *Federal work-study:* Total amount: $761,102; 375 jobs averaging $1820.

**ATHLETIC AWARDS** Total amount: $1,705,999 (52% need-based, 48% non-need-based).

**APPLYING FOR FINANCIAL AID** *Required financial aid forms:* FAFSA, institution's own form. *Financial aid deadline (priority):* 3/1. *Notification date:* 4/1. Students must reply by 5/1 or within 2 weeks of notification.

**CONTACT** Mr. Sean Smith, Director of Financial Aid, Westmont College, 955 La Paz Road, Santa Barbara, CA 93108, 805-565-6063 or toll-free 800-777-9011. *Fax:* 805-565-7157. *E-mail:* finaid@westmont.edu. *Website:* http://www.westmont.edu/.

# WEST TEXAS A&M UNIVERSITY
## Canyon, TX

| Tuition & fees (TX res): $6105 | Average undergraduate aid package: $7790 |
| --- | --- |

**ABOUT THE INSTITUTION** State-supported, coed. *Awards:* bachelor's, master's, and doctoral degrees. 68 undergraduate majors. *Total enrollment:* 8,972. Undergraduates: 7,133. Freshmen: 1,279. Federal methodology is used as a basis for awarding need-based institutional aid.

**UNDERGRADUATE EXPENSES for 2015–2016** *Application fee:* $40. *Tuition, state resident:* full-time $4863; part-time $50 per credit hour. *Tuition, nonresident:* full-time $6124; part-time $80 per credit hour. *Required fees:* full-time $1242; $74 per credit hour or $232 per term. Full-time tuition and fees vary according to course load, degree level, program, and student level. Part-time tuition and fees vary according to course load, degree level, program, and student level. *College room and board:* $7196. Room and board charges vary according to board plan and housing facility. *Payment plan:* Guaranteed tuition.

**FRESHMAN FINANCIAL AID (Fall 2014, est.)** 1,147 applied for aid; of those 80% were deemed to have need. 100% of freshmen with need received aid; of those 4% had need fully met. *Average percent of need met:* 59% (excluding resources awarded to replace EFC). *Average financial aid package:* $8467 (excluding resources awarded to replace EFC). 9% of all full-time freshmen had no need and received non-need-based gift aid.

**UNDERGRADUATE FINANCIAL AID (Fall 2014, est.)** 4,373 applied for aid; of those 82% were deemed to have need. 100% of undergraduates with need received aid; of those 3% had need fully met. *Average percent of need met:* 54% (excluding resources awarded to replace EFC). *Average financial aid package:* $7790 (excluding resources awarded to replace EFC). 10% of all full-time undergraduates had no need and received non-need-based gift aid.

**GIFT AID (NEED-BASED)** *Total amount:* $19,932,119 (59% federal, 25% state, 11% institutional, 5% external sources). *Receiving aid:* Freshmen: 56% (738); all full-time undergraduates: 49% (2,769). *Average award:* Freshmen: $6558; Undergraduates: $5460. *Scholarships, grants, and awards:* Federal Pell, FSEOG, state, private, college/university gift aid from institutional funds.

**GIFT AID (NON-NEED-BASED)** *Total amount:* $2,395,312 (63% institutional, 37% external sources). *Receiving aid:* Freshmen: 33% (438). Undergraduates: 22% (1,259). *Average award:* Freshmen: $1691. Undergraduates: $2082. *Scholarships, grants, and awards by category:* Academic interests/achievement: 2,674 awards ($1,531,139 total): agriculture, business, communication, computer science, education, engineering/technologies, English, general academic interests/achievements, health fields, humanities, mathematics, physical sciences, premedicine, social sciences. Creative arts/performance: 334 awards ($154,923 total): art/fine arts, cinema/film/broadcasting, dance, debating, journalism/publications, music, theater/drama. Special

*achievements/activities:* 507 awards ($213,729 total): cheerleading/drum major, community service, hobbies/interests, leadership, memberships, rodeo. *Special characteristics:* 474 awards ($283,047 total): children and siblings of alumni, children of faculty/staff, children of union members/company employees, children of workers in trades, first-generation college students, general special characteristics, handicapped students, international students, local/state students, out-of-state students, public servants, religious affiliation, veterans, veterans' children. *Tuition waivers:* Full or partial for employees or children of employees.
**LOANS** *Student loans:* $39,985,561 (76% need-based, 24% non-need-based). 59% of past graduating class borrowed through all loan programs. *Average indebtedness per student:* $20,682. *Average need-based loan:* Freshmen: $3407. Undergraduates: $4255. *Parent loans:* $1,644,311 (24% need-based, 76% non-need-based). *Programs:* Federal Direct (Subsidized and Unsubsidized Stafford, PLUS), state.
**WORK-STUDY** *Federal work-study:* Total amount: $269,293; 169 jobs averaging $2329. *State or other work-study/employment:* Total amount: $54,712 (100% need-based). 61 part-time jobs averaging $901.
**ATHLETIC AWARDS** Total amount: $1,958,713 (40% need-based, 60% non-need-based).
**APPLYING FOR FINANCIAL AID** *Required financial aid form:* FAFSA. *Financial aid deadline:* Continuous. *Notification date:* Continuous beginning 3/1. Students must reply within 2 weeks of notification.
**CONTACT** Marian Giesecke, Interim Director of Financial Aid, West Texas A&M University, WTAMU Box 60939, Canyon, TX 79016-0001, 806-651-2055 or toll-free 800-99-WTAMU. *Fax:* 806-651-2924. *E-mail:* mgiesecke@mail.wtamu.edu.
*Website:* http://www.wtamu.edu/.

---

# WEST VIRGINIA STATE UNIVERSITY
## Institute, WV

**CONTACT** Mrs. JoAnn L. Ross, Director of Student Financial Assistance, West Virginia State University, PO Box 1000, Ferrell Hall 324, Institute, WV 25112-1000, 304-204-4361 or toll-free 800-987-2112.
*Website:* http://www.wvstateu.edu/.

---

# WEST VIRGINIA UNIVERSITY
## Morgantown, WV

| Tuition & fees (WV res): $6960 | Average undergraduate aid package: $9060 |
| --- | --- |

**ABOUT THE INSTITUTION** State-supported, coed. *Awards:* bachelor's, master's, and doctoral degrees. 69 undergraduate majors. *Total enrollment:* 29,175. Undergraduates: 22,563. Freshmen: 4,868. Federal methodology is used as a basis for awarding need-based institutional aid.
**UNDERGRADUATE EXPENSES** for 2015–2016 *Application fee:* $60. *Tuition, state resident:* full-time $6960; part-time $290 per credit hour. *Tuition, nonresident:* full-time $20,424; part-time $851 per credit hour. Full-time tuition and fees vary according to location, program, and reciprocity agreements. Part-time tuition and fees vary according to course load, location, program, and reciprocity agreements. *College room and board:* $9582. Room and board charges vary according to board plan, housing facility, and location.
**FRESHMAN FINANCIAL AID (Fall 2014, est.)** 4,169 applied for aid; of those 84% were deemed to have need. 71% of freshmen with need received aid; of those 30% had need fully met. *Average percent of need met:* 72% (excluding resources awarded to replace EFC). *Average financial aid package:* $6860 (excluding resources awarded to replace EFC). 31% of all full-time freshmen had no need and received non-need-based gift aid.
**UNDERGRADUATE FINANCIAL AID (Fall 2014, est.)** 16,637 applied for aid; of those 63% were deemed to have need. 96% of undergraduates with need received aid; of those 38% had need fully met. *Average percent of need met:* 75% (excluding resources awarded to replace EFC). *Average financial aid package:* $9060 (excluding resources awarded to replace EFC). 21% of all full-time undergraduates had no need and received non-need-based gift aid.
**GIFT AID (NEED-BASED)** *Total amount:* $77,774,866 (34% federal, 12% state, 54% institutional). *Receiving aid:* Freshmen: 39% (1,869); all full-time undergraduates: 38% (7,929). *Average award:* Freshmen: $6460; Undergraduates: $6601.

---

*Scholarships, grants, and awards:* Federal Pell, FSEOG, state, private, college/university gift aid from institutional funds.
**GIFT AID (NON-NEED-BASED)** *Total amount:* $35,065,166 (59% state, 30% institutional, 11% external sources). *Receiving aid:* Freshmen: 49% (2,398). Undergraduates: 39% (8,219). *Average award:* Freshmen: $2580. Undergraduates: $2554.
*Scholarships, grants, and awards by category: Academic interests/achievement:* agriculture, architecture, area/ethnic studies, biological sciences, business, communication, computer science, education, engineering/technologies, English, foreign languages, general academic interests/achievements, health fields, home economics, humanities, international studies, library science, mathematics, military science, physical sciences, premedicine, religion/biblical studies, social sciences. *Creative arts/performance:* art/fine arts, debating, music, theater/drama. *Special achievements/activities:* general special achievements/activities, leadership. *Special characteristics:* children of faculty/staff, children of union members/company employees, children of workers in trades, ethnic background, general special characteristics, international students, local/state students, members of minority groups. *Tuition waivers:* Full or partial for employees or children of employees, senior citizens. *ROTC:* Army, Air Force.
**LOANS** *Student loans:* $110,039,050 (36% need-based, 64% non-need-based). 67% of past graduating class borrowed through all loan programs. *Average indebtedness per student:* $27,332. *Average need-based loan:* Freshmen: $3872. Undergraduates: $5214. *Parent loans:* $51,686,136 (100% non-need-based). *Programs:* Federal Direct (Subsidized and Unsubsidized Stafford, PLUS), Perkins, Federal Nursing, college/university.
**WORK-STUDY** *Federal work-study:* Total amount: $1,531,424; 875 jobs averaging $1874. *State or other work-study/employment:* Total amount: $2,122,490 (100% non-need-based). 1,089 part-time jobs averaging $1950.
**ATHLETIC AWARDS** Total amount: $5,515,424 (100% non-need-based).
**APPLYING FOR FINANCIAL AID** *Required financial aid forms:* FAFSA, state aid form. *Financial aid deadline:* 3/1. *Notification date:* Continuous beginning 3/15. Students must reply within 4 weeks of notification.
**CONTACT** Sandra Bennett, Executive Director of Financial Aid, West Virginia University, PO Box 6004, Morgantown, WV 26506-6004, 304-293-5242 or toll-free 800-344-9881. *Fax:* 304-293-4890. *E-mail:* sybennett@mail.wvu.edu.
*Website:* http://www.wvu.edu/.

---

# WEST VIRGINIA UNIVERSITY INSTITUTE OF TECHNOLOGY
## Montgomery, WV

| Tuition & fees (WV res): $6048 | Average undergraduate aid package: $7398 |
| --- | --- |

**ABOUT THE INSTITUTION** State-supported, coed. *Awards:* certificates and bachelor's degrees. 31 undergraduate majors. *Total enrollment:* 1,261. Undergraduates: 1,261. Freshmen: 264. Federal methodology is used as a basis for awarding need-based institutional aid.
**UNDERGRADUATE EXPENSES** for 2015–2016 *Tuition, state resident:* full-time $6048; part-time $252 per credit hour. *Tuition, nonresident:* full-time $15,192; part-time $633 per credit hour. Full-time tuition and fees vary according to program. Part-time tuition and fees vary according to course load and program. *College room and board:* $8902; *Room only:* $5192. Room and board charges vary according to board plan and housing facility.
**FRESHMAN FINANCIAL AID (Fall 2014, est.)** 227 applied for aid; of those 87% were deemed to have need. 98% of freshmen with need received aid; of those 15% had need fully met. *Average percent of need met:* 65% (excluding resources awarded to replace EFC). *Average financial aid package:* $7437 (excluding resources awarded to replace EFC). 16% of all full-time freshmen had no need and received non-need-based gift aid.
**UNDERGRADUATE FINANCIAL AID (Fall 2014, est.)** 973 applied for aid; of those 84% were deemed to have need. 91% of undergraduates with need received aid; of those 13% had need fully met. *Average percent of need met:* 76% (excluding resources awarded to replace EFC). *Average financial aid package:* $7398 (excluding resources awarded to replace EFC). 10% of all full-time undergraduates had no need and received non-need-based gift aid.
**GIFT AID (NEED-BASED)** *Total amount:* $3,479,068 (66% federal, 22% state, 12% external sources). *Receiving aid:* Freshmen: 60% (159); all full-time undergraduates: 47% (587). *Average award:* Freshmen: $5364; Undergraduates: $5095.

**Scholarships, grants, and awards:** Federal Pell, FSEOG, state, private, Federal Nursing.

**GIFT AID (NON-NEED-BASED) Total amount:** $801,020 (87% state, 13% external sources). **Receiving aid:** Freshmen: 17% (45). Undergraduates: 10% (128). **Average award:** Freshmen: $2045. Undergraduates: $2186. **Scholarships, grants, and awards by category:** Academic interests/achievement: general academic interests/achievements. Special achievements/activities: cheerleading/drum major. Special characteristics: 22 awards ($22,000 total): first-generation college students. **Tuition waivers:** Full or partial for senior citizens. **ROTC:** Army.

**LOANS Student loans:** $4,476,625 (44% need-based, 56% non-need-based). 67% of past graduating class borrowed through all loan programs. Average indebtedness per student: $20,893. **Average need-based loan:** Freshmen: $3764. Undergraduates: $3942. **Parent loans:** $961,823 (100% non-need-based). **Programs:** Federal Direct (Subsidized and Unsubsidized Stafford, PLUS), Perkins, college/university.

**WORK-STUDY Federal work-study:** Total amount: $42,592; 28 jobs averaging $1521. **State or other work-study/employment:** Total amount: $246,788 (100% non-need-based). 122 part-time jobs averaging $2023.

**ATHLETIC AWARDS** Total amount: $1,059,258 (100% non-need-based).

**APPLYING FOR FINANCIAL AID Required financial aid form:** FAFSA. **Financial aid deadline (priority):** 3/1. **Notification date:** Continuous beginning 4/1. Students must reply within 4 weeks of notification.

**CONTACT** Mr. Michael A. White, Director of Financial Aid Services, West Virginia University Institute of Technology, 405 Fayette Pike, Old Main, Room 206, Box 40, Montgomery, WV 25136, 304-442-3228 or toll-free 888-554-8324. Fax: 304-442-3052. E-mail: michael.white@mail.wvu.edu.
Website: http://www.wvutech.edu/.

# WEST VIRGINIA WESLEYAN COLLEGE
## Buckhannon, WV

| Tuition & fees: $28,792 | Average undergraduate aid package: $30,488 |
|---|---|

**ABOUT THE INSTITUTION** Independent United Methodist Church, coed. **Awards:** bachelor's and master's degrees. 62 undergraduate majors. **Total enrollment:** 1,511. Undergraduates: 1,390. Freshmen: 416. Federal methodology is used as a basis for awarding need-based institutional aid.

**UNDERGRADUATE EXPENSES for 2015–2016 Application fee:** $35. **Comprehensive fee:** $32,832 includes full-time tuition ($27,614), mandatory fees ($1178), and room and board ($4040). **College room only:** $4026. Full-time tuition and fees vary according to course load and student level. Room and board charges vary according to housing facility. Part-time tuition and fees vary according to course load.

**FRESHMAN FINANCIAL AID (Fall 2014, est.)** 378 applied for aid; of those 89% were deemed to have need. 100% of freshmen with need received aid; of those 39% had need fully met. **Average percent of need met:** 90% (excluding resources awarded to replace EFC). **Average financial aid package:** $28,054 (excluding resources awarded to replace EFC). 18% of all full-time freshmen had no need and received non-need-based gift aid.

**UNDERGRADUATE FINANCIAL AID (Fall 2014, est.)** 1,100 applied for aid; of those 90% were deemed to have need. 100% of undergraduates with need received aid; of those 53% had need fully met. **Average percent of need met:** 92% (excluding resources awarded to replace EFC). **Average financial aid package:** $30,488 (excluding resources awarded to replace EFC). 26% of all full-time undergraduates had no need and received non-need-based gift aid.

**GIFT AID (NEED-BASED) Total amount:** $19,015,909 (12% federal, 6% state, 82% institutional). **Receiving aid:** Freshmen: 81% (337); all full-time undergraduates: 73% (990). **Average award:** Freshmen: $21,893; Undergraduates: $21,187. **Scholarships, grants, and awards:** Federal Pell, FSEOG, state, private, college/university gift aid from institutional funds, Federal Nursing.

**GIFT AID (NON-NEED-BASED) Total amount:** $7,648,379 (26% state, 66% institutional, 8% external sources). **Receiving aid:** Freshmen: 15% (63). Undergraduates: 15% (207). **Average award:** Freshmen: $14,726. Undergraduates: $14,509. **Scholarships, grants, and awards by category:** Academic interests/achievement: English, general academic interests/achievements, physical sciences. Creative arts/performance: art/fine arts, music, performing arts, theater/drama. Special achievements/activities: community service, leadership, religious involvement. Special characteristics: children and siblings of alumni, children of faculty/staff, general special

characteristics, international students, relatives of clergy, religious affiliation. **Tuition waivers:** Full or partial for employees or children of employees.

**LOANS Student loans:** $9,049,974 (86% need-based, 14% non-need-based). 71% of past graduating class borrowed through all loan programs. Average indebtedness per student: $31,044. **Average need-based loan:** Freshmen: $7336. Undergraduates: $9603. **Parent loans:** $1,365,177 (100% non-need-based). **Programs:** Federal Direct (Subsidized and Unsubsidized Stafford, PLUS), Perkins, Federal Nursing.

**WORK-STUDY Federal work-study:** Total amount: $343,594; jobs available. **State or other work-study/employment:** Total amount: $90,554 (100% non-need-based). Part-time jobs available.

**ATHLETIC AWARDS** Total amount: $2,846,087 (42% need-based, 58% non-need-based).

**APPLYING FOR FINANCIAL AID Required financial aid form:** FAFSA. **Financial aid deadline (priority):** 2/15. **Notification date:** Continuous beginning 3/1.

**CONTACT** Susan George, Director of Financial Aid, West Virginia Wesleyan College, 59 College Avenue, Buckhannon, WV 26201, 304-473-8080 or toll-free 800-722-9933. E-mail: george_s@wvwc.edu.
Website: http://www.wvwc.edu/.

# WESTWOOD COLLEGE–ANAHEIM
## Anaheim, CA

**CONTACT** Financial Aid Office, Westwood College–Anaheim, 1551 South Douglass Road, Anaheim, CA 92806, 714-704-2721 or toll-free 877-840-8999.
Website: http://www.westwood.edu/.

# WESTWOOD COLLEGE–ANNANDALE CAMPUS
## Annandale, VA

**CONTACT** Financial Aid Office, Westwood College–Annandale Campus, 7619 Little River Turnpike, 5th Floor, Annandale, VA 22003, 706-642-3633 or toll-free 877-305-0049.
Website: http://www.westwood.edu/.

# WESTWOOD COLLEGE–ARLINGTON BALLSTON CAMPUS
## Arlington, VA

**CONTACT** Financial Aid Office, Westwood College–Arlington Ballston Campus, 4420 North Fairfax Drive, Arlington, VA 22203, 703-243-1662 or toll-free 877-268-5278.
Website: http://www.westwood.edu/.

# WESTWOOD COLLEGE–ATLANTA MIDTOWN
## Atlanta, GA

**CONTACT** Financial Aid Office, Westwood College–Atlanta Midtown, 1100 Spring Street, Suite 102, Atlanta, GA 30309, 404-745-9862 or toll-free 800-613-4595.
Website: http://www.westwood.edu/.

## WESTWOOD COLLEGE–ATLANTA NORTHLAKE
### Atlanta, GA

**CONTACT** Financial Aid Office, Westwood College–Atlanta Northlake, 2309 Parklake Drive, NE, Building 10, Atlanta, GA 30345, 404-962-2998 or toll-free 866-821-6145.
*Website:* http://www.westwood.edu/.

## WESTWOOD COLLEGE–CHICAGO DU PAGE
### Woodridge, IL

**CONTACT** Patty Zavala, Senior Student Finance Specialist, Westwood College–Chicago Du Page, 7155 Janes Avenue, Woodridge, IL 60517, 630-434-8244 or toll-free 866-721-7647.
*Website:* http://www.westwood.edu/.

## WESTWOOD COLLEGE–CHICAGO LOOP CAMPUS
### Chicago, IL

**CONTACT** Financial Aid Office, Westwood College–Chicago Loop Campus, 1 North State Street, Suite 1000, Chicago, IL 60602, 312-739-0890 or toll-free 800-693-5411.
*Website:* http://www.westwood.edu/.

## WESTWOOD COLLEGE–CHICAGO O'HARE AIRPORT
### Chicago, IL

**CONTACT** Financial Aid Office, Westwood College–Chicago O'Hare Airport, 8501 West Higgins Road, Suite 100, Chicago, IL 60631, 773-380-6801 or toll-free 866-235-2457.
*Website:* http://www.westwood.edu/.

## WESTWOOD COLLEGE–CHICAGO RIVER OAKS
### Calumet City, IL

**CONTACT** Financial Aid Office, Westwood College–Chicago River Oaks, 80 River Oaks Drive, Suite 111, Calumet City, IL 60409, 708-832-9760 or toll-free 888-549-4960.
*Website:* http://www.westwood.edu/.

## WESTWOOD COLLEGE–DENVER NORTH
### Denver, CO

**CONTACT** Admissions Office, Westwood College–Denver North, 7350 North Broadway, Denver, CO 80221, 800-875-6050 or toll-free 800-281-2978.
*Website:* http://www.westwood.edu/.

## WESTWOOD COLLEGE–DENVER SOUTH
### Aurora, CO

**CONTACT** Financial Aid Office, Westwood College–Denver South, 350 Blackhawk Street, Aurora, CO 80011, 303-934-1122 or toll-free 800-281-2978.
*Website:* http://www.westwood.edu/.

## WESTWOOD COLLEGE–INLAND EMPIRE
### Upland, CA

**CONTACT** Financial Aid Office, Westwood College–Inland Empire, 20 West 7th Street, Upland, CA 91786, 909-931-7599 or toll-free 866-221-5632.
*Website:* http://www.westwood.edu/.

## WESTWOOD COLLEGE–LOS ANGELES
### Los Angeles, CA

**CONTACT** Financial Aid Office, Westwood College–Los Angeles, 3250 Wilshire Boulevard, 4th Floor, Los Angeles, CA 90010, 213-382-2328 or toll-free 866-930-9256.
*Website:* http://www.westwood.edu/.

## WESTWOOD COLLEGE–SOUTH BAY CAMPUS
### Torrance, CA

**CONTACT** Financial Aid Office, Westwood College–South Bay Campus, 19700 South Vermont Avenue, Suite 100, Torrance, CA 90502, 310-522-2088 or toll-free 888-403-3308.
*Website:* http://www.westwood.edu/.

## WHEATON COLLEGE
### Wheaton, IL

| Tuition & fees: $31,900 | Average undergraduate aid package: $24,003 |
|---|---|

**ABOUT THE INSTITUTION** Independent nondenominational, coed. *Awards:* certificates, bachelor's, master's, and doctoral degrees. 40 undergraduate majors. *Total enrollment:* 2,914. Undergraduates: 2,432. Freshmen: 607. Both federal and institutional methodology are used as a basis for awarding need-based institutional aid.

**UNDERGRADUATE EXPENSES for 2015–2016** *Application fee:* $50. *Comprehensive fee:* $40,720 includes full-time tuition ($31,900) and room and board ($8820). *College room only:* $5120. Full-time tuition and fees vary according to program. Room and board charges vary according to board plan and housing facility. *Part-time tuition:* $1329 per credit hour. Part-time tuition and fees vary according to course load and program.

**FRESHMAN FINANCIAL AID (Fall 2014, est.)** 472 applied for aid; of those 70% were deemed to have need. 100% of freshmen with need received aid; of those 37% had need fully met. *Average percent of need met:* 90% (excluding resources awarded to replace EFC). *Average financial aid package:* $24,629 (excluding resources awarded to replace EFC). 26% of all full-time freshmen had no need and received non-need-based gift aid.

**UNDERGRADUATE FINANCIAL AID (Fall 2014, est.)** 1,607 applied for aid; of those 77% were deemed to have need. 100% of undergraduates with need received aid; of those 32% had need fully met. *Average percent of need met:* 89% (excluding resources awarded to replace EFC). *Average financial aid package:* $24,003 (excluding resources awarded to replace EFC). 19% of all full-time undergraduates had no need and received non-need-based gift aid.

**GIFT AID (NEED-BASED)** *Total amount:* $26,646,967 (10% federal, 2% state, 83% institutional, 5% external sources). *Receiving aid:* Freshmen: 54% (330); all full-time undergraduates: 52% (1,228). *Average award:* Freshmen: $20,791; Undergraduates: $20,255. *Scholarships, grants, and awards:* Federal Pell, FSEOG, state, private, college/university gift aid from institutional funds.

**GIFT AID (NON-NEED-BASED)** *Total amount:* $3,670,594 (77% institutional, 23% external sources). *Receiving aid:* Freshmen: 5% (31). Undergraduates: 5% (109). *Average award:* Freshmen: $5758. Undergraduates: $6428. *Scholarships, grants, and awards by category: Academic interests/achievement:* 911 awards ($3,317,495 total): biological sciences, business, computer science, education, engineering/technologies, English, foreign languages, general academic interests/achievements, health fields, humanities, mathematics, military science, physical sciences, premedicine, religion/biblical studies, social sciences. *Creative arts/performance:* 99 awards ($344,778 total): art/fine arts, music. *Special achievements/activities:* 69 awards ($335,947 total): general special achievements/activities. *Special characteristics:* 156 awards ($1,564,404 total): children and siblings of alumni, ethnic background, first-generation college students, general special characteristics, handicapped students, international students, members of minority groups. *ROTC:* Army, Air Force cooperative.

**LOANS** *Student loans:* $9,566,982 (84% need-based, 16% non-need-based). 57% of past graduating class borrowed through all loan programs. *Average indebtedness per student:* $25,939. *Average need-based loan:* Freshmen: $4533. Undergraduates: $4858. *Parent loans:* $3,222,087 (67% need-based, 33% non-need-based). *Programs:* Federal Direct (Subsidized and Unsubsidized Stafford, PLUS), Perkins.

**WORK-STUDY** *Federal work-study:* Total amount: $230,955; 184 jobs averaging $1227.

**APPLYING FOR FINANCIAL AID** *Required financial aid forms:* FAFSA, institution's own form. *Financial aid deadline (priority):* 2/15. *Notification date:* Continuous beginning 2/1.

**CONTACT** Ms. Karen Belling, Director of Financial Aid, Wheaton College, 501 College Avenue, Wheaton, IL 60187-5593, 630-752-5021 or toll-free 800-222-2419. *E-mail:* finaid@wheaton.edu.
*Website:* http://www.wheaton.edu/.

# WHEATON COLLEGE
## Norton, MA

| Tuition & fees: $46,423 | Average undergraduate aid package: $36,699 |
| --- | --- |

**ABOUT THE INSTITUTION** Independent, coed. *Awards:* bachelor's degrees. 41 undergraduate majors. *Total enrollment:* 1,587. Undergraduates: 1,587. Freshmen: 423. Institutional methodology is used as a basis for awarding need-based institutional aid.

**UNDERGRADUATE EXPENSES for 2015–2016** *Application fee:* $50. *Comprehensive fee:* $58,263 includes full-time tuition ($46,120), mandatory fees ($303), and room and board ($11,840). *College room only:* $6320. *Part-time tuition:* $1441 per credit hour. *Payment plan:* Tuition prepayment.

**FRESHMAN FINANCIAL AID (Fall 2014, est.)** 347 applied for aid; of those 84% were deemed to have need. 100% of freshmen with need received aid; of those 54% had need fully met. *Average percent of need met:* 94% (excluding resources awarded to replace EFC). *Average financial aid package:* $37,255 (excluding resources awarded to replace EFC). 29% of all full-time freshmen had no need and received non-need-based gift aid.

**UNDERGRADUATE FINANCIAL AID (Fall 2014, est.)** 1,171 applied for aid; of those 87% were deemed to have need. 100% of undergraduates with need received aid; of those 46% had need fully met. *Average percent of need met:* 92% (excluding resources awarded to replace EFC). *Average financial aid package:* $36,699 (excluding resources awarded to replace EFC). 26% of all full-time undergraduates had no need and received non-need-based gift aid.

**GIFT AID (NEED-BASED)** *Total amount:* $32,317,363 (5% federal, 1% state, 92% institutional, 2% external sources). *Receiving aid:* Freshmen: 68% (288); all full-time undergraduates: 64% (1,010). *Average award:* Freshmen: $32,756; Undergraduates: $31,090. *Scholarships, grants, and awards:* Federal Pell, FSEOG, state, private, college/university gift aid from institutional funds.

**GIFT AID (NON-NEED-BASED)** *Total amount:* $5,068,369 (95% institutional, 5% external sources). *Receiving aid:* Freshmen: 10% (43). Undergraduates: 6% (90).

*Average award:* Freshmen: $12,206. Undergraduates: $12,486. *Scholarships, grants, and awards by category: Academic interests/achievement:* 555 awards ($8,520,188 total): general academic interests/achievements. *Tuition waivers:* Full or partial for employees or children of employees. *ROTC:* Army cooperative.

**LOANS** *Student loans:* $9,123,864 (73% need-based, 27% non-need-based). 63% of past graduating class borrowed through all loan programs. *Average indebtedness per student:* $29,651. *Average need-based loan:* Freshmen: $4041. Undergraduates: $4969. *Parent loans:* $3,842,649 (100% non-need-based). *Programs:* Federal Direct (Subsidized and Unsubsidized Stafford, PLUS), Perkins, private loans, MEFA Loans.

**WORK-STUDY** *Federal work-study:* Total amount: $1,307,731; 771 jobs averaging $1670. *State or other work-study/employment:* Total amount: $476,082 (49% need-based, 51% non-need-based). 321 part-time jobs averaging $1650.

**APPLYING FOR FINANCIAL AID** *Required financial aid forms:* FAFSA, CSS Financial Aid PROFILE, noncustodial (divorced/separated) parent's statement, business/farm supplement, federal income tax form(s). *Financial aid deadline:* 2/1. *Notification date:* 4/1. Students must reply by 5/1.

**CONTACT** Ms. Susan Beard, Director of Financial Aid Programs, Wheaton College, 26 East Main Street, Norton, MA 02766, 508-286-8232 or toll-free 800-394-6003. *Fax:* 508-286-3787. *E-mail:* sfs@wheatonma.edu.
*Website:* http://www.wheatoncollege.edu/.

# WHEELING JESUIT UNIVERSITY
## Wheeling, WV

| Tuition & fees: $28,030 | Average undergraduate aid package: $24,604 |
| --- | --- |

**ABOUT THE INSTITUTION** Independent Roman Catholic (Jesuit), coed. *Awards:* certificates, bachelor's, master's, and doctoral degrees. 41 undergraduate majors. *Total enrollment:* 1,575. Undergraduates: 1,187. Freshmen: 252. Federal methodology is used as a basis for awarding need-based institutional aid.

**UNDERGRADUATE EXPENSES for 2015–2016** *Application fee:* $25. *Comprehensive fee:* $33,500 includes full-time tuition ($27,000), mandatory fees ($1030), and room and board ($5470). *College room only:* $3230. Room and board charges vary according to board plan, housing facility, and student level. *Part-time tuition:* $735 per credit hour.

**FRESHMAN FINANCIAL AID (Fall 2014, est.)** 229 applied for aid; of those 87% were deemed to have need. 100% of freshmen with need received aid; of those 39% had need fully met. *Average percent of need met:* 85% (excluding resources awarded to replace EFC). *Average financial aid package:* $25,267 (excluding resources awarded to replace EFC). 20% of all full-time freshmen had no need and received non-need-based gift aid.

**UNDERGRADUATE FINANCIAL AID (Fall 2014, est.)** 833 applied for aid; of those 85% were deemed to have need. 100% of undergraduates with need received aid; of those 36% had need fully met. *Average percent of need met:* 83% (excluding resources awarded to replace EFC). *Average financial aid package:* $24,604 (excluding resources awarded to replace EFC). 26% of all full-time undergraduates had no need and received non-need-based gift aid.

**GIFT AID (NEED-BASED)** *Total amount:* $3,580,499 (38% federal, 8% state, 54% institutional). *Receiving aid:* Freshmen: 52% (130); all full-time undergraduates: 45% (433). *Average award:* Freshmen: $8399; Undergraduates: $7422. *Scholarships, grants, and awards:* Federal Pell, FSEOG, state, private, college/university gift aid from institutional funds, Federal Nursing.

**GIFT AID (NON-NEED-BASED)** *Total amount:* $10,665,809 (2% federal, 4% state, 92% institutional, 2% external sources). *Receiving aid:* Freshmen: 76% (189). Undergraduates: 66% (634). *Average award:* Freshmen: $12,306. Undergraduates: $11,816. *Scholarships, grants, and awards by category: Academic interests/achievement:* 762 awards ($7,722,930 total): general academic interests/achievements, premedicine. *Creative arts/performance:* 49 awards ($130,500 total): music. *Special achievements/activities:* 67 awards ($259,045 total): community service, general special achievements/activities. *Special characteristics:* 207 awards ($1,292,297 total): children and siblings of alumni, children of faculty/staff, general special characteristics, religious affiliation. *Tuition waivers:* Full or partial for employees or children of employees.

**LOANS** *Student loans:* $6,706,009 (37% need-based, 63% non-need-based). 78% of past graduating class borrowed through all loan programs. *Average indebtedness*

*per student:* $29,131. *Average need-based loan:* Freshmen: $4444. Undergraduates: $4760. *Parent loans:* $899,175 (100% non-need-based). *Programs:* Federal Direct (Subsidized and Unsubsidized Stafford, PLUS), Perkins, Federal Nursing, alternative loans.

**WORK-STUDY** *Federal work-study:* Total amount: $198,439; 148 jobs averaging $2200. *State or other work-study/employment:* 130 part-time jobs averaging $2200.

**ATHLETIC AWARDS** Total amount: $2,213,786 (100% non-need-based).

**APPLYING FOR FINANCIAL AID** *Required financial aid forms:* FAFSA, institution's own form. *Financial aid deadline (priority):* 3/1. *Notification date:* Continuous beginning 3/15. Students must reply within 2 weeks of notification.

**CONTACT** Christie Tomczyk, Director of Financial Aid, Wheeling Jesuit University, 316 Washington Avenue, Wheeling, WV 26003-6295, 304-243-2304 or toll-free 800-624-6992 Ext. 2359. *Fax:* 304-243-4397. *E-mail:* finaid@wju.edu.
*Website:* http://www.wju.edu/.

# WHEELOCK COLLEGE
## Boston, MA

| Tuition & fees: $32,830 | Average undergraduate aid package: $22,967 |
|---|---|

**ABOUT THE INSTITUTION** Independent, coed, primarily women. *Awards:* certificates, bachelor's, and master's degrees. 14 undergraduate majors. *Total enrollment:* 1,331. Undergraduates: 869. Freshmen: 266. Federal methodology is used as a basis for awarding need-based institutional aid.

**UNDERGRADUATE EXPENSES** for 2015–2016 *Comprehensive fee:* $46,430 includes full-time tuition ($31,675), mandatory fees ($1155), and room and board ($13,600). *Part-time tuition:* $990 per credit hour.

**FRESHMAN FINANCIAL AID (Fall 2014, est.)** 244 applied for aid; of those 92% were deemed to have need. 100% of freshmen with need received aid; of those 15% had need fully met. *Average percent of need met:* 69% (excluding resources awarded to replace EFC). *Average financial aid package:* $25,443 (excluding resources awarded to replace EFC). 16% of all full-time freshmen had no need and received non-need-based gift aid.

**UNDERGRADUATE FINANCIAL AID (Fall 2014, est.)** 747 applied for aid; of those 93% were deemed to have need. 100% of undergraduates with need received aid; of those 14% had need fully met. *Average percent of need met:* 64% (excluding resources awarded to replace EFC). *Average financial aid package:* $22,967 (excluding resources awarded to replace EFC). 16% of all full-time undergraduates had no need and received non-need-based gift aid.

**GIFT AID (NEED-BASED)** *Total amount:* $13,253,636 (12% federal, 3% state, 81% institutional, 4% external sources). *Receiving aid:* Freshmen: 84% (225); all full-time undergraduates: 82% (691). *Average award:* Freshmen: $22,094; Undergraduates: $19,060. *Scholarships, grants, and awards:* Federal Pell, FSEOG, state, private, college/university gift aid from institutional funds.

**GIFT AID (NON-NEED-BASED)** *Total amount:* $2,270,461 (1% federal, 94% institutional, 5% external sources). *Receiving aid:* Freshmen: 9% (24). Undergraduates: 8% (67). *Average award:* Freshmen: $14,818. Undergraduates: $13,232. *Scholarships, grants, and awards by category:* Academic interests/achievement: general academic interests/achievements. *Tuition waivers:* Full or partial for employees or children of employees.

**LOANS** *Student loans:* $8,157,033 (74% need-based, 26% non-need-based). 85% of past graduating class borrowed through all loan programs. *Average indebtedness per student:* $46,690. *Average need-based loan:* Freshmen: $3109. Undergraduates: $4010. *Parent loans:* $2,516,597 (63% need-based, 37% non-need-based). *Programs:* Federal Direct (Subsidized and Unsubsidized Stafford, PLUS), Perkins, college/university.

**WORK-STUDY** *Federal work-study:* Total amount: $285,505; 198 jobs averaging $1800.

**APPLYING FOR FINANCIAL AID** *Required financial aid form:* FAFSA. *Financial aid deadline (priority):* 2/15. *Notification date:* Continuous beginning 3/15. Students must reply by 5/1.

**CONTACT** Roxanne Dumas, Director of Financial Aid, Wheelock College, 200 The Riverway, Boston, MA 02215-4176, 617-879-2443 or toll-free 800-734-5212. *Fax:* 617-879-2470. *E-mail:* finaid@wheelock.edu.
*Website:* http://www.wheelock.edu/.

# WHITMAN COLLEGE
## Walla Walla, WA

| Tuition & fees: $44,800 | Average undergraduate aid package: $34,254 |
|---|---|

**ABOUT THE INSTITUTION** Independent, coed. *Awards:* bachelor's degrees. 41 undergraduate majors. *Total enrollment:* 1,498. Undergraduates: 1,498. Freshmen: 395. Both federal and institutional methodology are used as a basis for awarding need-based institutional aid.

**UNDERGRADUATE EXPENSES** for 2015–2016 *Application fee:* $50. *Comprehensive fee:* $56,028 includes full-time tuition ($44,440), mandatory fees ($360), and room and board ($11,228). *College room only:* $5192. Room and board charges vary according to board plan and housing facility. *Part-time tuition:* $1852 per credit.

**FRESHMAN FINANCIAL AID (Fall 2014, est.)** 231 applied for aid; of those 76% were deemed to have need. 100% of freshmen with need received aid; of those 45% had need fully met. *Average percent of need met:* 93% (excluding resources awarded to replace EFC). *Average financial aid package:* $34,801 (excluding resources awarded to replace EFC). 29% of all full-time freshmen had no need and received non-need-based gift aid.

**UNDERGRADUATE FINANCIAL AID (Fall 2014, est.)** 796 applied for aid; of those 85% were deemed to have need. 100% of undergraduates with need received aid; of those 40% had need fully met. *Average percent of need met:* 92% (excluding resources awarded to replace EFC). *Average financial aid package:* $34,254 (excluding resources awarded to replace EFC). 31% of all full-time undergraduates had no need and received non-need-based gift aid.

**GIFT AID (NEED-BASED)** *Total amount:* $20,006,132 (5% federal, 1% state, 91% institutional, 3% external sources). *Receiving aid:* Freshmen: 44% (175); all full-time undergraduates: 46% (678). *Average award:* Freshmen: $29,099; Undergraduates: $28,484. *Scholarships, grants, and awards:* Federal Pell, FSEOG, state, private, college/university gift aid from institutional funds.

**GIFT AID (NON-NEED-BASED)** *Total amount:* $4,586,907 (96% institutional, 4% external sources). *Average award:* Freshmen: $10,159. Undergraduates: $9104. *Scholarships, grants, and awards by category:* Academic interests/achievement: general academic interests/achievements. *Creative arts/performance:* art/fine arts, debating, music, theater/drama. *Special characteristics:* ethnic background, first-generation college students, international students, veterans, veterans' children. *Tuition waivers:* Full or partial for employees or children of employees.

**LOANS** *Student loans:* $3,370,755 (81% need-based, 19% non-need-based). 49% of past graduating class borrowed through all loan programs. *Average indebtedness per student:* $19,147. *Average need-based loan:* Freshmen: $3869. Undergraduates: $4337. *Parent loans:* $1,320,525 (100% non-need-based). *Programs:* Federal Direct (Subsidized and Unsubsidized Stafford, PLUS), Perkins, alternative loans.

**WORK-STUDY** *Federal work-study:* Total amount: $931,733; 455 jobs averaging $1967. *State or other work-study/employment:* Total amount: $59,000 (100% need-based). 143 part-time jobs averaging $1846.

**APPLYING FOR FINANCIAL AID** *Required financial aid forms:* FAFSA, CSS Financial Aid PROFILE, noncustodial (divorced/separated) parent's statement. *Financial aid deadline:* 2/1 (priority: 11/15). *Notification date:* Continuous beginning 12/18. Students must reply within 2 weeks of notification.

**CONTACT** Tyson Harlow, Assistant Director, Whitman College, 345 Boyer Avenue, Walla Walla, WA 99362-2046, 509-527-5178 or toll-free 877-462-9448. *Fax:* 509-527-4967.
*Website:* http://www.whitman.edu/.

# WHITTIER COLLEGE
## Whittier, CA

| Tuition & fees: $41,636 | Average undergraduate aid package: $33,071 |
|---|---|

**ABOUT THE INSTITUTION** Independent, coed. *Awards:* bachelor's, master's, and doctoral degrees. 36 undergraduate majors. *Total enrollment:* 2,290. Undergraduates: 1,665. Freshmen: 388. Federal methodology is used as a basis for awarding need-based institutional aid.

**UNDERGRADUATE EXPENSES** for 2015–2016 *Application fee:* $50. *One-time required fee:* $200. *Comprehensive fee:* $53,881 includes full-time tuition

($41,246), mandatory fees ($390), and room and board ($12,245). **College room only:** $6720. Room and board charges vary according to board plan. **Part-time tuition:** $1720 per unit. Part-time tuition and fees vary according to course load.

**FRESHMAN FINANCIAL AID (Fall 2014, est.)** 333 applied for aid; of those 88% were deemed to have need. 100% of freshmen with need received aid; of those 24% had need fully met. **Average percent of need met:** 80% (excluding resources awarded to replace EFC). **Average financial aid package:** $34,377 (excluding resources awarded to replace EFC). 17% of all full-time freshmen had no need and received non-need-based gift aid.

**UNDERGRADUATE FINANCIAL AID (Fall 2014, est.)** 1,384 applied for aid; of those 92% were deemed to have need. 99% of undergraduates with need received aid; of those 16% had need fully met. **Average percent of need met:** 77% (excluding resources awarded to replace EFC). **Average financial aid package:** $33,071 (excluding resources awarded to replace EFC). 17% of all full-time undergraduates had no need and received non-need-based gift aid.

**GIFT AID (NEED-BASED) Total amount:** $33,468,797 (9% federal, 13% state, 77% institutional, 1% external sources). **Receiving aid:** Freshmen: 64% (247); all full-time undergraduates: 68% (1,122). **Average award:** Freshmen: $32,147; Undergraduates: $29,397. **Scholarships, grants, and awards:** Federal Pell, FSEOG, state, private, college/university gift aid from institutional funds.

**GIFT AID (NON-NEED-BASED) Total amount:** $5,571,617 (99% institutional, 1% external sources). **Receiving aid:** Freshmen: 12% (47). Undergraduates: 8% (134). **Average award:** Freshmen: $21,497. Undergraduates: $19,946. **Scholarships, grants, and awards by category:** Academic interests/achievement: general academic interests/achievements. Creative arts/performance: art/fine arts, music, theater/drama. Special characteristics: children and siblings of alumni, children of faculty/staff, international students. **Tuition waivers:** Full or partial for children of alumni, employees or children of employees. **ROTC:** Army cooperative.

**LOANS Student loans:** $10,736,192 (93% need-based, 7% non-need-based). 75% of past graduating class borrowed through all loan programs. Average indebtedness per student: $37,379. **Average need-based loan:** Freshmen: $4456. Undergraduates: $5614. **Parent loans:** $4,168,719 (93% need-based, 7% non-need-based). **Programs:** Federal Direct (Subsidized and Unsubsidized Stafford, PLUS), Perkins, alternative loans.

**WORK-STUDY Federal work-study:** Total amount: $961,690; 411 jobs averaging $2260. **State or other work-study/employment:** Total amount: $1,299,787 (92% need-based, 8% non-need-based). 464 part-time jobs averaging $1931.

**APPLYING FOR FINANCIAL AID Required financial aid form:** FAFSA. **Financial aid deadline:** 6/30 (priority: 3/1). **Notification date:** Continuous beginning 2/15. Students must reply within 2 weeks of notification.

**CONTACT** Mrs. Julie Aldama, Director of Financial Aid, Whittier College, 13406 East Philadelphia Street, Whittier, CA 90608-0634, 562-907-4285. Fax: 562-464-4560. E-mail: jaldama@whittier.edu. Website: http://www.whittier.edu/.

# WHITWORTH UNIVERSITY
## Spokane, WA

| Tuition & fees: $37,630 | Average undergraduate aid package: $31,373 |
| --- | --- |

**ABOUT THE INSTITUTION** Independent Presbyterian, coed. **Awards:** certificates, bachelor's, and master's degrees. 45 undergraduate majors. **Total enrollment:** 2,654. Undergraduates: 2,370. Freshmen: 619. Federal methodology is used as a basis for awarding need-based institutional aid.

**UNDERGRADUATE EXPENSES for 2015–2016 Comprehensive fee:** $47,908 includes full-time tuition ($36,734), mandatory fees ($896), and room and board ($10,278). Room and board charges vary according to board plan and housing facility. **Part-time tuition:** $1530 per credit hour. **Part-time fees:** $1530 per credit hour. Part-time tuition and fees vary according to course load.

**FRESHMAN FINANCIAL AID (Fall 2014, est.)** 539 applied for aid; of those 87% were deemed to have need. 100% of freshmen with need received aid; of those 18% had need fully met. **Average percent of need met:** 82% (excluding resources awarded to replace EFC). **Average financial aid package:** $33,144 (excluding resources awarded to replace EFC). 23% of all full-time freshmen had no need and received non-need-based gift aid.

**UNDERGRADUATE FINANCIAL AID (Fall 2014, est.)** 1,799 applied for aid; of those 89% were deemed to have need. 100% of undergraduates with need received

aid; of those 16% had need fully met. **Average percent of need met:** 80% (excluding resources awarded to replace EFC). **Average financial aid package:** $31,373 (excluding resources awarded to replace EFC). 26% of all full-time undergraduates had no need and received non-need-based gift aid.

**GIFT AID (NEED-BASED) Total amount:** $36,760,518 (8% federal, 8% state, 80% institutional, 4% external sources). **Receiving aid:** Freshmen: 75% (463); all full-time undergraduates: 69% (1,592). **Average award:** Freshmen: $24,618; Undergraduates: $22,974. **Scholarships, grants, and awards:** Federal Pell, FSEOG, state, private, college/university gift aid from institutional funds.

**GIFT AID (NON-NEED-BASED) Total amount:** $11,817,565 (1% federal, 96% institutional, 3% external sources). **Receiving aid:** Freshmen: 9% (53). Undergraduates: 7% (152). **Average award:** Freshmen: $19,447. Undergraduates: $16,897. **Scholarships, grants, and awards by category:** Academic interests/achievement: 1,884 awards ($26,824,424 total): general academic interests/achievements, military science. Creative arts/performance: 184 awards ($694,625 total): art/fine arts, journalism/publications, music, theater/drama. Special characteristics: 554 awards ($1,435,134 total): children and siblings of alumni, ethnic background, international students, members of minority groups. **Tuition waivers:** Full or partial for employees or children of employees, senior citizens. **ROTC:** Army cooperative.

**LOANS Student loans:** $11,745,722 (81% need-based, 19% non-need-based). 69% of past graduating class borrowed through all loan programs. Average indebtedness per student: $26,132. **Average need-based loan:** Freshmen: $4178. Undergraduates: $4963. **Parent loans:** $4,372,295 (42% need-based, 58% non-need-based). **Programs:** Federal Direct (Subsidized and Unsubsidized Stafford, PLUS), Perkins.

**WORK-STUDY Federal work-study:** Total amount: $2,130,353; 863 jobs averaging $2329. **State or other work-study/employment:** Total amount: $309,555 (100% need-based). 88 part-time jobs averaging $3300.

**APPLYING FOR FINANCIAL AID Required financial aid form:** FAFSA. **Financial aid deadline (priority):** 3/1. **Notification date:** Continuous beginning 3/15.

**CONTACT** Ms. Wendy Z. Olson, Director of Financial Aid, Whitworth University, 300 West Hawthorne Road, Spokane, WA 99251-0001, 509-777-4306 or toll-free 800-533-4668. Fax: 509-777-4601. E-mail: wolson@whitworth.edu. Website: http://www.whitworth.edu/.

# WICHITA STATE UNIVERSITY
## Wichita, KS

| Tuition & fees (KS res): $7265 | Average undergraduate aid package: $7684 |
| --- | --- |

**ABOUT THE INSTITUTION** State-supported, coed. **Awards:** certificates, associate, bachelor's, master's, and doctoral degrees. 56 undergraduate majors. **Total enrollment:** 15,003. Undergraduates: 11,979. Freshmen: 1,481. Federal methodology is used as a basis for awarding need-based institutional aid.

**UNDERGRADUATE EXPENSES for 2015–2016 Application fee:** $30. **Tuition, state resident:** full-time $5869; part-time $195.65 per credit hour. **Tuition, nonresident:** full-time $13,903; part-time $463.45 per credit hour. **Required fees:** full-time $1396; $46.55 per credit hour. Full-time tuition and fees vary according to course level, course load, degree level, program, and student level. Part-time tuition and fees vary according to course level, course load, degree level, program, and student level. **College room and board:** $8373. Room and board charges vary according to board plan and housing facility.

**FRESHMAN FINANCIAL AID (Fall 2013)** 1,137 applied for aid; of those 46% were deemed to have need. 99% of freshmen with need received aid; of those 75% had need fully met. **Average percent of need met:** 58% (excluding resources awarded to replace EFC). **Average financial aid package:** $5812 (excluding resources awarded to replace EFC). 38% of all full-time freshmen had no need and received non-need-based gift aid.

**UNDERGRADUATE FINANCIAL AID (Fall 2013)** 7,560 applied for aid; of those 59% were deemed to have need. 97% of undergraduates with need received aid; of those 66% had need fully met. **Average percent of need met:** 63% (excluding resources awarded to replace EFC). **Average financial aid package:** $7684 (excluding resources awarded to replace EFC). 15% of all full-time undergraduates had no need and received non-need-based gift aid.

**GIFT AID (NEED-BASED) Total amount:** $18,610,877 (95% federal, 4% state, 1% external sources). **Receiving aid:** Freshmen: 32% (383); all full-time undergraduates: 34% (2,845). **Average award:** Freshmen: $4400; Undergraduates: $4314.

*Scholarships, grants, and awards:* Federal Pell, FSEOG, state, private, college/university gift aid from institutional funds, Bureau of Indian Affairs Grants.
**GIFT AID (NON-NEED-BASED) Total amount:** $9,238,604 (1% federal, 1% state, 87% institutional, 11% external sources). *Receiving aid:* Freshmen: 26% (318). Undergraduates: 16% (1,354). *Average award:* Freshmen: $2430. Undergraduates: $1911. *Scholarships, grants, and awards by category: Academic interests/achievement:* area/ethnic studies, biological sciences, business, communication, computer science, education, engineering/technologies, English, foreign languages, general academic interests/achievements, health fields, humanities, international studies, mathematics, physical sciences, premedicine, social sciences. *Creative arts/performance:* applied art and design, art/fine arts, creative writing, dance, debating, journalism/publications, music, performing arts, theater/drama. *Special achievements/activities:* cheerleading/drum major, general special achievements/activities, leadership, memberships. *Special characteristics:* adult students, children of faculty/staff, first-generation college students, international students, members of minority groups, veterans. *Tuition waivers:* Full or partial for employees or children of employees, senior citizens.
**LOANS** *Student loans:* $45,432,463 (48% need-based, 52% non-need-based). 68% of past graduating class borrowed through all loan programs. *Average indebtedness per student:* $23,534. *Average need-based loan:* Freshmen: $3267. Undergraduates: $4292. *Parent loans:* $764,119 (100% non-need-based). *Programs:* Federal Direct (Subsidized and Unsubsidized Stafford, PLUS), Perkins.
**WORK-STUDY** *Federal work-study:* jobs available. *State or other work-study/employment:* Total amount: $89,700 (100% need-based). Part-time jobs available.
**ATHLETIC AWARDS** Total amount: $2,146,796 (100% non-need-based).
**APPLYING FOR FINANCIAL AID** *Required financial aid forms:* FAFSA, institution's own form. *Financial aid deadline (priority):* 3/1. *Notification date:* Continuous beginning 3/15. Students must reply within 2 weeks of notification.
**CONTACT** Sheelu M. Surender, Director of Financial Aid, Wichita State University, 1845 Fairmount Street, Wichita, KS 67260-0024, 316-978-5337 or toll-free 800-362-2594. *Fax:* 316-978-3396. *E-mail:* sheelu.surender@wichita.edu. *Website:* http://www.wichita.edu/.

# WIDENER UNIVERSITY
## Chester, PA

| Tuition & fees: $39,830 | Average undergraduate aid package: $29,545 |
|---|---|

**ABOUT THE INSTITUTION** Independent, coed. *Awards:* associate, bachelor's, master's, and doctoral degrees. 74 undergraduate majors. *Total enrollment:* 5,985. Undergraduates: 3,437. Freshmen: 739. Both federal and institutional methodology are used as a basis for awarding need-based institutional aid.
**UNDERGRADUATE EXPENSES** for 2015–2016 *Application fee:* $35. *Comprehensive fee:* $52,418 includes full-time tuition ($39,052), mandatory fees ($778), and room and board ($12,588). *College room only:* $6552. Full-time tuition and fees vary according to class time, course load, and program. Room and board charges vary according to board plan and housing facility. *Part-time tuition:* $1300 per credit hour.
**FRESHMAN FINANCIAL AID (Fall 2014, est.)** 703 applied for aid; of those 91% were deemed to have need. 100% of freshmen with need received aid; of those 41% had need fully met. *Average percent of need met:* 81% (excluding resources awarded to replace EFC). *Average financial aid package:* $32,294 (excluding resources awarded to replace EFC). 9% of all full-time freshmen had no need and received non-need-based gift aid.
**UNDERGRADUATE FINANCIAL AID (Fall 2014, est.)** 2,506 applied for aid; of those 92% were deemed to have need. 100% of undergraduates with need received aid; of those 20% had need fully met. *Average percent of need met:* 77% (excluding resources awarded to replace EFC). *Average financial aid package:* $29,545 (excluding resources awarded to replace EFC). 66% of all full-time undergraduates had no need and received non-need-based gift aid.
**GIFT AID (NEED-BASED) Total amount:** $53,871,581 (9% federal, 5% state, 84% institutional, 2% external sources). *Receiving aid:* Freshmen: 85% (620); all full-time undergraduates: 78% (2,235). *Average award:* Freshmen: $27,300; Undergraduates: $23,917. *Scholarships, grants, and awards:* Federal Pell, FSEOG, state, private, college/university gift aid from institutional funds, Federal Nursing.
**GIFT AID (NON-NEED-BASED) Total amount:** $7,728,952 (1% federal, 95% institutional, 4% external sources). *Receiving aid:* Freshmen: 83% (611). Undergrad-

uates: 72% (2,059). *Average award:* Freshmen: $22,340. Undergraduates: $20,604. *Scholarships, grants, and awards by category: Academic interests/achievement:* 2,394 awards ($43,213,620 total): biological sciences, business, communication, computer science, education, engineering/technologies, English, foreign languages, general academic interests/achievements, health fields, humanities, international studies, mathematics, military science, physical sciences, premedicine, social sciences. *Creative arts/performance:* 66 awards ($193,000 total): dance, music. *Special achievements/activities:* 59 awards ($287,500 total): community service, general special achievements/activities, leadership. *Special characteristics:* 124 awards ($2,294,370 total): adult students, children of faculty/staff, ethnic background, international students. *Tuition waivers:* Full or partial for employees or children of employees, senior citizens. *ROTC:* Army, Naval cooperative, Air Force cooperative.
**LOANS** *Student loans:* $26,727,779 (95% need-based, 5% non-need-based). *Average need-based loan:* Freshmen: $3695. Undergraduates: $4600. *Parent loans:* $7,636,850 (96% need-based, 4% non-need-based). *Programs:* Federal Direct (Subsidized and Unsubsidized Stafford, PLUS), Perkins.
**WORK-STUDY** *Federal work-study:* Total amount: $2,274,836; 1,634 jobs averaging $1400. *State or other work-study/employment:* Total amount: $410,765 (100% non-need-based). Part-time jobs available.
**APPLYING FOR FINANCIAL AID** *Required financial aid form:* FAFSA. *Financial aid deadline (priority):* 2/15. *Notification date:* Continuous beginning 3/15. Students must reply within 4 weeks of notification.
**CONTACT** Thomas K. Malloy, Director of Student Financial Services, Widener University, One University Place, Chester, PA 19013-5792, 610-499-4161 or toll-free 888-WIDENER. *Fax:* 610-499-4687. *E-mail:* finaidmc@mail.widener.edu. *Website:* http://www.widener.edu/.

# WILBERFORCE UNIVERSITY
## Wilberforce, OH

**CONTACT** Director of Financial Aid, Wilberforce University, 1055 North Bickett Road, Wilberforce, OH 45384, 937-708-5727 or toll-free 800-367-8568. *Fax:* 937-376-4752. *Website:* http://www.wilberforce.edu/.

# WILEY COLLEGE
## Marshall, TX

**CONTACT** Mr. Alan D. Jackson Jr., Director of Financial Aid, Wiley College, 711 Wiley Avenue, Marshall, TX 75670-5199, 903-927-3217 or toll-free 800-658-6889. *E-mail:* adjackson2@wileyc.edu. *Website:* http://www.wileyc.edu/.

# WILKES UNIVERSITY
## Wilkes-Barre, PA

| Tuition & fees: $31,262 | Average undergraduate aid package: $24,265 |
|---|---|

**ABOUT THE INSTITUTION** Independent, coed. *Awards:* bachelor's, master's, and doctoral degrees. 37 undergraduate majors. *Total enrollment:* 4,562. Undergraduates: 2,360. Freshmen: 559. Federal methodology is used as a basis for awarding need-based institutional aid.
**UNDERGRADUATE EXPENSES** for 2015–2016 *Application fee:* $40. *Comprehensive fee:* $44,070 includes full-time tuition ($29,750), mandatory fees ($1512), and room and board ($12,808). *College room only:* $7704. Room and board charges vary according to board plan and housing facility. *Part-time tuition:* $826 per credit hour. *Part-time fees:* $68 per credit hour.
**FRESHMAN FINANCIAL AID (Fall 2014, est.)** 523 applied for aid; of those 94% were deemed to have need. 100% of freshmen with need received aid; of those 10% had need fully met. *Average percent of need met:* 75% (excluding resources awarded to replace EFC). *Average financial aid package:* $25,626 (excluding resources awarded to replace EFC). 6% of all full-time freshmen had no need and received non-need-based gift aid.

UNDERGRADUATE FINANCIAL AID (Fall 2014, est.) 1,908 applied for aid; of those 94% were deemed to have need. 100% of undergraduates with need received aid; of those 10% had need fully met. **Average percent of need met:** 73% (excluding resources awarded to replace EFC). **Average financial aid package:** $24,265 (excluding resources awarded to replace EFC). 4% of all full-time undergraduates had no need and received non-need-based gift aid.

**GIFT AID (NEED-BASED) Total amount:** $33,972,020 (12% federal, 10% state, 77% institutional, 1% external sources). **Receiving aid:** Freshmen: 87% (487); all full-time undergraduates: 79% (1,752). **Average award:** Freshmen: $21,586; Undergraduates: $18,937. **Scholarships, grants, and awards:** Federal Pell, FSEOG, state, private, college/university gift aid from institutional funds.

**GIFT AID (NON-NEED-BASED) Total amount:** $1,923,123 (6% federal, 92% institutional, 2% external sources). **Receiving aid:** Freshmen: 73% (407). Undergraduates: 66% (1,463). **Average award:** Freshmen: $14,271. Undergraduates: $11,645. **Scholarships, grants, and awards by category:** Academic interests/achievement: general academic interests/achievements. Creative arts/performance: performing arts, theater/drama. Special achievements/activities: general special achievements/activities, leadership. Special characteristics: children of faculty/staff. **Tuition waivers:** Full or partial for employees or children of employees. **ROTC:** Army cooperative, Air Force.

**LOANS Student loans:** $19,372,486 (92% need-based, 8% non-need-based). 86% of past graduating class borrowed through all loan programs. Average indebtedness per student: $38,082. **Average need-based loan:** Freshmen: $4074. Undergraduates: $4743. **Parent loans:** $4,672,195 (80% need-based, 20% non-need-based). **Programs:** Federal Direct (Subsidized and Unsubsidized Stafford, PLUS), Perkins, Federal Nursing, state, college/university, Gulf Oil Loan Fund, Rulison Evans Loan Fund.

**WORK-STUDY Federal work-study:** Total amount: $2,690,051; jobs available. **State or other work-study/employment:** Part-time jobs available.

**APPLYING FOR FINANCIAL AID Required financial aid form:** FAFSA. **Financial aid deadline (priority):** 3/1. **Notification date:** Continuous.

**CONTACT** Melanie Wade, Vice President of Enrollment Services, Wilkes University, 84 West South Street, Wilkes-Barre, PA 18766, 570-408-4000 or toll-free 800-945-5378 Ext. 4400. Fax: 570-408-3000. E-mail: melanie.wade@wilkes.edu Website: http://www.wilkes.edu/.

# WILLAMETTE UNIVERSITY
## Salem, OR

| Tuition & fees: $44,076 | Average undergraduate aid package: $33,934 |
| --- | --- |

**ABOUT THE INSTITUTION** Independent United Methodist, coed. **Awards:** bachelor's, master's, and doctoral degrees. 41 undergraduate majors. **Total enrollment:** 3,060. Undergraduates: 2,375. Freshmen: 553. Federal methodology is used as a basis for awarding need-based institutional aid.

**UNDERGRADUATE EXPENSES for 2015–2016 Application fee:** $50. **Comprehensive fee:** $54,896 includes full-time tuition ($43,760), mandatory fees ($316), and room and board ($10,820). Full-time tuition and fees vary according to course load. Room and board charges vary according to board plan and housing facility. **Part-time tuition:** $5470 per course. Part-time tuition and fees vary according to course load. **Payment plan:** Tuition prepayment.

**FRESHMAN FINANCIAL AID (Fall 2014, est.)** 467 applied for aid; of those 79% were deemed to have need. 100% of freshmen with need received aid; of those 34% had need fully met. **Average percent of need met:** 84% (excluding resources awarded to replace EFC). **Average financial aid package:** $34,279 (excluding resources awarded to replace EFC). 32% of all full-time freshmen had no need and received non-need-based gift aid.

**UNDERGRADUATE FINANCIAL AID (Fall 2014, est.)** 1,444 applied for aid; of those 86% were deemed to have need. 100% of undergraduates with need received aid; of those 32% had need fully met. **Average percent of need met:** 84% (excluding resources awarded to replace EFC). **Average financial aid package:** $33,934 (excluding resources awarded to replace EFC). 36% of all full-time undergraduates had no need and received non-need-based gift aid.

**GIFT AID (NEED-BASED) Total amount:** $33,488,175 (8% federal, 1% state, 88% institutional, 3% external sources). **Receiving aid:** Freshmen: 65% (359); all full-time undergraduates: 61% (1,219). **Average award:** Freshmen: $27,478; Undergraduates: $26,574. **Scholarships, grants, and awards:** Federal Pell, FSEOG, state, private, college/university gift aid from institutional funds.

**GIFT AID (NON-NEED-BASED) Total amount:** $12,866,120 (99% institutional, 1% external sources). **Receiving aid:** Freshmen: 18% (100). Undergraduates: 10% (200). **Average award:** Freshmen: $19,565. Undergraduates: $17,896. **Scholarships, grants, and awards by category:** Academic interests/achievement: general academic interests/achievements. Creative arts/performance: general creative arts/performance. Special achievements/activities: general special achievements/activities. Special characteristics: general special characteristics. **Tuition waivers:** Full or partial for employees or children of employees. **ROTC:** Army cooperative, Air Force cooperative.

**LOANS Student loans:** $10,936,553 (89% need-based, 11% non-need-based). 66% of past graduating class borrowed through all loan programs. Average indebtedness per student: $26,936. **Average need-based loan:** Freshmen: $5240. Undergraduates: $5757. **Parent loans:** $3,234,777 (91% need-based, 9% non-need-based). **Programs:** Federal Direct (Subsidized and Unsubsidized Stafford, PLUS), Perkins.

**WORK-STUDY Federal work-study:** Total amount: $2,130,031; jobs available. **State or other work-study/employment:** Part-time jobs available.

**APPLYING FOR FINANCIAL AID Required financial aid form:** FAFSA. **Financial aid deadline (priority):** 2/1. **Notification date:** 3/15. Students must reply by 5/1 or within 2 weeks of notification.

**CONTACT** Patty Hoban, Director of Financial Aid, Willamette University, 900 State Street, Salem, OR 97301-3931, 503-370-6273 or toll-free 877-542-2787. Fax: 503-370-6588. E-mail: phoban@willamette.edu. Website: http://www.willamette.edu/.

# WILLIAM CAREY UNIVERSITY
## Hattiesburg, MS

**CONTACT** Ms. Brenda Pittman, Associate Director of Financial Aid, William Carey University, 498 Tuscan Avenue, Hattiesburg, MS 39401-5499, 601-318-6153 or toll-free 800-962-5991. Website: http://www.wmcarey.edu/.

# WILLIAM JESSUP UNIVERSITY
## Rocklin, CA

| Tuition & fees: $26,480 | Average undergraduate aid package: $20,123 |
| --- | --- |

**ABOUT THE INSTITUTION** Independent nondenominational, coed. **Awards:** certificates, associate, bachelor's, and master's degrees. 19 undergraduate majors. **Total enrollment:** 1,212. Undergraduates: 1,146. Freshmen: 212. Federal methodology is used as a basis for awarding need-based institutional aid.

**UNDERGRADUATE EXPENSES for 2015–2016 Application fee:** $45. **Comprehensive fee:** $36,758 includes full-time tuition ($26,480) and room and board ($10,278). Full-time tuition and fees vary according to course load. Room and board charges vary according to board plan and housing facility. **Part-time tuition:** $1120 per credit. Part-time tuition and fees vary according to course load.

**FRESHMAN FINANCIAL AID (Fall 2014, est.)** 193 applied for aid; of those 90% were deemed to have need. 100% of freshmen with need received aid; of those 16% had need fully met. **Average percent of need met:** 70% (excluding resources awarded to replace EFC). **Average financial aid package:** $21,347 (excluding resources awarded to replace EFC). 13% of all full-time freshmen had no need and received non-need-based gift aid.

**UNDERGRADUATE FINANCIAL AID (Fall 2014, est.)** 857 applied for aid; of those 90% were deemed to have need. 100% of undergraduates with need received aid; of those 12% had need fully met. **Average percent of need met:** 65% (excluding resources awarded to replace EFC). **Average financial aid package:** $20,123 (excluding resources awarded to replace EFC). 16% of all full-time undergraduates had no need and received non-need-based gift aid.

**GIFT AID (NEED-BASED) Total amount:** $11,796,259 (19% federal, 23% state, 54% institutional, 4% external sources). **Receiving aid:** Freshmen: 84% (174); all full-time undergraduates: 81% (767). **Average award:** Freshmen: $18,393; Undergraduates: $16,497. **Scholarships, grants, and awards:** Federal Pell, FSEOG, state, private, college/university gift aid from institutional funds.

**GIFT AID (NON-NEED-BASED)** *Total amount:* $1,536,095 (81% institutional, 19% external sources). *Receiving aid:* Freshmen: 10% (20). Undergraduates: 7% (69). *Average award:* Freshmen: $8538. Undergraduates: $7249. *Scholarships, grants, and awards by category:* Academic interests/achievement: 670 awards ($3,096,409 total): area/ethnic studies, biological sciences, business, education, English, general academic interests/achievements, humanities, international studies, mathematics, religion/biblical studies, social sciences. *Creative arts/performance:* 183 awards ($513,367 total): applied art and design, art/fine arts, general creative arts/performance, music, performing arts, theater/drama. *Special achievements/activities:* 440 awards ($1,150,389 total): general special achievements/activities, leadership, religious involvement. *Special characteristics:* 515 awards ($1,711,483 total): adult students, children of faculty/staff, ethnic background, general special characteristics, international students, out-of-state students, previous college experience, relatives of clergy, siblings of current students, veterans, veterans' children. *Tuition waivers:* Full or partial for employees or children of employees. *ROTC:* Air Force cooperative.
**LOANS** *Student loans:* $6,391,453 (51% need-based, 49% non-need-based). 74% of past graduating class borrowed through all loan programs. *Average indebtedness per student:* $23,636. *Average need-based loan:* Freshmen: $3296. Undergraduates: $4465. *Parent loans:* $1,047,881 (48% need-based, 52% non-need-based). *Programs:* Federal Direct (Subsidized and Unsubsidized Stafford, PLUS).
**WORK-STUDY** *Federal work-study:* Total amount: $66,281; 123 jobs averaging $1551. *State or other work-study/employment:* Total amount: $150,000 (100% non-need-based). 87 part-time jobs averaging $1206.
**ATHLETIC AWARDS** Total amount: $1,778,431 (75% need-based, 25% non-need-based).
**APPLYING FOR FINANCIAL AID** *Required financial aid form:* FAFSA. *Financial aid deadline (priority):* 3/2. *Notification date:* Continuous beginning 3/2. Students must reply within 3 weeks of notification.
**CONTACT** Office of Financial Aid, William Jessup University, 333 Sunset Boulevard, Rocklin, CA 95765, 916-577-2233. *Fax:* 916-577-2230. *E-mail:* finaid@jessup.edu. *Website:* http://www.jessup.edu/.

## WILLIAM JEWELL COLLEGE
### Liberty, MO

| Tuition & fees: $32,330 | Average undergraduate aid package: $26,735 |
|---|---|

**ABOUT THE INSTITUTION** Independent, coed. *Awards:* certificates, bachelor's, and master's degrees (also offers evening program with significant enrollment not reflected in profile). 39 undergraduate majors. *Total enrollment:* 1,060. Undergraduates: 1,043. Freshmen: 265. Federal methodology is used as a basis for awarding need-based institutional aid.
**UNDERGRADUATE EXPENSES** for 2015–2016 *Comprehensive fee:* $41,210 includes full-time tuition ($31,730), mandatory fees ($600), and room and board ($8880). Full-time tuition and fees vary according to course load and program. Room and board charges vary according to board plan and housing facility. *Part-time tuition:* $930 per credit.
**FRESHMAN FINANCIAL AID (Fall 2014, est.)** 232 applied for aid; of those 81% were deemed to have need. 100% of freshmen with need received aid; of those 25% had need fully met. *Average percent of need met:* 77% (excluding resources awarded to replace EFC). *Average financial aid package:* $24,492 (excluding resources awarded to replace EFC). 13% of all full-time freshmen had no need and received non-need-based gift aid.
**UNDERGRADUATE FINANCIAL AID (Fall 2014, est.)** 845 applied for aid; of those 87% were deemed to have need. 100% of undergraduates with need received aid; of those 24% had need fully met. *Average percent of need met:* 79% (excluding resources awarded to replace EFC). *Average financial aid package:* $26,735 (excluding resources awarded to replace EFC). 14% of all full-time undergraduates had no need and received non-need-based gift aid.
**GIFT AID (NEED-BASED)** *Total amount:* $12,511,743 (13% federal, 3% state, 82% institutional, 2% external sources). *Receiving aid:* Freshmen: 71% (188); all full-time undergraduates: 68% (698). *Average award:* Freshmen: $21,517; Undergraduates: $19,646. *Scholarships, grants, and awards:* Federal Pell, FSEOG, state, college/university gift aid from institutional funds.
**GIFT AID (NON-NEED-BASED)** *Total amount:* $3,935,169 (1% state, 95% institutional, 4% external sources). *Receiving aid:* Freshmen: 71% (188). Undergraduates: 68% (696). *Average award:* Freshmen: $17,666. Undergraduates: $15,269. *Scholarships, grants, and awards by category:* Academic interests/

achievement: 758 awards ($10,352,675 total): general academic interests/achievements. *Creative arts/performance:* 130 awards ($433,725 total): dance, debating, journalism/publications, music, theater/drama. *Special achievements/activities:* 16 awards ($36,250 total): cheerleading/drum major, religious involvement. *Special characteristics:* 148 awards ($847,012 total): children and siblings of alumni, children of faculty/staff, siblings of current students. *Tuition waivers:* Full or partial for employees or children of employees. *ROTC:* Army cooperative.
**LOANS** *Student loans:* $5,484,206 (75% need-based, 25% non-need-based). 64% of past graduating class borrowed through all loan programs. *Average indebtedness per student:* $29,885. *Average need-based loan:* Freshmen: $4262. Undergraduates: $5298. *Parent loans:* $1,484,178 (85% need-based, 15% non-need-based). *Programs:* Federal Direct (Subsidized and Unsubsidized Stafford, PLUS), Perkins, Federal Nursing, alternative loans.
**WORK-STUDY** *Federal work-study:* Total amount: $1,222,592; 494 jobs averaging $2429. *State or other work-study/employment:* 146 part-time jobs averaging $359.
**ATHLETIC AWARDS** Total amount: $3,905,200 (61% need-based, 39% non-need-based).
**APPLYING FOR FINANCIAL AID** *Required financial aid form:* FAFSA. *Financial aid deadline (priority):* 3/1. *Notification date:* Continuous beginning 3/1. Students must reply within 2 weeks of notification.
**CONTACT** Mr. Daniel Holt, Director of Financial Aid and Scholarship Services, William Jewell College, 500 College Hill, Liberty, MO 64068, 816-415-5977 or toll-free 888-2JEWELL. *Fax:* 816-415-5006. *E-mail:* holtd@william.jewell.edu. *Website:* http://www.jewell.edu/.

## WILLIAM PATERSON UNIVERSITY OF NEW JERSEY
### Wayne, NJ

| Tuition & fees (NJ res): $12,244 | Average undergraduate aid package: $10,356 |
|---|---|

**ABOUT THE INSTITUTION** State-supported, coed. *Awards:* certificates, bachelor's, master's, and doctoral degrees. 60 undergraduate majors. *Total enrollment:* 11,048. Undergraduates: 9,586. Freshmen: 1,171. Federal methodology is used as a basis for awarding need-based institutional aid.
**UNDERGRADUATE EXPENSES** for 2015–2016 *Application fee:* $50. *Tuition, state resident:* full-time $7622; part-time $243.69 per credit hour. *Tuition, nonresident:* full-time $15,298; part-time $495.69 per credit hour. *Required fees:* full-time $4622; $144.81 per credit hour. Full-time tuition and fees vary according to course load and location. Part-time tuition and fees vary according to course load and location. *College room and board:* $10,670; *Room only:* $6700. Room and board charges vary according to board plan and housing facility.
**FRESHMAN FINANCIAL AID (Fall 2013)** 1,102 applied for aid; of those 82% were deemed to have need. 98% of freshmen with need received aid; of those 38% had need fully met. *Average financial aid package:* $10,647 (excluding resources awarded to replace EFC). 7% of all full-time freshmen had no need and received non-need-based gift aid.
**UNDERGRADUATE FINANCIAL AID (Fall 2013)** 6,972 applied for aid; of those 84% were deemed to have need. 98% of undergraduates with need received aid; of those 34% had need fully met. *Average financial aid package:* $10,356 (excluding resources awarded to replace EFC). 6% of all full-time undergraduates had no need and received non-need-based gift aid.
**GIFT AID (NEED-BASED)** *Total amount:* $33,150,500 (60% federal, 38% state, 2% institutional). *Receiving aid:* Freshmen: 56% (650); all full-time undergraduates: 49% (3,840). *Average award:* Freshmen: $8536; Undergraduates: $7877. *Scholarships, grants, and awards:* Federal Pell, FSEOG, state, private, college/university gift aid from institutional funds.
**GIFT AID (NON-NEED-BASED)** *Total amount:* $9,180,000 (2% federal, 1% state, 92% institutional, 5% external sources). *Receiving aid:* Freshmen: 25% (296). Undergraduates: 18% (1,425). *Average award:* Freshmen: $3841. Undergraduates: $5192. *Tuition waivers:* Full or partial for employees or children of employees, senior citizens. *ROTC:* Air Force cooperative.
**LOANS** *Student loans:* $58,000,000 (47% need-based, 53% non-need-based). 76% of past graduating class borrowed through all loan programs. *Average indebtedness per student:* $25,062. *Average need-based loan:* Freshmen: $3537. Undergrad-

uates: $4461. *Parent loans:* $7,000,000 (100% non-need-based). *Programs:* Federal Direct (Subsidized and Unsubsidized Stafford, PLUS), Perkins, Federal Nursing, state.
**WORK-STUDY** *Federal work-study:* jobs available. *State or other work-study/employment:* Part-time jobs available.
**APPLYING FOR FINANCIAL AID** *Required financial aid form:* FAFSA. *Financial aid deadline (priority):* 4/1. *Notification date:* Continuous beginning 3/15.
**CONTACT** Michael Corso, Director of Financial Aid, William Paterson University of New Jersey, 300 Pompton Road, Morris Hall, 1st Floor, Wayne, NJ 07470, 973-720-2202 or toll-free 877-WPU-EXCEL. *Fax:* 973-720-3133. *E-mail:* finaid@wpunj.edu. *Website:* http://www.wpunj.edu/.

# WILLIAM PEACE UNIVERSITY
## Raleigh, NC

| Tuition & fees: $25,850 | Average undergraduate aid package: $19,961 |
|---|---|

**ABOUT THE INSTITUTION** Independent Presbyterian Church (U.S.A.), coed. *Awards:* bachelor's degrees. 19 undergraduate majors. *Total enrollment:* 1,077. Undergraduates: 1,077. Freshmen: 280. Federal methodology is used as a basis for awarding need-based institutional aid.
**UNDERGRADUATE EXPENSES for 2015–2016** *Application fee:* $35. *Comprehensive fee:* $35,750 includes full-time tuition ($25,650), mandatory fees ($200), and room and board ($9900). Full-time tuition and fees vary according to class time and course load. *Part-time tuition:* $855 per credit hour. Part-time tuition and fees vary according to class time and course load.
**FRESHMAN FINANCIAL AID (Fall 2013)** 317 applied for aid; of those 93% were deemed to have need. 100% of freshmen with need received aid; of those 16% had need fully met. *Average percent of need met:* 66% (excluding resources awarded to replace EFC). *Average financial aid package:* $24,109 (excluding resources awarded to replace EFC). 7% of all full-time freshmen had no need and received non-need-based gift aid.
**UNDERGRADUATE FINANCIAL AID (Fall 2013)** 982 applied for aid; of those 93% were deemed to have need. 100% of undergraduates with need received aid; of those 13% had need fully met. *Average percent of need met:* 52% (excluding resources awarded to replace EFC). *Average financial aid package:* $19,961 (excluding resources awarded to replace EFC). 7% of all full-time undergraduates had no need and received non-need-based gift aid.
**GIFT AID (NEED-BASED)** *Total amount:* $12,199,655 (23% federal, 21% state, 55% institutional, 1% external sources). *Receiving aid:* Freshmen: 79% (260); all full-time undergraduates: 66% (717). *Average award:* Freshmen: $12,672; Undergraduates: $8202. *Scholarships, grants, and awards:* Federal Pell, FSEOG, state, private, college/university gift aid from institutional funds.
**GIFT AID (NON-NEED-BASED)** *Total amount:* $3,194,373 (94% institutional, 6% external sources). *Receiving aid:* Freshmen: 79% (260). Undergraduates: 64% (694). *Average award:* Freshmen: $13,095. Undergraduates: $10,903. *Scholarships, grants, and awards by category:* Academic interests/achievement: 785 awards ($6,669,394 total): general academic interests/achievements. Creative arts/performance: 18 awards ($26,750 total): art/fine arts, performing arts. Special achievements/activities: 117 awards ($448,000 total): community service, leadership. Special characteristics: 9 awards ($24,217 total): children and siblings of alumni, children of faculty/staff, siblings of current students. *Tuition waivers:* Full or partial for employees or children of employees. *ROTC:* Army cooperative, Naval cooperative, Air Force cooperative.
**LOANS** *Student loans:* $6,213,242 (49% need-based, 51% non-need-based). 82% of past graduating class borrowed through all loan programs. *Average indebtedness per student:* $32,000. *Average need-based loan:* Freshmen: $3479. Undergraduates: $3943. *Parent loans:* $1,566,694 (86% need-based, 14% non-need-based). *Programs:* Federal Direct (Subsidized and Unsubsidized Stafford, PLUS), alternative loans.
**WORK-STUDY** *Federal work-study:* 128 jobs averaging $2000. *State or other work-study/employment:* Part-time jobs available.
**APPLYING FOR FINANCIAL AID** *Required financial aid form:* FAFSA. *Financial aid deadline (priority):* 2/15. *Notification date:* Continuous beginning 3/1. Students must reply within 4 weeks of notification.

**CONTACT** Ms. Michelle Day, Director of Financial Aid, William Peace University, 15 East Peace Street, Raleigh, NC 27604, 919-508-2260. *Fax:* 919-508-2325. *E-mail:* michelle.day@peace.edu. *Website:* http://www.peace.edu/.

# WILLIAM PENN UNIVERSITY
## Oskaloosa, IA

**CONTACT** Cyndi Peiffer, Director of Financial Aid, William Penn University, 201 Trueblood Avenue, Oskaloosa, IA 52577-1799, 641-673-1060. *Fax:* 641-673-1115. *E-mail:* peifferc@wmpenn.edu. *Website:* http://www.wmpenn.edu/.

# WILLIAMS BAPTIST COLLEGE
## Walnut Ridge, AR

| Tuition & fees: $16,430 | Average undergraduate aid package: $17,732 |
|---|---|

**ABOUT THE INSTITUTION** Independent Southern Baptist, coed. *Awards:* associate and bachelor's degrees. 26 undergraduate majors. *Total enrollment:* 560. Undergraduates: 560. Freshmen: 164. Federal methodology is used as a basis for awarding need-based institutional aid.
**UNDERGRADUATE EXPENSES for 2015–2016** *Comprehensive fee:* $23,430 includes full-time tuition ($15,400), mandatory fees ($1030), and room and board ($7000). Room and board charges vary according to board plan. *Part-time tuition:* $640 per credit hour. Part-time tuition and fees vary according to course load.
**FRESHMAN FINANCIAL AID (Fall 2013)** 126 applied for aid; of those 78% were deemed to have need. 100% of freshmen with need received aid. *Average financial aid package:* $14,196 (excluding resources awarded to replace EFC).
**UNDERGRADUATE FINANCIAL AID (Fall 2013)** 392 applied for aid; of those 84% were deemed to have need. 100% of undergraduates with need received aid. *Average financial aid package:* $17,732 (excluding resources awarded to replace EFC).
**GIFT AID (NEED-BASED)** *Total amount:* $1,174,891 (98% federal, 2% state). *Receiving aid:* Freshmen: 48% (73); all full-time undergraduates: 54% (256). *Average award:* Freshmen: $4425; Undergraduates: $4447. *Scholarships, grants, and awards:* Federal Pell, FSEOG, state, private, college/university gift aid from institutional funds.
**GIFT AID (NON-NEED-BASED)** *Total amount:* $2,988,683 (34% state, 57% institutional, 9% external sources). *Receiving aid:* Freshmen: 64% (98). Undergraduates: 68% (324). *Scholarships, grants, and awards by category:* Academic interests/achievement: 418 awards ($1,593,086 total): biological sciences, business, education, general academic interests/achievements, humanities, religion/biblical studies. Creative arts/performance: 45 awards ($41,785 total): art/fine arts, music, theater/drama. Special achievements/activities: 11 awards ($7000 total): cheerleading/drum major. Special characteristics: 79 awards ($128,309 total): children of faculty/staff, international students, members of minority groups, relatives of clergy, religious affiliation. *Tuition waivers:* Full or partial for employees or children of employees, senior citizens. *ROTC:* Army cooperative.
**LOANS** *Student loans:* $1,839,158 (57% need-based, 43% non-need-based). 71% of past graduating class borrowed through all loan programs. *Average indebtedness per student:* $20,077. *Average need-based loan:* Freshmen: $2913. Undergraduates: $3650. *Parent loans:* $232,142 (100% non-need-based). *Programs:* Federal Direct (Subsidized and Unsubsidized Stafford, PLUS).
**WORK-STUDY** *Federal work-study:* 191 jobs averaging $1320. *State or other work-study/employment:* Total amount: $28,007 (100% non-need-based). 20 part-time jobs averaging $1400.
**ATHLETIC AWARDS** Total amount: $1,058,882 (100% non-need-based).
**APPLYING FOR FINANCIAL AID** *Required financial aid form:* FAFSA. *Financial aid deadline:* Continuous. *Notification date:* Continuous beginning 4/1. Students must reply within 2 weeks of notification.

**CONTACT** Mrs. Barbara Turner, Director of Financial Aid, Williams Baptist College, 60 West Fulbright Avenue, Walnut Ridge, AR 72476, 870-759-4112 or toll-free 800-722-4434. *Fax:* 870-759-4209. *E-mail:* bturner@wbcoll.edu. *Website:* http://www.wbcoll.edu/.

## WILLIAMS COLLEGE
### Williamstown, MA

| Tuition & fees: $48,310 | Average undergraduate aid package: $47,404 |
|---|---|

**ABOUT THE INSTITUTION** Independent, coed. *Awards:* bachelor's and master's degrees. 41 undergraduate majors. *Total enrollment:* 2,099. Undergraduates: 2,045. Freshmen: 546. Institutional methodology is used as a basis for awarding need-based institutional aid.

**UNDERGRADUATE EXPENSES for 2015–2016** *Application fee:* $65. *Comprehensive fee:* $61,070 includes full-time tuition ($48,030), mandatory fees ($280), and room and board ($12,760). *College room only:* $6460. Room and board charges vary according to board plan.

**FRESHMAN FINANCIAL AID (Fall 2014, est.)** 322 applied for aid; of those 81% were deemed to have need. 100% of freshmen with need received aid; of those 100% had need fully met. *Average percent of need met:* 100% (excluding resources awarded to replace EFC). *Average financial aid package:* $47,675 (excluding resources awarded to replace EFC).

**UNDERGRADUATE FINANCIAL AID (Fall 2014, est.)** 1,136 applied for aid; of those 88% were deemed to have need. 100% of undergraduates with need received aid; of those 100% had need fully met. *Average percent of need met:* 100% (excluding resources awarded to replace EFC). *Average financial aid package:* $47,404 (excluding resources awarded to replace EFC).

**GIFT AID (NEED-BASED)** *Total amount:* $44,499,407 (5% federal, 93% institutional, 2% external sources). *Receiving aid:* Freshmen: 48% (260); all full-time undergraduates: 50% (999). *Average award:* Freshmen: $43,460; Undergraduates: $43,689. *Scholarships, grants, and awards:* Federal Pell, FSEOG, state, private, college/university gift aid from institutional funds.

**GIFT AID (NON-NEED-BASED)** *Total amount:* $982,664 (1% federal, 99% external sources). *ROTC:* Air Force cooperative.

**LOANS** *Student loans:* $2,438,116 (51% need-based, 49% non-need-based). 34% of past graduating class borrowed through all loan programs. *Average indebtedness per student:* $12,627. *Average need-based loan:* Freshmen: $2731. Undergraduates: $2965. *Parent loans:* $2,551,830 (100% non-need-based). *Programs:* Federal Direct (Subsidized and Unsubsidized Stafford, PLUS), Perkins, college/university.

**WORK-STUDY** *Federal work-study:* Total amount: $887,210; 439 jobs averaging $1900. *State or other work-study/employment:* Total amount: $981,579 (84% need-based, 16% non-need-based). 467 part-time jobs averaging $1876.

**APPLYING FOR FINANCIAL AID** *Required financial aid forms:* FAFSA, CSS Financial Aid PROFILE, noncustodial (divorced/separated) parent's statement, signed copies of parents' and student's federal income tax returns. *Financial aid deadline:* 2/1. *Notification date:* 4/1. Students must reply by 5/1.

**CONTACT** Mr. Paul J. Boyer, Director of Financial Aid, Williams College, PO Box 37, Williamstown, MA 01267, 413-597-4181. *Fax:* 413-597-2999. *E-mail:* paul.j.boyer@williams.edu. *Website:* http://www.williams.edu/.

## WILLIAMSON CHRISTIAN COLLEGE
### Franklin, TN

**CONTACT** Jeanie Maguire, Director of Financial Aid, Williamson Christian College, 200 Seaboard Lane, Franklin, TN 37067, 615-771-7821. *Fax:* 615-771-7810. *E-mail:* info@williamsoncc.edu. *Website:* http://www.williamsoncc.edu/.

## WILLIAM WOODS UNIVERSITY
### Fulton, MO

| Tuition & fees: $22,160 | Average undergraduate aid package: $17,991 |
|---|---|

**ABOUT THE INSTITUTION** Independent Christian Church (Disciples of Christ), coed. *Awards:* certificates, associate, bachelor's, master's, and doctoral degrees. 35 undergraduate majors. *Total enrollment:* 2,031. Undergraduates: 1,006. Freshmen: 200. Federal methodology is used as a basis for awarding need-based institutional aid.

**UNDERGRADUATE EXPENSES for 2015–2016** *Comprehensive fee:* $31,120 includes full-time tuition ($21,370), mandatory fees ($790), and room and board ($8960). *College room only:* $4600. Full-time tuition and fees vary according to degree level and program. Room and board charges vary according to board plan and housing facility. *Part-time tuition:* $325 per credit hour. *Part-time fees:* $35 per term. Part-time tuition and fees vary according to course load, degree level, and program.

**FRESHMAN FINANCIAL AID (Fall 2014, est.)** 127 applied for aid; of those 82% were deemed to have need. 100% of freshmen with need received aid; of those 22% had need fully met. *Average percent of need met:* 70% (excluding resources awarded to replace EFC). *Average financial aid package:* $17,688 (excluding resources awarded to replace EFC). 24% of all full-time freshmen had no need and received non-need-based gift aid.

**UNDERGRADUATE FINANCIAL AID (Fall 2014, est.)** 639 applied for aid; of those 84% were deemed to have need. 100% of undergraduates with need received aid; of those 24% had need fully met. *Average percent of need met:* 74% (excluding resources awarded to replace EFC). *Average financial aid package:* $17,991 (excluding resources awarded to replace EFC). 23% of all full-time undergraduates had no need and received non-need-based gift aid.

**GIFT AID (NEED-BASED)** *Total amount:* $5,929,617 (23% federal, 4% state, 66% institutional, 7% external sources). *Receiving aid:* Freshmen: 52% (104); all full-time undergraduates: 63% (533). *Average award:* Freshmen: $14,008; Undergraduates: $13,048. *Scholarships, grants, and awards:* Federal Pell, FSEOG, state, private, college/university gift aid from institutional funds.

**GIFT AID (NON-NEED-BASED)** *Total amount:* $2,338,057 (2% state, 94% institutional, 4% external sources). *Receiving aid:* Freshmen: 10% (20). Undergraduates: 10% (83). *Average award:* Freshmen: $11,114. Undergraduates: $9375. *Scholarships, grants, and awards by category:* Academic interests/achievement: general academic interests/achievements, health fields. *Creative arts/performance:* art/fine arts, journalism/publications, performing arts, theater/drama. *Special achievements/activities:* general special achievements/activities, leadership. *Special characteristics:* children and siblings of alumni, children of faculty/staff, relatives of clergy, religious affiliation, siblings of current students. *Tuition waivers:* Full or partial for children of alumni, employees or children of employees, senior citizens. *ROTC:* Army cooperative, Naval cooperative, Air Force cooperative.

**LOANS** *Student loans:* $5,056,572 (68% need-based, 32% non-need-based). 71% of past graduating class borrowed through all loan programs. *Average indebtedness per student:* $21,260. *Average need-based loan:* Freshmen: $4205. Undergraduates: $5459. *Parent loans:* $2,295,595 (48% need-based, 52% non-need-based). *Programs:* Federal Direct (Subsidized and Unsubsidized Stafford, PLUS), Perkins, college/university.

**WORK-STUDY** *Federal work-study:* Total amount: $241,168; jobs available. *State or other work-study/employment:* Total amount: $142,002 (39% need-based, 61% non-need-based). Part-time jobs available.

**ATHLETIC AWARDS** Total amount: $645,377 (59% need-based, 41% non-need-based).

**APPLYING FOR FINANCIAL AID** *Required financial aid forms:* FAFSA, institution's own form. *Financial aid deadline (priority):* 3/1. *Notification date:* Continuous beginning 3/15. Students must reply within 2 weeks of notification.

**CONTACT** Deana Ready, Director of Student Financial Services, William Woods University, One University Avenue, Fulton, MO 65251, 573-592-4236 or toll-free 800-995-3159 Ext. 4221. *Fax:* 573-592-1180. *E-mail:* deana.ready@williamwoods.edu. *Website:* http://www.williamwoods.edu/.

# WILMINGTON COLLEGE
## Wilmington, OH

**CONTACT** Donna Barton, Coordinator of Financial Aid, Wilmington College, Pyle Center Box 1184, Wilmington, OH 45177, 937-382-6661 Ext. 466 or toll-free 800-341-9318. *Fax:* 937-383-8564.
*Website:* http://www.wilmington.edu/.

# WILMINGTON UNIVERSITY
## New Castle, DE

**CONTACT** J. Lynn Iocono, Director of Financial Aid, Wilmington University, 320 DuPont Highway, New Castle, DE 19720, 302-328-9437 or toll-free 877-967-5464. *Fax:* 302-328-5902.
*Website:* http://www.wilmu.edu/.

# WILSON COLLEGE
## Chambersburg, PA

| Tuition & fees: $24,380 | Average undergraduate aid package: $11,503 |
|---|---|

**ABOUT THE INSTITUTION** Independent Presbyterian Church (U.S.A.), coed, primarily women. **Awards:** associate, bachelor's, and master's degrees. 23 undergraduate majors. **Total enrollment:** 662. Undergraduates: 571. Freshmen: 70. Federal methodology is used as a basis for awarding need-based institutional aid.
**UNDERGRADUATE EXPENSES for 2015–2016 Comprehensive fee:** $35,080 includes full-time tuition ($23,745), mandatory fees ($635), and room and board ($10,700). **College room only:** $5390. Full-time tuition and fees vary according to program. Room and board charges vary according to board plan and housing facility. **Part-time tuition:** $2375 per course. **Part-time fees:** $55 per course; $56 per term. Part-time tuition and fees vary according to course load and program.
**FRESHMAN FINANCIAL AID (Fall 2014, est.)** 309 applied for aid; of those 93% were deemed to have need. 100% of freshmen with need received aid; of those 19% had need fully met. **Average percent of need met:** 76% (excluding resources awarded to replace EFC). **Average financial aid package:** $23,120 (excluding resources awarded to replace EFC). 2% of all full-time freshmen had no need and received non-need-based gift aid.
**UNDERGRADUATE FINANCIAL AID (Fall 2014, est.)** 440 applied for aid; of those 100% were deemed to have need. 100% of undergraduates with need received aid; of those 17% had need fully met. **Average percent of need met:** 40% (excluding resources awarded to replace EFC). **Average financial aid package:** $11,503 (excluding resources awarded to replace EFC). 3% of all full-time undergraduates had no need and received non-need-based gift aid.
**GIFT AID (NEED-BASED) Total amount:** $6,743,014 (15% federal, 9% state, 65% institutional, 11% external sources). **Receiving aid:** Freshmen: 89% (285); all full-time undergraduates: 48% (285). **Average award:** Freshmen: $17,429; Undergraduates: $19,127. **Scholarships, grants, and awards:** Federal Pell, FSEOG, state, private, college/university gift aid from institutional funds.
**GIFT AID (NON-NEED-BASED) Total amount:** $217,583 (89% institutional, 11% external sources). **Receiving aid:** Freshmen: 90% (288). Undergraduates: 74% (440). **Average award:** Freshmen: $7400. Undergraduates: $11,109. **Scholarships, grants, and awards by category:** Academic interests/achievement: biological sciences, business, communication, computer science, education, English, foreign languages, general academic interests/achievements, humanities, international studies, mathematics, physical sciences, premedicine, religion/biblical studies, social sciences. Creative arts/performance: music. Special achievements/activities: community service, general special achievements/activities, leadership. Special characteristics: adult students, children and siblings of alumni, children of current students, children of faculty/staff, international students, local/state students, relatives of clergy, religious affiliation, veterans, veterans' children. **Tuition waivers:** Full or partial for employees or children of employees. **ROTC:** Army cooperative.
**LOANS Student loans:** $4,273,375 (92% need-based, 8% non-need-based). 81% of past graduating class borrowed through all loan programs. *Average indebtedness per*

*student:* $30,423. **Average need-based loan:** Freshmen: $3559. Undergraduates: $4701. **Parent loans:** $1,258,076 (87% need-based, 13% non-need-based). **Programs:** Federal Direct (Subsidized and Unsubsidized Stafford, PLUS), Perkins.
**WORK-STUDY Federal work-study:** Total amount: $32,287; 27 jobs available. **State or other work-study/employment:** Total amount: $171,330 (40% need-based, 60% non-need-based). 120 part-time jobs available.
**APPLYING FOR FINANCIAL AID Required financial aid forms:** FAFSA, institution's own form. **Financial aid deadline (priority):** 4/30. **Notification date:** Continuous beginning 9/15.
**CONTACT** Ms. Linda Brittain, Dean of Financial Aid/Senior Enrollment Associate, Wilson College, 1015 Philadelphia Avenue, Chambersburg, PA 17201-1285, 717-262-2002 or toll-free 800-421-8402. *Fax:* 717-262-2530. *E-mail:* finaid@wilson.edu.
*Website:* http://www.wilson.edu/.

# WINGATE UNIVERSITY
## Wingate, NC

| Tuition & fees: $28,110 | Average undergraduate aid package: $21,022 |
|---|---|

**ABOUT THE INSTITUTION** Independent Baptist, coed. **Awards:** certificates, bachelor's, master's, and doctoral degrees. 39 undergraduate majors. **Total enrollment:** 3,034. Undergraduates: 1,952. Freshmen: 584. Federal methodology is used as a basis for awarding need-based institutional aid.
**UNDERGRADUATE EXPENSES for 2015–2016 Application fee:** $30. **Comprehensive fee:** $38,710 includes full-time tuition ($27,930), mandatory fees ($180), and room and board ($10,600). Room and board charges vary according to board plan. **Part-time tuition:** $870 per credit hour. Part-time tuition and fees vary according to course load.
**FRESHMAN FINANCIAL AID (Fall 2013)** 538 applied for aid; of those 88% were deemed to have need. 98% of freshmen with need received aid; of those 25% had need fully met. **Average percent of need met:** 76% (excluding resources awarded to replace EFC). **Average financial aid package:** $21,332 (excluding resources awarded to replace EFC). 21% of all full-time freshmen had no need and received non-need-based gift aid.
**UNDERGRADUATE FINANCIAL AID (Fall 2013)** 1,738 applied for aid; of those 91% were deemed to have need. 98% of undergraduates with need received aid; of those 32% had need fully met. **Average percent of need met:** 79% (excluding resources awarded to replace EFC). **Average financial aid package:** $21,022 (excluding resources awarded to replace EFC). 19% of all full-time undergraduates had no need and received non-need-based gift aid.
**GIFT AID (NEED-BASED) Total amount:** $26,370,517 (13% federal, 18% state, 68% institutional, 1% external sources). **Receiving aid:** Freshmen: 72% (465); all full-time undergraduates: 79% (1,538). **Average award:** Freshmen: $19,154; Undergraduates: $18,013. **Scholarships, grants, and awards:** Federal Pell, FSEOG, state, private, college/university gift aid from institutional funds.
**GIFT AID (NON-NEED-BASED) Total amount:** $7,164,810 (95% institutional, 5% external sources). **Receiving aid:** Freshmen: 12% (80). Undergraduates: 20% (385). **Average award:** Freshmen: $13,719. Undergraduates: $13,028. **Scholarships, grants, and awards by category:** Academic interests/achievement: general academic interests/achievements. Creative arts/performance: art/fine arts, music, theater/drama. Special characteristics: children and siblings of alumni, relatives of clergy. **Tuition waivers:** Full or partial for employees or children of employees. **ROTC:** Army cooperative, Air Force cooperative.
**LOANS Student loans:** $10,833,700 (68% need-based, 32% non-need-based). 53% of past graduating class borrowed through all loan programs. *Average indebtedness per student:* $29,939. **Average need-based loan:** Freshmen: $2990. Undergraduates: $3998. **Parent loans:** $4,424,965 (22% need-based, 78% non-need-based). **Programs:** Federal Direct (Subsidized and Unsubsidized Stafford, PLUS).
**WORK-STUDY Federal work-study:** jobs available. **State or other work-study/employment:** Part-time jobs available.
**ATHLETIC AWARDS** Total amount: $3,292,616 (45% need-based, 55% non-need-based).
**APPLYING FOR FINANCIAL AID Required financial aid forms:** FAFSA, state aid form. **Financial aid deadline (priority):** 5/1. **Notification date:** Continuous beginning 3/15. Students must reply within 3 weeks of notification.

**CONTACT** Teresa G. Williams, Director of Student Financial Planning, Wingate University, Campus Box 3001, Wingate, NC 28174, 704-233-8209 or toll-free 800-755-5550. *Fax:* 704-233-9396. *E-mail:* tgwilliam@wingate.edu. *Website:* http://www.wingate.edu/.

# WINONA STATE UNIVERSITY
## Winona, MN

| Tuition & fees (MN res): $8750 | Average undergraduate aid package: $7426 |
|---|---|

**ABOUT THE INSTITUTION** State-supported, coed. *Awards:* certificates, associate, bachelor's, master's, and doctoral degrees. 57 undergraduate majors. *Total enrollment:* 8,655. Undergraduates: 8,109. Freshmen: 1,648. Federal methodology is used as a basis for awarding need-based institutional aid.

**UNDERGRADUATE EXPENSES for 2015–2016** *Application fee:* $20. *Tuition, state resident:* full-time $6860; part-time $227 per credit. *Tuition, nonresident:* full-time $12,360; part-time $412 per credit. *Required fees:* full-time $1890. Full-time tuition and fees vary according to location, program, and reciprocity agreements. Part-time tuition and fees vary according to course load, location, program, and reciprocity agreements. *College room and board:* $7890. Room and board charges vary according to board plan, housing facility, and location.

**FRESHMAN FINANCIAL AID (Fall 2013)** 1,439 applied for aid; of those 70% were deemed to have need. 97% of freshmen with need received aid; of those 11% had need fully met. *Average percent of need met:* 48% (excluding resources awarded to replace EFC). *Average financial aid package:* $6733 (excluding resources awarded to replace EFC). 20% of all full-time freshmen had no need and received non-need-based gift aid.

**UNDERGRADUATE FINANCIAL AID (Fall 2013)** 5,913 applied for aid; of those 75% were deemed to have need. 98% of undergraduates with need received aid; of those 11% had need fully met. *Average percent of need met:* 50% (excluding resources awarded to replace EFC). *Average financial aid package:* $7426 (excluding resources awarded to replace EFC). 11% of all full-time undergraduates had no need and received non-need-based gift aid.

**GIFT AID (NEED-BASED)** *Total amount:* $15,567,176 (57% federal, 26% state, 10% institutional, 7% external sources). *Receiving aid:* Freshmen: 44% (725); all full-time undergraduates: 41% (3,005). *Average award:* Freshmen: $4675; Undergraduates: $4979. *Scholarships, grants, and awards:* Federal Pell, FSEOG, state, private, college/university gift aid from institutional funds.

**GIFT AID (NON-NEED-BASED)** *Total amount:* $3,516,023 (12% federal, 51% institutional, 37% external sources). *Receiving aid:* Freshmen: 9% (143). Undergraduates: 6% (413). *Average award:* Freshmen: $2066. Undergraduates: $3145. *Scholarships, grants, and awards by category: Academic interests/achievement:* 1,346 awards ($1,472,950 total): general academic interests/achievements. *Creative arts/performance:* 70 awards ($98,850 total): art/fine arts, debating, music, theater/drama. *Special characteristics:* 327 awards ($1,658,579 total): children and siblings of alumni, children of faculty/staff, local/state students, members of minority groups, out-of-state students. *Tuition waivers:* Full or partial for employees or children of employees. *ROTC:* Army cooperative.

**LOANS** *Student loans:* $48,860,568 (60% need-based, 40% non-need-based). 76% of past graduating class borrowed through all loan programs. *Average indebtedness per student:* $35,131. *Average need-based loan:* Freshmen: $3306. Undergraduates: $3968. *Parent loans:* $4,296,585 (30% need-based, 70% non-need-based). *Programs:* Federal Direct (Subsidized and Unsubsidized Stafford, PLUS), Perkins, state, college/university.

**WORK-STUDY** *Federal work-study:* 184 jobs averaging $2138. *State or other work-study/employment:* Total amount: $747,816 (100% need-based). 321 part-time jobs averaging $2330.

**ATHLETIC AWARDS** Total amount: $805,138 (39% need-based, 61% non-need-based).

**APPLYING FOR FINANCIAL AID** *Required financial aid form:* FAFSA. *Financial aid deadline:* Continuous. *Notification date:* 5/1. Students must reply within 3 weeks of notification.

**CONTACT** Cindy Groth, Counselor, Winona State University, PO Box 5838, Winona, MN 55987-5838, 507-457-5090 Ext. 5561 or toll-free 800-DIAL WSU. *Website:* http://www.winona.edu/.

# WINSTON-SALEM STATE UNIVERSITY
## Winston-Salem, NC

**CONTACT** Raymond Solomon, Director of Financial Aid Office, Winston-Salem State University, 601 Martin Luther King Jr. Drive, PO Box 19524, Winston-Salem, NC 27110-0003, 336-750-3299 or toll-free 800-257-4052. *Fax:* 336-750-3297. *Website:* http://www.wssu.edu/.

# WINTHROP UNIVERSITY
## Rock Hill, SC

| Tuition & fees (SC res): $13,812 | Average undergraduate aid package: $12,387 |
|---|---|

**ABOUT THE INSTITUTION** State-supported, coed. *Awards:* certificates, bachelor's, and master's degrees. 28 undergraduate majors. *Total enrollment:* 1,050. Undergraduates: 4,974. Freshmen: 1,019. Federal methodology is used as a basis for awarding need-based institutional aid.

**UNDERGRADUATE EXPENSES for 2015–2016** *Application fee:* $40. *Tuition, state resident:* full-time $13,812; part-time $576 per credit hour. *Tuition, nonresident:* full-time $26,738; part-time $1115 per credit hour. Full-time tuition and fees vary according to degree level, reciprocity agreements, and student level. Part-time tuition and fees vary according to degree level and student level. *College room and board:* $8182; *Room only:* $5135. Room and board charges vary according to board plan and housing facility.

**FRESHMAN FINANCIAL AID (Fall 2014, est.)** 947 applied for aid; of those 87% were deemed to have need. 100% of freshmen with need received aid; of those 18% had need fully met. *Average percent of need met:* 63% (excluding resources awarded to replace EFC). *Average financial aid package:* $13,733 (excluding resources awarded to replace EFC). 10% of all full-time freshmen had no need and received non-need-based gift aid.

**UNDERGRADUATE FINANCIAL AID (Fall 2014, est.)** 3,735 applied for aid; of those 87% were deemed to have need. 100% of undergraduates with need received aid; of those 13% had need fully met. *Average percent of need met:* 57% (excluding resources awarded to replace EFC). *Average financial aid package:* $12,387 (excluding resources awarded to replace EFC). 11% of all full-time undergraduates had no need and received non-need-based gift aid.

**GIFT AID (NEED-BASED)** *Total amount:* $25,213,585 (37% federal, 36% state, 24% institutional, 3% external sources). *Receiving aid:* Freshmen: 80% (812); all full-time undergraduates: 66% (2,914). *Average award:* Freshmen: $9441; Undergraduates: $8324. *Scholarships, grants, and awards:* Federal Pell, FSEOG, state, private, college/university gift aid from institutional funds, TEACH Grants.

**GIFT AID (NON-NEED-BASED)** *Total amount:* $12,723,621 (1% federal, 59% state, 37% institutional, 3% external sources). *Receiving aid:* Freshmen: 14% (146). Undergraduates: 9% (397). *Average award:* Freshmen: $6161. Undergraduates: $4976. *Scholarships, grants, and awards by category: Academic interests/achievement:* general academic interests/achievements. *Creative arts/performance:* art/fine arts, dance, music, performing arts, theater/drama. *Special characteristics:* children of faculty/staff. *Tuition waivers:* Full or partial for employees or children of employees, senior citizens. *ROTC:* Army cooperative, Air Force cooperative.

**LOANS** *Student loans:* $28,893,673 (76% need-based, 24% non-need-based). 74% of past graduating class borrowed through all loan programs. *Average indebtedness per student:* $32,165. *Average need-based loan:* Freshmen: $3382. Undergraduates: $4357. *Parent loans:* $5,610,715 (55% need-based, 45% non-need-based). *Programs:* Federal Direct (Subsidized and Unsubsidized Stafford, PLUS), Perkins, alternative loans.

**WORK-STUDY** *Federal work-study:* Total amount: $243,970; 171 jobs averaging $1427. *State or other work-study/employment:* Part-time jobs available.

**ATHLETIC AWARDS** Total amount: $2,143,162 (41% need-based, 59% non-need-based).

**APPLYING FOR FINANCIAL AID** *Required financial aid form:* FAFSA. *Financial aid deadline (priority):* 3/1. *Notification date:* Continuous beginning 4/1. Students must reply within 2 weeks of notification.

**CONTACT** Michelle K. Hare, Director of Financial Aid, Winthrop University, Sykes House, 638 Oakland Avenue, Rock Hill, SC 29733, 803-323-2189 or toll-free 800-763-0230. *Fax:* 803-323-2557. *E-mail:* finaid@winthrop.edu. *Website:* http://www.winthrop.edu/.

# WISCONSIN LUTHERAN COLLEGE
## Milwaukee, WI

| Tuition & fees: $25,960 | Average undergraduate aid package: $19,552 |
|---|---|

**ABOUT THE INSTITUTION** Independent Wisconsin Evangelical Lutheran Synod, coed. *Awards:* bachelor's and master's degrees. 39 undergraduate majors. *Total enrollment:* 1,178. Undergraduates: 1,070. Freshmen: 229. Federal methodology is used as a basis for awarding need-based institutional aid.

**UNDERGRADUATE EXPENSES for 2015–2016** *Comprehensive fee:* $34,860 includes full-time tuition ($25,810), mandatory fees ($150), and room and board ($8900). Full-time tuition and fees vary according to program. Room and board charges vary according to housing facility. *Part-time tuition:* $700 per credit. Part-time tuition and fees vary according to program.

**FRESHMAN FINANCIAL AID (Fall 2014, est.)** 207 applied for aid; of those 88% were deemed to have need. 100% of freshmen with need received aid; of those 17% had need fully met. *Average percent of need met:* 81% (excluding resources awarded to replace EFC). *Average financial aid package:* $22,097 (excluding resources awarded to replace EFC). 17% of all full-time freshmen had no need and received non-need-based gift aid.

**UNDERGRADUATE FINANCIAL AID (Fall 2014, est.)** 874 applied for aid; of those 90% were deemed to have need. 100% of undergraduates with need received aid; of those 14% had need fully met. *Average percent of need met:* 76% (excluding resources awarded to replace EFC). *Average financial aid package:* $19,552 (excluding resources awarded to replace EFC). 16% of all full-time undergraduates had no need and received non-need-based gift aid.

**GIFT AID (NEED-BASED)** *Total amount:* $11,647,596 (12% federal, 8% state, 78% institutional, 2% external sources). *Receiving aid:* Freshmen: 83% (183); all full-time undergraduates: 77% (755). *Average award:* Freshmen: $18,372; Undergraduates: $15,625. *Scholarships, grants, and awards:* Federal Pell, FSEOG, state, private, college/university gift aid from institutional funds.

**GIFT AID (NON-NEED-BASED)** *Total amount:* $1,750,126 (96% institutional, 4% external sources). *Receiving aid:* Freshmen: 10% (23). Undergraduates: 6% (62). *Average award:* Freshmen: $10,155. Undergraduates: $8845. *Scholarships, grants, and awards by category:* Academic interests/achievement: biological sciences, business, communication, computer science, education, general academic interests/achievements, health fields, international studies, mathematics, physical sciences, religion/biblical studies, social sciences. *Creative arts/performance:* art/fine arts, music, theater/drama. *Special achievements/activities:* general special achievements/activities, leadership. *Special characteristics:* adult students, children of faculty/staff, ethnic background, first-generation college students, international students, members of minority groups, out-of-state students, religious affiliation. *Tuition waivers:* Full or partial for employees or children of employees. *ROTC:* Air Force cooperative.

**LOANS** *Student loans:* $7,506,800 (71% need-based, 29% non-need-based). 88% of past graduating class borrowed through all loan programs. *Average indebtedness per student:* $26,896. *Average need-based loan:* Freshmen: $3170. Undergraduates: $4172. *Parent loans:* $1,633,580 (22% need-based, 78% non-need-based). *Programs:* Federal Direct (Subsidized and Unsubsidized Stafford, PLUS), state, private loans.

**WORK-STUDY** *Federal work-study:* Total amount: $434,282; jobs available. *State or other work-study/employment:* Total amount: $242,750 (47% need-based, 53% non-need-based). Part-time jobs available.

**APPLYING FOR FINANCIAL AID** *Required financial aid forms:* FAFSA, institution's own form. *Financial aid deadline (priority):* 3/1. *Notification date:* Continuous beginning 3/15. Students must reply within 2 weeks of notification.

**CONTACT** Mrs. Linda Loeffel, Director of Financial Aid, Wisconsin Lutheran College, 8800 West Bluemound Road, Milwaukee, WI 53226-4699, 414-443-8856. *Fax:* 414-443-8514. *E-mail:* financial.aid@wlc.edu.
*Website:* http://www.wlc.edu/.

# WITTENBERG UNIVERSITY
## Springfield, OH

| Tuition & fees: $38,090 | Average undergraduate aid package: $31,787 |
|---|---|

**ABOUT THE INSTITUTION** Independent Evangelical Lutheran Church, coed. *Awards:* bachelor's and master's degrees. 41 undergraduate majors. *Total enrollment:* 1,964. Undergraduates: 1,948. Freshmen: 516. Federal methodology is used as a basis for awarding need-based institutional aid.

**UNDERGRADUATE EXPENSES for 2015–2016** *Application fee:* $40. *Comprehensive fee:* $48,118 includes full-time tuition ($37,230), mandatory fees ($860), and room and board ($10,028). *College room only:* $5158. Room and board charges vary according to board plan and housing facility. *Part-time tuition:* $1241 per credit. Part-time tuition and fees vary according to course load.

**FRESHMAN FINANCIAL AID (Fall 2014, est.)** 484 applied for aid; of those 90% were deemed to have need. 100% of freshmen with need received aid; of those 23% had need fully met. *Average percent of need met:* 83% (excluding resources awarded to replace EFC). *Average financial aid package:* $33,733 (excluding resources awarded to replace EFC). 15% of all full-time freshmen had no need and received non-need-based gift aid.

**UNDERGRADUATE FINANCIAL AID (Fall 2014, est.)** 1,623 applied for aid; of those 90% were deemed to have need. 100% of undergraduates with need received aid; of those 21% had need fully met. *Average percent of need met:* 80% (excluding resources awarded to replace EFC). *Average financial aid package:* $31,787 (excluding resources awarded to replace EFC). 20% of all full-time undergraduates had no need and received non-need-based gift aid.

**GIFT AID (NEED-BASED)** *Total amount:* $36,727,178 (8% federal, 2% state, 88% institutional, 2% external sources). *Receiving aid:* Freshmen: 85% (438); all full-time undergraduates: 78% (1,453). *Average award:* Freshmen: $27,517; Undergraduates: $25,953. *Scholarships, grants, and awards:* Federal Pell, FSEOG, state, private, college/university gift aid from institutional funds, United Negro College Fund.

**GIFT AID (NON-NEED-BASED)** *Total amount:* $7,138,857 (97% institutional, 3% external sources). *Average award:* Freshmen: $20,714. Undergraduates: $18,495. *Scholarships, grants, and awards by category:* Academic interests/achievement: general academic interests/achievements. *Creative arts/performance:* art/fine arts, dance, music, theater/drama. *Special achievements/activities:* community service, general special achievements/activities, leadership. *Special characteristics:* adult students, children and siblings of alumni, children of faculty/staff, ethnic background, international students, members of minority groups, relatives of clergy, religious affiliation. *Tuition waivers:* Full or partial for minority students, children of alumni, employees or children of employees, adult students, senior citizens. *ROTC:* Army cooperative, Air Force cooperative.

**LOANS** *Student loans:* $14,833,559 (92% need-based, 8% non-need-based). 69% of past graduating class borrowed through all loan programs. *Average indebtedness per student:* $30,748. *Average need-based loan:* Freshmen: $5113. Undergraduates: $5287. *Parent loans:* $5,883,985 (94% need-based, 6% non-need-based). *Programs:* Federal Direct (Subsidized and Unsubsidized Stafford, PLUS), Perkins, college/university.

**WORK-STUDY** *Federal work-study:* Total amount: $1,393,784; jobs available. *State or other work-study/employment:* Total amount: $1,503,218 (67% need-based, 33% non-need-based). Part-time jobs available.

**APPLYING FOR FINANCIAL AID** *Required financial aid form:* FAFSA. *Financial aid deadline (priority):* 3/1. *Notification date:* Continuous beginning 3/1. Students must reply by 5/1.

**CONTACT** Mr. J. Randy Green, Executive Director of Financial Aid, Wittenberg University, PO Box 720, Springfield, OH 45501-0720, 937-327-7321 or toll-free 800-677-7558 Ext. 6314. *Fax:* 937-327-6379. *E-mail:* jgreen@wittenberg.edu.
*Website:* http://www.wittenberg.edu/.

# WOFFORD COLLEGE
## Spartanburg, SC

| Tuition & fees: $37,120 | Average undergraduate aid package: $33,209 |
| --- | --- |

**ABOUT THE INSTITUTION** Independent United Methodist Church, coed. *Awards:* bachelor's degrees. 35 undergraduate majors. *Total enrollment:* 1,608. Undergraduates: 1,607. Freshmen: 487. Federal methodology is used as a basis for awarding need-based institutional aid.

**UNDERGRADUATE EXPENSES for 2015–2016** *Application fee:* $35. *Comprehensive fee:* $47,850 includes full-time tuition ($37,120) and room and board ($10,730). *Part-time tuition:* $1475 per semester hour.

**FRESHMAN FINANCIAL AID (Fall 2014, est.)** 407 applied for aid; of those 78% were deemed to have need. 100% of freshmen with need received aid; of those 35% had need fully met. *Average percent of need met:* 85% (excluding resources awarded to replace EFC). *Average financial aid package:* $32,533 (excluding resources awarded to replace EFC). 25% of all full-time freshmen had no need and received non-need-based gift aid.

**UNDERGRADUATE FINANCIAL AID (Fall 2014, est.)** 1,187 applied for aid; of those 83% were deemed to have need. 100% of undergraduates with need received aid; of those 39% had need fully met. *Average percent of need met:* 86% (excluding resources awarded to replace EFC). *Average financial aid package:* $33,209 (excluding resources awarded to replace EFC). 26% of all full-time undergraduates had no need and received non-need-based gift aid.

**GIFT AID (NEED-BASED)** *Total amount:* $22,653,552 (6% federal, 19% state, 71% institutional, 4% external sources). *Receiving aid:* Freshmen: 65% (316); all full-time undergraduates: 62% (981). *Average award:* Freshmen: $29,541; Undergraduates: $29,598. *Scholarships, grants, and awards:* Federal Pell, FSEOG, state, private, college/university gift aid from institutional funds.

**GIFT AID (NON-NEED-BASED)** *Total amount:* $10,437,634 (20% state, 69% institutional, 11% external sources). *Receiving aid:* Freshmen: 17% (85). Undergraduates: 18% (277). *Average award:* Freshmen: $14,850. Undergraduates: $15,057. *Scholarships, grants, and awards by category:* Academic interests/achievement: general academic interests/achievements. Creative arts/performance: art/fine arts, music. Special achievements/activities: leadership. Special characteristics: children of faculty/staff, general special characteristics, local/state students, members of minority groups, relatives of clergy. *Tuition waivers:* Full or partial for employees or children of employees. *ROTC:* Army.

**LOANS** *Student loans:* $6,107,716 (69% need-based, 31% non-need-based). 45% of past graduating class borrowed through all loan programs. *Average indebtedness per student:* $24,999. *Average need-based loan:* Freshmen: $3325. Undergraduates: $4242. *Parent loans:* $2,377,752 (41% need-based, 59% non-need-based). *Programs:* Federal Direct (Subsidized and Unsubsidized Stafford, PLUS).

**WORK-STUDY** *Federal work-study:* Total amount: $146,600; 146 jobs averaging $843.

**ATHLETIC AWARDS** Total amount: $7,508,115 (49% need-based, 51% non-need-based).

**APPLYING FOR FINANCIAL AID** *Required financial aid form:* FAFSA. *Financial aid deadline (priority):* 3/1. *Notification date:* Continuous beginning 3/31. Students must reply by 5/1.

**CONTACT** Carolyn B. Sparks, Director of Financial Aid, Wofford College, 429 North Church Street, Spartanburg, SC 29303-3663, 864-597-4160. *Fax:* 864-597-4149. *E-mail:* finaid@wofford.edu.
*Website:* http://www.wofford.edu/.

# WOODBURY UNIVERSITY
## Burbank, CA

| Tuition & fees: N/R | Average undergraduate aid package: $23,356 |
| --- | --- |

**ABOUT THE INSTITUTION** Independent, coed. *Awards:* bachelor's and master's degrees. 17 undergraduate majors. *Total enrollment:* 1,607. Undergraduates: 1,357. Freshmen: 100. Federal methodology is used as a basis for awarding need-based institutional aid.

**FRESHMAN FINANCIAL AID (Fall 2014, est.)** 89 applied for aid; of those 88% were deemed to have need. 99% of freshmen with need received aid; of those 6% had

need fully met. *Average percent of need met:* 56% (excluding resources awarded to replace EFC). *Average financial aid package:* $23,700 (excluding resources awarded to replace EFC). 24% of all full-time freshmen had no need and received non-need-based gift aid.

**UNDERGRADUATE FINANCIAL AID (Fall 2014, est.)** 758 applied for aid; of those 96% were deemed to have need. 100% of undergraduates with need received aid; of those 2% had need fully met. *Average percent of need met:* 53% (excluding resources awarded to replace EFC). *Average financial aid package:* $23,356 (excluding resources awarded to replace EFC). 12% of all full-time undergraduates had no need and received non-need-based gift aid.

**GIFT AID (NEED-BASED)** *Total amount:* $14,828,457 (19% federal, 21% state, 59% institutional, 1% external sources). *Receiving aid:* Freshmen: 72% (76); all full-time undergraduates: 86% (722). *Average award:* Freshmen: $21,075; Undergraduates: $19,116. *Scholarships, grants, and awards:* Federal Pell, FSEOG, state, private, college/university gift aid from institutional funds.

**GIFT AID (NON-NEED-BASED)** *Total amount:* $1,150,658 (1% state, 98% institutional, 1% external sources). *Receiving aid:* Freshmen: 5% (5). Undergraduates: 2% (15). *Average award:* Freshmen: $10,108. Undergraduates: $10,096. *Scholarships, grants, and awards by category:* Academic interests/achievement: 595 awards ($5,583,071 total): architecture, business, general academic interests/achievements.

**LOANS** *Student loans:* $8,042,768 (94% need-based, 6% non-need-based). 92% of past graduating class borrowed through all loan programs. *Average indebtedness per student:* $40,699. *Average need-based loan:* Freshmen: $3507. Undergraduates: $4798. *Parent loans:* $3,866,905 (71% need-based, 29% non-need-based). *Programs:* Federal Direct (Subsidized and Unsubsidized Stafford, PLUS), Perkins, alternative loans.

**WORK-STUDY** *Federal work-study:* Total amount: $103,034; 108 jobs averaging $950.

**APPLYING FOR FINANCIAL AID** *Required financial aid forms:* FAFSA, institution's own form. *Financial aid deadline:* 4/3 (priority: 3/2). *Notification date:* Continuous beginning 4/1. Students must reply within 2 weeks of notification.

**CONTACT** Celeastia Williams, Director of Enrollment Services, Woodbury University, 7500 Glenoaks Boulevard, Burbank, CA 91510, 818-767-0888 Ext. 273 or toll-free 800-784-WOOD. *Fax:* 818-767-4816.
*Website:* http://www.woodbury.edu/.

# WORCESTER POLYTECHNIC INSTITUTE
## Worcester, MA

| Tuition & fees: $44,222 | Average undergraduate aid package: $33,762 |
| --- | --- |

**ABOUT THE INSTITUTION** Independent, coed. *Awards:* bachelor's, master's, and doctoral degrees. 51 undergraduate majors. *Total enrollment:* 6,381. Undergraduates: 4,235. Freshmen: 1,056. Both federal and institutional methodology are used as a basis for awarding need-based institutional aid.

**UNDERGRADUATE EXPENSES for 2015–2016** *Application fee:* $65. *One-time required fee:* $200. *Comprehensive fee:* $57,304 includes full-time tuition ($43,612), mandatory fees ($610), and room and board ($13,082). *College room only:* $7466. Room and board charges vary according to board plan and housing facility. *Part-time tuition:* $1211 per credit hour. Part-time tuition and fees vary according to course load. *Payment plan:* Tuition prepayment.

**FRESHMAN FINANCIAL AID (Fall 2013)** 948 applied for aid; of those 85% were deemed to have need. 100% of freshmen with need received aid; of those 54% had need fully met. *Average percent of need met:* 79% (excluding resources awarded to replace EFC). *Average financial aid package:* $34,302 (excluding resources awarded to replace EFC). 25% of all full-time freshmen had no need and received non-need-based gift aid.

**UNDERGRADUATE FINANCIAL AID (Fall 2013)** 3,015 applied for aid; of those 89% were deemed to have need. 99% of undergraduates with need received aid; of those 45% had need fully met. *Average percent of need met:* 77% (excluding resources awarded to replace EFC). *Average financial aid package:* $33,762 (excluding resources awarded to replace EFC). 31% of all full-time undergraduates had no need and received non-need-based gift aid.

**GIFT AID (NEED-BASED)** *Total amount:* $56,610,667 (5% federal, 2% state, 86% institutional, 7% external sources). *Receiving aid:* Freshmen: 73% (803); all full-

time undergraduates: 66% (2,551). *Average award:* Freshmen: $23,297; Undergraduates: $21,119. *Scholarships, grants, and awards:* Federal Pell, FSEOG, state, private, college/university gift aid from institutional funds.

**GIFT AID (NON-NEED-BASED)** *Total amount:* $22,453,932 (83% institutional, 17% external sources). *Receiving aid:* Freshmen: 34% (374). Undergraduates: 24% (932). *Average award:* Freshmen: $13,078. Undergraduates: $15,783. *Scholarships, grants, and awards by category: Academic interests/achievement:* 3,384 awards ($42,088,753 total): general academic interests/achievements, premedicine. *Special achievements/activities:* leadership. *Special characteristics:* 19 awards ($140,849 total): children of workers in trades. *Tuition waivers:* Full or partial for employees or children of employees. *ROTC:* Army, Naval cooperative, Air Force.

**LOANS** *Student loans:* $29,181,022 (44% need-based, 56% non-need-based). *Average need-based loan:* Freshmen: $2866. Undergraduates: $2617. *Parent loans:* $10,164,433 (100% non-need-based). *Programs:* Federal Direct (Subsidized and Unsubsidized Stafford, PLUS), Perkins, state, college/university.

**WORK-STUDY** *Federal work-study:* 700 jobs averaging $951.

**APPLYING FOR FINANCIAL AID** *Required financial aid forms:* FAFSA, CSS Financial Aid PROFILE, noncustodial (divorced/separated) parent's statement. *Financial aid deadline (priority):* 2/1. *Notification date:* 4/1. Students must reply by 5/1.

**CONTACT** Office of Financial Aid, Worcester Polytechnic Institute, 100 Institute Road, Worcester, MA 01609-2280, 508-831-5469. *Fax:* 508-831-5039. *E-mail:* finaid@wpi.edu.

*Website:* http://www.wpi.edu/.

---

# WORCESTER STATE UNIVERSITY
## Worcester, MA

| Tuition & fees (MA res): $8557 | Average undergraduate aid package: $11,055 |
| --- | --- |

**ABOUT THE INSTITUTION** State-supported, coed. *Awards:* certificates, bachelor's, and master's degrees. 27 undergraduate majors. *Total enrollment:* 6,350. Undergraduates: 5,563. Freshmen: 794. Federal methodology is used as a basis for awarding need-based institutional aid.

**UNDERGRADUATE EXPENSES for 2015–2016** *Application fee:* $50. *Tuition, state resident:* full-time $970; part-time $40.42 per credit hour. *Tuition, nonresident:* full-time $7050; part-time $293.75 per credit hour. *Required fees:* full-time $7587. Full-time tuition and fees vary according to class time, course load, degree level, and reciprocity agreements. Part-time tuition and fees vary according to class time, course load, degree level, and reciprocity agreements. *College room and board:* $11,255; *Room only:* $7735. Room and board charges vary according to board plan and housing facility.

**FRESHMAN FINANCIAL AID (Fall 2013)** 731 applied for aid; of those 71% were deemed to have need. 97% of freshmen with need received aid; of those 34% had need fully met. *Average percent of need met:* 77% (excluding resources awarded to replace EFC). *Average financial aid package:* $11,209 (excluding resources awarded to replace EFC). 3% of all full-time freshmen had no need and received non-need-based gift aid.

**UNDERGRADUATE FINANCIAL AID (Fall 2013)** 3,479 applied for aid; of those 73% were deemed to have need. 98% of undergraduates with need received aid; of those 39% had need fully met. *Average percent of need met:* 80% (excluding resources awarded to replace EFC). *Average financial aid package:* $11,055 (excluding resources awarded to replace EFC). 2% of all full-time undergraduates had no need and received non-need-based gift aid.

**GIFT AID (NEED-BASED)** *Total amount:* $9,469,642 (67% federal, 20% state, 13% institutional). *Receiving aid:* Freshmen: 58% (447); all full-time undergraduates: 49% (1,996). *Average award:* Freshmen: $4570; Undergraduates: $4696. *Scholarships, grants, and awards:* Federal Pell, FSEOG, state, private, college/university gift aid from institutional funds.

**GIFT AID (NON-NEED-BASED)** *Total amount:* $1,643,436 (22% state, 48% institutional, 30% external sources). *Receiving aid:* Freshmen: 30% (234). Undergraduates: 20% (829). *Average award:* Freshmen: $3911. Undergraduates: $2691. *Tuition waivers:* Full or partial for employees or children of employees, senior citizens. *ROTC:* Army cooperative, Naval cooperative, Air Force cooperative.

**LOANS** *Student loans:* $21,710,588 (37% need-based, 63% non-need-based). 80% of past graduating class borrowed through all loan programs. *Average indebtedness per student:* $25,654. *Average need-based loan:* Freshmen: $2779. Undergrad-

uates: $3151. *Parent loans:* $1,670,920 (100% non-need-based). *Programs:* Federal Direct (Subsidized and Unsubsidized Stafford, PLUS), Perkins, state.

**WORK-STUDY** *Federal work-study:* 200 jobs averaging $1500.

**APPLYING FOR FINANCIAL AID** *Required financial aid forms:* FAFSA, institution's own form. *Financial aid deadline:* 5/1 (priority: 3/1). *Notification date:* Continuous beginning 3/1. Students must reply within 2 weeks of notification.

**CONTACT** Ms. Jayne McGinn, Director of Financial Aid, Worcester State University, 486 Chandler Street, Worcester, MA 01602, 508-929-8058. *Fax:* 508-929-8194. *E-mail:* jayne.mcginn@worcester.edu.

*Website:* http://www.worcester.edu/.

---

# WRIGHT STATE UNIVERSITY
## Dayton, OH

| Tuition & fees (OH res): $8730 | Average undergraduate aid package: $10,400 |
| --- | --- |

**ABOUT THE INSTITUTION** State-supported, coed. *Awards:* certificates, associate, bachelor's, master's, and doctoral degrees. 111 undergraduate majors. *Total enrollment:* 16,842. Undergraduates: 12,682. Freshmen: 2,284. Federal methodology is used as a basis for awarding need-based institutional aid.

**UNDERGRADUATE EXPENSES for 2015–2016** *Application fee:* $30. *Tuition, state resident:* full-time $8730; part-time $394 per credit hour. *Tuition, nonresident:* full-time $16,910; part-time $770 per credit hour. Full-time tuition and fees vary according to course load, location, and reciprocity agreements. Part-time tuition and fees vary according to course load, location, and reciprocity agreements. *College room and board:* $9108; *Room only:* $5878. Room and board charges vary according to board plan, housing facility, and location.

**FRESHMAN FINANCIAL AID (Fall 2014, est.)** 1,981 applied for aid; of those 77% were deemed to have need. 99% of freshmen with need received aid; of those 19% had need fully met. *Average percent of need met:* 70% (excluding resources awarded to replace EFC). *Average financial aid package:* $10,735 (excluding resources awarded to replace EFC). 18% of all full-time freshmen had no need and received non-need-based gift aid.

**UNDERGRADUATE FINANCIAL AID (Fall 2014, est.)** 7,645 applied for aid; of those 83% were deemed to have need. 98% of undergraduates with need received aid; of those 14% had need fully met. *Average percent of need met:* 62% (excluding resources awarded to replace EFC). *Average financial aid package:* $10,400 (excluding resources awarded to replace EFC). 12% of all full-time undergraduates had no need and received non-need-based gift aid.

**GIFT AID (NEED-BASED)** *Total amount:* $36,292,003 (61% federal, 15% state, 22% institutional, 2% external sources). *Receiving aid:* Freshmen: 59% (1,326); all full-time undergraduates: 51% (5,020). *Average award:* Freshmen: $6636; Undergraduates: $6322. *Scholarships, grants, and awards:* Federal Pell, FSEOG, state, private, college/university gift aid from institutional funds, United Negro College Fund, Federal Nursing, Choose Ohio First scholarships.

**GIFT AID (NON-NEED-BASED)** *Total amount:* $8,239,301 (4% federal, 16% state, 74% institutional, 6% external sources). *Receiving aid:* Freshmen: 6% (144). Undergraduates: 4% (372). *Average award:* Freshmen: $3879. Undergraduates: $4234. *Scholarships, grants, and awards by category: Academic interests/achievement:* 3,370 awards ($9,473,071 total): area/ethnic studies, biological sciences, business, communication, computer science, education, engineering/technologies, English, foreign languages, general academic interests/achievements, health fields, humanities, international studies, mathematics, military science, physical sciences, premedicine, religion/biblical studies, social sciences. *Creative arts/performance:* 287 awards ($432,995 total): applied art and design, art/fine arts, cinema/film/broadcasting, creative writing, dance, general creative arts/performance, music, performing arts, theater/drama. *Special achievements/activities:* 842 awards ($3,836,352 total): cheerleading/drum major, community service, general special achievements/activities, leadership, memberships. *Special characteristics:* 871 awards ($3,324,292 total): adult students, children and siblings of alumni, children of educators, children of faculty/staff, ethnic background, first-generation college students, handicapped students, international students, members of minority groups, out-of-state students. *Tuition waivers:* Full or partial for employees or children of employees, senior citizens. *ROTC:* Army, Air Force.

**LOANS** *Student loans:* $75,865,549 (78% need-based, 22% non-need-based). 71% of past graduating class borrowed through all loan programs. *Average indebtedness per student:* $30,778. *Average need-based loan:* Freshmen: $3770. Undergrad-

uates: $4473. *Parent loans:* $3,968,120 (38% need-based, 62% non-need-based). *Programs:* Federal Direct (Subsidized and Unsubsidized Stafford, PLUS), Perkins, Federal Nursing, state, college/university, private loans. **WORK-STUDY** *Federal work-study:* Total amount: $4,305,952; 1,316 jobs averaging $3206. **ATHLETIC AWARDS** Total amount: $2,757,388 (36% need-based, 64% non-need-based). **APPLYING FOR FINANCIAL AID** *Required financial aid form:* FAFSA. *Financial aid deadline (priority):* 3/1. *Notification date:* Continuous beginning 3/15. **CONTACT** Raider Connect, Wright State University, 130 Student Union, 3640 Colonel Glenn Highway, Dayton, OH 45435, 937-775-4000 or toll-free 800-247-1770. *Fax:* 937-775-4410. *E-mail:* raiderconnect@wright.edu. *Website:* http://www.wright.edu/.

# XAVIER UNIVERSITY
## Cincinnati, OH

| Tuition & fees: $33,960 | Average undergraduate aid package: $20,540 |
|---|---|

**ABOUT THE INSTITUTION** Independent Roman Catholic, coed. *Awards:* certificates, associate, bachelor's, master's, and doctoral degrees. 73 undergraduate majors. *Total enrollment:* 6,538. Undergraduates: 4,633. Freshmen: 1,214. Federal methodology is used as a basis for awarding need-based institutional aid.
**UNDERGRADUATE EXPENSES** for 2015–2016 *Application fee:* $35. *Comprehensive fee:* $44,980 includes full-time tuition ($33,030), mandatory fees ($930), and room and board ($11,020). *College room only:* $6120. Full-time tuition and fees vary according to class time, course load, degree level, location, and program. Room and board charges vary according to board plan and housing facility. *Part-time tuition:* $635 per credit hour. *Part-time fees:* $9 per term. Part-time tuition and fees vary according to class time, course load, degree level, location, and program.
**FRESHMAN FINANCIAL AID (Fall 2013)** 1,107 applied for aid; of those 77% were deemed to have need. 100% of freshmen with need received aid; of those 19% had need fully met. *Average percent of need met:* 74% (excluding resources awarded to replace EFC). *Average financial aid package:* $20,827 (excluding resources awarded to replace EFC). 32% of all full-time freshmen had no need and received non-need-based gift aid.
**UNDERGRADUATE FINANCIAL AID (Fall 2013)** 3,051 applied for aid; of those 81% were deemed to have need. 100% of undergraduates with need received aid; of those 19% had need fully met. *Average percent of need met:* 72% (excluding resources awarded to replace EFC). *Average financial aid package:* $20,540 (excluding resources awarded to replace EFC). 36% of all full-time undergraduates had no need and received non-need-based gift aid.
**GIFT AID (NEED-BASED)** *Total amount:* $38,041,145 (9% federal, 2% state, 85% institutional, 4% external sources). *Receiving aid:* Freshmen: 65% (833); all full-time undergraduates: 57% (2,379). *Average award:* Freshmen: $16,374; Undergraduates: $15,745. *Scholarships, grants, and awards:* Federal Pell, FSEOG, state, private, college/university gift aid from institutional funds.
**GIFT AID (NON-NEED-BASED)** *Total amount:* $24,420,080 (94% institutional, 6% external sources). *Receiving aid:* Freshmen: 12% (148). Undergraduates: 9% (353). *Average award:* Freshmen: $15,210. Undergraduates: $13,774. *Scholarships, grants, and awards by category:* Academic interests/achievement: foreign languages, general academic interests/achievements, mathematics, military science, physical sciences, social sciences. Creative arts/performance: art/fine arts, music, performing arts, theater/drama. Special characteristics: children and siblings of alumni, international students, members of minority groups, siblings of current students. *Tuition waivers:* Full or partial for employees or children of employees, senior citizens. *ROTC:* Army, Air Force cooperative.
**LOANS** *Student loans:* $26,022,126 (66% need-based, 34% non-need-based). 67% of past graduating class borrowed through all loan programs. *Average indebtedness per student:* $34,365. *Average need-based loan:* Freshmen: $3831. Undergraduates: $4496. *Parent loans:* $8,450,346 (44% need-based, 56% non-need-based). *Programs:* Federal Direct (Subsidized and Unsubsidized Stafford, PLUS), Perkins.
**WORK-STUDY** *Federal work-study:* jobs available. *State or other work-study/employment:* Part-time jobs available.
**ATHLETIC AWARDS** Total amount: $3,451,047 (41% need-based, 59% non-need-based).

**APPLYING FOR FINANCIAL AID** *Required financial aid form:* FAFSA. *Financial aid deadline (priority):* 2/15. *Notification date:* Continuous beginning 3/1. Students must reply by 5/1. **CONTACT** Office of Financial Aid, Xavier University, 3800 Victory Parkway, Cincinnati, OH 45207-5111, 513-745-3142 or toll-free 877-XUADMIT. *Fax:* 513-745-2806. *Website:* http://www.xavier.edu/.

# XAVIER UNIVERSITY OF LOUISIANA
## New Orleans, LA

| Tuition & fees: $21,552 | Average undergraduate aid package: $20,947 |
|---|---|

**ABOUT THE INSTITUTION** Independent Roman Catholic, coed. *Awards:* bachelor's, master's, and doctoral degrees. 49 undergraduate majors. *Total enrollment:* 2,976. Undergraduates: 2,359. Freshmen: 579. Federal methodology is used as a basis for awarding need-based institutional aid.
**UNDERGRADUATE EXPENSES** for 2015–2016 *Application fee:* $25. *One-time required fee:* $150. *Comprehensive fee:* $30,052 includes full-time tuition ($19,100), mandatory fees ($2452), and room and board ($8500). Room and board charges vary according to housing facility. *Part-time tuition:* $800 per credit hour. *Part-time fees:* $150 per term. Part-time tuition and fees vary according to course load.
**FRESHMAN FINANCIAL AID (Fall 2013)** 657 applied for aid; of those 90% were deemed to have need. 100% of freshmen with need received aid; of those .3% had need fully met. *Average percent of need met:* 14% (excluding resources awarded to replace EFC). *Average financial aid package:* $21,750 (excluding resources awarded to replace EFC). 6% of all full-time freshmen had no need and received non-need-based gift aid.
**UNDERGRADUATE FINANCIAL AID (Fall 2013)** 2,216 applied for aid; of those 89% were deemed to have need. 100% of undergraduates with need received aid; of those 1% had need fully met. *Average percent of need met:* 13% (excluding resources awarded to replace EFC). *Average financial aid package:* $20,947 (excluding resources awarded to replace EFC). 4% of all full-time undergraduates had no need and received non-need-based gift aid.
**GIFT AID (NEED-BASED)** *Total amount:* $4,060,786 (90% federal, 10% state). *Receiving aid:* Freshmen: 57% (384); all full-time undergraduates: 54% (1,287). *Average award:* Freshmen: $5701; Undergraduates: $5694. *Scholarships, grants, and awards:* Federal Pell, FSEOG, state, private, college/university gift aid from institutional funds, United Negro College Fund.
**GIFT AID (NON-NEED-BASED)** *Total amount:* $8,016,556 (19% state, 81% institutional). *Receiving aid:* Freshmen: 80% (537). Undergraduates: 66% (1,558). *Average award:* Freshmen: $10,296. Undergraduates: $11,700. *Scholarships, grants, and awards by category:* Academic interests/achievement: biological sciences, business, communication, computer science, education, engineering/technologies, English, foreign languages, general academic interests/achievements, health fields, humanities, mathematics, physical sciences, premedicine, religion/biblical studies, social sciences. Creative arts/performance: art/fine arts, music. Special characteristics: children of faculty/staff, spouses of current students. *Tuition waivers:* Full or partial for employees or children of employees. *ROTC:* Army cooperative, Naval cooperative, Air Force cooperative.
**LOANS** *Student loans:* $8,447,874 (84% need-based, 16% non-need-based). 87% of past graduating class borrowed through all loan programs. *Average indebtedness per student:* $24,570. *Average need-based loan:* Freshmen: $5569. Undergraduates: $6667. *Parent loans:* $4,309,920 (100% non-need-based). *Programs:* Federal Direct (Subsidized and Unsubsidized Stafford, PLUS), Perkins.
**WORK-STUDY** *Federal work-study:* jobs available.
**ATHLETIC AWARDS** Total amount: $701,703 (100% non-need-based).
**APPLYING FOR FINANCIAL AID** *Required financial aid form:* FAFSA. *Financial aid deadline (priority):* 1/1. *Notification date:* Continuous beginning 4/1. Students must reply within 2 weeks of notification.
**CONTACT** Mrs. Emily Jones, Financial Aid Director, Xavier University of Louisiana, One Drexel Drive, New Orleans, LA 70125-1098, 504-520-7517 or toll-free 877-XAVIERU. *E-mail:* ejones@xula.edu. *Website:* http://www.xula.edu/.

# YALE UNIVERSITY
### New Haven, CT

| Tuition & fees: $47,600 | Average undergraduate aid package: $48,261 |
|---|---|

**ABOUT THE INSTITUTION** Independent, coed. *Awards:* certificates, bachelor's, master's, and doctoral degrees. 67 undergraduate majors. *Total enrollment:* 12,336. Undergraduates: 5,477. Freshmen: 1,360. Both federal and institutional methodology are used as a basis for awarding need-based institutional aid.

**UNDERGRADUATE EXPENSES** for 2015–2016 *Application fee:* $80. *Comprehensive fee:* $62,200 includes full-time tuition ($47,600) and room and board ($14,600). *College room only:* $8200. Room and board charges vary according to board plan.

**FRESHMAN FINANCIAL AID (Fall 2014, est.)** 821 applied for aid; of those 82% were deemed to have need. 100% of freshmen with need received aid; of those 100% had need fully met. *Average percent of need met:* 100% (excluding resources awarded to replace EFC). *Average financial aid package:* $48,926 (excluding resources awarded to replace EFC).

**UNDERGRADUATE FINANCIAL AID (Fall 2014, est.)** 2,962 applied for aid; of those 92% were deemed to have need. 100% of undergraduates with need received aid; of those 100% had need fully met. *Average percent of need met:* 100% (excluding resources awarded to replace EFC). *Average financial aid package:* $48,261 (excluding resources awarded to replace EFC).

**GIFT AID (NEED-BASED)** *Total amount:* $124,762,525 (4% federal, 92% institutional, 4% external sources). *Receiving aid:* Freshmen: 49% (673); all full-time undergraduates: 50% (2,722). *Average award:* Freshmen: $47,237; Undergraduates: $45,710. *Scholarships, grants, and awards:* Federal Pell, FSEOG, state, private, college/university gift aid from institutional funds, United Negro College Fund, Federal Nursing.

**GIFT AID (NON-NEED-BASED)** *Total amount:* $461,021 (100% external sources). *Tuition waivers:* Full or partial for employees or children of employees.

**ROTC:** Army cooperative, Naval, Air Force.

**LOANS** *Student loans:* $2,830,042 (40% need-based, 60% non-need-based). 16% of past graduating class borrowed through all loan programs. *Average indebtedness per student:* $14,853. *Average need-based loan:* Freshmen: $2072. Undergraduates: $2620. *Parent loans:* $2,862,530 (100% non-need-based). *Programs:* Federal Direct (Subsidized and Unsubsidized Stafford, PLUS), Perkins, state, college/university.

**WORK-STUDY** *Federal work-study:* Total amount: $1,796,138; jobs available. *State or other work-study/employment:* Total amount: $4,026,913 (100% need-based). Part-time jobs available.

**APPLYING FOR FINANCIAL AID** *Required financial aid forms:* FAFSA, CSS Financial Aid PROFILE, noncustodial (divorced/separated) parent's statement, federal income tax form(s). *Financial aid deadline:* 3/1. *Notification date:* 4/1. Students must reply by 5/1 or within 1 week of notification.

**CONTACT** Mr. Caesar T. Storlazzi, University Director of Financial Aid, Yale University, PO Box 208288, New Haven, CT 06520-8288, 203-432-0371. Fax: 203-777-6100. *E-mail:* sfs@yale.edu. *Website:* http://www.yale.edu/.

# YESHIVA AND KOLEL BAIS MEDRASH ELYON
### Monsey, NY

**CONTACT** Financial Aid Office, Yeshiva and Kolel Bais Medrash Elyon, 73 Main Street, Monsey, NY 10952, 845-356-7064.

# YESHIVA AND KOLLEL HARBOTZAS TORAH
### Brooklyn, NY

**CONTACT** Financial Aid Office, Yeshiva and Kollel Harbotzas Torah, 1049 East 15th Street, Brooklyn, NY 11230, 718-692-0208.

# YESHIVA BETH MOSHE
### Scranton, PA

**CONTACT** Financial Aid Office , Yeshiva Beth Moshe, 930 Hickory Street, Scranton, PA 18505-2124, 717-346-1747.

# YESHIVA COLLEGE OF THE NATION'S CAPITAL
### Silver Spring, MD

**CONTACT** Financial Aid Office, Yeshiva College of the Nation's Capital, 1216 Arcola Avenue, Silver Spring, MD 20902, 301-593-2534. *Website:* http://www.yeshiva.edu/.

# YESHIVA DERECH CHAIM
### Brooklyn, NY

**CONTACT** Financial Aid Office, Yeshiva Derech Chaim, 1573 39th Street, Brooklyn, NY 11218, 718-438-5426.

# YESHIVA D'MONSEY RABBINICAL COLLEGE
### Monsey, NY

**CONTACT** Financial Aid Office, Yeshiva D'Monsey Rabbinical College, 2 Roman Boulevard, Monsey, NY 10952, 914-352-5852.

# YESHIVA GEDOLAH IMREI YOSEF D'SPINKA
### Brooklyn, NY

**CONTACT** Financial Aid Office, Yeshiva Gedolah Imrei Yosef D'Spinka, 1466 56th Street, Brooklyn, NY 11219, 718-851-8721.

# YESHIVA GEDOLAH OF GREATER DETROIT
### Oak Park, MI

**CONTACT** Rabbi P. Rushnawitz, Executive Administrator , Yeshiva Gedolah of Greater Detroit, 24600 Greenfield Road, Oak Park, MI 48237-1544, 810-968-3360. Fax: 810-968-8613.

# YESHIVA GEDOLAH RABBINICAL COLLEGE
### Miami Beach, FL

**CONTACT** Financial Aid Office, Yeshiva Gedolah Rabbinical College, 1140 Alton Road, Miami Beach, FL 33139, 305-673-5664.

# YESHIVA GEDOLAH ZICHRON LEYMA
### Linden, NJ

**CONTACT** Financial Aid Office, Yeshiva Gedolah Zichron Leyma, 1000 Orchard Terrace, Linden, NJ 07036, 908-587-0502.

# YESHIVA KARLIN STOLIN RABBINICAL INSTITUTE
### Brooklyn, NY

**CONTACT** Mr. Daniel Ross, Financial Aid Administrator, Yeshiva Karlin Stolin Rabbinical Institute, 1818 Fifty-fourth Street, Brooklyn, NY 11204, 718-232-7800 Ext. 116. *Fax:* 718-331-4833.

# YESHIVA OF FAR ROCKAWAY DERECH AYSON RABBINICAL SEMINARY
### Far Rockaway, NY

**CONTACT** Financial Aid Office, Yeshiva of Far Rockaway Derech Ayson Rabbinical Seminary, 802 Hicksville Road, Far Rockaway, NY 11691, 718-327-7600. *Website:* http://www.yofr.org/.

# YESHIVA OF MACHZIKAI HADAS
### Brooklyn, NY

**CONTACT** Financial Aid Office, Yeshiva of Machzikai Hadas, 1321 43rd Street, Brooklyn, NY 11219, 718-853-2442.

# YESHIVA OF NITRA RABBINICAL COLLEGE
### Mount Kisco, NY

**CONTACT** Mr. Yosef Rosen, Financial Aid Administrator , Yeshiva of Nitra Rabbinical College, 194 Division Avenue, Mount Kisco, NY 10549, 718-384-5460. *Fax:* 718-387-9400.

# YESHIVA OF THE TELSHE ALUMNI
### Riverdale, NY

**CONTACT** Financial Aid Office, Yeshiva of the Telshe Alumni, 4904 Independence Avenue, Riverdale, NY 10471, 718-601-3523.

# YESHIVA OHR ELCHONON CHABAD/ WEST COAST TALMUDICAL SEMINARY
### Los Angeles, CA

**CONTACT** Ms. Hendy Tauber, Director of Financial Aid , Yeshiva Ohr Elchonon Chabad/West Coast Talmudical Seminary, 7215 Waring Avenue, Los Angeles, CA 90046-7660, 213-937-3763. *Fax:* 213-937-9456. *Website:* http://www.yoec.edu/.

# YESHIVAS BE'ER YITZCHOK
### Elizabeth, NJ

**CONTACT** Financial Aid Office, Yeshivas Be'er Yitzchok, 1391 North Avenue, Elizabeth, NJ 07208, 908-354-6057. *Website:* http://www.elizabethkollel.org/.

# YESHIVA SHAAREI TORAH OF ROCKLAND
### Suffern, NY

**CONTACT** Financial Aid Office, Yeshiva Shaarei Torah of Rockland, 91 West Carlton Road, Suffern, NY 10901, 845-352-3431.

# YESHIVA SHAAR HATORAH TALMUDIC RESEARCH INSTITUTE
### Kew Gardens, NY

**CONTACT** Mr. Yoel Yankelewitz, Executive Director, Financial Aid, Yeshiva Shaar Hatorah Talmudic Research Institute, 117-06 84th Avenue, Kew Gardens, NY 11418-1469, 718-846-1940.

# YESHIVAS NOVOMINSK
### Brooklyn, NY

**CONTACT** Financial Aid Office, Yeshivas Novominsk, 1569 47th Street, Brooklyn, NY 11219, 718-438-2727.

# YESHIVATH VIZNITZ
### Monsey, NY

**CONTACT** Financial Aid Office, Yeshivath Viznitz, Phyllis Terrace, PO Box 446, Monsey, NY 10952, 914-356-1010.

# YESHIVATH ZICHRON MOSHE
### South Fallsburg, NY

**CONTACT** Ms. Miryom R. Miller, Director of Financial Aid , Yeshivath Zichron Moshe, Laurel Park Road, South Fallsburg, NY 12779, 914-434-5240. *Fax:* 914-434-1009. *E-mail:* lehus@aol.com.

# YESHIVAT MIKDASH MELECH
### Brooklyn, NY

**CONTACT** Financial Aid Office, Yeshivat Mikdash Melech, 1326 Ocean Parkway, Brooklyn, NY 11230-5601, 718-339-1090.

# YESHIVA TORAS CHAIM
### Lakewood, NJ

**CONTACT** Financial Aid Office, Yeshiva Toras Chaim, 999 Ridge Avenue, Lakewood, NJ 08701, 732-942-3090.

# YESHIVA TORAS CHAIM TALMUDICAL SEMINARY
## Denver, CO

**CONTACT** Office of Financial Aid, Yeshiva Toras Chaim Talmudical Seminary, 1400 Quitman Street, Denver, CO 80204-1415, 303-629-8200.

# YESHIVA UNIVERSITY
## New York, NY

| Tuition & fees: $38,730 | Average undergraduate aid package: $31,534 |
| --- | --- |

**ABOUT THE INSTITUTION** Independent, coed. **Awards:** certificates, associate, bachelor's, master's, and doctoral degrees (Yeshiva College and Stern College for Women are coordinate undergraduate colleges of arts and sciences for men and women, respectively. Sy Syms School of Business offers programs at both campuses). 36 undergraduate majors. **Total enrollment:** 6,438. Undergraduates: 2,817. Freshmen: 828. Both federal and institutional methodology are used as a basis for awarding need-based institutional aid.

**UNDERGRADUATE EXPENSES** for 2015–2016 **Application fee:** $65. **Comprehensive fee:** $49,980 includes full-time tuition ($37,730), mandatory fees ($1000), and room and board ($11,250). Full-time tuition and fees vary according to student level. **Part-time tuition:** $1320 per credit hour.

**FRESHMAN FINANCIAL AID (Fall 2014, est.)** 669 applied for aid; of those 84% were deemed to have need. 99% of freshmen with need received aid; of those 35% had need fully met. **Average percent of need met:** 92% (excluding resources awarded to replace EFC). **Average financial aid package:** $33,744 (excluding resources awarded to replace EFC). 23% of all full-time freshmen had no need and received non-need-based gift aid.

**UNDERGRADUATE FINANCIAL AID (Fall 2014, est.)** 2,006 applied for aid; of those 83% were deemed to have need. 94% of undergraduates with need received aid; of those 27% had need fully met. **Average percent of need met:** 89% (excluding resources awarded to replace EFC). **Average financial aid package:** $31,534 (excluding resources awarded to replace EFC). 16% of all full-time undergraduates had no need and received non-need-based gift aid.

**GIFT AID (NEED-BASED) Total amount:** $36,861,688 (6% federal, 2% state, 92% institutional). **Receiving aid:** Freshmen: 59% (528); all full-time undergraduates: 50% (1,437). **Average award:** Freshmen: $27,364; Undergraduates: $31,534. **Scholarships, grants, and awards:** Federal Pell, FSEOG, state, private, college/university gift aid from institutional funds.

**GIFT AID (NON-NEED-BASED) Total amount:** $10,902,043 (100% institutional). **Receiving aid:** Freshmen: 19% (167). Undergraduates: 12% (330). **Average award:** Freshmen: $23,689. Undergraduates: $21,976. **Scholarships, grants, and awards by category:** Academic interests/achievement: general academic interests/achievements. **Tuition waivers:** Full or partial for employees or children of employees.

**LOANS Student loans:** $5,741,036 (93% need-based, 7% non-need-based). 46% of past graduating class borrowed through all loan programs. **Average indebtedness per student:** $22,769. **Average need-based loan:** Freshmen: $5916. Undergraduates: $6469. **Parent loans:** $1,696,938 (75% need-based, 25% non-need-based). **Programs:** Federal Direct (Subsidized and Unsubsidized Stafford, PLUS), Perkins, college/university.

**WORK-STUDY Federal work-study:** Total amount: $428,104; jobs available. **State or other work-study/employment:** Part-time jobs available.

**APPLYING FOR FINANCIAL AID Required financial aid form:** FAFSA. **Financial aid deadline (priority):** 2/1. **Notification date:** Continuous beginning 3/15.

**CONTACT** Marianela Cabral, Director of Student Aid Operations, Yeshiva University, 500 West 185th Street, Room 121, New York, NY 10033, 212-960-5399. *Fax:* 212-960-0037. *E-mail:* mcabral@yu.edu. *Website:* http://www.yu.edu/.

# YORK COLLEGE
## York, NE

**CONTACT** Brien Alley, Director of Financial Aid, York College, 1125 East 8th Street, York, NE 68467, 402-363-5624 or toll-free 800-950-9675. *Fax:* 402-363-5623. *E-mail:* balley@york.edu. *Website:* http://www.york.edu/.

# YORK COLLEGE OF PENNSYLVANIA
## York, PA

| Tuition & fees: $18,240 | Average undergraduate aid package: $13,707 |
| --- | --- |

**ABOUT THE INSTITUTION** Independent, coed. **Awards:** certificates, associate, bachelor's, master's, and doctoral degrees. 56 undergraduate majors. **Total enrollment:** 5,067. Undergraduates: 4,853. Freshmen: 1,091. Federal methodology is used as a basis for awarding need-based institutional aid.

**UNDERGRADUATE EXPENSES** for 2015–2016 **Comprehensive fee:** $28,400 includes full-time tuition ($16,480), mandatory fees ($1760), and room and board ($10,160). Full-time tuition and fees vary according to program. Room and board charges vary according to board plan and housing facility. **Part-time tuition:** $510 per credit hour.

**FRESHMAN FINANCIAL AID (Fall 2014, est.)** 1,022 applied for aid; of those 77% were deemed to have need. 100% of freshmen with need received aid; of those 27% had need fully met. **Average percent of need met:** 70% (excluding resources awarded to replace EFC). **Average financial aid package:** $14,074 (excluding resources awarded to replace EFC). 27% of all full-time freshmen had no need and received non-need-based gift aid.

**UNDERGRADUATE FINANCIAL AID (Fall 2014, est.)** 3,651 applied for aid; of those 81% were deemed to have need. 99% of undergraduates with need received aid; of those 24% had need fully met. **Average percent of need met:** 67% (excluding resources awarded to replace EFC). **Average financial aid package:** $13,707 (excluding resources awarded to replace EFC). 25% of all full-time undergraduates had no need and received non-need-based gift aid.

**GIFT AID (NEED-BASED) Total amount:** $22,077,134 (26% federal, 14% state, 57% institutional, 3% external sources). **Receiving aid:** Freshmen: 44% (480); all full-time undergraduates: 45% (1,948). **Average award:** Freshmen: $4830; Undergraduates: $5302. **Scholarships, grants, and awards:** Federal Pell, FSEOG, state, private, college/university gift aid from institutional funds.

**GIFT AID (NON-NEED-BASED) Total amount:** $4,796,965 (97% institutional, 3% external sources). **Receiving aid:** Freshmen: 72% (779). Undergraduates: 54% (2,358). **Average award:** Freshmen: $5597. Undergraduates: $4377. **Scholarships, grants, and awards by category:** Academic interests/achievement: 3,195 awards ($22,042,250 total): engineering/technologies, general academic interests/achievements. Creative arts/performance: 15 awards ($23,000 total): music. Special characteristics: 31 awards ($56,668 total): children and siblings of alumni, children of union members/company employees, international students, members of minority groups. **Tuition waivers:** Full or partial for employees or children of employees.

**LOANS Student loans:** $22,915,277 (46% need-based, 54% non-need-based). 79% of past graduating class borrowed through all loan programs. **Average indebtedness per student:** $35,669. **Average need-based loan:** Freshmen: $6274. Undergraduates: $7258. **Parent loans:** $7,398,696 (83% need-based, 17% non-need-based). **Programs:** Federal Direct (Subsidized and Unsubsidized Stafford, PLUS), Perkins, Federal Nursing, college/university.

**WORK-STUDY Federal work-study:** Total amount: $620,845; 311 jobs averaging $2090. **State or other work-study/employment:** Total amount: $17,600 (100% non-need-based). 8 part-time jobs averaging $2200.

**APPLYING FOR FINANCIAL AID Required financial aid form:** FAFSA. **Financial aid deadline:** Continuous. **Notification date:** Continuous beginning 2/1. Students must reply within 4 weeks of notification.

**CONTACT** Calvin Williams, Director of Financial Aid, York College of Pennsylvania, 441 Country Club Road, York, PA 17403, 717-849-1682 or toll-free 800-455-8018. *Fax:* 717-849-1685. *E-mail:* financialaid@ycp.edu. *Website:* http://www.ycp.edu/.

# YORK COLLEGE OF THE CITY UNIVERSITY OF NEW YORK
### Jamaica, NY

| Tuition & fees (NY res): $6447 | Average undergraduate aid package: $7436 |
|---|---|

**ABOUT THE INSTITUTION** State and locally supported, coed. *Awards:* bachelor's and master's degrees. 46 undergraduate majors. *Total enrollment:* 8,493. Undergraduates: 8,438. Freshmen: 994. Federal methodology is used as a basis for awarding need-based institutional aid.

**UNDERGRADUATE EXPENSES for 2015–2016 Application fee:** $65. *Tuition, state resident:* full-time $6030; part-time $260 per credit. *Tuition, non-resident:* full-time $12,840; part-time $535 per credit. *Required fees:* full-time $417; $208 per term. Full-time tuition and fees vary according to degree level and student level. Part-time tuition and fees vary according to degree level and student level.

**FRESHMAN FINANCIAL AID (Fall 2014, est.)** 706 applied for aid; of those 92% were deemed to have need. 96% of freshmen with need received aid; of those 100% had need fully met. *Average percent of need met:* 88% (excluding resources awarded to replace EFC). *Average financial aid package:* $8302 (excluding resources awarded to replace EFC).

**UNDERGRADUATE FINANCIAL AID (Fall 2014, est.)** 4,033 applied for aid; of those 92% were deemed to have need. 95% of undergraduates with need received aid; of those 96% had need fully met. *Average percent of need met:* 84% (excluding resources awarded to replace EFC). *Average financial aid package:* $7436 (excluding resources awarded to replace EFC). 1% of all full-time undergraduates had no need and received non-need-based gift aid.

**GIFT AID (NEED-BASED) Total amount:** $31,144,225 (45% federal, 55% state). *Receiving aid:* Freshmen: 61% (587); all full-time undergraduates: 68% (3,427). *Average award:* Freshmen: $8301; Undergraduates: $7219. *Scholarships, grants, and awards:* Federal Pell, FSEOG, state, private, college/university gift aid from institutional funds.

**GIFT AID (NON-NEED-BASED) Total amount:** $1,018,238 (100% institutional). *Receiving aid:* Freshmen: 35% (335). Undergraduates: 8% (383). *Average award:* Undergraduates: $831. *Tuition waivers:* Full or partial for employees or children of employees, senior citizens. *ROTC:* Army.

**LOANS Student loans:** $3,448,781 (78% need-based, 22% non-need-based). 9% of past graduating class borrowed through all loan programs. *Average indebtedness per student:* $4745. *Average need-based loan:* Freshmen: $1700. Undergraduates: $3169. *Programs:* Federal Direct (Subsidized and Unsubsidized Stafford, PLUS), Perkins.

**WORK-STUDY Federal work-study:** Total amount: $599,927; jobs available.

**APPLYING FOR FINANCIAL AID Required financial aid forms:** FAFSA, state aid form. *Financial aid deadline:* 6/30 (priority: 5/1). *Notification date:* Continuous beginning 2/15. Students must reply within 4 weeks of notification.

**CONTACT** Ms. Beverly Brown, Director of Student Financial Services, York College of the City University of New York, 94-20 Guy R. Brewer Boulevard, Jamaica, NY 11451-0001, 718-262-2240. *E-mail:* bbrown@york.cuny.edu. *Website:* http://www.york.cuny.edu/.

# YOUNG HARRIS COLLEGE
### Young Harris, GA

**ABOUT THE INSTITUTION** Independent United Methodist, coed. 30 undergraduate majors.

**GIFT AID (NEED-BASED) Scholarships, grants, and awards:** Federal Pell, FSEOG, state, private, college/university gift aid from institutional funds.

**GIFT AID (NON-NEED-BASED) Scholarships, grants, and awards by category:** *Creative arts/performance:* art/fine arts, music, performing arts, theater/drama. *Special characteristics:* children of faculty/staff.

**LOANS Programs:** Federal Direct (Subsidized and Unsubsidized Stafford, PLUS), college/university.

**APPLYING FOR FINANCIAL AID Required financial aid forms:** FAFSA, state aid form.

**CONTACT** Linda Adams, Director of Financial Aid, Young Harris College, 1 College Street, Young Harris, GA 30582, 706-379-5188 or toll-free 800-241-3754 (in-state). *Fax:* 706-379-4594. *E-mail:* leadams@yhc.edu. *Website:* http://www.yhc.edu/.

# YOUNGSTOWN STATE UNIVERSITY
### Youngstown, OH

| Tuition & fees (OH res): $8317 | Average undergraduate aid package: $8724 |
|---|---|

**ABOUT THE INSTITUTION** State-supported, coed. *Awards:* certificates, diplomas, associate, bachelor's, master's, and doctoral degrees. 148 undergraduate majors. *Total enrollment:* 12,545. Undergraduates: 11,348. Freshmen: 1,776. Federal methodology is used as a basis for awarding need-based institutional aid.

**UNDERGRADUATE EXPENSES for 2015–2016 Application fee:** $45. *Tuition, state resident:* full-time $7847; part-time $327 per credit. *Tuition, non-resident:* full-time $13,847; part-time $577 per credit. *Required fees:* full-time $470. Full-time tuition and fees vary according to course load. Part-time tuition and fees vary according to course load. *College room and board:* $8645. Room and board charges vary according to board plan and housing facility.

**FRESHMAN FINANCIAL AID (Fall 2013)** 1,790 applied for aid; of those 87% were deemed to have need. 100% of freshmen with need received aid; of those 11% had need fully met. *Average percent of need met:* 33% (excluding resources awarded to replace EFC). *Average financial aid package:* $8226 (excluding resources awarded to replace EFC). 9% of all full-time freshmen had no need and received non-need-based gift aid.

**UNDERGRADUATE FINANCIAL AID (Fall 2013)** 8,294 applied for aid; of those 86% were deemed to have need. 99% of undergraduates with need received aid; of those 8% had need fully met. *Average percent of need met:* 32% (excluding resources awarded to replace EFC). *Average financial aid package:* $8724 (excluding resources awarded to replace EFC). 9% of all full-time undergraduates had no need and received non-need-based gift aid.

**GIFT AID (NEED-BASED) Total amount:** $34,619,945 (78% federal, 13% state, 2% institutional, 7% external sources). *Receiving aid:* Freshmen: 66% (1,252); all full-time undergraduates: 58% (5,451). *Average award:* Freshmen: $5261; Undergraduates: $5261. *Scholarships, grants, and awards:* Federal Pell, FSEOG, state, private, college/university gift aid from institutional funds, Advanced Education Nursing Scholarships.

**GIFT AID (NON-NEED-BASED) Total amount:** $9,600,472 (3% federal, 12% state, 20% institutional, 65% external sources). *Receiving aid:* Freshmen: 26% (497). Undergraduates: 23% (2,189). *Average award:* Freshmen: $4001. Undergraduates: $3358. *Scholarships, grants, and awards by category:* *Academic interests/achievement:* biological sciences, business, communication, computer science, education, engineering/technologies, English, foreign languages, general academic interests/achievements, health fields, humanities, mathematics, military science, physical sciences, premedicine, religion/biblical studies, social sciences. *Creative arts/performance:* art/fine arts, creative writing, journalism/publications, music, performing arts, theater/drama. *Special achievements/activities:* cheerleading/drum major, community service, leadership, memberships, religious involvement. *Special characteristics:* adult students, children and siblings of alumni, children of faculty/staff, children of union members/company employees, children of workers in trades, children with a deceased or disabled parent, ethnic background, handicapped students, international students, local/state students, members of minority groups, out-of-state students, public servants, religious affiliation, spouses of deceased or disabled public servants, veterans, veterans' children. *Tuition waivers:* Full or partial for employees or children of employees, senior citizens. *ROTC:* Army, Air Force cooperative.

**LOANS** *Student loans:* $69,803,898 (43% need-based, 57% non-need-based). 73% of past graduating class borrowed through all loan programs. *Average indebtedness per student:* $30,481. *Average need-based loan:* Freshmen: $3193. Undergraduates: $3849. *Parent loans:* $35,903,614 (100% non-need-based). *Programs:* Federal Direct (Subsidized and Unsubsidized Stafford, PLUS), Perkins, Charles E. Schell Foundation loans, George W. Wright Student Aid loans, Rogers student loans.

**WORK-STUDY** *Federal work-study:* jobs available. *State or other work-study/employment:* Total amount: $4,053,878 (100% non-need-based). Part-time jobs available.

**ATHLETIC AWARDS** Total amount: $4,301,471 (100% non-need-based).

**APPLYING FOR FINANCIAL AID** *Required financial aid forms:* FAFSA, institution's own form. *Financial aid deadline (priority):* 2/15. *Notification date:* Continuous beginning 4/1. Students must reply within 4 weeks of notification.

**CONTACT** Barbara Greene, Manager of Financial Analysis and Reporting, Youngstown State University, One University Plaza, Youngstown, OH 44555, 330-941-3504 or toll-free 877-468-6978. *Fax:* 330-941-1659. *E-mail:* bgreene@ysu.edu. *Website:* http://www.ysu.edu/.

# Appendix

# State Scholarship and Grant Programs

Each state government has established one or more state-administered financial aid programs for qualified students. In many instances, these state programs are restricted to legal residents of the state. However, they often are available to out-of-state students who will be or are attending colleges or universities within the state. In addition to residential status, other qualifications frequently exist.

Gift aid and forgivable loan programs open to undergraduate students for all states and the District of Columbia are described on the following pages. They are arranged in alphabetical order, first by state name, then by program name. The annotation for each program provides information about the program, eligibility, and the contact addresses for applications or further information. Unless otherwise stated, this information refers to awards for 2014–15. Information is provided by the state-sponsoring agency in response to *Peterson's Annual Survey of Non-institutional Aid*, which was conducted between January 2015 and April 2015. Information is accurate when Peterson's receives it. However, it is always advisable to check with the sponsor to ascertain that the information remains correct.

You should write to the address given for each program to request that award details for 2016–17 be sent to you as soon as they are available. Descriptive information, brochures, and application forms for state scholarship programs are usually available from the financial aid offices of public colleges or universities within the specific state. High school guidance offices often have information and relevant forms for awards for which high school seniors may be eligible. Increasingly, state government agencies are putting state scholarship information on state government agency websites. In searching state government websites, however, you should be aware that the higher education agency in many states is separate from the state's general education office, which is often responsible only for elementary and secondary education. Also, the page at public university websites that provides information about student financial aid frequently has a list of state-sponsored scholarships and financial aid programs.

Names of scholarship programs are frequently used inconsistently or become abbreviated in popular usage. Many programs have variant names by which they are known. The program's sponsor has approved the title of the program that Peterson's uses in this guide, yet this name may differ from the program's official name or from its most commonly used name.

In addition to the grant aid and forgivable loan programs listed on the following pages, states may also offer internship or work-study programs, graduate fellowships and grants, or low-interest loans. If you are interested in learning more about these other kinds of programs, the state education office that supplies information or applications for the undergraduate scholarship programs listed here should be able to provide information about other kinds of higher education financial aid programs that are sponsored by the state.

# ALABAMA

## Air Force ROTC College Scholarship.
Scholarship program provides three- and four-year scholarships in three different types to high school seniors. All scholarship cadets receive a nontaxable monthly allowance (stipend) during the academic year. For more details refer to web site http://www.afrotc.com/scholarships/hsschol/types.php. *Award:* Scholarship for use in freshman, sophomore, junior, or senior years; renewable. *Award amount:* $9000–$15,000. *Number of awards:* 2000–4000. *Eligibility Requirements:* Applicant must be age 17-30 and enrolled or expecting to enroll full-time at a two-year or four-year institution or university. Applicant must have 3.0 GPA or higher. Available to U.S. citizens. Applicant or parent must meet one or more of the following requirements: Air Force experience; retired from active duty; disabled or killed as a result of military service; prisoner of war; or missing in action. *Application Requirements:* Application form, interview, test scores, transcript. **Deadline:** December 1.

Contact Ty Christian, Chief Air Force ROTC Advertising Manager, Air Force Reserve Officer Training Corps, 551 East Maxwell Boulevard, Maxwell Air Force Base, AL 36112-6106. *E-mail:* ty.christian@maxwell.af.mil. *Phone:* 334-953-2278. *Fax:* 334-953-4384. *Website:* http://www.afrotc.com/.

## Alabama G.I. Dependents Scholarship Program.
Scholarship pays for tuition, textbooks and laboratory fees for eligible dependents of Alabama disabled, prisoner-of-war, or missing-in-action veterans. Child or stepchild must initiate training before 26th birthday; age 30 deadline may apply in certain situations. No age deadline for spouses or widows. The veteran and the step child's parent must have been married prior the the child's 19th birthday. *Award:* Scholarship for use in freshman, sophomore, junior, or senior years; renewable. *Eligibility Requirements:* Applicant must be enrolled or expecting to enroll full- or part-time at a two-year or four-year or technical institution or university; resident of Alabama and studying in Alabama. Available to U.S. citizens. Applicant or parent must meet one or more of the following requirements: general military experience; retired from active duty; disabled or killed as a result of military service; prisoner of war; or missing in action. *Application Requirements:* Application form. **Deadline:** varies.

Contact Kayla Kyle, Program Manager, Alabama Department of Veterans Affairs, PO Box 1509, Montgomery, AL 36102-1509. *Phone:* 334-242-5077. *Fax:* 334-353-4078. *Website:* http://www.va.alabama.gov/.

## Alabama National Guard Educational Assistance Program.
Renewable award aids Alabama residents who are members of the Alabama National Guard and are enrolled in a nationally recognized accredited college in Alabama. Forms must be signed by a representative of the Alabama Military Department and financial aid officer. Recipient must be in a degree-seeking program. *Award:* Scholarship for use in freshman, sophomore, junior, senior, or graduate years; not renewable. *Award amount:* $25–$1000. *Number of awards:* up to 800. *Eligibility Requirements:* Applicant must be enrolled or expecting to enroll full- or part-time at a two-year or four-year or technical institution or university; resident of Alabama and studying in Alabama. Available to U.S. citizens. Applicant must have national guard experience. *Application Requirements:* Application form, financial need analysis. **Deadline:** continuous.

Contact Cheryl Newton, Grants Coordinator. *E-mail:* cheryl.newton@ache.alabama.gov. *Phone:* 334-242-2273. *Fax:* 334-242-2269. *Website:* http://www.ache.alabama.gov/.

## Alabama Student Assistance Program.
Scholarship award of $300 to $5000 per academic year given to undergraduate students residing in the state of Alabama and attending a college or university in Alabama. *Award:* Grant for use in freshman, sophomore, junior, or senior years; not renewable. *Award amount:* $300–$5000. *Number of awards:* up to 3500. *Eligibility Requirements:* Applicant must be enrolled or expecting to enroll full- or part-time at a two-year or four-year or technical institution or university; resident of Alabama and studying in Alabama. Available to U.S. citizens. *Application Requirements:* Application form, completion of the FAFSA, financial need analysis. **Deadline:** continuous.

Contact Cheryl Newton, Grants Coordinator. *E-mail:* cheryl.newton@ache.alabama.gov. *Phone:* 334-242-2273. *Fax:* 334-242-2269. *Website:* http://www.ache.alabama.gov/.

## Alabama Student Grant Program.
Nonrenewable awards available to Alabama residents for undergraduate study at certain independent colleges within the state. Both full and half-time students are eligible. Deadlines: September 15, January 15, and February 15. *Award:* Grant for use in freshman, sophomore, junior, or senior years; not renewable. *Award amount:* up to $1200. *Number of awards:* up to 3500. *Eligibility Requirements:* Applicant must be enrolled or expecting to enroll full- or part-time at a four-year institution or university; resident of Alabama and studying in Alabama. Available to U.S. citizens. *Application Requirements:* 5 proofs of Alabama residency, application form.

Contact Cheryl Newton, Grants Coordinator. *E-mail:* cheryl.newton@ache.alabama.gov. *Phone:* 334-242-2273. *Fax:* 334-242-2269. *Website:* http://www.ache.alabama.gov/.

## Police Officers and Firefighters Survivors Education Assistance Program-Alabama.
Provides tuition, fees, books, and supplies to dependents of full-time police officers and firefighters killed or totally disabled in the line of duty. Must attend an Alabama public college as an undergraduate. Must be Alabama resident. *Award:* Scholarship for use in freshman, sophomore, junior, or senior years; renewable. *Award amount:* $1600–$12,000. *Number of awards:* 15–30. *Eligibility Requirements:* Applicant must be enrolled or expecting to enroll full- or part-time at a two-year or four-year or technical institution or university; single; resident of Alabama and studying in Alabama. Available to U.S. citizens. *Application Requirements:* Application form, birth certificate, marriage license, death certificate, letter from medical doctor, transcript. **Deadline:** continuous.

Contact Cheryl Newton, Grants Coordinator. *E-mail:* cheryl.newton@ache.alabama.gov. *Phone:* 334-242-2273. *Fax:* 334-242-2269. *Website:* http://www.ache.alabama.gov/.

# ALASKA

## AlaskAdvantage Education Grant.
The Alaska legislature created the AlaskAdvantage Education Grant Program (AEG) to provide need-based financial assistance to eligible Alaska students attending qualifying postsecondary educational institutions in Alaska. Students apply by completing the FAFSA annually. *Award:* Grant for use in freshman, sophomore, junior, or senior years; not renewable. *Award amount:* $500–$3000. *Eligibility Requirements:* Applicant must be enrolled or expecting to enroll full- or part-time at a two-year or four-year institution or university; resident of Alaska

and studying in Alaska. Available to U.S. and non-U.S. citizens. *Application Requirements:* Completed FAFSA.

Contact Adam Weed, Special Programs Coordinator. *E-mail:* customer_service@acpe.state.ak.us. *Phone:* 907-465-6685. *Website:* http://www.acpe.alaska.gov.

**Alaska Performance Scholarship.** To qualify, students must take a specific, rigorous high school curriculum; earn a minimum 2.5 GPA; and do well on college or career readiness exam. Students apply by completing the FAFSA by the annual deadline. Awards can be used at any regionally accredited college or university in Alaska, or for approved career and technical education programs in the state. Students must use scholarship within 6 years of high school graduation. Students cannot receive award for more than 8 semesters. *Award:* Scholarship for use in freshman, sophomore, junior, senior, graduate, or postgraduate years; not renewable. *Award amount:* $500–$4755. *Eligibility Requirements:* Applicant must be enrolled or expecting to enroll full- or part-time at a two-year or four-year or technical institution or university; resident of Alaska and studying in Alaska. Applicant must have 2.5 GPA or higher. Available to U.S. and non-U.S. citizens. *Application Requirements:* FAFSA.

Contact Adam Weed, Special Programs Coordinator. *E-mail:* customer_service@acpe.state.ak.us. *Phone:* 907-465-6685. *Website:* http://www.acpe.alaska.gov.

# ARIZONA

**Leveraging Educational Assistance Partnership.** Grants to financially needy students, who enroll in and attend postsecondary education or training in Arizona schools. Program was formerly known as the State Student Incentive Grant or SSIG Program. *Award:* Grant for use in freshman, sophomore, junior, senior, or graduate years; not renewable. *Award amount:* $100–$2500. *Eligibility Requirements:* Applicant must be enrolled or expecting to enroll full- or part-time at a two-year or four-year or technical institution or university; resident of Arizona and studying in Arizona. Available to U.S. citizens. *Application Requirements:* Application form, financial need analysis, transcript. **Deadline:** April 30.

Contact Mila Zaporteza, Business Manager and LEAP Financial Aid Manager, Arizona Commission for Postsecondary Education, 2020 North Central Avenue, Suite 650, Phoenix, AZ 85004-4503. *E-mail:* mila@azhighered.gov. *Phone:* 602-258-2435 Ext. 102. *Fax:* 602-258-2483. *Website:* http://www.azhighered.gov/.

# ARKANSAS

**Arkansas Academic Challenge Scholarship Program.** Awards for Arkansas residents who are graduating high school seniors, currently enrolled college students and nontraditional students to study at an approved Arkansas institution. Must have at least a 2.5 GPA or 19 ACT composite score (or the equivalent). Renewable up to three additional years. *Award:* Scholarship for use in freshman, sophomore, junior, or senior years; renewable. *Award amount:* $1250–$4500. *Number of awards:* 30,000–35,000. *Eligibility Requirements:* Applicant must be enrolled or expecting to enroll full- or part-time at a two-year or four-year institution or university; resident of Arkansas and studying in Arkansas. Applicant must have 2.5 GPA or higher. Available to U.S. citizens. *Application Requirements:* Application form, application form may be submitted online (http://www.adhe.edu), financial need analysis, test scores, transcript. **Deadline:** June 1.

Contact Philip Axelroth, Financial Aid Program Coordinator. *Phone:* 501-371-2000. *Website:* http://www.adhe.edu/.

**Arkansas Governor's Scholars Program.** Awards for outstanding Arkansas high school seniors. Must be an Arkansas resident and have a high school GPA of at least 3.5 or have scored at least 27 on the ACT. Award is $4000 per year for four years of full-time undergraduate study. Applicants who attain 32 or above on ACT, 1410 or above on SAT and have an academic 3.5 GPA, or are selected as National Merit or National Achievement finalists may receive an award equal to tuition, mandatory fees, room, and board up to $10,000 per year at any Arkansas institution. *Award:* Scholarship for use in freshman, sophomore, junior, senior, or graduate years; renewable. *Award amount:* $4000–$10,000. *Number of awards:* 75–375. *Eligibility Requirements:* Applicant must be high school student; planning to enroll or expecting to enroll full-time at a two-year or four-year institution or university; resident of Arkansas and studying in Arkansas. Applicant must have 3.5 GPA or higher. Available to U.S. citizens. *Application Requirements:* Application form, application form may be submitted online (http://www.adhe.edu), community service, test scores, transcript. **Deadline:** February 1.

Contact Philip Axelroth, Financial Aid Program Coordinator. *Phone:* 501-371-2000. *Website:* http://www.adhe.edu/.

**Arkansas Single Parent Scholarship.** Scholarships are awarded to economically disadvantaged single parents who live anywhere in Arkansas or in Bowie County, Texas. Applicants must have custodial care of at least one minor child. Generally, applicants who have not yet received a 4-year degree are preferred. In some cases, applications from students pursuing a Master's degree will be considered. Application forms, award values, deadlines, and other requirements will vary by county. Visit http://www.aspsf.org for more information. *Award:* Scholarship for use in freshman, sophomore, junior, senior, or graduate years; not renewable. *Award amount:* $200–$1800. *Number of awards:* up to 2000. *Eligibility Requirements:* Applicant must be enrolled or expecting to enroll full- or part-time at a two-year or four-year or technical institution or university; single and resident of Arkansas, Texas. Available to U.S. and non-U.S. citizens. *Application Requirements:* Application form, application form may be submitted online (http://www.aspsf.org), essay, FAFSA Student Aid Report (SAR), financial need analysis, interview, recommendations or references, transcript. **Deadline:** varies.

Contact Ruthanne Hill, Executive Director, Arkansas Single Parent Scholarship Fund, 614 E Emma Ave Ste 119, Springdale, AR 72764. *E-mail:* rhill@aspsf.org. *Phone:* 479-927-1402 Ext. 11. *Website:* http://www.aspsf.org/.

**Law Enforcement Officers' Dependents Scholarship–Arkansas.** Scholarship for dependents, under 23 years old, of Arkansas law-enforcement officers killed or permanently disabled in the line of duty. Renewable award is a waiver of tuition, fees, and room at two- or four-year Arkansas institution. Submit birth certificate, death certificate, and claims commission report of findings of fact. Proof of disability from State Claims Commission may also be submitted. *Award:* Scholarship for use in freshman, sophomore, junior, or senior years; renewable. *Number of awards:* 27–32. *Eligibility Requirements:* Applicant must be enrolled or expecting to enroll full- or part-time at a two-year or four-year or technical institution or university; resident of Arkansas and studying in Arkansas. Available to U.S. citizens. *Application Requirements:* Application form. **Deadline:** continuous.

Contact Tara Smith, Director of Financial Aid, Arkansas Department of Higher Education, 114 East Capitol Avenue, Little Rock, AR 72201-3818. *E-mail:* taras@adhe.edu. *Phone:* 501-371-2000. *Fax:* 501-371-2001. *Website:* http://www.adhe.edu/.

**Military Dependent's Scholarship Program.** Renewable waiver of tuition, fees, room and board undergraduate students seeking a Bachelor's degree or certificate of completion at any public college, university or technical school in Arkansas who qualify as a spouse or dependent child of an Arkansas resident who has been declared to be missing in action, killed in action, a POW, or killed on ordnance delivery, or a veteran who has been declared to be 100 percent totally and permanently disabled during, or as a result of, active military service. *Award:* Scholarship for use in freshman, sophomore, junior, or senior years; renewable. *Number of awards:* 1–60. *Eligibility Requirements:* Applicant must be enrolled or expecting to enroll full-time at a two-year or four-year or technical institution or university; resident of Arkansas and studying in Arkansas. Available to U.S. citizens. Applicant or parent must meet one or more of the following requirements: general military experience; retired from active duty; disabled or killed as a result of military service; prisoner of war; or missing in action. *Application Requirements:* Application form, recommendations or references, report of casualty. **Deadline:** June 1.

Contact Tara Smith, Director of Financial Aid, Arkansas Department of Higher Education, 114 East Capitol Avenue, Little Rock, AR 72201-3818. *E-mail:* taras@adhe.edu. *Phone:* 501-371-2000. *Fax:* 501-371-2001. *Website:* http://www.adhe.edu/.

**Second Effort Scholarship.** Awarded to those scholars who achieved one of the 10 highest scores on the Arkansas High School Diploma Test (GED). Must be at least age 18 and not have graduated from high school. Students do not apply for this award, they are contacted by the Arkansas Department of Higher Education. *Award:* Scholarship for use in freshman, sophomore, junior, or senior years; renewable. *Award amount:* up to $1000. *Number of awards:* 10. *Eligibility Requirements:* Applicant must be enrolled or expecting to enroll full- or part-time at a two-year or four-year institution or university; resident of Arkansas and studying in Arkansas. Available to U.S. citizens. *Application Requirements:* Application

form, application form may be submitted online (http://www.adhe.edu). **Deadline:** varies.

Contact Philip Axelroth, Financial Aid Program Coordinator. *Phone:* 501-371-2000. *Website:* http://www.adhe.edu/.

# CALIFORNIA

**Cal Grant C.** Award for California residents who are enrolled in a short-term vocational training program. Program must lead to a recognized degree or certificate. Course length must be a minimum of 4 months and no longer than 24 months. Students must be attending an approved California institution and show financial need. *Award:* Grant for use in freshman or sophomore years; renewable. *Award amount:* $576–$3168. *Number of awards:* up to 7761. *Eligibility Requirements:* Applicant must be enrolled or expecting to enroll full- or part-time at a two-year or technical institution; resident of California and studying in California. Available to U.S. citizens. *Application Requirements:* Application form, financial need analysis, GPA verification. **Deadline:** March 2.

Contact Catalina Mistler, Chief, Program Administration and Services Division, California Student Aid Commission, PO Box 419026, Rancho Cordova, CA 95741-9026. *E-mail:* studentsupport@csac.ca.gov. *Phone:* 916-464-7268. *Fax:* 916-526-8004. *Website:* http://www.csac.ca.gov/.

**Child Development Teacher and Supervisor Grant Program.** Award is for those students pursuing an approved course of study leading to a Child Development Permit issued by the California Commission on Teacher Credentialing. In exchange for each year funding is received, recipients agree to provide one year of service in a licensed childcare center. Child and Family Studies; Education. *Award:* Grant for use in freshman, sophomore, junior, senior, or graduate years; renewable. *Award amount:* $1000–$2000. *Number of awards:* up to 300. *Eligibility Requirements:* Applicant must be enrolled or expecting to enroll full- or part-time at a two-year or four-year institution or university; resident of California and studying in California. Applicant or parent of applicant must have employment or volunteer experience in teaching/education. Available to U.S. citizens. *Application Requirements:* Application form, financial need analysis, GPA verification, recommendations or references. **Deadline:** April 16.

Contact Catalina Mistler, Chief, Program Administration and Services Division, California Student Aid Commission, PO Box 419026, Rancho Cordova, CA 95741-9026. *E-mail:* studentsupport@csac.ca.gov. *Phone:* 916-464-7268. *Fax:* 916-526-8004. *Website:* http://www.csac.ca.gov/.

**Competitive Cal Grant A.** Award for California residents who are not recent high school graduates attending an approved college or university within the state. Must show financial need and meet minimum 3.00 GPA requirement. *Award:* Grant for use in freshman, sophomore, junior, or senior years; renewable. *Award amount:* $5472–$12,192. *Number of awards:* 1000–2000. *Eligibility Requirements:* Applicant must be enrolled or expecting to enroll full- or part-time at a two-year or four-year institution or university; resident of California and studying in California. Applicant must have 3.0 GPA or higher. Available to U.S. citizens. *Application Requirements:* Application form, financial need analysis, GPA verification. **Deadline:** March 2.

Contact Catalina Mistler, Chief, Program Administration and Services Division, California Student Aid Commission, PO Box 419026, Rancho Cordova, CA 95741-9026. *E-mail:* studentsupport@csac.ca.gov. *Phone:* 916-464-7268. *Fax:* 916-526-8004. *Website:* http://www.csac.ca.gov/.

**Cooperative Agencies Resources for Education Program.** Renewable award available to California residents and individuals who are exempt from paying nonresident tuition. Individuals must be enrolled as a full-time student at a two-year publicly-funded California community college. EOPS students must fulfill program-specific income and educational disadvantage eligibility requirements. CARE students must be in EOPS, currently receive CalWORKs/TANF, have at least one child under fourteen years of age at time of acceptance into CARE program, be a single head of household, and age 18 or older. EOPS students may also qualify for CARE if their dependent child(ren) receive CalWORKs/TANF cash aid even if the the student (i.e., parent) is not a cash aid recipient. Contact local college EOPS/CARE office for an application and more information about supportive services and grants. To locate nearest community college campus, see http://californiacommunitycolleges.cccco.edu/AlphaList.aspx. *Award:* Grant for use in freshman or sophomore years; renewable. *Number of awards:* 10,000–

11,000. *Eligibility Requirements:* Applicant must be enrolled or expecting to enroll full-time at a two-year institution; single; resident of California and studying in California. Available to U.S. citizens. *Application Requirements:* Application form, financial need analysis, test scores, transcript. **Deadline:** continuous.

**Entitlement Cal Grant B.** Provide grant funds for access costs for low-income students in an amount not to exceed $1648 and tuition/fee expenses of up to $12,192. Must be California residents and enroll in an undergraduate academic program of not less than one academic year at a qualifying postsecondary institution. Must show financial need and meet the minimum 2.00 GPA requirement. *Award:* Grant for use in freshman, sophomore, junior, or senior years; renewable. *Award amount:* $700–$13,665. *Number of awards:* 61,340. *Eligibility Requirements:* Applicant must be enrolled or expecting to enroll full- or part-time at a two-year or four-year or technical institution or university; resident of California and studying in California. Available to U.S. citizens. *Application Requirements:* Application form, financial need analysis. **Deadline:** March 2.

Contact Catalina Mistler, Chief, Program Administration and Services Division, California Student Aid Commission, PO Box 419026, Rancho Cordova, CA 95741-9026. *E-mail:* studentsupport@csac.ca.gov. *Phone:* 916-464-7268. *Fax:* 916-526-8004. *Website:* http://www.csac.ca.gov/.

**Law Enforcement Personnel Dependents Scholarship.** Provides college grants to needy dependents of California law enforcement officers, officers and employees of the Department of Corrections and Department of Youth Authority, and firefighters killed or disabled in the line of duty. *Award:* Grant for use in freshman, sophomore, junior, or senior years; renewable. *Award amount:* $100–$13,665. *Eligibility Requirements:* Applicant must be enrolled or expecting to enroll full- or part-time at a two-year or four-year institution or university; resident of California and studying in California. Applicant or parent of applicant must have employment or volunteer experience in police/firefighting. Available to U.S. citizens. *Application Requirements:* Application form, birth certificate, death certificate of parents or spouse, police report, financial need analysis, transcript. **Deadline:** continuous.

Contact Catalina Mistler, Chief, Program Administration and Services Division, California Student Aid Commission, PO Box 419026, Rancho Cordova, CA 95741-9026. *E-mail:* studentsupport@csac.ca.gov. *Phone:* 916-464-7268. *Fax:* 916-526-8004. *Website:* http://www.csac.ca.gov/.

# COLORADO

**American Legion Auxiliary Department of Colorado Past Presidents' Parley Nurses Scholarship.** Open to children, spouses, grandchildren, and great-grandchildren of American Legion veterans, and veterans who served in the armed forces during eligibility dates for membership in the American Legion. Must be Colorado residents who have been accepted by an accredited school of nursing in Colorado. Nursing. *Award:* Scholarship for use in freshman, sophomore, junior, senior, or graduate years; not renewable. *Award amount:* $500–$1500. *Number of awards:* 3–5. *Eligibility Requirements:* Applicant must be enrolled or expecting to enroll full- or part-time at a four-year institution or university; resident of Colorado and studying in Colorado. Applicant or parent of applicant must be member of American Legion or Auxiliary. Available to U.S. citizens. Applicant or parent must meet one or more of the following requirements: general military experience; retired from active duty; disabled or killed as a result of military service; prisoner of war; or missing in action. *Application Requirements:* Application form, application form may be submitted online (http://alacolorado.com), essay, financial need analysis, recommendations or references. **Deadline:** April 1.

Contact Rhonda Larkowski, Department Secretary and Treasurer, American Legion Auxiliary Department of Colorado, 7465 East First Avenue, Suite D, Denver, CO 80230. *E-mail:* www.dept-sec@alacolorado.com. *Phone:* 303-367-5388. *Fax:* 303-367-5388. *Website:* http://www.alacolorado.com.

**Colorado Student Grant.** Grants for Colorado residents attending eligible public, private, or vocational institutions within the state. Students must complete a Free Application for Federal Student Aid (FAFSA) and qualify at 150% of Pell eligibility. Application deadlines vary by institution. Renewable award for undergraduates. Contact the financial aid office at the college/institution for application and more information. *Award:* Grant for use in freshman, sophomore, junior, or

senior years; not renewable. *Award amount:* $850–$5000. *Number of awards:* 50,000–70,000. *Eligibility Requirements:* Applicant must be enrolled or expecting to enroll full- or part-time at a two-year or four-year or technical institution or university; resident of Colorado and studying in Colorado. Available to U.S. citizens. *Application Requirements:* Application form, financial need analysis, student must have an active FAFSA on file at the institution. **Deadline:** continuous.

Contact Celina Duran, Financial Aid Administrator, Colorado Commission on Higher Education, 1560 Broadway, Suite 1600, Denver, CO 80202. *E-mail:* celina.duran@dhe.state.co.us. *Phone:* 303-866-2723. *Website:* http://highered.colorado.gov/cche/mission.html.

# CONNECTICUT

**AIFS-HACU Scholarships.** Scholarships to outstanding Hispanic students to study abroad with AIFS. Available to students attending HACU member schools. Students will receive scholarships of up to 50 percent of the full program fee. Students must meet all standard AIFS eligibility requirements. Deadlines: April 15 for fall, October 1 for spring, and March 15 for summer. *Award:* Scholarship for use in freshman, sophomore, junior, or senior years; not renewable. *Award amount:* $6000–$8000. *Number of awards:* up to 1. *Eligibility Requirements:* Applicant must be Hispanic; enrolled or expecting to enroll full-time at a two-year or four-year institution or university and must have an interest in international exchange. Applicant must have 3.0 GPA or higher. Available to U.S. and non-U.S. citizens. *Application Requirements:* Application form, essay, personal photograph, recommendations or references, transcript. *Fee:* $95. **Deadline:** varies.

Contact David Mauro, Admissions Counselor, American Institute for Foreign Study, 1 High Ridge Park, Stamford, CT 06905. *E-mail:* dmauro@aifs.com. *Phone:* 800-727-2437 Ext. 5163. *Fax:* 203-399-5463. *Website:* http://www.aifsabroad.com/.

**Connecticut Army National Guard 100% Tuition Waiver.** Program is for any active member of the Connecticut Army National Guard in good standing. Must be a resident of Connecticut attending any Connecticut state (public) university, community-technical college or regional vocational-technical school. The total number of available awards is unlimited. *Award:* Scholarship for use in freshman, sophomore, junior, or senior years; not renewable. *Award amount:* $16,000. *Eligibility Requirements:* Applicant must be age 17-65; enrolled or expecting to enroll full- or part-time at a two-year or four-year or technical insti tution or university; resident of Con necticut and studying in Connecticut. Available to U.S. and non-U.S. citizens. Applicant or parent must meet one or more of the following requirements: national guard experience; retired from active duty; disabled or killed as a result of military service; prisoner of war; or missing in action. *Application Require ments:* Application form. **Deadline:** July 1.

Contact Capt. Jeremy Lingenfelser, Education Services Officer, Connecticut Army National Guard, 360 Broad Street, Hartford, CT 06105-3795. *E-mail:* education@ct.ngb.army.mil. *Phone:* 860-524-4816. *Fax:* 860-524-4904. *Website:* http://ct.ng.mil/Pages/default.aspx.

**Governor's Scholarship Program— Need-Based Grant.** This program pro vides need-based grants to eligible Con necticut residents attending eligible institutions of higher education in Con necticut. Students must file a Free Appli cation for Federal Student Aid (FAFSA) by their college's deadline, if applicable. Students, as a result of filing the FAFSA must have an Expected Family Contri bution (EFC) equal to or less than the allowable annual EFC. There is no appli cation to fill out. *Award:* Grant for use in freshman, sophomore, junior, or senior years; not renewable. *Award amount:* $250–$3000. *Number of awards:* 17,374. *Eligibility Requirements:* Applicant must be enrolled or expecting to enroll full- or part-time at a two-year or four-year insti tution or university; resident of Con necticut and studying in Connecticut. Available to U.S. citizens. *Application Requirements:* Financial need analysis.

Contact Ms. Lynne Little, Financial Aid Consultant, Connecticut Office of Higher Education, 61 Woodland Street, Hartford, CT 06105. *E-mail:* gsp@ctohe.org. *Phone:* 860-947-1855. *Website:* http://www.ctohe.org.

**Governor's Scholarship Program— Need/Merit Scholarship.** This program provides scholarships to eligible Connecticut residents attending eligible institutions of higher education in Con necticut. Eligibility is based on a minimum SAT score of 1800, or a minimum ACT score of 27 and/or top 20% ranking in the students junior year high school class. Applications must be filed through the students high school

counseling office. In addition, all students must file a Free Application for Federal Student Aid (FAFSA) and, as a result, have an Expected Family Contribution (EFC) equal to or less than the annual allowable maximum EFC. Both the appli cation and FAFSA must be processed by February 15th. *Award:* Scholarship for use in freshman, sophomore, junior, or senior years; renewable. *Award amount:* $500–$4500. *Number of awards:* 7500. *Eligibility Requirements:* Applicant must be enrolled or expecting to enroll full- or part-time at a two-year or four-year insti tution or university; resident of Con necticut and studying in Connecticut. Available to U.S. citizens. *Application Requirements:* Application form, financial need analysis. **Deadline:** Feb ruary 15.

Contact Ms. Lynne Little, Student Financial Aid Consultant, Connecticut Office of Higher Education, 61 Woodland Street, Hartford, CT 06105. *E-mail:* gsp@ctohe.org. *Phone:* 860-947-1855. *Website:* http://www.ctohe.org.

**Minority Teacher Incentive Grant Program.** Program provides up to $5000 a year for two years of full-time study in a teacher preparation program for the junior or senior year at a Connecticut college or university. Applicant must be African-American, Hispanic/Latino, Asian American or Native American heritage and be nominated by the Education Dean Program graduates who teach in Con necticut public schools may be eligible for loan reimbursement stipends up to $2500 per year for up to four years. Education. *Award:* Grant for use in junior or senior years; renewable. *Award amount:* $2500–$5000. *Number of awards:* 64. *Eligibility Requirements:* Applicant must be American Indian/Alaska Native, Asian/ Pacific Islander, Black (non-Hispanic), Hispanic; enrolled or expecting to enroll full-time at a four-year institution or uni versity and studying in Connecticut. Available to U.S. citizens. *Application Requirements:* Application form. **Deadline:** October 1.

Contact Ms. Lynne Little, Executive Assistant, Connecticut Office of Higher Education, 61 Woodland Street, Hartford, CT 06105. *E-mail:* mtip@ctohe.org. *Phone:* 860-947-1855. *Fax:* 860-947-1838. *Website:* http://www.ctohe.org.

# DELAWARE

**Delaware Solid Waste Authority John P. ";Pat"; Healy Scholarship.** Award for legal residents of Delaware

who are U.S. citizens or eligible non-cit izens. Must be high school seniors or full-time college students in their freshman or sophomore years. Must major in either environmental engineering or environ mental sciences at a Delaware college. Selection based on financial need, aca demic performance, community and school involvement, and leadership ability. Engineering-Related Technol ogies; Environmental Science. *Award:* Scholarship for use in freshman or soph omore years; renewable. *Award amount:* $2000. *Number of awards:* 1. *Eligibility Requirements:* Applicant must be enrolled or expecting to enroll full-time at a two-year or four-year institution or university; resident of Delaware; studying in Del aware and must have an interest in lead ership. Applicant or parent of applicant must have employment or volunteer expe rience in community service. Applicant must have 3.0 GPA or higher. Available to U.S. citizens. *Application Requirements:* Application form, FAFSA, Student Aid Report (SAR), financial need analysis. **Deadline:** March 14.

Contact Ms. Carylin Brinkley, Program Administrator, Delaware Higher Education Office, 401 Federal Street, Suite 2, Dover, DE 19901. *E-mail:* cbrinkley@doe.k12.de.us. *Phone:* 302-735-4120. *Fax:* 302-739-5894. *Website:* http://www.doe.k12.de.us.

**Diamond State Scholarship.** Award for legal residents of Delaware who are U. S. citizens or eligible non-citizens. Must be enrolled as a full-time student in a degree program at a nonprofit, regionally accredited institution. Minimum 3.0 GPA required. High school seniors should rank in upper quarter of class and have a com bined score of at least 1800 on the SAT. *Award:* Scholarship for use in freshman year; renewable. *Award amount:* $1250. *Number of awards:* 50. *Eligibility Requirements:* Applicant must be high school student; planning to enroll or expecting to enroll full-time at a four-year institution or university and resident of Delaware. Applicant must have 3.0 GPA or higher. Available to U.S. citizens. *Application Requirements:* Application form, essay, test scores, transcript. **Deadline:** March 22.

Contact Ms. Carylin Brinkley, Program Administrator, Delaware Higher Education Office, 401 Federal Street, Suite 2, Dover, DE 19901. *E-mail:* cbrinkley@doe.k12.de.us. *Phone:* 302-735-4120. *Fax:* 302-739-5894. *Website:* http://www.doe.k12.de.us.

**Educational Benefits for Children of Deceased Veterans.** Award for children between the ages of 16 and 24 of deceased/MIA/POW veterans or state police officers. Must have been a resident of Delaware for 3 or more years prior to the date of application. If the applicant's parent is a member of the armed forces, the parent must have been a resident of Delaware at the time of death or decla ration of missing in action or prisoner of war status. Award will not exceed tuition and fees at a Delaware public college. *Award:* Grant for use in freshman, soph omore, junior, or senior years; renewable. *Award amount:* $7479–$14,421. *Eligi bility Requirements:* Applicant must be age 16-24; enrolled or expecting to enroll full-time at a two-year or four-year insti tution or university and resident of Del aware. Applicant or parent of applicant must have employment or volunteer expe rience in police/firefighting. Available to U.S. citizens. Applicant or parent must meet one or more of the following requirements: general military expe rience; retired from active duty; disabled or killed as a result of military service; prisoner of war; or missing in action. *Application Requirements:* Application form, verification of service-related death. **Deadline:** continuous.

Contact Ms. Carylin Brinkley, Program Administrator, Delaware Higher Education Office, 401 Federal Street, Suite 2, Dover, DE 19901. *E-mail:* cbrinkley@doe.k12.de.us. *Phone:* 302-735-4120. *Fax:* 302-739-5894. *Website:* http://www.doe.k12.de.us.

**Governor's Education Grant for Unemployed Adults.** Grants for unem ployed part-time undergraduate students attending Delaware College of Art and Design, Delaware State University, Del aware Technical and Community College, Goldey-Beacom College, University of Delaware, Wesley College, Widener Uni versity (Delaware Campus), or PolyTech Adult division , Sussex Tech Adult division, or Wilmington College. Must be at least 18 years old, and a resident of Delaware. *Award:* Grant for use in freshman, sophomore, junior, or senior years; not renewable. *Award amount:* $2000. *Number of awards:* up to 1000. *Eligibility Requirements:* Applicant must be enrolled or expecting to enroll part-time at a two-year or four-year or tech nical institution or university. Available to U.S. citizens. *Application Requirements:* Application form. **Deadline:** continuous.

Contact Ms. Carylin Brinkley, Program Administrator, Delaware Higher Education Office, 401 Federal Street,

Suite 2, Dover, DE 19901. *E-mail:* cbrinkley@doe.k12.de.us. *Phone:* 302-735-4120. *Fax:* 302-739-5894. *Website:* http://www.doe.k12.de.us.

**Governor's Education Grant for Working Adults.** Grants for part-time undergraduate students attending Del aware College of Art and Design, Del aware State University, Delaware Technical and Community College, Goldey-Beacom College, University of Delaware, Wesley College, Widener Uni versity (Delaware Campus), PolyTech Adulte division, Sussex Tech Adult division, or Wilmington College. Must be at least 18 years old, a resident of Del aware, and employed by a company in Delaware that contributes to the Blue Collar Training Fund Program. *Award:* Grant for use in freshman, sophomore, junior, or senior years; not renewable. *Award amount:* $2000. *Number of awards:* up to 100. *Eligibility Require ments:* Applicant must be enrolled or expecting to enroll full- or part-time at a two-year or four-year or technical insti tution or university; resident of Delaware and studying in Delaware. Available to U. S. and non-U.S. citizens. *Application Requirements:* Application form. **Deadline:** varies.

Contact Ms. Carylin Brinkley, Program Administrator, Delaware Higher Education Office, 401 Federal Street, Suite 2, Dover, DE 19901. *E-mail:* cbrinkley@doe.k12.de.us. *Phone:* 302-735-4120. *Fax:* 302-739-5894. *Website:* http://www.doe.k12.de.us.

**Scholarship Incentive Program (ScIP).** Award for legal residents of Del aware who are U.S. citizens or eligible non-citizens. Must demonstrate sub stantial financial need and enroll full-time in an undergraduate degree program at a nonprofit, regionally accredited institution in Delaware or Pennsylvania. Minimum 2.5 GPA required. *Award:* Grant for use in freshman, sophomore, junior, senior, or graduate years; not renewable. *Award amount:* $700–$2200. *Number of awards:* 700–2200. *Eligibility Requirements:* Applicant must be enrolled or expecting to enroll full-time at a two-year or four-year institution or university; resident of Delaware and studying in Delaware, Pennsylvania. Applicant must have 2.5 GPA or higher. Available to U.S. citizens. *Application Requirements:* Application form, FAFSA, financial need analysis, transcript. **Deadline:** April 15.

Contact Ms. Carylin Brinkley, Program Administrator, Delaware Higher Education Office, 401 Federal Street, Suite 2, Dover, DE 19901. *E-mail:*

cbrinkley@doe.k12.de.us. *Phone:* 302-735-4120. *Fax:* 302-739-5894. *Website:* http://www.doe.k12.de.us.

**State Tuition Assistance.** You must enlist in the Delaware Air or Army National Guard to be eligible for this scholarship award. Award providing tuition assistance for any member of the Air or Army National Guard attending a Delaware two-year or four-year college. Awards are renewable. Applicant's minimum GPA must be 2.0. *Award:* Scholarship for use in freshman, soph omore, junior, or senior years; renewable. *Award amount:* $1–$10,000. *Number of awards:* 1–200. *Eligibility Requirements:* Applicant must be enrolled or expecting to enroll full- or part-time at a two-year or four-year institution or university and studying in Delaware. Available to U.S. citizens. Applicant or parent must meet one or more of the following require ments: national guard experience; retired from active duty; disabled or killed as a result of military service; prisoner of war; or missing in action. *Application Require ments:* Application form, transcript.

Contact Robert Csizmadia, State Tuition Assistance Manager, Delaware National Guard, 1st Regiment Road, Wilmington, DE 19808-2191. *E-mail:* robert.csizmadia@us.army.mil. *Phone:* 302-326-7012. *Fax:* 302-326-7029. *Website:* http://www. delawarenationalguard.com/.

# DISTRICT OF COLUMBIA

**American Council of the Blind Scholarships.** Merit-based award available to undergraduate students who are legally blind in both eyes. Submit cer tificate of legal blindness and proof of acceptance at an accredited postsecondary institution. *Award:* Scholarship for use in freshman, sophomore, junior, or senior years; renewable. *Award amount:* $1000–$2500. *Number of awards:* 16–20. *Eligi bility Requirements:* Applicant must be visually impaired and enrolled or expecting to enroll full- or part-time at a four-year institution or university. Applicant must be visually impaired. Applicant must have 3.5 GPA or higher. Available to U.S. citizens. *Application Requirements:* Application form, driver's license, essay, evidence of legal blindness, proof of post-secondary school accep tance, recommendations or references, transcript. **Deadline:** March 1.

Contact Tatricia Castillo, Scholarship Coordinator, American Council of the Blind, 1155 15th Street, NW, Suite 1004, Washington, DC 20005. *E-mail:*

tcastillo@acp.org. *Phone:* 202-467-5081. *Fax:* 202-467-5085. *Website:* http://www. acb.org/.

**American Indian Nurse Scholarship Program.** The current goal is to grant a $1,500 scholarship each semester, as long as the student remains in academic good standing. The scholarship money is restricted to tuition and specific academic expenses. Health Administration; Nursing. *Award:* Scholarship for use in freshman, sophomore, junior, senior, graduate, or postgraduate years; renewable. *Award amount:* $500–$1500. *Number of awards:* 5–10. *Eligibility Requirements:* Applicant must be American Indian/Alaska Native and enrolled or expecting to enroll full-time at a two-year or four-year or technical institution or university. Applicant must have 2.5 GPA or higher. Available to U.S. citizens. *Application Requirements:* Application form, driver's license, financial need analysis, personal photograph, recommendations or references, transcript. **Deadline:** continuous.

**Bureau of Indian Education Grant Program.** Grants are provided to supplement financial assistance to eligible American Indian/Alaska Native students entering college seeking a Baccalaureate degree. A student must be a member of, or at least one-quarter degree Indian blood descendent of a member of an American Indian tribe who are eligible for the special programs and services provided by the United States through the Bureau of Indian Affairs to Indians because of their status as Indians. *Award:* Grant for use in freshman year; not renewable. *Eligibility Requirements:* Applicant must be American Indian/Alaska Native; high school student and planning to enroll or expecting to enroll full-time at a two-year or four-year institution or university. Available to U.S. citizens. *Application Requirements:* Application form, recommendations or references, test scores, transcript. **Deadline:** varies.

Contact Paulina Bell, Office Automation Assistant. *Phone:* 202-208-6123. *Fax:* 202-208-3312. *Website:* http://www.bie.edu/.

**Central Intelligence Agency Undergraduate Scholarship Program.** Need and merit-based award for students with minimum 3.0 GPA, who are interested in working for the Central Intelligence Agency upon graduation. Renewable for four years of undergraduate study. Must apply in senior year of high school or sophomore year in college. For further information refer to web site http://www.cia.gov. Accounting; Business/Consumer Services; Computer Science/Data Processing; Economics; Electrical Engineering/Electronics; Foreign Language; Geography; Graphics/ Graphic Arts/Printing; International Studies; Political Science; Surveying, Surveying Technology, Cartography, or Geographic Information Science. *Award:* Scholarship for use in freshman, sophomore, junior, or senior years; renewable. *Award amount:* up to $18,000. *Eligibility Requirements:* Applicant must be enrolled or expecting to enroll full-time at a four-year institution or university. Applicant must have 3.0 GPA or higher. Available to U.S. citizens. *Application Requirements:* Application form, financial need analysis, recommendations or references, resume, test scores, transcript. **Deadline:** November 1.

Contact Van Patrick, Chief, College Relations. *E-mail:* ivanilp0@ucia.gov. *Phone:* 703-613-8388. *Fax:* 703-613-7676. *Website:* http://www.cia.gov/.

**Harry S. Truman Scholarship.** Scholarships for U.S. citizens or U.S. nationals who are college or university students with junior-level academic standing and who wish to attend professional or graduate school to prepare for careers in government or the nonprofit and advocacy sectors. Candidates must be nominated by their institution. Public service and leadership record considered. Visit web site http://www.truman.gov for further information and application. Political Science; Public Policy and Administration. *Award:* Scholarship for use in junior year; renewable. *Award amount:* $30,000. *Number of awards:* 65. *Eligibility Requirements:* Applicant must be enrolled or expecting to enroll full-time at a four-year institution or university and must have an interest in leadership. Available to U.S. citizens. *Application Requirements:* Application form, interview, policy proposal, recommendations or references. **Deadline:** February 5.

Contact Tonji Wade, Program Officer, Harry S. Truman Scholarship Foundation, 712 Jackson Place, NW, Washington, DC 20006. *E-mail:* office@truman.gov. *Phone:* 202-395-4831. *Fax:* 202-395-6995. *Website:* http://www.truman.gov/.

**Montgomery GI Bill (Active Duty) Chapter 30.** Award provides up to thirty-six months of education benefits to eligible veterans for college, business school, technical courses, vocational courses, correspondence courses, apprenticeships/job training, or flight training. Must be an eligible veteran with an Honorable Discharge and have high school diploma or GED before applying for benefits. *Award:* Scholarship for use in freshman, sophomore, junior, senior, or graduate years; renewable. *Eligibility Requirements:* Applicant must be enrolled or expecting to enroll full- or part-time at a two-year or four-year or technical institution or university. Available to U.S. citizens. Applicant or parent must meet one or more of the following requirements: general military experience; retired from active duty; disabled or killed as a result of military service; prisoner of war; or missing in action. *Application Requirements:* Application form, proof of active military service of at least 2 years. **Deadline:** continuous.

Contact Keith Wilson, Director, Education Service. *Phone:* 888-442-4551. *Website:* http://www.gibill.va.gov/.

**Montgomery GI Bill (Selected Reserve).** Educational assistance program for members of the selected reserve of the Army, Navy, Air Force, Marine Corps and Coast Guard, as well as the Army and Air National Guard. Available to all reservists and National Guard personnel who commit to a six-year obligation, and remain in the Reserve or Guard during the six years. Award is renewable. Monthly benefit is $309 for up to thirty-six months for full-time. *Award:* Scholarship for use in freshman, sophomore, junior, senior, or postgraduate years; renewable. *Eligibility Requirements:* Applicant must be enrolled or expecting to enroll full- or part-time at a two-year or four-year or technical institution or university. Available to U.S. citizens. Applicant or parent must meet one or more of the following requirements: general military experience; retired from active duty; disabled or killed as a result of military service; prisoner of war; or missing in action. *Application Requirements:* Application form, proof of military service of six years in the reserve or guard. **Deadline:** continuous.

Contact Keith Wilson, Director, Education Service. *Phone:* 888-442-4551. *Website:* http://www.gibill.va.gov/.

**Reserve Education Assistance Program.** The program provides educational assistance to members of National Guard and reserve components. Selected Reserve and Individual Ready Reserve (IRR) who are called or ordered to active duty service in response to a war or national emergency as declared by the president or Congress are eligible. For further information see web site http://

www.GIBILL.va.gov. *Award:* Scholarship for use in freshman, sophomore, junior, senior, graduate, or postgraduate years; renewable. *Eligibility Requirements:* Applicant must be enrolled or expecting to enroll full- or part-time at a two-year or four-year or technical institution or university. Available to U.S. citizens. Applicant or parent must meet one or more of the following requirements: general military experience; retired from active duty; disabled or killed as a result of military service; prisoner of war; or missing in action. *Application Requirements:* Application form. **Deadline:** continuous.

Contact Keith Wilson, Director, Education Service. *Phone:* 888-442-4551. *Website:* http://www.gibill.va.gov/.

**Survivors and Dependents Educational Assistance (Chapter 35)-VA.** Monthly $860 benefits for up to 45 months. Must be spouses or children under age 26 of current veterans missing in action or of deceased or totally and permanently disabled (service-related) service persons. For more information visit the following web site http://www.gibill.va.gov. *Award:* Scholarship for use in freshman, sophomore, junior, or senior years; renewable. *Eligibility Requirements:* Applicant must be enrolled or expecting to enroll full- or part-time at a two-year or four-year or technical institution or university. Available to U.S. and non-U.S. citizens. Applicant or parent must meet one or more of the following requirements: general military experience; retired from active duty; disabled or killed as a result of military service; prisoner of war; or missing in action. *Application Requirements:* Application form, proof of parent or spouse's qualifying service. **Deadline:** continuous.

Contact Keith Wilson, Director, Education Service. *Phone:* 888-442-4551. *Website:* http://www.gibill.va.gov/.

# FLORIDA

**Access to Better Learning and Education Grant.** Grant program provides tuition assistance to Florida undergraduate students enrolled in degree programs at eligible private Florida colleges or universities. Must be a U.S. citizen or eligible non-citizen and must meet Florida residency requirements. The participating institution determines application procedures, deadlines, and student eligibility. An eligible student must complete and submit the FAFSA in order to receive program funding. For more details, visit the web site at http://www.FloridaStu

dentFinancialAid.org/SSFAD/home/uamain.htm. *Award:* Grant for use in freshman, sophomore, junior, or senior years; renewable. *Award amount:* up to $1500. *Eligibility Requirements:* Applicant must be enrolled or expecting to enroll full-time at a four-year institution or university; resident of Florida and studying in Florida. Available to U.S. citizens. *Application Requirements:* Application form.

**First Generation Matching Grant Program.** Need-based grants to Florida resident undergraduate students who are enrolled in state universities and community colleges in Florida and whose parents have not earned baccalaureate degrees. Available state funds are contingent upon matching contributions from private sources on a dollar-for-dollar basis. Institutions determine application procedures, deadlines, and student eligibility. For more details, visit the web site at http://www.FloridaStudentFinancialAid.org/SSFAD/home/uamain.htm. *Award:* Grant for use in freshman, sophomore, junior, or senior years; renewable. *Eligibility Requirements:* Applicant must be enrolled or expecting to enroll full- or part-time at a two-year or four-year institution or university; resident of Florida and studying in Florida. Available to U.S. citizens. *Application Requirements:* Application form, financial need analysis.

**Florida Bright Futures Scholarship Program.** Three lottery-funded scholarships reward Florida high school graduates for high academic achievement. Program is comprised of the following three awards: Florida Academic Scholars Award, Florida Medallion Scholars Award and Florida Gold Seal Vocational Scholars Award. An eligible student must complete and submit the FAFSA in order to receive program funding. For more details, visit the web site at http://www.FloridaStudentFinancialAid.org/SSFAD/home/uamain.htm. *Award:* Scholarship for use in freshman, sophomore, junior, or senior years; renewable. *Eligibility Requirements:* Applicant must be high school student; planning to enroll or expecting to enroll full- or part-time at a two-year or four-year or technical institution or university; resident of Florida and studying in Florida. Applicant must have 3.0 GPA or higher. Available to U.S. citizens. *Application Requirements:* Application form, application form may be submitted online, community service, test scores, transcript.

**Florida Postsecondary Student Assistance Grant.** Scholarships to

degree-seeking, resident, undergraduate students who demonstrate substantial financial need and are enrolled in eligible degree-granting private colleges and universities not eligible under the Florida Private Student Assistance Grant. FSAG is a decentralized program, and each participating institution determines application procedures, deadlines and student eligibility. Number of awards varies. For more details, visit the web site at http://www.FloridaStudentFinancialAid.org/SSFAD/home/uamain.htm. *Award:* Grant for use in freshman, sophomore, junior, or senior years; renewable. *Award amount:* $200–$2610. *Eligibility Requirements:* Applicant must be enrolled or expecting to enroll full-time at a two-year or four-year institution or university; resident of Florida and studying in Florida. Available to U.S. citizens. *Application Requirements:* Financial need analysis.

**Florida Private Student Assistance Grant.** Grants for Florida residents who are U.S. citizens or eligible non-citizens attending eligible private, nonprofit, four-year colleges and universities in Florida. Must be a full-time student and demonstrate substantial financial need. For renewal, must have earned a minimum cumulative GPA of 2.0 at the last institution attended. For more details, visit the web site at http://www.FloridaStudentFinancialAid.org/SSFAD/home/uamain.htm. *Award:* Grant for use in freshman, sophomore, junior, or senior years; renewable. *Award amount:* $200–$2610. *Eligibility Requirements:* Applicant must be enrolled or expecting to enroll full-time at a four-year institution or university; resident of Florida and studying in Florida. Available to U.S. citizens. *Application Requirements:* Application form, financial need analysis.

**Florida Public Student Assistance Grant.** Grants for Florida residents, U.S. citizens or eligible non-citizens who attend state universities and public community colleges and demonstrate substantial financial need. For renewal, must have earned a minimum cumulative GPA of 2.0 at the last institution attended. For more details, visit the web site at http://www.FloridaStudentFinancialAid.org/SSFAD/home/uamain.htm. *Award:* Grant for use in freshman, sophomore, junior, or senior years; renewable. *Award amount:* $200–$2610. *Eligibility Requirements:* Applicant must be enrolled or expecting to enroll full- or part-time at a two-year or four-year institution or university; resident of Florida and studying in Florida. Available to U.S. citizens. *Application*

*Requirements:* Application form, financial need analysis.

**Florida Space Research Program.** Grants for faculty researchers from Florida public and private universities and community colleges. One-time award for aerospace and technology research. Submit research proposal with budget. Aviation/Aerospace; Earth Science; Materials Science, Engineering, and Metallurgy; Mathematics; Mechanical Engineering. *Award:* Grant for use in junior, senior, graduate, or postgraduate years; not renewable. *Award amount:* $12,500–$25,000. *Number of awards:* 13–15. *Eligibility Requirements:* Applicant must be enrolled or expecting to enroll full- or part-time at a two-year or four-year institution or university; resident of Florida and studying in Florida. Available to U.S. citizens. *Application Requirements:* Application form, application form may be submitted online (http://floridaspacegrant.org/programs/research/), proposal with budget. **Deadline:** May 30.

Contact Dr. Jaydeep Mukherjee, FSGC Director, NASA Florida Space Grant Consortium, PO Box 160650, 12354 Research Parkway, Room 218, Orlando, FL 32826. *E-mail:* fsgc@ucf.edu. *Phone:* 407-823-6177. *Website:* http://www.floridaspacegrant.org/.

**Florida Student Assistance Grant-Career Education.** Need-based grant program available to Florida residents enrolled in certificate programs of 450 or more clock hours at participating community colleges or career centers operated by district school boards. FSAG-CE is a decentralized state of Florida program, which means that each participating institution determines application procedures, deadlines, student eligibility, and award amounts. For more details, visit the web site at http://www.FloridaStudentFinancialAid.org/SSFAD/home/uamain.htm. *Award:* Grant for use in freshman, sophomore, junior, or senior years; renewable. *Award amount:* $200–$2610. *Eligibility Requirements:* Applicant must be enrolled or expecting to enroll full- or part-time at a two-year or technical institution; resident of Florida and studying in Florida. Available to U.S. citizens. *Application Requirements:* Application form may be submitted online, financial need analysis.

**Florida Work Experience Program.** Need-based program providing eligible Florida residents work experiences that will complement and reinforce their educational and career goals. Must maintain GPA of 2.0. Postsecondary institution will determine applicant's eligibility, number of hours to be worked per week, and the award amount. For more details, visit the web site at http://www.FloridaStudentFinancialAid.org/SSFAD/home/uamain.htm. *Award:* Grant for use in freshman, sophomore, junior, or senior years; renewable. *Eligibility Requirements:* Applicant must be enrolled or expecting to enroll full- or part-time at a two-year or four-year institution or university; resident of Florida and studying in Florida. Available to U.S. citizens. *Application Requirements:* Financial need analysis.

**Jose Marti Scholarship Challenge Grant Fund.** Award available to Hispanic-American students who were born in, or whose parent was born in a Hispanic country. Must be a Florida resident, be enrolled full-time in Florida at an eligible school, and have a GPA of 3.0 or above. Must be U.S. citizen or eligible non-citizen. FAFSA must be processed by May 15. For more details, visit the web site at http://www.FloridaStudentFinancialAid.org/SSFAD/home/uamain.htm. *Award:* Scholarship for use in freshman, sophomore, junior, or senior years; renewable. *Award amount:* $2000. *Eligibility Requirements:* Applicant must be of Hispanic heritage; high school student; planning to enroll or expecting to enroll full-time at a two-year or four-year institution or university; resident of Florida and studying in Florida. Applicant must have 3.0 GPA or higher. Available to U.S. citizens. *Application Requirements:* Application form, financial need analysis. **Deadline:** April 1.

**Mary McLeod Bethune Scholarship.** Renewable award to Florida residents with a GPA of 3.0 or above, who will attend Bethune-Cookman University, Edward Waters College, Florida A&M University, or Florida Memorial University. Must not have previously received a baccalaureate degree. Must demonstrate financial need as specified by the institution. For more details, visit the web site at http://www.FloridaStudentFinancialAid.org/SSFAD/home/uamain.htm. *Award:* Scholarship for use in freshman, sophomore, junior, or senior years; renewable. *Award amount:* $3000. *Eligibility Requirements:* Applicant must be enrolled or expecting to enroll full-time at a four-year institution or university; resident of Florida and studying in Florida. Applicant must have 3.0 GPA or higher. Available to U.S. citizens. *Application Requirements:* Financial need analysis.

**Rosewood Family Scholarship Fund.** Renewable award for eligible direct descendants of African-American Rosewood families affected by the incident of January 1923. Must not have previously received a baccalaureate degree. For more details, visit the web site at http://www.FloridaStudentFinancialAid.org/SSFAD/home/uamain.htm. *Award:* Scholarship for use in freshman, sophomore, junior, or senior years; renewable. *Award amount:* up to $6100. *Number of awards:* up to 50. *Eligibility Requirements:* Applicant must be enrolled or expecting to enroll full- or part-time at a two-year or four-year or technical institution or university and studying in Florida. Available to U.S. citizens. *Application Requirements:* Application form, documentation of Rosewood ancestry, financial need analysis. **Deadline:** April 1.

**Scholarships for Children & Spouses of Deceased or Disabled Veterans .** Renewable scholarships for children and spouses of deceased or disabled veterans. Children must be between the ages of 16 and 22, and attend an eligible Florida postsecondary institution and enrolled at least part-time. Must ensure that the Florida Department of Veterans Affairs certifies the applicant's eligibility. Must maintain GPA of 2.0. For more details, visit the web site at http://www.FloridaStudentFinancialAid.org/SSFAD/home/uamain.htm. *Award:* Scholarship for use in freshman, sophomore, junior, or senior years; renewable. *Eligibility Requirements:* Applicant must be age 16-22; enrolled or expecting to enroll full- or part-time at a two-year or four-year or technical institution or university; resident of Florida and studying in Florida. Available to U.S. citizens. Applicant or parent must meet one or more of the following requirements: general military experience; retired from active duty; disabled or killed as a result of military service; prisoner of war; or missing in action. *Application Requirements:* Application form. **Deadline:** April 1.

**William L. Boyd IV Florida Resident Access Grant.** Renewable awards to Florida undergraduate residents attending an eligible private, nonprofit Florida college or university. Postsecondary institution will determine applicant's eligibility. Renewal applicant must have earned a minimum institutional GPA of 2.0. An eligible student must complete and submit the FAFSA in order to receive program funding. For more details, visit the web site at http://www.FloridaStudentFinancialAid.org/SSFAD/home/

uamain.htm. *Award:* Grant for use in freshman, sophomore, junior, or senior years; renewable. *Award amount:* up to $3000. *Eligibility Requirements:* Applicant must be enrolled or expecting to enroll full-time at a four-year institution or university; resident of Florida and studying in Florida. Available to U.S. citizens. *Application Requirements:* Application form.

## GEORGIA

**Georgia HOPE Scholarship Program.** Scholarship and Grant program for Georgia residents who are college undergraduates to attend an accredited two or four-year Georgia institution. Pays a percentage of actual undergraduate tuition charged at public postsecondary institutions. Percentage paid will vary from year to year. At private postsecondary institutions in Georgia, students may receive up to $3600 per year for full-time study or $1800 per year for part-time. Minimum 3.0 GPA required. Renewable if student maintains grades. See http://www.GAcollege411.org for full details. *Award:* Scholarship for use in freshman, sophomore, junior, or senior years; renewable. *Award amount:* up to $6000. *Number of awards:* 200,000–230,000. *Eligibility Requirements:* Applicant must be enrolled or expecting to enroll full- or part-time at a two-year or four-year institution or university; resident of Georgia and studying in Georgia. Applicant must have 3.0 GPA or higher. Available to U.S. citizens. *Application Requirements:* Application form, high schools must report transcripts to GSFC. **Deadline:** continuous.

Contact Tracy Ireland, Vice President, Georgia Student Finance Commission, 2082 East Exchange Place, Suite 100, Tucker, GA 30084. *E-mail:* tracyi@gsfc.org. *Phone:* 800-505-4732. *Website:* http://www.GAcollege411.org/.

**Georgia Public Safety Memorial Grant.** Award for children of Georgia Public Safety Officers, prison guards, fire fighters, law enforcement officers or emergency medical technicians killed or permanently disabled in the line of duty. Must attend an accredited postsecondary Georgia school. Complete the Public Safety Memorial Grant application. *Award:* Grant for use in freshman, sophomore, junior, or senior years; not renewable. *Award amount:* $2000. *Number of awards:* 20–40. *Eligibility Requirements:* Applicant must be enrolled or expecting to enroll full-time at a two-year or four-year or technical institution

or university; resident of Georgia and studying in Georgia. Available to U.S. citizens. *Application Requirements:* Application form, selective service registration. **Deadline:** continuous.

Contact Caylee French, Division Director, Georgia Student Finance Commission, 2082 East Exchange Place, Suite 100, Tucker, GA 30084. *E-mail:* cayleef@gsfc.org. *Phone:* 770-724-9244. *Website:* http://www.GAcollege411.org/.

**Georgia Tuition Equalization Grant (GTEG).** Award for Georgia residents pursuing undergraduate study at an accredited two- or four-year Georgia private postsecondary institution. *Award:* Grant for use in freshman, sophomore, junior, or senior years; not renewable. *Number of awards:* 1–35,000. *Eligibility Requirements:* Applicant must be learning disabled; Hispanic; enrolled or expecting to enroll full-time at a two-year or four-year institution or university; resident of Georgia and studying in Georgia. Applicant must be learning disabled. Available to U.S. citizens. *Application Requirements:* Application form, application form may be submitted online (http://www.gacollege411.org), social security number.

Contact Ms. Caylee French, Director, Student Aid Services, Georgia Student Finance Commission, 2082 East Exchange Place, Suite 100, Tucker, GA 30084. *E-mail:* cayleef@gsfc.org. *Phone:* 770-724-9244. *Fax:* 770-724-9249. *Website:* http://www.GAcollege411.org/.

**Physicians for Rural Areas Assistance Program.** Service repayable medical school scholarship for a maximum of $20,000 per year for four years available to Georgia residents enrolled in U.S. accredited medical school. Repay by practicing medicine for one year in rural Georgia for each year that the scholarship is received. Service payment begins upon completion of residency training. Health and Medical Sciences. *Award:* Scholarship for use in freshman, sophomore, junior, or senior years; renewable. *Award amount:* up to $20,000. *Number of awards:* 20–25. *Eligibility Requirements:* Applicant must be enrolled or expecting to enroll full-time at an institution or university and resident of Georgia. Available to U.S. citizens. *Application Requirements:* Application form, essay, financial need analysis, interview, personal photograph, proof of GA residency, test scores, transcript. **Deadline:** June 1.

Contact Ms. Pamela Smith, Administration Manager, Georgia Board for Physician Workforce, 2 Peachtree

Street, NW, 36th Floor, Atlanta, GA 30303. *E-mail:* psmith@dch.ga.gov. *Phone:* 404-232-7972. *Website:* http://www.gbpw.georgia.gov/.

## HAWAII

**Hawaii State Student Incentive Grant.** Grants are given to residents of Hawaii who are enrolled in a participating Hawaiian state school. Funds are for undergraduate tuition only. Applicants must submit a financial need analysis. *Award:* Grant for use in freshman, sophomore, junior, or senior years; renewable. *Award amount:* $200–$2000. *Number of awards:* 470. *Eligibility Requirements:* Applicant must be enrolled or expecting to enroll full- or part-time at a two-year or four-year or technical institution or university; resident of Hawaii and studying in Hawaii. Available to U.S. citizens. *Application Requirements:* Application form, financial need analysis. **Deadline:** continuous.

Contact Janine Oyama, Financial Aid Specialist, Hawaii State Postsecondary Education Commission, University of Hawaii, Honolulu, HI 96822. *Phone:* 808-956-6066.

## ILLINOIS

**Golden Apple Scholars of Illinois.** Applicants must be between the ages of 16 and 21 and maintain a GPA of 2.5. Eligible applicants must be residents of Illinois studying in Illinois. Recipients must agree to teach in an Illinois school school of need for 5 years. Education. *Award:* Scholarship for use in freshman, sophomore, junior, or senior years; renewable. *Award amount:* $23,000. *Number of awards:* 100–175. *Eligibility Requirements:* Applicant must be age 16-21; enrolled or expecting to enroll full-time at a two-year or four-year institution or university; resident of Illinois and studying in Illinois. Available to U.S. citizens. *Application Requirements:* Application form, application form may be submitted online (http://www.golde napple.org), essay, interview, personal photograph, recommendations or references, social security card, test scores, transcript.

Contact Ms. Patricia Kilduff, Director of Recruitment and Placement. *E-mail:* kilduff@goldenapple.org. *Phone:* 312-477-7515. *Website:* http://www.goldenapple.org/.

**Grant Program for Dependents of Police, Fire, or Correctional Officers.** Awards available to Illinois residents who are dependents of police, fire, and correctional officers killed or disabled in line of duty. Provides for tuition and fees at approved Illinois institutions. Number of grants and individual dollar amount awarded vary. *Award:* Grant for use in freshman, sophomore, junior, senior, graduate, or postgraduate years; renewable. *Eligibility Requirements:* Applicant must be enrolled or expecting to enroll full- or part-time at a two-year or four-year or technical institution or university; resident of Illinois and studying in Illinois. Available to U.S. citizens. *Application Requirements:* Application form, proof of status. **Deadline:** varies.

**Higher Education License Plate Program-HELP.** Grants for students who attend Illinois colleges for which the special collegiate license plates are available. The Illinois Secretary of State issues the license plates, and part of the proceeds are used for grants for undergraduate students attending these colleges, to pay tuition and mandatory fees. *Award:* Grant for use in freshman, sophomore, junior, or senior years; not renewable. *Eligibility Requirements:* Applicant must be enrolled or expecting to enroll full- or part-time at a two-year or four-year institution or university; resident of Illinois and studying in Illinois. Available to U.S. citizens. *Application Requirements:* Application form, financial need analysis. **Deadline:** varies.

**Illinois College Savings Bond Bonus Incentive Grant Program.** Program offers Illinois college savings bond holders a grant for each year of bond maturity payable upon bond redemption if at least 70 percent of proceeds are used to attend college in Illinois. The amount of grant will depend on the amount of the bond, ranging from a $40 to $440 grant per $5000 of the bond. Applications are accepted between August 1 and May 30 of the academic year in which the bonds matured, or in the academic year immediately following maturity. *Award:* Grant for use in freshman, sophomore, junior, senior, graduate, or postgraduate years; not renewable. *Eligibility Requirements:* Applicant must be enrolled or expecting to enroll full- or part-time at a two-year or four-year or technical institution or university and studying in Illinois. Available to U.S. citizens. *Application Requirements:* Application form. **Deadline:** varies.

**Illinois Monetary Award Program.** Awards to Illinois residents enrolled in a minimum of 3 hours per term in a degree program at an approved Illinois institution. See web site for complete list of participating schools. Must demonstrate financial need, based on the information provided on the Free Application for Federal Student Aid. Number of grants and the individual dollar amount awarded vary. Deadline: As soon as possible after January 1 of the year in which the student will enter college. *Award:* Grant for use in freshman, sophomore, junior, or senior years; renewable. *Award amount:* $2599. *Eligibility Requirements:* Applicant must be enrolled or expecting to enroll full- or part-time at a two-year or four-year or technical institution or university; resident of Illinois and studying in Illinois. Available to U.S. citizens. *Application Requirements:* FAFSA online, financial need analysis. **Deadline:** varies.

**Illinois National Guard Grant Program.** Active duty members of the Illinois National Guard, or who are within 12 months of discharge, and who have completed one full year of service are eligible. May be used for study at Illinois two- or four-year public colleges for a maximum of the equivalent of four academic years of full-time enrollment. Deadlines: October 1 of the academic year for full year, March 1 for second/third term, or June 15 for the summer term. *Award:* Grant for use in freshman, sophomore, junior, senior, or graduate years; renewable. *Eligibility Requirements:* Applicant must be enrolled or expecting to enroll full- or part-time at a two-year or four-year institution or university; resident of Illinois and studying in Illinois. Available to U.S. citizens. Applicant or parent must meet one or more of the following requirements: national guard experience; retired from active duty; disabled or killed as a result of military service; prisoner of war; or missing in action. *Application Requirements:* Application form, documentation of service. **Deadline:** varies.

**Illinois Special Education Teacher Tuition Waiver.** Teachers or students who are pursuing a career in special education as public, private or parochial preschool, elementary or secondary school teachers in Illinois may be eligible for this program. This program will exempt such individuals from paying tuition and mandatory fees at an eligible institution, for up to four years. The individual dollar amount awarded are subject to sufficient annual appropriations by the Illinois General Assembly. Special Education. *Award:* Scholarship for use in freshman, sophomore, junior, senior, or graduate years; renewable. *Eligibility Requirements:* Applicant must be enrolled or expecting to enroll full- or part-time at a four-year institution or university; resident of Illinois and studying in Illinois. Available to U.S. citizens. *Application Requirements:* Application form. **Deadline:** March 1.

**Illinois Veteran Grant Program-IVG.** Awards qualified veterans and pays eligible tuition and fees for study in Illinois public universities or community colleges. Program eligibility units are based on the enrolled hours for a particular term, not the dollar amount of the benefits paid. Applications are available at college financial aid office and can be submitted any time during the academic year for which assistance is being requested. *Award:* Grant for use in freshman, sophomore, junior, senior, or graduate years; renewable. *Eligibility Requirements:* Applicant must be enrolled or expecting to enroll full- or part-time at a two-year or four-year institution or university; resident of Illinois and studying in Illinois. Available to U.S. citizens. Applicant or parent must meet one or more of the following requirements: general military experience; retired from active duty; disabled or killed as a result of military service; prisoner of war; or missing in action. *Application Requirements:* Application form. **Deadline:** continuous.

**MIA/POW Scholarship.** Any Spouse, natural child, adopted child, or any step child of a veteran. Child must attend school prior to 26th birthday. No age limit for spouse. Veteran must be MIA, POW, died as the result of service connected disability determined by the U.S. Department of Veterans' Affairs or is 100% service connected disabled permanent and total established by the U.S. Department of Veterans' Affairs. Veteran must have been an Illinois resident at time of entry into service or became an Illinois resident within 6 months after entering service. Scholarship is equivalent to four full years of college, including summer terms. Based on a point system with 120 points as the maximum. Applicant has 12 years to utilize scholarship from the date they begin using it. *Award:* Scholarship for use in freshman, sophomore, junior, or senior years; renewable. *Eligibility Requirements:* Applicant must be enrolled or expecting to enroll full- or part-time at a two-year or four-year institution or university; married; resident of Illinois and studying in Illinois. Available to U.S. citizens. Applicant must have general military experience. *Application*

*Requirements:* Application form. **Deadline:** continuous.

Contact Ms. Tracy Kimmel, Grants Section, Illinois Department of Veterans' Affairs, 833 South Spring Street, Springfield, IL 62794-9432. *Phone:* 217-782-3564. *Fax:* 217-782-4161. *Website:* http://www.state.il.us/agency/dva.

**Minority Teachers of Illinois Scholarship Program.** Award for minority students intending to become school teachers; teaching commitment attached to receipt. Number of scholarships and the individual dollar amounts vary. Education; Special Education. *Award:* Scholarship for use in freshman, sophomore, junior, senior, graduate, or postgraduate years; renewable. *Award amount:* up to $5000. *Eligibility Requirements:* Applicant must be American Indian/Alaska Native, Asian/Pacific Islander, Black (non-Hispanic), Hispanic; enrolled or expecting to enroll full- or part-time at a two-year or four-year institution or university; resident of Illinois and studying in Illinois. Available to U.S. citizens. *Application Requirements:* Application form, transcript. **Deadline:** March 1.

**Veterans' Children Educational Opportunities.** $250 award for each child aged 10 to 18 of a veteran who died or became totally disabled as a result of active duty. Must be Illinois resident studying in Illinois. Death must be service-connected. Disability must be rated 100 percent for two or more years. *Award:* Grant for use in freshman year; not renewable. *Award amount:* $250. *Eligibility Requirements:* Applicant must be age 10-18; enrolled or expecting to enroll full- or part-time at a two-year or four-year institution or university; single; resident of Illinois and studying in Illinois. Available to U.S. citizens. Applicant must have general military experience. *Application Requirements:* Application form. **Deadline:** June 30.

Contact Tracy Kimmel, Grants Section, Illinois Department of Veterans' Affairs, 833 South Spring Street, Springfield, IL 62794-9432. *Phone:* 217-782-3564. *Fax:* 217-782-4161. *Website:* http://www.state.il.us/agency/dva.

# INDIANA

**Child of Disabled Veteran Grant or Purple Heart Recipient Grant.** Free tuition at Indiana state-supported colleges or universities for children of disabled veterans or Purple Heart recipients. Must submit form DD214 or service record. Covers tuition and mandatory fees. *Award:* Grant for use in freshman, sophomore, junior, senior, graduate, or postgraduate years; renewable. *Eligibility Requirements:* Applicant must be enrolled or expecting to enroll full- or part-time at a two-year or four-year institution or university; resident of Indiana and studying in Indiana. Available to U.S. citizens. Applicant or parent must meet one or more of the following requirements: general military experience; retired from active duty; disabled or killed as a result of military service; prisoner of war; or missing in action. *Application Requirements:* Application form, FAFSA. **Deadline:** continuous.

Contact Jon Brinkley, State Service Officer, Indiana Department of Veterans Affairs, 302 West Washington Street, Room E-120, Indianapolis, IN 46204-2738. *E-mail:* jbrinkley@dva.in.gov. *Phone:* 317-232-3910. *Fax:* 317-232-7721. *Website:* http://www.in.gov/dva.

**Department of Veterans Affairs Free Tuition for Children of POW/MIA's in Vietnam.** Renewable award for residents of Indiana who are the children of veterans declared missing in action or prisoner-of-war after January 1, 1960. Provides tuition at Indiana state-supported institutions for undergraduate study. *Award:* Grant for use in freshman, sophomore, junior, senior, graduate, or postgraduate years; renewable. *Eligibility Requirements:* Applicant must be enrolled or expecting to enroll full- or part-time at a two-year or four-year institution or university; resident of Indiana and studying in Indiana. Available to U.S. citizens. Applicant or parent must meet one or more of the following requirements: general military experience; retired from active duty; disabled or killed as a result of military service; prisoner of war; or missing in action. *Application Requirements:* Application form. **Deadline:** continuous.

Contact Jon Brinkley, State Service Officer, Indiana Department of Veterans Affairs, 302 West Washington Street, Room E-120, Indianapolis, IN 46204-2738. *E-mail:* jbrinkley@dva.in.gov. *Phone:* 317-232-3910. *Fax:* 317-232-7721. *Website:* http://www.in.gov/dva.

**Frank O'Bannon Grant Program.** A need-based, tuition-restricted program for students attending Indiana public, private, or proprietary institutions seeking a first undergraduate degree. Students (and parents of dependent students) who are U.S. citizens and Indiana residents must file the FAFSA yearly by the March 10 deadline. *Award:* Grant for use in freshman, sophomore, junior, or senior years; not renewable. *Award amount:* $200–$10,992. *Number of awards:* 48,408–70,239. *Eligibility Requirements:* Applicant must be enrolled or expecting to enroll full-time at a two-year or four-year or technical institution or university; resident of Indiana and studying in Indiana. Available to U.S. citizens. *Application Requirements:* Application form, FAFSA, financial need analysis. **Deadline:** March 10.

**Hoosier Scholar Award.** A $500 non renewable award. Based on the size of the senior class, one to three scholars are selected by the guidance counselors of each accredited high school in Indiana. The award is based on academic merit and may be used for any educational expense at an eligible Indiana institution of higher education. *Award:* Scholarship for use in freshman year; not renewable. *Award amount:* $500. *Number of awards:* 666–840. *Eligibility Requirements:* Applicant must be high school student; planning to enroll or expecting to enroll full-time at a two-year or four-year institution or university; resident of Indiana and studying in Indiana. Applicant must have 3.5 GPA or higher. Available to U.S. citizens. *Application Requirements:* Application form, recommendations or references. **Deadline:** March 10.

Contact Ada Sparkman, Program Coordinator, State Student Assistance Commission of Indiana (SSACI), 150 West Market Street, Suite 500, Indianapolis, IN 46204-2805. *Phone:* 317-232-2350. *Fax:* 317-232-3260. *Website:* http://www.in.gov/ssaci.

**Indiana National Guard Supplemental Grant.** The award is a supplement to the Indiana Higher Education Grant program. Applicants must be members of the Indiana National Guard. All Guard paperwork must be completed prior to the start of each semester. The FAFSA must be received by March 10. Award covers certain tuition and fees at select public colleges. *Award:* Grant for use in freshman, sophomore, junior, or senior years; not renewable. *Award amount:* $20–$7110. *Number of awards:* 503–925. *Eligibility Requirements:* Applicant must be enrolled or expecting to enroll full- or part-time at a two-year or four-year institution or university; resident of Indiana and studying in Indiana. Available to U.S. citizens. Applicant or parent must meet one or more of the following requirements: national guard experience; retired from active duty; disabled or killed as a result of military service; prisoner of war; or missing in action. *Application Requirements:* Application form. **Deadline:** March 10.

Contact Kathryn Moore, Grants Counselor, State Student Assistance Commission of Indiana (SSACI), 150 West Market Street, Suite 500, Indianapolis, IN 46204-2805. *E-mail:* kmoore@ssaci.in.gov. *Phone:* 317-232-2350. *Fax:* 317-232-2360. *Website:* http://www.in.gov/ssaci.

**Indiana Nursing Scholarship Fund.** Need-based tuition funding for nursing students enrolled full- or part-time at an eligible Indiana institution. Must be a U.S. citizen and an Indiana resident and have a minimum 2.0 GPA or meet the minimum requirements for the nursing program. Upon graduation, recipients must practice as a nurse in an Indiana health care setting for two years. Nursing. *Award:* Scholarship for use in freshman, sophomore, junior, or senior years; not renewable. *Award amount:* $200–$5000. *Number of awards:* 490–690. *Eligibility Requirements:* Applicant must be enrolled or expecting to enroll full- or part-time at a two-year or four-year institution or university; resident of Indiana and studying in Indiana. Available to U.S. citizens. *Application Requirements:* Application form, FAFSA, financial need analysis. **Deadline:** continuous.

Contact Yvonne Heflin, Director, Special Programs, State Student Assistance Commission of Indiana (SSACI), 150 West Market Street, Suite 500, Indianapolis, IN 46204-2805. *Phone:* 317-232-2350. *Fax:* 317-232-3260. *Website:* http://www.in.gov/ssaci.

**National Guard Scholarship Extension Program.** A scholarship extension applicant is eligible for a tuition scholarship under Indiana Code 21-13-5-4 for a period not to exceed the period of scholarship extension the applicant served on active duty as a member of the National Guard (mobilized and deployed). Must apply not later than one (1) year after the applicant ceases to be a member of the Indiana National Guard. Applicant should apply through the education officer of their last unit of assignment. *Award:* Grant for use in freshman, sophomore, junior, or senior years; renewable. *Eligibility Requirements:* Applicant must be enrolled or expecting to enroll full- or part-time at a two-year or four-year technical institution or university and studying in Indiana. Available to U.S. citizens. Applicant must have national guard experience. *Application Requirements:* Application form. **Deadline:** continuous.

Contact Pamela Moody, National Guard Education Officer, Indiana Department of Veterans Affairs, 302 West Washington Street, Room E-120, Indianapolis, IN 46204. *E-mail:* pamela.moody@in.ngb.army.mil. *Phone:* 317-964-7017. *Fax:* 317-232-7721. *Website:* http://www.in.gov/dva.

**National Guard Tuition Supplement Program.** Applicant must be a member of the Indiana National Guard, in active drilling status, who has not been AWOL during the last 12 months, does not possess a Bachelor's degree, possesses the requisite academic qualifications, meets the requirements of the state-supported college or university, and meets all National Guard requirements. *Award:* Grant for use in freshman, sophomore, junior, or senior years; renewable. *Eligibility Requirements:* Applicant must be enrolled or expecting to enroll full- or part-time at a two-year or four-year or technical institution or university and studying in Indiana. Available to U.S. citizens. Applicant must have national guard experience. *Application Requirements:* Application form, FAFSA. **Deadline:** continuous.

Contact Jon Brinkley, State Service Officer. *E-mail:* jbrinkley@dva.in.gov. *Phone:* 317-232-3910. *Fax:* 317-232-7721. *Website:* http://www.in.gov/dva.

**Part-Time Grant Program.** Program is designed to encourage part-time undergraduates to start and complete their Associate or Baccalaureate degrees or certificates by subsidizing part-time tuition costs. It is a term-based award that is based on need. State residency requirements must be met and a FAFSA must be filed. Eligibility is determined at the institutional level subject to approval by SSACI. *Award:* Grant for use in freshman, sophomore, junior, or senior years; not renewable. *Award amount:* $20–$4000. *Number of awards:* 4680–6700. *Eligibility Requirements:* Applicant must be enrolled or expecting to enroll part-time at a two-year or four-year or technical institution or university; resident of Indiana and studying in Indiana. Available to U.S. citizens. *Application Requirements:* Application form, financial need analysis. **Deadline:** continuous.

**Resident Tuition for Active Duty Military Personnel.** Applicant must be a nonresident of Indiana serving on active duty and stationed in Indiana and attending any state-supported college or university. Dependents remain eligible for the duration of their enrollment, even if the active duty person is no longer in Indiana. Entitlement is to the resident tuition rate. *Award:* Grant for use in freshman, sophomore, junior, senior, graduate, or postgraduate years; renewable. *Eligibility Requirements:* Applicant must be enrolled or expecting to enroll full- or part-time at a two-year or four-year or technical institution or university and studying in Indiana. Available to U.S. citizens. Applicant or parent must meet one or more of the following requirements: Air Force, Army, Marine Corps, or Navy experience; retired from active duty; disabled or killed as a result of military service; prisoner of war; or missing in action. *Application Requirements:* Application form. **Deadline:** continuous.

Contact Jon Brinkley, State Service Officer. *E-mail:* jbrinkley@dva.in.gov. *Phone:* 317-232-3910. *Fax:* 317-232-7721. *Website:* http://www.in.gov/dva.

**Tuition and Fee Remission for Children and Spouses of National Guard Members.** Award to an individual whose father, mother or spouse was a member of the Indiana National Guard and suffered a service-connected death while serving on state active duty (which includes mobilized and deployed for federal active duty). The student must be eligible to pay the resident tuition rate at the state-supported college or university and must possess the requisite academic qualifications. *Award:* Grant for use in freshman, sophomore, junior, or senior years; renewable. *Eligibility Requirements:* Applicant must be enrolled or expecting to enroll full- or part-time at a two-year or four-year or technical institution or university and studying in Indiana. Available to U.S. citizens. Applicant or parent must meet one or more of the following requirements: national guard experience; retired from active duty; disabled or killed as a result of military service; prisoner of war; or missing in action. *Application Requirements:* Application form, FAFSA. **Deadline:** continuous.

Contact R. Martin Umbarger, Adjutant General, Indiana Department of Veterans Affairs, 2002 South Holt Road, Indianapolis, IN 46241. *E-mail:* r.martin.umbarger@in.ngb.army.mil. *Phone:* 317-247-3559. *Fax:* 317-247-3540. *Website:* http://www.in.gov/dva.

**Twenty-first Century Scholars Gear Up Summer Scholarship.** Grant of up to $3000 that pays for summer school tuition and regularly assessed course fees (does not cover other costs such as text books or room and board). *Award:* Scholarship for use in freshman, sophomore, junior, or senior years; not renewable. *Award amount:* up to $3000. *Number of* *awards:* 1. *Eligibility Requirements:* Applicant must be enrolled or expecting to enroll full-time at a two-year or four-year institution or university; resident of Indiana and studying in Indiana. Available to U.S. citizens. *Application Require ments:* Application form, must be in twenty-first century scholars program, high school diploma. **Deadline:** varies.

# IOWA

**All Iowa Opportunity Scholarship.** Students attending eligible Iowa colleges and universities may receive awards of up to $7824. Minimum 2.5 GPA. Priority will be given to students who participated in the Federal TRIO Programs or grad uated from alternative high schools or alternative high school programs. Applicant must enroll within two aca demic years of graduating from high school. Maximum individual awards cannot exceed more than the resident tuition and fee rate at Iowa Regent Uni versities. *Award:* Scholarship for use in freshman or sophomore years; not renewable. *Number of awards:* 200–800. *Eligibility Requirements:* Applicant must be enrolled or expecting to enroll full- or part-time at a two-year or four-year or technical institution or university; resident of Iowa and studying in Iowa. Applicant must have 2.5 GPA or higher. Available to U.S. citizens. *Application Requirements:* Application form, financial need analysis. **Deadline:** March 1.

Contact Todd Brown, Executive Officer 2, Iowa College Student Aid Commission, 430 E Grand Avenue, FL 3, Des Moines, IA 50309-1920. *E-mail:* grants@iowacollegeaid.gov. *Phone:* 877-272-4456. *Fax:* 515-725-3401. *Website:* http://www.iowacollegeaid.gov/.

**Iowa Grants.** Statewide need-based program to assist high-need Iowa resi dents. Recipients must demonstrate a high level of financial need to receive awards ranging from $100 to $1000. Awards are prorated for students enrolled for less than full-time. Awards must be used at Iowa postsecondary institutions. *Award:* Grant for use in freshman, sophomore, junior, or senior years; not renewable. *Award amount:* $100–$1000. *Number of awards:* 1000–3000. *Eligibility Requirements:* Applicant must be enrolled or expecting to enroll full- or part-time at a two-year or four-year or technical institution or uni versity; resident of Iowa and studying in Iowa. Available to U.S. citizens. *Appli cation Requirements:* Application form, financial need analysis. **Deadline:** con tinuous.

Contact Todd Brown, Executive Officer 2, Iowa College Student Aid Commission, 430 E Grand Avenue, FL 3, Des Moines, IA 50309-1920. *E-mail:* grants@iowacollegeaid.gov. *Phone:* 877-272-4456. *Fax:* 515-725-3401. *Website:* http://www.iowacollegeaid.gov/.

**Iowa National Guard Education Assistance Program.** Program pro vides postsecondary grant assistance to members of Iowa National Guard Units. Must study at a postsecondary institution in Iowa. *Award:* Grant for use in freshman, sophomore, junior, or senior years; not renewable. *Number of awards:* 700–1500. *Eligibility Requirements:* Applicant must be enrolled or expecting to enroll full- or part-time at a two-year or four-year or technical institution or uni versity; resident of Iowa and studying in Iowa. Available to U.S. citizens. Applicant must have national guard expe rience. *Application Requirements:* Appli cation form, application form may be submitted online (http://www.iowacol legeaid.gov). **Deadline:** July 1.

Contact Todd Brown, Executive Officer 2, Iowa College Student Aid Commission, 430 E Grand Avenue, FL 3, Des Moines, IA 50309-1920. *E-mail:* todd.brown@iowa.gov. *Phone:* 877-272-4456. *Fax:* 515-725-3401. *Website:* http://www.iowacollegeaid.gov/.

**Iowa Tuition Grant Program.** Program assists students who attend inde pendent postsecondary institutions in Iowa. Iowa residents currently enrolled, or planning to enroll, for at least 3 semester hours at one of the eligible Iowa postsecondary institutions may apply. Awards currently range from $100 to $5000. Grants may not exceed the dif ference between independent college and university tuition fees and the average tuition fees at the three public Regent uni versities. *Award:* Grant for use in freshman, sophomore, junior, or senior years; not renewable. *Award amount:* $100–$5000. *Number of awards:* 16,500–19,000. *Eligibility Requirements:* Applicant must be enrolled or expecting to enroll full- or part-time at a two-year or four-year institution or university; res ident of Iowa and studying in Iowa. Available to U.S. citizens. *Application Requirements:* Application form, financial need analysis. **Deadline:** July 1.

Contact Todd Brown, Executive Officer 2, Iowa College Student Aid Commission, 430 E Grand Avenue, FL 3, Des Moines, IA 50309-1920. *E-mail:* todd.brown@iowa.gov. *Phone:* 877-272-

4456. *Fax:* 515-725-3401. *Website:* http://www.iowacollegeaid.gov/.

**Iowa Vocational-Technical Tuition Grant Program.** Program provides need-based financial assistance to Iowa residents enrolled in career education (vocational-technical), and career option programs at Iowa area community col leges. Grants range from $150 to $1200, depending on the length of the program, financial need, and available funds. *Award:* Grant for use in freshman or soph omore years; not renewable. *Award amount:* $150–$1200. *Number of awards:* 2500–3500. *Eligibility Requirements:* Applicant must be enrolled or expecting to enroll full- or part-time at a two-year or technical institution; resident of Iowa and studying in Iowa. Available to U.S. cit izens. *Application Requirements:* Appli cation form, financial need analysis. **Deadline:** July 1.

Contact Todd Brown, Executive Officer 2, Iowa College Student Aid Commission, 430 E Grand Avenue, FL 3, Des Moines, IA 50309-1920. *E-mail:* todd.brown@iowa.gov. *Phone:* 515-725-3405. *Fax:* 515-725-3401. *Website:* http://www.iowacollegeaid.gov/.

# KANSAS

**Kansas Educational Benefits for Children of MIA, POW, and Deceased Veterans of the Vietnam War.** Scholarship awarded to students who are children of veterans. Must show proof of parent's status as missing in action, prisoner-of-war, or killed in action in the Vietnam War. Kansas residence required of veteran at time of entry to service. Must attend a state-supported postsecondary school. *Award:* Schol arship for use in freshman, sophomore, junior, or senior years; not renewable. *Number of awards:* 1. *Eligibility Require ments:* Applicant must be enrolled or expecting to enroll full-time at a two-year or four-year or technical institution or uni versity and studying in Kansas. Available to U.S. citizens. Applicant or parent must meet one or more of the following requirements: general military expe rience; retired from active duty; disabled or killed as a result of military service; prisoner of war; or missing in action. *Application Requirements:* Application form, birth certificate, school acceptance letter, military discharge of veteran. **Deadline:** varies.

Contact Wayne Bollig, Program Director. *E-mail:* wbollig@kcva.org. *Phone:* 785-296-3976. *Fax:* 785-296-1462. *Website:* http://www.kcva.org/.

**Kansas Ethnic Minority Scholarship.** Scholarship program designed to assist financially needy, academically competitive students who are identified as members of any of the following ethnic/racial groups: African-American, American Indian or Alaskan Native, Asian or Pacific Islander, or Hispanic. Priority is given to applicants who are freshmen. Students must be Kansas residents attending postsecondary institutions in Kansas. For more details refer to web site http://www.kansasregents.org/students/student_financial_aid/scholarships_and_grants. *Award:* Scholarship for use in freshman, sophomore, junior, or senior years; renewable. *Award amount:* up to $1850. *Eligibility Requirements:* Applicant must be American Indian/Alaska Native, Asian/Pacific Islander, Black (non-Hispanic), Hispanic; enrolled or expecting to enroll full-time at a two-year or four-year institution or university; resident of Kansas and studying in Kansas. Applicant must have 3.0 GPA or higher. Available to U.S. citizens. *Application Requirements:* Application form, financial need analysis, test scores. *Fee:* $12. **Deadline:** May 1.

Contact Diane Lindeman, Director of Student Financial Assistance, Kansas Board of Regents, 1000 SW Jackson, Suite 520, Topeka, KS 66612. *E-mail:* dlindeman@ksbor.org. *Phone:* 785-296-3517. *Fax:* 785-296-0983. *Website:* http://www.kansasregents.org/.

**Kansas Nursing Service Scholarship Program.** This is a service scholarship loan program available to students attending two-year or four-year public and private postsecondary institutions as well as vocational technical schools with nursing education programs. Students can be pursuing either LPN or RN licensure. This is a service obligation scholarship, therefore students must agree to work in the field of nursing one year for each year they have received the scholarship or must repay the amount of the scholarship award that they received plus interest. Students must be Kansas residents attending a postsecondary institution in Kansas. For more information, please visit our web site: http://www.kansasregents.org/students/student_financial_aid/scholarships_and_grants. Nursing. *Award:* Scholarship for use in freshman, sophomore, junior, or senior years; renewable. *Award amount:* $2500–$3500. *Eligibility Requirements:* Applicant must be enrolled or expecting to enroll full-time at a two-year or four-year or technical institution or university.

Available to U.S. citizens. *Application Requirements:* Application form, application form may be submitted online (http://www.kansasregents.org/students/student_financial_aid/scholarships_and_grants), financial need analysis. *Fee:* $12. **Deadline:** May 1.

Contact Diane Lindeman, Director of Student Financial Assistance, Kansas Board of Regents, 1000 SW Jackson, Suite 520, Topeka, KS 66612. *E-mail:* dlindeman@ksbor.org. *Phone:* 785-296-3517. *Fax:* 785-296-0983. *Website:* http://www.kansasregents.org/.

**Kansas Teacher Service Scholarship.** Scholarship to encourage talented students to enter the teaching profession and teach in Kansas in specific curriculum areas or in underserved areas of Kansas. Students must be Kansas residents attending a postsecondary institution in Kansas. For more details, refer to web site http://www.kansasregents.org. Education. *Award:* Scholarship for use in junior, senior, or graduate years; renewable. *Award amount:* $2206–$5514. *Eligibility Requirements:* Applicant must be enrolled or expecting to enroll full- or part-time at a four-year institution or university. Applicant must have 3.0 GPA or higher. Available to U.S. citizens. *Application Requirements:* Application form, application form may be submitted online (http://kansasregents.org/student_financial_aid), essay, financial need analysis, recommendations or references, resume, test scores, transcript. *Fee:* $12. **Deadline:** May 1.

Contact Diane Lindeman, Director of Student Financial Assistance, Kansas Board of Regents, 1000 SW Jackson, Suite 520, Topeka, KS 66612. *E-mail:* dlindeman@ksbor.org. *Phone:* 785-296-3517. *Fax:* 785-296-0983. *Website:* http://www.kansasregents.org/.

**Ted and Nora Anderson Scholarships.** Scholarship of $250 for each semester (one year only) given to the children of American Legion members or Auxiliary members who are holding membership for the past three consecutive years. Children of a deceased member can also apply. Parent of the applicant must be a veteran. Must be high school seniors or college freshmen or sophomores in a Kansas institution. Scholarship for use at an approved college, university, or trade school in Kansas. Must maintain a C average in college. *Award:* Scholarship for use in freshman or sophomore years; not renewable. *Award amount:* $250–$500. *Number of awards:* 4. *Eligibility Requirements:* Applicant must be enrolled

or expecting to enroll full-time at a two-year or four-year or technical institution or university; resident of Kansas and studying in Kansas. Applicant or parent of applicant must be member of American Legion or Auxiliary. Available to U.S. citizens. Applicant or parent must meet one or more of the following requirements: general military experience; retired from active duty; disabled or killed as a result of military service; prisoner of war; or missing in action. *Application Requirements:* Application form, essay, financial need analysis, personal photograph, recommendations or references, transcript. **Deadline:** February 15.

Contact Jim Gravenstein, Chairman, Scholarship Committee, American Legion Department of Kansas, 1314 SW Topeka Boulevard, Topeka, KS 66612. *Phone:* 785-232-9315. *Fax:* 785-232-1399. *Website:* http://www.ksamlegion.org/.

# KENTUCKY

**College Access Program (CAP) Grant.** Award for U.S. citizens and Kentucky residents seeking their first undergraduate degree. Applicants enrolled in sectarian institutions are not eligible. Must submit Free Application for Federal Student Aid to demonstrate financial need. Funding is limited. Awards are made on a first-come, first-serve basis. *Award:* Grant for use in freshman, sophomore, junior, or senior years; not renewable. *Award amount:* up to $1900. *Number of awards:* 35,000–45,000. *Eligibility Requirements:* Applicant must be enrolled or expecting to enroll full- or part-time at a two-year or four-year or technical institution or university; resident of Kentucky and studying in Kentucky. Available to U.S. citizens. *Application Requirements:* Application form may be submitted online (http://www.fafsa.ed.gov), FAFSA. **Deadline:** continuous.

Contact Sheila Roe, Program Coordinator, Kentucky Higher Education Assistance Authority (KHEAA), PO Box 798, Frankfort, KY 40602-0798. *E-mail:* sroc@khcaa.com. *Phone:* 800-928-8926 Ext. 67393. *Fax:* 502-696-7373. *Website:* http://www.kheaa.com/.

**Department of Veterans Affairs Tuition Waiver-KY KRS 164-507.** Scholarship available to college students who are residents of Kentucky under the age of 26. *Award:* Scholarship for use in freshman, sophomore, junior, or senior years; not renewable. *Number of awards:* 400. *Eligibility Requirements:* Applicant must be enrolled or expecting to enroll full- or part-time at a two-year or four-year institution or university and resident of Kentucky. Available to U.S. citizens. *Application Requirements:* Application form. **Deadline:** varies.

Contact Barbara Sipek, Tuition Waiver Coordinator. *E-mail:* barbaraa.sipek@ky. gov. *Phone:* 502-595-4447. *Website:* http: //www.veterans.ky.gov/.

**Early Childhood Development Scholarship.** Awards scholarship with conditional service commitment for part-time students currently employed by participating ECD facility or providing training in ECD for an approved organization. For more information, visit web site http://www.kheaa.com. Child and Family Studies; Education. *Award:* Scholarship for use in freshman, sophomore, junior, or senior years; not renewable. *Award amount:* up to $1800. *Number of awards:* 500–800. *Eligibility Requirements:* Applicant must be enrolled or expecting to enroll part-time at a two-year or four-year institution or university; resident of Kentucky and studying in Kentucky. Available to U.S. citizens. *Application Requirements:* Application form, application form may be submitted online (http://www.kheaa.com), FAFSA, financial need analysis. **Deadline:** continuous.

Contact Danny Prather, Program Coordinator, Kentucky Higher Education Assistance Authority (KHEAA), PO Box 798, Frankfort, KY 40602-0798. *E-mail:* danprather@kheaa.com. *Phone:* 800-928-8926 Ext. 67399. *Fax:* 502-696-7373. *Website:* http://www.kheaa.com/.

**Environmental Protection Scholarship.** Renewable awards for college juniors, seniors, and graduate students for in-state tuition, fees, room and board, and a book allowance at a Kentucky public university. Minimum 3.0 GPA required. Must work full-time for the Kentucky Department for Environmental Protection upon graduation (six months for each semester of scholarship support received). Interview required. Program not generally appropriate for non-residents. Biology; Chemical Engineering; Civil Engineering; Earth Science; Environmental Science; Hydrology; Mechanical Engineering; Natural Sciences. *Award:* Scholarship for use in junior, senior, or graduate years; renewable. *Award amount:* $10,000–$15,000. *Number of awards:* 1–4. *Eligibility Requirements:* Applicant must be enrolled or expecting to enroll full-time at a four-year institution or university and studying in Kentucky. Applicant must have 3.0 GPA or higher. Available to U.S. and non-U.S. citizens. *Application*

*Requirements:* Application form, essay, interview, recommendations or references, transcript, valid work permit for non-citizens. **Deadline:** February 15.

Contact James Kipp, Scholarship Program Coordinator, Kentucky Energy and Environment Cabinet, 233 Mining/ Mineral Resources Building, Lexington, KY 40506-0107. *E-mail:* kipp@uky.edu. *Phone:* 859-257-1299. *Fax:* 859-323-1049. *Website:* http://www.eec.ky.gov/.

**Go Higher Grant.** Need-based grant for adult students pursuing their first undergraduate degree. Completion of the FAFSA is required. *Award:* Grant for use in freshman, sophomore, junior, or senior years; not renewable. *Award amount:* up to $1000. *Number of awards:* 100–300. *Eligibility Requirements:* Applicant must be enrolled or expecting to enroll full- or part-time at a two-year or four-year or technical institution or university; resident of Kentucky and studying in Kentucky. Available to U.S. citizens. *Application Requirements:* Application form, FAFSA. **Deadline:** continuous.

Contact Sheila Roe, Grant Program Coordinator, Kentucky Higher Education Assistance Authority (KHEAA), PO Box 798, Frankfort, KY 40206-0798. *E-mail:* sroe@kheaa.com. *Phone:* 800-928-8926 Ext. 67393. *Website:* http://www.kheaa. com/.

**Kentucky Educational Excellence Scholarship (KEES).** Annual award based on yearly high school GPA and highest ACT or SAT score received by high school graduation. Awards are renewable, if required cumulative GPA is maintained at a Kentucky postsecondary school. Must be a Kentucky resident, and a graduate of a Kentucky high school. Low-income students who qualify for the free/reduced lunch program at least one year of high school may receive supplemental awards for passing scores on Advanced Placement (AP) or International Baccalaureate (IB) exams. *Award:* Scholarship for use in freshman, sophomore, junior, or senior years; renewable. *Award amount:* $125–$2500. *Number of awards:* 65,000–70,000. *Eligibility Requirements:* Applicant must be enrolled or expecting to enroll full- or part-time at a two-year or four-year or technical institution or university; resident of Kentucky and studying in Kentucky. Available to U. S. citizens. *Application Requirements:* Data submitted by KY high schools, test scores. **Deadline:** continuous.

Contact Becky Gilpatrick, Director of Student Aid Services, Kentucky Higher Education Assistance Authority (KHEAA), PO Box 798, Frankfort, KY

40602. *E-mail:* rgilpatrick@kheaa.com. *Phone:* 800-928-8926 Ext. 67394. *Fax:* 502-696-7373. *Website:* http://www. kheaa.com/.

**Kentucky National Guard Tuition Award.** Provides tuition assistance for active members of the Kentucky National Guard to attend a Kentucky college or university. Guard members may apply through their unit. *Award:* Grant for use in freshman, sophomore, junior, or senior years; not renewable. *Number of awards:* 1000–1500. *Eligibility Requirements:* Applicant must be enrolled or expecting to enroll full- or part-time at a two-year or four-year or technical institution or university; resident of Kentucky and studying in Kentucky. Available to U.S. citizens. Applicant must have national guard experience. *Application Requirements:* Application form, application form may be submitted online (http://ky.ngb. army.mil/tuitionstudent), must meet military standards, be eligible for positive personnel actions and have basic training completed. **Deadline:** continuous.

**Kentucky Office of Vocational Rehabilitation.** Grant provides services necessary to secure employment. Eligible individual must possess physical or mental impairment that results in a substantial impediment to employment; benefit from vocational rehabilitation services in terms of an employment outcome; and require vocational rehabilitation services to prepare for, enter, or retain employment. *Award:* Grant for use in freshman, sophomore, junior, senior, graduate, or postgraduate years; renewable. *Eligibility Requirements:* Applicant must be enrolled or expecting to enroll full- or part-time at a two-year or four-year or technical institution or university. *Application Requirements:* Application form, eligibility for OVR services and in proper priority category, financial need analysis, interview, transcript. **Deadline:** continuous.

Contact Charles Puckett, Program Administrator, Kentucky Office of Vocational Rehabilitation, 600 West Cedar Street, Suite 2E, Louisville, KY 40202. *E-mail:* marianu.spencer@mail. state.ky.us. *Phone:* 502-595-4173. *Fax:* 502-564-2358. *Website:* http://www.ovr. ky.gov/.

**Kentucky Transportation Cabinet Civil Engineering Scholarship Program.** Scholarships awarded to qualified Kentucky residents who wish to study civil engineering at University of Kentucky, Western Kentucky University, University of Louisville or Kentucky

State University. Applicant should be a graduate of an accredited Kentucky high school or a Kentucky resident. Scholarship recipients are given opportunities to work for the Cabinet during summers and job opportunities upon graduation within the state of KY. Civil Engineering. *Award:* Scholarship for use in freshman, sophomore, junior, or senior years; renewable. *Award amount:* $10,600–$44,000. *Number of awards:* 15–25. *Eligibility Requirements:* Applicant must be enrolled or expecting to enroll full-time at a four-year institution or university; resident of Kentucky and studying in Kentucky. Applicant must have 3.0 GPA or higher. Available to U.S. and non-U.S. citizens. *Application Requirements:* Application form, essay, interview, recommendations or references, test scores, transcript. **Deadline:** March 1.

Contact Cherie Mertz, Scholarship Program Coordinator, Kentucky Transportation Cabinet, 200 Mero Street, 6th Floor West, Frankfort, KY 40622. *E-mail:* Cherie.Mertz@ky.gov. *Website:* http://transportation.ky.gov/Education/Pages/Scholarships.aspx.

**Kentucky Tuition Grant (KTG).** Grants available to Kentucky residents who are full-time undergraduates at an independent college within the state. Based on financial need. Must submit FAFSA. *Award:* Grant for use in freshman, sophomore, junior, or senior years; not renewable. *Award amount:* $200–$3000. *Number of awards:* 11,500–12,500. *Eligibility Requirements:* Applicant must be enrolled or expecting to enroll full-time at a two-year or four-year institution or university; resident of Kentucky and studying in Kentucky. Available to U.S. citizens. *Application Requirements:* Application form may be submitted online (http://www.fafsa.ed.gov), FAFSA. **Deadline:** continuous.

Contact Sheila Roe, Grant Program Coordinator, Kentucky Higher Education Assistance Authority (KHEAA), PO Box 798, Frankfort, KY 40602-0798. *E-mail:* sroe@kheaa.com. *Phone:* 800-928-8926 Ext. 67393. *Fax:* 502-696-7373. *Website:* http://www.kheaa.com/.

**Mary Jo Young Scholarship.** Provides financial assistance for tuition and textbook expenses incurred by Kentucky high school students taking college/dual credit coursework. *Award:* Scholarship for use in freshman year; not renewable. *Award amount:* $125–$840. *Number of awards:* 700–900. *Eligibility Requirements:* Applicant must be high school student; planning to enroll or expecting to

enroll part-time at a two-year or four-year or technical institution or university; resident of Kentucky and studying in Kentucky. Applicant must have 2.5 GPA or higher. Available to U.S. citizens. *Application Requirements:* Application form, application form may be submitted online (http://www.kheaa.com). **Deadline:** May 1.

Contact Danny Prather, Program Coordinator, Kentucky Higher Education Assistance Authority (KHEAA), PO Box 798, Frankfort, KY 40602-0798. *E-mail:* danprather@kheaa.com. *Phone:* 800-938-8926 Ext. 67399. *Fax:* 502-696-7373. *Website:* http://www.kheaa.com/.

**Touchstone Energy All "A" Classic Scholarship.** Award of $1000 for senior student in good standing at a Kentucky high school which is a member of the All Classic. Applicant must be a U.S. citizen and must plan to attend a postsecondary institution in Kentucky in the upcoming year as a full-time student and be drug free. *Award:* Scholarship for use in freshman year; not renewable. *Award amount:* $1000. *Number of awards:* 12. *Eligibility Requirements:* Applicant must be high school student; planning to enroll or expecting to enroll full-time at a two-year or four-year or technical institution or university; resident of Kentucky and studying in Kentucky. Available to U.S. citizens. *Application Requirements:* Application form, essay, personal photograph, recommendations or references, transcript. **Deadline:** December 3.

Contact David Cowden, Chairperson, Scholarship Committee, Kentucky Touchstone Energy Cooperatives, 1320 Lincoln Road, Lewisport, KY 42351. *E-mail:* allaclassic@alltel.net. *Phone:* 859-744-4812. *Website:* http://www.ekpc.coop.

# LOUISIANA

**Louisiana National Guard State Tuition Exemption Program.** Renewable award for college undergraduates to receive tuition exemption upon satisfactory performance in the Louisiana National Guard. Applicant must attend a state-funded institution in Louisiana, be a resident and registered voter in Louisiana, meet the academic and residency requirements of the university attended, and provide documentation of Louisiana National Guard enlistment. The exemption can be used for up to 15 semesters. Minimum 2.5 GPA required. *Award:* Scholarship for use in freshman, sophomore, junior, or senior years;

renewable. *Eligibility Requirements:* Applicant must be enrolled or expecting to enroll full- or part-time at a two-year or four-year or technical institution or university; resident of Louisiana and studying in Louisiana. Applicant must have 2.5 GPA or higher. Available to U.S. citizens. Applicant or parent must meet one or more of the following requirements: national guard experience; retired from active duty; disabled or killed as a result of military service; prisoner of war; or missing in action. *Application Requirements:* Application form, test scores, transcript. **Deadline:** continuous.

Contact Jona Hughes, Education Services Officer, Louisiana National Guard, Joint Task Force LA, Building 35, Jackson Barracks, JI-PD, New Orleans, LA 70146-0330. *E-mail:* hughesj@la-arng.ngb.army.mil. *Phone:* 504-278-8531 Ext. 8304. *Fax:* 504-278-8025. *Website:* http://geauxguard.com/organization/joint-force-headquarters-jfhq-la/.

**Rockefeller State Wildlife Scholarship.** For college undergraduates with a minimum of 60 credit hours who are majoring in Forestry, Wildlife, or Marine Science, and for college graduate students who are majoring in Forestry, Wildlife, or Marine Science. College undergraduates must have a grade point average of at least 2.50 to apply. College graduate students must have a grade point average of at least 3.00 in order to apply. Renewable up to three years as an undergraduate and two years as a graduate student. Biology; Marine Biology; Marine/Ocean Engineering; Natural Resources; Oceanography. *Award:* Scholarship for use in freshman, sophomore, junior, senior, graduate, or postgraduate years; renewable. *Award amount:* $2000–$3000. *Number of awards:* 20–30. *Eligibility Requirements:* Applicant must be enrolled or expecting to enroll full-time at a four-year institution or university; resident of Louisiana and studying in Louisiana. Applicant must have 2.5 GPA or higher. Available to U.S. citizens. *Application Requirements:* Application form, application form may be submitted online (http://www.osfa.la.gov for Rockefeller app), FAFSA, test scores, transcript. **Deadline:** July 1.

Contact Bonnie Lavergne, Public Information, Louisiana Office of Student Financial Assistance, PO Box 91202, Baton Rouge, LA 70821-9202. *E-mail:* custserv@osfa.la.gov. *Phone:* 800-259-5626 Ext. 7714. *Fax:* 225-612-6508. *Website:* http://www.osfa.la.gov/.

**Taylor Opportunity Program for Students Honors Level.** Program awards 8 semesters or 12 terms of tuition to any Louisiana State postsecondary institution plus $400 stipend per semester. Program awards 8 semesters or 12 terms of an amount equal to the weighted average public tuition to students attending a LAICU (Louisiana Association of Independent Colleges and Universities) institution plus $400 stipend per semester. Program awards 8 semesters or 12 terms of an amount equal to the weighted average public tuition to two out-of-state Institutions for Hearing Impaired Students: Gallaudet University and Rochester Institute of Technology plus $400 stipend per semester. Program awards $1744 per year to Approved Proprietary and Cosmetology schools plus a stipend of $800 per year. When you submit the FAFSA, you have automatically applied for all four levels of TOPS, for Federal Pell Grants and Go Grants and for Federal Student Loans. Please do not send separate letters of application to the TOPS office. *Award:* Scholarship for use in freshman, sophomore, junior, or senior years; renewable. *Award amount:* $836–$6736. *Number of awards:* 9661. *Eligibility Requirements:* Applicant must be enrolled or expecting to enroll full-time at a two-year or four-year or technical institution or university; resident of Louisiana and studying in Louisiana. Applicant must have 3.0 GPA or higher. Available to U.S. citizens. *Application Requirements:* Application form, application form may be submitted online (http://www.osfa.la.gov), FAFSA, test scores, transcript. **Deadline:** July 1.

**Taylor Opportunity Program for Students Opportunity Level.** Program awards 8 semesters or 12 terms of tuition to any Louisiana State postsecondary institution. Program awards 8 semesters or 12 terms of an amount equal to the weighted average public tuition to students attending a LAICU (Louisiana Association of Independent Colleges and Universities) institution. Program awards 8 semesters or 12 terms of an amount equal to the weighted average public tuition to two out-of-state Institutions for Hearing Impaired Students: Gallaudet University and Rochester Institute of Technology. Program awards $1744 per year to Approved Proprietary and Cosmetology schools. When you submit the FAFSA, you have automatically applied for all four levels of TOPS, and for Federal Pell Grants and Go Grants. Please do not send separate letters of application to the TOPS office. *Award:* Scholarship

for use in freshman, sophomore, junior, or senior years; renewable. *Award amount:* $436–$5936. *Number of awards:* 24,633. *Eligibility Requirements:* Applicant must be enrolled or expecting to enroll full-time at a two-year or four-year or technical institution or university; resident of Louisiana and studying in Louisiana. Applicant must have 2.5 GPA or higher. Available to U.S. citizens. *Application Requirements:* Application form, application form may be submitted online (http://www.osfa.la.gov), FAFSA, test scores, transcript. **Deadline:** July 1.

**Taylor Opportunity Program for Students Performance Level.** Program awards 8 semesters or 12 terms of tuition to any Louisiana State postsecondary institution plus $200 stipend per semester. Program awards 8 semesters or 12 terms of an amount equal to the weighted average public tuition to students attending a LAICU (Louisiana Association of Independent Colleges and Universities) institution plus $200 stipend per semester. Program awards 8 semesters or 12 terms of an amount equal to the weighted average public tuition to two out-of-state Institutions for Hearing Impaired Students: Gallaudet University and Rochester Institute of Technology plus $200 stipend per semester. Program awards $1744 plus $400 per year to Approved Proprietary and Cosmetology schools. When you submit the FAFSA, you have automatically applied for all four levels of TOPS, for Federal Pell Grants and Go Grants and for Federal Student Loans. Please do not send separate letters of application to the TOPS office. *Award:* Scholarship for use in freshman, sophomore, junior, or senior years; renewable. *Award amount:* $636–$6336. *Number of awards:* 11,928. *Eligibility Requirements:* Applicant must be enrolled or expecting to enroll full-time at a two-year or four-year or technical institution or university; resident of Louisiana and studying in Louisiana. Applicant must have 3.0 GPA or higher. Available to U.S. citizens. *Application Requirements:* Application form, application form may be submitted online (http://www.osfa.la.gov), FAFSA, test scores, transcript. **Deadline:** July 1.

**Taylor Opportunity Program for Students Tech Level.** Program awards an amount equal to tuition for up to 4 semesters and two summers of technical training at a Louisiana postsecondary institution that offers a vocational or technical education certificate or diploma program, or a non-academic degree program; or up to $1744 to an approved

Proprietary or Cosmetology school. Must have completed the TOPS Opportunity core curriculum or the TOPS Tech core curriculum, must have achieved a 2.50 grade point average over the core curriculum only, and must have achieved an ACT score of 17 or an SAT score of 810. Program awards an amount equal to the weighted average public tuition for technical programs to students attending a LAICU private institution for technical training. When you submit the FAFSA, you have automatically applied for all four levels of TOPS, for Federal Pell Grants and Go Grants and Federal Student Loans. Please do not send separate letters of application to the TOPS office. *Award:* Scholarship for use in freshman or sophomore years; renewable. *Award amount:* $436–$3985. *Number of awards:* 1671. *Eligibility Requirements:* Applicant must be enrolled or expecting to enroll full-time at a technical institution; resident of Louisiana and studying in Louisiana. Applicant must have 2.5 GPA or higher. Available to U.S. citizens. *Application Requirements:* Application form, application form may be submitted online (http://www.osfa.la.gov), FAFSA, test scores, transcript. **Deadline:** July 1.

## MAINE

**American Legion Auxiliary Department of Maine Daniel E. Lambert Memorial Scholarship.** Scholarships to assist young men and women in continuing their education beyond high school. Must demonstrate financial need, must be a resident of the State of Maine, U.S. citizen, and parent must be a veteran. *Award:* Scholarship for use in freshman year; not renewable. *Award amount:* $1000. *Number of awards:* up to 2. *Eligibility Requirements:* Applicant must be high school student; planning to enroll or expecting to enroll full-time at a four-year institution or university and resident of Maine. Available to U.S. citizens. Applicant or parent must meet one or more of the following requirements: general military experience; retired from active duty; disabled or killed as a result of military service; prisoner of war; or missing in action. *Application Requirements:* Application form, financial need analysis. **Deadline:** May 1.

Contact Mary Wells, Education Chairman. *E-mail:* aladeptsecme@verizon.net. *Phone:* 207-532-6007. *Website:* http://www.mainelegion.org/.

**American Legion Auxiliary Department of Maine Past Presi-**

**dents' Parley Nurses Scholarship.** One-time award for child, grandchild, sister, or brother of veteran. Must be resident of Maine and wishing to continue education at accredited school in medical field. Must submit photo, doctor's statement, and evidence of civic activity. Minimum 3.5 GPA required. Health and Medical Sciences; Nursing. *Award:* Scholarship for use in freshman, sophomore, junior, or senior years; not renewable. *Award amount:* $300. *Number of awards:* 1. *Eligibility Requirements:* Applicant must be enrolled or expecting to enroll full-time at a two-year or four-year or technical institution or university and resident of Maine. Applicant or parent of applicant must have employment or volunteer experience in community service. Applicant must have 2.5 GPA or higher. Available to U.S. citizens. Applicant or parent must meet one or more of the following requirements: general military experience; retired from active duty; disabled or killed as a result of military service; prisoner of war; or missing in action. *Application Requirements:* Application form, doctor's statement, personal photograph, recommendations or references, transcript. **Deadline:** March 31.

Contact Mary Wells, Education Chairman. *E-mail:* aladeptsecme@ verizon.net. *Phone:* 207-532-6007. *Website:* http://www.mainelegion.org/.

**Early College for ME.** Scholarship for high school students who in their junior year have not made plans for college but are academically capable of success in college. Recipients are selected by their school principal or Guidance Director. Students must be entering a Maine Community College. Refer to web site http://www.mccs.me.edu/our-programs/programs-for-high-school-students/early-college/ *Award:* Scholarship for use in freshman or sophomore years; renewable. *Award amount:* $2000. *Number of awards:* 250–500. *Eligibility Requirements:* Applicant must be high school student; planning to enroll or expecting to enroll full-time at a two-year institution; resident of Maine and studying in Maine. Available to U.S. citizens. *Application Requirements:* Application form, financial need analysis, recommendations or references, transcript. **Deadline:** varies.

Contact Mercedes Pour, State Director, Early College for ME, Maine Community College System, 6 Fundy Road, Suite 300, Falmouth, ME 04105. *E-mail:*

mpour@mccs.me.edu. *Phone:* 207-699-4897. *Website:* http://www.mccs.me.edu/.

**Maine Rural Rehabilitation Fund Scholarship Program.** One-time scholarship open to Maine residents enrolled in or accepted by any school, college, or university. Must be full-time and demonstrate financial need. Those opting for a Maine institution given preference. Major must lead to an agricultural career. Minimum 3.0 GPA required. Agribusiness; Agriculture; Animal/Veterinary Sciences. *Award:* Scholarship for use in freshman, sophomore, junior, senior, graduate, or postgraduate years; not renewable. *Award amount:* $800–$2000. *Number of awards:* 10–20. *Eligibility Requirements:* Applicant must be enrolled or expecting to enroll full-time at a two-year or four-year or technical institution or university and resident of Maine. Applicant must have 3.0 GPA or higher. Available to U.S. citizens. *Application Requirements:* Application form, driver's license, financial need analysis, transcript. **Deadline:** June 15.

Contact Jane Aiudi, Director of Marketing. *E-mail:* jane.aiudi@maine. gov. *Phone:* 207-287-7628. *Fax:* 207-287-5576. *Website:* http://www.maine. gov/agriculture.

**State of Maine Grant Program.** Scholarship for residents of Maine, attending an eligible school in Maine, Connecticut, Massachusetts, New Hampshire, Rhode Island, or Vermont. Award based on need. Students attending out-of-state institutions must be participating in the New England Regional Tuition Break Program to be eligible. Students must apply annually. Complete free application for Federal Student Aid to apply. One-time award for undergraduate study. For further information see web site http://www.famemaine.com. *Award:* Grant for use in freshman, sophomore, junior, or senior years; not renewable. *Award amount:* $200–$1000. *Number of awards:* up to 22,005. *Eligibility Requirements:* Applicant must be enrolled or expecting to enroll full- or part-time at a two-year or four-year or technical institution or university; resident of Maine and studying in Connecticut, Maine, Massachusetts, New Hampshire, Rhode Island, Vermont. Available to U.S. citizens. *Application Requirements:* Application form, FAFSA, financial need analysis. **Deadline:** May 1.

Contact Claude Roy, Education Services Officer, Finance Authority of Maine, 5 Community Drive, Augusta, ME 04332. *E-mail:* education@famemaine.

com. *Phone:* 207-620-3507. *Website:* http://www.famemaine.com/.

**Tuition Waiver Programs.** Provides tuition waivers for children and spouses of EMS personnel, firefighters, and law enforcement officers who have been killed in the line of duty and for students who were foster children under the custody of the Department of Human Services when they graduated from high school. Waivers valid at the University of Maine System, the Maine Technical College System, and Maine Maritime Academy. Applicant must reside and study in Maine. *Award:* Grant for use in freshman, sophomore, junior, or senior years; renewable. *Number of awards:* up to 30. *Eligibility Requirements:* Applicant must be enrolled or expecting to enroll full- or part-time at a two-year or four-year institution or university; resident of Maine and studying in Maine. Applicant or parent of applicant must have employment or volunteer experience in police/firefighting. Available to U.S. citizens. *Application Requirements:* Application form, letter from the Department of Human Services documenting that applicant is in their custody and residing in foster care at the time of graduation from high school or its equivalent. **Deadline:** continuous.

Contact Claude Roy, Education Services Officer, Finance Authority of Maine, 5 Community Drive, Augusta, ME 04332. *E-mail:* education@famemaine. com. *Phone:* 207-620-3507. *Website:* http://www.famemaine.com/.

**Veterans Dependents Educational Benefits-Maine.** Tuition waiver award for dependent children who have not reached their 22nd birthday or spouses of veterans permanently and totally disabled resulting from service-connected disability; died from a service-connected disability; at time of death was totally and permanently disabled due to service-connected disability, but whose death was not related to the service-connected disability; or member of the Armed Forces on active duty who has been listed for more than 90 days as missing in action, captured or forcibly detained or interned in the line of duty. Benefits apply only to the University of Maine System, Maine community colleges and Maine Maritime Academy. Must be high school graduate. Must submit with application proof of veteran's VA disability along with dependent verification paperwork such as birth, marriage, or adoption certificate and proof of enrollment in degree program. *Award:* Scholarship for use in freshman, soph omore, junior, or senior years; not renewable. *Eligibility Requirements:* Applicant must be enrolled or expecting to enroll full- or part-time at a two-year or four-year institution or university; res ident of Maine and studying in Maine. Available to U.S. citizens. Applicant or parent must meet one or more of the fol lowing requirements: general military experience; retired from active duty; dis abled or killed as a result of military service; prisoner of war; or missing in action. *Application Requirements:* Appli cation form, see application.

Contact Mrs. Paula Gagnon, Office Associate II, Maine Veterans Services, State House Station 117, Augusta, ME 04333-0117. *E-mail:* mainebvs@maine. gov. *Phone:* 207-430-6035. *Fax:* 207-626-4471. *Website:* http://www.maine. gov/dvem/bvs.

# MARYLAND

**Charles W. Riley Fire and Emergency Medical Services Tuition Reimbursement Program.** Award intended to reimburse members of rescue organizations serving Maryland commu nities for tuition costs of course work towards a degree or certificate in fire service or medical technology. Must attend a two- or four-year school in Maryland. Minimum 2.0 GPA. The schol arship is worth up to $6500. Fire Sci ences; Health and Medical Sciences; Trade/Technical Specialties. *Award:* Scholarship for use in freshman, soph omore, junior, or senior years; not renewable. *Award amount:* up to $6500. *Number of awards:* up to 150. *Eligibility Requirements:* Applicant must be enrolled or expecting to enroll full- or part-time at a two-year or four-year institution or uni versity; resident of Maryland and studying in Maryland. Applicant or parent of applicant must have employment or volunteer experience in police/fire fighting. Available to U.S. citizens. *Appli cation Requirements:* Application form, transcript, tuition receipt, proof of enrollment. **Deadline:** July 1.

Contact Maura Sappington, Office of Student Financial Assistance, Maryland State Higher Education Commission, 839 Bestgate Road, Suite 400, Annapolis, MD 21401-3013. *E-mail:* msapping@mhec. state.md.us. *Phone:* 410-260-4569. *Fax:* 410-260-3203. *Website:* http://www. mhec.state.md.us/.

**Delegate Scholarship Program-Maryland.** Delegate scholarships help Maryland residents attending Maryland degree-granting institutions, certain career schools, or nursing diploma schools. May attend out-of-state institution if Maryland Higher Education Commission deems major to be unique and not offered at a Maryland institution. Free Application for Federal Student Aid may be required. Stu dents interested in this program should apply by contacting their legislative dis trict delegate. *Award:* Scholarship for use in freshman, sophomore, junior, or senior years; not renewable. *Award amount:* $200–$8650. *Number of awards:* up to 3500. *Eligibility Requirements:* Applicant must be enrolled or expecting to enroll full- or part-time at a two-year or four-year or technical institution or university; resident of Maryland and studying in Maryland. Available to U.S. citizens. *Application Requirements:* Application form, FAFSA. **Deadline:** continuous.

Contact Monica Wheatley, Office of Student Financial Assistance, Maryland State Higher Education Commission, 839 Bestgate Road, Suite 400, Annapolis, MD 21401-3013. *E-mail:* osfamail@mhec. state.md.us. *Phone:* 800-974-1024. *Fax:* 410-260-3200. *Website:* http://www. mhec.state.md.us/.

**Distinguished Scholar Award-Maryland.** Renewable award for Maryland students enrolled full-time at Maryland institutions. National Merit Scholar Finalists automatically offered award. Others may qualify for the award in satisfying criteria of a minimum 3.7 GPA or in combination with high test scores, or for Talent in Arts competition in categories of music, drama, dance, or visual arts. Must maintain annual 3.0 GPA in college for award to be renewed. *Award:* Scholarship for use in freshman, sophomore, junior, or senior years; renewable. *Award amount:* up to $3000. *Number of awards:* up to 1400. *Eligibility Requirements:* Applicant must be high school student; planning to enroll or expecting to enroll full-time at a two-year or four-year institution or university; res ident of Maryland and studying in Maryland. Available to U.S. citizens. *Application Requirements:* Application form, test scores, transcript.

Contact Tamika McKelvin, Program Administrator, Maryland State Higher Education Commission, 839 Bestgate Road, Suite 400, Annapolis, MD 21401-3013. *E-mail:* tmckelvi@mhec.state.md. us. *Phone:* 410-260-4546. *Fax:* 410-260-3200. *Website:* http://www.mhec.state. md.us/.

**Distinguished Scholar Community College Transfer Program.** Schol arship available for Maryland residents who have completed 60 credit hours or an associate degree at a Maryland com munity college and are transferring to a Maryland four-year institution. *Award:* Scholarship for use in freshman or soph omore years; renewable. *Award amount:* $3000. *Number of awards:* 127. *Eligibility Requirements:* Applicant must be enrolled or expecting to enroll full-time at a two-year institution; resident of Maryland and studying in Maryland. Available to U.S. citizens. *Application Requirements:* Application form, transcript. **Deadline:** March 1.

Contact Maura Sappington, Program Manager, Maryland State Higher Education Commission, 839 Bestgate Road, Suite 400, Annapolis, MD 21401-3013. *E-mail:* msapping@mhec.state.md. us. *Phone:* 410-260-4569. *Fax:* 410-260-3203. *Website:* http://www.mhec.state. md.us/.

**Edward T. Conroy Memorial Schol arship Program.** Scholarship for dependents of deceased or 100 percent disabled U.S. Armed Forces personnel; the son, daughter, or surviving spouse of a victim of the September 11, 2001 terrorist attacks who died as a result of the attacks on the World Trade Center in New York City, the attack on the Pentagon in Vir ginia, or the crash of United Airlines Flight 93 in Pennsylvania; a POW/MIA of the Vietnam Conflict or his/her son or daughter; the son, daughter or surviving spouse (who has not remarried) of a state or local public safety employee or vol unteer who died in the line of duty; or a state or local public safety employee or volunteer who was 100 percent disabled in the line of duty. Must be Maryland res ident at time of disability. Submit appli cable VA certification. Must be at least 16 years of age and attend Maryland insti tution. *Award:* Scholarship for use in freshman, sophomore, junior, or senior years; renewable. *Award amount:* $7200–$9000. *Number of awards:* up to 121. *Eli gibility Requirements:* Applicant must be age 16-24; enrolled or expecting to enroll full- or part-time at a two-year or four-year institution or university; resident of Maryland and studying in Maryland. Applicant or parent of applicant must have employment or volunteer experience in police/firefighting. Available to U.S. citizens. Applicant or parent must meet one or more of the following require ments: general military experience; retired from active duty; disabled or killed as a result of military service; prisoner of war; or missing in action. *Application Requirements:* Application form, birth and death certificate, disability papers. **Deadline:** July 15.

Contact Linda Asplin, Office of Student Financial Assistance, Maryland State Higher Education Commission, 839 Bestgate Road, Suite 400, Annapolis, MD 21401-3013. *E-mail:* lasplin@mhec.state.md.us. *Phone:* 410-260-4563. *Fax:* 410-260-3203. *Website:* http://www.mhec.state.md.us/.

**Graduate and Professional Scholarship Program-Maryland.** Graduate and professional scholarships provide need-based financial assistance to students attending a Maryland school of medicine, dentistry, law, pharmacy, social work, or nursing. Funds are provided to specific Maryland colleges and universities. Students must demonstrate financial need and be Maryland residents. Contact institution financial aid office for more information. Dental Health/Services; Health and Medical Sciences; Law/Legal Services; Nursing; Social Services. *Award:* Scholarship for use in freshman, sophomore, junior, or senior years; renewable. *Award amount:* $1000–$5000. *Number of awards:* up to 584. *Eligibility Requirements:* Applicant must be enrolled or expecting to enroll full- or part-time at a four-year institution or university; resident of Maryland and studying in Maryland. Available to U.S. citizens. *Application Requirements:* Application form, contact institution financial aid office, financial need analysis. **Deadline:** March 1.

Contact Monica Wheatley, Program Manager, Maryland State Higher Education Commission, 839 Bestgate Road, Suite 400, Annapolis, MD 21401. *E-mail:* mwheatle@mhec.state.md.us. *Phone:* 410-260-4560. *Fax:* 410-260-3202. *Website:* http://www.mhec.state.md.us/.

**Howard P. Rawlings Educational Excellence Awards Educational Assistance Grant.** Award for Maryland residents accepted or enrolled in a full-time undergraduate degree or certificate program at a Maryland institution or hospital nursing school. Must submit financial aid form by March 1. Must earn 2.0 GPA in college to maintain award. *Award:* Grant for use in freshman, sophomore, junior, or senior years; renewable. *Award amount:* $400–$2700. *Number of awards:* 15,000–30,000. *Eligibility Requirements:* Applicant must be enrolled or expecting to enroll full-time at a two-year or four-year institution or university; resident of Maryland and studying in Maryland. Available to U.S. citizens. *Application Requirements:* Application

form, financial need analysis. **Deadline:** March 1.

**Howard P. Rawlings Educational Excellence Awards Guaranteed Access Grant.** Award for Maryland resident enrolling full-time in an undergraduate program at a Maryland institution. Must be under 21 at time of first award and begin college within one year of completing high school in Maryland with a minimum 2.5 GPA. Must have an annual family income less than 130 percent of the federal poverty level guideline. *Award:* Grant for use in freshman, sophomore, junior, or senior years; renewable. *Award amount:* $400–$14,800. *Number of awards:* up to 1000. *Eligibility Requirements:* Applicant must be enrolled or expecting to enroll full-time at a two-year or four-year institution or university; resident of Maryland and studying in Maryland. Applicant must have 3.5 GPA or higher. Available to U.S. citizens. *Application Requirements:* Application form, financial need analysis, transcript. **Deadline:** March 1.

Contact Theresa Lowe, Office of Student Financial Assistance, Maryland State Higher Education Commission, 839 Bestgate Road, Suite 400, Annapolis, MD 21401-3013. *E-mail:* osfamail@mhec.state.md.us. *Phone:* 410-260-4555. *Fax:* 410-260-3200. *Website:* http://www.mhec.state.md.us/.

**Janet L. Hoffmann Loan Assistance Repayment Program.** Provides assistance for repayment of loan debt to Maryland residents working full-time in nonprofit organizations and state or local governments. Must submit Employment Verification Form and Lender Verification Form. Education; Law/Legal Services; Nursing; Social Services; Therapy/Rehabilitation. *Award:* Grant for use in freshman, sophomore, junior, or senior years; not renewable. *Award amount:* $1500–$10,000. *Number of awards:* up to 700. *Eligibility Requirements:* Applicant must be enrolled or expecting to enroll full-time at a four-year institution or university; resident of Maryland and studying in Maryland. Applicant or parent of applicant must have employment or volunteer experience in government/politics. Available to U.S. citizens. *Application Requirements:* Application form, IRS 1040 form, transcript. **Deadline:** September 30.

Contact Tamika McKelvin, Office of Student Financial Assistance, Maryland State Higher Education Commission, 839 Bestgate Road, Suite 400, Annapolis, MD 21401. *E-mail:* tmckelvil@mhec.state.

md.us. *Phone:* 410-260-4546. *Fax:* 410-260-3203. *Website:* http://www.mhec.state.md.us/.

**J.F. Tolbert Memorial Student Grant Program.** Awards of $500 granted to Maryland residents attending a private career school in Maryland. The scholarship deadline continues. *Award:* Grant for use in freshman or sophomore years; not renewable. *Award amount:* $500. *Number of awards:* 522. *Eligibility Requirements:* Applicant must be enrolled or expecting to enroll full-time at a technical institution; resident of Maryland and studying in Maryland. Available to U.S. citizens. *Application Requirements:* Application form, financial need analysis. **Deadline:** continuous.

Contact Glenda Hamlet, Office of Student Financial Assistance, Maryland State Higher Education Commission, 839 Bestgate Road, Suite 400, Annapolis, MD 21401-3013. *E-mail:* osfamail@mhec.state.md.us. *Phone:* 800-974-1024. *Fax:* 410-260-3200. *Website:* http://www.mhec.state.md.us/.

**Part-Time Grant Program-Maryland.** Funds provided to Maryland colleges and universities. Eligible students must be enrolled on a part-time basis (6 to 11 credits) in an undergraduate degree program. Must demonstrate financial need and also be Maryland resident. Contact financial aid office at institution for more information. *Award:* Grant for use in freshman, sophomore, junior, or senior years; renewable. *Award amount:* $200–$1500. *Number of awards:* 1800–9000. *Eligibility Requirements:* Applicant must be enrolled or expecting to enroll part-time at a two-year or four-year institution or university; resident of Maryland and studying in Maryland. Available to U.S. citizens. *Application Requirements:* Application form, financial need analysis. **Deadline:** March 1.

Contact Monica Wheatley, Program Manager, Maryland State Higher Education Commission, 839 Bestgate Road, Suite 400, Annapolis, MD 21401. *E-mail:* mwheatle@mhec.state.md.us. *Phone:* 410-260-4560. *Fax:* 410-260-3202. *Website:* http://www.mhec.state.md.us/.

**Senatorial Scholarships-Maryland.** Renewable award for Maryland residents attending a Maryland degree-granting institution, nursing diploma school, or certain private career schools. May be used out-of-state only if Maryland Higher Education Commission deems major to be unique and not offered at Maryland institution. The scholarship value is $400 to

$7000. *Award:* Scholarship for use in freshman, sophomore, junior, or senior years; renewable. *Award amount:* $400–$7000. *Number of awards:* up to 7000. *Eligibility Requirements:* Applicant must be enrolled or expecting to enroll full- or part-time at a two-year or four-year or technical institution or university; resident of Maryland and studying in Maryland. Available to U.S. citizens. *Application Requirements:* Application form, financial need analysis, test scores. **Deadline:** March 1.

Contact Monica Wheatley, Office of Student Financial Assistance, Maryland State Higher Education Commission, 839 Bestgate Road, Suite 400, Annapolis, MD 21401-3013. *E-mail:* osfamail@mhec.state.md.us. *Phone:* 800-974-1024. *Fax:* 410-260-3200. *Website:* http://www.mhec.state.md.us/.

**Tuition Reduction for Non-Resident Nursing Students.** Available to nonresidents of Maryland who attend a two-year or four-year public institution in Maryland. It is renewable provided student maintains academic requirements designated by institution attended. Recipient must agree to serve as a full-time nurse in a hospital or related institution for two to four years. Nursing. *Award:* Scholarship for use in freshman, sophomore, junior, or senior years; renewable. *Eligibility Requirements:* Applicant must be enrolled or expecting to enroll full- or part-time at a two-year or four-year institution and studying in Maryland. Available to U.S. citizens. *Application Requirements:* Application form. **Deadline:** varies.

Contact Robert Parker, Director. *E-mail:* rparker@mhec.state.md.us. *Phone:* 410-260-4558. *Website:* http://www.mhec.state.md.us/.

**Tuition Waiver for Foster Care Recipients.** Applicant must be a high school graduate or GED recipient and under the age of 21. Must either have resided in a foster care home in Maryland at the time of high school graduation or GED reception, or until 14th birthday, and been adopted after 14th birthday. Applicant, if status approved, will be exempt from paying tuition and mandatory fees at a public college in Maryland. *Award:* Grant for use in freshman, sophomore, junior, senior, or graduate years; renewable. *Eligibility Requirements:* Applicant must be enrolled or expecting to enroll full- or part-time at a two-year or four-year institution or university; resident of Maryland and studying in Maryland. Available to U.S. citizens. *Application Requirements:*

Application form, financial need analysis, must inquire at financial aid office of schools. **Deadline:** March 1.

Contact Robert Parker, Director. *E-mail:* rparker@mhec.state.md.us. *Phone:* 410-260-4558. *Website:* http://www.mhec.state.md.us/.

**Veterans of the Afghanistan and Iraq Conflicts Scholarship Program.** Provides financial assistance to Maryland resident U.S. Armed Forces personnel who served in Afghanistan or Iraq conflicts and their children or spouses who are attending Maryland institutions. *Award:* Scholarship for use in freshman, sophomore, junior, or senior years; renewable. *Award amount:* $8850. *Number of awards:* 123. *Eligibility Requirements:* Applicant must be enrolled or expecting to enroll full- or part-time at a two-year or four-year institution or university; resident of Maryland and studying in Maryland. Available to U.S. citizens. Applicant or parent must meet one or more of the following requirements: general military experience; retired from active duty; disabled or killed as a result of military service; prisoner of war; or missing in action. *Application Requirements:* Application form, birth certificate/marriage certificate, documentation of military order, financial need analysis. **Deadline:** March 1.

Contact Linda Asplin, Program Administrator, Maryland State Higher Education Commission, 839 Bestgate Road, Suite 400, Annapolis, MD 21401-3013. *E-mail:* lasplin@mhec.state.md.us. *Phone:* 410-260-4563. *Fax:* 410-260-3203. *Website:* http://www.mhec.state.md.us/.

**Workforce Shortage Student Assistance Grant Program.** Scholarship of $4000 available to students who will be required to major in specific areas and will be obligated to serve in the state of Maryland after completion of degree. *Award:* Scholarship for use in freshman, sophomore, junior, or senior years; renewable. *Award amount:* $4000. *Number of awards:* 1300. *Eligibility Requirements:* Applicant must be enrolled or expecting to enroll full- or part-time at a two-year or four-year institution or university; resident of Maryland and studying in Maryland. Available to U.S. citizens. *Application Requirements:* Application form, certain majors require additional documentation, essay, financial need analysis, recommendations or references, resume, transcript. **Deadline:** July 1.

Contact Maura Sappington, Program Manager, Maryland State Higher

Education Commission, 839 Bestgate Road, Suite 400, Annapolis, MD 21401-3013. *E-mail:* msapping@mhec.state.md.us. *Phone:* 410-260-4569. *Fax:* 410-260-3203. *Website:* http://www.mhec.state.md.us/.

# MASSACHUSETTS

**Agnes M. Lindsay Scholarship.** Scholarships for students with demonstrated financial need who are from rural areas of Massachusetts and attend public institutions of higher education in Massachusetts. Deadline varies. *Award:* Scholarship for use in freshman, sophomore, junior, or senior years; not renewable. *Eligibility Requirements:* Applicant must be enrolled or expecting to enroll full-time at a two-year or four-year institution or university; resident of Massachusetts and studying in Massachusetts. Available to U.S. citizens. *Application Requirements:* Application form, financial need analysis. **Deadline:** varies.

Contact Robert Brun, Director of Scholarships and Grants. *E-mail:* osfa@osfa.mass.edu. *Phone:* 617-727-9420. *Fax:* 617-727-0667. *Website:* http://www.osfa.mass.edu/.

**Christian A. Herter Memorial Scholarship.** Renewable award for Massachusetts residents who are in the tenth and eleventh grades, and whose socio-economic backgrounds and environment may inhibit their ability to attain educational goals. Must exhibit severe personal or family-related difficulties, medical problems, or have overcome a personal obstacle. Provides up to 50 percent of the student's calculated need, as determined by federal methodology, at the college of their choice within the continental United States. *Award:* Scholarship for use in freshman, sophomore, junior, or senior years; renewable. *Award amount:* up to $15,000. *Number of awards:* 25. *Eligibility Requirements:* Applicant must be high school student; planning to enroll or expecting to enroll full-time at a two-year or four-year or technical institution or university and resident of Massachusetts. Applicant must have 2.5 GPA or higher. Available to U.S. citizens. *Application Requirements:* Application form, community service, financial need analysis, interview, recommendations or references. **Deadline:** February 1.

Contact Robert Brun, Director of Scholarships and Grants. *E-mail:* osfa@osfa.mass.edu. *Phone:* 617-727-9420. *Fax:* 617-727-0667. *Website:* http://www.osfa.mass.edu/.

**DSS Adopted Children Tuition Waiver.** Need-based tuition waiver for Massachusetts residents who are full-time undergraduate students. Must attend a Massachusetts public institution of higher education and be under 24 years of age. File the FAFSA after January 1. Contact school financial aid office for more information. *Award:* Scholarship for use in freshman, sophomore, junior, or senior years; renewable. *Eligibility Requirements:* Applicant must be enrolled or expecting to enroll full-time at a two-year or four-year institution and resident of Massachusetts. Available to U.S. and non-Canadian citizens. *Application Requirements:* Application form, FAFSA, financial need analysis. **Deadline:** varies.

Contact Robert Brun, Director of Scholarships and Grants. *E-mail:* osfa@osfa.mass.edu. *Phone:* 617-727-9420. *Fax:* 617-727-0667. *Website:* http://www.osfa.mass.edu/.

**Early Childhood Educators Scholarship Program.** Scholarship to provide financial assistance for currently employed early childhood educators and providers who enroll in an associate or bachelor degree program in Early Childhood Education or related programs. Awards are not based on financial need. Individuals taking their first college-level ECE course are eligible for 100 percent tuition, while subsequent ECE courses are awarded at 50 percent tuition. Can be used for one class each semester. Education. *Award:* Scholarship for use in freshman, sophomore, junior, or senior years; not renewable. *Award amount:* $150–$3600. *Eligibility Requirements:* Applicant must be enrolled or expecting to enroll full- or part-time at a four-year institution or university. Available to U.S. citizens. *Application Requirements:* Application form. **Deadline:** July 1.

Contact Robert Brun, Director of Scholarships and Grants. *E-mail:* osfa@osfa.mass.edu. *Phone:* 617-727-9420. *Fax:* 617-727-0667. *Website:* http://www.osfa.mass.edu/.

**John and Abigail Adams Scholarship.** Scholarship to reward and inspire student achievement, attract more high-performing students to Massachusetts public higher education, and provide families of college-bound students with financial assistance. Must be a U.S. citizen or an eligible non-citizen. There is no application process for the scholarship. Students who are eligible will be notified in the fall of their senior year in high school. *Award:* Scholarship for use in freshman year; not renewable. *Eligibility Requirements:* Applicant must be high school student; planning to enroll or expecting to enroll full-time at a two-year or four-year institution or university; resident of Massachusetts and studying in Massachusetts. Applicant must have 3.0 GPA or higher. Available to U.S. citizens. *Application Requirements:* **Deadline:** varies.

Contact Robert Brun, Director of Scholarships and Grants. *E-mail:* osfa@osfa.mass.edu. *Phone:* 617-727-9420. *Fax:* 617-727-0667. *Website:* http://www.osfa.mass.edu/.

**Massachusetts Assistance for Student Success Program.** Provides need-based financial assistance to Massachusetts residents to attend undergraduate postsecondary institutions in Connecticut, Maine, Massachusetts, New Hampshire, Pennsylvania, Rhode Island, Vermont, and District of Columbia. High school seniors may apply. Expected Family Contribution (EFC) should be $3850. Timely filing of FAFSA required. *Award:* Grant for use in freshman, sophomore, junior, or senior years; not renewable. *Award amount:* $300–$1600. *Number of awards:* 50,000–57,000. *Eligibility Requirements:* Applicant must be enrolled or expecting to enroll full-time at a two-year or four-year or technical institution or university; resident of Massachusetts and studying in Connecticut, District of Columbia, Maine, Massachusetts, New Hampshire, Pennsylvania, Rhode Island, Vermont. Available to U.S. citizens. *Application Requirements:* FAFSA, financial need analysis. **Deadline:** May 1.

Contact Robert Brun, Director of Scholarships and Grants. *E-mail:* osfa@osfa.mass.edu. *Phone:* 617-727-9420. *Fax:* 617-727-0667. *Website:* http://www.osfa.mass.edu/.

**Massachusetts Cash Grant Program.** A need-based grant to assist with mandatory fees and non-state supported tuition. This supplemental award is available to Massachusetts residents, who are undergraduates at public two-year, four-year colleges and universities in Massachusetts. Must file FAFSA before May 1. Contact college financial aid office for information. *Award:* Grant for use in freshman, sophomore, junior, or senior years; not renewable. *Eligibility Requirements:* Applicant must be enrolled or expecting to enroll full-time at a two-year or four-year institution or university and resident of Massachusetts. Available to U.S. citizens. *Application Requirements:* Application form, FAFSA, financial need analysis. **Deadline:** continuous.

Contact Robert Brun, Director of Scholarships and Grants. *E-mail:* osfa@osfa.mass.edu. *Phone:* 617-727-9420. *Fax:* 617-727-0667. *Website:* http://www.osfa.mass.edu/.

**Massachusetts Gilbert Matching Student Grant Program.** Grants for permanent Massachusetts residents attending an independent, regionally accredited Massachusetts school or school of nursing full-time. Must be U.S. citizen and permanent legal resident of Massachusetts. File the Free Application for Federal Student Aid after January 1. Contact college financial aid office for complete details and deadlines. *Award:* Grant for use in freshman, sophomore, junior, or senior years; not renewable. *Award amount:* $200–$2500. *Eligibility Requirements:* Applicant must be enrolled or expecting to enroll full-time at a four-year institution or university; resident of Massachusetts and studying in Massachusetts. Available to U.S. citizens. *Application Requirements:* FAFSA, financial need analysis. **Deadline:** varies.

Contact Robert Brun, Director of Scholarships and Grants, Massachusetts Office of Student Financial Assistance, 454 Broadway, Suite 200, Revere, MA 02151. *E-mail:* rbrun@osfa.mass.edu. *Phone:* 617-727-9420. *Fax:* 617-727-0667. *Website:* http://www.osfa.mass.edu/

**Massachusetts Part-Time Grant Program.** Award for permanent Massachusetts residents who have enrolled part-time for at least one year in a state-approved postsecondary school. The recipient must not have a Bachelor's degree. FAFSA must be filed before May 1. Contact college financial aid office for further information. *Award:* Grant for use in freshman, sophomore, junior, or senior years; not renewable. *Award amount:* $200–$1150. *Number of awards:* 200. *Eligibility Requirements:* Applicant must be enrolled or expecting to enroll part-time at a two-year or four-year or technical institution or university and resident of Massachusetts. Available to U.S. citizens. *Application Requirements:* Application form, FAFSA, financial need analysis. **Deadline:** varies.

Contact Robert Brun, Director of Scholarships and Grants. *E-mail:* osfa@osfa.mass.edu. *Phone:* 617-727-9420. *Fax:* 617-727-0667. *Website:* http://www.osfa.mass.edu/.

**Massachusetts Public Service Grant Program.** Scholarships for children and/or spouses of deceased members of fire, police, and corrections departments, who were killed in the line of duty. Awards Massachusetts residents attending Massachusetts institutions. Applicant should have not received a prior Bachelor's degree or its equivalent. *Award:* Grant for use in freshman, sophomore, junior, or senior years; not renewable. *Award amount:* $910–$1714. *Eligibility Requirements:* Applicant must be enrolled or expecting to enroll full-time at a four-year institution or university; resident of Massachusetts and studying in Massachusetts. Applicant or parent of applicant must have employment or volunteer experience in police/firefighting. Available to U.S. citizens. Applicant must have general military experience. *Application Requirements:* Application form, copy of birth certificate, copy of veteran's death certificate, financial need analysis. **Deadline:** May 1.

**New England Regional Student Program-Tuition Break.** Tuition discount for residents of six New England states (Connecticut, Maine, Massachusetts, New Hampshire, Rhode Island, Vermont). Students pay reduced out-of-state tuition at public colleges or universities in other New England states when enrolling in certain majors not offered at public institutions in home state. Details are available at http://www.nebhe.org/tuitionbreak. *Award:* Scholarship for use in freshman, sophomore, junior, senior, or graduate years; renewable. *Eligibility Requirements:* Applicant must be enrolled or expecting to enroll full- or part-time at a two-year or four-year institution or university; resident of Connecticut, Maine, Massachusetts, New Hampshire, Rhode Island, Vermont and studying in Connecticut, Maine, Massachusetts, New Hampshire, Rhode Island, Vermont. Available to U.S. citizens. *Application Requirements:* College application for admission. **Deadline:** continuous.

Contact Wendy Lindsay, Senior Director of Regional Student Program, New England Board of Higher Education, 45 Temple Place, Boston, MA 02111. *E-mail:* tuitionbreak@nebhe.org. *Phone:* 617-533-9511. *Fax:* 617-357-9588. *Website:* http://www.nebhe.org/.

**Paraprofessional Teacher Preparation Grant.** Grant providing financial aid assistance to Massachusetts residents, who are currently employed as paraprofessionals in Massachusetts public schools and wish to obtain higher education and become certified as full-time teachers. Education. *Award:* Grant for use in freshman, sophomore, junior, or senior years; not renewable. *Award amount:* $250–$7500. *Eligibility Requirements:* Applicant must be enrolled or expecting to enroll full- or part-time at a two-year or four-year institution or university and resident of Massachusetts. Available to U.S. citizens. *Application Requirements:* Application form, FAFSA. **Deadline:** August 1.

Contact Robert Brun, Director of Scholarships and Grants. *E-mail:* osfa@osfa.mass.edu. *Phone:* 617-727-9420. *Fax:* 617-727-0667. *Website:* http://www.osfa.mass.edu/.

# MICHIGAN

**American Legion Auxiliary Department of Michigan Medical Career Scholarship.** Award for training in Michigan as registered nurse, licensed practical nurse, physical therapist, respiratory therapist, or in any medical career. Must be child, grandchild, great-grandchild, wife, or widow of honorably discharged or deceased veteran who has served during the eligibility dates for American Legion membership. Must be Michigan resident attending a Michigan school. Health and Medical Sciences; Nursing; Therapy/Rehabilitation. *Award:* Scholarship for use in freshman year; not renewable. *Award amount:* $500. *Number of awards:* 10–20. *Eligibility Requirements:* Applicant must be high school student; planning to enroll or expecting to enroll full-time at a two-year or four-year or technical institution or university; resident of Michigan and studying in Michigan. Available to U.S. citizens. Applicant must have general military experience. *Application Requirements:* Application form, financial need analysis, recommendations or references, transcript, veteran's discharge papers, copy of pages 1 and 2 of federal income tax return. **Deadline:** March 15.

**American Legion Auxiliary Department of Michigan Memorial Scholarship.** Scholarship for daughter, granddaughter, and great-granddaughter of any honorably discharged or deceased veteran of U.S. wars or conflicts. Must be Michigan resident for minimum of one year, female between 16 and 21 years, and attend college in Michigan. Must include copy of military discharge and copy of parent or guardian's IRS 1040 form. *Award:* Scholarship for use in freshman or sophomore years; not renewable. *Award amount:* $500. *Number of awards:* 10–20. *Eligibility Requirements:* Applicant must be age 16-21; enrolled or expecting to enroll full-time at a two-year or four-year or technical institution or university; female; resident of Michigan and studying in Michigan. Available to U.S. citizens. Applicant must have general military experience. *Application Requirements:* Application form, discharge papers, financial need analysis, recommendations or references, transcript. **Deadline:** March 15.

**American Legion Auxiliary Department of Michigan Scholarship for Non-Traditional Student.** Applicant must be a dependent of a veteran. Must be one of the following: nontraditional student returning to classroom after some period of time in which their education was interrupted, student over the age of 22 attending college for the first time to pursue a degree, or student over the age of 22 attending a trade or vocational school. Applicants must be Michigan residents only and attend Michigan institution. Judging based on need, character/leadership, scholastic standing, and initiative/goal. *Award:* Scholarship for use in freshman, sophomore, junior, or senior years; renewable. *Award amount:* $500. *Number of awards:* 1. *Eligibility Requirements:* Applicant must be age 23-99; enrolled or expecting to enroll full- or part-time at a two-year or four-year or technical institution or university; resident of Michigan and studying in Michigan. Available to U.S. citizens. Applicant must have general military experience. *Application Requirements:* Application form, copy of veteran's discharge papers, financial need analysis, transcript. **Deadline:** March 15.

**Michigan Competitive Scholarship.** Renewable awards for Michigan resident to pursue undergraduate study at a Michigan institution. Awards limited to tuition. Must maintain at least a 2.0 grade point average and meet the college's academic progress requirements. Must file Free Application for Federal Student Aid. *Award:* Scholarship for use in freshman, sophomore, junior, or senior years; renewable. *Award amount:* $575. *Eligibility Requirements:* Applicant must be enrolled or expecting to enroll full- or part-time at a two-year or four-year institution or university; resident of Michigan and studying in Michigan. Available to U.S. citizens. *Application Requirements:* Application form, financial need analysis, test scores. **Deadline:** March 1.

**Michigan Tuition Grant.** Need-based program. Students must be Michigan resi dents and attend a Michigan private, non profit, degree-granting college. Must file the Free Application for Federal Student Aid and meet the college's academic progress requirements. *Award:* Grant for use in freshman, sophomore, junior, or senior years; renewable. *Award amount:* $1512. *Eligibility Requirements:* Applicant must be enrolled or expecting to enroll full- or part-time at a four-year institution or university; resident of Michigan and studying in Michigan. Available to U.S. citizens. *Application Requirements:* Financial need analysis. **Deadline:** July 1.

**Tuition Incentive Program.** Award for Michigan residents who receive or have received Michigan Medicaid for required period of time through the Department of Human Services. Scholarship provides two years tuition towards an associate degree at a Michigan college or university and $2000 total assistance for third and fourth years. Must apply before graduating from high school or earning a general education development diploma and before age 20. *Award:* Grant for use in freshman, sophomore, junior, or senior years; renewable. *Eligibility Requirements:* Applicant must be enrolled or expecting to enroll full- or part-time at a two-year or four-year institution or university; resident of Michigan and studying in Michigan. Available to U.S. citizens. *Application Requirements:* Application form, Medicaid eligibility for specified period of time. **Deadline:** continuous.

# MINNESOTA

**Leadership, Excellence, and Dedicated Service Scholarship.** Scholarship provides a maximum of thirty $1000 to selected high school seniors who become a member of the Minnesota National Guard and complete the application process. The award recognizes demonstrated leadership, community services and potential for success in the Minnesota National Guard. *Award:* Scholarship for use in freshman year; not renewable. *Award amount:* $1000. *Number of awards:* up to 30. *Eligibility Requirements:* Applicant must be high school student; planning to enroll or expecting to enroll full- or part-time at a two-year or four-year or technical institution or university; resident of Minnesota and must have an interest in leadership. Applicant or parent of applicant must have employment or volunteer experience in community service. Available to U.S. citizens. Applicant or parent must meet one or more of the following requirements: national guard experience; retired from active duty; disabled or killed as a result of military service; prisoner of war; or missing in action. *Application Requirements:* Essay, recommendations or references, resume, transcript. **Deadline:** March 15.

Contact Barbara O'Reilly, Education Services Officer. *E-mail:* barbara. oreilly@mn.ngb.army.mil. *Phone:* 651-282-4508. *Website:* http://www. minnesotanationalguard.org/.

**Minnesota GI Bill Program.** Provides financial assistance to eligible Minnesota veterans and non-veterans who have served 5 or more years cumulatively as a member of the National Guard or Reserves, and served on or after September 11, 2001. Surviving spouses and children of service members who have died or have a total and permanent disability and who served on or after September 11, 2001, may also be eligible. Full-time students may receive up to $1000 per term, and part-time students up to $500 per term up to $3,000 per year. Maximum lifetime benefit is $10,000. *Award:* Scholarship for use in freshman, sophomore, junior, senior, graduate, or postgraduate years; not renewable. *Award amount:* up to $3000. *Eligibility Requirements:* Applicant must be enrolled or expecting to enroll full- or part-time at a two-year or four-year or technical institution or university; resident of Minnesota and studying in Minnesota. Available to U.S. citizens. Applicant or parent must meet one or more of the following requirements: general military experience; retired from active duty; disabled or killed as a result of military service; prisoner of war; or missing in action. *Application Requirements:* Application form, application form may be submitted online (http://www.getreadyforcollege. org), financial need analysis, military records. **Deadline:** continuous.

**Minnesota Indian Scholarship.** Scholarship for Minnesota residents who are one-fourth or more American Indian ancestry and attending an eligible Minnesota postsecondary institution. Maximum award is $4000 for undergraduate students and $6000 for graduate students. Scholarships are limited to 3 years for certificate or AA/AS programs, 5 years for Bachelor's degree programs, and 5 years for graduate programs. Applicants must maintain satisfactory academic progress, not be in default on student loans, and be eligible to receive Pell or State Grant and have remaining need.

Undergraduates must be enrolled on a least a 3/4-time basis. *Award:* Scholarship for use in freshman, sophomore, junior, senior, graduate, or postgraduate years; not renewable. *Award amount:* up to $6000. *Number of awards:* 500–600. *Eligibility Requirements:* Applicant must be American Indian/Alaska Native; enrolled or expecting to enroll full- or part-time at a two-year or four-year or technical institution or university; resident of Minnesota and studying in Minnesota. Available to U.S. citizens. *Application Requirements:* American Indian ancestry documentation, application form, financial need analysis. **Deadline:** continuous.

**Minnesota Reciprocal Agreement.** Renewable tuition waiver for Minnesota residents. Waives all or part of non-resident tuition surcharge at public institutions in Illinois, Indiana, Iowa, Kansas, Michigan, Missouri, Nebraska, North Dakota, South Dakota, Wisconsin and Manitoba. Deadline: last day of academic term. *Award:* Scholarship for use in freshman, sophomore, junior, senior, graduate, or postgraduate years; renewable. *Award amount:* up to $10,000. *Eligibility Requirements:* Applicant must be enrolled or expecting to enroll full- or part-time at a two-year or four-year or technical institution or university; resident of Minnesota and studying in Illinois, Indiana, Iowa, Kansas, Manitoba, Michigan, Missouri, Nebraska, North Dakota, South Dakota, Wisconsin. Available to U.S. citizens. *Application Requirements:* Application form. **Deadline:** continuous.

Contact Jodi Rouland, Program Assistant. *E-mail:* jodi.rouland@state.mn. us. *Phone:* 651-355-0614. *Fax:* 651-642-0675. *Website:* http://www.ohe.state.mn. us.

**Minnesota State Grant Program.** Need-based grant program available for Minnesota residents attending Minnesota colleges. Student covers 50% of cost with remainder covered by Pell Grant, parent contribution and state grant. Students apply with FAFSA and colleges administer the program on campus. *Award:* Grant for use in freshman, sophomore, junior, or senior years; not renewable. *Award amount:* $100–$10,450. *Number of awards:* 71,000–105,000. *Eligibility Requirements:* Applicant must be enrolled or expecting to enroll full- or part-time at a two-year or four-year or technical institution or university; resident of Minnesota and studying in Minnesota. Available to U.S. citizens. *Application Requirements:*

Application form, financial need analysis. **Deadline:** continuous.

**Minnesota State Veterans' Dependents Assistance Program.** Tuition assistance to dependents of persons considered to be prisoner-of-war or missing in action after August 1, 1958. Must be Minnesota resident attending Minnesota two- or four-year school. *Award:* Scholarship for use in freshman, sophomore, junior, or senior years; renewable. *Award amount:* up to $250. *Eligibility Requirements:* Applicant must be enrolled or expecting to enroll full- or part-time at a two-year or four-year institution; resident of Minnesota and studying in Minnesota. Available to U.S. citizens. Applicant or parent must meet one or more of the following requirements: general military experience; retired from active duty; disabled or killed as a result of military service; prisoner of war; or missing in action. *Application Requirements:* Application form. **Deadline:** continuous.

Contact Ginny Dodds, Manager. *E-mail:* ginny.dodds@state.mn.us. *Phone:* 651-355-0610. *Website:* http://www.ohe.state.mn.us.

**Postsecondary Child Care Grant Program-Minnesota.** Grant available for students not receiving MFIP (TANF). Based on financial need. Cannot exceed actual child care costs or maximum award chart (based on income). Must be Minnesota resident. For use at Minnesota two- or four-year school, including public technical colleges. Available until student has attended college for the equivalent of four full-time academic years. *Award:* Grant for use in freshman, sophomore, junior, or senior years; not renewable. *Award amount:* $100–$2800. *Number of awards:* 2500–3000. *Eligibility Requirements:* Applicant must be enrolled or expecting to enroll full- or part-time at a two-year or four-year or technical institution or university; resident of Minnesota and studying in Minnesota. Available to U.S. citizens. *Application Requirements:* Application form, financial need analysis. **Deadline:** continuous.

Contact Brenda Larter, Program Administrator, Minnesota Office of Higher Education, 1450 Energy Park Drive, Suite 350, St. Paul, MN 55108-5227. *E-mail:* brenda.larter@state.mn.us. *Phone:* 651-355-0612. *Fax:* 651-642-0675. *Website:* http://www.ohe.state.mn.us.

**Safety Officers' Survivor Grant Program.** Grant for eligible survivors of Minnesota public safety officers killed in the line of duty. Safety officers who have been permanently or totally disabled in the line of duty are also eligible. Must be used at a Minnesota institution participating in State Grant Program. Write for details. Must submit proof of death or disability and Public Safety Officers Benefit Fund Certificate. Must apply for renewal each year. Five-year limit on awards. *Award:* Grant for use in freshman, sophomore, junior, senior, or graduate years; not renewable. *Award amount:* up to $10,450. *Number of awards:* 1. *Eligibility Requirements:* Applicant must be enrolled or expecting to enroll full- or part-time at a two-year or four-year or technical institution or university; resident of Minnesota and studying in Minnesota. Applicant or parent of applicant must have employment or volunteer experience in police/firefighting. Available to U.S. citizens. *Application Requirements:* Application form, proof of death or disability. **Deadline:** continuous.

Contact Brenda Larter, Program Administrator. *E-mail:* brenda.larter@state.mn.us. *Phone:* 651-355-0612. *Fax:* 651-642-0675. *Website:* http://www.ohe.state.mn.us.

# MISSISSIPPI

**Higher Education Legislative Plan (HELP).** Eligible applicant must be resident of Mississippi and apply for the first time as a freshman and/or sophomore student who graduated from high school within the immediate past two years. Must demonstrate need as determined by the results of the FAFSA, documenting an average family adjusted gross income of $36,500 or less over the prior two years. Must be enrolled full-time at a Mississippi college or university, have a GPA of 2.5, have completed a specific high school core curriculum, and have scored 20 on the ACT. *Award:* Scholarship for use in freshman, sophomore, junior, or senior years; not renewable. *Award amount:* up to $6660. *Eligibility Requirements:* Applicant must be enrolled or expecting to enroll full-time at a two-year or four-year institution or university; resident of Mississippi and studying in Mississippi. Applicant must have 2.5 GPA or higher. Available to U.S. citizens. *Application Requirements:* Application form, application form may be submitted online (http://www.mississippi.edu/financialaid), FAFSA, specific high school curriculum, residency documentation, financial need analysis, test scores, transcript. **Deadline:** March 31.

**Law Enforcement Officers/Firemen Scholarship.** Financial assistance to dependent children and spouses of any Mississippi law enforcement officer, full-time fire fighter or volunteer fire fighter who has suffered fatal injuries or wounds or become permanently and totally disabled as a result of injuries or wounds which occurred in the performance of the official and appointed duties of his or her office. This financial assistance is offered as an eight semester tuition and room scholarship at any state-supported college or university in Mississippi. *Award:* Scholarship for use in freshman, sophomore, junior, or senior years; not renewable. *Award amount:* up to $10,664. *Eligibility Requirements:* Applicant must be enrolled or expecting to enroll full-time at a four-year institution or university; resident of Mississippi and studying in Mississippi. Applicant or parent of applicant must have employment or volunteer experience in police/firefighting. Available to U.S. citizens. *Application Requirements:* Application form, application form may be submitted online (http://www.mississippi.edu/financialaid), residency documentation; documentation of parent's death/disability in line of duty. **Deadline:** continuous.

**Mississippi Eminent Scholars Grant.** Award for an entering freshmen or as a renewal for sophomore, junior or senior, who are residents of Mississippi. Applicants must achieve a GPA of 3.5 and must have scored 29 on the ACT. Must enroll full-time at an eligible Mississippi college or university. *Award:* Grant for use in freshman, sophomore, junior, or senior years; not renewable. *Award amount:* up to $2500. *Eligibility Requirements:* Applicant must be enrolled or expecting to enroll full-time at a two-year or four-year institution or university; resident of Mississippi and studying in Mississippi. Applicant must have 3.5 GPA or higher. Available to U.S. citizens. *Application Requirements:* Application form, application form may be submitted online (http://www.mississippi.edu/financialaid), residency documentation, test scores, transcript. **Deadline:** September 15.

**Mississippi Resident Tuition Assistance Grant.** Must be a resident of Mississippi enrolled full-time at an eligible Mississippi college or university. Must maintain a minimum 2.5 GPA each semester. MTAG awards may be up to $500 per academic year for freshman and sophomores and $1000 per academic year for juniors and seniors. *Award:* Grant for use in freshman, sophomore, junior, or senior years; not renewable. *Award* *amount:* $17–$1000. *Eligibility Requirements:* Applicant must be enrolled or expecting to enroll full-time at a two-year or four-year institution or university; resident of Mississippi and studying in Mississippi. Applicant must have 2.5 GPA or higher. Available to U.S. citizens. *Application Requirements:* Application form, application form may be submitted online (http://www.mississippi.edu/financi alaid), residency documentation, test scores, transcript. **Deadline:** Sep tember 15.

## MISSOURI

**Access Missouri Financial Assistance Program.** Need-based program that provides awards to students who are enrolled full-time and have an expected family contribution (EFC) of $12,000 or less based on their Free Application for Federal Student Aid (FAFSA). Awards vary depending on EFC and the type of postsecondary school. *Award:* Grant for use in freshman, sophomore, junior, or senior years; not renewable. *Eligibility Requirements:* Applicant must be enrolled or expecting to enroll full-time at a two-year or technical institution or university; resident of Missouri and studying in Mis souri. Applicant must have 2.5 GPA or higher. Available to U.S. citizens. *Application Requirements:* FAFSA on file by April 1.

**Lillie Lois Ford Scholarship Fund.** Two awards of $1000 each are given each year to one boy and one girl. Applicant must have attended a full session of Mis souri Boys/Girls State or Missouri Cadet Patrol Academy. Must be a Missouri res ident below age 21, attending an accredited college/university as a full-time student. Must be an unmarried descendant of a veteran having served at least 90 days on active duty in the Army, Air Force, Navy, Marine Corps, or Coast Guard of the United States. *Award:* Schol arship for use in freshman year; not renewable. *Award amount:* $1000. *Number of awards:* 2. *Eligibility Requirements:* Applicant must be high school student; planning to enroll or expecting to enroll full-time at a two-year or four-year institution or university; single and res ident of Missouri. Available to U.S. cit izens. Applicant or parent must meet one or more of the following requirements: general military experience; retired from active duty; disabled or killed as a result of military service; prisoner of war; or missing in action. *Application Require*

*ments:* Application form, copy of the veteran's discharge certificate, financial need analysis, test scores. **Deadline:** April 20.

Contact John Doane, Chairman, Education and Scholarship Committee, American Legion Department of Missouri, PO Box 179, Jefferson City, MO 65102-0179. *Phone:* 417-924-8186. *Website:* http://www.missourilegion.org/.

**Marguerite Ross Barnett Memorial Scholarship.** Scholarship was estab lished for students who are employed while attending school part-time. Must be enrolled at least half-time but less than full-time at a participating Missouri post secondary school, be employed and com pensated for at least 20 hours per week, be 18 years of age, be a Missouri resident and a U.S. citizen or a permanent resident. *Award:* Scholarship for use in freshman, sophomore, junior, or senior years; renewable. *Eligibility Requirements:* Applicant must be enrolled or expecting to enroll part-time at a two-year or four-year or technical institution or university; resident of Missouri and studying in Mis souri. Applicant must have 2.5 GPA or higher. Available to U.S. citizens. *Application Requirements:* FAFSA on file by August 1. **Deadline:** August 1.

**Missouri Higher Education Academic Scholarship (Bright Flight).** Program encourages top-ranked high school seniors to attend approved Mis souri postsecondary schools. Must be a Missouri resident and a U.S. citizen or permanent resident. Must have a com posite score on the ACT or SAT in the top 5 percent of all Missouri students taking those tests. Students with scores in the top 3 percent are eligible for an annual award of up to $3000 (up to $1500 each semester). Students with scores in the top 4% and 5% are eligible for an annual award of up to $1000 (up to $500 each semester). Award amounts, and the avail ability of the award for students in the 4% and 5%, are subject to change based on the amount of funding allocated for the program in the legislative session. *Award:* Scholarship for use in freshman, soph omore, junior, or senior years; renewable. *Award amount:* $1000–$3000. *Eligibility Requirements:* Applicant must be enrolled or expecting to enroll full-time at a two-year or four-year or technical institution or university; resident of Missouri and studying in Missouri. Applicant must have 2.5 GPA or higher. Available to U.S. citizens. *Application Requirements:* Test scores.

## MONTANA

**Montana Higher Education Opportunity Grant.** This grant is awarded based on need to undergraduate students attending either part-time or full-time who are residents of Montana and attending participating Montana schools. Awards are limited to the most needy students. A specific major or program of study is not required. This grant does not need to be repaid, and students may apply each year. Apply by filing FAFSA by March 1 and contacting the financial aid office at the admitting college. *Award:* Grant for use in freshman, sophomore, junior, or senior years; not renewable. *Award amount:* $400–$600. *Number of awards:* up to 800. *Eligibility Requirements:* Applicant must be enrolled or expecting to enroll full- or part-time at a two-year or four-year insti tution or university; resident of Montana and studying in Montana. Available to U. S. citizens. *Application Requirements:* FAFSA, financial need analysis. **Deadline:** March 1.

Contact Jamie Dushin, Budget Analyst, Montana University System, Office of Commissioner of Higher Education, PO Box 203101, Helena, MT 59620-3101. *E-mail:* jdushin@mgslp. state.mt.us. *Phone:* 406-444-0638. *Fax:* 406-444-1869. *Website:* http://www. scholarship.mt.gov/.

**Montana Tuition Assistance Program-Baker Grant.** Need-based grant for Montana residents attending par ticipating Montana schools who have earned at least $2575 during the previous calendar year. Must be enrolled full-time. Grant does not need to be repaid. Award covers the first undergraduate degree or certificate. Apply by filing FAFSA by March 1 and contacting the financial aid office at the admitting college. *Award:* Grant for use in freshman, sophomore, junior, or senior years; not renewable. *Award amount:* $100–$1000. *Number of awards:* 1000–3000. *Eligibility Requirements:* Applicant must be enrolled or expecting to enroll full-time at a two-year or four-year institution or university; res ident of Montana and studying in Montana. Available to U.S. citizens. *Application Requirements:* Application form, FAFSA, financial need analysis, resume. **Deadline:** March 1.

Contact Jamie Dushin, Budget Analyst, Montana University System, Office of Commissioner of Higher Education, PO Box 203101, Helena, MT 59620-3101. *E-mail:* jdushin@mgslp. state.mt.us. *Phone:* 406-444-0638. *Fax:*

406-444-1869. *Website:* http://www.scholarship.mt.gov/.

**Montana University System Honor Scholarship.** Scholarship will be awarded annually to high school seniors graduating from accredited Montana high schools. The MUS Honor Scholarship is a four year renewable scholarship that waives the tuition and registration fee at one of the Montana University System campuses or one of the three community colleges (Flathead Valley in Kalispell, Miles in Miles City or Dawson in Glendive). The scholarship must be used within 9 months after high school graduation. Applicant must have a minimum GPA of 3.4. *Award:* Scholarship for use in freshman, sophomore, junior, or senior years; renewable. *Award amount:* $4000–$6000. *Number of awards:* up to 200. *Eligibility Requirements:* Applicant must be high school student; planning to enroll or expecting to enroll full-time at a two-year or four-year institution or university; resident of Montana and studying in Montana. Applicant must have 3.5 GPA or higher. Available to U.S. citizens. *Application Requirements:* Application form, college acceptance letter, test scores, transcript. **Deadline:** March 15.

Contact Sheila Newlun, Grants and Scholarship Coordinator. *E-mail:* snewlun@montana.edu. *Phone:* 406-444-0638. *Fax:* 406-444-1869. *Website:* http://www.scholarship.mt.gov/.

## NEBRASKA

**Nebraska Opportunity Grant.** Available to undergraduates attending a participating postsecondary institution in Nebraska. Must demonstrate financial need. Nebraska residency required. Awards determined by each participating institution. Student must complete the Free Application for Federal Student Aid (FAFSA) to apply. Contact financial aid office at institution for additional information. *Award:* Grant for use in freshman, sophomore, junior, or senior years; not renewable. *Award amount:* $100–$4034. *Eligibility Requirements:* Applicant must be enrolled or expecting to enroll full- or part-time at a two-year or four-year or technical institution or university; resident of Nebraska and studying in Nebraska. Available to U.S. citizens. *Application Requirements:* Application form, application form may be submitted online (http://www.fafsa.ed.gov), financial need analysis. **Deadline:** continuous.

Contact Mr. J. Ritchie Morrow, Financial Aid Coordinator, Nebraska's Coordinating Commission for Postsecondary Education, 140 North 8th Street, Suite 300, PO Box 95005, Lincoln, NE 68509-5005. *E-mail:* Ritchie. Morrow@nebraska.gov. *Phone:* 402-471-2847. *Fax:* 402-471-2886. *Website:* http://www.ccpe.state.ne.us/.

## NEVADA

**Governor Guinn Millennium Scholarship.** Scholarship for Nevada residents. Student must graduate from a public or private high school within Nevada with a minimum GPA of 3.25. Must complete core curriculum. Maximum award is $10,000. Student must acknowledge award and use it within 6 years of high school graduation. *Award:* Scholarship for use in freshman, sophomore, junior, or senior years; renewable. *Award amount:* up to $10,000. *Number of awards:* 1. *Eligibility Requirements:* Applicant must be enrolled or expecting to enroll full-time at a two-year or four-year institution or university; resident of Nevada and studying in Nevada. Available to U.S. citizens. *Application Requirements:* Application form may be submitted online (http://nevadatreasurer.gov), high schools determine eligibility; student must accept award. **Deadline:** varies.

Contact Linda English, Executive Director. *E-mail:* info@nevadatreasurer.gov. *Phone:* 702-486-3889. *Fax:* 702-486-3246. *Website:* http://www.nevadatreasurer.gov/.

## NEW HAMPSHIRE

**Scholarships for Orphans of Veterans.** Scholarship to provide financial assistance (room, board, books and supplies) to children of parents who served in World War II, Korean Conflict, Vietnam (Southeast Asian Conflict) or the Gulf Wars, or any other operation for which the armed forces expeditionary medal or theater of operations service medal was awarded to the veteran. Must be between the ages of 16 and 25 to qualify and be residents of New Hampshire studying at New Hampshire colleges and universities. *Award:* Scholarship for use in freshman, sophomore, junior, or senior years; renewable. *Award amount:* $1500–$2500. *Number of awards:* 1–10. *Eligibility Requirements:* Applicant must be age 16-25; enrolled or expecting to enroll full-time at a two-year or four-year institution or university; resident of New Hampshire and studying in New Hampshire. Available to U.S. citizens. Applicant or parent must meet one or more of the following requirements: general military experience; retired from active duty; disabled or killed as a result of military service; prisoner of war; or missing in action. *Application Requirements:* Application form. **Deadline:** September 1.

Contact Mrs. Pat Moquin, Program Assistant, N.H. Department of Education, Division of Higher Education - Higher Education Commission, 101 Pleasant Street, Concord, NH 03301. *E-mail:* patricia.moquin@doe.nh.gov. *Phone:* 603-271-0289. *Fax:* 603-271-1953. *Website:* http://www.education.nh.gov/highered.

## NEW JERSEY

**Law Enforcement Officer Memorial Scholarship.** Scholarships for full-time undergraduate study at approved New Jersey institutions for the dependent children of New Jersey law enforcement officers killed in the line of duty. Value of scholarship will be established annually. Deadline varies. *Award:* Scholarship for use in freshman, sophomore, junior, or senior years; renewable. *Eligibility Requirements:* Applicant must be enrolled or expecting to enroll full-time at a two-year or four-year institution or university; resident of New Jersey and studying in New Jersey. Applicant or parent of applicant must have employment or volunteer experience in police/firefighting. Available to U.S. citizens. *Application Requirements:* Application form. **Deadline:** varies.

Contact Alice McPaul, Assistant Director of Special Grants and Scholarships, New Jersey Higher Education Student Assistance Authority (HESAA), PO Box 540, Trenton, NJ 08625. *Phone:* 609-588-3266. *Fax:* 609-588-2228. *Website:* http://www.hesaa.org/.

**New Jersey Student Tuition Assistance Reward Scholarship II.** Must earn an Associate degree from the home New Jersey county college as an NJ STARS recipient and graduate with a cumulative GPA of 3.25 or higher. Family income (taxable and untaxed income) must be less than $250,000 as derived from the FAFSA.

Contact Jossette Greene, Program Officer, Trenton, NJ 08625. *Phone:* 609-584-4480. *Fax:* 609-588-2228. *Website:* http://www.hesaa.org/.

**New Jersey War Orphans Tuition Assistance.** $500 scholarship to children of those service personnel who died while in the military or due to service-connected disabilities, or who are officially listed as missing in action by the U.S. Department of Defense. Must be a resident of New Jersey for at least one year immediately preceding the filing of the application and be between the ages of 16 and 21 at the time of application. *Award:* Scholarship for use in freshman, sophomore, junior, or senior years; renewable. *Award amount:* $500. *Eligibility Requirements:* Applicant must be age 16-21; enrolled or expecting to enroll full-time at a four-year institution or university and resident of New Jersey. Available to U.S. citizens. Applicant or parent must meet one or more of the following requirements: general military experience; retired from active duty; disabled or killed as a result of military service; prisoner of war; or missing in action. *Application Requirements:* Application form, transcript. **Deadline:** varies.

Contact Patricia Richter, Grants Manager, New Jersey Department of Military and Veterans Affairs, PO Box 340, Trenton, NJ 08625-0340. *E-mail:* patricia.richter@njdmava.state.nj.us. *Phone:* 609-530-6854. *Fax:* 609-530-6970. *Website:* http://www.state.nj.us/military.

**New Jersey World Trade Center Scholarship.** Scholarship was established by the legislature to aid the dependent children and surviving spouses of New Jersey residents who were killed in the terrorist attacks, or who are missing and officially presumed dead as a direct result of the attacks; applies to instate and out-of-state institutions for students seeking undergraduate degrees. *Award:* Scholarship for use in freshman, sophomore, junior, or senior years; not renewable. *Award amount:* up to $6500. *Eligibility Requirements:* Applicant must be enrolled or expecting to enroll full-time at a two-year or four-year institution or university and resident of New Jersey. Available to U.S. citizens. *Application Requirements:* Application form. **Deadline:** varies.

Contact Alice McPaul, Assistant Director of Special Grants and Scholarships, New Jersey Higher Education Student Assistance Authority (HESAA), PO Box 540, Trenton, NJ 08625. *E-mail:* gjoachim@hesaa.org. *Phone:* 609-588-3266. *Fax:* 609-588-7389. *Website:* http://www.hesaa.org/.

**NJ Student Tuition Assistance Reward Scholarship.** Students must enroll in a full-time course of study at their home county colleges. The award covers tuition charges for up to 18 credit hours per term. *Award:* Scholarship for use in freshman or sophomore years;

renewable. *Award amount:* $500–$2600. *Eligibility Requirements:* Applicant must be enrolled or expecting to enroll full-time at a two-year institution; resident of New Jersey and studying in New Jersey. Applicant must have 3.0 GPA or higher. Available to U.S. citizens. *Application Requirements:* Application form, FAFSA, transcript. **Deadline:** varies.

Contact Ms. Jossette Greene, Program Officer, New Jersey Higher Education Student Assistance Authority (HESAA), PO Box 540, Trenton, NJ 08625. *E-mail:* cmuka@hessa.org. *Phone:* 609-584-4480. *Fax:* 609-588-2228. *Website:* http://www.hesaa.org/.

**Part-Time Tuition Aid Grant for County Colleges.** Provides financial aid to eligible part-time undergraduate students enrolled for 9 to 11 credits at New Jersey community colleges. *Award:* Grant for use in freshman or sophomore years; not renewable. *Award amount:* $546 $1900. *Eligibility Requirements:* Applicant must be enrolled or expecting to enroll part-time at a two-year institution; resident of New Jersey and studying in New Jersey. Available to U.S. citizens. *Application Requirements:* Application form, financial need analysis. **Deadline:** varies.

Contact Larry Sharp, Director of Grants and Scholarships, New Jersey Higher Education Student Assistance Authority (HESAA), PO Box 540, Trenton, NJ 08625. *Phone:* 609-584-4480. *Fax:* 609-588-2228. *Website:* http://www.hesaa.org/.

**POW-MIA Tuition Benefit Program.** Free undergraduate college tuition provided to any child born or adopted before or during the period of time his or her parent was officially declared a prisoner of war or person missing in action after January 1, 1960. The POW-MIA must have been a New Jersey resident at the time he or she entered the service. Child of veteran must attend either a public or private institution in New Jersey. A copy of DD 1300 must be furnished with the application. Minimum 2.5 GPA required. *Award:* Scholarship for use in freshman, sophomore, junior, or senior years; renewable. *Eligibility Requirements:* Applicant must be enrolled or expecting to enroll full-time at a two-year or four-year or technical institution or university; resident of New Jersey and studying in New Jersey. Applicant must have 2.5 GPA or higher. Available to U.S. citizens. Applicant or parent must meet one or more of the following requirements: general military experience; retired from

active duty; disabled or killed as a result of military service; prisoner of war; or missing in action. *Application Requirements:* Application form, copy of DD 1300, transcript. **Deadline:** varies.

Contact Patricia Richter, Grants Manager, New Jersey Department of Military and Veterans Affairs, PO Box 340, Trenton, NJ 08625-0340. *E-mail:* patricia.richter@njdmava.state.nj.us. *Phone:* 609-530-6854. *Fax:* 609-530-6970. *Website:* http://www.state.nj.us/military.

**Survivor Tuition Benefits Program.** The scholarship provides tuition fees for spouses and dependents of law enforcement officers, fire, or emergency services personnel killed in the line of duty. Eligible recipients may attend any independent institution in the state; however, the annual value of the grant cannot exceed the highest tuition charged at a New Jersey public institution. *Award:* Scholarship for use in freshman, sophomore, junior, or senior years; renewable. *Eligibility Requirements:* Applicant must be enrolled or expecting to enroll full- or part-time at a two-year or four-year institution or university; resident of New Jersey and studying in New Jersey. Applicant or parent of applicant must have employment or volunteer experience in police/firefighting. Available to U.S. citizens. *Application Requirements:* Application form. **Deadline:** varies.

Contact Alice McPaul, Assistant Director of Special Grants and Scholarships, New Jersey Higher Education Student Assistance Authority (HESAA), PO Box 540, Trenton, NJ 08625. *E-mail:* cmuka@hesaa.org. *Phone:* 609-588-3266. *Fax:* 609-588-2228. *Website:* http://www.hesaa.org/.

**Tuition Aid Grant.** The program provides grants to eligible undergraduate students attending participating in-state institutions. *Award:* Grant for use in freshman, sophomore, junior, or senior years; not renewable. *Award amount:* $1012–$11,550. *Eligibility Requirements:* Applicant must be enrolled or expecting to enroll full-time at a two-year or four-year institution or university; resident of New Jersey and studying in New Jersey. Available to U.S. citizens. *Application Requirements:* Application form, application form may be submitted online (http://www.hesaa.org), financial need analysis. **Deadline:** varies.

Contact Larry Sharp, Director of Grants and Scholarships, New Jersey Higher Education Student Assistance Authority (HESAA), PO Box 540,

Trenton, NJ 08625. *Phone:* 609-584-4480. *Fax:* 609-588-2228. *Website:* http://www.hesaa.org/.

**Veterans Tuition Credit Program-New Jersey.** Award for New Jersey res ident veterans who served in the armed forces between December 31, 1960, and May 7, 1975. Must have been a New Jersey resident at time of induction or dis charge or for two years immediately prior to application. *Award:* Scholarship for use in freshman, sophomore, junior, or senior years; renewable. *Award amount:* $200–$400. *Eligibility Requirements:* Applicant must be enrolled or expecting to enroll full- or part-time at a two-year or four-year or technical institution or university and resident of New Jersey. Available to U.S. citizens. Applicant or parent must meet one or more of the following requirements: general military expe rience; retired from active duty; disabled or killed as a result of military service; prisoner of war; or missing in action. *Application Requirements:* Application form. **Deadline:** varies.

Contact Patricia Richter, Grants Manager, New Jersey Department of Military and Veterans Affairs, PO Box 340, Trenton, NJ 08625-0340. *E-mail:* patricia.richter@njdmava.state.nj.us. *Phone:* 609-530-6854. *Fax:* 609-530-6970. *Website:* http://www.state.nj.us/military.

# NEW MEXICO

**Children of Deceased Veterans Scholarship-New Mexico.** Award for New Mexico residents who are children of veterans killed as a result of service, prisoner of war, or veterans missing in action. Must be between ages 16 and 26. For use at New Mexico schools for under graduate study. Must submit parent's death certificate and DD form 214. *Award:* Scholarship for use in freshman, sophomore, junior, or senior years; not renewable. *Award amount:* $300. *Number of awards:* up to 50. *Eligibility Require ments:* Applicant must be age 16-26; enrolled or expecting to enroll full- or part-time at a two-year or four-year or technical institution or university; resident of New Mexico and studying in New Mexico. Available to U.S. citizens. Applicant or parent must meet one or more of the following requirements: general military experience; retired from active duty; disabled or killed as a result of military service; prisoner of war; or missing in action. *Application Require ments:* Application form, death certif

icate or notice of casualty, DD form 214, transcript. **Deadline:** continuous.

Contact Mr. Alan Martinez, Deputy Cabinet Secretary, New Mexico Department of Veterans' Services, PO Box 2324, Santa Fe, NM 87504. *E-mail:* alan.martinez@state.nm.us. *Phone:* 505-827-6300. *Fax:* 505-827-6372. *Website:* http://www.dvs.state.nm.us/.

**College Affordability Grant.** Grant available to New Mexico students with financial need who do not qualify for other state grants and scholarships to attend and complete educational programs at a New Mexico public college or uni versity. Student must have unmet need after all other financial aid has been awarded. Student may not be receiving any other state grants or scholarships. Renewable upon satisfactory academic progress. *Award:* Grant for use in freshman, sophomore, junior, or senior years; renewable. *Award amount:* up to $1000. *Number of awards:* 1. *Eligibility Requirements:* Applicant must be enrolled or expecting to enroll full- or part-time at a two-year or four-year institution or uni versity; resident of New Mexico and studying in New Mexico. Available to U. S. citizens. *Application Requirements:* Application form, FAFSA, financial need analysis. **Deadline:** continuous.

Contact Tashina Acker, Director of Financial Aid, New Mexico Commission on Higher Education, 1068 Cerrillos Road, Santa Fe, NM 87505-1650. *E-mail:* tashina.banks-moore@state.nm.us. *Phone:* 505-476-6549. *Fax:* 505-476-6511. *Website:* http://www.hed.state.nm.us/.

**Legislative Endowment Scholar-ships.** Renewable scholarships to provide aid for undergraduate students with substantial financial need who are attending public postsecondary institu tions in New Mexico. Four-year schools may award up to $2500 per academic year, two-year schools may award up to $1000 per academic year. Deadlines varies. *Award:* Scholarship for use in freshman, sophomore, junior, or senior years; renewable. *Award amount:* $1000–$2500. *Number of awards:* 1. *Eligibility Requirements:* Applicant must be enrolled or expecting to enroll full- or part-time at a two-year or four-year institution or uni versity; resident of New Mexico and studying in New Mexico. Available to U. S. citizens. *Application Requirements:* Application form, FAFSA, financial need analysis. **Deadline:** varies.

Contact Tashina Moore, Director of Financial Aid, New Mexico Commission on Higher Education, 1068 Cerrillos

Road, Santa Fe, NM 87505-1650. *E-mail:* tashina.banks-moore@state.nm.us. *Phone:* 505-475-6549. *Fax:* 505-476-6511. *Website:* http://www.hed.state.nm.us/.

**Legislative Lottery Scholarship.** Renewable Scholarship for New Mexico high school graduates or GED recipients who plan to attend an eligible New Mexico public college or university. Must be enrolled full-time and maintain 2.5 GPA. *Award:* Scholarship for use in freshman year; renewable. *Number of awards:* 1. *Eligibility Requirements:* Applicant must be high school student; planning to enroll or expecting to enroll full-time at a four-year institution or uni versity; resident of New Mexico and studying in New Mexico. Applicant must have 3.5 GPA or higher. Available to U.S. citizens. *Application Requirements:* Application form, FAFSA. **Deadline:** varies.

Contact Tashina Moore, Director of Financial Aid, New Mexico Commission on Higher Education, 1068 Cerrillos Road, Santa Fe, NM 87505. *E-mail:* tashina.banks-moore@state.nm.us. *Phone:* 505-476-6549. *Fax:* 505-476-6511. *Website:* http://www.hed.state.nm.us/.

**New Mexico Competitive Schol-arship.** Scholarships for non-residents or non-citizens of the United States to encourage out-of-state students who have demonstrated high academic achievement in high school to enroll in public four-year universities in New Mexico. Renewable for up to four years. For details visit http://fin.hed.state.nm.us. *Award:* Scholarship for use in freshman year; renewable. *Eli gibility Requirements:* Applicant must be high school student; planning to enroll or expecting to enroll full-time at a four-year institution or university and studying in New Mexico. Available to Canadian and non-U.S. citizens. *Application Require ments:* Application form, essay, recom mendations or references, test scores. **Deadline:** varies.

Contact Tashina Moore, Director of Financial Aid, New Mexico Commission on Higher Education, 1068 Cerrillos Road, Santa Fe, NM 87505. *E-mail:* tashina.banks-moore@state.nm.us. *Phone:* 505-476-6549. *Fax:* 505-476-6511. *Website:* http://www.hed.state.nm.us/.

**New Mexico Scholars' Program.** Renewable award program created to encourage New Mexico high school stu dents to attend public postsecondary insti tutions or the following private colleges in

New Mexico: College of Santa Fe, St. John's College, College of the Southwest. For details visit http://fin.hed.state.nm.us. *Award:* Scholarship for use in freshman year; renewable. *Number of awards:* 1. *Eligibility Requirements:* Applicant must be high school student; planning to enroll or expecting to enroll full-time at a two-year or four-year institution; resident of New Mexico and studying in New Mexico. Available to U.S. citizens. *Application Requirements:* Application form, FAFSA, financial need analysis, test scores. **Deadline:** varies.

Contact Tashina Moore, Director of Financial Aid, New Mexico Commission on Higher Education, 1068 Cerrillos Road, Santa Fe, NM 87505-1650. *E-mail:* tashina.banks-moore@state.nm.us. *Phone:* 505-476-6549. *Fax:* 505-476-6511. *Website:* http://www.hed.state.nm.us/.

**New Mexico Student Incentive Grant.** Grant created to provide aid for undergraduate students with substantial financial need who are attending public colleges or universities or the following eligible colleges in New Mexico: College of Santa Fe, St. John's College, College of the Southwest, Institute of American Indian Art, Crownpoint Institute of Technology, Dine College and Southwestern Indian Polytechnic Institute. Part-time students are eligible for pro-rated awards. *Award:* Grant for use in freshman, sophomore, junior, or senior years; not renewable. *Award amount:* $200–$2500. *Number of awards:* 1. *Eligibility Requirements:* Applicant must be enrolled or expecting to enroll full- or part-time at a two-year or four-year or technical institution or university; resident of New Mexico and studying in New Mexico. Available to U.S. citizens. *Application Requirements:* Application form, FAFSA, financial need analysis. **Deadline:** varies.

Contact Tashina Moore, Director of Financial Aid, New Mexico Commission on Higher Education, 1068 Cerrillos Road, Santa Fe, NM 87505-1650. *E-mail:* tashina.banks-moore@state.nm.us. *Phone:* 505-476-6549. *Fax:* 505-476-6511. *Website:* http://www.hed.state.nm.us/.

**New Mexico Vietnam Veteran Scholarship.** Award for Vietnam veterans who have been New Mexico residents for a minimum of ten years and are attending state-funded postsecondary schools. Must have been awarded the Vietnam Campaign medal. Must submit DD 214 and discharge papers. *Award:*

Scholarship for use in freshman, sophomore, junior, or senior years; renewable. *Award amount:* $3500–$4000. *Number of awards:* 100. *Eligibility Requirements:* Applicant must be enrolled or expecting to enroll full- or part-time at a two-year or four-year or technical institution or university; resident of New Mexico and studying in New Mexico. Available to U. S. citizens. Applicant or parent must meet one or more of the following requirements: general military experience; retired from active duty; disabled or killed as a result of military service; prisoner of war; or missing in action. *Application Requirements:* Application form, copy of DD Form 214. **Deadline:** continuous.

Contact Mr. Alan Martinez, Deputy Cabinet Secretary, New Mexico Department of Veterans' Services, PO Box 2324, Santa Fe, NM 87504. *E-mail:* alan.martinez@state.nm.us. *Phone:* 505-827-6300. *Fax:* 505-827-6372. *Website:* http://www.dvs.state.nm.us/.

**NM Lottery Success Scholarship.** Scholarship to the residents of New Mexico. Applicant must be graduate from a New Mexico public (or accredited private) high school or receive a GED. Must enroll full-time in a Baccalaureate degree program and meet state determined eligibility requirements. Scholarship begins second semester of enrollment. See scholarship.unm.edu for details. *Award:* Scholarship for use in freshman year; renewable. *Eligibility Requirements:* Applicant must be enrolled or expecting to enroll full-time at a four-year institution or university and resident of New Mexico. Available to U.S. citizens. *Application Requirements:* **Deadline:** varies.

**Vietnam Veterans' Scholarship Program.** Renewable scholarship program created to provide aid for Vietnam veterans who are undergraduate and graduate students attending public postsecondary institutions or select private colleges in New Mexico. Private colleges include: College of Santa Fe, St. John's College and College of the Southwest. *Award:* Scholarship for use in freshman, sophomore, junior, or senior years; renewable. *Number of awards:* 1. *Eligibility Requirements:* Applicant must be enrolled or expecting to enroll full-time at a two-year or four-year institution; resident of New Mexico and studying in New Mexico. Available to U.S. citizens. Applicant or parent must meet one or more of the following requirements: general military experience; retired from active duty; disabled or killed as a result

of military service; prisoner of war; or missing in action. *Application Requirements:* Application form, certification by the NM Veteran's commission. **Deadline:** varies.

Contact Tashina Moore, Director of Financial Aid, New Mexico Commission on Higher Education, 1068 Cerrillos Road, Santa Fe, NM 87505-1650. *E-mail:* tashina.banks-moore@state.nm.us. *Phone:* 505-476-6549. *Fax:* 505-476-6511. *Website:* http://www.hed.state.nm.us/.

# NEW YORK

**Alexander and Maude Hadden Scholarship.** Youth Foundation offers exceptional students with financial need an award of $2500 to $4000 per year which is renewable for four years at the foundation's discretion. Minimum GPA of 3.5 required, community service and extra curricular activities expected. Must write Foundation for information and application request form. *Award:* Scholarship for use in freshman, sophomore, junior, or senior years; renewable. *Award amount:* $2500–$4000. *Number of awards:* 90–108. *Eligibility Requirements:* Applicant must be enrolled or expecting to enroll full-time at a four-year institution or university. Applicant or parent of applicant must have employment or volunteer experience in community service. Applicant must have 3.5 GPA or higher. Available to U.S. citizens. *Application Requirements:* Application form, community service, essay, financial need analysis, recommendations or references, test scores, transcript. **Deadline:** February 29.

Contact Ms. Johanna Lee, Executive Administrator. *E-mail:* YouthFdn@aol.com. *Phone:* 212-840-6291. *Fax:* 212-840-6747. *Website:* http://fdnweb.org/youthfdn.

**DAAD University Summer Course Grant.** Scholarships are awarded to full-time degree students of Canadian or U.S. colleges, sophomore/2nd year and higher, for the pursuit of summer courses at universities in Germany. It is open to applicants of any major but there is a prerequisite of at least two years of college level German or the equivalent German language fluency. Courses are three to four weeks in duration, take place at many locations in Germany (universities), are taught in German, and topics include German language, literature, current affairs, political science, history, culture, arts, film and media, economics, linguistics, law, translation and interpretation, and test prep for German language proficiency examinations. The scholarship is approximately €850 to cover course fees, and room and board in whole or in part, with an additional international travel reimbursement ranging from €300 to €450. Accommodations are arranged by the host institution. Foreign Language. *Award:* Grant for use in sophomore, junior, senior, or graduate years; not renewable. *Eligibility Requirements:* Applicant must be enrolled or expecting to enroll full-time at a four-year institution or university and must have an interest in German language/culture. Available to U.S. and non-U.S. citizens. *Application Requirements:* Application form, essay, recommendations or references, resume, transcript. **Deadline:** December 15.

Contact Katrin Kempiners, Information Officer. *E-mail:* daadny@daad.org. *Phone:* 212-758-3223. *Website:* http://www.daad.org/.

**New York Aid for Part-Time Study (APTS).** Renewable scholarship provides tuition assistance to part-time undergraduate students who are New York residents, meet income eligibility requirements and are attending New York accredited institutions. Deadline varies. Must be U.S. citizen. *Award:* Grant for use in freshman, sophomore, junior, or senior years; renewable. *Award amount:* up to $2000. *Eligibility Requirements:* Applicant must be enrolled or expecting to enroll part-time at a two-year or four-year institution or university; resident of New York and studying in New York. Available to U.S. citizens. *Application Requirements:* Application form, financial need analysis. **Deadline:** varies.

**New York Memorial Scholarships for Families of Deceased Police Officers, Fire Fighters, and Peace Officers.** Renewable scholarship for children, spouses and financial dependents of deceased fire fighters, volunteer firefighters, police officers, peace officers and emergency medical service workers who died in the line of duty. Provides up to the cost of SUNY educational expenses. *Award:* Scholarship for use in freshman, sophomore, junior, or senior years; renewable. *Eligibility Requirements:* Applicant must be enrolled or expecting to enroll full-time at a four-year institution or university; resident of New York and studying in New York. Available to U.S. citizens. *Application Requirements:* Application form,

financial need analysis, transcript. **Deadline:** May 1.

**New York State Aid to Native Americans.** Award for enrolled members of a New York State tribe and their children who are attending or planning to attend a New York State college and who are New York State residents. Deadlines: July 15 for the fall semester, December 31 for the spring semester, and May 20 for summer session. *Award:* Scholarship for use in freshman, sophomore, junior, or senior years; renewable. *Award amount:* $85–$2000. *Eligibility Requirements:* Applicant must be American Indian/Alaska Native; enrolled or expecting to enroll full- or part-time at a two-year or four-year or technical institution or university; resident of New York and studying in New York. Available to U.S. citizens. *Application Requirements:* Application form, financial need analysis, recommendations or references, transcript. **Deadline:** varies.

**New York State Tuition Assistance Program.** Award for New York state residents attending a New York postsecondary institution. Must be full-time student in approved program with tuition over $200 per year. Must show financial need and not be in default in any other state program. Renewable award of $500 to $5000 dependent on family income and tuition charged. *Award:* Grant for use in freshman, sophomore, junior, or senior years; renewable. *Award amount:* $500–$5000. *Number of awards:* 350,000–360,000. *Eligibility Requirements:* Applicant must be enrolled or expecting to enroll full-time at a two-year or four-year institution or university; resident of New York and studying in New York. Available to U.S. citizens. *Application Requirements:* Application form, financial need analysis. **Deadline:** May 1.

**New York Vietnam/Persian Gulf/Afghanistan Veterans Tuition Awards.** Scholarship for veterans who served in Vietnam, the Persian Gulf, or Afghanistan. Must be a New York resident attending a New York institution. Must establish eligibility by September 1. *Award:* Scholarship for use in freshman, sophomore, junior, or senior years; renewable. *Eligibility Requirements:* Applicant must be enrolled or expecting to enroll full- or part-time at a two-year or four-year or technical institution or university; resident of New York and studying in New York. Available to U.S. citizens. Applicant or parent must meet one or more of the following require

ments: general military experience; retired from active duty; disabled or killed as a result of military service; prisoner of war; or missing in action. *Application Requirements:* Application form, financial need analysis. **Deadline:** May 1.

**Regents Award for Child of Veteran.** Award for students whose parent, as a result of service in U.S. Armed Forces during war or national emergency, died; suffered a 40 percent or more disability; or is classified as missing in action or a prisoner of war. Veteran must be current New York State resident or have been so at time of death. Student must be a New York resident, attending, or planning to attend, college in New York State. Must establish eligibility before applying for payment. *Award:* Scholarship for use in freshman, sophomore, junior, or senior years; not renewable. *Award amount:* up to $450. *Eligibility Requirements:* Applicant must be enrolled or expecting to enroll full-time at a two-year or four-year institution or university; resident of New York and studying in New York. Available to U.S. citizens. Applicant or parent must meet one or more of the following requirements: general military experience; retired from active duty; disabled or killed as a result of military service; prisoner of war; or missing in action. *Application Requirements:* Application form, proof of eligibility. **Deadline:** May 1.

Contact Rita McGivern, Student Information, New York State Higher Education Services Corporation, 99 Washington Avenue, Room 1320, Albany, NY 12255. *E-mail:* rmcgivern@hesc.com. *Website:* http://www.hesc.com/.

**Scholarship for Academic Excellence.** Renewable award for New York residents. Scholarship winners must attend a college or university in New York. 2000 scholarships are for $1500 and 6000 are for $500. The selection criteria used are based on Regents test scores or rank in class or local exam. Must be U.S. citizen or permanent resident. *Award:* Scholarship for use in freshman year; renewable. *Award amount:* $500–$1500. *Number of awards:* up to 8000. *Eligibility Requirements:* Applicant must be high school student; planning to enroll or expecting to enroll full-time at a two-year or four-year institution or university; resident of New York and studying in New York. Available to U.S. citizens. *Application Requirements:* Application form. **Deadline:** December 19.

Contact Lewis Hall, Supervisor. *E-mail:* scholar@mail.nysed.gov. *Phone:*

518-486-1319. *Fax:* 518-486-5346. *Website:* http://www.highered.nysed.gov/.

**Scholarships for Academic Excellence.** Renewable awards of up to $1500 for academically outstanding New York State high school graduates planning to attend an approved postsecondary institution in New York State. For full-time study only. Contact high school guidance counselor to apply. *Award:* Scholarship for use in freshman, sophomore, junior, or senior years; renewable. *Award amount:* $500–$1500. *Number of awards:* up to 8000. *Eligibility Requirements:* Applicant must be high school student; planning to enroll or expecting to enroll full-time at a four-year institution or university; resident of New York and studying in New York. Available to U.S. citizens. *Application Requirements:* Application form. **Deadline:** varies.

Contact Rita McGivern, Student Information, New York State Higher Education Services Corporation, 99 Washington Avenue, Room 1320, Albany, NY 12255. *E-mail:* scholarship@hesc.com. *Website:* http://www.hesc.com/.

**World Trade Center Memorial Scholarship.** Renewable awards of up to the cost of educational expenses at a State University of New York four-year college. Available to the children, spouses and financial dependents of victims who died or were severely disabled as a result of the September 11, 2001 terrorist attacks on the U.S. and the rescue and recovery efforts. *Award:* Scholarship for use in freshman, sophomore, junior, or senior years; renewable. *Eligibility Requirements:* Applicant must be enrolled or expecting to enroll full-time at a four-year institution or university and studying in New York. Available to U.S. and non-U.S. citizens. *Application Requirements:* Application form, financial need analysis, recommendations or references, transcript. **Deadline:** May 1.

# NORTH CAROLINA

**North Carolina Community College Grant Program.** Grants are available to North Carolina residents who demonstrate financial need and are enrolled at NC community colleges. The applicant must:

Contact Trae Brookins, Scholarship and Grant Manager, North Carolina State Education Assistance Authority, PO Box 13663, Research Triangle Park, NC 27709-3663. *E-mail:* tbrookins@ncseaa.edu. *Phone:* 919-248-4650. *Fax:* 919-248-6650. *Website:* http://www.ncseaa.edu/.

**North Carolina Division of Services for the Blind Rehabilitation Services.** Financial assistance is available for North Carolina residents who are blind or visually impaired and who require vocational rehabilitation to help find employment. Tuition and other assistance provided based on need. Open to U.S. citizens and legal residents of United States. Applicants goal must be to work after receiving vocational services. To apply, contact the local DSB office and apply for vocational rehabilitation services. *Award:* Scholarship for use in freshman, sophomore, junior, or senior years; renewable. *Eligibility Requirements:* Applicant must be visually impaired; enrolled or expecting to enroll full-time at a two-year or four-year or technical institution or university and resident of North Carolina. Applicant must be visually impaired. Available to U.S. citizens. *Application Requirements:* Application form, financial need analysis, interview, proof of eligibility. **Deadline:** continuous.

Contact JoAnn Strader, Chief of Rehabilitation Field Services, North Carolina Division of Services for the Blind, 2601 Mail Service Center, Raleigh, NC 27699-2601. *E-mail:* joann.strader@ncmail.net. *Phone:* 919-733-9700. *Fax:* 919-715-8771. *Website:* http://www.ncdhhs.gov/.

**North Carolina National Guard Tuition Assistance Program.** Scholarship for members of the North Carolina Air and Army National Guard who will remain in the service for two years following the period for which assistance is provided. Must reapply for each academic period. For use at approved North Carolina institutions. *Award:* Grant for use in freshman, sophomore, junior, senior, or graduate years; not renewable. *Award amount:* up to $2000. *Eligibility Requirements:* Applicant must be enrolled or expecting to enroll full- or part-time at a two-year or four-year or technical institution or university; resident of North Carolina and studying in North Carolina. Available to U.S. citizens. Applicant or parent must meet one or more of the following requirements: national guard experience; retired from active duty; disabled or killed as a result of military service; prisoner of war; or missing in action. *Application Requirements:* Application form. **Deadline:** varies.

Contact Anne Gildhouse, Education Services Officer. *E-mail:* anne.gildhouse@nc.ngb.army.mil. *Phone:* 919-

664-6000. *Fax:* 919-664-6520. *Website:* http://www.nc.ngb.army.mil/.

**North Carolina Sheriffs' Association Undergraduate Criminal Justice Scholarships.** One-time award for full-time North Carolina resident undergraduate students majoring in criminal justice at a University of North Carolina school. Priority given to child of any North Carolina law enforcement officer. Letter of recommendation from county sheriff required. Criminal Justice/Criminology; Law Enforcement/Police Administration. *Award:* Scholarship for use in freshman, sophomore, junior, or senior years; not renewable. *Award amount:* $1000–$2000. *Number of awards:* up to 10. *Eligibility Requirements:* Applicant must be enrolled or expecting to enroll full-time at a four-year institution or university; resident of North Carolina and studying in North Carolina. Applicant or parent of applicant must have employment or volunteer experience in police/firefighting. Available to U.S. citizens. *Application Requirements:* Application form, financial need analysis, recommendations or references, statement of career goals, transcript. **Deadline:** continuous.

Contact Nolita Goldston, Assistant, Scholarship and Grant Division, North Carolina State Education Assistance Authority, PO Box 13663, Research Triangle Park, NC 27709. *E-mail:* ngoldston@ncseaa.edu. *Phone:* 919-549-8614. *Fax:* 919-248-4687. *Website:* http://www.ncseaa.edu/.

**North Carolina Veterans Scholarships Class I-A.** Scholarships for children of certain deceased, disabled or POW/MIA veterans. Award value is $4500 per nine-month academic year in private colleges and junior colleges. No limit on number awarded each year. *Award:* Scholarship for use in freshman, sophomore, junior, or senior years; renewable. *Award amount:* $4500. *Eligibility Requirements:* Applicant must be enrolled or expecting to enroll full-time at a two-year or four-year or technical institution or university; resident of North Carolina and studying in North Carolina. Available to U.S. citizens. Applicant or parent must meet one or more of the following requirements: general military experience; retired from active duty; disabled or killed as a result of military service; prisoner of war; or missing in action. *Application Requirements:* Application form, financial need analysis, interview, transcript. **Deadline:** continuous.

Contact Charles Smith, Assistant Secretary. *E-mail:* charlie.smith@ncmail. net. *Phone:* 919-733-3851. *Fax:* 919-733-2834. *Website:* http://www.doa.state.nc. us/vets/va.htm.

**North Carolina Veterans Scholarships Class I-B.** Awards for children of veterans rated by USDVA as 100 percent disabled due to wartime service as defined in the law, and currently or at time of death drawing compensation for such dis ability. Parent must have been a North Carolina resident at time of entry into service. Duration of the scholarship is four academic years (8 semesters) if used within 8 years. No limit on number awarded each year. *Award:* Scholarship for use in freshman, sophomore, junior, or senior years; renewable. *Award amount:* $1500. *Eligibility Requirements:* Applicant must be enrolled or expecting to enroll full- or part-time at a two-year or four-year or technical institution or uni versity; resident of North Carolina and studying in North Carolina. Available to U.S. citizens. Applicant or parent must meet one or more of the following requirements: general military expe rience; retired from active duty; disabled or killed as a result of military service; prisoner of war; or missing in action. *Application Requirements:* Application form, financial need analysis, interview, transcript. **Deadline:** continuous.

Contact Charles Smith, Assistant Secretary. *E-mail:* charlie.smith@ncmail. net. *Phone:* 919-733-3851. *Fax:* 919-733-2834. *Website:* http://www.doa.state.nc. us/vets/va.htm.

**North Carolina Veterans Scholarships Class II.** Awards for children of veterans rated by USDVA as much as 20 percent but less than 100 percent disabled due to wartime service as defined in the law, or awarded Purple Heart Medal for wounds received. Parent must have been a North Carolina resident at time of entry into service. Duration of the scholarship is four academic years (8 semesters) if used within 8 years. Free tuition and exemption from certain mandatory fees as set forth in the law in Public, Community and Tech nical Colleges. *Award:* Scholarship for use in freshman, sophomore, junior, or senior years; renewable. *Award amount:* $4500. *Number of awards:* up to 100. *Eli gibility Requirements:* Applicant must be enrolled or expecting to enroll full- or part-time at a two-year or four-year or technical institution or university; resident of North Carolina and studying in North Carolina. Available to U.S. citizens. Applicant or parent must meet one or more of the following requirements:

general military experience; retired from active duty; disabled or killed as a result of military service; prisoner of war; or missing in action. *Application Require ments:* Application form, financial need analysis, interview, transcript. **Deadline:** March 1.

Contact Charles Smith, Assistant Secretary. *E-mail:* charlie.smith@ncmail. net. *Phone:* 919-733-3851. *Fax:* 919-733-2834. *Website:* http://www.doa.state.nc. us/vets/va.htm.

**North Carolina Veterans Scholarships Class III.** Awards for children of a deceased war veteran, who was honorably discharged and who does not qualify under any other provision within this syn opsis or veteran who served in a combat zone or waters adjacent to a combat zone and received a campaign badge or medal and who does not qualify under any other provision within this synopsis. Duration of the scholarship is four academic years (8 semesters) if used within 8 years. *Award:* Scholarship for use in freshman, sophomore, junior, or senior years; renewable. *Award amount:* $4500. *Number of awards:* up to 100. *Eligibility Requirements:* Applicant must be enrolled or expecting to enroll full- or part-time at a two-year or four-year or technical insti tution or university; resident of North Carolina and studying in North Carolina. Available to U.S. citizens. Applicant or parent must meet one or more of the fol lowing requirements: general military experience; retired from active duty; dis abled or killed as a result of military service; prisoner of war; or missing in action. *Application Requirements:* Appli cation form, financial need analysis, interview, transcript. **Deadline:** March 1.

Contact Charles Smith, Assistant Secretary. *E-mail:* charlie.smith@ncmail. net. *Phone:* 919-733-3851. *Fax:* 919-733-2834. *Website:* http://www.doa.state.nc. us/vets/va.htm.

**North Carolina Veterans Scholarships Class IV.** Awards for children of veterans, who were prisoner of war or missing in action. Duration of the schol arship is four academic years (8 semesters) if used within 8 years. No limit on number awarded each year. Award value is $4500 per nine-month academic year in private colleges and junior col leges. *Award:* Scholarship for use in freshman, sophomore, junior, or senior years; renewable. *Award amount:* $4500. *Eligibility Requirements:* Applicant must be enrolled or expecting to enroll full- or part-time at a two-year or four-year or technical institution or university; resident of North Carolina and studying in North

Carolina. Available to U.S. citizens. Applicant or parent must meet one or more of the following requirements: general military experience; retired from active duty; disabled or killed as a result of military service; prisoner of war; or missing in action. *Application Require ments:* Application form, financial need analysis, interview, transcript. **Deadline:** continuous.

Contact Charles Smith, Assistant Secretary. *E-mail:* charlie.smith@ncmail. net. *Phone:* 919-733-3851. *Fax:* 919-733-2834. *Website:* http://www.doa.state.nc. us/vets/va.htm.

**Training Support for Youth with Disabilities.** Public service program that helps persons with disabilities obtain competitive employment. To qualify: student must have a mental, physical or learning disability that is an impediment to employment. A Rehabilitation Coun selor along with the eligible student indi vidually develops a rehabilitation program to achieve an employment outcome which requires post secondary training. Financial assistance is based on NC Division of Vocational Rehabilitation demonstrated financial need and type of program in which the student enrolls. *Award:* Grant for use in freshman, soph omore, junior, or senior years; renewable. *Eligibility Requirements:* Applicant must be hearing impaired, learning disabled, physically disabled, or visually impaired; enrolled or expecting to enroll full- or part-time at a two-year or four-year or technical institution or university and res ident of North Carolina. Applicant must be hearing impaired, learning disabled, physically disabled, or visually impaired. Available to U.S. citizens. *Application Requirements:* Application form, financial need analysis, interview, medical and psychological records, must be under an Individualized Plan for Employment, test scores, transcript. **Deadline:** continuous.

Contact Stephanie Hanes, Program Specialist for Transition. *E-mail:* stephanie.hanes@dhhs.nc.gov. *Phone:* 919-855-3576. *Website:* http://www.dhhs. state.nc.us/.

**University of North Carolina Need-Based Grant.** Applicants must be enrolled in at least 6 credit hours at one of sixteen UNC system universities. Eligi bility based on need; award varies, con sideration for grant automatic when FAFSA is filed. Late applications may be denied due to insufficient funds. *Award:* Grant for use in freshman, sophomore, junior, or senior years; renewable. *Eligi bility Requirements:* Applicant must be enrolled or expecting to enroll full- or part-time at an institution or university; resident of North Carolina and studying in North Carolina. Available to U.S. citizens. *Application Requirements:* Application form, FAFSA, financial need analysis. **Deadline:** varies.

Contact Bill Carswell, Manager of Scholarship and Grant Division, North Carolina State Education Assistance Authority, PO Box 13663, Research Triangle Park, NC 27709. *E-mail:* carswellb@ncseaa.edu. *Phone:* 919-549-8614. *Fax:* 919-248-4687. *Website:* http://www.ncseaa.edu/.

## NORTH DAKOTA

**North Dakota Academic Scholarship.** This scholarship rewards high schools students from ND for taking rigorous coursework in high school. Applicants must earn a cumulative high school GPA of 3.0 and have a minimum ACT score of 24. Full-time enrollment is defined as 12 credits per semester in year 1, and 15 credits in subsequent years. Full-time enrollment must be maintained to qualify. A minimum cumulative college GPA of 2.75 is required to renew the scholarship. This scholarship is based on merit. Awards are $750/sem. or $600/qtr. up to a total of $6,000. Students have up to 6 years following high school to utilize the scholarship. *Award:* Scholarship for use in freshman, sophomore, junior, or senior years; renewable. *Award amount:* $6000. *Number of awards:* up to 10,000. *Eligibility Requirements:* Applicant must be high school student; planning to enroll or expecting to enroll full-time at a two-year or four-year institution or university; resident of North Dakota and studying in North Dakota. Applicant must have 3.0 GPA or higher. Available to U.S. citizens. *Application Requirements:* Application form, application form may be submitted online (http://www.dpi.state.nd.us), test scores, transcript. **Deadline:** June 1.

Contact Brenda Zastoupil, Director of Financial Aid, North Dakota University System, 1815 Schafer Street, Suite 202, Bismarck, ND 58501. *E-mail:* ndfinaid@ndus.edu. *Phone:* 701-224-2541. *Fax:* 701-224-5707. *Website:* http://www.ndus.edu/.

**North Dakota Career and Technical Education Scholarship.** The ND Career and Technical Education Scholarship's goal is to reward students taking rigorous courses in high school, to increase awareness of career and technical programs, and to retain students within ND. The scholarship has an ACT or WorkKeys exam score requirement, a GPA requirement, and a specific high school course list that must be completed to qualify. Full-time enrollment is defined as 12 credits per semester in year 1, and 15 credits in subsequent years. Full-time enrollment must be maintained to qualify. A minimum cumulative college GPA of 2.75 is required to renew the scholarship. This scholarship is based on merit. Awards are $750/sem. or $600/qtr. up to a total of $6,000. Students have up to 6 years following high school to utilize the scholarship. *Award:* Scholarship for use in freshman, sophomore, junior, or senior years; renewable. *Award amount:* $6000. *Number of awards:* up to 10,000. *Eligibility Requirements:* Applicant must be high school student; planning to enroll or expecting to enroll full-time at a two-year or four-year institution or university; resident of North Dakota and studying in North Dakota. Applicant must have 3.0 GPA or higher. Available to U.S. citizens. *Application Requirements:* Application form, application form may be submitted online (http://www.dpi.state.nd.us), test scores, transcript. **Deadline:** June 1.

Contact Brenda Zastoupil, Director of Financial Aid, North Dakota University System, 1815 Schafer Street, Suite 202, Bismarck, ND 58501. *E-mail:* ndfinaid@ndus.edu. *Phone:* 701-224-2541. *Fax:* 701-224-5707. *Website:* http://www.ndus.edu/.

**North Dakota Indian Scholarship Program.** The North Dakota Indian Scholarship program was established to provide scholarship awards to Native American students attending qualifying colleges or universities within North Dakota. Students must be ND residents as defined by the college, enrolled full-time (limited exceptions), and maintain a GPA of at least 2.0. Awards are available to both undergraduate and graduate students. Students who maintain a 3.50 GPA qualify for the scholarship based on merit. Students who have a GPA lower than 3.50 must show unmet need. The minimum required GPA is 2.0. The priority application date is July 15. Not all eligible applicants are awarded due to limited appropriations. *Award:* Scholarship for use in freshman, sophomore, junior, senior, graduate, or postgraduate years; not renewable. *Award amount:* $1200–$1800. *Number of awards:* 230–270. *Eligibility Requirements:* Applicant must be American Indian/Alaska Native; enrolled or expecting to enroll full-time at a two-year or four-year or technical institution or university; resident of North Dakota and studying in North Dakota. Available to U.S. citizens. *Application Requirements:* Application form, financial need analysis, proof of tribal enrollment, transcript. **Deadline:** July 15.

Contact Brenda Zastoupil, Director of Financial Aid, North Dakota University System, 1815 Schafer Street, Suite 202, Bismarck, ND 58501. *E-mail:* ndfinaid@ndus.edu. *Phone:* 701-224-2541. *Fax:* 701-224-5707. *Website:* http://www.ndus.edu/.

**North Dakota Scholars Program.** The purpose of the ND Scholars Scholarship is to retain within ND, the brightest and best students who are pursuing post-secondary education. The scholarship amount equates to the tuition charged at the Scholar's eligible institution, not to exceed the highest regular resident undergraduate tuition rate in the NDUS system. This program provides merit-based, full-tuition scholarships to ND high school graduates who attend a qualifying college within ND. High school juniors who score in the top 95th percentile of all ND ACT test-takers prior to July 1 of the year preceding their freshman year of college will be considered as a candidate for this award. Not all eligible students will qualify due to limited appropriations. Students are ranked based on ACT test scores. This scholarship is renewable for up to three years. Recipients must be enrolled at qualifying institutions in ND at full-time status (12 cr. minimum per semester) and must maintain a cumulative GPA of 3.50. Only 40-50 new awards are made each year to new students. In addition to eligible students receiving a regular full tuition scholarship, freshmen also receive a one-time stipend of $2000. *Award:* Scholarship for use in freshman, sophomore, junior, or senior years; renewable. *Award amount:* $4637–$8336. *Number of awards:* 40–50. *Eligibility Requirements:* Applicant must be high school student; planning to enroll or expecting to enroll full-time at a two-year or four year institution or university; resident of North Dakota and studying in North Dakota. Available to U.S. citizens. *Application Requirements:* ACT , test scores.

Contact Brenda Zastoupil, Director of Financial Aid, North Dakota University System, 1815 Schafer Street, Suite 202, Bismarck, ND 58501. *E-mail:* ndfinaid@ndus.edu. *Phone:* 701-224-2541. *Fax:* 701-224-5707. *Website:* http://www.ndus.edu/.

**North Dakota State Student Incentive Grant Program.** The North Dakota State Grant is the premier need-based state grant in North Dakota. The North Dakota State Grant supports ND residents attending an eligible college or university within North Dakota in a program of study that is at least one year in length. The FAFSA is required annually with an April 15th deadline. Awards are available for up to 8 full-time equivalent semesters or 12 full-time equivalent quarters of undergraduate study. Students must meet the SAP guide lines of their institution and meet all title IV eligibility criteria, including having verification complete, if required. *Award:* Grant for use in freshman, sophomore, junior, or senior years; not renewable. *Award amount:* $412–$1648. *Number of awards:* 7000–7500. *Eligibility Require ments:* Applicant must be enrolled or expecting to enroll full- or part-time at a two-year or four-year institution or uni versity; resident of North Dakota and studying in North Dakota. Available to U. S. citizens. *Application Requirements:* Application form may be submitted online (http://fafsa.gov), FAFSA. **Deadline:** April 15.

Contact Brenda Zastoupil, Director of Financial Aid, North Dakota University System, 1815 Schafer Street, Suite 202, Bismarck, ND 58501. *E-mail:* ndfinaid@ ndus.edu. *Phone:* 701-224-2541. *Fax:* 701-224-5707. *Website:* http://www.ndus. edu/.

# OHIO

**Ohio College Opportunity Grant.** OCOG provides grant money to Ohio res idents who demonstrate the highest levels of financial need (as determined by the results of the FAFSA) who are enrolled at Ohio public university main campuses (not regional campuses or community col leges), Ohio private, non-profit colleges or universities, Ohio private, for-profit institutions or eligible Pennsylvania insti tutions. *Award:* Grant for use in freshman, sophomore, junior, or senior years; not renewable. *Award amount:* up to $2568. *Eligibility Requirements:* Applicant must be enrolled or expecting to enroll full- or part-time at a four-year institution or uni versity; resident of Ohio and studying in Ohio, Pennsylvania. Available to U.S. cit izens. *Application Requirements:* Appli cation form may be submitted online(https://fafsa.ed.gov/), FAFSA. **Deadline:** October 1.

Contact Tamika Braswell, Program Manager, Ohio Board of Regents, Ohio Board of Regents, 25 South Front Street,

Columbus, OH 43215. *E-mail:* ocog_ admin@regents.state.oh.us. *Phone:* 614-728-8862. *Fax:* 614-752-5903. *Website:* http://www.ohiohighered.org.

**Ohio Environmental Science & Engineering Scholarships.** Merit-based, non-renewable, tuition-only schol arships awarded to undergraduate stu dents admitted to Ohio state or private colleges and universities. Must be able to demonstrate knowledge of, and com mitment to, careers in environmental sci ences or environmental engineering. Environmental Science. *Award:* Schol arship for use in senior year; not renewable. *Award amount:* $1250–$2500. *Number of awards:* 18. *Eligibility Requirements:* Applicant must be enrolled or expecting to enroll full- or part-time at a two-year or four-year institution or uni versity and studying in Ohio. Applicant must have 3.0 GPA or higher. Available to U.S. citizens. *Application Requirements:* Application form, application form may be submitted online(https://mc04.manu scriptcentral.com/oas), community service, essay, recommendations or refer ences, resume, self-addressed stamped envelope with application, transcript. **Deadline:** April 15.

Contact Dr. Stephen McConoughey, Chief Executive Officer, Ohio Academy of Science/Ohio Environmental Education Fund, 1500 West Third Avenue, Suite 228, Columbus, OH 43212-2817. *E-mail:* smcconoughey@ohiosci. org. *Phone:* 614-488-2228. *Fax:* 614-488-7629. *Website:* http://www.ohiosci.org/.

**Ohio National Guard Scholarship Program.** Scholarships are for under graduate studies at an approved Ohio post-secondary institution. Applicants must enlist for six or three years of Selective Service Reserve Duty in the Ohio National Guard. Scholarship pays 100% instructional and general fees for public institutions and an average of cost of public universities is available for private schools. May reapply up to four years of studies (12 quarters or 8 semesters) for six year enlistment and two years of studies (6 quarters or 4 semesters) for three year enlistment. Deadlines: July 1 (fall), November 1 (winter quarter/spring semester), February 1 (spring quarter), April 1 (summer). *Award:* Scholarship for use in freshman, sophomore, junior, or senior years; not renewable. *Award amount:* up to $4006. *Number of awards:* up to 3500. *Eligibility Requirements:* Applicant must be enrolled or expecting to enroll full- or part-time at a two-year or four-year or technical insti tution or university; resident of Ohio and

studying in Ohio. Available to U.S. cit izens. Applicant must have national guard experience. *Application Requirements:* Application form. **Deadline:** varies.

Contact Mrs. Toni Davis, Grants Administrator, Ohio National Guard, 2825 West Dublin Granville Road, ONGSP, Columbus, OH 43235-2789. *E-mail:* toni.davis7@us.army.mil. *Phone:* 614-336-7143. *Fax:* 614-336-7318. *Website:* http://www.ongsp.org/.

**Ohio Safety Officers College Memorial Fund.** Renewable award cov ering up to full tuition is available to children and surviving spouses of peace officers, other safety officers and fire fighters killed in the line of duty in any state. Children must be under 26 years of age. Dollar value of each award varies. Must be an Ohio resident and enroll full-time or part-time at an Ohio college or university. Any spouse/child of a member of the armed services of the U.S., who has been killed in the line duty during Oper ation Enduring Freedom, Operation Iraqi Freedom or a combat zone designated by the President of the United States. Dollar value of each award varies. *Award:* Schol arship for use in freshman, sophomore, junior, or senior years; renewable. *Eligi bility Requirements:* Applicant must be enrolled or expecting to enroll full- or part-time at a two-year or four-year insti tution or university; resident of Ohio and studying in Ohio. Available to U.S. cit izens. *Application Requirements:* **Deadline:** continuous.

Contact Amber Brady, Program Manager, Ohio Board of Regents, 25 South Front Street, Columbus, OH 43215. *E-mail:* osom_admin@regents.state.oh. us. *Phone:* 614-752-9528. *Fax:* 614-752-5903. *Website:* http://www.ohiohighered. org.

**Ohio War Orphans Scholarship.** Aids Ohio residents attending an eligible college in Ohio. Must be between the ages of 16 and 25, the child of a disabled or deceased veteran, and enrolled full-time. Renewable up to five years. Amount of award varies. Must include Form DD214. *Award:* Scholarship for use in freshman, sophomore, junior, or senior years; renewable. *Eligibility Requirements:* Applicant must be age 16-25; enrolled or expecting to enroll full-time at a two-year or four-year institution or university; res ident of Ohio and studying in Ohio. Available to U.S. citizens. Applicant or parent must meet one or more of the fol lowing requirements: general military experience; retired from active duty; dis abled or killed as a result of military service; prisoner of war; or missing in action. *Application Requirements:* Application form, Form DD214. **Deadline:** July 1.

Contact Amber Brady, Program Manager, Ohio Board of Regents, Ohio Board of Regents, 25 South Front Street, Columbus, OH 43215. *E-mail:* wo_admin@regents.state.oh.us. *Phone:* 614-752-9528. *Fax:* 614-752-5903. *Website:* http://www.ohiohighered.org.

## OKLAHOMA

**Academic Scholars Program.** Awards for students of high academic ability to attend institutions in Oklahoma. Renewable up to four years. ACT or SAT scores must fall between 99.5 and 100th percentiles, or applicant must be designated as a National Merit scholar or finalist. Oklahoma public institutions can also select institutional nominees. *Award:* Scholarship for use in freshman, sophomore, junior, senior, or graduate years; renewable. *Award amount:* $1800–$5500. *Eligibility Requirements:* Applicant must be high school student; planning to enroll or expecting to enroll full-time at a two-year or four-year institution or university and studying in Oklahoma. Available to U.S. citizens. *Application Requirements:* Application form, test scores, transcript. **Deadline:** continuous.

**Future Teacher Scholarship-Oklahoma.** Open to outstanding Oklahoma high school graduates who agree to teach in shortage areas. Must rank in top 15 percent of graduating class or score above 85th percentile on ACT or similar test, or be accepted in an educational program. Students nominated by institution. Reapply to renew. Must attend college/university in Oklahoma. Education. *Award:* Scholarship for use in freshman, sophomore, junior, senior, or graduate years; not renewable. *Award amount:* $500–$1500. *Eligibility Requirements:* Applicant must be enrolled or expecting to enroll full- or part-time at a two-year or four-year institution or university; resident of Oklahoma and studying in Oklahoma. Available to U.S. citizens. *Application Requirements:* Application form, essay, test scores, transcript. **Deadline:** varies.

**Oklahoma Tuition Aid Grant.** Award for Oklahoma residents enrolled at an Oklahoma institution at least part-time each semester in a degree program. May be enrolled in two- or four-year or approved vocational-technical institution. Award for students attending public institutions or private colleges. Application is made through FAFSA. *Award:* Grant for use in freshman, sophomore, junior, or senior years; not renewable. *Award amount:* $1000–$1300. *Eligibility Requirements:* Applicant must be enrolled or expecting to enroll full- or part-time at a two-year or four-year or technical institution or university; resident of Oklahoma and studying in Oklahoma. Available to U.S. citizens. *Application Requirements:* Application form, FAFSA, financial need analysis. **Deadline:** varies.

Contact Mrs. Linette McMurtrey, Scholarship Programs Coordinator. *E-mail:* lmcmurtrey@osrhe.edu. *Phone:* 405-225-9131. *Website:* http://www.okhighered.org/.

**Regional University Baccalaureate Scholarship.** Renewable award for Oklahoma residents attending one of 11 participating Oklahoma public universities. Must have an ACT composite score of at least 30 or be a National Merit semifinalist or commended student. In addition to the award amount, each recipient will receive a resident tuition waiver from the institution. Must maintain a 3.25 GPA. Deadlines vary depending upon the institution attended. *Award:* Scholarship for use in freshman, sophomore, junior, or senior years; renewable. *Award amount:* $3000. *Eligibility Requirements:* Applicant must be enrolled or expecting to enroll full-time at an institution or university; resident of Oklahoma and studying in Oklahoma. Available to U.S. citizens. *Application Requirements:* Application form. **Deadline:** varies.

## OREGON

**American Legion Auxiliary Department of Oregon Department Grants.** One-time award for educational use in the state of Oregon. Must be a resident of Oregon who is the child or widow of a veteran or the wife of a disabled veteran. *Award:* Grant for use in freshman, sophomore, junior, or senior years; not renewable. *Award amount:* $1000. *Number of awards:* 2. *Eligibility Requirements:* Applicant must be enrolled or expecting to enroll full- or part-time at a two-year or four-year or technical institution or university and resident of Oregon. Available to U.S. citizens. Applicant or parent must meet one or more of the following requirements: general military experience; retired from active duty; disabled or killed as a result of military service; prisoner of war; or missing in action. *Application Require-*

*ments:* Application form, essay, financial need analysis, interview, recommendations or references, test scores, transcript. **Deadline:** March 10.

Contact Virginia Biddle, Secretary/Treasurer, American Legion Auxiliary Department of Oregon, PO Box 1730, Wilsonville, OR 97070. *E-mail:* alaor@pcez.com. *Phone:* 503-682-3162. *Fax:* 503-685-5008. *Website:* http://www.alaoregon.org/.

**American Legion Auxiliary Department of Oregon Nurses Scholarship.** One-time award for Oregon residents who are in their senior year of high school, who are the children of veterans who served during eligibility dates for American Legion membership. Must enroll in a nursing program. Contact local units for application. Nursing. *Award:* Scholarship for use in freshman year; not renewable. *Award amount:* $1500. *Number of awards:* 1. *Eligibility Requirements:* Applicant must be high school student; planning to enroll or expecting to enroll full- or part-time at a four-year institution or university and resident of Oregon. Available to U.S. citizens. Applicant or parent must meet one or more of the following requirements: general military experience; retired from active duty; disabled or killed as a result of military service; prisoner of war; or missing in action. *Application Requirements:* Application form, essay, financial need analysis, interview, transcript. **Deadline:** May 15.

Contact Virginia Biddle, Secretary/Treasurer, American Legion Auxiliary Department of Oregon, PO Box 1730, Wilsonville, OR 97070. *E-mail:* alaor@pcez.com. *Phone:* 503-682-3162. *Fax:* 503-685-5008. *Website:* http://www.alaoregon.org/.

**Better A Life Scholarship.** Scholarship award available to single parents age 17-25. High schools seniors must have at least 3.0 GPA and college students must have at least a 2.5 GPA. For use at Oregon public and nonprofit colleges and universities. Applicants may not already possess a Bachelor's degree. May reapply for one additional year of funding. FAFSA is required. *Award:* Scholarship for use in freshman, sophomore, junior, or senior years; not renewable. *Eligibility Requirements:* Applicant must be age 17-25; enrolled or expecting to enroll full- or part-time at a two-year or four-year institution or university; single and studying in Oregon. Available to U.S. citizens. *Application Requirements:* Application form, FAFSA, transcript. **Deadline:** March 1.

**Dorothy Campbell Memorial Scholarship.** Renewable award for female Oregon high school graduates with a minimum 2.75 GPA. Must submit essay describing strong, continuing interest in golf and the contribution that sport has made to applicant's development. Must have played on high school golf team (including intramural), if available, and planning to enroll or already enrolled at a four-year Oregon public or nonprofit college. FAFSA required. *Award:* Scholarship for use in freshman, sophomore, junior, or senior years; renewable. *Eligibility Requirements:* Applicant must be enrolled or expecting to enroll full-time at a four-year institution; female; resident of Oregon; studying in Oregon and must have an interest in golf. Available to U.S. citizens. *Application Requirements:* Application form, essay, FAFSA, financial need analysis, transcript. **Deadline:** March 1.

**Glenn Jackson Scholars Scholarships.** Renewable award for Oregon graduating high school seniors who are dependents of employees or retirees of Oregon Department of Transportation or Parks and Recreation Department. Employees must have worked in their department at least three years as of the March 1 scholarship deadline. FAFSA required. Scholarship is automatically renewable if renewal criteria met. *Award:* Scholarship for use in freshman, sophomore, junior, or senior years; renewable. *Eligibility Requirements:* Applicant must be high school student; planning to enroll or expecting to enroll full- or part-time at a two-year or four-year institution or university and resident of Oregon. Applicant or parent of applicant must be affiliated with Oregon Department of Transportation Parks and Recreation. Available to U.S. citizens. *Application Requirements:* Activity chart, FAFSA, application form, essay, financial need analysis, recommendations or references, transcript. **Deadline:** March 1.

**Laurence R. Foster Memorial Scholarship.** One-time award to students enrolled or planning to enroll in a public health degree program. First preference given to those working in the public health field and those pursuing a graduate degree in public health. Undergraduates entering junior or senior year health programs may apply if seeking a public health career, and not private practice. Applicants from diverse environments preferred. Additional essays required. Public Health. *Award:* Scholarship for use in junior, senior, or graduate years; not renewable. *Eligibility Requirements:*

Applicant must be enrolled or expecting to enroll full- or part-time at a four-year institution. Available to U.S. citizens. *Application Requirements:* Activity chart, FAFSA, application form, essay, financial need analysis, recommendations or references, transcript. **Deadline:** March 1.

**Oregon Scholarship Fund Community College Student Award.** Scholarship open to students enrolled or planning to enroll at least half time in Oregon community college programs. Recipients may reapply for one additional year. FAFSA is required. *Award:* Scholarship for use in freshman or sophomore years; not renewable. *Eligibility Requirements:* Applicant must be enrolled or expecting to enroll full- or part-time at a two-year institution and studying in Oregon. Available to U.S. citizens. *Application Requirements:* Activity chart, FAFSA, application form, essay, financial need analysis, transcript. **Deadline:** March 1.

**Oregon Scholarship Fund Transfer Student Award.** Award open to Oregon residents who are currently enrolled in their second year at an Oregon community college and are planning to transfer to a four-year college in Oregon. Prior recipients may apply for one additional year. Must enroll at least half-time. FAFSA is required. *Award:* Scholarship for use in junior or senior years; not renewable. *Eligibility Requirements:* Applicant must be enrolled or expecting to enroll full- or part-time at a four-year institution or university; resident of Oregon and studying in Oregon. Available to U.S. citizens. *Application Requirements:* Activity chart, FAFSA, application form, essay, financial need analysis, transcript. **Deadline:** March 1.

**Oregon Trucking Association Safety Management Council Scholarship.** One-time award available to a child of an Oregon Trucking Association member, or child of an employee of OTA member. Applicants must be graduating high school seniors from an Oregon high school planning to attend a public or non profit college or university. Oregon residency is not required. *Award:* Scholarship for use in freshman year; not renewable. *Eligibility Requirements:* Applicant must be high school student and planning to enroll or expecting to enroll full-time at a four-year institution. Applicant or parent of applicant must be affiliated with Oregon Trucking Association. Available to U.S. citizens. *Application Requirements:* Activity chart, application form, essay, financial need analysis, recommen

dations or references, transcript. **Deadline:** March 1.

**Oregon Veterans' Education Aid.** To be eligible, veteran must have actively served in U.S. armed forces 90 days and been discharged under honorable conditions. Must be U.S. citizen and Oregon resident. Korean War veteran or received campaign or expeditionary medal or ribbon awarded by U.S. armed forces for services after June 30, 1958. Full-time students receive up to $150 per month, and part-time students receive up to $100 per month for a maximum of 36 months. Length of benefits depend on length of service. Payments contingent upon available funding. *Award:* Grant for use in freshman, sophomore, junior, senior, graduate, or postgraduate years; not renewable. *Award amount:* $3600–$5400. *Number of awards:* 1–200. *Eligibility Requirements:* Applicant must be enrolled or expecting to enroll full- or part-time at a two-year or four-year or technical institution or university; resident of Oregon and studying in Oregon. Available to U.S. citizens. Applicant must have general military experience. *Application Requirements:* Application form, certified copy of DD Form 214. **Deadline:** continuous.

Contact Loriann Sheridan, Veterans Programs Consultant, Oregon Department of Veterans' Affairs, 700 Summer Street, NE, Salem, OR 97301-1289. *E-mail:* sheridl@odva.state.or.us. *Phone:* 503-373-2264. *Fax:* 503-373-2393. *Website:* http://www.oregon.gov/odva.

**Peter Connacher Memorial Scholarship.** Renewable award for American prisoners-of-war and their descendants. Written proof of prisoner-of-war status and discharge papers from the U.S. Armed Forces must accompany application. Statement of relationship between applicant and former prisoner-of-war is required. Oregon residency preferred but not required. FAFSA required. *Award:* Scholarship for use in freshman, sophomore, junior, senior, or graduate years; renewable. *Eligibility Requirements:* Applicant must be enrolled or expecting to enroll full-time at a two-year or four-year institution. Available to U.S. citizens. Applicant or parent must meet one or more of the following requirements: general military experience; retired from active duty; disabled or killed as a result of military service; prisoner of war; or missing in action. *Application Requirements:* Application form, essay, financial need analysis, military discharge papers, documentation of POW status, FAFSA, transcript. **Deadline:** March 1.

# PENNSYLVANIA

**Pennsylvania State Grant.** Award for Pennsylvania residents attending an approved postsecondary institution as undergraduates in a program of at least two years duration. Renewable for up to eight semesters if applicants show continued need and academic progress. Must submit FAFSA. Number of awards granted varies annually. Scholarship value is $200 to $4348. Deadlines: May 1 and August 1. *Award:* Grant for use in freshman, sophomore, junior, or senior years; renewable. *Award amount:* $200–$4011. *Eligibility Requirements:* Applicant must be enrolled or expecting to enroll full- or part-time at a two-year or four-year or technical institution or university and resident of Pennsylvania. Available to U.S. citizens. *Application Requirements:* Application form, FAFSA, financial need analysis. **Deadline:** varies.

Contact Keith New, Director of Public Relations, Pennsylvania Higher Education Assistance Agency, 1200 North Seventh Street, Harrisburg, PA 17102-1444. *Phone:* 717-720-2509. *Fax:* 717-720-3903. *Website:* http://www.pheaa.org/.

**Postsecondary Education Gratuity Program.** The program offers waiver of tuition and fees for children of Pennsylvania police officers, firefighters, rescue or ambulance squad members, corrections facility employees, or National Guard members who died in line of duty after January 1, 1976. *Award:* Grant for use in freshman, sophomore, junior, or senior years; renewable. *Eligibility Requirements:* Applicant must be enrolled or expecting to enroll full-time at a two-year or four-year institution or university; resident of Pennsylvania and studying in Pennsylvania. Available to U.S. citizens. Applicant or parent must meet one or more of the following requirements: national guard experience; retired from active duty; disabled or killed as a result of military service; prisoner of war; or missing in action. *Application Requirements:* Application form. **Deadline:** August 1.

Contact Keith New, Director of Public Relations. *E-mail:* knew@pheaa.org. *Phone:* 717-720-2509. *Website:* http://www.pheaa.org/.

# RHODE ISLAND

**Rhode Island State Grant Program.** Grants for residents of Rhode Island attending an accredited, Title-IV approved post secondary undergraduate program in the United States, Canada, or Mexico. Based on need as reported by the student and his or her family on the Free Application for Federal Student Aid (FAFSA). Renewable for up to four years if in good academic standing and student continues to meet financial need requirements. *Award:* Grant for use in freshman, sophomore, junior, or senior years; not renewable. *Award amount:* $250–$500. *Number of awards:* 10,000–20,000. *Eligibility Requirements:* Applicant must be enrolled or expecting to enroll full- or part-time at a two-year or four-year or technical institution or university and resident of Rhode Island. Available to U.S. citizens. *Application Requirements:* Application form, financial need analysis. **Deadline:** March 1.

Contact Mr. Michael Joyce, Director of Program Administration, Rhode Island Higher Education Assistance Authority, 560 Jefferson Boulevard, Suite 100, Warwick, RI 02886. *E-mail:* grants@riheaa.org. *Phone:* 401-736-1170. *Fax:* 401-736-3541. *Website:* http://www.riheaa.org/.

# SOUTH CAROLINA

**Educational Assistance for Certain War Veterans Dependents Scholarship-South Carolina.** Free tuition for South Carolina residents whose parent is a resident, wartime veteran, and meets one of these criteria. Must be awarded Purple Heart or Congressional Medal of Honor; permanently and totally disabled or killed as a result of military service; prisoner of war; or missing in action. Must be age 18 to 26 and enrolled or expecting to enroll full or part-time at a two-year or four-year technical institution or university in South Carolina. Complete information and qualifications for this award are on web site http://www.govoepp.state.sc.us. *Award:* Scholarship for use in freshman, sophomore, junior, or senior years; not renewable. *Eligibility Requirements:* Applicant must be age 18-26; enrolled or expecting to enroll full- or part-time at a two-year or four-year or technical institution or university; resident of South Carolina and studying in South Carolina. Available to U.S. citizens. Applicant or parent must meet one or more of the following requirements: general military experience; retired from active duty; disabled or killed as a result of military service; prisoner of war; or missing in action. *Application Requirements:* Application form, proof of qualification of veteran, transcript. **Deadline:** continuous.

Contact Adm. Dorian Sease-Phillips, Free Tuition Coordinator. *E-mail:* va@oepp.sc.gov. *Phone:* 803-647-2434. *Website:* http://va.sc.gov//benefits.html.

**Palmetto Fellows Scholarship Program.** Renewable award for qualified high school seniors in South Carolina to attend a four-year South Carolina institution. The scholarship must be applied directly towards the cost of attendance, less any other gift aid received. *Award:* Scholarship for use in freshman year; renewable. *Award amount:* $6700–$7500. *Number of awards:* 4846. *Eligibility Requirements:* Applicant must be high school student; planning to enroll or expecting to enroll full-time at a four-year institution or university; resident of South Carolina and studying in South Carolina. Applicant must have 3.5 GPA or higher. Available to U.S. citizens. *Application Requirements:* Application form, test scores, transcript. **Deadline:** December 15.

Contact Dr. Karen Woodfaulk, Director of Student Services, South Carolina Commission on Higher Education, 1333 Main Street, Suite 200, Columbia, SC 29201. *E-mail:* kwoodfaulk@che.sc.gov. *Phone:* 803-737-2244. *Fax:* 803-737-3610. *Website:* http://www.che.sc.gov/.

**South Carolina HOPE Scholarship.** A merit-based scholarship for eligible first-time entering freshman attending a four-year South Carolina institution. Minimum GPA of 3.0 required. Must be a resident of South Carolina. *Award:* Scholarship for use in freshman year; not renewable. *Award amount:* $2800. *Number of awards:* 2605. *Eligibility Requirements:* Applicant must be high school student; planning to enroll or expecting to enroll full-time at a four-year institution or university; resident of South Carolina and studying in South Carolina. Applicant must have 3.0 GPA or higher. Available to U.S. citizens. *Application Requirements:* Transcript. **Deadline:** continuous.

Contact Gerrick Hampton, Scholarship Coordinator, South Carolina Commission on Higher Education, 1333 Main Street, Suite 200, Columbia, SC 29201. *E-mail:* ghampton@che.sc.gov. *Phone:* 803-737-4544. *Fax:* 803-737-3610. *Website:* http://www.che.sc.gov/.

**South Carolina Need-Based Grants Program.** Award based on FAFSA. A student may receive up to $2500 annually for full-time and up to $1250 annually for part-time study. The grant must be applied directly towards the cost of college atten dance for a maximum of eight full-time equivalent terms. *Award:* Grant for use in freshman, sophomore, junior, senior, or graduate years; renewable. *Award amount:* $1250–$2500. *Number of awards:* 1–26,730. *Eligibility Requirements:* Applicant must be enrolled or expecting to enroll full- or part-time at a two-year or four-year or technical institution or university; resident of South Carolina and studying in South Carolina. Available to U.S. citizens. *Application Requirements:* Application form, financial need analysis. **Deadline:** continuous.

Contact Dr. Karen Woodfaulk, Director of Student Service, South Carolina Commission on Higher Education, 1333 Main Street, Suite 200, Columbia, SC 29201. *E-mail:* kwoodfaulk@che.sc.gov. *Phone:* 803-737-2244. *Fax:* 803-737-2297. *Website:* http://www.che.sc.gov/.

**South Carolina Tuition Grants Program.** Need-based grant set aside for 21 eligible independent colleges in South Carolina. Student must be a South Carolina resident. Must apply annually by submitting the Free Application for Federal Student Aid (FAFSA). Freshmen must graduate in top 75% of high school class OR score 900 on SAT/19 on ACT OR graduate with at least 2.0 on SC Uniform Grading Scale. Upperclassmen must pass a minimum of 24 credit hours annually. *Award:* Grant for use in freshman, sophomore, junior, or senior years; not renewable. *Award amount:* $100–$3000. *Eligibility Requirements:* Applicant must be enrolled or expecting to enroll full-time at a two-year or four-year institution or university; resident of South Carolina and studying in South Carolina. Available to U.S. citizens. *Application Requirements:* Application form, FAFSA. **Deadline:** June 30.

Contact Jessica Bagwell, Financial Aid Counselor, South Carolina Tuition Grants Commission, 115 Atrium Way, Suite 102, Columbia, SC 29223. *E-mail:* jessica@sctuitiongrants.org. *Phone:* 803-896-1120. *Fax:* 803-896-1126. *Website:* http://www.sctuitiongrants.com/.

# SOUTH DAKOTA

**South Dakota Opportunity Scholarship.** Renewable scholarship may be worth up to $5000 over four years to students who take a rigorous college-prep curriculum while in high school and stay in the state for their postsecondary education. *Award:* Scholarship for use in freshman, sophomore, junior, or senior years; renewable. *Award amount:* $1000. *Number of awards:* 1000. *Eligibility Requirements:* Applicant must be high school student; planning to enroll or expecting to enroll full-time at a two-year or four-year or technical institution or university; resident of South Dakota and studying in South Dakota. Applicant must have 3.0 GPA or higher. Available to U.S. citizens. *Application Requirements:* Application form, test scores, transcript. **Deadline:** September 1.

Contact Janelle Toman, Scholarship Committee, South Dakota Board of Regents, 306 East Capitol, Suite 200, Pierre, SD 57501-2545. *E-mail:* info@sdbor.edu. *Phone:* 605-773-3455. *Fax:* 605-773-2422. *Website:* http://www.sdbor.edu/.

# TENNESSEE

**Christa McAuliffe Scholarship Program.** Scholarship to assist and support Tennessee students who have demonstrated a commitment to a career in educating the youth of Tennessee. Offered to college seniors for a period of one academic year. Must have a minimum college GPA of 3.5. Must have attained scores on either the ACT or SAT which meet or exceed the national norms. Award is made on a periodic basis as funding becomes available. Education. *Award:* Scholarship for use in senior year; not renewable. *Award amount:* up to $500. *Number of awards:* up to 1. *Eligibility Requirements:* Applicant must be enrolled or expecting to enroll full-time at a four-year institution or university; resident of Tennessee and studying in Tennessee. Applicant must have 3.5 GPA or higher. Available to U.S. citizens. *Application Requirements:* Application form, application form may be submitted online (http://www.tn.gov/collegepays), essay, transcript. **Deadline:** April 1.

Contact Ms. Kathy Stripling, Grant and Scholarship Analyst, Tennessee Student Assistance Corporation, Parkway Towers, 404 James Robertson Parkway, Suite 1510, Nashville, TN 37243-0820. *E-mail:* kathy.stripling@tn.gov. *Phone:* 615-253-7480. *Fax:* 615-741-6101. *Website:* http://www.tn.gov/collegepays.

**Dependent Children Scholarship Program.** Scholarship for Tennessee residents who are dependent children of a Tennessee law enforcement officer, fireman, or an emergency medical service technician who have been killed or totally and permanently disabled while performing duties within the scope of such employment. The scholarship is awarded to full-time undergraduate students for a maximum of four academic years or the period required for the completion of the program of study. *Award:* Scholarship for use in freshman, sophomore, junior, or senior years; not renewable. *Award amount:* $3000–$30,000. *Number of awards:* up to 30. *Eligibility Requirements:* Applicant must be enrolled or expecting to enroll full-time at a two-year or four-year institution or university; resident of Tennessee and studying in Tennessee. Available to U.S. citizens. *Application Requirements:* Application form, application form may be submitted online (http://www.tn.gov/collegepays), FAFSA. **Deadline:** July 15.

Contact Ms. Kathy Stripling, Grant and Scholarship Analyst, Tennessee Student Assistance Corporation, Parkway Towers, 404 James Robertson Parkway, Suite 1510, Nashville, TN 37243-0820. *E-mail:* kathy.stripling@tn.gov. *Phone:* 615-253-7480. *Fax:* 615-741-6101. *Website:* http://www.tn.gov/collegepays.

**Helping Heroes Grant.** Provides assistance to Tennessee veterans who have been awarded the Iraq Campaign Medal, Afghanistan Campaign Medal, or Global War on Terrorism Expeditionary Medal (on or after 9/11/01) and who meet eligibility requirements for the program. Award is up to $2000 per year. For more information, visit http://www.TN.gov/collegepays. *Award:* Grant for use in freshman, sophomore, junior, or senior years; not renewable. *Award amount:* up to $2000. *Eligibility Requirements:* Applicant must be enrolled or expecting to enroll full- or part-time at a two-year or four-year institution or university. Available to U.S. citizens. Applicant must have general military experience. *Application Requirements:* Application form, application form may be submitted online (http://www.tn.gov/collegepays), DD-214. **Deadline:** September 1.

Contact Mr. Robert Biggers, Director of Lottery Programs, Tennessee Student Assistance Corporation, Parkway Towers, 404 James Robertson Parkway, Suite 1510, Nashville, TN 37243. *E-mail:* robert.biggers@tn.gov. *Phone:* 615-253-7453. *Fax:* 615-741-6101. *Website:* http://www.tn.gov/collegepays.

**HOPE with ASPIRE.** HOPE Scholarship of $2000 per semester (four-year institution) or $1000 per semester (two-year institution) with $750 supplement per semester. Must meet Tennessee HOPE Scholarship requirements and Adjusted Gross Income (AGI) attributable to the student must be $36,000 or less. *Award:* Scholarship for use in freshman, sophomore, junior, or senior years; renewable. *Award amount:* up to $5500. *Eligibility Requirements:* Applicant must be enrolled or expecting to enroll full- or part-time at a two-year or four-year institution or university; resident of Tennessee and studying in Tennessee. Applicant must have 3.0 GPA or higher. Available to U.S. citizens. *Application Requirements:* Application form, application form may be submitted online (http://www.fafsa. gov), financial need analysis. **Deadline:** September 1.

Contact Mr. Robert Biggers, Director of Lottery Scholarship Programs, Tennessee Student Assistance Corporation, Parkway Towers, 404 James Robertson Parkway, Suite 1510, Nashville, TN 37243-0820. *E-mail:* robert.biggers@tn.gov. *Phone:* 615-253-7453. *Fax:* 615-741-6101. *Website:* http://www.tn.gov/collegepays.

**Ned McWherter Scholars Program.** Award for Tennessee high school seniors with high academic ability. Must have minimum high school GPA of 3.5 and a score of 29 on the ACT or SAT equivalent. Must attend a college or university in Tennessee and be a permanent U.S. citizen. For more information, visit web site http://tn.gov/collegepays. *Award:* Scholarship for use in freshman, sophomore, junior, or senior years; not renewable. *Award amount:* up to $3000. *Number of awards:* up to 200. *Eligibility Requirements:* Applicant must be enrolled or expecting to enroll full-time at a two-year or four-year or technical institution or university; resident of Tennessee and studying in Tennessee. Applicant must have 3.5 GPA or higher. Available to U.S. citizens. *Application Requirements:* Application form, application form may be submitted online (http://www.tn.gov/collegepays), test scores, transcript. **Deadline:** February 15.

Contact Mrs. Kathy Stripling, Grants and Scholarship Analyst, Tennessee Student Assistance Corporation, 404 James Robertson Parkway, Suite 1510, Parkway Towers, Nashville, TN 37243-0820. *E-mail:* kathy.stripling@tn.gov. *Phone:* 615-253-7480. *Fax:* 615-741-6101. *Website:* http://www.tn.gov/collegepays.

**Tennessee Dual Enrollment Grant.** Grant for study at an eligible Tennessee postsecondary institution awarded to juniors and seniors in a Tennessee high school who have been admitted to undergraduate study while still pursuing a high school diploma. For more information, visit web site http://www.tn.gov/colleg

epays. *Award:* Grant for use in freshman year; renewable. *Award amount:* up to $1200. *Eligibility Requirements:* Applicant must be high school student; planning to enroll or expecting to enroll part-time at a two-year or four-year or technical institution or university; resident of Tennessee and studying in Tennessee. Available to U.S. citizens. *Application Requirements:* Application form, application form may be submitted online (http://www.tn.gov/collegepays). **Deadline:** September 1.

Contact Mr. Robert Biggers, Director of Lottery Scholarship Program, Tennessee Student Assistance Corporation, Parkway Towers, 404 James Robertson Parkway, Suite 1510, Nashville, TN 37243-0820. *E-mail:* robert.biggers@tn.gov. *Phone:* 615-253-7453. *Fax:* 615-741-1601. *Website:* http://www.tn.gov/collegepays.

**Tennessee Education Lottery Scholarship Program HOPE Access Grant.** Non-renewable award of $2750 for students at four-year colleges or $1750 for students at two-year colleges. Entering freshmen must have a minimum GPA of 2.75, ACT score of 18-20 (or SAT equivalent), and adjusted gross income attributable to the student must be $36,000 or less. Recipients will become eligible for Tennessee HOPE Scholarship by meeting HOPE Scholarship renewal criteria. *Award:* Scholarship for use in freshman, sophomore, junior, or senior years; not renewable. *Award amount:* up to $2750. *Eligibility Requirements:* Applicant must be enrolled or expecting to enroll full- or part-time at a two-year or four-year institution or university; resident of Tennessee and studying in Tennessee. Available to U.S. citizens. *Application Requirements:* Application form, application form may be submitted online (http://www.fafsa. gov), financial need analysis. **Deadline:** September 1.

Contact Mr. Robert Biggers, Director of Lottery Scholarship Programs, Tennessee Student Assistance Corporation, Parkway Towers, 404 James Robertson Parkway, Suite 1510, Nashville, TN 37243-0820. *E-mail:* robert.biggers@tn.gov. *Phone:* 615-253-7453. *Fax:* 615-741-6101. *Website:* http://www.tn.gov/collegepays.

**Tennessee Education Lottery Scholarship Program-HOPE with General Assembly Merit Scholarship (GAMS).** HOPE Scholarship of $2000 per semester (four-year institution) or $1000 per semester (two-year institution) with supplemental award of $500 per

semester. Entering freshmen must have 3.75 GPA and 29 ACT (1280 SAT). Must be a U.S. citizen and a resident of Tennessee. *Award:* Scholarship for use in freshman, sophomore, junior, or senior years; renewable. *Award amount:* up to $5000. *Eligibility Requirements:* Applicant must be enrolled or expecting to enroll full- or part-time at a two-year or four-year institution or university; resident of Tennessee and studying in Tennessee. Available to U.S. citizens. *Application Requirements:* Application form, application form may be submitted online (http://www.fafsa. gov). **Deadline:** September 1.

Contact Mr. Robert Biggers, Director of Lottery Scholarship Programs, Tennessee Student Assistance Corporation, Parkway Towers, 404 James Robertson Parkway, Suite 1510, Nashville, TN 37243-0820. *E-mail:* robert.biggers@tn.gov. *Phone:* 615-253-7453. *Fax:* 615-741-6101. *Website:* http://www.tn.gov/collegepays.

**Tennessee Education Lottery Scholarship Program Tennessee HOPE Scholarship.** Award amount is $2000 for per semester at four-year institutions and $1000 per semester at two-year institutions. Must be a Tennessee resident attending an eligible postsecondary institution in Tennessee. For more information, visit http://www.TN.gov/CollegePays. *Award:* Scholarship for use in freshman, sophomore, junior, or senior years; renewable. *Award amount:* $2000–$6000. *Eligibility Requirements:* Applicant must be enrolled or expecting to enroll full- or part-time at a two-year or four-year institution or university; resident of Tennessee and studying in Tennessee. Applicant must have 3.0 GPA or higher. Available to U.S. citizens. *Application Requirements:* Application form, application form may be submitted online (http://www.fafsa.gov). **Deadline:** September 1.

Contact Mr. Robert Biggers, Director of Lottery Scholarship Programs, Tennessee Student Assistance Corporation, Parkway Towers, 404 James Robertson Parkway, Suite 1510, Nashville, TN 37243-0820. *E-mail:* robert.biggers@tn.gov. *Phone:* 615-253-7453. *Fax:* 615-741-6101. *Website:* http://www.tn.gov/collegepays.

**Tennessee Education Lottery Scholarship Program Wilder-Naifeh Technical Skills Grant.** Award up to $2000 for students enrolled in a certificate or diploma program at a College of Applied Technology. Cannot be prior recipient of Tennessee HOPE Schol arship. For more information, visit http://www.TN.gov/CollegePays. *Award:* Grant for use in freshman or sophomore years; renewable. *Award amount:* up to $2000. *Eligibility Requirements:* Applicant must be enrolled or expecting to enroll full- or part-time at a technical institution; resident of Tennessee and studying in Tennessee. Available to U.S. citizens. *Application Requirements:* Application form, application form may be submitted online (http://www.fafsa.gov). **Deadline:** November 1.

Contact Mr. Robert Biggers, Director of Lottery Scholarship Programs, Tennessee Student Assistance Corporation, Parkway Towers, 404 James Robertson Parkway, Suite 1510, Nashville, TN 37243-0820. *E-mail:* robert.biggers@tn.gov. *Phone:* 615-253-7453. *Fax:* 615-741-6101. *Website:* http://www.tn.gov/collegepays.

**Tennessee HOPE Foster Child Tuition Grant.** Renewable tuition award available for recipients of the HOPE Scholarship or HOPE Access Grant. Student must have been in Tennessee state custody as a foster child for at least one year after reaching age 14. Award amount varies and shall not exceed the tuition and mandatory fees at an eligible Tennessee public postsecondary institution. For additional information, visit web site http://www.tn.gov/collegepays. *Award:* Scholarship for use in freshman, sophomore, junior, or senior years; renewable. *Eligibility Requirements:* Applicant must be enrolled or expecting to enroll full- or part-time at a two-year or four-year institution or university; resident of Tennessee and studying in Tennessee. Applicant must have 3.0 GPA or higher. Available to U.S. citizens. *Application Requirements:* Application form, application form may be submitted online (http://www.tn.gov/collegepays). **Deadline:** September 1.

Contact Mr. Robert Biggers, Director of Lottery Scholarship Programs, Tennessee Student Assistance Corporation, Parkway Towers, 404 James Robertson Parkway, Suite 1510, Nashville, TN 37243-0820. *E-mail:* robert.biggers@tn.gov. *Phone:* 615-253-7453. *Fax:* 615-741-6101. *Website:* http://www.tn.gov/collegepays.

**Tennessee Student Assistance Award.** Award to assist financially-needy Tennessee residents attending an approved college or university within the state. Complete a Free Application for Federal Student Aid form. FAFSA must be processed as soon as possible after January 1 for priority consideration. To apply, go to http://www.fafsa.gov. For more information, go to www.tn.gov/collegepays *Award:* Grant for use in freshman, sophomore, junior, or senior years; not renewable. *Award amount:* $100–$4000. *Number of awards:* 30,000–35,000. *Eligibility Requirements:* Applicant must be enrolled or expecting to enroll full- or part-time at a two-year or four-year or technical institution or university; resident of Tennessee and studying in Tennessee. Available to U.S. citizens. *Application Requirements:* Application form, application form may be submitted online (http://www.fafsa.gov), financial need analysis. **Deadline:** March 1.

Contact Ms. Leah Louallen, Director of Grants and Scholarship Programs, Tennessee Student Assistance Corporation, Parkway Towers, 404 James Robertson Parkway, Suite 1510, Nashville, TN 37243-0820. *E-mail:* leah.louallen@tn.gov. *Phone:* 615-253-7478. *Fax:* 615-741-6101. *Website:* http://www.tn.gov/collegepays.

## TEXAS

**Conditional Grant Program.** Renewable award to students who are considered economically disadvantaged based on federal guidelines. The maximum amount awarded per semester is $3000 not to exceed $6000 per academic year. Students already enrolled in an undergraduate program should have minimum GPA 2.5 and students newly enrolling should have minimum GPA 3.0. Civil Engineering; Computer Science/Data Processing; Occupational Safety and Health. *Award:* Grant for use in freshman, sophomore, junior, or senior years; renewable. *Award amount:* up to $6000. *Eligibility Requirements:* Applicant must be enrolled or expecting to enroll full-time at a four-year institution or university; resident of Texas and studying in Texas. Available to U.S. citizens. *Application Requirements:* Application form, essay, interview, recommendations or references, test scores, transcript. **Deadline:** March 1.

Contact Minnie Brown, Program Coordinator, Texas Department of Transportation, 125 East 11th Street, Austin, TX 78701-2483. *E-mail:* mbrown2@dot.state.tx.us. *Phone:* 512-416-4979. *Fax:* 512-416-4980. *Website:* http://www.txdot.gov/.

**Texas Educational Opportunity Grant (TEOG).** Provides grant aid to students with financial need attending public two-year colleges. For initial award, student must be enrolled at least half-time and awarded in the first 30 hours (or its equivalent) of an associate's degree or certificate program (excluding credits for dual enrollment or by examination). For renewal award, student must also maintain a minimum overall GPA of 2.50 and successfully complete a minimum of 75% of classes attempted during the school year. *Award:* Grant for use in freshman, sophomore, junior, or senior years; not renewable. *Award amount:* $1–$8000. *Eligibility Requirements:* Applicant must be enrolled or expecting to enroll full- or part-time at a two-year institution; resident of Texas and studying in Texas. Available to U.S. citizens. *Application Requirements:* FAFSA, financial need analysis.

**Texas National Guard Tuition Assistance Program.** Provides exemption from the payment of tuition to certain members of the Texas National Guard, Texas Air Guard or the State Guard. Must be Texas resident and attend school in Texas. Deadline varies. *Award:* Scholarship for use in freshman, sophomore, junior, or senior years; renewable. *Eligibility Requirements:* Applicant must be enrolled or expecting to enroll full- or part-time at a four-year institution or university; resident of Texas and studying in Texas. Available to U.S. citizens. Applicant or parent must meet one or more of the following requirements: national guard experience; retired from active duty; disabled or killed as a result of military service; prisoner of war; or missing in action. *Application Requirements:* Application form. **Deadline:** varies.

**Texas Professional Nursing Scholarships.** Award to provide financial assistance to encourage students to become Professional Nurses. Only in-state (Texas) colleges or universities may participate in the program. Both public and private, non-profit colleges or universities with professional nursing programs may participate in the programs. Nursing. *Award:* Scholarship for use in freshman, sophomore, junior, or senior years; not renewable. *Award amount:* $2500. *Eligibility Requirements:* Applicant must be enrolled or expecting to enroll full- or part-time at a two-year or four-year or technical institution; resident of Texas and studying in Texas. *Application Requirements:* Application form, financial need analysis.

**Texas Vocational Nursing Scholarships.** Awards to encourage individuals to pursue vocational nursing. Both public and private, non-profit colleges or universities with vocational nursing programs may participate in the programs. No individual award may be more than the student's financial need. The maximum award is $1500. Nursing. *Award:* Scholarship for use in freshman or sophomore years; not renewable. *Award amount:* $1500. *Eligibility Requirements:* Applicant must be enrolled or expecting to enroll full- or part-time at a two-year or technical institution; resident of Texas and studying in Texas. *Application Requirements:* Application form, financial need analysis.

**Top 10% Scholarship Program.** Encourage outstanding high school students who graduate within the top 10 percent of their high school graduating class to attend a public college or university in Texas. Students must demonstrate financial need and complete the FAFSA by the state priority deadline of March 15. Renewal award students must also maintain a minimum overall GPA of 3.25, successfully complete at least 30 SCH each year, and successfully complete at least 75% of the hours attempted each year. *Award:* Scholarship for use in freshman, sophomore, junior, or senior years; renewable. *Award amount:* $1–$600. *Eligibility Requirements:* Applicant must be enrolled or expecting to enroll full-time at a two-year or four-year or technical institution or university; resident of Texas and studying in Texas. Available to U.S. citizens. *Application Requirements:* FAFSA, financial need analysis.

**Toward EXcellence, Access, and Success (TEXAS) Grant.** Renewable aid for students enrolled at least three-quarter time in a public four-year college or university in Texas within sixteen months of graduation from high school. Must demonstrate financial need and have completed the Foundation, Recommended, or DAP Curriculum in high school. For renewal awards, must also maintain a minimum GPA of 2.5 and complete a minimum of 24 SCH's each year. Amount of award is determined by the financial aid office of each school. Priority FAFSA completion deadline is March 15. Contact the college/university financial aid office for additional eligibility information. *Award:* Grant for use in freshman, sophomore, junior, or senior years; renewable. *Award amount:* $1–$8000. *Eligibility Requirements:* Applicant must be enrolled or expecting to enroll full- or part-time at a four-year institution or university; resident of Texas and studying in Texas. Available to U.S.

citizens. *Application Requirements:* Financial need analysis, transcript.

**Tuition Equalization Grant (TEG) Program.** Renewable award for Texas residents enrolled at least three-quarter time at an independent college or university in Texas in a degree program that does not lead to ordination or licensure to preach. Non-residents who are National Merit Finalists and are receiving at least $1,000 in scholarships may also receive awards. Awards are based on financial need. Renewal awards also require the student to maintain a minimum overall college GPA of at least 2.5, complete at least 24 SCH's each year (18 SCH's for students in graduate programs), and complete a minimum of 75% of classes attempted each year. Priority deadline to complete the FAFSA is March 15. Must not be receiving athletic scholarship concurrently. Contact college/university financial aid office for application information. *Award:* Grant for use in freshman, sophomore, junior, senior, or graduate years; not renewable. *Award amount:* $1–$4875. *Eligibility Requirements:* Applicant must be enrolled or expecting to enroll full- or part-time at a two-year or four-year institution or university and studying in Texas. Available to U.S. citizens. *Application Requirements:* Financial need analysis.

## UTAH

**Higher Education Success Stipend Program.** Award available to students with substantial financial need for use at any of the participating Utah institutions. The student must be a Utah resident. Contact the financial aid office of the participating institution for requirements and deadlines. *Award:* Grant for use in freshman, sophomore, junior, or senior years; not renewable. *Award amount:* $300–$5000. *Number of awards:* 422–7028. *Eligibility Requirements:* Applicant must be enrolled or expecting to enroll full- or part-time at a two-year or four-year or technical institution or university; resident of Utah and studying in Utah. Available to U.S. citizens. *Application Requirements:* FAFSA, financial need analysis. **Deadline:** continuous.

Contact Mr. David Hughes, Manager of Student Aid Partnerships. *E-mail:* dhughes@utahsbr.edu. *Phone:* 801-321-7220. *Fax:* 801-321-7168. *Website:* http://www.uheaa.org/.

## VERMONT

**Vermont Incentive Grants.** Renewable grants for Vermont residents based on financial need. Must meet needs test. Must be college undergraduate or graduate student enrolled full-time at an approved post secondary institution. Only available to Vermont residents. *Award:* Grant for use in freshman, sophomore, junior, or senior years; renewable. *Award amount:* $500–$10,800. *Eligibility Requirements:* Applicant must be enrolled or expecting to enroll full-time at a two-year or four-year or technical institution or university and resident of Vermont. Available to U.S. citizens. *Application Requirements:* Application form, FAFSA, financial need analysis. **Deadline:** continuous.

**Vermont Non-Degree Student Grant Program.** Need-based, renewable grants for Vermont residents enrolled in non-degree programs in a college, vocational school, or high school adult program, that will improve employability or encourage further study. Award amounts vary. *Award:* Grant for use in freshman, sophomore, junior, or senior years; renewable. *Eligibility Requirements:* Applicant must be enrolled or expecting to enroll full- or part-time at a two-year or four-year or technical institution or university and resident of Vermont. Available to U.S. citizens. *Application Requirements:* Application form, financial need analysis. **Deadline:** continuous.

**Vermont Part-Time Student Grants.** For undergraduates carrying less than twelve credits per semester who have not received a Bachelor's degree. Must be a Vermont resident. Based on financial need. Complete Vermont Financial Aid Packet to apply. May be used at any approved post-secondary institution. *Award:* Grant for use in freshman, sophomore, junior, or senior years; renewable. *Award amount:* $250–$8100. *Eligibility Requirements:* Applicant must be enrolled or expecting to enroll part-time at a four-year institution or university and resident of Vermont. Available to U.S. citizens. *Application Requirements:* Application form, financial need analysis. **Deadline:** continuous.

## VIRGINIA

**Mary Marshall Practical Nursing Scholarship (LPN).** Awards for students who are accepted or enrolled as a full-time or part-time student in a practical school of nursing in the state of Virginia. Must be a Virginia resident for at least one year and have submitted a completed application form and a recommendation from the Director regarding scholastic attainment and financial need prior to June 30. Students pursuing a nursing degree not available in Virginia, are not eligible for the scholarship. Scholarship amount varies. Nursing. *Award:* Scholarship for use in freshman, sophomore, junior, or senior years; not renewable. *Award amount:* $600–$1200. *Number of awards:* 26–88. *Eligibility Requirements:* Applicant must be enrolled or expecting to enroll full- or part-time at a two-year or four-year or technical institution or university; resident of Virginia and studying in Virginia. Applicant must have 2.5 GPA or higher. Available to U.S. citizens. *Application Requirements:* Application form, driver's license, essay, financial need analysis, recommendations or references, transcript. **Deadline:** June 30.

Contact Miss. Sarahbeth Jones, Communications Specialist, Virginia Department of Health, Office of Minority Health and Health Equity, PO Box 2448, 109 Governor Street, Suite 1016-E, Richmond, VA 23218-2448. *E-mail:* IncentivePrograms@vdh.virginia.gov. *Phone:* 804-864-7422. *Fax:* 804-864-7440. *Website:* http://www.vdh.virginia.gov/.

**Mary Marshall Registered Nursing Scholarships.** Scholarship for Virginia residents who have been accepted or is enrollment as a full-time or part-time student in a school of nursing in the state of Virginia. Must demonstrate financial need, verified by the Financial Aid Office/authorized person at the applicant's nursing school. Must also be a resident of Virginia for at least one year and have a minimum 3.0 GPA in required courses. Must have submitted a completed application form and an official grade transcript to The Office of Minority Health and Public Health Policy prior to June 30. If no college courses attempted an official high school transcript or equivalent must be submitted. Nursing. *Award:* Scholarship for use in freshman, sophomore, junior, or senior years; not renewable. *Award amount:* $600–$2000. *Number of awards:* 28–95. *Eligibility Requirements:* Applicant must be enrolled or expecting to enroll full- or part-time at a two-year or four-year institution or university; resident of Virginia and studying in Virginia. Applicant must have 2.5 GPA or higher. Available to U.S. citizens. *Application Requirements:* Application form, driver's license, essay, financial need analysis,

recommendations or references, transcript. **Deadline:** June 30.

Contact Miss. Sarahbeth Jones, Communications Specialist, Virginia Department of Health, Office of Minority Health and Health Equity, PO Box 2448, 109 Governor Street, Suite 1016-E, Richmond, VA 23218-2448. *E-mail:* IncentivePrograms@vdh.virginia.gov. *Phone:* 804-864-7422. *Fax:* 804-864-7440. *Website:* http://www.vdh.virginia.gov/.

**State Department Federal Credit Union Annual Scholarship Program.** Scholarships available to members who are currently enrolled in a degree program and have completed 12 credit hours of coursework at an accredited college or university. Must have own account in good standing with SDFCU, have a minimum 2.5 GPA, submit official cumulative transcripts, and describe need for financial assistance to continue their education. Scholarship only open to members of State Department Federal Credit Union. *Award:* Scholarship for use in sophomore, junior, senior, or graduate years; not renewable. *Award amount:* $2500. *Eligibility Requirements:* Applicant must be enrolled or expecting to enroll full-time at a four-year institution or university. Applicant must have 2.5 GPA or higher. Available to U.S. and non-U.S. citizens. *Application Requirements:* Application form, entry in a contest, financial need analysis, personal statement, transcript. **Deadline:** April 29.

**Virginia Commonwealth Award.** Need-based award for undergraduate or graduate study at a Virginia public two- or four-year college, or university. Undergraduates must be Virginia residents. The application and awards process are administered by the financial aid office at the Virginia public institution where student is enrolled. Dollar value of each award varies. Contact financial aid office for application and deadlines. *Award:* Grant for use in freshman, sophomore, junior, or senior years; not renewable. *Eligibility Requirements:* Applicant must be enrolled or expecting to enroll full- or part-time at a two-year or four-year institution or university; resident of Virginia and studying in Virginia. Available to U.S. citizens. *Application Requirements:* Financial need analysis.

**Virginia Guaranteed Assistance Program.** Awards to undergraduate students proportional to their need, up to full tuition, fees and book allowance. Must be a graduate of a Virginia high school. High

school GPA of 2.5 required. Must be enrolled full-time in a public Virginia two- or four-year institution and demonstrate financial need. Must maintain minimum college GPA of 2.0 for renewal awards. *Award:* Grant for use in freshman, sophomore, junior, or senior years; not renewable. *Eligibility Requirements:* Applicant must be enrolled or expecting to enroll full-time at a two-year or four-year institution or university; resident of Virginia and studying in Virginia. Available to U.S. citizens. *Application Requirements:* Financial need analysis, transcript.

**Virginia Military Survivors and Dependents Education Program.** Scholarships for post-secondary students between ages 16 and 29 to attend Virginia state-supported institutions. Must be child or surviving spouse of veteran who has either been permanently or totally disabled due to war or other armed conflict; died as a result of war or other armed conflict; or been listed as a POW or MIA. Parent must also meet Virginia residency requirements. *Award:* Scholarship for use in freshman, sophomore, junior, senior, or graduate years; renewable. *Eligibility Requirements:* Applicant must be age 16-29; enrolled or expecting to enroll full-time at a two-year or four-year or technical institution or university; resident of Virginia and studying in Virginia. Available to U.S. citizens. Applicant or parent must meet one or more of the following requirements: general military experience; retired from active duty; disabled or killed as a result of military service; prisoner of war; or missing in action. *Application Requirements:* Application form, DD214 of service member, birth certificate of applicant, marriage certificate, acceptance letter from institution. **Deadline:** varies.

Contact Mrs. Doris Sullivan, Coordinator, Virginia Department of Veterans Services, 1351 Hershberger Road, Suite 220, Roanoke, VA 24012. *Phone:* 540-561-6625. *Fax:* 540-857-7573. *Website:* http://www.dvs.virginia.gov/.

**Virginia Tuition Assistance Grant Program (Private Institutions).** Awards for undergraduate students. Also available to graduate and first professional degree students pursuing a health-related degree program. Not to be used for religious study. Must be U.S. citizen or eligible non-citizen, Virginia domiciled, and enrolled full-time at an approved private, nonprofit college within Virginia. Information and application available from participating Virginia col leges financial aid office. Visit http://www.schev.edu and click on Financial Aid. *Award:* Grant for use in freshman, sophomore, junior, senior, or graduate years; renewable. *Award amount:* up to $3100. *Number of awards:* 22,000. *Eligibility Requirements:* Applicant must be enrolled or expecting to enroll full-time at a four-year institution or university; resident of Virginia and studying in Virginia. Available to U.S. citizens. *Application Requirements:* Application form. **Deadline:** July 31.

# WASHINGTON

**American Indian Endowed Scholarship.** Awarded to financially needy undergraduate and graduate students with close social and cultural ties with a Native-American community. Must be Washington resident and enrolled full-time at Washington public or private school. Must be committed to use education to return service to the state's American Indian community. *Award:* Scholarship for use in freshman, sophomore, junior, senior, graduate, or post graduate years; not renewable. *Award amount:* $500–$2000. *Number of awards:* 11–20. *Eligibility Requirements:* Applicant must be American Indian/Alaska Native; enrolled or expecting to enroll full-time at a two-year or four-year or technical institution or university; resident of Washington and studying in Washington. Available to U.S. citizens. *Application Requirements:* 2 written personal statements, one describing one's social and cultural ties to the American Indian community in WA state, and the other describing how one will use one's education to serve the American Indian community within the state of Washington, application form, recommendations or references, transcript. **Deadline:** February 1.

Contact Ann Voyles, Program Manager, Washington State Higher Education Coordinating Board, 917 Lakeridge Way, PO Box 43430, Olympia, WA 98504-3430. *E-mail:* annv@wsac.wa.gov. *Phone:* 360-753-7843. *Fax:* 360-704-6243.

**Passport to College Promise Scholarship.** Scholarship to encourage Washington residents to prepare for and succeed in college. Recipients must have spent at least one year in foster care after their 16th birthday and emancipated from care in Washington state. *Award:* Scholarship for use in freshman, sophomore, junior, or senior years; renewable. *Award*

*amount:* up to $4500. *Number of awards:* 1–400. *Eligibility Requirements:* Applicant must be age 18-26; enrolled or expecting to enroll full- or part-time at a two-year or four-year or technical institution or university; resident of Washington and studying in Washington. Available to U.S. citizens. *Application Requirements:* Application form, application form may be submitted online (http://www.wsac.wa.gov/sites/default/files/PassportConsentForm-2012.pdf), consent form, financial need analysis. **Deadline:** continuous.

Contact Ms. Dawn Cypriano-McAferty, Program Manager, Washington State Higher Education Coordinating Board, 917 Lakeridge Way SW, PO Box 43430, Olympia, WA 98504-3430. *E-mail:* passporttocollege@hecb.wa.gov. *Phone:* 888-535-0747 Ext. 5. *Fax:* 360-704-6246.

**Washington Award for Vocational Excellence (WAVE).** Award to honor vocational students from the legislative districts of Washington. Grants for up to two years of undergraduate resident tuition. Must be enrolled in Washington high school, skills center, or community or technical college at time of application. To be eligible to apply student must complete 360 hours in single vocational program in high school or one year at technical college. Contact principal, guidance counselor, or on-campus WAVE coordinator for more information. No new monetary scholarships awarded for 2011 and 2012 cohorts due to state budget cuts. Payments made during current fiscal year fulfill monetary commitments to cohorts awarded in 2010 and prior. *Award:* Scholarship for use in freshman, sophomore, junior, or senior years; renewable. *Number of awards:* 147. *Eligibility Requirements:* Applicant must be enrolled or expecting to enroll full- or part-time at a two-year or four-year or technical institution or university; resident of Washington and studying in Washington. Available to U.S. citizens. *Application Requirements:* Application form, recommendations or references.

Contact Terri Colbert, Program Specialist, Washington State Higher Education Coordinating Board, Workforce Training and Education Coordinating Board, PO Box 43105, Olympia, WA 98504-3105. *E-mail:* tcolbert@wtb.wa.gov. *Phone:* 360-709-4623. *Fax:* 360-586-5862.

**Washington Scholars Program.** Awards high school students from the leg

islative districts of Washington. Must enroll in college or university in Washington. Scholarships up to four years of full-time resident undergraduate tuition and fees. Student must not pursue a degree in theology. Contact principal or guidance counselor for more information. Requires nomination by high school principal and rank within the top 1 percent of his or her graduating senior class. Awards for new recipients selected for the 2011-2013 biennium are honorary recognition-only certificates. The monetary scholarship benefit has been suspended for new Washington Scholars during those years due to state budget cuts. Available funding is obligated to honoring residual, pre-existing monetary benefits awarded to scholarship-eligible recipients selected in 2010 and earlier. *Award:* Scholarship for use in freshman, sophomore, junior, or senior years; renewable. *Number of awards:* 147. *Eligibility Requirements:* Applicant must be high school student; planning to enroll or expecting to enroll full- or part-time at a two-year or four-year institution or university; resident of Washington and studying in Washington. Available to U.S. citizens. *Application Requirements:* Application form, community service, leadership activities, test scores, transcript. **Deadline:** January 22.

Contact Ann Voyles, Program Manager, Washington State Higher Education Coordinating Board, 917 Lakeridge Way, PO Box 43430, Olympia, WA 98504-3430. *E-mail:* annv@wsac.wa.gov. *Phone:* 360-753-7843. *Fax:* 360-704-6243.

**Washington State Need Grant Program.** The program helps Washington's lowest-income undergraduate students to pursue degrees, hone skills, or retrain for new careers. Students with family incomes equal to or less than 50 percent of the state median are eligible for up to 100 percent of the maximum grant. Students with incomes between 51-70% of the state median are prorated dependent on income. All grants are subject to funding. *Award:* Grant for use in freshman, sophomore, junior, or senior years; not renewable. *Award amount:* $176–$10,868. *Number of awards:* 74,000. *Eligibility Requirements:* Applicant must be enrolled or expecting to enroll full- or part-time at a two-year or four-year or technical institution or university; resident of Washington and studying in Washington. Available to U.S. citizens. *Application Requirements:* Application form, FAFSA, financial need analysis. **Deadline:** continuous.

# WEST VIRGINIA

**West Virginia Higher Education Grant Program.** Award available for West Virginia resident for one year immediately preceding the date of application, high school graduate or the equivalent, demonstrate financial need, and enroll as a full-time undergraduate at an approved university or college located in West Virginia or Pennsylvania. *Award:* Grant for use in freshman, sophomore, junior, or senior years; not renewable. *Award amount:* $300–$2600. *Number of awards:* 18,000–21,152. *Eligibility Requirements:* Applicant must be enrolled or expecting to enroll full-time at a two-year or four-year institution or university; resident of West Virginia and studying in Pennsylvania, West Virginia. Available to U.S. citizens. *Application Requirements:* Application form may be submitted online (http://www.fafsa.gov), FAFSA, financial need analysis. **Deadline:** April 15.

Contact Judy Smith, Senior Project Coordinator, West Virginia Higher Education Policy Commission-Student Services, 1018 Kanawha Boulevard East, Suite 700, Charleston, WV 25301-2827. *E-mail:* kee@hepc.wvnet.edu. *Phone:* 304-558-4618. *Fax:* 304-558-4622. *Website:* http://www.wvhepc.com.

# WISCONSIN

**Handicapped Student Grant-Wisconsin.** One-time award available to residents of Wisconsin who have severe or profound hearing or visual impairment. Must be enrolled at least half-time at a nonprofit institution. If the handicap prevents the student from attending a Wisconsin school, the award may be used out-of-state in a specialized college. Refer to web site for further details http://www. heab.state.wi.us. *Award:* Grant for use in freshman, sophomore, junior, or senior years; not renewable. *Award amount:* $250–$1800. *Eligibility Requirements:* Applicant must be hearing impaired or visually impaired; enrolled or expecting to enroll full- or part-time at a four-year institution or university and resident of Wisconsin. Applicant must be hearing impaired or visually impaired. Available to U.S. citizens. *Application Requirements:* Application form, financial need analysis. **Deadline:** continuous.

Contact Sandy Thomas, Program Coordinator, Wisconsin Higher Educational Aid Board, PO Box 7885, Madison, WI 53707-7885. *E-mail:* sandy. thomas@wi.gov. *Phone:* 608-266-0888.

*Fax:* 608-267-2808. *Website:* http://www. heab.wi.gov/.

**Minority Undergraduate Retention Grant-Wisconsin.** The grant provides financial assistance to African-American, Native-American, Hispanic, and former citizens of Laos, Vietnam, and Cambodia, for study in Wisconsin. Must be Wisconsin resident, enrolled at least half-time in Wisconsin Technical College System schools, non-profit independent colleges and universities, and tribal colleges. Refer to web site for further details http://www. heab.state.wi.us. *Award:* Grant for use in sophomore, junior, or senior years; not renewable. *Award amount:* $250–$2500. *Eligibility Requirements:* Applicant must be American Indian/Alaska Native, Asian/Pacific Islander, Black (non-Hispanic), Hispanic; enrolled or expecting to enroll full- or part-time at a two-year or four-year or technical institution or university; resident of Wisconsin and studying in Wisconsin. Available to U.S. and non-U.S. citizens. *Application Requirements:* Application form, financial need analysis. **Deadline:** continuous.

Contact Mary Lou Kuzdas, Program Coordinator, Wisconsin Higher Educational Aid Board, PO Box 7885, Madison, WI 53707-7885. *E-mail:* mary. kuzdas@wi.gov. *Phone:* 608-267-2212. *Fax:* 608-267-2808. *Website:* http://www. heab.wi.gov/.

**Talent Incentive Program Grant.** Grant assists residents of Wisconsin who are attending a nonprofit institution in Wisconsin, and who have substantial financial need. Must meet income criteria, be considered economically and educationally disadvantaged, and be enrolled at least half-time. Refer to web site for further details http://www.heab.state.wi. us. *Award:* Grant for use in freshman, sophomore, junior, or senior years; renewable. *Award amount:* $250–$1800. *Eligibility Requirements:* Applicant must be enrolled or expecting to enroll full- or part-time at a two-year or four-year or technical institution or university; resident of Wisconsin and studying in Wisconsin. Available to U.S. citizens. *Application Requirements:* Application form, financial need analysis, nomination by financial aid office. **Deadline:** continuous.

Contact Colette Brown, Program Coordinator, Wisconsin Higher Educational Aid Board, PO Box 7885, Madison, WI 53707-7885. *E-mail:* colette.brown@wi.gov. *Phone:* 608-266-1665. *Fax:* 608-267-2808. *Website:* http:// www.heab.wi.gov/.

**Veterans Education (VetEd) Reimbursement Grant.** The grant is for eligible Wisconsin veterans enrolled at approved schools who have not yet earned a BS/BA. Reimburses up to 120 credits or eight semesters at the UW Madison rate for the same number of credits taken in one semester or term. The number of credits or semesters is based on length of time serving on active duty in the armed forces (active duty for training does not apply). Application is due no later than 60 days after the course start date. The student must earn a 2.0 or better for the semester. An eligible veteran will have entered active duty as a Wisconsin resident or lived in state for twelve consecutive months since entering active duty. *Award:* Grant for use in freshman, sophomore, junior, or senior years; renewable. *Award amount:* up to $4000. *Number of awards:* up to 350. *Eligibility Requirements:* Applicant must be enrolled or expecting to enroll full- or part-time at a two-year or four-year or technical institution or university; resident of Wisconsin and studying in Minnesota, Wisconsin. Applicant must have 2.5 GPA or higher. Available to U.S. citizens. Applicant must have served in the Air Force, Army, Coast Guard, Marine Corps, or Navy. *Application Requirements:* Application form, certified Wisconsin veteran. **Deadline:** continuous.

Contact Mrs. Leslie Busby-Amegashie, Analyst, Wisconsin Department of Veterans Affairs (WDVA), PO Box 7843, Madison, WI 53707-7843. *E-mail:* leslie.busby-amegashie@dva. wisconsin.gov. *Phone:* 800-947-8387. *Fax:* 608-267-0403. *Website:* http://www. dva.state.wi.us/.

**Wisconsin Academic Excellence Scholarship.** Renewable award for high school seniors with the highest GPA in graduating class. Must be a Wisconsin resident attending a nonprofit Wisconsin institution full-time. Scholarship value is $2250 toward tuition each year for up to four years. Must maintain 3.0 GPA for renewal. Refer to your high school counselor for more details. *Award:* Scholarship for use in freshman year; renewable. *Award amount:* up to $2250. *Eligibility Requirements:* Applicant must be high school student; planning to enroll or expecting to enroll full-time at a two-year or four-year or technical institution or university; resident of Wisconsin and studying in Wisconsin. Applicant must have 3.0 GPA or higher. Available to U.S. citizens. *Application Requirements:* Application form, test scores, transcript. **Deadline:** continuous.

Contact Nancy Wilkison, Program Coordinator, Wisconsin Higher Educational Aid Board, PO Box 7885, Madison, WI 53707-7885. *E-mail:* nancy.wilkison@wi.gov. *Phone:* 608-267-2213. *Fax:* 608-267-2808. *Website:* http://www.heab.wi.gov/.

**Wisconsin Higher Education Grants (WHEG).** Grants for residents of Wisconsin enrolled at least half-time in degree or certificate programs at a University of Wisconsin Institution, Wisconsin Technical College or an approved Tribal College. Must show financial need. Refer to web site for further details http://www.heab.wi.gov. *Award:* Grant for use in freshman, sophomore, junior, or senior years; not renewable. *Award amount:* $250–$3000. *Eligibility Requirements:* Applicant must be enrolled or expecting to enroll full- or part-time at a two-year or four-year or technical institution or university; resident of Wisconsin and studying in Wisconsin. Available to U.S. citizens. *Application Requirements:* Application form, financial need analysis. **Deadline:** continuous.

Contact Sandra Thomas, Program Coordinator, Wisconsin Higher Educational Aid Board, PO Box 7885, Madison, WI 53707-7885. *E-mail:* sandy.thomas@heab.state.wi.us. *Phone:* 608-266-0888. *Fax:* 608-267-2808. *Website:* http://www.heab.wi.gov/.

**Wisconsin League for Nursing, Inc. Scholarship.** One-time award for Wisconsin residents who have completed half of an accredited Wisconsin school of nursing program. Financial need of student must be demonstrated. Scholarship applications are mailed by WLN office ONLY to Wisconsin nursing schools in January for distribution to students. Students interested in obtaining an application must contact their nursing school and submit completed applications to their school. Applications sent directly to WLN office will be returned to applicant. For further information visit web site http://www.wisconsinwln.org/Scholarships.htm. Nursing. *Award:* Scholarship for use in junior or senior years; not renewable. *Award amount:* $500–$1000. *Number of awards:* 11–35. *Eligibility Requirements:* Applicant must be enrolled or expecting to enroll full-time at a two-year or four-year or technical institution or university; resident of Wisconsin and studying in Wisconsin. Available to U.S. citizens. *Application Requirements:* Application form, essay, financial need analysis. **Deadline:** March 1.

Contact Mary Ann Tanner, Administrative Secretary. *E-mail:* wln@wisconsinwln.org. *Phone:* 888-755-3329. *Website:* http://www.wisconsinwln.org/.

**Wisconsin Native American/Indian Student Assistance Grant.** Grants for Wisconsin residents who are at least one-quarter American Indian. Must be attending a college or university within the state. Refer to web site for further details, http://www.heab.state.wi.us. *Award:* Grant for use in freshman, sophomore, junior, or senior years; not renewable. *Award amount:* $250–$1100. *Eligibility Requirements:* Applicant must be American Indian/Alaska Native; enrolled or expecting to enroll full- or part-time at a two-year or four-year or technical institution or university; resident of Wisconsin and studying in Wisconsin. Available to U.S. citizens. *Application Requirements:* Application form, financial need analysis. **Deadline:** continuous.

Contact Sandra Thomas, Program Coordinator, Wisconsin Higher Educational Aid Board, PO Box 7885, Madison, WI 53707-7885. *E-mail:* sandy.thomas@wi.gov. *Phone:* 608-266-0888. *Fax:* 608-267-2808. *Website:* http://www.heab.wi.gov/.

# WYOMING

**Douvas Memorial Scholarship.** Available to Wyoming residents who are first-generation Americans. Must be between 18 and 22 years old. Must be used at any Wyoming public institution of higher education for study in freshman year. *Award:* Scholarship for use in freshman year; not renewable. *Award amount:* $500. *Number of awards:* 2. *Eligibility Requirements:* Applicant must be age 18-22; enrolled or expecting to enroll full- or part-time at a two-year or four-year institution or university; resident of Wyoming and studying in Wyoming. Available to U.S. citizens. *Application Requirements:* Application form. **Deadline:** April 30.

Contact Stephanie Brady, Social Studies Consultant, Wyoming Department of Education, 2300 Capitol Avenue, Hathaway Building, 2nd Floor, Cheyenne, WY 82002. *E-mail:* stephanie.brady@wyo.gov. *Phone:* 307-777-3793. *Fax:* 307-777-6234. *Website:* http://edu.wyoming.gov/.

**Hathaway Scholarship.** Scholarship for Wyoming students to pursue postsecondary education within the state. Award ranges from $840 to $1680 per semester. Deadline varies. *Award:* Scholarship for use in freshman, sophomore, junior, senior, or graduate years; renewable. *Award amount:* $840–$1680. *Eligibility Requirements:* Applicant must be enrolled or expecting to enroll full- or part-time at a two-year or four-year institution or university; resident of Wyoming and studying in Wyoming. Applicant must have 2.5 GPA or higher. Available to U.S. citizens. *Application Requirements:* Application form, application form may be submitted online(varies by college), test scores, transcript. **Deadline:** varies.

Contact Mr. Bradley Barker III, Hathaway Scholarship Consultant, Wyoming Department of Education, 2300 Capitol Avenue, Hathaway Building, 2nd Floor, Cheyenne, WY 82002. *E-mail:* bradley.barker@wyo.gov. *Phone:* 307-777-6226. *Fax:* 307-777-6234. *Website:* http://edu.wyoming.gov/.

**Superior Student in Education Scholarship-Wyoming.** Scholarship available each year to sixteen Wyoming high school graduates who plan to teach in Wyoming. The award covers costs of undergraduate tuition at the University of Wyoming or any Wyoming community college. Education. *Award:* Scholarship for use in freshman, sophomore, junior, or senior years; renewable. *Award amount:* $1000. *Number of awards:* 16–16. *Eligibility Requirements:* Applicant must be enrolled or expecting to enroll full-time at a two-year or four-year institution or university; resident of Wyoming and studying in Wyoming. Applicant must have 3.0 GPA or higher. Available to U.S. citizens. *Application Requirements:* Application form, recommendations or references, test scores, transcript. **Deadline:** October 31.

Contact Tammy Mack, Assistant Director, Scholarships, University of Wyoming, Department 3335, 1000 East University Avenue, Laramie, WY 82071. *E-mail:* FinAid@uwyo.edu. *Phone:* 307-766-2412. *Fax:* 307-766-3800. *Website:* http://www.uwyo.edu/scholarships.

**Vietnam Veterans Award-Wyoming.** Scholarship available to Wyoming residents who served in the armed forces between August 5, 1964 and May 7, 1975, and received a Vietnam service medal. *Award:* Scholarship for use in freshman, sophomore, junior, or senior years; renewable. *Eligibility Requirements:* Applicant must be enrolled or expecting to enroll full- or part-time at a two-year or four-year institution or university and resident of Wyoming. Available to U.S. citizens. Applicant or parent must meet one or more of the following requirements: general military experience; retired from active duty; disabled or killed as a result of military service; prisoner of war; or missing in action. *Application Require*

*ments:* Application form. **Deadline:** continuous.

Contact Tammy Mack, Assistant Director, Scholarships, University of Wyoming, Department 3335, 1000 East

University Avenue, Laramie, WY 82071. *E-mail:* FinAid@uwyo.edu. *Phone:* 307-766-2412. *Fax:* 307-766-3800. *Website:* http://www.uwyo.edu/scholarships.

# Indexes

# Non-Need Scholarships for Undergraduates

## Academic Interests/Achievements

### Agriculture

Abilene Christian University, TX
Alabama Agricultural and Mechanical University, AL
Angelo State University, TX
Arkansas State University, AR
Auburn University, AL
Austin Peay State University, TN
Berry College, GA
California Polytechnic State University, San Luis Obispo, CA
California State Polytechnic University, Pomona, CA
California State University, Bakersfield, CA
California State University, Chico, CA
California State University, Fresno, CA
California State University, Stanislaus, CA
Cameron University, OK
Clemson University, SC
Dickinson State University, ND
Dordt College, IA
Eastern Michigan University, MI
Eastern New Mexico University, NM
Ferris State University, MI
Florida Agricultural and Mechanical University, FL
Florida Southern College, FL
Fort Hays State University, KS
Fort Valley State University, GA
Illinois State University, IL
Iowa State University of Science and Technology, IA
Keystone College, PA
Langston University, OK
Lincoln University, MO
Louisiana State University and Agricultural & Mechanical College, LA
Louisiana Tech University, LA
Lubbock Christian University, TX
Michigan State University, MI
Middle Tennessee State University, TN
Mississippi State University, MS
Montana State University, MT
Morehead State University, KY
Murray State University, KY
New Mexico State University, NM
North Carolina Agricultural and Technical State University, NC
North Carolina State University, NC
Northwestern Oklahoma State University, OK
Northwest Missouri State University, MO
The Ohio State University, OH
Oklahoma State University, OK
Post University, CT
Purdue University, IN
Sam Houston State University, TX
South Dakota State University, SD
Southeast Missouri State University, MO
Southern Illinois University Carbondale, IL
State University of New York College of Environmental Science and Forestry, NY

Stephen F. Austin State University, TX
Sul Ross State University, TX
Tennessee Technological University, TN
Texas A&M University, TX
Texas A&M University–Commerce, TX
Texas Christian University, TX
Texas State University, TX
Texas Tech University, TX
Truman State University, MO
Tuskegee University, AL
University of Alaska Fairbanks, AK
The University of Arizona, AZ
University of Arkansas, AR
University of California, Davis, CA
University of California, Riverside, CA
University of Connecticut, CT
University of Delaware, DE
University of Florida, FL
University of Georgia, GA
University of Idaho, ID
University of Maryland, College Park, MD
University of Maryland Eastern Shore, MD
University of Massachusetts Amherst, MA
University of Minnesota, Crookston, MN
University of Minnesota, Twin Cities Campus, MN
University of Missouri, MO
University of Nebraska–Lincoln, NE
University of Nevada, Reno, NV
University of New Hampshire, NH
The University of Tennessee, TN
The University of Tennessee at Martin, TN
The University of Texas at San Antonio, TX
University of the District of Columbia, DC
University of Vermont, VT
The University of Virginia's College at Wise, VA
University of Wisconsin–River Falls, WI
University of Wisconsin–Stevens Point, WI
University of Wyoming, WY
Utah State University, UT
Vermont Technical College, VT
Washington State University, WA
Western Illinois University, IL
Western Kentucky University, KY
West Texas A&M University, TX
West Virginia University, WV

### Architecture

Auburn University, AL
Ball State University, IN
Boston Architectural College, MA
California Baptist University, CA
California Polytechnic State University, San Luis Obispo, CA
California State Polytechnic University, Pomona, CA
California State University, Bakersfield, CA
Calvin College, MI
City College of the City University of New York, NY
Clemson University, SC
College of Staten Island of the City University of New York, NY

Cooper Union for the Advancement of Science and Art, NY
Drury University, MO
Eastern Michigan University, MI
Fairmont State University, WV
Ferris State University, MI
Florida Agricultural and Mechanical University, FL
Georgia Institute of Technology, GA
Hampton University, VA
Howard University, DC
Idaho State University, ID
Illinois Institute of Technology, IL
Iowa State University of Science and Technology, IA
James Madison University, VA
Kent State University, OH
Lawrence Technological University, MI
Louisiana State University and Agricultural & Mechanical College, LA
Louisiana Tech University, LA
Marywood University, PA
Miami University, OH
Mississippi State University, MS
Missouri Western State University, MO
Montana State University, MT
New Jersey Institute of Technology, NJ
The Ohio State University, OH
Oklahoma State University, OK
Portland State University, OR
Robert Morris University Illinois, IL
Savannah College of Art and Design, GA
Southern California Institute of Architecture, CA
Southern Illinois University Carbondale, IL
State University of New York College of Environmental Science and Forestry, NY
Texas A&M University, TX
Texas Tech University, TX
Tuskegee University, AL
The University of Arizona, AZ
University of Arkansas, AR
University of Colorado Boulder, CO
University of Florida, FL
University of Houston, TX
University of Idaho, ID
University of Illinois at Chicago, IL
The University of Kansas, KS
University of Maryland, College Park, MD
University of Massachusetts Amherst, MA
University of Michigan, MI
University of Minnesota, Twin Cities Campus, MN
University of Nebraska–Lincoln, NE
University of Nevada, Las Vegas, NV
The University of North Carolina at Charlotte, NC
University of Oklahoma, OK
University of Oregon, OR
University of South Florida, FL
The University of Tennessee, TN
The University of Texas at Arlington, TX
The University of Texas at San Antonio, TX
University of Utah, UT
University of Washington, WA

University of Wisconsin–Stevens Point, WI
University of Wyoming, WY
Utah State University, UT
Washington State University, WA
Washington University in St. Louis, MO
West Virginia University, WV
Woodbury University, CA

### Area/Ethnic Studies

Arkansas State University, AR
Augustana College, IL
Binghamton University, State University of
    New York, NY
Birmingham-Southern College, AL
California State University, Chico, CA
California State University, Fresno, CA
California State University, Fullerton, CA
California State University, Stanislaus, CA
Calvin College, MI
City College of the City University of New
    York, NY
The College of New Rochelle, NY
College of Staten Island of the City
    University of New York, NY
Drew University, NJ
Eastern Washington University, WA
Edgewood College, WI
Florida Agricultural and Mechanical
    University, FL
Fort Hays State University, KS
Fort Lewis College, CO
Furman University, SC
Indiana State University, IN
Indiana University of Pennsylvania, PA
Iowa State University of Science and
    Technology, IA
Kean University, NJ
Kent State University, OH
Middle Tennessee State University, TN
Mississippi State University, MS
Montana State University, MT
New Jersey Institute of Technology, NJ
New Mexico State University, NM
Oakland University, MI
The Ohio State University, OH
Ohio University, OH
Ohio University–Chillicothe, OH
Ohio University–Eastern, OH
Ohio University–Lancaster, OH
Ohio University–Southern Campus, OH
Ohio University–Zanesville, OH
Oklahoma State University, OK
Old Dominion University, VA
Ouachita Baptist University, AR
Portland State University, OR
Purchase College, State University of New
    York, NY
Saint Louis University, MO
San Diego State University, CA
Sonoma State University, CA
South Dakota State University, SD
Southern Illinois University Carbondale, IL
State University of New York at New Paltz,
    NY
State University of New York at Oswego,
    NY
State University of New York at Plattsburgh,
    NY
State University of New York College at
    Geneseo, NY
Stetson University, FL
Stockton University, NJ
Stony Brook University, State University of
    New York, NY
The University of Alabama, AL
University of Arkansas, AR

University of California, Davis, CA
University of California, Irvine, CA
University of California, Riverside, CA
University of Colorado Boulder, CO
University of Houston, TX
The University of Kansas, KS
University of Michigan, MI
University of Minnesota, Twin Cities
    Campus, MN
University of Missouri, MO
University of Oklahoma, OK
University of South Carolina, SC
The University of Texas at San Antonio, TX
University of Utah, UT
University of Vermont, VT
University of Wisconsin–Eau Claire, WI
University of Wisconsin–Green Bay, WI
University of Wisconsin–La Crosse, WI
University of Wisconsin–River Falls, WI
University of Wyoming, WY
Warner Pacific College, OR
Washington State University, WA
Wayne State University, MI
Western Illinois University, IL
West Virginia University, WV
Wichita State University, KS
William Jessup University, CA
Wright State University, OH

### Biological Sciences

Abilene Christian University, TX
Alabama Agricultural and Mechanical
    University, AL
Alaska Pacific University, AK
Albany College of Pharmacy and Health
    Sciences, NY
Albany State University, GA
Albertus Magnus College, CT
Alderson Broaddus University, WV
Angelo State University, TX
Arkansas State University, AR
Arkansas Tech University, AR
Armstrong State University, GA
Auburn University, AL
Augustana College, IL
Augustana College, SD
Austin College, TX
Austin Peay State University, TN
Averett University, VA
Ball State University, IN
Belhaven University, MS
Bellarmine University, KY
Belmont University, TN
Bemidji State University, MN
Bethel College, KS
Binghamton University, State University of
    New York, NY
Biola University, CA
Birmingham-Southern College, AL
Bloomfield College, NJ
Bloomsburg University of Pennsylvania, PA
Blue Mountain College, MS
Bluffton University, OH
Boise State University, ID
Bowie State University, MD
Bowling Green State University, OH
Brenau University, GA
Buena Vista University, IA
Buffalo State College, State University of
    New York, NY
Butler University, IN
Caldwell University, NJ
California Lutheran University, CA
California Polytechnic State University, San
    Luis Obispo, CA

California State Polytechnic University,
    Pomona, CA
California State University, Bakersfield, CA
California State University, Chico, CA
California State University, Fresno, CA
California State University, Fullerton, CA
California State University, Los Angeles, CA
California State University, San Bernardino,
    CA
California State University, Stanislaus, CA
Calvin College, MI
Cameron University, OK
Campbellsville University, KY
Carroll University, WI
Carson-Newman University, TN
Case Western Reserve University, OH
Castleton State College, VT
Centenary College of Louisiana, LA
Central College, IA
Central Methodist University, MO
Central Michigan University, MI
Chapman University, CA
Christopher Newport University, VA
The Citadel, The Military College of South
    Carolina, SC
City College of the City University of New
    York, NY
Clarion University of Pennsylvania, PA
Clarkson University, NY
Clemson University, SC
Cleveland State University, OH
Coastal Carolina University, SC
Coe College, IA
Coker College, SC
The College at Brockport, State University
    of New York, NY
College of Charleston, SC
The College of Idaho, ID
The College of New Rochelle, NY
College of Saint Mary, NE
College of Staten Island of the City
    University of New York, NY
The Colorado College, CO
Colorado Mesa University, CO
Colorado State University–Pueblo, CO
Columbia College, MO
Columbus State University, GA
Concordia University Chicago, IL
Concordia University, Nebraska, NE
Concordia University Texas, TX
Dakota Wesleyan University, SD
Dallas Baptist University, TX
Davidson College, NC
Delta State University, MS
Denison University, OH
DeSales University, PA
Dickinson State University, ND
Dordt College, IA
Drew University, NJ
Drury University, MO
D'Youville College, NY
East Carolina University, NC
Eastern Illinois University, IL
Eastern Michigan University, MI
Eastern New Mexico University, NM
Eastern Washington University, WA
East Stroudsburg University of
    Pennsylvania, PA
East Texas Baptist University, TX
Elizabethtown College, PA
Elmhurst College, IL
Elon University, NC
Emporia State University, KS
Evangel University, MO
Fairmont State University, WV
Ferris State University, MI

Florida Agricultural and Mechanical University, FL
Florida Gulf Coast University, FL
Florida Southern College, FL
Fordham University, NY
Fort Hays State University, KS
Fort Lewis College, CO
Framingham State University, MA
Francis Marion University, SC
Friends University, KS
Frostburg State University, MD
Furman University, SC
Gannon University, PA
Gardner-Webb University, NC
George Fox University, OR
Georgia College & State University, GA
Georgia Institute of Technology, GA
Georgian Court University, NJ
Georgia Southern University, GA
Glenville State College, WV
Governors State University, IL
Grambling State University, LA
Grand View University, IA
Greenville College, IL
Grove City College, PA
Guilford College, NC
Hamline University, MN
Hampden-Sydney College, VA
Hampshire College, MA
Hampton University, VA
Hardin-Simmons University, TX
Hawai`i Pacific University, HI
Henderson State University, AR
Hillsdale College, MI
Howard Payne University, TX
Howard University, DC
Huntingdon College, AL
Huntington University, IN
Husson University, ME
Idaho State University, ID
Illinois State University, IL
Indiana State University, IN
Indiana University of Pennsylvania, PA
Indiana University–Purdue University Fort Wayne, IN
Iowa State University of Science and Technology, IA
Jacksonville State University, AL
James Madison University, VA
Jefferson College of Health Sciences, VA
John Carroll University, OH
Johnson C. Smith University, NC
Juniata College, PA
Kansas Wesleyan University, KS
Kean University, NJ
Kennesaw State University, GA
Kent State University, OH
King's College, PA
Kutztown University of Pennsylvania, PA
Lake Erie College, OH
La Sierra University, CA
Lebanon Valley College, PA
Lees-McRae College, NC
Lee University, TN
Lewis-Clark State College, ID
Liberty University, VA
Lincoln University, PA
Lindenwood University, MO
Lindsey Wilson College, KY
Linfield College, OR
Lipscomb University, TN
Lock Haven University of Pennsylvania, PA
Long Island University–LIU Post, NY
Longwood University, VA

Louisiana State University and Agricultural & Mechanical College, LA
Louisiana Tech University, LA
Loyola Marymount University, CA
Lycoming College, PA
Lynn University, FL
Maine Maritime Academy, ME
Malone University, OH
Manhattan College, NY
Mansfield University of Pennsylvania, PA
Marquette University, WI
Marymount Manhattan College, NY
Marymount University, VA
Maryville University of Saint Louis, MO
Marywood University, PA
Massachusetts College of Liberal Arts, MA
The Master's College and Seminary, CA
Mayville State University, ND
McKendree University, IL
McMurry University, TX
Mercer University, GA
Meredith College, NC
Michigan State University, MI
Middle Tennessee State University, TN
Midwestern State University, TX
Millersville University of Pennsylvania, PA
Millikin University, IL
Mills College, CA
Minnesota State University Moorhead, MN
Minot State University, ND
Mississippi State University, MS
Mississippi University for Women, MS
Missouri University of Science and Technology, MO
Missouri Valley College, MO
Missouri Western State University, MO
Molloy College, NY
Montana State University, MT
Montana State University Billings, MT
Montclair State University, NJ
Moravian College, PA
Morehead State University, KY
Murray State University, KY
Muskingum University, OH
Newberry College, SC
New England College, NH
New Jersey Institute of Technology, NJ
New Mexico Highlands University, NM
New Mexico State University, NM
North Carolina Central University, NC
North Carolina State University, NC
North Central College, IL
Northeastern Illinois University, IL
Northeastern State University, OK
Northern Illinois University, IL
Northern Kentucky University, KY
Northern Michigan University, MI
Northern State University, SD
Northwestern Oklahoma State University, OK
Northwest Missouri State University, MO
Northwest Nazarene University, ID
Oakland University, MI
The Ohio State University, OH
Ohio University, OH
Ohio University–Chillicothe, OH
Ohio University–Eastern, OH
Ohio University–Lancaster, OH
Ohio University–Southern Campus, OH
Ohio University–Zanesville, OH
Oklahoma Baptist University, OK
Oklahoma State University, OK
Oklahoma Wesleyan University, OK
Old Dominion University, VA
Oral Roberts University, OK

Ouachita Baptist University, AR
Pace University, NY
Pacific University, OR
Piedmont College, GA
Pine Manor College, MA
Pittsburg State University, KS
Point Loma Nazarene University, CA
Post University, CT
Purchase College, State University of New York, NY
Quincy University, IL
Randolph College, VA
Regis University, CO
Rochester Institute of Technology, NY
Rockford University, IL
Rockhurst University, MO
Sacred Heart University, CT
Saginaw Valley State University, MI
St. Ambrose University, IA
Saint Augustine's University, NC
St. Cloud State University, MN
St. Edward's University, TX
Saint Francis University, PA
St. John Fisher College, NY
St. John's University, NY
Saint Louis University, MO
Samford University, AL
Sam Houston State University, TX
San Diego State University, CA
Savannah State University, GA
Schreiner University, TX
Seton Hill University, PA
Shepherd University, WV
Shippensburg University of Pennsylvania, PA
Siena College, NY
Skidmore College, NY
Slippery Rock University of Pennsylvania, PA
Sonoma State University, CA
South Dakota School of Mines and Technology, SD
South Dakota State University, SD
Southeastern Oklahoma State University, OK
Southeast Missouri State University, MO
Southern Illinois University Carbondale, IL
Southern Oregon University, OR
Southwestern College, KS
Southwestern Oklahoma State University, OK
State University of New York at Fredonia, NY
State University of New York at New Paltz, NY
State University of New York at Oswego, NY
State University of New York at Plattsburgh, NY
State University of New York College at Geneseo, NY
State University of New York College at Old Westbury, NY
State University of New York College at Potsdam, NY
State University of New York College of Environmental Science and Forestry, NY
Stephen F. Austin State University, TX
Stetson University, FL
Stockton University, NJ
Stony Brook University, State University of New York, NY
Sul Ross State University, TX
Tabor College, KS
Tennessee Technological University, TN

Texas A&M University, TX
Texas A&M University–Commerce, TX
Texas Christian University, TX
Texas Lutheran University, TX
Texas Tech University, TX
Texas Wesleyan University, TX
Texas Woman's University, TX
Thiel College, PA
Thomas More College, KY
Thomas University, GA
Towson University, MD
Trevecca Nazarene University, TN
Trinity Christian College, IL
Truman State University, MO
Union College, KY
Union University, TN
The University of Akron, OH
The University of Alabama, AL
The University of Alabama in Huntsville, AL
University of Alaska Anchorage, AK
University of Alaska Fairbanks, AK
The University of Arizona, AZ
University of Arkansas, AR
University of California, Davis, CA
University of California, Irvine, CA
University of California, Riverside, CA
University of California, San Diego, CA
University of Central Oklahoma, OK
University of Colorado Boulder, CO
University of Colorado Denver, CO
University of Connecticut, CT
University of Dallas, TX
University of Dayton, OH
University of Delaware, DE
University of Denver, CO
University of Evansville, IN
University of Great Falls, MT
University of Houston, TX
University of Houston–Clear Lake, TX
University of Idaho, ID
University of Illinois at Springfield, IL
The University of Kansas, KS
University of Louisville, KY
University of Maine at Augusta, ME
University of Maine at Fort Kent, ME
University of Mary Hardin-Baylor, TX
University of Maryland, Baltimore County, MD
University of Maryland, College Park, MD
University of Mary Washington, VA
University of Massachusetts Amherst, MA
University of Massachusetts Dartmouth, MA
University of Massachusetts Lowell, MA
University of Memphis, TN
University of Michigan, MI
University of Michigan–Dearborn, MI
University of Michigan–Flint, MI
University of Minnesota, Crookston, MN
University of Minnesota, Twin Cities Campus, MN
University of Mississippi, MS
University of Missouri, MO
University of Missouri–St. Louis, MO
The University of Montana, MT
The University of Montana Western, MT
University of Montevallo, AL
University of Nebraska at Omaha, NE
University of Nebraska–Lincoln, NE
University of Nevada, Las Vegas, NV
University of Nevada, Reno, NV
University of New Hampshire, NH
University of New Hampshire at Manchester, NH
University of New Orleans, LA

University of North Carolina at Asheville, NC
The University of North Carolina at Greensboro, NC
The University of North Carolina Wilmington, NC
University of Northern Colorado, CO
University of Northern Iowa, IA
University of North Georgia, GA
University of Oklahoma, OK
University of Oregon, OR
University of Pittsburgh at Bradford, PA
University of Pittsburgh at Johnstown, PA
University of Portland, OR
University of Puget Sound, WA
University of Richmond, VA
University of Rio Grande, OH
University of St. Francis, IL
University of St. Thomas, MN
University of St. Thomas, TX
University of South Carolina, SC
University of South Carolina Aiken, SC
The University of South Dakota, SD
University of Southern Indiana, IN
University of South Florida, FL
The University of Tampa, FL
The University of Tennessee at Chattanooga, TN
The University of Tennessee at Martin, TN
The University of Texas at Arlington, TX
The University of Texas at Brownsville, TX
The University of Texas at Dallas, TX
The University of Texas at El Paso, TX
The University of Texas at San Antonio, TX
The University of Texas–Pan American, TX
The University of Toledo, OH
The University of Tulsa, OK
University of Utah, UT
The University of Virginia's College at Wise, VA
University of West Florida, FL
University of West Georgia, GA
University of Wisconsin–Eau Claire, WI
University of Wisconsin–Green Bay, WI
University of Wisconsin–La Crosse, WI
University of Wisconsin–Parkside, WI
University of Wisconsin–River Falls, WI
University of Wisconsin–Stevens Point, WI
University of Wisconsin–Superior, WI
University of Wisconsin–Whitewater, WI
University of Wyoming, WY
Utah State University, UT
Valdosta State University, GA
Valley City State University, ND
Virginia Commonwealth University, VA
Virginia Military Institute, VA
Virginia State University, VA
Walla Walla University, WA
Warner Pacific College, OR
Wartburg College, IA
Washburn University, KS
Washington State University, WA
Washington University in St. Louis, MO
Wayland Baptist University, TX
Waynesburg University, PA
Wayne State College, NE
Wayne State University, MI
Webster University, MO
Wesleyan College, GA
Western Carolina University, NC
Western Illinois University, IL
Western Kentucky University, KY
Western Oregon University, OR
Western Washington University, WA
West Virginia University, WV
Wheaton College, IL

Wichita State University, KS
Widener University, PA
William Jessup University, CA
Williams Baptist College, AR
Wilson College, PA
Wisconsin Lutheran College, WI
Wright State University, OH
Xavier University of Louisiana, LA
Youngstown State University, OH

**Business**
Abilene Christian University, TX
Adelphi University, NY
Adrian College, MI
Alaska Pacific University, AK
Albertus Magnus College, CT
Albion College, MI
Alderson Broaddus University, WV
Alliant International University–San Diego, CA
American Jewish University, CA
Anderson University, SC
Angelo State University, TX
Arkansas State University, AR
Arkansas Tech University, AR
Auburn University, AL
Augustana College, IL
Augustana College, SD
Austin College, TX
Austin Peay State University, TN
Averett University, VA
Ball State University, IN
Baylor University, TX
Belhaven University, MS
Bellarmine University, KY
Belmont University, TN
Bemidji State University, MN
Berry College, GA
Binghamton University, State University of New York, NY
Birmingham-Southern College, AL
Bloomfield College, NJ
Bloomsburg University of Pennsylvania, PA
Blue Mountain College, MS
Boise State University, ID
Bowie State University, MD
Bowling Green State University, OH
Brenau University, GA
Bucknell University, PA
Buena Vista University, IA
Buffalo State College, State University of New York, NY
Butler University, IN
California Lutheran University, CA
California Polytechnic State University, San Luis Obispo, CA
California State Polytechnic University, Pomona, CA
California State University, Bakersfield, CA
California State University, Chico, CA
California State University, Fresno, CA
California State University, Fullerton, CA
California State University, Los Angeles, CA
California State University, Monterey Bay, CA
California State University, San Bernardino, CA
California State University, Stanislaus, CA
Calvin College, MI
Cameron University, OK
Campbellsville University, KY
Carroll University, WI
Carson-Newman University, TN
Case Western Reserve University, OH
Castleton State College, VT
Cedar Crest College, PA

Centenary College of Louisiana, LA
Central College, IA
Central Methodist University, MO
Central Michigan University, MI
Champlain College, VT
Christopher Newport University, VA
The Citadel, The Military College of South Carolina, SC
Clarion University of Pennsylvania, PA
Clarkson University, NY
Clemson University, SC
Cleveland State University, OH
Coastal Carolina University, SC
Coe College, IA
The College at Brockport, State University of New York, NY
College of Charleston, SC
The College of Idaho, ID
The College of New Rochelle, NY
The College of Saint Rose, NY
College of Staten Island of the City University of New York, NY
Colorado Mesa University, CO
Colorado School of Mines, CO
Colorado State University–Pueblo, CO
Columbia College, MO
Columbus State University, GA
Concordia University Ann Arbor, MI
Concordia University Chicago, IL
Concordia University, Nebraska, NE
Concordia University Texas, TX
Concord University, WV
Cornerstone University, MI
Creighton University, NE
Dakota State University, SD
Dakota Wesleyan University, SD
Dallas Baptist University, TX
Davidson College, NC
Delta State University, MS
DeSales University, PA
Dickinson State University, ND
Dordt College, IA
Dowling College, NY
Drury University, MO
D'Youville College, NY
East Carolina University, NC
Eastern Illinois University, IL
Eastern Michigan University, MI
Eastern New Mexico University, NM
Eastern University, PA
Eastern Washington University, WA
East Stroudsburg University of Pennsylvania, PA
East Texas Baptist University, TX
ECPI University, VA
Elizabethtown College, PA
Elmhurst College, IL
Elon University, NC
Emmanuel College, GA
Emory University, GA
Emporia State University, KS
Endicott College, MA
Evangel University, MO
Fairmont State University, WV
Felician College, NJ
Five Towns College, NY
Flagler College, FL
Florida Agricultural and Mechanical University, FL
Florida Atlantic University, FL
Florida Gulf Coast University, FL
Florida Institute of Technology, FL
Florida Southern College, FL
Fordham University, NY

Fort Hays State University, KS
Fort Lewis College, CO
Fort Valley State University, GA
Francis Marion University, SC
Fresno Pacific University, CA
Frostburg State University, MD
Furman University, SC
Gannon University, PA
Gardner-Webb University, NC
George Fox University, OR
Georgia College & State University, GA
Georgian Court University, NJ
Georgia Regents University, GA
Georgia Southern University, GA
Glenville State College, WV
Golden Gate University, CA
Gonzaga University, WA
Goshen College, IN
Governors State University, IL
Grambling State University, LA
Grand Valley State University, MI
Grand View University, IA
Grove City College, PA
Hamline University, MN
Hampton University, VA
Hardin-Simmons University, TX
Hawai`i Pacific University, HI
Hillsdale College, MI
Hillsdale Free Will Baptist College, OK
Howard Payne University, TX
Howard University, DC
Huntington University, IN
Husson University, ME
Idaho State University, ID
Illinois Institute of Technology, IL
Illinois State University, IL
Indiana State University, IN
Indiana University of Pennsylvania, PA
Iowa State University of Science and Technology, IA
Iowa Wesleyan College, IA
Jacksonville State University, AL
James Madison University, VA
John Carroll University, OH
Juniata College, PA
Kansas Wesleyan University, KS
Kean University, NJ
Kennesaw State University, GA
Kent State University, OH
Kent State University at Geauga, OH
Kent State University at Stark, OH
Kentucky Christian University, KY
King's College, PA
Kutztown University of Pennsylvania, PA
Lake Erie College, OH
Langston University, OK
La Sierra University, CA
Lawrence Technological University, MI
Lee University, TN
Lehigh University, PA
Lewis-Clark State College, ID
Liberty University, VA
Lincoln University, PA
Lindenwood University, MO
Lindsey Wilson College, KY
Linfield College, OR
Lipscomb University, TN
Lock Haven University of Pennsylvania, PA
Long Island University–LIU Post, NY
Longwood University, VA
Louisiana State University and Agricultural & Mechanical College, LA
Louisiana Tech University, LA
Loyola Marymount University, CA
Lubbock Christian University, TX

Lycoming College, PA
Lynn University, FL
Lyon College, AR
Maine Maritime Academy, ME
Malone University, OH
Manhattan College, NY
Maranatha Baptist University, WI
Marquette University, WI
Marymount University, VA
Maryville University of Saint Louis, MO
Marywood University, PA
Massachusetts College of Liberal Arts, MA
The Master's College and Seminary, CA
Mayville State University, ND
McKendree University, IL
McMurry University, TX
Mercer University, GA
Meredith College, NC
Methodist University, NC
Michigan State University, MI
Michigan Technological University, MI
Middle Tennessee State University, TN
Midwestern State University, TX
Millersville University of Pennsylvania, PA
Millikin University, IL
Millsaps College, MS
Milwaukee School of Engineering, WI
Minnesota State University Moorhead, MN
Minot State University, ND
Misericordia University, PA
Mississippi State University, MS
Mississippi University for Women, MS
Missouri University of Science and Technology, MO
Missouri Valley College, MO
Missouri Western State University, MO
Molloy College, NY
Monmouth University, NJ
Montana State University, MT
Montana State University Billings, MT
Montana Tech of The University of Montana, MT
Montclair State University, NJ
Moravian College, PA
Morehead State University, KY
Mount Mary University, WI
Murray State University, KY
Newberry College, SC
New England College, NH
New Jersey Institute of Technology, NJ
New Mexico Highlands University, NM
New Mexico State University, NM
North Carolina Agricultural and Technical State University, NC
North Carolina Central University, NC
North Carolina State University, NC
North Central College, IL
Northeastern Illinois University, IL
Northeastern State University, OK
Northern Illinois University, IL
Northern Kentucky University, KY
Northern Michigan University, MI
Northern State University, SD
Northwestern Oklahoma State University, OK
Northwest Missouri State University, MO
Northwest Nazarene University, ID
Oakland University, MI
The Ohio State University, OH
Ohio University, OH
Ohio University–Chillicothe, OH
Ohio University–Eastern, OH
Ohio University–Lancaster, OH
Ohio University–Southern Campus, OH
Ohio University–Zanesville, OH

Ohio Wesleyan University, OH
Oklahoma Baptist University, OK
Oklahoma City University, OK
Oklahoma State University, OK
Oklahoma Wesleyan University, OK
Old Dominion University, VA
Olivet College, MI
Oral Roberts University, OK
Ouachita Baptist University, AR
Pace University, NY
Pacific University, OR
Peirce College, PA
Piedmont College, GA
Pittsburg State University, KS
Point Loma Nazarene University, CA
Portland State University, OR
Post University, CT
Providence College, RI
Quincy University, IL
Regent University, VA
Robert Morris University Illinois, IL
Rochester College, MI
Rochester Institute of Technology, NY
Rockford University, IL
Rockhurst University, MO
Sacred Heart University, CT
Saginaw Valley State University, MI
St. Andrews University, NC
St. Bonaventure University, NY
St. Catherine University, MN
St. Cloud State University, MN
St. Edward's University, TX
Saint Francis University, PA
St. John Fisher College, NY
St. John's University, NY
Saint Louis University, MO
Saint Martin's University, WA
St. Thomas Aquinas College, NY
Salisbury University, MD
Samford University, AL
Sam Houston State University, TX
San Diego State University, CA
Santa Clara University, CA
Savannah State University, GA
Schreiner University, TX
Seton Hill University, PA
Shenandoah University, VA
Shepherd University, WV
Shippensburg University of Pennsylvania, PA
Siena College, NY
Slippery Rock University of Pennsylvania, PA
Sonoma State University, CA
South Dakota State University, SD
Southeastern Louisiana University, LA
Southeastern Oklahoma State University, OK
Southeast Missouri State University, MO
Southern Illinois University Carbondale, IL
Southern Illinois University Edwardsville, IL
Southern Oregon University, OR
Southwestern College, KS
Southwestern Oklahoma State University, OK
Southwestern University, TX
State University of New York at Fredonia, NY
State University of New York at New Paltz, NY
State University of New York at Oswego, NY
State University of New York at Plattsburgh, NY

State University of New York College at Geneseo, NY
State University of New York College at Potsdam, NY
Stephen F. Austin State University, TX
Stetson University, FL
Stockton University, NJ
Stony Brook University, State University of New York, NY
Suffolk University, MA
Sul Ross State University, TX
Susquehanna University, PA
Tennessee Technological University, TN
Texas A&M International University, TX
Texas A&M University, TX
Texas A&M University–Commerce, TX
Texas Christian University, TX
Texas Lutheran University, TX
Texas State University, TX
Texas Tech University, TX
Texas Wesleyan University, TX
Texas Woman's University, TX
Thiel College, PA
Thomas More College, KY
Thomas University, GA
Towson University, MD
Trevecca Nazarene University, TN
Trinity Christian College, IL
Truman State University, MO
Tuskegee University, AL
Union University, TN
The University of Akron, OH
The University of Alabama, AL
The University of Alabama at Birmingham, AL
The University of Alabama in Huntsville, AL
University of Alaska Anchorage, AK
The University of Arizona, AZ
University of Arkansas, AR
University of California, Davis, CA
University of California, Irvine, CA
University of California, Riverside, CA
University of California, San Diego, CA
University of Central Oklahoma, OK
University of Colorado Boulder, CO
University of Colorado Denver, CO
University of Connecticut, CT
University of Dallas, TX
University of Dayton, OH
University of Delaware, DE
University of Denver, CO
University of Evansville, IN
University of Florida, FL
University of Georgia, GA
University of Great Falls, MT
University of Houston, TX
University of Houston–Clear Lake, TX
University of Houston–Downtown, TX
University of Idaho, ID
University of Illinois at Chicago, IL
University of Illinois at Springfield, IL
University of Indianapolis, IN
The University of Iowa, IA
The University of Kansas, KS
University of Louisville, KY
University of Maine at Augusta, ME
University of Maine at Fort Kent, ME
University of Mary Hardin-Baylor, TX
University of Maryland, College Park, MD
University of Maryland Eastern Shore, MD
University of Mary Washington, VA
University of Massachusetts Amherst, MA
University of Massachusetts Dartmouth, MA
University of Massachusetts Lowell, MA
University of Memphis, TN

University of Michigan, MI
University of Michigan–Dearborn, MI
University of Michigan–Flint, MI
University of Minnesota, Twin Cities Campus, MN
University of Mississippi, MS
University of Missouri, MO
University of Missouri–St. Louis, MO
The University of Montana, MT
The University of Montana Western, MT
University of Montevallo, AL
University of Nebraska at Omaha, NE
University of Nebraska–Lincoln, NE
University of Nevada, Las Vegas, NV
University of Nevada, Reno, NV
University of New Hampshire, NH
University of New Hampshire at Manchester, NH
University of New Orleans, LA
University of North Carolina at Asheville, NC
The University of North Carolina at Chapel Hill, NC
The University of North Carolina at Charlotte, NC
The University of North Carolina at Greensboro, NC
The University of North Carolina Wilmington, NC
University of Northern Colorado, CO
University of Northern Iowa, IA
University of North Florida, FL
University of North Georgia, GA
University of Oklahoma, OK
University of Oregon, OR
University of Pittsburgh at Bradford, PA
University of Pittsburgh at Johnstown, PA
University of Portland, OR
University of Puget Sound, WA
University of Rio Grande, OH
University of St. Thomas, MN
University of St. Thomas, TX
University of South Alabama, AL
University of South Carolina, SC
University of South Carolina Aiken, SC
The University of South Dakota, SD
University of Southern Indiana, IN
University of South Florida, FL
The University of Tennessee, TN
The University of Tennessee at Chattanooga, TN
The University of Tennessee at Martin, TN
The University of Texas at Arlington, TX
The University of Texas at Brownsville, TX
The University of Texas at Dallas, TX
The University of Texas at El Paso, TX
The University of Texas at San Antonio, TX
The University of Texas–Pan American, TX
The University of Toledo, OH
The University of Tulsa, OK
University of Utah, UT
University of Vermont, VT
The University of Virginia's College at Wise, VA
University of Washington, WA
University of West Florida, FL
University of West Georgia, GA
University of Wisconsin–Eau Claire, WI
University of Wisconsin–Green Bay, WI
University of Wisconsin–La Crosse, WI
University of Wisconsin–Parkside, WI
University of Wisconsin–River Falls, WI
University of Wisconsin–Stevens Point, WI
University of Wisconsin–Stout, WI
University of Wisconsin–Superior, WI
University of Wisconsin–Whitewater, WI

University of Wyoming, WY
Utah State University, UT
Valley City State University, ND
Valparaiso University, IN
Virginia Commonwealth University, VA
Virginia Military Institute, VA
Walla Walla University, WA
Warner Pacific College, OR
Wartburg College, IA
Washburn University, KS
Washington & Jefferson College, PA
Washington State University, WA
Washington University in St. Louis, MO
Wayland Baptist University, TX
Waynesburg University, PA
Wayne State College, NE
Wayne State University, MI
Webber International University, FL
Webster University, MO
West Chester University of Pennsylvania, PA
Western Carolina University, NC
Western Illinois University, IL
Western Kentucky University, KY
Western Oregon University, OR
Western Washington University, WA
West Texas A&M University, TX
West Virginia University, WV
Wheaton College, IL
Wichita State University, KS
Widener University, PA
William Jessup University, CA
Williams Baptist College, AR
Wilson College, PA
Wisconsin Lutheran College, WI
Woodbury University, CA
Wright State University, OH
Xavier University of Louisiana, LA
Youngstown State University, OH

**Communication**
Abilene Christian University, TX
Adelphi University, NY
Alaska Pacific University, AK
Albertus Magnus College, CT
Albion College, MI
Alderson Broaddus University, WV
Alliant International University–San Diego, CA
Angelo State University, TX
Arkansas State University, AR
Auburn University, AL
Augustana College, IL
Augustana College, SD
Austin College, TX
Austin Peay State University, TN
Ball State University, IN
Baylor University, TX
Belhaven University, MS
Bemidji State University, MN
Berry College, GA
Bethel College, KS
Biola University, CA
Birmingham-Southern College, AL
Bloomsburg University of Pennsylvania, PA
Boise State University, ID
Bowie State University, MD
Bowling Green State University, OH
Brenau University, GA
Buffalo State College, State University of New York, NY
Butler University, IN
California Lutheran University, CA
California Polytechnic State University, San Luis Obispo, CA

California State University, Bakersfield, CA
California State University, Chico, CA
California State University, Fresno, CA
California State University, Fullerton, CA
California State University, Los Angeles, CA
California State University, Stanislaus, CA
Calvin College, MI
Cameron University, OK
Campbellsville University, KY
Case Western Reserve University, OH
Castleton State College, VT
Cedar Crest College, PA
Centenary College of Louisiana, LA
Central College, IA
Central Methodist University, MO
Central Michigan University, MI
Champlain College, VT
Christopher Newport University, VA
City College of the City University of New York, NY
Clarion University of Pennsylvania, PA
Clarkson University, NY
Clemson University, SC
Cleveland State University, OH
Coastal Carolina University, SC
The College at Brockport, State University of New York, NY
College of Charleston, SC
The College of New Rochelle, NY
The College of Saint Rose, NY
College of Staten Island of the City University of New York, NY
Colorado Mesa University, CO
Colorado State University–Pueblo, CO
Columbia College, MO
Columbus State University, GA
Concordia University Chicago, IL
Concordia University, Nebraska, NE
Concordia University Texas, TX
Concord University, WV
Cornerstone University, MI
Dakota State University, SD
Dallas Baptist University, TX
DeSales University, PA
Dickinson State University, ND
Dordt College, IA
Drury University, MO
East Carolina University, NC
East Central University, OK
Eastern Illinois University, IL
Eastern Michigan University, MI
Eastern New Mexico University, NM
Eastern Washington University, WA
East Stroudsburg University of Pennsylvania, PA
East Texas Baptist University, TX
Elizabethtown College, PA
Elmhurst College, IL
Elon University, NC
Emmanuel College, GA
Emporia State University, KS
Evangel University, MO
Ferris State University, MI
Flagler College, FL
Florida Agricultural and Mechanical University, FL
Florida Southern College, FL
Fordham University, NY
Fort Hays State University, KS
Fort Lewis College, CO
Franklin Pierce University, NH
Frostburg State University, MD
Furman University, SC
Gardner-Webb University, NC
George Fox University, OR

Georgetown College, KY
Georgia Southern University, GA
Goshen College, IN
Governors State University, IL
Grambling State University, LA
Grand Valley State University, MI
Grand View University, IA
Grove City College, PA
Hamline University, MN
Hampton University, VA
Harding University, AR
Hardin-Simmons University, TX
Hastings College, NE
Hawai'i Pacific University, HI
Hofstra University, NY
Howard Payne University, TX
Howard University, DC
Huntington University, IN
Idaho State University, ID
Illinois State University, IL
Indiana State University, IN
Indiana University of Pennsylvania, PA
Iowa State University of Science and Technology, IA
Ithaca College, NY
Jacksonville State University, AL
John Carroll University, OH
Juniata College, PA
Kansas Wesleyan University, KS
Kean University, NJ
Kennesaw State University, GA
Kent State University, OH
Kent State University at Stark, OH
King's College, PA
Kutztown University of Pennsylvania, PA
Lake Erie College, OH
Lee University, TN
Lehigh University, PA
Lewis-Clark State College, ID
Liberty University, VA
Lincoln University, PA
Lindenwood University, MO
Linfield College, OR
Lipscomb University, TN
Lock Haven University of Pennsylvania, PA
Long Island University–LIU Brooklyn, NY
Louisiana State University and Agricultural & Mechanical College, LA
Loyola Marymount University, CA
Lubbock Christian University, TX
Lycoming College, PA
Lynn University, FL
Malone University, OH
Mansfield University of Pennsylvania, PA
Marquette University, WI
Marymount University, VA
Marywood University, PA
Massachusetts College of Liberal Arts, MA
Mayville State University, ND
Michigan State University, MI
Middle Tennessee State University, TN
Midwestern State University, TX
Millersville University of Pennsylvania, PA
Millikin University, IL
Milwaukee School of Engineering, WI
Minnesota State University Moorhead, MN
Minot State University, ND
Mississippi State University, MS
Mississippi University for Women, MS
Missouri Valley College, MO
Missouri Western State University, MO
Molloy College, NY
Monmouth University, NJ
Montana State University, MT
Montana State University Billings, MT

Montclair State University, NJ
Morehead State University, KY
Mount Mary University, WI
Murray State University, KY
Newberry College, SC
New England College, NH
New Jersey Institute of Technology, NJ
New Mexico Highlands University, NM
New Mexico State University, NM
North Central College, IL
Northeastern Illinois University, IL
Northeastern State University, OK
Northern Illinois University, IL
Northern Kentucky University, KY
Northern Michigan University, MI
Northern State University, SD
Northwestern Oklahoma State University, OK
Northwest Missouri State University, MO
Northwest Nazarene University, ID
The Ohio State University, OH
Ohio University, OH
Ohio University–Chillicothe, OH
Ohio University–Eastern, OH
Ohio University–Lancaster, OH
Ohio University–Southern Campus, OH
Ohio University–Zanesville, OH
Oklahoma City University, OK
Oklahoma State University, OK
Old Dominion University, VA
Olivet College, MI
Oral Roberts University, OK
Ouachita Baptist University, AR
Pace University, NY
Pacific University, OR
Patrick Henry College, VA
Pittsburg State University, KS
Point Loma Nazarene University, CA
Post University, CT
Queens University of Charlotte, NC
Quincy University, IL
Regent University, VA
Rochester Institute of Technology, NY
Rockhurst University, MO
St. Ambrose University, IA
St. Cloud State University, MN
St. Edward's University, TX
Saint Francis University, PA
St. John's University, NY
Saint Louis University, MO
St. Thomas Aquinas College, NY
Sam Houston State University, TX
San Diego State University, CA
Seton Hill University, PA
Shepherd University, WV
Shippensburg University of Pennsylvania, PA
Siena College, NY
Simpson University, CA
Slippery Rock University of Pennsylvania, PA
Sonoma State University, CA
South Dakota State University, SD
Southeastern Louisiana University, LA
Southeastern Oklahoma State University, OK
Southeast Missouri State University, MO
Southern Illinois University Carbondale, IL
Southwestern College, KS
Southwestern Oklahoma State University, OK
State University of New York at Fredonia, NY
State University of New York at New Paltz, NY

State University of New York at Oswego, NY
State University of New York at Plattsburgh, NY
State University of New York College at Geneseo, NY
State University of New York College at Potsdam, NY
Stephen F. Austin State University, TX
Stetson University, FL
Tabor College, KS
Tennessee Technological University, TN
Texas A&M International University, TX
Texas A&M University–Commerce, TX
Texas Christian University, TX
Texas Tech University, TX
Texas Wesleyan University, TX
Texas Woman's University, TX
Thomas More College, KY
Towson University, MD
Trevecca Nazarene University, TN
Trinity Christian College, IL
Truman State University, MO
Union University, TN
The University of Akron, OH
The University of Alabama, AL
The University of Alabama at Birmingham, AL
The University of Alabama in Huntsville, AL
University of Alaska Anchorage, AK
University of Arkansas, AR
University of California, Davis, CA
University of California, Irvine, CA
University of California, San Diego, CA
University of Central Oklahoma, OK
University of Colorado Boulder, CO
University of Colorado Denver, CO
University of Connecticut, CT
University of Dayton, OH
University of Delaware, DE
University of Denver, CO
University of Evansville, IN
University of Florida, FL
University of Houston, TX
University of Idaho, ID
University of Illinois at Springfield, IL
University of Indianapolis, IN
The University of Kansas, KS
University of Maine at Fort Kent, ME
University of Mary Hardin-Baylor, TX
University of Maryland, College Park, MD
University of Massachusetts Amherst, MA
University of Memphis, TN
University of Michigan, MI
University of Michigan–Dearborn, MI
University of Michigan–Flint, MI
University of Minnesota, Twin Cities Campus, MN
University of Mississippi, MS
University of Missouri, MO
University of Missouri–St. Louis, MO
University of Montevallo, AL
University of Nebraska at Kearney, NE
University of Nebraska at Omaha, NE
University of Nevada, Las Vegas, NV
University of Nevada, Reno, NV
University of New Hampshire at Manchester, NH
University of North Carolina at Asheville, NC
The University of North Carolina at Chapel Hill, NC
The University of North Carolina at Greensboro, NC

The University of North Carolina Wilmington, NC
University of Northern Colorado, CO
University of Northern Iowa, IA
University of Oklahoma, OK
University of Pittsburgh at Bradford, PA
University of Pittsburgh at Johnstown, PA
University of Portland, OR
University of Puget Sound, WA
University of Rio Grande, OH
University of St. Francis, IL
University of St. Thomas, TX
University of South Carolina, SC
University of South Carolina Aiken, SC
The University of South Dakota, SD
University of South Florida, FL
The University of Tennessee, TN
The University of Tennessee at Chattanooga, TN
The University of Tennessee at Martin, TN
The University of Texas at Arlington, TX
The University of Texas at Brownsville, TX
The University of Texas at El Paso, TX
The University of Texas at San Antonio, TX
The University of Texas–Pan American, TX
The University of Toledo, OH
The University of Tulsa, OK
University of Utah, UT
University of West Florida, FL
University of West Georgia, GA
University of Wisconsin–Eau Claire, WI
University of Wisconsin–Green Bay, WI
University of Wisconsin–La Crosse, WI
University of Wisconsin–Parkside, WI
University of Wisconsin–River Falls, WI
University of Wisconsin–Stevens Point, WI
University of Wisconsin–Superior, WI
University of Wisconsin–Whitewater, WI
University of Wyoming, WY
Utah State University, UT
Valdosta State University, GA
Valley City State University, ND
Waldorf College, IA
Walla Walla University, WA
Warner Pacific College, OR
Wartburg College, IA
Washburn University, KS
Washington State University, WA
Washington University in St. Louis, MO
Wayland Baptist University, TX
Waynesburg University, PA
Wayne State College, NE
Wayne State University, MI
Webster University, MO
Western Carolina University, NC
Western Illinois University, IL
Western Kentucky University, KY
Western Washington University, WA
West Texas A&M University, TX
West Virginia University, WV
Wichita State University, KS
Widener University, PA
Wilson College, PA
Wisconsin Lutheran College, WI
Wright State University, OH
Xavier University of Louisiana, LA
Youngstown State University, OH

**Computer Science**
Adelphi University, NY
Albany State University, GA
Albertus Magnus College, CT
Alderson Broaddus University, WV
Alliant International University–San Diego, CA
Angelo State University, TX

Arkansas State University, AR
Arkansas Tech University, AR
Armstrong State University, GA
Auburn University, AL
Augustana College, IL
Augustana College, SD
Austin Peay State University, TN
Baylor University, TX
Bemidji State University, MN
Binghamton University, State University of
    New York, NY
Birmingham-Southern College, AL
Bloomfield College, NJ
Bloomsburg University of Pennsylvania, PA
Boise State University, ID
Bowie State University, MD
Bowling Green State University, OH
Buena Vista University, IA
Buffalo State College, State University of
    New York, NY
Butler University, IN
California Lutheran University, CA
California Polytechnic State University, San
    Luis Obispo, CA
California State Polytechnic University,
    Pomona, CA
California State University, Chico, CA
California State University, Fullerton, CA
California State University, Los Angeles, CA
California State University, San Bernardino,
    CA
California State University, Stanislaus, CA
Calvin College, MI
Cameron University, OK
Campbellsville University, KY
Carroll University, WI
Case Western Reserve University, OH
Central College, IA
Central Methodist University, MO
Central Michigan University, MI
Champlain College, VT
Christopher Newport University, VA
City College of the City University of New
    York, NY
Clarion University of Pennsylvania, PA
Clarkson University, NY
Clemson University, SC
Cleveland State University, OH
Coastal Carolina University, SC
The College at Brockport, State University
    of New York, NY
College of Charleston, SC
College of Saint Benedict, MN
College of Staten Island of the City
    University of New York, NY
Colorado Mesa University, CO
Colorado School of Mines, CO
Colorado State University–Pueblo, CO
Columbia College, MO
Columbus State University, GA
Concordia University Chicago, IL
Concordia University, Nebraska, NE
Concordia University Texas, TX
Dakota State University, SD
Dallas Baptist University, TX
Delta State University, MS
DeSales University, PA
Dickinson State University, ND
Dordt College, IA
Drew University, NJ
Drury University, MO
East Carolina University, NC
Eastern Illinois University, IL
Eastern Michigan University, MI
Eastern New Mexico University, NM

Eastern Washington University, WA
East Stroudsburg University of
    Pennsylvania, PA
ECPI University, VA
Elizabeth City State University, NC
Elizabethtown College, PA
Elmhurst College, IL
Elon University, NC
Emporia State University, KS
Evangel University, MO
Fairmont State University, WV
Ferris State University, MI
Florida Agricultural and Mechanical
    University, FL
Fontbonne University, MO
Fort Hays State University, KS
Francis Marion University, SC
Frostburg State University, MD
Furman University, SC
Gardner-Webb University, NC
George Fox University, OR
Georgia College & State University, GA
Georgia Institute of Technology, GA
Georgia Regents University, GA
Georgia Southern University, GA
Golden Gate University, CA
Graceland University, IA
Grambling State University, LA
Grand Valley State University, MI
Hampton University, VA
Harding University, AR
Hardin-Simmons University, TX
Howard University, DC
Huntingdon College, AL
Huntington University, IN
Husson University, ME
Idaho State University, ID
Illinois State University, IL
Indiana State University, IN
Indiana Tech, IN
Indiana University of Pennsylvania, PA
Iowa State University of Science and
    Technology, IA
Jacksonville State University, AL
James Madison University, VA
John Carroll University, OH
Johnson C. Smith University, NC
Juniata College, PA
Kansas Wesleyan University, KS
Kean University, NJ
Kennesaw State University, GA
Kent State University, OH
Kentucky State University, KY
Keystone College, PA
King's College, PA
Kutztown University of Pennsylvania, PA
Lawrence Technological University, MI
Liberty University, VA
Lincoln University, PA
Lindenwood University, MO
Linfield College, OR
Lock Haven University of Pennsylvania, PA
Long Island University–LIU Post, NY
Longwood University, VA
Louisiana State University and Agricultural
    & Mechanical College, LA
Louisiana Tech University, LA
Lubbock Christian University, TX
Lycoming College, PA
Manhattan College, NY
Marywood University, PA
Massachusetts College of Liberal Arts, MA
Mayville State University, ND
McMurry University, TX
Meredith College, NC

Michigan State University, MI
Middle Tennessee State University, TN
Midwestern State University, TX
Millersville University of Pennsylvania, PA
Mills College, CA
Milwaukee School of Engineering, WI
Minnesota State University Moorhead, MN
Minot State University, ND
Misericordia University, PA
Mississippi State University, MS
Mississippi University for Women, MS
Missouri University of Science and
    Technology, MO
Missouri Valley College, MO
Missouri Western State University, MO
Monmouth University, NJ
Montana State University, MT
Montana State University Billings, MT
Montana Tech of The University of
    Montana, MT
Moravian College, PA
Morningside College, IA
Murray State University, KY
Muskingum University, OH
Neumont University, UT
New England College, NH
New Jersey Institute of Technology, NJ
New Mexico Highlands University, NM
New Mexico State University, NM
North Carolina Central University, NC
North Central College, IL
Northeastern Illinois University, IL
Northeastern State University, OK
Northern Illinois University, IL
Northern Kentucky University, KY
Northern Michigan University, MI
Northern State University, SD
Northwestern Oklahoma State University,
    OK
Northwest Missouri State University, MO
Northwest Nazarene University, ID
The Ohio State University, OH
Ohio University, OH
Ohio University–Chillicothe, OH
Ohio University–Eastern, OH
Ohio University–Lancaster, OH
Ohio University–Southern Campus, OH
Ohio University–Zanesville, OH
Oklahoma Baptist University, OK
Oklahoma State University, OK
Oklahoma Wesleyan University, OK
Old Dominion University, VA
Ouachita Baptist University, AR
Pace University, NY
Peirce College, PA
Pittsburg State University, KS
Portland State University, OR
Post University, CT
Purchase College, State University of New
    York, NY
Purdue University, IN
Quincy University, IL
Regent University, VA
Robert Morris University Illinois, IL
Rochester College, MI
Rochester Institute of Technology, NY
Rockford University, IL
Rockhurst University, MO
Rollins College, FL
Sacred Heart University, CT
Saginaw Valley State University, MI
St. Cloud State University, MN
St. Edward's University, TX
Saint Francis University, PA
St. John's University, NY

Saint Louis University, MO
Saint Michael's College, VT
St. Thomas Aquinas College, NY
Samford University, AL
Sam Houston State University, TX
San Diego State University, CA
Savannah State University, GA
Seton Hill University, PA
Shepherd University, WV
Shippensburg University of Pennsylvania, PA
Siena College, NY
Skidmore College, NY
Slippery Rock University of Pennsylvania, PA
Sonoma State University, CA
South Dakota School of Mines and Technology, SD
South Dakota State University, SD
Southeastern Louisiana University, LA
Southeastern Oklahoma State University, OK
Southeast Missouri State University, MO
Southern Illinois University Carbondale, IL
Southwestern College, KS
Southwestern Oklahoma State University, OK
State University of New York at Fredonia, NY
State University of New York at Oswego, NY
State University of New York at Plattsburgh, NY
State University of New York College at Geneseo, NY
State University of New York College at Potsdam, NY
State University of New York Polytechnic Institute, NY
Stephen F. Austin State University, TX
Stetson University, FL
Stockton University, NJ
Stony Brook University, State University of New York, NY
Tennessee Technological University, TN
Texas A&M University, TX
Texas A&M University–Commerce, TX
Texas Tech University, TX
Texas Woman's University, TX
Thiel College, PA
Thomas More College, KY
Towson University, MD
Trinity Christian College, IL
Truman State University, MO
Tuskegee University, AL
Union University, TN
The University of Akron, OH
The University of Alabama, AL
The University of Alabama at Birmingham, AL
The University of Alabama in Huntsville, AL
University of Alaska Anchorage, AK
University of Arkansas, AR
University of California, Davis, CA
University of California, Irvine, CA
University of California, San Diego, CA
University of California, Santa Cruz, CA
University of Central Oklahoma, OK
University of Colorado Boulder, CO
University of Connecticut, CT
University of Dayton, OH
University of Delaware, DE
University of Denver, CO
University of Evansville, IN
University of Florida, FL

University of Great Falls, MT
University of Houston, TX
University of Houston–Clear Lake, TX
University of Idaho, ID
University of Illinois at Springfield, IL
The University of Kansas, KS
University of Maine at Fort Kent, ME
University of Mary Hardin-Baylor, TX
University of Maryland, Baltimore County, MD
University of Maryland, College Park, MD
University of Maryland Eastern Shore, MD
University of Mary Washington, VA
University of Massachusetts Amherst, MA
University of Massachusetts Dartmouth, MA
University of Massachusetts Lowell, MA
University of Michigan, MI
University of Michigan–Dearborn, MI
University of Michigan–Flint, MI
University of Minnesota, Twin Cities Campus, MN
University of Mississippi, MS
University of Missouri, MO
University of Missouri–St. Louis, MO
The University of Montana, MT
University of Nebraska at Omaha, NE
University of Nebraska–Lincoln, NE
University of Nevada, Las Vegas, NV
University of Nevada, Reno, NV
University of New Hampshire, NH
University of New Hampshire at Manchester, NH
University of North Carolina at Asheville, NC
The University of North Carolina at Charlotte, NC
The University of North Carolina at Greensboro, NC
The University of North Carolina Wilmington, NC
University of Northern Iowa, IA
University of North Florida, FL
University of Oklahoma, OK
University of Pittsburgh at Bradford, PA
University of Pittsburgh at Johnstown, PA
University of Portland, OR
University of Puget Sound, WA
University of Richmond, VA
University of Rio Grande, OH
University of St. Thomas, TX
University of South Alabama, AL
University of South Carolina, SC
University of South Carolina Aiken, SC
The University of South Dakota, SD
University of South Florida, FL
The University of Tennessee, TN
The University of Tennessee at Martin, TN
The University of Texas at Arlington, TX
The University of Texas at Brownsville, TX
The University of Texas at Dallas, TX
The University of Texas at El Paso, TX
The University of Texas at San Antonio, TX
The University of Texas–Pan American, TX
The University of Tulsa, OK
University of Utah, UT
University of Vermont, VT
The University of Virginia's College at Wise, VA
University of Washington, WA
University of West Florida, FL
University of West Georgia, GA
University of Wisconsin–Eau Claire, WI
University of Wisconsin–La Crosse, WI
University of Wisconsin–River Falls, WI
University of Wisconsin–Stevens Point, WI
University of Wisconsin–Stout, WI

University of Wisconsin–Superior, WI
University of Wisconsin–Whitewater, WI
University of Wyoming, WY
Utah State University, UT
Valley City State University, ND
Virginia Commonwealth University, VA
Virginia Military Institute, VA
Virginia State University, VA
Wartburg College, IA
Washburn University, KS
Washington State University, WA
Washington University in St. Louis, MO
Waynesburg University, PA
Wayne State College, NE
Wayne State University, MI
Webster University, MO
Western Illinois University, IL
Western Oregon University, OR
Western Washington University, WA
West Texas A&M University, TX
West Virginia University, WV
Wheaton College, IL
Wichita State University, KS
Widener University, PA
Wilson College, PA
Wisconsin Lutheran College, WI
Wright State University, OH
Xavier University of Louisiana, LA
Youngstown State University, OH

**Education**
Abilene Christian University, TX
Alaska Pacific University, AK
Albany State University, GA
Albertus Magnus College, CT
Alderson Broaddus University, WV
Alliant International University–San Diego, CA
Anderson University, SC
Angelo State University, TX
Antioch University Midwest, OH
Arkansas State University, AR
Arkansas Tech University, AR
Armstrong State University, GA
Auburn University, AL
Augustana College, IL
Augustana College, SD
Austin College, TX
Austin Peay State University, TN
Averett University, VA
Ball State University, IN
The Baptist College of Florida, FL
Baylor University, TX
Belhaven University, MS
Bellarmine University, KY
Bemidji State University, MN
Berklee College of Music, MA
Berry College, GA
Binghamton University, State University of New York, NY
Birmingham-Southern College, AL
Bloomfield College, NJ
Bloomsburg University of Pennsylvania, PA
Blue Mountain College, MS
Boise State University, ID
Bowling Green State University, OH
Brenau University, GA
Buena Vista University, IA
Buffalo State College, State University of New York, NY
Butler University, IN
California Lutheran University, CA
California Polytechnic State University, San Luis Obispo, CA
California State Polytechnic University, Pomona, CA

California State University, Bakersfield, CA
California State University, Chico, CA
California State University, Fresno, CA
California State University, Fullerton, CA
California State University, Los Angeles, CA
California State University, San Bernardino, CA
California State University, Stanislaus, CA
Calvin College, MI
Cameron University, OK
Campbellsville University, KY
Carroll University, WI
Carson-Newman University, TN
Castleton State College, VT
Catawba College, NC
Centenary College of Louisiana, LA
Central College, IA
Central Methodist University, MO
Central Michigan University, MI
Champlain College, VT
Charlotte Christian College and Theological Seminary, NC
Christopher Newport University, VA
Cincinnati Christian University, OH
City College of the City University of New York, NY
Clarion University of Pennsylvania, PA
Clemson University, SC
Cleveland State University, OH
Coastal Carolina University, SC
The College at Brockport, State University of New York, NY
College of Charleston, SC
The College of Idaho, ID
The College of New Rochelle, NY
College of Saint Mary, NE
The College of Saint Rose, NY
College of Staten Island of the City University of New York, NY
Colorado Mesa University, CO
Colorado State University–Pueblo, CO
Columbia College, MO
Columbus State University, GA
Concordia University Ann Arbor, MI
Concordia University Chicago, IL
Concordia University, Nebraska, NE
Concordia University Texas, TX
Concord University, WV
Cornerstone University, MI
Creighton University, NE
Dakota State University, SD
Dakota Wesleyan University, SD
Dallas Baptist University, TX
Davidson College, NC
Delta State University, MS
DeSales University, PA
Dickinson State University, ND
Dominican College, NY
Dordt College, IA
Dowling College, NY
Drury University, MO
Duquesne University, PA
D'Youville College, NY
East Carolina University, NC
Eastern Illinois University, IL
Eastern Michigan University, MI
Eastern New Mexico University, NM
Eastern Washington University, WA
East Stroudsburg University of Pennsylvania, PA
East Texas Baptist University, TX
Elizabeth City State University, NC
Elizabethtown College, PA
Elmhurst College, IL
Elon University, NC

Emmanuel College, GA
Emporia State University, KS
Endicott College, MA
Evangel University, MO
Fairmont State University, WV
Felician College, NJ
Ferris State University, MI
Five Towns College, NY
Flagler College, FL
Florida Agricultural and Mechanical University, FL
Florida Gulf Coast University, FL
Florida Southern College, FL
Fort Hays State University, KS
Fort Lewis College, CO
Framingham State University, MA
Francis Marion University, SC
Frostburg State University, MD
Furman University, SC
Gannon University, PA
Gardner-Webb University, NC
George Fox University, OR
Georgia College & State University, GA
Georgian Court University, NJ
Georgia Regents University, GA
Georgia Southern University, GA
Glenville State College, WV
Goshen College, IN
Governors State University, IL
Grambling State University, LA
Grand Valley State University, MI
Grand View University, IA
Grove City College, PA
Hamline University, MN
Hampden-Sydney College, VA
Hampton University, VA
Hardin-Simmons University, TX
Henderson State University, AR
Hillsdale College, MI
Hillsdale Free Will Baptist College, OK
Howard Payne University, TX
Howard University, DC
Huntington University, IN
Husson University, ME
Idaho State University, ID
Illinois State University, IL
Indiana State University, IN
Indiana University of Pennsylvania, PA
Iowa State University of Science and Technology, IA
Iowa Wesleyan College, IA
Jacksonville State University, AL
James Madison University, VA
John Carroll University, OH
Juniata College, PA
Kansas Wesleyan University, KS
Kean University, NJ
Kennesaw State University, GA
Kent State University, OH
Kent State University at Geauga, OH
Kent State University at Stark, OH
Kentucky Christian University, KY
King's College, PA
Kutztown University of Pennsylvania, PA
LaGrange College, GA
Lake Erie College, OH
Langston University, OK
La Sierra University, CA
Lawrence Technological University, MI
Lees-McRae College, NC
Lee University, TN
Lewis-Clark State College, ID
Liberty University, VA
Lincoln University, PA
Lindenwood University, MO

Lindsey Wilson College, KY
Linfield College, OR
Lipscomb University, TN
Lock Haven University of Pennsylvania, PA
Long Island University–LIU Brooklyn, NY
Long Island University–LIU Post, NY
Longwood University, VA
Louisiana State University and Agricultural & Mechanical College, LA
Louisiana Tech University, LA
Loyola Marymount University, CA
Lubbock Christian University, TX
Lycoming College, PA
Malone University, OH
Mansfield University of Pennsylvania, PA
Marquette University, WI
Maryville University of Saint Louis, MO
Marywood University, PA
Massachusetts College of Liberal Arts, MA
The Master's College and Seminary, CA
Mayville State University, ND
McMurry University, TX
Mercer University, GA
Meredith College, NC
Methodist University, NC
Metropolitan State University, MN
Metropolitan State University of Denver, CO
Miami University, OH
Michigan State University, MI
Middle Tennessee State University, TN
Midwestern State University, TX
Millersville University of Pennsylvania, PA
Millikin University, IL
Minnesota State University Moorhead, MN
Minot State University, ND
Misericordia University, PA
Mississippi State University, MS
Mississippi University for Women, MS
Missouri University of Science and Technology, MO
Missouri Valley College, MO
Missouri Western State University, MO
Molloy College, NY
Monmouth University, NJ
Montana State University, MT
Montana State University Billings, MT
Montclair State University, NJ
Morehead State University, KY
Mount Mary University, WI
Murray State University, KY
Newberry College, SC
New England College, NH
New Jersey Institute of Technology, NJ
New Mexico Highlands University, NM
New Mexico State University, NM
North Carolina Central University, NC
North Carolina State University, NC
North Central College, IL
Northeastern Illinois University, IL
Northeastern State University, OK
Northern Illinois University, IL
Northern Kentucky University, KY
Northern Michigan University, MI
Northern State University, SD
Northwestern Oklahoma State University, OK
Northwest Missouri State University, MO
Northwest Nazarene University, ID
Oakland University, MI
The Ohio State University, OH
Ohio University, OH
Ohio University–Chillicothe, OH
Ohio University–Eastern, OH
Ohio University–Lancaster, OH
Ohio University–Southern Campus, OH

Ohio University–Zanesville, OH
Ohio Wesleyan University, OH
Oklahoma Baptist University, OK
Oklahoma City University, OK
Oklahoma State University, OK
Oklahoma Wesleyan University, OK
Old Dominion University, VA
Olivet College, MI
Oral Roberts University, OK
Ouachita Baptist University, AR
Pace University, NY
Pacific University, OR
Piedmont College, GA
Pine Manor College, MA
Pittsburg State University, KS
Point Loma Nazarene University, CA
Portland State University, OR
Post University, CT
Purdue University, IN
Queens University of Charlotte, NC
Quincy University, IL
Randolph College, VA
Regent University, VA
Rochester College, MI
Rockford University, IL
Rockhurst University, MO
Sacred Heart University, CT
Saginaw Valley State University, MI
St. Bonaventure University, NY
St. Catherine University, MN
St. Cloud State University, MN
St. Edward's University, TX
Saint Francis University, PA
St. John's University, NY
Saint Louis University, MO
Saint Martin's University, WA
St. Mary's College of Maryland, MD
St. Thomas Aquinas College, NY
Salisbury University, MD
Samford University, AL
Sam Houston State University, TX
San Diego State University, CA
Schreiner University, TX
Seton Hill University, PA
Shepherd University, WV
Shippensburg University of Pennsylvania, PA
Siena College, NY
Slippery Rock University of Pennsylvania, PA
Sonoma State University, CA
South Dakota State University, SD
Southeastern Louisiana University, LA
Southeastern Oklahoma State University, OK
Southeast Missouri State University, MO
Southern Illinois University Carbondale, IL
Southern Illinois University Edwardsville, IL
Southern Oregon University, OR
Southwestern Oklahoma State University, OK
State University of New York at Fredonia, NY
State University of New York at New Paltz, NY
State University of New York at Oswego, NY
State University of New York at Plattsburgh, NY
State University of New York College at Cortland, NY
State University of New York College at Geneseo, NY
State University of New York College at Potsdam, NY

Stephen F. Austin State University, TX
Stetson University, FL
Stockton University, NJ
Sul Ross State University, TX
Tennessee Technological University, TN
Texas A&M International University, TX
Texas A&M University, TX
Texas A&M University–Commerce, TX
Texas Christian University, TX
Texas Lutheran University, TX
Texas State University, TX
Texas Tech University, TX
Texas Wesleyan University, TX
Texas Woman's University, TX
Thiel College, PA
Thomas More College, KY
Thomas University, GA
Towson University, MD
Trevecca Nazarene University, TN
Trinity Christian College, IL
Truett-McConnell College, GA
Truman State University, MO
Union University, TN
The University of Akron, OH
The University of Alabama, AL
The University of Alabama in Huntsville, AL
University of Alaska Anchorage, AK
The University of Arizona, AZ
University of Arkansas, AR
University of California, Irvine, CA
University of California, Riverside, CA
University of Central Oklahoma, OK
University of Colorado Boulder, CO
University of Colorado Denver, CO
University of Connecticut, CT
University of Dallas, TX
University of Dayton, OH
University of Delaware, DE
University of Evansville, IN
University of Florida, FL
University of Georgia, GA
University of Great Falls, MT
University of Houston, TX
University of Houston–Clear Lake, TX
University of Idaho, ID
University of Illinois at Springfield, IL
The University of Kansas, KS
University of Louisville, KY
University of Maine at Fort Kent, ME
University of Mary Hardin-Baylor, TX
University of Maryland, Baltimore County, MD
University of Maryland, College Park, MD
University of Maryland Eastern Shore, MD
University of Mary Washington, VA
University of Massachusetts Amherst, MA
University of Massachusetts Dartmouth, MA
University of Massachusetts Lowell, MA
University of Memphis, TN
University of Michigan, MI
University of Michigan–Dearborn, MI
University of Michigan–Flint, MI
University of Minnesota, Twin Cities Campus, MN
University of Mississippi, MS
University of Missouri, MO
University of Missouri–St. Louis, MO
The University of Montana, MT
The University of Montana Western, MT
University of Montevallo, AL
University of Nebraska at Omaha, NE
University of Nebraska–Lincoln, NE
University of Nevada, Las Vegas, NV
University of Nevada, Reno, NV
University of New Hampshire, NH

University of New Orleans, LA
University of North Carolina at Asheville, NC
The University of North Carolina at Chapel Hill, NC
The University of North Carolina at Charlotte, NC
The University of North Carolina at Greensboro, NC
The University of North Carolina at Pembroke, NC
The University of North Carolina Wilmington, NC
University of Northern Colorado, CO
University of Northern Iowa, IA
University of North Florida, FL
University of North Georgia, GA
University of Oklahoma, OK
University of Oregon, OR
University of Pittsburgh at Bradford, PA
University of Pittsburgh at Johnstown, PA
University of Portland, OR
University of Rio Grande, OH
University of St. Francis, IL
University of St. Thomas, MN
University of St. Thomas, TX
University of South Carolina, SC
University of South Carolina Aiken, SC
The University of South Dakota, SD
University of Southern Indiana, IN
University of South Florida, FL
The University of Tennessee, TN
The University of Tennessee at Chattanooga, TN
The University of Tennessee at Martin, TN
The University of Texas at Arlington, TX
The University of Texas at Brownsville, TX
The University of Texas at El Paso, TX
The University of Texas at San Antonio, TX
The University of Texas–Pan American, TX
University of the District of Columbia, DC
The University of Toledo, OH
The University of Tulsa, OK
University of Utah, UT
University of Vermont, VT
The University of Virginia's College at Wise, VA
University of Washington, WA
University of West Florida, FL
University of West Georgia, GA
University of Wisconsin–Eau Claire, WI
University of Wisconsin–Green Bay, WI
University of Wisconsin–La Crosse, WI
University of Wisconsin–Parkside, WI
University of Wisconsin–River Falls, WI
University of Wisconsin–Stevens Point, WI
University of Wisconsin–Stout, WI
University of Wisconsin–Superior, WI
University of Wisconsin–Whitewater, WI
University of Wyoming, WY
Utah State University, UT
Valdosta State University, GA
Valley City State University, ND
VanderCook College of Music, IL
Virginia Commonwealth University, VA
Walla Walla University, WA
Warner Pacific College, OR
Wartburg College, IA
Washburn University, KS
Washington State University, WA
Washington University in St. Louis, MO
Wayland Baptist University, TX
Waynesburg University, PA
Wayne State College, NE
Wayne State University, MI
Webster University, MO

Western Carolina University, NC
Western Illinois University, IL
Western Kentucky University, KY
Western Oregon University, OR
Western Washington University, WA
West Texas A&M University, TX
West Virginia University, WV
Wheaton College, IL
Wichita State University, KS
Widener University, PA
William Jessup University, CA
Williams Baptist College, AR
Wilson College, PA
Wisconsin Lutheran College, WI
Wright State University, OH
Xavier University of Louisiana, LA
Youngstown State University, OH

### Engineering/Technologies

Abilene Christian University, TX
Alabama Agricultural and Mechanical University, AL
Arkansas State University, AR
Arkansas Tech University, AR
Armstrong State University, GA
Auburn University, AL
Austin College, TX
Averett University, VA
Ball State University, IN
Baylor University, TX
Bemidji State University, MN
Berklee College of Music, MA
Binghamton University, State University of New York, NY
Birmingham-Southern College, AL
Bluefield State College, WV
Boise State University, ID
Boston University, MA
Bowie State University, MD
Bowling Green State University, OH
Bucknell University, PA
Buffalo State College, State University of New York, NY
Butler University, IN
California Baptist University, CA
California Polytechnic State University, San Luis Obispo, CA
California State Polytechnic University, Pomona, CA
California State University, Chico, CA
California State University, Fresno, CA
California State University, Fullerton, CA
California State University, Los Angeles, CA
Calvin College, MI
Cameron University, OK
Case Western Reserve University, OH
Centenary College of Louisiana, LA
Central Michigan University, MI
Champlain College, VT
Christian Brothers University, TN
Christopher Newport University, VA
The Citadel, The Military College of South Carolina, SC
City College of the City University of New York, NY
Clarkson University, NY
Clemson University, SC
Cleveland State University, OH
College of Charleston, SC
College of Saint Benedict, MN
The College of Saint Rose, NY
College of Staten Island of the City University of New York, NY
Colorado Mesa University, CO
Colorado School of Mines, CO

Colorado State University–Pueblo, CO
Cooper Union for the Advancement of Science and Art, NY
Dordt College, IA
East Carolina University, NC
Eastern Illinois University, IL
Eastern Michigan University, MI
Eastern New Mexico University, NM
Eastern Washington University, WA
ECPI University, VA
Elizabethtown College, PA
Elon University, NC
Emporia State University, KS
Evangel University, MO
Fairmont State University, WV
Ferris State University, MI
Florida Agricultural and Mechanical University, FL
Florida Atlantic University, FL
Florida Gulf Coast University, FL
Florida Institute of Technology, FL
Fort Hays State University, KS
Framingham State University, MA
Frostburg State University, MD
Furman University, SC
Gannon University, PA
Geneva College, PA
George Fox University, OR
Georgia Institute of Technology, GA
Georgia Southern University, GA
Gonzaga University, WA
Graceland University, IA
Grambling State University, LA
Grand Valley State University, MI
Greenville College, IL
Grove City College, PA
Hampton University, VA
Harding University, AR
Hofstra University, NY
Howard University, DC
Idaho State University, ID
Illinois Institute of Technology, IL
Illinois State University, IL
Indiana State University, IN
Indiana Tech, IN
Indiana University of Pennsylvania, PA
Indiana University–Purdue University Fort Wayne, IN
Iowa State University of Science and Technology, IA
James Madison University, VA
Johns Hopkins University, MD
Johnson C. Smith University, NC
Kean University, NJ
Kent State University, OH
King's College, PA
Langston University, OK
Lawrence Technological University, MI
Lehigh University, PA
Lewis-Clark State College, ID
Liberty University, VA
Lindenwood University, MO
Lipscomb University, TN
Loras College, IA
Louisiana State University and Agricultural & Mechanical College, LA
Louisiana Tech University, LA
Loyola Marymount University, CA
Maine Maritime Academy, ME
Marquette University, WI
Mercer University, GA
Miami University, OH
Michigan State University, MI
Middle Tennessee State University, TN
Midwestern State University, TX

Milwaukee School of Engineering, WI
Minnesota State University Moorhead, MN
Mississippi State University, MS
Missouri University of Science and Technology, MO
Missouri Western State University, MO
Montana State University, MT
Montana State University Billings, MT
Montana Tech of The University of Montana, MT
Morehead State University, KY
Murray State University, KY
Muskingum University, OH
New England College, NH
New Jersey Institute of Technology, NJ
New Mexico Highlands University, NM
New Mexico State University, NM
North Carolina Agricultural and Technical State University, NC
North Carolina State University, NC
Northern Illinois University, IL
Northern Kentucky University, KY
Northern Michigan University, MI
Northwest Nazarene University, ID
Oakland University, MI
The Ohio State University, OH
Ohio University, OH
Ohio University–Chillicothe, OH
Ohio University–Eastern, OH
Ohio University–Lancaster, OH
Ohio University–Southern Campus, OH
Ohio University–Zanesville, OH
Oklahoma Christian University, OK
Oklahoma State University, OK
Old Dominion University, VA
Oral Roberts University, OK
Ouachita Baptist University, AR
Philadelphia University, PA
Pittsburg State University, KS
Point Loma Nazarene University, CA
Portland State University, OR
Purdue University, IN
Rice University, TX
Rochester Institute of Technology, NY
Rockhurst University, MO
Rollins College, FL
Saginaw Valley State University, MI
St. Ambrose University, IA
St. Cloud State University, MN
Saint Francis University, PA
Saint Louis University, MO
Saint Martin's University, WA
St. Thomas Aquinas College, NY
Sam Houston State University, TX
San Diego State University, CA
Santa Clara University, CA
Savannah State University, GA
Seattle Pacific University, WA
Shepherd University, WV
Sonoma State University, CA
South Dakota School of Mines and Technology, SD
South Dakota State University, SD
Southeastern Oklahoma State University, OK
Southeast Missouri State University, MO
Southern Illinois University Carbondale, IL
Southwestern Oklahoma State University, OK
State University of New York at New Paltz, NY
State University of New York at Plattsburgh, NY
State University of New York College at Potsdam, NY

State University of New York College of
Environmental Science and Forestry, NY
State University of New York Polytechnic
Institute, NY
Stony Brook University, State University of
New York, NY
Suffolk University, MA
Tennessee Technological University, TN
Texas A&M International University, TX
Texas A&M University, TX
Texas A&M University–Commerce, TX
Texas Christian University, TX
Texas Tech University, TX
Trinity Christian College, IL
Tuskegee University, AL
Union University, TN
The University of Akron, OH
The University of Alabama, AL
The University of Alabama at Birmingham,
AL
The University of Alabama in Huntsville,
AL
University of Alaska Anchorage, AK
University of Alaska Fairbanks, AK
The University of Arizona, AZ
University of Arkansas, AR
University of California, Davis, CA
University of California, Irvine, CA
University of California, Riverside, CA
University of California, San Diego, CA
University of Colorado Boulder, CO
University of Colorado Denver, CO
University of Connecticut, CT
University of Dayton, OH
University of Delaware, DE
University of Denver, CO
University of Evansville, IN
University of Florida, FL
University of Hartford, CT
University of Houston, TX
University of Idaho, ID
The University of Iowa, IA
The University of Kansas, KS
University of Louisville, KY
University of Maryland, Baltimore County,
MD
University of Maryland, College Park, MD
University of Maryland Eastern Shore, MD
University of Massachusetts Amherst, MA
University of Massachusetts Dartmouth, MA
University of Massachusetts Lowell, MA
University of Memphis, TN
University of Michigan, MI
University of Michigan–Dearborn, MI
University of Michigan–Flint, MI
University of Minnesota, Twin Cities
Campus, MN
University of Mississippi, MS
University of Missouri, MO
University of Missouri–St. Louis, MO
University of Nebraska at Omaha, NE
University of Nebraska–Lincoln, NE
University of Nevada, Las Vegas, NV
University of Nevada, Reno, NV
University of New Hampshire, NH
University of New Hampshire at
Manchester, NH
University of New Orleans, LA
University of North Carolina at Asheville,
NC
The University of North Carolina at
Charlotte, NC
The University of North Carolina
Wilmington, NC
University of North Florida, FL
University of Oklahoma, OK

University of Pittsburgh at Bradford, PA
University of Pittsburgh at Johnstown, PA
University of Portland, OR
University of Rochester, NY
University of South Carolina, SC
University of South Carolina Aiken, SC
University of Southern Indiana, IN
University of South Florida, FL
The University of Tennessee, TN
The University of Tennessee at Chattanooga,
TN
The University of Tennessee at Martin, TN
The University of Texas at Arlington, TX
The University of Texas at Brownsville, TX
The University of Texas at Dallas, TX
The University of Texas at El Paso, TX
The University of Texas at San Antonio, TX
The University of Texas–Pan American, TX
The University of Toledo, OH
The University of Tulsa, OK
University of Utah, UT
University of Vermont, VT
University of Washington, WA
University of West Florida, FL
University of Wisconsin–Green Bay, WI
University of Wisconsin–Parkside, WI
University of Wisconsin–Stevens Point, WI
University of Wisconsin–Stout, WI
Utah State University, UT
Valley City State University, ND
Valparaiso University, IN
Virginia Commonwealth University, VA
Virginia Military Institute, VA
Virginia State University, VA
Walla Walla University, WA
Wartburg College, IA
Washburn University, KS
Washington State University, WA
Washington University in St. Louis, MO
Wayne State University, MI
Webb Institute, NY
Western Illinois University, IL
Western Kentucky University, KY
Western Washington University, WA
West Texas A&M University, TX
West Virginia University, WV
Wheaton College, IL
Wichita State University, KS
Widener University, PA
Wright State University, OH
Xavier University of Louisiana, LA
York College of Pennsylvania, PA
Youngstown State University, OH

**English**
Abilene Christian University, TX
Alaska Pacific University, AK
Albertus Magnus College, CT
Alliant International University–San Diego,
CA
Angelo State University, TX
Arkansas State University, AR
Armstrong State University, GA
Auburn University, AL
Augustana College, IL
Augustana College, SD
Austin College, TX
Austin Peay State University, TN
Averett University, VA
Ball State University, IN
Baylor University, TX
Belhaven University, MS
Bemidji State University, MN
Berry College, GA
Binghamton University, State University of
New York, NY

Birmingham-Southern College, AL
Bloomfield College, NJ
Bloomsburg University of Pennsylvania, PA
Blue Mountain College, MS
Boise State University, ID
Bowling Green State University, OH
Brenau University, GA
Butler University, IN
California Lutheran University, CA
California Polytechnic State University, San
Luis Obispo, CA
California State University, Chico, CA
California State University, Fresno, CA
California State University, Fullerton, CA
California State University, Los Angeles, CA
California State University, Stanislaus, CA
Calvin College, MI
Cameron University, OK
Campbellsville University, KY
Case Western Reserve University, OH
Castleton State College, VT
Cedar Crest College, PA
Centenary College of Louisiana, LA
Central Methodist University, MO
Central Michigan University, MI
Christopher Newport University, VA
City College of the City University of New
York, NY
Clarion University of Pennsylvania, PA
Clemson University, SC
Cleveland State University, OH
Coastal Carolina University, SC
Coe College, IA
The College at Brockport, State University
of New York, NY
College of Charleston, SC
The College of Idaho, ID
The College of New Rochelle, NY
The College of Saint Rose, NY
College of Staten Island of the City
University of New York, NY
Colorado Mesa University, CO
Colorado State University–Pueblo, CO
Columbia College, MO
Columbus State University, GA
Concordia University Chicago, IL
Concordia University, Nebraska, NE
Concordia University Texas, TX
Concord University, WV
Cornerstone University, MI
Dakota State University, SD
Dallas Baptist University, TX
Delta State University, MS
Denison University, OH
DeSales University, PA
Dickinson State University, ND
Dordt College, IA
Drew University, NJ
Drury University, MO
D'Youville College, NY
East Carolina University, NC
Eastern Illinois University, IL
Eastern Michigan University, MI
Eastern New Mexico University, NM
Eastern Washington University, WA
East Stroudsburg University of
Pennsylvania, PA
East Texas Baptist University, TX
Elizabethtown College, PA
Elmhurst College, IL
Emmanuel College, GA
Emporia State University, KS
Evangel University, MO
Fairmont State University, WV
Felician College, NJ
Flagler College, FL

Florida Agricultural and Mechanical University, FL
Fontbonne University, MO
Fort Hays State University, KS
Fort Lewis College, CO
Framingham State University, MA
Francis Marion University, SC
Frostburg State University, MD
Furman University, SC
Gannon University, PA
Gardner-Webb University, NC
George Fox University, OR
Georgian Court University, NJ
Georgia Southern University, GA
Glenville State College, WV
Governors State University, IL
Graceland University, IA
Grambling State University, LA
Grand Valley State University, MI
Grand View University, IA
Grove City College, PA
Hamline University, MN
Hampshire College, MA
Harding University, AR
Hardin-Simmons University, TX
Hillsdale College, MI
Hillsdale Free Will Baptist College, OK
Houghton College, NY
Howard Payne University, TX
Howard University, DC
Huntington University, IN
Husson University, ME
Idaho State University, ID
Illinois State University, IL
Indiana State University, IN
Indiana University of Pennsylvania, PA
Iowa State University of Science and Technology, IA
Iowa Wesleyan College, IA
Jacksonville State University, AL
James Madison University, VA
John Carroll University, OH
Kansas Wesleyan University, KS
Kean University, NJ
Kennesaw State University, GA
Kent State University, OH
King's College, PA
Kutztown University of Pennsylvania, PA
Lake Erie College, OH
La Sierra University, CA
Lebanon Valley College, PA
Lewis-Clark State College, ID
Liberty University, VA
Lincoln University, PA
Lindenwood University, MO
Lindsey Wilson College, KY
Linfield College, OR
Lipscomb University, TN
Lock Haven University of Pennsylvania, PA
Long Island University–LIU Post, NY
Longwood University, VA
Louisiana State University and Agricultural & Mechanical College, LA
Louisiana Tech University, LA
Loyola Marymount University, CA
Lubbock Christian University, TX
Lycoming College, PA
Marquette University, WI
Marymount University, VA
Maryville University of Saint Louis, MO
Marywood University, PA
Massachusetts College of Liberal Arts, MA
Mayville State University, ND
McMurry University, TX
Mercer University, GA

Meredith College, NC
Methodist University, NC
Michigan State University, MI
Middle Tennessee State University, TN
Midwestern State University, TX
Millersville University of Pennsylvania, PA
Millikin University, IL
Minnesota State University Moorhead, MN
Minot State University, ND
Mississippi State University, MS
Mississippi University for Women, MS
Missouri University of Science and Technology, MO
Missouri Valley College, MO
Missouri Western State University, MO
Molloy College, NY
Montana State University, MT
Montana State University Billings, MT
Montclair State University, NJ
Mount Mary University, WI
Murray State University, KY
New England College, NH
New Mexico Highlands University, NM
New Mexico State University, NM
North Carolina Central University, NC
North Central College, IL
Northeastern Illinois University, IL
Northeastern State University, OK
Northern Illinois University, IL
Northern Kentucky University, KY
Northern Michigan University, MI
Northern State University, SD
Northwestern Oklahoma State University, OK
Northwest Missouri State University, MO
Northwest Nazarene University, ID
Oakland University, MI
The Ohio State University, OH
Ohio University, OH
Ohio University–Chillicothe, OH
Ohio University–Eastern, OH
Ohio University–Lancaster, OH
Ohio University–Southern Campus, OH
Ohio University–Zanesville, OH
Oklahoma Baptist University, OK
Oklahoma State University, OK
Old Dominion University, VA
Olivet College, MI
Ouachita Baptist University, AR
Pace University, NY
Pacific University, OR
Piedmont College, GA
Pittsburg State University, KS
Purchase College, State University of New York, NY
Quincy University, IL
Randolph College, VA
Regent University, VA
Rockford University, IL
Rockhurst University, MO
Sacred Heart University, CT
St. Catherine University, MN
St. Cloud State University, MN
St. Edward's University, TX
Saint Francis University, PA
St. John Fisher College, NY
St. John's University, NY
Saint Louis University, MO
Saint Mary's College of California, CA
St. Thomas Aquinas College, NY
Samford University, AL
Sam Houston State University, TX
San Diego State University, CA
Savannah State University, GA
Schreiner University, TX

Seton Hill University, PA
Shepherd University, WV
Shippensburg University of Pennsylvania, PA
Siena College, NY
Sierra Nevada College, NV
Slippery Rock University of Pennsylvania, PA
Sonoma State University, CA
South Dakota State University, SD
Southeastern Louisiana University, LA
Southeastern Oklahoma State University, OK
Southeast Missouri State University, MO
Southern Illinois University Carbondale, IL
Southern Oregon University, OR
Southwestern Oklahoma State University, OK
State University of New York at Fredonia, NY
State University of New York at New Paltz, NY
State University of New York at Oswego, NY
State University of New York at Plattsburgh, NY
State University of New York College at Geneseo, NY
State University of New York College at Potsdam, NY
Stephens College, MO
Stetson University, FL
Stony Brook University, State University of New York, NY
Sul Ross State University, TX
Tennessee Technological University, TN
Texas A&M International University, TX
Texas A&M University–Commerce, TX
Texas Christian University, TX
Texas State University, TX
Texas Tech University, TX
Texas Wesleyan University, TX
Texas Woman's University, TX
Thiel College, PA
Thomas More College, KY
Thomas University, GA
Towson University, MD
Trevecca Nazarene University, TN
Trinity Christian College, IL
Truman State University, MO
Union University, TN
The University of Akron, OH
The University of Alabama, AL
The University of Alabama in Huntsville, AL
University of Alaska Anchorage, AK
University of Arkansas, AR
University of California, Davis, CA
University of California, Irvine, CA
University of California, Riverside, CA
University of Central Oklahoma, OK
University of Colorado Boulder, CO
University of Colorado Denver, CO
University of Connecticut, CT
University of Dayton, OH
University of Delaware, DE
University of Evansville, IN
University of Houston, TX
University of Idaho, ID
University of Illinois at Springfield, IL
The University of Kansas, KS
University of Louisville, KY
University of Maine at Fort Kent, ME
University of Mary Hardin-Baylor, TX

University of Maryland, Baltimore County, MD
University of Maryland, College Park, MD
University of Maryland Eastern Shore, MD
University of Mary Washington, VA
University of Massachusetts Amherst, MA
University of Massachusetts Lowell, MA
University of Memphis, TN
University of Michigan, MI
University of Michigan–Flint, MI
University of Minnesota, Twin Cities Campus, MN
University of Mississippi, MS
University of Missouri, MO
University of Missouri–St. Louis, MO
The University of Montana, MT
The University of Montana Western, MT
University of Montevallo, AL
University of Nebraska at Omaha, NE
University of Nebraska–Lincoln, NE
University of Nevada, Las Vegas, NV
University of Nevada, Reno, NV
University of New Hampshire, NH
University of New Hampshire at Manchester, NH
University of New Orleans, LA
University of North Carolina at Asheville, NC
The University of North Carolina at Chapel Hill, NC
The University of North Carolina at Greensboro, NC
The University of North Carolina Wilmington, NC
University of Northern Colorado, CO
University of North Georgia, GA
University of Oklahoma, OK
University of Oregon, OR
University of Pittsburgh at Bradford, PA
University of Pittsburgh at Johnstown, PA
University of Portland, OR
University of Puget Sound, WA
University of Rio Grande, OH
University of St. Thomas, MN
University of St. Thomas, TX
University of South Carolina, SC
University of South Carolina Aiken, SC
The University of South Dakota, SD
University of South Florida, FL
The University of Tampa, FL
The University of Tennessee at Chattanooga, TN
The University of Tennessee at Martin, TN
The University of Texas at Arlington, TX
The University of Texas at Brownsville, TX
The University of Texas at El Paso, TX
The University of Texas at San Antonio, TX
The University of Texas–Pan American, TX
The University of Toledo, OH
The University of Tulsa, OK
University of Utah, UT
University of Vermont, VT
The University of Virginia's College at Wise, VA
The University of West Alabama, AL
University of West Georgia, GA
University of Wisconsin–Eau Claire, WI
University of Wisconsin–La Crosse, WI
University of Wisconsin–Parkside, WI
University of Wisconsin–River Falls, WI
University of Wisconsin–Stevens Point, WI
University of Wisconsin–Superior, WI
University of Wisconsin–Whitewater, WI
Utah State University, UT
Valley City State University, ND
Virginia Military Institute, VA

Walla Walla University, WA
Warner Pacific College, OR
Wartburg College, IA
Washburn University, KS
Washington State University, WA
Washington University in St. Louis, MO
Wayland Baptist University, TX
Waynesburg University, PA
Wayne State College, NE
Wayne State University, MI
Webster University, MO
Wesleyan College, GA
Western Carolina University, NC
Western Illinois University, IL
Western Kentucky University, KY
Western Oregon University, OR
Western Washington University, WA
West Texas A&M University, TX
West Virginia University, WV
West Virginia Wesleyan College, WV
Wheaton College, IL
Wichita State University, KS
Widener University, PA
William Jessup University, CA
Wilson College, PA
Wright State University, OH
Xavier University of Louisiana, LA
Youngstown State University, OH

**Foreign Languages**
Abilene Christian University, TX
Adelphi University, NY
Albertus Magnus College, CT
Alliant International University–San Diego, CA
Angelo State University, TX
Armstrong State University, GA
Auburn University, AL
Augustana College, IL
Augustana College, SD
Austin College, TX
Austin Peay State University, TN
Averett University, VA
Ball State University, IN
Baylor University, TX
Belhaven University, MS
Bemidji State University, MN
Binghamton University, State University of New York, NY
Birmingham-Southern College, AL
Bloomsburg University of Pennsylvania, PA
Boise State University, ID
Bowling Green State University, OH
Buffalo State College, State University of New York, NY
Butler University, IN
California Lutheran University, CA
California Polytechnic State University, San Luis Obispo, CA
California State University, Bakersfield, CA
California State University, Chico, CA
California State University, Fresno, CA
California State University, Fullerton, CA
California State University, Los Angeles, CA
California State University, San Bernardino, CA
California State University, Stanislaus, CA
Calvin College, MI
Cameron University, OK
Case Western Reserve University, OH
Castleton State College, VT
Centenary College of Louisiana, LA
Central College, IA
Central Methodist University, MO
Central Michigan University, MI
Centre College, KY

Charlotte Christian College and Theological Seminary, NC
Christopher Newport University, VA
City College of the City University of New York, NY
Clarion University of Pennsylvania, PA
Clemson University, SC
Coastal Carolina University, SC
Coe College, IA
The College at Brockport, State University of New York, NY
College of Charleston, SC
The College of Idaho, ID
The College of New Rochelle, NY
The College of Saint Rose, NY
College of Staten Island of the City University of New York, NY
Colorado Mesa University, CO
Colorado State University–Pueblo, CO
Concordia University Chicago, IL
Concordia University Texas, TX
Cornerstone University, MI
Davidson College, NC
Delta State University, MS
Denison University, OH
DeSales University, PA
Dickinson State University, ND
Dordt College, IA
Drew University, NJ
Drury University, MO
East Carolina University, NC
Eastern Illinois University, IL
Eastern Michigan University, MI
Eastern New Mexico University, NM
Eastern Washington University, WA
East Stroudsburg University of Pennsylvania, PA
Edgewood College, WI
Elizabethtown College, PA
Elmhurst College, IL
Emporia State University, KS
Evangel University, MO
Flagler College, FL
Florida Agricultural and Mechanical University, FL
Fordham University, NY
Fort Hays State University, KS
Frostburg State University, MD
Furman University, SC
Gannon University, PA
Gardner-Webb University, NC
George Fox University, OR
Georgia Southern University, GA
Grambling State University, LA
Grand Valley State University, MI
Grove City College, PA
Hamline University, MN
Hardin-Simmons University, TX
Hillsdale College, MI
Howard University, DC
Idaho State University, ID
Illinois State University, IL
Indiana State University, IN
Indiana University of Pennsylvania, PA
Iowa State University of Science and Technology, IA
John Carroll University, OH
Johnson C. Smith University, NC
Juniata College, PA
Kansas Wesleyan University, KS
Kean University, NJ
Kennesaw State University, GA
Kent State University, OH
Kent State University at Stark, OH
King's College, PA
Kutztown University of Pennsylvania, PA

Lake Erie College, OH
La Sierra University, CA
Lindenwood University, MO
Linfield College, OR
Lock Haven University of Pennsylvania, PA
Louisiana State University and Agricultural
   & Mechanical College, LA
Louisiana Tech University, LA
Loyola Marymount University, CA
Lubbock Christian University, TX
Lycoming College, PA
Manhattan College, NY
Marquette University, WI
Marywood University, PA
McMurry University, TX
Mercer University, GA
Meredith College, NC
Methodist University, NC
Michigan State University, MI
Middle Tennessee State University, TN
Midwestern State University, TX
Millersville University of Pennsylvania, PA
Millikin University, IL
Mississippi State University, MS
Missouri Western State University, MO
Monmouth College, IL
Montana State University, MT
Montana State University Billings, MT
Montclair State University, NJ
Moravian College, PA
Newberry College, SC
New Mexico Highlands University, NM
New Mexico State University, NM
North Central College, IL
Northeastern Illinois University, IL
Northeastern State University, OK
Northern Illinois University, IL
Northern Kentucky University, KY
Northern Michigan University, MI
Northern State University, SD
Northwestern Oklahoma State University,
   OK
Northwest Missouri State University, MO
Oakland University, MI
The Ohio State University, OH
Ohio University, OH
Ohio University–Chillicothe, OH
Ohio University–Eastern, OH
Ohio University–Lancaster, OH
Ohio University–Southern Campus, OH
Ohio University–Zanesville, OH
Oklahoma Baptist University, OK
Oklahoma State University, OK
Old Dominion University, VA
Olivet College, MI
Ouachita Baptist University, AR
Pace University, NY
Pacific University, OR
Piedmont College, GA
Pittsburg State University, KS
Portland State University, OR
Regent University, VA
Rockford University, IL
Rockhurst University, MO
St. Ambrose University, IA
St. Catherine University, MN
St. Edward's University, TX
St. John Fisher College, NY
St. John's University, NY
Saint Louis University, MO
St. Thomas Aquinas College, NY
Samford University, AL
Sam Houston State University, TX
San Diego State University, CA
Seton Hill University, PA

Shippensburg University of Pennsylvania,
   PA
Siena College, NY
Sonoma State University, CA
South Dakota State University, SD
Southeastern Louisiana University, LA
Southeast Missouri State University, MO
Southern Illinois University Carbondale, IL
Southern Oregon University, OR
Southwestern Oklahoma State University,
   OK
State University of New York at Fredonia,
   NY
State University of New York at New Paltz,
   NY
State University of New York at Oswego,
   NY
State University of New York College at
   Geneseo, NY
State University of New York College at
   Potsdam, NY
Stetson University, FL
Stony Brook University, State University of
   New York, NY
Suffolk University, MA
Sul Ross State University, TX
Tennessee Technological University, TN
Texas A&M International University, TX
Texas A&M University–Commerce, TX
Texas Christian University, TX
Texas Tech University, TX
Texas Wesleyan University, TX
Texas Woman's University, TX
Towson University, MD
Truman State University, MO
Union University, TN
The University of Akron, OH
The University of Alabama, AL
The University of Alabama in Huntsville,
   AL
University of Arkansas, AR
University of California, Davis, CA
University of California, Irvine, CA
University of Central Oklahoma, OK
University of Colorado Boulder, CO
University of Connecticut, CT
University of Dallas, TX
University of Dayton, OH
University of Delaware, DE
University of Evansville, IN
University of Houston, TX
University of Idaho, ID
The University of Kansas, KS
University of Louisville, KY
University of Maine at Fort Kent, ME
University of Mary Hardin-Baylor, TX
University of Maryland, Baltimore County,
   MD
University of Maryland, College Park, MD
University of Mary Washington, VA
University of Massachusetts Dartmouth, MA
University of Michigan, MI
University of Michigan–Dearborn, MI
University of Michigan–Flint, MI
University of Minnesota, Twin Cities
   Campus, MN
University of Mississippi, MS
University of Missouri, MO
University of Missouri–St. Louis, MO
The University of Montana, MT
University of Montevallo, AL
University of Nebraska at Omaha, NE
University of Nebraska–Lincoln, NE
University of Nevada, Las Vegas, NV
University of Nevada, Reno, NV

University of New Hampshire, NH
University of New Orleans, LA
The University of North Carolina at
   Greensboro, NC
The University of North Carolina
   Wilmington, NC
University of Oklahoma, OK
University of Oregon, OR
University of Portland, OR
University of Puget Sound, WA
University of St. Thomas, TX
University of South Carolina, SC
The University of South Dakota, SD
University of South Florida, FL
The University of Texas at Arlington, TX
The University of Texas at Brownsville, TX
The University of Texas at San Antonio, TX
The University of Toledo, OH
The University of Tulsa, OK
University of Utah, UT
University of Vermont, VT
University of West Georgia, GA
University of Wisconsin–Eau Claire, WI
University of Wisconsin–La Crosse, WI
University of Wisconsin–Parkside, WI
University of Wisconsin–River Falls, WI
University of Wisconsin–Stevens Point, WI
University of Wisconsin–Whitewater, WI
Utah State University, UT
Valparaiso University, IN
Virginia Commonwealth University, VA
Virginia Military Institute, VA
Walla Walla University, WA
Wartburg College, IA
Washburn University, KS
Washington State University, WA
Washington University in St. Louis, MO
Wayne State College, NE
Wayne State University, MI
Webster University, MO
Western Illinois University, IL
Western Kentucky University, KY
Western Oregon University, OR
Western Washington University, WA
West Virginia University, WV
Wheaton College, IL
Wichita State University, KS
Widener University, PA
Wilson College, PA
Wright State University, OH
Xavier University, OH
Xavier University of Louisiana, LA
Youngstown State University, OH

**Health Fields**
Alabama Agricultural and Mechanical
   University, AL
Alaska Pacific University, AK
Albany College of Pharmacy and Health
   Sciences, NY
Albany State University, GA
Alderson Broaddus University, WV
Allen College, IA
Antioch University Midwest, OH
Arkansas State University, AR
Arkansas Tech University, AR
Armstrong State University, GA
Auburn University, AL
Augustana College, SD
Austin College, TX
Austin Peay State University, TN
Averett University, VA
Ball State University, IN
Bastyr University, WA
Baylor University, TX

Bellarmine University, KY
Belmont University, TN
Bemidji State University, MN
Binghamton University, State University of New York, NY
Birmingham-Southern College, AL
Bloomfield College, NJ
Bloomsburg University of Pennsylvania, PA
Blue Mountain College, MS
Boise State University, ID
Bowling Green State University, OH
Brenau University, GA
Buffalo State College, State University of New York, NY
Butler University, IN
Caldwell University, NJ
California Baptist University, CA
California Polytechnic State University, San Luis Obispo, CA
California State University, Bakersfield, CA
California State University, Chico, CA
California State University, Fresno, CA
California State University, Fullerton, CA
California State University, Los Angeles, CA
California State University, San Bernardino, CA
California State University, Stanislaus, CA
Calvin College, MI
Cameron University, OK
Campbellsville University, KY
Carroll University, WI
Case Western Reserve University, OH
Castleton State College, VT
Centenary College of Louisiana, LA
Central College, IA
Central Methodist University, MO
Central Michigan University, MI
Champlain College, VT
Christian Brothers University, TN
Clarion University of Pennsylvania, PA
Clemson University, SC
Cleveland State University, OH
The College at Brockport, State University of New York, NY
College of Charleston, SC
The College of New Rochelle, NY
College of Staten Island of the City University of New York, NY
Colorado Mesa University, CO
Colorado State University–Pueblo, CO
Columbus State University, GA
Concordia University, Nebraska, NE
Concordia University Texas, TX
Dakota Wesleyan University, SD
Davidson College, NC
Delta State University, MS
DeSales University, PA
Dickinson State University, ND
Dominican College, NY
Drury University, MO
D'Youville College, NY
East Carolina University, NC
Eastern Illinois University, IL
Eastern Michigan University, MI
Eastern New Mexico University, NM
Eastern Washington University, WA
East Stroudsburg University of Pennsylvania, PA
East Texas Baptist University, TX
ECPI University, VA
Elizabethtown College, PA
Elmhurst College, IL
Emmanuel College, GA
Emporia State University, KS
Endicott College, MA
Evangel University, MO

Fairmont State University, WV
Felician College, NJ
Ferris State University, MI
Florida Agricultural and Mechanical University, FL
Florida Gulf Coast University, FL
Florida Southern College, FL
Fort Hays State University, KS
Francis Marion University, SC
Friends University, KS
Frostburg State University, MD
Furman University, SC
Gardner-Webb University, NC
George Fox University, OR
Georgian Court University, NJ
Georgia Regents University, GA
Georgia Southern University, GA
Governors State University, IL
Grambling State University, LA
Grand Valley State University, MI
Grand View University, IA
Hamline University, MN
Hampden-Sydney College, VA
Hampton University, VA
Harding University, AR
Hardin-Simmons University, TX
Hawai`i Pacific University, HI
Hillsdale College, MI
Hillsdale Free Will Baptist College, OK
Houston Baptist University, TX
Howard University, DC
Huntington University, IN
Husson University, ME
Idaho State University, ID
Illinois State University, IL
Indiana State University, IN
Indiana University of Pennsylvania, PA
Iowa State University of Science and Technology, IA
Iowa Wesleyan College, IA
Jacksonville State University, AL
James Madison University, VA
Jefferson College of Health Sciences, VA
John Carroll University, OH
Juniata College, PA
Kean University, NJ
Kennesaw State University, GA
Kent State University, OH
Kent State University at Geauga, OH
Kent State University at Stark, OH
Kentucky Christian University, KY
Keystone College, PA
King's College, PA
LaGrange College, GA
Lakeview College of Nursing, IL
Langston University, OK
Lewis-Clark State College, ID
Lindenwood University, MO
Linfield College, OR
Lock Haven University of Pennsylvania, PA
Long Island University–LIU Brooklyn, NY
Long Island University–LIU Post, NY
Louisiana Tech University, LA
Lycoming College, PA
Malone University, OH
Mansfield University of Pennsylvania, PA
Marquette University, WI
Marymount University, VA
Maryville University of Saint Louis, MO
Marywood University, PA
Massachusetts College of Liberal Arts, MA
Mayville State University, ND
Medical University of South Carolina, SC
Mercy College of Health Sciences, IA
Mercy College of Ohio, OH
Michigan State University, MI

Middle Tennessee State University, TN
Midwestern State University, TX
Millersville University of Pennsylvania, PA
Millikin University, IL
Milwaukee School of Engineering, WI
Minnesota State University Moorhead, MN
Minot State University, ND
Misericordia University, PA
Mississippi State University, MS
Mississippi University for Women, MS
Missouri Valley College, MO
Missouri Western State University, MO
Molloy College, NY
Monmouth University, NJ
Montana State University, MT
Montana State University Billings, MT
Montana Tech of The University of Montana, MT
Moravian College, PA
Morehead State University, KY
Murray State University, KY
Nebraska Methodist College, NE
New England College, NH
New Mexico Highlands University, NM
New Mexico State University, NM
Northeastern State University, OK
Northern Illinois University, IL
Northern Kentucky University, KY
Northern Michigan University, MI
Northwestern Oklahoma State University, OK
Northwest Missouri State University, MO
Northwest Nazarene University, ID
Oakland University, MI
The Ohio State University, OH
Ohio University, OH
Ohio University–Chillicothe, OH
Ohio University–Eastern, OH
Ohio University–Lancaster, OH
Ohio University–Southern Campus, OH
Ohio University–Zanesville, OH
Oklahoma Baptist University, OK
Oklahoma City University, OK
Oklahoma Wesleyan University, OK
Old Dominion University, VA
Oral Roberts University, OK
Oregon Health & Science University, OR
Ouachita Baptist University, AR
Pace University, NY
Pacific University, OR
Peirce College, PA
Piedmont College, GA
Pittsburg State University, KS
Point Loma Nazarene University, CA
Purdue University, IN
Queens University of Charlotte, NC
Quincy University, IL
Robert Morris University Illinois, IL
Rochester Institute of Technology, NY
Rockhurst University, MO
Sacred Heart University, CT
Saginaw Valley State University, MI
St. Ambrose University, IA
St. Catherine University, MN
St. Cloud State University, MN
St. Edward's University, TX
Saint Francis Medical Center College of Nursing, IL
Saint Francis University, PA
St. John's University, NY
Saint Louis University, MO
Salisbury University, MD
Samford University, AL
San Diego State University, CA
Shepherd University, WV
Siena College, NY

Slippery Rock University of Pennsylvania, PA
Sonoma State University, CA
South Dakota State University, SD
Southeast Missouri State University, MO
Southern Illinois University Carbondale, IL
Southern Illinois University Edwardsville, IL
Southern Oregon University, OR
Southwestern College, KS
Southwestern Oklahoma State University, OK
State University of New York at Plattsburgh, NY
State University of New York College at Old Westbury, NY
Stephen F. Austin State University, TX
Stockton University, NJ
Stony Brook University, State University of New York, NY
Sul Ross State University, TX
Tennessee Technological University, TN
Texas A&M International University, TX
Texas A&M University, TX
Texas A&M University–Commerce, TX
Texas Christian University, TX
Texas Wesleyan University, TX
Texas Woman's University, TX
Thomas Jefferson University, PA
Thomas University, GA
Towson University, MD
Trinity Christian College, IL
Truett-McConnell College, GA
Truman State University, MO
Union College, KY
Union University, TN
The University of Akron, OH
The University of Alabama at Birmingham, AL
The University of Alabama in Huntsville, AL
University of Alaska Anchorage, AK
University of Arkansas, AR
University of California, Davis, CA
University of California, Irvine, CA
University of Central Oklahoma, OK
University of Colorado Boulder, CO
University of Connecticut, CT
University of Dayton, OH
University of Delaware, DE
University of Evansville, IN
University of Florida, FL
University of Hartford, CT
University of Houston, TX
University of Idaho, ID
University of Indianapolis, IN
The University of Kansas, KS
University of Louisville, KY
University of Maine at Fort Kent, ME
University of Mary Hardin-Baylor, TX
University of Maryland, College Park, MD
University of Maryland Eastern Shore, MD
University of Massachusetts Amherst, MA
University of Massachusetts Boston, MA
University of Massachusetts Dartmouth, MA
University of Massachusetts Lowell, MA
University of Memphis, TN
University of Michigan, MI
University of Michigan–Flint, MI
University of Minnesota, Twin Cities Campus, MN
University of Mississippi, MS
University of Missouri, MO
University of Missouri–St. Louis, MO
The University of Montana, MT

University of Nebraska–Lincoln, NE
University of Nevada, Las Vegas, NV
University of Nevada, Reno, NV
University of New Hampshire, NH
University of North Carolina at Asheville, NC
The University of North Carolina at Chapel Hill, NC
The University of North Carolina at Charlotte, NC
The University of North Carolina at Greensboro, NC
The University of North Carolina Wilmington, NC
University of Northern Colorado, CO
University of North Florida, FL
University of North Georgia, GA
University of Oregon, OR
University of Pittsburgh at Bradford, PA
University of Pittsburgh at Johnstown, PA
University of Portland, OR
University of Rio Grande, OH
University of St. Francis, IL
University of St. Thomas, TX
University of South Carolina, SC
University of Southern Indiana, IN
University of South Florida, FL
The University of Tennessee, TN
The University of Tennessee at Martin, TN
The University of Texas at Arlington, TX
The University of Texas at Brownsville, TX
The University of Texas at El Paso, TX
The University of Texas Health Science Center at Houston, TX
The University of Texas–Pan American, TX
University of the District of Columbia, DC
The University of Toledo, OH
The University of Tulsa, OK
University of Utah, UT
University of Vermont, VT
The University of Virginia's College at Wise, VA
University of Washington, WA
University of West Georgia, GA
University of Wisconsin–Eau Claire, WI
University of Wisconsin–Green Bay, WI
University of Wisconsin–La Crosse, WI
University of Wisconsin–Parkside, WI
University of Wisconsin–River Falls, WI
University of Wisconsin–Stevens Point, WI
University of Wisconsin–Superior, WI
Utah State University, UT
Valdosta State University, GA
Valparaiso University, IN
Virginia Commonwealth University, VA
Warner Pacific College, OR
Washburn University, KS
Washington State University, WA
Washington University in St. Louis, MO
Waynesburg University, PA
Wayne State College, NE
Wayne State University, MI
Western Illinois University, IL
Western Kentucky University, KY
Western Washington University, WA
West Texas A&M University, TX
West Virginia University, WV
Wheaton College, IL
Wichita State University, KS
Widener University, PA
William Woods University, MO
Wisconsin Lutheran College, WI
Wright State University, OH
Xavier University of Louisiana, LA
Youngstown State University, OH

**Home Economics**

Auburn University, AL
Averett University, VA
Baylor University, TX
Bowling Green State University, OH
Buffalo State College, State University of New York, NY
California Polytechnic State University, San Luis Obispo, CA
Carson-Newman University, TN
Central Michigan University, MI
College of Staten Island of the City University of New York, NY
East Carolina University, NC
Eastern Illinois University, IL
Eastern Michigan University, MI
Eastern New Mexico University, NM
Fort Hays State University, KS
Fort Valley State University, GA
Framingham State University, MA
George Fox University, OR
Grambling State University, LA
Illinois State University, IL
Indiana University of Pennsylvania, PA
Iowa State University of Science and Technology, IA
Jacksonville State University, AL
Lipscomb University, TN
Louisiana State University and Agricultural & Mechanical College, LA
Louisiana Tech University, LA
Marywood University, PA
Michigan State University, MI
Middle Tennessee State University, TN
Mississippi State University, MS
Mississippi University for Women, MS
Montana State University, MT
Montclair State University, NJ
Murray State University, KY
New Mexico State University, NM
Northeastern State University, OK
Northwest Missouri State University, MO
The Ohio State University, OH
Ohio University, OH
Ohio University–Chillicothe, OH
Ohio University–Eastern, OH
Ohio University–Lancaster, OH
Ohio University–Southern Campus, OH
Ohio University–Zanesville, OH
Oklahoma State University, OK
Ouachita Baptist University, AR
Pittsburg State University, KS
Point Loma Nazarene University, CA
St. Catherine University, MN
Samford University, AL
Sam Houston State University, TX
Seton Hill University, PA
Shepherd University, WV
South Dakota State University, SD
Southeast Missouri State University, MO
Southern Illinois University Carbondale, IL
State University of New York at Plattsburgh, NY
Stephen F. Austin State University, TX
Tennessee Technological University, TN
Texas State University, TX
Texas Tech University, TX
Texas Woman's University, TX
The University of Akron, OH
The University of Alabama, AL
University of Arkansas, AR
University of California, Davis, CA
University of Central Oklahoma, OK
University of Idaho, ID
University of Maryland Eastern Shore, MD

University of Minnesota, Twin Cities
Campus, MN
University of Missouri, MO
University of Nebraska at Omaha, NE
University of Nebraska–Lincoln, NE
The University of North Carolina at
Greensboro, NC
University of Northern Colorado, CO
The University of Tennessee at Chattanooga,
TN
The University of Tennessee at Martin, TN
University of Vermont, VT
University of Wisconsin–Stevens Point, WI
University of Wisconsin–Stout, WI
Utah State University, UT
Washington State University, WA
Wayne State College, NE
Western Illinois University, IL
Western Kentucky University, KY
West Virginia University, WV

**Humanities**

Alaska Pacific University, AK
Albertus Magnus College, CT
Alderson Broaddus University, WV
Alliant International University–San Diego,
CA
Angelo State University, TX
Arkansas State University, AR
Arkansas Tech University, AR
Armstrong State University, GA
Auburn University, AL
Augustana College, IL
Augustana College, SD
Austin College, TX
Austin Peay State University, TN
Averett University, VA
Ball State University, IN
Baylor University, TX
Belhaven University, MS
Bemidji State University, MN
Berry College, GA
Binghamton University, State University of
New York, NY
Birmingham-Southern College, AL
Bloomfield College, NJ
Bloomsburg University of Pennsylvania, PA
Blue Mountain College, MS
Boise State University, ID
Bowling Green State University, OH
Brenau University, GA
Buena Vista University, IA
Butler University, IN
California Lutheran University, CA
California Polytechnic State University, San
Luis Obispo, CA
California State Polytechnic University,
Pomona, CA
California State University, Bakersfield, CA
California State University, Chico, CA
California State University, Fresno, CA
California State University, Fullerton, CA
California State University, Stanislaus, CA
Calvin College, MI
Campbellsville University, KY
Carroll University, WI
Case Western Reserve University, OH
Castleton State College, VT
Centenary College of Louisiana, LA
Central College, IA
Central Methodist University, MO
Central Michigan University, MI
Christopher Newport University, VA
The Citadel, The Military College of South
Carolina, SC

City College of the City University of New
York, NY
Clarion University of Pennsylvania, PA
Clarkson University, NY
Clemson University, SC
Cleveland State University, OH
Coastal Carolina University, SC
The College at Brockport, State University
of New York, NY
College of Charleston, SC
The College of Idaho, ID
The College of New Rochelle, NY
The College of Saint Rose, NY
College of Staten Island of the City
University of New York, NY
College of the Holy Cross, MA
Colorado Mesa University, CO
Columbia College, MO
Columbus State University, GA
Concordia University, Nebraska, NE
Cornerstone University, MI
Dallas Baptist University, TX
Delta State University, MS
DeSales University, PA
Dickinson State University, ND
Dordt College, IA
Drew University, NJ
Drury University, MO
D'Youville College, NY
East Carolina University, NC
Eastern Illinois University, IL
Eastern Michigan University, MI
Eastern New Mexico University, NM
Eastern Washington University, WA
East Texas Baptist University, TX
Elizabethtown College, PA
Elmhurst College, IL
Emory University, GA
Emporia State University, KS
Evangel University, MO
Fairmont State University, WV
Flagler College, FL
Florida Agricultural and Mechanical
University, FL
Florida Gulf Coast University, FL
Fort Hays State University, KS
Fort Lewis College, CO
Francis Marion University, SC
Fresno Pacific University, CA
Frostburg State University, MD
Furman University, SC
Gannon University, PA
Gardner-Webb University, NC
George Fox University, OR
Georgia College & State University, GA
Georgia Southern University, GA
Grambling State University, LA
Grand Valley State University, MI
Hamline University, MN
Hampshire College, MA
Hardin-Simmons University, TX
Hillsdale College, MI
Howard University, DC
Idaho State University, ID
Illinois State University, IL
Indiana State University, IN
Indiana University of Pennsylvania, PA
Iowa State University of Science and
Technology, IA
Jacksonville State University, AL
James Madison University, VA
Juniata College, PA
Kean University, NJ
Kennesaw State University, GA
Kent State University, OH
Kent State University at Geauga, OH

Kentucky Christian University, KY
King's College, PA
Kutztown University of Pennsylvania, PA
Lake Erie College, OH
Lawrence Technological University, MI
Lewis-Clark State College, ID
Lincoln University, PA
Lindenwood University, MO
Linfield College, OR
Longwood University, VA
Louisiana State University and Agricultural
& Mechanical College, LA
Loyola Marymount University, CA
Lubbock Christian University, TX
Lycoming College, PA
Massachusetts College of Liberal Arts, MA
Middle Tennessee State University, TN
Midwestern State University, TX
Millersville University of Pennsylvania, PA
Millikin University, IL
Minot State University, ND
Mississippi State University, MS
Mississippi University for Women, MS
Missouri University of Science and
Technology, MO
Missouri Valley College, MO
Missouri Western State University, MO
Molloy College, NY
Monmouth University, NJ
Montana State University, MT
Montana State University Billings, MT
Montclair State University, NJ
Mount Mary University, WI
Murray State University, KY
Newberry College, SC
New England College, NH
New Jersey Institute of Technology, NJ
New Mexico Highlands University, NM
New Mexico State University, NM
North Carolina State University, NC
North Central College, IL
Northeastern State University, OK
Northern Illinois University, IL
Northern State University, SD
Northwest Missouri State University, MO
Oakland University, MI
The Ohio State University, OH
Ohio University, OH
Ohio University–Chillicothe, OH
Ohio University–Eastern, OH
Ohio University–Lancaster, OH
Ohio University–Southern Campus, OH
Ohio University–Zanesville, OH
Oklahoma Baptist University, OK
Oklahoma State University, OK
Old Dominion University, VA
Ouachita Baptist University, AR
Pace University, NY
Pacific University, OR
Piedmont College, GA
Point Loma Nazarene University, CA
Portland State University, OR
Post University, CT
Purchase College, State University of New
York, NY
Purdue University, IN
Quincy University, IL
Regent University, VA
Rensselaer Polytechnic Institute, NY
Rockhurst University, MO
Sacred Heart University, CT
St. Catherine University, MN
St. Edward's University, TX
Saint Francis University, PA
St. John Fisher College, NY
St. John's University, NY

Saint Louis University, MO
Saint Martin's University, WA
Saint Mary's College of California, CA
St. Thomas Aquinas College, NY
Salisbury University, MD
Samford University, AL
Sam Houston State University, TX
San Diego State University, CA
Savannah State University, GA
Seton Hill University, PA
Shepherd University, WV
Shippensburg University of Pennsylvania, PA
Siena College, NY
Sonoma State University, CA
South Dakota State University, SD
Southeastern Louisiana University, LA
Southeast Missouri State University, MO
Southern Illinois University Carbondale, IL
Southwestern University, TX
State University of New York at Fredonia, NY
State University of New York at Oswego, NY
State University of New York at Plattsburgh, NY
State University of New York College at Geneseo, NY
State University of New York College at Potsdam, NY
Stetson University, FL
Stockton University, NJ
Tabor College, KS
Tennessee Technological University, TN
Texas A&M University–Commerce, TX
Texas Christian University, TX
Texas Tech University, TX
Texas Wesleyan University, TX
Texas Woman's University, TX
Thomas University, GA
Trinity Christian College, IL
Truman State University, MO
Union University, TN
The University of Akron, OH
The University of Alabama in Huntsville, AL
University of Alaska Anchorage, AK
The University of Arizona, AZ
University of Arkansas, AR
University of California, Davis, CA
University of California, Irvine, CA
University of California, Riverside, CA
University of California, Santa Cruz, CA
University of Central Oklahoma, OK
University of Colorado Boulder, CO
University of Colorado Denver, CO
University of Connecticut, CT
University of Dayton, OH
University of Delaware, DE
University of Denver, CO
University of Evansville, IN
University of Great Falls, MT
University of Houston, TX
University of Houston–Clear Lake, TX
University of Idaho, ID
University of Illinois at Springfield, IL
The University of Kansas, KS
University of Maine at Fort Kent, ME
University of Mary Hardin-Baylor, TX
University of Maryland, Baltimore County, MD
University of Maryland, College Park, MD
University of Mary Washington, VA
University of Massachusetts Amherst, MA
University of Massachusetts Dartmouth, MA

University of Massachusetts Lowell, MA
University of Memphis, TN
University of Michigan, MI
University of Michigan–Flint, MI
University of Minnesota, Twin Cities Campus, MN
University of Mississippi, MS
University of Missouri, MO
University of Missouri–St. Louis, MO
The University of Montana, MT
The University of Montana Western, MT
University of Nebraska–Lincoln, NE
University of Nevada, Las Vegas, NV
University of New Hampshire, NH
University of New Hampshire at Manchester, NH
The University of North Carolina at Charlotte, NC
The University of North Carolina at Greensboro, NC
The University of North Carolina Wilmington, NC
University of North Georgia, GA
University of Oklahoma, OK
University of Oregon, OR
University of Pittsburgh at Bradford, PA
University of Pittsburgh at Johnstown, PA
University of Portland, OR
University of Puget Sound, WA
University of Rio Grande, OH
University of St. Thomas, MN
University of St. Thomas, TX
University of South Alabama, AL
University of South Carolina, SC
University of South Carolina Aiken, SC
The University of South Dakota, SD
University of Southern Indiana, IN
University of South Florida, FL
The University of Tennessee, TN
The University of Tennessee at Martin, TN
The University of Texas at Arlington, TX
The University of Texas at El Paso, TX
The University of Texas at San Antonio, TX
The University of Toledo, OH
University of Utah, UT
University of Vermont, VT
The University of Virginia's College at Wise, VA
University of West Georgia, GA
University of Wisconsin–Eau Claire, WI
University of Wisconsin–Green Bay, WI
University of Wisconsin–La Crosse, WI
University of Wisconsin–River Falls, WI
University of Wisconsin–Stevens Point, WI
University of Wisconsin–Superior, WI
University of Wisconsin–Whitewater, WI
Utah State University, UT
Valley City State University, ND
Virginia Commonwealth University, VA
Virginia Military Institute, VA
Walla Walla University, WA
Warner Pacific College, OR
Wartburg College, IA
Washburn University, KS
Washington & Jefferson College, PA
Washington State University, WA
Washington University in St. Louis, MO
Waynesburg University, PA
Wayne State College, NE
Wayne State University, MI
Webster University, MO
Western Oregon University, OR
Western Washington University, WA
West Texas A&M University, TX
West Virginia University, WV

Wheaton College, IL
Wichita State University, KS
Widener University, PA
William Jessup University, CA
Williams Baptist College, AR
Wilson College, PA
Wright State University, OH
Xavier University of Louisiana, LA
Youngstown State University, OH

**International Studies**
Albertus Magnus College, CT
Alliant International University–San Diego, CA
Angelo State University, TX
Armstrong State University, GA
Augustana College, SD
Austin College, TX
Austin Peay State University, TN
Ball State University, IN
Baylor University, TX
Belhaven University, MS
Bemidji State University, MN
Binghamton University, State University of New York, NY
Birmingham-Southern College, AL
Bloomsburg University of Pennsylvania, PA
Boise State University, ID
Bowling Green State University, OH
Buena Vista University, IA
Butler University, IN
California Lutheran University, CA
California Polytechnic State University, San Luis Obispo, CA
California State University, Chico, CA
California State University, San Bernardino, CA
California State University, Stanislaus, CA
Calvin College, MI
Carroll University, WI
Case Western Reserve University, OH
Central College, IA
Central Michigan University, MI
City College of the City University of New York, NY
Clarion University of Pennsylvania, PA
Clemson University, SC
Coastal Carolina University, SC
The College at Brockport, State University of New York, NY
College of Staten Island of the City University of New York, NY
Columbus State University, GA
Concordia University Texas, TX
Davidson College, NC
D'Youville College, NY
East Carolina University, NC
Eastern Illinois University, IL
Eastern Washington University, WA
Elizabethtown College, PA
Elmhurst College, IL
Evangel University, MO
Fairmont State University, WV
Fort Hays State University, KS
Frostburg State University, MD
Furman University, SC
Gannon University, PA
George Fox University, OR
Georgetown College, KY
Georgia College & State University, GA
Georgia Southern University, GA
Golden Gate University, CA
Grand Valley State University, MI
Hamline University, MN
Hampden-Sydney College, VA

Hampshire College, MA
Henderson State University, AR
Hillsdale College, MI
Howard University, DC
Idaho State University, ID
Illinois State University, IL
Indiana University of Pennsylvania, PA
Iowa State University of Science and
    Technology, IA
James Madison University, VA
Juniata College, PA
Kean University, NJ
Kennesaw State University, GA
Kent State University, OH
Kentucky Christian University, KY
Keuka College, NY
Kutztown University of Pennsylvania, PA
Lake Erie College, OH
Lawrence Technological University, MI
Lehigh University, PA
Lindenwood University, MO
Linfield College, OR
Lock Haven University of Pennsylvania, PA
Long Island University–LIU Brooklyn, NY
Long Island University–LIU Post, NY
Longwood University, VA
Louisiana Tech University, LA
Loyola Marymount University, CA
Lycoming College, PA
Lynn University, FL
Maryville University of Saint Louis, MO
Mercer University, GA
Methodist University, NC
Michigan State University, MI
Middle Tennessee State University, TN
Midwestern State University, TX
Millikin University, IL
Minnesota State University Moorhead, MN
Mississippi State University, MS
Molloy College, NY
Monmouth University, NJ
Montclair State University, NJ
Morehead State University, KY
Murray State University, KY
New England College, NH
New Jersey Institute of Technology, NJ
North Central College, IL
Northern Illinois University, IL
Northern Kentucky University, KY
Northern Michigan University, MI
Northern State University, SD
The Ohio State University, OH
Ohio University, OH
Ohio University–Chillicothe, OH
Ohio University–Eastern, OH
Ohio University–Lancaster, OH
Ohio University–Southern Campus, OH
Ohio University–Zanesville, OH
Oklahoma State University, OK
Old Dominion University, VA
Ouachita Baptist University, AR
Portland State University, OR
Post University, CT
Quincy University, IL
Rochester Institute of Technology, NY
Rockhurst University, MO
St. Ambrose University, IA
St. Cloud State University, MN
St. Edward's University, TX
Saint Francis University, PA
Saint Louis University, MO
Saint Martin's University, WA
Saint Mary's College of California, CA
Samford University, AL
San Diego State University, CA
Siena College, NY

South Dakota State University, SD
Southeast Missouri State University, MO
Southern Illinois University Carbondale, IL
Southwestern University, TX
State University of New York at Fredonia,
    NY
State University of New York at New Paltz,
    NY
State University of New York at Oswego,
    NY
State University of New York at Plattsburgh,
    NY
State University of New York College at
    Cortland, NY
State University of New York College at
    Geneseo, NY
Stony Brook University, State University of
    New York, NY
Tennessee Technological University, TN
Texas A&M International University, TX
Texas A&M University–Commerce, TX
Texas Christian University, TX
Texas State University, TX
Texas Tech University, TX
Texas Wesleyan University, TX
Thomas University, GA
Trinity Christian College, IL
Union University, TN
The University of Akron, OH
University of Arkansas, AR
University of California, Davis, CA
University of California, Irvine, CA
University of Colorado Boulder, CO
University of Colorado Denver, CO
University of Connecticut, CT
University of Dayton, OH
University of Delaware, DE
University of Denver, CO
University of Evansville, IN
University of Houston, TX
University of Illinois at Springfield, IL
The University of Kansas, KS
University of Mary Hardin-Baylor, TX
University of Maryland, College Park, MD
University of Mary Washington, VA
University of Memphis, TN
University of Michigan, MI
University of Michigan–Dearborn, MI
University of Michigan–Flint, MI
University of Minnesota, Twin Cities
    Campus, MN
University of Mississippi, MS
University of Missouri, MO
University of Missouri–St. Louis, MO
The University of Montana, MT
University of Nebraska–Lincoln, NE
University of Nevada, Las Vegas, NV
The University of North Carolina at
    Greensboro, NC
The University of North Carolina
    Wilmington, NC
University of North Florida, FL
University of Oklahoma, OK
University of Oregon, OR
University of Puget Sound, WA
University of St. Francis, IL
University of St. Thomas, MN
University of St. Thomas, TX
University of South Alabama, AL
University of South Carolina, SC
University of South Florida, FL
The University of Tampa, FL
The University of Tennessee, TN
The University of Texas at Arlington, TX
The University of Texas at Brownsville, TX
The University of Texas at El Paso, TX

The University of Texas at San Antonio, TX
The University of Toledo, OH
The University of Tulsa, OK
University of Utah, UT
University of Vermont, VT
University of Wisconsin–Eau Claire, WI
University of Wisconsin–La Crosse, WI
University of Wisconsin–River Falls, WI
University of Wisconsin–Stevens Point, WI
University of Wisconsin–Stout, WI
Utah State University, UT
Villanova University, PA
Virginia Military Institute, VA
Washburn University, KS
Washington State University, WA
Washington University in St. Louis, MO
Waynesburg University, PA
Wayne State University, MI
Webster University, MO
Western Illinois University, IL
West Virginia University, WV
Wichita State University, KS
Widener University, PA
William Jessup University, CA
Wilson College, PA
Wisconsin Lutheran College, WI
Wright State University, OH

**Library Science**
Arkansas State University, AR
Blue Mountain College, MS
California Polytechnic State University, San
    Luis Obispo, CA
Clarion University of Pennsylvania, PA
College of Staten Island of the City
    University of New York, NY
East Carolina University, NC
Illinois State University, IL
Iowa State University of Science and
    Technology, IA
Kent State University, OH
Kutztown University of Pennsylvania, PA
Lindenwood University, MO
Lock Haven University of Pennsylvania, PA
Long Island University–LIU Post, NY
Mayville State University, ND
Mississippi State University, MS
North Carolina Central University, NC
Northeastern State University, OK
Northwestern Oklahoma State University,
    OK
Sam Houston State University, TX
Texas Woman's University, TX
The University of Alabama, AL
University of Houston, TX
University of Idaho, ID
University of Illinois at Springfield, IL
University of Maryland, College Park, MD
University of Michigan, MI
University of Minnesota, Twin Cities
    Campus, MN
University of Missouri, MO
The University of North Carolina at
    Greensboro, NC
University of South Carolina, SC
University of South Florida, FL
The University of Tennessee, TN
The University of Toledo, OH
University of Wisconsin–Eau Claire, WI
Utah State University, UT
Valdosta State University, GA
Valley City State University, ND
Virginia Polytechnic Institute and State
    University, VA
Wayne State University, MI
Western Illinois University, IL

Western Kentucky University, KY
Western Washington University, WA
West Virginia University, WV

**Mathematics**
Abilene Christian University, TX
Adelphi University, NY
Alabama Agricultural and Mechanical
    University, AL
Alaska Pacific University, AK
Albany State University, GA
Albertus Magnus College, CT
Albion College, MI
Alderson Broaddus University, WV
Angelo State University, TX
Arkansas State University, AR
Armstrong State University, GA
Ashland University, OH
Auburn University, AL
Augustana College, IL
Augustana College, SD
Austin Peay State University, TN
Averett University, VA
Ball State University, IN
Baylor University, TX
Belhaven University, MS
Bemidji State University, MN
Binghamton University, State University of
    New York, NY
Birmingham-Southern College, AL
Bloomfield College, NJ
Bloomsburg University of Pennsylvania, PA
Blue Mountain College, MS
Bluffton University, OH
Boise State University, ID
Bowie State University, MD
Bowling Green State University, OH
Bucknell University, PA
Buena Vista University, IA
Buffalo State College, State University of
    New York, NY
Butler University, IN
California Lutheran University, CA
California Polytechnic State University, San
    Luis Obispo, CA
California State Polytechnic University,
    Pomona, CA
California State University, Bakersfield, CA
California State University, Chico, CA
California State University, Fresno, CA
California State University, Fullerton, CA
California State University, Los Angeles, CA
California State University, San Bernardino,
    CA
California State University, San Marcos, CA
California State University, Stanislaus, CA
Calvin College, MI
Cameron University, OK
Campbellsville University, KY
Carroll University, WI
Carson-Newman University, TN
Case Western Reserve University, OH
Castleton State College, VT
Centenary College of Louisiana, LA
Central College, IA
Central Methodist University, MO
Central Michigan University, MI
Christopher Newport University, VA
City College of the City University of New
    York, NY
Clarion University of Pennsylvania, PA
Clarkson University, NY
Clemson University, SC
Cleveland State University, OH
Coastal Carolina University, SC

Coe College, IA
The College at Brockport, State University
    of New York, NY
College of Charleston, SC
The College of Idaho, ID
The College of New Rochelle, NY
College of Saint Benedict, MN
College of Saint Mary, NE
The College of Saint Rose, NY
College of Staten Island of the City
    University of New York, NY
The Colorado College, CO
Colorado Mesa University, CO
Colorado School of Mines, CO
Colorado State University–Pueblo, CO
Columbia College, MO
Columbus State University, GA
Concordia University Chicago, IL
Concordia University, Nebraska, NE
Concordia University, St. Paul, MN
Concordia University Texas, TX
Concord University, WV
Cornerstone University, MI
Dakota State University, SD
Dakota Wesleyan University, SD
Dallas Baptist University, TX
Davidson College, NC
Delta State University, MS
Denison University, OH
DeSales University, PA
Dickinson State University, ND
Dordt College, IA
Dowling College, NY
Drew University, NJ
Drury University, MO
Duke University, NC
D'Youville College, NY
East Carolina University, NC
Eastern Illinois University, IL
Eastern Michigan University, MI
Eastern New Mexico University, NM
Eastern Washington University, WA
East Stroudsburg University of
    Pennsylvania, PA
East Texas Baptist University, TX
Elizabeth City State University, NC
Elizabethtown College, PA
Elmhurst College, IL
Elon University, NC
Emporia State University, KS
Evangel University, MO
Fairmont State University, WV
Ferris State University, MI
Florida Agricultural and Mechanical
    University, FL
Florida Gulf Coast University, FL
Fort Hays State University, KS
Fort Lewis College, CO
Framingham State University, MA
Francis Marion University, SC
Frostburg State University, MD
Furman University, SC
Gannon University, PA
Gardner-Webb University, NC
George Fox University, OR
Georgian Court University, NJ
Georgia Regents University, GA
Georgia Southern University, GA
Glenville State College, WV
Governors State University, IL
Grambling State University, LA
Grand Valley State University, MI
Grand View University, IA
Greenville College, IL
Grove City College, PA

Hamline University, MN
Hampshire College, MA
Hardin-Simmons University, TX
Henderson State University, AR
Hillsdale College, MI
Howard Payne University, TX
Howard University, DC
Huntingdon College, AL
Huntington University, IN
Idaho State University, ID
Illinois State University, IL
Indiana State University, IN
Indiana University of Pennsylvania, PA
Iowa State University of Science and
    Technology, IA
Jacksonville State University, AL
James Madison University, VA
John Carroll University, OH
Juniata College, PA
Kansas Wesleyan University, KS
Kean University, NJ
Kennesaw State University, GA
Kent State University, OH
King's College, PA
Knox College, IL
Kutztown University of Pennsylvania, PA
Lake Erie College, OH
Lawrence Technological University, MI
Lebanon Valley College, PA
Lees-McRae College, NC
Lewis-Clark State College, ID
Liberty University, VA
Lincoln University, PA
Lindenwood University, MO
Lindsey Wilson College, KY
Linfield College, OR
Lipscomb University, TN
Lock Haven University of Pennsylvania, PA
Long Island University–LIU Post, NY
Longwood University, VA
Louisiana State University and Agricultural
    & Mechanical College, LA
Louisiana Tech University, LA
Loyola Marymount University, CA
Lycoming College, PA
Malone University, OH
Manhattan College, NY
Manhattanville College, NY
Mansfield University of Pennsylvania, PA
Marquette University, WI
Marymount University, VA
Maryville University of Saint Louis, MO
Marywood University, PA
Massachusetts College of Liberal Arts, MA
The Master's College and Seminary, CA
Mayville State University, ND
McMurry University, TX
Meredith College, NC
Michigan State University, MI
Middle Tennessee State University, TN
Midwestern State University, TX
Millersville University of Pennsylvania, PA
Millikin University, IL
Mills College, CA
Minnesota State University Moorhead, MN
Minot State University, ND
Mississippi State University, MS
Mississippi University for Women, MS
Missouri University of Science and
    Technology, MO
Missouri Valley College, MO
Missouri Western State University, MO
Molloy College, NY
Monmouth University, NJ
Montana State University, MT

Montana State University Billings, MT
Montana Tech of The University of Montana, MT
Montclair State University, NJ
Moravian College, PA
Mount Mary University, WI
Murray State University, KY
Muskingum University, OH
Newberry College, SC
New England College, NH
New Jersey Institute of Technology, NJ
New Mexico Highlands University, NM
New Mexico State University, NM
North Carolina State University, NC
North Central College, IL
Northeastern Illinois University, IL
Northeastern State University, OK
Northern Illinois University, IL
Northern Kentucky University, KY
Northern Michigan University, MI
Northern State University, SD
Northwestern Oklahoma State University, OK
Northwest Missouri State University, MO
Northwest Nazarene University, ID
The Ohio State University, OH
Ohio University, OH
Ohio University–Chillicothe, OH
Ohio University–Eastern, OH
Ohio University–Lancaster, OH
Ohio University–Southern Campus, OH
Ohio University–Zanesville, OH
Oklahoma Baptist University, OK
Oklahoma State University, OK
Old Dominion University, VA
Ouachita Baptist University, AR
Pace University, NY
Pacific University, OR
Piedmont College, GA
Pittsburg State University, KS
Point Loma Nazarene University, CA
Purchase College, State University of New York, NY
Purdue University, IN
Quincy University, IL
Randolph College, VA
Regent University, VA
Regis University, CO
Rensselaer Polytechnic Institute, NY
Rochester College, MI
Rochester Institute of Technology, NY
Rockford University, IL
Rockhurst University, MO
Rollins College, FL
Sacred Heart University, CT
Saginaw Valley State University, MI
St. Catherine University, MN
St. Cloud State University, MN
St. Edward's University, TX
Saint Francis University, PA
St. John Fisher College, NY
St. John's University, NY
Saint Louis University, MO
Saint Mary's College of California, CA
Saint Michael's College, VT
St. Thomas Aquinas College, NY
Samford University, AL
Sam Houston State University, TX
San Diego State University, CA
Savannah State University, GA
Schreiner University, TX
Seton Hill University, PA
Shepherd University, WV
Shippensburg University of Pennsylvania, PA
Siena College, NY

Skidmore College, NY
Sonoma State University, CA
South Dakota School of Mines and Technology, SD
South Dakota State University, SD
Southeastern Louisiana University, LA
Southeastern Oklahoma State University, OK
Southeast Missouri State University, MO
Southern Illinois University Carbondale, IL
Southern Oregon University, OR
Southwestern Oklahoma State University, OK
Southwestern University, TX
State University of New York at Fredonia, NY
State University of New York at New Paltz, NY
State University of New York at Oswego, NY
State University of New York at Plattsburgh, NY
State University of New York College at Cortland, NY
State University of New York College at Geneseo, NY
State University of New York College at Potsdam, NY
Stephen F. Austin State University, TX
Stetson University, FL
Stockton University, NJ
Stony Brook University, State University of New York, NY
Suffolk University, MA
Tennessee Technological University, TN
Texas A&M International University, TX
Texas A&M University, TX
Texas A&M University–Commerce, TX
Texas Christian University, TX
Texas Lutheran University, TX
Texas Tech University, TX
Texas Wesleyan University, TX
Texas Woman's University, TX
Thiel College, PA
Thomas More College, KY
Thomas University, GA
Towson University, MD
Trinity Christian College, IL
Truman State University, MO
Union College, KY
Union University, TN
The University of Akron, OH
The University of Alabama, AL
The University of Alabama at Birmingham, AL
The University of Alabama in Huntsville, AL
University of Alaska Anchorage, AK
University of Alaska Fairbanks, AK
University of Arkansas, AR
University of California, Davis, CA
University of California, Irvine, CA
University of California, Riverside, CA
University of California, San Diego, CA
University of California, Santa Cruz, CA
University of Central Oklahoma, OK
University of Colorado Boulder, CO
University of Colorado Denver, CO
University of Connecticut, CT
University of Dallas, TX
University of Dayton, OH
University of Delaware, DE
University of Denver, CO
University of Evansville, IN
University of Great Falls, MT
University of Houston, TX

University of Houston–Clear Lake, TX
University of Idaho, ID
University of Illinois at Springfield, IL
The University of Kansas, KS
University of Louisville, KY
University of Maine at Augusta, ME
University of Maine at Fort Kent, ME
University of Mary Hardin-Baylor, TX
University of Maryland, Baltimore County, MD
University of Maryland, College Park, MD
University of Maryland Eastern Shore, MD
University of Mary Washington, VA
University of Massachusetts Amherst, MA
University of Massachusetts Dartmouth, MA
University of Massachusetts Lowell, MA
University of Memphis, TN
University of Michigan, MI
University of Michigan–Dearborn, MI
University of Michigan–Flint, MI
University of Minnesota, Twin Cities Campus, MN
University of Mississippi, MS
University of Missouri, MO
University of Missouri–St. Louis, MO
The University of Montana, MT
The University of Montana Western, MT
University of Montevallo, AL
University of Nebraska at Omaha, NE
University of Nebraska–Lincoln, NE
University of Nevada, Las Vegas, NV
University of Nevada, Reno, NV
University of New Hampshire, NH
University of New Orleans, LA
University of North Carolina at Asheville, NC
The University of North Carolina at Chapel Hill, NC
The University of North Carolina at Charlotte, NC
The University of North Carolina at Greensboro, NC
The University of North Carolina Wilmington, NC
University of Northern Colorado, CO
University of Northern Iowa, IA
University of North Georgia, GA
University of Oklahoma, OK
University of Oregon, OR
University of Pittsburgh at Bradford, PA
University of Pittsburgh at Johnstown, PA
University of Portland, OR
University of Puget Sound, WA
University of Richmond, VA
University of Rio Grande, OH
University of St. Thomas, MN
University of St. Thomas, TX
University of South Carolina, SC
University of South Carolina Aiken, SC
The University of South Dakota, SD
University of Southern Indiana, IN
University of South Florida, FL
The University of Tennessee at Chattanooga, TN
The University of Tennessee at Martin, TN
The University of Texas at Arlington, TX
The University of Texas at Brownsville, TX
The University of Texas at Dallas, TX
The University of Texas at El Paso, TX
The University of Texas at San Antonio, TX
The University of Texas–Pan American, TX
The University of Toledo, OH
The University of Tulsa, OK
University of Utah, UT
University of Vermont, VT

The University of Virginia's College at Wise, VA
University of West Florida, FL
University of West Georgia, GA
University of Wisconsin–Eau Claire, WI
University of Wisconsin–La Crosse, WI
University of Wisconsin–Parkside, WI
University of Wisconsin–River Falls, WI
University of Wisconsin–Stevens Point, WI
University of Wisconsin–Stout, WI
University of Wisconsin–Superior, WI
University of Wisconsin–Whitewater, WI
Utah State University, UT
Valdosta State University, GA
Valley City State University, ND
Virginia Commonwealth University, VA
Virginia Military Institute, VA
Virginia State University, VA
Walla Walla University, WA
Warner Pacific College, OR
Wartburg College, IA
Washburn University, KS
Washington State University, WA
Washington University in St. Louis, MO
Wayland Baptist University, TX
Waynesburg University, PA
Wayne State College, NE
Wayne State University, MI
West Chester University of Pennsylvania, PA
Western Carolina University, NC
Western Illinois University, IL
Western Kentucky University, KY
Western Oregon University, OR
Western Washington University, WA
West Texas A&M University, TX
West Virginia University, WV
Wheaton College, IL
Wichita State University, KS
Widener University, PA
William Jessup University, CA
Wilson College, PA
Wisconsin Lutheran College, WI
Wright State University, OH
Xavier University, OH
Xavier University of Louisiana, LA
Youngstown State University, OH

**Military Science**

Alabama Agricultural and Mechanical University, AL
Angelo State University, TX
Arkansas State University, AR
Arkansas Tech University, AR
Armstrong State University, GA
Austin Peay State University, TN
Ball State University, IN
Baylor University, TX
Boise State University, ID
Boston College, MA
Boston University, MA
Bowie State University, MD
Bowling Green State University, OH
California Polytechnic State University, San Luis Obispo, CA
California State University, Fullerton, CA
Cameron University, OK
Carson-Newman University, TN
Central Michigan University, MI
The Citadel, The Military College of South Carolina, SC
Claremont McKenna College, CA
Clarion University of Pennsylvania, PA
Clarkson University, NY
Clemson University, SC

The College at Brockport, State University of New York, NY
College of Saint Benedict, MN
College of the Holy Cross, MA
Colorado School of Mines, CO
Columbus State University, GA
Creighton University, NE
Dickinson College, PA
East Carolina University, NC
Eastern New Mexico University, NM
Eastern Washington University, WA
Elizabeth City State University, NC
Elon University, NC
Florida Agricultural and Mechanical University, FL
Florida Institute of Technology, FL
Fort Hays State University, KS
Fort Valley State University, GA
Furman University, SC
Georgia Southern University, GA
Gonzaga University, WA
Grambling State University, LA
Howard University, DC
Idaho State University, ID
Illinois State University, IL
Indiana University of Pennsylvania, PA
Iowa State University of Science and Technology, IA
Jacksonville State University, AL
James Madison University, VA
John Carroll University, OH
Kent State University, OH
Lawrence Technological University, MI
Lehigh University, PA
Lincoln University, MO
Lindenwood University, MO
Longwood University, VA
Louisiana State University and Agricultural & Mechanical College, LA
Louisiana Tech University, LA
Manhattan College, NY
Mercer University, GA
Methodist University, NC
Michigan State University, MI
Michigan Technological University, MI
Middle Tennessee State University, TN
Mississippi State University, MS
Missouri University of Science and Technology, MO
Missouri Valley College, MO
Missouri Western State University, MO
Montana State University, MT
Morehead State University, KY
Murray State University, KY
New Mexico State University, NM
North Carolina State University, NC
Northern Michigan University, MI
Northwest Nazarene University, ID
The Ohio State University, OH
Ohio University, OH
Ohio University–Chillicothe, OH
Ohio University–Eastern, OH
Ohio University–Lancaster, OH
Ohio University–Southern Campus, OH
Ohio University–Zanesville, OH
Oklahoma State University, OK
Old Dominion University, VA
Olivet Nazarene University, IL
Pittsburg State University, KS
Providence College, RI
Purdue University, IN
Rensselaer Polytechnic Institute, NY
Rochester Institute of Technology, NY
Saint Augustine's University, NC
St. Edward's University, TX

St. John's University, NY
Saint Louis University, MO
Sam Houston State University, TX
San Diego State University, CA
Santa Clara University, CA
Savannah State University, GA
Siena College, NY
South Dakota School of Mines and Technology, SD
South Dakota State University, SD
Southeast Missouri State University, MO
Southern Illinois University Carbondale, IL
Stephen F. Austin State University, TX
Stetson University, FL
Tennessee Technological University, TN
Texas Christian University, TX
Texas State University, TX
Texas Tech University, TX
Texas Wesleyan University, TX
Truman State University, MO
Union University, TN
The University of Akron, OH
The University of Alabama, AL
The University of Arizona, AZ
University of Arkansas, AR
University of Central Oklahoma, OK
University of Colorado Boulder, CO
University of Dayton, OH
University of Delaware, DE
University of Florida, FL
University of Houston, TX
University of Idaho, ID
The University of Iowa, IA
The University of Kansas, KS
University of Louisville, KY
University of Maryland, College Park, MD
University of Massachusetts Amherst, MA
University of Memphis, TN
University of Miami, FL
University of Michigan, MI
University of Minnesota, Twin Cities Campus, MN
University of Mississippi, MS
The University of Montana, MT
University of New Hampshire, NH
The University of North Carolina at Charlotte, NC
University of Northern Colorado, CO
University of North Georgia, GA
University of Oklahoma, OK
University of Oregon, OR
University of Portland, OR
University of Rochester, NY
University of San Francisco, CA
The University of Scranton, PA
University of South Alabama, AL
University of South Carolina, SC
The University of South Dakota, SD
University of South Florida, FL
The University of Tampa, FL
The University of Tennessee, TN
The University of Tennessee at Chattanooga, TN
The University of Tennessee at Martin, TN
The University of Texas at Arlington, TX
The University of Texas at El Paso, TX
The University of Texas–Pan American, TX
University of Utah, UT
University of Vermont, VT
University of West Florida, FL
University of Wisconsin–La Crosse, WI
University of Wisconsin–Stevens Point, WI
Villanova University, PA
Virginia Commonwealth University, VA
Virginia Military Institute, VA

Washington State University, WA
Washington University in St. Louis, MO
Wayne State University, MI
Western Illinois University, IL
Western Kentucky University, KY
West Virginia University, WV
Wheaton College, IL
Whitworth University, WA
Widener University, PA
Wright State University, OH
Xavier University, OH
Youngstown State University, OH

**Physical Sciences**

Abilene Christian University, TX
Adelphi University, NY
Alabama Agricultural and Mechanical
    University, AL
Alaska Pacific University, AK
Albany College of Pharmacy and Health
    Sciences, NY
Albertus Magnus College, CT
Alderson Broaddus University, WV
Angelo State University, TX
Arkansas State University, AR
Arkansas Tech University, AR
Armstrong State University, GA
Ashland University, OH
Auburn University, AL
Augustana College, IL
Augustana College, SD
Austin College, TX
Austin Peay State University, TN
Averett University, VA
Ball State University, IN
Baylor University, TX
Bellarmine University, KY
Bemidji State University, MN
Binghamton University, State University of
    New York, NY
Birmingham-Southern College, AL
Bloomfield College, NJ
Bloomsburg University of Pennsylvania, PA
Blue Mountain College, MS
Bluffton University, OH
Boise State University, ID
Bowling Green State University, OH
Bucknell University, PA
Buffalo State College, State University of
    New York, NY
Butler University, IN
California Lutheran University, CA
California Polytechnic State University, San
    Luis Obispo, CA
California State Polytechnic University,
    Pomona, CA
California State University, Bakersfield, CA
California State University, Chico, CA
California State University, Fresno, CA
California State University, Fullerton, CA
California State University, Los Angeles, CA
California State University, San Bernardino,
    CA
California State University, Stanislaus, CA
Calvin College, MI
Cameron University, OK
Campbellsville University, KY
Carroll University, WI
Case Western Reserve University, OH
Centenary College of Louisiana, LA
Central College, IA
Central Methodist University, MO
Central Michigan University, MI
Chapman University, CA
Christopher Newport University, VA
Clarion University of Pennsylvania, PA

Clarkson University, NY
Clemson University, SC
Cleveland State University, OH
Coastal Carolina University, SC
Coe College, IA
The College at Brockport, State University
    of New York, NY
College of Charleston, SC
The College of Idaho, ID
The College of New Rochelle, NY
College of Saint Benedict, MN
College of Staten Island of the City
    University of New York, NY
The Colorado College, CO
Colorado Mesa University, CO
Colorado School of Mines, CO
Colorado State University–Pueblo, CO
Columbia College, MO
Columbus State University, GA
Concordia University, Nebraska, NE
Concordia University Texas, TX
Concord University, WV
Cornerstone University, MI
Dallas Baptist University, TX
Davidson College, NC
Delta State University, MS
Denison University, OH
DeSales University, PA
Dickinson State University, ND
Dordt College, IA
Drew University, NJ
Drury University, MO
East Carolina University, NC
Eastern Illinois University, IL
Eastern Michigan University, MI
Eastern New Mexico University, NM
Eastern Washington University, WA
East Stroudsburg University of
    Pennsylvania, PA
East Texas Baptist University, TX
Elizabethtown College, PA
Elmhurst College, IL
Elon University, NC
Emory University, GA
Emporia State University, KS
Evangel University, MO
Fairmont State University, WV
Florida Agricultural and Mechanical
    University, FL
Florida Atlantic University, FL
Florida Gulf Coast University, FL
Florida Southern College, FL
Fort Hays State University, KS
Fort Lewis College, CO
Framingham State University, MA
Frostburg State University, MD
Furman University, SC
Gardner-Webb University, NC
George Fox University, OR
Georgia College & State University, GA
Georgia Institute of Technology, GA
Georgian Court University, NJ
Governors State University, IL
Graceland University, IA
Grambling State University, LA
Grand Valley State University, MI
Grand View University, IA
Greenville College, IL
Grove City College, PA
Hamline University, MN
Hampshire College, MA
Hampton University, VA
Hardin-Simmons University, TX
Hillsdale College, MI
Houghton College, NY
Howard Payne University, TX

Howard University, DC
Idaho State University, ID
Illinois State University, IL
Indiana State University, IN
Indiana University of Pennsylvania, PA
Iowa State University of Science and
    Technology, IA
Jacksonville State University, AL
James Madison University, VA
John Carroll University, OH
Juniata College, PA
Kansas Wesleyan University, KS
Kean University, NJ
Kennesaw State University, GA
Kent State University, OH
King's College, PA
Kutztown University of Pennsylvania, PA
Lake Erie College, OH
Lawrence Technological University, MI
Lebanon Valley College, PA
Lewis-Clark State College, ID
Lincoln University, PA
Lindenwood University, MO
Linfield College, OR
Lock Haven University of Pennsylvania, PA
Loras College, IA
Louisiana State University and Agricultural
    & Mechanical College, LA
Louisiana Tech University, LA
Loyola Marymount University, CA
Lubbock Christian University, TX
Lycoming College, PA
Mansfield University of Pennsylvania, PA
Marietta College, OH
Marquette University, WI
Massachusetts College of Liberal Arts, MA
The Master's College and Seminary, CA
Mayville State University, ND
McMurry University, TX
Meredith College, NC
Michigan State University, MI
Middle Tennessee State University, TN
Midwestern State University, TX
Millersville University of Pennsylvania, PA
Millikin University, IL
Mills College, CA
Minnesota State University Moorhead, MN
Misericordia University, PA
Mississippi State University, MS
Mississippi University for Women, MS
Missouri University of Science and
    Technology, MO
Missouri Valley College, MO
Missouri Western State University, MO
Montana State University, MT
Montana State University Billings, MT
Montana Tech of The University of
    Montana, MT
Montclair State University, NJ
Moravian College, PA
Morehead State University, KY
Murray State University, KY
Muskingum University, OH
Newberry College, SC
New Jersey Institute of Technology, NJ
New Mexico Highlands University, NM
New Mexico State University, NM
North Carolina Central University, NC
North Carolina State University, NC
North Central College, IL
Northeastern Illinois University, IL
Northeastern State University, OK
Northern Illinois University, IL
Northern Kentucky University, KY
Northern Michigan University, MI
Northern State University, SD

Northwestern Oklahoma State University, OK
Northwest Missouri State University, MO
Northwest Nazarene University, ID
Oberlin College, OH
The Ohio State University, OH
Ohio University, OH
Ohio University–Chillicothe, OH
Ohio University–Eastern, OH
Ohio University–Lancaster, OH
Ohio University–Southern Campus, OH
Ohio University–Zanesville, OH
Oklahoma Baptist University, OK
Oklahoma State University, OK
Old Dominion University, VA
Ouachita Baptist University, AR
Pace University, NY
Pacific University, OR
Pittsburg State University, KS
Portland State University, OR
Purdue University, IN
Quincy University, IL
Randolph College, VA
Regis University, CO
Rhodes College, TN
Rochester Institute of Technology, NY
Rockford University, IL
Rockhurst University, MO
Rollins College, FL
Sacred Heart University, CT
Saginaw Valley State University, MI
St. Catherine University, MN
St. Cloud State University, MN
St. Edward's University, TX
St. John Fisher College, NY
St. John's University, NY
Saint Louis University, MO
Saint Mary's College of California, CA
Salisbury University, MD
Samford University, AL
Sam Houston State University, TX
San Diego State University, CA
Savannah State University, GA
Schreiner University, TX
Seton Hill University, PA
Shepherd University, WV
Shippensburg University of Pennsylvania, PA
Siena College, NY
Skidmore College, NY
Slippery Rock University of Pennsylvania, PA
Sonoma State University, CA
South Dakota School of Mines and Technology, SD
South Dakota State University, SD
Southeastern Oklahoma State University, OK
Southeast Missouri State University, MO
Southern Illinois University Carbondale, IL
Southern Oregon University, OR
Southwestern College, KS
Southwestern Oklahoma State University, OK
State University of New York at Fredonia, NY
State University of New York at New Paltz, NY
State University of New York at Oswego, NY
State University of New York at Plattsburgh, NY
State University of New York College at Cortland, NY

State University of New York College at Geneseo, NY
State University of New York College at Old Westbury, NY
State University of New York College at Potsdam, NY
State University of New York College of Environmental Science and Forestry, NY
Stephen F. Austin State University, TX
Stetson University, FL
Stockton University, NJ
Stony Brook University, State University of New York, NY
Tennessee Technological University, TN
Texas A&M International University, TX
Texas A&M University, TX
Texas A&M University–Commerce, TX
Texas Christian University, TX
Texas Lutheran University, TX
Texas Tech University, TX
Texas Wesleyan University, TX
Texas Woman's University, TX
Thiel College, PA
Thomas More College, KY
Thomas University, GA
Towson University, MD
Trevecca Nazarene University, TN
Trinity Christian College, IL
Truman State University, MO
Union College, KY
Union University, TN
The University of Akron, OH
The University of Alabama, AL
The University of Alabama in Huntsville, AL
University of Alaska Fairbanks, AK
The University of Arizona, AZ
University of Arkansas, AR
University of California, Irvine, CA
University of California, Riverside, CA
University of California, San Diego, CA
University of California, Santa Cruz, CA
University of Central Oklahoma, OK
University of Colorado Boulder, CO
University of Colorado Denver, CO
University of Connecticut, CT
University of Dallas, TX
University of Dayton, OH
University of Delaware, DE
University of Denver, CO
University of Evansville, IN
University of Great Falls, MT
University of Houston, TX
University of Idaho, ID
University of Indianapolis, IN
University of Jamestown, ND
The University of Kansas, KS
University of Mary Hardin-Baylor, TX
University of Maryland, Baltimore County, MD
University of Maryland, College Park, MD
University of Maryland Eastern Shore, MD
University of Mary Washington, VA
University of Massachusetts Amherst, MA
University of Massachusetts Dartmouth, MA
University of Memphis, TN
University of Michigan, MI
University of Michigan–Dearborn, MI
University of Michigan–Flint, MI
University of Minnesota, Twin Cities Campus, MN
University of Mississippi, MS
University of Missouri, MO
University of Missouri–St. Louis, MO
The University of Montana, MT

The University of Montana Western, MT
University of Montevallo, AL
University of Nebraska at Omaha, NE
University of Nebraska–Lincoln, NE
University of Nevada, Las Vegas, NV
University of Nevada, Reno, NV
University of New Hampshire, NH
University of New Orleans, LA
University of North Carolina at Asheville, NC
The University of North Carolina at Greensboro, NC
The University of North Carolina Wilmington, NC
University of Northern Colorado, CO
University of Northern Iowa, IA
University of North Georgia, GA
University of Oklahoma, OK
University of Oregon, OR
University of Pittsburgh at Bradford, PA
University of Pittsburgh at Johnstown, PA
University of Portland, OR
University of Puget Sound, WA
University of Richmond, VA
University of Rio Grande, OH
University of St. Thomas, MN
University of St. Thomas, TX
University of South Carolina, SC
University of South Carolina Aiken, SC
University of South Florida, FL
The University of Tennessee at Chattanooga, TN
The University of Tennessee at Martin, TN
The University of Texas at Arlington, TX
The University of Texas at Brownsville, TX
The University of Texas at Dallas, TX
The University of Texas at El Paso, TX
The University of Texas at San Antonio, TX
The University of Toledo, OH
The University of Tulsa, OK
University of Utah, UT
University of Vermont, VT
The University of Virginia's College at Wise, VA
University of West Florida, FL
University of West Georgia, GA
University of Wisconsin–Eau Claire, WI
University of Wisconsin–Green Bay, WI
University of Wisconsin–La Crosse, WI
University of Wisconsin–Parkside, WI
University of Wisconsin–River Falls, WI
University of Wisconsin–Stevens Point, WI
University of Wisconsin–Stout, WI
University of Wisconsin–Superior, WI
University of Wisconsin–Whitewater, WI
Utah State University, UT
Valdosta State University, GA
Valley City State University, ND
Valparaiso University, IN
Virginia Commonwealth University, VA
Virginia Military Institute, VA
Virginia State University, VA
Warner Pacific College, OR
Wartburg College, IA
Washburn University, KS
Washington State University, WA
Washington University in St. Louis, MO
Wayland Baptist University, TX
Waynesburg University, PA
Wayne State College, NE
Wayne State University, MI
Western Illinois University, IL
Western Kentucky University, KY
Western Oregon University, OR
Western Washington University, WA

West Texas A&M University, TX
West Virginia University, WV
West Virginia Wesleyan College, WV
Wheaton College, IL
Wichita State University, KS
Widener University, PA
Wilson College, PA
Wisconsin Lutheran College, WI
Wright State University, OH
Xavier University, OH
Xavier University of Louisiana, LA
Youngstown State University, OH

## Premedicine

Albany College of Pharmacy and Health
    Sciences, NY
Albertus Magnus College, CT
Alderson Broaddus University, WV
American Jewish University, CA
Angelo State University, TX
Arkansas State University, AR
Auburn University, AL
Augustana College, SD
Austin College, TX
Averett University, VA
Baylor University, TX
Belhaven University, MS
Bemidji State University, MN
Binghamton University, State University of
    New York, NY
Birmingham-Southern College, AL
Blue Mountain College, MS
Bluffton University, OH
Boise State University, ID
Butler University, IN
California State University, Bakersfield, CA
California State University, Stanislaus, CA
Calvin College, MI
Campbellsville University, KY
Carroll University, WI
Case Western Reserve University, OH
Centenary College of Louisiana, LA
Central College, IA
Central Methodist University, MO
Central Michigan University, MI
Christopher Newport University, VA
City College of the City University of New
    York, NY
Clarion University of Pennsylvania, PA
Clemson University, SC
Cleveland State University, OH
Coe College, IA
The College at Brockport, State University
    of New York, NY
College of Charleston, SC
The College of Idaho, ID
The College of New Rochelle, NY
The College of Saint Rose, NY
College of Staten Island of the City
    University of New York, NY
Colorado State University–Pueblo, CO
Concordia University, Nebraska, NE
Concord University, WV
Dakota Wesleyan University, SD
Dallas Baptist University, TX
Davidson College, NC
Delta State University, MS
DeSales University, PA
Dickinson State University, ND
Dordt College, IA
Drury University, MO
D'Youville College, NY
Eastern Illinois University, IL
Eastern New Mexico University, NM
Eastern Washington University, WA
Elizabethtown College, PA

Elmhurst College, IL
Elon University, NC
Emory & Henry College, VA
Emporia State University, KS
Evangel University, MO
Florida Agricultural and Mechanical
    University, FL
Fort Hays State University, KS
Fort Valley State University, GA
Francis Marion University, SC
Frostburg State University, MD
Furman University, SC
Gannon University, PA
Gardner-Webb University, NC
Grambling State University, LA
Grand Valley State University, MI
Hamline University, MN
Hampden-Sydney College, VA
Hardin-Simmons University, TX
Hillsdale College, MI
Hobart and William Smith Colleges, NY
Howard Payne University, TX
Howard University, DC
Idaho State University, ID
Illinois State University, IL
Indiana State University, IN
Indiana University of Pennsylvania, PA
Indiana University–Purdue University Fort
    Wayne, IN
Iowa State University of Science and
    Technology, IA
James Madison University, VA
John Carroll University, OH
Juniata College, PA
Kansas Wesleyan University, KS
Kean University, NJ
Kennesaw State University, GA
Kent State University, OH
Kentucky Christian University, KY
King's College, PA
Liberty University, VA
Lindenwood University, MO
Lindsey Wilson College, KY
Lipscomb University, TN
Lock Haven University of Pennsylvania, PA
Long Island University–LIU Post, NY
Louisiana State University and Agricultural
    & Mechanical College, LA
Lycoming College, PA
Malone University, OH
Mayville State University, ND
McMurry University, TX
Middle Tennessee State University, TN
Midwestern State University, TX
Millikin University, IL
Mills College, CA
Minnesota State University Moorhead, MN
Mississippi State University, MS
Missouri University of Science and
    Technology, MO
Missouri Valley College, MO
Missouri Western State University, MO
Montana State University Billings, MT
Moravian College, PA
Murray State University, KY
Muskingum University, OH
New Jersey Institute of Technology, NJ
North Central College, IL
Northeastern State University, OK
Northern Kentucky University, KY
Northern Michigan University, MI
Northwestern Oklahoma State University,
    OK
Northwest Nazarene University, ID
The Ohio State University, OH
Ohio University, OH

Ohio University–Chillicothe, OH
Ohio University–Eastern, OH
Ohio University–Lancaster, OH
Ohio University–Southern Campus, OH
Ohio University–Zanesville, OH
Oklahoma Baptist University, OK
Oklahoma State University, OK
Ouachita Baptist University, AR
Pacific University, OR
Piedmont College, GA
Providence College, RI
Quincy University, IL
Randolph College, VA
Rochester Institute of Technology, NY
Rockford University, IL
Rockhurst University, MO
Sacred Heart University, CT
St. Catherine University, MN
St. Edward's University, TX
St. John's University, NY
Saint Louis University, MO
Saint Martin's University, WA
Samford University, AL
Schreiner University, TX
Shepherd University, WV
Siena College, NY
Sonoma State University, CA
South Dakota State University, SD
Southeastern Louisiana University, LA
Southeast Missouri State University, MO
Southern Illinois University Carbondale, IL
Southwestern University, TX
State University of New York at Oswego,
    NY
State University of New York at Plattsburgh,
    NY
State University of New York College at
    Geneseo, NY
State University of New York College of
    Environmental Science and Forestry, NY
Stephen F. Austin State University, TX
Stetson University, FL
Tennessee Technological University, TN
Texas A&M International University, TX
Texas A&M University, TX
Texas A&M University–Commerce, TX
Texas Christian University, TX
Texas Lutheran University, TX
Texas Tech University, TX
Texas Wesleyan University, TX
Texas Woman's University, TX
Thomas More College, KY
Thomas University, GA
Trine University, IN
Trinity Christian College, IL
Truman State University, MO
Union University, TN
The University of Akron, OH
The University of Alabama, AL
University of Arkansas, AR
University of California, Davis, CA
University of California, Irvine, CA
University of California, Riverside, CA
University of California, San Diego, CA
University of Colorado Boulder, CO
University of Colorado Denver, CO
University of Connecticut, CT
University of Dallas, TX
University of Dayton, OH
University of Delaware, DE
University of Evansville, IN
University of Great Falls, MT
University of Hartford, CT
University of Houston, TX
University of Idaho, ID
The University of Kansas, KS

University of Louisville, KY
University of Mary Hardin-Baylor, TX
University of Maryland, College Park, MD
University of Massachusetts Amherst, MA
University of Memphis, TN
University of Michigan, MI
University of Michigan–Flint, MI
University of Minnesota, Twin Cities
    Campus, MN
University of Mississippi, MS
University of Missouri, MO
University of Missouri–St. Louis, MO
The University of Montana, MT
The University of Montana Western, MT
University of Nebraska at Omaha, NE
University of Nebraska–Lincoln, NE
University of Nevada, Las Vegas, NV
University of North Carolina at Asheville,
    NC
The University of North Carolina at
    Greensboro, NC
The University of North Carolina
    Wilmington, NC
University of North Georgia, GA
University of Oregon, OR
University of Pittsburgh at Bradford, PA
University of Pittsburgh at Johnstown, PA
University of Portland, OR
University of Puget Sound, WA
University of St. Francis, IL
University of St. Thomas, TX
University of South Carolina, SC
The University of South Dakota, SD
University of Southern Indiana, IN
University of South Florida, FL
The University of Tennessee at Martin, TN
The University of Texas–Pan American, TX
The University of Toledo, OH
The University of Tulsa, OK
University of Vermont, VT
The University of Virginia's College at
    Wise, VA
University of West Georgia, GA
University of Wisconsin–Eau Claire, WI
University of Wisconsin–Green Bay, WI
University of Wisconsin–Parkside, WI
University of Wisconsin–River Falls, WI
University of Wisconsin–Stevens Point, WI
University of Wisconsin–Whitewater, WI
Utah State University, UT
Virginia Military Institute, VA
Virginia State University, VA
Wartburg College, IA
Washburn University, KS
Washington State University, WA
Washington University in St. Louis, MO
Wayne State College, NE
Wayne State University, MI
Western Kentucky University, KY
Western Oregon University, OR
Western Washington University, WA
West Texas A&M University, TX
West Virginia University, WV
Wheaton College, IL
Wheeling Jesuit University, WV
Wichita State University, KS
Widener University, PA
Wilson College, PA
Worcester Polytechnic Institute, MA
Wright State University, OH
Xavier University of Louisiana, LA
Youngstown State University, OH

**Religion/Biblical Studies**
Abilene Christian University, TX

Alaska Bible College, AK
Alaska Pacific University, AK
Albertus Magnus College, CT
Alderson Broaddus University, WV
Anderson University, SC
Augustana College, IL
Augustana College, SD
Austin College, TX
Averett University, VA
The Baptist College of Florida, FL
Baylor University, TX
Belhaven University, MS
Belmont University, TN
Berry College, GA
Birmingham-Southern College, AL
Bloomfield College, NJ
Bloomsburg University of Pennsylvania, PA
Blue Mountain College, MS
Butler University, IN
California Baptist University, CA
California Lutheran University, CA
California State University, Bakersfield, CA
California State University, Fullerton, CA
Calvin College, MI
Campbellsville University, KY
Carson-Newman University, TN
Case Western Reserve University, OH
Centenary College of Louisiana, LA
Central Christian College of the Bible, MO
Central College, IA
Central Methodist University, MO
Central Michigan University, MI
Charlotte Christian College and Theological
    Seminary, NC
Cincinnati Christian University, OH
The Citadel, The Military College of South
    Carolina, SC
The College of Idaho, ID
The College of New Rochelle, NY
Columbia College, MO
Concordia University Ann Arbor, MI
Concordia University Chicago, IL
Concordia University, Nebraska, NE
Concordia University, St. Paul, MN
Concordia University Texas, TX
Concordia University Wisconsin, WI
Cornerstone University, MI
The Criswell College, TX
Crossroads Bible College, IN
Dallas Baptist University, TX
Davidson College, NC
DeSales University, PA
Dordt College, IA
Drew University, NJ
Eastern Michigan University, MI
Eastern New Mexico University, NM
Eastern University, PA
East Texas Baptist University, TX
Elizabethtown College, PA
Elmhurst College, IL
Elon University, NC
Emmanuel College, GA
Emory & Henry College, VA
Evangel University, MO
Faulkner University, AL
Felician College, NJ
Flagler College, FL
Florida Gulf Coast University, FL
Florida Southern College, FL
Fort Hays State University, KS
Friends University, KS
Furman University, SC
Gannon University, PA
Gardner-Webb University, NC
Geneva College, PA

George Fox University, OR
Grand View University, IA
Grove City College, PA
Hamline University, MN
Harding University, AR
Hardin-Simmons University, TX
Hastings College, NE
Heritage Christian University, AL
Hillsdale College, MI
Hillsdale Free Will Baptist College, OK
Houghton College, NY
Houston Baptist University, TX
Howard Payne University, TX
Howard University, DC
Indiana University of Pennsylvania, PA
James Madison University, VA
John Carroll University, OH
Kansas Wesleyan University, KS
Kent State University, OH
Kentucky Christian University, KY
King's College, PA
La Sierra University, CA
Lebanon Valley College, PA
Lee University, TN
Liberty University, VA
Lindenwood University, MO
Lindsey Wilson College, KY
Linfield College, OR
Lipscomb University, TN
Loyola Marymount University, CA
Lubbock Christian University, TX
Lycoming College, PA
Malone University, OH
Maranatha Baptist University, WI
Marymount University, VA
Marywood University, PA
The Master's College and Seminary, CA
McKendree University, IL
McMurry University, TX
Mercer University, GA
Meredith College, NC
Methodist University, NC
Mid-Atlantic Christian University, NC
Milligan College, TN
Mississippi State University, MS
Missouri Baptist University, MO
Missouri Western State University, MO
Montclair State University, NJ
Nebraska Christian College, NE
Newberry College, SC
North Central College, IL
Northwest Nazarene University, ID
Oklahoma Baptist University, OK
Oklahoma Christian University, OK
Oklahoma City University, OK
Oklahoma Wesleyan University, OK
Oral Roberts University, OK
Ouachita Baptist University, AR
Piedmont College, GA
Point Loma Nazarene University, CA
Quincy University, IL
Randolph-Macon College, VA
Regent University, VA
Rochester College, MI
Rockhurst University, MO
St. Ambrose University, IA
St. Edward's University, TX
Saint Francis University, PA
Saint Louis University, MO
Saint Mary's College of California, CA
St. Thomas Aquinas College, NY
Samford University, AL
San Diego State University, CA
Schreiner University, TX
Seton Hill University, PA

Siena College, NY
Southeast Missouri State University, MO
Southern Illinois University Carbondale, IL
Southwestern College, KS
Stetson University, FL
Texas Christian University, TX
Texas Wesleyan University, TX
Thiel College, PA
Thomas More College, KY
Trevecca Nazarene University, TN
Trinity Christian College, IL
Trinity College of Florida, FL
Truett-McConnell College, GA
Union University, TN
The University of Arizona, AZ
University of California, Davis, CA
University of Connecticut, CT
University of Dayton, OH
University of Delaware, DE
University of Evansville, IN
University of Great Falls, MT
University of Indianapolis, IN
The University of Kansas, KS
University of Mary Hardin-Baylor, TX
University of Mary Washington, VA
University of Massachusetts Dartmouth, MA
University of Minnesota, Twin Cities
   Campus, MN
University of Mississippi, MS
University of Missouri, MO
The University of North Carolina at
   Greensboro, NC
University of Portland, OR
University of St. Thomas, MN
University of St. Thomas, TX
University of South Carolina, SC
University of South Florida, FL
The University of Tulsa, OK
University of Wisconsin–Eau Claire, WI
Valparaiso University, IN
Walla Walla University, WA
Warner Pacific College, OR
Wartburg College, IA
Washburn University, KS
Washington University in St. Louis, MO
Wayland Baptist University, TX
Waynesburg University, PA
Wesleyan College, GA
Western Illinois University, IL
West Virginia University, WV
Wheaton College, IL
William Jessup University, CA
Williams Baptist College, AR
Wilson College, PA
Wisconsin Lutheran College, WI
Wright State University, OH
Xavier University of Louisiana, LA
Youngstown State University, OH

**Social Sciences**

Abilene Christian University, TX
Alabama Agricultural and Mechanical
   University, AL
Alaska Pacific University, AK
Albany State University, GA
Albertus Magnus College, CT
Alderson Broaddus University, WV
Alliant International University–San Diego,
   CA
Angelo State University, TX
Arkansas State University, AR
Arkansas Tech University, AR
Ashland University, OH
Auburn University, AL
Augustana College, IL
Augustana College, SD

Austin College, TX
Austin Peay State University, TN
Ball State University, IN
Baylor University, TX
Belhaven University, MS
Belmont University, TN
Bemidji State University, MN
Bethel College, KS
Binghamton University, State University of
   New York, NY
Birmingham-Southern College, AL
Bloomfield College, NJ
Bloomsburg University of Pennsylvania, PA
Blue Mountain College, MS
Boise State University, ID
Bowling Green State University, OH
Buffalo State College, State University of
   New York, NY
Butler University, IN
California Lutheran University, CA
California Polytechnic State University, San
   Luis Obispo, CA
California State Polytechnic University,
   Pomona, CA
California State University, Bakersfield, CA
California State University, Chico, CA
California State University, Fresno, CA
California State University, Fullerton, CA
California State University, Los Angeles, CA
California State University, San Bernardino,
   CA
California State University, Stanislaus, CA
Calvin College, MI
Cameron University, OK
Campbellsville University, KY
Carroll University, WI
Case Western Reserve University, OH
Centenary College of Louisiana, LA
Central College, IA
Central Methodist University, MO
Central Michigan University, MI
Champlain College, VT
Christopher Newport University, VA
City College of the City University of New
   York, NY
Clarion University of Pennsylvania, PA
Clarkson University, NY
Clemson University, SC
Cleveland State University, OH
Coastal Carolina University, SC
The College at Brockport, State University
   of New York, NY
College of Charleston, SC
The College of Idaho, ID
The College of New Rochelle, NY
The College of Saint Rose, NY
College of Staten Island of the City
   University of New York, NY
Colorado Mesa University, CO
Colorado State University–Pueblo, CO
Columbia College, MO
Concordia University, Nebraska, NE
Concordia University Texas, TX
Concord University, WV
Cornerstone University, MI
Dallas Baptist University, TX
Davidson College, NC
Delta State University, MS
DeSales University, PA
Dickinson State University, ND
Dordt College, IA
Dowling College, NY
Drew University, NJ
Drury University, MO
D'Youville College, NY
East Carolina University, NC

Eastern Illinois University, IL
Eastern Michigan University, MI
Eastern New Mexico University, NM
Eastern Washington University, WA
East Stroudsburg University of
   Pennsylvania, PA
East Texas Baptist University, TX
Elizabethtown College, PA
Elmhurst College, IL
Elon University, NC
Emporia State University, KS
Evangel University, MO
Fairmont State University, WV
Flagler College, FL
Florida Agricultural and Mechanical
   University, FL
Florida Atlantic University, FL
Florida Gulf Coast University, FL
Florida Southern College, FL
Fort Hays State University, KS
Fort Lewis College, CO
Fort Valley State University, GA
Francis Marion University, SC
Fresno Pacific University, CA
Frostburg State University, MD
Furman University, SC
Gannon University, PA
Gardner-Webb University, NC
George Fox University, OR
Georgia College & State University, GA
Georgia Southern University, GA
Glenville State College, WV
Governors State University, IL
Grambling State University, LA
Grand Valley State University, MI
Grand View University, IA
Grove City College, PA
Hamline University, MN
Hampshire College, MA
Hardin-Simmons University, TX
Hawai`i Pacific University, HI
Hillsdale College, MI
Howard Payne University, TX
Howard University, DC
Husson University, ME
Idaho State University, ID
Illinois State University, IL
Indiana State University, IN
Indiana University of Pennsylvania, PA
Iowa State University of Science and
   Technology, IA
Iowa Wesleyan College, IA
Jacksonville State University, AL
James Madison University, VA
John Carroll University, OH
Juniata College, PA
Kansas Wesleyan University, KS
Kean University, NJ
Kennesaw State University, GA
Kent State University, OH
Kent State University at Stark, OH
King's College, PA
Lake Erie College, OH
Lebanon Valley College, PA
Lewis-Clark State College, ID
Lincoln University, PA
Lindenwood University, MO
Linfield College, OR
Lock Haven University of Pennsylvania, PA
Long Island University–LIU Post, NY
Longwood University, VA
Louisiana Tech University, LA
Loyola Marymount University, CA
Lubbock Christian University, TX
Lycoming College, PA
Malone University, OH

Marymount University, VA
Marywood University, PA
Massachusetts College of Liberal Arts, MA
The Master's College and Seminary, CA
Mayville State University, ND
McMurry University, TX
Michigan State University, MI
Middle Tennessee State University, TN
Midwestern State University, TX
Millersville University of Pennsylvania, PA
Minnesota State University Moorhead, MN
Minot State University, ND
Misericordia University, PA
Mississippi State University, MS
Missouri University of Science and
    Technology, MO
Missouri Valley College, MO
Missouri Western State University, MO
Molloy College, NY
Monmouth University, NJ
Montana State University, MT
Montana State University Billings, MT
Montclair State University, NJ
Morehead State University, KY
Mount Mary University, WI
Newberry College, SC
New England College, NH
New Mexico Highlands University, NM
New Mexico State University, NM
North Carolina Central University, NC
North Carolina State University, NC
North Central College, IL
Northeastern Illinois University, IL
Northeastern State University, OK
Northern Illinois University, IL
Northern Kentucky University, KY
Northern Michigan University, MI
Northern State University, SD
Northwestern Oklahoma State University,
    OK
Northwest Missouri State University, MO
Northwest Nazarene University, ID
The Ohio State University, OH
Ohio University, OH
Ohio University–Chillicothe, OH
Ohio University–Eastern, OH
Ohio University–Lancaster, OH
Ohio University–Southern Campus, OH
Ohio University–Zanesville, OH
Oklahoma Baptist University, OK
Oklahoma State University, OK
Old Dominion University, VA
Ouachita Baptist University, AR
Pace University, NY
Pacific University, OR
Piedmont College, GA
Pittsburg State University, KS
Point Loma Nazarene University, CA
Portland State University, OR
Post University, CT
Purchase College, State University of New
    York, NY
Quincy University, IL
Randolph College, VA
Regent University, VA
Rochester Institute of Technology, NY
Rockford University, IL
Rockhurst University, MO
St. Catherine University, MN
St. Cloud State University, MN
St. Edward's University, TX
Saint Francis University, PA
St. John's University, NY
Saint Louis University, MO
St. Thomas Aquinas College, NY

Salisbury University, MD
Samford University, AL
Sam Houston State University, TX
San Diego State University, CA
Savannah State University, GA
Schreiner University, TX
Seton Hill University, PA
Shepherd University, WV
Shippensburg University of Pennsylvania,
    PA
Siena College, NY
Slippery Rock University of Pennsylvania,
    PA
Sonoma State University, CA
South Dakota State University, SD
Southeastern Louisiana University, LA
Southeastern Oklahoma State University,
    OK
Southeast Missouri State University, MO
Southern Illinois University Carbondale, IL
Southern Oregon University, OR
Southwestern College, KS
Southwestern Oklahoma State University,
    OK
Southwestern University, TX
State University of New York at Fredonia,
    NY
State University of New York at Oswego,
    NY
State University of New York at Plattsburgh,
    NY
State University of New York College at
    Genesco, NY
State University of New York College at
    Potsdam, NY
Stetson University, FL
Stockton University, NJ
Stony Brook University, State University of
    New York, NY
Tennessee Technological University, TN
Texas A&M International University, TX
Texas A&M University–Commerce, TX
Texas Christian University, TX
Texas Tech University, TX
Texas Wesleyan University, TX
Texas Woman's University, TX
Thomas More College, KY
Thomas University, GA
Trevecca Nazarene University, TN
Trinity Christian College, IL
Truman State University, MO
Union University, TN
The University of Akron, OH
The University of Alabama, AL
The University of Alabama in Huntsville,
    AL
University of Alaska Anchorage, AK
University of Arkansas, AR
University of California, Davis, CA
University of California, Irvine, CA
University of California, Riverside, CA
University of California, San Diego, CA
University of California, Santa Cruz, CA
University of Central Missouri, MO
University of Central Oklahoma, OK
University of Colorado Boulder, CO
University of Colorado Denver, CO
University of Connecticut, CT
University of Dayton, OH
University of Delaware, DE
University of Denver, CO
University of Evansville, IN
University of Great Falls, MT
University of Houston, TX
University of Houston–Clear Lake, TX

University of Idaho, ID
University of Illinois at Springfield, IL
The University of Kansas, KS
University of Maine at Fort Kent, ME
University of Mary Hardin-Baylor, TX
University of Maryland, Baltimore County,
    MD
University of Maryland, College Park, MD
University of Maryland Eastern Shore, MD
University of Mary Washington, VA
University of Massachusetts Amherst, MA
University of Massachusetts Dartmouth, MA
University of Memphis, TN
University of Michigan, MI
University of Michigan–Dearborn, MI
University of Michigan–Flint, MI
University of Minnesota, Twin Cities
    Campus, MN
University of Mississippi, MS
University of Missouri, MO
University of Missouri–St. Louis, MO
The University of Montana, MT
The University of Montana Western, MT
University of Montevallo, AL
University of Nebraska at Omaha, NE
University of Nebraska–Lincoln, NE
University of Nevada, Las Vegas, NV
University of New Orleans, LA
University of North Carolina at Asheville,
    NC
The University of North Carolina at
    Greensboro, NC
The University of North Carolina
    Wilmington, NC
University of Northern Colorado, CO
University of Northern Iowa, IA
University of Oklahoma, OK
University of Oregon, OR
University of Pittsburgh at Bradford, PA
University of Pittsburgh at Johnstown, PA
University of Portland, OR
University of Puget Sound, WA
University of Rio Grande, OH
University of St. Francis, IL
University of St. Thomas, MN
University of St. Thomas, TX
University of South Carolina, SC
University of South Carolina Aiken, SC
The University of South Dakota, SD
University of Southern Indiana, IN
University of South Florida, FL
The University of Tampa, FL
The University of Tennessee, TN
The University of Tennessee at Martin, TN
The University of Texas at Arlington, TX
The University of Texas at Brownsville, TX
The University of Texas at San Antonio, TX
The University of Texas–Pan American, TX
The University of Toledo, OH
The University of Tulsa, OK
University of Utah, UT
University of Vermont, VT
The University of Virginia's College at
    Wise, VA
University of West Florida, FL
University of West Georgia, GA
University of Wisconsin–Eau Claire, WI
University of Wisconsin–Green Bay, WI
University of Wisconsin–La Crosse, WI
University of Wisconsin–River Falls, WI
University of Wisconsin–Stevens Point, WI
University of Wisconsin–Superior, WI
University of Wisconsin–Whitewater, WI
Utah State University, UT
Valdosta State University, GA

Valley City State University, ND
Warner Pacific College, OR
Wartburg College, IA
Washburn University, KS
Washington State University, WA
Washington University in St. Louis, MO
Wayland Baptist University, TX
Waynesburg University, PA
Wayne State College, NE
Wayne State University, MI
West Chester University of Pennsylvania, PA
Western Illinois University, IL
Western Kentucky University, KY
Western Oregon University, OR
Western Washington University, WA
West Texas A&M University, TX
West Virginia University, WV
Wheaton College, IL
Wichita State University, KS
Widener University, PA
William Jessup University, CA
Wilson College, PA
Wisconsin Lutheran College, WI
Wright State University, OH
Xavier University, OH
Xavier University of Louisiana, LA
Youngstown State University, OH

## Creative Arts/Performance

### Applied Art and Design
Arcadia University, PA
Auburn University, AL
Belhaven University, MS
Belmont University, TN
Bemidji State University, MN
Bloomfield College, NJ
Bowie State University, MD
Brenau University, GA
Brooks Institute, CA
Buffalo State College, State University of New York, NY
Butler University, IN
California Baptist University, CA
California Institute of the Arts, CA
California Polytechnic State University, San Luis Obispo, CA
California State University, Chico, CA
Calvin College, MI
Castleton State College, VT
Central Michigan University, MI
Chatham University, PA
City College of the City University of New York, NY
Clemson University, SC
Cleveland Institute of Art, OH
Colby-Sawyer College, NH
The College of New Rochelle, NY
College of Staten Island of the City University of New York, NY
Colorado State University–Pueblo, CO
Concordia University, Nebraska, NE
Converse College, SC
Dominican University, IL
East Carolina University, NC
Eastern Illinois University, IL
Eastern Michigan University, MI
Eastern New Mexico University, NM
East Stroudsburg University of Pennsylvania, PA
Emmanuel College, GA
Fashion Institute of Technology, NY
Ferris State University, MI
Flagler College, FL

Florida Agricultural and Mechanical University, FL
Fort Hays State University, KS
Friends University, KS
Graceland University, IA
Grand Valley State University, MI
Grand View University, IA
Greenville College, IL
Hamline University, MN
Hardin-Simmons University, TX
Hofstra University, NY
Howard University, DC
Huntington University, IN
Illinois Institute of Technology, IL
Illinois State University, IL
Indiana State University, IN
Indiana University of Pennsylvania, PA
Iowa State University of Science and Technology, IA
Kean University, NJ
Keene State College, NH
Kent State University, OH
Kutztown University of Pennsylvania, PA
Lafayette College, PA
Laguna College of Art & Design, CA
La Sierra University, CA
Lindenwood University, MO
Lindsey Wilson College, KY
Louisiana State University and Agricultural & Mechanical College, LA
Louisiana Tech University, LA
Loyola Marymount University, CA
Lycoming College, PA
Massachusetts College of Liberal Arts, MA
Mercyhurst University, PA
Meredith College, NC
Minneapolis College of Art and Design, MN
Mississippi College, MS
Mississippi State University, MS
Missouri Valley College, MO
Missouri Western State University, MO
Montserrat College of Art, MA
Morehead State University, KY
Mount Mary University, WI
New England College, NH
New Jersey Institute of Technology, NJ
New Mexico State University, NM
Northeastern State University, OK
Northern Illinois University, IL
Northern Michigan University, MI
Northwest College of Art & Design, WA
Notre Dame de Namur University, CA
Ohio University, OH
Ohio University–Chillicothe, OH
Ohio University–Eastern, OH
Ohio University–Lancaster, OH
Ohio University–Southern Campus, OH
Ohio University–Zanesville, OH
Ohio Wesleyan University, OH
Oklahoma Baptist University, OK
Oklahoma Christian University, OK
Oklahoma City University, OK
Old Dominion University, VA
Oral Roberts University, OK
Otis College of Art and Design, CA
Rhode Island School of Design, RI
Ringling College of Art and Design, FL
Robert Morris University Illinois, IL
Rochester Institute of Technology, NY
Sacred Heart University, CT
St. Cloud State University, MN
Salisbury University, MD
San Diego State University, CA
Santa Fe University of Art and Design, NM
Savannah College of Art and Design, GA
Schreiner University, TX

Seton Hill University, PA
Shepherd University, WV
Slippery Rock University of Pennsylvania, PA
Sonoma State University, CA
Southern Illinois University Carbondale, IL
Southwestern Oklahoma State University, OK
State University of New York at Fredonia, NY
State University of New York College at Geneseo, NY
Stetson University, FL
Stockton University, NJ
Texas A&M University–Commerce, TX
Texas Christian University, TX
Texas State University, TX
Texas Tech University, TX
Texas Woman's University, TX
Trinity Christian College, IL
The University of Akron, OH
University of Alaska Fairbanks, AK
University of Bridgeport, CT
University of California, San Diego, CA
University of Central Oklahoma, OK
University of Colorado Denver, CO
University of Delaware, DE
University of Idaho, ID
University of Illinois at Chicago, IL
The University of Kansas, KS
University of Maryland, College Park, MD
University of Massachusetts Dartmouth, MA
University of Nebraska at Kearney, NE
University of Nevada, Las Vegas, NV
The University of North Carolina at Chapel Hill, NC
University of North Carolina School of the Arts, NC
University of Northern Iowa, IA
University of North Georgia, GA
University of Oregon, OR
University of St. Francis, IL
University of St. Thomas, TX
University of South Florida, FL
The University of Texas at El Paso, TX
University of West Florida, FL
University of West Georgia, GA
University of Wisconsin–Parkside, WI
University of Wisconsin–Stevens Point, WI
University of Wisconsin–Stout, WI
University of Wyoming, WY
Utah State University, UT
Valley City State University, ND
Virginia Polytechnic Institute and State University, VA
Virginia State University, VA
Washington State University, WA
Washington University in St. Louis, MO
Wayne State College, NE
Western Illinois University, IL
Western Washington University, WA
Wichita State University, KS
William Jessup University, CA
Wright State University, OH

### Art/Fine Arts
Abilene Christian University, TX
Adelphi University, NY
Adrian College, MI
Alabama Agricultural and Mechanical University, AL
Alaska Pacific University, AK
Albertus Magnus College, CT
Albion College, MI
Albright College, PA
Alderson Broaddus University, WV

Alma College, MI
Alverno College, WI
Anderson University, IN
Anderson University, SC
Angelo State University, TX
Arcadia University, PA
Arizona State University at the Tempe
 campus, AZ
Arkansas State University, AR
Armstrong State University, GA
Ashland University, OH
Auburn University, AL
Augustana College, IL
Augustana College, SD
Austin College, TX
Austin Peay State University, TN
Averett University, VA
Barclay College, KS
Baylor University, TX
Belhaven University, MS
Bellarmine University, KY
Belmont University, TN
Bemidji State University, MN
Berry College, GA
Bethany Lutheran College, MN
Bethel College, KS
Bethel University, MN
Binghamton University, State University of
 New York, NY
Birmingham-Southern College, AL
Bloomfield College, NJ
Bluefield College, VA
Blue Mountain College, MS
Bluffton University, OH
Boise State University, ID
Boston University, MA
Bowie State University, MD
Bowling Green State University, OH
Bradley University, IL
Brenau University, GA
Brevard College, NC
Brigham Young University, UT
Brooks Institute, CA
Bucknell University, PA
Buena Vista University, IA
Buffalo State College, State University of
 New York, NY
Butler University, IN
Caldwell University, NJ
California Baptist University, CA
California Institute of the Arts, CA
California Lutheran University, CA
California Polytechnic State University, San
 Luis Obispo, CA
California State University, Bakersfield, CA
California State University, Chico, CA
California State University, Fresno, CA
California State University, Fullerton, CA
California State University, Los Angeles, CA
California State University, San Bernardino,
 CA
California State University, Stanislaus, CA
Calumet College of Saint Joseph, IN
Calvin College, MI
Cameron University, OK
Campbellsville University, KY
Campbell University, NC
Canisius College, NY
Cardinal Stritch University, WI
Carnegie Mellon University, PA
Carroll College, MT
Carroll University, WI
Carson-Newman University, TN
Case Western Reserve University, OH
Castleton State College, VT

Cedar Crest College, PA
Centenary College of Louisiana, LA
Central College, IA
Central Michigan University, MI
Central Washington University, WA
Chapman University, CA
Chatham University, PA
Christian Brothers University, TN
Christopher Newport University, VA
City College of the City University of New
 York, NY
Clarion University of Pennsylvania, PA
Clarke University, IA
Clemson University, SC
Cleveland Institute of Art, OH
Cleveland State University, OH
Coastal Carolina University, SC
Coe College, IA
Coker College, SC
Colby-Sawyer College, NH
The College at Brockport, State University
 of New York, NY
College of Charleston, SC
The College of Idaho, ID
The College of New Jersey, NJ
The College of New Rochelle, NY
College of Saint Benedict, MN
College of Saint Mary, NE
The College of Saint Rose, NY
College of Staten Island of the City
 University of New York, NY
Colorado Mesa University, CO
Colorado State University, CO
Colorado State University-Pueblo, CO
Columbia College, MO
Columbus College of Art & Design, OH
Columbus State University, GA
Concordia College, MN
Concordia University Ann Arbor, MI
Concordia University, Nebraska, NE
Concord University, WV
Cooper Union for the Advancement of
 Science and Art, NY
Cornell College, IA
Cornish College of the Arts, WA
Creighton University, NE
Culver-Stockton College, MO
Cumberland University, TN
Dakota Wesleyan University, SD
Dallas Baptist University, TX
Davidson College, NC
Delta State University, MS
DePaul University, IL
Dickinson State University, ND
Doane College, NE
Dominican University, IL
Drake University, IA
Drew University, NJ
Drury University, MO
East Carolina University, NC
Eastern Illinois University, IL
Eastern Michigan University, MI
Eastern New Mexico University, NM
Eastern Washington University, WA
East Stroudsburg University of
 Pennsylvania, PA
Eckerd College, FL
Edgewood College, WI
Elizabethtown College, PA
Elmhurst College, IL
Elon University, NC
Emmanuel College, GA
Emory & Henry College, VA
Emory University, GA
Emporia State University, KS

Endicott College, MA
Eureka College, IL
Evangel University, MO
Fairmont State University, WV
Ferris State University, MI
Flagler College, FL
Florida Agricultural and Mechanical
 University, FL
Florida Gulf Coast University, FL
Florida Southern College, FL
Fontbonne University, MO
Fort Hays State University, KS
Fort Lewis College, CO
Francis Marion University, SC
Franklin College, IN
Friends University, KS
Frostburg State University, MD
Furman University, SC
Gardner-Webb University, NC
George Fox University, OR
Georgetown College, KY
Georgia College & State University, GA
Georgian Court University, NJ
Georgia Regents University, GA
Georgia Southern University, GA
Georgia Southwestern State University, GA
Gordon College, MA
Goucher College, MD
Grand Valley State University, MI
Grand View University, IA
Greensboro College, NC
Greenville College, IL
Gustavus Adolphus College, MN
Hamline University, MN
Hanover College, IN
Harding University, AR
Hardin-Simmons University, TX
Hartwick College, NY
Hastings College, NE
Henderson State University, AR
Hendrix College, AR
Hillsdale College, MI
Hobart and William Smith Colleges, NY
Hofstra University, NY
Hollins University, VA
Hope College, MI
Houghton College, NY
Houston Baptist University, TX
Howard Payne University, TX
Howard University, DC
Huntington University, IN
Idaho State University, ID
Illinois College, IL
Illinois State University, IL
Illinois Wesleyan University, IL
Indiana State University, IN
Indiana University of Pennsylvania, PA
Indiana University–Purdue University Fort
 Wayne, IN
Iowa State University of Science and
 Technology, IA
Iowa Wesleyan College, IA
Jacksonville State University, AL
Jacksonville University, FL
James Madison University, VA
John Brown University, AR
Juniata College, PA
Kalamazoo College, MI
Kansas City Art Institute, MO
Kean University, NJ
Keene State College, NH
Kennesaw State University, GA
Kent State University, OH
Kentucky State University, KY
Kentucky Wesleyan College, KY

Kenyon College, OH
King University, TN
Knox College, IL
Kutztown University of Pennsylvania, PA
Lafayette College, PA
LaGrange College, GA
Laguna College of Art & Design, CA
Lake Erie College, OH
La Sierra University, CA
Lewis-Clark State College, ID
Lewis University, IL
Lincoln University, MO
Lindenwood University, MO
Lipscomb University, TN
Lock Haven University of Pennsylvania, PA
Long Island University–LIU Brooklyn, NY
Long Island University–LIU Post, NY
Longwood University, VA
Louisiana Tech University, LA
Loyola Marymount University, CA
Loyola University Chicago, IL
Loyola University New Orleans, LA
Lubbock Christian University, TX
Lycoming College, PA
Lynchburg College, VA
Lyon College, AR
Mansfield University of Pennsylvania, PA
Marietta College, OH
Marlboro College, VT
Marshall University, WV
Marymount Manhattan College, NY
Maryville College, TN
Maryville University of Saint Louis, MO
Marywood University, PA
Massachusetts College of Liberal Arts, MA
McMurry University, TX
Mercer University, GA
Mercyhurst University, PA
Meredith College, NC
Messiah College, PA
Miami University, OH
Michigan State University, MI
Michigan Technological University, MI
Midwestern State University, TX
Millersville University of Pennsylvania, PA
Milligan College, TN
Millikin University, IL
Millsaps College, MS
Minneapolis College of Art and Design, MN
Minnesota State University Mankato, MN
Minnesota State University Moorhead, MN
Minot State University, ND
Mississippi College, MS
Mississippi State University, MS
Mississippi University for Women, MS
Missouri Southern State University, MO
Missouri Valley College, MO
Missouri Western State University, MO
Molloy College, NY
Monmouth College, IL
Montana State University, MT
Montana State University Billings, MT
Montclair State University, NJ
Montserrat College of Art, MA
Morehead State University, KY
Morningside College, IA
Mount Marty College, SD
Mount Mary University, WI
Mount Mercy University, IA
Mount St. Joseph University, OH
Mount St. Mary's University, MD
Muhlenberg College, PA
Murray State University, KY
Muskingum University, OH
Nazareth College of Rochester, NY
New England College, NH

New Jersey Institute of Technology, NJ
Newman University, KS
New Mexico Highlands University, NM
New Mexico State University, NM
North Carolina Central University, NC
North Central College, IL
Northeastern Illinois University, IL
Northeastern State University, OK
Northern Arizona University, AZ
Northern Illinois University, IL
Northern Kentucky University, KY
Northern State University, SD
Northland College, WI
Northwest College of Art & Design, WA
Northwestern Oklahoma State University, OK
Northwest Missouri State University, MO
Notre Dame de Namur University, CA
Notre Dame of Maryland University, MD
Oglethorpe University, GA
Ohio University, OH
Ohio University–Chillicothe, OH
Ohio University–Eastern, OH
Ohio University–Lancaster, OH
Ohio University–Southern Campus, OH
Ohio University–Zanesville, OH
Ohio Wesleyan University, OH
Oklahoma Baptist University, OK
Oklahoma City University, OK
Oklahoma State University, OK
Old Dominion University, VA
Olivet College, MI
Olivet Nazarene University, IL
Oral Roberts University, OK
Otis College of Art and Design, CA
Otterbein University, OH
Ouachita Baptist University, AR
Pacific Lutheran University, WA
Pacific University, OR
Park University, MO
Piedmont College, GA
Point Loma Nazarene University, CA
Portland State University, OR
Purchase College, State University of New York, NY
Queens University of Charlotte, NC
Quincy University, IL
Reinhardt University, GA
Rhode Island College, RI
Rhode Island School of Design, RI
Rhodes College, TN
Rice University, TX
Ringling College of Art and Design, FL
Roanoke College, VA
Roberts Wesleyan College, NY
Rochester Institute of Technology, NY
Rockford University, IL
Rollins College, FL
Rosemont College, PA
Sacred Heart University, CT
The Sage Colleges, NY
Saginaw Valley State University, MI
St. Ambrose University, IA
St. Catherine University, MN
St. Cloud State University, MN
St. Edward's University, TX
Saint Francis University, PA
Saint John's University, MN
St. John's University, NY
Saint Louis University, MO
Saint Mary's University of Minnesota, MN
Saint Michael's College, VT
St. Norbert College, WI
St. Olaf College, MN
Saint Xavier University, IL
Salve Regina University, RI

Sam Houston State University, TX
San Diego State University, CA
San Francisco Art Institute, CA
San Jose State University, CA
Santa Fe University of Art and Design, NM
Savannah College of Art and Design, GA
School of the Art Institute of Chicago, IL
School of the Museum of Fine Arts, Boston, MA
School of Visual Arts, NY
Schreiner University, TX
Seattle Pacific University, WA
Seattle University, WA
Seton Hill University, PA
Shawnee State University, OH
Shepherd University, WV
Shippensburg University of Pennsylvania, PA
Sierra Nevada College, NV
Simpson College, IA
Slippery Rock University of Pennsylvania, PA
Sonoma State University, CA
South Dakota State University, SD
Southeastern Louisiana University, LA
Southeastern Oklahoma State University, OK
Southern Illinois University Carbondale, IL
Southern Illinois University Edwardsville, IL
Southern Oregon University, OR
Southern Utah University, UT
Southwest Baptist University, MO
Southwestern Oklahoma State University, OK
Southwestern University, TX
Spring Arbor University, MI
State University of New York at Fredonia, NY
State University of New York at New Paltz, NY
State University of New York at Plattsburgh, NY
State University of New York College at Cortland, NY
State University of New York College at Geneseo, NY
State University of New York College at Potsdam, NY
Sterling College, KS
Stetson University, FL
Stevenson University, MD
Stockton University, NJ
Sul Ross State University, TX
Syracuse University, NY
Temple University, PA
Tennessee Technological University, TN
Texas A&M International University, TX
Texas A&M University–Commerce, TX
Texas A&M University–Corpus Christi, TX
Texas Christian University, TX
Texas State University, TX
Texas Tech University, TX
Texas Wesleyan University, TX
Texas Woman's University, TX
Thomas More College, KY
Thomas University, GA
Towson University, MD
Transylvania University, KY
Trinity Christian College, IL
Trinity University, TX
Truman State University, MO
Union University, TN
The University of Akron, OH
The University of Alabama, AL

The University of Alabama at Birmingham, AL
The University of Alabama in Huntsville, AL
University of Alaska Anchorage, AK
University of Alaska Fairbanks, AK
The University of Arizona, AZ
University of Arkansas, AR
University of California, Irvine, CA
University of California, Riverside, CA
University of California, Santa Cruz, CA
University of Central Oklahoma, OK
University of Colorado Boulder, CO
University of Colorado Denver, CO
University of Connecticut, CT
University of Dallas, TX
University of Dayton, OH
University of Delaware, DE
University of Denver, CO
University of Evansville, IN
University of Florida, FL
University of Hartford, CT
University of Houston, TX
University of Houston–Clear Lake, TX
University of Idaho, ID
University of Illinois at Chicago, IL
University of Illinois at Springfield, IL
University of Indianapolis, IN
University of Jamestown, ND
The University of Kansas, KS
University of La Verne, CA
University of Louisville, KY
University of Maine, ME
University of Mary Hardin-Baylor, TX
University of Maryland, Baltimore County, MD
University of Maryland, College Park, MD
University of Maryland Eastern Shore, MD
University of Mary Washington, VA
University of Massachusetts Amherst, MA
University of Massachusetts Dartmouth, MA
University of Massachusetts Lowell, MA
University of Memphis, TN
University of Michigan, MI
University of Michigan–Dearborn, MI
University of Michigan–Flint, MI
University of Minnesota, Twin Cities Campus, MN
University of Mississippi, MS
University of Missouri, MO
University of Missouri–Kansas City, MO
University of Missouri–St. Louis, MO
University of Mobile, AL
The University of Montana Western, MT
University of Montevallo, AL
University of Mount Olive, NC
University of Mount Union, OH
University of Nebraska at Kearney, NE
University of Nebraska at Omaha, NE
University of Nebraska–Lincoln, NE
University of Nevada, Las Vegas, NV
University of Nevada, Reno, NV
University of New Hampshire, NH
University of North Alabama, AL
University of North Carolina at Asheville, NC
The University of North Carolina at Chapel Hill, NC
The University of North Carolina at Greensboro, NC
The University of North Carolina at Pembroke, NC
The University of North Carolina Wilmington, NC
University of Northern Iowa, IA

University of North Florida, FL
University of Oklahoma, OK
University of Oregon, OR
University of Puget Sound, WA
University of Redlands, CA
University of Rhode Island, RI
University of Richmond, VA
University of Rio Grande, OH
University of St. Francis, IL
University of St. Thomas, TX
University of Science and Arts of Oklahoma, OK
University of South Alabama, AL
University of South Carolina, SC
University of South Carolina Aiken, SC
The University of South Dakota, SD
University of Southern California, CA
University of Southern Indiana, IN
University of Southern Mississippi, MS
University of South Florida, FL
The University of Tampa, FL
The University of Tennessee, TN
The University of Tennessee at Chattanooga, TN
The University of Tennessee at Martin, TN
The University of Texas at Austin, TX
The University of Texas at Brownsville, TX
The University of Texas at El Paso, TX
The University of Texas at San Antonio, TX
The University of Texas–Pan American, TX
University of the Incarnate Word, TX
The University of Toledo, OH
The University of Tulsa, OK
University of Utah, UT
University of Valley Forge, PA
University of Washington, WA
University of West Florida, FL
University of West Georgia, GA
University of Wisconsin–Eau Claire, WI
University of Wisconsin–Green Bay, WI
University of Wisconsin–La Crosse, WI
University of Wisconsin–Oshkosh, WI
University of Wisconsin–Parkside, WI
University of Wisconsin–River Falls, WI
University of Wisconsin–Stout, WI
University of Wisconsin–Whitewater, WI
University of Wyoming, WY
Utah State University, UT
Valdosta State University, GA
Valley City State University, ND
Valparaiso University, IN
Virginia Commonwealth University, VA
Virginia Polytechnic Institute and State University, VA
Virginia State University, VA
Virginia Wesleyan College, VA
Wabash College, IN
Wake Forest University, NC
Warren Wilson College, NC
Wartburg College, IA
Washburn University, KS
Washington College, MD
Washington State University, WA
Washington University in St. Louis, MO
Wayland Baptist University, TX
Waynesburg University, PA
Wayne State College, NE
Wayne State University, MI
Webster University, MO
Wesleyan College, GA
West Chester University of Pennsylvania, PA
Western Carolina University, NC
Western Illinois University, IL
Western Kentucky University, KY

Western Michigan University, MI
Western Oregon University, OR
Western State Colorado University, CO
Western Washington University, WA
Westmont College, CA
West Texas A&M University, TX
West Virginia University, WV
West Virginia Wesleyan College, WV
Wheaton College, IL
Whitman College, WA
Whittier College, CA
Whitworth University, WA
Wichita State University, KS
William Jessup University, CA
William Peace University, NC
Williams Baptist College, AR
William Woods University, MO
Wingate University, NC
Winona State University, MN
Winthrop University, SC
Wisconsin Lutheran College, WI
Wittenberg University, OH
Wofford College, SC
Wright State University, OH
Xavier University, OH
Xavier University of Louisiana, LA
Youngstown State University, OH

**Cinema/Film/Broadcasting**
Adelphi University, NY
Arkansas State University, AR
Arkansas Tech University, AR
Auburn University, AL
Ball State University, IN
Baylor University, TX
Bemidji State University, MN
Binghamton University, State University of New York, NY
Biola University, CA
Bloomfield College, NJ
Bowling Green State University, OH
Brenau University, GA
Brooks Institute, CA
Butler University, IN
California Baptist University, CA
California Institute of the Arts, CA
California Polytechnic State University, San Luis Obispo, CA
California State University, Chico, CA
California State University, Fullerton, CA
Calvin College, MI
Cameron University, OK
Castleton State College, VT
Central Michigan University, MI
Chapman University, CA
City College of the City University of New York, NY
The College at Brockport, State University of New York, NY
The College of New Rochelle, NY
College of Staten Island of the City University of New York, NY
Colorado State University–Pueblo, CO
DeSales University, PA
Eastern Illinois University, IL
Eastern Michigan University, MI
Eastern New Mexico University, NM
Eastern Washington University, WA
Emory University, GA
Five Towns College, NY
Flagler College, FL
Florida Agricultural and Mechanical University, FL
Florida State University, FL
Fort Hays State University, KS

George Fox University, OR
Georgia Southern University, GA
Grand Valley State University, MI
Harding University, AR
Hastings College, NE
Henderson State University, AR
Hofstra University, NY
Hollins University, VA
Howard University, DC
Huntington University, IN
Illinois State University, IL
Ithaca College, NY
James Madison University, VA
Kean University, NJ
Keene State College, NH
Kent State University, OH
Lafayette College, PA
Liberty University, VA
Lindenwood University, MO
Long Island University–LIU Brooklyn, NY
Long Island University–LIU Post, NY
Loyola Marymount University, CA
Massachusetts College of Liberal Arts, MA
Milligan College, TN
Minneapolis College of Art and Design, MN
Minnesota State University Moorhead, MN
Minot State University, ND
Mississippi State University, MS
Missouri Valley College, MO
Missouri Western State University, MO
Montana State University, MT
Montclair State University, NJ
Morningside College, IA
Muhlenberg College, PA
New Mexico State University, NM
North Central College, IL
Northwestern Oklahoma State University, OK
Northwest Missouri State University, MO
Ohio University, OH
Ohio University–Chillicothe, OH
Ohio University–Eastern, OH
Ohio University–Lancaster, OH
Ohio University–Southern Campus, OH
Ohio University–Zanesville, OH
Old Dominion University, VA
Oral Roberts University, OK
Purchase College, State University of New York, NY
Quincy University, IL
Regent University, VA
Rhode Island College, RI
Rochester Institute of Technology, NY
Sacred Heart University, CT
St. Cloud State University, MN
St. John's University, NY
Saint Joseph's College, IN
Saint Mary's College of California, CA
San Diego State University, CA
Santa Fe University of Art and Design, NM
Savannah College of Art and Design, GA
Sonoma State University, CA
Southern Illinois University Carbondale, IL
Southwestern College, KS
Stony Brook University, State University of New York, NY
Sul Ross State University, TX
Texas Christian University, TX
Texas Woman's University, TX
Towson University, MD
Trevecca Nazarene University, TN
Union University, TN
The University of Alabama, AL
University of California, Irvine, CA
University of California, San Diego, CA
University of California, Santa Cruz, CA

University of Central Florida, FL
University of Colorado Boulder, CO
The University of Kansas, KS
University of La Verne, CA
University of Maryland, Baltimore County, MD
University of Memphis, TN
University of Michigan, MI
University of Michigan–Dearborn, MI
University of Mississippi, MS
University of Missouri, MO
University of Montevallo, AL
University of Mount Union, OH
University of Nebraska–Lincoln, NE
University of Nevada, Las Vegas, NV
The University of North Carolina at Greensboro, NC
The University of North Carolina at Pembroke, NC
University of North Carolina School of the Arts, NC
The University of North Carolina Wilmington, NC
University of Oklahoma, OK
University of Pittsburgh at Bradford, PA
University of South Florida, FL
The University of Tennessee at Chattanooga, TN
The University of Tennessee at Martin, TN
University of Utah, UT
University of Wisconsin–Whitewater, WI
University of Wyoming, WY
Virginia Polytechnic Institute and State University, VA
Wartburg College, IA
Washburn University, KS
Washington State University, WA
Western Illinois University, IL
Western Kentucky University, KY
Western Washington University, WA
Westminster College, PA
West Texas A&M University, TX
Wright State University, OH

**Creative Writing**

Alderson Broaddus University, WV
Arkansas Tech University, AR
Auburn University, AL
Augustana College, IL
Augustana College, SD
Austin Peay State University, TN
Belhaven University, MS
Bemidji State University, MN
Binghamton University, State University of New York, NY
Bowling Green State University, OH
Brenau University, GA
Bucknell University, PA
California Institute of the Arts, CA
California Lutheran University, CA
California Polytechnic State University, San Luis Obispo, CA
California State University, Chico, CA
Calumet College of Saint Joseph, IN
Calvin College, MI
Cameron University, OK
Campbell University, NC
Carroll College, MT
Case Western Reserve University, OH
Central College, IA
Central Michigan University, MI
Chapman University, CA
City College of the City University of New York, NY
Cleveland State University, OH
Coe College, IA

Coker College, SC
Colby-Sawyer College, NH
The College at Brockport, State University of New York, NY
The College of New Rochelle, NY
College of Staten Island of the City University of New York, NY
Colorado Mesa University, CO
Colorado State University, CO
Columbia College, MO
Davidson College, NC
Delta State University, MS
Dickinson State University, ND
Drew University, NJ
Drury University, MO
Duke University, NC
Eastern Illinois University, IL
Eastern Michigan University, MI
Eastern New Mexico University, NM
Eastern Washington University, WA
Eckerd College, FL
Edgewood College, WI
Emmanuel College, GA
Emporia State University, KS
Fairmont State University, WV
Florida Agricultural and Mechanical University, FL
Fontbonne University, MO
Fort Hays State University, KS
Frostburg State University, MD
Furman University, SC
Goddard College, VT
Graceland University, IA
Grove City College, PA
Hamline University, MN
Hampshire College, MA
Hardin-Simmons University, TX
Hobart and William Smith Colleges, NY
Hollins University, VA
Hope College, MI
Huntington University, IN
Illinois State University, IL
Kent State University, OH
Kentucky Wesleyan College, KY
Kenyon College, OH
Knox College, IL
Lafayette College, PA
Lewis-Clark State College, ID
Long Island University–LIU Brooklyn, NY
Louisiana Tech University, LA
Loyola Marymount University, CA
Lycoming College, PA
Malone University, OH
Meredith College, NC
Michigan State University, MI
Midwestern State University, TX
Minnesota State University Moorhead, MN
Mississippi State University, MS
Morningside College, IA
New England College, NH
New Mexico State University, NM
Northeastern Illinois University, IL
Northern Illinois University, IL
Northland College, WI
Notre Dame de Namur University, CA
The Ohio State University, OH
Oklahoma State University, OK
Old Dominion University, VA
Plymouth State University, NH
Purchase College, State University of New York, NY
Rockhurst University, MO
Sacred Heart University, CT
St. Cloud State University, MN
St. John's University, NY
St. Thomas Aquinas College, NY

San Diego State University, CA
Santa Fe University of Art and Design, NM
Savannah College of Art and Design, GA
Siena College, NY
Sonoma State University, CA
Southern Illinois University Carbondale, IL
Southern Oregon University, OR
State University of New York College at Geneseo, NY
Stockton University, NJ
Susquehanna University, PA
Texas Christian University, TX
Texas Wesleyan University, TX
The University of Akron, OH
The University of Alabama, AL
University of Alaska Fairbanks, AK
University of California, Irvine, CA
University of California, Riverside, CA
University of California, Santa Cruz, CA
University of Colorado Boulder, CO
University of Houston, TX
University of Idaho, ID
The University of Kansas, KS
University of Louisville, KY
University of Maryland, Baltimore County, MD
University of Michigan, MI
University of Michigan–Dearborn, MI
University of Mississippi, MS
University of Missouri, MO
University of Missouri–St. Louis, MO
The University of Montana, MT
University of Montevallo, AL
University of Nebraska at Omaha, NE
University of Nevada, Las Vegas, NV
The University of North Carolina Wilmington, NC
University of Oregon, OR
University of Redlands, CA
The University of South Dakota, SD
University of Southern Indiana, IN
University of South Florida, FL
The University of Tampa, FL
The University of Tennessee at Martin, TN
The University of Texas at San Antonio, TX
University of Utah, UT
The University of Virginia's College at Wise, VA
University of Wisconsin–Stevens Point, WI
University of Wisconsin–Whitewater, WI
University of Wyoming, WY
Ursinus College, PA
Virginia Polytechnic Institute and State University, VA
Wabash College, IN
Warren Wilson College, NC
Washington College, MD
Washington State University, WA
Washington University in St. Louis, MO
Wayne State College, NE
Webster University, MO
Western Illinois University, IL
Western Washington University, WA
Wichita State University, KS
Wright State University, OH
Youngstown State University, OH

**Dance**

Adelphi University, NY
Alma College, MI
Angelo State University, TX
Arizona State University at the Tempe campus, AZ
Augustana College, SD
Ball State University, IN

Belhaven University, MS
Binghamton University, State University of New York, NY
Birmingham-Southern College, AL
Boise State University, ID
Bowling Green State University, OH
Brenau University, GA
Bucknell University, PA
Butler University, IN
California Institute of the Arts, CA
California Polytechnic State University, San Luis Obispo, CA
California State University, Bakersfield, CA
California State University, Chico, CA
California State University, Fullerton, CA
Canisius College, NY
Case Western Reserve University, OH
Cedar Crest College, PA
Centenary College of Louisiana, LA
Central Michigan University, MI
Chapman University, CA
Cleveland State University, OH
Coker College, SC
The College at Brockport, State University of New York, NY
College of Staten Island of the City University of New York, NY
The College of Wooster, OH
Colorado Mesa University, CO
Colorado State University, CO
Columbus State University, GA
Concordia University, Nebraska, NE
Cornish College of the Arts, WA
Creighton University, NE
DeSales University, PA
Drexel University, PA
Duquesne University, PA
East Carolina University, NC
Eastern Michigan University, MI
Eastern New Mexico University, NM
Eastern University, PA
Emmanuel College, GA
Florida Agricultural and Mechanical University, FL
Florida State University, FL
Fordham University, NY
Fort Hays State University, KS
Friends University, KS
Georgian Court University, NJ
Goucher College, MD
Graceland University, IA
Grambling State University, LA
Grand Valley State University, MI
Grand View University, IA
Gustavus Adolphus College, MN
Hastings College, NE
Hawai'i Pacific University, HI
Henderson State University, AR
Hendrix College, AR
Hobart and William Smith Colleges, NY
Hofstra University, NY
Hollins University, VA
Hope College, MI
Howard University, DC
Huntingdon College, AL
Idaho State University, ID
Indiana University of Pennsylvania, PA
Ithaca College, NY
James Madison University, VA
The Juilliard School, NY
Kansas Wesleyan University, KS
Kean University, NJ
Keene State College, NH
Kennesaw State University, GA
Kent State University, OH

Knox College, IL
Kutztown University of Pennsylvania, PA
Lafayette College, PA
Lake Erie College, OH
Lees-McRae College, NC
Lindenwood University, MO
Long Island University–LIU Brooklyn, NY
Long Island University–LIU Post, NY
Manhattanville College, NY
Marymount Manhattan College, NY
McKendree University, IL
Mercyhurst University, PA
Methodist University, NC
Middle Tennessee State University, TN
Milligan College, TN
Millikin University, IL
Mississippi State University, MS
Missouri Valley College, MO
Missouri Western State University, MO
Montana State University, MT
Montclair State University, NJ
Morningside College, IA
Muhlenberg College, PA
Murray State University, KY
New Mexico State University, NM
Nicholls State University, LA
Northeastern Illinois University, IL
Northeastern State University, OK
Northern Illinois University, IL
Northwest Missouri State University, MO
Oakland University, MI
The Ohio State University, OH
Ohio University, OH
Ohio University–Chillicothe, OH
Ohio University–Eastern, OH
Ohio University–Lancaster, OH
Ohio University–Southern Campus, OH
Ohio University–Zanesville, OH
Ohio Wesleyan University, OH
Oklahoma City University, OK
Old Dominion University, VA
Pace University, NY
Pacific Lutheran University, WA
Palm Beach Atlantic University, FL
Plymouth State University, NH
Purchase College, State University of New York, NY
Rhode Island College, RI
Robert Morris University Illinois, IL
Rockford University, IL
Sacred Heart University, CT
St. Ambrose University, IA
St. John's University, NY
Saint Joseph's College, IN
Saint Mary's College of California, CA
St. Olaf College, MN
Sam Houston State University, TX
San Diego State University, CA
Santa Clara University, CA
Santa Fe University of Art and Design, NM
Savannah College of Art and Design, GA
Shenandoah University, VA
Slippery Rock University of Pennsylvania, PA
Sonoma State University, CA
Southeastern Oklahoma State University, OK
Southern Illinois University Carbondale, IL
Southern Illinois University Edwardsville, IL
Southwestern College, KS
State University of New York at Fredonia, NY
State University of New York College at Geneseo, NY

State University of New York College at
  Potsdam, NY
Stephens College, MO
Sterling College, KS
Stockton University, NJ
Texas A&M International University, TX
Texas Christian University, TX
Texas Tech University, TX
Texas Wesleyan University, TX
Texas Woman's University, TX
Towson University, MD
Trine University, IN
The University of Akron, OH
The University of Alabama, AL
University of Alaska Anchorage, AK
The University of Arizona, AZ
University of California, Irvine, CA
University of California, Riverside, CA
University of California, San Diego, CA
University of Colorado Boulder, CO
University of Dubuque, IA
University of Florida, FL
University of Great Falls, MT
University of Hartford, CT
University of Houston, TX
University of Idaho, ID
The University of Kansas, KS
University of Louisville, KY
University of Maryland, Baltimore County,
  MD
University of Maryland, College Park, MD
University of Mary Washington, VA
University of Massachusetts Amherst, MA
University of Memphis, TN
University of Michigan, MI
University of Missouri–St. Louis, MO
The University of Montana, MT
University of Nebraska–Lincoln, NE
University of Nevada, Las Vegas, NV
University of New Hampshire, NH
University of North Alabama, AL
The University of North Carolina at
  Greensboro, NC
University of North Carolina School of the
  Arts, NC
University of Northern Colorado, CO
University of Oklahoma, OK
University of Oregon, OR
University of Richmond, VA
University of South Carolina, SC
University of Southern Mississippi, MS
University of South Florida, FL
The University of Texas–Pan American, TX
University of Utah, UT
The University of West Alabama, AL
University of Wisconsin–Green Bay, WI
University of Wisconsin–Stevens Point, WI
University of Wyoming, WY
Virginia Commonwealth University, VA
Virginia State University, VA
Wayne State University, MI
Western Illinois University, IL
Western Kentucky University, KY
Western Michigan University, MI
Western Oregon University, OR
Western Washington University, WA
Westmont College, CA
West Texas A&M University, TX
Wichita State University, KS
Widener University, PA
William Jewell College, MO
Winthrop University, SC
Wittenberg University, OH
Wright State University, OH

## Debating

Abilene Christian University, TX
Alderson Broaddus University, WV
Arkansas State University, AR
Augustana College, IL
Austin Peay State University, TN
Ball State University, IN
Baylor University, TX
Berry College, GA
Bethany Lutheran College, MN
Bethel College, KS
Bethel University, MN
Boise State University, ID
Bowling Green State University, OH
California Baptist University, CA
California Polytechnic State University, San
  Luis Obispo, CA
California State University, Chico, CA
Cameron University, OK
Carroll College, MT
Carson-Newman University, TN
Cedarville University, OH
The College of Idaho, ID
The College of New Rochelle, NY
College of Saint Mary, NE
College of Staten Island of the City
  University of New York, NY
Concordia College, MN
Concordia University, CA
Concordia University, Nebraska, NE
Culver-Stockton College, MO
Doane College, NE
Dordt College, IA
Drury University, MO
Eastern Illinois University, IL
Eastern Michigan University, MI
Eastern New Mexico University, NM
Emory University, GA
Emporia State University, KS
Evangel University, MO
Fairmont State University, WV
Ferris State University, MI
Fort Hays State University, KS
George Fox University, OR
Gonzaga University, WA
Gustavus Adolphus College, MN
Harding University, AR
Hastings College, NE
Hawai'i Pacific University, HI
Henderson State University, AR
Hillsdale College, MI
Idaho State University, ID
Illinois State University, IL
Kentucky Christian University, KY
Lewis & Clark College, OR
Lewis-Clark State College, ID
Liberty University, VA
Lindenwood University, MO
Linfield College, OR
Louisiana Tech University, LA
Loyola University Chicago, IL
Malone University, OH
Marist College, NY
McKendree University, IL
Mercer University, GA
Methodist University, NC
Michigan State University, MI
Middle Tennessee State University, TN
Mississippi State University, MS
Monmouth College, IL
Muskingum University, OH
North Central College, IL
Northeastern State University, OK
Northern Illinois University, IL
Northwestern Oklahoma State University,
  OK

Northwest Missouri State University, MO
Northwest Nazarene University, ID
Northwest University, WA
Ohio University, OH
Ohio University–Chillicothe, OH
Ohio University–Eastern, OH
Ohio University–Lancaster, OH
Ohio University–Southern Campus, OH
Ohio University–Zanesville, OH
Pacific Lutheran University, WA
Pacific University, OR
Patrick Henry College, VA
Piedmont College, GA
Point Loma Nazarene University, CA
Regis University, CO
St. John's University, NY
Saint Joseph's University, PA
Saint Mary's College of California, CA
Samford University, AL
San Diego State University, CA
Santa Clara University, CA
Savannah College of Art and Design, GA
South Dakota State University, SD
Southeastern Oklahoma State University,
  OK
Southern Illinois University Carbondale, IL
Southwest Baptist University, MO
Sterling College, KS
Tennessee Technological University, TN
Texas Wesleyan University, TX
Towson University, MD
Trinity University, TX
Truman State University, MO
Union University, TN
The University of Akron, OH
The University of Alabama, AL
University of Alaska Anchorage, AK
University of Denver, CO
University of Indianapolis, IN
The University of Kansas, KS
University of Louisville, KY
University of Michigan–Dearborn, MI
University of Mississippi, MS
University of Missouri–Kansas City, MO
University of Nebraska at Kearney, NE
University of Nebraska at Omaha, NE
University of Nevada, Las Vegas, NV
University of Northern Iowa, IA
University of Oklahoma, OK
University of Oregon, OR
University of Puget Sound, WA
University of Redlands, CA
University of South Carolina, SC
The University of South Dakota, SD
University of Southern California, CA
University of South Florida, FL
The University of Texas at San Antonio, TX
University of the Pacific, CA
University of Vermont, VT
University of West Georgia, GA
University of Wisconsin–Eau Claire, WI
University of Wyoming, WY
Vanguard University of Southern California,
  CA
Washburn University, KS
Wayne State University, MI
Webster University, MO
Western Illinois University, IL
Western Kentucky University, KY
West Texas A&M University, TX
West Virginia University, WV
Whitman College, WA
Wichita State University, KS
William Jewell College, MO
Winona State University, MN

**Journalism/Publications**

Abilene Christian University, TX
Alaska Pacific University, AK
Albright College, PA
Alderson Broaddus University, WV
Angelo State University, TX
Arkansas State University, AR
Arkansas Tech University, AR
Auburn University, AL
Augustana College, SD
Austin Peay State University, TN
Averett University, VA
Ball State University, IN
Baylor University, TX
Belhaven University, MS
Bemidji State University, MN
Berry College, GA
Bethany Lutheran College, MN
Binghamton University, State University of
    New York, NY
Biola University, CA
Boise State University, ID
Bowling Green State University, OH
Brenau University, GA
Brooks Institute, CA
Butler University, IN
California Baptist University, CA
California Lutheran University, CA
California Polytechnic State University, San
    Luis Obispo, CA
California State University, Chico, CA
California State University, Fresno, CA
California State University, Fullerton, CA
California State University, Los Angeles, CA
California State University, San Bernardino,
    CA
Calvin College, MI
Cameron University, OK
Campbellsville University, KY
Campbell University, NC
Carroll University, WI
Carson-Newman University, TN
Central Michigan University, MI
The Citadel, The Military College of South
    Carolina, SC
Cleveland State University, OH
The College at Brockport, State University
    of New York, NY
The College of New Rochelle, NY
College of Staten Island of the City
    University of New York, NY
Colorado Mesa University, CO
Colorado State University–Pueblo, CO
Concord University, WV
Cornerstone University, MI
Delta State University, MS
Dickinson State University, ND
Dordt College, IA
Eastern Illinois University, IL
Eastern New Mexico University, NM
Eastern Washington University, WA
Elon University, NC
Emmanuel College, GA
Fairmont State University, WV
Faulkner University, AL
Ferris State University, MI
Florida Agricultural and Mechanical
    University, FL
Fort Hays State University, KS
Fort Valley State University, GA
Franklin College, IN
Frostburg State University, MD
Georgia College & State University, GA
Glenville State College, WV
Grand Valley State University, MI

Hamline University, MN
Harding University, AR
Hardin-Simmons University, TX
Hastings College, NE
Hawai'i Pacific University, HI
Henderson State University, AR
Hillsdale College, MI
Hofstra University, NY
Howard University, DC
Huntington University, IN
Idaho State University, ID
Indiana University of Pennsylvania, PA
Iowa State University of Science and
    Technology, IA
Ithaca College, NY
Jacksonville State University, AL
James Madison University, VA
John Brown University, AR
Kent State University, OH
Kent State University at Stark, OH
Lees-McRae College, NC
Lehigh University, PA
LeMoyne-Owen College, TN
Liberty University, VA
Lincoln University, MO
Lipscomb University, TN
Lock Haven University of Pennsylvania, PA
Long Island University–LIU Brooklyn, NY
Long Island University–LIU Post, NY
Louisiana State University and Agricultural
    & Mechanical College, LA
Louisiana Tech University, LA
Loyola Marymount University, CA
Loyola University Chicago, IL
Lubbock Christian University, TX
Malone University, OH
Mansfield University of Pennsylvania, PA
Massachusetts College of Liberal Arts, MA
Michigan State University, MI
Middle Tennessee State University, TN
Midwestern State University, TX
Mississippi State University, MS
Mississippi University for Women, MS
Missouri Southern State University, MO
Missouri Valley College, MO
Missouri Western State University, MO
Morehead State University, KY
Morningside College, IA
Murray State University, KY
Muskingum University, OH
New Jersey Institute of Technology, NJ
Newman University, KS
New Mexico State University, NM
North Central College, IL
Northeastern Illinois University, IL
Northeastern State University, OK
Northern Illinois University, IL
Northwestern Oklahoma State University,
    OK
Northwest Missouri State University, MO
Nyack College, NY
Oglethorpe University, GA
The Ohio State University, OH
Ohio University, OH
Ohio University–Chillicothe, OH
Ohio University–Eastern, OH
Ohio University–Lancaster, OH
Ohio University–Southern Campus, OH
Ohio University–Zanesville, OH
Oklahoma Christian University, OK
Oklahoma State University, OK
Old Dominion University, VA
Olivet College, MI
Oral Roberts University, OK
Ouachita Baptist University, AR

Pacific University, OR
Patrick Henry College, VA
Piedmont College, GA
Regent University, VA
Rhode Island College, RI
Robert Morris University Illinois, IL
Rochester College, MI
St. Ambrose University, IA
St. Bonaventure University, NY
St. Cloud State University, MN
St. Edward's University, TX
St. John's University, NY
Samford University, AL
San Diego State University, CA
Savannah College of Art and Design, GA
Schreiner University, TX
Siena College, NY
Sonoma State University, CA
South Dakota State University, SD
Southern Illinois University Carbondale, IL
Southern Oregon University, OR
Southwestern College, KS
State University of New York at Plattsburgh,
    NY
State University of New York College at
    Geneseo, NY
Stephen F. Austin State University, TX
Stockton University, NJ
Stony Brook University, State University of
    New York, NY
Suffolk University, MA
Sul Ross State University, TX
Tabor College, KS
Texas A&M University, TX
Texas A&M University–Commerce, TX
Texas Christian University, TX
Texas Lutheran University, TX
Texas State University, TX
Texas Tech University, TX
Texas Wesleyan University, TX
Texas Woman's University, TX
Trinity Christian College, IL
Union University, TN
The University of Akron, OH
The University of Alabama, AL
University of Arkansas, AR
University of California, San Diego, CA
University of Central Oklahoma, OK
University of Colorado Boulder, CO
University of Florida, FL
University of Houston, TX
University of Idaho, ID
The University of Kansas, KS
University of La Verne, CA
University of Mary Washington, VA
University of Massachusetts Amherst, MA
University of Memphis, TN
University of Michigan, MI
University of Michigan–Dearborn, MI
University of Michigan–Flint, MI
University of Mississippi, MS
University of Missouri, MO
The University of Montana, MT
University of Montevallo, AL
University of Mount Union, OH
University of Nebraska at Kearney, NE
University of Nebraska at Omaha, NE
University of Nebraska–Lincoln, NE
University of Nevada, Las Vegas, NV
University of Nevada, Reno, NV
University of North Alabama, AL
The University of North Carolina at Chapel
    Hill, NC
University of Oklahoma, OK
University of Oregon, OR

University of Pittsburgh at Johnstown, PA
University of St. Thomas, MN
University of South Alabama, AL
University of South Carolina, SC
University of South Carolina Aiken, SC
University of South Florida, FL
The University of Tampa, FL
The University of Tennessee at Chattanooga, TN
The University of Tennessee at Martin, TN
The University of Texas at Arlington, TX
The University of Texas at El Paso, TX
The University of Texas–Pan American, TX
University of Utah, UT
The University of Virginia's College at Wise, VA
University of West Georgia, GA
University of Wisconsin–Eau Claire, WI
University of Wisconsin–Green Bay, WI
University of Wisconsin–Whitewater, WI
University of Wyoming, WY
Utah State University, UT
Valdosta State University, GA
Valley City State University, ND
Virginia Polytechnic Institute and State University, VA
Wabash College, IN
Wartburg College, IA
Washburn University, KS
Washington State University, WA
Wayland Baptist University, TX
Wayne State College, NE
Wayne State University, MI
Webber International University, FL
Western Illinois University, IL
Western Kentucky University, KY
Western Washington University, WA
West Texas A&M University, TX
Whitworth University, WA
Wichita State University, KS
William Jewell College, MO
William Woods University, MO
Youngstown State University, OH

**Music**

Abilene Christian University, TX
Adelphi University, NY
Adrian College, MI
Agnes Scott College, GA
Alabama Agricultural and Mechanical University, AL
Alabama State University, AL
Alaska Bible College, AK
Alaska Pacific University, AK
Albany State University, GA
Albion College, MI
Albright College, PA
Alcorn State University, MS
Alderson Broaddus University, WV
Allegheny Wesleyan College, OH
Alma College, MI
Alverno College, WI
Anderson University, IN
Anderson University, SC
Andrews University, MI
Angelo State University, TX
Anna Maria College, MA
Arizona Christian University, AZ
Arizona State University at the Tempe campus, AZ
Arkansas State University, AR
Armstrong State University, GA
Ashland University, OH
Auburn University, AL
Augustana College, IL
Augustana College, SD

Austin College, TX
Austin Peay State University, TN
Ave Maria University, FL
Averett University, VA
Baldwin Wallace University, OH
Ball State University, IN
The Baptist College of Florida, FL
Barclay College, KS
Baylor University, TX
Belhaven University, MS
Bellarmine University, KY
Belmont University, TN
Beloit College, WI
Bemidji State University, MN
Benedictine University, IL
Berklee College of Music, MA
Berry College, GA
Bethany College, WV
Bethany Lutheran College, MN
Bethel College, KS
Bethel University, MN
Binghamton University, State University of New York, NY
Biola University, CA
Birmingham-Southern College, AL
Bluefield College, VA
Blue Mountain College, MS
Bluffton University, OH
Boise State University, ID
Boston University, MA
Bowie State University, MD
Bowling Green State University, OH
Bradley University, IL
Brenau University, GA
Brevard College, NC
Bridgewater College, VA
Brigham Young University, UT
Bucknell University, PA
Buena Vista University, IA
Buffalo State College, State University of New York, NY
Butler University, IN
Cairn University, PA
Caldwell University, NJ
California Baptist University, CA
California Institute of the Arts, CA
California Lutheran University, CA
California Polytechnic State University, San Luis Obispo, CA
California State University, Bakersfield, CA
California State University, Chico, CA
California State University, East Bay, CA
California State University, Fresno, CA
California State University, Fullerton, CA
California State University, Los Angeles, CA
California State University, San Bernardino, CA
California State University, Stanislaus, CA
Calvin College, MI
Cameron University, OK
Campbellsville University, KY
Campbell University, NC
Canisius College, NY
Capital University, OH
Cardinal Stritch University, WI
Carleton College, MN
Carnegie Mellon University, PA
Carroll College, MT
Carroll University, WI
Carson-Newman University, TN
Case Western Reserve University, OH
Castleton State College, VT
Catawba College, NC
The Catholic University of America, DC
Cedarville University, OH
Centenary College of Louisiana, LA

Central College, IA
Central Methodist University, MO
Central Michigan University, MI
Central Washington University, WA
Centre College, KY
Chapman University, CA
Chatham University, PA
Chowan University, NC
Christopher Newport University, VA
Cincinnati Christian University, OH
The Citadel, The Military College of South Carolina, SC
City College of the City University of New York, NY
Clarion University of Pennsylvania, PA
Clarke University, IA
Clear Creek Baptist Bible College, KY
Cleveland Institute of Music, OH
Cleveland State University, OH
Coastal Carolina University, SC
Coe College, IA
Coker College, SC
The College at Brockport, State University of New York, NY
College of Charleston, SC
The College of Idaho, ID
The College of New Jersey, NJ
The College of New Rochelle, NY
College of Saint Benedict, MN
College of Saint Mary, NE
The College of Saint Rose, NY
The College of St. Scholastica, MN
College of Staten Island of the City University of New York, NY
College of the Holy Cross, MA
The College of William and Mary, VA
The College of Wooster, OH
Colorado Mesa University, CO
Colorado State University, CO
Colorado State University–Pueblo, CO
Columbia College, MO
Columbus State University, GA
Concordia College, MN
Concordia University, CA
Concordia University Ann Arbor, MI
Concordia University Chicago, IL
Concordia University, Nebraska, NE
Concordia University, St. Paul, MN
Concordia University Texas, TX
Concordia University Wisconsin, WI
Concord University, WV
Converse College, SC
Corban University, OR
Cornell College, IA
Cornerstone University, MI
Cornish College of the Arts, WA
Covenant College, GA
Creighton University, NE
Culver-Stockton College, MO
Cumberland University, TN
Dakota State University, SD
Dakota Wesleyan University, SD
Dallas Baptist University, TX
Davidson College, NC
Delaware State University, DE
Delta State University, MS
DePaul University, IL
Dickinson State University, ND
Doane College, NE
Dordt College, IA
Drake University, IA
Drew University, NJ
Drexel University, PA
Drury University, MO
Duquesne University, PA
East Carolina University, NC

East Central University, OK
Eastern Illinois University, IL
Eastern Kentucky University, KY
Eastern Michigan University, MI
Eastern New Mexico University, NM
Eastern University, PA
Eastern Washington University, WA
East Stroudsburg University of
    Pennsylvania, PA
East Texas Baptist University, TX
Eckerd College, FL
Edgewood College, WI
Elizabeth City State University, NC
Elizabethtown College, PA
Elmhurst College, IL
Elon University, NC
Emmanuel College, GA
Emory & Henry College, VA
Emory University, GA
Emporia State University, KS
Endicott College, MA
Eureka College, IL
Evangel University, MO
Fairmont State University, WV
Faulkner University, AL
Fayetteville State University, NC
Ferris State University, MI
Five Towns College, NY
Florida Agricultural and Mechanical
    University, FL
Florida Atlantic University, FL
Florida Gulf Coast University, FL
Florida Institute of Technology, FL
Florida Southern College, FL
Florida State University, FL
Fordham University, NY
Fort Hays State University, KS
Fort Lewis College, CO
Fort Valley State University, GA
Francis Marion University, SC
Franklin & Marshall College, PA
Franklin College, IN
Fresno Pacific University, CA
Friends University, KS
Frostburg State University, MD
Furman University, SC
Gannon University, PA
Gardner-Webb University, NC
Geneva College, PA
George Fox University, OR
Georgetown College, KY
Georgia College & State University, GA
Georgia Regents University, GA
Georgia Southern University, GA
Georgia Southwestern State University, GA
Gettysburg College, PA
Glenville State College, WV
Gonzaga University, WA
Gordon College, MA
Goshen College, IN
Goucher College, MD
Graceland University, IA
Grambling State University, LA
Grand Valley State University, MI
Grand View University, IA
Greensboro College, NC
Greenville College, IL
Grove City College, PA
Guilford College, NC
Gustavus Adolphus College, MN
Hamline University, MN
Hampden-Sydney College, VA
Hampton University, VA
Hanover College, IN
Harding University, AR

Hardin-Simmons University, TX
Hartwick College, NY
Hastings College, NE
Hawai'i Pacific University, HI
Heidelberg University, OH
Henderson State University, AR
Hendrix College, AR
Hillsdale College, MI
Hillsdale Free Will Baptist College, OK
Hobart and William Smith Colleges, NY
Hofstra University, NY
Hollins University, VA
Hood College, MD
Hope College, MI
Houghton College, NY
Houston Baptist University, TX
Howard Payne University, TX
Howard University, DC
Huntingdon College, AL
Huntington University, IN
Huston-Tillotson University, TX
Idaho State University, ID
Illinois College, IL
Illinois State University, IL
Illinois Wesleyan University, IL
Indiana State University, IN
Indiana University of Pennsylvania, PA
Indiana University–Purdue University Fort
    Wayne, IN
Iona College, NY
Iowa State University of Science and
    Technology, IA
Iowa Wesleyan College, IA
Ithaca College, NY
Jackson State University, MS
Jacksonville State University, AL
Jacksonville University, FL
James Madison University, VA
John Brown University, AR
Johnson C. Smith University, NC
The Juilliard School, NY
Juniata College, PA
Kalamazoo College, MI
Kansas Wesleyan University, KS
Kean University, NJ
Keene State College, NH
Kennesaw State University, GA
Kent State University, OH
Kent State University at Stark, OH
Kentucky Christian University, KY
Kentucky State University, KY
Kentucky Wesleyan College, KY
Kenyon College, OH
King University, TN
Knox College, IL
Kutztown University of Pennsylvania, PA
Lafayette College, PA
LaGrange College, GA
Lake Erie College, OH
Lancaster Bible College, PA
Langston University, OK
La Sierra University, CA
Lawrence University, WI
Lebanon Valley College, PA
Lee University, TN
Lehigh University, PA
Le Moyne College, NY
LeMoyne-Owen College, TN
Lenoir-Rhyne University, NC
Lewis & Clark College, OR
Lewis-Clark State College, ID
Lewis University, IL
Liberty University, VA
Lincoln Memorial University, TN
Lincoln University, MO

Lincoln University, PA
Lindenwood University, MO
Lindsey Wilson College, KY
Linfield College, OR
Lipscomb University, TN
Lock Haven University of Pennsylvania, PA
Long Island University–LIU Brooklyn, NY
Long Island University–LIU Post, NY
Longwood University, VA
Loras College, IA
Louisiana State University and Agricultural
    & Mechanical College, LA
Louisiana Tech University, LA
Loyola Marymount University, CA
Loyola University Chicago, IL
Lubbock Christian University, TX
Luther College, IA
Lycoming College, PA
Lynchburg College, VA
Lynn University, FL
Lyon College, AR
Malone University, OH
Manchester University, IN
Manhattan College, NY
Manhattan School of Music, NY
Mansfield University of Pennsylvania, PA
Maranatha Baptist University, WI
Marian University, WI
Marietta College, OH
Marist College, NY
Martin Luther College, MN
Maryville College, TN
Maryville University of Saint Louis, MO
Marywood University, PA
Massachusetts College of Liberal Arts, MA
The Master's College and Seminary, CA
Mayville State University, ND
McKendree University, IL
McMurry University, TX
McNally Smith College of Music, MN
Mercer University, GA
Mercyhurst University, PA
Meredith College, NC
Messiah College, PA
Methodist University, NC
Metropolitan State University of Denver, CO
Miami University, OH
Michigan State University, MI
Middle Tennessee State University, TN
Midwestern State University, TX
Millersville University of Pennsylvania, PA
Milligan College, TN
Millikin University, IL
Millsaps College, MS
Mills College, CA
Minnesota State University Moorhead, MN
Minot State University, ND
Mississippi College, MS
Mississippi State University, MS
Mississippi University for Women, MS
Missouri Baptist University, MO
Missouri Southern State University, MO
Missouri University of Science and
    Technology, MO
Missouri Valley College, MO
Missouri Western State University, MO
Molloy College, NY
Monmouth College, IL
Montana State University, MT
Montana State University Billings, MT
Montclair State University, NJ
Montreat College, NC
Moravian College, PA
Morehead State University, KY
Morningside College, IA

Mount Aloysius College, PA
Mount Marty College, SD
Mount Mary University, WI
Mount Mercy University, IA
Mount St. Joseph University, OH
Mount Saint Mary's University, CA
Muhlenberg College, PA
Murray State University, KY
Muskingum University, OH
Nazareth College of Rochester, NY
Newberry College, SC
New England Conservatory of Music, MA
Newman University, KS
New Mexico Highlands University, NM
New Mexico State University, NM
The New School for Jazz and Contemporary
 Music, NY
Nicholls State University, LA
North Carolina Agricultural and Technical
 State University, NC
North Carolina Central University, NC
North Central College, IL
Northeastern Illinois University, IL
Northeastern State University, OK
Northern Arizona University, AZ
Northern Illinois University, IL
Northern Kentucky University, KY
Northern Michigan University, MI
Northern State University, SD
Northland College, WI
Northwest Christian University, OR
Northwestern Oklahoma State University,
 OK
Northwestern University, IL
Northwest Missouri State University, MO
Northwest Nazarene University, ID
Northwest University, WA
Notre Dame de Namur University, CA
Nova Southeastern University, FL
Nyack College, NY
Oakland University, MI
Oberlin College, OH
Occidental College, CA
Oglethorpe University, GA
The Ohio State University, OH
Ohio University, OH
Ohio University–Chillicothe, OH
Ohio University–Eastern, OH
Ohio University–Lancaster, OH
Ohio University–Southern Campus, OH
Ohio University–Zanesville, OH
Ohio Wesleyan University, OH
Oklahoma Baptist University, OK
Oklahoma Christian University, OK
Oklahoma City University, OK
Oklahoma State University, OK
Oklahoma Wesleyan University, OK
Old Dominion University, VA
Olivet College, MI
Olivet Nazarene University, IL
Oral Roberts University, OK
Otterbein University, OH
Ouachita Baptist University, AR
Our Lady of the Lake University of San
 Antonio, TX
Pacific Lutheran University, WA
Pacific University, OR
Palm Beach Atlantic University, FL
Park University, MO
Patrick Henry College, VA
Peabody Conservatory of The Johns Hopkins
 University, MD
Philander Smith College, AR
Piedmont College, GA
Pittsburg State University, KS
Plymouth State University, NH

Point Loma Nazarene University, CA
Portland State University, OR
Presbyterian College, SC
Purchase College, State University of New
 York, NY
Purdue University, IN
Queens College of the City University of
 New York, NY
Queens University of Charlotte, NC
Quincy University, IL
Regis University, CO
Reinhardt University, GA
Rhode Island College, RI
Rhodes College, TN
Rice University, TX
Roanoke College, VA
Robert Morris University Illinois, IL
Roberts Wesleyan College, NY
Rochester College, MI
Rockford University, IL
Rockhurst University, MO
Rogers State University, OK
Rollins College, FL
Roosevelt University, IL
Rowan University, NJ
Sacred Heart University, CT
Saginaw Valley State University, MI
St. Ambrose University, IA
Saint Augustine's University, NC
St. Bonaventure University, NY
St. Catherine University, MN
St. Cloud State University, MN
Saint John's University, MN
St. John's University, NY
Saint Joseph's College, IN
Saint Louis University, MO
Saint Martin's University, WA
Saint Mary's College of California, CA
Saint Mary's University of Minnesota, MN
St. Norbert College, WI
St. Olaf College, MN
Saint Xavier University, IL
Salem College, NC
Salisbury University, MD
Samford University, AL
Sam Houston State University, TX
San Diego State University, CA
San Francisco Conservatory of Music, CA
Santa Clara University, CA
Santa Fe University of Art and Design, NM
Savannah College of Art and Design, GA
Schreiner University, TX
Seattle University, WA
Seton Hill University, PA
Shenandoah University, VA
Shepherd University, WV
Shippensburg University of Pennsylvania,
 PA
Siena College, NY
Simpson College, IA
Simpson University, CA
Skidmore College, NY
Slippery Rock University of Pennsylvania,
 PA
Sonoma State University, CA
South Dakota State University, SD
Southeastern Louisiana University, LA
Southeastern Oklahoma State University,
 OK
Southeast Missouri State University, MO
Southern Illinois University Carbondale, IL
Southern Illinois University Edwardsville,
 IL
Southern Oregon University, OR
Southern Utah University, UT
Southwest Baptist University, MO

Southwestern Christian College, TX
Southwestern College, KS
Southwestern Oklahoma State University,
 OK
Southwestern University, TX
State University of New York at Fredonia,
 NY
State University of New York at New Paltz,
 NY
State University of New York at Plattsburgh,
 NY
State University of New York College at
 Cortland, NY
State University of New York College at
 Geneseo, NY
State University of New York College at
 Potsdam, NY
Stephen F. Austin State University, TX
Stephens College, MO
Sterling College, KS
Stetson University, FL
Stockton University, NJ
Stony Brook University, State University of
 New York, NY
Sul Ross State University, TX
Susquehanna University, PA
Syracuse University, NY
Tabor College, KS
Tarleton State University, TX
Taylor University, IN
Temple University, PA
Tennessee State University, TN
Tennessee Technological University, TN
Tennessee Wesleyan College, TN
Texas A&M International University, TX
Texas A&M University–Commerce, TX
Texas Christian University, TX
Texas Lutheran University, TX
Texas State University, TX
Texas Tech University, TX
Texas Wesleyan University, TX
Texas Woman's University, TX
Thiel College, PA
Thomas University, GA
Tiffin University, OH
Towson University, MD
Transylvania University, KY
Trevecca Nazarene University, TN
Trine University, IN
Trinity Christian College, IL
Trinity University, TX
Troy University, AL
Truett-McConnell College, GA
Truman State University, MO
Tulane University, LA
Tusculum College, TN
Tuskegee University, AL
Union College, KY
Union College, NE
Union University, TN
The University of Akron, OH
The University of Alabama, AL
The University of Alabama at Birmingham,
 AL
The University of Alabama in Huntsville,
 AL
University of Alaska Anchorage, AK
University of Alaska Fairbanks, AK
The University of Arizona, AZ
University of Arkansas, AR
University of Bridgeport, CT
University of California, Irvine, CA
University of California, Riverside, CA
University of California, Santa Cruz, CA
University of Central Florida, FL
University of Central Oklahoma, OK

University of Charleston, WV
University of Colorado Boulder, CO
University of Colorado Denver, CO
University of Connecticut, CT
University of Dayton, OH
University of Delaware, DE
University of Denver, CO
University of Dubuque, IA
University of Evansville, IN
The University of Findlay, OH
University of Florida, FL
University of Georgia, GA
University of Hartford, CT
University of Houston, TX
University of Idaho, ID
University of Illinois at Chicago, IL
University of Illinois at Springfield, IL
University of Indianapolis, IN
The University of Iowa, IA
University of Jamestown, ND
The University of Kansas, KS
University of La Verne, CA
University of Louisville, KY
University of Maine at Augusta, ME
University of Maine at Farmington, ME
University of Mary Hardin-Baylor, TX
University of Maryland, Baltimore County, MD
University of Maryland, College Park, MD
University of Maryland Eastern Shore, MD
University of Mary Washington, VA
University of Massachusetts Amherst, MA
University of Massachusetts Lowell, MA
University of Memphis, TN
University of Miami, FL
University of Michigan, MI
University of Michigan–Flint, MI
University of Mississippi, MS
University of Missouri, MO
University of Missouri–Kansas City, MO
University of Missouri–St. Louis, MO
University of Mobile, AL
The University of Montana, MT
University of Montevallo, AL
University of Mount Union, OH
University of Nebraska at Kearney, NE
University of Nebraska at Omaha, NE
University of Nebraska–Lincoln, NE
University of Nevada, Las Vegas, NV
University of Nevada, Reno, NV
University of New Hampshire, NH
University of New Orleans, LA
University of North Alabama, AL
University of North Carolina at Asheville, NC
The University of North Carolina at Chapel Hill, NC
The University of North Carolina at Charlotte, NC
The University of North Carolina at Greensboro, NC
University of North Carolina School of the Arts, NC
The University of North Carolina Wilmington, NC
University of Northern Colorado, CO
University of Northern Iowa, IA
University of North Florida, FL
University of North Georgia, GA
University of Oklahoma, OK
University of Oregon, OR
University of Portland, OR
University of Puget Sound, WA
University of Redlands, CA
University of Rhode Island, RI

University of Richmond, VA
University of Rio Grande, OH
University of Rochester, NY
University of St. Francis, IL
University of St. Thomas, MN
University of St. Thomas, TX
University of San Diego, CA
University of Science and Arts of Oklahoma, OK
University of South Alabama, AL
University of South Carolina, SC
University of South Carolina Aiken, SC
The University of South Dakota, SD
University of Southern California, CA
University of Southern Maine, ME
University of Southern Mississippi, MS
University of South Florida, FL
The University of Tampa, FL
The University of Tennessee at Chattanooga, TN
The University of Tennessee at Martin, TN
The University of Texas at Arlington, TX
The University of Texas at Brownsville, TX
The University of Texas at El Paso, TX
The University of Texas at San Antonio, TX
The University of Texas–Pan American, TX
University of the Cumberlands, KY
University of the Incarnate Word, TX
University of the Pacific, CA
The University of Toledo, OH
The University of Tulsa, OK
University of Utah, UT
University of Valley Forge, PA
University of Vermont, VT
University of Virginia, VA
The University of Virginia's College at Wise, VA
University of Washington, WA
The University of West Alabama, AL
University of West Florida, FL
University of West Georgia, GA
University of Wisconsin–Eau Claire, WI
University of Wisconsin–Green Bay, WI
University of Wisconsin–La Crosse, WI
University of Wisconsin–Parkside, WI
University of Wisconsin–River Falls, WI
University of Wisconsin–Stevens Point, WI
University of Wisconsin–Stout, WI
University of Wisconsin–Whitewater, WI
University of Wyoming, WY
Utah State University, UT
Valdosta State University, GA
Valley City State University, ND
Valparaiso University, IN
VanderCook College of Music, IL
Vanguard University of Southern California, CA
Virginia Commonwealth University, VA
Virginia Military Institute, VA
Virginia Polytechnic Institute and State University, VA
Virginia State University, VA
Virginia Union University, VA
Virginia Wesleyan College, VA
Wabash College, IN
Wagner College, NY
Waldorf College, IA
Walla Walla University, WA
Warner Pacific College, OR
Wartburg College, IA
Washburn University, KS
Washington College, MD
Washington State University, WA
Wayland Baptist University, TX
Waynesburg University, PA

Wayne State College, NE
Wayne State University, MI
Webber International University, FL
Webster University, MO
Wesleyan College, GA
West Chester University of Pennsylvania, PA
Western Carolina University, NC
Western Illinois University, IL
Western Kentucky University, KY
Western Michigan University, MI
Western New England University, MA
Western Oregon University, OR
Western State Colorado University, CO
Western Washington University, WA
Westminster College, MO
Westminster College, PA
Westmont College, CA
West Texas A&M University, TX
West Virginia University, WV
West Virginia Wesleyan College, WV
Wheaton College, IL
Wheeling Jesuit University, WV
Whitman College, WA
Whittier College, CA
Whitworth University, WA
Wichita State University, KS
Widener University, PA
William Jessup University, CA
William Jewell College, MO
Williams Baptist College, AR
Wilson College, PA
Wingate University, NC
Winona State University, MN
Winthrop University, SC
Wisconsin Lutheran College, WI
Wittenberg University, OH
Wofford College, SC
Wright State University, OH
Xavier University, OH
Xavier University of Louisiana, LA
York College of Pennsylvania, PA
Youngstown State University, OH

**Performing Arts**
Adelphi University, NY
Albertus Magnus College, CT
Albion College, MI
Alderson Broaddus University, WV
Alma College, MI
Anderson University, SC
Angelo State University, TX
Arkansas State University, AR
Auburn University, AL
Augustana College, SD
Austin Peay State University, TN
Ball State University, IN
Belhaven University, MS
Belmont University, TN
Bemidji State University, MN
Binghamton University, State University of New York, NY
Birmingham-Southern College, AL
Bloomfield College, NJ
Bluefield College, VA
Bluffton University, OH
Boise State University, ID
Bowling Green State University, OH
Brenau University, GA
Bucknell University, PA
Buffalo State College, State University of New York, NY
Butler University, IN
California Institute of the Arts, CA
California Lutheran University, CA

California Polytechnic State University, San Luis Obispo, CA
California State University, Chico, CA
California State University, Fullerton, CA
Calvin College, MI
Cameron University, OK
Capital University, OH
Carroll College, MT
Carroll University, WI
Case Western Reserve University, OH
Castleton State College, VT
Cedar Crest College, PA
Centenary College of Louisiana, LA
Central Michigan University, MI
Chapman University, CA
Christian Brothers University, TN
Christopher Newport University, VA
City College of the City University of New York, NY
Clemson University, SC
Cleveland State University, OH
Coastal Carolina University, SC
Coe College, IA
College of Charleston, SC
The College of Idaho, ID
College of Staten Island of the City University of New York, NY
Colorado Mesa University, CO
Columbus State University, GA
Concordia University Ann Arbor, MI
Corban University, OR
Cornell College, IA
Creighton University, NE
Cumberland University, TN
Davidson College, NC
Delta State University, MS
DePaul University, IL
DeSales University, PA
Doane College, NE
Drexel University, PA
East Carolina University, NC
East Central University, OK
Eastern Illinois University, IL
Eastern Michigan University, MI
Eastern New Mexico University, NM
Edgewood College, WI
Elizabeth City State University, NC
Elizabethtown College, PA
Elon University, NC
Emerson College, MA
Emmanuel College, GA
Endicott College, MA
Eureka College, IL
Flagler College, FL
Florida Agricultural and Mechanical University, FL
Florida Atlantic University, FL
Fort Hays State University, KS
Fort Lewis College, CO
Franklin College, IN
Franklin Pierce University, NH
Fresno Pacific University, CA
Friends University, KS
Frostburg State University, MD
Gannon University, PA
Georgetown College, KY
Goucher College, MD
Grambling State University, LA
Greenville College, IL
Hamline University, MN
Hardin-Simmons University, TX
Hastings College, NE
Heidelberg University, OH
Henderson State University, AR
Hobart and William Smith Colleges, NY
Hofstra University, NY

Houghton College, NY
Howard University, DC
Huntingdon College, AL
Idaho State University, ID
Illinois State University, IL
Indiana State University, IN
Indiana University of Pennsylvania, PA
Ithaca College, NY
The Juilliard School, NY
Juniata College, PA
Kalamazoo College, MI
Kean University, NJ
Kennesaw State University, GA
Kent State University, OH
Kent State University at Stark, OH
Kentucky Christian University, KY
Kentucky State University, KY
Kentucky Wesleyan College, KY
King University, TN
Lafayette College, PA
Lake Erie College, OH
Lees-McRae College, NC
Lehigh University, PA
Liberty University, VA
Lincoln University, MO
Lindenwood University, MO
Lock Haven University of Pennsylvania, PA
Long Island University–LIU Brooklyn, NY
Long Island University–LIU Post, NY
Louisiana State University and Agricultural & Mechanical College, LA
Louisiana Tech University, LA
Loyola Marymount University, CA
Lubbock Christian University, TX
Manhattanville College, NY
Marietta College, OH
Marymount Manhattan College, NY
Massachusetts College of Liberal Arts, MA
Metropolitan State University of Denver, CO
Michigan State University, MI
Michigan Technological University, MI
Minot State University, ND
Mississippi State University, MS
Mississippi University for Women, MS
Missouri Valley College, MO
Missouri Western State University, MO
Molloy College, NY
Montclair State University, NJ
Mount Aloysius College, PA
Mount Marty College, SD
Muhlenberg College, PA
New Jersey Institute of Technology, NJ
New Mexico Highlands University, NM
New Mexico State University, NM
Northeastern Illinois University, IL
Northeastern State University, OK
Northern Illinois University, IL
Notre Dame de Namur University, CA
Nova Southeastern University, FL
Nyack College, NY
Oakland University, MI
Oglethorpe University, GA
The Ohio State University, OH
Ohio University, OH
Ohio University–Chillicothe, OH
Ohio University–Eastern, OH
Ohio University–Lancaster, OH
Ohio University–Southern Campus, OH
Ohio University–Zanesville, OH
Ohio Wesleyan University, OH
Oklahoma Baptist University, OK
Oklahoma City University, OK
Old Dominion University, VA
Olivet Nazarene University, IL
Ouachita Baptist University, AR
Pace University, NY

Purchase College, State University of New York, NY
Robert Morris University Illinois, IL
Rockford University, IL
Rockhurst University, MO
Sacred Heart University, CT
St. Andrews University, NC
Saint Augustine's University, NC
St. Bonaventure University, NY
St. Cloud State University, MN
Saint Louis University, MO
Saint Mary's College of California, CA
Saint Michael's College, VT
Samford University, AL
San Diego State University, CA
Santa Fe University of Art and Design, NM
Savannah College of Art and Design, GA
Seattle Pacific University, WA
Seton Hill University, PA
Shawnee State University, OH
Shenandoah University, VA
Shepherd University, WV
Siena College, NY
Slippery Rock University of Pennsylvania, PA
Sonoma State University, CA
South Dakota State University, SD
Southeastern Oklahoma State University, OK
Southeast Missouri State University, MO
Southern Illinois University Carbondale, IL
Southwestern College, KS
State University of New York at Fredonia, NY
State University of New York College at Geneseo, NY
State University of New York College at Potsdam, NY
Stephens College, MO
Stockton University, NJ
Tabor College, KS
Temple University, PA
Texas A&M International University, TX
Texas A&M University, TX
Texas A&M University–Commerce, TX
Texas Christian University, TX
Texas Tech University, TX
Texas Wesleyan University, TX
Tiffin University, OH
Towson University, MD
Trinity Christian College, IL
The University of Akron, OH
The University of Alabama at Birmingham, AL
University of Alaska Anchorage, AK
The University of Arizona, AZ
University of California, Irvine, CA
University of California, San Diego, CA
University of Colorado Boulder, CO
University of Colorado Denver, CO
University of Dubuque, IA
University of Florida, FL
University of Hartford, CT
University of Houston, TX
University of Idaho, ID
University of Illinois at Chicago, IL
The University of Kansas, KS
University of La Verne, CA
University of Maine at Fort Kent, ME
University of Maryland, Baltimore County, MD
University of Maryland, College Park, MD
University of Maryland Eastern Shore, MD
University of Miami, FL
University of Michigan, MI
University of Michigan–Flint, MI

University of Mississippi, MS
University of Missouri–Kansas City, MO
University of Mobile, AL
The University of Montana, MT
University of Nebraska at Omaha, NE
University of Nebraska–Lincoln, NE
University of Nevada, Las Vegas, NV
University of New Hampshire, NH
The University of North Carolina at Charlotte, NC
The University of North Carolina at Greensboro, NC
University of North Carolina School of the Arts, NC
University of Northern Colorado, CO
University of Oklahoma, OK
University of Oregon, OR
University of Portland, OR
University of Richmond, VA
University of Rochester, NY
University of St. Francis, IL
University of St. Thomas, TX
University of South Florida, FL
The University of Tampa, FL
The University of Tennessee at Chattanooga, TN
The University of Texas at Brownsville, TX
The University of Texas at El Paso, TX
The University of Toledo, OH
The University of Tulsa, OK
University of Utah, UT
The University of Virginia's College at Wise, VA
University of Washington, WA
University of West Georgia, GA
University of Wisconsin–Eau Claire, WI
University of Wisconsin–Stevens Point, WI
University of Wyoming, WY
Utah State University, UT
Valdosta State University, GA
Valparaiso University, IN
Virginia Commonwealth University, VA
Virginia Polytechnic Institute and State University, VA
Virginia State University, VA
Wartburg College, IA
Washburn University, KS
Washington College, MD
Washington State University, WA
Wayne State College, NE
Wayne State University, MI
Western Illinois University, IL
Western New Mexico University, NM
Western Oregon University, OR
Western State Colorado University, CO
Western Washington University, WA
West Virginia Wesleyan College, WV
Wichita State University, KS
Wilkes University, PA
William Jessup University, CA
William Peace University, NC
William Woods University, MO
Winthrop University, SC
Wright State University, OH
Xavier University, OH
Youngstown State University, OH

**Theater/Drama**
Abilene Christian University, TX
Adelphi University, NY
Adrian College, MI
Alabama State University, AL
Alaska Pacific University, AK
Albertus Magnus College, CT
Albion College, MI

Albright College, PA
Alderson Broaddus University, WV
Alma College, MI
Anderson University, SC
Angelo State University, TX
Arcadia University, PA
Arizona State University at the Tempe campus, AZ
Arkansas State University, AR
Arkansas Tech University, AR
Ashland University, OH
Auburn University, AL
Augustana College, IL
Augustana College, SD
Austin College, TX
Austin Peay State University, TN
Averett University, VA
Ball State University, IN
Baylor University, TX
Belhaven University, MS
Belmont Abbey College, NC
Berry College, GA
Bethany Lutheran College, MN
Bethel College, KS
Bethel University, MN
Binghamton University, State University of New York, NY
Biola University, CA
Birmingham-Southern College, AL
Bloomfield College, NJ
Bluefield College, VA
Blue Mountain College, MS
Boise State University, ID
Boston University, MA
Bowling Green State University, OH
Bradley University, IL
Brenau University, GA
Brevard College, NC
Brigham Young University, UT
Bucknell University, PA
Buena Vista University, IA
Buffalo State College, State University of New York, NY
Butler University, IN
California Baptist University, CA
California Institute of the Arts, CA
California Lutheran University, CA
California Polytechnic State University, San Luis Obispo, CA
California State University, Bakersfield, CA
California State University, Chico, CA
California State University, Fresno, CA
California State University, Fullerton, CA
California State University, Los Angeles, CA
California State University, San Bernardino, CA
Calumet College of Saint Joseph, IN
Calvin College, MI
Cameron University, OK
Campbellsville University, KY
Campbell University, NC
Cardinal Stritch University, WI
Carroll College, MT
Carroll University, WI
Case Western Reserve University, OH
Castleton State College, VT
Catawba College, NC
The Catholic University of America, DC
Cedar Crest College, PA
Centenary College of Louisiana, LA
Central College, IA
Central Methodist University, MO
Central Michigan University, MI
Central Washington University, WA
Centre College, KY

Chapman University, CA
Christopher Newport University, VA
Clarion University of Pennsylvania, PA
Clarke University, IA
Clemson University, SC
Cleveland State University, OH
Coastal Carolina University, SC
Coe College, IA
Coker College, SC
The College at Brockport, State University of New York, NY
College of Charleston, SC
The College of Idaho, ID
The College of New Rochelle, NY
College of Saint Benedict, MN
College of Staten Island of the City University of New York, NY
The College of William and Mary, VA
The College of Wooster, OH
Colorado Mesa University, CO
Colorado State University, CO
Columbus State University, GA
Concordia College, MN
Concordia University, CA
Concordia University Ann Arbor, MI
Concordia University, Nebraska, NE
Concordia University, St. Paul, MN
Concord University, WV
Converse College, SC
Cornell College, IA
Cornish College of the Arts, WA
Creighton University, NE
Culver-Stockton College, MO
Cumberland University, TN
Dakota Wesleyan University, SD
Davidson College, NC
DePaul University, IL
DeSales University, PA
Dickinson State University, ND
Doane College, NE
Dordt College, IA
Drake University, IA
Drew University, NJ
Drexel University, PA
Drury University, MO
East Central University, OK
Eastern Illinois University, IL
Eastern Michigan University, MI
Eastern New Mexico University, NM
Eastern Washington University, WA
East Stroudsburg University of Pennsylvania, PA
East Texas Baptist University, TX
Eckerd College, FL
Edgewood College, WI
Elizabethtown College, PA
Elmhurst College, IL
Elon University, NC
Emmanuel College, GA
Emory & Henry College, VA
Emory University, GA
Emporia State University, KS
Eureka College, IL
Evangel University, MO
Fairmont State University, WV
Faulkner University, AL
Ferris State University, MI
Five Towns College, NY
Flagler College, FL
Florida Agricultural and Mechanical University, FL
Florida Southern College, FL
Florida State University, FL
Fontbonne University, MO
Fort Hays State University, KS

Fort Lewis College, CO
Francis Marion University, SC
Franklin College, IN
Franklin Pierce University, NH
Fresno Pacific University, CA
Friends University, KS
Frostburg State University, MD
Furman University, SC
Gannon University, PA
Gardner-Webb University, NC
George Fox University, OR
Georgetown College, KY
Georgia Southern University, GA
Georgia Southwestern State University, GA
Gordon College, MA
Goshen College, IN
Goucher College, MD
Graceland University, IA
Grambling State University, LA
Grand Valley State University, MI
Grand View University, IA
Greensboro College, NC
Guilford College, NC
Gustavus Adolphus College, MN
Hamline University, MN
Hanover College, IN
Hardin-Simmons University, TX
Hastings College, NE
Henderson State University, AR
Hendrix College, AR
Hillsdale College, MI
Hillsdale Free Will Baptist College, OK
Hofstra University, NY
Hollins University, VA
Hope College, MI
Howard Payne University, TX
Howard University, DC
Huntington University, IN
Idaho State University, ID
Illinois College, IL
Illinois State University, IL
Illinois Wesleyan University, IL
Indiana State University, IN
Indiana University of Pennsylvania, PA
Indiana University–Purdue University Fort
    Wayne, IN
Iowa State University of Science and
    Technology, IA
Ithaca College, NY
Jacksonville State University, AL
Jacksonville University, FL
James Madison University, VA
John Brown University, AR
The Juilliard School, NY
Juniata College, PA
Kansas Wesleyan University, KS
Kean University, NJ
Keene State College, NH
Kennesaw State University, GA
Kent State University, OH
Kent State University at Stark, OH
Kentucky Christian University, KY
King University, TN
Knox College, IL
Lafayette College, PA
LaGrange College, GA
Lake Erie College, OH
La Sierra University, CA
Lees-McRae College, NC
Lee University, TN
Lehigh University, PA
Lewis-Clark State College, ID
Lewis University, IL
Lincoln University, MO
Lindenwood University, MO
Linfield College, OR

Lipscomb University, TN
Long Island University–LIU Brooklyn, NY
Long Island University–LIU Post, NY
Longwood University, VA
Louisiana State University and Agricultural
    & Mechanical College, LA
Louisiana Tech University, LA
Loyola Marymount University, CA
Loyola University Chicago, IL
Lubbock Christian University, TX
Lycoming College, PA
Lynchburg College, VA
Lyon College, AR
Malone University, OH
Marietta College, OH
Marist College, NY
Marquette University, WI
Maryville College, TN
Massachusetts College of Liberal Arts, MA
Mayville State University, ND
McMurry University, TX
Mercer University, GA
Messiah College, PA
Methodist University, NC
Metropolitan State University of Denver, CO
Miami University, OH
Michigan State University, MI
Michigan Technological University, MI
Middle Tennessee State University, TN
Midwestern State University, TX
Milligan College, TN
Millikin University, IL
Millsaps College, MS
Minnesota State University Moorhead, MN
Minot State University, ND
Mississippi State University, MS
Mississippi University for Women, MS
Missouri Baptist University, MO
Missouri Southern State University, MO
Missouri University of Science and
    Technology, MO
Missouri Valley College, MO
Missouri Western State University, MO
Molloy College, NY
Monmouth College, IL
Montana State University, MT
Montana State University Billings, MT
Montclair State University, NJ
Morehead State University, KY
Morningside College, IA
Mount Marty College, SD
Mount Mercy University, IA
Muhlenberg College, PA
Murray State University, KY
Muskingum University, OH
Nazareth College of Rochester, NY
Newberry College, SC
New England College, NH
New England Conservatory of Music, MA
New Jersey Institute of Technology, NJ
Newman University, KS
New Mexico State University, NM
Niagara University, NY
North Carolina Central University, NC
North Central College, IL
Northeastern Illinois University, IL
Northeastern State University, OK
Northern Arizona University, AZ
Northern Illinois University, IL
Northern Kentucky University, KY
Northern Michigan University, MI
Northern State University, SD
Northwestern Oklahoma State University,
    OK
Northwest Missouri State University, MO
Notre Dame de Namur University, CA

Nyack College, NY
Oglethorpe University, GA
The Ohio State University, OH
Ohio University, OH
Ohio University–Chillicothe, OH
Ohio University–Eastern, OH
Ohio University–Lancaster, OH
Ohio University–Southern Campus, OH
Ohio University–Zanesville, OH
Ohio Wesleyan University, OH
Oklahoma Baptist University, OK
Oklahoma Christian University, OK
Oklahoma City University, OK
Oklahoma State University, OK
Old Dominion University, VA
Olivet Nazarene University, IL
Otterbein University, OH
Ouachita Baptist University, AR
Pace University, NY
Pacific Lutheran University, WA
Pacific University, OR
Palm Beach Atlantic University, FL
Park University, MO
Piedmont College, GA
Plymouth State University, NH
Point Loma Nazarene University, CA
Portland State University, OR
Providence College, RI
Purchase College, State University of New
    York, NY
Queens College of the City University of
    New York, NY
Queens University of Charlotte, NC
Rhode Island College, RI
Rhodes College, TN
Rider University, NJ
Rochester College, MI
Rockford University, IL
Rockhurst University, MO
Rogers State University, OK
Rollins College, FL
Roosevelt University, IL
Sacred Heart University, CT
The Sage Colleges, NY
Saginaw Valley State University, MI
St. Ambrose University, IA
St. Andrews University, NC
St. Cloud State University, MN
St. Edward's University, TX
Saint John's University, MN
Saint Joseph's College, IN
Saint Joseph's University, PA
Saint Louis University, MO
Saint Martin's University, WA
Saint Mary's College of California, CA
Saint Mary's University of Minnesota, MN
Saint Michael's College, VT
St. Norbert College, WI
St. Olaf College, MN
Salisbury University, MD
Samford University, AL
Sam Houston State University, TX
San Diego State University, CA
Santa Clara University, CA
Santa Fe University of Art and Design, NM
Savannah College of Art and Design, GA
Schreiner University, TX
Seattle University, WA
Seton Hill University, PA
Shenandoah University, VA
Shepherd University, WV
Shippensburg University of Pennsylvania,
    PA
Siena College, NY
Simpson College, IA

Slippery Rock University of Pennsylvania, PA
Sonoma State University, CA
South Dakota State University, SD
Southeastern Louisiana University, LA
Southeastern Oklahoma State University, OK
Southeast Missouri State University, MO
Southern Illinois University Carbondale, IL
Southern Illinois University Edwardsville, IL
Southern Oregon University, OR
Southern Utah University, UT
Southwest Baptist University, MO
Southwestern College, KS
Southwestern Oklahoma State University, OK
Southwestern University, TX
State University of New York at Fredonia, NY
State University of New York at New Paltz, NY
State University of New York at Plattsburgh, NY
State University of New York College at Geneseo, NY
State University of New York College at Potsdam, NY
Stephen F. Austin State University, TX
Stephens College, MO
Sterling College, KS
Stetson University, FL
Stockton University, NJ
Sul Ross State University, TX
Susquehanna University, PA
Syracuse University, NY
Tabor College, KS
Tarleton State University, TX
Taylor University, IN
Texas A&M University, TX
Texas A&M University–Commerce, TX
Texas Christian University, TX
Texas Lutheran University, TX
Texas State University, TX
Texas Tech University, TX
Texas Wesleyan University, TX
Texas Woman's University, TX
Thiel College, PA
Thomas More College, KY
Tiffin University, OH
Towson University, MD
Transylvania University, KY
Trinity Christian College, IL
Trinity College of Florida, FL
Trinity University, TX
Troy University, AL
Truman State University, MO
Union College, KY
Union University, TN
The University of Akron, OH
The University of Alabama, AL
The University of Alabama at Birmingham, AL
University of Alaska Fairbanks, AK
The University of Arizona, AZ
University of Arkansas, AR
University of California, Irvine, CA
University of California, Riverside, CA
University of California, Santa Cruz, CA
University of Central Florida, FL
University of Central Oklahoma, OK
University of Colorado Boulder, CO
University of Colorado Denver, CO
University of Connecticut, CT
University of Dallas, TX

University of Delaware, DE
University of Denver, CO
University of Dubuque, IA
University of Evansville, IN
The University of Findlay, OH
University of Florida, FL
University of Hartford, CT
University of Houston, TX
University of Idaho, ID
University of Illinois at Chicago, IL
University of Illinois at Springfield, IL
University of Indianapolis, IN
University of Jamestown, ND
The University of Kansas, KS
University of La Verne, CA
University of Louisville, KY
University of Maine at Farmington, ME
University of Maryland, Baltimore County, MD
University of Maryland, College Park, MD
University of Maryland Eastern Shore, MD
University of Mary Washington, VA
University of Massachusetts Amherst, MA
University of Miami, FL
University of Michigan, MI
University of Michigan–Flint, MI
University of Mississippi, MS
University of Missouri, MO
University of Missouri–St. Louis, MO
The University of Montana, MT
University of Montevallo, AL
University of Mount Union, OH
University of Nebraska at Omaha, NE
University of Nebraska–Lincoln, NE
University of Nevada, Las Vegas, NV
University of Nevada, Reno, NV
University of New Hampshire, NH
University of New Orleans, LA
University of North Carolina at Asheville, NC
The University of North Carolina at Chapel Hill, NC
The University of North Carolina at Greensboro, NC
University of North Carolina School of the Arts, NC
The University of North Carolina Wilmington, NC
University of Northern Colorado, CO
University of Northern Iowa, IA
University of Oklahoma, OK
University of Oregon, OR
University of Pittsburgh at Johnstown, PA
University of Portland, OR
University of Puget Sound, WA
University of Rhode Island, RI
University of Richmond, VA
University of St. Thomas, TX
University of Science and Arts of Oklahoma, OK
University of South Alabama, AL
University of South Carolina, SC
University of South Carolina Aiken, SC
The University of South Dakota, SD
University of Southern California, CA
University of Southern Indiana, IN
University of Southern Maine, ME
University of Southern Mississippi, MS
University of South Florida, FL
The University of Tampa, FL
The University of Tennessee at Chattanooga, TN
The University of Tennessee at Martin, TN
The University of Texas at Arlington, TX
The University of Texas at El Paso, TX

The University of Texas–Pan American, TX
University of the Incarnate Word, TX
The University of Toledo, OH
The University of Tulsa, OK
University of Utah, UT
University of Vermont, VT
The University of Virginia's College at Wise, VA
The University of West Alabama, AL
University of West Florida, FL
University of West Georgia, GA
University of Wisconsin–Eau Claire, WI
University of Wisconsin–Green Bay, WI
University of Wisconsin–La Crosse, WI
University of Wisconsin–Parkside, WI
University of Wisconsin–River Falls, WI
University of Wisconsin–Stevens Point, WI
University of Wisconsin–Whitewater, WI
University of Wyoming, WY
Utah State University, UT
Valdosta State University, GA
Valley City State University, ND
Valparaiso University, IN
Vanguard University of Southern California, CA
Virginia Commonwealth University, VA
Virginia Polytechnic Institute and State University, VA
Virginia Wesleyan College, VA
Wabash College, IN
Wagner College, NY
Waldorf College, IA
Walla Walla University, WA
Warner Pacific College, OR
Wartburg College, IA
Washburn University, KS
Washington College, MD
Washington State University, WA
Wayland Baptist University, TX
Waynesburg University, PA
Wayne State College, NE
Wayne State University, MI
Webster University, MO
Wesleyan College, GA
West Chester University of Pennsylvania, PA
Western Carolina University, NC
Western Illinois University, IL
Western Kentucky University, KY
Western Michigan University, MI
Western Oregon University, OR
Western Washington University, WA
Westminster College, PA
Westmont College, CA
West Texas A&M University, TX
West Virginia University, WV
West Virginia Wesleyan College, WV
Whitman College, WA
Whittier College, CA
Whitworth University, WA
Wichita State University, KS
Wilkes University, PA
William Jessup University, CA
William Jewell College, MO
Williams Baptist College, AR
William Woods University, MO
Wingate University, NC
Winona State University, MN
Winthrop University, SC
Wisconsin Lutheran College, WI
Wittenberg University, OH
Wright State University, OH
Xavier University, OH
Youngstown State University, OH

# Special Achievements/Activities

**Cheerleading/Drum Major**

Abilene Christian University, TX
Anderson University, SC
Angelo State University, TX
Arkansas State University, AR
Ashland University, OH
Auburn University, AL
Augustana College, SD
Belhaven University, MS
Bellarmine University, KY
Belmont University, TN
Bethel College, KS
Bluefield College, VA
Bluefield State College, WV
Boise State University, ID
Brenau University, GA
Brevard College, NC
California Baptist University, CA
Cameron University, OK
Campbellsville University, KY
Campbell University, NC
Carroll College, MT
Central Methodist University, MO
Cleveland State University, OH
Coastal Carolina University, SC
Coker College, SC
Columbus State University, GA
Concordia University, Nebraska, NE
Culver-Stockton College, MO
Dakota Wesleyan University, SD
Delta State University, MS
Dickinson State University, ND
Drexel University, PA
Drury University, MO
East Central University, OK
Eastern Kentucky University, KY
Emmanuel College, GA
Evangel University, MO
Fairmont State University, WV
Faulkner University, AL
Florida Agricultural and Mechanical
    University, FL
Fort Hays State University, KS
Francis Marion University, SC
Friends University, KS
Gardner-Webb University, NC
Georgia Institute of Technology, GA
Georgia Southern University, GA
Glenville State College, WV
Graceland University, IA
Grambling State University, LA
Grand View University, IA
Harding University, AR
Hastings College, NE
Hawai`i Pacific University, HI
Henderson State University, AR
Hofstra University, NY
Houston Baptist University, TX
Howard University, DC
Huntingdon College, AL
Huntington University, IN
Idaho State University, ID
James Madison University, VA
Kansas Wesleyan University, KS
Kentucky Christian University, KY
Kentucky State University, KY
Langston University, OK
Lawrence Technological University, MI
Lees-McRae College, NC
Lee University, TN
Lenoir-Rhyne University, NC
Lewis University, IL
Liberty University, VA
Lincoln Memorial University, TN

Lincoln University, MO
Lindenwood University, MO
Lindsey Wilson College, KY
Lipscomb University, TN
Long Island University–LIU Brooklyn, NY
Louisiana Tech University, LA
Lubbock Christian University, TX
Lyon College, AR
Malone University, OH
Maryville University of Saint Louis, MO
McKendree University, IL
Methodist University, NC
Middle Tennessee State University, TN
Midwestern State University, TX
Milligan College, TN
Mississippi State University, MS
Missouri Baptist University, MO
Missouri Southern State University, MO
Missouri Valley College, MO
Missouri Western State University, MO
Montana State University Billings, MT
Morehead State University, KY
Morningside College, IA
Newberry College, SC
New Mexico State University, NM
Nicholls State University, LA
Northeastern State University, OK
Northern Kentucky University, KY
Northern Michigan University, MI
Northwestern Oklahoma State University,
    OK
Northwest Missouri State University, MO
Nyack College, NY
The Ohio State University, OH
Oklahoma Baptist University, OK
Oklahoma Christian University, OK
Oklahoma City University, OK
Oklahoma State University, OK
Old Dominion University, VA
Olivet Nazarene University, IL
Oral Roberts University, OK
Ouachita Baptist University, AR
Quincy University, IL
Robert Morris University Illinois, IL
Rocky Mountain College, MT
Rogers State University, OK
St. Ambrose University, IA
St. Edward's University, TX
Saint Francis University, PA
St. John's University, NY
Saint Joseph's College, IN
Saint Louis University, MO
Samford University, AL
Sam Houston State University, TX
San Diego State University, CA
Seton Hill University, PA
Southeastern Louisiana University, LA
Southeastern Oklahoma State University,
    OK
Southeast Missouri State University, MO
Southern Illinois University Carbondale, IL
Southwestern College, KS
Southwestern Oklahoma State University,
    OK
Stephen F. Austin State University, TX
Sterling College, KS
Stetson University, FL
Tabor College, KS
Temple University, PA
Tennessee Technological University, TN
Tennessee Wesleyan College, TN
Texas A&M University–Commerce, TX
Texas Wesleyan University, TX
Tiffin University, OH
Trine University, IN
Tusculum College, TN

Union College, KY
Union University, TN
The University of Alabama, AL
The University of Alabama at Birmingham,
    AL
The University of Alabama in Huntsville,
    AL
University of Arkansas, AR
University of Delaware, DE
University of Great Falls, MT
University of Houston, TX
University of Idaho, ID
University of Louisville, KY
University of Mary Hardin-Baylor, TX
University of Maryland, College Park, MD
University of Massachusetts Amherst, MA
University of Memphis, TN
University of Miami, FL
University of Mississippi, MS
University of Missouri, MO
University of Missouri–St. Louis, MO
The University of Montana, MT
University of Nebraska at Kearney, NE
University of Nebraska–Lincoln, NE
University of Nevada, Las Vegas, NV
University of North Alabama, AL
The University of North Carolina
    Wilmington, NC
University of North Georgia, GA
University of Rio Grande, OH
University of St. Francis, IL
University of Science and Arts of Oklahoma,
    OK
University of South Carolina, SC
University of South Carolina Aiken, SC
University of Southern Mississippi, MS
The University of Tennessee at Chattanooga,
    TN
The University of Tennessee at Martin, TN
The University of Texas at Arlington, TX
The University of Texas at El Paso, TX
The University of Texas at San Antonio, TX
The University of Texas–Pan American, TX
University of the Cumberlands, KY
The University of Toledo, OH
The University of Tulsa, OK
University of Utah, UT
The University of West Alabama, AL
University of Wyoming, WY
Virginia Polytechnic Institute and State
    University, VA
Virginia State University, VA
Waldorf College, IA
Washburn University, KS
Wayland Baptist University, TX
Webber International University, FL
West Texas A&M University, TX
West Virginia University Institute of
    Technology, WV
Wichita State University, KS
William Jewell College, MO
Williams Baptist College, AR
Wright State University, OH
Youngstown State University, OH

**Community Service**

Adelphi University, NY
Agnes Scott College, GA
Alaska Pacific University, AK
Albertus Magnus College, CT
Allen College, IA
Alliant International University–San Diego,
    CA
Alvernia University, PA
Alverno College, WI
Arcadia University, PA

Arizona Christian University, AZ
Arkansas State University, AR
Armstrong State University, GA
Augustana College, SD
Austin College, TX
Ball State University, IN
Baylor University, TX
Bellarmine University, KY
Beloit College, WI
Benedictine University, IL
Bentley University, MA
Berry College, GA
Bethany College, WV
Bethel University, MN
Binghamton University, State University of
New York, NY
Biola University, CA
Bloomfield College, NJ
Boise State University, ID
Bradley University, IL
Brenau University, GA
Brevard College, NC
Caldwell University, NJ
California Lutheran University, CA
California Polytechnic State University, San
Luis Obispo, CA
California State University, Bakersfield, CA
California State University, Chico, CA
California State University, Fresno, CA
California State University, Los Angeles, CA
California State University, San Bernardino,
CA
California State University, Stanislaus, CA
Calvin College, MI
Castleton State College, VT
Cedar Crest College, PA
Centenary College of Louisiana, LA
Central College, IA
Centre College, KY
Chaminade University of Honolulu, HI
Christopher Newport University, VA
The Citadel, The Military College of South
Carolina, SC
City College of the City University of New
York, NY
Clark University, MA
Clemson University, SC
Coe College, IA
Colby-Sawyer College, NH
The College at Brockport, State University
of New York, NY
The College of New Rochelle, NY
College of Saint Elizabeth, NJ
College of Saint Mary, NE
The College of Saint Rose, NY
College of Staten Island of the City
University of New York, NY
The College of Wooster, OH
Colorado State University–Pueblo, CO
Columbia College, MO
Columbus State University, GA
Concord University, WV
Creighton University, NE
Dallas Baptist University, TX
Davidson College, NC
DePaul University, IL
DePauw University, IN
DeSales University, PA
Dordt College, IA
Eastern New Mexico University, NM
Eastern University, PA
ECPI University, VA
Edgewood College, WI
Elon University, NC
Emmanuel College, MA

Endicott College, MA
Eureka College, IL
Florida Agricultural and Mechanical
University, FL
Florida Gulf Coast University, FL
Florida Southern College, FL
Fontbonne University, MO
Frostburg State University, MD
Furman University, SC
Gannon University, PA
Georgia Southern University, GA
Golden Gate University, CA
Goshen College, IN
Grand View University, IA
Greensboro College, NC
Hamline University, MN
Hampshire College, MA
Hawai`i Pacific University, HI
Hendrix College, AR
Hillsdale College, MI
Hobart and William Smith Colleges, NY
Hollins University, VA
Houghton College, NY
Houston Baptist University, TX
Howard Payne University, TX
Huntingdon College, AL
Illinois Institute of Technology, IL
Illinois State University, IL
Indiana University of Pennsylvania, PA
Iona College, NY
Iowa State University of Science and
Technology, IA
John Carroll University, OH
John Paul the Great Catholic University, CA
Juniata College, PA
Kennesaw State University, GA
Kent State University, OH
Kent State University at Stark, OH
Kentucky Christian University, KY
Keuka College, NY
King's College, PA
Knox College, IL
Kutztown University of Pennsylvania, PA
Lake Erie College, OH
La Salle University, PA
Lasell College, MA
Lawrence University, WI
Lewis & Clark College, OR
Lewis-Clark State College, ID
Lewis University, IL
Lindenwood University, MO
Linfield College, OR
Lipscomb University, TN
Lock Haven University of Pennsylvania, PA
Longwood University, VA
Loyola Marymount University, CA
Loyola University Chicago, IL
Lycoming College, PA
Manhattan College, NY
Manhattanville College, NY
Marymount University, VA
Maryville College, TN
Maryville University of Saint Louis, MO
Marywood University, PA
McKendree University, IL
Mercer University, GA
Mercy College of Health Sciences, IA
Mercyhurst University, PA
Meredith College, NC
Michigan State University, MI
Millersville University of Pennsylvania, PA
Milligan College, TN
Millikin University, IL
Millsaps College, MS
Minnesota State University Moorhead, MN

Misericordia University, PA
Missouri Valley College, MO
Missouri Western State University, MO
Molloy College, NY
Montana Tech of The University of
Montana, MT
Montclair State University, NJ
Morehead State University, KY
Morningside College, IA
Mount Carmel College of Nursing, OH
Mount Marty College, SD
Mount St. Joseph University, OH
Mount Saint Mary's University, CA
Muskingum University, OH
New England College, NH
New Jersey Institute of Technology, NJ
Newman University, KS
Niagara University, NY
Nichols College, MA
North Central College, IL
Northeastern State University, OK
Northern Kentucky University, KY
Northwest Christian University, OR
Notre Dame de Namur University, CA
Notre Dame of Maryland University, MD
Nyack College, NY
Oglethorpe University, GA
Oklahoma State University, OK
Old Dominion University, VA
Olivet College, MI
Oral Roberts University, OK
Otterbein University, OH
Pace University, NY
Pacific University, OR
Patrick Henry College, VA
Piedmont College, GA
Pitzer College, CA
Portland State University, OR
Principia College, IL
Providence College, RI
Queens University of Charlotte, NC
Quincy University, IL
Randolph College, VA
Ringling College of Art and Design, FL
Robert Morris University Illinois, IL
Rochester Institute of Technology, NY
Rockford University, IL
Rockhurst University, MO
Rosemont College, PA
Sacred Heart University, CT
The Sage Colleges, NY
Saginaw Valley State University, MI
St. Andrews University, NC
St. Catherine University, MN
St. Cloud State University, MN
St. Edward's University, TX
St. John Fisher College, NY
St. John's University, NY
St. Joseph's College, Long Island Campus,
NY
St. Joseph's College, New York, NY
Saint Joseph's University, PA
St. Lawrence University, NY
St. Louis College of Pharmacy, MO
Saint Louis University, MO
Saint Martin's University, WA
St. Olaf College, MN
St. Thomas Aquinas College, NY
Schreiner University, TX
Shippensburg University of Pennsylvania,
PA
Siena College, NY
Simmons College, MA
Simpson College, IA
Simpson University, CA

Slippery Rock University of Pennsylvania, PA
Sonoma State University, CA
South Dakota State University, SD
Southern Illinois University Carbondale, IL
Southern Oregon University, OR
Southwestern College, KS
Spring Hill College, AL
State University of New York at Plattsburgh, NY
State University of New York College at Cortland, NY
State University of New York College at Geneseo, NY
State University of New York College at Potsdam, NY
State University of New York College of Environmental Science and Forestry, NY
State University of New York College of Technology at Delhi, NY
Stetson University, FL
Stockton University, NJ
Stony Brook University, State University of New York, NY
Suffolk University, MA
Texas A&M University, TX
Texas Tech University, TX
Texas Wesleyan University, TX
Thomas More College, KY
Towson University, MD
Trinity Christian College, IL
Trinity College of Florida, FL
Tulane University, LA
Tusculum College, TN
Union College, KY
Union College, NE
Union University, TN
Unity College, ME
The University of Akron, OH
The University of Alabama, AL
The University of Alabama in Huntsville, AL
University of Alaska Fairbanks, AK
University of Arkansas, AR
University of California, Irvine, CA
University of California, San Diego, CA
University of Charleston, WV
University of Chicago, IL
University of Colorado Boulder, CO
University of Connecticut, CT
University of Delaware, DE
University of Denver, CO
University of Florida, FL
University of Hartford, CT
University of Houston, TX
University of Houston–Clear Lake, TX
University of Houston–Downtown, TX
University of Illinois at Springfield, IL
University of Indianapolis, IN
University of Jamestown, ND
The University of Kansas, KS
University of La Verne, CA
University of Louisville, KY
University of Maine at Presque Isle, ME
University of Mary Hardin-Baylor, TX
University of Massachusetts Dartmouth, MA
University of Massachusetts Lowell, MA
University of Michigan, MI
University of Michigan–Dearborn, MI
University of Michigan–Flint, MI
University of Mississippi, MS
University of Missouri–St. Louis, MO
University of Nebraska–Lincoln, NE
University of Nevada, Las Vegas, NV
University of New Hampshire, NH
University of New Orleans, LA

University of North Carolina at Asheville, NC
The University of North Carolina at Chapel Hill, NC
The University of North Carolina at Greensboro, NC
University of North Florida, FL
University of North Georgia, GA
University of Puget Sound, WA
University of Richmond, VA
University of St. Francis, IL
University of South Carolina, SC
University of South Carolina Aiken, SC
University of Southern Maine, ME
The University of Tennessee at Chattanooga, TN
The University of Texas at Arlington, TX
The University of Texas–Pan American, TX
University of the Cumberlands, KY
The University of Toledo, OH
The University of Tulsa, OK
University of Valley Forge, PA
University of Vermont, VT
The University of Virginia's College at Wise, VA
University of West Georgia, GA
University of Wisconsin–Eau Claire, WI
University of Wisconsin–Green Bay, WI
University of Wisconsin–La Crosse, WI
University of Wisconsin–Parkside, WI
University of Wisconsin–Stout, WI
Ursuline College, OH
Vanderbilt University, TN
Virginia Polytechnic Institute and State University, VA
Virginia State University, VA
Virginia Wesleyan College, VA
Wabash College, IN
Warren Wilson College, NC
Washburn University, KS
Washington State University, WA
Waynesburg University, PA
Webb Institute, NY
Webster University, MO
Wesleyan College, GA
Western Illinois University, IL
Western Oregon University, OR
Western Washington University, WA
West Texas A&M University, TX
West Virginia Wesleyan College, WV
Wheeling Jesuit University, WV
Widener University, PA
William Peace University, NC
Wilson College, PA
Wittenberg University, OH
Wright State University, OH
Youngstown State University, OH

### Hobbies/Interests

Angelo State University, TX
Arkansas Tech University, AR
Bethany College, WV
California State Polytechnic University, Pomona, CA
California State University, Chico, CA
California State University, San Bernardino, CA
Capital University, OH
Centenary College of Louisiana, LA
The College at Brockport, State University of New York, NY
The College of New Rochelle, NY
College of Staten Island of the City University of New York, NY
Colorado Mesa University, CO
Corban University, OR

Eastern Nazarene College, MA
Eastern New Mexico University, NM
Emmanuel College, GA
Florida Institute of Technology, FL
Hawai'i Pacific University, HI
Hollins University, VA
Houghton College, NY
Illinois Institute of Technology, IL
Indiana University of Pennsylvania, PA
Lake Erie College, OH
Michigan State University, MI
Millsaps College, MS
Missouri Valley College, MO
Missouri Western State University, MO
Montana Tech of The University of Montana, MT
New Jersey Institute of Technology, NJ
New Mexico State University, NM
The Ohio State University, OH
Quincy University, IL
Sacred Heart University, CT
St. John's University, NY
Saint Martin's University, WA
San Diego State University, CA
Siena College, NY
South Dakota State University, SD
Southern Oregon University, OR
State University of New York College at Cortland, NY
Stephen F. Austin State University, TX
Texas Tech University, TX
Union College, KY
The University of Alabama, AL
University of Houston, TX
University of Louisville, KY
University of Michigan–Flint, MI
University of Minnesota, Twin Cities Campus, MN
University of South Alabama, AL
The University of Toledo, OH
University of Wisconsin–Eau Claire, WI
Virginia State University, VA
West Texas A&M University, TX

### Junior Miss

Arkansas Tech University, AR
Belhaven University, MS
Bethel University, MN
Birmingham-Southern College, AL
Bluefield State College, WV
Campbellsville University, KY
Carroll University, WI
Cedar Crest College, PA
Concordia University Texas, TX
Georgetown College, KY
Georgia Southern University, GA
Goshen College, IN
Grambling State University, LA
Grand View University, IA
Gustavus Adolphus College, MN
Huntingdon College, AL
Kansas Wesleyan University, KS
Kentucky Wesleyan College, KY
Lawrence Technological University, MI
Lewis-Clark State College, ID
Lindenwood University, MO
Lindsey Wilson College, KY
Louisiana Tech University, LA
McDaniel College, MD
Mississippi State University, MS
Mississippi University for Women, MS
Missouri Valley College, MO
Morehead State University, KY
Muskingum University, OH
New Mexico State University, NM
Northeastern State University, OK

Oklahoma City University, OK
Roberts Wesleyan College, NY
South Dakota State University, SD
Spring Arbor University, MI
Stetson University, FL
Tennessee Wesleyan College, TN
Texas A&M University–Commerce, TX
Texas Lutheran University, TX
The University of Alabama, AL
The University of Alabama at Birmingham, AL
The University of Alabama in Huntsville, AL
University of Central Oklahoma, OK
University of Idaho, ID
University of Louisville, KY
University of Mississippi, MS
University of Montevallo, AL
University of North Carolina at Asheville, NC
The University of North Carolina at Greensboro, NC
University of South Alabama, AL
University of the District of Columbia, DC
The University of West Alabama, AL
University of Wyoming, WY
Waldorf College, IA
Wartburg College, IA
Washington State University, WA

**Leadership**

Abilene Christian University, TX
Adelphi University, NY
Agnes Scott College, GA
Alabama State University, AL
Alaska Pacific University, AK
Albertus Magnus College, CT
Alcorn State University, MS
Alderson Broaddus University, WV
Allen College, IA
Alliant International University–San Diego, CA
Alvernia University, PA
American Jewish University, CA
American University, DC
Anderson University, IN
Anderson University, SC
Andrews University, MI
Angelo State University, TX
Arcadia University, PA
Arizona Christian University, AZ
Arizona State University at the Downtown Phoenix campus, AZ
Arizona State University at the Polytechnic campus, AZ
Arizona State University at the Tempe campus, AZ
Arizona State University at the West campus, AZ
Arkansas State University, AR
Arkansas Tech University, AR
Ashland University, OH
Auburn University, AL
Augustana College, IL
Augustana College, SD
Austin College, TX
Austin Peay State University, TN
Ave Maria University, FL
Averett University, VA
Azusa Pacific University, CA
Babson College, MA
Baldwin Wallace University, OH
Ball State University, IN
Barclay College, KS
Bard College, NY

Baylor University, TX
Becker College, MA
Belhaven University, MS
Bellarmine University, KY
Belmont University, TN
Beloit College, WI
Bemidji State University, MN
Benedictine University, IL
Berry College, GA
Bethany College, WV
Bethel University, MN
Binghamton University, State University of New York, NY
Biola University, CA
Birmingham-Southern College, AL
Bloomfield College, NJ
Bluefield State College, WV
Blue Mountain College, MS
Bluffton University, OH
Boise State University, ID
Boston Architectural College, MA
Bowdoin College, ME
Bowling Green State University, OH
Bradley University, IL
Brenau University, GA
Brevard College, NC
Brigham Young University, UT
Bryn Mawr College, PA
Bucknell University, PA
Buena Vista University, IA
California Lutheran University, CA
California Polytechnic State University, San Luis Obispo, CA
California State Polytechnic University, Pomona, CA
California State University, Bakersfield, CA
California State University, Chico, CA
California State University, Fresno, CA
California State University, Fullerton, CA
California State University, Monterey Bay, CA
California State University, San Marcos, CA
California State University, Stanislaus, CA
Calumet College of Saint Joseph, IN
Calvin College, MI
Cameron University, OK
Campbellsville University, KY
Capital University, OH
Carnegie Mellon University, PA
Carroll College, MT
Carroll University, WI
Carson-Newman University, TN
Case Western Reserve University, OH
Catawba College, NC
Cedar Crest College, PA
Cedarville University, OH
Central Methodist University, MO
Central Michigan University, MI
Central Washington University, WA
Champlain College, VT
Chatham University, PA
Chowan University, NC
Christian Brothers University, TN
Christopher Newport University, VA
Cincinnati Christian University, OH
The Citadel, The Military College of South Carolina, SC
City College of the City University of New York, NY
Claremont McKenna College, CA
Clarion University of Pennsylvania, PA
Clarke University, IA
Clarkson University, NY
Clemson University, SC
Coker College, SC

Colby-Sawyer College, NH
The College at Brockport, State University of New York, NY
The College of Idaho, ID
College of Mount Saint Vincent, NY
The College of New Rochelle, NY
College of Saint Elizabeth, NJ
College of Saint Mary, NE
College of Staten Island of the City University of New York, NY
Colorado Mesa University, CO
Colorado State University–Pueblo, CO
Columbia College, MO
Columbia International University, SC
Columbus State University, GA
Concordia University Texas, TX
Concord University, WV
Corban University, OR
Covenant College, GA
Creighton University, NE
Culver-Stockton College, MO
Cumberland University, TN
Dallas Baptist University, TX
Davidson College, NC
Delta State University, MS
DePaul University, IL
Dickinson State University, ND
Dordt College, IA
Drury University, MO
Duke University, NC
Eastern Illinois University, IL
Eastern Michigan University, MI
Eastern Nazarene College, MA
Eastern New Mexico University, NM
Eastern University, PA
East Stroudsburg University of Pennsylvania, PA
East Texas Baptist University, TX
Elmira College, NY
Elon University, NC
Embry-Riddle Aeronautical University–Daytona, FL
Emmanuel College, GA
Emmanuel College, MA
Emmaus Bible College, IA
Emory University, GA
Emporia State University, KS
Endicott College, MA
Eureka College, IL
Evangel University, MO
Fairmont State University, WV
Faulkner University, AL
Flagler College, FL
Florida Agricultural and Mechanical University, FL
Florida Gulf Coast University, FL
Florida Institute of Technology, FL
Florida Southern College, FL
Fontbonne University, MO
Fort Hays State University, KS
Fort Lewis College, CO
Franklin Pierce University, NH
Friends University, KS
Frostburg State University, MD
Furman University, SC
Gallaudet University, DC
Gannon University, PA
George Fox University, OR
Georgetown College, KY
Georgia Institute of Technology, GA
Georgia Southern University, GA
Georgia Southwestern State University, GA
Golden Gate University, CA
Gonzaga University, WA
Gordon College, MA

Graceland University, IA
Grambling State University, LA
Greensboro College, NC
Greenville College, IL
Grove City College, PA
Hamline University, MN
Hampden-Sydney College, VA
Hampshire College, MA
Hampton University, VA
Harding University, AR
Hawai`i Pacific University, HI
Henderson State University, AR
Hendrix College, AR
Hilbert College, NY
Hillsdale College, MI
Hobart and William Smith Colleges, NY
Hofstra University, NY
Hollins University, VA
Hood College, MD
Hope International University, CA
Houghton College, NY
Houston Baptist University, TX
Howard Payne University, TX
Howard University, DC
Husson University, ME
Illinois Institute of Technology, IL
Illinois State University, IL
Indiana University of Pennsylvania, PA
Indiana University–Purdue University Fort
    Wayne, IN
Iowa State University of Science and
    Technology, IA
Ithaca College, NY
Jackson State University, MS
Jacksonville State University, AL
Jacksonville University, FL
James Madison University, VA
John Carroll University, OH
John Paul the Great Catholic University, CA
Juniata College, PA
Kalamazoo College, MI
Keene State College, NH
Kennesaw State University, GA
Kent State University, OH
Kentucky Christian University, KY
Kentucky Wesleyan College, KY
Keuka College, NY
King's College, PA
Kutztown University of Pennsylvania, PA
LaGrange College, GA
Lancaster Bible College, PA
Langston University, OK
Lasell College, MA
La Sierra University, CA
Lee University, TN
Le Moyne College, NY
Lenoir-Rhyne University, NC
Lewis & Clark College, OR
Lewis-Clark State College, ID
Lewis University, IL
Liberty University, VA
Life University, GA
LIM College, NY
Lindenwood University, MO
Lindsey Wilson College, KY
Linfield College, OR
Lipscomb University, TN
Lock Haven University of Pennsylvania, PA
Long Island University–LIU Brooklyn, NY
Long Island University–LIU Post, NY
Longwood University, VA
Loyola Marymount University, CA
Loyola University Chicago, IL
Loyola University New Orleans, LA
Lubbock Christian University, TX
Lycoming College, PA

Lynn University, FL
MacMurray College, IL
Malone University, OH
Manchester University, IN
Manhattan College, NY
Manhattanville College, NY
Mansfield University of Pennsylvania, PA
Marlboro College, VT
Mary Baldwin College, VA
Marymount Manhattan College, NY
Marymount University, VA
Maryville College, TN
Maryville University of Saint Louis, MO
Marywood University, PA
Massachusetts College of Liberal Arts, MA
Massachusetts Maritime Academy, MA
The Master's College and Seminary, CA
McDaniel College, MD
McKendree University, IL
Mercer University, GA
Mercyhurst University, PA
Meredith College, NC
Merrimack College, MA
Messiah College, PA
Methodist University, NC
Metropolitan State University of Denver, CO
Miami University, OH
Michigan State University, MI
Middle Tennessee State University, TN
Midwestern State University, TX
Millsaps College, MS
Mills College, CA
Minnesota State University Mankato, MN
Misericordia University, PA
Mississippi College, MS
Mississippi State University, MS
Mississippi University for Women, MS
Missouri Southern State University, MO
Missouri State University, MO
Missouri Valley College, MO
Missouri Western State University, MO
Molloy College, NY
Monmouth University, NJ
Montana State University, MT
Montana Tech of The University of
    Montana, MT
Montclair State University, NJ
Montreat College, NC
Moravian College, PA
Morehead State University, KY
Morningside College, IA
Morrisville State College, NY
Mount Aloysius College, PA
Mount Marty College, SD
Mount Mary University, WI
Mount Mercy University, IA
Mount St. Joseph University, OH
Mount Saint Mary College, NY
Mount Saint Mary's University, CA
Muskingum University, OH
National University, CA
New England College, NH
New Jersey Institute of Technology, NJ
Newman University, KS
New Mexico State University, NM
Nicholls State University, LA
Nichols College, MA
North Carolina Central University, NC
North Carolina State University, NC
Northeastern Illinois University, IL
Northeastern State University, OK
Northern Arizona University, AZ
Northern Illinois University, IL
Northern Kentucky University, KY
Northern Michigan University, MI
Northern State University, SD

Northland College, WI
Northwest Christian University, OR
Northwestern Oklahoma State University,
    OK
Northwest Missouri State University, MO
Northwest Nazarene University, ID
Northwest University, WA
Notre Dame de Namur University, CA
Notre Dame of Maryland University, MD
Nova Southeastern University, FL
Nyack College, NY
Occidental College, CA
The Ohio State University, OH
Ohio Wesleyan University, OH
Oklahoma Baptist University, OK
Oklahoma City University, OK
Oklahoma State University, OK
Oklahoma Wesleyan University, OK
Old Dominion University, VA
Olivet College, MI
Oral Roberts University, OK
Oregon Institute of Technology, OR
Oregon State University, OR
Otterbein University, OH
Pace University, NY
Pacific Lutheran University, WA
Palm Beach Atlantic University, FL
Patrick Henry College, VA
Peirce College, PA
Piedmont College, GA
Pine Manor College, MA
Pitzer College, CA
Portland State University, OR
Presbyterian College, SC
Prescott College, AZ
Principia College, IL
Purdue University, IN
Queens University of Charlotte, NC
Quincy University, IL
Randolph College, VA
Regent University, VA
Regis University, CO
Reinhardt University, GA
Rice University, TX
Robert Morris University Illinois, IL
Rochester College, MI
Rochester Institute of Technology, NY
Rockford University, IL
Rockhurst University, MO
Rogers State University, OK
Rosemont College, PA
Sacred Heart University, CT
The Sage Colleges, NY
Saginaw Valley State University, MI
St. Ambrose University, IA
St. Andrews University, NC
St. Catherine University, MN
St. Cloud State University, MN
St. Edward's University, TX
Saint Francis University, PA
St. John's University, NY
St. Joseph's College, Long Island Campus,
    NY
St. Joseph's College, New York, NY
St. Lawrence University, NY
St. Louis College of Pharmacy, MO
Saint Louis University, MO
Saint Martin's University, WA
Saint Mary's College of California, CA
Saint Mary's University of Minnesota, MN
St. Thomas Aquinas College, NY
St. Thomas University, FL
Salem College, NC
Samford University, AL
Sam Houston State University, TX
San Diego State University, CA

San Jose State University, CA
Schreiner University, TX
Seattle University, WA
Shepherd University, WV
Shippensburg University of Pennsylvania, PA
Siena College, NY
Simpson College, IA
Simpson University, CA
Slippery Rock University of Pennsylvania, PA
Sonoma State University, CA
South Dakota State University, SD
Southeastern Louisiana University, LA
Southeastern Oklahoma State University, OK
Southeast Missouri State University, MO
Southern Illinois University Carbondale, IL
Southern Oregon University, OR
Southern Utah University, UT
Southwestern College, KS
Southwestern Oklahoma State University, OK
Southwestern University, TX
State University of New York at Fredonia, NY
State University of New York at Plattsburgh, NY
State University of New York College at Cortland, NY
State University of New York College at Geneseo, NY
State University of New York College at Potsdam, NY
State University of New York College of Agriculture and Technology at Cobleskill, NY
State University of New York College of Environmental Science and Forestry, NY
State University of New York Maritime College, NY
Stephen F. Austin State University, TX
Stephens College, MO
Stetson University, FL
Stockton University, NJ
Stony Brook University, State University of New York, NY
Suffolk University, MA
Sul Ross State University, TX
Susquehanna University, PA
Taylor University, IN
Texas A&M University, TX
Texas A&M University–Commerce, TX
Texas Christian University, TX
Texas Lutheran University, TX
Texas State University, TX
Texas Tech University, TX
Texas Wesleyan University, TX
Thiel College, PA
Thomas More College, KY
Trinity Christian College, IL
Trinity College, CT
Trinity College of Florida, FL
Troy University, AL
Truett-McConnell College, GA
Truman State University, MO
Tusculum College, TN
Union College, KY
Union College, NE
Union University, TN
Unity College, ME
The University of Akron, OH
The University of Alabama at Birmingham, AL

The University of Alabama in Huntsville, AL
University of Alaska Anchorage, AK
University of Arkansas, AR
University of California, Irvine, CA
University of California, San Diego, CA
University of California, Santa Cruz, CA
University of Central Florida, FL
University of Central Oklahoma, OK
University of Charleston, WV
University of Chicago, IL
University of Colorado Boulder, CO
University of Colorado Colorado Springs, CO
University of Connecticut, CT
University of Dayton, OH
University of Delaware, DE
University of Denver, CO
University of Evansville, IN
University of Florida, FL
University of Houston, TX
University of Houston–Clear Lake, TX
University of Houston–Downtown, TX
University of Idaho, ID
University of Illinois at Springfield, IL
The University of Iowa, IA
University of Jamestown, ND
The University of Kansas, KS
University of La Verne, CA
University of Louisville, KY
University of Maine, ME
University of Maine at Augusta, ME
University of Maine at Farmington, ME
University of Mary Hardin Baylor, TX
University of Mary Washington, VA
University of Massachusetts Amherst, MA
University of Massachusetts Boston, MA
University of Memphis, TN
University of Miami, FL
University of Michigan, MI
University of Michigan–Dearborn, MI
University of Michigan–Flint, MI
University of Minnesota, Crookston, MN
University of Minnesota, Twin Cities Campus, MN
University of Mississippi, MS
University of Missouri–Kansas City, MO
The University of Montana, MT
University of Montevallo, AL
University of Mount Olive, NC
University of Nebraska at Kearney, NE
University of Nebraska at Omaha, NE
University of Nebraska–Lincoln, NE
University of Nevada, Las Vegas, NV
University of New England, ME
University of New Hampshire, NH
University of New Orleans, LA
University of North Alabama, AL
University of North Carolina at Asheville, NC
The University of North Carolina at Chapel Hill, NC
The University of North Carolina at Greensboro, NC
The University of North Carolina Wilmington, NC
University of Northern Iowa, IA
University of North Florida, FL
University of North Georgia, GA
University of Oklahoma, OK
University of Pittsburgh at Johnstown, PA
University of Puget Sound, WA
University of Rochester, NY
University of St. Francis, IL
University of St. Thomas, TX

University of San Diego, CA
University of South Alabama, AL
University of South Carolina, SC
University of South Carolina Aiken, SC
The University of South Dakota, SD
University of Southern California, CA
University of Southern Indiana, IN
University of Southern Mississippi, MS
The University of Tampa, FL
The University of Tennessee at Martin, TN
The University of Texas at Arlington, TX
The University of Texas at Austin, TX
The University of Texas at Dallas, TX
The University of Texas at El Paso, TX
The University of Texas–Pan American, TX
University of the Cumberlands, KY
University of the Incarnate Word, TX
University of the Pacific, CA
The University of Toledo, OH
The University of Tulsa, OK
University of Utah, UT
University of Valley Forge, PA
University of Vermont, VT
University of Washington, WA
The University of West Alabama, AL
University of West Florida, FL
University of West Georgia, GA
University of Wisconsin–Eau Claire, WI
University of Wisconsin–Green Bay, WI
University of Wisconsin–La Crosse, WI
University of Wisconsin–Oshkosh, WI
University of Wisconsin–Parkside, WI
University of Wisconsin–River Falls, WI
University of Wisconsin–Stevens Point, WI
University of Wisconsin–Stout, WI
University of Wisconsin–Whitewater, WI
University of Wyoming, WY
Ursinus College, PA
Ursuline College, OH
Utah State University, UT
Vanderbilt University, TN
Virginia Military Institute, VA
Virginia Polytechnic Institute and State University, VA
Virginia State University, VA
Virginia Wesleyan College, VA
Wabash College, IN
Wake Forest University, NC
Waldorf College, IA
Walla Walla University, WA
Warner Pacific College, OR
Warren Wilson College, NC
Wartburg College, IA
Washburn University, KS
Washington State University, WA
Wayland Baptist University, TX
Wayne State College, NE
Wayne State University, MI
Webber International University, FL
Webb Institute, NY
Webster University, MO
Wells College, NY
Wesleyan College, GA
West Chester University of Pennsylvania, PA
Western Illinois University, IL
Western Kentucky University, KY
Western Oregon University, OR
Western State Colorado University, CO
Western Washington University, WA
Westminster College, MO
Westmont College, CA
West Texas A&M University, TX
West Virginia University, WV
West Virginia Wesleyan College, WV

Wichita State University, KS
Widener University, PA
Wilkes University, PA
William Jessup University, CA
William Peace University, NC
William Woods University, MO
Wilson College, PA
Wisconsin Lutheran College, WI
Wittenberg University, OH
Wofford College, SC
Worcester Polytechnic Institute, MA
Wright State University, OH
Youngstown State University, OH

**Memberships**

Adelphi University, NY
Albright College, PA
Alvernia University, PA
American University, DC
Anderson University, SC
Angelo State University, TX
Arcadia University, PA
Arkansas Tech University, AR
Auburn University, AL
Austin Peay State University, TN
Averett University, VA
Benedictine University, IL
Birmingham-Southern College, AL
Blue Mountain College, MS
Boston University, MA
California State University, Chico, CA
California State University, San Bernardino, CA
California State University, Stanislaus, CA
Carroll University, WI
Carson-Newman University, TN
Cedar Crest College, PA
Chaminade University of Honolulu, HI
Charlotte Christian College and Theological Seminary, NC
Christian Brothers University, TN
City Vision University, MO
Clarion University of Pennsylvania, PA
The College of New Rochelle, NY
Corban University, OR
Dallas Baptist University, TX
Delta State University, MS
Eastern Michigan University, MI
Eastern New Mexico University, NM
Eastern University, PA
Emmanuel College, GA
Emporia State University, KS
Ferris State University, MI
Flagler College, FL
Florida Institute of Technology, FL
Georgia Southern University, GA
Gonzaga University, WA
Grand View University, IA
Greenville College, IL
Grove City College, PA
Hamline University, MN
Hastings College, NE
Hawai`i Pacific University, HI
Houghton College, NY
Howard University, DC
Illinois Institute of Technology, IL
Kennesaw State University, GA
Lewis University, IL
LIM College, NY
Lock Haven University of Pennsylvania, PA
Longwood University, VA
Loyola Marymount University, CA
Loyola University Chicago, IL
MacMurray College, IL
Marymount University, VA
Massachusetts College of Liberal Arts, MA

Michigan State University, MI
Mississippi State University, MS
Missouri Baptist University, MO
Molloy College, NY
Montana Tech of The University of Montana, MT
Morrisville State College, NY
Murray State University, KY
Newman University, KS
New Mexico State University, NM
Northern Michigan University, MI
Northwestern Oklahoma State University, OK
Northwest Missouri State University, MO
Notre Dame of Maryland University, MD
Nova Southeastern University, FL
The Ohio State University, OH
Oklahoma State University, OK
Old Dominion University, VA
Olivet College, MI
Oral Roberts University, OK
Pace University, NY
Pacific University, OR
Patrick Henry College, VA
Peirce College, PA
Portland State University, OR
Quincy University, IL
Regent University, VA
Sacred Heart University, CT
St. Catherine University, MN
Saint Louis University, MO
Saint Mary's College of California, CA
San Diego State University, CA
Schreiner University, TX
Shawnee State University, OH
Siena College, NY
Sonoma State University, CA
South Dakota State University, SD
Southeastern Louisiana University, LA
Southeast Missouri State University, MO
Southern Oregon University, OR
Southwestern College, KS
State University of New York College at Geneseo, NY
State University of New York College of Environmental Science and Forestry, NY
Stephens College, MO
Tennessee Wesleyan College, TN
Texas A&M University, TX
Texas Christian University, TX
Texas Lutheran University, TX
Texas Tech University, TX
Texas Wesleyan University, TX
Thomas More College, KY
Towson University, MD
Union College, KY
Union University, TN
The University of Akron, OH
The University of Alabama at Birmingham, AL
University of Evansville, IN
University of Louisville, KY
University of Michigan–Dearborn, MI
University of Mississippi, MS
University of Missouri, MO
University of Missouri–St. Louis, MO
University of Nebraska at Omaha, NE
University of South Carolina, SC
The University of Tampa, FL
The University of Tennessee at Chattanooga, TN
The University of Texas–Pan American, TX
The University of Toledo, OH
University of Vermont, VT
University of Washington, WA
The University of West Alabama, AL

University of West Georgia, GA
University of Wisconsin–Eau Claire, WI
University of Wisconsin–La Crosse, WI
University of Wisconsin–Stout, WI
Virginia Polytechnic Institute and State University, VA
Warner Pacific College, OR
Washington State University, WA
Wayland Baptist University, TX
Webber International University, FL
Wesleyan College, GA
Western Kentucky University, KY
Western Washington University, WA
West Texas A&M University, TX
Wichita State University, KS
Wright State University, OH
Youngstown State University, OH

**Religious Involvement**

Adrian College, MI
Alaska Bible College, AK
Alaska Pacific University, AK
Albright College, PA
Alma College, MI
Alvernia University, PA
Amridge University, AL
Andrews University, MI
Anna Maria College, MA
Ashland University, OH
Augustana College, SD
Austin College, TX
Averett University, VA
Baylor University, TX
Bellarmine University, KY
Belmont University, TN
Berry College, GA
Bethany College, WV
Bethel University, MN
Birmingham-Southern College, AL
Blue Mountain College, MS
Brigham Young University, UT
Caldwell University, NJ
California Lutheran University, CA
Calvary Bible College and Theological Seminary, MO
Calvin College, MI
Campbellsville University, KY
Campbell University, NC
Canisius College, NY
Capital University, OH
Carroll College, MT
Carroll University, WI
Cedar Crest College, PA
Centenary College of Louisiana, LA
Central College, IA
Central Methodist University, MO
Chaminade University of Honolulu, HI
Charlotte Christian College and Theological Seminary, NC
Cincinnati Christian University, OH
The Citadel, The Military College of South Carolina, SC
The College at Brockport, State University of New York, NY
The College of New Rochelle, NY
College of Saint Mary, NE
The College of Wooster, OH
Columbia College, MO
Columbia International University, SC
Concordia University Texas, TX
Corban University, OR
The Criswell College, TX
Crossroads Bible College, IN
Dallas Baptist University, TX
Davidson College, NC
Drury University, MO

Earlham College, IN
Eastern Michigan University, MI
Eastern Nazarene College, MA
East Texas Baptist University, TX
Elizabethtown College, PA
Elon University, NC
Emmanuel College, GA
Emmaus Bible College, IA
Endicott College, MA
Eureka College, IL
Evangel University, MO
Faulkner University, AL
Flagler College, FL
Franciscan University of Steubenville, OH
Friends University, KS
Furman University, SC
Gardner-Webb University, NC
George Fox University, OR
Georgetown College, KY
Georgia Southern University, GA
Graceland University, IA
Grand View University, IA
Greensboro College, NC
Greenville College, IL
Grove City College, PA
Guilford College, NC
Harding University, AR
Hawai`i Pacific University, HI
Hendrix College, AR
Heritage Christian University, AL
Hillsdale Free Will Baptist College, OK
Houghton College, NY
Houston Baptist University, TX
Howard Payne University, TX
Howard University, DC
Huntington University, IN
John Paul the Great Catholic University, CA
Kentucky Christian University, KY
Kutztown University of Pennsylvania, PA
Lancaster Bible College, PA
Lee University, TN
Lewis University, IL
Lindsey Wilson College, KY
Lipscomb University, TN
Loyola Marymount University, CA
MacMurray College, IL
Malone University, OH
Maryville University of Saint Louis, MO
Mercyhurst University, PA
Methodist University, NC
Mid-Atlantic Christian University, NC
Millsaps College, MS
Mississippi College, MS
Missouri Baptist University, MO
Missouri Western State University, MO
Molloy College, NY
Monmouth College, IL
Moravian College, PA
Mount Marty College, SD
Mount St. Mary's University, MD
Newberry College, SC
New Jersey Institute of Technology, NJ
Newman University, KS
North Central College, IL
Northwest Christian University, OR
Northwest Nazarene University, ID
Northwest University, WA
Notre Dame of Maryland University, MD
Nyack College, NY
Oglethorpe University, GA
Oklahoma Baptist University, OK
Oklahoma City University, OK
Oklahoma Wesleyan University, OK
Olivet Nazarene University, IL
Oral Roberts University, OK

Pacific University, OR
Patrick Henry College, VA
Piedmont College, GA
Presbyterian College, SC
Principia College, IL
Queens University of Charlotte, NC
Randolph-Macon College, VA
Rosemont College, PA
Sacred Heart University, CT
Saint Francis University, PA
St. John's University, NY
Saint Louis University, MO
Saint Martin's University, WA
St. Olaf College, MN
Saint Xavier University, IL
Schreiner University, TX
Shenandoah University, VA
Siena College, NY
Simpson College, IA
Simpson University, CA
Southwest Baptist University, MO
Southwestern College, KS
Sterling College, KS
Stetson University, FL
Tabor College, KS
Tennessee Wesleyan College, TN
Texas Christian University, TX
Texas Lutheran University, TX
Texas Wesleyan University, TX
Thomas More College, KY
Trinity Christian College, IL
Trinity College of Florida, FL
Truett-McConnell College, GA
Union College, KY
Union College, NE
Union University, TN
The University of Alabama at Birmingham, AL
University of Great Falls, MT
University of Indianapolis, IN
University of Mary Hardin-Baylor, TX
University of Mobile, AL
The University of North Carolina at Charlotte, NC
The University of North Carolina at Greensboro, NC
University of Puget Sound, WA
University of St. Francis, IL
University of St. Thomas, TX
University of San Diego, CA
University of South Carolina, SC
The University of Tennessee at Chattanooga, TN
University of the Cumberlands, KY
University of the Incarnate Word, TX
University of the Pacific, CA
The University of Toledo, OH
University of Valley Forge, PA
The University of Virginia's College at Wise, VA
University of West Georgia, GA
University of Wisconsin–Stout, WI
Valdosta State University, GA
Virginia Polytechnic Institute and State University, VA
Virginia State University, VA
Virginia Wesleyan College, VA
Washington State University, WA
Wayland Baptist University, TX
Wesleyan College, GA
West Virginia Wesleyan College, WV
William Jessup University, CA
William Jewell College, MO
Youngstown State University, OH

### Rodeo

Angelo State University, TX
Boise State University, ID
California Polytechnic State University, San Luis Obispo, CA
Dickinson State University, ND
Eastern New Mexico University, NM
Fort Hays State University, KS
Hastings College, NE
Lewis-Clark State College, ID
Michigan State University, MI
Missouri Valley College, MO
Murray State University, KY
New Mexico State University, NM
Northwestern Oklahoma State University, OK
Oklahoma State University, OK
Sam Houston State University, TX
South Dakota State University, SD
Southeastern Oklahoma State University, OK
Southwestern Oklahoma State University, OK
Stephen F. Austin State University, TX
Texas A&M University, TX
Texas A&M University–Commerce, TX
Texas Tech University, TX
University of Idaho, ID
The University of Montana, MT
The University of Montana Western, MT
University of Nevada, Las Vegas, NV
The University of Tennessee at Martin, TN
The University of West Alabama, AL
University of Wyoming, WY
Washington State University, WA
West Texas A&M University, TX

## Special Characteristics

### Adult Students

Adelphi University, NY
Agnes Scott College, GA
Alaska Pacific University, AK
Allegheny College, PA
American University, DC
Anderson University, IN
Arkansas State University, AR
Augustana College, SD
Averett University, VA
Ball State University, IN
Bay Path University, MA
Bellarmine University, KY
Berry College, GA
Binghamton University, State University of New York, NY
Birmingham-Southern College, AL
Bloomfield College, NJ
Bluefield College, VA
California Baptist University, CA
California Lutheran University, CA
California State University, Chico, CA
Calvin College, MI
Campbellsville University, KY
Carroll University, WI
Cedar Crest College, PA
Christian Brothers University, TN
Coe College, IA
College of Saint Elizabeth, NJ
The College of Saint Rose, NY
College of Staten Island of the City University of New York, NY
Colorado Mesa University, CO
Colorado State University–Pueblo, CO
Columbia College, MO

Concordia University Texas, TX
Dowling College, NY
East Carolina University, NC
Eastern Washington University, WA
East Stroudsburg University of
    Pennsylvania, PA
ECPI University, VA
Elon University, NC
Emmanuel College, GA
Evangel University, MO
The Evergreen State College, WA
Fairmont State University, WV
Faulkner University, AL
Ferris State University, MI
Florida Gulf Coast University, FL
Fordham University, NY
Fort Hays State University, KS
Fort Lewis College, CO
Francis Marion University, SC
Franklin Pierce University, NH
Frostburg State University, MD
Gannon University, PA
Georgia College & State University, GA
Georgia Southern University, GA
Golden Gate University, CA
Grand Valley State University, MI
Grand View University, IA
Greensboro College, NC
Hampton University, VA
Hastings College, NE
Hollins University, VA
Houghton College, NY
Howard University, DC
Indiana University of Pennsylvania, PA
Iowa State University of Science and
    Technology, IA
Kent State University, OH
Kent State University at Stark, OH
Kentucky State University, KY
Lancaster Bible College, PA
La Sierra University, CA
Lincoln University, MO
Lipscomb University, TN
Lock Haven University of Pennsylvania, PA
Long Island University–LIU Post, NY
Loyola Marymount University, CA
Loyola University Chicago, IL
Maryville University of Saint Louis, MO
Mercer University, GA
Meredith College, NC
Messiah College, PA
Metropolitan State University of Denver, CO
Middle Tennessee State University, TN
Millsaps College, MS
Minnesota State University Moorhead, MN
Mississippi State University, MS
Mississippi University for Women, MS
Missouri Baptist University, MO
Missouri Western State University, MO
Monmouth University, NJ
Montana State University Billings, MT
Moravian College, PA
Morehead State University, KY
Mount St. Joseph University, OH
Murray State University, KY
New Jersey Institute of Technology, NJ
New Mexico State University, NM
North Central College, IL
Northeastern Illinois University, IL
Northern Illinois University, IL
Northern Kentucky University, KY
Northern State University, SD
Oakland University, MI
The Ohio State University, OH
Oklahoma Baptist University, OK
Oklahoma State University, OK

Palm Beach Atlantic University, FL
Piedmont College, GA
Portland State University, OR
Queens University of Charlotte, NC
Quincy University, IL
Randolph College, VA
Regis University, CO
Robert Morris University Illinois, IL
Rochester College, MI
Rogers State University, OK
Sacred Heart University, CT
The Sage Colleges, NY
Saginaw Valley State University, MI
St. Ambrose University, IA
St. Catherine University, MN
St. Edward's University, TX
Saint Francis University, PA
Salisbury University, MD
San Diego State University, CA
Siena College, NY
Simpson College, IA
Sonoma State University, CA
South Dakota School of Mines and
    Technology, SD
South Dakota State University, SD
Southeastern Louisiana University, LA
Southern Oregon University, OR
Spring Arbor University, MI
State University of New York College at
    Cortland, NY
State University of New York College at
    Geneseo, NY
State University of New York College at
    Potsdam, NY
Stephen F. Austin State University, TX
Stockton University, NJ
Texas A&M University–Commerce, TX
Texas Christian University, TX
Texas Wesleyan University, TX
Thomas More College, KY
Towson University, MD
Trinity Christian College, IL
Tusculum College, TN
Union College, KY
The University of Akron, OH
The University of Alabama at Birmingham,
    AL
University of Arkansas, AR
University of Connecticut, CT
University of Hartford, CT
University of Idaho, ID
The University of Kansas, KS
University of Louisville, KY
University of Maine at Fort Kent, ME
University of Maryland, College Park, MD
University of Maryland Eastern Shore, MD
University of Mary Washington, VA
University of Massachusetts Boston, MA
University of Massachusetts Dartmouth, MA
University of Memphis, TN
University of Michigan–Dearborn, MI
University of Michigan–Flint, MI
University of Mississippi, MS
University of Missouri, MO
University of Missouri–St. Louis, MO
University of Nebraska at Omaha, NE
University of Nevada, Las Vegas, NV
University of Nevada, Reno, NV
University of New Orleans, LA
University of North Carolina at Asheville,
    NC
The University of North Carolina at
    Greensboro, NC
University of Northern Colorado, CO
University of Pittsburgh at Bradford, PA
University of St. Francis, IL

University of South Carolina, SC
University of South Carolina Aiken, SC
The University of Tennessee at Martin, TN
The University of Texas at Dallas, TX
The University of Toledo, OH
University of Vermont, VT
University of West Georgia, GA
University of Wisconsin–Eau Claire, WI
University of Wisconsin–Green Bay, WI
University of Wisconsin–La Crosse, WI
University of Wisconsin–Parkside, WI
University of Wisconsin–Stevens Point, WI
University of Wisconsin–Stout, WI
University of Wisconsin–Whitewater, WI
University of Wyoming, WY
Washburn University, KS
Wesleyan College, GA
Western Kentucky University, KY
Western Oregon University, OR
Wichita State University, KS
Widener University, PA
William Jessup University, CA
Wilson College, PA
Wisconsin Lutheran College, WI
Wittenberg University, OH
Wright State University, OH
Youngstown State University, OH

**Children and Siblings of Alumni**
Adelphi University, NY
Adrian College, MI
Alaska Pacific University, AK
Albany College of Pharmacy and Health
    Sciences, NY
Albany State University, GA
Albion College, MI
Albright College, PA
Alliant International University–San Diego,
    CA
Alma College, MI
Alvernia University, PA
American University, DC
Aquinas College, MI
Arcadia University, PA
Arkansas State University, AR
Ashland University, OH
Auburn University, AL
Augustana College, IL
Augustana College, SD
Averett University, VA
Baldwin Wallace University, OH
Barclay College, KS
Bellarmine University, KY
Belmont University, TN
Bemidji State University, MN
Benedictine University, IL
Berklee College of Music, MA
Bethany College, WV
Bethel College, KS
Bethel University, MN
Binghamton University, State University of
    New York, NY
Birmingham-Southern College, AL
Bloomfield College, NJ
Blue Mountain College, MS
Bluffton University, OH
Boston University, MA
Bowling Green State University, OH
Bradley University, IL
Cabrini College, PA
California Lutheran University, CA
California Polytechnic State University, San
    Luis Obispo, CA
California State Polytechnic University,
    Pomona, CA

California State University, Monterey Bay, CA
Calumet College of Saint Joseph, IN
Calvary Bible College and Theological Seminary, MO
Calvin College, MI
Canisius College, NY
Capital University, OH
Cardinal Stritch University, WI
Carroll University, WI
Carson-Newman University, TN
Castleton State College, VT
The Catholic University of America, DC
Cedar Crest College, PA
Centenary College of Louisiana, LA
Central College, IA
Central Methodist University, MO
Central Michigan University, MI
Central Washington University, WA
Centre College, KY
Chapman University, CA
Chatham University, PA
Christian Brothers University, TN
Christopher Newport University, VA
The Citadel, The Military College of South Carolina, SC
City College of the City University of New York, NY
Clarion University of Pennsylvania, PA
Clarke University, IA
Clarkson University, NY
Coe College, IA
Coker College, SC
The College at Brockport, State University of New York, NY
The College of Idaho, ID
College of Mount Saint Vincent, NY
The College of New Rochelle, NY
College of Saint Benedict, MN
College of Saint Elizabeth, NJ
The College of Saint Rose, NY
The College of St. Scholastica, MN
College of Staten Island of the City University of New York, NY
Colorado State University–Pueblo, CO
Columbia College, MO
Columbia International University, SC
Concordia University Ann Arbor, MI
Concordia University Chicago, IL
Concordia University, Nebraska, NE
Concordia University Texas, TX
Converse College, SC
Corban University, OR
Cornell College, IA
The Criswell College, TX
Culver-Stockton College, MO
Curry College, MA
Delaware Valley University, PA
Delta State University, MS
DePauw University, IN
Dickinson College, PA
Doane College, NE
Dominican University, IL
Dordt College, IA
Dowling College, NY
Drake University, IA
Drexel University, PA
Drury University, MO
Duke University, NC
Duquesne University, PA
D'Youville College, NY
East Carolina University, NC
Eastern Kentucky University, KY
Eastern Michigan University, MI
Eastern Nazarene College, MA

Eastern New Mexico University, NM
Eastern University, PA
Eastern Washington University, WA
East Stroudsburg University of Pennsylvania, PA
East Texas Baptist University, TX
ECPI University, VA
Elmhurst College, IL
Emmanuel College, MA
Emmaus Bible College, IA
Emporia State University, KS
Endicott College, MA
Eureka College, IL
Evangel University, MO
Fairfield University, CT
Fairmont State University, WV
Faulkner University, AL
Ferris State University, MI
Florida Institute of Technology, FL
Florida Southern College, FL
Fordham University, NY
Fort Hays State University, KS
Fort Lewis College, CO
Francis Marion University, SC
Franklin College, IN
Franklin Pierce University, NH
Friends University, KS
George Fox University, OR
Georgetown College, KY
Georgia Southern University, GA
Georgia Southwestern State University, GA
Golden Gate University, CA
Gonzaga University, WA
Gordon College, MA
Graceland University, IA
Grambling State University, LA
Grand Valley State University, MI
Grand View University, IA
Greensboro College, NC
Greenville College, IL
Gustavus Adolphus College, MN
Gwynedd Mercy University, PA
Hamline University, MN
Hanover College, IN
Hardin-Simmons University, TX
Hartwick College, NY
Hastings College, NE
Henderson State University, AR
Hilbert College, NY
Hillsdale Free Will Baptist College, OK
Hobart and William Smith Colleges, NY
Hofstra University, NY
Hollins University, VA
Hood College, MD
Houghton College, NY
Howard Payne University, TX
Huntingdon College, AL
Illinois Institute of Technology, IL
Indiana State University, IN
Indiana University–Purdue University Fort Wayne, IN
Iona College, NY
Iowa State University of Science and Technology, IA
Iowa Wesleyan College, IA
Ithaca College, NY
Jackson State University, MS
Jacksonville State University, AL
James Madison University, VA
Kalamazoo College, MI
Kansas Wesleyan University, KS
Keene State College, NH
Kennesaw State University, GA
Kent State University, OH
Kent State University at Stark, OH

Kentucky Christian University, KY
Kentucky Wesleyan College, KY
Keuka College, NY
Keystone College, PA
King's College, PA
Lancaster Bible College, PA
Lasell College, MA
Lawrence University, WI
Lebanon Valley College, PA
Le Moyne College, NY
Lenoir-Rhyne University, NC
Lewis-Clark State College, ID
Lewis University, IL
Life University, GA
Lincoln Memorial University, TN
Lincoln University, PA
Lindenwood University, MO
Lindsey Wilson College, KY
Long Island University–LIU Brooklyn, NY
Long Island University–LIU Post, NY
Longwood University, VA
Louisiana Tech University, LA
Loyola Marymount University, CA
Loyola University New Orleans, LA
Luther College, IA
Lynn University, FL
MacMurray College, IL
Malone University, OH
Manchester University, IN
Mansfield University of Pennsylvania, PA
Maranatha Baptist University, WI
Marietta College, OH
Marshall University, WV
Maryville College, TN
Massachusetts Maritime Academy, MA
The Master's College and Seminary, CA
McKendree University, IL
Mercyhurst University, PA
Merrimack College, MA
Methodist University, NC
Michigan State University, MI
Michigan Technological University, MI
Mid-Atlantic Christian University, NC
Middle Tennessee State University, TN
Midwestern State University, TX
Millikin University, IL
Minot State University, ND
Misericordia University, PA
Mississippi College, MS
Mississippi State University, MS
Mississippi University for Women, MS
Missouri Baptist University, MO
Missouri State University, MO
Missouri University of Science and Technology, MO
Missouri Valley College, MO
Missouri Western State University, MO
Monmouth University, NJ
Montana State University, MT
Montana State University Billings, MT
Montana Tech of The University of Montana, MT
Montclair State University, NJ
Moravian College, PA
Morehead State University, KY
Morningside College, IA
Mount St. Joseph University, OH
Mount Saint Mary's University, CA
Muskingum University, OH
Nazareth College of Rochester, NY
Newberry College, SC
New England College, NH
Newman University, KS
New Mexico State University, NM
New York Institute of Technology, NY

Nichols College, MA
North Carolina Central University, NC
North Carolina State University, NC
Northeastern State University, OK
Northern Arizona University, AZ
Northern Kentucky University, KY
Northland College, WI
Northwest Missouri State University, MO
Northwest Nazarene University, ID
Notre Dame de Namur University, CA
Nyack College, NY
The Ohio State University, OH
Ohio University, OH
Ohio University–Chillicothe, OH
Ohio University–Lancaster, OH
Ohio University–Southern Campus, OH
Ohio University–Zanesville, OH
Ohio Wesleyan University, OH
Oklahoma Baptist University, OK
Oklahoma State University, OK
Oklahoma Wesleyan University, OK
Olivet College, MI
Oral Roberts University, OK
Oregon State University, OR
Otterbein University, OH
Ouachita Baptist University, AR
Pace University, NY
Pacific Lutheran University, WA
Pacific University, OR
Palm Beach Atlantic University, FL
Peirce College, PA
Penn State Abington, PA
Penn State Altoona, PA
Penn State Beaver, PA
Penn State Berks, PA
Penn State Brandywine, PA
Penn State Erie, The Behrend College, PA
Penn State Harrisburg, PA
Penn State Hazleton, PA
Penn State New Kensington, PA
Penn State York, PA
Pine Manor College, MA
Pittsburg State University, KS
Post University, CT
Principia College, IL
Quincy University, IL
Randolph-Macon College, VA
Regent University, VA
Rensselaer Polytechnic Institute, NY
Rhode Island College, RI
Roberts Wesleyan College, NY
Rochester College, MI
Rockford University, IL
Rosemont College, PA
Sacred Heart University, CT
The Sage Colleges, NY
St. Ambrose University, IA
St. Catherine University, MN
Saint Francis University, PA
St. John Fisher College, NY
Saint Joseph's College, IN
St. Joseph's College, Long Island Campus, NY
St. Joseph's College, New York, NY
Saint Joseph's University, PA
St. Lawrence University, NY
Saint Martin's University, WA
Saint Mary's College of California, CA
Saint Mary's University of Minnesota, MN
Saint Vincent College, PA
Salisbury University, MD
Salve Regina University, RI
San Diego State University, CA
Santa Clara University, CA
Seattle Pacific University, WA
Seattle University, WA

Seton Hill University, PA
Shimer College, IL
Shippensburg University of Pennsylvania, PA
Siena College, NY
Simmons College, MA
Simpson College, IA
Slippery Rock University of Pennsylvania, PA
Sonoma State University, CA
Southeastern Louisiana University, LA
Southeastern Oklahoma State University, OK
Southern Illinois University Carbondale, IL
Southern Utah University, UT
Southwestern Oklahoma State University, OK
State University of New York at Fredonia, NY
State University of New York College at Potsdam, NY
State University of New York College of Agriculture and Technology at Cobleskill, NY
State University of New York College of Environmental Science and Forestry, NY
Stephen F. Austin State University, TX
Sterling College, KS
Stetson University, FL
Suffolk University, MA
Sul Ross State University, TX
Susquehanna University, PA
Tabor College, KS
Taylor University, IN
Tennessee Technological University, TN
Tennessee Wesleyan College, TN
Texas A&M University–Commerce, TX
Texas Lutheran University, TX
Texas State University, TX
Texas Wesleyan University, TX
Thiel College, PA
Thomas More College, KY
Thomas University, GA
Towson University, MD
Trine University, IN
Trinity Christian College, IL
Trinity University, TX
Truman State University, MO
Union College, KY
Union University, TN
The University of Alabama at Birmingham, AL
University of Alaska Anchorage, AK
University of Arkansas, AR
University of Dayton, OH
University of Delaware, DE
University of Dubuque, IA
University of Evansville, IN
University of Great Falls, MT
University of Houston, TX
University of Idaho, ID
University of Illinois at Springfield, IL
The University of Iowa, IA
University of Jamestown, ND
The University of Kansas, KS
University of Louisville, KY
University of Maine, ME
University of Mary Hardin-Baylor, TX
University of Mary Washington, VA
University of Massachusetts Amherst, MA
University of Massachusetts Lowell, MA
University of Michigan–Dearborn, MI
University of Michigan–Flint, MI
University of Minnesota, Crookston, MN
University of Mississippi, MS
University of Missouri, MO

University of Missouri–Kansas City, MO
University of Missouri–St. Louis, MO
The University of Montana, MT
University of Mount Union, OH
University of Nebraska at Kearney, NE
University of Nebraska at Omaha, NE
University of Nebraska–Lincoln, NE
University of Nevada, Las Vegas, NV
University of Nevada, Reno, NV
University of New England, ME
University of New Hampshire, NH
University of New Orleans, LA
University of North Alabama, AL
University of North Carolina at Asheville, NC
The University of North Carolina at Greensboro, NC
The University of North Carolina at Pembroke, NC
University of Oklahoma, OK
University of Rhode Island, RI
University of Rio Grande, OH
University of Rochester, NY
University of St. Francis, IL
University of South Alabama, AL
University of South Carolina, SC
University of Southern California, CA
University of Southern Mississippi, MS
The University of Tampa, FL
The University of Tennessee at Chattanooga, TN
The University of Tennessee at Martin, TN
University of the Cumberlands, KY
University of the Incarnate Word, TX
The University of Toledo, OH
The University of Tulsa, OK
The University of West Alabama, AL
University of West Florida, FL
University of West Georgia, GA
University of Wisconsin–La Crosse, WI
University of Wyoming, WY
Upper Iowa University, IA
Ursinus College, PA
Ursuline College, OH
Utah State University, UT
Valley City State University, ND
Valparaiso University, IN
Virginia Military Institute, VA
Wake Forest University, NC
Warner Pacific College, OR
Wartburg College, IA
Washburn University, KS
Washington & Jefferson College, PA
Washington State University, WA
Wayland Baptist University, TX
Webber International University, FL
Webster University, MO
Wells College, NY
Wesleyan College, GA
Western Michigan University, MI
Western State Colorado University, CO
Westminster College, MO
Westminster College, PA
West Texas A&M University, TX
West Virginia Wesleyan College, WV
Wheaton College, IL
Wheeling Jesuit University, WV
Whittier College, CA
Whitworth University, WA
William Jewell College, MO
William Peace University, NC
William Woods University, MO
Wilson College, PA
Wingate University, NC
Winona State University, MN
Wittenberg University, OH

Wright State University, OH
Xavier University, OH
York College of Pennsylvania, PA
Youngstown State University, OH

### Children of Current Students

Alliant International University–San Diego, CA
Augustana College, SD
Barclay College, KS
Bethel College, KS
Bloomfield College, NJ
Blue Mountain College, MS
Caldwell University, NJ
California State Polytechnic University, Pomona, CA
Cardinal Stritch University, WI
Carroll University, WI
Central College, IA
College of Staten Island of the City University of New York, NY
Colorado State University–Pueblo, CO
Columbia College, MO
Curry College, MA
ECPI University, VA
Elmhurst College, IL
Emmanuel College, GA
Franklin Pierce University, NH
Hodges University, FL
Indiana Tech, IN
Lancaster Bible College, PA
Marymount University, VA
Misericordia University, PA
Missouri Baptist University, MO
Mount Aloysius College, PA
Mount Marty College, SD
Newman University, KS
New Mexico State University, NM
Northwest University, WA
Palm Beach Atlantic University, FL
Queens University of Charlotte, NC
Rockford University, IL
Sacred Heart University, CT
St. Catherine University, MN
Saint Francis University, PA
Texas Wesleyan University, TX
Truett-McConnell College, GA
Union College, KY
Union University, TN
The University of Alabama at Birmingham, AL
University of Alaska Anchorage, AK
University of Great Falls, MT
University of Hartford, CT
University of Valley Forge, PA
Upper Iowa University, IA
Wesleyan College, GA
Wilson College, PA

### Children of Educators

Agnes Scott College, GA
Allegheny College, PA
Amridge University, AL
Austin Peay State University, TN
Bard College, NY
Bennington College, VT
Bridgewater College, VA
Calvary Bible College and Theological Seminary, MO
Campbellsville University, KY
Canisius College, NY
Centenary College of Louisiana, LA
Chowan University, NC
Coe College, IA
The College of Idaho, ID

College of Staten Island of the City University of New York, NY
The College of Wooster, OH
Columbia College, MO
Columbus College of Art & Design, OH
Concordia University, Nebraska, NE
Dowling College, NY
Emmanuel College, GA
Emmanuel College, MA
Emory & Henry College, VA
Endicott College, MA
Evangel University, MO
Flagler College, FL
Franklin Pierce University, NH
Goshen College, IN
Governors State University, IL
Grand View University, IA
Hampden-Sydney College, VA
Hardin-Simmons University, TX
Hastings College, NE
Hendrix College, AR
Heritage Christian University, AL
Jacksonville University, FL
John Carroll University, OH
King's College, PA
Lees-McRae College, NC
Lipscomb University, TN
Long Island University–LIU Brooklyn, NY
Long Island University–LIU Post, NY
Lycoming College, PA
Lynn University, FL
Maranatha Baptist University, WI
Mary Baldwin College, VA
Mississippi State University, MS
Moravian College, PA
Mount St. Mary's University, MD
New England College, NH
Northwest University, WA
Nyack College, NY
Occidental College, CA
Oklahoma Wesleyan University, OK
Palm Beach Atlantic University, FL
Rockford University, IL
Rosemont College, PA
St. Ambrose University, IA
Saint Anselm College, NH
St. Catherine University, MN
Saint Francis University, PA
Saint Mary's College of California, CA
Salem College, NC
Seattle University, WA
Simpson College, IA
Sonoma State University, CA
Southern Illinois University Carbondale, IL
Tennessee Technological University, TN
Texas Christian University, TX
Texas Wesleyan University, TX
Trine University, IN
Trinity University, TX
Union University, TN
Unity College, ME
The University of Alabama at Birmingham, AL
University of Alaska Anchorage, AK
University of Dubuque, IA
University of Memphis, TN
University of St. Francis, IL
University of St. Thomas, MN
The University of Scranton, PA
The University of Tennessee at Martin, TN
Villanova University, PA
Wright State University, OH

### Children of Faculty/Staff

Abilene Christian University, TX

Adelphi University, NY
Adrian College, MI
Agnes Scott College, GA
Alaska Bible College, AK
Alaska Pacific University, AK
Albany College of Pharmacy and Health Sciences, NY
Alcorn State University, MS
Alderson Broaddus University, WV
Allegheny College, PA
Allen College, IA
Alliant International University–San Diego, CA
Alvernia University, PA
Alverno College, WI
American University, DC
Amridge University, AL
Anderson University, IN
Anderson University, SC
Andrews University, MI
Anna Maria College, MA
Aquinas College, MI
Arizona State University at the Downtown Phoenix campus, AZ
Arizona State University at the Polytechnic campus, AZ
Arizona State University at the Tempe campus, AZ
Arizona State University at the West campus, AZ
Arkansas State University, AR
Arkansas Tech University, AR
Ashland University, OH
Auburn University, AL
Augustana College, IL
Augustana College, SD
Austin College, TX
Austin Peay State University, TN
Ave Maria University, FL
Ball State University, IN
Barclay College, KS
Bard College, NY
Baylor University, TX
Bay Path University, MA
Becker College, MA
Belhaven University, MS
Bellarmine University, KY
Belmont Abbey College, NC
Belmont University, TN
Bemidji State University, MN
Benedictine University, IL
Bennington College, VT
Berklee College of Music, MA
Berry College, GA
Bethany College, WV
Bethany Lutheran College, MN
Bethel College, KS
Bethel University, MN
Binghamton University, State University of New York, NY
Biola University, CA
Birmingham-Southern College, AL
Bloomsburg University of Pennsylvania, PA
Bluefield College, VA
Blue Mountain College, MS
Bluffton University, OH
Boston University, MA
Bowdoin College, ME
Bowling Green State University, OH
Bradley University, IL
Brenau University, GA
Brevard College, NC
Bridgewater College, VA
Buena Vista University, IA
Cairn University, PA

Caldwell University, NJ
California Baptist University, CA
California Lutheran University, CA
California State University, Bakersfield, CA
California State University, Chico, CA
California State University, Stanislaus, CA
Calumet College of Saint Joseph, IN
Calvary Bible College and Theological
    Seminary, MO
Calvin College, MI
Cameron University, OK
Campbellsville University, KY
Campbell University, NC
Canisius College, NY
Capital University, OH
Cardinal Stritch University, WI
Carlos Albizu University, Miami Campus,
    FL
Carroll College, MT
Carroll University, WI
Case Western Reserve University, OH
Castleton State College, VT
The Catholic University of America, DC
Cedarville University, OH
Centenary College of Louisiana, LA
Central College, IA
Central Methodist University, MO
Central Michigan University, MI
Central Washington University, WA
Centre College, KY
Chaminade University of Honolulu, HI
Chowan University, NC
Cincinnati Christian University, OH
Clarion University of Pennsylvania, PA
Clarke University, IA
Clarkson University, NY
Clemson University, SC
Cleveland Institute of Art, OH
Cleveland Institute of Music, OH
Cleveland State University, OH
Coe College, IA
Coker College, SC
Colby-Sawyer College, NH
The College of Idaho, ID
College of Mount Saint Vincent, NY
The College of New Rochelle, NY
College of Saint Mary, NE
The College of Saint Rose, NY
The College of St. Scholastica, MN
College of Staten Island of the City
    University of New York, NY
College of the Holy Cross, MA
The College of Wooster, OH
The Colorado College, CO
Colorado State University, CO
Colorado State University–Pueblo, CO
Columbia College, MO
Columbia International University, SC
Columbus College of Art & Design, OH
Concordia University, CA
Concordia University Ann Arbor, MI
Concordia University Chicago, IL
Concordia University, Nebraska, NE
Concordia University, St. Paul, MN
Concordia University Texas, TX
Concord University, WV
Converse College, SC
Corban University, OR
Cornell College, IA
Cornerstone University, MI
Covenant College, GA
The Criswell College, TX
Crossroads Bible College, IN
Culver-Stockton College, MO
Cumberland University, TN
Curry College, MA

Dakota Wesleyan University, SD
Dallas Baptist University, TX
Delta State University, MS
Denison University, OH
DePaul University, IL
Dickinson College, PA
Dickinson State University, ND
Doane College, NE
Dominican College, NY
Dominican University, IL
Dordt College, IA
Dowling College, NY
Drury University, MO
Duquesne University, PA
D'Youville College, NY
East Carolina University, NC
East Central University, OK
Eastern Kentucky University, KY
Eastern Nazarene College, MA
Eastern University, PA
East Texas Baptist University, TX
Eckerd College, FL
ECPI University, VA
Edgewood College, WI
Elizabethtown College, PA
Elmira College, NY
Elms College, MA
Elon University, NC
Emmanuel College, GA
Emmanuel College, MA
Emmaus Bible College, IA
Emory & Henry College, VA
Emory University, GA
Emporia State University, KS
Eureka College, IL
Evangel University, MO
Fairfield University, CT
Fairmont State University, WV
Faulkner University, AL
Felician College, NJ
Flagler College, FL
Florida Institute of Technology, FL
Florida Southern College, FL
Fordham University, NY
Fort Hays State University, KS
Fort Lewis College, CO
Framingham State University, MA
Franciscan University of Steubenville, OH
Francis Marion University, SC
Franklin College, IN
Franklin Pierce University, NH
Fresno Pacific University, CA
Furman University, SC
Gardner-Webb University, NC
Geneva College, PA
George Fox University, OR
Georgetown College, KY
Georgetown University, DC
Georgia College & State University, GA
Georgian Court University, NJ
Glenville State College, WV
Golden Gate University, CA
Gonzaga University, WA
Gordon College, MA
Goshen College, IN
Graceland University, IA
Grambling State University, LA
Grand Valley State University, MI
Grand View University, IA
Greensboro College, NC
Greenville College, IL
Guilford College, NC
Gwynedd Mercy University, PA
Hampden-Sydney College, VA
Hampshire College, MA
Hampton University, VA

Hanover College, IN
Harding University, AR
Hardin-Simmons University, TX
Hartwick College, NY
Hastings College, NE
Heidelberg University, OH
Henderson State University, AR
Hendrix College, AR
Heritage Christian University, AL
Hillsdale College, MI
Hillsdale Free Will Baptist College, OK
Hofstra University, NY
Hollins University, VA
Hood College, MD
Hope International University, CA
Houghton College, NY
Houston Baptist University, TX
Howard Payne University, TX
Huntingdon College, AL
Huntington University, IN
Idaho State University, ID
Illinois College, IL
Illinois Institute of Technology, IL
Illinois State University, IL
Illinois Wesleyan University, IL
Indiana State University, IN
Indiana Tech, IN
Indiana University of Pennsylvania, PA
Iowa Wesleyan College, IA
Ithaca College, NY
Jackson State University, MS
Jacksonville University, FL
James Madison University, VA
John Carroll University, OH
Johns Hopkins University, MD
Johnson C. Smith University, NC
Juniata College, PA
Kansas Wesleyan University, KS
Kent State University, OH
Kent State University at Geauga, OH
Kent State University at Stark, OH
Kentucky Christian University, KY
Kentucky State University, KY
Kentucky Wesleyan College, KY
Keuka College, NY
King's College, PA
King University, TN
Knox College, IL
Kutztown University of Pennsylvania, PA
LaGrange College, GA
Lake Erie College, OH
Lancaster Bible College, PA
La Salle University, PA
Lasell College, MA
La Sierra University, CA
Lawrence Technological University, MI
Lawrence University, WI
Lebanon Valley College, PA
Lees-McRae College, NC
Lee University, TN
Lehigh University, PA
LeMoyne-Owen College, TN
Lenoir-Rhyne University, NC
Lewis & Clark College, OR
Lewis University, IL
Liberty University, VA
LIM College, NY
Lincoln Christian University, IL
Lincoln Memorial University, TN
Lincoln University, MO
Lincoln University, PA
Lindenwood University, MO
Lindsey Wilson College, KY
Linfield College, OR
Lipscomb University, TN
Long Island University–LIU Brooklyn, NY

Long Island University–LIU Post, NY
Louisiana Tech University, LA
Loyola Marymount University, CA
Loyola University New Orleans, LA
Lubbock Christian University, TX
Lycoming College, PA
Lynn University, FL
Lyon College, AR
MacMurray College, IL
Maine Maritime Academy, ME
Manchester University, IN
Manhattan College, NY
Maranatha Baptist University, WI
Marian University, WI
Marquette University, WI
Marshall University, WV
Mary Baldwin College, VA
Marymount University, VA
Maryville College, TN
Massachusetts College of Art and Design, MA
Massachusetts Maritime Academy, MA
The Master's College and Seminary, CA
Mayville State University, ND
McKendree University, IL
McMurry University, TX
McNally Smith College of Music, MN
MCPHS University, MA
Mercer University, GA
Mercy College, NY
Mercy College of Health Sciences, IA
Mercyhurst University, PA
Meredith College, NC
Merrimack College, MA
Messiah College, PA
Methodist University, NC
Miami University, OH
Michigan State University, MI
Mid-Atlantic Christian University, NC
Midwestern State University, TX
Milligan College, TN
Millikin University, IL
Millsaps College, MS
Milwaukee School of Engineering, WI
Minnesota State University Moorhead, MN
Minot State University, ND
Misericordia University, PA
Mississippi College, MS
Mississippi State University, MS
Mississippi University for Women, MS
Missouri Baptist University, MO
Missouri University of Science and Technology, MO
Missouri Valley College, MO
Monmouth University, NJ
Montana State University Billings, MT
Montana Tech of The University of Montana, MT
Montreat College, NC
Moravian College, PA
Morningside College, IA
Morrisville State College, NY
Mount Carmel College of Nursing, OH
Mount Marty College, SD
Mount Mary University, WI
Mount St. Joseph University, OH
Mount Saint Mary College, NY
Mount St. Mary's University, MD
Murray State University, KY
Nazareth College of Rochester, NY
Nebraska Christian College, NE
Nebraska Methodist College, NE
Newberry College, SC
New England College, NH
New Jersey Institute of Technology, NJ

Newman University, KS
New Mexico State University, NM
New York Institute of Technology, NY
Niagara University, NY
Nicholls State University, LA
Nichols College, MA
North Central College, IL
Northeastern Illinois University, IL
Northeastern State University, OK
Northern Illinois University, IL
Northern Kentucky University, KY
Northern Michigan University, MI
Northwest Christian University, OR
Northwestern Oklahoma State University, OK
Northwest Missouri State University, MO
Northwest Nazarene University, ID
Northwest University, WA
Norwich University, VT
Notre Dame de Namur University, CA
Nova Southeastern University, FL
Nyack College, NY
Occidental College, CA
Oglethorpe University, GA
The Ohio State University, OH
Ohio University, OH
Ohio University–Chillicothe, OH
Ohio University–Eastern, OH
Ohio University–Lancaster, OH
Ohio University–Southern Campus, OH
Ohio University–Zanesville, OH
Oklahoma Baptist University, OK
Oklahoma Christian University, OK
Oklahoma City University, OK
Oklahoma Wesleyan University, OK
Old Dominion University, VA
Olivet College, MI
Olivet Nazarene University, IL
Oral Roberts University, OK
Otterbein University, OH
Ouachita Baptist University, AR
Our Lady of the Lake University of San Antonio, TX
Pace University, NY
Pacific University, OR
Palm Beach Atlantic University, FL
Park University, MO
Patrick Henry College, VA
Peirce College, PA
Piedmont College, GA
Plymouth State University, NH
Presbyterian College, SC
Principia College, IL
Purdue University, IN
Queens University of Charlotte, NC
Quincy University, IL
Quinnipiac University, CT
Ramapo College of New Jersey, NJ
Randolph College, VA
Randolph-Macon College, VA
Regent University, VA
Regis University, CO
Rensselaer Polytechnic Institute, NY
Rhode Island School of Design, RI
Rhodes College, TN
Robert Morris University, PA
Robert Morris University Illinois, IL
Roberts Wesleyan College, NY
Rochester College, MI
Rochester Institute of Technology, NY
Rockford University, IL
Rockhurst University, MO
Rosemont College, PA
Sacred Heart University, CT
St. Ambrose University, IA

Saint Anselm College, NH
Saint Augustine's University, NC
St. Bonaventure University, NY
St. Catherine University, MN
St. Cloud State University, MN
St. Edward's University, TX
Saint Francis University, PA
St. John Fisher College, NY
St. John's College, NM
St. John's University, NY
Saint Joseph's College, IN
St. Joseph's College, Long Island Campus, NY
St. Joseph's College, New York, NY
Saint Joseph's University, PA
St. Louis College of Pharmacy, MO
Saint Louis University, MO
Saint Martin's University, WA
Saint Mary's College of California, CA
St. Mary's College of Maryland, MD
Saint Mary's University of Minnesota, MN
St. Norbert College, WI
Saint Vincent College, PA
Saint Xavier University, IL
Salem College, NC
Samford University, AL
San Diego State University, CA
Santa Clara University, CA
Santa Fe University of Art and Design, NM
Schreiner University, TX
Seattle Pacific University, WA
Seattle University, WA
Seton Hill University, PA
Shenandoah University, VA
Siena College, NY
Simpson College, IA
Simpson University, CA
Skidmore College, NY
Slippery Rock University of Pennsylvania, PA
Soka University of America, CA
Sonoma State University, CA
South Dakota State University, SD
Southeastern Louisiana University, LA
Southeast Missouri State University, MO
Southern Connecticut State University, CT
Southern Illinois University Carbondale, IL
Southern Illinois University Edwardsville, IL
Southwestern Christian College, TX
Southwestern College, KS
Southwestern University, TX
Spring Arbor University, MI
Springfield College, MA
Spring Hill College, AL
State University of New York at New Paltz, NY
State University of New York College at Potsdam, NY
Stephen F. Austin State University, TX
Stephens College, MO
Stetson University, FL
Stockton University, NJ
Stonehill College, MA
Suffolk University, MA
Susquehanna University, PA
Tabor College, KS
Taylor University, IN
Temple University, PA
Tennessee Technological University, TN
Tennessee Wesleyan College, TN
Texas A&M University, TX
Texas Christian University, TX
Texas Lutheran University, TX
Texas Tech University, TX

Texas Wesleyan University, TX
Thiel College, PA
Thomas College, ME
Thomas More College, KY
Thomas University, GA
Tiffin University, OH
Towson University, MD
Transylvania University, KY
Trevecca Nazarene University, TN
Trine University, IN
Trinity Christian College, IL
Trinity College of Florida, FL
Truett-McConnell College, GA
Truman State University, MO
Tulane University, LA
Tusculum College, TN
Tuskegee University, AL
Union College, KY
Union College, NY
Union University, TN
The University of Alabama at Birmingham, AL
University of Alaska Anchorage, AK
The University of Arizona, AZ
University of Arkansas, AR
University of Bridgeport, CT
University of Central Oklahoma, OK
University of Colorado Denver, CO
University of Connecticut, CT
University of Dallas, TX
University of Dayton, OH
University of Delaware, DE
University of Dubuque, IA
University of Evansville, IN
The University of Findlay, OH
University of Florida, FL
University of Great Falls, MT
University of Hartford, CT
University of Idaho, ID
University of Illinois at Springfield, IL
University of Indianapolis, IN
University of Jamestown, ND
The University of Kansas, KS
University of Louisville, KY
University of Maine at Augusta, ME
University of Maine at Farmington, ME
University of Maine at Fort Kent, ME
University of Maine at Presque Isle, ME
University of Mary Hardin-Baylor, TX
University of Maryland Eastern Shore, MD
University of Mary Washington, VA
University of Massachusetts Amherst, MA
University of Massachusetts Boston, MA
University of Massachusetts Dartmouth, MA
University of Massachusetts Lowell, MA
University of Memphis, TN
University of Miami, FL
University of Michigan, MI
University of Michigan–Dearborn, MI
University of Michigan–Flint, MI
University of Minnesota, Crookston, MN
University of Mississippi, MS
University of Missouri, MO
University of Missouri–St. Louis, MO
University of Mobile, AL
The University of Montana Western, MT
University of Montevallo, AL
University of Mount Olive, NC
University of Mount Union, OH
University of Nebraska at Kearney, NE
University of Nebraska at Omaha, NE
University of Nevada, Las Vegas, NV
University of New Hampshire, NH
University of New Hampshire at Manchester, NH
University of North Alabama, AL

University of North Carolina at Asheville, NC
The University of North Carolina at Chapel Hill, NC
The University of North Carolina at Greensboro, NC
University of Northern Colorado, CO
University of Notre Dame, IN
University of Oregon, OR
University of Pittsburgh, PA
University of Pittsburgh at Bradford, PA
University of Pittsburgh at Johnstown, PA
University of Portland, OR
University of Puget Sound, WA
University of Rio Grande, OH
University of Rochester, NY
University of St. Thomas, MN
University of St. Thomas, TX
University of San Diego, CA
University of Science and Arts of Oklahoma, OK
The University of Scranton, PA
University of South Alabama, AL
University of South Carolina, SC
University of Southern California, CA
University of Southern Indiana, IN
University of Southern Mississippi, MS
The University of Tampa, FL
The University of Tennessee at Chattanooga, TN
The University of Tennessee at Martin, TN
The University of Texas at Brownsville, TX
University of the Cumberlands, KY
University of the District of Columbia, DC
University of the Incarnate Word, TX
The University of Toledo, OH
The University of Tulsa, OK
University of Utah, UT
University of Valley Forge, PA
The University of West Alabama, AL
University of West Florida, FL
Ursinus College, PA
Ursuline College, OH
Utah State University, UT
Valley City State University, ND
Valparaiso University, IN
Vanguard University of Southern California, CA
Villanova University, PA
Virginia Military Institute, VA
Virginia Polytechnic Institute and State University, VA
Virginia Union University, VA
Virginia Wesleyan College, VA
Wabash College, IN
Wagner College, NY
Waldorf College, IA
Walla Walla University, WA
Warren Wilson College, NC
Wartburg College, IA
Washburn University, KS
Washington & Jefferson College, PA
Washington College, MD
Washington State University, WA
Wayland Baptist University, TX
Waynesburg University, PA
Wayne State College, NE
Wayne State University, MI
Webber International University, FL
Webster University, MO
Wesleyan College, GA
West Chester University of Pennsylvania, PA
Western Illinois University, IL
Western Michigan University, MI
Western New England University, MA

Westminster College, MO
Westmont College, CA
West Texas A&M University, TX
West Virginia University, WV
West Virginia Wesleyan College, WV
Wheeling Jesuit University, WV
Whittier College, CA
Wichita State University, KS
Widener University, PA
Wilkes University, PA
William Jessup University, CA
William Jewell College, MO
William Peace University, NC
Williams Baptist College, AR
William Woods University, MO
Wilson College, PA
Winona State University, MN
Winthrop University, SC
Wisconsin Lutheran College, WI
Wittenberg University, OH
Wofford College, SC
Wright State University, OH
Xavier University of Louisiana, LA
Youngstown State University, OH

**Children of Public Servants**
California State University, San Bernardino, CA
Central Washington University, WA
Chowan University, NC
College of Staten Island of the City University of New York, NY
Dowling College, NY
Framingham State University, MA
Georgia Southern University, GA
Governors State University, IL
Grambling State University, LA
Illinois Institute of Technology, IL
Louisiana Tech University, LA
Mercer University, GA
Mississippi State University, MS
Missouri Western State University, MO
Monmouth University, NJ
New Mexico State University, NM
Northern Kentucky University, KY
The Ohio State University, OH
Patrick Henry College, VA
Peirce College, PA
Robert Morris University Illinois, IL
St. Francis College, NY
Siena College, NY
Sonoma State University, CA
Southern Illinois University Carbondale, IL
Tennessee Technological University, TN
Texas Wesleyan University, TX
The University of Alabama at Birmingham, AL
University of Delaware, DE
University of Massachusetts Lowell, MA
University of Memphis, TN
University of Nevada, Las Vegas, NV
University of New Orleans, LA
The University of Texas at Dallas, TX
The University of Toledo, OH
University of Utah, UT
University of Wisconsin–Green Bay, WI
University of Wyoming, WY
Washington State University, WA
Western Washington University, WA

**Children of Union Members/Company Employees**
Adrian College, MI
Auburn University, AL
Averett University, VA
California State University, Bakersfield, CA
Calvin College, MI
Carroll College, MT

Chowan University, NC
Clarion University of Pennsylvania, PA
The College of New Rochelle, NY
The College of Saint Rose, NY
College of Staten Island of the City
    University of New York, NY
Columbia College, MO
Dowling College, NY
Eastern Washington University, WA
Emmanuel College, MA
Emporia State University, KS
Framingham State University, MA
Francis Marion University, SC
Frostburg State University, MD
Grand Valley State University, MI
Hofstra University, NY
Husson University, ME
Illinois State University, IL
Kennesaw State University, GA
Kent State University, OH
Kutztown University of Pennsylvania, PA
Marian University, WI
Massachusetts College of Art and Design,
    MA
Mercy College of Health Sciences, IA
Michigan State University, MI
Midwestern State University, TX
Millersville University of Pennsylvania, PA
Millikin University, IL
Missouri University of Science and
    Technology, MO
Missouri Western State University, MO
Montana State University Billings, MT
New Jersey Institute of Technology, NJ
New Mexico State University, NM
Northern Michigan University, MI
The Ohio State University, OH
Sacred Heart University, CT
St. Cloud State University, MN
Siena College, NY
Slippery Rock University of Pennsylvania,
    PA
Sonoma State University, CA
Stephen F. Austin State University, TX
Stephens College, MO
Stockton University, NJ
Stonehill College, MA
Texas Christian University, TX
Texas Wesleyan University, TX
Thomas More College, KY
The University of Alabama, AL
The University of Alabama at Birmingham,
    AL
University of Arkansas, AR
University of Connecticut, CT
University of Hartford, CT
University of Illinois at Springfield, IL
University of Louisville, KY
University of Massachusetts Boston, MA
University of Massachusetts Dartmouth, MA
University of Massachusetts Lowell, MA
University of Michigan–Flint, MI
University of Nevada, Las Vegas, NV
University of Northern Colorado, CO
University of Pittsburgh, PA
University of Pittsburgh at Bradford, PA
University of South Carolina, SC
The University of Tennessee at Chattanooga,
    TN
The University of Tennessee at Martin, TN
The University of Toledo, OH
University of Wisconsin–La Crosse, WI
University of Wisconsin–Parkside, WI
Western Kentucky University, KY
Western New England University, MA

Western Washington University, WA
West Texas A&M University, TX
West Virginia University, WV
York College of Pennsylvania, PA
Youngstown State University, OH

**Children of Workers in Trades**
Calvin College, MI
The College of New Rochelle, NY
College of Staten Island of the City
    University of New York, NY
Dowling College, NY
Grand Valley State University, MI
Huntingdon College, AL
Kennesaw State University, GA
Midwestern State University, TX
Missouri Western State University, MO
New Mexico State University, NM
The Ohio State University, OH
San Diego State University, CA
Siena College, NY
Sonoma State University, CA
South Dakota State University, SD
Texas Christian University, TX
The University of Alabama at Birmingham,
    AL
University of Arkansas, AR
University of Michigan, MI
University of South Carolina, SC
University of Wisconsin–Parkside, WI
Western Oregon University, OR
West Texas A&M University, TX
West Virginia University, WV
Worcester Polytechnic Institute, MA
Youngstown State University, OH

**Children with a Deceased or Disabled Parent**
The Baptist College of Florida, FL
Bay Path University, MA
California State University, San Bernardino,
    CA
Calvin College, MI
The Citadel, The Military College of South
    Carolina, SC
The College of New Jersey, NJ
College of Staten Island of the City
    University of New York, NY
Dickinson State University, ND
Elmhurst College, IL
Fairfield University, CT
Fordham University, NY
Georgia Institute of Technology, GA
Harding University, AR
Idaho State University, ID
Illinois State University, IL
Kentucky State University, KY
Lees-McRae College, NC
Lipscomb University, TN
Louisiana State University and Agricultural
    & Mechanical College, LA
Marian University, WI
Midwestern State University, TX
Millikin University, IL
New Mexico State University, NM
Northeastern State University, OK
Northern Kentucky University, KY
Santa Clara University, CA
Siena College, NY
Southern Illinois University Carbondale, IL
Texas Wesleyan University, TX
The University of Alabama at Birmingham,
    AL
University of Arkansas, AR
University of Hartford, CT
University of Louisville, KY
University of Massachusetts Dartmouth, MA

The University of Montana, MT
University of Nevada, Las Vegas, NV
University of New Orleans, LA
University of South Carolina, SC
The University of Tennessee at Chattanooga,
    TN
The University of Texas at Arlington, TX
University of Utah, UT
The University of Virginia's College at
    Wise, VA
Washington State University, WA
Youngstown State University, OH

**Ethnic Background**
Abilene Christian University, TX
Alaska Pacific University, AK
Albright College, PA
Alderson Broaddus University, WV
American University, DC
Anderson University, SC
Arkansas State University, AR
Armstrong State University, GA
Ashland University, OH
Auburn University, AL
Augustana College, IL
Augustana College, SD
Austin Peay State University, TN
Ball State University, IN
Bellarmine University, KY
Berry College, GA
Bethel College, KS
Bethel University, MN
Binghamton University, State University of
    New York, NY
Biola University, CA
Birmingham-Southern College, AL
Boise State University, ID
Buena Vista University, IA
California State University, Bakersfield, CA
California State University, Chico, CA
California University of Pennsylvania, PA
Calvin College, MI
Capital University, OH
Cedarville University, OH
Centenary College of Louisiana, LA
Central Michigan University, MI
Centre College, KY
Chaminade University of Honolulu, HI
Christian Brothers University, TN
Clemson University, SC
Coe College, IA
The College at Brockport, State University
    of New York, NY
The College of Saint Rose, NY
The College of St. Scholastica, MN
College of Staten Island of the City
    University of New York, NY
Colorado State University–Pueblo, CO
Columbia College, MO
Columbia International University, SC
Concordia University Ann Arbor, MI
Cornerstone University, MI
Dickinson State University, ND
Dowling College, NY
Drury University, MO
Duke University, NC
Duquesne University, PA
Earlham College, IN
East Carolina University, NC
Eastern Michigan University, MI
Eastern New Mexico University, NM
Eastern Washington University, WA
Elizabeth City State University, NC
Elmhurst College, IL
Elon University, NC

Emmanuel College, MA
Emmaus Bible College, IA
The Evergreen State College, WA
Fairfield University, CT
Fairmont State University, WV
Ferris State University, MI
Flagler College, FL
Florida Agricultural and Mechanical
    University, FL
Florida Gulf Coast University, FL
Fort Lewis College, CO
Franklin College, IN
Furman University, SC
Gannon University, PA
George Fox University, OR
Goshen College, IN
Grambling State University, LA
Grand View University, IA
Grove City College, PA
Gustavus Adolphus College, MN
Hamline University, MN
Hampden-Sydney College, VA
Hardin-Simmons University, TX
Hawai`i Pacific University, HI
Hope College, MI
Howard University, DC
Huntington University, IN
Idaho State University, ID
Indiana University of Pennsylvania, PA
Iowa State University of Science and
    Technology, IA
Johnson C. Smith University, NC
Juniata College, PA
Kennesaw State University, GA
Kent State University, OH
Kentucky Christian University, KY
Kentucky State University, KY
Kenyon College, OH
LaGrange College, GA
Langston University, OK
Lawrence University, WI
Lebanon Valley College, PA
Lenoir-Rhyne University, NC
Lesley University, MA
Lewis-Clark State College, ID
Lock Haven University of Pennsylvania, PA
Long Island University–LIU Brooklyn, NY
Long Island University–LIU Post, NY
Loyola Marymount University, CA
Lyon College, AR
Macalester College, MN
Marietta College, OH
Maryville University of Saint Louis, MO
Massachusetts Maritime Academy, MA
McMurry University, TX
Medical University of South Carolina, SC
Mercy College of Health Sciences, IA
Meredith College, NC
Methodist University, NC
Millsaps College, MS
Minot State University, ND
Mississippi University for Women, MS
Molloy College, NY
Montana State University Billings, MT
Morehead State University, KY
Muskingum University, OH
Nazareth College of Rochester, NY
New England College, NH
New Jersey Institute of Technology, NJ
New Mexico State University, NM
Northern Illinois University, IL
Northern State University, SD
Northland College, WI
Oakland University, MI
The Ohio State University, OH
Oklahoma State University, OK

Ouachita Baptist University, AR
Pacific University, OR
Portland State University, OR
Randolph-Macon College, VA
Rensselaer Polytechnic Institute, NY
Sacred Heart University, CT
The Sage Colleges, NY
St. Catherine University, MN
St. John Fisher College, NY
Saint Martin's University, WA
Saint Mary's University of Minnesota, MN
Shawnee State University, OH
Shepherd University, WV
Siena College, NY
Simpson College, IA
Slippery Rock University of Pennsylvania,
    PA
Sonoma State University, CA
South Dakota School of Mines and
    Technology, SD
South Dakota State University, SD
Southwestern University, TX
State University of New York at Fredonia,
    NY
State University of New York at New Paltz,
    NY
State University of New York College at
    Geneseo, NY
State University of New York College at
    Potsdam, NY
Stetson University, FL
Stockton University, NJ
Stony Brook University, State University of
    New York, NY
Taylor University, IN
Tennessee Technological University, TN
Texas A&M University–Commerce, TX
Texas Christian University, TX
Texas Wesleyan University, TX
Thomas University, GA
Towson University, MD
Trinity Christian College, IL
Truman State University, MO
Union University, TN
The University of Alabama at Birmingham,
    AL
The University of Arizona, AZ
University of Arkansas, AR
University of California, San Diego, CA
University of Central Oklahoma, OK
University of Dallas, TX
University of Delaware, DE
University of Great Falls, MT
University of Hartford, CT
University of Idaho, ID
University of Illinois at Springfield, IL
The University of Iowa, IA
The University of Kansas, KS
University of Louisville, KY
University of Maine at Augusta, ME
University of Maine at Fort Kent, ME
University of Maine at Presque Isle, ME
University of Mary Hardin-Baylor, TX
University of Massachusetts Dartmouth, MA
University of Michigan–Dearborn, MI
University of Minnesota, Crookston, MN
University of Mississippi, MS
University of Missouri, MO
University of Missouri–Kansas City, MO
University of Missouri–St. Louis, MO
University of Mount Union, OH
University of Nebraska at Kearney, NE
University of Nebraska at Omaha, NE
University of Nebraska–Lincoln, NE
University of Nevada, Las Vegas, NV
University of Nevada, Reno, NV

University of North Carolina at Asheville,
    NC
The University of North Carolina at
    Charlotte, NC
University of Northern Colorado, CO
University of St. Francis, IL
The University of Scranton, PA
University of South Carolina, SC
University of Southern Mississippi, MS
The University of Tennessee at Chattanooga,
    TN
The University of Tennessee at Martin, TN
The University of Texas at El Paso, TX
The University of Texas at San Antonio, TX
The University of Texas–Pan American, TX
The University of Toledo, OH
University of Utah, UT
University of Vermont, VT
The University of Virginia's College at
    Wise, VA
University of Wisconsin–Eau Claire, WI
University of Wisconsin–Green Bay, WI
University of Wisconsin–La Crosse, WI
University of Wisconsin–Parkside, WI
University of Wisconsin–Stevens Point, WI
University of Wisconsin–Whitewater, WI
University of Wyoming, WY
Valley City State University, ND
VanderCook College of Music, IL
Washburn University, KS
Wayland Baptist University, TX
Wayne State College, NE
Webster University, MO
Wesleyan College, GA
Western Carolina University, NC
Western Kentucky University, KY
Western Oregon University, OR
Western Washington University, WA
Westminster College, MO
Westmont College, CA
West Virginia University, WV
Wheaton College, IL
Whitman College, WA
Whitworth University, WA
Widener University, PA
William Jessup University, CA
Wisconsin Lutheran College, WI
Wittenberg University, OH
Wright State University, OH
Youngstown State University, OH

**First-Generation College Students**
Abilene Christian University, TX
Adrian College, MI
American University, DC
Angelo State University, TX
Arkansas State University, AR
Austin College, TX
Averett University, VA
Berry College, GA
Binghamton University, State University of
    New York, NY
Birmingham-Southern College, AL
Bluefield College, VA
Boise State University, ID
Bowie State University, MD
Brenau University, GA
Cabarrus College of Health Sciences, NC
California State University, Bakersfield, CA
California State University, Chico, CA
California State University, San Bernardino,
    CA
California State University, Stanislaus, CA
Calvin College, MI
Centenary College of Louisiana, LA
Centre College, KY

Champlain College, VT
Chowan University, NC
Christopher Newport University, VA
Clarion University of Pennsylvania, PA
The College at Brockport, State University of New York, NY
The College of Idaho, ID
College of Saint Mary, NE
College of Staten Island of the City University of New York, NY
Colorado Mesa University, CO
Colorado State University, CO
Colorado State University–Pueblo, CO
Columbia College, MO
Concordia University, CA
Creighton University, NE
Davidson College, NC
Dowling College, NY
Eastern New Mexico University, NM
Eastern Washington University, WA
Elon University, NC
Emmanuel College, GA
Emporia State University, KS
The Evergreen State College, WA
Fairfield University, CT
Fairmont State University, WV
Flagler College, FL
Florida Agricultural and Mechanical University, FL
Fort Lewis College, CO
Georgia Southern University, GA
Glenville State College, WV
Golden Gate University, CA
Graceland University, IA
Grove City College, PA
Guilford College, NC
Gustavus Adolphus College, MN
Hodges University, FL
Howard University, DC
Idaho State University, ID
Illinois State University, IL
Iowa State University of Science and Technology, IA
Kent State University, OH
Kent State University at Stark, OH
Kenyon College, OH
Kutztown University of Pennsylvania, PA
LaGrange College, GA
Lewis-Clark State College, ID
Long Island University–LIU Brooklyn, NY
Long Island University–LIU Post, NY
Loyola Marymount University, CA
Lyon College, AR
MacMurray College, IL
Meredith College, NC
Metropolitan State University of Denver, CO
Michigan State University, MI
Middle Tennessee State University, TN
Midwestern State University, TX
Millsaps College, MS
Minnesota State University Moorhead, MN
Mississippi State University, MS
Missouri Baptist University, MO
Missouri Western State University, MO
Monmouth University, NJ
Montana State University Billings, MT
Montana Tech of The University of Montana, MT
Montreat College, NC
Moravian College, PA
New Jersey Institute of Technology, NJ
Ohio University, OH
Ohio University–Chillicothe, OH
Ohio University–Lancaster, OH
Ohio University–Southern Campus, OH

Ohio University–Zanesville, OH
Oklahoma State University, OK
Ouachita Baptist University, AR
Pacific Lutheran University, WA
Pacific University, OR
Queens University of Charlotte, NC
Quincy University, IL
Rochester College, MI
The Sage Colleges, NY
St. John Fisher College, NY
Saint Joseph's University, PA
Saint Louis University, MO
Saint Vincent College, PA
Salisbury University, MD
San Diego State University, CA
Shawnee State University, OH
Sonoma State University, CA
South Dakota State University, SD
Southeastern Louisiana University, LA
Southeast Missouri State University, MO
Southern Illinois University Carbondale, IL
State University of New York at New Paltz, NY
Stephen F. Austin State University, TX
Stetson University, FL
Stockton University, NJ
Tennessee Technological University, TN
Texas A&M University, TX
Texas A&M University–Commerce, TX
Texas A&M University–Corpus Christi, TX
Texas Lutheran University, TX
Texas State University, TX
Texas Tech University, TX
Texas Wesleyan University, TX
Towson University, MD
Trinity Christian College, IL
Truman State University, MO
Union University, TN
The University of Alabama at Birmingham, AL
University of Arkansas, AR
University of California, San Diego, CA
University of California, Santa Cruz, CA
University of Central Florida, FL
University of Colorado Boulder, CO
University of Colorado Denver, CO
University of Delaware, DE
University of Great Falls, MT
University of Hartford, CT
University of Houston, TX
University of Idaho, ID
University of Illinois at Springfield, IL
The University of Iowa, IA
The University of Kansas, KS
University of Maryland Eastern Shore, MD
University of Massachusetts Boston, MA
University of Massachusetts Dartmouth, MA
University of Miami, FL
University of Michigan–Flint, MI
University of Minnesota, Crookston, MN
University of Mississippi, MS
University of Missouri, MO
The University of Montana Western, MT
University of Nebraska at Kearney, NE
University of Nebraska at Omaha, NE
University of Nevada, Las Vegas, NV
University of Nevada, Reno, NV
University of North Alabama, AL
University of North Carolina at Asheville, NC
University of North Florida, FL
University of St. Francis, IL
University of South Carolina, SC
University of South Carolina Aiken, SC
University of South Carolina Upstate, SC

The University of Texas at Arlington, TX
The University of Texas at Brownsville, TX
The University of Texas at San Antonio, TX
The University of Toledo, OH
University of Utah, UT
University of Vermont, VT
The University of West Alabama, AL
University of Wisconsin–Eau Claire, WI
University of Wisconsin–La Crosse, WI
University of Wisconsin–Stout, WI
University of Wyoming, WY
Virginia Polytechnic Institute and State University, VA
Washington State University, WA
Wesleyan College, GA
West Texas A&M University, TX
West Virginia University Institute of Technology, WV
Wheaton College, IL
Whitman College, WA
Wichita State University, KS
Wisconsin Lutheran College, WI
Wright State University, OH

**Handicapped Students**
Arkansas State University, AR
Bemidji State University, MN
Binghamton University, State University of New York, NY
Boise State University, ID
California State University, Chico, CA
California State University, Fresno, CA
California State University, San Bernardino, CA
Calvin College, MI
Central College, IA
Chowan University, NC
Clear Creek Baptist Bible College, KY
The College of St. Scholastica, MN
College of Staten Island of the City University of New York, NY
Colorado State University–Pueblo, CO
Dordt College, IA
East Carolina University, NC
Eastern Washington University, WA
East Stroudsburg University of Pennsylvania, PA
Elizabeth City State University, NC
Emmanuel College, MA
Emporia State University, KS
Fairmont State University, WV
Florida Gulf Coast University, FL
Fordham University, NY
Fort Lewis College, CO
Fort Valley State University, GA
Francis Marion University, SC
Gardner-Webb University, NC
Georgia Southern University, GA
Grand Valley State University, MI
Grove City College, PA
Hamline University, MN
Hardin-Simmons University, TX
Hofstra University, NY
Houghton College, NY
Howard University, DC
Idaho State University, ID
James Madison University, VA
Kennesaw State University, GA
Kent State University, OH
Kutztown University of Pennsylvania, PA
Lock Haven University of Pennsylvania, PA
Long Island University–LIU Brooklyn, NY
Long Island University–LIU Post, NY
Louisiana Tech University, LA
Loyola Marymount University, CA

Malone University, OH
Michigan State University, MI
Mid-Atlantic Christian University, NC
Middle Tennessee State University, TN
Midwestern State University, TX
Mississippi State University, MS
Morehead State University, KY
New Jersey Institute of Technology, NJ
New Mexico State University, NM
Northern Kentucky University, KY
Northern State University, SD
The Ohio State University, OH
Oklahoma State University, OK
Old Dominion University, VA
Ouachita Baptist University, AR
Portland State University, OR
Sacred Heart University, CT
St. Francis College, NY
San Diego State University, CA
Santa Clara University, CA
Shawnee State University, OH
Shepherd University, WV
Shippensburg University of Pennsylvania, PA
Sonoma State University, CA
South Dakota State University, SD
Southern Illinois University Carbondale, IL
State University of New York College at Potsdam, NY
Texas Christian University, TX
Texas State University, TX
Texas Tech University, TX
Texas Wesleyan University, TX
Towson University, MD
Union University, TN
The University of Akron, OH
The University of Alabama at Birmingham, AL
University of Arkansas, AR
University of California, San Diego, CA
University of Colorado Denver, CO
University of Connecticut, CT
University of Hartford, CT
University of Houston, TX
University of Idaho, ID
University of Illinois at Springfield, IL
The University of Iowa, IA
University of Mary Hardin-Baylor, TX
University of Massachusetts Amherst, MA
University of Memphis, TN
University of Michigan, MI
University of Michigan–Dearborn, MI
University of Michigan–Flint, MI
University of Mississippi, MS
University of Nebraska at Omaha, NE
University of Nebraska–Lincoln, NE
University of Nevada, Las Vegas, NV
University of New Hampshire, NH
University of North Alabama, AL
University of North Carolina at Asheville, NC
The University of North Carolina at Charlotte, NC
The University of North Carolina at Greensboro, NC
University of Northern Colorado, CO
University of South Carolina, SC
University of South Carolina Aiken, SC
The University of Tennessee at Chattanooga, TN
The University of Tennessee at Martin, TN
The University of Texas at Arlington, TX
The University of Texas at Dallas, TX
The University of Texas at San Antonio, TX
The University of Toledo, OH
University of Utah, UT

University of West Florida, FL
University of West Georgia, GA
University of Wisconsin–Green Bay, WI
University of Wisconsin–Stout, WI
University of Wisconsin–Whitewater, WI
University of Wyoming, WY
Washington State University, WA
Wesleyan College, GA
Western Carolina University, NC
Western Kentucky University, KY
Western Oregon University, OR
West Texas A&M University, TX
Wheaton College, IL
Wright State University, OH
Youngstown State University, OH

**International Students**
Adrian College, MI
Agnes Scott College, GA
Alaska Pacific University, AK
Albany College of Pharmacy and Health Sciences, NY
Alderson Broaddus University, WV
Allegheny College, PA
Alliant International University–San Diego, CA
Alverno College, WI
Anderson University, IN
Anderson University, SC
Andrews University, MI
Arizona State University at the Downtown Phoenix campus, AZ
Arizona State University at the Polytechnic campus, AZ
Arizona State University at the Tempe campus, AZ
Arizona State University at the West campus, AZ
Arkansas Tech University, AR
Armstrong State University, GA
Ashland University, OH
Augustana College, IL
Augustana College, SD
Austin College, TX
Averett University, VA
Ball State University, IN
Barclay College, KS
Bay Path University, MA
Belhaven University, MS
Bellarmine University, KY
Bemidji State University, MN
Benedictine University, IL
Bentley University, MA
Berry College, GA
Bethany College, WV
Bethel College, KS
Bethel University, MN
Binghamton University, State University of New York, NY
Biola University, CA
Birmingham-Southern College, AL
Bloomfield College, NJ
Bloomsburg University of Pennsylvania, PA
Bluffton University, OH
Boise State University, ID
Bowling Green State University, OH
Brenau University, GA
Brevard College, NC
Bridgewater College, VA
Bryant University, RI
Buena Vista University, IA
Buffalo State College, State University of New York, NY
California Baptist University, CA
California Institute of Integral Studies, CA
California Lutheran University, CA

California State University, Chico, CA
California University of Pennsylvania, PA
Calvin College, MI
Cameron University, OK
Campbellsville University, KY
Canisius College, NY
Capital University, OH
Cardinal Stritch University, WI
Carroll College, MT
Carroll University, WI
Castleton State College, VT
Centenary College of Louisiana, LA
Central College, IA
Central Methodist University, MO
Central Michigan University, MI
Champlain College, VT
Chowan University, NC
Cincinnati Christian University, OH
Clarkson University, NY
Clear Creek Baptist Bible College, KY
Coastal Carolina University, SC
Coe College, IA
Coker College, SC
The College at Brockport, State University of New York, NY
The College of Idaho, ID
College of Saint Benedict, MN
College of Saint Mary, NE
The College of St. Scholastica, MN
College of Staten Island of the City University of New York, NY
The College of Wooster, OH
The Colorado College, CO
Colorado Mesa University, CO
Colorado State University, CO
Colorado State University–Pueblo, CO
Columbia College, MO
Columbia International University, SC
Concordia College, MN
Concordia University Chicago, IL
Concordia University, Nebraska, NE
Corban University, OR
Cornerstone University, MI
Covenant College, GA
The Criswell College, TX
Culver-Stockton College, MO
Dickinson State University, ND
Dordt College, IA
Drake University, IA
Drury University, MO
Duke University, NC
Duquesne University, PA
East Central University, OK
Eastern Michigan University, MI
Eastern Nazarene College, MA
Eastern New Mexico University, NM
Eastern University, PA
East Stroudsburg University of Pennsylvania, PA
East Texas Baptist University, TX
Eckerd College, FL
Elizabeth City State University, NC
Elizabethtown College, PA
Elmira College, NY
Elon University, NC
Emmanuel College, GA
Emmanuel College, MA
Emmaus Bible College, IA
Emporia State University, KS
Endicott College, MA
Fairmont State University, WV
Ferris State University, MI
Florida Gulf Coast University, FL
Florida Institute of Technology, FL
Fort Hays State University, KS
Fort Lewis College, CO

Fort Valley State University, GA
Franciscan University of Steubenville, OH
Francis Marion University, SC
Franklin Pierce University, NH
Friends University, KS
Frostburg State University, MD
Furman University, SC
Gannon University, PA
George Fox University, OR
Golden Gate University, CA
Gonzaga University, WA
Gordon College, MA
Goshen College, IN
Graceland University, IA
Grambling State University, LA
Grand Valley State University, MI
Greensboro College, NC
Greenville College, IL
Gustavus Adolphus College, MN
Hamline University, MN
Hampden-Sydney College, VA
Hampton University, VA
Hanover College, IN
Harding University, AR
Hartwick College, NY
Harvey Mudd College, CA
Hastings College, NE
Hawai'i Pacific University, HI
Heidelberg University, OH
Henderson State University, AR
Hendrix College, AR
Hillsdale College, MI
Hollins University, VA
Hood College, MD
Houghton College, NY
Howard University, DC
Huntingdon College, AL
Huntington University, IN
Idaho State University, ID
Illinois College, IL
Illinois Institute of Technology, IL
Illinois Wesleyan University, IL
Indiana University of Pennsylvania, PA
Iowa State University of Science and
    Technology, IA
Iowa Wesleyan College, IA
Jacksonville University, FL
James Madison University, VA
Johnson C. Smith University, NC
Juniata College, PA
Kennesaw State University, GA
Kent State University, OH
Kentucky Christian University, KY
Keuka College, NY
Keystone College, PA
King's College, PA
Lancaster Bible College, PA
Lawrence University, WI
Lebanon Valley College, PA
Lees-McRae College, NC
Liberty University, VA
Life University, GA
Lincoln Christian University, IL
Lincoln University, MO
Lincoln University, PA
Linfield College, OR
Lipscomb University, TN
Lock Haven University of Pennsylvania, PA
Long Island University–LIU Brooklyn, NY
Long Island University–LIU Post, NY
Louisiana Tech University, LA
Loyola Marymount University, CA
Malone University, OH
Manchester University, IN
Marymount Manhattan College, NY

Marymount University, VA
Maryville University of Saint Louis, MO
The Master's College and Seminary, CA
Mayville State University, ND
McKendree University, IL
McMurry University, TX
Mercer University, GA
Meredith College, NC
Merrimack College, MA
Michigan State University, MI
Mid-Atlantic Christian University, NC
Middle Tennessee State University, TN
Midwestern State University, TX
Millersville University of Pennsylvania, PA
Millikin University, IL
Minot State University, ND
Mississippi University for Women, MS
Missouri Western State University, MO
Monmouth College, IL
Monmouth University, NJ
Montclair State University, NJ
Montreat College, NC
Moravian College, PA
Morehead State University, KY
Morningside College, IA
Mount Marty College, SD
Mount Mary University, WI
Nebraska Christian College, NE
Newberry College, SC
New England College, NH
New Jersey Institute of Technology, NJ
Newman University, KS
New Mexico State University, NM
North Central College, IL
Northern Illinois University, IL
Northern Michigan University, MI
Northern State University, SD
Northwestern University, IL
Northwest Nazarene University, ID
Northwest University, WA
Notre Dame of Maryland University, MD
Nyack College, NY
Ohio Wesleyan University, OH
Oklahoma Baptist University, OK
Oklahoma Christian University, OK
Oklahoma State University, OK
Oklahoma Wesleyan University, OK
Old Dominion University, VA
Olivet College, MI
Oral Roberts University, OK
Otterbein University, OH
Ouachita Baptist University, AR
Pacific Lutheran University, WA
Pacific University, OR
Palm Beach Atlantic University, FL
Peirce College, PA
Piedmont College, GA
Plymouth State University, NH
Portland State University, OR
Queens University of Charlotte, NC
Quinnipiac University, CT
Ramapo College of New Jersey, NJ
Randolph College, VA
Roberts Wesleyan College, NY
Rockford University, IL
Sacred Heart University, CT
St. Ambrose University, IA
St. Catherine University, MN
Saint Francis University, PA
Saint John's University, MN
Saint Joseph's University, PA
Saint Louis University, MO
Saint Martin's University, WA
Saint Mary's University of Minnesota, MN
St. Norbert College, WI

Schreiner University, TX
Seattle Pacific University, WA
Simpson College, IA
Sonoma State University, CA
South Dakota School of Mines and
    Technology, SD
South Dakota State University, SD
Southeast Missouri State University, MO
Southern Illinois University Carbondale, IL
Southern Oregon University, OR
Southwestern College, KS
Spring Arbor University, MI
State University of New York at Fredonia,
    NY
State University of New York at Plattsburgh,
    NY
State University of New York College of
    Environmental Science and Forestry, NY
Stetson University, FL
Stockton University, NJ
Tabor College, KS
Taylor University, IN
Tennessee Wesleyan College, TN
Texas A&M University, TX
Texas A&M University–Corpus Christi, TX
Texas Christian University, TX
Texas Wesleyan University, TX
Texas Woman's University, TX
Thiel College, PA
Thomas College, ME
Thomas More College, KY
Towson University, MD
Trinity University, TX
Truett-McConnell College, GA
Truman State University, MO
Tulane University, LA
Union University, TN
The University of Akron, OH
The University of Alabama, AL
The University of Alabama at Birmingham,
    AL
The University of Arizona, AZ
University of Arkansas, AR
University of Bridgeport, CT
University of California, Irvine, CA
University of California, Santa Cruz, CA
University of Central Oklahoma, OK
University of Charleston, WV
University of Colorado Denver, CO
University of Evansville, IN
University of Great Falls, MT
University of Hartford, CT
University of Houston, TX
University of Idaho, ID
University of Indianapolis, IN
The University of Kansas, KS
University of Maine at Augusta, ME
University of Maine at Fort Kent, ME
University of Maine at Presque Isle, ME
University of Mary Hardin-Baylor, TX
University of Miami, FL
University of Michigan, MI
University of Michigan–Dearborn, MI
University of Michigan–Flint, MI
University of Mississippi, MS
University of Missouri, MO
University of Missouri–St. Louis, MO
The University of Montana, MT
The University of Montana Western, MT
University of Montevallo, AL
University of Mount Union, OH
University of Nebraska at Kearney, NE
University of Nebraska at Omaha, NE
University of Nebraska–Lincoln, NE
University of Nevada, Las Vegas, NV

University of New Hampshire, NH
University of New Orleans, LA
University of North Carolina at Asheville, NC
The University of North Carolina at Chapel Hill, NC
The University of North Carolina at Greensboro, NC
University of Northern Colorado, CO
University of North Florida, FL
University of Oregon, OR
University of Puget Sound, WA
University of Redlands, CA
University of Rochester, NY
University of Science and Arts of Oklahoma, OK
University of South Carolina, SC
University of South Carolina Aiken, SC
The University of Tampa, FL
The University of Texas at Brownsville, TX
The University of Texas at Dallas, TX
The University of Texas at El Paso, TX
The University of Texas–Pan American, TX
The University of Toledo, OH
University of West Florida, FL
University of West Georgia, GA
University of Wisconsin–Eau Claire, WI
University of Wisconsin–La Crosse, WI
University of Wisconsin–Parkside, WI
University of Wisconsin–Stevens Point, WI
University of Wisconsin–Stout, WI
University of Wisconsin–Superior, WI
University of Wisconsin–Whitewater, WI
University of Wyoming, WY
Ursinus College, PA
Utah State University, UT
Valley City State University, ND
Valparaiso University, IN
Warner Pacific College, OR
Wartburg College, IA
Washburn University, KS
Washington & Jefferson College, PA
Washington State University, WA
Wayland Baptist University, TX
Webber International University, FL
Webster University, MO
Wells College, NY
Wesleyan College, GA
Wesleyan University, CT
Western Illinois University, IL
Western Kentucky University, KY
Western Michigan University, MI
Western Oregon University, OR
Western Washington University, WA
Westminster College, MO
Westminster College, PA
Westmont College, CA
West Texas A&M University, TX
West Virginia University, WV
West Virginia Wesleyan College, WV
Wheaton College, IL
Whitman College, WA
Whittier College, CA
Whitworth University, WA
Wichita State University, KS
Widener University, PA
William Jessup University, CA
Williams Baptist College, AR
Wilson College, PA
Wisconsin Lutheran College, WI
Wittenberg University, OH
Wright State University, OH
Xavier University, OH
York College of Pennsylvania, PA
Youngstown State University, OH

**Local/State Students**

Abilene Christian University, TX
Agnes Scott College, GA
Alaska Pacific University, AK
Albany State University, GA
Albertus Magnus College, CT
Allen College, IA
Alliant International University–San Diego, CA
Alvernia University, PA
American University, DC
Angelo State University, TX
Anna Maria College, MA
Arizona State University at the Downtown Phoenix campus, AZ
Arizona State University at the Polytechnic campus, AZ
Arizona State University at the Tempe campus, AZ
Arizona State University at the West campus, AZ
Arkansas State University, AR
Auburn University, AL
Augustana College, SD
Austin College, TX
Averett University, VA
Ball State University, IN
Barclay College, KS
Belhaven University, MS
Bellarmine University, KY
Benedictine University, IL
Berry College, GA
Bethany College, WV
Bethel College, KS
Binghamton University, State University of New York, NY
Birmingham-Southern College, AL
Bluefield College, VA
Boise State University, ID
Boston University, MA
Brevard College, NC
Bridgewater State University, MA
Brigham Young University, UT
Caldwell University, NJ
California Polytechnic State University, San Luis Obispo, CA
California State University, Bakersfield, CA
California State University, Chico, CA
California State University, Fresno, CA
California State University, Monterey Bay, CA
California State University, San Marcos, CA
California State University, Stanislaus, CA
Calvin College, MI
Carnegie Mellon University, PA
Catawba College, NC
Centenary College of Louisiana, LA
Central College, IA
Central Michigan University, MI
Central Washington University, WA
Chowan University, NC
Christian Brothers University, TN
Christopher Newport University, VA
The Citadel, The Military College of South Carolina, SC
City College of the City University of New York, NY
Clarion University of Pennsylvania, PA
Clarkson University, NY
Clemson University, SC
Coastal Carolina University, SC
Coker College, SC
The College of Idaho, ID
The College of St. Scholastica, MN
College of Staten Island of the City University of New York, NY

Colorado Mesa University, CO
Colorado Mountain College, CO
Colorado State University–Pueblo, CO
Columbia College, MO
Columbia International University, SC
Columbus College of Art & Design, OH
Concordia University, Nebraska, NE
The Criswell College, TX
Culver-Stockton College, MO
Davidson College, NC
DePaul University, IL
Dordt College, IA
Dowling College, NY
Duke University, NC
Eastern Washington University, WA
East Stroudsburg University of Pennsylvania, PA
Eckerd College, FL
Elizabethtown College, PA
Elmira College, NY
Emmanuel College, GA
Emmanuel College, MA
Emory University, GA
Endicott College, MA
Everglades University, FL
Everglades University, FL
Everglades University, FL
The Evergreen State College, WA
Fairmont State University, WV
Faulkner University, AL
Fayetteville State University, NC
Ferris State University, MI
Flagler College, FL
Florida Agricultural and Mechanical University, FL
Florida Gulf Coast University, FL
Florida Southern College, FL
Florida State University, FL
Fort Lewis College, CO
Franciscan University of Steubenville, OH
Franklin Pierce University, NH
Frostburg State University, MD
Furman University, SC
Gardner-Webb University, NC
Georgetown College, KY
Georgia College & State University, GA
Georgia Institute of Technology, GA
Georgian Court University, NJ
Georgia Southwestern State University, GA
Graceland University, IA
Grambling State University, LA
Grand Valley State University, MI
Greenville College, IL
Guilford College, NC
Hamline University, MN
Hawai`i Pacific University, HI
Hofstra University, NY
Hollins University, VA
Hood College, MD
Houghton College, NY
Howard Payne University, TX
Howard University, DC
Huntingdon College, AL
Huntington University, IN
Idaho State University, ID
Illinois Institute of Technology, IL
Indiana University–Purdue University Fort Wayne, IN
Iowa State University of Science and Technology, IA
Jacksonville State University, AL
James Madison University, VA
Jefferson College of Health Sciences, VA
John Carroll University, OH
Johns Hopkins University, MD
Juniata College, PA

Kennesaw State University, GA
Kent State University, OH
Kentucky Christian University, KY
Kentucky State University, KY
Kentucky Wesleyan College, KY
Kutztown University of Pennsylvania, PA
Lees-McRae College, NC
Lee University, TN
Lenoir-Rhyne University, NC
Liberty University, VA
Life University, GA
LIM College, NY
Lincoln Memorial University, TN
Lipscomb University, TN
Lock Haven University of Pennsylvania, PA
Longwood University, VA
Loyola Marymount University, CA
Lycoming College, PA
Lyon College, AR
Malone University, OH
Mansfield University of Pennsylvania, PA
Marian University, WI
Marist College, NY
Marshall University, WV
Marymount Manhattan College, NY
Marymount University, VA
Massachusetts Maritime Academy, MA
Mayville State University, ND
McDaniel College, MD
McMurry University, TX
Medical University of South Carolina, SC
Messiah College, PA
Methodist University, NC
Metropolitan State University of Denver, CO
Miami University, OH
Michigan State University, MI
Middle Tennessee State University, TN
Millsaps College, MS
Minot State University, ND
Mississippi State University, MS
Missouri State University, MO
Missouri Western State University, MO
Monmouth University, NJ
Montana State University, MT
Montana State University Billings, MT
Montana Tech of The University of
   Montana, MT
Montreat College, NC
Morehead State University, KY
Morningside College, IA
Morrisville State College, NY
Murray State University, KY
Muskingum University, OH
Newberry College, SC
New England College, NH
New Jersey Institute of Technology, NJ
New Mexico State University, NM
New York Institute of Technology, NY
Nicholls State University, LA
North Carolina State University, NC
Northeastern State University, OK
Northern Arizona University, AZ
Northern Kentucky University, KY
Northern State University, SD
Nyack College, NY
Ohio Wesleyan University, OH
Oklahoma Baptist University, OK
Oklahoma State University, OK
Old Dominion University, VA
Oral Roberts University, OK
Oregon State University, OR
Ouachita Baptist University, AR
Post University, CT
Queens College of the City University of
   New York, NY

Quincy University, IL
Randolph College, VA
Regis University, CO
Rice University, TX
Robert Morris University Illinois, IL
Rochester College, MI
Sacred Heart University, CT
Saginaw Valley State University, MI
Saint Augustine's University, NC
St. Bonaventure University, NY
St. Catherine University, MN
St. John Fisher College, NY
St. John's University, NY
St. Louis College of Pharmacy, MO
Saint Martin's University, WA
Saint Michael's College, VT
San Diego State University, CA
San Jose State University, CA
Santa Fe University of Art and Design, NM
Shawnee State University, OH
Shenandoah University, VA
Shepherd University, WV
Shippensburg University of Pennsylvania,
   PA
Siena College, NY
Slippery Rock University of Pennsylvania,
   PA
Smith College, MA
Sonoma State University, CA
South Dakota School of Mines and
   Technology, SD
Southern Illinois University Carbondale, IL
Southern Utah University, UT
Southwest Baptist University, MO
Southwestern Christian College, TX
Southwestern Oklahoma State University,
   OK
State University of New York at Fredonia,
   NY
State University of New York at New Paltz,
   NY
State University of New York College at
   Cortland, NY
State University of New York College at
   Geneseo, NY
State University of New York College at
   Potsdam, NY
State University of New York College of
   Agriculture and Technology at
   Cobleskill, NY
State University of New York College of
   Environmental Science and Forestry, NY
State University of New York Polytechnic
   Institute, NY
Stephen F. Austin State University, TX
Stetson University, FL
Stockton University, NJ
Sul Ross State University, TX
Swarthmore College, PA
Tabor College, KS
Tennessee State University, TN
Tennessee Technological University, TN
Texas A&M University, TX
Texas Christian University, TX
Texas State University, TX
Texas Wesleyan University, TX
Thiel College, PA
Thomas College, ME
Trinity Christian College, IL
Truett-McConnell College, GA
Tulane University, LA
Tusculum College, TN
Tuskegee University, AL
Unity College, ME
The University of Akron, OH

The University of Alabama in Huntsville,
   AL
University of Alaska Fairbanks, AK
University of Arkansas, AR
University of Bridgeport, CT
University of Colorado Boulder, CO
University of Connecticut, CT
University of Dayton, OH
University of Delaware, DE
University of Georgia, GA
University of Great Falls, MT
University of Hartford, CT
University of Houston, TX
University of Houston–Clear Lake, TX
University of Idaho, ID
The University of Iowa, IA
The University of Kansas, KS
University of Louisville, KY
University of Maine, ME
University of Maine at Augusta, ME
University of Maine at Presque Isle, ME
University of Mary Hardin-Baylor, TX
University of Mary Washington, VA
University of Massachusetts Dartmouth, MA
University of Michigan, MI
University of Michigan–Flint, MI
University of Minnesota, Crookston, MN
University of Minnesota, Twin Cities
   Campus, MN
University of Mississippi, MS
University of Missouri, MO
University of Missouri–Kansas City, MO
University of Missouri–St. Louis, MO
The University of Montana, MT
University of Mount Olive, NC
University of Nebraska at Kearney, NE
University of Nevada, Las Vegas, NV
University of New Hampshire, NH
University of New Orleans, LA
University of North Carolina at Asheville,
   NC
The University of North Carolina at
   Greensboro, NC
The University of North Carolina
   Wilmington, NC
University of Oregon, OR
University of Pittsburgh at Bradford, PA
University of Rio Grande, OH
University of South Alabama, AL
University of South Carolina, SC
University of Southern Mississippi, MS
The University of Texas at Austin, TX
The University of Texas at Dallas, TX
The University of Texas at El Paso, TX
The University of Texas at San Antonio, TX
The University of Texas–Pan American, TX
University of the Cumberlands, KY
University of Valley Forge, PA
The University of Virginia's College at
   Wise, VA
University of West Georgia, GA
University of Wisconsin–Eau Claire, WI
University of Wisconsin–La Crosse, WI
University of Wisconsin–Oshkosh, WI
University of Wisconsin–Parkside, WI
University of Wisconsin–River Falls, WI
University of Wisconsin–Stout, WI
University of Wisconsin–Whitewater, WI
University of Wyoming, WY
Utah State University, UT
Valdosta State University, GA
Vanderbilt University, TN
Virginia Military Institute, VA
Virginia Polytechnic Institute and State
   University, VA

Wake Forest University, NC
Warner Pacific College, OR
Warren Wilson College, NC
Washburn University, KS
Washington & Jefferson College, PA
Wayland Baptist University, TX
Wayne State College, NE
Webber International University, FL
Western Carolina University, NC
Western Kentucky University, KY
Western Michigan University, MI
Western Oregon University, OR
Western Washington University, WA
Westminster College, MO
West Texas A&M University, TX
West Virginia University, WV
Wilson College, PA
Winona State University, MN
Wofford College, SC
Youngstown State University, OH

**Married Students**

Alaska Bible College, AK
Auburn University, AL
Barclay College, KS
Binghamton University, State University of
    New York, NY
Blue Mountain College, MS
California State University, Chico, CA
Cincinnati Christian University, OH
The College at Brockport, State University
    of New York, NY
The College of Idaho, ID
College of Staten Island of the City
    University of New York, NY
Colorado State University–Pueblo, CO
Crossroads Bible College, IN
Eastern Washington University, WA
Emmanuel College, GA
Franklin Pierce University, NH
Georgia Southern University, GA
Heritage Christian University, AL
Howard University, DC
Indiana Tech, IN
Lancaster Bible College, PA
Lock Haven University of Pennsylvania, PA
Mid-Atlantic Christian University, NC
Montana Tech of The University of
    Montana, MT
Newman University, KS
New Mexico State University, NM
Northwest University, WA
Ouachita Baptist University, AR
Sonoma State University, CA
South Dakota School of Mines and
    Technology, SD
Texas Wesleyan University, TX
Truett-McConnell College, GA
The University of Alabama at Birmingham,
    AL
University of Arkansas, AR
The University of Kansas, KS
University of Nevada, Reno, NV
The University of North Carolina
    Wilmington, NC
University of Portland, OR
University of Valley Forge, PA

**Members of Minorities**

Abilene Christian University, TX
Alabama State University, AL
Alaska Pacific University, AK
Alice Lloyd College, KY
Allen College, IA
American University, DC
Anderson University, SC
Arkansas State University, AR

Ashland University, OH
Assumption College, MA
Augustana College, IL
Augustana College, SD
Austin Peay State University, TN
Azusa Pacific University, CA
Baldwin Wallace University, OH
Ball State University, IN
Bellarmine University, KY
Belmont University, TN
Bemidji State University, MN
Bentley University, MA
Berry College, GA
Bethel University, MN
Binghamton University, State University of
    New York, NY
Biola University, CA
Bluffton University, OH
Boise State University, ID
Boston University, MA
Bowling Green State University, OH
Bridgewater College, VA
Bridgewater State University, MA
Brigham Young University, UT
Bryant University, RI
California State Polytechnic University,
    Pomona, CA
California State University, Chico, CA
California University of Pennsylvania, PA
Calvin College, MI
Cameron University, OK
Capital University, OH
Carnegie Mellon University, PA
Carson-Newman University, TN
Centenary College of Louisiana, LA
Central College, IA
Central Connecticut State University, CT
Central Washington University, WA
Champlain College, VT
Cincinnati Christian University, OH
Clarion University of Pennsylvania, PA
Clarkson University, NY
Clemson University, SC
Coe College, IA
The College at Brockport, State University
    of New York, NY
The College of Idaho, ID
The College of New Jersey, NJ
The College of Saint Rose, NY
The College of St. Scholastica, MN
College of Staten Island of the City
    University of New York, NY
The College of Wooster, OH
Colorado Mesa University, CO
Colorado State University–Pueblo, CO
Columbia College, MO
Columbia International University, SC
Concordia University, Nebraska, NE
Cornerstone University, MI
Covenant College, GA
Creighton University, NE
Dickinson State University, ND
Dordt College, IA
Dowling College, NY
Drew University, NJ
Drury University, MO
Duquesne University, PA
East Central University, OK
Eastern Kentucky University, KY
Eastern Michigan University, MI
Eastern New Mexico University, NM
East Stroudsburg University of
    Pennsylvania, PA
Elizabeth City State University, NC
Elizabethtown College, PA
Elmhurst College, IL

Elon University, NC
Emporia State University, KS
Fairmont State University, WV
Ferris State University, MI
Flagler College, FL
Florida Gulf Coast University, FL
Franklin College, IN
Fresno Pacific University, CA
Gallaudet University, DC
Gannon University, PA
Gardner-Webb University, NC
George Fox University, OR
Georgetown College, KY
Georgia Institute of Technology, GA
Georgia Southern University, GA
Golden Gate University, CA
Gonzaga University, WA
Goshen College, IN
Governors State University, IL
Graceland University, IA
Grambling State University, LA
Grove City College, PA
Gustavus Adolphus College, MN
Hamline University, MN
Hampden-Sydney College, VA
Hampton University, VA
Hanover College, IN
Hilbert College, NY
Hofstra University, NY
Howard University, DC
Idaho State University, ID
Illinois State University, IL
Indiana State University, IN
Iowa State University of Science and
    Technology, IA
Ithaca College, NY
James Madison University, VA
Kennesaw State University, GA
Kent State University, OH
Kent State University at Stark, OH
Kentucky Christian University, KY
Lawrence Technological University, MI
Lebanon Valley College, PA
Lehigh University, PA
Le Moyne College, NY
Lenoir-Rhyne University, NC
Lewis-Clark State College, ID
Life University, GA
Lincoln Memorial University, TN
Linfield College, OR
Lipscomb University, TN
Lock Haven University of Pennsylvania, PA
Louisiana Tech University, LA
Loyola Marymount University, CA
Luther College, IA
Lyon College, AR
Malone University, OH
Manchester University, IN
Mansfield University of Pennsylvania, PA
Marietta College, OH
Marshall University, WV
Maryville College, TN
Maryville University of Saint Louis, MO
Massachusetts Maritime Academy, MA
Mayville State University, ND
Medical University of South Carolina, SC
Meredith College, NC
Methodist University, NC
Miami University, OH
Middle Tennessee State University, TN
Midwestern State University, TX
Minnesota State University Mankato, MN
Minnesota State University Moorhead, MN
Minot State University, ND
Misericordia University, PA
Mississippi University for Women, MS

Missouri State University, MO
Missouri University of Science and
    Technology, MO
Molloy College, NY
Monmouth University, NJ
Montana State University, MT
Montana State University Billings, MT
Morehead State University, KY
Morrisville State College, NY
Mount Carmel College of Nursing, OH
Mount St. Mary's University, MD
Murray State University, KY
Muskingum University, OH
New Jersey Institute of Technology, NJ
New Mexico State University, NM
Nicholls State University, LA
Northeastern State University, OK
Northern Arizona University, AZ
Northern Illinois University, IL
Northern Kentucky University, KY
Northern Michigan University, MI
Northern State University, SD
Northwest Missouri State University, MO
The Ohio State University, OH
Ohio University, OH
Ohio University–Chillicothe, OH
Ohio University–Eastern, OH
Ohio University–Lancaster, OH
Ohio University–Southern Campus, OH
Ohio University–Zanesville, OH
Ohio Wesleyan University, OH
Oklahoma Baptist University, OK
Old Dominion University, VA
Oregon State University, OR
Otterbein University, OH
Ouachita Baptist University, AR
Pine Manor College, MA
Portland State University, OR
Quincy University, IL
Rensselaer Polytechnic Institute, NY
Rhodes College, TN
Rice University, TX
Rider University, NJ
Sacred Heart University, CT
The Sage Colleges, NY
Saginaw Valley State University, MI
St. Ambrose University, IA
St. Bonaventure University, NY
St. John Fisher College, NY
Saint Joseph's University, PA
Saint Louis University, MO
Saint Martin's University, WA
Saint Mary's University of Minnesota, MN
Saint Michael's College, VT
Samford University, AL
Seattle University, WA
Shawnee State University, OH
Shepherd University, WV
Simpson College, IA
Simpson University, CA
Slippery Rock University of Pennsylvania,
    PA
Sonoma State University, CA
South Dakota School of Mines and
    Technology, SD
South Dakota State University, SD
Southeast Missouri State University, MO
Southern Illinois University Carbondale, IL
Southern Oregon University, OR
Southern Utah University, UT
Southwestern College, KS
Spring Arbor University, MI
State University of New York at Fredonia,
    NY

State University of New York at New Paltz,
    NY
State University of New York College at
    Cortland, NY
State University of New York College at
    Geneseo, NY
State University of New York College at
    Potsdam, NY
State University of New York College of
    Agriculture and Technology at
    Cobleskill, NY
State University of New York College of
    Environmental Science and Forestry, NY
State University of New York Polytechnic
    Institute, NY
Stetson University, FL
Stockton University, NJ
Tennessee State University, TN
Tennessee Technological University, TN
Tennessee Wesleyan College, TN
Texas A&M University–Commerce, TX
Texas Christian University, TX
Texas Wesleyan University, TX
Thomas Jefferson University, PA
Thomas More College, KY
Towson University, MD
Transylvania University, KY
Trine University, IN
Trinity Christian College, IL
Union College, KY
Union University, TN
Unity College, ME
The University of Akron, OH
The University of Alabama at Birmingham,
    AL
The University of Alabama in Huntsville,
    AL
University of Arkansas, AR
University of California, San Diego, CA
University of Central Oklahoma, OK
University of Dayton, OH
University of Delaware, DE
University of Evansville, IN
University of Florida, FL
University of Hartford, CT
University of Idaho, ID
The University of Kansas, KS
University of Louisville, KY
University of Maine, ME
University of Maine at Farmington, ME
University of Maine at Fort Kent, ME
University of Mary Hardin-Baylor, TX
University of Massachusetts Dartmouth, MA
University of Memphis, TN
University of Michigan, MI
University of Michigan–Dearborn, MI
University of Michigan–Flint, MI
University of Minnesota, Crookston, MN
University of Minnesota, Twin Cities
    Campus, MN
University of Mississippi, MS
University of Missouri, MO
University of Missouri–Kansas City, MO
University of Missouri–St. Louis, MO
The University of Montana Western, MT
University of Mount Union, OH
University of Nebraska at Kearney, NE
University of Nebraska at Omaha, NE
University of Nebraska–Lincoln, NE
University of Nevada, Las Vegas, NV
University of New Orleans, LA
The University of North Carolina at
    Charlotte, NC
University of Northern Iowa, IA
University of North Florida, FL

University of Oklahoma, OK
The University of Scranton, PA
University of South Alabama, AL
University of South Carolina, SC
University of South Carolina Aiken, SC
The University of South Dakota, SD
University of Southern Indiana, IN
The University of Tennessee at Martin, TN
The University of Texas at Dallas, TX
The University of Texas at El Paso, TX
The University of Texas at San Antonio, TX
The University of Toledo, OH
University of West Georgia, GA
University of Wisconsin–Eau Claire, WI
University of Wisconsin–Green Bay, WI
University of Wisconsin–La Crosse, WI
University of Wisconsin–Oshkosh, WI
University of Wisconsin–Parkside, WI
University of Wisconsin–River Falls, WI
University of Wisconsin–Stevens Point, WI
University of Wisconsin–Stout, WI
University of Wisconsin–Superior, WI
University of Wisconsin–Whitewater, WI
University of Wyoming, WY
Utah State University, UT
Valdosta State University, GA
Valley City State University, ND
Vanderbilt University, TN
Virginia Polytechnic Institute and State
    University, VA
Warner Pacific College, OR
Washington & Jefferson College, PA
Wayland Baptist University, TX
Wayne State College, NE
Webster University, MO
Western Carolina University, NC
Western Illinois University, IL
Western Kentucky University, KY
Western Washington University, WA
West Virginia University, WV
Wheaton College, IL
Whitworth University, WA
Wichita State University, KS
Williams Baptist College, AR
Winona State University, MN
Wisconsin Lutheran College, WI
Wittenberg University, OH
Wofford College, SC
Wright State University, OH
Xavier University, OH
York College of Pennsylvania, PA
Youngstown State University, OH

**Out-of-State Students**
Abilene Christian University, TX
Alaska Pacific University, AK
Allen College, IA
Anderson University, SC
Arizona State University at the Downtown
    Phoenix campus, AZ
Arizona State University at the Polytechnic
    campus, AZ
Arizona State University at the Tempe
    campus, AZ
Arizona State University at the West
    campus, AZ
Arkansas State University, AR
Arkansas Tech University, AR
Ashland University, OH
Auburn University, AL
Austin College, TX
Averett University, VA
Ball State University, IN
Bellarmine University, KY
Bemidji State University, MN

Benedictine University, IL
Berry College, GA
Bethany College, WV
Bethel University, MN
Binghamton University, State University of
  New York, NY
Bloomfield College, NJ
Bluefield College, VA
Bluffton University, OH
Boise State University, ID
Bridgewater College, VA
Buena Vista University, IA
Cabrini College, PA
California State University, Chico, CA
Calvin College, MI
Cameron University, OK
Capital University, OH
Carnegie Mellon University, PA
Centenary College of Louisiana, LA
Central College, IA
Central Michigan University, MI
Central Washington University, WA
Chowan University, NC
Christian Brothers University, TN
The Citadel, The Military College of South
  Carolina, SC
Cleveland State University, OH
Coastal Carolina University, SC
Coker College, SC
The College of Idaho, ID
The College of New Rochelle, NY
College of Saint Benedict, MN
The College of Saint Rose, NY
College of Staten Island of the City
  University of New York, NY
Colorado Mesa University, CO
Colorado State University–Pueblo, CO
Concordia University Ann Arbor, MI
Concordia University Wisconsin, WI
The Criswell College, TX
Davidson College, NC
Delaware State University, DE
Delta State University, MS
Dordt College, IA
East Central University, OK
Eastern Michigan University, MI
Eastern New Mexico University, NM
Elmira College, NY
Emory & Henry College, VA
Evangel University, MO
The Evergreen State College, WA
Fairmont State University, WV
Faulkner University, AL
Flagler College, FL
Florida Agricultural and Mechanical
  University, FL
Florida Gulf Coast University, FL
Florida Southern College, FL
Fort Lewis College, CO
Fort Valley State University, GA
Francis Marion University, SC
Franklin College, IN
Friends University, KS
Frostburg State University, MD
Gardner-Webb University, NC
George Fox University, OR
Georgetown College, KY
Georgia College & State University, GA
Georgia Institute of Technology, GA
Glenville State College, WV
Grambling State University, LA
Grand Valley State University, MI
Greenville College, IL
Gustavus Adolphus College, MN
Hamline University, MN
Hampden-Sydney College, VA

Hanover College, IN
Hardin-Simmons University, TX
Hawai`i Pacific University, HI
Heidelberg University, OH
Henderson State University, AR
Hollins University, VA
Idaho State University, ID
Iowa State University of Science and
  Technology, IA
Iowa Wesleyan College, IA
James Madison University, VA
Johnson C. Smith University, NC
Kent State University, OH
Kent State University at Geauga, OH
Kent State University at Stark, OH
Kentucky Wesleyan College, KY
King University, TN
Lewis-Clark State College, ID
Lincoln University, MO
Louisiana Tech University, LA
Loyola Marymount University, CA
Lynn University, FL
MacMurray College, IL
Manchester University, IN
Marian University, WI
Marymount Manhattan College, NY
Marymount University, VA
Maryville University of Saint Louis, MO
Mayville State University, ND
McMurry University, TX
Meredith College, NC
Miami University, OH
Michigan State University, MI
Minnesota State University Moorhead, MN
Minot State University, ND
Misericordia University, PA
Mississippi State University, MS
Mississippi University for Women, MS
Missouri Western State University, MO
Monmouth University, NJ
Montana State University Billings, MT
Montana Tech of The University of
  Montana, MT
Morehead State University, KY
Morningside College, IA
Morrisville State College, NY
Murray State University, KY
Nazareth College of Rochester, NY
New College of Florida, FL
New Jersey Institute of Technology, NJ
New Mexico State University, NM
Nicholls State University, LA
Northeastern State University, OK
Northern Michigan University, MI
Northwest Missouri State University, MO
Nyack College, NY
Oakland University, MI
The Ohio State University, OH
Oklahoma Baptist University, OK
Oklahoma State University, OK
Ouachita Baptist University, AR
Pacific Lutheran University, WA
Palm Beach Atlantic University, FL
Piedmont College, GA
Portland State University, OR
Ramapo College of New Jersey, NJ
Randolph-Macon College, VA
Robert Morris University Illinois, IL
Roberts Wesleyan College, NY
Rochester College, MI
Rockford University, IL
Rogers State University, OK
Sacred Heart University, CT
St. Ambrose University, IA
St. Bonaventure University, NY
St. Catherine University, MN

St. Cloud State University, MN
Saint Francis University, PA
Saint John's University, MN
Saint Martin's University, WA
Saint Michael's College, VT
Saint Vincent College, PA
Shepherd University, WV
Siena College, NY
Simpson University, CA
Slippery Rock University of Pennsylvania,
  PA
Sonoma State University, CA
South Dakota School of Mines and
  Technology, SD
Southeastern Louisiana University, LA
Southeastern Oklahoma State University,
  OK
Southeast Missouri State University, MO
Southwestern Oklahoma State University,
  OK
State University of New York at Fredonia,
  NY
State University of New York at Plattsburgh,
  NY
State University of New York College of
  Environmental Science and Forestry, NY
Stetson University, FL
Tabor College, KS
Tennessee Technological University, TN
Texas A&M University–Commerce, TX
Texas Tech University, TX
Texas Wesleyan University, TX
Thomas College, ME
Thomas More College, KY
Thomas University, GA
Transylvania University, KY
Trinity Christian College, IL
Truett-McConnell College, GA
Truman State University, MO
The University of Akron, OH
The University of Alabama, AL
The University of Alabama at Birmingham,
  AL
University of Arkansas, AR
University of California, Irvine, CA
University of California, Santa Cruz, CA
University of Colorado Denver, CO
University of Connecticut, CT
University of Dubuque, IA
University of Florida, FL
University of Houston, TX
University of Idaho, ID
University of Illinois at Springfield, IL
University of Indianapolis, IN
The University of Iowa, IA
The University of Kansas, KS
University of Louisville, KY
University of Maine at Farmington, ME
University of Maine at Presque Isle, ME
University of Mary Hardin-Baylor, TX
University of Maryland, College Park, MD
University of Massachusetts Lowell, MA
University of Michigan, MI
University of Michigan–Dearborn, MI
University of Mississippi, MS
University of Missouri, MO
University of Missouri–Kansas City, MO
University of Missouri–St. Louis, MO
The University of Montana, MT
The University of Montana Western, MT
University of Montevallo, AL
University of Nebraska at Kearney, NE
University of Nebraska at Omaha, NE
University of Nebraska–Lincoln, NE
University of Nevada, Las Vegas, NV
University of New Orleans, LA

University of North Alabama, AL
The University of North Carolina at Chapel
  Hill, NC
The University of North Carolina at
  Greensboro, NC
University of Northern Colorado, CO
University of North Florida, FL
University of Pittsburgh at Bradford, PA
University of Rio Grande, OH
University of Science and Arts of Oklahoma,
  OK
University of South Carolina, SC
University of Southern Indiana, IN
University of Southern Mississippi, MS
The University of Tennessee at Martin, TN
The University of Texas at Dallas, TX
The University of Texas at El Paso, TX
The University of Texas at San Antonio, TX
The University of Texas–Pan American, TX
The University of Toledo, OH
University of Utah, UT
University of West Florida, FL
University of Wisconsin–La Crosse, WI
University of Wisconsin–Stevens Point, WI
University of Wisconsin–Stout, WI
University of Wisconsin–Whitewater, WI
University of Wyoming, WY
VanderCook College of Music, IL
Virginia Military Institute, VA
Virginia Polytechnic Institute and State
  University, VA
Washington State University, WA
Wayne State College, NE
Webster University, MO
Western Kentucky University, KY
Western Michigan University, MI
Western Oregon University, OR
West Texas A&M University, TX
William Jessup University, CA
Winona State University, MN
Wisconsin Lutheran College, WI
Wright State University, OH
Youngstown State University, OH

**Parents of Current Students**
Barclay College, KS
Blue Mountain College, MS
Caldwell University, NJ
Cincinnati Christian University, OH
The College of New Rochelle, NY
College of Staten Island of the City
  University of New York, NY
Columbia College, MO
ECPI University, VA
Emmanuel College, GA
Franklin Pierce University, NH
Manchester University, IN
Maryville University of Saint Louis, MO
Millikin University, IL
Mississippi University for Women, MS
Missouri Baptist University, MO
Mount Aloysius College, PA
Mount Marty College, SD
Mount Mary University, WI
New England College, NH
Northwest University, WA
Rockford University, IL
St. Joseph's College, Long Island Campus,
  NY
St. Joseph's College, New York, NY
State University of New York at Fredonia,
  NY
Stephens College, MO
Texas Wesleyan University, TX
Truett-McConnell College, GA

The University of Alabama at Birmingham,
  AL
University of Great Falls, MT
University of Hartford, CT
University of Valley Forge, PA
Upper Iowa University, IA
Wesleyan College, GA

**Previous College Experience**
Abilene Christian University, TX
Alaska Pacific University, AK
American University, DC
Anna Maria College, MA
Austin College, TX
Bellarmine University, KY
Bemidji State University, MN
Bethel College, KS
Birmingham-Southern College, AL
Boise State University, ID
Brevard College, NC
Bridgewater College, VA
Calumet College of Saint Joseph, IN
Cedar Crest College, PA
Central College, IA
Clarion University of Pennsylvania, PA
Coker College, SC
The College at Brockport, State University
  of New York, NY
The College of New Rochelle, NY
The College of St. Scholastica, MN
College of Staten Island of the City
  University of New York, NY
Columbia College, MO
Dowling College, NY
Eastern Michigan University, MI
Elmira College, NY
Fairmont State University, WV
Ferris State University, MI
Florida Institute of Technology, FL
Gardner-Webb University, NC
Golden Gate University, CA
Hamline University, MN
Hastings College, NE
Hawai'i Pacific University, HI
Hendrix College, AR
Hollins University, VA
Howard University, DC
Huntington University, IN
Illinois College, IL
Illinois Institute of Technology, IL
Illinois State University, IL
Indiana State University, IN
Kent State University, OH
Kentucky Christian University, KY
Kentucky State University, KY
Lancaster Bible College, PA
Lees-McRae College, NC
Lewis-Clark State College, ID
Linfield College, OR
Lock Haven University of Pennsylvania, PA
Loyola Marymount University, CA
Manhattanville College, NY
McDaniel College, MD
McMurry University, TX
Meredith College, NC
Misericordia University, PA
Mississippi State University, MS
Missouri Western State University, MO
Monmouth University, NJ
Morehead State University, KY
Mount Mercy University, IA
New Mexico State University, NM
New York Institute of Technology, NY
Nicholls State University, LA
Northwest Missouri State University, MO

The Ohio State University, OH
Oklahoma State University, OK
Old Dominion University, VA
Otterbein University, OH
Ouachita Baptist University, AR
Palm Beach Atlantic University, FL
Rochester College, MI
St. Ambrose University, IA
Saint Francis University, PA
Saint Louis University, MO
San Diego State University, CA
Shepherd University, WV
Siena College, NY
Slippery Rock University of Pennsylvania,
  PA
Sonoma State University, CA
Southeast Missouri State University, MO
State University of New York at Fredonia,
  NY
State University of New York College at
  Potsdam, NY
State University of New York Polytechnic
  Institute, NY
Stephen F. Austin State University, TX
Stockton University, NJ
Texas A&M University–Commerce, TX
Texas Christian University, TX
Texas Wesleyan University, TX
Towson University, MD
Truman State University, MO
The University of Alabama at Birmingham,
  AL
University of Arkansas, AR
University of Bridgeport, CT
University of Hartford, CT
University of Houston, TX
The University of Kansas, KS
University of Louisville, KY
University of Massachusetts Dartmouth, MA
University of Michigan–Dearborn, MI
University of Mississippi, MS
University of Missouri–St. Louis, MO
University of Nevada, Las Vegas, NV
University of Oklahoma, OK
University of St. Thomas, TX
University of Science and Arts of Oklahoma,
  OK
The University of Toledo, OH
The University of West Alabama, AL
University of Wisconsin–Eau Claire, WI
University of Wisconsin–Stout, WI
Warren Wilson College, NC
Wartburg College, IA
Western Michigan University, MI
Western Washington University, WA
William Jessup University, CA

**Public Servants**
Arkansas Tech University, AR
Caldwell University, NJ
Central Washington University, WA
Chowan University, NC
College of Staten Island of the City
  University of New York, NY
Dowling College, NY
Georgia College & State University, GA
Grambling State University, LA
Grand Valley State University, MI
Hardin-Simmons University, TX
Hofstra University, NY
Kent State University at Stark, OH
Kentucky State University, KY
La Sierra University, CA
Lindenwood University, MO
Missouri Baptist University, MO

Missouri Western State University, MO
New Mexico State University, NM
Nicholls State University, LA
Patrick Henry College, VA
Peirce College, PA
Regent University, VA
Regis University, CO
St. Francis College, NY
St. Joseph's College, Long Island Campus, NY
St. Joseph's College, New York, NY
Southern Illinois University Carbondale, IL
Tennessee Technological University, TN
Texas Wesleyan University, TX
The University of Alabama at Birmingham, AL
University of Massachusetts Dartmouth, MA
University of Memphis, TN
University of Michigan–Dearborn, MI
University of New Orleans, LA
University of Oklahoma, OK
The University of Texas at Arlington, TX
The University of Texas at Dallas, TX
The University of Toledo, OH
Washington State University, WA
West Texas A&M University, TX
Youngstown State University, OH

**Relatives of Clergy**

Abilene Christian University, TX
Albion College, MI
American University, DC
Anderson University, IN
Arcadia University, PA
Ashland University, OH
Austin College, TX
Averett University, VA
Barclay College, KS
Benedictine University, IL
Bethany College, WV
Bethel College, KS
Bethel University, MN
Biola University, CA
Birmingham-Southern College, AL
Boston University, MA
Cairn University, PA
Caldwell University, NJ
California Baptist University, CA
California Lutheran University, CA
Calvary Bible College and Theological Seminary, MO
Campbellsville University, KY
Capital University, OH
Carson-Newman University, TN
Cedar Crest College, PA
Centenary College of Louisiana, LA
Central Methodist University, MO
Chowan University, NC
Clarke University, IA
Corban University, OR
Cornerstone University, MI
Dallas Baptist University, TX
Davidson College, NC
Dominican College, NY
Drury University, MO
Duquesne University, PA
Eastern University, PA
Elon University, NC
Emmanuel College, GA
Emmaus Bible College, IA
Eureka College, IL
Evangel University, MO
Faulkner University, AL
Florida Southern College, FL
Fresno Pacific University, CA
Friends University, KS

Furman University, SC
Gardner-Webb University, NC
George Fox University, OR
Georgetown College, KY
Gordon College, MA
Greensboro College, NC
Greenville College, IL
Hamline University, MN
Harding University, AR
Hardin-Simmons University, TX
Hawai`i Pacific University, HI
Heidelberg University, OH
Hendrix College, AR
Heritage Christian University, AL
Hillsdale Free Will Baptist College, OK
Hobart and William Smith Colleges, NY
Houghton College, NY
Houston Baptist University, TX
Howard Payne University, TX
Huntington University, IN
Kentucky Wesleyan College, KY
King's College, PA
LaGrange College, GA
Lancaster Bible College, PA
La Salle University, PA
La Sierra University, CA
Lees-McRae College, NC
Lenoir-Rhyne University, NC
Lindsey Wilson College, KY
Lipscomb University, TN
Lycoming College, PA
Malone University, OH
Maranatha Baptist University, WI
The Master's College and Seminary, CA
McMurry University, TX
Mercer University, GA
Merrimack College, MA
Methodist University, NC
Millikin University, IL
Misericordia University, PA
Mississippi College, MS
Missouri Baptist University, MO
Montreat College, NC
Moravian College, PA
Muskingum University, OH
Nebraska Christian College, NE
Newberry College, SC
New Jersey Institute of Technology, NJ
Niagara University, NY
North Central College, IL
Northwest Christian University, OR
Northwest Nazarene University, ID
Northwest University, WA
Nyack College, NY
Ohio Wesleyan University, OH
Oklahoma Baptist University, OK
Oklahoma City University, OK
Oklahoma Wesleyan University, OK
Olivet Nazarene University, IL
Oral Roberts University, OK
Otterbein University, OH
Ouachita Baptist University, AR
Pacific Lutheran University, WA
Pacific University, OR
Patrick Henry College, VA
Presbyterian College, SC
Queens University of Charlotte, NC
Randolph College, VA
Randolph-Macon College, VA
Rhodes College, TN
Roberts Wesleyan College, NY
Rochester College, MI
Rosemont College, PA
St. Bonaventure University, NY
St. John's University, NY
Saint Mary's College of California, CA

Salem College, NC
Samford University, AL
Schreiner University, TX
Seattle Pacific University, WA
Shenandoah University, VA
Siena College, NY
Simpson College, IA
Simpson University, CA
Southwest Baptist University, MO
Southwestern University, TX
Spring Arbor University, MI
Stonehill College, MA
Susquehanna University, PA
Tennessee Wesleyan College, TN
Texas Christian University, TX
Texas Wesleyan University, TX
Thiel College, PA
Transylvania University, KY
Trevecca Nazarene University, TN
Trinity College of Florida, FL
Truett-McConnell College, GA
Union University, TN
The University of Alabama at Birmingham, AL
University of Dubuque, IA
University of Indianapolis, IN
University of Jamestown, ND
University of Mary Hardin-Baylor, TX
University of Mobile, AL
University of Mount Union, OH
The University of North Carolina at Chapel Hill, NC
University of Portland, OR
University of the Cumberlands, KY
The University of Tulsa, OK
University of Valley Forge, PA
Ursuline College, OH
Valparaiso University, IN
Virginia Wesleyan College, VA
Warren Wilson College, NC
Wayland Baptist University, TX
Wesleyan College, GA
Westminster College, MO
West Virginia Wesleyan College, WV
William Jessup University, CA
Williams Baptist College, AR
William Woods University, MO
Wilson College, PA
Wingate University, NC
Wittenberg University, OH
Wofford College, SC

**Religious Affiliation**

Abilene Christian University, TX
Adrian College, MI
Agnes Scott College, GA
Alaska Pacific University, AK
Albertus Magnus College, CT
Alderson Broaddus University, WV
Anderson University, SC
Arcadia University, PA
Armstrong State University, GA
Ashland University, OH
Augustana College, IL
Augustana College, SD
Austin College, TX
Ave Maria University, FL
Averett University, VA
Azusa Pacific University, CA
Baldwin Wallace University, OH
The Baptist College of Florida, FL
Barclay College, KS
Bellarmine University, KY
Bethany College, WV
Bethel College, KS
Bethel University, MN

Birmingham-Southern College, AL
Bluefield College, VA
Blue Mountain College, MS
Bluffton University, OH
Boston University, MA
Bridgewater College, VA
Brigham Young University, UT
Buena Vista University, IA
Cabrini College, PA
Caldwell University, NJ
California Baptist University, CA
California Lutheran University, CA
Calumet College of Saint Joseph, IN
Calvary Bible College and Theological
    Seminary, MO
Calvin College, MI
Campbellsville University, KY
Canisius College, NY
Capital University, OH
Cardinal Stritch University, WI
Carroll College, MT
The Catholic University of America, DC
Cedarville University, OH
Centenary College of Louisiana, LA
Central College, IA
Central Methodist University, MO
Chaminade University of Honolulu, HI
Charlotte Christian College and Theological
    Seminary, NC
Chowan University, NC
Coe College, IA
The College at Brockport, State University
    of New York, NY
The College of St. Scholastica, MN
Columbia College, MO
Conception Seminary College, MO
Concordia University, CA
Concordia University Ann Arbor, MI
Concordia University Chicago, IL
Concordia University, Nebraska, NE
Concordia University, St. Paul, MN
Concordia University Texas, TX
Covenant College, GA
The Criswell College, TX
Culver-Stockton College, MO
Dakota Wesleyan University, SD
Dallas Baptist University, TX
Davidson College, NC
Doane College, NE
Dordt College, IA
Drury University, MO
Duquesne University, PA
Eastern Michigan University, MI
Eastern Nazarene College, MA
East Texas Baptist University, TX
Eckerd College, FL
Elizabethtown College, PA
Elmhurst College, IL
Elms College, MA
Emmanuel College, GA
Emmanuel College, MA
Emory University, GA
Emporia State University, KS
Endicott College, MA
Eureka College, IL
Evangel University, MO
Faulkner University, AL
Florida Southern College, FL
Fontbonne University, MO
Franciscan University of Steubenville, OH
Franklin College, IN
Fresno Pacific University, CA
Furman University, SC
Gannon University, PA
Geneva College, PA

George Fox University, OR
Georgetown College, KY
Georgian Court University, NJ
Georgia Regents University, GA
Georgia Southern University, GA
Graceland University, IA
Grand View University, IA
Greensboro College, NC
Greenville College, IL
Hamline University, MN
Hanover College, IN
Hardin-Simmons University, TX
Hastings College, NE
Hawai`i Pacific University, HI
Heidelberg University, OH
Hillsdale Free Will Baptist College, OK
Hood College, MD
Houghton College, NY
Howard Payne University, TX
Howard University, DC
Huntingdon College, AL
Huntington University, IN
Iona College, NY
Kennesaw State University, GA
Kentucky Christian University, KY
Kentucky Wesleyan College, KY
LaGrange College, GA
Lancaster Bible College, PA
La Sierra University, CA
Lees-McRae College, NC
Lenoir-Rhyne University, NC
Lewis University, IL
Liberty University, VA
Lindsey Wilson College, KY
Lipscomb University, TN
Loyola Marymount University, CA
Loyola University Chicago, IL
Luther College, IA
Lyon College, AR
Malone University, OH
Manchester University, IN
Mansfield University of Pennsylvania, PA
Marymount University, VA
Maryville College, TN
McKendree University, IL
McMurry University, TX
Meredith College, NC
Merrimack College, MA
Messiah College, PA
Methodist University, NC
Millsaps College, MS
Missouri Baptist University, MO
Missouri Western State University, MO
Molloy College, NY
Montreat College, NC
Moravian College, PA
Morningside College, IA
Mount Aloysius College, PA
Mount Marty College, SD
Muskingum University, OH
Newberry College, SC
New Jersey Institute of Technology, NJ
Northeastern State University, OK
Northwest Christian University, OR
Northwest Nazarene University, ID
Northwest University, WA
Notre Dame de Namur University, CA
Nyack College, NY
Ohio Wesleyan University, OH
Oklahoma Baptist University, OK
Oklahoma City University, OK
Oklahoma Wesleyan University, OK
Olivet College, MI
Olivet Nazarene University, IL
Ouachita Baptist University, AR

Our Lady of the Lake University of San
    Antonio, TX
Pacific Lutheran University, WA
Park University, MO
Presbyterian College, SC
Queens University of Charlotte, NC
Randolph College, VA
Reinhardt University, GA
Rhodes College, TN
Roberts Wesleyan College, NY
Rochester College, MI
Sacred Heart University, CT
St. Ambrose University, IA
St. Bonaventure University, NY
St. Catherine University, MN
St. Edward's University, TX
Saint Francis University, PA
St. John's University, NY
Saint Louis University, MO
Saint Michael's College, VT
Saint Vincent College, PA
Schreiner University, TX
Seattle Pacific University, WA
Seattle University, WA
Shenandoah University, VA
Siena College, NY
Simpson College, IA
Simpson University, CA
Southwest Baptist University, MO
Southwestern College, KS
Southwestern University, TX
Spring Arbor University, MI
State University of New York College at
    Geneseo, NY
Tabor College, KS
Taylor University, IN
Tennessee Wesleyan College, TN
Texas Christian University, TX
Texas Lutheran University, TX
Texas Wesleyan University, TX
Thiel College, PA
Thomas More College, KY
Transylvania University, KY
Trevecca Nazarene University, TN
Trinity Christian College, IL
Truett-McConnell College, GA
Union College, KY
Union University, TN
University of California, Riverside, CA
University of Dallas, TX
University of Dayton, OH
University of Dubuque, IA
University of Evansville, IN
University of Great Falls, MT
University of Hartford, CT
University of Indianapolis, IN
University of Jamestown, ND
University of Mary Hardin-Baylor, TX
University of Mount Olive, NC
The University of North Carolina at Chapel
    Hill, NC
The University of North Carolina at
    Greensboro, NC
University of Portland, OR
University of St. Francis, IL
University of St. Thomas, TX
University of San Diego, CA
The University of Scranton, PA
University of South Carolina, SC
The University of Tennessee at Chattanooga,
    TN
University of the Cumberlands, KY
University of the Pacific, CA
The University of Toledo, OH
The University of Tulsa, OK

Ursuline College, OH
Utah State University, UT
Valparaiso University, IN
VanderCook College of Music, IL
Vanguard University of Southern California, CA
Villanova University, PA
Virginia Wesleyan College, VA
Wake Forest University, NC
Waldorf College, IA
Warner Pacific College, OR
Warren Wilson College, NC
Wartburg College, IA
Washington State University, WA
Wayland Baptist University, TX
Wesleyan College, GA
Western Kentucky University, KY
Westminster College, MO
Westminster College, PA
West Texas A&M University, TX
West Virginia Wesleyan College, WV
Wheeling Jesuit University, WV
Williams Baptist College, AR
William Woods University, MO
Wilson College, PA
Wisconsin Lutheran College, WI
Wittenberg University, OH
Youngstown State University, OH

**Siblings of Current Students**

Albany College of Pharmacy and Health Sciences, NY
Albertus Magnus College, CT
Albright College, PA
Alliant International University–San Diego, CA
Alma College, MI
Alvernia University, PA
Ashland University, OH
Augustana College, IL
Augustana College, SD
Ave Maria University, FL
Baldwin Wallace University, OH
Barclay College, KS
Bay Path University, MA
Becker College, MA
Belmont University, TN
Beloit College, WI
Benedictine University, IL
Bethel College, KS
Bloomfield College, NJ
Blue Mountain College, MS
Bryant University, RI
Buena Vista University, IA
Cabrini College, PA
Caldwell University, NJ
California Baptist University, CA
Calvary Bible College and Theological Seminary, MO
Capital University, OH
Cardinal Stritch University, WI
Carroll College, MT
Carroll University, WI
Carson-Newman University, TN
The Catholic University of America, DC
Cedar Crest College, PA
Centenary College of Louisiana, LA
Central College, IA
Central Methodist University, MO
Chaminade University of Honolulu, HI
Chatham University, PA
Cincinnati Christian University, OH
Coe College, IA
The College of Idaho, ID
College of Mount Saint Vincent, NY
The College of New Rochelle, NY

The College of Saint Rose, NY
The College of St. Scholastica, MN
College of Staten Island of the City University of New York, NY
Columbia College, MO
Concordia University Ann Arbor, MI
Corban University, OR
Crossroads Bible College, IN
Curry College, MA
Doane College, NE
Dominican University, IL
Dowling College, NY
Drexel University, PA
Elizabethtown College, PA
Elmhurst College, IL
Elmira College, NY
Elms College, MA
Emmanuel College, GA
Emmanuel College, MA
Eureka College, IL
Faulkner University, AL
Felician College, NJ
Florida Institute of Technology, FL
Florida Southern College, FL
Fontbonne University, MO
Franciscan University of Steubenville, OH
Franklin College, IN
Franklin Pierce University, NH
Gonzaga University, WA
Greensboro College, NC
Greenville College, IL
Gustavus Adolphus College, MN
Gwynedd Mercy University, PA
Hanover College, IN
Harding University, AR
Hardin-Simmons University, TX
Hartwick College, NY
Hastings College, NE
Hilbert College, NY
Hood College, MD
Houghton College, NY
Howard Payne University, TX
Indiana Tech, IN
Iona College, NY
Iowa Wesleyan College, IA
Ithaca College, NY
James Madison University, VA
Johnson C. Smith University, NC
Kansas Wesleyan University, KS
Keuka College, NY
Keystone College, PA
King's College, PA
Lancaster Bible College, PA
Lasell College, MA
La Sierra University, CA
Lawrence University, WI
Lee University, TN
Lenoir-Rhyne University, NC
LIM College, NY
Long Island University–LIU Brooklyn, NY
Long Island University–LIU Post, NY
Lynn University, FL
MacMurray College, IL
Manchester University, IN
Marian University, WI
Marymount University, VA
McDaniel College, MD
Mercer University, GA
Merrimack College, MA
Methodist University, NC
Millikin University, IL
Misericordia University, PA
Missouri Baptist University, MO
Molloy College, NY
Montserrat College of Art, MA
Moravian College, PA

Mount Aloysius College, PA
Mount Marty College, SD
Mount Mary University, WI
Mount St. Mary's University, MD
Muskingum University, OH
Nazareth College of Rochester, NY
Newberry College, SC
New England College, NH
New Jersey Institute of Technology, NJ
Newman University, KS
Nichols College, MA
Northwest Christian University, OR
Northwest University, WA
Notre Dame of Maryland University, MD
Nyack College, NY
Oglethorpe University, GA
Oklahoma Wesleyan University, OK
Olivet College, MI
Oral Roberts University, OK
Otterbein University, OH
Palm Beach Atlantic University, FL
Park University, MO
Peirce College, PA
Pine Manor College, MA
Post University, CT
Providence College, RI
Queens University of Charlotte, NC
Quinnipiac University, CT
Randolph-Macon College, VA
Regent University, VA
Roberts Wesleyan College, NY
Rochester College, MI
Rockford University, IL
Rockhurst University, MO
Rosemont College, PA
Sacred Heart University, CT
Saint Anselm College, NH
St. Bonaventure University, NY
St. Catherine University, MN
Saint Francis University, PA
Saint Joseph's College, IN
St. Joseph's College, Long Island Campus, NY
St. Joseph's College, New York, NY
St. Lawrence University, NY
Saint Louis University, MO
Saint Martin's University, WA
Saint Michael's College, VT
St. Thomas Aquinas College, NY
Samford University, AL
Schreiner University, TX
Seton Hill University, PA
Simpson College, IA
Simpson University, CA
Springfield College, MA
Spring Hill College, AL
Stephens College, MO
Stonehill College, MA
Suffolk University, MA
Texas Wesleyan University, TX
Thiel College, PA
Thomas More College, KY
Trine University, IN
Truett-McConnell College, GA
Union College, KY
Union University, TN
The University of Alabama at Birmingham, AL
University of Dallas, TX
University of Dubuque, IA
University of Evansville, IN
University of Great Falls, MT
University of Hartford, CT
University of Jamestown, ND
University of New England, ME
University of St. Francis, IL

University of Saint Joseph, CT
The University of Scranton, PA
University of the Cumberlands, KY
The University of Tulsa, OK
University of Valley Forge, PA
Ursinus College, PA
Ursuline College, OH
Wagner College, NY
Wartburg College, IA
Waynesburg University, PA
Webber International University, FL
Wesleyan College, GA
Western New England University, MA
Westminster College, MO
William Jessup University, CA
William Jewell College, MO
William Peace University, NC
William Woods University, MO
Xavier University, OH

### Spouses of Current Students
Alaska Bible College, AK
Alliant International University–San Diego,
    CA
American University, DC
Augustana College, SD
The Baptist College of Florida, FL
Barclay College, KS
Bethel College, KS
Bloomfield College, NJ
Blue Mountain College, MS
Boise State University, ID
Caldwell University, NJ
Culvary Bible College and Theological
    Seminary, MO
Cardinal Stritch University, WI
Carroll College, MT
Carroll University, WI
Central Methodist University, MO
Cincinnati Christian University, OH
Clarion University of Pennsylvania, PA
The College of New Rochelle, NY
The College of St. Scholastica, MN
College of Staten Island of the City
    University of New York, NY
Columbia College, MO
Columbia International University, SC
Crossroads Bible College, IN
Curry College, MA
Elmhurst College, IL
Emmanuel College, GA
Fort Hays State University, KS
Franklin Pierce University, NH
Fresno Pacific University, CA
Hastings College, NE
Heritage Christian University, AL
Hodges University, FL
Huntingdon College, AL
Indiana Tech, IN
Kentucky Christian University, KY
Lancaster Bible College, PA
Lee University, TN
Manchester University, IN
Maranatha Baptist University, WI
Mid-Atlantic Christian University, NC
Missouri Baptist University, MO
Mount Aloysius College, PA
Mount Marty College, SD
Newman University, KS
New Mexico State University, NM
Northwest University, WA
Nyack College, NY
Palm Beach Atlantic University, FL
St. Catherine University, MN
Saint Francis University, PA

St. Joseph's College, Long Island Campus,
    NY
St. Joseph's College, New York, NY
St. Thomas Aquinas College, NY
Samford University, AL
Texas Wesleyan University, TX
Trinity College of Florida, FL
Truett-McConnell College, GA
Union University, TN
The University of Alabama at Birmingham,
    AL
University of Dubuque, IA
University of Great Falls, MT
University of Jamestown, ND
University of Mississippi, MS
University of Southern Indiana, IN
University of Valley Forge, PA
University of Wyoming, WY
Upper Iowa University, IA
Wesleyan College, GA
Xavier University of Louisiana, LA

### Spouses of Deceased or Disabled Public Servants
The College of New Rochelle, NY
College of Staten Island of the City
    University of New York, NY
Eastern Washington University, WA
Francis Marion University, SC
Grand Valley State University, MI
Louisiana Tech University, LA
Michigan State University, MI
Mississippi State University, MS
New Mexico State University, NM
Northeastern State University, OK
Northern Kentucky University, KY
Pace University, NY
Southern Illinois University Carbondale, IL
Texas Wesleyan University, TX
The University of Alabama, AL
The University of Alabama at Birmingham,
    AL
University of Connecticut, CT
University of South Carolina, SC
University of Utah, UT
Youngstown State University, OH

### Twins
Blue Mountain College, MS
Caldwell University, NJ
Calvin College, MI
The Catholic University of America, DC
Central College, IA
The College of Saint Rose, NY
Dowling College, NY
Drexel University, PA
Emmanuel College, GA
Lake Erie College, OH
Mount Aloysius College, PA
Ohio Wesleyan University, OH
Ouachita Baptist University, AR
Randolph College, VA
Sacred Heart University, CT
St. Joseph's College, Long Island Campus,
    NY
St. Joseph's College, New York, NY
St. Thomas Aquinas College, NY
Simpson College, IA
Sterling College, KS
Texas Wesleyan University, TX
Trine University, IN
Union University, TN
The University of Alabama at Birmingham,
    AL
University of Hartford, CT
Virginia Polytechnic Institute and State
    University, VA

Westminster College, MO

### Veterans
Adelphi University, NY
Adrian College, MI
Agnes Scott College, GA
Alliant International University–San Diego,
    CA
American University, DC
Amridge University, AL
Anderson University, SC
Arkansas State University, AR
Ashland University, OH
Augustana College, SD
Austin College, TX
Austin Peay State University, TN
Babson College, MA
Ball State University, IN
Baylor University, TX
Belmont University, TN
Beloit College, WI
Benedictine University, IL
Bennington College, VT
Berry College, GA
Binghamton University, State University of
    New York, NY
Birmingham-Southern College, AL
Bluefield College, VA
Boise State University, ID
Boston University, MA
Brown University, RI
Butler University, IN
Caldwell University, NJ
California Baptist University, CA
California Lutheran University, CA
California State University, Bakersfield, CA
California State University, San Bernardino,
    CA
California University of Pennsylvania, PA
Calvin College, MI
Cameron University, OK
Campbellsville University, KY
Carroll College, MT
Castleton State College, VT
The Catholic University of America, DC
Cedarville University, OH
Central College, IA
Central Washington University, WA
Chowan University, NC
Christian Brothers University, TN
City Vision University, MO
Claremont McKenna College, CA
Clarkson University, NY
Clemson University, SC
Cleveland Institute of Art, OH
Coe College, IA
Coker College, SC
Colgate University, NY
The College at Brockport, State University
    of New York, NY
The College of New Rochelle, NY
College of Staten Island of the City
    University of New York, NY
Columbia College, MO
Columbia International University, SC
Concordia University, Nebraska, NE
Concordia University, St. Paul, MN
Concordia University Texas, TX
Concord University, WV
Corban University, OR
The Criswell College, TX
The Culinary Institute of America, NY
Culver-Stockton College, MO
Dallas Baptist University, TX
Denison University, OH

DePaul University, IL
Dickinson College, PA
Dickinson State University, ND
Dowling College, NY
Drury University, MO
Duquesne University, PA
D'Youville College, NY
East Central University, OK
Eastern Nazarene College, MA
Eastern New Mexico University, NM
Eastern Washington University, WA
ECPI University, VA
Elizabeth City State University, NC
Elmhurst College, IL
Elmira College, NY
Elon University, NC
Emmanuel College, MA
Emory University, GA
Emporia State University, KS
Everglades University, FL
Everglades University, FL
Everglades University, FL
The Evergreen State College, WA
Fairfield University, CT
Fairmont State University, WV
Ferris State University, MI
Fort Hays State University, KS
Framingham State University, MA
Francis Marion University, SC
Frostburg State University, MD
Furman University, SC
Gannon University, PA
Georgetown College, KY
Georgia Institute of Technology, GA
Georgian Court University, NJ
Glenville State College, WV
Golden Gate University, CA
Gordon College, MA
Governors State University, IL
Grambling State University, LA
Grand Valley State University, MI
Grand View University, IA
Greensboro College, NC
Gwynedd Mercy University, PA
Hamline University, MN
Hampden-Sydney College, VA
Hampton University, VA
Hardin-Simmons University, TX
Hartwick College, NY
Hillsdale Free Will Baptist College, OK
Hodges University, FL
Hofstra University, NY
Hollins University, VA
Hope International University, CA
Houghton College, NY
Huntingdon College, AL
Huntington University, IN
Illinois Institute of Technology, IL
Indiana State University, IN
Iona College, NY
John Carroll University, OH
Kent State University, OH
Kent State University at Stark, OH
Kentucky State University, KY
Kentucky Wesleyan College, KY
King's College, PA
King University, TN
Knox College, IL
Lake Erie College, OH
Lancaster Bible College, PA
La Salle University, PA
Lasell College, MA
Lawrence University, WI
Lebanon Valley College, PA
Lees-McRae College, NC
Lewis University, IL

Liberty University, VA
Lindenwood University, MO
Long Island University–LIU Brooklyn, NY
Long Island University–LIU Post, NY
Louisiana Tech University, LA
Loyola Marymount University, CA
Lynn University, FL
MacMurray College, IL
Malone University, OH
Marian University, WI
Marymount Manhattan College, NY
Marymount University, VA
Maryville College, TN
Massachusetts College of Art and Design, MA
McDaniel College, MD
McKendree University, IL
McNally Smith College of Music, MN
Methodist University, NC
Metropolitan State University of Denver, CO
Michigan State University, MI
Michigan Technological University, MI
Midwestern State University, TX
Millikin University, IL
Minot State University, ND
Missouri Baptist University, MO
Missouri Southern State University, MO
Molloy College, NY
Monmouth College, IL
Monmouth University, NJ
Montana State University Billings, MT
Montana Tech of The University of Montana, MT
Montreat College, NC
Morehead State University, KY
Mount Mary University, WI
Nazareth College of Rochester, NY
New Jersey Institute of Technology, NJ
New Mexico State University, NM
New York Institute of Technology, NY
Nicholls State University, LA
Northern Illinois University, IL
Northern Kentucky University, KY
Nova Southeastern University, FL
Occidental College, CA
Oklahoma Baptist University, OK
Otterbein University, OH
Pace University, NY
Pacific University, OR
Park University, MO
Patrick Henry College, VA
Peirce College, PA
Portland State University, OR
Queens University of Charlotte, NC
Randolph-Macon College, VA
Regent University, VA
Robert Morris University, PA
Robert Morris University Illinois, IL
Rochester Institute of Technology, NY
Sacred Heart University, CT
The Sage Colleges, NY
Saginaw Valley State University, MI
St. Ambrose University, IA
St. Edward's University, TX
St. John's College, NM
Saint Joseph's University, PA
Saint Martin's University, WA
Saint Mary's College of California, CA
Saint Michael's College, VT
St. Thomas Aquinas College, NY
Samford University, AL
San Diego State University, CA
Savannah College of Art and Design, GA
Schreiner University, TX
Seattle Pacific University, WA
Shawnee State University, OH

Sierra Nevada College, NV
Sonoma State University, CA
South Dakota State University, SD
Southeastern Louisiana University, LA
Southeast Missouri State University, MO
Southern Connecticut State University, CT
Southern Illinois University Carbondale, IL
Stephen F. Austin State University, TX
Stephens College, MO
Stetson University, FL
Stonehill College, MA
Suffolk University, MA
Susquehanna University, PA
Temple University, PA
Texas A&M University, TX
Texas A&M University–Commerce, TX
Texas Christian University, TX
Texas Lutheran University, TX
Texas Tech University, TX
Texas Wesleyan University, TX
Thiel College, PA
Thomas College, ME
Thomas Jefferson University, PA
Thomas More College, KY
Thomas University, GA
Towson University, MD
Trinity Christian College, IL
Trinity University, TX
Union College, KY
Union University, TN
The University of Alabama at Birmingham, AL
University of Arkansas, AR
University of California, Riverside, CA
University of California, Santa Cruz, CA
University of Colorado Denver, CO
University of Connecticut, CT
University of Evansville, IN
University of Houston–Clear Lake, TX
University of Idaho, ID
University of Illinois at Springfield, IL
University of Indianapolis, IN
The University of Iowa, IA
University of Jamestown, ND
The University of Kansas, KS
University of Louisville, KY
University of Maryland Eastern Shore, MD
University of Massachusetts Amherst, MA
University of Massachusetts Boston, MA
University of Massachusetts Dartmouth, MA
University of Massachusetts Lowell, MA
University of Miami, FL
University of Michigan–Flint, MI
University of Mississippi, MS
University of Missouri–St. Louis, MO
The University of Montana, MT
The University of Montana Western, MT
University of Mount Olive, NC
University of Mount Union, OH
University of Nebraska at Kearney, NE
University of Nevada, Las Vegas, NV
University of New Orleans, LA
University of North Carolina at Asheville, NC
The University of North Carolina at Greensboro, NC
University of Northern Colorado, CO
University of Northern Iowa, IA
University of Oregon, OR
University of Pittsburgh at Bradford, PA
University of Puget Sound, WA
University of Rochester, NY
University of St. Francis, IL
The University of Scranton, PA
University of Southern Mississippi, MS
The University of Tampa, FL

The University of Texas at Dallas, TX
The University of Texas–Pan American, TX
The University of Toledo, OH
The University of Virginia's College at
    Wise, VA
University of West Florida, FL
University of Wisconsin–Green Bay, WI
University of Wisconsin–La Crosse, WI
University of Wisconsin–Stevens Point, WI
University of Wisconsin–Stout, WI
University of Wisconsin–Superior, WI
University of Wyoming, WY
Ursuline College, OH
Walla Walla University, WA
Washington & Jefferson College, PA
Washington State University, WA
Wayne State College, NE
Webber International University, FL
Wesleyan College, GA
Western Kentucky University, KY
Western Michigan University, MI
Western New Mexico University, NM
Western Oregon University, OR
Western Washington University, WA
West Texas A&M University, TX
Whitman College, WA
Wichita State University, KS
William Jessup University, CA
Wilson College, PA
Youngstown State University, OH

### Veterans' Children

Adrian College, MI
Agnes Scott College, GA
American University, DC
Anderson University, SC
Arkansas State University, AR
Ball State University, IN
Baylor University, TX
Belmont University, TN
Benedictine University, IL
Bennington College, VT
Berry College, GA
Binghamton University, State University of
    New York, NY
Birmingham-Southern College, AL
Bluefield College, VA
Boise State University, ID
Boston University, MA
Brevard College, NC
Brown University, RI
Butler University, IN
California Baptist University, CA
California Lutheran University, CA
California State University, San Bernardino,
    CA
Calvin College, MI
Cameron University, OK
The Catholic University of America, DC
Central College, IA
Central Washington University, WA
Chowan University, NC
Christian Brothers University, TN
Claremont McKenna College, CA
Coastal Carolina University, SC
Coe College, IA
Colgate University, NY
The College of Idaho, ID
The College of New Rochelle, NY
College of Staten Island of the City
    University of New York, NY
Columbia College, MO
Columbia International University, SC
Concordia University, Nebraska, NE
Concordia University, St. Paul, MN

Concordia University Texas, TX
Concord University, WV
Corban University, OR
The Culinary Institute of America, NY
Culver-Stockton College, MO
Dallas Baptist University, TX
DePaul University, IL
Dickinson College, PA
Dickinson State University, ND
Duquesne University, PA
East Central University, OK
Eastern Washington University, WA
ECPI University, VA
Elizabeth City State University, NC
Elmhurst College, IL
Emmanuel College, MA
Emory University, GA
Emporia State University, KS
The Evergreen State College, WA
Fairfield University, CT
Fairmont State University, WV
Fort Hays State University, KS
Fort Lewis College, CO
Francis Marion University, SC
Frostburg State University, MD
Georgetown College, KY
Georgia Institute of Technology, GA
Glenville State College, WV
Gordon College, MA
Grambling State University, LA
Grand Valley State University, MI
Gwynedd Mercy University, PA
Hampden-Sydney College, VA
Hampton University, VA
Hardin-Simmons University, TX
Hillsdale Free Will Baptist College, OK
Hobart and William Smith Colleges, NY
Hodges University, FL
Hofstra University, NY
Huntingdon College, AL
Huntington University, IN
Illinois Institute of Technology, IL
Iona College, NY
John Carroll University, OH
Kennesaw State University, GA
Kent State University, OH
King University, TN
Lake Erie College, OH
Lasell College, MA
Lawrence University, WI
Lewis University, IL
Lindenwood University, MO
Long Island University–LIU Brooklyn, NY
Long Island University–LIU Post, NY
Louisiana Tech University, LA
MacMurray College, IL
Marymount Manhattan College, NY
Marymount University, VA
Mayville State University, ND
McKendree University, IL
McNally Smith College of Music, MN
Michigan Technological University, MI
Midwestern State University, TX
Minot State University, ND
Missouri Baptist University, MO
Monmouth University, NJ
Montreat College, NC
Morehead State University, KY
New Jersey Institute of Technology, NJ
New Mexico State University, NM
Northern Kentucky University, KY
Occidental College, CA
Old Dominion University, VA
Peirce College, PA
Queens University of Charlotte, NC

Randolph-Macon College, VA
Sacred Heart University, CT
Saginaw Valley State University, MI
Saint Joseph's University, PA
St. Lawrence University, NY
Saint Martin's University, WA
Saint Mary's College of California, CA
Saint Michael's College, VT
San Diego State University, CA
Savannah College of Art and Design, GA
Seattle Pacific University, WA
Siena College, NY
South Dakota State University, SD
Southeastern Louisiana University, LA
Southern Illinois University Carbondale, IL
Stephen F. Austin State University, TX
Stephens College, MO
Stetson University, FL
Stonehill College, MA
Texas A&M University, TX
Texas A&M University–Commerce, TX
Texas Christian University, TX
Texas Lutheran University, TX
Texas Tech University, TX
Texas Wesleyan University, TX
Thomas College, ME
Thomas More College, KY
Trinity University, TX
Union College, KY
Union University, TN
The University of Alabama at Birmingham,
    AL
University of Arkansas, AR
University of California, Riverside, CA
University of California, San Diego, CA
University of Houston–Clear Lake, TX
University of Idaho, ID
University of Illinois at Springfield, IL
University of Louisville, KY
University of Maine at Augusta, ME
University of Maine at Farmington, ME
University of Maine at Presque Isle, ME
University of Miami, FL
University of Michigan–Flint, MI
University of Mount Olive, NC
University of Nebraska at Kearney, NE
University of Nebraska at Omaha, NE
University of Nebraska–Lincoln, NE
University of Nevada, Las Vegas, NV
University of North Carolina at Asheville,
    NC
The University of North Carolina at
    Greensboro, NC
University of Oregon, OR
University of Puget Sound, WA
University of St. Francis, IL
The University of Scranton, PA
University of Southern Indiana, IN
The University of Texas at Dallas, TX
The University of Texas–Pan American, TX
The University of Toledo, OH
The University of Virginia's College at
    Wise, VA
University of Wisconsin–La Crosse, WI
University of Wisconsin–Stout, WI
University of Wyoming, WY
Virginia Commonwealth University, VA
Virginia Polytechnic Institute and State
    University, VA
Washington & Jefferson College, PA
Washington State University, WA
Wayne State College, NE
Webster University, MO
Western Illinois University, IL
Western Kentucky University, KY

Western Oregon University, OR
West Texas A&M University, TX

Whitman College, WA
William Jessup University, CA

Wilson College, PA
Youngstown State University, OH

# Athletic Grants for Undergraduates

**Archery**
| | |
|---|---|
| Emmanuel College, GA | M,W |
| Texas A&M University, TX | W |
| University of the Cumberlands, KY | M,W |

**Baseball**
| | |
|---|---|
| Abilene Christian University, TX | M |
| Academy of Art University, CA | M |
| Adams State University, CO | M |
| Adelphi University, NY | M |
| Alabama State University, AL | M |
| Albany State University, GA | M |
| Alcorn State University, MS | M |
| Alice Lloyd College, KY | M |
| Anderson University, SC | M |
| Angelo State University, TX | M |
| Appalachian State University, NC | M |
| Arizona Christian University, AZ | M |
| Arizona State University at the Downtown Phoenix campus, AZ | M |
| Arizona State University at the Polytechnic campus, AZ | M |
| Arizona State University at the Tempe campus, AZ | M |
| Arizona State University at the West campus, AZ | M |
| Arkansas State University, AR | M |
| Arkansas Tech University, AR | M |
| Armstrong State University, GA | M |
| Ashland University, OH | M |
| Auburn University, AL | M |
| Auburn University at Montgomery, AL | M |
| Augustana College, SD | M |
| Austin Peay State University, TN | M |
| Azusa Pacific University, CA | M |
| Ball State University, IN | M |
| Barry University, FL | M |
| Baylor University, TX | M |
| Belhaven University, MS | M |
| Bellarmine University, KY | M |
| Belmont Abbey College, NC | M |
| Belmont University, TN | M |
| Bemidji State University, MN | M |
| Bethune-Cookman University, FL | M |
| Binghamton University, State University of New York, NY | M |
| Biola University, CA | M |
| Blessing-Rieman College of Nursing, IL | M,W |
| Bloomfield College, NJ | M |
| Bloomsburg University of Pennsylvania, PA | M |
| Bluefield College, VA | M |
| Bluefield State College, WV | M |
| Blue Mountain College, MS | M |
| Boston College, MA | M |
| Bowling Green State University, OH | M |
| Bradley University, IL | M |
| Brevard College, NC | M |
| Brigham Young University, UT | M |
| Bryant University, RI | M |
| Butler University, IN | M |

| | |
|---|---|
| Caldwell University, NJ | M |
| California Baptist University, CA | M |
| California Polytechnic State University, San Luis Obispo, CA | M |
| California State Polytechnic University, Pomona, CA | M |
| California State University, Chico, CA | M |
| California State University, Dominguez Hills, CA | M |
| California State University, Fresno, CA | M |
| California State University, Fullerton, CA | M |
| California State University, Los Angeles, CA | M |
| California State University, Monterey Bay, CA | M |
| California State University, Sacramento, CA | M |
| California State University, San Bernardino, CA | M |
| California State University, Stanislaus, CA | M |
| Calumet College of Saint Joseph, IN | M |
| Cameron University, OK | M |
| Campbellsville University, KY | M |
| Canisius College, NY | M |
| Cardinal Stritch University, WI | M |
| Carson-Newman University, TN | M |
| Catawba College, NC | M |
| Cedarville University, OH | M |
| Central Connecticut State University, CT | M |
| Central Methodist University, MO | M |
| Central Michigan University, MI | M |
| Central Washington University, WA | M |
| Chestnut Hill College, PA | M |
| Chowan University, NC | M |
| Christian Brothers University, TN | M |
| The Citadel, The Military College of South Carolina, SC | M |
| Clarion University of Pennsylvania, PA | M |
| Clarke University, IA | M |
| Coastal Carolina University, SC | M |
| Coker College, SC | M |
| College of Charleston, SC | M |
| The College of Idaho, ID | M |
| The College of Saint Rose, NY | M |
| College of the Ozarks, MO | M |
| The College of William and Mary, VA | M |
| Colorado Mesa University, CO | M |
| Colorado School of Mines, CO | M |
| Colorado State University–Pueblo, CO | M |
| Columbus State University, GA | M |
| Concordia University, CA | M |
| Concordia University, Nebraska, NE | M |
| Concordia University, St. Paul, MN | M |
| Concord University, WV | M |

| | |
|---|---|
| Corban University, OR | M |
| Cornerstone University, MI | M |
| Creighton University, NE | M |
| Culver-Stockton College, MO | M |
| Cumberland University, TN | M |
| Dakota State University, SD | M |
| Dallas Baptist University, TX | M |
| Davidson College, NC | M |
| Delaware State University, DE | M |
| Delta State University, MS | M |
| Dickinson State University, ND | M |
| Dixie State University, UT | M |
| Doane College, NE | M |
| Dominican College, NY | M |
| Dowling College, NY | M |
| Drury University, MO | M |
| East Carolina University, NC | M |
| East Central University, OK | M |
| Eastern Illinois University, IL | M |
| Eastern Kentucky University, KY | M |
| Eastern Michigan University, MI | M |
| Eastern New Mexico University, NM | M |
| East Stroudsburg University of Pennsylvania, PA | M |
| Eckerd College, FL | M |
| Elon University, NC | M |
| Embry-Riddle Aeronautical University–Daytona, FL | M |
| Emmanuel College, GA | M |
| Emporia State University, KS | M |
| Evangel University, MO | M |
| Fairfield University, CT | M |
| Fairmont State University, WV | M |
| Faulkner University, AL | M |
| Flagler College, FL | M |
| Florida Agricultural and Mechanical University, FL | M |
| Florida Atlantic University, FL | M |
| Florida Gulf Coast University, FL | M |
| Florida Institute of Technology, FL | M |
| Florida Southern College, FL | M |
| Florida State University, FL | M |
| Fordham University, NY | M |
| Fort Hays State University, KS | M |
| Francis Marion University, SC | M |
| Franklin Pierce University, NH | M |
| Friends University, KS | M |
| Furman University, SC | M |
| Gannon University, PA | M |
| George Mason University, VA | M |
| Georgetown College, KY | M |
| Georgetown University, DC | M |
| The George Washington University, DC | M |
| Georgia College & State University, GA | M |
| Georgia Institute of Technology, GA | M |
| Georgia Regents University, GA | M |
| Georgia Southern University, GA | M |
| Georgia Southwestern State University, GA | M |

| | | | | | |
|---|---|---|---|---|---|
| Georgia State University, GA | M | Manhattan College, NY | M | Nyack College, NY | M |
| Gonzaga University, WA | M | Mansfield University of | | Oakland University, MI | M |
| Goshen College, IN | M | Pennsylvania, PA | M | The Ohio State University, OH | M |
| Graceland University, IA | M | Marist College, NY | M | Ohio University, OH | M |
| Grambling State University, LA | M | Marshall University, WV | M | Oklahoma Baptist University, OK | M |
| Grand Valley State University, MI | M | Maryville University of Saint | | Oklahoma Christian University, OK | M |
| Grand View University, IA | M | Louis, MO | M | Oklahoma City University, OK | M |
| Harding University, AR | M | The Master's College and | | Oklahoma State University, OK | M |
| Hastings College, NE | M | Seminary, CA | M | Oklahoma Wesleyan University, OK | M |
| Hawai`i Pacific University, HI | M | Mayville State University, ND | M | Old Dominion University, VA | M |
| Hillsdale College, MI | M | McKendree University, IL | M | Olivet Nazarene University, IL | M |
| Hofstra University, NY | M | Mercer University, GA | M | Oral Roberts University, OK | M |
| Houston Baptist University, TX | M | Mercy College, NY | M | Oregon State University, OR | M |
| Huston-Tillotson University, TX | M | Merrimack College, MA | M | Our Lady of the Lake University | |
| Illinois Institute of Technology, IL | M | Miami University, OH | M | of San Antonio, TX | M |
| Illinois State University, IL | M | Michigan State University, MI | M | Pace University, NY | M |
| Indiana State University, IN | M | Middle Tennessee State | | Palm Beach Atlantic University, FL | M |
| Indiana University Bloomington, IN | M | University, TN | M | Park University, MO | M |
| Indiana University of | | Midland College, TX | M | Penn State University Park, PA | M |
| Pennsylvania, PA | M | Millersville University of | | Pepperdine University, CA | M |
| Indiana University–Purdue | | Pennsylvania, PA | M | Philadelphia University, PA | M |
| University Fort Wayne, IN | M | Milligan College, TN | M | Pittsburg State University, KS | M |
| Indiana University Southeast, IN | M | Minnesota State University | | Point Loma Nazarene University, CA | M |
| Indian River State College, FL | M | Mankato, MN | | Post University, CT | M |
| Inter American University of | | Minot State University, ND | M | Prairie View A&M University, TX | M |
| Puerto Rico, Bayamón Campus, PR | M | Mississippi State University, MS | M | Presbyterian College, SC | M |
| Iona College, NY | M | Missouri Baptist University, MO | M | Purdue University, IN | M |
| Jackson State University, MS | M | Missouri Southern State | | Purdue University Calumet, IN | M |
| Jacksonville State University, AL | M | University, MO | M | Queens College of the City | |
| Jacksonville University, FL | M | Missouri State University, MO | M | University of New York, NY | M |
| James Madison University, VA | M | Missouri University of Science | | Quincy University, IL | M |
| Kansas State University, KS | M | and Technology, MO | | Quinnipiac University, CT | M |
| Kansas Wesleyan University, KS | M | Missouri Valley College, MO | M | Radford University, VA | M |
| Kennesaw State University, GA | M | Missouri Western State | | Regis University, CO | M |
| Kent State University, OH | M | University, MO | M | Reinhardt University, GA | M |
| Kentucky State University, KY | M | Molloy College, NY | M | Rice University, TX | M |
| Kentucky Wesleyan College, KY | M | Monmouth University, NJ | M | Rider University, NJ | M |
| King University, TN | M | Montreat College, NC | M | Robert Morris University | |
| Kutztown University of | | Morehead State University, KY | M | Illinois, IL | M |
| Pennsylvania, PA | M | Morningside College, IA | M | Rockhurst University, MO | M |
| Lake Erie College, OH | M | Mount Marty College, SD | M | Rollins College, FL | M |
| Lamar University, TX | M | Mount Mercy University, IA | M | Sacred Heart University, CT | M |
| La Salle University, PA | M | Mount St. Mary's | | Saginaw Valley State University, | |
| Lee University, TN | M | University, MD | M | MI | M |
| Le Moyne College, NY | M | Murray State University, KY | M | St. Andrews University, NC | M |
| LeMoyne-Owen College, TN | M | Newberry College, SC | M | Saint Anselm College, NH | M |
| Lenoir-Rhyne University, NC | M | New Jersey Institute of | | Saint Augustine's | |
| Lewis-Clark State College, ID | M | Technology, NJ | | University, NC | M |
| Lewis University, IL | M | Newman University, KS | M | St. Bonaventure University, NY | M |
| Liberty University, VA | M | New Mexico Highlands University, | | St. Edward's University, TX | M |
| Lincoln Christian University, IL | M | NM | M | St. John's University, NY | M |
| Lincoln Memorial University, TN | M | New Mexico State University, NM | M | Saint Joseph's College, IN | M |
| Lincoln University, MO | M | New York Institute of | | Saint Joseph's University, | |
| Lincoln University, PA | M | Technology, NY | M | PA | M |
| Lindenwood University, MO | M | Niagara University, NY | M | Saint Leo University, FL | M |
| Lindsey Wilson College, KY | M | Nicholls State University, LA | M | Saint Louis University, MO | M |
| Lipscomb University, TN | M | North Carolina Agricultural and | | Saint Martin's University, | |
| Lock Haven University of | | Technical State University, NC | M | WA | M |
| Pennsylvania, PA | M | North Carolina Central | | St. Thomas Aquinas College, NY | M |
| Long Island University–LIU | | University, NC | M | St. Thomas University, FL | M |
| Brooklyn, NY | M | North Carolina State University, | | Samford University, AL | M |
| Long Island University–LIU | | NC | M | Sam Houston State University, TX | M |
| Post, NY | M | Northeastern State University, OK | M | San Diego State University, CA | M |
| Longwood University, VA | M | Northeastern University, MA | M | San Francisco State University, CA | M |
| Louisiana State University and | | Northern Illinois University, IL | M | San Jose State University, CA | M |
| Agricultural & Mechanical | | Northern Kentucky University, KY | M | Santa Clara University, CA | M |
| College, LA | M | Northern State University, SD | M | Savannah State University, GA | M |
| Louisiana Tech University, LA | M | Northwestern Oklahoma State | | Seton Hill University, PA | M |
| Loyola Marymount University, CA | M | University, OK | M | Shawnee State University, OH | M |
| Lubbock Christian University, TX | M | Northwest Missouri State | | Shepherd University, WV | M |
| Lynn University, FL | M | University, MO | M | Shippensburg University of | |
| Lyon College, AR | M | Northwest Nazarene University, ID | M | Pennsylvania, PA | M |
| Malone University, OH | M | Nova Southeastern University, FL | M | Siena College, NY | M |

| | |
|---|---|
| Simpson University, CA | M |
| Slippery Rock University of Pennsylvania, PA | M |
| South Dakota State University, SD | M |
| Southeastern Louisiana University, LA | M |
| Southeastern Oklahoma State University, OK | M |
| Southeast Missouri State University, MO | M |
| Southern Connecticut State University, CT | M |
| Southern Illinois University Carbondale, IL | M |
| Southern Illinois University Edwardsville, IL | M |
| Southwest Baptist University, MO | M |
| Spring Hill College, AL | M |
| Stanford University, CA | M |
| Stephen F. Austin State University, TX | M |
| Sterling College, KS | M |
| Stetson University, FL | M |
| Stonehill College, MA | M |
| Stony Brook University, State University of New York, NY | M |
| Tabor College, KS | M |
| Tarleton State University, TX | M |
| Taylor University, IN | M |
| Tennessee Wesleyan College, TN | M |
| Texas A&M International University, TX | M |
| Texas A&M University, TX | M |
| Texas A&M University–Corpus Christi, TX | M |
| Texas Christian University, TX | M |
| Texas Southern University, TX | M |
| Texas State University, TX | M |
| Texas Tech University, TX | M |
| Texas Wesleyan University, TX | M |
| Tiffin University, OH | M |
| Towson University, MD | M |
| Trevecca Nazarene University, TN | M |
| Trinity Christian College, IL | M |
| Troy University, AL | M |
| Truett-McConnell College, GA | M |
| Truman State University, MO | M |
| Tulane University, LA | M |
| Tusculum College, TN | M |
| Union College, KY | M |
| Union University, TN | M |
| University at Albany, State University of New York, NY | M |
| University at Buffalo, the State University of New York, NY | M |
| The University of Akron, OH | M |
| The University of Alabama, AL | M |
| The University of Alabama at Birmingham, AL | M |
| The University of Alabama in Huntsville, AL | M |
| The University of Arizona, AZ | M |
| University of Arkansas, AR | M |
| University of Bridgeport, CT | M |
| University of California, Davis, CA | M |
| University of California, Irvine, CA | M |
| University of California, Los Angeles, CA | M |
| University of California, Riverside, CA | M |

| | |
|---|---|
| University of California, Santa Barbara, CA | M |
| University of Central Arkansas, AR | M |
| University of Central Florida, FL | M |
| University of Central Missouri, MO | M |
| University of Central Oklahoma, OK | M |
| University of Charleston, WV | M |
| University of Cincinnati, OH | M |
| University of Connecticut, CT | M |
| University of Dayton, OH | M |
| University of Delaware, DE | M |
| University of Evansville, IN | M |
| The University of Findlay, OH | M |
| University of Florida, FL | M |
| University of Georgia, GA | M |
| University of Hartford, CT | M |
| University of Hawaii at Manoa, HI | M |
| University of Houston, TX | M |
| University of Illinois at Chicago, IL | M |
| University of Illinois at Springfield, IL | M |
| University of Indianapolis, IN | M |
| The University of Iowa, IA | M |
| University of Jamestown, ND | M |
| The University of Kansas, KS | M |
| University of Louisiana at Lafayette, LA | M |
| University of Louisville, KY | M |
| University of Maine, ME | M |
| University of Maryland, Baltimore County, MD | M |
| University of Maryland, College Park, MD | M |
| University of Massachusetts Amherst, MA | M |
| University of Massachusetts Lowell, MA | M |
| University of Memphis, TN | M |
| University of Miami, FL | M |
| University of Michigan, MI | M |
| University of Minnesota, Crookston, MN | M |
| University of Minnesota, Duluth, MN | M |
| University of Minnesota, Twin Cities Campus, MN | M |
| University of Mississippi, MS | M |
| University of Missouri, MO | M |
| University of Missouri–St. Louis, MO | M |
| University of Mobile, AL | M |
| University of Montevallo, AL | M |
| University of Nebraska at Kearney, NE | M |
| University of Nebraska Lincoln, NE | M |
| University of Nevada, Las Vegas, NV | M |
| University of Nevada, Reno, NV | M |
| University of New Haven, CT | M |
| University of New Orleans, LA | M |
| University of North Alabama, AL | M |
| University of North Carolina at Asheville, NC | M |
| The University of North Carolina at Chapel Hill, NC | M |
| The University of North Carolina at Charlotte, NC | M |
| The University of North Carolina at Greensboro, NC | M |
| The University of North Carolina at Pembroke, NC | M |

| | |
|---|---|
| The University of North Carolina Wilmington, NC | M |
| University of Northern Colorado, CO | M |
| University of North Florida, FL | M |
| University of North Georgia, GA | M |
| University of Notre Dame, IN | M |
| University of Oklahoma, OK | M |
| University of Oregon, OR | M |
| University of Pikeville, KY | M |
| University of Pittsburgh, PA | M |
| University of Portland, OR | M |
| University of Rhode Island, RI | M |
| University of Richmond, VA | M |
| University of Rio Grande, OH | M |
| University of St. Francis, IL | M |
| University of San Diego, CA | M |
| University of San Francisco, CA | M |
| University of Science and Arts of Oklahoma, OK | M |
| University of South Alabama, AL | M |
| University of South Carolina, SC | M |
| University of South Carolina Aiken, SC | M |
| University of South Carolina Upstate, SC | M |
| University of Southern California, CA | M |
| University of Southern Indiana, IN | M |
| University of Southern Mississippi, MS | M |
| University of South Florida, FL | M |
| The University of Tampa, FL | M |
| The University of Tennessee, TN | M |
| The University of Tennessee at Martin, TN | M |
| The University of Texas at Arlington, TX | M |
| The University of Texas at Austin, TX | M |
| The University of Texas at San Antonio, TX | M |
| The University of Texas–Pan American, TX | M |
| University of the Cumberlands, KY | M |
| University of the Incarnate Word, TX | M |
| University of the Pacific, CA | M |
| University of the Sciences, PA | M |
| The University of Toledo, OH | M |
| University of Utah, UT | M |
| University of Virginia, VA | M |
| The University of Virginia's College at Wise, VA | M |
| University of Washington, WA | M |
| The University of West Alabama, AL | M |
| University of West Florida, FL | M |
| University of West Georgia, GA | M |
| University of Wisconsin–Milwaukee, WI | M |
| University of Wisconsin–Parkside, WI | M |
| Upper Iowa University, IA | M |
| Utah Valley University, UT | M |
| Valdosta State University, GA | M |
| Valley City State University, ND | M |
| Valparaiso University, IN | M |
| Vanderbilt University, TN | M |
| Vanguard University of Southern California, CA | M |
| Villanova University, PA | M |
| Virginia Commonwealth University, VA | M |

Virginia Military Institute, VA — M
Virginia State University, VA — M
Wagner College, NY — M
Wake Forest University, NC — M
Waldorf College, IA — M
Washburn University, KS — M
Washington State University, WA — M
Wayland Baptist University, TX — M
Wayne State College, NE — M
Wayne State University, MI — M
Webber International University, FL — M
West Chester University of Pennsylvania, PA — M
Western Carolina University, NC — M
Western Illinois University, IL — M
Western Kentucky University, KY — M
Western Michigan University, MI — M
Western Oregon University, OR — M
West Texas A&M University, TX — M
West Virginia University, WV — M
West Virginia University Institute of Technology, WV — M
West Virginia Wesleyan College, WV — M
Wheeling Jesuit University, WV — M
Wichita State University, KS — M
William Jessup University, CA — M
William Jewell College, MO — M
Williams Baptist College, AR — M
William Woods University, MO — M
Wingate University, NC — M
Winona State University, MN — M
Winthrop University, SC — M
Wofford College, SC — M
Wright State University, OH — M
Xavier University, OH — M
Youngstown State University, OH — M

**Basketball**

Abilene Christian University, TX — M,W
Academy of Art University, CA — M,W
Adams State University, CO — M,W
Adelphi University, NY — M,W
Alabama State University, AL — M,W
Albany State University, GA — M,W
Alcorn State University, MS — M,W
Alice Lloyd College, KY — M,W
American University, DC — M,W
Anderson University, SC — M,W
Angelo State University, TX — M,W
Appalachian State University, NC — M,W
Arizona Christian University, AZ — M,W
Arizona State University at the Downtown Phoenix campus, AZ — M,W
Arizona State University at the Polytechnic campus, AZ — M,W
Arizona State University at the Tempe campus, AZ — M,W
Arizona State University at the West campus, AZ — M,W
Arkansas State University, AR — M,W
Arkansas Tech University, AR — M,W
Armstrong State University, GA — M,W
Ashland University, OH — M,W
Assumption College, MA — M,W
Auburn University, AL — M,W
Auburn University at Montgomery, AL — M,W
Augustana College, SD — M,W
Austin Peay State University, TN — M,W
Azusa Pacific University, CA — M,W
Ball State University, IN — M,W
Barry University, FL — M,W
Baylor University, TX — M,W

Belhaven University, MS — M,W
Bellarmine University, KY — M,W
Belmont Abbey College, NC — M,W
Belmont University, TN — M,W
Bemidji State University, MN — M,W
Bentley University, MA — M,W
Bethel College, KS — M,W
Bethune-Cookman University, FL — M,W
Binghamton University, State University of New York, NY — M,W
Biola University, CA — M,W
Blessing-Rieman College of Nursing, IL — M,W
Bloomfield College, NJ — M,W
Bloomsburg University of Pennsylvania, PA — M,W
Bluefield College, VA — M,W
Bluefield State College, WV — M,W
Blue Mountain College, MS — M,W
Boston College, MA — M,W
Boston University, MA — M,W
Bowie State University, MD — M,W
Bowling Green State University, OH — M,W
Bradley University, IL — M
Brenau University, GA — W
Brevard College, NC — M,W
Brigham Young University, UT — M,W
Bryant University, RI — M,W
Bucknell University, PA — M,W
Butler University, IN — M,W
Caldwell University, NJ — M,W
California Baptist University, CA — M,W
California Polytechnic State University, San Luis Obispo, CA — M,W
California State Polytechnic University, Pomona, CA — M,W
California State University, Bakersfield, CA — M
California State University, Chico, CA — M,W
California State University, Dominguez Hills, CA — M,W
California State University, Fresno, CA — M,W
California State University, Fullerton, CA — M,W
California State University, Long Beach, CA — M,W
California State University, Los Angeles, CA — M,W
California State University, Monterey Bay, CA — M,W
California State University, Sacramento, CA — M,W
California State University, San Bernardino, CA — M,W
California State University, Stanislaus, CA — M,W
Calumet College of Saint Joseph, IN — M,W
Cameron University, OK — M,W
Campbellsville University, KY — M,W
Canisius College, NY — M,W
Cardinal Stritch University, WI — M,W
Carroll College, MT — M,W
Carson-Newman University, TN — M,W
Catawba College, NC — M,W
Cedarville University, OH — M,W
Central Connecticut State University, CT — M,W
Central Methodist University, MO — M,W
Central Michigan University, MI — M,W
Central Washington University, WA — M,W

Chaminade University of Honolulu, HI — M,W
Chestnut Hill College, PA — M,W
Chowan University, NC — M,W
Christian Brothers University, TN — M,W
Cincinnati Christian University, OH — M,W
The Citadel, The Military College of South Carolina, SC — M
Clarion University of Pennsylvania, PA — M,W
Clarke University, IA — M,W
Clayton State University, GA — M,W
Cleveland State University, OH — M,W
Coastal Carolina University, SC — M,W
Coker College, SC — M,W
College of Charleston, SC — M,W
The College of Idaho, ID — M,W
College of Saint Mary, NE — W
The College of Saint Rose, NY — M,W
College of the Holy Cross, MA — M,W
College of the Ozarks, MO — M,W
The College of William and Mary, VA — M,W
Colorado Mesa University, CO — M,W
Colorado School of Mines, CO — M,W
Colorado State University, CO — M,W
Colorado State University–Pueblo, CO — M,W
Columbia College, MO — M,W
Columbia International University, SC — M,W
Columbus State University, GA — M,W
Concordia University, CA — M,W
Concordia University, Nebraska, NE — M,W
Concordia University, St. Paul, MN — M,W
Concord University, WV — M,W
Corban University, OR — M,W
Cornerstone University, MI — M,W
Creighton University, NE — M,W
Culver-Stockton College, MO — M,W
Cumberland University, TN — M,W
Dakota State University, SD — M,W
Dallas Baptist University, TX — M
Davidson College, NC — M,W
Delaware State University, DE — M,W
Delta State University, MS — M,W
DePaul University, IL — M,W
Dickinson State University, ND — M,W
Dixie State University, UT — M,W
Doane College, NE — M,W
Dominican College, NY — M,W
Dowling College, NY — M,W
Drake University, IA — M,W
Drexel University, PA — M,W
Drury University, MO — M,W
Duquesne University, PA — M,W
East Carolina University, NC — M,W
East Central University, OK — M,W
Eastern Illinois University, IL — M,W
Eastern Kentucky University, KY — M,W
Eastern Michigan University, MI — M,W
Eastern New Mexico University, NM — M,W
East Stroudsburg University of Pennsylvania, PA — M,W
Eckerd College, FL — M,W
Elon University, NC — M,W
Embry-Riddle Aeronautical University–Daytona, FL — M,W
Embry-Riddle Aeronautical University–Prescott, AZ — M
Emmanuel College, GA — M,W
Emporia State University, KS — M,W

| | |
|---|---|
| Evangel University, MO | M,W |
| The Evergreen State College, WA | M,W |
| Fairfield University, CT | M,W |
| Fairmont State University, WV | M,W |
| Faulkner University, AL | M,W |
| Fayetteville State University, NC | M,W |
| Ferris State University, MI | M,W |
| Flagler College, FL | M,W |
| Florida Agricultural and Mechanical University, FL | M,W |
| Florida Atlantic University, FL | M,W |
| Florida Gulf Coast University, FL | M,W |
| Florida Institute of Technology, FL | M,W |
| Florida National University, FL | M |
| Florida Southern College, FL | M,W |
| Florida State University, FL | M,W |
| Fordham University, NY | M,W |
| Fort Hays State University, KS | M,W |
| Fort Lewis College, CO | M,W |
| Fort Valley State University, GA | M,W |
| Francis Marion University, SC | M,W |
| Franklin Pierce University, NH | M,W |
| Friends University, KS | M,W |
| Furman University, SC | M,W |
| Gannon University, PA | M,W |
| George Mason University, VA | M,W |
| Georgetown College, KY | M,W |
| Georgetown University, DC | M,W |
| The George Washington University, DC | M,W |
| Georgia College & State University, GA | M,W |
| Georgia Institute of Technology, GA | M,W |
| Georgian Court University, NJ | M,W |
| Georgia Regents University, GA | M,W |
| Georgia Southern University, GA | M,W |
| Georgia Southwestern State University, GA | M,W |
| Georgia State University, GA | M,W |
| Gonzaga University, WA | M,W |
| Goshen College, IN | M,W |
| Governors State University, IL | M,W |
| Graceland University, IA | M,W |
| Grambling State University, LA | M,W |
| Grand Valley State University, MI | M,W |
| Grand View University, IA | M,W |
| Hampton University, VA | M,W |
| Harding University, AR | M,W |
| Hastings College, NE | M,W |
| Hawai`i Pacific University, HI | M,W |
| Hillsdale College, MI | M,W |
| Hofstra University, NY | M,W |
| Holy Family University, PA | M,W |
| Hope International University, CA | M,W |
| Houston Baptist University, TX | M,W |
| Howard University, DC | M,W |
| Humboldt State University, CA | M,W |
| Huston-Tillotson University, TX | M,W |
| Idaho State University, ID | M,W |
| Illinois State University, IL | M,W |
| Indiana State University, IN | M,W |
| Indiana University Bloomington, IN | M,W |
| Indiana University Northwest, IN | M,W |
| Indiana University of Pennsylvania, PA | M,W |
| Indiana University–Purdue University Fort Wayne, IN | M,W |
| Indiana University–Purdue University Indianapolis, IN | M,W |
| Indiana University South Bend, IN | M,W |
| Indiana University Southeast, IN | M,W |

| | |
|---|---|
| Indian River State College, FL | M,W |
| Inter American University of Puerto Rico, Bayamón Campus, PR | M,W |
| Inter American University of Puerto Rico, Guayama Campus, PR | M,W |
| Iona College, NY | M,W |
| Iowa State University of Science and Technology, IA | M,W |
| Jackson State University, MS | M,W |
| Jacksonville State University, AL | M,W |
| Jacksonville University, FL | M,W |
| James Madison University, VA | M,W |
| John Brown University, AR | M,W |
| Johnson C. Smith University, NC | M,W |
| Kansas State University, KS | M,W |
| Kansas Wesleyan University, KS | M,W |
| Kennesaw State University, GA | M,W |
| Kent State University, OH | M,W |
| Kentucky State University, KY | M,W |
| Kentucky Wesleyan College, KY | M,W |
| King University, TN | M,W |
| Kutztown University of Pennsylvania, PA | M,W |
| Lake Erie College, OH | M,W |
| Lamar University, TX | M,W |
| Langston University, OK | M,W |
| La Salle University, PA | M,W |
| Lawrence Technological University, MI | M,W |
| Lees-McRae College, NC | M,W |
| Lee University, TN | M,W |
| Lehigh University, PA | M,W |
| Le Moyne College, NY | M,W |
| LeMoyne-Owen College, TN | M,W |
| Lenoir-Rhyne University, NC | M,W |
| Lewis-Clark State College, ID | M,W |
| Lewis University, IL | M,W |
| Liberty University, VA | M,W |
| Life University, GA | M |
| Lincoln Christian University, IL | M,W |
| Lincoln Memorial University, TN | M,W |
| Lincoln University, MO | M,W |
| Lincoln University, PA | M,W |
| Lindenwood University, MO | M,W |
| Lindsey Wilson College, KY | M,W |
| Lipscomb University, TN | M,W |
| Lock Haven University of Pennsylvania, PA | M,W |
| Long Island University–LIU Brooklyn, NY | M,W |
| Long Island University–LIU Post, NY | M,W |
| Longwood University, VA | M,W |
| Louisiana State University and Agricultural & Mechanical College, LA | M,W |
| Louisiana Tech University, LA | M,W |
| Loyola Marymount University, CA | M,W |
| Loyola University Chicago, IL | M,W |
| Loyola University New Orleans, LA | M,W |
| Lubbock Christian University, TX | M,W |
| Lynn University, FL | M,W |
| Lyon College, AR | M,W |
| Malone University, OH | M,W |
| Manhattan College, NY | M,W |
| Mansfield University of Pennsylvania, PA | M,W |
| Marist College, NY | M,W |
| Marquette University, WI | M,W |
| Marshall University, WV | M,W |

| | |
|---|---|
| Maryville University of Saint Louis, MO | M,W |
| The Master's College and Seminary, CA | M,W |
| Mayville State University, ND | M,W |
| McKendree University, IL | M,W |
| Menlo College, CA | M,W |
| Mercer University, GA | M,W |
| Mercy College, NY | M,W |
| Merrimack College, MA | M,W |
| Miami University, OH | M,W |
| Michigan State University, MI | M,W |
| Michigan Technological University, MI | M,W |
| Middle Tennessee State University, TN | M,W |
| Midland College, TX | M,W |
| Midwestern State University, TX | M,W |
| Millersville University of Pennsylvania, PA | M,W |
| Milligan College, TN | M,W |
| Minnesota State University Mankato, MN | M,W |
| Minnesota State University Moorhead, MN | M,W |
| Minot State University, ND | M,W |
| Mississippi State University, MS | M,W |
| Missouri Baptist University, MO | M,W |
| Missouri Southern State University, MO | M,W |
| Missouri State University, MO | M,W |
| Missouri University of Science and Technology, MO | M,W |
| Missouri Valley College, MO | M,W |
| Missouri Western State University, MO | M,W |
| Molloy College, NY | M,W |
| Monmouth University, NJ | M,W |
| Montana State University, MT | M,W |
| Montana State University Billings, MT | M,W |
| Montana Tech of The University of Montana, MT | M,W |
| Montreat College, NC | M,W |
| Morehead State University, KY | M,W |
| Morningside College, IA | M,W |
| Mount Marty College, SD | M,W |
| Mount Mercy University, IA | M,W |
| Mount St. Mary's University, MD | M,W |
| Murray State University, KY | M,W |
| Newberry College, SC | M,W |
| New Jersey Institute of Technology, NJ | M,W |
| Newman University, KS | M,W |
| New Mexico Highlands University, NM | M,W |
| New Mexico State University, NM | M,W |
| New York Institute of Technology, NY | M,W |
| Niagara University, NY | M,W |
| Nicholls State University, LA | M,W |
| North Carolina Agricultural and Technical State University, NC | M,W |
| North Carolina Central University, NC | M,W |
| North Carolina State University, NC | M,W |
| Northeastern State University, OK | M,W |
| Northeastern University, MA | M,W |
| Northern Arizona University, AZ | M,W |
| Northern Illinois University, IL | M,W |
| Northern Kentucky University, KY | M,W |

| | | | | | |
|---|---|---|---|---|---|
| Northern Michigan University, MI | M,W | Saint Louis University, MO | M,W | Towson University, MD | M,W |
| Northern State University, SD | M,W | Saint Martin's University, WA | M,W | Trevecca Nazarene University, TN | M,W |
| Northwest Christian University, OR | M,W | Saint Michael's College, VT | M,W | Trinity Christian College, IL | M,W |
| Northwestern Oklahoma State University, OK | M,W | St. Thomas Aquinas College, NY | M,W | Troy University, AL | M,W |
| | | Samford University, AL | M,W | Truett-McConnell College, GA | M,W |
| Northwest Missouri State University, MO | M,W | Sam Houston State University, TX | M,W | Truman State University, MO | M,W |
| | | San Diego State University, CA | M,W | Tulane University, LA | M,W |
| Northwest Nazarene University, ID | M,W | San Francisco State University, CA | M,W | Tusculum College, TN | M,W |
| Northwest University, WA | M,W | San Jose State University, CA | M,W | Union College, KY | M,W |
| Nova Southeastern University, FL | M,W | Santa Clara University, CA | M,W | Union University, TN | M,W |
| Nyack College, NY | M,W | Savannah State University, GA | M,W | University at Albany, State University of New York, NY | M,W |
| Oakland University, MI | M,W | Seattle Pacific University, WA | M,W | | |
| The Ohio State University, OH | M,W | Seattle University, WA | M,W | University at Buffalo, the State University of New York, NY | M,W |
| Ohio University, OH | M,W | Seton Hill University, PA | M,W | | |
| Oklahoma Baptist University, OK | M,W | Shawnee State University, OH | M,W | The University of Akron, OH | M,W |
| Oklahoma Christian University, OK | M,W | Shepherd University, WV | M,W | The University of Alabama, AL | M,W |
| Oklahoma City University, OK | M,W | Shippensburg University of Pennsylvania, PA | M,W | The University of Alabama at Birmingham, AL | M,W |
| Oklahoma State University, OK | M,W | | | | |
| Oklahoma Wesleyan University, OK | M,W | Siena College, NY | M,W | The University of Alabama in Huntsville, AL | M,W |
| Old Dominion University, VA | M,W | Simpson University, CA | M,W | | |
| Olivet Nazarene University, IL | M,W | Slippery Rock University of Pennsylvania, PA | M,W | University of Alaska Anchorage, AK | M,W |
| Oral Roberts University, OK | M,W | | | University of Alaska Fairbanks, AK | M,W |
| Oregon State University, OR | M,W | South Dakota School of Mines and Technology, SD | M,W | The University of Arizona, AZ | M,W |
| Our Lady of the Lake University of San Antonio, TX | M,W | | | University of Arkansas, AR | M,W |
| | | South Dakota State University, SD | M,W | University of Bridgeport, CT | M,W |
| Pace University, NY | M,W | Southeastern Louisiana University, LA | M,W | University of California, Davis, CA | M,W |
| Palm Beach Atlantic University, FL | M,W | | | University of California, Irvine, CA | M,W |
| Park University, MO | M,W | Southeastern Oklahoma State University, OK | M,W | | |
| Penn State University Park, PA | M,W | | | University of California, Los Angeles, CA | M,W |
| Pepperdine University, CA | M,W | Southeast Missouri State University, MO | M,W | | |
| Philadelphia University, PA | M,W | | | University of California, Merced, CA | M,W |
| Philander Smith College, AR | M,W | Southern Connecticut State University, CT | M,W | | |
| Pittsburg State University, KS | M,W | | | University of California, Riverside, CA | M,W |
| Point Loma Nazarene University, CA | M,W | Southern Illinois University Carbondale, IL | M,W | | |
| Post University, CT | M,W | | | University of California, Santa Barbara, CA | M,W |
| Prairie View A&M University, TX | M,W | Southern Illinois University Edwardsville, IL | M,W | | |
| Presbyterian College, SC | M,W | | | University of Central Arkansas, AR | M,W |
| Providence College, RI | M,W | Southern Methodist University, TX | M,W | University of Central Florida, FL | M,W |
| Purdue University, IN | M,W | Southern Oregon University, OR | M,W | University of Central Missouri, MO | M,W |
| Purdue University Calumet, IN | M,W | Southern Utah University, UT | M,W | University of Central Oklahoma, OK | M,W |
| Queens College of the City University of New York, NY | M,W | Southwest Baptist University, MO | M,W | University of Charleston, WV | M,W |
| | | Southwestern College, KS | M,W | University of Cincinnati, OH | M,W |
| Quincy University, IL | M,W | Spring Hill College, AL | M,W | University of Colorado Boulder, CO | M,W |
| Quinnipiac University, CT | M,W | Stanford University, CA | M,W | University of Colorado Colorado Springs, CO | M,W |
| Radford University, VA | M,W | Stephen F. Austin State University, TX | M,W | | |
| Regis University, CO | M,W | | | University of Connecticut, CT | M,W |
| Reinhardt University, GA | M,W | Stephens College, MO | W | University of Dayton, OH | M,W |
| Rice University, TX | M,W | Sterling College, KS | M,W | University of Delaware, DE | M,W |
| Rider University, NJ | M,W | Stetson University, FL | M,W | University of Denver, CO | M,W |
| Robert Morris University, PA | M,W | Stonehill College, MA | M,W | University of Evansville, IN | M,W |
| Robert Morris University Illinois, IL | M,W | Stony Brook University, State University of New York, NY | M,W | The University of Findlay, OH | M,W |
| | | | | University of Florida, FL | M,W |
| Roberts Wesleyan College, NY | M,W | Syracuse University, NY | M,W | University of Georgia, GA | M,W |
| Rockhurst University, MO | M,W | Tabor College, KS | M,W | University of Great Falls, MT | M,W |
| Rocky Mountain College, MT | M,W | Tarleton State University, TX | M,W | University of Hartford, CT | M,W |
| Rollins College, FL | M,W | Taylor University, IN | M,W | University of Hawaii at Manoa, HI | M,W |
| Sacred Heart University, CT | M,W | Temple University, PA | M,W | University of Houston, TX | M,W |
| Saginaw Valley State University, MI | M,W | Tennessee State University, TN | M,W | University of Idaho, ID | M,W |
| | | Tennessee Wesleyan College, TN | M,W | University of Illinois at Chicago, IL | M,W |
| St. Andrews University, NC | M,W | Texas A&M International University, TX | M,W | | |
| Saint Anselm College, NH | M,W | | | University of Illinois at Springfield, IL | M,W |
| Saint Augustine's University, NC | M,W | Texas A&M University, TX | M,W | | |
| | | Texas A&M University–Commerce, TX | M,W | University of Indianapolis, IN | M,W |
| St. Bonaventure University, NY | M,W | | | The University of Iowa, IA | M,W |
| St. Edward's University, TX | M,W | Texas A&M University–Corpus Christi, TX | M,W | University of Jamestown, ND | M,W |
| St. Francis College, NY | M,W | | | The University of Kansas, KS | M,W |
| Saint Francis University, PA | M,W | Texas Christian University, TX | M,W | University of Louisiana at Lafayette, LA | M,W |
| St. John's University, NY | M,W | Texas Southern University, TX | M,W | | |
| Saint Joseph's College, IN | M,W | Texas State University, TX | M,W | University of Louisville, KY | M,W |
| Saint Joseph's University, PA | M,W | Texas Tech University, TX | M,W | University of Maine, ME | M,W |
| | | Texas Wesleyan University, TX | M,W | University of Maine at Augusta, ME | M,W |
| Saint Leo University, FL | M,W | Texas Woman's University, TX | W | University of Maryland, Baltimore County, MD | M,W |
| St. Louis College of Pharmacy, MO | M,W | Tiffin University, OH | M,W | | |

| | | | | | | |
|---|---|---|---|---|---|
| University of Maryland, College Park, MD | M,W | University of South Carolina, SC | M,W | Waldorf College, IA | M,W |
| University of Massachusetts Amherst, MA | M,W | University of South Carolina Aiken, SC | M,W | Warner Pacific College, OR | M,W |
| University of Massachusetts Lowell, MA | M,W | University of South Carolina Upstate, SC | M,W | Washburn University, KS | M,W |
| University of Memphis, TN | M,W | The University of South Dakota, SD | M,W | Washington State University, WA | M,W |
| University of Miami, FL | M,W | University of Southern California, CA | M,W | Wayland Baptist University, TX | M,W |
| University of Michigan, MI | M,W | University of Southern Indiana, IN | M,W | Wayne State College, NE | M,W |
| University of Michigan–Dearborn, MI | M,W | University of Southern Mississippi, MS | M,W | Wayne State University, MI | M,W |
| University of Minnesota, Crookston, MN | M,W | University of South Florida, FL | M,W | Webber International University, FL | M,W |
| University of Minnesota, Duluth, MN | M,W | The University of Tampa, FL | M,W | Weber State University, UT | M,W |
| University of Minnesota, Twin Cities Campus, MN | M,W | The University of Tennessee, TN | M,W | West Chester University of Pennsylvania, PA | M,W |
| University of Mississippi, MS | M,W | The University of Tennessee at Chattanooga, TN | M,W | Western Carolina University, NC | M,W |
| University of Missouri, MO | M,W | The University of Tennessee at Martin, TN | M,W | Western Illinois University, IL | M,W |
| University of Missouri–Kansas City, MO | M,W | The University of Texas at Arlington, TX | M,W | Western Kentucky University, KY | M,W |
| University of Missouri–St. Louis, MO | M,W | The University of Texas at Austin, TX | M,W | Western Michigan University, MI | M,W |
| University of Mobile, AL | M,W | The University of Texas at El Paso, TX | M,W | Western Oregon University, OR | M,W |
| The University of Montana, MT | M,W | The University of Texas at San Antonio, TX | M,W | Western State Colorado University, CO | M,W |
| The University of Montana Western, MT | M,W | The University of Texas–Pan American, TX | M,W | Western Washington University, WA | M,W |
| University of Montevallo, AL | M,W | University of the Cumberlands, KY | M,W | Westminster College, UT | M,W |
| University of Nebraska at Kearney, NE | M,W | University of the District of Columbia, DC | M,W | West Texas A&M University, TX | M,W |
| University of Nebraska–Lincoln, NE | M,W | University of the Incarnate Word, TX | M,W | West Virginia University, WV | M,W |
| University of Nevada, Las Vegas, NV | M,W | University of the Pacific, CA | M,W | West Virginia University Institute of Technology, WV | M,W |
| University of Nevada, Reno, NV | M,W | University of the Sciences, PA | M,W | West Virginia Wesleyan College, WV | M,W |
| University of New Hampshire, NH | M,W | The University of Toledo, OH | M,W | Wheeling Jesuit University, WV | M,W |
| University of New Haven, CT | M,W | The University of Tulsa, OK | M,W | Wichita State University, KS | M,W |
| University of New Orleans, LA | M,W | University of Utah, UT | M,W | William Jessup University, CA | M,W |
| University of North Alabama, AL | M,W | University of Vermont, VT | M,W | William Jewell College, MO | M,W |
| University of North Carolina at Asheville, NC | M,W | University of Virginia, VA | M,W | Williams Baptist College, AR | M,W |
| The University of North Carolina at Chapel Hill, NC | M,W | The University of Virginia's College at Wise, VA | M,W | William Woods University, MO | M,W |
| The University of North Carolina at Charlotte, NC | M,W | University of Washington, WA | M,W | Wingate University, NC | M,W |
| The University of North Carolina at Greensboro, NC | M,W | The University of West Alabama, AL | M,W | Winona State University, MN | M,W |
| The University of North Carolina at Pembroke, NC | M,W | University of West Florida, FL | M,W | Winthrop University, SC | M,W |
| The University of North Carolina Wilmington, NC | M,W | University of West Georgia, GA | M,W | Wofford College, SC | M,W |
| University of Northern Colorado, CO | M,W | University of Wisconsin–Green Bay, WI | M,W | Wright State University, OH | M,W |
| University of Northern Iowa, IA | M,W | University of Wisconsin–Madison, WI | M,W | Xavier University, OH | M,W |
| University of North Florida, FL | M,W | University of Wisconsin–Milwaukee, WI | M,W | Xavier University of Louisiana, LA | M,W |
| University of North Georgia, GA | M,W | University of Wisconsin–Parkside, WI | M,W | Youngstown State University, OH | M,W |
| University of North Texas, TX | M,W | University of Wyoming, WY | M,W | | |
| University of Notre Dame, IN | M,W | Upper Iowa University, IA | M,W | **Bowling** | |
| University of Oklahoma, OK | M,W | Ursuline College, OH | W | Adelphi University, NY | W |
| University of Oregon, OR | M,W | Utah State University, UT | M,W | Alabama State University, AL | W |
| University of Pikeville, KY | M,W | Utah Valley University, UT | M,W | Arkansas State University, AR | W |
| University of Pittsburgh, PA | M,W | Valdosta State University, GA | M,W | Bethune-Cookman University, FL | W |
| University of Portland, OR | M,W | Valley City State University, ND | M,W | Caldwell University, NJ | W |
| University of Rhode Island, RI | M | Valparaiso University, IN | M,W | Calumet College of Saint Joseph, IN | M,W |
| University of Richmond, VA | M,W | Vanderbilt University, TN | M,W | Campbellsville University, KY | M,W |
| University of Rio Grande, OH | M,W | Vanguard University of Southern California, CA | M,W | Cardinal Stritch University, WI | M,W |
| University of St. Francis, IL | M,W | Villanova University, PA | M,W | Chestnut Hill College, PA | W |
| University of St. Thomas, TX | M,W | Virginia Commonwealth University, VA | M,W | Chowan University, NC | W |
| University of San Diego, CA | M,W | Virginia Military Institute, VA | M | Clarke University, IA | M,W |
| University of San Francisco, CA | M,W | Virginia State University, VA | M,W | Culver-Stockton College, MO | M,W |
| University of Science and Arts of Oklahoma, OK | M,W | Virginia Union University, VA | M,W | Cumberland University, TN | M,W |
| University of South Alabama, AL | M,W | Wagner College, NY | M,W | Delaware State University, DE | W |
| | | Wake Forest University, NC | M,W | Emmanuel College, GA | M,W |
| | | | | Florida Agricultural and Mechanical University, FL | W |
| | | | | Graceland University, IA | M,W |
| | | | | Grambling State University, LA | W |
| | | | | Grand View University, IA | M,W |
| | | | | Hampton University, VA | W |
| | | | | Hastings College, NE | M,W |
| | | | | Howard University, DC | W |
| | | | | Jackson State University, MS | W |
| | | | | Johnson C. Smith University, NC | W |
| | | | | Kansas Wesleyan University, KS | M,W |
| | | | | Kentucky Wesleyan College, KY | W |
| | | | | Kutztown University of Pennsylvania, PA | W |

Lawrence Technological University, MI — M,W
Lincoln University, MO — W
Lindenwood University, MO — M,W
Lindsey Wilson College, KY — M,W
Long Island University–LIU Brooklyn, NY — W
McKendree University, IL — W
Missouri Baptist University, MO — M,W
Monmouth University, NJ — W
Newman University, KS — M,W
North Carolina Agricultural and Technical State University, NC — W
North Carolina Central University, NC — W
Post University, CT — W
Robert Morris University Illinois, IL — M,W
Sacred Heart University, CT — W
Saint Augustine's University, NC — W
Sam Houston State University, TX — W
Spring Hill College, AL — M,W
Stephen F. Austin State University, TX — W
Tabor College, KS — M,W
Texas Southern University, TX — W
Union College, KY — M,W
University of Nebraska–Lincoln, NE — W
University of Pikeville, KY — M,W
University of St. Francis, IL — M,W
University of South Florida, FL — M,W
University of the Cumberlands, KY — M,W
Ursuline College, OH — W
Valparaiso University, IN — W
Vanderbilt University, TN — W
Virginia State University, VA — W
Virginia Union University, VA — M,W
Waldorf College, IA — M,W
Webber International University, FL — M,W
West Texas A&M University, TX — M,W
Wichita State University, KS — M,W

**Cheerleading**

Adelphi University, NY — W
Alabama State University, AL — M,W
Anderson University, SC — W
Arkansas Tech University, AR — M,W
Ashland University, OH — W
Auburn University at Montgomery, AL — M,W
Austin Peay State University, TN — M,W
Baylor University, TX — M,W
Bellarmine University, KY — M,W
Biola University, CA — W
Brevard College, NC — W
Brigham Young University, UT — M,W
California Baptist University, CA — W
Cameron University, OK — M,W
Campbellsville University, KY — M,W
Cardinal Stritch University, WI — M,W
Carroll College, MT — M,W
Clayton State University, GA — W
Columbus State University, GA — M,W
Concordia University, CA — M,W
Concordia University, Nebraska, NE — W
Cornerstone University, MI — W
Culver-Stockton College, MO — M,W
Cumberland University, TN — M,W
Delaware State University, DE — M,W
Delta State University, MS — M,W
Doane College, NE — W

Drake University, IA — M,W
Drury University, MO — M,W
Eastern New Mexico University, NM — M,W
East Texas Baptist University, TX — M,W
Emmanuel College, GA — M,W
Emporia State University, KS — M,W
Faulkner University, AL — M,W
Friends University, KS — M,W
Gannon University, PA — W
Georgetown College, KY — M,W
Georgia Institute of Technology, GA — M,W
Graceland University, IA — M,W
Grambling State University, LA — M,W
Grand View University, IA — W
Hastings College, NE — W
Hawai`i Pacific University, HI — M,W
Hofstra University, NY — M,W
Houston Baptist University, TX — M,W
John Brown University, AR — M,W
Kansas Wesleyan University, KS — M,W
Kentucky State University, KY — W
King University, TN — M,W
Lee University, TN — M,W
Lenoir-Rhyne University, NC — M,W
Lewis University, IL — W
Liberty University, VA — M,W
Lincoln University, MO — W
Lindenwood University, MO — M,W
Lindsey Wilson College, KY — M,W
Maryville University of Saint Louis, MO — M,W
McKendree University, IL — M,W
Menlo College, CA — M,W
Middle Tennessee State University, TN — M,W
Midwestern State University, TX — M,W
Millersville University of Pennsylvania, PA — W
Mississippi State University, MS — M,W
Missouri Baptist University, MO — M,W
Missouri Valley College, MO — M,W
Montana State University, MT — M,W
Morehead State University, KY — M,W
Newberry College, SC — M,W
Newman University, KS — M,W
North Carolina State University, NC — M,W
Northwestern Oklahoma State University, OK — M,W
Northwest Missouri State University, MO — M,W
Oklahoma City University, OK — M,W
Oklahoma State University, OK — M,W
Old Dominion University, VA — M,W
Olivet Nazarene University, IL — M,W
Penn State University Park, PA — M,W
Pittsburg State University, KS — M,W
Presbyterian College, SC — M,W
Reinhardt University, GA — M,W
Robert Morris University Illinois, IL — M,W
Rocky Mountain College, MT — M,W
Saint Augustine's University, NC — W
Saint Joseph's College, IN — M,W
Sam Houston State University, TX — M,W
Savannah State University, GA — M,W
Southeastern Louisiana University, LA — M,W
Southeast Missouri State University, MO — M,W
Southern Methodist University, TX — M,W

Southern Utah University, UT — M,W
Southwestern College, KS — M,W
Stephen F. Austin State University, TX — M,W
Tabor College, KS — M,W
Tarleton State University, TX — M,W
Temple University, PA — M,W
Tennessee Wesleyan College, TN — M,W
Texas A&M University–Commerce, TX — M,W
Texas Wesleyan University, TX — M,W
Tiffin University, OH — M,W
Tusculum College, TN — W
Union College, KY — M,W
Union University, TN — W
The University of Alabama, AL — M,W
The University of Alabama in Huntsville, AL — M,W
University of Central Arkansas, AR — M,W
University of Central Florida, FL — M,W
University of Charleston, WV — W
University of Delaware, DE — M,W
University of Florida, FL — M,W
University of Great Falls, MT — M,W
University of Memphis, TN — M,W
University of Michigan, MI — M,W
University of Mississippi, MS — M,W
University of Mobile, AL — W
University of Nevada, Las Vegas, NV — M,W
University of North Alabama, AL — M,W
The University of North Carolina Wilmington, NC — W
University of Oklahoma, OK — M,W
University of Pikeville, KY — M,W
University of Rhode Island, RI — M,W
University of St. Francis, IL — M,W
University of Science and Arts of Oklahoma, OK — M,W
University of South Carolina, SC — M,W
University of South Carolina Upstate, SC — M,W
The University of Tennessee at Martin, TN — W
University of the Cumberlands, KY — M,W
University of the Incarnate Word, TX — W
University of Utah, UT — M,W
The University of West Alabama, AL — M,W
University of West Georgia, GA — W
University of Wyoming, WY — M,W
Waldorf College, IA — W
Washburn University, KS — M,W
Wayland Baptist University, TX — M,W
Wayne State University, MI — M,W
Webber International University, FL — M,W
Weber State University, UT — M,W
West Virginia University Institute of Technology, WV — M,W
William Jewell College, MO — M,W
Williams Baptist College, AR — W
William Woods University, MO — W
Wright State University, OH — M,W

**Crew**

Barry University, FL — W
Boston College, MA — W
Boston University, MA — M,W
California State University, Sacramento, CA — M,W
College of the Holy Cross, MA — W
Creighton University, NE — W
Drexel University, PA — M,W

| | |
|---|---|
| Duquesne University, PA | W |
| Eastern Michigan University, MI | W |
| Fairfield University, CT | M,W |
| Florida Institute of Technology, FL | M,W |
| Fordham University, NY | W |
| George Mason University, VA | W |
| Georgetown University, DC | M,W |
| The George Washington University, DC | M,W |
| Gonzaga University, WA | W |
| Indiana University Bloomington, IN | W |
| Jacksonville University, FL | M,W |
| Kansas State University, KS | W |
| La Salle University, PA | M,W |
| Lehigh University, PA | W |
| Loyola Marymount University, CA | W |
| Marist College, NY | W |
| Merrimack College, MA | W |
| Michigan State University, MI | W |
| Northeastern University, MA | M,W |
| Nova Southeastern University, FL | W |
| Oklahoma City University, OK | M,W |
| Old Dominion University, VA | W |
| Robert Morris University, PA | W |
| Saint Joseph's University, PA | M,W |
| San Diego State University, CA | W |
| Seattle Pacific University, WA | W |
| Southern Methodist University, TX | W |
| Stanford University, CA | M,W |
| Stetson University, FL | W |
| Syracuse University, NY | M,W |
| Temple University, PA | M,W |
| University at Buffalo, the State University of New York, NY | W |
| The University of Alabama, AL | W |
| University of California, Los Angeles, CA | W |
| University of Central Florida, FL | W |
| University of Charleston, WV | M,W |
| University of Delaware, DE | W |
| The University of Iowa, IA | W |
| The University of Kansas, KS | W |
| University of Louisville, KY | W |
| University of Massachusetts Amherst, MA | W |
| University of Miami, FL | W |
| University of Michigan, MI | W |
| The University of North Carolina at Chapel Hill, NC | W |
| University of Notre Dame, IN | W |
| University of Oklahoma, OK | W |
| University of Rhode Island, RI | M |
| University of San Diego, CA | W |
| University of Southern California, CA | W |
| The University of Tampa, FL | W |
| The University of Tennessee, TN | W |
| The University of Texas at Austin, TX | W |
| The University of Tulsa, OK | W |
| University of Virginia, VA | W |
| University of Washington, WA | M,W |
| Washington State University, WA | W |
| Western Washington University, WA | M,W |
| West Virginia University, WV | W |

**Cross-country running**

| | |
|---|---|
| Abilene Christian University, TX | M,W |
| Academy of Art University, CA | M,W |
| Adams State University, CO | M,W |
| Adelphi University, NY | M,W |
| Alabama State University, AL | M,W |
| Albany State University, GA | M,W |
| Alcorn State University, MS | M,W |
| American University, DC | M,W |
| Anderson University, SC | M,W |
| Angelo State University, TX | M,W |
| Appalachian State University, NC | M,W |
| Arizona Christian University, AZ | M,W |
| Arizona State University at the Downtown Phoenix campus, AZ | M,W |
| Arizona State University at the Polytechnic campus, AZ | |
| Arizona State University at the Tempe campus, AZ | M,W |
| Arizona State University at the West campus, AZ | M,W |
| Arkansas State University, AR | M,W |
| Arkansas Tech University, AR | W |
| Armstrong State University, GA | M |
| Ashland University, OH | M,W |
| Auburn University, AL | M,W |
| Auburn University at Montgomery, AL | M,W |
| Augustana College, SD | M,W |
| Austin Peay State University, TN | M,W |
| Azusa Pacific University, CA | M,W |
| Ball State University, IN | W |
| Baylor University, TX | M,W |
| Belhaven University, MS | M,W |
| Bellarmine University, KY | M,W |
| Belmont Abbey College, NC | M,W |
| Belmont University, TN | M,W |
| Bemidji State University, MN | W |
| Bethel College, KS | M,W |
| Bethune-Cookman University, FL | M,W |
| Binghamton University, State University of New York, NY | M,W |
| Biola University, CA | M,W |
| Bloomfield College, NJ | M,W |
| Bloomsburg University of Pennsylvania, PA | M,W |
| Bluefield College, VA | M,W |
| Bluefield State College, WV | M,W |
| Blue Mountain College, MS | M,W |
| Boston College, MA | M,W |
| Boston University, MA | M,W |
| Bowie State University, MD | M,W |
| Bowling Green State University, OH | M,W |
| Bradley University, IL | M,W |
| Brenau University, GA | W |
| Brevard College, NC | M,W |
| Brigham Young University, UT | M,W |
| Bryant University, RI | M,W |
| Bucknell University, PA | W |
| Butler University, IN | M,W |
| Caldwell University, NJ | M,W |
| California Baptist University, CA | M,W |
| California Polytechnic State University, San Luis Obispo, CA | M,W |
| California State Polytechnic University, Pomona, CA | M,W |
| California State University, Chico, CA | M,W |
| California State University, Fresno, CA | M,W |
| California State University, Fullerton, CA | M,W |
| California State University, Long Beach, CA | M,W |
| California State University, Los Angeles, CA | W |
| California State University, Monterey Bay, CA | M,W |

| | |
|---|---|
| California State University, Sacramento, CA | M,W |
| California State University, Stanislaus, CA | M,W |
| Calumet College of Saint Joseph, IN | M,W |
| Cameron University, OK | M |
| Campbellsville University, KY | M,W |
| Canisius College, NY | M,W |
| Cardinal Stritch University, WI | M,W |
| Carroll College, MT | M,W |
| Carson-Newman University, TN | M,W |
| Catawba College, NC | M,W |
| Cedarville University, OH | M,W |
| Central Connecticut State University, CT | M,W |
| Central Methodist University, MO | M,W |
| Central Michigan University, MI | M,W |
| Central Washington University, WA | M,W |
| Chaminade University of Honolulu, HI | M,W |
| Chestnut Hill College, PA | M,W |
| Chowan University, NC | M,W |
| Christian Brothers University, TN | M,W |
| Cincinnati Christian University, OH | M,W |
| The Citadel, The Military College of South Carolina, SC | M,W |
| Clarion University of Pennsylvania, PA | W |
| Clarke University, IA | M,W |
| Clayton State University, GA | M,W |
| Cleveland State University, OH | W |
| Coastal Carolina University, SC | M,W |
| Coker College, SC | M,W |
| College of Charleston, SC | M,W |
| The College of Idaho, ID | M,W |
| College of Saint Mary, NE | W |
| College of the Holy Cross, MA | W |
| The College of William and Mary, VA | M,W |
| Colorado Mesa University, CO | M,W |
| Colorado School of Mines, CO | M,W |
| Colorado State University, CO | M,W |
| Colorado State University Pueblo, CO | W |
| Columbia College, MO | M,W |
| Columbia International University, SC | M,W |
| Columbus State University, GA | M,W |
| Concordia University, CA | M,W |
| Concordia University, Nebraska, NE | M,W |
| Concordia University, St. Paul, MN | M,W |
| Concord University, WV | M,W |
| Corban University, OR | M,W |
| Cornerstone University, MI | M,W |
| Creighton University, NE | M,W |
| Culver-Stockton College, MO | M,W |
| Cumberland University, TN | M,W |
| Dakota State University, SD | M,W |
| Dallas Baptist University, TX | W |
| Davidson College, NC | M,W |
| Delaware State University, DE | M,W |
| Delta State University, MS | W |
| DePaul University, IL | M,W |
| Dickinson State University, ND | M,W |
| Dixie State University, UT | M,W |
| Doane College, NE | M,W |
| Dominican College, NY | M,W |
| Dowling College, NY | M,W |
| Drake University, IA | M,W |
| Drury University, MO | M,W |
| Duquesne University, PA | M,W |

| | | | | | |
|---|---|---|---|---|---|
| East Carolina University, NC | M,W | Indiana University of | | Marshall University, WV | M,W |
| East Central University, OK | M,W | Pennsylvania, PA | M,W | Maryville University of Saint | |
| Eastern Illinois University, IL | M,W | Indiana University–Purdue | | Louis, MO | M,W |
| Eastern Kentucky University, KY | M,W | University Fort Wayne, IN | M,W | The Master's College and | |
| Eastern Michigan University, MI | M,W | Indiana University–Purdue | | Seminary, CA | M,W |
| Eastern New Mexico University, NM | M,W | University Indianapolis, IN | M,W | McKendree University, IL | M,W |
| East Stroudsburg University of | | Inter American University of | | Mercer University, GA | M,W |
| Pennsylvania, PA | M,W | Puerto Rico, Bayamón | | Merrimack College, MA | M,W |
| Elon University, NC | M,W | Campus, PR | M,W | Miami University, OH | M,W |
| Embry-Riddle Aeronautical | | Inter American University of | | Michigan State University, MI | M,W |
| University–Daytona, FL | M,W | Puerto Rico, Guayama | | Michigan Technological | |
| Embry-Riddle Aeronautical | | Campus, PR | M,W | University, MI | |
| University–Prescott, AZ | M,W | Iona College, NY | M,W | Middle Tennessee State | |
| Emmanuel College, GA | M,W | Iowa State University of Science | | University, TN | M,W |
| Emporia State University, KS | M,W | and Technology, IA | M,W | Midwestern State University, TX | W |
| Evangel University, MO | M,W | Jackson State University, MS | M,W | Millersville University of | |
| Fairfield University, CT | M,W | Jacksonville State University, AL | M,W | Pennsylvania, PA | W |
| Fairmont State University, WV | M,W | Jacksonville University, FL | W | Milligan College, TN | M,W |
| Fayetteville State University, NC | M,W | James Madison University, VA | W | Minnesota State University | |
| Ferris State University, MI | M,W | John Brown University, AR | M,W | Mankato, MN | M,W |
| Flagler College, FL | M,W | Johnson C. Smith University, NC | M,W | Minnesota State University | |
| Florida Agricultural and | | Kansas State University, KS | M,W | Moorhead, MN | M,W |
| Mechanical University, FL | M,W | Kansas Wesleyan University, KS | M,W | Minot State University, ND | M,W |
| Florida Gulf Coast University, FL | M,W | Kennesaw State University, GA | M,W | Mississippi State University, MS | M,W |
| Florida Institute of Technology, | | Kent State University, OH | M,W | Missouri Baptist University, MO | M,W |
| FL | M,W | Kentucky State University, KY | M,W | Missouri Southern State | |
| Florida Southern College, FL | M,W | Kentucky Wesleyan College, KY | M,W | University, MO | M,W |
| Florida State University, FL | M,W | King University, TN | M,W | Missouri State University, MO | W |
| Fordham University, NY | M,W | Kutztown University of | | Missouri University of Science | |
| Fort Hays State University, KS | M,W | Pennsylvania, PA | M,W | and Technology, MO | M,W |
| Fort Lewis College, CO | M,W | Lake Erie College, OH | M,W | Missouri Valley College, MO | M,W |
| Francis Marion University, SC | M,W | Lamar University, TX | M,W | Molloy College, NY | M,W |
| Friends University, KS | M,W | La Salle University, PA | M,W | Monmouth University, NJ | M,W |
| Furman University, SC | M,W | Lawrence Technological | | Montana State University, MT | M,W |
| Gannon University, PA | M,W | University, MI | M,W | Montana State University | |
| George Mason University, VA | M,W | Lees-McRae College, NC | M,W | Billings, MT | M,W |
| Georgetown College, KY | M,W | Lee University, TN | M,W | Montreat College, NC | M,W |
| Georgetown University, DC | M,W | Lehigh University, PA | M,W | Morehead State University, KY | M,W |
| The George Washington | | Le Moyne College, NY | M,W | Morningside College, IA | M,W |
| University, DC | M,W | LeMoyne-Owen College, TN | M,W | Mount Marty College, SD | M,W |
| Georgia College & State | | Lenoir-Rhyne University, NC | M,W | Mount Mercy University, IA | M,W |
| University, GA | M,W | Lewis-Clark State College, ID | M,W | Mount St. Mary's | |
| Georgia Institute of Technology, | | Lewis University, IL | M,W | University, MD | M,W |
| GA | M,W | Liberty University, VA | M,W | Murray State University, KY | W |
| Georgian Court University, NJ | M,W | Life University, GA | W | Newberry College, SC | M,W |
| Georgia Regents University, GA | M,W | Lincoln Memorial University, TN | M,W | New Jersey Institute of | |
| Georgia Southern University, GA | W | Lincoln University, MO | W | Technology, NJ | M,W |
| Georgia Southwestern State | | Lincoln University, PA | M,W | Newman University, KS | M,W |
| University, GA | W | Lindenwood University, MO | M,W | New Mexico Highlands University, | |
| Georgia State University, GA | M | Lindsey Wilson College, KY | M,W | NM | M,W |
| Gonzaga University, WA | M,W | Lipscomb University, TN | M,W | New Mexico State University, NM | M,W |
| Goshen College, IN | M,W | Lock Haven University of | | New York Institute of | |
| Governors State University, IL | M,W | Pennsylvania, PA | M,W | Technology, NY | M,W |
| Graceland University, IA | M,W | Long Island University–LIU | | Niagara University, NY | M,W |
| Grand Valley State University, MI | M,W | Brooklyn, NY | M,W | Nicholls State University, LA | M,W |
| Grand View University, IA | M,W | Long Island University–LIU | | North Carolina Agricultural and | |
| Hampton University, VA | M,W | Post, NY | M,W | Technical State University, NC | M,W |
| Harding University, AR | M,W | Longwood University, VA | M,W | North Carolina Central | |
| Hastings College, NE | M,W | Louisiana State University and | | University, NC | M,W |
| Hawai`i Pacific University, HI | M,W | Agricultural & Mechanical | | North Carolina State University, | |
| Hillsdale College, MI | M,W | College, LA | M,W | NC | M,W |
| Hofstra University, NY | M,W | Louisiana Tech University, LA | M,W | Northeastern University, MA | M,W |
| Holy Family University, PA | M,W | Loyola Marymount University, CA | M,W | Northern Arizona University, AZ | M,W |
| Hope International University, CA | M,W | Loyola University Chicago, IL | M,W | Northern Kentucky University, KY | M,W |
| Houston Baptist University, TX | M,W | Lubbock Christian University, TX | M,W | Northern Michigan University, MI | W |
| Howard University, DC | M,W | Lynn University, FL | W | Northern State University, SD | M,W |
| Humboldt State University, CA | M,W | Lyon College, AR | M,W | Northwest Christian University, OR | M,W |
| Huston-Tillotson University, TX | M | Malone University, OH | M,W | Northwestern Oklahoma State | |
| Idaho State University, ID | M,W | Manhattan College, NY | M,W | University, OK | M,W |
| Illinois Institute of Technology, IL | M,W | Mansfield University of | | Northwest Missouri State | |
| Illinois State University, IL | M,W | Pennsylvania, PA | M,W | University, MO | M,W |
| Indiana State University, IN | M,W | Marist College, NY | M,W | Northwest Nazarene University, ID | M,W |
| Indiana University Bloomington, IN | M,W | Marquette University, WI | M,W | Northwest University, WA | M,W |

| | | | | | |
|---|---|---|---|---|---|
| Nova Southeastern University, FL | M,W | Seton Hill University, PA | M,W | The University of Alabama at Birmingham, AL | W |
| Nyack College, NY | M,W | Shawnee State University, OH | M,W | The University of Alabama in Huntsville, AL | M,W |
| Oakland University, MI | M,W | Shippensburg University of Pennsylvania, PA | M,W | University of Alaska Anchorage, AK | M |
| The Ohio State University, OH | M,W | Siena College, NY | M,W | University of Alaska Fairbanks, AK | M,W |
| Ohio University, OH | M,W | Simpson University, CA | M,W | The University of Arizona, AZ | M,W |
| Oklahoma Baptist University, OK | M,W | Slippery Rock University of Pennsylvania, PA | M,W | University of Arkansas, AR | M,W |
| Oklahoma Christian University, OK | M,W | Soka University of America, CA | M,W | University of Bridgeport, CT | M,W |
| Oklahoma State University, OK | M,W | South Dakota School of Mines and Technology, SD | M,W | University of California, Davis, CA | M,W |
| Oklahoma Wesleyan University, OK | M,W | South Dakota State University, SD | M,W | University of California, Irvine, CA | M,W |
| Olivet Nazarene University, IL | M,W | Southeastern Louisiana University, LA | M,W | University of California, Los Angeles, CA | M,W |
| Oral Roberts University, OK | M,W | Southeastern Oklahoma State University, OK | W | University of California, Merced, CA | |
| Oregon State University, OR | W | Southeast Missouri State University, MO | M,W | University of California, Riverside, CA | M,W |
| Our Lady of the Lake University of San Antonio, TX | M,W | Southern Connecticut State University, CT | M,W | University of California, Santa Barbara, CA | M,W |
| Pace University, NY | M,W | Southern Illinois University Carbondale, IL | M,W | University of Central Arkansas, AR | M,W |
| Palm Beach Atlantic University, FL | W | Southern Illinois University Edwardsville, IL | M,W | University of Central Florida, FL | W |
| Park University, MO | M,W | Southern Methodist University, TX | W | University of Central Missouri, MO | M,W |
| Penn State University Park, PA | M,W | Southern Utah University, UT | M,W | University of Central Oklahoma, OK | W |
| Pepperdine University, CA | M,W | Southwest Baptist University, MO | M,W | University of Charleston, WV | W |
| Pittsburg State University, KS | M,W | Southwestern College, KS | M,W | University of Cincinnati, OH | M,W |
| Point Loma Nazarene University, CA | W | Spring Hill College, AL | M,W | University of Colorado Boulder, CO | M,W |
| Post University, CT | M,W | Stanford University, CA | M,W | University of Colorado Colorado Springs, CO | M,W |
| Prairie View A&M University, TX | M,W | Stephen F. Austin State University, TX | M,W | University of Connecticut, CT | M,W |
| Presbyterian College, SC | M,W | Stephens College, MO | W | University of Dayton, OH | M,W |
| Providence College, RI | M,W | Sterling College, KS | M,W | University of Delaware, DE | W |
| Purdue University, IN | M,W | Stetson University, FL | M,W | University of Evansville, IN | M,W |
| Purdue University Calumet, IN | M,W | Stonehill College, MA | M,W | The University of Findlay, OH | M,W |
| Queens College of the City University of New York, NY | M,W | Stony Brook University, State University of New York, NY | | University of Florida, FL | M,W |
| Quincy University, IL | M,W | Syracuse University, NY | M,W | University of Georgia, GA | M,W |
| Quinnipiac University, CT | M,W | Tabor College, KS | M,W | University of Hartford, CT | M,W |
| Radford University, VA | M,W | Tarleton State University, TX | M,W | University of Houston, TX | M,W |
| Regis University, CO | M,W | Taylor University, IN | M,W | University of Idaho, ID | M,W |
| Reinhardt University, GA | M,W | Temple University, PA | M,W | University of Illinois at Chicago, IL | M,W |
| Rice University, TX | M,W | Tennessee State University, TN | M,W | University of Indianapolis, IN | M,W |
| Rider University, NJ | M,W | Tennessee Wesleyan College, TN | M,W | The University of Iowa, IA | M,W |
| Robert Morris University Illinois, IL | M,W | Texas A&M International University, TX | M,W | University of Jamestown, ND | M,W |
| Roberts Wesleyan College, NY | M,W | Texas A&M University, TX | M,W | The University of Kansas, KS | M,W |
| Rockhurst University, MO | W | Texas A&M University–Commerce, TX | M,W | University of Louisiana at Lafayette, LA | M,W |
| Rocky Mountain College, MT | M,W | Texas A&M University–Corpus Christi, TX | M,W | University of Louisville, KY | M,W |
| Sacred Heart University, CT | M,W | Texas Christian University, TX | M,W | University of Maine, ME | M,W |
| Saginaw Valley State University, MI | M,W | Texas Southern University, TX | M,W | University of Maryland, Baltimore County, MD | M,W |
| St. Andrews University, NC | M,W | Texas State University, TX | M,W | University of Maryland, College Park, MD | W |
| Saint Anselm College, NH | M,W | Texas Tech University, TX | M,W | University of Massachusetts Amherst, MA | M,W |
| Saint Augustine's University, NC | M,W | Texas Wesleyan University, TX | M,W | University of Massachusetts Lowell, MA | M,W |
| St. Bonaventure University, NY | M,W | Tiffin University, OH | M,W | University of Memphis, TN | M,W |
| St. Francis College, NY | M,W | Towson University, MD | W | University of Miami, FL | M,W |
| Saint Francis University, PA | M,W | Trinity Christian College, IL | M,W | University of Michigan, MI | M,W |
| St. John's University, NY | W | Troy University, AL | M,W | University of Michigan–Dearborn, MI | M,W |
| Saint Joseph's College, IN | M,W | Truett-McConnell College, GA | M,W | University of Minnesota, Duluth, MN | M,W |
| Saint Joseph's University, PA | M,W | Truman State University, MO | M,W | University of Minnesota, Twin Cities Campus, MN | M,W |
| Saint Leo University, FL | M,W | Tulane University, LA | M,W | University of Mississippi, MS | M,W |
| St. Louis College of Pharmacy, MO | M,W | Tusculum College, TN | M,W | University of Missouri, MO | M,W |
| Saint Louis University, MO | M,W | Union College, KY | M,W | University of Missouri–Kansas City, MO | M,W |
| Saint Martin's University, WA | M,W | Union University, TN | W | University of Mobile, AL | M,W |
| St. Thomas Aquinas College, NY | M,W | University at Albany, State University of New York, NY | M,W | The University of Montana, MT | M,W |
| St. Thomas University, FL | M,W | University at Buffalo, the State University of New York, NY | M,W | | |
| Samford University, AL | M,W | The University of Akron, OH | M,W | | |
| Sam Houston State University, TX | M,W | The University of Alabama, AL | M,W | | |
| San Diego State University, CA | W | | | | |
| San Francisco State University, CA | M,W | | | | |
| San Jose State University, CA | M,W | | | | |
| Santa Clara University, CA | M,W | | | | |
| Savannah College of Art and Design, GA | M,W | | | | |
| Savannah State University, GA | M,W | | | | |
| Seattle Pacific University, WA | M,W | | | | |
| Seattle University, WA | M,W | | | | |

ATHLETIC GRANTS FOR UNDERGRADUATES

| | |
|---|---|
| University of Nebraska at Kearney, NE | M,W |
| University of Nebraska–Lincoln, NE | M,W |
| University of Nevada, Las Vegas, NV | W |
| University of Nevada, Reno, NV | W |
| University of New Hampshire, NH | M,W |
| University of New Haven, CT | M,W |
| University of New Orleans, LA | M,W |
| University of North Alabama, AL | M,W |
| University of North Carolina at Asheville, NC | M,W |
| The University of North Carolina at Chapel Hill, NC | M,W |
| The University of North Carolina at Charlotte, NC | M,W |
| The University of North Carolina at Greensboro, NC | M,W |
| The University of North Carolina at Pembroke, NC | M,W |
| The University of North Carolina Wilmington, NC | M,W |
| University of Northern Colorado, CO | W |
| University of Northern Iowa, IA | M,W |
| University of North Florida, FL | M,W |
| University of North Georgia, GA | W |
| University of North Texas, TX | M,W |
| University of Notre Dame, IN | M,W |
| University of Oklahoma, OK | M,W |
| University of Oregon, OR | M,W |
| University of Pikeville, KY | M,W |
| University of Pittsburgh, PA | M,W |
| University of Portland, OR | M,W |
| University of Rhode Island, RI | M,W |
| University of Richmond, VA | M,W |
| University of Rio Grande, OH | M,W |
| University of St. Francis, IL | M,W |
| University of San Diego, CA | M,W |
| University of San Francisco, CA | M,W |
| University of South Alabama, AL | M,W |
| University of South Carolina, SC | W |
| University of South Carolina Aiken, SC | W |
| University of South Carolina Upstate, SC | M,W |
| The University of South Dakota, SD | M,W |
| University of Southern California, CA | W |
| University of Southern Indiana, IN | M,W |
| University of Southern Mississippi, MS | W |
| University of South Florida, FL | M,W |
| The University of Tampa, FL | M,W |
| The University of Tennessee at Chattanooga, TN | M,W |
| The University of Tennessee at Martin, TN | M,W |
| The University of Texas at Arlington, TX | M,W |
| The University of Texas at Austin, TX | M,W |
| The University of Texas at El Paso, TX | M,W |
| The University of Texas at San Antonio, TX | M,W |
| The University of Texas–Pan American, TX | M,W |
| University of the Cumberlands, KY | M,W |
| University of the District of Columbia, DC | W |

| | |
|---|---|
| University of the Incarnate Word, TX | M,W |
| University of the Pacific, CA | W |
| The University of Toledo, OH | M,W |
| The University of Tulsa, OK | M,W |
| University of Utah, UT | W |
| University of Vermont, VT | M,W |
| University of Virginia, VA | M,W |
| The University of Virginia's College at Wise, VA | M,W |
| University of Washington, WA | M,W |
| The University of West Alabama, AL | M,W |
| University of West Florida, FL | M,W |
| University of West Georgia, GA | M,W |
| University of Wisconsin–Green Bay, WI | M,W |
| University of Wisconsin–Madison, WI | M,W |
| University of Wisconsin–Milwaukee, WI | M,W |
| University of Wisconsin–Parkside, WI | M,W |
| University of Wyoming, WY | M,W |
| Upper Iowa University, IA | W |
| Ursuline College, OH | W |
| Utah State University, UT | M,W |
| Utah Valley University, UT | M,W |
| Valdosta State University, GA | M,W |
| Valley City State University, ND | M,W |
| Valparaiso University, IN | M,W |
| Vanderbilt University, TN | M,W |
| Vanguard University of Southern California, CA | M,W |
| Villanova University, PA | M,W |
| Virginia Commonwealth University, VA | M,W |
| Virginia Military Institute, VA | M,W |
| Virginia State University, VA | M,W |
| Virginia Union University, VA | M,W |
| Wagner College, NY | M,W |
| Wake Forest University, NC | M,W |
| Waldorf College, IA | M,W |
| Warner Pacific College, OR | M,W |
| Washington State University, WA | M,W |
| Wayland Baptist University, TX | M,W |
| Wayne State College, NE | M,W |
| Wayne State University, MI | M,W |
| Webber International University, FL | M,W |
| West Chester University of Pennsylvania, PA | M,W |
| Western Carolina University, NC | M,W |
| Western Illinois University, IL | M,W |
| Western Kentucky University, KY | M,W |
| Western Michigan University, MI | W |
| Western Oregon University, OR | M,W |
| Western State Colorado University, CO | M,W |
| Western Washington University, WA | M,W |
| Westminster College, UT | M,W |
| West Texas A&M University, TX | M,W |
| West Virginia University, WV | W |
| West Virginia University Institute of Technology, WV | M,W |
| West Virginia Wesleyan College, WV | M,W |
| Wheeling Jesuit University, WV | M,W |
| Wichita State University, KS | M,W |
| William Jessup University, CA | M,W |
| William Jewell College, MO | M,W |
| Williams Baptist University, AR | M,W |
| William Woods University, MO | M,W |
| Wingate University, NC | M,W |

| | |
|---|---|
| Winona State University, MN | M,W |
| Winthrop University, SC | M,W |
| Wofford College, SC | M,W |
| Wright State University, OH | M,W |
| Xavier University, OH | M,W |
| Youngstown State University, OH | M,W |

**Equestrian sports**

| | |
|---|---|
| Auburn University, AL | W |
| Baylor University, TX | W |
| California State University, Fresno, CA | W |
| Delaware State University, DE | W |
| Maryville College, TN | M,W |
| New Mexico State University, NM | W |
| Oklahoma State University, OK | W |
| St. Andrews University, NC | M,W |
| Savannah College of Art and Design, GA | M,W |
| Seton Hill University, PA | W |
| South Dakota State University, SD | W |
| Southern Methodist University, TX | W |
| Texas A&M University, TX | W |
| Texas Christian University, TX | W |
| Tiffin University, OH | M,W |
| University of Georgia, GA | W |
| University of Great Falls, MT | M,W |
| University of Minnesota, Crookston, MN | W |
| University of South Carolina, SC | W |
| The University of Tennessee at Martin, TN | W |
| West Texas A&M University, TX | W |

**Fencing**

| | |
|---|---|
| Cleveland State University, OH | M,W |
| New Jersey Institute of Technology, NJ | M,W |
| The Ohio State University, OH | M,W |
| Penn State University Park, PA | M,W |
| Queens College of the City University of New York, NY | W |
| St. John's University, NY | M,W |
| Stanford University, CA | M,W |
| Temple University, PA | W |
| The University of North Carolina at Chapel Hill, NC | M,W |
| University of Notre Dame, IN | M,W |
| Wayne State University, MI | M,W |

**Field hockey**

| | |
|---|---|
| Adelphi University, NY | W |
| American University, DC | W |
| Appalachian State University, NC | W |
| Ball State University, IN | W |
| Bellarmine University, KY | W |
| Bloomsburg University of Pennsylvania, PA | W |
| Boston College, MA | W |
| Boston University, MA | W |
| Bryant University, RI | W |
| Bucknell University, PA | W |
| Central Michigan University, MI | W |
| College of the Holy Cross, MA | W |
| The College of William and Mary, VA | W |
| Davidson College, NC | W |
| Drexel University, PA | W |
| East Stroudsburg University of Pennsylvania, PA | W |
| Fairfield University, CT | W |
| Franklin Pierce University, NH | W |
| Georgetown University, DC | W |
| Hofstra University, NY | W |

| | |
|---|---|
| Indiana University of Pennsylvania, PA | W |
| James Madison University, VA | W |
| Kent State University, OH | W |
| Kutztown University of Pennsylvania, PA | W |
| La Salle University, PA | W |
| Lehigh University, PA | W |
| Liberty University, VA | W |
| Lindenwood University, MO | W |
| Lock Haven University of Pennsylvania, PA | W |
| Long Island University–LIU Brooklyn, NY | W |
| Long Island University–LIU Post, NY | W |
| Longwood University, VA | W |
| Mansfield University of Pennsylvania, PA | W |
| Mercy College, NY | W |
| Merrimack College, MA | W |
| Miami University, OH | W |
| Michigan State University, MI | W |
| Millersville University of Pennsylvania, PA | W |
| Missouri State University, MO | W |
| Monmouth University, NJ | W |
| Newberry College, SC | W |
| Northeastern University, MA | W |
| The Ohio State University, OH | W |
| Ohio University, OH | W |
| Old Dominion University, VA | W |
| Pace University, NY | W |
| Penn State University Park, PA | W |
| Providence College, RI | W |
| Quinnipiac University, CT | W |
| Rider University, NJ | W |
| Robert Morris University Illinois, IL | W |
| Sacred Heart University, CT | W |
| Saint Anselm College, NH | W |
| Saint Francis University, PA | W |
| Saint Joseph's University, PA | W |
| Saint Louis University, MO | W |
| Seton Hill University, PA | W |
| Shippensburg University of Pennsylvania, PA | W |
| Siena College, NY | W |
| Slippery Rock University of Pennsylvania, PA | W |
| Southern Connecticut State University, CT | W |
| Stanford University, CA | W |
| Stonehill College, MA | W |
| Syracuse University, NY | W |
| Temple University, PA | W |
| Towson University, MD | W |
| University at Albany, State University of New York, NY | W |
| University of California, Davis, CA | W |
| University of Connecticut, CT | W |
| University of Delaware, DE | W |
| The University of Iowa, IA | W |
| University of Louisville, KY | W |
| University of Maine, ME | W |
| University of Maryland, College Park, MD | W |
| University of Massachusetts Amherst, MA | W |
| University of Massachusetts Lowell, MA | W |

| | |
|---|---|
| University of Michigan, MI | W |
| University of New Hampshire, NH | W |
| The University of North Carolina at Chapel Hill, NC | W |
| University of Richmond, VA | W |
| University of the Pacific, CA | W |
| University of Vermont, VT | W |
| University of Virginia, VA | W |
| Villanova University, PA | W |
| Virginia Commonwealth University, VA | W |
| Wake Forest University, NC | W |
| West Chester University of Pennsylvania, PA | W |

**Football**

| | |
|---|---|
| Abilene Christian University, TX | M |
| Adams State University, CO | M |
| Alabama State University, AL | M |
| Albany State University, GA | M |
| Alcorn State University, MS | M |
| Angelo State University, TX | M |
| Appalachian State University, NC | M |
| Arizona Christian University, AZ | M |
| Arizona State University at the Downtown Phoenix campus, AZ | M |
| Arizona State University at the Polytechnic campus, AZ | M |
| Arizona State University at the Tempe campus, AZ | M |
| Arizona State University at the West campus, AZ | M |
| Arkansas State University, AR | M |
| Arkansas Tech University, AR | M |
| Ashland University, OH | M |
| Auburn University, AL | M |
| Augustana College, SD | M |
| Austin Peay State University, TN | M |
| Azusa Pacific University, CA | M |
| Ball State University, IN | M |
| Baylor University, TX | M |
| Belhaven University, MS | M |
| Bemidji State University, MN | M |
| Bethel College, KS | M |
| Bethune-Cookman University, FL | M |
| Blessing-Rieman College of Nursing, IL | M |
| Bloomsburg University of Pennsylvania, PA | M |
| Bluefield College, VA | M |
| Boston College, MA | M |
| Bowie State University, MD | M |
| Bowling Green State University, OH | M |
| Brevard College, NC | M |
| Brigham Young University, UT | M |
| Bryant University, RI | M |
| Bucknell University, PA | M |
| California Polytechnic State University, San Luis Obispo, CA | M |
| California State University, Fresno, CA | M |
| California State University, Sacramento, CA | M |
| Campbellsville University, KY | M |
| Carroll College, MT | M |
| Carson-Newman University, TN | M |
| Catawba College, NC | M |
| Central Methodist University, MO | M |
| Central Michigan University, MI | M |
| Central Washington University, WA | M |
| Chestnut Hill College, PA | M |
| Chowan University, NC | M |

| | |
|---|---|
| The Citadel, The Military College of South Carolina, SC | M |
| Clarion University of Pennsylvania, PA | M |
| Coastal Carolina University, SC | M |
| College of the Holy Cross, MA | M |
| The College of William and Mary, VA | M |
| Colorado Mesa University, CO | M |
| Colorado School of Mines, CO | M |
| Colorado State University, CO | M |
| Colorado State University–Pueblo, CO | M |
| Concordia University, Nebraska, NE | M |
| Concordia University, St. Paul, MN | M |
| Concord University, WV | M |
| Culver-Stockton College, MO | M |
| Cumberland University, TN | M |
| Dakota State University, SD | M |
| Davidson College, NC | M |
| Delaware State University, DE | M |
| Delta State University, MS | M |
| Dickinson State University, ND | M |
| Dixie State University, UT | M |
| Doane College, NE | M |
| Duquesne University, PA | M |
| East Carolina University, NC | M |
| East Central University, OK | M |
| Eastern Illinois University, IL | M |
| Eastern Kentucky University, KY | M |
| Eastern Michigan University, MI | M |
| Eastern New Mexico University, NM | M |
| East Stroudsburg University of Pennsylvania, PA | M |
| Elon University, NC | M |
| Emporia State University, KS | M |
| Evangel University, MO | M |
| Fairmont State University, WV | M |
| Faulkner University, AL | M |
| Fayetteville State University, NC | M |
| Ferris State University, MI | M |
| Florida Agricultural and Mechanical University, FL | M |
| Florida Atlantic University, FL | M |
| Florida Institute of Technology, FL | M |
| Florida State University, FL | M |
| Fordham University, NY | M |
| Fort Hays State University, KS | M |
| Fort Lewis College, CO | M |
| Fort Valley State University, GA | M |
| Friends University, KS | M |
| Furman University, SC | M |
| Gannon University, PA | M |
| Georgetown College, KY | M |
| Georgia Institute of Technology, GA | M |
| Georgia Southern University, GA | M |
| Georgia State University, GA | M |
| Graceland University, IA | M |
| Grambling State University, LA | M |
| Grand Valley State University, MI | M |
| Grand View University, IA | M |
| Hampton University, VA | M |
| Harding University, AR | M |
| Hastings College, NE | M |
| Hillsdale College, MI | M |
| Houston Baptist University, TX | M |
| Howard University, DC | M |
| Humboldt State University, CA | M |
| Idaho State University, ID | M |
| Illinois State University, IL | M |
| Indiana State University, IN | M |

| | |
|---|---|
| Indiana University Bloomington, IN | M |
| Indiana University of Pennsylvania, PA | M |
| Iowa State University of Science and Technology, IA | M |
| Jackson State University, MS | M |
| Jacksonville State University, AL | M |
| James Madison University, VA | M |
| Johnson C. Smith University, NC | M |
| Kansas State University, KS | M |
| Kansas Wesleyan University, KS | M |
| Kennesaw State University, GA | M |
| Kent State University, OH | M |
| Kentucky State University, KY | M |
| Kentucky Wesleyan College, KY | M |
| Kutztown University of Pennsylvania, PA | M |
| Lake Erie College, OH | M |
| Lamar University, TX | M |
| Langston University, OK | M |
| Lehigh University, PA | M |
| Lenoir-Rhyne University, NC | M |
| Liberty University, VA | M |
| Lincoln University, MO | M |
| Lincoln University, PA | M |
| Lindenwood University, MO | M |
| Lindsey Wilson College, KY | M,W |
| Lock Haven University of Pennsylvania, PA | M |
| Long Island University–LIU Post, NY | M |
| Louisiana State University and Agricultural & Mechanical College, LA | M |
| Louisiana Tech University, LA | M |
| Lyon College, AR | M |
| Malone University, OH | M |
| Marshall University, WV | M |
| Mayville State University, ND | M |
| McKendree University, IL | M |
| Merrimack College, MA | M |
| Miami University, OH | M |
| Michigan State University, MI | M |
| Michigan Technological University, MI | M |
| Middle Tennessee State University, TN | M |
| Midwestern State University, TX | M |
| Millersville University of Pennsylvania, PA | M |
| Minnesota State University Mankato, MN | M |
| Minnesota State University Moorhead, MN | M |
| Minot State University, ND | M |
| Mississippi State University, MS | M |
| Missouri Baptist University, MO | M |
| Missouri Southern State University, MO | M |
| Missouri State University, MO | M |
| Missouri University of Science and Technology, MO | M |
| Missouri Valley College, MO | M |
| Missouri Western State University, MO | M |
| Monmouth University, NJ | M |
| Montana State University, MT | M |
| Montana Tech of The University of Montana, MT | M |
| Morningside College, IA | M |
| Murray State University, KY | M |
| Newberry College, SC | M |

| | |
|---|---|
| New Mexico Highlands University, NM | M |
| New Mexico State University, NM | M |
| Nicholls State University, LA | M |
| North Carolina Agricultural and Technical State University, NC | M |
| North Carolina Central University, NC | M |
| North Carolina State University, NC | M |
| Northeastern State University, OK | M |
| Northern Arizona University, AZ | M |
| Northern Illinois University, IL | M |
| Northern Michigan University, MI | M |
| Northern State University, SD | M |
| Northwestern Oklahoma State University, OK | M |
| Northwest Missouri State University, MO | M |
| The Ohio State University, OH | M |
| Ohio University, OH | M |
| Oklahoma Baptist University, OK | M |
| Oklahoma State University, OK | M |
| Old Dominion University, VA | M |
| Olivet Nazarene University, IL | M |
| Oregon State University, OR | M |
| Pace University, NY | M |
| Penn State University Park, PA | M |
| Pittsburg State University, KS | M |
| Prairie View A&M University, TX | M |
| Presbyterian College, SC | M |
| Purdue University, IN | M |
| Quincy University, IL | M |
| Reinhardt University, GA | M |
| Rice University, TX | M |
| Robert Morris University, PA | M |
| Robert Morris University Illinois, IL | M |
| Rocky Mountain College, MT | M |
| Sacred Heart University, CT | M |
| Saginaw Valley State University, MI | M |
| Saint Anselm College, NH | M |
| Saint Augustine's University, NC | M |
| Saint Joseph's College, IN | M |
| Samford University, AL | M |
| Sam Houston State University, TX | M |
| San Diego State University, CA | M |
| San Jose State University, CA | M |
| Savannah State University, GA | M |
| Seton Hill University, PA | M |
| Shepherd University, WV | M |
| Shippensburg University of Pennsylvania, PA | M |
| Slippery Rock University of Pennsylvania, PA | M |
| South Dakota School of Mines and Technology, SD | M |
| South Dakota State University, SD | M |
| Southeastern Louisiana University, LA | M |
| Southeastern Oklahoma State University, OK | M |
| Southeast Missouri State University, MO | M |
| Southern Connecticut State University, CT | M |
| Southern Illinois University Carbondale, IL | M |
| Southern Methodist University, TX | M |
| Southern Oregon University, OR | M |
| Southern Utah University, UT | M |

| | |
|---|---|
| Southwest Baptist University, MO | M |
| Southwestern College, KS | M |
| Stanford University, CA | M |
| Stephen F. Austin State University, TX | M |
| Sterling College, KS | M |
| Stonehill College, MA | M |
| Stony Brook University, State University of New York, NY | M |
| Syracuse University, NY | M |
| Tabor College, KS | M |
| Tarleton State University, TX | M |
| Taylor University, IN | M |
| Temple University, PA | M |
| Tennessee State University, TN | M |
| Texas A&M University, TX | M |
| Texas A&M University–Commerce, TX | M |
| Texas Christian University, TX | M |
| Texas Southern University, TX | M |
| Texas State University, TX | M |
| Texas Tech University, TX | M |
| Tiffin University, OH | M |
| Towson University, MD | M |
| Troy University, AL | M |
| Truman State University, MO | M |
| Tulane University, LA | M |
| Tusculum College, TN | M |
| Union College, KY | M |
| University at Albany, State University of New York, NY | M |
| University at Buffalo, the State University of New York, NY | M |
| The University of Akron, OH | M |
| The University of Alabama, AL | M |
| The University of Arizona, AZ | M |
| University of Arkansas, AR | M |
| University of California, Davis, CA | M |
| University of California, Los Angeles, CA | M |
| University of Central Arkansas, AR | M |
| University of Central Florida, FL | M |
| University of Central Missouri, MO | M |
| University of Central Oklahoma, OK | M |
| University of Charleston, WV | M |
| University of Cincinnati, OH | M |
| University of Colorado Boulder, CO | M |
| University of Connecticut, CT | M |
| University of Delaware, DE | M |
| The University of Findlay, OH | M |
| University of Florida, FL | M |
| University of Georgia, GA | M |
| University of Hawaii at Manoa, HI | M |
| University of Houston, TX | M |
| University of Idaho, ID | M |
| University of Indianapolis, IN | M |
| The University of Iowa, IA | M |
| University of Jamestown, ND | M |
| The University of Kansas, KS | M |
| University of Louisiana at Lafayette, LA | M |
| University of Louisville, KY | M |
| University of Maine, ME | M |
| University of Maryland, College Park, MD | M |
| University of Massachusetts Amherst, MA | M |
| University of Memphis, TN | M |
| University of Miami, FL | M |
| University of Michigan, MI | M |
| University of Minnesota, Crookston, MN | M |

| | |
|---|---|
| University of Minnesota, Duluth, MN | M |
| University of Minnesota, Twin Cities Campus, MN | M |
| University of Mississippi, MS | M |
| University of Missouri, MO | M |
| The University of Montana, MT | M |
| The University of Montana Western, MT | M |
| University of Nebraska at Kearney, NE | M |
| University of Nebraska–Lincoln, NE | M |
| University of Nevada, Las Vegas, NV | M |
| University of Nevada, Reno, NV | M |
| University of New Hampshire, NH | M |
| University of New Haven, CT | M |
| University of North Alabama, AL | M |
| The University of North Carolina at Chapel Hill, NC | M |
| The University of North Carolina at Charlotte, NC | M |
| The University of North Carolina at Pembroke, NC | M |
| University of Northern Colorado, CO | M |
| University of Northern Iowa, IA | M |
| University of North Texas, TX | M |
| University of Notre Dame, IN | M |
| University of Oklahoma, OK | M |
| University of Oregon, OR | M |
| University of Pikeville, KY | M |
| University of Pittsburgh, PA | M |
| University of Rhode Island, RI | M |
| University of Richmond, VA | M |
| University of St. Francis, IL | M |
| University of South Alabama, AL | M |
| University of South Carolina, SC | M |
| The University of South Dakota, SD | M |
| University of Southern California, CA | M |
| University of Southern Mississippi, MS | M |
| University of South Florida, FL | M |
| The University of Tennessee, TN | M |
| The University of Tennessee at Chattanooga, TN | M |
| The University of Tennessee at Martin, TN | M |
| The University of Texas at Austin, TX | M |
| The University of Texas at El Paso, TX | M |
| The University of Texas at San Antonio, TX | M |
| University of the Cumberlands, KY | M |
| University of the Incarnate Word, TX | M |
| The University of Toledo, OH | M |
| The University of Tulsa, OK | M |
| University of Utah, UT | M |
| University of Virginia, VA | M |
| The University of Virginia's College at Wise, VA | |
| University of Washington, WA | M |
| The University of West Alabama, AL | M |
| University of West Georgia, GA | M |
| University of Wisconsin–Madison, WI | M |
| University of Wyoming, WY | M |
| Upper Iowa University, IA | M |
| Utah State University, UT | M |

| | |
|---|---|
| Valdosta State University, GA | M |
| Valley City State University, ND | M |
| Vanderbilt University, TN | M |
| Villanova University, PA | M |
| Virginia Military Institute, VA | M |
| Virginia Polytechnic Institute and State University, VA | M |
| Virginia State University, VA | M |
| Virginia Union University, VA | M |
| Wagner College, NY | M |
| Wake Forest University, NC | M |
| Waldorf College, IA | M |
| Washburn University, KS | M |
| Washington State University, WA | M |
| Wayland Baptist University, TX | M |
| Wayne State College, NE | M |
| Wayne State University, MI | M |
| Webber International University, FL | M |
| Weber State University, UT | M |
| West Chester University of Pennsylvania, PA | M |
| Western Carolina University, NC | M |
| Western Illinois University, IL | M |
| Western Kentucky University, KY | M |
| Western Michigan University, MI | M |
| Western Oregon University, OR | M |
| Western State Colorado University, CO | M |
| West Texas A&M University, TX | M |
| West Virginia University, WV | M |
| West Virginia Wesleyan College, WV | M |
| William Jewell College, MO | M |
| Wingate University, NC | M |
| Winona State University, MN | M |
| Wofford College, SC | M |
| Youngstown State University, OH | M |

## Golf

| | |
|---|---|
| Abilene Christian University, TX | M |
| Academy of Art University, CA | M,W |
| Adams State University, CO | M,W |
| Adelphi University, NY | M,W |
| Alabama State University, AL | M,W |
| Alcorn State University, MS | M,W |
| Anderson University, SC | M,W |
| Angelo State University, TX | W |
| Appalachian State University, NC | M,W |
| Arizona Christian University, AZ | M,W |
| Arizona State University at the Downtown Phoenix campus, AZ | M,W |
| Arizona State University at the Polytechnic campus, AZ | M,W |
| Arizona State University at the Tempe campus, AZ | M,W |
| Arizona State University at the West campus, AZ | M,W |
| Arkansas State University, AR | M,W |
| Arkansas Tech University, AR | M,W |
| Armstrong State University, GA | M,W |
| Ashland University, OH | M,W |
| Auburn University, AL | M,W |
| Augustana College, SD | M,W |
| Austin Peay State University, TN | M,W |
| Ball State University, IN | M,W |
| Barry University, FL | M,W |
| Baylor University, TX | M,W |
| Belhaven University, MS | M,W |
| Bellarmine University, KY | M,W |
| Belmont Abbey College, NC | M,W |
| Belmont University, TN | M,W |
| Bemidji State University, MN | M,W |
| Bethel College, KS | M,W |

| | |
|---|---|
| Bethune-Cookman University, FL | M,W |
| Binghamton University, State University of New York, NY | M |
| Biola University, CA | M,W |
| Bluefield College, VA | M |
| Bluefield State College, WV | M |
| Blue Mountain College, MS | M,W |
| Boston College, MA | M,W |
| Bowling Green State University, OH | M,W |
| Bradley University, IL | M,W |
| Brevard College, NC | M,W |
| Brigham Young University, UT | M,W |
| Bryant University, RI | M |
| Butler University, IN | M,W |
| California Baptist University, CA | M,W |
| California Polytechnic State University, San Luis Obispo, CA | M,W |
| California State University, Bakersfield, CA | M |
| California State University, Chico, CA | M,W |
| California State University, Dominguez Hills, CA | M |
| California State University, Fresno, CA | M,W |
| California State University, Fullerton, CA | M,W |
| California State University, Monterey Bay, CA | M,W |
| California State University, Sacramento, CA | M |
| California State University, San Bernardino, CA | M |
| California State University, Stanislaus, CA | M |
| Calumet College of Saint Joseph, IN | M,W |
| Cameron University, OK | M,W |
| Campbellsville University, KY | M,W |
| Canisius College, NY | M |
| Cardinal Stritch University, WI | M,W |
| Carroll College, MT | M,W |
| Carson Newman University, TN | M |
| Catawba College, NC | M,W |
| Cedarville University, OH | M |
| Central Connecticut State University, CT | M,W |
| Central Michigan University, MI | W |
| Chaminade University of Honolulu, HI | M |
| Chestnut Hill College, PA | M |
| Chowan University, NC | M,W |
| Christian Brothers University, TN | M,W |
| Cincinnati Christian University, OH | M |
| The Citadel, The Military College of South Carolina, SC | W |
| Clarion University of Pennsylvania, PA | M,W |
| Clarke University, IA | M,W |
| Clayton State University, GA | M |
| Cleveland State University, OH | M |
| Coastal Carolina University, SC | M,W |
| Coker College, SC | M,W |
| College of Charleston, SC | M,W |
| The College of Idaho, ID | M,W |
| College of Saint Mary, NE | W |
| The College of William and Mary, VA | M,W |
| Colorado Mesa University, CO | M,W |
| Colorado State University, CO | M,W |
| Colorado State University–Pueblo, CO | M,W |

| | |
|---|---|
| Columbia College, MO | M,W |
| Columbia International University, SC | M |
| Columbus State University, GA | M,W |
| Concordia University, Nebraska, NE | M,W |
| Concordia University, St. Paul, MN | M,W |
| Concord University, WV | M,W |
| Corban University, OR | M,W |
| Cornerstone University, MI | M,W |
| Creighton University, NE | M,W |
| Culver-Stockton College, MO | M,W |
| Cumberland University, TN | M,W |
| Dallas Baptist University, TX | W |
| Davidson College, NC | M |
| Delta State University, MS | M |
| DePaul University, IL | M |
| Dickinson State University, ND | M,W |
| Dixie State University, UT | M,W |
| Doane College, NE | M,W |
| Dominican College, NY | M |
| Dowling College, NY | M |
| Drake University, IA | M |
| Drexel University, PA | M |
| Drury University, MO | M,W |
| East Carolina University, NC | M,W |
| East Central University, OK | M |
| Eastern Illinois University, IL | M,W |
| Eastern Kentucky University, KY | M,W |
| Eastern Michigan University, MI | M,W |
| Eckerd College, FL | M,W |
| Elon University, NC | M,W |
| Embry-Riddle Aeronautical University–Daytona, FL | M,W |
| Embry-Riddle Aeronautical University–Prescott, AZ | M,W |
| Emmanuel College, GA | M,W |
| Evangel University, MO | M,W |
| Fairfield University, CT | M,W |
| Fairmont State University, WV | M,W |
| Faulkner University, AL | M,W |
| Fayetteville State University, NC | M |
| Ferris State University, MI | M,W |
| Flagler College, FL | M,W |
| Florida Agricultural and Mechanical University, FL | M,W |
| Florida Atlantic University, FL | M,W |
| Florida Gulf Coast University, FL | M,W |
| Florida Institute of Technology, FL | M,W |
| Florida Southern College, FL | M,W |
| Florida State University, FL | M,W |
| Fordham University, NY | M |
| Fort Hays State University, KS | M,W |
| Fort Lewis College, CO | M |
| Fort Valley State University, GA | M |
| Francis Marion University, SC | M |
| Friends University, KS | M |
| Furman University, SC | W |
| Gannon University, PA | M,W |
| George Mason University, VA | M |
| Georgetown College, KY | M,W |
| Georgetown University, DC | M,W |
| The George Washington University, DC | M |
| Georgia College & State University, GA | M |
| Georgia Institute of Technology, GA | M |
| Georgia Regents University, GA | M,W |
| Georgia Southern University, GA | M |
| Georgia Southwestern State University, GA | M |
| Georgia State University, GA | M,W |

| | |
|---|---|
| Governors State University, IL | M,W |
| Graceland University, IA | M,W |
| Grand Valley State University, MI | M,W |
| Grand View University, IA | M,W |
| Hampton University, VA | M,W |
| Harding University, AR | M,W |
| Hastings College, NE | M,W |
| Hawai`i Pacific University, HI | M |
| Hofstra University, NY | M,W |
| Hope International University, CA | M,W |
| Houston Baptist University, TX | M,W |
| Idaho State University, ID | W |
| Illinois State University, IL | M,W |
| Indiana State University, IN | W |
| Indiana University Bloomington, IN | M,W |
| Indiana University of Pennsylvania, PA | M |
| Indiana University–Purdue University Fort Wayne, IN | M,W |
| Indiana University–Purdue University Indianapolis, IN | M,W |
| Iona College, NY | M |
| Iowa State University of Science and Technology, IA | M,W |
| Jackson State University, MS | M,W |
| Jacksonville State University, AL | M,W |
| Jacksonville University, FL | M,W |
| James Madison University, VA | M,W |
| John Brown University, AR | M |
| Johnson C. Smith University, NC | M |
| Kansas State University, KS | M,W |
| Kansas Wesleyan University, KS | M,W |
| Kennesaw State University, GA | M,W |
| Kent State University, OH | M,W |
| Kentucky State University, KY | M |
| Kentucky Wesleyan College, KY | M,W |
| King University, TN | M,W |
| Kutztown University of Pennsylvania, PA | W |
| Lake Erie College, OH | M,W |
| Lamar University, TX | M,W |
| La Salle University, PA | M,W |
| Lee University, TN | M,W |
| Lehigh University, PA | M,W |
| Le Moyne College, NY | M,W |
| LeMoyne-Owen College, TN | M,W |
| Lenoir-Rhyne University, NC | M,W |
| Lewis-Clark State College, ID | M,W |
| Lewis University, IL | M,W |
| Liberty University, VA | M |
| Lincoln Memorial University, TN | M,W |
| Lincoln University, MO | M,W |
| Lindenwood University, MO | M,W |
| Lindsey Wilson College, KY | M,W |
| Lipscomb University, TN | M,W |
| Long Island University–LIU Brooklyn, NY | M,W |
| Longwood University, VA | M,W |
| Louisiana State University and Agricultural & Mechanical College, LA | M,W |
| Louisiana Tech University, LA | M |
| Loyola Marymount University, CA | M |
| Loyola University Chicago, IL | M,W |
| Lubbock Christian University, TX | M,W |
| Lynn University, FL | M,W |
| Lyon College, AR | M,W |
| Malone University, OH | M,W |
| Manhattan College, NY | M |
| Marquette University, WI | M |
| Marshall University, WV | M,W |
| Maryville University of Saint Louis, MO | M,W |

| | |
|---|---|
| The Master's College and Seminary, CA | M |
| McKendree University, IL | M,W |
| Menlo College, CA | M,W |
| Mercer University, GA | M,W |
| Merrimack College, MA | W |
| Miami University, OH | M |
| Michigan State University, MI | M,W |
| Middle Tennessee State University, TN | M |
| Midland College, TX | M |
| Midwestern State University, TX | M,W |
| Millersville University of Pennsylvania, PA | M,W |
| Milligan College, TN | M,W |
| Minnesota State University Mankato, MN | M,W |
| Minnesota State University Moorhead, MN | W |
| Mississippi State University, MS | M,W |
| Missouri Baptist University, MO | M,W |
| Missouri Southern State University, MO | M |
| Missouri State University, MO | M,W |
| Missouri Valley College, MO | M,W |
| Missouri Western State University, MO | M,W |
| Monmouth University, NJ | M,W |
| Montana State University, MT | W |
| Montana Tech of The University of Montana, MT | M,W |
| Montreat College, NC | M |
| Morehead State University, KY | M,W |
| Morningside College, IA | M,W |
| Mount Marty College, SD | M,W |
| Mount Mercy University, IA | M,W |
| Murray State University, KY | M,W |
| Newberry College, SC | M,W |
| Newman University, KS | M,W |
| New Mexico State University, NM | M,W |
| Niagara University, NY | M,W |
| Nicholls State University, LA | M,W |
| North Carolina Central University, NC | M |
| North Carolina State University, NC | M,W |
| Northeastern State University, OK | M,W |
| Northern Arizona University, AZ | W |
| Northern Illinois University, IL | M,W |
| Northern Kentucky University, KY | M,W |
| Northern Michigan University, MI | M,W |
| Northwest Christian University, OR | M,W |
| Northwestern Oklahoma State University, OK | M,W |
| Northwest Missouri State University, MO | W |
| Northwest Nazarene University, ID | M,W |
| Nova Southeastern University, FL | M,W |
| Nyack College, NY | M |
| Oakland University, MI | M,W |
| The Ohio State University, OH | M,W |
| Ohio University, OH | M,W |
| Oklahoma Baptist University, OK | M,W |
| Oklahoma Christian University, OK | M |
| Oklahoma City University, OK | M,W |
| Oklahoma State University, OK | M,W |
| Oklahoma Wesleyan University, OK | M,W |
| Old Dominion University, VA | M,W |
| Olivet Nazarene University, IL | M |
| Oral Roberts University, OK | M,W |
| Oregon State University, OR | M,W |
| Our Lady of the Lake University of San Antonio, TX | M |

| | | | | | |
|---|---|---|---|---|---|
| Park University, MO | W | Spring Hill College, AL | M,W | University of Houston, TX | M,W |
| Penn State University Park, PA | M,W | Stanford University, CA | M,W | University of Idaho, ID | M,W |
| Pepperdine University, CA | M,W | Stephen F. Austin State | | University of Illinois at | |
| Philadelphia University, PA | M | University, TX | M,W | Springfield, IL | M,W |
| Pittsburg State University, KS | M | Stephens College, MO | W | University of Indianapolis, IN | M,W |
| Point Loma Nazarene University, CA | W | Sterling College, KS | M,W | The University of Iowa, IA | M,W |
| Post University, CT | M,W | Stetson University, FL | M,W | University of Jamestown, ND | M,W |
| Prairie View A&M University, TX | M,W | Tarleton State University, TX | W | The University of Kansas, KS | M,W |
| Presbyterian College, SC | M,W | Taylor University, IN | M,W | University of Louisiana at | |
| Purdue University, IN | M,W | Temple University, PA | M | Lafayette, LA | M |
| Purdue University Calumet, IN | M | Tennessee State University, TN | M | University of Louisville, KY | M,W |
| Quincy University, IL | M,W | Tennessee Wesleyan College, TN | M,W | University of Maryland, College | |
| Quinnipiac University, CT | W | Texas A&M International | | Park, MD | M,W |
| Radford University, VA | M,W | University, TX | M,W | University of Massachusetts | |
| Regis University, CO | M,W | Texas A&M University, TX | M,W | Lowell, MA | M |
| Reinhardt University, GA | M | Texas A&M University– | | University of Memphis, TN | M,W |
| Rice University, TX | M | Commerce, TX | M,W | University of Miami, FL | W |
| Rider University, NJ | M | Texas A&M University– | | University of Michigan, MI | M,W |
| Robert Morris University, PA | M,W | Corpus Christi, TX | W | University of Minnesota, | |
| Robert Morris University | | Texas Christian University, TX | M,W | Crookston, MN | M,W |
| Illinois, IL | M,W | Texas Southern University, TX | M,W | University of Minnesota, Twin | |
| Roberts Wesleyan College, NY | M | Texas State University, TX | M,W | Cities Campus, MN | M,W |
| Rockhurst University, MO | M,W | Texas Tech University, TX | M,W | University of Mississippi, MS | M,W |
| Rocky Mountain College, MT | M,W | Texas Wesleyan University, TX | M,W | University of Missouri, MO | M,W |
| Rollins College, FL | M,W | Tiffin University, OH | M,W | University of Missouri– | |
| Sacred Heart University, CT | M,W | Towson University, MD | M,W | Kansas City, MO | M,W |
| Saginaw Valley State University, | | Trevecca Nazarene University, TN | M,W | University of Missouri–St. | |
| MI | M | Trinity Christian College, IL | M | Louis, MO | M,W |
| St. Andrews University, NC | M,W | Troy University, AL | M,W | University of Mobile, AL | M,W |
| Saint Anselm College, NH | M | Truett-McConnell College, GA | M,W | The University of Montana, MT | W |
| Saint Augustine's | | Truman State University, MO | W | University of Montevallo, AL | M,W |
| University, NC | M | Tulane University, LA | W | University of Nebraska at | |
| St. Bonaventure University, NY | M | Tusculum College, TN | M | Kearney, NE | M,W |
| St. Edward's University, TX | M,W | Union College, KY | M,W | University of Nebraska– | |
| St. Francis College, NY | M,W | Union University, TN | M | Lincoln, NE | M,W |
| Saint Francis University, PA | M,W | University at Albany, State | | University of Nevada, Las Vegas, | |
| St. John's University, NY | M,W | University of New York, NY | W | NV | M |
| Saint Joseph's College, IN | M,W | The University of Akron, OH | M,W | University of Nevada, Reno, NV | M,W |
| Saint Joseph's University, | | The University of Alabama, AL | M,W | University of New Orleans, LA | M |
| PA | M | The University of Alabama at | | University of North Alabama, AL | M |
| Saint Leo University, FL | M,W | Birmingham, AL | M,W | The University of North Carolina | |
| Saint Martin's University, | | The University of Arizona, AZ | M,W | at Chapel Hill, NC | M,W |
| WA | M,W | University of Arkansas, AR | M,W | The University of North Carolina | |
| St. Thomas University, FL | M,W | University of California, Davis, | | at Charlotte, NC | M |
| Samford University, AL | M,W | CA | M,W | The University of North Carolina | |
| Sam Houston State University, TX | M,W | University of California, | | at Greensboro, NC | |
| San Diego State University, CA | M,W | Irvine, CA | M,W | The University of North Carolina | |
| San Jose State University, CA | M,W | University of California, Los | | at Pembroke, NC | M,W |
| Santa Clara University, CA | M,W | Angeles, CA | M,W | The University of North Carolina | |
| Savannah College of Art and | | University of California, | | Wilmington, NC | M,W |
| Design, GA | M,W | Riverside, CA | M | University of Northern Colorado, | |
| Savannah State University, GA | M,W | University of California, Santa | | CO | M,W |
| Seattle University, WA | M,W | Barbara, CA | M | University of Northern Iowa, IA | M,W |
| Seton Hill University, PA | W | University of Central Arkansas, AR | M,W | University of North Florida, FL | M |
| Shawnee State University, OH | M | University of Central Florida, FL | M,W | University of North Georgia, GA | M,W |
| Shepherd University, WV | M | University of Central Missouri, MO | M | University of North Texas, TX | M,W |
| Siena College, NY | M,W | University of Central Oklahoma, OK | M,W | University of Notre Dame, IN | M,W |
| Simpson University, CA | M,W | University of Charleston, WV | M,W | University of Oklahoma, OK | M,W |
| South Dakota School of Mines and | | University of Cincinnati, OH | M,W | University of Oregon, OR | M,W |
| Technology, SD | M,W | University of Colorado Boulder, CO | M,W | University of Pikeville, KY | M,W |
| South Dakota State University, SD | M,W | University of Colorado Colorado | | University of Rhode Island, RI | M |
| Southeastern Louisiana | | Springs, CO | M,W | University of Richmond, VA | M,W |
| University, LA | M | University of Connecticut, CT | M | University of St. Francis, IL | M,W |
| Southeastern Oklahoma State | | University of Dayton, OH | M | University of St. Thomas, TX | M,W |
| University, OK | M | University of Delaware, DE | M,W | University of San Diego, CA | M |
| Southern Illinois University | | University of Denver, CO | M,W | University of San Francisco, CA | M,W |
| Carbondale, IL | M,W | University of Evansville, IN | M,W | University of South Alabama, AL | M,W |
| Southern Illinois University | | The University of Findlay, OH | M,W | University of South Carolina, SC | M,W |
| Edwardsville, IL | M,W | University of Florida, FL | M,W | University of South Carolina | |
| Southern Methodist University, TX | M,W | University of Georgia, GA | M,W | Aiken, SC | M |
| Southern Utah University, UT | M,W | University of Great Falls, MT | M,W | University of South Carolina | |
| Southwest Baptist University, MO | M,W | University of Hartford, CT | M,W | Upstate, SC | M,W |
| Southwestern College, KS | M,W | University of Hawaii at Manoa, HI | M,W | The University of South Dakota, SD | W |

| | |
|---|---|
| University of Southern California, CA | M,W |
| University of Southern Indiana, IN | M,W |
| University of Southern Mississippi, MS | M,W |
| University of South Florida, FL | M,W |
| The University of Tampa, FL | M,W |
| The University of Tennessee, TN | M,W |
| The University of Tennessee at Chattanooga, TN | M,W |
| The University of Tennessee at Martin, TN | M |
| The University of Texas at Arlington, TX | M |
| The University of Texas at Austin, TX | M,W |
| The University of Texas at El Paso, TX | M |
| The University of Texas at San Antonio, TX | M,W |
| The University of Texas– Pan American, TX | M,W |
| University of the Cumberlands, KY | M,W |
| University of the Incarnate Word, TX | M,W |
| University of the Pacific, CA | M |
| The University of Toledo, OH | M,W |
| The University of Tulsa, OK | M,W |
| University of Utah, UT | M |
| University of Virginia, VA | M |
| University of Washington, WA | M,W |
| The University of West Alabama, AL | M,W |
| University of West Florida, FL | M,W |
| University of West Georgia, GA | M,W |
| University of Wisconsin– Green Bay, WI | M,W |
| University of Wisconsin– Madison, WI | M,W |
| University of Wisconsin– Parkside, WI | M |
| University of Wyoming, WY | M,W |
| Upper Iowa University, IA | M,W |
| Ursuline College, OH | W |
| Utah State University, UT | M |
| Utah Valley University, UT | M,W |
| Valdosta State University, GA | M |
| Valley City State University, ND | M,W |
| Valparaiso University, IN | M,W |
| Vanderbilt University, TN | M,W |
| Virginia Commonwealth University, VA | M |
| Virginia Military Institute, VA | M |
| Virginia Polytechnic Institute and State University, VA | M |
| Virginia State University, VA | M,W |
| Virginia Union University, VA | M |
| Wagner College, NY | M,W |
| Wake Forest University, NC | M,W |
| Waldorf College, IA | M,W |
| Warner Pacific College, OR | M,W |
| Washburn University, KS | M |
| Washington State University, WA | M,W |
| Wayland Baptist University, TX | M,W |
| Wayne State College, NE | M,W |
| Wayne State University, MI | M,W |
| Webber International University, FL | M,W |
| Weber State University, UT | M,W |
| West Chester University of Pennsylvania, PA | M,W |
| Western Carolina University, NC | M,W |
| Western Illinois University, IL | M |
| Western Kentucky University, KY | M,W |

| | |
|---|---|
| Western Michigan University, MI | W |
| Western Washington University, WA | M,W |
| Westminster College, UT | M,W |
| West Texas A&M University, TX | M,W |
| West Virginia University, WV | M |
| West Virginia University Institute of Technology, WV | M |
| West Virginia Wesleyan College, WV | M,W |
| Wheeling Jesuit University, WV | M,W |
| Wichita State University, KS | M,W |
| William Jessup University, CA | M |
| William Jewell College, MO | M,W |
| Williams Baptist College, AR | M |
| William Woods University, MO | M,W |
| Wingate University, NC | M,W |
| Winona State University, MN | M,W |
| Winthrop University, SC | M,W |
| Wofford College, SC | M,W |
| Wright State University, OH | M |
| Xavier University, OH | M,W |
| Youngstown State University, OH | M,W |

## Gymnastics

| | |
|---|---|
| Arizona State University at the Downtown Phoenix campus, AZ | W |
| Arizona State University at the Polytechnic campus, AZ | W |
| Arizona State University at the Tempe campus, AZ | M,W |
| Arizona State University at the West campus, AZ | W |
| Auburn University, AL | W |
| Azusa Pacific University, CA | W |
| Ball State University, IN | W |
| Bowling Green State University, OH | W |
| Brigham Young University, UT | W |
| California State University, Sacramento, CA | W |
| Central Michigan University, MI | W |
| The College of William and Mary, VA | M,W |
| Eastern Michigan University, MI | W |
| Gannon University, PA | W |
| The George Washington University, DC | W |
| Illinois State University, IL | W |
| Iowa State University of Science and Technology, IA | W |
| Kent State University, OH | W |
| King University, TN | M,W |
| Lindenwood University, MO | W |
| Louisiana State University and Agricultural & Mechanical College, LA | W |
| Michigan State University, MI | W |
| North Carolina State University, NC | W |
| Northern Illinois University, IL | W |
| The Ohio State University, OH | M,W |
| Oregon State University, OR | W |
| Penn State University Park, PA | M,W |
| Quinnipiac University, CT | W |
| San Jose State University, CA | W |
| Seattle Pacific University, WA | W |
| Southeast Missouri State University, MO | W |
| Southern Connecticut State University, CT | W |
| Southern Utah University, UT | W |
| Stanford University, CA | M,W |
| Temple University, PA | W |
| Texas Woman's University, TX | W |
| Towson University, MD | W |

| | |
|---|---|
| The University of Alabama, AL | W |
| University of Alaska Anchorage, AK | W |
| The University of Arizona, AZ | W |
| University of Arkansas, AR | W |
| University of Bridgeport, CT | W |
| University of California, Davis, CA | W |
| University of California, Los Angeles, CA | W |
| University of California, Santa Barbara, CA | M,W |
| University of Denver, CO | W |
| University of Florida, FL | W |
| University of Georgia, GA | W |
| University of Illinois at Chicago, IL | M,W |
| The University of Iowa, IA | M,W |
| University of Michigan, MI | M,W |
| University of Minnesota, Twin Cities Campus, MN | M,W |
| University of Missouri, MO | W |
| University of Nebraska– Lincoln, NE | M,W |
| University of New Hampshire, NH | W |
| The University of North Carolina at Chapel Hill, NC | W |
| University of Oklahoma, OK | M,W |
| University of Pittsburgh, PA | W |
| University of Utah, UT | W |
| University of Washington, WA | W |
| Utah State University, UT | W |
| West Chester University of Pennsylvania, PA | W |
| Western Michigan University, MI | W |
| West Virginia University, WV | W |

## Ice hockey

| | |
|---|---|
| Arizona State University at the Downtown Phoenix campus, AZ | M |
| Arizona State University at the Polytechnic campus, AZ | M |
| Arizona State University at the Tempe campus, AZ | M |
| Arizona State University at the West campus, AZ | M |
| Bemidji State University, MN | M,W |
| Bentley University, MA | M |
| Boston College, MA | M,W |
| Boston University, MA | M,W |
| Bowling Green State University, OH | M |
| Canisius College, NY | M |
| Clarkson University, NY | M,W |
| College of the Holy Cross, MA | M |
| The Colorado College, CO | M |
| Ferris State University, MI | M |
| Lindenwood University, MO | M,W |
| Merrimack College, MA | M,W |
| Miami University, OH | M |
| Michigan State University, MI | M |
| Michigan Technological University, MI | M |
| Minnesota State University Mankato, MN | M,W |
| Niagara University, NY | M |
| Northeastern University, MA | M,W |
| Northern Michigan University, MI | M |
| The Ohio State University, OH | M,W |
| Penn State University Park, PA | M,W |
| Providence College, RI | M,W |
| Quinnipiac University, CT | M,W |
| Rensselaer Polytechnic Institute, NY | M,W |
| Robert Morris University, PA | M,W |
| Sacred Heart University, CT | M |

| | | | | | |
|---|---|---|---|---|---|
| St. Lawrence University, NY | M,W | Gannon University, PA | W | Roberts Wesleyan College, NY | M,W |
| Syracuse University, NY | W | George Mason University, VA | W | Rockhurst University, MO | M,W |
| The University of Alabama in Huntsville, AL | M | Georgetown College, KY | W | Sacred Heart University, CT | M,W |
| | | Georgetown University, DC | M,W | St. Andrews University, NC | M,W |
| University of Alaska Anchorage, AK | M | Georgian Court University, NJ | W | Saint Anselm College, NH | M,W |
| University of Alaska Fairbanks, AK | M | Hofstra University, NY | M,W | St. Bonaventure University, NY | W |
| University of Connecticut, CT | M,W | Holy Family University, PA | W | Saint Francis University, PA | W |
| University of Denver, CO | M | Howard University, DC | W | St. John's University, NY | M |
| University of Maine, ME | M,W | Indiana University of Pennsylvania, PA | W | Saint Joseph's University, PA | M,W |
| University of Massachusetts Amherst, MA | M | Iona College, NY | W | Saint Leo University, FL | M,W |
| University of Massachusetts Lowell, MA | M | Jacksonville University, FL | M,W | San Diego State University, CA | W |
| | | James Madison University, VA | W | Savannah College of Art and Design, GA | M,W |
| University of Michigan, MI | M | Johns Hopkins University, MD | M,W | Seton Hill University, PA | M,W |
| University of Minnesota, Duluth, MN | M,W | Kennesaw State University, GA | W | Shepherd University, WV | W |
| | | Kutztown University of Pennsylvania, PA | W | Shippensburg University of Pennsylvania, PA | W |
| University of Minnesota, Twin Cities Campus, MN | M,W | Lake Erie College, OH | M,W | Siena College, NY | M,W |
| University of New Hampshire, NH | M,W | La Salle University, PA | W | Slippery Rock University of Pennsylvania, PA | W |
| University of Notre Dame, IN | M | Lawrence Technological University, MI | M,W | Southern Connecticut State University, CT | W |
| University of Vermont, VT | M,W | Lees-McRae College, NC | M,W | Stanford University, CA | W |
| University of Wisconsin–Madison, WI | M,W | Lehigh University, PA | M,W | Stetson University, FL | W |
| Western Michigan University, MI | M | Le Moyne College, NY | M,W | Stonehill College, MA | W |
| | | Lenoir-Rhyne University, NC | M,W | Stony Brook University, State University of New York, NY | M,W |
| **Lacrosse** | | Liberty University, VA | W | | |
| Adams State University, CO | M,W | Lincoln Memorial University, TN | M,W | Syracuse University, NY | M,W |
| Adelphi University, NY | M,W | Lindenwood University, MO | M,W | Temple University, PA | W |
| American University, DC | W | Lock Haven University of Pennsylvania, PA | W | Tennessee Wesleyan College, TN | M,W |
| Bellarmine University, KY | M | | | Tiffin University, OH | W |
| Belmont Abbey College, NC | M,W | Long Island University–LIU Brooklyn, NY | W | Towson University, MD | M,W |
| Binghamton University, State University of New York, NY | M,W | Long Island University–LIU Post, NY | M,W | Truett-McConnell College, GA | W |
| Bloomsburg University of Pennsylvania, PA | W | Longwood University, VA | W | Tusculum College, TN | M,W |
| Boston College, MA | W | Lynn University, FL | M | University at Albany, State University of New York, NY | M,W |
| Boston University, MA | W | Manhattan College, NY | M,W | University of Bridgeport, CT | W |
| Brevard College, NC | M,W | Marist College, NY | M,W | University of California, Davis, CA | W |
| Bryant University, RI | M,W | Marquette University, WI | M,W | University of Cincinnati, OH | W |
| Bucknell University, PA | M,W | McKendree University, IL | W | University of Colorado Boulder, CO | W |
| Caldwell University, NJ | W | Mercer University, GA | M,W | University of Delaware, DE | M,W |
| California State University, Fresno, CA | W | Mercy College, NY | M,W | University of Denver, CO | M,W |
| Canisius College, NY | M,W | Merrimack College, MA | M,W | The University of Findlay, OH | W |
| Catawba College, NC | M,W | Millersville University of Pennsylvania, PA | W | University of Florida, FL | W |
| Central Connecticut State University, CT | W | Missouri Baptist University, MO | M,W | University of Hartford, CT | M |
| Central Michigan University, MI | W | Molloy College, NY | M,W | University of Louisville, KY | W |
| Chestnut Hill College, PA | M,W | Monmouth University, NJ | M,W | University of Maryland, Baltimore County, MD | M,W |
| Chowan University, NC | W | Mount St. Mary's University, MD | M,W | University of Maryland, College Park, MD | M,W |
| Clarke University, IA | M,W | Newberry College, SC | W | | |
| Coastal Carolina University, SC | W | New York Institute of Technology, NY | M | University of Massachusetts Amherst, MA | M,W |
| Coker College, SC | M,W | Niagara University, NY | W | | |
| The College of Saint Rose, NY | M | Northern Michigan University, MI | W | University of Massachusetts Lowell, MA | M,W |
| College of the Holy Cross, MA | M,W | Nyack College, NY | W | University of Michigan, MI | M,W |
| The College of William and Mary, VA | W | The Ohio State University, OH | M,W | University of Michigan–Dearborn, MI | M |
| Colorado Mesa University, CO | M,W | Old Dominion University, VA | W | | |
| Concordia University, CA | M,W | Pace University, NY | M,W | University of Minnesota, Duluth, MN | M,W |
| Davidson College, NC | W | Penn State University Park, PA | M,W | | |
| Dominican College, NY | M,W | Philadelphia University, PA | W | University of New Hampshire, NH | W |
| Dowling College, NY | M,W | Post University, CT | M,W | University of New Haven, CT | W |
| Drexel University, PA | M,W | Presbyterian College, SC | W | The University of North Carolina at Chapel Hill, NC | M,W |
| Duquesne University, PA | W | Providence College, RI | M | | |
| East Stroudsburg University of Pennsylvania, PA | W | Queens College of the City University of New York, NY | W | University of Notre Dame, IN | M,W |
| Elon University, NC | W | Quinnipiac University, CT | M,W | University of Oregon, OR | W |
| Emmanuel College, GA | M,W | Radford University, VA | W | University of Pikeville, KY | W |
| Fairfield University, CT | M,W | Regis University, CO | W | University of Richmond, VA | M,W |
| Florida Institute of Technology, FL | M,W | Reinhardt University, GA | M,W | University of Southern California, CA | W |
| Florida Southern College, FL | M,W | Robert Morris University, PA | M,W | The University of Tampa, FL | M |
| Fort Lewis College, CO | W | Robert Morris University Illinois, IL | M,W | University of the Cumberlands, KY | M,W |

| | |
|---|---|
| University of the District of Columbia, DC | M,W |
| University of Vermont, VT | M,W |
| University of Virginia, VA | M,W |
| Ursuline College, OH | W |
| Vanderbilt University, TN | W |
| Villanova University, PA | M,W |
| Virginia Military Institute, VA | M |
| Virginia Polytechnic Institute and State University, VA | W |
| Wagner College, NY | M,W |
| West Chester University of Pennsylvania, PA | W |
| Westminster College, UT | M,W |
| West Virginia Wesleyan College, WV | W |
| Wheeling Jesuit University, WV | M,W |
| Wingate University, NC | M,W |

**Riflery**

| | |
|---|---|
| The Citadel, The Military College of South Carolina, SC | M,W |
| Columbus State University, GA | M,W |
| Emmanuel College, GA | M,W |
| Georgia Southern University, GA | W |
| Hillsdale College, MI | M,W |
| Jacksonville State University, AL | M,W |
| Lindenwood University, MO | M,W |
| Morehead State University, KY | M,W |
| Murray State University, KY | M,W |
| North Carolina State University, NC | M,W |
| Texas Christian University, TX | W |
| The University of Akron, OH | W |
| University of Alaska Fairbanks, AK | M,W |
| University of Memphis, TN | M,W |
| University of Mississippi, MS | W |
| University of Nebraska–Lincoln, NE | W |
| University of Nevada, Reno, NV | M,W |
| University of North Georgia, GA | M,W |
| The University of Tennessee at Martin, TN | M,W |
| Virginia Military Institute, VA | M,W |
| West Virginia University, WV | M,W |

**Rugby**

| | |
|---|---|
| Central Washington University, WA | M,W |
| Eastern Illinois University, IL | W |
| Lee University, TN | M,W |
| Life University, GA | M,W |
| Lindenwood University, MO | M,W |
| Quinnipiac University, CT | W |
| The University of North Carolina at Pembroke, NC | M |
| West Chester University of Pennsylvania, PA | W |
| Wheeling Jesuit University, WV | M |

**Sailing**

| | |
|---|---|
| Hampton University, VA | M,W |

**Skiing (cross-country)**

| | |
|---|---|
| Michigan Technological University, MI | M,W |
| Montana State University, MT | M,W |
| Northern Michigan University, MI | M,W |
| University of Alaska Anchorage, AK | M,W |
| University of Alaska Fairbanks, AK | M,W |
| University of Colorado Boulder, CO | M,W |
| University of Denver, CO | M,W |
| University of New Hampshire, NH | M,W |
| University of Utah, UT | M,W |
| University of Vermont, VT | M,W |

| | |
|---|---|
| University of Wisconsin–Green Bay, WI | M,W |

**Skiing (downhill)**

| | |
|---|---|
| The College of Idaho, ID | M,W |
| Montana State University, MT | M,W |
| Rocky Mountain College, MT | M,W |
| Saint Anselm College, NH | M,W |
| University of Alaska Anchorage, AK | M,W |
| University of Colorado Boulder, CO | M,W |
| University of Denver, CO | M,W |
| University of New Hampshire, NH | M,W |
| University of Utah, UT | M,W |
| University of Vermont, VT | M,W |
| Westminster College, UT | M,W |

**Soccer**

| | |
|---|---|
| Abilene Christian University, TX | W |
| Academy of Art University, CA | M,W |
| Adams State University, CO | M,W |
| Adelphi University, NY | M,W |
| Alabama State University, AL | W |
| Alcorn State University, MS | W |
| American University, DC | M,W |
| Anderson University, SC | M,W |
| Angelo State University, TX | W |
| Appalachian State University, NC | M,W |
| Arizona Christian University, AZ | M,W |
| Arizona State University at the Downtown Phoenix campus, AZ | W |
| Arizona State University at the Polytechnic campus, AZ | W |
| Arizona State University at the Tempe campus, AZ | W |
| Arizona State University at the West campus, AZ | W |
| Arkansas State University, AR | W |
| Armstrong State University, GA | W |
| Ashland University, OH | W |
| Auburn University, AL | W |
| Auburn University at Montgomery, AL | M,W |
| Augustana College, SD | W |
| Austin Peay State University, TN | W |
| Azusa Pacific University, CA | M,W |
| Ball State University, IN | W |
| Barry University, FL | M,W |
| Baylor University, TX | W |
| Belhaven University, MS | M,W |
| Bellarmine University, KY | M,W |
| Belmont Abbey College, NC | M,W |
| Belmont University, TN | M,W |
| Bemidji State University, MN | W |
| Bethel College, KS | M,W |
| Binghamton University, State University of New York, NY | M,W |
| Biola University, CA | M,W |
| Blessing-Rieman College of Nursing, IL | M,W |
| Bloomfield College, NJ | M,W |
| Bloomsburg University of Pennsylvania, PA | M,W |
| Bluefield College, VA | M,W |
| Boston College, MA | M,W |
| Boston University, MA | M,W |
| Bowling Green State University, OH | M,W |
| Bradley University, IL | M |
| Brenau University, GA | W |
| Brevard College, NC | M,W |
| Brigham Young University, UT | W |
| Bryant University, RI | M,W |
| Bucknell University, PA | M,W |
| Butler University, IN | M,W |
| Caldwell University, NJ | M,W |

| | |
|---|---|
| California Baptist University, CA | M,W |
| California Polytechnic State University, San Luis Obispo, CA | M,W |
| California State Polytechnic University, Pomona, CA | M,W |
| California State University, Bakersfield, CA | M |
| California State University, Chico, CA | M,W |
| California State University, Dominguez Hills, CA | M,W |
| California State University, Fresno, CA | W |
| California State University, Fullerton, CA | M,W |
| California State University, Long Beach, CA | W |
| California State University, Los Angeles, CA | M,W |
| California State University, Monterey Bay, CA | M,W |
| California State University, Sacramento, CA | M,W |
| California State University, San Bernardino, CA | M,W |
| California State University, Stanislaus, CA | M,W |
| Calumet College of Saint Joseph, IN | M,W |
| Campbellsville University, KY | M,W |
| Canisius College, NY | M,W |
| Cardinal Stritch University, WI | M,W |
| Carroll College, MT | M,W |
| Carson-Newman University, TN | M,W |
| Catawba College, NC | M,W |
| Cedarville University, OH | M,W |
| Central Connecticut State University, CT | M,W |
| Central Methodist University, MO | M,W |
| Central Michigan University, MI | W |
| Central Washington University, WA | W |
| Chaminade University of Honolulu, HI | M,W |
| Chestnut Hill College, PA | M,W |
| Chowan University, NC | M,W |
| Christian Brothers University, TN | M,W |
| Cincinnati Christian University, OH | M,W |
| The Citadel, The Military College of South Carolina, SC | W |
| Clarion University of Pennsylvania, PA | W |
| Clarke University, IA | M,W |
| Clayton State University, GA | M,W |
| Cleveland State University, OH | M |
| Coastal Carolina University, SC | M,W |
| Coker College, SC | M,W |
| College of Charleston, SC | M,W |
| The College of Idaho, ID | M,W |
| College of Saint Mary, NE | W |
| The College of Saint Rose, NY | M,W |
| College of the Holy Cross, MA | M,W |
| The College of William and Mary, VA | M,W |
| The Colorado College, CO | W |
| Colorado Mesa University, CO | M,W |
| Colorado School of Mines, CO | M,W |
| Colorado State University, CO | W |
| Colorado State University–Pueblo, CO | M,W |
| Columbia College, MO | M,W |
| Columbia International University, SC | M,W |

| | | | | | |
|---|---|---|---|---|---|
| Columbus State University, GA | W | Harding University, AR | M,W | Manhattan College, NY | M,W |
| Concordia University, CA | M,W | Hartwick College, NY | M | Mansfield University of | |
| Concordia University, Nebraska, NE | M,W | Hastings College, NE | M,W | Pennsylvania, PA | W |
| Concordia University, St. Paul, MN | W | Hawai`i Pacific University, HI | M,W | Marist College, NY | M,W |
| Concord University, WV | M,W | Hofstra University, NY | M,W | Marquette University, WI | M,W |
| Corban University, OR | M,W | Holy Family University, PA | M,W | Marshall University, WV | M,W |
| Cornerstone University, MI | M,W | Hope International University, CA | M,W | Marymount California University, | |
| Creighton University, NE | M,W | Houston Baptist University, TX | M,W | CA | M |
| Culver-Stockton College, MO | M,W | Howard University, DC | M,W | Maryville University of Saint | |
| Cumberland University, TN | M,W | Humboldt State University, CA | M,W | Louis, MO | M,W |
| Dallas Baptist University, TX | W | Huston-Tillotson University, TX | M,W | The Master's College and | |
| Davidson College, NC | M,W | Idaho State University, ID | W | Seminary, CA | M,W |
| Delaware State University, DE | W | Illinois Institute of Technology, IL | M,W | McKendree University, IL | M,W |
| Delta State University, MS | M,W | Illinois State University, IL | W | Menlo College, CA | M,W |
| DePaul University, IL | M,W | Indiana State University, IN | W | Mercer University, GA | M,W |
| Dixie State University, UT | M,W | Indiana University Bloomington, IN | M,W | Mercy College, NY | M,W |
| Doane College, NE | M,W | Indiana University of | | Merrimack College, MA | M,W |
| Dominican College, NY | M,W | Pennsylvania, PA | W | Miami University, OH | M,W |
| Dowling College, NY | M,W | Indiana University–Purdue | | Michigan State University, MI | M,W |
| Drake University, IA | M,W | University Fort Wayne, IN | M,W | Michigan Technological | |
| Drexel University, PA | M,W | Indiana University–Purdue | | University, MI | W |
| Drury University, MO | M,W | University Indianapolis, IN | M,W | Middle Tennessee State | |
| Duquesne University, PA | M,W | Inter American University of | | University, TN | W |
| East Carolina University, NC | W | Puerto Rico, Guayama | | Midwestern State University, TX | M,W |
| East Central University, OK | W | Campus, PR | M | Millersville University of | |
| Eastern Illinois University, IL | M,W | Iona College, NY | M,W | Pennsylvania, PA | M,W |
| Eastern Michigan University, MI | W | Iowa State University of Science | | Milligan College, TN | M,W |
| Eastern New Mexico University, NM | M,W | and Technology, IA | W | Minnesota State University | |
| East Stroudsburg University of | | Jackson State University, MS | W | Mankato, MN | W |
| Pennsylvania, PA | M,W | Jacksonville State University, AL | W | Minnesota State University | |
| Eckerd College, FL | M,W | Jacksonville University, FL | M,W | Moorhead, MN | W |
| Elon University, NC | M,W | James Madison University, VA | M,W | Mississippi State University, MS | W |
| Embry-Riddle Aeronautical | | John Brown University, AR | M,W | Missouri Baptist University, MO | M,W |
| University–Daytona, FL | M,W | Kansas Wesleyan University, KS | M,W | Missouri Southern State | |
| Embry-Riddle Aeronautical | | Kennesaw State University, GA | W | University, MO | M,W |
| University–Prescott, AZ | M,W | Kent State University, OH | W | Missouri State University, MO | M,W |
| Emmanuel College, GA | M,W | Kentucky Wesleyan College, KY | M,W | Missouri University of Science | |
| Emporia State University, KS | W | King University, TN | M,W | and Technology, MO | W |
| The Evergreen State College, WA | M,W | Kutztown University of | | Missouri Valley College, MO | M,W |
| Fairfield University, CT | M,W | Pennsylvania, PA | W | Missouri Western State | |
| Faulkner University, AL | M,W | Lake Erie College, OH | M,W | University, MO | W |
| Ferris State University, MI | W | Lamar University, TX | W | Molloy College, NY | M,W |
| Flagler College, FL | M,W | La Salle University, PA | M,W | Monmouth University, NJ | M,W |
| Florida Gulf Coast University, FL | M,W | Lawrence Technological | | Montana State University | |
| Florida Institute of Technology, | | University, MI | M,W | Billings, MT | W |
| FL | M,W | Lees-McRae College, NC | M,W | Montreat College, NC | M,W |
| Florida Southern College, FL | M,W | Lee University, TN | M,W | Morehead State University, KY | W |
| Florida State University, FL | W | Le Moyne College, NY | M,W | Morningside College, IA | M,W |
| Fordham University, NY | M,W | Lenoir-Rhyne University, NC | M,W | Mount Marty College, SD | M,W |
| Fort Hays State University, KS | M,W | Lewis University, IL | M,W | Mount Mercy University, IA | M,W |
| Fort Lewis College, CO | M,W | Liberty University, VA | M,W | Mount St. Mary's | |
| Francis Marion University, SC | M,W | Lincoln Christian University, IL | M,W | University, MD | W |
| Franklin Pierce University, NH | M,W | Lincoln Memorial University, TN | M,W | Murray State University, KY | W |
| Friends University, KS | M,W | Lincoln University, PA | W | Newberry College, SC | M,W |
| Furman University, SC | M,W | Lindenwood University, MO | M,W | New Jersey Institute of | |
| Gannon University, PA | M,W | Lindsey Wilson College, KY | M,W | Technology, NJ | M,W |
| George Mason University, VA | M,W | Lipscomb University, TN | M,W | Newman University, KS | M,W |
| Georgetown College, KY | M,W | Lock Haven University of | | New Mexico Highlands University, | |
| Georgetown University, DC | M,W | Pennsylvania, PA | M,W | NM | W |
| The George Washington | | Long Island University–LIU | | New Mexico State University, NM | W |
| University, DC | M,W | Brooklyn, NY | M,W | New York Institute of | |
| Georgia College & State | | Long Island University–LIU | | Technology, NY | M,W |
| University, GA | W | Post, NY | M,W | Niagara University, NY | M,W |
| Georgian Court University, NJ | M,W | Longwood University, VA | M,W | Nicholls State University, LA | W |
| Georgia Southern University, GA | M,W | Louisiana State University and | | North Carolina State University, | |
| Georgia Southwestern State | | Agricultural & Mechanical | | NC | M,W |
| University, GA | M,W | College, LA | W | Northeastern State University, OK | M,W |
| Georgia State University, GA | M,W | Loyola Marymount University, CA | M,W | Northeastern University, MA | M,W |
| Gonzaga University, WA | M,W | Loyola University Chicago, IL | M,W | Northern Arizona University, AZ | W |
| Goshen College, IN | M,W | Lubbock Christian University, TX | M,W | Northern Illinois University, IL | M,W |
| Graceland University, IA | M,W | Lynn University, FL | M,W | Northern Kentucky University, KY | M,W |
| Grand Valley State University, MI | W | Lyon College, AR | M,W | Northern Michigan University, MI | M,W |
| Grand View University, IA | M,W | Malone University, OH | M,W | Northern State University, SD | W |

| | | | | | |
|---|---|---|---|---|---|
| Northwest Christian University, OR | M,W | San Diego State University, CA | M,W | University at Buffalo, the State University of New York, NY | M,W |
| Northwestern Oklahoma State University, OK | W | San Francisco State University, CA | M,W | The University of Akron, OH | M,W |
| Northwest Missouri State University, MO | W | San Jose State University, CA | M,W | The University of Alabama, AL | W |
| Northwest Nazarene University, ID | W | Santa Clara University, CA | M,W | The University of Alabama at Birmingham, AL | M,W |
| Northwest University, WA | M,W | Savannah College of Art and Design, GA | M,W | The University of Alabama in Huntsville, AL | M,W |
| Nova Southeastern University, FL | M,W | Seattle Pacific University, WA | M,W | The University of Arizona, AZ | W |
| Nyack College, NY | M,W | Seattle University, WA | M,W | University of Arkansas, AR | W |
| Oakland University, MI | M,W | Seton Hill University, PA | M,W | University of Bridgeport, CT | M,W |
| The Ohio State University, OH | M,W | Shawnee State University, OH | M,W | University of California, Davis, CA | M,W |
| Ohio University, OH | W | Shepherd University, WV | M,W | University of California, Irvine, CA | M,W |
| Oklahoma Christian University, OK | M,W | Shippensburg University of Pennsylvania, PA | M,W | University of California, Los Angeles, CA | M,W |
| Oklahoma City University, OK | M,W | Siena College, NY | M,W | University of California, Merced, CA | M,W |
| Oklahoma State University, OK | W | Simpson University, CA | M,W | University of California, Riverside, CA | M,W |
| Oklahoma Wesleyan University, OK | M,W | Slippery Rock University of Pennsylvania, PA | M,W | University of California, Santa Barbara, CA | M,W |
| Old Dominion University, VA | M,W | Soka University of America, CA | M,W | University of Central Arkansas, AR | M,W |
| Olivet Nazarene University, IL | M,W | South Dakota State University, SD | W | University of Central Florida, FL | M,W |
| Oral Roberts University, OK | M,W | Southeastern Louisiana University, LA | W | University of Central Missouri, MO | W |
| Oregon State University, OR | M,W | Southeast Missouri State University, MO | W | University of Central Oklahoma, OK | W |
| Our Lady of the Lake University of San Antonio, TX | M,W | Southern Connecticut State University, CT | M,W | University of Charleston, WV | M,W |
| Pace University, NY | W | Southern Illinois University Edwardsville, IL | M,W | University of Cincinnati, OH | M,W |
| Palm Beach Atlantic University, FL | M,W | Southern Methodist University, TX | M,W | University of Colorado Boulder, CO | W |
| Park University, MO | M,W | Southern Oregon University, OR | W | University of Colorado Colorado Springs, CO | M,W |
| Penn State University Park, PA | M,W | Southern Utah University, UT | W | University of Connecticut, CT | M,W |
| Pepperdine University, CA | W | Southwest Baptist University, MO | W | University of Dayton, OH | M,W |
| Philadelphia University, PA | M,W | Southwestern College, KS | M,W | University of Delaware, DE | M,W |
| Point Loma Nazarene University, CA | M,W | Spring Hill College, AL | M,W | University of Denver, CO | M,W |
| Post University, CT | M,W | Stanford University, CA | M,W | University of Evansville, IN | M,W |
| Prairie View A&M University, TX | W | Stephen F. Austin State University, TX | W | The University of Findlay, OH | M,W |
| Presbyterian College, SC | M,W | Stephens College, MO | W | University of Florida, FL | W |
| Providence College, RI | M,W | Sterling College, KS | M,W | University of Georgia, GA | W |
| Purdue University, IN | W | Stetson University, FL | M,W | University of Great Falls, MT | M,W |
| Purdue University Calumet, IN | M,W | Stonehill College, MA | M,W | University of Hartford, CT | M,W |
| Queens College of the City University of New York, NY | M,W | Stony Brook University, State University of New York, NY | M,W | University of Hawaii at Manoa, HI | W |
| Quincy University, IL | M,W | Syracuse University, NY | M,W | University of Houston, TX | W |
| Quinnipiac University, CT | M,W | Tabor College, KS | M,W | University of Idaho, ID | W |
| Radford University, VA | M,W | Taylor University, IN | M,W | University of Illinois at Chicago, IL | M |
| Regis University, CO | M,W | Temple University, PA | M,W | University of Illinois at Springfield, IL | M,W |
| Reinhardt University, GA | M,W | Tennessee Wesleyan College, TN | M,W | University of Indianapolis, IN | M,W |
| Rice University, TX | W | Texas A&M International University, TX | M,W | The University of Iowa, IA | |
| Rider University, NJ | M,W | Texas A&M University, TX | W | University of Jamestown, ND | M,W |
| Robert Morris University, PA | M,W | Texas A&M University–Commerce, TX | W | The University of Kansas, KS | W |
| Robert Morris University Illinois, IL | M,W | Texas A&M University–Corpus Christi, TX | W | University of Louisville, KY | M,W |
| Roberts Wesleyan College, NY | M,W | Texas Christian University, TX | W | University of Maine, ME | W |
| Rockhurst University, MO | M,W | Texas Southern University, TX | W | University of Maine at Augusta, ME | W |
| Rocky Mountain College, MT | M,W | Texas State University, TX | W | University of Maryland, Baltimore County, MD | M,W |
| Rollins College, FL | M,W | Texas Tech University, TX | W | University of Maryland, College Park, MD | M,W |
| Sacred Heart University, CT | M,W | Texas Wesleyan University, TX | M,W | University of Massachusetts Amherst, MA | M,W |
| Saginaw Valley State University, MI | M,W | Texas Woman's University, TX | W | University of Massachusetts Lowell, MA | M,W |
| St. Andrews University, NC | M,W | Tiffin University, OH | M,W | University of Memphis, TN | M,W |
| Saint Anselm College, NH | M,W | Towson University, MD | W | University of Miami, FL | W |
| St. Bonaventure University, NY | M,W | Trevecca Nazarene University, TN | M,W | University of Michigan, MI | M,W |
| St. Edward's University, TX | M,W | Trinity Christian College, IL | M,W | University of Minnesota, Crookston, MN | W |
| St. Francis College, NY | M | Troy University, AL | W | University of Minnesota, Duluth, MN | W |
| Saint Francis University, PA | M,W | Truett-McConnell College, GA | M,W | University of Minnesota, Twin Cities Campus, MN | W |
| St. John's University, NY | M,W | Truman State University, MO | M,W | | |
| Saint Joseph's College, IN | M,W | Tulane University, LA | W | | |
| Saint Joseph's University, PA | M,W | Tusculum College, TN | M,W | | |
| Saint Leo University, FL | M,W | Union College, KY | M,W | | |
| St. Louis College of Pharmacy, MO | M,W | Union University, TN | M,W | | |
| Saint Louis University, MO | M,W | University at Albany, State University of New York, NY | M,W | | |
| Saint Martin's University, WA | W | | | | |
| St. Thomas Aquinas College, NY | M,W | | | | |
| St. Thomas University, FL | M,W | | | | |
| Samford University, AL | W | | | | |
| Sam Houston State University, TX | W | | | | |

| | | | | | | |
|---|---|---|---|---|---|---|
| University of Mississippi, MS | W | University of the Cumberlands, KY | M,W | Wofford College, SC | M,W |
| University of Missouri, MO | W | University of the District of | | Wright State University, OH | M,W |
| University of Missouri– | | Columbia, DC | M | Xavier University, OH | M,W |
| Kansas City, MO | M,W | University of the Incarnate | | Youngstown State University, OH | W |
| University of Missouri–St. | | Word, TX | M,W | | |
| Louis, MO | M,W | University of the Pacific, CA | W | **Softball** | |
| University of Mobile, AL | M,W | The University of Toledo, OH | W | Abilene Christian University, TX | W |
| The University of Montana, MT | W | The University of Tulsa, OK | M,W | Academy of Art University, CA | W |
| University of Montevallo, AL | M,W | University of Utah, UT | W | Adams State University, CO | W |
| University of Nebraska– | | University of Vermont, VT | M,W | Adelphi University, NY | W |
| Lincoln, NE | W | University of Virginia, VA | M,W | Alabama State University, AL | W |
| University of Nevada, Las Vegas, | | University of Washington, WA | M,W | Albany State University, GA | W |
| NV | M,W | The University of West Alabama, AL | M,W | Alcorn State University, MS | W |
| University of Nevada, Reno, NV | W | University of West Florida, FL | M,W | Anderson University, SC | W |
| University of New Hampshire, NH | M,W | University of West Georgia, GA | W | Angelo State University, TX | W |
| University of New Haven, CT | M,W | University of Wisconsin– | | Appalachian State University, NC | W |
| University of North Alabama, AL | W | Green Bay, WI | M,W | Arizona Christian University, AZ | W |
| University of North Carolina at | | University of Wisconsin– | | Arizona State University at the | |
| Asheville, NC | M,W | Madison, WI | M,W | Downtown Phoenix campus, AZ | W |
| The University of North Carolina | | University of Wisconsin– | | Arizona State University at the | |
| at Chapel Hill, NC | M,W | Milwaukee, WI | M,W | Polytechnic campus, AZ | W |
| The University of North Carolina | | University of Wisconsin– | | Arizona State University at the | |
| at Charlotte, NC | M,W | Parkside, WI | M,W | Tempe campus, AZ | W |
| The University of North Carolina | | University of Wyoming, WY | W | Arizona State University at the | |
| at Greensboro, NC | M,W | Upper Iowa University, IA | M,W | West campus, AZ | W |
| The University of North Carolina | | Ursuline College, OH | W | Arkansas Tech University, AR | W |
| at Pembroke, NC | M,W | Utah State University, UT | W | Armstrong State University, GA | W |
| The University of North Carolina | | Utah Valley University, UT | W | Ashland University, OH | W |
| Wilmington, NC | M,W | Valdosta State University, GA | W | Auburn University, AL | W |
| University of Northern Colorado, | | Valparaiso University, IN | M,W | Auburn University at Montgomery, | |
| CO | W | Vanderbilt University, TN | W | AL | W |
| University of Northern Iowa, IA | W | Vanguard University of Southern | | Augustana College, SD | W |
| University of North Florida, FL | M,W | California, CA | M,W | Austin Peay State University, TN | W |
| University of North Georgia, GA | M,W | Villanova University, PA | M,W | Azusa Pacific University, CA | W |
| University of North Texas, TX | W | Virginia Commonwealth | | Ball State University, IN | W |
| University of Notre Dame, IN | M,W | University, VA | M,W | Barry University, FL | W |
| University of Oklahoma, OK | W | Virginia Military Institute, VA | M | Baylor University, TX | W |
| University of Oregon, OR | W | Virginia Polytechnic Institute | | Belhaven University, MS | W |
| University of Pikeville, KY | M,W | and State University, VA | M,W | Bellarmine University, KY | W |
| University of Pittsburgh, PA | M,W | Wagner College, NY | W | Belmont Abbey College, NC | W |
| University of Portland, OR | M,W | Wake Forest University, NC | M,W | Belmont University, TN | W |
| University of Rhode Island, RI | M,W | Waldorf College, IA | M,W | Bemidji State University, MN | W |
| University of Richmond, VA | W | Warner Pacific College, OR | M,W | Bethune-Cookman University, FL | W |
| University of Rio Grande, OH | M | Washburn University, KS | W | Binghamton University, State | |
| University of St. Francis, IL | M,W | Washington State University, WA | W | University of New York, NY | W |
| University of St. Thomas, TX | M,W | Wayland Baptist University, TX | M,W | Biola University, CA | W |
| University of San Diego, CA | M,W | Wayne State College, NE | W | Bloomfield College, NJ | W |
| University of San Francisco, CA | M,W | Webber International University, | | Bloomsburg University of | |
| University of Science and Arts | | FL | M,W | Pennsylvania, PA | W |
| of Oklahoma, OK | M,W | Weber State University, UT | W | Bluefield College, VA | W |
| University of South Alabama, AL | W | West Chester University of | | Bluefield State College, WV | W |
| University of South Carolina, SC | M,W | Pennsylvania, PA | M,W | Blue Mountain College, MS | W |
| University of South Carolina | | Western Carolina University, NC | W | Boston College, MA | W |
| Aiken, SC | M,W | Western Illinois University, IL | M,W | Boston University, MA | W |
| University of South Carolina | | Western Michigan University, MI | M,W | Bowie State University, MD | W |
| Upstate, SC | M,W | Western Oregon University, OR | W | Bowling Green State University, OH | W |
| The University of South Dakota, SD | W | Western State Colorado | | Bradley University, IL | W |
| University of Southern | | University, CO | W | Brenau University, GA | W |
| California, CA | W | Western Washington University, WA | M,W | Brevard College, NC | W |
| University of Southern Indiana, IN | M,W | Westminster College, UT | M,W | Brigham Young University, UT | W |
| University of Southern | | West Texas A&M University, TX | M,W | Bryant University, RI | W |
| Mississippi, MS | W | West Virginia University, WV | M,W | Bucknell University, PA | W |
| University of South Florida, FL | M,W | West Virginia University | | Butler University, IN | W |
| The University of Tampa, FL | M,W | Institute of Technology, WV | M,W | Caldwell University, NJ | W |
| The University of Tennessee, TN | W | West Virginia Wesleyan College, WV | M,W | California Baptist University, CA | W |
| The University of Tennessee at | | Wheeling Jesuit University, WV | M,W | California Polytechnic State | |
| Chattanooga, TN | W | William Jessup University, CA | M,W | University, San Luis Obispo, CA | W |
| The University of Tennessee at | | William Jewell College, MO | M,W | California State University, | |
| Martin, TN | W | Williams Baptist College, AR | M,W | Bakersfield, CA | W |
| The University of Texas at | | William Woods University, MO | M,W | California State University, | |
| Austin, TX | W | Wingate University, NC | M,W | Chico, CA | W |
| The University of Texas at San | | Winona State University, MN | W | California State University, | |
| Antonio, TX | W | Winthrop University, SC | M,W | Dominguez Hills, CA | W |

| | | | |
|---|---|---|---|
| California State University, Fresno, CA | W | East Carolina University, NC | W |
| California State University, Fullerton, CA | W | East Central University, OK | W |
| California State University, Long Beach, CA | W | Eastern Illinois University, IL | W |
| | | Eastern Kentucky University, KY | W |
| California State University, Monterey Bay, CA | W | Eastern Michigan University, MI | W |
| | | Eastern New Mexico University, NM | W |
| California State University, Sacramento, CA | W | East Stroudsburg University of Pennsylvania, PA | W |
| California State University, San Bernardino, CA | W | Eckerd College, FL | W |
| | | Elon University, NC | M,W |
| California State University, Stanislaus, CA | W | Embry-Riddle Aeronautical University–Daytona, FL | W |
| Calumet College of Saint Joseph, IN | W | Embry-Riddle Aeronautical University–Prescott, AZ | W |
| Cameron University, OK | W | Emmanuel College, GA | W |
| Campbellsville University, KY | W | Emporia State University, KS | W |
| Canisius College, NY | W | Evangel University, MO | W |
| Cardinal Stritch University, WI | W | Fairfield University, CT | W |
| Carroll College, MT | W | Fairmont State University, WV | W |
| Carson-Newman University, TN | W | Faulkner University, AL | W |
| Catawba College, NC | W | Fayetteville State University, NC | W |
| Cedarville University, OH | W | Ferris State University, MI | W |
| Central Connecticut State University, CT | W | Flagler College, FL | W |
| | | Florida Agricultural and Mechanical University, FL | W |
| Central Methodist University, MO | W | | |
| Central Michigan University, MI | W | Florida Atlantic University, FL | W |
| Central Washington University, WA | W | Florida Gulf Coast University, FL | W |
| Chaminade University of Honolulu, HI | W | Florida Institute of Technology, FL | W |
| Chestnut Hill College, PA | W | Florida Southern College, FL | W |
| Chowan University, NC | W | Florida State University, FL | W |
| Christian Brothers University, TN | W | Fordham University, NY | W |
| Clarion University of Pennsylvania, PA | W | Fort Hays State University, KS | W |
| | | Fort Lewis College, CO | W |
| Clarke University, IA | W | Francis Marion University, SC | W |
| Cleveland State University, OH | W | Franklin Pierce University, NH | W |
| Coastal Carolina University, SC | W | Friends University, KS | W |
| Coker College, SC | W | Furman University, SC | W |
| College of Charleston, SC | W | Gannon University, PA | W |
| The College of Idaho, ID | W | George Mason University, VA | W |
| College of Saint Mary, NE | W | Georgetown College, KY | W |
| The College of Saint Rose, NY | W | Georgetown University, DC | W |
| College of the Holy Cross, MA | W | Georgia College & State University, GA | W |
| Colorado Mesa University, CO | W | | |
| Colorado School of Mines, CO | W | Georgia Institute of Technology, GA | W |
| Colorado State University, CO | W | Georgian Court University, NJ | W |
| Colorado State University–Pueblo, CO | W | Georgia Regents University, GA | W |
| | | Georgia Southern University, GA | W |
| Columbia College, MO | W | Georgia Southwestern State University, GA | W |
| Columbus State University, GA | W | | |
| Concordia University, CA | W | Georgia State University, GA | W |
| Concordia University, Nebraska, NE | W | Goshen College, IN | W |
| Concordia University, St. Paul, MN | W | Graceland University, IA | W |
| Concord University, WV | W | Grambling State University, LA | W |
| Corban University, OR | W | Grand Valley State University, MI | W |
| Cornerstone University, MI | W | Grand View University, IA | W |
| Creighton University, NE | W | Hampton University, VA | W |
| Culver-Stockton College, MO | W | Harding University, AR | W |
| Cumberland University, TN | W | Hastings College, NE | W |
| Dakota State University, SD | W | Hawai`i Pacific University, HI | W |
| Delaware State University, DE | W | Hillsdale College, MI | W |
| Delta State University, MS | W | Hofstra University, NY | W |
| DePaul University, IL | W | Holy Family University, PA | W |
| Dickinson State University, ND | W | Hope International University, CA | W |
| Dixie State University, UT | W | Houston Baptist University, TX | W |
| Doane College, NE | W | Humboldt State University, CA | W |
| Dominican College, NY | W | Huston-Tillotson University, TX | W |
| Dowling College, NY | W | Idaho State University, ID | W |
| Drake University, IA | W | Illinois State University, IL | W |
| Drexel University, PA | W | Indiana State University, IN | W |
| Drury University, MO | W | Indiana University Bloomington, IN | W |

| | |
|---|---|
| Indiana University of Pennsylvania, PA | W |
| Indiana University–Purdue University Fort Wayne, IN | W |
| Indiana University–Purdue University Indianapolis, IN | W |
| Indian River State College, FL | W |
| Inter American University of Puerto Rico, Bayamón Campus, PR | M,W |
| Inter American University of Puerto Rico, Guayama Campus, PR | M,W |
| Iona College, NY | W |
| Iowa State University of Science and Technology, IA | W |
| Jackson State University, MS | W |
| Jacksonville State University, AL | W |
| Jacksonville University, FL | W |
| James Madison University, VA | W |
| Johnson C. Smith University, NC | W |
| Kansas Wesleyan University, KS | W |
| Kennesaw State University, GA | W |
| Kent State University, OH | W |
| Kentucky State University, KY | W |
| Kentucky Wesleyan College, KY | W |
| King University, TN | W |
| Kutztown University of Pennsylvania, PA | W |
| Lake Erie College, OH | W |
| La Salle University, PA | W |
| Lees-McRae College, NC | W |
| Lee University, TN | W |
| Lehigh University, PA | W |
| Le Moyne College, NY | W |
| LeMoyne-Owen College, TN | W |
| Lenoir-Rhyne University, NC | W |
| Lewis University, IL | W |
| Liberty University, VA | W |
| Lincoln Memorial University, TN | W |
| Lincoln University, MO | W |
| Lincoln University, PA | W |
| Lindenwood University, MO | W |
| Lindsey Wilson College, KY | W |
| Lipscomb University, TN | W |
| Lock Haven University of Pennsylvania, PA | W |
| Long Island University–LIU Brooklyn, NY | W |
| Long Island University–LIU Post, NY | W |
| Longwood University, VA | W |
| Louisiana State University and Agricultural & Mechanical College, LA | W |
| Louisiana Tech University, LA | W |
| Loyola Marymount University, CA | W |
| Loyola University Chicago, IL | W |
| Lubbock Christian University, TX | W |
| Lynn University, FL | W |
| Lyon College, AR | W |
| Malone University, OH | W |
| Manhattan College, NY | W |
| Mansfield University of Pennsylvania, PA | W |
| Marist College, NY | W |
| Marshall University, WV | W |
| Maryville University of Saint Louis, MO | W |
| Mayville State University, ND | W |
| McKendree University, IL | W |
| Menlo College, CA | W |
| Mercer University, GA | W |

| | |
|---|---|
| Mercy College, NY | W |
| Merrimack College, MA | W |
| Miami University, OH | W |
| Michigan State University, MI | W |
| Middle Tennessee State University, TN | W |
| Midland College, TX | W |
| Midwestern State University, TX | W |
| Millersville University of Pennsylvania, PA | W |
| Milligan College, TN | W |
| Minnesota State University Mankato, MN | W |
| Minnesota State University Moorhead, MN | W |
| Minot State University, ND | W |
| Mississippi State University, MS | W |
| Missouri Baptist University, MO | W |
| Missouri Southern State University, MO | W |
| Missouri State University, MO | W |
| Missouri University of Science and Technology, MO | W |
| Missouri Valley College, MO | W |
| Missouri Western State University, MO | W |
| Molloy College, NY | W |
| Monmouth University, NJ | W |
| Montreat College, NC | W |
| Morehead State University, KY | W |
| Morningside College, IA | W |
| Mount Marty College, SD | W |
| Mount Mercy University, IA | W |
| Mount St. Mary's University, MD | W |
| Murray State University, KY | W |
| Newberry College, SC | W |
| Newman University, KS | W |
| New Mexico Highlands University, NM | W |
| New Mexico State University, NM | W |
| New York Institute of Technology, NY | W |
| Niagara University, NY | W |
| Nicholls State University, LA | W |
| North Carolina Agricultural and Technical State University, NC | W |
| North Carolina Central University, NC | W |
| North Carolina State University, NC | W |
| Northeastern State University, OK | W |
| Northern Illinois University, IL | W |
| Northern Kentucky University, KY | W |
| Northern State University, SD | W |
| Northwest Christian University, OR | W |
| Northwestern Oklahoma State University, OK | W |
| Northwest Missouri State University, MO | W |
| Northwest Nazarene University, ID | W |
| Northwest University, WA | W |
| Nova Southeastern University, FL | W |
| Nyack College, NY | W |
| Oakland University, MI | W |
| The Ohio State University, OH | W |
| Ohio University, OH | W |
| Oklahoma Baptist University, OK | W |
| Oklahoma Christian University, OK | W |
| Oklahoma City University, OK | W |
| Oklahoma State University, OK | W |
| Oklahoma Wesleyan University, OK | W |
| Olivet Nazarene University, IL | W |
| Oregon State University, OR | W |
| Our Lady of the Lake University of San Antonio, TX | W |
| Pace University, NY | W |
| Palm Beach Atlantic University, FL | W |
| Park University, MO | W |
| Penn State Hazleton, PA | W |
| Penn State University Park, PA | W |
| Philadelphia University, PA | W |
| Pittsburg State University, KS | W |
| Post University, CT | W |
| Prairie View A&M University, TX | W |
| Presbyterian College, SC | W |
| Providence College, RI | W |
| Purdue University, IN | W |
| Purdue University Calumet, IN | W |
| Queens College of the City University of New York, NY | W |
| Quincy University, IL | W |
| Quinnipiac University, CT | W |
| Radford University, VA | W |
| Regis University, CO | W |
| Reinhardt University, GA | W |
| Rider University, NJ | W |
| Robert Morris University, PA | W |
| Robert Morris University Illinois, IL | W |
| Rockhurst University, MO | W |
| Rollins College, FL | W |
| Sacred Heart University, CT | W |
| Saginaw Valley State University, MI | W |
| St. Andrews University, NC | W |
| Saint Anselm College, NH | W |
| Saint Augustine's University, NC | W |
| St. Bonaventure University, NY | W |
| St. Edward's University, TX | W |
| Saint Francis University, PA | W |
| St. John's University, NY | W |
| Saint Joseph's College, IN | W |
| Saint Joseph's University, PA | W |
| Saint Leo University, FL | W |
| St. Louis College of Pharmacy, MO | W |
| Saint Louis University, MO | W |
| Saint Martin's University, WA | W |
| St. Thomas Aquinas College, NY | W |
| St. Thomas University, FL | W |
| Samford University, AL | W |
| Sam Houston State University, TX | W |
| San Diego State University, CA | W |
| San Francisco State University, CA | W |
| San Jose State University, CA | W |
| Santa Clara University, CA | W |
| Savannah State University, GA | W |
| Seattle University, WA | W |
| Seton Hill University, PA | W |
| Shawnee State University, OH | M |
| Shepherd University, WV | W |
| Shippensburg University of Pennsylvania, PA | W |
| Siena College, NY | W |
| Simpson University, CA | W |
| Slippery Rock University of Pennsylvania, PA | W |
| South Dakota State University, SD | W |
| Southeastern Louisiana University, LA | W |
| Southeastern Oklahoma State University, OK | W |
| Southeast Missouri State University, MO | W |
| Southern Connecticut State University, CT | W |
| Southern Illinois University Carbondale, IL | W |
| Southern Illinois University Edwardsville, IL | W |
| Southern Oregon University, OR | W |
| Southern Utah University, UT | W |
| Southwest Baptist University, MO | W |
| Southwestern College, KS | W |
| Spring Hill College, AL | W |
| Stanford University, CA | W |
| Stephen F. Austin State University, TX | W |
| Stephens College, MO | W |
| Sterling College, KS | W |
| Stetson University, FL | W |
| Stonehill College, MA | W |
| Stony Brook University, State University of New York, NY | W |
| Syracuse University, NY | W |
| Tabor College, KS | W |
| Tarleton State University, TX | W |
| Taylor University, IN | W |
| Tennessee Wesleyan College, TN | W |
| Texas A&M International University, TX | W |
| Texas A&M University, TX | W |
| Texas A&M University–Corpus Christi, TX | W |
| Texas Southern University, TX | W |
| Texas State University, TX | W |
| Texas Tech University, TX | W |
| Texas Wesleyan University, TX | W |
| Texas Woman's University, TX | W |
| Tiffin University, OH | W |
| Towson University, MD | W |
| Trevecca Nazarene University, TN | W |
| Trinity Christian College, IL | W |
| Troy University, AL | W |
| Truett-McConnell College, GA | W |
| Truman State University, MO | W |
| Tusculum College, TN | W |
| Union College, KY | W |
| Union University, TN | W |
| University at Albany, State University of New York, NY | W |
| University at Buffalo, the State University of New York, NY | W |
| The University of Akron, OH | W |
| The University of Alabama, AL | W |
| The University of Alabama at Birmingham, AL | W |
| The University of Alabama in Huntsville, AL | W |
| The University of Arizona, AZ | W |
| University of Arkansas, AR | W |
| University of Bridgeport, CT | W |
| University of California, Davis, CA | W |
| University of California, Los Angeles, CA | W |
| University of California, Riverside, CA | W |
| University of California, Santa Barbara, CA | W |
| University of Central Arkansas, AR | W |
| University of Central Florida, FL | W |
| University of Central Missouri, MO | W |
| University of Central Oklahoma, OK | W |
| University of Charleston, WV | W |

| | |
|---|---|
| University of Colorado Colorado Springs, CO | W |
| University of Connecticut, CT | W |
| University of Dayton, OH | W |
| University of Delaware, DE | W |
| University of Evansville, IN | W |
| The University of Findlay, OH | W |
| University of Florida, FL | W |
| University of Georgia, GA | W |
| University of Hartford, CT | W |
| University of Hawaii at Manoa, HI | W |
| University of Houston, TX | W |
| University of Illinois at Chicago, IL | W |
| University of Illinois at Springfield, IL | W |
| University of Indianapolis, IN | W |
| The University of Iowa, IA | W |
| University of Jamestown, ND | W |
| The University of Kansas, KS | W |
| University of Louisiana at Lafayette, LA | W |
| University of Louisville, KY | W |
| University of Maine, ME | W |
| University of Maryland, Baltimore County, MD | W |
| University of Maryland, College Park, MD | W |
| University of Massachusetts Amherst, MA | W |
| University of Massachusetts Lowell, MA | W |
| University of Michigan, MI | W |
| University of Michigan–Dearborn, MI | W |
| University of Minnesota, Crookston, MN | W |
| University of Minnesota, Duluth, MN | W |
| University of Minnesota, Twin Cities Campus, MN | W |
| University of Mississippi, MS | W |
| University of Missouri, MO | W |
| University of Missouri–Kansas City, MO | W |
| University of Missouri–St. Louis, MO | W |
| University of Mobile, AL | W |
| The University of Montana, MT | W |
| University of Nebraska at Kearney, NE | W |
| University of Nebraska–Lincoln, NE | W |
| University of Nevada, Las Vegas, NV | W |
| University of Nevada, Reno, NV | W |
| University of New Haven, CT | W |
| University of North Alabama, AL | W |
| The University of North Carolina at Chapel Hill, NC | W |
| The University of North Carolina at Charlotte, NC | W |
| The University of North Carolina at Greensboro, NC | W |
| The University of North Carolina at Pembroke, NC | W |
| The University of North Carolina Wilmington, NC | W |
| University of Northern Colorado, CO | W |
| University of Northern Iowa, IA | W |
| University of North Florida, FL | W |
| University of North Georgia, GA | W |
| University of North Texas, TX | W |
| University of Notre Dame, IN | W |
| University of Oklahoma, OK | W |
| University of Oregon, OR | W |
| University of Pikeville, KY | W |
| University of Pittsburgh, PA | W |
| University of Rhode Island, RI | W |
| University of Rio Grande, OH | W |
| University of St. Francis, IL | W |
| University of San Diego, CA | W |
| University of Science and Arts of Oklahoma, OK | W |
| University of South Alabama, AL | W |
| University of South Carolina, SC | W |
| University of South Carolina Aiken, SC | W |
| University of South Carolina Upstate, SC | W |
| The University of South Dakota, SD | W |
| University of Southern Indiana, IN | W |
| University of Southern Mississippi, MS | W |
| University of South Florida, FL | W |
| The University of Tampa, FL | W |
| The University of Tennessee, TN | W |
| The University of Tennessee at Chattanooga, TN | W |
| The University of Tennessee at Martin, TN | W |
| The University of Texas at Arlington, TX | W |
| The University of Texas at Austin, TX | W |
| The University of Texas at San Antonio, TX | W |
| University of the Cumberlands, KY | W |
| University of the Incarnate Word, TX | W |
| University of the Pacific, CA | W |
| University of the Sciences, PA | W |
| The University of Toledo, OH | W |
| The University of Tulsa, OK | W |
| University of Utah, UT | W |
| University of Virginia, VA | W |
| The University of Virginia's College at Wise, VA | W |
| University of Washington, WA | W |
| The University of West Alabama, AL | W |
| University of West Florida, FL | W |
| University of West Georgia, GA | W |
| University of Wisconsin–Green Bay, WI | W |
| University of Wisconsin–Madison, WI | W |
| University of Wisconsin–Parkside, WI | W |
| Upper Iowa University, IA | W |
| Ursuline College, OH | W |
| Utah State University, UT | W |
| Utah Valley University, UT | W |
| Valdosta State University, GA | W |
| Valley City State University, ND | W |
| Valparaiso University, IN | W |
| Vanguard University of Southern California, CA | W |
| Villanova University, PA | W |
| Virginia State University, VA | W |
| Virginia Union University, VA | W |
| Wagner College, NY | W |
| Waldorf College, IA | W |
| Washburn University, KS | W |
| Wayne State College, NE | W |
| Wayne State University, MI | W |
| Webber International University, FL | W |
| Weber State University, UT | W |
| West Chester University of Pennsylvania, PA | W |
| Western Carolina University, NC | W |
| Western Illinois University, IL | W |
| Western Kentucky University, KY | W |
| Western Michigan University, MI | W |
| Western Oregon University, OR | W |
| Western Washington University, WA | W |
| West Texas A&M University, TX | W |
| West Virginia University Institute of Technology, WV | W |
| West Virginia Wesleyan College, WV | W |
| Wheeling Jesuit University, WV | W |
| Wichita State University, KS | W |
| William Jessup University, CA | W |
| William Jewell College, MO | W |
| Williams Baptist College, AR | W |
| William Woods University, MO | W |
| Wingate University, NC | W |
| Winona State University, MN | W |
| Winthrop University, SC | W |
| Wright State University, OH | W |
| Youngstown State University, OH | W |

**Squash**

| | |
|---|---|
| Drexel University, PA | M,W |
| Fordham University, NY | M |
| University of Great Falls, MT | W |
| University of Rochester, NY | M |

**Swimming and diving**

| | |
|---|---|
| Adams State University, CO | M,W |
| Adelphi University, NY | M,W |
| Arizona State University at the Downtown Phoenix campus, AZ | M,W |
| Arizona State University at the Polytechnic campus, AZ | M,W |
| Arizona State University at the Tempe campus, AZ | M,W |
| Arizona State University at the West campus, AZ | M,W |
| Ashland University, OH | M,W |
| Auburn University, AL | M,W |
| Azusa Pacific University, CA | W |
| Ball State University, IN | M,W |
| Bellarmine University, KY | M,W |
| Binghamton University, State University of New York, NY | M,W |
| Biola University, CA | M,W |
| Bloomsburg University of Pennsylvania, PA | M,W |
| Boston College, MA | M,W |
| Boston University, MA | M,W |
| Bowling Green State University, OH | W |
| Brenau University, GA | W |
| Brigham Young University, UT | M,W |
| Bryant University, RI | M,W |
| Bucknell University, PA | M,W |
| California Baptist University, CA | M,W |
| California Polytechnic State University, San Luis Obispo, CA | M,W |
| California State University, Bakersfield, CA | M,W |
| California State University, Fresno, CA | W |
| Campbellsville University, KY | M,W |
| Canisius College, NY | M,W |
| Carson-Newman University, TN | M,W |
| Catawba College, NC | M,W |
| Central Connecticut State University, CT | W |

| | |
|---|---|
| Clarion University of Pennsylvania, PA | M,W |
| Cleveland State University, OH | M,W |
| College of Charleston, SC | M,W |
| The College of Idaho, ID | M,W |
| College of Saint Mary, NE | W |
| The College of Saint Rose, NY | M,W |
| College of the Holy Cross, MA | W |
| Colorado Mesa University, CO | M,W |
| Colorado State University, CO | W |
| Concordia University, CA | M,W |
| Davidson College, NC | M,W |
| Delta State University, MS | M,W |
| Drexel University, PA | M,W |
| Drury University, MO | M,W |
| Duquesne University, PA | W |
| East Carolina University, NC | M,W |
| Eastern Illinois University, IL | M,W |
| Eastern Michigan University, MI | M,W |
| East Stroudsburg University of Pennsylvania, PA | M,W |
| Emmanuel College, GA | M,W |
| Fairfield University, CT | M,W |
| Fairmont State University, WV | M,W |
| Florida Agricultural and Mechanical University, FL | M,W |
| Florida Gulf Coast University, FL | W |
| Florida Institute of Technology, FL | M,W |
| Florida Southern College, FL | M,W |
| Florida State University, FL | M,W |
| Fordham University, NY | M,W |
| Gannon University, PA | M,W |
| George Mason University, VA | M,W |
| Georgetown University, DC | W |
| The George Washington University, DC | M,W |
| Georgia Institute of Technology, GA | M,W |
| Georgia Southern University, GA | W |
| Grand Valley State University, MI | M,W |
| Hillsdale College, MI | W |
| Howard University, DC | M,W |
| Illinois Institute of Technology, IL | M,W |
| Illinois State University, IL | W |
| Indiana University Bloomington, IN | M,W |
| Indiana University of Pennsylvania, PA | M,W |
| Indiana University–Purdue University Indianapolis, IN | M,W |
| Indian River State College, FL | M,W |
| Inter American University of Puerto Rico, Bayamón Campus, PR | M,W |
| Iona College, NY | M,W |
| Iowa State University of Science and Technology, IA | M,W |
| James Madison University, VA | M,W |
| King University, TN | M,W |
| Kutztown University of Pennsylvania, PA | W |
| Lake Erie College, OH | M,W |
| La Salle University, PA | M,W |
| Lehigh University, PA | M,W |
| Le Moyne College, NY | M,W |
| Lenoir-Rhyne University, NC | M,W |
| Lewis University, IL | M,W |
| Liberty University, VA | W |
| Life University, GA | W |
| Lindenwood University, MO | M,W |
| Lindsey Wilson College, KY | M,W |
| Lock Haven University of Pennsylvania, PA | W |

| | |
|---|---|
| Long Island University–LIU Brooklyn, NY | W |
| Long Island University–LIU Post, NY | W |
| Louisiana State University and Agricultural & Mechanical College, LA | M,W |
| Loyola Marymount University, CA | W |
| Lynn University, FL | W |
| Malone University, OH | M,W |
| Manhattan College, NY | M,W |
| Marist College, NY | M,W |
| Marshall University, WV | W |
| Maryville University of Saint Louis, MO | W |
| Merrimack College, MA | W |
| Miami University, OH | M,W |
| Michigan State University, MI | M,W |
| Millersville University of Pennsylvania, PA | W |
| Milligan College, TN | M,W |
| Minnesota State University Mankato, MN | W |
| Minnesota State University Moorhead, MN | W |
| Missouri State University, MO | M,W |
| Missouri University of Science and Technology, MO | M |
| Morningside College, IA | M,W |
| Mount St. Mary's University, MD | W |
| New Jersey Institute of Technology, NJ | M,W |
| New Mexico State University, NM | W |
| Niagara University, NY | M,W |
| North Carolina Agricultural and Technical State University, NC | W |
| North Carolina State University, NC | M,W |
| Northeastern University, MA | W |
| Northern Arizona University, AZ | W |
| Northern Illinois University, IL | M,W |
| Northern Michigan University, MI | M,W |
| Northern State University, SD | W |
| Nova Southeastern University, FL | M,W |
| Oakland University, MI | M,W |
| The Ohio State University, OH | M,W |
| Ohio University, OH | W |
| Old Dominion University, VA | M,W |
| Oregon State University, OR | W |
| Pace University, NY | M,W |
| Penn State University Park, PA | M,W |
| Pepperdine University, CA | W |
| Purdue University, IN | M,W |
| Queens College of the City University of New York, NY | M,W |
| Rice University, TX | W |
| Rider University, NJ | M,W |
| Sacred Heart University, CT | W |
| Saginaw Valley State University, MI | M,W |
| St. Bonaventure University, NY | M,W |
| St. Francis College, NY | M,W |
| Saint Francis University, PA | M,W |
| Saint Leo University, FL | M,W |
| Saint Louis University, MO | M,W |
| San Diego State University, CA | W |
| San Jose State University, CA | W |
| Savannah College of Art and Design, GA | M,W |
| Seattle University, WA | M,W |
| Shippensburg University of Pennsylvania, PA | M,W |

| | |
|---|---|
| Siena College, NY | W |
| Soka University of America, CA | M,W |
| South Dakota State University, SD | M,W |
| Southern Connecticut State University, CT | M,W |
| Southern Illinois University Carbondale, IL | M,W |
| Southern Methodist University, TX | M,W |
| Stanford University, CA | M,W |
| Stony Brook University, State University of New York, NY | W |
| Tabor College, KS | M,W |
| Texas A&M University, TX | M,W |
| Texas Christian University, TX | M,W |
| Tiffin University, OH | M,W |
| Towson University, MD | M,W |
| Truman State University, MO | W |
| Tulane University, LA | W |
| Union College, KY | M,W |
| University at Buffalo, the State University of New York, NY | M,W |
| The University of Akron, OH | W |
| The University of Alabama, AL | M,W |
| University of Alaska Fairbanks, AK | W |
| The University of Arizona, AZ | M,W |
| University of Arkansas, AR | W |
| University of Bridgeport, CT | M,W |
| University of California, Davis, CA | W |
| University of California, Los Angeles, CA | W |
| University of California, Santa Barbara, CA | M,W |
| University of Charleston, WV | M,W |
| University of Cincinnati, OH | M,W |
| University of Connecticut, CT | M,W |
| University of Delaware, DE | W |
| University of Denver, CO | M,W |
| University of Evansville, IN | M,W |
| The University of Findlay, OH | M,W |
| University of Florida, FL | M,W |
| University of Georgia, GA | M,W |
| University of Hawaii at Manoa, HI | M,W |
| University of Houston, TX | W |
| University of Idaho, ID | W |
| University of Illinois at Chicago, IL | M,W |
| University of Indianapolis, IN | M,W |
| The University of Iowa, IA | M,W |
| The University of Kansas, KS | W |
| University of Louisville, KY | M,W |
| University of Maine, ME | W |
| University of Maryland, Baltimore County, MD | M,W |
| University of Massachusetts Amherst, MA | M,W |
| University of Miami, FL | M,W |
| University of Michigan, MI | M,W |
| University of Minnesota, Twin Cities Campus, MN | M,W |
| University of Missouri, MO | M,W |
| University of Missouri–St. Louis, MO | M,W |
| University of Nebraska at Kearney, NE | W |
| University of Nebraska–Lincoln, NE | W |
| University of Nevada, Las Vegas, NV | M,W |
| University of Nevada, Reno, NV | W |
| University of New Hampshire, NH | W |
| University of North Carolina at Asheville, NC | W |

| | |
|---|---|
| The University of North Carolina at Chapel Hill, NC | M,W |
| The University of North Carolina Wilmington, NC | M,W |
| University of Northern Colorado, CO | W |
| University of Northern Iowa, IA | W |
| University of North Florida, FL | W |
| University of North Texas, TX | W |
| University of Notre Dame, IN | M,W |
| University of Pittsburgh, PA | M,W |
| University of Rhode Island, RI | W |
| University of Richmond, VA | W |
| University of San Diego, CA | W |
| University of South Carolina, SC | M,W |
| The University of South Dakota, SD | M,W |
| University of Southern California, CA | M,W |
| The University of Tampa, FL | M,W |
| The University of Tennessee, TN | M,W |
| The University of Texas at Austin, TX | M,W |
| University of the Cumberlands, KY | M,W |
| University of the Incarnate Word, TX | M,W |
| University of the Pacific, CA | M,W |
| The University of Toledo, OH | W |
| University of Utah, UT | M,W |
| University of Vermont, VT | W |
| University of Virginia, VA | M,W |
| University of West Florida, FL | W |
| University of Wisconsin–Green Bay, WI | M,W |
| University of Wisconsin–Madison, WI | M,W |
| University of Wisconsin–Milwaukee, WI | M,W |
| University of Wyoming, WY | M,W |
| Ursuline College, OH | W |
| Valparaiso University, IN | M,W |
| Vanderbilt University, TN | W |
| Villanova University, PA | W |
| Virginia Military Institute, VA | M |
| Virginia Polytechnic Institute and State University, VA | M,W |
| Wagner College, NY | W |
| Washington State University, WA | W |
| Wayne State University, MI | M,W |
| West Chester University of Pennsylvania, PA | M,W |
| Western Illinois University, IL | M,W |
| Western Kentucky University, KY | M,W |
| Western State Colorado University, CO | W |
| West Virginia University, WV | M,W |
| West Virginia University Institute of Technology, WV | M,W |
| West Virginia Wesleyan College, WV | M,W |
| Wheeling Jesuit University, WV | M,W |
| William Jewell College, MO | M,W |
| Wingate University, NC | M,W |
| Wright State University, OH | M,W |
| Xavier University, OH | M,W |
| Youngstown State University, OH | W |

**Table tennis**

| | |
|---|---|
| Inter American University of Puerto Rico, Bayamón Campus, PR | M,W |
| Lindenwood University, MO | M,W |
| Texas Wesleyan University, TX | M,W |

**Tennis**

| | |
|---|---|
| Abilene Christian University, TX | M,W |
| Academy of Art University, CA | W |
| Adelphi University, NY | M,W |
| Alabama State University, AL | M,W |
| Albany State University, GA | W |
| Alcorn State University, MS | M,W |
| Anderson University, SC | M,W |
| Appalachian State University, NC | M,W |
| Arizona Christian University, AZ | M,W |
| Arizona State University at the Downtown Phoenix campus, AZ | W |
| Arizona State University at the Polytechnic campus, AZ | W |
| Arizona State University at the Tempe campus, AZ | W |
| Arizona State University at the West campus, AZ | W |
| Arkansas State University, AR | W |
| Arkansas Tech University, AR | W |
| Armstrong State University, GA | M,W |
| Ashland University, OH | W |
| Auburn University, AL | M,W |
| Auburn University at Montgomery, AL | M,W |
| Augustana College, SD | M,W |
| Austin Peay State University, TN | M,W |
| Azusa Pacific University, CA | M,W |
| Ball State University, IN | M,W |
| Barry University, FL | M,W |
| Baylor University, TX | M,W |
| Belhaven University, MS | M,W |
| Bellarmine University, KY | M,W |
| Belmont Abbey College, NC | M,W |
| Belmont University, TN | M,W |
| Bemidji State University, MN | W |
| Bethel College, KS | M,W |
| Bethune-Cookman University, FL | M,W |
| Binghamton University, State University of New York, NY | M,W |
| Biola University, CA | M,W |
| Bloomfield College, NJ | M |
| Bloomsburg University of Pennsylvania, PA | M,W |
| Bluefield College, VA | M,W |
| Bluefield State College, WV | M,W |
| Boston College, MA | M,W |
| Boston University, MA | W |
| Bowie State University, MD | W |
| Bowling Green State University, OH | W |
| Bradley University, IL | W |
| Brenau University, GA | W |
| Brevard College, NC | M,W |
| Brigham Young University, UT | M,W |
| Bryant University, RI | M,W |
| Butler University, IN | M,W |
| Caldwell University, NJ | M,W |
| California Polytechnic State University, San Luis Obispo, CA | M,W |
| California State University, Bakersfield, CA | W |
| California State University, Fresno, CA | M,W |
| California State University, Fullerton, CA | W |
| California State University, Long Beach, CA | W |
| California State University, Los Angeles, CA | W |
| California State University, Sacramento, CA | M,W |
| California State University, Stanislaus, CA | W |
| Calumet College of Saint Joseph, IN | M,W |
| Cameron University, OK | M,W |
| Campbellsville University, KY | M,W |
| Cardinal Stritch University, WI | M,W |
| Carson-Newman University, TN | M,W |
| Catawba College, NC | M,W |
| Cedarville University, OH | M,W |
| Chaminade University of Honolulu, HI | W |
| Chestnut Hill College, PA | M,W |
| Chowan University, NC | M,W |
| Christian Brothers University, TN | M,W |
| The Citadel, The Military College of South Carolina, SC | M |
| Clarion University of Pennsylvania, PA | W |
| Clayton State University, GA | W |
| Cleveland State University, OH | W |
| Coastal Carolina University, SC | M,W |
| Coker College, SC | M,W |
| College of Charleston, SC | M,W |
| The College of Idaho, ID | W |
| College of Saint Mary, NE | W |
| The College of William and Mary, VA | M,W |
| Colorado Mesa University, CO | M,W |
| Colorado State University, CO | W |
| Colorado State University–Pueblo, CO | M,W |
| Columbus State University, GA | M,W |
| Concordia University, CA | M,W |
| Concordia University, Nebraska, NE | M,W |
| Concord University, WV | M,W |
| Creighton University, NE | M,W |
| Cumberland University, TN | M,W |
| Dallas Baptist University, TX | W |
| Davidson College, NC | M,W |
| Delaware State University, DE | W |
| Delta State University, MS | M,W |
| DePaul University, IL | M,W |
| Dixie State University, UT | W |
| Dowling College, NY | M,W |
| Drake University, IA | M,W |
| Drexel University, PA | M,W |
| Drury University, MO | M,W |
| Duquesne University, PA | M,W |
| East Carolina University, NC | M,W |
| East Central University, OK | M,W |
| Eastern Illinois University, IL | M,W |
| Eastern Kentucky University, KY | M,W |
| Eastern Michigan University, MI | W |
| East Stroudsburg University of Pennsylvania, PA | W |
| Eckerd College, FL | M,W |
| Elon University, NC | M,W |
| Embry-Riddle Aeronautical University–Daytona, FL | M,W |
| Emmanuel College, GA | M,W |
| Emporia State University, KS | M,W |
| Evangel University, MO | M,W |
| Fairfield University, CT | M,W |
| Fairmont State University, WV | M,W |
| Fayetteville State University, NC | W |
| Ferris State University, MI | M,W |
| Flagler College, FL | M,W |
| Florida Agricultural and Mechanical University, FL | M,W |
| Florida Gulf Coast University, FL | M,W |
| Florida Institute of Technology, FL | M,W |
| Florida Southern College, FL | M,W |
| Florida State University, FL | M,W |
| Fordham University, NY | M,W |
| Fort Hays State University, KS | M,W |

| | |
|---|---|
| Fort Valley State University, GA | M,W |
| Francis Marion University, SC | M,W |
| Franklin Pierce University, NH | M,W |
| Friends University, KS | M,W |
| Furman University, SC | M,W |
| George Mason University, VA | M,W |
| Georgetown College, KY | M,W |
| Georgetown University, DC | W |
| The George Washington University, DC | M,W |
| Georgia College & State University, GA | M,W |
| Georgia Institute of Technology, GA | M,W |
| Georgian Court University, NJ | W |
| Georgia Regents University, GA | M,W |
| Georgia Southern University, GA | M,W |
| Georgia Southwestern State University, GA | M,W |
| Georgia State University, GA | M,W |
| Gonzaga University, WA | M,W |
| Goshen College, IN | M,W |
| Graceland University, IA | M,W |
| Grambling State University, LA | W |
| Grand Valley State University, MI | M,W |
| Grand View University, IA | M,W |
| Hampton University, VA | M,W |
| Harding University, AR | M,W |
| Hastings College, NE | M,W |
| Hawai`i Pacific University, HI | M,W |
| Hillsdale College, MI | W |
| Hofstra University, NY | M,W |
| Holy Family University, PA | W |
| Hope International University, CA | M,W |
| Howard University, DC | M,W |
| Idaho State University, ID | M,W |
| Illinois State University, IL | M,W |
| Indiana University Bloomington, IN | M,W |
| Indiana University of Pennsylvania, PA | W |
| Indiana University–Purdue University Fort Wayne, IN | M,W |
| Indiana University–Purdue University Indianapolis, IN | M,W |
| Iowa State University of Science and Technology, IA | W |
| Jackson State University, MS | M,W |
| Jacksonville State University, AL | M,W |
| James Madison University, VA | M,W |
| John Brown University, AR | M,W |
| Johnson C. Smith University, NC | M,W |
| Kansas State University, KS | W |
| Kansas Wesleyan University, KS | M,W |
| Kennesaw State University, GA | M,W |
| Kentucky Wesleyan College, KY | W |
| King University, TN | M,W |
| Kutztown University of Pennsylvania, PA | M,W |
| Lamar University, TX | M,W |
| La Salle University, PA | M,W |
| Lees-McRae College, NC | M,W |
| Lee University, TN | M,W |
| Lehigh University, PA | M,W |
| Le Moyne College, NY | M,W |
| LeMoyne-Owen College, TN | M,W |
| Lenoir-Rhyne University, NC | M,W |
| Lewis-Clark State College, ID | M,W |
| Lewis University, IL | M,W |
| Liberty University, VA | M,W |
| Lincoln Memorial University, TN | M,W |
| Lincoln University, MO | W |
| Lindenwood University, MO | M,W |
| Lindsey Wilson College, KY | M,W |

| | |
|---|---|
| Lipscomb University, TN | M,W |
| Long Island University–LIU Brooklyn, NY | W |
| Long Island University–LIU Post, NY | W |
| Longwood University, VA | M,W |
| Louisiana State University and Agricultural & Mechanical College, LA | M,W |
| Louisiana Tech University, LA | W |
| Loyola Marymount University, CA | M,W |
| Lynn University, FL | M,W |
| Manhattan College, NY | W |
| Marist College, NY | M,W |
| Marquette University, WI | M,W |
| Marshall University, WV | W |
| Maryville University of Saint Louis, MO | W |
| McKendree University, IL | M,W |
| Mercer University, GA | M,W |
| Merrimack College, MA | M,W |
| Miami University, OH | W |
| Michigan State University, MI | M,W |
| Michigan Technological University, MI | M,W |
| Middle Tennessee State University, TN | M,W |
| Midwestern State University, TX | M,W |
| Millersville University of Pennsylvania, PA | M,W |
| Milligan College, TN | M,W |
| Minnesota State University Mankato, MN | M,W |
| Minnesota State University Moorhead, MN | W |
| Mississippi State University, MS | M,W |
| Missouri Baptist University, MO | M,W |
| Missouri Southern State University, MO | W |
| Missouri Valley College, MO | M,W |
| Missouri Western State University, MO | W |
| Molloy College, NY | W |
| Monmouth University, NJ | M,W |
| Montana State University, MT | M,W |
| Montreat College, NC | M,W |
| Morehead State University, KY | M,W |
| Morningside College, IA | M,W |
| Mount Marty College, SD | W |
| Mount St. Mary's University, MD | M,W |
| Murray State University, KY | M,W |
| Newberry College, SC | M,W |
| New Jersey Institute of Technology, NJ | M,W |
| Newman University, KS | M,W |
| New Mexico State University, NM | M,W |
| New York Institute of Technology, NY | M,W |
| Niagara University, NY | M,W |
| Nicholls State University, LA | W |
| North Carolina Agricultural and Technical State University, NC | W |
| North Carolina Central University, NC | M,W |
| North Carolina State University, NC | M,W |
| Northeastern State University, OK | W |
| Northern Arizona University, AZ | M,W |
| Northern Illinois University, IL | M,W |
| Northern Kentucky University, KY | M,W |
| Northwest Missouri State University, MO | M,W |

| | |
|---|---|
| Nova Southeastern University, FL | W |
| Oakland University, MI | W |
| The Ohio State University, OH | M,W |
| Oklahoma Baptist University, OK | M,W |
| Oklahoma State University, OK | M,W |
| Oklahoma Wesleyan University, OK | M,W |
| Old Dominion University, VA | M,W |
| Olivet Nazarene University, IL | M,W |
| Oral Roberts University, OK | M,W |
| Our Lady of the Lake University of San Antonio, TX | M,W |
| Palm Beach Atlantic University, FL | M,W |
| Penn State University Park, PA | M,W |
| Pepperdine University, CA | M,W |
| Philadelphia University, PA | M,W |
| Point Loma Nazarene University, CA | M,W |
| Post University, CT | M,W |
| Prairie View A&M University, TX | M,W |
| Presbyterian College, SC | M,W |
| Purdue University, IN | M,W |
| Purdue University Calumet, IN | M,W |
| Queens College of the City University of New York, NY | M,W |
| Quincy University, IL | M,W |
| Quinnipiac University, CT | M,W |
| Radford University, VA | M,W |
| Reinhardt University, GA | M,W |
| Rice University, TX | M,W |
| Rider University, NJ | M,W |
| Robert Morris University Illinois, IL | W |
| Roberts Wesleyan College, NY | M,W |
| Rockhurst University, MO | M,W |
| Rollins College, FL | M,W |
| Sacred Heart University, CT | M,W |
| Saginaw Valley State University, MI | W |
| St. Andrews University, NC | M,W |
| Saint Anselm College, NH | M,W |
| St. Bonaventure University, NY | M,W |
| St. Edward's University, TX | M,W |
| St. Francis College, NY | M,W |
| Saint Francis University, PA | M,W |
| St. John's University, NY | M,W |
| Saint Joseph's College, IN | M,W |
| Saint Joseph's University, PA | M,W |
| Saint Leo University, FL | M,W |
| St. Louis College of Pharmacy, MO | M,W |
| Saint Louis University, MO | M,W |
| St. Thomas University, FL | M,W |
| Samford University, AL | M,W |
| Sam Houston State University, TX | W |
| San Diego State University, CA | M,W |
| San Jose State University, CA | W |
| Santa Clara University, CA | M,W |
| Savannah College of Art and Design, GA | M,W |
| Savannah State University, GA | W |
| Seton Hill University, PA | M,W |
| Shawnee State University, OH | M,W |
| Shepherd University, WV | M,W |
| Shippensburg University of Pennsylvania, PA | M,W |
| Siena College, NY | M,W |
| Slippery Rock University of Pennsylvania, PA | W |
| South Dakota State University, SD | M,W |
| Southeastern Louisiana University, LA | W |
| Southeastern Oklahoma State University, OK | M,W |

| School | |
|---|---|
| Southeast Missouri State University, MO | W |
| Southern Illinois University Carbondale, IL | M,W |
| Southern Illinois University Edwardsville, IL | M,W |
| Southern Methodist University, TX | M,W |
| Southern Utah University, UT | M,W |
| Southwest Baptist University, MO | M,W |
| Southwestern College, KS | M,W |
| Spring Hill College, AL | M,W |
| Stanford University, CA | M,W |
| Stephen F. Austin State University, TX | W |
| Stephens College, MO | W |
| Stetson University, FL | M,W |
| Stonehill College, MA | M,W |
| Stony Brook University, State University of New York, NY | M,W |
| Syracuse University, NY | W |
| Tabor College, KS | M,W |
| Tarleton State University, TX | W |
| Taylor University, IN | M,W |
| Temple University, PA | M,W |
| Tennessee State University, TN | M,W |
| Tennessee Wesleyan College, TN | M,W |
| Texas A&M University, TX | M,W |
| Texas A&M University–Corpus Christi, TX | M,W |
| Texas Christian University, TX | M,W |
| Texas Southern University, TX | M,W |
| Texas State University, TX | W |
| Texas Tech University, TX | M,W |
| Tiffin University, OH | M,W |
| Towson University, MD | W |
| Troy University, AL | M,W |
| Truman State University, MO | M,W |
| Tulane University, LA | M,W |
| Tusculum College, TN | M,W |
| Union College, KY | M,W |
| University at Albany, State University of New York, NY | W |
| University at Buffalo, the State University of New York, NY | M,W |
| The University of Akron, OH | W |
| The University of Alabama, AL | M,W |
| The University of Alabama at Birmingham, AL | M,W |
| The University of Alabama in Huntsville, AL | M,W |
| The University of Arizona, AZ | M,W |
| University of Arkansas, AR | M,W |
| University of California, Davis, CA | M,W |
| University of California, Irvine, CA | M,W |
| University of California, Los Angeles, CA | M,W |
| University of California, Santa Barbara, CA | M,W |
| University of Central Arkansas, AR | W |
| University of Central Florida, FL | M,W |
| University of Central Oklahoma, OK | W |
| University of Charleston, WV | M,W |
| University of Cincinnati, OH | W |
| University of Colorado Boulder, CO | W |
| University of Connecticut, CT | M,W |
| University of Dayton, OH | M,W |
| University of Delaware, DE | M,W |
| University of Denver, CO | M,W |
| University of Evansville, IN | W |
| The University of Findlay, OH | M,W |
| University of Florida, FL | M,W |

| School | |
|---|---|
| University of Georgia, GA | M,W |
| University of Hartford, CT | M,W |
| University of Hawaii at Manoa, HI | M,W |
| University of Houston, TX | W |
| University of Idaho, ID | M,W |
| University of Illinois at Chicago, IL | M,W |
| University of Illinois at Springfield, IL | M,W |
| University of Indianapolis, IN | M,W |
| The University of Iowa, IA | M,W |
| The University of Kansas, KS | W |
| University of Louisiana at Lafayette, LA | M,W |
| University of Louisville, KY | M,W |
| University of Maryland, Baltimore County, MD | M,W |
| University of Massachusetts Amherst, MA | W |
| University of Memphis, TN | M,W |
| University of Miami, FL | M,W |
| University of Michigan, MI | M,W |
| University of Minnesota, Crookston, MN | W |
| University of Minnesota, Duluth, MN | W |
| University of Minnesota, Twin Cities Campus, MN | M,W |
| University of Mississippi, MS | M,W |
| University of Missouri, MO | W |
| University of Missouri–Kansas City, MO | M,W |
| University of Missouri–St. Louis, MO | M,W |
| University of Mobile, AL | M,W |
| The University of Montana, MT | M,W |
| University of Montevallo, AL | W |
| University of Nebraska at Kearney, NE | M,W |
| University of Nebraska–Lincoln, NE | M,W |
| University of Nevada, Las Vegas, NV | M,W |
| University of Nevada, Reno, NV | M,W |
| University of New Haven, CT | W |
| University of New Orleans, LA | M,W |
| University of North Alabama, AL | M,W |
| University of North Carolina at Asheville, NC | M,W |
| The University of North Carolina at Chapel Hill, NC | M,W |
| The University of North Carolina at Charlotte, NC | M,W |
| The University of North Carolina at Greensboro, NC | M,W |
| The University of North Carolina at Pembroke, NC | W |
| The University of North Carolina Wilmington, NC | M,W |
| University of Northern Colorado, CO | M,W |
| University of Northern Iowa, IA | W |
| University of North Florida, FL | M,W |
| University of North Georgia, GA | M,W |
| University of Notre Dame, IN | M,W |
| University of Oklahoma, OK | M,W |
| University of Oregon, OR | M,W |
| University of Pikeville, KY | M,W |
| University of Pittsburgh, PA | M,W |
| University of Portland, OR | M,W |
| University of Rhode Island, RI | W |
| University of Richmond, VA | M,W |
| University of St. Francis, IL | M,W |

| School | |
|---|---|
| University of San Diego, CA | M,W |
| University of San Francisco, CA | M,W |
| University of South Alabama, AL | M,W |
| University of South Carolina, SC | M,W |
| University of South Carolina Aiken, SC | M,W |
| University of South Carolina Upstate, SC | M,W |
| The University of South Dakota, SD | W |
| University of Southern California, CA | M,W |
| University of Southern Indiana, IN | M,W |
| University of Southern Mississippi, MS | M,W |
| University of South Florida, FL | M,W |
| The University of Tampa, FL | W |
| The University of Tennessee, TN | M,W |
| The University of Tennessee at Chattanooga, TN | M,W |
| The University of Tennessee at Martin, TN | W |
| The University of Texas at Arlington, TX | M,W |
| The University of Texas at Austin, TX | M,W |
| The University of Texas at El Paso, TX | W |
| The University of Texas at San Antonio, TX | M,W |
| The University of Texas–Pan American, TX | M,W |
| University of the Cumberlands, KY | M,W |
| University of the District of Columbia, DC | M,W |
| University of the Incarnate Word, TX | M,W |
| University of the Pacific, CA | M,W |
| The University of Toledo, OH | M,W |
| The University of Tulsa, OK | M,W |
| University of Utah, UT | M,W |
| University of Virginia, VA | M,W |
| The University of Virginia's College at Wise, VA | M,W |
| University of Washington, WA | M,W |
| The University of West Alabama, AL | M,W |
| University of West Florida, FL | M,W |
| University of West Georgia, GA | W |
| University of Wisconsin–Green Bay, WI | M,W |
| University of Wisconsin–Madison, WI | M,W |
| University of Wisconsin–Milwaukee, WI | W |
| University of Wyoming, WY | W |
| Upper Iowa University, IA | W |
| Ursuline College, OH | W |
| Utah State University, UT | M,W |
| Valdosta State University, GA | M,W |
| Valparaiso University, IN | M,W |
| Vanderbilt University, TN | M,W |
| Virginia Commonwealth University, VA | M,W |
| Virginia Military Institute, VA | M |
| Virginia Polytechnic Institute and State University, VA | M,W |
| Virginia State University, VA | M,W |
| Virginia Union University, VA | M,W |
| Wagner College, NY | M,W |
| Wake Forest University, NC | M,W |
| Washburn University, KS | M,W |
| Washington State University, WA | W |
| Wayne State University, MI | M,W |

| | |
|---|---|
| Webber International University, FL | M,W |
| Weber State University, UT | M,W |
| West Chester University of Pennsylvania, PA | M,W |
| Western Carolina University, NC | W |
| Western Illinois University, IL | M,W |
| Western Kentucky University, KY | M,W |
| Western Michigan University, MI | M,W |
| West Virginia University, WV | W |
| West Virginia Wesleyan College, WV | M,W |
| Wichita State University, KS | M,W |
| William Jewell College, MO | M,W |
| William Woods University, MO | M,W |
| Wingate University, NC | M,W |
| Winona State University, MN | W |
| Winthrop University, SC | M,W |
| Wofford College, SC | M,W |
| Wright State University, OH | M,W |
| Xavier University, OH | M,W |
| Xavier University of Louisiana, LA | M,W |
| Youngstown State University, OH | M,W |

## Track and field

| | |
|---|---|
| Abilene Christian University, TX | M,W |
| Academy of Art University, CA | M,W |
| Adams State University, CO | M,W |
| Adelphi University, NY | M,W |
| Alabama State University, AL | M,W |
| Albany State University, GA | M,W |
| Alcorn State University, MS | M,W |
| American University, DC | M,W |
| Anderson University, SC | M,W |
| Angelo State University, TX | M,W |
| Appalachian State University, NC | M,W |
| Arizona Christian University, AZ | M,W |
| Arizona State University at the Downtown Phoenix campus, AZ | M,W |
| Arizona State University at the Polytechnic campus, AZ | M,W |
| Arizona State University at the Tempe campus, AZ | M,W |
| Arizona State University at the West campus, AZ | M,W |
| Arkansas State University, AR | M,W |
| Ashland University, OH | M,W |
| Auburn University, AL | M,W |
| Augustana College, SD | M,W |
| Austin Peay State University, TN | W |
| Azusa Pacific University, CA | M,W |
| Ball State University, IN | W |
| Baylor University, TX | M,W |
| Bellarmine University, KY | M,W |
| Belmont Abbey College, NC | M,W |
| Belmont University, TN | M,W |
| Bemidji State University, MN | W |
| Bethel College, KS | M,W |
| Bethune-Cookman University, FL | M,W |
| Binghamton University, State University of New York, NY | M,W |
| Biola University, CA | M,W |
| Bloomsburg University of Pennsylvania, PA | M,W |
| Bluefield College, VA | M,W |
| Boston College, MA | M,W |
| Boston University, MA | M,W |
| Bowie State University, MD | M,W |
| Bowling Green State University, OH | W |
| Bradley University, IL | M,W |
| Brenau University, GA | W |
| Brevard College, NC | M,W |
| Brigham Young University, UT | M,W |
| Bryant University, RI | M,W |

| | |
|---|---|
| Butler University, IN | M,W |
| Caldwell University, NJ | M,W |
| California Baptist University, CA | M,W |
| California Polytechnic State University, San Luis Obispo, CA | M,W |
| California State Polytechnic University, Pomona, CA | M,W |
| California State University, Bakersfield, CA | M,W |
| California State University, Chico, CA | M,W |
| California State University, Dominguez Hills, CA | W |
| California State University, Fresno, CA | M,W |
| California State University, Fullerton, CA | M,W |
| California State University, Long Beach, CA | M,W |
| California State University, Los Angeles, CA | M,W |
| California State University, Sacramento, CA | M,W |
| California State University, Stanislaus, CA | M,W |
| Calumet College of Saint Joseph, IN | M,W |
| Campbellsville University, KY | M,W |
| Cardinal Stritch University, WI | M,W |
| Carroll College, MT | M,W |
| Carson-Newman University, TN | M,W |
| Cedarville University, OH | M,W |
| Central Connecticut State University, CT | M,W |
| Central Methodist University, MO | M,W |
| Central Michigan University, MI | M,W |
| Central Washington University, WA | M,W |
| Christian Brothers University, TN | M,W |
| The Citadel, The Military College of South Carolina, SC | M,W |
| Clarion University of Pennsylvania, PA | W |
| Clarke University, IA | M,W |
| Clayton State University, GA | M,W |
| Cleveland State University, OH | W |
| Coastal Carolina University, SC | M,W |
| Coker College, SC | M,W |
| The College of Idaho, ID | M,W |
| The College of Saint Rose, NY | M,W |
| College of the Holy Cross, MA | W |
| The College of William and Mary, VA | M,W |
| Colorado Mesa University, CO | M,W |
| Colorado School of Mines, CO | M,W |
| Colorado State University, CO | M,W |
| Colorado State University–Pueblo, CO | W |
| Concordia University, CA | M,W |
| Concordia University, Nebraska, NE | M,W |
| Concordia University, St. Paul, MN | M,W |
| Concord University, WV | M,W |
| Corban University, OR | M,W |
| Cornerstone University, MI | M,W |
| Culver-Stockton College, MO | M,W |
| Dakota State University, SD | M,W |
| Dallas Baptist University, TX | W |
| Davidson College, NC | M,W |
| Delaware State University, DE | M,W |
| DePaul University, IL | M,W |
| Dickinson State University, ND | M,W |
| Doane College, NE | M,W |
| Dominican College, NY | M,W |
| Drake University, IA | M,W |

| | |
|---|---|
| Drury University, MO | M,W |
| Duquesne University, PA | M,W |
| East Carolina University, NC | M,W |
| Eastern Illinois University, IL | M,W |
| Eastern Kentucky University, KY | M,W |
| Eastern Michigan University, MI | M,W |
| Eastern New Mexico University, NM | M,W |
| East Stroudsburg University of Pennsylvania, PA | M,W |
| Elon University, NC | W |
| Embry-Riddle Aeronautical University–Daytona, FL | M,W |
| Emmanuel College, GA | M,W |
| Emporia State University, KS | M,W |
| Evangel University, MO | M,W |
| The Evergreen State College, WA | M,W |
| Fayetteville State University, NC | W |
| Ferris State University, MI | M,W |
| Florida Agricultural and Mechanical University, FL | M,W |
| Florida Institute of Technology, FL | M,W |
| Florida Southern College, FL | M,W |
| Florida State University, FL | M,W |
| Fordham University, NY | M,W |
| Fort Hays State University, KS | M,W |
| Fort Valley State University, GA | M,W |
| Friends University, KS | M,W |
| Furman University, SC | M,W |
| George Mason University, VA | M,W |
| Georgetown College, KY | M,W |
| Georgetown University, DC | M,W |
| Georgia Institute of Technology, GA | M,W |
| Georgian Court University, NJ | M,W |
| Georgia Southern University, GA | W |
| Georgia State University, GA | W |
| Gonzaga University, WA | M,W |
| Goshen College, IN | M,W |
| Graceland University, IA | M,W |
| Grambling State University, LA | M,W |
| Grand Valley State University, MI | M,W |
| Grand View University, IA | M,W |
| Hampton University, VA | M,W |
| Harding University, AR | M,W |
| Hastings College, NE | M,W |
| Hillsdale College, MI | M,W |
| Holy Family University, PA | M,W |
| Hope International University, CA | M,W |
| Houston Baptist University, TX | M,W |
| Howard University, DC | M,W |
| Humboldt State University, CA | M,W |
| Huston-Tillotson University, TX | M,W |
| Idaho State University, ID | M,W |
| Illinois State University, IL | M,W |
| Indiana State University, IN | M,W |
| Indiana University Bloomington, IN | M,W |
| Indiana University of Pennsylvania, PA | M,W |
| Indiana University–Purdue University Fort Wayne, IN | W |
| Inter American University of Puerto Rico, Bayamón Campus, PR | M,W |
| Inter American University of Puerto Rico, Guayama Campus, PR | M,W |
| Iona College, NY | M,W |
| Iowa State University of Science and Technology, IA | M,W |
| Jackson State University, MS | M,W |
| Jacksonville University, FL | W |
| James Madison University, VA | W |

| | | | | | |
|---|---|---|---|---|---|
| Johnson C. Smith University, NC | M,W | Montreat College, NC | M,W | Saint Martin's University, WA | M,W |
| Kansas State University, KS | M,W | Morehead State University, KY | M,W | Samford University, AL | M,W |
| Kansas Wesleyan University, KS | M,W | Morningside College, IA | M,W | Sam Houston State University, TX | M,W |
| Kennesaw State University, GA | M,W | Mount Marty College, SD | M,W | San Diego State University, CA | W |
| Kent State University, OH | M,W | Mount Mercy University, IA | M,W | San Francisco State University, CA | W |
| Kentucky State University, KY | M,W | Mount St. Mary's University, MD | M,W | San Jose State University, CA | W |
| Kentucky Wesleyan College, KY | M,W | Murray State University, KY | W | Santa Clara University, CA | M,W |
| King University, TN | M,W | New Mexico State University, NM | W | Savannah College of Art and Design, GA | M,W |
| Kutztown University of Pennsylvania, PA | M,W | Niagara University, NY | W | Savannah State University, GA | M,W |
| Lake Erie College, OH | M,W | Nicholls State University, LA | M,W | Seattle Pacific University, WA | M,W |
| Lamar University, TX | M,W | North Carolina Agricultural and Technical State University, NC | M,W | Seattle University, WA | M,W |
| Langston University, OK | M,W | North Carolina Central University, NC | M,W | Seton Hill University, PA | M,W |
| La Salle University, PA | M,W | North Carolina State University, NC | M,W | Shippensburg University of Pennsylvania, PA | M,W |
| Lees-McRae College, NC | M,W | Northeastern University, MA | M,W | Slippery Rock University of Pennsylvania, PA | M,W |
| Lee University, TN | M,W | Northern Arizona University, AZ | M,W | Soka University of America, CA | M,W |
| Lehigh University, PA | M,W | Northern Michigan University, MI | W | South Dakota School of Mines and Technology, SD | M,W |
| Le Moyne College, NY | M,W | Northern State University, SD | M,W | South Dakota State University, SD | M,W |
| Lenoir-Rhyne University, NC | M,W | Northwest Christian University, OR | M,W | Southeastern Louisiana University, LA | M,W |
| Lewis University, IL | M,W | Northwest Missouri State University, MO | M,W | Southeast Missouri State University, MO | M,W |
| Liberty University, VA | M,W | Northwest Nazarene University, ID | M,W | Southern Connecticut State University, CT | M,W |
| Lincoln University, MO | M,W | Northwest University, WA | M,W | Southern Illinois University Carbondale, IL | M,W |
| Lincoln University, PA | M,W | Nova Southeastern University, FL | M,W | Southern Illinois University Edwardsville, IL | M,W |
| Lindenwood University, MO | M,W | Oakland University, MI | M,W | Southern Oregon University, OR | M,W |
| Lindsey Wilson College, KY | M,W | The Ohio State University, OH | M,W | Southern Utah University, UT | M,W |
| Lipscomb University, TN | M,W | Ohio University, OH | W | Southwest Baptist University, MO | M,W |
| Lock Haven University of Pennsylvania, PA | M,W | Oklahoma Baptist University, OK | M,W | Southwestern College, KS | M,W |
| Long Island University–LIU Brooklyn, NY | M,W | Oklahoma Christian University, OK | M,W | Spring Hill College, AL | M,W |
| Louisiana State University and Agricultural & Mechanical College, LA | M,W | Oklahoma City University, OK | M,W | Stanford University, CA | M,W |
| | | Oklahoma State University, OK | M,W | Stephen F. Austin State University, TX | M,W |
| Louisiana Tech University, LA | M,W | Oklahoma Wesleyan University, OK | M,W | Sterling College, KS | M,W |
| Loyola University Chicago, IL | M,W | Olivet Nazarene University, IL | M,W | Stonehill College, MA | M,W |
| Malone University, OH | M,W | Oral Roberts University, OK | M,W | Stony Brook University, State University of New York, NY | M,W |
| Manhattan College, NY | M,W | Oregon State University, OR | W | Syracuse University, NY | M,W |
| Mansfield University of Pennsylvania, PA | M,W | Our Lady of the Lake University of San Antonio, TX | M,W | Tabor College, KS | M,W |
| Marist College, NY | M,W | Park University, MO | M,W | Tarleton State University, TX | M,W |
| Marquette University, WI | M,W | Penn State University Park, PA | M,W | Taylor University, IN | M,W |
| Marshall University, WV | M,W | Philander Smith College, AR | M,W | Temple University, PA | W |
| Maryville University of Saint Louis, MO | M,W | Pittsburg State University, KS | M,W | Tennessee State University, TN | M,W |
| The Master's College and Seminary, CA | M,W | Point Loma Nazarene University, CA | W | Tennessee Wesleyan College, TN | M,W |
| | | Post University, CT | M,W | Texas A&M University, TX | M,W |
| McKendree University, IL | M,W | Prairie View A&M University, TX | M,W | Texas A&M University–Commerce, TX | M,W |
| Merrimack College, MA | M,W | Providence College, RI | M,W | Texas Christian University, TX | M,W |
| Miami University, OH | M,W | Purdue University, IN | M,W | Texas Southern University, TX | M,W |
| Michigan State University, MI | M,W | Queens College of the City University of New York, NY | M,W | Texas State University, TX | M,W |
| Michigan Technological University, MI | M,W | Quinnipiac University, CT | W | Texas Tech University, TX | M,W |
| Middle Tennessee State University, TN | M,W | Radford University, VA | W | Texas Wesleyan University, TX | M,W |
| | | Rice University, TX | M,W | Tiffin University, OH | M,W |
| Millersville University of Pennsylvania, PA | W | Rider University, NJ | M,W | Towson University, MD | W |
| Milligan College, TN | M,W | Robert Morris University Illinois, IL | M,W | Trevecca Nazarene University, TN | M,W |
| Minnesota State University Mankato, MN | M,W | Roberts Wesleyan College, NY | M,W | Trinity Christian College, IL | M,W |
| | | Rocky Mountain College, MT | M,W | Troy University, AL | M,W |
| Minnesota State University Moorhead, MN | M,W | Sacred Heart University, CT | M,W | Truman State University, MO | M,W |
| Minot State University, ND | M,W | Saginaw Valley State University, MI | M,W | Tulane University, LA | W |
| Mississippi State University, MS | M,W | Saint Augustine's University, NC | M,W | Union College, KY | M,W |
| Missouri Baptist University, MO | M,W | St. Francis College, NY | M,W | University at Albany, State University of New York, NY | M,W |
| Missouri Southern State University, MO | M,W | Saint Francis University, PA | M,W | University at Buffalo, the State University of New York, NY | M,W |
| Missouri State University, MO | W | St. John's University, NY | W | | |
| Missouri University of Science and Technology, MO | M,W | Saint Joseph's College, IN | M,W | | |
| Missouri Valley College, MO | M,W | Saint Joseph's University, PA | M,W | | |
| Molloy College, NY | M,W | Saint Leo University, FL | M,W | The University of Akron, OH | M,W |
| Monmouth University, NJ | M,W | St. Louis College of Pharmacy, MO | M,W | The University of Alabama, AL | M,W |
| Montana State University, MT | M,W | Saint Louis University, MO | M,W | | |

| | |
|---|---|
| The University of Alabama at Birmingham, AL | W |
| The University of Alabama in Huntsville, AL | M,W |
| The University of Arizona, AZ | M,W |
| University of Arkansas, AR | M,W |
| University of California, Davis, CA | M,W |
| University of California, Irvine, CA | M,W |
| University of California, Los Angeles, CA | M,W |
| University of California, Santa Barbara, CA | M,W |
| University of Central Arkansas, AR | M,W |
| University of Central Florida, FL | W |
| University of Central Missouri, MO | M,W |
| University of Charleston, WV | M,W |
| University of Cincinnati, OH | M,W |
| University of Colorado Boulder, CO | M,W |
| University of Colorado Colorado Springs, CO | M,W |
| University of Connecticut, CT | M,W |
| University of Dayton, OH | W |
| University of Delaware, DE | W |
| The University of Findlay, OH | M,W |
| University of Florida, FL | M,W |
| University of Georgia, GA | M,W |
| University of Great Falls, MT | M,W |
| University of Hawaii at Manoa, HI | W |
| University of Houston, TX | M,W |
| University of Idaho, ID | M,W |
| University of Illinois at Chicago, IL | M,W |
| University of Indianapolis, IN | M,W |
| The University of Iowa, IA | M,W |
| University of Jamestown, ND | M,W |
| The University of Kansas, KS | M,W |
| University of Louisiana at Lafayette, LA | M,W |
| University of Louisville, KY | M,W |
| University of Maine, ME | M,W |
| University of Maryland, Baltimore County, MD | M,W |
| University of Maryland, College Park, MD | W |
| University of Massachusetts Amherst, MA | M,W |
| University of Massachusetts Lowell, MA | M,W |
| University of Memphis, TN | M,W |
| University of Miami, FL | M,W |
| University of Michigan, MI | M,W |
| University of Minnesota, Duluth, MN | M,W |
| University of Minnesota, Twin Cities Campus, MN | M,W |
| University of Mississippi, MS | M,W |
| University of Missouri, MO | M,W |
| University of Missouri–Kansas City, MO | M,W |
| University of Mobile, AL | M,W |
| The University of Montana, MT | M,W |
| University of Nebraska at Kearney, NE | M,W |
| University of Nebraska–Lincoln, NE | M,W |
| University of Nevada, Las Vegas, NV | W |
| University of Nevada, Reno, NV | W |
| University of New Hampshire, NH | M,W |
| University of New Haven, CT | M,W |
| University of New Orleans, LA | M,W |

| | |
|---|---|
| University of North Carolina at Asheville, NC | M,W |
| The University of North Carolina at Chapel Hill, NC | M,W |
| The University of North Carolina at Charlotte, NC | M,W |
| The University of North Carolina at Greensboro, NC | M,W |
| The University of North Carolina at Pembroke, NC | M,W |
| The University of North Carolina Wilmington, NC | M,W |
| University of Northern Colorado, CO | M,W |
| University of Northern Iowa, IA | M,W |
| University of North Florida, FL | M,W |
| University of North Texas, TX | M,W |
| University of Notre Dame, IN | M,W |
| University of Oklahoma, OK | M,W |
| University of Oregon, OR | M,W |
| University of Pikeville, KY | M,W |
| University of Pittsburgh, PA | M,W |
| University of Portland, OR | M,W |
| University of Rhode Island, RI | M,W |
| University of Richmond, VA | W |
| University of Rio Grande, OH | M,W |
| University of St. Francis, IL | M,W |
| University of San Diego, CA | W |
| University of San Francisco, CA | W |
| University of South Alabama, AL | M,W |
| University of South Carolina, SC | M,W |
| University of South Carolina Upstate, SC | M,W |
| The University of South Dakota, SD | M,W |
| University of Southern California, CA | M,W |
| University of Southern Mississippi, MS | M,W |
| University of South Florida, FL | M,W |
| The University of Tennessee, TN | M,W |
| The University of Tennessee at Chattanooga, TN | M,W |
| The University of Texas at Arlington, TX | M,W |
| The University of Texas at Austin, TX | M,W |
| The University of Texas at El Paso, TX | M,W |
| The University of Texas at San Antonio, TX | M,W |
| The University of Texas–Pan American, TX | M,W |
| University of the Cumberlands, KY | M,W |
| University of the District of Columbia, DC | W |
| University of the Incarnate Word, TX | M,W |
| The University of Toledo, OH | W |
| The University of Tulsa, OK | M,W |
| University of Utah, UT | W |
| University of Vermont, VT | M,W |
| University of Virginia, VA | M,W |
| University of Washington, WA | M,W |
| The University of West Alabama, AL | M,W |
| University of West Georgia, GA | W |
| University of Wisconsin–Madison, WI | M,W |
| University of Wisconsin–Milwaukee, WI | M,W |
| University of Wisconsin–Parkside, WI | M,W |
| University of Wyoming, WY | M,W |
| Upper Iowa University, IA | W |

| | |
|---|---|
| Ursuline College, OH | W |
| Utah State University, UT | M,W |
| Utah Valley University, UT | M,W |
| Valley City State University, ND | M,W |
| Valparaiso University, IN | M,W |
| Vanderbilt University, TN | W |
| Vanguard University of Southern California, CA | M,W |
| Villanova University, PA | M,W |
| Virginia Commonwealth University, VA | M,W |
| Virginia Military Institute, VA | M,W |
| Virginia Polytechnic Institute and State University, VA | M,W |
| Virginia State University, VA | M,W |
| Virginia Union University, VA | M,W |
| Wagner College, NY | M,W |
| Wake Forest University, NC | M,W |
| Waldorf College, IA | M,W |
| Warner Pacific College, OR | M,W |
| Washington State University, WA | M,W |
| Wayland Baptist University, TX | M,W |
| Wayne State College, NE | M,W |
| Wayne State University, MI | W |
| Webber International University, FL | M,W |
| Weber State University, UT | M,W |
| West Chester University of Pennsylvania, PA | M,W |
| Western Carolina University, NC | M,W |
| Western Illinois University, IL | M,W |
| Western Kentucky University, KY | M,W |
| Western Michigan University, MI | W |
| Western Oregon University, OR | M,W |
| Western State Colorado University, CO | M,W |
| Western Washington University, WA | M,W |
| Westminster College, UT | M,W |
| West Texas A&M University, TX | M,W |
| West Virginia University, WV | W |
| West Virginia Wesleyan College, WV | M,W |
| Wheeling Jesuit University, WV | M,W |
| Wichita State University, KS | M,W |
| William Jessup University, CA | M,W |
| William Jewell College, MO | M,W |
| William Woods University, MO | M,W |
| Wingate University, NC | M,W |
| Winona State University, MN | W |
| Winthrop University, SC | M,W |
| Wofford College, SC | M,W |
| Wright State University, OH | W |
| Xavier University, OH | M,W |
| Youngstown State University, OH | M,W |

## Volleyball

| | |
|---|---|
| Abilene Christian University, TX | W |
| Academy of Art University, CA | W |
| Adams State University, CO | W |
| Adelphi University, NY | W |
| Alabama State University, AL | W |
| Albany State University, GA | W |
| Alcorn State University, MS | W |
| American University, DC | W |
| Anderson University, SC | W |
| Angelo State University, TX | W |
| Appalachian State University, NC | W |
| Arizona Christian University, AZ | W |
| Arizona State University at the Downtown Phoenix campus, AZ | W |
| Arizona State University at the Polytechnic campus, AZ | W |
| Arizona State University at the Tempe campus, AZ | W |

| | |
|---|---|
| Arizona State University at the West campus, AZ | W |
| Arkansas State University, AR | W |
| Arkansas Tech University, AR | W |
| Armstrong State University, GA | W |
| Ashland University, OH | W |
| Auburn University, AL | W |
| Augustana College, SD | W |
| Austin Peay State University, TN | W |
| Azusa Pacific University, CA | W |
| Ball State University, IN | M,W |
| Barry University, FL | W |
| Baylor University, TX | W |
| Belhaven University, MS | W |
| Bellarmine University, KY | W |
| Belmont Abbey College, NC | M,W |
| Belmont University, TN | W |
| Bemidji State University, MN | W |
| Bethel College, KS | W |
| Bethune-Cookman University, FL | W |
| Binghamton University, State University of New York, NY | W |
| Biola University, CA | W |
| Blessing-Rieman College of Nursing, IL | M,W |
| Bloomfield College, NJ | W |
| Bluefield College, VA | M,W |
| Boston College, MA | W |
| Bowie State University, MD | W |
| Bowling Green State University, OH | W |
| Bradley University, IL | W |
| Brenau University, GA | W |
| Brevard College, NC | W |
| Brigham Young University, UT | M,W |
| Bryant University, RI | W |
| Bucknell University, PA | W |
| Butler University, IN | W |
| Caldwell University, NJ | W |
| California Baptist University, CA | M,W |
| California Polytechnic State University, San Luis Obispo, CA | W |
| California State Polytechnic University, Pomona, CA | W |
| California State University, Bakersfield, CA | W |
| California State University, Chico, CA | W |
| California State University, Dominguez Hills, CA | W |
| California State University, Fresno, CA | W |
| California State University, Fullerton, CA | W |
| California State University, Long Beach, CA | M,W |
| California State University, Los Angeles, CA | W |
| California State University, Monterey Bay, CA | W |
| California State University, Sacramento, CA | W |
| California State University, San Bernardino, CA | W |
| California State University, Stanislaus, CA | W |
| Calumet College of Saint Joseph, IN | M,W |
| Cameron University, OK | W |
| Campbellsville University, KY | W |
| Canisius College, NY | W |
| Cardinal Stritch University, WI | M,W |
| Carroll College, MT | W |
| Carson-Newman University, TN | W |
| Catawba College, NC | W |
| Cedarville University, OH | W |
| Central Connecticut State University, CT | W |
| Central Methodist University, MO | W |
| Central Michigan University, MI | W |
| Central Washington University, WA | W |
| Chaminade University of Honolulu, HI | W |
| Chestnut Hill College, PA | W |
| Chowan University, NC | W |
| Christian Brothers University, TN | W |
| Cincinnati Christian University, OH | M,W |
| The Citadel, The Military College of South Carolina, SC | W |
| Clarion University of Pennsylvania, PA | W |
| Clarke University, IA | M,W |
| Cleveland State University, OH | W |
| Coastal Carolina University, SC | W |
| Coker College, SC | M,W |
| College of Charleston, SC | W |
| The College of Idaho, ID | W |
| College of Saint Mary, NE | W |
| The College of Saint Rose, NY | W |
| College of the Holy Cross, MA | W |
| College of the Ozarks, MO | W |
| The College of William and Mary, VA | W |
| Colorado Mesa University, CO | W |
| Colorado School of Mines, CO | W |
| Colorado State University, CO | W |
| Colorado State University–Pueblo, CO | W |
| Columbia College, MO | W |
| Columbus State University, GA | W |
| Concordia University, CA | M,W |
| Concordia University, Nebraska, NE | W |
| Concordia University, St. Paul, MN | W |
| Concord University, WV | W |
| Corban University, OR | W |
| Cornerstone University, MI | W |
| Creighton University, NE | W |
| Culver-Stockton College, MO | M,W |
| Cumberland University, TN | W |
| Dakota State University, SD | W |
| Dallas Baptist University, TX | W |
| Davidson College, NC | W |
| Delaware State University, DE | W |
| DePaul University, IL | W |
| Dickinson State University, ND | W |
| Dixie State University, UT | W |
| Doane College, NE | W |
| Dominican College, NY | W |
| Dowling College, NY | W |
| Drake University, IA | W |
| Drury University, MO | W |
| Duquesne University, PA | W |
| East Carolina University, NC | W |
| East Central University, OK | W |
| Eastern Illinois University, IL | W |
| Eastern Kentucky University, KY | W |
| Eastern Michigan University, MI | W |
| Eastern New Mexico University, NM | W |
| Eckerd College, FL | W |
| Elon University, NC | M,W |
| Embry-Riddle Aeronautical University–Daytona, FL | W |
| Embry-Riddle Aeronautical University–Prescott, AZ | W |
| Emmanuel College, GA | M,W |
| Emporia State University, KS | W |
| Evangel University, MO | W |
| The Evergreen State College, WA | W |
| Fairfield University, CT | W |
| Fairmont State University, WV | W |
| Faulkner University, AL | W |
| Fayetteville State University, NC | W |
| Ferris State University, MI | W |
| Flagler College, FL | W |
| Florida Agricultural and Mechanical University, FL | W |
| Florida Atlantic University, FL | W |
| Florida Gulf Coast University, FL | W |
| Florida Institute of Technology, FL | W |
| Florida Southern College, FL | W |
| Florida State University, FL | W |
| Fordham University, NY | W |
| Fort Hays State University, KS | W |
| Fort Lewis College, CO | W |
| Fort Valley State University, GA | W |
| Francis Marion University, SC | W |
| Franklin Pierce University, NH | W |
| Friends University, KS | W |
| Furman University, SC | W |
| Gannon University, PA | W |
| George Mason University, VA | M,W |
| Georgetown College, KY | W |
| Georgetown University, DC | W |
| The George Washington University, DC | W |
| Georgia College & State University, GA | W |
| Georgia Institute of Technology, GA | W |
| Georgian Court University, NJ | W |
| Georgia Southern University, GA | W |
| Georgia State University, GA | W |
| Gonzaga University, WA | W |
| Goshen College, IN | W |
| Governors State University, IL | W |
| Graceland University, IA | M,W |
| Grambling State University, LA | W |
| Grand Valley State University, MI | W |
| Grand View University, IA | M,W |
| Hampton University, VA | W |
| Harding University, AR | W |
| Hastings College, NE | W |
| Hawai`i Pacific University, HI | W |
| Hillsdale College, MI | W |
| Hofstra University, NY | W |
| Holy Family University, PA | W |
| Hope International University, CA | M,W |
| Houston Baptist University, TX | W |
| Howard University, DC | W |
| Humboldt State University, CA | W |
| Huston-Tillotson University, TX | W |
| Idaho State University, ID | W |
| Illinois Institute of Technology, IL | W |
| Illinois State University, IL | W |
| Indiana State University, IN | W |
| Indiana University Bloomington, IN | W |
| Indiana University of Pennsylvania, PA | W |
| Indiana University–Purdue University Fort Wayne, IN | M,W |
| Indiana University–Purdue University Indianapolis, IN | W |
| Indiana University Southeast, IN | W |
| Indian River State College, FL | W |
| Inter American University of Puerto Rico, Bayamón Campus, PR | M,W |
| Iona College, NY | W |

| | | | | | | |
|---|---|---|---|---|---|
| Iowa State University of Science and Technology, IA | W | Midland College, TX | W | Our Lady of the Lake University of San Antonio, TX | W |
| Jackson State University, MS | W | Midwestern State University, TX | W | Pace University, NY | W |
| Jacksonville State University, AL | W | Millersville University of Pennsylvania, PA | W | Palm Beach Atlantic University, FL | W |
| Jacksonville University, FL | W | Milligan College, TN | W | Park University, MO | M,W |
| James Madison University, VA | W | Minnesota State University Mankato, MN | W | Penn State University Park, PA | M,W |
| John Brown University, AR | W | | | Pepperdine University, CA | M,W |
| Johnson C. Smith University, NC | W | Minnesota State University Moorhead, MN | W | Philadelphia University, PA | W |
| Kansas State University, KS | W | Minot State University, ND | W | Philander Smith College, AR | W |
| Kansas Wesleyan University, KS | W | Mississippi State University, MS | W | Pittsburg State University, KS | W |
| Kennesaw State University, GA | W | Missouri Baptist University, MO | M,W | Point Loma Nazarene University, CA | W |
| Kent State University, OH | W | Missouri Southern State University, MO | W | Post University, CT | W |
| Kentucky State University, KY | W | Missouri State University, MO | W | Prairie View A&M University, TX | W |
| Kentucky Wesleyan College, KY | W | Missouri University of Science and Technology, MO | W | Presbyterian College, SC | W |
| King University, TN | M,W | | | Providence College, RI | W |
| Kutztown University of Pennsylvania, PA | W | Missouri Valley College, MO | M,W | Purdue University, IN | W |
| Lake Erie College, OH | W | Missouri Western State University, MO | W | Purdue University Calumet, IN | W |
| Lamar University, TX | W | Molloy College, NY | W | Queens College of the City University of New York, NY | W |
| La Salle University, PA | W | Montana State University, MT | W | | |
| Lawrence Technological University, MI | W | Montana State University Billings, MT | W | Quincy University, IL | M,W |
| Lees-McRae College, NC | M,W | Montana Tech of The University of Montana, MT | W | Quinnipiac University, CT | W |
| Lee University, TN | W | | | Radford University, VA | W |
| Lehigh University, PA | W | Montreat College, NC | W | Regis University, CO | W |
| Le Moyne College, NY | W | Morehead State University, KY | W | Reinhardt University, GA | W |
| LeMoyne-Owen College, TN | W | Morningside College, IA | W | Rice University, TX | W |
| Lenoir-Rhyne University, NC | W | Mount Marty College, SD | W | Rider University, NJ | W |
| Lewis-Clark State College, ID | W | Mount Mercy University, IA | W | Robert Morris University, PA | W |
| Lewis University, IL | M,W | Murray State University, KY | W | Robert Morris University Illinois, IL | M,W |
| Liberty University, VA | W | Newberry College, SC | W | | |
| Lincoln Christian University, IL | W | New Jersey Institute of Technology, NJ | M,W | Roberts Wesleyan College, NY | W |
| Lincoln Memorial University, TN | W | | | Rockhurst University, MO | W |
| Lincoln University, PA | W | Newman University, KS | W | Rocky Mountain College, MT | W |
| Lindenwood University, MO | M,W | New Mexico Highlands University, NM | W | Rollins College, FL | W |
| Lindsey Wilson College, KY | W | | | Sacred Heart University, CT | W |
| Lipscomb University, TN | W | New Mexico State University, NM | W | Saginaw Valley State University, MI | W |
| Lock Haven University of Pennsylvania, PA | W | New York Institute of Technology, NY | W | | |
| Long Island University–LIU Brooklyn, NY | W | Niagara University, NY | W | Saint Anselm College, NH | W |
| | | Nicholls State University, LA | W | Saint Augustine's University, NC | W |
| Long Island University–LIU Post, NY | W | North Carolina Agricultural and Technical State University, NC | W | St. Edward's University, TX | W |
| Louisiana State University and Agricultural & Mechanical College, LA | W | | | St. Francis College, NY | W |
| | | North Carolina Central University, NC | W | Saint Francis University, PA | M,W |
| Louisiana Tech University, LA | W | North Carolina State University, NC | W | St. John's University, NY | W |
| Loyola Marymount University, CA | W | | | Saint Joseph's College, IN | W |
| Loyola University Chicago, IL | M,W | Northeastern University, MA | W | Saint Leo University, FL | W |
| Lubbock Christian University, TX | W | Northern Arizona University, AZ | W | St. Louis College of Pharmacy, MO | W |
| Lynn University, FL | W | Northern Illinois University, IL | W | Saint Louis University, MO | W |
| Lyon College, AR | W | Northern Kentucky University, KY | W | Saint Martin's University, WA | W |
| Malone University, OH | W | Northern Michigan University, MI | W | | |
| Manhattan College, NY | W | Northern State University, SD | W | St. Thomas Aquinas College, NY | W |
| Marist College, NY | W | Northwest Christian University, OR | W | St. Thomas University, FL | W |
| Marquette University, WI | W | Northwestern Oklahoma State University, OK | W | Samford University, AL | W |
| Marshall University, WV | W | | | Sam Houston State University, TX | W |
| Maryville University of Saint Louis, MO | W | Northwest Missouri State University, MO | W | San Diego State University, CA | W |
| | | | | San Francisco State University, CA | W |
| The Master's College and Seminary, CA | W | Northwest Nazarene University, ID | W | San Jose State University, CA | W |
| Mayville State University, ND | W | Northwest University, WA | W | Santa Clara University, CA | W |
| McKendree University, IL | M,W | Nova Southeastern University, FL | W | Savannah State University, GA | W |
| Menlo College, CA | W | Nyack College, NY | W | Seattle Pacific University, WA | W |
| Mercer University, GA | W | Oakland University, MI | W | Seattle University, WA | W |
| Mercy College, NY | W | The Ohio State University, OH | M,W | Seton Hill University, PA | W |
| Merrimack College, MA | W | Ohio University, OH | W | Shawnee State University, OH | M,W |
| Miami University, OH | W | Oklahoma City University, OK | W | Shepherd University, WV | W |
| Michigan State University, MI | W | Oklahoma Wesleyan University, OK | W | Shippensburg University of Pennsylvania, PA | W |
| Michigan Technological University, MI | W | Olivet Nazarene University, IL | W | | |
| | | Oral Roberts University, OK | W | Siena College, NY | W |
| Middle Tennessee State University, TN | W | Oregon State University, OR | W | Simpson University, CA | W |
| | | | | Slippery Rock University of Pennsylvania, PA | W |
| | | | | South Dakota School of Mines and Technology, SD | W |
| | | | | South Dakota State University, SD | W |

| | | | | | | | |
|---|---|---|---|---|---|---|---|
| Southeastern Louisiana University, LA | W | University of California, Davis, CA | W | University of Montevallo, AL | W |
| Southeastern Oklahoma State University, OK | W | University of California, Irvine, CA | M,W | University of Nebraska at Kearney, NE | W |
| Southeast Missouri State University, MO | W | University of California, Los Angeles, CA | M,W | University of Nebraska–Lincoln, NE | W |
| Southern Connecticut State University, CT | W | University of California, Merced, CA | M,W | University of Nevada, Las Vegas, NV | W |
| Southern Illinois University Carbondale, IL | W | University of California, Riverside, CA | W | University of Nevada, Reno, NV | W |
| Southern Illinois University Edwardsville, IL | W | University of California, Santa Barbara, CA | M,W | University of New Hampshire, NH | W |
| Southern Methodist University, TX | W | University of Central Arkansas, AR | W | University of New Haven, CT | W |
| Southern Oregon University, OR | W | University of Central Florida, FL | W | University of New Orleans, LA | W |
| Southern Utah University, UT | W | University of Central Missouri, MO | W | University of North Alabama, AL | W |
| Southwest Baptist University, MO | W | University of Central Oklahoma, OK | W | University of North Carolina at Asheville, NC | W |
| Southwestern College, KS | W | University of Charleston, WV | M,W | The University of North Carolina at Chapel Hill, NC | W |
| Spring Hill College, AL | W | University of Cincinnati, OH | W | The University of North Carolina at Charlotte, NC | W |
| Stanford University, CA | M,W | University of Colorado Boulder, CO | W | The University of North Carolina at Greensboro, NC | W |
| Stephen F. Austin State University, TX | W | University of Colorado Colorado Springs, CO | W | The University of North Carolina at Pembroke, NC | W |
| Stephens College, MO | W | University of Connecticut, CT | W | The University of North Carolina Wilmington, NC | W |
| Sterling College, KS | W | University of Dayton, OH | W | University of Northern Colorado, CO | W |
| Stetson University, FL | W | University of Delaware, DE | W | University of Northern Iowa, IA | W |
| Stonehill College, MA | W | University of Denver, CO | W | University of North Florida, FL | W |
| Stony Brook University, State University of New York, NY | W | University of Evansville, IN | W | University of North Texas, TX | W |
| Syracuse University, NY | W | The University of Findlay, OH | W | University of Notre Dame, IN | W |
| Tabor College, KS | W | University of Florida, FL | W | University of Oklahoma, OK | W |
| Tarleton State University, TX | W | University of Georgia, GA | W | University of Oregon, OR | W |
| Taylor University, IN | W | University of Great Falls, MT | W | University of Pikeville, KY | W |
| Temple University, PA | W | University of Hartford, CT | W | University of Pittsburgh, PA | W |
| Tennessee Wesleyan College, TN | W | University of Hawaii at Manoa, HI | M,W | University of Portland, OR | W |
| Texas A&M International University, TX | W | University of Houston, TX | W | University of Rhode Island, RI | W |
| Texas A&M University, TX | W | University of Idaho, ID | W | University of Rio Grande, OH | W |
| Texas A&M University–Commerce, TX | W | University of Illinois at Chicago, IL | W | University of St. Francis, IL | W |
| Texas A&M University–Corpus Christi, TX | W | University of Illinois at Springfield, IL | W | University of St. Thomas, TX | W |
| Texas Christian University, TX | W | University of Indianapolis, IN | W | University of San Diego, CA | W |
| Texas Southern University, TX | W | The University of Iowa, IA | W | University of San Francisco, CA | W |
| Texas State University, TX | W | University of Jamestown, ND | W | University of South Alabama, AL | W |
| Texas Tech University, TX | W | The University of Kansas, KS | W | University of South Carolina, SC | W |
| Texas Wesleyan University, TX | W | University of Louisiana at Lafayette, LA | W | University of South Carolina Aiken, SC | W |
| Texas Woman's University, TX | W | University of Louisville, KY | W | University of South Carolina Upstate, SC | W |
| Tiffin University, OH | W | University of Maine, ME | W | The University of South Dakota, SD | W |
| Towson University, MD | W | University of Maryland, Baltimore County, MD | W | University of Southern California, CA | M,W |
| Trevecca Nazarene University, TN | W | University of Maryland, College Park, MD | W | University of Southern Indiana, IN | W |
| Trinity Christian College, IL | W | University of Massachusetts Lowell, MA | W | University of Southern Mississippi, MS | W |
| Troy University, AL | W | University of Memphis, TN | W | University of South Florida, FL | W |
| Truett-McConnell College, GA | W | University of Miami, FL | W | The University of Tampa, FL | W |
| Truman State University, MO | W | University of Michigan, MI | W | The University of Tennessee, TN | W |
| Tulane University, LA | W | University of Michigan–Dearborn, MI | W | The University of Tennessee at Chattanooga, TN | W |
| Tusculum College, TN | W | University of Minnesota, Crookston, MN | W | The University of Tennessee at Martin, TN | W |
| Union College, KY | W | University of Minnesota, Duluth, MN | W | The University of Texas at Arlington, TX | W |
| Union University, TN | W | University of Minnesota, Twin Cities Campus, MN | W | The University of Texas at Austin, TX | W |
| University at Albany, State University of New York, NY | W | University of Mississippi, MS | W | The University of Texas at El Paso, TX | W |
| University at Buffalo, the State University of New York, NY | W | University of Missouri, MO | W | The University of Texas at San Antonio, TX | W |
| The University of Akron, OH | W | University of Missouri–Kansas City, MO | W | The University of Texas–Pan American, TX | W |
| The University of Alabama, AL | W | University of Missouri–St. Louis, MO | W | University of the Cumberlands, KY | W |
| The University of Alabama at Birmingham, AL | W | University of Mobile, AL | W | University of the Incarnate Word, TX | W |
| The University of Alabama in Huntsville, AL | W | The University of Montana, MT | W | | |
| University of Alaska Anchorage, AK | W | The University of Montana Western, MT | W | | |
| University of Alaska Fairbanks, AK | W | | | | |
| The University of Arizona, AZ | W | | | | |
| University of Arkansas, AR | W | | | | |
| University of Bridgeport, CT | W | | | | |

| | |
|---|---|
| University of the Pacific, CA | M,W |
| University of the Sciences, PA | W |
| The University of Toledo, OH | W |
| The University of Tulsa, OK | W |
| University of Utah, UT | W |
| University of Virginia, VA | W |
| The University of Virginia's College at Wise, VA | W |
| University of Washington, WA | W |
| The University of West Alabama, AL | W |
| University of West Florida, FL | W |
| University of West Georgia, GA | W |
| University of Wisconsin–Green Bay, WI | W |
| University of Wisconsin–Madison, WI | W |
| University of Wisconsin–Milwaukee, WI | W |
| University of Wisconsin–Parkside, WI | W |
| University of Wyoming, WY | W |
| Upper Iowa University, IA | W |
| Ursuline College, OH | W |
| Utah State University, UT | W |
| Utah Valley University, UT | W |
| Valdosta State University, GA | W |
| Valley City State University, ND | W |
| Valparaiso University, IN | W |
| Vanguard University of Southern California, CA | W |
| Villanova University, PA | W |
| Virginia Commonwealth University, VA | W |
| Virginia State University, VA | W |
| Virginia Union University, VA | W |
| Wake Forest University, NC | W |
| Waldorf College, IA | W |
| Warner Pacific College, OR | W |
| Washburn University, KS | W |
| Washington State University, WA | W |
| Wayland Baptist University, TX | W |
| Wayne State College, NE | W |
| Wayne State University, MI | W |
| Webber International University, FL | M,W |
| Weber State University, UT | W |
| West Chester University of Pennsylvania, PA | W |
| Western Carolina University, NC | W |
| Western Illinois University, IL | W |
| Western Kentucky University, KY | W |
| Western Michigan University, MI | W |
| Western Oregon University, OR | W |
| Western State Colorado University, CO | W |
| Western Washington University, WA | W |
| Westminster College, UT | W |
| West Texas A&M University, TX | W |
| West Virginia University, WV | W |
| West Virginia University Institute of Technology, WV | W |
| West Virginia Wesleyan College, WV | W |
| Wheeling Jesuit University, WV | W |
| Wichita State University, KS | W |
| William Jessup University, CA | W |
| William Jewell College, MO | W |
| Williams Baptist College, AR | W |
| William Woods University, MO | W |
| Wingate University, NC | W |
| Winona State University, MN | W |
| Winthrop University, SC | W |
| Wofford College, SC | W |
| Wright State University, OH | W |

| | |
|---|---|
| Xavier University, OH | W |
| Youngstown State University, OH | W |

**Water polo**

| | |
|---|---|
| Arizona State University at the Downtown Phoenix campus, AZ | W |
| Arizona State University at the Polytechnic campus, AZ | W |
| Arizona State University at the Tempe campus, AZ | W |
| Arizona State University at the West campus, AZ | W |
| California Baptist University, CA | M,W |
| California State University, Bakersfield, CA | W |
| California State University, Long Beach, CA | M,W |
| California State University, Monterey Bay, CA | W |
| Concordia University, CA | M,W |
| Fordham University, NY | M |
| Gannon University, PA | M,W |
| The George Washington University, DC | M |
| Hartwick College, NY | W |
| Indiana University Bloomington, IN | W |
| Iona College, NY | W |
| Lindenwood University, MO | M,W |
| Loyola Marymount University, CA | M,W |
| Marist College, NY | W |
| Pepperdine University, CA | M |
| St. Francis College, NY | M,W |
| San Diego State University, CA | W |
| San Jose State University, CA | W |
| Santa Clara University, CA | M,W |
| Siena College, NY | W |
| Stanford University, CA | M,W |
| University of California, Davis, CA | M,W |
| University of California, Irvine, CA | M,W |
| University of California, Los Angeles, CA | M,W |
| University of California, Santa Barbara, CA | M,W |
| University of Hawaii at Manoa, HI | W |
| University of Maryland, College Park, MD | W |
| University of Michigan, MI | W |
| University of Southern California, CA | M,W |
| University of the Pacific, CA | M,W |
| Wagner College, NY | W |

**Weight lifting**

| | |
|---|---|
| Inter American University of Puerto Rico, Bayamón Campus, PR | M |
| Lindenwood University, MO | M,W |
| South Dakota State University, SD | M,W |

**Wrestling**

| | |
|---|---|
| Adams State University, CO | M |
| American University, DC | M |
| Anderson University, SC | M |
| Appalachian State University, NC | M |
| Arizona State University at the Downtown Phoenix campus, AZ | M |
| Arizona State University at the Polytechnic campus, AZ | M |
| Arizona State University at the Tempe campus, AZ | M |
| Arizona State University at the West campus, AZ | M |

| | |
|---|---|
| Ashland University, OH | M |
| Augustana College, SD | M |
| Belmont Abbey College, NC | M |
| Binghamton University, State University of New York, NY | M |
| Bloomsburg University of Pennsylvania, PA | M |
| Bucknell University, PA | M |
| California Baptist University, CA | M |
| California Polytechnic State University, San Luis Obispo, CA | M |
| California State University, Bakersfield, CA | M |
| Calumet College of Saint Joseph, IN | M |
| Campbellsville University, KY | M,W |
| Carson-Newman University, TN | M |
| Central Michigan University, MI | M |
| The Citadel, The Military College of South Carolina, SC | M |
| Clarion University of Pennsylvania, PA | M |
| Cleveland State University, OH | M |
| Coker College, SC | M |
| Colorado Mesa University, CO | M |
| Colorado School of Mines, CO | M |
| Colorado State University–Pueblo, CO | M |
| Concordia University, Nebraska, NE | M |
| Cumberland University, TN | M |
| Davidson College, NC | M |
| Dickinson State University, ND | M |
| Drexel University, PA | M |
| Eastern Michigan University, MI | M |
| East Stroudsburg University of Pennsylvania, PA | M |
| Embry-Riddle Aeronautical University–Prescott, AZ | M |
| Emmanuel College, GA | M,W |
| Fort Hays State University, KS | M |
| Gannon University, PA | M |
| George Mason University, VA | M |
| Graceland University, IA | M |
| Grand View University, IA | M |
| Hastings College, NE | M |
| Hofstra University, NY | M |
| Indiana University Bloomington, IN | M |
| Iowa State University of Science and Technology, IA | M |
| Kansas Wesleyan University, KS | M |
| Kent State University, OH | M |
| King University, TN | M,W |
| Kutztown University of Pennsylvania, PA | M |
| Lake Erie College, OH | M |
| Lehigh University, PA | M |
| Life University, GA | M,W |
| Lindenwood University, MO | M,W |
| Lindsey Wilson College, KY | M |
| Lock Haven University of Pennsylvania, PA | M |
| Lyon College, AR | M,W |
| Maryville University of Saint Louis, MO | M |
| McKendree University, IL | M,W |
| Menlo College, CA | M,W |
| Michigan State University, MI | M |
| Millersville University of Pennsylvania, PA | M |
| Minnesota State University Mankato, MN | M |
| Minnesota State University Moorhead, MN | M |

| | | | | | |
|---|---|---|---|---|---|
| Missouri Baptist University, MO | M,W | Stanford University, CA | M | University of Northern Colorado, CO | M |
| Missouri Valley College, MO | M,W | Tiffin University, OH | M | University of Northern Iowa, IA | M |
| Morningside College, IA | M | Truett-McConnell College, GA | M | University of Oklahoma, OK | M |
| Newberry College, SC | M | Truman State University, MO | M | University of Pittsburgh, PA | M |
| Newman University, KS | M | University at Buffalo, the State University of New York, NY | M | The University of Tennessee at Chattanooga, TN | M |
| North Carolina State University, NC | M | University of Central Missouri, MO | M | University of the Cumberlands, KY | M,W |
| Northern Illinois University, IL | M | University of Central Oklahoma, OK | M | University of Virginia, VA | M |
| Northern State University, SD | M | The University of Findlay, OH | M | University of Wisconsin–Madison, WI | M |
| The Ohio State University, OH | M | University of Great Falls, MT | M | University of Wisconsin–Parkside, WI | M |
| Ohio University, OH | M | University of Indianapolis, IN | M | University of Wyoming, WY | M |
| Oklahoma City University, OK | M,W | The University of Iowa, IA | M | Upper Iowa University, IA | M |
| Oklahoma State University, OK | M | University of Jamestown, ND | M,W | Utah Valley University, UT | M |
| Old Dominion University, VA | M | University of Maryland, College Park, MD | M | Virginia Military Institute, VA | M |
| Oregon State University, OR | M | University of Michigan, MI | M | Waldorf College, IA | M,W |
| Penn State University Park, PA | M | University of Minnesota, Twin Cities Campus, MN | M | Wayland Baptist University, TX | M,W |
| Purdue University, IN | M | University of Missouri, MO | M | Western State Colorado University, CO | M |
| Rider University, NJ | M | University of Nebraska at Kearney, NE | M | West Virginia University, WV | M |
| Sacred Heart University, CT | M | University of Nebraska–Lincoln, NE | M | West Virginia University Institute of Technology, WV | M |
| San Francisco State University, CA | M | | | | |
| Seton Hill University, PA | M | The University of North Carolina at Chapel Hill, NC | M | Wheeling Jesuit University, WV | M |
| Shippensburg University of Pennsylvania, PA | M | The University of North Carolina at Pembroke, NC | M | Williams Baptist College, AR | M |
| Simpson University, CA | M | | | | |
| South Dakota State University, SD | M | | | | |
| Southern Illinois University Edwardsville, IL | M | | | | |
| Southern Oregon University, OR | M | | | | |

# Co-Op Programs

Adelphi University, NY
Adventist University of Health Sciences, FL
Alabama State University, AL
Albany State University, GA
Alcorn State University, MS
Allen College, IA
Alma College, MI
American University, DC
Anderson University, SC
Andrews University, MI
Anna Maria College, MA
Antioch University Midwest, OH
Aquinas College, MI
Arcadia University, PA
Arizona Christian University, AZ
Arizona State University at the Downtown Phoenix campus, AZ
Arizona State University at the Polytechnic campus, AZ
Arizona State University at the Tempe campus, AZ
Arizona State University at the West campus, AZ
Armstrong State University, GA
Ashland University, OH
Athens State University, AL
Auburn University, AL
Auburn University at Montgomery, AL
Augustana College, SD
Austin Peay State University, TN
Averett University, VA
Azusa Pacific University, CA
Ball State University, IN
Bastyr University, WA
Bates College, ME
Bay Path University, MA
Beacon College, FL
Becker College, MA
Bellarmine University, KY
Belmont Abbey College, NC
Belmont University, TN
Berkeley College–New York City Campus, NY
Bethany College, WV
Bethany Lutheran College, MN
Bethune-Cookman University, FL
Biola University, CA
Birmingham-Southern College, AL
Bloomsburg University of Pennsylvania, PA
Bluefield College, VA
Boston University, MA
Bowie State University, MD
Bowling Green State University, OH
Bradley University, IL
Buffalo State College, State University of New York, NY
Butler University, IN
Cabarrus College of Health Sciences, NC
Cabrini College, PA
Caldwell University, NJ
California Christian College, CA
California College of the Arts, CA
California Institute of Technology, CA
California Institute of the Arts, CA
California Lutheran University, CA
California Polytechnic State University, San Luis Obispo, CA
California State Polytechnic University, Pomona, CA
California State University, Chico, CA

California State University, Dominguez Hills, CA
California State University, Fresno, CA
California State University, Fullerton, CA
California State University, Los Angeles, CA
California State University, Monterey Bay, CA
California State University, San Bernardino, CA
California State University, Stanislaus, CA
California University of Pennsylvania, PA
Calumet College of Saint Joseph, IN
Canisius College, NY
Capital University, OH
Cardinal Stritch University, WI
Carlos Albizu University, Miami Campus, FL
Carroll College, MT
Case Western Reserve University, OH
Castleton State College, VT
The Catholic University of America, DC
Cedarville University, OH
Central College, IA
Central Connecticut State University, CT
Central Methodist University, MO
Central Washington University, WA
Centre College, KY
Champlain College, VT
Chatham University, PA
Chowan University, NC
Christendom College, VA
Christian Brothers University, TN
Cincinnati Christian University, OH
The Citadel, The Military College of South Carolina, SC
Clarion University of Pennsylvania, PA
Clarke University, IA
Clarkson University, NY
Clayton State University, GA
Cleveland State University, OH
Coastal Carolina University, SC
The College at Brockport, State University of New York, NY
College of Biblical Studies–Houston, TX
College of Charleston, SC
The College of Idaho, ID
The College of New Rochelle, NY
College of the Atlantic, ME
Colorado School of Mines, CO
Colorado State University, CO
Colorado State University–Pueblo, CO
Columbia College, MO
Columbia International University, SC
Columbus State University, GA
Concordia College, MN
Concord University, WV
Corban University, OR
Cornell University, NY
Cornish College of the Arts, WA
Cumberland University, TN
Dakota State University, SD
Delaware State University, DE
Delta State University, MS
DeSales University, PA
Dickinson State University, ND
Dixie State University, UT
Doane College, NE
Dominican College, NY
Drake University, IA
Drexel University, PA

Drury University, MO
East Carolina University, NC
Eastern Connecticut State University, CT
Eastern Kentucky University, KY
Eastern Michigan University, MI
Eastern New Mexico University, NM
Edgewood College, WI
Elmhurst College, IL
Embry-Riddle Aeronautical University–Daytona, FL
Embry-Riddle Aeronautical University–Prescott, AZ
Emory & Henry College, VA
Emory University, GA
Emporia State University, KS
Endicott College, MA
Eureka College, IL
Everglades University, FL
Fairmont State University, WV
Farmingdale State College, NY
Fayetteville State University, NC
Ferris State University, MI
Flagler College, FL
Florida Agricultural and Mechanical University, FL
Florida Atlantic University, FL
Florida Gulf Coast University, FL
Florida Institute of Technology, FL
Florida National University, FL
Florida State University, FL
Fontbonne University, MO
Fordham University, NY
Framingham State University, MA
Franciscan University of Steubenville, OH
Franklin College, IN
Friends University, KS
Frostburg State University, MD
Gannon University, PA
Geneva College, PA
George Mason University, VA
Georgetown College, KY
The George Washington University, DC
Georgia Institute of Technology, GA
Georgia Regents University, GA
Georgia Southern University, GA
Georgia State University, GA
Gordon College, MA
Graceland University, IA
Grambling State University, LA
Grand Valley State University, MI
Grand View University, IA
Greenville College, IL
Guilford College, NC
Gustavus Adolphus College, MN
Gwynedd Mercy University, PA
Hampton University, VA
Hanover College, IN
Harding University, AR
Hawai'i Pacific University, HI
Heidelberg University, OH
Hendrix College, AR
Hilbert College, NY
Hodges University, FL
Hofstra University, NY
Holy Family University, PA
Houghton College, NY
Howard University, DC
Humboldt State University, CA
Husson University, ME
Huston-Tillotson University, TX

Idaho State University, ID
Illinois Institute of Technology, IL
Illinois State University, IL
Indiana State University, IN
Indiana University Bloomington, IN
Indiana University East, IN
Indiana University Northwest, IN
Indiana University of Pennsylvania, PA
Indiana University–Purdue University Fort Wayne, IN
Indiana University–Purdue University Indianapolis, IN
Inter American University of Puerto Rico, Bayamón Campus, PR
Inter American University of Puerto Rico, Guayama Campus, PR
Iowa State University of Science and Technology, IA
Iowa Wesleyan College, IA
Jackson State University, MS
Jacksonville State University, AL
Jacksonville University, FL
Jefferson College of Health Sciences, VA
John Carroll University, OH
Johnson C. Smith University, NC
Kansas City Art Institute, MO
Kansas State University, KS
Kansas Wesleyan University, KS
Kean University, NJ
Keene State College, NH
Kennesaw State University, GA
Kent State University, OH
Kentucky Christian University, KY
Kentucky State University, KY
Kentucky Wesleyan College, KY
Keuka College, NY
Keystone College, PA
King University, TN
Lamar University, TX
Langston University, OK
La Salle University, PA
Lasell College, MA
Lawrence Technological University, MI
Lees-McRae College, NC
Lee University, TN
Lehigh University, PA
Lehman College of the City University of New York, NY
LeMoyne-Owen College, TN
Liberty University, VA
Life University, GA
LIM College, NY
Lincoln University, MO
Lindsey Wilson College, KY
Lock Haven University of Pennsylvania, PA
Long Island University–LIU Brooklyn, NY
Long Island University–LIU Post, NY
Loras College, IA
Louisiana State University and Agricultural & Mechanical College, LA
Loyola Marymount University, CA
Loyola University Chicago, IL
Loyola University New Orleans, LA
Lynn University, FL
Maine Maritime Academy, ME
Manhattan College, NY
Marian University, WI
Marist College, NY
Marquette University, WI
Marshall University, WV
Maryville University of Saint Louis, MO
Massachusetts College of Liberal Arts, MA
Massachusetts Institute of Technology, MA
Massachusetts Maritime Academy, MA
The Master's College and Seminary, CA
Mayville State University, ND

McKendree University, IL
Medgar Evers College of the City University of New York, NY
Mercer University, GA
Mercy College, NY
Meredith College, NC
Merrimack College, MA
Messiah College, PA
Miami University, OH
Michigan State University, MI
Michigan Technological University, MI
Millersville University of Pennsylvania, PA
Milligan College, TN
Minnesota State University Mankato, MN
Minot State University, ND
Misericordia University, PA
Mississippi State University, MS
Missouri Southern State University, MO
Missouri State University, MO
Missouri University of Science and Technology, MO
Missouri Valley College, MO
Monmouth University, NJ
Montana State University Billings, MT
Montana Tech of The University of Montana, MT
Montclair State University, NJ
Montreat College, NC
Moravian College, PA
Morehead State University, KY
Morrisville State College, NY
Mount Holyoke College, MA
Mount Marty College, SD
Mount St. Joseph University, OH
Mount Saint Mary College, NY
Mount Saint Mary's University, CA
Murray State University, KY
Naropa University, CO
National University, CA
Nazareth College of Rochester, NY
New College of Florida, FL
New Jersey City University, NJ
New Jersey Institute of Technology, NJ
Newman University, KS
New Mexico Highlands University, NM
New Mexico Institute of Mining and Technology, NM
New Mexico State University, NM
New York Institute of Technology, NY
New York University, NY
Niagara University, NY
Nicholls State University, LA
Nichols College, MA
North Carolina Agricultural and Technical State University, NC
North Carolina Central University, NC
North Carolina State University, NC
Northeastern Illinois University, IL
Northeastern State University, OK
Northeastern University, MA
Northern Arizona University, AZ
Northern Illinois University, IL
Northern Kentucky University, KY
Northern Michigan University, MI
Northern State University, SD
Northland College, WI
Northwest Christian University, OR
Northwestern Oklahoma State University, OK
Northwestern University, IL
Northwest Nazarene University, ID
Northwest University, WA
Norwich University, VT
Oakland University, MI
Oglethorpe University, GA
The Ohio State University, OH

Ohio University, OH
Oklahoma Baptist University, OK
Oklahoma City University, OK
Oklahoma Wesleyan University, OK
Old Dominion University, VA
Olivet College, MI
Olivet Nazarene University, IL
Oregon State University, OR
Otis College of Art and Design, CA
Our Lady of the Lake University of San Antonio, TX
Pace University, NY
Pacific Lutheran University, WA
Patrick Henry College, VA
Peirce College, PA
Penn State University Park, PA
Pennsylvania College of Technology, PA
Philander Smith College, AR
Piedmont College, GA
Portland State University, OR
Post University, CT
Prairie View A&M University, TX
Purdue University, IN
Purdue University Calumet, IN
Ramapo College of New Jersey, NJ
Reed College, OR
Regis University, CO
Reinhardt University, GA
Rensselaer Polytechnic Institute, NY
Rhode Island School of Design, RI
Rhodes College, TN
Rider University, NJ
Robert Morris University, PA
Roberts Wesleyan College, NY
Rochester Institute of Technology, NY
Rockhurst University, MO
Roger Williams University, RI
Rose-Hulman Institute of Technology, IN
Rowan University, NJ
Rutgers, The State University of New Jersey, Camden, NJ
Rutgers, The State University of New Jersey, Newark, NJ
Rutgers, The State University of New Jersey, New Brunswick, NJ
Sacred Heart University, CT
The Sage Colleges, NY
Saginaw Valley State University, MI
Saint Augustine's University, NC
St. Francis College, NY
Saint Joseph's University, PA
Saint Louis University, MO
Saint Martin's University, WA
St. Mary's College of Maryland, MD
Saint Mary's University of Minnesota, MN
Saint Vincent College, PA
Salisbury University, MD
San Francisco State University, CA
Santa Clara University, CA
Savannah State University, GA
School of the Art Institute of Chicago, IL
Shepherd University, WV
Shimer College, IL
Shippensburg University of Pennsylvania, PA
Simpson College, IA
Soka University of America, CA
South Dakota School of Mines and Technology, SD
South Dakota State University, SD
Southern California Institute of Architecture, CA
Southern Connecticut State University, CT
Southern Illinois University Carbondale, IL
Southern Illinois University Edwardsville, IL

Southern Methodist University, TX
Southern Oregon University, OR
Southern Utah University, UT
Southwest Baptist University, MO
State University of New York at New Paltz, NY
State University of New York at Oswego, NY
State University of New York at Plattsburgh, NY
State University of New York College of Agriculture and Technology at Cobleskill, NY
State University of New York College of Environmental Science and Forestry, NY
State University of New York Polytechnic Institute, NY
Stephen F. Austin State University, TX
Stephens College, MO
Stevenson University, MD
Stony Brook University, State University of New York, NY
Stratford University, MD
Stratford University, VA
Stratford University, VA
Stratford University, VA
Stratford University, VA
Suffolk University, MA
Syracuse University, NY
Tabor College, KS
Tarleton State University, TX
Taylor University, IN
Temple University, PA
Tennessee State University, TN
Texas A&M University, TX
Texas A&M University–Commerce, TX
Texas A&M University–Corpus Christi, TX
Texas Southern University, TX
Texas Tech University, TX
Texas Woman's University, TX
Thiel College, PA
Thomas Aquinas College, CA
Thomas More College, KY
Towson University, MD
Trine University, IN
Trinity Christian College, IL
Trinity College of Florida, FL
Truman State University, MO
Tulane University, LA
Union College, NE
Union University, TN
Unity College, ME
University at Buffalo, the State University of New York, NY
The University of Akron, OH
The University of Alabama, AL
The University of Alabama at Birmingham, AL
The University of Alabama in Huntsville, AL
University of Alaska Anchorage, AK
University of Alaska Fairbanks, AK
The University of Arizona, AZ
University of Arkansas, AR
University of Bridgeport, CT
University of California, Santa Barbara, CA
University of California, Santa Cruz, CA
University of Central Arkansas, AR
University of Central Florida, FL
University of Central Oklahoma, OK
University of Charleston, WV
University of Cincinnati, OH
University of Colorado Boulder, CO
University of Colorado Colorado Springs, CO

University of Colorado Denver, CO
University of Connecticut, CT
University of Dayton, OH
University of Denver, CO
University of Evansville, IN
The University of Findlay, OH
University of Florida, FL
University of Georgia, GA
University of Hartford, CT
University of Hawaii at Manoa, HI
University of Houston, TX
University of Houston–Clear Lake, TX
University of Idaho, ID
University of Illinois at Chicago, IL
University of Illinois at Springfield, IL
University of Indianapolis, IN
The University of Iowa, IA
University of Jamestown, ND
The University of Kansas, KS
University of Louisiana at Lafayette, LA
University of Louisville, KY
University of Maine, ME
University of Maine at Fort Kent, ME
University of Maine at Machias, ME
University of Maine at Presque Isle, ME
University of Maryland, Baltimore County, MD
University of Maryland, College Park, MD
University of Maryland University College, MD
University of Massachusetts Amherst, MA
University of Massachusetts Boston, MA
University of Massachusetts Dartmouth, MA
University of Massachusetts Lowell, MA
University of Memphis, TN
University of Miami, FL
University of Michigan, MI
University of Michigan–Dearborn, MI
University of Michigan–Flint, MI
University of Minnesota, Crookston, MN
University of Minnesota, Duluth, MN
University of Minnesota, Twin Cities Campus, MN
University of Mississippi, MS
University of Missouri, MO
University of Missouri–Kansas City, MO
University of Missouri–St. Louis, MO
The University of Montana, MT
The University of Montana Western, MT
University of Mount Union, OH
University of Nebraska–Lincoln, NE
University of Nevada, Las Vegas, NV
University of New England, ME
University of New Haven, CT
University of New Orleans, LA
University of North Alabama, AL
The University of North Carolina at Charlotte, NC
The University of North Carolina at Pembroke, NC
The University of North Carolina Wilmington, NC
University of Northern Colorado, CO
University of Northern Iowa, IA
University of North Florida, FL
University of North Georgia, GA
University of North Texas, TX
University of Oklahoma, OK
University of Oregon, OR
University of Pennsylvania, PA
University of Pittsburgh, PA
University of Puget Sound, WA
University of Rhode Island, RI
University of Rio Grande, OH
University of Rochester, NY

University of San Francisco, CA
University of South Alabama, AL
University of South Carolina, SC
University of South Carolina Aiken, SC
University of South Carolina Upstate, SC
The University of South Dakota, SD
University of Southern California, CA
University of Southern Indiana, IN
University of Southern Maine, ME
University of Southern Mississippi, MS
University of South Florida, FL
The University of Tampa, FL
The University of Tennessee, TN
The University of Tennessee at Chattanooga, TN
The University of Tennessee at Martin, TN
The University of Texas at Arlington, TX
The University of Texas at Austin, TX
The University of Texas at Dallas, TX
The University of Texas at El Paso, TX
The University of Texas at San Antonio, TX
The University of Texas–Pan American, TX
University of the Cumberlands, KY
University of the District of Columbia, DC
University of the Incarnate Word, TX
University of the Pacific, CA
University of the Sciences, PA
The University of Toledo, OH
University of Utah, UT
University of Vermont, VT
University of Virginia, VA
The University of Virginia's College at Wise, VA
University of Washington, WA
University of Washington, Bothell, WA
University of Washington, Tacoma, WA
The University of West Alabama, AL
University of West Florida, FL
University of West Georgia, GA
University of Wisconsin–Eau Claire, WI
University of Wisconsin–La Crosse, WI
University of Wisconsin–Madison, WI
University of Wisconsin–Milwaukee, WI
University of Wisconsin–Oshkosh, WI
University of Wisconsin–Stevens Point, WI
University of Wisconsin–Stout, WI
University of Wisconsin–Superior, WI
University of Wisconsin–Whitewater, WI
Upper Iowa University, IA
Ursinus College, PA
Ursuline College, OH
Utah State University, UT
Utah Valley University, UT
Valdosta State University, GA
Valley City State University, ND
Valparaiso University, IN
Vanderbilt University, TN
Vassar College, NY
Vermont Technical College, VT
Villa Maria College, NY
Villanova University, PA
Virginia Commonwealth University, VA
Virginia Polytechnic Institute and State University, VA
Virginia State University, VA
Virginia Union University, VA
Waldorf College, IA
Walla Walla University, WA
Warner Pacific College, OR
Warren Wilson College, NC
Washburn University, KS
Washington State University, WA
Washington University in St. Louis, MO
Wayne State College, NE
Wayne State University, MI

Webber International University, FL
Weber State University, UT
Webster University, MO
Wentworth Institute of Technology, MA
Wesleyan College, GA
Western Carolina University, NC
Western Kentucky University, KY
Western Michigan University, MI
Western Washington University, WA
Westminster College, MO
Westminster College, UT

West Texas A&M University, TX
West Virginia University Institute of
    Technology, WV
Wheaton College, MA
Whitman College, WA
Whitworth University, WA
Wichita State University, KS
Widener University, PA
Wilkes University, PA
William Jewell College, MO
William Peace University, NC

Winthrop University, SC
Wittenberg University, OH
Worcester Polytechnic Institute, MA
Wright State University, OH
Xavier University, OH
Xavier University of Louisiana, LA
York College of Pennsylvania, PA
York College of the City University of New
    York, NY
Youngstown State University, OH

# ROTC Programs

* program is offered at another college's campus

Le Moyne College, NY*
LeMoyne-Owen College, TN*
Lenoir-Rhyne University, NC*
Lewis-Clark State College, ID*
Lewis University, IL*
Liberty University, VA*
Lincoln University, MO*
Lincoln University, PA*
Lindenwood University, MO*
Linfield College, OR*
Lipscomb University, TN*
Louisiana State University and Agricultural
    & Mechanical College, LA
Louisiana Tech University, LA
Loyola Marymount University, CA
Loyola University Chicago, IL*
Loyola University New Orleans, LA*
Lubbock Christian University, TX*
Lynn University, FL*
Macalester College, MN*
Malone University, OH*
Manhattan College, NY
Maranatha Baptist University, WI*
Marquette University, WI
Mary Baldwin College, VA*
Marywood University, PA*
Massachusetts Institute of Technology, MA
The Master's College and Seminary, CA*
Mayville State University, ND*
McKendree University, IL*
Mercy College, NY*
Meredith College, NC*
Merrimack College, MA*
Miami University, OH
Michigan State University, MI
Michigan Technological University, MI
Middle Tennessee State University, TN*
Midwestern State University, TX*
Millsaps College, MS*
Milwaukee School of Engineering, WI*
Minnesota State University Moorhead, MN*
Misericordia University, PA*
Mississippi State University, MS
Mississippi University for Women, MS*
Missouri University of Science and
    Technology, MO
Monmouth University, NJ*
Montana State University, MT
Montclair State University, NJ
Morrisville State College, NY*
Mount Carmel College of Nursing, OH*
Mount Holyoke College, MA*
Mount Mary University, WI*
Mount St. Joseph University, OH*
National University, CA*
Nazareth College of Rochester, NY*
Nebraska Methodist College, NE*
New England College, NH*
New Jersey City University, NJ*
New Jersey Institute of Technology, NJ
New Mexico State University, NM
New York Institute of Technology, NY*
New York University, NY*
Nichols College, MA*
North Carolina Agricultural and Technical
    State University, NC
North Carolina Central University, NC
North Carolina State University, NC
North Central College, IL*
Northeastern Illinois University, IL*
Northeastern University, MA*
Northern Arizona University, AZ
Northern Illinois University, IL*
Northern Kentucky University, KY*
Northwestern University, IL*

Northwest University, WA*
Norwich University, VT
Oakland University, MI*
Occidental College, CA*
Oglethorpe University, GA*
The Ohio State University, OH
Ohio University, OH
Ohio Wesleyan University, OH*
Oklahoma Baptist University, OK*
Oklahoma Christian University, OK*
Oklahoma City University, OK*
Oklahoma State University, OK
Olivet College, MI*
Oral Roberts University, OK*
Oregon State University, OR
Pace University, NY*
Pacific University, OR*
Penn State Abington, PA*
Penn State Altoona, PA
Penn State Brandywine, PA*
Penn State Hazleton, PA*
Penn State New Kensington, PA*
Penn State University Park, PA
Penn State Wilkes-Barre, PA*
Penn State Worthington Scranton, PA*
Pepperdine University, CA*
Plymouth State University, NH*
Point Loma Nazarene University, CA*
Pomona College, CA*
Portland State University, OR*
Princeton University, NJ*
Purdue University, IN
Quinnipiac University, CT*
Ramapo College of New Jersey, NJ*
Reed College, OR*
Regis University, CO*
Rensselaer Polytechnic Institute, NY
Rhodes College, TN*
Rice University, TX*
Robert Morris University, PA*
Roberts Wesleyan College, NY*
Rochester Institute of Technology, NY
Rose-Hulman Institute of Technology, IN
Rutgers, The State University of New Jersey,
    Camden, NJ*
Rutgers, The State University of New Jersey,
    Newark, NJ
Rutgers, The State University of New Jersey,
    New Brunswick, NJ
The Sage Colleges, NY
Saint Augustine's University, NC*
St. Catherine University, MN*
St. Edward's University, TX*
St. Francis College, NY*
St. John Fisher College, NY*
Saint Joseph's University, PA
St. Lawrence University, NY*
St. Louis College of Pharmacy, MO*
Saint Louis University, MO
Saint Martin's University, WA*
Saint Mary's College, IN*
Saint Michael's College, VT*
St. Thomas Aquinas College, NY*
Saint Vincent College, PA*
Salem College, NC*
Salisbury University, MD*
Samford University, AL*
San Diego State University, CA
San Francisco State University, CA*
San Jose State University, CA
Santa Clara University, CA*
Scripps College, CA*
Seattle Pacific University, WA*
Seattle University, WA*
Shepherd University, WV*

Siena College, NY*
Skidmore College, NY*
Smith College, MA*
South Dakota State University, SD
Southeast Missouri State University, MO
Southern Connecticut State University, CT*
Southern Illinois University Carbondale, IL
Southern Illinois University Edwardsville,
    IL*
Southern Methodist University, TX*
Spelman College, GA*
Spring Hill College, AL*
Stanford University, CA*
State University of New York at Oswego,
    NY*
State University of New York College at
    Cortland, NY*
State University of New York College at
    Geneseo, NY*
State University of New York College at Old
    Westbury, NY*
State University of New York College at
    Potsdam, NY*
State University of New York College of
    Environmental Science and Forestry, NY*
State University of New York College of
    Technology at Canton, NY*
State University of New York Polytechnic
    Institute, NY*
Stephens College, MO*
Stevenson University, MD*
Stony Brook University, State University of
    New York, NY*
Syracuse University, NY
Temple University, PA*
Tennessee State University, TN
Texas A&M University, TX
Texas A&M University–Commerce, TX*
Texas Christian University, TX
Texas Lutheran University, TX*
Texas Southern University, TX*
Texas State University, TX
Texas Tech University, TX
Texas Wesleyan University, TX*
Texas Woman's University, TX*
Thomas More College, KY*
Tiffin University, OH*
Towson University, MD*
Transylvania University, KY*
Trine University, IN*
Trinity University, TX*
Troy University, AL
Tufts University, MA*
Tulane University, LA
Union College, NY*
University at Albany, State University of New
    York, NY*
The University of Akron, OH*
The University of Alabama, AL
The University of Alabama at Birmingham,
    AL*
University of Alaska Anchorage, AK
The University of Arizona, AZ
University of Arkansas, AR
University of California, Berkeley, CA
University of California, Davis, CA*
University of California, Irvine, CA*
University of California, Los Angeles, CA
University of California, Riverside, CA*
University of California, Santa Barbara, CA*
University of California, Santa Cruz, CA*
University of Central Florida, FL
University of Central Missouri, MO*
University of Chicago, IL*
University of Cincinnati, OH

---

* program is offered at another college's campus

University of Colorado Boulder, CO
University of Colorado Denver, CO*
University of Connecticut, CT
University of Dallas, TX*
University of Dayton, OH*
University of Delaware, DE
University of Denver, CO*
The University of Findlay, OH*
University of Florida, FL
University of Georgia, GA
University of Hartford, CT*
University of Hawaii at Manoa, HI
University of Hawaii–West Oahu, HI*
University of Houston, TX
University of Houston–Downtown, TX*
University of Idaho, ID*
University of Illinois at Chicago, IL*
The University of Iowa, IA
The University of Kansas, KS
University of Louisville, KY
University of Mary Hardin-Baylor, TX*
University of Maryland, Baltimore County, MD*
University of Maryland, College Park, MD
University of Massachusetts Amherst, MA
University of Massachusetts Boston, MA*
University of Massachusetts Lowell, MA
University of Memphis, TN
University of Miami, FL
University of Michigan, MI
University of Michigan–Dearborn, MI
University of Minnesota, Crookston, MN*
University of Minnesota, Duluth, MN
University of Minnesota, Twin Cities Campus, MN
University of Mississippi, MS
University of Missouri, MO
University of Missouri–Kansas City, MO*
University of Missouri–St. Louis, MO*
University of Mobile, AL*
University of Montevallo, AL*
University of Mount Union, OH*
University of Nebraska–Lincoln, NE
University of Nevada, Las Vegas, NV
University of New Hampshire, NH
University of New Hampshire at Manchester, NH*
University of New Haven, CT*
University of New Orleans, LA*
The University of North Carolina at Chapel Hill, NC
The University of North Carolina at Charlotte, NC
The University of North Carolina at Greensboro, NC*
The University of North Carolina at Pembroke, NC
University of Northern Colorado, CO
University of North Texas, TX
University of Notre Dame, IN
University of Oklahoma, OK
University of Oregon, OR*
University of Pennsylvania, PA*
University of Pittsburgh, PA
University of Pittsburgh at Greensburg, PA*
University of Portland, OR
University of Rochester, NY*
University of St. Thomas, MN
University of St. Thomas, TX*
University of San Diego, CA*
University of San Francisco, CA*
The University of Scranton, PA*
University of South Alabama, AL
University of South Carolina, SC
University of Southern California, CA

University of Southern Maine, ME*
University of Southern Mississippi, MS
University of South Florida, FL
The University of Tampa, FL*
The University of Tennessee, TN
The University of Texas at Arlington, TX*
The University of Texas at Austin, TX
The University of Texas at Dallas, TX*
The University of Texas at San Antonio, TX
University of the District of Columbia, DC*
University of the Incarnate Word, TX*
University of the Pacific, CA*
University of the Sciences, PA*
The University of Toledo, OH*
The University of Tulsa, OK*
University of Utah, UT
University of Virginia, VA
University of Washington, WA
University of Washington, Bothell, WA*
University of Washington, Tacoma, WA*
The University of West Alabama, AL*
University of West Florida, FL
University of West Georgia, GA*
University of Wisconsin–Madison, WI
University of Wisconsin–Milwaukee, WI*
University of Wisconsin–Stout, WI*
University of Wisconsin–Superior, WI*
University of Wisconsin–Whitewater, WI
University of Wyoming, WY
Utah State University, UT
Utah Valley University, UT*
Utica College, NY*
Valdosta State University, GA
Valparaiso University, IN*
Vanderbilt University, TN*
Vanguard University of Southern California, CA*
Villanova University, PA*
Virginia Military Institute, VA
Virginia Polytechnic Institute and State University, VA
Warner Pacific College, OR*
Washburn University, KS*
Washington & Jefferson College, PA*
Washington State University, WA
Washington University in St. Louis, MO*
Wayland Baptist University, TX*
Wayne State University, MI*
Weber State University, UT*
Webster University, MO*
Wentworth Institute of Technology, MA*
Wesleyan University, CT*
West Chester University of Pennsylvania, PA*
Western Kentucky University, KY*
Western New England University, MA*
Westfield State University, MA*
Westminster College, MO*
Westminster College, UT*
West Virginia University, WV
Wheaton College, IL*
Widener University, PA*
Wilkes University, PA
Willamette University, OR*
William Jessup University, CA*
William Paterson University of New Jersey, NJ*
William Peace University, NC*
Williams College, MA*
William Woods University, MO*
Wingate University, NC*
Winthrop University, SC*
Wittenberg University, OH*
Worcester Polytechnic Institute, MA
Worcester State University, MA*

Wright State University, OH
Xavier University, OH*
Xavier University of Louisiana, LA*
Yale University, CT
Youngstown State University, OH*

**Army**
Adelphi University, NY*
Agnes Scott College, GA*
Alabama State University, AL*
Alaska Pacific University, AK*
Albany State University, GA
Albright College, PA*
Alcorn State University, MS
Allen College, IA*
Alma College, MI*
Alvernia University, PA*
Alverno College, WI*
American University, DC*
Amherst College, MA*
Anderson University, SC*
Appalachian State University, NC
Aquinas College, MI*
Arizona State University at the Downtown Phoenix campus, AZ*
Arizona State University at the Polytechnic campus, AZ*
Arizona State University at the Tempe campus, AZ
Arizona State University at the West campus, AZ*
Arkansas State University, AR
Arkansas Tech University, AR*
Armstrong State University, GA
Ashland University, OH*
Assumption College, MA*
Auburn University, AL
Auburn University at Montgomery, AL
Augustana College, SD*
Austin Peay State University, TN
Azusa Pacific University, CA
Babson College, MA*
Baldwin Wallace University, OH*
Ball State University, IN
Barnard College, NY*
Barry University, FL*
Baruch College of the City University of New York, NY*
Baylor University, TX
Bay Path University, MA*
Becker College, MA*
Belhaven University, MS*
Bellarmine University, KY*
Belmont Abbey College, NC*
Belmont University, TN*
Benedictine University, IL*
Bentley University, MA*
Bethany Lutheran College, MN*
Bethel University, MN*
Bethune-Cookman University, FL*
Binghamton University, State University of New York, NY*
Biola University, CA*
Birmingham-Southern College, AL*
Bloomfield College, NJ*
Bloomsburg University of Pennsylvania, PA
Boston College, MA*
Boston University, MA
Bowie State University, MD
Bowling Green State University, OH
Bradley University, IL
Brandeis University, MA*
Bridgewater State University, MA*
Brigham Young University, UT
Brown University, RI*

---

* program is offered at another college's campus

Bryant University, RI*
Bucknell University, PA
Buena Vista University, IA
Buffalo State College, State University of New York, NY*
Butler University, IN
Cabrini College, PA*
Caldwell University, NJ*
California Baptist University, CA
California Institute of Technology, CA*
California Lutheran University, CA*
California Polytechnic State University, San Luis Obispo, CA
California State Polytechnic University, Pomona, CA
California State University, Dominguez Hills, CA
California State University, Fresno, CA
California State University, Fullerton, CA
California State University, Long Beach, CA
California State University, Los Angeles, CA*
California State University, Sacramento, CA*
California State University, San Bernardino, CA
California State University, San Marcos, CA*
California University of Pennsylvania, PA
Calvary Bible College and Theological Seminary, MO*
Calvin College, MI*
Cameron University, OK
Campbellsville University, KY*
Canisius College, NY
Capital University, OH
Carroll College, MT
Carson-Newman University, TN
Case Western Reserve University, OH
Castleton State College, VT
Catawba College, NC*
The Catholic University of America, DC
Cazenovia College, NY*
Cedar Crest College, PA*
Cedarville University, OH*
Central Connecticut State University, CT*
Central Methodist University, MO*
Central Michigan University, MI
Central Washington University, WA
Centre College, KY*
Chaminade University of Honolulu, HI*
Champlain College, VT*
Chapman University, CA*
Chatham University, PA*
Christian Brothers University, TN*
Christopher Newport University, VA
The Citadel, The Military College of South Carolina, SC
City College of the City University of New York, NY
Claremont McKenna College, CA
Clarion University of Pennsylvania, PA*
Clarke University, IA*
Clarkson University, NY
Clark University, MA*
Clayton State University, GA
Cleveland State University, OH*
Coastal Carolina University, SC
Coe College, IA
Colby College, ME*
Colby-Sawyer College, NH*
The College at Brockport, State University of New York, NY
The College of Idaho, ID*
The College of New Jersey, NJ*
College of Saint Benedict, MN*
College of Saint Mary, NE*

The College of Saint Rose, NY*
College of the Holy Cross, MA*
College of the Ozarks, MO
The College of William and Mary, VA
The Colorado College, CO*
Colorado School of Mines, CO
Colorado State University, CO
Colorado State University–Pueblo, CO
Columbia College, MO*
Columbia University, NY*
Columbia University, School of General Studies, NY*
Columbus State University, GA
Concordia College, MN*
Concordia University, Nebraska, NE*
Concordia University, St. Paul, MN*
Concordia University Texas, TX*
Cooper Union for the Advancement of Science and Art, NY*
Corban University, OR*
Cornell University, NY
Cornerstone University, MI*
Covenant College, GA*
Creighton University, NE
Cumberland University, TN
Curry College, MA*
Dallas Baptist University, TX*
Dartmouth College, NH*
Davidson College, NC
Delaware State University, DE
Delta State University, MS
Denison University, OH*
DePaul University, IL
DePauw University, IN*
DeSales University, PA*
Dickinson College, PA
Dixie State University, UT
Doane College, NE*
Dowling College, NY*
Drake University, IA*
Drexel University, PA
Drury University, MO*
Duquesne University, PA
East Carolina University, NC
Eastern Connecticut State University, CT*
Eastern Illinois University, IL
Eastern Kentucky University, KY
Eastern Michigan University, MI
Eastern University, PA*
East Stroudsburg University of Pennsylvania, PA
Eckerd College, FL*
Edgewood College, WI*
Elmhurst College, IL*
Elmira College, NY
Elms College, MA*
Elon University, NC
Embry-Riddle Aeronautical University–Daytona, FL
Embry-Riddle Aeronautical University–Prescott, AZ
Emmanuel College, MA*
Emory University, GA*
Endicott College, MA*
Evangel University, MO*
Fairfield University, CT*
Fairmont State University, WV
Farmingdale State College, NY*
Faulkner University, AL*
Fayetteville State University, NC*
Ferris State University, MI*
Fisher College, MA*
Florida Agricultural and Mechanical University, FL
Florida Atlantic University, FL

Florida Institute of Technology, FL
Florida Southern College, FL
Florida State University, FL
Fontbonne University, MO*
Fordham University, NY
Fort Valley State University, GA
Franciscan University of Steubenville, OH
Francis Marion University, SC
Franklin & Marshall College, PA*
Franklin College, IN*
Franklin Pierce University, NH*
Furman University, SC
Gannon University, PA
Geneva College, PA*
George Mason University, VA
Georgetown College, KY*
Georgetown University, DC
The George Washington University, DC*
Georgia College & State University, GA*
Georgia Institute of Technology, GA
Georgia Regents University, GA
Georgia Southern University, GA
Georgia State University, GA
Gettysburg College, PA*
Gonzaga University, WA
Gordon College, MA*
Goucher College, MD*
Grambling State University, LA
Grand View University, IA*
Greensboro College, NC*
Gustavus Adolphus College, MN*
Hamilton College, NY*
Hamline University, MN*
Hampden-Sydney College, VA*
Hampshire College, MA*
Hampton University, VA
Harvard University, MA*
Harvey Mudd College, CA*
Hawai`i Pacific University, HI*
Heidelberg University, OH*
Hendrix College, AR*
Hilbert College, NY*
Hobart and William Smith Colleges, NY*
Hofstra University, NY
Holy Family University, PA*
Hood College, MD
Hope College, MI*
Hope International University, CA*
Houghton College, NY*
Houston Baptist University, TX*
Howard University, DC
Huntingdon College, AL*
Husson University, ME
Huston-Tillotson University, TX*
Idaho State University, ID
Illinois Institute of Technology, IL
Illinois State University, IL
Illinois Wesleyan University, IL*
Indiana State University, IN
Indiana University Bloomington, IN
Indiana University Kokomo, IN
Indiana University Northwest, IN
Indiana University of Pennsylvania, PA
Indiana University–Purdue University Fort Wayne, IN
Indiana University–Purdue University Indianapolis, IN
Indiana University South Bend, IN*
Indiana University Southeast, IN*
Inter American University of Puerto Rico, Bayamón Campus, PR*
Inter American University of Puerto Rico, Guayama Campus, PR*
Iona College, NY*

---

* program is offered at another college's campus

Iowa State University of Science and
Technology, IA
Ithaca College, NY*
Jackson State University, MS
Jacksonville State University, AL
Jacksonville University, FL
James Madison University, VA
John Brown University, AR*
John Carroll University, OH
Johns Hopkins University, MD
Johnson C. Smith University, NC
Kalamazoo College, MI*
Kansas State University, KS
Kean University, NJ*
Keene State College, NH*
Kennesaw State University, GA*
Kent State University, OH
Kent State University at Geauga, OH*
Kent State University at Stark, OH*
Kentucky State University, KY*
Kentucky Wesleyan College, KY*
Keystone College, PA*
The King's College, NY*
King's College, PA
Kutztown University of Pennsylvania, PA*
Lafayette College, PA*
Lakeview College of Nursing, IL*
Langston University, OK*
La Roche College, PA*
La Salle University, PA*
Lehigh University, PA
Lehman College of the City University of
New York, NY*
Le Moyne College, NY*
LeMoyne-Owen College, TN*
Lenoir-Rhyne University, NC*
Lewis & Clark College, OR*
Lewis-Clark State College, ID*
Lewis University, IL*
Liberty University, VA
Lincoln University, MO
Lincoln University, PA*
Lindenwood University, MO
Lipscomb University, TN*
Lock Haven University of Pennsylvania, PA
Longwood University, VA
Loras College, IA*
Louisiana State University and Agricultural
& Mechanical College, LA
Louisiana Tech University, LA*
Loyola Marymount University, CA*
Loyola University Chicago, IL
Loyola University New Orleans, LA*
Lubbock Christian University, TX*
Lycoming College, PA*
Macalester College, MN*
Maine Maritime Academy, ME*
Malone University, OH*
Manhattan College, NY*
Mansfield University of Pennsylvania, PA*
Maranatha Baptist University, WI
Marian University, WI
Marist College, NY
Marquette University, WI
Marshall University, WV
Mary Baldwin College, VA
Marymount University, VA*
Maryville University of Saint Louis, MO*
Marywood University, PA*
Massachusetts Institute of Technology, MA
Massachusetts Maritime Academy, MA*
The Master's College and Seminary, CA*
Mayville State University, ND*
McDaniel College, MD
McKendree University, IL*

Mercer University, GA
Mercy College, NY*
Meredith College, NC*
Miami University, OH*
Michigan State University, MI
Michigan Technological University, MI
Mid-Atlantic Christian University, NC*
Middlebury College, VT*
Middle Tennessee State University, TN
Millersville University of Pennsylvania, PA
Millsaps College, MS*
Mills College, CA*
Milwaukee School of Engineering, WI*
Minnesota State University Mankato, MN
Minnesota State University Moorhead, MN*
Misericordia University, PA*
Mississippi State University, MS
Mississippi University for Women, MS*
Missouri Baptist University, MO*
Missouri State University, MO
Missouri University of Science and
Technology, MO
Missouri Valley College, MO
Missouri Western State University, MO
Molloy College, NY*
Monmouth College, IL*
Monmouth University, NJ*
Montana State University, MT
Montana State University Billings, MT
Montclair State University, NJ
Moravian College, PA*
Morehead State University, KY
Morningside College, IA*
Morrisville State College, NY*
Mount Carmel College of Nursing, OH*
Mount Holyoke College, MA*
Mount Marty College, SD*
Mount St. Joseph University, OH*
Mount Saint Mary College, NY*
Mount St. Mary's University, MD*
Muhlenberg College, PA*
Murray State University, KY
National University, CA*
Nazareth College of Rochester, NY*
Nebraska Methodist College, NE*
Newberry College, SC
New England College, NH*
New Jersey City University, NJ*
New Jersey Institute of Technology, NJ*
New Mexico State University, NM
New York Institute of Technology, NY*
New York University, NY*
Niagara University, NY
Nichols College, MA*
North Carolina Agricultural and Technical
State University, NC
North Carolina Central University, NC
North Carolina State University, NC
North Central College, IL*
Northeastern Illinois University, IL*
Northeastern State University, OK
Northeastern University, MA
Northern Arizona University, AZ
Northern Illinois University, IL
Northern Kentucky University, KY*
Northern Michigan University, MI
Northwestern University, IL*
Northwest Missouri State University, MO
Northwest Nazarene University, ID
Northwest University, WA*
Norwich University, VT
Notre Dame of Maryland University, MD*
Occidental College, CA*
The Ohio State University, OH
Ohio University, OH

Ohio Wesleyan University, OH*
Oklahoma Christian University, OK*
Oklahoma City University, OK*
Oklahoma State University, OK
Old Dominion University, VA
Olivet Nazarene University, IL
Oregon State University, OR
Our Lady of the Lake University of San
Antonio, TX*
Pace University, NY*
Pacific Lutheran University, WA
Pacific University, OR*
Palm Beach Atlantic University, FL*
Park University, MO
Penn State Abington, PA*
Penn State Altoona, PA
Penn State Berks, PA*
Penn State Brandywine, PA*
Penn State Erie, The Behrend College, PA
Penn State Harrisburg, PA*
Penn State Hazleton, PA
Penn State Lehigh Valley, PA*
Penn State University Park, PA
Penn State Wilkes-Barre, PA*
Penn State Worthington Scranton, PA*
Pennsylvania College of Technology, PA
Pepperdine University, CA*
Philander Smith College, AR*
Pittsburg State University, KS
Plymouth State University, NH*
Point Loma Nazarene University, CA*
Pomona College, CA*
Prairie View A&M University, TX
Pratt Institute, NY*
Presbyterian College, SC
Princeton University, NJ
Providence College, RI
Purdue University, IN
Purdue University Calumet, IN
Queens College of the City University of
New York, NY*
Quinnipiac University, CT*
Radford University, VA
Ramapo College of New Jersey, NJ*
Randolph-Macon College, VA*
Regent University, VA*
Regis University, CO*
Rensselaer Polytechnic Institute, NY
Rhode Island College, RI*
Rhode Island School of Design, RI*
Rhodes College, TN*
Rice University, TX*
Rider University, NJ*
Robert Morris University, PA
Robert Morris University Illinois, IL*
Roberts Wesleyan College, NY*
Rochester Institute of Technology, NY
Rockhurst University, MO*
Rocky Mountain College, MT*
Roger Williams University, RI*
Rose-Hulman Institute of Technology, IN
Rowan University, NJ*
Rutgers, The State University of New Jersey,
Camden, NJ*
Rutgers, The State University of New Jersey,
Newark, NJ
Rutgers, The State University of New Jersey,
New Brunswick, NJ
Sacred Heart University, CT*
The Sage Colleges, NY
Saint Anselm College, NH*
Saint Augustine's University, NC
St. Bonaventure University, NY
St. Catherine University, MN*
St. Edward's University, TX*

---

* program is offered at another college's campus

St. Francis College, NY*
Saint Francis University, PA
St. John Fisher College, NY*
Saint John's University, MN
St. John's University, NY
Saint Joseph's University, PA*
St. Lawrence University, NY*
Saint Leo University, FL
St. Louis College of Pharmacy, MO*
Saint Louis University, MO*
Saint Martin's University, WA*
Saint Mary's College, IN*
Saint Mary's University of Minnesota, MN*
Saint Michael's College, VT*
St. Norbert College, WI
Saint Vincent College, PA*
Salem College, NC*
Salisbury University, MD
Salve Regina University, RI*
Samford University, AL*
Sam Houston State University, TX
San Diego State University, CA
San Francisco State University, CA*
San Jose State University, CA*
Santa Clara University, CA
Savannah State University, GA
Scripps College, CA*
Seattle Pacific University, WA*
Seattle University, WA
Seton Hill University, PA*
Shippensburg University of Pennsylvania, PA
Siena College, NY
Simmons College, MA*
Skidmore College, NY*
Slippery Rock University of Pennsylvania, PA
Smith College, MA*
South Dakota School of Mines and Technology, SD
South Dakota State University, SD
Southeastern Louisiana University, LA*
Southern Connecticut State University, CT*
Southern Illinois University Carbondale, IL
Southern Illinois University Edwardsville, IL
Southern Methodist University, TX
Southern Oregon University, OR
Southern Utah University, UT
Southwest Baptist University, MO*
Spelman College, GA*
Spring Hill College, AL*
Stanford University, CA*
State University of New York at Oswego, NY*
State University of New York College at Cortland, NY*
State University of New York College at Geneseo, NY*
State University of New York College at Old Westbury, NY*
State University of New York College at Potsdam, NY*
State University of New York College of Environmental Science and Forestry, NY*
State University of New York College of Technology at Canton, NY*
State University of New York Maritime College, NY*
State University of New York Polytechnic Institute, NY*
Stephen F. Austin State University, TX
Stephens College, MO*
Stetson University, FL*
Stevenson University, MD*
Stockton University, NJ*
Stonehill College, MA

Stony Brook University, State University of New York, NY
Suffolk University, MA*
Susquehanna University, PA*
Syracuse University, NY
Tarleton State University, TX
Temple University, PA
Tennessee State University, TN*
Texas A&M International University, TX
Texas A&M University, TX
Texas A&M University–Corpus Christi, TX
Texas Christian University, TX
Texas Lutheran University, TX*
Texas Southern University, TX
Texas State University, TX
Texas Tech University, TX
Texas Wesleyan University, TX*
Texas Woman's University, TX*
Thomas More College, KY*
Tiffin University, OH*
Towson University, MD*
Transylvania University, KY*
Trevecca Nazarene University, TN*
Trinity College, CT*
Trinity University, TX*
Troy University, AL
Truman State University, MO
Tufts University, MA*
Tulane University, LA
Union College, NY*
Union University, TN*
Unity College, ME*
University at Albany, State University of New York, NY
University at Buffalo, the State University of New York, NY*
The University of Akron, OH
The University of Alabama, AL
The University of Alabama at Birmingham, AL
The University of Alabama in Huntsville, AL*
University of Alaska Anchorage, AK
University of Alaska Fairbanks, AK
The University of Arizona, AZ
University of Arkansas, AR
University of California, Berkeley, CA
University of California, Davis, CA
University of California, Irvine, CA
University of California, Los Angeles, CA
University of California, Riverside, CA*
University of California, Santa Barbara, CA
University of California, Santa Cruz, CA*
University of Central Arkansas, AR
University of Central Florida, FL
University of Central Missouri, MO
University of Central Oklahoma, OK
University of Charleston, WV
University of Chicago, IL*
University of Cincinnati, OH
University of Colorado Boulder, CO
University of Colorado Colorado Springs, CO
University of Colorado Denver, CO*
University of Connecticut, CT
University of Dallas, TX*
University of Dayton, OH
University of Delaware, DE
University of Denver, CO*
University of Dubuque, IA
University of Evansville, IN*
The University of Findlay, OH*
University of Florida, FL
University of Georgia, GA
University of Hartford, CT*
University of Hawaii at Manoa, HI

University of Hawaii–West Oahu, HI*
University of Houston, TX
University of Houston–Downtown, TX*
University of Idaho, ID
University of Illinois at Chicago, IL
University of Indianapolis, IN*
The University of Iowa, IA
The University of Kansas, KS
University of La Verne, CA*
University of Louisiana at Lafayette, LA
University of Louisville, KY
University of Maine, ME
University of Maine at Augusta, ME*
University of Mary Hardin-Baylor, TX
University of Maryland, Baltimore County, MD*
University of Maryland, College Park, MD
University of Mary Washington, VA*
University of Massachusetts Amherst, MA
University of Massachusetts Boston, MA*
University of Massachusetts Dartmouth, MA*
University of Massachusetts Lowell, MA
University of Memphis, TN
University of Miami, FL
University of Michigan, MI
University of Michigan–Dearborn, MI
University of Michigan–Flint, MI*
University of Minnesota, Twin Cities Campus, MN
University of Mississippi, MS
University of Missouri, MO
University of Missouri–Kansas City, MO
University of Missouri–St. Louis, MO
University of Mobile, AL*
The University of Montana, MT
University of Montevallo, AL*
University of Mount Union, OH
University of Nebraska at Kearney, NE
University of Nebraska–Lincoln, NE
University of Nevada, Las Vegas, NV
University of Nevada, Reno, NV
University of New England, ME*
University of New Hampshire, NH
University of New Hampshire at Manchester, NH*
University of New Haven, CT
University of New Orleans, LA*
University of North Alabama, AL
The University of North Carolina at Chapel Hill, NC
The University of North Carolina at Charlotte, NC
The University of North Carolina at Greensboro, NC*
The University of North Carolina at Pembroke, NC
University of Northern Colorado, CO
University of Northern Iowa, IA
University of North Florida, FL
University of North Georgia, GA
University of North Texas, TX
University of Notre Dame, IN
University of Oklahoma, OK
University of Oregon, OR
University of Pennsylvania, PA*
University of Pikeville, KY
University of Pittsburgh, PA
University of Pittsburgh at Bradford, PA*
University of Pittsburgh at Greensburg, PA*
University of Portland, OR
University of Puget Sound, WA*
University of Rhode Island, RI
University of Richmond, VA
University of Rochester, NY*

---

* program is offered at another college's campus

University of St. Francis, IL*
University of St. Thomas, MN*
University of St. Thomas, TX*
University of San Diego, CA*
University of San Francisco, CA
The University of Scranton, PA
University of South Alabama, AL
University of South Carolina, SC
University of South Carolina Upstate, SC*
The University of South Dakota, SD
University of Southern California, CA
University of Southern Indiana, IN
University of Southern Maine, ME*
University of Southern Mississippi, MS*
University of South Florida, FL
The University of Tampa, FL
The University of Tennessee, TN
The University of Tennessee at Chattanooga, TN
The University of Tennessee at Martin, TN
The University of Texas at Arlington, TX
The University of Texas at Austin, TX
The University of Texas at Dallas, TX*
The University of Texas at San Antonio, TX
The University of Texas Health Science Center at Houston, TX*
The University of Texas–Pan American, TX
University of the District of Columbia, DC*
University of the Incarnate Word, TX*
University of the Sciences, PA*
The University of Toledo, OH
University of Utah, UT
University of Vermont, VT
University of Virginia, VA
The University of Virginia's College at Wise, VA
University of Washington, WA
University of Washington, Bothell, WA*
University of Washington, Tacoma, WA*
University of West Florida, FL
University of Wisconsin–Eau Claire, WI
University of Wisconsin–Green Bay, WI*
University of Wisconsin–La Crosse, WI
University of Wisconsin–Madison, WI
University of Wisconsin–Milwaukee, WI*
University of Wisconsin–Oshkosh, WI
University of Wisconsin–Parkside, WI*
University of Wisconsin–River Falls, WI
University of Wisconsin–Stevens Point, WI
University of Wisconsin–Stout, WI
University of Wisconsin–Whitewater, WI
University of Wyoming, WY
Ursuline College, OH*
Utah State University, UT
Utah Valley University, UT
Utica College, NY
Valparaiso University, IN*
Vanderbilt University, TN
Vermont Technical College, VT*
Villanova University, PA
Virginia Commonwealth University, VA*
Virginia Military Institute, VA
Virginia Polytechnic Institute and State University, VA
Virginia State University, VA
Virginia Union University, VA*
Virginia Wesleyan College, VA*
Wagner College, NY*
Wake Forest University, NC
Washburn University, KS
Washington & Jefferson College, PA
Washington and Lee University, VA*
Washington State University, WA
Washington University in St. Louis, MO
Wayland Baptist University, TX*

Waynesburg University, PA*
Wayne State College, NE
Wayne State University, MI
Weber State University, UT
Webster University, MO*
Wentworth Institute of Technology, MA*
Wesleyan College, GA*
West Chester University of Pennsylvania, PA
Western Illinois University, IL
Western Kentucky University, KY
Western Michigan University, MI
Western New England University, MA
Western Oregon University, OR
Westfield State University, MA*
Westminster College, MO*
Westminster College, UT*
West Virginia University, WV
West Virginia University Institute of Technology, WV
Wheaton College, IL
Wheaton College, MA*
Whittier College, CA*
Whitworth University, WA*
Widener University, PA
Wilkes University, PA*
Willamette University, OR*
William Jewell College, MO*
William Peace University, NC*
Williams Baptist College, AR*
William Woods University, MO*
Wingate University, NC*
Winona State University, MN*
Winthrop University, SC*
Wittenberg University, OH*
Wofford College, SC
Worcester Polytechnic Institute, MA
Worcester State University, MA*
Wright State University, OH
Xavier University, OH
Xavier University of Louisiana, LA*
Yale University, CT*
York College of the City University of New York, NY
Youngstown State University, OH

## Naval

Arizona State University at the Downtown Phoenix campus, AZ*
Arizona State University at the Polytechnic campus, AZ*
Arizona State University at the Tempe campus, AZ
Arizona State University at the West campus, AZ*
Armstrong State University, GA*
Auburn University, AL
Babson College, MA*
Barnard College, NY*
Belmont University, TN*
Boston College, MA*
Boston University, MA
California State University, San Marcos, CA*
The Catholic University of America, DC*
Chatham University, PA*
Christian Brothers University, TN*
The Citadel, The Military College of South Carolina, SC
Clark University, MA*
Clayton State University, GA*
The College at Brockport, State University of New York, NY*
The College of Saint Rose, NY*
College of the Holy Cross, MA
Columbia College, MO*
Columbia University, NY

Columbia University, School of General Studies, NY
Cornell University, NY
Drexel University, PA*
Duquesne University, PA*
Eastern Michigan University, MI*
Edgewood College, WI*
Embry-Riddle Aeronautical University–Daytona, FL
Emory University, GA*
Farmingdale State College, NY*
Florida Agricultural and Mechanical University, FL
Florida State University, FL*
Fordham University, NY*
Georgetown University, DC*
The George Washington University, DC
Georgia Institute of Technology, GA
Georgia State University, GA*
Hampton University, VA
Harvard University, MA
Houston Baptist University, TX*
Husson University, ME*
Huston-Tillotson University, TX*
Illinois Institute of Technology, IL
Indiana University South Bend, IN*
Iowa State University of Science and Technology, IA
Jacksonville University, FL
Lewis-Clark State College, ID*
Lincoln University, MO*
Louisiana State University and Agricultural & Mechanical College, LA*
Loyola Marymount University, CA*
Loyola University Chicago, IL*
Loyola University New Orleans, LA*
Macalester College, MN*
Maine Maritime Academy, ME
Marquette University, WI
Mary Baldwin College, VA*
Massachusetts Institute of Technology, MA
Massachusetts Maritime Academy, MA
Miami University, OH
Milwaukee School of Engineering, WI*
Molloy College, NY*
Montclair State University, NJ
Mount Carmel College of Nursing, OH*
North Carolina State University, NC
Northeastern University, MA*
Northwestern University, IL
Norwich University, VT
The Ohio State University, OH
Old Dominion University, VA
Oregon State University, OR
Penn State University Park, PA
Point Loma Nazarene University, CA*
Prairie View A&M University, TX
Princeton University, NJ*
Purdue University, IN
Queens College of the City University of New York, NY*
Regent University, VA*
Regis University, CO*
Rensselaer Polytechnic Institute, NY
Rice University, TX
Rochester Institute of Technology, NY*
Rutgers, The State University of New Jersey, Newark, NJ
Rutgers, The State University of New Jersey, New Brunswick, NJ
St. John Fisher College, NY*
Saint Joseph's University, PA*
St. Louis College of Pharmacy, MO*
Saint Mary's College, IN*
San Diego State University, CA

---

* program is offered at another college's campus

Savannah State University, GA
Seattle Pacific University, WA*
Seattle University, WA*
Spelman College, GA*
Stanford University, CA*
State University of New York Maritime
    College, NY
Stephens College, MO*
Stony Brook University, State University of
    New York, NY*
Temple University, PA*
Tennessee State University, TN*
Texas A&M University, TX
Texas Southern University, TX*
Tufts University, MA*
Tulane University, LA
Union College, NY*
The University of Arizona, AZ
University of California, Berkeley, CA
University of California, Davis, CA*
University of California, Los Angeles, CA
University of California, Santa Cruz, CA*
University of Colorado Boulder, CO
University of Florida, FL
University of Houston, TX*
University of Idaho, ID
University of Illinois at Chicago, IL*

The University of Kansas, KS
University of Maine, ME*
University of Maryland, College Park, MD*
University of Massachusetts Boston, MA*
University of Memphis, TN
University of Michigan, MI
University of Michigan–Dearborn, MI
University of Minnesota, Twin Cities
    Campus, MN
University of Mississippi, MS
University of Missouri, MO
University of Nebraska–Lincoln, NE
University of New Orleans, LA*
The University of North Carolina at Chapel
    Hill, NC
University of North Florida, FL*
University of Notre Dame, IN
University of Oklahoma, OK
University of Pennsylvania, PA
University of Pittsburgh, PA*
University of Rochester, NY
University of St. Thomas, MN*
University of San Diego, CA
University of South Carolina, SC
University of Southern California, CA
University of South Florida, FL
The University of Tampa, FL*

The University of Texas at Austin, TX
University of Utah, UT
University of Virginia, VA
University of Washington, WA
University of Washington, Bothell, WA*
University of Washington, Tacoma, WA*
University of Wisconsin–Madison, WI
University of Wisconsin–Milwaukee, WI*
Vanderbilt University, TN
Villanova University, PA
Virginia Military Institute, VA
Virginia Polytechnic Institute and State
    University, VA
Washburn University, KS*
Washington State University, WA*
Weber State University, UT*
Western Oregon University, OR*
Westminster College, UT*
Widener University, PA*
William Peace University, NC*
William Woods University, MO*
Worcester Polytechnic Institute, MA*
Worcester State University, MA*
Xavier University of Louisiana, LA*
Yale University, CT

* program is offered at another college's campus

# Tuition Waivers

## Adult Students
Albright College, PA
Bluefield State College, WV
Caldwell University, NJ
Campbellsville University, KY
Cedarville University, OH
Clarke University, IA
Coe College, IA
Creighton University, NE
DeSales University, PA
Elmira College, NY
Faulkner University, AL
Greensboro College, NC
Hastings College, NE
Hilbert College, NY
Lewis University, IL
Lipscomb University, TN
Lynchburg College, VA
Marist College, NY
Mercyhurst University, PA
Messiah College, PA
Mississippi College, MS
Montreat College, NC
New England College, NH
Randolph College, VA
Roanoke College, VA
St. Andrews University, NC
St. John's University, NY
Southeastern Oklahoma State University, OK
Trinity College, CT
University of Dayton, OH
University of Evansville, IN
University of Hawaii at Manoa, HI
Utah State University, UT
Virginia Wesleyan College, VA
Webber International University, FL
Wittenberg University, OH

## Children of Alumni
Adelphi University, NY
Adrian College, MI
Aquinas College, MI
Ashland University, OH
Baldwin Wallace University, OH
Bay Path University, MA
Cabrini College, PA
Caldwell University, NJ
Calumet College of Saint Joseph, IN
The Catholic University of America, DC
Cedar Crest College, PA
Central Methodist University, MO
Central Michigan University, MI
Clarke University, IA
College of Saint Elizabeth, NJ
Columbia College, MO
Concordia University Chicago, IL
Curry College, MA
Delta State University, MS
Dickinson State University, ND
Drake University, IA
Drexel University, PA
Drury University, MO
D'Youville College, NY
Eastern University, PA
Emmanuel College, MA
Florida Southern College, FL
Grambling State University, LA
Grand View University, IA
Henderson State University, AR

Hilbert College, NY
Hillsdale College, MI
Hillsdale Free Will Baptist College, OK
Huntingdon College, AL
Huntington University, IN
Iona College, NY
Ithaca College, NY
Jackson State University, MS
Johnson C. Smith University, NC
Kansas Wesleyan University, KS
Kentucky Wesleyan College, KY
Langston University, OK
Lasell College, MA
Lewis University, IL
Lincoln Memorial University, TN
Lincoln University, PA
Louisiana Tech University, LA
MacMurray College, IL
McKendree University, IL
Michigan Technological University, MI
Mid-Atlantic Christian University, NC
Minneapolis College of Art and Design, MN
Minot State University, ND
Mississippi State University, MS
Missouri Baptist University, MO
Missouri State University, MO
Morehead State University, KY
Morningside College, IA
Morrisville State College, NY
Murray State University, KY
Nazareth College of Rochester, NY
Nebraska Christian College, NE
New England College, NH
Oklahoma State University, OK
Pacific Lutheran University, WA
Peirce College, PA
Pine Manor College, MA
Saint Joseph's College, IN
Saint Louis University, MO
Saint Martin's University, WA
Simpson College, IA
Southeastern Oklahoma State University, OK
Southern Illinois University Carbondale, IL
Southern Utah University, UT
Suffolk University, MA
Texas Lutheran University, TX
Truman State University, MO
Union University, TN
University of Alaska Fairbanks, AK
University of Charleston, WV
University of Evansville, IN
The University of Findlay, OH
University of Louisiana at Lafayette, LA
University of Minnesota, Duluth, MN
University of Mississippi, MS
University of Mount Union, OH
University of Nebraska at Omaha, NE
University of New England, ME
University of St. Francis, IL
The University of South Dakota, SD
University of Southern Mississippi, MS
The University of Toledo, OH
University of Wisconsin–Whitewater, WI
University of Wyoming, WY
Utah State University, UT
Warner Pacific College, OR
Webber International University, FL
Webb Institute, NY
Western Kentucky University, KY

Westminster College, MO
Whittier College, CA
William Woods University, MO
Wittenberg University, OH

## Minority Students
Dickinson State University, ND
Drury University, MO
Fort Lewis College, CO
Hilbert College, NY
Huntington University, IN
Illinois State University, IL
Lock Haven University of Pennsylvania, PA
Mayville State University, ND
Minot State University, ND
Montana State University, MT
Montana Tech of The University of Montana, MT
Morehead State University, KY
Morrisville State College, NY
Nazareth College of Rochester, NY
Saint Joseph's College, IN
Shepherd University, WV
Slippery Rock University of Pennsylvania, PA
Southeastern Oklahoma State University, OK
Texas Southern University, TX
University at Buffalo, the State University of New York, NY
University of Evansville, IN
University of Hawaii at Manoa, HI
University of Maine at Augusta, ME
University of Maine at Farmington, ME
University of Maine at Presque Isle, ME
The University of Montana, MT
The University of Montana Western, MT
University of Rhode Island, RI
University of Wisconsin–La Crosse, WI
Utah State University, UT
Webb Institute, NY
Western Washington University, WA
Wittenberg University, OH

## Senior Citizens
Adams State University, CO
Adelphi University, NY
Albany State University, GA
Albertus Magnus College, CT
Albright College, PA
Alvernia University, PA
Andrews University, MI
Arkansas State University, AR
Arkansas Tech University, AR
Armstrong State University, GA
Ashland University, OH
Athens State University, AL
Auburn University at Montgomery, AL
Austin Peay State University, TN
Averett University, VA
Ball State University, IN
Baruch College of the City University of New York, NY
Becker College, MA
Bellarmine University, KY
Belmont University, TN
Bemidji State University, MN
Berry College, GA
Bethany Lutheran College, MN
Bethel College, KS
Bloomfield College, NJ

Bloomsburg University of Pennsylvania, PA
Bluefield College, VA
Bluefield State College, WV
Bob Jones University, SC
Boise State University, ID
Bowie State University, MD
Bowling Green State University, OH
Bradley University, IL
Brevard College, NC
Bridgewater College, VA
Bridgewater State University, MA
Cabrini College, PA
Caldwell University, NJ
California State University, Chico, CA
California State University, Dominguez Hills, CA
California State University, East Bay, CA
California State University, Fullerton, CA
California State University, Long Beach, CA
California State University, Monterey Bay, CA
California State University, San Bernardino, CA
California State University, San Marcos, CA
Calumet College of Saint Joseph, IN
Cameron University, OK
Campbellsville University, KY
Capital University, OH
Carroll College, MT
Carson-Newman University, TN
Castleton State College, VT
Cedarville University, OH
Central Connecticut State University, CT
Central Michigan University, MI
Central Washington University, WA
Chestnut Hill College, PA
Chowan University, NC
Christopher Newport University, VA
The Citadel, The Military College of South Carolina, SC
City College of the City University of New York, NY
Clarion University of Pennsylvania, PA
Clarke University, IA
Clayton State University, GA
Clemson University, SC
Cleveland State University, OH
Coastal Carolina University, SC
Coe College, IA
The College at Brockport, State University of New York, NY
The College of New Jersey, NJ
College of Saint Elizabeth, NJ
College of Saint Mary, NE
The College of St. Scholastica, MN
College of Staten Island of the City University of New York, NY
The College of William and Mary, VA
Colorado State University–Pueblo, CO
Columbia College, MO
Concordia University Chicago, IL
Connecticut College, CT
Corban University, OR
Covenant College, GA
Creighton University, NE
Culver-Stockton College, MO
Dakota State University, SD
Dakota Wesleyan University, SD
Delaware State University, DE
Delta State University, MS
DeSales University, PA
Dickinson College, PA
Dickinson State University, ND
Dixie State University, UT
Doane College, NE
Dominican College, NY

Drake University, IA
Duquesne University, PA
D'Youville College, NY
East Carolina University, NC
East Central University, OK
Eastern Illinois University, IL
Eastern Kentucky University, KY
Eastern New Mexico University, NM
East Stroudsburg University of Pennsylvania, PA
Elmhurst College, IL
Elms College, MA
Emmanuel College, GA
Emporia State University, KS
Eureka College, IL
The Evergreen State College, WA
Fashion Institute of Technology, NY
Fayetteville State University, NC
Florida Agricultural and Mechanical University, FL
Florida Atlantic University, FL
Florida Institute of Technology, FL
Florida State University, FL
Fort Valley State University, GA
Framingham State University, MA
Francis Marion University, SC
Franklin College, IN
Franklin Pierce University, NH
Friends University, KS
Frostburg State University, MD
Gannon University, PA
George Fox University, OR
George Mason University, VA
Georgia College & State University, GA
Georgia Institute of Technology, GA
Georgia Southern University, GA
Georgia State University, GA
Governors State University, IL
Graceland University, IA
Grambling State University, LA
Grand View University, IA
Greensboro College, NC
Greenville College, IL
Hanover College, IN
Harding University, AR
Henderson State University, AR
Hilbert College, NY
Hillsdale Free Will Baptist College, OK
Hofstra University, NY
Holy Family University, PA
Hood College, MD
Husson University, ME
Idaho State University, ID
Illinois State University, IL
Indiana State University, IN
Indiana University of Pennsylvania, PA
Indiana University–Purdue University Fort Wayne, IN
John Carroll University, OH
Juniata College, PA
Kansas Wesleyan University, KS
Kean University, NJ
Keene State College, NH
Kennesaw State University, GA
Kent State University, OH
Kent State University at Geauga, OH
Kent State University at Stark, OH
Kentucky State University, KY
Kentucky Wesleyan College, KY
Keystone College, PA
King's College, PA
King University, TN
Kutztown University of Pennsylvania, PA
LaGrange College, GA
Lake Erie College, OH
Lamar University, TX

La Roche College, PA
Lebanon Valley College, PA
Lee University, TN
Lenoir-Rhyne University, NC
Lewis-Clark State College, ID
Lincoln Christian University, IL
Lincoln Memorial University, TN
Lincoln University, MO
Lindenwood University, MO
Lindsey Wilson College, KY
Linfield College, OR
Lock Haven University of Pennsylvania, PA
Longwood University, VA
Louisiana Tech University, LA
Loyola University Chicago, IL
Loyola University New Orleans, LA
Lynchburg College, VA
MacMurray College, IL
Malone University, OH
Mansfield University of Pennsylvania, PA
Marian University, WI
Marquette University, WI
Marshall University, WV
Marymount California University, CA
Marymount Manhattan College, NY
Marymount University, VA
Maryville University of Saint Louis, MO
Marywood University, PA
Massachusetts College of Art and Design, MA
Massachusetts College of Liberal Arts, MA
Mayville State University, ND
Merrimack College, MA
Messiah College, PA
Metropolitan State University, MN
Michigan Technological University, MI
Mid-Atlantic Christian University, NC
Midland College, TX
Midwestern State University, TX
Millersville University of Pennsylvania, PA
Minnesota State University Mankato, MN
Minnesota State University Moorhead, MN
Minot State University, ND
Mississippi State University, MS
Missouri Baptist University, MO
Missouri Southern State University, MO
Missouri State University, MO
Missouri Western State University, MO
Molloy College, NY
Monmouth University, NJ
Montana State University, MT
Montana State University Billings, MT
Montana Tech of The University of Montana, MT
Montclair State University, NJ
Morehead State University, KY
Morningside College, IA
Morrisville State College, NY
Mount Mary University, WI
Mount St. Joseph University, OH
Murray State University, KY
New England College, NH
New Jersey City University, NJ
New Mexico Highlands University, NM
New Mexico Institute of Mining and Technology, NM
New Mexico State University, NM
New York Institute of Technology, NY
Niagara University, NY
North Central College, IL
Northeastern Illinois University, IL
Northern Kentucky University, KY
Northern Michigan University, MI
Northern State University, SD
Northwestern Oklahoma State University, OK

Northwest Missouri State University, MO
Notre Dame de Namur University, CA
Oakland University, MI
The Ohio State University, OH
Ohio University, OH
Ohio University–Eastern, OH
Oklahoma Baptist University, OK
Oklahoma Wesleyan University, OK
Old Dominion University, VA
Pace University, NY
Park University, MO
Penn State Abington, PA
Penn State Altoona, PA
Penn State Beaver, PA
Penn State Berks, PA
Penn State Brandywine, PA
Penn State Erie, The Behrend College, PA
Penn State Greater Allegheny, PA
Penn State Harrisburg, PA
Penn State Hazleton, PA
Penn State Lehigh Valley, PA
Penn State New Kensington, PA
Penn State Schuylkill, PA
Penn State University Park, PA
Penn State Wilkes-Barre, PA
Penn State Worthington Scranton, PA
Penn State York, PA
Plymouth State University, NH
Point Loma Nazarene University, CA
Portland State University, OR
Post University, CT
Prairie View A&M University, TX
Presbyterian College, SC
Purdue University, IN
Queens College of the City University of
    New York, NY
Quincy University, IL
Radford University, VA
Ramapo College of New Jersey, NJ
Roanoke College, VA
Roberts Wesleyan College, NY
Rockhurst University, MO
Rogers State University, OK
Rosemont College, PA
St. Andrews University, NC
St. Bonaventure University, NY
St. Catherine University, MN
St. Cloud State University, MN
St. John's University, NY
St. Joseph's College, Long Island Campus,
    NY
St. Joseph's College, New York, NY
St. Mary's College of Maryland, MD
St. Olaf College, MN
Salisbury University, MD
San Francisco State University, CA
Savannah State University, GA
Seattle Pacific University, WA
Shawnee State University, OH
Shepherd University, WV
Shimer College, IL
Shippensburg University of Pennsylvania,
    PA
Simpson College, IA
Skidmore College, NY
Slippery Rock University of Pennsylvania,
    PA
South Dakota School of Mines and
    Technology, SD
South Dakota State University, SD
Southeastern Oklahoma State University,
    OK
Southeast Missouri State University, MO
Southern Connecticut State University, CT
Southern Illinois University Carbondale, IL

Southern Illinois University Edwardsville,
    IL
Southern Oregon University, OR
Southern Utah University, UT
Southwestern College, KS
State University of New York College at Old
    Westbury, NY
State University of New York College of
    Agriculture and Technology at
    Cobleskill, NY
Stephen F. Austin State University, TX
Sterling College, KS
Stockton University, NJ
Suffolk University, MA
Taylor University, IN
Tennessee Technological University, TN
Texas A&M International University, TX
Texas A&M University–Commerce, TX
Texas A&M University–Corpus Christi, TX
Texas Southern University, TX
Texas Tech University, TX
Texas Woman's University, TX
Thomas More College, KY
Tiffin University, OH
Towson University, MD
Trevecca Nazarene University, TN
Trine University, IN
Trinity College of Florida, FL
Truman State University, MO
Union College, NY
The University of Akron, OH
University of Alaska Fairbanks, AK
University of Arkansas, AR
University of Bridgeport, CT
University of Central Arkansas, AR
University of Central Florida, FL
University of Charleston, WV
University of Colorado Boulder, CO
University of Connecticut, CT
University of Dayton, OH
University of Delaware, DE
University of Denver, CO
University of Evansville, IN
The University of Findlay, OH
University of Florida, FL
University of Georgia, GA
University of Hartford, CT
University of Hawaii at Manoa, HI
University of Houston–Clear Lake, TX
University of Houston–Downtown, TX
University of Idaho, ID
University of Illinois at Chicago, IL
University of Illinois at Springfield, IL
University of Louisville, KY
University of Maine, ME
University of Maine at Augusta, ME
University of Maine at Farmington, ME
University of Maine at Fort Kent, ME
University of Maine at Presque Isle, ME
University of Maryland, Baltimore County,
    MD
University of Maryland Eastern Shore, MD
University of Maryland University College,
    MD
University of Mary Washington, VA
University of Massachusetts Amherst, MA
University of Massachusetts Dartmouth, MA
University of Massachusetts Lowell, MA
University of Memphis, TN
University of Michigan–Dearborn, MI
University of Michigan–Flint, MI
University of Minnesota, Crookston, MN
University of Minnesota, Twin Cities
    Campus, MN
University of Mississippi, MS

University of Missouri, MO
University of Missouri–St. Louis, MO
The University of Montana, MT
The University of Montana Western, MT
University of Mount Union, OH
University of Nevada, Reno, NV
University of New Hampshire at
    Manchester, NH
University of New Haven, CT
University of New Orleans, LA
University of North Alabama, AL
The University of North Carolina at
    Charlotte, NC
University of North Florida, FL
University of North Georgia, GA
University of North Texas, TX
University of Oklahoma, OK
University of Pikeville, KY
University of Pittsburgh at Greensburg, PA
University of Rhode Island, RI
University of Rio Grande, OH
University of St. Thomas, MN
University of St. Thomas, TX
University of Science and Arts of Oklahoma,
    OK
The University of Scranton, PA
University of South Carolina, SC
University of South Carolina Aiken, SC
University of South Carolina Upstate, SC
The University of South Dakota, SD
University of Southern Mississippi, MS
University of South Florida, FL
The University of Tennessee, TN
The University of Tennessee at Chattanooga,
    TN
The University of Tennessee at Martin, TN
The University of Texas at Austin, TX
The University of Texas at Dallas, TX
University of the Cumberlands, KY
University of the District of Columbia, DC
University of the Incarnate Word, TX
University of Utah, UT
University of Virginia, VA
The University of Virginia's College at
    Wise, VA
University of Washington, WA
University of Washington, Bothell, WA
University of Washington, Tacoma, WA
University of West Florida, FL
University of West Georgia, GA
University of Wisconsin–Green Bay, WI
University of Wisconsin–Milwaukee, WI
University of Wisconsin–Whitewater, WI
University of Wyoming, WY
Utah State University, UT
Villanova University, PA
Virginia State University, VA
Virginia Wesleyan College, VA
Washburn University, KS
Washington State University, WA
Wayne State University, MI
Webber International University, FL
Weber State University, UT
Wells College, NY
Wesleyan College, GA
West Chester University of Pennsylvania,
    PA
Western Connecticut State University, CT
Western Illinois University, IL
Western Kentucky University, KY
Western Michigan University, MI
Western New England University, MA
Western State Colorado University, CO
Westfield State University, MA
West Virginia University, WV

West Virginia University Institute of
 Technology, WV

Whitworth University, WA

Wichita State University, KS

Widener University, PA

William Paterson University of New Jersey,
 NJ

Williams Baptist College, AR

William Woods University, MO

Winthrop University, SC

Wittenberg University, OH

Worcester State University, MA

Wright State University, OH

Xavier University, OH

York College of the City University of New
 York, NY

Youngstown State University, OH

# Tuition Payment Alternatives

| | |
|---|---|
| Abilene Christian University, TX | I,P |
| Academy of Art University, CA | I |
| Adams State University, CO | D,I |
| Adelphi University, NY | D,I,P |
| Adrian College, MI | I |
| Adventist University of Health Sciences, FL | D,I |
| Agnes Scott College, GA | I |
| Alabama Agricultural and Mechanical University, AL | G,I |
| Alabama State University, AL | D |
| Alaska Pacific University, AK | D,I |
| Albany College of Pharmacy and Health Sciences, NY | I |
| Albany State University, GA | I |
| Albertus Magnus College, CT | I |
| Albion College, MI | D,I |
| Albright College, PA | I |
| Alcorn State University, MS | I |
| Alderson Broaddus University, WV | I |
| Alice Lloyd College, KY | I |
| Allegheny College, PA | I |
| Allen College, IA | D |
| Alma College, MI | D,I |
| Alvernia University, PA | I |
| Alverno College, WI | D,I |
| American Baptist College of American Baptist Theological Seminary, TN | D |
| American Jewish University, CA | I |
| American University, DC | I,P |
| Amherst College, MA | D,I |
| Amridge University, AL | G,I |
| Anderson University, IN | I |
| Anderson University, SC | I |
| Andrews University, MI | I |
| Appalachian State University, NC | I |
| Aquinas College, MI | D,I |
| Arizona Christian University, AZ | I |
| Arizona State University at the Downtown Phoenix campus, AZ | I |
| Arizona State University at the Polytechnic campus, AZ | I |
| Arizona State University at the Tempe campus, AZ | I |
| Arizona State University at the West campus, AZ | I |
| Arkansas State University, AR | I |
| Arkansas Tech University, AR | D,I |
| Ashland University, OH | I |
| Assumption College, MA | G |
| Athens State University, AL | I |
| Auburn University, AL | I |
| Auburn University at Montgomery, AL | I |
| Augustana College, IL | I,P |
| Augustana College, SD | I |
| Austin College, TX | I |
| Austin Peay State University, TN | I |
| Ave Maria University, FL | I |
| Averett University, VA | I |
| Azusa Pacific University, CA | I |
| Babson College, MA | I |
| Baldwin Wallace University, OH | D,I |
| Ball State University, IN | I |
| Baptist University of the Americas, TX | I |
| Barclay College, KS | I |
| Bard College, NY | I,P |
| Barnard College, NY | D,I,P |

| | |
|---|---|
| Baruch College of the City University of New York, NY | D,I |
| Bates College, ME | I,P |
| Baylor University, TX | I |
| Bay Path University, MA | I |
| Beacon College, FL | I |
| Becker College, MA | G,I |
| Belhaven University, MS | I |
| Bellarmine University, KY | |
| Belmont Abbey College, NC | D,I |
| Belmont University, TN | D,I |
| Beloit College, WI | I |
| Bemidji State University, MN | I |
| Bennington College, VT | I |
| Bentley University, MA | I |
| Berkeley College–New York City Campus, NY | G,I |
| Berry College, GA | I |
| Bethany College, WV | I |
| Bethany Lutheran College, MN | I |
| Bethel College, KS | D,I |
| Bethel University, MN | I,P |
| Bethune-Cookman University, FL | I |
| Binghamton University, State University of New York, NY | I |
| Biola University, CA | I |
| Birmingham-Southern College, AL | I |
| Blessing Rieman College of Nursing, IL | I |
| Bloomfield College, NJ | D,I |
| Bloomsburg University of Pennsylvania, PA | I |
| Bluefield College, VA | I |
| Bluefield State College, WV | I |
| Blue Mountain College, MS | D,I |
| Bluffton University, OH | I |
| Bob Jones University, SC | I |
| Boise State University, ID | I |
| Boston Architectural College, MA | D |
| Boston College, MA | I |
| Boston University, MA | I,P |
| Bowdoin College, ME | D,I |
| Bowie State University, MD | D,I |
| Bowling Green State University, OH | I |
| Bradley University, IL | D,I |
| Brandeis University, MA | I,P |
| Brenau University, GA | I |
| Brevard College, NC | I |
| Bridgewater College, VA | I |
| Bridgewater State University, MA | I |
| Brown University, RI | I |
| Bryant University, RI | I |
| Bucknell University, PA | I,P |
| Buena Vista University, IA | I |
| Buffalo State College, State University of New York, NY | I |
| Butler University, IN | I |
| Cabarrus College of Health Sciences, NC | I |
| Cabrini College, PA | I |
| Cairn University, PA | I |
| Caldwell University, NJ | I |
| California Baptist University, CA | I |
| California Christian College, CA | I |
| California College of the Arts, CA | I |
| California Institute of Integral Studies, CA | I |
| California Institute of Technology, CA | D,I |

| | |
|---|---|
| California Institute of the Arts, CA | I |
| California Lutheran University, CA | I |
| California Polytechnic State University, San Luis Obispo, CA | I |
| California State Polytechnic University, Pomona, CA | D,I |
| California State University, Chico, CA | D,I |
| California State University, Dominguez Hills, CA | I |
| California State University, East Bay, CA | I |
| California State University, Fresno, CA | I |
| California State University, Fullerton, CA | D,I |
| California State University, Long Beach, CA | I |
| California State University, Los Angeles, CA | I |
| California State University, Monterey Bay, CA | I |
| California State University, San Bernardino, CA | I |
| California State University, Stanislaus, CA | I |
| California University of Pennsylvania, PA | I |
| Calumet College of Saint Joseph, IN | D,G |
| Calvary Bible College and Theological Seminary, MO | I |
| Calvin College, MI | I,P |
| Cameron University, OK | I |
| Campbellsville University, KY | I |
| Campbell University, NC | I |
| Canisius College, NY | D,I |
| Capital University, OH | I |
| Cardinal Stritch University, WI | I |
| Carleton College, MN | I |
| Carlos Albizu University, Miami Campus, FL | I |
| Carroll College, MT | I |
| Carroll University, WI | I |
| Carson-Newman University, TN | D,I |
| Case Western Reserve University, OH | I |
| Castleton State College, VT | I |
| Catawba College, NC | I |
| The Catholic University of America, DC | I |
| Cazenovia College, NY | I |
| Cedar Crest College, PA | D,I |
| Cedarville University, OH | I |
| Centenary College of Louisiana, LA | I |
| Central College, IA | I |
| Central Connecticut State University, CT | I |
| Central Methodist University, MO | I |
| Central Michigan University, MI | I |
| Central Washington University, WA | I |
| Centre College, KY | I |
| Chaminade University of Honolulu, HI | I |
| Champlain College, VT | I,P |
| Chapman University, CA | D,I,P |
| Chatham University, PA | I |
| Chestnut Hill College, PA | D,I |
| Chowan University, NC | I |
| Christendom College, VA | I |
| Christian Brothers University, TN | I |
| Christopher Newport University, VA | I |

*D* = deferred payment system; *G* = guaranteed tuition rate; *I* = installment payments; *P* = prepayment locks in tuition rate

929

| | |
|---|---|
| Cincinnati Christian University, OH | I |
| City College of the City University of New York, NY | D |
| City Vision University, MO | I |
| Claremont McKenna College, CA | I |
| Clarion University of Pennsylvania, PA | D,I |
| Clarke University, IA | D,I |
| Clarkson University, NY | I |
| Clark University, MA | I,P |
| Clemson University, SC | I |
| Cleveland Institute of Art, OH | I |
| Cleveland Institute of Music, OH | I |
| Cleveland State University, OH | I |
| Coastal Carolina University, SC | I |
| Coe College, IA | I |
| Coker College, SC | I |
| Colby College, ME | I |
| Colby-Sawyer College, NH | I |
| Colgate University, NY | D,I,P |
| The College at Brockport, State University of New York, NY | D,I |
| College of Biblical Studies–Houston, TX | D,I |
| The College of New Jersey, NJ | I |
| The College of New Rochelle, NY | I |
| College of Saint Benedict, MN | I |
| College of Saint Elizabeth, NJ | I |
| College of Saint Mary, NE | D,I |
| The College of Saint Rose, NY | I |
| The College of St. Scholastica, MN | I |
| College of the Atlantic, ME | I |
| College of the Holy Cross, MA | I |
| College of the Ozarks, MO | I |
| The College of William and Mary, VA | G,I |
| The College of Wooster, OH | I |
| The Colorado College, CO | I |
| Colorado Mesa University, CO | I |
| Colorado School of Mines, CO | I |
| Colorado State University–Pueblo, CO | D,I |
| Columbia College, MO | D,G,I |
| Columbia International University, SC | I |
| Columbia University, NY | I |
| Columbia University, School of General Studies, NY | I,P |
| Columbus College of Art & Design, OH | D,I |
| Conception Seminary College, MO | I |
| Concordia College, MN | I |
| Concordia University, CA | I |
| Concordia University Ann Arbor, MI | I |
| Concordia University Chicago, IL | I |
| Concordia University, Nebraska, NE | I |
| Concordia University, St. Paul, MN | I |
| Concordia University Texas, TX | I |
| Concord University, WV | I |
| Connecticut College, CT | I |
| Converse College, SC | I |
| Cooper Union for the Advancement of Science and Art, NY | I |
| Corban University, OR | I |
| Cornell College, IA | I |
| Cornell University, NY | I |
| Cornerstone University, MI | I |
| Cornish College of the Arts, WA | I |
| Covenant College, GA | I |
| Creighton University, NE | I |
| Culver-Stockton College, MO | I |
| Cumberland University, TN | I |
| Curry College, MA | I |
| Dakota State University, SD | D,I |
| Dallas Baptist University, TX | D,I |
| Dartmouth College, NH | I,P |
| Delaware State University, DE | D |

| | |
|---|---|
| Delta State University, MS | I |
| Denison University, OH | I |
| DePaul University, IL | D,I |
| DePauw University, IN | I |
| DeSales University, PA | D,I |
| Dickinson College, PA | I |
| Dickinson State University, ND | I |
| Dixie State University, UT | I |
| Doane College, NE | I |
| Dominican College, NY | D,I |
| Dominican University, IL | D |
| Dowling College, NY | I |
| Drake University, IA | I |
| Drew University, NJ | D,I,P |
| Drexel University, PA | I |
| Drury University, MO | D,I,P |
| Duquesne University, PA | D,I |
| D'Youville College, NY | D,G,I |
| Earlham College, IN | D,I,P |
| East Carolina University, NC | D,I |
| East Central University, OK | G |
| Eastern Connecticut State University, CT | I |
| Eastern Illinois University, IL | G,I |
| Eastern Kentucky University, KY | I |
| Eastern Michigan University, MI | I |
| Eastern New Mexico University, NM | I |
| Eastern University, PA | I |
| Eastern Washington University, WA | I |
| East Stroudsburg University of Pennsylvania, PA | I |
| East Texas Baptist University, TX | I |
| Eckerd College, FL | I |
| Edgewood College, WI | I |
| Elizabeth City State University, NC | I |
| Elizabethtown College, PA | I |
| Elmhurst College, IL | I |
| Elmira College, NY | I,P |
| Elms College, MA | I |
| Elon University, NC | I |
| Embry-Riddle Aeronautical University–Daytona, FL | I |
| Embry-Riddle Aeronautical University–Prescott, AZ | I |
| Emerson College, MA | I |
| Emmanuel College, GA | I |
| Emmanuel College, MA | I |
| Emory & Henry College, VA | D,I |
| Emory University, GA | I |
| Emporia State University, KS | D,I |
| Endicott College, MA | I,P |
| Eureka College, IL | I |
| Evangel University, MO | I |
| Everglades University, FL | I |
| The Evergreen State College, WA | I |
| Excelsior College, NY | I |
| Fairfield University, CT | I |
| Fairmont State University, WV | I |
| Farmingdale State College, NY | I |
| Fashion Institute of Technology, NY | I |
| Faulkner University, AL | D,I |
| Fayetteville State University, NC | I |
| Felician College, NJ | I |
| Ferris State University, MI | I |
| Fisher College, MA | I |
| Five Towns College, NY | I |
| Flagler College, FL | I |
| Florida Agricultural and Mechanical University, FL | P |
| Florida Atlantic University, FL | D,I,P |
| Florida Institute of Technology, FL | I |
| Florida National University, FL | G,I,P |
| Florida Southern College, FL | I |
| Florida State University, FL | I,P |
| Fontbonne University, MO | I |

| | |
|---|---|
| Fordham University, NY | I |
| Fort Lewis College, CO | I |
| Fort Valley State University, GA | I |
| Framingham State University, MA | I,P |
| Franciscan University of Steubenville, OH | I |
| Francis Marion University, SC | I |
| Franklin & Marshall College, PA | D,I |
| Franklin College, IN | I |
| Franklin Pierce University, NH | I |
| Franklin W. Olin College of Engineering, MA | I |
| Freed-Hardeman University, TN | I |
| Fresno Pacific University, CA | I |
| Friends University, KS | I |
| Frostburg State University, MD | D,I |
| Furman University, SC | I |
| Gallaudet University, DC | D,I |
| Gannon University, PA | D,I |
| Gardner-Webb University, NC | I |
| Geneva College, PA | I |
| George Fox University, OR | I |
| George Mason University, VA | D,I |
| Georgetown College, KY | I |
| Georgetown University, DC | I |
| The George Washington University, DC | G,I |
| Georgia College & State University, GA | I |
| Georgia Institute of Technology, GA | D |
| Georgian Court University, NJ | I |
| Georgia Southern University, GA | I |
| Gettysburg College, PA | I |
| Goddard College, VT | I |
| Goldfarb School of Nursing at Barnes-Jewish College, MO | I |
| Gonzaga University, WA | D,I |
| Gordon College, MA | I |
| Goshen College, IN | I |
| Goucher College, MD | I,P |
| Governors State University, IL | D,G,I |
| Graceland University, IA | I |
| Grambling State University, LA | D,I |
| Grand Valley State University, MI | D,I |
| Grand View University, IA | I |
| Greensboro College, NC | I |
| Grinnell College, IA | I |
| Guilford College, NC | I |
| Gustavus Adolphus College, MN | I,P |
| Gwynedd Mercy University, PA | I |
| Hamilton College, NY | I |
| Hamline University, MN | I |
| Hampden-Sydney College, VA | I |
| Hampshire College, MA | I |
| Hampton University, VA | D,I |
| Hanover College, IN | I |
| Harding University, AR | I,P |
| Hardin-Simmons University, TX | G,I |
| Hartwick College, NY | I |
| Harvard University, MA | I,P |
| Harvey Mudd College, CA | I |
| Hastings College, NE | I |
| Haverford College, PA | I,P |
| Hawai`i Pacific University, HI | I |
| Heidelberg University, OH | I |
| Hendrix College, AR | I |
| Heritage Christian University, AL | I |
| Hilbert College, NY | I |
| Hillsdale College, MI | I,P |
| Hillsdale Free Will Baptist College, OK | I |
| Hobart and William Smith Colleges, NY | I,P |
| Hodges University, FL | I |
| Hofstra University, NY | G,I |
| Hollins University, VA | I,P |

*D* = deferred payment system; *G* = guaranteed tuition rate; *I* = installment payments; *P* = prepayment locks in tuition rate

|  | |
|---|---|
| Holy Family University, PA | D,I |
| Hood College, MD | I |
| Hope College, MI | I |
| Hope International University, CA | I |
| Houghton College, NY | I |
| Houston Baptist University, TX | I |
| Howard Payne University, TX | I |
| Howard University, DC | I |
| Humboldt State University, CA | I |
| Huntingdon College, AL | D,G,I |
| Huntington University, IN | I |
| Husson University, ME | I,P |
| Huston-Tillotson University, TX | D,I |
| Idaho State University, ID | I |
| Illinois College, IL | D,I |
| Illinois Institute of Technology, IL | I |
| Illinois State University, IL | G,I |
| Illinois Wesleyan University, IL | I |
| Indiana State University, IN | D,I |
| Indiana Tech, IN | D,I |
| Indiana University Bloomington, IN | D,I |
| Indiana University East, IN | D,I |
| Indiana University Kokomo, IN | D,I |
| Indiana University Northwest, IN | D,I |
| Indiana University of Pennsylvania, PA | D,I |
| Indiana University–Purdue University Fort Wayne, IN | D,I |
| Indiana University–Purdue University Indianapolis, IN | D |
| Indiana University South Bend, IN | D,I |
| Indiana University Southeast, IN | D,I |
| Indian River State College, FL | D,I |
| Inter American University of Puerto Rico, Bayamón Campus, PR | D |
| Inter American University of Puerto Rico, Guayama Campus, PR | D |
| Iona College, NY | I |
| Iowa State University of Science and Technology, IA | D,I |
| Iowa Wesleyan College, IA | D,I |
| Ithaca College, NY | I |
| Jackson State University, MS | D,I |
| Jacksonville State University, AL | I |
| Jacksonville University, FL | D |
| John Brown University, AR | I |
| John Carroll University, OH | D,I |
| John Paul the Great Catholic University, CA | G |
| Johns Hopkins University, MD | I |
| Johnson C. Smith University, NC | I |
| The Juilliard School, NY | I |
| Juniata College, PA | I |
| Kalamazoo College, MI | I |
| Kansas City Art Institute, MO | I |
| Kansas State University, KS | D,I |
| Kansas Wesleyan University, KS | I |
| Kean University, NJ | I |
| Keene State College, NH | I |
| Kennesaw State University, GA | D |
| Kent State University, OH | I |
| Kent State University at Geauga, OH | I |
| Kent State University at Stark, OH | I |
| Kentucky Christian University, KY | I |
| Kentucky State University, KY | I |
| Kentucky Wesleyan College, KY | D,I |
| Kenyon College, OH | I |
| Keuka College, NY | I |
| Keystone College, PA | D,I |
| The King's College, NY | D,I |
| King's College, PA | I |
| King University, TN | I |
| Knox College, IL | I |
| Kutztown University of Pennsylvania, PA | D,I |

|  | |
|---|---|
| Lafayette College, PA | I |
| LaGrange College, GA | I |
| Laguna College of Art & Design, CA | I |
| Lake Erie College, OH | I |
| Lakeview College of Nursing, IL | I |
| Lamar University, TX | G,I |
| Langston University, OK | G,I,P |
| La Roche College, PA | I |
| La Salle University, PA | D,I |
| Lasell College, MA | I |
| La Sierra University, CA | I |
| Lawrence Technological University, MI | I |
| Lawrence University, WI | I |
| Lebanon Valley College, PA | I |
| Lees-McRae College, NC | I |
| Lee University, TN | D |
| Lehigh University, PA | I,P |
| Lehman College of the City University of New York, NY | I |
| Le Moyne College, NY | D,I |
| LeMoyne-Owen College, TN | I |
| Lesley University, MA | I |
| LeTourneau University, TX | I |
| Lewis & Clark College, OR | I |
| Lewis-Clark State College, ID | D |
| Lewis University, IL | I |
| Liberty University, VA | I |
| Life University, GA | I |
| LIM College, NY | I |
| Lincoln Christian University, IL | D,I |
| Lincoln Memorial University, TN | I |
| Lincoln University, MO | D,I |
| Lincoln University, PA | D,G,I |
| Lindenwood University, MO | D,I |
| Lindsey Wilson College, KY | I |
| Linfield College, OR | I |
| Lipscomb University, TN | I |
| Lock Haven University of Pennsylvania, PA | I |
| Long Island University–LIU Brooklyn, NY | I |
| Long Island University–LIU Post, NY | I |
| Longwood University, VA | I |
| Loras College, IA | I |
| Louisiana State University and Agricultural & Mechanical College, LA | D |
| Louisiana Tech University, LA | D,I |
| Loyola Marymount University, CA | D,I |
| Loyola University Chicago, IL | D,I |
| Loyola University Maryland, MD | I |
| Loyola University New Orleans, LA | I |
| Lubbock Christian University, TX | I |
| Luther College, IA | I |
| Lycoming College, PA | I |
| Lynchburg College, VA | I,P |
| Lynn University, FL | D,I |
| Lyon College, AR | I |
| Macalester College, MN | I |
| MacMurray College, IL | D |
| Maine Maritime Academy, ME | I |
| Malone University, OH | I |
| Manchester University, IN | I |
| Manhattan College, NY | D,I |
| Manhattan School of Music, NY | D,I |
| Manhattanville College, NY | D,I |
| Mansfield University of Pennsylvania, PA | D,I |
| Maranatha Baptist University, WI | I |
| Marian University, WI | I |
| Marietta College, OH | I |
| Marist College, NY | I |
| Marquette University, WI | I |

|  | |
|---|---|
| Marshall University, WV | I |
| Martin Luther College, MN | I |
| Mary Baldwin College, VA | I |
| Marymount California University, CA | I |
| Marymount Manhattan College, NY | I |
| Marymount University, VA | I |
| Maryville College, TN | I |
| Maryville University of Saint Louis, MO | D,I |
| Marywood University, PA | D,I |
| Massachusetts College of Art and Design, MA | I |
| Massachusetts College of Liberal Arts, MA | I |
| Massachusetts Institute of Technology, MA | I |
| The Master's College and Seminary, CA | I |
| Mayville State University, ND | I |
| McDaniel College, MD | I,P |
| McKendree University, IL | D,I |
| McMurry University, TX | I |
| McNally Smith College of Music, MN | D,I,P |
| MCPHS University, MA | I |
| Medgar Evers College of the City University of New York, NY | D,I |
| Menlo College, CA | I |
| Mercer University, GA | I |
| Mercy College, NY | I |
| Mercy College of Health Sciences, IA | I |
| Mercyhurst University, PA | I |
| Merrimack College, MA | I |
| Messiah College, PA | I |
| Miami University, OH | I |
| Michigan State University, MI | D |
| Michigan Technological University, MI | D,I |
| Mid-Atlantic Christian University, NC | D |
| Middlebury College, VT | P |
| Middle Tennessee State University, TN | I |
| Midland College, TX | D,I |
| Midwestern State University, TX | I |
| Millersville University of Pennsylvania, PA | I |
| Milligan College, TN | I |
| Millikin University, IL | I |
| Millsaps College, MS | I |
| Mills College, CA | I |
| Milwaukee School of Engineering, WI | I |
| Minneapolis College of Art and Design, MN | I |
| Minnesota State University Mankato, MN | I |
| Minnesota State University Moorhead, MN | I |
| Minot State University, ND | I |
| Misericordia University, PA | D,I |
| Mississippi College, MS | I |
| Mississippi State University, MS | I,P |
| Mississippi University for Women, MS | I |
| Missouri Baptist University, MO | I |
| Missouri Southern State University, MO | I |
| Missouri State University, MO | D |
| Missouri University of Science and Technology, MO | I |
| Missouri Western State University, MO | I |
| Molloy College, NY | D,I |
| Monmouth College, IL | I |
| Monmouth University, NJ | I |
| Monroe College, NY | I,P |
| Montana State University, MT | D,I |

*D* = deferred payment system; *G* = guaranteed tuition rate; *I* = installment payments; *P* = prepayment locks in tuition rate

| | | | | | |
|---|---|---|---|---|---|
| Montana State University Billings, MT | I | Oglethorpe University, GA | I,P | Regis University, CO | D,I |
| Montana Tech of The University of Montana, MT | I | The Ohio State University, OH | I | Rensselaer Polytechnic Institute, NY | I |
| Montclair State University, NJ | I | Ohio University, OH | G,I | Rhode Island College, RI | I |
| Montreat College, NC | I | Ohio University–Eastern, OH | I | Rhode Island School of Design, RI | I |
| Montserrat College of Art, MA | I | Ohio Wesleyan University, OH | I | Rhodes College, TN | I |
| Moravian College, PA | I | Oklahoma Baptist University, OK | I | Rice University, TX | I |
| Morehead State University, KY | D,I | Oklahoma Christian University, OK | I | Ringling College of Art and Design, FL | I |
| Morningside College, IA | I | Oklahoma City University, OK | D,I | Roanoke College, VA | I |
| Morrisville State College, NY | D,I | Oklahoma State University, OK | G,I | Robert Morris University, PA | D,I |
| Mount Carmel College of Nursing, OH | I | Oklahoma Wesleyan University, OK | D,I | Robert Morris University Illinois, IL | I |
| Mount Holyoke College, MA | I | Old Dominion University, VA | D,I | Roberts Wesleyan College, NY | I |
| Mount Marty College, SD | I | Olivet Nazarene University, IL | I | Rochester Institute of Technology, NY | D,I,P |
| Mount Mary University, WI | I | Oral Roberts University, OK | I | Rockford University, IL | I |
| Mount Mercy University, IA | I | Otterbein University, OH | I | Rockhurst University, MO | D,I |
| Mount St. Joseph University, OH | D,I | Ouachita Baptist University, AR | D,I | Rocky Mountain College, MT | I |
| Mount Saint Mary College, NY | I | Our Lady of the Lake University of San Antonio, TX | D,I | Rogers State University, OK | I |
| Mount Saint Mary's University, CA | I | Pace University, NY | I | Roger Williams University, RI | D,G,I |
| Mount St. Mary's University, MD | I | Pacific Lutheran University, WA | I | Rollins College, FL | I |
| Muhlenberg College, PA | I | Pacific University, OR | D,I | Rose-Hulman Institute of Technology, IN | I,P |
| Murray State University, KY | I | Palm Beach Atlantic University, FL | I | Rosemont College, PA | I |
| Naropa University, CO | I | Patrick Henry College, VA | D,I | Rowan University, NJ | D,I |
| Nazarene Bible College, CO | I | Peabody Conservatory of The Johns Hopkins University, MD | I | Rutgers, The State University of New Jersey, Camden, NJ | I |
| Nazareth College of Rochester, NY | I | Peirce College, PA | D,I | |  |
| Nebraska Christian College, NE | D,I | Penn State Abington, PA | D,I | Rutgers, The State University of New Jersey, Newark, NJ | I |
| Nebraska Methodist College, NE | I | Penn State Altoona, PA | D,I | |  |
| Neumont University, UT | I | Penn State Beaver, PA | D,I | Rutgers, The State University of New Jersey, New Brunswick, NJ | I |
| Newberry College, SC | G,I | Penn State Berks, PA | D,I | |  |
| New College of Florida, FL | I | Penn State Brandywine, PA | D,I | Sacred Heart University, CT | I |
| New England College, NH | I | Penn State Erie, The Behrend College, PA | D,I | The Sage Colleges, NY | I |
| New Jersey City University, NJ | D | | | Saginaw Valley State University, MI | I |
| New Jersey Institute of Technology, NJ | D,I | Penn State Greater Allegheny, PA | D,I | St. Andrews University, NC | I |
| | | Penn State Harrisburg, PA | D,I | Saint Anthony College of Nursing, IL | D,I |
| Newman University, KS | I | Penn State Hazleton, PA | D,I | Saint Augustine's University, NC | D |
| New Mexico Highlands University, NM | I | Penn State Lehigh Valley, PA | D,I | |  |
| New Mexico State University, NM | D,I | Penn State New Kensington, PA | D,I | St. Catherine University, MN | I |
| New York Institute of Technology, NY | I | Penn State Schuylkill, PA | D,I | St. Cloud State University, MN | I |
| New York School of Interior Design, NY | I | Penn State University Park, PA | D,I | St. Edward's University, TX | I |
| | | Penn State Wilkes-Barre, PA | D,I | Saint Francis Medical Center College of Nursing, IL | I |
| New York University, NY | D,I,P | Penn State Worthington Scranton, PA | D,I | |  |
| Niagara University, NY | D,I | Penn State York, PA | D,I | St. John Fisher College, NY | D,I |
| Nicholls State University, LA | D,I | Pennsylvania College of Technology, PA | D | St. John's College, MD | I,P |
| Nichols College, MA | I | Pepperdine University, CA | I | St. John's College, NM | I |
| North Carolina Central University, NC | I | Philadelphia University, PA | D,I | Saint John's University, MN | I |
| | | Philander Smith College, AR | D,I | St. John's University, NY | I |
| North Carolina State University, NC | I | Piedmont College, GA | I | Saint Joseph's College, IN | G,I |
| North Central College, IL | I | Pine Manor College, MA | I | St. Joseph's College, Long Island Campus, NY | D,I |
| Northeastern Illinois University, IL | D,G | Pittsburg State University, KS | I | |  |
| Northeastern State University, OK | G | Pitzer College, CA | D,I | St. Joseph's College, New York, NY | D,I |
| Northeastern University, MA | I | Plymouth State University, NH | I | |  |
| Northern Arizona University, AZ | G,I | Point Loma Nazarene University, CA | I | Saint Joseph's University, PA | I |
| Northern Kentucky University, KY | I | Pomona College, CA | I | St. Lawrence University, NY | I,P |
| Northern Michigan University, MI | D,I | Portland State University, OR | I | Saint Leo University, FL | D,I |
| Northern State University, SD | I | Post University, CT | I,P | St. Louis College of Pharmacy, MO | D |
| Northland College, WI | G,I | Prairie View A&M University, TX | G,I | Saint Louis University, MO | I |
| Northwest Christian University, OR | I | Presbyterian College, SC | I | Saint Martin's University, WA | I |
| Northwest College of Art & Design, WA | D,I | Princeton University, NJ | D,I | Saint Mary's College, IN | I |
| | | Principia College, IL | I | Saint Mary's College of California, CA | I,P |
| Northwestern Oklahoma State University, OK | I | Providence College, RI | I | |  |
| | | Purchase College, State University of New York, NY | I | St. Mary's College of Maryland, MD | I |
| Northwestern University, IL | I | |  | |  |
| Northwest Missouri State University, MO | D,I | Purdue University, IN | I | Saint Mary's University of Minnesota, MN | I |
| | | Purdue University Calumet, IN | I | |  |
| Northwest Nazarene University, ID | I,P | Queens College of the City University of New York, NY | I | Saint Michael's College, VT | I |
| Northwest University, WA | I | |  | St. Norbert College, WI | D,I |
| Notre Dame de Namur University, CA | I | Quincy University, IL | I | St. Olaf College, MN | I |
| Notre Dame of Maryland University, MD | D,I | Quinnipiac University, CT | I | St. Thomas Aquinas College, NY | I |
| | | Radford University, VA | I | St. Thomas University, FL | I |
| Nova Southeastern University, FL | D,I | Ramapo College of New Jersey, NJ | I | Saint Vincent College, PA | I |
| Nyack College, NY | I | Randolph College, VA | I | Salem College, NC | I |
| Oakland University, MI | D,I | Randolph-Macon College, VA | I | Salisbury University, MD | I |
| Oberlin College, OH | I | Reed College, OR | I | Salve Regina University, RI | I |
| | | Regent University, VA | I | |  |

*D* = deferred payment system; *G* = guaranteed tuition rate; *I* = installment payments; *P* = prepayment locks in tuition rate

| | | | | | |
|---|---|---|---|---|---|
| Samford University, AL | I | State University of New York College at Cortland, NY | I | Trinity University, TX | I |
| Sam Houston State University, TX | G,I | State University of New York College at Geneseo, NY | D,I | Troy University, AL | I |
| San Diego State University, CA | I | | | Truett-McConnell College, GA | I |
| San Francisco Art Institute, CA | I | State University of New York College at Old Westbury, NY | I | Truman State University, MO | I |
| San Francisco Conservatory of Music, CA | I | State University of New York College at Potsdam, NY | I | Tufts University, MA | I,P |
| San Francisco State University, CA | I | | | Tulane University, LA | I,P |
| Santa Clara University, CA | I | State University of New York College of Agriculture and Technology at Cobleskill, NY | D,I | Tuskegee University, AL | I |
| Sarah Lawrence College, NY | I | | | Union College, KY | I |
| Savannah College of Art and Design, GA | I | State University of New York College of Environmental Science and Forestry, NY | D,I | Union College, NE | I |
| | | | | Union College, NY | I |
| Savannah State University, GA | I | | | Union University, TN | D,I |
| School of the Art Institute of Chicago, IL | I | State University of New York College of Technology at Canton, NY | D,I | Unity College, ME | I |
| | | | | Universidad Teológica del Caribe, PR | D |
| School of the Museum of Fine Arts, Boston, MA | I | State University of New York College of Technology at Delhi, NY | I | University at Buffalo, the State University of New York, NY | I |
| Schreiner University, TX | I | | | The University of Akron, OH | I |
| Scripps College, CA | I,P | State University of New York Maritime College, NY | I | The University of Alabama, AL | D,I |
| Seattle Pacific University, WA | D,I | | | The University of Alabama at Birmingham, AL | I |
| Seattle University, WA | D,I | State University of New York Polytechnic Institute, NY | I | | |
| Seton Hill University, PA | I | | | The University of Alabama in Huntsville, AL | I |
| Sewanee: The University of the South, TN | G,I | Stephen F. Austin State University, TX | G,I | University of Alaska Fairbanks, AK | D,I |
| Shawnee State University, OH | I | Stephens College, MO | I | The University of Arizona, AZ | G,I |
| Shenandoah University, VA | I | Sterling College, KS | I | University of Arkansas, AR | I |
| Shepherd University, WV | I | Stetson University, FL | I | University of Bridgeport, CT | D,I |
| Shimer College, IL | I | Stevenson University, MD | D,I | University of California, Berkeley, CA | I |
| Shippensburg University of Pennsylvania, PA | I | Stockton University, NJ | D,I | | |
| | | Stonehill College, MA | I,P | University of California, Davis, CA | D |
| Siena College, NY | I | Stony Brook University, State University of New York, NY | I | University of California, Irvine, CA | I |
| Sierra Nevada College, NV | I | | | University of California, Riverside, CA | D |
| Simmons College, MA | I | Stratford University, MD | I | | |
| Simpson College, IA | I | Stratford University, VA | I | University of California, Santa Barbara, CA | I |
| Simpson University, CA | D | Stratford University, VA | I | | |
| Skidmore College, NY | I,P | Stratford University, VA | I | University of California, Santa Cruz, CA | I |
| Slippery Rock University of Pennsylvania, PA | I | Stratford University, VA | I | University of Central Arkansas, AR | I |
| | | Suffolk University, MA | D,I | University of Central Florida, FL | D,P |
| Smith College, MA | I,P | Sul Ross State University, TX | I | University of Central Missouri, MO | D,I |
| Soka University of America, CA | D,I | Susquehanna University, PA | I,P | University of Central Oklahoma, OK | D,G |
| Sonoma State University, CA | I | Swarthmore College, PA | I | University of Charleston, WV | I |
| South Dakota School of Mines and Technology, SD | I | Syracuse University, NY | I,P | University of Chicago, IL | I,P |
| | | Tabor College, KS | I | University of Cincinnati, OH | I |
| South Dakota State University, SD | D,I | Tarleton State University, TX | G,I | University of Colorado Boulder, CO | D |
| Southeastern Louisiana University, LA | I | Taylor University, IN | I | University of Colorado Colorado Springs, CO | I |
| | | Temple University, PA | I | | |
| Southeastern Oklahoma State University, OK | G,I | Tennessee Technological University, TN | D | University of Colorado Denver, CO | D,I |
| | | | | University of Connecticut, CT | D,I |
| Southeast Missouri State University, MO | D,I | Tennessee Wesleyan College, TN | I | University of Dallas, TX | I |
| | | Texas A&M International University, TX | I | University of Dayton, OH | D,I,P |
| Southern Connecticut State University, CT | D,I | | | University of Delaware, DE | I |
| | | Texas A&M University, TX | G,I | University of Denver, CO | D,I |
| Southern Illinois University Carbondale, IL | G,I | Texas A&M University–Commerce, TX | G,I | University of Dubuque, IA | I |
| | | | | University of Evansville, IN | I |
| Southern Illinois University Edwardsville, IL | G,I | Texas A&M University–Corpus Christi, TX | G,I | The University of Findlay, OH | I |
| | | | | University of Florida, FL | D |
| Southern Methodist University, TX | I,P | Texas Christian University, TX | I | University of Great Falls, MT | I |
| Southern Oregon University, OR | D,I | Texas Lutheran University, TX | I | University of Hartford, CT | I,P |
| Southern Utah University, UT | I | Texas Southern University, TX | D,G,I | University of Hawaii at Manoa, HI | I |
| Southwest Baptist University, MO | I | Texas State University, TX | G,I | University of Hawaii–West Oahu, HI | I |
| Southwestern College, KS | I | Texas Tech University, TX | I | | |
| Southwestern University, TX | I | Texas Wesleyan University, TX | D,I | University of Houston, TX | D,G,I |
| Spelman College, GA | D,I | Texas Woman's University, TX | I | University of Houston–Clear Lake, TX | D,I |
| Spring Arbor University, MI | I | Thiel College, PA | I | | |
| Springfield College, MA | I | Thomas Aquinas College, CA | I | University of Houston–Downtown, TX | I |
| Spring Hill College, AL | I | Thomas More College, KY | D,I | | |
| Stanford University, CA | I | Tiffin University, OH | D,I | University of Idaho, ID | D,I |
| State University of New York at Fredonia, NY | I | Towson University, MD | I | University of Illinois at Chicago, IL | G,I |
| | | Transylvania University, KY | I | | |
| State University of New York at New Paltz, NY | I | Trevecca Nazarene University, TN | I,P | University of Illinois at Springfield, IL | G,I |
| | | Trine University, IN | I | University of Indianapolis, IN | I |
| State University of New York at Oswego, NY | I | Trinity Christian College, IL | I | The University of Iowa, IA | I |
| | | Trinity College, CT | I | University of Jamestown, ND | I |
| State University of New York at Plattsburgh, NY | D,I | Trinity College of Florida, FL | I | The University of Kansas, KS | G,I |
| | | | | University of La Verne, CA | D,I |

---

*D* = deferred payment system; *G* = guaranteed tuition rate; *I* = installment payments; *P* = prepayment locks in tuition rate

| | | | | | |
|---|---|---|---|---|---|
| University of Louisville, KY | I | University of Oregon, OR | I | University of Wisconsin–Green Bay, WI | I |
| University of Maine, ME | I | University of Pennsylvania, PA | I,P | University of Wisconsin–La Crosse, WI | I |
| University of Maine at Augusta, ME | I | University of Pikeville, KY | I | University of Wisconsin–Milwaukee, WI | I |
| University of Maine at Farmington, ME | I | University of Pittsburgh, PA | D,I | University of Wisconsin–Stevens Point, WI | D,I |
| University of Maine at Fort Kent, ME | I | University of Pittsburgh at Bradford, PA | I | University of Wisconsin–Superior, WI | I |
| University of Maine at Presque Isle, ME | D,I | University of Pittsburgh at Greensburg, PA | I | University of Wisconsin–Whitewater, WI | I |
| University of Mary Hardin-Baylor, TX | I | University of Pittsburgh at Johnstown, PA | I | University of Wyoming, WY | I |
| University of Maryland, Baltimore County, MD | I | University of Portland, OR | D,I | Upper Iowa University, IA | I |
| University of Maryland, College Park, MD | D,I | University of Puget Sound, WA | D,I | Ursuline College, OH | I |
| University of Maryland Eastern Shore, MD | D,I | University of Redlands, CA | I | Utah State University, UT | D |
| University of Maryland University College, MD | I | University of Rhode Island, RI | I | Utah Valley University, UT | D,I |
| University of Mary Washington, VA | I | University of Richmond, VA | I | Valdosta State University, GA | I |
| University of Massachusetts Amherst, MA | I | University of Rochester, NY | I,P | Valley City State University, ND | I |
| University of Massachusetts Dartmouth, MA | I | University of St. Francis, IL | D,I | Valparaiso University, IN | I,P |
| University of Massachusetts Lowell, MA | I | University of Saint Joseph, CT | I | Vanderbilt University, TN | I,P |
| University of Memphis, TN | I | University of St. Thomas, MN | I | VanderCook College of Music, IL | I |
| University of Miami, FL | I | University of St. Thomas, TX | D,I | Vanguard University of Southern California, CA | I |
| University of Michigan, MI | I | University of San Diego, CA | I | Vassar College, NY | I |
| University of Michigan–Dearborn, MI | I | University of San Francisco, CA | I | Vermont Technical College, VT | I |
| University of Michigan–Flint, MI | I | University of Science and Arts of Oklahoma, OK | G,I | Villa Maria College, NY | I |
| University of Minnesota, Crookston, MN | I | The University of Scranton, PA | I | Villanova University, PA | I |
| University of Minnesota, Duluth, MN | I | University of South Alabama, AL | I | Virginia Commonwealth University, VA | I |
| University of Minnesota, Twin Cities Campus, MN | I | University of South Carolina, SC | D | Virginia Military Institute, VA | I |
| University of Missouri, MO | I | University of South Carolina Aiken, SC | D | Virginia State University, VA | I |
| University of Missouri–Kansas City, MO | I | University of South Carolina Upstate, SC | D | Virginia Union University, VA | D,I |
| University of Missouri–St. Louis, MO | I | The University of South Dakota, SD | D | Virginia Wesleyan College, VA | I |
| University of Mobile, AL | I | University of Southern California, CA | I,P | Wabash College, IN | I,P |
| The University of Montana, MT | I | University of Southern Indiana, IN | I | Wagner College, NY | I |
| The University of Montana Western, MT | D,I | University of Southern Maine, ME | I | Waldorf College, IA | D,I |
| University of Mount Union, OH | I,P | University of Southern Mississippi, MS | I | Warner Pacific College, OR | D,I |
| University of Nebraska at Kearney, NE | I | University of South Florida, FL | I | Warren Wilson College, NC | I |
| University of Nebraska–Lincoln, NE | I | The University of Tampa, FL | I | Wartburg College, IA | I |
| University of Nevada, Las Vegas, NV | D | The University of Tennessee, TN | I | Washburn University, KS | I |
| University of New England, ME | I | The University of Tennessee at Chattanooga, TN | I | Washington & Jefferson College, PA | D,I,P |
| University of New Hampshire, NH | I | The University of Tennessee at Martin, TN | D,I | Washington and Lee University, VA | I |
| University of New Hampshire at Manchester, NH | I | The University of Texas at Arlington, TX | G,I | Washington College, MD | I,P |
| University of New Haven, CT | I | The University of Texas at Austin, TX | G,I | Washington University in St. Louis, MO | I,P |
| University of North Alabama, AL | I | The University of Texas at Dallas, TX | G,I | Wayland Baptist University, TX | I |
| University of North Carolina at Asheville, NC | I | The University of Texas at San Antonio, TX | D,I | Waynesburg University, PA | I |
| The University of North Carolina at Chapel Hill, NC | I | The University of Texas Health Science Center at Houston, TX | I | Wayne State College, NE | I |
| The University of North Carolina at Charlotte, NC | I | The University of Texas–Pan American, TX | I | Wayne State University, MI | I |
| The University of North Carolina at Greensboro, NC | I | University of the Cumberlands, KY | G,I | Webber International University, FL | I |
| The University of North Carolina at Pembroke, NC | I | University of the District of Columbia, DC | D,I | Webb Institute, NY | I |
| The University of North Carolina Wilmington, NC | I | University of the Incarnate Word, TX | I | Weber State University, UT | I |
| University of Northern Colorado, CO | I | University of the Pacific, CA | D | Webster University, MO | I |
| University of Northern Iowa, IA | I | The University of Toledo, OH | I | Wellesley College, MA | I,P |
| University of North Florida, FL | I | The University of Tulsa, OK | I | Wells College, NY | I |
| University of North Texas, TX | G,I | University of Utah, UT | D,I | Wentworth Institute of Technology, MA | I |
| University of Notre Dame, IN | I | University of Valley Forge, PA | I | Wesleyan College, GA | D,I |
| University of Oklahoma, OK | G,I | University of Vermont, VT | I | Wesleyan University, CT | I |
| | | University of Virginia, VA | I | West Chester University of Pennsylvania, PA | I |
| | | The University of Virginia's College at Wise, VA | D,I | Western Connecticut State University, CT | I |
| | | The University of West Alabama, AL | I | Western Illinois University, IL | G,I |
| | | University of West Florida, FL | D,P | Western Kentucky University, KY | I |
| | | University of Wisconsin–Eau Claire, WI | I | Western Michigan University, MI | I |
| | | | | Western New England University, MA | I,P |
| | | | | Western Oregon University, OR | G |
| | | | | Western State Colorado University, CO | D,I |
| | | | | Western Washington University, WA | I |
| | | | | Westfield State University, MA | I |
| | | | | Westminster College, MO | I |
| | | | | Westminster College, UT | D,I |
| | | | | Westmont College, CA | I |

*D* = deferred payment system; *G* = guaranteed tuition rate; *I* = installment payments; *P* = prepayment locks in tuition rate

| | | | | | |
|---|---|---|---|---|---|
| West Texas A&M University, TX | G,I | Willamette University, OR | I,P | Wittenberg University, OH | I |
| West Virginia University, WV | I | William Jessup University, CA | D | Wofford College, SC | I |
| West Virginia University Institute of Technology, WV | I | William Jewell College, MO | I | Worcester Polytechnic Institute, MA | D,I,P |
| West Virginia Wesleyan College, WV | I | William Paterson University of New Jersey, NJ | I | Worcester State University, MA | I |
| Wheaton College, IL | D,I | William Peace University, NC | I | Wright State University, OH | I |
| Wheaton College, MA | I,P | Williams Baptist College, AR | I | Xavier University, OH | D,I |
| Wheelock College, MA | I | Williams College, MA | I | Xavier University of Louisiana, LA | I |
| Whitman College, WA | D | William Woods University, MO | I | Yale University, CT | I |
| Whittier College, CA | I | Wilson College, PA | I | Yeshiva University, NY | I |
| Whitworth University, WA | I | Wingate University, NC | I | York College of Pennsylvania, PA | I |
| Wichita State University, KS | I | Winona State University, MN | I | York College of the City University of New York, NY | I |
| Widener University, PA | I | Winthrop University, SC | I | Youngstown State University, OH | I |
| Wilkes University, PA | D,I | Wisconsin Lutheran College, WI | I | | |

---

$D$ = deferred payment system; $G$ = guaranteed tuition rate; $I$ = installment payments; $P$ = prepayment locks in tuition rate

*Peterson's*® *How to Get Money for College 2016*